1999

44TH EDITION

INTERNATIONAL TELEVISION & VIDEO ALMANAC

Editorial Director
TRACY STEVENS

Editor
PATRICIA KEEGAN NICOLESCU

Canadian Editor
PATRICIA THOMPSON

QUIGLEY PUBLISHING COMPANY, INC.
159 WEST 53RD STREET • NEW YORK, NY 10019
6639 LA JOLLA BLVD., LA JOLLA, CA 92037

(619) 459-1159

1999 44th Edition
INTERNATIONAL TELEVISION & VIDEO ALMANAC

ISSN: 0539-0761
ISBN: 0-900610-64-6

PRINTED IN THE UNITED STATES OF AMERICA

TABLE OF CONTENTS

THE YEAR IN REVIEW

BY PATRICIA KEEGAN NICOLESCU AND TRACY STEVENS

The competition from relatively new networks, the the introduction of digital TV and the pressure on the networks to win back viewers who have defected to cable have the broadcast networks chasing their tails. Television as it was known, has been shaken up; more precisely, the old networks have continued to feel the pressure build.

NBC managed to stay in first place, but with the end of "Seinfeld" and the rising cost of its star programs ("ER," at $13 million per episode, and "Mad About You," at $1 million apiece per episode to its stars, Helen Hunt and Paul Reiser), the network's long term future is more uncertain. The cost of staying in first place has been a steady diet of lower priced news magazines, with Dateline airing five nights per week and considerable belt tightening elsewhere. Warner Bros. will continue to receive $13 million per episode, 22 episodes per season for the next three years. Per annum, that represents $286,000,000 for one show — which is more than double NBC's profits for 1996-1997. Most executives agree that NBC had little choice without either "Seinfeld" or Monday Night Football to guarantee ratings and advertising revenue.

The networks continue to promote themselves relentlessly with NBC touting it's "Must See TV" and ABC covering America with its high concept, low art, yellow and black ads promoting the essential goodness of television. Of the 'Big Three', ABC came in last in the ratings in spite of (or perhaps because of) their advertising campaign. Slogans such as "TV is good" and "Without a TV, how would you know where to put the sofa" did little to help the network's sagging ratings.

Keeping the stars around by meeting their salary demands seemed easier to do than winning back the viewers who have turned to the more diverse and original entertainment found on cable. With programming that includes more movies, more news shows and specialty channels devoted to music and children's programming, basic cable ratings hit a combined 28.9 in the first quarter of 1998 – an all time high. In the third quarter, the top 35 basic cable networks averaged a 23.8 rating/44 share. This was an intimidating figure by anyone's measure, but especially for the six networks, which experienced a 10% decrease in their ratings from the third quarter of 1997 and a 9% decrease in primetime viewership for the past quarter.

The networks also managed to pit themselves against their affiliates over the issue of compensation and program exclusivity. In May of 1998, the big three proposed to cut down on the $600 million program carriage payments to affiliates as a way of lowering costs. But, with stations having to bare the costs of building digital facilities, the idea was not well received by the affiliates.

For the 1998-99 season, the majority of the networks have invested more in their primetime programming. CBS has equity stakes in more than half its shows, NBC owns a stake in 40% of its shows and UPN invested in 46% of its fall shows. With the exception of ABC who will own just 29% down from 44% in the 1997-1998 season, all major networks will continue to attempt to collect more of the revenues created by network hits.

Lowell "Bud" Paxson's switch from infomercial to broadcast television, was met with both skepticism and excitement. In late 1997, the founder of the Home Shopping Network announced a unique kind of network, the seventh, that would develop programming with Focus On the Family, a conservative Christian group. And, from 1 to 6 A.M., the network was scheduled to broadcast five uninterrupted hours of Christian programming. In May of 1998, Paxson paid Tele-Communications Inc. $27 million to carry Pax Net in small town and rural "white areas." This allows Paxson to broadcast without having to purchase additional stations. A week before launching, in August of 1998, the network announced a name change from Pax Net to Pax TV. Pax TV premiered August 31, 1998, with 20% original programming and the unique ability to be seen on both broadcast and cable. According to Mr. Paxson, the new network which will show "family friendly" programming such as "Touched By An Angel," "Dr. Quinn, Medicine Woman" and "Diagnosis Murder," that will reach more than 80% of U.S. TV households in the near future.

Although Pax TV's design to show only "wholesome" fare may have been influenced by the publicly stated, personal beliefs of Mr. Paxson, a born-again Christian, the trend to create "family-friendly" fare in order to increase ratings was visible on all the networks. WB was especially hungry for the attention of teens and young adults. For the 1998 Fall Season, the network added "Felicity," a one hour drama about the life of a female college freshman to its popular slate of teen oriented shows such as "Dawson's Creek," and "Buffy the Vampire Slayer". The strategy proved successful, as WB was the only network to experience ratings growth for the 1997-98 season.

The FCC's approval of the V-chip, in March of 1998 was a reminder of the important role young viewers play for the networks and the advertisers. The technology will allow parents to block out programming they deem unsuitable for their children. Although broadcasters have been slow to add the letter rating system that's been in use since the fall of 1997, and have only done so when pressured by lawmakers, parent groups and the White House, the V-chip may prove an excellent device in winning young viewers. Giving parents a simple ratings system and dispelling any doubt as to the appropriateness of a program allows the parent to let youngsters view a program from start to finish. Family or child friendly television may not necessarily attract more viewers, but may instead guarantee more hours of viewing.

The link between television and other communication mediums may have been accelerated or at least exposed by the White House sex scandal involving President Clinton and intern, Monica Lewinsky. Although newspapers and television were abuzz with speculations and analysis, the independent counsel Kenneth Starr's report containing the findings from his investigation and including testimony from both Ms. Lewinsky and President Clinton, appeared in its entirety on the internet. Sites and servers were set up to deal solely with developments in the Clinton-Lewinsky case, and CNN's site and Fox News online had their capacity limits challenged. The story's dominance on the broadcast networks and the cable news channels brought to the fore the American public's fascination with sex. The proof was in the ratings, the news executives claimed, and greenlighted endless hours of news programming devoted to dissecting the minutiae of the scandal. When ABC, CBS, NBC, CNN, MSNBC, CNBC, Fox News, C-SPAN, and Court TV aired the President's testimony in late September, the executives explained the airing of all 4 hours of the testimony not as news, but as an historical event that needed to be brought to the public. Television history was indeed made when the words "oral sex" could be heard repeated on the evening news. Surprisingly, the numerous polls conducted showed that the majority of Americans, as well as media critics, considered the coverage of the Clinton-Lewinsky story excessive and trashy.

All of this has further served to highlight the public's simultaneous attraction to and revulsion for the media reminiscent of the reaction to coverage of the Princess of Wales in life and in death. This conflict will likely continue as the public's appetite for scandal equals its ensuing moral outrage at those who work to satiate that appetite. Programmers find themselves in a quandary, trying to satisfy a group of viewers who clamor for the V-chip while sending the "Jerry Springer Show" to ratings heaven.

DTV or Digital TV, was scheduled to premiere in November of 1998. Although in March of 1998, the FCC approved a second channel for every TV station that would broadcast digital TV, there was still no consensus between ABC, CBS, NBC and Fox as to what kind of format to use for digital broadcasting. The format is composed of the number of scanning lines of 480, 720 or 1080 and the lines presented on the screen, interlaced or progressive. The higher number of scanning lines, interlaced or progressive, are defined as high-standard definition, or HDTV, the lowest number offers a standard-definition SDTV format. On November 1st, ABC became the first commercial network to deliver a national HDTV broadcast, "101 Dalmations," using a 720-line progressive version, and on the 8th of the month, CBS broadcast the NFL in HDTV using the 1080 interlace picture format.

Digital technology also had an effect on cable broadcasters. In 1997, the number of new cable networks was 94; by January 1998, the number reached 100. In April, Disney/ABC Cable Network launched Toon Disney, featuring Disney animated programming. Designed for a digital tier, the new network also has analogue carriage and is offered to those operators that already carry The Disney Channel. Disney also talked of at least four digital networks. Lifetime Television was also aiming for the digital tier, recognizing that this technology would allow viewers to choose when they want to see a program.

Satellite operators failed to win legislation in 1998 that would have allowed them to transmit local broadcast signals. The Congress did authorize local-into-local service and thwarted the must-carry requirements that would have forced satellite operators to carry all the stations in the markets they were serving. It is widely believed that local-into-local will become law in 1999. Although local-into-local service allows satellite TV to compete with cable by giving satellite operators local broadcast signals, the cable industry considers this development less dangerous than the extension of rate regulations, which are supposed to expire in the Spring of 1999.

Polls conducted throughout 1998 indicated that the majority of the viewing public had little understanding and even less interest in television's digital revolution. Set-top converters and other hardware that will require any capital outlay will likely take some time to catch on as there is currently insufficient programming in the digital medium to warrant the investment for the public.

As we move toward the millennium, the original three broadcast networks and their newer counterparts are experiencing a rate of viewer attrition that neither technology nor programming can forestall. The networks face increasing competition from satellite and cable. Cable networks can produce more original programming designed to target a narrower, niche audience for a lower price. The cost of entry into the television market has been dropping steadily as programming can be locally produced and distributed on low-overhead cable channels nationwide. While that programming may not attract a wide audience, it does serve to further fragment the viewership that once pledged its allegiance to the the networks. Soon, broadcast television will face an additional challenge from video-on-demand and improved internet connections that will provide adequate bandwidth for computer users to watch movies over the internet.

Television, a medium that was once hailed as a unifying force, has become ever more fractionalized. Long gone are the days when a weekly program could reliably command a 40 share. Even ""Seinfeld"", which was undoubtedly the most popular show of the 1990's, had ratings that would have barely cracked the top 20 in the 1970's.

While opinions differ as to the cause of the decline, all agree that cable television plays a part. However, to attribute the Networks' demise to cable is to overlook the fact that a major cause for the decline has been the choice of programming. CBS, ABC, NBC and even the new networks have pursued the 18-49 demographic, long considered advertising gold, to the exclusion of all else. By marginalizing viewers over 50 and under 18, they have lost most of America's largest demographic – the baby-boomers. The networks have also lost their young viewers to Nickelodeon, MTV and the Disney Channel. And, in chasing the same demographic, the Big Three have largely lost their individual identities.

So, the Networks are faced with a choice as we enter the second century of television: adopt the successful formula of cable, producing lower cost entertainment that caters to a niche audience or return to programming that has broader appeal than the white, 18-49 demographic. Whether they can win back their audience from cable or whether they can attract a broad base of viewers in a multilingual, multicultural America is a question that will be answered in the coming millennium as television is invented anew.

TELEVISION, VIDEO, CABLE AND SATELLITE STATISTICS

THE UNITED STATES TELEVISION INDUSTRY AT A GLANCE

Number of TV Households: 98 million.
Total Number of Commercial Television Stations: 1,561.
Top-Rated Network, 1997-98 Television Season: NBC.
Number of Basic Cable Subscribers: 64.8 million.
Top Cable MSO: TCI (14 million subscribers).
Number of DTH Satellite Subscribers: 7.47 million.
Top DTH Service Provider: DirecTV (2.8 million subscribers).
Number of VCRs: 82.91 million.
Number of Video Stores: 28,000.
Average Video Rental Price: $2.75.
Basic Window of Time from Theatrical Release to Video Release: 5 months, 23 days.
Basic Window of Time from Video Release to Pay-Per-View Release: 45 days.
Number of DVD Players Sold to Consumers: 144,000.

THE TELEVISION RATINGS SYSTEM

TV-Y—Suitable for children of all ages.
TV-Y7—Suitable for children over age 7.
TV-G—General Audience—Mainly suitable for all ages.
TV-PG—May contain some material unsuitable for young children.
TV-14—May contain material unsuitable for children under 14.
TV-MA—Specifically designed for adults and unsuitable for children under 17.
The following ratings are appended to the above ratings to further clarify content.
S—Sexual content.
V—Violence.
L—Language.
D—Rough Dialogue.
FV—Fantasy Violence.

TOP MEDIA GROUPS

All figures in billions, unless otherwise noted.

	Revenue	Operating Cash Flow	Operating Income
Time Warner Inc.	24.620	5.412	2.728
The Walt Disney Co.	22.473	7.1	4.312
Viacom	13.2	1.7	752.8 (millions)
News Corp. Ltd.	12.8	1.401	1.8
Sony Corp.	15.609	2.02	1.565
Tele-Communications Inc.	7.570	2.975	685 (millions)

TOP CABLE MULTIPLE SYSTEMS OPERATORS

The top ten Multiple System Operators service 75% of the estimated 65.8 million cable subscribers.

Systems Operators	Subscribers (in millions)
Tele-Communications, Inc.	15.7
Time Warner Cable	12.6
MediaOne	4.9
Comcast Cable Comm., Inc.	4.3
Cox Communications	3.2
Cablevision Systems Corp.	2.8
Adelphia Communications.	1.9
Jones Intercable	1.4
Century Communications Corp.	1.3
Marcus Cable	1.2

BROADCAST, CABLE & SATELLITE STATISTICS

COMMERCIAL TELEVISION STATIONS

	VHF	UHF	TOTAL
1970	501	176	677
1980	516	218	734
1990	547	545	1,092
1991	547	551	1,098
1992	551	567	1,118
1993	552	585	1,137
1994	561	584	1,145
1995	562	599	1,163
1996	554	620	1,174
1997	558	619	1,177
1998	562	642	1,204

U.S. DIRECT TO HOME (DTH) SATELLITE SUBSCRIBERS

	TOTAL DTH	TOTAL DBS	C-BAND	DIRECTV	PRIMESTAR	ECHOSTAR	ALPHASTAR	USSB
1994	2,555,293	390,000	2,165,293	200,000	190,000	N/A	N/A	N/A
1995	4,335,376	1980000	2,355,376	1,100,000	880,000	N/A	N/A	N/A
1996	6,342,766	4,040,000	2,302,766	2,135,000	1,600,000	285,000	20,000	N/A
1997*	7,472,051	5,305,000	2,167,051	2,800,000	1,790,000	715,000	51,000	138,000

CABLE COMPARED TO SATELLITE

	Television Households	Cable Households	Satellite Households
1994	94,200,000	58,750,000	2,555,000
1995	95,400,000	60,460,000	4,335,000
1996	95,900,000	62,580,000	6,343,000
1997	97,000,000	64,800,000	7,342.000
1998	98,000,000	65,810,000	N/A

CONSUMER OWNERSHIP & SUBSCRIPTION STATISTICS

TELEVISION USAGE

	Total U.S. Households	TV Households	% with TV
1970	61,410,000	58,500,000	95.3
1980	77,900,000	76,300,000	97.9
1990	93,760,000	92,100,000	98.2
1991	94,800,000	93,100,000	98.2
1992	93,680,000	92,100,000	98.3
1993	94,710,000	93,100,000	98.3
1994	95,860,000	94,200,000	98.3
1995	97,060,000	95,400,000	98.3
1996	97,540,000	95,900,000	98.3
1997	99,666.000	97,000,000	98.4
1998	99,680,000	98,000,000	98.3

TELEVISION SETS

	In Home	Avg. # Sets Per Household	Avg. # Sets Per Multi-Set Household
1970	81,040,000	1.39	2.20
1980	128,190,000	1.68	2.36
1990	193,320,000	2.10	2.68
1991	193,200,000	2.08	2.67
1992	192,480,000	2.09	2.67
1993	200,565,000	2.15	2.72
1994	211,443,000	2.24	2.77
1995	217,067,000	2.28	2.80
1996	222,753,000	2.32	2.82
1997	228,740,000	2.36	2.84
1998	235,010,000	2.40	2.89

COLOR TV & MULTI-SET HOUSEHOLDS

	Color TV Households	%	Multi-Set Households	%
1970	20,910,000	35.7	18,840,000	32.2
1980	63,350,000	83.0	38,260,000	50.1
1985	77,660,000	93.2	48,220,000	56.8
1990	90,070,000	97.8	60,140,000	65.3
1991	91,300,000	98.3	60,040,000	64.5
1992	90,810,000	98.6	59,990,000	65.1
1993	91,520,000	98.3	62,560,000	67.2
1994	93,260,000	99.0	66,130,000	70.2
1995	94,446,000	99.0	67,639,000	70.9
1996	95,230,000	99.3	69,720,000	72.7
1997	95,510,000	99.5	71,780,000	74.0
1998	97,510,000	99.5	72,420,000	73.9

CABLE & VCR

	Cable Households	%	Pay Cable Households	%	VCR Households	%
1970	3,900,000	6.7	—	—	—	—
1980	15,200,000	19.9	5,200,000	6.8	840,000	1.1
1985	36,340,000	42.8	21,840,000	25.7	17,744,000	20.9
1990	51,900,000	56.4	27,120,000	29.4	63,181,000	68.6
1991	54,860,000	58.9	27,040,000	29.0	66,939,000	71.9
1992	55,490,000	60.2	25,990,000	28.2	69,075,000	75.0
1993	57,200,000	61.4	25,850,000	27.8	71,780,000	77.1
1994	58,750,000	62.4	26,070,000	27.7	74,420,000	79.0
1995	60,460,000	63.4	27,100,000	28.4	77,270,000	81.0
1996	62,580,000	65.3	30,360,000	31.7	78,830,000	82.2
1997	64,800,000	66.1	31,620,000	32.6	81,670,000	84.2
1998	65,810,000	67.2	34,090,000	34.8	82,910,000	84.6

VIEWING HABITS

TIME SPENT VIEWING

	1970	1980	1990	1993-94	1994-95	1995-96	1996-1997
Hours Viewing Television	5:56	6:36	6:53	7:16	7:17	7:11	7:12

PER-PERSON PER DAY ANNUAL AVERAGES

	1990	1991	1992	1993	1994	1995	1996	1997
Men	3:51	4:01	4:02	4:04	4:02	4:02	3:58	3:56
Women	4:28	4:36	4:40	4:41	4:39	4:38	4:34	4:33
Teens	3:15	3:16	3:10	3:07	3:05	3:02	2:49	2:54
Children	3:18	3:11	3:08	3:07	3:06	3:07	2:59	3:03

NETWORK TELEVISION COST TRENDS

DAYTIME (M-F)—AVERAGE PROGRAM

	# of Households Viewing Per Average Min.	Cost Per 30 Sec.	Cost Per 1000 Homes
1970	4,880,000	$4,000	$0.82
1975	5,550,000	5,200	0.94
1980	5,530,000	10,000	1.81
1985	5,460,000	14,700	2.69
1990	4,340,000	10,700	2.46
1991	4,350,000	10,400	2.39
1992	4,210,000	10,400	2.45
1993	4,420,000	11,100	2.50
1994	4,420,000	13,800	3.12
1995	3,890,000	12,900	3.32
1996	3,950,000	13,600	3.44
1997	3,830,000	14,800	3.85

NIGHTIME (M-S)—AVERAGE PROGRAM

	# of Households Viewing Per Average Min.	Cost Per 30 Sec.	Cost Per 1000 Homes
1970	11,430,000	$24,000	$2.10
1975	13,500,000	32,200	2.39
1980	15,240,000	57,900	3.79
1985	14,510,000	94,700	6.52
1990	12,540,000	122,200	9.74
1991	11,810,000	106,400	9.00
1992	12,020,000	93,700	7.79
1993	11,070,000	92,700	8.37
1994	12,710,000	97,200	7.64
1995	10,860,000	95,500	8.79
1996	9,940,000	101,400	10.20
1997	9,530,000	106,500	11.18

EARLY EVENING NEWS (M-F)—AVERAGE PROGRAM

	# of Households Viewing Per Average Min.	Cost Per 30 Sec.	Cost Per 1000 Homes
1975	9,790,000	$12,400	$1.27
1980	11,490,000	25,700	2.23
1985	10,870,000	42,800	3.94
1990	9,570,000	51,800	5.41
1991	10,180,000	47,400	4.65
1992	9,420,000	43,400	4.61
1993	9,870,000	46,300	4.69
1994	10,600,000	47,200	4.45
1995	8,670,000	49,600	5.72
1996	8,680,000	46,000	5.30
1997	8,390,000	46,600	5.55

LATE EVENING (M-F)—AVERAGE PROGRAM

	# of Households Viewing Per Average Min.	Cost Per 30 Sec.	Cost Per 1000 Homes
1975	5,170,000	$8,300	$1.61
1980	4,420,000	11,900	2.70
1985	4,260,000	14,700	3.45
1990	3,080,000	21,500	6.97
1991	2,970,000	16,500	5.57
1992	2,780,000	13,200	4.75
1993	2,970,000	15,800	5.31
1994	4,230,000	24,100	5.70
1995	3,660,000	23,600	6.43
1996	3,370,000	26,700	7.93
1997	3,270,000	24,500	7.48

Sources: A.C. Nielsen, TV Bureau of Advertising, FCC, MPAA.

1998-1999 PRIME TIME PROGRAMS

ABC-TV

Series Title	Day	Hr.	Mins.	Supplier	Production Principals	Cast Regulars & Semi-Regulars
ABC Thursday Night Movie	Thu	9:00	120	Various	Various	Various
America's Funniest	Sat	8:00	60	Vin di Bona Productions		Daisy Fuentes, John Fugelsang
Boy Meets World	Fri	8:30	30	Michael Jacobs/ Touchstone	Michael Jacobs, Bob Tischler, Karen MacCain, Jeff Menell, Bob Nelson	Ben Savage,Danielle Fishel, Rider Strong, Will Friedle, Matthew Lawrence, William Russ, Betsy Randle, Lindsay Ridgeway, William Daniels
Brother's Keeper	Fri	9:30	30	Studios USA	Jonathan Axelrod, James Widdoes and Donald Todd	William Ragsdale, Justin Cooper, Sean O'Bryan, Bess Meyer
Cupid	Sat	10:00	60	Mandalay/ Columbia Tristar	Scott Winant, Joe Voci, Scott Sanders	Jeremy Piven, Paula Marshall, Jeffrey D. Sams
Dharma & Greg	Wed	8:00	30	Chuck Lorre/ 20th Century Fox TV	Chuck Lorre, Dottie Dartland, Erwin More, Brian Medavoy	Jenna Elfman, Thomas Gibson
The Drew Carey Show	Wed	9:00	30	Warner Bros. TV	Bruce Helford, Clay Graham	Drew Carey, Ryan Stiles, Christa Miller, Diedrich Bader.
Fantasy Island	Sat	9:00	60	Columbia TriStar	Barry Sonnenfeld, Barry Josephson	Malcolm McDowell, Louis Lombardi, Edward Hibbert, Madchen Amick, Fyvush Finkel, Sylvia Sydney
Home Improvement	Tue	8:00	30	Disney	Carmen Finestra, David McFadzean and Matt Williams	Tim Allen, Patricia Richardson, Earl Hindman, Zachery Ty Bryan, Jonathan Taylor Thomas
The Hughleys	Tue	8:30	30	Greenblatt-Janollari	Chris Rock, Robert Greenblatt, David Janollari, Matt Wickline	D. L. Hughley, Elise Neal, Ashley Monique Clark, Dee Jay Daniels, Eric Allan Kramer, Marietta Deprima, John Henton
Monday Night Football	Mon	8:00	180	ABC Sports		Boomer Esiason, Al Michaels, Dan Dierdorf
NYPD Blue	Tue	10:00	60	Steven Bochco Prods.	Steven Bochco, David Milch, Mark Tinker, Mike Robin	Dennis Franz, Jimmy Smits, James McDaniel, Gail O'Grady, Kim Delaney, Nicholas Turturro, Sharon Lawrence
The Practice	Sun	10:00	60	20th Century Fox	David E. Kelley	Dylan McDermott, Lara Flynn Boyle, Michael Badalucco, Lisa Gay Hamilton, Camryn Manheim
Sabrina, The Teenage Witch	Fri	9:00	30	Viacom Prods.	Paula Hart, Nell Scovell	Melissa Joan Hart, Beth Broderick, Caroline Rhea, Nate Richert
The Secret Lives of Men	Wed	9:30	30	Witt-Thomas-Harris	Paul Junger Witt, Susan Harris, Tony Thomas, Nina Wass	Peter Gallagher, Brad Whitford, Mitch Rouse, Sofia Milos
Spin City	Tue	9:00	30	UBU Prods./Dreamworks	Gary David Goldberg	Michael J. Fox, Richard Kind, Barry Bostwick, Connie Britton
Sports Night	Tue	9:30	30	Imagine/Touchstone	Brian Grazer, Ron Howard, Tony Krantz, Aaron Sorkin, Rob Scheidlinger	Peter Krause, Felicity Huffman, Josh Charles, Joshua Malina, Sabrina Lloyd, Robert Guillaume
20/20	Sun	9:00	60	ABC News		Barbara Walters, Hugh Downs, Sam Donaldson, Diane Sawyer David Stossel, Connie Chung
	Wed	10:00	60			
	Fri	10:00	60			
Two Guys, a Girl and a Pizza Place	Wed	8:30	30	Infront Prods./ 20th Century	Danny Jacobson, Marjorie Weitzman	Traylor Howard, Ryan Reynolds, Richard Ruccolo, Jennifer Westfeldt
Two of A Kind	Fri	8:00	30	Warner Bros.	Tom Miller, Bob Boyett, Michael Warren, Howard Adler, Bob Griffard	Mary Kate Olsen, Ashley Olsen, Orlando Brown
Vengeance Unlimited	Thu	8:00	60	Warner Bros.	John McNamara, David Simkins James Frawley	Michael Madsen, Kathleen York
The Wonderful World of Disney	Sun	7:00	120	Disney/Jacobs Prod.	Various	Various

CBS-TV

Series Title	Day	Hr.	Mins.	Supplier	Production Principals	Cast Regulars & Semi-Regulars
The Benben Show	Mon	9:30	30	Warner Bros./CBS	Brian Benben, Robert Borden	Brian Benben, Charles Esten, Lisa Thornhill, Wendell Pierce, Luis Ramos
Buddy Faro	Fri	9:00	60	Spelling	Mark Frost, Charles Haid	Dennis Farina, Frank Whaley, Allison Smith
Candid Camera	Fri	8:30	30	Candid Camera Prod./CBS		Peter Funt, Suzanne Somers
CBS Sunday Night Movie	Sun	9:00	120	Various	Various	Various
CBS Tuesday Night Movie	Tue	9:00	120	Various	Various	Various
Chicago Hope	Wed.	10:00	60	Twentieth Television David E. Kelley Prods.	John Tinker, Bill D'Elia	Adam Arkin, Christine Lahti, Roxanne Hart, Mark Harmon, Hector Elizondo, Peter Berg.
Cosby	Mon	8:00	30	Carsey-Werner Prods./LLC/Bill Cosby	Dr. Wiliam H. Cosby, Marcy Carsey, Tom Werner, Caryn Mandabach, Peter Tortorici	Bill Cosby, Phylicia Rashad, Doug E. Doug
Diagnosis Murder	Thu	9:00	60	Fred Silverman Co./Dean Hargrove Prods./Viacom	Fred Silverman, Dean Hargrove, Dick van Dyke, Tom Chehak	Dick van Dyke, Charlie Schlatter, Barry Van Dyke, Victoria Powell, Michael Tucci
Early Edition	Sat	8:00	60	Columbia TriStar/CBS	Bob Brush, Dean Hargrove	Kyle Chandler, Shanesia Davis Williams, Fisher Stevens
Everybody Loves Raymond	Mon	9:00	30	Worldwide Pants/HBO Independent Prods.	Phil Rosenthal, Stu Smiley	Ray Romano, Patricia Heaton, Doris Roberts, Peter Boyle, Brad Garrett
48 Hours	Thu	10:00	60	CBS News	Susan Virinksy	Dan Rather, Harold Dow, Phil Jones, Erin Moriarty, Richard Schlesinger
JAG	Tue	8:00	60	Belisarius/Paramount	Donald Bellisario	David James Elliott, Catherine Bell, Patrick Labyorteaux, John M. Jackson
Kids Say the Darndest Things	Fri	8:00	30	LMNO Prod./CBS	Eric Schotz	Bill Cosby
King of Queens	Mon	8:30	30	Columbia TriStar/CBS	Michael Weithorn	Kevin James, Leah Remini, Jerry Stiller, Lisa Rieffel
L.A. Docs	Mon	10:00	60	Columbia TriStar/CBS	John Lee Hancock,	Ken Olin, Matt Craven, Rick Roberts Mark Johnson, Sheryl Lee
Maggie Winters	Wed	8:30	30	Greenblatt-Janollari/CBS	Bob Greenblatt, David Janollari, Kari Lizer	Faith Ford, Jenny Robertson, Alex Kapp, Vincent Ventresca, Brian Haley, Shirley Knight
Martial Law	Sat	9:00	60	Twentieth Television/CBS	Carlton Cuse, Stanley Tong, Andre Morgan	Sammo Hung
The Nanny	Wed	8:00	30	Columbia TriStar/Sternin/Fraser Ink	Robert Sternin, Prudence Fraser, Peter Marc Jacobsen	Fran Drescher, Charles Shaughnessy, Lauren Lane, Nicholle Tom, Madeline Zima
Nash Bridges	Fri	10:00	60	Rysher Entertainment	Carlton Cuse, Don Johnson	Don Johnson, Cheech Marin
Promised Land	Thu	8:00	60	CBS & Moonwater Prods.	Martha Williamson	Gerald McRaney, Wendy Phillips, Celeste Holm, Austin O'Brien Sarah Schuab, Eddie Karr
60 Minutes	Sun	7:00	60	CBS News	Don Hewitt	Mike Wallace, Morley Safer, Ed Bradley, Steve Kroft, Lesley Stahl, Andy Rooney
To Have and to Hold	Wed	9:00	60	Greenblatt-Janollari/CBS	Bob Greenblatt, David Janollari, Scott Shepherd	Moira Kelly, Jason Beghe, Stephen Largay, Jason Wiles, Steven Lee, Finola Flanagan, John Cullum
Touched by an Angel	Sun	8:00	60	CBS & Moonwater Prods.	Martha Williamson	Della Reese, Roma Downey, John Dye
Walker, Texas Ranger	Sat	10:00	60	Amadea Film Prods./CBS	Chuck Norris, Aaron Norris	Chuck Norris, Clarence Gilyard, Sheree J. Wilson, Floyd Red Crow Westerman

Fox

Series Title	Day	Hr.	Mins.	Supplier	Production Principals	Cast Regulars & Semi-Regulars
Ally McBeal	Mon	9:00	60	20th Century Fox TV/ David E. Kelley Prods.	David E. Kelley	Calista Flockhart, Gil Bellows, Greg Germann
America's Most Wanted: America Fights Back	Sat	9:00	60	STF Prods./Twentieth Television	Lance Heflin	John Walsh
Beverly Hills 90210	Wed	8:00	60	Spelling TV	Aaron Spelling, E. Duke Vincent, Paul Waigner, Steve Wasserman, Jessica Kelin, Larry Molin	Jason Priestley, Jennie Garth, Ian Ziering, Brian Austin Green, Tori Spelling, Tiffani-Amber Thiessen
Brimstone	Tue	9:00	60	Warner Bros. TV	Chad Hoffman, Cyrus Voris, Ethan Reiff	Peter Horton
Cops	Sat	8:00	60	Foxlab/Barbour/Langley	John Langley	Various
Costello	Tue	8:30	30	Wind Dancer/Touchstone	C. Finestra, D. McFadzean, M. Williams, S. Costello, C. Holliday	Sue Costello, Dan Lauria
Getting Personal	Fri	8:30	30	20th Century	Jeff Greenstein, Jeff Strauss	John Cryer, Vivica A. Fox, Duane Martin, Elliott Gould, Nancy Cassaro, Reggie Hayes
Holding the Baby	Sun	7:30	30	20th C./Granada TV	Howard Morris	Jon Patrick Walker, Jennifer Westfeldt, Rom Leibman
Hollyweird	Thu	9:00	60	USA Network	Shaun Cassidy, Wes Craven,	
King of the Hill	Tue	8:00	30	20th Century	Howard Klein, Mark McJimsy, Brent Forrester	Mike Judge, Kathy Najimy, Pamela Segall, Ashley Gardner
Living in Captivity	Fri	8:00	30	Shukovsky-English Ent.	Tom Palmer	Dondre Whitfield, Kira Arne, Lenny Venito, Mia Kotet
Melrose Place	Mon	8:00	60	Spelling TV	Aaron Spelling, Frank South, E. Duke Vincent, Charles Pratt	Josie Bissett, Thomas Calabro, Heather Locklear, Marcia Cross, Grant Show, Andrew Shue
Millenium	Fri	9:00	60	20th Century Fox TV	Chris Carter, Jorge Zamacona, John P. Kousakis	Lance Henriksen, Megan Gallagher, Bill Smitrovich
Party of Five	Wed	9:00	60	Columbia TriStar	Amy Lippman, Christopher Keyser, Ken Topolsky	Matthew Fox, Neve Campbell, Scott Wolf, Lacey Chabert, Taylor Porter, Paula Devicq
The Simpsons	Sun	8:00	30	Gracie Films/Twentieth TV	James L. Brooks, Matt Groening, Bill Oakley	Dan Castellaneta, Julie Kavner, Nancy Cartwright, Harry Shearer
That 70's Show	Sun	8:30	30	Carsey-Werner	Tom Werner, Marcy Carsey, Bonnie Turner, Mark Brazill	Topher Grace, Mila Kunis, Ashton Kutcher, Danny Masterson
World's Funniest	Sun	7:00	30	Brad Lachman Prod.		Various
World's Wildest Police Videos	Thu	8:00	60	20th Century Fox TV		Various
The X-Files	Sun	9:00	60	Twentieth TV	Chris Carter, R.W. Goodwin, Howard Gordon	David Duchovny, Gillian Anderson

NBC-TV

Series Title	Day	Hr.	Mins.	Supplier	Production Principals	Cast Regulars & Semi-Regulars
All My Life	Thu	8:30	30	Bright/Kauffman/Crane Warner Bros.	Kevin S. Bright, Marta Kauffman David Krane	Christina Applegate, George Dzundza, Rafer Weigel, Eric Lloyd, John Lehr, Jennifer Milmore
Caroline in the City	Mon	9:00	30	CBS Productions/ Barron/Pennette	Fred Barron, Marco Pennette,	Lea Thompson, Eric Lutes, Amy Pietz, Dotti Dartland, Malcomb Gets
Conrad Bloom	Mon	8:30	30	NBC Studios	Marco Penette, Pamela Putch	Mark Feuerstein, Linda Lavin, Paula Newsome, Jenica Bergere, Steve Landesberg
Dateline NBC	Mon	10:00	60	NBC News	Neal Shapiro	Jane Pauley, Stone Phillips, Jon Scott, Deborah Roberts
	Tue	10:00	60			
	Wed	8:00	60			
	Fri	9:00	60			
	Sun	7:00	60			
Encore! Encore!	Tue	8:30	30	Paramount	Peter Casey	Nathan Lane, Joan Plowright, Molly Price, Ernie Sabella

ER	Thu	10:00	60	Warner Bros./Amblin	Michael Crichton, John Wells, Lydia Woodard, Carol Flint	Anthony Edwards, George Clooney, Gloria Reuben, Noah Wyle, Eriq La Salle, Julianna Margulies
Frasier	Thu	9:00	30	Grub Street Prods./ Paramount TV	David Angell, Peter Casey, David Lee, Christopher Lloyd	Kelsey Grammer, John Mahoney, David Hyde Pierce, Peri Gilpin, Jane Leeves
Friends	Thu	8:00	30	Bright-Kauffman-Crane Prods./Warner Bros. TV	Kevin S. Bright, Marta Kauffman, David Crane, Michael Borkow	Jennifer Aniston, Courteney Cox, Lisa Kudrow, Matt LeBlanc, Matthew Perry, David Schwimmer
Homicide: Life on the Streets	Fri	10:00	60	NBC Prods./Baltimore Pictures/Fatima Prods./ MCEG Sterling Inc.	Barry Levinson, Tom Fontana	Richard Belzer, Andre Braugher, Clark Johnson, Yaphett Kotto, Kyle Secor, Melissa Leo, Reed Diamond
Just Shoot Me	Tue	9:00	30	Brillstein-Grey Comms.	Bernie Brillstein, Brad Grey	Laura San Giacomo, George Segal, David Spade, Wendie Malick
Law & Order	Wed	10:00	60	Wolf Films/Studios USA	Dick Wolf, Rene Balcer, Ed Sherin	Jerry Orbach, Sam Waterston, S. Epatha Merkerson, Benjamin Bratt
Mad About You	Tue	8:00	30	Columbia Tristar	Danny Jacobson, Larry Charles, Paul Reiser, Richard Day	Paul Reiser, Helen Hunt, Anne Elizabeth Ramsay, Leila Kenzle, John Pankow
NBC Sunday Night Movie	Sun	9:00	120	Various	Various	Various
NewsRadio	Wed	9:30	30	Brillstein-Grey Comm.	Paul Simms, Brad Grey, Bernie Brillstein	Dave Foley, Vicki Lewis, Phil Hartman, Stephen Root, Andy Dick, Maura Tierney, Khandi Alexander
The Pretender	Sat	9:00	60	20th/NBC Studios	Steven Long Mitchell, Tommy Thompson, Craig Van Sickle	Michael T. Weiss, Andrea Parker, Patrick Bauchau
Profiler	Sat	10:00	60	NBC Studios	Ian Sander, Kim Moses, Nancy Miller	Ally Walker, Robet Davi
Suddenly Susan	Mon	8:00	30	Warner Bros. TV	Gary Dontzig, Steven Peterman	Brooke Shields, Judd Nelson, Kathy Griffin, Nestor Carbonell, David Strickland, Barbara Barrie
3rd Rock From the Sun	Wed	9:00	30	Carsey-Werner Prods.	Terrie Turner, Bonnie Turner	John Lithgow, Jane Curtin, French Stewart, Kristen Johnston, Joseph Gordon Levitt
Trinity	Fri	8:00	60	Warner Bros.	John Wells	Tate Donovan, Charlotte Ross, Justin Louis, Sam Trammell, Bonnie Root, Kim Raver, Alicia Coppola
Veronica's Closet	Thu	9:30	30	Warner Bros.	Kevin S. Bright, Marta Kauffman, David Crane	Kirstie Alley, Dan Cortese, Kathy Najimy, Ron Silver, Wallace Langham
Will & Grace	Mond	9:30	30	NBC Studios	Max Mutchnick, Dave Kahan	Eric McCormack, Debra Messing, Megan Mullally, Sean P. Hayes
Wind on Water	Sat	8:00	60	NBC Studios	Zalman King, Charles Rosen, Stuart Sheslow	Bo Derek, Lee Horsley, William Gregory Lee, Brian Gross, Shawn Christian, Jacinda Barrett, Matthew Stephen Liu, Matt George
Working	Tue	9:30	30	NBC Studios	Michael Davidoff, Bill Rosenthal	Fred Savage, Maurice Godin, Sarah Knowlton, Arden Myrin

UPN

Series Title	Day	Hr.	Mins.	Supplier	Production Principals	Cast Regulars & Semi-Regulars
Clueless	Tue	8:30	30	Paramount Network TV	Amy Heckerling, Tim O'Donnell	Rachel Blanchard, Stacey Dash, Michael Lerner
DiResta	Mon	8:30	30	Paramount TV	Matt Goldman, Sean O'Brien	John DiResta, Leila Kenzle
Guys Like Us	Mon	8:00	30	Columbia TriStar	David W. Duclon, Dan Schnieder	Maestro Harrell, Bumper Robinson, Chris Hardwick
Legacy	Fri	8:00	60	Atlantis Comm.	Chris Abbott, Joel Blasberg	Brett Cullen, Jeremy Garrett,
Love Boat: The Next Wave	Fri	9:00	60	Spelling	Aaron Spelling, E. Duke Vincent	Robert Urich, Corey Parker, Phil Morris, Stacey Travis
Malcolm & Eddie	Mon	9:30	30	Columbia TriStar	Kim Weiskopf, Joel Madison	Malcolm-Jamal Warner, Eddie Griffin
Mercy Point	Tue	9:00	60	Columbia Tristar/Mandalay	Joe Vocci, Scott Sanders	Joe Morton, Maria Del Mar, Alexandra Wilson
Moesha	Tue	8:00	30	Big Ticket TV	Ralph Farquhar, Sara V. Finney, Vida Spears	Brandy Norwood, William Allen, Young, Marcus T. Paulk

Secret Diaries of Desmond Pfeiffer	Mon	9:00	30	Paramount TV	Mort Nathan, Barry Fanaro	Chi McBride, Max Baker, Dann Florek
Seven Days	Wed	8:00	60	Paramount TV	Chris Crowe	Jonathan LaPaglia
Star Trek: Voyager	Wed	9:00	60	Paramount TV	Rick Berman, Jeri Taylor	Kate Mulgrew, Robert Beltran, Roxann Dawson, Jennifer Lien, Robert Duncan McNeill
Way Out There Movie	Thu	8:00	120	Various	Various	Various

WB

Series Title	Day	Hr.	Mins.	Supplier	Production Principals	Cast Regulars & Semi-Regulars
The Army Show	Sun	9:30	30	Castle Rock	J.J. Wall	John Sencio, Harry Sylvester
Buffy the Vampire Slayer	Tue	8:00	60	20th Century Fox	Joss Whedon	Sarah Michelle Gellar, Anthony Stewart Head, Nicholas Brendon
Charmed	Wed	9:00	60	Spelling Ent.	Constance M. Burge	Shannon Doherty
Dawson's Creek	Wed	8:00	60	Columbia TriStar TV	Kevin Williamson	James Van Der Beek, Katie Holmes, Michelle Williams, Joshua Jackson
Felicity	Tue	9:00	60	Imagine/Touchstone	Ron Howard, T. Krantz, J. Abrams, M. Reeves	Keri Russell
For Your Love	Thu	9:00	30	Warner Bros. TV	Yvette Lee Bowser	Holly Robinson Peete
Hyperion Bay	Mon	9:00	60	Warner Bros. TV	Joseph Dougherty	Mark Paul Gosselaar, Dylan Neal, Sydney Penny
The Jamie Foxx Show	Thu	8:30	30	Warner Bros. TV	Bentley Evans, Marcus King	Jami Foxx, Garret Morris
Seventh Heaven	Sun Mon	7:00 8:00	60 60	Aaron Spelling	Aaron Spelling, E. Duke Vincent, Brenda Hampton	Stephen Collins, David Gallagher, Catherine Hicks, Barry Watson
Sister, Sister	Sun	8:00	30	Paramount Network TV & dePasse Entertainment	Suzanne de Passe, Brian Pollack, Suzanne Coston, Mert Rich	Tim Reid, Jackee Harry, Tia Mowry, Tamera Mowry, Marques Houston
Smart Guy	Sun	8:30	30	Walt Disney TV	Suzanne de Passe	Taj Mowry
The Steve Harvey Show	Thu	9:30	30	WB TV & Brillstein-Grey Comm.	Bernie Brillstein, Brad Grey,	Steve Harvey, Cedric the Entertainer
Unhappily Ever After	Sun	9:00	30	Touchstone	Ron Leavitt, Arthur Silver, Marcy Vosburgh, David Caplan	Geoff Pierson, Stephanie Hodge, Kevin Connolly, Nikki Cox
The Wayans Bros.	Thu	8:00	30	Warner Bros. TV	Phil Kelard, Tom Moore, Josh Goldstein, Eric Gould	Shawn Wayans, Marlon Wayans, John Witherspoon

EMMY AWARDS

The Academy of Television Arts & Sciences awards Primetime Emmys. The National Academy of Television Arts & Sciences awards the Daytime Emmys. Listings for both can be found under Television Organizations. Programs are listed in bold face or in quotes; episodes are in italics.

1997-98 PRIMETIME ACADEMY AWARDS

OUTSTANDING COMEDY SERIES
Frasier, Grub Street Prods. in association with Paramount Network Television. NBC.

OUTSTANDING DRAMA SERIES
The Practice, David E. Kelley Productions in association with Twentieth Century Fox. ABC.

OUTSTANDING MINISERIES
From the Earth to the Moon, Programming in association with Imagine Entertainment and Clavius Base. HBO.

OUTSTANDING MADE FOR TELEVISION MOVIE
Don King: Only in America, Thomas Carter Co Productions in association with HBO Pictures. HBO.

OUTSTANDING VARIETY, MUSIC OR COMEDY SPECIAL
The 1997 Tony Awards, A Tony Award Production. CBS.

OUTSTANDING VARIETY, MUSIC OR COMEDY SERIES
Late Show With David Letterman, Worldwide Pants Inc. CBS.

OUTSTANDING PERFORMANCE IN A VARIETY OR MUSIC PROGRAM
Billy Crystal, "The 70th Annual Academy Awards." ABC

OUTSTANDING ANIMATED PROGRAM (FOR PROGRAMMING ONE HOUR OR LESS)
The Simpsons, *(Trash of the Titans)*. Gracie Films in association with 20th Television Fox.

OUTSTANDING LEAD ACTRESS IN A COMEDY SERIES
Helen Hunt, "Mad About You." In Front Productions and Nuance Productions in association with TriStar Television. NBC.

OUTSTANDING LEAD ACTOR IN A COMEDY SERIES
Kelsey Grammer, "Frasier." Grub Street Productions in association with Paramount. NBC.

OUTSTANDING LEAD ACTRESS IN A DRAMA SERIES
Christine Lahti, "Chicago Hope." David E. Kelley Productions in association with Century Fox Television CBS.

OUTSTANDING LEAD ACTOR IN A DRAMA SERIES
Andre Braugher, "Homicide." NBC Studios in association with Baltimore Pictures and Fatima Productions. NBC.

OUTSTANDING LEAD ACTRESS IN A MINISERIES OR SPECIAL
Ellen Barkin, "Before Women Had Wings." Harpo Films Inc. ABC.

OUTSTANDING LEAD ACTOR IN A MINISERIES OR SPECIAL
Gary Sinise, "George Wallace." A Mark Carliner Production TNT.

OUTSTANDING SUPPORTING ACTRESS IN A COMEDY SERIES
Lisa Kudrow, "Friends." Bright/Kauffman/Crane Productions in association with Warner Bros Television. NBC.

OUTSTANDING SUPPORTING ACTOR IN A COMEDY SERIES
David Hyde Pierce, "Frasier." Grub Street Productions in association with Paramount. NBC.

OUTSTANDING SUPPORTING ACTRESS IN A DRAMA SERIES
Camryn Manheim, "The Practice." David E. Kelley Productions in association with Twentieth Century Fox. ABC.

OUTSTANDING SUPPORTING ACTOR IN A DRAMA SERIES
Gordon Clapp, "NYPD Blue." Steven Bochco Productions. ABC.

OUTSTANDING SUPPORTING ACTRESS IN A MINISERIES OR SPECIAL
Mare Winningham, "George Wallace." A Mark Carliner Production. TNT.

OUTSTANDING SUPPORTING ACTOR IN A MINISERIES OR A SPECIAL
George C Scott, "12 Angry Men." MGM Worldwide Television Showtime.

OUTSTANDING GUEST ACTRESS IN A COMEDY SERIES
Carol Burnett, "Mad About You." In Front Productions and Nuance Productions in association with TriStar Television. NBC.

OUTSTANDING GUEST ACTOR IN A COMEDY SERIES
Mel Brooks, "Mad About You." In Front Productions and Nuance Productions in association with TriStar Television. NBC.

OUTSTANDING GUEST ACTRESS IN A DRAMA SERIES
Cloris Leachman, "Promised Land." CBS Productions in association with Moonwater Productions. CBS.

OUTSTANDING GUEST ACTOR IN A DRAMA SERIES
John Larroquette, "The Practice." David E Kelley in association with Twentieth Century Fox. ABC.

OUTSTANDING ACHIEVEMENT IN DIRECTING FOR A DRAMA SERIES (TIE)
Mark Tinker, "Brooklyn South" *(Pilot)*. Steven Bochco Productions. CBS.
Paris Barclay "NYPD" *(Lost Israel Part 2)*. Steven Bochco Productions. ABC.

OUTSTANDING ACHIEVEMENT IN DIRECTING FOR A COMEDY SERIES
Todd Holland, "The Larry Sanders Show." Brillstein/Grey Entertainment, Partners with Boundaries Productions. HBO.

OUTSTANDING ACHIEVEMENT IN DIRECTING FOR A MINISERIES OR A SPECIAL
John Frankenheimer, "George Wallace." A Mark Carliner Production. TNT.

OUTSTANDING ACHIEVEMENT IN DIRECTING FOR A VARIETY OR MUSIC PROGRAM
Louis J Horvitz, "The 70th Annual Academy Awards." Academy of Motion Pictures Arts & Sciences. ABC.

OUTSTANDING ACHIEVEMENT IN WRITING FOR A COMEDY SERIES
Peter Tolan, Gary Shandling, "The Larry Sanders Show." (FLIP) Brillstein/Grey Entertainment, Partners with Boundaries Productions. HBO.

OUTSTANDING ACHIEVEMENT IN WRITING FOR A DRAMA SERIES
Nicholas Wooton, David Milch, Bill Clark, "NYPD" *(Lost Israel, Part 2)*. Steven Bochco Productions. ABC.

OUTSTANDING ACHIEVEMENT IN WRITING FOR A MINISERIES OR A SPECIAL
Kario Salem, "Don King: Only in America." A Thomas Carter Co Production in association with HBO Pictures. HBO

OUTSTANDING ACHIEVEMENT IN WRITING FOR A VARIETY OR MUSIC PROGRAM
Eddie Feldmann, Dennis Miller, David Feldman, Leah Krinsky, Jim Hanna, David Weiss, Jose Arroyo, "Dennis Miller Live." Happy Family Productions. HBO.

OUTSTANDING ACHIEVEMENT IN COSTUME DESIGN FOR A SERIES
Dan Moore, "The Magnificent Seven" *(Working Girls)*. Trilogy Entertainment. CBS.

OUTSTANDING ACHIEVEMENT IN COSTUME DESIGN FOR A MINISERIES OR A SPECIAL
Ann Hollowood, "Merlin" *(Part 1)*. Hallmark Entertainment. NBC.

OUTSTANDING ACHIEVEMENT IN COSTUME DESIGN FOR A VARIETY OR MUSIC PROGRAM
Jane Ruhm, "Tracey Takes On...," Takes On Productions, Inc. HBO.

OUTSTANDING ACHIEVEMENT IN COSTUMING FOR A SERIES
LuEllyn Harper, "Newsradio." Brillstein-Grey Communications. NBC.

OUTSTANDING INDIVIDUAL ACHIEVEMENT IN COSTUMING FOR A MINISERIES OR SPECIAL
Amy Stofsky, "The Pentagon Wars." A Howard Meltze/Entertainment Group Production in association with Jersey Films and HBO NYC. HBO.

OUTSTANDING ACHIEVEMENT IN MAIN TITLE DESIGN
Kasumi Mihori, Billy Pittard, Ed Sullivan, Title Designers, "The Wonderful World of Disney." Walt Disney Television. ABC.

OUTSTANDING ACHIEVEMENT IN MAKEUP FOR A SERIES
Todd A. McIntosh, John Vulich, John Maldonado, John Wheaton, Gerald Quist, Margi Latinopoulos, Dayne Johnson, Alan Friedman, Craig Reardon, Michael Blake, Robin Beauchesne, Brigette Myre-Ellis, Mark Shostrom, "Buffy the Vampire Slayer." (Surprise/Innocence) Mutant Enemy/Kuzui Enterprises/Sanddollar Productions in association with Twentieth Century Fox TV. WB.

OUTSTANDING ACHIEVEMENT IN MAKEUP FOR A MINISERIES OR SPECIAL
Aileen Seaton, Mark Coulier, "Merlin." Hallmark Entertainment. NBC.

OUTSTANDING ACHIEVEMENT IN HAIRSTYLING FOR A SERIES
Audree Futterman, "Tracey takes On...," Takes on Productions Inc. HBO.

OUTSTANDING ACHIEVEMENT IN HAIRSTYLING FOR A MINISERIES, MOVIE OR A SPECIAL
Vicky Phillips, Lynda Gurasich, "From the Earth to the Moon." HBO Programming in association with Imagine Entertainment and Clavius Base. HBO.

OUTSTANDING ACHIEVEMENT IN CASTING FOR A SERIES
Lou Digiaimo, Pat Moran C.S.A., Brett Goldstein, Casting Executives, "Homicide: Life on the Streets."NBC Studios in association with Baltimore Pictures and Fatima Productions. NBC.

OUTSTANDING ACHIEVEMENT IN CASTING FOR A MINISERIES OR A SPECIAL
Meg Liberman, C.S.A, Marc Hirschfeld, C.S.A, Sharon Klein, Mark Fincannon, Lisa Mae Wells Fincannon, Craig Fincannon, Casting Executives, Deborah Brown, Casting Executive NY, "From the Earth to the Moon." HBO Programming in association with Imagine Entertainment and Clavius Base. HBO.

OUTSTANDING ACHIEVEMENT IN SPECIAL VISUAL EFFECTS FOR A SERIES
Pedro Pires, "Yo-Yo Ma Inspired By Bach" (The Sound of the Carceri). Rhombus Media Production in co-production with TVOntario, Thirteen/WNET in NY, BBC Television. PBS.

OUTSTANDING ACHIEVEMENT IN SPECIAL VISUAL EFFECTS FOR A MINISERIES OR A MOVIE
Tim Webber, Stefan Lange, Matthew Cope, Richard Conway, Tim Greenwood, George Roper, Murray Bytler, Angus Wilson, Pedro Sabrosa, William Bartlett, Avtar Bains, "Merlin" (Part 1). Hallmark Entertainment. NBC.

OUTSTANDING ACHIEVEMENT IN SOUND EDITING FOR A SERIES
Walter Newman, Darren Wright, Rick Camera, Darleen Stoker-Kageyama, Cathy Flynn-Morris, Tom Harris, Michael D Ditrick, Casey Crabtree, James Bailey, Foley Artist, "ER" (Exodus). Constant c Productions, Amblin Television in association with Warner Bros Television. NBC

OUTSTANDING ACHIEVEMENT IN SOUND EDITING FOR A MINISERIES OR A SPECIAL
Michael Graham, Greg Schorer, Kristi Johns, Suzanne Angel, Bill Bell, Mark Friedgen, Bob Costanza, Rob Webber, Gary Macheel, rick Steele, Lou Thomas, Adriane Marfiak, Anton Holden, Michael Lyle, David Eichhorn, Mark Steele, Tim Terusa, Rusty Tinsley, Kim Naves, Tim Chilton, Jill Schachne, Foley Artist, "Rough Riders" (Part 2). An Affinity Entertainment, Esparza/Katz Production in association with Larry Levinson Productions. TNT.

OUTSTANDING ACHIEVEMENT IN SOUND MIXING FOR A DRAMA SERIES
Russell Fager, Rusty Russell Smith, William Freesh, "Chicago Hope" (Brian Salad Surgery). David E. Kelley Productions in association with 20 Century Fox Television. CBS.

OUTSTANDING ACHIEVEMENT IN SOUND MIXING FOR A VARIETY OR MUSIC SERIES OR A SPECIAL
Edward J. Greene, Tom Vicari, Robert Douglass Patrick Baltzell, "The 70th Annual Academy Awards." Academy of Motion Picture Arts & Sciences. ABC.

OUTSTANDING ACHIEVEMENT IN SOUND MIXING FOR A COMEDY SERIES OR A SPECIAL
Paul Lewis, Nello Torri, Kurt Kassulke, Peter R. Kelsey, "Ally McBeal" (Boy to the World). David E. Kelley Productions in association with 20th Century Fox Television. FOX.

OUTSTANDING ACHIEVEMENT IN SOUND MIXING FOR A DRAMA MINISERIES OR SPECIAL
Russell Williams II, David E. Fluhr, Adam Jenkins, "12 Angry Men." MGM Worldwide Television. Showtime.

OUTSTANDING ACHIEVEMENT IN MUSIC COMPOSITION FOR A SERIES
Christopher Beck, "Buffy the Vampire Slayer" (Becoming — Part 1). A Mutant Enemy Inc/Kuzui Enterprises/Sanddollar Productions in association with 20th Century Fox Television WB.

OUTSTANDING ACHIEVEMENT IN MUSIC COMPOSITION FOR A MINISERIES OR A MOVIE
Bruce Broughton, "Glory & Honor." American Filmworks Inc in association with TNT. TNT.

OUTSTANDING ACHIEVEMENT IN MAIN TITLE THEME MUSIC
Maribeth Derry, Tom Snow, Robbie Buchanan, Richard Barton Lewis, "Fame LA," Syndicated Trilogy Entertainment Group. Syndicated.

OUTSTANDING ACHIEVEMENT IN MUSIC DIRECTION
Bill Conti, "The 70th Annual Academy Award." Academy of Motion Pictures Arts & Sciences. ABC.

OUTSTANDING ACHIEVEMENT IN MUSIC & LYRICS
Alf Clausen, Ken Keeler, "The Simpsons." Your Checkin In, A Musical Tribute to the Betty Ford Center. Gracie Films in association with Twentieth Century Fox Television. FOX.

OUTSTANDING ACHIEVEMENT IN ART DIRECTION FOR A VARIETY OR MUSIC PROGRAM
Randy Ser, Edward L Rubin, Julie Kaye Fanton, "Rodgers & Hammerstein's Cinderella." Citadel Entertainment, Storyline Entertainment, Brownhouse Productions in sociation with Walt Disney Television. ABC

OUTSTANDING ACHIEVEMENT IN ART DIRECTION FOR A SERIES
Graeme Murray, Greg Loewen Shirley Ingret, "The X-Files" (The Post Modern Prometheus). Ten Thirteen Productions in association with 20th Century Fox Television. FOX.

OUTSTANDING ACHIEVEMENT IN ART DIRECTION FOR A MINISERIES OR A SPECIAL
John King, Roger Hall, Mike Boone, Karen Brooks, "Merlin" (Part 1). Hallmark Entertainment. NBC.

OUTSTANDING ACHIEVEMENT IN EDITING FOR A SERIES—SINGLE-CAMERA PRODUCTION
Heather MacDougall, "The X-Files" (Kill Switch). Ten Thirteen Productions in association with 20th Century Fox Television. FOX.

OUTSTANDING ACHIEVEMENT IN EDITING FOR A SERIES—MULTI-CAMERA PRODUCTION
Ron Volk, "Frasier" (Room Service). Grub Street Productions in association with Paramount. NBC.

OUTSTANDING ACHIEVEMENT IN EDITING FOR A MINISERIES OR A SPECIAL — SINGLE-CAMERA PRODUCTION
Eric Sears, "Gia." A Marvin Worth Production in association with Citadel Entertainment/Kahn Power Pictures and HBO Pictures. HBO.

OUTSTANDING ACHIEVEMENT IN EDITING FOR A MINISERIES OR A SPECIAL—MULTI-CAMERA PRODUCTION
Richard Daws, Jason Porthouse, "Stomp Out Loud." Yes/No Productions, Ltd/Yellow House Film Company/HBO. HBO.

17

OUTSTANDING ACHIEVEMENT IN CINEMATOGRAPHY FOR A SERIES
Constantine Makris, "Law & Order" *(Stalker)*. Wolf Films in association with Universal Television. NBC.

OUTSTANDING ACHIEVEMENT IN CINEMATOGRAPHY FOR A MINISERIES OR A SPECIAL
Eric Van Haran Norman., "What the Deaf Man Heard." Hallmark Hall of Fame production. CBS

OUTSTANDING ACHIEVEMENT IN LIGHTING DIRECTION (ELECTRONIC) FOR A COMEDY SERIES
Donald A. Morgan, "Home Improvement" *(A Night to Remember)*. Wind Dancer Production in Association with Touchstone Television. ABC.

OUTSTANDING ACHIEVEMENT IN LIGHTING DIRECTION (ELECTRONIC) FOR A DRAMA SERIES, VARIETY PROGRAM, MINI-SERIES OR SPECIAL
Robert Dickinson, Andy O'Reilly, Matt Ford Bob Barnhart, "The 70th Annual Academy Awards." Academy of Motion Picture Arts & Sciences. ABC.

OUTSTANDING TECHNICAL DIRECTION/CAMERA/VIDEO FOR A SERIES
Gene Crowe, Dave Chameides, Hank Geving, Larry Heider, Bob Heighton, Don Lenzer, Bill Philbin, Chuck Reilly, John O'Brien, "ER" *(Ambush)*. Constant c Productions, Amblin Television in association with Warner Bros Television.

OUTSTANDING ACHIEVEMENT IN TECHNICAL DIRECTION/CAMERA/VIDEO FOR A SPECIAL
Ron Washburn, Emmett Loughran, Miguel Armstrong, Juan Barrera, Jim Covello, John Feher, Manny Gutierrez, Jake Ostroff, David Smith, William Steinberg, "The Metropolitan Opera Presents Carmen." The Metropolitan Opera Association. PBS

OUTSTANDING ACHIEVEMENT IN CHOREOGRAPHY
Marguerite Derricks, Peggy Holmes, "Fame LA" *(Pilot)*. Trilogy Entertainment Group. Syndicated.

OUTSTANDING ACHIEVEMENT IN CINEMATOGRAPHY FOR NON-FICTION PROGRAMMING (TIE)
Richard Chisolm, Paul Goldsmith, Buddy Squires, Jerry Cotts, Nick Caloyianis, Jon Else, "National Geographic Special: America's Endangered Species: Don't Say Goodbye. NBC.
Jim Dutcher, "Wolves at Our Door." Dutcher Films for The Discovery Channel. Discovery Channel.

OUTSTANDING ACHIEVEMENT IN SOUND MIXING FOR NON-FICTION PROGRAMMING
Jamie Dutcher, "Wolves at Our Door." Dutcher Films for The Discovery Channel. Discovery Channel.

OUTSTANDING CLASSICAL MUSIC-DANCE PROGRAM
Yo-Yo Ma Inspired By Bach, A Rhombus Media Production in co-production with TVOntario, Thirteen/WNET in NY, BBC Television. PBS.

OUTSTANDING NON-FICTION SERIES
The American Experience, David Grubb Productions in association with The American Experience. Margaret Drain, David Grub. PBS.

OUTSTANDING NON-FICTION SPECIAL
Discovery Sunday — Vietnam POWs: Stories of Survival, A KnightScenes Inc Production for Discovery Channel. Bob Reid, Jacinda A Davis, Brian Leonard. Discovery Channel.

OUTSTANDING CHILDREN'S PROGRAM
Muppets Tonight, The Jim Henson Company. Brian Henson, Dick Blasucci, Executive Producers. Disney Channel.

OUTSTANDING COMMERCIAL
Apple Computer, Think Different. TBWA Chiat/Day, Ad Agency.

DAYTIME PROGRAMMING

OUTSTANDING DRAMA SERIES
All My Children, Executive Producer: Francesca James. ABC.

OUTSTANDING CHILDREN'S SERIES
Sesame Street, Executive Producer: Michael Loman. PBS.

OUTSTANDING CHILDREN'S SPECIAL
In His Father's Shoes, Executive Producer: Louis Gossett Jr. PBS.

OUTSTANDING CHILDREN'S ANIMATED PROGRAM
Arthur, Executive Producer: Micheline Charest. PBS.

OUTSTANDING TALK SHOW
The Rosie O'Donnell Show, Executive Producer: Rosie O'Donnell. Syndicated.

OUTSTANDING LEAD ACTRESS IN A DRAMA SERIES
Cynthia Watros, "Guiding Light." CBS.

OUTSTANDING LEAD ACTOR IN A DRAMA SERIES
Eric Braeden, "The Young & the Restless." CBS.

OUTSTANDING SUPPORTING ACTRESS IN A DRAMA SERIES
Julia Barr, "All My Children." ABC.

OUTSTANDING SUPPORTING ACTOR IN A DRAMA SERIES
Steve Burton, "General Hospitall." ABC.

OUTSTANDING YOUNGER ACTRESS IN A DRAMA SERIES
Sarah Brown, "General Hospital." ABC.

OUTSTANDING YOUNGER ACTOR IN A DRAMA SERIES
Jonathan Jackson, "General Hospital." ABC.

OUTSTANDING PERFORMER IN AN ANIMATED PROGRAM
Bill Nye, "Disney Presents: Bill Nye the Science Guy." Syndicated.

OUTSTANDING GAME/AUDIENCE PARTICIPATION SHOW
JEOPARDY, Executive Producer: Merv Griffin. Syndicated.

OUTSTANDING TALK SHOW HOST (TIE)
Rosie O'Donnell, "The Rosie O'Donnell Show." Syndicated.
Oprah Winfrey, "The Oprah Winfrey Show." Syndicated.

OUSTANDING, DRAMA SERIES DIRECTING TEAM
Heather Hill, Sally McDonald, Mike Denney, Kathryn Foster, Sally McDonald, "The Young & the Restless." CBS.

OUTSTANDING DRAMA SERIES WRITING TEAM
Agnes Nixon, Lorraine Broderick, Victoria Miller, Craig Carlson, Hal Corley, Frederick Johnson, Jeff Beldner, Christina Covino, Peggy Sloane, Karen L. Lewis, Elizabeth Smith, Michelle Patrick, Bettina F. Bradbury, Judith Donato, Kathleen Klein, Jane Owen Murphy, Caroline Franz, Charlotte Gibson, "All My Children." ABC.

NATIONAL AND INTERNATIONAL AWARDS

GOLDEN GLOBE AWARDS

BEST SERIES—DRAMA
The X-Files, 20th Century Fox, Ten Thirteen Prods. FOX.

BEST ACRESS IN A DRAMA SERIES
Christine Lahti, "Chicago Hope". CBS.

BEST ACTOR IN A DRAMA SERIES
Anthony Edwards, "ER". NBC.

BEST SERIES—MUSICAL OR COMEDY
Ally McBeal, David E. Kelley Productions. FOX.

BEST ACTRESS IN A MUSICAL OR COMEDY SERIES
Calista Flockhart, "Ally McBeal". FOX.

BEST ACTOR IN A MUSICAL OR COMEDY SERIES
Michael J Fox, "Spin City". ABC.

BEST MINISERIES OR TELEFILM
George Wallace, A Mark Carliner Production. TNT.

BEST ACTRESS IN A MINISERIES OR TELEFILM
Alfre Woodard, "Miss Evers Boys". HBO.

BEST ACTOR IN A MINISERIES OR TELEFILM
Ving Rhames, "Don King: Only in America". HBO.

BEST SUPPORTING ACTRESS IN A SERIES, MINISERIES OR TELEFILM
Angelina Jolie, "George Wallace". TNT.

BEST SUPPORTING ACTOR IN A SERIES, MINISERIES OR TELE-FILM
George C Scott, "12 Angry Men". Showtime.

DIRECTORS GUILD OF AMERICA AWARDS

BEST COMEDY SERIES
Andy Ackerman, "Seinfeld" *(The Betrayal)*. Castle Rock Entertainment, NBC.

BEST DRAMATIC SERIES
Barbara Kopple, "Homicide: Life on the Street" *(The Documentary)*. Baltimore Pictures. NBC.

BEST DRAMATIC SPECIAL
John Herzfeld, "Don King: Only in America".

BEST MUSICAL OR VARIETY PROGRAM
Louis Horvitz, "The Kennedy Center Honors" New Liberty Productions in association with Don Mischer Productions. CBS.

BEST CHILDREN'S PROGRAM
Brian Robbins, "First Time" (Nickelodeon's Sports Theater with Shaquille O'Neal). NICKELODEON.

BEST DAYTIME DRAMA SERIES
Scott McKinsey, "General Hospital" *(Episode 8883)*.

HONOREE LIFE ACHIEVEMENT IN SPORTS
Craig Janoff.

HONOREE LIFE ACHIEVEMENT IN NEWS
Robert E. Vitarelli.

WRITERS GUILD AWARDS

BEST ORIGINAL LONGFORM
The Summer of Ben Tyler, Teleplay by Robert Inman. ABC.

BEST ADAPTED LONG FORM
Bastard out of Carolina, Teleplay by Anne Meredit.

BEST EPISODIC DRAMA
Entrapment, "Law & Order". Teleplay by Rene Balcer & Richard Sweren. NBC.

BEST EPISODIC COMEDY
The Fatigues, "Seinfeld". Gregg Kavet & Andy Robin Castle Rock Television. NBC.

BEST VARIETY, MUSICAL AWARD, TRIBUTE, SPECIAL EVENT
HBO Comedy Hour: Dennis Miller Citizen Arcane, Written by Dennis Miller. HBO.

BEST DAYTIME SERIAL
General Hospital, Written by Meg Bennett, Richard Culliton, Karen Harris, Craig Heller, Janet Iacobuzio, Elizabeth Korte, Bill Levinson, Eleanor Mancusi, Patrick Mulcahey, Lynda Myles, Judith Pinsker, Mary Ryan, Courtney Simon, Michele Val Jean, Christopher Whitsell, Garin Wolf. ABC.

BEST CHILDREN'S SCRIPT (TIE)
The Song of the Zubble-Wump, (The Wubbulous World of Dr Seuss), David Stephen Cohen, Nickelodeon.
Elmo Saves Christmas, (Sesame Street), Christine Ferraro, Tony Geiss. PBS

BEST DOCUMENTARY—SPECIAL EVENTS (TIE)
CBS News Sunday Morning, (Diana, Princess of Wales), Written by Thomas A Harris CBS.
CBS Evening News with Dan Rather, (The Conviction of Timothy McVeigh), Writen by Jerry Cipriano, Paul Fischer, Tom Phillips. CBS.

BEST DOCUMENTARY—OTHER THAN CURRENT EVENTS
The Secret White House Tapes (An Investigative Report), Written by Carol L Fleisher and William Doyle.. A&E.

BEST TV NEWS ANALYSIS, FEATURE OR COMMENTARY
48 Hours, Written by Greg Kandra. CBS.

BRITISH ACADEMY OF FILM & TELEVISION ARTS AWARDS

BEST SINGLE DRAMA
No Child of Mine, Peter Kosminsky, Guy Hibbert.

BEST DRAMA SERIES
Jonathan Creek, Susan Belbin, David Renwick

BEST DRAMA SERIAL
Holding On, David Snodin, Adrian Shergold, Tony Marchant.

BEST FACTUAL SERIES
The Nazis - A Warning from History, Laurence Rees

BEST LIGHT ENTERTAINMENT (PROGRAM OR SERIES)
The Fast Show, Charlie Higson, Paul Whitehouse, Mark Mylod.

BEST COMEDY (PROGRAM OR SERIES)
I'm Alan Patridge, Armando Iannucci, Dominic Brigstocke,Peter Baynham, Steve Coogan .

THE HUW WELDON AWARD FOR BEST ARTS PROGRAM OR SERIES
Gilbert & George (The South Bank Show), Gerald Fox.

THE ALAN CLARKE AWARD FOR OUTSTANDING CONTRIBU-TION TO TELEVISION
Rugby Union (Sky), Martin Turner.

THE FLAHERTY DOCUMENTARY AWARD
The Grave (True Stories), Belinda Giles.

BEST ACTRESS
Daniela Nardini, "This Life".

BEST ACTOR
Simon Russell Beale, "A Dance to the Music of Time".

BEST LIGHT ENTERTAINMENT PERFORMANCE
Paul Whitehouse, "The Fast Show"

BEST COMEDY PERFORMANCE
Steve Coogan, "I'm Alan Patridge.

BEST NEWS AND CURRENT AFFAIRS JOURNALISM
Valentina 's Story (Panorama), Mike Robinson.

BEST SPORTS/EVENTS COVERAGE IN REAL TIME
Rugby Union (Sky), Martin Turner.

BEST INTERNATIONAL TELEVISION PROGRAMME
Friends, Bright/Kauffman/Crane Productions in association with Warner Bros Television.

THE RICHARD DIMBLEBY AWARD
David Dimbleby.

THE DENNIS POTER AWARD
Kay Mellor.

THE LEW GRADE AWARD
A Touch of Frost.

Nielsen TV Index Ranking
Top Primetime Programs

The rating represents the percentage of 95.4 million tv households. The share is the percentage of tv sets in use turned to a show. Ratings are for the 36 week season, 9/17/97 to 5/20/98.

Rank	Program Name	Network	Rating/Share	Rank	Program Name	Network	Rating/Share
1	Seinfeld	NBC	22.0/33	50	Cybill	CBS	8.3/13
2	ER	NBC	20.7/34	50	Kids Say the Darndest Things	CBS	8.3/16
3	Veronica's Closet	NBC	16.8/26	50	Nanny	CBS	8.3/14
4	Friends	NBC	16.4/27	54	George & Leo	CBS	8.2/12
5	NFL Monday Night Football	ABC	15.0/26	54	Magnificent Seven	CBS	8.2/15
6	Touched By An Angel	CBS	14.4/22	54	Something So Right	ABC	8.2/13
7	60 Minutes	CBS	13.9/24	57	Ally McBeal	FOX	8.1/12
8	Union Square	NBC	13.6/21	57	Candid Camera	CBS	8.1/15
9	CBS Sunday Movie	CBS	13.3/21	57	48 Hours	CBS	8.1/13
10	Frasier	NBC	12.0/18	57	Over the Top	ABC	8.1/13
10	Home Improvement	ABC	12.0/18	57	Party of Five	FOX	8.1/13
10	Just Shoot Me	NBC	12.0/19	62	Newsradio	NBC	8.0/13
13	Dateline NBC-Tue	NBC	11.5/20	62	Sabrina-Teenage Witch	ABC	8.0/14
13	NFL Monday Showcase	ABC	11.5/18	62	Working	NBC	8.0/12
15	Dateline NBC-Mon	NBC	11.4/19	65	Nash Bridges	CBS	7.9/15
16	Drew Carey Show	ABC	11.1/17	65	Suddenly Susan	NBC	7.9/13
16	Fox NFL Sunday-Post (MN)	FOX	11.1/18	65	That's Life	ABC	7.9/12
18	20/20	ABC	10.9/20	65	Wonderful World of Disney	ABC	7.9/13
19	NYPD Blue	ABC	10.8/18	69	Damon-Preview	FOX	7.8/12
19	Primetime Live	ABC	10.8/18	69	Early Edition	CBS	7.8/14
19	X-Files	FOX	10.8/16	69	Grace Under Fire	ABC	7.8/13
22	Fox NFL Sun-Post Game (PM)	FOX	10.7/18	69	Murphy Brown	CBS	7.8/12
23	Law and Order	NBC	10.2/17	69	Naked Truth	NBC	7.8/12
24	20/20-Mon	ABC	10.0/15	74	Dateline- 8P Fri	NBC	7.7/14
25	Diagnosis Murder	CBS	9.8/15	74	Dateline NBC-Sun	NBC	7.7/13
25	King of the Hill	FOX	9.8/15	74	Dr. Quinn Medicine Woman	CBS	7.7/15
27	Mad About You	NBC	9.7/16	77	America's Funniest Home Videos	ABC	7.6/12
28	Cosby	CBS	9.5/15	77	Homicide: Life On the Street	NBC	7.6/14
28	Dateline NBC-Fri	NBC	9.5/17	77	3rd Rock From the Sun-Wed	NBC	7.6/12
28	Dharma & Greg	ABC	9.5/15	80	Boy Meets World	ABC	7.5/14
28	NBC Sunday Night Movie	NBC	9.5/15	80	Fired Up	NBC	7.5/11
32	Hiller & Diller	ABC	9.3/15	80	For Your Love	NBC	7.5/12
32	The Simpsons	FOX	9.3/15	80	Melrose Place	FOX	7.5/11
32	Walker, Texas Ranger	CBS	9.3/17	84	The Closer	CBS	7.4/11
35	Dateline NBC 8P Sunday	NBC	9.2/15	84	Pretender	NBC	7.4/13
35	Everybody Loves Raymond	CBS	9.2/14	84	Public Eye-Bryant Gumbel	CBS	7.4/12
37	Soul Man	ABC	9.1/14	84	Sabrina-Teenage Witch-8:00 PM	ABC	7.4/14
38	Lateline	NBC	9.0/14	88	Michael Hayes	CBS	7.3/11
39	Chicago Hope	CBS	8.9/15	89	The Practice	ABC	7.3/13
39	Jag	CBS	8.9/14	90	Style & Substance	CBS	7.1/11
39	Promised Land	CBS	8.9/14	91	Jenny	NBC	7.0/10
42	Ellen	ABC	8.8/14	91	Unsolved Mysteries	CBS	7.0/13
42	Two Guys, A Girl and A Pizza Pl	ABC	8.8/14	91	You Wish	ABC	7.0/13
44	ABC Sunday Night Movie	ABC	8.5/13	94	Brooklyn South	CBS	6.9/12
44	3rd Rock From the Sun	NBC	8.5/13	94	World's Wildest Police Videos	FOX	6.9/11
44	20/20-Thurs	ABC	8.5/14	96	Dellaventura	CBS	6.8/12
47	Caroline In the City	NBC	8.4/13	96	Profiler	NBC	6.8/13
47	CBS Tuesday Movie	CBS	8.4/14	96	Teen Angel	ABC	6.8/12
47	Spin City	ABC	8.4/14	99	Cops 2	FOX	6.5/12
50	Beverly Hills, 90210	FOX	8.3/14	99	Men Behaving Badly	NBC	6.5/10
				101	AMW: America Fights Back	FOX	6.4/12

INTERNATIONAL FILM & TV
FESTIVALS AND MARKETS

JANUARY

BRUSSELS INTERNATIONAL FILM FESTIVAL
30 Chausee de Louvain, B-1030 Brussels, Belgium. Tel: (32 2) 218 1055. FAX: (32 2) 218 6627.

CINEASIA
Jon Margolis, Cinema Expo International, 244 W. 49th Street, Ste. 200, New York, NY 10019. Tel: (212) 246-6460. FAX: (212) 265-6428. email: sunshine@maestro.com

CINEQUEST (THE SAN JOSE FILM FESTIVAL)
Mike Rabehl, P.O. Box 720040, San Jose, CA 95172. Tel: (408) 995-6305. FAX: (408) 995-5713. email: sjfilmfest@aol.com URL: http://www.cinequest.com

CLERMONT-FERRAND SHORT FILM FESTIVAL
26 rue des Jacobins, 63000 Clermont-Ferrand, France. Tel: (33 73) 91 65 73. FAX: (33 73) 92 11 93.

FAJR INTERNATIONAL FILM FESTIVAL
Farhang Cinema, Dr. Shariati Avenue, Gholhak, Tehran 19139 Iran. Tel: (98 21) 205 2088. FAX: (98 21) 267 082.

FILMFESTIVAL MAX OPHULS PRIZE
Mainzerstrasse 8, 6600 Saarbrucken, Germany. Tel: (49 681) 329 452. FAX: (49 681) 905 1943.

FIPA (FESTIVAL INTERNATIONAL DE PROGRAMMES AUDIOVISUEL)
Faubourg St. Honore, 75008 Paris, France. Tel: (33 1) 45 61 01 66. FAX: (33 1) 40 74 07 96.

INTERNATIONAL FILM FESTIVAL OF INDIA
Ministry of Information & Broadcasting, Government of India, Lok Nayak Bhavan, Khan Market, New Delhi 110003. Tel: (91 11) 461 5963. FAX: (91 11) 469 4920.

KIDFILM FESTIVAL, U.S.A. FILM FESTIVAL
Alonso Duralde, 2917 Swiss Ave., Dallas, TX 75204. Tel: (214) 821-6300. FAX: (214) 821-6364. URL: http://www.usafilmfestival.com

NATPE
2425 Olympic Blvd., Suite 550E, Santa Monica, CA 90404. Tel: (310) 453-4440. FAX: (310) 453-5258.

NORTEL PALM SPRINGS INTERNATIONAL FILM FESTIVAL
Paola Fracero, P.O. Box 2230, Palm Springs, CA 92263. Tel: (760) 322-2930. FAX: (760) 322-4087.

ROTTERDAM INTERNATIONAL FILM FESTIVAL
P.O. Box 21696, 3001 AR Rotterdam, Netherlands. Tel: (31 10) 411 8080. FAX: (31 10) 413 5132.

SUNDANCE FILM FESTIVAL
Nicole Guillernet, P.O. Box 16450, Salt Lake City, UT 84116 (801) 328-FILM, (310) 394-4662. FAX: (801) 575 5175. email: sundance@xmission.com URL: http://www.sundance.org

TROMSO INTERNATIONAL FILM FESTIVAL
Georgernes Verft 3, 5011 Bergen, Norway. Tel: (475) 5532 2590. FAX: (475) 5532 3740.

FEBRUARY

ASPEN SHORTFEST
P.O. Box 8910, Aspen, CO 81611. Tel: (910) 925-6882. FAX: (910) 925-1967.

AMERICAN FILM MARKET
Ms. Brady Craine, AMFA, 10850 Wilshire Blvd., 9th Flr., Los Angeles, CA 90024. Tel: (310) 446-1000. FAX: (310) 446-1600. email: info@afma.com URL: http://www.afma.com

BERLIN INTERNATIONAL FILM FESTIVAL
Budapesterstrasse 50, 10787 Berlin, Germany. Tel: (49 30) 254 890. FAX: (49 30) 2548 9249.

BRUSSELS CARTOON & ANIMATED FILM FESTIVAL, FOLIOSCOPE
rue de la Rhetorique 19, B-1060 Brussels, Belgium. Tel: (32 2) 534 4125. FAX: (32 2) 534 2279.

FANTASPORTO (OPPORTO INTERNATIONAL FILM FESTIVAL)
Rua da Constituicao 311, 4200 Porto, Portugal. Tel: (35 11) 550 8990. FAX: (35 11) 550 8210.

GOTHENBURG FILM FESTIVAL
Box 7079, 40232 Gothenburg, Sweden. Tel: (46 31) 410 546. FAX: (46 31) 410 063.

HUNGARIA FILM WEEK
Magyar Filmunio, Varosiglieti Sasor 38, 1068 Budapest, Hungary (36 1) 269 7760. FAX: (36 1) 268 0070.

MIAMI FILM FESTIVAL
444 Brickell Avenue, Miami, FL 33131. Tel: (305) 377-3456. FAX: (305) 577-9768.

MILIA
MIDEM Organisation, 179 ave. Victor Hugo, 75016 Paris, France. Tel: (33 1) 4434 4444. FAX: (33 1) 4434 4400.

MONTE CARLO TELEVISION FESTIVAL & MARKET
Boulevard Louis II, 98000 Monaco.

PORTLAND INTERNATIONAL FILM FESTIVAL
Northwest Film Center, 1219 S.W. Park Ave., Portland, OR 97205. Tel: (503) 221-1156. FAX: (503) 294-0874.

MARCH

BERGAMO FILM MEETING
Via Pascoli 3, 24121 Bergamo, Italy. Tel: (39 35) 234011. FAX: (39 35) 233129.

BRUSSELS INTERNATIONAL FESTIVAL OF FANTASY, THRILLER & SCIENCE FICTION FILMS
111 avenue de la Reine, 1210 Brussels, Belgium. Tel: (32 2) 201 1713. FAX: (32 2) 201 1469.

CARTAGENA FILM FESTIVAL
P.O. Box 1834, Cartagena, Colombia. Tel: (57 53) 600 966. FAX: (57 53) 600 970.

CLEVELAND INTERNATIONAL FILM FESTIVAL
David W. Wittkowsky, c/o The Cleveland Film Society, 1621 Euclid Ave., Ste. 428, Cleveland, OH 44115. Tel: (216) 623-0400. FAX: (216) 623-0101. URL: http://www.clevefilmfest.org

DUBLIN FILM FESTIVAL
1 Suffolk Street, Dublin 2, Ireland. Tel: (353 1) 679 2937. FAX: (353 1) 679 2939.

FRIBOURG FILM FESTIVAL
rue de Locarno 8, 1700 Fribourg, Switzerland. Tel: (41 37) 222 232. FAX: (41 37) 227 950.

INTERNATIONAL WOMEN'S FILM FESTIVAL
Maison des Arts, Place Salvador Allende, 94000 Creteil, France. Tel: (33 1) 4980 3998. FAX: (33 1) 4399 0410.

LOCAL HEROES INTERNATIONAL SCREEN FESTIVAL
10022-103 St., Edmonton, Alberta T5J 0X2, Canada. Tel: (403) 421-4084. FAX: (403) 425-8090.

LONDON LESBIAN & GAY FILM FESTIVAL
National Film Theatre, South Bank, Waterloo, London SE1 8XT, England. Tel: (44 171) 815 1323. FAX: (44 171) 633 0786.

NEW DIRECTORS/NEW FILMS
The Film Society of Lincoln Center, 70 Lincoln Center Plaza, New York, NY 10023. Tel: (212) 875-5610. FAX: (212) 875-5636.

NEW ENGLAND FILM & VIDEO FESTIVAL
Devon Damonte, Boston Film/Video Foundation, 1126 Boylston St., Ste. 201, Boston, MA 02215. Tel: (617) 536-1540. FAX: (617) 536-3576. email: bfvf@aol.com URL: http://www.actwin.com/bfvf

SAN FRANCISCO ASIAN AMERICAN INTERNATIONAL FILM FESTIVAL
346 Ninth St., San Francisco, CA 94103. Tel: (415) 863-0814. FAX: (415) 863-7428.

SANTA BARBARA INTERNATIONAL FILM FESTIVAL
Diane M. Durst, 1216 State St., Ste. 710, Santa Barbara, CA 93101. Tel: (805) 963-0023. FAX: (805) 962-2524. email: sbiff@west.net URL: http://www.west.net/~sbiff3

SHOWEST
Daniel Wheatcroft, 116 North Robertson, Suite 708, Los Angeles, CA 90048. Tel: (310) 652-1093. FAX: (310) 657 4758. email: showest@aol.com. URL: http://www.showest.org

APRIL

ACADEMIC FILM OLOMUC
Krizkiveskeho 8, 771 47 Olomuc, Czech Republic. Tel: (42 68) 5508 277. FAX: (42 68) 26 476.

BALTIMORE FILM FESTIVAL
10 Art Museum Drive, Baltimore, MD 21218. Tel: (410) 889-1993. FAX: (410) 889-2567.

BLACK FILMWORKS
Black Filmmakers Hall of Fame, P.O. Box 28055, Oakland, CA 94606. Tel: (510) 465-0804. FAX: (510) 839-9858.

CAPE TOWN INTERNATIONAL FILM FESTIVAL
c/o University of Cape Town, Private Bag, Rondebosch 7700, Cape Town, South Africa. Tel: (27 21) 238 257. FAX: (27 21) 242 355.

CHICAGO LATINO CINEMA
c/o Columbia College, 600 South Michigan Ave., Chicago, IL 60605. Tel: (312) 431-1330. FAX: (312) 360-0629.

COGNAC INTERNATIONAL FILM FESTIVAL OF THE THRILLER
c/o Promo 2000, 36 rue Perriet, 92200 Neuilly-sur-Seine, France. Tel: (33 1) 4640 5500. FAX: (33 1) 4640 5539.

FESTIVAL OF FRENCH CINEMA
Tel Aviv Cinematheque, 2 Sprintzak St., Tel Aviv, Israel.

HONG KONG INTERNATIONAL FILM FESTIVAL
Festivals Office, Level 7, Administration Bldg., Hong Kong Cultural Centre, 10 Salisbury Rd., Tsimshatsui, Kowloon, Hong Kong. Tel: (852) 734 2903. FAX: (852) 366 5206.

INTERNATIONAL CINEMA WEEK
Via S. Giacomo alla Pignano. 6, 37121 Verona, Italy. Tel: (39 45) 800 6778. FAX: (39 45) 590 624.

INTERNATIONAL ELECTRONIC CINEMA FESTIVAL
P.O. Box 1451, 1820 Montreux, Switzerland. Tel: (41 21) 963 3220. FAX: (41 21) 963 8851.

INTERNATIONAL SHORT FILM FESTIVAL OBERHAUSEN
Grillostrasse 34, 46045 Oberhausen, Germany. Tel: (49 208) 825 2625. FAX: (49 208) 825 5413.

ISTANBUL INTERNATIONAL FILM FESTIVAL
Istiklal Caddest 146, Luvr Apt. Beyoglu, 80070 Istanbul, Turkey. Tel: (901) 293 31 33. FAX: (901) 249 77 71.

LILLE INTERNATIONAL FESTIVAL OF SHORT & DOCUMENTARY FILMS
58, rue du port, 59800 Lille, France. Tel: (33 03) 2015 4825. FAX: (33 03) 2015 4523.

LOS ANGELES INTERNATIONAL ANIMATION CELEBRATION
28024 Dorothy Dr., Agoura Hills, CA 91301. Tel: (818) 991-2884. FAX: (818) 991-3773.

MIP – TV
MIDEM Organisation, BP 572, 11 rue du Colonel Pierre Avia, 75726 Paris Cedex 15, France. Tel: (33 1) 4190 4400. FAX: (33 1) 4190 4409.

RIVERTOWN: MINNEAPOLIS/ ST. PAUL INTERNATIONAL FILM FESTIVAL
425 Ontario St. S.E., Minneapolis, MN 55414. Tel: (612) 627-4432. FAX: (612) 627-4111.

SAN FRANCISCO INTERNATIONAL FILM FESTIVAL
Peter Scarlet, 1521 Eddy Street, San Francisco, CA 94115. Tel: (415) 929-5000. FAX: (415) 921-5032. email: sfiff@sfiff.org. URL: http://www.sfiff.org

SINGAPORE INTERNATIONAL FILM FESTIVAL
169 Kim Seng Road, Singapore 0923. Tel: (65) 738 7567. FAX: (65) 738 7578.

USA FILM FESTIVAL
2917 Swiss Ave., Dallas, TX 75204. Tel: (214) 821-6300. FAX: (214) 821-6364.

WORLDFEST – HOUSTON
2700 Post Oak Blvd., Ste. 1798, Houston, TX 77056. Tel: (713) 965-9955. FAX: (713) 965-9960. email: worldfest@aol.com. URL: http://www.world-fest.com

MAY

BRIGHTON FESTIVAL
21-22 Old Steine, Brighton, BN1 1EL, England. Tel: (44 1273) 713 875. FAX: (44 1273) 622 453.

CANNES FILM FESTIVAL
99 Boulevard Malesherbes, 75008 Paris, France. Tel: (33 1) 45 61 66 00. FAX: (33 1) 45 61 97 60.

ETHNOGENRE FILM FESTIVAL
184 Dorchester Rd., Rochester,NY 14610. Tel: (716) 288-2152. FAX: (716) 288-2156.

GOLDEN PRAGUE INTERNATIONAL TV FESTIVAL
Czechoslovak TV, Kaveci Hory 140 70, Prague 4, Czech Republic. Tel: (14 22) 6121 2882. FAX: (14 22) 6121 2891.

HUMAN RIGHTS WATCH INTERNATIONAL FILM FESTIVAL
485 Fifth Ave., New York, NY 10017. Tel: (212) 972-8400. Tel: (212) 972-0905.

INDEPENDENT FILM DAYS
Filmburo Augsburg, Schroeckstrasse 6, 86152 Augsburg, Germany. Tel: (49 821) 153 077. FAX: (49 821) 155 518.

INTERNATIONAL SHORT FILM FESTIVAL – KRACOW
c/o Apollo Film, ul. Pychowicka 7, 30-364 Kracow, Poland. (48 12) 672 340. FAX: (48 12) 671 552.

PHILADELPHIA FESTIVAL OF WORLD CINEMA
Susan Sheppard, Int'l House of Philadelphia, 3701 Chestnut St., Philadelphia, PA 19104. Tel: (215) 895-6542. FAX: (215) 895-6562. email: pfwc@libertynet.org. URL: http://www.liber-tynet.org/ihouse

PRIX DANUBE
Mylneska Dolina, 845 45 Bratislava, Slovakia. Tel: (42 7) 727 448. FAX: (42 7) 729 440.

SEATTLE INTERNATIONAL FILM FESTIVAL
Darryl Macdonald, c/o Egyptian Theatre, 801 E. Pine St., Seattle, WA 98122. Tel: (206) 324-9996. FAX: (206) 324-9998. email: mail@seattlefilm.com. URL: http://www.seattlefilm.com

JUNE

AFI LOS ANGELES INTERNATIONAL FILM FESTIVAL
c/o American Film Institute, 2021 N. Western Ave., Los Angeles, CA 90027. Tel: (213) 856-7707. FAX: (213) 462-4049. URL http://www.afionline.org

AUSTRIAN FILM DAYS
Austrian Film Office, Columbusgasse 2, 1100 Vienna, Austria. (43 1) 604 0126. FAX: (43 1) 602 0795.

BANFF TELEVISION FESTIVAL
P.O. Box 219, Suite 9000, Banff, Alberta TOL OCO, Canada. (403) 678-9260. FAX: (403) 678-9269.

BELLARIA FILM FESTIVAL
Viale Paolo Guidi 108, 47041 Bellaria Igea Marina (RN), Italy. Tel: (39 541) 347 186. FAX: (39 541) 347 186.

CINEMA EXPO INTERNATIONAL
244 West 49th Street, New York, NY 10019. Tel: (212) 246-6460. FAX: (212) 265-6428.

DONOSTIA SCREENINGS
c/o Euroaim, 210 avenue Winston Churchill, B-1180 Brussels, Belgium. Tel: (32 2) 346 1500. FAX: (32 2) 346 3842.

DYLAN DOG HORROR FILMS
Via M. Buonarotti 38, 20145 Milan, Italy. Tel: (39 2) 4800 2877. FAX: (39 2) 4801 1937.

FESTIVAL OF FESTIVALS
10 Kamennoostrovsky Ave., St. Petersburg 197101, Russia. Tel: (7 812) 238 5811. FAX: (7 812) 232 8881.

FLORIDA FILM FESTIVAL
Sigrid Tiedtke, 1300 S. Orlando Ave., Maitland, FL 32751. Tel: (407) 629-1088. FAX: (407) 629-6870. email: filmfest@gate.net. URL: http://www.enzign.org

FRENCH AMERICAN FILM WORKSHOP
10 Montee de la Tour, Villeneuve Les Avignon, France. Tel: (33) 9025 9323. FAX: (33) 9025 9324.

INTERNATIONAL ADVERTISING FILM FESTIVAL
c/o 2nd floor, Woolverstone House, 61-62 Berners St., London W1P 3AE, England. Tel: (44 171) 636 6122. FAX: (44 171) 636 6086.

LA ROCHELLE INTERNATIONAL FILM FESTIVAL
16 rue Saint Sabin, 75011 Paris, France. Tel: (33 1) 4806 1666. FAX: (33 1) 4806 1540.

LONDON JEWISH FILM FESTIVAL
South Bank, Waterloo, London SE1 8XT, England. Tel: (44 171) 815 1322. FAX: (44 171) 633 0786.

MARKETSKAYA
c/o Seineva Organisation, 10 rue de la Boetie, 75008 Paris, France. Tel: (33 1) 5376 1628. FAX: (33 1) 4561 9427.

MELBOURNE INTERNATIONAL FILM FESTIVAL
P.O. Box 2206, Fitzroy Mail Centre, Victoria 3065, Australia (61 3) 9417 2011. FAX: (61 3) 9417 3804.

MIDNIGHT SUN FILM FESTIVAL
Malminkatu 36 B 102, Helsinki, Finland. Tel: (35 80) 685 2242. FAX: (35 80) 694 5560.

THE MONTREAL INTERNATIONAL FESTIVAL OF NEW CINEMA & VIDEO
3726 Blvd. St. Laurent, Montreal, Quebec H2X 2V8, Canada. Tel: (514) 843-4725. FAX: (514) 843-4631.

MUNICH FILM FESTIVAL
Kaiserstrasse 39, 80801 Munich, Germany. Tel: (49 89) 381 9040. FAX: (49 89) 381 90427.

MYSTFEST (INTERNATIONAL MYSTERY FILM FESTIVAL)
Centro Cultural Polivalente, Piazza Della Repubblica 34, 47033 Catolica (FO), Italy. Tel: (39 541) 967 802. FAX: (39 541) 967 803.

NEWARK BLACK FILM FESTIVAL
The Newark Museum Assn., 49 Washington St., P.O. Box 540, Newark, NJ 07101. Tel: (201) 596-6637. FAX: (201) 642-0459.

NORWEGIAN SHORT FILM FESTIVAL
Storengveien 8B, N-1342 Jar, Norway. Tel: (47 67) 122 013. FAX: (47 67) 124 865.

PESARO FILM FESTIVAL
Via Villefranca 20, 00185 Rome, Italy. Tel: (39 6) 445 6643. FAX: (39 6) 491 163.

SAN FRANCISCO LESBIAN & GAY FILM FESTIVAL AND MARKET
Frameline, 346 Ninth St., San Francisco, CA 94103 (415) 703-8658. FAX: (415) 861-1404

SYDNEY FILM FESTIVAL
Paul Byrnes, P.O. Box 950, Glebe, NSW 2037, Australia. Tel: (61 2) 660 3844. FAX: (61 2) 692 8793.

TROIA INTERNATIONAL FILM FESTIVAL
Troia, 2902 Setubal Codex, Portugal. Tel: (35 165) 441 21.

VUE SUR LES DOCS
3 Square Stalingrad, 13001 Marseille, France. Tel: (33 91) 91 84 40 17. FAX: (33 91) 9184 3834.

JULY

ASIAN AMERICAN INTERNATIONAL FILM FESTIVAL
Asian Cinevision, 32 E. Broadway, New York, NY 10002. Tel: (212) 925-8685. FAX: (212) 925-8157.

AUCKLAND INTERNATIONAL FILM FESTIVAL
P.O. Box 9544, Wellington, New Zealand. Tel: (64 4) 385 0162. FAX: (64 4) 801 7304.

CAMBRIDGE FILM FESTIVAL
Cambridge Arts Cinema, 8 Market Passage, Cambridge CB2 2PF, England. Tel: (44 1223) 352 001. FAX: (44 1223) 462 555.

DURBAN INTERNATIONAL FILM FESTIVAL
U. of Natal, King George V Ave., Durban 4001, South Africa. (27 31) 811 3978. FAX: (27 31) 261 7107.

HOMETOWN VIDEO FESTIVAL
Buske Group, 30001 J Street, Sacramento, CA 95816. Tel: (916) 441-6277. FAX: (916) 441-7670.

INTERNATIONAL FILM FESTIVAL OF GIJON
Paseo de Begona 24, Entreselvo, 33205 Gijon, Spain. Tel: (34 85) 343 735. FAX: (34 85) 354 152.

JERUSALEM FILM FESTIVAL
P.O. Box 8561, Jerusalem, Israel. Tel: (97 22) 724 131. FAX: (97 22) 733 076.

KARLOVY VARY FILM FESTIVAL
Ministry of Culture, Nadace, Valdstejnsska 12, 11811 Prague 1, Czech Republic. Tel: (42 2) 513 2473. FAX: (42 2) 530 542.

PHILAFILM
IAMPTP, 215 South Broad St., Philadelphia, PA 19107. Tel: (215) 977-2831. FAX: (215) 546-8055.

SHORT & DOCUMENTARY FILM FESTIVAL
Farhang Cinema, Dr. Shariati Ave., Gholbak, Tehran 19139, Iran. Tel: (98 21) 265 086. FAX: (98 21) 678 155.

TAORMINA INTERNATIONAL FILM FESTIVAL
Via Pirandello 31, 98039 Taormina, Italy. Tel: (39 942) 211 42. FAX: (39 942) 233 48.

VEVEY INTERNATIONAL COMEDY FILM FESTIVAL
Buureau du Festival du Film de Comedie, La Greneyye, Grand Place 29, CH-1800 Vevey, Switzerland. Tel: (41 21) 922 2027. FAX: (41 21) 922 2024.

WELLINGTON FILM FESTIVAL
P.O. Box 9544, Te Aro, Wellington, New Zealand. Tel: (64 4) 385 0162. FAX: (64 4) 801 7304.

WINE COUNTRY FILM FESTIVAL
Stephen Ashton, P.O. Box 303, Glen Ellen, CA 95442. Tel: (707) 996-2536. FAX: (707) 996-6964.

AUGUST

ALEXANDRIA FILM FESTIVAL
9 Oraby Street, Cairo, Eqypt. Tel: (20 2) 578 0042. FAX: (20 2) 768 727.

BRISBANE INTERNATIONAL FILM FESTIVAL
Level 3, Hoyts Regent Bldg., 167 Queen St. Mall, Brisbane, Queensland 4000, Australia. Tel: (61 73) 220 0333. FAX: (61 73) 220 0400.

DRAMBUIE EDINBURGH FILM FESTIVAL
88 Lothian Road, Edinburgh EH3 9BZ, Scotland. Tel: (44 131) 228 4051. FAX: (44 131) 228 5501.

ESPOO CINE FILM FESTIVAL
P.O. Box 95, 02101 Espoo, Finland. Tel: (35 80) 466 599. FAX: (35 80) 466 458.

GIFFONI INTERNATIONAL FILM FESTIVAL
Piazza Umberto 1, 84095 Giffoni Valle Piana (Salerno), Italy (39 89) 868 544. FAX: (39 89) 866 111.

GRAMADO CINEMA FESTIVAL
Avenida des Hortensias 2029, Cap. 9567, 1000 Gramado, R.G. Sul, Brazil. Tel: (55 54) 286 2335. FAX: (55 54) 286 2397.

INTERNATIONAL ANIMATION FESTIVAL IN JAPAN-HIROSHIMA
4-17 Kalo-machi, Naka-ku, Hirshima 730, Japan. Tel: (81 82) 245 0245. FAX: (81 82) 245 1246.

LOCARNO INTERNATIONAL FILM FESTIVAL
Via della Posta 6, Cassella Postale, 6600 Locarno, Switzerland (41 93) 310 232. FAX: (41 93) 317 465.

MONTREAL WORLD FILM FESTIVAL
Serge Losique, 1432 de Bleury St., Montreal, Quebec, Canada H3A 2J1. Tel: (514) 848-3883. FAX: (514) 848-3886.

NORWEGIAN INTERNATIONAL FILM FESTIVAL
P.O. Box 145, 5501 Haugesund, Norway. Tel: (47 52) 734 430. FAX: (52) 734 420.

ODENSE INTERNATIONAL FILM FESTIVAL
Vindegade 18, DK-5000 Odense C, Denmark. Tel: (45) 6613 1372. FAX: (45) 6591 4318.

WEEKLY MAIL/GUARDIAN FILM FESTIVAL
P.O. Box 2601245, Excom 2023, South Africa. Tel: (27 11) 331 1712. FAX: (27 11) 331 3339.

SEPTEMBER

AMERICA FILM FESTIVAL
Museumstrasse 31, A-6020 Innsbruck, Austria. Tel: (43 512) 580 723. FAX: (43 512) 581 762.

ASPEN FILMFEST
110 E. Hallam St., Ste. 102, Aspen, CO 81611. Tel: (303) 925-6882. FAX: (303) 925-1967.

ATLANTIC FILM FESTIVAL
1541 Barrington St., Suite 326, Halifax, Nova Scotia, Canada. Tel: (902) 422-3456. FAX: (902) 422-4006.

BANCO NACIONAL INTERNATIONAL FILM FESTIVAL
Rua Voluntarios de Patria 97, Botafogo, Rio de Janeiro 22270, Brazil. Tel: (55 21) 286 8505. FAX: (55 21) 286 4029.

BOSTON FILM FESTIVAL
333 Victory Rd., Quincy, MA 02171. Tel: (617) 471-1778. FAX: (617) 479-0778.

BRITISH SHORT FILM FESTIVAL
Room 313, BBC Threshold House, 65-69 Shepherds Bush Green, London W12 7RJ, England. Tel: (44 181) 743 8000. FAX: (44 181) 740 8540.

CAIRO INTERNATIONAL CHILDREN'S FILM FESTIVAL
17 Kasr El Nil St., Cairo, Eqypt. Tel: (202) 3923 562. FAX: (202) 3938 979.

COPENHAGEN FILM FESTIVAL
Bulowsvej 50A, DK-1870 Frederiksberg C, Copenhagen, Denmark. Tel: (45) 3537 2507. FAX: (45) 3135 5758.

DEAUVILLE FESTIVAL OF AMERICAN FILMS
c/o Promo, 36 rue Perriet, 92200 Neuilly-sur-Seine, France (33 1) 4640 5500. FAX: (33 1) 4640 5539.

EUROPACINEMA FESTIVAL
Via Giulia 66, 00186 Rome, Italy. Tel: (39 6) 686 7581. FAX: (39 6) 688 05417.

FEMINALE – INTERNATIONAL WOMEN'S FILM FESTIVAL
Luxemburgerstrasse 72, D-50674 Cologne, Germany. Tel: (49 221) 416 066. FAX: (49 221) 417 568.

FESTIVAL INTERNATIONAL DE CINEMA FIGUEIRA DA FOZ
Partado dos Correios 50407, 1709 Lisbon Codex, Portugal. Tel: (35 11) 346 9556. FAX: (35 11) 342 0890.

FESTIVAL INTERNATIONAL DU FILM FRANCOPHONE
175 rue des Brasseurs, 5000 Namur, Belgium. Tel: (32 81) 241 236. FAX: (32 81) 241 164.

HAIFA INTERNATIONAL FILM FESTIVAL
142 Hanassi Ave., Haifa 34633, Israel. Tel: (97 24) 386 246. FAX: (97 24) 384 327.

HAMBURG FILM FESTIVAL
Friedensallee 7, 22765 Hamburg, Germany. Tel: (49 40) 3982 6210. FAX: (49 40) 3982 6211.

HELSINKI FILM FESTIVAL – LOVE AND ANARCHY
Unioninkatu 10 A 27, SF-00130 Helsinki, Finland. Tel: (35 80) 629 528. FAX: (35 80) 631 450.

INDEPENDENT FEATURE FILM MARKET
104 West 29th St., 12th Flr., New York, NY 10011. Tel: (212) 465-8200. FAX: (212) 465-8525. URL: http://www.ifp.org

INTERNATIONAL CHILDREN'S FILM FESTIVAL
Deutsches Filmmuseum, Schaumainkai 41, 60596 Frankfurt-am-Main, Germany. Tel: (49 69) 2123 3369. FAX: (49 69) 2123 7881.

INTERNATIONAL FILM FORUM "ARSENALS"
Marstalulela 14, P.O. Box 626, LV-1047 Riga, Latvia. Tel: (37 12) 221 620. FAX: (37 12) 882 0445.

MAGDEBURG INTERNATIONAL FILM FESTIVAL
Coquistrasse 18A, D-39104 Magdeburg, Germany. Tel: (49 391) 401 0875. FAX: (49 391) 48668.

NETHERLANDS FILM FESTIVAL
Hoogt 4, 3512 GW Utrecht, Netherlands. Tel: (31 30) 2 322 684. FAX: (31 30) 2 313 200.

NEW YORK FILM FESTIVAL
Film Society of Lincoln Center, 70 Lincoln Center Plaza, New York, NY 10023. Tel: (212) 875-5638. FAX: (212) 875-5636. email: filmlinc@dti.net. URL: http://www.filmlinc.com

OTTAWA INTERNATIONAL ANIMATION FESTIVAL
2 Daly Ave., Ottaa, Ontario K1N 6E2, Canada. Tel: (613) 232-6727. FAX: (613) 232-6315.

PRIX ITALIA
c/o RAI, Viale Mazzini 14, 00195 Rome, Italy. Tel: (39 6) 3751 4996. FAX: (39 6) 3613 3401.

SAN SEBASTIAN INTERNATIONAL FILM FESTIVAL
Plaza de Okendo s/n, Donostioa-San Sebastian 20080, Spain. Tel: (34 43) 481 212. FAX: (34 43) 481 212.

SANTA FE DE BOGOTA FESTIVAL
Calle 26 No. 4-92, Apartedo Aereo 23398, Santa Fe de Bogota, Colombia. Tel: (57 1) 282 5196. FAX: (57 1) 342 2872.

TELLURIDE FESTIVAL
Stella Pence, c/o National Film Preserve Ltd., Box B1156, Hanover, NH 03755. Tel: (603) 643-1255. FAX: (603) 643-5938. email: tellufilm@aol.com. URL: http://www.telluridemm.com/filmfest.html

TOKYO INTERNATIONAL FILM FESTIVAL
4th Floor, Landic Ginza Bldg. II, 1-6-5 Ginza, Chuo-Ku, Tokyo 104, Japan. Tel: (81 3) 3563 6305. FAX: (81 3) 3563 6310.

TORONTO INTERNATIONAL FILM FESTIVAL
2 Carlton, Toronto, Ontario M5B 1J3, Canada. Tel: (416) 967-7371. FAX: (416) 967-9477.

VANCOUVER INTERNATIONAL FILM FESTIVAL
Ste. 410-1008 Homer St., Vancouver B.C. V6B 2X1, Canada. Tel: (604) 685 0260. FAX: (604) 688 8221.

VENICE FILM FESTIVAL (BIENNALE)
Mostra Internazionale d'Arte Cinematografica, La Biennale, San Marco, Ca Giustinian, 30124 Venice, Italy. Tel: (39 41) 521 8711. FAX: (39 41) 523 6374. Telex: 410685 BLE-VE-1.

OCTOBER

BIRMINGHAM INTERNATIONAL FILM AND TELEVISION FESTIVAL
c/o Central Independent TV, Central House, Broad Street, Birmingham B1 2JP, England. Tel: (44 121) 634 4213. FAX: (44 121) 634 4392.

CHICAGO INTERNATIONAL FILM FESTIVAL
Michael Kutza, 32 W. Randolph St., Ste. 600, Chicago, IL 60601. Tel: (312) 425-9400. FAX: (312) 425-0944. email: filmfest@wwa.com. URL: http://www.chicago.ddbn.com/filmfest

CORK FILM FESTIVAL
Festival Office, Hatfield House, Tobin St., Cork, Ireland. Tel: (353 21) 271 711. FAX: (535 21) 275 945.

DENVER INTERNATIONAL FILM FESTIVAL
Ron Henderson, 1430 Lorimer Sq., Ste. 201, Denver, CO 80202. Tel: (303)595-3456. FAX: (303) 595-0956.

FLANDERS INTERNATIONAL FILM FESTIVAL
Kortrijksesteenweg 1104, B-9051 Ghent, Belgium. Tel: (32 9) 221 8946. FAX: (32 9) 221 9074.

GENEVA FILM FESTIVAL
Case Postale 561, CH-1211 Geneva 11, Switzerland. Tel: (41 22) 321 5466. FAX: (41 22) 321 9862.

HAMPTONS INTERNATIONAL FILM FESTIVAL
3 Newtown Mews, East Hampton, NY 11937. Tel: (516) 324-4600.

INDEPENDENT FILM DAYS
Filmburo Augsburg, Schroeckstrasse 6, 86152 Augsburg, Germany. Tel: (49 821) 153 079. FAX: (49 821) 349 5218.

INTERNATIONAL FILMFESTIVAL MANNHEIM – HEIDELBERG
Collini Center, Galerie, D-68161 Mannheim, Germany. Tel: (49 621) 102 943. FAX: (49 621) 291 564.

INTERNATIONAL HOFER FILMTAGE
c/o Heinz Badewitz, Lothstrasse 28, 80335 Munich, Germany. Tel: (49 89) 129 7422. FAX: (49 89) 123 6868.

ISRAEL FILM FESTIVAL
IsraFest Foundation, 6404 Wilshire Blvd., Suite 1151, Los Angeles CA 90048. Tel: (213) 966-4166. FAX: (213) 658-6346.

LEEDS INTERNATIONAL FILM FESTIVAL
19 Wellington Street, Leeds LS1 4DG, England. Tel: (44 113) 247 8389. FAX: (44 113) 247 8397.

LOS ANGELES INTERNATIONAL FILM FESTIVAL
AFI Festivals, 2021 N. Western Ave., Los Angeles, CA 90027. Tel: (213) 856-7707. FAX: (213) 462-4049.

MARGARET MEAD FILM FESTIVAL
American Museum of Natural History, 79th St. & Central Park West, New York, NY 10024. Tel: (212) 769-5305. FAX: (212) 769-5329.

MIFED
Mrs. Elena Lloyd, E.A. Fiera Internazionale di Milano, Largo Dommodossola 1, 20145 Milano, Italy. Tel: (39 2) 48012 912 x 2920. FAX: (39 2) 49977 020.

MILL VALLEY FILM FESTIVAL
Mark Fishkin, 38 Miller Ave., Ste. 6, Mill Valley CA 94941. (415) 383-5256. FAX: (415) 383-8606. email: finc@well.com. URL: http://www.finc.org

MIPCOM
MIDEM Organisation, 179 avenue Victor Hugo, 75016 Paris, France. Tel: (33 1) 4434 4444. FAX: (33 1) 4434 4400

MONTPELLIER FESTIVAL OF MEDITERRANEAN CINEMA
6 rue Vieille-Aguillerie, 34000 Montpellier, France. Tel: (33) 6766 3636. FAX: (33) 6766 3637.

NORWICH FESTIVAL OF WOMEN FILMMAKERS
Cinema City, St. Andrews St., Norwich NR2 4AD, England. Tel: (44 163) 622 047.

NYON – VISIONS DU REEL
Case Postale 2320, CH-1260, Nyon Switzerland. Tel: (41 22) 3 616 060. FAX: (41 22) 3 617 071.

PORDENONE SILENT FILM FESTIVAL
c/o La Cineteca del Friuli, Via Osoppo 26, 33013 (UD) Italy. Tel: (39 432) 980 458. FAX: (39 432) 970 542.

SAN JUAN CINEMAFEST
P.O. Box 4543, San Juan, Puerto Rico 00902. Tel: (809) 721-6125. FAX: (809) 723-6412.

SAO PAULO INTERNATIONAL FILM FESTIVAL
Al. Lorena 937, CJ 303, 01424-001 Sao Paulo, Brazil. Tel: (55 11) 883 5137. FAX: (55 11) 853 7936.

SHOTS IN THE DARK
Broadway, 14 Broad Street, Nottingham, NG1 3 AL, England. Tel: (44 115) 952 6600. FAX: (44 115) 952 6622.

SHOWEAST
Mitch Neuhauser, NATO ShowEast, 244 W. 49th Street, Ste. 200, New York, NY 10019. (212) 246-6460. FAX: (212) 265-6428.

SITGES FANTASY FILM FESTIVAL
Calle Rossello 257, 3E, 08008 Barcelona, Spain. Tel: (34 3) 415 3938. FAX: (34 3) 237 6521.

SPORTEL
6040 Boulevard East, Ste. 27C, West New York, NJ 07093. Tel: (201) 869-4022. FAX: (201) 869-4335.

UPPSALA INTERNATIONAL SHORT FILM FESTIVAL
Box 1746, S-75147, Uppsala, Sweden. Tel: (46 18) 120 025. FAX: (46 18) 121 350.

VALENCIA FILM FESTIVAL
Plaza del Arzobispo, 2 Bajo, 46003 Valencia, Spain. Tel: (34 96) 392 1506. FAX: (34 96) 391 5156.

VALLADOLID INTERNATIONAL FILM FESTIVAL
P.O. Box 646, 47080 Valladolid, Spain. Tel: (34 83) 305 700. FAX: (34 83) 309 835.

VIENNALE (VIENNA INTERNATIONAL FILM FESTIVAL)
Stiftgasse 6, A-1070 Vienna, Austria. Tel: (43 1) 526 5947. FAX: (43 1) 934 172.

WARSAW FILM FESTIVAL
P.O. Box 816, 00-950 Warsaw 1, Poland. Tel: (48 22) 635 7591.

YAMAGATA INTERNATIONAL DOCUMENTARY FILM FESTIVAL
Kitagawa Building, 4th floor, 6-42 Kagurazaka Shinjuku-ku, Tokyo 162, Japan. Tel: (81 3) 3266 9704. FAX: (81 3) 3266 9700.

NOVEMBER

AMERICAS FILM FESTIVAL
19th & Constitution Ave., NW, Washington DC 20006. Tel: (202) 458-6379. FAX: (202) 458-3122.

AMIENS INTERNATIONAL FILM FESTIVAL
36 rue de Noyon, 8000 Amiens, France. Tel: (33) 2291 0144. FAX: (33) 2292 5304.

ANNUAL SPAA CONFERENCE
Southern Cross Hotel, 131 Exhibition St., Melbourne 3001, Australia. Tel: (61 3) 262 2277. FAX: (61 3) 262 2323.

BRITISH FILM FESTIVAL
8 Passage Digard, 50100 Cherbourg, France. Tel: (33) 9338 94. FAX: (33) 0120 78.

CAIRO INTERNATIONAL FILM FESTIVAL
17 Kasr El Nir Street, Cairo, Egypt. Tel: (20 2) 392 3962. FAX: (20 2) 392 3562.

CHILDREN'S FILM FESTIVAL
Filmburo Augsberg, Schroekstr. 6, 86152 Augsberg, Germany. Tel: (49 821) 153 079. FAX: (49 821) 349 5218.

DUISBERG FILM WEEK
Am Konig-Heinrich-Platz, D-47049, Guisberg, Germany. Tel: (49 203) 283 4187. FAX: (49 203) 283 4130.

FESTIVAL DEI POPOLI
Via Castellani 8, 50122 Firenze, Italy. Tel: (39 55) 294 353. FAX: (39 55) 213 698.

FESTIVAL DES 3 CONTINENTS
19 Passage Pmmeraye, BP-3306, 44033 Nantes Cedex 01, France. Tel: (33) 4069 7414. FAX: (33) 4073 5522.

FESTIVAL INTERNATIONAL DU FILM JUIF ET ISRAELIEN DE MONTPELLIER
500 Boulevard d'Antigone, 34000 Montpellier, France. Tel: (33) 6715 0872. FAX: (33) 6715 0872.

FESTIVAL INTERNAZIONALE CINEMA GIOVANI
Via Monte di Pieta 1, 10120 Torino, Italy. Tel: (39 11) 562 3309. FAX: (39 11) 562 9796.

FESTIVAL SINATRON INDONESIA
Sekretariat Pantap, Kedoya Center, Jl. Perjuangan-Block II No. 1, Kebon Jeruk, Jakarta 11063, Indonesia. Tel: (62 21) 533 0467. FAX: (62 21) 533 0467.

FORT LAUDERDALE INTERNATIONAL FILM FESTIVAL
2633 East Sunrise Blvd., Fort Lauderdale, FL 33304-3205.

HAWAII INTERNATIONAL FILM FESTIVAL
Christian Gaines, 100 Bishop St., Suite 745, Pacific Tower, Honolulu, HI 96813. Tel: (808) 528-3456. FAX: (808) 528-1410. URL: http://www.hiff.org

HEARTLAND FILM FESTIVAL
613 N. East Street, Indianapolis, IN 46202. Tel: (317) 464-9405. FAX: (317) 635-4201.

HOLLAND ANIMATION FILM FESTIVAL
Hoogt 4, 3512 GW Utrecht, The Netherlands. Tel: (31 30) 312 216. FAX: (31 30) 312 940.

INTERNATIONAL ANIMATED FILM FESTIVAL
Rua 62, No. 251 4501 Espinho Codex, Portugal. Tel: (35 12) 721 611. FAX: (35 12) 726 015.

INTERNATIONAL THESSALONIKI FILM FESTIVAL
36 Sina Street, GR 10672 Athens, Greece. Tel: (30 1) 361 0418. FAX: (30 1) 362 1023.

JUNIOR DUBLIN FILM FESTIVAL
Irish Film Centre, 6 Eustace St., Dublin 2, Ireland. Tel: (353 1) 677 7095. FAX: (353 1) 677 8755.

LONDON FILM FESTIVAL
London Film Festival, South Bank, London SE1 8XT, England. Tel: (44 171) 815 1322. FAX: (44 171) 633 0786.

NEW YORK EXPOSITION OF SHORT FILM & VIDEO
New York Expo, 532 La Guardia Place, Box 330, New York, NY. Tel: (212) 505-7742.

NORDIC FILM DAYS LUBECK
D-23539 Lubeck, Germany. Tel: (49 451) 122 4105. FAX: (49 451) 122 7197.

NORTHWEST FILM & VIDEO FESTIVAL
N.W. Film Center, 1219 S.W. Park Ave., Portland, OR 97205. Tel: (503) 221-1156. FAX: (503) 226-4842.

OULU INTERNATIONAL CHILDREN'S FILM FESTIVAL
Torikatu 8, 90100 Oulu, Finland. Tel: (35 881) 314 1735. FAX: (35 881) 314 1730.

PUERTO RICO INTERNATIONAL FILM FESTIVAL
70 Mayaguez St., Ste. B-1 Hato Rey, Puerto Rico 00918. Tel: (809) 764-7044. FAX: (809) 763-4997.

RAINDANCE FILM SHOWCASE & MARKET
81 Berwick St., London W1V 3PF, England. Tel: (44 171) 437 3991. FAX: (44 171) 439 2243.

SARASOTA FRENCH FILM FESTIVAL
5555 North Tamiami Trail, Sarasota, FL 34243. Tel: (813) 351-9010. FAX: (813) 351-5796

TAIPEI GOLDEN HORSE FILM FESTIVAL
Room 7F, No. 45 Chilin Rd., Taipei 104, Taiwan. Tel: (88 62) 567 5861. FAX: (88 62) 531 8966.

TYNESIDE EUROPEAN FILM FESTIVAL
Tyneside Cinema, 10 Pilgrim St., Newcastle-upon-Tyne NE1 6QG, England. Tel: (44 191) 232 8289. FAX: (44 191) 221 0535.

WELSH INTERNATIONAL FILM FESTIVAL
Unit 8C, Cefn Llan, Aberystwyth, Dyfed SY23 3AH, Wales. Tel: (19 70) 617 995. FAX: (19 70) 617 942.

WORLDFEST – CHARLESTON
2700 Post Oak Blvd., Ste. 1798, Houston, TX 77056. Tel: (713) 965-9955. FAX: (713) 965-9960. email: worldfest@aol.com URL: http://www.world-fest.com

DECEMBER

ESSEN INTERNATIONAL FESTIVAL OF FILMS FOR CHILDREN
Baumstrasse 24, D-45128 Essen, Germany. Tel: (49 201) 794 951. FAX: (49 201) 794 952.

FESTIVAL OF INTERNATIONAL CINEMA STUDENTS
FFICS Secretariat, c/o Tokyo Agency Inc., 4-8-18 Akasaka, Minato-ku, Tokyo 107, Japan. Tel: (81 3) 3475 3855. FAX: (81 3) 5411 0382.

INTERNATIONAL DOCUMENTARY FILMFESTIVAL AMSTERDAM (IFDA)
Kleine Gartmenplantsoen 10, 1017 RR Amsterdam, The Netherlands. Tel: (49 20) 627 3329. FAX: (49 20) 638 5388.

MIP ASIA SCREENINGS & CONFERENCES
Reed Midem Organisation, 179 Victor Hugo, 75116 Paris, France. Tel: (33 1) 4434 4444. FAX: (33 1) 4434 4400.

NOIR IN FESTIVAL
Via dei Coronari 44, 00186 Rome, Italy. Tel: (39 6) 683 3844. FAX: (39 6) 686 7902.

RENCONTRES DU CINEMA ITALIEN D'ANNECY
Banlieu Scene Nationale, 1 rue Jean Jaures-BP 294, 74007 Annecy Cedex, France. Tel: (33) 5033 4400. FAX: (33) 5051 8209.

ENTERTAINMENT INDUSTRY MERGERS

(SEPTEMBER 1, 1997—OCTOBER 15, 1998)

The following list of mergers and acquisitions shows information current as of October, 1998. Since that date, some pending mergers may have been completed. Pending acquisitions do not have effective dates.

Date Announced	Date Effective	Acquisition Target	Target Country	Acquired by	Acquiror Country	Status
			September, 1997			
09/01/97	10/29/97	E-Plus Mobilfunk GmbH (Otelo)	Germany	Otelo Communications GmbH	Germany	Completed
09/01/97	09/01/97	JMB Pty Ltd-PMFM and 94.5 FM	Australia	Austereo Ltd (Village Roadshow)	Australia	Completed
09/01/97		WGNT-TV,Portsmouth,VA	U.S.	Paramount Stations Group	U.S.	Pending
09/02/97	01/26/98	Cablevision Sys-Cable Systems	U.S.	Mediacom LLC	U.S.	Completed
09/03/97		Bimcom (Cable & Wireless PLC)	U.K.	GN Store Nord A/S	Denmark	Pending
09/03/97		Martin Dawes Communications	U.K.	Scottish Telecom	U.K.	Pending
09/03/97	08/29/97	Gaylord Entertainment Company	U.S.	Richard C. Blum & Assoc.	U.S.	Completed
09/03/97		Oulun Puhelin	Finland	Finnet 11 (Finnet)	Finland	Pending
09/04/97	12/30/97	Cinergi Pictures Entertainment	U.S.	Valdina Corp. NV	U.S.	Completed
09/04/97		Classic Sports Network Inc	U.S.	ESPN Inc (Capital Cities/ABC)	U.S.	Pending
09/04/97	10/15/97	KENS-TV, San Antonio,TX	U.S.	AH Belo Corp	U.S.	Completed
09/05/97	09/05/97	GP Film Services	U.K.	VFG PLC	U.K.	Completed
09/05/97		Petracom Holdings Inc.	U.S.	Quorum Broadcasting Inc.	U.S.	Pending
09/08/97	09/08/97	MTV	Finland	Tidnings Marieberg AB	Sweden	Completed
09/08/97	09/08/97	Monarchy BV	Netherlands	Fox Filmed Ent (News Corp)	U.S.	Completed
09/08/97	09/08/97	Six Street Studios Pty Ltd	South Africa	Abacus Technology Holdings Ltd	South Africa	Completed
09/08/97		Synergy Broadcasting Inc .	U.S.	Jacor Communications Inc.	U.S.	Pending
09/09/97	11/01/97	Cie Generale de Video-Commun	France	Canal Plus SA	France	Completed
09/09/97	05/01/98	New Regency Productions Inc.	U.S.	Fox Filmed Ent (News Corp)	U.S.	Completed
09/09/97		Procono Television	Spain	Supercanal SA	Argentina	Pending
09/10/97		Travel Channel (Paxson Commun)	U.S.	Discovery Communications Inc	U.S.	Pending
09/11/97	11/17/97	Capitol Industries-10 Theaters	U.S.	Regal Cinemas Inc	U.S.	Completed
09/11/97		Cottonwood Communications LLC	U.S.	GOCOM Television	U.S.	Pending
09/11/97	09/11/97	Mandalay Television	U.S.	Lion's Gate Entertainment Corp	Canada	Completed
09/11/97		WKBN-TV,Youngstown,OH	U.S.	GOCOM Television	U.S.	Completed
09/12/97	09/12/97	AlphaNet Telecom Inc	Canada	Indosat PT (Indonesia)	Indonesia	Completed
09/12/97		Cinepix Film Properties Inc.	Canada	Lion's Gate Entertainment Corp	Canada	Intended
09/12/97		Ten Group (Oltec Ltd/CanWest)	Australia	Telecasters North Queensland	Australia	Pending
09/12/97	09/12/97	United Artists-Theaters (5)	U.S.	Clearview Cinema Group Inc.	U.S.	Completed
09/12/97	09/12/97	Via Digital	Spain	Direct TV	U.S.	Completed
09/16/97		ABC Cinemas-20 City Centres	U.K.	Seeking Buyer		S. Buyer
09/16/97	11/04/97	All American Communications	U.S.	Pearson PLC	U.K.	Completed
09/16/97		KXGR TV-46,Tuscon,AZ (Sungilt)	U.S.	Paxson Communications Corp.	U.S.	Pending
09/16/97		WFAY TV-62,Raleigh,NC	U.S.	Paxson Communications Corp.	U.S.	Pending
09/16/97		WKRP TV-29,Charleston,NC	U.S.	Paxson Communications Corp.	U.S.	Pending
09/18/97		Educ Media Australia-Bus Asts	Australia	Entertainment World Ltd.	Australia	Pending
09/18/97		TV3 (Budapest Communications)	Hungary	Investor Group	Bermuda	Pending
09/22/97	10/21/97	USA Network	U.S.	Seagram Co Ltd.	Canada	Completed
09/24/97	09/23/97	Carmike Cinemas Inc	U.S.	Investor	U.S.	Completed
09/24/97	09/24/97	Cox Communications Inc-Sun	U.S.	Mediacom LLC	U.S.	Completed
09/24/97		Electric Pictures Ltd	U.K.	Alliance Communications Corp.	Canada	Completed
09/24/97	01/12/98	Jones Cable Fund 1-B/C Venture	U.S.	Mediacom LLC	U.S.	Completed
09/26/97		Antena 3 Television	Spain	Recoletos Cia Editorial SA	Spain	Pending
09/26/97	12/10/97	Movie City 8,Edison,NJ	U.S.	Clearview Cinema Group Inc.	U.S.	Completed
09/26/97	12/10/97	Movie City 5,Woodbridge,NJ	U.S.	Clearview Cinema Group Inc	U.S.	Completed
09/26/97		Prime Cable of Chicago	U.S.	Prime Cable Corp/Carlyle Group	U.S.	Pending
09/26/97		SBC Communications-Cable TV	U.S.	Prime Cable Corp/Carlyle Group	U.S.	Pending
09/29/97	09/29/97	United Artists-Theaters	Mexico	GC Cos	U.S.	Completed
09/30/97	09/30/97	Asia Satellite Telecommun Hldg	Hong Kong	Cable & Wireless PLC	U.K	Completed
09/30/97	12/01/97	Euronews	France	Independent Television News	U.K.	Completed
09/30/97	09/30/97	Harmony Holdings Inc	U.S.	Children's Broadcasting Corp	U.S.	Completed
09/30/97		Metrocable	U.S.	Definition Ltd	U.S.	Pending
09/30/97	09/30/97	Supercanal Holding SA	Argentina	Multicanal SA (Grupo Clarin)	Argentina	Completed
			October, 1997			
10/01/97	05/14/98	Cineplex Odeon Corp	Canada	Sony Retail Ent (Sony Corp)	U.S.	Completed
10/01/97	10/01/97	Lake Dillon Cinema Movie	U.S.	Trans-Lux Colorado (Trans-Lux)	U.S.	Completed
10/01/97	10/01/97	National Cable Acquisition	U.S.	Olympus Capital Corp	U.S.	Completed
10/03/97	10/03/97	Fit TV Cable Network	U.S.	Liberty Networks	U.S.	Completed
10/03/97		Jones Intercable-Broward Cable	U.S.	Comcast Corp	U.S.	Pending
10/07/97		Roslyn Trio Multiplex Cinema	U.S.	Clearview Cinema Group Inc	U.S.	Pending
10/07/97		WRBW-TV,Orlando,Florida	U.S.	United Television Inc	U.S.	Pending
10/09/97	12/04/97	Act III Theatres Inc	U.S.	Kohlberg Kravis Roberts & Co	U.S.	Completed
10/10/97	10/28/97	Fintelco SA	Argentina	Multicanal SA (Grupo Clarin)	Argentina	Completed
10/10/97		Fintelco SA	Argentina	Cablevision SA	Chile	Pending

Date Announced	Date Effective	Acquisition Target	Target Country	Acquired By	Acquiror Country	Status
10/10/97	10/10/97	Ulster Television	U.K.	CanWest Global Communications	Canada	Completed
10/13/97		Moonlighting Filmmakers	South Africa	Carrig Diamonds Ltd	South Africa	Pending
10/13/97		Penguin Films	South Africa	Carrig Diamonds Ltd	South Africa	Pending
10/14/97		Pacific Title & Art Studio	U.S.	Safeguard Scientifics Mirage Entertainment Sciences	U.S.	Pending
10/14/97	02/17/98	UTV Cable Network	Thailand	Intl Broadcasting Corp Ltd	Thailand	Completed
10/15/97	10/15/97	Ray-Art Studios	U.S.	Investor Group	U.S.	Completed
10/15/97		Television Interactive del	Mexico	Investor Group	U.K.	Pending
10/16/97		CNBC Europe (NBC/RCA/GE)	U.K.	European Business News	U.K.	Intended
10/16/97	03/03/98	KXAS-TV,Dallas,Texas	U.S.	KNSD-TV,CA (NBC/RCA/GE)	U.S.	Completed
10/16/97	01/30/98	Mandeville Cable Partners	Argentina	Cablevision SA de Argentina	Argentina	Completed
10/17/97	10/17/97	Asia Bdcstg & Commun Network	Thailand	United Communication Industry	Thailand	Completed
10/17/97	10/17/97	Satellite Media Services	U.K.	Gold and Appel	U.S.	Completed
10/17/97	10/17/97	Sega Channel	U.S.	Entertainment Online	U.K.	Completed
10/17/97	02/12/98	Universal Studios-TV assets	U.S.	HSN Inc	U.S.	Completed
10/20/97	10/20/97	TV Cable,Cable DU-KE,Multivisi	Argentina	Multicanal SA (Grupo Clarin)	Argentina	Completed
10/21/97	12/08/97	Windlight Studios Inc	U.S.	Nelvana Ltd	Canada	Completed
10/22/97	10/22/97	Phase II Broadcasting Inc	U.S.	Sinclair Broadcast Group Inc	U.S.	Completed
10/23/97	10/23/97	Grosso-Jacobson Companies	U.S.	Producers Entertainment Group	U.S.	Completed
10/23/97		XTV Ltd (Tele-Cine Cell Group)	U.K.	Tele-Cine Cell Group PLC	U.K.	Pending
10/27/97	01/20/98	TeleDanmark A/S (Denmark)	Denmark	Ameritech Corp	U.S.	Completed
10/28/97		Gym Vision Pty Ltd-Gym Vision	Australia	Media Entertainment Group Ltd	Australia	Pending
10/29/97	12/04/97	Celcore Inc	U.S.	DSC Communications Corp	U.S.	Completed
10/30/97	10/30/97	Sun Cable	Philippines	Sky Cable Corp	Philippines	Completed
10/31/97	10/31/97	Of Sound Mind	U.S.	Marquee Entertainment Inc	U.S.	Completed

November, 1997

Date Announced	Date Effective	Acquisition Target	Target Country	Acquired By	Acquiror Country	Status
11/03/97	01/05/98	Broadband Networks Inc	Canada	Northern Telecom Ltd (BCE Inc)	Canada	Completed
11/03/97	02/03/98	Regional Cablesystems Inc	Canada	Canadian Satellite Commun Inc	Canada	Completed
11/06/97	04/28/98	Digital Television Services	U.S.	Pegasus Communications Corp	U.S.	Completed
11/06/97		Pegasus Comm-Cable Systems	U.S.	Avalon Partners	U.S.	Pending
11/06/97		WJCB-TV,Norfolk,Virgina	U.S.	Paxson Communications Corp	U.S.	Pending
11/06/97		WPMC-TV,Knoxville,Tennessee	U.S.	Paxson Communications Corp	U.S.	Intended
11/10/97		Advanced Electronic Sdn Bhd	Malaysia	Cable-Vision Corp Sdn Bhd	Malaysia	Pending
11/10/97		CTV Television Network Ltd	Canada	Baton Broadcasting Inc	Canada	Pending
11/10/97	11/10/97	Metro-Goldwyn-Mayer Inc	U.S.	Tracinda Corp	U.S.	Completed
11/11/97	11/11/97	CTV Television Network Ltd	Canada	Baton Broadcasting Inc	Canada	Completed
11/11/97		Citadel Entertainment Inc	U.S.	Alliance Communications Corp	Canada	Pending
11/11/97	11/11/97	GOCOM Television	U.S.	GOCOM Comm.(Bain Capital Inc)	U.S.	Completed
11/11/97		Southland Theaters-Theaters (2)	U.S.	Clearview Cinema Group Inc	U.S.	Pending
11/11/97		ST Research	U.S.	Daedalus Enterprises Inc	U.S.	Pending
11/11/97		Time Warner Cable-Cable System	U.S.	Cable One Inc	U.S.	Pending
11/13/97		Telekabel NV (NUON)	Netherlands	United and Philips Comm	Netherlands	Pending
11/13/97	01/21/98	WHSW-TV,Baltimore,Maryland	U.S.	United Television Inc	U.S.	Completed
11/14/97		CJM Ent-Movie Theaters (27)	U.S.	Clearview Cinema Group Inc	U.S.	Pending
11/14/97		Lakeland Group Television Inc	U.S.	Sinclair Broadcast Group Inc	U.S.	Pending
11/14/97	11/14/97	TV Quattro	Romania	Metromedia Intl Telecom	U.S.	Completed
11/17/97	01/22/98	CanalSatelite (Sogecable)	Spain	Warner Bros Inc	U.S.	Completed
11/17/97	03/02/98	KBGE-TV,Seattle,Washington	U.S.	Paxson Communications Corp	U.S.	Completed
11/17/97	03/02/98	ValueVision Intl-Stn (2),Oregon	U.S.	Paxson Communications Corp	U.S.	Completed
11/19/97	08/12/98	Telemundo Group Inc	U.S.	Liberty Media Apollo Group Inc. Bastion Capital Corp. Sony Pictures Entertainment	U.S.	Completed
11/19/97	04/13/98	Time Warner Inc-Cable Systems	U.S.	Morgan Stanley Capital Renaissance Media Partners LLC	U.S.	Completed
11/20/97		Fifth Avenue Channel Inc	U.S.	Tel-Com Wireless Cable TV Corp	U.S.	Pending
11/20/97		Hungarian Satellite and Cable	U.S.	Shareholders	U.S.	Pending
11/20/97		WPMC-TV,Knoxville,Tennessee	U.S.	Paxson Communications Corp	U.S.	Intended
11/21/97		British Sky Broadcasting	U.K.	Seeking Buyer	Unknown	
11/24/97	12/29/97	Cinamerica Theatres LP	U.S.	WestStar Holdings Inc	U.S.	Completed
11/24/97		Mountain Brook Cablevision Inc	U.S.	Marcus Cable Co	U.S.	Pending
11/24/97	11/24/97	Nelson Ferman-Theaters (2)	U.S.	Clearview Cinema Group Inc	U.S.	Completed
11/26/97	11/26/97	Channel Nine Network	Argentina	Prime Television Ltd	Australia	Completed
11/27/97		WFXG-TV (Augusta Family)	U.S.	Retlaw Enterprises Inc	U.S.	Pending
11/27/97	11/27/97	WXTX-TV,Columbus,Georgia	U.S.	Retlaw Enterprises Inc	U.S.	Completed
11/28/97	11/28/97	TV Azteca	Mexico	Ricardo Salinas Pliega	Mexico	Completed

December, 1997

Date Announced	Date Effective	Acquisition Target	Target Country	Acquired By	Acquiror Country	Status
12/01/97	12/01/97	Fast Forward Inc	U.S.	VDI Media	U.S.	Completed
12/01/97		Telelatino Network	Canada	Shaw Communications Inc	Canada	Pending
12/02/97	08/14/98	Groupe Videotron-Alberta Cable	Canada	Videon Cablesystems Inc	Canada	Completed
12/03/97	01/15/98	CDR-Epic Film Library	France	PolyGram Filmed Entertainment	U.S.	Completed
12/03/97		Max Media Properties LLC-Radio	U.S.	Sinclair Broadcast Group Inc	U.S.	Pending
12/03/97		Szczecinska Telewizja Kablowa	Poland	PTK-Szczecin (@Entertainment)	Poland	Pending
12/04/97	12/04/97	Adelphia Comm-NY,NC Cable Sys	U.S.	Time Warner Entertain-Advance	U.S.	Completed
12/04/97	12/04/97	Idan Cable Systems Ltd	Israel	Investor Group	Israel	Completed
12/04/97	01/02/98	La Red Television Network	Chile	TV Azteca	Mexico	Completed

Date Announced	Date Effective	Acquisition Target	Target Country	Acquired By	Acquiror Country	Status
12/04/97		WSYT-TV,WNYS-TV,6 others	U.S.	Sinclair Broadcast Group Inc	U.S.	Pending
12/08/97	04/01/98	Marcus Cable-DE,MD Cable TV	U.S.	Comcast Corp	U.S.	Completed
12/08/97		Scripps Howard Production	U.S.	Seeking Buyer	Unknown	S. Buyer
12/09/97		Asia Business News (Singapore)	Singapore	CNBC Asia (Natl Bdcstg Co Inc)	Hong Kong	Pending
12/09/97		European Business News	U.K.	CNBC Europe (NBC/RCA/GE)	U.K.	Pending
12/09/97		TCI Comm. (Tele-Comm)	U.S.	Century Communications Corp	U.S.	Pending
12/10/97	12/10/97	Arabsat-Satellite	India	India	India	Completed
12/10/97	12/10/97	Kenya Television Network	Kenya	East African Standard	Kenya	Completed
12/11/97	05/08/98	Guetschoff Theatre-Theatres (6)	U.S.	Marcus Theatre Corp (Marcus)	Canada	Completed
12/11/97		TCI Communications Inc-South	U.S.	US WEST Media-IL&MI Cable Sys	U.S.	Pending
12/12/97	12/19/97	Casema (Vision Networks NV)	Netherlands	France Telecom SA (France)	France	Completed
12/14/97	12/14/97	Channel Nine Network	Argentina	Torneos y Competencias SA	Argentina	Completed
12/16/97	03/02/97	Integrated Tele Prod-Services	U.S.	InterVoice Inc	U.S.	Completed
12/16/97	02/01/98	MovieVision Inc	U.S.	SIMS Communications Inc	U.S.	Completed
12/17/97	12/17/97	Grupo Saba	Mexico	TV Azteca	Mexico	Completed
12/17/97	04/27/98	Landmark Theatre Corp	U.S.	Silver Cinemas International	U.S.	Completed
12/20/97		Cineplex Odeon-Film Dstbn	Canada	Seeking Buyer	Unknown	S. Buyer
12/20/97	05/01/98	PerfecTV	Japan	JSkyB (News Corp,Softbank,Fuji)	Japan	Completed
12/24/97		Kings Road Entertainment Inc	U.S.	Morgan Kent	U.S.	Pending
12/29/97	12/28/97	Multicanal Participacoes SA	Brazil	Banco Bradesco de Investimento	Brazil	Completed
12/30/97	12/30/97	AlphaStar Television Network	U.S.	Champion Holding Co	U.S.	Completed
12/31/97	12/31/97	MY TV	S. Korea	SK Business Group	S. Korea	Completed

January, 1998

Date Announced	Date Effective	Acquisition Target	Target Country	Acquired By	Acquiror Country	Status
01/02/98	01/02/98	DirecTv Inc	U.S.	Digital Television Services	U.S.	Completed
01/02/98	01/02/98	LIN Television Corp	U.S.	Mario Gabelli	U.S.	Completed
01/05/98		Filmove Laborate Barrandov	Czech	Republic Seeking Buyer	Unknown	S. Buyer
01/06/98	01/06/98	Global Television Networks Inc	U.S.	Hungarian Broadcasting Corp	U.S.	Completed
01/06/98		Newsforce (UK) Ltd	U.K.	France Telecom SA (France)	France	Intended
01/06/98	03/31/98	Phoenix Network Inc	U.S.	Qwest Communications Corp	U.S.	Completed
01/09/98	01/09/98	Gedeon Communications	France	Canal Plus SA	France	Completed
01/12/98		Isla Communications (Asiacom)	Philippines	Deutsche Telekom AG (Germany)	Germany	Pending
01/13/98	01/13/98	E! Online (CNET Inc,E!)	U.S.	E! Entertainment Television	U.S.	Completed
01/13/98		WLAJ-TV,Lansing,Michigan	U.S.	Freedom Communications Inc	U.S.	Pending
01/13/98	07/15/98	WWMT-TV Kalamazoo,Michigan	U.S.	Freedom Communications Inc	U.S.	Completed
01/15/98	08/03/98	Busse Broadcasting Corp	U.S.	Gray Communications Systems	U.S.	Completed
01/15/98	01/15/98	Rural Missouri Cable TV	U.S.	Rapid Communications Partners	U.S.	Completed
01/16/98	01/16/98	Funbag Animation Studios	Canada	PolyGram Filmed Entertainment	U.S.	Completed
01/20/98	01/20/98	Ardman Broadcasting-Towers (5)	U.S.	OmniAmerica Communications Inc	U.S.	Completed
01/20/98	05/27/98	Regal Cinemas Inc	U.S.	Kohlberg Kravis Roberts & Co. Hicks Muse Tate & Furst, Inc.	U.S.	Completed
01/20/98	01/20/98	Via Digital	Spain	Galaxy Latin America DTH	Venezuela	Completed
01/21/98		Cineplex Odeon Corp-Millburn	U.S.	Clearview Cinema Group Inc	U.S.	Pending
01/23/98		CF-Nrthn Ontario Cable TV Sys	Canada	Regional Cablesystems Inc	Canada	Pending
01/23/98		Regional Cabl-Quebec Cable Div	Canada	Groupe Videotron Ltee	Canada	Pending
01/26/98		Christian Commun-WCFC TV-38	U.S.	Paxson Communications Corp	U.S.	Pending
01/26/98		Sinclair Broadcast Gp Stn (3)	U.S.	Entertainment Communications	U.S.	Pending
01/27/98	05/31/98	Intl Broadcasting Corp Ltd	Thailand	Universal Cable Television	Thailand	Completed
01/27/98		Tele-Comm-CT Cable TV Prop	U.S.	Cablevision Systems Corp	U.S.	Pending
01/27/98	01/27/98	Gilat Satellite Networks Ltd	Israel	Investor Group	Israel	Completed
01/28/98	01/28/98	Comunicacoes por Cabo-Certain	Portugal	Televisao por Cabo SA	Portugal	Completed
01/28/98		Hoyts Cinemas Ltd-Hoyts Centre	Australia	Village Entertainment Property	Australia	Pending
01/30/98		Multimedia Cablevision-Cable		TCI Communications (Tele-Comm)	U.S.	Pending

February, 1998

Date Announced	Date Effective	Acquisition Target	Target Country	Acquired By	Acquiror Country	Status
02/02/98	02/02/98	American Multi-Cinema Inc-Gulf	U.S.	Entertainment Properties Trust	U.S.	Completed
02/02/98	02/02/98	Millburn Cinemas,Millburn,NJ	U.S.	Clearview Cinema Group Inc	U.S.	Completed
02/02/98	02/02/98	STAR Satellite TV and Radio	U.S.	New Visual Entertainment	U.S.	Completed
02/02/98	03/09/98	United Artists-Manhasset	U.S.	Clearview Cinema Group Inc	U.S.	Completed
02/02/98	03/09/98	United Artists-Babylon	U.S.	Clearview Cinema Group Inc	U.S.	Completed
02/03/98		Sinclair Bdcst-WPTZ-TV,WNNE-TV	U.S.	STC Broadcasting Inc	U.S.	Pending
02/04/98	02/04/98	Community TV Corp	U.S.	Harron Commmunications Corp	U.S.	Completed
02/04/98		Spice Entertainment Cos Inc	U.S.	Playboy Enterprises Inc	U.S.	Pending
02/05/98		WFHL-TV,Decatur,Illinois	U.S.	Paxson Communications Corp	U.S.	Pending
02/05/98		Comcast UK Cable Partners Ltd	Bermuda	NTL Inc	U.S.	Pending
02/06/98	06/23/98	Broadcast Communications PLC	U.K.	Endemol Entertainment BV	Netherlands	Completed
02/11/98		Antena 3 Television	Spain	Seeking Buyer	Unknown	S Buyer
02/11/98	02/11/98	Blue Sky Networks	South Africa	Usko Ltd	South Africa	Completed
02/17/98		Canal 9	Spain	Seeking Buyer	Unknown	S Buyer
02/17/98		JV-Hoyts Cinames Ltd,Endeavor	Australia	Hoyts Cinemas Ltd	Australia	Pending
02/18/98		Citra Imaji Kreatif PT	Indonesia	Rajawali Citra Televisi Indone	Indonesia	Pending
02/18/98		Superstar/Netlink Group LLC	U.S.	United Video Satellite Group	U.S.	Pending
02/19/98		Fox Children's Network (Fox)	U.S.	Fox Kids Worldwide Inc	U.S.	Pending
02/20/98	07/02/98	Sunrise Television-WPTZ-TV,oth	U.S.	Hearst-Argyle Television Inc	U.S.	Completed
02/20/98	05/29/98	SFX Broadcasting Inc	U.S.	Capstar Broadcasting Partners	U.S.	Completed
02/23/98		Atlantic 252 (CLT-UFA)	U.K.	Seeking Buyer	Unknown	S Buyer
02/23/98		RTL Country (CTL-UFA)	U.K.	Seeking Buyer	Unknown	S Buyer
02/23/98	07/01/98	Sullivan Broadcast Holdings	U.S.	Sinclair Broadcast Group Inc	U.S.	Completed

Date Announced	Date Effective	Acquisition Target	Target Country	Acquired By	Acquiror Country	Status
02/23/98	02/23/98	Ulster Television	U.K.	CanWest Global Communications	Canada	Completed
02/27/98	06/15/98	Lancit Media Entertainment Ltd	U.S.	RCN Corp	U.S.	Completed

March, 1998

Date Announced	Date Effective	Acquisition Target	Target Country	Acquired By	Acquiror Country	Status
03/02/98	03/31/98	Fitto Entertainment Holdings	Hong Kong	Investor	Hong Kong	Completed
03/02/98		Tirrenia Studios	Italy	Cecchi Gori Communication	Italy	Pending
03/03/98	05/14/98	RTL 9 (CLT-UFA/Bertelsmann AG)	Luxembourg	Groupe AB SA	France	Completed
03/04/98		Marcus Cable Co-Connecticut	U.S.	TMC Holdings Ltd	Canada	Pending
03/09/98		5th Dimension Commun-Satellite	Canada	New Frontier Media Inc	U.S.	Pending
03/09/98		MultiMedios America	Argentina	Torneos y Competencias SA	Argentina	Pending
03/10/98		Cabletel LLC	Israel	Tevel Broadcast International	Israel	Pending
03/11/98	03/11/98	Canal 4 Multivision	Costa Rica	TV Azteca	Mexico	Completed
03/11/98	03/11/98	Zlin Film Studio (Bonton Group)	Czech Rep.	Bonton Group	Czech Rep.	Completed
03/12/98		Cable TV Fund-Palmdale System	U.S.	Jones Intercable Inc	U.S.	Pending
03/12/98		Cable TV Fund-Littlerock Sys	U.S.	Jones Intercable Inc	U.S.	Pending
03/12/98		Supercable Sevilla	Spain	Supercable Valencia	Spain	Pending
03/13/98	03/13/98	Video Services Corp	U.S.	Sandler Capital Management	U.S.	Completed
03/16/98	03/16/98	N Oakland Cablevision,TVC	U.S.	FrontierVision Oper Partners	U.S.	Completed
03/17/98	03/17/98	East African TV Network	Kenya	African Broadcasting Ltd	Kenya	Completed
03/17/98	03/20/98	Sky Channel	Australia	Totalizator Agency Board	Australia	Completed
03/20/98	03/20/98	Time Warner	U.S.	Citibank NA (Citicorp)	U.S.	Completed
03/20/98	03/20/98	WPXP TV-67,West Palm Beach,FL	U.S.	Paxson Communications Corp	U.S.	Completed
03/23/98	03/23/98	BET Holdings Inc	U.S.	Mario Gabelli	U.S.	Completed
03/26/98		Asia Television	Hong Kong	Rupert Murdoch	U.S.	Pending
03/27/98		Outdoor Life	U.S.	Fox/Liberty Networks	U.S.	Pending
03/27/98		Speedvision	U.S.	Fox/Liberty Networks	U.S.	Pending
03/31/98		Baton Broadcasting Inc	Canada	Electrohome Broadcasting Ltd	Canada	Pending
03/31/98	07/31/98	Cable One Inc-Cable Sys (14)	U.S.	Classic Communications Inc	U.S.	Completed
03/31/98		KHON-TV, WVUE-TV	U.S.	Emmis Broadcasting Corp	U.S.	Pending
03/31/98		WALA-TV, WLUK-TV	U.S.	Emmis Broadcasting Corp	U.S.	Completed
03/31/98	07/31/98	Marcus Cable-MO,LA,TX,OK Cable	U.S.	Cable One Inc	U.S.	Completed
03/31/98		Natl Film Dvlp,Film Negara	Malaysia	Investor Group	U.S.	Pending
03/31/98		WTHI-TV,WFTX-TV (Wabash Valley)	U.S.	Emmis Broadcasting Corp	U.S.	Pending
03/31/98	03/27/98	WOAC-TV,Cleveland,Ohio	U.S.	Shop at Home Inc	U.S.	Completed

April, 1998

Date Announced	Date Effective	Acquisition Target	Target Country	Acquired By	Acquiror Country	Status
04/03/98	04/03/98	Marcus Cable Co	U.S.	Paul Allen	U.S.	Completed
04/04/98	04/04/98	Golden Harvest Entertainment	Hong Kong	Village Roadshow Corp Ltd	Australia	Completed
04/06/98		Tele-Cine Cell Group PLC	U.K.	Todd-AO Europe Holding Co Ltd	U.K.	Completed
04/07/98	04/07/98	VHD Entertainment (Grupo Video)	Mexico	Grupo Video Visa, SA de CV	Mexico	Completed
04/08/98		Cable Televisio de Catalunya	Spain	Cableuropa	Spain	Completed
04/10/98		Abrams Gentile Entertainment	U.S.	MSH Entertainment Corp	U.S.	Pending
04/10/98		WSYX-TV,Columbus,Ohio	U.S.	Sinclair Broadcast Group Inc	U.S.	Pending
04/10/98		Pacific Video Canada	Canada	Command Post & Transfer Corp	Canada	Completed
04/15/98		Cable & Wireless North America	U.S.	Telecom Italia (IT Treasury)	Italy	Pending
04/16/98	04/16/98	Ascent Entertainment Group	U.S.	Leon G. Cooperman	U.S.	Completed
04/16/98		Marcus Cable Co-Television	U.S.	Triax Midwest Associates	U.S.	Pending
04/16/98		Television Tokyo Channel 12-	Japan	Toshiba Corp	Japan	Pending
04/17/98		Galaxie TV Network	Czech	Global Television Networks Inc	U.S.	Pending
04/17/98		Jones Intercable Inc-Suburban	U.S.	TCI Communications (Tele-Comm)	U.S.	Intended
04/17/98		TCI Commun-Cable TV Props (4)	U.S.	TW Fanch-one Co	U.S.	Pending
04/20/98	04/20/98	Television Federal SA	Argentina	Enfisur SA (Editorial Atlantid)	Argentina	Completed
04/22/98		Broadcast Communications Ltd	N. Zealand	Seeking Buyer	Unknown	S Buyer
04/23/98		Time Warner Inc-Wade Commun	U.S.	Inner City Broadcasting	U.S.	Pending
04/23/98		Zoetermeer Cable Network	Netherlands	France Telecom SA (France)	France	Pending
04/24/98	07/06/98	Globalstar LP	U.S.	Loral Space & Communications	U.S.	Completed
04/24/98		United Video Satellite-Superst	U.S.	Primestar Partners LP	U.S.	Pending
04/27/98	06/11/98	Metromedia China Corp	China	VDC Corporation Ltd	U.S.	Completed
04/27/98		Sunbow Entertainment LLC	U.S.	Sony Wonder (Sony Corp)	U.S.	Pending
04/28/98		TCI Music (Tele-Communications)	U.S.	Much Music (MuchMusic,Rainbow	U.S.	Pending
04/28/98	04/28/98	TeleUno (Spelling Entertainment)	U.S.	Sony Pictures Entertainment	U.S.	Completed
04/28/98		Westinghouse Communications	U.S.	RSL Communications Ltd	Bermuda	Pending
04/29/98		Valleyfield Transvision Inc	Canada	Cogeco Cable Inc	Canada	Pending
04/30/98		Western Canadian	Canada	Regional Cable TV (Western)	Canada	Pending

May, 1998

Date Announced	Date Effective	Acquisition Target	Target Country	Acquired By	Acquiror Country	Status
05/04/98		Spectrum Cablevison LP	U.S.	Hector Communications Corp	U.S.	Pending
05/04/98		WALB-TV,Albany,GA	U.S.	Cosmos Broadcasting Corp	U.S.	Pending
05/04/98	08/03/98	WEAU-TV,Eau Claire,WI (Busse)	U.S.	Cosmos Broadcasting Corp	U.S.	Completed
05/05/98	05/05/98	Fireworks Entertainment Inc	Canada	CanWest Global Communications	Canada	Completed
05/05/98		KMEG-TV (Maine Radio & TV Co)	U.S.	Waitt Broadcasting Corp	U.S.	Pending
05/05/98		Prime South Diversified Inc	U.S.	Cox Commun (Cox Enterprises)	U.S.	Pending
05/06/98		Max's Film AB	Sweden	Private Media Group Ltd	U.S.	Pending
05/07/98	05/07/98	MDS-2 Channel	U.S.	SuperChannels of Las Vegas	U.S.	Completed
05/07/98		WWAY-TV,Wilmington,NC	U.S.	Cosmos Broadcasting Corp	U.S.	Pending
05/12/98		Look Tele (Quebec) Inc	Canada	Look TV (Ontario) Inc	Canada	Pending
05/13/98		Undisclosed DIRECTV Providers	U.S.	Pegasus Communications Corp	U.S.	Pending

Date Announced	Date Effective	Acquisition Target	Target Country	Acquired By	Acquiror Country	Status
05/21/98	05/21/98	Cineplex Odeon Films (Cineplex)	Canada	Alliance Communications Corp	Canada	Completed
05/21/98		PolyGram Filmed Entertainment	U.S.	Seeking Buyer	Unknown	S Buyer
05/22/98	06/16/98	Fireworks Entertainment Inc	Canada	CanWest Global Communications	Canada	Completed
05/25/98		Hearst-Argyle Television Inc	U.S.	Hearst-Argyle Television Inc	U.S.	Intended
05/25/98		Jones Intercable Inc	U.S.	Comcast Corp	U.S.	Intended
05/25/98		Jones Intercable Inc	U.S.	Comcast Corp	U.S.	Pending
05/25/98		Jones Entertainment,Jones Edu	U.S.	Comcast Corp	U.S.	Pending
05/26/98		All American Cables & Radio	U.S.	WorldPort Communications Inc	U.S.	Pending
05/26/98		Asia Television	Hong Kong	Dragon Viceroy	Hong Kong	Pending
05/26/98		Court TV Cable Network	U.S.	Time Warner/Liberty Media	U.S.	Pending
05/26/98		Deutsche Telekom-Cable TV	Germany	Shareholders	Germany	Pending
05/26/98		Pulitzer Publishing-Radio/TV	U.S.	Hearst-Argyle Television Inc	U.S.	Pending
05/27/98		KEVN Inc (USA Broadcasting)	U.S.	Mission TV LLC	U.S.	Pending
05/27/98	05/27/98	Umoya Communications (Pty) Ltd	S. Africa	African Media Entertainment	S. Africa	Completed
05/29/98	07/29/98	Blockbuster Italy (Blockbuster)	Italy	Medusa (Fininvest SpA)	Italy	Completed

June, 1998

Date Announced	Date Effective	Acquisition Target	Target Country	Acquired By	Acquiror Country	Status
06/01/98	06/01/98	Satellite Image Systems	U.S.	Insurdata Inc	U.S.	Completed
06/03/98		Australis Media Pty Ltd-Set	Australia	Foxtel Pty (Telstra,News Corp)	Australia	Pending
06/03/98		News/Sports Microwave Rental	U.S.	Guardian Technologies Intl Inc	U.S.	Pending
06/03/98	03/03/98	Worldwide Television News Corp	U.S.	Associated Press	U.S.	Completed
06/04/98		Cable Michigan Inc	U.S.	Avalon Cable	U.S.	Pending
06/04/98		International Movie Group Inc	Canada	Lion's Gate Entertainment Corp	Canada	Pending
06/04/98		Mercom Inc (C-TEC Corp)	U.S.	Cable Michigan Inc	U.S.	Pending
06/04/98	06/04/98	3DV Systems (Rafael Dvlp)	Israel	Vision-Sciences Inc	U.S.	Completed
06/09/98	06/09/98	CNET Inc	U.S.	NBC	U.S.	Completed
06/09/98	06/09/98	Multicanal SA (Grupo Clarin)	Argentina	Grupo Clarin	Argentina	Completed
06/09/98	07/06/98	People's Choice TV-Video Asts	U.S.	OnePoint Communications Corp	U.S.	Completed
06/10/98		Central de Video SA de CV	Mexico	Technicolor Video Services	U.S.	Pending
06/10/98		Kabel Media	Germany	Sueweda Elektronische Medien	Germany	Pending
06/10/98		Stereovision	U.S.	New Visual Entertainment Inc	U.S.	Pending
06/11/98		National Screen Service Ltd	U.K.	Carlton Communications PLC	U.K.	Pending
06/12/98		All Post Inc-Certain Assets	U.S.	VDI Media	U.S.	Pending
06/15/98	06/15/98	Topaz Broadcasting Inc	U.S.	Regent Bdcstg of Victorville	U.S.	Completed
06/16/98	06/16/98	Z Spanish Media Corp	U.S.	Chancellor Media Corp	U.S.	Completed
06/16/98	04/01/98	Smyrna Cable TV	U.S.	Vista Broadband Communications	U.S.	Completed
06/18/98		Termite Art Productions	U.S.	Lions Gate Media Division	Canada	Pending
06/19/98	07/16/98	Golden Harvest Entertainment	Hong Kong	Investor Group	China	Completed
06/19/98		Tribune-Atlanta,New Orleans TV	U.S.	Seeking Buyer	Unknown	S Buyer
06/25/98		General Instr-TV Encoding Sys	U.S.	TVN Entertainment Corp	U.S.	Pending
06/29/98		Consoldiated Theatres Inc-Comp	U.S.	Entertainment Properties Trust	U.S.	Pending
06/29/98		Odyssey Channel	U.S.	Hallmark Ent/Jim Henson Co.	U.S.	Pending
06/29/98	06/29/98	Phones 4U Cellular Services BV	U.K.	Libertel (Vodaphone Group)	Netherlands	Completed
06/29/98		Raleigh Grand 16,Raleigh,NC	U.S.	Entertainment Properties Trust	U.S.	Pending
06/29/98	06/29/98	State Cable-ME, NH Cable TV	U.S.	FrontierVision Oper Partners	U.S.	Completed
06/30/98	06/30/98	Cable TV Fund 14B Ltd-Surfside	U.S.	Undisclosed Acquiror	Unknown	Completed
06/30/98	06/30/98	Jones Spacelink-Indiana Cable	U.S.	Undisclosed Acquiror	Unknown	Completed

July, 1998

Date Announced	Date Effective	Acquisition Target	Target Country	Acquired By	Acquiror Country	Status
07/01/98	07/01/98	Hampton Town Center,Norfolk,VA	U.S.	Entertainment Properties Trust	U.S.	Completed
07/02/98		RTL 4 Holding SA	Netherlands	CLT-UFA (Cie Luxembourgeoise)	Germany	Pending
07/02/98	07/02/98	USA Networks	U.S.	Tele-Communications Inc	U.S.	Completed
07/06/98	07/06/98	Cinecitta (Ente Gestione Cinem)	Italy	Vittorio Cecchi Gori	Italy	Completed
07/06/98	07/06/98	Two Way TV Ltd	U.K.	Cable & Wireless PLC	U.K.	Completed
07/07/98		Grupo Gallego del Cable	Spain	Inversiones Gallegas del Cable	Spain	Pending
07/07/98		KAVU-TV,Victoria,Texas	U.S.	Saga Communications Inc	U.S.	Pending
07/07/98		LIN Television Corp	U.S.	Chancellor Media Corp	U.S.	Pending
07/07/98	07/07/98	Railway Film Centre Ltd	Canada	Rainmaker Entertainment Group	Canada	Completed
07/08/98	07/08/98	Cine Principal	Spain	Ayuntamiento de Sabadell	Spain	Completed
07/08/98	07/08/98	Patagonik Film Group	Argentina	Investor Group	Argentina	Completed
07/10/98	07/10/98	ECTV (Century Communications)	Australia	Austar	Australia	Completed
07/10/98	07/10/98	East Coast TV-Pay TV Assets	Australia	Austar Entertainment Pty Ltd	Australia	Completed
07/10/98		Muvico Theatres-Pompano 18	U.S.	Entertainment Properties Trust	U.S.	Pending
07/10/98	07/10/98	Peoples Choice TV Corp-Video	U.S.	OnePoint Communications Corp	U.S.	Completed
07/10/98		XYZ Entertainment Pty Ltd	Australia	UIH Asia/Pacific Commun	U.S.	Pending
07/10/98	07/10/98	XYZ Entertainment Pty Ltd	Australia	Austar	Australia	Completed
07/13/98	07/13/98	International Theatre,Kowloon	Hong Kong	Undisclosed Acquiror	Unknown	Completed
07/15/98	07/15/98	Cable TV Fund 12-A-Cable Sys	U.S.	Undisclosed Acquiror	Unknown	Completed
07/15/98		DDD Cablevision	U.S.	Resort World Enterprises Inc	U.S.	Pending
07/16/98		Rysher Entertinment Inc	U.S.	Seeking Buyer	Unknown	S Buyer
07/17/98	07/17/98	Cablevisa SA,Multicable SA	El Salvador	Chispa Dos Inc	Cayman	Completed
07/17/98	07/17/98	Legacy Releasing	U.S.	Wealden Corp	U.S.	Completed
07/20/98		Atlantis Communications Inc	Canada	Alliance Communications Corp	Canada	Pending
07/20/98		Helkon Media Group	Germany	Endemol Entertainment BV	Netherlands	Pending
07/20/98	07/20/98	TCI Cablevision,TV Cable	U.S.	Friendship Cable of Texas	U.S.	Completed
07/21/98	08/07/98	Cigar Television Network Inc	U.S.	Reliant Corp	U.S.	Completed
07/21/98	07/21/98	Digital Broadcasting Co	U.K.	Pearson Television (Pearson)	U.K.	Completed
07/21/98	07/21/98	KOFY-TV,San Francisco,CA	U.S.	Granite Broadcasting Corp	U.S.	Completed

Date Announced	Date Effective	Acquisition Target	Target Country	Acquired By	Acquiror Country	Status
07/22/98	07/22/98	Atlas Air Film & Media Service	Germany	Kinowelt Medien AG	Germany	Completed
07/22/98		Telecomunicaciones SA	Mexico	Grupo Televisa SA de CV	Mexico	Pending
07/22/98		Regal Powder Springs Movie	U.S.	Entertainment Properties Trust	U.S.	Pending
07/22/98		Via Digital	Spain	CanalSatelite (Sogecable)	Spain	Pending
07/22/98		United Artists Theater	U.S.	Forest City Enterprises Inc	U.S.	Intended
07/23/98	07/23/98	Pandora Investment SA	Luxembourg	Gaylord Entertainment Company	U.S.	Completed
07/24/98		Hungarian Broadcasting-Adult	U.S.	Shareholders	U.S.	Pending
07/27/98		CBS Eye on People	U.S.	Discovery Communications Inc	U.S.	Pending
07/27/98		Primedia Broadcast Group	U.S.	Chancellor Media Corp	U.S.	Pending
07/27/98		WUPW-TV,Toledo,Ohio (Raycom)	U.S.	Sunrise Television Corp	U.S.	Pending
07/28/98	07/28/98	Flamingo Film	Germany	Endemol Entertainment BV	Netherlands	Completed
07/29/98	07/29/98	Jones Intercable-Cable Sys,FL	U.S.	Olympus Capital Corp	U.S.	Completed
07/29/98		Television del Valle de Mexico	Mexico	TV Azteca	Mexico	Pending
07/30/98		Cable Televisio de Catalunya	Spain	Investor Group	Spain	Pending
07/30/98		Hollywood Entertainment Corp	U.S.	Investor Group	U.S.	Pending

August, 1998

Date Announced	Date Effective	Acquisition Target	Target Country	Acquired By	Acquiror Country	Status
08/03/98	08/03/98	Cablodistribution De La Cote	Canada	Groupe Videotron Ltee	Canada	Completed
08/03/98	08/03/98	Le Cable De Riviere-Du-Loup	Canada	Groupe Videotron Ltee	Canada	Completed
08/03/98	08/03/98	Tele-Cable Charlevoix (1977)	Canada	Groupe Videotron Ltee	Canada	Completed
08/04/98	08/04/98	Deutsche Sportfernsehen	Germany	Kirch-Gruppe	Germany	Completed
08/04/98	08/04/98	Pescado Oy AB	Finland	MTV	Finland	Completed
08/06/98		Metro-Goldwyn-Mayer Inc	U.S.	Seeking Buyer	Unknown	Intended
08/06/98	08/06/98	Spectrum Cablevision LP-4580	U.S.	Loretel Systems Inc	U.S.	Completed
08/10/98		Hunan International TV	China	AmTec Inc	U.S.	Pending
08/10/98		KTVF-TV,KXLR-FM,KCBF-AM	U.S.	Ackerley Group Inc	U.S.	Pending
08/10/98	08/10/98	Kabelkom (Time Warner Inc)	Hungary	Telekabel NV (NUON)	Netherlands	Completed
08/10/98		Primestar Partners LP	U.S.	News Corp./TCI	U.S.	Pending
08/10/98		United Group TV	Ukraine	Investor Group	Ukraine	Pending
08/10/98		WMHO-TV,Albany,New York	U.S.	Sinclair Broadcast Group Inc	U.S.	Pending
08/17/98	10/28/98	Birmingham Cable Corp	U.S.	TeleWest PLC	U.S.	Completed
08/17/98	08/17/98	Cable Properties Inc.	U.S.	DF Cablevision LP	U.S.	Completed
08/17/98		KGBT-TV, Harlingen,TX	U.S.	Cosmos Broadcasting Corp	U.S.	Pending
08/17/98	09/04/98	Westwood Studios Inc.	U.S.	Electronic Arts Inc	U.S.	Completed
08/18/98	08/18/98	Metronome (TeleDanmark A/S)	Denmark	Endemol Entertainment BV	Holland	Completed
08/19/98	08/19/98	Kids Can Press Ltd		Nelvana Ltd	U.S./Canada	Completed
08/19/98		Metro-Goldwyn-Mayer Inc.	U.S.	Tracinda Corp.	U.S.	Pending
08/20/98	08/20/98	Nevada Filmakers Inc.	U.S.	Universal Marketing and Ent.	U.S.	Completed
08/20/98	08/20/98	North Arundel CATV	U.S.	Millennium Digital Media	U.S.	Completed
08/21/98		Channel 9 South Australia Pty	Australia	Southern Cross Broadcasting	Australia	Pending
08/21/98		Ken Crane's-DVD,Laserdisc Ops	U.S.	Image Entertainment Inc.	U.S.	Pending
08/21/98		KCPQ-TV,Seattle,Washington	U.S.	Meredith Corp.	U.S.	Pending
08/21/98	08/21/98	WNEQ-TV,Buffalo,New York	U.S.	Sinclair Broadcast Group Inc.	U.S.	Completed
08/21/98		National Film Development		Seeking Buyer	Unknown	S Buyer
08/21/98	08/24/98	Pramer SRL	Argentina	TCI International Holdings Inc	U.S.	Completed
08/21/98		WGNX-TV,Atlanta,Georgia	U.S.	Meredith Corp.	U.S.	Pending
08/23/98		MediaOne Grp-Broadband Sys	U.S.	Northland Cable Television	U.S.	Pending
08/24/98	08/24/98	Coaxial Communications-Cable	U.S.	Insight Communications Co LP	U.S.	Completed
08/24/98		KCRA-TV,Sacramento,California	U.S.	Hearst-Argyle Television Inc	U.S.	Pending
08/24/98	08/24/98	McKibben Communications	U.S.	GlobeComm Systems Inc	U.S.	Completed
08/24/98		Tele-Commun International (TCI)	U.S.	Liberty Media (Tele-Commun)	U.S.	Pending
08/25/98		KVIQ-TV,Eureka,California	U.S.	Ackerley Group Inc.	U.S.	Pending
08/26/98		Loews Cineplex-Theaters (24)	U.S.	Cablevision Systems Corp.	U.S.	Pending
08/26/98	08/26/98	TVI	U.S.	Media Capital	U.S.	Completed
08/27/98		Loews Cineplex-Theaters (7)	U.S.	Cablevision Systems Corp.	U.S.	Pending
08/28/98	08/28/98	Century City Walk,Glen Waverly	U.S.	Village Roadshow Corp Ltd.	Australia	Completed
08/28/98	10/26/98	Foghound Studios (Pty) Ltd.		AME Commercial Filmmakers	Australia	Completed
08/28/98	08/28/98	Hollywood Entertainment,AZ		Star Entertainment Group Inc		Completed
08/28/98	10/26/98	Quayle Properties (Pty) Ltd	Australia	AME Commercial Filmmakers	Australia	Completed
08/31/98	08/31/98	FSN Cable Ltd.	U.S.	Moffat Communications Ltd.	U.S.	Completed
08/31/98		High Definition Oberhausen	Germany	Gravity & DLIN		Pending

September, 1998

Date Announced	Date Effective	Acquisition Target	Target Country	Acquired By	Acquiror Country	Status
09/01/98		TV3 (Ireland) Television	Ireland	ACT Venture Capital Ltd.	Ireland	Pending
09/01/98	09/01/98	Televisoras Provinciales SA	Argentina	Editorial Atlantida SA	Argentina	Completed
09/03/98	09/03/98	Win TV-Productions BV	Holland	Endemol Entertainment BV	Holland	Completed
09/04/98		Enstar Income Program IV-1 LP	U.S.	Madison Partnership Liquidity	U.S.	Completed
09/04/98		Globo Cabo Participacoes SA	Brazil	Multicanal Participacoes SA	Brazil	Pending
09/04/98	09/04/98	Vision Electronics Co	U.S.	TelePartners LLC	U.S.	Completed
09/07/98		Kabelmedia Holding GmbH	Germany	Investor Group		Pending
09/08/98		Guy Gannett Commun-TV Assets		Sinclair Broadcast Group Inc.	U.S.	Pending
09/08/98		WOKR-TV,Rochester,New York	U.S.	Ackerley Group Inc.	U.S.	Pending
09/08/98	09/08/98	WIVT-TV,Binghamton,New York	U.S.	Ackerley Group Inc.	U.S.	Completed
09/09/98		Manchester United PLC	U.K.	British Sky Broadcasting	U.K.	Pending
09/10/98	09/10/98	Craftsman & Scribes Creative	U.S.	Select Media Communications	U.S.	Completed
09/11/98	09/11/98	Digital Research Corp.	U.S.	American International Inds.	U.S.	Completed
09/11/98	09/11/98	Electronic Pictures Inc.	U.S.	American International Inds.	U.S.	Completed
09/11/98	09/11/98	Modern Film Effects Inc.	U.S.	American International Inds.	U.S.	Completed
09/15/98		ACTV Inc.	U.S.	Liberty Media	U.S.	Pending
09/15/98	09/15/98	Big 4 Ranch Inc.	U.S.	Reading Entertainment Inc.	U.S.	Completed

Date Announced	Date Effective	Acquisition Target	Target Country	Acquired By	Acquiror Country	Status
09/16/98		TeleWest PLC	U.S.	MediaOne (US WEST Media Group)	U.S.	Pending
09/18/98	09/18/98	Cecchi Gori Maedia Holding	Italy	Fin.Ma.Vi (Cecchi Gori)	Italy	Completed
09/18/98	09/18/98	Fin.Ma.Vi (Cecchi Gori)	Italy	Investor Group		Completed
09/18/98	09/18/98	MSCL Inc	U.S.	Four Media Company	U.S.	Completed
09/18/98		Metro-Goldwyn-Mayer Inc-Films	U.S.	ProSieben Media AG	Germany	Pending
09/21/98	09/21/98	Bruce Austin Productions	U.S.	New Visual Entertainment Inc.	U.S.	Completed
09/22/98	09/22/98	CinemaxX AG	Germany	Investor		Completed
09/22/98		DirecTV Japan	Japan	Hughes Electronics Corp.	U.S.	Pending
09/24/98		CBS TeleNoticias (CBS Corp)	U.S.	Medcom	U.S.	Pending
09/24/98	09/24/98	Cinema Complex, Cary, NC	U.S.	Konover Property Trust Inc.	U.S.	Completed
09/28/98	09/28/98	ODS Technologies	U.S.	United Video Satellite Group	U.S.	Completed
09/28/98	10/02/98	Primetime PLC	Australia	Southern Star Group Ltd	Australia	Completed
09/29/98	09/29/98	Midwest Commun Tech Inc.U.S.	Black Box Corp.		U.S.	Completed
09/29/98	09/28/98	Spanish Telecommunications		Capital Comm. CDPQ (Caisse de)	Canada	Completed
09/29/98		Teleport London International	U.K.	Kingston Communications (Hull)	U.K.	Pending
09/30/98		Spice Entertainment-Spice Hot		Califa Entertainment	U.S.	Pending

October, 1998

Date Announced	Date Effective	Acquisition Target	Target Country	Acquired By	Acquiror Country	Status
10/01/98	10/01/98	Wet 'N Wild	U.S.	Universal Studios Inc.	U.S.	Completed
10/02/98		Highlight Communications AG	Germany	ABN AMRO Ventures BV	Netherlands	Pending
10/05/98	10/05/98	SND		CLT-UFA (Cie Luxembourgeoise)	Luxembourg	Completed
10/06/98	10/06/98	Cogeno Cable-Cable System, BC	Canada	Shaw Communications Inc.	Canada	Completed
10/07/98	10/07/98	Undisclosed Brazilian Pay (3)	Brazil	Canbras Communications Corp	Brazil	Completed
10/07/98		Jacor Communications Inc. U.S.	Clear Channel Communications		U.S.	Pending
10/12/98	11/06/98	TM3 Fernseh GmbH & Co KG	Germany	News Corp Ltd.	U.K.	Completed
10/14/98	10/14/98	Cine-Cinema (Multithematiques)	France	Communication Developpement	France	Completed
10/14/98	10/14/98	Cine-Classique	France	Communication Developpement	France	Completed
10/14/98	10/14/98	Jimmy (Multithematiques)	France	Communication Developpement	France	Completed
10/14/98		Multicanal SA (Grupo Clarin)	Argentina	Seeking Buyer		S Buyer
10/14/98	10/14/98	Planete (Multithematique)	France	Communication Developpement	France	Completed
10/15/98		Loxley Video Post (Bangkok) Co.	Thailand	Video Animation Co.		Pending

WHO'S WHO

IN THE ENTERTAINMENT WORLD

■

A

AARON, PAUL
Director, Producer, Writer.
THEATRE: B'way: Salvation, Paris Is Out, '70 Girls '70, Love Me Love My Children, That's Entertainment, The Burnt Flowerbed.
PICTURES: A Different Story, A Force of One, Deadly Force, Maxie.
TELEVISION: Movies: The Miracle Worker, Thin Ice, Maid in America, When She Says No, Save the Dog!, In Love and War, Laurel Avenue (creator, co-writer, exec. prod.), Under One Roof (co-creator, co-writer, exec. prod.), Grand Avenue (creator, exec. prod.).

AARON, ROY H.
Executive, Entertainment Industry Consultant. b. Los Angeles, CA, April 8, 1929. e. UC Berkeley, BA; USC, LLB. Attorney in L.A. law firm of Pacht, Ross, Warne, Bernhard & Sears (1957-78). Joined Plitt Companies in 1978 as sr. v.p. & gen. counsel. In 1980 was named pres. & CEO of Plitt Theatres, Inc. and related Plitt companies. 1985-93, pres. & CEO of Showscan Corp. 1993, business consultant, pres. of Plitt Entertainment Group Inc. & chmn. of Pacific Leisure Entertainment Group, L.L.C. Chmn. & CEO Intra-Asia Ent. Corp., 1997-.

ABARBANEL, SAM X.
Producer, Writer, Publicist. b. Jersey City, NJ, March 27, 1914. e. Cornell U. of Illinois, B.S. 1935. Newspaperman in Chicago before joining NY exploitation dept. of Republic, then to studio as asst. publicity director. WWII in Europe with 103rd Div. After war became independent publicist and producer. Formed own co. in Spain, 1966. A founder of the Publicists Guild in Hollywood.
PICTURES: Producer/Co-Prod./Exec. Prod./Assoc. Prod.: Argyle Secrets, Prehistoric Women (also co-s.p.), Golden Mistress, Gunfighters of Casa Grande, Son of Gunfighter, Narco Men, Last Day of War (also co-s.p.), Summer-time Killers (also co-s.p).

ABEND, SHELDON
Executive. b. New York, NY, June 13, 1929. Maritime Labor-Rel. Negotiator, 1954-56; chmn., Maritime Union, 1954-56. Head, exec. dir. Authors' Research Co. (est. 1957) representing estates of deceased authors. Ind't literary negotiator: CC films, A.A.P., RKO General Inc., David O. Selznick, 7 Arts, Warner Bros., 1959-65. Pres. American Play Co. Inc. & Century Play Co. Inc., 1961-present. Est. Million Dollar Movie Play Library, 1962. Pres. Amer. Literary Consultants, est. 1965. Exec. v.p. Chantec Enterprises Inc. 1969-72. Mktg. literary cons. for Damon Runyon Estate. Copyright analyst and literary rights negotiator, United Artists Corp. Founder and chmn., Guild for Author's Heirs, 1970-72. Literary negotiator and prod. cons. for Robert Fryer, 1972. Founder, Copyright Royalty Co. for Authors' Heirs, 1974. Copyright consultant, Films, Inc. 1975; literary agent for Bway. play, Chicago, 1975. Owner of 53 classic RKO motion pictures for the non-theatrical markets, distributed by Films, Inc. Revived publishing of Damon Runyon stories in quality paperback. Published Cornell Woolrich mystery stories-all prod. by Alfred Hitchcock for TV & motion pictures, 1976. Assoc. prod. of film, Why Would I Lie?, 1978. Originator of Million Dollar Movie Book Theatre and Million Dollar Movie Sound Track Co., 1980. Assoc. prod. of B'way revival, Shanghai Gesture, 1981. Publ. 5 Cornell Woolrich books owned by S. Abend, 1982-83. Co-authored, The Guardians, 1985 and Romance of the Forties by Damon Runyon, 1986. Founder and pres. American Concerts, Inc. and American Theatre Collections, Inc., 1985. Published Into the Night by Cornell Woolrich. Packaged m.p. Bloodhounds of Broadway, 1988; co-author s.p. Ultimate Deman; stage adapt. of Bloodhounds of Broadway, Madam La Gimp, 1990. Exec. prod. adaptation of Cornell Woolrich stories for TV and movies. Won landmark copyright case before U.S. Supreme Court protecting Woolrich estate, also affecting other deceased authors, songwriters and their copyright renewals of their work, 1990. Acquired Damon Runyon copyrights, 1992. Guys & Dolls handbook published by Viking, 1993.

ABRAHAM, F. MURRAY
Actor. r.n. Fahrid Murray Abraham. b. Pittsburgh, PA, Oct. 24, 1939. e. U. of Texas, 1959-61; trained for stage at Herbert Berghof Studios with Uta Hagen. First NY acting job was as Macy's Santa Claus. Stage debut in Los Angeles in The Wonderful Ice Cream Suit, 1965. New York debut in The Fantasticks, 1966. Full professor of theatre at CUNY Brooklyn College. Honorary Doctorate, Ryder College.
THEATER: Antigone (NYSF, 1982), Uncle Vanya (Obie, LaMamma, etc.), The Golem (NYSF), Madwoman of Chaillot, Othello, Cyrano, A Life in the Theatre, Sexual Perversity in Chicago, Duck Variations, The David Show, Adaptation/Next, Don't Drink the Water, And Miss Reardon Drinks a Little, Where Has Tommy Flowers Gone?, A Christmas Carol, The Seagull, Landscape of the Body, 6 Rms Riv Vu, Survival of St. Joan, Scuba Duba, Teibele & Her Demon, The Ritz, Legend, Bad Habits, Frankie & Johnnie in the Claire De Lune, Twelfth Night, Macbeth, A Midsummer's Night Dream, Waiting for Godot, King Lear, Angels in America: Millenium Aproaches/Perestroika, Little Murders, A Month in the Country; also 5 Children's musicals, Theatreworks.
PICTURES: They Might Be Giants (debut, 1971), Serpico, The Prisoner of 2nd Avenue, The Sunshine Boys, All the President's Men, The Ritz, Madman, The Big Fix, Scarface, Amadeus (Academy Award, 1984), The Name of the Rose, Slipstream, The Favorite, Russicum (The Third Solution), The Betrothed, An Innocent Man, Beyond the Stars, Eye of the Widow, The Bonfire of the Vanities, Cadence, Mobsters, National Lampoon's Loaded Weapon 1, By the Sword, Last Action Hero, Sweet Killing, The Final Card, Surviving the Game, Nostradamus, Jamila, Quiet Flows the Dawn, Money, Dillinger and Capone, Mighty Aphrodite.
TELEVISION: Movies: Sex and the Married Woman, A Season of Giants, Journey to the Center of the Earth. Series: Love of Life, How to Survive a Marriage. Mini-Series: Marco Polo, Dream West. Guest: Kojak, All in the Family. Specials: Largo Desolato.

ABRAHAMS, JIM
Producer, Writer, Director. b. Milwaukee, WI, May 10, 1944. e. U. of Wisconsin. Former private investigator. 1971, with friends David and Jerry Zucker, opened the Kentucky Fried Theatre in Madison, WI, a multimedia show specializing in live improvisational skits mixed with videotaped and film routines and sketches, with the threesome writing and appearing in most. Opened new theatre in Los Angeles in 1972 and developed large following. Co-wrote, co-dir., and co-exec. prod. TV series Police Squad!
PICTURES: With Zuckers: The Kentucky Fried Movie (co-s.p.), Airplane! (co-dir., co-exec. prod., co-s.p.), Top Secret! (co-dir., co-s.p.), Ruthless People (co-dir.). Also: Big Business (dir.), The Naked Gun (exec. prod., co-s.p.), Cry-Baby (co-exec. prod.), Welcome Home Roxy Carmichael (dir.), The Naked Gun 2-1/2 (co-exec. prod.), Hot Shots! (dir., co-s.p.), Hot Shots Part Deux!. (dir., co-s.p.), Naked Gun 33 1/3: The Final Insult (co-exec. prod.), Mafia (dir.).
TELEVISION: Movies: First do No Harm (dir.).

ABRAHAMS, MORT
Producer. b. New York, NY. Dir. programming, prod., NTA, 1958-60. Exec. prod. Cooga Mooga Prod. Inc., 1960-61. Prod.: Target, The Corruptors 1961, Route 66, 1962-63; writer TV shows, 1963-64. Prod., Kraft Suspense Theatre, 1965; prod., Man from U.N.C.L.E., 1965-66; exec. v.p., APJAC Prod., 1966; v.p. in chg. of prod., Rastar Prods., 1969; exec. prod. American Film Theatre & v.p. Ely Landau Organization, in charge of West Coast prod., 1971-74. Member of Faculty and prod.-in-residence, Center for Advanced Film and TV Studies of A.F.I. Vice-pres. Alph Productions, 1993-present.
PICTURES: Assoc. Prod.: Doctor Dolittle, Planet of the Apes, Goodbye Mr. Chips. Exec. Prod.: Luther, Homecoming, The Man in the Glass Booth, The Greek Tycoon, Hopscotch, The Chosen (exec. in chg. prod.), Beatlemania (exec. in chg. prod.), The Deadly Game, Arch of Triumph, The Holcroft Covenant, Seven Hours to Judgment (prod.).

ACKERMAN, ANDY
Director, Producer, Editor.
TELEVISION: *Series Dir.*: Cheers (also co-prod., editor, Emmy Award, 1988, 1991), Wings, Seinfeld (also prod., Directors' Guild Award, 1997-98), Frasier, Almost Perfect, Suddenly Susan, Jenny, LateLine (also prod.).

ACKERMAN, BETTYE
Actress. b. Cottageville, SC, Feb. 28, 1928. e. Columbia U., 1948-52. Taught dancing, 1950-54.
THEATER: No Count Boy, 1954; Tartuffe, Sophocles' Antigone and Oedipus at Colonus, The Merchant of Venice.
PICTURES: Face of Fire, Rascal, Ted & Venus, Pre-Hysteria II.
TELEVISION: *Movies:* Companions in Nightmare, A Day for Thanks on Walton's Mountain, Confessions of a Married Man. *Series:* Ben Casey. *Guest:* Alcoa Premiere, Alfred Hitchcock Presents, Perry Mason, Breaking Point, Hope-Chrysler Theatre, Bonanza, FBI Story, Mannix, Ironside, Medical Center, Columbo, Sixth Sense, Heat of Anger, Return to Peyton Place, The Rookies, Barnaby Jones, Police Story, Gunsmoke, Harry O, Streets of San Francisco, S.W.A.T., Petrocelli, Wonder Woman, Police Woman, Chips, 240-Robert, The Waltons, Dynasty, Falcon Crest, Me and Mom, Trapper John M.D.

ACKLAND, JOSS
Actor. b. London, England, Feb. 29, 1928. e. Central Sch. of Speech Training & Dramatic Art. Spent time in Central Africa as a tea planter. Over 400 TV appearances. Autobiography, I Must Be in There Somewhere.
THEATER: The Old Vic (3 yrs.), Mermaid Theatre (artistic dir., 3 yrs.); Hotel in Amsterdam, Jorrocks Come as You Are, The Collaborators, A Streetcar Named Desire, The Madras House, Captain Brassbound's Conversion, Never the Sinner, Henry IV Parts I & II, Peter Pan (dramatic & musical versions), A Little Night Music, Evita, The Visit, etc.
PICTURES: Seven Days to Noon, Crescendo, Trecolonne in Cronaca, The House That Dripped Blood, The Happiness Cage, Villain, England Made Me, The Black Windmill, S.P.Y.S, The Little Prince, Royal Flash, Operation Daybreak, Who Is Killing the Great Chefs of Europe, Saint Jack, The Apple, Rough Cut, Lady Jane, A Zed and Two Noughts, The Sicilian, White Mischief, To Kill a Priest, It Couldn't Happen Here, Lethal Weapon 2, The Hunt for Red October, Object of Beauty, Bill and Ted's Bogus Journey, The Palermo Connection, The Mighty Ducks, Nowhere to Run, Mother's Boys, The Princess and the Goblin (voice), Miracle on 34th Street, Giorgino, Mad Dogs and Englishmen, A Kid in the Court of King Arthur, Occhio Pinocchio, Daisies in December, To the Ends of Time, Mighty Ducks 3, Surviving Picasso, Deadly Voyage, Firelight.
TELEVISION: *Movies/Specials:* Queenie, Shadowlands, The Man Who Lived at the Ritz, A Quiet Conspiracy, Jekyll and Hyde, First and Last, A Murder of Quality, A Woman Named Jackie, Ashenden, Voices in the Garden, Queenie, The Bible, Citizen X.

ADAM, KEN
Art Director, Prod. Designer. b. Berlin, Germany, Feb. 5, 1921. e. St. Pauls Sch., London; London U., student of architecture. 6 years war service as RAF pilot. In 1947 entered motion picture industry as draughtsman for movie, This Was a Woman.
PICTURES: *Art Dir.:* The Devil's Pass, Soho Incident, Around the World in 80 Days. *Prod. Designer:* Spin a Dark Web, Night of the Demon, Gideon's Day, The Angry Hills, Beyond This Place, The Rough and the Smooth, In the Nick, Let's Get Married, Trials of Oscar Wilde, Dr. No, Sodom and Gomorrah, In the Cool of the Day, Dr. Strangelove, Goldfinger, Woman of Straw, Thunderball, The Ipcress File, Funeral in Berlin, You Only Live Twice, Chitty Chitty Bang Bang, Goodbye Mr. Chips, The Owl and the Pussycat, Diamonds Are Forever, Sleuth, The Last of Sheila, Barry Lyndon (Acad. Award, 1975), Madam Kitty, The Seven Percent Solution, The Spy Who Loved Me, Moonraker, Pennies From Heaven (visual consult., assoc. prod.), King David, Agnes of God, Crimes of the Heart, The Deceivers, Dead-Bang, The Freshman, The Doctor, Company Business, Undercover Blues, Addams Family Values, The Madness of King George (Acad. Award, 1994), Boys on the Side, Bogus, In & Out, The Out of Towners.

ADAMS, BROOKE
Actress. b. New York, NY, Feb. 8, 1949. e. H.S. of Performing Arts; Inst. of American Ballet. Studied with Lee Strasberg. Made professional debut at six in Finian's Rainbow. Worked steadily in summer stock and TV until age 18. After hiatus resumed acting career.
THEATER: Petrified Forest, Split, Key Exchange, Linda Her, Over Mother's Dead Body, Old Neighborhood, Heidi Chronicles, Lost in Yonkers. *Director:* Two Faced. Helps run small summer theater upstate NY.
PICTURES: Shock Waves (Death Corps), Car Wash, Days of Heaven, Invasion of the Body Snatchers, Cuba, A Man a Woman and a Bank, Tell Me a Riddle, Utilities, The Dead Zone, Almost You, Key Exchange, The Stuff, Man on Fire, The Unborn, Gas Food Lodging, The Baby Sitter's Club.
TELEVISION: *Movies:* F. Scott Fitzgerald and the Last of the Belles, The Daughters of Joshua Cabe Return, James Dean, Who is the Black Dahlia?, Murder on Flight 502, Lace, Haunted, Special People, Lace II, The Lion of Africa, Bridesmaids, Sometimes They Come Back, The Last Hit, Gun, Song of the Succubus. *Specials:* Paul Reiser: Out on a Whim. *Series:* O.K. Crackerby. *Pilot:* A Girl's Life, Nero Wolfe, The Lords of Flatbush. *Guest:* Kojak, Family, Police Woman, Moonlighting, Tony Randall Show, Bob Newhart Show.

ADAMS, CATLIN
Actress, Director. r.n. Barab. b. Los Angeles, CA, Oct. 11, 1950. Began career as actress then studied directing at American Film Institute. Made directorial debut with, Wanted: The Perfect Guy. Also directed Little Shiny Shoes (short, written and prod. with Melanie Mayron), Stolen: One Husband (TV).
THEATER: Safe House, Scandalous Memories, Dream of a Blacklisted Actor, The Candy Store, Ruby Ruby Sam Sam, Bermuda Avenue Triangle (dir.).
PICTURES: *Actress:* The Jerk, The Jazz Singer. *Director:* Sticky Fingers (also co-s.p., co-prod.).
TELEVISION: *Movies:* Panic in Echo Park, Freaky Friday. *Guest:* thirtysomething. *Series:* Square Pegs. *Specials:* How to Survive the 70's and Maybe Even Bump into a Little Happiness, She Loves Me She Loves Me Not.

ADAMS, DON
Actor. b. New York, NY, April 13, 1926. Won Arthur Godfrey talent contest. Was nightclub impressionist before starting in TV.
PICTURES: The Nude Bomb, Jimmy the Kid, Back to the Beach.
TELEVISION: *Series:* Perry Como's Kraft Music Hall, The Bill Dana Show, Tennessee Tuxedo (voice), Get Smart (3 Emmy Awards, 2 Clio Awards), The Partners, Don Adams' Screen Test, Three Times Daley, Inspector Gadget (voice), Check It Out!, Get Smart (1995). *Movies:* The Love Boat, Get Smart Again!

ADAMS, EDIE
Actress, Singer. r.n. Edith Elizabeth Enke. b. Kingston, PA, April 16, 1927. e. Juilliard Sch. of Music, Columbia Sch. of Drama.
THEATER: *NY:* Wonderful Town, Lil Abner (Tony Award), Mame.
PICTURES: The Apartment, Lover Come Back, Call Me Bwana, It's a Mad Mad Mad Mad World, Under the Yum Yum Tree, Love With the Proper Stranger, The Best Man, Made in Paris, The Oscar, The Honey Pot, Up in Smoke, The Happy Hooker Goes Hollywood, Boxoffice.
TELEVISION: *Movies:* Evil Roy Slade, Return of Joe Forrester, Superdome, Fast Friends, Make Me an Offer, A Cry for Love, Ernie Kovacs' Between the Laughter. *Series:* Ernie in Kovacsland, The Ernie Kovacs Show (1952-54, 1955-56), The Chevy Show, Take a Good Look (panelist), Here's Edie, The Edie Adams Show. *Guest:* Miss U.S. Television, Three to Get Ready, Kovacs on the Corner, Kovacs Unlimited, Jack Paar, Ed Sullivan Show, Perry Como Show, Pat Boone Show, G.E. Theatre, Colgate Comedy House, Dinah Shore Show, Palace, Bob Hope Show. *Specials:* Cinderella, Tales of the City.

ADAMS, GERALD DRAYSON
Writer. b. Winnipeg, Manitoba, June 26, 1900. e. Oxford U. Export exec. 1925-30; literary agt. 1931-45. Member of Screen Writers' Guild.
PICTURES: Magnificent Rogue, Plunderers, Gallant Legion, Big Steal, Dead Reckoning, Battle of Apache Pass, Son of Ali Baba, Flaming Feather, Flame of Araby, Lady from Texas, Steel Town, Untamed, Frontier, Duel at Silver Creek, Princess of the Nile, Three Young Texans, Gambler from Natchez, Wings of the Hawk, Between Midnight and Dawn, Taza Son of Cochise, Gambler from Natchez, Chief Crazy Horse, Golden Horde, Prince Who Was a Thief, Sea Hornet, Three Bad Sisters, Duel on the Mississippi, Black Sleep, War Drums, Gun Brothers, Affair in Reno, Frontier Rangers, Gold Glory & Custer, Kissin' Cousins, Harum Scarum.
TELEVISION: *Series:* Maverick, G.E. Theatre, Northwest Passage, Broken Arrow, Cheyenne, 77 Sunset Strip.

ADAMS, JOEY LAUREN
Actress. b. Little Rock, AR, Jan. 6, 1971.
PICTURES: Dazed and Confused (debut, 1993), Coneheads, The Program, Sleep with Me, S.F.W., The Pros & Cons of Breathing, Mallrats, Drawing Flies, Bio-Dome, Michael, Chasing Amy (Chicago Crits. Award, Most Promising New Actress, 1997), A Cool Dry Place, Bruno, Guy Gets Kid.
TELEVISION: *Series:* Top of the Heap, Vinnie & Bobby.

ADAMS, JULIE
Actress. r.n. Betty May Adams. b. Waterloo, IA, Oct. 17, 1926. e. jr. coll., Little Rock, AK. Coll. dramatics.
PICTURES: Red Hot and Blue (debut, 1949), The Dalton Gang, Crooked River, Hostile Country, West of the Brazos, Colorado Ranger, Fast on the Draw, Marshal of Heldorado. *As Julie Adams:* Hollywood Story, Finders Keepers, Bend of the River, Bright Victory, Treasure of Lost Canyon, Horizons West, Lawless Breed, Mississippi Gambler, Man From the Alamo, The Stand of Apache River, Wings of the Hawk, The Creature From the Black Lagoon, Francis Joins the WACS, The Looters, One Desire, The Private War of Major Benson, Six Bridges to Cross, Away All Boats, Four Girls in Town, Slim Carter, Slaughter on 10th Avenue, Tarawa Beachhead, Gunfight at Dodge City, Raymie, Underwater City, Tickle Me, Valley of Mystery, The Last Movie, McQ, Psychic Killer, The Wild McCullochs, Killer Inside Me, Goodbye Franklin High, The Fifth Floor, Black Roses.
TELEVISION: *Movies:* The Trackers, Go Ask Alice, Code Red, Backtrack, The Conviction of Kitty Dodds. *Series:* Yancy Derringer, General Hospital, The Jimmy Stewart Show, Code Red, Capitol. *Guest:* Murder She Wrote.

ADAMS, MASON
Actor. b. New York, NY, Feb. 26, 1919. e. U. Wisconsin. B.A., 1940; M.A., 1941. Trained for stage at Neighborhood Playhouse. Began on radio in 1946, spending nearly two decades in starring role of Pepper Young's Family. Made B'way. debut in, Get Away Old Man, 1943.
THEATER: Career Angel, Public Relations, Violet, Shadow of My Enemy, Inquest, The Sign in Sidney Brustein's Window, Tall Story, The Trial of the Catonsville Nine, Foxfire, Checking Out, Danger Memory, The Day Room, The Rose Quartet.
PICTURES: God Told Me To, Raggedy Ann and Andy (voice), Northstar, The Final Conflict, F/X, Toy Soldiers, Son-in-Law, Houseguest, Touch, Hudson River Blues.
TELEVISION: Movies: The Deadliest Season, And Baby Makes Six, The Shining Season, Flamingo Road, The Revenge of the Stepford Wives, The Kid with the Broken Halo, Adam, Passions, Solomon Northrup's Odyssey, The Night They Saved Christmas, Who is Julia?, Under Siege, Rage of Angels: The Story Continues, Perry Mason, Jonathan: The Boy Nobody Wanted, Buying a Landslide, Assault at West Point, Not of This Earth. Series: Lou Grant, Morningstar/Eveningstar, Knight and Daye, Murder One.

ADAMS, MAUD
Actress. r.n. Maud Wikstrum. b. Lulea, Sweden, Feb. 12, 1945. Formerly a model. Acting debut as model in, The Boys in the Band.
PICTURES: The Boys in the Band, The Christian Licorice Store, U-Turn, Mahoney's Estate, The Man With the Golden Gun, Rollerball, Killer Force, The Merciless Man, Tattoo, Octopussy, Target Eagle, Jane and the Lost City, The Women's Club, A Man of Passion, The Favorite, Soda Cracker, Deadly Intent, Angel III, The Kill Reflex, Forbidden Sun, Favorite, Ringer.
TELEVISION: Movies: Big Bob Johnson and His Fantastic Speed Circus, The Hostage Tower, Playing for Time, Nairobi Affair, The Case of the Wicked Wives. Series: Chicago Story, Emerald Point, N.A.S. and many notable guest appearances.

ADAMS, TONY
Producer. b. Dublin, Ireland, Feb. 15, 1953. Began career as asst. to dir. John Boorman and was associated with Burt Reynolds prior to joining Blake Edwards as a prod., 1971. Then president, The Blake Edwards Entertainment; Pres. & CEO, The Blake Edwards Company, 1988.
PICTURES: Assoc. Prod.: Return of the Pink Panther, The Pink Panther Strikes Again. Exec. Prod.: Revenge of the Pink Panther. Prod.: ``10'', S.O.B., Victor/Victoria, Trail of the Pink Panther, Curse of the Pink Panther, The Man Who Loved Women, Micki & Maude, That's Life, A Fine Mess, Blind Date, Sunset, Skin Deep, Switch, Son of the Pink Panther.
TELEVISION: Julie Andrews (series and specials), Justin Case, Peter Gunn, Julie.

ADDISON, JOHN
Composer. b. West Chobham, Surrey, England, March 16, 1920. e. Wellington and Royal Coll. of Music. Entered motion picture industry in 1948. Professor, Royal Coll. of Music, 1948-53. Member of bd. of govs. of AMPAS, 1980-89.
THEATER: The Amazons, Popkiss, The Entertainer, The Chairs, Luther, Midsummer Night's Dream, The Broken Heart, The Workhouse Donkey, Hamlet, Semi-Detached, The Seagull, Saint Joan of the Stockyards, Listen to the Mockingbird, Cranks (revue), Antony & Cleopatra, I Claudius, Twelfth Night, Bloomsbury, Antony and Cleopatra (LA Theatre Centre). Ballets: Carte Blanche (at Sadlers Wells and Edinburgh Fest.), Cat's Cradle (Marquis de Cuevas, Paris, Monte Carlo).
PICTURES: Seven Days to Noon, The Man Between, The Maggie, Make Me An Offer, Private's Progress, Reach for the Sky, Lucky Jim, I Was Monty's Double, Carlton Brown of the F. O., The Entertainer, School for Scoundrels, A Taste of Honey, The Loneliness of the Long Distance Runner, Tom Jones (Academy. Award, Grammy Award, 1963), Guns at Batasi, Girl With Green Eyes, The Loved One, Torn Curtain, A Fine Madness, I Was Happy Here, The Honey Pot, Smashing Time, The Charge of the Light Brigade, Start the Revolution Without Me, Country Dance (Brotherly Love), Mr. Forbush and the Penguins, Sleuth, Luther, Dead Cert, Ride a Wild Pony, Seven-Per-Cent Solution, Swashbuckler, Joseph Andrews, A Bridge Too Far (Brit. Acad. Anthony Asquith Award), The Pilot, High Point, Strange Invaders, Grace Quigley, Code Name: Emerald, To Die For.
TELEVISION: Movies: Sambo and the Snow Mountains, Detective, Hamlet, The Search for Ulysses, Way of the World, Back of Beyond, Black Beauty, The Bastard, Deadly Price of Paradise, Love's Savage Fury, Like Normal People, The French Atlantic Affair, Mistress of Paradise, Eleanor: First Lady of The World, Charles and Diana: A Royal Love Story, Mail Order Bride, Thirteen at Dinner, Dead Man's Folly, Mr. Boogedy, Something in Common, Firefighter, Amazing Stories, Bride of Boogedy, Strange Voices. Series: Nero Wolfe, Murder She Wrote (Emmy Award). Mini-series: Centennial, Pearl, Ellis Island, Beryl Markham: A Shadow on the Sun, Phantom of the Opera.

ADELMAN, GARY
Executive. b. Los Angeles, CA, March 16, 1944. e. California State U., Long Beach State Coll. Asst. dir. on feature, The Masterpiece, 1969; assoc. prod. on The Candy Snatchers. Produced first feature film, The Severed Arm, 1974. Assisted Winston Hock in development of 3-D process, 1975. Pres. & COO of Monarch Prods, 1976-93. Post-prod. consultant for Jerry Gross Organization. Founder and partial owner of New Image Releasing Inc., a prod. & dist. co., 1983. Had post of secty./treas. then named v.p., chg. prod., All-American Group, 1987. Assoc. prod. on Nobody's Perfect, 1990.

ADELMAN, JOSEPH A.
Executive. b. Winnipeg, Manitoba, Canada, Dec. 27, 1933. e. NYU, B.A., 1954; Harvard Law Sch., J.D., graduated cum laude, 1957. Attorney, United Artists Corp., New York, 1958; named west coast counsel, Hollywood, 1964; named exec. asst. to the v.p. in charge of prod. 1968; named v.p., west coast business and legal affairs, 1972. Appointed exec. v.p., Association of Motion Pictures and Television Producers, 1977. Appointed v.p. in chg. of business affairs, Paramount Pictures Corp., 1979. Co-founder and exec. v.p. Kidpix, Inc., since 1984; founder and CEO of Kidpix Theaters Corp,. since 1985. Appointed sr. v.p. for business/legal affairs, Color Systems Technology, Inc. 1986. Named pres. of CST Entertainment, 1987. Appointed mng. dir., Broadway Video Entertainment, 1990. CEO, Intl. Entertainment Enterprises 1991. Admitted to NY, California and U.S. Supreme Court bars. Member: Phi Beta Kappa, American Bar Association, Los Angeles Copyright Society, Academy of Motion Picture Arts and Sciences, National Assn. of Television Programming Executives. On bd. of dirs., AMPTP, 1969-1979; bd. of trustees, Theatre Authority, 1970-79. Recipient of Alumni Achievement Award, NYU, 1982

ADELSON, GARY
Producer. b. 1954. e. UCLA, B.A. Son of Merv Adelson. Joined Lorimar Prods. 1970 as prod. asst. on TV movie Helter Skelter. In 1989, formed Adelson/Baumgarten Prods. with Craig Baumgarten.
PICTURES: The Last Starfighter, The Boy Who Could Fly, In The Mood, Tap, Hard to Kill, Hook, Universal Soldier, Nowhere to Run, Blank Check, It Could Happen to You, Jade, Rolling Thunder, The Shooter.
TELEVISION: Helter Skelter (asst. prod.), Sybil (assoc. prod.), Eight Is Enough (prod.), The Blue Knight (prod.). Exec. prod.: Too Good To Be True, Our Family Business, Cass Malloy, John Steinbeck's The Winter of Our Discontent, Lace, Detective in the House, Lace II, Critical Choices, The Hunchback, Love in Another Town. Series: Spies.

ADELSON, MERV
Producer. b. Los Angeles, CA, Oct. 23, 1929. e. UCLA. Pres., Markettown Builders Emporium, Las Vegas, 1953-63. Managing partner Paradise Dev., 1958-. Pres. Realty Holdings, 1962-. Bd. chmn., Lorimar Inc., 1969-86. Bd. dirs. chmn. & CEO, Lorimar Telepictures, 1986-.
PICTURES: Twilight's Last Gleaming, The Choirboys, Who Is Killing the Great Chefs of Europe?, Avalanche Express, The Big Red One.
TELEVISION: Movies/Mini-Dir.: Sybil, A Man Called Intrepid, The Blue Knight, Helter-Skelter. Series: The Waltons, Eight Is Enough, Dallas, Kaz, The Waverly Wonders, Knots Landing.

ADJANI, ISABELLE
Actress, Producer. b. Gennevilliers, France, June 27, 1955.
PICTURES: Faustine and the Beautiful Summer, The Slap, The Story of Adele H. (Acad. Award nom.), The Tenant, Barocco, Violette and Francois, The Driver, Nosferatu—The Vampire, Bronte Sisters, Clara et les Chics Types, Possession, Quartet, Next Year If All Goes Well, One Deadly Summer, Antonieta, Deadly Circuit, Subway, Ishtar, Camille Claudel (also co-prod.; Acad. Award nom.), Toxic Affair, Queen Margot, Diabolique.

ADLER, ALLEN
Executive Producer. b. New York, NY, 1946. e. Princeton U., B.A.; Harvard Business Sch., M.B.A. Started with Standard & Poor's Inter-Capital then joined Alan Hirschfield at American Diversified Enterprises. Moved to Columbia Pictures as corporate officer, 1973; named sr. v.p., Columbia, 1979. Teamed with Daniel Melnick in IndieProd Co., 1981. Exec. prod., Making Love.

ADLON, PERCY
Director, Writer, Producer. b. Munich, Germany, June 1, 1935. e. Munich Univ. m. Eleonore Adlon, with whom he has worked on several film projects. Created more than forty tv documentaries.
PICTURES: Celeste, The Last Five Days (dir. only), The Swing, Sugarbaby, Bagdad Cafe, Rosalie Goes Shopping, Salmonberries, Younger and Younger, Hotel Adlon, Eat Your Heart Out (prod. only).
TELEVISION: The Guardian and His Poet (Adolf Grimme Award).

AFFLECK, BEN
Actor, Writer, Director. b. Berkeley, CA, Aug. 15, 1972. Began acting at age 8.
PICTURES: *Actor:* School Ties (debut, 1992), Buffy the Vampire Slayer, Dazed and Confused, Mallrats, I Killed My Lesbian Wife Hunger Her on a Meak Hook and Now I Have a Three-Picture Deal at Disney (dir. only), Glory Daze, Office Killer, Chasing Amy, Going All the Way, Good Will Hunting (also s.p., Acad. Award, Golden Globe Award, Best Screenplay, 1997), Phantoms, Armageddon, Shakespeare in Love, Forces of Nature, Dogma, Daddy and Them, 200 Cigarettes.
TELEVISION: *Series:* Voyage of the Mimi, Against the Grain, Lifestories: Families in Crisis. *Movies:* Hands of a Stranger, Daddy.

AGAR, JOHN
Actor. b. Chicago, IL, Jan. 31, 1921. In service WWII.
PICTURES: Fort Apache (debut, 1948), Adventure in Baltimore, I Married a Communist, Sands of Iwo Jima, She Wore a Yellow Ribbon, Breakthrough, Woman on Pier 13, Magic Carpet, Along the Great Divide, Woman of the North Country, Man of Conflict, Bait, Rocket Man, Shield for Murder, Golden Mistress, Revenge of the Creature, Hold Back Tomorrow, Tarantula, Star in the Dust, The Lonesome Trail, The Mole People, Flesh and the Spur, Daughter of Dr. Jekyll, Cavalry Command, The Brain from Planet Arous, Attack of the Puppet People, Ride a Violent Mile, Joe Butterfly, Jet Attack, Frontier Gun, Invisible Invaders, Raymie, Hand of Death, Lisette, Journey to the 7th Planet, Of Love and Desire, The Young and the Brave, Law of the Lawless, Stage to Thunder Rock, Young Fury, Waco, Johnny Reno, Curse of the Swamp Creature, Zontar: The Thing from Venus, Women of the Prehistoric Planet, St. Valentine's Day Massacre, Big Jake, Chisum, King Kong, Perfect Bride, Miracle Mile, Nightbreed, Fear, Invasion of Privacy, Body Bags, Pandora Directive (CD-ROM).

AGOGLIA, JOHN J.
Executive. Worked for 14 years for CBS Entertainment in New York, becoming v.p. business affairs. Joined NBC in 1979 as v.p., program and talent negotiations; named sr. v.p. business affairs NBC, 1980; exec. v.p. NBC Prods., 1984; exec. v.p., business affairs NBC-TV Network, 1986; in charge of foreign marketing relating to NBC Productions products, 1987; pres. of NBC Enterprises, 1990; pres. of NBC Prods., 1993.

AGUTTER, JENNY
Actress. b. Taunton, Devonshire, England, Dec. 20, 1952. e. Elmhurst Ballet Sch. Received Variety Club of Great Britain Most Promising Artiste Award, 1971.
THEATER: School for Scandal, Rooted, Arms and the Man, The Ride Across Lake Constance, The Tempest, Spring Awakening, Hedda, Betrayal. Member, Royal Shakespeare Co.-King Lear, Arden of Taversham, The Body. Breaking the Silence, Shrew (Los Angeles), Love's Labour's Lost, Mothers and Daughters.
PICTURES: East of Sudan (debut, 1964), Ballerina (tv in U.S.), Gates of Paradise, Star!, I Start Counting, Walkabout, The Railway Children, Logan's Run, The Eagle Has Landed, Equus (BAFTA Award, 1977), Dominique, China 9 Liberty 37, The Riddle of the Sands, Sweet William, The Survivor, Amy, An American Werewolf in London, Secret Places, Dark Tower, King of the Wind, Dark Man, Child's Play 2, Freddie as F.R.O. 7 (voice), Blue Juice.
TELEVISION: *Movies:* The Great Mr. Dickens, The Wild Duck, The Cherry Orchard, The Snow Goose (Emmy Award, 1972), As Many as Are Here Present, A War of Children, The Man in the Iron Mask, A House in Regent Place, There's Love and Dove, Kiss Me and Die, A Legacy, The Waiting Room, Six Million Dollar Man, School Play, The Mayflower, Voyage of the Pilgrims, Beulah Land, Love's Labour's Lost, This Office Life, Magnum, The Two Ronnies, Silas Marner, The Twilight Zone, Murder She Wrote, No a Penny More Not a Penny Less, Dear John, The Equalizer, The Outsiders, Breaking the Code, Boon, Love Hurts, Heartbeat, The Buccaneers, September, Bramwell: Our Brave Boys, Bramwell: Loose Women. *Mini-series:* A Respectable Trade.

AIELLO, DANNY
Actor. b. New York, NY, June 20, 1936.
THEATER: Lampost Reunion (Theatre World Award), Wheelbarrow Closers, Gemini (Obie Award), Knockout, The Floating Light Bulb, Hurlyburly (LA Drama Critics Award), The House of Blue Leaves.
PICTURES: Bang the Drum Slowly (debut, 1973), The Godfather Part II, The Front, Fingers, Blood Brothers, Defiance, Hide in Plain Sight, Fort Apache the Bronx, Chu Chu and the Philly Flash, Deathmask, Once Upon a Time in America, Old Enough, The Purple Rose of Cairo, Key Exchange, The Protector, The Stuff, Radio Days, The Pick-Up Artist, Man on Fire, Moonstruck, The January Man, Crack in the Mirror, Do the Right Thing (LA, Chicago & Boston Film Critics Awards; Acad. Award nom.), Russicum (The Third Solution), Harlem Nights, Jacob's Ladder, Once Around, Hudson Hawk, The Closer, 29th Street, Ruby, Mistress, The Cemetery Club, The Pickle, Me and the Kid, The Professional, Ready to Wear (Pret-a-Porter), City Hall, Power of Attorney, He Ain't Heavy, Two Much, 2 Days in the Valley, Mojave Moon, Brooklyn State of Mind, Bring Me The Head of Mavis Davis.
TELEVISION: *Movies:* The Last Tenant, Lovey: A Circle of Children Part 2, A Question of Honor, Blood Feud, Lady Blue, Daddy, Alone in the Neon Jungle, The Preppie Murder. *Mini Series:* The Last Don. *Series:* Lady Blue, Dellaventura (also prod). *Specials:* Family of Strangers (Emmy Award), Lieberman in Love.

AIMEE, ANOUK
Actress. r.n. Francoise Soyra Dreyfus. b. Paris, France, April 27, 1932. Studied dancing at Marseilles Opera, acting at Bauer-Therond dramatic school, Paris. Started in films as teenager billed as Anouk.
PICTURES: La Maison Sous la Mer (debut, 1946), La Fleur de l'age, Les Amants De Verone, The Golden Salamander, Noche de Tormenta, Le Rideau Cramoisi, The Man Who Watched the Trains Go By (Paris Express), Contraband Spain, Forever My Heart, Les Mauvaises Rencontres, Ich Suche Dich, Nina, Stresemann, Pot Bouille, Montparnasse 19, Tous Peuvent Me Tuer, Le Tete Contre Les Murs, The Journey, Les Dragueurs, La Dolce Vita, Le Farceur, Lola, L'Imprevu, Quai Notre-Dame, Il Giudizio Universale, Sodom and Gomorrah, Les Grand Chemins, 8 1/2, Il Terrorista, Il Successo, Liola, Le Voci Bianche, La Fuga, La Stagione del Nostro Amore, A Man and a Woman (Acad. Award nom.), Lo Sacandalo, Il Morbidonne, Un Soir Un Train, The Model Shop, Justine, The Appointment, Si C'Etait d Refaire, Mon Premier Amour, Salto nel Vuoto (Leap Into the Void), Tragedy of a Ridiculous Man, What Makes David Run?, Le General de l'Armee Morte, Success is the Best Revenge, Viva la Vie, A Man and A Woman: 20 Years Later, Arrivederci e Grazie, La Table Tournante, The House of the Lord, Dr. Bethune, Rabbit Face, Ready to Wear (Pret-a-Porter), Ruptures, Marmottes, LA Without a Map.
TELEVISION: Voices in the Garden.

ALBECK, ANDY
Executive. b. U.S.S.R., Sept. 25, 1921. Industry career began in 1939 with Columbia Pictures Intl. Corp. Central Motion Picture Exchange, 1947. Eagle Lion Classics, Inc., 1949. Joined UA in intl. dept., functioning in the area of operations, 1951. After filling a number of key posts, named asst. treas., 1970; v.p. of UA and its subsidiary, UA Broadcasting, Inc., 1972; pres. of UA Broadcasting, 1973; sr. v.p. operations, 1976; UA Corp. pres. & chief exec. officer in 1978. Retired, 1981.

ALBERGHETTI, ANNA MARIA
Singer, Actress. b. Pesaro, Italy, May 15, 1936. d. Daniele Alberghetti, cellist. Concert debut in 1948 in Pesaro, then toured Italy, Scandinavia, Spain; Am. debut Carnegie Hall, 1950, sang with NY Philharmonic Society, Phila. Symphony, on television. Made B'way debut in Carnival, 1962 (Tony Award).
PICTURES: The Medium (debut, 1951), Here Comes the Groom, The Stars Are Singing, The Last Command, Duel at Apache Wells, Ten Thousand Bedrooms, Cinderfella.
TELEVISION: *Guest:* Toast of the Town, Cavalcade of Stars, Arthur Murray Show, Bob Hope, Eddie Fisher, Red Skelton, Dinah Shore, Desilu Playhouse, G.E. Theatre, Chevy Show, Dupont Show, Voice of Firestone, Colgate Hour, Climax, Loretta Young, Ford Jubilee, Perry Como.

ALBERT, EDDIE
Actor. r.n. Eddie Albert Heimberger. b. Rock Island, IL, April 22, 1908. e. U. of Minnesota. Son is actor Edward Albert. Performer on Radio NBC.
THEATER: *B'way:* Brother Rat, Say Darling, The Music Man, Room Service, The Boys from Syracuse, Seven Year Itch, Our Town, No Hard Feelings, Reuben Reuben, Miss Liberty, You Can't Take It With You.
PICTURES: Brother Rat (debut, 1938), On Your Toes, Four Wives, Brother Rat and a Baby, Angel from Texas, My Love Came Back, Dispatch from Reuter's, Four Mothers, The Wagons Roll at Night, Out of the Fog, Thieves Fall Out, The Great Mr. Nobody, Treat 'em Rough, Eagle Squadron, Ladies' Day, Lady Bodyguard, Bombadier, Strange Voyage, Rendezvous With Annie, Perfect Marriage, Smash-Up, Time Out of Mind, Hit Parade of 1947, Dude Goes West, You Gotta Stay Happy, Fuller Brush Girl, You're in the Navy Now, Meet Me After the Show, Carrie, Actors and Sin, Roman Holiday (Acad. Award nom.), Girl Rush, I'll Cry Tomorrow, Oklahoma!, Attack, Teahouse of the August Moon, The Sun Also Rises, The Joker is Wild, Orders to Kill, Gun Runners, The Roots of Heaven, Beloved Infidel, The Young Doctors, Two Little Bears, Madison Avenue, Who's Got the Action?, The Longest Day, Captain Newman M.D., Miracle of the White Stallions, The Party's Over, Seven Women, The Heartbreak Kid (Acad. Award nom.), McQ, The Take, The Longest Yard, Escape to Witch Mountain, The Devil's Rain, Hustle, Whiffs, Birch Interval, Moving Violations, Yesterday, The Concorde — Airport 79, Foolin' Around, How to Beat the High Cost of Living, Take This Job and Shove It, Yes Giorgio, Dreamscape, The Act, Stitches, Head Office, The Big Picture, Brenda Starr.
TELEVISION: *Movies/Specials:* The Yeagers, Benjamin Franklin, The Borrowers, Killer Bees, Nutcracker, Anything Goes, Crash, The Word, Evening in Byzantium, Pirates Key, Living in Paradise, Oklahoma Dolls, The Plan, Peter and Paul, Goliath Awaits, Concord, Beyond Witch Mountain, Rooster, Demon Murder Case, Coalfire, In Like Flynn, Dress Gray, Mercy or Murder?, War and Remembrance, Return to Green Acres, The Girl from Mars, The Barefoot Executive. *Series:* Leave It To Larry, Nothing But the Best, Saturday Night Revue, Green Acres, Switch!, Falcon Crest, General Hospital. *Guest:* The Fall Guy, Love Boat, Highway to Heaven, Falcon Crest, Murder She Wrote, thirtysomething, Ray Bradbury Theatre, Twilight Zone, Time Trax, Golden Palace, Dr. Quinn–Medicine Woman.

ALBERT, EDWARD
Actor. b. Los Angeles, CA, Feb. 20, 1951. e. UCLA. Son of actor Eddie Albert and late actress Margo. Was prod. asst. on Patton in Spain. Has appeared with father on radio and TV shows. Is photographer and has exhibited work in L.A.
THEATER: Room Service, Our Town, The Glass Menagerie, Hamlet.
PICTURES: The Fool Killer (debut, 1965), Wild Country, Butterflies Are Free, Forty Carats, Midway, The Domino Principle, Purple Taxi, The Greek Tycoon, When Time Ran Out, The Squeeze, Galaxy of Terror, Butterfly, The House Where Evil Dwells, A Time to Die, Ellie, Getting Even (Hostage: Dallas), Distortions, Terminal Entry, The Rescue, Mind Games, Fist Fighter, Shoot Fighter, Fight to the Death, Broken Trust, The Ice Runner, Demon Keeper, Guarding Tess.
TELEVISION: Movies: Killer Bees, Death Cruise, The Millionaire, Silent Victory: The Kitty O'Neil Story, Black Beauty, Blood Feud, The Girl from Mars, Sight Unseen, Body Language. Series: The Yellow Rose, Falcon Crest. Host: Viva, Different Point of View, On Call. Mini-Series: The Last Convertible. Specials: Daddy Can't Read, Orson Welles' Great Mysteries (BBC). Guest: Beauty and the Beast, Houston Knights, Murder She Wrote, Police Story, Hitchhiker, The Love Boat, The Rookies.

ALBRIGHT, LOLA
Actress. b. Akron, OH, July 20, 1925. e. Studied piano 12 years. Switchboard operator and stenographer NBC; stenographer with WHAM and bit player; photographers' model. Made screen debut in The Pirate, 1947.
PICTURES: The Pirate (debut, 1947), Easter Parade, Julia Misbehaves, The Girl From Jones Beach, Tulsa, Champion, Bodyhold, Beauty on Parade, The Good Humor Man, When You're Smiling, Sierra Passage, The Killer That Stalked New York, Arctic Flight, The Silver Whip, The Treasure of Ruby Hills, The Magnificent Matador, The Tender Trap, The Monolith Monsters, Pawnee, Oregon Passage, Seven Guns to Mesa, A Cold Wind in August, Kid Galahad, Joy House (The Love Cage), Lord Love a Duck, The Way West, Where Were You When the Lights Went Out?, The Impossible Years, The Money Jungle.
TELEVISION: Movies: Helicopter Spies, How I Spent My Summer Vacation, Delta County USA, Terraces. Series: Peter Gunn, Peyton Place. Guest: Switch, The Eddie Capra Mysteries, Quincy, Airwolf.

ALCAINE, JOSE LUIS
Cinematographer. b. Tangier, Algeria, Dec. 26, 1938. e. Spanish Cinema Sch., Madrid. After graduation joined Madrid's Studio Moros doing commercials.
PICTURES: El Puente, El Sur, Taseo, Rustlers' Rhapsody, Bluebeard Bluebeard, Women on the Verge of a Nervous Breakdown, The Mad Monkey, Tie Me Up Tie Me Down, Ay Carmela, Lovers, Ham Ham, Sevillanas, The Age of Beauty, The Bird of Happiness, Golden Balls, Intruder, The Tit & the Moon, La Pasion.Turca, Libertarias, Tramway to Malvarrosa, In Praise of Older Women, Two Much, La Pistola de Mi Hermano.

ALDA, ALAN
Actor, Writer, Director r.n. Alphonso D'Abruzzo b. New York, NY, Jan. 28, 1936. e. Fordham U., 1956. Son of actor Robert Alda. Studied at Cleveland Playhouse on Ford Foundation Grant; performed with Second City, then on TV in That Was The Week That Was. For work as director, writer and actor on M*A*S*H won 5 Emmys, 2 Writers Guild Awards, 3 Directors Guild Awards, 6 Golden Globes, 7 People's Choice Awards, Humanitas Award (for Writing).
THEATER: B'way: Only in America, The Owl and The Pussycat, Purlie Victorious, Fair Game For Lovers (Theatre World Award), The Apple Tree (Tony nom.), Jake's Women (Tony Award nom.). London: Our Town.
PICTURES: Gone Are The Days (debut, 1963), Paper Lion, The Extraordinary Seaman, Jenny, The Moonshine War, The Mephisto Waltz, To Kill a Clown, Same Time Next Year, California Suite, The Seduction of Joe Tynan (also s.p.), The Four Seasons (also dir., s.p.), Sweet Liberty (also dir., s.p.), A New Life (also dir., s.p.), Crimes and Misdemeanors (D.W. Griffith Award, NY Film Critics Award), Betsy's Wedding (also dir., s.p.), Whispers in the Dark, Manhattan Murder Mystery, Canadian Bacon, Flirting With Disaster, Everyone Says I Love You, Murder at 1600.
TELEVISION: Movies: The Glass House, Playmates, Isn't It Shocking?, Kill Me If You Can (Emmy nom.), And the Band Played On, Jake's Women, White Mile. Series: That Was the Week That Was, M*A*S*H (11 years), Scientific American Frontiers (PBS, host). Series creator: We'll Get By, The Four Seasons. Specials: Free to Be You and Me, 6 Rms Riv Vu (also dir.), Life's Big Questions (host). Guest: Phil Silvers Show, The Nurses, Route 66, Trials of O'Brien, Coronet Blue, Carol Burnet Show. Pilots: Where's Everett, Higher and Higher.

ALDREDGE, THEONI V.
Costume Designer. b. Salonika, Greece, Aug. 22, 1932. m. actor Tom Aldredge. e. American School, Athens; Goodman Theatre School, Chicago, 1949-52.
THEATER: B'way: Sweet Bird of Youth, That Championship Season, Sticks and Bones, Two Gentlemen of Verona, A Chorus Line, Annie (Tony Award), Ballroom, Much Ado About Nothing, Barnum (Tony Award), Dream Girls, Woman of the Year, Onward Victoria, La Cage aux Folles (Tony Award), 42nd Street, Merlin, Private Lives, The Corn is Green, The Rink, Blithe Spirit, Chess, Gypsy, Oh Kay!, The Secret Garden, High Rollers.
PICTURES: You're A Big Boy Now, No Way to Treat a Lady, Uptight, Last Summer, I Never Sang for My Father, Promise at Dawn, The Great Gatsby (Acad. Award, 1974), Network, Semi-Tough, The Cheap Detective, The Fury, Eyes of Laura Mars (Sci Fi. Acad. Honor), The Champ, The Rose, Can't Stop the Music, Circle of Two, Loving Couples, A Change of Seasons, Middle Age Crazy, Rich and Famous, Annie, Monsignor, Ghostbusters, Moonstruck, We're No Angels, Stanley & Iris, Other People's Money, Milk Money, The First Wives Club, Mrs. Winterbourne, Addams Family Values, The Mirror Has Two Faces.

ALEANDRO, NORMA
Actress. b. Buenos Aires, Argentina, May 2, 1936. Sister is actress Maria Vaner. As child, performed with parents in theater troupe. In Argentina performed in every theatrical genre and epoch and also directed. Has written & published short stories (1986), poems and the screenplay for Argentinian film, Los Heroderos. Was in exile in Uruguay (18 months) and Spain 1976-82 because of the military junta in Argentina. Before exile had made 12 films; after return in 1982 starred in theatre and 7 films.
THEATER: U.S.: About Love and Other Stories (one-woman show, toured South America, then at La Mama and later off-B'way at Public Theater 1986); The Senorita of Tacna (written for her by Mario Vargas-Llosa, 1987).
PICTURES: The Official Story (Cannes Film Fest. Award, 1986), Gaby: A True Story (Acad. Award nom.), Cousins, Vital Signs, The Tombs.
TELEVISION: Movies: Autumn Sun, Dark Holiday, One Man's War.

ALEXANDER, JANE
Actress. r.n. Jane Quigley. b. Boston, MA, Oct. 28, 1939. e. Sarah Lawrence Coll., U. of Edinburgh. m. director Edwin Sherin. Mother of actor Jace Alexander. Stage career includes appearances on B'way; at Arena Stage, Washington D.C.; Kennedy Center, D.C.; Music Center, L.A.; and Shakespeare Festival at Stamford, Conn. Appointed chairwoman of the National Endowment for the Arts, 1993.
THEATER: NY: The Great White Hope (Tony & Theatre World Awards, 1969), 6 Rms Riv Vu, Find Your Way Home, Hamlet, The Heiress, First Monday in October, Goodbye Fidel, Losing Time, Monday After the Miracle, Old Times, Night of the Iguana, Approaching Zanzibar, Shadowlands, The Visit, The Sisters Rosensweig.
PICTURES: The Great White Hope (debut, 1970), A Gunfight, The New Centurions, All the President's Men, The Betsy, Kramer vs. Kramer, Brubaker, Night Crossing, Testament, City Heat, Square Dance, Sweet Country, Glory.
TELEVISION: Movies: Welcome Home Johnny Bristol, Miracle on 34th St., This is the West That Was, Death Be Not Proud, Eleanor and Franklin, Eleanor and Franklin: The White House Years, A Circle of Children, Lovey: A Circle of Children Part II, A Question of Love, Playing for Time (Emmy Award), In the Custody of Strangers, When She Says No, Calamity Jane, Malice in Wonderland, Blood & Orchids, In Love and War, Open Admissions, A Friendship in Vienna, Daughter of the Streets, Stay the Night. Specials: Mountain View, A Marriage: Georgia O'Keeffe and Alfred Stieglitz. Pilot: New Year.

ALEXANDER, JASON
Actor. r.n. Jay Scott Greenspan. b. Newark, NJ, Sept. 23, 1959. e. Boston Univ.
THEATER: NY: Merrily We Roll Along, Forbidden Broadway, The Rink, Personals, Stop the World, Light Up the Sky, Broadway Bound, Jerome Robbins' Broadway (Tony, Drama Desk & Outer Critics' Circle Awards, 1989), Accomplice. Regional: Give 'em Hell Harry.
PICTURES: The Burning (debut, 1981), Brighton Beach Memoirs, The Mosquito Coast, Pretty Woman, White Palace, Jacob's Ladder, I Don't Buy Kisses Anymore, Coneheads, The Paper, North, Blankman, For Better or Worse (also dir.), The Last Supper, Dunston Checks In, The Hunchback of Notre Dame (voice), Love! Valour! Compassion!.
TELEVISION: Movies: Senior Trip, Rockabye, Favorite Son, Bye Bye Birdie. Series: E/R, Everything's Relative, Seinfeld, Duckman (voice). Guest: Newhart, Dream On. Special: Sexual Healing.

ALEXANDER, RALPH
Executive. Began career with Universal Pictures in sales, 1949. Had various sls. jobs with 20th Century Fox and Lorimar. Appointed v.p., theatrical foreign sls., Filmway Pictures, 1981-82. Appoined v.p., sls, for Latin America & Southeast Asia, Embassy Pictures Intl., 1982-84. Named exec. v.p., multi-media foreign sls. for Robert Meyers Intl., 1984. Joined Dino De Laurentiis Corp. as intl. sls. dir. in chg. all foreign sls. theatrical and ancillary rights except tv., 1985. Promoted to v.p., intl. sls., DEG, 1986. Appointed pres. mktg. and sales, Kings Road Intl., 1989. Joined Scotti Bros. Pictures as pres. intl. sales and mktg., 1989.

ALIN, MORRIS
Editor, Writer, Publicist, Lyricist. e. City Coll. of New York. Entered motion picture industry as auditor of Hunchback of Notre Dame roadshow oper., 1924. Appointed asst. sls. prom. mgr. Universal, 1926-27; slsmn., Universal, 1927. Named assoc. editor The Distributor, MGM publication, 1927; editor, 1928-33; writer, publicist, MGM Studio, 1933-34; writer, publicist, Hollywood, New York, 1935-38. Rejoined Universal, Progress (Univ. publication) editor, 1938; senior publicist and Progress editor, Universal, 1961-67. Twice winner of International Competition on Industrial Journalism. Editor Enterprise Press, 1968. Member: exec., Enterprise Press, 1973; American Guild of Authors and Composers; American Society of Composers, Authors and Publishers; National Academy of Popular Music; Motion Picture Pioneers.

ALLAND, WILLIAM
Producer. b. Delmar, DE, March 4, 1916. e. Baltimore. Acted in semi-professional groups: actor, stage mgr., Orson Welles' Mercury Theatre; asst. prod., Mercury Theatre radio series. Served in U.S. Air Force, WWII; then radio writer. Prod: Universal, 1952; Paramount, 1960; Allied Artists, 1963.
PICTURES: Actor: Citizen Kane (also dialogue dir.), Macbeth. Producer: The Raiders, Flesh and Fury, Stand At Apache River, It Came From Outer Space, The Lawless Breed, Creature From The Black Lagoon, Johnny Dark, This Island Earth, Dawn At Socorro, Four Guns To The Border, Chief Crazy Horse, Revenge Of The Creature, Tarantula, The Creature Walks Among Us, The Mole People, Gun for a Coward, Land Unknown, Deadly Mantis, The Lady Takes a Flyer, As Young As We Are, The Party Crashers, Colossus of New York, Raw Wind in Eden, The Space Children, Look In Any Window (also dir.), The Lively Set, Treasure of the Lost Canyon, The Rare Breed, The Black Castle, Battle Over Citizen Kane.
(d. Nov. 10, 1997).

ALLEN, COREY
Director, Actor. r.n. Alan Cohen. b. Cleveland, OH, June 29, 1934. e. UCLA, 1951-54; UCLA law sch. 1954-55. Actor turned dir. starred in Oscar-winning UCLA student film, appeared in 20 plays at Players Ring, Players Gallery and other L.A. theaters. TV: Perry Mason, Alfred Hitchcock Presents. With partner John Herman Shaner, prod. Freeway Circuit Theatre. Led Actors Workshop with actor Guy Stockwell for 10 years.
PICTURES: Actor: Rebel Without a Cause, Key Witness, Sweet Bird of Youth, Private Property, Party Girl, The Chapman Report. Director: The Erotic Adventures of Pinocchio, Thunder and Lightning, Avalanche.
TELEVISION: Movies: See the Man Run, Cry Rape!, Yesterday's Child, Stone (pilot), Man in the Santa Claus Suit, The Return of Frank Cannon, Code Name: Foxfire (pilot), Brass, Destination America, Beverly Hills Cowgirl Blues, The Last Fling, Ann Jillian Story, Stalking Back. Series Dir.: This is the Life, Mannix, High Chaparral, Dr. Kildare, Streets of San Francisco (DGA nom.), Ironside, Barnaby Jones, Police Woman, Rockford Files, Quincy, Dallas, Lou Grant, McClain's Law, Family Novak, T.J. Hooker, Paper Chase: The Second Year, Hill Street Blues (Emmy), Road Home, Deep Space Nine. Pilots: Man Undercover, Capitol, Simon and Simon, Whiz Kids, Murder She Wrote, Code Name: Foxfire, Star Trek: The Next Generation. Unsub.

ALLEN, DAYTON
Performer. b. New York, NY, Sept. 24, 1919. e. Mt. Vernon H.S. Motion picture road shows, 1936-40. Disc jockey, WINS, N.Y., 1940-41. Writer, vaudeville comedy bits, 1941-45, then radio comic, puppeteer and voices. In television since 1948, film commercials and shows. Acted in the film The Cotton Club.
TELEVISION: (voices): Terrytoons, Deputy Dwag, Heckle & Jeckle, Lancelot Link: Secret Chimp, Lariat Sam, Oaky Doky, Bonny Maid Varieties, Howdy Doody, Jack Barry's Winky Dink, The Steve Allen Show. 130 Dayton Allen 5 min. shows (synd.).

ALLEN, DEBBIE
Actress, Choreographer. b. Houston, TX, Jan. 16, 1950. e. Howard U. Sister is actress Phylicia Rashad.
THEATER: Ti-Jean and His Brothers (debut, 1972), Purlie, Raisin, Ain't Misbehavin', West Side Story (revival), Sweet Charity (revival, Tony Award, 1986), Carrie (choreographer).
PICTURES: The Fish That Saved Pittsburgh (1979), Fame, Ragtime, Jo Jo Dancer Your Life is Calling, Blank Check.

TELEVISION: Movies: The Greatest Thing That Almost Happened, Ebony—Ivory and Jade, Women of San Quentin, Celebrity, Polly-Comin' Home (dir.), Stompin' at the Savoy (also dir.). Series: The Jim Stafford Show, 3 Girls 3, Fame (series; 3 Emmys as choreographer, 1 nom. as actress), A Different World (prod., dir), In the House. Mini-Series: Roots-The Next Generation. Specials: Ben Vereen-His Roots, Loretta Lynn in Big Apple Country, Texaco Star Theater—Opening Night, The Kids from Fame, John Schneider's Christmas Holiday, A Tribute to Martin Luther King Jr.—A Celebration of Life, Motown Returns to the Apollo, The Debbie Allen Special (also dir., chor.), Sinbad Live (Afros and Bell Bottoms), Academy Awards (choreographer: 1991-96).

ALLEN, DEDE
Film Editor. r.n. Dorothea Carothers Allen b. Cleveland, OH, 1924. Started as messenger at Columbia Pictures, moved to editing dept., then to commercials and features. Theatrical Production v.p. then pres. at Warner Brothers, 1992-1997. A.C.E. Honorary Lifetime Achievement Award, 1994.
PICTURES: Odds Against Tomorrow (1959), The Hustler, America America, Bonnie and Clyde, Rachel Rachel, Alice's Restaurant, Little Big Man, Slaughterhouse 5, Serpico, Night Moves, Dog Day Afternoon (Acad. award nom.), The Missouri Breaks, Slap Shot, The Wiz, Reds (also exec. prod. Acad. award nom.), Harry and Son, Mike's Murder, The Breakfast Club, Off Beat, The Milagro Beanfield War (co-ed.), Let It Ride (co-ed.), Henry and June, The Addams Family.

ALLEN, IOAN
Executive. b. Stafford, England, Oct. 25, 1938. e. Rossall School and Dartmouth Naval College, England. Artist mgmt. and record prod., 1964-1969. Responsible for origination and devt. of Dolby Stereo film program. Past Fellow of Society of Motion Picture & Television Engineers, Audio Engineering Society and the British Kinematographic Sound & Television Society. Pres., Intl. Theatre Equipment Assn. U.S. correspondent on the Intl. Standards Org. cinematographic subcommittee. Adjunct prof., USC School of Cinema-Television. Vice pres., Dolby Laboratories. Recipient: Acad. Scientific & Technical Awards, 1979 & 1987. Acad. award for work in Dolby Laboratories film program, 1989; Samuel L. Warner Award for contribution to motion picture sound, 1985.

ALLEN, JAY PRESSON
Writer, Producer. r.n. Jacqueline Presson. b. Fort Worth, TX, March 3, 1922. m. prod. Lewis M. Allen.
THEATER: Writer:The First Wife, The Prime of Miss Jean Brodie, Forty Carats, Tru (also dir.), The Big Love (also dir.).
PICTURES: Writer: Marnie, The Prime of Miss Jean Brodie, Cabaret, Travels with My Aunt, Funny Lady, Just Tell Me What You Want (also prod.), It's My Turn (exec. prod. only), Prince of the City (also exec. prod.), Deathtrap (also exec. prod.).
TELEVISION: Series: Family (creator), Hot House (also exec. prod.).

ALLEN, JOAN
Actress. b. Rochelle, IL, Aug. 20, 1956. Founding member of Steppenwolf Theatre Co., in Chicago where she performed in over 20 shows.
THEATER: Chicago: A Lesson from Aloes, Three Sisters, The Miss Firecracker Contest, Cloud 9, Balm in Gilead, Fifth of July, Reckless, Earthly Possessions. Off B'way: The Marriage of Bette and Boo, And a Nightingale Sang (Clarence Derwent, Drama Desk, Outer Critics' Circle and Theatre World Awards). B'way.: Burn This (debut, 1987; Tony Award), The Heidi Chronicles.
PICTURES: Compromising Positions (debut, 1985), Manhunter, Peggy Sue Got Married, Tucker: The Man and His Dream, In Country, Ethan Frome, Searching for Bobby Fischer, Josh and S.A.M., Mad Love, Nixon, The Crucible, The Ice Storm.
TELEVISION: Movie: Without Warning: The James Brady Story. Mini-Series: Evergreen. Specials: All My Sons.

ALLEN, KAREN
Actress. b. Carrollton, IL, Oct. 5, 1951. e. George Washington U., U. of Maryland. Auditioned for theatrical company in Washington, DC and won a role in Saint, touring with it for 7 months. Spent several years with Washington Theatre Laboratory Co. Moved to NY, acted in student films at NYU and studied acting at Theatre Institute with Lee Strasberg.
THEATER: NY: Monday After the Miracle (B'way debut, 1982; Theatre World Award), Extremities, The Miracle Worker, The Country Girl. Williamstown (MA) Theatre: Tennessee Williams-- A Celebration, The Glass Menagerie.
PICTURES: National Lampoon's Animal House (debut, 1978), Manhattan, The Wanderers, Cruising, A Small Circle of Friends, Raiders of the Lost Ark, Shoot the Moon, Split Image, Until September, Starman, Terminus, The Glass Menagerie, Backfire, Scrooged, Animal Behavior, Secret Places of the Heart, Sweet Talker, Exile, Malcolm X, The Sandlot, Ghost in the Machine.
TELEVISION: Movies: Lovey: A Circle of Children Part II, Secret Weapon, Challenger, Voyage, Down Home. Guest: Alfred Hitcock Presents (1986). Mini-Series: East of Eden.

ALLEN, LEWIS M.
Producer. b. Berryville, VA, June 27, 1922. e. Univ. of VA. m. writer-producer Jay Presson Allen.
PICTURES: *Prod./Exec. prod./Co-prod.*:The Connection, The Balcony, Lord of the Flies, Fahrenheit 451, The Queen, Fortune and Men's Eyes, Never Cry Wolf, 1918, Valentine's Day, Swimming to Cambodia, O.C. & Stiggs, End of the Line, Miss Firecracker.

ALLEN, NANCY
Actress. b. New York, NY, June 24, 1950. e. H.S. Performing Arts, N.Y.
PICTURES: The Last Detail (debut, 1973), Carrie, I Wanna Hold Your Hand, 1941, Home Movies, Dressed to Kill, Blow Out, Strange Invaders, The Buddy System, The Philadelphia Experiment, The Last Victim (Forced Entry), Not for Publication, Terror in the Aisles, Sweet Revenge, Robocop, Poltergeist III, Limit Up, Robocop 2, Robocop 3.
TELEVISION: *Movies*: The Gladiator, Memories of Murder, Acting on Impulse, The Man Who Wouldn't Die.

ALLEN, REX
Actor. b. Wilcox, AZ, Dec. 31, 1922. e. Wilcox H.S., 1939. Vaudeville & radio actor, WLS, Chicago, 5 yrs. Was rodeo star appearing in shows through U.S.
PICTURES: Arizona Cowboy, Hills of Oklahoma, Under Mexicali Stars, Thunder in God's Country, Rodeo King & the Senorita, I Dream of Jeannie, Last Musketeer, South Pacific Trail, Old Overland Trail, Down Laredo Way, Phantom Stallion, For the Love of Mike, Tomboy and the Champ. Narrator: The Legend of Lobo, The Incredible Journey, Charlotte's Web.
TELEVISION: *Series*: Frontier Doctor, Five Star Jubilee.*Guest*: Perry Como Special. *Voice only*: commercials, Wonderful World of Color.

ALLEN, STEVE
Performer. b. New York, NY, Dec 26, 1921. e. Arizona St. Univ. m. actress Jayne Meadows. U.S. Army 1942. Radio shows, Los Angeles. TV, N.Y., 1950. On NY stage in The Mikado. Composer or lyricist of numerous songs including This Could Be the Start of Something Big, Pretend You Don't See Her, South Rampart St. Parade, Picnic, Houseboat, On the Beach, Sleeping Beauty, Bell Book and Candle, Gravy Waltz, Impossible; score for B'way musical Sophie; score for TV musicals: The Bachelor, and Alice in Wonderland.
AUTHOR: Fourteen For Tonight, Steve Allen's Bop Fables, The Funny Men, Wry On the Rocks, The Girls on the Tenth Floor, The Question Man, Mark It and Strike It, Not All of Your Laughter, Not All of Your Tears, Bigger Than a Breadbox, A Flash of Swallows, The Wake, Princess Snip-Snip and the Puppykittens, Curses, Schmock-Schmock!, Meeting of Minds, Ripoff, Meeting of Minds-Second Series, Rip-off, Explaining China, The Funny People, Talk Show Murders, Beloved Son: Story of the Jesus Cults, More Funny People, How To Make a Speech and How To Be Funny, Murder on the Glitter Box, The Passionate Non-smoker's Bill of Rights, Dumbth and 81 Ways to Make Americans Smarter, Murder in Manhattan, Steve Allen on the Bible, Religion and Morality, The Public Hating, Murder in Vegas, Hi-Ho Steverino!: My Adventures in the Wonderful Wacky World of TV, The Murder Game, More Steve Allen on the Bible, Religion & Morality Book II, Make 'em Laugh, Reflections, Murder on the Atlantic, The Man Who Turned Back the Clock and Other Short Stories, Die Laughing.
PICTURES: Down Memory Lane (debut, 1949), I'll Get By, The Benny Goodman Story, The Big Circus, College Confidential, Don't Worry We'll Think of a Title, Warning Shot, Where Were You When the Lights Went Out?, The Comic, The Sunshine Boys, Heart Beat, Amazon Women on the Moon, Great Balls of Fire!, The Player, Casino.
TELEVISION: *Movies*: Now You See It Now You Don't, Stone, The Gossip Columnist. *Series*: The Steve Allen Show (1950-52), Songs for Sale, Talent Patrol, What's My Line, Steve Allen Show, Tonight, Steve Allen Show (1956-61), (1962-64), (1964-67), I've Got a Secret, Steve Allen Comedy Hour (1967), Steve Allen Show (1967-69), I've Got a Secret (1972-73) Steve Allen's Laugh Back, Meeting of Minds, Steve Allen Comedy Hour (1980-81), Life's Most Embarrassing Moments. *Mini-Series*: Rich Man Poor Man.

ALLEN, TIM
Actor. r.n. Timothy Allen Dick. b. Denver, CO, June 13, 1953. e. W. Michigan Univ., Univ. of Detroit, studied acting. Worked as creative dir. for adv. agency before becoming stand up comedian. Made stand up tv debut on Showtime Comedy Club All-Stars, 1988. Author: Don't Stand Close to a Naked Man (1994).
PICTURES: Comedy's Dirtiest Dozen, The Santa Clause, Toy Story (voice), Jungle2Jungle.
TELEVISION: *Series*: Home Improvement. *Specials*: Tim Allen: Men Are Pigs (also writer), Tim Allen Rewrites America (also exec. prod., writer).

ALLEN, WILLIAM
Executive. e. USC Cinema/TV Sch., Pepperdine Univ. 1979. Exec. trainee in CBS Entertainment division, eventually serving as assoc. program exec. in the Comedy Series Programming Dept.; mngr./dir. of the CBS Comedy Program Development. Dept. Joined MTM as sr. v.p., Comedy Programming, 1986-87; sr. v.p. creative affairs, 1987-88; exec. v.p. MTM Television, 1989-1991; pres., MTM Television, 1992.

ALLEN, WOODY
Actor, Director, Writer. r.n. Allan Stewart Konigsberg. b. New York, NY, Dec. 1, 1935. e. NYU, 1953; City Coll. NY, 1953. Began writing comedy at age 17, contributing to various magazines (Playboy, New Yorker) and top TV comedy shows incl. Sid Caesar (1957), Art Carney (1958-59), Herb Shriner (1953). Appeared in nightclubs starting in 1961 as stand-up comic; later performed as a jazz musician at Michael's Pub, NY. Special Award, Berlin Film Fest., 1975.
AUTHOR: Getting Even, Without Feathers, Side Effects.
THEATER: *Author*. Play It Again Sam (also actor), Don't Drink The Water, The Floating Lightbulb, Central Park West (from Death Defying Acts).
PICTURES: *Actor-Screenplay*: What's New Pussycat?, What's Up Tiger Lily? (also dubbed and compiled footage; assoc. prod.), Casino Royale (actor only). Play It Again Sam. *Director/Screenplay/Actor*: Take the Money and Run, Bananas, Everything You Always Wanted to Know About Sex* But Were Afraid to Ask, Sleeper, Love and Death, The Front (actor only), Annie Hall (Acad. Awards for Best Director and Original Screenplay, 1977), Interiors (dir., s.p. only), Manhattan, Stardust Memories, A Midsummer Night's Sex Comedy, Zelig, Broadway Danny Rose, The Purple Rose of Cairo (dir., s.p. only), Hannah and Her Sisters (Acad. Award for Best Original Screenplay, 1986), Radio Days (dir., s.p., narrator only), September (dir., s.p. only), King Lear (actor only), Another Woman (dir., s.p. only), New York Stories (Oedipus Wrecks segment), Crimes and Misdemeanors, Alice (dir., s.p. only), Scenes From a Mall (actor only), Shadows and Fog, Husbands and Wives, Manhattan Murder Mystery, Bullets Over Broadway (dir., s.p. only), Mighty Aphrodite, Everyone Says I Love You (dir. & actor), Deconstructing Harry, Wild Man Blues, Celebrity.
TELEVISION: *Movies*: Don't Drink the Water (also dir., writer), The Sunshine Boys. *Specials*: The Best on Record, Gene Kelly in New York New York, The Woody Allen Special (also writer, co-dir.), Woody Allen Looks at 1967 (Kraft Music Hall; also writer), Plimpton: Did You Hear the One About ...? *Guest*: Hullabaloo, Andy Williams, Hippodrome.

ALLEY, KIRSTIE
Actress. b. Wichita, KS, Jan. 12, 1955. m. actor Parker Stevenson. e. KS State U., U. of Kansas. On L.A. stage in Cat on a Hot Tin Roof.
PICTURES: Star Trek II: The Wrath of Khan (debut, 1982), Blind Date, Champions, Runaway, Summer School, Shoot to Kill, Loverboy, Look Who's Talking, Madhouse, Sibling Rivalry, Look Who's Talking Too, Look Who's Talking Now, Village of the Damned, It Takes Two, Deconstructing Harry.
TELEVISION: *Movies*: Sins of the Past, A Bunny's Tale, Stark: Mirror Image, Prince of Bel Air, Infidelity, David's Mother (Emmy Award, 1994). *Series*: Masquerade, Cheers (Emmy Award, 1991), Untitled, Veronica's Closet. *Mini-Series*: North and South, North and South Book II. *Guest*: The Love Boat, The Hitchhiker.

ALLYSON, JUNE
Actress. r.n. Ella Geisman. b. Westchester, NY, Oct. 7, 1917. Started as chorus girl. Voted one of ten top money-making stars in Motion Picture Herald-Fame poll, 1955.
THEATER: *B'way*: Sing Out the News, Panama Hattie, Best Foot Forward, 40 Carats. *Tour*: No No Nanette.
PICTURES: Best Foot Forward (debut, 1943), Girl Crazy, Thousands Cheer, Meet the People, Two Girls and a Sailor, Music For Millions, Her Highness and the Bellboy, The Sailor Takes a Wife, Two Sisters From Boston, Till the Clouds Roll By, Secret Heart, High Barbaree, Good News, The Bride Goes Wild, The Three Musketeers, Words and Music, Little Women, The Stratton Story, Meet the People, Reformer and the Redhead, Right Cross, Too Young to Kiss, Girl in White, Battle Circus, Remains to be Seen, Executive Suite, Glenn Miller Story, Woman's World, Strategic Air Command, The Shrike, McConnell Story, Opposite Sex, You Can't Run Away From It, Interlude, My Man Godfrey, Stranger in My Arms, They Only Kill Their Masters, Blackout, That's Entertainment III.
TELEVISION: *Movies*: See the Man Run, Letters from Three Lovers, Curse of the Black Widow, Vega$, Three on a Date, The Kid With the Broken Halo. *Series*: DuPont Show With June Allyson. *Guest*: Murder She Wrote, Misfits of Science. *Special*: 20th Century Follies.

ALMODOVAR, PEDRO
Director, Writer. b. La Mancha, Spain, Sept. 25, 1951. Grew up in Calzada de Calatrava. At 17 moved to Madrid where worked 10 years for telephone co. while writing comic strips and articles for underground newspapers and working as actor with independent theater co., Los Goliardos. Upon the end of Francoist repression in 1975, made Super-8 experimental films starring friends. Wrote fiction, sang with rock band and created character of porn star, Patty Diphusa, whose fictionalized confessions he published in the magazine La Luna.
PICTURES: Pepi Lucy Bom and Other Girls on the Heap (debut, 1980), Labyrinth of Passion, Dark Habits, What Have I Done to Deserve This?, Matador, Law of Desire, Women on the Verge of a Nervous Breakdown, Tie Me Up! Tie Me Down!, High Heels, Kika, The Flower of My Secret, Live Flesh.

ALMOND, PAUL
Producer, Director, Writer. b. Montreal, Canada, April 26, 1931. e. McGill U., Balliol Coll., Oxford U. 1954-66, produced and directed over a hundred television dramas in Toronto, London, N.Y., and Hollywood.
PICTURES: Backfire, Isabel, Act of the Heart, Journey, Final Assignment, Ups and Downs, Captive Hearts, The Dance Goes On.

ALONSO, MARIA CONCHITA
Actress, Singer. b. Cuba, 1957. Family moved to Venezuela when she was five. 1971, named Miss Teenager of the World. 1975, Miss Venezuela. 6th runner up, Miss World. Appeared in four feature films and 10 soap operas before coming to U.S. Recorded several albums as singer: 5 gold albums, 1 platinum, 3 Grammy noms.
THEATER: Aurora. B'way: Kiss of the Spider Woman.
PICTURES: Fear City, Moscow on the Hudson, Touch and Go, A Fine Mess, Extreme Prejudice, The Running Man, Colors, Vampire's Kiss, Predator 2, McBain, The House of the Spirits, Roosters, Caught, For Which He Stands, Acts of Betrayal.
TELEVISION: Movies: Teamster Boss: The Jackie Presser Story, MacShayne: The Final Roll of the Dice, Texas. Also: An American Cousin (RAI mini-series), The Gun, Sudden Terror, Fx. Specials: Viva Miami!, The Night of the Super Sounds (host). Guest: One of the Boys, Chicago Hope.

ALONZO, JOHN A
Cinematographer, Director. b. Dallas, TX, 1934.
PICTURES: Bloody Mama, Vanishing Point, Harold and Maude, Get to Know Your Rabbit, Lady Sings the Blues, Sounder, Pete-n-Tillie, Hit, The Naked Ape, Conrack, Chinatown, Farewell My Lovely, The Fortune, I Will ... I Will ... For Now, Once Is Not Enough, The Bad News Bears, Black Sunday, Beyond Reason, Close Encounters of the Third Kind (addtl. photog.), Which Way Is Up?, Casey's Shadow, FM (dir. only), The Cheap Detective, Norma Rae, Tom Horn, Back Roads, Zorro the Gay Blade, Blue Thunder, Cross Creek, Scarface, Out of Control, Terror in the Aisles, Runaway, Jo Jo Dancer Your Life Is Calling, Nothing in Common, 50 Years of Action, Real Men, Overboard, Physical Evidence, Steel Magnolias, Internal Affairs, The Guardian, Navy Seals, Housesitter, Cool World, The Meteor Man, Clifford, The Grass Harp.
TELEVISION: Champions: A Love Story, Belle Star (also dir.), Blinded By the Light (also dir.), The Kid From Nowhere (also dir.), Roots: The Gift, Knights of the City, World War II, When Lions Roared. Specials: High Def.

ALTERMAN, JOSEPH GEORGE
Executive. b. New Haven, CT., Dec. 17, 1919. e. Wesleyan U., B.A., 1942; Inst. for Organization Management, Yale U., 1957-59. Exec. assist., SoundScriber Corp., 1945-48. District mgr., Industrial Luncheon Service, 1948-55. Asst. secretary and admin. secretary, Theatre Owners of America, 1955; exec. dir. and vice pres., Natl. Assn. of Theatre Owners, 1966. Exec. v.p. COMPO., 1970. Retired 1988 from NATO. Consultant m.p. industry, conventions and meetings. Chmn., bd. govs., Institute for Learning in Retirement, Albertus Magnus College.

ALTMAN, ROBERT
Director, Writer, Producer. b. Kansas City, MO, Feb. 20, 1925. e. U. of Missouri. Early film writer credits: Bodyguard (co-story), Corn's-a-Poppin (co-s.p.). Made industrial films and documentaries for the Calvin Company in Kansas City, before dir. first indept. feature in 1957. Received D.W. Griffith Lifetime Achievement Award from Directors Guild of America, 1994.
THEATER: NY: Two By South, Come Back to the Five and Dime Jimmy Dean Jimmy Dean. Operas: The Rake's Progress, McTeague.
PICTURES: Director: The Delinquents (also s.p., prod.), The James Dean Story (also co-prod., edit.), Countdown, That Cold Day in the Park, M*A*S*H (Cannes Film Fest. Golden Palm Award, 1970; Acad. Award nom.), Brewster McCloud, McCabe & Mrs. Miller (also co-s.p.), Images (also s.p.), The Long Goodbye, Thieves Like Us (also co-s.p.), California Split (also co-prod.), Nashville (also prod.; NY Film Critics, Natl. Society of Film Critics & Natl. Board of Review Awards for Best Director & Picture, 1975; Acad. Award noms. for dir. & picture), Buffalo Bill and the Indians: Or Sitting Bull's History Lesson (also co-s.p., prod.), Three Women (also s.p., prod.), A Wedding (also co-s.p., prod., co-story), Quintet (also co-s.p., prod., co-story), A Perfect Couple (also co-s.p., prod.), Health (also co-s.p., prod.), Popeye, Come Back to the Five and Dime Jimmy Dean Jimmy Dean, Streamers (also co-prod.), Secret Honor (also prod.), Fool for Love, Beyond Therapy (also co-s.p.), O.C. and Stiggs (also co-prod.), Aria (dir. Les Boreades sequence; also s.p.), Vincent & Theo, The Player (BAFTA & Cannes Film Fest. Awards for Best Director, 1991; Acad. Award nom.), Short Cuts (also co-s.p.; Acad. Award nom. for dir.), Ready to Wear/Pret-a-Porter (also co-s.p.). Producer: The Late Show, Welcome to L.A., Remember My Name, Rich Kids, Mrs. Parker and the Vicious Circle, Kansas City.
TELEVISION: Series: Director/Writer &/or Producer: The Roaring Twenties, The Millionaire, Bonanza, Bus Stop, Combat, Kraft Mystery Theatre (Nightmare in Chicago: Once Upon a Savage Night), The Gallant Men (pilot). Specials: Two by South (also prod.), The Laundromat, The Dumb Waiter (also prod.), Tanner '88 (also co-exec. prod.; Emmy Award for dir. episode The Boiler Room, 1989), The Room, The Real McTeague, Black and Blue. Movie: The Caine Mutiny Court-Martial (also co-prod.).

ALVARADO, TRINI
Actress. b. New York, NY, 1967. e. Fordham U. m. actor Robert McNeill. Began performing at age 7 as flamenco dancer with her parents' troupe. Prof. acting debut at 9 in stage musical Becca.
THEATER: Runaways, Yours Anne, Maggie Magalita, I Love You—I Love You Not, Reds, The Magic Show, Godspell.
PICTURES: Rich Kids (debut, 1989), Times Square, Mrs. Soffel, Sweet Lorraine, Satisfaction, The Chair, Stella, American Blue Note, The Babe, American Friends, Little Women, Frighteners.
TELEVISION: Movies: Dreams Don't Die, Prisoner Without a Name, Nitti. Specials: Private Contentment, Unicorn Tales, A Movie Star's Daughter, Stagestruck, Sensibility and Sense. Guest: Kay O'Brien, Kate and Allie.

ALVIN, JOHN
Actor. r.n. John Alvin Hoffstadt. b. Chicago, IL, Oct. 24, 1917. e. Pasadena Playhouse, CA. Attended Morgan Park Military Acad. On radio Chicago & Detroit; on N.Y. stage Leaning on Letty, Life of the Party. Screen debut 1944 in Destination Tokyo. Under contract four years to Warner Bros., featured in 25 films.
PICTURES: Destination Tokyo, Objective Burma, San Antonio, The Beast With Five Fingers, Night and Day, Cheyenne, Missing Women, Two Guys From Texas, Bold Frontiersman, Train to Alcatraz, Shanghai Chest, Carrie, April In Paris, Roughly Speaking, The Very Thought of You, Shadow of a Woman, Three Strangers, Romance on the High Seas, Torpedo Alley, Irma La Douce, Marnie, Inside Daisy Clover, The Legend of Lylah Clare, They Shoot Horses Don't They?, They Call Me Mr. Tibbs, Somewhere in Time, Beethoven's 2nd, Milk Money.
TELEVISION: Meet Millie, Burns and Allen, Death Valley Days, Asphalt Jungle, Climax, Dragnet, Jack Benny Show, My Three Sons, The Texan, Adventures in Paradise, Rawhide, Rifleman, Omnibus, Wells Fargo, Alfred Hitchcock, Mannix, I Spy, Legend of Lizzie Borden, All in the Family, McDuff, Lineup, My Favorite Husband, Family Affair, Get Smart, The Incredible Hulk, The Lucy Show, Ironside, Nightstalker, M*A*S*H, Lou Grant Show, Hart to Hart, Yellow Rose, Dennis the Menace (2 Hour Pilot), Murder She Wrote, Monster Squad, House of Evil, Aftermath, General Hospital, Starsky & Hutch, Policewoman, Amazing Stories, Capitol, Passions, The Quest, Visions/KCET, Rachel Sweet Rachel, Swallows Came Back, Return to Green Acres, Moving Target, From Out of the Night, The Walkers, The Bold and the Beautiful.

AMATEAU, ROD
Director. b. New York, NY, Dec. 20, 1923. U.S. Army, 1941. 20th Century-Fox, 2nd unit dir.
PICTURES: The Statue, Where Does It Hurt?, The Wilby Conspiracy, Drive-In, Lovelines, Garbage Pail Kids (also s.p., prod.), Sunset (story only).
TELEVISION: Movies: Uncommon Valor, High School U.S.A., Swimsuit (prod.). Series: Schlitz Playhouse of Stars, Four Star Playhouse, General Electric Theatre, Private Secretary, Dennis Day Show, Lassie, Ray Milland Show, Bob Cummings Show, Burns & Allen Show (also prod.), Dobie Gillis.

AMES, LOUIS B.
Executive. b. St. Louis, MO, Aug. 9, 1918. e. Washington U., St. Louis. m. Jetti Ames. Began as music consultant and staff dir. of musical programs for NBC; appt. music dir., WPIX, 1948; program mgr., WPIX, 1951. Assoc. prod., Today, NBC TV, 1954. Feature editor Home, 1957. Adm.-prod. NBC Opera, 1958. Dir. cultural prog. N.Y. World's Fair, 1960-63; dir. RCA Pavillion, N.Y. World's Fair, 1963-65; dir., Nighttime, TV, 1966; dir. of programming N.W. Ayer & Sons, Inc., 1969. Mgr. Station Services, Television Information Office. NY, 1973.

AMIEL, JON
Director, Producer. b. London, England, 1948. e. Cambridge. Was in charge of the Oxford & Cambridge Shakespeare Co., then literary mgr. for Hamptead Theatre Club where he started directing. Became story edit. for BBC, then director.
PICTURES: Silent Twins, Queen of Hearts, Tune in Tomorrow, Sommersby, Copycat.
TELEVISION: A Sudden Wrench, Gates of Gold, Busted, Tandoori Nights (series), The Singing Detective (mini-series).

AMIN, MARK
Executive. Chairman & Acting CEO, TriMark Pictures.
PICTURES: *Exec. prod.*: The Servants of the Twilight, Whore, Into the Sun, Interceptor, Philadelphia Experiment II, Leprechaun, Extreme Justice, Deadfall, Separate Lives, Night of the Running Man, Million to Juan, Frank and Jesse, Dangerous Touch, Love and a .45, Two Guys Talkin' About Girls, The Maddening, Leprechaun 3, Iron Eagle IV, Evolver, Aurora:Operation Intercept, A Kid in King Arthur's Court, Kicking and Screaming, Sometimes They Come Back, Pinocchio's Revenge, Never Ever, Crossworlds, Eve's Bayou, Underworld, Sprung, Star Kid, Chairman of the Board.

AMIS, SUZY
Actress. b. Oklahoma City, OK, Jan. 5, 1962. e. Heritage Hall, Oklahoma City. At 16 was introduced on the Merv Griffin Show by Eileen Ford whose modeling agency she worked for, as "The Face of the Eighties." After modeling and living in Europe, made film debut in Fandango (1985). Off-B'way debut: Fresh Horses (Theatre World Award).
PICTURES: Fandango, The Big Town, Plain Clothes, Rocket Gibraltar, Twister, Where the Heart Is, Rich in Love, Watch It, The Ballad of Little Jo, Two Small Bodies, Blown Away, The Usual Suspects, Nadja, One Good Turn, Titanic, Last Stand at Saber River, The Ex, Cadillac Ranch, Firestorm.
TELEVISION: *Movies*: The Beneficiary, Dead by Midnight.

AMOS, JOHN
Actor. b. Newark, NJ, Dec. 27, 1941. e. East Orange H.S., Colorado State U, Long Beach City Col. Inducted as honorary Master Chief Petty Officer in U.S. Navy 1993. Worked as professional football player, social worker (heading the Vera Institute of Justice in NY), and advertising copywriter before writing television comedy material (for the Leslie Uggams Show) and performing as stand-up comedian in Greenwich Village. Has also dir. theatre with Bahamian Rep. Co. Artistic dir., John Harms Theatre, Englewood, NJ.
THEATER: *L.A.*: Norman Is That You?, Master Harold...And the Boys, Split Second, The Emperor Jones. *B'way*: Tough to Get Help. NYSF: Twelfth Night. *Off-B'way*: The Past is the Past. *Regional*: Fences, Halley's Comet (also writer). *Foreign*: Life and Death of a Buffalo Sodier.
PICTURES: Vanishing Point (debut, 1971), Sweet Sweetback's Baadasssss Song, The World's Greatest Athlete, Let's Do It Again, Touched By Love, The Beastmaster, Dance of the Dwarfs, American Flyers, Coming to America, Lock Up, Die Hard 2, Ricochet, Two Evil Eyes (The Black Cat), Mac, Night Trap (Mardi Gras for the Devil).
TELEVISION: *Movies*: The President's Plane is Missing, Future Cop, Cops and Robin, Willa, Alcatraz-The Whole Shocking Story, Bonanza-the Next Generation. *Series*: Mary Tyler Moore, The Funny Side, Maude, Good Times, Hunter, South by Southwest, 704 Hauser. *Mini-Series*: Roots. *Pilots*: Clippers, 704 Hauser Street; many guest appearances incl. Bill Cosby Show, Love American Style, Sanford and Son, The Love Boat, Cosby Show. *Special*: Without a Pass.

ANDERSON, DAVID LEROY
Special Effects.
PICTURES: Shocker, Beyond the Law, Alien 3, Loaded Weapon 1, The Nutty Professor, Men in Black (Acad. Award, Best Makeup, 1997).

ANDERSON, GERRY
Hon. F.B.K.S., Producer, Director, Writer. b. London, England, 1929. Entered industry in 1946. Chmn./man. dir. Gerry Anderson Productions, Ltd. Over 320 pictures produced for TV worldwide. Co-founded Anderson Burr Pictures, 1981. Prod. Terrahawks in association with London Weekend Television, 1982; second series, Terrahawks, 1984. Space Police pilot for series in assoc. with TVS, 1985-6. Dick Spanner stop motion series for Channel Four, 1987. Entered commercials as a dir.: numerous commercials incl. Royal Bank of Scotland, Children's World, Domestos, Shout, Scotch Tape, etc. Anglo Russian Cartoon Series Astro Force and lecture tour An Evening with Garry Anderson, 1992.

PICTURES: Thunderbirds Are Go, Thunderbird 6, Journey to the Far Side of the Sun.
TELEVISION: *Series*: The Adventures of Twizzle, Torchy the Battery Boy, Four Feather Falls, Supercar, Fireball XL5, Stingray, Thunderbirds, Captain Scarlet, Joe 90, The Secret Service, The Protectors, UFO, Space 1999, Terrahawks, Dick Spanner, Space Precinct, Lavender Castle.

ANDERSON, HARRY
Actor. b. Newport, RI, Oct. 14, 1952. m. actress-magician Leslie Pollack. Performed magic show prior to plays at Oregon Shakespeare Festival. Also opening act for Kenny Rogers, Debbie Reynolds and Roger Miller in Las Vegas. Owner of magic shop in Ashland OR. Received Stage Magician of Year Award, National Acad. of Magician Arts and Sciences.
PICTURE: The Escape Artist.
TELEVISION: *Movies*: Spies, Lies and Naked Thighs; The Absent-Minded Professor, Stephen King's It. *Series*: Night Court (Emmy nom.), Our Time, Dave's World. *Guest*: Cheers, The Tonight Show, David Letterman, Saturday Night Live, Wil Shriner. *Specials*: Comic Relief, Harry Anderson's Sideshow (also exec. prod., writer), Comic Relief II, The Best of Gleason, Magic with the Stars, Nell Carter: Never Too Old to Dream, Hello Sucker.

ANDERSON, J. WAYNE
Executive. b. Clifton Forge, VA, Feb. 19, 1947. e. USA Signal School (1965-67); USN Service Schools (1967). USMC, 1965-69; opened and operated 1st military 35mm m.p. theatre, DaNang, Vietnam, 1967-69. R/C Theatres, dist. mgr., 1971-75; v.p., 1976-83; pres./COO, 1983-present. Bd. of dirs., Maryland Permanent Bank & Trust co., 1988-present; chmn., 1992-present. Member of NATO, bd. of dirs., 1987-present; technical advancement committee, 1981-present; chmn., 1991-present. Inter-Society for the Enhancement of Theatrical Presenation, 1986-present. Huntsman bd. of dirs., 1979-83; pres., 1982-83. Member: NRA, 1970-life; Will Rogers Inst., 1988-present; Presidential Task Force, 1990-life.

ANDERSON, KEVIN
Actor. b. Illinois, Jan. 13, 1960. e. Goodman School. Member of Chicago's Steppenwolf Theatre where he starred in Orphans. Moved with the play when it transferred to New York (1985) and later starred in the London production, as well as the film version.
THEATER: *NY*: Orphans (Theatre World Award), Moonchildren, Brilliant Tracers, Orpheus Descending. *London*: Sunset Boulevard.
PICTURES: Risky Business (debut, 1983), Pink Nights, A Walk on the Moon, Orphans, Miles From Home, In Country, Sleeping With the Enemy, Liebestraum, Hoffa, The Night We Never Met, Rising Sun, A Thousand Acres, Eye of God, Firelight, A Thousand Acres.
TELEVISION: *Movies*: Orpheus Descending, The Wrong Man. *Special*: Hale the Hero. *Series*: Nothing Sacred.

ANDERSON, LONI
Actress. b. St. Paul, MN, Aug. 5. 1946. e. U. of Minnesota. Taught school before acting.
PICTURES: Stroker Ace, The Lonely Guy (cameo), All Dogs Go to Heaven (voice), Munchie.
TELEVISION: *Movies*: The Magnificent Magnet of Mesa, Three on a Date, The Jayne Mansfield Story, Sizzle, Country Gold, My Mother's Secret Life, A Letter to Three Wives, Stranded, Necessity, A Whisper Kills, Too Good to Be True, Sorry Wrong Number, Coins in the Fountain, White Hot: The Mysterious Murder of Thelma Todd, The Price She Paid, Gambler V: Playing for Keeps. *Series*: WKRP in Cincinnati, Partners in Crime, Easy Street, Nurses. *Specials*: Christmas in Opryland, Shaun Cassidy Special, Bob Hope specials, etc.

ANDERSON, MELISSA SUE
Actress. b. Berkeley, CA, Sept. 26, 1962. Took up acting at suggestion of a dancing teacher. Did series of commercials; guest role in episode of Brady Bunch; episode of Shaft. Gained fame as Mary Ingalls on Little House on the Prairie series (Emmy nom.).
PICTURES: Happy Birthday to Me, Chattanooga Choo Choo, Dead Men Don't Die.
TELEVISION: *Movies*: Little House on the Prairie (pilot), The Loneliest Runner, James at 15 (pilot), Survival of Dana, Midnight Offerings, Advice to the Lovelorn, An Innocent Love, First Affair, Dark Mansions. *Series*: Little House on the Prairie. *Specials*: Which Mother is Mine? (Emmy Award, 1980).

ANDERSON, MICHAEL
Director. b. London, England, Jan. 30, 1920. e. France, Germany. Ent. motion picture industry as actor, 1936. Son is actor Michael Anderson Jr.

PICTURES: Private Angelo (debut, 1949; co-dir. with Peter Ustinov), Waterfront, Hell Is Sold Out, Night Was Our Friend, Will Any Gentleman?, The Dam Busters, 1984, Around the World in 80 Days, Yangtse Incident (Battle Hell), Chase a Crooked Shadow, Shake Hands With the Devil (also prod.), The Wreck of the Mary Deare, All the Fine Young Cannibals, The Naked Edge, Flight From Ashiya, Wild and Wonderful, Operation Crossbow, The Quiller Memorandum, The Shoes of the Fisherman, Pope Joan, Doc Savage: The Man of Bronze, Conduct Unbecoming, Logan's Run, Orca, Dominique (Avenging Spirit), Murder By Phone, Second Time Lucky, Separate Vacations, Jeweller's Shop, Millenium.
TELEVISION: Movies: Regina Vs. Nelles, The Sea Wolf, Harry Oakes, Rugged Gold, Captain's Courageous, 20,000 Leagues Under the Sea. Mini-Series: The Martian Chronicles, Sword of Gideon, Young Catherine.

ANDERSON, MICHAEL, JR.
Actor. b. London, England, Aug. 6, 1943. Father is director Michael Anderson. Ent. films as child actor, 1954.
PICTURES: The Moonraker, Tiger Bay, The Sundowners, In Search of the Castaways, Play It Cool, Reach For Glory, Greatest Story Ever Told, Dear Heart, Major Dundee, The Glory Guys, The Sons of Katie Elder, The Last Movie, Logan's Run.
TELEVISION: Movies: The House That Would Not Die, In Search of America, The Family Rico, The Daughters of Joshua Cabe, Coffee Tea or Me? Shootout in a One-Dog Town, Kiss Me Kill Me, The Million Dollar Face, Making of a Male Model, Love Leads the Way. Series: The Monroes. Mini-Series: Washington Behind Closed Doors, The Martian Chronicles.

ANDERSON, PAUL THOMAS
Director, Writer, Producer. b. Studio City, CA, Jan. 1, 1970. LA Film Crits. Award, New Generation, 1997.
PICTURES: Dir.: The Dirk Diggler Story (also s.p.), Cigarettes and Coffee (also s.p.), Hard Eight (also s.p.), Boogie Nights (also s.p., prod.), Lennon.

ANDERSON, RICHARD
Actor. b. Long Branch, NJ, Aug. 8, 1926. e. University H.S., W. Los Angeles. Served in U.S. Army, WWII. Began acting career in summer theatre in Santa Barbara and Laguna Playhouse where spotted by MGM executives who signed him to six year contract. Appeared in 26 films for MGM before leaving studio. Spokesperson for Kiplinger Washington Letter since 1985.
PICTURES: 12 O'Clock High, The People Against O'Hara, Scaramouche, The Story of Three Loves, Escape from Fort Bravo, Forbidden Planet, The Search for Bridey Murphy, Paths of Glory, The Long Hot Summer, Curse of the Faceless Man, Compulsion, A Gathering of Eagles, Johnny Cool, Seven Days in May, Seconds, The Ride to Hangman's Tree, Tora! Tora! Tora!, Macho Callahan, Doctors' Wives, Play It As It Lays, The Honkers, The Player, The Glass Shield, An American in Saigon, Gettysburg.
TELEVISION: Movies: Along Came a Spider, Kane & Abel, The Return of the Six Million Dollar Man and the Bionic Woman, Pearl, Perry Mason Returns, Hoover vs. the Kennedys, Eminent Domain, Danger High, Stranger on My Land, The Bionic Showdown: The Six Million Dollar Man & The Bionic Woman (also co-prod.), Return of the Six Million Dollar Man and the Bionic Woman III, Kung Fu Revisted, Bionic Breakdown: The Six Million Dollar Man & The Bionic Woman (exec. prod.), Bionic Ever After? (also co-exec. prod.), A Lake In The Woods. Series: Mama Rosa, Bus Stop, The Lieutenant, Perry Mason, Dan August, The Six Million Dollar Man, The Bionic Woman (Emmy nom.), Dynasty, Cover-Up. Guest: Ironside, The Big Valley, Mannix, My Friend Tony, The Mod Squad, Land of the Giants, The FBI, Gunsmoke.

ANDERSON, RICHARD DEAN
Actor. b. Minneapolis, MN, Jan. 23, 1950. Planned to become professional hockey player. Became a street mime and jester. Performed with his own rock band, Ricky Dean and Dante.
PICTURES: Young Doctors in Love, Ordinary Heroes, Odd Jobs, Firehouse, Fallout (voice).
TELEVISION: Movies: In the Eyes of a Stranger, Through the Eyes of a Killer, MacGyver: Lost Treasure of Atlantis (also co-exec. prod.), MacGyver: Trail to Doomsday, Beyond Betrayal, Past the Bleachers. Series: General Hospital (1976-81), Seven Brides for Seven Brothers, Emerald Point N.A.S., MacGyver, Legend. x, Stargate SG-1. Mini-series: Pandora's Clock.

ANDERSON, SYLVIA.
Producer, Writer (Pinewood Studios). b. London, England. e. London U. Entered m.p. ind. 1960. First pub. novel, Love and Hisses. UK rep for Home Box Office of America.
PICTURES: Thunderbird Six (prod.), Thunderbirds Are Go.
TELEVISION: Creator &/or Prod.: Space 1999, UFO, Thunderbirds, Journey Throught the Black Sun, Destination Moonbase Alpha, Alien Attack.

ANDERSON, WILLIAM H.
Producer. b. Utah, Oct. 12, 1911. e. Compton Coll. Firestone Rubber Co.; Universal Credit Co. Prod. & Member of Bd. of dirs. at Walt Disney Prods.
PICTURES: Old Yeller, Swiss Family Robinson, The Happiest Millionaire, The Computer Wore Tennis Shoes, The Barefoot Executive, $1,000,000 Duck, Superdad, The Strongest Man in the World, The Apple Dumpling Gang, Treasure of Matecumbe, The Shaggy D.A., The Moonspinners, Third Man on the Mountain, A Tiler Walks, The One And Only Genuine Original Family Band, The Biscuit Eater.
TELEVISION: Series: Zorro, Pop Warner Football. (Wonderful World of Disney) Movies: Zorro, Texas John Slaughter, Daniel Boone, The Swamp Fox, Johnny Shiloh, Mooncussers, Bristle Face, The Scarecrow of Romney Marsh, The Legend of Young Dick Turpin, Willie and the Yank, A Boy Called Nuthin', The Young Loner, The Wacky Zoo of Morgan City, The Mystery of Dracula's Castle, The Bull from the Sky (co-prod.), Great Sleeping Bear Sled Dog Race (co-prod.).
(d. Dec. 28, 1998)

ANDERSSON, BIBI
Actress. b. Stockholm, Sweden, Nov. 11, 1935. e. Royal Dramatic Theatre School (Kungliga Dramatiska Teatern).
PICTURES: Dum-Bom (debut, 1953), Sir Arne's Treasure, Smiles of a Summer Night, The Seventh Seal, Wild Strawberries, The Magician, Brink of Life, The Face, The Devil's Eye, Square of Violence, Pleasure Garden, The Swedish Mistress, Not to Mention These Women, My Sister My Love, Persona, Duel at Diablo, A Question of Rape, Black Palm Trees, The Girls, Story of a Woman, The Passion of Anna, The Kremlin Letter, The Touch, Scenes From a Marriage, It Is Raining on Santiago, Blondy (Vortex), The Hounds of Spring, I Never Promised You a Rose Garden, An Enemy of the People, Quintet, The Concorde: Airport '79, Prosperous Times, The Marmalade Revolution, Black Crows, Exposed, The Hill on the Other Side of the Moon, Babette's Feast, Manika, Fordringsagare.
TELEVISION: Rabies, Wallenberg—A Hero's Story, Tul Julia.

ANDRESS, URSULA
Actress. b. Bern, Switzerland, Mar. 19, 1936. To Rome as teen where she landed roles in Italian Films.
PICTURES: Sins of Casanova (debut, 1954), An American in Rome, The Tempest Has Gone, La Catena dell'Odio, Anyone Can Play, Dr. No, Four For Texas, Fun in Acapulco, Nightmare in the Sun, She, The Tenth Victim, What's New Pussycat?, Up to His Ears, Once Before I Die, The Blue Max, Casino Royale, The Southern Star, Perfect Friday, Red Sun, Africa Express, Scaramouche, The Sensuous Nurse, Slave of the Cannibal God, Tigers in Lipstick, The Fifth Musketeer, Primitive Desires, Four Tigers in Lipstick, Clash of the Titans, Reporters, Mexico in Flames, Liberte/Egalite/Choucroute, Class Reunion.
TELEVISION: Movies: Man Against the Mob. Series: Falcon Crest. Mini-Series: Peter the Great.

ANDREWS, ANTHONY
Actor, Producer. b. London, England, Dec. 1, 1948. e. Royal Masonic Sch., Herts. Regional stage debut, 1967.
PICTURES: Take Me High/Hot Property (debut, 1973), Operation Daybreak, Under the Volcano, The Holcroft Covenant, The Second Victory, The Lighthorsemen, Hanna's War, Lost in Siberia, Haunted (also co-prod.).
TELEVISION: A Beast With Two Backs, Upstairs Downstairs, A War of Children, Romeo and Juliet, QB VII, Ivanhoe, The Scarlet Pimpernel, Danger UXB, Brideshead Revisited, Sparkling Cyanide, A.D., Bluegrass, Suspicion, The Woman He Loved, Columbo Goes to the Guillotine, Danielle Steel's Jewels, Strange Case of Dr. Jekyll and Mr. Hyde, Hands of a Murderer, Heartstones, Mothertime.

ANDREWS, JULIE
Actress, Singer. r.n. Julia Wells. b. Walton-on-Thames, England. Oct. 1, 1935. m. dir./writer Blake Edwards. Debut, England Starlight Roof Revue London Hippodrome, 1948. Author of Mandy, Last of the Really Great Whangdoodles, 1973.
THEATER: NY: The Boy Friend, My Fair Lady, Camelot, Putting It Together, Victor/Victoria.
PICTURES: Mary Poppins (debut, 1964; Acad. Award), The Americanization of Emily, The Sound of Music (Acad. Award nom.), Hawaii, Torn Curtain, Thoroughly Modern Millie, Star!, Darling Lili, The Tamarind Seed, ``10,'' S.O.B, Victor/Victoria (Acad. Award nom.), The Man Who Loved Women, That's Life, Duet For One, A Fine Romance.
TELEVISION: Movies: Our Sons. Series: The Julie Andrews Hour (1972-73), Julie. Specials: High Tor, Julie and Carol at Carnegie Hall, The Julie Andrews Show, An Evening with Julie Andrews and Harry Belafonte, The World of Walt Disney, Julie and Carol at Lincoln Center, Julie on Sesame Street, Julie Andrews' Christmas Special, Julie and Dick in Covent Garden, Julie Andrews and Jackie Gleason Together, Julie Andrews: My Favorite Things, Julie Andrews:The Sound of Christmas, Julie and Carol: Together Again.

ANDREWS, NAVEEN
Actor. b. Enland, 1971. e. Guildhall School of Music and Drama.
PICTURES: London Kills Me, Wild West, True Love and Chaos, Kama Sutra: A Tale of Love, The English Patient, Mighty Joe Young.
TELEVISION: Double Vision, The Buddha of Suburbia, The Peacock Spring.

ANGELOPOULOS, THEO
Director, Writer, Producer, Actor. b. Athens, Greece, April 17, 1935.
PICTURES: Reconstruction, Days of 36, The Travelling Players, The Hunters, Alexander the Great, Voyage to Kythera (Cannes Film Fest. Award, Best Screenplay, 1984), The Beekeeper, Landscape in the Mist, The Suspended Step of the Stork, The Gaze of Odysseus (Cannes Film Fest. Award, Jury Prize, 1995), Lumiere and Company, Eternity and a Day (Cannes Film Fest. Award, Palm D'Or, 1998).

ANGERS, AVRIL
Actress, Comedienne, Singer. b. Liverpool, England, April 18. Stage debut at age of 14; screen debut in 1947 in Lucky Mascot (The Brass Monkey).
THEATER: The Mating Game, Cockie, Murder at the Vicarage, Little Me, Norman, Is That You?, Blithe Spirit, Oklahoma!, Gigi, The Killing of Sister George, Cards on the Table, When We Are Married, Cinderella, Easy Virtue, Post Mortem, Crazy for You.
PICTURES: Miss Pilgrim's Progress, Don't Blame the Stork, Women Without Men, Green Man, Devils of Darkness, Be My Guest, Three Bites of the Apple, The Family Way, Two a Penny, The Best House in London, Staircase, There's a Girl in My Soup, Forbush and the Penguins, Gollocks, Confessions of a Driving Instructor, Dangerous Davies.
TELEVISION: How Do You View, Friends and Neighbors, Dear Dotty, Holiday Town, Charlie Fainsbarn Show, Arthur Askey Show, All Aboard, The Gold Hunter, Bob Monkhouse Show, Before The Fringe, Hudd, Coronation Street, Dick Emery Show, Dad's Army, Bright Boffins, The More We Are Together, The Millionairess, Liver Birds, Looks Familiar, No Appointment Necessary, The Songwriters, All Creatures Great and Small, Coronation Concert, Minder, Smuggler, Just Liz, Give Us a Clue, Are You Being Served, Trelawney of the Wells, Cat's Eye, C.A.B., Rude Health, Victoria Wood Playhouse, Common As Muck.

ANHALT, EDWARD
Writer. b. New York, NY, March 28, 1914. e. Columbia U.
PICTURES: Crime Doctor's Diary, Gentleman From Nowhere, Avalanche, Strange Voyage, Bulldog Drummond Strikes Back, Panic in the Streets (Acad. Award for Best Original Story, 1950), Red Mountain, The Member of the Wedding (also prod.), The Sniper (Acad. award nom.), My Six Convicts, Eight Iron Men, Not as a Stranger, The Pride and the Passion, The Young Lions, In Love and War, The Restless Years, The Sins of Rachel Cade, The Young Savages, Girls Girls Girls, A Girl Named Tamiko, Wives and Lovers, Becket (Acad. Award for Best Adapted Screenplay, 1964), The Satan Bug, Boeing-Boeing, Hour of the Gun, In Enemy Country, The Boston Strangler, The Madwoman of Chaillot, Jeremiah Johnson, The Man in the Glass Booth, Luther, Escape to Athena, Green Ice, The Holcroft Covenant.
TELEVISION: A Time for Killing, Madame X, Peter the Great, QB VII, Contract on Cherry Street, Day That Christ Died, The Neon Empire, The Take, Alexander the Great, The Life and Times of Santa Claus, The Apostles.

ANISTON, JENNIFER
Actress. b. Sherman Oaks, CA, Feb. 11, 1969. e. NY High School of the Performing Arts. Daughter of actor John Aniston. Started training as a drama student in high school. In 1987, after graduation, appeared in For Dear Life and Dancing on Checker's Grave (off B'way.). Made television debut on Molloy, 1989.
PICTURES: Leprechaun, Dream for an Insomniac, She's the One, 'Til There Was You, Picture Perfect, The Object of My Affection.
TELEVISION: Movies: How I Spent My Summer, Camp Cucamonga. Series: Molloy (debut), Ferris Bueller, The Edge, Muddling Through, Friends. Guest: Quantum Leap, Herman's Head, The Larry Sanders Show, Burke's Law, Partners.

ANN-MARGRET
Actress, Singer, Dancer. r.n. Ann-Margret Olsson. b. Valsjobyn, Sweden, April 28, 1941. e. New Trier H.S., Winnetka, IL; Northwestern U. m. Roger Smith, actor, dir., prod. Radio shows, toured with band; worked with George Burns in Las Vegas. TV debut, Jack Benny Show, 1961.
PICTURES: Pocketful of Miracles (debut, 1961), State Fair, Bye Bye Birdie, Viva Las Vegas, Kitten With a Whip, The Pleasure Seekers, Bus Riley's Back in Town, Once A Thief, The Cincinnati Kid, Made in Paris, Stagecoach, The Swinger, Murderer's Row, The Prophet, The Tiger and the Pussycat, Rebus, Criminal Affair, RPM, C. C. & Company, Carnal Knowledge (Acad. Award nom.), The Outside Man, The Train Robbers, Tommy (Acad. Award nom.), The Last Remake of Beau Geste, The Twist, Joseph Andrews, The Cheap Detective, Magic, The Villain, Middle Age Crazy, I Ought To Be in Pictures, Lookin' to Get Out, The Return of the Soldier, Twice in a Lifetime, 52 Pick-up, A Tiger's Tail, A New Life, Newsies, Grumpy Old Men, Grumpier Old Men.
TELEVISION: Movies: Who Will Love My Children?, A Streetcar Named Desire, The Two Mrs. Grenvilles, Our Sons, Nobody's Children, Following Her Heart, Blue Rodeo. Mini-Series: Queen, Scarlett, Seduced By Madness: The Diane Borchardt Story. Specials: The Ann-Margret Show, From Hollywood With Love, Dames at Sea, When You're Smiling, Ann-Margret Smith, Ann-Margret Olsson, Memories of Elvis, Rhinestone Cowgirl, Hollywood Movie Girls.

ANNAUD, JEAN-JACQUES
Writer, Director. b. Draveil, France, Oct. 1, 1943. Began career as film dir. in French army, making educational pictures. Also directed 500 commercials. Received 1989 cinema prize from French Acad. for career's work. Directed IMAX film Wings of Courage.
PICTURES: Director: Black and White in Color (also s.p., winner of Best Foreign Language Film Oscar, 1978), Coup de Tete (Hothead), Quest for Fire (Cesar Award for best dir., 1982), The Name of the Rose, The Bear (also co-s.p.: Cesar Award for best dir., 1989), The Lover, Wings of Courage, Seven Years In Tibet. Writer: Black and White In Color, Too Shy to Try.

ANSARA, MICHAEL
Actor. b. Lowell, MA, April 15, 1922. e. Pasadena Playhouse. Served in U.S. Army; then summer stock, little theatre, road shows.
PICTURES: Soldiers Three, Only the Valiant, The Robe, Julius Caesar, Sign of the Pagan, Bengal Brigade, New Orleans Uncensored, Diane, Lone Ranger, Sol Madrid, Daring Game, Dear Dead Delilah, The Bears and I, Mohammad Messenger of God, The Manitou, Gas, Access Code, Knights of the City. Lethal (KGB: The Secret War).
TELEVISION: Series: Broken Arrow, Law of the Plainsman, Buck Rogers in the 25th Century. Mini-Series: Centennial. Guest: The Westerner, Lost in Space, Simon and Simon, Gavilan, George Burns Comedy Week, Hunter, Hardcastle and McCormick. Movies: How I Spent My Summer Vacation, Powderkeg, A Call to Danger, Ordeal, Shootout in a One-Dog Town, Barbary Coast, The Fantastic World of D.C. Collins.

ANSPACH, SUSAN
Actress. b. New York, NY, Nov. 23, 1945. e. Catholic U., Washington, DC. After school returned to NY and in 3 years had performed in 11 B'way and off-B'way prods. Moved to Los Angeles and entered films.
PICTURES: The Landlord (debut, 1970), Five Easy Pieces, Play It Again Sam, Blume in Love, The Big Fix, Running, The Devil and Max Devlin, Gas, Montenegro, Misunderstood, Blue Monkey, Into the Fire, Blood Red, Back to Back.
TELEVISION: Movies: I Want to Keep My Baby, The Secret Life of John Chapman, Rosetti & Ryan, Mad Bull, The Last Giraffe, Portrait of an Escort, The First Time, Deadly Encounter, Cagney & Lacey: The Return. Series: The Yellow Rose, The Slap Maxwell Story. Mini-Series: Space.

ANSPAUGH, DAVID
Director, Producer. b. Decatur, IN, Sept. 24, 1946. e. Indiana U., 1965-70; U. of Southern CA, 1974-76. School teacher, Aspen, CO, 1970-74.
PICTURES: Director: Hoosiers (debut, 1986), Fresh Horses, Rudy, Moonlight and Valentino.
TELEVISION: Movies: Deadly Care, In the Company of Darkness. Series: Hill St. Blues (assoc. prod. 1980-81; prod.-dir. 1981-82; prod.-dir. 1983-84, dir. 1985. DGA Award: 1983, 2 Emmy Awards for producing: 1982, 1983), St. Elsewhere (dir.), Miami Vice (dir.).

ANTHONY, LYSETTE
Actress. b. London, England, 1963. Stage work incl. Bristol Old Vic, 1988-90.
PICTURES: Krull, The Emperor's New Clothes, Without a Clue, 29 Days in February, Switch, Husbands and Wives, The Pleasure Principle, Look Who's Talking Now, The Advocate, Dr. Jekyll and Ms. Hyde, Dead Cold, Dracula: Dead and Loving It.
TELEVISION: Movies/Specials: Ivanhoe, Oliver Twist, Dombey and Son, Jemima Shore, Night Train to Murder, The Bretts, Princess Daisy, The Lady and the Highwayman (Dangerous Love), Jack the Ripper, A Ghost in Monte Carlo, Sweet Danger. Series: Lovejoy (BBC), Three Up Two Down (BBC), Campion, Dark Shadows.

ANTHONY, MICHELE
Executive. e. George Washington U.; USC, J.D. Currently exec. v.p. of Sony Music Entertainment. Bd. member: The Rock and Roll Hall of Fame, Tock the Vote, Sloan Kettering Cancer Center.

ANTHONY, TONY
Actor, Producer, Writer. b. Clarksburg, WV, Oct. 16, 1939. e. Carnegie Mellon.
PICTURES: Force of Impulse, Pity Me Not, The Wounds of Hunger, A Stranger in Town, The Stranger Returns, A Stranger in Japan, Come Together, Blindman, Pete Pearl and the Pole, Let's Talk About Men, Get Mean, Treasure of the Four Crowns, Comin' at Ya, For Better or For Worse.

ANTON, SUSAN
Actress. b. Oak Glen, CA, Oct. 12, 1950. Concert & night club singer. Country album & single Killin' Time went top 10 on Country charts, received Gold Record in Japan. Made B'way debut in Hurlyburly, 1985. Also in The Will Rogers Follies. Off-B'way in X-mas a Go-Go. 1992, hon. chmn. of Amer. Cancer Soc., Calif. Special Olympics, & hon. capt. U.S. Woman's Olympic Volleyball Team..
PICTURES: Goldengirl, Spring Fever, Cannonball Run II, Options (cameo), Making Mr. Right, Lena's Holiday.
TELEVISION: Movies: The Great American Beauty Contest. Guest: Quantum Leap, Blossom, Murder She Wrote, Night Court, The Famous Teddy Z, Circus of the Stars. Series: Stop Susan Williams (Cliff Hangers), Presenting Susan Anton.

ANTONIO, LOU
Actor, Writer, Producer, Director. b. Oklahoma City, OK. e. U. of OK. Two Emmy Nominations for TV Movies.
THEATER: Actor: The Buffalo Skinner (Theatre World Award), The Girls of Summer, The Good Soup, The Garden of Sweets, Andorra, The Lady of the Camellias, The Ballad of the Sad Cafe, Ready When You Are, C.B. Director: Private Lives (w Taylor/Burton).
PICTURES: Actor: The Strange One, Splendor in the Grass, America America, Hawaii, Cool Hand Luke, The Phynx. Also: Mission Batangas (s.p.), Micki and Maude (exec. prod.).
TELEVISION: Movies: Lanigan's Rabbi, Someone I Touched, Something for Joey, The Girl in the Empty Grave, The Critical List, Silent Victory-The Kitty O'Neil Story, A Real American Hero, The Contender, We're Fighting Back, Something So Right, A Good Sport, Threesome, Rearview Mirror, Face to Face, The Outside Woman (also prod.), Dark Holiday (also exec. prod.), Between Friends, Mayflower Madam, One Terrific Guy, Pals, 13 at Dinner, This Gun for Hire, Lies Before Kisses, The Last Prostitute, The Rape of Dr. Willis, A Taste for Killing, Nightmare in the Daylight. Series: Snoop Sisters, Dog and Cat, Making It, Piece of Blue Sky, The Power and the Glory, Danny Thomas Hour, Partners in Crime, Sole Survivor, Where the Ladies Go, Star Trek. Director: Mini-Series: Rich Man, Poor Man (co-dir.), Breaking Up Is Hard to Do, The Star Maker. Guest: Picket Fences (also dir.), Chicago Hope (also dir.).

ANTONIONI, MICHELANGELO
Director, Writer. b. Ferrara, Italy, Sept. 29, 1912. e. Centro Spiremintale di Cinematografia; degree in economics. Film critic on local newspaper; film critic with Corriere Padano, 1936-40; script writer for Un Pilota Ritorna, I due Foscari and asst. dir. for Les Visiteurs du Soir, 1942; with Italia Libera and on edit. staff of Cinema, 1944-45. First films as dir. were short documentaries including: Gente del Po (1943-47), N.U., L'Amorosa Menzogna, Superstizione, Sette canne un vestito, followed by latter works La Villa dei Mostri, La Funivia del Faloria, Kumbha Mela, Roma, Noto—Mandorli—Vulcano—Stromboli—Carnevale. Recipient of: Palme d'Or, 1987; Prix Lumiere, 1990; h.c. degree, Univ. of Berkeley, 1993; honorary Academy Award, 1995; Legion d'Honneur, Paris 1996 and many others. Prof. at Cornell Univ., NY.
PICTURES: Director/Writer: Story of a Love Affair (feature debut as dir., 1950), The Vanquished, Lady Without Camelias (Camille Without Camelias), Love in the City (segment: When Love Fails), The Girl Friends, The Outcry, I Am a Camera, L'Avventura, The Night, Eclipse, The Red Desert, I Tre Volti/Three Faces of a Woman (dir. only; segment: Prefazione), Blow-Up (Acad. Award nom. for dir.), Zabriskie Point, Chung Kuo (documentary), The Passenger, The Oberwald Mystery, Identification of a Woman, The Crew, Beyond the Clouds (co-dir., co-s.p., with Wim Wenders), Just to Be Together.

ANTONOWSKY, MARVIN
Executive. b. New York, NY, Jan. 31, 1929. e. City Coll. of New York, B.A., M.B.A. Joined Kenyon and Eckhart in 1957 for which was media research dir. then mktg. svcs. Became v.p. in charge of media research and spot buying at J. Walter Thompson, 1965. Joined ABC-TV as v.p. in charge of research, 1969. Left to become v.p. in charge of programming at NBC-TV. Became sr. v.p., Universal-TV, 1976. Joined Columbia Pictures as pres., mktg. & research, 1979. Rejoined MCA/Universal Pictures as pres, mktg., 1983. Formed Marvin Antonowsky & Assoc., mktg. consultancy firm, 1989. Rejoined Columbia Pictures in 1990 as exec. v.p. and asst. to chmn. Joined Price Entertainment as exec. v.p., 1993.

ANWAR, GABRIELLE
Actress. b. Laleham, England, 1970.
PICTURES: Manifesto (debut, 1989), If Looks Could Kill, Wild Hearts Can't Be Broken, Scent of a Woman, For Love or Money, The Three Musketeers, Body Snatchers, Things to Do in Denver When You're Dead, Innocent Lies, The Grave.
TELEVISION: Movies: First Born, In Pursuit of Honor, The Ripper, White Chapel, Nevada, Sub Down. Specials: The Storyteller, Summer's Lease, Dead-End for Delia (Fallen Angels).

APFEL, EDWIN R.
Writer, Executive. b. New York, NY, Jan. 2, 1934. e. Franklin and Marshall Coll., B.A., 1955. Mktg. exec.: Metro-Goldwyn-Mayer, Verve Records, Embassy Pictures. Freelance copywriter. Writer of, Edward R. Murrow: This Reporter, Amer. Masters (PBS), 1990. Council member, WGA East, 1992.

APPLEGATE, CHRISTINA
Actress. b. Hollywood, CA, Nov. 25, 1972.
PICTURES: Jaws of Satan (debut, 1980), Streets, Don't Tell Mom the Babysitter's Dead, Across the Moon, Wild Bill, Nowhere.
TELEVISION: Movies: Grace Kelly, Dance 'til Dawn. Series: Washingtoon, Heart of the City, Married... With Children. Guest: Quincy M.E., Charles in Charge, The New Leave It to Beaver, Amazing Stories, 21 Jump Street.

APTED, MICHAEL
Director, Producer. b. Aylesbury, England, Feb. 10, 1941. e. Cambridge. Broke into show business at Granada TV in England in early 1960's as trainee, researcher and finally director. By 1965, was prod.-dir. for local programs and current affairs then staff drama dir. for TV series, plays and serials. In late 1960's, left Granada to freelance.
PICTURES: Triple Echo, Stardust, The Squeeze, Agatha, Coal Miner's Daughter, Continental Divide, Gorky Park, Firstborn, Bring on the Night, 28 Up, Critical Condition, Gorillas in the Mist, Class Action, 35 Up, Thunderheart, Incident at Oglala, Bram Stoker's Dracula (exec. prod. only), Blink, Nell, Moving the Mountain, Extreme Measures.
TELEVISION: Director: Seven Up, Big Breadwinner Hogg (series), Seven Plus Seven, The Lovers (series), Another Sunday and Sweet F.A., Follyfoot, Joy The Style of the Countess, The Reporters, The Collection, Stronger Than the Sun, Buggins' Ermine, Jackpoint, Kisses at 50, High Kampf, Poor Girl, Wednesday Love, Ptang Yang Kipperbang, The Long Way Home, My Life and Times, Crossroads, New York News (pilot), Always Outnumbered. Exec. Prod: Criminal Justice, Age 7 in America, Intruders, Strapped.

ARAKI, GREGG
Director, Editor, Producer, Writer. b. Los Angeles, CA.
PICTURES: Three Bewildered People In The Night, The Living End, Totally F***ed Up, The Doom Generation, Nowhere.

ARAU, ALFONSO
Director, Actor. b. Mexico, 1933. e. Univ. of Mexico. Studied drama there and with Saki Sano in Mexico; UCLA film school; studied pantomime in Paris.
PICTURES: Actor: The Wild Bunch, El Topo, Scandalous John, Run Cougar Run, Tivoli, Posse, Used Cars, Romancing the Stone, Three Amigos, Walker, Camino Largo a Tijuana. Director: The Barefoot Eagle (also actor), Clazonian Inspector, Mojado Power (Wetback Power), Chido One, Like Water for Chocolate (Mexico's Ariel Award), A Walk in the Clouds.
TELEVISION: Movies: Stones for Ibarra, Dynamite and Gold. Series: El Show de Arau.

ARCAND, DENYS
Director. b. Deschambault, Quebec, Canada, June 25, 1941. e. U. of Montreal, 1963. While still history student, co-prod. Seul ou avec D'Autres (1962). Joined National Film Board of Canada, where he began making documentary shorts (Champlain, Les Montrealistes and La Route de l'ouest) forming a trilogy dealing with colonial Quebec. In 1970 socio-political doc. about Quebec textile workers, On Est au Coton, generated controversy resulting in the NFB banning film until 1976.
PICTURES: On Est au Coton (doc.), Un Maudite Galette (1st fiction feature, 1971). Dir. &/or Writer: Seoul ou Avec D'autres, Entre la Mer et L'eau Douce, Quebec: Duplessis et Apres... (doc.), Dirty Money, Rejeanne Padovani, Gina, Comfort and Indifference, Le Crime d'Ovide Plouffe, The Decline of the American Empire, Night Zoo (actor only), Jesus of Montreal (Cannes Film Fest. jury prize, 1989), Leolo (actor only), Montreal Sextet (also actor), Love and Human Remains, Poverty and Other Delights.
TELEVISION: Series: Duplessis (s.p.), Empire Inc. (dir.), Murder in the Family(mini).

ARCHER, ANNE
Actress. b. Los Angeles, CA, Aug. 25, 1947. Daughter of actress Marjorie Lord and actor John Archer. m. Terry Jastrow, TV network sports producer-director and pres. Jack Nicklaus Prods.
THEATER: A Coupla White Chicks Sitting Around Talking (off-B'way, 1981), Les Liaisons Dangereuses (Williamstown Fest., 1988).
PICTURES: The Honkers (debut, 1972), Cancel My Reservation, The All-American Boy, Trackdown, Lifeguard, Paradise Alley, Good Guys Wear Black, Hero at Large, Raise the Titanic, Green Ice, Waltz Across Texas (also co-story), The Naked Face, Too Scared to Scream, The Check Is in the Mail, Fatal Attraction (Acad. Award nom.), Love at Large, Narrow Margin, Eminent Domain, Patriot Games, Body of Evidence, Family Prayers, Short Cuts, Clear and Present Danger, There Goes My Baby (narrator), Mojave Moon.

TELEVISION: *Movies*: The Blue Knight, The Mark of Zorro, The Log of the Black Pearl, A Matter of Wife...and Death, The Dark Side of Innocence, Harold Robbins' The Pirate, The Sky's No Limit, A Different Affair, A Leap of Faith, The Last of His Tribe, Nails, Jane's House, Because Mommy Works (also co-prod.), The Man in the Attic. *Series*: Bob and Carol and Ted and Alice, The Family Tree, Falcon Crest. *Mini-Series*: Seventh Avenue. *Special*: Leslie's Folly.

ARCHERD, ARMY
Columnist, TV commentator. r.n. Armand Archerd. b. New York, NY, Jan. 13, 1922. e. UCLA, grad. '41, U.S. Naval Academy Post Graduate Sch., 1943. m. actress Selma Archerd. Started as usher at Criterion Theatre, N.Y., while in high school. After grad. UCLA, worked at Paramount studios before entering Navy. Joined AP Hollywood bureau 1945, Herald-Express, Daily Variety as columnist, 1953. M.C. Hollywood premieres, Emmys and Academy Awards. Pres., found., Hollywood Press Club. Awards from Masquers, L.A. Press Club, Hollywood Foreign Press Club, and Newsman of the Year award from Publicists Guild, 1970; Movie Game. Co-host on TV series, People's Choice. Received Hollywood Women's Press Club Man of the Year Award, 1987.

ARDANT, FANNY
Actress. b. Monte Carlo, March 22, 1949. Majored in political science in college. Served a 5-year apprenticeship in the French theater acting in Polyeucte, Esther, The Mayor of Santiago, Electra and Tete d'Or. TV debut in Les Dames de la Cote.
PICTURES: Les Chiens (debut, 1979), Les uns et les Autres, The Woman Next Door, The Ins and Outs, Life Is a Novel, Confidentially Yours, Benevenuta, Desire, Swann in Love, Love Unto Death, Les Enrages, L'Ete Prochain, Family Business, Affabulazione, Melo, The Family, La Paltoquet, Three Sisters, Australia, Pleure pas My Love, Adventure of Catherine C., Afraid of the Dark, Rien Que des Mensonges, La Femme du Deserteur, Amok, Colonel Chabert, Beyond the Clouds, Ridicule, Elizabeth I.

ARGENTO, DARIO
Director, Writer. b. Rome, Italy, 1940. Son of prod. Salvatore Argento.
PICTURES: *Writer/Co-s.p.*: Today It's Me...Tomorrow It's You, Cemetery Without Crosses, Once Upon a Time in the West, Commandos, Zero Probability, The Five Man Army, One Night at Dinner, Sex Revoultion, Legion of the Damned, Seasons of Love .*Also Dir./Prod./Co-Prod.*: Bird With the Crystal Plumage, Cat O'Nine Tails (also story), Four Flies on Grey Velvet, Five Days in Milan, Deep Red, Suspiria (also music), Dawn of the Dead (also music), Inferno (also story), Tenebrae Unsane (also story), Creepers, Demons, Demons 2: The Nightmare is Back, Opera (Terror at the Opera), The Church (also story), Two Evil Eyes (episode: The Black Cat), Devil's Daughter, Innocent Blood (actor only), Trauma, Stendhal's Syndrome, The Wax Mask, Phantom of the Opera.
TELEVISION: *Series*: Door Into Darkness (It.).

ARKIN, ADAM
Actor. b. Brooklyn, NY, Aug. 19, 1956. Father is actor Alan Arkin. Made acting debut in short film prod. by father, People Soup.
THEATER: I Hate Hamlet (Theatre World Award), Four Dogs and a Bone.
PICTURES: Made for Each Other, Baby Blue Marine, Improper Channels (s.p.), Under the Rainbow, Chu Chu and the Philly Flash, Full Moon High, The Doctor.
TELEVISION: *Movies*: It Couldn't Happen to a Nicer Guy, All Together Now, In the Line of Duty: Hunt for Justice. *Series*: Busting Loose, Teachers Only, Tough Cookies, A Year in the Life, Northern Exposure, Chicago Hope. *Mini-Series*: Pearl. *Specials*: Mark Twain's America: Tom Edison, The Fourth Wise Man.

ARKIN, ALAN
Actor, Director, b. New York, NY, March 26, 1934. e. Los Angeles City Col., Los Angeles State Col., Bennington (VT) Col. m. Barbara Dana, actress-author. Father of actor Adam Arkin. Was member of folk singing group The Tarriers, then one of the original members of Chicago's Second City improvisational group. Directed short films T.G.I.F., People Soup (Acad. Award nom.). Author: Tony's Hard Work Day, The Lemming Condition, Halfway Through the Door, The Clearing, Some Fine Grandpa.
THEATER: *B'way*: Enter Laughing (Tony & Theatre World Awards, 1963), Luv. *Off-B'way*: Second City, Man Out Loud, From the Second City. *Director*: Eh?, Little Murders, White House Murder Case (Obie Award), Joan of Lorraine, Rubbers and Yanks Three, The Sunshine Boys, The Sorrows of Stephen, Room Service.
PICTURES: Calypso Heat Wave (debut, 1957), The Russians Are Coming The Russians Are Coming (Golden Globe Award, Acad. Award nom.), Woman Times Seven, Wait Until Dark, Inspector Clouseau, The Heart Is a Lonely Hunter (NY Film Critics Award, Acad. Award nom.), Popi, The Monitors, Catch-22, Little Murders (also dir.), Deadhead Miles, Last of the Red Hot Lovers, Freebie and the Bean, Rafferty and the Gold Dust Twins, Hearts of the West (NY Film Critics Award), The 7 Per Cent Solution, Fire Sale

(also dir.), The In-Laws (also exec. prod.), The Magician of Lublin, Simon, Improper Channels, Chu Chu and the Philly Flash, Full Moon High, The Last Unicorn (voice), The Return of Captain Invincible, Joshua Then and Now, Bad Medicine, Big Trouble, Coupe de Ville, Edward Scissorhands, Havana, The Rocketeer, Glengarry Glen Ross, Indian Summer, So I Married an Axe Murderer, North, The Jerky Boys, Steal Big Steal Little, Mother Night, Grosse Point Blank, Gattaca, The Slums of Beverly Hills, Jakob the Liar, Arigo (also dir. & s.p.).
TELEVISION: *Movies*: The Defection of Simas Kurdirka, The Other Side of Hell, A Deadly Business, Escape from Sobibor, Cooperstown, Taking the Heat, Doomsday Gun.*Series*: Harry, Chicago Hope. *Guest*: East Side/West Side, St. Elsewhere. *Specials*: The Love Song of Barney Kempinski, The Fourth Wise Man, A Matter of Principle, Fay (pilot; dir.), Twigs (dir.), The Emperor's New Clothes (Faerie Tale Theatre), The Visit (Trying Times; dir.), The Boss (Trying Times; dir.), Necessary Parties (also co-s.p., co-prod.).

ARKOFF, SAMUEL Z.
Producer, Executive. b. Fort Dodge, IA, June 12, 1918. e. U. of Colorado, U. of Iowa, Loyola U. Law Sch. Chmn. & pres. of the Samuel Z. Arkoff Company (formed 1980) and Arkoff Int'l Pictures (formed 1981). Served in USAF as cryptographer WWII. Exec. prod. of The Hank McCune Show, 1948-51. Co-founder American Releasing, 1954, and American International Pictures, 1955. Pres. and chmn. of bd. AIP until 1979. Named with partner James H. Nicholson, Producers of the Year by Allied States Assoc. of MP Theatre Owners, 1963. Named Master Showmen of the Decade by the Theatre Owners of America, 1964. Along with Nicholson, named Pioneers of the Year by the Foundation of the MP Pioneers, Inc., 1971. Since appointment in 1973, has served as intl. v.p. of Variety Clubs Intl. V.p., Permanent Charities Committee. Member of the bd. of Trustees of Loyola Marymount U., L.A., 1979. Hollywood Walk of Fame Star, 1993. Author of Flying Through Hollywood By the Seat of My Pants, with Richard Trubo.
PICTURES: *Exec. Prod./Producer*: Reform School Girl, Motorcycle Gang, Machine Gun Kelly, The Bonnie Parker Story, The Fall of the House of Usher, The Pit and the Pendulum, Tales of Terror, Master of The World, Premature Burial, Panic in the Year Zero, The Raven, Beach Party, Haunted Palace, Comedy of Terrors, Bikini Beach, Masque of the Red Death, Muscle Beach Party, Pajama Party Tomb of Ligeia, Wild Angels, Devil's Angels, The Trip, Three in the Attic, Wild in the Streets, The Oblong Box, Scream and Scream Again, Murders in the Rue Morgue, Cry of the Banshee, Bloody Mama, Wuthering Heights, The Abominable Dr. Phibes, Frogs, Blacula, Dillinger, Heavy Traffic, Hennessy, Cooley High, Food of the Gods, Futureworld, The Great Scout and Cathouse Thursday, The Land That Time Forgot, The People That Time Forgot, At the Earth's Core, Island of Dr. Moreau, Our Winning Season, The Amityville Horror, C.H.O.M.P.S., Dressed to Kill, How to Beat the High Cost of Living, The Final Terror, Up the Creek, I Was a Teenage Werewolf, I Was a Teenage Frankenstein, Amazing Colossal Man, Force 10 From Navarone, California Dreaming, Coffy, Foxy Brown, War of the Colossal Beast, Beast With a Million Eyes, Dementia 13, Mad Max, X The Man With X-ray Eyes, How to Make a Monster.

ARKUSH, ALLAN
Director. b. Jersey City, NJ, April 30, 1948. e. Franklin & Marshall, NYU. Film Sch. With New World Pictures as film, music and trailer editor, 1974-79. Co-dir. Hollywood Boulevard and Death Sport and was 2nd unit dir. of Grand Theft Auto before directing on own. Dir. rock videos with Bette Midler and Mick Jagger, Elvis Costello, Christine McVie.
PICTURES: Hollywood Boulevard (co-dir., co-edit.), Deathsport (co-dir.), Rock 'n' Roll High School (also story), Heartbeeps, Get Crazy, Caddyshack II, Shake Rattle and Rock.
TELEVISION: *Movies*: XXX & OOOs (co-exec. prod.), Young at Heart, Desert Breeze (co-exec. prod.), Elvis Meets Nixon (dir.). *Series*: Fame, St. Elsewhere, L.A. Law, Moonlighting (Emmy nom.), Shannon's Deal (spv. prod.), Tattinger's, Twilight Zone, Mann & Machine, I'll Fly Away, Middle Ages, Johnny Bago, Central Park West (co-exec. prod.), Ally McBeal, The Visitor, Timecop, Players, Ally McBeal, The Visitor, Timecop, Players. *Pilots*: The Bronx Zoo, Capital News (prod.), Parenthood (co-exec. prod.), Body of Evidence, Moon Over Miami (exec. prod.).

ARLEDGE, ROONE
Executive. b. Forest Hills, NY, July 8, 1931. e. Columbia U. Entered industry with Dumont Network in 1952. Joined U.S. Army, 1953, serving at Aberdeen Proving Ground in Maryland, prod. and dir. radio programs. Joined NBC, held various production positions, 1954. Went to ABC TV, 1960; named v.p. in charge of ABC Sports, 1964; created ABC's Wide World of Sports, 1961; named pres. of ABC News, 1968; pres. of ABC News and Sports, 1977. Holds four George Foster Peabody Awards for sports reporting; 19 Emmy awards.

ARLING, ARTHUR E.
Cinematographer. b. Missouri, Sept. 2, 1906. e. N.Y. Inst. of Photography. Entered motion picture industry working for Fox studio as asst. cameraman, 1927; 2nd cameraman 1931; operative cameraman on Gone With the Wind which won the Academy Award for technicolor photography 1939. Lt. Comdr. U.S.N.R., WWII. Member: Amer. Soc. of Cinematographers.
PICTURES: The Yearling (Academy Award, 1946), Homestretch, Captain from Castile, Mother Was a Freshman, You're My Everything, Wabash Avenue, My Blue Heaven, Call Me Mister, Belles on Their Toes, The Glass Slipper, Three for the Show, Love Me or Leave Me, I'll Cry Tomorrow, Ransom, Great American Pastime, Tammy & the Bachelor, Pay the Devil, Story of Ruth, Pillow Talk, Lover Come Back, Notorious Landlady, Boys Night Out, My Six Loves, Ski Party, Once Before I Die.

ARMSTRONG, BESS
Actress. b. Baltimore, MD, Dec. 11, 1953. e. Brown U. m. producer John Fiedler.
PICTURES: The House of God (debut, 1979), The Four Seasons, Jekyll and Hyde—Together Again, High Road to China, Jaws 3-D, Nothing in Common, Second Sight, Mother Mother, The Skateboard Kid.
TELEVISION: Movies: Getting Married, How to Pick Up Girls, Walking Through the Fire, 11th Victim, This Girl for Hire, Lace, Take Me Home Again, She Stood Alone: The Tailhook Scandal, Stolen Innocence. Series: On Our Own, All is Forgiven, Married People, My So-Called Life. Special: Barefoot in the Park.

ARMSTRONG, GILLIAN
Director. b. Melbourne, Australia, Dec. 18, 1950. e. Swinburne Coll. Among 1st class in dirs. course at National Aust. Film & TV School, Sydney. Worked as art dir. on a number of films. Dir. numerous shorts (One Hundred a Day, The Singer and the Dancer) and documentaries (A Busy Kind of Bloke, Bingo Bridesmaids and Braces) before turning to features.
PICTURES: My Brilliant Career (Australian Film Inst. Award), Starstruck, Mrs. Soffel, Hard to Handle, High Tide, Fires Within, The Last Days of Chez Nous, Little Women, Not 14 Again, Oscar & Lucinda.

ARMSTRONG, GORDON
Executive. b. East Orange, NJ, Nov. 26, 1937. e. Arizona State U., graduate studies at NYU. Joined 20th Century-Fox as nat. pub. dir., 1970. Was appointed dir. of adv.-pub.-promo. for Dino De Laurentiis Corp., 1975; became vice pres., worldwide marketing for the company, 1978. Named v.p., adv.-pub.-promo., Universal Pictures, 1970; exec. v.p., mktg. MCA Recreation, 1984; pres. mktg., Morgan Creek Prods., 1991. Pres., Entertainment Marketing Group, 1993. V.p., sales and mktg., ATTICA Cybernetics ,1995; v.p., sales and mktg., Doubleclick Network, 1996.

ARNALL, ELLIS GIBBS
Lawyer, executive. b. Newnan, GA, March 20, 1907. e. Mercer U., U. of the South, A.B. 1928, D.C.L. 1947; U. of Georgia LL.B. 1931; Atlanta Law Sch., LL.D 1941; Piedmont Coll., LL.D 1943; Bryant Coll., LL.D. 1948. Georgia state rep. from Coweta County, 1936-38; asst. Attorney-General (GA), 1938-42; Attorney-General (GA), 1942-43; Governor of GA, 1943-47. Pres. Dixie Life Insurance Co; pres., Columbus Natl Life Insurance Co; sr. member, law firm Arnall Golden & Gregory; pres. Georgia State Jr. Chamber of Commerce ,1939. Author: The Shore Dimly Seen (1946), What The People Want (1948). Member, U.S. Natl. Com. on UNESCO; member, U.S. delegation to 4th annual conference UNESCO, Paris, 1949. SIMPP pres., 1948 & 1952; pres. Indept. Film Prod. Export Corp., 1953. Bd. of dir., exec. com., U.S. Nat'l Comm. for UNESCO, 1964-65; AMPAS.

ARNAZ, JR., DESI
Actor, Singer. b. Los Angeles, CA, Jan. 19, 1953. e. Beverly Hills H.S. Son of Lucille Ball and Desi Arnaz. Sister is actress Lucie Arnaz. Gained fame as rock singer and musician with the Dino, Desi and Billy group. Video: A Day at the Zoo. Regional theatre includes Sunday in New York, Grease, Promises Promises, Alone Together, I Love My Wife, Is There Life After High School?, Love Letters, The Boys Next Door.
PICTURES: Red Sky at Morning (debut, 1971), Marco, Billy Two Hats, Joyride, A Wedding, House of the Long Shadows, The Mambo Kings.
TELEVISION: Movies: Mr. & Mrs. Bo Jo Jones, Voyage of the Yes, She Lives, Having Babies, Flight to Holocaust, Black Market Baby, To Kill a Cop, The Courage and the Passion, How to Pick Up Girls, Crisis in Mid-Air, Gridlock, Advice to the Lovelorn, The Night the Bridge Fell Down. Series: Here's Lucy, Automan. Guest: The Love Boat, Fantasy Island, Paul Reiser: Out on a Whim, Matlock.

ARNAZ, LUCIE
Actress. b. Los Angeles, CA, July 17, 1951. Daughter of Lucille Ball and Desi Arnaz. m. actor Laurence Luckinbill. Brother is actor Desi Arnaz Jr. B'way: They're Playing Our Song (Theatre World Award), Lost in Yonkers. National touring companies: Whose Life is It Anyway?, Educating Rita, My One and Only, Social Security. Nightclubs: Lucie Arnaz-Latin Roots, Irving Berlin in Concert-In Sicily.
PICTURES: Billy Jack Goes to Washington, The Jazz Singer, Second Thoughts.
TELEVISION: Movies: Who is the Black Dahlia, The Mating Season, The Washington Mistress, Who Gets the Friends? Series: Here's Lucy, The Lucy Arnaz Show, Sons and Daughters. Pilot: One More Try. Specials: Lucy & Desi: A Home Movie (host, co-exec. prod., co-dir.).

ARNESS, JAMES
Actor. r.n. James Aurness. b. Minneapolis, MN, May 26, 1923. e. Beloit Coll. Brother of actor Peter Graves. Served in U.S. Army; worked in advertising, real estate. Started in films in late 1940's appearing under his real name.
PICTURES: The Farmer's Daughter (debut 1947), Roses Are Red, The Man From Texas, Battleground, Sierra, Two Lost Worlds, Wyoming Mail, Wagon Master, Double Crossbones, Stars in My Crown (1st billing as James Arness), Cavalry Scout, Belle le Grand, Iron Man, The People Against O'Hara, The Girl in White, The Thing, Carbine Williams, Hellgate, Big Jim McLain, Horizons West, Lone Hand, Ride the Man Down, Island in the Sky, Veils of Bagdad, Hondo, Her Twelve Men, Them!, Many Rivers to Cross, Flame of the Islands, The Sea Chase, The First Travelling Saleslady, Gun the Man Down, Alias Jesse James (cameo).
TELEVISION: Movies: The Macahans, The Alamo: 13 Days to Glory, Gunsmoke: Return to Dodge, Red River, Gunsmoke: The Last Apache, Gunsmoke: To the Last Man, Gunsmoke: The Long Ride (also exec. prod.). Series: Gunsmoke (20 years), How the West Was Won, McClain's Law. Mini-Series: How the West Was Won.

ARNOLD, EDDY
Singer. b. Henderson, TN, May 15, 1918. Radio performer, Nashville, TN. Recording star since 1946; records include That's How Much I Love You, Anytime, Bouquet of Roses (on the Country Music charts longer than any record in the history of country music), Make the World Go Away. Holds the record for most Country Records on the charts. Elected to Country Music Hall of Fame, 1966; Entertainer of the Year, 1967; Pioneer Award from Acad. of Country Music, 1984; President's Award from Songwriter's Guild, 1987.
TELEVISION: Series: Eddy Arnold Show (1952-3), Eddy Arnold Time, Eddy Arnold Show (1956), The Kraft Music Hall (1967-71). Hosted Music from the Land, Tonight Show, more than 20 specials.

ARNOLD, TOM
Actor. b. Ottumwa, IA, June 3, 1959.
PICTURES: Freddy's Dead: The Final Nightmare, Hero, Undercover Blues, True Lies, Nine Months, Big Bully, Carpool, The Stupids, Hacks, Touch, McHale's Navy (also co-prod.)
TELEVISION: Series: The Roseanne Barr Show, Roseanne (also prod.), The Jackie Thomas Show (also creator, exec. prod.), Tom, The Tom Show (also creator, exec. prod.). Movies: Backfield in Motion, Body Bags, The Woman Who Loved Elvis. Guest: The Ben Stiller Show, Saturday Night Live, The Larry Sanders Show, High Society, The Naked Truth.

ARNOW, TED J.
Executive. b. Brooklyn, NY. e. St. Johns U., Washington and Lee U. Served as dir. of recreation for 262nd General Hospital in Panama. Veteran of over 50 yrs. in amusement industry. Was v.p. for adv., pub., & promo. for Loew's Theatres. Member: Motion Picture Pioneers, Variety Clubs, Will Rogers Hospital. Former pres. of AMPA (Assoc. M.P. Advertisers). Retired.

ARQUETTE, PATRICIA
Actress. b. Chicago, IL, April 8, 1968. m. actor Nicolas Cage. Sister of actress Rosanna Arquette and actors Richmond, Alexis and David Arquette. Prof. debut in children's version of Story Theatre. Studied acting with Milton Katselis.
PICTURES: A Nightmare on Elm Street 3: Dream Warriors (debut, 1987), Pretty Smart, Time Out, Far North, Prayer of the Rollerboys, The Indian Runner, Ethan Frome, Trouble Bound, Inside Monkey Zetterland, True Romance, Holy Matrimony, Ed Wood, Beyond Rangoon, Infinity, Flirting With Disaster, The Secret Agent, Nightwatch.
TELEVISION: Movies: Daddy, Dillinger, Wildflower, Betrayed by Love. Special: The Girl With the Crazy Brother. Guest: The Edge (Indian Poker), thirtysomething, Tales From the Crypt.

ARQUETTE, ROSANNA
Actress. b. New York, NY, Aug. 10, 1959. Granddaughter of humorist Cliff Arquette (Charlie Weaver). Daughter of actor-producer Lewis Arquette. Sister of actress Patricia Arquette and actors Richmond, Alexis and David Arquette. Prof. debut in children's version of Story Theatre. Studied acting in San Francisco. Role in LA play led to bit parts on tv then regular role as Shirley Jones' teenage daughter on series Shirley (1979).
PICTURES: More American Graffiti (debut, 1979), Gorp, S.O.B., Baby It's You, Off the Wall, The Aviator, Desperately Seeking Susan, Silverado, After Hours, 8 Million Ways To Die, Nobody's Fool, Amazon Women on the Moon, The Big Blue, New York Stories (Life Lessons), Flight of the Intruder, Wendy Cracked a Walnut, The Linguini Incident, Fathers and Sons, Nowhere to Run, Pulp Fiction, Search and Destroy, Gone Fishin, Crash, Liar.
TELEVISION: *Movies*: Having Babies II, The Dark Secret of Harvest Home, Zuma Beach, The Ordeal of Patty Hearst, A Long Way Home, The Wall, The Executioner's Song, Johnny Belinda, One Cooks the Other Doesn't, The Parade, Survival Guide, Promised a Miracle, Sweet Revenge, Separation, Son of the Morning Star, Black Rainbow, In the Deep Woods, The Wrong Man, Nowhere to Hide. *Series*: Shirley. *Specials*: Mom and Dad Can't Hear Me, A Family Tree (Trying Times).

ARTHUR, BEATRICE
Actress. r.n. Bernice Frankel. b. New York, NY, May 13, 1926. Franklin Inst. of Sciences & Art. Studied with Erwin Piscator at New School for Social Research; first stage role as Lysistrata; professional stage debut in Dog Beneath the Skin, 1947.
THEATER: Gas, Yerma, No Exit, Six Characters in Search of an Author, The Taming of the Shrew, (1948) The Owl and the Pussycat, The Threepenny Opera (1953 revival), The ShoeString Revue, What's the Rush?, Nature's Way, Ulysses in Nighttown, Gay Divorcee, Fiddler on the Roof, Mame (Tony Award, 1966), The Floating Light Bulb, Night of the 100 Stars.
PICTURES: That Kind of Woman, Lovers and Other Strangers, Mame, History of the World Part I.
TELEVISION: Once Upon a Time (debut, 1951), Numerous guest appearances. *Series*: Caesar's Hour, Maude (Emmy Award, 1977), Amanda's, Golden Girls (Emmy Award, 1988). *Specials*: All Star Gala at Ford's Theater (host), Jay Leno's Family Comedy Hour. *Movie*: My First Love.

ARTHUR, KAREN
Director. b. Omaha, NB, Aug. 24, 1941. Ballet dancer, choreographer and musical comedy singer, dancer and actress, 1950-68; actress, film, tv and theatre, 1968-75; film, tv director, 1970-95.
PICTURES: *Actress*: A Guide for the Married Man, Winning. *Director*: Legacy (1975, Int'l Film Critics & Josef Von Sternberg Awards, 1975), The Mafu Cage, Lady Beware.
TELEVISION: *Movies*: Charleston, Victims for Victims: The Theresa Saldana Story (Christopher Award), A Bunny's Tale, The Rape of Richard Beck, Evil in Clear River (Christopher Award), Cracked Up, Bridge to Silence, Fall from Grace, Bump in the Night, Shadow of a Doubt, The Secret, The Disappearance of Christina, Against Their Will: Women in Prison. *Mini-Series*: Love and Betrayal: The Mia Farrow Story, Crossings, Return to Eden, The Jacksons: An American Dream, Dead by Sunset. *Pilots*: Tin Man, Blue Bayou. *Episodes*: Rich Man Poor Man Book II, Emerald Point, Boone, Two Marriages, Hart to Hart, Remington Steele, Cagney & Lacey (Emmy Award, 1985).

ARTZ, BOB
Theatre executive. b. Spokane, WA, Aug 21, 1946. e., B.T.A. Pasadena Playhouse College of Theatre Arts. Began in 1968 as doorman, became asst. mgr. to mgr. with National General Theatre Corporation. Joined Plitt Theatres in 1978 as dist. mgr. and ad/pub. dir., West Coast. Joined General Cinema Theatres in 1986 as reg. mktg. dir., Western region. Became dir., film mktg. in 1993. National dir., Entertainment Mktg. & Operations in 1996. Dir. client svc's., Global Cinema Network, 1998. Member: Variety Club, Film Information Council, Pasadena PlayHouse Alumni & Assoc (life mem.).

ASH, RENE
Producer. b. Brussels, Belgium, March 14, 1939. e. U. of Omaha. Employed with I.A.T.S.E. 1968-1979, prior to which was assoc. editor, Greater Amusements. Eastern v.p. of Pub. Guild, 1973-1981; editor-in-chief, Backstage, 1979-80; pres., Cinereal Pictures, 1984-85; co-pres., Eagle Films Corp., 1985-94; pres. Rea Film Prods. Author of various articles published in foreign film magazines and The Film Editor in Motion Pictures & Television. Member of the Pub. Guild since 1968.

ASHER, JANE
Actress. b. London, England, April 5, 1946.
PICTURES: Mandy (Crash of Silence; debut, 1952), Third Party Risk, Dance Little Lady, Adventure in the Hopfields, The Quatermass Experiment (The Creeping Unknown), Charley Moon, Greengage Summer (Loss of Innocence), The Girl in the Headlines (The Model Murder Case), The Masque of the Red Death, Alfie, The Winter's Tale, Deep End, The Buttercup Chain, Henry VIII and His Six Wives (from the BBC series the Six Wives of Henry VIII), Runners, Success Is the Best Revenge, Dream Child, Paris By Night, Closing Numbers.
TELEVISION: *Movies/Specials*: Brideshead Revisited, Voyage 'Round My Father, East Lynne, The Mistress, Wish Me Luck, Tonight at 8:30, The Volunteer. *Mini-series*: The Choir.

ASHLEY, JOHN
Actor, Producer. r.n. John Atchley. b. Kansas City, MO, Dec. 25, 1934. e. Oklahoma State U., B.A., 1956. Career started in Tulsa Little Theatre, 1956.
PICTURES: Dragstrip Girl (debut, 1957), Motorcycle Gang, Suicide Battalion, Beach Party, How to Stuff a Wild Bikini.
TELEVISION: *Movie*: Something is Out There (co-exec. prod.). *Series*: Straightaway. *Guest*: Men of Annapolis, Sheriff of Cochise, Frontier Doctor, Matinee Theatre, Jefferson Drum. *Series Prod*: The A-Team, Werewolf, Hardball, Raven, Walker: Texas Ranger.
(d. Oct. 3, 1997)

ASHLEY, ELIZABETH
Actress. b. Ocala, FL, Aug. 30, 1939. e. Studied ballet LA State U., 1957-58; grad. Neighborhood Playhouse, 1961. Author: Postcards From the Road.
THEATER: Take Her She's Mine (1962 Tony & Theatre World Awards), The Highest Tree, Barefoot in the Park, Ring 'Round the Bathtub, The Skin of Our Teeth, Legend, Cat on a Hot Tin Roof (B'way revival), Caesar and Cleopatra, Agnes of God, The Milk Train Doesn't Stop Here Anymore, When She Danced.
PICTURES: The Carpetbaggers (debut, 1964), Ship of Fools, The Third Day, The Marriage of a Young Stockbroker, Paperback Hero, Golden Needles, Rancho DeLuxe, 92 in the Shade, The Great Scout and Cathouse Thursday, Coma, Windows, Paternity, Split Image, Dragnet, Vampire's Kiss, Dangerous Curves, Lost Memories.
TELEVISION: *Movies*: Harpy, The Face of Fear, When Michael Calls, Second Chance, The Heist, Your Money or Your Wife, The Magician, One of My Wives is Missing, The War Between the Tates, A Fire in the Sky, Svengali, He's Fired She's Hired, Stagecoach, Warm Hearts Cold Feet, The Two Mrs. Grenvilles, Blue Bayou, Reason for Living: The Jill Ireland Story, Love and Curses... and All That Jazz, In the Best Interest of the Children. *Series*: Evening Shade. *Pilot*: Tom and Joann. *Guest*: Miami Vice, Hunter, Murder She Wrote, B.L. Stryker.

ASHTON, JOHN
Actor. b. Springfield, MA, Feb. 22, 1948. e. USC, BA in theatre.
THEATER: The Last Meeting of the Knights of the White Magnolia (L.A. Drama Critics Circle Award), True West (Drama-Logue Award), A Flea in Her Ear (L.A. Drama Critics Circle Award).
PICTURES: Oh God!, Breaking Away, Borderline, Honky Tonk Freeway, Adventures of Buckaroo Banzai, Beverly Hills Cop, The Last Resort, King Kong Lives, Some Kind of Wonderful, Beverly Hills Cop II, She's Having a Baby, Midnight Run, I Want to Go Home, Curly Sue, Little Big League, Trapped in Paradise, The Shooter, Fast Money, Meet the Deedles, Instinct.
TELEVISION: *Movies*: Elvis and the Beauty Queen, A Death in California, The Deliberate Stranger, I Know My First Name is Steven, Dirty Work, Stephen King's The Tommyknockers. *Series*: Dallas, Breaking Away, Hardball, The Day Lincoln Was Shot. *Mini-Series*: The Rhinemann Exchange. Love Lies and Murder. *Guest*: M*A*S*H*, Police Squad!, The Twilight Zone.

ASNER, EDWARD
Actor. b. Kansas City, MO, Nov. 15, 1929. e. U. of Chicago, where affiliated with campus acting group. Served two years with U.S. Army in France. Returned to Chicago to join Playwright's Theatre Club. Moved to NY and joined NY Shakespeare Festival, 1960 and American Shakespeare Festival, 1961. In 1961, moved to Hollywood to become active in films and tv. National pres. Screen Actors Guild, 1981-85. Prod. tv & feature projects through his company, Quince. Winner of numerous humanitarian awards.
THEATER: *B'way*: Face of a Hero, Born Yesterday (debut, 1989). *Off-B'way*: Ivanov, Threepenny Opera, Legend of Lovers, The Tempest, Venice Preserved.
PICTURES: Kid Gallahad (debut, 1962), The Slender Thread, The Satan Bug, The Venetian Affair, El Dorado, Gunn, Change of Habit, Halls of Anger, They Call Me Mister Tibbs, The Todd Killings, Skin Game, The Wrestler, Gus, Teach Our Children, Americas in Transition, Fort Apache-The Bronx, O'Hara's Wife, Daniel, Pinocchio and the Emperor of the Night (voice), Moon Over Parador (cameo), JFK, Happily Ever After (voice), Cat's Don't Dance (voice), Earth and the American Dream, Down on the Waterfront, Prep, 187: Documented, The Long Way Home, Hard Rain.

TELEVISION: *Movies*: Fanfare for a Death Scene, The Doomsday Flight, Daughter of the Mind, The House on Greenapple Road, The Old Man Who Cried Wolf, The Last Child, They Call It Murder, Haunts of the Very Rich, The Police Story, The Girl Most Likely To..., The Imposter, Death Scream, Hey I'm Alive, Life and Assassination of the Kingfish, The Gathering, The Family Man, The Marva Collins Story, A Small Killing, A Case of Libel, Anatomy of an Illness, Vital Signs, Kate's Secret, The Christmas Star, Cracked Up, A Friendship in Vienna, Not a Penny More Not a Penny Less, Good Cops Bad Cops, Switched at Birth, Silent Motive, Yes Virginia There Is a Santa Claus, Cruel Doubt, Gypsy, Heads, Dog's Best Friend, Higher Education, The Story of Santa Claus, Payback. *Series*: Slattery's People, The Mary Tyler Moore Show (3 Emmy Awards: 1971, 1972, 1975), Lou Grant (2 Emmy Awards: 1978, 1980), Off the Rack, The Bronx Zoo, The Trials of Rosie O'Neill, Fish Police (voice), Hearts Afire, Gargoyles, Thunder Alley, Spider-Man, Freakazoid, Bruno the Kid (voice), Batman: Gotham Knights, Ask Harriet, The Closer. *Mini-Series*: Rich Man Poor Man (Emmy Award, 1976), Roots (Emmy Award, 1977), Tender Is the Night. *Guest*: Gunsmoke, Hawaii Five-O, Roseanne, Mad About You, The Practice and numerous others.

ASPEL, SIR MICHAEL

Radio/TV Presenter. b. London, England, Jan. 12, 1933. Entered industry in 1954 as actor/presenter for BBC Radio, and announcer/newsreader for BBC TV. Presentations incl: Miss World, Crackerjack, Give Us A Clue, Ask Aspel, Family Favourites, Child's Play, ITV Telethon 1988, 1990 & 1992, Aspel and Company, This Is Your Life, BAFTA Awards, Strange ... But True?, Caught on Camera, Light Camera Action, ITN's V.E. Day Programme 1995, Blockbusters. Received OBE in 1993.

ASSANTE, ARMAND

Actor. b. New York, NY, Oct. 4, 1949. e. American Acad. of Dramatic Arts. Appeared with regional theatre groups incl. Arena Stage, DC; Long Wharf, New Haven; Actor's Theatre of Louisville.
THEATER: B'way: Boccaccio, Comedians, Romeo and Juliet, Kingdoms. Off-B'way: Why I Went Crazy, Rubbers, The Beauty Part, Lake of the Woods, Yankees 3 Detroit 0.
PICTURES: Paradise Alley, Prophecy, Little Darlings, Private Benjamin, Love and Money, I the Jury, Unfaithfully Yours, Belizaire the Cajun, The Penitent, Animal Behavior, Q & A, Eternity, The Marrying Man, The Mambo Kings, 1492: Conquest of Paradise, Hoffa, Fatal Instinct, Trial by Jury, Judge Dredd, Striptease.
TELEVISION: *Movies*: Human Feelings, Lady of the House, The Pirate, Sophia Loren-Her Own Story, Rage of Angels, Why Me?, A Deadly Business, Stranger in My Bed, Hands of a Stranger, Jack the Ripper, Passion and Paradise, Fever, Blind Justice, Kidnapped, Gotti (Emmy Award, 1997). *Series*: The Doctors (1975). *Mini-Series*: Napoleon and Josephine: A Love Story, Evergreen, The Odyssey.

ASSEYEV, TAMARA

Producer. e. Marymont College; UCLA, MA, theatre arts. Began career as asst. to Roger Corman, working on 8 films with him. In 1967 started to produce films independently. Then co-produced films with Alex Rose, starting with Drive-In. In 1966 at 24, became youngest member of Producers Guild of Amer. Member: Costume Council, LA City Museum; founding member, LA Museum of Contemporary Art.
PICTURES: The Wild Racers, Paddy, The Arousers, The History of Atlantic Records. Co-prod. with Ms. Rose: Drive-In, I Wanna Hold Your Hand, Big Wednesday, Norma Rae.
TELEVISION: *Movies*: Exec. prod.: Penalty Phase, After the Promise, A Shadow on the Sun (also actress), The Secret Life of Kathy McCormick, The Hijacking of the Achille Lauro, Murder By Moonlight.

ASTIN, JOHN

Actor. b. Baltimore, MD, March 30, 1930. e. Washington and Jefferson Coll., Washington Drama Sch., Johns Hopkins U., grad. BA, U. of Minnesota Graduate School. Father of actors Sean and Mackenzie Astin. Theatre debut on Off-B'way stage, Threepenny Opera. B'way debut, Major Barbara. Dir., co-prod., A Sleep of Prisoners, Phoenix Theatre. Did voices in cartoons, commercials, 1955-59. Prod. & dir. short subject Prelude.
THEATER: The Cave Dwellers, Ulysses in Nighttown, Tall Story, Lend Me a Tenor, H.M.S. Pinafore.
PICTURES: The Pusher (debut, 1958), West Side Story, That Touch of Mink, Move Over Darling, The Wheeler Dealers, The Spirit is Willing, Candy, Viva Max!, Bunny O'Hare, Get to Know Your Rabbit, Every Little Crook and Nanny, The Brothers O'Toole, Freaky Friday, National Lampoon's European Vacation, Body Slam, Teen Wolf Too, Return of the Killer Tomatoes, Night Life, Gremlins 2, Killer Tomatoes Eat France, Stepmonster, The Silence of the Hams, Frighteners, Harrison Bergeron.

TELEVISION: *Movies*: Two on a Bench, Evil Roy Slade, Skyway to Death, Only with Married Men, The Dream Makers, Operation Petticoat (also dir.), Rossetti and Ryan: Men Who Love Women (dir. only), Huck and the King of Hearts. *Series*: I'm Dickens... He's Fenster, The Addams Family, The Pruitts of Southampton, Operation Petticoat, Mary, The Addams Family (voice for animated series), The Adventures of Brisco County Jr. *Guest*: Batman, The Flying Nun, Bonanza, Odd Couple, Night Gallery, Partridge Family, Police Woman, Love Boat, Night Court. *Specials*: Harry Anderson's Sideshow, Halloween With the Addams Family. *Pilots*: Phillip and Barbara, Ethel Is an Elephant.

ASTIN, MACKENZIE

Actor. b. Los Angeles, CA, May 12, 1973. Parents are actors John Astin and Patty Duke. Brother is Sean Astin.
PICTURES: The Garbage Pail Kids Movie, Widow's Kiss, Iron Will, Wyatt Earp, In Love and War, Dream for an Insomniac, The Evening Star, The Last Days of Disco.
TELEVISION: The Facts of Life, Lois Gibbs and the Love Canal, I Dream of Jeannie: 15 Years Later, A Child Lost Forever.

ASTIN, SEAN

Actor. b. Santa Monica, Feb. 25, 1971. Parents are actors John Astin and Patty Duke. Brother is actor Mackenzie Astin. First acting job at 7 opposite mother in Afterschool Special, Please Don't Hit Me Mom. Dir. short films On My Honor, Kangaroo Court (Acad. Award nom.). On LA stage in Lone Star.
PICTURES: The Goonies (debut, 1985), White Water Summer, Like Father Like Son, Staying Together, The War of the Roses, Memphis Belle, The Willies, Toy Soldiers, Encino Man, Where the Day Takes You, Rudy, Safe Passage, The Low Life.
TELEVISION: *Movies*: The Rules of Marriage, The Brat Patrol. *Pilot*: Just Our Luck.

ATHERTON, WILLIAM

Actor. b. New Haven, CT, June 30, 1947. While in high school became youngest member of Long Wharf Theatre Co. Given scholarship to Pasadena Playhouse; then switched to Carnegie Tech Sch. of Drama in 1965. In college years toured with USO prods in Europe and in stock and industrial shows. Came to NY where first prof. job was in nat'l co. of Little Murders.
THEATER: The House of Blue Leaves, The Basic Training of Pavlo Hummel, The Sign in Sidney Brustein's Window, Suggs (Theatre World Award, Outer Circle Critics Award, Drama Desk Award), Rich and Famous, Passing Game, Happy New Year, The American Clock, Three Acts of Recognition, The Caine Mutiny Court-Martial, Child's Play, Loco Motives.
PICTURES: The New Centurions (debut, 1972), Class of '44, The Sugarland Express, The Day of the Locust, The Hindenburg, Looking for Mr. Goodbar, Ghostbusters, Real Genius, No Mercy, Frank and Jesse, Die Hard, Die Hard 2, Grim Prairie Tales, Oscar, The Pelican Brief, Bio-Dome, Hoods, Executive Power, Mad City..
TELEVISION: *Movies*: Tomorrow's Child, Malibu, Intrigue, Buried Alive, Diagnosis of Murder, Chrome Soldiers, Robin Cook's Virus, Broken Trust. *Mini-Series*: Centennial. *Guest*: The Equalizer, Twilight Zone, Murder She Wrote, Tales From the Crypt, *Special*: The House of Mirth.

ATKINS, CHRISTOPHER

Actor. b. Rye, NY, Feb. 21, 1961. e. Dennison U., Ohio. Early modeling jobs before being hired for theatrical film debut in The Blue Lagoon (1980).
PICTURES: The Blue Lagoon, The Pirate Movie, A Night in Heaven, Beaks, Mortuary Academy, Listen to Me, Shakma, King's Ransom, Outrage, Dracula Rising, Die Watching, Exchange Lifeguards, A Bullet Down Under, Trigger Fast, Project Shadowchaser III, It's My Party, Mutual Needs, The Day October Died.
TELEVISION: *Movies*: Child Bride of Short Creek, Secret Weapons, Fatal Charm, Guns of Honor. *Series*: Dallas. *Guest*: The Black Stallion. *Also*: The Black Rose, Miami Killer, The Floating Outfit, Deadman's Island, Angel Flight Down.

ATKINSON, ROWAN

Actor, Writer. b. England, Jan. 6, 1955. e. Newcastle U., Oxford.
THEATER: Rowan Atkinson in Revue (also writer), Not in Front of an Audience, The Nerd, Rowan Atkinson at the Atkinson (also writer; NY), Mime Gala, The Sneeze.
PICTURES: The Secret Policeman's Ball (also co-s.p.), Fundamental Frolics, The Secret Policeman's Other Ball, Dead on Time, Never Say Never Again, The Appointments of Dennis Jennings, The Tall Guy, The Witches, Hot Shots Part Deux, Four Weddings and a Funeral, The Lion King (voice), Mr. Bean, Lion King: Simba's Pride.
TELEVISION: *Series*: Not the Nine O'Clock News (also writer; BAFTA Award for acting), Blackadder, Blackadder II, Blackadder the Third, Mr Bean, Blackadder Goes Forth, The Thin Blue Line. *Specials*: Canned Laughter, Just for Laughs II, Live from London, Blackadder's Christmas Carol, Blackadder: The Cavalier Years, The Driven Man, Mr. Bean Rides Again.

ATTENBOROUGH, BARON RICHARD (SAMUEL)

Actor, Producer, Director. 1993, Life Peer of Richmond Upon Thames; Kt 1976; CBE 1967. b. Cambridge, England, Aug. 29, 1923. e. Wyggeston Grammar Sch., Leicester; Leverhulme Scholarship to Royal Acad. of Dramatic Art, 1941 (Bancroft Medal). m. Sheila Beryl Grant Sim, 1945. Stage debut in Ah Wilderness (Palmers Green, 1941). West End debut in Awake and Sing (1942), then The Little Foxes, Brighton Rock. Joined RAF, 1943; seconded to RAF Film Unit, and appeared in training film Journey Together, 1945; demobilized, 1946. Returned to stage, 1949, in The Way Back (Home of the Brave), To Dorothy a Son, Sweet Madness, The Mousetrap (original cast: 1952-54), Double Image, The Rape of the Belt. Formed Beaver Films with Bryan Forbes, 1959; formed Allied Film Makers, 1960.
PICTURES: *Actor*. In Which We Serve (debut, 1942), Schweik's New Adventures, The Hundred Pound Window, Journey Together, A Matter of Life and Death (Stairway to Heaven), School for Secrets (Secret Flight), The Man Within (The Smugglers), Dancing With Crime, Brighton Rock (Young Scarface), London Belongs to Me (Dulcimer Street), The Guinea Pig, The Lost People, Boys in Brown, Morning Departure (Operation Disaster), Hell Is Sold Out, The Magic Box, Gift Horse (Glory at Sea), Father's Doing Fine, Eight O'Clock Walk, The Ship That Died of Shame, Private's Progress, The Baby and the Battleship, Brothers in Law, The Scamp, Dunkirk, The Man Upstairs, Sea of Sand (Desert Patrol), Danger Within (Breakout), I'm All Right Jack, Jet Storm, SOS Pacific, The Angry Silence (also co-prod.), The League of Gentlemen, Only Two Can Play, All Night Long, The Dock Brief (Trial & Error), The Great Escape, Seance on a Wet Afternoon (also prod.; San Sebastian Film Fest. & Brit. Acad. Awards for Best Actor), The Third Secret, Guns at Batasi (Brit. Acad. Award), The Flight of the Phoenix, The Sand Pebbles (Golden Globe Award), Dr. Dolittle (Golden Globe Award), The Bliss of Mrs Blossom, Only When I Larf, The Magic Christian, David Copperfield (TV in U.S.), The Last Grenade, A Severed Head, Loot, 10 Rillington Place, Ten Little Indians (And Then There Were None), Rosebud, Brannigan, Conduct Unbecoming, The Chess Players, The Human Factor, Jurassic Park, Miracle on 34th Street, Hamlet, The Lost World: Jurassic Park, Elizabeth I. *Producer*. Whistle Down the Wind, The L-Shaped Room. *Director*: Oh! What a Lovely War (also prod.); 16 Intl. Awards incl. Golden Globe and BAFTA UN Award), Young Winston (Golden Globe), A Bridge Too Far (Evening News Best Drama Award, 1977), Magic, Gandhi (also prod.; 8 Oscars, 5 BAFTA Awards, 5 Golden Globes, DGA Award, 1982), A Chorus Line, Cry Freedom (also prod.; Berlinale Kamera, 1987; BFI Award for Tech. Achievement), Chaplin (also prod.), Shadowlands (also prod.; BAFTA Award for Best British Film of 1993), In Love and War (also prod.), Grey Owl (also prod.)

ATTENBOROUGH, SIR DAVID

Broadcaster. b. London, England, May 8, 1926. Brother of Baron Richard Attenborough. e. Wyggeston Sch., Leicester; Clare Coll., Cambridge. Early career, editor in educational publishing house. Ent. BBC-TC, 1952. Prod. Zoo Quest series, Travellers Tales, Adventure and other prog., travel, Eastward with Attenborough, The Tribal Eye, Life on Earth, The Living Planet, The First Eden, The Trials of Life. Controller BBC-2, 1965-68; Dir. of Prog. BBC-TV, 1969-72. Received Desmond Davis Award, 1970 and a Fellowship, 1979. Narrator of A Zed and Two Noughts, Survival Island (also writer), Cities of the Wild (also writer).

AUBERJONOIS, RENE

Actor. b. New York, NY, June 1, 1940. e. attended Carnegie Mellon U.
THEATER: Dark of the Moon, Beyond the Fringe, Tartuffe, King Lear, Fire, Julius Caesar, Charley's Aunt, Coco (Tony Award, 1970), Tricks, The Ruling Class, Twelfth Night, The Good Doctor (Tony nom.), Break a Leg, The New York Idea, Every Good Boy Deserves Favor, Richard III, The Misanthrope, Flea in Her Ear, Big River (Tony nom.), Metamorphosis, City of Angels (Tony nom.).
PICTURES: Lilith (debut, 1964), Petulia, M*A*S*H*, Brewster McCloud, McCabe and Mrs. Miller, Pete 'n Tillie, Images, Hindenberg, The Big Bus, King Kong, Eyes of Laura Mars, Where the Buffalo Roam, The Last Unicorn (voice), 3:15, Walker, Police Academy 5: Assignment Miami Beach, My Best Friend is a Vampire, The Little Mermaid (voice), The Feud, Star Trek VI: The Undiscovered Country (unbilled), The Player, Little Nemo (voice), The Ballad of Little Jo, Burning Down the House, Los Locos, Snide and Prejudice.
TELEVISION: *Movies*: The Birdmen, Shirts/Skins, Panache, The Secret of Harvest Home, Wild Wild West Revisited, More Wild Wild West, Smoky Mountain Christmas, The Christmas Star, Gore Vidal's Billy the Kid, Longarm, A Connecticut Yankee in King Arthur's Court, Absolute Strangers, Ned Blessing: The True Story of My Life, Wild Card. *Series*: Benson (Emmy nom.), Star Trek: Deep Space Nine. *Mini-Series*: The Rhineman Exchange. *Specials*: Faerie Tale Theatre (The Frog Prince, Sleeping Beauty), King Lear, Legend of Sleepy Hollow (Emmy nom.), Fort Necessity, Incident at Vichy, The Booth, The Cask of Amontillado, Ashenden (BBC), The Lost Language of Cranes (BBC). *Episode Director*: Marble Head Manor, Star Trek: Deep Space Nine.

AUDRAN, STEPHANE

Actress. b. Versailles, France, Nov. 8, 1938. Former wife of French star Jean-Louis Trintignant and director Claude Chabrol.
PICTURES: Les Cousins (debut under direction of Chabrol, 1959), Les Bonnes Femmes, Bluebeard, The Third Lover, Six in Paris, The Champagne Murders, Les Biches, La Femme Infidele, The Beast Must Die, The Lady in the Car, Le Boucher, Without Apparent Motive, Dead Pigeon on Beethoven Street, La Rupture, Just Before Nightfall, The Discreet Charm of the Bourgeoisie, Blood Wedding, The Devil's Advocate, Le Cri de Couer, Vincent Francois Paul and the Others, The Black Bird (U.S. film debut), Ten Little Indians, The Silver Bears, Eagle's Wing, The Big Red One, Coup de Torchon (Clean Slate), La Cage aux Folles III: The Wedding, Cop au Vin, Babette's Feast, Seasons of Pleasure, Faceless, Body-To-Body, Sons, Manika: The Girl Who Lived Twice, Quiet Days in Clichy, Mass in C Minor, Betty, Poulet au Vinaigre, Au Petit Marguery, Arlette, Maximum Risk.
TELEVISION: Mistral's Daughter, The Blood of Others, The Sun Also Rises, Poor Little Rich Girl: The Barbara Hutton Story, Champagne Charlie, Petit, Un Printemps de Chien.

AUERBACH, NORBERT T.

Executive. b. Vienna, Austria, 1923. e. UCLA, business administration. Served with U.S. Army Intelligence in Europe during WWII. Entered motion picture industry after grad., 1946. First asst. dir. at Service Studios in CA. Moved to N.Y. to join domestic sales dept. of Film Classics. Joined Columbia Pictures in foreign dept. In 1950 assigned to Paris office, where remained for over decade, except for 18 mos. in Portugal as mgr. Returned to Paris in 1953 and filled number of exec. sls. positions for Columbia, ultimately rising to continental mgr. Left Columbia to produce films in France, 1961. Resumed career in dist. as continental mgr. at Paris office of United Artists. Returned to prod. to make The Thief of Paris, 1966. Joined Seven Arts Prods. heading theatrical and TV sls. operations in Paris, 1967. When Seven Arts acquired Warner Bros., he became continental sls. mgr. for Warners in Paris. Set up European prod. and dist. org. for CBS Cinema Center Films, operating from London, 1968. Moved to L.A. as v.p., foreign mgr. for CCF, 1972. Returned to London to be consultant in prod. and dist., 1973. Rejoined UA as sls. mgr. for Europe and the Middle East, 1977; named sr. v.p. & foreign mgr., 1978; named pres. & COO, Jan. 1981; pres. & CEO, Feb. 1981. Co-pres., United Int'l Pictures, London, until 1982. Acting pres. and chief exec. officer of Almi Distribution Corp., 1982. Formed packaging and financing Co., Eliktra, Inc., 1983. Now Almi consultant, exec. v.p. American Screen Co.

AUGUST, BILLE

Director. b. Brede, Denmark, Nov. 9, 1948. e. trained in advertising photography, Danish Film School, grad. 1971, cinematography. As cinematographer shot: Miesta ei voi raiskata (Men Can't Be Raped), Karleken, The Grass is Singing. Became dir. 1978 with short Kim G. and dramas for Danish TV.
PICTURES: Honning Maane/In My Life (also sp.), Zappa (also s.p.), Twist and Shout (also s.p.), Pelle the Conquerer (also s.p.), The Best Intentions (Cannes Film Festival Palm d'Or Award, 1992), The House of the Spirits, Smilla's Sense of Snow

AUMONT, JEAN-PIERRE

Actor. b. Paris, France, Jan. 5, 1911. e. Conservatoire of Drama. Roles French stage and films. In 1943 enlisted in Free French Army. Film debut, Jean de la Lune, 1932.
THEATER: *U.S.*: Tovarich, Incident at Vichy, Hostile Witness, Carnival, Camino Real, Murderous Angels, Gigi, A Talent for Murder.
PICTURES: Hotel du Nord, Assignment in Brittany, The Cross of Lorraine, Heartbeat, Song of Scheherazade, Siren of Atlantis, Affairs of a Rogue, Wicked City, Lili, Life Begins Tomorrow, Gay Adventure, Charge of the Lancers, Hilda Crane, The Seventh Sin, John Paul Jones, The Enemy General, The Devil at 4 O'Clock, Carnival of Crime, Five Miles to Midnight, Cauldron of Blood, Castle Keep, Day for Night, Turn the Other Cheek, The Happy Hooker, Mahogany, Catherine & Co., Entire Days Among the Trees, Cat and Mouse, Blackout, Two Solitudes, Something Short of Paradise, Nana, Sweet Country, The Free Frenchman, Senso, A Star for Two, Becoming Colette, Giorgino, Jefferson in Paris.
TELEVISION: Sins, Windmills of the Gods, A Tale of Two Cities, Young Indiana Jones.

AURELIUS, GEORGE M.

Executive. b. Grasston, MN, Sept. 16, 1911. e. U. of Minnesota. Entered motion picture industry in 1927 as usher Finkelstein & Ruben, St. Paul; asst. mgr. 1929-30. To Warner Theatres, New York, 1931; mgr. Moss' B'way. Minnesota Amusement Co., 1932-41. City mgr. Publix-Rickards-Nace; Paramount-Nace Theatres, Tucson, Ariz. 1941-46. V.p. ABC Theatres of Arizona, Inc., 1949-67; pres. ABC North Central Theatres, Inc., 1967-72; v.p., ABC Intermountain Theatres, Inc., & v.p. ABC Theatres of California, Inc. 1972-1974. Mgmt. Consulting and ShoWest Convention & Trade Show since 1975, named exec. dir., 1979. Retired 1985.

AUSTIN, RAY
Baron Devere-Austin of Delvin, Lord of Bradwell. **Producer, Director, Writer**. b. London, England, Dec. 5, 1932. Has written, produced and directed many TV series, specials and movies. Lecturer, film & tv techniques, etc., 1978-93. Lecturer U. of VA.
PICTURES: Virgin Witches, House of the Living Dead, Fun & Games (One Woman And A 1,000 Men).
TELEVISION: Series: Dir.: Avengers, The Champions, Department S, Randall & Hopkirk, Ugliest Girl in Town, Journey into the Unknown, Magnum P.I., Simon and Simon, House Calls, Kings Crossing, Fall Guy, Lime Street (pilot), Spencer for Hire, Haven Help Us, JAG. Prod./Dir.: The Perfumed Garden. Director: It's the Only Way to Go, Fun and Games, Space 1999, New Avengers, Hawaii Five-O, Sword of Justice, Webb, Barnaby Jones, Hardy Boys, Wonder Woman, Salvage, B.J. and the Bear, Hart to Hart, The Yeagers, Man Called Sloane, From Here to Eternity, Bad Cats, Westworld, Tales of the Gold Monkey (2-hr. pilot), The Return of the Man from U.N.C.L.E. Dir./Writer: Randall & Hopkirk, Black Beauty, Zany Adventures of Robin Hood, The Master, Hart to Hart (series), V, Air Wolf, Lime Street (pilot and episodes), Spenser for Hire (several episodes), Magnum P.I. (season premiere 2-hr. episode); Return of the Six Million Dollar Man (pilot); Our House (episodes), Dirty Dozen, Alfred Hitchcock Presents, A Fine Romance, Zorro, Boys of Twilight, Crossroads, Highlander, High Tide, Heaven Help Us. Writer: Department S (also prod.).

AUTANT-LARA, CLAUDE
Director. b. Luzerches, France, Aug. 5, 1901. Began career as scenic designer for French films in early 1920s, then asst. dir. to Rene Clair. First solo venture experimental film, 1923; in Hollywood, dir., Parlor, Bedroom and Bath, Incomplete Athlete, 1930-32.
PICTURES: Nana (actor only), Construire un feu, Pur sang, .Le Fils du royal, Buster se marie, Un Chien serieux, Le Plombier amoureux, La Peur des coups, Monsieur le duc, Invite monsieur a diner, Le Gendarme est sans pitie, L'Athlete incomplet, Ciboulette (also writer), My Partner Mr. Davis, Fric-Frac, Le Mariage de chiffon, Lettres d'amour, Love Story, Sylvia and the Ghost, Devil in the Flesh, Oh Amelia!, The Red Inn (also writer), The Seven Deadly Sins (also writer), Le Bon Dieu sans confession, The Red and the Black (also writer), The Game of Love (also writer), Marguerite de la nuit (also writer), Four Bags Full, Love Is My Profession, Le Joueur, The Green Mare, Le Bois des amants, Les Regates de San Francisco, Vive Henri IV... vive l'amour, Thou Shalt Not Kill, The Story of Monte Crisco, Enough Rope, Black Humor, Le Magot de Josefa (also writer), A Woman in White, Une Femme en blanc se revolte, The Oldest Profession, Flash 29 (actor only), (Le Franciscain de Bourges, Les Patates (also writer), Le Rouge et le blanc.

AUTEUIL, DANIEL
Actor. b. Algeria, Jan. 24, 1950. Parents were lyric opera singers in roving troupe. Lived in Avignon. Performed in Amer. prod. in Paris of Godspell. Then did musical comedy for 2 years. Provided voice of baby for French print of U.S. film Look Who's Talking.
PICTURES: L'Aggression/Sombres Vacanes, Attention Les Yeaux, La Nuit de Saint-Germain des Pres, Monsieur Papa, L'Amour Viole (Rape of Love), Les Heroes n'ont pas Froid aux Oreilles, A Nous Deux, Bete Mais Discipline, Les Sous-Doues, La Banquiere, Clara et les Chic Types, Men Prefer Fat Girls, Pour 100 Briques t'as Plus Rien Maintentant, Que les Gros Salaires Levent le Doigt!!!, L'Indic, P'tit Con, The Beast, L'Arbalete, Palace, L'Amour en Douce, Jean de Florette, Manon of the Spring, Romuald and Juliette (Mama There's a Man in Your Bed), A Few Days With Me, My Life is Hell, L'Elegant Criminel, Un Coeur en Hiver (A Heart in Winter), Ma Saison Preferee (My Favorite Season), Queen Margot, The Separation, Un Femme Francais, According to Pereira, The Eighth Day (Best actor, Cannes 1996), Thieves, Death in Therapy, Lucie Aubrac, On Guard.

AUTRY, GENE
Actor. b. Tioga, TX, Sept. 29, 1907. Railroad telegrapher at Sapulpa, OK, 1925. Became radio singer and recording artist (Columbia Records), 1928. Made screen debut at Mascot Pictures (later became Republic) as screen's first singing cowboy, 1934. Starred in 89 feature films and 91 half hour TV films. The Gene Autry Show, 1950-55. Formed Flying A Productions, produced Annie Oakley, The Range Rider, Buffalo Bill, Jr. and Adventures of Champion TV series. Wrote or co-wrote over two hundred songs, recorded 635 records, has 12 Gold Records, and 6 platinum records, including all-time best seller, Rudolph the Red-Nosed Reindeer. Voted top money making Western star 1937-42, and in top Western stars 1936, 1946-54; first Western star to be in top ten money makers from 1939-42. Star of Madison Square Garden Rodeo first in 1940. Served in U.S.A.A.F. as flight officer, 1942-45; on USO tour overseas 3 mos. Immediately thereafter resumed radio career with former sponsor, the Wm. Wrigley Co.; formed Gene Autry Productions, Inc. Composed & recorded song Here Comes Santa Claus; Be Honest With Me (Acad. Award nom.). Owner KSCA FM radio station, California Angels baseball team. Chmn. of the bd of Gene Autry Western Heritage Museum. The only entertainer with five stars on the Hollywood Walk of Fame for radio, recordings, movies, tv and live performances, theatrical and rodeo. Hosted Melody Ranch Theatre on the Nashville Network, 1988-89. TV Specials incl. Biography, 1994; Gene Autry: Melody of the West, 1995.

PICTURES: In Old Santa Fe (debut, 1934), Tumbling Tumbleweeds, The Singing Vagabond, The Big Show, Oh Susannah, The Old Corral, Boots and Saddles, Manhattan Merry-Go-Round, Gold Mine in the Sky, Rhythm of the Saddle, Mexicali Rose, In Old Monterey, South of the Border, Rancho Grande, Melody Ranch, Back in the Saddle, Sierra Sue, Stardust on the Sage, Sioux City Sue, Saddle Pals, Robin Hood of Texas, The Last Round-Up, The Cowboy and the Indians, Cow Town, Mule Train, The Blazing Sun, Valley of Fire, Apache Country, Barbed Wire, Wagon Team, Saginaw Trail, Last of the Pony Riders, Alias Jesse James (cameo), many others.
(d. Oct. 2, 1998)

AVALON, FRANKIE
Singer, Actor. b. Philadelphia, PA, Sept 18, 1940. e. South Philadelphia H.S. r.n. Francis Thomas Avalone. Trumpet prodigy age 9 yrs. Recording contract, Chancellor Records, Inc., 1957; Gold Record: Venus 1959; Gold Album: Swingin' on a Rainbow, 1959.
PICTURES: Jamboree (debut, 1957), Guns of the Timberland, The Alamo, Alakazam the Great (voice), Voyage to the Bottom of the Sea, Sail a Crooked Ship, Panic in the Year Zero, Beach Party, The Castilian, Drums of Africa, Operation Bikini, Bikini Beach, Pajama Party, Muscle Beach Party, How to Stuff a Wild Bikini, Beach Blanket Bingo, Ski Party, I'll Take Sweden, Sgt. Deadhead, Dr. Goldfoot and the Bikini Machine, Fireball 500, The Million Eyes of Su-Muru, Skidoo, Horror House, The Take, Grease, Back to the Beach, Troop Beverly Hills.
TELEVISION: Series: Easy Does It... Starring Frankie Avalon. Guest: Ed Sullivan, Perry Como, Pat Boone, Arthur Murray, Dick Clark Shows, Milton Berle, Golden Circle Spectacular, Dinah Shore Show, Steve Allen Show, The Patty Duke Show, Hullabaloo, Happy Days.

AVEDON, DOE
Actress, b. Old Westbury, NY, 1928. Bookkeeper, then actress.
THEATER: Young and the Fair, My Name Is Aquilon.
PICTURES: The High and the Mighty, Deep in My Heart, The Boss.
TELEVISION: Series: Big Town.

AVILDSEN, JOHN G.
Director, Cinematographer, Editor. b. Chicago, IL, Dec. 21, 1935. m. actress Tracy Brooks Swope. e. NYU. After service in Army made film with friend, Greenwich Village Story, then joined ad agency to write, direct, photograph & edit industrial films. Entered motion picture industry as ass't cameraman on Below the Hill, followed with prod. mgr. job on two Italian films made in U.S. Afterwards, made first theatrical short, Smiles. Asst. dir., Black Like Me; prod. mgr., Mickey One, Una Moglie Americana; 2nd unit dir., Hurry Sundown. Produced, photographed & edited a short, Light—Sound—Diffuse. Returned to industry to make industrial films for ad agencies before resuming theatrical career.
PICTURES: Dir./photo./edit.: Turn on to Love (debut), Out of It (assoc. prod., dir. of photog.), Sweet Dreams (aka Okay, Bill), Guess What We Learned in School Today?, Joe, Cry Uncle, The Stoolie, Save the Tiger, W. W. and the Dixie Dancekings, Foreplay, Rocky (Acad. Award, 1976), Slow Dancing in the Big City (also prod.), The Formula, Neighbors (also supv. edit.), Traveling Hopefully (documentary; Acad. Award nom.), A Night in Heaven, The Karate Kid, The Karate Kid: Part II, Happy New Year, For Keeps, Lean On Me, The Karate Kid Part III (also co-edit.), Rocky V (also co-edit.), The Power of One, Steal This Video Abbie Hoffman (documentary), 8 Seconds, Save The Everglades (documentary).
TELEVISION: From No House to Options House (2 On the Town, Emmy Award).

AVNET, JON
Producer, Director. b. Brooklyn, NY, Nov. 17, 1949. e. U. of PA, Sarah Lawrence Coll. Began career as director of off-B'way prods. Produced and directed low-budget film, Confusion's Circle, which brought a directing fellowship at American Film Institute. Joined Weintraub/Heller Prods. as assoc. prod., where met Steve Tisch, with whom formed Tisch/Avnet Prods. Formed Avnet/Kerner Co., 1986.
PICTURES: Checkered Flag or Crash (assoc. prod.), Outlaw Blues (assoc. prod.). Producer: Coast to Coast, Risky Business, Deal of the Century (exec. prod.), Less Than Zero, Men Don't Leave, Funny About Love, Fried Green Tomatoes (also dir., co-s.p.), The Mighty Ducks, The Mighty Ducks II, The Mighty Ducks III, The Three Musketeers (co-exec. prod.), When a Man Loves a Woman, The War (also dir.), Miami Rhapsody (co-exec. prod.), Up Close and Personal (also dir.), George of the Jungle.
TELEVISION: Producer: No Other Love, Homeward Bound, Prime Suspect, Something So Right, Silence of the Heart, Calendar Girl Murders, Call to Glory (pilot and series), The Burning Bed, In Love and War (also exec. prod.), Between Two Women (also dir., co-s.p.), Naomi and Wynona: Love Can Build a Bridge. Exec. Prod.: Side By Side, My First Love, Breaking Point, O Do You Know the Muffin Man?, Heatwave, Backfield in Motion, The Nightman, The Switch, For Their Own Good.

AXEL, GABRIEL
Director. b. Denmark, 1918. e. France, then studied acting at Danish National Conservatory. Returned to France where joined the Paris theater co. of Louis Jouvet as stagehand. Worked as actor in Copenhagen Boulevard theater where made directing debut. Went on to dir. Danish TV, mostly classic plays.
PICTURES: Golden Mountains (debut, 1957), Crazy Paradise, The Red Mantle, Danish Blue, Babette's Feast (also s.p.; Acad. Award for Best Foreign-Language Feature, 1988), Christian (also s.p.), Prince of Jutland (Royal Deceit; also s.p.), Lumiere & Company. *Actor*: The Reluctant Sadist, Love Me Darling, and numerous other Danish films. *Writer*: Crazy Paradise, The Red Mantle, Det Kaere legetoj, Bebette's Feast.

AXELMAN, ARTHUR
Executive. b. Philadelphia, PA, Dec. 10, 1944. e. Florida Atlantic U., B.A., 1969. Entered NY offices of William Morris Agency, June 1972; transferred to Bev. Hills offices, 1976, as literary agent. Founded company's original TV Movie dept., 1977; appointed v.p. in 1980; sr. v.p. in 1991. Among clients represented while overseeing network sales, negotiation, packaging, development, etc. of some 100 TV movies have been EMI TV, Bob Banner, Edward S. Feldman, Lee Grant, Thom Mount, Edward Anhalt, Zev Braun, Marvin Worth, Gilbert Cates, Jerry London, Jeremy Kagan, Dick Berg, Patty Duke, Finnegan-Pinchuk Prods.

AXELROD, GEORGE
Writer, Producer, Director. b. New York, NY, June 9, 1922. Stage mgr., actor, summer stock, 1940-41; radio writer, 1941-52.
AUTHOR: *Novels*: Beggar's Choice, Blackmailer; co-writer, nightclub musical: All About Love, 1951. *Memoirs*: Where Am I Now When I Need Me?
THEATER: *B'way*: The Seven Year Itch, Will Success Spoil Rock Hunter?, Visit to a Small Planet, Once More with Feeling, Goodbye Charlie (also dir.).
PICTURES: *Writer*: Phffft, The Seven Year Itch, Bus Stop, Breakfast at Tiffany's, The Manchurian Candidate (also co-prod.), Paris When It Sizzles (also co-prod.), How to Murder Your Wife, Lord Love a Duck (also dir., prod.), The Secret Life of an American Wife (also dir., prod.), The Lady Vanishes, The Holcroft Covenant, The Fourth Protocol.

AXELROD, JONATHAN
Writer, Producer. b. New York, NY, July 9, 1952. Stepson of writer George Axelrod. Started as on-set "gofer" before writing screenplays. V.p. primetime drama dev., ABC Entertainment,1978-80; v.p. exec. dir. in charge dev. ABC Ent., 1980-82. Exec. v.p., Columbia Pictures TV, 1983-85. Pres. New World Pictures, 1985-87. Co-owner, Camden Artists, 1987-. Exec. v.p. Ventura Entertainment Group, 1989. Pres. & CEO Producers Entertainment Group, 1990-93. Exec. Prod. of Hollywood Detective series. Formed Axelrod Woddoes Productions, 1994.
TELEVISION: *Exec. Prod*.: Dave's World, Can't Hurry Love, A Day With, Manhattan Match, Late Bloomer.

AYKROYD, DAN
Actor, Writer. b. Ottawa, Canada, July 1, 1952. m. actress Donna Dixon. Member of Toronto Co. of Second City Theater. Worked as mgr. of Club 505, after-hours Toronto nightclub 1970-73. Performed and recorded (Briefcase Full of Blues, Made in America) with John Belushi as the Blues Brothers. Co-owner, Hard Rock Cafe.
PICTURES: Love at First Sight (debut, 1977; also co-s.p.), Mr. Mike's Mondo Video, 1941, The Blues Brothers (also co-s.p.), Neighbors, It Came From Hollywood, Doctor Detroit, Trading Places, Twilight Zone—The Movie, Indiana Jones and the Temple of Doom (cameo), Ghostbusters (also co-s.p.), Nothing Lasts Forever, Into the Night, Spies Like Us (also co-s.p.), One More Saturday Night (exec. prod. only), Dragnet (also co-s.p.), The Couch Trip, The Great Outdoors, Caddyshack II, My Stepmother Is an Alien, Ghostbusters II (also co-s.p.), Driving Miss Daisy (Acad. Award nom.), Loose Cannons, Nothing But Trouble (also dir., s.p.), Masters of Menace, My Girl, This Is My Life, Sneakers, Chaplin, Coneheads (also co-s.p.), My Girl 2, North, Exit to Eden, Tommy Boy, Casper (cameo), Canadian Bacon (cameo), Getting Away With Murder, Sgt. Bilko, Celtic Pride, My Fellow Americans, Grosse Pointe Blank.
TELEVISION: Coming Up Rosie (Canada), Saturday Night Live 1975-79 (writer and performer; Emmy Award for writing: 1977). Steve Martin's Best Show Ever (performer, writer). *Guest*: Tales From the Crypt. *Series*: Soul Man.

AYRES, LEW
Actor. b. Minneapolis, MN, Dec. 28, 1908. Toured Mexico with own orchestra, then with Henry Halstead's Orchestra. Served as medical corpsman & asst. chaplain WWII.
PICTURES: The Sophomore (debut, 1929), The Kiss, All Quiet on the Western Front, Common Clay, East is West, Doorway to Hell, Up for Murder, Many a Slip, Spirit of Notre Dame, Heaven on Earth, Impatient Maiden, Night World, Okay America, State Fair, Don't Bet on Love, My Weakness, Cross Country Cruise, Let's Be Ritzy, She Learned About Sailors, Servants' Entrance, Lottery Lover, Silk Hat Kid, Leathernecks Have Landed, Panic on the Air, Shakedown, Lady Be Careful, Murder With Pictures, The Crime Nobody Saw, Last Train From Madrid, Hold 'Em Navy,

King of the Newsboys, Scandal Street, Holiday, Rich Man Poor Girl, Young Dr. Kildare (and subsequent film series), Spring Madness, Ice Follies of 1939, Broadway Serenade, These Glamour Girls, The Golden Fleecing, Maisie Was a Lady, Fingers at the Window, Dark Mirror, Unfaithful, Johnny Belinda (Acad. Award nom.), The Capture, New Mexico, No Escape, Donovan's Brain, Altars to the East (also dir., prod., narrator), Advise and Consent, The Carpetbaggers, The Biscuit Eater, The Man, Battle for the Planet of the Apes, End of the World, Damien-Omen II, Battlestar Galactica.
TELEVISION: *Movies*: Hawaii Five-O (pilot), Marcus Welby M.D. (pilot), Earth II, She Waits, The Stranger, The Questor Tapes, Heatwave, Francis Gary Powers, Suddenly Love, Salem's Lot, Letters from Frank, Reunion, Of Mice and Men, Under Siege, Hart to Hart: Crimes of the Hart. *Series*: Frontier Justice (host), Lime Street.

AZARIA, HANK
Actor. b. Forest Hills, NY, April 25, 1964. e. Tufts Univ.
PICTURES: Pretty Woman, Cool Blue, Quiz Show, Now and Then, Heat, The Birdcage, Grosse Pointe Blank, Anastasia (voice), Mystery Alaska, Homegrown, Godzilla.
TELEVISION: *Series*: The Simpsons (voice), Herman's Head, If Not for You. *Guest*: Fresh Prince of Bel-Air, Growing Pains, Mad About You.

AZNAVOUR, CHARLES
Singer, Songwriter, Actor. r.n. Shahnour Varenagh Aznavourian. b. Paris, France, May 22, 1924. Studied dance and drama as a child and was performing at the age of 10. Encouraged by Edith Piaf, became one of France's leading performers by the mid-1950s and an international concert star by the 1970s. Has also composed music for film.
PICTURES: Adieu Cherie (1947), C'est arrive a 36 Chandelles, Les Dragueurs, Shoot the Piano Player, Le testament d'Orphee, Le Passage du Rhin, Un taxi pour Tobrouk, Horace 62, Tempo di Roma, Les Quatres Verites, Le Rat'd Amerique, Pourquoi Paris?, Paris in August, Candy, The Games, The Adventurers, The Blockhouse, Ten Little Indians, The Twist, Sky Riders, Ciao Les Mecs, The Tin Drum, The Magic Mountain, Hatter's Ghosts, What Makes David Run?, Edith and Marcel, Long Live Life!, Mangeclous, Friend to Friend, Il Maestro, Double Game.

B

BABENCO, HECTOR
Director. b. Buenos Aires, Argentina, Feb. 7, 1946. Early years spent in Mar del Plata. Left home at 17 and traveled throughout Europe for 8 years working as a writer, house-painter, salesman, and, in Rome, as an extra at Cinecitta. Moved to Sao Paulo, Brazil where he made several short documentaries, before turning to features in 1975.
PICTURES: Rei Da Noite (King of the Night; debut, 1975), Lucio Flavio—Passageiro da Agonia, Pixote (also co-s.p.), Kiss of the Spider Woman, Ironweed, Besame Mucho (prod. only), At Play in the Fields of the Lord (also co-s.p.).

BACALL, LAUREN
Actress. r.n. Betty Joan. b. New York, NY, Sept. 16, 1924. e. American Acad. Dram. Arts. Was m. Jason Robards, late Humphrey Bogart. *Autobiographies*: By Myself (1979), Now (1994).
THEATER: *B'way*: Cactus Flower, Goodbye Charlie, Applause (Tony Award), Woman of the Year (Tony Award). *Foreign*: Sweet Bird of Youth. *Tour*: Wonderful Town.
PICTURES: To Have and Have Not (debut, 1944), Two Guys From Milwaukee (cameo), Confidential Agent, The Big Sleep, Dark Passage, Key Largo, Young Man With a Horn, Bright Leaf, How to Marry a Millionaire, Woman's World, Cobweb, Blood Alley, Written on the Wind, Designing Woman, Gift of Love, Flame Over India, Shock Treatment, Sex and the Single Girl, Harper, Murder on the Orient Express, The Shootist, Health, The Fan, Appointment With Death, Mr. North, Innocent Victim, Misery, A Star for Two, All I Want for Christmas, My Fellow Americans, Le Jour et La Nuit, Ready to Wear (Pret-a-Porter), The Mirror Has Two Faces (Golden Globe Award, 1996; Screen Actors Guild Award), My Fellow Americans.
TELEVISION: *Movies*: Perfect Gentlemen, Dinner at Eight, A Little Piece of Sunshine (BBC), The Portrait, From the Mixed Up Files of Mrs. Basil E. Frankweiler. *Specials*: The Girls in Their Summer Dresses, Blithe Spirit, The Petrified Forest, Applause, Bacall on Bogart, A Foreign Field (BBC).

BACH, CATHERINE
Actress. b. Warren, Ohio, March 1, 1954.
PICTURES: The Midnight Man, Thunderbolt and Lightfoot, Hustle, Cannonball Run II, Tunnels (Criminal Act), Music City Blues, Driving Force, Street Justice.
TELEVISION: *Series*: The Dukes of Hazzard (1979-85), The Dukes (cartoon, voice), African Skies. Guest on many specials. *Movies*: Matt Helm, Strange New World, Murder in Peyton Place, White Water Rebels, Masters of Menace, Rage & Honor, The Nutt House, The Dukes of Hazard Reunion.

BACHARACH, BURT
Composer, Conductor, Arranger. b. Kansas City, MO, May 12, 1928. e. McGraw U., Mannes Sch. of Music, Music Acad. of the West. Studied with composers Darius Milhaud, Henry Cowell, and Bohuslav Martinu. Has conducted for Marlene Dietrich, Vic Damone. As a performer albums include: Burt Bacharach; Futures, Man! His Songs. Book: The Bacharach-David Song Book (1978).
THEATER: Promises Promises (Tony Award, 1969).
PICTURES: Lizzie, The Sad Sack, The Blob, Country Music Holiday, Love in a Goldfish Bowl, Wives and Lovers, Who's Been Sleeping in My Bed?, Send Me No Flowers, A House Is Not a Home, What's New Pussycat?, Alfie, Made in Paris, After the Fox, Promise Her Anything, Casino Royale, The April Fools, Butch Cassidy and the Sundance Kid (2 Acad. Awards: Best Original Score & Best Song: Raindrops Keep Fallin' on My Head; 1969), Something Big, Lost Horizon, Together?, Arthur (Acad. Award for Best Song: Arthur's Theme; 1981), Night Shift, Best Defense, Tough Guys, Baby Boom, Arthur 2 on the Rocks, Love Hurts, Austin Powers—International Man of Mystery (actor only).
TELEVISION: Special: Singer Presents Burt Bacharach (Emmy Award for Best Variety Special, 1971).

BACK, LEON B.
Exhibitor. b. Philadelphia, PA, Oct. 23, 1912. e. Johns Hopkins U., B.E., 1932; U. of Baltimore, LL.B., 1933. Entered motion picture industry as mgr. for Rome Theatres, Inc., Baltimore, Md., 1934; booker, ass't buyer, 1936; ass't to gen. mgr. 1939; U.S. Navy 1944-46; v.p., gen. mgr., Rome Theatres, 1946. Allied MPTO of Md. 1952-55; nat'l dir. Allied States, 1952-55; nat'l secy. 1954. Pres. NATO of Maryland 1969-80. Pres. USO Council, Greater Baltimore 1969-75. Chmn., bd. of trustees, Employees Benefit Trust for Health & Welfare Council of Central Maryland, 1970-79.

BACON, KEVIN
Actor. b. Philadelphia, PA, July 8, 1958. m. actress Kyra Sedgwick. Studied at Manning St. Actor's Theatre. Apprentice at Circle-in-the-Square in N.Y. B'way debut in Slab Boys with Sean Penn. Narrated short film A Little Vicious.
THEATER: B'way: Slab Boys. Off-B'way: Getting Out (debut), Album, Forty Deuce (Obie Award), Poor Little Lambs, Flux, Men Without Dates, The Author's Voice, Loot, Road, Spike Heels.
PICTURES: National Lampoon's Animal House (debut, 1978), Starting Over, Hero at Large, Friday the 13th, Only When I Laugh, Forty Deuce, Diner, Footloose, Enormous Changes at the Last Minute, Quicksilver, White Water Summer (Rites of Summer), End of the Line, Planes Trains and Automobiles, She's Having a Baby, Criminal Law, The Big Picture, Tremors, Flatliners, Queens Logic, He Said/She Said, Pyrates, JFK, A Few Good Men, The Air Up There, The River Wild, Murder in the First, Apollo 13, Balto (voice), Sleepers, Picture Perfect, Telling Lies in America, Digging to China, Wild Things.
TELEVISION: Movies: The Gift, The Demon Murder Case, The Tender Age (The Little Sister), Lemon Sky, Losing Chase (dir. only). Series: Search for Tomorrow, The Guiding Light. Specials: Mr. Roberts.

BADHAM, JOHN
Director. b. Luton, England, Aug. 25, 1939. Raised in Alabama. e. Yale U., B.A.; Yale Drama School, M.F.A. Sister is actress Mary Badham. Landed first job at Universal Studio mailroom; later was Universal tour guide, a casting dir. and assoc. prod. to William Sackheim. Twice nominated for Emmy Awards for TV movies. Recipient of George Pal Award.
PICTURES: The Bingo Long Traveling All-Stars and Motor Kings (debut 1976), Saturday Night Fever, Dracula (Best Horror Film award, Science Fiction/Fantasy Academy), Whose Life Is It Anyway? (San Rafael Grand Prize), Blue Thunder, War Games (Best Directing award, Science Fiction/Fantasy Academy), American Flyers, Short Circuit, Stakeout (also exec. prod.), Disorganized Crime (exec. prod. only), Bird on a Wire, The Hard Way, Point of No Return, Another Stakeout (also exec. prod.), Drop Zone (also exec. prod.), Nick of Time (also prod.).
TELEVISION: Movies: Night Gallery (assoc. prod. only), Neon Ceiling (assoc. prod. only), The Impatient Heart, Isn't It Shocking?, The Law, The Gun, Reflections of Murder, The Godchild, The Keegans, Relentless: Mind of a Killer (co-exec. prod. only). Series episodes: The Senator (also assoc. prod.), Kung Fu, Night Gallery, Streets of San Francisco, The Doctors, Owen Marshall - Counsellor at Law, Sunshine, Nichols, Sarge, The Sixth Sense, Cannon.

BAILEY, JOHN
Cinematographer. b. Moberly, MO, Aug. 10, 1942. m. film editor Carol Littleton. e. U. of Santa Clara, Loyola U., U.S.C., U. of Vienna. Lecturer, American Film Institute, 1982, 1984, 1994.
PICTURES: Premonition, End of August, Legacy, The Mafu Cage (visual consult.), Boulevard Nights, Winter Kills (add. photog.), American Gigolo, Ordinary People, Honky Tonk Freeway, Continental Divide, Cat People, That Championship Season, Without a Trace, The Big Chill, Racing With the Moon, The Pope of Greenwich Village, Mishima, Silverado, Crossroads, Brighton Beach Memoirs, Light of Day, Swimming to Cambodia, Tough Guys Don't Dance (visual consult.), Vibes, The Accidental Tourist, My Blue Heaven, The Search for Signs of Intelligent Life in the Universe (also dir.), A Brief History of Time, Groundhog Day, In the Line of Fire, China Moon (dir. only), Nobody's Fool, Mariette in Ecstasy (dir. only), Extreme Measures, As Good As It Gets.
TELEVISION: Battered, City in Fear, Always Outnumbered.

BAILEY, ROBIN
Actor. b. Hucknall (Nottingham), England, Oct. 5, 1919. e. Henry Mellish School, Nottingham. In Barrets of Wimpole Street, with Theatre Royal, Nottingham, 1938.
PICTURES: School for Secrets (1946), Private Angelo, Portrait of Clare, His Excellency, Gift Horse, Folly to Be Wise, Single Handed, Sailor of the King, The Young Lovers, For Better—For Worse, Catch Us If You Can, The Whisperers, Spy with a Cold Nose, You Only Live Twice, The Eliminator, Blind Terror, Down by the Riverside, Nightmare Rally, The Four Feathers, Jane and the Lost City, Number 27.
TELEVISION: Olive Latimer's Husband, Seven Deadly Sins, The Power Game, Public Eye, Person to Person, Troubleshooters, Armchair Theatre, Split Level, The Newcomers, Discharge of Trooper Lusby, Brett, Owen M.D., Solidarity, General Hospital, Murder Must Advertise, Vienna 1900, Justice, The Pallisers, The Couch, Way of the World, Upstairs, Downstairs, Walk with Destiny, North and South, A Legacy, The Velvet Glove, Crown Court, Took and Co., The Good Companions, Cupid's Darts, Sorry, I'm a Stranger Here Myself, Call My Bluff, Jane, Potter, Tales from a Long Room, Sharing Time, Bleak House, Charters and Caldicott, Looks Familiar, On Stage, Rumpole of the Bailey, I Didn't Know You Cared, Number 27, Tinniswood's North Country, Tales From Hollywood, Bed, Dalziel and Pascoe.

BAIO, SCOTT
Actor. b. New York, NY, Sept. 22, 1961. Started career at 9 doing commercials and voice-overs.
PICTURES: Bugsy Malone, Skatetown USA, Foxes, Zapped!, I Love New York, Detonator.
TELEVISION: Series: Blansky's Beauties, Happy Days, Who's Watching the Kids?, We're Movin' (host), Joanie Loves Chachi, Charles in Charge (also dir.), Luke Was There, Baby Talk, Diagnosis Murder. Specials: Luke Was There, Muggsy, Stoned, How to Be a Man, Gemini, The Truth About Alex. Guest: Hotel, The Fall Guy, Full House, Can't Hurry Love. Movies: The Boy Who Drank Too Much, Senior Trip, Alice in Wonderland, Perry Mason: The Case of the Fatal Fashion, Mixed Blessings. Director: Lassie, Out of This World, First Time Out, Wayans Brothers, Jamie Foxx Show, Nick Freno; Licensed Teacher.

BAKER, BLANCHE
Actress. r.n. Blanche Garfein. b. New York, NY, Dec. 20, 1956. Daughter of actress Carroll Baker and dir. Jack Garfein. e. Wellesley, Coll., studied acting with Uta Hagen. Acting debut, White Marriage, Yale Repertory Co. (1978), Regional Theater. B'way debut in Lolita (1981).
PICTURES: The Seduction of Joe Tynan (debut, 1979), French Postcards, Sixteen Candles, Raw Deal, Cold Feet, Nobody's Child, Shakedown, The Handmaid's Tale, Livin' Large, Bum Rap, Dead Funny.
TELEVISION: Movies: Mary and Joseph, The Day the Bubble Burst, The Awakening of Candra, Nobody's Child. Mini-Series: Holocaust (Emmy Award, 1978). Specials: Romeo & Juliet.

BAKER, CARROLL
Actress. b. Johnstown, PA, May 28, 1931. e. schools there and St. Petersburg (FL) Junior Coll. Career started as dancer in nightclubs. Actors' Studio N.Y. Made stage debut in Escapade, then acted in All Summer Long. Autobiography: Baby Doll.
PICTURES: Easy to Love (debut, 1953), Giant, Baby Doll, The Big Country, But Not for Me, The Miracle, Bridge to the Sun, Something Wild, How the West Was Won, The Carpetbaggers, Station Six Sahara, Cheyenne Autumn, The Greatest Story Ever Told, Sylvia, Mister Moses, Harlow, Jack of Diamonds, The Sweet Body of Deborah, Paranoia, A Quiet Place to Kill, Captain Apache, The Harem, Honeymoon, My Father's Wife, Bloodbath (The Sky Is Falling), Andy Warhol's Bad, The World is Full of Married Men, Watcher in the Woods, Star 80, The Secret Diary of Sigmund Freud, Native Son, Ironweed, Red Monarch, Kindergarten Cop, Blonde Fist, Cybereden, Undercurrent, Skeletons, Just Your Luck, The Game, Nowhere to Go.
TELEVISION: Movies: Hitler's SS: Portrait in Evil, On Fire, Judgement Day: The John List Story, Men Don't Tell, A Kiss to Die For, North Shore Fish, Heart Full of Rain, Big Guns Talk: The Story of the Western. Specials: Rain, On Fire, Sharing Time, Coward's: What Mad Pursuit. Guest: Tales from the Crypt, L.A. Law.

BAKER, DIANE
Actress. b. Hollywood, CA, Feb. 25, 1938. e. USC.
PICTURES: The Diary of Anne Frank (debut, 1959), The Best of Everything, Journey to the Center of the Earth, Tess of the Storm Country, The Wizard of Baghdad, Hemingway's Adventures of a Young Man, 300 Spartans, Nine Hours to Rama, Stolen Hours, The Prize, Straight Jacket, Marnie, Mirage, Sands of Beersheba, The Horse in the Grey Flannel Suit, Krakatoa — East of Java, Baker's Hawk, The Pilot, The Silence of the Lambs, The Closer, The Joy Luck Club, Twenty Bucks, Imaginary Crimes, The Net, The Cable Guy, Murder at 1600.
TELEVISION: Movies: Dangerous Days of Kiowa Jones, Trial Run, The D.A.: Murder One, The Old Man Who Cried Wolf, Do You Take This Stranger?, Sarge: The Badge or the Cross, Congratulations It's a Boy!, A Little Game, Killer By Night, Police Story (pilot), A Tree Grows in Brooklyn, The Dream Makers, The Last Survivors, Fugitive Family, The Haunted, Perry Mason: The Case of the Heartbroken Bride, About Sarah. Series: Here We Go Again. Mini-Series: The Blue and the Gray.

BAKER, DYLAN
Actor. b. Syracuse, NY. e. Southern Methodist Univ. (BFA), Yale Sch. of Drama (MFA).
THEATER: *B'way:* Eastern Standard (Theatre World Award), La Bete (Tony nom.). *Off-B'way:* Not About Heroes (Obie Award).
PICTURES: Ishtar (debut, 1987), Planes Trains and Automobiles, The Wizard of Loneliness, The Long Walk Home, Delirious, Passed Away, Love Potion No. 9, The Last of the Mohicans, Life With Mikey, Radioland Murders, Disclosure, The Stars Fell on Henrietta, True Blue.
TELEVISION: *Movies:* A Case of Deadly Force, The Murder of Mary Phagan, Judgment, Love Honor and Obey: The Last Mafia Marriage, Forbidden Territory: Stanley's Search for Livingstone. *Series:* Murder One, Feds. *Mini-Series:* Return to Lonesome Dove. *Guest:* Spenser: For Hire, Miami Vice, Law and Order, The Cosby Mysteries, Northern Exposure.

BAKER, GEORGE
Actor, Writer. b. Varna, Bulgaria, April 1, 1931. e. Lancing College, Sussex. Stage debut Deal Repertory Theatre, 1946.
AUTHOR: The Fatal Spring, Imaginary Friends, Going for Broke, The Marches of Wales, The Hopkins, Just a Hunch, Sister, Dear Sister, From Doom With Death, Mouse in the Corner, The Strawberry Tree, Talking About Mira Beau, Dead on Time, The Last Silence.
PICTURES: The Intruder (debut, 1953), The Dam Busters, The Ship That Died of Shame, Woman for Joe, The Extra Day, The Feminine Touch, A Hill in Korea (Hell in Korea), No Time for Tears, These Dangerous Years (Dangerous Youth), The Moonraker, Tread Softly Stranger, Lancelot and Guinevere (Sword of Lancelot), Curse of the Fly, Mister Ten Per Cent, Goodbye Mr. Chips, Justine, The Executioners, On Her Majesty's Secret Service, A Warm December, The Fire Fighters, The Spy Who Loved Me, Thirty-Nine Steps, A Nightingale Sang in Berkeley Square, Hopscotch, North Sea Hijack (ffolkes), For Queen and Country, Simisola.
TELEVISION: Fan Show, Ron Raudell's programme 1956, Guinea Pig, Death of a Salesman, The Last Troubadour, The Square Ring, Nick of the River, Mary Stuart, Probation Officers, Far Away Music, It Happened Like This, Boule de Suif, Maigret, Zero One, Rupert Henzau, Miss Memory, Any Other Business, The Navigators, Common Ground, Alice, The Queen and Jackson, The Big Man Coughed and Died, Up and Down, Call My Bluff, The Baron, St. Patrick, Love Life, Seven Deadly Virtues, The Prisoner, The Sex Games, Z Cars, Paul Temple, Candida, Fenn Street, Man Outside, The Persuaders, Main Chance, Ministry of Fear, Bowler, Voyage in the Dark, Dial M for Murder, Zodiac, The Survivors, I, Claudius, Print Out, Goodbye, Darling, Chinese Detective, Triangle, Minder, Hart to Hart, Goodbye Mr. Chips, Woman of Substance, The Bird Fancier, Robin of Sherwood, Time after Time, If Tomorrow Comes, Coast to Coast, Dead Head, The Canterville Ghost, Room at the Bottom, Ruth Rendell Mysteries (From Doon With Death; adap.), Journey's End, No Job for a Lady, Little Lord Fauntleroy.

BAKER, JOE DON
Actor. b. Groesbeck, TX, Feb. 12, 1936. e. North Texas State Coll., B.B.A., 1958. Began career on N.Y. stage, in Marathon 33 and Blues for Mr. Charlie. L.A. stage in The Caine Mutiny Court Martial.
PICTURES: Cool Hand Luke (debut, 1967), Guns of the Magnificent Seven, Adam at Six A.M., Wild Rovers, Welcome Home Soldier Boys, Junior Bonner, Walking Tall, Charley Varrick, The Outfit, Golden Needles, Mitchell, Framed, Checkered Flag or Crash, Speedtrap, The Pack, Wacko, Joysticks, The Natural, Fletch, Getting Even (Hostage Dallas), The Living Daylights, The Killing Time, Leonard Part 6, Criminal Law, The Children, Cape Fear, The Distinguished Gentleman, Reality Bites, Panther, The Underneath, Congo, The Grass Harp, Goldeneye.
TELEVISION: *Movies:* Mongo's Back in Town, That Certain Summer, To Kill a Cop, Power, The Abduction of Kari Swenson, Edge of Darkness (BBC mini-series), Defrosting the Fridge (BBC), Citizen Cohn, Complex of Fear. *Series:* Eischeid. *Guest:* In the Heat of the Night.

BAKER, KATHY
Actress. B. Midland, TX, June 8, 1950. Raised in Albuquerque, NM. e. UC/Berkeley. Stage debut in San Francisco premiere of Fool for Love, won Obie and Theatre World Awards for New York debut in same. Also appeared in Desire Under the Elms, Aunt Dan and Lemon.
PICTURES: The Right Stuff (debut, 1983), Street Smart (Natl. Society of Film Critics Award), Permanent Record, A Killing Affair, Clean and Sober, Jacknife, Dad, Mr. Frost, Edward Scissorhands, Article 99, Jennifer Eight, Mad Dog and Glory, To Gillian on Her 37th Birthday, Inventing the Abbotts.
TELEVISION: *Series:* Picket Fences (2 Emmy Awards: 1993, 1995). *Movies:* Nobody's Child, The Image, One Special Victory, Lush Life. *Guest:* Amazing Stories.

BAKER, RICK
Makeup Artist, Performer. b. Binghamton, NY, Dec. 8, 1950. Started as assist. to makeup artist Dick Smith before creating his own designs in 1972. Frequent film appearances in makeup, usually as gorillas. Worked on Michael Jackson's video Thriller.
PICTURES: *Actor:* The Thing With Two Heads, King Kong, The Kentucky Fried Movie, The Incredible Shrinking Woman, Into the Night. *Makeup Design:* Shlock, Zebra Force, It's Alive, The Incredible Melting Man, Star Wars (2nd unit), It Lives Again, The Howling (consultant), Funhouse, An American Werewolf in London (Acad. Award, 1981), Videodrome, Greystoke: The Legend of Tarzan Lord of the Apes (also costume design; Acad. Award nom.), Ratboy, Harry and the Hendersons (Acad. Award, 1987), Coming to America (Acad. Award nom.), Gorillas in the Mist (also assoc. prod.), Missing Link, Wolf, Ed Wood (Acad. Award, 1994), Batman and Robin, Mighty Joe Young, Batman Forever (also designed monster bat), Escape From L.A. The Nutty Professor (Acad. Award, 1996), Men in Black (Acad. Award, Best Makeup, 1997), A Thousand Acres, The Devil's Advocate, Critical Care, Mighty Joe Young. *Other:* Tanya's Island (beast design), Starman (transformation scenes), Cocoon (consultant), My Science Project (Tyrannosaurus Rex sequences consultant), Max My Love (chimpanzee consultant), Gremlins 2: The New Batch (co-prod., f/x supervisor), Baby's Day Out (baby f/x), Just Cause (special bodies), Little Panda (panda suits).
TELEVISION: *Movies:* The Autobiography of Miss Jane Pittman (Emmy Award), An American Christmas Carol, Something Is Out There. *Makeup Design: Series:* Werewolf, Beauty and the Beast, Harry and the Hendersons.

BAKER, ROY
Producer, Director. b. London, England. e. Lycaee Corneille, Rouen; City of London School. Ass't dir. with Gainsborough 1934-40; served in Army 1940-46.
PICTURES: Operation Disaster, Don't Bother to Knock, Inferno, One That Got Away, A Night to Remember, The Singer Not the Song, Flame in the Streets, Quartermass and the Pit, The Anniversary, Vampire Lovers, Dr. Jekyll and Mr. Hyde, Asylum (Paris Grand Prize), Seven Golden Vampires.
TELEVISION: The Human Jungle, The Saint, Gideon's Way, The Baron, The Avengers, The Champions, Department S., The Persuaders, Danger UXB, Minder.

BAKER, DR. WILLIAM F.
Executive. b. 1944. e. Case Western Reserve U., B.A., M.A., Ph.D. Began broadcasting career in Cleveland while still a student. Joined Scripps-Howard Broadcasting, 1971. Joined Group W as v.p. and general mgr., WJZ-TV, 1978; served as pres. and CEO, Group W Productions; pres. of Group W. Television, 1979; chmn., Group W Satellite Communications, 1981. Carried Explorers Club flag to top of world, becoming one of few in history to visit both North and South Poles, 1983. Appointed pres. and CEO, WNET/Thirteen, NY PBS station, 1987. Pres., NY Chapter, Natl. Acad. Television Arts & Sciences. Recipient of 4 Emmy Awards, 2 Columbia Dupont Journalism Awards. Author of, Down the Tube, 1998.

BAKER, WILLIAM M.
Executive. b. Newark, NJ, Dec. 26, 1939. e. University of Virginia 1961. Joined FBI in 1965. From 1987 to 1989, took a haitus from the FBI to serve as dir. of Public Affairs for the CIA. Retired from position as asst. dir., Criminal Investigative Division of FBI in 1991. Currently pres. and COO Motion Picture Assoc. and exec. v.p., Motion Picture Assoc. of America.

BAKSHI, RALPH
Animator, Writer, Director. b. Haifa, Israel, Oct. 29, 1938. Began career at Terrytoons at age 18 as cell painter and animator, then creative dir. 1965, headed Paramount Cartoons, 1967. Pres., Bakshi Prods. Inc., 1973-.
PICTURES: *Dir./S.P./Writer:* Fritz the Cat, Heavy Traffic, Coonskin. *Also Prod/Co-prod.:* Wizards, The Lord of the Rings, American Pop, Hey Good Lookin', Fire and Ice, Cool World.
TELEVISION: Mighty Mouse: The New Adventures (dir., prod.) This Ain't Bebop (Amer. Playhouse, dir., s.p.), The Cool and the Crazy (dir., writer).

BAKULA, SCOTT
Actor. b. St. Louis, MO, Oct. 9, 1955. e. Kansas Univ.
THEATER: *NY:* Marilyn: An American Fable, Three Guys Naked from the Waist Down, Romance/Romance (Tony nom.). *LA:* Nite Club Confidential.
PICTURES: Sibling Rivalry, Necessary Roughness, Color of Night, A Passion to Kill, My Family/Mi Familia, Lord of Illusions, Cats Don't Dance (voice), Major League: Back to the Minors.
TELEVISION: *Movies:* The Last Fling, An Eye for an Eye, In the Shadow of a Killer, Mercy Mission: The Rescue of Flight 771, Nowhere to Hide, The Invaders. *Series:* Gung Ho, Eisenhower & Lutz, Quantum Leap (Emmy noms., Golden Globe Award), Murphy Brown, Mr. & Mrs. Smith.

BALABAN, BOB
Actor, Director. b. Chicago, IL, Aug. 16, 1945. Began studying with Second City troupe while still in high school. Attended Colgate U. and NYU while appearing on Broadway in Plaza Suite.
THEATER: You're a Good Man Charlie Brown, The Inspector General, Who Wants to Be the Lone Ranger?, The Basic Training of Pavlo Hummel, The Children, The White House Murder Case, Some of My Best Friends, The Three Sisters, The Boys Next Door, Speed-the-Plow, Some Americans Abroad.
PICTURES: *Actor*: Midnight Cowboy (debut, 1969), Me Natalie, The Strawberry Statement, Catch-22, Making It, Bank Shot, Report to the Commissioner, Close Encounters of the Third Kind, Girlfriends, Altered States, Prince of the City, Absence of Malice, Whose Life Is It Anyway?, 2010, In Our Hands (doc.), End of the Line, Dead-Bang, Alice, Little Man Tate, Bob Roberts, For Love or Money, Greedy, Pie in the Sky, Deconstructing Harry, Waiting For Guffman. *Director*: Parents, My Boyfriend's Back, The Last Good Time (also co-s.p.).
TELEVISION: *Movies*: Marriage: Year One, The Face of Fear, Unnatural Pursuits, The Late Shift. *Series*: Miami Vice, Late Shift, Seinfeld. *Director*: Tales From the Darkside, Amazing Stories, Penn & Teller's Invisible Thread, Eerie Indiana.

BALDWIN, ADAM
Actor. b. Chicago, IL, Feb. 27, 1962. While in high school in Winnetka, was chosen by dir. Tony Bill for role in My Bodyguard. Made stage debut in Album, Chicago.
PICTURES: My Bodyguard (debut, 1980), Ordinary People, D.C. Cab, Reckless, Hadley's Rebellion, Bad Guys, 3:15, Full Metal Jacket, The Chocolate War, Cohen and Tate, Next of Kin, Predator 2, Guilty By Suspicion, Radio Flyer, Where the Day Takes You, Deadbolt, Bitter Harvest, Eight Hundred Leagues Down the Amazon, Wyatt Earp, Independence Day.
TELEVISION: *Movies*: Off Sides, Poison Ivy, Welcome Home Bobby, Murder in High Places, Cruel Doubt, Cold Sweat, Sawbones. *Special*: The Last Shot.

BALDWIN, ALEC
Actor. r.n. Alexander Rae Baldwin III. b. Massapequa, NY, April 3, 1958. e. George Washington U., NYU. m. actress Kim Basinger. Brother of actors Stephen, William and Daniel Baldwin. Trained at Lee Strasberg Theatre Inst. and with Mira Rostova, Elaine Aiken. Started career in daytime TV on serial The Doctors. Member, The Creative Coalition.
THEATER: A Midsummer Night's Dream, The Wager, Summertree, A Life in the Theatre (Hartman), Study in Scarlet (Williamstown). *NY*: Loot (B'way debut; Theatre World Award, 1986), Serious Money, Prelude to a Kiss, A Streetcar Named Desire.
PICTURES: Forever Lulu (debut, 1987), She's Having a Baby, Beetlejuice, Married to the Mob, Working Girl, Talk Radio, Great Balls of Fire!, The Hunt for Red October, Miami Blues, Alice, The Marrying Man, Prelude to a Kiss, Glengarry Glen Ross, Malice, The Getaway, The Shadow, Heaven's Prisoners (also exec. prod.), The Juror, Looking For Richard, Ghosts of Mississippi, The Edge.
TELEVISION: *Movies*: Sweet Revenge, Love on the Run, Dress Gray, The Alamo: 13 Days to Glory. *Series*: The Doctors (1980-2), Cutter to Houston, Knots Landing. *Guest*: Hotel, Saturday Night Live.

BALDWIN, DANIEL
Actor. b. Long Island, NY, 1961. e. Nassau Comm. Col., Ball St. Univ. Brother of actors Alec, William and Stephen Baldwin.
PICTURES: Born on the Fourth of July, Harley Davidson and the Marlboro Man, Knight Moves, Car 54 Where Are You?, Lone Justice, Mullholland Drive.
TELEVISION: *Movies*: Too Good to Be True, L.A. Takedown, The Heroes of Desert Storm, Ned Blessing: The True Story of My Life, Attack of the 50 Foot Woman. *Series*: Sydney, Homicide: Life on the Street. *Specials*: Curse of the Corn People. *Guest*: Family Ties, Charles in Charge, The Larry Sanders Show.

BALDWIN, STEPHEN
Actor. b. Long Island, NY, 1966. Brother of actors Alec, William and Daniel Baldwin. Stage debut in Off-B'way prod., Out of America.
PICTURES: The Beast, Born on the Fourth of July, Last Exit to Brooklyn, Crossing the Bridge, Bitter Harvest, Posse, New Eden, 8 Seconds, Threesome, A Simple Twist of Fate, Mrs. Parker and the Vicious Circle, Fall Time, The Usual Suspects, Under the Hula Moon, Bio-Dome, Fled.
TELEVISION: *Movies*: Jury Duty: The Comedy, Dead Weekend. *Series*: The Young Riders. *Specials*: The Lawrenceville Stories, In a New Light: Sex Unplugged (co-host). *Guest*: Family Ties, Kate and Allie, China Beach.

BALDWIN, WILLIAM
Actor. b. Massapequa, NY, Feb. 21, 1963. e. SUNY/Binghamton. Degree in political science; worked in Washington on staff of rep. Thomas J. Downey. Brother of actors Alec, Stephen and Daniel Baldwin. With Ford Model agency, appearing in tv ads while studying acting. Member, The Creative Coalition.
PICTURES: Born on the Fourth of July (debut, 1989), Internal Affairs, Flatliners, Backdraft, Three of Hearts, Sliver, A Pyromaniac's Love Story, Fair Game, Curdled, Virus.
TELEVISION: *Movie*: The Preppie Murder.

BALE, CHRISTIAN
Actor. b. Pembrokeshire, Wales, Jan. 30, 1974. Acting debut at age 9 in U.S. Pac-Man commercial. London stage debut following year in The Nerd.
PICTURES: Empire of the Sun, Land of Faraway, Henry V, Newsies, Swing Kids, Prince of Jutland, Little Women, Pocahontas (voice), The Secret Agent, The Portrait of a Lady, Metroland, Velvet Goldmine, All the Little Animals, A Midsummer Night's Dream.
TELEVISION: *Specials/Movies*: Heart of the Country (BBC), Anastasia: The Mystery of Anna (U.S.), Treasure Island (released theatrically in U.K.), A Murder of Quality.

BALLARD, CARROLL
Director. b. Los Angeles, Oct. 14, 1937. e. UCLA. Prod. of 1967 film Harvest. Camera operator on Star Wars.
PICTURES: The Black Stallion (debut, 1979), Never Cry Wolf, Nutcracker: The Motion Picture, Wind, Fly Away Home.

BALLARD, KAYE
Actress. r.n. Catherine Gloria Balotta. b. Cleveland, OH, Nov. 20, 1926. Began career as impressionist-singer-actress, toured vaudeville. 17 recordings incl.: The Fanny Brice Story, Peanuts, Oklahoma (w/ Nelson Eddy), Unsung Sondheim, Then & Again. Appeared in short film Walking to Waldheim.
THEATER: Three to Make Ready, Carnival, Molly, The Pirates of Penzance, Hey Ma It's Me, Working 42nd Street at Last, Chicago, Touch & Go (London), Nymph Errant (concert version), Hello Dolly, She Stoops to Conquer, Funny Girl, High Spirits, Crazy Words Crazy Times: The Cole Porter-Irving Berlin Revue, Beloved Enemies.
PICTURES: The Girl Most Likely, A House is Not a Home, Which Way to the Front?, The Ritz, Freaky Friday, Falling in Love Again, Pandemonium, Tiger Warsaw, Modern Love, Eternity, The Missing Elephant (Due South).
TELEVISION: *Movies*: The Dream Merchants, Alice in Wonderland. *Series*: Henry Morgan's Great Talent Hunt, The Perry Como Show, The Mothers-in-Law, The Doris Day Show, The Steve Allen Comedy Hour, What a Dummy. Guest appearances incl. over 100 spots on The Tonight Show. *Pilot*: Makin' Out.

BALLHAUS, MICHAEL
Cinematographer. b. Berlin, Germany, Aug. 5, 1935.
PICTURES: Deine Zartlichkeiten, Two of Us, Whity, Beware of a Holy Whore, Tschetan, The Indian Boy, The Bitter Tears of Petra von Kant, Fox and His Friends, Mother Kusters Goes to Heaven, Summer Guests, Satan's Brew, I Only Want You To Love Me, Adolf and Marlene, Chinese Roulette, Bolweiser (The Stationmaster's Wife), Willie and the Chinese Cat, Women in New York, Despair, The Marriage of Maria Braun, Germany in Autumn, German Spring, The Uprising, Big and Little, Malou, Looping, Baby It's You, Friends and Husbands, Dear Mr. Wonderful, Magic Mountain, Edith's Diary, Aus der Familie der Panzereschen, The Autograph, Heartbreakers, Old Enough, Reckless, After Hours, Under the Cherry Moon, The Color of Money, The Glass Menagerie, Broadcast News, The House on Carroll Street, The Last Temptation of Christ, Working Girl, Dirty Rotten Scoundrels, The Fabulous Baker Boys, GoodFellas, Postcards from the Edge, Guilty by Suspicion, What About Bob?, The Mambo Kings, Bram Stoker's Dracula, The Age of Innocence, Quiz Show, Outbreak, Sleepers, Air Force One, Primary Colors, The Wild, Wild West.

BANCROFT, ANNE
Actress. r.n. Anna Maria Italiano. b. New York, NY, Sept. 17, 1931. m. actor-comedian Mel Brooks. e. American Acad. of Dramatic Arts. Acting debut on TV, Studio One as Anne Marno in Torrents of Spring.
THEATER: Two For the Seesaw (Tony Award, Theatre World Award; 1958), The Miracle Worker (Tony Award, 1960), Mother Courage, The Devils, A Cry of Players, Golda, Duet For One, Mystery of the Rose Bouquet, The Little Foxes.
PICTURES: Don't Bother to Knock (debut, 1952), Tonight We Sing, Treasure of the Golden Condor, The Kid from Left Field, Gorilla at Large, Demetrius and the Gladiators, The Raid, New York Confidential, Life in the Balance, The Naked Street, The Last Frontier, Walk the Proud Land, Nightfall, The Restless Breed, The Girl in Black Stockings, The Miracle Worker (Acad. Award for Best Actress, 1962), The Pumpkin Eater, The Slender Thread, Seven Women, The Graduate, Young Winston, The Prisoner of Second Avenue, The Hindenburg, Lipstick, Silent Movie, The Turning Point, Fatso (also dir., s.p.), The Elephant Man, To Be or Not to Be, Garbo Talks, Agnes of God, 'night Mother, 84 Charing Cross Road, Torch Song Trilogy, Bert Rigby You're a Fool, Honeymoon in Vegas, Love Potion No. 9, Point of No Return, Malice, Mr. Jones, How to Make an American Quilt, Home for the Holidays, Dracula–Dead & Loving It, The Sunchaser, Great Expectations, Critical Care, G.I. Jane.
TELEVISION: *Movies*: Broadway Bound, Oldest Living Confederate Widow Tells All, The Mother, Homecoming. *Mini-Series*: Jesus of Nazareth, Marco Polo. *Specials*: I'm Getting Married, Annie and the Hoods, Annie: The Women in the Life of a Man (also dir.; Emmy Award for Best Variety Special, 1970), Mrs. Cage, The Mother.

BAND, ALBERT
Producer, Director. b. Paris, France, May 7, 1924. e. Lyceum Louis le Grand, won French-English Literature Prize 1938. Entered m.p. industry as cutter Pathe Lab.; prod. ass't to John Huston at MGM. First screen credit adaptation Red Badge of Courage novel; first direction, The Young Guns. Formed Maxim Prods., Inc., Sept. 1956. Recently formed Albert Band Intl. Prods., Inc.
PICTURES: The Young Guns, I Bury the Living, Face of Fire, The Avenger, Grand Canyon Massacre, The Tramplers, The Hellbenders (prod. only), A Minute to Pray a Second to Die, Little Cigars, Mansion of the Doomed, Dracula's Dog, She Came to the Valley, Metalstorm: The Destruction of Jared-Syn, Swordkill, Buy and Cell (exec. prod. only), Troll, Terrorvision, Ghoulies II, Robot Jox, Trancers III; Honey, I Blew Up the Kid; Pet Shop, Oblivion, Oblivion 2: Backlash, Zarkorr! The Invader.

BAND, CHARLES
Producer, Director. b. Los Angeles, CA, Dec. 27, 1951. e. Overseas Sch. of Rome. Son of Albert Band. Formed Media Home Ent., 1978; formed Empire Ent., 1983; formed Full Moon Ent., 1988; formed Moonbeam Productions, 1993.
PICTURES: Prod.: Mansion of the Doomed, Cinderella, End of the World, Laserblast, Fairytales, Swordkill, Dungeonmaster, Puppet Master 4, Eliminators. Dir./Prod.: Crash, Parasite, Metalstorm, Trancers, Pulsepounders, Meridian (Kiss of the Beast), Crash & Burn, Trancers II, Dr. Mordrid, Dollman vs. Demonic Toys, Hideous, The Creeps. Exec. Prod.: Tourist Trap, Day Time Ended, Ghoulies, Re-Animator, Zone Troopers, Troll, Terrorvision, Crawlspace, Dolls, From Beyond, The Caller, Spellcaster, Cellar Dweller, Ghoulies II, Enemy Territory, Deadly Weapon, Robot Jox, Prison, Buy & Cell, Ghost Town, Catacombs, Arena, Puppet Master, Shadowzone, Puppet Master II, The Pit and the Pendulum, Subpecies, Puppet Master III, Arcade, Dollman, Netherworld, Bad Channels, Trancers III, Shrunken Heads, Oblivion, Seed People, Bad Channels, Robot Wars, Subspecies II, Mandroid, Invisible, Prehysteria, Remote, Dragonworld, Beanstalk, Pet Shop, Prehysteria II, Curse IV: The Ultimate Sacrifice, Bloodstone: Subspecies II, Puppet Master 5, Lurking Fear, Trancers 5, Castle Freak, Oblivion 2: Backlash, Magic in the Mirror.

BANDERAS, ANTONIO
Actor. b. Malaga, Spain, Aug. 10, 1960. e. School of Dramatic Art, Malaga. Moved to Madrid in 1981 where he made his stage debut in Los Tarantos. Other theatre incl.: The City and the Dogs, Daughter of the Air, The Tragedy of Edward II of England.
PICTURES: Labyrinth of Passion (debut, 1982), Pesantas Positzas, Y Del Seguro... Libranos Senor!, Pestanas Positzas, El Senor Galindez, El Caso Almeria, Los Zancos, Casa Cerrado, La Corte de Faraon, Requiem por un Campesino Espanol, 27 Horas, Puzzle, Matador, Asi Como Habian Sido, Law of Desire, The Pleasure of Killing, Baton Rouge, Bajarse Al Moro, Women on the Verge of a Nervous Breakdown, Si Te Dicen Que Cai, Tie Me Up! Tie Me Down!, Contra el Viento, La Blanca Paloma, Truth or Dare, The Mambo Kings, Philadelphia, Dispara, Of Love and Shadows, The House of the Spirits, Interview With the Vampire, Miami Rhapsody, Desperado, Four Rooms, Never Talk to Strangers, Two Much, Assassins, Evita.
TELEVISION: La llave de Hierro, Fragmentos de Interior, La Mujer de Tu Vida.

BANDY, MARY LEA
Director, Dept. of Film, Museum of Modern Art. b. Evanston, IL, June 16, 1943. e. Stanford U., B.A., 1965. Asst. editor, Harry Abrams and Museum of Modern Art dir., 1980-93; chief Curator 1993-. Dept. of Film, Museum of Modern Art Editor of MOMA film publications incl.: Rediscovering French Film (1983). Member: Advisory Bd., AFI's National Center for Preservation of Film and Video; Film Advisory Comm., American Federation of Arts; Advisory Comm. on Film, Japan Society; Advisory Comm., NY State Motion Picture and Television. Co-pres., National Alliance of Media Arts Center, 1986-88. Bd. mem.: Intl. Film Seminars; MacDowell Colony; Natl. Film Preservation Bd.; Library of Congress; Advisory Board, Film Foundation; Bd. of dirs., Third World Newsreel.

BANERJEE, VICTOR
Actor. b. Calcutta, India, Oct. 15, 1946. Was instrumental in forming the first Screen Extras Union in India, presently founding secretary. Won international recognition for A Passage to India. On stage in: Pirates of Penzance, An August Requiem (dir., 1981), Desert Song, Godspell.
PICTURES: The Chess Players (debut), Hullabaloo, Madhurban, Tanaya, Pratidan, Prarthana, Dui Prithri, Kalyug, Arohan, Jaipur Junction (German), A Passage to India, Foreign Body, The Home and the World, Hard to Be a God, Bitter Moon, Mahaprithivi.
TELEVISION: Movie: Dadah Is Death.

BANNEN, IAN
Actor. b. Airdrie, Scotland, June 29, 1928. Early career Shakespeare Memorial Theatre (now RSC), Stratford-on-Avon. THEATER: A View From the Bridge, The Iceman Cometh, Long Days Journey Into Night, Sergeant Musgrave's Dance. Royal Shakespeare Thea. Co. 1961-62. Toys in the Attic, Hamlet, As You Like It (with Vanessa Redgrave), Romeo and Juliet, Othello, The Blood Knot, Devil's Disciple, The Iceman Cometh, Hedda Gabler, Translations (Drama Critics Award, 1981); Riverside Mermaid Theatres, 1983; Moon for the Misbegotten (London, Boston, Broadway), All My Sons.
PICTURES: Private's Progress (debut, 1956), The Third Key (The Long Arm), Battle Hell (Yangtse Incident), Miracle in Soho, The Birthday Present, Behind the Mask, A Tale of Two Cities, She Didn't Say No, The French Mistress, Carlton-Browne of the F.O. (Man in Cocked Hat), On Friday at 11, A French Mistress, The Risk (Suspect), Macbeth, Station Six Sahara, Psyche 59, Mister Moses, Rotten to the Core, The Hill, The Flight of the Phoenix (Acad. Award nom.), Penelope, Sailor From Gibraltar, Lock Up Your Daughters!, Too Late the Hero, The Deserter, Fright, Doomwatch, The Offence (BAFTA nom.), The Macintosh Man, The Driver's Seat, The Voyage, Bite the Bullet, From Beyond the Grave, Sweeney!, Inglorious Bastards, Ring of Darkness, The Watcher in the Woods, Eye of the Needle, Night Crossing, Gandhi, The Prodigal, Gorky Park, Defense of the Realm, Lamb, Hope and Glory (BAFTA nom.), The Courier, The Match, Ghost Dad, Crossing the Line (The Big Man), George's Island, The Gamble, Damage, A Pin for the Butterfly, Braveheart, Dead Sea Reels, Something to Believe In, Waking Ned Devine.
TELEVISION: Johnny Belinda, Jane Eyre, Jesus of Nazareth, Tinker Tailor Soldier Spy, Dr. Jekyll and Mr. Hyde, Fifteen Streets, Murder in Eden, Ashenden, Uncle Vanya, The Sound and the Silence, The Treaty, Doctor Finlay, The Politician's Wife, Original Sin.

BANNER, BOB
Producer, Director. b. Ennis, TX, Aug. 15, 1921. e. Southern Methodist U., B.A., 1939-43; Northwestern U., M.A., 1946-48. U.S. Naval Reserve 1943-46. Faculty, Northwestern U., 1948-50. Staff dir., NBC-TV in Chicago, 1949-50. Pres., Bob Banner Assocs. Visiting Prof.: Southern Methodist U.
TELEVISION: Movies: Mongo's Back in Town, The Last Survivors, Journey From Darkness, My Sweet Charlie, Bud and Lou, Yes Virginia There is a Santa Claus, Crash Landing, With Murder in Mind, The Sea Wolf, Angel Flight Down. Series: Almost Anything Goes, Solid Gold, Star Search, It's Showtime at the Apollo, Uptown Comedy Club. Specials: Garroway at Large (dir.), Fred Waring Show (prod., dir.), Omnibus (dir.), Nothing But the Best (prod. dir.), Dave Garroway Show (prod. dir), Dinah Shore Show, Garry Moore Show (exec. prod.), Candid Camera TV Show (exec. prod.), Carnegie Hall Salutes Jack Benny (exec. prod.), Julie & Carol at Carnegie Hall, Carol & Co., Jimmy Dean Show, Calamity Jane, Once Upon a Mattress, The Entertainers, Kraft Summer Music Hall, Carol & Co., Ice Follies, Carol Burnett Show, Peggy Fleming at Madison Square Garden, John Davidson at Notre Dame, Here's Peggy Fleming, Peggy Fleming at Sun Valley, The American West of John Ford, Love! Love! Love!—Hallmark Hall of Fame, To Europe with Love, Peggy Fleming Visits the Soviet Union, Perry Como's Lake Tahoe Holiday, Perry Como's Christmas In Mexico, Perry Como's Hawaiian Holiday, Perry Como's Spring In New Orleans, Don Ho Show, Perry Como Las Vegas Style, Perry Como's Christmas in Austria, All-Star Anything Goes, Peggy Fleming and Holiday on Ice at Madison Square Garden, Julie Andrews, One Step Into Spring, Leapin' Lizards, It's Liberace, Perry Como's Easter By The Sea, Ford Motor Company's 75th Anniversary; Gift of Music, specials starring Bob Hope, Julie Andrews, Andy Williams, Los Angeles Music Center 25th Anniversay, Amazing Music Series, Happy Birthday George Gershwin.

BAR, JACQUES JEAN LOUIS
Executive, Producer, Exhibitor. b. Chateauroux, France, Sept. 12, 1921. e. Lycees Lakanal and Saint Louis, France. Formed Citae-Films S.A., 1947; CIPRA in assoc. with MGM, 1961; S.C.B., Bourges, 8 cinemas; S.C.M., Le Mans, 9 cinemas. Hollywood films incl.: Bridge to the Sun, Once A Thief, Guns for San Sebastian. Prod. 57 films in France, Spain, Italy, Switzerland, Japan and Brazil 1948-89.
PICTURES: Where the Hot Wind Blows, Bridge to the Sun, Rififi in Tokyo, A Very Private Affair, Swordsmen of Siena, Monkey in Winter, The Turfist, Any Number Can Win, The Day and the Hour, Joy House, Guns for San Sebastian, Last Known Address, The Homecoming, Dancing Machine, The Candidate, Once a Thief, My Father the Hero.

BARANSKI, CHRISTINE
Actress. b. Buffalo, NY, May 2, 1952. e. Juilliard Sch. of Music & Dramatic Arts.
THEATER: NY: Private Lives, One Crack Out, Says I Says He, Shadow of a Gunman, Hide and Seek (B'way debhut, 1980), Company, Coming Attractions, Operation Midnight Climax, A Midsummer Night's Dream (Obie Award, 1982), Sally and Marsha, The Real Thing (Tony Award, 1984), Hurlyburly, It's Only a Play, The House of Blue Leaves, Rumors (Tony Award, 1989), Elliot Loves, Nick and Nora, Lips Together Teeth Apart, The Loman Family Picnic.
PICTURES: Soup for One (debut, 1982), Lovesick, Crackers, Nine 1/2 Weeks, Legal Eagles, The Pick-Up Artist, Reversal of Fortune, The Night We Never Met, Life With Mikey, Addams Family Values, New Jersey Drive, Jeffrey, Birdcage, Odd Couple II, The Ref.
TELEVISION: Series: Cybill (Emmy Award, 1995). Movie: Playing for Time, To Dance With the White Dog. Special: The Addams Chronicles.

BARBEAU, ADRIENNE
Actress. b. Sacramento, CA, June 11, 1947. e. Foothill Col.
THEATER: B'way: Fiddler on the Roof, Grease (Tony nom., Theatre World Award). L.A.: Women Behind Bars, Strange Snow, Pump Boys & Dinettes, Drop Dead. Canadian Premiere: Lost in Yonkers. Regional: Love Letters, Best Little Whorehouse in Texas.
PICTURES: The Fog, Cannonball Run, Escape From New York, Swamp Thing, Creepshow, The Next One, Back to School, Open House, Two Evil Eyes, Cannibal Women & the Avocado Jungle of Death, Father Hood.
TELEVISION: Movies: The Great Houdinis, Having Babies, Red Alert, Return to Fantasy Island, Crash, Someone's Watching Me!, The Darker Side of Terror, The Top of the Hill, Valentine Magic on Love Island, Tourist, Charlie and the Great Balloon Chase, Seduced, Bridge Across Time, Blood River, Double Crossed, The Burden of Proof, The Parsley Garden, Jailbreakers, Bram Stoker's Burial of the Rats. Guest: Quincy, 8 Is Enough, Tony Orlando and Dawn, The David Frost Special, Bobby Vinton Show, FBI, Head of the Class, Love Boat, Hotel, Twlight Zone, Murder She Wrote, Dream On, Daddy Dearest, The Carlin Show, Babylon 5. Series: Maude, Batman (voice).

BARBER, FRANCES
Actress. b. Wolverhampton, England, May 13, 1957. e. Bangor U.; grad. studies in theatre, Cardiff U. Stage experience with fringe theaters including improvisational troupe Hull Truck Theatre Company, Glasgow Citizens and Tricycle Theatre (Killburn) before joining Royal Shakespeare Co. (Camille, Hamlet).
PICTURES: The Missionary (debut, 1982), A Zed and Two Noughts, White City, Castaway, Prick Up Your Ears, Sammy and Rosie Get Laid, We Think the World of You, The Grasscutter, Separate Bedrooms, Young Soul Rebels, Secret Friends; Soft Top, Hard Shoulder; Germaine and Benjamin, Giorgino, Tea, Photographing Fairies.
TELEVISION: Clem, Jackie's Story, Home Sweet Home, Flame to the Phoenix, Reilly, Ace of Spies, Those Glory Glory Days; Hard Feelings, Behaving Badly, The Nightmare Years, The Leaving of Liverpool, Three Steps to Heaven, A Royal Scandal, The Ice House. Mini-Series: Rhodes, Real Women.

BARBER, GARY
Executive Producer. COO, Morgan Creek Prod.; pres. Morgan Creek Int'l.
PICTURES: Midnight Crossing, Communion, Young Guns II, Pacific Heights, Robin Hood: Prince of Thieves, Freejack, White Sands, The Crush, True Romance, Imaginary Crimes, Ace Ventura: Pet Detective, Chasers, Silent Fall, Trial by Jury, Ace Ventura: When Nature Calls, Two if by Sea, Big Bully, Diabolique, Bad Moon, Wild America, Incognito, Major League: Back to the Minors.

BARBERA, JOSEPH R.
Executive. b. New York, NY, Mar. 24, 1911. e. NYU, American Institute of Banking. After schooling joined Irving Trust Co. in N.Y.; started submitting cartoon drawings to leading magazines selling one to Collier's. Joined Van Buren Assocs. as sketch artist, later going to work in animation dept. of MGM Studios. At MGM met William Hanna, who became his lifelong business associate. Made first animated short together in 1937, starting the famous Tom & Jerry series which they produced for 20 years. Left MGM in 1957 to form Hanna-Barbera Productions to make cartoons for TV. Hanna-Barbera became a subsidiary of Taft Ent. Co. in 1968 with both men operating the studio under long-term agreements with Taft. Taft and the studio were sold to Great American Broadcasting, 1988. Hanna-Barbera Prods. acquired by Turner Bdcstg. System, 1991; Barbera is co-founder, chmn. Team received Governor's Award from the Acad. of Television Arts & Sciences, 1988.
PICTURES: Hey There It's Yogi Bear, A Man Called Flintstone, Charlotte's Web, C.H.O.M.P.S., Heidi's Song, Jetsons: The Movie, The Flintstones (exec. prod. of live action film; also cameo appearance).

BARBOUR, ALAN G.
Writer, Editor, Publisher. b. Oakland, CA, July 25, 1933. e. Rutgers U. m. Catherine Jean Callovini, actress, Teacher, AADA, American Mime Theatre. U.S. Army, worked as computer programmer. Formed Screen Facts Press in 1963, Screen Facts Magazine. Compiled, edited: The Serials of Republic, The Serials of Columbia, Great Serial Ads, The B Western, Serial Showcase, Hit the Saddle, The Wonderful World of B-Films, Days of Thrills and Adventure, Serial Quarterly, Serial Pictorial, Karloff—A Pictorial History, Errol Flynn—A Pictorial Biography, A Pictorial History of the Serial, A Thousand and One Delights, Cliffhanger, The Old-Time Radio Quiz Book. Direct Mktg. Div., RCA Records. Mgr., A & R, RCA, BMGVideo Club.

BARBOUR, MALCOLM
Executive. b. London, England, May 3, 1934. e. Radley Coll., Oxford, England, A.B., Columbia Coll. At National Broadcasting Co., was press info. asst., 1958-59; asst. magazine ed., 1959-62; assoc. mag. ed., 1962-64; sr. mag. ed., 1964-65; mgr. of magazine pub., 1965-67. Pub. mgr., Buena Vista, 1967-68; relations, Buena Vista, 1969. Eastern story ed., Walt Disney Prod., 1968-69; dir. of adv. & pub. Partner, Producers Creative Services, 1976-79. Pres., The International Picture Show, 1980-81 (Tim Conway comedies The Billion Dollar Hobo and They Went That-A-Way & That-A-Way; Slayer. Distributor: Soldier of Orange, The Magic of Lassie, The Visitor, etc.). Pres., Barbour/Langley Productions, 1982-present. Prod., Geraldo Rivera specials: American Vice, Innocence Lost, Sons of Scarface, Murder: Live from Death Row, Satan Worship. Prod., Jack Anderson specials. Writer, prod., Cocaine Blues. Co-screenplay, P.O.W. The Escape. Exec. producer: Cops, Code 3, Inside the KGB, Cop Files, Deadly Sins (also writer).

BARCLAY, PARIS
Director, Actor.
PICTURES: America's Dream, Don't Be a Menace to South Central While Drinking Your Juice in the Hood.
TELEVISION: Movies: The Cherokee Kid (also actor). Series: NYPD Blue (Emmy Award, 1998), Diagnosis: Murder, ER, Sliders, Clueless, Brooklyn South.

BARDEN, EARL
Executive. b. 1941. e. Whitworth Coll. Hist./Educ., 1963. Began career as doorman at Yakima Theatre, Yakima, WA. Became gen'l mgr. of Yakima Theatres, Inc., 1968. VP, 1979. Pres. Yakima Audio Svcs. Co., 1974.

BARDOT, BRIGITTE
Actress. b. Paris, France, Sept. 28, 1934. e. Paris Conservatory. Studied ballet, before becoming model. Studied acting with Rene Simon. On stage in L'Invitation au Chateau. Awarded French Legion of Honor, 1985. Active in the movement to preserve endangered animals. Created the Brigitte Bardot Foundation for animal protection, April 1986.
PICTURES: Le Trou Normand (debut, 1952), Nanina la Fille san Voiles, Les Dents Longues, Act of Love, Le Portrait de Son Pere, Royal Affairs in Versailles, Tradita, Le Fils de Caroline Cherie, Helen of Troy, Futures Vedettes, Les Grandes Maneuvres, Doctor at Sea, La Lumiere d'En Face (The Light Across the Street), Cette Sacre Gamine (Mam'zelle Pigalle), Mi Figlio Nerone, En Effeuillant la Marguerite (Please Mr. Balzac), The Bride is Much Too Beautiful, And God Created Woman, Une Parisienne, The Night Heaven Fell, En Cas de Malheur, Le Femme et le Pantin, Babette Goes to War, Come Dance With Me, La Verite (The Truth), La Bride sur le Cou, Les Amours Celebres, A Very Private Affair, Love on a Pillow, Contempt, A Ravishing Idiot, Dear Brigitte, Viva Maria, Masculine-Feminine, Two Weeks in September, Spirits of the Dead (Histories Extraordinaires), Shalako, Les Femmes, L'Ours et la Poupee, Les Novices, Boulevard du Rhum (Rum Runner), Les Petroleuses (The Legend of Frenchie King), Ms. Don Juan, L'Historie Tres Bonne et Tres Joyeuse de Colinot Troussechemise.

BARE, RICHARD L.
Producer, Director. b. Turlock, CA. Started as dir. for Warners. SDG Best Dir. TV award, 1959. Author of The Film Director (Macmillan, 1971). Pres., United National Film Corp.
PICTURES: Director: Smart Girls Don't Talk, Flaxy Martin, This Side of the Law, House Across The Street, This Rebel Breed, Girl on the Run, Return of Frontiersman. Dir./Prod./Writer: Wicked Wicked, Story of Chang & Eng, City of Shame, Sudden Target, Purple Moon.
TELEVISION: 77 Sunset Strip, Maverick, So This is Hollywood, The Islanders, Dangerous Robin, This Rebel Breed, Twilight Zone, Bus Stop, Adventures in Paradise, The Virginian, Kraft Theatre, Run For Your Life, Green Acres, Faraday and Son, Westwind.

BAREN, HARVEY M.
Executive. b. New York, NY, Nov. 25, 1931. e. State U. of New York. Served in U.S. Army, 1952-54. United Artists Corp., 1954-59 (contract dept., print dept., booker—NY branch). Asst. to general sls. mgr., Magna Pictures Corp., 1959-61. Road show mgr., nat'l. sls. coordinator, 20th Century-Fox, 1961-71. Asst. general sls. manager, Allied Artists Pictures, 1971-79. V.p., gen. sls. mgr., Nat'l. Screen Service, 1978-79. V.p., gen. sls. mgr., Cannon Pictures, 1979-80. Pres. of Summit Feature Distributors, 1980. Exec. v.p., dir., MGM/UA Classics, 1983. Joined New Century/Vista as v.p., sls. admin, 1986. Pres., Sea Movies Inc., 1991.

BARENHOLTZ, BEN
Executive. b. Kovel, Poland, Oct. 5, 1935. Asst. theatre mngr., RKO Bushwick, Brooklyn, 1959-60. Mngr., Village Theatre, NY, 1966-68. Owner, operator, Elgin Cinema, 1968-75; originated Midnight Movie concept with El Topo. Pres., owner., Libra Film Corp., 1972-84. V.p.& partner, Circle Releasing (which launched and distributed The Family Game, Therese, Blood Simple and prod. Raising Arizona) 1984-1992. Pres., Barenholtz Prods. Inc.
PICTURES: Exec. Prod.: Miller's Crossing, Barton Fink, Cheat, White Man's Burden (Bleeding Hearts), Georgia.

BARISH, KEITH
Producer. b. Los Angeles, CA. Background in finance. Founded Keith Barish Prods., 1979. In partnership with Taft Broadcasting Co., Entertainment Div., 1984-88. Founder and chmn. of Planet Hollywood. Appeared in film Last Action Hero.
PICTURES: Exec. prod.: Endless Love, Sophie's Choice (prod.), Kiss Me Goodbye, Misunderstood, Nine 1/2 Weeks, Big Trouble in Little China, Light of Day (prod.), The Running Man, The Monster Squad, Ironweed (prod.), The Serpent and the Rainbow, Her Alibi, Firebirds, The Fugitive, U.S. Marshals.
TELEVISION: Movie: A Streetcar Named Desire (exec. prod.).

BARKER, BOB
TV host. b. Darrington, WA, Dec. 12. e. Springfield Central H.S., Drury Coll. News writer, announcer, disc jockey KTTS until 1949. News editor, staff announcer, Station WWPG. Pres. Bob Barker Prod., Inc. Started as M.C. for both Miss USA Pageant and Miss Universe Pageant, 1966. First time as M.C. of both Rose Bowl Parade and Pillsbury Bakeoff. Series, 1970.
TELEVISION: Emcee or host: The End of the Rainbow, Truth or Consequences (daytime: 1956-65; nighttime synd: 1966-74), Lucky Pair (prod.), That's My Line (1980-1), The Price Is Right (exec. prod. & m.c.; 1972-; received several Emmy Awards as host). Narrator: 500 Festival Parade, Indianapolis 1969-81.

BARKER, CLIVE
Writer, Producer, Director. b. Liverpool, England, Oct. 5, 1952. e. Liverpool Univ. Moved to London at twenty-one, forming theatre company. Began writing short stories which were subsequently published as Books of Blood (Vols. 1-3 & Vols. 4-6). Author of: Novels: Damnation Game, Weaveworld, The Great and Secret Show, Imajica, The Thief of Always, Everville, Sacrament. Books: Clive Barker: Illustrator, The Art of Clive Barker, Incarnations. Plays: History of the Devil, Colossus, Frankenstein In Love. Painter with exhibitions in NY, California.
PICTURES: Rawhead Rex (from his story), Transmutations (from his story), Hellraiser (dir., s.p.: from his novella The Hellbound Heart), Hellbound: Hellraiser II (co-exec. prod.; from his story), Nightbreed (dir., s.p.; from his novel Cabal), Sleepwalkers (actor), Hellraiser III: Hell on Earth (exec. prod.; from his story), Candyman (exec. prod.; from his story The Forbidden), Candyman: Farewell to the Flesh (exec. prod.; from his story), Lord of Illusions (dir., s.p., co-prod.; from his story The Last Illusion).

BARKER, MICHAEL W.
Executive. B.b. Nuremberg, Germany, Jan. 9, 1954. e. U. of Texas at Austin, B.S. in International Communications, 1976. Joined Films Inc. 1979-80; then United Artists 1980-83, first as non-theatrical sls. mngr., then as nat'l. sls. mngr. of UA Classics. Co-founder and v.p., sls. & mktg. for Orion Classics, a div. of Orion, 1983-1992. Co-founder and co-pres., Sony Pictures Classics, 1992-present. Member bd. of dirs. of BAFTA NY, and Independent Features Project.

BARKETT, STEVE
Actor, Director, Producer, Film Editor, Writer. b. Oklahoma City, OK, Jan. 1, 1950. Exhibited and scored over 52 feature length classic silent films 1966-1968 as dir. of two film series at the Oklahoma Art Center and Science and Arts Foundation, prior to coming to LA in 1970. Toured in stage prod. 1971-72: Pajama Tops, Winnie the Pooh. Exec. in several non-theatrical releasing cos., incl. Independent Film Associates and Thunderbird Films. Active in film preservation and restoration work on early silent and sound films, 1968-1974. Founded The Hollywood Book and Poster Company, 1978; established The Nautilus Film Co., 1978. Founded and operated Capt. Nemo's Video, 1985-87; co-wrote and performed 42 episodes of Capt. Nemo's Video Review for radio, 1987.

PICTURES: Actor: The Egyptians are Coming, Corpse Grinders, Dillinger, Night Caller, Cruise Missile, Beverly Hills Vampire, Wizard of the Demon Sword, Bikini Drive-In, Cyber Zone, Hard Bounty, Masseuse, Star Hunter, Rapid Assault. Prod./Dir./S.P./Edit.: Collecting, Empire of the Dark, Angels of Death. Also Actor: The Movie People, Cassavetes, The Aftermath, Angels of Death, Empire of the Dark. Actor/FX: Dark Universe, Dinosaur Island, Attack of the 60's Centerfold, Invisible Mom. FX Only: Warlords, Sorceress. Editor only: Hurricane Express.

BARKIN, ELLEN
Actress. b. Bronx, NY, Apr. 16, 1954. e. Hunter Coll.; Actors Studio.
THEATER: Irish Coffee (debut, Ensemble Studio Theatre), Shout Across the River, Killings Across the Last, Tobacco Road, Extremities, Eden Court.
PICTURES: Diner (debut, 1982), Tender Mercies, Daniel, Eddie and the Cruisers, Harry and Son, The Adventures of Buckaroo Banzai Across the Eighth Dimension, Enormous Changes at the Last Minute, Terminal Choice, Desert Bloom, Down by Law, The Big Easy, Siesta, Made in Heaven (unbilled), Sea of Love, Johnny Handsome, Switch, Man Trouble, Mac, This Boy's Life, Into the West, Bad Company, Wild Bill, Mad Dog Time, Fear and Loathing in Las Vegas, Popcorn, Dairy Queens.
TELEVISION: Movies: Kent State, We're Fighting Back, Parole, Terrible Joe Moran, Act of Vengeance, Clinton and Nadine, Before Women Had Wings (Emmy Award, 1998). Series: Search for Tomorrow. Special: Faerie Tale Theatre (The Princess Who Never Laughed), Before Women Had Wings.

BARLOW, PHIL
Executive. President, Buena Vista Pictures Distribution.

BARNHOLTZ, BARRY
Executive. b. St. Louis, MO, Oct. 12, 1945. e. California State U., Northridge; USC; UCLA; WLAU, studied law. Concert promotions in So. Calif. 1963-71. With Medallion TV as v.p. in chg. sls. Barnholtz Organization, representing ind't. prod. cos. for feature films for cable. Founder, sr. v.p. of Vidmark Inc., and Trimark Films.

BARONE, TRACY
Producer. b. Nov. 1, 1962. m. actor Paul Michael Glaser.
PICTURES: Writer's Block (writer). Exec prod.: Money Train, My Fellow Americans, Rosewood.

BARR, ANTHONY
Producer, Director, Actor. r.n. Morris Yaffe. b. St. Louis, MO, March 14, 1921. e. Washington U., B.S. 1942. Actor, asst. stage mgr., 1944-46; stage mgr., Katherine Dunham Dancers, 1946-47. Teacher, actor, dir. in chg. Film Actors' Workshop, Professional Theatre Workshop, Hollywood. V.p. current prime time series, ABC-TV. V.p., current dramatic program production, CBS-TV; v.p., CBS Entertainment Prods. Author of Acting for the Camera, 1982.
THEATER: Jacobowsky and the Colonel, Winters' Tale, Embezzled Heaven.
PICTURES: Actor: People Against O'Hara, Border Incident, The Hollywood Story, The Mozart Story. Co-prod.: Dime with a Halo.
TELEVISION: Director: Art Linkletter's Houseparty, About Faces. Assoc. dir.: Climax, Shower of Stars. Producer.: Climax, Summer Studio One. Assoc. prod.: Climax, Playhouse 90, Pursuit, G.E. Theatre, The Law and Mr. Jones, Four-Star.

BARR, JULIA
Actress. b. Ft. Wayne, IN, Feb. 8, 1949.
PICTURES: I, the Jury.
TELEVISION: Series: All My Children (Emmy Awards, 1990, 1998), Ryan's Hope.

BARRAULT, MARIE-CHRISTINE
Actress. b. Paris, France, March 21, 1944. m. dir. Roger Vadim.
PICTURES: My Night at Maud's, Le Distrait (The Daydreamer), Lancelot of the Lake, The Aspern Papers, Les Intrus, La Famille Grossfeld, Chloe in the Afternoon, John Glueckstadt, Cousin Cousine (Acad. Award nom.), By the Tennis Courts, Perceval, The Medusa Touch, Tout est a nous, Femme Entre Chien et Loup, Ma Cherie, Stardust Memories, Table for Five, Josephs Tochter, A Love in Germany, Les Mots Pour le Dire, Swann in Love, Grand Piano, Prisonnieres, Un Etae de orages, Savage State, Necessary Love.

BARRETT, RONA
News Correspondent b. New York, NY, Oct. 8, 1936. e. NYU (communications major). Created the column, Rona Barrett's Young Hollywood, which led to featured column in 1960 in Motion Picture Magazine and a nationally syndicated column distributed to 125 newspapers by the North American Newspaper Alliance. Turned to TV; initial appearances on ABC Owned Stations in 5 cities, providing two-minute reports for local newscasts. Resulted in Dateline Hollywood a network morning prog., co-hosted by Joanna Barnes. 1969, created first daily syndicated TV news segment for Metromedia. 1975, became arts and entertainment editor for ABC's Good Morning America. 1980, joined NBC News. Publ. and exec. editor, newsletter, The Rona Barrett Report. 1985, pres., Rona Barrett Enterprises, Inc.; sr. corresp., Entertainment Tonight; Mutual Radio Network. 1988, creator of original novels for television, for NBC prods. Appeared in films Sextette, An Almost Perfect Affair.

BARRIE, BARBARA
Actress. b. Chicago, IL, May 23, 1931. e. U. of TX, B.F.A., 1953. Trained for stage at Herbert Berghof Studio. NY stage debut, The Wooden Dish, 1955. Author of, Lone Star (1990), Adam Zigzag (1994), Second Act (1997).
THEATER: The Crucible, The Beaux Stratagem, The Taming of the Shrew, Conversations in the Dark, All's Well That Ends Well, Happily Never After, Horseman Pass By, Company, The Selling of the President, The Prisoner of Second Avenue, The Killdeer, California Suite, Big and Little, Isn't It Romantic, Torch Song Trilogy, Fugue, After-play.
PICTURES: Giant (debut, 1956), The Caretakers, One Potato Two Potato (best actress, Cannes Film Fest, 1964), The Bell Jar, Breaking Away (Acad. nom.), Private Benjamin, Real Men, End of the Line, The Passage.
TELEVISION: Movies: Tell Me My Name, Summer of My German Soldier, To Race the Wind, The Children Nobody Wanted, Not Just Another Affair, Two of a Kind, The Execution, Vital Signs, Winnie, My First Love, Guess Who's Coming for Christmas?, The Odd Couple: Together Again, My Breast. Series: Love of Life, Diana, Barney Miller, Breaking Away, Tucker's Witch, Reggie, Double Trouble, Love of Life, Big City Story, Suddenly Susan. Mini-Series: 79 Park Avenue, Backstairs at the White House, Roots: The Next Generation, Scarlett. Guest: Ben Casey, The Fugitive, Dr. Kildare, Alfred Hitchcock Presents, The Defenders, Mary Tyler Moore Show, Lou Grant, Trapper John, M.D., Babes, Kojak, Island Son, thirtysomething. Specials: To Be Young Gifted and Black, Barefoot in the Park, What's Alan Watching?, Lovejoy: The Lost Colony, My Summer As a Girl.

BARRON, ARTHUR RAY
Executive. b. Mt. Lake, MN, July 12, 1934. e. San Diego State U. 1956-60, B.S. Accounting. Certified public acc't, Calif., 1960. Coopers & Lybrand, 1960-63; Desilu Productions, Inc., 1963-67. V.p. finance and admin., Paramount TV, 1967-70; v.p. finance, Paramount Pictures Corp., 1970; sr. v.p. finance and admin., 1971; exec. v.p., finance & admin., 1974; exec. v.p 1980. Exec. v.p., Gulf & Western Industries, entertainment & communications group, 1983; promoted to pres., 1984-88. Chmn, Time Warner Enterprises, 1990.

BARRY, GENE
Actor. r.n. Eugene Klass. b. New York, NY. e. New Utrecht H.S., Brooklyn.
BROADWAY: Rosalinda, Catherine Was Great, Happy As Larry, Bless You All, The Would-Be Gentleman, La Cage aux Folles (Tony nom.).
PICTURES: Atomic City (debut, 1952), The Girls of Pleasure Island, The War of the Worlds, Those Redheads From Seattle, Alaska Seas, Red Garters, Naked Alibi, Soldier of Fortune, The Purple Mask, The Houston Story, Back From Eternity, China Gate, The 27th Day, Forty Guns, Thunder Road, Hong Kong Confidential, Maroc 7, Subterfuge, The Second Coming of Suzanne, Guyana: Cult of the Damned.
TELEVISION: Movies: Prescription Murder, Istanbul Express, Do You Take This Stranger?, The Devil and Miss Sarah, Ransom for Alice!, A Cry for Love, The Girl the Gold Watch and Dynamite, Adventures of Nellie Bly, Turn Back the Clock. Mini-Series: Aspen. Series: Our Miss Brooks, Bat Masterson, Burke's Law (1963-66), The Name of the Game, Burke's Law (1994-95).

BARRY, JOHN
Composer, Arranger, Conductor. r.n. John Barry Prendergast. b. York, England, 1933. Started as rock 'n' roll trumpeter. Artist and prod., CBS Records.
PICTURES: Beat Girl, Never Let Go, The L-Shaped Room, The Amorous Mr. Prawn, From Russia With Love, Seance on a Wet Afternoon, Zulu, Goldfinger, The Ipcress File, The Knack, King Rat, Mister Moses, Thunderball, The Chase, Born Free (2 Acad. Awards: Best Music Scoring and Best Song: title song, 1966), The Wrong Box, The Quiller Memorandum, The Whisperers, Deadfall, You Only Live Twice, Petulia, The Lion in Winter (Acad. Award, 1968), Midnight Cowboy, The Appointment, On Her Majesty's Secret Service, Monte Walsh, The Last Valley, They Might Be Giants, Murphy's War, Walkabout, Diamonds Are Forever, Mary Queen of Scots, Alice's Adventures in Wonderland, The Public Eye (Follow Me), A Doll's House, The Tamarind Seed, The Dove, The Man With the Golden Gun, The Day of the Locust, Robin and Marian, King Kong, The Deep, The Betsy, Hanover Street, Moonraker, The Black Hole, Starcrash, Game of Death, Raise the Titanic, Somewhere in Time, Inside Moves, Touched By Love, Body Heat, The Legend of the Lone Ranger, Frances, Hammett, High Road to China, Octopussy, The Golden Seal, Mike's Murder, Until September, The Cotton Club, A View to a Kill, Jagged Edge, Out of Africa (Acad. Award, 1985), Howard the Duck, Peggy Sue Got Married, The Living Daylights, Hearts of Fire, Masquerade, A Killing Affair, Dances With Wolves (Acad. Award, 1990), Chaplin, Indecent Proposal, Deception, My Life, The Specialist.
TELEVISION: Elizabeth Taylor in London, Sophia Loren in Rome.

BARRYMORE, DREW
Actress. b. Los Angeles, CA, Feb. 22, 1975. Father is actor John Barrymore, Jr. (John Drew Barrymore). At 11 months appeared in first commercial. Author of Little Girl Lost (1990).
PICTURES: Altered States (debut, 1980), E.T.: The Extra Terrestrial, Firestarter, Irreconcilable Differences, Cat's Eye, See You in the Morning, Far From Home, No Place to Hide, Waxwork II, Poison Ivy, Motorama, Doppelganger, Wayne's World 2, Bad Girls, Inside the Goldmine, Boys on the Side, Mad Love, Batman Forever, Everyone Says I Love You, Scream, Wishful Thinking, All She Wanted, Best Man, Never Been Kissed (also prod.), Home Fries, The Wedding Singer, Ever After: A Cinderella Story, Planet Ice (voice).
TELEVISION: Movies: Bogie, Suddenly Love, Babes in Toyland, Conspiracy of Love, The Sketch Artist, Guncrazy (also released theatrically), The Amy Fisher Story. Series: 2000 Malibu Road. Specials: Disneyland's 30th Anniversary, Night of 100 Stars II, Con Sawyer and Hucklemary Finn, 15 & Getting Straight.

BARRYMORE, JOHN DREW
Actor. r.n. John Blythe Barrymore Jr. b. Beverly Hills, CA, June 4, 1932. e. St. John's Military Acad., various public and private schools. Son of actors John Barrymore and Delores Costello. Daughter is actress Drew Barrymore. Started acting at age 18 under the name John Barrymore Jr.
PICTURES: Sundowners (debut, 1950), High Lonesome, Quebec, The Big Night, Thunderbirds, While the City Sleeps, Shadow on the Window, Never Love a Stranger, High School Confidential, Night of the Quarter Moon, The Cossacks, The Night They Killed Rasputin, The Pharaoh's Woman, The Trojan Horse, The Centurion, Invasion 1700, War of the Zombies.

BART, PETER
Executive. b. Martha's Vineyard, MA, July 24, 1932. e. Swarthmore Coll. and The London School of Economics. Eight years as corrp. for New York Times and wrote for such magazines as Harper's, The Atlantic, Saturday Review, etc. Joined Paramount Pictures in 1965. Named exec. ass't. to Robert Evans, exec. in charge of world-wide prod. Appointed v.p. prod. Resigned 1973 to develop and produce own films for Paramount. Appointed pres. Lorimar Films, 1978. Resigned, 1979, to be indept. prod. 1983, joined MGM as sr. v.p., prod., m.p. div. Resigned, 1985, to be indep. prod. Editor, Variety. Author of novels: Thy Kingdom Come (1983), Destinies (1979), Fade Out.
PICTURES: Producer: Islands in the Stream, Fun with Dick and Jane, Revenge of the Nerds (exec. prod.), Youngblood, Revenge of the Nerds II.

BARTEK, STEVE
Composer, orchestrator. Co-founded musical group Oingo Boingo with composer Danny Elfman. With group performed in film Back to School.
PICTURES: Composer: Guilty as Charged, Cabin Boy, Coldblooded, Romy and Michele's High School Reunion, Meet the Deedles (also act.). Orchestrator: Forbidden Zone, Beetlejuice, Batman, Nightbreed, Darkman, Edward Scissorhands, Batman Returns, Tim Burton's The Nightmare Before Christmas. Also songs: Sommersby, Dolores Claiborne, Black Beauty , To Die For, Dead Presidents, The Frighteners.

BARTEL, PAUL
Director, Writer, Actor. b. New York, NY, Aug. 6, 1938. e. UCLA, B.A. At 13 spent summer working at UPA Cartoons. Later at UCLA won acting and playwriting awards and prod. animated and doc. films. Awarded Fulbright schl. to study film dir. at Centro Sperimentale di Cinematografia in Rome where dir. short Progetti (presented Venice Fest., 1962). Then at Army Pictorial Center, L.I. City. Asst. dir. military training films. After discharge from army worked for Hearst Metrotone News as writer-dir. monthly news doc. series, Horizontes for U.S. Information Agency. The Naughty Nurse. Appeared in 1984 short film Frankenweenie.
PICTURES: Actor: Hi Mom!, Private Parts (also dir. debut), Big Bad Mama (2nd unit. dir. only), Death Race 2000, Cannonball (also dir., co-s.p.), Eat My Dust!, Hollywood Boulevard, Grand Theft Auto, Mr. Billion, Piranha, Rock 'n' Roll High School, Heart Like a Wheel, Eating Raoul (also dir., s.p.), Trick or Treats, White Dog, Get Crazy, Not for Publication (also dir., s.p.), Lust in the Dust (dir. only), Into the Night, Sesame Street Presents Follow That Bird, Chopping Mall, Killer Party, The Longshot (dir. only), Munchies, Amazon Women on the Moon, Mortuary Academy, Out of the Dark (also exec. prod.), Scenes From the Class Struggle in Beverly Hills (also dir., s.p.), Pucker Up and Bark Like a Dog, Far Out Man, Gremlins 2: The New Batch, The Pope Must Die, Liquid Dreams, Desire and Hell at Sunset Motel, Posse, Grief, The Jerky Boys, The Usual Suspects, Red Ribbon Blues, Basquiat.
TELEVISION: Actor: Alfred Hitchcock Presents, Fame, L.A. Law, Acting on Impulse (movie), A Bucket of Blood (movie). Director: Amazing Stories (The Secret Cinema, Gershwin's Truck; also writer, actor), The Hustler of Muscle Beach, Clueless (2 episodes).

BARTKOWIAK, ANDRZEJ
Cinematographer. b. Lodz, Poland, 1950. Attended Polish Film School. Moved to US in 1972, gaining experience in TV commercials and low-budget features. Protege of Sidney Lumet, for whom did several Pictures.
PICTURES: Deadly Hero, Prince of the City, Deathtrap, The Verdict, Daniel, Terms of Endearment, Garbo Talks, Prizzi's Honor, The Morning After, Power, Nuts, Twins, Q&A, Hard Promises, A Stranger Among Us, Falling Down, Guilty As Sin, Speed, A Good Man in Africa, Losing Isaiah, Species, Jade, The Mirror Has Two Faces, Dante's Peak, The Devil's Advocate, U.S. Marshals.

BARTY, BILLY
Actor. b. Millsboro, PA, Oct. 25, 1924. e. LA City Col., LA State U. Began performing at age 3 appearing as Mickey Rooney's little brother in the Mickey McGuire shorts. Founded Little People of America, 1957; Billy Barty Foundation, 1975.
PICTURES: Golddigers of 1933, Footlight Parade, Roman Scandals, Gift of Gab, A Midsummer Night's Dream, Nothing Sacred, The Clown, The Undead, Billy Rose's Jumbo, Roustabout, Harum Scarum, Pufnstuf, The Day of the Locust, The Amazing Dobermans, W.C. Fields and Me, Foul Play, Firepower, Hardly Working, Under the Rainbow, Night Patrol, Legend, Tough Guys, Body Slam, Rumplestiltskin, Willow, Lobster Man From Mars, UHF, The Rescuers Down Under (voice), Life Stinks, The Naked Truth, Radioland Murders, Burn Hollywood Burn, I/O Error.
TELEVISION: Movies: Punch and Jody, Twin Detectives. Series: Ford Festival, The Spike Jones Show, Circus Boy, Club Oasis, Ace Crawford—Private Eye, Vendetta, Secrets of a Mafia Bride.

BARUCH, RALPH M.
Executive. b. Frankfurt, Germany, Aug. 5, 1923. e. The Sorbonne. m. Jean Ursell de Mountford. Administrative aide, SESAC, Inc. 1944-48. Account exec., DuMont Television Network, 1950-54. Account exec., CBS Films, 1954; account supr., 1957; dir. int'l sales, 1959; CBS Group President 1961-70. Pres. and CEO Viacom International, 1971-1983; chmn. 1983-87. Currently a consultant to Viacom International. Trustee of Lenox Hill Hospital. Chmn. Emeritus of the Nat'l Academy of Cable Programming and recipient of the Academy's first Governor's Award. Past-pres., the International Radio & Television Society and was honored by an IRTS gold medal award. Founder and fellow of the International Council of the Nat'l Academy of Television Arts & Sciences. Recipient of an Emmy Award. Former dir., Exec. Committee of the Nat'l Cable Television Assoc. Co-founder of C-Span. Recipient of the Vanguard Award, three NCTA President's Awards and NCTA Chmn. of the Year Award. Chmn. of the USIA's Television Communications Board of Advisors under Pres. Reagan. Elected to the Broadcasting/Cable Hall of Fame in 1992. Appointed to New York City Cultural Affairs Advisory Comm. Member of New York Yacht Club.

BARWOOD, HAL
Writer, Producer, Director. e. U. of Southern California Sch. of Cinema. Has written scripts in collaboration with Matthew Robbins. Barwood branched out into producing with Corvette Summer, 1978 and directing with Warning Sign, 1985.
PICTURES: Screenplays (all with Robbins): The Sugarland Express, The Bingo Long Traveling All-Stars and Motor Kings, MacArthur, Corvette Summer (also prod.), Dragonslayer (also prod.), Warning Sign (also dir.).

BARYSHNIKOV, MIKHAIL
Dancer, Actor. b. Riga, Latvia, Jan. 27, 1948. Joined Kirov Ballet, Leningrad, 1969-74; defected to U.S. With American Ballet Theatre 1974-78; New York City Ballet Company 1978-79; named dir. of the American Ballet Theatre. B'way stage debut, Metamorphosis (1989).
PICTURES: The Turning Point (debut, 1977; Acad. Award nom.), That's Dancing!, White Nights (also co-choreog.), Dancers (also choreog.), Company Business, The Cabinet of Dr. Ramirez.
TELEVISION: Baryshnikov at the White House (Emmy Award, 1979), Bob Hope on the Road to China, Baryshnikov on Broadway (Emmy Award, 1980), AFI Salute to Fred Astaire, Baryshnikov in Hollywood (Emmy Award, 1980), AFI Salute to Gene Kelly, David Gordon's Made in USA, All Star Gala at Ford's Theater, Dance in America: Baryshnikov Dances Balanchine (Emmy Award, 1989).

BASCH, BUDDY
Print Media Syndicater, Publicist, Producer. b. South Orange, NJ, June 28, 1922. e. Columbia U. Began career as youngest radio editor in U.S. at 15. Has since written for nat'l mags, syndicates, wire services, and newspapers. Edit. & pub. Top Hit Club News for 7 yrs. Joined Donahue and Coe 1940 on m.p. accounts, U.S. Army in Europe 1942-45. 1945-67, own publicity and promotion office, working on m.p. company accounts and stars such as Burl Ives, Dinah Shore, Tony Martin, Danny Kaye, Peter Lorre, Tony Bennett, Gloria De Haven, McGuire Sisters, Rhonda Fleming, Sammy Davis, Jr., Anna Maria Alberghetti, Polly Bergen, Meyer Davis, The Beatles, Glenn Miller and Tommy Dorsey Orchestras. Produced many shows for radio, TV and stage in New York, Newark, Chicago, Hartford. Asst. to publisher, The Brooklyn Eagle 1962. 1966, formed Buddy Basch Feature Syndicate, covering assignments on show business,

travel, health, medicine, food, human interest and general subjects for such pulications as N.Y. Daily News, A.P., Grit Magazine, Travel/Holiday, Frontier Magazine, Kaleidoscope, True, United Features, Gannett Westchester-Rockland Newspapers, Bergen (NJ) Record, Argosy, N.A.N.A., Womens' News Service, Today Magazine, Christian Science Monitor, New York Post, Inflight Magazine, Deseret News, California Canadian and Diversion. Provided Associated Press with worldwide exclusives on a number of national and intl. events. Member: Friars Club since 1959; Admission Comm. and House Comm. Organized & appointed permanent chmn. of VIP Reception and Security for Friars luncheons and dinners since 1970. Served as chmn. of Elections (6 times). Contributing ed. Friars Epistle.

BASINGER, KIM
Actress. b. Athens, GA, Dec. 8, 1953. e. Neighborhood Playhouse. m. actor Alec Baldwin. Began career as Ford model in New York.
PICTURES: Hard Country (debut, 1981), Mother Lode, Never Say Never Again, The Man Who Loved Women, The Natural, Fool for Love, 9-1/2 Weeks, No Mercy, Blind Date, Nadine, My Stepmother is an Alien, Batman, The Marrying Man, Final Analysis, Cool World, The Real McCoy, Wayne's World 2, The Getaway, L.A. Confidential (Acad. Award, Golden Globe Award, Best Supporting Actress).
TELEVISION: Movies: Dog and Cat (pilot), The Ghost of Flight 401, Katie: Portrait of a Centerfold, Killjoy. Series: Dog and Cat, From Here to Eternity. Mini-Series: From Here to Eternity. Guest: Charlie's Angels.

BASS, RONALD
Writer. b. Los Angeles, CA. e. Yale, Harvard Law School. Entered industry as entertainment lawyer, while writing novels: The Perfect Thief, Lime's Crisis, The Emerald Illusion.
PICTURES: Writer &/or prod.: Code Name: Emerald, Black Widow, Gardens of Stone, Rain Man (Academy Award, 1988), Sleeping With the Enemy, The Joy Luck Club, When a Man Loves a Woman, Dangerous Minds, Waiting to Exhale, My Best Friend's Wedding (also prod.), What Dreams May Come, Snow Falling on Cedars, Good Nigh Moon, The Entrapment, Die Hard 4, How Stella Got Her Groove Back.
TELEVISION: Series: Dangerous Minds, Moloney.

BASSETT, ANGELA
Actress. b. New York, NY, Aug. 16, 1958. Moved to St. Petersburg, FL, at 5 yrs. old. e. Yale.
THEATER: B'way: Ma Rainey's Black Bottom, Joe Turner's Come and Gone. Off-B'way: Colored People's Time, Antigone, Black Girl, Henry IV Part 1. Regional: Beef No Chicken.
PICTURES: F/X (debut, 1986), Kindergarten Cop, Boyz N the Hood, City of Hope, Critters 4, Innocent Blood, Malcolm X, Passion Fish, What's Love Got to Do With It (Acad. Award nom., Golden Globe Award), Strange Days, Waiting to Exhale, Vampire in Brooklyn, Panther, Contact, Wings Against the Wind, How Stella Got Her Groove Back, Supernova, Cosm.
TELEVISION: Movies: Line of Fire: The Morris Dees Story, The Jacksons: An American Dream. Guest: Cosby Show, 227, thirtysomething, Tour of Duty, Equal Justice.

BATEMAN, JASON
Actor. b. Rye, NY, Jan. 14, 1969. Brother of actress Justine Bateman. Son of prod.-theatrical mgr. Kent Bateman. Started career in commercials until cast in Little House on the Prairie at 12 (1981).
PICTURES: Teen Wolf Too, Necessary Roughness, Breaking the Rules.
TELEVISION: Movies: The Fantastic World of D.C. Collins, The Thanksgiving Promise, Can You Feel Me Dancing, The Bates Motel, Moving Target, A Taste for Killing, Confessions: Two Faces of Evil, This Can't Be Love, Hart to Hart: Secrets of the Hart. Series: Little House on the Prairie, Silver Spoons, It's Your Move, Valerie (Valerie's Family, The Hogan Family), Simon, Chicago Sons. Mini-Series: Robert Kennedy and His Times. Specials: Just a Little More Love, Candid Camera: Eat! Eat! Eat!

BATEMAN, JUSTINE
Actress. b. Rye, NY, Feb. 19, 1966. Brother is actor Jason Bateman.
THEATER: Lulu, Self-Storage, The Crucible, Love Letters, Carnal Knowledge, Speed-the-Plow.
PICTURES: Satisfaction, The Closer, Primary Motive, Deadbolt, The Night We Never Met, God's Lonely Man, Kiss & Tell, Bucket of Blood.
TELEVISION: Movies: Right to Kill?, Family Ties Vacation, Can You Feel Me Dancing?, The Fatal Image, In the Eyes of a Stranger, The Hunter, Terror in the Night, Another Woman. Series: Family Ties, Men Behaving Badly. Guest: Tales from the Dark Side, One to Grow On, It's Your Move, Glitter, Lois & Clark. Specials: First the Egg, Whatta Year... 1986, Fame Fortune and Romance, Candid Camera: Eat! Eat! Eat!, Merry Christmas Baby, A Century of Women.

BATES, ALAN
Actor. b. Allestree, Derbyshire, England, Feb. 17, 1934. e. Herbert Strutt Grammar Sch.; after natl. service with the RAF studied at RADA with Albert Finney, Peter O'Toole and Tom Courtenay. Professional stage debut 1955 with the Midland Theatre Co. in You and Your Wife.
THEATER: London: The Mulberry Tree, Look Back in Anger (also NY, Moscow), Long Day's Journey Into Night, Poor Richard, Richard III, In Celebration, Hamlet, Butley (also NY; Tony Award, 1973), The Taming of the Shrew, Life Class, Otherwise Engaged, The Seagull, Stage Struck, A Patriot for Me, One for the Road, Victoria Station, Dance of Death, Yonadab, Melon, Much Ado About Nothing, Ivanov, Stages, The Showman, Simply Disconnected, Fortune's Fool, Life Support.
PICTURES: The Entertainer (debut, 1960), Whistle Down the Wind, A Kind of Loving, The Caretaker (The Guest), The Running Man, Nothing But the Best, Zorba the Greek, Georgy Girl, King of Hearts, Far From the Madding Crowd, The Fixer (Acad. Award nom.), Women in Love, Three Sisters, The Go-Between, A Day in the Death of Joe Egg, Impossible Object (Story of a Love Story), Butley, In Celebration, Royal Flash, An Unmarried Woman, The Shout, The Rose, Nijinsky, Quartet, The Return of the Soldier, Britannia Hospital, The Wicked Lady, Duet for One, A Prayer for the Dying, We Think the World of You, Mr. Frost, Hamlet, Force Majeure, Dr. M (Club Extinction), Shuttlecock, Secret Friends, Silent Tongue, Losing Track, The Grotesque, Varya.
TELEVISION: The Thug, A Memory of Two Mondays, The Jukebox, The Square Ring, The Wind and the Rain, Look Back in Anger, Three on a Gasring, Duel for Love, A Hero for Our Time, Plaintiff & Defendant, Two Sundays, The Collection, The Mayor of Casterbridge, The Trespasser, Very Like a Whale, Voyage Round My Father, An Englishman Abroad, Separate Tables, Dr. Fischer of Geneva, One for the Road, Pack of Lies, 102 Boulevard Haussmann, Unnatural Pursuits, Hard Times, Oliver's Travels, Hard Times, Nicholas' Gift.

BATES, KATHY
Actress. b. Memphis, TN, June 28, 1948. e. S. Methodist U. Regional theatre incl. D.C. and Actor's Theatre in Louisville.
THEATER: Vanities (Off-B'way debut, 1976), Semmelweiss, Crimes of the Heart, The Art of Dining, Goodbye Fidel (B'way debut, 1980), Chocolate Cake and Final Placement, Fifth of July, Come Back to the 5 & Dime Jimmy Dean Jimmy Dean, 'night Mother (Tony nom., Outer Critics Circle Award), Two Masters: The Rain of Terror, Curse of the Starving Class, Frankie and Johnny in the Clair de Lune (Obie, L.A. Drama Critics Award), The Road to Mecca.
PICTURES: Taking Off (debut, 1971), Straight Time, Come Back to the 5 & Dime Jimmy Dean Jimmy Dean, Two of a Kind, Summer Heat, My Best Friend is a Vampire, Arthur 2 on the Rocks, Signs of Life, High Stakes (Melanie Rose), Men Don't Leave, Dick Tracy, White Palace, Misery (Acad. Award, Golden Globe & Chicago Film Critics Awards, 1990), At Play in the Fields of the Lord, Fried Green Tomatoes, Shadows and Fog, The Road to Mecca, Prelude to a Kiss, Used People, A Home of Our Own, North, Dolores Claiborne, Angus, Diabolique, The War at Home, Titanic, Swept from the Sea, Primary Colors, The Water Boy, Bruno.
TELEVISION: Movies: Johnny Bull, No Place Like Home, Roe vs. Wade, Hostages, Curse of the Starving Class. Mini-Series: Murder Ordained, The Stand, The Night Shift (Golden Globe Award, 1997). Guest: The Love Boat, St. Elsewhere, Cagney and Lacey, L.A. Law, China Beach. Special: Talking With (also dir.).

BATTY, PETER
Producer, Director, Writer. b. Sunderland, England, June 18, 1931. e. Bede Grammar Sch. and Queen's Coll., Oxford. Feature-writer both sides Atlantic 1954-58. Joined BBC TV 1958 dir. short films. Edited Tonight programme 1963-4. Exec. prod. ATV 1964-68. Awarded Grand Prix for doc. at 1965 Venice and Leipzig festivals. Official entries 1970 and 1971 San Francisco and Melbourne festivals. Nominated Int'l. Emmy, 1986. Own company since 1968 prod. TV specials, commercials.
TELEVISION: The Quiet Revolution, The Big Freeze, The Katanga Affair, Sons of the Navvy Man, The Fall and Rise of the House of Krupp, The Road to Suez, The Suez Affair, Battle for the Desert, Vietnam Fly-In, The Plutocrats, The Aristocrats, Battle for Cassino, Battle for the Bulge, Birth of the Bomb, Search for the Super, Operation Barbarossa, Farouk: Last of the Pharaohs, Superspy, Spy Extraordinary, Sunderland's Pride and Passion, A Rothschild and His Red Gold, The World of Television, The Story of Wine, The Rise and Rise of Laura Ashley, The Gospel According to Saint Michael, Battle for Warsaw, Battle for Dien Bien Phu, Nuclear Nightmares. A Turn Up in A Million, Il Poverello, Swindle!, The Algerian War, Fonteyn and Nureyev: The Perfect Partnership, The Divided Union, A Time for Remembrance, Swastika Over British Soil. Contributed 6 episodes to Emmy-winning World at War series.

BAUER, STEVEN
Actor. b. Havana, Cuba, Dec. 2, 1956. Moved with family to Miami at age 3. e. Miami Dade Jr. Coll. where studied acting. Breakthrough came with selection for role in Que Pasa U.S.A.? for Public TV. Signed by Columbia TV and moved to California.
PICTURES: Scarface, Thief of Hearts, Running Scared, The Beast, Wildfire, Gleaming the Cube, Bloody Murder!, Raising Cain, Woman of Desire, Improper Conduct, Stranger by Night, Wild Side.
TELEVISION: Movies: Doctors' Private Lives, She's in the Army Now, Nichols and Dymes, An Innocent Love, Sword of Gideon, Sweet Poison, False Arrest, Drive Like Lightning. Series: Wiseguy. Mini-Series: Drug Wars: The Camarena Story. Guest: The Rockford Files, From Here to Eternity, One Day at a Time, Hill Street Blues.

BAUM, MARTIN
Executive. b. New York, NY, March 2, 1924. Pres., ABC Pictures. Previously partner Baum & Newborn Theatrical Agency. Head of West Coast office General Artists Corp.; head of m.p. dept., Ashley Famous Agency. Pres., Martin Baum Agency. Sr. exec. v.p. Creative Management Assoc. Pres., Optimus Productions, Inc., prod.: Bring Me the Head of Alfredo Garcia, The Wilby Conspiracy, The Killer Elite. Partner with Michael Ovitz, Ron Meyer, Rowland Perkins, Bill Haber in Creative Artists Agency, Inc.

BAUMGARTEN, CRAIG
Executive. b. Aug. 27, 1949. Partner in independent prod. co., New America Cinema. Joined Paramount Pictures as prod. exec.; named v.p., prod. In 1980 went to Keith Barish Prods., of which was pres. three years. In 1983 appt. exec. v.p. & exec. asst. to the pres. & CEO, Columbia Pictures; resigned 1985. Joined Lorimar Motion Pictures as pres. Joined 20th Century Fox m.p. div. as exec. v.p. of prod., 1987; resigned. Formed Adelson/Baumgarten Prods. with Gary Adelson, 1989. Co-Prod.: Hard to Kill, Hook, Universal Soldier, Nowhere to Run, Blank Check, It Could Happen to You, Jade, The Shooter, Esmeralda, Michael Hayes. Formed Baumgarten/Prophet Entertainment Inc., 1994.

BAXTER, BILLY
Executive. b. New York, NY, Feb. 8, 1926. e. Holy Cross, 1948. Mgr., Ambassador Brokerage Group, Albany, 1957-58. Bill Doll & Co., 1959-63. Organ., prod., radio show, Earl Wilson Celebrity Column, 1962; prod. B'way show, Mandingo, with Franchot Tone, 1962. Dir. of promotion, spec. events, Rumrill Ad Agency, 1963-64; dir. of promotion, exploitation, Landau Co., 1964-65; dir. of adv. and pub., Rizzoli Co., 1965-66. Consultant on special events to the Philip Morris Corp. and American Express.
PICTURES: Co-prod.: Love and Anarchy, Daughters-Daughters, Outrageous, One Man, Dawn of the Dead. Prod.: Diary of the Cannes Film Festival with Rex Reed, 1980. Prod./dir.: documentaries: Artists of the Old West, Remington & Russell, Buffalo Bill Cody (1988).

BAXTER, KEITH
Actor. b. Monmouthshire, Wales, April 29, 1933. e. Wales, entered Royal Acad. of Dramatic Art in 1951. 1952-55 in national service; returned to RADA. Did years of repertory work in Dublin, Croydon, Chichester, London's West End, and New York. Biggest stage hit in Sleuth, both London and NY. Later in Corpse (London, NY).
PICTURES: The Barretts of Wimpole Street, Peeping Tom, Chimes at Midnight, With Love in Mind, Ash Wednesday, Berlin Blues.
TELEVISION: For Tea on Sunday, Hold My Hand Soldier, Saint Joan, Mini-Series: Merlin.

BAXTER, MEREDITH
Actress. b. Los Angeles, CA, June 21, 1947. e. Interlochen Arts Academy. On stage in Guys and Dolls, Butterflies Are Free, Vanities, Country Wife, Talley's Folly, Love Letters, Diaries of Adam & Eve.
PICTURES: Ben, Stand Up and Be Counted, Bittersweet Love, All the President's Men, Jezebel's Kiss.
TELEVISION: Movies: Cat Creature, The Stranger Who Looks Like Me, Target Risk, The Imposter, The Night That Panicked America, Little Women, The Family Man, Beulah Land, Two Lives of Carol Letner, Take Your Best Shot, The Rape of Richard Beck, Kate's Secret, The Long Journey Home (also co-exec. prod.), Winnie: My Life in the Institution, She Knows Too Much, The Kissing Place, Burning Bridges, Bump in the Night, A Mother's Justice, A Woman Scorned: The Betty Broderick Story, Her Final Fury: Betty Broderick—The Last Chapter, Darkness Before Dawn (also co-exec. prod.), For the Love of Aaron, One More Mountain, My Breast (also co-exec. prod.), Betrayed: A Story of Three Women (also co-exec. prod.). Series: The Interns, Bridget Loves Bernie, Family, Family Ties, The Faculty. Specials: The Diaries of Adam and Eve, Vanities, Other Mothers (Afterschool Special).

BAXTER, STANLEY
Actor. b. Glasgow, Scotland, May, 1926. e. Hillhead H.S., Glasgow. Principal comedian in Howard & Wyndham pantomimes. Summer revues. Televised regularly on BBC-TV, and also frequent broadcaster. M.P. debut in Geordie, 1955.
THEATER: The Amorous Prawn, On the Brighter Side, Chase Me Comrade (Australia), Cinderella, What the Butler Saw, Phil The Fluter, Mother Goose Pantomime seasons 1970-74. Jack & The Beanstalk, Cinderella, Mother Goose, Aladdin, Cinderella.
PICTURES: Geordie (debut, 1955), Very Important Person, Crooks Anonymous, The Fast Lady, Father Came Too, Joey Boy.
TELEVISION: Baxter on (series) 1964; The Confidence Course, The World of Stanley Baxter, Stanley Baxter Show, Time for Baxter, The Stanley Baxter Big Picture Show, The Stanley Baxter Moving Picture Show, Part III, Stanley Baxter's Christmas Box, Bing Crosby's Merrie Olde Christmas, Stanley Baxter's Greatest Hits, Baxter on Television, Stanley Baxter Series, The Stanley Baxter Hour, Children's Royal, Stanley Baxter's Christmas Hamper, Stanley Baxter's Picture Annual 1986; Mr. Majeika (series, 1988-89), Fitby, Stanley Baxter Is Back.

BAY, MICHAEL
Director. b. 1964. e. Wesleyan U.; Pasadena's Art Center College of Design. Worked on advertisements and created music videos for Tina Turner, Meatloaf, Lionel Richie, Wilson Phillips. Recipient of the Gold Lion for The Best Beer campaign for Miller Lite; Silver Lion & Grand Prix Clio for Commercial of the Year, for the Got Milk/AaronBurr commercial; Commercial Dir. of the Year, Directors Guild of America, 1995.
PICTURES: Vengeance (actor only), Bad Boys, The Rock, Armageddon (also prod.).

BEACHAM, STEPHANIE
Actress. b. Casablanca, Morocco, Feb. 28, 1947. e. RADA. On London stage in The Basement, On Approval, London Cuckolds, etc.
PICTURES: The Games, Tam Lin, The Nightcomers, Dracula A.D., And Now the Screaming Stars, House of Whipcord, Schizo, The Confessional, Horror Planet (Inseminoid), The Wolves of Willoughby Chase, Troop Beverly Hills, Wedding Bell Blues.
TELEVISION: Movies/Specials: Napoleon & Josephine: A Love Story, Lucky/Chances, Secrets, To Be the Best, Foreign Affairs, Marked Personal, Jane Eyre, A Sentimental Education, A Change of Place.Series: Tenko (PBS), The Colbys, Dynasty, Sister Kate, SeaQuest DSV, Beverly Hills, 90210, Riders.

BEALS, JENNIFER
Actress. b. Chicago, IL, Dec. 19, 1963. Started as fashion model before making film debut in small role in My Bodyguard, 1980.
PICTURES: My Bodyguard, Flashdance, The Bride, Split Decisions, Vampire's Kiss, Layover, Rider in the Dark, The Lizard's Tale, Sons, Jackal's Run, A Reasonable Doubt, Dr. M, Blood and Concrete, In the Soup, Day of Atonement, Caro Diario, Mrs. Parker and the Vicious Circle, Arabian Knight (voice), Devil in a Blue Dress, Four Rooms.
TELEVISION: Movies: Terror Strikes the Class Reunion, Indecency, Night Owl. Series: 2000 Malibu Road. Specials: The Picture of Dorian Grey, Cinderella (Faerie Tale Theatre).

BEAN, ORSON
Actor. r.n. Dallas Burrows. b. Burlington, VT, July 22, 1928. Performed in nightclubs as comic and on Broadway (Never Too Late, Will Success Spoil Rock Hunter?, Subways are for Sleeping, Roar of the Grease Paint, the Smell of the Crowd, Ilya Darling.) Author of Me and the Orgone. Founder, administrator, dir. 15th St. School, NY.
PICTURES: How to Be Very Very Popular (debut, 1955), Anatomy of a Murder, Lola, Forty Deuce, Innerspace, Instant Karma.
TELEVISION: Series: The Blue Angel (host), I've Got a Secret (panelist), Keep Talking, To Tell the Truth (panelist), Mary Hartman Mary Hartman, One Life to Live, Dr. Quinn: Medicine Woman. Special: Arsenic and Old Lace.

BEAN, SEAN
Actor. b. Sheffield, Yorkshire, England, Apr. 17, 1958.
THEATER: Romeo and Juliet, Fair Maid of the West, Midsummer Night's Dream, Who Knew Mackenzie and Gone, Deathwatch, Last Days of Mankind.
PICTURES: Winter Flight, Caravaggio, Stormy Monday, War Requeim, The Field, Patriot Games. Shopping, Black Beauty, Goldeneye, When Saturday Comes, Leo Tolstoy's Anna Karenina, Ronin, Bravo Two Zero, Airborne.
TELEVISION: Troubles, Small Zones, 15 Street, My Kingdom for a Horse, Winter Flight, Samson & Delilah, The True Bride, Prince, Tell Me That You Love Me, Clarissa, Scarlett, Jacob, The "Sharpe" teleplays.

BEART, EMMANUELLE
Actress. b. Gassin, France, Aug. 14, 1965. Moved to Montreal at age 15. Returned to France and enrolled in drama school.
THEATER: La Repetition ou l'Amour Puni, La Double Inconstance.
PICTURES: Premiers Desirs, L'Enfant Trouve, L'Amour en Douce, Manon of the Spring, Date With an Angel, A Gauche en Sortant de L'Ascenseur, Les Enfants du Desordre, Capitaine Fracasse, La Belle Noiseuse, J'Embrasse Pas, Un Coeur en Hiver (A Heart in Winter), Ruptures, Divertimento, L'Enfer (Hell), Une Femme Francaise, Nelly & Mr. Arnaud, Mission: Impossible, Voleur de Vie, Don Juan.
TELEVISION: Zacharius, Raison Perdue.

BEATTY, NED
Actor. b. Lexington, KY, July 6, 1937. Worked at Barter Theatre in Virginia appearing in over 70 plays, 1957-66; with Arena Stage, Washington D.C. 1963-71. Made Bway debut in The Great White Hope.
PICTURES: Deliverance (debut, 1972), The Life and Times of Judge Roy Bean, The Thief Who Came to Dinner, The Last American Hero, White Lightning, Nashville, W.W. and the Dixie Dance Kings, All the President's Men, The Big Bus, Network, Mikey and Nicky, Silver Streak, Exorcist II: The Heretic, Gray Lady Down, The Great Georgia Bank Hoax, Superman, Alambrista!, Promises in the Dark, 1941, Wise Blood, American Success Company, Hopscotch, The Incredible Shrinking Woman, Superman II, The Toy, Touched, Stroker Ace, Back to School, The Big Easy, The Fourth Protocol, The Trouble With Spies, Switching Channels, Rolling Vengeance, The Unholy, Midnight Crossing, After the Rain, Purple People Eater, Physical Evidence, Time Trackers, Big Bad John, Chattahoochee, A Cry in the Wild, Repossessed, Blind Vision, Going Under, Hear My Song, Prelude to a Kiss, Ed and His Dead Mother, Rudy, Black Water, Radioland Murders, Just Cause.
TELEVISION: Movies: Footsteps, Marcus-Nelson Murders, Dying Room Only, The Execution of Private Slovik, Attack on Terror: The FBI vs. the Ku Klux Klan, The Deadly Tower, Tail Gunner Joe, Lucan, A Question of Love, Friendly Fire, Guyana Tragedy: The Story of Jim Jones, All God's Children, The Violation of Sarah McDavid, Splendor in the Grass, Pray TV, A Woman Called Golda, Kentucky Woman, Hostage Flight, Go Toward the Light, Spy, Last Train Home, Back to Hannibal, The Tragedy of Flight 103: The Inside Story, Trial: The Price of Passion, T Bone N Weasel. Series: Szysznyk, The Boys, Homicide: Life on the Street. Guest: Murder She Wrote, M*A*S*H, Rockford Files, Alfred Hitchcock, B.L. Stryker, Roseanne. Mini-Series: Celebrity, The Last Days of Pompeii, Robert Kennedy and His Times. Special: Our Town (1977).

BEATTY, WARREN
Actor., Producer, Director, Writer. r.n. Henry Warren Beaty. b. Richmond, VA, March 30, 1937. e. Northwestern U. Sister is actress Shirley MacLaine. m. actress Annette Bening. Studied with Stella Adler. Small roles on television; on stage in Compulsion (winter stock, North Jersey Playhouse); B'way debut: A Loss of Roses (Theatre World Award).
PICTURES: Splendor in the Grass (debut, 1961), The Roman Spring of Mrs. Stone, All Fall Down, Lilith, Mickey One, Promise Her Anything, Kaleidoscope, Bonnie and Clyde (also prod.), The Only Game in Town, McCabe and Mrs. Miller, $ (Dollars), The Parallax View, Shampoo (also prod., co-s.p.), The Fortune, Heaven Can Wait (also prod., co-dir., co-s.p.), Reds (also prod., dir., co-s.p.; Acad. Award for Best dir., 1981), Ishtar (also prod.), Dick Tracy (also prod., dir.), Bugsy (also co-prod.), Love Affair (also prod, co-s.p.).
TELEVISION: Series: The Many Loves of Dobie Gillis (1959-60). Guest: Kraft Television Theatre, Studio One, Suspicion, Alcoa Presents, One Step Beyond, Wagon Train.

BECK, ALEXANDER J.
Executive. b. Ung. Brod, Czechoslovakia, Nov. 5, 1926. e. Charles U., Prague; NYU. Owns 500 features and westerns for foreign distribution and library of 1400 shorts, importer and exporter. Pres., chmn. of bd. Alexander Beck Films, 1955. Formed Albex Films and A.B. Enterprises, 1959; formed & pres., Beckman Film Corp., 1960; formed Alexander Beck Productions, 1964. In 1969 formed Screencom Int'l Corp., 1986, formed Beck Int'l Corp., 1987; formed Challenger Pictures Corp., 1988.

BECK, JACKSON
Actor, announcer, narrator. b. New York, NY. TV and radio commercials, children's records, comm. industrial films; Narrator.

BECK, MICHAEL
Actor. b. Memphis, TN, Feb. 4, 1949. e. Millsaps Coll. on football scholarship (quarterback). Became active in college theatre. In 1971 attended Central Sch. of Speech and Drama, London; studied 3 years, following which toured England with repertory companies for 2 years. Returned to U.S.; cast as lead in independent film, Madman (shot in Israel in 1977).
PICTURES: Madman, The Warriors, Xanadu, Megaforce, War Lords of the 21st Century, The Golden Seal, Triumphs of a Man Called Horse, Final Judgment, Forest Warrior.
TELEVISION: *Movies*: Mayflower: the Pilgrim's Adventure, Alcatraz: The Whole Shocking Story, Fly Away Home, The Last Ninja, Rearview Mirror, Chiller, Blackout, Only One Survived, The Reckoning, Houston: Legend of Texas, Deadly Game, Deadly Aim, Stranger at My Door, Fade to Black. *Series*: Houston Knights. *Mini-Series*: Holocaust, Celebrity.

BECKER, HAROLD
Director. b. New York, NY. Dir. documentaries, Eugene Atget Interview with Bruce Gordon, Blind Gary Davis, Signet, Ivanhoe Donaldson.
PICTURES: The Ragman's Daughter (debut, 1972), The Onion Field, The Black Marble, Taps, Vision Quest, The Boost, Sea of Love, Malice (also co-prod.), City Hall (also co-prod.), Mercury Rising.

BEDELIA, BONNIE
Actress. b. New York, NY, March 25, 1946. e. Hunter Coll.
THEATER: Enter Laughing, The Playroom, My Sweet Charlie (Theatre World Award).
PICTURES: The Gypsy Moths (debut, 1969), They Shoot Horses Don't They?, Lovers and Other Strangers, The Strange Vengeance of Rosalie, The Big Fix, Heart Like a Wheel, Death of an Angel, Violets Are Blue, The Boy Who Could Fly, The Stranger, Die Hard, The Prince of Pennsylvania, Fat Man and Little Boy, Die Hard 2, Presumed Innocent, Needful Things.
TELEVISION: *Movies*: Then Came Bronson, Sandcastles, A Time for Love, Hawkins on Murder (Death and the Maiden), Message to My Daughter, Heatwave!, A Question of Love, Walking Through the Fire, Salem's Lot, Tourist, Fighting Back, Million Dollar Infield, Memorial Day, Alex: The Life of a Child, The Lady from Yesterday, Somebody Has to Shoot the Picture, Switched at Birth, A Mother's Right: The Elizabeth Morgan Story, The Fire Next Time, Judicial Consent, Legacy of Sin: The William Coit Story. *Series*: Love of Life (1961-67), The New Land. *Special*: The Gift. Guest: Fallen Angels (The Quiet Room).

BEGLEY, ED, JR.
Actor. b. Los Angeles, CA, Sept. 16, 1949. Son of late actor Ed Begley. Debut in a guest appearance on My Three Sons at 17. On NY stage in The Cryptogram.
PICTURES: The Computer Wore Tennis Shoes (debut, 1970), Now You See Him Now You Don't, Showdown, Superdad, Cockfighter, Stay Hungry, Citizens Band (Handle With Care), Blue Collar, The One and Only, Goin' South, Hardcore, Battlestar Gallactica, The In-Laws, The Concorde: Airport '79, Private Lessons, Cat People, Eating Raoul, Get Crazy, This Is Spinal Tap, Streets of Fire, Protocol, Transylvania 6-5000, Amazon Women on the Moon, The Accidental Tourist, Scenes From the Class Struggle in Beverly Hills, She-Devil, Meet the Applegates, Dark Horse, Greedy, Even Cowgirls Get the Blues, Renaissance Man, The Pagemaster, Batman Forever, The Lay of the Land.
TELEVISION: *Movies*: Family Flight, Amateur Night at the Dixie Bar and Grill, Elvis, Hot Rod, A Shining Season, Rascals and Robbers - The Secret Adventures of Tom Sawyer and Huck Finn, Tales of the Apple Dumpling Gang, Voyagers, Not Just Another Affair, Still the Beaver, An Uncommon Love, Insight/The Clearing House, Roman Holiday, Spies Lies & Naked Thighs, Not a Penny More Not a Penny Less, In the Best Inerest of the Child, The Big One: The Great Los Angeles Earthquake, Chance of a Lifetime, The Story Lady, In the Line of Duty: Siege at Marion, Exclusive, Running Mates. Cooperstown, World War II: When Lions Roared, Columbo: Undercover, Incident at Deception Ridge, The Shaggy Dog. *Series*: Roll Out, St. Elsewhere (1982-88), Parenthood, Winnetka Road. Guest: Room 222, Love American Style, Happy Days, Columbo, M*A*S*H, Barnaby Jones, Doris Day Show, Mary Hartman Mary Hartman, Faerie Tale Theatre, Meego. *Specials*: Mastergate, Partners.

BELAFONTE, HARRY
Actor, Singer, Producer. b. New York, NY, March 1, 1927. Trained for stage at the Actors Studio, New Sch. for Social Research and American Negro Theatre. Professional debut, Royal Roost nightclub, N.Y., Village Vanguard, 1950. Broadway debut: John Murray Anderson's Almanac, 1953. Recording, concert artist. Emmy Award for Tonight With Harry Belafonte, 1961.
THEATER: Juno and the Paycock, John Murray Anderson's Almanac. (Tony Award, 1953), Three for Tonight, A Night With Belafonte, To Be Young Gifted and Black (prod.), Asinamali (co-prod.).

PICTURES: Bright Road (debut, 1953), Carmen Jones, Island in the Sun, Odds Against Tomorrow, The World the Flesh and the Devil, The Angel Levine, Buck and the Preacher, Uptown Saturday Night (also prod.), Beat Street (prod. only), The Player, Ready to Wear (Pret-a-Porter), White Man's Burden, Kansas City (NY Society of Film Critics Award, 1997).
TELEVISION: *Movie*: Grambling's White Tiger. Many variety specials. *Series*: Sugar Hill Times.

BELAFONTE, SHARI
Actress. b. New York, NY, Sept. 22, 1954. e. Carnegie-Mellon U., BFA, 1976. Daughter of actor-singer Harry Belafonte. Worked as publicist's asst. at Hanna Barbera Prods. before becoming successful model (appearing on more than 200 magazine covers and in numerous TV commercials).
PICTURES: If You Could See What I Hear, Time Walker, Murder One Murder Two, The Player, Fire—Ice & Dynamite, Mars.
TELEVISION: *Movies*: The Night the City Screamed, The Midnight Hour, Kate's Secret, Perry Mason: The Case of the All-Star Assassin, French Silk, Heidi Chronicles, Babylon V. *Host*: Big Hex of Little Lulu, AM Los Angeles, Living the Dream: a Tribute to Dr. Martin Luther King Jr., Lifestyles with Robin Leach and Shari Belafonte, First Edition, The Caribbean with Shari Belafonte. *Series*: Hotel. *Pilot*: Velvet, Beyond Reality. *Guest*: Hart to Hart, Code Red, Trapper John M.D., Different Strokes, The Love Boat, Matt Houston.

BELFER, HAL B.
Executive Producer, Director, Choreographer. b. Los Angeles, CA, Feb. 16. e. USC; U. of CA (writing). Head of choreography depts. at both 20th Century-Fox and Universal Studios. Dir. of entertainment, in Las Vegas, Riviera and Flamingo Hotels. Prod., musical shows for Mexico City, Aruba, Puerto Rico, Montreal, Las Vegas. Dir., TV commercials and industrials. H.R. Pufnstuf TV series. Prod., dir., choreographer, Premore, Inc. Develop TV specials and sitcom, tape and film. Exec. prod.: Once Upon a Tour and Dora's World, Rose on Broadway, Secret Sleuth, Inn by the Side of the Road, Imagine That! Special staging Tony The Pony Series and prod., segment of What a Way to Run a Railroad; TV specials. Talent dev't. programs, Universal Studios, 20th Century-Fox. Personal mgr. and show packager. 1982, exec. prod.: Enchanted Inn (TV Special), Cameo Music Hall I; stage mgr.: Promises, Promises, A Chorus Line (Sahara Hotel, Las Vegas). Created: Hal Belfer Associates Talent and Production Consultant; Convention Destination & Services Consultant.

BEL GEDDES, BARBARA
Actress. r.n. Barbara Geddes Lewis. b. New York, NY, Oct 31, 1922. Father was Norman Bel Geddes, scenic designer. B'way debut in Out of the Frying Pan. Toured USO camps in Junior Miss, 1941; voted Star of Tomorrow, 1949. Author-illustrator children's books: I Like to Be Me (1963), So Do I (1972). Also designer of greeting cards for George Caspari Co.
THEATER: Out of the Frying Pan, Deep Are the Roots, Burning Bright, The Moon Is Blue, Living Room, Cat on a Hot Tin Roof, The Sleeping Prince, Silent Night Holy Night, Mary Mary, Everything in the Garden, Finishing Touches.
PICTURES: The Long Night (debut, 1947), I Remember Mama (Acad Award nom.), Blood on the Moon, Caught, Panic in the Streets, Fourteen Hours, Vertigo, The Five Pennies, Five Branded Women, By Love Possessed, Summertree, The Todd Killings.
TELEVISION: Live TV in 1950s: Robert Montgomery Presents (The Philadelphia Story), Schlitz Playhouse of the Stars; several Alfred Hitchcock Presents episodes (incl. Lamb to the Slaughter), Our Town. *Series*: Dallas (Emmy Award, 1980).

BELL, TOM
Actor. b. Liverpool, England, 1932. Early career in repertory and on West End stage. First TV appearance in Promenade.
PICTURES: The Concrete Jungle (The Criminal; debut, 1960), Echo of Barbara, Payroll, The Kitchen, H.M.S. Defiant (Damn the Defiant!), A Prize of Arms, The L-Shaped Room, Ballad in Blue (Blues for Lovers), He Who Rides a Tiger, Sands of Beersheba, In Enemy Country, The Long Day's Dying, Lock Up Your Daughters, All the Right Noises, The Violent Enemy, Quest for Love, Straight on Till Morning, Royal Flash, The Sailor's Return, Stronger Than the Sun, The Innocent, Wish You Were Here, Resurrected, The Magic Toy Shop, The Krays, Let Him Have It, Angels, Seconds Out, Feast of July, Swept for the Sea, Preaching to the Perverted, The Boxer, Swing.
TELEVISION: No Trams to Lime Street, Love on the Dole, A Night Out, The Seekers, Long Distance Blue, Summer Lightning, Hard Travelling, White Knight, The Virginian, The Rainbow, Prime Suspect 3, *Mini-Series*: The Cinder Path, No Bananas, The Great Kandinsky.

BELLAMY, EARL
Producer, Director. b. Minneapolis, MN, March 11, 1917. e. Los
Angeles City Coll. President, The Bellamy Productions Co.
PICTURES: Seminole Uprising (debut, 1955), Blackjack
Ketchum: Desperado, Toughest Gun in Tombstone, Stagecoach
to Dancers' Rock (also prod.), Fluffy, Gunpoint, Munster Go
Home!, Incident at Phantom Hill, Three Guns for Texas,
Backtack, Sidecar Racers, Seven Alone, Part 2: Walking Tall,
Against a Crooked Sky, Sidewinder 1, Speedtrap, Magnum
Thrust.
TELEVISION: Bachelor Father, Wells Fargo, Lone Ranger,
Alcoa Premiere, Arrest and Trial, The Virginian, The Crusaders,
Schlitz Playhouse, Rawhide, The Donna Reed Show, Andy
Griffith Show, Wagon Train, Laramie, Laredo, I Spy, Mod Squad,
Medical Center.

BELLFORT, JOSEPH
Executive. b. New York, NY, Sept. 20, 1912. e. NYU, Brooklyn
Law Sch. Joined RKO Service Corp., 1930; trans. to RKO Radio
Pictures, legal dept., 1942; joined RKO Fgn. dept., 1944; han-
dled Far Eastern division, 1946; then asst. to European gen.
mgr.; gen. European mgr., 1949-1958. Gen. sales mgr. Nat'l
Screen Service, 1959. Home office supv., Europe & Near East,
20th Century-Fox, 1963; home office intl. mgr., 20th Century-
Fox, 1966; asst. v.p. & foreign mgr. 20th Cent.-Fox, 1967; v.p.
20th Century-Fox, Intl. Corp. & Inter-America, Inc. 1968; named
sr. v.p., 1975. Resigned from Fox, 1977, to become v.p., Motion
Picture Export Assn. of America in New York. Retired 1983.

BELLFORT, TOM
Sound.
PICTURES: Rumble Fish, The Cotton Club, The Journey of
Natty Gann, Seize the Day, Tucker: The Man and His Dream,
The Godfather: Part III, Bingo!, The Last Supper, One Fine Day,
Titanic (Acad. Award, Best Sound Editing, 1997).

BELLOCCHIO, MARCO
Director, Writer. b. Piacenza, Italy, Nov. 9, 1939. e. Academy of
Cinematografia, Rome (studying acting, then film directing);
Slade School of Fine Arts, London 1959-63.
PICTURES: Fist in His Pocket (debut, 1965), China Is Near,
Amore e Rabbia (segment: Discutiamo Discutiamo), Nel Nome
del Padre (In the Name of the Father), Slap the Monster on the
Front Page (also co-s.p.), Madmen to Be Released, Triumphal
March, Il Gabbiano (The Seagull), The Film Machine, Leap Into
the Void, The Eyes and the Mouth, Henry IV, Devil in the Flesh,
The Sabba's Vision, The Conviction, The Butterfly's Dream,
Broken Dreams, The Prince of Homburg.

BELMONDO, JEAN-PAUL
Actor. b. Neuilly-sur-Seine, France, April 9, 1933. e. private
drama school of Raymond Girard, and the Conservatoire d'Art
Dramatique. Formed a theater group with Annie Girardot and
Guy Bedos.
THEATER: (Jean Marais' production) Caesar and Cleopatra,
Treasure Party, Oscar, Kean, Cyrano de Bergerac, Tailleur pour
Dames, La Puce a L'Oreille.
PICTURES: A Pied a Cheval et en Voiture (By Foot Horse and
Car), Look Pretty and Shut Up, Drole de Dimanche, Les
Tricheurs, Les Copains du Dimanche, Charlotte et Son Jules, A
Double Tour, Breathless, Classe Tous Risques, Moderato
Cantabile, La Francaise et l'Amour, Les Distractions,
Mademoiselle Ange, La Novice, Two Women, La Viaccia, Une
Femme Est une Femme, Leon Morin Pretre, Les Amours
Celebres, Un Singe en Hiver, Le Doulos, L'Aine des Ferchaux,
La Mer A Boire, Banana Peel, That Man From Rio, Cent Mille
Dollars au Soleil, Echappement Libre, La Chasse a l'Homme,
Dieu a Choisi Paris, Weekend a Zuydcocte, Par Un Beau Matin
d'Ete, Up to His Ears, Is Paris Burning?, Casino Royale, The
Thief of Paris, Pierrot le Fou, The Brain, Love Is a Funny Thing,
Mississippi Mermaid, Borsalino, A Man I Like, The Burglars,
Tender Scoundrel, Inheritor, Stavisky, Fear Over the City,
L'Animal, The Professional, Ace of Aces, The Vultures, Happy
Easter, Hold Up, Le Solitaire, Itinerary of a Spoiled Child (also
prod.), L'Inconnu dans la Maison, Les Miserables, Les Cent et
une Nuits, Desire, Une chance sur deux.

BELSON, JERRY
Producer, Director, Writer. With Garry Marshall, writer of The
Dick Van Dyke Show, prod. of The Odd Couple. Co-authoring the
Broadway play The Roast (1980).
PICTURES: How Sweet It Is (prod., s.p.), The Grasshopper
(s.p., prod.), Smile (s.p.), Fun With Dick and Jane (s.p.), Smokey
and the Bandit II (s.p.), Student Bodies (exec. prod.), The End
(s.p.), Jekyll and Hyde Together Again (dir.), Surrender (dir.,
s.p.), For Keeps (prod.), Always (co-s.p.).
TELEVISION: Series: The Dick Van Dyke Show, The Odd
Couple, The Tracey Ullman Show (co-creator, co-exec. prod.;
Emmy Awards). Special: Billy Crystal: Midnight Train to Moscow
(co-writer; Emmy Award).

BELUSHI, JAMES
Actor. b. Chicago, IL, June 15, 1954. e. DuPage Coll., Southern
Illinois U. Brother was late actor John Belushi. Began at
Chicago's Second City Theatre.
THEATER: Sexual Perversity in Chicago, The Pirates of
Penzance, True West, Conversations With My Father, Baal.
PICTURES: Thief (debut, 1981), Trading Places, The Man with One
Red Shoe, Salvador, About Last Night, Jumpin' Jack Flash, Little
Shop of Horrors, Number One With a Bullet (co-s.p. only), The
Principal, Real Men, Red Heat, Who's Harry Crumb? (cameo), K-9,
Homer and Eddie, Wedding Band (cameo), Taking Care of
Business, Mr. Destiny, The Palermo Connection, Only the Lonely,
Masters of Menace (cameo), Curly Sue, Once Upon a Crime, Diary
of a Hitman (cameo), Traces of Red, Last Action Hero (cameo), The
Pebble and the Penguin (voice), Destiny Turns on the Radio,
Separate Lives, Canadian Bacon (cameo), Race the Sun, Jingle All
the Way, Gold in the Streets, Retroactive, Bad Baby (voice), Living
in Peril, Gang Related, Wag the Dog, The Florentine.
TELEVISION: Movies: Royce, Parallel Lives, Sahara. Series:
Who's Watching the Kids?, Working Stiffs, Saturday Night Live,
Mighty Ducks, Superman, It's Good to Be King, Total Security.
Mini-Series: Wild Palms. Specials: The Joseph Jefferson
Awards, The Best Legs in the 8th Grade, Cinemax's Comedy
Experiment's Birthday Boy (also prod., writer).

BELZER, RICHARD
Actor, Comedian. b. Bridgeport, CT, Aug. 4, 1944.
PICTURES: The Groove Tube (debut, 1974), Fame, Author
Author, Night Shift, Scarface, America, Flicks, The Wrong Guys,
Freeway, Fletch Lives, The Big Picture, The Bonfire of the
Vanities, Off and Running, Mad Dog and Glory, Girl 6, Get on
the Bus.
TELEVISION: Movies: Not of This Earth, Prince for a Day.
Series: The Late Show (host), Homicide: Life on the Street.
Specials: On Location: Richard Belzer in Concert (also writer),
Belzer on Broadway (also writer, exec. prod.).

BENBEN, BRIAN
Actor. b. Winchester, VA, June 18. Raised in Marlboro, NY. m.
actress Madeleine Stowe. In regional and alternative theatre
before making B'way debut in Slab Boys.
TELEVISION: Series: The Gangster Chronicles, Kay O'Brien,
Dream On (Cable ACE Award, 1992). Special: Conspiracy: The
Trial of the Chicago 8.
PICTURES: Clean and Sober (debut, 1988), Dangerous
Obsession (Mortal Sins), I Come in Peace, Radioland Murders.

BENDICK, ROBERT
Indep. documentary prod., dir. b. New York, NY, Feb. 8, 1917.
e. NYU, White School Photography. U.S. Air Force, W.W.II.
Documentary and still cameraman before joining CBS Television
as cameraman and dir., 1940; rejoined CBS Television as dir.
special events, 1946; promoted dir. news & special events; act-
ing program dir. 1947; resigned 1951. Collaborated with Jeanne
Bendick on: Making the Movies, Electronics for Young People,
Television Works Like This, Filming Works Like This, 1971. Prod.
Peabody Award-winning U.N. show The U.N. in Action. V.p.,
Cinerama Prod. Co-prod., This Is Cinerama; co-dir., Cinerama
Holiday; prod., Dave Garroway Show Today and Wide Wide
World, 1955-56. NBC prod. dir. C.V. Whitney Pict., 1956; Merian
C. Cooper Ent., 1957; prod. NBC, 1958. Prod.: Garroway Today
Show, Bob Hope 25 Yrs. of Life Show, 1961; Bell Telephone
Threshold Science Series, Groucho Marx, Merrily We Roll
Along, US Steel Opening New York World's Fair, 1964; First
Look Series 1965 (Ohio St. Award); also dir. American
Sportsman, ABC; prod., pilot, Great American Dream Machine
(NET) (Emmy Award, 1971 and 1972); co-exec. prod., Dick
Cavett—Feeling Good, 1975. Pres. Bendick Assoc. Inc.; prod. of
education audio-visual systems. Bd. of Govs., NY Academy of
TV Arts and Science. 1976, co-author with Jeanne Bendick, TV
Reporting. Consultant, Warner Qube Cable Co. Prod., dir., Fight
for Food (PBS), 1978. Program consultant to Times-Mirror Cable
Co., L.A. Prod. segment ABC 20/20. Member awards committee,
National TV Acad. Arts & Science. Co-author with Jeanne
Bendick of Eureka It's Television (1993). Inducted into Natl. TV
Academy Arts & Science, NY chapter, Silver Circle, 1994. Co-
author with Jeanne Bendick of Markets
—From Barter to Bar Codes, 1998.

BENEDICT, DIRK
Actor. r.n. Dirk Niewoehner. b. Helena, MT, March 1, 1945. e.
Whitman Coll., Walla Walla, WA. Enrolled in John Fernald
Academy of Dramatic Arts, Rochester, MI, after which had sea-
son with Seattle Repertory Theatre; also in summer stock at Ann
Arbor, MI. Made B'way debut in Abelard and Heloise, 1970.
Author: Confessions of a Kamikaze Cowboy, And Then We Went
Fishing. Film debut, Georgia, Georgia, 1972.
PICTURES: Sssssss, W, Battlestar Galactica, Scavenger Hunt,
Ruckus, Underground Aces, Body Slam, Blue Tornado, Shadow
Force, Cahoots, Tales From the Crypt Presents Demon Knight,
Alaska, The Feminine Touch.
TELEVISION: Movies: Journey from Darkness, The Georgia
Peaches, Scruples, Trenchcoat in Paradise. Series: Chopper
One, Battlestar Galactica, The A Team. Guest: Love Boat,
Murder She Wrote, Hawaii Five-O.

BENEDICT, PAUL
Actor, Director. b. Silver City, NM, Sept. 17, 1938. Acted with the Theatre Company of Boston, Arena Stage, D.C.; Trinity Rep.; Providence; Playhouse in the Park, Cincinnati; Center Stage, Baltimore; A.R.T., Cambridge.
THEATER: NY: Little Murders, The White House Murder Case, Bad Habits, It's Only a Play, Richard III, The Play's the Thing. LA: The Unvarnished Truth, It's Only a Play. Director: Frankie & Johnnie in the Clair de Lune, Bad Habits, The Kathy and Mo Show, Beyond Therapy, Geniuses, Any Given Day.
PICTURES: The Virgin President, They Might Be Giants (debut, 1971), The Gang that Couldn't Shoot Straight, Cold Turkey, Taking Off, Up the Sandbox, Deadhead Miles, Jeremiah Johnson, The Front Page, Mandingo, The Goodbye Girl, Billy in the Lowlands, The Man With Two Brains, This Is Spinal Tap, Arthur 2 on the Rocks, Cocktail, The Chair, The Freshman, Sibling Rivalry, The Addams Family, Waiting for Guffman.
TELEVISION: Movies: Hustling, Baby Cakes, Attack of the 50 Ft. Woman. Series: Sesame Street (1969-74), The Jeffersons, Mama Malone. Mini-Series: The Blue and the Gray. Guest: Kojak, Maude, All in the Family, Harry-O, Seinfeld.

BENIGNI, ROBERTO
Actor, Writer, Director, Producer. b. Misericordia, Arezzo, Italy, Oct. 27, 1952.
PICTURES: Berlinguer ti voglio bene (also s.p.), Giorni cantati, Chiedo asilo (also s.p.), Clair de femme, La Luna, In the Pope's Eye, Il Minestrone, Tu mi turbi (also s.p., dir.), F.F.S.S. cioe che mi hai portato a fare sopra Posillipo se non mi vuoi piu bene, Nothing Left to Do But Cry (also s.p., dir.), Coffee and Cigarettes, Down by Law, The Little Devil (also s.p., dir.), The Voice of the Moon, Johnny Toothpick (also s.p., dir.), Night on Earth, Son of the Pink Panther, The Monster (also s.p., dir., prod.), Life Is Beautiful (also s.p., dir.), Asterix and Obelix vs. Caesar.

BENING, ANNETTE
Actress. b. Topeka, KS, May 29, 1958. Raised in San Diego. e. San Francisco St. Univ. m. actor Warren Beatty. Acted with San Francisco's American Conservatory Theatre.
THEATER: Coastal Disturbances (Tony Award nom., Theatre World & Clarence Derwent Awards), Spoils of War.
PICTURES: The Great Outdoors (debut, 1988), Valmont, Postcards from the Edge, The Grifters (Natl. Society of Film Critics Award, Acad. Award nom., 1990), Guilty by Suspicion, Regarding Henry, Bugsy, Love Affair, The American President, Richard III, Mars Attacks.
TELEVISION: Movies: Manhunt for Claude Dallas, Hostage. Guest: Miami Vice, Wiseguy. Pilot: It Had to Be You.

BENJAMIN, RICHARD
Actor, Director. b. New York, NY, May 22, 1939. e. Northwestern U. m. actress Paula Prentiss.
THEATER: (Central Park productions) The Taming of the Shrew, As You Like It; toured in Tchin Tchin, A Thousand Clowns, Barefoot in the Park, The Odd Couple. Star Spangled Girl (B'way debut; Theatre World Award, 1966). Also: The Little Black Book, The Norman Conquests, Barefoot in the Park (dir. only; London prod).
PICTURES: Actor: Goodbye Columbus, Catch-22, Diary of a Mad Housewife, The Marriage of a Young Stockbroker, The Steagle, Portnoy's Complaint, The Last of Sheila, Westworld, The Sunshine Boys (Golden Globe Award), House Calls, Love at First Bite, Scavenger Hunt, The Last Married Couple in America, Witches' Brew, How to Beat the High Cost of Living, First Family, Saturday the 14th, Deconstructing Harry. Director: My Favorite Year, Racing with the Moon, City Heat, The Money Pit, Little Nikita, My Stepmother Is an Alien, Downtown, Mermaids, Made in America, Milk Money, Mrs. Winterbourne.
TELEVISION: Movies: No Room to Run (Australia), Packin' It In. Series: He and She (with Paula Prentiss, 1967), Quark. Special: Arthur Miller's Fame.

BENNETT, ALAN
Author, Actor. b. Leeds, England, May 9, 1934. e. Oxford U. With Jonathan Miller, Dudley Moore and Peter Cook co-authored and starred in satirical revue Beyond the Fringe in London (1961) and on B'way (special Tony Award, 1963).
THEATER: Forty Years On (actor, author), Getting On, Habeas Corpus (also actor), The Old Country, Enjoy, Kafka's Dick, Single Spies (also dir.), The Madness of George III.
PICTURES: Actor: Pleasure at Her Majesty's, The Secret Policeman's Other Ball, Long Shot, Dream Child (voice), Little Dorrit. Writer: A Private Function, Prick Up Your Ears, The Madness of King George, The Wind in the Willows (voice), In Love And War.
TELEVISION: Famous Gossips, On the Margin (also actor), An Evening With, A Day Out, Sunset Across the Bay, A Little Outing, A Visit from Miss Prothero, Me—I'm Afraid of Virginia Woolf, Doris and Doreen, The Old Crowd, Afternoon Off, All Day on the Sands, The Insurance Man, Talking Heads (6 TV monologues), One Fine Day, Our Winnie, A Woman of No Importance, Rolling Home, Marks, An Englishman Abroad, Intensive Care (also actor), 102 Boulevard Haussmann, Poetry in Motion.

BENNETT, BRUCE
Actor. r.n. Herman Brix. b. Tacoma, WA, May 19, 1909. e. U. of Washington.
PICTURES: My Son Is Guilty, Lone Wolf Keeps a Date, Atlantic Convoy, Sabotage, Underground Agent, The More the Merrier, Sahara, Mildred Pierce, The Man I Love, A Stolen Life, Nora Prentiss, Cheyenne, Dark Passage, Treasure of the Sierra Madre, Smart Girls Don't Talk, Task Force, The Second Face, The Great Missouri Raid, Angels in the Outfield, Sudden Fear, Dream Wife, Dragonfly Squadron, Robber's Roost, Big Tipoff, Hidden Guns, Bottom of the Bottle, Strategic Air Command, Danger Signal, Silver River, Younger Brothers, Without Honor, Mystery Street, The Last Outpost, Three Violent People, The Outsider, Deadhead Miles, The Clones.

BENNETT, HARVE
Producer. r.n. Harve Fischman. b. Chicago, IL, Aug. 17, 1930. e. UCLA. Quiz Kids radio show, 5 yrs.; newspaper columnist, drama critic; freelance writer; Assoc. prod., CBS-TV; freelance TV writer; prod. of special events. CBS-TV; dir., Television film commercials; program exec., ABC, vice pres., programs west coast, ABC-TV. Pres., Bennett-Katleman. Productions at Columbia Studios.
PICTURES: Star Trek II: The Wrath of Khan (exec. prod., co-story), Star Trek IV: The Voyage Home (prod., co-s.p.), Star Trek V: The Final Frontier (prod., co-story).
TELEVISION: Movies: A Woman Named Golda (exec. prod., Emmy Award), The Jesse Owens Story (exec. prod.), Crash Landing: The Rescue of Flight 232 (writer). Series: Mod Squad (prod., writer), The Young Rebels (creator-writer), Six Million Dollar Man (exec. prod.), Bionic Woman (exec. prod.). American Girls (exec. prod.). From Here to Eternity, Salvage 1, Time Trax (exec. prod.). Mini-Series: Rich Man Poor Man.

BENNETT, HYWEL
Actor, Director. b. Garnant, South Wales, Apr. 8, 1944. Early career National Youth Theatre where he played many leading Shakespearean roles followed by extensive work in British theatre. 1971-81: directed numerous stage productions.
PICTURES: The Family Way (debut, 1967), Drop Dead My Love, Twisted Nerve, The Virgin Soldiers, The Buttercup Chain, Loot, Percy, Endless Night, Alice in Wonderland, Murder Elite, War Zone, Deadline, Deadly Advice.
TELEVISION: Where The Buffalo Roam, Malice Aforethought, Tinker Tailor Soldier Spy (series), Artemis 81, Myself A Mandarin, Frankie and Johnnie, Check Point Chiswick, Twilight Zone, The Idiot, The Traveller, Death of a Teddy Bear, Three's One, Pennies From Heaven, Shelley (series), The Critic, The Consultant, Absent Friends, The Secret Agent, A Mind to Kill, Virtual Murder, The Other Side of Paradise.

BENNIS, JEFFREY D.
Executive. e. Penn. State U and U. Conn., MBA. Started with Clairol, Inc., Hair and Skin Care Divs. as marketing dir. VP Marketing/Programming of Rifkin & Assocs., 1991-94. Elected to bds. of Nat'l Cable TV Assoc. and C-SPAN in 1995. Pres. and COO, Rifkin & Assocs., 1994-.

BENSON, HUGH
Producer. Exec. Prod., Screen Gems; exec. prod., MGM Television. On staff Col.-TV, pilots and long form.
PICTURES: Nightmare Honeymoon (prod.), Logan's Run (assoc. prod.), Billy Jack Goes to Washington (prod.).
TELEVISION: Producer: Contract On Cherry St., Child Stealers, Goldie and the Boxer, A Fire in the Sky, Shadow Riders, Confessions of a Lady Cop, The Dream Merchants, Goldie and the Boxer Go to Hollywood, Goliath Awaits, The Blue and the Gray, Hart to Hart, Master of Ballantrae, Anna Karenina, The Other Lover, I Dream of Jeannie 15 Yrs. Later, Miracle of the Heart: A Boy's Town Story, Crazy Like a Fox, In the Heat of the Night (pilot and series), Daughter of the Streets, Back to Hannibal: Tom and Huck Return, Danielle Steele's Fine Things, Danielle Steele's Changes, Shadow of a Stranger, Diana: Her True Story, Danielle Steele's Message From 'Nam, A Season of Hope, Liz: The Elizabeth Taylor Story.

BENSON, ROBBY
Actor, Writer, Director. r.n. Robert Segal. b. Dallas, TX, Jan. 21, 1956. m. actress Karla DeVito. Father is Jerry Segal, novelist and screenwriter, mother is Ann Benson, veteran of Dallas stage and nat'l summer stock and nat'l spokesperson for Merrill Lynch. Appeared in commercials and summer stock at age 5. B'way debut at age 12 in Zelda. Made dir. debut with White Hot (a.k.a. Crack in the Mirror), 1989. Composed music for Diana Ross, Karla DeVito and soundtrack of film The Breakfast Club.
THEATER: NY: Zelda, The Rothschilds, Dude, The Pirates of Penzance. Regional: Oliver!, Evita, The King and I, King of Hearts, Do Black Patent Leather Shoes Really Reflect Up?

PICTURES: Jory (debut, 1973), Jeremy, Lucky Lady, Ode to Billy Joe, One on One (also co-s.p. with father), The End, Ice Castles, Walk Proud (also co-s.p. & co-composer with father), Die Laughing (also prod., co-s.p., co-composer), Tribute, National Lampoon Goes to the Movies, The Chosen, Running Brave, Harry and Son, City Limits, Rent-a-Cop, White Hot (also dir.), Modern Love (also dir., s.p., composed songs), Beauty and the Beast (voice), Betrayal of the Dove (s.p. only), At Home with the Webbers, Deadly Exposure.
TELEVISION: Movies: Death Be Not Proud, The Death of Richie, Remember When, Virginia Hill Story, All the Kind Strangers, Two of a Kind, California Girls, Invasion of Privacy, Homewrecker, Precious Victims. Specials: Our Town, The Last of Mrs. Lincoln. Series: Search for Tomorrow, Tough Cookies. Guest: One Day at a Time, Alfred Hitchcock Presents. Writer: Animsed. Episode dir.: True Confessions, Thunder Alley, Evening Shade, Good Advice, Muddling Through, Monty, Dream On, Friends, Family Album, Ellen. Pilot dir.: Bringing Up Jack, George Wendt Show, Game Nigh, Commonlaw, Family Beat, Style & Substance, Sabrina the Teenage Witch (also episodes), The Naked Truth.

BENTON, ROBERT

Writer, Director. b. Waxahachie, TX, 1932. e. U. of Texas, B.A. Was art dir. and later consulting ed. at Esquire Magazine where he met David Newman, a writer-editor, and formed writing partnership. Together wrote a monthly column for Mademoiselle (10 years). Made dir. debut with Bad Company, 1972.
THEATER: It's a Bird... It's a Plane... It's Superman (libretto), Oh! Calcutta (one sketch).
PICTURES: Co-writer (with Newman): Bonnie and Clyde, There Was a Crooked Man, What's Up, Doc?, Superman (with Mario Puzo and Tom Mankiewicz). Dir./Writer: Bad Company, The Late Show, Kramer vs. Kramer (Acad. Awards for Best Dir. and Adapted Screenplay, 1979), Still of the Night, Places in the Heart (Acad. Award for Best Original Screenplay, 1984), Nadine, The House on Carroll Street (co-exec. prod. only), Billy Bathgate (dir. only), Nobody's Fool.

BERENGER, TOM

Actor. b. Chicago, IL, May 31, 1950. e. U. of Missouri (drama). Studied acting at H.B. Studios. Acted in regional theatres and off-off-Broadway. Plays include Death Story, The Country Girl, National Anthems, The Rose Tattoo, Electra, Streetcar Named Desire, End as a Man (Circle Rep.).
PICTURES: The Sentinel (debut, 1977), Looking for Mr. Goodbar, In Praise of Older Women, Butch and Sundance: The Early Days, The Dogs of War, Beyond the Door, The Big Chill, Eddie and the Cruisers, Fear City, Rustler's Rhapsody, Platoon (Acad. Award nom.), Someone to Watch Over Me, Shoot to Kill, Betrayed, Last Rites, Major League, Born on the Fourth of July, Love at Large, The Field, Shattered, At Play in the Fields of the Lord, Sniper, Sliver, Gettysburg, Major League 2, Chasers, Last of the Dogmen, The Substitute.
TELEVISION: Movies: Johnny We Hardly Knew Ye, The Avenging Angel, Body Language. Series: One Life to Live (1975-76). Mini-Series: Flesh and Blood, If Tomorrow Comes. Special: Dear America: Letters Home From Vietnam (reader).

BERENSON, MARISA

Actress. b. New York, NY, Feb. 15, 1947. Granddaughter of haute couture fashion designer Schiaparelli. Great niece of art critic and historian Bernard Berenson. Former model.
PICTURES: Death in Venice (debut, 1971), Cabaret, Barry Lyndon, Casanova & Co., Killer Fish, S.O.B., The Secret Diary of Sigmund Freud, La Tete Dans Le Sac, L'Arbalete, Desire, Quel Treno da Vienna, Il Giardino Dei Cigliegi, Winds of the South, White Hunter Black Heart, Night of the Cyclone, The Cherry Orchard, Flagrant Desire, Tonka; Rich, belles, etc.
TELEVISION: Movies: Tourist, Playing for Time, Notorious. Mini-Series: Sins, Hemingway. Also: Lo Scialo, Blue Blood, Have a Nice Night, L'Enfant Des Loups, Oceano, Hollywood Detective, Bel Ami, Murder She Wrote (guest).

BERESFORD, BRUCE

Director, Writer. b. Sydney, Australia, Aug. 16, 1940. e. U. of Sydney, B.A. 1962. Worked as teacher in London, 1961. Film editor, East Nigerian Film Unit, 1966; sect. and head of prod., British Film Inst. Production Board, 1966-71.
PICTURES: Director: The Adventures of Barry McKenzie (also co-s.p.), Barry McKenzie Holds His Own (also prod., co-s.p.), Don's Party, The Getting of Wisdom, Money Movers, Breaker Morant (also s.p.), The Club, Puberty Blues, Tender Mercies, King David, The Fringe Dwellers (also s.p.), Crimes of the Heart, Aria (sequence), Her Alibi, Driving Miss Daisy, Mister Johnson (also co-s.p.), Black Robe, Rich in Love, A Good Man in Africa, Silent Fall, The Last Dance, Paradise Road (also s.p.), Double Jeopardy.
TELEVISION: Movie: Curse of the Starving Class (writer, exec. prod.)

BERG, DICK

Writer, Producer. b. New York, NY. e. Lehigh U. 1942; Harvard Business Sch. 1943. Prior to 1960 writer for TV shows Playhouse 90 Studio One, Robert Montgomery Presents, Kraft Television Playhouse. Prod., writer for Universal Studios, 1961-69; exec. prod., The Chrysler Theatre, Alcoa Premiere, Checkmate. Created and wrote Staccato (series). Prod., writer of over 50 TV movies via his Stonehenge Prods, 1971-85. TV films won 15 Emmies, 23 nominations. Twice elected pres. National Acad. of Television Arts and Sciences.
PICTURES: Prod.: Counterpoint, House of Cards, Banning Shoot (also s.p.), Fresh Horses.
TELEVISION: Prod. and/or writer: Movies: Rape and Marriage: The Rideout Case, An Invasion of Privacy, Thief, Footsteps, Firehouse, American Geisha, Class of '63, Louis Armstrong, Chicago Style, Everybody's Baby: The Rescue of Jessica McClure (exec. prod.), White Mile, Pronto. Mini-Series: A Rumor of War, The Martian Chronicles, The Word, Space, Wallenberg: A Hero's Story.

BERG, JEFF

Executive. b. Los Angeles, CA, May 26, 1947. e. U of California, Berkeley, B.A., 1969. V.P., head lit. div., Creative Mgt. Associates, Los Angeles, 1969-75; v.p., m.p. dept., International Creative Associates, 1975-80; pres., 1980-. Dir., Joseph Intl. Industries. Named chmn. ICM.

BERG, PETER

Actor. b. New York, NY, 1964. e. Malcalester Col., St. Paul, MN.
PICTURES: Miracle Mile, Heart of Dixie, Race for Glory, Shocker, Genuine Risk, Crooked Hearts, Late for Dinner, A Midnight Clear,Aspen Extreme, Fire in the Sky, Girl 6, The Great White Hype, Cop Land, Very Bad Things (writer, dir. only).
TELEVISION: Movies: Rise and Walk: The Dennis Byrd Story, The Last Seduction (also released theatrically). Series: Chicago Hope.

BERGEN, CANDICE

Actress. b. Beverly Hills, CA, May 9, 1946. e. U. of PA. m. late dir. Louis Malle. Father was late ventriloquist Edgar Bergen. Modeled during college; freelance photo-journalist. Autobiography: Knock Wood (1984). B'way debut in Hurlyburly.
PICTURES: The Group (debut, 1966), The Sand Pebbles, The Day the Fish Came Out, Live for Life, The Magus, The Adventurers, Getting Straight, Soldier Blue, Carnal Knowledge, The Hunting Party, T. R. Baskin, 11 Harrowhouse, The Wind and the Lion, Bite the Bullet, The Domino Principle, A Night Full of Rain, Oliver's Story, Starting Over (Acad. Award nom.), Rich and Famous, Gandhi, Stick.
TELEVISION: Movies: Arthur the King, Murder: By Reason of Insanity, Mayflower Madam. Series: Murphy Brown (5 Emmy Awards: 1989, 1990, 1992, 1994, 1995). Mini-Series: Hollywood Wives. Specials: Woody Allen Special, Moving Day (Trying Times).

BERGEN, POLLY

Singer, Actress. r.n. Nellie Burgin b. Bluegrass, TN, July 14, 1930. e. Compton Jr. Coll., CA. Prof. debut radio at 14; in light opera, summer stock; sang with orchestra and appeared in night clubs; Columbia recording star. Bd. chmn. Polly Bergen Co.; chmn. Culinary Co., Inc.; co-chmn. Natl. Business Council for Equal Rights Amendment. Humanitarian Award: Asthmatic Research Inst. & Hosp., 1971; Outstanding Mother's Award, 1984.
THEATRE: B'way.: John Murray Anderson's Almanac, Champagne Complex, First Impressions, Top Man, Plaza Suit, Love Letters.
PICTURES: At War With the Army (debut, 1950), That's My Boy, Warpath, The Stooge, Half a Hero, Cry of the Hunted, Arena, Fast Company, Escape from Fort Bravo, Belle Sommers, Cape Fear, The Caretakers, Move Over Darling, Kisses for My President, A Guide for the Married Man, Making Mr. Right, Mother Mother, Cry-Baby, Dr. Jekyll and Ms. Hyde, Once Upon a Time... When We Were Colored, For Hope.
TELEVISION: Movies: Death Cruise, Murder on Flight 502, Telethon, How to Pick Up Girls, The Million Dollar Face, Born Beautiful, Velvet, Addicted to His Love, She Was Marked For Murder, The Haunting of Sarah Hardy, My Brother's Wife, Lightning Field, Lady Against the Odds, Perry Mason: The Case of the Skin-Deep Scandal, Leave of Absence (also story, co-exec. prod.), Hand In the Glove, Blink Of an Eye, The Surrogate, For Hope. Series: Pepsi-Cola Playhouse (host 1954-55), To Tell the Truth (panelist), The Polly Bergen Show, Baby Talk. Mini-Series: 79 Park Avenue, The Winds of War, War and Remembrance. Guest: G.E. Theatre, Schlitz Playhouse, Playhouse 90, Studio One, Perry Como, Ed Sullivan Show, Bob Hope Show, Bell Telephone, Wonderful World of Entertainment, Dinah Shore Show, Dean Martin Show, Andy Williams Show, Red Skelton Show, Mike Douglas Show. Special: The Helen Morgan Story (Emmy Award, 1958).

BERGER, HELMUT
Actor. r.n. Helmut Steinberger. b. Salzburg, Austria, May 29, 1943. e. Feldkirk College and U. of Perugia. First film, small role in Luchino Visconti's The Witches (Le Streghe) in 1966.
PICTURES: The Young Tigers, The Damned, Do You Know What Stalin Did To Women?, The Garden of the Finzi-Continis, Dorian Gray, A Butterfly with Bloody Wings, The Greedy Ones, The Strange Love Affair, Ludwig, Ash Wednesday, Conversation Piece, The Romantic Englishwoman, Orders to Kill, Madam Kitty, Merry-Go-Round, Code Name: Emerald, The Glass Heaven, Faceless, The Betrothed, The Godfather Part III, Once Arizona, Ludwig 1881, Exit II - Transfigured Night, Still Waters, Die 120 Tage von Bottrop.

BERGER, RICHARD L.
Executive. b. Tarrytown, NY, Oct. 25, 1939. e. Cornell U., UCLA 1963, B.S. In 1964 joined acct. dept., 20th Century-Fox; promoted to exec. position in Fox-TV; was dir. of programming, then v.p. of programs.; asst. v.p. prod. 20th-Fox. Left in 1975 to join CBS-TV as v.p. dramatic development. Returned to 20th-Fox in 1977 as v.p., domestic prod., 20th Century-Fox Pictures. Joined Disney as pres. Walt Disney Pictures; resigned 1984. Named sr. v.p., United Artists Corp., promoted to pres. MGM/UA Film Group, 1988.

BERGER, SENTA
Actress. b. Vienna, Austria, May 13, 1941. Studied ballet, then acting at Vienna's Reinhardt Seminar. Debuted in German films as teen.
PICTURES: Die Lindenwirtin vom Donanstrand (debut, 1957), The Journey, Katia, The Good Soldier Schweik, The Secret Ways, Sherlock Holmes and the Deadly Necklace, The Testament of Dr. Mabuse, The Victors, Major Dundee, The Glory Guys, Cast a Giant Shadow, Bang! Bang! You're Dead, The Poppy Is Also a Flower, The Quiller Memorandum, To Commit a Murder, The Treasure of San Gennaro, The Ambushers, Diabolically Yours, If It's Tuesday This Must Be Belgium, De Sade, When Women Had Tails, Percy, The Scarlet Letter, Merry-Go-Round, White Mafia, The Swiss Conspiracy, Cross of Iron, Nest of Nipers, The Two Lives of Mattia Pascal, The Flying Devils, Swiss Cheese, Am I Beautiful?.

BERGERAC, JACQUES
Actor. b. Biarritz, France, May 26, 1927. Career includes Five Minutes With Jacques Bergerac on radio; in the theatre, on tour in Once More with Feeling; on most major network TV shows.
PICTURES: Twist of Fate, The Time is Now, Strange Intruder, Come Away With Me, Les Girls, Gigi, Man and His Past, Thunder in the Sun, Hypnotic Eye, A Sunday in Summer, Fear No More, Achilles, A Global Affair, Taffy and the Jungle Hunter, The Emergency Operation, Lady Chaplin, The Last Party, One Plus One.

BERGIN, PATRICK
Actor. b. Ireland, 1954.
PICTURES: Those Glory Glory Days, Taffin, The Courier, Mountains of the Moon, Sleeping With the Enemy,.Love Crimes, Highway to Hell, Patriot Games, Map of the Human Heart, Double Cross, Soft Deceit, Lawnmower Man 2: Beyond Cyberspace, Whitechapel, The Proposition, The Island on Bird Street, Taxman, The Lost World, Eye of the Beholder.
TELEVISION: Movies: Act of Betrayal, Robin Hood, They, Frankenstein, Triple Cross; Stolen Women, Captured Hearts;. Robert Ludlum's The Apocalypse Watch, The Ripper. Specials: Morphine and Dolly Mixtures (BBC), The Real Carlotte. Guest: Twilight Zone: Lost Classics.

BERGMAN, ALAN
Songwriter. b. Brooklyn, NY. e. U. of North Carolina, UCLA. m. Marilyn Bergman with whom he collaborates.
THEATER: Ballroom, Something More, The Lady and the Clarinet.
PICTURES: Lyrics: Harlow, Harper, In the Heat of the Night, Fitzwilly, The Thomas Crown Affair (Acad. Award for Best Song: The Windmills of Your Mind, 1968), John and Mary, The Happy Ending, Gaily Gaily, The Magic Garden of Stanley Sweetheart, Move, Pieces of Dreams, Wuthering Heights, Doctor's Wives, Sometimes a Great Notion, Pete 'n' Tillie, The Life and Times of Judge Roy Bean, Breezy, 40 Carats, The Way We Were (Acad. Award for title song, 1973), Summer Wishes Winter Dreams, Harry and Walter Go to New York, Ode to Billy Joe, A Star Is Born, Same Time Next Year, The Promise, And Justice for All, A Change of Seasons, Back Roads, Author Author, Yes Giorgio, Best Friends, Tootsie, Never Say Never Again, Yentl (Academy Award for song score, 1983), The Man Who Loved Women, Micki and Maude, The January Man, Major League, Shirley Valentine, Welcome Home, Switch, For the Boys, Sabrina, Bogus.
TELEVISION: Queen of the Stardust Ballroom (Emmy Award), Hollow Image, Sybil (Emmy Award). Themes: Bracken's World, Maude, The Sandy Duncan Show, Good Times, Alice, The Dumplings, Nancy Walker Show, The Powers That Be, Brooklyn Bridge, etc.

BERGMAN, ANDREW
Writer, Director, Producer. b. Queens, NY, Feb. 20, 1945. e. Harpur Coll., magna cum laude; U. of Wisconsin, Ph.D, history, 1970. Worked as publicist at United Artists. Author: We're in the Money, a study of Depression-era films, and the mysteries: The Big Kiss-Off of 1944, Hollywood and Levine, Sleepless Nights. Also wrote Broadway comedy, Social Security.
PICTURES: Writer: Blazing Saddles, The In Laws, So Fine (also dir.) Oh God You Devil, Fletch, The Freshman (also dir.), Soapdish, Honeymoon in Vegas (also dir.), It Could Happen to You (dir. only), The Scout, Striptease (also dir.), Isn't She Great? Exec. Prod.: Chances Are, Undercover Blues, Little Big League.

BERGMAN, INGMAR
Writer, Director. b. Uppsala, Sweden, July 14, 1918. e. Stockholm U. Directed university play prods.; wrote & dir. Death of Punch, 1940; first theatrical success, dir., Macbeth, 1940; writer-dir., Svensk Film-industri, 1942-present; first s.p., Frenzy, 1943; first directorial assignment, Crisis, 1945; chief prod., Civic Malmo, 1956-60. Directed Swedish prod. Hamlet for stage at Brooklyn Acad. of Music, 1988.
PICTURES: Writer: Torment, Woman Without a Face, Eva, The Last Couple Out, Pleasure Garden, Best Intentions, Sunday's Children. Dir./Writer: Crisis It Rains on Our Love, A Ship to India, Night is My Future (dir. only), Port of Call, The Devil's Wanton, Three Strange Loves, To Joy, This Can't Happen Here (dir. only), Summer Interlude (Illicit Interlude), Secrets of Women, Summer With Monika, The Naked Night (Sawdust and Tinsel), A Lesson in Love, Dreams (Journey Into Autumn), Smiles of a Summer Night, The Seventh Seal, Wild Strawberries, Brink of Life, The Magician, The Virgin Spring (dir. only), The Devil's Eye, Through a Glass Darkly, Winter Light, The Silence, All These Women, Persona, Stimulantia (episode), Hour of the Wolf, Shame, The Ritual, The Passion of Anna, The Touch, Cries and Whispers, Scenes from a Marriage, The Magic Flute, Face to Face, The Serpent's Egg, Autumn Sonata, From the Life of the Marionettes, Fanny and Alexander, After the Rehearsal.
U.S. TELEVISION: The Lie.

BERGMAN, MARILYN
Songwriter. b. Brooklyn, NY. e. NYU. m. Alan Bergman with whom she collaborates. Became pres. of ASCAP, 1994.
THEATER: Ballroom, Something More, The Lady and the Clarinet.
PICTURES: Lyrics: Harlow, Harper, In the Heat of the Night, Fitzwilly, The Thomas Crown Affair (Acad. Award for Best Song: The Windmills of Your Mind, 1968), John and Mary, The Happy Ending, Gaily Gaily, The Magic Garden of Stanley Sweetheart, Move, Pieces of Dreams, Wuthering Heights, Doctor's Wives, Sometimes a Great Notion, Pete 'n' Tillie, The Life and Times of Judge Roy Bean, Breezy, 40 Carats, The Way We Were (Acad. Award for title song, 1973), Summer Wishes Winter Dreams, Harry and Walter Go to New York, Ode to Billy Joe, A Star Is Born, Same Time Next Year, The Promise, And Justice for All, A Change of Seasons, Back Roads, Author Author, Yes Giorgio, Best Friends, Tootsie, Never Say Never Again, Yentl (Academy Award for song score, 1983), The Man Who Loved Women, Micki and Maude, The January Man, Major League, Shirley Valentine, Welcome Home, Switch, For the Boys.
TELEVISION: Queen of the Stardust Ballroom (Emmy Award), Hollow Image, Sybil (Emmy Award). Themes: Bracken's World, Maude, The Sandy Duncan Show, Good Times, Alice, The Dumplings, Nancy Walker Show, The Powers That Be, Brooklyn Bridge, etc.

BERKOFF, STEVEN
Actor, Director, Writer. b. London, England, Aug. 3, 1937. e. studied drama in London and Paris. Founder of London Theatre Group. Author of plays; East, West, Greek Decadence, Sink the Belgrano, Kvetch (London, NY). Staged, adapted and toured with: Kafka's In the Penal Colony, The Trial and Metamorphosis; Agamemnon, The Fall of the House of Usher. Starred in Hamlet and Macbeth. NY theater: Dir.: Kvetch (also writer, actor), Coriolanus, Metamorphosis (starring Baryshnikov). Also dir. Roman Polanski in Metamorphosis in Paris.
PICTURES: Actor: Nicholas and Alexandra, A Clockwork Orange, Barry Lyndon, The Passenger, Outland, McVicar, Octopussy, Beverly Hills Cop, Rambo: First Blood II, Revolution, Underworld, Absolute Beginners, Under the Cherry Moon, The Krays, Decadence (also dir., s.p.), Fair Game.
TELEVISION: Beloved Family, Knife Edge, War and Remembrance, A Season of Giants, Intruders.

BERLE, MILTON
Actor. r.n. Milton Berlinger. b. New York, NY, July 12, 1908. e. Professional Children's Sch., N.Y. Early appearances as child actor incl. film Tillie's Punctured Romance. In vaudeville; on N.Y. stage (Ziegfeld Follies 1936, Life Begins at 8:40, etc.): nightclubs; concurrently on radio & screen. Author: Out of My Trunk (1945), Earthquake (1959), Milton Berle: An Autobiography (1974).

PICTURES: New Faces of 1937, Radio City Revels, Tall Dark and Handsome, Sun Valley Serenade, Rise and Shine, A Gentleman at Heart, Whispering Ghosts, Over My Dead Body, Margin for Error, Always Leave Them Laughing, Let's Make Love, The Bellboy (cameo), It's a Mad Mad Mad Mad World, The Loved One, The Oscar, Don't Worry We'll Think of a Title, The Happening, Who's Minding the Mint?, Where Angels Go... Trouble Follows, For Singles Only, Can Hieronymus Merkin Ever Forget Mercy Humppe and Find True Happiness?, Lepke, Won Ton Ton the Dog Who Saved Hollywood, The Muppet Movie, Cracking Up, Broadway Danny Rose, Driving Me Crazy, Storybook, Legend of Forrest Tucker.
TELEVISION: Movies: Seven in Darkness, Evil Roy Slade, Legend of Valentino, Side By Side. Series: Texaco Star Theatre, Kraft Music Hall TV Show, Jackpot Bowling, Milton Berle Show. Guest: Doyle Against the House, Dick Powell Show, Chrysler TV special, Lucy Show, F Troop, Batman, Love Boat, many others.

BERLINGER, WARREN
Actor. b. Brooklyn, NY, Aug. 31, 1937. e. Columbia U.
THEATER: Annie Get Your Gun, The Happy Time, Bernardine, Take A Giant Step, Anniversary Waltz, Roomful of Roses, Blue Denim (Theatre World Award), Come Blow Your Horn, How To Succeed in Business Without Really Trying, (London) Who's Happy Now?, California Suite (1977-78 tour), Lead Me a Tenor-Toup.
PICTURES: Teenage Rebel, Three Brave Men, Blue Denim, Because They're Young, Platinum High School, The Wackiest Ship in the Army, All Hands on Deck, Billie, Spinout, Thunder Alley, Lepke, The Four Deuces, I Will I Will... for Now, Harry and Walter Go to New York, The Shaggy D.A., The Magician of Lublin, The Cannonball Run, The World According to Garp, Going Bananas, Outlaw Force, Ten Little Indians, Hero, Crime and Punishment, Feminine Touch, That Thing You Do!, Dear God.
TELEVISION: Movies: The Girl Most Likely To..., The Red Badge of Courage, Ellery Queen, Wanted: The Sundance Woman, Sex and the Single Parent, The Other Woman, Trial By Jury, Death Hits the Jackspot. Series: Secret Storm (serial), The Joey Bishop Show, The Funny Side, A Touch of Grace, Operation Petticoat, Small & Frye, Shades of L.A. Guest: Alcoa, Goodyear, Armstrong, Matinee Theatre, The London Palladium, Kilroy, Bracken's World, Columbo, Friends.

BERMAN, BRUCE
Executive. b. New York, NY, April 25, 1952. e. California Inst. of the Arts Film School; UCLA, magna cum laude, history degree 1975; Georgetown Law School and California Bar, 1978. Entered motion picture industry while in law school, as assistant to Jack Valenti, MPAA. Assistant to Peter Guber, Casablanca Filmworks, 1979. Assistant to Sean Daniel & Joel Silver, Universal Pictures, 1979; v.p. prod., Universal, 1982. V.p. prod., Warner Bros., 1984; sr. v.p., prod.,1988; pres., Theatrical Prod.,1989; pres., Worldwide Prod., 1991-96. Founded Plan B Ent., an independent motion picture prod. co., funded by Warner Bros., Inc., 1996.

BERMAN, JOEL P.
Executive. b. Forest Hills, NY, Dec. 3, 1951. e. Ohio University, BS communications, 1973. Acct. exec., Petry Television, NY, 1976-79. Dir. ad sales, Westwood One, NY, 1979-80. East. div. mgr., Paramount Pictures Domestic Television, NY, 1981-84, VP, East. reg. mgr., 1985-87. Sr. VP/sales mgr., GTG Marketing, NY, 1987-89. Back to Paramount Pics. Domestic TV, VP, off-network and features, 1989-90, Sr. VP/nat'l sales mgr., 1990-92, Exec. VP/sales and mktng., LA, 1992-94, pres. of distribution, 1994-97, co-pres., 1997-present.

BERMAN, PANDRO S.
Producer. b. Pittsburgh, PA, March 28, 1905. Son of late Harry M. Berman, gen. mgr. Universal, FBO. Asst. dir. film ed., FBO; film & title ed. Columbia Studios; chief film ed. RKO, later asst. to William Le Baron & David Selznick; became prod. 1931 (RKO). A Champion of Champions Prod. in Fame ratings. Joined MGM 1940.
PICTURES: What Price Hollywood?, Symphony of Six Million, Morning Glory, The Gay Divorcee, Of Human Bondage, Roberta, Alice Adams, The Informer, Quality Street, Top Hat, Follow the Fleet, Winterset, Stage Door, Vivacious Lady, Carefree, Room Service, Gunga Din, Bachelor Mother, The Hunchback of Notre Dame, Ziegfeld Girl, Honky Tonk, Rio Rita, The Seventh Cross, National Velvet, Dragon Seed, The Picture of Dorian Grey, Marriage Is a Private Affair, Undercurrent, Sea of Grass, The Three Musketeers, Madame Bovary, Father of the Bride, Father's Little Dividend, The Prisoner of Zenda, Ivanhoe, All the Brothers Were Valiant, Knights of the Round Table, The Long Long Trailer, Blackboard Jungle, Bhowani Junction, Tea and Sympathy, Something of Value, The Brothers Karamazov, The Reluctant Debutante, Butterfield 8, Sweet Bird of Youth, The Prize, A Patch of Blue, Justine, Move.

BERMAN, RICK
Producer. r.n. Richard Keith Berman. b. Dec. 25, 1944. e. Univ. of Wisconsin-Madison, BA in speech, 1963-67.
PICTURES: Star Trek: Generations (also story), Star Trek: First Contact (also story), Star Trek: The Experience, Star Trek: IMAX, Star Trek IX (also Story).
TELEVISION: Series: Star Trek: The Next Generation, Star Trek: Deep Space Nine, Star Trek: Voyager.

BERMAN, STEVEN H.
Executive. b. Middletown, OH, March 22, 1952. e. Ohio U., B.F.A. in playwriting, 1974; USC, Annenberg Sch. of Communication studied management, 1977. Special research projects Paramount and ABC TV, 1977. Account exec., Gardner Advertising, 1978. Devt. exec., CBS Television, 1979-82; dir. of comedy devt., CBS Television, 1982-84; five years at CBS in series devt., comedy and drama. Vice pres., dramatic devt., Columbia Pictures TV, 1984-85; sr. v.p., Creative Affairs, Columbia Pictures TV, 1985-87; exec. v.p., Columbia TV, div. of Columbia Entertainment TV, 1987-90; ind. prod., Columbia Pictures TV, 1990-present.

BERNARD, MARVIN A.
Executive. b. New York, NY, Oct. 1, 1934. e. NYU. Lab technician
to v.p. in charge of sales, Rapid Film Technique, Inc., 1949-63; developed technological advances in film rejuvenation and preservation, responsible for public underwriting; real estate sales & investments in Bahamas, then with Tishman Realty (commercial leasing div.), 1964-69; est. B-I-G Capital Properties; v.p. and operating head of International Filmtreat 1970-1973; authored Film Damaged Control Chart, a critical analysis of film care and repair, 1971; founded Filmlife Inc. with latest chemical/mechanical and technical advancement in field of film rejuvenation and preservation. Bd. chmn. and chief executive officer of Filmlife Inc., m. p. film rejuvenation, storage and distribution company, 1973-75. Elected president in addition to remaining bd. chairman, Feb. 1975. Consultant to National Archives of U.S. on m.p. preservation, 1979. Dev. m.p. rejuvenation and preservation for 8mm and S8mm, 1981. Introduced this technology to private home movie use before and after transfer to videotape, 1986. Active mem. of awards comm. for tech. achievements, National Acad. TV Arts & Sciences, 1987. Recognition as leading authority and m.p. conservator from Intl. Communications Industries Assn. (ICIA), 1988. Filmlife became 1st national film to video transfer lab in U.S., 1989. Elected to Princeton Film Preservation Group. Established Film/Video Hospital, repairing broken tapes & videocassettes, 1990.

BERNARD, TOM
Executive. Co-President, Sony Pictures Classics.

BERNHARD, HARVEY
Producer. b. Seattle, WA, March 5, 1924. e. Stanford U. In real estate in Seattle, 1947-50; started live lounge entertainment at the Last Frontier Hotel, Las Vegas, 1950. Partner with Sandy Howard, 1958-60; v.p. in chg. prod., David L. Wolper Prods., dividing time between TV and feature films, 1961-68; with MPC, v.p., chg. prod., 1968-70. Now pres. of Harvey Bernhard Ent., Inc.
PICTURES: The Mack (1973), The Omen, Damien—Omen II, The Final Conflict, The Beast Within, Ladyhawke (exec. prod.), The Goonies (prod.), The Lost Boys.
TELEVISION: Movies: Omen IV: The Awakening.

BERNHARD, SANDRA
Actress, Comedian, Singer. b. Flint, MI, June 6, 1955. Moved to Scottsdale, AZ at 10. Began career in Los Angeles 1974 as stand-up comedian while supporting herself as manicurist in Beverly Hills. Has written articles for Vanity Fair, Interview, Spin, recorded and written lyrics for debut album I'm Your Woman (1985) and starred in one-woman off-B'way show Without You I'm Nothing (1988). Published collection of essays, short stories and memoirs, Confessions of a Pretty Lady (1988). Frequent guest on Late Night with David Letterman and Robin Byrd Show.
PICTURES: Cheech and Chong's Nice Dreams (debut, 1981), The King of Comedy, Sesame Street Presents: Follow That Bird, The Whoopee Boys, Track 29, Heavy Petting, Without You I'm Nothing, Hudson Hawk, Inside Monkey Zetterland, Dallas Doll, Somewhere in the City, Lover Girl.
TELEVISION: Movies: Freaky Friday. Series: The Richard Pryor Show, Roseanne.

BERNSEN, CORBIN
Actor. b. North Hollywood, CA, Sept. 7, 1954. e. UCLA, B.A. theater arts; M.F.A playwriting. m. actress Amanda Pays. Son of actress Jeanne Cooper. Teaching asst. at UCLA while working on playwriting degree. 1981 studied acting in NY while supporting self as carpenter and model (Winston cigarettes). Built own theater in loft. Formed theatre co. Theatre of the Night.

PICTURES: Three the Hard Way (debut, 1974), Eat My Dust!, King Kong, S.O.B., Hello Again, Bert Rigby You're a Fool, Major League, Disorganized Crime, Shattered, Frozen Assets, The Killing Box, Savage Land, Major League 2, Trigger Fast, A Brilliant Disguise, The New Age, Radioland Murders, Tales From the Hood, The Great White Hype, The Dentist, Menno's Mind, Circuit Breaker, An American Affair, Recipe for Revenge, The Misadventures of Margaret, Drop Dead, Beings, Major League: Back to the Minors.
TELEVISION: Movies: Breaking Point, Line of Fire: The Morris Dees Story, Dead on the Money, Grass Roots, Love Can Be Murder, Beyond Suspicion, I Know My Son is Alive, Where Are My Children?, Voice From Within, Dangerous Intentions, In the Heat of the Night: By Duty Bound, Bloodhounds, The Cape, Tidalwave: No Escape, Loyal Opposition: Terror in the White House. Series: Ryan's Hope, L.A. Law, A Whole New Ballgame, The Cape. Guest: Anything But Love, Roc, The Larry Sanders Show, Love and War, The Nanny, Night Watch, Seinfeld, Dear John.

BERNSEN, HARRY
Producer, Executive. b. Chicago, IL, June 14, 1935. Served in US Marine Corp., 1953-55. Had own agency, Continental Management, 1956-70. Became prod., 1970.
THEATER: Producer: Beyond the Rainbow, The Boys in Autumn.
PICTURES: Producer/Assoc. prod.: Fool's Parade, Something Big, Three the Hard Way, Take a Hard Ride, Fatal Inheritance.
TELEVISION: Movies: Exec. prod.: The Awakening Land, ABC After School Specials.

BERNSTEIN, ARMYAN
Director, Writer, Producer.
PICTURES: Thank God It's Friday (s.p.), One From the Heart (co-s.p.), Windy City (dir. s.p.), Cross My Heart (dir., co-s.p.), Satisfaction (co-exec. prod.), The Commitments (co-exec. prod.), A Midnight Clear (co-exec. prod.), The Baby-sitters Club (co-exec. prod.), Airforce One, A Thousand Acres, Playing God (exec. prod.), Disturbing Behaviour (prod.), For the Love of the Game, End of Days (prod.).

BERNSTEIN, BOB
Executive. Began public relations career 1952 at DuMont TV Network, followed by 2 yrs. as press agent for Liberace. With Billboard Magazine as review editor 3 yrs. Joined Westinghouse Bdg. Co. as p.r. dir., 1959. In 1963 named p.r. dir. for Triangle Publications, serving in various capacities to 1971. Joined Viacom Intl. as dir. of information services. In 1975 formed own co., March Five Inc., p.r. and promotion firm.

BERNSTEIN, ELMER
Composer, Conductor. b. New York, NY, April 4, 1922. e. Scholarship, Juilliard; Walden Sch., NYU., U.S. Army Air Force radio unit. After war 3 yrs. recitals, musical shows, United Nations radio dept. Pres., Young Musicians Found. 1st v.p. Academy of Motion Picture Arts & Sciences; co-chmn. music branch. Music dir. Valley Symphony. Recording artist, United Artists. More than 90 major films. Pres. of Composers & Lyricists Guild of America.
THEATER: How Now Dow Jones?
PICTURES: Never Wave at a WAC, Sudden Fear, Robot Monster, Cat Women of the Moon, It's a Dog's Life, Man With the Golden Arm, Storm Fear, The View From Pompey's Head, The Ten Commandments, Fear Strikes Out, Desire Under the Elms, Drango, The Naked Eye, Sweet Smell of Success, The Tin Star, Anna Lucasta, The Buccaneer, God's Little Acre, Kings Go Forth, Some Came Running, The Miracle, The Story on Page One, From the Terrace, The Magnificent Seven, The Rat Race, By Love Possessed, The Commancheros, Summer and Smoke, The Young Doctors, Birdman of Alcatraz, Walk on the Wild Side, A Girl Named Tamiko, To Kill a Mockingbird, The Great Escape, The Caretakers, Hud, Kings of the Sun, Rampage, Love With the Proper Stranger, The Carpetbaggers, Four Days in November, The World of Henry Orient, The Hallelujah Trail, The Reward, Seven Women, Cast a Giant Shadow, Hawaii, Thoroughly Modern Millie (Acad. Award, 1967), I Love You Alice B. Toklas, The Scalphunters, True Grit, The Gypsy Moths, Midas Run, Where's Jack?, Cannon for Cordoba, The Liberation of L.B. Jones, A Walk in the Spring Rain, Doctor's Wives, See No Evil, Big Jake, The Magnificent Seven Ride, Cahill U.S. Marshall, McQ., Gold, The Trial of Billy Jack, Report to the Commissioner, From Noon Till Three, The Incredible Sarah, The Shootist, Slap Shot, National Lampoon's Animal House, Bloodbrothers, Meatballs, The Great Santini, Saturn 3, The Blues Brothers, Airplane!, Zulu Dawn, Going Ape, Stripes, An American Werewolf in London, Honky Tonk Freeway, The Chosen, Five Days One Summer, Airplane II: The Sequel, Spacehunter, Trading Places, Class, Bolero, Ghostbusters, The Black Cauldron, Spies Like Us, Legal Eagles, Three Amigos, Amazing Grace and Chuck, Leonard Part 6, Da, Funny Farm, The Good Mother, Slipstream, My Left Foot, The Grifters, The Field, Oscar, A Rage in Harlem, Rambling Rose, Cape Fear (adapt.), The Babe, The Cemetery Club, Mad Dog and Glory, Lost in Yonkers, The Age of Innocence, The Good Son, I Love Trouble, Roommates, Canadian Bacon, Devil in a Blue Dress, Buddy, Hoodlums, The Rainmaker, Twilight, The Deep End of the Ocean, The Wild Wild West.

TELEVISION: Movies: Gulag, Guyana Tragedy, Today's FBI, Rough Riders. Series: Julia, Owen Marshall, Ellery Queen, Serpico, The Chisholms. Specials: Hollywood: The Golden Years, The Race for Space: Parts I & II, D-Day, The Making of the President—1960 (Emmy Award), Hollywood and the Stars, Voyage of the Brigantine Yankee, Crucifiction of Jesus, NBC Best Sellers Theme (1976). Mini-series: A Personal Journey with Martin Scorsese Through American Movies.

BERNSTEIN, FRED
Executive. Was sr. v.p. of business affairs and pres. of world-wide prod. for Columbia Pictures in 1980's before serving as sr. v.p. of MCA Inc.'s Motion Picture Group, 1987-94. Named pres. of Coumbia TriStar Motion Pictures, 1994.

BERNSTEIN, JACK B.
Executive. b. New York, NY, May 6, 1937. e. City U. of New York, B.A., sociology. U.S. Army-Europe, 1956-58; research bacteriol-ogist, 1959-61. Entered industry in 1962 with S.I.B. Prods., Paramount, as v.p. gen. mgr.; 1964-66, v.p. gen. mgr. C.P.I. Prods.; 1966-73, prod. mgr. asst. dir., free lance. 1973-1982, assoc. prod. exec. prod. at several studios. 1983-86, v.p. world-wide prod., Walt Disney Pictures; 1987, sr. v.p., worldwide prod., United Artists Pictures; 1988-90, sr. v.p. worldwide prod., MGM Pictures. Member: DGA, Friars, Academy of MP Arts & Sciences, Academy of TV Arts & Sciences, AFI.
PICTURES: Asst. dir. Hearts of the West. Prod. mngr.: Silver Streak. Assoc. prod.: The Other Side of Midnight, The Fury, Butch and Sundance: The Early Days, Six Pack, Unfaithfully Yours. Exec. prod.: North Dallas Forty, Monsignor, The Beast Within. Co-prod.: The Mambo Kings, Under Siege.

BERNSTEIN, JAY
Producer, Personal manager. b. Oklahoma City, OK. e. Pomona Coll. 1963-76, pres. of Jay Bernstein Public Relations, representing over 600 clients. Formed Jay Bernstein Enterprises, acting as personal manager for Farrah Fawcett, Suzanne Somers, Kristy McNichol, Susan Hayward, Donald Sutherland, Bruce Boxleitner, Robert Conrad, Susan Saint James, Robert Blake, William Shatner, Linda Evans, Cicely Tyson, etc. Past pres., Bernstein Thompson Entertainment Complex, entertainment and personal mgt. firm.
PICTURES: Exec. prod.: Sunburn, Nothing Personal.
TELEVISION: Exec. prod. Movies: The Return of Mike Hammer, Mickey Spillane's Margin for Murder, Wild—Wild—West Revisited, More Wild—Wild West, Murder Me Murder You, More Than Murder, The Return of Mike Hammer, Murder Takes All, The Diamond Trap, Final Notice, Double Jeopardy, Come Die with Me: A Mickey Spillane's Mike Hammer Mystery. Series: Bring 'Em Back Alive, Mike Hammer, Houston Knights.

BERNSTEIN, WALTER
Director, Writer. b. New York, NY. Aug. 20, 1919. e. Dartmouth. Wrote for NY Magazine; in W.W.II was roving correspondent for Yank Magazine. Returned to NY after war. Wrote TV scripts; published Keep Your Head Down (collection of articles).
PICTURES: Writer. Kiss the Blood Off My Hands (co-s.p.), That Kind of Woman, Heller in Pink Tights, A Breath of Scandal (co-s.p.), Paris Blues, The Magnificent Seven (uncredited), Fail Safe, The Money Trap, The Train, The Molly Maguires, The Front, Semi-Tough, The Betsy (co-s.p.), An Almost Perfect Affair, Yanks, Little Miss Marker (dir. debut), The House on Carroll Street.

BERNSTEIN, WILLIAM
Executive. b. New York, NY, Aug. 30, 1933. e. New York U., B.A. 1954; Yale U., L.L.B. 1959. Joined United Artists as an attorney in 1959; v.p.; business affairs, 1967-72; promoted to sr. v.p., 1972. Executive v.p., Orion Pictures, 1978-91. Pres. and CEO Orion Pictures, 1991-92. Exec. v.p., Paramount Pictures 1992-present. Member, A.B.A., A.M.P.A.S.

BERRI, CLAUDE
Director, Actor, Producer. r.n. Claude Langmann. b. Paris, France, July 1, 1934. Started as actor, playing roles in French films and on stage in the 1950s. Began dir. career with short film Jeanine, followed by Le Poulet (The Chicken; also prod.) Acad. Award for best live action short (subject, 1965). 1963, created Renn Productions. 1973, became partner in AMLF distribution co.
PICTURES: Director: The Two of Us (feature debut, 1967), Marry Me Marry Me (also s.p., actor), Le Pistonne (The Man with Connections), Le Cinema de Papa (Cinema of My Father; also prod.), Le Sex Shop (also s.p.), Male of the Century (also s.p., actor), The First Time (also s.p.), Tess (prod.) Inspecteur la Bavure (prod.), Je Vous Aime (prod., s.p.), In a Wild Moment, Je Vous Aime (I Love You), Le Maitre d' Ecole (The Schoolmaster; also prod., s.p.), A Quarter to Two Before Jesus Christ (prod.), L'Africain (prod.), Banzai (prod.), L'Homme Blesse (prod.), Tchao Pantin (also prod., s.p.), Jean la Florette, Manon of the Spring, The Bear (exec. prod.), Valmont (exec. prod.), Uranus (also s.p., prod.), Germinal (also prod., co-s.p.), Queen Margot (prod.), La Separation (prod.), French Twist (exec. prod.), Les Trois Freres (prod., actor), Arlette (prod.), The Ogre (prod.), Didier (Prod.), Le Pari (exec. prod.), Lucie Aubrac (s.p.), Asterix and Obelix vs. Ceasar (prod.).

BERRIDGE, ELIZABETH
Actress. b. New Rochelle, NY, May 2, 1962. Studied acting at Lee Strasberg Inst., Warren Robertson Theatre Workshop.
THEATER: *NY:* The Vampires, The Incredibly Famous Willy Rivers, Outside Waco, Ground Zero Club, Cruise Control, Sorrows and Sons, Crackwalker, Coyote Ugly, Briar Patch. *Regional:* Tuesday's Child, Hedda Gabler, Lulu, Venus and Thumbtacks.
PICTURES: Natural Enemies, The Funhouse, Amadeus, Smooth Talk, Five Corners, When the Party's Over.
TELEVISION: *Movies:* Silence of the Heart, Home Fires Burning, Montana. *Series:* One of the Boys, The Powers That Be, The John Larroquette Show.

BERRY, HALLE
Actress. b. Cleveland, OH, 1968. Named Miss Teen Ohio, Miss Teen All-American, runner up to Miss U.S.A.
PICTURES: Jungle Fever, Strictly Business, The Last Boy Scout, Boomerang, Father Hood, The Program, The Flintstones, Losing Isaiah, Race the Sun, Girl 6, Executive Decision, Rich Man's Wife, B.A.P.S., Bulworth, Why Do Fools Fall in Love.
TELEVISION: *Movie:* Solomon and Sheba. *Mini-Series:* Queen, The Wedding.

BERRY, JOHN
Director. b. New York, NY, 1917. Directed films in Hollywood mid and late '40s; went abroad during McCarthy era in U.S. where worked in French film industry. Later went to London to do stage work, acting as well as directing. Returned to U.S. to do stage work; returned to Hollywood to do TV.
PICTURES: Cross My Heart, From This Day Forward, Miss Susie Slagle's, Casbah, Tension, He Ran All the Way, CCa Va Barder, The Great Lover, Je Suis un Sentimental, Tamango, On Que Mambo, Claudine, Maya, The Bad News Bears Go to Japan, Thieves, Il y a maldonne, 'Round Midnight (actor only), A Man in Love (actor only), La Voyage a Paimpol (also prod.), Captive in the Land (also prod.), Hantises (actor).
TELEVISION: One Drink at a Time, Farewell Party, Mr. Broadway, Sister Sister (also prod.), Angel on My Shoulder, Honeyboy, Legitimate Defense.

BERRY, KEN
Actor. b. Moline, IL, Nov. 3, 1933.
PICTURES: Two for the Seesaw, Hello Down There, Herbie Rides Again, The Cat from Outer Space.
TELEVISION: *Movies:* Wake Me When the War Is Over, The Reluctant Heroes, Every Man Needs One, Letters from Three Lovers, Love Boat II. *Series:* The Ann Sothern Show, Bob Newhart Show (1962), F Troop, Mayberry RFD, Ken Berry Wow Show, Mama's Family. *Guest:* Dick Van Dyke Show, Hazel, Lucy Show, Carol Burnett, Sonny & Cher, etc.

BERTINELLI, VALERIE
Actress. b. Wilmington, DE, April 23, 1960. m. musician Eddie Van Halen. Dramatic training at Tami Lynn Academy of Artists in California. Made early TV appearances in the series, Apple's Way, in commercials, and in public service announcements. Started own prod. company to acquire properties for self.
PICTURE: Number One with a Bullet.
TELEVISION: *Movies:* Young Love First Love, The Promise of Love, The Princess and the Cabbie, I Was a Mail Order Bride, The Seduction of Gina, Shattered Vows, Silent Witness, Rockabye, Pancho Barnes, In a Child's Name, What She Doesn't Know, Murder of Innocence. *Mini-Series:* I'll Take Manhattan. *Specials:* The Secret of Charles Dickens, The Magic of David Copperfield. *Series:* One Day at a Time, Sydney, Cafe Americain.

BERTOLUCCI, BERNARDO
Director, Writer, b. Parma, Italy, May 16, 1940. e. Rome U. Son of Attilio Bertolucci, poet and film critic. At age 20 worked as asst. dir. to Pier Paolo Pasolini on latter's first film, Accatone. Made debut film, The Grim Reaper, from script by Pasolini, 1962; published poetry book, In Cerca del Mistero, 1962. Directed and wrote 3-part TV documentary, La vie del Petrolio for Ital. Oil co. in Iran, 1965-66. Collaborated on s.p. for Ballata de un Milliardo, Sergio Leone's Once Upon a Time in the West, L'inchiesta. Prod.: Sconcerto Rock, La Con Te Non Ci Sto Piu, Lost and Found.
PICTURES: *Dir./Writer:* The Grim Reaper, Before the Revolution, Love and Rage (episode: Agony), Partner, The Spider's Strategem, The Conformist, Last Tango in Paris, 1900, Luna, Tragedy of a Ridiculous Man, The Last Emperor (Acad. Awards for Best Dir. & Screenplay, 1987), The Sheltering Sky, Little Buddha, Stealing Beauty, L'Assedio.

BESSON, LUC
Director, Writer, Producer. b. Paris, France, March 18, 1959. Formed Les Films de Loups, which later changed name to Les Films de Dauphins.
PICTURES: Le Dernier Combat (dir., prod., s.p.), Le Grand Carnaval (2nd unit dir.), Subway (dir., prod., s.p.), Kamikaze (prod., s.p.), Taxi Boy (tech. advis.), The Big Blue (dir., s.p., lyrics, camera op.), La Femme Nikita (dir., s.p., song), The Professional (dir., prod., s.p.), The Fifth Element (dir.), Taxi (s.p., prod.), Joan of Arc (dir.), Nil by Mouth (prod., BAFTA Award, Outstanding Brit. Film, 1997).

BEST, BARBARA
Publicist. b. San Diego, CA, Dec. 2, 1921. e. U. of Southern California, AB, 1943. Pub., 20th Century-Fox, 1943-49; reporter, San Diego Journal, 1950 Stanley Kramer Co. 1950-53; own agency, Barbara Best & Associates, 1953-66; exec. v.p. Jay Bernstein Public rel., 1966; Freeman and Best, 1967-74; Barbara Best Inc. publ. rel. 1975-85; Barbara Best Personal Management, 1997. Retired, 1998.

BEST, JAMES
Actor. r.n. Jules Guy. b. Corydon, IN, July 26, 1926. Magazine model; on stage in European roadshow cast of My Sister Eileen. Served as M.P. with USAAF, WWII.
PICTURES: One Way Street (debut, 1950), Commanche Territory, Winchester 73, Peggy, Kansas Raiders, Air Cadet, Cimarron Kid, Target Unknown, Apache Drums, Ma & Pa Kettle at the Fair, Steel Town, Francis Goes to West Point, Battle at Apache Pass, Flat Top, About Face, The Beast from 20000 Fathoms, Seminole, The President's Lady, City of Bad Men, Column South, Riders to the Stars, The Raid, The Caine Mutiny, Return from the Sea, They Rode West, Seven Angry Men, The Eternal Sea, A Man Called Peter, Forbidden Planet, Calling Homicide, When Gangland Strikes, Come Next Spring, Gaby, The Rack, Man on the Prowl, Hot Summer Night, Last of the Badmen, Verboten!, The Naked and the Dead, The Left Handed Gun, Cole Younger—Gunfighter, The Killer Shrews, Ride Lonesome, Cast a Long Shadow, The Mountain Road, Shock Corridor, Black Gold, The Quick Gun, Black Spurs, Shenandoah, Three on a Couch, First to Fight, Firecreek, The Brain Machine, Sounder, Ode to Billy Joe, Gator (also assoc. prod.), Nickelodeon, Rolling Thunder, The End (also assoc. prod.), Hooper.
TELEVISION: *Movies:* Run Simon Run, Savages, The Runaway Barge, The Savage Bees, The Dukes of Hazzard: Reunion! *Guest:* Alfred Hitchcock Presents, Twilight Zone, The Andy Griffith Show, Hawkins, Enos, In the Heat of the Night, etc. *Series:* Dukes of Hazzard. *Mini-Series:* Centennial.

BETHUNE, ZINA
Actress, Dancer, Singer. b. New York, NY, Feb. 17, 1950. New York City Ballet (Balanchine), Zina Bethune & Company Dance Theatre, Bethune Theatredanse. Special performance at the White House and Kennedy Center.
THEATER: *Bway:* Most Happy Fella, Grand Hotel. National tours: Sweet Charity, Carnival, Oklahoma!, Damn Yankees, Member of the Wedding, The Owl and The Pussycat, Nutcracker.
PICTURES: Sunrise At Campobello, Who's That Knocking at My Door, The Boost.
TELEVISION: *Movies:* Party of Five, Nutcracker: Money Madness Murder (also choreographer) . *Series:* The Nurses, The Guiding Light, Love of Life. *Guest:* Lancer, Cains Hundred, Naked City, Route 66, Little Women, Santa Barbara, Judy Garland Show, Jackie Gleason Show, Gunsmoke, Dr. Kildare, Emergency, Planet of The Apes, Police Story, Chips, Hardy Boys, Dirty Dancing. *Specials:* The Gymnast (An ABC Afterschool Special), Heart Dancing, From the Heart.

BETTGER, LYLE
Actor b. Philadelphia, PA, Feb. 13, 1915. e. Haverford School, Philadelphia, American Acad. of Dramatic Art, N.Y. m. Mary Rolfe, actress. Started in summer stock; in road cos. of Brother Rat, Man Who Came to Dinner.
THEATER: John Loves Mary, Love Life, Eve of St. Mark, The Male Animal, Sailor Beware, The Moon is Down.
PICTURES: No Man of Her Own, Union Station, First Legion, Greatest Show on Earth, The Denver & Rio Grande, Vanquished, Forbidden, The Great Sioux Uprising, All I Desire, Drums Across the River, Destry, Carnival Story, Sea Chase, Showdown at Abilene, Gunfight at OK Corral, Town Tamer, Johnny Reno, Nevada Smith, Return of The Gunfighter, Impasse, The Hawaiians, The Seven Minutes.
TELEVISION: Court of Last Resort, Grand Jury, Hawaii 5-0, Police Story, Bonanza, Combat, Gunsmoke, etc.

BEVILLE, HUGH M., JR.
Executive; b. April 18, 1908. e. Syracuse U., NYU (MBA). To NBC 1930 statistician, chief statistician; research mgr., dir., research. U.S. Army 1942-46. Dir. of research and planning for NBC then v.p., planning and research, 1956; v.p., planning, 1964; consultant, 1968. Professor Business Admin., Southampton Coll., 1968. Exec. dir., Broadcast Rating Council, 1971-82. Author, cons., contributing ed., TV/Radio Age, 1982-85. Author of Audience Ratings; Radio, Television, Cable, 1985, Elected member, Research Hall of Fame, 1986.

BEY, TURHAN
Actor. b. Vienna, Austria, March 30, 1922. Came to U.S. in 1930's studying acting at Ben Bard's School of Dramatic Arts, Pasadena Playhouse.

PICTURES: Footsteps in the Dark (debut, 1941), Burma Convoy, Raiders of the Desert, Shadows on the Stairs, The Gay Falcon, Junior G-Men of the Air (serial), The Falcon Takes Over, A Yank on the Burma Road, Bombay Clipper, Drums of the Congo, Destination Unknown, Arabian Nights, The Unseen Enemy, The Mummy's Tomb, Danger in the Pacific, Adventures of Smilin' Jack (serial), White Savage, The Mad Ghoul, Background to Danger, Follow the Boys, The Climax, Dragon Seed, Bowery to Broadway, Ali Baba and the 40 Thieves, Frisco Sal, Sudan, Night in Paradise, Out of the Blue, The Amazing Mr. X, Adventures of Casanova, Parole Inc., Song of India, Prisoners of the Casbah, Stolen Identity (prod. only), Healer, Possessed by the Night, The Skateboard Kid II, Virtual Combat.
TELEVISION: Guest: Seaquest, Murder She Wrote, Babylon 5

BEYMER, RICHARD
Actor. r.n. George Richard Beymer, Jr., b. Avoca, IA, Feb. 21, 1939. e. N. Hollywood H.S., Actors Studio. Performer, KTLA, Sandy Dreams, Fantastic Studios, Inc., 1949, Playhouse 90.
PICTURES: Indiscretion of an American Wife (debut, 1953), So Big, Johnny Tremain, The Diary of Anne Frank, High Time, West Side Story, Bachelor Flat, Five Finger Exercise, Hemingway's Adventures of a Young Man, The Longest Day, The Stripper, Grass (Scream Free!), Cross Country, Silent Night Deadly Night 3: Better Watch Out, My Girl 2.
TELEVISION: Movies: Generation, With a Vengeance. Guest: The Virginian, Walt Disney (Boston Tea Party), Dr. Kildare, Man from U.N.C.L.E., Moonlighting, Murder She Wrote, The Bronx Zoo. Series: Paper Dolls, Twin Peaks.

BIALIK, MAYIM
Actress. b. Dec. 12, 1976.
PICTURES: Pumpkinhead (debut, 1988), Beaches.
TELEVISION: Movies: Blossom in Paris, Don't Drink the Water. Series: Blossom. Specials: Earth Day Special, Sea World Mother Earth Celebration (host), Surviving a Break-Up, The Kingdom Chums: Original Top Ten (voice), I Hate the Way I Look, For Our Children: The Concert (host). Pilot: Molly. Guest: Webster, Facts of Life, MacGyver, Empty Nest, The John Larroquette Show.

BICK, JERRY
Producer. b. New York, NY, April 26, 1923. e. Columbia U., Sorbonne. Taught English at U. of Georgia, before entering film industry in pub. dept. of MGM, N.Y. Opened own literary agency in Hollywood after stint with MCA. Began career as producer in London; debut film, Michael Kohlhaas, 1969. 1986-89, exec. v.p. worldwide prod., Heritage Entertainment.
PICTURES: The Long Goodbye, Thieves Like Us, Russian Roulette, The Big Sleep, Against All Odds (exec. prod.), Swing Shift.

BIEHN, MICHAEL
Actor. b. Anniston, AL, July 31, 1956. Raised in Lincoln, NB, and Lake Havisu, AZ. At 18 years moved to Los Angeles and studied acting with Vincent Chase. First professional job in 1977 in TV pilot for Logan's Run.
PICTURES: Grease (debut, 1978), Coach, Hog Wild, The Fan, The Lords of Discipline, The Terminator, Aliens, The Seventh Sign, Rampage, In a Shallow Grave, The Abyss, Navy Seals, Time Bomb, K2, DeadFall, Tombstone, Deep Red, Jade.
TELEVISION: Movies: Zuma Beach, A Fire in the Sky, China Rose, Deadly Intentions, A Taste for Killing, Strapped. Series: The Runaways. Guest: Logan's Run, Hill Street Blues, Police Story, Family Pilots: James at 15, The Paradise Connection.

BIGELOW, KATHRYN
Director, Writer. b. 1951. e. SF Art Inst., Columbia. Studied to be painter before turning to film with short Set-Up, 1978. Was script supervisor on Union City; appeared in film Born in Flames.
PICTURES: The Loveless (feature debut as co-dir. with Monty Montgomery, 1981; also co-s.p.), Near Dark (also co-s.p.), Blue Steel (also co-s.p.), Point Break, Strange Days, Undertow (s.p.).
TELEVISION: Mini-Series: Wild Palms (co-dir.).

BIKEL, THEODORE
Actor. b. Vienna, Austria, May 2, 1924. Moved to Palestine (Israel) as teen where he made stage debut in Tevye the Milkman. Studied acting at Royal Academy of Dramatic Arts in London. London stage debut in 1948. Autobiography: Theo (1995).
THEATER: Tonight in Samarkland, The Lark, The Rope Dancers, The Sound of Music, Cafe Crown, Fiddler on the Roof.
PICTURES: The African Queen, Melba, Desperate Moment, The Divided Heart, The Little Kidnappers, The Vintage, The Pride and the Passion, The Enemy Below, Fraulein, The Defiant Ones (Acad. Award nom.), I Want to Live, The Angry Hills, The Blue Angel, A Dog of Flanders, My Fair Lady, Sands of the Kalahari, The Russians Are Coming the Russians Are Coming, Sweet November, My Side of the Mountain, Darker Than Amber, 200 Motels, The Little Ark, Prince Jack, Dark Tower, See You in the Morning, Shattered, Crisis in the Kremlin, My Family Treasure, Benefit of the Doubt, Shadow Conspiracy.
TELEVISION: Movies: The Eternal Light, Look Up and Live, Who Has Seen the Wind?, The Diary of Anne Frank, Killer by Night, Murder on Flight 502, Victory at Entebbe, Christine Cromwell: Things That Go Bump in the Night, The Final Days, Babylon 5: In the Beginning. Mini-series: Testimony of Two Men, Loose Change.

BILBY, KENNETH W.
Executive. b. Salt Lake City, UT, Oct. 7, 1918. e. Columbia U; U. of Arizona, B.A. With N.Y. Herald-Tribune, 1947-50. Author of New Star in the Near East, 1950. Pub. rel. rep. to RCA Victor, Camden, NJ, 1950-54. Exec. v.p. National Broadcasting Co., N.Y., 1954-60. V.p. public affairs, RCA, 1960-62; exec. v.p., 1962-75; exec. v.p. corporate affairs, 1976-present.

BILL, TONY
Director, Producer, Actor. b. San Diego, CA, Aug. 23, 1940. e. Notre Dame U. Founded Bill/Phillips Prods. with Julia and Michael Phillips, 1971-73; Tony Bill Prods. 1973-92; Barnstorm Films, 1993-. Acad. of M.P. Arts & Sciences, bd. of govs., bd of trustees, chmn. prods. branch.
PICTURES: Director: My Bodyguard (debut, 1980), Six Weeks, Five Corners (also co-prod.), Crazy People, Untamed Heart (also co-prod.), A Home of Our Own. Prod.: Hearts of the West (exec. prod.), Harry and Walter Go to New York, Boulevard Nights (exec. prod.), Going in Style, Little Dragons (also actor). Co-producer: Deadhead Miles, Steelyard Blues, The Sting (Acad. Award for Best Picture, 1973), Taxi Driver. Actor: Come Blow Your Horn (debut, 1963), Soldier in the Rain, Marriage on the Rocks, None But the Brave, You're a Big Boy Now, Ice Station Zebra, Never a Dull Moment, Castle Keep, Flap, Shampoo, Heartbeat, Pee-wee's Big Adventure, Less Than Zero.
TELEVISION: Director: Dirty Dancing (pilot), Love Thy Neighbor, Next Door, One Christmas, Oliver Twist, A Chance of Snow. Actor: Movies: Haunts of the Very Rich, Having Babies II, The Initiation of Sarah, With This Ring, Are You in the House Alone?, Portrait of an Escort, Freedom, Washington Mistress, Running Out, The Killing Mind. Series: What Really Happened to the Class of '65?. Mini-Series: Washington Behind Closed Doors. Guest: Alfred Hitchcock Presents (Night Caller, 1985). Special: Lee Oswald - Assassin (BBC).

BILLS, ELMER E.
Executive. b. Salisbury, MO, July 12, 1936. e. University of Missouri, B.S. Partner B & B Theatres, Inc.

BILSON, BRUCE
Director. b. Brooklyn, NY, May 19, 1928. e. UCLA, BA, Theater Arts, 1950. m. actress Renne Jarrett. Father was prod. George Bilson; son is prod.-dir. Danny Bilson, daughter is prod. Julie Ahlberg. Asst. film ed. 1951-55; USAF photo unit 1952-53; asst. dir. 1955-65. Dir. since 1965 of more than 390 TV shows.
PICTURES: The North Avenue Irregulars, Chattanooga Choo Choo.
TELEVISION: Movies/pilots: The Odd Couple, The Dallas Cowboys Cheerleaders, BJ and the Bear, The Misadventures of Sheriff Lobo, Half Nelson, Finder of Lost Loves, The Girl Who Came Gift Wrapped, The Ghosts of Buxley Hall, The New Gidget, Barefoot in the Park, The Bad News Bears, Harper Valley PTA. Series: The Sentinel, Touched by an Angel, Viper, The Flash, Dinosaurs, Barney Miller, Get Smart (Emmy Award, 1968), Andy Griffith Show (asst. dir.), Route 66 (asst. dir.), The Baileys of Balboa (also assoc. prod.), Hogan's Heroes, House Calls, Alice, Private Benjamin, Life With Lucy, Spenser: For Hire, Hotel, Dallas, Hawaii Five-O, Dynasty, The Fall Guy, Nightingales.

BINDER, STEVE
Producer, Director, Writer. b. Los Angeles, CA, Dec. 12. e. Univ. of Southern California. 1960-61, announcer in Austria and Germany with AFN, Europe. Prof. of Cinema, Univ. Southern CA. Mem.: DGA, Producers Guild of America, Writers Guild of America, NARAS, ATAS.
PICTURES: Director: The T.A.M.I. Show, Give 'Em Hell Harry!, Melissa, Father Guido Sarducci Goes to College.
TELEVISION: Prod./Dir.: Soupy Sales Show, Jazz Scene U.S.A., Hullabaloo, The Danny Kaye Show, Hallelujah Leslie!, TJ's, Petula, America, A Funny Thing Happened on the Way to the White House, Comedy of the 60's, Don Kirshner's Rock Concert, Olivia Newton-John, Norman Corwin Theater, Mac Davis Series, The Big Show, Primetime Emmy's, Motown Revue, Peggy Fleming Special, Dorothy Hammil Special, Shields & Yarnell Series (also writer) The Magic Castle Special, Star Wars Holiday Special, Father Guido Sarducci at UCSB, A Tribute to Sam Kinison, Smhatar, Jane Fonda In Search of the Missing Smhatar, Steve Allen Show (1963-65, 1973), Elvis Presley Comeback Special, Barry Manilow Special (also exec. prod., writer, Emmy Award, 1977), Diana Ross '81, Ringling Bros & Barnum Bailey Circus (also writer), Pee-wee's Playhouse (exec. prod., writer), Barry Manilow Big Fun on Swing Street, Pee-wee's Playhouse Christmas Special, A Tribute to Sam Kinison, Diana Ross at Wembley, Diana Ross Sings Jazzy Blues, Diana Ross—World Tour, Diana Ross in Central Park (Cable Ace Award, also writer), Diana Ross (also writer), The International Special Olimpics, 65th Anniversary of the Grand Ole Opry, The First Annual ESPY Awards, Liza Minneli, Lucy in London, Fiesta Texas, Eddie Rabbit Special, One Night With You, Disney's First Lady of Magic (exec. prod.). Exec. Prod./Writer:: Soul Train Music Awards, Zoobilee Zoo, Disney's Greatest Hits on Ice, Disney's Alladin on Ice, Disney's Beauty and the Beast on Ice, Innocent Love (MOW), The Chevy Chase Show, SK8 TV, On the Television Series, Tales From the Whoop, The Beach Boys Summer Series, Television's Greatest Performances.

BINOCHE, JULIETTE
Actress. b. Paris, France, March 9, 1964. e. Natl Schl. of Dramatic Art, Paris. Began acting career while in school, performing on stage. In 1984, after some small roles in films and TV prods., appeared in Jean-Luc Godard's, Je Vous Salue Marie. In 1985, gained recognition at the Cannes Film Festival for her role in Andre Techine's Rendez-Vous.
PICTURES: Liberty Bell, Le Meilleur de la Vie, Adieu Blaireau, La Vie de la Familie, Je Vous Salue Marie, Les Nanas, Rendez-Vous, Mauvais Sang, Mon Beau-Frere a Tue Ma Soeur, The Unbearable Lightness of Being, Un Tour de Manege, Les Amants du Pont-Neuf, Mara (Women & Men), Wuthering Heights, Damage, Three colors: Blue, Le Hussard Sur le Toit, The English Patient (Acad. Award, 1996; BAFTA), A Couch in New York.

BIONDI, JR. FRANK J.
Executive. b. Jan. 9, 1945. e. Princeton U.; Harvard U., MBA (1968). Various investment banking positions, 1968-74. Asst. treas. Children's TV Workshop 1974-78. V.p. programming HBO 1978-82; pres. HBO 1983, then chmn. & chief exec. off. Joined Coca-Cola Co. as exec. v.p., entertainment business arm, 1984. Resigned 1987 to join Viacom International as pres. and CEO. Pres., MCA, 1996.

BIRCH, THORA
Actress. b. California. Began acting at age 4. First appeared in commericals.
PICTURES: Paradise, All I Want for Christmas, Patriot Games, Hocus Pocus, Monkey Trouble, Clear and Present Danger, Now and Then, Alaska.
TELEVISION: Series: Parenthood, Day by Day. Guest: Amen, Doogie Howser M.D.

BIRKIN, JANE
Actress. b. London, England, Dec. 14, 1946. Daughter is actress Charlotte Gainsbourg. Sister of dir.-writer Andrew Birkin. Was subject of Agnes Vardas` 1988 documentary Jane B. par Agnes V.
PICTURES: Blow-Up, Kaleidoscope, Wonderwall, Les Chemins de Katmandou, La Piscine, Cannabis, Romance of a Horse Thief, Trop jolies pour etre honnetes, Dark Places, Projection Privee, La Moutarde me monte au nex, Le Mouton Enrage, 7 Morts sur Ordonnance, Catherine et Cie, La Course a l'echalote, Je T'Aime Moi Non Plus, Seriex comme let plaisir, Le Diable au Coeur, L'Animal, Death on the Nile, Au bout du bout du banc, Melancolie Baby, La Miel, La Fille Prodigue, Evil Under the Sun, L'Ami de Vincent, Circulez u'a rien a voir, Love on the Ground, le Garde du Corps, The Pirate, Beethoven's Nephew, Dust, Leave All Fair, la Femme de ma vie, Comedie!, Kung Fu Master (also story), Soigne ta droite, Daddy Nostalgia, Between the Devil and the Deep Blue Sea.

BIRNBAUM, ROGER
Producer, Executive. b. Teaneck, NJ. e. Univ. of Denver. Was v.p. of both A&M Records and Arista records before becoming m.p. prod.. Headed Guber/Peters Company, then named pres. of worldwide prod., United Artists; pres. of worldwide prod. and exec. v.p. of 20th Century Fox. Left Fox in 1993 to become co-founder of Caravan Pictures.
PICTURES: Prod./Exec. Prod.: The Sure Thing, Young Sherlock Homes, Who's That Girl, The Three Musketeers, Angie, Angels in the Outfield, A Low Down Dirty Shame, Houseguest, Tall Tale, While You Were Sleeping, Dead Presidents, Powder, Celtic Pride, The Beautician and the Beast, G.I. Jane, Gone Fishin', Grosse Pointe Blank, Washington Square, Metro, Rocket Man, A Small Miracle, Flash, Holy Man, Six Days Seven Nights.

BIRNEY, DAVID
Actor. b. Washington, DC, April 23, 1940. e. Dartmouth Coll., B.A., UCLA, M.A. Phd. Southern Utah St. (hon.). Following grad. sch. and the Army spent 2 yrs. in regional theatre, Amer. Shakespeare Festival, Lincoln Center Repertory Theatre, Great Lakes Theatre Festival, Mark Taper Forum, Shakespeare Theatre Washington DC, Hartford Stage Co., Barter Theatre, to N.Y. where appeared in Lincoln Center prod. of Summertree (Theatre World Award). Appeared for two yrs. on TV daytime series, Love Is a Many Splendored Thing, doing other stage roles in same period. Theatre panelist, Natl. Endowment for the Arts; bd. mem., Hopkins Center, Dartmouth College; bd. of Foundation for Biomedical Research.
THEATER: Comedy of Errors (NY debut; NY Shakespeare Fest). NY & Regional: Amadeus, Benefactors, Anthony & Cleopatra, Man and Superman, Macbeth, Hamlet, Richard II, III, Romeo & Juliet, Much Ado About Nothing, King John, Titus Andronicus, Major Barbara, Biko Inquest, Playboy of the Western World, The Miser, Antigone, My Fair Lady, Camelot, Love Letters, Present Laughter, Twelfth Night, Talley's Folley, Rumors, Social Security, Enemy of the People, Mark Twain's The Diaries of Adam & Eve.
PICTURES: Caravan to Vaccares, Trial by Combat, Oh God Book II, Prettykill, Nightfall.

TELEVISION:
TELEVISION: Movies: Murder or Mercy, Bronk, Serpico: The Deadly Game, Someone's Watching Me!, High Midnight, Only With Married Men, OHMS, Mom The Wolfman & Me, The Five of Me, The Long Journey Home (also co-exec. prod.), Love and Betrayal, Always Remember I Love You, Touch and Die, Keeping Secrets, The Champions. Series: Bridget Loves Bernie, Serpico, St. Elsewhere, Glitter, Live Shot, Beyond 2000 (host), Raising Kids (host), Great American TV Poll (host). Mini-Series: Night of the Fox, Seal Morning, Adam's Chronicles, Testimony of Two Men, Master of the Game, Valley of the Dolls, The Bible. Specials: Missing: Have You Seen This Person? Drop Everything and Read, 15 and Getting Straight, Mark Twain's The Diaries of Adam and Eve (co-prod.), St. Joan. Guest appearances in series & anthology shows.

BISHOP, LARRY
Actor.
MOVIES: Wild in the Street, The Savage Seven, The Devil's Eight, Angel Unchained, Chrome and Hot Leather, Shanks, How Come Nobody's on Our Side?, The Big Fix, Hey Good Lookin' (voice), The Sting II, Mad Dog Time (also dir., prod., writer), Underworld (also writer).

BISSET, JACQUELINE
Actress. b. Weybridge, England, September 13, 1944. e. French Lycaee, London. After photographic modeling made film debut in The Knack, 1965.
PICTURES: The Knack... and How to Get It (debut, 1965), Cul de Sac, Two For The Road, Casino Royale, The Cape Town Affair, The Sweet Ride, The Detective, Bullitt, The First Time, Secret World, Airport, The Grasshopper, The Mephisto Waltz, Believe in Me, Stand Up and Be Counted, The Life & Times of Judge Roy Bean, The Thief Who Came to Dinner, Day for Night, Le Manifique, Murder on the Orient Express, End of the Game, The Spiral Staircase, St. Ives, Sunday Woman, The Deep, The Greek Tycoon, Secrets, Who Is Killing the Great Chefs of Europe?, Together? (I Love You I Love You You), When Time Ran Out, Rich and Famous, Inchon, Class, Under the Volcano, High Season, Scenes From the Class Struggle in Beverly Hills, La Maison de Jade, Wild Orchid, The Maid, A Judgment in Stone.
TELEVISION: Movies: Forbidden, Anna Karenina, Choices, Leave of Absence. Mini-Series: Napoleon and Josephine: A Love Story.

BLACK, ALEXANDER F.
Publicist. b. New Rochelle, NY, Dec. 27, 1918. e. Brown U., BA, 1940. Joined Universal 1941. U.S. Navy 1942-45, Lt. Sr. Grade. Rejoined Universal 1946 serving in various capacities in Foreign Department, becoming dir. of foreign publicity for Universal International Films, Inc. in 1967. Named exec. in chg. intl. pro-motion for MCA-TV, 1974.

BLACK, KAREN
Actress. b. Park Ridge, IL, July 1, 1942. r.n. Karen Ziegler. e. Northwestern U. Left school for NY to join the Hecscher House, appearing in several Shakespearean plays. In 1965 starred in Playroom, which ran only 1 month but won her NY Drama Critic nom. as best actress.
THEATER: Happily Never After, Keep It in the Family, Come Back to the Five and Dime Jimmy Dean Jimmy Dean.
PICTURES: You're a Big Boy Now (debut, 1966), Hard Contact, Easy Rider, Five Easy Pieces (Acad. Award nom.), Drive He Said, A Gunfight, Born To Win, Cisco Pike, Portnoy's Complaint, The Pyx, Little Laura and Big John, Rhinoceros, The Outfit, The Great Gatsby, Airport 1975, Law and Disorder, Day of the Locust, Nashville, Family Plot, Crime and Passion, Burnt Offerings, Capricorn One, Killer Fish, In Praise of Older Women, The Squeeze, The Last Word, Chanel Solitaire, Come Back to the Five and Dime Jimmy Dean Jimmy Dean, Killing Heat (The Grass is Singing), Can She Bake a Cherry Pie?, Martin's Day, Bad Manners (Growing Pains), Cut and Run (Amazon: Savage Adventure), Invaders from Mars, Flight of the Spruce Goose, It's Alive III, Hostage, Eternal Evil, The Invisible Kid, Out of the Dark, Homer and Eddie, Night Angel, Miss Right, Dixie Lanes, Sister City, Zapped Again, Twisted Justice, Over Exposure, The Children, Mirror Mirror, Haunting Fear, Quiet Fire, Children of the Night, Hotel Oklahoma, Killer's Edge, Club Fed, Evil Spirits, Moon Over Miami, The Legend of the Rollerblade 7, Hitz (Judgment), FInald Judgment (Mrs. Sorrel), Caged Fear, Bound & Gagged: A Love Story, The Player, Rubin & Ed, The Trust, The Double O Kid, Sister Island, Plan 10 From Outer Space, The Wacky Adventures of Dr. Boris & Mrs. Duluth, Odyssey, Every Minute Is Goodbye, A Thousand Stars, Children of the Corn III: The Fever, Crime Time.
TELEVISION: Movies: Trilogy of Terror, The Strange Possession of Mrs. Oliver, Mr. Horn, Power, Where the Ladies Go, Because He's My Friend, Full Circle Again (Canadian TV). Guest: In the Heat of the Night.

BLACK, NOEL
Director. b. Chicago, IL, June 30, 1937. e. UCLA, B.A., 1959; M.A. 1964. Made short film Skaterdater and won numerous awards including the Cannes' Grand Prix for Best Short Film.
PICTURES: Pretty Poison (debut, 1968), Cover Me Babe, Jennifer on My Mind, Mirrors, A Man a Woman and a Bank, Private School, Mischief (s.p., exec. prod.).
TELEVISION: Trilogy: The American Boy, The World Beyond, I'm a Fool, The Golden Honeymoon, The Electric Grandmother, The Doctors Wilde, Meet the Munceys, Eyes of the Panther, The Hollow Boy, Swan's Crossing, The Baby Sitter's Club, Doplhin Cove. Movies: Mulligan's Stew, The Other Victim, Prime Suspect, Happy Endings, Quarterback Princess, Promises to Keep, A Time to Triumph, My Two Loves, Conspiracy of Love, The Town Bully. Mini-series: Deadly Intentions.

BLACK, STANLEY
Composer, Conductor, Musical director. OBE. b. London, Eng. Resident conductor, BBC, 1944-52. Musical director 105 feature films and Pathe Newsreel music: Music dir. Associated British Film Studios 1958-64. Guest conductor, Royal Philharmonic Orchestra and London Symphony. Orchestra; many overseas conducting engagements including (1977) Boston Pops and Winnipeg Symphony. Associated conductor Osaka Philharmonic Orchestra. Exclusive recording contract with Decca Record Co. since 1944.
PICTURES: Crossplot, The Long the Short and The Tall, Rattle of a Simple Man, The Young Ones, Hell Is a City, Top Secret, Valentino.

BLACKMAN, HONOR
Actress. b. London, England, 1926. Stage debut. The Gleam 1946.
PICTURES: Fame Is the Spur (debut, 1947), Quartet, Daughter of Darkness, A Boy A Girl and a Bike, Diamond City, Conspirator, So Long at the Fair, Set a Murderer, Green Grow the Rushes, Come Die My Love, Rainbow Jacket, Outsiders, Delavine Affair, Three Musketeers, Breakaway, Homecoming, Suspended Alibi, Dangerous Drugs, A Night to Remember, The Square Peg, A Matter of Who, Present Laughter, The Recount, Serena, Jason & the Golden Fleece, Goldfinger, The Secret of My Success, Moment to Moment, Life at the Top, A Twist of Sand, Shalako, Struggle for Rome, Twinky (Lola), The Last Grenade, The Virgin and the Gypsy, Fright, Something Big, Out Damned Spot, Summer, Cat and the Canary.
TELEVISION: African Patrol, The Witness, Four Just Men, Probation Officer series, Top Secret, Ghost Squad, Invisible Man, The Saint, The Avengers series, Voice of the Heart, The Upper Hand (series).

BLADES, RUBEN
Actor, Composer, Singer, Writer. b. Panama City, Panama, July 16, 1948. e. U. of Panama (law and political science, 1974), Harvard U., L.L.M., 1985. Has recorded more than 14 albums, winning 3 Grammy Awards (1986, 1988, 1997). With his band Seis del Solar has toured U.S., Central America and Europe. President of Panama's Papa Egoro political party.
PICTURES: Actor: The Last Fight (debut 1982), Crossover Dreams (also co-s.p.), Critical Condition, The Milagro Beanfield War, Fatal Beauty, Homeboy, Disorganized Crime, The Lemon Sisters, Mo' Better Blues, The Two Jakes, Predator 2, Homeboy, The Super, Life With Mikey, A Million to Juan, Color of Night. Music: Beat Street, Oliver & Company, Caminos Verdes (Venezuela), Q&A, Scorpion Spring, The Devil's Own, The Chinese Box, The Cradle Will Rock.
TELEVISION: Guest: Sesame Street. Movies: Dead Man Out (ACE Award), One Man's War, The Josephine Baker Story (Emmy nom.), Crazy from the Heart (Emmy nom.), The Heart of the Deal, Miracle on I-880.

BLAIN, GERARD
Actor, Director. b. Paris, France, Oct. 23, 1930. Began his professional career in 1943 as an extra in Marcel Carne's The Children of Paradise. Appeared on stage in Marcel Pagnol's Topaze (1944). Military service in a parachute regiment. In 1955 Julien Duvivier gave him his first major role in Voici le Temps des Assassins (Murder a la Carte). By 1969 had appeared in more than 30 stage and film roles before becoming a dir. and co-author.
PICTURES: Actor: Voice le temps des assassins, Les Mistons, Giovani mariti, Charlotte et son Jules, Le Beau Serge, Les Cousins, Match contre la mort, Il Gobbo, I Delfini, L'Oro di Roma, Hatari!, Les Vierges, La Smania addosso, La Bonne soupe, Un Amore, Joe Caligula, Negresco -- Eine toedliche Affaere, Un homme de trop, Le Pelican (also dir.), Der Amerikanische Freund, Un dimance de flic, Pas de vieux os, Poussiere d'ange, Der Schnee der Anden, L'Enfant de l'hiver, Jour apres jour, Faut-il aimer Mathilde?, Chasse gardee. Director: Les Amis (also s.p.), Un enfant dans la foule, Un second souffle, Le Rebelle, Pierre et Djemila (also s.p.).

BLAIR, JANET
Actress. b. Blair, PA, April 23, 1921. r.n. Martha Janet Lafferty. With Hal Kemp's Orchestra; toured in South Pacific, 1950-52.
PICTURES: Three Girls About Town (debut, 1941), Blondie Goes to College, Two Yanks in Trinidad, Broadway, My Sister Eileen, Something to Shout About, Once Upon a Time, Tonight and Every Night, Tars and Spars, Gdallant Journey, The Fabulous Dorseys, I Love Trouble, The Black Arrow, Fuller Brush Man, Public Pigeon No. 1, Boys Night Out, Burn Witch Burn, The One and Only Genuine Original Family Band, Won Ton Ton the Dog Who Saved Hollywood.
TELEVISION: Series: Leave it to the Girls (panelist), Caesar's Hour, The Chevy Show, The Smith Family. Special: Arabian Nights, Tom Sawyer. Guest: Bell Telephone Hour, Ed Sullivan, Murder She Wrote, etc.

BLAIR, LINDA
Actress. b. St. Louis, MO, Jan. 22, 1959. Model and actress on TV commercials before going into films.
PICTURES: The Sporting Club (debut, 1971), The Exorcist, Airport '75, Exorcist II: The Heretic, Roller Boogie, Wild Horse Hank, Hell Night, Ruckus, Chained Heat, Savage Streets, Savage Island, Red Heat, Night Patrol, Night Force, Silent Assassins, Grotesque (also prod.), Witchery, The Chilling, Bad Blood, Moving Target, Up Your Alley, Repossessed, Aunt Millie's Will, Zapped Again, Dead Sleep, Double Blast, Temptress, Prey of the Jaguar.
TELEVISION: Movies: Born Innocent, Sarah T.--Portrait of a Teenage Alcoholic, Sweet Hostage, Victory at Entebbe, Stranger in Our House, Calendar Girl Cop Killer? The Bambi Bembenek Story, Perry Mason: The Case of the Heartbroken Bride. Guest: Fantasy Island, Murder She Wrote.

BLAIR, STEWART
Executive. b. Scotland. e. Univ. of Glasgow. Was v.p. of Chase Manhattan Bank N.A. in NY, before joining Tele-Communications Inc. in 1981. Served as vice-chmn. & CEO of United Artists Entertainment Company. 1992, appointed chmn. and CEO of United Artists Theatre Circuit Inc.; removed, 1996. Bd. member of Foundation of Motion Picture Pioneers, exec. v.p. of Will Rogers Memorial Fund.

BLAKE, JEFFREY
Executive. President, Sony Pictures Releasing.

BLAKE, ROBERT
Actor. r.n. Michael Gubitosi. b. Nutley, NJ, Sept. 18, 1933. Started as a child actor in Our Gang comedies as Mickey Gubitosi, also appeared as Little Beaver in Red Ryder series. Later was Hollywood stunt man in Rumble on the Docks and The Tijuana Story. First adult acting job was at the Gallery Theater in Hatful of Rain.
PICTURES: I Love You Again (debut, 1940, as Bobby Blake), Andy Hardy's Double Life, China Girl, Mokey, Salute to the Marines, Slightly Dangerous, The Big Noise, Lost Angel, Red Ryder series (as Little Beaver), Meet the People, Dakota, The Horn Blows at Midnight, Pillow to Post, The Woman in the Window, A Guy Could Change, Home on the Range, Humoresque, In Old Sacramento, Out California Way, The Last Round-Up, Treasure of the Sierra Madre, The Black Rose, Blackout (also co-prod.), Apache War Smoke, Treasure of the Golden Condor, Veils of Bagdad, The Rack, Screaming Eagles, Three Violent People, Beast of Budapest, Revolt in the Big House, Pork Chop Hill, The Purple Gang, Town Without Pity, PT 109, The Greatest Story Ever Told, The Connection, This Property Is Condemned, In Cold Blood, Tell Them Willie Boy is Here, Ripped-Off, Corky, Electra Glide in Blue, Busting, Coast to Coast, Second-Hand Hearts, Money Train.
TELEVISION: Series: The Richard Boone Show, Barretta (Emmy Award, 1975), Hell Town (also exec. prod.). Movies: The Big Black Pill (also creator & exec. prod.), The Monkey Mission (also creator & exec. prod.), Of Mice and Men (also exec. prod.), Blood Feud, Murder 1--Dancer 3 (also exec. prod.), Heart of a Champion: The Ray Mancini Story, Judgment Day: The John List Story. Guest: One Step Beyond, Have Gun Will Travel, Bat Masterson.

BLAKELY, SUSAN
Actress. b. Frankfurt, Germany, Sept. 7, 1948, where father was stationed in Army. Studied at U. of Texas. m. prod., media consultant Steve Jaffe. Became top magazine and TV commercial model in N.Y.
PICTURES: Savages (debut, 1972), The Way We Were, The Lords of Flatbush, The Towering Inferno, Report to the Commissioner, Shampoo, Capone, Dreamer, The Concorde—Airport '79, Over the Top, Dream a Little Dream, My Mom's a Werewolf, Russian Holiday, Seven Sundays.

TELEVISION: *Series*: Falcon Crest, The George Carlin Show. *Mini-Series*: Rich Man Poor Man. *Movies*: Secrets, Make Me an Offer, A Cry For Love, The Bunker, The Oklahoma City Dolls, Will There Really Be A Morning?, The Ted Kennedy Jr. Story, Blood & Orchids, April Morning, Fatal Confession: A Father Dowling Mystery, Broken Angel, Hiroshima Maiden, Ladykillers, Sight Unseen, The Incident, End Run, Dead Reckoning, Murder Times Seven, And the Sea Will Tell, Sight Unseen, Blackmail, Wildflower, Against Her Will: An Incident in Baltimore, Intruders, No Child of Mine, Honor Thy Father and Mother: The True Story of the Menendez Murders, Color Me Perfect, Co-ed Call Girl, Race Against Fear. *Special*: Torn Between Two Fathers. *Guest*: Step by Step. *Pilot*: Dad's a Dog.

BLAKLEY, RONEE
Actress, Singer. b. Stanley, ID, 1946. Wrote and performed songs for 1972 film Welcome Home Soldier Boys.
PICTURES: Nashville (debut, 1975; Acad. Award nom.), The Private Files of J. Edgar Hoover, The Driver, Renaldo and Clara, Good Luck Miss Wyckoff (Secret Yearnings/The Sin), The Baltimore Bullet, A Nightmare on Elm Street, Return to Salem's Lot, Student Confidential, Someone to Love.

BLANC, MICHEL
Actor. b. France, 1952.
PICTURES: Que la Fete Commence, The Tenant, Les Bronzes, The Adolescent, Les Bronzes font du Ski, Le Cheval d'Orgueil, Walk in the Shadow, Les Fugitives, Evening Dress, Menage, I Hate Actors!, Story of Women, Monsieur Hire, Chambre a Part, Strike It Rich, Uranus, Merci la Vie, Prospero's Books, The Favor the Watch and the Very Big Fish, Ready to Wear (Pret-a-Porter), Grosse Fatigue (also dir., s.p.), The Monster, The Grand Dukes.

BLANCHETT, CATE
Actress. e. National Institute of Dramatic Art, Australia.
THEATER: Top Girls, Kafka Dances, Oleanna, Hamlet, Sweet Phoebe, The Tempest, The Blind Giant is Dancing.
PICTURES: Police Rescue, Parklands, Paradise Road, Thank God He Met Lizzie, Oscar and Lucinda, Pushing Tin, Elizabeth I, Dreamtime Alice, The Talented Mr. Ripley, An Ideal Husband.
TELEVISION: *Movie*: Heartland, Bordertown. *Guest*: G.P., Police Rescue.

BLANCO, RICHARD M.
Executive. b. Brooklyn, NY. e. electrical engineering, Wentworth Institute. J.C., 1925-27; bus. admin., U. of CA, 1939-40; U.S. Govt. Coll., 1942. Superv. Technicolor Corp., 1931-56; organ. and operator Consumer Products, Kodachrome film process., Technicolor, 1956-62; dir. of MP Govt. and theatre sales, NY & DC, 1963-65; gen. mgr. of Technicolor Florida photo optns. at Kennedy Space Center.; prod. doc. & educ. films for NASA, 1965; v.p. of tv div., Technicolor Corp. of America; 1967 elected corporate v.p. Technicolor, Inc.; 1971 pres., Technicolor Graphic Services, Inc.; 1974, elected chmn. of bd. of Technicolor Graphic Services; 1977, elected to bd. of dirs. of Technicolor Inc.

BLANK, MIKE
Executive. e. U. Michigan, 1933. Began career as poster clerk for Pathe, 1927. Head of const., maint., concessions, Central States Theatres, 1933. US Navy, 1942, in charge of visual ed. for 7th Naval Dist. in Miami. Pres., CEO, chmn., Central States 1950. B. V. Sturdivant Award, NATO/ShoWest, 1990.

BLANK, MYRON
Circuit executive. b. Des Moines, IA, Aug. 30, 1911. e. U. of Michigan. Son of A. H. Blank, circuit operator. On leaving coll. joined father in operating Tri-States and Central States circuits. On leave 1943-46 in U.S. Navy, officer in charge visual educ. Now pres. Central States Theatre Corp.; pres. TOA, 1955; chmn. bd. TOA Inc. 1956-57; exec. chmn. of NATO. Pres. of Greater Des Moines Comm. Built Anne Blank Child Guidance Center-Raymond Blank Hospital for Children. Endowed chair for gifted and talented children at Univ. of Iowa; permanent scholarship at Wertzman Inst., Israel. Sturdevant Award from NATO, Humanitarian Award from Variety Club in 1980. Partial scholarship for 80 students annually for 3-week seminar at Univ. of Iowa.

BLATT, DANIEL
Producer. e. Philips Andover Acad., Duke U., Northwestern U Sch. of Law.Indt. prod. since 1976; prior posts: resident counsel, ABC Pictures; exec. v.p. Palomar Pictures.
PICTURES: I Never Promised You a Rose Garden, Independence Day, Cujo, Restless, The Boost.
TELEVISION: *Movies*: Circle of Children, Zuma Beach, The Children Nobody Wanted, Sadat, V—The Final Battle, Badge of the Assassin, Raid on Entebbe, Sacred Vows, A Winner Never Quits, Sworn to Silence, Common Ground. *Series*: V, Against the Law.

BLATTY, WILLIAM PETER
Writer, Director, Producer. b. New York, NY, Jan. 7, 1928. e. George Washington U., Seattle U. Worked as editor for U.S. Information Bureau, publicity dir. for USC and Loyola U. before becoming novelist and screenwriter. Novels include John Goldfarb Please Come Home (filmed), Twinkle Twinkle Killer Kane, The Exorcist, Legion (filmed as Exorcist III).
PICTURES: The Man From the Diner's Club, A Shot in the Dark, Promise Her Anything, What Did You Do in the War Daddy?, Gunn, The Great Bank Robbery, Darling Lili, The Exorcist (also prod.; Academy Award for Best Adapted Screenplay, 1973), The Ninth Configuration (a.k.a. Twinkle Twinkle Killer Kane; also dir., prod.), The Exorcist III (also dir.), Dimiter (dir.).

BLAU, MARTIN
Executive. b. New York, NY, June 6, 1924. e. Ohio U., 1948. Employed on newspapers in OH, TX, WV. Pub. dept., Columbia Pictures, 1951; asst. pub. mgr. 1959; pub. mgr., Columbia Int'l, 1961; admin. asst. to v.p. of adv. & pub. Columbia Pictures, 1966. Dir. adv. and publicity, Columbia Pictures Int'l, 1970; v.p.; 1971; sr. v.p., 1985. Retired, 1988.

BLAY, ANDRE
Executive. In 1979, sold Magnetic Video to 20th Century Fox, named pres., CEO, 20th Century Fox Home Video; 1982, formed The Blay Corporation; 1982, joined with Norman Lear and Jerry Perenchio, founders of Embassy Communications, as chairman and CEO of Embassy Home Entertainment; 1986, when Embassy sold to Nelson Group, left to form Palisades Entertainment Group with Elliott Kastner.
PICTURES: *Exec. Prod.*: Prince of Darkness, They Live, Jack's Back, Homeboy, Braindamage, The Blob, A Chorus of Disapproval, Village of the Damned (prod.).

BLECKNER, JEFF
Director, Producer. b. Brooklyn, NY, Aug. 12, 1943. e. Amherst College, BA., 1965; Yale Sch. of Drama, MFA 1968. Taught drama at Yale, also participated in the theater co. 1965-68. 1968-75 theater dir. NY Shakespeare Fest. Public Theatre (2 Drama Desk Awards, Tony nom. for Sticks and Bones); Basic Training of Pavlo Hummel (Obie Award, 1971), The Unseen Hand (Obie Award). Began TV career directing The Guiding Light, 1975.
TELEVISION: Hill Street Blues (Emmy Award, DGA Award, 1983), Concealed Enemies (Emmy Award, 1984), Daddy, I'm Their Momma Now (Emmy nom.), Do You Remember Love (Christopher, Humanitas, Peabody Awards, Emmy nom.), Fresno, Terrorist on Trial, Brotherly Love, My Father My Son, Favorite Son, Mancuso F.B.I. (exec. prod.), Lifestories (exec. prod.), Last Wish, In Sickness and In Health, The Round Table (pilot), 7th Avenue (pilot), Serving In Silence (Emmy nom.), A Father For Charlie, Any Day Now. *Mini-series*: In The Best of Families, Beast, The Advocate's Devil, Blackout Effect.

BLEES, ROBERT
Writer, Producer. b. Lathrop, MO, June 9, 1925. e. Dartmouth, Phi Beta Kappa. Writer/photographer, Time and Life Magazines. Fiction: Cosmopolitan, etc. Exec. boards of Writers Guild, Producers Guild. Executive consultant, QM Prods.; BBC (England). Trustee, Motion Picture & TV Fund. Expert witness, copyright and literary litigation, U.S. Federal Court, California Superior Court.
PICTURES: Magnificent Obsession, Autumn Leaves, The Glass Web.
TELEVISION: *Producer*: Combat!, Bonanza, Bus Stop, Kraft Theater. Writer also: Alfred Hitchcock, Cannon, Barnaby Jones, Harry O, Columbo. *Co-creator*: The New Gidget.

BLEIER, EDWARD
Executive. b. New York, NY, October 16, 1929. e. Syracuse U., 1951, C.U.N.Y., grad. courses. Reporter/sportscaster: Syracuse and NY newspapers/stations: 1947-50. Prog. service mgr., DuMont Television Network, 1951; v.p., radio-television-film, Tex McCrary, Inc. 1958. American Broadcasting Company, 1952\-57; 1959-68 v.p. in chg. pub. relations (marketing, advertising, publicity), & planning, broadcast div.; v.p. in chg. of daytime sales & programming; v.p./gen. sales mgr., ABC-TV Network. U.S. Army Psy. War School; Ex-chmn., TV Committee, NASL; Trustee, NATAS; founder-dir. & vice-chmn., International TV Council (NATAS); past-pres., IRTS; trustee, Keystone Center for Scientific & Environmental Policy, Council on Foreign Relations; ATAS; AMPAS; guest lecturer at universities. Chmn., Steering comm., Aspen B'dcaster's Conference. 1969-present: Warner Bros. Inc.: Pres, pay-TV, cable & network features.

BLETHYN, BRENDA
Actress. b. Ramsgate, Kent, England, Feb. 20, 1946.
PICTURES: The Witches, A River Runs Through It, Secrets & Lies (Acad. Award. nom.; Golden Globe Award, 1997; L.A. Film Critics Award; BAFTA Award), Remember Me?, Girls Night, Music From Another Room, Remember Me?, In the Winter Dark, Little Voice, Keeping Time.
TELEVISION: *Movies*: Grown-Ups, King Lear, Henry VI (Part One), The Bullion Boys. *Series*: Chance In a Million, The Labours of Erica, Outside Edge. *Mini-series*: The Buddha of Suburbia. *Guest*: The Minister.

BLIER, BERTRAND
Director. b. Paris, France, 1939. Son of late actor Bernard Blier. Served as asst. dir. to Georges Lautner, John Berry, Christian-Jaque, Denys de la Paatelliere and Jean Delannoy for two years before dir. debut.
PICTURES: Hitler Connais Pas (debut, 1963), Breakdown, C'Est une Valse (s.p. only), Going Places, Femme Fatales (Calmos), Get Out Your Handkerchiefs (Academy Award for Best Foreign-Language Film, 1978), Buffet Froid, Beau-pere, My Best Friend's Girl, Notre Historie, Menage, Too Beautiful for You, Thank You Life, Patrick Deware (actor only), 1-2-3 Sun, Mon Homme.

BLOCK, WILLARD
Executive. b. New York, NY, March 18, 1930.; e. Columbia Coll., Columbia U. Law Sch., 1952. Counter-Intelligence Corps., U.S. Army, 1952-54, account exec., Plus Marketing, Inc. 1954-55; joined sales staff, NBC Television Network, 1955-57; sales staff, CBS Enterprises, Inc., 1957; intl. sales mgr, 1960; dir., intl. sales, 1965; v.p., 1967; v.p., Viacom Enterprises, 1971; pres., 1972; v.p. MCA-TV, 1973; v.p., gen. mgr., Taft, H-B International, Inc.; pres. Willard Block, Ltd.; 1979, named pres., Viacom Enterprises; 1982-89, pres. Viacom Worldwide Ltd.; 1989, retired. Currently consultant to Sumitomo Corp., TCI, Int'l. Telecommunications, Jupiter Telecommunications, Ltd. Past consultant & mem. bd. dirs, Starsight Telecast.

BLOODWORTH-THOMASON, LINDA
Producer, Writer. b. Poplar Bluff, MO, April 15, 1947. With husband Harry Thomason co-owner of Mozark Productions.
TELEVISION: Series; M*A*S*H (writer), Rhoda (writer), Flithy Rich (prod.), Lime Street (co-exec. prod., creator), Designing Women (co-exec. prod., creator, writer), Evening Shade (co-exec. prod., creator, writer), Women of the House. Pilots: Dribble (prod.), Over and Out (writer), London and Davis in New York (prod.).

BLOOM, CLAIRE
Actress. r.n. Claire Blume. b. London, England, Feb. 15, 1931.e. Guildhall School of Music & Drama, Central Sch. To U.S. in 1940 during London evacuation. Returned to England in 1943. Stage debut with Oxford Rep 1946 in It Depends What You Mean. Author: Limelight and After: The Education of an Actress (1982).
THEATER: The White Devil (London debut), The Lady's Not for Burning, Ring Round the Moon, A Streetcar Named Desire; at Stratford-on-Avon, Old Vic seasons, etc. B'way: Rashomon, A Doll's House, Hedda Gabler, Vivat Vivat Regina, Cherry Orchard, Long Day's Journey Into Night.
PICTURES: The Blind Goddess (debut, 1948), Limelight, Innocents in Paris, The Man Between, Richard III, Alexander the Great, The Brothers Karamazov, The Buccaneer, Look Back in Anger, The Royal Game (Schachnovelle/ Brainwashed), The Wonderful World of the Brothers Grimm, The Chapman Report, The Haunting, 80000 Suspects, High Infidelity, Il Maestro di Vigevano, The Outrage, The Spy Who Came in From the Cold, Charly, The Illustrated Man, Three Into Two Won't Go, A Severed Head, Red Sky at Morning, A Doll's House, Islands in the Stream, Clash of the Titans, Deja Vu, Sammy and Rosie Get Laid, Crimes and Misdemeanors, The Princess and the Goblin (voice), Mighty Aphrodite, Daylight, Wrestling With Alligators.
TELEVISION: Specials/Movies (US/UK): Cyrano de Bergerac, Caesar and Cleopatra, Misalliance, Anna Karenina, Wuthering Heights, Ivanov, Wessex Tales, An Imaginative Woman, A Legacy, In Praise of Love, The Orestaia, Henry VIII, Backstairs at the White House, Brideshead Revisited, Hamlet, Cymbeline, King John, Ann and Debbie, The Going Up of David Lev, Ellis Island, Separate Tables, Florence Nightingale, The Ghost Writer, Time and the Conways, Shadowlands, Liberty, Promises to Keep, The Belle of Amherst, Hold the Dream, Anastasia, Queenie, Intimate Contact, Beryl Markham: A Shadow on the Sun, Oedipus the King, The Lady and the Highwayman, The Camomile Lawn, The Mirror Crack'd From Side to Side, It's Nothing Personal, Barbara Taylor Bradford's Remember., Family Money, Imogen's Face

BLOOM, MARCIE
Executive. Co-President, Sony Pictures Classics.

BLOOM, VERNA
Actress. b. Lynn, MA, Aug. 7, 1938. e. Boston U. Studied drama at Uta Hagen-Herbert Berghof School. Performed with small theatre groups all over country; then started repertory theatre in Denver.
THEATER: B'way: Marat/Sade, Brighton Beach Memoirs. Off B'way.: Messiah, Bits and pieces, The Cherry Orchard.
PICTURES: Medium Cool (debut, 1969), The Hired Hand, High Plains Drifter, Badge 373, National Lampoon's Animal House, Honkytonk Man, After Hours, The Journey of Natty Gann, The Last Temptation of Christ.
TELEVISION: Movies: Where Have All the People Gone?, Sarah T.: Portrait of a Teenage Alcoholic, The Blue Knight, Contract on Cherry Street, Playing for Time, Rivkin-Bounty Hunter, Gibbsville.

BLOUNT, LISA
Actress. b. Fayetteville, AK, July 1, 1957. e. Univ. of AK. Auditioned for role as extra in film September 30, 1955 and was chosen as the female lead.
PICTURES: September 30, 1955, Dead and Buried, An Officer and a Gentleman, Cease Fire, What Waits Below, Radioactive Dreams, Prince of Darkness, Nightflyers, South of Reno,Out Cold, Great Balls of Fire, Blind Fury, Femme Fatale, Cut and Run, Stalked.
TELEVISION: Series: Sons and Daughters. Pilot: Off Duty. Movies: Murder Me Murder You, Stormin' Home, The Annihilator, Unholy Matrimony, In Sickness and in Health, An American Story, Murder Between Friends, Judicial Consent. Guest: Moonlighting, Magnum P.I., Starman, Murder She Wrote, Hitchhiker, Picket Fences.

BLUM, HARRY N.
Executive. b. Cleveland, OH, Oct. 3, 1932. e. U. of Michigan, B.B.A., LL.B. Toy & hobby industry exec., gen. mngr. Lionel division of General Mills, mngt. consultant, and venture capital mngr. before entering industry. Now heads The Blum Group, entertainment financing, packaging, production and worldwide distrib.
PICTURES: Executive Action (assoc. prod.), The Land That Time Forgot (assoc. prod.), At the Earth's Core (assoc. prod.), Drive-In (assoc. prod.), Diamonds (exec. prod.), The Bluebird (assoc. prod.), Obsession (prod.), Skateboard (prod.), The Magician of Lublin (exec. prod.), Duran Duran—Arena (exec. prod.), Young Lady Chatterly II (exec. prod.), Eminent Domain (exec. prod.).

BLUM, MARK
Actor. b. Newark, NJ, May 14, 1950. Studied drama at U. of Minnesota and U. of Pennsylvania. Also studied acting with Andre Gregory, Aaron Frankel and Daniel Seltzer. Extensive Off-B'way work after debut in The Cherry Orchard (1976).
THEATER: NY: Green Julia, Say Goodnight Gracie, Table Settings, Key Exchange, Loving Reno, Messiah, It's Only a Play, Little Footsteps, Cave of Life, Gus & Al (Obie Award), Lost in Yonkers (Broadway). Regional: Brothers (New Brunswick, NJ), Close Ties (Long Wharf), The Cherry Orchard (Long Wharf), Iago in Othello (Dallas). Mark Taper Forum: American Clock, Wild Oats, Moby Dick Rehearsed and An American Comedy.
PICTURES: Lovesick, Desperately Seeking Susan, Just Between Friends, Crocodile Dundee, Blind Date, The Presidio, Worth Winning, Emma & Elvis, The Low Life, Miami Rhapsody, Denise Calls Up, Sudden Manhattan, Stag.
TELEVISION: Series: Sweet Surrender, Capitol News. Pilot: Critical Condition. Guest: Miami Vice, St. Elsewhere, Roseanne. Movies: Condition: Critical, Indictment: The McMartin Trial.

BLUMOFE, ROBERT F.
Producer. b. New York, NY, Sept. 23, 1909. e. Columbia Coll., AB, Columbia U. Sch. of Law, JD. v.p., West Coast oper., U.A., 1953-66; indept. prod., pres. RFB Enterprises, Inc; American Film Institute, dir., AFI—West, 1977-81. Now indep. prod.

BLUTH, DON
Animator, Director, Producer, Writer. b. El Paso, TX, Sept. 13, 1938.e. Brigham Young U. Animator with Walt Disney Studios 1956 and 1971-79; animator with Filmation 1967; Co-founder and dir. with Gary Goldman and John Pomery, Don Bluth Productions, 1979-85; animator, Sullivan Studios, 1986. Joined Fox Animation as dir./prod., 1995.
PICTURES: Animation director: Robin Hood, The Rescuers, Pete's Dragon, Xanadu. Director/Co-Producer: The Secret of NIMH (also co-s.p.), An American Tail, The Land Before Time, All Dogs Go to Heaven (also co-story), Rock-a-Doodle, Hans Christian Andersen's Thumbelina (also s.p.), A Troll in Central Park, The Pebble and the Penguin (presenter).
TELEVISION: Banjo the Woodpile Cat (prod., dir., story, music and lyrics).

BLYTH, ANN
Actress. b. Mt. Kisco, NY, Aug. 16, 1928. e. New Wayburn's Dramatic Sch. On radio in childhood; with San Carlos Opera Co. 3 years; Broadway debut in Watch on the Rhine.
PICTURES: Chip Off the Old Block (debut, 1944), The Merry Monahans, Babes on Swing Street, Bowery to Broadway, Mildred Pierce (Acad. Award nom.), Swell Guy, Brute Force, Killer McCoy, A Woman's Vengeance, Another Part of the Forest, Mr. Peabody and the Mermaid, Red Canyon, Once More My Darling, Free for All, Top o' the Morning, Our Very Own, The Great Caruso, Katie Did It, Thunder on the Hill, I'll Never Forget You, Golden Horde, One Minute to Zero, The World in His Arms, Sally and Saint Anne, All the Brothers Were Valiant, Rose Marie, The Student Prince, King's Thief, Kismet, Slander, The Buster Keaton Story, The Helen Morgan Story.
TELEVISION: Guest: Lux Video Theatre (A Place in the Sun).

BOCHCO, STEVEN
Producer, Writer. b. New York, NY, Dec. 16, 1943. m. actress Barbara Bosson. e. Carnegie Tech, MFA. Won MCA fellowship in college, joined U-TV as apprentice. Awards incl. Humanitas, NAACP Image, Writers Guild, George Foster Peabody, & Edgar Allen Poe Awards.
PICTURES: Co-Writer: The Counterfeit Killer, Silent Running.
TELEVISION: Writer and story ed.: Name of the Game, Columbo, McMillan and Wife; Delvecchio (writer-prod.), Paris (exec. prod.), Richie Brockelman (co-creator), Turnabout (writer), Invisible Man (writer), Vampire (writer), Hill St. Blues (creator, prod., writer; Emmys 1981, 1982, 1983, 1984), Every Stray Dog and Kid (exec. prod.), Bay City Blues (exec. prod., writer, creator), L.A. Law (Emmy Awards: 1987, 1989), Hooperman, Cop Rock, NYPD Blue (Emmy Award, 1995), Byrds of Paradise, Murder One, Public Morals, Total Security (prod.), Brooklyn South (prod.).

BOCHNER, HART
Actor, Director. b. Toronto, Ontario, Oct. 3, 1956. Son of actor Lloyd Bochner. e. U. of. San Diego. Wrote, prod., dir. short film The Buzz (1992) starring Jon Lovitz.
PICTURES: Islands in the Stream (debut, 1977), Breaking Away, Terror Train, Rich and Famous, The Wild Life, Supergirl, Making Mr. Right, Die Hard, Apartment Zero, Mr. Destiny, Mad at the Moon, Fellow Traveller, Batman: Mask of the Phantasm (voice), The Innocent. Dir.: High School High, PCU, The Breakup.
TELEVISION: Movies: Having It All, Complex of Fear. Mini-Series: Haywire, East of Eden, The Sun Also Rises, War and Remembrance, And the Sea Will Tell, Children of the Dust. Special: Teach 109.

BOCHNER, LLOYD
Actor. b. Toronto, Canada, July 29, 1924. Father of actor Hart Bochner.
PICTURES: Drums of Africa, The Night Walker, Sylvia, Tony Rome, Point Blank, The Detective, The Horse in the Gray Flannel Suit, Tiger By the Tail, Ulzana's Raid, The Man in the Glass Booth, The Lonely Lady, Millenium, The Naked Gun 2 1/2, Morning Glory, It Seemed Like A G ood Idea At The Time, Hot Touch, The Crystal Cage, Berlin Lady, Landslide, Lolita's Affair, The Dozier Case, Fine Gold.
TELEVISION: Series: One Man's Family, Hong Kong, The Richard Boone Show, Dynasty. Movies: Scalplock, Stranger on the Run, Crowhaven Farm, They Call It Murder, Satan's School for Girls, Richie Brockelman: Missing 24 Hours, Terraces, Immigrants, A Fire in the Sky, The Best Place to Be, The Golden Gate Murders, Mary and Joseph: A Story of Faith, Mazes & Monsters, Blood Sport, Race For the Bomb, Double Agent, Eagle One, Our Man Flint. Guest: Fantasy Island, Masquerade, The A-Team, Hotel, Crazy Like a Fox, Greatest Heroes of the Bible, Murder She Wrote, Designing Women, Hart To Hart, Who's The Boss, Golden Girls, The Love Boat, etc..

BODE, RALF
Cinematographer. b. Berlin, Germany. Attended Yale where was actor with drama school and acquired degree in directing. Received on-job training teaching combat photography and making films for Army at Ft. Monmouth. First professional job in films was gaffer on Harry, followed by long association with dir. John G. Avildsen, for whom served as gaffer and lighting designer on Guess What We Learned in School Today, Joe, and Cry Uncle. Later dir. of photography for Avildsen on Inaugural Ball and as East Coast dir. phot. for Rocky.
PICTURES: There is No. 13, Saturday Night Fever, Slow Dancing in the Big City, Rich Kids, Coal Miner's Daughter, Dressed to Kill, Raggedy Man, A Little Sex, Gorky Park, First Born, Bring on the Night, Violets Are Blue, Critical Condition, The Big Town, The Accused, Distant Thunder, Cousins, Uncle Buck, One Good Cop, Love Field, Made in America, George Balanchine's The Nutcracker, Bad Girls, Safe Passage, Don Juan DeMarco, A Simple Wish, The Big Green, Women Without Implants.
TELEVISION: PBS Theatre in America, lighting designer and dir. of photo. Also many TV commercials. Movie: Gypsy, A Streetcar Named Desire, Cinderella.

BOETTICHER, BUDD
Director, Writer. Producer. r.n. Oscar Boetticher, Jr. b. Chicago, IL, July 29, 1916. e. Culver Military Acad., Ohio State U. bull-fighter Novillero; then technical dir., Blood and Sand, 1941; asst. dir., Hal Roach studios and Columbia 1941-44; became feature dir. at Columbia in 1944; dir. Eagle Lion, 1946; dir., Universal; independ. prod., 1954. Autobiography: When in Disgrace.
PICTURES: As Oscar Boetticher: Behind Locked Doors, Assigned to Danger, Black Midnight, Killer Shark, Wolf Hunters. As Budd Boetticher: The Bullfighter and the Lady (also co-story), The Sword of D'Artagnan, The Cimarron Kid, Bronco Busters, Red Ball Express, Horizons West, City Beneath the Sea, Seminole, The Man from the Alamo, Wings of the Hawk, East of Sumatra, The Magnificent Matador (also story), The Killer Is Loose, Seven Men From Now, Decision at Sundown, The Tall T, Buchanan Rides Alone, Ride Lonesome (also prod.), Westbound, The Rise and Fall of Legs Diamond, Comanche Station (also prod.), Arruza (also prod., co-s.p.), A Time For Dying (also s.p.), My Kingdom For a... (also s.p.).
TELEVISION: Movies: Big Guns Talk: The Story of the Western (actor only).

BOGARDE, SIR DIRK
Actor. b. Hampstead, London, March 28, 1921. r.n. Derek Van Den Bogaerde. e. Allen Glens Coll., Glasgow & University Coll., London. Knighted, Feb. 1992. Started theatrical career with Amersham Repertory Co., then London stage; in Army in WWII. Commandeur des arts et des Lettres, France, 1990. Hon. Doc. Lit.: St. Andrews Univ., Sussex Univ. Top ten British star: 1953-54, 1956-64; number one British money-making star 1955, 1957, 1958, 1959; Variety Club Award—Best Performance 1961-64.
THEATER: U.K.: Power With Glory (1947), Point of Departure, The Shaughraun, The Vortex, Summertime, Jezebel.
PICTURES: Come on George (debut as extra, 1939), Dancing With Crime, Esther Waters, Quartet, Once a Jolly Swagman, Dear Mr. Prohack, Boys in Brown, The Blue Lamp, So Long at the Fair, Blackmailed, Woman in Question, Hunted (Stranger in Between), Penny Princess, The Gentle Gunman, Appointment in London, Desperate Moment, They Who Dare, The Sleeping Tiger, Doctor in the House, For Better or Worse, The Sea Shall Not Have Them, Simba, Doctor at Sea, Cast a Dark Shadow, Spanish Gardener, Ill Met by Moonlight (Night Ambush), Doctor at Large, Campbell's Kingdom, A Tale of Two Cities, The Wind Cannot Read, The Doctor's Dilemma, Libel, The Angel Wore Red, Song Without End, The Singer Not the Song, Victim, H.M.S. Defiant (Damn the Defiant), We Joined the Navy (cameo), The Password Is Courage, I Could Go on Singing, The Mind Benders, The Servant (BFA Award, 1964), Hot Enough for June (Agent 8 3/4), Doctor in Distress, The High Bright Sun (McGuire Go Home), King and Country, Darling (BFA Award, 1965), Modesty Blaise, Accident, Our Mother's House, Sebastian, The Fixer, Justine, Oh! What a Lovely War, The Damned, Death in Venice, The Serpent (Night Flight From Moscow), The Night Porter, Permission to Kill, Providence, A Bridge Too Far, Despair, Daddy Nostalgia.
TELEVISION: The Little Moon of Alban, Blithe Spirit, Upon This Rock, The Patricia Neal Story, May We Borrow Your Husband?, The Vision.
AUTHOR: A Postillion Struck by Lightning (1977), Snakes and Ladders (1978), An Orderly Man (1983), Backcloth, A Particular Friendship, Great Meadow, A Short Walk From Harrods. Novels: A Gentle Occupation, Voices in the Garden, West of Sunset, Jericho, A Period of Adjustment, Cleared For Take Off (autobiography).

BOGART, PAUL
Director. b. New York, NY, Nov. 13, 1919. Puppeteer-actor with Berkeley Marionettes 1946-48; TV stage mgr., assoc. dir. NBC 1950-52. Won numerous Christopher Awards; recipient homage from French Festival Internationale Programmes Audiovisuelle, Cannes '91.
PICTURES: Marlowe (debut, 1969), Halls of Anger, Skin Game, Cancel My Reservation, Class of '44 (also prod.), Mr. Ricco, Oh God! You Devil, Torch Song Trilogy.
TELEVISION: Series: U.S. Steel Hour, Kraft Theatre, Armstrong Circle Theatre, Goodyear Playhouse, The Defenders (Emmy Award, 1965), All in the Family (Emmy Award, 1978), The Golden Girls (Emmy Award, 1986). Specials: Ages of Man, Mark Twain Tonight, The Final War of Ollie Winter, Dear Friends (Emmy Award, 1968), Secrets, Shadow Game (Emmy Award, 1970), The House Without a Christmas Tree, Look Homeward Angel, The Country Girl, Double Solitaire, The War Widow, The Thanksgiving Treasure; The Adams Chronicles, Natica Jackson. Movies: In Search of America, Tell Me Where It Hurts, Winner Take All, Nutcracker: Money, Madness and Murder, Broadway Bound, The Gift of Love, The Heidi Chronicles.

BOGDANOVICH, PETER
Director, Producer, Writer, Actor. b. Kingston, NY, July 30, 1939. e. Collegiate Sch., Stella Adler Theatre Sch., N.Y. 1954-58. Stage debut, Amer. Shakespeare Festival, Stratford, CT, followed by N.Y. Shakespeare Festival, 1958. Off-Bway: dir./prod.: The Big Knife, Camino Real, Ten Little Indians, Rocket to the Moon, Once in a Lifetime. Film critic and feature writer, Esquire, New York Times, Village Voice, Cahiers du Cinema, Los Angeles Times,New York Magazine, Vogue, Variety, etc. 1961–. Owner: The Holly Moon Company Inc. (L.A.), 1992-present. LA Film Crits. Career Achievement Award, 1997.
PICTURES: Voyage to the Planet of the Prehistoric Women (dir., s.p., narrator; billed as Derek Thomas), The Wild Angels (2nd unit dir., co-s.p., actor). Director: Targets (also prod., co-s.p., actor), The Last Picture Show (also co-s.p; N.Y. Film Critics' Award, best s.p., British Academy Award, best s.p. 1971), Directed by John Ford (also s.p., interviewer), What's Up Doc? (also prod., co-s.p.; Writer's Guild of America Award, best s.p., 1972), Paper Moon (also prod.; Silver Shell, Mar del Plata, Spain 1973), Daisy Miller (also prod.; Best Director, Brussels Festival, 1974), At Long Last Love (also prod., s.p.), Nickelodeon (also co-s.p.), Saint Jack (also co-s.p., actor; Pasinetti Award, Critics Prize, Venice Festival, 1979), Opening Night (actor only), They All Laughed (also co-s.p.), Mask, Illegally Yours (also prod.), Texasville (also co-prod., s.p.), Noises Off (also co-exec. prod.), The Thing Called Love. Actor: Jean Renior, The Battle Over Citizen Kane, Ben Johnson: Third Cowboy on the Right, Mr. Jealousy, Highball, 54.

TELEVISION: *Movies*: To Sir with Love 2 (dir.), The Price of Heaven (dir.). *Special*: The Great Professional: Howard Hawks (co-dir., writer, interviewer; BBC). *Series*: CBS This Morning (weekly commentary; 1987-89). *Mini-series*: Bella Mafia. *Guest*: Northern Exposure (actor), to Sir With Love 2, The Price of Heaven.
AUTHOR: The Cinema of Orson Welles (1961), The Cinema of Howard Hawks (1962), The Cinema of Alfred Hitchcock, (1963), John Ford (1968; enlarged 1978), Fritz Lang in America, (1969), Allan Dwan—The Last Pioneer (1971), Pieces of Time (1973, enlarged 1985), The Killing of the Unicorn: Dorothy Stratten: 1960-1980 (1984), This Is Orson Welles (1992). Also edit., intro. writer to annual Year and a Day Engagement Calendar (1991-).

BOGOSIAN, ERIC
Actor, Writer. b. Woburn, MA, Apr. 24, 1953. e. studied 2 years at U. of Chicago, then Oberlin, theater degree, 1976. In high school, acted in plays with Fred Zollo (now prod.) and Nick Paleologus (now MA congressman). Moved to NY and worked briefly as gofer at Chelsea Westside Theater. Then joined downtown performance space, the Kitchen, first acting in others pieces, then creating his own incl. character Ricky Paul, a stand-up comedian in punk clubs. Theater pieces include: The New World, Men Inside, Voices of America, FunHouse, Drinking in America (Drama Desk and Obie Awards), Talk Radio, Sex Drugs Rock & Roll, Pounding Nails in the Floor With My Forehead (Obie Award), SubUrbia (author only). Author of Notes From Underground.
PICTURES: Special Effects, Talk Radio (also s.p.; Silver Bear Award 1988 Berlin Film Fest.), Sex Drugs Rock & Roll (also s.p.), Naked in New York, Dolores Claiborne, Under Siege 2: Dark Territory, Arabian Knight (voice), Beavis and Butt-Head Do America (voice), Suburbia (s.p. only), Deconstructing Harry.
TELEVISION: *Guest*: Miami Vice, Twilight Zone, Law & Order, The Larry Sanders Show. *Movies*: The Caine Mutiny Court Martial, Last Flight Out, Witch Hunt. *Special*: Drinking in America.

BOLAM, JAMES
Actor. b. Sunderland, England. Entered motion picture industry, 1960.
PICTURES: The Kitchen, A Kind of Loving, Loneliness of the Long Distance Runner, HMS Defiant, Murder Most Foul, In Celebration, Clockwork Mice, Stella Does Tricks, Island on Bird Street.
TELEVISION: Likely Lads, When The Boat Comes In, Only When I Laugh, The Beiderbecke Affair, Father Matthews Daughter, Room at the Bottom, Andy Capp, The Beiderbecke Tapes, The Beiderbecke Connection, Second Thoughts, Have Your Cake, The Missing Postman, The Stalker's Apprentice.

BOLOGNA, JOSEPH
Actor, Writer. b. Brooklyn, NY., Dec. 30, 1938. e. Brown U. m. actress-writer Renee Taylor. Service in Marine Corps and on discharge joined ad agency, becoming dir.-prod. of TV commercials. Collaborated with wife on short film, 2, shown at 1966 N.Y. Film Festival. Together they wrote Lovers and Other Strangers, B'way play, in which both also acted; wrote s.p. for film version. Both wrote and starred in Made for Each Other, and created and wrote TV series, Calucci's Dept.
PICTURES: Lovers and Other Strangers (co.-s.p. only), Made for Each Other (also co.-s.p.), Cops and Robbers, Mixed Company, The Big Bus , Chapter Two, My Favorite Year, Blame It on Rio , The Woman in Red, Transylvania 6-5000, It Had to Be You (also co-dir., co-s.p.), Coupe de Ville, Jersey Girl, Alligator II: The Mutation, Love Is All There Is, Heaven Before I Die.
TELEVISION: *Series*: Calucci's Dept. (creator, co-writer only), Rags to Riches, Top of the Heap. *Movies*: Honor Thy Father, Woman of the Year (also co-writer), Torn Between Two Lovers, One Cooks The Other Doesn't, Copacabana, A Time To Triumph, Prime Target, Thanksgiving Day, Citizen Cohn, The Danger of Love: The Carolyn Warmus Story, Revenge of the Nerds IV: Nerds in Love, The Don's Analyst. *Special*: Acts of Love and Other Comedies (Emmy Award, 1974). *Mini-Series*: Sins.

BONANNO, LOUIE
Actor. a.k.a. Louix Dor Dempriey. b. Somerville, MA, Dec. 17, 1961. e. Bentley Coll., Waltham, MA, BS-economics, finance; AS accountancy, 1983. In Who's Who Among Students in American Univ. & Colleges; Who's Who Among Rising Young Americans. Moved to NY, 1983 to study at Amer. Acad. of Dramatic Arts. Toured U.S. 1985-86 as Dangermouse for MTV/Nickelodeon. Stand-up comedian 1987-89. Stage debut in The Head, 1990.
PICTURES: Sex Appeal (debut, 1986), Wimps, Student Affairs, Cool as Ice, Auntie Lee's Meat Pies.
TELEVISION: *Series*: Eisenhower & Lutz, 227, Tour of Duty, TV 101, Santa Barbara, New York Story.

BONET, LISA
Actress. b. Los Angeles, CA, Nov. 16, 1967. First gained recognition on The Cosby Show as Denise Huxtable at the age of 15.
PICTURES: Angel Heart, Dead Connection, Bank Robber, New Eden.
TELEVISION: *Series*: The Cosby Show, A Different World. *Guest*: Tales From the Dark Side. *Special*: Don't Touch.

BONET, NAI
Actress, Producer. Worked in entertainment field since age of 13, including opera, films, TV, stage, night clubs and records.
PICTURES: *Actress*: The Soul Hustlers, The Seventh Veil, Fairy Tales, The Soul of Nigger Charlie, The Spy with the Cold Nose, John Goldfarb Please Come Home, Nocturna (also s.p.), Hoodlums, (also s.p.).
TELEVISION: Johnny Carson Show, Merv Griffin Show, Joe Franklin Show, Beverly Hillbillies, Tom Snyder Show.

BONHAM-CARTER, HELENA
Actress. b. London, England, May 26, 1966. Great granddaughter of Liberal Prime Minister Lord Asquith. e. Westminster. Appeared on BBC in A Pattern of Roses; seen by dir. Trevor Nunn who cast her in Lady Jane, 1986, theatrical film debut. On London stage in Trelawny of the Wells.
PICTURES: Lady Jane, A Room with a View, Maurice (cameo), Francesco, La Mascheral (The Mask), Getting It Right, Hamlet, Where Angles Fear to Tread, Howards End, Mary Shelley's Frankenstein, Mighty Aphrodite, Margaret's Museum, Twelfth Night, Shadow Play, The Wings of the Dove (LA Film Crits. Award, Best Actress, 1997), Keep the Aspidistra Flying, The Theory of Flight, The Revengers of Comedy, Fight Club.
TELEVISION: *Guest*: Miami Vice, Simply Fabulous. *Movies*: A Hazard of Hearts (U.S.), The Vision, Beatrix Potter, Fatal Deception: Mrs. Lee Harvey Oswald, Dancing Queen. *Series*: The Great War (voice). *Mini-Series*: Merlin.

BOOKMAN, ROBERT
Executive. b. Los Angeles, CA, Jan. 29, 1947. e. U. of California, Yale Law Sch. Motion picture literary agent, IFA 1972-74, ICM 1974-79. 1979-84, ABC Motion Pictures v.p., worldwide production; 1984-6, Columbia Pictures, exec. v.p., world-wide prod. 1986, Creative Artists Agency, as motion picture literary and directors' agent.

BOONE, PAT
Singer, Actor. b. Jacksonville, FL, June 1, 1934. e. David Lipscomb Coll., North Texas State Coll., grad. magna cum laude, Columbia U. Winner of Ted Mack's Amateur Hour TV show; joined Arthur Godfrey TV show, 1955. Most promising new male star, Motion Picture Daily-Fame Poll 1957. One of top ten moneymaking stars, M.P. Herald-Fame Poll, 1957. Daughter is singer Debby Boone. Author: Twixt Twelve and Twenty, Between You & Me and the Gatepost, The Real Christmas, A New Song, others.
RECORDINGS: Ain't That a Shame, I Almost Lost My Mind, Friendly Persuasion, Love Letters in the Sand, April Love, Tutti Frutti, many others.
PICTURES: Bernardine (debut, 1957), April Love, Mardi Gras, Journey to the Center of the Earth, All Hands on Deck, State Fair, The Main Attraction, The Yellow Canary, The Horror of It All, Never Put It in Writing, Goodbye Charlie, The Greatest Story Ever Told, The Perils of Pauline, The Cross and the Switchblade, Roger and Me.
TELEVISION: *Series*: Arthur Godfrey and His Friends, The Pat Boone-Chevy Showroom (1957-60), The Pat Boone Show (1966-8). *Movie*: The Pigeon.

BOORMAN, JOHN
Director, Producer, Writer. b. London, England, Jan. 18, 1933. Wrote film criticism at age of 17 for British publications incl. Manchester Guardian; founder TV Mag. Day By Day; served in National Service in Army; Broadcaster and BBC radio film critic 1950-54; film editor Independent Television News; prod. documentaries for Southern Television; joined BBC, headed BBC Documentary Film Unit 1960-64, indep. doc. about D.W. Griffith; chmn. Natl. Film Studios of Ireland 1975-85; governor Brit. Film Inst. 1985-.
PICTURES: *Director*: Catch Us If You Can (Having a Wild Weekend; debut, 1965), Point Blank, Hell in the Pacific, Leo the Last (also co-s.p., Cannes Film Fest. Award, Best Director 1970), Deliverance (also prod.; 2 Acad. Award noms.), Zardoz (also prod., s.p.), Exorcist II: The Heretic (also co-prod.), Excalibur (also exec. prod., co-s.p., Cannes Film Fest. Award, Best Art. Contribution, 1981), Danny Boy (exec. prod. only), The Emerald Forest (also prod.), Hope and Glory (also prod., s.p., actor; 3 Acad. Award noms., Nat'l Film Critics Awards for dir., s.p.; L.A. Film Critics Awards for picture, s.p., dir.; U.K. Critics Awards for picture), Where the Heart Is (also prod., co-s.p.), I Dreamt I Woke Up (also s.p., actor), Two Nudes Bathing (also s.p., prod.), Beyond Rangoon (also co-prod.), The General (also s.p., prod.).
TELEVISION: *Series*: Citizen '63 (dir.), The Newcomers (dir.).

BOOTH, MARGARET
Film editor. b. Los Angeles, CA, 1898. Awarded honorary Oscar, 1977.
PICTURES: Why Men Leave Home, Husbands and Lovers, Bridge of San Luis Rey, New Moon, Susan Lenox, Strange Interlude, Smilin' Through, Romeo and Juliet, Barretts of Wimpole Street, Mutiny on the Bounty, Camille, etc. Supervising editor on Owl and the Pussycat, The Way We Were, Funny Lady, Murder by Death, The Goodbye Girl, California Suite, The Cheap Detective (also assoc. prod.), Chapter Two (also assoc. prod.), The Toy (assoc. prod. only), Annie, The Slugger's Wife (exec. prod. only).

BOOTHE, POWERS
Actor. b. Snyder, TX, June 1, 1949. e. Southern Methodist U. On B'way in Lone Star.
PICTURES: The Goodbye Girl, Cruising, Southern Comfort, A Breed Apart, Red Dawn, The Emerald Forest, Extreme Prejudice, Stalingrad, Rapid Fire, Tombstone, Blue Sky, Sudden Death, Nixon, U-Turn.
TELEVISION: *Series*: Skag, Philip Marlowe. *Movies*: Skag, Plutonium Incident, Guyana Tragedy—The Story of Jim Jones (Emmy Award, 1980), A Cry for Love, Into the Homeland, Family of Spies, By Dawn's Early Light, Wild Card, Marked for Murder, Web of Deception, The Spree. *Mini-Series*: True Women.

BORGE, VICTOR
Comedian, Pianist. b. Copenhagen, Denmark, Jan. 3, 1909. Child prodigy at age 8. Awarded scholarship to study in Berlin and Vienna. Later became humorous concert artist. Wrote and starred in musical plays and films in Denmark. Fled Nazis in 1940, came to America. Appeared on Bing Crosby radio show, concert and nightclub tours, tv variety shows. One-man Broadway shows: Comedy in Music, 1953, 1965, 1977, 1989. Guest conductor with major symphonies around the world. Recent recording, The Two Sides of Victor Borge. Author: My Favorite Intermissions and My Favorite Comedies in Music. Awarded Medal of Honor by Statue of Liberty Centennial Comm. Knighted by 5 Scandinavian countries, honored by U.S. Congress and U.N. Created Thanks to Scandinavia Scholarship Fund, Dana College, Univ. of Conn., SUNY—Purchase Scholarships. Recent video: Onstage with Victor Borge.

BORGNINE, ERNEST
Actor. b. Hamden, CT, Jan. 24, 1917. e. Randall Sch. of Dramatic Art, Hartford, CT. Joined Barter Theatre in Virginia. Served in U.S. Navy; then little theatre work, stock companies; on Broadway in Harvey, Mrs. McThing; many TV appearances. Honors: 33rd Degree of the Masonic Order, Order of the Grand Cross, from same. Named honorary Mayor of Universal City Studios.
PICTURES: China Corsair (debut, 1951), The Mob, Whistle at Eaton Falls, From Here to Eternity, The Stranger Wore a Gun, Demetrius & the Gladiators, Johnny Guitar, Bounty Hunter, Vera Cruz, Bad Day at Black Rock, Marty (Acad. Award for Best Actor, 1955), Run for Cover, Violent Saturday, Last Command, Square Jungle, Catered Affair, Jubal, Best Things in Life are Free, Three Brave Men, The Vikings, Badlanders, Torpedo Run, Rabbit Trap, Season of Passion, Man on a String, Pay or Die, Go Naked in the World, Barabbas, McHale's Navy, Flight of the Phoenix, The Oscar, Chuka, The Dirty Dozen, Ice Station Zebra, Legend of Lylah Clare, The Split, The Wild Bunch, The Adventurers, Suppose They Gave a War and Nobody Came?, A Bullet for Sandoval, Bunny O'Hare, Willard, Rain for a Dusty Summer, Hannie Caulder, The Revengers, Ripped Off, The Poseidon Adventure, Emperor of the North Pole, The Neptune Factor, Manhunt, Law and Disorder, Sunday in the Country, The Devil's Rain, Hustle, Shoot, Love By Appointment, The Greatest, Crossed Swords, Convoy, Strike Force, Diary of Madam X, The Black Hole, The Double McGuffin, The Ravagers, When Time Ran Out, High Risk, Super Fuzz, Escape from New York, Deadly Blessing, Young Warriors, Codename: Wild Geese, Skeleton Coast, Spike of Bensonhurst, The Opponent, Any Man's Death, Laser Mission, Turnaround, Captain Henkel, Real Men Don't Eat Gummy Bears, Moving Target, The Last Match, Mistress, All Dogs Go to Heaven 2 (voice) McHale's Navy.
TELEVISION: *Series*: McHale's Navy, Air Wolf, The Single Guy. *Movies*: Sam Hill: Who Killed the Mysterious Mr. Foster?, The Trackers, Twice in a Lifetime, Future Cop, Jesus of Nazareth, Fire!, The Ghost of Flight 401, Cops and Robin, All Quiet on the Western Front, Blood Feud, Carpool, Love Leads the Way, Last Days of Pompeii, The Dirty Dozen: The Next Mission, Alice in Wonderland, The Dirty Dozen: The Deadly Mission, Treasure Island (Ital. TV), The Dirty Dozen: The Fatal Mission, Jake Spanner-Private Eye, Appearances, The Burning Shore, Mountain of Diamonds (Ital TV). *Guest*: Philco Playhouse, General Electric Theater, Wagon Train, Laramie, Zane Grey Theater, Alcoa Premiere, The Love Boat, Little House on the Prairie, Murder She Wrote, Home Improvement. *Specials*: Billy the Kid, Legend in Granite: The Vince Lombardi Story.

BORIS, ROBERT
Writer, Director. b. NY, NY, Oct. 12, 1945. Screenwriter before also turning to direction with Oxford Blues, 1984.
PICTURES: *Writer*: Electra Glide in Blue, Some Kind of Hero, Doctor Detroit, Oxford Blues (also dir.), Steele Justice (dir.), Buy and Cell (dir.).
TELEVISION: Birds of Prey, Blood Feud, Deadly Encounter, Izzy and Moe, Frank and Jesse (also dir.).

BORODINSKY, SAMUEL
Executive. b. Brooklyn, NY, Oct. 25, 1941. e. Industrial Sch. of Arts & Photography. Expert in film care and rejuvenation. Now exec. v.p., Filmtreat International Corp. Previously with Modern Film Corp. (technician) and Comprehensive Filmtreat, Inc. & International Filmtreat (service manager).

BOSCO, PHILIP
Actor. b. Jersey City, NJ, Sept. 26, 1930. e. Catholic U., Washington, DC, BA. drama, 1957. Studied for stage with James Marr, Josephine Callan and Leo Brady. Consummate stage actor (in over 100 plays, 61 in NY) whose career spans the classics (with NY Shakespeare Fest. and American Shakespeare Fest, CT.), 20 plays with Arena Stage 1957-60, to modern classics as a resident actor with Lincoln Center Rep. Co. in the 1960s, winning Tony and Drama Desk Awards for the farce Lend Me a Tenor, 1988. Recipient: Clarence Derwent Award for General Excellence, Outer Critics Circle Award & Obie for Lifetime Achievement.
THEATER: Auntie Mame (B'way debut, City Center revival, 1958), Measure for Measure, The Rape of the Belt (Tony nom.), Donnybrook, Richard III, The Alchemist, The East Wind, The Ticket of Leave Man, Galileo, Saint Joan, Tiger at the Gates, Cyrano de Bergerac, Be Happy for Me, King Lear, The Miser, The Time of Your Life, Camino Real, Operation Sidewinder, Amphitryon, In the Matter of J. Robert Oppenheimer, The Good Woman of Setzuan, The Playboy of the Western World, An Enemy of the People, Antigone, Mary Stuart, The Crucible, Enemies, Mrs. Warren's Profession, Henry V, The Threepenny Opera, Streamers, Stages, The Biko Inquest, Whose Life Is It Anyway? A Month in the Country, Don Juan in Hell, Inadmissible Evidence, Ah! Wilderness, Man and Superman, Major Barbara, The Caine Mutiny Court Martial, Heartbreak House (Tony nom.), Come Back Little Sheba, Loves of Anatol, Be Happy for Me, Master Class, You Never Can Tell, A Man for All Seasons, Devil's Disciple, Lend Me a Tenor (Tony Award, 1989), The Miser, Breaking Legs, An Inspector Calls, The Heiress, Moon Over Buffalo.
PICTURES: Requiem for a Heavyweight, A Lovely Way to Die, Trading Places, The Pope of Greenwich Village, Walls of Glass, Heaven Help Us, Flanagan, The Money Pit, Children of a Lesser God, Suspect, Three Men and a Baby, Another Woman, Working Girl, The Luckiest Man in the World, Dream Team, Blue Steel, Quick Change, True Colors, FX2, Shadows and Fog, Straight Talk, Angie, Milk Money, Nobody's Fool, Safe Passage, It Takes Two, My Best Friend's Wedding, Critical Care, Frank Lloyd Wright (voice).
TELEVISION: *Series*: TriBeCa. *Mini-series*: LIBERTY!: The American Revolution. *Specials*: Prisoner of Zenda, An Enemy of the People, A Nice Place to Visit, Read Between the Lines (Emmy Award). *Guest*: Nurses, Trials of O'Brien, Law and Order, Spenser: For Hire, The Equalizer, Against the Law, Janek. *Movies*: Echoes in the Darkness, Second Effort, Internal Affairs, Murder in Black and White, The Return of Eliot Ness, Against the Wall, The Forget-Me-Not Murders, Attica: Line of Fire, Janek: A Silent Betrayal, Young at Heart, Carriers.

BOSLEY, TOM
Actor. b. Chicago, IL, Oct. 1, 1927. e. DePaul U. Had roles on radio in Chicago and in stock productions before moving to New York. Appeared off-Broadway and on road before signed to play lead in Fiorello! for George Abbott on Broadway. First actor to win Tony, Drama Critics, ANTA and Newspaper Guild awards in one season for that role.
PICTURES: Love with the Proper Stranger, The World of Henry Orient, Divorce American Style, Yours Mine and Ours, The Secret War of Harry Frigg, To Find a Man, Mixed Company, Gus, O'Hara's Wife, Million Dollar Mystery, Wicked Stepmother.
TELEVISION: *Specials*: Alice in Wonderland (1953), Arsenic and Old Lace, The Drunkard, Profiles in Courage. *Guest*: Focus, Naked City, The Right Man, The Nurses, Route 66, The Perry Como Show. *Series*: That Was the Week That Was, The Debbie Reynolds Show, The Dean Martin Show, Sandy Duncan Show, Wait Til Your Father Gets Home (voice), Happy Days, That's Hollywood (narrator), Murder She Wrote, Father Dowling Mysteries. *Movies*: Marcus Welby M.D.: A Matter of Humanities (pilot), Night Gallery, A Step Out of Line, Vanished, Congratulations It's a Boy!, Mr. & Mrs. Bo Jo Jones, Streets of San Francisco (pilot), No Place to Run, Miracle on 34th Street, The Girl Who Came Gift Wrapped, Death Cruise, Who Is the Black Dahlia?, Last Survivors, The Night That Panicked America, Love Boat, Testimony of 2 Men, Black Market Baby, With This Ring, The Bastard, The Triangle Factory Fire Scandal, The Castaways on Gilligan's Island, The Rebels, Return of the Mod Squad, For the Love of It, Jesse Owens Story, Fatal Confession: A Father Dowling Mystery, The Love Boat: A Valentine Voyage.

BOSTWICK, BARRY
Actor. b. San Mateo, CA, Feb. 24, 1945. e. USIU Sch. of Performing Arts, San Diego, BFA in acting; NYU Grad. Sch. of the Arts. Made prof. stage debut while in coll. working with Walter Pidgeon in Take Her She's Mine. Joined APA Phoenix Rep. Co. making his B'way debut in Cock-A-Doodle Dandy.
THEATER: Salvation, House of Leather, Soon, The Screens, Colette, Grease (created role of Danny Zuko, 1972), They Knew What They Wanted, The Robber Bridegroom (Tony Award, 1977), She Loves Me, L'Historie du Soldat, Nick and Nora.
PICTURES: The Rocky Horror Picture Show, Movie Movie, Megaforce, Eight Hundred Leagues Down the Amazon, Weekend at Bernie's 2, Spy Hard.

TELEVISION: *Series*: Foul Play, Dads. *Movies*: The Chadwick Family, The Quinns, Murder By Natural Causes, Once Upon a Family, Moviola—The Silent Lovers, Red Flag: The Ultimate Game, Summer Girl, An Uncommon Love, Deceptions, Betrayed by Innocence, Body of Evidence, Addicted to His Love, Parent Trap III, Till We Meet Again, Challenger, Captive, Between Love and Hate, Praying Mantis, Danielle Steel's Once in a Lifetime, The Return of Hunter, The Secretary. *Mini-Series*: Scruples, George Washington, I'll Take Manhattan, War and Remembrance. *Specials*: A Woman of Substance, You Can't Take It With You, Working.

BOSUSTOW, NICK
Producer. b. Los Angeles, CA, March 28, 1940. e. Menlo Coll., CA, administration. MCA, intl. sales, 1963. Pres., Stephen Bosustow Productions, 1967. Pres., ASIFA-West. Pres., Bosustow Entertainment Inc., 1973. Founded Animation Consultants International, 1995.
PICTURES: Is It Always Right to Be Right?(Acad. award) The Legend of John Henry (Acad. award nom.).
TELEVISION: *Specials*: The Incredible Book Escape, Misunderstood Monsters, A Tale of Four Wishes, Wrong Way Kid (Emmy, 1984). *Series*: The Hayley Mills Story Book.

BOSWALL, JEFFERY
Producer, Director, Writer. b. Brighton, England, 1931. e. Taunton House School, Montpelier Coll., Brighton. Started career as an ornithologist for the Royal Society for the Protection of Birds. Joined BBC in 1958 as radio prod., moving to TV 1964 making films in diverse locations (Ethiopia and Antarctica). Contributed to 50 films as wildlife cameraman. Co-founder of British Library of Wildlife Sounds. 1987: returned to RSPB. Head of Film and Video Unit, 1987. 1992, sr. lecturer in Biological Film & Video, Derby Univ. Chairmanship BKSTS Intl Wildlife Filmmakers' Symposium.
AUTHOR: Birds for All Seasons. Ed. Look and Private Lives. Contrib.: Times, Countryman, the Field, Wildlife and Countryside, BBC Wildlife, Scientific Film, Journal of the Society of Film and TV Arts, Image Technology. Has written for scientific journals and writes annual update for Encyclopedia Britannica on ornithology.
TELEVISION: 18 films in the Private Lives series of which 4 (about the Kingfisher, Cuckoo, Starling and Jackass Penguin) won intl awards. Animal Olympians, Birds For All Seasons, Where the Parrots Speak Mandarin, Wildlife Safari to Ethiopia.

BOTTOMS, JOSEPH
Actor. b. Santa Barbara, CA, April 22, 1954. Brother of Sam and Timothy Bottoms. Did plays in jr. high school in Santa Barbara and then with community theatre.
PICTURES: The Dove (debut, 1974), Crime and Passion, The Black Hole, Cloud Dancer, King of the Mountain, Blind Date, Open House, Born to Race, Inner Sanctum.
TELEVISION: *Movies*: Trouble Comes to Town, Unwed Father, Stalk the Wild Child, The Intruder Within, Side By Side: The True Story of the Osmond Family, I Married Wyatt Earp, The Sins of Dorian Gray, Time Bomb, Braker, Island Sons, Cop Killer, Gunsmoke: To the Last Man, Treacherous Crossing, Liar's Edge. *Mini-Series*: Holocaust, Celebrity. *Special*: Winesburg Ohio. *Guest*: Owen Marshall, Murder She Wrote.

BOTTOMS, SAM
Actor. b. Santa Barbara, CA, Oct. 17, 1955. Brother of Timothy, Joseph and Ben Bottoms. Co-prod. documentary Picture This.
Appeared in documentary Hearts of Darkness.
PICTURES: The Last Picture Show (debut, 1971), Class of '44, Zandy's Bride, Up From the Depths, The Outlaw Josey Wales, Apocalypse Now, Bronco Billy, Hunter's Blood, Gardens of Stone, After School, Hearts of Darkness: A Filmmaker's Apocalypse, Picture This--The Times of Peter Bogdanovich in Archer City Texas, Ragin' Cajun, Dolly Dearest, In 'n Out, North of Chiang Mai, Prime Risk, The Trust, Sugar Hill, Sunny Side Up, Project Showchaser 3000, Angel Blue.
TELEVISION: *Series*: Santa Barbara. *Movies*: Savages, Cage Without a Key, Desperate Lives, Island Sons, The Witching of Ben Wagner, Zooman. *Mini-Series*: East of Eden, Return to Eden. *Guest*: Greatest Heroes of the Bible, Murder She Wrote, Marcus Welby M.D., Doc Elliot, Eddie Capra, Lucas Tanner, 21 Jump Street, X Files.

BOTTOMS, TIMOTHY
Actor. b. Santa Barbara, CA, Aug. 30, 1951. Brother of actors Joseph and Sam Bottoms. Early interest in acting; was member of S.B. Madrigal Society, touring Europe in 1967. Sang and danced in West Side Story local prod. With brother Sam co-prod. documentary Picture This about making of the Last Picture Show and Texasville.
PICTURES: Johnny Got His Gun (debut, 1971), The Last Picture Show, Love and Pain and the Whole Damn Thing, The Paper Chase, The White Dawn, The Crazy World of Julius Vrooder, Operation Daybreak, A Small Town in Texas, Rollercoaster, The Other Side of the Mountain: Part 2, Hurricane, The High Country, Tin Man, The Census Taker, Hambone and Hillie, In the Shadow of Kilimanjaro, The Sea Serpent, The Fantasist, Invaders from Mars, The Drifter, Mio in the Land of Faraway, Return to the River Kwai, A Case of Law, Texasville, Istanbul, I'll Met By Moonlight, Top Dog.

TELEVISION: *Special*: Look Homeward Angel. *Mini-Series*: The Money Changers, East of Eden. *Movies*: The Story of David, The Gift of Love, A Shining Season, Escape, Perry Mason: The Case of the Notorious Nun. Island Sons. *Series*: Land of the Lost.

BOUCHEZ, ELODIE
Actress.
PICTURES: Stan the Flasher, The Stolen Diary, Tango, Good Old Daze, Les mots de l'amour, The Wild Reeds, Those Were the Days, Clubbed to Death, Mademoiselle Personne, Full Speed, The Proprietor, Fire in Paradise, La divine poursuite, Le ciel est a nous, The Dreamlife of Angels (Cannes Film Fest. Award, Best Actress, 1998), Louise (Take 2), J'aimerais pas crever un dimanche, Zonzon, Les Kidnappeurs.

BOUQUET, CAROLE
Actress. b. Neuilly-sur-Seine, France, Aug. 18, 1957. e. Sorbonne, Paris, Paris Conservatoire. Also model for Chanel No. 5 perfume.
PICTURES: That Obscure Object of Desire (debut, 1977), Buffet Froid, Il Cappotto di Astrakan, For Your Eyes Only, Bingo Bongo, Mystere, Nemo, Le Bon Roi Dagobert, Rive Droite Rive Gauche, Special Police, Double Messieurs, Le Mal d'aimer, Jenatsch, Bunker Palace Hotel, New York Stories, Too Beautiful for You, Against Oblivion, Tango, Women in Skirts, Grosse Fatigue, A Business Affair, Lucie Aubrac, In All Innocence.
TELEVISION: *Mini-series:* Le Rouge et le Noir.

BOUTSIKARIS, DENNIS
Actor. b. Newark, NJ, Dec. 21, 1952. e. Hampshire Col.
THEATER: *Off-B'way*: Another Language (debut, 1975), Funeral March for a One Man Band, All's Well That Ends Well, Nest of the Wood Grouse, Cheapside, Rum and Coke, The Boys Next Door, Sight Unseen. *B'way*: Filomena, Bent, Amadeus.
PICTURES: The Exterminator, Very Close Quarters, Batteries Not Included, Crocodile Dundee II, The Dream Team, Talent for the Game, The Boy Who Cried Bitch, Boys on the Side, Chasing the Dragon, Surviving Picasso, Blue Vision.
TELEVISION: *Series*: Nurse, Stat, The Jackie Thomas Show, Misery Loves Company. *Movies:* Rappaccini's Daughter, Internal Affairs, Thunderboat Row, The Keys, Love Lies and Murder, The Hit Man, Victim of Love: The Shannon Mohr Story, The Yarn Princess, Tonya & Nancy: The Inside Story, Beyond Betrayal, Love and Betrayal: The Mia Farrow Story, The Three Lives of Karen, Survival on the Mountain. *Mini Series*: The Last Don. *Guest*: Murphy Brown, Law & Order, The Burning Zone, ER.

BOWIE, DAVID
Singer, Actor. b. Brixton, South London, England, Jan. 8, 1947. r.n. David Robert Jones. m. model-actress Iman. Broadway debut: The Elephant Man (1980).
PICTURES: The Virgin Soldiers (debut, 1969), Ziggy Stardust and the Spiders from Mars (1973; U.S. release 1983), The Man Who Fell to Earth, Just a Gigolo, Radio On, Christiane F, Cat People (performed song), The Hunger, Yellowbeard (cameo), Merry Christmas Mr. Lawrence, Into the Night, Absolute Beginners (also songs), Labyrinth (also songs), When the Wind Blows (songs), The Last Temptation of Christ, Imagine—John Lennon, The Linguini Incident, Twin Peaks: Fire Walk With Me, Basquiat.
TELEVISION: *Specials*: Christmas With Bing Crosby, The Midnight Special, Glass Spider Tour.

BOWSER, EILEEN
Curator, Film Archivist, Historian. b. Ohio, Jan. 18, 1928. e. Marietta Coll., B.A., 1950; U. of North Carolina, M.A., history of art, 1953. Joined Dept. of Film, Museum of Modern Art, 1954. Curator, Dept. of Film (1976-1993). Organized major exhib. of the films of D.W. Griffith, Carl-Theodor Dreyer, Art of the Twenties, recent acquisitions and touring shows. On exec. comm. of Federation Internationale des Archives du Film 1969-91, v.p. FIAF 1977-85; pres. FIAF Documentation Commission 1972-81. Film Archives Advisory Comm. since 1971. Assoc. of Univ. Seminars on Cinema and Interdisciplinary Interpretation. Publications: The Transformation of Cinema: 1907-15, Vol II, History of the American Film Series, The Movies, David Wark Griffith, Biograph Bulletins 1908-1912. A Handbook for Film Archives. Has written numerous articles on film history.

BOXLEITNER, BRUCE
Actor. b. Elgin, IL, May 12, 1950. m. actress Melissa Gilbert. After high school enrolled in Chicago's Goodman Theatre, staging productions and working with lighting and set design in addition to acting.
PICTURES: Six-Pack Annie, The Baltimore Bullet, Tron, The Crystal Eye, Breakaway, Diplomatic Immunity, Kuffs, The Babe.
TELEVISION: *Series*: How the West Was Won, Bring 'Em Back Alive, Scarecrow and Mrs. King, Babylon 5. *Movies*: The Chadwick Family, A Cry for Help, The Macahans, Kiss Me—Kill Me, Murder at the World Series, Happily Ever After, Wild Times, Kenny Rogers as The Gambler, Fly Away Home, Bare Essence, I Married Wyatt Earp, Kenny Rogers as The Gambler: The Adventure Continues, Passion Flower, Angel in Green, Kenny Rogers as the Gambler: The Legend Continues, Red River, The Town Bully, From the Dead of Night, The Road Raiders, Till We Meet Again, Murderous Vision, The Secret, Perfect Family, Double Jeopardy (also co-exec. prod.), House of Secrets, Gambler V: Playing for Keeps, Danielle Steel's Zoya. *Mini-Series*: How the West Was Won, East of Eden, The Last Convertible. *Special*: Wyatt Earp: Return to Tombstone.

BOYER, PHIL
TV Executive. b. Portland, OR, Dec. 13, 1940. e. Sacramento State U. Began broadcasting career as 12-year-old in Portland, establishing nation's first youth radio facility—a 5-watt facility in the basement of his home. At 16 began working at KPDQ, Portland; two years later joined KPTV, Portland, as announcer. In 1960 joined KEZI-TV, Eugene, OR, heading prod. and prog. depts. In 1965 named staff prod.-dir. for KCRA, TV, Sacramento, CA, becoming prod. mgr. in 1967 and prog. mgr. in 1969. In 1972 joined KNBC-TV, Los Angeles, as prog. dir. In 1974 named v.p., programming, of ABC Owned TV Stations; 1977, v.p.-gen. mgr., WLS-TV, Chicago; 1979, v.p.-gen. mgr. of WABC-TV, NY, 1981; v.p., gen mgr., ABC-owned TV station div.; 1984, joined ABC Video Enterprises as v.p. intl. dev.; 1986-97 sr. v.p., intl and prog. dev., CC/ABC Video Ent.

BOYES, CHRISTOPHER
Sound.
PICTURES: Rush, Terminator 2: Judgment Day, Bingo!, Single White Female, Jurassic Park, Under Siege 2: Dark Territory, The Rock, Broken Arrow, Eraser, Titanic (Acad. Award, Best Sound Effects Editing, 1997), Volcano, The Lost World: Jurassic Park, Con Air.

BOYETT, ROBERT LEE
Producer. e. Duke U., B.A.; Col. U., M.A., marketing. Began career in entertainment media and mkt. research at Grey Advertising, Inc. Was program development consultant for PBS. In 1973 joined ABC as dir. of prime time series TV, East Coast. In 1975 named ABC TV v.p. & asst. to v.p. programs for West Coast. In 1977 joined Paramount Pictures in newly created position of v.p., exec. asst. to pres. & chief operating officer. 1979, joined Miller-Milkis-Boyett Productions to produce for Paramount Television.
TELEVISION: *Exec. prod.:* Laverne and Shirley, Happy Days, Bosom Buddies, Mork and Mindy, Valerie, Perfect Strangers, Family Matters, Meego, Step By Step, Full House, Family Matters, Going Places, The Family Man, Getting By, On Our Own, Two-N-Two Together, Hogan Family.

BOYLE, BARBARA D.
Executive. b. New York, NY. e. U. of California, Berkeley, B.A., 1957; UCLA, J.D., 1960. Named to bar: California, 1961; New York, 1964; Supreme Court, 1964. Atty. in busn. affairs dept. & corp. asst. secty., American Intl. Pictures, Los Angeles, 1965-67; partner in entertainment law firm, Cohen & Boyle, L.A., 1967-74; exec. v.p. & gen. counsel, COO, New World Pictures, L.A., 1974-82. Sr. v.p. worldwide prod., Orion Pictures, L.A., 1982-86; exec. v.p., prod., RKO Pictures, L.A., 1986-87. President, Sovereign Pictures, L.A., 1988-92; Boyle-Taylor Prods., 1993-. Exec. prod: Eight Men Out, Battle Rocket. Prod.: Mrs. Munch, Phenomenon, Instinct. Co-chmn. 1979-80, Entertainment Law Symposium Advisory Committee, UCLA Law Sch. Member, AMPAS, Women in Film (pres., 1977-78, mem. of bd., chairperson 1981-84), Women Entertainment Lawyers Assn., California Bar Assn., N.Y. State Bar Assn., Beverly Hills Bar Assn., Hollywood Women's Political Committee, American Film Institute. Bd. mem.: Women Director's Workshop, Independent Feature Project/West (pres. 1994-), Los Angeles Women's Campaign Fund. Founding mem. UCLA Sch. of Law's Entertainment Advisory Council (& co-chairperson 1979 & 80).

BOYLE, LARA FLYNN
Actress. b. Davenport, IA, Mar. 24, 1970. e. Chicago Academy for the Visual and Performing Arts. First studied acting at the Piven Theatre. Professional debut at age 15 in tv mini-series Amerika.
PICTURES: Poltergeist III (debut, 1988), How I Got Into College, Dead Poets Society, May Wine, The Rookie, The Dark Backward, Mobsters, Wayne's World, Where the Day Takes You, The Temp, Eye of the Storm, Equinox, Red Rock West, Threesome, Baby's Day Out, The Road to Wellville, Farmer & Chase, Cafe Society, The Big Squeeze, Afterglow.
TELEVISION: *Series:* Twin Peaks, The Practice. *Mini-Series:* Amerika. *Movies:* Terror on Highway 91, Gang of Four, The Preppie Murder, The Hidden Room, Past Tense, Jacob.

BOYLE, PETER
Actor. b. Philadelphia, PA, Oct. 18, 1933. e. LaSalle Coll. Was monk in Christian Bros. order before leaving in early 60s to come to N.Y. Acted in off-Broadway shows and joined The Second City in Chicago. Also did TV commercials.
THEATER: *NY:* Shadow of Heroes, Paul Sills' Story Theatre, The Roast, True West, Snow Orchid.
PICTURES: The Virgin President (debut, 1968), The Monitors, Medium Cool, Joe, Diary of a Mad Housewife, T.R. Baskin, The Candidate, Steelyard Blues, Slither, The Friends of Eddie Coyle, Kid Blue, Ghost in the Noonday Sun, Crazy Joe, Young Frankenstein, Taxi Driver, Swashbuckler, F.I.S.T., The Brink's Job, Hardcore, Beyond the Poseidon Adventure, Where the Buffalo Roam, In God We Trust, Outland, Hammett, Yellowbeard, Johnny Dangerously, Turk 182, Surrender, Walker, The In Crowd, Red Heat, The Dream Team, Speed Zone, Funny, Men of Respect, Solar Crisis, Kickboxer 2, Honeymoon in Vegas, Nervous Ticks, Malcolm X, The Shadow, The Santa Clause, Bulletproof Heart, Born to Be Wild, While You Were Sleeping, That Darn Cat.

TELEVISION: *Series:* Comedy Tonight, Joe Bash, Everybody Loves Raymond. *Mini-Series:* From Here to Eternity. *Movies:* The Man Who Could Talk to Kids, Tail Gunner Joe, Echoes in the Darkness, Disaster at Silo 7, Guts and Glory: The Rise and Fall of Oliver North, Challenger, In the Line of Duty: Street War, Taking the Heat, Royce. *Specials:* 27 Wagons Full of Cotton, Conspiracy: The Trial of the Chicago Eight. *Guest:* Cagney & Lacey, Midnight Caller, X-Files (Emmy Award, 1996). *Pilot:* Philly Heat.

BRABOURNE, LORD JOHN
Producer. b. London, England, Nov. 9, 1924.
PICTURES: Harry Black and the Tiger, Sink the Bismarck, H.M.S. Defiant (Damn the Defiant!), Othello, The Mikado, Up the Junction, Romeo and Juliet, Dance of Death, Peter Rabbit and Tales of Beatrix Potter, Murder on the Orient Express, Death on the Nile, Stories from a Flying Trunk, The Mirror Crack'd, Evil Under the Sun, A Passage to India, Little Dorrit.

BRACCO, LORRAINE
Actress. b. Brooklyn, NY, Oct. 2, 1955. m. actor Edward James Olmos. At 16 began modelling for Wilhelmina Agency appearing in Mademoiselle, Seventeen, Teen magazine. Moved to Paris where modelling career continued and led to TV commercials. After making her film debut in Duo sur Canape became a disc jockey on Radio Luxembourg, Paris. 1983 produced a TV special on fashion and music. In Lincoln Center workshop performance of David Rabe's Goose and Tom Tom, 1986.
PICTURES: Cormorra, The Pick-up Artist, Someone to Watch Over Me, Sing, The Dream Team, On a Moonlit Night, Good Fellas (Acad. Award nom.), Talent for the Game, Switch, Medicine Man, Radio Flyer, Traces of Red, Being Human, The Basketball Diaries, Hackers, The Liars, Ladies Room.
TELEVISION: *Movies:* Scam, Getting Gotti, Lifeline, The Taking of Pelham One-Two-Three.

BRACKEN, EDDIE
Actor. b. New York, NY, Feb. 7, 1920. e. Prof. Children's Sch. for Actors, N.Y. m. Connie Nickerson, actress. Vaudeville & night club singer: stage debut in Lottery, 1930.
THEATER: Lady Refuses, Iron Men, So Proudly We Hail, Brother Rat, What A Life, Too Many Girls, Seven Year Itch, Shinbone Alley, Teahouse of the August Moon, You Know I Can't Hear You When The Water's Running, The Odd Couple, Never Too Late, Sunshine Boys, Hotline to Heaven, Hello Dolly, Damn Yankees, Sugar Babies, Show Boat, The Wizard of Oz, It Runs in the Family, These Golden Years, No No Nanette.
PICTURES: Too Many Girls (debut, 1940), Life With Henry, Reaching for the Sun, Caught in the Draft, The Fleet's In, Sweater Girl, Star Spangled Rhythm, Happy Go Lucky, Young and Willing, The Miracle of Morgan's Creek, Hail the Conquering Hero, Rainbow Island, Bring on the Girls, Duffy's Tavern, Hold That Blonde, Out of This World, Ladies' Man, Fun on a Weekend, The Girl From Jones Beach, Summer Stock, Two Tickets to Broadway, About Face, We're Not Married, Slight Case of Larceny, Wild Wild World (narrator), Shinbone Alley (voice), National Lampoon's Vacation, Oscar, Home Alone 2: Lost in New York, Rookie of the Year, Baby's Day Out, The Brave Little Toaster (voice).
TELEVISION: *Series:* I've Got a Secret (panelist), Make the Connection (panelist), Masquerade Party (host, 1957). *Guest:* Goodyear Playhouse, Studio One, Climax, Murder She Wrote, Blacke's Magic, Amazing Stories, Tales of the Dark Side, Golden Girls, Wise Guy, Empty Nest, Monsters. *Movies:* The American Clock, Assault at West Point.

BRADEN, WILLIAM
Executive, Producer. b. Alberta, Canada. e. U.S., Canada, and abroad. Began career as stuntman in Hollywood, and has worked in all aspects of industry Worked for Elliott Kastner as prod. exec. and with Jeffrey Bloom, of Feature Films, Inc., as prod. and v.p. in chg. of prod. Also with Dunatai Corp., as head of film and TV prod. With Completion Bond Co. one yr. as prod. exec., Australia then with Filmaker Completion as pres. 4 years. Now indep. prod.
PICTURES: Pyramid (assoc. prod., prod. supv.), Russian Roulette (prod. exec.), 92 in the Shade (prod. exec.), Breakheart Pass (prod. exec.), Dogpound Shuffle (asst. dir.), Dublin Murders (supvr. re-edit), He Wants Her Back (prod.), Goldengirl (prod. exec.), Running Scared (prod.), Death Valley (asst. dir.), The Seduction (prod. exec.), Slapstick of Another Kind (prod. exec.).
TELEVISION: Requiem for a Planet (series, prod./creator). *Specials:* Nothing Great is Easy (exec. prod.), King of the Channel (exec. prod.), I Believe (prod.), If My People... (prod.), America: Life in the Family (dir./prod.). Also various Movies of the Week for networks and many industrial and doc. films.

BRADFORD, JESSE
Actor. b. May 28, 1979. Made first appearance as infant in Q-tip commercial.
PICTURES: Falling in Love (debut, 1984), Prancer, Presmued Innocent, My Blue Heaven, The Boy Who Cried Bitch, King of the Hill, Far From Home: The Adventures of Yello Dog, Hackers, Romeo & Juliet.
TELEVISION: *Movie:* The Boys. *Special:* Classified Love. *Guest:* Tribeca.

BRADLEY, ED
Newscaster. b. Philadelphia, Pa., June 22, 1941. e. Cheyney State Coll, B.S. Worked way up through the ranks as local radio reporter in Philadelphia 1963-67 and NY 1967-71. Joined CBS News as stringer in Paris bureau, 1971; then Saigon bureau. Named CBS news correspondent, 1973. Became CBS News White House corr. and anchor of CBS Sunday Night News, 1976-81; principal corr. and anchor, CBS Reports, 1978-81; co-editor and reporter 60 Minutes since 1980. Recipient: Alfred I. duPont-Columbia University and Overseas Press Club Awards, George Foster Peabody and Ohio State Awards, George Polk Award.
TELEVISION: Special reports: What's Happened to Cambodia, The Boat People, The Boston Goes to China, Blacks in America—With All Deliberate Speed, Return of the CIA, Miami... The Trial That Sparked the Riot (Emmy Award), The Saudis, Too Little Too Late (Emmy Award), Murder—Teenage Style (Emmy Award, 1981), In the Belly of the Beast (Emmy Award, 1982), Lena (Emmy Award, 1982).

BRAEDEN, ERIC
Actor. r.n. Hans Gudegast. b. Kiel, Germany, Apr. 3, 1941. Awarded Federal Medal of Honor by pres. of Germany for promoting positive, realistic image of Germans in America.
PICTURES: Morituri, Dayton's Devils, 100 Rifles, Colossus: The Forbin Project, Escape from the Planet of the Apes, Lady Ice, The Adulteress, The Ultimate Thrill, Herbie Goes to Monte Carlo, The Ambulance, Titanic, Meet the Deedles.
TELEVISION: Series: The Rat Patrol, The Young and the Restless (People's Choice Award, Soap Opera Award, 2 Emmy noms., Emmy Award, 1998). Movies: Honeymoon With a Stranger, The Mask of Sheba, The Judge and Jake Wyler, Death Race, Death Scream, The New Original Wonder Woman (pilot), Code Name: Diamond Head, Happily Ever After, The Power Within, The Aliens Are Coming, The Case of the Wicked Wives. Mini-series: Jackie Collins' Lucky Chances.

BRAGA, SONIA
Actress. b. Maringa, Parana, Brazil, 1950. Began acting at 14 on live children's program on Brazilian TV, Gardin Encantado. Stage debut at 17 in Moliere's Jorge Dandin, then in Hair! Starred in many Brazilian soap operas including Gabriella, as well as a prod. of Sesame Street in Sao Paulo.
PICTURES: The Main Road, A Moreninha, Captain Bandeira Vs. Dr. Moura Brasil, Mestica, The Indomitable Slave, The Couple, Dona Flor and Her Two Husbands, Gabriella, I Love You, A Lady in the Bus, Kiss of the Spider Woman, The Milagro Beanfield War, Moon Over Parador, The Rookie, Roosters.
TELEVISION: Movies: The Man Who Broke 1000 Chains, The Last Prostitute, The Burning Season. Guest: The Cosby Show, Tales From the Crypt.

BRANAGH, KENNETH
Actor, Director, Producer, Author. b. Belfast, Northern Ireland, Dec. 10, 1960. Moved to Reading, England at age 9. e. RADA. Went from drama school into West End hit Another Country, followed by Gamblers, The Madness, Francis. Royal Shakespeare Co.: Love Labors Lost, Hamlet, Henry V. Left Royal Shakespeare Company to form his own Renaissance Theater Co. with actor David Parfitt for which he wrote a play Public Enemy (also produced Off-B'way), wrote-directed Tell Me Honestly, directed Twelfth Night, produced-directed-starred in Romeo & Juliet, and played Hamlet, Benedick and Touchstone in a sold-out nationwide tour and London season. L.A.: King Lear, A Midsummer Night's Dream. Author: Beginning (1990). Received BAFTA's Michael Balcon Award for Outstanding Contribution to Cinema (1993). Made short film Swan Song (Acad. Award nom.).
PICTURES: High Season (debut, 1987), A Month in the Country, Henry V (also dir., adapt.; BAFTA & Natl. Board of Review Awards for Best Dir., 1989), Dead Again (also dir.), Peter's Friends (also dir., prod.), Swing Kids, Much Ado About Nothing (also dir., adapt.), Mary Shelley's Frankenstein (also dir., co-prod.), In the Bleak Mid-Winter (dir., s.p. only), Anne Frank Remembered (narrator), Othello, Hamlet (also dir, prod..).
TELEVISION: The Boy in the Bush (series), The Billy Plays, Maybury, To the Lighthouse, Coming Through, Ghosts, The Lady's Not For Burning, Fortunes of War (mini-series) Thompson (series), Strange Interlude, Look Back in Anger.

BRANDAUER, KLAUS MARIA
Actor, Director. r.n. Klaus Maria Steng. b. Bad Ausse, Steiermark, Austria, June 22, 1944. m. film and TV dir.-screenwriter Karin Mueller. e. Acad. of Music and Dramatic Arts, Stuttgart, W. Germany. Was established in the German and Austrian theater before film debut.
PICTURES: The Salzburg Connection (debut, 1972), Mephisto (Cannes Film Fest. Award, 1981). Never Say Never Again, Colonel Redl, Out of Africa, The Lightship, Streets of Gold, Burning Secret, Hanussen, Hitlerjunge Salomon, Das Spinnennetz (The Spider's Web) The French Revolution, The Russia House, White Fang, The Resurrected, Seven Minutes (also dir.), Becoming Colette, Felidae (voice), Marco and the Magician (also dir.), Die Wand (dir. only).
TELEVISION: Quo Vadis?

BRANDIS, JONATHAN
Actor. b. Danbury, CT, April 13, 1976. Started as print model at age 4; followed by several tv commercials.
PICTURES: Fatal Attraction, Stepfather 2, Never Ending Story II: The Next Chapter, Ladybugs, Sidekicks, Ride with the Devil, Outside Providence.
TELEVISION: Series: SeaQuest DSV, Aladdin (voice). Movies: Poor Little Rich Girl, Stephen King's IT, SeaQuest DSV, Good King Wenceslas, Born Free: A New Adventure, Her Last Chance, Fall Into Darkness, Two Came Back. Guest: Murder, She Wrote, L.A. Law, The Wonder Years, Alien Nation, The Flash, Saved by the Bell: The College Years.

BRANDO, MARLON
Actor. b. Omaha, NB, April 3, 1924. Sister is actress Jocelyn Brando. e. Shattuck Military Acad., Faribault, MN. Studied acting at New School's Dramatic Workshop, NY, with Stella Adler; played stock in Sayville, Long Island. Broadway debut: I Remember Mama, followed by Truckline Cafe, Candida, A Flag Is Born, A Streetcar Named Desire. Voted one of top ten Money-Making Stars, M.P. Herald-Fame poll, 1954-55. Autobiography: Brando: Songs My Mother Taught Me (1994).
PICTURES: The Men (debut, 1950), A Streetcar Named Desire, Viva Zapata!, Julius Caesar, The Wild One, On the Waterfront (Academy Award, 1954), Desiree, Guys and Dolls, The Teahouse of the August Moon, Sayonara, The Young Lions, The Fugitive Kind, One-Eyed Jacks (also dir.), Mutiny on the Bounty, The Ugly American, Bedtime Story, The Saboteur—Code Name: Morituri, The Chase, The Appaloosa, A Countess From Hong Kong, Reflections in a Golden Eye, Candy, The Night of the Following Day, Burn!, The Nightcomers, The Godfather (Academy Award, 1972), Last Tango in Paris, The Missouri Breaks, Superman, Apocalypse Now, The Formula, A Dry White Season, The Freshman, Christopher Columbus: The Discovery, Don Juan DeMarco, Divine Rapture, The Island of Dr. Moreau, The Brave.
TELEVISION: Mini-Series: Roots: The Next Generations (Emmy Award, 1979).

BRANDON, MICHAEL
Actor. b. Brooklyn, NY. e. AADA. Appeared on B'way in Does Tiger Wear a Necktie?
PICTURES: Lovers and Other Strangers, Jennifer on My Mind, Four Flies on Grey Velvet, Heavy Traffic (voice), FM, Promises in the Dark, A Change of Seasons, Rich and Famous.
TELEVISION: Series: Emerald Point, Dempsey & Makepeace, Home Fires. Movies: The Impatient Heart, The Strangers in 7A, The Third Girl From the Left, Hitchhike!, The Red Badge of Courage, Queen of the Stardust Ballroom, Cage Without a Key, James Dean, Scott Free, Red Alert, The Comedy Company, A Vacation in Hell, A Perfect Match, Between Two Brothers, The Seduction of Gina, Deadly Messages, Rock 'n' Roll Mom, Dynasty: The Reunion, Not in My Family, Moment of Truth: Murder or Memory?

BRANDT, RICHARD PAUL
Executive. b. New York, NY, Dec. 6, 1927. e. Yale U., BS, Phi Beta Kappa. Chmn. Trans Lux Corp.; chmn., Brandt Theatres; dir.; Presidential Realty Corp.; chmn. emeritus & trustee, American Film Institute; trustee, American Theatre Wing; member, Tony Awards Management Comm.; vice-chmn. & trustee, College of Santa Fe.

BRAUGHER, ANDRE
Actor. b. Chicago, IL, July 1, 1962.
PICTURES: Glory, Striking Distance, Primal Fear, Get on the Bus, Thick as Thieves, City of Angels, A Better Way to Die.
TELEVISION: Movies: Kojak: Fatal Flaw, Kojak: Ariana, Kojak: None So Blind, Murder in Mississippi, Somebody Has to Shoot the Picture, The Court-Martial of Jackie Robinson, Simple Justice, Class of '61, Without Warning: Terror in the Towers, The Tuskegee Airmen. Series: Kojak, Homicide: Life in the Street (Emmy Award, 1998).

BRAUNSTEIN, GEORGE GREGORY
Producer. b. New York, NY, May 23, 1947. e. Culver Military Acad., U. of California, B.A., biology, chemistry, 1970. U. W.L.A. Law School, J.D. 1987. Father is Jacques Braunstein (Screen Televideo Prods. At War with the Army, Young Lions, etc.)
PICTURES: Train Ride to Hollywood, Fade to Black, Surf II, And God Created Woman, Out Cold, Don't Tell Her It's Me.

BRAVERMAN, CHARLES
Producer, Director. b. Los Angeles, CA, March 3, 1944. e. Los Angeles City Coll., U. of Southern California, B.A. m. Kendall Carly Browne, actress. Child actor, 1950-57. Two time Emmy winner.
PICTURES: Dillinger, Soylent Green, Same Time Next Year (all montages, titles), Can't Stop the Music (titles), Hit and Run (prod./dir.), The Hank Gather Story.

TELEVISION: An American Time Capsule, The Smothers Brothers Racing Team Special, How to Stay Alive, David Hartman... Birth and Babies, Breathe a Sigh of Relief, The Television Newsman, Getting Married, The Making of a Live TV Show, Televisionland, Nixon: Checkers to Watergate, Braverman's Condensed Cream of Beatles, Two Cops, Peanuts to the Presidency: The Jimmy Carter Campaign, The Making of Beatlemania, Willie Nelson Plays Lake Tahoe, Tony Bennett Sings, What's Up, America?, The Big Laff Off, Engelbert at the MGM Grand, Oscar's First 50 Years, Frankie Valli Show, The Sixties, Showtime Looks at 1981, Roadshow, Kenny Rodger's America, St. Elsewhere, DTV (Disney Channel), Crazy Like a Fox, Dreams, The Richard Lewis Special, Prince of Bel Air, Brotherhood of Justice, The Wizard; Heart of the City, Rags to Riches, The New Mike Hammer, Sledge Hammer!, Gabriel's Fire, Life Goes On, Beverly Hills 90210, FBI: Untold Stories, Final Shot: The Hank Gathers Story, Melrose Place, Northern Exposure (DGA nom.), Haunted Lives II.

BRECHER, IRVING
Writer, Director. b. New York, NY, Jan. 17, 1914. e. Roosevelt H.S. in Yonkers. Yonkers Herald reporter; network programs writer for Milton Berle, Willie Howard, Al Jolson, etc., m.p. writer since 1937. On B'way in Sweet Charity, 1942.
PICTURES: At the Circus, Go West, Du Barry Was a Lady, Shadow of the Thin Man, Best Foot Forward, Meet Me in St. Louis, Summer Holiday, Yolanda and the Thief, Life of Riley (also dir.), Somebody Loves Me (also dir.), Cry for Happy, Sail a Crooked Ship (also dir.), Bye Bye Birdie.
TELEVISION: The People's Choice, The Life of Riley.

BREGMAN, MARTIN
Producer, Writer. b. New York, NY, May 18, 1931. m. actress Cornelia Sharpe. e. Indiana U., NYU. Began career as business and personal mgr. to Barbra Streisand, Faye Dunaway, Candice Bergen, Al Pacino, etc. Chairman NY Advisory Council for Motion Pictures, Radio and TV (co-founder, 1974).
PICTURES: Producer. Serpico, Dog Day Afternoon, The Next Man, The Seduction of Joe Tynan, Simon, The Four Seasons, Eddie Macon's Run, Venom, Scarface, Sweet Liberty, Real Men, A New Life, Sea of Love, Nesting, Betsy's Wedding, Whispers in the Dark, The Real McCoy, Carlito's Way, The Shadow, Gold Diggers: The Secret of Bear Mountain, Matilda (exec. prod.), Nothing to Lose, The Bone Collector.
TELEVISION: Prod.: S*H*E (movie), The Four Seasons (series).

BRENNAN, EILEEN
Actress. b. Los Angeles, CA, Sept. 3, 1935. e. Georgetown U., American Acad. of Dramatic Arts, N.Y. Daughter of silent film actress Jean Manahan. Big break came with lead in off-Broadway musical, Little Mary Sunshine (Obie & Theatre World Awards, 1960).
THEATER: The Miracle Worker (tour), Hello Dolly! (Broadway), and revivals of The King and I, Guys and Dolls, Camelot, Bells Are Ringing; also An Evening with Eileen Brennan, A Couple of White Chicks Sitting Around Talking.
PICTURES: Divorce American Style (debut, 1967), The Last Picture Show (BAFTA nom.), Scarecrow, The Sting, Daisy Miller, At Long Last Love, Hustle, Murder by Death, FM, The Cheap Detective, The Last of the Cowboys (The Great Smokey Roadblock), Private Benjamin (Acad. Award nom.), Pandemonium, The Funny Farm, Clue, Sticky Fingers, Rented Lips, The New Adventures of Pippi Longstocking, It Had to Be You, Stella, Texasville, White Palace, Joey Takes a Cab, I Don't Buy Kisses Anymore, Reckless, Pants on Fire, Nuncio's Second Cousin, Changing Bad Habits, Boy's Life 2.
TELEVISION: Series: Rowan & Martin's Laugh-In, All My Children, 13 Queens Boulevard, A New Kind of Family, Private Benjamin (Emmy Award, 1981), Off the Rack, 7th Heaven. Specials: Working, In Search of Dr. Seuss. Movies: Playmates, My Father's House, The Night That Panicked America, The Death of Richie, When She Was Bad..., My Old Man, When the Circus Came to Town, Incident at Crestridge, Going to the Chapel, Deadly Intentions... Again?, Taking Back My Life: The Nancy Ziegenmeyer Story, Poisoned by Love: The Kern County Murders, Precious Victims, My Name Is Kate, Take Me Home Again, Freaky Friday, Trail of Tears, Toothless. Mini-Series: The Blue Knight, Black Beauty. Guest: Taxi, Magnum P.I., Newhart, All in the Family, Murder She Wrote, Blossom, Mad About You, Veronica's Closet, numerous others.

BRENNEMAN, AMY
Actress. b. Connecticut, 1964.
PICTURES: Bye Bye Love, Casper, Heat, Fear, Daylight, Nevada (also prod.), Lesser Prophets, Friends and Neighbors.
TELEVISION: Middle Ages, NYPD Blue, ATF.

BREST, MARTIN
Director. b. Bronx, NY, Aug. 8, 1951. e. NYU Sch. of Film. m. prod. Lisa Weinstein. Made award-winning short subject, Hot Dogs for Gauguin (featuring Danny DeVito). Accepted into fellowship program at American Film Institute, making first feature, Hot Tomorrows (dir., prod., s.p.), as AFI project. Appeared in Fast Times at Ridgemont High, Spies Like Us. Produced film Josh and S.A.M.
PICTURES: Going in Style (also s.p.), Beverly Hills Cop, Midnight Run (also prod.), Scent of a Woman (also prod.).

BRIALY, JEAN-CLAUDE
Actor. b. Aumale, Algeria, March 30, 1933. e. Strasbourg U. (philosophy) also attended drama classes at Strasbourg Conservatoire. Made several short films with Jacques Rivette and Jean-Luc Godard. Appeared in several French TV movies.
PICTURES: Paris Does Strange Things, Elevator to the Gallows, Les Cousins, Three Faces of Sin, A Woman Is a Woman, Seven Capitol Sins, The Devil and Ten Commandments, Two Are Guilty, Nutty Naughty Chateau, Carless Love, Male Hunt, Circle of Love, King of Hearts, The Oldest Profession, Shock Troops, The Bride Wore Black, Claire's Knee, A Murder is a Murder, The Phantom of Liberty, Catherine et Cie, The Accuser, L'Annee Sainte, Robert and Robert, Eglantine, Les Violets Clos, L'oiseau Rare, Un Amour De Pluie, Bobo Jacco, L'oeil Du Maitre, La Banquiere, La Nuit de Varennes, Cap Canaille, Le Demon Dan L'Isle, Edith and Marcel, Sarah, Stella, The Crime, Papy Fait de la Resistance, Pinot, Simple Flic, Comedie dété, My New Partner 2, No Fear-No Die, August, Pakt mit dem Tod, The Monster, Queen Margot, The Son of Gascogne, A French Woman, A Hundred and One Nights, Shadow Play, Beaumarchais the Scoundrel.

BRICKMAN, MARSHALL
Writer, Director. b. Rio de Janeiro, Brazil, Aug. 25, 1941. e. U. of Wisconsin. Banjoist, singer, writer with folk groups The Tarriers and The Journeymen before starting to write for TV. Appeared in films Funny and That's Adequate.
PICTURES: Co-writer (with Woody Allen): Sleeper, Annie Hall (Acad. Award, 1977), Manhattan, Manhattan Murder Mystery. Dir./Writer: Simon (dir. debut, 1980), Lovesick, The Manhattan Project (also prod.). Co-Writer: For the Boys, Intersection.
TELEVISION: Writer: Candid Camera 1966, The Tonight Show 1966-70. Specials: Johnny Carson's Repertory Co. in an Evening of Comedy (1969), Woody Allen Special, Woody Allen Looks at 1967. Prod.: Dick Cavett Show (1970-72, Emmy Award).

BRICKMAN, PAUL
Writer, Director. b. Chicago, IL. e. Claremont Men's Coll. Worked as camera asst., then story analyst at Paramount, Columbia, and Universal.
PICTURES: Handle With Care (Citizen's Band; assoc. prod., s.p.), The Bad News Bears in Breaking Training (s.p.), Risky Business, (dir., s.p.), Deal of the Century (s.p., co-exec. prod.), That's Adequate (interviewee), Men Don't Leave (dir., co-s.p.).

BRIDGES, ALAN
Director. b. England, Sept. 28, 1927. Started dir. for the BBC before moving into feature films.
PICTURES: An Act of Murder (debut, 1965), Invasion, Shelley, The Hireling, Out of Season, Summer Rain, The Return of the Soldier, The Shooting Party, Displaced Persons, Apt Pupil, Secret Places of the Heart, Fire Princess.
TELEVISION: The Father, Dial M For Murder, The Intrigue, The Ballade of Peckham Rye, The Initiation, Alarm Call: Z Cars, The Fontenay Murders, The Brothers Karamazov, The Idiot, Days to Come, Les Miserables, Born Victim, The Wild Duck, The Lie, Brief Encounter, Forget Me Not Lane, Double Echo, Saturday—Sunday—Monday, Crown Matrimonial.

BRIDGES, BEAU
Actor. r.n. Lloyd Vernet Bridges III. b. Hollywood, CA, Dec. 9, 1941. e. UCLA; U. of Hawaii. Father is actor Lloyd Bridges, brother is actor Jeff Bridges.
PICTURES: Force of Evil (debut, 1948), No Minor Vices, The Red Pony, Zamba, The Explosive Generation, Village of the Giants, The Incident, For Love of Ivy, Gaily Gaily, The Landlord, Adam's Woman, The Christian Licorice Store, Hammersmith Is Out, Child's Play, Your Three Minutes Are Up, Lovin' Molly, The Other Side of the Mountain, Dragonfly (One Summer Love), Swashbuckler, Two-Minute Warning, Greased Lightning, Norma Rae, The Fifth Musketeer, The Runner Stumbles, Silver Dream Racer, Honky Tonk Freeway, Night Crossing, Love Child, Heart Like a Wheel, The Hotel New Hampshire, The Killing Time, The Wild Pair (also dir.), Seven Hours to Judgement (also dir.), The Iron Triangle, Signs of Life, The Fabulous Baker Boys, The Wizard, Daddy's Dyin'...Who's Got the Will?, Married to It, Sidekicks.
TELEVISION: Movies: The Man Without a Country, The Stranger Who Looks Like Me, Medical Story, The Four Feathers, Shimmering Light, The President's Mistress, The Child Stealer, The Kid from Nowhere (also dir.), Dangerous Company, Witness for the Prosecution, The Red-Light Sting, Alice in Wonderland, Outrage!, Fighting Choice, The Thanksgiving Promise (also dir., co-prod.), Everybody's Baby: The Rescue of Jessica McClure, Just Another Secret, Women & Men: Stories of Seduction (The Man in the Brooks Brothers Shirt), Guess Who's Coming for Christmas?, Without Warning: The James Brady Story (Emmy Award, 1992), Wildflower, Elvis and the Colonel, The Man With 3 Wives, The Positively True Adventures of the Alleged Texas Cheerleader-Murdering Mom (Emmy Award, 1993), Secret Sins of the Fathers (also dir.), Kissinger and Nixon, Losing Chase. Series: Ensign O'Toole, United States, Harts of the West. Mini-series: The Second Civil War (Emmy Award, 1997). Guest: Sea Hunt, Ben Casey, Dr. Kildare, Mr. Novak, Combat, Eleventh Hour, Cimarron Strip, Amazing Stories, The Outer Limits.

BRIDGES, JEFF

Actor. b. Los Angeles, CA, Dec. 4, 1949. Appeared as infant in 1950 film The Company She Keeps. Made acting debut at eight in the TV series Sea Hunt starring his father, Lloyd Bridges. Studied acting at Herbert Berghof Studio, NY. Mil. service in Coast Guard reserves. Brother is actor-dir. Beau Bridges. Composed and performed song for film John and Mary. Named Male Star of the Year (1990) by NATO.

PICTURES: Halls of Anger (debut, 1970), The Yin and Yang of Mr. Go, The Last Picture Show (Acad. Award nom.), Fat City, Bad Company, The Iceman Cometh, The Last American Hero, Lolly-Madonna XXX, Thunderbolt and Lightfoot (Acad. Award nom.), Hearts of the West, Rancho Deluxe, Stay Hungry, King Kong, Somebody Killed Her Husband, The American Success Company, Winter Kills, Heaven's Gate, Cutter's Way (Cutter and Bone), Tron, The Last Unicorn (voice only), Kiss Me Goodbye, Against All Odds, Starman (Acad. Award nom.), Jagged Edge, 8 Million Ways to Die, The Morning After, Nadine, Tucker: The Man and His Dream, See You in the Morning, Cold Feet, The Fabulous Baker Boys, Texasville, The Fisher King, The Vanishing, American Heart (also co-prod.), Fearless, Blown Away, Wild Bill, White Squall, The Mirror Has Two Faces, The Big Lebowski, Arlington Road.

TELEVISION: *Movies*: Silent Night, Lonely Night; In Search of America, The Thanksgiving Promise (cameo). *Special*: Faerie Tale Theatre (Rapunzel). *Guest*: Lloyd Bridges Show, The FBI, Most Deadly Game.

BRIDGES, LLOYD

Actor. b. San Leandro, CA, January 15, 1913. e. UCLA. Went into stock from college dramatics. Formed off-B'way theater, the Playroom Club. With wife taught drama at private sch. in Darien, CT when signed stock contract with Columbia. B'way stage: Dead Pigeon, Oh Men! Oh Women!, Heart Song, Cactus Flower, Man of La Mancha.

PICTURES: They Dare Not Love, Honolulu Lu, The Lone Wolf Takes a Chance, Cadets on Parade, Son of Davy Crockett, I Was a Prisoner of Devil's Island, Here Comes Mr. Jordan, The Medico of Painted Sprgins, Our Wife, Two Latins From Manhattan, Harmon of Michigan, Three Girls About Town, The Royal Mounted Patrol, Harvard Here I Come, You Belong to Me, The Wife Takes a Flyer, Underground Agent, North of the Rockies, West of Tombstone, Blondie Goes to College, Sing for Your Supper, Shut My Big Mouht, Canal Zone, Stand By All Networks, Tramp Tramp Tramp, Alias Boston Blackie, Hello Annapolis, Sweetheart of the Fleet, Meet the Stewarts, Flight Lieutenant, Riders of the Northland, Atlantic Convoy, The Talk of the Town, Spirit of Stanford, A Man's World, Pardon My Gun, Commandos Strike at Dawn, Sahara, The Heat's On, Hail to the Rangers, The Crime Doctor's Strangest Case, Destroyer, Two-Man Submarine, Louisiana Hayride, Once Upon a Time, She's a Soldier Too, The Master Race, Saddle Leather Law, A Walk in the Sun, Strange Confession, Secret Agent X-9 (serial), Miss Susie Slage's, Abilene Town, Canyon Passage, Ramrod, The Trouble With Women, Unconquered, Secret Service Investigator, Sixteen Fathoms Deep, Moonrise, Red Canyon, Hideout, Home of the Brave, Calamity Jane and Sam Bass, Trapped, Rocketship XM, Try and Get Me (The Sound of Fury), The White Tower, Colt .45, Little Big Horn, Three Steps North, The Whistle at Eaton Falls, Last of the Comanches, High Noon, Plymouth Adventure, The Tall Texan, The Kid From Left Field, City of Bad Men, The Limping Man, Pride of the Blue Grass, Apache Woman, Wichita, The Deadly Game (Third Party Risk), Wetbacks, The Rainmaker, Ride Out for Revenge, The Goddess, Around the World Under the Sea, Attack on the Iron Coast, The Daring Game, The Happy Ending, To Find a Man, Running Wild, Deliver Us From Evil, The Fifth Musketeer, Bear Island, Airplane!, Airplane II: The Sequel, Weekend Warriors, The Wild Pair, Tucker: The Man and His Dream, Cousins, Winter People, Joe Versus the Volcano, Hot Shots!, Honey I Blew Up the Kid, Hot Shots Part Deux!, Blown Away.

TELEVISION: *Series*: Police Story, Sea Hunt, The Lloyd Bridges Show, The Loner, San Francisco International Airport, Joe Forrester, Paper Dolls, Capitol News, Harts of the West. *Movies*: Tragedy in a Temporary Town, The Fortress, The People Next Door, Paper Dolls, Silent Night, Lonley Night, The Thanksgiving Promise, She Was Marked For Murder, Cross of Fire, Leona Helmsley: The Queen of Mean, In the Nick of Time, Devlin, Secret Sins of the Father, The Other Woman. *Mini-series*: Roots, Disaster on the Coastliner, East of Eden, Movieola, The Blue and the Gray, George Washington, Dress Gray, North & South Book II. *Special*: Cinderella... Frozen in Time, Nothing Lasts Forever. *Guest*: Bigelow Theatre, Kraft Suspense Theatre, Robt. Montgomery Present, CBS Playhouse, Alcoa Hour, Philco Playhouse, U.S. Steel Hour, Playhouse 90.
(d. March 10, 1998)

BRIGHT, RICHARD

Actor. b. Brooklyn, NY, June 11. e. trained for stage with Frank Corsaro, John Lehne and Paul Mann.

THEATER: The Balcony (1959), The Beard, The Salvation of St. Joan, Gogol, The Basic Training of Pavlo Hummel, Richard III, Kid Twist, Short Eyes as well as regional theater.

PICTURES: Odds Against Tomorrow, Lion's Love, Panic in Needle Park, The Getaway, Pat Garrett and Billy the Kid, The Godfather, The Godfather II, Rancho Deluxe, Marathon Man,

Citizens Band, Looking For Mr. Goodbar, On the Yard, Hair, The Idolmaker, Vigilante, Two of a Kind, Once Upon a Time in America, Crackers, Crimewave, Cut and Run, Brighton Beach Memoirs, 52-Pick-up, Time Out, Red Head, The Godfather III, Who's the Man, The Ref, Sweet Nothing, Ripper, Jaded, Beautiful Girls, Night Falls of Manhattan, OK Garage.

TELEVISION: *Series*: Lamp Unto My Feet, Armstrong Circle Theater, The Verdict Is Yours, Kraft Television Theatre, Studio One, Cagney and Lacey, Beacon Hill, Hill Street Blues, From These Roots. *Movies*: A Death of Innocence, The Connection, The Gun, Cops and Robin, Sizzle, There Must Be A Pony, Penalty Phase. *Mini-series*: From Here to Eternity, Skag, Calm of Sunset, Witness to the Mob.

BRIGHT, RICHARD S.

Executive. b. New Rochelle, NY, Feb. 28, 1936. e. Hotchkiss Sch., 1953-54; Wharton Sch. of Finance, U. of Pennsylvania, 1954-58. With U.S. Army Finance Corp., 1959-60. Was corporate exec. prior to founding Persky-Bright Organization in 1973, private investment group to finance films. Now bd. chmn, Persky-Bright Productions, Inc.

THEATER: A History of the American Film, Album (Off-B'way, co-prod.).

PICTURES: Last Detail, Golden Voyage of Sinbad, For Pete's Sake, California Split, The Man Who Would Be King, Funny Lady, The Front, and Equus. Financing/production services for: Hard Times, Taxi Driver, Missouri Breaks, Bound for Glory, Sinbad and the Eye of the Tiger, Hair, Body Heat, Still of the Night. Exec. prod.: Tribute.

TELEVISION: The President's Mistress (co-prod.).

BRILLSTEIN, BERNIE

Producer, Talent Manager. b. New York, NY. 1931. e. NYU, B.S. advertising. Manager whose clients have incl. Lorne Michaels, John Belushi, Jim Henson and the Muppets. Chairman and chief exec. officer, Lorimar Film Entertainment. Founder, chmn., pres., The Brillstein Company. Former co-partner of Brillstein-Grey Entertainment and Brillstein-Grey Communications.

PICTURES: *Exec. Prod.*: The Blues Brothers, Up the Academy, Continental Divide, Neighbors, Doctor Detroit, Ghostbusters, Spies Like Us, Summer Rental, Armed and Dangerous, Dragnet, Ghostbusters II, Hexed, The Celluloid Closet, Cat and Mouse, Happy Gilmore, The Cable Guy, Bulletproof, Dirty Work, The Replacement Killers.

TELEVISION: *Exec. prod.*: Burns and Schreiber Comedy Hour, Buckshot, Open All Night, Show Business, Sitcom, Buffalo Bill, Jump, The Faculty, The Real Ghostbusters (exec. consultant), It's Garry Shandling's Show, The Days and Nights of Molly Dodd, The "Slap" Maxwell Show, The Boys (pilot), The Wickedest Witch, Normal Life, The Larry Sanders Show, Newsradio, Def Comedy Jam—Prime Time, Hightower 411, Just Shoot Me, The Naked Truth, The Steve Harvey Show, Mr. Show, Just Shoot Me.

BRIMLEY, WILFORD

Actor. b. Salt Lake City, UT, Sept. 27, 1934. Formerly a blacksmith, ranch hand and racehorse trainer; began in films as an extra and stuntman. Also acted as A. Wilford Brimley. Original member of L.A. Actors Theatre.

PICTURES: True Grit, Lawman, The China Syndrome, The Electric Horseman, Brubaker, Borderline, Absence of Malice, Death Valley, The Thing, Tender Mercies, Tough Enough, High Road to China, 10 to Midnight, Hotel New Hampshire, Harry and Son, The Stone Boy, The Natural, Country, Cocoon, Remo Williams: The Adventure Begins, American Justice, End of the Line, Cocoon: The Return, Eternity, The Firm, Hard Target, Last of the Dogmen, My Fellow Americans, In & Out.

TELEVISION: *Movies*: The Oregon Trail, The Wild Wild West Revisited, Amber Waves, Roughnecks, Rodeo Girl, The Big Black Pill, Ewoks: The Battle for Endor, Murder in Space, Thompson's Last Run, Act of Vengeance, Gore Vidal's Billy the Kid, Blood River, Tom Clancy's Op Center. *Series*: Our House, Boys of Twilight. *Guest*: The Waltons.

BRINKLEY, DAVID

TV news correspondent. b. Wilmington, NC, July 10, 1920. e. U. of North Carolina; Vanderbilt U. Started writing for hometown newspaper. Joined United Press before entering Army, WWII. After discharge in 1943, joined NBC News in Washington as White House corr. for many years with late Chet Huntley on NBC Nightly News. Then began David Brinkley's Journal. Moved to ABC to host This Week with David Brinkley.

BRISKIN, MORT

Producer, Writer. b. Oak Park, IL, 1919. e. U. of Southern California; attended Harvard and Northwestern law schools, being admitted to the bar at 20. Practiced law before entering m.p. industry in management with such stars as Mickey Rooney. Turned to production and also wrote screenplays for 16 of his 29 films. Created nine TV series and was prod. or exec. prod. of some 1,350 TV segments of which he wrote more than 300.

PICTURES: The River, The Magic Face, No Time for Flowers, The Second Woman, Quicksand, The Big Wheel, The Jackie Robinson Story, Ben, Willard, Walking Tall, Framed.

TELEVISION: Sheriff of Cochise, U.S. Marshal, The Texan, Grand Jury, The Walter Winchell File, Official Detective, Whirlybirds.

BRITTANY, MORGAN
Actress. r.n. Suzanne Cupito. b. Hollywood, CA, Dec. 5, 1951.
PICTURES: Gypsy, The Birds, Marnie, Yours Mine and Ours, Gable and Lombard, Sundown: The Vampire in Retreat, The Prodigal, Last Action Hero, The Saint.
TELEVISION: Series: Dallas, Glitter, Melrose Place. Guest: B. L. Stryker. Movies: Amazing Howard Hughes, Delta County U.S.A., The Initiation of Sarah, Samurai, Stunt Seven, Death on the Freeway, The Dream Merchants, Moviola: The Scarlett O'Hara War, The Wild Women of Chastity Gulch, LBJ: The Early Years, Perry Mason: The Case of the Scandalous Scoundrel, National Lampoon's Favorite Deadly Sins.

BROADBENT, JIM
Actor, Writer. b. England. Member of the National Theatre and the Royal Shakespeare Company. Wrote and starred in short film A Sense of History (Clermont-Ferrand Intl. Film Fest. Award).
THEATER: The Recruiting Officer, A Winter's Tale, The Government Inspector, A Flea in Her Ear, Goose Pimples.
PICTURES: The Shout (debut, 1978), The Passage, Breaking Glass, The Dogs of War, Time Bandits, Brazil, The Good Father, Superman IV: The Quest for Peace, Life Is Sweet, Enchanted April, The Crying Game, Widow's Peak, The Wedding Gift, Princess Caraboo, Bullets Over Broadway, Rough Magic, The Secret Agent, Richard III, The Borrowers, Little Voice, The Avengers.
TELEVISION: Not the Nine O'Clock News, Gone to Seed, Sense of History (also writer), Murder Most Horrid, Gone to the Dogs, Only Fools and Horses, The Victoria Wood Show, Silas Marner, Blackladder, Birth of a Nation, The Peter Principles and many notable guest appearances.

BROADHEAD, PAUL E.
Executive. e. Univ. of MS. Founder of Paul Broadhead & Assocs. real estate development. 1984, sold his interests in that company. Became chmn. of bd. of Theatre Properties, Cinemark USA.

BROADNAX, DAVID
Actor, Producer, Writer. b. Columbus, GA, Dec. 16.
PICTURES: Actor: The Landlord, Come Back Charleston Blue, Sharpies (also prod., co-s.p.), Zombie Island Massacre (also prod., story).
TELEVISION: As the World Turns, Another World, Edge of Night, Love Is a Many Splendored Thing, Search for Tomorrow, Saturday Night Live.

BROCKMAN, MICHAEL
Executive. b. Brooklyn, NY, Nov. 19, 1938. e. Ithaca Coll. Became v.p., daytime programming, ABC Entertainment, 1974; later v.p., tape prod. operations and admin. Left to become v.p., daytime programs, NBC Entertainment, 1977-1980. Became v.p. programs, Lorimar Prods. 1980-82; v.p. daytime and children's prog. CBS Entertainment, 1982-89. 1986, title changed to v.p. daytime, children's and late night. Became pres. ABC daytime, children's & late night entertainment 1989-90. Joined Mark Goodson Prods. as v.p. 1991. Became sr. v.p. in 1993. Pres., M. Brockman Broadcast Inc., 1995.

BRODERICK, MATTHEW
Actor, Producer, Director. b. New York, NY, Mar. 21, 1962. Son of late actor James Broderick and writer-dir./artist Patricia Broderick. Acted in a workshop prod. of Horton Foote's Valentine's Day with his father (1979).
THEATER: NY: Torch Song Trilogy, Brighton Beach Memoirs (Tony & Theatre World Awards, 1983), Biloxi Blues, The Widow Claire, How to Succeed in Business Without Really Trying (Tony Award, 1995).
PICTURES: Max Dugan Returns (debut, 1983), WarGames, Ladyhawke, 1918, On Valentine's Day, Ferris Bueller's Day Off, Project X, Biloxi Blues, Torch Song Trilogy, Glory, Family Business, The Freshman, Out on a Limb, The Night We Never Met, The Lion King (voice), The Road to Wellville, Mrs. Parker and the Vicious Circle, Arabian Knight (voice), Infinity (also dir., co-prod.), The Cable Guy, Infinity (also dir.), Addicted to Love, Walking to the Waterline, Lion King II: Simba Pride (voice), Godzilla, Election.
TELEVISION: Specials: Master Harold... and the Boys, Cinderella (Faerie Tale Theatre), The Year of the Generals (voice), A Simple Melody. Movie: A Life in the Theatre. Guest: Lou Grant.

BRODNEY, OSCAR
Writer. b. Boston, MA, 1906. e. Boston U., LL.B., 1927; Harvard, LL.M., 1928. Atty., MA Bar, 1928-35.
PICTURES: She Wrote the Book, If You Knew Susie, Are You With It?, For the Love of Mary, Mexican Hayride, Arctic Manhunt, Yes Sir, That's My Baby, Double Crossbones, Gal Who Took the West, South Sea Sinner, Comanche Territory, Harvey, Frenchie, Francis Goes to the Races, Little Egypt, Francis Covers the Big Town, Willie and Joe Back at the Front, Scarlet Angel, Francis Goes to West Point, Walking My Baby Back Home, Sign of the Pagan, Black Shield of Falworth, Captain Lightfoot, The Spoilers, Purple Mask, Lady Godiva, Day of Fury, Star in the Dust, Tammy and the Bachelor, When Hell Broke Loose, Bobbikins (also prod.), Tammy Tell Me True, The Right Approach, All Hands on Deck, Tammy and the Doctor, The Brass Bottle, I'd Rather Be Rich.

BRODSKY, JACK
Producer. b. Brooklyn, NY, July 3, 1932. e. George Washington H.S. Writer for N.Y. Times. Joined 20th-Fox publicity in N.Y. in 1956. Left in 1961 to head national ad-pub for Filmways. Joined Rastar Productions to work on Funny Girl; later named v.p. in charge of prod. In 1976 named v.p. in chg. film prod. prom., Rogers & Cowan; 1978, Columbia Pictures v.p. of adv., pub., promo.; 1979, named exec. v.p. of Michael Douglas' Big Stick Productions; 1983; joined 20th-Fox as exec. v.p., worldwide adv., pub., exploit. Resigned 1985 to resume career as prod..
PICTURES: Harry & Walter Go to New York (actor only), Two Minute Warning (actor only), Little Murders, Everything You Always Wanted To Know About Sex But Were Afraid to Ask (exec. prod.), Summer Wishes Winter Dreams, The Jewel of the Nile, Dancers (co-exec. prod., actor), King Ralph, Scenes From a Mall (actor), Rookie of the Year (co-exec. prod.).
AUTHOR: The Cleopatra Papers, with Nat Weiss.

BROKAW, CARY
Executive, Producer. b. Los Angeles, CA, June 21, 1951. e. Univ. of CA/Berkeley, UCLA Grad. Sch. Worked at several positions at 20th Century Fox before serving as exec. v.p. for Cineplex Odeon Corp. 1983 became co-chmn., pres. of Island Alive; 1985, became co-chmn., pres. & CEO of Island Pictures. 1987, formed Avenue Pictures; 1991, became pres. & CEO for Avenue Entertainment Group.
PICTURES: Executive Producer: Trouble in Mind, Down by Law, Nobody's Fool, Slamdance, Pascali's Island, Signs of Life, Cold Feet, Drugstore Cowboy, After Dark My Sweet, The Object of Beauty, Sex Drugs Rock & Roll, The Player, American Heart. Producer: Short Cuts, Restoration, Voices From a Locked Room, Graceland.
TELEVISION: Movies: In the Eyes of a Stranger, Amelia Earhart: The Final Flight, See Jane Run, Stranger in Town, Two Mothers for Zachary, Tell Me No Secrets, The Almost Perfect Bank Robbery, Path to Paradise. Series: The Player.

BROKAW, NORMAN R.
Executive. b. New York, NY, April 21, 1927. Joined William Morris Agency as trainee in 1943; junior agent, 1948; sr. agent, company exec. in m.p. and TV, 1951; 1974, v.p., William Morris Agency, World Wide all areas. 1981, named exec. v.p. & mem. of bd., William Morris Agency, worldwide; 1986, named co-chmn. of bd., WMA, worldwide. 1989, named pres. & CEO, William Morris Inc. worldwide. 1991, named Chmn. of Board of CEO. Member Acad. of TV Arts & Sciences, AMPAS. Member bd. of dir. of Cedars-Sinai Medical Center, Los Angeles; pres., The Betty Ford Cancer Center. Clients include former President and Mrs. Gerald R. Ford, Bill Cosby, Gen. Alexander Haig, Priscilla Presley, Andy Griffith, Dr. C. Everett Koop, Marcia Clark, Christopher Darden.

BROKAW, TOM
TV Host, Anchorman. b. Yankton, S.D., Feb. 6, 1940. e. U. of South Dakota. Newscaster, weatherman, staff announcer KTIV, Sioux City, IA, 1960-62. Joined KMTV, NBC affiliate in Omaha, in 1962; 1965, joined WSB-TV, Atlanta. Worked in L.A. bureau of NBC News, anchored local news shows for KNBC, NBC station (1966-73). In 1973 named NBC News' White House correspondent; was anchor of NBC Saturday Night News. Named host of Today show in August, 1976. In 1982 co-anchor, NBC Nightly News. Co-anchor 1993 series NBC newsmagazine, Now With Tom Brokaw & Katie Couric. Special: Conversation with Mikhail S. Gorbachev.

BROLIN, JAMES
Actor, Producer, Director. b. Los Angeles, CA, July 18, 1940. r.n. James Bruderlin. e. UCLA. Son is actor Josh Brolin. Debut in Bus Stop (TV series); named most promising actor of 1970 by Fame and Photoplay magazines. Winner, Emmy and Golden Globe Awards. Also nominated for 3 additional Emmys and 2 Golden Globes.
PICTURES: Take Her She's Mine (debut, 1963), John Goldfarb Please Come Home, Goodbye Charlie, Dear Brigitte, Von Ryan's Express, Morituri, Fantastic Voyage, Way ... Way Out, The Cape Town Affair, Our Man Flint, The Boston Strangler, Skyjacked, Westworld, Gable and Lombard, The Car, Capricorn One, The Amityville Horror, Night of the Juggler, High Risk, Pee-wee's Big Adventure, Bad Jim, Super High Score, Ted & Venus, Gas Food Lodging, Cheatin' Hearts (also exec. prod.), Back Stab, Savate, Relative Fear, Parallel Lives, Indecent Behavior, The Expert, Tracks of a Killer, Lewis and Clark and George, Blood Money, My Brother's War, Haunted Sea, Goodbye America.
TELEVISION: Series: Marcus Welby M.D. (Emmy Award, 1970), Hotel, Angel Falls, Extreme. Movies: Marcus Welby M.D. (A Matter of Humanities), Short Walk to Daylight, Class of '63, Trapped, Steel Cowboys, The Ambush Murders, Mae West, White Water Rebels, Cowboy, Beverly Hills Cowgirl Blues, Hold the Dream, Intimate Encounters, Voice of the Heart, Finish Line, Nightmare on the 13th Floor, And the Sea Will Tell, Deep Dark Secrets, The Sands of Time, Visions of Murder, Gunsmoke: The Long Ride, The Calling, Parallel Lives, A Perry Mason Mystery: The Case of the Grimacing Governor, Terminal Virus. Special: City Boy (PBS). Director: Hotel (12 episodes), The Young Riders, Hijacked: Flight 285, Pensacola Wings of Gold, Beyond Belief, Fact or Fiction.

BROMHEAD, DAVID M.
Executive. b. Teaneck, NJ, Jan. 7, 1960. e. Leighton Park Sch., Reading, England, 1973-78. Overseas sls. exec., Rank Film Dist., 1980; joined New World Pictures, 1984, dir. intl. dist.; named dir., TV dist., 1986.

BRON, ELEANOR
Actress, Writer. b. Stanmore, Middlesex, England, 1938. Started career in Establishment Club, London, and on American tour. Leading lady on British TV show Not So Much a Programme—More a Way of Life. Author of Double Take, The Pillowbook of Eleanor Bron, Life and Other Punctures. Translator of Desdemona—If You Had Only Spoken, by Christine Bruckner.
THEATER: The Doctor's Dilemma, Howards End, The Prime of Miss Jean Brodie, Hedda Gabler, The Duchess of Malfi, The Madwoman of Chaillot, Uncle Vanya, A Delicate Balance, A Perfect Ganesh, Dona Rosita, The Cherry Orchard, A Month In the Country.
PICTURES: Help!, Alfie, Two for the Road, Bedazzled, The Turtle Diary, Thank You All Very Much, Women in Love, The Millstone, Little Dorrit, Black Beauty, A Little Princess, Saint-Ex, Deadly Advice.
TELEVISION: Movies: The Day Christ Died, The Attic: The Hiding of Anne Frank, Intrigue, Changing Step, The Blue Boy. Series: Where Was Spring? (also co-wrote), After That This. Guest: Rumpole of the Bailey, Yes Minister, Absolutely Fabulous.

BRONDFIELD, JEROME
Writer. b. Cleveland, OH, Dec. 9, 1913. e. Ohio State U., 1936. Reporter, ed. on Columbus Dispatch, Associated Press, story ed., script head, RKO Pathe, Oct., 1944; writer, dir. & supvr. of many doc. shorts incl. This Is America series; TV writer; short story writer; collab. s.p., Below the Sahara; s.p. Louisiana Territory; doc. film writer. Author: Woody Hayes, The 100-Yard War, Knute Rockne, The Man and the Legend. Sr. editor, Scholastic, Inc.

BRONFMAN, EDGAR, JR.
Executive. Joined Seagram 1982 as asst. to officeof the pres.; served as mng. dir. of Seagram Europe until he was appointed pres. of The House of Seagram, 1984-88; became pres. & COO in 1989. June 1994 named pres. & CEO of The Seagram Company Ltd. Upon acquisition of MCA Inc. was named acting chairman, 1995.

BRONSON, CHARLES
Actor. r.n. Charles Buchinsky. b. Ehrenfeld, PA, Nov. 3, 1921. Worked as a coal miner. Served in Air Force (1943-46) as tail gunner on B29s in Pacific. Studied acting at Pasadena Playhouse. Started in films billed under real name. Guest in numerous TV shows in addition to those below.
PICTURES: You're in the Navy Now (debut, 1951), The People Against O'Hara, The Mob, Red Skies of Montana, My Six Convicts, The Marrying Kind, Pat and Mike, Diplomatic Courier, Bloodhounds of Broadway, House of Wax, The Clown, Miss Sadie Thompson, Crime Wave, Tennessee Champ, Riding Shotgun, Apache, Drum Beat (lst billing as Charles Bronson), Vera Cruz, Big House U.S.A., Target Zero, Jubal, Run of the Arrow, Machine Gun Kelly, Gang War, Showdown at Boot Hill, When Hell Broke Loose, Ten North Frederick, Never So Few, The Magnificent Seven, Master of the World, A Thunder of Drums, X-15, Kid Galahad, The Great Escape, Four for Texas, The Sandpiper, The Battle of the Bulge, This Property Is Condemned, The Dirty Dozen, Villa Rides, Guns for San Sebastian, Farewell Friend, Once Upon a Time in the West, Rider on the Rain, You Can't Win Em All, The Family, Cold Sweat, Twinky (Lola), Someone Behind the Door, Red Sun, Chato's Land, The Mechanic, The Valachi Papers, The Stone Killer, Chino, Mr. Majestyk, Death Wish, Breakout, Hard Times, Breakheart Pass, From Noon Till Three, St. Ives, The White Buffalo, Telefon, Love and Bullets, Caboblanco, Borderline, Death Hunt, Death Wish II, Ten to Midnight, The Evil That Men Do, Death Wish 3, Murphy's Law, Assassination, Death Wish 4: The Crackdown, Messenger of Death, Kinjite: Forbidden Subjects, The Indian Runner, Death Wish V: The Face of Death, Family of Cops II & III.
TELEVISION: Series: Man With a Camera, Empire, Travels of Jamie McPheeters. Guest: Philco Playhouse (Adventure in Java), Medic, A Bell for Adano, Gunsmoke, Have Gun Will Travel, Meet McGraw, The FBI, The Fugitive, The Virginian. Movies: Raid on Entebbe, Act of Vengeance, Yes Virginia There Is a Santa Claus, The Sea Wolf, Donato and Daughter, A Family of Cops.

BROOK, PETER
Director. b. London, England, March 21, 1925. e. Magdalen Coll., Oxford. To London 1943 to dir. his first play, Doctor Faustus; other stage incl. Man and Superman, Marat/Sade, A Midsummer Night's Dream, etc.
PICTURES: The Beggar's Opera (debut, 1953), Moderato Cantabile (also co-s.p.), Lord of the Flies (also s.p., edit), The Persecution and Assassination of Jean-Paul Marat as Performed by the Inmates of the Asylum of Charenton Under the Direction of the Marquis de Sade, Tell Me Lies (also prod.), King Lear (also s.p.), Meetings With Remarkable Men (also s.p.), The Tragedy of Carmen, Swann in Love (s.p. only), The Mahabharata.

BROOKS, ALBERT
Director, Writer, Actor. r.n. Albert Einstein. b. Los Angeles, CA, July 22, 1947. e. Carnegie Tech. Son of late comedian Harry Einstein (Parkyakarkus). Brother is performer Bob Einstein. Sports writer KMPC, L.A. 1962-63. Recordings: Comedy Minus One, A Star is Bought (Grammy nom.).
PICTURES: Actor: Taxi Driver, Real Life (also dir., co-s.p.), Private Benjamin, Modern Romance (also dir., co-s.p.), Twilight Zone—The Movie, Terms of Endearment (voice), Unfaithfully Yours, Lost in America (also dir., co-s.p.), Broadcast News (Acad. Award nom.), Defending Your Life (also dir., s.p.), I'll Do Anything, The Scout (also co-s.p.), Mother (also dir.; NY Society of Film Critics Award, Natl Society of Film Critics Award for best s.p., 1997), Doctor Dolittle, Out of Sight.
TELEVISION: Series: Dean Martin Presents the Golddiggers, Saturday Night Live (prod., dir. short films 1975-76), Hot Wheels (voices), The Associates (wrote theme song). Specials: Milton Berle's Mad Mad Mad World of Comedy, General Electric's All-Star Anniversary. Guest: Love American Style, The Odd Couple, Ed Sullivan Show, Tonight Show, The Simpsons, others.

BROOKS, JAMES L.
Director, Producer, Writer. b. North Bergen, NJ, May 9, 1940. e. NYU. Copyboy for CBS News, N.Y.; promoted to newswriter. 1965 moved to L.A. to work for David Wolper's documentary prod. co. In 1969 conceived idea for series, Room 222; formed partnership with fellow writer Allan Burns. Together they created Mary Tyler Moore Show in 1970. 1977, established prod. co. on Paramount lot with other writers, producing and creating the series, The Associates and Taxi. Formed Gracie Films. Directed play Brooklyn Laundry, in L.A.
PICTURES: Real Life (actor), Starting Over (s.p., co-prod.), Modern Romance (actor), Terms of Endearment (dir., prod., s.p.; Acad. Awards for Best Picture, Dir. and Screenplay, 1983), Broadcast News (dir., prod., s.p.), Big (co-prod.), Say Anything (exec. prod.), The War of the Roses (co-prod.), I'll Do Anything (dir., prod., s.p.), Jerry Macguire.
TELEVISION: Movie: Thursday's Game (writer, prod., 1971). Series: The Mary Tyler Moore Show (co-creator, writer, exec. prod.; 2 Emmy Awards for writing: 1971, 1977; 3 Emmy Awards as exec. prod.: 1975, 1976, 1977), Rhoda (writer, prod.), The New Lorenzo Music Show (writer), Lou Grant (co-exec. prod.). Series (co-creator, and/or exec. prod.): Taxi (3 Emmy Awards as exec. prod.: 1979, 1980, 1981), Cindy, The Associates, Cheers, Tracey Ullman Show (Emmy Award as exec. prod., 1989), The Simpsons (2 Emmy Awards as exec. prod.: 1990, 1991), Sibs, Phenom, The Critics.

BROOKS, JOSEPH
Producer, Director, Writer, Composer, Conductor. Well-known for composing music for TV commercials before turning to producing, directing, writing and scoring theatrical feature, You Light Up My Life, in 1977. Winner of 21 Clio Awards (advertising industry), Grammy, Golden Globe, People's Choice, Amer. Music Awards; created music for 100 commercials. Has also composed for theatrical films. Winner of Cannes Film Festival Advertising Award.
PICTURES: Scores: The Garden of the Finzi-Continis, Marjoe, Jeremy, The Lords of Flatbush. Prod.-Dir.-Writer-Composer: You Light Up My Life (Academy Award for Best Song: title song, 1977), If Ever I See You Again (also actor).

BROOKS, MEL
Writer, Director, Actor. b. Brooklyn, NY, June 28, 1926. r.n. Melvin Kaminsky. m. actress Anne Bancroft. e. VA Military Inst. 1944. U.S. Army combat engineer 1944-46. As child, did impressions and was amateur drummer and pianist. First appearance as actor in play Separate Rooms in Red Bank, NJ. Was also social dir. of Grossinger's Resort in the Catskills. Became writer for Sid Caesar on TV's Broadway Review and Your Show of Shows. Teamed with Carl Reiner for comedy record albums: The 2000 Year Old Man, The 2000 and 13 Year Old Man. Founded Brooksfilms Ltd., 1981. Won Academy Award for Best Short Subject (animated): The Critic (dir., s.p., narrator). Co-writer of Shinbone Alley.
THEATER: Writer: New Faces of 1952 (sketches), Shinbone Alley (book), All-American (book).
PICTURES: New Faces (co-s.p.), The Producers (dir., s.p.; Academy Award for Best Original Screenplay, 1968), The Twelve Chairs (dir., s.p., actor), Blazing Saddles (dir., co-s.p., actor), Young Frankenstein (dir., co-s.p.; Acad. Award nom. for s.p.), Silent Movie (dir., co-s.p., actor), Frances (exec.-prod), High Anxiety (dir., prod., co-s.p., actor), The Muppet Movie (actor), History of the World Part 1 (dir., prod., s.p., actor, lyrics), To Be or Not To Be (exec-prod., actor), Spaceballs (dir., prod., co-s.p., actor), My Favorite YEar (exec.-prod.), Look Who's Talking Too (voice), Life Stinks (dir., prod., co-s.p., actor), Robin Hood: Men in Tights (dir., prod., co-s.p., actor), The Silence of the Hams (actor), The Little Rascals (actor), They Fly II (exec.-prod.), Dracula: Dead and Loving It (dir., prod., co-s.p., actor). Exec. Prod.: The Elephant Man, The Doctor and the Devils, The Fly, 84 Charing Cross Road, Solarbabies, The Vagrant.
TELEVISION: Special: The Sid bCaesar-Imogene Coca-Carl Reiner-Howard Morris Special (co-writer; Emmy Award, 1967). Series: Get Smart (co-creator, co-writer), When Things Were Rotten (co-creator, co- writer, prod.), The Nutt House (prod., co-writer). Guest: Mad About You (Emmy Award, 1997).

BROSNAN, PIERCE
Actor. b. Navan, County Meath, Ireland, May 16, 1953. Left County Meath, Ireland for London at 11. Worked as commercial illustrator, then joined experimental theater workshop and studied at the Drama Center. On London stage (Wait Until Dark, The Red Devil Battery Sign, Filumenia, etc.)
PICTURES: The Mirror Crack'd (debut, 1980), The Long Good Friday, Nomads, The Fourth Protocol, Taffin, The Deceivers, Mister Johnson, The Lawnmower Man, Entangled, Mrs. Doubtfire, Love Affair, Goldeneye, Mars Attacks, The Mirror Has Two Faces, Dante's Peak.
TELEVISION: Series: Remington Steele, Frame-Up (NBC Friday Night Mystery). Movies/Specials: Murphy's Stroke, The Manions of America, Nancy Astor, Noble House, Around the World in 80 Days, The Heist, Murder 101, Victim of Love, Live Wire, Death Train (Detonator), The Broken Chain, Don't Talk to Strangers, Alistair MacLean's Night Watch.

BROUGH, WALTER
Producer, Writer. b. Phila. PA, Dec. 19, 1935. e. La Salle U. (B.A.), USC (M.A.). Began career with Stage Society Theatre, LA. Currently CEO, Orb Enterprises, Inc.
PICTURES: Gabriella, A New Life, No Place to Hide, Run Wild Run Free, The Desperadoes, Funeral for an Assassin (also prod.), On a Dead Man's Chest (also prod.), Jed and Sonny (also prod.).
TELEVISION: Doctor Kildare, The Fugitive, Branded, Name of the Game, Mannix, Mission Impossible, The Magician, Man From Atlantis, Police Story, Wildside, Heart of the City (also prod.), Thunder Guys (pilot), Spencer for Hire (also co-prod.), Law & Harry McGraw, New Mission Impossible (also co-prod.), Over My Dead Body, Hunter, Tequila & Bonetti, Sirens.

BROUGHTON, BRUCE
Composer. b. Los Angeles, CA , March 8, 1945. e. U. of Southern California, B.M., 1967. Music supvr., CBS-TV, 1967-77. Since then has been freelance composer for TV and films. Member of Academy of TV Arts & Sciences Society of Composers & Lyricists (past pres.), AMPAS (governor). Nominated 17 times for Emmy. Nominated for Grammy for Young Sherlock Holmes.
PICTURES: The Prodigal, The Ice Pirates, Silverado (Acad. Award nom.), Young Sherlock Holmes, Sweet Liberty, The Boy Who Could Fly, Square Dance, Harry and the Hendersons, Monster Squad, Big Shots, Cross My Heart, The Rescue, The Presidio, Last Rites, Moonwalker, Jacknife, Betsy's Wedding, Narrow Margin, The Rescuers Down Under, All I Want for Christmas, Honey I Blew Up the Kid, Stay Tuned, Homeward Bound: The Incredible Journey, So I Married an Axe Murderer, For Love or Money, Tombstone, Holy Matrimony, Baby's Day Out, Miracle on 34th Street, Infinity, Carried Away, House Arrest, Homeward Bound II: Lost in San Francisco, The Shadow Conspiracy, A Simple Wish, One Tough Cop, Krippendorf's Tribe, Lost in Space.
TELEVISION: Series: Hawaii Five-0, Gunsmoke, Quincy, How the West Was Won, Logan's Run, The Oregon Trail, Buck Rogers (Emmy Award), Dallas (Emmy Award), Dinosaurs (theme), Capitol Critters (theme), Tiny Toon Adventures (Emmy Award). Movies: The Paradise Connection, Desperate Voyage, The Return of Frank Cannon, Desperate Lives, Killjoy, One Shoe Makes It Murder, The Master of Ballantrae, MADD, The Candy Lightner Story, Cowboy, A Thanksgiving Promise, The Old Man and the Sea, O Pioneers! (Emmy Award). Mini-Series: The Blue and the Gray, The First Olympics—Athens: 1896 (Emmy Award), George Washington II, True Women.

BROUMAS, JOHN G.
Executive. b. Youngstown, OH, Oct. 12, 1917. e. Youngstown. Usher, Altoona Publix Theatres, 1933, usher to asst. mgr., Warner Thea. 1934-39; mgr. Grand 1939-40; mgr. Orpheum 1940-41. WWII active, Officer Chemical Corps, commanding officer 453rd Chem. Battalion (Reserve); Life member Reserve Officers Assoc.; Gen. mgr. Pitts & Roth Theatres 1946-54; pres., Broumas Theatres; v.p. NATO, 1969; bd. of dir. of NATO of VA, MD, D.C.; pres., Broumas Theatre Service 1954-82; bd. chmn., Showcase Theatres 1965-82; past pres. & bd. chmn. Maryland Theatre Owners; v.p. & bd. of dir., Virginia Theatre Owners; bd. of dir. NATO of D.C.; pres. B.C. Theatres; Past dir. and mem. Motion Picture Pioneers; Advisory Council: Will Rogers Memorial Hospital; Washington, D.C. Variety Club, Tent No. 11, bd. of gov. 1959, 1st asst. chief. barker, 1964 & 71, chief barker 1965-66, 1972, and 1978-79, and bd. chmn., 1980; lecturer, Georgetown Univ., 1972-; Life Patron, Variety Clubs Int'l, 1978 Life Liner, Variety Clubs Intl.; member: Screen Actors Guild. 1994.

BROWN, BLAIR
Actress. b. Washington, DC, 1948. e. National Theatre Sch. of Canada.
THEATER: NY: The Threepenny Opera (NY Shakespeare Fest), Comedy of Errors, The Secret Rapture, Arcadia. Acted with Old Globe, San Diego; Stratford, Ont. Shakespeare Fest.; Guthrie Theatre MN; Arena Stage, Wash.; Long Wharf, New Haven; Shaw Festival.

PICTURES: The Paper Chase, The Choirboys, One-Trick Pony, Altered States, Continental Divide, A Flash of Green, Stealing Home, Strapless, Passed Away, Good Policeman.
TELEVISION: Series: The Days and Nights of Molly Dodd, Talk It Over (discussion). Mini-series: Captains and the Kings, James Michener's Space, Arthur Hailey's Wheels, Kennedy. Movies: The 3,000 Mile Chase, The Quinns, And I Alone Survived, The Child Stealer, The Bad Seed, Hands of a Stranger, Eleanor and Franklin: The White House Years, Extreme Close-Up, Those Secrets, Majority Rule, Rio Shannon (pilot), The Day My Parents Ran Away, Moment of Truth: To Walk Again, The Gift of Love. Specials: School for Scandal, The Skin of Your Teeth, Lethal Innocence, Oregon Trail, The Quinns, Space.

BROWN, BRYAN
Actor. b. Sydney, Australia, June 23, 1947. m. actress Rachel Ward. Began acting professionally in Sydney. Worked in repertory theatres in England with the National Theatre of Great Britain. Returned to Australia to work in films while continuing stage work with Theatre Australia.
PICTURES: Love Letters From Teralba Road (debut, 1977), The Irishman, Weekend of Shadows, Newsfront, Third Person Plural, Money Movers, Palm Beach, Cathy's Child, The Odd Angry Shot, Breaker Morant, Blood Money, Stir, Winter of Our Dreams, Far East, Give My Regards to Broad Street, Parker (Bones), The Empty Beach, F/X, Tai-Pan, Rebel, The Good Wife, Cocktail, Gorillas in the Mist, Shall We Dance, FX2 (also co-exec. prod.), Sweet Talker (also co-wrote story), Prisoners of the Sun, Blame It on the Bellboy, The Chart of Jimmy Balcksmith, Age of Treason, Dead Heart, On the Border.
TELEVISION: Mini-Series: Against the Wind, A Town Like Alice, The Thorn Birds. Movies: The Shiralee (Aust.), Dead in the Water, Devlin, The Last Hit, Eureka Stockade, Full Body Massage, Twisted Tales, 20,000 Leagues Under the Sea, Dogboys.

BROWN, CLANCY
Actor. b. Ohio. e. Northwestern Univ.
PICTURES: Bad Boys (debut, 1983), The Adventures of Buckaroo Banzai, The Bride, Highlander, Extreme Prejudice, Shoot to Kill, Season of Fear, Blue Steel, Waiting for the Light, Ambition, Past Midnight, Pet Sematary II, Thunder Alley, The Shawshank Redemption, Dead Man Walking, Donor Unknown, Female Perversions, Starship Troopers, Flubber.
TELEVISION: Series: Earth 2, ER. Movies: Johnny Ryan, Love Lies & Murder, Cast a Deadly Spell, Desperate Rescue: The Cathy Mahone Story, Bloodlines, Last Light, The Patron Saint of Liars.

BROWN, DAVID
Executive, Producer. b. New York, NY, July 28, 1916. m. writer-editor Helen Gurley Brown. e. Stanford U., A.B., 1936; Columbia U. Sch. of Journalism, M.S., 1937. Apprentice reporter, copy-editing, San Francisco News & Wall Street Journal, 1936; night ed. asst. drama critic, Fairchild Publications, N.Y., 1937-39; edit. dir. Milk Research Council, N.Y., 1939-40; assoc. ed., Street & Smith Publ., N.Y., 1940-43; assoc. ed., exec. ed., then ed.-in-chief, Liberty Mag., N.Y., 1943-49; edit. dir., nat'l education campaign, Amer. Medical Assn., 1949; assoc. ed., mng. ed., Cosmopolitan Mag., N.Y., 1949-52; contrib. stories & articles to many nat'l mags.; man. ed., story dept., 20th-Fox, L.A., Jan., 1952; story ed. & head of scenario dept., 1953-56; appt'd. member of exec. staff of Darryl F. Zanuck, 1956; mem. of exec. staff, 20th-Fox studios, and exec. studio story editor, 1956-60; Prod. 20th-Fox Studios, Sept. 1960-62; Editorial v.p. New American Library of World Literature, Inc., 1963-64; exec. story opers., 20th Century-Fox, 1964-67; vp. of story operations, 1967; exec. v.p., creative optns. and mem. bd. of dir., 1969-71. Exec. v.p., mem. bd. of directors Warner Bros., 1971-72; partner and dir., The Zanuck/Brown Co., 1972-88. Pres., Manhattan Project Ltd., 1988-; mem., bd. of trustees, American Film Institute, 1972-80. Recipient with Richard D. Zanuck of the Mo. Pic. Acad. of Arts & Sciences' Irving G. Thalberg Memorial Award. Books: Brown's Guide to Growing Gray, Delacorte, Let Me Entertain You, Morrow, The Rest of Your Life is the Best of Your Life, Barricade.
PICTURES: Ssssssss, The Sting (Academy Award for Best Picture, 1973), The Sugarland Express, The Black Windmill, Willie Dynamite, The Girl from Petrovka, The Eiger Sanction, Jaws, MacArthur, Jaws 2, The Island, Neighbors, The Verdict, Cocoon, Target, Cocoon: The Return, Driving Miss Daisy (exec. prod.), The Player, A Few Good Men, The Cemetery Club, Watch It, Canadian Bacon, The Saint, Kiss the Girls, Kiss the Girls, The Saint, Deep Impact, Angela's Ashes.

BROWN, GEORG STANFORD
Actor, Director. b. Havana, Cuba, June 24, 1943. Acted on stage with the New York Shakespeare Fest. in the 1960s. Gained fame as one of the rookie cops in the 1970s TV series, The Rookies, before turning to TV directing.
THEATER: All's Well That Ends Well, Measure for Measure, Macbeth, Murderous Angels, Hamlet, Detective Story.
PICTURES: The Comedians, Dayton's Devils, Bullitt, Colossus: The Forbin Project, The Man, Black Jack (Wild in the Sky), Stir Crazy, House Party 2.

TELEVISION: *Series*: The Rookies. *Movies*: The Young Lawyers, Ritual of Evil, The Rookies (pilot), Dawn: Portrait of a Teenage Runaway, The Night the City Screamed, The Kid With the Broken Halo, In Defense of Kids, The Jesse Owens Story, Murder Without Motive. *Dir. of movies*: Grambling's White Tiger, Kids Like These, Alone in the Neon Jungle, Stuck With Each Other, Father & Son: Dangerous Relations. *Dir. of episodes*: Charlie's Angels, Starsky and Hutch, Dynasty, Hill Street Blues, Great American Hero, Cagney & Lacey (Emmy Award, 1986).

BROWN, HIMAN
M.P. Producer, Director, b. New York, NY, July 21, 1910. e. City Coll. of New York, St. Lawrence U. Radio & TV package prod. since 1927 include: Inner Sanctum, Thin Man, Bulldog Drummond, Dick Tracy, Terry and the Pirates, Joyce Jordan MD, Grand Central Station, CBS Radio Mystery Theatre, pres. Production Center, Inc.
PICTURES: The Thin Man, Nero Wolfe, Bulldog, Drummond, That Night, Violators, The Stars Salute, The Price of Silence, The Road Ahead.

BROWN, JIM
Actor. b. St. Simons Island, GA, Feb. 17, 1936. e. Manhasset H.S., Syracuse U. For nine years played football with Cleveland Browns; in 1964 won Hickock Belt as Professional Athlete of the year. Founder, Black Economic Union.
PICTURES: Rio Conchos (debut, 1964), The Dirty Dozen, Ice Station Zebra, The Split, Riot, Dark Of The Sun, 100 Rifles, Kenner, El Condor, The Phynx, ... tick ... tick ... tick ..., The Grasshopper, Slaughter, Black Gunn, I Escaped from Devil's Island, The Slams, Slaughter's Big Rip-Off, Three the Hard Way, Take a Hard Ride, Adios Amigo, Mean Johnny Barrows, Kid Vengeance, Fingers, One Down Two to Go (also exec. prod.), Richard Pryor: Here and Now (exec. prod. only), Pacific Inferno (also exec. prod.), Abducted, The Running Man, I'm Gonna Git You Sucka, L.A. Heat, Crack House, Twisted Justice, The Divine Enforcer, Original Gangstas, Mars Attacks.
TELEVISION: *Movie*: Lady Blue.

BROWNE, ROSCOE LEE
Actor, Director, Writer. b. Woodbury, NJ, May 2, 1925. e. Lincoln U., PA; postgraduate studies in comparative literature and French at Middlebury Coll., VT, Columbia U., N.Y. Taught French and lit. at Lincoln U. until 1952. National sales rep. for Schenley Import Corp. 1946-56; United States' intl. track star and a member of ten A.A.U. teams. Twice American champion in the 1000-yard indoor competition, twice all-American and, in 1951 in Paris, ran the fastest 800 meters in the world for that year. Professional acting debut, 1956, in Julius Caesar at the NY Shakespeare Fest.; published poet and short story writer. Trustee: Millay Colony Arts, NY; Los Angeles Free Public Theatre.
THEATER: *NY*: The Ballad of the Sad Cafe, The Cool World, General Seeger, Tiger Tiger Burning Bright!, The Old Glory, A Hand Is on the Gate (dir., actor), My One and Only. Off-Broadway: The Connection, The Blacks, Aria da Capo, Benito Cereno (Obie Award), Joe Turner's Come and Gone (L.A., S.F., Pittsburgh), Two Trains Running.
PICTURES: The Connection (debut, 1961), Black Like Me, The Comedians, Uptight, Topaz, The Liberation of L. B. Jones, Cisco Pike, The Cowboys, The World's Greatest Athlete, Superfly T.N.T., The Ra Expeditions (narrator), Uptown Saturday Night, Logan's Run, Twilight's Last Gleaming, Nothing Personal, Legal Eagles, Jumpin' Jack Flash, Oliver & Company (voice), Moon 44, The Mambo Kings, Naked in New York, Brother Minister: The Assassination of Malcolm X (narrator), Babe (voice), The Pompatus of Love, Last Summer in the Hamptons, Dear God.
TELEVISION: *Series*: McCoy, Miss Winslow and Son, Soap, Falcon Crest. *Movies*: The Big Ripoff, Dr. Scorpion, Lady in a Corner, Columbo: Rest in Peace Mrs. Columbo, Meeting of Minds (Peabody Award), A Connecticut Yankee in King Arthur's Court (Peabody Award). *Guest*: All in the Family, Maude, Barney Miller, Soap, Head of the Class, The Cosby Show (Emmy Award, 1986), Falcon Crest. *Mini-Series*: King, Space.

BROWNING, KIRK
TV Director. b. New York, NY, March 28, 1921. e. Brooks School, Andover, MA, Avon Old Farms, Avon, CT., and Cornell U. 1940. Reporter for News-Tribune in Waco, TX; with American Field Service, 1942-45; adv. copywriter for Franklin Spier, 1945-48; became floor mgr. NBC-TV 1949; app't asst. dir. NBC-TV Opera Theatre in 1951 directing NBC Opera Theatre, TV Recital Hall, and Toscanini Simulcasts.
TELEVISION: Trial of Mary Lincoln, Jascha Heifetz Special, Harry and Lena, NBC Opera Theatre, Producers Showcase, Evening with Toscanini, Bell Telephone, The Flood, Beauty and the Beast, Lizzie Borden, World of Carl Sandburg, La Gioconda (Emmy Award, 1980), Big Blonde, Working, Ian McKellan Acting Shakespeare, Fifth of July, Alice in Wonderland, Live From the Met—Centennial.

BROWNLOW, KEVIN
Film Historian, Writer, Director, Film Editor. b. Crowborough, England, June 2, 1938. e. University College Sch. Asst. ed./editor, World Wide Pictures, London, 1955-61; film editor, Samaritan Films, 1961-65; film editor, Woodfall Films, 1965-68. Dir., Thames Television 1975-90. Dir., Photoplay Productions 1990-present.
PICTURES: It Happened Here (dir. with Andrew Mollo) 1964, Charge of the Light Brigade (editor), Winstanley (with Andrew Mollo), Napoleon (restoration of 1927 film, re-released 1980).
TELEVISION: Charm of Dynamite (dir., ed.), All with David Gill: Hollywood (dir., writer), Unknown Chaplin (dir., prod.; Emmy Award), Buster Keaton: A Hard Act to Follow (prod.; 2 Emmy Awards), Harold Lloyd—The Third Genius, D.W. Griffith: Father of Film, Cinema Europe—The Other Hollywood.
AUTHOR: How It Happened Here (1968), The Parade's Gone By... (1968), Adventures with D.W. Griffith (editor, 1973), The War the West and the Wilderness (1979), Hollywood: The Pioneers (1980), Napoleon: Abel Gance's Classic Film (1983), Behind the Mask of Innocence (1990), David Lean—A Biography (1996).

BRUBAKER, JAMES D.
Producer. b. Hollywood, CA, March 30, 1937. e. Eagle Rock H.S. Transportation coordinator for 15 years before becoming unit prod. mgr., 1978-84. Then assoc. prod., exec. prod. & prod. Prod. tv movie, Runnng Mates.
PICTURES: *Assoc. Prod.*: True Confessions, Rocky III, Rhinestone. Unit Prod. Mgr.: New York New York, Comes a Horseman, Uncle Joe Shannon, Rocky II, Raging Bull, True Confessions (also assoc. prod.), Rocky III (also assoc. prod.), Staying Alive, Rhinestone (also assoc. prod.), K-9, Problem Child, Mr. Baseball. *Exec. Prod.*: The Right Stuff, Beer, Rocky IV, Cobra, Over the Top, Problem Child (also prod. mgr.), Brain Donors (also prod. mgr.), A Walk in the Clouds, Liar Liar.

BRUCE, BRENDA
Actress. b. Manchester, England, 1918. e. privately. London stage debut: 1066 and All That.
THEATER: Gently Does It (1953), This Year Next Year, Happy Days, Woman in a Dressing Gown, Victor Eh!, Merry Wives of Windsor, The Revenger's Tragedy, Little Murders, Winter's Tale, Pericles, Twelfth Night, Hamlet.
PICTURES: Millions Like Us (debut, 1944), Night Boat to Dublin, I See a Dark Stranger (The Adventuress), They Came to a City, Carnival, Piccadilly Incident, While the Sun Shines, When the Bough Breaks, My Brother's Keeper, Don't Ever Leave Me, The Final Test, Law and Disorder, Behind the Mask, Peeping Tom, Nightmare, The Uncle, That'll Be the Day.
TELEVISION: Mary Britton series, Nearer to Heaven, Wrong Side of the Park, The Lodger, The Monkey and the Mohawk, Love Story, A Piece of Resistance, Give the Clown His Supper, Knock on Any Door, The Browning Version, Death of a Teddy Bear, Softly, Softly, The Girl, Happy, Family at War, Budgie.

BRUCKHEIMER, BONNIE
Producer. b. Brooklyn, NY. Started in advertising and public relations eventually working for treasurer of Columbia Pictures. Later worked as asst. to Arthur Penn and Ross Hunter. Became partner with Bette Midler in All Girl Productions, 1985.
PICTURES: Big Business (assoc. prod.), Beaches, Stella, For the Boys, Hocus Pocus, Man of the House, That Old Feeling.
TELEVISION: *Movie*: Gypsy (exec. prod.).

BRUCKHEIMER, JERRY
Producer. b. Detroit, MI. e. U. of Arizona. Was art dir./prod. of TV commercials before becoming prod. of films. 1983, formed Don Simpson/Jerry Bruckheimer Prods. with the late Don Simpson and entered into deal with Paramount Pictures to produce; company moved over to Walt Disney in early 1990's. Formed Jerry Bruckheimer Films in 1997.
PICTURES: *Assoc. Prod.*: The Culpepper Cattle Company, Rafferty and the Gold Dust Twins. *Producer*: Farewell My Lovely, March or Die, Defiance, American Gigolo, Thief, Cat People (exec. prod.), Young Doctors in Love, Flashdance, Thief of Hearts, Beverly Hills Cop, Top Gun, Beverly Hills Cop II, Days of Thunder, The Ref, Bad Boys, Crimson Tide, Dangerous Minds, The Rock, Con Air (prod.).
TELEVISION: *Exec Prod*: Dangerous Minds (series).

BRYAN, DORA
Actress. b. Southport, Lancashire, England, Feb. 7, 1924. e. Council Sch. Stage debut 1935.
PICTURES: Once Upon a Dream, (debut, 1947), The Fallen Idol, No Room at the Inn, Blue Lamp, Cure for Love, Now Barabas, The Ringer, Women of Twilight, The Quiet Woman, The Intruder, You Know What Sailors Are, Mad About Men, See How They Run, Cockleshell Heroes, Child in the House, Green Man, Carry on Sergeant, Operation Bullshine, Desert Mice, The Night We Got the Bird, A Taste of Honey, Two a Penny, Apartment Zero, Up to Front.
TELEVISION: Virtual Murder, Casualty, Presenting Frank Subbs, Heartbeat, Both Ends Meet, Mothers Ruin.

BUCHHOLZ, HORST
Actor. b. Berlin, Germany, Dec. 4, 1933. e. high school. In radio and stage plays. Started in films dubbing foreign movies. Work with Berlin's Schiller Theatre result in film debut in French film.
PICTURES: Marianne (debut, 1955), Emil and the Detectives, Himmel Ohne Sterne (Sky Without Stars), Regine, Teenage Wolfpack, The King in Shadow, The Confessions of Felix Krull, The Legend of Robinson Crusoe, Mompti, Endstation Liebe, Nasser Asphalt, Resurrection, Das Totenschiff, Tiger Bay (English-language debut, 1959), The Magnificent Seven, Fanny, One Two Three, Nine Hours to Rama, The Empty Canvas, Andorra, Marco the Magnificent, That Man in Istanbul, Johnny Banco, Cervantes (The Young Rebel), L'Astragale, How When and With Whom, La Sauveur, La Columba non deve Volare, The Great Waltz, The Catamount Killing, Women in Hospital, The Amazing Captain Nemo, From Hell to Victory, Avalanche Express, Aphrodite, Sahara, Fear of Falling, Code Name: Emerald, And the Violins Stopped Playing, Escape From Paradise, Aces: Iron Eagle III, Far Away So Close.
TELEVISION: *Movies*: The Savage Bees, Raid on Entebbe, Return to Fantasy Island, Berlin Tunnel 21, Family Affairs, The Lion of Granada, Come Back to Kampen. *Mini-Series*: The French Atlantic Affair.

BUCKLEY, BETTY
Actress. b. Fort Worth, TX, July 3, 1947. e. Texas Christian U., BA. Studied acting with Stella Adler. NY Stage debut: 1776 (1969); London debut: Promises Promises. Appeared in interactive short film Race for Your Life.
THEATER: Johnny Pott, What's a Nice Country Like You Doing in a State Like This?, Pippin, I'm Getting My Act Together and Taking It on the Road, Cats (Tony Award, 1983), Juno's Swans, The Mystery of Edwin Drood, Song and Dance, Carrie, The Fourth Wall, The Perfectionist, Sunset Boulevard (London/B'way; Olivier Award nom.).
PICTURES: Carrie (debut, 1976), Tender Mercies, Wild Thing, Frantic, Another Woman, Rain Without Thunder, Wyatt Earp.
TELEVISION: *Series*: Eight is Enough. *Movies*: The Ordeal of Bill Carney, Roses Are for the Rich, The Three Wishes of Billy Grier, Babycakes, Bonnie & Clyde: The True Story (Emmy nom.), Betrayal of Trust. *Specials*: Bobby and Sarah, Salute to Lady Liberty, Taking a Stand (Afterschool Special; Emmy nom.), Stephen Sondheim Carnegie Hall Gala. *Mini-Series*: Evergreen. *Guest*: L.A. Law, Tribeca.

BUCKLEY, DONALD
Executive. b. New York, NY, June 28, 1955. e. C.W. Post Coll, NY, Sch. of Visual Arts. Ad. mgr., United Artists Theatres, 1975-78. Acct. exec., Grey Advertising, 1978-80. Joined Warner Bros. in 1980 as NY adv. mgr.; 1986; promoted to east. dir. of adv./promo. for WB; 1988, named eastern dir. of adv. and publicity; 1991, promoted to v.p., East Coast Adv. & Publicity; 1996, promoted to v.p., Adv. & Publicity, v.p., WB On-Line; 1997, promoted to senior v.p., Theatrical Marketing & New Media.

BUFF, CONRAD
Editor.
PICTURES: The Empires Strikes Back, Raiders of the Lost Ark, Poltergeist, E.T. the Extra-Terrestrial, Return of the Jedi, Jagged Edge, Solarbabies, Spaceballs, Short Circuit 2, The Abyss, Side Out, Terminator 2: Judgment Day, Jennifer Eight, The Getaway, True Lies, Species, Titanic (Acad. Award, 1997), Dante's Peak, Switchback, Arlington Road.

BUJOLD, GENEVIEVE
Actress. b. Montreal, Canada, July 1, 1942. e. Montreal Conservatory of Drama. Worked in a Montreal cinema as an usher; American TV debut: St. Joan.
THEATER: The Barber of Seville, A Midsummer Night's Dream, A House...A Day.
PICTURES: La Guerre est Finie, La Fleur de L'Age, Entre La Mer et L'eau Douce, King of Hearts, The Thief of Paris, Isabel, Anne of the Thousand Days, Act of the Heart, The Trojan Women, The Journey, Kamouraska, Earthquake, Swashbuckler, Obsession, Alex and the Gypsy, Another Man Another Chance, Coma, Murder by Decree, Final Assignment, The Last Flight of Noah's Ark, Monsignor, Tightrope, Choose Me, Trouble in Mind, The Moderns, Dead Ringers, False Identity, Secret Places of the Heart, A Paper Wedding, An Ambush of Ghosts, Mon Amie Max.
TELEVISION: *Specials*: Saint Joan, Antony and Cleopatra. *Movies*: Mistress of Paradise, Red Earth White Earth.

BULLOCK, SANDRA
Actress. b. Arlington, VA, 1964. e. East Carolina Univ., drama major. Raised in Germany; studied piano in Europe. First prof. acting job in NY in Off-B'way prod. No Time Flat.
PICTURES: Who Shot Patakango?, Love Potion No. 9, When the Party's Over, The Vanishing, The Thing Called Love, Demolition Man, Speed, Me and the Mob, While You Were Sleeping, The Net, Two If by Sea, A Time to Kill, In Love and War, Speed 2 Cruise Control.
TELEVISION: *Series*: Working Girl. *Movies*: The Preppie Murder, Bionic Showdown: The Six Million Dollar Man and the Bionic Woman, Jackie Collins' Lucky/Chances.

BURGHOFF, GARY
Actor. b. Bristol, CT, May 24, 1943. Winner of Student Hallmark Award while in high school, 1961. Also wildlife artist, with work exhibited in many U.S. galleries.
THEATER: *NY*: You're a Good Man Charlie Brown, The Nerd. *Also*: Finian's Rainbow, Bells Are Ringing, Sound of Music, The Boy Friend, Romanoff and Juliet, Whose Life Is It Anyway?
PICTURES: M*A*S*H*, B.S. I Love You, Small Kill (also co-dir.).
TELEVISION: *Series*: The Don Knotts Show, M*A*S*H (Emmy Award, 1977). *Guest*: Good Guys, Name of the Game, Love American Style, Fernwood 2-Night, Sweepstakes, Love Boat, Fantasy Island. *Movies*: The Man in the Santa Claus Suit, Casino. *Special*: Twigs.

BURKE, ALFRED
Actor. b. London, England, February 28, 1918.
PICTURES: Touch and Go, The Man Upstairs, The Angry Silence, Moment of Danger, The Man Inside, No Time To Die, Children of the Damned, The Nanny, One Day in the Life of Ivan Denisovitch, Law and Disorder, Yangtse Incident, Interpol, Bitter Victory.
TELEVISION: The Crucible, Mock Auction, Parole, No Gun, No Guilt, The Big Knife, Parnell, The Strong Are Lonely, Home of the Brave, The Birthday Party, The Watching Eye, Public Eye (series).

BURKE, DELTA
Actress. b. Orlando, FL, July 30, 1956. e. LAMDA. m. actor Gerald McRaney. Competed in Miss America contest as Miss Florida, prior to studying acting in England.
TELEVISION: *Series*: The Chisholms, Filthy Rich, 1st & Ten, Designing Women, Delta (also co-exec. prod.), Women of the House (also exec. prod.). *Movies*: Charleston, A Last Cry for Help, Mickey Spillane's Mike Hammer: Murder Me Murder You, A Bunny's Tale, Where the Hell's That Gold?!!? Love and Curses... And All That Jazz (also co-exec. prod.), Day-O, Simon & Simon: In Trouble Again, A Promise to Carolyn, Melanie Darron.
PICTURES: Maternal Instincts.

BURNETT, CAROL
Actress, Singer, Producer, Director. b. San Antonio, TX, April 26, 1933. e. Hollywood H.S., UCLA. Daughter is actress Carrie Hamilton. Introduced comedy song "I Made a Fool of Myself Over John Foster Dulles," 1957; regular performer Garry Moore Show, 1959-62. Recipient outstanding commedienne award Am. Guild Variety Artists, 5 times; TV Guide award for outstanding female performer 1961, 62, 63; Peabody Award, 1963; 5 Golden Globe awards for outstanding comedienne of year; Woman of Year award Acad. TV Arts and Scis. Voted one of the world's 20 most admired women in 1977 Gallup Poll. First Annual Television Critics Award for Outstanding Performance, 1977. Best Actress Award at San Sebastian Film Fest. for film A Wedding, 1978. Inducted Acad. of Television Arts and Sciences Hall of Fame, 1985. *Author*: Once Upon a Time (1986).
THEATER: *NY*: Once Upon a Mattress (debut, 1959; Theatre World Award), Fade Out-Fade In, Moon Over Buffalo. *Regional*: Calamity Jane, Plaza Suite, I Do I Do, Same Time Next Year.
PICTURES: Who's Been Sleeping in My Bed? (debut, 1963), Pete 'n' Tillie, The Front Page, A Wedding, H.E.A.L.T.H., The Four Seasons, Chu Chu and the Philly Flash, Annie, Noises Off.
TELEVISION: *Movies*: The Grass Is Always Greener Over the Septic Tank, Friendly Fire, The Tenth Month, Life of the Party: The Story of Beatrice, Between Friends, Hostage, Seasons of the Heart. *Series*: Stanley, Pantomime Quiz, The Garry Moore Show (Emmy Award, 1962), The Entertainers, The Carol Burnett Show (1967-78; in syndication as Carol Burnett & Friends), Carol Burnett & Company, Carol & Company, The Carol Burnett Show (1991). *Mini-Series*: Fresno. *Specials*: Julie & Carol at Carnegie Hall, Carol and Company (Emmy Award for previous 2 specials, 1963), An Evening with Carol Burnett, Calamity Jane, Once Upon a Mattress, Carol + 2, Julie & Carol at Lincoln Center, 6 Rms Riv Vu, Twigs, Sills & Burnett at the Met, Dolly & Carol in Nashville, All-Star Party for Carol Burnett, Burnett Discovers Domingo, The Laundromat, Carol Carl Whoopi & Robin, Julie & Carol—Together Again, The Carol Burnett Show: A Reunion (also co-exec. prod.), Men Movies & Carol. *Guest*: Twilight Zone, The Jack Benny Program, Get Smart, The Lucy Show, Fame, Magnum P.I., Mad About You (Emmy Award, 1997), Grace, Happy Birthday Elizabeth.

BURNETT, CHARLES
Director, Writer, Cinematographer. b. Vicksburg, MI, 1944. e. LA Community Col., UCLA.
PICTURES: *Director*: Killer of Sheep (also prod., s.p., photog., edit.), My Brother's Wedding (also prod., s.p., photog.), To Sleep With Anger (also s.p.), The Glass Shield (also s.p.). Cinematographer: Bless Their Little Hearts (also s.p.), Guest of Hotel Astoria.

BURNS, EDWARD J.
Actor, Director, Producer. b. Valley Stream, NY, Jan. 28, 1968.
PICTURES: *Actor/prod./dir./s.p.*: The Brothers McMullen, She's the One, No Looking Back, Saving Private Ryan (actor only).

BURNS, KEN
Producer, Director, Cinematographer, Writer. b. July 29, 1953. e. Hampshire Col. Prod. and dir. of the following documentaries: Brooklyn Bridge (also photog., edit.; Acad. Award nom.), The Shakers: Hands to Work Hearts to God (also co-writer), The Statue of Liberty (also photog.; Acad. Award nom.), Huey Long (also co-writer), Thomas Hart Benton (also photog.), The Congress, The Civil War (also photog., co-writer; numerous awards incl. Peabody and Emmy), Lindbergh (co-prod. only), Empire of the Air: The Men Who Made Radio (also photog., music dir.), Baseball (co- writer, prod., dir.). Co-author: Shakers: Hands to Work Hearts to God: The History and Visions of the United Society of Believers in Christ's Second Appearance from 1774 to Present, The Civil War: An Illustrated History, Baseball: An Illustrated History. Appeared in film Gettysburg.

BURNS, RALPH
Musical Conductor, Composer. b. Newton, MA, June 29, 1922. PICTURES: Lenny, Cabaret (Academy Award, 1972), Lucky Lady, New York New York, Movie Movie, All That Jazz (Academy Award, 1979), Urban Cowboy, Annie, My Favorite Year, Jinxed, Kiss Me Goodbye, Star 80, National Lampoon's Vacation, Perfect, Bert Rigby You're a Fool.
TELEVISION: *Specials*: Baryshnikov on Broadway, Liza and Goldie Special. *Movies*: Ernie Kovacs—Between the Laughter, After the Promise, Sweet Bird of Youth.

BURRILL, TIMOTHY
Producer, Executive. b. North Wales, June 8, 1931. e. Eton Coll., Sorbonne U., Paris. Grenadier Guards 2 yrs, then London Shipping Co. Ent. m.p. ind. as resident prod. mgr. Samaritan Films working on shorts, commercials, documentaries, 1954. Ass't. dir.: The Criminal, The Valiant Years (TV series), On The Fiddle, Reach for Glory, War Lover. Prod. mgr: The Cracksman, Night Must Fall, Lord Jim, Yellow Rolls Royce, The Heroes of Telemark, Resident prod. with World Film Services. 1970 prod. two films on pop music for Anglo-EMI. 1972 first prod. administrator National Film School in U.K. 1974 Post prod. administrator The Three Musketeers. Prod. TV Special The Canterville Ghost; assoc. prod, That Lucky Touch; UK Administrator, The Prince and the Pauper; North American Prod. controller, Superman; 1974-1983 council member of BAFTA; mng. dir., Allied Stars (Breaking Glass, Chariots of Fire); 1979-80 V. chmn. Film BAFTA; 1980-83 chmn. BAFTA; 1981-92, Gov. National Film School, executive BFTPA mem. Cinematograph Films Council. 1982-88 Gov Royal National Theatre; 1987-93, chmn., Film Asset Developments, Formed Burrill Prods, 1979-; chmn. First Film Foundation. Exec. member PACT, 1991. Vice-chmn. (film) PACT, 1993.
PICTURES: *Prod.*: Privilege, Oedipus the King, A Severed Head, Three Sisters, Macbeth (assoc. prod.), Alpha Beta, Tess (co-prod.), Pirates of Penzance (co-prod.), Supergirl, The Fourth Protocol, To Kill a Priest (co-prod.), Return of the Musketeers (tv in U.S.), Valmont, The Rainbow Thief, The Lover, Bitter Moon, Sweet Killing.

BURROWS, JAMES
Director, Producer. b. Los Angeles, CA, Dec. 30, 1940. e. Oberlin, B.A.; Yale, M.F.A. Son of late Abe Burrows, composer, writer, dir. Directed off-B'way.
PICTURE: Partners.
TELEVISION: *Series: Dir.*: Mary Tyler Moore, Bob Newhart, Laverne and Shirley, Rhoda, Phyllis, Tony Randall Show, Betty White Show, Taxi (2 Emmy Awards: 1980, 1981), Lou Grant, Cheers (also prod.; 4 Emmy Awards as prod.: 1983, 1984, 1989, 1991; 2 Emmy Awards as dir.: 1983, 1991), Dear John, Night Court, All is Forgiven (also exec. prod.), The Fanelli Boys, Frasier (Emmy Award, 1994), Friends, NewsRadio, Men Behaving Badly, Chicago Sons. *Movie*: More Than Friends.

BURROWS, ROBERTA
Executive. e. Brandeis U; Academia, Florence, Italy. Career includes freelance writing for natl. magazines: GQ, Italian Bazaar, US, Family Circle. Dir. of pub. for Howard Stein Enterprises and with Rogers & Cowan and Billings Associates. Joined Warner Bros. as sr. publicist 1979; named dir. east coast publicity, 1986. Resigned 1989 to dev. novelty products. Proj. coordinator at Orion Pictures in NY for The Silence of the Lambs, Little Man Tate, Married to It, Bill & Ted's Bogus Journey. Columnist, Max publication.

BURSTYN, ELLEN
Actress. r.n. Edna Rae Gilhooley. b. Detroit, MI, Dec. 7, 1932. Majored in art; was fashion model in Texas at 18. Moved to Montreal as dancer; then N.Y. to do TV commercials (under the name of Ellen McRae), appearing for a year on the Jackie Gleason show (1956-57). In 1957 turned to dramatics and won lead in B'way show, Fair Game. Then went to Hollywood to do TV and films. Returned to N.Y. to study acting with Lee Strasberg; worked in TV serial, The Doctors. Co-artistic dir. of Actor's Studio. 1982-88. Pres. Actors Equity Assn. 1982-85. On 2 panels of Natl. Endowment of the Arts and Theatre Advisory Council (NY).

THEATER: *NY*: Same Time Next Year (Tony Award, 1975), 84 Charing Cross Road, Shirley Valentine, Shimada. L.A.: Love Letters. Regional: The Trip to Bountiful.
PICTURES: *As Ellen McRae*: For Those Who Think Young (debut, 1964), Goodbye Charlie, Pit Stop. *As Ellen Burstyn*: Tropic of Cancer, Alex in Wonderland, The Last Picture Show, The King of Marvin Gardens, The Exorcist, Harry and Tonto, Alice Doesn't Live Here Anymore (Academy Award, 1974), Providence, A Dream of Passion, Same Time Next Year, Resurrection, Silence of the North, The Ambassador, In Our Hands (doc.), Twice in a Lifetime, Hanna's War, Dying Young, The Color of Evening, The Cemetery Club, When a Man Loves a Woman, Roommates, The Baby-sitters Club, How to Make an American Quilt, The Spitfire Grill, Liar.
TELEVISION: *Movies*: Thursday's Game, The People Vs. Jean Harris, Surviving, Act of Vengeance, Into Thin Air, Something in Common, Pack of Lies, When You Remember Me, Mrs. Lambert Remembers Love, Taking Back My Life: The Nancy Ziegenmeyer Story, Grand Isle, Shattered Trust: The Shari Karney Story, Getting Out, Getting Gotti, Trick of the Eye, My Brother's Keeper, Follow the River. *Special*: Dear America: Letters Home From Vietnam (reader). *Series*: The Doctors, The Ellen Burstyn Show. *Guest*: Cheyenne, Dr. Kildare, 77 Sunset Strip, Perry Mason, The Iron Horse.

BURTON, KATE
Actress. b. Geneva, Switzerland, Sept. 10, 1957. e. Brown Univ. (B.A.), Yale Drama Sch. Daughter of late Richard Burton. m. stage manager Michael Ritchie. Worked at Yale Repertory Theatre, Hartford, Stage Co., the Hartman, Huntington Theatre, Williamstown, Berkshire Theatre festivals, The O'Neil Playwright's Conference, Pray Street Theatre.
THEATER: Present Laughter (debut, 1982; Theatre World Award), Alice in Wonderland, Winners, The Accrington Pals, Doonesbury, The Playboy of the Western World, Wild Honey, Measure For Measure, Some Americans Abroad (Drama Desk nom.), Jake's Women, London Suite, Company.
PICTURES: Big Trouble in Little China (debut, 1986), Life With Mikey, August, First Wives Club, Looking for Richard, The Ice Storm.
TELEVISION: *Mini-Series*: Ellis Island, Evergreen. *Movies*: Alice in Wonderland, Uncle Tom's Cabin, Love Matters, Mistrial, Notes For My Daughter, Ellen Foster. *Series*: Home Fires, Monty.

BURTON, LEVAR
Actor. b. Landstuhl, W. Germany, Feb. 16, 1957. e. U. of Southern California. Signed to play role of Kunta Kinte in TV mini-series, Roots, while still in school. Has hosted Public TV children's shows, Rebop, and Reading Rainbow.
PICTURES: Looking for Mr. Goodbar, The Hunter, The Supernaturals, Star Trek: Generations, Star Trek: First Contact.
TELEVISION: *Mini-Series*: Roots. *Special*: Almos' a Man. *Movies*: Billy: Portrait of a Street Kid, Battered, One in a Million: The Ron Leflore Story, Dummy, Guyana Tragedy: The Story of Jim Jones, The Acorn People, Grambling's White Tiger, Emergency Room, The Jesse Owens Story, A Special Friendship, Roots: The Gift, Firestorm: 72 Hours in Oakland, Parallel Lives. *Series*: Star Trek: The Next Generation, Reading Rainbow (PBS; host, co-exec. prod.).

BURTON, STEVE
Actor. b. Indianapolis, IN, June 28, 1970.
PICTURES: Red Sun Rising, CyberTracker CyberTracker 2.
TELEVISION: *Series*: Out of This World, Days of Our Lives, General Hospital (Emmy Award, 1998).

BURTON, TIM
Director, Producer. b. Burbank, CA, Aug. 25, 1958. Cartoonist since grade school in suburban Burbank. Won Disney fellowship to study animation at California Institute of the Arts. At 20 went to Burbank to work as apprentice animator on Disney lot, working on such features as The Fox and the Hound, The Black Cauldron. Made Vincent, 6-minute stop-motion animation short on his own which was released commercially in 1982 and won several film fest. awards. Also made Frankenweenie, 29 minute live-action film. Appeared in film Singles. Wrote and illustrated children's book based on The Nightmare Before Christmas.
PICTURES: *Director*: Pee-wee's Big Adventure, Beetlejuice, Batman, Edward Scissorhands (also co-story), Batman Returns (also co-prod.), Ed Wood (also co-prod.), Mars Attacks (also prod.). *Co-Prod.*: The Nightmare Before Christmas (also story), Cabin Boy, James and the Giant Peach, Mars Attacks (also prod.).
TELEVISION: *Episode Director*: Aladdin (Faerie Tale Theatre), Alfred Hitchcock Presents, Amazing Stories (Family Dog). *Exec. Prod. for animated series*: Beetlejuice, Family Dog.

BUSBY, Ann
Executive. Senior v.p., MCA Motion Picture Group.

BUSCEMI, STEVE
Actor. b. Brooklyn, NY, 1957. Started as standup comedian in New York City, also wrote and acted in numerous one-act plays in collaboration with Mark Boone Jr. Acted in many plays by John Jesurun and worked briefly with the Wooster Group; worked as fireman. Studied acting at Lee Strasberg Inst. in NY.
PICTURES: The Way It Is/Eurydice in the Avenue, No Picnic, Parting Glances, Sleepwalk, Heart, Kiss Daddy Good Night, Call Me, Force of Circumstance, Vibes, Heart of Midnight, Bloodhounds of Broadway, Borders, New York Stories (Life Lessons), Slaves of New York, Mystery Train, Tales from the Dark Side, Miller's Crossing, King of New York, Zandalee, Barton Fink, Billy Bathgate, Crisscross, In the Soup, Reservoir Dogs, Trusting Beatrice, Rising Sun, Twenty Bucks, Ed and His Dead Mother, The Hudsucker Proxy, Floundering, Airheads, Me and the Mob, Pulp Fiction, Billy Madison, Desperado, Somebody to Love, The Search for One-Eye Jimmy, Living in Oblivion, Things to Do in Denver When You're Dead, Pistolero, Fargo, Kansas City, Trees Lounge, John Carpenter's Escape From L.A., Con Air, The Impostors, The Big Lebowski, The Wedding Singer, Armageddon, Louis et Frank.
TELEVISION: Mini-Series: Lonesome Dove. Movie: The Last Outlaw. Guest: Miami Vice, The Equalizer, L.A. Law, Mad About You, Homicide: Life on the Streets.

BUSCH, H. DONALD
Exhibitor. b. Philadelphia, PA, Sept. 21, 1935. e. U. of Pennsylvania, physics, math, 1956; law school, 1959. Practiced law, anti-trust & entertainment, 1960-87. 1984, pres., Budco Theatres, Inc. 1975-87. Pres., Busch, Grafman & Von Dreusche, P.C. 1987. Pres. & CEO, AMC Philadelphia, Inc., 1986-96. NATO chmn.,1990-91; chmn. emeritus, 1992. Showeast, gen. chmn., 1990-93. Will Rogers Memorial Fund, dir. Pres. of NATO of Pennsylvania, 1988. Motion Picture Pioneers, Inc., dir., 1995

BUSEY, GARY
Actor, Musician. b. Goose Creek, TX, June 29, 1944. e. Coffeyville Jr. Coll. A.B., 1963; attended Kansas State Coll, Okla. State U. Played drums with the Rubber Band 1963-70. Also drummer with Leon Russell, Willie Nelson (as Teddy Jack Eddy).
PICTURES: Angels Hard as They Come (debut, 1971), Didn't You Hear?, Dirty Little Billy, The Magnificent Seven Ride, The Last American Hero, Lolly Madonna XXX, Hex, Thunderbolt and Lightfoot, The Gumball Rally, A Star Is Born, Straight Time, Big Wednesday, The Buddy Holly Story (Natl. Society of Film Critics Award; Acad. Award nom., 1978), Foolin' Around, Carny, Barbarosa, D.C. Cab, The Bear, Insignificance, Stephen King's Silver Bullet, Let's Get Harry, Eye of the Tiger, Lethal Weapon, Bulletproof, Act of Piracy, Predator 2, My Heroes Have Always Been Cowboys, Hider in the House, Point Break, The Player, Under Siege, South Beach, The Firm, Rookie of the Year. Surviving the Game, Chasers, Breaking Point, Drop Zone, Man With a Gun, Black Sheep, Carried Away, Rough Riders, Rough Draft, Steel Sharks, Deadly Current, Warriors.
TELEVISION: Series: The Texas Wheelers, Bonanza. Guest: High Chaparral (debut, 1970), Gunsmoke, Saturday Night Live, The Hitchhiker (ACE Award). Movies: Bloodsport, The Execution of Private Slovik, The Law, Wild Texas Wind, Chrome Soldiers. Mini-Series: A Dangerous Life, The Neon Empire.

BUSFIELD, TIMOTHY
Actor. b. Lansing, MI, June 12, 1957. e. East Tennessee State U; Actor's Theatre of Louisville (as apprentice and resident). Founded Fantasy Theatre in Sacramento, 1986, a professional acting co., which performs in Northern CA schools, providing workshops on playwriting for children and sponsors annual Young Playwrights contest.
THEATER: Richard II, Young Playwrights Festival (Circle Rep.), A Tale Told, Getting Out (European tour), Green Mountain Guilds Children Theatre, Mass Appeal, The Tempest, A Few Good Men (B'way). Founded & co-prod. The "B" Theatre, 1992, prods. Mass Appeal, Hidden in This Picture.
PICTURES: Stripes, Revenge of the Nerds, Revenge of the Nerds II, Field of Dreams, Sneakers, The Skateboard Kid, Striking Distance, Little Big League, Quiz Show.
TELEVISION: Series: Reggie, Trapper John M.D., thirtysomething (Emmy Award, 1991; also dir. 3 episodes), Byrds of Paradise, Champs. Guest: Family Ties, Matlock, Paper Chase, Love American Style, After M.A.S.H, Hotel. Movies: Strays, Calendar Girl-Cop-Killer?: The Bambi Bembenek Story, Murder Between Friends, In the Shadow of Evil, In the Line of Duty: Kidnapped.

BUTTONS, RED
Actor. r.n. Aaron Chwatt. b. New York, NY, Feb. 5, 1919. Attended Evander Child H.S. in the Bronx. Singer at the age of 13; comic, Minsky's. Served in U.S. Army, during WWII; in Army stage prod. and film version of Winged Victory. Received Golden Globe Award noms. for Harlow and They Shoot Horses Don't They?; Best Comedian Award for The Red Buttons Show. Performed in most major Variety nightclubs shows.
PICTURES: Winged Victory (1944, debut), 5 Rue Madeleine, Footlight Varieties of 1951, Sayonara (Acad. Award for Best Supporting Actor, 1957; also Golden Globe Award), Imitation General, The Big Circus, One Two Three, The Longest Day, Gay Purr-ee (voice), Five Weeks in a Balloon, Hatari!, A Ticklish

Affair, Your Cheatin' Heart, Harlow, Up From the Beach, Stagecoach, They Shoot Horses Don't They?, Who Killed Mary What's 'er Name?, The Poseidon Adventure, Gable and Lombard, Viva Knievel!, Pete's Dragon, Movie Movie, C.H.O.M.P.S., When Time Ran Out..., 18 Again!, The Ambulance, It Could Happen to You, Off Your Rocker.
TELEVISION: Series: The Red Buttons Show (1952-55), The Double Life of Henry Phyfe, Knots Landing, Rosanne, Bill Cosby, E.R.. Movies: Breakout, The New Original Wonder Woman, Louis Armstrong: Chicago Style, Telethon, Vega$, The Users, Power, The Dream Merchants, Leave 'Em Laughing, Reunion at Fairborough, Alice in Wonderland, Hansel & Gretel. Barefoot Boy With Cheek, Hold It, The Admiral Had a Wife, Winged Victory, Tender Trap, Play It Again Sam, The Teahouse of the August Moon, Red Buttons on Broadway, Finian's Rainbow.

BUZZI, RUTH
Actress. b. Westerly, RI, July 24, 1939. e. Pasadena Playhouse Col. of Theatre Arts. On Country Music charts with You Oughta Hear the Song. Has received 5 Emmy nominations; Golden Globe winner, AGVA Variety Artist of the Year, 1977, Rhode Island Hall of Fame, Presidential commendation for outstanding artist in the field of entertainment, 1980, NAACP Image Award.
THEATER: Sweet Charity (Broadway), 4 off-Broadway shows incl. A Man's A Man, Little Mary Sunshine, Cinderella, Wally's Cafe, 18 musical revues and Las Vegas club act.
PICTURES: Record City, Freaky Friday, The Apple Dumpling Gang Rides Again, The North Avenue Irregulars, The Villain, Surf Two, Skatetown USA, Chu Chu and the Philly Flash, The Being, The Bad Guys, Dixie Lanes, Up Your Alley, Diggin' Up Business, My Mom's a Werewolf, It's Your Life Michael Angelo, The Trouble Makers (orig. title: The Fight Before Christmas).
TELEVISION: Series: Rowan & Martin's Laugh-In, The Steve Allen Comedy Hour, Donny & Marie, The Lost Saucer, Betsy Lee's Ghost Town Jamboree, Carol Burnett's The Entertainers, Days of Our Lives, Sesame Street; semi-regular on 12 other series including Flip, Tony Orlando & Dawn, That Girl, Glen Campbell's Goodtime Hour, Leslie Uggums Show, The Dean Martin Variety Hour; guest on many TV series and specials including Medical Center, Adam 12, Trapper John M.D., Love Boat, They Came from Outer Space, Major Dad, Alice, Here's Lucy, Saved by the Bell, etc. Movie: In Name Only. Many cartoon voice-over series and over 150 on-camera commercials.

BYGRAVES, MAX
Comedian, Actor. b. London, England, October 16, 1922. e. St. Joseph's R.C. School, Rotherhithe. After RAF service, touring revues and London stage. TV debut in 1953, with own show. Autobiography: I Wanna Tell You A Story, 1976. Novel: The Milkman's on His Way, 1977. Received O.B.E., New Year's Honours 1983.
PICTURES: Skimpy in the Navy (debut, 1949), Bless 'em All, Nitwits on Parade, Tom Brown's Schooldays, Charley Moon, A Cry from the Streets, Bobbikins, Spare the Rod, The Alf Garnett Saga.
TELEVISION: Roamin' Holiday (series).

BYRD, CARUTH C.
Production Executive. b. Dallas, TX, March 25, 1941. e. Trinity U, San Antonio. Multi-millionaire businessman, chmn. of Caruth C. Byrd Enterprises, Inc., who entered entertainment industry forming Communications Network Inc. in 1972. Was principal investor in film Santee (1972) and in 1973 formed Caruth C. Byrd Prods. to make theatrical features. 1983, chmn., Lone Star Pictures. 1987, formed Caruth C. Byrd Television. Formed Caruth C. Byrd Entertainment Inc. May, 1989. Concerts incl. Tom Jones, Natalie Cole, B.J. Thomas, Tammy Wynette, Seals & Croft, Eddie Rabbit, Helen Reddy, Jim Stafford, Tanya Tucker and many more.
PICTURES: Murph the Surf, The Monkeys of Bandapur (both exec. prod.), Santee, Sudden Death, Hollywood High II, Lone Star Country, Trick or Treats.
TELEVISION: Fishing Fever, Kids Are People Too, Tribute to Mom and Dad, Back to School, Texas 150: A Celebration Special.

BYRNE, DAVID
Actor, Singer, Director. b. Dumbarton, Scotland, May 14, 1952. Moved to Baltimore at 7. e. Rhode Island Sch. of Design studying photography, performance and video, and Maryland Inst. Coll. of Art 1971-72. Prod. and dir. music videos. Awarded MTV's Video Vanguard Award, 1985. Best known as the lead singer and chief songwriter of Talking Heads. Composed and performed original score for choreographer Twyla Tharp's The Catherine Wheel (B'way). Wrote music for Robert Wilson's The Knee Plays.
PICTURES: Stop Making Sense (conceived and stars in concert film), True Stories (dir., s.p., narrator), The Last Emperor (music, Academy Award, 1987), Married to the Mob (music), Heavy Petting, Between the Teeth (also co-dir.). Also contributed music to such films as Times Square, The Animals' Film, King of Comedy, America is Waiting, Revenge of the Nerds, Down and Out in Beverly Hills, Dead End Kids, Cross My Heart, Somebody Is Waiting.
TELEVISION: A Family Tree (Trying Times), Alive From Off-Center (also composed theme), Survival Guides; Rolling Stone Magazine's 20 Years of Rock and Roll.

BYRNE, GABRIEL
Actor. b. Dublin, Ireland, 1950. e. University Coll., Ireland. Worked as archaeologist, then taught Spanish at girls' school. Participated in amateur theater before acting with Ireland's Focus Theatre, an experimental rep. co. and joining Dublin's Abbey Theatre Co. Cast in long-running TV series the Riordans. Also worked with National Theater in London. Author: Pictures in My Head (1994).
PICTURES: On a Paving Stone Mounted, The Outsider, Excalibur, Hanna K, The Keep, Defence of the Realm, Gothic, Lionheart, Siesta, Hello Again, Julia and Julia, A Soldier's Tale, The Courier, Miller's Crossing, Shipwrecked, Dark Obsession (Diamond Skulls), Cool World, Point of No Return, Into the West (also assoc. prod.), A Dangerous Woman, In the Name of the Father (co-prod. only), Prince of Jutland, A Simple Twist of Fate, Trial by Jury, Little Women, The Usual Suspects, Frankie Starlight, Dead Man, Last of the High Kings (also co-s.p.), Mad Dog Time, Somebody Is Waiting, The End of Violence, Toby's Story, Polish Wedding, This Is the Sea, Man in the Iron Mask, Quest for Camelot.
TELEVISION: Series: The Riordan's, Branken. Movies/Specials: Wagner, The Search for Alexander the Great, Treatment, Joyce, Mussolini, Christopher Columbus, Lark in the Clear Air (also dir., writer), Buffalo Girls, Weapons of Mask Destruction.

BYRNES, EDD
Actor. b. New York, NY, July 30, 1933. e. Harren H.S. Prof. debut, Joe E. Brown's Circus Show. Author of Edd Byrnes: Kookie No More.
THEATER: Tea and Sympathy, Picnic, Golden Boy, Bus Stop, Ready When You Are C.B., Storm in Summer.
PICTURES: Reform School Girl, Darby's Rangers, Up Periscope, Marjorie Morningstar, Yellowstone Kelly, Girl on the Run, The Secret Invasion, Wicked Wicked, Grease, Stardust, Go Kill and Come Back, Payment in Blood, Troop Beverly Hills.
TELEVISION: Series: 77 Sunset Strip, Sweepstake$. Has appeared in over 300 TV shows incl.: Matinee Theatre, Crossroads, Jim Bowie, Wire Service, Navy Log, Oh Susanna!, Throb, Rags to Riches, Murder She Wrote. Movies: The Silent Gun, Mobile Two, Telethon, Vega$, Twirl.

BYRON, KATHLEEN
Actress. b. London, England, Jan. 11, 1922. e. London U., Old Vic. co. student, 1942. Screen debut in Young Mr. Pitt, 1943.
PICTURES: Silver Fleet, Black Narcissus, Matter of Life and Death, Small Back Room, Madness of the Heart, Reluctant Widow, Prelude to Fame, Scarlet Thread, Tom Brown's Schooldays, Four Days, Hell Is Sold Out, I'll Never Forget You, Gambler and the Lady, Young Bess, Night of the Silvery Moon, Profile, Secret Venture, Hand in Hand, Night of the Eagle, Hammerhead, Wolfshead, Private Road, Twins of Evil, Craze, Abdication, One of Our Dinosaurs Is Missing, The Elephant Man, From a Far Country, Emma, Remembering Sister Ruth (documentary).
TELEVISION: The Lonely World of Harry Braintree, All My Own Work, Emergency Ward 10, Probation Officer, Design for Murder, Sergeant Cork, Oxbridge 2000, The Navigators, The Worker, Hereward the Wake, Breaking Point, Vendetta, Play To Win, Who Is Sylvia, Portrait of a Lady, Callan, You're Wrecking My Marriage, Take Three Girls, The Confession of Mariona Evans, Paul Temple, The Worker, The Moonstone, The Challengers, The Golden Bowl, The Edwardians, The New Life, Menace, The Rivals of Sherlock Holmes, The Brontes, On Call, Edward VII, Sutherland's Law, Crown Court, Anne of Avonlea, Heidi, Notorious Woman, General Hospital, North & South, Angelo, Within these Walls, Jubilee, Z Cars, Tales from the Supernatural, Secret Army, An Englishman's Castle, The Professionals, Forty Weeks, Emmerdale Farm, Blake Seven, The Minders, Together, Hedda Gabler, Nancy Astor, God Speed Co-operation, Take Three Women, Reilly, Memoirs of Sherlock Holmes, Moon And Son, The Bill, Casualty, Portrait of a Marriage, Gentlemen & Players, The Frighteners.

BYRUM, JOHN
Writer, Director. b. Winnetka, IL, March 14, 1947. e. New York U. Film School. First job as gofer on industrial films and cutting dailies for underground filmmakers. Went to England where wrote 1st s.p., Comeback. From 1970-73, was in NY writing and re-writing scripts for low-budget films.
PICTURES: Writer: Mahogany, Inserts (also dir.) Harry and Walter Go to New York, Heart Beat (also dir.), Sphinx, Scandalous, The Razor's Edge (also dir.), The Whoopee Boys (also dir.), The War at Home (also dir.).
TELEVISION: Movie: Murder in High Places (dir., writer). Series: Alfred Hitchcock Presents (1985), Middle Ages (creator, writer, exec. prod.), South of Sunset (creator, writer, exec. prod.), Winnetka Road (creator, writer, exec. prod.).

C

CAAN, JAMES
Actor. b. Bronx, NY, March 26, 1940. e. Hofstra U. Studied with Sanford Meisner at the Neighborhood Playhouse. Appeared off-B'way in La Ronde, 1961. Also on B'way in Mandingo, Blood Sweat and Stanley Poole.
PICTURES: Irma La Douce (debut, 1963), Lady in a Cage, The Glory Guys, Red Line 7000, El Dorado, Games, Countdown, Journey to Shiloh, Submarine X-1, The Rain People, Rabbit Run, T.R. Baskin, The Godfather (Acad. Award nom.), Slither, Cinderella Liberty, The Gambler, Freebie and the Bean, The Godfather Part II, Funny Lady, Rollerball, The Killer Elite, Harry and Walter Go To New York, Silent Movie, A Bridge Too Far, Another Man Another Chance, Comes a Horseman, Chapter Two, Hide in Plain Sight (also dir.), Thief, Bolero, Kiss Me Goodbye, Gardens of Stone, Alien Nation, Dick Tracy, Misery, The Dark Backward, For the Boys, Honeymoon in Vegas, The Program, Flesh & Bone, A Boy Called Hate, Things to Do in Denver When You're Dead, Bottle Rocket, Eraser, Bulletproof, Poodle Springs, Mickey Blue Eyes.
TELEVISION: Much series guest work (Naked City, Route 66, Wagon Train, Ben Casey, Alfred Hitchcock Presents, etc.) 1962-69. Movie: Brian's Song (Emmy nom.).

CACOYANNIS, MICHAEL
Producer, Director, Writer. b. Limassoc, Cyprus, June 11, 1922. Studied law in London, admitted to bar at age 21. Became a producer of BBC's wartime Greek programs while attending dramatic school. After acting on the stage in England, left in 1952 for Greece, where he made his first film, Windfall in Athens, with his own script. While directing Greek classical plays, he continued making films.
PICTURES: Director/Writer: Windfall in Athens (Sunday Awakening; debut, 1954), Stella, Girl in Black, A Matter of Dignity (The Final Lie), Our Last Spring (Eroica), The Wastrel, Electra, Zorba the Greek, The Day the Fish Came Out, The Trojan Women, Attila '74, Iphigenia, Sweet Country, Up Down and Sideways, Varya.

CAESAR, SID
Actor. b. Yonkers, NY, Sept. 8, 1922. Studied saxophone at Juilliard School; then appeared in service revue Tars and Spars. Cast by prod. Max Liebman in B'way revue Make Mine Manhattan in 1948. Voted best comedian in M.P. Daily's TV poll, 1951, 1952. Best Comedy Team (with Imogene Coca) in 1953. Received Sylvania Award, 1958. Formed Shelbrick Corp. TV, 1959. Appeared in B'way musical Little Me (1962), Off-B'way & B'way revue Sid Caesar & Company (1989). Author: Where Have I Been? (autobiography, 1982).
PICTURES: Tars and Spars (debut, 1945), The Guilt of Janet Ames, It's a Mad Mad Mad Mad World, The Spirit Is Willing, The Busy Body, A Guide for the Married Man, Airport 1975, Silent Movie, Fire Sale, Grease, The Cheap Detective, The Fiendish Plot of Dr. Fu Manchu, History of the World Part 1, Grease 2, Over the Brooklyn Bridge, Cannonball Run II, Stoogemania, The Emperor's New Clothes.
TELEVISION: Series: Admiral Broadway Revue, Your Show of Shows (Emmy Award for Best Actor, 1952), Caesar's Hour (Emmy Award for Best Comedian, 1956), Sid Caesar Invites You (1958), As Caesar Sees It, The Sid Caesar Show. Movies: Flight to Holocaust, Curse of the Black Widow, The Munsters' Revenge, Found Money, Love Is Never Silent, Alice in Wonderland, Freedom Fighter, Side By Side, The Great Mom Swap. Guest: U.S. Steel Hour, G.E. Theatre, The Ed Sullivan Show, Carol Burnett Show, Lucy Show, That's Life, Love American Style, When Things Were Rotten, The Love Boat, Amazing Stories, others. Specials: Tiptoe Through TV, Variety—World of Show Biz, Sid Caesar and Edie Adams Together, The Sid Caesar Imogene Coca Carl Reiner Howard Morris Special, Christmas Snow.

CAGE, NICOLAS
Actor. b. Long Beach, CA, Jan. 7, 1964. r.n. Nicholas Coppola. Nephew of dir. Francis Ford Coppola. Joined San Francisco's American Conservatory Theatre at age 15. While attending Beverly Hills High School won role on tv pilot Best of Times.
PICTURES: Fast Times at Ridgemont High (debut, 1982; billed as Nicholas Coppola), Valley Girl, Rumble Fish, Racing with the Moon, The Cotton Club, Birdy, The Boy in Blue, Peggy Sue Got Married, Raising Arizona, Moonstruck, Vampire's Kiss, Fire Birds, Wild at Heart, Tempo di Mecidere (Time to Kill), Zandalee, Honeymoon in Vegas, Amos & Andrew, DeadFall, Red Rock West, Guarding Tess, It Could Happen to You, Trapped in Paradise, Kiss of Death, Leaving Las Vegas (Academy Award, Chicago Film Critics Award, Nat'l Society of Film Critics Award; Golden Globe Award), The Rock, Con Air, Face/Off, Tom Slick: Monster Hunter, 8mm, City of Angels, Snake Eyes, Defective Detective, Bringing Out the Dead.

CAINE, MICHAEL
Actor. r.n. Maurice Micklewhite. b. London, England, March 14, 1933. Asst. stage mgr. Westminster Rep. (Sussex, UK 1953); Lowestoft Rep. 1953-55. London stage: The Room, The Dumbwaiter, Next Time I'll Sing For You (1963). Author: Michael Caine's Moving Picture Show or: Not Many People Know This Is the Movies, Acting on Film, What's It All About? (autobiography, 1993). Awarded C.B.E., 1992. Video: Michael Caine—Acting on Film.
PICTURES: A Hill in Korea (debut, 1956; aka Hell in Korea), How to Murder A Rich Uncle, The Key, Two-Headed Spy, Blind Spot, Breakout (Danger Within), Foxhole in Cairo, Bulldog Breed, The Day the Earth Caught Fire, Solo for Sparrow, Zulu, The Ipcress File, Alfie (Acad. Award nom.), The Wrong Box, Gambit, Funeral in Berlin, Hurry Sundown, Woman Times Seven, Billion Dollar Brain, Deadfall, The Magus, Play Dirty, The Italian Job, The Battle of Britain, Too Late the Hero, The Last Valley, Get Carter, Kidnapped, Zee and Company (X,Y & Zee), Pulp, Sleuth (Acad. Award nom.), The Black Windmill, The Destructors (The Marseille Contract), The Wilby Conspiracy, Peeper, The Romantic Englishwoman, The Man Who Would Be King, Harry and Walter Go to New York, The Eagle Has Landed, A Bridge Too Far, The Silver Bears, The Swarm, California Suite, Ashanti, Beyond the Poseidon Adventure, The Island, Dressed to Kill, The Hand, Victory, Deathtrap, Educating Rita (Acad. Award nom.), Beyond the Limit, Blame It on Rio, The Jigsaw Man, The Holcroft Covenant, Hannah and Her Sisters (Academy Award for Best Supporting Actor, 1986), Water, Sweet Liberty, Mona Lisa, Half Moon Street, Jaws—The Revenge, The Whistle Blower, The Fourth Protocol (also exec. prod.), Surrender, Without a Clue, Dirty Rotten Scoundrels, A Shock to the System, Mr. Destiny, Bullseye!, Noises Off, The Muppet Christmas Carol, On Deadly Ground, Bullet in Beijing, Blood & Wine, Shadow Run, Little Voice, Curtain Call.
TELEVISION: Series: Rickles (1975). In more than 100 British teleplays 1957-63 incl. The Compartment, The Playmates, Hobson's Choice, Funny Noises with Their Mouths, The Way with Reggie, Luck of the Draw, Hamlet, The Other Man. Movies: Jack the Ripper, Jekyll and Hyde, Blue Ice, World War II: When Lions Roared, 20,000 League under the Sea, Mandela and De Klerk.

CALHOUN, RORY
Actor. r.n. Francis Timothy McCown. b. Los Angeles, CA, Aug. 8, 1922. e. Santa Cruz H.S. Worked as logger, miner, cowpuncher, firefighter before becoming actor.
PICTURES: (as Frank McCown): Something for the Boys (debut, 1944), The Bullfighters, Sunday Dinner for a Soldier, Nob Hill, The Great John L, Where Do We Go From Here?; (as Rory Calhoun): The Red House, Adventure Island, That Hagen Girl, Miraculous Journey, Massacre River, Sand, Return of the Frontiersman, A Ticket to Tomahawk, County Fair, Rogue River, I'd Climb the Highest Mountain, Meet Me After the Show, With a Song in My Heart, Way of a Gaucho, The Silver Whip, Powder River, How to Marry a Millionaire, Yellow Tomahawk, River of No Return, A Bullet Is Waiting, Dawn at Socorro, Four Guns to the Border, The Looters, Ain't Misbehavin', Treasure of Pancho Villa, The Spoilers, Red Sundown, Raw Edge, Flight to Hong Kong, Utah Blaine, Hired Gun, The Domino Kid, The Big Caper, Ride Out for Revenge, Apache Territory, The Saga of Hemp Brown, Thunder in Carolina (Hard Drivin'), The Colossus of Rhodes, Marco Polo, Treasure of Monte Cristo (The Secret of Monte Cristo), Gun Hawk, The Young and the Brave, A Face in the Rain (also co-exec. prod.), Black Spurs, Young Fury, Operation Delilah, Finger on the Trigger, Our Man in Baghdad, The Emerald of Artatama, Apache Uprising, Dayton's Devils, Operation Cross Eagles, Night of the Lepus, Blood Black and White, Won Ton Ton the Dog Who Saved Hollywood, Mule Feathers, Kino the Padre on Horseback, Love and the Midnight Auto Supply, Just Not the Same Without You, Bitter Heritage, The Main Event, Motel Hell, Angel, Rollerblade Warriors, Avenging Angel, Hell Comes to Frogtown, Bad Jim, Fists of Steel, Pure Country.
TELEVISION: Series: U.S. Camera, The Texan, Capitol. Mini-Series: The Blue and the Gray, The Rebels. Movies: Flight to Holocaust, Flatbed Annie and Sweetie Pie: Lady Truckers. Guest: The Road Ahead, Day Is Done, Bet the Wild Queen, Zane Grey Theater, Killer Instinct, Land's End (pilot), Champion, Hart to Hart, Police Woman, Movin' On, Alias Smith & Jones.

CALLAN, MICHAEL
Actor, Singer, Dancer. b. Philadelphia, PA, Nov. 22, 1935. Singer, dancer, Philadelphia nightclubs; to New York in musicals including The Boy Friend and West Side Story; dancer at Copacabana nightclub; in short-run plays, Las Vegas: That Certain Girl, Love Letters.
PICTURES: They Came to Cordura (debut, 1958) The Flying Fontaines, Because They're Young, Pepe, Mysterious Island, Gidget Goes Hawaiian, 13 West Street, Bon Voyage, The Interns, The Victors, The New Interns, Cat Ballou, You Must Be Joking!, The Magnificent Seven Ride!, Frasier the Sensuous Lion, Lepke, The Photographer, The Cat and The Canary, Record City, Double Exposure (also prod.), Chained Heat, Freeway, Leprechaun III, Hello Muddah—Hello Fadduh (prod. only).
TELEVISION: Series: Occasional Wife, Superboy. Guest: Murder She Wrote, Superboy, etc. Movies: In Name Only, Donner Pass: The Road to Survival, Last of the Great Survivors. Mini-Series: Blind Ambition, Scruples.

CALLEY, JOHN
Executive. b. New Jersey, 1930. Was dir. of nighttime programming and dir. of programming sales at NBC, 1951-57; prod. exec. & TV prod., Henry Jaffe Enterprises, 1957; in charge of radio & tv for Ted Bates Adv. Agency, 1958; 1960-69, Filmways Inc., exec. v.p. & prod.; 1970, exec. v.p. in chg. of worldwide prod., Warner Bros.; pres. of Warner Bros. 1975-80. Retired from industry for 13 yrs. 1993 appointed pres. of United Artists.

CALLOW, SIMON
Actor, Writer, Director. b. London, June 15, 1949. e. Queens, U. of Belfast. The Drama Centre. Originated role of Mozart in London premiere of Amadeus and Burgess/Chubb in Single Spies. Author: Being an Actor, Acting in Restoration Comedy, Charles Laughton: A Difficult Actor, Shooting the Actor, Orson Welles: The Road to Xanadu.
THEATER: London: Plumber's Progress, The Doctor's Dilemma, Soul of the White Ant, Blood Sports, The Resistible Rise of Arturo Ui, Amadeus, Restoration, The Beastly Beatitudes of Balthazar B, Titus Andronicus (Bristol Old Vic), Faust. Shakespeare's Sonnets. Director: Loving Reno, The Infernal Machine (also translator); Jacques and His Master (also trans.; L.A.), Single Spies, Shades, My Fair Lady (Natl. tour), Shirley Valentine (London, NY), Carmen Jones.
PICTURES: Amadeus, A Room With a View, The Good Father, Maurice, Manifesto, Postcards From the Edge, Mr. and Mrs. Bridge, The Ballad of the Sad Cafe (dir. only), Howards End (unbilled), Four Weddings and a Funeral, Street Fighter, Jefferson in Paris, Ace Ventura: When Nature Calls, James and the Giant Peach, The Scarlet Tunic.
TELEVISION: Man of Destiny, La Ronde, All the World's a Stage, Wings of Song, The Dybbuk, Instant Enlightenment, Chance of a Lifetime (series), David Copperfield, Honour, Profit and Pleasure, Old Flames, Revolutionary Witness: Palloy, The Woman in White.

CALVET, CORINNE
Actress. r.n. Corinne Dibos. b. Paris, France, April 30, 1925. e. U. of Paris School of Fine Arts, Comedie Francaise. On French stage and radio; screen debut in French films, then to U.S. in 1949. Author: Has Corinne Been a Good Little Girl?, The Kirlian Aura.
PICTURES: La Part de L'Ombre (debut, 1946), Nous ne Sommes pas Maries, Petrus, La Chateau de la Derniere Chance, Rope of Sand (U.S. debut), When Willie Comes Marching Home, My Friend Irma Goes West, Quebec, On the Riviera, Peking Express, Sailor Beware, Thunder in the East, What Price Glory?, Powder River, Flight to Tangier, The Far Country, So This Is Paris, The Adventures of Casanova (Sins of Casanova), The Girls of San Frediano, Four Women in the NIhgt, Bonnes a Tuer (One Step to Eternity), Napoleon, Plunderers of Painted Flats, Bluebeard's Ten Honeymoons, Hemingway's Adventures of a Young Man, Apache Uprising, Pound, Too Hot to Handle, Dr. Heckle and Mr. Hype, The Sword and the Sorcerer, Side Roads.
TELEVISION: Movies: The Phantom of Hollywood, She's Dressed to Kill, The French Atlantic Affair.

CAMERON, JAMES
Director, Writer. b. Kapuskasing, Ontario, Canada, Aug. 16, 1954. e. Fullerton Junior Col. (physics). 1990, formed Lightstorm Entertainment.
PICTURES: Piranha II—The Spawning (dir.), The Terminator (dir., s.p.), Rambo: First Blood Part II (co-s.p.), Aliens (dir., s.p.), The Abyss (dir., s.p.), Terminator 2: Judgment Day (dir., co-s.p., prod.), Point Break (exec. prod.), True Lies (dir., co-s.p., prod.), Strange Days (co-prod., co-s.p., story), Titanic (dir., prod., story, Acad. Award, Golden Globe Award, Best Pic., Best Dir., Best Film Edit., 1997).

CAMERON, JOANNA
Actress, Director. r.n. Patricia Cameron. b. Aspen, CO, Sept. 20, 1951. e. U. of California, Sorbonne, Pasadena Playhouse, 1968. Guinness Record: Most network programmed TV commercials. TV Director: Various commercials, CBS Preview Special, closed circuit program host U.S.N., all TV equipped ships–actress and dir. Documentaries: Razor Sharp (prod., dir.), El Camino Real (dir., prod.).
PICTURES: How To Commit Marriage (debut), P.S. I Love You, Pretty Maids All in a Row.
TELEVISION: Movies: The Great American Beauty Contest, Night Games, It Couldn't Happen to a Nicer Guy, High Risk, Swan Song. Series: Isis. Guest: The Survivors, Love American Style, Daniel Boone, Mission Impossible, The Partners, Search, Medical Center, Name of the Game, The Bold Ones, Marcus Welby, Petrocelli, Columbo, Switch, MacMillan, Spiderman. Specials: Bob Hope Special, Bob Hope 25th NBC Anniversary Special.

CAMERON, KIRK
Actor. b. Canoga Park, CA, Oct. 12, 1970. m. actress Chelsea Noble. Sister is actress Candace Cameron. Started doing TV commercials at age 9.
PICTURES: The Best of Times, Like Father, Like Son, Listen to Me, You Lucky Dog.
TELEVISION: Series: Two Marriages, Growning Pains, Kirk. Movies: Goliath Awaits, Starflight: The Plane That Couldn't Land, A Little Piece of Heaven, Star Struck, The Computer Wore Tennis Shoes. Specials: The Woman Who Willed a Miracle, Andrea's Story. Ice Capades with Kirk Cameron.

CAMP, COLLEEN
Actress. b. San Francisco, CA, 1953. Spent 2 years as a bird trainer at Busch Gardens before being noticed by an agent and cast on TV. TV debut on The Dean Martin Show. Assoc. prod. on Martha Coolidge's film The City Girl. Sang several songs in They All Laughed and made Billboard charts with song One Day Since Yesterday.
PICTURES: Battle for the Planet of the Apes (debut, 1973), Swinging Cheerleaders, Death Game (The Seducers), Funny Lady, Smile, The Gumball Rally, Cats in a Cage, Game of Death, Apocalypse Now, Cloud Dancer, They All Laughed, The Seduction, Valley Girl, Smokey and the Bandit III, Rosebud Beach Hotel, The Joy of Sex, Police Academy II, Doin' Time, D.A.R.Y.L., Clue, Walk Like a Man, Illegally Yours, Track 29, Wicked Stepmother, My Blue Heaven, Wayne's World, The Vagrant, Un-Becoming Age, Sliver, Last Action Hero, Greedy, Naked in New York, Die Hard With a Vengeance, The Baby-sitter's Club, Three Wishes, Pulp Fiction, House Arrest, The Ice Storm, Speed 2: Cruise Control.
TELEVISION: Movies: Amelia Earhart, Lady of the House, Sisterhood, Addicted to His Love, Backfield in Motion, For Their Own Good, The Right to Remain Silent. Mini-Series: Rich Man Poor Man Book II. Series: Dallas. Guest: Happy Days, Dukes of Hazzard, WKRP in Cincinnati, Magnum PI, Murder She Wrote, Tales from the Crypt. Guest: George Burns Comedy Week. Special: Going Home Again.

CAMP, JOE
Producer, Director, Writer. b. St. Louis, MO, Apr. 20, 1939. e. U. of Mississippi, B.B.A. Acct. exec. McCann-Erickson Advt., Houston 1961-62; owner Joe Camp Real Estate 1962-64; acct. exec. Norsworthy-Mercer, Dallas 1964-69; dir. TV commercials; founder and pres. Mulberry Square Prods, 1971-present. Author: Underdog.
PICTURES: Dir./Prod./Writer: Benji, Hawmps, For the Love of Benji, The Double McGuffin, Oh Heavenly Dog, Benji the Hunted.
TELEVISION: Specials: The Phenomenon of Benji (dir., writer, prod.), Benji's Very Own Christmas Story (dir., prod., writer), Benji at Work (prod., writer), Benji at Marineland (dir., writer), Benji Zax and the Alien Prince (dir.).

CAMPANELLA, TOM
Executive. b. Houston, TX, 1944. e. City U. of NY. Joined Paramount Pictures 1968 as asst. business mgr.; later worked for corporate div. and Motion Picture Group. Named exec. dir., nat'l adv. 1979, made v.p., nat'l adv. 1982, appt. sr. v.p., adv., for M.P. Group. of Paramount, 1984. Appointed exec. v.p., adv. & promo., 1990.

CAMPBELL, BRUCE
Actor, Producer. b. Birmingham, MI, 1958.
PICTURES: The Evil Dead (debut, 1983; also exec. prod.), Crimewave (also co-prod.), Evil Dead 2 (also co-prod.), Maniac Cop, Moontrap, Darkman, Maniac Cop 2, Sundown: The Vampire in Retreat, Mindwarp, Lunatics: A Love Story (also prod.), Waxwork II: Lost in Time, Army of Darkness (also co-prod.), The Hudsucker Proxy, The Demolitionist, Congo, Assault on Dome 4, Menno's Mind, John Carpenter's Escape From L.A., Running Time, McHale's Navy, The Ice Rink, Texas Blood Money.
TELEVISION: Series: The Adventures of Brisco County Jr., Timecop. Guest: Xena. Movies: Tornado!, Missing Links, The Love Bug, In the Line of Duty: Blaze of Glory, Goldrush: A Real Life Alaskan Adventure.

CAMPBELL, GLEN
Actor, Singer. b. Delight, AK, April 22, 1936. After forming local band became studio guitarist in Hollywood on records for such performers as Frank Sinatra and Elvis Presley. Won two Grammy awards for record By the Time I Get to Phoenix, 1967. Appeared frequently on Shindig on TV.
PICTURES: The Cool Ones, True Grit, Norwood, Any Which Way You Can, Rock a Doodle (voice).
TELEVISION: Series: The Smothers Brothers Comedy Hour, The Glen Campbell Goodtime Hour, The Glen Campbell Music Show; many specials. Movie: Strange Homecoming.

CAMPBELL, MICHAEL L.
Executive. b. Knoxville, TN, Jan. 22, 1954. Worked for White Stores, Inc. in a management position until 1982. Founded first theatre venture, Premiere Cinemas in 1982. Premiere grew to 150 screens and was sold to Cinemark in 1989. Founded Regal Cinemas in 1989. President and CEO Regal Cinemas, Inc which has more than 3,200 screens (1998). Named Coopers & Lybrand regional entreprenuer of the year, 1993. Dir. NATO and serves on NATO executive committee.

CAMPBELL, NEVE
Actress. b. Guelph, Ontario, Canada, Oct. 3, 1973.
PICTURES: Paint Cans, The Dark, Love Child, The Craft, Scream, Simba's Pride (voice), Scream 2, Hairshirt, Wild Things, 54.
TELEVISION: Series: Catwalk, Party of Five. Movies: Web of Deceit, Baree, I Know My Son is Alive, The Forget-Me-Not Murders, The Canterville Ghost. Guest: The Kids in the Hall, Are You Afraid of the Dark?, Mad TV, Saturday Night Live.

CAMPBELL, WILLIAM
Actor. b. Newark, NJ, Oct. 30, 1926. e. Feagin Sch. of Drama. Appeared in summer stock; B'way before film debut.
PICTURES: The Breaking Point (debut, 1950), Breakthrough, Inside the Walls of Folsom Prison, Operation Pacific, The People Against O'Hara, Holiday for Sinners, Battle Circus, Small Town Girl, Code Two, The Big Leaguer, Escape from Fort Bravo, The High and the Mighty, The Fast and the Furious, Man Without a Star, Cell 2455— Death Row, Battle Cry, Running Wild, Man in the Vault, Backlash, Love Me Tender, Walk the Proud Land, Eighteen and Anxious, The Naked and the Dead, Money Women and Guns, The Sheriff of Fractured Jaw, Natchez Train, Night of Evil, The Young Racers, The Secret Invasion, Dementia 13, Hush Hush Sweet Charlotte, Blood Bath, Track of the Vampire, Pretty Maids All in a Row, Black Gunn, Dirty Mary Crazy Larry.
TELEVISION: Series: Cannonball, Dynasty, Crime Story. Pilot: The Heat: When You Lie Down With Dogs. Movie: Return of the Six Million Dollar Man and the Bionic Woman.

CAMPION, JANE
Director, Writer. b. Wellington, New Zealand, 1955. e. Victoria Univ. of Wellington (BA, anthropology, 1975), Sydney Coll. of Arts (BA, painting, 1979). Attendend Australian Sch. of Film & TV in early 1980's, where she debuted as dir. & writer with short film Peel (1982; Palme d'Or at Cannes Film Fest., 1986). Other short films: A Girl's Own Story, Passionless Moments, After Hours, Two Friends, Mishaps of Seduction & Conquest.
PICTURES: Director/Writer: Sweetie (feature debut, 1989; Australian Film Awards for Best Director & Film; LA Film Critics New Generation Award, American Indept. Spirit Award), An Angel at My Table (Venice Film Fest. Silver Lion Award, Indept. Spirit Award), The Piano (Academy Award, WGA, LA Film Critics, NY Film Critics, & Natl. Society of Film Critics Awards for best screenplay; LA Film Critics & NY Film Critics Awards for best director; Cannes Film Fest. Award for best film), The Portrait of a Lady, Holy Smoke.
TELEVISION: Series: Episode director: Dancing Daze.

CANBY, VINCENT
Journalist, Critic. b. Chicago, IL, July 27, 1924. e. Dartmouth Coll. Navy officer during WWII. Worked on newspapers in Paris and Chicago. Joined Quigley Publications in 1951 in editorial posts on Motion Picture Herald. Reporter for Weekly Variety 1959-1965. Joined New York Times film news staff, 1965; named film critic, 1969. Author: Living Quarters (1975); End of the War (play, 1978); Unnatural Scenery (1979); After All (play, 1981); The Old Flag (1984).

CANNELL, STEPHEN J.
Writer, Producer. b. Los Angeles, CA, Feb. 5, 1942. e. U. of Oregon, B.A., 1964. After coll. worked at father's decorating firm for 4 years while writing scripts in evening. Sold 1st script for Adam 12, 1966. Asked to serve as head writer at Universal Studios. Chief exec. officer, Stephen J. Cannell Prods. TV prod. co. he formed 1979. Also formed The Cannell Studios, parent co. 1986. Natl. chmn., Orton Dyslexia Society. Received Mystery Writers award 1975; 4 Writers Guild Awards. Acted in films: Identity Crisis, Posse.
TELEVISION: The Rockford Files (creator, writer, prod.; Emmy Award), The Jordan Chance, The Duke, Stone, 10 Speed and Brownshoe, Nightside, Midnight Offerings, The Greatest American Hero, The Quest, Them. Prod.: The A-Team, Hardcastle and McCormick, The Rousters, Riptide, Brothers-in-Law, Creator/Prod.: Baa Baa Black Sheep, Richie Brockelman, Hunter, Wise Guy, 21 Jump Street, J.J. Starbuck, Sonny Spoon, Sirens (co-exec. prod.), Unsub (exec. prod., writer, pilot), Booker (exec. prod.), Top of the Hill (exec. prod.), Scene of the Crime (exec.-prod., creator), The Commish, The Hat Squad, Traps, Greyhounds (exec. prod., writer), Hawkeye, Marker (exec. prod., creator), Renegade (exec. prod., creator), U.S. Customs Classified (exec. prod., host).

CANNON, DYAN
Actress. r.n. Samille Diane Friesen. b. Tacoma, WA, Jan. 4, 1937. e. U. of Washington. Studied with Sanford Meisner. Modelled before becoming actress. Directed, produced and wrote short film Number One (Acad. Award nom.).
THEATER: *B'way*: The Fun Couple, Ninety-Day Mistress. *Tour*: How to Succeed in Business Without Really Trying.
PICTURES: The Rise and Fall of Legs Diamond (debut, 1960), This Rebel Breed, Bob & Carol & Ted & Alice (Acad. Award nom.), Doctors' Wives, The Anderson Tapes, The Love Machine, The Burglars, Such Good Friends, Shamus, The Last of Sheila, Child Under a Leaf, Heaven Can Wait (Acad. Award nom.), Revenge of the Pink Panther, Honeysuckle Rose, Coast To Coast, Deathtrap, Author Author, Caddyshack II, The End of Innocence (also dir., prod., s.p.), The Pickle, Out to Sea, That Darn Cat.
TELEVISION: *Mini-Series*: Master of the Game. *Movies*: The Virginia Hill Story, Lady of the House, Having It All, Arthur the King, Jenny's War, Rock 'n' Roll Mom, Jailbirds, Christmas in Connecticut, Based on an Untrue Story, A Perry Mason Mystery: The Case of the Jealous Jokester. *Guest*: Playhouse 90.

CANNON, WILLIAM
Writer, Producer, Director. b. Toledo, OH, Feb. 11, 1937. e. Columbia Coll., B.A., 1959; M.B.A., 1962. Wrote, prod., dir., Square Root of Zero, Locarno and San Francisco Film Festivals, 1963-65. Distrib., at Doran Enterprises, Ltd. Publisher of Highlife and Movie Digest, 1978 and The Good Guys, 1987. Co-inventor: Cardz (TM), 1988. Author: Authorship: The Dynamic Principles of Writing Creatively, 1993; The Veteran, (novel) 1974; The Trojan Head (play), 1997.
THEATER: *Off-B'Way*: Death of a Salesman, Pirates of Penzance, 1960.
PICTURES: *Writer*: Skidoo, Brewster McCloud, Hex.
TELEVISION: *Writer*: Knots Landing, Heaven on Earth.

CANOVA, DIANA
Actress. b. West Palm Beach, FL, June 1, 1952. r.n. Diana Rivero. Daughter of actress Judy Canova and musician Filberto Rivero. NY theater: They're Playing Our Song (1981). People's Choice award, favorite female performer, 1981. On B'way in, Company. In film, The First Nudie Musical.
TELEVISION: *Series*: Dinah and Her New Best Friends, Soap, I'm a Big Girl Now, Foot in the Door, Throb, Home Free. *Guest*: Ozzie's Girls (debut), Happy Days, Love Boat, Fantasy Island, Hotel, Chico and the Man, Barney Miller, Murder She Wrote. *Movies*: The Love Boat II, With This Ring, Death of Ocean View Park, Night Partners.

CANTON, ARTHUR H.
Motion Picture Producer. b. New York, NY. e. NYU, Columbia U. Capt. USAF. Pres., Canton-Weiner Films, indep. foreign films importers, 1947; Van Gogh (Academy Award for best 2-reel short subject, 1949); MGM Pictures, eastern div. publicity mgr., executive liaison, advertising-publicity, Independent Productions; public relations executive, v.p.; pres., Blowitz, Thomas & Canton Inc., 1964; pres., Arthur H. Canton Co. Inc.; prod. exec., Warner Bros., 1968-70; advertising-publicity v.p., Columbia Pictures, 1971; exec. v.p. of advertising and publicity, Billy Jack Productions, 1974-76. Co-founder of Blowitz & Canton Co. Inc., 1976, chmn of bd. Pres. of Arthur H. Canton Co. Member Academy of Motion Picture Arts and Sciences. Now exec. v.p. of Filmroos.

CANTON, MARK
Executive. b. New York, NY, June 19, 1949. e. UCLA, 1978. v.p.; m.p. dev., MGM; 1979, exec. v.p., JP Organization; 1980, v.p. prod., Warner Bros.; named sr. v.p., 1983 and pres. worldwide theatrical prod. div., 1985; v.p. worldwide m.p. production, 1989; appointed chmn. of Columbia Pictures, 1991. Promoted to chmn. of Columbia TriStar Motion Pictures, 1994. Resigned, 1996.

CAPRA, FRANK, JR.
Executive. Son of famed director Frank Capra. Served in various creative capacities on TV series (Zane Grey Theatre, Gunsmoke, The Rifleman, etc.). Associate producer on theatrical films (Planet of the Apes, Play It Again Sam, Marooned, etc.). Joined Avco Embassy Pictures, 1981, as v.p., worldwide production. In July, 1981, became pres. of A-E. Resigned May, 1982 to become indep. producer. Now with Pinehurst Industry Studios, NC.
PICTURES: *Producer*: Tom Sawyer (assoc. prod.), Billy Jack Goes to Washington, Born Again, The Black Marble, An Eye for an Eye, Vice Squad, Firestarter, Marie, Waterproof. *Exec. prod.*: Death Before Dishonor.

CAPSHAW, KATE
Actress. b. Ft. Worth, TX, 1953. r.n. Kathleen Sue Nail. e. U. of Missouri. m. director Steven Spielberg. Taught school before moving to New York to try acting.
PICTURES: A Little Sex (debut, 1982), Indiana Jones and the Temple of Doom, Best Defense, Dreamscape, Windy City, Power, SpaceCamp, Black Rain, Love at Large, My Heroes Have Always Been Cowboys, Love Affair, Just Cause, Duke of Groove (short), How to Make an American Quilt, The Locusts.
TELEVISION: *Series*: The Edge of Night, Black Tie Affair. *Movies*: Missing Children: A Mother's Story, The Quick and the Dead, Her Secret Life, Internal Affairs, Next Door.

CARA, IRENE
Singer, Actress. b. New York, NY, March 18, 1959. Off-B'way shows include The Me Nobody Knows, Lotta. On B'way in Maggie Flynn, Ain't Misbehavin', Via Galactica. Received Academy Award for co-writing theme song from Flashdance, 1983.
THEATER: *B'way.*: Maggie Flynn, The Me Nobody Knows, Via Galactica, Got to Go Disco. *Off-B'way.*: Ain't Misbehavin'. *Regional*: Lotta, The Wiz, Jesus Christ Superstar. *Foreign*: Mo' Magic.
PICTURES: Aaron Loves Angela, Sparkle, Fame, D.C. Cab, City Heat, Certain Fury, Killing 'em Softly, Paradiso, Busted Up, Maximum Security, Happily Ever After (voice), The Magic Voyage (voice).
TELEVISION: *Series*: Hearts are Wild, Love of Life, The Electric Company. *Mini-Series*: Roots—The Next Generation. *Movies*: Guyana Tragedy, Sisters, For Us the Living, Gabriel's Fire. *Special*: Tribute to Martin Luther King, Jr., Bob Hope Thanksgiving Special, Tribute to Ray Charles.

CARDIFF, JACK
Cinematographer, Director. b. Yarmouth, Eng., Sept. 18, 1914. Early career as child actor, before becoming cinematographer, then dir. in 1958.
PICTURES: *Cinematographer*: A Matter of Life and Death (Stairway to Heaven), Black Narcissus (Acad. Award, 1947), The Red Shoes, Scott of the Antarctic, Black Rose, Under Capricorn, Pandora and the Flying Dutchman, The African Queen, The Magic Box, The Master of Ballantrae, The Barefoot Contessa, The Brave One, War and Peace, Legend of the Lost, The Prince and the Showgirl, The Vikings, The Journey, Fanny, Scalawag, Crossed Swords (The Prince and the Pauper), Death on the Nile, Avalanche Express, The Fifth Musketeer, A Man a Woman and a Bank, The Awakening, The Dogs of War, Ghost Story, The Wicked Lady, Scandalous, Conan the Destroyer, Cat's Eye, Rambo: First Blood II, Blue Velvet, Tai-Pan, Million Dollar Mystery. *Director*: Intent to Kill (debut, 1958), Beyond This Place, Scent of Mystery, Sons and Lovers, My Geisha, The Lion, The Long Ships, Young Cassidy (co-dir.), The Liquidator, Dark of the Sun, Girl on a Motorcycle, Penny Gold, The Mutations, Ride a Wild Pony.
TELEVISION: *Cinematographer*: The Far Pavillions, The Last Days of Pompeii.

CARDINALE, CLAUDIA
Actress. b. Tunis, No. Africa, April 15, 1939. Raised in Italy. Studied acting at Centro Sperimentale film school in Rome. Debuted 1956 in short French film Anneaux d'Or.
PICTURES: Goha (feature debut, 1957), Big Deal on Madonna Street, The Facts of Murder, Upstairs and Downstairs, The Battle of Austerlitz, Il Bell' Antonio, Rocco and His Brothers, Senilita, Girl With a Suitcase, The Love Makers, Cartouche, The Leopard, 8 1/2, Bebo's Girl, The Pink Panther, Circus World, Time of Indifference, The Magnificent Cuckold, Sandra, Blindfold, Lost Command, The Professionals, Don't Make Waves, Mafia, The Queens, Day of the Owl, The Hell With Heroes, Once Upon a Time in the West, A Fine Pair, The Butterfly Affair, The Red Tent, The Legend of Frenchy King, Conversation Piece, Escape to Athena, The Salamander, Careless, Immortal Bachelor, History, The French Revolution, Hiver '54, L'abbe Pierre, Mother, 588 Rue Paradis, Women Only Have One Thing on Their Minds...
TELEVISION: Princess Daisy, Jesus of Nazareth.

CAREY, HARRY JR.
Actor. b. Saugus, CA, May 16, 1921. e. Newhall, CA, public school, Black Fox Military Acad., Hollywood. m. Marilyn Fix. Son of Harry Carey. Appeared in Railroads on Parade at 1939-40 NY World's Fair. Summer stock, Skowhegan, ME., with father; page boy, NBC, New York; U.S. Navy 1942-45. Author of Company of Heroes - My Life as an Actor in the John Ford Stock Co.
PICTURES: Rolling Home (debut, 1946), Pursued, Red River, Three Godfathers, She Wore a Yellow Ribbon, Wagonmaster, Rio Grande, Copper Canyon, Warpath, Wild Blue Yonder, Monkey Business, San Antone, Island in the Sky, Gentlemen Prefer Blondes, Beneath the 12-Mile Reef, Silver Lode, The Outcast, Long Gray Line, Mister Roberts, House of Bamboo, The Great Locomotive Chase, The Searchers, The River's Edge, Rio Bravo, The Great Imposter, Two Rode Together, Alvarez Kelly, Bandolero, The Undefeated, Dirty Dingus Magee, Big Jake, Something Big, One More Train To Rob, Cahill: U.S. Marshal, Take a Hard Ride, Nickelodeon, The Long Riders, Endangered Species, Mask, Crossroads, The Whales of August, Cherry 2000, Illegally Yours, Breaking In, Bad Jim, Back to the Future Part III, The Exorcist III, Tombstone.

TELEVISION: *Movies*: Black Beauty, The Shadow Riders, Wild Times, Once Upon a Texas Train, Last Stand at Saber River. *Guest*: Gunsmoke, Rifleman, Laramie, Wagon Train, Have Gun Will Travel, John Ford's America, Legends of the American West. Disney *Series*: Spin & Marty. *Special*: Wyatt Earp: Return to Tombstone.

CARIOU, LEN
Actor. b. Winnipeg, Manitoba, Canada, Sept. 30, 1939. e. St. Paul's Col.
THEATER: *NY stage*: House of Atreus, Henry V, Applause (Theatre World Award), Night Watch, A Sorrow Beyond Dreams, Up from Paradise, A Little Night Music, Cold Storage, Sweeney Todd—The Demon Barber of Fleet Street (Tony Award), Master Class, Dance a Little Closer, Teddy & Alice, Measure for Measure, Mountain, The Speed of Darkness, Papa.
PICTURES: Drying Up the Streets, A Little Night Music, One Man, The Four Seasons, There Were Times Dear, Lady in White, Getting In, Never Talk to Strangers, Executive Decision.
TELEVISION: *Movies*: Who'll Save Our Children?, Madame X, The Four Seasons, Louisiana, Surviving, Killer in the Mirror, Miracle on Interstate 880, Class of '61, The Sea Wolf, Witness to the Execution, Love on the Run, The Man in the Attic, A Dream Is a Wish Your Heart Makes: The Annette Funicello Story, Derby, The Summer of Ben Tyler. *Series*: Swift Justice. *Specials*: The Master Builder, Juno and the Paycock, Kurt Vonnegut's Monkey House (All the King's Men).

CARLIN, GEORGE
Actor, Comedian. b. New York, NY, May 12, 1937. Stand-up comedian and recording artist. Recipient of 1972 Grammy Award for Best Comedy Album: FM & AM; 1993 Grammy Award for Best Comedy Album: Jammin'. Has released 15 comedy albums between 1960-90. Has guested on many TV shows including Talent Scouts, On B'way Tonight, Merv Griffin Show, Saturday Night Live. *Author*: Sometimes a Little Brain Damage Can Help (1984), Braindroppings (1997).
PICTURES: With Six You Get Eggroll, Car Wash, Americathon (narrator), Outrageous Fortune, Bill & Ted's Excellent Adventure, Bill and Ted's Bogus Journey, The Prince of Tides, Dogma.
TELEVISION: *Series*: Kraft Summer Music Hall, That Girl, Away We Go, Tony Orlando and Dawn, Shining Time Station, The George Carlin Show. *Movies*: Justin Case, Working Trash. *Specials*: George Carlin: Jammin' in New York, also appeared in 10 HBO comedy specials.

CARLINER, MARK
Producer.
PICTURES: Viva Max!, Heaven Help Us, Crossroads.
TELEVISION: *Movies*: A Death of Innocence, Revenge, Strangers in 7A, Nightmare, The Phoenix (pilot), Disaster at Silo 7 (also story), Stalin, George Wallace (Emmy Award, 1998). *Series*: The Phoenix. *Mini-series*: The Shining, Storm of the Century.

CARLINO, LEWIS JOHN
Writer, Director. b. New York, NY, Jan. 1, 1932. e. U. of Southern California. Early interest in theatre, specializing in writing 1-act plays. Winner of Obie award (off-B'way play). Won Rockefeller Grant for Theatre, the Int'l. Playwriting Competition from British Drama League, Huntington Hartford Fellowship.
THEATER: Cages, Telemachus Clay, The Exercise, Double Talk, Objective Case, Used Car for Sale, Junk Yard.
PICTURES: *Writer*: Seconds, The Brotherhood, The Fox (co-s.p.), A Reflection of Fear, The Mechanic (also prod.), Crazy Joe, The Sailor Who Fell From Grace With the Sea (also dir.), I Never Promised You a Rose Garden (co-s.p.), The Great Santini (also dir.), Resurrection, Class (dir. only), Haunted Summer.
TELEVISION: Honor Thy Father, In Search of America, Where Have All the People Gone?

CARLTON, RICHARD
Executive. b. New York, NY, Feb. 9, 1919. e. Columbia U., Pace Inst. Columbia Pictures 1935-41; U.S. Army 1941-45; National Screen Serv. 1945-51; Sterling Television 1951-54; U.M. & M. TV Corp. 1955; v.p. in charge of sales, Trans-Lux Television Corp., 1956; exec. v.p., Television Affiliates Corp., 1961; exec. v.p. Trans-Lux Television Corp.; v.p. Entertainment Div. Trans-Lux Corp., 1966. Pres., Schnur Appel, TV, Inc. 1970; Deputy Director, American Film Institute, 1973. Pres., Carlton Communications Corporation, 1982; exec. dir., International Council, National Academy of Television Arts and Sciences, 1983-93. Became writer/consultant, 1994.

CARLYLE, ROBERT
Actor. b. Glasgow, Scotland, April 14, 1961.
PICTURES: Silent Scream, Riff-Raff, Safe, Being Human, Priest, Go Now, Trainspotting, Carla's Song, Face, The Full Monty (BAFTA Award, Best Actor, 1997), Ravenous, Plunkett & MaCleane, Angela's Ashes.
TELEVISION: *Series*: Hamish Macbeth. *Mini-series*: Looking After Jo Jo.

CARMEN, JULIE
Actress. b. New York, NY, Apr. 4, 1954. Studied acting at Neighborhood Playhouse. On NY stage in The Creation of the Universe, Cold Storage, Zoot Suit. Also acted with INTAR and the New Conservatory Theater. Recipient of 1992 National Council of La Raza Pioneer Award.
PICTURES: Night of the Juggler, Gloria, Man on the Wall, Comeback, Blue City, The Penitent, The Milagro Beanfield War, Fright Night 2, Kiss Me a Killer, Paint It Black, Cold Heaven, In the Mouth of Madness, Africa.
TELEVISION: *Series*: Condo, Falcon Crest. *Mini-Series*: True Women. *Movies*: Can You Hear the Laughter?: The Story of Freddie Prinze, Three Hundred Miles for Stephanie, She's in the Army Now, Fire on the Mountain, Neon Empire, Manhunt: Search for the Night Stalker, Billy the Kid, Drug Wars: The Cocaine Cartel, Finding the Way Home, Curacao, The Omen, Gargantua. *Mini-Series*: True Women.

CARMICHAEL, IAN
Actor. b. Hull, England, June 18, 1920. e. Scarborough Coll., Bromsgrove Sch. Stage debut: R.U.R. 1939. B'way debut: Boeing-Boeing (1965). One of the top ten British money making stars Motion Picture Herald Fame Poll 1957, 1958.
PICTURES: Bond Street (debut, 1948), Trottie True (Gay Lady), Mr. Prohack, Time Gentlemen Please, Ghost Ship!, Miss Robin Hood, Meet Mr. Lucifer, Betrayed, The Colditz Story, Storm Over the Nile, Simon and Laura, Private's Progress, The Big Money, Brothers in Law, Lucky Jim, Happy Is the Bride, Left Right and Center, I'm All Right Jack, School for Scoundrels, Light Up the Sky, Double Bunk, The Amorous Prawn, Hide and Seek, Heavens Above, The Case of the 44's, Smashing Time, The Magnificent Seven Deadly Sins, From Beyond the Grave, The Lady Vanishes, Dark Obsession (Diamond Skulls).
TELEVISION: New Faces, Twice Upon a Time, Passing Show, Tell Her The Truth, Lady Luck, Give My Regards to Leicester Square, Jill Darling, Don't Look Now, Regency Room, Globe Revue, Off the Record, Here and Now, The Girl at the Next Table, Gilt and Gingerbread, The Importance of Being Earnest, Simon and Laura, 90 Years On, The World of Wooster (series), The Last of the Big Spenders, The Coward Revue, Odd Man In, Bachelor Father (series), Lord Peter Wimsey (series), Alma Mater, Comedy Tonight, Song by Song, Country Calendar, Down at the Hydro, Obituaries, Strathblair, The Great Kandinsky. *Guest*: Under The Hammer, Bramwell.

CARNEY, ART
Actor. b. Mt. Vernon, NY, Nov. 4, 1918. Started as band singer with the Horace Heidt Orchestra. On many radio shows before and after war. Served in U.S. Army, 1944-45. Regular on Morey Amsterdam's radio show which eventually moved to television.
THEATER: The Rope Dancers. B'way: Take Her She's Mine, The Odd Couple, Lovers, The Prisoner of Second Avenue.
PICTURES: Pot o' Gold (debut, 1941), The Yellow Rolls Royce, A Guide for the Married Man, Harry and Tonto (Academy Award for Best Actor, 1974), W. W. and the Dixie Dancekings, Won Ton Ton the Dog Who Saved Hollywood, The Late Show, Scott Joplin, House Calls, Movie Movie, Ravagers, Sunburn, Going in Style, Defiance, Roadie, Steel, St. Helens, Take This Job and Shove It, Better Late Than Never, Firestarter, The Naked Face, The Muppets Take Manhattan, Night Friend, Last Action Hero.
TELEVISION: *Series*: The Morey Amsterdam Show, Cavalcade of Stars, Henry Morgan's Great Talent Hunt, The Jackie Gleason Show (1951-55; 2 Emmy Awards: 1953, 1954), The Honeymooners (Emmy Award, 1955), The Jackie Gleason Show (1956-57), The Jackie Gleason Show (1966-70; 2 Emmy Awards: 1967, 1968), Lanigan's Rabbi. *Guest*: Studio One, Kraft Theatre, Playhouse 90, Alfred Hitchcock Presents (Safety for the Witness), Sid Caesar Show, Twilight Zone (Night of the Meek), Bob Hope Chrysler Theater (Timothy Heist), Danny Kaye Show, Men From Shiloh, Batman, Carol Burnett Show, Jonathan, Winters Show, Faerie Tale Theatre (The Emperor's New Clothes). *Specials*: Peter and the Wolf, Harvey, Our Town, Charley's Aunt, Art Carney Meets the Sorcerer's Apprentice, Very Important People, Jane Powell Special: Young at Heart, Man in the Dog Suit, The Great Santa Claus Switch. *Movies*: The Snoop Sisters, Death Scream, Katherine, Letters From Frank, Terrible Joe Moran (Emmy Award, 1984), The Night They Saved Christmas, A Doctor's Story, Izzy and Moe, Blue Yonder, Where Pigeons Go to Die.

CARNEY, FRED
Producer, Director. b. Brooklyn, NY, June 10, 1914. e. Mt. Vernon H.S., 1932. Actor on B'way & summer stock; prod. mgr. for radio show, Truth or Consequences; asst. to prod.-dir of Kraft TV Theatre, 3 yrs.; dir., Kraft, Pond's Show; creator-prod., Medical Horizons; dir., Lux Video Theatre; prod. commercials at Cunningham & Walsh. Assoc. Prod. Everybody's Talking for ABC-TV. Ass't. exec. dir., Hollywood Chpt., Nat'l Acad. TV; Assoc. prod. 40th Acad. Award show, ABC-TV Arts & Sciences.

CARON, GLENN GORDON
Writer, Director, Producer. Started as tv writer for James L. Brooks, Steve Gordon. Prod. of tv series Breaking Away. Formed prod. co., Picturemaker Productions, 1985.
PICTURES: *Director*: Clean and Sober (debut, 1988), Wilder Napalm, Love Affair.
TELEVISION: *Series*: Moonlighting (creator, prod., writer).

CARON, LESLIE
Actress, Dancer. b. Paris, France, July 1, 1931. e. Convent of Assumption, Paris; Nat'l Conservatory of Dance, Paris 1947-50; joined Roland Petit's Ballet des Champs Elysees where she was spotted by Gene Kelly who chose her as his co-star in An American in Paris. Also with Ballet de Paris.
THEATER: Orvet, Ondine, Gigi (London), 13 Rue de l'Amour, The Rehearsal, Women's Games, On Your Toes, One For the Tango.
PICTURES: An American in Paris (debut, 1951), The Man With a Cloak, Glory Alley, The Story of Three Loves, Lili (Acad. Award nom.; BFA Award), The Glass Slipper, Daddy Long Legs, Gaby, Gigi, The Doctor's Dilemma, The Man Who Understood Women, The Subterraneans, Austerlitz, Fanny, Guns of Darkness, Three Fables of Love, The L-Shaped Room (Acad. Award nom.; BFA Award), Father Goose, A Very Special Favor, Promise Her Anything, Is Paris Burning?, Head of the Family, The Beginners, Madron, Chandler, Purple Night, Valentino, The Man Who Loved Women, Golden Girl, Contract, Imperative, The Unapproachable, Dangerous Moves, Warriors and Prisoners, Courage Mountain, Damage, Funny Bones, Let It Be Me, The Reef.
TELEVISION: *Mini-Series*: QB VIII, Master of the Game. *Guest*: Love Boat, Tales of the Unexpected, Carola, Falcon Crest. *Movie*: The Man Who Lived at the Ritz. *Special*: The Sealed Train. *Series*: The Great War.

CARPENTER, CARLETON
Actor. b. Bennington, VT, July 10, 1926 e. Bennington H.S., Northwestern U. (summer scholarship). Began career with magic act, clubs, camps, hospitals in New Eng.; then toured with carnival; first N.Y. stage appearance in Bright Boy. Appeared in nightclubs, radio; as magazine model. TV debut, Campus Hoopla show. Screen debut Lost Boundaries (also wrote song for film, I Wouldn't Mind). Member: SAG, AFTRA, AEA, ASCAP, Dramatists Guild, Mystery Writers of Amer. (ex.-treas., bd. mem.).
THEATER: *NY*: Career Angel, Three To Make Ready, The Magic Touch, The Big People, Out of Dust, John Murray Anderson's Almanac, Hotel Paradiso, Box of Watercolors, A Stage Affair, Greatest Fairy Story Ever Told, Something for the Boys, Boys in the Band, Dylan, Hello Dolly!, Light Up the Sky, Murder at Rutherford House, Rocky Road, Apollo of Bellac, Sweet Adaline, Geo. White's Scandals, Life on the L.I.E. Miss Stanwyck is Still in Hiding, Good Ole Fashioned Revue, What is Turning Gilda So Grey?, Crazy for You, Many Thousands Gone.
PICTURES: Lost Boundries (debut, 1949), Summer Stock, Father of the Bride, Three Little Words, Two Weeks With Love, The Whistle at Eaton Falls, Fearless Fagan, Sky Full of Moon, Vengeance Valley, Up Periscope, Take the High Ground, Some of My Best Friends Are..., The Prowler, Simon, Byline, Cauliflower Cupids, The Bar, Carnegie Hall.
TELEVISION: Over 6,000 shows (live & filmed) since 1945.

CARPENTER, JOHN
Director, Writer, Composer. b. Carthage, NY, Jan. 16, 1948. e. Western Kentucky U., U. of Southern California. At U.S.C. became involved in film short, Resurrection of Bronco Billy, which won Oscar as best live-action short of 1970. Also at U.S.C. began directing what ultimately became Dark Star, science fiction film that launched his career.
PICTURES: *Director*: Dark Star (also co-s.p., music), Assault on Precinct 13 (also s.p., music), Halloween (also s.p., music), The Fog (also co-s.p., music), Escape from New York (also co-s.p., music), The Thing, Christine (also music), Starman, Big Trouble in Little China (also music), Prince of Darkness (also music, and s.p. as Martin Quatermass), They Live (also music, and s.p. as Frank Armitage), Memoirs of an Invisible Man, In the Mouth of Madness (also co-music), Village of the Damned (also s.p., co-music), Escape From L.A, Vampires, (also s.p. and music), Meltdown (also s.p. only). *Also*: Eyes of Laura Mars (co-sp., co-story), Halloween II (co- s.p., co-prod., co-music), Halloween III: Season of the Witch (co-prod., co-music), The Philadelphia Experiment (co-exec. prod.), Black Moon Rising (co-s.p., story), The Silence of the Hams (actor).
TELEVISION: *Movies* (director): Elvis, Someone Is Watching Me (also writer), John Carpenter Presents Body Bags (also co-exec. prod., actor). Movies (writer): Zuma Beach, El Diablo, Blood River.

CARPENTER, ROBERT L.
Executive. b. Memphis, TN, March 20, 1927. Joined Universal Pictures in 1949 as booker in Memphis exchange; promoted to salesman, 1952, then branch mgr., 1958; 1963 named Los Angeles branch mgr. 1971, moved to New York to become asst. to gen. sales mgr. Named gen. sales mgr. 1972, replacing Henry H. Martin when latter became pres. of Universal. Left in 1982 to become consultant and producer's rep. 1984, joined Cannon Releasing Corp. as east. div. mgr. Left in 1989 to become consultant and producers rep.

CARPENTER, RUSSELL
Cinematographer, Actor.
PICTURES: The Wizard of Speed and Time (also actor), Lady in White, Critters 2: The Main Course, Cameron's Closet, Solar Crisis, Lionheart, Death Warrant, The Perfect Weapon, The Lawnmower Man, Pet Sematary II, Hard Target, True Lies, The Indian in the Cupboard, T2 3D: Battle Across Time, Titanic (Acad. Award, Chicago Film Crits. Award, Best Cinematography, 1997), Ghosts, Money Talks, The Negotiator.
TELEVISION: *Movies*: Attack of the 50 Ft. Woman.

CARR, MARTIN
Producer, Director, Writer. b. New York, NY, Jan. 20, 1932. e. Williams Coll. Recepient of: 5 Emmys, 3 Peabody awards, 2 DuPont Col. Journalism awards, Robert F. Kennedy award, Sidney Hillman award, Writers Guild Award.
TELEVISION: PBS Smithsonian World (exec. prod.). For CBS prod., wrote and dir. CBS Reports: Hunger in America, The Search for Ulysses, Gauguin in Tahiti, Five Faces of Tokyo, Dublin Through Different Eyes. For NBC prod., wrote and dir. NBC White Paper: Migrant, NBC White Paper: This Child Is Rated X. Also directed drama, dance, music, opera specials and daytime serial for CBS-TV. ABC Close-Up. The Culture Thieves. PRS Global Paper: Waging Peace, ABC News 20/20; NBC, The Human Animal.

CARRADINE, DAVID
Actor. b. Hollywood, CA, Dec. 8, 1936. e. San Francisco State U. Son of late actor John Carradine. Brother of actors Keith and Robert Carradine. Began career in local repertory; first TV on Armstrong Circle Theatre and East Side, West Side; later TV includes Shane series and Kung Fu; N.Y. stage in The Deputy, Royal Hunt of the Sun (Theatre World Award).
PICTURES: Taggart, Bus Riley's Back in Town, The Violent Ones, Young Billy Young, The McMasters, Heaven with a Gun, The Bood Buys and the Bad Guys, Macho Callahan, Boxcar Bertha, Mean Streets, House of Dracula's Daughter, Death Race 2000, Cannonball, Bound for Glory, Thunder and Lightning, A Look at Liv, The Serpent's Egg, Dray Lady Down, Deathsport, Fast Charlie the Moonbeam Rider, Circle of Iron, Cloud Dancer, The Long Rides, Americana, Trick or Treats, Safari 3000, Q, Lone Wolf McQuade, The Warrior and the Sorceress, Rio Abajo, A Distant Scream, Armed Response, P.O.W. the Escape, The Misfit Brigade, Wizards of the Lost Kingdom II, Warlords, Open Fire, Fatal Secret, Crime Zone, Animal Protector, Thry This One for Size, Tropical Snow, Sundown: The Vampire in Retreat, Nowhere to Run, The Mad Bunch, Las Huellas del lince, Crime of Crimes, Thing Big, Sonny Boy, Night Children, Midnight Fear, Future Zone, Future Force, Evil Toons, Dune Warriors, Bird on a Wire, Karate Cop, Field of Fire, Capital Punishment, Waxwork II: Lost in Time, Night Rhythms, Martial Law, Double Trouble, Distant Justice, Animal Instincts, Roadside Prophets, Kill Zine, Dead Center, The Rage, Full Blast, Crossroads of Destiny, Light Speed, Drop-Dead, The New Swiss Family Robinson, American Reel.
TELEVISION: *Movies*: Maybe I'll Come Home in the Spring, Kung Fu (1972 pilot), Mr. Horn, Johnny Belinda, Gaugin the Savage, High Noon Part II, Jealousy, The Bad Seed, Kung Fu: The Movie, Oceans of Fire, Six Against the Rock, The Cover Girl & the Cop, I Saw What You Did, The Cover Girl and the Cop, Deadly Surveillance, Brotherhood of the Gun, The Gambler Returns: Luck of the Draw, Kung Fu: The Legend Continues, The Eagle and the Horse, Lost Treasure of Dos Santos, Last Stand at Saber River. *Mini-series*: North & South Books I & II. *Series*: Shane, Kung Fu, Kung Fu: The Legend Continues. Guest: Darkroom, Amazing Stories.

CARRADINE, KEITH
Actor. b. San Mateo, CA, Aug. 8, 1949. e. Colorado State U. Daughter is actress Martha Plimpton. Son of late actor John Carradine, brother of David and Robert Carradine. First break in rock opera Hair.
THEATER: Wake Up It's Time to Go to Bed, Foxfire, The Will Rogers Follies.
PICTURES: A Gunfight (debut, 1971), McCabe and Mrs. Miller, Hex, Emperor of the North Pole, Thieves Like Us, Antoine et Sebastien, Run Joe Run, Idaho Transfer, Nashville (also composed songs; Acad. Award for best song: I'm Easy, 1975), You and Me, Lumiere, Welcome to L.A. (also composed songs), Duellists, Pretty Baby, Sgt. Pepper's Lonely Heart Club Band (cameo), Old Boyfriends, An Almost Perfect Affair, The Long Riders, Southern Comfort, Choose Me, Maria's Lovers (also composed song), Trouble in Mind, The Inquiry (The Investigation), Backfire, The Moderns, Street of No Return, Cold Feet, Daddy's Dyin'...Who's Got the Will?, The Ballad of the Sad Cafe, Crisscross, The Bachelor, Andre, Mrs. Parker and the Vicious Circle, The Tie That Binds, Wild Bill, A Thousand Acres.
TELEVISION: *Movies*: Man on a String, Kung Fu, The Godchild, A Rumor of War, Scorned and Swindled, A Winner Never Quits, Murder Ordained, Eye on the Sparrow, Blackout, Stones for Ibarra, My Father My Son, The Revenge of Al Capone, Judgment, Payoff, In the Best of Families: Marriage Pride & Madness, Is There Life Out There?, Trial by Fire *Mini-Series*: Chiefs. *Guest*: Bonanza, Love American Style.

CARRADINE, ROBERT
Actor. b. Hollywood, CA, March 24, 1954. Son of late actor John Carradine; brother of Keith and David Carradine.
PICTURES: The Cowboys (debut, 1972), Mean Streets, Aloha Bobby and Rose, Jackson County Jail, The Pom Pom Girls, Cannonball, Massacre at Central High, Joyride, Orca, Blackout, Coming Home, The Long Riders, The Big Red One, Heartaches, Tag: The Assassination Game, Wavelength, Revenge of the Nerds, Just the Way You Are, Number One With a Bullet, Revenge of the Nerds II: Nerds in Paradise, Buy and Cell, All's Fair, Rude Awakening, The Player, Bird of Prey, Escape From L.A.
TELEVISION: Series: The Cowboys. Movies: Footsteps, Rolling Man, Go Ask Alice, The Hatfields and the McCoys, The Survival of Dana, The Sun Also Rises, Monte Carlo, The Liberators, I Saw What You Did, The Incident, Clarence, Doublecrossed, Revenge of the Nerds III: The Next Generation, Body Bags, The Disappearance of Christina, Revenge of the Nerds IV: Nerds in Love (also co-prod.), A Part of the Family. Guest: Alfred Hitchcock Presents (1985), The Hitchhiker, Twilight Zone (1986). Specials: Disney's Totally Minnie, As Is.

CARRERA, BARBARA
Actress. b. Nicaragua, Dec. 31, 1951. Fashion model before film career; had part in film Puzzle of a Downfall Child.
PICTURES: The Master Gunfighter, Embryo, The Island of Dr. Moreau, When Time Ran Out, Condorman, I the Jury, Lone Wolf McQuade, Never Say Never Again, Wild Geese II, The Underachievers, Love at Stake, Wicked Stepmother, Loverboy, Spanish Rose, Night of the Archer, Tryst, Oh No Not Her (Love Is All There Is), Moscow Connection, Ghost Ships of the Kalahari, Love Is All There Is, Illusion of Infinity.
TELEVISION: Mini-Series: Centennial, Masada, Emma: Queen of the South Seas. Series: Dallas. Movies: Sins of the Past, Murder in Paradise, Lakota Moon, The Rockford Files. Guest: Fortune Hunter

CARRERE, TIA
Actress. r.n. Althea Janairo. b. Honolulu, HI, 1967. Was prof. model before turning to acting. Received NATO/ShoWest award for Female Star of 1994.
PICTURES: Zombie Nightmare (debut, 1987), Aloha Summer, Fatal Mission, Instant Karma, Showdown in Little Tokyo, Harley Davidson and the Marlboro Man, Wayne's World, Rising Sun, Wayne's World 2, True Lies, Jury Duty, My Generation, The Immortals, Hollow Point, Kull the Conqueror, Scar City, 20 Dates.
TELEVISION: Series: General Hospital. Mini-Series: James Clavell's Noble House. Movies: The Road Raiders, Fine Gold, Natural Enemy. Guest: The A-Team, MacGyver, Tales From the Crypt.

CARREY, JIM
Actor. b. Newmarket, Ontario, Canada, Jan. 17, 1962. Began performing act at Toronto comedy clubs while teenager. Moved to LA at 19, performing at the Comedy Store.
PICTURES: Finders Keepers (debut, 1984), Once Bitten, Peggy Sue Got Married, The Dead Pool, Earth Girls Are Easy, Pink Cadillac, High Strung, Ace Ventura: Pet Detective (also co-s.p.), The Mask, Dumb and Dumber, Batman Forever, Ace Ventura: When Nature Calls, The Cable Guy, Liar Liar.
TELEVISION: Series: The Duck Factory, In Living Color. Movies: Mickey Spillane's Mike Hammer—Murder Takes All, Doin' Time on Maple Drive. Special: Jim Carrey's Unnatural Act. Canadian TV: Introducing Janet, Copper Mountain: A Club Med Experience.

CARROLL, DIAHANN
Actress, Singer. r.n. Carol Diahann Johnson. b. Bronx, NY, July 17, 1935. r.n. Carol Diahann Johnson. m. singer Vic Damone. Started singing as teen, winning 1st place on tv's Chance of a Lifetime talent show resulting in engagement at Latin Quarter nightclub in New York. Autobiography: Diahann! (1986).
THEATER: B'way: House of Flowers, No Strings (Tony Award, 1962), Agnes of God.
PICTURES: Carmen Jones (debut, 1954), Porgy and Bess, Goodbye Again, Paris Blues, Hurry Sundown, The Split, Claudine (Acad. Award nom.), The Five Heartbeats, Eve's Bayou.
TELEVISION: Series: Julia, The Diahann Carroll Show, Dynasty. Movies: Death Scream, I Know Why the Caged Bird Sings, Sister Sister, From the Dead of Night, Murder in Black and White, A Perry Mason Mystery: The Case of the Lethal Lifestyle. The Sweetest Gift. Mini-Series: Roots: The Next Generations; many specials; guest appearances incl. The Naked City, Andy Williams, Judy Garland, Dean Martin Shows.

CARROLL, GORDON
Producer. b. Baltimore, MD, Feb. 2, 1928. e. Princeton U. Advtg. exec., Foote, Cone & Belding, 1954-58; Ent. industry, Seven Arts Prods., 1958-61; v.p., prod., Jalem Prods., 1966-1969; independent producer to present.
PICTURES: How to Murder Your Wife, Luv, Cool Hand Luke, The April Fools, Pat Garrett and Billy the Kid, Alien, Blue Thunder, The Best of Times, Aliens, Red Heat, Alien 3, Alien: Resurrection.

CARROLL, PAT
Actress. b. Shreveport, LA, May 5, 1927. e. Immaculate Heart Coll., L.A, Catholic U., Washington, DC. Joined U.S. Army in capacity of Civilian Actress Technician. Night club entertainer in N.Y., 1950.
THEATER: Catch a Star (debut, 1955), Gertrude Stein Gertrude Stein (Drama Desk, Outer Critics Circle, Grammy Awards), Dancing in the End Zone, The Show Off. Shakespeare Theatre at the Folger: Romeo and Juliet (Helen Hayes Award), The Merry Wives of Windsor (Helen Hayes Award), Mother Courage (Helen Hayes Award), H.M.S. Pinafore, Volpone.
PICTURES: With Six You Get Eggroll, The Brothers O'Toole, The Last Resort, The Little Mermaid (voice).
TELEVISION: Series: Red Buttons Show, Saturday Night Revue, Caesar's Hour (Emmy Award, 1957), Masquerade Party (panelist), Keep Talking, You're in the Picture (panelist), Danny Thomas Show, Getting Together, Busting Loose, The Ted Knight Show, She's the Sheriff. Specials: Cinderella, Gertrude Stein. Guest: Carol Burnett, Danny Kaye, Red Skelton, many others. Movie: Second Chance.

CARSEY, MARCY
Producer. b. Weymouth, MA, Nov. 21, 1944. e. Univ. NH. Was actress in tv commercials, tour guide at Rockefeller Center. Served as exec. story editor, Tomorrow Ent., 1971-74; sr. v.p. for prime time series, ABC-TV, 1978-71; founded Carsey Prods., 1981; owner, Carsey-Werner Co., 1982-.
TELEVISION: Series (exec. prod.): Oh Madeline, The Cosby Show, A Different World, Roseanne, Chicken Soup, Grand, Davis Rules, Frannie's Turn, You Bet Your Life (synd.), Grace Under Fire, Cybill, Cosby (1996-), Men Behaving Badly, Townies, Damon. Pilots: Callahan, I Do I Don't. Special: Carol Carl Whoopi and Robin. Movie: Single Bars Single Women.

CARSON, JEANNIE
Actress. b. Yorkshire, England, 1928. Became Amer. citizen, 1966. Founded Hyde Park Festival Theatre with husband William "Biff" McGuire, 1979. Has taught a musical drama class at U. of WA. Awards: TV Radio Mirror, 1st Recipient of the Variety Club Theatre Award in England.
THEATER: U.K.: Ace of Clubs, Love From Judy, Starlight Roof, Casino Reviews, Aladdin. U.S.: The Sound of Music, Blood Red Roses, Finian's Rainbow (revival). Tours: Camelot, 110 in the Shade, Cactus Flower. Also extensive work with the Seattle Repertory Theatre as actress, and dir. with Seattle Bathhouse Theatre.
PICTURES: A Date with a Dream (debut, 1948), Love in Pawn, As Long as They're Happy, An Alligator Named Daisy, Mad Little Island (Rockets Galore), Seven Keys.
TELEVISION: Best Foot Forward, Little Women, Berkeley Square, The Rivals, Frank Sinatra Show, Heidi, What Every Woman Knows, Jimmy Durante Show, Pat Boone Show, A Kiss for Cinderella. Series: Hey Jeannie, Jeannie Carson Show.

CARSON, JOHNNY
Host, Comedian. b. Corning, IA, Oct. 23, 1925. e. U. of Nebraska, B.A. 1949. U.S. Navy service during WWII; announcer with station KFAB, Lincoln, Neb.; WOW radio-TV, Omaha, 1948; announcer, KNXT-TV, Los Angeles, 1950; then hosted own program, Carson's Cellar (1951-53); latter resulted in job as writer for Red Skelton Show. 1958 guest hosting for Jack Paar on The Tonight Show led to his becoming regular host 4 years later. President, Carson Productions. Recipient: ATAS Governor's Award, 1980. Author: Happiness Is a Dry Martini (1965).
PICTURES: Movies: Looking for Love, Cancel My Reservation.
TELEVISION: Series: Earn Your Vacation (emcee; 1954), The Johnny Carson Show (daytime, 1955; later moved to nighttime, 1955-56), Who Do You Trust? (1957-62), The Tonight Show Starring Johnny Carson (1962-92). Guest: Playhouse 90, U.S. Steel Hour, Get Smart, Here's Lucy, etc. Pilot: Johnny Come Lately.

CARTER, CHRIS
Producer, Composer, Writer, Director. b. Bellflower, CA, Oct. 13, 1957.
PICTURES: The X Files: Fight the Future.
TELEVISION: Producer/Composer/Writer/Director: In the Shadow of the Sun, The B.R.A.T. Patrol, Rags to Riches (co-prod. only), Millenium (also creator), The X-Files (also creator), X-Files: The Movie.

CARTER, DIXIE
Actress. b. McLemoresville, TN, May 25, 1939. m. actor Hal Holbrook. e. U. of Tennessee, Knoxville, Rhodes Coll.; Memphis, Memphis State U. Off-B'way debut, A Winter's Tale with NY Shakespeare Fest (1963). London debut, Buried Inside Extra (1983). Lincoln Center musicals: The King & I, Carousel, The Merry Widow. Video: Dixie Carter's Unworkout.
THEATER: Pal Joey (1976 revival), Jesse and the Bandit Queen (Theatre World Award), Fathers and Sons, Taken in Marriage, A Coupla White Chicks Sitting Around Talking, Buried Inside Extra, Sextet, Pal Joey.
PICTURE: Going Berserk.
TELEVISION: Series: The Edge of Night, On Our Own, Out of the Blue, Filthy Rich, Diff'rent Strokes, Designing Women. Movies: OHMS, The Killing of Randy Webster, Dazzle, Gambler V: Playing for Keeps, A Perry Mason Mystery: The Case of the Lethal Lifestyle, Gone in the Night.

CARTER, JACK
Actor, r.n. Jack Chakrin. b. New York, NY, June 24, 1923. e. New Utrecht H.S., Brooklyn Coll., Feagin Sch. of Dramatic Arts. Worked as comm. artist for adv. agencies. Debut B'way in Call Me Mister, 1947; starred in TV Jack Carter Show, NBC Sat. Nite Revue. Hosted first televised Tony Awards. Seen on most major variety, dram. programs, incl. Ed Sullivan Show. Emmy nom. 1962 for Dr. Kildare seg. Played most major nightclubs. On B'way in Top Banana, Mr. Wonderful, Dir. several Lucy Shows. TV incl. specials, HA Comedy Special, Top Banana, Girl Who Couldn't Lose.
PICTURES: The Horizontal Lieutenant, Viva Las Vegas, The Extraordinary Seaman, The Resurrection of Zachary Wheeler, Red Nights, Hustle, The Amazing Dobermans, Alligator, The Octagon, History of the World Part 1, Heartbeeps (voice), The Arena, Deadly Embrace, In the Heat of Passion, Social Suicide, The Opposite Sex, W.A.R., Natl. Lampoon's Last Resort.
TELEVISION: Series: American Minstrels of 1949, Cavalcade of Stars, The Jack Carter Show. Movies: The Lonely Profession, The Family Rico, The Sex Symbol, The Great Houdinis, The Last Hurrah, Human Feelings, Rainbow, The Gossip Columnist, The Hustler of Muscle Beach, For the Love of It. Guest: Blossom, Empty Nest, Nurses, Murder She Wrote, Time Trax, Burke's Law, New Adventures of Superman.

CARTER, LYNDA
Actress. b. Phoenix, AZ. r.n. Lynda Jean Cordoba. e. Arcadia H.S. Wrote songs and sang professionally in Ariz. from age of 15; later toured 4 yrs. with rock 'n roll band. Won beauty contests in Ariz. and became Miss World-USA 1973. Dramatic training with Milton Katselas, Greta Seacat, and Sandra Seacat.
PICTURE: Lightning in a Bottle.
TELEVISION: Series: Wonder Woman, Hawkeye. Specials: The New Original Wonder Woman Specials; 5 variety specials, Hawkeye. Movies: The New Original Wonder Woman, A Matter of Wife... and Death, Baby Brokers, Last Song, Hotline, Rita Hayworth: The Love Goddess, Stillwatch (also exec. prod.), Mickey Spillane's Mike Hammer, Murder Takes All, Danielle Steel's Daddy, Posing: Inspired By 3 Real Stories, She Woke Up Pregnant, A Secret Between Friends, Family Blessings, A Prayer in the Dark.

CARTER, NELL
Actress. b. Birmingham, AL. Sept. 13, 1948.
THEATER: Hair, Dude, Don't Bother Me I Can't Cope, Jesus Christ Superstar, Ain't Misbehavin' (Tony & Theatre World Awards, 1978), Ain't Misbehaving (1988 revival), Hello Dolly! (L.A.).
PICTURES: Hair, Quartet, Back Roads, Modern Problems, Bebe's Kids (voice), The Grass Harp, The Crazysitter, The Proprietor, Fakin' Da Funk.
TELEVISION: Series: Lobo, Gimme a Break, You Take the Kids, Hangin' With Mr. Cooper. Specials: Baryshnikov on Broadway, The Big Show, An NBC Family Christmas, Ain't Misbehavin' (Emmy Award), Christmas in Washington, Nell Carter, Never Too Old To Dream, Morton's By the Bay (pilot). Movies: Cindy, Maid for Each Other, Final Shot: The Hank Gathers Story.

CARTLIDGE, WILLIAM
Director, Producer. b. England, June 16, 1942. e. Highgate Sch. Ent. m.p. ind. 1959. Early career in stills dept., Elstree Studio. Later worked as an asst. dir. on The Young Ones, Summer Holiday, The Punch & Judy Man, The Naked Edge. As 1st asst. dir. on such pictures as Born Free, Alfie, You Only Live Twice, The Adventurers, Young Winston, Friends. As assoc. prod., Paul and Michelle, Seven Nights in Japan, The Spy Who Loved Me, Moonraker. Prod.: Educating Rita, Not Quite Paradise, Consuming Passions, Dealers, The Playboys. Producer of Haunted, Incognito.

CARTWRIGHT, VERONICA
Actress. b. Bristol, Eng., 1949. m. writer-dir. Richard Compton. Sister is actress Angela Cartwright. Began career as child actress. On stage in, The Hands of Its Enemies (Mark Taper Forum, LA 1984), The Triplet Connection (off-B'way).
PICTURES: In Love and War (debut, 1958), The Children's Hour, The Birds, Spencer's Mountain, One Man's Way, Inserts, Goin' South, Invasion of the Body Snatchers, Alien, Nightmares, The Right Stuff, My Man Adam, Flight of the Navigator, Wisdom, The Witches of Eastwick, Valentino Returns, False Identity, Man Trouble, Candyman: Farewell to the Flesh.
TELEVISION: Series: Daniel Boone. Guest: Leave It to Beaver, Twilight Zone. Mini-series: Robert Kennedy and His Times. Movies: Guyana Tragedy—The Story of Jim Jones, The Big Black Pill, Prime Suspect, Intimate Encounters, Desperate for Love, A Son's Promise, Hitler's Daughter, Dead in the Water, It's Nothing Personal, My Brother's Keeper. Specials: Who Has Seen the Wind?, Bernice Bobs Her Hair, Tell Me Not the Mournful Numbers (Emmy Award), Joe Dancer, Abby My Love, On Hope.

CARUSO, DAVID
Actor. b. Queens, NY, Jan. 7, 1956.
PICTURES: Without Warning (debut, 1980), An Officer and a Gentleman, First Blood, Thief of Hearts, Blue City, China Girl, Twins, King of New York, Hudson Hawk, Mad Dog and Glory, Kiss of Death, Jade.
TELEVISION: Series: N.Y.P.D. Blue, Michael Hayes (also prod.). Movies: Crazy Times, The First Olmypics—Athens 1896, Into the Homeland, Rainbow Drive, Mission of the Shark, Judgment Day: The John List Story. Guest: Crime Story, Hill Street Blues.

CARVER, STEVE
Director. b. Brooklyn, NY, April 5, 1945. e. U. of Buffalo; Washington U., MFA. Directing, writing fellow, Film Inst. Center for Advanced Studies, 1970. (Writer, dir. films Patent and the Tell-Tale Heart). Teacher of filmmaking art and photo. Florissant Valley Col., MO 1966-68. News photographer, UPI. Instructor, film and photography, Metropolitan Ed. Council in the Arts; St. Louis Mayor's Council on the Arts, Give a Damn (dir., prod.); asst. dir. Johnny Got His Gun; writer, editor with New World Pictures. Member: Sierra Club, Natl. Rifle Assn.
PICTURES: Arena, Big Bad Mama, Capone, Drum, Fast Charlie, The Moonbeam Rider, Steel, An Eye for an Eye, Lone Wolf McQuade (also prod.), Oceans of Fire, Jocks (also co-s.p.), Bulletproof (also co-s.p.), River of Death, Crazy Joe, The Wolves.

CARVEY, DANA
Actor. b. Missoula, MT, Apr. 2, 1955. e. San Francisco State Coll. Won San Francisco Stand-Up Comedy Competition which led to work as stand-up comedian in local S.F., then L.A. comedy clubs. TV debut as Mickey Rooney's grandson on series, One of the Boys, 1982. Received American Comedy Award (1990, 1991) as TV's Funniest Supporting Male Performer.
PICTURES: Halloween II, Racing With the Moon, This is Spinal Tap, Tough Guys, Moving, Opportunity Knocks, Wayne's World, Wayne's World 2, Clean Slate, The Road to Wellville, Trapped in Paradise, The Shot.
TELEVISION: Series: One of the Boys, Blue Thunder, Saturday Night Live (Emmy Award, 1993), The Dana Carvey Show. Specials: Superman's 50th Anniversary (host), Salute to Improvisation, Wayne & Garth's Saturday Night Live Music a Go-Go. Guest: The Larry Sanders Show. Pilots: Alone at Last, Whacked Out.

CASEY, BERNIE
Actor. b. Wyco, WV, June 8, 1939. e. Bowling Green U. Played pro-football with San Francisco 49ers and L.A. Rams.
PICTURES: Guns of the Magnificent Seven (debut, 1969), Tick...Tick...Tick, Boxcar Bertha, Black Gunn, Hit Man, Cleopatra Jones, Maurie, Cornbread Earl and Me, The Man Who Fell to Earth, Dr. Black/Mr. Hyde, Brothers, Sharky's Machine, Never Say Never Again, Revenge of the Nerds, Spies Like Us, Steele Justice, Rent-a-Cop, I'm Gonna Git You Sucka, Backfire, Bill and Ted's Excellent Adventure, Another 48 HRS, Under Siege, The Cemetery Club, Street Knight, The Glass Shield.
TELEVISION: Series: Harris and Company, Bay City Blues. Movies: Brian's Song, Gargoyles, Panic on the 5:22, Mary Jane Harper Cried Last Night, It Happened at Lake Wood Manor, Ring of Passion, Love is Not Enough, Sophisticated Gents, Hear No Evil, The Fantastic World of D.C. Collins. Mini-Series: Roots—The Next Generations, The Martian Chronicles.

CASS, PEGGY
Actress. b. Boston, MA, May 21, 1924.
THEATER: B'way: Burlesque, Bernardine, Auntie Mame (Tony & Theatre World Awards, 1957), A Thurber Carnival, Don't Drink the Water, Front Page, Plaza Suite, Last of the Red Hot Lovers, Once a Catholic, 42nd Street, The Octette Bridge Club, Light Up the Sky, 100,000 Frenchmen.
PICTURES: The Marrying Kind (debut, 1952), Auntie Mame (Acad. Award nom.), Gidget Goes Hawaiian, The Age of Consent, If It's Tuesday This Must Be Belgium, Paddy.
TELEVISION: Series: The Jack Paar Show, Keep Talking, The Hathaways, To Tell the Truth, The Doctors (1978-79), Women in Prison. Movie: Danielle Steel's Zoya. Guest: Garry Moore Show, Barbara Stanwyck Show, Tales from the Darkside, Major Dad.

CASSAVETES, NICK
Actor, Director, Writer. b. New York, NY, May 21, 1959. Son of director/actor John Cassavetes and actress Gena Rowlands.
PICTURES: A Woman Under the Influence, Mask, The Wraith, Quiet Cool, Black Moon Rising, Assault of the Killer Bimbos, Blind Fury, Backstreet Dreams, Delta Force 3: The Killing Game, Twogether, Sins of the Night, Sins of Desire, Body of Influence, Class of 1999 II: The Substitute, Mrs. Parker and the Vicious Circle, Just Like Dad, Black Rose of Harlem, Face/Off, Life. Director: Unhook the Stars, She's So Lovely.
TELEVISION: Movies: Reunion, Shooter.

CASSEL, ALVIN I.
Executive. b. New York , NY, July 26. e. U. of Michigan, B.A., 1938. Capt. in U.S. Army European Theatre, 1941-45. Surveyed Central Africa for MGM, 1946-50, then assumed duties as asst. mgr. for MGM South Africa. Continued with MGM in West Indies, 1950-51 and Philippines, 1951-57. In 1957 joined Universal as mgr./supvr. for Southeast Asia; back to MGM in 1963 as supvr. S.E. Asia; 1967, with CBS Films as Far East supvr. In 1972, established Cassel Films to secure theatrical films for foreign distributors, principally in Far East. 1979, consultant for Toho-Towa and the Toho Co. of Japan and other Far East distributors.

CASSEL, JEAN-PIERRE
Actor. b. Paris, France, Oct. 27, 1932. Began as dancer, attracting attention of Gene Kelly at Left Bank nightspot, resulting in film debut. Also appeared in plays before becoming established as leading French screen star.
PICTURES: The Happy Road (debut, 1956), A Pied a Cheval et en Voiture, Le Desorde et la Nuit, Love Is My Profession, The Love Game, The Joker, Candide, The Five-Day Lover, Seven Capital Sins, La Gamberge, The Elusive Corporal, Arsene Lupin contre Arsene Lupin, Cyrano and D'Artagnan, The Beautiful Swindlers, The Male Companion, High Infidelity, La Ronde, Les Fetes Galantes, Those Magnificent Men in Their Flying Machines, Is Paris Burning?, Anyone Can Play, The Killing Game, The Bear and the Doll, Oh! What a Lovely War, The Army of the Shadows, The Break Up, The Boat on the Grass, Baxter!, Malpertuis, The Discreet Charm of the Bourgeoisie, The Three Musketeers, Le Mouton Enrage, Murder on the Orient Express, The Twist, That Lucky Touch, No Time for Breakfast, The Four Musketeers, Les Oeufs Brouilles, The Meetings of Anna, Who Is Killing the Great Chefs of Europe?, Alice, Chouans! Grandeson, From Hell to Victory, La Ville des Silence, The Green Jacket, Ehrengard, La Vie Continue, Portrait of a Nude Woman, The Trout, Viva le Sociale! Tranches de Vie, Mangeclous, The Return of the Musketeers, Mr. Frost, Vincent & Theo, Tha Maid, The Favor the Watch and the Very Big Fish, Lieutenant Lorena, Love and Tiny Toes, Between Heaven and Earth, Coup de Jeune, The Secret Coach of 13, Petain, Blue Helmet, Metisse, Cha Forte Com Limao, L'Enfer, Ready to Wear (Pret-a-Porter), La Ceremonie (A Judgment in Stone), The Ice Rink.
TELEVISION: La Lune d'Omaha, Liberty, A Matter of Convenience, Sentimental Journey, Tu Crois Pa si Bien Dire, Casanova, The Burning Shore, Warburg, Young Indiana Jones Chronicles, From Earth and Blood, Elissa Rhais, The Fatal Image, The Phantom of the Opera, Cave of the Golden Rose, Notorious, Tatort - Eine Todsichere Falle, Flairs Ennemis, Un Printemps de Chien. Mini-series: The Secret of the Sahara, La Misere des Riches, Disperatamente Giulia

CASSEL, SEYMOUR
Actor. b. Detroit, MI, Jan. 22, 1937. As a boy travelled with a troupe of burlesque performers including his mother. After high school appeared in summer stock in Michigan. Studied acting at American Theatre Wing and Actor's Studio. After joining a workshop taught by John Cassavetes, began a long creative association with the director-actor. On B'way, in The World of Suzy Wong, The Disenchanted.
PICTURES: Murder Inc., Shadows, Too Late Blues, Juke Box Racket, The Killers, The Sweet Ride, Coogan's Bluff, Faces (Acad. Award nom.), The Revolutionary, Minnie and Moskowitz, Black Oak Conspiracy, Death Game (The Seducers), The Killing of a Chinese Bookie, The Last Tycoon, Scott Joplin, Opening Night, Valentino, Convoy, California Dreaming, Ravagers, Sunburn, The Mountain Men, King of the Mountain, I'm Almost Not Crazy..., John Cassavetes–The Man and His Work (doc.), Love Streams, Eye of the Tiger, Survival Game, Tin Men, Johnny Be Good, Plain Clothes, Colors, Track 29, Wicked Stepmother, Dick Tracy, White Fang, Cold Dog Soup, Mobsters, Diary of a Hitman, Honeymoon in Vegas, In the Soup, Trouble Bound, Indecent Proposal, Boiling Point, Chain of Desire, Chasers, There Goes My Baby, When Pigs Fly, Hand Gun, It Could Happen to You, Tollbooth, Dark Side of Genius, Imaginary Crimes, Things I Never Told You, Dead Presidents, The Last Home Run, Dream for an Insomniac, Four Rooms, Cameleone.
TELEVISION: Movies: The Hanged Man, Angel on My Shoulder, Blood Feud, I Want to Live, Beverly Hills Madame, Sweet Bird of Youth, My Shadow, Dead in the Water, Face of a Stranger. Pilot: Rose City. Special: Partners. Series: Good Company.

CASSIDY, DAVID
Actor, Singer. b. New York, NY, April 12, 1950. Son of late actor Jack Cassidy; brother of Shaun and Patrick. Composed and performed theme song for The John Larroquette Show.
THEATER: B'way: The Fig Leaves Are Falling (debut, 1968), Joseph and the Amazing Technicolor Dreamcoat, Blood Brothers. Regional: Little Johnny Jones, Tribute. London: Time.
PICTURES: Instant Karma, The Spirit of '76.
TELEVISION: Series: The Partridge Family, David Cassidy-Man Undercover. Movie: The Night the City Screamed. Guest: The Mod Squad, Bonanza, Adam-12, Ironside, Marcus Welby M.D., Police Story (Emmy nom.), The Love Boat, Alfred Hitchcock Presents, The Flash.

CASSIDY, JOANNA
Actress. b. Camden, NJ, Aug. 2, 1944. e. Syracuse U.
PICTURES: Bullitt (debut, 1968), Fools, The Laughing Policeman, The Outfit, Bank Shot, The Stepford Wives, Stay Hungry, The Late Show, Stunts, The Glove, Our Winning Season, Night Games, Blade Runner, Under Fire, Club Paradise, The Fourth Protocol, Who Framed Roger Rabbit, 1969, The Package, Where the Heart Is, Don't Tell Mom the Babysitter's Dead, All-American Murder, May Wine, Vampire in Brooklyn, Chain Reaction.
TELEVISION: Series: Shields and Yarnell, The Roller Girls, 240-Robert, Family Tree, Buffalo Bill, Code Name: Foxfire, Hotel Malibu. Movies: She's Dressed to Kill, Reunion, Invitation to Hell, The Children of Times Square, Pleasures, A Father's Revenge, Nightmare at Bitter Creek, Wheels of Terror, Grass Roots, Taking Back My Life, Live! From Death Row, Perfect Family, Barbarians at the Gate, Stephen King's The Tommyknockers, The Rockford Files: I Still Love L.A, Sleep Baby Sleep. Mini-Series: Hollywood Wives. Special: Roger Rabbit and the Secrets of Toontown (host), Other Mothers (Afterschool Special). Pilot: Second Stage. Guest: Taxi, Love Boat, Hart to Hart, Charlie's Angels, Lou Grant.

CASSIDY, PATRICK
Actor. b. Los Angeles, CA, Jan. 4, 1961. Son of late actor Jack Cassidy and actress-singer Shirley Jones.
THEATER: NY: The Pirates of Penzance, Leader of the Pack, Assassins. Regional: Conrack.
PICTURES: Off the Wall, Just the Way You Are, Fever Pitch, Nickel Mountain, Love at Stake, Longtime Companion, I'll Do Anything.
TELEVISION: Series: Bay City Blues, Dirty Dancing. Movies: Angel Dusted, Midnight Offerings, Choices of the Heart, Christmas Eve, Dress Gray, Something in Comon, Follow Your Heart, Three on a Match, How the West Was Fun. Mini-Series: Napoleon and Josephine: A Love Story. Pilot: The Six of Us.

CASTLE, NICK
Writer, Director. b. Los Angeles, CA, Sept. 21, 1947. e. Santa Monica Coll., U. of Southern California film sch. Son of late film and TV choreographer Nick Castle Sr. Appeared as child in films Anything Goes, Artists and Models. Worked with John Carpenter and other USC students on Acad. Award-winning short, The Resurrection of Bronco Billy.
PICTURES: Skatedown USA (s.p.), Tag: The Assassination Game (Kiss Me Kill Me; dir., s.p.), Escape from New York (co-s.p.), The Last Starfighter (dir.), The Boy Who Could Fly (dir.), Tap (dir., s.p.), Hook (co-story), Dennis the Menace (dir.), Major Payne (dir.), Mr. Wrong (dir.).

CATES, GILBERT
Director, Producer. r.n. Gilbert Katz. b. New York, NY, June 6, 1934. e. Syracuse U. Brother is dir.-prod. Joseph Cates. Began TV career as guide at NBC studios in N.Y., working way up to prod. and dir. of game shows (Camouflage, Haggis Baggis, Mother's Day, etc.). Created Hootenanny and packaged and directed many TV specials. Pres. Directors Guild of America 1983-87. Awarded DGA's Robert B. Aldrich award 1989. Dir. short film The Painting.
THEATER: Director: Tricks of the Trade, Voices, The Price (Long Wharf Theatre). Producer: Solitaire/Double Solitaire, The Chinese and Mr. Fish, I Never Sang for My Father, You Know I Can't Hear You When the Water's Running.
PICTURES: Rings Around the World (debut, 1966), I Never Sang for My Father (also prod.), Summer Wishes Winter Dreams, One Summer Love (Dragonfly; also prod.), The Promise, The Last Married Couple in America, Oh God!—Book II (also prod.), Backfire.
TELEVISION: Specials: Prod. &/or Dir. unless otherwise noted: International Showtime (1963-65 exec. prod.), Electric Showcase Specials, Academy Awards (prod. 1990-95, 1997-98; Emmy Award, 1991), After the Fall. Movies: To All My Friends on Shore, The Affair, Johnny, We Hardly Knew Ye, The Kid from Nowhere, Country Gold, Hobson's Choice, Burning Rage, Consenting Adult, Fatal Judgement, My First Love, Do You Know the Muffin Man, Call Me Anna, Absolute Strangers (exec. prod.), In My Daughter's Name (co-exec. prod.), Confessions: Two Faces of Evil, To Life: America Celebrates Israel's 50th.

CATES, JOSEPH
Producer, Director. r.n. Joseph Katz. b. Aug. 10, 1924. e. NYU. Brother is dir. Gilbert Cates. Father of actress Phoebe Cates. One of first producers and dirs. of live TV with Look Upon a Star, 1947. Prod., Jackie Gleason Cavalcade of Stars, game shows, ($64,000 Question, $64,000 Challenge, Stop the Music, Haggis Baggis), NBC Spectaculars (1955-60), High Button Shoes, The Bachelor, Accent on Love, Gene Kelly, Ethel Merman, Victor Borge, Yves Montand shows.
THEATER: Prod. on B'way: What Makes Sammy Run?, Joe Egg, Spoon River Anthology, Gantry, Her First Roman.
PICTURES: Director: Who Killed Teddy Bear?, The Fat Spy, Girl of the Night.

TELEVISION: *Series*: International Showtime (Don Ameche Circuses). Prod.-dir. of spectaculars and special programs, 1955-88: Johnny Cash, David Copperfield, Steve Martin; Anne Bancroft: The Woman in the Life of Man (Emmy Award as exec. prod., 1970), Jack Lemmon and Fred Astaire: S'Wonderful S'Marvelous S'Gershwin (Emmy Award as exec. prod., 1972), Annual Ford Theater Salutes to the President, Country Music Awards Show, Miss Teen Age America, Junior Miss pageants, Tony Awards 1992, International Emmies, The Ford Theatre Salute to the President, The 1993 Monte Carlo Circus Festival, Comedy Zone. *Movies*: Prod.: The Quick and the Dead, The Last Days of Frank and Jessie James, The Last Married Couple in America, The Cradle Will Fall, Special People.

CATES, PHOEBE
Actress. b. New York, NY, July 16, 1962. e. Juilliard. Father is prod-dir. Joseph Cates. m. actor Kevin Kline. Dance prodigy and fashion model before launching acting career. NY stage debut The Nest of the Wood Grouse (1984).
PICTURES: Paradise (debut, 1982), Fast Times at Ridgemont High, Private School, Gremlins, Date With an Angel, Bright Lights Big City, Shag, Heart of Dixie, I Love You to Death (unbilled), Gremlins 2: The New Batch, Drop Dead Fred, Bodies Rest and Motion, My Life's in Turnaround, Princess Caraboo.
TELEVISION: *Movies*: Baby Sister, Lace, Lace II. *Special*: Largo Desolato.

CATON-JONES, MICHAEL
Director. b. Broxburn, Scotland, 1958.
PICTURES: Scandal (debut, 1989), Memphis Belle, Doc Hollywood (also cameo), This Boy's Life, Rob Roy (also exec. prod.).

CATTRALL, KIM
Actress. b. Liverpool, Eng., Aug. 21, 1956. e. American Acad. of Dramatic Arts, N.Y. Started stage career in Canada's Off-B'way in Vancouver and Toronto; later performed in L.A. in A View from the Bridge, Agnes of God, Three Sisters, etc. On B'way in Wild Honey. Chicago Goodman Theatre in the Misanthrope. Regional: Miss Julie (Princeton).
PICTURES: Rosebud (debut 1975), The Other Side of the Mountain Part II, Tribute, Ticket to Heaven, Porky's, Police Academy, Turk 182, City Limits, Hold-Up, Big Trouble in Little China, Mannequin, Masquerade, Midnight Crossing, Palais Royale, Honeymoon Academy, The Return of the Musketeers, Brown Bread Sandwiches, Bonfire of the Vanities, Star Trek VI: The Undiscovered Country, Split Second, Double Vision, Breaking Point, Unforgettable, Live Nude Girls, Where Truth Lies, Baby Geniuses, Revenant.
TELEVISION: *Series*: Angel Falls, Sex and the City. *Movies*: Good Against Evil, The Bastard, The Night Rider, The Rebels, The Gossip Columnist, Sins of the Past, Miracle in the Wilderness, Running Delilah, Above Suspicion, The Heidi Chronicles, Two Golden Balls, Outer Limits. *Mini-Series*: Scruples, Wild Palms, Tom Clancy's Op Center, Invasion, Creature.

CAULFIELD, MAXWELL
Actor. b. Glasgow, Scotland, Nov. 23, 1959. m. actress Juliet Mills. First worked as a dancer at a London nightclub. After coming to NY in 1978, ran the concession stand at the Truck and Warehouse Theatre. Won a Theatre World Award for Class Enemy.
THEATER: Entertaining Mr. Sloane, Salonika, Journey's End, Sleuth, The Elephant Man, An Inspector Calls, Sweet Bird of Youth, The Woman In Black.
PICTURES: Grease 2, Electric Dreams, The Boys Next Door, The Supernaturals, Sundown: The Vampire in Retreat, Mind Games, Alien Intruder, Midnight Witness, Ipi/Tombi, In a Moment of Passion, Calendar Girl, Gettysburg, Inevitable Grace, Empire Records, Prey of the Jaguar, Oblivion 2: Backlash, The Real Blonde.
TELEVISION: *Series*: Dynasty, The Colbys, All My Children, Spider Man (voice). *Movies*: The Parade, Till We Meet Again, Blue Bayou, Dynasty: The Reunion.

CAVANAUGH, ANDREW
Executive. Held positions with Norton Simon, Inc. and Equitable Life Insurance Co. before joining Paramount Pictures in 1984 as v.p., human resources. 1985, appt. sr. v.p., administration, mng. personnel depts. on both coasts. Also oversees corp. admin. function for Paramount.

CAVANI, LILIANA
Director. b. near Modena, in Emilia, Italy, Jan. 12, 1937. e. U. of Bologna, diploma in classic literature, 1960; Ph.D. in linguistics. In 1960 took courses at Centro Sperimentale di Cinematografia in Rome where made short films Incontro Notturno and L'Evento. 1961 winner of RAI sponsored contest and started working for the new second Italian TV channel, 1962-66 directing progs. of serious political and social nature incl. History of 3rd Reich, Women in the Resistance, Age of Stalin, Philippe Petain–Trial at Vichy (Golden Lion Venice Fest.), Jesus My Brother, Day of Peace, Francis of Assisi. Has also directed operas Wozzeck, Iphigenia in Tauris and Medea on stage; also dir. opera liriche: Cardillac, Jenufa, Traviata, Vestale, Cena Delle Beffe, Iphigenia in Tauride, Medea.
PICTURES: Galileo, I Cannibali, Francesco d'Assissi, L'Ospite, Milarepa, Night Porter, Beyond Good and Evil, The Skin, Oltre la Porta, The Berlin Affair, Francesco, Sans Pouvoir le Dire.

CAVETT, DICK
Actor, Writer. b. Kearny, NE, Nov. 19, 1936. e. Yale U. Acted in TV dramas and Army training films. Was writer for Jack Paar and his successors on the Tonight Show. Also wrote comedy for Merv Griffin, Jerry Lewis, Johnny Carson. In 1967 began performing own comedy material in night clubs. On TV starred in specials Where It's At (ABC Stage 67) and What's In. Author of, Cavett (with Christopher Porter) 1974.
THEATER: *B'way*: Otherwise Engaged, Into the Woods.
PICTURES: Annie Hall, Power Play, Health, Simon, A Nightmare on Elm Street 3, Beetlejuice, Moon Over Parador, After School, Funny, Year of the Gun, Forrest Gump.
TELEVISION: *Series*: This Morning (ABC daytime talk show, 1968), The Dick Cavett Show (ABC primetime talk show, summer 1969), The Dick Cavett Show (ABC late night talk show, 1969-72: Emmy Award, 1972), ABC Late Night (talk show, 1973-74; Emmy Award, 1974), The Dick Cavett Show (CBS primetime variety; 1975), Dick Cavett Show (talk show: PBS, 1977-82; USA, 1985-86; CBS, 1986), The Edge of Night (1983), The Dick Cavett Show (CNBC talk show: 1989).

CAZENOVE, CHRISTOPHER
Actor. b. Winchester, Eng., Dec. 17, 1945. m. Angharad Rees. e. Eton, Oxford U., trained at Bristol Old Vic Theatre School.
THEATER: Hamlet (1969), The Lionel Touch, My Darling Daisy, The Winslow Boy, Joking Apart, In Praise of Rattigan, The Life and Poetry of T.S. Eliot, The Sound of Music, Goodbye Fidel (B'way debut, 1980).
PICTURES: There's a Girl in My Soup, Royal Flash, East of Elephant Rock, The Girl in Blue Velvet, Zulu Dawn, Eye of the Needle, From a Far Country, Heat and Dust, Until September, Mata Hari, The Fantasist, Hold My Hand I'm Dying, Three Men and a Little Lady, Aces: Iron Eagle III, The Proprietor.
TELEVISION: *Series*: The Regiment, The Duchess of Duke Street, Dynasty, A Fine Romance, Tales From the Crypt. *Specials/Movies*: The Rivals of Sherlock Holmes (1971), Affairs of the Heart, Jennie: Lady Randolph Churchill, The Darkwater Hall Mystery, Ladykillers—A Smile Is Sometimes Worth a Million, The Red Signal, Lou Grant, The Letter, Jenny's War, Lace 2, Kane and Abel, Windmills of the Gods, Shades of Love, Souvenir, The Lady and the Highwayman, Tears in the Rain, Ticket to Ride (A Fine Romance), To Be the Best.

CELENTINO, LUCIANO
Producer, Director, Writer. b. Naples, Italy, 1940. e. Rome, Paris, London. Ent. ind. 1959. Wrote, prod., dir. many plays incl: Infamita di Questa Terra, Black Destiny, Honour, Stranger's Heart, Youth's Sin, Wanda Lontano Amore. Stage musicals such as Songs...Dots...And Fantasies, Night Club's Appointment, Filumena, Serenada, Mamma. Since 1964, film critic of Il Meridionale Italiano. From 1962, co-writer and first asst. director to Luigi Capuano and Vittorio De Sica. In 1972, formed own company, Anglo-Fortunato Films. Co-wrote, prod., dir. Blood Money. Dir. Bandito (in Italy). Wrote and dir. Toujours, Parole, Jackpot; 1988: Panache (dir.), 1989: Was There a Way Out? (prod., wrote, dir.), Hobo.

CELLAN-JONES, JAMES
Director. b. Swansea, Wales, July 13, 1931. e. St. John's Coll., Cambridge. Best known for his adaptations of classic novels for the BBC and PBS (shown on Masterpiece Theatre). Won Nymphe d'Or at Monaco Festival.
PICTURE: The Nelson Affair, Chou Chou, Une Vie de Debussy.
TELEVISION: The Scarlet and the Black, The Forsythe Saga, Portrait of a Lady, The Way We Live Now, Solo, The Roads to Freedom, Eyeless In Gaza, The Golden Bowl, Jennie (DGA series award), Caesar and Cleopatra, The Adams Chronicles, The Day Christ Died, The Ambassadors, Unity Mitford, Oxbridge Blues (also prod.), Sleeps Six (also prod.), The Comedy of Errors, Fortunes of War, You Never Can Tell, Arms and the Man, A Little Piece of Sunshine, A Perfect Hero (also prod.), The Gravy Train Goes East, Maigret, Harnessing Peacocks, Brighton Belles.

CHABROL, CLAUDE
Director. b. Paris, France, June 24, 1930. Worked as newsman for Fox, then writer for Cahiers du Cinema. A founding director of the French New Wave.
PICTURES: Le Beau Serge, The Cousins, A Double Tour, Les Bonnes Femmes, Les Godelureaux, The Third Lover, Seven Capital Sins, Ophelia, Landru, Le Tigre Aime la Chair Fraiche, Marie-Chantal Contre le Docteur Kah, Le Tigre Se Parfume a la Dunamite, Paris vu par... Chabrol, La Ligne de Demarcation, The Champagne Murders, The Route to Corinth, Les Biches, Le Femme Infidele, This Man Must Die, Le Boucher, La Rapture, Ten Days' Wonder, Just Before Nightfall, Dr. Popaul, Les Noces Rouges, Nada, The Blood of Others, The Horse of Pride, Alouette je te plumera, Poulet au Vinaigre, Inspector Lavardin, Masques, Le Cri du Hibou, Story of Women, Clichy Days (Quiet Days in Clichy), The Lark (actor only), Doctor M (Club Extinction), Madame Bovary, Betty, Through the Eyes of Vichy, L'Enfer (Hell; also s.p.), A Judgment in Stone (also co-s.p.), Rien Ne Va Plus.

CHAKERES, MICHAEL H.
Executive. b. Ohio. e. Wittenberg U, 1935. Pres. and chmn. of bd. of Chakeres Theatres of Ohio and Kentucky. U.S. Army AF 1942-45. Bd. of Dir.: National NATO, NATO of Ohio, Will Rogers Hospital, Motion Picture Pioneers, Society National Bank, Wittenberg U., Springfield Foundation, Variety Club of Palm Beach, Tent No. 65. Member: Masonic Temple, Scottish Rite, I.O.O.F., AHEPA, Leadership 100, ARCHON-Order of St. Andrew, Rotary Club, City of Hope, University Club.

CHAKIRIS, GEORGE
Actor. b. Norwood, OH, Sept. 16, 1933. Entered m.p. industry as chorus dancer.
PICTURES: Song of Love (debut, 1947), The Great Caruso, The 5000 Fingers of Dr. T, Give a Girl a Break, Gentlemen Prefer Blondes, There's No Business Like Show Business, White Christmas, Brigadoon, The Girl Rush, Meet Me in Las Vegas, Under Fire (1st acting role), West Side Story (Academy Award for Best Supporting Actor, 1961), Two and Two Make Six, Diamond Head, Bebo's Girl, Kings of the Sun, Flight From Ashiya, 633 Squadron, McGuire Go Home! (The High Bright Sun), Is Paris Burning?, The Young Girls of Rochefort, The Big Cube, The Day the Hot Line Got Hot, Why Not Stay for Breakfast?, Jekyll and Hyde... Together Again, Pale Blood.
TELEVISION: *Series*: Dallas (1985-86). *Guest*: Fantasy Island, CHiPs, Matt Houston, Scarecrow and Mrs. King, Hell Town, Murder She Wrote. *Movie*: Return to Fantasy Island. *Specials*: You're the Top, Highways of Melody, Kismet, Notorious Woman (PBS).

CHAMBERLAIN, RICHARD
Actor. r.n. George Richard Chamberlain. b. Los Angeles, CA, March 31, 1935. Studied voice, LA Conservatory of Music 1958; acting with Jeff Corey. Founding mem. City of Angels, LA Theater Company. Became TV star in Dr. Kildare series, 1961-66. Founded prod. co. Cham Enterprises. Had hit record Three Stars Will Shine Tonight (them from Dr. Kildare) in 1962.
THEATER: Breakfast at Tiffany's, Night of the Iguana, Fathers & Sons, Blithe Spirit.
PICTURES: The Secret of the Purple Reef (debut, 1960), A Thunder of Drums, Twilight of Honor, Joy in the Morning, Petulia, The Madwoman of Chaillot, Julius Caesar, The Music Lovers, Lady Caroline Lamb, The Three Musketeers, The Towering Inferno, The Four Musketeers, The Slipper and the Rose, The Swarm, The Last Wave, Murder by Phone (Bells), King Solomon's Mines, Alan Quartermain and the Lost City of Gold, The Return of the Musketeers (tv in U.S.), Bird of Prey.
TELEVISION: *Specials*: Hamlet, Portrait of a Lady, The Woman I Love, The Lady's Not for Burning. *Movies*: F. Scott Fitzgerald and the Last of the Belles, The Count of Monte Cristo, The Man in the Iron Mask, Cook and Perry: The Race to the Pole, Wallenberg: A Hero's Story, Casanova, Aftermath: A Test of Love, The Night of the Hunter, Ordeal in the Arctic, The Thorn Birds: The Missing Year, All the Winters that Have Been. *Mini-Series*: Centennial, Shogun, The Thorn Birds, Dream West, The Bourne Identity. *Series*: Dr. Kildare, Island Son (also co-exec. prod.). *Host*: The Astronomers. *Guest*: Gunsmoke, Thriller, The Deputy, Alfred Hitchcock Presents, The Lost Daughter.

CHAMBERS, EVERETT
Producer, Writer, Director. b. Montrose, CA; Aug. 19, 1926. e. New School For Social Research, Dramatic Workshop, N.Y. Entered industry as actor; worked with Fred Coe as casting dir. and dir., NBC, 1952-57; Author: Producing TV Movies.
PICTURES: *Actor*: Too Late Blues. Writer: Tess of the Storm Country, Run Across the River, The Kiss (short; dir.: Acad. Award nom.), The Lollipop Cover (also prod., dir.; Acad. award, Chicago Film Fest.), Private Duty Nurses, A Girl to Kill For.
TELEVISION: *Series*: *Producer*: Johnny Staccato (also writer), Target the Corrupters, The Dick Powell Theatre, The Lloyd Bridges Show (also writer), Peyton Place, Columbo, Future Cop, Timeslip (exec. prod., writer), Lucan (also writer), Airwolf, Partners in Crime, Rin Tin Tin K-9 Cop (also creative consultant). *Movies*: Beverly Hills Madam, A Matter of Sex (exec. prod., 1985 Christopher & A.W.R.T. Awards), Will There Really Be a Morning?, Berlin Tunnel 21 (sprv. prod.), Night Slaves (also writer), Moon of the Wolf, Trouble Comes to Town, The Great American Beauty Contest, Can Ellen Be Saved? (also writer), Jigsaw John, Street Killing, Nero Wolfe, Twin Detectives (also writer), The Girl Most Likely to..., Sacrifice the Queen, Paris Conspiracy, Family Secret, Incident in a Small Town (spv. prod.). *Co-writer*: The Perfect Town for Murder, Last Chance (pilot).

CHAMPION, JOHN C.
Director, Producer, Writer. b. Denver, CO, Oct. 13, 1923. e. Stanford U., Wittenberg Coll. a. Lee R. Champion, Supreme Court judge. Entered m.p. in Fiesta; did some radio work; in stock at MGM briefly; co-pilot Western Air Lines, Inc., 1943; served in U.S. Army Air Force, air transport command pilot 1943-45; public relations officer AAF; writer & prod. for Allied Artists; v.p. prod. Commander Films Corp.: press. Champion Pictures, Inc.; prod., MGM, Warner, Paramount, Universal. Member: SAG, SWG, SIMPP, SPG; TV Academy, Prod. Writer. Mirisch-U.A.; prod. TV Laramie series; created McHales Navy; author, novel, The Hawks of Noon, 1965; National Cowboy Hall of Fame Award, 1976.

PICTURES: Panhandle, Stampede, Hellgate, Dragonfly Squadron, Shotgun, Zero Hour, The Texican, Attack on the Iron Coast, Submarine X-1, The Last Escape, Brother of the Wind, Mustang Country (dir-prod-writer).

CHAMPION, MARGE
Dancer, Actress, Choreographer. b. Los Angeles, CA, Sept. 2, 1921. r.n. Marjorie Celeste Belcher. e. Los Angeles public schools. Father was Ernest Belcher, ballet master. Was model for Snow White for Disney's animated feature. Debuted in films as Marjorie Bell. Made debut in 1947, with former husband Gower Champion as dancing team; team was signed by MGM; voted Star of Tomorrow, 1952. Received Lifetime Achievement award from the American Dance Foundation, 1997.
THEATER: Blossom Time, Student Prince (LA Civic Opera), Dark of the Moon. Beggar's Holiday (NY), 3 for Tonight (NY), nvitation to a March (tour). Director: Stepping Out, Lute Song (Berkshire Theatre Fest, 1989), She Loves Me, No No Nanette.
PICTURES: Honor of the West (debut, 1939), The Story of Vernon and Irene Castle, Sorority House, Mr. Music, Show Boat, Lovely to Look At, Everything I Have Is Yours, Give a Girl a Break, Three for the Show, Jupiter's Darling, The Swimmer, The Party, The Cockeyed Cowboys of Calico County. *Choreographer only*: The Day of the Locust, Whose Life Is It Anyway?.
TELEVISION: *Series*: Admiral Broadway Revue, Marge and Gower Champion Show. *Guest*: GE Theatre, Chevy Show, Bell Telephone Hour, Ed Sullivan, Shower of Stars, Fame. *Movie*: Queen of the Stardust Ballroom (choreographer; Emmy Award, 1975).

CHAN, JACKIE
Actor, Director, Writer. r.n. Chan Kwong-Sang. b. Hong Kong, Apr. 7, 1955. Trained in acrobatics, mime and martial arts at Peking Opera Sch. Was child actor in several films; later became stuntman before being launched as action star by prod.-dir. Lo Wei.
PICTURES: Little Tiger From Canton, New Fist of Fury, Shaolin Wooden Men, To Kill With Intrigue, Snake in the Eagle's Shadow, Snake & Crane Arts of Shaolin, Magnificent Bodyguards, Drunken Master (Drunk Monkey in the Tiger's Eyes), Spiritual Kung Fu, The Fearless Hyena, Dragon Fist, The Young Master (also dir., co-s.p.), Half a Loaf of Kung Fu, The Big Brawl, The Cannonball Run, Dragon Lord (also dir., co-s.p.), Winners and Sinners, The Fearless Hyena Part 2, Cannonball Run II, Project A (also co-dir., co-s.p.), Wheels on Meals, My Lucky Stars, The Protector, Twinkle Twinkle Lucky Stars, Heart of the Dragon (First Mission), Police Story (also dir., co-s.p.), Armour of God (also dir., co-s.p.), Project A Part 2 (also dir., co-s.p.), Dragons Forever, Police Story II (also dir., co-s.p.), Mr. Canton and Lady Rose (Miracle; also dir., co-s.p.), Armour of God II: Operation Condor (also dir., co-s.p.), Island of Fire, Twin Dragons, Police Story III: Super Cop (also dir., co-s.p.), City Hunter, Crime Story, Project S, Drunken Master II, Rumble in the Bronx, Thunderbolt, First Strike, Burn Hollywood Burn, Mr. Nice Guy, Rush Hour, Who Am I?.

CHANCELLOR, JOHN
TV Anchorman, News Reporter. b. Chicago, IL, 1927. e. U. of Illinois. After military service joined Chicago Sun-Times (1948) and after two years moved to NBC News as Midwest corr. In 1948, assigned to Vienna bureau. Subsequently reported from London; was chief of Moscow bureau before appt. as host of Today program for one year (1961). Left NBC 1965-67 to become dir. of Voice of America. In recent yrs. anchorman for special coverage of moon landings, political conventions, inaugurations etc. Anchorman, NBC Nightly News, 1970-82. Now sr. commentator, NBC News, delivering news commentaries on NBC Nightly News.

CHANNING, CAROL
Actress. b. Seattle, WA, Jan. 31, 1921. e. Bennington Coll.
THEATER: B'way: Gentlemen Prefer Blondes, Lend an Ear (Theatre World Award), Hello Dolly! (Tony Award, 1964), Show Girl, Lorelei. Tour: Legends.
PICTURES: Paid in Full (debut, 1950), The First Traveling Saleslady, Thoroughly Modern Millie (Acad. Award nom.), Skidoo, Shinbone Alley (voice), Sgt. Pepper's Lonely Hearts Club Band (cameo), Happily Ever After (voice), Hans Christian Andersen's Thumbelina (voice), Edie & Pen.
TELEVISION: *Specials*: Svengali and the Blonde, Three Men on a Horse, Crescendo, The Carol Channing Special. *Guest*: Omnibus, George Burns Show, Lucy Show, Carol Burnett Show, The Love Boat.

CHANNING, STOCKARD
Actress. r.n. Susan Williams Antonia Stockard. b. New York, NY, Feb. 13, 1944. e. Radcliffe Coll., B.A., 1965. With Theater Co. of Boston, experimental drama company, 1967.
THEATER: Two Gentlemen of Verona, No Hard Feelings, Vanities (Mark Taper Forum, LA), They're Playing Our Song, The Lady and the Clarinet, Golden Age, The Rink, Joe Egg (Tony Award, 1985), Love Letters, Woman in Mind, House of Blue Leaves, Six Degrees of Separation, Four Baboons Adoring the Sun.

PICTURES: The Hospital (debut, 1971), Up the Sandbox, The Fortune, The Big Bus, Sweet Revenge, Grease, The Cheap Detective, The Fish That Saved Pittsburgh, Safari 3000, Without a Trace, Heartburn, The Men's Club, A Time of Destiny, Staying Together, Meet the Applegates, Married to It, Six Degrees of Separation (Acad. Award nom.), Bitter Moon, Smoke, To Wong Foo—Thanks for Everything—Julie Newmar, Up Close and Personal, Moll Flanders, Edie and Pen, The First Wives Club, Practical Magic, Baby Dance, Twilight.
TELEVISION: Series: Stockard Channing in Just Friends, The Stockard Channing Show. Movies: The Girl Most Likely To..., Lucan, Silent Victory: The Kitty O'Neil Story, Not My Kid, The Room Upstairs, Echoes in the Darkness, The Perfect Witness, David's Mother, An Unexpected Family, Lily Dale, The Prosecutors, An Unexpected Life. Guest: Medical Center, Trying Times (The Sad Professor). Special: Tidy Endings.

CHAPIN, DOUG
Producer. Began career as actor; then switched to film production, making debut with When a Stranger Calls, 1979.
PICTURES: Pandemonium, American Dreamer, What's Love Got to Do With It, Love! Valour! Compassion!.
TELEVISION: Movies: All Lies End in Murder, Belle Starr, Missing Pieces, Second Sight, When A Stranger Calls Back. Series: Tim Conway's Funny America.

CHAPLIN, CHARLES S.
Executive. b. Toronto, Ont., Canada, June 24, 1911. Studied law. Entered m.p. ind. in 1930 as office boy with United Artists; then office mgr. booker, St. John, N.B., 1933; br. mgr. 1935; to Montreal in same capacity, 1941; 1945-62, Canadian gen. mgr.; v.p. Canadian sls. mgr., 7 Arts Prod., 1962; CEO, v.p., dir. TV sls., Europe-Africa, Middle East-Socialist countries, 1968-70; v.p., WB-7 Arts, 1970-72; exec. v.p. intl. film dist., NTA (Canada) Ltd., Toronto Intl. Film Studios, 1972-80; pres., Charles Chaplin Enterprises, specializing in theatrical and TV sls. and prod. Pres.: B'nai Brith, Toronto Bd. of Trade, various charitable org., many trade assns., past pres. Canadian M.P. Dist. Assn., Chmn. m.p. section Com. Chest, chmn. publ. rel. comm. & past-chmn., M.P. Industry Council; Natl. Board Council Christians & Jews, etc. Representing many indept. producers in Europe, Canada, Far East, South America, etc.

CHAPLIN, GERALDINE
Actress. b. Santa Monica, CA, July 3, 1944. e. Royal Ballet School, London. Father was actor-director Charles Chaplin. Starred in over 20 European productions, including seven with Spanish filmmaker, Carlos Saura. On NY stage in The Little Foxes.
PICTURES: Limelight (debut, 1952), Par un Beau Matin d'Ete, Doctor Zhivago, Andremo in Citta, A Countess from Hong Kong, Stranger in the House (Cop-Out), I Killed Rasputin, Peppermint Frappe, Stres es Tres Tres, Honeycomb, Garden of Delights, The Hawaiians, Sur un Arbre Perche, Z.P.G. (Zero Population Growth), Innocent Bystanders, La Casa sin Fronteras, Ana and the Wolves, The Three Musketeers, Le Marriage a la Mode, The Four Musketeers, Summer of Silence, Nashville, Elisa My Love, Noroit, Buffalo Bill and the Indians or Sitting Bull's History Lesson, Welcome to L.A., Cria, In Memorium, Une Page d'Amour, Roseland, Remember My Name, Los Ojos Vendados, The Masked Bride, L'Adoption, A Wedding, The Mirror Crack'd, Le Voyage en Douce, Bolero, Life Is a Bed of Roses, Love on the Ground, The Moderns, White Mischief, Mama Turns 100, The Return of the Musketeers (tv in U.S.), I Want to Go Home, The Children, Buster's Bedroom, Chaplin, The Age of Innocence, Words Upon the Window Pane, Home for the Holidays, Jane Eyre, Crimetime, The Eyes of Asia, Mother Theresa: In the Name of God's Poor.
TELEVISION: Specials: The Corsican Brothers, My Cousin Rachel, The House of Mirth, A Foreign Field. Mini-Series: The World, The Odyssey. Movie: Duel of Hearts, Gulliver's Travels.

CHAPLIN, SAUL
Musical Director, Producer. b. Brooklyn, NY, Feb. 19, 1912. e. NYU, 1929-34. Wrote vaudeville material, 1933-36; songwriter Vitaphone Corp.; other, 1934-40; Columbia, 1940-48; MGM, from 1948; songs include: Bei Mir Bist Du Schoen, Shoe Shine Boy, Anniversary Song.
PICTURES: Scoring/Musical Director/Arranger: Argentine Nights, Crazy House, Countess of Monte Cristo, An American in Paris (Acad. Award, 1951), Lovely to Look At, Give a Girl a Break, Kiss Me Kate, Seven Brides for Seven Brothers (Acad. Award, 1954), Jupiter's Darling, Interrupted Melody, High Society. Producer: Les Girls (assoc. prod.), Merry Andrew (assoc. prod.), Can-Can (assoc. prod.), West Side Story (Acad. Award, 1961), The Sound of Music (assoc. prod.), Star! (prod.), Man of La Mancha (assoc. prod.), That's Entertainment II (co-prod.).
(d. Nov. 15, 1997)

CHAPMAN, MICHAEL
Cinematographer, Director. b. New York, NY, Nov. 21, 1935. m. writer-dir. Amy Jones. Early career in N.Y. area working on documentaries before becoming camera operator for cinematographer Gordon Willis on The Godfather, Klute, End of the Road, The Landlord. Also camera operator on Jaws.
PICTURES: Cinematographer: The Last Detail, White Dawn, Taxi Driver, The Front, The Next Man, Fingers, The Last Waltz, Invasion of the Body Snatchers, Hardcore, The Wanderers, Raging Bull, Dead Men Don't Wear Plaid, Personal Best, The Man With Two Brains, Shoot to Kill, Scrooged, Ghostbusters II, Quick Change, Kindergarten Cop, Whispers in the Dark, Rising Sun, The Fugitive, Space Jam. Director: All the Right Moves, The Clan of the Cave Bear.
TELEVISION: Death Be Not Proud, King, Gotham. Dir.: The Annihilator (pilot).

CHARBONNEAU, PATRICIA
Actress. b. Valley Stream, Long Island, NY, 1959. Stage appearances with Actors Theatre of Louisville, KY. Also in NY in My Sister in This House.
PICTURES: Desert Hearts, Manhunter, Stalking Danger, Call Me, Shakedown, Brain Dead, Captive, The Owl, K2, Portraits of a Killer.
TELEVISION: Series: Crime Story. Pilots: C.A.T. Squad, Dakota's Way. Guest: Spenser: For Hire, The Equalizer, Wiseguy, UNSUB, Matlock. Movies: Disaster at Silo 7, Desperado: Badlands Justice.

CHAREST, MICHELINE
Producer.
PICTURES: Bonjour Timothy, The Whole of the Moon, The Sleep Room.
TELEVISION: Series: The Wonderful Wizard of Oz, Arthur (Emmy Award, 1998), Lassie, The Country Mouse and the City Mouse Adventures, Emily of the New Moon. Mini-series: Million Dollar Babies.

CHARISSE, CYD
Dancer, Actress. r.n. Tula Ellice Finklea. b. Amarillo, TX, March 8, 1921. e. Hollywood Prof. Sch. m. Tony Martin, singer. Toured U.S. & Europe with Ballet Russe starting at age 13. Began in films as bit player using the name Lily Norwood. Signed contract with MGM in 1946. Named Star of Tomorrow 1948. B'way debut 1991 in Grand Hotel.
PICTURES: Something to Shout About (debut, 1943; billed as Lily Norwood), Mission to Moscow; Ziegfeld Follies (1st film billed as Cyd Charisse), The Harvey Girls, Three Wise Fools, Till the Clouds Roll By, Fiesta, Unfinished Dance, On an Island with You, Words and Music, Kissing Bandit, Tension, East Side West Side, Mark of the Renegade, Wild North, Singin' in the Rain, Sombrero, The Band Wagon, Brigadoon, Deep in My Heart, It's Always Fair Weather, Meet Me in Las Vegas, Silk Stockings, Twilight for the Gods, Party Girl, Five Golden Hours, Black Tights, Two Weeks in Another Town, The Silencers, Maroc 7, Won Ton Ton the Dog Who Saved Hollywood, Warlords of Atlantis, That's Entertainment III.
TELEVISION: Movies: Portrait of an Escort, Swimsuit, Cinderalla Summer; many specials.

CHARLES, MARIA
Actress. b. London, England, Sept. 22, 1929. Trained at RADA. London stage debut 1946 in Pick Up Girl.
THEATER: London: Women of Twilight, The Boy Friend, Divorce Me Darling!, Enter A Free Man, They Don't Grow on Trees, Winnie the Pooh, Jack the Ripper, The Matchmaker, Measure for Measure, Annie (1979-80), Fiddler on the Roof, Steaming, Peer Gynt, The Lower Depths, When We Are Married, Follies, Party Piece, School for Scandal, Driving Miss Daisy, Hay Fever, Blithe Spirit. Dir.: Owl and the Pussycat. Dir./prod.: The Boy Friend, 40, Starting Here Starting Now.
PICTURES: Folly To Be Wise, The Deadly Affair, Eye of the Devil, Great Expectations, The Return of the Pink Panther, Cuba, Victor/Victoria, Savage Hearts, The Fool.
TELEVISION: The Likes of 'Er, The Moon and the Yellow River, Down Our Street, Easter Passion, Nicholas Nickleby, The Voice of the Turtle, The Fourth Wall, The Good Old Days, Turn Out the Lights, Angel Pavement, The Ugliest Girl in Town, Other Peoples Houses, Rogues Gallery, The Prince and the Pauper, Crown Court, Bar Mitzvah Boy, Secret Army, Agony, Never the Twain, La Ronde, Shine of Harvey Moon, Sheppey, La Ronde, Brideshead Revisited, A Perfect Spy, Casualty, The Fallout Guy, Lovejoy, Anna, Agony Again.

CHARTOFF, ROBERT
Producer. b. New York, NY., Aug. 26, 1933. e. Union College, A.B.; Columbia U., LL.B. Met Irwin Winkler through mutual client at William Morris Agency (N.M.) and established Chartoff-Winkler Prods. Currently pres., Chartoff Prods., Inc.
PICTURES: Double Trouble, Point Blank, The Split, They Shoot Horses Don't They?, The Strawberry Statement, Leo the Last, Believe in Me, The Gang That Couldn't Shoot Straight, The New Centurions, Up the Sandbox, The Mechanic, Thumb Tripping, Busting, The Gambler, S*P*Y*S, Breakout, Nickelodeon, Rocky, New York New York, Valentino, Comes a Horseman, Uncle Joe Shannon, Rocky II, Raging Bull, True Confessions, Rocky III, The Right Stuff, Rocky IV, Beer, Rocky V, Straight Talk.

CHASE, BRANDON
Producer, Director. President MPA Feature Films, Inc.; news-caster-news director NBC-TV 1952-57. Executive director Mardi Gras Productions, Inc. and member of Board of Directors. Now pres., Group I Films, Ltd., and V.I. Prods., Ltd.
PICTURES: The Dead One, The Sinner and the Slave Girl, Bourbon Street Shadows, Verdict Homicide, Face of Fire, Four for the Morgue, Mission To Hell, The Wanton, Harlow, Girl In Trouble, Threesome, Wild Cargo, Alice in Wonderland, The Models, The Four of Us, Against All Odds, The Giant Spider Invasion, House of 1000 Pleasures, The Rogue, Eyes of Dr. Chaney, Alligator, Crash!, Take All of Me, The Psychic, UFOs Are Real, The Actresses, The Sword and the Sorcerer, Alligator II.
TELEVISION: Wild Cargo (series prod.-dir.); This Strange and Wondrous World (prod.-dir.), Linda Evans: Secrets to Stay Young Forever.

CHASE, CHEVY
Actor. r.n. Cornelius Crane Chase. b. New York, NY, Oct. 8, 1943. e. Bard Coll.; B.A. Studied audio research at CCS Institute. Worked as writer for Mad Magazine 1969. Teamed with Kenny Shapiro and Lane Sarasohn while still in school to collaborate on material for underground TV, which ultimately became off-off-Broadway show and later movie called Groove Tube. Co-wrote and starred in Saturday Night Live on TV, winning 2 Emmys as continuing single performance by a supporting actor and as writer for show. Wrote Paul Simon Special (Emmy Award, 1977).
PICTURES: The Groove Tube (debut, 1974), Tunnelvision, Foul Play, Caddyshack, Oh Heavenly Dog, Seems Like Old Times, Under the Rainbow, Modern Problems, National Lampoon's Vacation, Deal of the Century, Fletch, National Lampoon's European Vacation, Sesame Street Presents Follow That Bird (cameo), Spies Like Us, Three Amigos!, The Couch Trip (cameo), Funny Farm, Caddyshack II, Fletch Lives, National Lampoon's Christmas Vacation, L.A. Story (cameo), Nothing But Trouble, Memoirs of an Invisible Man, Hero (unbilled), Last Action Hero (cameo), Cops and Robbersons, Man of the House, Vegas Vacation, State & Maine, Fletch 3, Dirty Work.
TELEVISION: Series: Saturday Night Live, The Chevy Chase Show.

CHASE, STANLEY
Producer. b. Brooklyn, NY, May 3. e. NYU, B.A.; Columbia U, postgraduate. m. actress/artist Dorothy Rice. Began career as assoc. prod. of TV show Star Time; story dept., CBS-TV; then produced plays Off-B'way and on B'way, winner Tony and Obie awards for The Threepenny Opera. Joined ABC-TV as dir. in chg. programming; prod., Universal Pictures & TV; exec. consultant, Metromedia Producers Org.; prod. & exec. Alan Landsburg Productions. Formed Stanley Chase Productions, Inc. in 1975, which heads as pres.
THEATER: B'way Producer: The Potting Shed, The Cave Dwellers, A Moon for the Misbegotten, European Tour: Free and Easy. Off-B'way: The Threepenny Opera.
PICTURES: The Hell with Heroes, Colossus: The Forbin Project, Welcome to Blood City, High-Ballin', Fish Hawk, The Guardian, Mack the Knife.
TELEVISION: Inside Danny Baker (pilot), Al Capp special (prod., writer), Happily Ever After (pilot; prod., writer), Bob Hope Presents the Chrysler Theatre series, Jigsaw (pilot), Fear on Trial (Emmy nom.), Courage of Kavik: The Wolf Dog (exec. prod.), An American Christmas Carol, Grace Kelly.

CHASMAN, DAVID
Executive. b. New York, NY, Sept. 28, 1925. e. Sch. of Industrial Art, 1940-43; Academie De La Grande-Chaumiere, 1949-50. Monroe Greenthal Co., Inc. 1950-53; Grey Advertising Agency, Inc., 1953-60. Freelance consultant to industry 1950-60; worked on pictures for UA, 20th-Fox, Columbia, Samuel Goldwyn, City Film; Adv. mgr. United Artists, 1960; exec. dir. adv., United Artists, 1962; exec. production, United Artists, London, 1964; v.p. in prod. United Artists, 1969; v.p. of west coast operations, U.A. 1970; sr. v.p. in charge of prod., U.A. 1972; president, Convivium Productions Inc., 1974. Joined Columbia 1977, named exec. v.p. worldwide theatrical prod. 1979. Joined MGM 1980; named exec. v.p.-worldwide theatrical prod.
PICTURES: Exec. prod.: Brighton Beach Memoirs, The Secret of My Success.

CHAUDHRI, AMIN QAMAR
Director, Producer, Cinematographer, Editor. b. Punjab, India, April 18, 1942. e. Hampstead Polytechnic, London, City U. of New York. Pres., Filmart Enterprises Ltd. & Filmart Int'l Ltd., Pres./CEO, Continental Film Group Ltd. Pres./CEO, Continental Entertainment Group, Ltd., Heron Int'l Pictures, Ltd.
PICTURES: Director: Kashish, Khajuraho, Eternal, Urvasi, Konarak, The Land of Buddha. Producer: Night Visitors, Diary of a Hit Man, The Master Mechanic. Producer/Director: Once Again, An Unremarkable Life, Tiger Warsaw, The Last Day of School, Gunga Din, Golden Chute, Wings of Grey, Call It Sleep, The Bookie. Cinematography: Right On, Sweet Vengeance, The Hopefuls, The Wicked Die Slow, Who Says I Can't Ride a Rainbow, Black Rodeo, Medium Is the Message, Death of a Dunbar Girl, Kashish, The Last Day of School.
TELEVISION: Reflections of India (prod.-dir.), Wild Wild East (camera), Nehru (edit.), Medium is the Message (photog.), America... Amerika (prod., dir.).

CHAYKIN, MAURY
Actor. b. Brooklyn, NY, July 27, 1949. e. Univ. of Buffalo. Formed theatre co. Swamp Fox; later acted with Buffalo rep. co., Public Theatre in NY. Moved to Toronto in 1980.
PICTURES: The Kidnapping of the President, Death Hunt, Soup for One, Of Unknown Origin, Harry and Son, Highpoint, Mrs. Soffel, Turk 182!, Meatballs III, The Bedroom Window, Wild Thing, Stars and Bars, Caribe, Iron Eagle II, Twins, Millenium, Breaking In, Where the Heart Is, Mr. Destiny, Dances With Wolves, George's Island, My Cousin Vinny, Leaving Normal, The Adjuster, Hero, Sommersby, Money for Nothing, Josh and S.A.M., Beethoven's 2nd, Camilla, Whale Music (Genie Award), Unstrung Heroes, Devil in a Blue Dress, Cutthroat Island, Love and Death on Long Island, Pale Saints, Strip Search, The Sweet Hereafter, A Life Less Ordinary, Mouse Hunt, Jerry & Tom, Mystery Alaska.
TELEVISION: Special: Canada's Sweetheart: The Saga of Hal Banks (Nellie Award). Series: Emily of New Moon. Movies: If Looks Could Kill, Northern Lights.

CHELSOM, PETER
Director, Writer. b. Blackpool, England. Studied acting at London's Central School of Drama. Acted with Royal Shakespeare Co., Royal Natl. Theatre, Royal Court Theatre. Dir. at Central School of Drama, taught acting at Actors Ints. and at Cornell Univ. Wrote and directed short film Treacle for Channel 4/British Screen. Director of many commercials for television in London and U.S.
PICTURES: Hear My Song (dir., story, co-s.p.), Funny Bones (dir., co-prod., co-s.p.).

CHEN, JOAN
Actress. r.n. Chen Chong. b. Shanghai, China, 1961. Studied acting with actress Zhang Rei Fang at Shanghai Film Studio. Debuted as teenager in Chinese films. Moved to U.S. in 1981.
PICTURES: Little Flower, Awakening, Dim Sum: A Little Bit of Heart, Tai-Pain, The Last Emperor, The Blood of Heroes, Turtle Beach, When Sleeping Dogs Lie, Night Stalker, Heaven and Earth, Golden Gate, On Deadly Ground, Temptation of a Monk, Deadlock, The Hunted, Red Rose/White Rose, Judge Dredd, Wild Side, Precious Find.
TELEVISION: Series: Twin Peaks. Movie: Shadow of a Stranger. Guest: Miami Vice.

CHER
Singer, Actress. r.n. Cherilyn Sarkisian. b. El Centro, CA, May 20, 1946. Began singing as backup singer for Crystals and Ronettes then with former husband Sonny Bono in 1965; first hit record I Got You Babe, sold 3 million copies. Made two films and then debuted nightclub musical-comedy act in 1969. CBS comedy-variety series started as summer show in 1971; became regular series the following December. NY stage debut: Come Back to the Five and Dime Jimmy Dean Jimmy Dean (1982).
PICTURES: Wild on the Beach (debut, 1965), Good Times, Chastity, Come Back to the Five and Dime Jimmy Dean Jimmy Dean, Silkwood, Mask (Cannes award), The Witches of Eastwick, Suspect, Moonstruck (Academy Award), Mermaids, The Player, Ready to Wear (Pret- a-Porter), Faithful.
TELEVISION: Series: Sonny & Cher Comedy Hour (1971-74), Cher, The Sonny and Cher Show (1976-77). Specials: Cher, Cher... Special, Cher and Other Fantasies, Cher: A Celebration at Caesar's Palace, Cher at the Mirage. Movie: If These Walls Could Talk (also dir.). Guest: Shindig, Hullabaloo, Hollywood Palace, The Man from U.N.C.L.E., Laugh-In, Glen Campbell, Love American Style.

CHERMAK, CY
Producer, Writer. b. Bayonne, NJ, Sept. 20, 1929. e. Brooklyn Coll., Ithaca Coll.
TELEVISION: Writer, prod., exec. prod.: Ironside, The Virginian, The New Doctors, Amy Prentiss, Kolchak: The Night Stalker, Barbary Coast, CHiPS. Movie: Murder at the World Series (prod., s.p.).

CHERNIN, PETER
Executive. Chairman, Fox, Inc. Formerly pres., Fox Broadcasting.

CHERTOK, JACK
Producer. b. Atlanta, GA, July 13, 1906. Began career as script clerk, MGM; later asst. cameraman, asst. dir., head of music dept., short subjects prod. (including Crime Does Not Pay, Robert Benchley, Pete Smith series). Feature prod. MGM 1939-42 (The Penalty, Joe Smith, American, Kid Glove Killer, The Omaha Trail, Eyes in the Night, etc.). In 1942, apptd. Hollywood prod. chief, Co-Ord. Inter-Amer. Affairs, serving concurrently with regular studio work. Left MGM in 1942 and prod. for Warner Bros. to late 1944; Produced The Corn is Green and Northern Pursuit for Warner Bros. Pres. Jack Chertok TV, Inc.
TELEVISION: Prod.: My Favorite Martian, The Lone Ranger, Sky King, Cavalcade, Private Secretary, My Living Doll, Western Marshal, The Lawless Years.

CHETWYND, LIONEL
Executive, Writer, Director. b. London, England. m. actress Gloria Carlin. Emigrated to Canada, 1948. e. Sir George Williams U., Montreal, BA, economics; BCL-McGill U., Montreal. Graduate Work-Law, Trinity Coll. Oxford. Admitted to bar, Province of Quebec, 1968. C.B.C., TV-Public Affairs and Talks, 1961-1965. CTV network 1965-67. Controller commercial TV and film rights, Expo '67. Freelance writer and consultant 1961-68. Asst. mng. dir. Columbia Pictures (U.K.) Ltd. London 1968-72. Asst. mng. dir. Columbia-Warner UK, 1971. Story and book for musical Maybe That's Your Problem, 1971-1973. Then Bleeding Great Orchids (staged London, and Off-B'way). Also wrote The American 1776, official U.S. Bi-centennial film and We the People/200 Constitutional Foundation. Former mem. of NYU grad. film sch. faculty, lecturer on screenwriting at Frederick Douglass Ctr. Harlem. Mem of Canadian Bar Assc. Served on bd. of gov., Commission on Battered Children, and the Little League.
PICTURES: *Director and/or Writer:* The Apprenticeship of Duddy Kravitz (Acad. Award nom.), Morning Comes, Two Solitudes (also prod.), Grand Award Salonika), Quintet, The Hanoi Hilton, Redline, The Hot Touch.
TELEVISION: *Producer and/or Writer:* Johnny We Hardly Knew Ye (George Washington Honor Medal, Freedom Fdn.), It Happened One Christmas, Goldenrod, A Whale for the Killing , Miracle on Ice (Christopher Award), Escape From Iran: The Canadian Caper, Sadat (NAACP Image Award), Children in the Crossfire, To Heal a Nation (also exec. prod.), Evil in Clear River (exec. prod. only, Christopher Award), So Proudly We Hail (also exec. prod.), The Godfather Wars, The Heroes of Desert Storm, Reverse Angle (also exec. prod.), Doom's Day Gun, The Bible... Moses, The Bible... Jacob, The Bible... Joseph (Emmy award), The Man Who Captured Eichmann, Kissinger & Nixon (also exec. prod.), Ruby Ridge, An American Tragedy, The Doom's Day Gun, Freefall, Goldenrod.

CHINICH, MICHAEL
Producer. b. New York, NY. e. Boston U. Began career as casting agent in N.Y.; moved to L.A. to join MCA-Universal Pictures as executive in casting. Named head of feature film casting; then prod. v.p.
PICTURES: *Casting dir.:* Dog Day Afternoon, Coal Miner's Daughter, Animal House, Melvin and Howard, The Blues Brothers, Mask, Midnight Run, Twins, Ghostbusters II, Kindergarten Cop, Dave, Junior, The Late Shift, Father's Day. *Exec. Prod.:* Pretty in Pink, Ferris Bueller's Day Off, Some Kind of Wonderful, Planes Trains and Automobiles (co-exec. prod.), Commandments (prod.).

CHOMSKY, MARVIN J.
Director, Producer. b. Bronx, NY, May 23, 1929. e. Syracuse U., B.S.; Stanford U., M.A. Started in theatre business at early age as art dir. with such TV credits as U.S. Steel Hour, Playhouse 90, Studio One, etc. Later worked with Herbert Brodkin who advanced him to assoc. prod. with such TV shows as The Doctors and The Nurses. Brought to Hollywood in 1965 as assoc. prod. for Talent Associates, producing series of TV pilots. Art dir.: The Bubble.
PICTURES: Evel Knievel, Murph the Surf, Mackintosh and T.J., Good Luck Miss Wycoff, Tank.
TELEVISION: *Series:* The Wild Wild West, Gunsmoke, Star Trek, Then Came Bronson. *Movies:* Assault on the Wayne, Mongo's Back in Town, Family Flight, Fireball Forward, Female Artillery, The Magician, The F.B.I. Story: The F.B.I. Vs. Alvin Karpas, Mrs. Sundance, Attack on Terror: The F.B.I. Vs. the Ku Klux Klan, Kate McShane, Brink's: The Great Robbery, Law and Order, A Matter of Wife and Death, Victory at Entebbe, Little Ladies of the Night, Roots (co-dir.), Danger in Paradise, Holocaust (Emmy Award, 1978), Hollow Image, King Crab, Attica (Emmy Award, 1980), Inside the Third Reich (Emmy Award, 1982), My Body My Child, The Nairobi Affair, I Was a Mail Order Bride, Robert Kennedy and His Times, Evita Peron (also prod.), Peter the Great (also prod.; Emmy Award as prod., 1986), The Deliberate Stranger (also prod.), Anastasia: The Mystery of Anna (also prod.), Billionaire Boys Club (also spv. prod.), Angel in Green, I'll Be Home for Christmas (also prod.), Brotherhood of the Rose (also prod.), Telling Secrets, Strauss Dynasty (also prod.), Hurricane Andrew (also prod.), Catherine the Great (also prod.).

CHONG, RAE DAWN
Actress. b. Edmonton Alta, Canada, Feb. 28, 1961. Father is director-comedian Tommy Chong. Debut at 12 in The Whiz Kid of Riverton (TV). B'way debut 1991 in Oh Kay!
PICTURES: Stony Island (debut, 1978), Quest for Fire, Beat Street, The Corsican Brothers, Choose Me, Fear City, City Limits, American Flyers, Commando, The Color Purple, Soul Man, The Squeeze, The Principal, Walking After Midnight, Tales From the Darkside, Far Out Man, The Borrower, Amazon, Chaindance, Time Runner, When the Party's Over, In Exile, Boulevard, Boca, Hideaway, The Break, Starlight, Mask of Death, Waiting for the Man, Goodbye America.
TELEVISION: *Movies:* The Top of the Hill, Badge of the Assassin, Curiosity Kills, Prison Stories: Women on the Inside, Father & Son: Dangerous Relations, Thing I Forgot to Remember. *Series:* Nitecap, Martian Law.

CHONG, TOMMY
Actor, Writer, Director. b. Edmonton, Alta., Canada, May 24, 1938. Daughter is actress Rae Dawn Chong. Was guitar player with various Canadian rhythm and blues combinations, before teaming with Richard (Cheech) Marin in improvisational group. Has made comedy recordings.
PICTURES: Up in Smoke, Cheech and Chong's Next Movie (also dir., co-s.p.), Cheech and Chong's Nice Dreams (also dir., co-s.p.), Things Are Tough All Over, It Came from Hollywood, Still Smokin', Yellowbeard, The Corsican Brothers (also dir., s.p.), After Hours, Tripwire (cameo), Far Out Man (also dir., s.p.), The Spirit of 76, FernGully (voice), National Lampoon's Senior Trip, McHale's Navy.
TELEVISION: Trial and Error (co-exec. prod.).

CHOOLUCK, LEON
Producer, Director. b. New York, NY, March 19, 1920. e. City Coll. of New York, 1938. Production, distribution, editing Consolidated Film Industries Ft. Lee 1936-40; staff sgt., Army Pictorial Service as news photographer 1941-45; prod. for Regal Films (Fox) Clover Prods. (Col.), Hugo Haas Prods. and Orbit Pro. (Col), 1957-58; dir. Highway Patrol, 1958. Prod. mgr., Captain Sinbad, prod. sprv. Encyclopedia Britannica Films, in Spain, 1964; prod. supv., U.S. Pictures, Battle of the Bulge; v.p. Fouad Said Cinemobile Systems, 1969-70; ABC Pictures 1970-71 (Grissom Gang, Kotch). 1983-present, consultant, intl. film services.
PICTURES: Hell on Devil's Island, Plunder Road, Murder by Contract, City of Fear (prod.), The Fearmakers, Day of the Outlaw, Bramble Bush, Rise and Fall of Legs Diamond (assoc. prod.), Studs Lonigan, Three Blondes in His Life (dir.), El Cid, Midas Run (assoc. prod.), Payday; Three the Hard Way, Take a Hard Ride, Apocalypse Now, Loving Couples, Square Dance, Wonders of China (Disney Circlevision Epcot).
TELEVISION: Prod. supv.: 1/4 hr. Fireside Theatre, Stoney Burke, The Outer Limits (assoc. prod.), I Spy (assoc. prod.), Lock Up (dir.). *Specials:* Strange Homecoming, James Mitchener's Dynasty, Judge Horton and the Scottsboro Boys, Pearl, A Rumor of War, Murder in Texas, Love Boat, Dynasty, Breakdown (Alfred Hitchcock), On Wings of Eagles.

CHOW, RAYMOND
O.B.E. Producer. b. Hong Kong, 1927. e. St. John's U., Shanghai. Worked for Hong Kong Standard; then joined the Hong Kong office of the U.S. Information Service. In 1959 joined Shaw Brothers as head of publicity, became head of production before leaving in 1970 to start Golden Harvest to produce Chinese-language films in Hong Kong. Kung-fu films featuring Bruce Lee put Harvest into int'l market. Started English-language films in 1977, beginning with The Amsterdam Kill and The Boys in Company C. Named Showman of the Year 1984 by NATO. Awarded O.B.E. in 1988.
PICTURES: Armour of God, The Big Boss (and subsequent Bruce Lee films), The Cannonball Run (and Part II), High Road to China, Lassiter, Miracles, Mr. Boo (a.k.a. The Private Eyes; and many subsequent Michael Hui films), Painted Faces, Police Story (and Part II), Project A (and Part II), Rouge, The Story of the Flying Fox, Love on the Rooftops, A Show of Force, China O'Brien (and Part II), Teenage Mutant Ninja Turtles (and Part II), Lord of East China Sea, The Reincarnation of Golden Lotus, Summer Snow, Rumble in the Bronx, Lost & Found, Viva Erotica, The Stunt Woman, Hold You Tight, The Soong Sisters, Kitchen.

CHRISTIANSEN, ROBERT W.
Producer. b. Porterville, CA. e. Bakersfield Coll. Spent 3 years in Marine Corps. Worked on Hollywood Reporter in circulation and advertising. Joined Cinema Center Films; prod. asst. on Monte Walsh and Hail Hero. Co-produced first feature in 1970, Adam at Six A.M., with Rick Rosenberg, with whom co-produced all credits listed.
PICTURES: Adam at Six A.M., Hide in Plain Sight.
TELEVISION: *Features:* Suddenly Single, The Glass House, Gargoyles, A Brand New Life, The Man Who Could Talk to Kids, The Autobiography of Miss Jane Pittman, I Love You...Goodbye, Queen of the Stardust Ballroom, Born Innocent, A Death in Canaan, Strangers, Robert Kennedy and His Times, Kids Don't Tell, As Summers Die, Gore Vidal's Lincoln, Red Earth, White Earth, The Heist, A House of Secrets and Lies, The Last Hit, Heart of Darkness, Tad, Kingfish: A Story of Huey P. Long, Redwood Curtain.

CHRISTIE, JULIE
Actress. b. Chukua, Assam, India, April 14, 1941. Father had tea plantation in India. e. in Britian, at 16 studied art in France, then attended Central Sch. of Music & Drama in London. 3 yrs. with Frinton-on-Sea Rep., before TV debut in A for Andromeda. Birmingham Rep.; Royal Shakespeare Co.; East European and American tour. NY stage: Uncle Vanya. London stage: Old Times.
PICTURES: Crooks Anonymous (debut, 1962), Fast Lady, Billy Liar, Young Cassidy, Darling (Academy Award & BFA Award, 1965), Dr. Zhivago, Farenheit 451, Far From the Madding Crowd, Petulia, In Search of Gregory, The Go-Between, McCabe and Mrs. Miller, Don't Look Now, Shampoo, Nashville (cameo), Demon Seed, Heaven Can Wait, Memoirs of a Survivor, The Return of the Soldier, Heat and Dust, Golddiggers, Power, Miss Mary, La Memoire tatouree (Secret Obsession), Fools of Fortune, Dragonheart, Hamlet, Afterglow (NY Film Crits. Circle Award, Best Actress, 1997; Academy Award nom.).
TELEVISION: Debut: A is for Andromeda (UK series, 1962), Sins of the Fathers (Italian TV), Separate Tables, Dadah Is Death (Amer. TV debut, 1988), The Railway Station Man.

CHRISTOPHER, DENNIS
Actor. b. Philadelphia, PA, Dec. 2, 1955. e. Temple U. NY stage debut, Yentl the Yeshiva Boy (1974). Other NY theater: Dr. Needle and the Infectious Laughter Epidemic, The Little Foxes, Brothers, Exmass, A Pound on Demand, Advice from a Caterpillar. Regional theater incl. Balm in Gilead, American Buffalo. Appeared in 1991 short The Disco Years.
PICTURES: Blood and Lace, Didn't You Hear?, The Young Graduates, Fellini's Roma, Salome, 3 Women, September 30, 1955, A Wedding, California Dreaming, The Last Word, Breaking Away, Fade to Black, Chariots of Fire, Don't Cry It's Only Thunder, Alien Predator, Flight of the Spruce Goose, Jake Speed, Friends, A Sinful Life, Circuitry Man, Dead Women in Lingerie, Doppelganger, Circuitry Man II: Plughead Rewired.
TELEVISION: *Movies*: The Oregon Trail, Stephen King's IT, False Arrest, Willing to Kill: The Texas Cheerleader Story, Curacao, Deadly Invasion: The Killer Bee Nightmare. *Specials*: Bernice Bobs Her Hair, Jack and the Beanstalk (Faerie Tale Theatre), Cristabel. *Guest*: Trapper John M.D., Tales of the Unexpected, Stingray, Cagney & Lacey, Moonlighting, Hooperman, The Equalizer, Matlock, Murder She Wrote, Monsters, Civil Wars, Dark Justice, The Watcher, The Cosby Mysteries.

CHRISTOPHER, JORDAN
Actor, Musician. b. Youngstown, OH. Oct. 23, 1941. e. Kent State U. Led rock 'n' roll group, The Wild Ones. B'way debut, Black Comedy, 1967.
PICTURES: Return of the Seven, The Fat Spy, The Tree, Angel Angel Down We Go, Pigeons, Brainstorm, Star 80, That's Life!
TELEVISION: *Series*: Secrets of Midland Heights.

CHUNG, CONNIE
TV News Anchor. r.n. Constance Yu-Hwa Chung. m. anchor Maury Povich. b. Washington, D.C., Aug. 20, 1946. e. U. of Maryland, B.S. Entered field 1969 as copy person, writer then on-camera reporter for WTTG-TV, Washington; 1971, named Washington corr., CBS News; 1976, anchor KNXT, Los Angeles; 1983, anchor, NBC News at Sunrise; anchor, NBC Saturday Nightly News and news specials; 1989 moved to CBS as anchor, Sunday Night Evening News; anchor and reporter, Saturday Night with Connie Chung (later Face ot Face With Connie Chung), 1989-90. Received Emmy Award for Shot in Hollywood (1987), Interview With Marlon Brando (1989); 2 additional Emmy Awards: 1986, 1990. Became co-anchor, with Dan Rather, of CBS Evening News, 1993-95. Prime time series: Eye to Eye With Connie Chung, 1993. Many other awards incl. Peabody, 2 LA Emmy Awards, Golden Mike, Women in Business Award, etc.

CHURCH, THOMAS HADEN
Actor. b. March 31, 1960
PICTURES: Tombstone, Tales From the Crypt Presents: Demon Knight, George of the Jungle, One Night, Free Money, Scotch and Milk (prod.).
TELEVISION: *Series*: Wings, Ned and Stacey. *Movies*: Fugitive Nights: Danger in the Desert. *Guest*: China Beach, Cheers, Booker, 21 Jump Street, Flying Blind, Partners. *Mini-series*: Mr. Murder.

CILENTO, DIANE
Actress. b. Queensland, Australia, April 2, 1934. e. Toowoomba. Went to New York and finished schooling and then American Acad. of Dramatic Art. First theatre job at 16; toured U.S. with Barter Co.; returned to London and joined Royal Acad. of Dramatic Art; several small parts and later repertory at Manchester's Library Theatre.
THEATER: *London stage*: Tiger at the Gates (also NY: Theatre World Award), The Third Secret, The Four Seasons, The Bonne Soup, Heartbreak House. NY: The Big Knife, Orpheus, Altona, Castle in Sweden, Naked, Marys, I've Seen You Cut Lemons.
PICTURES: Wings of Danger (Dead on Course; debut, 1952), Moulin Rouge, Meet Mr. Lucifer, All Halloween, The Angel Who Pawned Her Harp, The Passing Stranger, Passage Home, The Woman for Joe, The Admirable (Paradise Lagoon), The Truth About Women, Jet Storm, Stop Me Before I Kill! (The Full Treatment), I Thank a Fool, The Naked Edge, Tom Jones (Acad. Award nom.), Rattle of a Simple Man, The Third Secret, The Agony and the Ecstacy, Hombre, Negatives, Z.P.G. (Zero Population Growth), Hitler: The Last Ten Days, The Wicker Man, The Tiger Lily, The Boy Who Had Everything, Duet for Four.
TELEVISION: La Belle France (series), Court Martial, Blackmail, Dial M for Murder, Rogues Gallery, Rain, Lysistrata, The Kiss of Blood, For the Term of His Natural Life.

CIMINO, MICHAEL
Writer, Director. b. New York, NY, 1943. e. Yale U. BFA, MFA. Was tv commecial director before becoming screen writer.
PICTURES: Silent Running (co-s.p.), Magnum Force (co-s.p.). Director: Thunderbolt and Lightfoot (also s.p.), The Deer Hunter (also co-wrote story, co-prod.; Academy Awards for Best Picture & Director, 1978.), Heaven's Gate (also s.p.), Year of the Dragon (also co-s.p.), The Sicilian (also co-prod.), Desperate Hours (also co-prod.), The Sunchasers (also co-s.p., co-prod.).

CIPES, ARIANNE ULMER
Executive. b. New York, NY, July 25, 1937. e. Royal Acad. of Dramatic Art, London, U. of London. Daughter of film dir. Edgar G. Ulmer. Actress, then production and dubbing, Paris; CDC, Rome; Titra, New York; 1975-77, v.p., Best Intl Films (intl film distributor), Los Angeles; 1977 co-founder and sr. v.p./sales & services of Producers Sales Organization; 1981, named exec. v.p., American Film Marketing Assn.; 1982, founded AUC Films, consulting and intl. and domestic sales-prods. rep.; pres. of the Edgar G. Ulmer Preservation Corp.

CIPES, JAY H.
Executive. b. Mt. Vernon, NY, Dec. 14, 1928. e. Cornell U. 1960-66, indt producer-packager-distributor European features for U.S. TV sales; 1967, prod., 20th Century-Fox TV; 1970, prod., Four Star TV; 1971, mktg. exec. Technicolor, Inc.; 1973, v.p., mktg. Technicolor, Inc.; 1979 sr. v.p., dir. worldwide mktg, Technicolor, Inc. Professional Film Division. 1992, indt. consultant to prod. & post-prod. facilities.

CLAPP, GORDON
Actor. b. Canada, Sept. 24, 1948.
PICTURES: Running, Return of the Secaucus 7, Matewan, Eight Men Out, Termini Station, Gross Anatomy, April One, Badge of Betrayal.
TELEVISION: *Movies*: The Other Kingdom, Letting Go, The Right of the People, Hands of a Stranger, Small Sacrifices, Family of Spies, Blind Faith, The Secret Life of Archie's Wife, Fever, Mission of the Shark: The Saga of the U.S.S. Indianapolis, Bonds of Love, Kiss of a Killer, Family of Strangers, In the Line of Duty: Ambush in Waco, Her Hidden Truth, Abandoned and Deceived, The Morrison Murders. *Mini-series*: Evergreen. *Series*: Check It Out, NYPD Blue (Emmy Award, 1998).

CLARK, BILL
Producer.
TELEVISION: *Series*: NYPD Blue (Emmy Award, 1998), Brooklyn South.

CLARK, BOB
Director, Writer, Producer. b. New Orleans, LA, Aug. 5.
PICTURES: *Director*: The She Man, The Emperor's New Clothes, Children Shouldn't Play with Dead Things (credited as Benjamin Clark), Deathdream (Dead of Night), Deranged (prod. only), Black Christmas (Silent Night Evil Night), Breaking Point, Murder by Decree, Tribute, Porky's (also s.p., prod.), Porky's II—The Next Day (also s.p., prod.), A Christmas Story (also s.p., prod.), Rhinestone, Turk 182, From the Hip (also co-s.p.), Loose Cannons (also co-s.p.), It Runs in the Family (also co-s.p.), Baby Geniuses.
TELEVISION: *Movies*: The American Clock, Stolen Memories, Secrets from the Rose Garden, Fudge-A-Mania, Derby, Ransom of the Red Chief. *Series episode*: Amazing Stories (Remote Control Man).

CLARK, CANDY
Actress. b. Norman, OK, June 20. Was successful model in N.Y. before landing role in Fat City, 1972. Off-B'way debut 1981: A Couple of White Chicks Sitting Around Talking; followed by It's Raining on Hope Street. Appeared in short Blind Curve.
PICTURES: Fat City (debut, 1972), American Graffiti (Acad. Award nom.), I Will I Will... For Now, The Man Who Fell To Earth, Citizens Band (Handle With Care), The Big Sleep, When You Comin' Back Red Ryder, More American Graffiti, National Lampoon Goes to the Movies, Q, Blue Thunder, Amityville 3-D, Hambone and Hillie, Cat's Eye, At Close Range, The Blob, Original Intent, Deuce Coupe, Cool as Ice, Buffy the Vampire Slayer, Radioland Murders.
TELEVISION: *Movies*: James Dean, Amateur Night at the Dixie Bar and Grill, Where the Ladies Go, Rodeo Girl, Johnny Belinda, Cocaine and Blue Eyes, The Price She Paid.

CLARK, DANE
Actor. b. New York, NY, Feb. 18, 1915. e. Cornell U., St. John's. In radio series 2 yrs.; on N.Y. stage (Of Mice and Men, Dead End, The Country Girl, Brecht on Brecht, The Number, The Fragile Fox, A Thousand CLowns, Mike Downstairs, etc.). Natl. Co. of Two for the Seesaw.
PICTURES: The Glass Key (debut, 1942), Sunday Punch, Pride of the Yankees, Tennessee Johnson, Action in the North Atlantic, Destination Tokyo, The Very Thought of You, Hollywood Canteen, Pride of the Marines, God Is My Co-Pilot, Her Kind of Man, A Stolen Life, That Way With Women, Deep Valley, Embraceable You, Moonrise, Whiplash, Without Honor, Backfire, Barricade, Never Trust a Gambler, Fort Defiance, Highly Dangerous, Gambler and the Lady, Go Man Go, Blackout, Paid to Kill, Thunder Pass, Port of Hell, Toughest Man Alive, Massacre, The Man is Armed, Outlaw's Son, Blood Song, The Woman Inside, Last Rites.
TELEVISION: *Series*: Wire Service, Bold Venture, Perry Mason (1973-4). *Specials*: No Exit, The Closing Door, The French Atlantic Affair. *Guest*: Twilight Zone, I Spy, Mod Squad, Cannon, Hawaii 5-O, Murder She Wrote, Police Story, Highway to Heaven, The Rookies, many others. *Movies*: The Face of Fear, The Family Rico, Say Goodbye Maggie Cole, The Return of Joe Forrester, Murder on Flight 502, James Dean, Condominium. *Mini-Series*: Once an Eagle, The French Atlantic Affair.
(d. Sept. 11, 1998)

CLARK, DICK
Performer; Chairman, CEO, dick Clark Prods., Inc. b. Mt. Vernon, NY, Nov. 30, 1929. e. Syracuse U. graduated 1951, summer announcer WRUN, Utica 1949, staff announcer WOLF, Syracuse 1950. After grad. 1951, took regular job with WOLF. Rejoined WRUN, Utica, then joined WKTV, Utica. Announcer WFIL Philadelphia 1952. Formed Dick Clark productions 1956, TV and motion picture production with in-person concert division, cable TV programing dept. Host of two weekly synd. radio programs: U.S. Music Survey and Rock Roll & Remember. Founder and principal owner of Unistar Communications Group. Took company public in January, 1987 (NASDAQ: DCPI), serves as chmn. & CEO. Received Emmy Lifetime Achievement Award, 1994.
PICTURES: *Actor.* Because They're Young (debut, 1960), The Young Doctors, Killers Three. *Producer.* Psychout, The Savage Seven, Remo Williams: The Adventure Begins.
TELEVISION: *Host:* American Bandstand (also exec. prod.; Emmy Award as exec. prod., 1982-83), The Dick Clark Beechnut Show, Dick Clark's World of Talent, Record Years, Years of Rock. $25,000 Pyramid (3 Emmy Awards as host: 1979, 1985, 1986), $100,000 Pyramid, The Challengers. *Producer:* Where The Action Is, Swinging Country, Happening, Get It Together, Shebang, Record Years, Years of Rock. *Executive Producer:* American Music Awards, Academy of Country Music Awards, Dick Clark's New Year's Rockin' Eve, ACE Awards, Daytime Emmy Awards, Golden Globe Awards, Soap Opera Awards, Superstars and Their Moms, Caught in the Act (pilot). *Series:* TV's Bloopers & Practical Jokes, Puttin' on the Hits, Puttin' on the Kids, Dick Clark's Nitetime, Inside America, In Person From the Palace, Getting in Touch, Live! Dick Clark Presents!, VH-1's Best of American Bandstand, Strange Truth: Fact or Fiction, Primetime Country, No Relation, The Weird Al Show, Meet Hanson. *Movies:* Elvis, Man in the Santa Claus Suit, Murder in Texas, Reaching for the Stars, The Demon Murder Case, The Woman Who Willed a Miracle (Emmy Award, 1983), Birth of the Beatles, Copacabana, Promised a Miracle, The Town Bully, Liberace, Backtrack, Death Dreams, Elvis and the Colonel, Secret Sins of the Father, Deep Family Secrets. *Specials:* Live Aid—An All-Star Concert for African Relief, Farm Aid III, Super Bloopers & New Practical Jokes, American Bandstand's 33 1/3 Celebration, America Picks the No. 1 Songs, You Are the Jury, Thanks for Caring, Supermodel of the World, Freedom Festival '89, What About Me I'm Only Three, 1992 USA Music Challenge, The Good Doctor, TV Censored Bloopers '98, Motown 40: The Music Is Forever.
WRITER: Your Happiest Years, 1959; Rock, Roll & Remember, 1976; To Goof or Not to Goof, 1963; Dick Clark's Easygoing Guide to Good Grooming, 1986; The History of American Bandstand, 1986, Dick Clark's American Bandstand, 1997.

CLARK, DUNCAN C.
Executive. b. Sutton, Surrey, England. Entered industry in 1972. Appointed dir. of publicity and adv., CIC, Jan. 1979, taking up similar post in 1981 for United Artists. On formation of U.I.P. in 1982, appt. dir., pub. and adv., & deputy mng. dir., 1983. 1987 appt. v.p. adv. & pub., Columbia Pictures Intl (NY). In 1987, sr. v.p. intl marketing for Columbia (Burbank); appt. sr. v.p., Columbia Tri-Star Film Distribs., Inc., (NY). Relocated to corp. headquarters in Culver City, 1991. Appointed exec. v.p. Worldwide Marketing, 1994. In 1996, appointed presdient Columbia TriStar Film Distributors Intl.

CLARK, GREYDON
Producer, Director, Writer. b. Niles, MI, Feb. 7, 1943. e. Western Michigan U., B.A., theatre arts, 1963. Heads own company, World Amusement Corp., Sherman Oaks, CA.
PICTURES: *Director:* Danse Macabre, Satan's Sadists (actor only), Hell's Bloody Devils (actor only), The Blood Seekers (actor only), The Bad Bunch (also writer, actor), Black Shampoo (also writer), Satan's Cheerleaders, Hi-Riders (also writer), Angels' Revenge (also prod., writer), Without Warning (also prod.), The Return, Wacko (also prod.), Joysticks, Final Justice, Uninvited, Skinheads (also prod., writer), Out of Sight Out of Mind, The Forbidden Dance, Killer Instinct, Dark Future (also prod.).
TELEVISION: *Series:* Star Games.

CLARK, HILARY J.
Executive. e. U. of Southern California, B.A., 1976. Began industry career 1978 as ad-pub admin. in co-op adv. dept., Buena Vista Dist. Co. Promoted to mgr. of natl. field pub & promo., 1980. Acted as unit publicist on numerous films (Explorers, Sylvester, Swing Shift, Twilight Zone, Crossroads, etc.) before returning to BV 1986 as natl. pub. dir. for Walt Disney Pictures. Became exec. dir. of Natl. Publicity for Disney and Touchstone Pictures, 1988; v.p. Intl. Publicity for Buena Vista Intl., 1990.

CLARK, MATT
Actor, Director. b. Washington, DC, Nov. 25, 1936.
THEATER: *NY:* A Portrait of the Artist as a Young Man, The Subject Was Roses, The Trial of the Catonsville Nine; *Regional:* One Flew Over the Cuckoo's Nest, Tonight We Improvise.
PICTURES: Black Like Me (debut, 1964), In the Heat of the Night, Will Penny, The Bridge at Remagen, Macho Callahan, Homer (co-s.p. only), Monte Walsh, The Beguiled, The Grissom Gang, The Cowboys, The Culpepper Cattle Company, The Great Northfield Minnesota Raid, Jeremiah Johnson, The Life and Times of Judge Roy Bean, Emperor of the North Pole, The Laughing Policeman, Pat Garrett and Billy the Kid, White Lightning, The Terminal Man, Hearts of the West, Outlaw Blues, Kid Vengeance, The Driver, Dreamer, Brubaker, An Eye for an Eye, Legend of the Lone Ranger, Ruckus, Some Kind of Hero, Honkytonk Man, Love Letters, The Adventures of Buckaroo Banzai, Country, Tuff Turf, Return to Oz, Let's Get Harry, Da (dir. only), The Horror Show, Back to the Future Part III, Cadence, Class Action, Frozen Assets, Fortunes of War, The Harvest, Candyman: Farewell to the Flesh, Mother, Hacks.
TELEVISION: *Series:* Dog and Cat, The Jeff Foxworthy Show. *Mini-Series:* The Winds of War, War and Remembrance, Trilogy of Special Terror II. *Movies:* The Execution of Private Slovik, The Great Ice Rip-Off, Melvin Purvis: G-Man, This is the West That Was, The Kansas City Massacre, Dog and Cat (pilot), Lacy and the Mississippi Queen, The Last Ride of the Dalton Gang, The Children Nobody Wanted, In the Custody of Strangers, Love Mary, Out of the Darkness, The Quick and the Dead, The Gambler III: The Legend Continues, Terror on Highway 91, Blind Witness, Deceptions, Dead Before Dawn, Barbarians at the Gate, A Season of Hope, Raven Hawk. *Specials:* Shadow of Fear, Andrea's Story. *Pilots:* The Big Easy, Highway Honeys, Traveling Man. *Guest:* Hardcastle and McCormick, Midnight Caller, Bodies of Evidence. *Director:* Midnight Caller, My Dissident Mom (Schoolbreak Special).

CLARK, PETULA
Actress, Singer. b. Ewell, Surrey, England, Nov. 15, 1932. On British stage in The Sound of Music, Candida, Someone Like You (also composer, co-writer). B'way debut in Blood Brothers (1993). Starred in own BBC TV series 1967-8. Winner of two Grammy Awards, 1964 (Best Rock and Roll Recording: Downtown), 1965 (Best Contemporary R & R Vocal Performance Female: I Know a Place).
PICTURES: Medal for the General (debut, 1944), Strawberry Roan, Murder in Reverse, I Know Where I'm Going, London Town (My Heart Goes Crazy), Vice Versa, Easy Money, Here Come the Huggets, Vote for Hugget, Don't Ever Leave Me, The Huggets Abroad, The Romantic Age (Naughty Arlette), Dance Hall, White Corridors, Madame Louise, The Card (The Promoter), Made In Heaven, The Gay Dog, The Runaway Bus, The Happiness of Three Women, Track the Man Down, That Woman Opposite (City After Midnight), Six-Five Special, A Couteaux Tires (Daggers Drawn), Questi Pazzi Pazzi Italiani, The Big T.N.T. Show, Finian's Rainbow, Goodbye Mr. Chips, Never Never Land.

CLARK, SUSAN
Actress. r.n. Nora Golding. b. Sarnid, Ontario, Canada, March 8, 1943. Trained at Royal Acad. of Dramatic Art, London and Stella Adler Academy.
PICTURES: Banning (debut, 1967), Coogan's Bluff, Madigan, Tell Them Willie Boy Is Here, Colossus: The Forbin Project, Skullduggery, Skin Game, Valdez Is Coming, Showdown, The Midnight Man, Airport 1975, Night Moves, The Apple Dumpling Gang, The North Avenue Irregulars, Murder by Decree, City on Fire, Promises in the Dark, Double Negative, Nobody's Perfekt, Porky's.
TELEVISION: *Series:* Webster, Emily of New Moon. *Movies:* Something for a Lonely Man, The Challengers, The Astronaut, Trapped, Babe (Emmy Award, 1976), McNaughton's Daughter, Amelia Earhart, Jimmy B. and Andre (also co-prod.), The Choice, Maid in America (also co-prod.), Snowbound: The Jim and Jennifer Stolpa Story, Tonya and Nancy: The Inside Story, Butterbox Babies. *Specials:* Hedda Gabler, Double Solitaire.

CLAYBURGH, JILL
Actress. b. New York, NY, April 30, 1944. m. playwright David Rabe. e. Sarah Lawrence Coll. 1966. Former member of Charles Playhouse, Boston.
THEATER: The Nest (*off-B'way*), The Rothschilds, Jumpers, Pippin, In the Boom Boom Room, Design For Living.
PICTURES: The Wedding Party (debut, 1969), The Telephone Book, Portnoy's Complaint, The Thief Who Came to Dinner, Terminal Man, Gable and Lombard, Silver Streak, Semi-Tough, An Unmarried Woman (Acad. Award nom.), Luna, Starting Over (Acad. Award nom.), It's My Turn, First Monday in October, I'm Dancing as Fast as I Can, Hannah K, Where Are The Children?, Shy People, Beyond the Ocean, Whispers in the Dark, Rich in Love, Day of Atonement, Naked in New York, Going All the Way, Fools Rush In.

TELEVISION: *Series*: Search For Tomorrow. *Movies*: The Snoop Sisters (Female Instinct), Miles To Go, Hustling, The Art of Crime, Griffin and Phoenix, Who Gets the Friends?, Fear Stalk, Unspeakable Acts, Reason for Living: The Jill Ireland Story, Trial: The Price of Passion, Firestorm: 72 Hours in Oakland, Honor Thy Father and Mother: The True Story of the Menedez Murders, For the Love of Nancy, The Face on the Milk Carton, Crowned & Dangerous, Sins of the Mind. *Guest*: Medical Center, Rockford Files, Saturday Night Live.

CLEESE, JOHN
Actor, Writer. b. Weston-Super-Mare, England, Oct. 27, 1939. e. Clifton Coll., Cambridge U. Began acting with Cambridge University Footlights revue. With classmate Graham Chapman wrote for British TV. Co-creator of Monty Python's Flying Circus. Co-author (with psychiatrist Robin Skynner): Families and How to Survive Them (1983), Life and How to Survive It (1995).
PICTURES: Interlude (debut, 1968), The Bliss of Mrs. Blossom, The Best House in London, The Rise and Rise of Michael Rimmer (also co-s.p.), The Magic Christian (also co-s.p.), The Statue, And Now for Something Completely Different (also co-s.p.), Monty Python and the Holy Grail (also co-s.p.), The Life of Brian (also co-s.p.), The Great Muppet Caper, Time Bandits, The Secret Policeman's Other Ball, Monty Python Live at the Hollywood Bowl (also co-s.p.), Monty Python's The Meaning of Life (also co-s.p.), Yellowbeard, Privates on Parade, Silverado, Clockwise, A Fish Called Wanda (also co-s.p., exec. prod., BAFTA Award, Writer's Guild of America nom., Oscar nom.), The Big Picture (cameo), Erik the Viking, An American Tail: Fievel Goes West (voice), Splitting Heirs, Mary Shelley's Frankenstein, The Swan Princess (voice), Rudyard Kipling's The Jungle Book, George of the Jungle.
TELEVISION: *Special*: Taming of the Shrew. *Series*: The Frost Report, At Last the 1948 Show, Monty Python's Flying Circus, Fawlty Towers. *Guest*: Cheers (Emmy Award, 1987).

CLEMENS, BRIAN
Writer, Producer, Director. b. Croydon, England. Early career in advertising then wrote BBC TV play. Later TV filmed series as writer, script editor and features. Script editor Danger Man; Won Edgar Allen Poe Award for Best TV Thriller of 1962 (Scene of the Crime for U.S. Steel Hour). Various plays for Armchair Theatre; ATV Drama 70; Love Story. Winner two Edgar Allan Poe Awards, Cinema Fantastique Award for best s.p.
PICTURES: The Tell-Tale Heart, Station Six-Sahara, The Peking Medallion, And Soon The Darkness, The Major, When The Wind Blows, See No Evil, Dr. Jekyll and Sister Hyde, Golden Voyage of Sinbad, Watcher in the Woods, Stiff, Highlander 2, Justine (France), Bugs (UK).
TELEVISION: *Wrote and prod.*: The Avengers (2 Emmy noms.), The New Avengers, The Professionals, Escapade (U.S.), Perry Mason, Loose Cannon, Fther Dowling..

CLENNON, DAVID
Actor. b. Waukegan, IL. e. Univ. of Notre Dame, Yale Drama School.
THEATER: *Off-B'way.*: The Unseen Hand, Forensic and the Navigators, As You Like It, Little Eyolf, Welcome to Andromeda, Medal of Honor Rag, The Cherry Orchard. *Regional*: Saved, Blood Knot, Loot, Marat/Sade, Beyond Therapy, others.
PICTURES: The Paper Chase, Bound for Glory, The Greatest, Coming Home, Gray Lady Down, Go Tell the Spartans, On the Yard, Being There, Hide in Plain Sight, Missing, The Escape Artist, The Thing, Ladies and Gentlemen the Fabulous Stains, The Right Stuff, Hannah K., Star 80, Falling in Love, Sweet Dreams, Legal Eagles, He's My Girl, The Couch Trip, Betrayed, Downtown, Man Trouble, Light Sleeper, Matinee, Two Crimes (Dos Crimenes), Grace of My Heart.
TELEVISION: *Series*: Rafferty, Park Place, thirtysomething, Almost Perfect. *Movies*: The Migrants, Crime Club, Helter Skelter, Gideon's Trumpet, Marriage is Alive and Well, Reward, Special Bulletin, Best Kept Secrets, Blood and Orchids, Conspiracy: The Trial of the Chicago 8, Nurses on the Line: The Crash of Flight 7, Black Widow Murders, Original Sins, Tecumseh: The Last Warrior. *Guest*: Alfred Hitchcock Presents, Murder She Wrote, Barney Miller, Dream On (Emmy Award, 1993). *Special*: The Seagull.

CLIFFORD, GRAEME
Director. b. England. Worked as film editor on such films as Don't Look Now, The Rocky Horror Picture Show, The Man Who Fell to Earth, F.I.S.T., The Postman Always Rings Twice, before turning to directing.
PICTURES: Frances, Burke & Wills, Gleaming the Cube, Deception, Past Tense.
TELEVISION: The New Avengers, Barnaby Jones, Faerie Tale Theatre, The Turn of the Screw, Twin Peaks, Crossroads.

CLOONEY, GEORGE
Actor. b. Augusta, KY, 1962. Father is tv newscaster-host Nick Clooney. Aunt is singer Rosemary Clooney. e. Northern KY Univ.
PICTURES: Return to Horror High, Return of the Killer Tomatoes, Red Surf, Unbecoming Age, The Harvest, One Fine Day, Full Tilt Boogie, From Dusk Till Dawn, Batman and Robin, The Peacemaker, The Thin Red Line, Out of Sight.
TELEVISION: *Series*: The Facts of Life, Roseanne, Sunset Beat, Baby Talk, Sisters, Bodies of Evidence, ER. *Guest*: Hunter, Murder She Wrote, The Golden Girls, The Building, Friends, South Park (voice).

CLOONEY, ROSEMARY
Singer, Actress. b. Maysville, KY, May 23, 1928. Was singer with sister Betty on radio and with Tony Pastor's band. Won first place on Arthur Godfrey's Talent Scouts in early 1950's. Had first million selling record in 1951 with Come on-a My House. Son is actor Miguel Ferrer. *Autobiography:* This for Remembrance (1977).
PICTURES: The Stars Are Singing (debut, 1953), Here Come the Girls, Red Garters, White Christmas, Deep in My Heart, Radioland Murders.
TELEVISION: *Series*: Songs for Sale, The Johnny Johnston Show, The Rosemary Clooney Show (1956-57), The Lux Show Starring Rosemary Clooney (1957-58). *Movie:* Sister Margaret and the Saturday Night Ladies. *Guest:* Ed Sullivan, Steve Allen, Perry Como's Kraft Music Hall, Red Skelton, Dick Powell Show, Bing Crosby, Hardcastle and McCormick, ER. *Special:* Danny Kaye: A Legacy of Laughter.

CLOSE, GLENN
Actress. b. Greenwich, CT, Mar. 19, 1947. e. Coll. of William and Mary. Began performing with a repertory group Fingernails, then toured country with folk-singing group Up With People. Professional debut at Phoenix Theatre, New York. Also accomplished musical performer (lyric soprano).
THEATER: *NY*: Love for Love, Rules of the Game, Member of the Wedding, Rex, Uncommon Women and Others, The Crucifer of Blood, Wine Untouched, The Winter Dancers, Barnum, Singular Life of Albert Nobbs (Obie Award), The Real Thing (Tony Award, 1984), Childhood, Joan of Arc at the Stake, Benefactors, Death and the Maiden (Tony Award, 1992), Sunset Boulevard (Tony Award, 1995). *Regional*: King Lear, Uncle Vanya, The Rose Tattoo, A Streetcar Named Desire, Brooklyn Laundry, Sunset Boulevard.
PICTURES: The World According to Garp (debut, 1982), The Big Chill, The Natural, The Stone Boy, Greystoke: The Legend of Tarzan Lord of the Apes (dubbed voice), Jagged Edge, Maxie, Fatal Attraction, Light Years (voice), Dangerous Liaisons, Immediate Family, Reversal of Fortune, Hamlet, Meeting Venus, Hook (cameo), The Paper, The House of the Spirits, Anne Frank Remembered (voice), Mary Reilly, Mars Attacks!, 101 Dalmatians, Paradise Road, Airforce One, In & Out, Cookie's Fortune, Tarzan (voice).
TELEVISION: *Movies*: Too Far To Go, The Orphan Train, Something About Amelia, Stones for Ibarra, Sarah: Plain and Tall, Skylark (also co-exec. prod.), Serving in Silence: The Margarethe Cammermeyer Story (Emmy Award, 1995; also co-exec. prod.), In the Gloaming. *Specials*: The Elephant Man, Broken Hearts Broken Homes (host, co-exec. prod.).

COATES, ANNE V.
Film editor, Producer. b. Reigate, Surrey, Eng. e. Bartrum Gables Coll. m. late dir. Douglas Hickox. Worked as nurse at East Grinstead Plastic Surgery Hospital. Recipient of 1995 A.C.E. Career Achievement award.
PICTURES: Pickwick Papers, Grand National Night, Forbidden Cargo, To Paris With Love, The Truth About Women, The Horse's Mouth, Tunes of Glory, Don't Bother to Knock, Lawrence of Arabia (Academy Award, 1962; also ACE nom.), Becket (Acad. Award & ACE noms.), Young Cassidy, Those Magnificent Men in Their Flying Machines (co-ed.), Hotel Paridiso, Great Catherine, The Bofors Guns, The Adventurers, Friends, The Public Eye, The Nelson Affair, 11 Harrowhouse, Murder on the Orient Express (BAFTA nom.), Man Friday, Aces High, The Eagle Has Landed, The Medusa Touch (prod. & sprv. ed.), The Legacy, The Elephant Man (Acad. Award nom., BAFTA nom.), The Bushido Blade, Ragtime (co-ed.), The Pirates of Penzance, Greystoke: The Legend of Tarzan Lord of the Apes, Lady Jane, Raw Deal, Masters of the Universe, Farewell to the King (co-ed.), Listen to Me, I Love You to Death, What About Bob?, Chaplin, In the Line of Fire (Acad. Award nom., A.C.E. nom., BAFTA nom., G.B.F.E. award), Pontiac Moon, Congo, Striptease, Out to Sea, Out of Sight.

COBE, SANDY

Executive, Producer, Distributor. b. New York, NY, Nov. 30, 1928. e. Tulane U., B.A., fine arts. U.S. Army WWII & Korea, combat photographer; produced 11 features for Artmark Pictures, N.Y. General Studios, exec. v.p., distribution; First Cinema Releasing Corp., pres. Formed Sandy Cobe Productions, Inc., producer, packager, European features for U.S. theatrical & television. 1974 pres., Intercontinental Releasing Corporation, domestic and foreign distribution of theatrical features; 1989, named chmn. of bd. and CEO. Member, dir. of bd., American Film Marketing Assn., Dir. of bd., Scitech Corp. USA, 14 year mem., Academy of Television Arts and Sciences, 32nd degree Mason, Shriner, Variety Club Int'l. Special commendations from: Mayor of Los Angeles, California State Senate, City and County of L.A., California Assembly and Senate, and Governor of CA.
PICTURES: Terror on Tour (prod.), Access Code (exec. prod.), A.R.C.A.D.E. (prod.), Terminal Entry (exec. prod.), Open House (prod.).

COBE, SHARYON REIS

Executive, Producer. b. Honolulu, HI, e. U. of Hawaii, Loyola Marymount U. Dancer Fitzgerald, & Sample, N.Y. United Air Lines, N.Y.; v.p., story editor, Gotham Publishing N.Y.; v.p., distribution-foreign sales, World Wide Film Distributors, L.A.; pres. and chief operating officer, Intercontinental Releasing Corp., L.A. Member of Variety Clubs Intl., Industry Rltns. Com., Amer. Film Mktg. Assoc., Indpt. Feature Projects West. (tent 25), Women in Film.
PICTURES: Home Sweet Home (prod. mgr.), To All a Good Night (assoc. prod.), Access Code (co-prod.), Terminal Entry (prod.), Open House (exec. in chg. of prod.).

COBLENZ, WALTER

Producer.
PICTURES: The Candidate, All the President's Men, The Onion Field, The Legend of the Lone Ranger, Strange Invaders, Sister Sister, 18 Again!, For Keeps, The Babe, Money Talks.
TELEVISION: *Movie*: Jack Reed: Badge of Honor, House of Secrets, Not Our Son, A Dream for Christmas. *Series*: Apples Way. *Mini Series*: The Blue Knight.

COBURN, JAMES

Actor. b. Laurel, NB, Aug. 31, 1928. e. Los Angeles City Coll., where he studied drama. Also studied with Stella Adler in NY for 5 years. Served in U.S. Army. First acting role in coast production of Billy Budd. Later to New York, where he worked on TV commercials, then in live teleplays on Studio One, GE Theatre, Robert Montgomery Presents. Summer stock in Detroit before returning to Hollywood. Commercial: Remington Rand.
PICTURES: Ride Lonesome (debut, 1959), Face of a Fugitive, The Magnificent Seven, Hell Is for Heroes, The Great Escape, Charade, The Americanization of Emily, The Loved One, Major Dundee, A High Wind in Jamaica, Our Man Flint, What Did You Do in the War Daddy?, Dead Heat on a Merry-Go-Round, In Like Flint, Waterhole No. 3, The President's Analyst, Duffy, Candy, Hard Contract, Last of the Mobile Hot-Shots, The Carey Treatment, The Honkers, Duck You Sucker, Pat Garrett and Billy the Kid, The Last of Sheila, Harry in Your Pocket, A Reason to Live—A Reason to Die, The Internecine Project, Bite the Bullet, Hard Times, Sky Riders, The Last Hard Men, Midway, Cross of Iron, California Suite (cameo), The Muppet Movie, Goldengirl, Firepower, The Baltimore Bullet, Loving Couples, Mr. Patman, High Risk, Looker, Martin's Day, Death of a Soldier, Phoenix Fire, Walking After Midnight, Train to Heaven, Young Guns II, Hudson Hawk, The Player, Hugh Hefner: Once Upon a Time (narrator), Deadfall, Sister Act 2: Back in the Habit, Maverick, The Nutty Professor, Eraser, Keys to Tulsa, Affliction.
TELEVISION: *Series*: Klondike, Acapulco, Darkroom (host), Hollywood Stuntmakers (host), Fifth Corner. *Movies*: Draw!, Sins of the Fathers, Malibu, The Dain Curse, Valley of the Dolls, Crash Landing: The Rescue of Flight 232, The Hit List, Greyhounds, The Avenging Angel, Ray Alexander: A Menu for Murder, The Set Up. *Specials*: Pinocchio (Faerie Tale Theater), Mastergate. *Pilot*: Silver Fox.

COCA, IMOGENE

Actress. b. Philadelphia, PA, Nov. 18, 1908. p. the late Joe Coca, orchestra leader, and Sadie Brady, vaudevillian. At 11, debut tap dancer in New York vaudeville; solo dancer B'way musicals; as comedienne, in New Faces of 1934; with former husband, Bob Burton, in Straw Hat Revue in 1939, and others through 1942. New York night clubs, Cafe Society and Le Ruban Bleu, Palmer House, Chicago; Park Plaza, St. Louis, and at Tamiment resort. Seen on early experimental TV telecasts in 1939.1949 to TV via B'way Revue, co-starring with Sid Caesar. Emmy Award, 1951. Returned to B'way in Musical On the Twentieth Century.
PICTURES: Under the Yum Yum Tree, Promises! Promises!, Rabbit Test, National Lampoon's Vacation, Nothing Lasts Forever, Buy and Cell.

TELEVISION: *Series*: Buzzy Wuzzy (host, 1948), Admiral Broadway Revue (1949), Your Show of Shows (1950-54). Imogene Coca Show (1954-55), Sid Caesar Invites You (1958), Grindl (1963-64), It's About Time (1966-67). Special: Ruggles of Red Gap. *Guest*: Fireside Theatre, Hollywood Palace, Love American Style, Moonlighting. *Movies*: Alice in Wonderland, Return of the Beverly Hillbillies, Papa Was a Preacher.

COCCHI, JOHN

Writer, Critic. b. Brooklyn, NY, June 19, 1939. e. Fort Hamilton H.S., 1957; Brooklyn College, A.A.S., 1961. U.S. Army, 1963-65. Puritan Film Labs, manager, 1967-69. Independent-International Pictures, biographer-researcher, 1969. Boxoffice Magazine, critic, reporter, columnist, 1970-79. Co-author: The American Movies Reference Book (Prentice-Hall). Contributor: Screen Facts, Film Fan Monthly, Films in Review. Actor in: The Diabolical Dr. Ongo, Thick as Thieves, Captain Celluloid vs. the Film Pirates. Worked on dubbing: Dirtymouth, 1970. Author of film books incl. The Westerns: a Movie Quiz Book, Second Feature, Best of the B Films. Now free lance writer, researcher, agent. Recent credits: contributor to books, 500 Best American Films, 500 Best British and Foreign-Language Films. Consultant to Killiam Shows, Prof. Richard Brown, Photofest, Star Magazine; research chief for American Movie Classics channel, 1984-present; Global Producers Group associate.

COCHRAN, BARBARA

Executive, Writer. b. Akron, OH, June 16 1945. e. Swarthmore, BA English Lit., 1967. Columbia U., MA journalism, 1968. Various positions and finally managing ed., Washington *Times*, 1968-79. VP news, NPR, 1979-83. Political ed., NBC, 1983-85. Exec. prod., NBC's *Meet the Press*, 1985-89. VP news/Wash. bureau chief, CBS news, 1989-95. Exec. prod. for political coverage, CBS, 1996. Pres., Radio-Television News Directors Assoc., 1997-.

COEN, ETHAN

Producer, Writer. b. St. Louis Park, MN, Sep. 21, 1957. e. Princeton U. Co-wrote s.p. with brother, Joel, XYZ Murders (renamed Crimewave)
PICTURES: *Producer/Co-Writer*: Blood Simple (also co-edited under pseudonym Roderick James), Raising Arizona, Miller's Crossing, Barton Fink, The Hudsucker Proxy, Fargo (Best dir., Cannes; original s.p. Acad. Award, 1996; Chicago Film Critics Award for s.p.; LA Film Critics Award for s.p.: BAFTA for achievment in dir.), The Naked Man, The Big Lebowski.

COEN, GUIDO

Producer, Executive. In 1959 became production exec. Twickenham Studios, 1963 Appt. a dir. there, then producer and executive prod. series pictures for Fortress Films and Kenilworth Films.
PICTURES: One Jump Ahead, Golden Link, The Hornet's Nest, Behind the Headlines, Murder Reported, There's Always a Thursday, Date with Disaster, The End of the Line, The Man Without a Body, Woman Eater, Kill Her Gently, Naked Fury, Operation Cupid, Strictly Confidential, Dangerous Afternoon, Jungle Street, Strongroom, Penthouse, Baby Love, One Brief Summer, Burke and Hare, Au Pair Girls, Intimate Games.

COEN, JOEL

Director, Writer. b. St. Louis Park, MN, Nov. 29, 1954. e. Simon's Rock College, MA; studied film at NYU. m. actress Frances McDormand. Was asst. editor on Fear No Evil and Evil Dead. Co-wrote with brother, Ethan, s.p. for XYZ Murders (renamed Crime Wave.) Cameo role in film Spies Like Us, 1985.
PICTURES: *Director/Co-Writer*: Blood Simple (also co-editor, under pseudonym Roderick Jaynes), Raising Arizona, Miller's Crossing, Barton Fink (also co-editor, as Roderick Jaynes), The Hudsucker Proxy, Fargo (Best director, Cannes 1996; original s.p. Acad. Award, 1997; Chicago Film Critics Award for s.p.; amd dir.; LA Film Critics Award for s.p.; BAFTA for achievement in dir.), The Big Lebowski.

COHEN, ELLIS A.

Producer, Writer. b. Baltimore, MD, Sept. 15, 1945. e. Baltimore Jr. Coll., A.A. 1967, Univ. of W. LA, mini-law sch., 1992. 1963, talent coord., Cerebral Palsy Telethon, WBAL-TV, Baltimore; 1964, p.r. asst. Campbell-Ewald Adv. Agency, L.A.; 1966, retail mgr.; 1968-69, talent booking; 1968, journalist & ed.; 1969-72, p.r. & adv. Camera Mart, NY; 1972-74, creator & ed.-in-chief, TV/NY Magazine; 1974-76 dir., worldwide pub./adv., William Morris Agency. 1973-74, prod., NY Emmy Awards Telecast; WOR-TV (prod.), chmn., exec. prod. of TV Academy Celebrity drop-in luncheon series; 1972, talent coordinator Bob Hope's Celebrity Flood Relief Telethon; 1976, exec. prod., Democratic Nat'l Conv. Gala. 1978, acc. exec., Solters & Roskin P.R., L.A.; 1978, dir. of TV Network Boxing Events, Don King Prod., NY; 1979, prod., Henry Jaffe Ent., Inc.; 1980, prod.-writer, CBS Entertainment & pres. Ellis A. Cohen Prods. Since 1983, pres., Hennessey Ent., Ltd. Author: Avenue of the Stars, (novel 1990), Dangerous Evidence (1995). Member: WGA, Producers Guild of America, World Affairs Council, Friars Club, Amer. Newspaper Guild, Intl. Press Corp., Israeli Press Corp., Acad. of TV Arts & Sciences, SAG. Comm. Public Interest for NYC; Natl. Writers Union, and many others.
TELEVISION: *Movies*: Producer: Aunt Mary (also story); First Steps, Love Mary, Dangerous Evidence (also story). *Specials*: NY Area Emmy Awards (1973-74).

COHEN, IRWIN R.
Exhibition Executive. b. Baltimore, MD, Sept. 4, 1924. e. U. of Baltimore, (LLB) 1948, admitted to Maryland and U.S. Bar same year. Active limited practice. R/C Theatres outgrowth of family business started in 1932. One of founders of Key Bank and Trust, chairman of board Loan Comm., director and member of exec. comm. Pres. NATO of Virginia 1976-78, chairman 1978-80. Director, member of exec. comm., treasurer, former chairman of finance comm. National NATO. Member of Motion Picture Pioneers, Will Rogers Hospital, and various other orgs.

COHEN, LARRY
Director, Producer, Writer. b. New York, NY, July 15, 1946. e. CCNY. Started as writer for TV series incl. Kraft Mystery Theatre, The Defenders, Arrest and Trial. Creator of series Branded, The Invaders, Cool Million, Blue Light, Cop Talk.
PICTURES: *Dir./prod./s.p.*: Daddy's Gone A-Hunting (co-s.p.), El Condor, Bone, Black Caesar, It's Alive, Demon, The Private Files of J. Edgar Hoover, It Lives Again, Success (story), Full Moon High, Q, I The Jury, Perfect Strangers, The Man Who Wasn't There (story), Special Effects, Scandalous (story), The Stuff (exec. prod.), Spies Like Us (actor), It's Alive III: Island of the Alive (exec. prod.), Return to Salem's Lot (exec. prod.), Best Seller, Deadly Illusion, Maniac Cop, Wicked Stepmother (exec. prod.), Maniac Cop II, The Ambulance, The Apparatus, Guilty As Sin, Original Gangstas, Invasion of Privacy (writer), The Ex, Misbegotten.
TELEVISION: *Movies: Writer*: Cool Million, Man on the Outside, Shootout in a One Dog Town (co-writer, story) Desperado: Avalanche at Devil's Ridge, As Good as Dead (also dir., prod.), 87th Precint–Ice. *Series: Writer*: NYPD Blue, 87th Precinct Heatwave.

COHEN, PAUL
Executive. b. New York, NY, Apr. 16, 1948. e. Hofstra U.; New School for Social Research; Jungian Inst. NY. Started in industry as exec. prod., distributor, screenwriter, producer for Masada Prods. Served as v.p. of Grand Slam Prods., exec. prod. for Moonbeam Assocs. Head of Analysis Films, 1976-84. Founded Aries Film Releasing, 1989, becoming pres. & CEO. Professor, Florida State Univ., 1995-97. Currently pres., Stratosphere Entertainment; oversaw Stratosphere's acquisition of The Thief, One Tough Cop, Bandits, Six Ways to Sunday, Divine Trash, The Last Big Thing, The Inheritors.
PICTURES: Caligula, My Brilliant Career, Maniac, Basket Case, The Chosen, Butterfly, The Innocent, Mephisto, The Icicle Thief, My Twentieth Century, Superstar: The Life and Times of Andy Warhol, Overseas, The Story of Boys and Girls, Thank You and Goodnight, Lovers, Bad Lieutenant.

COHEN, ROB
Producer, Director. b. Cornwall-on-the-Hudson, NY, March 12, 1949. e. Harvard U. BA. Formerly exec. v.p. in chg of m.p. and TV for Motown. Started as dir. of m.p. for TV at 20th Century-Fox. Joined Motown at age of 24 to produce films. Headed own production co. 1985, appt. pres., Keith Barish Prods.
PICTURES: Mahogany (prod.), The Bingo Long Traveling All-Stars (prod.), Scott Joplin (prod.), Almost Summer (prod.), Thank God It's Friday (prod.), The Wiz (prod.), A Small Circle of Friends (dir.), Scandalous (dir., co-s.p.), The Razor's Edge (prod.), The Legend of Billie Jean (prod.), Light of Day (co-prod.), The Witches of Eastwick (co-exec. prod.), The Monster Squad (co-exec. prod.), Ironweed (co-exec. prod.), The Running Man (co-exec. prod.), The Serpent and the Rainbow (exec. prod.), Disorganized Crime (exec. prod.), Bird on a Wire (prod.), The Hard Way (prod.), Dragon: The Bruce Lee Story (dir., co-s.p., actor), Dragonheart, Daylight, The Rat Pack.
TELEVISION: Miami Vice (dir.), Cuba and Claude (exec. prod.), Vanishing Son (exec. prod.).

COHEN, ROBERT B.
Executive. e. George Washington U., B.A., Southern Texas Sch. of Law. 1980-84. Atty. for Pillsbury Madison's Sutro and for Greenberg, Glusker, Fields, Clamans and Machtinger (L.A.). Was asst. gen. counsel for Columbia Pictures. Joined Paramount 1985 as sr. atty. for M.P. Group. to oversee legal functions for assigned feature films; 1988 named v.p. in charge of legal affairs, Motion Picture Group of Paramount; 1990, named sr. v.p. legal affairs, motion picture group, Paramount.

COHEN, SID
Executive. e. Univ. of RI Col. of Business. Served as western div. mngr. for WB tv distrib. in 1970's. 1979-84, v.p. feature planning & sls. develop. for domestic tv distrib. div. of Paramount Pictures Corp. There he created the first satellite- delivered feature-film package for free over-the-air tv on a regularly scheduled natl. basis. 1985-91, pres. of domestic tv distrib. at King World Prods. Sept. 1991, became pres. of MGM Domestic TV Distrib.

COHN, ROBERT
Producer. b. Avon, NJ, Sept. 6, 1920. e. U. of Michigan, B.A., 1941. p. Jack Cohn. Joined Columbia as asst. dir. In WWII, as Signal Corps film cutter. Air Corps Training Lab. unit mgr., combat aerial m.p. camera man with 13th A.A.F. Awarded: DFC, Air Medal & 3 clusters, Purple Heart. Assoc. prod. Lone Wolf In London, 1947; prod. Adventures in Silverado, 1948, all Col. Headed Robert Cohn prod. unit at Columbia, pres. International Cinema Guild. Columbia European prod.: exec. Columbia Studios. Hollywood: formed Robert Cohn Prod.
PICTURES: Black Eagle, Rusty Leads the Way, Palomino, Kazan, Killer That Stalked New York, The Barefoot Mailman, Mission Over Korea, The Interns, The New Interns, The Young Americans.

COLBY, RONALD
Producer, Director, Writer. b. New York, NY. e. Hofstra U., NYU. Began career as playwright at Cafe La Mama and Caffe Cino; performed in off-B'way shows; spent year as actor-writer in residence at Pittsburgh Playhouse. Served as dialogue coach and asst. to Francis Coppola; was v.p. of Zoetrope Studios. Directed several documentaries and short films.
PICTURES: Finian's Rainbow (act. only), The Rain People (prod.), Hammett (prod.), Some Kind of Wonderful (exec. prod.), She's Having a Baby (exec. prod.), Jailbait (co-prod.).
TELEVISION: Margaret Bourke-White (co-prod.), Lush Life (co-prod.).

COLE, GARY
Actor. b. Park Ridge, IL, Sept. 20. e. Illinois State, theater major. Dropped out of coll. after 3 years and moved to Chicago where he tended bar, painted houses and worked with Steppenwolf Theatre group. In 1979 helped to form Remains Theatre, left in 1986 to become ensemble member of Steppenwolf.
PICTURES: Lucas, In the Line of Fire, The Brady Bunch Movie.
TELEVISION: *Series*: Midnight Caller, American Gothic. *Movies*: Heart of Steel, Fatal Vision, Vital Signs, Those She Left Behind, The Old Man and the Sea, Son of the Morning Star, The Switch, When Love Kills: The Seduction of John Hearn, A Time to Heal, Fall from Grace. *Mini-Series*: Echoes in the Darkness.

COLE, GEORGE
Actor. b. London, Eng., Apr. 22, 1925. e. secondary sch. Surrey. Stage debut in White Horse Inn, 1939; motion picture debut in Cottage to Let, 1941.
PICTURES: Henry V, Quartet, My Brother's Keeper, Laughter in Paradise, Scrooge, Lady Godiva Rides Again, Who Goes There (Passionate Sentry), Morning Departure (Operation Disaster), Top Secret (Mr. Potts Goes to Moscow), Happy Family, Will Any Gentleman, Apes of the Rock, The Intruder, Happy Ever After (Tonight's the Night), Our Girl Friday (Adventures of Sadie), Belles of St. Trinian's, Prize of Gold, Where There's a Will, Constant Husband, Quentin Durward, The Weapon, It's a Wonderful Life, Green Man, Bridal Path, Too Many Crooks, Blue Murder at St. Trinians, Don't Panic Chaps, Dr. Syn, One Way Pendulum, Legend of Young Dick Turpin, The Great St. Trinian's Train Robbery, Cleopatra, The Green Shoes, Vampire Lovers, Fright, The Bluebird, Mary Reilly.
TELEVISION: Life of Bliss, A Man of Our Times, Don't Forget To Write, The Good Life. *Series*: Minder, Root Into Europe, My Good Friend, An Independent Man, Dad.

COLEMAN, DABNEY
Actor. b. Austin, TX, Jan. 3, 1932. e. VA Military Inst. 1949-51; U. Texas 1951-57; Neighborhood Playhouse School Theater 1958-60.
PICTURES: The Slender Thread (debut, 1965), This Property Is Condemned, The Scalphunters, The Trouble With Girls, Downhill Racer, I Love My Wife, Cinderella Liberty, The Dove, The Towering Inferno, The Other Side of the Mountain, Bite the Bullet, The Black Streetfighter, Midway, Rolling Thunder, Viva Knievel, North Dallas Forty, Nothing Personal, How to Beat the High Cost of Living, Melvin and Howard, Nine to Five, On Golden Pond, Modern Problems, Young Doctors in Love, Tootsie, WarGames, The Muppets Take Manhattan, Cloak and Dagger, The Man with One Red Shoe, Dragnet, Hot to Trot, Where the Heart Is, Short Time, Meet the Applegates, There Goes the Neighborhood, Amos & Andrew, The Beverly Hillbillies, Clifford.
TELEVISION: *Movies*: Brotherhood of the Bell, Savage, Dying Room Only, The President's Plane is Missing, Bad Ronald, Attack on Terror: The FBI Versus the Ku Klux Klan, Returning Home, Kiss Me Kill Me, Maneaters Are Loose!, More Than Friends, Apple Pie, When She Was Bad, Murrow, Guilty of Innocence, Sworn To Silence (Emmy Award, 1987), Baby M, Maybe Baby, Never Forget, Columbo and the Murder of a Rock Star, Judicial Consent, In the Line of Duty: Kidnapped, Devil's Food. *Mini-Series*: Fresno. *Series*: That Girl, Bright Promise, Mary Hartman Mary Hartman, Apple Pie, Forever Fernwood, Buffalo Bill, The Slap Maxwell Story, Drexell's Class, Madman of the People. *Special*: Plaza Suite, Texan.

COLEMAN, GARY
Actor. b. Zion, IL, Feb. 8, 1968. Gained fame as star of TV's Diff'rent Strokes.
PICTURES: On the Right Track, Jimmy the Kid.
TELEVISION: *Series*: Diff'rent Strokes. *Guest*: America 2-Night, Good Times, The Jeffersons, Lucy Moves to NBC, The Big Show, etc., Martin, Married... With Children, Fresh Prince of Bel-Air, The Steve Allen Show. *Movies*: *Actor/Producer*: The Kid from Left Field, Scout's Honor, The Kid With the Broken Halo; The Kid with the 200 I.Q., The Fantastic World of D.C. Collins, Playing With Fire.

COLEMAN, NANCY
Actress. b. Everett, WA, Dec. 30, 1912. e. U. of Washington. In radio serials; on NY stage in Susan and God, Liberty Jones, Desperate Hours, 1955; American Theatre Guild Rep. Co. tour of Europe and So. America, 1961.
PICTURES: Dangerously They Live, Kings Row (debut, 1941), The Gay Sisters, Desperate Journey, Edge of Darkness, In Our Time, Devotion, Her Sister's Secret, Violence, Mourning Becomes Electra, That Man from Tangier, Slaves.
TELEVISION: Valiant Lady, Producers Showcase, Kraft Theatre, Philco Playhouse, Robert Montgomery Presents, Lux Theatre, Alcoa Hour, Theatre Guild Playhouse, Play of the Week, Silver Theatre, Adams Chronicles. *Series*: Ryan's Hope.

COLEMAN, THOMAS J.
Executive. b. Connecticut, Apr. 13, 1950. e. Boston U. Pres., Twalzo Music Corp., 1972-73; v.p., natl. sls. mgr., United Intl. Pictures, 1973-74; founded Atlantic Releasing Corp., 1974; Atlantic Television, Inc., 1981. All Atlantic corps. consolidated into Atlantic Entertainment Group, 1986. Co. has distributed over 100 films and produced 30 features and TV movies. Sold Atlantic, March, 1989. Formed Independent Entertainment Group, named chmn. Feb., 1992 formed Rocket Pictures.
PICTURES: *Producer or Exec. Prod.*: Valley Girl, Alphabet City, Roadhouse, Night of the Comet, Starchaser, Teen Wolf, Extremities, The Men's Club, Modern Girls, Nutcracker, Teen Wolf Too, Cop, Patty Hearst, 1969, Bad Golf Made Easier, Fluke, A New York Minute, Cannes Man, The Love Master.

COLER, JOEL H.
Executive. b. Bronx, NY, July 27, 1931. e. Syracuse U., B.A., journalism. Worked as adv. asst. NBC; acct. exec. Grey advertising. Joined 20th Century-Fox 1964 as adv. coordinator Fox Intl.; 1967, named intl. adv./pub. mgr. 1974, named v.p. dir., intl. adv./pub. Nov. 1990, named v.p. publicity/promotions Fox Intl. 1991, v.p. Worldwide Distrib. Services. 1984, memb. L.A. Olympic Org. Com. Left Fox in 1992 to form Joel Coler & Friends intl. mktg. consultants. Memb. L.A. Philarmonic Business & Professional Com.

COLIN, MARGARET
Actress. b. Brooklyn, NY, 1958. Raised on Long Island. Studied acting at Stella Adler Conservatory, Juilliard, Hofstra U. Left Hofstra to pursue acting career in Manhattan where she was cast in daytime TV series The Edge of Night. NY Theatre incl. work at Ensemble Studio, Geva Theatre and Manhattan Theatre Club (Aristocrats, Sight Unseen).
PICTURES: Pretty in Pink, Something Wild, Like Father Like Son, Three Men and a Baby, True Believer, Martians Go Home, The Butcher's Wife, Amos & Andrew, Terminal Velocity, Independence Day, The Devil's Own.
TELEVISION: *Movies*: Warm Hearts Cold Feet, The Return of Sherlock Holmes, The Traveling Man, Good Night Sweet Wife: A Murder in Boston, In the Shadow of Evil. *Series*: The Edge of Night, As the World Turns, Foley Square, Leg Work, Sibs. *Guest*: Chicago Hope.

COLLERAN, BILL
Producer, Director. b. Edgerton, WI, Nov. 6, 1922. Story department 20th Century-Fox 1945-46; Director Louis de Rochemont 1946-50; stage mgr. NBC 1951; assoc. dir. The Hit Parade 1952-53; dir. The Hit Parade, various TV specs. 1954-56; dir. Cinerama Windjammer film 1956; tv specs. with Bing Crosby, Frank Sinatra, Debbie Reynolds 1957-60; exec. Prod. Judy Garland Show, Dean Martin Show, 1965-66; dir. Richard Burton's Hamlet film; prod. Popendipity ABC-TV spec. and various other TV specs. and series 1967-77. 1978-83, prod., dir., writer for Hill-Eubanks Group and Little Joey, Inc.; 1984-86, dir. music video for Simba; developing film and TV projects for own production co. 1988, semi-retired.

COLLET, CHRISTOPHER
Actor. b. New York, NY, March 13, 1968. Started acting in commercials as teenager.
THEATER: *NY*: Off-B'way: Coming of Age in SoHo, An Imaginary Life, Unfinished Stories. B'way: Torch Song Trilogy, Spoils of War. Regional: The Lion in Winter, The Old Boy, Pterodactyls.
PICTURES: Sleepaway Camp (debut, 1983), Firstborn, The Manhattan Project, Prayer of the Rollerboys.

COLLINS, GARY
Actor. b. Boston, MA, Apr. 30, 1938.
TELEVISION: *Series*: The Wackiest Ship in the Army, The Iron Horse, Sixth Sense, Born Free, Hour Magazine (host), Home. *Movies*: Quarantined, Getting Away from It All, Houston We've Got a Problem, The Night They Took Miss Beautiful, The Kid From Left Field, Jacqueline Susann's Valley of the Dolls, Danielle Steel's Secrets. *Mini-Series*: Roots.
PICTURES: The Pigeon That Took Rome, The Longest Day, Cleopatra, Stranded, Angel in My Pocket, Airport, Killer Fish, Hangar 18.

COLLINS, JOAN
Actress. b. London, Eng., May 23, 1933. e. Francis Holland Sch., London. Sister is writer Jackie Collins. Made stage debut in A Doll's House, Arts Theatre 1946. Author: Past Imperfect (autobiography, 1978), Katy, A Fight For Life, Joan Collins Beauty Book, Prime Time, Love & Desire & Hate, My Secrets, Too Damn Famous. On London, LA and NY stage in Private Lives. Video: Secrets of Fitness and Beauty (also exec. prod.)
PICTURES: I Believe in You (debut, 1951), Lady Godiva Rides Again, Judgment Deferred, Decameron Nights, Cosh Boy, The Square Ring, Turn the Key Softly, Our Girl Friday (Adventures of Sadie), The Good Die Young, Land of the Pharaohs, Virgin Queen, Girl in the Red Velvet Swing, Opposite Sex, Sea Wife, Island in the Sun, Wayward Bus, Stopover Tokyo, The Bravados, Rally Round the Flag Boys, Seven Thieves, Esther and the King, Road to Hong Kong, Warning Shot, Can Hieronymus Merkin Ever Forget Mercy Humppe and Find True Happiness?, If It's Tuesday This Must Be Belgium, Subterfuge, The Executioner, Up in the Cellar, Quest for Love, Inn of the Frightened People, Fear in the Night, Tales from the Crypt, Tales That Witness Madness, Dark Places, Alfie Darling, The Devil Within Her, The Bawdy Adventures of Tom Jones, Empire of the Ants, The Big Sleep, The Stud, Zero to Sixty, The Bitch, Game of Vultures, Sunburn, Homework, Nutcracker, Decadence, In the Bleak Mid-Winter, Decadence, In The Bleak Midwinter, Annie: A Royal Adventure, The Line King: Al Hirschfeld.
TELEVISION: *Series*: Dynasty, Pacific Palisades. *Movies*: The Cartier Affair, The Making of a Male Model, Her Life as a Man, Paper Dolls, The Wild Women of Chastity Gulch, Drive Hard Drive Fast, Dynasty: The Reunion. *Specials*: Hansel and Gretel (Faerie Tale Theater), Mama's Back, Hidden Hollywood: Treasures from the 20th Century Fox Film Vaults (Host). *Mini-Series*: The Moneychangers, Sins, Monte Carlo (also exec. prod.).

COLLINS, PAULINE
Actress. b. Exmouth, Devon, Eng., Sept. 3, 1940. m. actor John Alderton (Thomas on Upstairs, Downstairs). e. Central School of Speech and Drama. Stage debut A Gazelle in Park Lane (Windsor, 1962). Best known to US audiences as Sarah in Upstairs, Downstairs.
THEATER: Passion Flower Hotel (London debut, 1965), The Erpingham Camp, The Happy Apple, The Importance of Being Earnest, The Night I Chased the Women with an Eel, Come as You Are, Judies, Engaged, Confusions, Romantic Comedy, Woman in Mind, Shirley Valentine (in London won Olivier Award as best actress, in NY won Tony, Drama Desk and Outer Critics Circle Awards).
PICTURES: Secrets of a Windmill Girl, Shirley Valentine, City of Joy, My Mother's Courage.
TELEVISION: *Series*: Upstairs Downstairs, Thomas and Sarah, Forever Green, No—Honestly (all with husband), Tales of the Unexpected, Knockback, Tropical Moon Over Dorking.

COLLINS, STEPHEN
Actor. b. Des Moines, IA, Oct. 1, 1947. Appeared off-B'way in several Joseph Papp productions before B'way debut in Moonchildren, followed by No Sex We're British, The Ritz, Loves of Anatol, Censored Scenes from King Kong. Off-B'way: Twelfth Night, The Play's the Thing, Beyond Therapy, One of the Guys, The Old Boy, Putting It Together. Author of play Super Sunday (Williamstown Fest.), and novel Eye Contact (1994).
PICTURES: All the President's Men, Between the Lines, The Promise, Fedora, Star Trek: The Motion Picture, Loving Couples, Brewster's Millions, Jumpin' Jack Flash, Choke Canyon, The Big Picture, Stella, My New Gun, The First Wives Club, An Unexpected Life.
TELEVISION: *Series*: Tales of the Gold Monkey, Tattinger's (revamped as Nick & Hillary), Working it Out, Seventh Heaven. *Movies*: Brink's: The Great Robbery, The Henderson Monster, Dark Mirror, Threesome, Weekend War, A Woman Scorned: The Betty Broderick Story, Her Final Fury: Betty Broderick--The Last Chapter, The Disappearance of Nora, Barbara Taylor Bradford's Remember, A Family Divided, On Seventh Avenue, The Babysitter's Seduction, An Unexpected Family. *Mini-Series*: The Rhinemann Exchange, Hold the Dream, Inside the Third Reich, Chiefs, The Two Mrs. Grenvilles, A Woman Named Jackie, Scarlett.

COLT, MARSHALL
Actor, Writer. b. New Orleans, LA, Oct. 26. e. Tulane U., B.S. Physics; Pepperdine U., M.A. Clinical Psychology; Fielding Inst., PhD. candidate student, Clinical Psychology. Combat tour in Southeast Asia during Vietnam War. Captain, U.S. Naval Reserve. Stage productions: (Hotel Universe, Who's Afraid of Virginia Woolf?, Zoo Story, Killer's Head, etc.).
PICTURES: Bimbo (short), North Dallas Forty, Those Lips, Those Eyes, Jagged Edge, Flowers in the Attic, Illegally Yours, Deceptions.
TELEVISION: *Guest*: Family, Paper Chase, Streets of San Francisco, Barnaby Jones, Murder She Wrote. *Series*: McClain's Law, Lottery! *Movies*: Colorado C-1, Sharon: Portrait of a Mistress, Once an Eagle, To Heal a Nation, Mercy or Murder, Guilty of Innocence.

COLTRANE, ROBBIE
Actor. b. Glasgow, Scotland, 1950. Ent. ind. 1977.
THEATER: San Quentin theatre workshop, Oxford Theatre Group, Citizens Theatre, Traverse Theatre, Borderline Theatre, Hampstead Theatre, Bush Theatre; one man shows: Your Obedient Servant,Mistero Buffo.
PICTURES: Bad Business (dir.); Flash Gordon, Death Watch, Subway Riders, Britannia Hospital, Scrubbers, Ghost Dance, Krull, National Lampoon's European Vacation, Caravaggio, Defence of the Realm, Chinese Boxes, The Supergrass, Mona Lisa, Eat the Rich, Bert Rigby You're a Fool, Wonderland (The Fruit Machine), Let It Ride, Henry V, Slipstream, Nuns on the Run, Perfectly Normal, The Pope Must Die, Triple Bogey on a Par 5 Hole, Oh What a Night, The Adventures of Huck Finn, Goldeneye, Buddy.
TELEVISION: 1981 Take Two, Seven Deadly Sins, Keep It in the Family, Kick Up The Eighties, The Green Door, The Sheep Stealer, House With Green Shutters, The Lost Tribe, Alfresco, Laugh? I Nearly Paid My Licence Fee, Comic Strip Presents Five Go Mad in Dorset, Beat Generation, Susie, Gino, The Bullshitters, Miner's Strike, Tutti Frutti, Danny the Champion of the World (theatrical release in Europe), Jealousy (also dir., co-writer), Space Sluts From Planet Sex, French and Aunders, The Lenny Henry Show, Robbie Coltrane Special, Mistero Buffo (series), Alive & Kicking, The Secret Ingredients, The Bogie Man, Rednose of Courage, A Tour of the Western Isles, Coltrane in a Cadillac (also co-writer), Cracker (BAFTA & Cable ACE Awards).

COLUMBUS, CHRIS
Director,Writer. b. Spangler, PA, 1959. Grew up in Ohio. Started making short super 8 films in high school, studied screenwriting at New York U. Film Sch., graduated 1980. Sold first s.p., Jocks, while at college. Wrote for and developed TV cartoon series, Galaxy High School.
PICTURES: *Writer*: Reckless, Gremlins, The Goonies, Young Sherlock Holmes, Heartbreak Hotel, Little Nemo: Adventures in Slumberland (co-s.p.), Fantastic Four. *Director*: Adventures in Babysitting (debut, 1987), Heartbreak Hotel (also s.p.), Home Alone, Only the Lonely (also s.p.), Home Alone 2: Lost in New York, Mrs. Doubtfire (uncredited), Nine Months (also co-prod.), Jingle All the Way, (also prod.), The Interpreter, Good Night Moon.
TELEVISION: Amazing Stories, Twilight Zone, Alfred Hitchcock Presents.

COMDEN, BETTY
Writer. b. Brooklyn, NY, May 3, 1917. e. Erasmus Hall, NYU sch. of ed., B.S. Nightclub performer and writer with The Revuers, 1939-44. NY City Mayor's Award Art and Culture, 1978. Named to Songwriters Hall of Fame, 1980. NYU Alumnae Assn.'s Woman of Achievement award, 1987. Kennedy Center Honors for Life Achievement, 1991.
THEATER: With Adolph Green: writer book, sketches & lyrics for B'way shows: On the Town (book, lyrics, actress, 1944), Billion Dollar Baby (bk., Lyrics), Bonanza Bound! (bk., lyrics), Two on the Aisle (sketches and lyrics), Wonderful Town (lyrics; Tony Award, 1953), Peter Pan (lyrics), Bells Are Ringing (bk., lyrics), Say Darling (lyrics), A Party With Comden and Green (bk., lyrics, star; 1959 and 1977); Do Re Mi (lyrics), Subways Are For Sleeping (bk., lyrics), Fade Out-Fade In (bk., lyrics), Leonard Bernstein's Theatre Songs, Hallelujah, Baby (lyrics; Tony Award, 1968), Applause (book; Tony Award, 1970), Lorelei (revision to book), By Bernstein (book and some lyrics), On the Twentieth Century (2 Tony Awards, book and lyrics, 1978); A Doll's Life (bk., lyrics), The Will Rogers Follies (Tony Award, 1991). Actress only: Isn't It Romantic.
PICTURES: *Writer with Adolph Green*: Good News, Take Me Out to the Ballgame (lyrics), On the Town, Barkleys of Broadway, Singin' in the Rain, The Band Wagon, It's Always Fair Weather (also lyrics), Auntie Mame, Bells Are Ringing (also lyrics), What a Way to Go, The Addams Family (lyrics). *Actress*: Greenwich Village, Garbo Talks, Slaves of New York.

COMO, PERRY
Singer. r.n. Pierino Como. b. Canonsburg, PA, May 18, 1912. e. Canonsburg local schools. Barber at 15; joined Carlone Band, then Ted Weems Orchestra, 1936-42; played many night clubs; records for RCA Victor. Voted Best Male vocalist M.P. Daily, TV poll, 1952-56; radio poll, 1954. Best TV performer M.P.D. Fame poll 1957. Recipient of Emmy Awards: Best Male Singer (1954, 1955), Best Emcee (1955), Best Male Personality (1956), Best Actor in a Musical or Variety Show (1956).
PICTURES: Something for the Boys (debut, 1944), Doll Face, If I'm Lucky, Words and Music.
TELEVISION: *Series*: The Chesterfield Supper Club, The Perry Como Show (1950-61), The Kraft Music Hall (1961-63); numerous annual holiday specials.

COMPTON, JOYCE
Actress. b. Lexington, KY, Jan. 27, 1907. e. Tulsa U. r.n. Olivia Joyce Compton. Screen debut in Ankles Preferred.
PICTURES: The Awful Truth, Spring Madness, Sky Murder, Turnabout, A Southern Yankee, If I Had a Million, Christmas in Connecticut, Artists and Models Abroad, Rustlers of Red Dog, The White Parade, Wild Party, Three Sisters, Sorry Wrong Number, Mighty Joe Young, Grand Canyon, Jet Pilot, The Persuader, Girl in the Woods, many others.
(d. Oct. 13, 1998)

CONAWAY, JEFF
Actor. b. New York, NY, Oct. 5, 1950. Started in show business at the age of 10 when he appeared in B'way production, All the Way Home. Later toured in Critics Choice before turning to fashion modeling. Toured with musical group, 3 1/2, as lead singer and guitarist. Entered theatre arts program at NYU. Film debut at 19 in Jennifer on My Mind.
THEATER: Grease, The News.
PICTURES: Jennifer on My Mind (debut, 1971), The Eagle Has Landed, Pete's Dragon, I Never Promised You a Rose Garden, Grease, The Patriot, Elvira: Mistress of the Dark, Cover Girl, Tale of Two Sisters, The Banker, The Sleeping Car, A Time to Die, Total Exposure, Mirror Images, Sunset Strip, Bikini Summer II, Almost Pregnant, L.A. Goddess, It's Showtime, In a Moment of Passion, Alien Intruder, 2002: The Rape of Eden.
TELEVISION: *Series*: Taxi, Wizards and Warriors, Berrenger's, The Bold and the Beautiful, Babylon 5, Crusade: The Babylon Project. *Guest*: From Sea to Shining Sea (1974), Joe Forrester, The Mary Tyler Moore Show, Happy Days, Movin' On, Barnaby Jones, Kojak, Mickey Spillane's Mike Hammer. *Movies*: Having Babies, Delta County, U.S.A., Breaking Up Is Hard to Do, For the Love of It, Nashville Grab, The Making of a Male Model, Bay Coven, The Dirty Dozen: The Fatal Mission, Ghost Writer, Eye of the Storm.

CONDON, CHRIS J.
Producer, Director, Motion Equipment Designer. b. Chicago, IL, Dec. 7, 1922. e. Davidson Inst., U. of Southern California. U.S. Air Force 1943-46. Founded Century Precision Optics, 1948. Designed Athenar telephoto lenses, Century Super wide-angle lenses and Duplikins. Co-founded StereoVision International, Inc. 1969 specializing in films produced in new 3-D process. Member SMPTE. Lecturer and consultant on motion picture optics and 3-D motion picture technology.
PICTURES: The Wild Ride, The Surfer, Girls, Airline, The New Dimensions.

CONN, ROBERT A.
Executive. b. Philadelphia, PA, Jan. 16, 1926. e. Lehigh U. 1944; U. of Pennsylvania, 1948. 1st Lt. Days of Eden Army Security Agency, 1944-46, 1951-52; band & act. dept., MCA, 1952-53; dir. of adv. & prom. Official Films NY 1954; head of Official Films Philadelphia sales office serving PA, Baltimore, Washington, Cleveland and Detroit, 1956. Eastern Reg. Sls. Mgr. Flamingo Films, 1957; acct. exec. Dunnan and Jeffrey, Inc., 1961; v.p., Dunnan and Jeffrey, 1962; pres., adv. mgr., Suburban Knitwear Co., 1963; exec. v.p. Rogal Travel Service, 1964-68. 1968-78, pres. RAC Travel, Inc., Jenkintown, PA. and pres. Royal Palm Travel, Inc. Palm Beach, Florida, 1978; Rosenbluth Travel Service, 1979; v.p., natl. retail mktg., E.F. Hutton & Co. (N.Y.), 1983.

CONNELLY, JENNIFER
Actress. b. New York, NY, Dec. 12, 1970. e. Yale, Stamford U.
PICTURES: Once Upon a Time in America (debut, 1983), Creepers, Labyrinth, Seven Minutes in Heaven, Etoile, Some Girls, The Hot Spot, Career Opportunities, The Rocketeer, Of Love and Shadows (De Amor y de Sombra), Higher Education, Mulholland Falls, Far Harbor, Inventing the Abbotts, Waking the Dead, Dark City.
TELEVISION: *Movie*: The Heart of Justice.

CONNERY, SEAN
Actor. b. Edinburgh, Scotland, Aug. 25, 1930. r.n. Thomas Connery. Worked as a lifeguard and a model before landing role in chorus of London prod. of South Pacific, 1953. Prod. dir., The Bowler and the Bonnet (film doc.), I've Seen You Cut Lemons (London stage). Director of Tantallon Films Ltd. (First production: Something Like the Truth). Recipient of Golden Globe Cecil B. Demille Award, 1996.
PICTURES: No Road Back (debut, 1957), Time Lock, Hell Drivers, Action of the Tiger, Another Time Another Place, Darby O'Gill and the Little People, Tarzan's Greatest Adventure, Frightened City, On the Fiddle (Operation Snafu), The Longest Day, Dr. No, From Russia With Love, Marnie, Woman of Straw, Goldfinger, The Hill, Thunderball, A Fine Madness, You Only Live Twice, Shalako, The Molly Maguires, The Red Tent, The Anderson Tapes, Diamonds Are Forever, The Offence, Zardoz, Murder on the Orient Express, The Terrorists, The Wind and the Lion, The Man Who Would Be King, Robin and Marian, The Next Man, A Bridge Too Far, The Great Train Robbery, Meteor, Cuba, Outland, Time Bandits, Wrong Is Right, Five Days One Summer, Sword of the Valiant, Never Say Never Again, Highlander, The Name of the Rose, The Untouchables (Academy Award, best supporting actor, 1987), The Presidio, Memories of Me (cameo), Indiana Jones and the Last Crusade, Family Business, The Hunt for Red October, The Russia House, Robin Hood: Prince of Thieves (cameo), Highlander 2: The Quickening, Medicine Man (also exec. prod.), Rising Sun (also exec. prod.), A Good Man in Africa, Just Cause (also exec. prod.), First Knight, Dragonheart (voice), The Rock, The Avengers, Entrapment.
TELEVISION: Requiem for a Heavyweight, Anna Christie, Boy with the Meataxe, Women in Love, The Crucible, Riders to the Sea, Colombe, Adventure Story, Anna Karenina, Macbeth (Canadian TV).

CONNICK, HARRY, JR.
Musician, Actor. b. New Orleans, LA, Sept. 11, 1967. Began performing with Bourbon Street jazz combos at age 6. Studied classical piano. Albums: Harry Connick, 20, When Harry Met Sally..., Lofty's Roach Souffle, We are in Love (Grammy Award, 1991), Blue Light Red Light, 25, Eleven, When My Heart Finds Christmas, She, Star Turtle. Acting debut in Memphis Belle (1990). B'way debut 1990 in An Evening with Harry Connick Jr.
PICTURES: When Harry Met Sally... (special musical performances and arrangements), Memphis Belle, The Godfather Part III (performed theme song), Little Man Tate, Sleepless in Seattle (performed song), Copycat, Independence Day, Excess Baggage, Hope Floats.
TELEVISION: Specials: Swingin' Out Live, The New York Big Band Concert, The Harry Connick Jr. Christmas Special. Guest: Cheers, Mad TV.

CONNORS, MIKE
Actor. r.n. Krekor Ohanian. b. Fresno, CA, Aug. 15, 1925. e. UCLA. Film debut in Sudden Fear (1952) as Touch Connors.
PICTURES: Sudden Fear (debut, 1952), Sky Commando, 49th Man, Island in the Sky, Day of Triumph, Five Guns West, The Twinkle in God's Eye, Oklahoma Woman, Swamp Woman, The Day the World Ended, The Ten Commandments, Flesh and Spur, Shake Rattle and Rock, Voodoo Woman, Live Fast Die Young, Suicide Battalion, Panic Button, Seed of Violence, Good Neighbor Sam, Where Love Has Gone, Harlow, Situation Hopeless–But Not Serious, Stagecoach, Kiss the Girls and Make Them Die, Avalanche Express, Nightkill, Too Scared to Scream, Fist Fighter, Friend to Friend.
TELEVISION: Series: Tightrope, Mannix (Golden Globe Award), Today's FBI, Crimes of the Century (host). Movies: High Midnight, Beg Borrow or Steal, The Killer Who Wouldn't Die, Revenge for a Rape, Long Journey Back, The Death of Ocean View Park, Casino, Hart to Hart Returns. Mini-Series: War and Remembrance.

CONRAD, ROBERT
Actor, Director. r.n. Conrad Robert Falk. b. Chicago, IL, March 1, 1935. e. public schools, Northwestern U. Prof. debut, nightclub singer. Formed Robert Conrad Productions, 1966 (later A Shane Productions, then Black Sheep Productions).
PICTURES: Thundering Jets (debut, 1958), Palm Springs Weekend, Young Dillinger, The Bandits (also dir.), Murph the Surf (Live a Little Steal a Lot), The Lady in Red, Wrong Is Right, Moving Violations, Uncommon Courage, Jingle All the Way, The Wild Wild West.
TELEVISION: Series: Hawaiian Eye, Wild Wild West, The D.A., Assignment Vienna, Baa Baa Black Sheep, The Duke, A Man Called Sloane, High Mountain Rangers, Jesse Hawkes, Search and Rescue. Guest: Lawman, Maverick, 77 Sunset Strip. Mini-Series: Centennial. Movies: Weekend of Terror, The D.A.: Conspiracy to Kill, Five Desperate Women, Adventures of Nick Carter, The Last Day, Smash-Up on Interstate 5, Wild Wild West Revisited, Breaking Up Is Hard To Do, More Wild Wild West, Coach of the Year, Will: G. Gordon Liddy, Confessions of a Married Man, Hard Knox, Two Fathers' Justice, Assassin, Charley Hannah, The Fifth Missile, One Police Plaza, High Mountain Rangers (also dir., co-story), Glory Days (also dir.), Anything to Survive, Mario and the Mob, Sworn to Vengeance, Two Fathers: Justice for the Innocent, Search and Rescue.

CONSTANTINE, MICHAEL
Actor. b. Reading, PA, May 22, 1927.
PICTURES: The Hustler, Hawaii, Skidoo, Justine, If It's Tuesday This Must Be Belgium, Peeper, Voyage of the Damned, The North Avenue Irregulars, Pray for Death, In the Mood, Prancer, Dead Fall, My Life, The Juror, Stephen King's Thinner.
TELEVISION: Series: Hey Landlord, Room 222 (Emmy Award, 1970), Sirota's Court. Mini-Series: 79 Park Avenue, Roots: The Next Generations. Movies: Suddenly Single, Deadly Harvest, Say Goodbye Maggie Cole, The Bait, Death Cruise, The Night That Panicked America, Conspiracy of Terror, Wanted: The Sundance Woman, The Pirate, Crisis in Mid-Air, The Love Tapes, Evita Peron, My Palikari, Finder of Lost Loves, Leap of Faith, Because Mommy Works. Numerous guest appearances.

CONTE, JOHN
Actor, Singer. b. Palmer, MA, Sept. 15, 1915. e. Lincoln H.S., Los Angeles. Actor, Pasadena Playhouse; radio anncr., m.c.; Armed Forces, WWII. Pres. KMIR-TV, Channel 36, Desert Empire Television Corp., Palm Springs, NBC Affiliate.
THEATER: On B'way in Windy City, Allegro, Carousel, Arms and the Girl.
PICTURES: Thousands Cheer, Lost in a Harem, Trauma, Man With the Golden Arm, The Carpetbaggers.
TELEVISION: Series: Van Camp's Little Show (1950-52), Mantovani. Specials: Max Liebman Spectaculars and dramatic shows, host and star of NBC Matinee Theatre, TV Hour of Stars.

CONTI, BILL
Composer. b. Providence, RI, April 13, 1942. Studied piano at age 7, forming first band at age 15. e. Louisiana State U., Juilliard School of Music. Moved to Italy with jazz trio where scored first film, Candidate for a Killing. Was: music supvr. on Blume in Love for Paul Mazursky.
PICTURES: Harry and Tonto, Next Stop Greenwich Village, Rocky, Handle With Care, Slow Dancing in the Big City, An Unmarried Woman, F.I.S.T., The Big Fix, Paradise Alley, Uncle Joe Shannon, Rocky II, A Man a Woman and A Bank, Goldengirl, The Seduction of Joe Tynan, The Formula, Gloria, Private Benjamin, Carbon Copy, Victory, For Your Eyes Only, I The Jury, Rocky III, Neighbors, Split Image, Bad Boys, That Championship Season, Unfaithfully Yours, The Right Stuff (Academy Award, 1983), Mass Appeal, The Karate Kid, The Bear, Big Trouble, Gotcha, Beer, Nomads, F/X, The Karate Kid II, A Prayer for the Dying, Masters of the Universe, Baby Boom, Broadcast News, For Keeps, A Night in the Life of Jimmy Reardon, Betrayed, Cohen and Tate, Big Blue, Lean On Me, The Karate Kid Part III, Lock Up, The Fourth War, Backstreet Dreams, Rocky V, Necessary Roughness, Year of the Gun, A Captive in the Land, The Adventures of Huck Finn, Bound By Honor, By the Sword, Rookie of the Year, 8 Seconds, Bushwhacked, Spy Hard.
TELEVISION: Kill Me If You Can, Stark, North and South, The Pirate, Smashup on Interstate 5, Papa & Me, Napoleon and Josephine, Murderers Among Us: The Simon Wiesenthal Story. Series themes: Cagney and Lacy, Dynasty, Falcon Crest, The Colbys, Kenya, Heartbeat, Lifestyles of the Rich and Famous, Emerald Point N.A.S., Dolphin Cove, The Elite, Instant Recall, Inside Edition.

CONTI, TOM
Actor. b. Paisley, Scotland, Nov. 22, 1941. Trained at Royal Scottish Academy of Music, Glasgow. Did repertory work in Scotland before London stage debut appearing with Paul Scofield in Savages, 1973.
THEATER: London: Devil's Disciple, Whose Life Is It Anyway?, They're Playing Our Song, Romantic Comedy, Two Into One, Italian Straw Hat, Jeffrey Bernard is Unwell, Present Laughter. Director: Before the Party, The Housekeeper. NY: Whose Life Is It Anyway? (Tony Award, 1979), Last Licks (dir.), Present Laughter (dir.), Chapter Two.
PICTURES: Galileo (debut, 1975), Eclipse, The Duellists, The Haunting of Julia (Full Circle), Merry Christmas Mr. Lawrence, Reuben Reuben (Acad. Award nom.), American Dreamer, Miracles, Saving Grace, Beyond Therapy, The Gospel According to Vic, That Summer of White Roses, Shirley Valentine, Someone Else's America, Subdown, Something to Believe in.
TELEVISION: Mother of Men (1959), The Glittering Prizes, Madame Bovery, Treats, The Norman Conquests, The Wall, Nazi Hunter, The Quick and the Dead, Roman Holiday, The Dumb Waiter, Faerie Tale Theater (The Princess and the Pea), Fatal Judgement, Blade on the Feather, Voices Within: The Lives of Truddi Chase, The Wright Verdicts (series).

CONVERSE, FRANK
Actor. b. St. Louis, MO, May 22, 1938. e. Carnegie-Mellon. Early training on stage in New York. Active in repertory theatres. Two seasons with Amer. Shakespeare Fest.

111

THEATER: The Seagull, Death of a Salesman, Night of the Iguana, A Man for All Seasons, The House of Blue Leaves, First One Asleep Whistle, Arturo Ui, The Philadelphia Story (1980 revival), Brothers, A Streetcar Named Desire (1988 revival), Design for Living, The Crucible, Hobson's Choice, The Ride Down Mount Morgan, etc.
PICTURES: Hurry Sundown, Hour of the Gun, The Rowdyman, The Pilot, The Bushido Blade, Spring Fever, Everybody Wins, Primary Motive.
TELEVISION: Movies: Dr. Cook's Garden, A Tattered Web, In Tandem, Killer on Board, Cruise Into Terror, Sgt. Matlovich Vs. the U.S. Air Force, Marilyn: The Untold Story, The Miracle of Kathy Miller, Anne of Green Gables—The Sequel, Alone in the Neon Jungle. Guest: Mod Squad, Medical Center, Wonderworks, Guests of the Nation. Series: Coronet Blue, N.Y.P.D., Movin' On, The Family Tree, Dolphin Cove, One Life to Live.

CONWAY, GARY
Actor. r.n. Gareth Carmody. b. Boston, MA, Feb. 4, 1936. e. U. of California at L.A. As college senior was chosen for title role in Teen-Age Frankenstein. After graduating served in military at Ford Ord, CA. In 1960 began contract with Warner Bros., appearing in films and TV. Has also appeared on stage. Has given several one-man shows as painter and is represented in public and private collections.
PICTURES: I Was a Teenage Frankenstein, Young Guns of Texas, Once Is Not Enough, The Farmer (also prod.), American Ninja (also s.p.), Over The Top, American Ninja III: Blood Hunt (s.p.).
TELEVISION: Series: Burke's Law, Land of the Giants. Movie: The Judge and Jake Wyler. Guest: 77 Sunset Strip, Columbo, Police Story, Love Boat.

CONWAY, KEVIN
Actor. b. New York, NY, May 29, 1942.
THEATER: Actor: One Flew Over the Cuckoo's Nest, When You Comin' Back Red Ryder? (Obie & Drama Desk Awards), Of Mice and Men, Moonchildren, Life Class, Saved, The Elephant Man, Other Places, King John (NYSF), Other People's Money (Outer Critics Circle Award; also L.A. prod.), The Man Who Fell in Love with His Wife, Ten Below, On the Waterfront. Director: Mecca, Short Eyes (revival), One Act Play Fest (Lincoln Center), The Milk Train Doesn't Stop Here Anymore (revival), The Elephant Man (tour), Other People's Money (Chicago, L.A. & S.F.).
PICTURES: Believe in Me, Portnoy's Complaint, Slaughterhouse Five, Shamus, F.I.S.T., Paradise Alley, The Fun House, Flashpoint, Homeboy, The Sun and the Moon (dir., prod.), Funny Farm, One Good Cop, Rambling Rose, Jennifer Eight, Gettysburg, The Quick and the Dead, Lawnmower Man II, Looking for Richard.
TELEVISION: Series: All My Children. Movies: Johnny We Hardly Knew Ye, The Deadliest Season, Rage of Angels, The Lathe of Heaven, Attack on Fear, Something About Amelia, Jesse, When Will I Be Loved?, Breaking the Silence, The Whipping Boy. Specials: The Scarlet Letter, The Elephant Man, Calm at Sunset. Mini-Series: Streets of Laredo.

CONWAY, TIM
Actor. b. Willoughby, OH, Dec. 15, 1933. e. Bowling Green State U. After 2 yrs. Army service joined KYW-TV in Cleveland as writer-director and occasional performer. Comedienne Rose Marie discovered him and arranged audition for the Steve Allen Show on which he became regular. In 1962 signed for McHale's Navy, series. Also has done night club appearances.
PICTURES: McHale's Navy (debut, 1964), McHale's Navy Joins the Air Force, The World's Greatest Athlete, The Apple Dumpling Gang, Gus, The Shaggy D.A., Billion Dollar Hobo, The Apple Dumpling Gang Rides Again, The Prize Fighter, The Private Eyes (also co-s.p.), Cannonball Run II, The Longshot, Dear God.
TELEVISION: Series: The Steve Allen Show, McHale's Navy, Rango, The Tim Conway Show (1970), The Tim Conway Comedy Hour, The Carol Burnett Show (3 Emmy Awards as actor: 1973, 1977, 1978; Emmy Award as writer: 1976), The Tim Conway Show (1980-81), Ace Crawford: Private Eye, Tim Conway's Funny America. Guest: Hollywood Palace, and shows starring Garry Moore, Carol Burnett, Red Skelton, Danny Kaye, Dean Martin, Cher, Doris Day, Coach (Emmy Award, 1996). Movie: Roll Freddy Roll.

COOGAN, KEITH
Actor. b. Palm Springs, CA, Jan. 13, 1970. e. Santa Monica City Col. Grandson of late actor Jackie Coogan. Formerly acted as Keith Mitchell. Appeared in shorts All Summer in a Day and The Great O'Grady.
PICTURES: The Fox and the Hound (voice), Adventures in Babysitting, Hiding Out, Under the Boardwalk, Cousins, Cheetah, Book of Love, Toy Soldiers, Don't Tell Mom the Babysitter's Dead, Forever, In the Army Now, Life 101, The Power Within, A Reason to Believe, Downhill Willy, Ivory Tower.
TELEVISION: Series: The MacKenzies of Paradise Cove, The Waltons, Gun Shy. Movies: A Question of Love, Million Dollar Infield, Kid With the Broken Halo, Battered, Memorial Day, Spooner. Specials: Wrong Way Kid, The Treasure of Alpheus T. Winterborn, Rascal, Over the Limit, A Town's Revenge. Guest: Growing Pains, Silver Spoons, Fame, CHips, The Love Boat, Mork and Mindy, 21 Jump Street, 8 is Enough, Fantasy Island, Just the Ten of Us, Sibs, Tales From the Crypt, others. Pilots: Norma Rae, Apple Dumpling Gang, Wonderland Cove.

COOK, FIELDER
Director, Producer. b. Atlanta, GA. e. Washington & Lee U., B.A.; U. of Birmingham, Eng., post grad. Served with 7th Amphibious Force, WWII.
PICTURES: Patterns (debut, 1956), Home Is the Hero, A Big Hand for the Little Lady (also prod.), How to Save a Marriage and Ruin Your Life, Prudence and the Pill, Eagle in a Cage, From the Mixed Up Files of Mrs. Basil E. Frankweiler.
TELEVISION: Movies: Sam Hill: Who Killed the Mysterious Mr. Foster?, Goodbye Raggedy Ann (also exec. prod.), The Homecoming, Miracle on 34th Street, This is the West That Was, Miles to Go Before I Sleep, Judge Horton and the Scottsboro Boys, Beauty and the Beast, A Love Affair: The Eleanor and Lou Gehrig Story, Too Far to Go (also released theatrically), I Know Why the Caged Bird Sings, Gaugin the Savage, Family Reunion, Will There Really Be a Morning?, Why Me?, A Special Friendship. Mini-Series: Evergreen. Specials: The Hands of Carmac Joyce, Teacher Teacher, The Rivalry, Valley Forge, The Price (Emmy Award), Harvey, Brigadoon (also prod.; 2 Emmy Awards), Seize the Day, Third and Oak: The Pool Hall, A Member of the Wedding. Pilots: Ben Casey, The 11th Hour, The Waltons.

COOK, RICHARD
Executive. b. Bakersfield, CA, Aug. 20, 1950. e. USC. Began career 1971 as Disneyland sls. rep.; promoted 1974 to mgr. of sls. Moved to studio in 1977 as mgr., pay TV and non-theatrical releases. 1980, named asst. domestic sls. mgr., for Buena Vista; 1981 promoted to v.p. & asst. gen. sls. mgr.; 1984, promoted to v.p. & gen. sls. mgr., B.V.; 1985, appt. sr. v.p., domestic distribution. 1988: appt. pres. Buena Vista Pictures Distribution. 1994, pres., Worldwide Marketing, Buena Vista Pictures Marketing. 1996 named chmn., Walt Disney Motion Picture Group.

COOKE, ALISTAIR
Journalist, Broadcaster. b. Manchester, Eng., Nov. 20, 1908. e. Jesus Coll., Cambridge U.; Yale U.; Harvard U. Film crit. of BBC 1934-37. London corr. NBC 1936-37. BBC commentator in U.S. since 1937. Weekly 15 min. talk on radio show, Letter From America, starting in 1946. Chief Amer. corr., Manchester Guardian, 1948-72; English narrator, The March of Time, 1938-39. Became U.S. citizen in 1941. Peabody award winner for International reporting, 1952, 1973-83. Hon. Knighthood, KBE, 1973.
AUTHOR: Douglas Fairbanks, Garbo & The Night Watchmen, A Generation on Trial, One Man's America, Christmas Eve, The Vintage Mencken, etc. America, 1973; Six Men, 1977; Talk About America, 1968; The Americans, 1979; Above London (with Robert Cameron), 1980; Masterpieces, 1981; The Patient Has the Floor, 1986, America Observed, 1988; Fun and Games with Alistair Cooke, 1995.
PICTURES: Narrator: Sorrowful Jones, The Three Faces of Eve, Hitler—The Last Ten Days
TELEVISION: Series: Omnibus (host; 1952-61), m.c. prod. U.N.'s International Zone (host, prod.; Emmy Award, 1958); Masterpiece Theatre (host, 1971-92). Special doc.: America: A Personal History of The United States (writer and narrator; 5 Emmy Awards, 1973; Franklin Medal, Royal Society of Arts, 1973).

COOLIDGE, MARTHA
Director, Writer, Producer. b. New Haven, CT, Aug. 17, 1946. e. Rhode Island Sch. of Design. NYU Inst. of Film and TV grad. sch. m. writer Michael Backes. Dir. short films while in school. Wrote and prod. daily children's tv show Magic Tom in Canada Worked on commercials and political doc. film crews. Prod., dir. and writer of docs. which have won festival awards, including Passing Quietly Through; David: Off and On (American Film Fest.), Old Fashioned Woman (CINE Golden Eagle Award, Blue Ribbon Award, American film festival), Bimbo (short), Magic Tom in Canada. First feature film Not a Pretty Picture (won Blue Ribbon Award, Amer. Film Fest.) Helped start assn. of Indep. Video and Filmmakers, Inc. As an AFI/Academy Intern worked with Robert Wise on his film Audrey Rose, 1976. Wrote orig. story that was filmed as the The Omega Connection. DGA, member of bd. of dirs.; WIF, member bd. of dirs. Acted in film Beverly Hills Cop III.
PICTURES: The City Girl, Valley Girl, Joy of Sex, Real Genius, Plain Clothes, That's Adequate (interviewee), Rambling Rose (IFP Spirit Award, 1991), Lost in Yonkers, Angie, Three Wishes, Out to Sea.
TELEVISION: The Twilight Zone, Sledge Hammer (pilot), House and Home (pilot). Movies: Trenchcoat in Paradise, Bare Essentials, Crazy in Love.

COONEY, JOAN GANZ
Executive, Producer. b. Phoenix, AZ, Nov. 30, 1929. e. U. of Arizona. After working as a reporter in Phoenix, moved to NY in 1953 where she wrote soap-opera summaries at NBC. Then was publicist for U.S. Steel Hour. Became producer of live weekly political TV show Court of Reason (Emmy Award) and documentaries (Poverty, Anti-Poverty and the Poor) before founding Children's Television Workshop and Sesame Street in 1969. Currently chmn., exec. committe, CTW.

COOPER, BEN
Actor. b. Hartford, CT, Sept. 30, 1933. e. Columbia U. On stage in Life with Father (1942); over 3200 radio, TV appearances starting from 1945.
PICTURES: Side Street (debut, 1950), Thunderbirds, The Woman They Almost Lynched, A Perilous Journey, Sea of Lost Ships, Flight Nurse, The Outcast, Johnny Guitar, Jubilee Trail, Hell's Outpost, The Eternal Sea, The Last Command, Headline Hunters, Finghting Chance, The Rose Tattoo, Rebel in Town, A Strange Adventure, Duel at Apache Wells, Outlaw's Son, Chartroose Caboose, The Raiders, Gunfight at Comanche Creek, Arizona Raiders, Waco, The Fastest Gun Alive, Red Tomahawk, One More Train to Rob, Support Your Local Gunfighter, Lighting Jack.

COOPER, HAL
Director, Performer. b. New York, NY, Feb. 22, 1923. e. U. of Michigan. m. Marta Salcido; child actor in various radio prog. starting in 1932; featured Bob Emery's Rainbow House, Mutual, 1936-46; asst. dir. Dock St. Theatre, Charleston, SC, 1946-48.
TELEVISION: Your School Reporter, TV Baby Sitter, The Magic Cottage (writer, prod.). *Director:* Valiant Lady, Search for Tomorrow, Portia Faces Life, Kitty Foyle (also assoc. prod.), Indictment (also prod.), The Happy Time (also assoc. prod.), For Better or Worse (also prod.), The Clear Horizon, Surprise Package (also assoc. prod.), Dick Van Dyke Show, The Art Linkletter Show (also prod.), The Object Is, Death Valley Days, I Dream of Jeannie, That Girl, I Spy, Hazel, Gidget, Gilligan's Island, NYPD, Mayberry, Courtship of Eddie's Father, My World and Welcome to It, The Brady Bunch, The Odd Couple, Mary Tyler Moore, All in the Family. *Exec. prod./Director:* Maude, Phyl and Mikky, Love, Sidney, Gimme a Break, Empty Nest, Dear John, The Powers That Be.

COOPER, JACKIE
Actor, Director, Producer. b. Los Angeles, CA, Sept. 15, 1922. Began theatrical career at age of 3 as m.p. actor; was member of Our Gang comedies (first short was Boxing Gloves in 1929). First starring role in 1931 in Skippy. Worked at every major studio, always with star billing. At 20 enlisted in Navy. After three-yr. tour of duty went to N.Y. to work in live TV. Appeared in 3 plays on B'way stage and in Mr. Roberts on natl. tour and in London. Directed as well as acted in live and filmed TV. Served as v.p. in chg. of TV prod. for Screen Gems, 1964-69, when resigned to return to acting, directing, producing. 2 Emmy Awards for directing M*A*S*H and The White Shadow. Retired 1989.
PICTURES: Fox Movietone Follies (feature debut, 1929), Sunny Side Up, Skippy (Acad. Award nom.), Young Donovan's Kid, Sooky, The Champ, When a Feller Needs a Friend, Divorce in the Family, Broadway to Hollywood, The Bowery, Lone Cowboy, Treasure Island, Peck's Bad Boy, Dinky, O'Shaughnessy's Boy, Tough Guy, The Devil Is a Sissy, Boy of the Streets, White Banners, Gangster's Boy, That Certain Age, Newsboys' Home, Scouts to the Rescue (serial), Spirit of Culver, Streets of New York, What a Life, Two Bright Boys, The Big Guy, The Return of Frank James, Seventeen, Gallant Sons, Life With Henry, Ziegfeld Girl, Glamour Boy, Her First Beau, Syncopation, Men of Texas, The Navy Comes Through, Where Are Your Children?, Stork Bites Man, Kilroy Was Here, French Leave, Everything's Ducky, The Love Machine, Stand Up and Be Counted (dir. only), Chosen Survivors, Superman, Superman II, Superman III, Superman IV: The Quest for Peace, Surrender.
TELEVISION: *Series:* People's Choice (also directed 71 episodes), Hennessey (also dir. 91 epsiodes), Dean Martin Comedy World (host), Mobile One. *Movies:* Shadow on the Land, Maybe I'll Come Home in the Spring, The Astronaut, The Day the Earth Moved, The Invisible Man, Mobile Two, Operation Petticoat. *Director:* Having Babies III, Rainbow, White Mama, Rodeo Girl, Sex and the Single Parent, The Ladies, Deacon Street Deer, Perfect Gentlemen, Marathon, Leave 'Em Laughing, Rosie (also prod.), Glitter, The Night They Saved Christmas, Izzy and Moe.

COOPER, JEANNE
Actress. r.n. Wilma Jean Cooper. b. Taft, CA, Oct. 25. e. College of the Pacific, Pasadena Playhouse. Son is actor Corbin Bernsen. Recipient: 3 Soap Opera Update MVP Awards, Soap Opera Digest, Pasadena Playhouse Woman of the Year and Hollywood Entertainment Museum Award.
THEATER: The Miracle Worker, Plain and Fancy, Picnic, On the Town, The Big Knife, Tonight at 8:30, Dark Side of the Moon, Plaza Suite.
PICTURES: Man From the Alamo, The Redhead From Wyoming, The Houston Story, Red Nightmare, Plunder Road, 9 Steps to Danger, The Intruder, House of Women, 13 West Street, Let No Man Write My Epitaph, The Glory Guys, Tony Rome, The Boston Strangler, There Was a Crooked Man, Kansas City Bomber, All-American Boy, Frozen Assets.
TELEVISION: *Series:* Bracken's World, The Young and the Restless (1973-). *Movie:* Sweet Hostage, Beyond Suspicion. *Guest:* Perry Mason, The Twilight Zone, Wanted: Dead or Alive, Gunsmoke, The Big Valley, L.A. Law, and numerous others.

COOPER, SHELDON
Executive. e. Indiana U. Joined WGN Television, 1950 holding various positions in prod. including floor mgr., dir., prod.; 1961, named mgr. prod.; 1961 became exec. prod. for station; 1964, named asst. prog. mgr.; 1965, mgr. of dept.; 1966, v.p. prog. dev. with WGN Continental Productions Co.; elected to bd. of dir., Continental Broadcasting Co. and appointed station mgr., WGN TV, April 1974.; 1975, named v.p. and gen. mrg., WGN Continental Broadcasting.; 1977, dir., broadcasting; 1979, pres. and gen. mgr., WGN Television; 1982, chief exec. of newly formed Tribune Entertainment Co. and dir. of Tribune Co. Syndicate, Inc., 1982-present. One of founders of Operation Prime Time, consortium of independent stations. Awarded Emmys: 1960 as television's man of the year behind the cameras and 1964 for continuing excellence as writer, prod., executive, WGN TV. Chmn., Assoc. of Independent TV Stations, Inc. (INTV), 1980 and 1981; National v.p., Muscular Dystrophy Assoc.; 1980, on bd. National Assoc. of TV Prog. Executives (NATPE); first v.p., Chicago chap. Acad. of TV Arts and Sciences; v.p., trustee of national chap.

COOPERMAN, ALVIN
Producer. b. Brooklyn, NY. Prod., Untouchables, 1961-63; exec. dir., Shubert Theatre Ent. 1963; v.p., special programs, NBC, 1967-68; exec. v.p., Madison Square Garden Center, 1968-72; pres., Madison Square Garden Center, Inc.; founder , Madison Sq. Garden Prods. and Network; chmn. of the board, Athena Communications Corp.; pres., NY Television Academy, 1987-89.
TELEVISION: *Producer:* Romeo and Juliet (Emmy nom.), Pele's Last Game, The Fourth King, Amahl and the Night Visitors, Live from Studio 8H—A Tribute to Toscanini (Emmy Award), Live from Studio 8H—An Evening with Jerome Robbins and the New York City Ballet (Emmy Award), Live from Studio 8H—Caruso Remembered, Ain't Misbehavin' (Emmy nom., NAACP Image Award), Pope John Paul II, My Two Loves, Safe Passage, Family Album, U.S.A. (26 half hrs.), Witness to Survival (26 half hrs.), Mobs and Mobsters, Follow The River, Susan B. Anthony Slept Here (docu.).

COPELAND, STEWART
Composer. b. Alexandria, Egypt, July 16, 1952. Drummer and singer for The Police. Member of pop group, Animal Logic.
PICTURES: Rumble Fish, Out of Bounds, Wall Street, Talk Radio, Sge's Having a Baby, See No Evil Hear No Evil, Riff-Raff, Hidden Agenda, The First Power, Men at Work, Highlander II: The Quickening, Taking Care of Business, Wide Sargasso Sea, Bank Robber, Airborne, Raining Stones, Surviving the Game, Decadence, Fresh, Rapa Nui, Silent Fall, The Girl You Want, The Pallbearer, Boys, The Leopard Son, O Que E Isso Companheiro?, Little Boy Blue, Gridlock'd, Good Burger, Welcome to Woop-Woop.
TELEVISION: *Series:* The Equalizer, TV 101, Afterburn, Babylon 5. *Movies:* White Dwarf, Tyson The Taking of Pelham One Two Three.

COPPOLA, FRANCIS FORD
Director, Writer, Producer. b. Detroit, MI, April 7, 1939. Raised in NYC. Son of late composer Carmine Coppola. Sister is actress Talia Shire. e. Hofstra U, B.A.: 1958; UCLA, 1958-68, M.F.A., cinema. While at UCLA was hired as asst. to Roger Corman as dialogue dir., sound man and assoc. prod. 1969; est. American Zoetrope, (later Zoetrope Studios), a prod. center in San Francisco. Publisher, City (magazine, 1975-6). Appeared in documentary Hearts of Darkness: A Filmmaker's Apocalypse.
PICTURES: Tonight for Sure (dir.), The Playgirls and the Bellboy (co-dir., co-s.p. of addtl. sequences for U.S. version), Premature Burial (asst. dir.), Tower of London (dialog. dir.), Battle Beyond the Sun (adapt.), The Young Races (sound, 2nd unit dir.), The Terror (assoc. prod., 2nd unit dir.), Dementia 13 (dir., s.p.), Is Paris Burning? (co-s.p.), This Property Is Condemned (co-s.p.), You're a Big Boy Now (dir., s.p.), The Wild Races (2nd unit dir.), Reflections in a Golden Eye (s.p.), Finian's Rainbow (dir.), The Rain People (dir., s.p.), Patton (co-s.p.; Academy Award, 1970), THX 1138 (exec. prod.), The Godfather (dir., co-s.p.; Academy Award for Best Screenplay, 1972), American Graffiti (exec. prod.), The Great Gatsby (s.p.), The Conversation (dir., co-prod., s.p.), The Godfather Part II (dir., co-s.p., prod.; Academy Awards for Best Picture, Director & Screenplay, 1974), Apocalypse Now (dir., prod., co-s.p., cameo), The Black Stallion (exec. prod.), Kagemusha (co-exec. prod.), One From the Heart (dir., co-s.p.), Hammett (exec. prod.), The Escape Artist (co-exec. prod.), The Black Stallion Returns (exec. prod.), The Outsiders (dir.), Rumble Fish (dir., exec. prod., co-s.p.), The Cotton Club (dir., co-s.p.), Mishima (co-exec. prod.), Peggy Sue Got Married (dir.), Gardens of Stone (dir., co-prod.), Tough Guys Don't Dance (co-exec. prod.), Lionheart (exec. prod.), Tucker: The Man and His Dream (dir.), New York Stories (Life Without Zoe; dir., co-s.p.), The Godfather Part III (dir., co-s.p., prod.), Wind (co-exec. prod.), Bram Stoker's Dracula (dir., co-prod.), The Secret Garden (exec. prod.), Mary Shelley's Frankenstein (prod.), Don Juan DeMarco (exec. prod.), My Family/Mi Familia (prod.), Haunted (exec. prod.), Jack, Buddy (exec. prod.)..
TELEVISION: *Movies:* The People (exec. prod.), White Dwarf (co- prod), Tecumseh: The Last Warrior (co-exec. prod.). *Special:* Rip Van Winkle (Faerie Tale Theatre; dir.). *Series:* The Outsiders (exec. prod.).

CORBIN, BARRY
Actor. b. Dawson County, TX, Oct. 16, 1940. e. Texas Tech. Univ.
PICTURES: Urban Cowboy, Stir Crazy, Any Which Way You Can, Dead and Buried, The Night the Lights Went Out in Georgia, The Best Little Whorehouse in Texas, Six Pack, Honkytonk Man, The Ballad of Gregorio Cortez, WarGames, The Man Who Loved Women, Hard Traveling, What Comes Around, My Science Project, Nothing in Common, Under Cover, Off the Mark, Permanent Record, Critters 2: The Main Course, It Takes Two, Who is Harry Crumb?, Short Time, Ghost Dad, The Hot Spot, Career Opportunities, Solo, Kiss and Tell, Curdled.
TELEVISION: Series: Boone, Spies, Northern Exposure, The Big Easy. Mini-Series: The Thorn Birds, Lonesome Dove. Movies: Rage, This House Possessed, The Killing of Randy Webster, Murder in Texas, Bitter Harvest, A Few Days in Weasel Creek, Fantasies, Prime Suspect, Travis McGee, Flight #90: Disaster on the Potomac, The Jesse Owens Story, Fatal Vision, I Know My First Name is Steven, Last Flight Out, The Chase, Conagher, Siringo, The Keys, Robin Cook's Virus, Moon Shot, Deadly Family Secrets, My Son Is Easy, Columbo: A Trace of Murder, The Hired Heart. Guest: Mash, Call to Glory, Murder She Wrote, Hill Street Blues, Matlock, Murphy Brown, Ellen, The Drew Carrey Show.

CORD, ALEX
Actor. r.n. Alexander Viespi. b. Floral Park, NY, May 3, 1933. Early career in rodeo; left to become actor. Studied at Shakespeare Academy (Stratford, Conn.) and Actor's Studio (N.Y.). Spent two yrs. in summer stock; in 1961 went on tour with Stratford Shakespeare Co. Author of novel Sandsong. Co-founder of Chuckers for Charity polo team which has raised more than $2 million for various charities. Champion rodeo team roper and cutting horse rider.
PICTURES: Synanon (debut, 1965), Stagecoach, A Minute to Pray A Second to Die, The Brotherhood, Stiletto, The Last Grenade, The Dead Are Alive, Chosen Survivors, Inn of the Damned, Sidewinder One, Grayeagle, Jungle Warriors, Street Asylum.
TELEVISION: Series: W.E.B., Cassie & Company, Airwolf. Movies: The Scorpio Letters, Hunter's Man; Genesis II, Fire !, Beggerman Thief, Goliath Awaits, The Dirty Dozen: The Fatal Mission.

CORDAY, BARBARA
Executive. b. New York, NY, Oct. 15, 1944. Began career as publicist in N.Y. and L.A. Turned to writing for TV; named v.p., ABC-TV, in chg. of comedy series development. 1982-84, headed own production co. in association with Columbia Pictures TV; June, 1984-87 pres.; Columbia Pictures TV; 1988, appointed CBS Entertainment, exec. v.p. primetime programs. Member: Caucus of Writers, Producers & Directors; Hollywood Women's Coalition.
TELEVISION: Writer: American Dream (pilot), Cagney and Lacey (also co-creator).

COREY, JEFF
Actor. b. New York, NY, Aug. 10, 1914. e. Feagin Sch. of Dram. Art. On stage in Leslie Howard prod. of Hamlet, 1936; Life and Death of an American, In the Matter of J. Robert Oppenheimer, Hamlet-Mark Taper Forum, King Lear, Love Suicide at Schofield Barracks.
PICTURES: All That Money Can Buy, Syncopation, The Killers, Ramrod, Joan of Arc, Roughshod, Black Shadows, Bagdad, Outriders, The Devil and Daniel Webster, My Friend Flicka, Canyon City, Singing Guns, Seconds, In Cold Blood, Golden Bullet, Boston Strangler, True Grit, Butch Cassidy and The Sundance Kid, Beneath the Planet of the Apes, Getting Straight, Little Big Man, They Call Me Mister Tibbs, Clear and Present Danger, High Flying Love, Catlow, Something Evil, Premonition, Shine, Rooster, Oh God!, Butch and Sundance: The Early Days, Up River, Conan the Destroyer, Cognac, Messenger of Death, Bird on a Wire, The Judas Project, Deception, Beethoven's 2nd, Surviving the Game, Color of Night, Home of the Brave.
TELEVISION: Guest: The Untouchables, The Beachcomber,, Outer Limits, Channing, The Doctors and the Nurses, Perry Mason, Gomer Pyle, Wild Wild West, Run for Your Life, Bonanza, Iron Horse, Judd for Defense, Garrisons Gorillas, Gunsmoke, Hawaii Five O, Star Trek, The Psychiatrist, Night Gallery, Alias Smith and Jones, Sixth Sense, Hawkins, Owen Marshall, Police Story, Bob Newhart Show, Six Million Dollar Man, Doctors Hospital, Starsky and Hutch, Land of the Free, Kojak, McCloud, Captains Courageous, Bionic Woman, Barney Miller, One Day at a Time, The Pirate, Lou Grant, The Powers of Jonathan Starr, Cry for the Strangers, Today's FBI, Knots Landing, Archie Bunker's Place, Faerie Tale Theatre, Night Court, Helltown, Morning Star/Evening Star, New Love American Style, Starman, The A Team, Jessamene, Wolf, Jake and the Fatman, Rose and the Jackal, To My Daughter, Payoff, Sinatra, The Marshal, Home Court, Picket Fences, Murphy Brown, Nothing Sacred. Movies: A Deadly Silence, The Balcony, Yellow Canary, Lady in a Cage.

CORMAN, GENE
Producer. r.n. Eugene H. Corman. b. Detroit, MI, Sept. 24, 1927. e. Stanford U. Went to work for MCA as agent 1950-57; left to produce his first feature film, Hot Car Girl. Partner with brother Roger in Corman Company and New World Distributors. Vice pres. 20th Century Fox Television, 1983-87; exec. v.p. worldwide production, 21st Century Film Corp.
PICTURES: Attack of the Giant Leeches, Not of This Earth, Blood and Steel, Valley of the Redwoods, Secret of the Purple Reef, Beast from Haunted Cave, Cat Burglar, The Intruder, Tobruk, You Can't Win Em All, Cool Breeze, Hit Man, The Slams, Von Richthofen and Brown, I Escaped from Devil's Island, Secret Invasion, Vigilante Force, F.I.S.T. (exec. prod.), The Big Red One, If You Could See What I Hear, Paradise, A Man Called Sarge.
TELEVISION: What's In It For Harry, A Woman Called Golda (Emmy and Christopher Awards as prod.), Mary and Joseph, a Love Story, Blood Ties.

CORMAN, ROGER WILLIAM
Executive, Director, Producer, Writer, Distributor. b. Detroit, MI, April 5, 1921. e. Stanford U. 1947; Oxford U., England 1950. U.S. Navy 1944; 20th Century-Fox, production dept., 1948, story analyst 1948-49; Literary agent, 1951-52; story, s.p., assoc. prod., Highway Dragnet. Formed Roger Corman Prod. and Filmgroup. Prod. over 200 feature films and dir. over 60 of them. Formed production-releasing company, org., New World Pictures, Inc., 1970. Formed prod. co., Concorde, 1984; distribution co., New Horizons, 1985. On TV acted in film Body Bags. Recipient of LA Film Critics Award for Career Achievement, 1997.
PICTURES: Director: Five Guns West (dir. debut, 1955), Apache Woman, Swamp Women, The Day the World Ended, The Oklahoma Woman, The Gunslinger, It Conquered the World, Not of This Earth, Naked Paradise (Thunder Over Hawaii), Attack of the Crab Monsters, Rock All Night, Teenage Doll, Carnival Rock, Sorority Girl, Saga of the Viking Women and Their Voyage to the Waters of the Great Sea Serpent, The Undead, War of the Satellites, She Gods of Shark Reef, Machine Gun Kelly, Teenage Caveman, I Mobster, A Bucket of Blood, The Wasp Woman, Ski Troop Attack, House of Usher, The Little Shop of Horrors, The Last Woman on Earth, Creature From the Haunted Sea, Atlas, The Pit and the Pendulum, The Intruder, The Premature Burial, Tales of Terror, Tower of London, The Raven, The Terror, X—The Man With the X Ray Eyes, The Haunted Palace, The Young Racers, The Secret Invasion, The Masque of the Red Death, Tomb of Ligeia, The Wild Angels, The St. Valentine's Day Massacre, The Trip, Target: Harry (credited as Henry Neill), Bloody Mama, Gas-s-s-s, Von Richtofen and Brown, Frankenstein Unbound. Producer: Boxcar Bertha, Big Bad Mama, Death Race 2000, Eat My Dust, Capone, Jackson County Jail, Fighting Mad, Thunder & Lightning, Grand Theft Auto, I Never Promised You A Rose Garden, Deathsport, Avalanche, Battle Beyond the Stars, St. Jack, Love Letters, Smokey Bites the Dust, Galaxy of Terror, Slumber Party Massacre Part II, Death Stalker, Barbarian Queen, Munchies, Stripped To Kill, Big Bad Mama II, Daddy's Boys, Lords of the Deep (also actor), The Terror Within, Two to Tango, Time Trackers, Heroes Stand Alone, Bloodfist, Silk 2, Edgar Allan Poe's The Masque of Red Death, Haunted Symphony, Midnight Tease. Exec. Prod.: Black Scorpion, Black Scorpion 2, Not of This Earth, Not Like Us, Sweet Revenge (co-exec. prod.), The Drifter, Singles, Crime Zone, Watcher, The Lawless Land, Stripped to Kill 2, Hollywood Boulevard II, Rock and Roll High School Forever, Bloodfist II (prod.), One Night Stand (exec. prod.). Actor: The Godfather Part II, Cannonball, The Howling, The State of Things, Swing Shift, The Silence of the Lambs, Philadelphia., Apollo 13.
TELEVISION: Movie Series: Roger Corman Presents (exec. prod.). Movie: The Second Civil War.
AUTHOR: How I Made a Hundred Movies in Hollywood and Never Lost a Dime.

CORNELL, JOHN
Producer, Director, Writer. b. Kalgoorlie, Western Australia, 1941. m. actress Delvene Delancy. Grew up Bunbury. e. studied pharmacy for two years in Perth. Won internship at Western Australian Newspapers at 19, becoming columnist then London editor at 26. As Melbourne prod. of TV show, A Current Affair, discovered bridge rigger Paul Hogan. Put him on show, became his manager and formed JP Productions with him in 1972. Prod. and appeared on The Paul Hogan Show. Formed movie co. with Hogan, Rimfire Films.
PICTURES: Crocodile Dundee (prod., co-s.p.), Crocodile Dundee II (prod., dir., editor), Almost an Angel (dir., prod.).

CORNFELD, STUART
Producer. b. Los Angeles, CA. e. U. of California, Berkeley. Entered America Film Institute's Center for Advanced Film Studies as producing fellow, 1975. Joined Brooksfilm as asst. to Mel Brooks on High Anxiety. Assoc. prod., History of the World Part I.
PICTURES: Fatso, The Elephant Man, (exec. prod.), Fast Times at Richmont High (actor only), National Lampoon's European Vacation (co-prod.), Girls Just Want to Have Fun (exec. prod.), The Fly, Moving, The Fly II (exec. prod.), Hider in the House (co-prod.), Darkman (actor only), Kafka, Wilder Napalm, Mimic (co-exec. prod.).

CORRI, ADRIENNE
Actress. r.n. Adrienne Riccoboni. b. Glasgow, Scotland, Nov. 13, 1933. e. RADA at 13; parts in several stage plays including The Human Touch. Numerous TV appearances.
PICTURES: The Romantic Age (Naughty Arlette; debut, 1949), The River, Quo Vadis, The Little Kidnappers, The Sinners, Devil Girl From Mars, Meet Mr. Callaghan, Lease of Life, Make Me an Offer, Triple Blackmail, The Feminine Touch, Behind the Headlines, The Shield of Faith, Three Men in a Boat, Second Fiddle, The Surgeon's Knife, The Big Chance, Corridors of Blood, The Rough and the Smooth (Portrait of a Sinner), The Tell-Tale Heart, Sword of Freedom, The Hellfire, Dynamite Jack, Sword of Lancelot, A Study in Terror, Bunny Lake Is Missing, Doctor Zhivago, Woman Times Seven, The Viking Queen, Africa—Texas Style!, The File of the Golden Goose, Cry Wolf, Moon Zero Two, Vampire Circus, A Clockwork Orange, Madhouse, Rosebud, Revenge of the Pink Panther, The Human Factor.

CORT, BUD
Actor. r.n. Walter Edward Cox. b. New Rochelle, NY, March 29, 1950. e. NYU School of the Arts. Stage debut in Wise Child, B'way. L.A. theatre includes Forget-Me-Not Lane, August 11 1947, Endgame (Dramalogue Award), Demon Wine, The Seagull, He Who Gets Slapped. Founding member of L.A. Classical Theatre. Theatrical film debut as extra in Up the Down Staircase 1967. Television debut in The Doctors.
PICTURES: Sweet Charity, M*A*S*H, Gas-s-s-s, The Traveling Executioner, Brewster McCloud, Harold and Maude, Die Laughing, Why Shoot the Teacher?, She Dances Alone, Hysterical, Electric Dreams (voice), Love Letters, The Secret Diary of Sigmund Freud, Maria's Lovers, Invaders from Mars, Love at Stake, The Chocolate War, Out of the Dark, Brain Dead, Going Under, Ted and Venus (also dir., co-s.p.), Girl in the Cadillac, Heat (uncredited), Theodore Rex, Sweet Jane, I Woke Up Early the Day I Died, Dogma.
TELEVISION: Special: Bernice Bobs Her Hair. Guest: Faerie Tale Theatre (The Nightingale), The Hitchhiker (Made for Each Other), The New Twilight Zone, Midnight Caller, Gun. Movies: Brave New World, The Bates Motel, and The Band Played On, Jitters.

CORT, ROBERT W.
Executive. e. U. of Pennsylvania (Phi Beta Kappa). Moved into feature prod. after having worked primarily in marketing/advertising. Joined Columbia Pictures as v.p., 1976; elevated to v.p., adv./pub./promo. Named exec. v.p. of mktg. for 20th-Fox, 1980. Moved into feature prod. as senior v.p., 1981. In 1983 named exec. v.p., prod., 20th-Fox Prods. 1985, joined Interscope Communications as pres.
PICTURES: Prod.: Critical Condition, Outrageous Fortune, Revenge of the Nerds II, Three Men and a Baby, The Seventh Sign, Cocktail, Bill & Ted's Excellent Adventure (exec. prod.), Renegades (exec. prod.), Blind Fury (exec. prod.), An Innocent Man, The First Power (exec. prod.), Bird on a Wire, Arachnophobia, Three Man and a Little Lady, Eve of Destruction, Class Action, Bill & Ted's Bogus Journey, Paradise, The Hand That Rocks the Cradle, The Cutting Edge, FernGully, The Gun in Betty Lou's Handbag, Out on a Limb, Jersey Girl, Holy Matrimony, Imaginary Crimes, Operation Dumbo Drop, The Tie That Binds, Mr. Holland's Opus, The Associate (exec. prod.), Snow White (exec.), The Odd Couple II.
TELEVISION: Movies (co-exec. prod.): A Mother's Courage (Emmy Award), A Part of the Family, Body Language.

CORTESE, VALENTINA
Actress. b. Milan, Italy, Jan. 1, 1924. Started career at 15 in Orizzonte Dipinto while studying at Rome Acad. of Dramatic Art. Following several appearances in European films brought to Hollywood by 20th Century-Fox, 1949; billed in U.S. films as Valentina Cortesa. Experience on dramatic stage in variety of roles inc. Shakespeare, O'Neill, Shaw.
PICTURES: Orizzonte Dipinto (debut, 1940), Primo Amore, A Yank in Rome, A Bullet for Stefano, Les Miserables, The Glass Mountain (English-language debut, 1950), Black Magic, Malaya, Thieves Highway, Shadow of the Eagle, The House on Telegraph Hill, Secret People, Lulu, Forbidden Women (Angels of Darkness), The Barefoot Contessa, Le Amiche, Magic Fire, Calabuch, Barabbas, The Evil Eye, The Visit, The Possessed, Juliet of the Spirits, Black Sun, The Legend of Lylah Clare, The Secret of Santa Vittoria, First Love, Give Her the Moon, The Assassination of Trotsky, Brother Sun Sister Moon, Day for Night (Acad. Award nom.), Tendre Dracula, Widow's Nest, When Time Ran Out, La Ferdinanda, Blue Tango, The Adventures of Baron Munchausen, The Betrothed, Young Toscanini, Buster's Bedroom, Sparrow.

CORTEZ, STANLEY
Director of Photography. r.n. Stanislaus Krantz. b. New York, NY, Nov. 4, 1908. e. NYU. Brother was late actor Ricardo Cortez. Began working with portrait photographers (Steichen, Pirie MacDonald, Bachrach, etc.), N.Y. Entered film indust. with Paramount; to Hollywood as camera asst. and later 2nd cameraman, various studios; pioneer in use of montage. Served Signal Corps WWII. Received Film Critics of Amer. award for work on Magnificent Ambersons. Under personal contract to David O. Selznick, Orson Welles, Walter Wanger, David Wolper. Contributor, Encyclopedia Britannica.

PICTURES: Four Days Wonder, The Forgotten Women, Alias the Deacon, Love Honor and Oh Baby!, Meet the Wildcat, The Black Cat, Badlands of Dakota, Bombay Clipper, Eagle Squadron, The Magnificent Ambersons (Acad. Award nom.), Flesh and Fantasy, Since You Went Away (Acad. Award. nom.) Smash Up—The Story of a Woman, Secret Beyond the Door, Man on the Eiffel Tower, The Admiral Was a Lady, Fort Defiance, Abbott & Costello Meet Captain Kidd, Stronghold, Diamond Queen, Neanderthal Man, Shark River, Riders to the Stars, The Night of the Hunter, Man from Del Rio, Three Faces of Eve, Top Secret Affair, The Angry Red Planet, Thunder in the Sun, Dinosaurus, Back Street, Shock Corridor, Nightmare in the Sun, The Naked Kiss, Young Dillinger, Ghost in the Invisible Bikini, Blue, The Bridge at Remagen, Another Man Another Chance, Damien: Omen II (special photog.), When Time Ran Out (special photog.).
(d. Dec. 23, 1997)

CORWIN, BRUCE CONRAD
Exhibitor. b. Los Angeles, CA, June 11, 1940. e. Wesleyan U. Pres., Metropolitan Theatres Corp.; Past pres., Variety Children's Charities Tent 25; Board of Trustees U.C.S.B. Foundation; pres. emeritus, L.A. Children's Museum; chmn., Coro Natl. Board of Governors; Past President of the Foundation of Motion Picture Pioneers and Pioneer of the Year, 1977.

CORWIN, NORMAN
Writer, Producer, Director. b. Boston, MA, May 3, 1910. Sports ed. Greenfield, Mass. Daily Recorder, 1926-29; radio ed., news commentator, Springfield Republican & Daily News, 1929-36; prog. dir., CBS, 1938. Author of Thirteen by Corwin, More by Corwin, Untitled & Other Plays, The Plot to Overthrow Christmas, Dog in the Sky, Overkill and Megalove, Prayer for the 70's, Holes in a Stained Glass Window, Trivializing America; taught courses at UCLA, USC, San Diego State U. Faculty, U.S.C. Sch. of Journalism, 1980-.; sec., M.P. Academy Foundation, 1985. First v.p., Motion Picture Acad., 1989. Inducted into Radio Hall of Fame, Chicago Museum, 1993. Writer-host Academy Leaders (PBS). Chmn. Doc. Award Com., Motion Picture Acad. 1965-91; elected to bd. of gov., 1980; first v.p., 1988-89; chmn., writers' exec. comm., M.P. Academy; co-chmn. scholarship com., M.P. Academy; mem.: Film Advisory Bd.; bd. of trustees, Advisory Board, Filmex; bd. of dirs., WGA. Books incl. Directors Guild Oral History, Years of the Electric Ear, Norman Corwin's Letters.
THEATER: The Rivalry, The World of Carl Sandburg, The Hyphen, Overkill and Megalove, Cervantes. Together Tonight: Jefferson Hamilton and Burr.
PICTURES: Once Upon a Time, The Blue Veil, The Grand Design, Scandal in Scourie, Lust for Life (Acad. Award nom. best adapt. s.p.), The Story of Ruth.
TELEVISION: Inside the Movie Kingdom, The FDR series, The Plot to Overthrow Christmas, Norman Corwin Presents, The Court Martial of General Yamashita, Network at 50.

COSBY, BILL
Actor, Comedian. b. Philadelphia, PA, July 12, 1938. e. Temple U., U. of Mass., Ed.D. Served in United States Navy Medical Corps. Started as night club entertainer.
AUTHOR: The Wit and Wisdom of Fat Albert, Bill Cosby's Personal Guide to Power Tennis, Fatherhood, Time Flies.
COMEDY ALBUMS: Bill Cosby Is a Very Funny Fellow... Right! (Grammy Award, 1964), I Started Out As a Child (Grammy Award, 1965), Why Is There Air? (Grammy Award, 1966), Wonderfulness (Grammy Award, 1967), Revenge (Grammy Award, 1967), To Russell My Brother Whom I Slept With (Grammy Award, 1969), Bill Cosby Is Not Himself These Days, Rat Own Rat Own Rat Own, My Father Confused Me... What Must I Do? What Must I Do?, Disco Bill, Bill's Best Friend, Cosby and the Kids, It's True It's True, Bill Cosby - Himself, 200 MPH, Silverthroat, Hooray for the Salvation Army Band, 8:15 12:15, For Adults Only, Bill Cosby Talks to Kids About Drugs, Inside the Mind of Bill Cosby.
RADIO: The Bill Cosby Radio Program.
PICTURES: Hickey and Boggs (debut, 1972), Man and Boy, Uptown Saturday Night, Let's Do It Again, Mother Jugs and Speed, A Piece of the Action, California Suite, The Devil and Max Devlin, Bill Cosby Himself, Leonard Part VI (also co-prod., story), Ghost Dad, The Meteor Man, Jack, 4 Little Girls.
TELEVISION: Series: I Spy (3 Emmy Awards for Best Actor: 1966, 1967, 1968), The Bill Cosby Show (1969-71), The New Bill Cosby Show (1972-73), Fat Albert and the Cosby Kids, Cos, The New Fat Albert Show (Emmy Award, 1981), The Cosby Show (1984-92), A Different World (exec. prod. only), You Bet Your Life, Here and Now (exec. prod. only), The Cosby Mysteries, Cosby (also prod., 1996-), Kids Say the Darndest Things. Specials: The Bill Cosby Special, The Second Bill Cosby Special, Fat Albert Easter Special (voice), Cosby Salutes Alvin Ailey. Movies: To All My Friends on Shore (also exec. prod., story, music), Top Secret, The Cosby Mysteries (also co-exec. prod.), I Spy Returns (also co-exec. prod.).

COSMATOS, GEORGE PAN
Director, Producer, Writer. b. Tuscany, Italy, Jan. 4, 1947. e. London U., London Film School. Asst. on such films as Exodus, Zorba the Greek.
PICTURES: *Director*: Restless (also co-prod., s.p.), Massacre in Rome (also co-s.p.), The Cassandra Crossing (also co-s.p.), Escape to Athena (also co-s.p.), Of Unknown Origin, Rambo: First Blood Part II, Cobra, Leviathan, Tombstone, Shadow Conspiracy.

COSTA-GAVRAS (CONSTANTIN)
Director, Writer. r.n. Konstantinos Gavras. b. Athens, Greece, Feb. 13, 1933. French citizen. e. Studied at the Sorbonne; Hautes Etudes Cinematographique, (IDHEC). Was leading ballet dancer in Greece before the age of 20. Worked as second, then first assistant to Marcel Ophuls, Rene Clair, Rene Clement and Jacques Demy. Pres. of the Cinematheque Francaise, 1982-87. Appeared as actor in film Madame Rosa.
PICTURES: *Director*: The Sleeping Car Murders (also s.p.; debut, 1965), Un Homme De Trop/Shock Troops (also s.p.), Z (also co-s.p.; 2 Acad. Award noms.), The Confession, State of Siege (also co- s.p.), Special Section (also co-s.p.), Clair de Femme (also s.p.), Missing (also co-s.p.; Acad. Award for Best Adapted s.p., 1982; Palm d'Or at Cannes Film Fest.), Hannah K. (also prod.), Spies Like Us (actor only), Family Business (also s.p.), Betrayed, Music Box (Golden Bear, Berlin Festival, 1989), The Little Apocalypse, Lumiere & Company, Mad City.

COSTNER, KEVIN
Actor. b. Lynwood, CA, Jan. 18, 1955. e. CA. State U, Fullerton majored in marketing. Acted with South Coast Actors' Co-op, community theater gp. while at coll. After grad. took marketing job which lasted 30 days. Early film work in low budget exploitation film, Sizzle Beach, 1974. Then one line as Luther Adler in Frances. Role in The Big Chill was edited from final print. 1989, set up own prod. co. Tig Prods. at Raleigh Studios.
PICTURES: Sizzle Beach U.S.A., Shadows Run Black, Night Shift, Chasing Dreams, Table for Five, Testament, Stacy's Knights, The Gunrunner, Fandango, Silverado, American Flyers, The Untouchables, No Way Out, Bull Durham, Field of Dreams, Revenge (also exec. prod.), Dances With Wolves (also dir., co-prod.; Academy Awards for Best Picture & Director, 1990), Robin Hood: Prince of Thieves, JFK, The Bodyguard (also co-prod.), A Perfect World, Wyatt Earp (also co-prod.), Rapa Nui (co-prod. only), The War, Waterworld (also co-prod.), Tin Cup.
TELEVISION: *Special*: 500 Nations (co-exec. prod., host)

COUNTER, J. NICHOLAS III
Executive. Pres., Alliance of Motion Picture and Television Producers.

COURIC, KATIE
Newcaster. b. Arlington, VA, Jan. 7, 1957. e. Univ. of VA. Started as desk asst. at ABC News, then assignment editor for CNN, reporter for WTVJ, NBC affiliate in Miami. Moved to NBC's Washington D.C. station WRC. Became natl. correspondent for The Today Show, 1989, then co-host in 1991. Served as co-host of Macy's Thanksgiving Day Parade, 1991-present. Co-host of nighttime series Now With Tom Brokaw & Katie Couric.

COURTENAY, TOM
Actor. b. Hull, England, Feb. 25, 1937 e. University Coll., London, Royal Acad. of Dramatic Art, 1960-61; Old Vic.
THEATER: Billy Liar, Andorra, Hamlet, She Stoops to Conquer, Otherwise Engaged (N.Y. debut), The Dresser, Poison Pen, Uncle Vanya, Moscow Stations, etc.
PICTURES: The Loneliness of the Long Distance Runner (debut, 1962), Private Potter, Billy Liar, King and Country, Operation Crossbow, King Rat, Doctor Zhivago (Acad. Award nom.), The Night of the Generals, The Day the Fish Came Out, A Dandy in Aspic, Otley, One Day in the Life of Ivan Denisovich, Catch Me a Spy, The Dresser (Acad. Award nom.), Happy New Year, Leonard Part VI, Let Him Have It, The Last Butterfly.
TELEVISION: *Series*: The Lads, Ghosts, Private Potter. *Movies/Specials*: I Heard the Owl Call My Name, Jesus of Nazareth, Absent Friends, Chekhov in Yalta, Redemption, The Old Curiosity Shop.

COURTLAND, JEROME
Actor, Producer, Director. b. Knoxville, TN, Dec. 27, 1926. Began career in 40s as actor, then turned to directing and producing.
PICTURES: *Actor*: Kiss and Tell, Man from Colorado, Battleground, The Barefoot Mailman, The Bamboo Prison, Tonka, Black Spurs. *Director*: Run, Cougar, Run, Diamond on Wheels. *Producer*: Escape to Witch Mountain, Ride a Wild Pony, Return from Witch Mountain, Pete's Dragon.
TELEVISION: *Actor*: The Saga of Andy Burnett, Tonka. *Director*: Hog Wild (also co-prod.), Harness Fever. Knots Landing, Dynasty, Hotel, Love Boat, Fantasy Island.

COUTARD, RAOUL
Cinematographer. b. Paris, France, Sept. 16, 1924. Spent 4 years in Vietnam working for French Military Info. Service, later a civilian photographer for Time and Paris-Match. During WWII worked in photo labs. After war returned to France and formed prod. co. making documentaries. Joined Jean-Luc Godard as his cinematographer on Breathless (1960). His use of hand-held camera and natural light established him as a seminal cameraman of the French New Wave, working with Godard, Truffaut and later with Costa Gavras. Director: Hoa Binh (1971).
PICTURES: Breathless, Shoot the Piano Player, Lola, Jules and Jim, The Army Game, My Life to Live, Love at Twenty (segment), Les Carabiniers, Contempt, Alphaville, The Soft Skin, Male Companion, Pierrot le Fou, Made in USA, Weekend, Sailor From Gibraltar, The Bride Wore Black, Z, The Confession, Le Crabe Tambour, Passion, First Name: Carmen, Dangerous Moves, Salt on the Skin, La Garce, Max My Love, Burning Beds, Let Sleeping Cops Lie, Bethune: The Making of a Hero.

COWAN, WARREN J.
Publicist. b. New York, NY, Mar. 13. e. Townsend Harris H.S., UCLA, graduated 1941. Entered public relations, 1941, with Alan Gordon & Associates; three yrs. Air Force; joined Henry C. Rogers office in 1945; became partner, 1949, and changed name to Rogers & Cowan Public Relations; advisor, Rogers & Cowan, Inc., 1960; pres., Rogers & Cowan, Inc., 1964; named bd. chmn., 1983. Retired as Rogers & Cowan chmn. in 1992. 1994, started new P.R. company, Warren Cowan & Assocs. Served as natl. communications chmn. for United Way of America. On advisory bd. of the Natl. Assoc. of Film Commissioners; 2nd Decade Council of American Film Inst. On bd. L.A. County High School for the Arts, Scott Newman Center, Young Musicians Foundation.

COX, ALEX
Director, Writer. b. Liverpool, England, Dec. 15, 1954. Studied law at Oxford U. where he dir. and acted in plays for school drama society. Studied film prod. Bristol U. Received Fulbright Scholarship to study at UCLA film school, 1981.
PICTURES: Repo Man (also s.p.), Sid and Nancy (also co-s.p.), Straight to Hell (also co-s.p.), Walker (also co-editor), Highway Patrolman, The Glimmer Man, Floundering (actor only), Dead Beat (actor only), The Queen of the Night (actor only), The Winner (also actor), Death and the Compass (also actor), Perdita Durango (actor only), Waldo's Hawaiian Holiday.

COX, BRIAN
Actor. b. Dundee, Scotland, June 1, 1946. e. London Acad. of Music & Dramatic Art. Acted with Royal Lyceum Edinburgh and Birmingham Rep. Theatre; also season with Royal Shakespeare Company. Video: Acting and Tragedy. Author: The Lear Diaries, Salem in Moscow.
THEATER: The Master Builder, King Lear, Richard III, Fashion, Rat in the Skull (Olivier Award; also B'way), Titus Andronicus (Olivier Award), Penny for a Song, Misalliance, St. Nicholas, Skylight.
PICTURES: Nicholas and Alexandra, In Celebration, Manhunter, Shoot for the Sun, Hidden Agenda, Prince of Jutland, Iron Will, Rob Roy, Braveheart, Chain Reaction, The Boxer, Desperate Measures, Food For Ravens.
TELEVISION: Inspector Morse, Therese Raquin, Pope John Paul II, Florence Nightingale, Beryl Markham: A Shadow on the Sun, Murder by Moonlight, Six Characters in Search of an Author, Picasso, The Negotiator, The Big Battalions, Bach, Bothwell, Churchill's People, Master of Ballantrae, Lost Language of Cranes, The Changeling, Secret Weapon.

COX, COURTENEY
Actress. b. Birmingham, AL, June 15, 1964. Left AL to pursue modelling career in NY. Dir. Brian DePalma selected her to be the young woman who jumps out of audience and dances with Bruce Springsteen in his music video Dancing in the Dark. This break led to featured role in short-lived TV series Misfits of Science (1985-86).
PICTURES: Masters of the Universe, Down Twisted, Cocoon: The Return, Mr. Destiny, Blue Desert, Shaking the Tree, The Opposite Sex, Ace Ventura—Pet Detective, Scream.
TELEVISION: *Series*: Misfits of Science, Family Ties, The Trouble With Larry, Friends. *Movies*: I'll Be Home for Christmas, Roxanne: The Prize Pulitzer, Till We Meet Again, Curiosity Kills, Battling for Baby, Topper, Sketch Artist II: Hands That See.

COX, RONNY
Actor. b. Cloudcroft, NM, July 23, 1938. e. Eastern New Mexico Univ.
PICTURES: The Happiness Cage (debut, 1972), Deliverance, Hugo the Hippo (voice), Bound for Glory, The Car, Gray Lady Down, Harper Valley P.T.A., The Onion Field, Taps, The Beast Within, Some Kind of Hero, Courage (Raw Courage), Beverly Hills Cop, Vision Quest, Hollywood Vice Squad, Steele Justice, Beverly Hills Cop II, Robocop, One Man Force, Loose Cannons, Martians Go Home!, Total Recall, Scissors, Captain America, Past Midnight, Murder at 1600.

TELEVISION: *Series*: Apple's Way, Spencer, St. Elsewhere, Cop Rock, Sweet Justice. *Movies*: The Connection, A Case of Rape, Who Is the Black Dahlia?, Having Babies, Corey: For the People, The Girl Called Hatter Fox, Lovey: A Circle of Children Part II, Transplant, When Hell Was in Session, Fugitive Family, Courage of Kavik: The Wolf Dog, The Last Song, Alcatraz—The Whole Shocking Story, Fallen Angel, Two of a Kind, The Jesse Owens Story, The Abduction of Kari Swenson, Baby Girl Scott, In the Line of Duty: The FBI Murders, The Comeback, When We Were Young, With Murder in Mind, Perry Mason: The Case of the Heartbroken Bride, A Part of the Family. *Mini-Series*: Favorite Son. *Specials*: Our Town, Chicago 7 Trial.

COYOTE, PETER
Actor. r.n. Peter Cohon. b. New York, NY, 1942. Studied with San Francisco Actors Workshop. Theatre includes The Minstrel Show (dir.), Olive Pits (also co-writer), The Red Snake, True West, The Abduction of Kari Swenson, Baby Girl Scott.
PICTURES: Die Laughing (debut, 1980), Tell Me a Riddle, Southern Comfort, The Pursuit of D.B. Cooper, E.T.: The Extra Terrestrial, Endangered Species, Timerider, Cross Creek, Slayground, Stranger's Kiss, Heartbreakers, The Legend of Billie Jean, Jagged Edge, Outrageous Fortune, A Man in Love, Stacking, Heart of Midnight, The Man Inside, Crooked Hearts, Exposure, Bitter Moon, Kika, That Eye The Sky, Moonlight and Valentino, Unforgettable, Sphere, Patch Adams.
TELEVISION: *Movies*: Alcatraz: The Whole Shocking Story, The People vs. Jean Harris, Isabel's Choice, Best Kept Secrets, Scorned and Swindled, Time Flyer, Child's Cry, Sworn to Silence, Echoes in the Darkness, Unconquered, A Seduction in Travis County, Living a Lie, Keeper of the City, Breach of Conduct. Buffalo Girls. *Special*: Abraham Lincoln: A New Birth of Freedom (voice).

CRAIG, MICHAEL
Actor. r.n. Michael Gregson. b. Poona, India, Jan. 27, 1929. At 16 joined Merchant Navy. 1949, returned to England and made stage debut in repertory. Entered industry as extra in 1949.
PICTURES: Passport to Pimlico (debut, 1949), The Magic Box, The Cruel Sea, Malta Story, The Love Lottery, Passage Home, The Black Tent, Yield to the Night, Eye-Witness, House of Secrets, High Tide At Noon, Sea of Sand, Sapphire, Upstairs and Downstairs, The Angry Silence, Cone of Silence, Doctor In Love, Mysterious Island, Payroll, No My Darling Daughter, A Pair of Briefs, A Life for Ruth, The Iron Maiden, Captive City, Summer Flight, Stolen Flight, Of a Thousand Delights, Life at the Top, Modesty Blaise, Star!, Twinky, The Royal Hunt of the Sun, Brotherly Love (Country Dance), A Town Called Bastard, The Fourth Mrs. Anderson, Vault of Horror, Inn of the Damned, Ride a Wild Pony, The Irishman, Turkey Shoot, Stanley, Appointment With Death.
TELEVISION: *Movie*: Spoiled, Tartuffe. *Series*: G.P. Guest: Doctor Who, The Professionals, Shoestring. *Mini-Series*: The Timeless Land.

CRAIN, JEANNE
Actress. b. Barstow, CA, May 25, 1925. Model; crowned Miss Long Beach of 1941: Camera Girl of 1942.
PICTURES: The Gang's All Here (debut, 1943), Home in Indiana, In the Meantime Darling, Winged Victory, State Fair, Leave Her to Heaven, Margie, Centennial Summer, You Were Meant for Me, Apartment for Peggy, Letter to Three Wives, The Fan, Pinky, Cheaper by the Dozen, I'll Get By (cameo), Take Care of My Little Girl, People Will Talk, Model and the Marriage Broker, Belles on Their Toes, O. Henry's Full House, City of Bad Men, Dangerous Crossing, Vicki, Duel in the Jungle, Man Without a Star, The Second Greatest Sex, Gentlemen Marry Brunettes, Fastest Gun Alive, Tattered Dress, The Joker is Wild, Guns of the Timberland, Queen of the Nile, Twenty Plus Two, Madison Avenue, Pontius Pilate, Hot Rods to Hell, The Night God Screamed, Skyjacked, .

CRAMER, DOUGLAS S.
Executive. e. Northwestern U., Sorbonne, U. of Cincinnati, B.A.; Columbia U.M.F.A. m. Joyce Haber, columnist. Taught at Carnegie Inst. of Tech., 1954-55; Production asst. Radio City Music Hall 1950-51; MGM Script Dept. 1952; Manag. Dir. Cincinnati Summer Playhouse 1953-54. TV supvr. Procter and Gamble 1956-59; Broadcast supvr. Ogilvy Benson and Mather adv. 1959-62; v.p. program dev. ABC-TV 1962-66; v.p. program dev. 20 Cent.-Fox TV 1966; exec. v.p. in chg. of prod., Paramount TV, 1968-71; exec. v.p. Aaron Spelling Prods. 1976-89; pres. Douglas S. Cramer Co, 1989-.
THEATER: Call of Duty, Love is a Smoke, Whose Baby Are You, Last Great Dish.
PICTURES: *Exec. prod.*: Sleeping Together.
TELEVISION: *Exec. prod.*: Bridget Loves Bernie, QB VII, Dawn: Portrait of a Teenage Runaway, Nightmare in Badham County, Sex Symbol, Danielle Steel's Fine Things, Kaleidoscope, Changes, Message from Nam, Daddy, Palamino, Once in a Lifetime, The Ring, Zoya: Trade Winds, Lake Success, Wonder Woman. *Co-exec. prod.*: Love Boat (1977-86), Vegas (1978-81), Dynasty, Matt Houston, Hotel, Colbys.

CRAVEN, GEMMA
Actress. b. Dublin, Ireland, June 1, 1950. e. Loretto Coll. Studied acting at Bush Davies School. London stage debut, Fiddler on the Roof (1970).
THEATER: *London*: Audrey, Trelawny, Dandy Dick, They're Playing Our Song, Song and Dance, Loot, A Chorus of Disapproval, Three Men on a Horse, Jacobowsky and the Colonel, The Magistrate, South Pacific, The London Vertigo, Private Lives, Present Laughter.
PICTURES: Kingdom of Gifts, Why Not Stay for Breakfast, The Slipper and the Rose, Wagner, Double X: The Name of the Game, Words Upon the Windowpane, Still Life.
TELEVISION: Pennies From Heaven, Must Wear Tights, She Loves Me, Song by Song by Noel Coward, Song by Song by Alan Jay Lerner, East Lynne, Robin of Sherwood, Treasure Hunt, Gemma Girls and Gershwin, Boon, The Bill, The Marshal.

CRAVEN, WES
Director, Writer. b. Cleveland, OH, Aug. 2, 1939. e. Wheaton Coll., B.A.; Johns Hopkins, M.A., philosophy. Worked as humanities prof. prior to film.
PICTURES: The Last House on the Left (also s.p., ed.), The Hills Have Eyes (also s.p., ed.), Deadly Blessing, Swamp Thing (also s.p.), A Nightmare on Elm Street (also s.p.), The Hills Have Eyes Part II (also s.p.), Deadly Friend, A Nightmare on Elm Street III: Dream Warriors (co-s.p., co-exec. prod. only), The Serpent and the Rainbow, Shocker (also exec. prod., s.p.), The People Under the Stairs (also s.p., co-exec. prod.), Wes Craven's New Nightmare (also actor, s.p.), Vampire in Brooklyn, The Fear (actor only), Scream.
TELEVISION: *Series*: Twilight Zone (1985, 2 episodes: Word Play, A Little Peace and Quiet, Shatterday, Chameleon, Dealer's Choice, The Road Less Traveled, Pilgrim Soul). The People Next Door (exec. prod.). *Movies*: A Stranger in Our House, Invitation to Hell, Chiller, Casebusters, Night Visions (also exec. prod., co-writer), Laurel Canyon (exec. prod. only), Body Bags (actor only).

CRAWFORD, MICHAEL
O.B.E. Actor. r.n. Michael Dumbell-Smith. b. Salisbury, England, Jan.19, 1942. Early career as boy actor in children's films, as a boy soprano in Benjamin Britten's Let's Make an Opera and on radio. Later star of TV's Not So Much a Programme, More a Way of Life. Solo albums: Songs from the Stage and Screen, With Love, Performs Andrew Lloyd Weber, A Touch of Music in the Night. Appeared for MGM Grand in production EFX.
THEATER: Come Blow Your Horn, Traveling Light, The Anniversary, White Lies and Black Comedy (N.Y.), No Sex Please We're British, Billy, Same Time Next Year, Flowers for Algernon, Barnum, The Phantom of the Opera (London: Laurence Olivier Award; New York: Tony, Drama Desk, Drama League & Outer Circle Critics Awards, 1988; also L.A.), The Music of Andrew Lloyd Weber (U.S., Canada, U.K. & Australia).
PICTURES: Soap Box Derby (debut, 1957), Blow Your Own Trumpet, A French Mistress, Two Living One Dead, Two Left Feet, The War Lover, The Knack... and How to Get It, A Funny Thing Happened on the Way to the Forum, The Jokers, How I Won the War, Hello Dolly!, The Games, Hello-Goodbye, Alice's Adventures in Wonderland, Condorman, Once Upon a Forest (voice).
TELEVISION: Still Life, Destiny, Byron, Move After Checkmate, Three Barrelled Shotgun, Home Sweet Honeycomb, Some Mothers Do 'ave 'em, Chalk and Cheese, BBC Play for Today, Private View, Barnum.

CRENNA, RICHARD
Actor. b. Los Angeles, CA, Nov. 30, 1927. e. Belmont H.S., USC.
RADIO: Boy Scout Jamboree, A Date With Judy, The Hardy Family, The Great Gildersleeve, Burns & Allen, Our Miss Brooks.
PICTURES: Red Skies of Montana (debut, 1951), Pride of St. Louis, It Grows on Trees, Our Miss Brooks, Over-Exposed, John Goldfarb Please Come Home, Made in Paris, The Sand Pebbles, Wait Until Dark, Star!, Midas Run, Marooned, The Deserter, Doctors' Wives, Red Sky at Morning, Catlow, A Man Called Noon, Dirty Money (Un Flic), Jonathan Livingston Seagull (voice), Breakheart Pass, The Evil, Wild Horse Hank, Death Ship, Stone Cold Dead, Body Heat, First Blood, Table for Five, The Flamingo Kid, Rambo: First Blood Part II, Summer Rental, Rambo III, Leviathan, Hot Shots! Part Deux, A Pyromaniac's Love Story (unbilled), Jade, Sabrina.
TELEVISION: *Series*: Our Miss Brooks, The Real McCoys, Slattery's People, All's Fair, It Takes Two, Pros & Cons. *Movies*: Footsteps, Thief, Passions, A Case of Deadly Force, The Day the Bubble Burst, Centennial, The Rape of Richard Beck (Emmy Award, 1985), Doubletake, The Price of Passion, Police Story: The Freeway Killings, Plaza Suite, Kids Like These, On Wings of Eagles, Internal Affairs, Blood Brothers: The Case of the Hillside Stranglers, Murder in Black and White, Stuck with Each Other, Montana, Last Flight Out, Murder Times Seven, And the Sea Will Tell, Intruders, Terror on Track 9, A Place to Be Loved, The Forget-Me-Not Murders, Jonathan Stone: Threat of Innocence, Janek: A Silent Betrayal, In the Name of Love: A Texas Tragedy.

CRICHTON, CHARLES
Director. b. Wallasey, England, Aug. 6, 1910. e. Oundle & Oxford.
PICTURES: For Those in Peril (debut, 1944), Painted Boats (The Girl on the Canal), Dead of Night (Golfing segment), Hue and Cry, Against the Wind, Another Shore, Train of Events (Orchestra Conductor segment), Dance Hall, The Lavender Hill Mob, Hunted (The Stranger in Between), The Titfield Thunderbolt, The Love Lottery, The Divided Heart, Man in the Sky (Decision Against Time), Floods of Fear (also s.p.), The Battle of the Sexes, The Boy Who Stole a Million (also co-s.p.), The Third Secret, He Who Rides a Tiger, Tomorrow's Island (also s.p.), A Fish Called Wanda (also story; 2 Acad. Award noms.).
TELEVISION: The Wild Duck, Danger Man, The Avengers, Man in a Suitcase, The Strange Report, Shirley's World, Black Beauty, The Protectors, Space 1999, Return of the Saint, Dick Turpin 1 & 2 Series, Smuggler, Video Arts Shorts.

CRICHTON, MICHAEL
Writer, Director. r.n. John Michael Crichton. b. Chicago, IL, Oct. 23, 1942. e. Harvard U. Medical School (M.D.), 1969. Postdoctoral fellow, Salk Inst. for Biological Sciences, La Jolla, 1969-70. Visiting writer, MIT, 1988. Recipient Edgar Award, Mystery Writers Amer.: A Case of Need (1968), The Great Train Robbery (1980). Named medical writer of year, Assn. of Amer. Med. Writers: Five Patients (1970). Received Scientific and Technical Achievement Academy Award, 1995.
AUTHOR: Novels: (as John Lange): Odds On, Scratch One, Easy Go (The Last Tomb), The Venom Business, Zero Cool, Grave Descend, Drug of Choice, Binary. (as Jeffery Hudson): A Case of Need (filmed as The Carey Treatment). (as Michael Douglas, with brother Douglas Crichton): Dealing or the Berkeley-to-Boston Forty-Brick Lost-Bag Blues (filmed). (as Michael Crichton): The Andromeda Strain (filmed), The Terminal Man (filmed), The Great Train Robbery, Eaters of the Dead, Congo, Sphere, Jurassic Park, Rising Son, Disclosure, The Lost World, Airframe (filmed), The Lost World (filmed). Non-Fiction (as Michael Crichton): Five Patients, Jasper Johns, Electronic Life, Travels, The Lost World (filmed), Spare, Airframe, The 13th Warrior.
PICTURES: Westworld (dir., s.p.), Coma (dir., s.p.), The Great Train Robbery (dir., s.p.), Looker (dir., s.p.), Runaway (dir., s.p.), Physical Evidence (dir.), Jurassic Park (co-s.p.), Rising Sun (co-s.p.), Disclosure (co-prod.), Congo (co-s.p.), Twister (co- s.p., co-prod.).
TELEVISION: Movie: Pursuit (dir.; based on Binary). Series: ER (creator, co-exec. prod.; Emmy Award, 1996). Pilot: ER (Writers Guild Award, 1996).

CRIST, JUDITH
Journalist, Critic. b. New York, NY, May 22, 1922. e. Hunter College, Columbia U. School of Journalism. Joined NY Herald Tribune, serving as reporter, arts editor, assoc. drama critic, film critic. Contributing editor Columbia Magazine. Continued as film critic for NY World Journal Tribune, NBC-TV Today Show, New York Magazine, NY Post, Saturday Review, TV Guide, WWOR-TV. Teaches at Col. Grad. School of Journalism.
AUTHOR: The Private Eye the Cowboy and the Very Naked Girl, Judith Crist's TV Guide to the Movies, Take 22: Moviemakers on Moviemaking.

CRISTALDI, FRANCO
Producer. b. Turin, Italy, Oct. 3, 1924. Owner, prod. Vides Cinematografica; President of Italian Producer's Union.
PICTURES: White Nights, The Strawman, The Challenge, Big Deal On Madonna Street, Kapo, The Dauphins, Salvatore Giuliano, The Assassin, Divorce Italian Style, The Organizer, Bebo's Girl, Seduced and Abandoned, Time of Indifference, Sandra, A Rose for Every-One, China Is Near, A Quiet Couple, The Red Tent, New Paradise Cinema.
TELEVISION: Marco Polo.

CROMWELL, JAMES
Actor. b. Los Angeles, CA, Jan. 27, 1940. e. Carnegie Mellon Univ. Father was director John Cromwell, mother was actress Kate Johnson.
PICTURES: Murder by Death, The Cheap Detective, The Man With Two Brains, House of God, Tank, Revenge of the Nerds, Oh God You Devil, Explorers, A Fine Mess, Revenge of the Nerds II: Nerds in Paradise, The Rescue, Pink Cadillac, The Runnin' Kind, The Babe, Romeo Is Bleeding, Babe, Eraser, The People vs. Larry Flynt, Star Trek: First Contact, L.A. Confidential, The Education of Little Tree, Winter, Deep Impact, Babe: Pig in the City, Species 2, Snow Falling on Cedars, The Green Mile, The General's Daughter.
TELEVISION: Series: All in the Family, Hot L Baltimore, The Nancy Walker Show, The Last Precinct, Easy Street, Mama's Boy. Mini-Series: Once an Eagle. Movies: The Girl in the Empty Grave, Deadly Game, A Christmas Without Snow, The Wall, Sprague, The Shaggy Dog. Guest: M*A*S*H, Dallas, L.A. Law, Star Trek: The Next Generation, Hill Street Blues.

CRONENBERG, DAVID
Writer, Director. b. Toronto, Ont., May 15, 1943. e. U. of Toronto. In college produced two short movies on 16mm. 1971, to Europe on a Canadian Council grant where in 1975 he shot his first feature, They Came From Within (Shivers).
PICTURES: Director: Transfer (also prod, s.p. and edit.), From the Drain (also s.p. and edit.), Stereo, Crimes of the Future, Jim Ritchie Sculptor, They Came From Within (Shivers; also s.p.), Rabid (also s.p.), Fast Company, The Brood (also s.p.), Scanners (also s.p.), Videodrome, The Dead Zone, The Fly (also co-s.p., cameo), Dead Ringers (also co-prod., co-s.p.), Naked Lunch (also s.p.), M. Butterfly, Crash, eXistenZ (also s.p. and prod.). Actor: Into the Night, Nightbreed, Trial by Jury, Blue, Henry & Verlin, Trial By Jury, To Die For, Blood and Donuts, The Stupids, Extreme Measures.
TELEVISION: Movie: Moonshine Highway.

CRONKITE, WALTER
Correspondent. b. St. Joseph, MO, Nov. 4, 1916. e. U. of Texas. Reporter and editor Scripps-Howard News Service, TX; radio reporter; U.P. correspondent. WW II corres. British Isles, N. Africa. Foreign Correspondent, France, Belgium, Netherlands, Soviet Union. Joined CBS as Washington news correspondent, 1950; anchorman and mng. editor, CBS Evening News, 1962-81; special correspondent, CBS News, 1981-present. Many TV shows including You Are There, Twentieth Century, Eyewitness to History: CBS Reports: 21st Century, Walter Cronkite's Universe. Past nat'l pres. & mem. bd. Trustees, Acad. TV Arts & Sciences. Mng. editor of CBS Evening News 1963-81. Special correspondent, Children of Apartheid, Walter Cronkite at Large, Cronkite Remembers. Chairman, Cronkite Ward & Company, which has produced more than 25 award winning documentary hours for the Discovery Channel, PBS and others, 1993-98. Host/commentator of The Cronkite Reports, on the Discovery Channel which investigates current, global news issues. Other Cronkite Ward & Co. productions: Great Books series for the Learning Channel and Understanding: Science programs for the Discovery Channel. Supplied voice for 1995 B'way revival of How to Succeed in Business Without Really Trying. Autobiography, A Reporter's Life, 1996.

CRONYN, HUME
Actor, Writer, Director. b. London, Ont., Canada, July 18, 1911. Was married to late actress Jessica Tandy. e. Ridley Coll., McGill U., Amer. Acad. of Dramatic Art.
THEATER: N.Y.: Actor: High Tor, Escape This Night, Three Men on a Horse, Boy Meets Girl, Three Sisters, Mr. Big, The Survivors, Now I Lay Me Down to Sleep (dir.), Hilda Crane (dir.), The Fourposter (dir.), Madam Will You Walk, The Honeys, A Day by the Sea, The Man in the Dog Suit, The Egghead (dir.), Triple Play (dir. and toured with wife), Big Fish Little Fish (also in London), The Miser, The Three Sisters, Hamlet, The Physicists, Slow Dance on The Killing Ground (prod.), appeared at the White House, Hear America Speaking, Richard III, The Miser, A Delicate Balance (1966 and tour, 1967), Hadrian VII (tour), Caine Mutiny Court Martial, Promenade All, Krapp's Last Tape, Happy Days, Act Without Words, Many Faces Of Love (concert recital), Noel Coward in Two Keys (National tour), Merchant of Venice and A Midsummer Night's Dream (Stratford Festival Theatre). Canada: The Gin Game (with Miss Tandy; Long Wharf Thea., New Haven, B'way, 1977, co-prod. with Mike Nichols; also toured U.S., Toronto, London, U.S.S.R., 1978-79). Also: Foxfire (co-author, actor, at Stratford, Ont., 1980, Minneapolis, 1981 and N.Y., 1982-83); Traveler in the Dark (Amer. Repertory Theatre, Cambridge, MA), Foxfire (Ahmanson, LA 1985-86), The Petition (NY 1986).
PICTURES: Shadow of a Doubt (debut, 1943), Phantom of the Opera, The Cross of Lorraine, Lifeboat, The Seventh Cross (Acad. Award nom.), Main Street After Dark, The Sailor Takes a Wife, A Letter for Evie, The Green Years, The Postman Always Rings Twice, Ziegfeld Follies, The Secret Heart (narrator), The Beginning or the End, Brute Force, Rope (adapt. only), The Bride Goes Wild, Top o' the Morning, Under Capricorn (adapt. only), People Will Talk, Crowded Paradise, Sunrise at Campobello, Cleopatra, Hamlet, Gaily Gaily, The Arrangement, There Was a Crooked Man, Conrack, The Parallax View, Honky Tonk Freeway, Rollover, The World According to Garp, Impulse, Brewster's Millions, Cocoon, Batteries Not Included, Cocoon: The Return, The Pelican Brief, Camilla, Marvin's Room.
TELEVISION: Series: The Marriage. Movies: The Dollmaker (co-writer only), Foxfire (also co-writer), Day One, Age-old Friends, Christmas on Division Street, Broadway Bound (Emmy Award, 1992), To Dance With the White Dog (Emmy Award, 1994), Alone, Twelve Angry Men (Emmy nom., 1997), Love on the Land.

CROSBY, CATHY LEE
Actress. b. Los Angeles, CA. e. Grad. of U. of Southern California. Studied with Lee Strasberg. Author of Let The Magic Begin.
THEATER: Downside Risk, Almost Perfect (Off-B'way debut), Jellyroll Shoes, They Shoot Horses, Don't They? (wrote, dir. starred in 1st theatrical adapt. Hollywood Amer. Legion), Zoot Suit—The Real Story (writer, dir., actress, adapt., Beverly Hills).
PICTURES: The Laughing Policeman (debut, 1973), Trackdown, The Dark, Coach, Training Camp (s.p.), San Sebastian (s.p.), Call Me By My Rightful Name, The Player.
TELEVISION: Movies: Wonder Woman, Keefer, Roughnecks, World War III, Intimate Strangers, One Child, North & South III: Heaven and Hell, Untamed Love (also co-exec. prod.), When the Cradle Falls, Treasure of Dos Santos. Series: That's Incredible. Specials: A Spectacular Evening in Egypt, Battle of the Network Stars, Circus of the Stars, Bob Hope Specials, Get High on Yourself, Bob Hope: USO Tour of Lebanon & the Mediterranean.

CROSBY, KATHRYN
Actress. r.n. Olive Kathryn Grandstaff. b. Houston, TX. e. U. of Texas, Queen of Angels Sch. of Nursing, Immaculate Heart Col. m. late actor-singer Bing Crosby. Author: Bing and Other Things, My Life With Bing.
THEATER: Mama's Baby Boy, The Enchanted, Sunday in New York, The Guardsman, Guys and Dolls, Same Time Next Year, The Crucible, Cyrano de Bergerac, Tonight at 8:30, The Cocktail Hour, Oh Coward, I Do I Do, The Heiress, The Seagull, Hello Dolly, State Fair, The Music Man, Lion In Winter, and many others.
PICTURES: Forever Female, Rear Window, Living It Up, Sabrina, Arrowhead, Casanova's Big Night, Unchained, Cell 2455 Death Row, Tight Spot, Five Against the House, Reprisal, Guns of Fort Petticoat, The Phenix City Story, Wild Party, Mister Cory, Gunman's Walk, The Librarian, Anatomy of a Murder, The Brothers Rico, Operation Mad Ball, The Seventh Voyage of Sinbad, The Big Circus, The Wild Party.
TELEVISION: Guest: Bob Hope Chrysler Theatre, Bing Crosby Christmas Specials, Suspense Theatre, Ben Casey, The Kathryn Crosby Show (KPIX-TV, San Francisco). Movie: The Initiation of Sarah.

CROSBY, MARY
Actress. b. Los Angeles, CA, Sept. 14, 1959. e. U. TX; American Conservatory Theatre. Daughter of performers Kathryn Crosby and the late Bing Crosby. Formerly acted as Mary Frances Crosby. Appeared from an early age in several TV variety specials with her parents. On stage in: Rome & Juliet, A Gentleman of Verona (L.A.), As You Like It (L.A.), The Seagull (L.A.).
PICTURES: The Last Plane Out, The Ice Pirates, Tapeheads, Body Chemistry, Corporate Affairs, Eating, The Berlin Conspiracy, Desperate Motive (Distant Cousins).
TELEVISION: Series: Brothers and Sisters, Dallas. Movies: With This Ring, A Guide for the Married Woman, Midnight Lace, Golden Gate, Confessions of a Married Man, Final Jeopardy, Stagecoach, Johnann Strauss: The King Without a Crown. Mini-Series: Pearl, Hollywood Wives, North and South Book II. Pilot: Golden Gate, The Big Easy, Cover Up. Specials: Goldilocks, Bing Crosby's Christmas Show (1970-73, 1976-77), Battle of the Network Stars, The 21st Annual Academy of Country Music Awards, Crazy Dan, Tube Test Two, Best Sellers: Men Who Hate Women and the Wome Who Love Them. Guest: Knots Landing, The Love Boat, The Fall Guy, Hotel, In the Heat of the Night, Murder She Wrote, Beverly Hills 90210, and many others.

CROSS, BEN
Actor. r.n. Bernard Cross. b. London, England, Dec. 16, 1947. e. Royal Acad. of Dramatic Art. Worked as stagehand, prop-master, and master carpenter with Welsh Natl. Opera and as set builder, Wimbledon Theatre.
THEATER: The Importance of Being Earnest (Lancaster, debut, 1972), I Love My Wife, Privates on Parade, Chicago, Lydie Breeze (NY debut, 1982), Caine Mutiny Court Martial.
PICTURES: A Bridge Too Far (debut, 1977), Chariots of Fire, The Unholy, The Goldsmith's Shop, Paperhouse, The House of the Lord, Eye of the Widow, Haunted Symphony, The Ascent, First Knight, Turbulence.
TELEVISION: Movies/Specials: Melancholy Hussar of the German Legion (1973, BBC), The Flame Trees of Thika, The Citadel, The Far Pavilions, Coming Out of the Ice, The Assisi Underground, Arthur Hailey's Strong Medicine, Steal the Sky, Pursuit, Twist of Fate, Nightlife, She Stood Alone, Diamond Fleece, Live Wire, Deep Trouble, Cold Sweat. Series: Dark Shadows (1991).

CROUSE, LINDSAY
Actress. b. New York, NY, May 12, 1948. Daughter of playwright Russel Crouse. e. Radcliffe.
THEATER: With Circle Repertory Co. N.Y.: Hamlet, Twelfth Night, Richard II, Childe Byron, Reunion (Obie Award). NY: Serenading Louie, The Shawl, The Stick Wife, The Homecoming (B'way debut; Theatre World Award). With L.A. Matrix Theatre Co.: The Tavern, Habeus Corpus.

PICTURES: All the President's Men (debut, 1976), Slap Shot, Between the Lines, Prince of the City, The Verdict, Daniel, Iceman, Places in the Heart (Acad. award nom.), House of Games, Communion, Desperate Hours, Being Human, Bye Bye Love, The Indian in the Cupboard, The Arrival, The Juror, Prefontaine.
TELEVISION: Movies: Eleanor and Franklin, Chantilly Lace, Final Appeal, Out of Darkness, Parallel Lives, Traps. Mini-Series: The Kennedys of Massachusetts. Specials: Kennedy's Children, Lemon Sky, Between Mother and Daughter, If These Walls Could Talk. Guest: Colombo, Murder She Wrote, LA Law, Hill Street Blues, Civil Wars, Law and Order, E.R. Series: American Nuclear (pilot), NYPD Blue, Millenium.

CROWE, CAMERON
Writer, Director. b. Palm Springs, CA, July 13, 1957. e. Calif. St. Univ., San Diego. Began career as journalist and editor for Rolling Stone. Adapted his book Fast Times at Ridgemont High into Writers Guild Award-nominated screenplay for 1982 film.
PICTURES: American Hot Wax (actor). Writer: Fast Times at Ridgemont High, The Wild Life (also co-prod.), Say Anything (also dir.), Singles (also dir.), Singles (also dir.), Jerry Maguire (dir. & prod. only).
TELEVISION: Series: Fast Times (creative consultant).

CROWE, KEN
Executive. b. Sewickley, PA, Sept. 3, 1939. e. San Diego U. CPA, public accounting, Coopers & Lybrand, 1968-77. Mann Theatres, treas./CFO, 1977-86; Paramount Mann Theatres, sr. v.p./CFO, 1986-88. Cinamerica Theatres, exec. v.p./CFO, 1988-present. Member of Motion Picture Pioneers, AICPA, FEI, Variety Club of So. Calif and Sertoma.

CROWE, RUSSELL
Actor. b. New Zealand, 1964. Raised in Australia. Worked as professional musician while appearing on Australian stage in Bad Boy Johnny and the Profits of Doom, Blood Brothers, Rocky Horror Show.
PICTURES: For the Moment, The Silver Brumby, Hammers Over the Anvil, Prisoners of the Sun, Love in Limbo, For the Moment, Proof (Australian Film Inst. Award), The Efficiency Expert, Romper Stomper (Australian Film Inst. Award), The Quick and the Dead, The Sum of Us, Virtuosity, Rough Magic, No Way Back, Breaking Up, L.A. Confidential, Heaven's Burning, Breaking Up, Mystery Alaska.

CROWN, DANIEL
Executive. Pres., Crown Theatres, S. Norwalk, CT., 1990-. Bd. or dirs., NY Yankees, 1985-. Other bds.: Lenox Hill Hosp., Mt. Sinai Children's Ctr. Fdn., Jerusalem Fdn., Jewish Nat'l. Fund, New York, NY. Member NATO, 1991-.

CRUEA, EDMOND D.
Executive. b. Jersey City, NJ, June 3. Joined Grand Natl. Pictures, LA, 1935; Monogram Pictures, 1938-41, LA & Seattle; U.S. Army Signal Corps., 1942-46; Monogram Pictures, Seattle, 1946; branch mgr. & district mgr. Allied Artists, 1950-65 (Seattle, Portland, San Francisco, LA); v.p. & gen. sls. mgr., Allied Artists, 1965-71; dir. distbn., Abkco Films div. of Abkco Industries Inc., 1971-73; pres. Royal Dist. Corp, 1974; joined Film Ventures Intl. 1976 as exec. v.p. succeeding to pres. & COO in 1976. Co-founded New Image Releasing Inc., 1982, as pres. & CEO. 1985, v.p. theatrical, Cinetel Films; 1987 theatrical distbn. cons., Sony Pictures (NY), Sony Video Softwear plus and Shining Armour Commun (London). Acquisitions & distbn. cons. to Columbia TriStar Home Video, Triumph Pictures and Healing Arts Documentary Prods.; 1995, chmn. and CEO Global International Films Inc.; 1996, pres. Capstone films; cons. to Intic Productions.

CRUISE, TOM
Actor. r.n. Thomas Cruise Mapother IV. b. Syracuse, NY, July 3, 1962. m. actress Nicole Kidman. Acted in high school plays; secured role in dinner theatre version of Godspell. Studied acting at Neighborhood Playhouse, before landing small part in Endless Love. Received American Cinema Award for Distinguished Achievement in Film, 1991.
PICTURES: Endless Love (debut, 1981), Taps, Losin' It, The Outsiders, Risky Business, All the Right Moves, Legend, Top Gun, The Color of Money, Cocktail, Rain Man, Born on the 4th of July (Golden Globe Award; Acad. Award nom., 1989), Days of Thunder (also co-wrote story), Far and Away, A Few Good Men, The Firm, Interview With the Vampire, Mission: Impossible, Jerry Macguire (Golden Globe Award, 1997), Eyes Wide Shut.
TELEVISION: Director: The Frightening Framis (episode of series Fallen Angels).

CRYER, JON
Actor. b. New York, NY, Apr. 16, 1965. Son of actor David Cryer and songwriter-actress Gretchen Cryer. On B'way stage in Brighton Beach Memoirs.
PICTURES: No Small Affair (debut, 1984), Pretty in Pink, Morgan Stewart's Coming Home, O.C. and Stiggs, Superman IV: The Quest for Peace, Hiding Out, Dudes, Penn and Teller Get Killed, Hot Shots!, The Pompatus of Love, Plan B, Went to Coney Island on a Mission from God...Back By 5, Die Wholesale, Holy Man.
TELEVISION: Series: The Famous Teddy Z, Partners, It's Good to Be King, Getting Personal. Special: Kurt Vonnegut's Monkey House. Movie: Heads.

CRYSTAL, BILLY
Actor, Writer, Producer, Director. b. Long Island, NY, Mar. 14, 1947. e. Marshall U., Nassau Commun. Col., NYU (BFA in tv & film direction). Father, Jack, produced jazz concerts; family owned Commodore jazz record label. Worked with Alumni Theatre Group at Nassau Commun. College. Later teamed with two friends (billed as We the People, Comedy Jam, 3's Company) and toured coffee houses and colleges. Became stand-up comedian on own, appearing at Catch a Rising Star, The Comedy Story and on TV. Album: Mahvelous!. Book: Absolutely Mahvelous!
PICTURES: Rabbit Test (debut, 1978), Animalympics (voice), This Is Spinal Tap, Running Scared, The Princess Bride, Throw Mama From the Train, Memories of Me (also co-prod., co-s.p.), When Harry Met Sally..., City Slickers (also exec. prod.), Mr. Saturday Night (also dir., prod., co-s.p.), City Slickers II: The Legend of Curly's Gold (also prod., co-s.p.), Forget Paris (also dir., prod., co-s.p.), Hamlet, Father's Day, Deconstructing Harry, My Giant, Analyze This.
TELEVISION: Series: Soap, The Billy Crystal Comedy Hour (also writer), Saturday Night Live (also writer), Sessions (creator, exec. prod. only). Guest: Saturday Night Live with Howard Cosell, Tonight Show, Dinah, Mike Douglas Show, That Was the Year That Was, All in the Family, Love Boat. Specials include: Battle of the Network Stars, Billy Crystal: A Comic's Line (also writer), A Comedy Salute to Baseball (also writer), On Location: Billy Crystal - Don't Get Me Started (also dir., writer), The Three Little Pigs (Faerie Tale Theatre), The Lost Minutes of Billy Crystal, Midnight Train to Moscow (also exec. prod., co-writer; Emmy Award 1990). Movies: SST—Death Flight, Human Feelings, Breaking Up Is Hard to Do, Enola Gay: The Men the Mission and the Atomic Bomb. Host: Grammy Awards (Emmy Awards for hosting, 1988, 1989), Academy Awards (Emmy Award for hosting, 1991, 1997; Emmy Award for co-writing, 1992).

CULBERG, PAUL S.
Executive. b. Chicago, IL, June 14, 1942. Began career in record industry, holding positions with Elektra Records & Wherehouse Record; 1977-80; v.p. sls. mktg., Cream Records.; 1980-82, dir. sls. Paramount Home Video; 1982, v.p. sls. mktg., Media Home Entertainment; 1984-89, pres., New World Video; 1989-present, COO, RCA Columbia/TriStar Home Video.

CULKIN, MACAULAY
Actor. b. New York, NY, Aug. 26, 1980. Acting debut at 4 yrs. old in Bach Babies at NY's Symphony Space. Appeared in several TV commercials. Studied ballet at George Ballanchine's School of American Ballet and danced in NY productions of H.M.S. Pinafore and The Nutcracker. Received Comedy Award and Youth in Film Award for role in Home Alone. Appeared in Michael Jackson video Black and White.
THEATER: NY: Afterschool Special, Mr. Softee, Buster B. and Olivia.
PICTURES: Rocket Gibraltar (debut, 1988), See You in the Morning, Uncle Buck, Jacob's Ladder, Home Alone, Only the Lonely, My Girl, Home Alone 2: Lost in New York, The Good Son, George Balanchine's The Nutcracker, Getting Even With Dad, The Pagemaster, Richie Rich.
TELEVISION: Guest: The Equalizer, Saturday Night Live, Bob Hope Christmas Special.

CULLUM, JOHN
Actor. b. Knoxville, TN, Mar. 2, 1930. e. Univ. of TN. Son is actor John David (J.D.) Cullum.
THEATER: NY: Camelot, On a Clear Day You Can See Forever (Theatre World Award, Tony nom.), Hamlet, Man of La Mancha, 1776, Shenandoah (Tony Award, Drama Desk & Outer Circle Critics Awards, 1975), The Trip Back Down, On the Twentieth Century (Tony Award, 1978), Deathtrap, Private Lives, Doubles, The Boys in Autumn, Aspects of Love, Showboat.
PICTURES: All the Way Home, 1776, The Prodigal, The Act, Marie, Sweet Country.
TELEVISION: Series: Buck James, Northern Exposure. Guest: Quantum Leap (also dir.). Movies: The Man Without a Country, The Day After, Shoot Down, With a Vengeance.

CULP, ROBERT
Actor, Writer, Director. b. Berkeley, CA, Aug. 16, 1930. e. Stockton, College of the Pacific, Washington U., San Francisco State. To N.Y. to study with Herbert Berghof (played Potzo in 1st U.S. prod. of Waiting for Godot. Starred in off-Bway prod. He Who Gets Slapped. Best Actor of the Year in an off-Bway Play; motion picture debut, 1962; P.T. 109. Television guest appearances in Rawhide, Wagon Train, Bob Hope Presents the Chrysler Theatre; wrote and acted in Rifleman, Cain's Hundred, The Dick Powell Show.
THEATER: Bway.: The Prescott Proposals, A Clearing in the Woods, Diary of a Scoundrel.
PICTURES: PT 109 (debut, 1963), Sunday in New York, Rhino!, Bob & Carol & Ted & Alice, The Grove, Hannie Caulder, Hickey & Boggs (also dir., uncredited co-s.p.), A Name for Evil, The Castaway Cowboy, Inside Out (Golden Heist), Sky Riders, Breaking Point, The Great Scout and Cathouse Thursday, Goldengirl, National Lampoon Goes to the Movies, Turk 182!, Big Bad Mama II, Silent Night Deadly Night 3: Better Watch Out, Pucker Up and Bark Like a Dog, Timebomb, The Pelican Brief, Panther.
TELEVISION: Series: Trackdown, I Spy (also wrote pilot and 6 shows; Emmy noms. as writer and actor), The Greatest American Hero (also wrote 2 shows). Guest: The Cosby Show. Movies: Sammy The Way Out Seal, The Raiders, The Hanged Man, See the Man Run, A Cold Night's Death, Outrage!, Houston We've Got a Problem, Strange Homecoming, A Cry for Help, Flood, Spectre, Last of the Good Guys, Women in White, Hot Rod, The Dream Merchants, The Night the City Screamed, Killjoy, Thou Shalt Not Kill, Her Life as a Man, The Calendar Girl Murders, Brothers-in-Law, The Blue Lightning, The Gladiator, The Key to Rebecca, Combat High, Voyage of Terror: The Achille Lauro Affair, Columbo Goes to College, I Spy Returns.

CUMMINS, PEGGY
Actress. b. Prestatyn, North Wales, Dec. 18, 1925. e. Alexandra Sch., Dublin, Gate Theatre, Dublin. Starred in Let's Pretend on London Stage 1938, followed by Junior Miss, Alice in Wonderland, Peter Pan.
PICTURES: Dr. O'Dowd (debut, 1939), Salute John Citizen, Old Mother Riley—Detective, Welcome Mr. Washington, English Without Tears (Her Man Gilbey), The Late George Apley, Moss Rose, Green Grass of Wyoming, Escape, That Dangerous Age (If This Be Sin), Gun Crazy, My Daughter Joy (Operation X), Who Goes There (Passionate Sentry), Street Corner (Both Sides of the Law), Meet Mr. Lucifer, Always a Bride, The Love Lottery, To Dorothy a Son (Cash on Delivery), The March Hare, Carry on Admiral, Night of the Demon, Hell Drivers, The Captain's Table, Your Money or Your Wife, Dentist in the Chair, In the Doghouse.
TELEVISION: The Human Jungle, Looks Familiar.

CUNNINGHAM, SEAN S.
Producer, Director. b. New York, NY, Dec. 31 1941. e. Franklin & Marshall, B.A.; Stanford U., M.F.A. Worked briefly as actor, moving into stage-managing. Became producer of Mineola Theatre (Long Island, NY) and took several productions to B'way. Formed Sean S. Cunningham Films, Ltd., 1971. Produced commercials, industrial film, documentaries, features.
PICTURES: Together (prod., dir.), Last House on the Left (prod.), The Case of the Full Moon Murders (prod.), Here Come the Tigers (prod., dir.), Kick (prod., dir.), Friday the 13th (prod., dir.), A Stranger Is Watching (prod., dir.), Spring Break (prod., dir.), The New Kids (prod., dir.), House (prod.), House II: The Second Story (prod.), Deepstar Six (prod., dir.), The Horror Show (House III; prod.), House IV (prod.), My Boyfriend's Back (prod.), Jason Goes to Hell: The Final Friday (prod.).

CURLEY, JOHN J
Executive. b. Dec. 31, 1938. e. Dickinson Coll., BA, 1960; Columbia U., MS, 1963. Reporter, editor Associated Press, 1961-69. With Gannett Co., Inc., 1969-; pres. mid-Atlantic newspaper group Gannett Co., Inc, 1980-82; sr. v.p., Gannett Co., Inc, 1983-84; pres., 1984-; COO, 1984-86; CEO, 1986-; chmn., and bd. dirs., 1989-.

CURRY, TIM
Actor. b. Cheshire, England, Apr. 19, 1946. e. Birmingham U. Albums: Read My Lips, Fearless, Simplicity.
THEATER: Hair, A Midsummer Night's Dream, The Rocky Horror Show, Travesties, Amadeus (Tony nom.), The Pirates of Penzance, Me and My Girl (U.S. tour), The Art of Success, My Favorite Year (Tony nom.).
PICTURES: The Rocky Horror Picture Show (debut, 1975), The Shout, Times Square, Annie, The Ploughman's Lunch, Blue Money, Clue, Legend, Pass the Ammo, The Hunt for Red October, Oscar, FernGully... The Last Rainforest (voice), Passed Away, Home Alone 2: Lost in New York, National Lampoon's Loaded Weapon 1, The Three Musketeers, The Shadow, Lovers' Knot, The Pebble and the Penguin (voice), Congo, The Muppet Treasure Island, Lover's Knot, McHale's Navy.
TELEVISION: Movies: Oliver Twist, Stephen King's IT. Voice work—series: Peter Pan and the Pirates (Emmy Award, 1991), Captain Planet and the Planeteers, Fish Police, Over the Top. Specials: The Life of Shakespeare, Three Men in a Boat, Rock Follies, City Sugar. Guest: Dinosaurs (voice), Earth 2.

CURTIN, JANE
Actress. b. Cambridge, MA, Sept. 6, 1947. e. Northeastern U. On stage in Proposition, Last of the Red Hot Lovers, Candida. Author, actress off-B'way musical revue Pretzel 1974-75.
PICTURES: Mr. Mike's Mondo Video, How to Beat the High Cost of Living, O.C. and Stiggs, Coneheads.
TELEVISION: *Series*: Saturday Night Live (1974-79), Kate & Allie (Emmy Awards: 1984, 1985), Working It Out. *Movies*: What Really Happened to the Class of '65, Divorce Wars—A Love Story, Suspicion, Maybe Baby, Common Ground. *Special*: Candida.

CURTIS, DAN
Producer, Director. b. Bridgeport, CT, Aug. 12, 1928. e. U. of Bridgeport, Syracuse U., B.A. Was sales exec. for NBC and MCA before forming own company, Dan Curtis Productions, which he now heads. Producer/owner of CBS Golf Classic (1963-73).
PICTURES: *Dir./Prod.*: House of Dark Shadows, Night of Dark Shadows, Burnt Offerings (also co-s.p.), Me and the Kid.
TELEVISION: *Series*: *Producer*: Dark Shadows (ABC daytime serial, 1966-71), Dark Shadows (prime time series, 1991). *Movies*: *Director*: The Night Stalker, Frankenstein, The Picture of Dorian Gray, The Last Ride of the Dalton Gang, The Long Days of Summer, Mrs. R's Daughter, Intruders (also co-exec. prod.). *Prod./Dir.*: The Night Strangler, The Norliss Tapes, Scream of the Wolf, Dracula, Melvin Purvis: G-Man, The Turn of the Screw, The Great Ice-Rip Off, Trilogy of Terror, Kansas City Massacre, Curse of the Black Widow, When Every Day Was the Fourth of July (also co-story), The Love Letter. *Mini-Series (prod./dir.)*: The Winds of War, War and Remembrance (also co-writer).

CURTIS, JAMIE LEE
Actress. b. Los Angeles, CA, Nov. 22, 1958. e. Choat Rosemary Hall, CT; Univ. of the Pacific. m. actor-director Christopher Guest. Daughter of Janet Leigh and Tony Curtis. While in school won contract with Universal Studios appearing in small parts in several tv shows.
PICTURES: Halloween (debut, 1978), The Fog, Prom Night, Terror Train, Halloween II, Roadgames, Trading Places, Love Letters, Grandview USA, Perfect, Amazing Grace and Chuck, A Man in Love, Dominick and Eugene, A Fish Called Wanda, Blue Steel, Queens Logic, My Girl, Forever Young, My Girl 2, Mother's Boys, True Lies, House Arrest, Death Fish II, Halloween: H2O, Homegrown, Virus.
TELEVISION: *Special*: Tall Tales (Annie Oakley). *Series*: Operation Petticoat (1977-78), Anything But Love (also, dir., Golden Globe Award). *Movies*: Operation Petticoat (pilot), She's in the Army Now, Death of a Centerfold: The Dorothy Stratten Story, Money on the Side, As Summers Die, The Heidi Chronicles, Nicholas' Gift. *Pilot*: Callahan. *Guest*: Quincy, Nancy Drew Mysteries.

CURTIS, TONY
Actor. r.n. Bernard Schwartz. b. New York, NY, June 3, 1925. e. Seward Park H.S. Daughter is actress Jamie Lee Curtis. In U.S. Navy, amateur dramatics, N.Y., started Empire Players Theatre, Newark, NJ. With Dramatic Workshop, Cherry Lane Theatre, Junior Drama workshop of Walt Whitman School. First prod. work with Stanley Woolf Players. Made m.p. debut unbilled in Criss-Cross; signed with U-I. Star of Tomorrow, 1953. Author: Tony Curtis: The Autobiography (1993).
PICTURES: Criss Cross (debut, 1948), City Across the River, The Lady Gambles, Johnny Stool Pigeon, Francis, Sierra, I Was a Shoplifter, Winchester 73, Sierra, Kansas Raiders, Prince Who Was a Thief, Flesh and Fury, Son of Ali Baba, No Room for the Groom, Houdini, All American, Forbidden, Beachhead, Johnny Dark, Black Shield of Falworth, 6 Bridges to Cross, So This Is Paris, Purple Mask, Square Jungle, Rawhide Years, Trapeze, Mister Cory, Midnight Story, Sweet Smell of Success, The Vikings, Kings Go Forth, The Defiant Ones (Acad. Award nom.), The Perfect Furlough, Some Like It Hot, Operation Petticoat, Who Was That Lady?, The Rat Race, Spartacus, Pepe (cameo), The Great Impostor, The Outsider, Taras Bulba, 40 Pounds of Trouble, The List of Adrian Messenger, Captain Newman, M.D., Paris When it Sizzles, Wild and Wonderful, Sex and the Single Girl, Goodbye Charlie, The Great Race, Boeing-Boeing, Chamber of Horrors (cameo), Not With My Wife You Don't!, Arrivederci Baby!, Don't Make Waves, On My Way to the Crusades I Met a Girl Who—(The Chastity Belt), The Boston Strangler, Rosemary's Baby (voice), Those Daring Young Men in Their Jaunty Jalopies (Monte Carlo or Bust), Suppose They Gave a War and Nobody Came, You Can't Win 'Em All, Lepke, The Last Tycoon, Casanova & Co., The Manitou, The Bad News Bears Go to Japan, Sextette, Little Miss Marker, The Mirror Crack'd, Brainwaves, King of the City, Insignificance, Club Life, The Last of Philip Banter, Balboa, Midnight, Lobster Man From Mars, The High-Flying Mermaid, Prime Target, Center of the Web, Naked in New York, The Reptile Man, The Immortals, The Celluloid Closet.
TELEVISION: *Series*: The Persuaders, McCoy, Vega$, Hollywood Babylon (host). *Movies*: The Third Girl from the Left, The Count of Monte Cristo, Vega$, The Users, Moviola: The Scarlett O'Hara War, Inmates: A Love Story, Harry's Back, The Million Dollar Face, Mafia Princess, Murder in Three Acts, Portrait of a Showgirl, Tarzan in Manhattan, Thanksgiving Day, Christmas in Connecticut, A Perry Mason Mystery: The Case of the Grimacing Governor.

CUSACK, JOAN
Actress. b. Evanston, IL, Oct. 11, 1962. Brother is actor John Cusack. e. U. of Wisconsin, Madison. Studied acting at Piven Theatre Workshop, Evanston, IL. While in coll. joined The Ark, local improvisational comedy group.
THEATER: Road, Brilliant Traces (Theatre World Award for both), Cymbeline, The Celestial Alphabet Event, 'Tis Pity She's a Whore, A Midsummer Night's Dream.
PICTURES: My Bodyguard (debut, 1980), Class, Sixteen Candles, Grandview U.S.A., The Allnighter, Broadcast News, Stars and Bars, Married to the Mob, Working Girl (Acad. Award nom.), Say Anything..., Men Don't Leave, My Blue Heaven, The Cabinet of Dr. Ramirez, Hero, Toys, Addams Family Values, Corrina Corrina, Nine Months, Mr. Wrong, Grosse Pointe Blank, A Smile Like Yours, In & Out (NY Film Crits. Circle Award, Best Supporting Actress, 1997).
TELEVISION: *Series*: Saturday Night Live (1985-86). *Special*: The Mother.

CUSACK, JOHN
Actor. b. Evanston, IL, June 28, 1966. Sister is actress Joan Cusack. Member of Piven Theatre Workshop in Evanston for 10 years beginning when he was 9 years old. Appeared on several tv commercials as teen. Formed Chicago theatrical company, New Criminals.
PICTURES: Class (debut, 1983), Sixteen Candles, Grandview U.S.A., The Sure Thing, The Journey of Natty Gann, Better Off Dead, Stand By Me, One Crazy Summer, Hot Pursuit, Eight Men Out, Tapeheads, Say Anything..., Fat Man and Little Boy, The Grifters, True Colors, Shadows and Fog, Roadside Prophets, The Player, Bob Roberts, Map of the Human Heart, Money for Nothing, Bullets Over Broadway, The Road to Wellville, Floundering, City Hall, Grosse Pointe Blank (also co-prod. & s.p.), Con Air, Midnight in the Garden of Good and Evil, Anastasia (voice), This Is My Father, The Thin Red Line, Pushing Tin, Chicago Cab, Arigo (also prod.), High Fidelity (also s.p.), The Cradle Will Rock.
TELEVISION: *Movies*: Eastwood on Eastwood. *Mini-Series*: Baseball (voice).

CZERNY, HENRY
Actor. b. Toronto, Canada, 1959. Began acting career performing in musicals at Humberside collegiate in Toronto.
PICTURES: I Love a Man in Uniform, Cold Sweat, Buried on Sunday, Anchor Zone, Clear and Present Danger, Notes From Underground, The Michelle Apartments, The Interview, When Night Is Falling, Mission Impossible, Promise the Moon, Kayla, The Ice Storm, Glory & Honor.
TELEVISION: *Movies*: Deadly Matrimony, A Town Torn Apart, Lifeline to Victory, The Boys of St. Vincent, Ultimate Betrayal, Choices of the Heart: The Margaret Sanger Story, For Hope. *Guest*: Street Legal, Counterstrike, Kung Fu: The Legend Continues.

D

D'ABO, OLIVIA
Actress. b. England. Parents, singer Michael d'Abo, actress Maggie London.
THEATER: *LA*: Scenes From an Execution, It's a Girl.
PICTURES: Conan the Destroyer, Bolero, Bullies, Into the Fire, Beyond the Stars, The Spirit of 76, Point of No Return, Wayne's World 2, Bank Robber, Greedy, Clean Slate, The Last Good Time, The Big Green, Kicking and Screaming.
TELEVISION: *Series*: The Wonder Years, The Single Guy. *Movies*: Not My Kid, Crash Course, Midnight's Child.

DAFOE, WILLEM
Actor. r.n. William Dafoe. b. Appleton, WI, July 22, 1955. Worked with experimental group Theatre X on the road before coming to New York. Built sets and debuted with the Wooster Group at the Performing Garage playing (literally) a chicken heart in Elizabeth Le Compte's Nayatt School. Current member of the Wooster Group, performing with them frequently in U.S. and Europe. For them appeared in independent film The Communists Are Comfortable.
PICTURES: Heaven's Gate (debut, 1980), The Loveless, The Hunger, Streets of Fire, Roadhouse 66, To Live and Die in L.A., Platoon (Acad. Award nom.), Off Limits, The Last Temptation of Christ, Mississippi Burning, Triumph of the Spirit, Born on the Fourth of July, Cry-Baby, Wild at Heart, Flight of the Intruder, White Sands, Light Sleeper, Body of Evidence, Faraway So Close!, Clear and Present Danger, Tom and Viv, The Night and the Moment, The English Patient, Speed 2: Cruise Control, Affliction, Lulu on the Bridge.

DAHL, ARLENE
Actress, Writer, Designer. b. Minneapolis, MN, Aug. 11, 1928. e. MN Business Coll.; U. of Minnesota, summers 1941-44; Minneapolis. Coll. of Music. m. Marc A. Rosen. Mother of actor Lorenzo Lamas. At age 8, played heroine of children's adventure serials on radio. Internationally syndicated beauty columnist, Chgo. Tribune-N.Y. News Syndicate, 1951-71; Pres. Arlene Dahl Enterprises, 1951-75; Sleepwear Designer, A.N. Saab & Co., 1952-57; Natl. Beauty Advisor, Sears Roebuck & Co., 1970-75; v.p. Kenyon & Eckhart Advg. Agcy., pres., Women's World Div., Kenyon-Eckhart, 1967-72; Fashion Consultant, O.M.A. 1975-78, Int'l. Director of S.M.E.I., 1973-76, Designer, Vogue Patterns 1978-85. Pres., Dahlia Parfums Inc., 1975-80, pres., Dahlia Prods., 1978-81: pres. Dahlmark Prods. 1981-. Honrs. include: 8 Motion Picture Laurel Awards, 1948-63; Hds. of Fame Award, 1971, Woman of the Year, N.Y. Adv. Council, 1969. Mother of the Year, 1979; Coup de Chapeau, Deauville Film Fest 1983. Received star on Hollywood Walk of Fame. Lifetime Achievement Award Filmfest 1994.
THEATER: B'way: Mr. Strauss Goes to Boston (debut, 1946), Cyrano de Bergerac, Applause. Major US tours include: Questionable Ladies, The King and I, One Touch of Venus, I Married an Angel, Mame, Pal Joey, Bell Book and Candle, The Camel Bell, Life With Father, A Little Night Music, Lilliom, Marriage Go Round, Blithe Spirit, Forty Carats, Dear Liar, Murder Among Friends.
PICTURES: My Wild Irish Rose (debut, 1947), The Bride Goes Wild, A Southern Yankee, Ambush, Reign of Terror (The Black Book), Scene of the Crime, The Outriders, Three Little Words, Watch the Birdie, Inside Straight, No Questions Asked, Caribbean, Jamaica Run, Desert Legion, Here Come the Girls, Sangaree, The Diamond Queen, Wicked as They Come, Fortune is a Woman, Bengal Brigade, Woman's World, Slightly Scarlet, She Played With Fire, Journey to the Center of the Earth, Kisses for My President, Les Ponyettes, DuBle en Liasse, Le Chemin du Katmandu. The Landraiders, A Place to Hide, Night of the Warrior.
TELEVISION: Max Factor Playhouse, Lux Television Theater, Pepsi Cola Playhouse, Opening Night, Arlene Dahl's Beauty Spot, Hostess, Model of the Year Show, Arlene Dahl's Starscope, Arlene Dahl's Lovescopes, One Life to Live (1981-84), Night of One Hundred Stars, Happy Birthday Hollywood, Who Killed Max Thorn?, Love Boat, Love American Style, Fantasy Island, Burke's Law, Renegade.
WRITER: Always Ask a Man, 1965, Your Beautyscope, 1969, Secrets of Hair Care, 1971, Secrets of Skin Care, 1973, Your Beautyscope 1977-78, Beyond Beauty, 1980, Lovescopes, 1983.

DAHL, JOHN
Director, Writer. b. Montana. e. Univ. of MT, Montana St. In collaboration with David Warfield made 30 minute rock musical, Here Come the Pugs and indept. feature, The Death Mutants.
PICTURES: Private Investigations (co-s.p.), Kill Me Again (dir., co-s.p.), Red Rock West (dir., co-s.p.), The Last Seduction (dir.), Unforgettable (dir., co-s.p.)

DALE, JIM
Actor. b. Rothwell, Northhamptonshire, England, Aug. 15, 1935. Debut as solo comedian at the Savoy, 1951. Joined National Theatre Co. in 1969 playing in Love's Labour's Lost, The Merchant of Venice, The National Health, The Card. Has written songs and music for films: Twinky, Shalako, Joseph Andrews, Georgy Girl (Acad. Award nom.). Many TV appearances. Director: Asprin and Elephants. In TV movie, The American Clock.
THEATER: U.S.: Mark Taper Forum: Comedians, Scapino. N.Y.: Theater: Taming of the Shrew, Scapino, Barnum (Tony and Drama Desk Awards, 1980), Joe Egg (Tony Award nom.), Me and My Girl, Privates on Parade, Travels With My Aunt.
PICTURES: Six-Five Special (debut, 1958), Raising the Wind, Nurse on Wheels, The Iron Maiden, Carry on Cabby, Carry on Jack, Carry on Spying, Carry on Cleo, The Big Job, Carry on Cowboy, Carry on Screaming, Don't Lose Your Head, The Winter's Tale, The Plank, Follow That Camel, Carry on Doctor, Lock Up Your Daughters, Carry on Again Doctor, The National Health, Digby—The Biggest Dog in the World, Joseph Andrews, Pete's Dragon, Hot Lead Cold Feet, Unidentified Flying Oddball, Scandalous, Carry on Columbus.

DALEY, ROBERT
Producer. e. UCLA. Began career in pictures at Universal International and TV at Desilu.
PICTURES: Play Misty For Me, Dirty Harry (exec. prod.), Joe Kidd, High Plains Drifter, Breezy, Magnum Force, Thunderbolt and Lightfoot, The Eiger Sanction, The Outlaw Josey Wales, The Enforcer, The Gauntlet, Every Which Way But Loose, Escape from Alcatraz (exec. prod.), Any Which Way You Can (exec. prod.), Bronco Billy (exec. prod.), Stick (exec. prod.), Real Genius (exec. prod.).
TELEVISION: The Untouchables, Ben Casey, The FBI, 12 O'Clock High, The Invaders, etc.

DALSIMER, SUSAN
Executive. Editor for E.P. Dutton before joining Lorimar Prods., as v.p. of east coast development. Left to become consultant for original programming at Home Box Office. 1987, named v.p., creative affairs, east coast, for Warner Bros. 1994, v.p., publishing for Miramax Films.

DALTON, TIMOTHY
Actor. b. Colwyn Bay, No. Wales, March 21, 1946. Started acting at Natl. Youth Theatre, then studied at RADA. Prof. stage debut in Richard III and As You Like It at Birmingham Rep.
THEATER: Coriolanus, The Merchant of Venice, Richard III, The Doctor's Dilemma, St. Joan, Macbeth, Henry IV, Henry V, The Samaritan, Black Comedy, White Liars, Lunatic Lover and Poet, Love Letters (1991).
PICTURES: The Lion in Winter (debut, 1968), Cromwell, The Voyeur, Wuthering Heights, Mary Queen of Scots, Permission to Kill, Sextette, Agatha, Flash Gordon, El Hombre Que Supo Amar, Anthony and Cleopatra, Chanel Solitaire, The Doctor and the Devils, The Living Daylights, Brenda Starr, Hawks, Licence to Kill, The King's Whore, The Rocketeer, Naked in New York, Saltwater Moose, The Beautician and the Beast.
TELEVISION: Mini-Series: Centennial, Mistral's Daughter, Sins, Scarlett, Framed. Movies: The Master of Ballantrae, Lie Down With Lions, Field of Blood. Specials: The Three Princes, Five Finger Exercise, Candida, Daerie Tale Theater: The Emperor's New Clothes (narr.), Nature: In The Company of Wolves (docu.). Series: Sat'day While Sunday, Judge Dee, Hooked International, Charlie's Angels: Fallen Angel, Tales From the Crypt: Werewolf Concerto, Survival Factor Series (narr.).

DALTREY, ROGER
Singer, Actor. b. London, England, March 1, 1944. Lead vocalist with The Who.
PICTURES: Woodstock, Tommy, Lisztomania, The Legacy, The Kids Are Alright, McVicar (also prod.), Mack the Knife, The Teddy Bear Habit, Father Jim, If Looks Could Kill, Buddy's Song, Lightning Jack.
TELEVISION: Movie: Forgotten Prisoners: The Amnesty Files.

DALY, ANN
Executive. Pres., Domestic Home Video, Buena Vista Home Video.

DALY, JIM
Executive Director. b. 1938. Managing director of Film and Television division which includes: Pinewood Studios, Rank Film Laboratories, Odeon Cinemas, Rank Film Distributors, Deluxe Hollywood, Deluxe Toronto, Rank Advertising Films, Rank Theatres, Rank Video Services, Rank Video Services America, Rank Video Services Europe, Film House Company, Rank Brimar, Rank Cintel, Strand Lighting, Rank Taylor Hobson. Appt. exec. dir., Rank Org., 1982.

DALY, JOHN
Executive. b. London, England, July 16, 1937. After working in journalism joined Royal Navy. On leaving Service after three years, trained as underwriter with an Assurance Company. In 1966 became David Hemmings manager and in 1967 formed the Hemdale Company with Hemmings (who later sold interest) Chmn. Hemdale Holdings Ltd.
PICTURES: Images, Sunburn (co-prod., co-s.p.), High Risk, Going Ape, Deadly Force, Carbon Copy, Yellowbeard, The Terminator, The Falcon and the Snowman, Salvador, River's Edge, At Close Range, Hoosiers, Platoon, Best Seller, Shag (exec. prod.), Vampire's Kiss (exec. prod.), Miracle Mile (prod.), Criminal Law (co-exec. prod.), War Party (prod.), The Boost, Out Cold (exec. prod.), Staying Together (exec. prod.).

DALY, ROBERT A.
Executive. b. New York, NY, Dec. 8, 1936. e. Brooklyn Coll., Hunter Coll. Joined CBS-TV in 1955; dir. of program acct.; dir. of research and cost planning; dir. of business affairs. Later named v.p., business affairs, NY; exec. v.p. of network on April, 1976. Named president, CBS Entertainment, Oct. 1977. In Oct. 1979 became responsible for CBS Theatrical Films as well as the TV operation. In 1981, appointed chmn. of bd. and co-CEO of Warner Bros.; 1982, named chmn. of bd. and CEO; 1994, named chmn. of bd. and co-CEO, sharing office with Terry Semel; 1995, also named chmn. and co-CEO of the Warner Bros. Music Group.

DALY, TIM
Actor. b. New York, NY, March 1, 1956. m. actress Amy Van Nostrand. Son of late actor James Daly, brother of actress Tyne Daly. e. Bennington Coll., B.A. Acted in summer stock while in college. Moved to NY where had own rock and roll band. Has performed in cabaret at Williamstown Theater Festival.

THEATER: Fables for Friends, Oliver Oliver, Mass Appeal, Bus Stop, Coastal Disturbances (Theatre World Award).
PICTURES: Diner, Just the Way You Are, Made in Heaven, Spellbinder, Love or Money, Year of the Comet, Caroline at Midnight, Dr. Jekyll and Ms. Hyde, Denise Calls Up, The Associate.
TELEVISION: *Special*: The Rise and Rise of Daniel Rocket. *Mini-Series*: I'll Take Manhattan, Queen. *Series*: Ryan's Four, Almost Grown, Wings. *Movies*: I Married a Centerfold, Mirrors, Red Earth White Earth, In the Line of Duty: Ambush in Waco, Dangerous Heart, Witness to the Execution. *Guest*: Midnight Caller, Hill Street Blues, Alfred Hitchcock Presents.

DALY, TYNE
Actress. r.n. Ellen Tyne Daly. b. Madison, WI, Feb. 21, 1946. Daughter of late actor James Daly and actress Hope Newell; brother is actor Timothy Daly.
THEATER: The Butter and Egg Man, That Summer That Fall, Skirmishes, The Black Angel, Rimers of Eldritch, Ashes, Three Sisters, Come Back Little Sheba (L.A., 1987), Gypsy (Tony Award, 1990), Queen of the Stardust Ballroom, The Seagull, On the Town, Call Me Madam (in concert).
PICTURES: John and Mary, Angel Unchained, Play It As It Lays, The Adulteress, The Enforcer, Telefon, Speedtrap, Zoot Suit, The Aviator, Movers & Shakers, The Lay of the Land, Vig, Autumn Heart.
TELEVISION: *Series*: Cagney & Lacey (4 Emmy Awards), Christy (Emmy Award, 1996). *Movies*: In Search of America, A Howling in the Woods, Heat of Anger, The Man Who Could Talk to Kids, Larry, The Entertainer, Better Late Than Never, Intimate Strangers, The Women's Room, A Matter of Life or Death, Your Place or Mine, Kids Like These, Stuck With Each Other, The Last to Go, Face of a Stranger, Columbo: A Bird in the Hand, Scattered Dreams: The Kathryn Messenger Story, The Forget-Me-Not Murders, Columbo: Undercover, Cagney & Lacey: The Return, Cagney & Lacey: Together Again, Bye Bye Birdie. *Guest*: Medical Center, Columbo, Ray Bradbury Theatre, Wings.

DAMON, MARK
Executive, Actor. b. Chicago, IL, April 22, 1933. e. UCLA, B.A. literature, M.A. business administration. Actor: 1958 under contract to 20th Century Fox, 1960 winner Golden Globe Award-Newcomer of the Year; early career includes The Fall of The House of Usher, The Longest Day; 1961 moved to Italy, stayed 16 years appearing in leading roles in 50 films; 1974 head of foreign dept. for PAC, a leading film distributor in Italy; 1976 returned to the U.S. as exec. prod. of The Choirboys and in charge of its foreign distribution; 1979 founder and pres. of Producers Sales Organization, intl. distribution org. 1987 formed Vision Int'l.; 1993, formed MDP Worlwide, intl. prod. & distrib. co.
PICTURES: *Exec. prod. or prod.*: The Arena, The Choirboys, The Neverending Story, Das Boot, Nine 1/2 Weeks, Short Circuit, Flight of the Navigator, Lost Boys, High Spirits, Bat 21 (co-prod.), Diary of a Hit Man, Wild Orchid, Wild Orchid II: Two Shades of Blue, Stalingrad, The Jungle Book, The Jungle Book 2, The Blackout, The Winner, Orgazmo, Loved, Deceiver (also actor), Eye of the Beholder. *Actor*: Inside Detroit, Screaming Eagles, Between Heaven and Hell, Young and Dangerous, The Party Crashers, Life Begins at 17, House of Usher, This Rebel Breed, The Reluctant Saint, The Longest Day (uncredited), Beauty and the Beast, The Young Racers, Black Christmas, Pedro el Cruel, Son of Cleopatra, Hundred Horsemen, Ringo and His Golden Pistol, Agente segreto 777 operzione Mistero, Dio—come ti amo, One for All, Train for Durango, Death Does Not Count the Dollars, Johnny Yuma, Morti non si contano I, Kill and Pray, School Girl Killer, Anzio, Long Live Robin Hood, The Norman Swordsman, La Spada Normanna, Posate le pistole reverendo, Leoni di Petersburgo, Monta in sella figlio di...!, The Devil's Wedding Night, Little Mother, Crypt of the Living Death, Byleth, There Is No 13, Lo matas tu o lo mato yo, Do I Kill You or Do You Kill Me?, Stuck on You.

DAMON, MATT
Actor, Writer. b. Cambridge, MA, Oct. 8, 1970. Chicago Film Crits. Award, Most Promising New Actor, 1997.
PICTURES: *Actor*: Mystic Pizza (debut, 1988), School Ties, Geronimo: An American Legend, Courage Under Fire, Glory Daze, Chasing Amy, The Rainmaker, Good Will Hunting (also s.p., Acad. Award, Golden Globe Award, Best Screenplay, 1997), Rounders, Saving Private Ryan, The Talented Mr. Ripley, Dogma, All the Pretty Horses, Planet Ice (voice).
TELEVISION: *Movies*: Rising Son, The Good Old Boys.

DAMONE, VIC
Singer, Actor. r.n. Vito Farinola. b. Brooklyn, NY, June 12, 1928. m. actress-singer Diahann Carroll. e. Lafayette H.S., Brooklyn. Winner Arthur Godfrey talent show, 1947; then night clubs, radio, theatres. U.S. Army, 1951-53.
PICTURES: Rich Young and Pretty (debut, 1951), The Strip, Athena, Deep in My Heart, Hit the Deck, Kismet, Hell to Eternity.
TELEVISION: *Series*: The Vic Damone Show (1956-57), Lively Ones (1962-63), The Vic Damone Show (1967).

DAMSKI, MEL
Director. b. New York, NY, July 21, 1946. e. Colgate U., AFI. Worked as reporter, journalism professor. USC Cinema instructor.
PICTURES: Yellowbeard, Mischief, Happy Together.
TELEVISION: *Series*: M*A*S*H, Lou Grant, Dolphin Cove. *Movies*: Long Journey Back, The Child Stealer, Word of Honor, The Legend of Walks Far Woman, American Dream, For Ladies Only, Making the Grade, An Invasion of Privacy, Badge of the Assassin, A Winner Never Quits, Attack on Fear, Hero in the Family, Murder by the Book, Hope Division, The Three Kings, Everybody's Baby: The Rescue of Jessica McClure, Back to the Streets of San Francisco.

DANA, BILL
Actor, Writer. b. Quincy, MA, Oct. 5, 1924. In night clubs and on TV.
PICTURES: The Busy Body, The Barefoot Executive, The Nude Bomb (also s.p.).
TELEVISION: *Series*: The Steve Allen Show (performer, head writer, 1961), The Bill Dana Jose Jimenez Show (star, writer), Spike Jones Show (prod., writer, performer), Milton Berle Show (prod., writer, performer), No Soap Radio, Zorro and Son, All in the Family (writer). *Movies*: The Snoop Sisters, Rosetti & Ryan: Men Who Love Women, A Guide for the Married Woman, Murder in Texas. *Actor*: Facts of Life, Too Close for Comfort, Golden Girls, Hollywood Palace, St. Elsewhere.

DANCE, CHARLES
Actor. b. Worcestershire, England, Oct. 10, 1946. e. Plymouth Coll. Art., Leicester Coll. of Art (graphic design degree). After first working as a West End theatre stagehand, made acting debut in 1970 in a touring company of It's a Two-Foot-Six-Inches-above-the Ground World. Worked in provincial repertory theaters. Joined the Royal Shakespeare Company 1975-80: Hamlet, Richard III, As You Like It. Lead in Henry V (1975, N.Y.), Coriolanus (Paris, London, Stratford).
THEATER: Plenty, McGuffin, revival of Irma La Douce (West End), Turning Over (London's Bush Theatre).
PICTURES: The Spy Who Loved Me (debut, 1977), For Your Eyes Only, Plenty, The Golden Child, Good Morning Babylon, White Mischief, The Hidden City, Pascali's Island, Alien 3, The Valley of Stone, Last Action Hero, China Moon, Century, Kabloonak, Exquisite Tenderness, Shortcut to Paradise, Undertow, Michael Collins, Space Truckers, In the Presence of Mine Enemies.
TELEVISION: Very Like a Whale, The McGuffin, The Jewel in the Crown, Lightning Always Strikes Twice, Edward VII, The Fatal Spring, Little Eyolf, Frost in May, Nancy Astor, Saigon—The Last Day, Out On a Limb, BBC's The Secret Servant, Rainy Day Woman, Out of the Shadows, First Born, Goldeneye, Rebecca, Phantom of the Opera (mini-series), Darling of the Gods.

D'ANGELO, BEVERLY
Actress. b. Columbus, OH, Nov. 15, 1954. Studied visual arts and was exchange student in Italy before working as cartoonist for Hanna-Barbera Studios in Hollywood. Toured Canada's coffeehouse circuit as singer and appeared with rock band called Elephant. Joined Charlotte Town Festival Company. B'way debut in rock musical, Rockabye Hamlet. Off-B'way: Simpatico (Theatre World Award).
PICTURES: The Sentinel (debut 1977), Annie Hall, First Love, Every Which Way But Loose, Hair, Highpoint, Coal Miner's Daughter, Honky Tonk Freeway, Paternity, National Lampoon's Vacation, Finders Keepers, National Lampoon's European Vacation, Big Trouble, Maid to Order, In the Mood, Aria, Trading Hearts, High Spirits, National Lampoon's Christmas Vacation, Daddy's Dyin', Pacific Heights (unbilled), The Miracle, The Pope Must Die, Man Trouble, Lonely Hearts, Lightning Jack, Eye for an Eye, Edie and Pen, Pterodactyl Woman from Beverly Hills, Vegas Vacation.
TELEVISION: *Mini-Series*: Captains and the Kings. *Movies*: A Streetcar Named Desire, Doubletake, Slow Burn, Hands of a Stranger, Trial: The Price of Passion, A Child Lost Forever, The Switch, Judgment Day: The John List Story, Jonathan Stone: Threat of Innocence, Menendez: A Killing in Beverly Hills. *Special*: Sleeping Beauty (Faerie Tale Theater).

DANES, CLAIRE
Actress. b. New York, NY, April 12, 1979. e. Professional Performing Arts School, NY; Lee Strasberg Studio. Acting career began with off-off-B'way appearances in Happiness, Punk Ballet and Kids on Stage.
PICTURES: Dreams of Love (debut), Thirty (short), The Pesky Suitor (short), Little Women, Romeo and Juliet, To Gillian on Her 37th Birthday, Polish Wedding, U-Turn.
TELEVISION: *Series*: My So Called Life. *Guest*: Law and Order. *Movies*: No Room for Opal, The Coming Out of Heidi Leiter.

DANGERFIELD, RODNEY
Actor, Comedian. r.n. Jacob Cohen. b. Babylon, NY, Nov. 22, 1921. Performer in nightclubs as Jack Roy 1941-51. Worked as businessman 1951-63, before becoming stand-up comedian. Founder Dangerfields' Nightclub, 1969. Regular appearances on Dean Martin Show, 1972-73. Appeared in TV movie Benny and Barney: Las Vegas Undercover.
PICTURES: The Projectionist, Caddyshack, Easy Money (also co-s.p.), Back to School, Moving, Rover Dangerfield (voice, exec. prod., s.p., co-story, co-wrote songs), Ladybugs, Natural Born Killers, Casper (cameo), Meet Wally Sparks (also co-s.p.).

DANIEL, SEAN
Executive. b. Aug. 15, 1951. e. California Inst. of Arts film school. BFA, 1973. Was journalist for Village Voice before starting m.p. career as documentary filmmaker and asst. dir. for New World Pictures. In 1976 joined Universal Pictures as prod. exec.; 1979, named v.p., then pres., production. Resigned March, 1989 to become pres., The Geffen Co., film div.; resigned from Geffen, Nov. 1989. 1990, with Jim Jacks started own prod. co. Alphaville, in partnership with Universal Pictures.
PICTURES: Pure Luck, American Me, CB4, Hard Target, Heart and Souls, Tombstone, Michael.

DANIELS, JEFF
Actor. b. Athens, Georgia. Feb. 19, 1955. e. Central Michigan U. Apprentice with Circle Repertory Theatre, New York. Established Purple Rose Theatre Co. in Chelsea, Michigan. Playwright: The Kingdom's Coming, The Vast Difference.
THEATER: Brontosaurus, Short-Changed Review, The Farm, Fifth of July, Johnny Got His Gun (Obie Award), Lemon Sky, The Three Sisters, The Golden Age, Redwood Curtain.
PICTURES: Ragtime (debut, 1981), Terms of Endearment, The Purple Rose of Cairo, Marie, Heartburn, Something Wild, Radio Days, The House on Carroll Street, Sweet Hearts Dance, Checking Out, Arachnophobia, Welcome Home Roxy Carmichael, Love Hurts, The Butcher's Wife, There Goes the Neighborhood, Rain Without Thunder, Gettysburg, Speed, Terminal Velocity, Dumb & Dumber, 2 Days in the Valley, Fly Away Home, 101 Dalmations, Trial and Error.
TELEVISION: Movies: A Rumor of War, Invasion of Privacy, The Caine Mutiny Court Martial, No Place Like Home, Disaster in Time, Teamster Boss: The Jackie Presser Story, Redwood Curtain. Specials: Fifth of July, The Visit (Trying Times). Guest: Breaking Away (pilot), Hawaii 5-0.

DANIELS, PAUL
TV performer, Magician. b. South Bank, England, April 6, 1938. Early career starring in British and overseas theatres. 1983, Magician Of The Year Award by Hollywood's Academy of Magical Arts. 1985, his BBC TV special awarded Golden Rose of Montreux trophy. Presenter of Every Second Counts and Paul Daniels Magic Show. Devised children's TV series, Wizbit and radio series Dealing With Daniels, Secret Magic and Game Show Wipeout.

DANIELS, WILLIAM
Actor. b. Brooklyn, NY, Mar 31, 1927. e. Northwestern U. m. actress Bonnie Bartlett. Traveled around NY area as part of The Daniels Family song and dance troupe. Appeared with family on experimental TV in 1941. Stage debut in Life with Father. Brought to national attention in A Thousand Clowns in original B'way play and film version.
THEATER: The Zoo Story, On a Clear Day You Can See Forever, 1776, Dear Me, The Sky Is Falling, A Little Night Music.
PICTURES: Ladybug Ladybug, A Thousand Clowns, Two for the Road, The Graduate, The President's Analyst, Marlowe, 1776, The Parallax View, Black Sunday, Oh God!, The One and Only, Sunburn, The Blue Lagoon, All Night Long, Reds, Blind Date, Her Alibi, Magic Kid.
TELEVISION: Series: Captain Nice, The Nancy Walker Show, Freebie and the Bean, Knight Rider (voice), St. Elsewhere (Emmy Awards, 1985, 1986), Boy Meets World. Guest: East Side/West Side, For the People, Toma, The Rockford Files. Movies: Rooster, Rehearsal for a Murder, Murdock's Gang, A Case of Rape, Sarah T.—Portrait of a Teenage Alcoholic, One of Our Own, Francis Gary Powers, Killer on Board, The Bastard, Big Bob Johnson and His Fantastic Speed Circus, Sgt. Matlovich Vs. the U.S. Air Force, The Rebels, City in Fear, Damien: The Leper Priest, Million Dollar Face, Drop Out Father, The Little Match Girl, Knight Rider 2000 (voice), Back to the Streets of San Francisco. Mini-series: Blind Ambition, The Adams Chronicles, The Lottery.

DANNER, BLYTHE
Actress. b. Philadelphia, PA, Feb. 3, 1943. e. Bard Coll. m. writer-prod. Bruce Paltrow. Daughter is actress Gwyneth Paltrow. Appeared in repertory cos. in U.S. before Lincoln Center productions of Cyrano de Bergerac, Summertree, and The Miser (Theatre World Award for last).
THEATER: NY: Butterflies Are Free (Tony Award, 1971), Major Barbara, Twelfth Night, The Seagull, Ring Around The Moon, Betrayal, Blithe Spirit, A Streetcar Named Desire, Much Ado About Nothing, Sylvia. Williamstown: Picnic.

PICTURES: To Kill a Clown (debut, 1972), 1776, Lovin' Molly, Hearts of the West, Futureworld, The Great Santini, Man Woman and Child, Brighton Beach Memoirs, Another Woman, Mr. and Mrs. Bridge, Alice, The Prince of Tides, Husbands and Wives, To Wong Foo—Thanks for Everything—Julie Newmar, Homage, The Myth of Fingerprints.
TELEVISION: Movies: Dr. Cook's Garden, F. Scott Fitzgerald and The Last of the Belles, Sidekicks, A Love Affair: The Eleanor and Lou Gehrig Story, Too Far to Go, Eccentricities of a Nightingale, Are You in the House Alone?, Inside the Third Reich, In Defense of Kids, Helen Keller: The Miracle Continues, Guilty Conscience, Money Power Murder, Judgment, Never Forget, Cruel Doubt, Getting Up and Going Home, Oldest Living Confederate Widow Tells All, Leave of Absence. Series: Adam's Rib, Tattingers (revamped as Nick & Hillary). Specials: To Confuse the Angel, George M, To Be Young Gifted and Black, The Scarecrow., Kiss Kiss Dahlings.

DANSON, TED
Actor, Producer. b. San Diego, CA, Dec. 29, 1947. e. Kent Sch., Stanford U., Carnegie-Mellon U, 1972. m. actress Mary Steenburgen. Studied at Actors Inst. New York stage debut, The Real Inspector Hound, 1972; mgr. and teacher, Actors Inst., L.A., 1978. Tv debut, The Doctors. Founded Amer. Oceans Campaign; bd. mem. Futures for Children.
PICTURES: The Onion Field (debut, 1979), Body Heat, Creepshow, Little Treasure, Just Between Friends, A Fine Mess, Three Men and a Baby, Cousins, Dad, Three Men and a Little Lady, Made in America, Getting Even With Dad, Pontiac Moon (also co-exec. prod.), Loch Ness, Mumford, Tom and Jerry, Homegrown.
TELEVISION: An Affectionate Look at Fatherhood (special). Series: Somerset, Cheers (2 Emmy Awards: 1990, 1993), Ink (also co-exec. prod.). Movies: The Women's Room, Once Upon a Spy, Our Family Business, Cowboy, Something About Amelia, When the Bough Breaks (also prod.), We Are the Children, Mercy Mission: The Rescue of Flight 771, On Promised Land, Fight For Justice, The Canterville Ghost, Gulliver's Travels, Thanks of a Grateful Nation. Guest: Laverne & Shirley, Magnum P.I., Taxi, Saturday Night Live.

DANTE, JOE
Director. b. Morristown, NJ. Managing editor for Film Bulletin before going to Hollywood to work in advertising, creating campaigns for many films. Became protege of Roger Corman, co-directing Hollywood Boulevard. Edited film Grand Theft Auto; co-wrote story for Rock 'n' Roll High School.
PICTURES: Director: Piranha (also co-editor), The Howling (also co-editor), Twilight Zone-The Movie (dir. segment), Gremlins, Explorers, Innerspace, Amazon Women on the Moon (co-dir.), The 'Burbs, Gremlins II (also cameo), Matinee. Actor: Cannonball, Slumber Party Massacre, Eating Raoul, Sleepwalkers, Beverly Hills Cop III, The Silence of the Hams.
TELEVISION: Amazing Stories, Eerie Indiana. Movie: Runaway Daughters.

D'ANTONI, PHILIP
Producer, Director. b. New York, NY, Feb. 19, 1929. e. Fordham U., business administration. Joined CBS in mailroom, advanced into prod., sales development, prog. analysis, mkt. rsrch. Became indep. radio-TV repr. in 1954 for two years; then joined Mutual Broadcasting as sales manager; later, exec. v.p. Resigned in 1962 to form own prod. co. Made theatrical film debut with Bullitt as prod.; directing debut with The Seven Ups. Heads D'Antoni Prods.
PICTURES: Producer: Bullitt, The French Connection (Acad. Award for Best Picture, 1971). Prod.-Dir.: The Seven Ups.
TELEVISION: Movin' On (series) Elizabeth Taylor in London, Sophia Loren in Rome, Melina Mercouri in Greece, Jack Jones Special, This Proud Land. Movies: Mr. Inside/Mr. Outside, The Connection, Strike Force, In Tandem, Rubber Gun Squad, Cabo.

DANZ, FREDRIC A.
Executive. b. Seattle, WA, Feb. 28, 1918. Is chmn. of Sterling Recreation Organization Co., Seattle. Member, Foundation of M.P. Pioneers; v.p., Variety Club Intl.

DANZA, TONY
Actor, Producer. b. Brooklyn, NY, April 21, 1951. e. U. of Dubuque, IA on a wrestling scholarship. After grad. professional boxer before tested for role in TV pilot (Fast Lane Blues) which he won. Back to New York and fighting until called to coast to appear as Tony Banta in Taxi series. On L.A. & NY Stage: Wrong Turn at Lungfish.
PICTURES: Hollywood Knights, Going Ape, Cannonball Run II, She's Out of Control, Mob Justice, Angels in the Outfield, The Jerky Boys (co-exec. prod. only), Noah.
TELEVISION: Series: Taxi, Who's the Boss, Baby Talk (voice), The Mighty Jungle (voice), George (co-exec. prod. only), Hudson Street (also co-exec. prod.), The Tony Danza Show (also prod.). Movies: Murder Can Hurt You!, Doing Life (also exec. prod.), Single Bars Single Women, Freedom Fighter (also co-exec. prod.), The Whereabouts of Jenny (also co-exec. prod.), Dead and Alive (also co-exec. prod.), Deadly Whispers, Garbage Picking Field Goal Kicking etc., 12 Angry Men, The Girl Gets Moe, A Brooklyn State of Mind.

D'ARBANVILLE-QUINN, PATTI
Actress. b. New York, NY, 1951. Grew up in Greenwich Village. Landed first job as baby in Ivory Soap commercials. In early teens worked as disc jockey where discovered by Andy Warhol and cast in small role in film Flesh. Moved to Paris at 15 where she became successful model and was featured in book *Scavullo on Beauty*. Made film debut in Gerard Brach's 1969 film La Maison. Fluent in French, worked in French films until 1973 when moved to Los Angeles. Won Dramalogue Award for John Patrick Shanley's Italian-American Reconciliation (L.A., 1987).
PICTURES: La Maison, La Saigne, The Crazy American Girl, Rancho DeLuxe, Bilitis, Big Wednesday, The Main Event, Time After Time, The Fifth Floor, Hog Wild, Modern Problems, Contract: Kill, The Boys Next Door, Real Genius, Call Me, Fresh Horses, Wired.
TELEVISION: *Movies*: Crossing the Mob, Blind Spot. *Mini-Series*: Once an Eagle, New York Undercover. *Guest*: Crime Story, R.E.L.A.X., Tough Cookies, Charlie's Angels, Barnaby Jones, Miami Vice, Murder She Wrote.

DARBY, KIM
Actress. r.n. Deborah Zerby. b. Hollywood, CA, July 8, 1948. e. Swanson's Ranch Sch., Van Nuys H.S. Studied at the Desilu Workshop in Hollywood. Professional debut on the Mr. Novak TV series; screen debut as extra in Bye Bye Birdie.
PICTURES: Bus Riley's Back in Town, The Restless Ones, True Grit, Generation, Norwood, The Strawberry Statement, The Grissom Gang, The One and Only, Better Off Dead, Teen Wolf Too, Halloween: The Curse of Michael Myers.
TELEVISION: *Movies*: The Karate Killers, Ironside (pilot), The People, Streets of San Francisco (pilot), Don't Be Afraid of the Dark, Story of Pretty Boy Floyd, This Was the West That Was, Flatbed Annie & Sweetiepie: Lady Truckers, Enola Gay, Embassy. *Mini-Series*: Rich Man Poor Man, The Last Convertible. *Guest*: Eleventh Hour, Gunsmoke. *Special*: Flesh and Blood.

DARK, JOHN
Producer. Pres. of J.D.Y.T. Producciones S.L., Coin Film City.
PICTURES: Light Up the Sky, Wind of Change, Loss of Innocence (Greengage Summer), The 7th Dawn, Casino Royale, Half a Sixpence, Bachelor of Arts, There's a Girl in My Soup, From Beyond the Grave, Madhouse, Land That Time Forgot, At the Earth's Core, The People That Time Forgot, Warlords of Atlantis, Arabian Adventure, Slayground, Shirley Valentine, Stepping Out.

DARREN, JAMES
Actor. b. Philadelphia, PA, June 8, 1936. e. Thomas Jefferson h.s., South Philadelphia h.s. Studied acting with Stella Adler, NYC.
PICTURES: Rumble on the Docks (debut, 1956), The Brothers Rico, The Tijuana Story, Operation Mad Ball, Gunman's Walk, Gidget, The Gene Krupa Story, Because They're Young, All the Young Men, Let No Man Write My Epitaph, Guns of Navarone, Gidget Goes Hawaiian, Diamond Head, Gidget Goes to Rome, For Those Who Think Young, The Lively Set, Venus in Furs, The Boss' Son.
TELEVISION: *Series*: The Time Tunnel, T.J. Hooker. *Guest*: Police Story, Hawaii Five-0, Vega$, Baa Baa Blacksheep, One Day at a Time. *Movies*: City Beneath the Sea, Police Story, The Lives of Jenny Dolan, Turnover Smith, Scruples. *Episode Director*: T.J. Hooker, The A Team, Stingray, Werewolf, Hardball, Hunter, Tequila and Bonetti, Raven, Silk Stalkings, Walker: Texas Ranger, Renegade, Nowhere Man, Beverly Hills 90210, Savannah, Melrose Place..

DARRIEUX, DANIELLE
Actress. b. Bordeaux, France, May 1, 1917. e. Lycee LaTour, Conservatoire de Musique.
THEATER: Coco, The Ambassador (B'way).
PICTURES: Le Bal (debut, 1932), La Crise Est Finis, Mayerling, Tarass Boulba, Port Arthur, Un Mauvais Garcon, Club de Femmes, Abus de Confiance, Mademoiselle ma Mere, The Rage of Paris, Katia, Retour a l'Aube, Battlement de Coeur, Premier Rendezvous, Caprices, Adieu Cherie, Au Petit Bonheur, Bethsabee, Ruy Blas, Jean de la Lune, Occupe-toi d'Amelie, La Ronde, Rich Young and Pretty, Five Fingers, Le Plaisir, La Verite sur Bebe Donge, Adorable Creatures, Le Bon Dieu sans Confession, The Earrings of Madame De, Le Rouge et le Noir, Bonnes a Tuer, Napoleon, Alexander the Great, A Friend of the Family, Loss of Innocence (Greengage Summer), Les Lions sont Laches, Les Bras de lat Nuit, Bluebeard (Landru), Patate, Le Coup de Grace, L'Or du Duc, Le Dimanche de la Vie, The Young Girls of Rochefort, La Maison de Campagne, Scene of the Crime, A Few Days With me.

DARTNALL, GARY
Executive. b. Whitchurch, England, May 9, 1937. e. Kings Col., Taunton. Overseas div., Associate British Pathe. European rep., 1958-60; Middle & Far East rep., Lion Intl. Films; U.S. rep., 1962; pres. Lion Intl. 1963; U.S. rep., Alliance Intl. Films Distributors Ltd., and London Indept. Prods. Ltd.; pres. Alliance Intl. Films Corp. and Dartnall Films Ltd., 1966; mng. dir., Overseas div. Walter Reade Org., 1969; pres. EMI Film Distribs., 1971; vice chmn. EMI TV Programs Inc.; pres. EMI Videograms Inc., 1979; pres. VHO Programs Inc. & VHD Disc Mfg. Co, 1980; chmn. Thorn EMI Cinemas; CEO, Thorn EMI Screen Entertainment Ltd. 1987; acquired Southbrook Intl. TV and formed Palladium Inc., chmn. & CEO.

DASSIN, JULES
Director, Writer, Actor. b. Middletown, CT, Dec. 18, 1911. Was married to late actress Melina Mercouri. Actor on dramatic stage several years; radio writer. Joined MGM, 1940, as dir. short subjects; later dir. features.
PICTURES: *Director*: Nazi Agent, Affairs of Martha, Reunion in France, Young Ideas, The Canterville Ghost, A Letter for Evie, Two Smart People, Brute Force, The Naked City, Thieves' Highway, Night and the City, Rififi (also co-s.p., actor), He Who Must Die (also co-s.p.), Where the Hot Wind Blows (also co-s.p.), Never on Sunday (also actor, prod., s.p.), Phaedra (also prod., co-s.p., actor), Topkapi (also prod.), 10:30 p.m. Summer (also prod., co-s.p.), Survival (also co-prod.), Uptight (also prod., co-s.p.), Promise at Dawn (also actor, prod., s.p.), The Rehearsal, A Dream of Passion (also s.p., prod.), Circle of Two.
PLAYS: Ilya Darling, Medicine Show, Magdalena, Joy to the World, Isle of Children, Two's Company, Heartbreak House, Threepenny Opera, Sweet Bird of Youth, A Month in the Country, Who's Afraid of Virginia Woolf?, The Road to Mecca, Death of a Salesman.

DAVENPORT, NIGEL
Actor. b. Cambridge, England, May 23, 1928. e. Trinity Coll., Oxford. Began acting after stint in British military at 18 years. First 10 years of professional career in theatre. Majority of screen work in British films in 1960s and 70s.
PICTURES: Look Back in Anger (debut, 1959), Desert Mice, Peeping Tom, The Entertainer, Lunch Hour, In the Cool of the Day, Operation Snatch, Return to Sender, Ladies Who Do, The Third Secret, Sands of the Kalahari, A High Wind in Jamaica, Where the Spies Are, Life at the Top, A Man for All Seasons, Sebastian, The Strange Affair, Play Dirty, Sinful Davey, The Virgin Soldiers, The Royal Hunt of the Sun, The Mind of Mr. Soames, The Last Valley, No Blade of Grass, Villain, Mary Queen of Scots, L'Attentat, Living Free, Charley-One-Eye, Phase IV, La Regenta, Stand Up Virgin Soldiers, The Island of Dr. Moreau, Zulu Dawn, The Omega Connection, Nighthawks, Chariots of Fire, Greystoke: The Legend of Tarzan Lord of the Apes, Caravaggio, Without a Clue, The Circus Trap.
TELEVISION: A Christmas Carol, Dracula, The Picture of Dorian Gray, The Ordeal of Dr. Mudd, Masada, The Upper Crust.

DAVIAU, ALLEN
Cinematographer. b. New Orleans, LA, June 14, 1942. Started as still photographer and stage lighting designer. Received Gold Clio Award for Tackle (Levi's 501).
PICTURES: Harry Tracy, E.T.: The Extra-Terrestrial (Acad. Award nom.), Twilight Zone: The Movie (co-photog.), Indiana Jones and the Temple of Doom (Calif. unit), The Falcon and the Snowman, The Color Purple (Acad. Award nom.), Harry and the Hendersons, Empire of the Sun (Acad. Award nom.; BAFTA & ASC Awards), Avalon (Acad. Award nom.), Defending Your Life, Bugsy (Acad. Award nom.; ASC Award), Fearless, Congo.
TELEVISION: *Movies*: Streets of L.A., Rage, Legs. *Specials*: The Boy Who Drank Too Much. *Series*: Amazing Stories (pilot).

DAVID, KEITH
Actor. b. New York, NY, June 4, 1954. e. Juilliard.
THEATER: *NY*: The Pirates of Penzance, A Midsummer Night's Dream, Waiting for Godot, Miss Waters to You, La Boheme, Coriolanus, Titus Andronicus, A Map of the World, The Haggadah, Alec Wilder: Clues to a Life, Boesman & Lena, Jelly's Last Jam, Hedda Gabler, Seven Guitars.
PICTURES: The Thing, Platoon, Hot Pursuit, Braddock: Missing in Action III, Off Limits, Stars and Bars, Bird, They Live, Road House, Always, Men at Work, Marked for Death, Final Analysis, Article 99, Reality Bites, The Puppet Masters, The Quick and the Dead, Clockers, Dead Presidents, Johns, Dead Cold (prod.), Marked Man (prod.), Daddy's Girl (prod.), The Dentist (prod.), The Nurse (prod.), The Stranger In The House (prod.), Voodoo (exec. prod.), Serial Killer (prod./dir.), Flipping, Larger than Life, Eye for an Eye, Johns, Hercules (voice), Fallout (voice), Executive Target, Volcano, Armageddon, There's Something About Mary.
TELEVISION: *Movies*: Ladykillers, Murder in Black and White, There Are No Children Here, Vanishing Point, Murder She Wrote: South by Southwest, Don King: Only in America, The Tiger Woods Story. *Series*: Spawn. *Mini-Series*: Roots: The Next Generations. *Special*: Hallelujah. *Guest*: The Equalizer, A Man Called Hawk, New York Undercover.

DAVID, PIERRE

Executive, Producer. b. Montreal, Canada, May 17, 1944. e. U. of Montreal. Joined radio station CJMS 1966 as pub. rel. & spec. events dir., 1969, while running Mutual Broadcasting Network of Canada's live entertainment div., created new film dist. co. Mutual Films. 1972 added prod. unit and as prod. or exec. prod., prod. and dist. 19 French language. Canadian films. With filmmaker Roger Corman est. Mutual Pictures of Canada, Ltd to dist. films in English Canada; 1978 teamed Mutual Films with Victor Solnicki and Claude Heroux to prod. English language films. Pioneered 3-picture concept for Canadian m.p. investors. Moved to L.A. 1983 where became pres., Film Packages Intl. where prod. exec. on Platoon. Then joined Larry Thompson Org. as partner involved in dev. and/or prod. of m.p., Jan., 1987, named chmn. of bd. and chief exec. officer, Image Org., Inc. intl. dist. co. formed by David and Rene Malo. Also pres. Lance Entertainment, prod. co.
PICTURES: *Prod.*: The Brood, Hog Wild, Scanners, Dirty Tricks, Gas, The Funny Farm, Visiting Hours, Videodrome, Going Berserk, Of Unknown Origin, Covergirl, Breaking All the Rules, For Those I Loved, Blind-Fear (co-prod.), The Perfect Bride, Hot Pursuit, The Perfect Weapon, Bounty Tracker, Distant Cousins, Deep Cover, Marital Outlaw, Stalked, Open Fire, The Force, The Secretary, Scanner Cop 2, The Wrong Woman. *Exec. Prod.*: Quiet Cool, Scanners II: The New Order, Desire and Hell at Sunset Motel, Martial Law, Scanners III, Dolly Dearest, Mission of Justice, Deadbolt, Internal Affairs, Twin Sisters, Pin, The Neighbor, The Paperboy. *Prod.-Dir.*: Scanner Cop.

DAVIDOVICH, LOLITA

Actress. b. Ontario, Canada, 1961. Also acted under the name Lolita David.
PICTURES: Class, Adventures in Babysitting, The Big Town, Blaze, The Object of Beauty, JFK, The Inner Circle, Raising Cain, Leap of Faith, Boiling Point, Younger and Younger, Cobb, For Better or Worse, Now and Then, Jungle 2 Jungle, Touch, Gods and Monsters, Mystery Alaska.
TELEVISION: *Movies*: Two Fathers' Justice, Prison Stories: Women on the Inside (Parole Board), Keep the Change, Indictment: The McMartin Trial, McMartin Trial, Dead Silence.

DAVIDSON, JOHN

Actor, Singer. b. Pittsburgh, PA, Dec. 13, 1941. e. Denison U. In numerous school stage prods. before coming to N.Y. in 1964 to co-star with Bert Lahr in B'way show, Foxy. Signed as regular on The Entertainers with Carol Burnett.
PICTURES: The Happiest Millionaire, The One and Only Genuine Original Family Band, The Concorde—Airport '79, The Squeeze, Edward Scissorhands.
TELEVISION: *Special*: The Fantasticks. *Guest*: The FBI, The Interns, Owen Marshall, The Tonight Show, (also frequent guest host). *Series*: The Entertainers, Kraft Summer Music Hall, The John Davidson Show (1969), The Girl With Something Extra, The John Davidson Show (1976), The John Davidson Talk Show (1980), That's Incredible, New Hollywood Squares, Time Machine (game show), Incredible Sunday, The $100,000 Pyramid. *Movies*: Coffee Tea or Me?, Shell Game, Roger & Harry: The Mitera Target, Dallas Cowboys Cheerleaders II.

DAVIDSON, MARTIN

Director, Writer. b. New York, NY, Nov. 7, 1939.
PICTURES: The Lords of Flatbush, Almost Summer, Hero at Large, Eddie and the Cruisers, Heart of Dixie (also exec. prod.), Hard Promises.
TELEVISION: *Series*: Our Family Honor, Call to Glory, Law and Order, My Life and Times, Picket Fences, Chicago Hope. *Movies*: Long Gone, A Murderous Affair: The Carolyn Warmus Story, Follow the River.

DAVIDTZ, EMBETH

Actress. b. Trenton, New Jersey, 1966.
PICTURES: Sweet Murder, Mutator, Schindler's List, Army of Darkness, Murder in the First, Feast of July, Matilda, Fallen, The Gingerbread Man.
TELEVISION: A Private Life, 'Till Death Us Do Part, Deadly Matrimony, The Garden of Redemption.

DAVIES, JOHN HOWARD

Producer, Director. b. London, England, March 9, 1939. e. Haileybory, I.S.C. and Grenoble Univ. Former child actor played leading roles in Oliver Twist, The Rocking Horse Winner, Tom Brown's Schooldays.
TELEVISION: *Prod./Dir.*: Monty Python's Flying Circus, Steptoe and Son, Fawlty Towers, The Good Life, The Goodies, The Other One, No Job for a Lady, Mr. Bean.

DAVIS, ANDREW

Director. b. Chicago, IL. e. Univ. of IL. Former journalist and photographer before landing job as asst. cameraman on 1969 film Medium Cool. Was dir. of photog. on several TV commercials and documentaries.
PICTURES: Lepke (dir. of photog.), Stony Island (dir., prod., co-s.p.), Over the Edge (dir. of photog.), Angel (dir. of photog.), Beat Street (co-s.p.). *Director*: The Final Terror, Code of Silence, Above the Law (also co-prod., co-story), The Package, Under Siege, The Fugitive, Steal Big Steal Little (also co-prod., co-s.p., co-story), Chain Reaction, Volcano (prod. only).

DAVIS, CARL

Composer. b. New York, NY, Oct. 28, 1936. e. Queens Coll., Bard Coll. and New England Coll. of Music. Worked as pianist with Robert Shaw Chorale and wrote music for revue Diversions (1958) and Twists (London), Moved to England 1961 writing incidental music for Joan Littlewood's Theatre Workshop Co., Royal Shakespeare Co. and National Theatre. Other theater music includes Jonathan Miller's Tempest, Forty Years On, and the musical The Vackees. Best known for composing new scores for silent classics (Napoleon, The Crowd, Greed, Intolerance, etc.) for screenings at which he conducts and for Thames TV The Silents series. Concert work: Paul McCartney's Liverpool Oratorio.
PICTURES: The Bofors Gun, Up Pompeii, Rentadick, Man Friday, The Sailor's Return, Birth of the Beatles, The French Lieutenant's Woman, Praying Mantis, The Aerodrome, Champions, Weather in the Streets, George Stevens: A Filmmaker's Journey, King David, The Rainbow, Scandal, Girl in a Swing, Fragments of Isabella, Frankenstein Unbound, Diary of a Madman, Raft of the Medusa, The Voyage, Liberation, Widow's Peak, Anne Frank Remembered.
TELEVISION: That Was the Week That Was, Hollywood, the Pioneers, World at War, Mayor of Casterbridge, Lorna Doone, Unknown Chaplin, Buster Keaton—A Hard Act to Follow, Treasure Island, The Snow Goose, Our Mutual Friend, Naked Civil Servant, Silas Marner, The Accountant, Secret Life of Ian Fleming, Why Lockerbie?, Buried Mirro, A Christmas Carol, Royal Collection, Hotel du Lac, Black Velvet Gown, Lie Down With Lions, The Return of the Native. *Mini-series*: Pride & Prejudice, Oliver's Travels, Cinema Europe: The Other Hollywood, Real Women.

DAVIS, COLIN

Executive. Held executive positions in Canada in adv., bdcst., & p.r. with several companies, including Procter & Gamble, Young & Rubicam. Joined MCA TV Canada as v.p. & gen. mgr., 1977. Named dir. intl. sls., 1978. In 1986 appt. pres., MCA TV Int'l.

DAVIS, FRANK I.

Executive. b. Poolesville, MD, Feb. 18, 1919. e. U. of Maryland, A.B., 1941; Harvard Law School, LL.B., 1948. Law firm, Donovan, Leisure, Newton, Lombard and Irvine, 1948-50; v.p., gen. counsel, Vanguard Films, 1951; v.p., gen. counsel, Selznick Releasing Org., 1951-53; pres., The Selznick Company, 1953-55; v.p., Famous Artists Corp., 1956-62; v.p. George Stevens Productions Inc., 1962-65; exec. prod., The Greatest Story Ever Told; v.p. in charge of m.p. affairs, Seven Arts, 1966; exec. in chg. talent and exec. asst. to v.p. in chg. prod., MGM, 1967; dir. m.p. business affairs, MGM, 1970; v.p., business affairs, MGM, 1972; sr. v.p., motion picture business affairs, MGM/UA, 1983, exec. v.p., business affairs, MGM Pictures, 1986-88; sr. exec. v.p., business affairs, Pathe Entertainment Inc., 1989-90; sr. exec. v.p. of bus. affairs, MGM, 1990.

DAVIS, GEENA

Actress. r.n. Virginia Elizabeth Davis. b. Wareham, MA, Jan. 21, 1957. e. Boston U. Acted with Mount Washington Repertory Theatre Co., NH. Was NY model before winning role Tootsie, 1982.
PICTURES: Tootsie (debut, 1982), Fletch, Transylvania 6-5000, The Fly, Beetlejuice, The Accidental Tourist (Acad. Award, supporting actress, 1988), Earth Girls Are Easy, Quick Change, Thelma & Louise, A League of Their Own, Hero, Angie, Speechless (also prod.), Cutthroat Island, The Long Kiss Goodnight.
TELEVISION: *Series*: Buffalo Bill (also wrote one episode), Sara. *Movie*: Secret Weapons. *Guest*: Family Ties, Riptide, Remington Steele, Saturday Night Live, Trying Times (The Hit List).

DAVIS, GEORGE W.

Art Director. b. Kokomo, IN, April 17, 1914. e. U. of Southern California.
PICTURES: The Ghost and Mrs. Muir, House of Stranger, All About Eve, David and Bathsheba, The Robe (Acad. Award, 1953), Love Is a Many-Splendored Thing, Funny Face, The Diary of Anne Frank (Acad. Award, 1959), The Time Machine, Butterfield 8, Cimarron, Period of Adjustment, Mutiny on the Bounty, The Wonderful World of the Brothers Grimm, Twilight of Honor, How the West Was Won, The Americanization of Emily, The Unsinkable Molly Brown, A Patch of Blue, Mr. Buddwing, Point Blank, The Shoes of the Fisherman, The Gypsy Moths, Brewster McCloud, Wild Rovers, etc

DAVIS, JOHN

Executive, Producer. e. Bowdoin Col., Harvard Bus. Sch. Served as v.p. at 20th Century Fox before forming Davis Entertainment.
PICTURES: Predator, Three O'Clock High, License to Drive, Little Monsters, The Last of the Finest, Shattered, Storyville, The Firm, The Thing Called Love, Fortress, Gunmen, Grumpy Old Men, Richie Rich, The Hunted, Waterworld, The Grass Harp, Courage Under Fire, Daylight, Out to Sea.
TELEVISION: *Movies*: Tears and Laughter: The Joan and Melissa Rivers Story, The Last Outlaw, This Can't Be Love.

DAVIS, JUDY
Actress. b. Perth, Australia, 1955. m. actor Colin Friels. Left convent school as teenager to become a singer in a rock band. Studied at West Australia Inst. of Technology and National Inst. of Dramatic Art, Sydney. Worked with theatre companies in Adelaide and Sydney and at Royal Court Theatre, London. Los Angeles stage debut Hapgood.
PICTURES: High Rolling (debut, 1977), My Brilliant Career, Hoodwink, Heatwave, Winter of Our Dreams, The Final Option, A Passage to India (Acad. Award nom.), Kangaroo, High Tide, Georgia, Alice, Impromtu, Barton Fink, Naked Lunch, Where Angels Fear to Tread, Husbands and Wives (Acad. Award nom.), On My Own (Australian Film Inst. Award), The Ref, The New Age, Absolute Power, Deconstructing Harry, Blood and Wine, Celebrity.
TELEVISION: Rocket to the Moon, A Woman Called Golda, One Against the Wind, Serving in Silence: The Margarethe Cammermeyer Story (Emmy Award, 1995), The Echo of Thunder.

DAVIS, LUTHER.
Writer, Producer. b. New York, NY, Aug. 29, 1921. e. Yale, B.A.
THEATER: Writer. Kiss Them for Me, Kismet (Tony Award), Timbuktu! (also prod.), Grand Hotel (Tony nom.). Co-Prod.: Eden Court, Not About Heroes.
PICTURES: Writer. The Hucksters, B.F.'s Daughter, Black Hand, A Lion Is in the Streets, The Gift of Love, Holiday for Lovers, The Wonders of Aladdin, Lady in a Cage (also prod.), Across 110th Street.
TELEVISION: Writer/Prod.: Kraft Suspense Theatre and many pilots for series (Run for Your Life, The Silent Force, Eastside, Westside, etc.). Specials: Arsenic and Old Lace, The People Trap (prod.). Movies: Daughter of the Mind, The Old Man Who Cried Wolf.

DAVIS, MAC
Singer, Songwriter, Actor. b. Lubbock, TX, Jan 21, 1942. e. Emory U., Georgia State Coll. Employed as ditch digger, service station attendant, laborer, probation officer and record company salesman before gaining fame as entertainer-singer in 1969. Recording artist and composer of many popular songs. On B'way 1992 in The Will Rogers Follies.
PICTURES: North Dallas Forty, Cheaper to Keep Her, The Sting II.
TELEVISION: Series: The Mac Davis Show. Movies: Brothers-In-Law, What Price Victory?, Blackmail.

DAVIS, MARTIN S.
Executive. b. New York, NY, Feb. 5, 1927. U.S. Army, 1943-46; joined Samuel Goldwyn Prod., Inc., 1946; with pub. dept. Allied Artists, 1955; Paramount Pictures, 1958. as dir. sales and mktg. then dir. adv., pub. expl. 1960; v.p. in chg. of home office and asst. to pres.; 1963; exec. v.p. 1966; exec. comm. & bd. of dir. Member of Bd., Gulf & Western, 1967, named sr. v.p. 1969; elected exec. v.p. and mem. exec. comm. Gulf & Western, 1974; elected CEO and chmn. of bd. and chmn. exec. comm. 1983; CEO & mng. partner Wellspring Associates, LLC, 1995. Member: bd. trustees, Montefiore Medical Center, Thomas Jefferson Memorial Foundation; Chmn,. NYC Chap, Natl. Multiple Sclerosis Society; bd. of trustees Carnegie Hall. Co-chmn. of Corp. Advisory Committee of the Barbara Bush Foundation for Family Literacy. Bd. of dirs., National Amusements, Inc.

DAVIS, OSSIE
Actor, Writer, Director. b. Cogdell, GA, Dec. 18, 1917. e. Howard U., Washington, DC. m. actress Ruby Dee. Studied acting in N.Y. with Rose McLendon Players, made to Broadway debut in 1946 in Jeb. For years thereafter was one of best-known black actors on Bway stage in: Anna Lucasta, Jamaica, The Green Pastures, Wisteria Tree, A Raisin in the Sun, I'm Not Rappaport. Wrote and starred in Purlie Victorious, repeating role for film version. Directed and appeared with Ms. Dee in her musical Take It From the Top. Co-hosted Ossie Davis and Ruby Dee Story Hour on radio (3 years). Published plays: Purlie Victorious, Langston, Escape to Freedom, Curtain Call, Mr. Aldredge, Sir.
PICTURES: Actor. No Way Out, Fourteen Hours, The Joe Louis Story, Gone Are the Days, The Cardinal, Shock Treatment, The Hill, Man Called Adam, The Scalphunters, Sam Whiskey, Slaves, Let's Do It Again, Hot Stuff, House of God, Harry and Son, Avenging Angel, School Daze, Do the Right Thing, Joe Versus the Volcano, Jungle Fever, Gladiator, Malcolm X (voice), Grumpy Old Men, The Client, I'm Not Rappaport, Get on the Bus. Director: Cotton Comes to Harlem (also co-s.p.), Black Girl, Gordon's War, Countdown at Kusini (also actor, prod.), Get on the Bus, Doctor Dolittle.
TELEVISION: Writer. East Side/West Side, The Eleventh Hour. Guest: Name of the Game, Night Gallery, Bonanza, etc. Specials: Martin Luther King: The Dream and the Drum, With Ossie and Ruby (also co-prod.), Today is Ours (writer, dir.). Movies: All God's Children, Don't Look Back, Roots: The Next Generations, King, Teacher Teacher, The Ernest Green Story, Ray Alexander: A Taste for Justice, Ray Alexander: A Menu for Murder, The Android Affair. Series: B.L. Stryker, Evening Shade, John Grisham's The Client. Mini-Series: Queen, Stephen King's The Stand, Miss Evers' Boys.

DAVIS, PETER
Author, Filmmaker. b. Santa Monica, CA, Jan. 2, 1937. e. Harvard Coll., 1955-57. Parents were screenwriter Frank Davis, and novelist-screenwriter Tess Slesinger. Writer-interviewer, Sextant Prods., FDR Series, 1964-65. Host: The Comers, PBS 1964-65. Author: Hometown (1982), Where Is Nicaragua? (1987), If You Came This Way (1995), articles for Esquire, NY Times Mag., The Nation, NY Woman, TV Guide.
PICTURES: Hearts and Minds (prod., dir.; Acad. Award, best documentary, 1975; Prix Sadoul, 1974), Jack (writer/prod.).
TELEVISION: Writer-prod.: Hunger in America (assoc. prod., WGA Award, 1968), The Heritage of Slavery, The Battle of East St. Louis, (Saturday Review Award, 1970; 2 Emmy nom.), The Selling of the Pentagon (WGA, Emmy, Peabody, George Polk, Ohio State, Sat. Review Awards, 1971), 60 Minutes (segment prod.), Middletown (series, prod., Dupont Citation, Emmy noms. 1983), The Best Hotel on Skidrow (ACE Award noms., 1992).

DAVIS, PRESTON A.
Executive. b. Norfolk, VA. Served in US Army. 1976, joined ABC as engineer in Washington DC, later becoming sprv. of Electronic News Gathering; 1979, became tech. mngr. of ENG; 1983, named tech. mngr. then manager of ENG for southeast region, Atlanta; 1986, promoted to gen. mngr. ENG Operations, New York; 1988, named v.p. TV Operations, Broadcast Operations & Engineering, East Coast; 1993, named pres. of Broadcast Operations and Engineering for ABC Television Network Group.

DAVIS, ROGER H.
Executive. Chairman, Motion Picture and Television Fund.

DAVIS, SAMMI
Actress. b. Kidderminster, Worcestershire, England, June 21, 1964. Convent-educated before taking drama course. Performed in stage prods. with local drama society in Midlands, then Birmingham Rep. and Big Brum Theatre Co. Plays include The Home Front, The Apple Club, Nina Days, Databased, Choosey Susie. London stage debut: A Collier's Friday.
PICTURES: Mona Lisa, Lionheart, Hope and Glory, A Prayer for the Dying, Consuming Passions, The Lair of the White Worm, The Rainbow, The Horseplayer, Shadow of China, Four Rooms, Death Do Us Part, Assignment Berlin.
TELEVISION: Auf Wiedersehn Pet, The Day After the Fair, Pack of Lies, Chernobyl: The Final Warning, The Perfect Bride, Indecency, Spring Awakening. Series: Homefront.

DAVISON, BRUCE
Actor. b. Philadelphia, PA, June 28, 1946. e. Pennsylvania State U., NYU. debut, Lincoln Center Repertory prod. of Tiger at the Gates, 1967.
THEATER: NY: King Lear (Lincoln Center), The Elephant Man, Richard III (NY Shakespeare Fest.), The Glass Menagerie, The Cocktail Hour. Regional: Streamers (LA Critics Award), The Caine Mutiny Court-Martial, The Normal Heart, To Kill a Mockingbird, A Life in the Theatre, The Front Page, Downside, Breaking the Silence.
PICTURES: Last Summer (debut, 1969), The Strawberry Statement, Willard, Been Down So Long It Looks Like Up To Me, The Jerusalem File, Ulzana's Raid, Mame, Mother Jugs and Speed, Grand Jury, Short Eyes, Brass Target, French Quarter, High Risk, A Texas Legend, Lies, Crimes of Passion, Spies Like Us, The Ladies Club, The Misfit Brigade, Longtime Companion (NY Film Critics, Natl. Society of Film Critics, & Golden Globe Awards, 1990; Acad. Award nom.), Steel and Lace, Short Cuts, An Ambush of Ghosts, Six Degrees of Separation, Far From Home: The Adventures of Yellow Dog, The Cure, The Baby-sitters Club, Homage, Grace of My Heart, The Crucible.
TELEVISION: Movies: Owen Marshall: Counsellor at Law (A Pattern of Morality), The Affair, The Last Survivors, Deadman's Curve, Summer of My German Soldier, Mind Over Murder, The Gathering, Tomorrow's Child, Ghost Dancing, Poor Little Rich Girl: The Barbara Hutton Story, Lady in a Corner, Stolen: One Husband, Live! From Death Row, Desperate Choices: To Save My Child, A Mother's Revenge, Someone Else's Child, Down Out and Dangerous, The Color of Justice, Hidden in Silence. Specials: Taming of the Shrew, The Lathe of Heaven, The Wave. Guest: Medical Center, Marcus Welby, Love American Style, Police Story, Lou Grant, Murder She Wrote, Alfred Hitchcock Presents (1985), Amazing Stories. Series: Hunter, Harry and the Hendersons.

DAVISON, DALE
Executive. b. North Hollywood, CA, March 21, 1955. e. U.C.L.A., B.A., 1978. Entered the motion picture industry in 1973 working for Pacific Theatres. Employed with Great Western Theatres 1974-77 as manager, dir. of concessions, and asst. vice pres. Partner with Great Western Theatres, 1978-1984. Founder and CEO, CinemaCal Enterprises, Inc., 1985-present.

127

DAVISON, JON

Producer. b. Haddonfield, NJ, July 21, 1949. e. NYU Film School. 1972, joined New World Pictures as natl. dir. of publ./adv.; 1972, named in charge of prod.; 1980, became indep. prod.
PICTURES: Hollywood Boulevard, Grand Theft Auto, Piranha, Airplane!, White Dog, Twilight Zone—The Movie (episode), Top Secret! Robocop, Robocop 2, Trapped in Paradise, Starship Troopers.

DAWBER, PAM

Actress, Singer. b. Detroit, MI, Oct. 18, 1954. m. actor Mark Harmon. e. Farmington H.S., Oakland Community Coll. Worked as model and did commercials. First professional performance as singer in Sweet Adeleine at Goodspeed Opera House, East Haddam, CT.
THEATER: Regional: My Fair Lady, The Pirates of Penzance, The Music Man, She Loves Me, Love Letters.
PICTURES: A Wedding, Stay Tuned.
TELEVISION: Series: Mork and Mindy, My Sister Sam. Movies: The Girl the Gold Watch and Everything, Remembrance of Love, Through Naked Eyes, Last of the Great Survivors, This Wife For Hire, Wild Horses, Quiet Victory: The Charlie Wedemeyer Story, Do You Know the Muffin Man, The Face of Fear, The Man With 3 Wives, Web of Deception, Trail of Tears. Specials: Kennedy Center Honors, Salute to Andy Gibb, Night of the 100 Stars, 3rd Annual TV Guide Special.

DAY, DORIS

Singer, Actress. r.n. Doris Kappelhoff. b. Cincinnati, OH, April 3, 1924. e. dancing, singing. Toured as dancer; radio and band singer; screen debut in Romance on the High Seas, 1948. Voted one of Top Ten Money-Making Stars in Motion Picture Herald-Fame poll, 1951-52. Best female vocalist. M. P. Daily radio poll, 1952.
PICTURES: Romance on the High Seas (debut, 1948), My Dream is Yours, It's a Great Feeling, Young Man With a Horn, Tea for Two, Storm Warning, West Point Story, Lullaby of Broadway, On Moonlight Bay, I'll See You in My Dreams, Starlift, The Winning Team, April in Paris, By the Light of the Silvery Moon, Calamity Jane, Lucky Me, Young at Heart, Love Me or Leave Me, The Man Who Knew Too Much, Julie, The Pajama Game, Teacher's Pet, Tunnel of Love, It Happened to Jane, Pillow Talk (Acad. Award nom.), Please Don't Eat the Daisies, Midnight Lace, Lover Come Back, That Touch of Mink, Bill Rose's Jumbo, The Thrill of It All, Move Over Darling, Send Me No Flowers, Do Not Disturb, Glass Bottom Boat, Caprice, The Ballad of Josie, Where Were You When the Lights Went Out?, With Six You Get Eggroll.
TELEVISION: Series: The Doris Day Show (1968-73), Doris Day's Best Friends (educational cable show; 1985-86).

DAY, LARAINE

Actress. r.n. Laraine Johnson. b. Roosevelt, UT, Oct. 13, 1920. e. Long Beach Polytechic H.S., Paramount Studio School. In school dramatics; with Players Guild, Long Beach, Calif.; toured in church prod. Conflict; Professionally on stage in Lost Horizon, The Women, Time of the Cuckoo, Angel Street.
PICTURES: Stella Dallas (debut, 1937 as Laraine Johnson), Scandal Sheet, Border G-Man, Young Dr. Kildare (and subsequent series), And One Was Beautiful, My Son My Son, Foreign Correspondent, The Trial of Mary Dugan, The Bad Man, Unholy Partners, Fingers at the Window, Journey for Margaret, Mr. Lucky, The Story of Dr. Wassell, Bride by Mistake, Those Endearing Young Charms, Keep Your Powder Dry, The Locket, Tycoon, My Dear Secretary, I Married a Communist (Woman on Pier 13), Without Honor, The High and the Mighty, Toy Tiger, Three for Jamie Dawn, The Third Voice, Painted Desert, Sergeant Madden, Arizona Legion, Tarzan Finds A Son, I Take This Woman, Kathleen, Yank On the Burma Road.
TELEVISION: Appearances include Climax, Playhouse 90, Alfred Hitchcock, Wagon Train, Let Freedom Ring, Name of the Game, FBI, Sixth Sense, Medical Center, Murder on Flight 504 (movie), Fantasy Island, Love Boat, Lou Grant, Airwolf, Hotel, Murder She Wrote.

DAY, ROBERT

Director. b. England, Sept. 11, 1922. Started as cinematographer before turning to direction.
PICTURES: Director: The Green Man (debut, 1956), Stranger's Meeting, Grip of the Strangler (The Haunted Strangler), First Man Into Space, Bobbikins, Two-Way Stretch, Tarzan the Magnificent (also co-s.p.), The Rebel (Call Me Genius), Corridors of Blood, Operation Snatch, Tarzan's Three Challenges (also co-s.p.), She, Tarzan and the Valley of Gold, Tarzan and the Great River, Tarzan and the Jungle Boy (prod. only), The Man with Bogart's Face.
TELEVISION: Pilots include: Banion, Kodiak, Dan August, Sunshine, Switch, Logan's Run, Kingston, Dallas, Matlock. Movies include: Ritual of Evil, The House of Greenapple Road, In Broad Daylight, Having Babies, The Grass Is Always Greener Over the Septic Tank, Peter and Paul, Running Out, Scruples, Cook and Peary—The Race to the Pole, Hollywood Wives, The Lady from Yesterday, Diary of a Perfect Murder, Celebration, Higher Ground, Walking Through the Fire.

DAY-LEWIS, DANIEL

Actor. b. London, England, April 29, 1957. Son of late C. Day-Lewis, poet laureate of Eng., and actress Jill Balcon. Grandson of late Sir Malcolm Balcon who prod. Hitchcock's Brit. films. e. Bristol Old Vic. Theatre School. First professional job at 12 as ruffian scratching cars with broken bottle in film, Sunday Bloody Sunday. Then acted with Bristol Old Vic and Royal Shakespeare Co.
THEATER: London: Dracula, Funny Peculiar, Troilus & Cressida, A Midsummer Night's Dream, Class Enemy, Edward II, Look Back in Anger, Another Country, Romeo and Juliet The Futurists Hamlet.
PICTURES: Gandhi, The Bounty, A Room With a View, My Beautiful Laundrette, The Unbearable Lightness of Being, Stars and Bars, Nanou, Ever Smile New Jersey, My Left Foot (Acad. Award, 1989; also BAFTA, NY Film Critics, L.A. Film Critics, Natl. Society of Film Critics Awards), The Last of the Mohicans, The Age of Innocence, In the Name of the Father, The Crucible, The Boxer.
TELEVISION: BBC Movies/Specials: Eddie Shoestring, Artemis 11, The Lost Traveller, The Sugar House, Beyond the Glass, Thenk You P.G. Woodhouse, Dangerous Corner, A Frost in May, How Many Miles to Babylon?, My Brother Jonathan, The Insurance Man, History of Hamlet (host).

DEAKINS, ROGER

Cinematographer. b. Devon, England, May 24, 1949. Accepted into National Film School in 1972. Working as professional filmmaker from 1975 directing and photographing documentary films including Around the World With Ridgeway, Zimbabwe, Eritrea—Behind the Lines, When the World Changed, Worlds Apart S.E. Nuba, Worlds Apart Rajgonds. Photographed first feature, Another Time Another Place in 1982.
PICTURES: 1984, The Innocent, Sid & Nancy, Shadey, Defense of the Realm, White Mischief, Personal Services, Stormy Monday, Pascali's Island, The Kitchen Toto, Mountains of the Moon, Air America, The Long Walk Home, Barton Fink, Homicide, Thunderheart, Passion Fish, The Secret Garden, The Hudsucker Proxy, The Shawshank Redemption (Acad. Award nom.; ASC Award), Dead Man Walking, Fargo, Courage Under Fire, Kundun, Martial Law, The Big Lebowski.

DEAN, EDDIE

Actor. r.n. Edgar Dean Glosup. b. Posey, TX, July 9, 1907. 1930-33 in radio throughout middle west; 1934 National Barn Dance, Station WLS; 1935 on CBS & NBC with same program. Featured male singer on TV KTLA Western Varieties 1944-55. Came to Hollywood in 1936; since then has starred in many westerns. Featured performer in western series for PRC in 1945. Voted one of the ten best money making Western Stars in Motion Picture Herald-Fame Poll 1936-47; recording artists, personal appearances, rodeos, fairs, etc.; 1966 v.p. Academy of Country & Western Music; 1967-68 on Bd. of Dir. of Academy of Western Music, Calif. Winner, Pioneer Award of Academy of Country Music, 1978. In 1983 named ACM v.p.; also v.p. in 1985. Recorded video cassette 1986, A Tribute to Eddie Dean. Recipient of two gold records in 1995 for co-writing of "Hillbilly Heaven"; 1997, Living Legend Award from the Country Music Organizations of America.

DEAN, JIMMY

Performer. b. Plainview, TX, Aug. 10, 1928. Joined armed forces, 1946-49; first appeared in various clubs in Wash., 1949; then appeared on Town and Country Jamboree; toured Caribbean and Europe with his troupe; appeared in Las Vegas. TNN/Music City News Country Music Awards, Song-writer of the Year Awards.
SONGS: Composer: Big Bad John, Little Black Book, I.O.U., To a Sleeping Beauty, PT-109, Dear Ivan.
PICTURES: Diamonds Are Forever, Big Bad John.
TELEVISION: Series: The Jimmy Dean Show (1957; 1963-66), Daniel Boone, J.J. Starbuck. Specials: Sunday Night at the Palladium (London), Celebrities Offstage. Movies: The Ballad of Andy Crocker, Rolling Man, The City.

DEAN, MORTON

Television Newsman. b. Fall River, MA, Aug. 22, 1935. e. Emerson Coll. News dir., N.Y. Herald Tribune Net, 1957; corr. WBZ, 1960, corr. WCBS-TV, 1964; anchor, WCBW-TV News, 1967; corr., CBS News, 1967; anchor, CBS Sunday Night News, 1975; anchor, Sunday edition CBS Evening News, 1976; co-anchor, Independent Network News, 1985.

DEARDEN, JAMES

Writer, Director, b. London, England, Sept. 14, 1949. Son of late British director Basil Dearden. e. New Coll., Oxford U. Entered film industry in 1967 as production runner. After editing commercials and documentaries, and working as asst. dir., wrote, prod. and dir. first short film, The Contraption (Silver Bear Award, 1978 Berlin Film Fest.). 1978, began dir. commercials and made short, Panic (Cert. of Merit, 1980 Chicago Film Fest.). 1979, made 45-min film Diversion, which became basis for Fatal Attraction (Gold Plaque, best short drama, 1980 Chicago Film Fest.).
PICTURES: Fatal Attraction (s.p.), Pascali's Island (dir., s.p.), A Kiss Before Dying (dir., s.p.), Rogue Trader (dir., s.p., prod.).
TELEVISION: The Cold Room (dir., writer, Special Jury Prize, dir., 1985 Fest. Intl. d'Avoriaz du Film Fantastique).

De BONT, JAN
Cinematographer, Director. b. Holland, Oct. 22, 1943.Trained at Amsterdam Film Acad. Recipient of Kodak Camera Award and Rembrandt Award.
PICTURES: *Cinematographer:* Turkish Delight, Keetje Tippel, Max Heuelaar, Soldier of Orange, Private Lessons (U.S. debut, 1981), Roar, I'm Dancing as Fast as I Can, Cujo, All the Right Moves, Bad Manners, The Fourth Man, Mischief, The Jewel of the Nile, Flesh + Blood, The Clan of the Cave Bear, Ruthless People, Who's That Girl, Leonard Part 6, Die Hard, Bert Rigby You're a Fool, Black Rain, The Hunt for Red October, Flatliners, Shining Through, Basic Instinct, Lethal Weapon 3. *Director:* Speed (debut, 1994), Twister, Speed 2: Cruise Control (also s.p., story). *Producer:* S.L.C. Punk!, Zero Hour, Like a Hole in the Head, Cosm.
TELEVISION (Photography): *Movie:* The Ray Mancini Story. *Episode:* Tales From the Crypt (Split Personality).

De BROCA, PHILIPPE
Director, Writer. b. Paris, France, March 15, 1933. e. Paris Technical School of Photography and Cinematography.
PICTURES: *Director/Writer:* Les Jeux de l'Amour (The Love Game), The Joker, The Five Day Lovers, Seven Capitol Sins (dir. segment only), Cartouche (also actor), Les Veinards (segment), That Man From Rio, Male Companion (Un Monsieur de Compagnie), Les Tribulations d'un Chinois en Chine (Up to His Ears), King of Hearts (also prod.), Devil by the Tail, Give Her the Moon, Chere Louise, Le Magnifique, Dear Inspector (also s.p.), The Skirt Chaser, Someone's Stolen the Thigh of Jupiter, The African, Louisiana (TV in U.S.), The Gypsy, Chouans! (dir., co-s.p.), Scheherazade.

De CAMP, ROSEMARY
Actress. b. Prescott AZ, Nov. 14, 1913.
PICTURES: Cheers for Miss Bishop (debut, 1941), Hold Back the Dawn, Jungle Book, Yankee Doodle Dandy, Eyes in the Night, THe Commandos Strike at Dawn, Smith of Minnesota, Without Men, This is the Army, The Merry Monahans, Bowery to Broadway, Blood on the Sun, Practically Yours, Rhapsody in Blue, Pride of the Marines, Danger Signal, Too Young to Know, From This Day Forward, Nora Prentiss, Night Unto Night, The Life of Riley, Look for the Silver Lining, Story of Seabiscuit, The Big Hangover, Night Into Morning, On Moonlight Bay, Scandal Sheet, Treasure of Lost Canyon, By the Light of the Silvery Moon, Main Street to Broadway, So This Is Love, Many Rivers to Cross, Strategic Air Command, 13 Ghosts, Saturday the 14th.
TELEVISION: *Series:* The Life of Reilly (with Jackie Gleason), The Bob Cummings Show, That Girl. *Guest:* Death Valley Days, Partridge Family, Love American Style, Police Story, Rockford Files, Days of Our Lives, Misadventures of Sheriff Lobo, Love Boat, B.J. & the Bear. *Mini-Series:* Blind Ambition. *Movie:* The Time Machine.

De CAPRIO, AL
Producer, Director. e. Brooklyn Tech., NYU. Started as radio engineer, cameraman, tech. dir., prod. & dir. CBS; dir. series episodes of Sgt. Bilko, Car 54 Where Are You?, Musical specials for ABC, CBS, NBC; v.p. exec. prod. dir., MPO Videotronics, Pres. World Wide Videotape; retired.

DECHERD, ROBERT WILLIAM
Newspaper & Broadcasting Executive. b. April 9, 1951. e. Harvard U., AB cum laude, 1973. Exec. v.p., Dallas Morning News, 1980-83. Exec. v.p. A.H. Belo Corp., 1981-84; pres., COO, 1985-86; chmn., CEO, 1987-94; chmn., pres., CEO & bd. dirs., 1994-. Pres.: Dallas Symphony Assn., 1979-80; Dallas Symphony Found., 1984-86; St. Mark's Sch., Tex., 1988-91. Chmn.: Dallas Parks Found., 1985-87; Dallas Soc. Profl. Journalists, 1978. Trustee:
Tomas Rivera Ctr., 1992-. Incorporator, pres.. Freedom of Info. Found., 1978. Mem.: Tex., Soc. of Archs (hon.); Newspaper assn. Am. (exec. bd., 1992-). Recipient of: Disting. Svc. award Dallas Jaycees, 1985; Am. Newspaper Exec. of Yr. award Adweek mag., 1985; citation of honor Am. Inst. Arch., 1988; Seymour Preston award Nat. Assn. Ind. Schs. Coun. Advancement and Support Edn., 1989; James Madison award Freedom of Info. Found. Tex., 1989; Henry Cohn Humanitarian award Anti-Defamation League, 1992.

De CARLO, YVONNE
Actress. b. Vancouver, B.C., Sept. 1, 1922. e. June Roper School of Dance, Britsh Columbia; Fanchon & Marco, Hollywood. Specialty dancing at Florentine Gardens, Earl Carroll's; motion picture debut in This Gun for Hire, 1942. One-woman club act and 7-person club act. Autobiography, Yvonne (1987).
THEATER: B'way: Follies.
PICTURES: This Gun for Hire (debut, 1942), Harvard Here I Come, Youth on Parade, Road to Morocco, Let's Face It, The Crystal Ball, Salute for Three, For Whom the Bell Tolls, True to Life, So Proudly We Hail, The Deerslayer, Practically Yours, Salome Where She Danced, Frontier Gal, Brute Force, Song of Scheherazade, Slave Girl, Black Bart, Casbah, River Lady,

Criss Cross, Gal Who Took the West, Calamity Jane and Sam Bass, Buccaneer's Girl, The Desert Hawk, Tomahawk, Hotel Sahara, Silver City, Scarlet Angel, San Francisco Story, Hurricane Smith, Sombrero, Sea Devils, Fort Algiers, Captain's Paradise, Border River, Passion, Tonight's the Night, Shotgun, Magic Fire, Flame of the Islands, Ten Commandments, Raw Edge, Death of a Scoundrel, Band of Angels, Timbuktu, McLintock!, A Global Affair, Law of the Lawless, Munster Go Home, Hostile Guns, The Power, Arizona Bushwhackers, The Seven Minutes, Play Dead, It Seemed Like a Good Idea at the Time, Won Ton Ton the Dog Who Saved Hollywood, Blazing Stewardesses, Satan's Cheerleaders, Nocturna, Silent Scream, Guyana Cult of the Damned, The Man With Bogart's Face, Liar's Moon, American Gothic, Cellar Dweller, Mirror Mirror, Oscar, The Naked Truth.
TELEVISION: *Series:* The Munsters. *Movies:* The Girl on the Late Late Show, The Mark of Zorro, The Munsters' Revenge, A Masterpiece of Murder. *Guest:* Bonanza, Man From U.N.C.L.E., Murder She Wrote, Hollywood Sign (special), Johnny Carson, Merv Griffin, Steve Allen, David Frost, Perry Como, Tales from the Crypt, Dream On.

De CORDOVA, FREDERICK
Director. b. New York, NY, Oct. 27, 1910. e. Northwestern U., B.S. 1931. Gen. stage dir. Shubert enterprises, N.Y., 1938-41; same for Alfred Bloomingdale Prods., N.Y., and prod. Louisville (Ky.) Amphitheatre 1942-43. Dir., program planning, Screen Gems, 1964. Author: Johnny Came Lately, 1988.
PICTURES: *Dialogue Director:* San Antonio, Janie, Between Two Worlds. *Director:* Too Young to Know (debut, 1945), Her Kind of Man, That Way with Women, Love and Learn, Always Together, Wallflower, For the Love of Mary, The Countess of Monte Cristo, Illegal Entry, The Gal Who Took the West, Buccaneer's Girl, Peggy, The Desert Hawk, Bedtime for Bonzo, Katie Did It, Little Egypt, Finders Keepers, Here Come the Nelsons, Yankee Buccaneer, Bonzo Goes to College, Column South, I'll Take Sweden, Frankie and Johnny.
TELEVISION: *Series* (prod., dir.): The Burns and Allen Show, December Bride, Mr. Adams and Eve, George Gobel Show, The Jack Benny Program, The Smothers Bros. Show, My Three Sons (dir.), Tonight Show (prod.; 6 Emmy Awards).

DeCUIR, JR., JOHN F.
Art Director, Production Designer. b. Burbank, CA, Aug. 4, 1941. e. U. of Southern California, bachelor of architecture, 1965. Son of John F. De Cuir, Sr. 1966-68, U.S. Coast Guard (holds commission with rank of Lt. Commander, USCGR). 1968-72, project designer, Walt Disney World, Walt Disney Prods. 1972-74, dir. of design, Six Flags Corp. 1974-9, project designer, EPCOT, Walt Disney Prods. 1980-86, pres., John F. De Cuir, Jr. Design Consultants, Inc.; 1987-pres., Cinematix Inc.
PICTURES: *Illustrator:* Cleopatra, The Honey Pot. Design Concepts: The Agony and the Ecstasy. *Art Director:* Raise the Titanic, Ghosbusters. *Special Effects Consultant:* Dead Men Don't Wear Plaid, Monsignor. *Producer:* Jazz Club, The Baltimore Clipper, The Building Puzzle. Prod. *Designer:* Fright Night, Top Gun, Apt Pupil, Elvira Mistress of the Dark, Turner & Hooch, True Identity, Sleepwalkers, Sister Act 2: Back in the Habit.
TELEVISION: *Art Director:* Frank Sinatra Special—Old Blue Eyes Is Back, Annual Academy Awards Presentation 1971, Double Agent. *Production Design:* Double Switch, Earth * Star Voyager.

DEE, RUBY
Actress. b. Cleveland, OH, Oct. 27, 1924. r.n. Ruby Ann Wallace. e. Hunter Coll. m. actor-dir.-writer Ossie Davis. Worked as apprentice at Amer. Negro Theatre, 1941-44, studied at Actor's Workshop. Stage appearances include Jeb, Anna Lucasta, The World of Sholom Aleichem, A Raisin in the Sun, Purlie Victorious, Wedding Band, Boseman and Lena, Hamlet, Checkmates.
PICTURES: No Way Out, The Jackie Robinson Story, The Tall Target, Go Man Go!, Edge of the City, St. Louis Blues, Take a Giant Step, Virgin Island, A Raisin in the Sun, Gone Are the Days, The Balcony, The Incident, Up Tight, Buck and the Preacher, Black Girl, Countdown at Kusini, Cat People, Do the Right Thing, Love at Large, Jungle Fever, Cop and a Half, Just Cause, A Simple Wish.
TELEVISION: *Movies:* Deadlock, The Sheriff, It's Good to Be Alive, I Know Why the Caged Bird Sings, All God's Children, The Atlanta Child Murders, Go Tell it on the Mountain, Windmills of the Gods, The Court-Martial of Jackie Robinson, Decoration Day (Emmy Award, 1991), The Ernest Green Story. *Specials:* Actor's Choice, Seven Times Monday, Go Down Moses, Twin-Bit Gardens, Wedding Band, To Be Young Gifted and Black, Long Day's Journey into Night, Edgar Allan Poe: Terror of the Soul (narrator). *Mini-Series:* Roots: The Next Generation, Gore Vidal's Lincoln, The Stand. *Series:* Peyton Place, With Ossie and Ruby, Middle Ages.

DEE, SANDRA
Actress. r.n. Alexandra Zuck. b. Bayonne, NJ, April 23, 1942. Modeled, Harry Conover and Huntington Hartford Agencies, N.Y., 1954-56; signed long term exclusive contract, U-I, 1957. PICTURES: Until They Sail (debut, 1957), The Reluctant Debutante, The Restless Years, Stranger in My Arms, Imitation of Life, Gidget, The Wild and the Innocent, A Summer Place, The Snow Queen (voice), Portrait in Black, Romanoff and Juliet, Come September, Tammy Tell Me True, If a Man Answers, Tammy and the Doctor, Take Her She's Mine, I'd Rather Be Rich, That Funny Feeling, A Man Could Get Killed, Doctor You've Got to Be Kidding!, Rosie, The Dunwich Horror.
TELEVISION: Movies: The Daughters of Joshua Cabe, Houston We've Got a Problem, The Manhunter, Fantasy Island (pilot). Guest: Steve Allen Show, Night Gallery, Love American Style, Police Woman.

DEELEY, MICHAEL
Producer. b. London, England, August 6, 1932. Ent. m.p. ind. 1951 and TV, 1967, as alt. dir. Harlech Television Ltd. Film editor, 1951-58. MCA-TV 1958-61, later with Woodfall as prod. and assoc. prod. Assoc. prod. The Knack, The White Bus, Ride of the Valkyrie. Great Western Investments Ltd.; 1972; Great Western Festivals Ltd.; 1973, mng. dir. British Lion Films Ltd. 1975, purchased BLF, Ltd. Appt. man. dir. EMI Films Ltd., 1977; pres., EMI Films, 1978, Member Film Industry Interim Action Committee, 1977-82; Deputy Chairman, British Screen Advisory Council, 1985. Appt. Chief Executive Officer, Consolidated Television Production & Distribution Inc., 1984. PICTURES: Prod.: One Way Pendulum, Robbery, The Italian Job, Long Days Dying (exec. prod.), Where's Jack, Sleep Is Lovely, Murphy's War, The Great Western Express, Conduct Unbecoming, The Man Who Fell to Earth, Convoy, The Deer Hunter (Acad. Award for Best Picture, 1978), Blade Runner. TELEVISION: Movie: A Gathering of Old Men (exec. prod.).

DE FINA, BARBARA
Producer. Started as prod. asst. before working at various jobs for such filmmakers as Woody Allen and Sidney Lumet. Became assoc. prod. of development for King/Hitzig Prods., working on Happy Birthday Gemini, Cattle Annie and Little Britches. Was unit mgr./assoc. prod. on Prince of the City. First worked with Martin Scorsese on The King of Comedy as unit mgr. Produced music video Bad.
PICTURES: Producer: The Color of Money, The Last Temptation of Christ, New York Stories (segment: Life Lessons), GoodFellas (exec. prod.), The Grifters (exec. prod.), Cape Fear, Mad Dog and Glory, The Age of Innocence, Casino, Kicked in the Head, Kundun.

DEGENERES, ELLEN
Actress. b. New Orleans, LA, Jan 26, 1958.
PICTURES: Wisecracks, Coneheads, Mr. Wrong, Goodbye Lover.
TELEVISION: Series: Open House, Laurie Hill, Ellen (also prod.). Guest: Roseanne.

De HAVILLAND, OLIVIA
Actress b. Tokyo, Japan, July 1, 1916. e. California schools and Notre Dame Convent, Belmont. Acting debut, Max Reinhardt's stage prod., A Midsummer Night's Dream; going to Warner Bros. for film debut in m.p. version, 1935. Recipient: The Snake Pit (NY Film Critics & Look Awards), The Heiress (NY Film Critics, Women's Natl. Press Club & Look Awards). Autobiography: Every Frenchman Has One (1962).
THEATER: A Midsummer Night's Dream (Hollywood Bowl). B'way: Romeo and Juliet (1951), A Gift of Time. U.S. Tour: Candida (1951-52).
PICTURES: A Midsummer Night's Dream (debut, 1935), Alibi Ike, The Irish in Us, Captain Blood, Anthony Adverse, The Charge of the Light Brigade, Call It a Day, It's Love I'm After, The Great Garrick, Gold is Where You Find It, The Adventures of Robin Hood, Four's a Crowd, Hard to Get, Wings of the Navy, Dodge City, The Private Lives of Elizabeth and Essex, Gone With the Wind, Raffles, My Love Came Back, Santa Fe Trail, Strawberry Blonde, Hold Back the Dawn, They Died With Their Boots On, The Male Animal, In This Our Life, Princess O'Rourke, Thank Your Lucky Stars, Government Girl, The Well Groomed Bride, To Each His Own (Acad. Award, 1946), Devotion, Dark Mirror, The Snake Pit, The Heiress (Acad. Award, 1949), My Cousin Rachel, That Lady, Not as a Stranger, Ambassador's Daughter, Proud Rebel, Libel, Light in the Piazza, Lady in a Cage, Hush ... Hush Sweet Charlotte, The Adventurers, Pope Joan, Airport '77, The Swarm, The Fifth Musketeer.
TELEVISION: Special: Noon Wine (Stage 67). Movies & Miniseries: The Screaming Woman, Roots: The Next Generations, Murder is Easy, Charles & Diana: A Royal Romance, North & South Book II, Anastasia, The Woman He Loved.

DELANY, DANA
Actress. b. New York, NY, March 13, 1956. e. Phillips Acad., Wesleyan U.
THEATER: B'way: Translations, A Life. Off-B'way: Blood Moon.
PICTURES: Almost You, Where the River Runs Black, Masquerade, Moon Over Parador, Patty Hearst, Housesitter, Light Sleeper, Batman: Mask of the Phantasm (voice), Tombstone, Exit to Eden, Live Nude Girls, Fly Away Home, Wide Awake.
TELEVISION: Series: Love of Life, As the World Turns, Sweet Surrender, China Beach (2 Emmy Awards: 1989, 1992). Guest: Moonlighting, Magnum P.I. Movies: A Promise to Keep, Donato and Daughter, The Enemy Within, Choices of the Heart: The Margaret Sanger Story, For Hope, The Patron St. of Liars. Mini-Series: Wild Palms, True Women. Specials: Texan, Fallen Angels (Good Housekeeping), The Rescuers.

De LAURENTIIS, DINO
Producer, Executive. b. Torre Annunziata, Italy, Aug. 8, 1919. Took part in Rome Experimental Film Center; dir., prod. chmn. of the bd. and CEO, De Laurentiis Entertainment Group Inc.; founded in 1984 the DEG Film Studios in Wilmington, NC. Resigned 1988. Started Dino De Laurentiis Communications, 1990.
PICTURES: L'amore Canta, Il Bandito, La Figlia del Capitano, Riso Amaro, La Lupa, Anna, Ulysses, Mambo, La Strada, Gold of Naples, War and Peace, Nights of Cabiria, The Tempest, Great War, Five Branded Women, Everybody Go Home, Under Ten Flags, The Best of Enemies, The Unfaithfuls, Barabbas, The Bible, Operation Paradise, The Witches, The Stranger, Diabolik, Anzio, Barbarella, Waterloo, The Valachi Papers, The Stone Killer, Serpico, Death Wish, Mandingo, Three Days of the Condor, Drum, Face to Face, Buffalo Bill and the Indians, King Kong, The Shootist, Orca, White Buffalo, The Serpent's Egg, King of the Gypsies, The Brink's Job, Hurricane, Flash Gordon, Halloween II, Ragtime, Conan the Barbarian, Fighting Back, Amityville II: The Possession, Halloween III: Season of the Witch, The Dead Zone, Amityville 3-D, Firestarter, The Bounty, Conan the Destroyer, Stephen King's Cat's Eye, Red Sonja, Year of the Dragon, Marie, Stephen King's Silver Bullet, Raw Deal, Maximum Overdrive, Tai-Pan, Blue Velvet, The Bedroom Window, Crimes of the Heart, King Kong Lives, Million Dollar Mystery, Weeds, Desperate Hours, Kuffs, Once Upon a Crime, Body of Evidence, Army of Darkness, Unforgettable, Assassins, Dragonheart.
TELEVISION: Movie: Solomon and Sheba.

De LAURENTIIS, RAFFAELLA
Producer. Daughter of Dino De Laurentiis. Began career as prod. asst. on father's film Hurricane. Independent prod..
PICTURES: Beyond the Reef, Conan the Barbarian, Conan the Destroyer, Dune, Tai-Pan, Prancer, Dragon: The Bruce Lee Story, Trading Mom, Dragonheart, Backdraft (exec. prod.), Daylight (exec. prod.), Kull the Conqueror.
TELEVISION: Series: Vanishing Son.

De La VARRE, ANDRE, JR.
Producer, Director. b. Vienna, Austria, Oct. 26, 1934. Prod. Grand Tour travelogues; prod. of promotion films for KLM, Swissair, tourist offices, recent productions: Bicentennial films for state of Virginia, city of Charleston, NY state; winner, Atlanta Film Festival, Sunset Travel Film Festival; Burton Holmes Travelogue subjects; Corporate Incentive Videos, V-P-R Educational Films; prod., director, lecturer, narrator.

DEL BELSO, RICHARD
Marketing Executive. b. Albany, NY, Aug. 9, 1939. e. Fordham U, 1961, NYU, 1965. Began career in adv./research dept. at Benton & Bowles Advertising, NY. Served as research dept. group head for Kenyon and Eckhart; group head for Grudin/Appell/Haley Research Co. (now known as A/H/F/ Marketing Research, Inc.). Two years as assoc. dir. of mktg., research for Grey Advertising (N.Y.). Joined MCA/Universal in 1976 as assoc. dir., mktg. research. In 1980 named v.p. & dir. of mktg. research for Warner Bros; became worldwide v.p. of mktg. research, 1984; named sr. v.p. worldwide theatrical film market research, 1990.

De LELLIS, BOB
Executive. President, 20th Century Fox Home Entertainment.

De LINE, DONALD
Executive. President, Touchstone Pictures.

DELON, ALAIN
Actor. b. Sceaux, France, Nov. 8, 1935. Discovered by Yves Allegret. Served in French Navy as a Marine. Worked as cafe waiter, heavy-load carrier.
PICTURES: When a Woman Gets Involved (debut, 1957), Be Beautiful and Keep Quiet, 3 Murderesses, Christine, Le Chemin Des Ecoliers, Plein Soleil (Purple Noon), Quelle Joie de Vivre!, Rocco and His Brothers, Famous Loves, Eclipse, The Leopard, The Devil and the 10 Commandments, Any Number Can Win, The Black Tulip, The Felines (Joy House), L'Insoumis (also prod., co-s.p.), The Yellow Rolls Royce, Once a Thief, Lost Command, Is Paris Burning?, Texas Across the River, The Adventurers, Spirits of the Dead, Samurai,

Diabolically Yours, Girl on a Motorcycle, Goodbye Friend, The Swimming Pool, Jeff (also prod.), The Sicilian Clan, Borsalino, The Red Circle, Madly (also prod.), Doucement Les Basses, Red Sun, The Widow Cuderc, Assassination of Trotsky, Dirty Money, The Teacher, Scorpio, Shock Treatment, The Burning Barn, Big Guns, Two Men in the City, La Race des Seigneurs, Les Seins de Glace, Borsalino & Company (also prod.), Zorro, Police Story, The Gypsy, Mr. Klein (also prod.), Like a Boomerang (also prod., s.p.), The Gang (also exec. prod.), Armaggedon, L'Homme Presse, Mort d'un Pourri (also s.p.), Attention Les Enfants Regardent, The Concorde - Airport 79, The Doctor, Teheran 43, Three Men to Destroy (also prod.), For a Cop's Honor (also dir, s.p., prod.), The Shock (also s.p.), The Cache (also prod., dir., s.p.), Swann in Love, Our Story, Military Police (also exec. prod., s.p.), The Passage (also prod.), Let Sleeping Cops Lie (also prod., co-s.p.), New Wave, Dancing Machine, The Return of Casanova, Un Crime... L'Ours en Peluche.

DELPY, JULIE
Actress. b. Paris, France, 1970. Made acting debut as teenager for dir. Jean-Luc Godard.
PICTURES: Detective (debut, 1985) Bad Blood, King Lear, Beatrice, The Dark Night, Europa Europa, Voyager, The Three Musketeers, White, Killing Zoe, Younger and Younger, Before Sunrise, The Treat, LA Without a Map
TELEVISION: Movies: The Passion of Ayn Rand.

DEL ROSSI, PAUL R.
Executive. b. Winchester, MA, Oct. 19, 1942. e. Harvard Coll, 1964; Harvard Business Sch., 1967. Sr. v.p., The Boston Co., 1977-1980; sr. consultant, Arthur D. Little, Inc.; presently pres. & CEO, General Cinema Theatres.

DELORA, JENNIFER
Actress, Writer, Producer. b. Kingston, NY, March 2, 1962. e. Amer. Acad. Dramatic Arts, 1982. Antioch U., BA, 1993. CA Coast U., MA, 1995; PhD, 1997. Artistic Dir., LA Bridges Theatre Co. of the Deaf, 1993-present. Top industry technical advisor for projects involving deafness, 1995-present. Member AFTRA, SAG, ATAS, Amer. Bd. of Disability Analysts, Nat'l Assoc. of the Deaf, Deaf Artists of Amer., Deaf Entertainment Guild, Amer. Psych. Assoc.
PICTURES: Actor: Bad Girls' Dormitory, Young Nurses in Love, Robot Holocaust, New York's Finest, Deranged, Sexpot, Cleo/Leo, Frankenhooker, Deadly Manor, Bedroom Eyes II, Suburban Commando. Tech. Advisor: 413 Hope Street, His Bodyguard, Copland, Tango & Flush.
TELEVISION: Movies: Breaking Through, Blue Rodeo. Tech. Advisor: 7th Heaven.

DeLUCA, MICHAEL
Executive, Writer. b. Brooklyn, Aug., 1965. Left NYU to take intern job at New Line Cinema; became story editor before becoming production exec. in 1989. 1993 named pres. of production of New Line.
PICTURES: Writer: Freddy's Dead: The Final Nightmare, In the Mouth of Madness, Judge Dredd (story), B.A.P.S. (exec. prod.).

De LUISE, DOM
Comedian, Actor. b. Brooklyn, NY, Aug. 1, 1933. e. Tufts Coll. m. actress Carol Arthur. Sons: Peter, Michael, David. Spent two seasons with Cleveland Playhouse. Launched TV career on The Garry Moore Show with character, Dominick the Great, a bumbling magician.
THEATER: Little Mary Sunshine, Another Evening With Harry Stoones, All in Love, Half-Past Wednesday, Too Much Johnson, The Student Gypsy, Last of the Red Hot Lovers, Here's Love, Little Shop of Horrors, Die Fledermus (NY Met. Opera: 2 seasons), Peter and the Wolf.
PICTURES: Fail Safe (debut, 1964), Diary of a Bachelor, The Glass Bottom Boat, The Busy Body, What's So Bad About Feeling Good?, Norwood, The Twelve Chairs, Who Is Harry Kellerman...?, Every Little Crook and Nanny, Blazing Saddles, The Adventure of Sherlock Holmes' Smarter Brother, Silent Movie, The World's Greatest Lover, The End, The Cheap Detective, Sextette, The Muppet Movie, Hot Stuff (also dir.), The Last Married Couple in America, Fatso, Wholly Moses, Smokey and the Bandit II, History of the World Part I, The Cannonball Run, The Best Little Whorehouse in Texas, The Secret of NIMH (voice), Cannonball Run II, Johnny Dangerously, Haunted Honeymoon, An American Tail (voice), Spaceballs (voice), A Taxi Driver in New York, Going Bananas, Oliver & Company (voice), All Dogs Go To Heaven (voice), Loose Cannons, Driving Me Crazy, Fievel Goes West (voice), Munchie (voice), The Skateboard Kid (voice), Happily Ever After (voice), Robin Hood: Men in Tights, The Silence of the Hams, A Troll in Central Park (voice), All Dogs Go to Heaven 2 (voice).
TELEVISION: Series: The Entertainers, The Dean Martin Summer Show, Dom DeLuise Show, The Barrum-Bump Show, The Glenn Campbell Goodtime Hour, The Dean Martin Show, Lotsa Luck, Dom DeLuise Show (synd.), The New Candid Camera, Fievel's American Tails (voice). Movies: Evil Roy Slade, Only With Married Men, Happy (also exec. prod.), Don't Drink the Water, The Tin Soldier. Guest: The Munsters, Please Don't Eat the Daisies, Ghost and Mrs. Muir, Medical Center, Amazing Stories, Easy Street, B.L. Stryker, Burke's Law, Murphy Brown, Beverly Hills 90210.

del VALLE, JOHN
Publicist. b. San Francisco, CA, March 23, 1904. e. U. of California. Adv., edit. staff various newspapers including asst. drama ed. S.F. Call-Bulletin, L.A. Mirror; adv.-publicity dir. San Francisco Fox Theatre 1933-36; publicist, Paramount Studio, 1936-42; dir. pub., adv. Arnold Prod. 1946; Chaplin Studios, 1947; Nat Holt Prod., 1948-52; Editor, TV Family mag., N.Y., 1952-53; adv. pub. dir. Century Films, 1954; pub. rel. Academy M.P. Arts & Sciences, 1965; publicist, various U.A. indep. film prod., 1955-56; unit publicist, Paramount, 1956; TC-F 1957-62, Para., 1962-63; Universal 1964-65; Mirisch Corp.-UA Filming, Hawaii, 1965; pub. rel. and editor, Atomics Int'l div. North American Rockwell, 1966-71; present, freelance writer. NY Times Op. Ed. (1985), Gourmet Mag. (1989), others.

DEMME, JONATHAN
Director, Writer, Producer. b. Rockville Centre, NY, Feb. 22, 1944. e. U. of Florida. First job in industry as usher; was film critic for college paper, The Florida Alligator and the Coral Gable Times. Did publicity work for United Artists, Avco Embassy; sold films for Pathe Contemporary Films; wrote for trade paper, Film Daily, 1966-68. Moved to England in 1969; musical co-ordinator on Irving Allen's EyeWitness in 1970. In 1972 co-prod and co-wrote first film, Angels Hard As They Come. Appeared in film Into the Night.
PICTURES: Hot Box (prod., co-s.p.), Black Mama White Mama (story). Director: Caged Heat (also s.p.), Crazy Mama (also s.p.), Fighting Mad (also s.p.), Citizen's Band (Handle With Care), Last Embrace, Melvin and Howard, Swing Shift, Stop Making Sense, Something Wild (also co-prod.), Swimming to Cambodia, Married to the Mob, Miami Blues (prod. only), The Silence of the Lambs (Acad. Award, 1991), Cousin Bobby, Philadelphia (also co-prod.), Devil in a Blue Dress (exec. prod. only).
TELEVISION: Specials: Who Am I This Time?, Accumation With Talking plus Water Motor, Survival Guides, A Family Tree (Trying Times series, PBS), Haiti: Dreams of Democracy. Movie: Women & Men 2 (A Domestic Dilemma; prod. only).

DE MORNAY, REBECCA
Actress. b. Santa Rosa, CA, Aug. 29, 1962. Spent childhood in Europe, graduating from high school in Austria. Returned to America, enrolling at Lee Strasberg's Los Angeles Institute; apprenticed at Zoetrope Studios.
THEATER: Born Yesterday (Pasadena Playhouse), Marat/Sade (Williamstown Fest.).
PICTURES: Risky Business, Testament, The Slugger's Wife, Runaway Train, The Trip to Bountiful, Beauty and the Beast, And God Created Woman, Feds, Dealers, Backdraft, The Hand That Rocks the Cradle, Guilty as Sin, The Three Musketeers, Never Talk to Strangers, The Winner, Thick As Thieves, High Life.
TELEVISION: Movies: The Murders in the Rue Morgue, By Dawn's Early Light, An Inconvenient Woman, Blindside, Getting Out, The Shining, The Con.

DEMPSEY, PATRICK
Actor. b. Lewiston, ME, Jan. 13, 1966. e. St. Dominic Regional h.s. in Lewiston where he became State downhill skiing champion. Juggling, magic and puppetry led to performances before Elks clubs and community orgs. Cast by Maine Acting Co. in On Golden Pond. In 1983 acted in Torch Song Trilogy in San Francisco and toured in Brighton Beach Memoirs. NY Theatre debut, 1991 in The Subject Was Roses.
PICTURES: Heaven Help Us (debut, 1985), Meatballs III, Can't Buy Me Love, In the Mood, In a Shallow Grave, Some Girls, Loverboy, Coupe de Ville, Happy Together, Run, Mobsters, For Better and For Worse (R.S.V.P.), Face the Music, Bank Robber, With Honors, Outbreak, Hugo Pool, The Treat, There Is No Fish Food in Heaven, Me and Will, Denial.
TELEVISION: Movies: A Fighting Choice, JFK: Reckless Youth, Bloodknot. Series: Fast Times at Ridgemont High. Special: Merry Christmas Baby.

De MUNN, JEFFREY
Actor. b. Buffalo, NY, April 25, 1947. e. Union Col. Studied acting at Old Vic Theatre in Bristol, Eng.
THEATER: NY: Comedians, A Prayer for My Daughter, Modigliani, Augusta, Hands of Its Enemy, Chekhov Sketchbook, A Midsummer Night's Dream, Total Abandon, Country Girl, Bent, K-2, Sleight of Hand, Spoils of War, One Shoe Off, Hedda Gabler, Gunshy.
PICTURES: You Better Watch Out (Christmas Evil), The First Deadly Sin, Resurrection, Ragtime, I'm Dancing as Fast as I Can, Frances, Windy City, Enormous Changes at the Last Minute, Warning Sign, The Hitcher, The Blob, Betrayed, Blaze, Newsies, Eyes of an Angel, The Shawshank Redemption, Safe Passage, Killer, Phenomenon, Turbulence, Rocket Man, Harvest, The X-Files, Rocket Man, Harvest, Blackwood (X-Files).
TELEVISION: Movies: The Last Tenant, Sanctuary of Fear, King Crab, Word of Honor, I Married Wyatt Earp, The Face of Rage, Sessions, When She Says No, Windmills of the Gods, Lincoln, Doubletake, A Time to Live, Who Is Julia?, Young Harry Houdini, Price of Justice, Switch, Elysian Fields, The Haunted, Treacherous Crossing, Jonathan: The Boy Nobody Wanted, Barbarians at the Gate, Crash: The Fate of Flight 1502, Settle the Score, Under the Influence, Betrayal of Trust, Citizen X, Down Came a Blackbird, Hiroshima, Almost Golden: The Jessica Savitch Story, A Christmas Memory, Path to Paradise, Black Cat Run, Storm of the Century. Specials: Mourning Becomes Electra, Peacemaker (Triple Play II), Sensiblity and Sense, The Joy That Kills, Teacher, Pigeon Feathers, Many Mansions, Wild Jackasses, Ebbie. Mini-series: Night Sins, Liberty! The American Revolution.

DENCH, DAME JUDI
Actress. b. York, England, Dec. 9, 1934. Studied for stage at Central Sch. of Speech and Drama. Theatre debut Old Vic, 1957. Created a Dame in 1988 Honours List. Recent Theatre: Cymbeline, Juno and the Paycock, A Kind of Alaska, The Cherry Orchard, The Plough and the Stars, Importance of Being Earnest, Pack of Lies, Mr. and Mrs. Nobody, Antony and Cleopatra, The Sea, Coriolanus, The Gift of the Gorgon, The Seagull. Director: Much Ado About Nothing, Look Back in Anger, Boys from Syracuse, Romeo and Juliet, Absolute Hell, A Little Night Music.
PICTURES: The Third Secret (debut, 1964), He Who Rides a Tiger, A Study in Terror, Four in the Morning, A Midsummer Night's Dream (RSC Prod.), Luther, Dead Cert, Wetherby, A Room With a View, 84 Charing Cross Road, A Handful of Dust, Henry V, Jack and Sarah, Goldeneye, Mrs. Brown (BAFTA Award, Golden Globe Award, Chicago Film Crits. Award, Best Actress, 1997).
TELEVISION: Major Barbara, Pink String and Sealing Wax, Talking to a Stranger, The Funambulists, Age of Kings, Jackanory, Hilda Lessways, Luther, Neighbours, Parade's End, Marching Song, On Approval, Days to Come, Emilie, The Comedy of Errors (RSC Prod.), Macbeth (RSC Prod.), Langrishe Go Down, On Giant's Shoulders, Love in a Cold Climate, Village Wooing, A Fine Romance (series), The Cherry Orchard, Going Gently, Saigon—Year of the Cat, Ghosts, Behaving Badly, Torch, Can You Hear Me Thinking?, Absolute Hell, As Time Goes By (series).

DENEAU, SIDNEY, G.
Sales executive. Head film buyer Fabian Theatres; U.S. Army 1942-46; gen. mgr. Schine Theatres 1947; v.p., gen. sales mgr., Selznick Releasing Orgn., 1949; 1956; v.p. asst. gen. sls. mgr., Para. Film Dist., 1958; exec. v.p., Rugoff Theatres, 1964. Resigned, September, 1969 to engage in own theatre consultant business.

DENEUVE, CATHERINE
Actress. r.n. Catherine Dorleac. b. Paris, France, Oct. 22, 1943. Sister was the late Francoise Dorleac. Made screen debut as teen using adopting mother's maiden name.
PICTURES: Les Collegiennes (debut, 1956), Wild Roots of Love, L'homme a Femmes, The Doors Slam, La Parisiennes (segment: Sophie), Vice and Virtue, Satan Leads the Dance, Vacances Portugaises, Les Plus Belles Escroqueries du Monde, The Umbrellas of Cherbourg (Cannes Film Fest. Award, 1964), Male Hunt (La Chasse a l'Homme), Male Companion, La Costanza della Ragione, Repulsion, Le Chant du Monde, La Vie de Chateau (A Matter of Resistance), Who Wants to Sleep?, Les Creatures, The Young Girls of Rochefort, Belle de Jour (Venice Film Fest. Award, 1967), Benjamin, Manon 70, Mayerling, La Chamade (Heartbeat), The April Fools, Mississippi Mermaid, Don't Be Blue, Tristana, Donkey Skin, Henri Langolis, Liza, It Only Happens to Others, Dirty Money, Melampo, The Slightly Pregnant Man, Touche Pas a la Femme Blanche, La Grande Bourgeoise, Zig-Zag, La Femme aux Bottes Rouges, Hustle, Lovers Like Us, Act of Agression, The Beach Hut, Second Chance, March or Die, Ecoute voir, L'Argent des Autres, When I Was a Kid I Didn't Dare, Anima Persa, An Adventure for Two, Ils Sont Grandes ces Petits, Courage--Let's Run, The Last Metro, Je vous Aime, Choice of Arms, Hotel des Ameriques, Reporters, Daisy Chain, Le Choc, The African, The Hunger, Le Bon Plaisir, Fort Saganne, Love Songs, Let's Hope It's a Girl, Le Mauvaise Herbe, Scene of the Crime, Agent Trouble, A Strange Place to Meet (also prod.), Hotel Panique, The Man Who Loved Zoos, Frequency Murder, Helmut Newton: Frames From the Edge (doc.), The White Queen, Indochine (Acad. Award nom.), Ma Saison Preferee (My Favorite Season), The Chess Game, The Convent.

DENHAM, MAURICE
O.B.E., 1992: Actor. b. Beckenham, Kent, England, Dec. 23, 1909. e. Tonbridge Sch. Started theatrical career with repertory com. 1934. Served in W.W.II. Played in numerous plays, films & radio shows.
PICTURES: Blanche Fury, London Belongs To Me, It's Not Cricket, Traveller's Joy, Landfall, Spider and the Fly, No Highway in the Sky, The Net, Time Bomb, Street Corner (Both Sides of the Law), Million Pound Note (Man With a Million), Eight O'Clock Walk, Purple Plain, Simon and Laura, 23 Paces to Baker Street, Checkpoint, Carrington V.C. (Court Martial), Doctor at Sea, Night of the Demon, Man With a Dog, Barnacle Bill, The Captain's Table, Our Man in Havana, Sink the Bismark, Two-Way Stretch, Greengage Summer, Invasion, Quartette, The Mark, HMS Defiant, The Very Edge, Paranoiac, The Set Up, Penang, The King's Breakfast, Downfall, Hysteria, The Uncle, Operation Crossbow, Legend of Dick Turpin, The Alphabet Murders, The Night Callers, The Nanny, Those Magnificent Men in Their Flying Machines, Heroes of Telemark, After the Fox, The Torture Garden, The Long Duel, The Eliminator, Danger Route, Attack on the Iron Coast, The Best House in London, Negatives, The Midas Run, Some Girls Do, The Touch of Love, The Virgin and the Gypsy, Bloody Sunday, Countess Dracula, Nicholas and Alexandra, The Day of the Jackal, Luther, Shout at the Devil, Julia, The Recluse, From a Far Country, Mr. Love, The Chain, Monsignor Quixote, Murder on the Orient Express, 84 Charing Cross Road.

TELEVISION: Uncle Harry, Day of the Monkey, Miss Mabel, Angel Pavement, The Paraguayan Harp, The Wild Bird, Soldier Soldier, Changing Values, Maigret, The Assassins, Saturday Spectacular, Vanishing Act, A Chance in Life, Virtue, Somerset Maugham, Three of a Kind, Sapper, Pig in the Middle, Their Obedient Servants, Long Past Glory, Devil in The Wind, Any Other Business, The Retired Colourman, Sherlock Holmes (series), Blackmail, Knock on Any Door, Danger Man, Dr. Finley's Casebook, How to Get Rid of Your Husband, Talking to a Stranger, A Slight Ache, From Chekhov with Love, Home Sweet Honeycomb, St. Joan, Julius Caesar, Golden Days, Marshall Petain, The Lotus Eaters, Fall of Eagles, Carnforth Practice. The Unofficial Rose, Omnibus, Balzac, Loves Labour Lost, Angels, Huggy Bear, The Portrait, The Crumbles Murder, A Chink In The Wall, Porridge, For God's Sake, Bosch, Marie Curie, Upchat Line, Secret Army, My Son, My Son, Edward and Mrs. Simpson, Gate of Eden, Potting Shed, Double Dealer, Minder, Agatha Christie Hour, Chinese Detective, The Old Men at the Zoo, The Hope and the Glory, Luther, Love Song, Mr. Palfrey, The Black Tower, Boon, Rumpole, All Passions Spent, Trial of Klaus Barbie, Miss Marple, Tears in the Rain, Behaving Badly, Seeing in the Dark, Inspector Morse: Fat Chance, La Nonna, Lovejoy, Memento Mori, Sherlock Holmes, The Last Vampire, Peak Pratice, Bed, The Bill, Prisoner In Time, Pie In The Sky.

De NIRO, ROBERT
Actor. b. New York, NY, Aug. 17, 1943. Studied acting with Stella Adler and Lee Strasberg; 1988, formed Tribeca Film Center in NY. Co-Prod. of film Thunderheart.
THEATER: One Night Stand of a Noisy Passenger (Off-B'way), Cuba and His Teddy Bear (Public Theater and B'way; Theatre World Award).
PICTURES: The Wedding Party (debut, 1969), Greetings, Sam's Song (The Swap), Bloody Mama, Hi Mom, Born to Win, Jennifer on My Mind, The Gang That Couldn't Shoot Straight, Bang the Drum Slowly, Mean Streets, The Godfather Part II (Acad. Award, best supporting actor, 1974), Taxi Driver, The Last Tycoon, New York New York, 1900, The Deer Hunter, Raging Bull (Acad. Award, 1980), True Confessions, The King of Comedy, Once Upon a Time in America, Falling in Love, Brazil, The Mission, Angel Heart, The Untouchables, Midnight Run, Jacknife, We're No Angels, Stanley and Iris, GoodFellas, Awakenings, Guilty by Suspicion, Backdraft, Cape Fear, Mistress (also co-prod.), Night and the City, Mad Dog and Glory, This Boy's Life, A Bronx Tale (also dir., co-prod.), Mary Shelley's Frankenstein, Casino, Heat, Marvin's Room (also exec. prod.), The Fan, Sleepers, Stolen Flower, Copland, Great Expectations, Ronin.
TELEVISION: Specials: Night of 100 Stars, Dear America: Letters Home From Vietnam (reader).

DENNEHY, BRIAN
Actor. b. Bridgeport, CT, July 9, 1939. e. Columbia U. In Marine Corps five years, including Vietnam. After discharge in 1965 studied with acting coaches in N.Y., while working at part time jobs as a salesman, bartender, truck driver.
THEATER: Streamers, Galileo (Goodman Th.), The Cherry Orchard, Translations.
PICTURES: Looking for Mr. Goodbar, Semi-Tough, F.I.S.T., Foul Play, 10, Butch and Sundance: The Early Days, Little Miss Marker, Split Image, First Blood, Never Cry Wolf, Gorky Park, Finders Keepers, River Rat, Cocoon, Silverado, Twice in a Lifetime, F/X, Legal Eagles, The Check Is in the Mail, Best Seller, The Belly of an Architect, Return to Snowy River Part II, Miles From Home, Cocoon: The Return, The Last of the Finest, Presumed Innocent, FX2, Gladiator, Seven Minutes, Tommy Boy, The Stars Fell on Henrietta, Midnight Movie, Romeo and Juliet.
TELEVISION: Series: Big Shamus Little Shamus, Star of the Family, Birdland. Movies: Johnny We Hardly Knew Ye, It Happened at Lake Wood Manor, Ruby and Oswald, A Death in Canaan, A Real American Hero, Silent Victory: The Kitty O'Neil Story, The Jericho Mile, Dummy, The Seduction of Miss Leona, A Rumor of War, Fly Away Home, Skokie, I Take These Men, Blood Feud, Off Sides, Acceptable Risks, Private Sessions, The Lion of Africa, A Father's Revenge, Day One, Perfect Witness, Pride and Extreme Prejudice, Rising Son, A Killing in a Small Town, In Broad Daylight, The Burden of Proof, To Catch a Killer, Diamond Fleece, Teamster: The Jackie Presser Story, Deadly Matrimony, Foreign Affairs, Murder in the Heartland, Prophet of Evil: The Ervil LeBaron Story, Final Appeal, Jack Reed: Badge of Honor (also co-exec. prod.), Leave of Absence, Jack Reed: Search for Justice (also dir., co-writer). Mini-Series: Evergreen. Guest: M*A*S*H, Lou Grant, Cagney and Lacey, Hunter, Tall Tales (Annie Oakley). Special: Dear America: Letter Home From Vietnam (reader).

DENVER, BOB
Actor. b. New Rochelle, NY, Jan. 9, 1935. e. Loyola U.
PICTURES: A Private's Affair, Take Her She's Mine, For Those Who Think Young, Who's Minding the Mint? The Sweet Ride, Did You Hear the One About the Travelling Saleslady?, Back to the Beach.
TELEVISION: Series: The Many Loves of Dobie Gillis, Gilligan's Island, The Good Guys, Dusty's Trail. Movies: Rescue from Gilligan's Island, The Castaways on Gilligan's Island, The Harlem Globetrotters on Gilligans Island, The Invisible Woman, High School USA, Bring Me the Head of Dobie Gillis. Also: Far Out Space Nuts, Scamps.

DENVER, JOHN
Singer, Actor. r.n. Henry John Deutschendorf. b. Roswell, NM, Dec. 31, 1943. Records, concerts, nightclubs.
PICTURES: Oh, God!, Fire and Ice (narrator).
TELEVISION: *Specials:* An Evening with John Denver (Emmy Award for Outstanding Special, 1975), Rocky Mountain Christmas, John Denver and the Muppets, Rocky Mountain Holiday, Salute to Lady Liberty, Jacques Costeau--The First 75 Years, Julie Andrews...The Sound of Christmas, John Denver's Christmas in Aspen. *Movies:* The Christmas Gift, Foxfire, Higher Ground (co-exec. prod., co-music, actor).
(d. Oct. 12, 1997)

De PALMA, BRIAN
Director, Writer, Producer. b. Newark, NJ, Sept. 11, 1940. e. Columbia U.,B.A.; Sarah Lawrence, M.A. While in college made series of shorts, including Wotan's Wake, winner of Rosenthal Foundation Award for best film made by American under 25. Also judged most popular film of Midwest Film Festival (1963); later shown at San Francisco Film Festival. Dir.: The Responsive Eye (doc., 1966).
PICTURES: *Director:* Murder a La Mod (also s.p., edit.), Greetings (also co-s.p. ed.), The Wedding Party (also co-s.p., co-prod., ed.), Hi Mom (also co-story, s.p.), Dionysus in '69 (also co-prod., co-photog., co-ed.), Get To Know Your Rabbit, Sisters (also co-s.p.), Phantom of the Paradise (also co-s.p.), Obsession (also co-story), Carrie, The Fury, Home Movies (also s.p., co-prod.), Dressed to Kill (also s.p.), Blow Out (also s.p.), Scarface, Body Double (also prod., s.p.), Wiseguys, The Untouchables, Casualties of War, The Bonfire of the Vanities (also prod.), Raising Cain (also s.p.), Carlito's Way, Mission: Impossible.

DEPARDIEU, GÉRARD
Actor. b. Chateauroux, France, Dec. 27, 1948. Studied acting at Theatre National Populaire in Paris. Made film debut at 16 in short by Roger Leenhardt (Le Beatnik et Le Minet). Acted in feature film by Agnes Varda (uncompleted).
PICTURES: Le Cri du Cormoran le Soir au-dessis des Jonques, Nathalie Granger, A Little Sun in Cold Water, Le Tueur, L'Affaire Dominici, Au Renedez-vous de la mort joyeuse, La Scoumone, Rude Journee our la Reine, Deux Hommes dans la Ville, The Holes, Going Places, Stavisky, Woman of the Granges, Vincent Francois Paul and the Others, The Wonderful Crook, 7 Morts sur ordonnance, Maitresse, Je t'Aime Moi Non Plus, The Last Woman, 1900, Barocco, Rene la Canne, Baxter Vera Baxter, The Truck, Tell Him I Love Him, At Night All Cats are Gray, Get Out Your Handkerchiefs, The Left-Handed Woman, Bye Bye Monkey, Violanta, Le Sucre, Les Chiens, L'Ingorgo, Buffet Froid, Temporale Rosy, Mon Oncle d'Amerique, Loulou, The Last Metro, Inspector Blunder, I Love You, Choice of Arms, The Woman Next Door, Le Chevre. The Return of Martin Guerre, The Big Brother, Danton, The Moon in the Gutter, Les Comperes (also co-prod.), Fort Saganne, Le Tartuffe (also dir., co-s.p), Rive Droie Rive Gauche, Police, One Woman or Two, Menage, Ru du depart, Jean De Florette (also co-prod.), Under Satan's Sun (also co-prod.), A Strange Place for an Enounter (also co-prod.), Camille Claudel (also co-prod.), Dreux, Too Beautiful for You (also co-prod.), I Want to Go Home, Cyrano de Bergerac (also co-prod), Green Card, Uranus, Thanks for Life, Mon Pere ce Heros (My Father the Hero), 1492: Conquest of Paradise, Tous les Matins du Monde (All the Mornings of the World), Helas Pour Moi (Oh Woe is Me), Une Pure Formalite (A Pure Formality), Germinal, My Father the Hero, Colonel Chabert, La Machine, Elisa, Les Anges Gardiens, The Horseman on the Roof, Bogus, Le Garcu, She's So Lovely (exec.prod. only), Hamlet.

DEPP, JOHNNY
Actor. b. Owensboro, KY, June 9, 1963. Raised in Miramar, FL. Played lead guitar with band The Kids, with whom he moved to L.A. in 1983. With no prior acting experience made film debut in A Nightmare on Elm Street.
PICTURES: A Nightmare on Elm Street (debut, 1984), Private Resort, Platoon, Cry-Baby, Edward Scissorhands, Freddy's Dead: The Final Nightmare (cameo), Benny & Joon, What's Eating Gilbert Grape?, Arizona Dream, Ed Wood, Don Juan DeMarco, Dead Man, Nick of Time, Divine Rapture, Donnie Brasco, The Brave (also dir.), The Astronauts Wife, Just to Be Together, Fear and Loathing in Las Vegas.
TELEVISION: *Series:* 21 Jump Street. *Movie:* Slow Burn. *Guest:* Lady Blue.

DEREK, BO
Actress. r.n. Mary Cathleen Collins. b. Torrance, CA., Nov. 20, 1956. Discovered by actor-turned-filmmaker John Derek, whom she married.
PICTURES: Orca (debut, 1977), 10, A Change of Seasons, Fantasies (And Once Upon a Time), Tarzan the Ape Man (also prod.), Bolero (also prod.), Ghosts Can't Do It (also prod.), Hot Chocolate, Sognando la California (California Dreaming), Woman of Desire, Tommy Boy.
TELEVISION: *Movie:* Shattered Image, Wind on Water.

DERN, BRUCE
Actor. b. Chicago, IL, June 4, 1936. e. U. of Pennsylvania. Daughter is actress Laura Dern. Studied acting with Gordon Phillips, member, Actor's Studio, 1959 after N.Y. debut in Shadow of a Gunman. Broadway: Sweet Bird of Youth, Orpheus Descending, Strangers. Film Awards: Natl. Society of Film Critics (Drive He Said, 1971), People's Choice (Coming Home, 1978), Genie (Middle Age Crazy, 1980), Silver Bear (That Championship Season, 1982).
PICTURES: Wild River (debut, 1960), Marnie, Hush...Hush Sweet Charlotte, The Wild Angels, The St. Valentine's Day Massacre, Waterhole No. 3, The Trip, The War Wagon, Psych-Out, Rebel Rousers, Hang 'Em High, Will Penny, Number One, Castle Keep, Support Your Local Sheriff, They Shoot Horses Don't They?, Cycle Savages, Bloody Mama, The Incredible Two-Headed Transplant, Drive He Said, Silent Running, Thumb Tripping, The Cowboys, The King of Marvin Gardens, The Laughing Policeman, The Great Gatsby, Smile, Posse, Family Plot, Won Ton Ton the Dog Who Saved Hollywood, The Twist (Folies Bourgeoises), Black Sunday, Coming Home (Acad. Award nom.), The Driver, Middle Age Crazy, Tattoo, Harry Tracy: Desperado, That Championship Season, On the Edge, The Big Town, World Gone Wild, 1969, The 'Burbs, After Dark My Sweet, Diggstown, Wild Bill, Down Periscope, Mulholland Falls, Last Man Standing.
TELEVISION: *Series:* Stoney Burke. *Mini-Series:* Space. *Movies:* Sam Hill: Who Killed the Mysterious Mr. Foster?, Toughlove, Roses Are for the Rich, Uncle Tom's Cabin, Trenchcoat in Paradise, The Court-Martial of Jackie Robinson, Into the Badlands, Carolina Skeletons, It's Nothing Personal, Deadman's Revenge, Amelia Earhart: The Final Flight, A Mother's Prayer. *Guest:* Naked City, Ben Casey, The Virginian, Twelve O'Clock High, The Big Valley, Gunsmoke, The FBI, Land of the Giants, Saturday Night Live, Fallen Angels (Murder Obliquely).

DERN, LAURA
Actress. b. Los Angeles, CA, Feb. 10, 1967. Daughter of actors Diane Ladd and Bruce Dern. At age 5 appeared with mother on daytime serial The Secret Storm. Was an extra in several of her father's films and her mother's Alice Doesn't Live Here Anymore. Studied acting at RADA appearing on stage in Hamlet, A Midsummer Night's Dream.
THEATER: *NY:* The Palace of Amateurs. *LA:* Brooklyn Laundry.
PICTURES: White Lightning (debut, 1973), Alice Doesn't Live Here Anymore, Foxes, Ladies and Gentlemen: The Fabulous Stains, Teachers, Mask, Smooth Talk, Blue Velvet, Haunted Summer, Fat Man and Little Boy, Wild at Heart, Rambling Rose (Acad. Award nom.), Jurassic Park, A Perfect World, Devil Inside, Citizen Ruth.
TELEVISION: *Movies:* Happy Endings, Three Wishes of Billy Greer, Afterburn (Golden Globe Award), Down Came a Blackbird. *Special:* The Gift (dir., co-story only). *Guest:* Fallen Angels (Murder Obliquely).

DE SANTIS, GREGORY JOSEPH
Producer, Writer, Director. b. Los Angeles, CA, July 12, 1955. e. Durham Univ.; Canaan Coll. Pres., Millennium Mulitmedia.
PICTURES: *Prod.:* The Companion, Car Trouble, Pass the Buck, Die Sister Die!, Diary of a Surfing Film, Firepower, The Forest.
TELEVISION: *Prod.:* Volleyball: A Sport Come of Age, The Nature Series, Caribou Crossing, California Day, Midnight Son, Lightning, Mysterious River.

DESCHANEL, CALEB
Cinematographer, Director. b. Philadelphia, PA, Sept. 21, 1944. m. actress Mary Jo Deschanel. e. Johns Hopkins U., U. of Southern California Film Sch. Studied at Amer. Film Inst., interned under Gordon Willis then started making commercials, short subjects, docs.
PICTURES: *Cinematographer:* More American Graffiti, Being There, The Black Stallion, Apocalypse Now (2nd unit photog.), The Right Stuff, Let's Spend the Night Together (co-cinematographer), The Natural, The Slugger's Wife, It Could Happen to You, Flying Wild. *Director:* The Escape Artist, Crusoe.

De TOTH, ANDRE
Writer, Director, Producer. b. Hungary. Dir.-writer European films, 1931-39; U.S. assoc. Alexander Korda prod., 1940; dir. Columbia, 1943; assoc. David Selznick, 1943; assoc. Hunt Stromberg-UA, 1944-45; staff dir., Enterprise 1946-47; dir., 20th-Fox, 1948-49; collab. story, The Gunfighter; assoc., Sam Spiegel, Horizon Pictures, Columbia, 1962; Harry Saltzman, Lowndes Prod., U.A. 1966-68; National General, 1969-70.
PICTURES: Passport to Suez, None Shall Escape, Pitfall, Slattery's Hurricane, Springfield Rifle, Thunder Over the Plains, House of Wax, The Stranger Wore a Gun, Bounty Hunter, Tanganyika, The Indian Fighter, Monkey on My Back, Two Headed Spy, Day of the Outlaw, Man on a String, Morgan The Pirate, The Mongols, Gold for the Caesars, Billion Dollar Brain (exec. prod. only), Play Dirty (also exec. prod.), El Condor (prod. only), The Dangerous Game.

DEUTCH, HOWARD
Director. b. New York, NY. e. Ohio State U. m. actress Lea Thompson. Son of music publisher Murray Deutch. Spent almost 10 yrs. working in various film media, including music videos and film trailer advertising, before feature directorial debut with Pretty in Pink, 1986.
PICTURES: Pretty in Pink, Some Kind of Wonderful, The Great Outdoors, Article 99, Getting Even With Dad, Grumpier Old Men, The Odd Couple II.
TELEVISION: *Series*: Tales from the Crypt (2 episodes; ACE Award for Dead Right), Caroline in the City.

DEUTCHMAN, IRA J.
Executive. b. Cherry Point, NC, March 24, 1953. e. Northwestern U., B.S., majoring in film. Began career with Cinema 5, Ltd. serving, 1975-79, as non-theatrical sls. mgr.; dir. theatrical adv./pub./dir. acquisitions. Joined United Artists Classics, 1981 as dir. of adv./pub. 1982, left to become one of the founding partners in Cinecom Intl. Films, where headed mktg./dist. div. from inception. Resigned, Jan. 1989 to form the Deutchman Company, Inc., a production company and marketing consultancy firm. Founded and served as pres. of Fine Line Features, a division of New Line Cinema, and sr. v.p. of parent corp, 1991-95. Currenly, pres. of Redeemable Features, a New York-based prod. company. Adjunct prof. Columbia U. film dept. On advisory bds. Sundance U.S. Film Festival and the Sundance Institute.
PICTURES: *Exec. Prod.*: Swimming to Cambodia, Matewan (assoc. prod.), Miles From Home (co-exec. prod.), Scenes from the Class Struggle in Beverly Hills, Straight Out of Brooklyn, Waterland, The Ballad of Little Jo, Mrs. Parker and the Vicious Circle. *Producer*: Kiss Me Guida, 54, The Hairy Bird, Way Past Cool.

DEUTCHMAN, LAWRENCE SCOT
Executive. b. Bronx, NY, Dec. 10, 1960. e. Rutgers U. Wrote, prod. & dir. Mythbusters campaign. 1986-92, various positions: Entertainment Industries Council, Inc.; wrote, prod., co-dir. That's a Wrap campaign. 1986-88, board member, Public Interest Radio & Television Educational Society. 1987-88, wrote, exec. prod., post-prod. sprv., Buckle Up educational & music video (CINE Golden Eagle). 1989: EIC: An Industry in Action (writer, prod., dir.); Campaigns: Natl. Red Ribbon, Office for Substance Abuse Prevention (writer, dir., exec. prod.), Stop the Madness (co-writer, prod.). 1990, developed: Vince & Larry: The Amazing Crash Test Dummies (series, NBC), Drug Proofing Your Kids (TV special); Campaigns: Alcoholism Runs in Families, Texas Prevention Partnership (dir., exec. prod.), They Do as You Do (writer, exec. prod.). 1991: The Inhalant Problem in Texas docum. (co-exec prod.), Inhalants: The Silent Epidemic award-winning drama (writer, co-exec. prod.), KBVO Fox Kids Club segments (writer, prod., set designer), The Incredible Crash Dummies toy property (co-creator), Ollie Odorfree property (creator). 1992-present: Pres., Dynamic Commun. Intl. Inc.; v.p. prod. & mktg., EIC. 1993: Hollywood Gets M.A.D.D. TV special (co-prod., TBS, TNT, synd.). 1994: Dinorock Time TV series (exec. prod., writer.); 1994-present, s.r., vp. prod. & mktg, EIC.

DEUTSCH, STEPHEN
Producer. b. Los Angeles, CA, June 30, 1946. e. UCLA, B.A.; Loyola Law Sch., 1974. Son of late S. Sylvan Simon. Stepson of Armand Deutsch. Private law practice before joining Rastar 1976 as asst. to Ray Stark; 1977, sr. v.p., Rastar; prod. head for SLM Inc. Film Co. entered independent prod. 1978.
PICTURES: Somewhere in Time, All the Right Moves, Russkies (co-exec. prod.), She's Out of Control, Bill & Ted's Excellent Adventure (exec. prod.), Lucky Stiff, Bill and Ted's Bogus Journey (co-exec. prod.), Body of Evidence (exec. prod.).

DEVANE, WILLIAM
Actor. b. Albany, NY, Sept. 5, 1939. Appeared in some 15 productions with N.Y. Shakespeare Festival, also B'way & off-B'way shows before heading to California for films and TV.
PICTURES: The Pursuit of Happiness (debut, 1970), The 300 Hundred Year Weekend, Lady Liberty, McCabe and Mrs. Miller, Glory Boy (My Old Man's Place), Irish Whiskey Rebellion, Report to the Commissioner, Family Plot, Marathon Man, Bad News Bears in Breaking Training, Rolling Thunder, The Dark, Yanks, Honky Tonk Freeway, Testament, Hadley's Rebellion, Vital Signs.
TELEVISION: *Series*: From Here to Eternity, Knots Landing, Phenom, The Monroes. *Movies*: Crime Club, The Bait, Fear on Trial, Red Alert, Black Beauty, Red Flag: The Ultimate Game, The Other Victim, Jane Doe, With Intent to Kill, Timestalker, Murder C.O.D., Nightmare in Columbia County, Obsessed, The President's Child. Prophet of Evil: The Ervil LeBaron Story, Rubdown, For the Love of Nancy, Falling From the Sky!: Flight 174, Robin Cook's Virus, Alistair MacLean's Night Watch. *Special*: The Missiles of October. *Mini-Series*: A Woman Named Jackie, Knot's Landing: Back to the Cul-de-Sac, Doomsday Rock.

De VITO, DANNY
Actor, Director, Producer. b. Asbury Park, NJ, Nov. 17, 1944. m. actress Rhea Perlman. e. Oratory Prep Sch. Studied at American Acad. of Dramatic Arts. Wilfred Acad. of Hair and Beauty Culture. At 18 worked as hair dresser for 1 yr. at his sister's shop. NY stage in The Man With a Flower in His Mouth (debut, 1969), Down the Morning Line, The Line of Least Existence, The Shrinking Bride, Call Me Charlie, Comedy of Errors, Merry Wives of Windsor (NYSF). Three By Pirandello. Performance in One Flew Over the Cuckoo's Nest led to casting in the film version. Prod. short films: The Sound Sleeper (1973), Minestrone (1975).
PICTURES: Lady Liberty (debut, 1971), Hurry Up or I'll Be 30, Scalawag, One Flew Over the Cuckoo's Nest, Deadly Hero, The Van, The World's Greatest Lover, Goin' South, Going Ape, Terms of Endearment, Romancing the Stone, Johnny Dangerously, The Jewel of the Nile, Head Office, Wiseguys, Ruthless People, My Little Pony (voice), Tin Men, Throw Momma from the Train (also dir.), Twins, The War of the Roses (also dir.), Other People's Money, Batman Returns, Hoffa (also dir., co-prod.), Jack the Bear, Last Action Hero (voice), Look Who's Talking Now (voice), Reality Bites (co-prod. only), Renaissance Man, Pulp Fiction (co-exec. prod. only), Junior, Get Shorty (also co-prod.), Sunset Park (prod.), Matilda (also dir., co-prod.), Mars Attacks, Hercules (voice), L.A. Confidential, Space Jam. (voice), Gattaca (prod. only).
TELEVISION: *Series*: Taxi (Emmy & Golden Globe Awards, 1981; also dir. episodes), Mary (dir. only). Movies: Valentine, The Ratings Game (also dir.). Specials: All the Kids Do It (Afterschool Special), A Very Special Christmas Party, Two Daddies? (voice), What a Lovely Way to Spend an Evening (dir.), The Selling of Vince DeAngelo (dir.). Guest: Police Woman, Saturday Night Live, Amazing Stories (also dir.), The Simpsons (voice).

DEVLIN, DEAN
Actor, Writer, Producer. b. Aug. 27, 1962. Began career as an actor, appearing in numerous film and television projects, as well as B'way production of There Must Be a Pony. Met Roland Emmerich while acting in Moon 44. Joined Emmerich as a partner at Centropolis Films. Prod. TV series, The Visitor, 1997.
PICTURES: *Actor*: My Bodyguard, The Wild Life, Real Genius, City Limits, Moon 44, Martians Go Home, Total Exposure. *Writer/Producer*: Stargate, Independence Day, Godzilla, The Mark. *Writer*: Universal Soldier.
TELEVISION: *Series creator*: The Visitor. *Series actor*: Hard Copy, Generations.

De WITT, JOYCE
Actress. b. Wheeling, WV, April 23, 1949. e. Ball State U., B.A., theatre; UCLA, MFA in acting. Classically trained, worked in theater since 13 as actress and dir.
TELEVISION: *Series*: Three's Company. *Guest*: Baretta, The Tony Randall Show, Most Wanted, Risko, Finder of Lost Loves. *Movies*: With This Ring, Spring Fling.

DEY, SUSAN
Actress. b. Pekin, IL, Dec. 10, 1952. Signed as magazine teen model at age 15. Made professional TV debut at 17, appearing in The Partridge Family 1970.
PICTURES: Skyjacked (debut, 1972), First Love, Looker, Echo Park, That's Adequate.
TELEVISION: *Series*: The Partridge Family, Loves Me Loves Me Not, Emerald Point N.A.S., L.A. Law, Love and War. *Movies*: Terror on the Beach, Cage Without a Key, Mary Jane Harper Cried Last Night, Little Women, The Comeback Kid, The Gift of Life, Malibu, Sunset Limousine, I Love You Perfect, Bed of Lies, Lies and Lullabies (also co-prod.), Whose Child Is This? The War for Baby Jessica, Beyond Betrayal, Deadly Love.

DE YOUNG, CLIFF
Actor. b. Inglewood, CA, Feb. 12, 1947. e. California State Coll., Illinois State U. On stage in Hair, Sticks and Bones, Two By South, The Three Sisters, The Orphan.
PICTURES: Harry and Tonto, Blue Collar, Shock Treatment, Independence Day, The Hunger, Reckless, Protocol, Secret Admirer, F/X, Flight of the Navigator, Fear, Pulse, Rude Awakening, Glory, Flashback, Crackdown, Dr. Giggles, Carnosaur II, Final Frontier, The Craft, The Substitute, Suicide Kings.
TELEVISION: *Series*: Sunshine, Robocop, Relativity. *Special*: Sticks and Bones. *Mini-Series*: Centennial, Master of the Game, Captains and the Kings, King, Robert Kennedy and His Times, Andersonville, Seduced By Madness, The Last Don. *Movies*: Sunshine, The 3000 Mile Chase, The Lindbergh Kidnapping Case, Scared Straight: Another Story, Invasion of Privacy, The Seeding of Sarah Burns, The Night That Panicked America, This Girl for Hire, The Awakening of Candra, Deadly Intentions, Sunshine Christmas, Fun and Games, Where Pigeons Go to Die, Fourth Story, Criminal Behavior, Love Can Be Murder, The Tommyknockers, Precious Victims, Heaven & Hell: North and South Book III, JAG, Element of Truth, The Westing Game, Nails, George Wallace, The Westing Game.

DIAMANT, LINCOLN
Executive, Biographer, Historian. b. New York, NY, Jan. 25, 1923. e. Columbia Coll., A.B. cum laude 1943. Cofounder, Columbia U. radio station. WKCR-FM; served in Wash. as prod., Blue Network (NBC), then in NY as CBS newswriter; 1949 joined World Pub. Co. as adv. and promo. dir.; 1952-69 worked in creative/TV dept. McCann-Erickson, Grey, then Ogilvy & Mather ad agencies (winning 6 Clio Awards). Prod. Lend Us Your Ears (Met. Museum Art broadcast series); founder, pres., Spots Alive, Inc., broadcast adv. consultants, 1969; Author, The Broadcast Communications Dictionary, Anatomy of a Television Commercial, Television's Classic Commercials, biography of Bernard Romans, Chaining the Hudson (Sons of Revolution Book Award), Stamping Our History, Yankee Doodle Days. Contrib., to Effective Advertising, to Messages and Meaning; New Routes to English; columnist Back Stage/Shoot. Member, Broadcast Pioneers, Acad. TV Arts & Sciences; v.p. Broadcast Advertising Producer's Society of America. Adjunct faculty member, Pace U., Hofstra U. Fellow, Royal Society of Arts.

DIAMOND, NEIL
Singer, Songwriter. b. Brooklyn, NY, Jan. 24, 1941. Many concert tours.
PICTURES: Jonathan Livingston Seagull (music), Every Which Way But Loose (music), The Last Waltz (actor), The Jazz Singer (actor, music).
TELEVISION: Specials: Neil Diamond... Hello Again, I Never Cared for the Sound of Being Alone, I'm Glad You're Here With Me Tonight, Greatest Hits Live, Neil Diamond's Christmas Special, Neil Diamond... Under a Tennessee Moon.

DIAZ, CAMERON
Actress. Began career as model for Elite. Feature debut was in The Mask. Received ShoWest 1996 Female Star of Tomorrow Award.
PICTURES: The Mask, The Last Supper, Keys to Tulsa, Feeling Minnesota, Head Above Water, She's the One, Head Above Water, My Best Friend's Wedding, A Life Less Ordinary, There's Something About Mary, Very Bad Things.

DI CAPRIO, LEONARDO
Actor. b. Hollywood, CA, Nov. 11, 1974. Started acting at age 15 in commercials and educational films. Appeared in short film The Foot Shooting Party.
PICTURES: Critters III (debut, 1991), Poison Ivy, This Boy's Life, What's Eating Gilbert Grape? (Natl. Board of Review, Chicago Film Critics & LA Film Critics Awards, Acad. Award nom.), The Quick and the Dead, The Basketball Diaries, Total Eclipse, Marvin's Room, Romeo and Juliet, Titanic.
TELEVISION: Series: Growing Pains, Parenthood.

DICKERSON, ERNEST
(A.S.C.): Cinematographer, Director. b. Newark, NJ, 1952. e. Howard U., architecture, NYU, grad. film school. First job, filming surgical procedures for Howard U. medical school. At NYU film school shot classmate Spike Lee's student films Sarah, and Joe's Bed Stuy Barbershop: We Cut Heads. Also shot Nike commercial and several music videos including Bruce Springsteen's Born in the U.S.A., Patti LaBelle's Stir It Up and Miles Davis' Tutu; and Branford Marsalis' Royal Garden Blues directed by Spike Lee. Admitted into Amer. Soc. of Cinematographers in 1989.
PICTURES: Cinematographer: The Brother From Another Planet, She's Gotta Have It (also cameo), Krush Groove, School Daze, Raw, Do the Right Thing, Def By Temptation, The Laser Man, Mo' Better Blues, Jungle Fever, Sex Drugs Rock & Roll, Cousin Bobby (co-photog.), Malcolm X. Director: Juice (also co-s.p., story), Surviving the Game, Tales Fromt he Crypt Presents Demon Knight.
TELEVISION: Do it Acapella (dir.; PBS).

DICKINSON, ANGIE
Actress. r.n. Angeline Brown. b. Kulm, ND, Sept. 30, 1931. e. Immaculate Heart Coll., Glendale Coll., secretarial course. Beauty contest winner.
PICTURES: Lucky Me (debut in bit part, 1954), Man With the Gun, The Return of Jack Slade, Tennessee's Partner, The Black Whip, Hidden Guns, Tension at Table Rock, Gun the Man Down, Calypso Joe, China Gate, Shoot Out at Medicine Bend, Cry Terror, I Married a Woman, Rio Bravo, The Bramble Bush, Ocean's 11, A Fever in the Blood, The Sins of Rachel Cade, Jessica, Rome Adventure, Captain Newman M.D., The Killers, The Art of Love, Cast a Giant Shadow, The Chase, The Poppy is Also a Flower, The Last Challenge, Point Blank, Sam Whiskey, Some Kind of a Nut, Young Billy Young, Pretty Maids All in a Row, The Resurrection of Zachary Wheeler, The Outside Man, Big Bad Mama, Klondike Fever, Dressed to Kill, Charlie Chan and the Curse of the Dragon Queen, Death Hunt, Big Bad Mama II, Even Cowgirls Get the Blues, The Maddening, Sabrina, The Sun—The Moon and The Stars.
TELEVISION: Series: Police Woman, Cassie & Co. Movies: The Love War, Thief, See the Man Run, The Norliss Tapes, Pray for the Wildcats, A Sensitive Passionate Man, Overboard, The Suicide's Wife, Dial M for Murder, One Shoe Makes It Murder, Jealousy, A Touch of Scandal, Stillwatch, Police Story: The Freeway Killings, Once Upon a Texas Train, Prime Target, Treacherous Crossing, Danielle Steel's Remembrance, Deep Family Secrets. Mini-Series: Pearl, Hollywood Wives, Wild Palms. Special: Ira Geshwin at 100.

DICKINSON, WOOD
Executive, Exhibitor. r.n. Glen Wood Dickinson III. b. Fairway, KS, Sept. 14, 1952. e. Texas Christian U (BFA Communications, MA Film). CEO and pres. Dickinson, Inc. and Dickinson Operating Company, Inc., commonly known as Dickinson Theatres.

DILLER, BARRY
Executive. b. San Francisco, CA, Feb. 2, 1942. Joined ABC in April, 1966, as asst. to v.p. in chg. programming. In 1968, made exec. asst. to v.p. in chg. programming and dir. of feature films. In 1969, named v.p., feature films and program dev., east coast. In 1971, made v.p., Feature Films and Circle Entertainment, a unit of ABC Entertainment, responsible for selecting, producing and scheduling The Tuesday Movie of the Week, The Wednesday Movie of the Week, and Circle Film original features for airing on ABC-TV, as well as for acquisition and scheduling of theatrical features for telecasting on ABC Sunday Night Movie and ABC Monday Night Movie. In 1973, named v.p. in chg. of prime time TV for ABC Entertainment. In 1974 joined Paramount Pictures as bd. chmn. and chief exec. officer. 1983, named pres. of Gulf & Western Entertainment and Communications Group, while retaining Paramount titles. Resigned from Paramount in 1984 to join 20th Century-Fox as bd. chmn. and chief. exec. officer. Named chmn. & CEO of Fox, Inc. (comprising 20th Fox Film Corp., Fox TV Stations & Fox Bdcstg. Co.), Oct., 1985. Named to bd., News Corp. Ltd., June, 1987. Resigned from Fox in Feb., 1992. Named CEO of QVC Network Inc. TV shopping concern. Resigned QVC in 1995. CEO and bd. chair, Silver King Communications, Inc, Aug. 1995. Bd. chairman, Home Shopping Network, Nov. 1995.

DILLER, PHYLLIS
Comedienne, Actress. b. Lima, OH, July 17, 1917. r.n. Phyllis Ada Driver. e. Sherwood Music Sch.; Bluffton Coll., OH, 1938-39. Started as publicist at San Francisco radio station before becoming nightclub comic at the age of 37.
Recordings: Phyllis Diller Laughs, Are You Ready for Phyllis Diller?, Great Moments of Comedy, Born to Sing. Performed with many U.S. symphonies, 1971-90.
AUTHOR: Phyllis Diller's Housekeeping Hints, Phyllis Diller's Marriage Manual, Phyllis Diller's The Complete Mother, The Joys of Aging and How to Avoid Them.
THEATER: Hello Dolly! (B'way), Everybody Loves Opal, Happy Birthday, The Dark at the Top of the Stairs, Subject to Change, The Wizard of Oz, Nunsense, Cinderella.
PICTURES: Splendor in the Grass (debut, 1961), Boy Did I Get a Wrong Number!, The Fat Spy, Mad Monster Party (voice), Eight on the Lam, Did You Hear the One About the Traveling Saleslady?, The Private Navy of Sgt. O'Farrell, The Adding Machine, The Sunshine Boys (cameo), A Pleasure Doing Business, Pink Motel, Pucker Up and Bark Like a Dog, Dr. Hackenstein, Friend to Friend, The Nutcracker Prince (voice), The Boneyard, Wisecracks, Happily Ever After (voice), The Perfect Man, The Silence of the Hams.
TELEVISION: Series: Showstreet, The Pruitts of Southampton, The Beautiful Phyllis Diller Show. Specials: The Phyllis Diller Special, An Evening With Phyllis Diller, Phyllis Diller's 102nd Birthday Party. Guest: Laugh In, Love American Style, The Muppet Show, The Love Boat, CHiPs, etc.

DILLMAN, BRADFORD
Actor. b. San Francisco, CA, April 14, 1930. m. actress-model Suzy Parker. e. Yale U., 1951. Studied at Actors Studio. Author: Inside the New York Giants, Are You Anybody?
THEATER: The Scarecrow (1953), Third Person, Long Day's Journey into Night (premiere; Theatre World Award), The Fun Couple.
PICTURES: A Certain Smile (debut, 1958), In Love and War, Compulsion, Crack in the Mirror, Circle of Deception, Sanctuary, Francis of Assisi, A Rage to Live, The Plainsman, Sergeant Ryker, Helicopter Spies, Jigsaw, The Bridge at Remagen, Suppose They Gave a War and Nobody Came, Brother John, The Mephisto Waltz, Escape from the Planet of the Apes, The Resurrection of Zachary Wheeler, The Iceman Cometh, The Way We Were, Chosen Survivors, 99 and 44/100% Dead, Gold, Bug, Mastermind, The Enforcer, The Lincoln Conspiracy, Amsterdam Kill, The Swarm, Piranha, Love and Bullets, Guyana: Cult of the Damned, Sudden Impact, Treasure of the Amazon, Man Outside, Lords of the Deep, Heroes Stand Alone.
TELEVISION: Series: Court-Martial, King's Crossing, Dynasty. Movies: Fear No Evil, Black Water Gold, Longstreet, Five Desperate Women, Revenge, Eyes of Charles Sand, The Delphi Bureau, Moon of the Wolf, Deliver Us From Evil, Murder or Mercy, Disappearance of Flight 412, Adventures of the Queen, Force Five, Widow, Street Killing, Kingston: The Power Play, The Hostage Heart, Jennifer: A Woman's Story, Before and After, The Memory of Eva Ryker, Tourist, The Legend of Walks Far Woman, Covenant, Heart of Justice.

135

DILLON, KEVIN
Actor. b. Mamaroneck, NY, Aug. 19, 1965. Younger brother of actor Matt Dillon. Stage work includes Dark at the Top of the Stairs, The Indian Wants the Bronx.
PICTURES: No Big Deal, Heaven Help Us, Platoon, Remote Control, The Rescue, The Blob, War Party, Immediate Family, The Doors, A Midnight Clear, No Escape.
TELEVISION: Movie: When He's Not a Stranger. Special: Dear America: Letters Home from Vietnam (reader). Guest: Tales From the Crypt.

DILLON, MATT
Actor. b. New Rochelle, NY, Feb. 18, 1964. Discovered at age 14 in junior high school by casting dir. who cast him in Over the Edge. Brother is actor Kevin Dillon.
THEATER: NY: The Boys of Winter (B'way debut, 1985).
PICTURES: Over the Edge (debut, 1979), Little Darlings, My Bodyguard, Liar's Moon, Tex, The Outsiders, Rumble Fish, The Flamingo Kid, Target, Rebel, Native Son, The Big Town, Kansas, Bloodhounds of Broadway, Drugstore Cowboy, A Kiss Before Dying, Singles, Mr. Wonderful, The Saint of Fort Washington, Golden Gate, To Die For, Frankie Starlight, Beautiful Girls, Grace of My Heart, Albino Alligator, In & Out.
TELEVISION: Movie: Women & Men 2: In Love There Are No Rules (Return to Kansas City). Specials: The Great American Fourth of July and Other Disasters, Dear America: Letters Home From Vietnam (reader).

DILLON, MELINDA
Actress. b. Hope, AR, Oct. 13, 1939. e. Chicago Sch. of Drama, Art Inst., Goodman Theatre. Launched career on Broadway in original prod. of Who's Afraid of Virginia Woolf? (Theatre World Award, Tony Award nom., Drama Critics Award).
THEATER: Story Theater, You Know I Can't Hear You When The Water's Running, A Way of Life, Our Town
PICTURES: The April Fools (debut, 1969), Bound for Glory (People's Choice Award), Slap Shot, Close Encounters of the Third Kind (Acad. Award nom.), F.I.S.T., Absence of Malice (Acad. Award nom.), A Christmas Story, Songwriter, Harry and the Hendersons, Staying Together, Spontaneous Combustion, Capt. America, The Prince of Tides, Sioux City, To Fong Woo–Thanks for Everything Julie Newmar, How to Make an American Quilt, Dorothy Day, The Effects of Magic.
TELEVISION: Series: Paul Sills Story Theatre. Guest: Twilight Zone, The Defenders, Bonanza, East Side West Side, The Paul Sand Show, The Jeffersons, Good Morning America, The Today Show, Dick Cavett Show, Dinah Shore Show, Picket Fences, The Client, Texarkana. Mini-Series: Space. Movies: Critical List, Transplant, Marriage is Alive and Well, The Shadow Box, Fallen Angel, Hellinger's Law, Right of Way, Shattered Spirits, Shattered Innocence, Nightbreaker, Judgment Day: The John List Story, State of Emergency, Confessions: Two Faces of Evil, Naomi & Wynonna: Love Can Build a Bridge.

DINDAL, MARK
Animator, director. b. Columbus, OH.
PICTURES: The Fox and the Hound, Mickey's Christmas Carol, The Black Cauldron, The Great Mouse Detective, Oliver & Company, The Little Mermaid, The Rocketeer, Cats Don't Dance (voice, dir., writer), Kingdom of the Sun (dir.).

DiNOVI, DENISE
Producer. b. Canada. Started as journalist, reporter, film critic in Toronto before entering film industry as unit publicist. 1980, joined Montreal's Film Plan production co. as co-prod., assoc. prod. and exec. in charge of prod. working on such movies as Visiting Hours, Going Berserk, Videodrome. Became exec. v.p. of prod. at New World, then head of Tim Burton Prods., 1989-92.
PICTURES: Heathers, Edward Scissorhands, Meet the Applegates, Batman Returns, The Nightmare Before Christmas, Cabin Boy, Little Women, Ed Wood, James and the Giant Peach, Practical Magic, Almost Heroes, Messge in a Bottle.

Di PIETRA, ROSEMARY
Executive. Joined Paramount Pictures in 1976, rising through ranks to become director-corporate administration. 1985, promoted to exec. dir.-corporate administration.

DISHY, BOB
Actor. b. Brooklyn, NY. e. Syracuse U.
THEATER: Damn Yankees, From A to Z, Second City, Flora the Red Menace, By Jupiter, Something Different, The Goodbye People, The Good Doctor, The Unknown Soldier at His Wife, The Creation of the World and Other Business, An American Millionaire, Sly Fox, Murder at Howard Johnson's, Grown Ups, Cafe Crown.
PICTURES: The Tiger Makes Out, Lovers and Other Strangers, The Big Bus, I Wonder Who's Killing Her Now?, The Last Married Couple in America, First Family, Author! Author!, Brighton Beach Memoirs, Critical Condition, Stay Tuned, Used People, My Boyfriend's Back, Don Juan DeMarco, Jungle to Jungle.
TELEVISION: Series: That Was the Week That Was. Specials: Story Theatre (dir.), The Cafeteria. Guest: The Comedy Zone. Movies: It Couldn't Happen to a Nicer Guy, Thicker Than Blood: The Larry McLinden Story.

DISNEY, ROY E.
Producer, Director, Writer, Cameraman, Film editor. b. Los Angeles, CA, Jan. 10, 1930. e. Pomona Coll., CA. 1951 started as page, NBC-TV. Asst. film editor Dragnet TV series. 1952-78, Walt Disney Prods., Burbank, Calif., various capacities; vice chmn. of the board, The Walt Disney Co.; bd. chmn., Shamrock Holdings, Inc., bd. dir., Walt Disney Co.
PICTURES: Perri, Mysteries of the Deep, Mustang (dir.), Pacific High, The Fantasy Film Worlds of George Pal (actor), The Wonderful Ice Cream Suit (prod.).
TELEVISION: Walt Disney's Wonderful World of Color, The Hound That Thought He Was A Raccoon, Sancho, The Homing Steer, The Silver Fox and Sam Davenport, Wonders of the Water World, Legend of Two Gypsy Dogs, Adventure in Wildwood Heart, The Postponed Wedding, Zorro series, An Otter in the Family, My Family is a Menagerie, Legend of El Blanco, Pancho, The Fastest Paw in the West, The Owl That Didn't Give A Hoot, Varda the Peregrine Falcon, Cristobalito, The Calypso Colt, Three Without Fear, Hamade and the Pirates, Chango, Guardian of the Mayan Treasure, Nosey the Sweetest Skunk in the World, Mustang!, Call It Courage, Ringo the Refugee Raccoon, Shokee the Everglades Panther, Deacon the High-Noon Dog, Wise One, Whale's Tooth, Track of African Bongo, Dorsey the Mail-Carrying Dog.

DIXON, BARBARA
Executive. b. Pasadena CA. e. USC, grad. degree from Johns Hopkins U. Served as staff member of Senate Judiciary Committee and was dir. of legislation for Sen. Birch Bayh, 1974-79. Left to become dir. of Office of Government & Public Affairs of Natl. Transportation Safety Board. Named v.p., Fratelli Group, p.r. firm in Washington; took leave of absence in 1984 to serve as deputy press secty. to Democratic V.P. candidate, Geraldine Ferraro. In 1985 joined Motion Picture Assn. of America as v.p. for public affairs.

DIXON, DONNA
Actress. b. Alexandria, VA, July 20, 1957. m. actor-writer Dan Aykroyd. e. Studied anthropology and medicine, Mary Washington U. Left to become a model, both on magazine covers and in TV commercials (Vitalis, Max Factor, Gillette).
PICTURES: Dr. Detroit, Twilight Zone--The Movie, Spies Like Us, The Couch Trip, It Had To Be You, Speed Zone, Lucky Stiff, Wayne's World.
TELEVISION: Series: Bosom Buddies, Berrenger's. Movies: Mickey Spillane's Margin for Murder, No Man's Land, Beverly Hills Madam. Specials: Women Who Rate a "10," The Shape of Things, The Rodney Dangerfield Show: I Can't Take it No More.

DIXON, WHEELER WINSTON
Educator, Writer, Filmmaker. b. New Brunswick, NJ, March 12, 1950. e. Rutgers U. In 1960s asst. writer for Time/Life publications; also writer for Interview magazine. 1976, directed TV commercials in NY. One season with TVTV, Los Angeles, as post-prod. suprv. 1978, formed Deliniator Films, Inc., serving as exec. prod./dir. Since 1988 has directed film program at Univ. of Nebraska, holds rank of tenured full prof. and chair, Film Studies Prog.; received Rockefeller Foundation grant. Prod., dir. with Gwendolyn Audrey-Foster: Women Who Made the Movies (video). Prod/Dir: What Can I Do?, Squatters. 1992, guest programmer at the British Film Inst./Natl. Film Theatre. 1993, Distinguished Teaching Award. Invited lecturer at Yale, 1995; invited lecturer at New School for Social Research, 1997. Series ed. for SUNY Press Cultural Studies in Cinema/Video (20 vol.)
AUTHOR: The 'B' Directors, 1985; The Cinematic Vision of F. Scott Fitzgerald, 1986; PRC: A History of Producer's Releasing Corp., 1986; books on Freddie Francis, Terence Fisher, Reginald Le Borg, 1992-93; The Early Film Criticism of Francois Truffaut; Re-Viewing British Cinema, 1900-92; It Looks at You: The Returned Gaze of Cinema, 1995; The Films of Jean-Luc Godard, 1997; The Exploding Eye: A Revisionary History of 1960s American Experimental Cinema, 1997.

DMYTRYK, EDWARD
Director. b. Grand Forks, B.C., Canada, Sept. 4, 1908. Entered employ Paramount 1923, working as messenger after school. Film editor 1930-39. One of the ``Hollywood Ten'' who was held in contempt by the House UnAmerican Activities Comm. 1947. The only one to recant. Autobiography: It's a Hell of a Life But Not a Bad Living (1979).
PICTURES: The Hawk (debut, 1935), Television Spy, Emergency Squad, Golden Gloves, Mystery Sea Raider, Her First Romance, The Devil Commands, Under Age, Sweetheart of the Campus, The Blonde From Singapore, Confessions of Boston Blackie, Secrets of the Lone Wolf, Counter-Espionage, Seven Miles From Alcatraz, Hilter's Children, The Falcon Strikes Back, Behind the Rising Sun, Captive Wild Woman Tender Comrade, Murder My Sweet, Back to Bataan, Cornered, Till the End of Time, Crossfire (Acad. Award nom.), So Well Remembered, Obsession (The Hidden Room), Give Us This Day, Mutiny, The Sniper, Eight Iron Men, The Juggler, The Caine Mutiny, Broken Lance, The End of the Affair, The Left Hand of God, Soldier of Fortune, The Mountain (also prod.), Raintree County, The Young Lions, Warlock (also prod.), The Blue Angel, The Reluctant Saint (It.), Walk on the Wild Side, The Carpetbaggers, Where Love Has Gone, Mirage, Alvarez Kelly, Shalako, Anzio, Bluebeard, The Human Factor, He Is My Brother.

DOBSON, KEVIN
Actor. b. New York, NY, March 18, 1943.
PICTURES: Love Story, Bananas, Klute, The Anderson Tapes, The French Connection, Carnal Knowledge, Midway, All Night Long.
TELEVISION: Series: Kojak, Shannon, Knots Landing (also dir. 9 episodes), F/X: The Series. Movies: The Immigrants, Transplant, Orphan Train, Hardhat and Legs, Reunion, Mark I Love You, Mickey Splillane's Margin for Murder, Money Power Murder (also prod.), Casey's Gift: For Love of a Child, Sweet Revenge, Fatal Friendship, Dirty Work, House of Secrets and Lies, The Conviction of Kitty Dodds, If Someone Had Known, Crimes of Passion: Voice from the Grave, Nobody Lives Forever. Mini-series: Knots Landing: Back to the Cul-de-Sac. Guest: The Nurses, The Doctors, Greatest Heroes of the Bible.

DOCTOROW, ERIC
Executive. Pres., Home Video Division of Viacom, Inc. Worldwide Video.

DOERFLER, RONALD J.
Executive. e. Fairleigh Dickinson Univ. Became CPA in 1967. 1972, received M.B.A. from Fairleigh Dickinson. Joined Capital Cities 1969 as asst. controller. Became treas. in 1977; v.p. & CFO, 1980. 1983, named sr. v.p.,.then sr. v.p. & CFO.

DOHERTY, SHANNEN
Actress. b. Memphis, TN, April 12, 1971. On stage in The Mound Builders.
PICTURES: Night Shift, The Secret of NIMH (voice), Girls Just Want to Have Fun, Heathers, Freeze Frame, Mall Rats, Nowhere.
TELEVISION: Series: Little House on the Prairie, Our House, Beverly Hills 90210. Movies: The Other Lover, Obsessed, Blindfold, Jailbreakers, A Burning Passion: The Margaret Mitchell Story, Gone in the Night, Friends 'Til the End, Sleeping with the Devil, The Ticket. Mini-Series: Robert Kennedy and His Times. Pilot: His and Hers. Guest: 21 Jump Street, Cagney and Lacey, Highway to Heaven, Life Goes On, The Dennis Miller Show, Parker Lewis Can't Lose.

DOLAN, CHARLES F.
Executive. b. Cleveland, OH, Oct. 16, 1926. e. John Carroll U. Established Teleguide Inc., early 1960s. Found. Sterling Manhattan Cable, mid 1960s. Found. Home Box Office Inc., early 1970s; after sale of HBO to Time Life Inc., organized Cablevision Systems Corp., 1973; presently, chmn. Chmn., Natl Acad. of TV Arts & Sci. Bd. govs., Natl Hockey League. Bd. dirs.: Madison Square Garden Prop.; St. Francis Hospital, NY. Mng. dir., Metropolitan Opera of NY. Trustee, Fairfield U, CT.

DOLAN, JAMES L.
Executive. Began working at Cablevision in the 1970s, in construction, field sales & collections depts.; named asst. gen mngr. of Cablevision of Chicago, late 1970's. Early 1980s, as Cablevision v.p., found. & mngd. WKNR-AM, Cleveland; also oversaw weekly TV mag. Total. During the 1980s, corp. dir. advt., at Rainbow, & v.p. for advt. sales at Cablevision. CEO, Rainbow Media Holdings, Inc., 1993-1995. CEO, Cablevision Systems Corp., 1995-; also on bd. dirs., & exec. com. On bd. & exec. com., Natl Cable TV Assn., & chair., music licensing com. On bd. dirs., Hazelden NY & Cable Labs, CO. Hon. co-chair, LI Film & TV Found.

DOLGEN, JONATHAN L.
Executive. b. New York, NY, April 27, 1945. e. Cornell U., NYU Sch. of Law. Began career with Wall Street law firm, Fried, Frank, Harris, Shriver & Jacobson. In 1976 joined Columbia Pictures Industries as asst. gen. counsel and deputy gen. counsel. 1979, named sr. v.p. in chg. of worldwide business affairs; 1980, named exec. v.p. Joined Columbia m.p. div., 1981; named pres. of Columbia Pay-Cable & Home Entertainment Group. Also pres. Columbia Pictures domestic operations, overseeing Music Group. 1985, joined 20th-Fox in newly created position of sr. exec. v.p. for telecommunications. Became pres. of Sony Motion Picture Group, 1991. Appointed chmn. Viacom Entertainment Group, 1994.

DONAHUE, ELINOR
Actress. b. Tacoma, WA, April 19, 1937.
PICTURES: Mr. Big, Tenth Avenue Angel, Unfinished Dance, Three Daring Daughters, Love is Better Than Ever, Girls Town, Pretty Woman, Freddy's Dead: The Final Nightmare.
TELEVISION: Series: Father Knows Best, The Andy Griffith Show, Many Happy Returns, The Odd Couple, Mulligan's Stew, Please Stand By, Days of Our Lives,The New Adventures of Beans Baxter, Get a Life. Pilot: The Grady Nutt Show. Guest: One Day at a Time, Sweepstakes$, The Golden Girls. Movies: In Name Only, Gidget Gets Married, Mulligan's Stew (pilot), Doctors' Private Lives, Condominium, High School U.S.A. Special: Father Knows Best Reunion.

DONAHUE, PHIL
Television Host. b. Cleveland, OH, Dec. 21, 1935. e. Notre Dame, BBA. m. actress Marlo Thomas. Worked as check sorter, Albuquerque Natl. Bank, 1957, then as announcer at KYW-TV & AM, Cleveland; news dir. WABJ radio, Adrian, MI; morning newscaster WHIO-TV. Interviews with Jimmy Hoffa and Billy Sol Estes picked up nationally by CBS. Host of Conversation Piece, phone-in talk show. Debuted The Phil Donahue Show, daytime talk show in Dayton, Ohio, 1967. Syndicated 2 years later. Moved to Chicago, 1974. Host, Donahue, now in 165 outlets in U.S. In 1979 a mini-version of show became 3-times-a-week segment on NBC's Today Show. Winner of several Emmys. Books: Donahue: My Own Story (1980), The Human Animal (1985).

DONAHUE, TROY
Actor. r.n. Merle Johnson, Jr. b. New York, NY, Jan. 27, 1937. e. Bayport H.S., N.Y. Military Acad. Columbia U., Journalism. Directed, wrote, acted in school plays. Summer stock, Bucks County Playhouse, Sayville Playhouse; contract, Warner Brothers, 1959.
PICTURES: Man Afraid (debut, 1957), The Tarnished Angels, This Happy Feeling, The Voice in the Mirror, Live Fast Die Young, Monster on the Campus, Summer Love, Wild Heritage, The Perfect Furlough, Imitation of Life, A Summer Place, The Crowded Sky, Parrish, Susan Slade, Rome Adventure, Palm Springs Weekend, A Distant Trumpet, My Blood Runs Cold, Blast-Off! (Those Fantastic Flying Fools), Come Spy With Me, Sweet Savior, Cockfighter, Seizure, The Godfather Part II, Tin Man, Grandview U.S.A., Low Blow, Cyclone, Deadly Prey, American Revenge, Dr. Alien (I Was a Teenage Sex Mutant), Sexpot, Hard Rock Nightmare, Bad Blood, John Travis, Solar Survivor, The Chilling, The Housewarming, Deadly Spy Games, Assault of the Party Nerds, Deadly Diamonds, Deadly Embrace, Cry-Baby, Double Trouble.
TELEVISION: Series: Hawaiian Eye, Surfside 6. Guest: Matt Houston. Movies: Split Second to an Epitaph, The Loneliest Profession, Malibu.

DONALDSON, ROGER
Director. b. Ballarat, Australia, Nov. 15, 1945. Emigrated to New Zealand at 19. Established still photography business; then began making documentaries. Directed Winners and Losers, a series of short dramas for NZ-TV.
PICTURES: Sleeping Dogs (also prod.), Smash Palace (also s.p. prod.), The Bounty, Marie, No Way Out, Cocktail, Cadillac Man (also prod.), White Sands, The Getaway, Species, Dante's Peak.

DONEN, STANLEY
Director, Producer, Choreographer. b. Columbia, SC, April 13, 1924. e. USC. Former dancer, B'way debut 1940 in chorus of Pal Joey starring Gene Kelly. Assisted Kelly as choreog. on stage prod. of Best Foot Forward; hired by MGM to repeat duties in film version. Choreographer or co-choreographer on such films as Cover Girl, Holiday in Mexico, This Time for Keeps, A Date With Judy, Take Me Out to the Ballgame (also co-story credit). Honorary Acad. Award, 1997.
PICTURES: Director: On the Town (debut, 1949; co-dir. with Gene Kelly), Royal Wedding, Singin' in the Rain (co-dir., co-choreog. with Gene Kelly), Fearless Fagan, Love Is Better Than Ever, Give a Girl a Break (also co-choreog.), Seven Brides for Seven Brothers, Deep in My Heart (also co-choreog.), It's Always Fair Weather (co-dir., co-choreog. with Gene Kelly), Funny Face, The Pajama Game (co-dir., co-prod. with George Abbott), Kiss Them for Me. Director-Producer: Indiscreet, Damn Yankees (co-dir., co-prod. with George Abbott), Once More With Feeling, Surprise Package, The Grass Is Greener, Charade, Arabesque, Two for the Road, Bedazzled, Staircase, The Little Prince, Lucky Lady (dir. only), Movie Movie, Saturn 3, Blame It on Rio.
TELEVISION: Actor: The Making of Seven Brides for Seven Brothers, The Hollywood Fashion Machine.

DONIGER, WALTER
Writer, Director, Producer. b. New York NY. e. Valley Forge Military Academy, Duke U., Harvard U. Graduate Business Sch. Entered m.p. business as writer later writer-prod-dir. Wrote documentaries in Army Air Forces M.P. Unit in W.W.II. WGA award nominee and other awards.
PICTURES: Rope of Sand, Desperate Search, Cease Fire, Safe At Home (dir.), House of Women (dir.), Duffy of San Quentin (dir.), Along the Great Divide, Tokyo Joe, Alaska Seas, Steel Cage (dir.), Steel Jungle (dir.), Hold Back the Night, Guns of Fort Petticoat, Unwed Mother (dir.), Stone Cold (exec. prod., s.p.).
TELEVISION: Series: Delvecchio, Mad Bull, Switch, Moving On, Baa Baa Blacksheep, McCloud, The Man and the City, Sarge, Owen Marshall, Peyton Place, Mr. Novak, The Greatest Show on Earth, Travels of Jaimie McPheeters, Outlaws, Hong Kong, Checkmate, Bat Masterson, The Web, Bold Venture, Tombstone Territory, Maverick, Rough Riders, Lockup, Dick Powell, The Survivors, Bracken's World, Bold Ones, Kung Fu, Barnaby Jones, Marcus Welby, Lucas Tanner, etc.

DONNELLY, DONAL
Actor. b. Bradford, England, July 6, 1931. Studied for theatre at the Dublin Gate Theatre.
THEATER: *NY Theatre*: Philadelphia Here I Come (B'way debut, 1966), Joe Egg, Sleuth (NY and U.S. tour), The Elephant Man, The Faith-Healer, The Chalk Garden, My Astonishing Self, Big Maggie, Execution of Justice, Sherlock's Last Case, Ghetto, Dancing at Lughnasa, Translations.
PICTURES: Rising of the Moon (1957), Gideon's Day, Shake Hands With the Devil, Young Cassidy, The Knack, Up Jumped a Swagman, The Mind of Mr. Soames, Waterloo, The Dead, The Godfather Part III, Squanto: A Warrior's Tale, Korea.
TELEVISION: Juno and the Paycock (BBC, 1958), Home Is the Hero, The Venetian Twins, The Plough and the Stars, Playboy of the Western World, Sergeant Musgrave's Dance, Yes-Honestly (series).

DONNELLY, RALPH E.
Executive. b. Lynbrook, NY, Jan. 20, 1932. e. Bellmore, NY public school; W. C. Mepham H.S., 1949. Worked for Variety (publication) as writer, 1950; Long Island Press as daily columnist, 1953, as gen. mgr.; later film buyer; in 1973 left to become independent buyer and booker for Creative Films; film buyer and v.p., RKO/Stanley Warner Theatres, 1976-79; pres. & gen. mgr. for Cinema 5 Ltd. circuit, N.Y., 1980-87; 1987-93, exec. v.p. City Cinemas, N.Y. Now chmn. of Cinema Connection.

DONNER, CLIVE
Director. b. London, England,, Jan 21, 1926. Ent. m.p. ind. 1942. Asst. film ed. Denham Studios, 1942. Dir. London stage: The Formation Dancers, The Front Room Boys, Kennedy's Children (also NY). *Film editor*: A Christmas Carol (Scrooge), The Card (The Promoter), Genevieve, Man With a Million (The Million Pound Note), The Purple Plain, I Am a Camera.
PICTURES: The Secret Place (debut, 1957), Heart of a Child, Marriage of Convenience, The Sinister Man, Some People, The Caretaker (The Guest), Nothing But the Best, What's New Pussycat?, Luv, Here We Go Round the Mulberry Bush (also prod.), Alfred the Great, Old Dracula (Vampira), The Nude Bomb, Charlie Chan and the Curse of the Dragon Queen, Stealing Heaven.
TELEVISION: Danger Man, Sir Francis Drake, Mighty and Mystical, British Institutions, Tempo, Spectre, The Thief of Baghdad, Oliver Twist, Rogue Male, The Scarlet Pimpernel, Arthur the King, To Catch a King, Three Hostages, She Fell Among Thieves, A Christmas Carol, Dead Man's Folly, Babes in Toyland, Not a Penny More Not a Penny Less, Coup de Foudre (Love at First Sight), Terror Strikes the Class Reunion (For Better or Worse), Charlemagne.

DONNER, RICHARD
Director. b. New York, NY, 1939. Began career as actor off-B'way. Worked with director Martin Ritt on TV production of Maugham's Of Human Bondage. Moved to California 1958, directing commercials, industrial films and documentaries. First TV drama: Wanted: Dead or Alive.
PICTURES: X-15 (debut, 1961), Salt and Pepper, Twinky (Lola), The Omen, Superman, Inside Moves, The Final Conflict (exec. prod. only), The Toy (also exec. prod.), Ladyhawke (also prod.), The Goonies (also prod.), Lethal Weapon (also prod.), The Lost Boys (exec. prod. only), Scrooged (also prod.), Lethal Weapon 2 (also prod.), Delirious (exec. prod. only), Radio Flyer, Lethal Weapon 3 (also prod.), Free Willy (co-exec. prod. only), Maverick (also prod.), Tales From the Crypt Presents Demon Knight (co-exec. prod. only), Assassins (also prod.), Conspiracy Theory (also prod.), Free Willy 3: The Rescue (exec. prod.), Lethal Weapon 4.
TELEVISION: *Series episodes:* Have Gun Will Travel, Perry Mason, Cannon, Get Smart, The Fugitive, Kojak, Bronk, Gilligan's Island, Man From U.N.C.L.E., Wild Wild West, Tales From the Crypt, Two Fisted Tales, Twilight Zone, The Banana Splits, Combat. *Movies*: Lucas Tanner (pilot), Sarah T.: Portrait of a Teen-Age Alcoholic, Senior Year, A Shadow in the Streets, Tales From the Crypt (exec. prod.; also dir. episode: Dig That Cat... He's Real Gone).

D'ONOFRIO, VINCENT PHILLIP
Actor. b. Brooklyn, NY, 1960. Studied acting with the American Stanislavsky Theatre in NY, appearing in Of Mice and Men, The Petrified Forest, Sexual Perversity in Chicago, and The Indian Wants the Bronx.
THEATER: *B'way*: Open Admissions.
PICTURES: The First Turn On! (debut, 1984), Full Metal Jacket, Adventures in Babysitting, Mystic Pizza, Signs of Life, The Blood of Heroes, Crooked Hearts, Dying Young, Fires Within, Naked Tango, JFK, The Player, Desire, Household Saints, Mr. Wonderful, Being Human, Ed Wood, Imaginary Crimes, Stuart Saves His Family, Strange Days, Feeling Minnesota, Men in Black.

DONOHOE, AMANDA
Actress. b. London, England, June 29, 1962. e. Francis Holland Sch. for Girls, Central Sch. of Speech & Drama. Member of Royal Exchange Theatre in Manchester. B'way debut 1995 in Uncle Vanya.
PICTURES: Foreign Body (debut, 1986), Castaway, The Lair of the White Worm, The Rainbow, Tank Malling, Diamond Skulls (Dark Obsession), Paper Mask, The Madness of King George, Liar Liar, Writer's Block, I'm Losing You.
TELEVISION: *Series*: L.A. Law (Golden Globe Award). *Movies*: Married to Murder, Shame, It's Nothing Personal (also co-exec. prod.), The Substitute, Shame II: The Secret (also co-exec. prod.). *Special*: Game Set and Match (Mystery!). *Guest:* The Hidden Room, Murder Most Horrid, Frasier.

DONOVAN, ARLENE
Producer. b. Kentucky. e. Stratford Coll., VA. Worked in publishing before entering industry as asst. to late dir. Robert Rosen on Cocoa Beach, uncompleted at his death. Worked as story editor, Columbia Pictures. 1969-82, literary head of m.p. dept. for ICM; involved in book publishing as well as stage and screen projects.
PICTURES: Still of the Night, Places in the Heart, Nadine, The House on Carroll Street (co-exec. prod.), Billy Bathgate, Nobody's Fool, Twilight.

DONOVAN, HENRY B.
Executive, Producer. b. Boston, MA. Entered m.p. ind. for RKO Pathe Studios, property master, special effects dir., unit mgr., asst. dir., prod. mgr.; worked on over 320 pictures; Harry Sherman, Hopalong Cassidy features (for Paramount). 10 yrs., U.S. Army Signal Corps, as head of dept. of California studios prod. training m.p.; pres.: Telemount Pictures, Inc. Prod., dir., writer Cowboy G Men (TV series). Wrote: Corkscrewed (novel), 7 Zane Grey westerns for Paramount. Founder and Chairman of SCOA & SCOW Corp.
PICTURES: Hopalong Cassidy Features, Gone with the Wind, Becky Sharp, Our Flag (dir.), Magic Lady (13 one-reel features), others. Cowboy G Men (prod., writer; 39 films).
TELEVISION: programming, financing, distribution. Global Scope; International TV; Dist., Financing, programming; sls. consultant, Intl. TV & motion pictures. Cable TV & distribution & program development, collector of movie memorabilia; DBS TV programming & financing: production software. Worldwide TV consultant. Created Silicon Valley for satellite B.D. Frontier Lawyer: Historical United States of America.

DONOVAN, TATE
Actor. b. New York, NY, 1964. Raised in New Jersey. Studied acting at USC. Worked as still photographer for two Mutual of Omaha documentaries.
THEATER: Ruffian on the Stair, The American Plan, The Rhythm of Torn Stars, Bent. B'way: Picnic.
PICTURES: SpaceCamp, Clean and Sober, Dead Bang, Memphis Belle, Love Potion No. 9, Ethan Frome, Equinox, Holy Matrimony, Murder at 1600, Hercules (voice).
TELEVISION: *Series*: Partners. *Movies*: Not My Kid, Into Thin Air, A Case of Deadly Force, Nutcracker: Money Madness Murder. *HBO Special*: Vietnam War Stories.

DOOHAN, JAMES
Actor. b. Vancouver, B.C., Canada, March 3, 1920. WWII capt. in Royal Canadian Artillery. 1946 won scholarship to Neighborhood Playhouse in NY and later taught there. 1953, returned to Canada to live in Toronto, becoming engaged in acting career on radio, TV and in film. Then to Hollywood and chief fame as Chief Engineer Scott in TV series, Star Trek.
PICTURES: The Wheeler Dealers, The Satan Bug, Bus Riley's Back in Town, Pretty Maids All in a Row, Star Trek—The Motion Picture, Star Trek II: The Wrath of Khan, Star Trek III: The Search for Spock, Star Trek IV: The Voyage Home, Star Trek V: The Final Frontier, Star Trek VI: The Undiscovered Country, Double Trouble, National Lampoon's Loaded Weapon 1, Star Trek: Generations.
TELEVISION: *Series*: Star Trek. *Guest*: Hazel, Bonanza, The Virginia, Gunsmoke, Peyton Place, The Fugitive, Marcus Welby MD, Ben Casey, Bewitched, Fantasy Island, etc. Movie: Scalplock.

DOOLEY, PAUL
Actor. b. Parkersburg, WV, Feb. 22, 1928. Began career on NY stage in Threepenny Opera. Later member of Second City. B'way credits include The Odd Couple, Adaptation/Next, The White House Murder Case, Hold Me, etc. Co-creator and writer for The Electric Company on PBS. Owns co. called All Over Creation.
PICTURES: What's So Bad About Feeling Good? (debut, 1968), The Out-of-Towners, Death Wish, The Gravy Train, Slap Shot, A Wedding, A Perfect Couple, Breaking Away, Rich Kids, Popeye, Health (also co-s.p.), Paternity, Endangered Species, Kiss Me Goodbye, Strange Brew, Going Berserk, Sixteen Candles, Big Trouble, O.C. and Stiggs, Monster in the Closet, Last Rites, Flashback, Shakes the Clown, The Player, My Boyfriend's Back, A Dangerous Woman, The Underneath, God's Lonely Man.

TELEVISION: *Specials*: Faerie Tale Theater, The Firm, Traveler's Rest, Tales of the City. *Movies*: The Murder of Mary Phagan, Lip Service, Guts and Glory: The Rise and Fall of Oliver North, When He's Not a Stranger, The Court Martial of Jackie Robinson, Guess Who's Coming for Christmas?, White Hot: The Mysterious Murder of Thelma Todd, Cooperstown, Mother of the Bride, State of Emergency, The Computer Wore Tennis Shoes. *Series*: The Dom DeLuise Show, Coming of Age. *Guest:* Dream On, ALF, The Golden Girls, thirtysomething, Mad About You, Evening Shade, Coach, Wonder Years, The Boys, L.A. Law, The Mommies, Star Trek: Deep Space Nine, many others.

DORAN, LINDSAY
Executive. b. Los Angeles, CA. e. U. of California at Santa Cruz. Moved to London where was contributing author to The Oxford Companion to Film and the World Encyclopedia of Film. Returned to U.S. to write and produce documentaries and children's programs for Pennsylvania public affairs station WPSX-TV. Career in m.p. industry began in story dept. at Embassy Pictures which she joined in 1979; 1982 promoted to dir. of development; then v.p., creative affairs. 1985, joined Paramount Pictures as v.p., production, for MP Group. 1987, promoted to senior v.p., production. 1989, appointed pres., Mirage Productions. Pres. and COO, United Artists Pictures, 1996-.

DORFF, STEPHEN
Actor. b. July 29, 1973. Started acting at age 9.
PICTURES: The Gate (debut, 1987), The Power of One, An Ambush of Ghosts, Judgment Night, Rescue Me, BackBeat, S.F.W., Reckless, Innocent Lies, I Shot Andy Warhol, City of Industry.
TELEVISION: *Series*: What a Dummy. *Movies*: I Know My First Name Is Steven, Always Remember I Love You, Do You Know the Muffin Man?, A Son's Promise. *Guest*: Empty Nest, Roseanne, The Outsiders, Married...With Children, Empty Nest.

DORTORT, DAVID
Executive Producer. b. New York, NY, Oct. 23, 1916. e. City Coll. of New York. Served U.S. Army, 1943-46. Novelist and short story writer, 1943-49. Also TV writer. Now pres. of Xanadu Prods., Aurora Enterprises, Inc., and Bonanza Ventures, Inc. & Pres. TV branch, WGA, West, 1954-55; TV-radio branch, 1955-57; v.p. PGA, 1967; pres. 1968. Chmn., Caucus for Producers, Writers and Directors, 1973-75. Pres., PGA, 1980-81; campaign dir., Permanent Charities Comm. 1980-81; chmn., Interguild Council 1980-81. Received WGA/West noms. for TV work on An Error in Chemistry (Climax), and The Ox-Bow Incident (20th Century Fox Hour). Author: novels include Burial of the Fruit, The Post of Honor.
PICTURES: The Lusty Men, Reprisal, The Big Land, Cry in the Night, Clash by Night, Going Bananas (exec. prod.).
TELEVISION: *Creator and exec. prod.*: Bonanza, High Chaparral, The Chisholms, Hunter's Moon, Bonanza: Legends of the Ponderosa. *Producer:* The Restless Gun, The Cowboys. *Creator, story and exec. prod.*: Bonanza: The Next Generation. *Exec. prod.*: Bonanza: The Return, Bonanza: Under Attack.

DOUGHERTY, MARION
Executive. e. Penn St. U. Gained fame as casting director. Casting dir. on series Naked City, Route 66. Formed own co. in 1965. Acted as co-exec. prod. on Smile, 1975. In 1977 named v.p. in chg. talent for Paramount Pictures. In 1979 joined Warner Bros. as sr. v.p. in chg. talent to work with production dept. and producers and directors.
CASTING: A Little Romance, Urban Cowboy, Honky Tonk Freeway, Reds, Firefox, Honkytonk Man, The World According to Garp, Sudden Impact, The Man With Two Brains, The Killing Fields, Swing Shift, The Little Drummer Girl, Lethal Weapon (also 2 & 3), Batman, Batman Returns, Forever Young, Falling Down.

DOUGLAS, ILLEANA
Actress. Grandfather was actor Melvyn Douglas. Directed short films The Perfect Woman (Aspen Film Fest. prize, 1994), Boy Crazy—Girl Crazier.
THEATER: *NY*: Takes on Women, As Sure as You Live, Black Eagles.
PICTURES: Hello Again, New York Stories (Life Lessons), GoodFellas, Guilty By Suspicion, Cape Fear, Alive, Household Saints, Grief, Quiz Show, Search and Destroy, To Die For, Grace of My Heart, Picture Perfect.

DOUGLAS, KIRK
Actor, Producer, Director. r.n. Issur Danielovitch (changed to Demsky). b. Amsterdam, NY, Dec. 9, 1916. m. Anne Buydens, pres. of Bryna Prod. Co. Father of Michael, Joel, Peter, Eric. e. St. Lawrence U, B.A, AADA. Stage debut in New York: Spring Again. U.S. Navy during W.W.II; resumed stage work. Did radio soap operas. Signed by Hal B. Wallis for film debut. Autobiography: The Ragman's Son (1988). Novels: Dance With the Devil, The Secret, Last Tango in Brooklyn. Recipient of U.S. Presidential Medal of Freedom, 1981. Career achievement award, National Board of Review, 1989. Received AFI Lifetime Achievement Award, 1991.

THEATER: Spring Again, Three Sisters, Kiss and Tell, Trio, The Wind is Ninetry, Star in the Window, Man Bites Dog, One Flew Over the Cuckoo's Nest, The Boys of Autumn.
PICTURES: The Strange Love of Martha Ivers (debut, 1946), Out of the Past, I Walk Alone, Mourning Becomes Electra, The Walls of Jericho, My Dear Secretary, Letter to Three Wives, Champion, Young Man with a Horn, The Glass Menagerie, Ace in the Hole (The Big Carnival), Along the Great Divide, Detective Story, The Big Trees, The Big Sky, Bad and the Beautiful, Story of Three Loves, The Juggler, Act of Love, 20,000 Leagues Under the Sea, Ulysses, Man Without a Star, The Racers, The Indian Fighter (also prod.), Lust for Life, Top Secret Affair, Gunfight at the OK Corral, Paths of Glory, The Vikings (also prod.), Last Train from Gun Hill, The Devil's Disciple, Strangers When We Meet, Spartacus (also prod.), The Last Sunset, Town Without Pity, Lonely Are the Brave (also prod.), Two Weeks in Another Town, The Hook, List of Adrian Messenger (also prod.), For Love or Money, Seven Days in May (also prod.), In Harm's Way, The Heroes of Telemark, Cast a Giant Shadow, Is Paris Burning?, The Way West, The War Wagon, A Lovely Way to Die, The Brotherhood (also prod.), The Arrangement, There Was a Crooked Man, A Gunfight, Summertree (prod. only), The Light at the Edge of the World (also prod.), Catch Me a Spy, Scalawag (also dir., prod.), Master Touch, Once is Not Enough, Posse (also dir., prod.), The Chosen, The Fury, The Villain, Saturn III, Home Movies, The Final Countdown, The Man from Snowy River, Eddie Macon's Run, Tough Guys, Oscar, Welcome to Veraz, Greedy, A Century of Cinema, The Films of John Frankenheimer, A Song for David.
TELEVISION: *Movies*: Mousey, The Money Changers, Draw! (HBO), Victory at Entebbe, Remembrance of Love, Amos, Queenie, Inherit the Wind, The Secret, Take Me Home Again. *Guest*: The Lucy Show, Tales From the Crypt (Yellow). *Specials*: Legend of Silent Night, Dr. Jekyll & Mr. Hyde.

DOUGLAS, MICHAEL
Actor, Producer. b. New Brunswick, NJ, Sept 25, 1944. p. Kirk Douglas and Diana Dill. e. Black Fox Military Acad., Choate, U. of California. Worked as asst. director on Lonely Are the Brave, Heroes of Telemark, Cast a Giant Shadow; after TV debut in The Experiment (CBS Playhouse), appeared off-Broadway in City Scene, Pinkville (Theatre World Award). Produced 1993 Off-B'way show The Best of Friends.
PICTURES: Hail Hero (debut, 1969), Adam at 6 A.M., Summertree, Napoleon and Samantha, One Flew Over the Cuckoo's Nest (co-prod. only; Acad. Award for Best Picture, 1975), Coma, The China Syndrome (also prod.), Running (also exec. prod.), It's My Turn, The Star Chamber, Romancing the Stone (also prod.), Starman (exec. prod. only), A Chorus Line, The Jewel of the Nile (also prod.), Fatal Attraction, Wall Street (Acad. Award; Natl. Board of Review Award, 1987), Black Rain, The War of the Roses, Flatliners (co-exec. prod. only), Shining Through, Radio Flyer (co-exec. prod. only), Basic Instinct, Falling Down, Made in America (co-exec. prod. only), Disclosure, The American President, The Ghost and the Darkness, Face/Off (exec. prod. only), The Game.
TELEVISION: *Series*: Streets of San Francisco. *Guest*: The FBI, Medical Center. *Movies*: Streets of San Francisco (pilot), When Michael Calls.

DOUGLAS, MIKE
TV host. r.n. Michael Delaney Dowd, Jr. b. Chicago, IL, Aug. 11, 1925. Started career singing with bands in and around Chicago. 1950-54 featured singer with Kay Kyser's band. In 1953 became host of WGN-TV's Hi Ladies in Chicago; also featured on WMAQ-TV, NBC, Chicago, as singer and host. Moved to Hollywood in late '50s, working as piano bar singer. In 1961 hired as host for new show on station KYW-TV in Cleveland, owned by Westinghouse Bdg. Co., featuring celebrity guests. This became the Mike Douglas Show which was later nationally syndicated and moved base of operations to Philadelphia, then Los Angeles. Ran 21 years til Mid-1982. Books: The Mike Douglas Cookbook (1969), Mike Douglas My Story (1978), When the Going Gets Tough.
PICTURES: Gator, Nasty Habits, The Incredible Shrinking Woman.

DOUMANIAN, JEAN
Producer.
PICTURES: Oxen, Bullets Over Broadway (exec. prod.), Mighty Aphrodite (exec. prod.), Everyone Says I Love You (exec. prod.), Deconstructing Harry, Story of a Bad Boy, Elements, Wild Man Blues.

DOURIF, BRAD
Actor. b. Huntington, WV, March 18, 1950. Studied with Stanford Meisner. Stage actor, three years with Circle Repertory Co., NY (When You Comin' Back Red Ryder?), before films and TV.
PICTURES: Split, One Flew Over the Cuckoo's Nest (Acad. Award nom., Golden Globe & BAFTA Awards, 1975), Group Portrait with Lady, Eyes of Laura Mars, Wise Blood, Heaven's Gate, Ragtime, Dune, Impure Thoughts, Istanbul, Blue Velvet, Fatal Beauty, Child's Play, Mississippi Burning, Medium Rare, The Exorcist: 1990, Spontaneous Combustion, Grim Prairie Tales, Sonny Boy, Graveyard Shift, Child's Play II, Hidden Agenda, Dead Certain, Jungle Fever, The Horseplayer, Body Parts, Child's Play 3, Common Bonds, Scream of Stone, Critters 4, London Kills Me, Diary of the Hurdy Gurdy Man, Murder Blues, Final Judgment, Amos & Andrew, Trauma, Color of Night, Murder in the First.

TELEVISION: *Movies*: Sgt. Matlovitch vs. the U.S. Air Force, Guyana Tragedy—The Story of Jim Jones, I Desire, Vengeance: The Story of Tony Cimo, Rage of Angels: The Story Continues, Desperado: The Outlaw Wars, Class of '61, Escape From Terror: The Teresa Stamper Story, Escape to Witch Mountain. *Mini-Series*: Studs Lonigan, Wild Palms. *Specials*: Mound Builders, The Gardener's Son. *Guest*: Miami Vice, The Hitchhiker, Spencer for Hire, Tales of the Unexpected, Moonlighting, The Equalizer, Murder She Wrote, Babylon 5, Voyager.

DOWN, LESLEY-ANNE
Actress. b. London, England, March 17, 1954. At age of 10 modeled for TV and film commercials, leading to roles in features. Film debut at 14 in The Smashing Bird I Used to Know (billed as Lesley Down).
THEATER: Great Expectations, Hamlet, etc.
PICTURES: The Smashing Bird I Used to Know (debut, 1969), All the Right Noises, Countess Dracula, Assault, Pope Joan, Scalawag, From Beyond the Grave, Brannigan, The Pink Panther Strikes Again, The Betsy, A Little Night Music, The Great Train Robbery, Hanover Street, Rough Cut, Sphinx, Nomads, Scenes from the Goldmine, Mardi Gras for the Devil, Death Wish V: The Face of Death, Munchie Stikes Back, The Unfaithful, Beastmaster III, The Secret Agent Club, Meet Wally Sparks.
TELEVISION: *Series*: Upstairs, Downstairs, Dallas, Sunset Beach. *Movies*: Agatha Christie's Murder is Easy, Hunchback of Notre Dame, The One and Only Phyllis Dixey, Arch of Triumph, Indiscreet, Lady Killers, Night Walk, Family of Cops. *Mini-Series*: North and South Books I & II & III, Last Days of Pompeii. *Specials*: Unity Mitford,. Heartbreak House. *Pilots*: Shivers, 1775.

DOWNEY, ROBERT, JR.
Actor. b. New York, NY, April 4, 1965. Father is indep. filmmaker Robert Downey. Film debut at age 5 in his father's film Pound.
PICTURES: Pound (debut, 1970), Greaser's Palace, Jive, Up the Academy, Baby Its You, Firstborn, Tuff Turf, Weird Science, To Live and Die in L.A., Back to School, America, The Pick-Up Artist, Less Than Zero, Johnny B. Good, Rented Lips, 1969, True Believer, Chances Are, That's Adequate, Air America, Too Much Sun, Soapdish, Chaplin (Acad. Award nom., BAFTA Award), Hail Caesar, Heart and Souls, The Last Party (also writer), Short Cuts, Natural Born Killers, Only You, Restoration, Danger Zone, Home for the Holidays, Richard III, Two Girls & A Guy, One Night Stand, Hugo Pool, Blue Vision, The Gingerbread Man, U.S. MarshalsA Guy and Two Girls.
TELEVISION: *Series*: Saturday Night Live. *Mini-Series*: Mussolini: The Untold Story. *Special*: Dear America (reader). *Movie*: Mr. Willowby's Christmas Tree.

DOWNS, HUGH
Broadcaster. b. Akron, OH, Feb. 14, 1921. e. Bluffton Coll., 1938. Wayne U., 1941. Col. U., N.Y., 1955; Supervisor of Science Programming, NBC's Science Dept. one yr.; science consultant for Westinghouse Labs., Ford Foundation, etc.; chmn. of bd., Raylin Prods., Inc. Today, Chairman, U.S. Committee for UNICEF. Chm. of bd. of governors, National Space Society. Books: Thirty Dirty Lies about Old, Rings Around Tomorrow, School of Stars, Yours Truly Hugh Downs, On Camera: My Ten Thousand Hours on Television, Perspectives, Fifty to Forever.
TELEVISION: *Series*: Kukla Fran & Ollie (announcer), Home, Sid Caesar (announcer), The Jack Paar Show, Concentration, The Tonight Show (announcer, 1962), Today. *Host*: 20/20, Over-Easy (Emmy Award, 1981), Live From Lincoln Center.
RADIO: NBC's Monitor, ABC's Perspectives.

DOYLE, KEVIN
Executive. b. Sydney, Australia, June 21, 1933. e. N. Sydney Tech. HS., Aust. Jr. exec., asst. adv. & pub. div., 20th Century-Fox, Aust.; 1947-59; adv. & pub. dir., Columbia Pictures Aust., 1960-66; intl. advertising ad/pub. mgr.; Columbia Pictures Int'l, N.Y. 1966; intl. pub./promo. mgr., 1980; 1987, Columbia Int'l. rep., Coca-Cola promotions/mktg. sub-committee; int'l pub./promo. mgr. Columbia Tri-Star Film Distributors Inc., 1988; int'l pub./promo. dir. Columbia/Tri-Star Film distrib. Inc. 1990. Retired 1992.

DOYLE-MURRAY, BRIAN
Actor, Writer. b. Chicago, IL., Oct. 31. Brother is comedian Bill Murray. Started as member of Chicago's Second City improv. troupe, before joining the Organic Theatre of Chicago and the Boston Shakespeare Co. Appeared Off-B'way in The National Lampoon Show and on radio on weekly National Lampoon Show.
PICTURES: Caddyshack (also co-s.p.), Modern Problems, National Lampoon's Vacation, Sixteen Candles, The Razor's Edge, Legal Eagles, Club Paradise (also co-s.p.), Scrooged, The Experts, How I Got Into College, Ghostbusters II, National Lampoon's Christmas Vacation, Nothing But Trouble, JFK, Wayne's World, Groundhog Day, Cabin Boy, Jury Duty, Multiplicity, Waiting for Guffman, As Good As It Gets, Casper: A Spirited Beginning, Dennis the Menace 2, Doctor Dolittle (voice).
TELEVISION: *Series*: Saturday Night Live (also writer), Get a Life, Good Sports, Bakersfield P.D., The Martin Short Show, The George Wendt Show. *Movies*: Babe Ruth, My Brother's Keeper, Frosty Returns (voice). *Special*: Texan.

DRAGOTI, STAN
Director. b. New York, NY, Oct. 4, 1932. e. Cooper Union and Sch. of Visual Arts. 1959 hired as sketch at ad agency, promoted to sr. art dir., later TV dept. and art dir. of Young & Rubicam. Studied acting HB Studios. Directed Clio awarding-winning TV commercials (including I Love New York campaign).
PICTURES: Dirty Little Billy (debut, 1972; also co-prod., co-s.p.), Love at First Bite, Mr. Mom, The Man With One Red Shoe, She's Out of Control, Necessary Roughness.

DRAI, VICTOR
Producer. b. Casablanca, Morocco, July 25, 1947. e. Lycee de Port Lyautey, 1957-63. In real estate in Los Angeles 1976-82; clothing designer/mfg. in Paris, France, 1969-76. Began producing features in 1984, The Woman in Red.
PICTURES: The Man with One Red Shoe, The Bride, Weekend at Bernie's, Folks!, Weekend at Bernie's II.

DRAZEN, LORI
Executive. Began career as asst. to dir. of adv. for Orion Pictures; creative dept. mgr., Kenyon & Eckhardt; gen. mgr., Seiniger Advertising; joined Warner Bros. 1985 as v.p., world-wide adv. & pub. services.

DREYFUSS, RICHARD
Actor. b. Brooklyn, NY, Oct. 29, 1947. e. Beverly Hills H.S.; San Fernando Valley State Coll. 1965-67. Prof. career began at Gallery Theatre (L.A.) in In Mama's House. Co-Exec. Prod. of film Quiz Show.
THEATER: Journey to the Day, Incident at Vichy, People Need People, Enemy Line, Whose Little Boy Are You, But Seriously, Major Barbara, The Time of Your Life, The Hands of Its Enemy (L.A.), The Normal Heart, Death and the Maiden, others.
PICTURES: The Graduate, Valley of the Dolls, The Young Runaways, Hello Down There, Dillinger, American Graffiti, The Second Coming of Suzanne, The Apprenticeship of Duddy Kravitz, Jaws, Inserts, Close Encounters of the Third Kind, The Goodbye Girl (Acad. Award, 1977), The Big Fix (also co-prod.) The Competition, Whose Life Is It Anyway?, The Buddy System, Down and Out in Beverly Hills, Stand by Me, Tin Men, Stakeout, Nuts, Moon Over Parador, Let It Ride, Always, Postcards from the Edge, Once Around, Rosencrantz and Guildenstern Are Dead, What About Bob?, Lost in Yonkers, Another Stakeout, Silent Fall, The Last Word, The American President, Mr. Holland's Opus, James and the Giant Peach, Night Falls on Manhattan, Mad Dog Time, The Call of the Wild (narr.), A Fine and Private Place, Krippendorf's Tribe.
TELEVISION: *Series*: Karen. *Host*: American Chronicles. *Guest*: Love on a Rooftop, Occasional Wife, The Big Valley, Room 222, Judd for the Defense, The Bold Ones. *Special*: Funny You Don't Look 200 (host, co-prod., co-writer). *Movies*: Two for the Money, Victory at Entebbe, Prisoner of Honor (also prod.), Lincoln (voice), The Universal Story, Frank Capra's American Dream, Oliver Twist.

DRESCHER, FRAN
Actress. b. Queens, NY, Sept. 30, 1957. e. Queen's College.
PICTURES: Saturday Night Fever (debut), American Hot Wax, Gorp, The Hollywood Knights, Ragtime, Cadillac Man, Serious Money, It Had to Be You, This is Spinal Tap, Car 54, Where are You?, Jack, The Beautician and the Beast.
TELEVISION: *Series*: Princesses, The Nanny (Golden Globe nom., also co-creator, writer. prod.). *Movies*: Stranger In Our House, Rock 'n' Roll Mom, Love & Betrayal, Wedding Band, Without Warning: Terror In the Towers.

DRIVER, MINNIE
Actress. r. n. Amelia Driver. b. England, Jan. 31, 1970. e. Bedales School, Petersfield, Hants.
PICTURES: Circle of Friends, GoldenEye, Baggage, Big Night, Sleepers, Grosse Pointe Blank, Good Will Hunting, Tarzan (voice), The Governess, Hard Rain.
TELEVISION: *Series*: God on the Rocks, Mr. Wroe's Virgins. *Mini-Series*: The Politician's Wife. *Guest*: Lovejoy. *Movies*: Merry Christmas George Bailey, That Sunday.

DROMGOOLE, PATRICK
Director, Producer, Executive. b. Iqueque, Chile, Aug. 30, 1930; e. Dulwich Coll., University Coll., Oxford. Joined BBC Radio as dir. 1954, later directing TV plays for BBC and ABC, incl. Armchair Theatre, Frontier, Dracula, Mystery Imagination. Joined HTV as West Country Programme Controller, 1968; dir. award-winning dramas; Thick as Thieves, Machine Gunner. Developed Company's drama output and promoted policy of international pre-sales with such dramas as Jamaica Inn, Separate Tables, Catholics, Smuggler, Into the Labyrinth, Kidnapped, Robin of Sherwood, Arch of Triumph, Mr. Halpern and Mr. Johnson, Jenny's War, Codename Kyril, The Diamond Trap, Wall of Tyranny, Strange Interlude, The Woman He Loved, Grand Larceny, Suspicion, Maigret, September. Made Fellow of RTS, 1978; chief exec. HTV Group since 1988. Fellow of RSA, 1989.

THEATER: *Director*: incl. first plays of Charles Wood, Joe Orton, David Halliwell, Colin Welland; Peter O'Toole in Man and Superman.
PICTURES: Two Vale South, Hidden Face, Dead Man's Chest, Anthony Purdy Esq., Point of Dissent, The Actors, King of the Wind (exec. prod.), Visage du Passe (dir.), Meutres en Douce, The Canterville Ghost, The Little Match Girl (exec. prod.), Sunday Pursuit (exec. prod.), The Last Butterfly (assoc. prod.).
TELEVISION: *Movie*: Machine Gunner. *Mini-series*: Kidnapped, Return to Treasure Island. *Series*: Smuggler, Into the Labyrinth, Public Eye.

DRURY, JAMES
Actor. b. New York, NY, April 18, 1934. e. New York U. Acting debut at age 8 in biblical play for children at Greenwich Settlement Playhouse. Performed on stage while youngster. Signed by MGM in 1955, working one day in each of seven movies that year, including Blackboard Jungle. Then got two-year contract at 20th-Fox. Gained fame as hero of TV series, The Virginian, which had nine-year run.
PICTURES: Forbidden Planet, Love Me Tender, Bernardine, Toby Tyler, Pollyana, Ten Who Dared, Ride the High Country, The Young Warriors.
TELEVISION: *Series*: The Virginian, Firehouse. *Movies*: Breakout, Alias Smith and Jones, The Devil and Miss Sarah, The Gambler Returns: Luck of the Draw.

DUBAND, WAYNE
Executive. b. Sydney, Australia, Feb. 13, 1947. Joined Warner Bros. 1969 as mgr. trainee in Australia. 1973, transferred to South Africa as mgr. dir.; 1977 gen. mgr. of CIC/Warner Bros. joint venture, also managing the CIC theatre operation there. 1980, named exec. asst. to Myron D. Karlin, pres. WB Intl., in Burbank. 1981, mgr. dir. of Warner/Columbia joint venture in France. 1985, appt. v.p. of sls. for WB Intl. division. 1987, appt. senior v.p. for Warner Bros. Intl. division. 1992, appt. pres. Intl. Theatrical div., WB Intl.

DUBE, JACKSON E.
Executive. b. New York, NY. e. U. of North Carolina. m. Pat Lavelle, actress. USAF 1942-45 Radar-Gunner, AAF, Italy. Writer: Television and Sponsor Magazine 1947-48; reviews of recorded music. 1947-51, Consol Film Inds. Penthouse Prods. Dist.: E. sales mgr. Atlas Tel. Corp. 1951-54; v.p & gen. mgr., Craftsman Film Greatest Fights of the Century 1954; vp, Conquest Prods. CBS Net. Docus. 1954-57. TV and radio dir. Cote Fischer & Rogow Adv., 1957-59; exec. vp, Bon Ami Film; dist.: UA Feats. abroad 1959-63; prod's rep. Le Vien Prods.—Finest Hours King's Story; Eastern sales mgr. Desilu, 1964-67; exec. vp, UCC Films; dist. RKO feature Library abroad, 1969-70; pres. JED Rrns. Corp. Dist. London Films, Rank chidren's features, 1967-88. Consultant: New Century Ent., Windsor Pdns., Rurner Program Services, 1985-88. Agent for Weiss Global, Medallion TV Enterprises, Turner International, Morin International, 1988-92. Agent for Aries S.A. and Sidney Beckerman Prods. Agent for Otto Preminger Films Ltd. JED Productions Corp. owner or partner in remake rights to 125 US feature motion pictures 1992 to present.

DUBS, ARTHUR R.
Executive, Producer, Director, Writer, President and Owner of Pacific International Enterprises, b. Medford, OR, Feb. 26, 1930. e. Southern Oregon State Coll. Founded Pacific International Enterprises, 1969.
PICTURES: *Producer-Director*: American Wilderness, Vanishing Wilderness, Wonder of It All. *Exec. Prod.*: Challenge to Be Free. *Prod.*: Adventures of the Wilderness Family, Wilderness Family Part 2 (also s.p.), Mountain Family Robinson (also s.p.), Across the Great Divide, Sacred Ground, Mystery Mansion, Dream Chasers (also co-dir.). *Co-Prod.*: Windwalker.

DUCHOVNY, DAVID
Actor. b. New York, NY, Aug. 7, 1960. e. Yale. Was teaching asst. at Yale before landing first acting job in beer commercial.
PICTURES: Working Girl (debut, 1988), New Year's Day, Bad Influence, Julia Has Two Lovers, Don't Tell Mom the Babysitter's Dead, The Rapture, Ruby, Venice/Venice, Chaplin, Kalifornia, Playing God.
TELEVISION: *Series*: Twin Peaks, The X Files (Golden Globe Award, 1997). *Movies*: Red Shoe Diaries 2: Double Dare, Baby Snatcher, Red Shoe Diaries 3: Another Woman's Lipstick, Red Shoe Diaries 6: How I Met My Husband.

DUDELHEIM, HANS RUDOLF
Communications Executive. b. Berlin, Germany, June 17, 1927. e. Sch. of Photography Berlin, School of Radio & TV NY. Film editor, ABC, 1951-66. Prod/Dir/Edit.: Cinema Arts Assn. 1966-90; served as pres. Founder, 1961, Cinema Arts Film Soc. Editor of documentaries: Saga of Western Man, Comrade Student, Sublimated Birth (also prod.), Kent State, Sigmund Freud, IBM Motivation Project, The Forgotten Pioneers of Hollywood, Painting With Love. *Producer*: Sesame Street, 60 Minutes: Ranaissance Community, American Dream Machine, Voyage of the Barba Negra. Presently film and video consultant. Instructor at New School For Social Reserach.

DUDLEY, ANNE
Composer. b. Chatham, Kent, England, May 7, 1956.
PICTURES: Hiding Out, Buster, The Misadventures of Mr. Wilt, The Mighty Quinn, Zwei Frauen, Say Anything..., The Pope Must Die, The Miracle, Knight Moves, The Crying Game, Felidae, When Saturday Comes, The Grotesque, Hollow Reed, The Full Monty (Acad. Award, 1997), American History X.
TELEVISION: *Series*: Jeeves and Wooster, Ngaio Marsh's Alleyn Mysteries, Anna Lee.

DUDIKOFF, MICHAEL
Actor. b. Torrance, CA, Oct. 8, 1954.
PICTURES: Making Love, I Ought to Be in Pictures, Tron, Bachelor Party, Bloody Birthday, American Ninja, Radioactive Dreams, Avenging Force, American Ninja II: The Confrontation, Platoon Leader, River of Death, American Ninja 4: The Annihilation, Midnight Ride, Human Shield, Rescue Me, Virtual Assassin, Shooter, Executive Command, Bounty Hunters II, Crash Dive, Moving Target, Soldier Boyz, Cyberjack, Chain of Command..
TELEVISION: *Mini-Series*: North and South Book II. *Movie*: The Woman Who Sinned. *Series*: Star of the Family, Cobra. *Pilot*: Sawyer and Finn. *Guest*: Happy Days, Dallas.

DUFFY, JAMES E.
Executive. b. Decatur, IL, April 2, 1926. e. Beloit Coll. Radio announcer, then reporter; joined publicity dept., ABC in 1949; named dir. of adv. & promo., then account exec. for Central division of ABC Radio Network; dir. of sales ABC Radio, 1957; central div. account exec., ABC TV Network, 1955; natl. dir. of Sales, ABC Radio central division, 1960; v.p., ABC Radio Network, 1961; exec. v.p. & natl. dir. of sales, 1962; v.p. in charge of sales, ABC TV Network, 1963; pres., ABC TV Network, 1970-85; pres., communications, 1985-86; v.p. Capital Cities/ABC, Inc.; pres., communications, ABC Network & Bdgst. Divisions.

DUFFY, PATRICK
Actor. b. Townsend, MT, March 17, 1949. e. U. of Washington. Became actor-in-residence in state of Washington, where performed with various statefunded groups. Acted off-B'way Taught mime and movement classes in summer camp in Seattle. Moved to L.A. and began TV acting career.
PICTURE: Vamping (also co-exec prod.).
TELEVISION: *Specials*: The Last of Mrs. Lincoln, Freedom Festival '89 (host). *Movies*: The Stranger Who Looks Like Me, Hurricane, Man From Atlantis, Enola Gay, Cry for the Strangers, Strong Medicine, Alice in Wonderland, Too Good to Be True, Unholy Matrimony, Murder C.O.D, Children of the Bride, Danielle Steel's Daddy, Texas. *Series*: Man from Atlantis, Dallas, Step By Step. *Guest*: Switch, George Burns' Comedy Week.

DUGAN, DENNIS
Actor, Director. b. Wheaton, IL, Sept. 5, 1946. Studied acting at Goodman Theatre School.
THEATER: *NY*: A Man's Man, The House of Blue Leaves. *LA*: Once in a Lifetime, Rainbows for Sale, Estonia, The Dining Room, The Kitchen.
PICTURES: Night Call Nurses, The Day of the Locust, Night Moves, Smile, Harry and Walter Go to New York, Norman ... Is That You?, Unidentified Flying Oddball, The Howling, Water, Can't Buy Me Love, She's Having a Baby, The New Adventures of Pippi Longstocking, Parenthood, Problem Child (also dir.), Brain Donors (dir. only), Happy Gilmore (dir. only), Happy Gilmore (also dir.), Beverly Hills Ninja (dir. only).
TELEVISION: *Series*: Richie Brockelman: Private Eye, Empire, Shadow Chasers. *Movies*: Death Race, The Girl Most Likely To..., Last of the Good Guys, Country Gold, The Toughest Man in the World, Columbo: Butterfly in Shades of Grey. *Mini-Series*: Rich man Poor Man. *Guest*: Hooperman, Moonlighting, M*A*S*H, The Rockford Files, Scene of the Crime, Making a Living, Hill Street Blues. *Pilots*: Alice, Father O Father, Did You Hear About Josh and Kelly?, Full House, Channel 99. *Director*: Hunter, Sonny Spoon, Wiseguy, Moonlighting, The Shaggy Dog (movie), L.A. Law, Columbo, Picket Fences, NYPD Blue, Chicago Hope.

DUGGAN, ERVIN S.
Executive. Started as reporter for the Washington Post in early 1960's. As member of President Lydon Johnson's staff helped define government's role in supporting public broadcasting with the Public Broadcasting Act of 1967. Served as special asst. to Senators Lloyd Bentsen and Adlai Stevenson III, Health Education and Welfare Secretary Joseph Califano; and as member of the State Dept. Policy Planning Staff. 1981-90, managed communications and consulting firm. Served 4 years as Commissioner of the Federal Communications Commission. Feb. 1994 joined PBS as pres. and CEO.

DUIGAN, JOHN
Director, Writer.b. Hartley Wintney, Hampshire, England, June 19, 1949. Lived in England and Malaysia before moving to Sydney, Australia. e. Univ. of Melbourne, philosophy, M.A. Taught for several years at Univ. of Melbourne and Latrobe U. before entering films. Directed and wrote experimental short, The Firm Man (1974). Novels: Badge, Players, Room to Move.
PICTURES: *Dir.-Writer*: Trespassers, Mouth to Mouth, Winter of Our Dreams (Australian Writers Guild Award), Far East, The Year My Voice Broke (Australian Acad. Award for best dir., s.p.) Romero (dir. only), Flirting, Wide Sargasso Sea, Sirens (also actor), The Journey of August King, The Leading Man, Lawn Dogs, Molly.
TELEVISION: *Mini-Series*: Vietnam (co-dir.). *Movie*: Fragments of War: The Story of Damien Parer.

DUKAKIS, OLYMPIA
Actress. b. Lowell, MA, June 20, 1931. m. actor Louis Zorich. e. Boston U., B.A., M.F.A. Founding mem. of The Charles Playhouse, Boston, establishing summer theatre 1957-60. Taught acting at NYU; 1967-70 as instructor, 1974-83 as master teacher, and at Yale U. 1976. With husband conceived and guided artistic dev. of Whole Theatre of Monclair, NJ, 1977-90; producing artistic dir. Adapted plays for her co. and dir. theater there; also at Williamstown Theatre Fest. and Delaware Summer Fest. Appeared in more than 100 plays on B'way, Off-B'way and in regional and summer theater.
THEATER: Who's Who in Hell, The Aspern Papers, Night of the Iguana, The Breaking Wall, Curse of the Starving Class, Snow Orchid, The Marriage of Bette and Boo (Obie Award), Social Security.
PICTURES: Lilith, Twice a Man, John and Mary, Made for Each Other, Death Wish, Rich Kids, The Wanderers, The Idolmaker, National Lampoon Goes to the Movies, Flanagan, Moonstruck (Acad. Award, best supporting actress, 1987), Working Girl, Look Who's Talking, Steel Magnolias, Dad, In the Spirit, Look Who's Talking Too, The Cemetery Club, Over the Hill, Look Who's Talking Now, Naked Gun 33 1/3: The Final Insult (cameo), I Love Trouble, Jeffrey, Mighty Aphrodite, Mr. Holland's Opus, Picture Perfect.
TELEVISION: *Specials*: The Rehearsal, Sisters, Last Act is a Solo, A Century of Women. *Series*: Search for Tomorrow, One of the Boys. *Movies*: Nicky's World, The Neighborhood, FDR-The Last Year, King of America, Lucky Day, Fire in the Dark, Sinatra, Young at Heart. *Mini-Series*: Tales of the City.

DUKE, BILL
Actor, Director. b. Poughkeepsie, NY, Feb. 26, 1943. e. Boston Univ., NY Univ. Sch. of the Arts. Recieved AFI Best Young Director Award for short The Hero (Gold Award, Houston Film Festival). Has written poetry, short stories for children. Member bd. of dirs. American Film Institute.
PICTURES: *Actor*: Car Wash, American Gigolo, Commando, Predator, No Man's Land, Action Jackson, Bird on a Wire, Street of No Return, Menace II Society, Payback. *Director*: A Rage in Harlem, Deep Cover, The Cemetery Club, Sister Act 2: Back in the Habit, America's Dream, Hoodlums (also exec. prod.).
TELEVISION: *Actor: Movies*: Love is Not Enough, Sgt. Matlovich Vs. the U.S. Air Force. *Series*: Palmerstown U.S.A. *Director: Series*: A Man Called Hawk, Cagney & Lacey, Hill Street Blues, Miami Vice, Dallas. *Specials*: The Killing Floor, A Raisin in the Sun, The Meeting. *Movie*: Johnnie Mae Gibson.

DUKE, PATTY
Actress. r.n. Anna Marie Duke. b. New York, NY, Dec. 14, 1946. e. Quintano Sch. for Young Professionals. Mother of actors Sean and Mackenzie Astin. Pres., Screen Actors Guild, 1985-88. *Author*: Surviving Sexual Assault (1983), Call Me Anna (1987).
THEATER: The Miracle Worker (Theatre World Award), Isle of Children.
PICTURES: I'll Cry Tomorrow (debut as extra 1955), The Goddess, Happy Anniversary, The 4-D Man, The Miracle Worker (Acad. Award, best supporting actress, 1962), Billie, Valley of the Dolls, Me Natalie, The Swarm, By Design, Something Special, Prelude to a Kiss, Harvest of Fire.
TELEVISION: *Series*: The Brighter Day, The Patty Duke Show, It Takes Two, Hail to the Chief, Karen's Song, Amazing Grace. *Guest*: Armstrong Circle Theatre, The SS Andrea Doria, U.S. Steel Hour, All's Fair. *Specials*: The Prince and the Pauper, Wuthering Heights, Swiss Family Robinson, Meet Me in St. Louis, The Power and the Glory. *Movies*: My Sweet Charlie (Emmy Award, 1970), Two on a Bench, If Tomorrow Comes, She Waits, Deadly Harvest, Nightmare, Look What's Happened to Rosemary's Baby, Fire!, Rosetti & Ryan: Men Who Love Women, Curse of the Black Widow, Killer on Board, The Storyteller, Having Babies III, A Family Upside Down, Women in White, Hanging by a Thread, Before and After, The Miracle Worker (Emmy Award, 1980), The Women's Room, Mom The Wolfman and Me, The Babysitter, Violation of Sarah McDavid, Something So Right, September Gun, Best Kept Secrets, Fight for Life, Perry Mason: The Case of the Avenging Angel, A Time to Triumph, Fatal Judgment, Everybody's Baby: The Rescue of Jessica McClure, Amityville: The Evil Escapes, Call Me Anna, Always Remember I Love You, Absolute Strangers, Last Wish, Grave Secrets: The Legacy of Hilltop Drive, A Killer Among Friends, Family of Strangers, No Child of Mine, A Matter of Justice, One Woman's Courage, Cries From the Heart, When the Vows Break, Race Against Time: The Search for Sarah, The Disappearing Act, A Christmas Memory. *Mini-Series*: Captains and the Kings (Emmy Award, 1977), George Washington.

DUKES, DAVID
Actor. b. San Francisco, CA, June 6, 1945. With The American Consevatory Theatre in San Francisco, The CA Shakespeare Festival in Los Gatos, The Alley Theater in Houston, The San Diego Shakespeare Festival, The Matrix Theatre Co. in L.A., and many others.
THEATER: *B'way*: The School for Wives, Don Juan, The Great God Brown, Chemin de Fer, The Visit, Holiday, The Play's the Thing, Love for Love, Rules of the Game, Travesties, Dracula, Bent, Frankenstein, Amadeus, M. Butterfly, Love Letters, Someone Who'll Watch Over Me, Broken Glass.
PICTURES: The Strawberry Statement, Call Me Mister Tibbs!, The Wild Party, A Little Romance, The First Deadly Sin, Only When I Laugh, Without a Trace, The Men's Club, Rawhead Rex, Catch the Heat, Date With an Angel, Deadly Intent, See You in the Morning, Under Surveillance, The Rutanga Tapes, The Handmaid's Tale, Me and the Kid, Slappy and the Stinkers, Fled.
TELEVISION: *Series*: Beacon Hill, All That Glitters, Sisters, The Mommies, Pauly. *Mini-Series*: 79 Park Avenue, George Washington, Kane & Abel, Space, The Winds of War, War and Remembrance, Look at it This Way. *Specials*: Strange Interlude, Cat on a Hot Tin Roof. *Movies*: Valley Forge, The Norming of Jack 243, A Fire in the Sky, The Triangle Factory Fire, How the West Was Won, Some Kind of Miracle, Mayflower—The Pilgrim Adventure, Margaret Sanger— Portrait of a Rebel, Miss All-American Beauty, Sentimental Journey, Darlin' Clementine, Snowkill, Held Hostage: The Sis and Jerry Levin Story, The Josephine Baker Story, Turn Back the Clock, Wife—Mother—Murderer, She Woke Up, Spies Look at It This Way (BBC), And The Band Played On, The Surrogate, Norma Jean & Marilyn, Last Stand at Saber River, The Love Letter. *Guest*: All in the Family, The Jeffersons, Once Day at a Time, Barney Miller, Hawaii 5-0, Police Story, Police Woman, Cannon, etc.

DULLEA, KEIR
Actor. b. Cleveland, OH, May 30, 1936. e. Rutgers Univ., San Francisco State Coll., Sanford Meisner's Neighborhood Playhouse. Acted as resident juvenile at the Totem Pole Playhouse in PA. NY theatre debut in the revue Sticks and Stones, 1956; appeared in stock co. prods. at the Berkshire Playhouse and Philadelphia's Hedgerow Theatre, 1959; off-Broadway debut in Season of Choice, 1969. Won San Francisco Film Festival Award for performance in film David and Lisa, 1963.
THEATER: Dr. Cook's Garden, Butterflies Are Free, Cat on a Hot Tin Roof, P.S. Your Cat is Dead, The Other Side of Paradise.
PICTURES: The Hoodlum Priest (debut, 1961), David and Lisa, The Thin Red Line, Mail Order Bride, The Naked Hours, Bunny Lake Is Missing, Madame X, The Fox, 2001: A Space Odyssey, De Sade, Pope Joan, Paperback Hero, Il Diavolo nel Cervello, Paul and Michelle, Black Christmas (Silent Night Evil Night), Leopard in the Snow, Welcome to Blood City, The Haunting of Julia (Full Circle), Because He's My Friend, The Next One, Brainwaves, Blind Date, 2010, Oh What a Night.
TELEVISION: *Movies*: Black Water Gold, Law and Order, Legend of the Golden Gun, Brave New World, The Hostage Tower, No Place to Hide. *Special*: Mrs. Miniver.

DUNAWAY, FAYE
Actress. b. Bascom, FL, Jan. 14, 1941. e. Texas, Arkansas, Utah, Germany, U. of Florida. Awarded a Fulbright scholarship in theatre. Boston U. of Fine Applied Arts. With Lincoln Center Rep. Co. for 3 years. NY Stage: A Man for All Seasons, After the Fall, Hogan's Goat (Theatre World Award), The Curse of an Aching Heart.
PICTURES: Hurry Sundown (debut, 1967), The Happening, Bonnie and Clyde, The Thomas Crown Affair, The Extraordinary Seaman, A Place for Lovers, The Arrangement, Puzzle of a Downfall Child, Little Big Man, The Deadly Trap, Doc, Oklahoma Crude, The Three Musketeers, Chinatown, The Towering Inferno, The Four Musketeers, Three Days of the Condor, Network (Acad. Award, 1976), Voyage of the Damned, Eyes of Laura Mars, The Champ, The First Deadly Sin, Mommie Dearest, The Wicked Lady, Ordeal by Innocence, Supergirl, Barfly, Midnight Crossing, Burning Secret, The Handmaid's Tale, Wait Until Spring Bandini, The Gamble, On a Moonlit Night, Scorchers, Double Edge, The Temp, Arizona Dream, Don Juan DeMarco, Drunks, Dunston Checks In, Albino Alligator, The Chamber.
TELEVISION: *Movies*: The Woman I Love, The Disappearance of Aimee, Evita, Peron, 13 at Dinner, Beverly Hills Madam, The Country Girl, Casanova, The Raspberry Ripple, Cold Sassy Tree, Silhouette, Columbo: It's All in the Game (Emmy Award, 1994), A Family Divided. *Mini-Series*: Ellis Island, Christopher Columbus. *Specials*: Hogan's Goat, After the Fall, Supergirl: The Making of the Movie (host), Inside the Dream Factory (host). *Series*: It Had to Be You.

DUNCAN, LINDSAY
Actress. Stage actress with National Theatre, Royal Shakespeare Company.
THEATER: Plenty, The Provok'd Wife, The Prince of Homburg, Top Girls, Progress, The Merry Wives of Windsor, Les Liaisons Dangereuses (RSC, West End, Broadway; Theatre World Award), Cat On A Hot Tin Roof, Hedda Gabler, A Midsummer Night's Dream, Cryptogram.
PICTURES: Loose Connections, Samson & Delilah, Prick Up Your Ears, Manifesto, The Reflecting Skin, Body Parts, City Hall, A Midsummer Night's Dream.
TELEVISION: *Movies*: Reilly, Ace of Spies, A Year in Provence, The Rector's Wife. *Mini-series*: Dead Head, Traffik, A Year in Provence, G.B.H., Jake's Progress, The History of Tom Jones A Foundling. *Guest*: The Storyteller: Greek Myths, The New Avengers, Colin's Sandwich, Tecx.

DUNCAN, SANDY
Actress. b. Henderson, TX, Feb. 20, 1946. m. singer-dancer Don Correia. e. Len Morris Coll.
THEATER: The Music Man (NY debut, 1965); The Boyfriend, Ceremony of Innocence (Theatre World Award), Your Own Thing, Canterbury Tales, Peter Pan, Five Six Seven Eight Dance!, My One and Only.
PICTURES: $1,000,000 Duck, Star Spangled Girl, The Cat from Outer Space, Rock a Doodle (voice), The Swan Princess (voice).
TELEVISION: Series: Funny Face, The Sandy Duncan Show, Valerie's Family (later called The Hogan Family). Movies: My Boyfriend's Back, Miracle on Interstate 880. Mini-Series: Roots. Specials: Pinocchio, Sandy in Disneyland, The Sandy Duncan Special.

DUNING, GEORGE
Composer, Conductor, Arranger. b. Richmond, IN, Feb. 25, 1908. e. Cincinnati Conservatory of Music, U. of Cincinnati. Music dir. Aaron Spelling Prods., 1970-71, Bobby Sherman Show, Movies of the Week. Board of Directors, ASCAP, 1969-83. V.P. ASCAP, 1977-79. Society for Preservation of Film Music Career Achievement Award, 1987; Indiana Composer of the Year, 1993.
PICTURES: Down to Earth, The Guilt of Janet Ames, Johnny O'Clock, To the Ends of the Earth, Jolson Sings Again, The Eddy Duchin Story, From Here to Eternity, Picnic, Pal Joey, Cowboy, The Last Angry Man, The World of Susie Wong, Devil at 4 O'Clock, The Notorious Landlady, Toys in the Attic, Ensign Pulver, Dear Brigitte, Any Wednesday, Terror in the Wax Museum, The Man with Bogart's Face.
TELEVISION: No Time for Sergeants, Wendy and Me, The Farmer's Daughter, Big Valley, The Long Hot Summer, The Second Hundred Years, Star Trek, Mannix, Then Came Bronson.

DUNLAP, RICHARD D.
Producer, Director. b. Pomona, CA, Jan. 30, 1923. e. Yale U., B.A., 1944; M.F.A., 1948. U.S. Navy 1943-46; Instructor, English dept., Yale U., 1947-48; Prod.-dir., Kraft TV Theatre, 3 years; Dir, Assoc. Prod., Omnibus, 3 seasons; Dir., 25 half-hr. Dramatic Film Shows. Frank Sinatra Specials, Prod.-Dir., 11 Academy Award Shows, 4 Emmy Award Shows.

DUNNE, DOMINICK
Producer. Writer. b. Hartford, CT, Oct. 29, 1925. e. Canterbury Sch., 1944; Williams Col., 1949. Son is actor-prod. Griffin Dunne. Began career as stage manager at NBC-TV; then produced shows for CBS Studio One. Later exec. prod. at 20th-Fox TV, v.p. at Four Star. Novels: The Winners, The Two Mrs. Grenvilles, People Like Us, An Inconvenient Woman, A Season in Purgatory, Fatal Charms, The Mansions of Limbo.
PICTURES: The Boys in the Band (exec. prod.), The Panic in Needle Park, Play It as It Lays, Ash Wednesday.

DUNN, KEVIN
Actor. b. Chicago, IL, 1956.
PICTURES: Mississippi Burning, Ghostbusters II (uncredited), Taken Away, Marked for Death, Blue Steel, The Bonfire of the Vanities, Hot Shots!, Only the Lonely, Chaplin, 1492: Conquest of Paradise, Dave, Little Big League, Mad Love, Nixon, Commandments, Chain Reaction, Edwards and Hunt, The Sixth Man, Picture Perfect, Almost Heroes, Godzilla, Snake Eyes, Small Soldiers.
TELEVISION: Series: Jack & Mike, Arsenio. Movies: Night of Courage, Blind Faith, Double Edge, Shadow of a Doubt, The Four Diamonds, Unforgivable, The Second Civil War, On the Edge of Innocence. Guest: Cheers, Roseanne, 21 Jump Street, Seinfeld.

DUNNE, GRIFFIN
Actor, Producer. b. New York, NY, June 8, 1955. Son of prod.-writer Dominick Dunne. foremerly m. actress Carey Lowell. Formed Double Play Prods. with Amy Robinson. Studied at Neighborhood Playhouse and with Uta Hagen. On Stage in Album, Marie and Bruce, Coming Attractions, Hotel Play, Search and Destroy (B'way debut; Theatre World Award).
PICTURES: Actor: The Other Side of the Mountain (debut, 1975), Chilly Scenes of Winter (also prod.), The Fan, American Werewolf in London, Cold Feet, Almost You, Johnny Dangerously, After Hours (also co-prod., Golden Globe nom.), Who's That Girl, Amazon Women on the Moon, Big Blue, Me and Him, Once Around (also co-prod.), My Girl, Straight Talk, Big Girls Don't Cry... They Get Even, The Pickle, Naked in New York, Quiz Show, I Like It Like That, Search and Destroy. Producer only: Baby It's You, Running on Empty, White Palace. Director/Writer: Duke of Groove (short, Oscar nom.).
TELEVISION: Movies: The Wall, Secret Weapon, Love Matters, The Android Affair, Love Matters (Ace nom.). Specials: Lip Service, Trying Times: Hunger Chic, Partners. Pilot: Graham.

DURNING, CHARLES
Actor. b. Highland Falls, NY, Feb. 28, 1923. e. NYU. Studied acting on the G.I. Bill. Prof. stage debut, 1960. Made several appearances with Joseph Papp's NY Shakespeare Festival.

THEATER: That Championship Season, Knock Knock, Au Pair Man, In the Boom Boom Room, The Happy Time, Indians, Cat on a Hot Tin Roof (Tony Award, 1990), Queen of the Stardust Ballroom, Inherit the Wind.
PICTURES: Harvey Middleman—Fireman (debut, 1965), I Walk the Line, Hi Mom!, The Pursuit of Happiness, Dealing: or the Berkeley-to- Boston Forty-Brick Lost-Bag Blues, Deadhead Miles, Sisters, The Sting, The Front Page, Dog Day Afternoon, The Hindenburg, Breakheart Pass, Harry and Walter Go to New York, Twilight's Last Gleaming, The Choirboys, An Enemy of the People, The Fury, The Greek Tycoon, Tilt, The Muppet Movie, North Dallas Forty, Starting Over, When a Stranger Calls, Die Laughing, The Final Countdown, True Confessions, Sharky's Machine, The Best Little Whorehouse in Texas (Acad. Award nom.), Tootsie, To Be or Not to Be (Acad. Award nom.), Two of a Kind, Hadley's Rebellion, Mass Appeal, Stick, The Man With One Red Shoe, Stand Alone, Big Trouble, Tough Guys, Where the River Runs Black, Solarbabies, Happy New Year, The Rosary Murders, A Tiger's Tail, Cop, Far North, Cat Chaser, Dick Tracy, V. I. Warshawski, Brenda Starr, Etolie, Fatal Sky, The Music of Chance, The Hudsucker Proxy, I.Q., Home for the Holidays, The Last Supper, The Grass Harp, Spy Hard, One Fine Day.
TELEVISION: Series: Another World (1972), The Cop and the Kid, Eye to Eye, Evening Shade. Mini-Series: Captains and the Kings, Studs Lonigan, The Kennedys of Massachusetts, A Woman of Independent Means. Specials: The Rivalry, The Dancing Bear, Working, Mr. Roberts, Side by Side (pilot), P.O.P. (pilot), Eye to Eye, Tales from Hollywood, Normandy (narrator), Texan, Leslie's Folly. Movies: The Connection, The Trial of Chaplain Jensen, Queen of the Stardust Ballroom, Switch, Special Olympics, Attica, Perfect Match, Crisis at Central High, The Best Little Girl in the World, Dark Night of the Scarecrow, Death of a Salesman, Kenny Rogers as The Gambler III—The Legend Continues, The Man Who Broke 1000 Chains, Case Closed, Unholy Matrimony, Prime Target, It Nearly Wasn't Christmas, Dinner at Eight, The Return of Eliot Ness, The Story Lady, The Water Engine, Roommates. Guest: Madigan, All in the Family, Barnaby Jones, Hawaii Five-O, Amazing Stories.

DURWOOD, RICHARD M.
Executive. b. Kansas City, MO, Aug. 18, 1929. e. Brown U., A.B. Pres. Crown Cinema Corp. Member: Motion Picture Assn. of Kansas City (pres.), United Motion Pictures Assn. (pres. 1972-73), Young NATO (chmn., 1968-69), Past Chief Barker, Tent No. 8. Past mem., exec. comm., National NATO. Sr. v.p., and on bd. of dirs. of American Movie Classics, 1952-1976,

DURWOOD, STANLEY H.
Executive. b. 1920. e. Harvard Coll., B.S. Air Force navigator 3 years. Chmn. of bd. AMC Entertainment Inc. Member: Harvard Club of Kansas City; Harvard Club of New York. On board of United Missouri Bankshares. Recipient of: Salah M. Hassanein Humanitarian award, 1989; University of Missouri, Kansas City, Chancellor's medal, 1994; Foundation of Motion Picture Pioneers "Pioneer of the Year" award, 1995.

DUSSAULT, NANCY
Actress. b. Pensacola, FL, Jun. 30, 1936. e. Northwestern U.
THEATER: B'way: Street Scene, The Mikado, The Cradle Will Rock, Do Re Mi (Theatre World Award), Sound of Music, Carousel, Fiorello, The Gershwin Years, Into the Woods. L.A. stage: Next in Line.
PICTURE: The In-Laws, The Nurse.
TELEVISION: Special: The Beggars Opera. Host: Good Morning America. Series: The New Dick Van Dyke Show, Too Close for Comfort (The Ted Knight Show).

DUTTON, CHARLES S.
Actor. b. Baltimore, MD, Jan. 30, 1951. e. Towson St., Yale Sch. of Drama.
THEATER: Yale Rep: The Works, Beef No Chicken, Astopovo, Othello. NY: Ma Rainey's Black Bottom (Theatre World Award, 1983), Joe Turner's Come and Gone, The Piano Lesson.
PICTURES: No Mercy, Crocodile Dundee II, Jacknife, An Unremarkable Life, Q & A, Mississippi Masala, Alien3, The Distinguished Gentleman, Menace II Society, Rudy, Foreign Student, A Low Down Dirty Shame, Cry the Beloved Country, Nick of Time, The Last Dance, A Time to Kill, Get on the Bus.
TELEVISION: Series: Roc. Guest: Miami Vice, The Equalizer, Cagney and Lacey. Movies: Apology, The Murder of Mary Phagan, Jack Reed: Search for Justice, The Piano Lesson, Zooman. Special: Runaway.

DUVALL, ROBERT
Actor. b. San Diego, CA, Jan. 5, 1931. e. Principia College, IL. Studied at the Neighborhood Playhouse, NY.
THEATER: Off-B'way: The Days and Nights of Bee Bee Fenstermaker, Call Me By My Rightful Name, A View From the Bridge (Obie Award, 1965). B'way: Wait Until Dark, American Buffalo.

PICTURES: To Kill a Mockingbird (debut, 1962), Captain Newman M.D., Nightmare in the Sun, The Chase, Countdown, The Detective, Bullitt, True Grit, The Rain People, M*A*S*H, The Revolutionary, THX-1138, Lawman, The Godfather, Tomorrow, The Great Northfield Minnesota Raid, Joe Kidd, Lady Ice, Badge 373, The Outfit, The Conversation, The Godfather Part II, Breakout, The Killer Elite, The Seven Percent Solution, Network, We're Not the Jet Set (dir., co-prod. only), The Eagle Has Landed, The Greatest, The Betsy, Invasion of the Body Snatchers (cameo), Apocalypse Now, The Great Santini, True Confessions, The Pursuit of D.B. Cooper, Tender Mercies (Acad. Award, 1983; also co-prod, songwriter), Angelo My Love (dir., prod., s.p. only), The Stone Boy, The Natural, Bellizaire the Cajun (cameo; also creative consultant), The Lightship, Let's Get Harry, Hotel Colonial, Colors, The Handmaid's Tale, A Show of Force, Days of Thunder, Rambling Rose, Convicts, Newsies, Falling Down, The Plague, Geronimo: An American Legend, Wrestling Ernest Hemingway, The Paper, Something to Talk About, The Stars Fell on Henrietta, The Scarlet Letter, A Family Thing (also co-prod.), Sling Blade, Phenomenon, The Apostle (also s.p., dir., exec. prod., Chicago Film Crits. Award, LA Film Crits. Award, Best Actor, 1997), Deep Impact, The Gingerbread Man, A Civil Action.
TELEVISION: Fame Is the Name of the Game, The Terry Fox Story, Stalin. Mini-Series: Ike, Lonesome Dove. Guest: Great Ghost Tales, The Outer Limits, Naked City, Route 66, The Defenders, Alfred Hitchcock Presents, Twilight Zone, Combat, Wild Wild West, The FBI, Mod Squad.

DUVALL, SHELLEY
Actress, Producer. b. Houston, TX, July 7, 1949. Founded Think Entertainment, TV prod. co. Appeared in 1984 short film Frankenweenie.
PICTURES: Brewster McCloud (debut, 1970), McCabe and Mrs. Miller, Thieves Like Us, Nashville, Buffalo Bill and the Indians, Three Women (Cannes Fest. Award, 1977), Annie Hall, The Shining, Popeye, Time Bandits, Roxanne, Suburban Commando, The Underneath, Portrait of a Lady, Changing Habits.
TELEVISION: Actress: Bernice Bobs Her Hair, Lily, Twilight Zone, Mother Goose Rock 'n' Rhyme, Faerie Tale Theatre (Rumpelstiltskin, Rapunzel), Tall Tales and Legends (Darlin' Clementine). Exec. Producer: Faerie Tale Theatre, Tall Tales and Legends, Nightmare Classics, Dinner at Eight (movie), Mother Goose Rock 'n' Rhyme, Stories from Growing Up, Backfield in Motion (movie), Bedtime Stories, Mrs. Piggle-Wiggle.

DYSART, RICHARD A.
Actor. b. Brighton, MA, March 30, 1929. e. Emerson Coll., B.S., M.S., L.L.D.(honorary). Univ. of Maine, PhD (honorary). Trustee Gallaudet Univ, DC. Bd. of Dir, American Judicature Society.
THEATER: B'way: in A Man for All Seasons, All in Good Time, The Little Foxes, A Place without Doors, That Championship Season, Another Part of the Forest. Off-B'way: in The Quare Fellow, Our Town, Epitaph for George Dillon, Six Characters in Search of an Author.
PICTURES: Petulia, The Lost Man, The Sporting Club, The Hospital, The Terminal Man, The Crazy World of Julius Vrooder, The Day of the Locust, The Hindenberg, Prophecy, Meteor, Being There, An Enemy of the People, The Thing, The Falcon and the Snowman, Mask, Warning Signs, Pale Rider, Wall Street, Back to the Future Part III, Hard Rain.
TELEVISION: Movies: The Autobiography of Miss Jane Pittman, Gemini Man, It Happened One Christmas, First You Cry, Bogie, The Ordeal of Dr. Mudd, Churchill and the Generals (BBC), People Vs. Jean Harris, Bitter Harvest, Missing, Last Days of Patton, Children--A Mother's Story, Malice in Wonderland, Day One, Bobby and Marilyn: Her Final Affair, Truman, A Child Is Missing, Spawn. Specials: Sandburg's Lincoln, Jay Leno's Family Comedy Hour, Concealed Enemies, Charlie Smith and the Fritter Tree, Moving Target. Mini-Series: War and Remembrance. Series: L.A. Law (Emmy Award, 1992).

DZUNDZA, GEORGE
Actor. b. Rosenheim, Germany, 1945. Spent part of childhood in displaced-persons camps before he was moved to Amsterdam in 1949. Came to NY in 1956 where he attended St. John's U. as speech and theater major.
THEATER: King Lear (NY Shakespeare Fest., debut, 1973), That Championship Season (tour, 1973), Mert and Phil, The Ritz, Legend, A Prayer for My Daughter.
PICTURES: The Happy Hooker, The Deer Hunter, Honky Tonk Freeway, Streamers, Best Defense, No Mercy, No Way Out, The Beast, Impulse, White Hunter Black Heart, The Butcher's Wife, Basic Instinct, Crimson Tide, Dangerous Minds, That Darn Cat, Species II.
TELEVISION: Series: Open All Night, Road Rovers (voice), Superman (voice), Law and Order, Batman: Gotham Knights (voice). Movies: The Defection of Simas Kudirka, Salem's Lot, Skokie, A Long Way Home, The Face of Rage, The Last Honor of Kathryn Beck, When She Says No, The Rape of Richard Beck, Brotherly Love, The Execution of Raymond Graham, Something is Out There, The Ryan White Story, Terror on Highway 91, What She Doesn't Know, The Enemy Within, The Babymaker: The Dr. Cecil Jacobson Story, The Limbic Region. Guest: Starsky and Hutch, The Waltons.

E

EASTWOOD, CLINT
Actor, Producer, Director. b. San Francisco, CA, May 31, 1930; e. Oakland Technical H.S., Los Angeles City Coll. Worked as a lumberjack in Oregon before being drafted into the Army, Special Services 1950-54. Then contract player at Universal Studios. Starred in TV series Rawhide, 1958-65. Formed Malpaso Productions, 1969. Made a Chevalier des Lettres by French gov., 1985. Mayor, Carmel, CA, 1986-88. Best Director for Bird: Hollywood Foreign Press Assoc., Orson Award. Made Commandeur de Ordre des Arts & Lettres by French Government, 1994. Received Irving G. Thalberg Award, 1995. Received American Film Institute Life Achievement Award, 1996.
PICTURES: Revenge of the Creature (debut, 1955), Francis in the Navy, Lady Godiva, Tarantula, Never Say Goodbye, Away All Boats, The First Traveling Saleslady, Star in the Dust, Escapade in Japan, Ambush at Cimarron Pass, Lafayette Escadrille, A Fistful of Dollars, For a Few Dollars More, The Witches, The Good The Bad and The Ugly, Hang 'Em High, Coogan's Bluff, Where Eagles Dare, Paint Your Wagon, Kelly's Heroes, Two Mules For Sister Sara, Beguiled, Play Misty For Me (also dir.), Dirty Harry, Joe Kidd, Breezy (dir. only), High Plains Drifter (also dir.), Magnum Force, Thunderbolt & Lightfoot, The Eiger Sanction (also dir.), The Outlaw Josey Wales (also dir.), The Enforcer, The Gauntlet (also dir.), Every Which Way But Loose, Escape from Alcatraz, Bronco Billy (also dir.), Any Which Way You Can, Firefox (also dir., prod.), Honky Tonk Man (also dir., prod.), Sudden Impact (also dir., prod.), Tightrope (also prod.), City Heat, Pale Rider (also dir., prod.), Heartbreak Ridge (also dir., prod.), The Dead Pool (also prod.), Bird (dir. only), Thelonius Monk: Straight, No Chaser (exec. prod. only), Pink Cadillac, White Hunter Black Heart (also dir., prod.), The Rookie (also dir.), Unforgiven (also dir., prod.)/ Acad. Awards for Best Picture & Director; L.A. Film Critics Awards for Best Actor, Director & Picture; Natl. Society of Film Critics Awards for Best Director & Picture; Golden Globe Award for Best Director; DGA Award, 1992), In the Line of Fire, A Perfect World (also dir.), Casper (cameo), The Bridges of Madison County (also dir., prod.), The Stars Fell on Henrietta (co-prod. only), Absolute Power (also dir., prod.).
TELEVISION: Series: Rawhide. Specials: Fame Fortune and Romance, Happy Birthday Hollywood, Clint Eastwood: The Man From Malpaso, Don't Pave Main Street: Carmel's Heritage, Salute to Martin Scorcese, Big Guns Talk: Story of the Western, Eastwood on Eastwood. Dir.: Amazing Stories (Vanessa in the Garden). Guest: Navy Log, Maverick, Mr. Ed, Danny Kaye Show.

EBERSOL, DICK
Executive. 1968, started at ABC as Olympic Television researcher; 1974, joined NBC as dir. of weekend late- night programming; named v.p. late night programming; 1977, became v.p. of Comedy Variety and Event Programming; 1981-85, served as exec. prod. of series Saturday Night Live; 1983, formed his own production company, No Sleep Productions, creating Friday Night Videos, Saturday Night's Main Event, Later With Bob Costas; 1989, named pres. of NBC Sports; served as exec. prod. of NBC's coverage of the 1992 Barcelona Summer Olympics, and the 1996 Atlanta Summer Olympics.

EBERTS, JOHN DAVID (JAKE)
Producer, Financier. b. Montreal, Canada, July 10, 1941. e. McGill Univ, Harvard. President Goldcrest, founder & CEO 1976-83, 1985-6; 1984 joined Embassy Communications Intl. 1985 founded and chief exec. of Allied Filmmakers. Film Prods. Award of Merit 1986; Evening Standard Special Award 1987. Publication: My Indecision Is Final (1990).
PICTURES: Chariots of Fire, Gandhi, Another Country, Local Hero, The Dresser, Cal, The Emerald Forest, The Name of the Rose, Hope and Glory, Cry Freedom, The Adventures of Baron Munchausen, Driving Miss Daisy, Dances With Wolves, Black Robe, Get Back, City of Joy, A River Runs Through It, Super Mario Bros., No Escape, Arabian Knight.

EBSEN, BUDDY
Actor. r.n. Christian Ebsen, Jr. b. Belleville, IL, April 2, 1908. e. U. of Florida, Rollins Coll. Won first Broadway role as dancer in Ziegfeld's Whoopee in 1928. Sister, Vilma, became dancing partner and they played nightclubs and did road tours. Went to Hollywood and appeared in Broadway Melody of 1936 with Vilma then in many musicals as single. Later became dramatic actor and appeared on TV. Co-wrote title song for film Behave Yourself.
PICTURES: Broadway Melody of 1936 (debut, 1935), Born to Dance, Captain January, Banjo on My Knee, Yellow Jack, Girl of the Golden West, My Lucky Star, Broadway Melody of 1938, Four Girls in White, Parachute Battalion, They Met in Argentina, Sing Your Worries Away, Thunder in God's Country, Night People, Red Garters, Davy Crockett--King of the Wild Frontier, Davy Crockett and the River Pirates, Between Heaven and Hell, Attack!, Breakfast at Tiffany's, The Interns, Mail Order Bride, The One and Only Genuine Original Family Band, The Beverly Hillbillies.

TELEVISION: *Series*: Davy Crockett, Northwest Passage, The Beverly Hillbillies, Barnaby Jones, Matt Houston. *Guest*: Hawaii Five-O, Gunsmoke. *Movies*: Stone Fox, The Daughters of Joshua Cabe, Horror at 37000 Feet, Smash-Up on Interstate 5, The President's Plane is Missing, Leave Yesterday Behind, The Paradise Connection, Fire on the Mountain, The Return of the Beverly Hillbillies, The Bastard, Tom Sawyer, Stone Fox, Working Trash. *Special*: The Legend of the Beverly Hillbillies.
THEATER: Flying Colors, Yokel Boy, The Male Animal, Ziegfeld Follies, Take Her She's Mine, Our Town, The Best Man.

ECKERT, JOHN M.

Producer, Production Executive. b. Chatham, Ontario, Canada, e. Ryerson Polytechnical Inst., 1968-71 (film major). Member: DGA, DGC.
PICTURES: Power Play (assoc. prod.), Running (co-prod.), Middle Age Crazy (co-prod.), Dead Zone (unit prod. mgr.), Cats Eye (exec. in charge of prod.), Silver Bullet (assoc. prod.), The Incubus, Home Is Where the Heart Is (prod.), Millenium (suprv. prod.), Deep Sleep (prod.), Car 54 Where Are You? (s.p. prod.), Legends of the Fall (unit prod. mngr.), The Scarlet Letter (unit prod. mngr.), Flying Wild (assoc. prod.), Booty Call (co-prod.), The Big Hit (exec. prod), The Big Hit.
TELEVISION: Terry Fox Story (assoc. prod.), Special People (prod., Christopher Award), Danger Bay (series supv. prod.), 1985-87), Family Pictures (unit prod. mngr.), Getting Gotti (prod.).

EDELMAN, RANDY

Composer. b. Patterson, NJ, June 10, 1947.
PICTURES: Feds, Twins, Troop Beverly Hills, Ghostbusters II, Quick Change, Come See the Paradise, Kindergarten Cop, V.I. Warshawski, Drop Dead Fred, Eyes of an Angel, The Distinguished Gentleman, Beethoven, My Cousin Vinny, The Last of the Mohicans (Golden Globe nom.), Gettysburg, Dragon: The Bruce Lee Story, Beethoven's 2nd, Tall Tale, Pontiac Moon, Greedy, Angels in the Outfield, The mas, Billy Madison, While you Were Sleeping, The Indian in the Cupboard, The Big Green, Down Periscope, Diabolique, The Quest, Dragonheart, Daylight, Anaconda, Gone Fishin', The Chipmunk Adventure, Executive Action, The Big Green, Leave It To Beaver, For Richer or Poorer, Six Days Seven Nights.
TELEVISION: A Doctor's Story, Dennis the Menace, Citizen X. Series: MacGyver, The Adventures of Brisco County Jr.

EDEN, BARBARA

Actress. b. Tucson, AZ, Aug. 23, 1934. r.n. Barbara Jean Huffman. e. San Francisco Conservatory of Music. Pres. Mi-Bar Productions. Dir. Security National Bank of Chicago.
PICTURES: Back From Eternity (debut, 1956), The Wayward Girl, A Private's Affair, From the Terrace, Twelve Hours to Kill, Flaming Star, All Hands on Deck, Voyage to the Bottom of the Sea, Five Weeks in a Balloon, Swingin' Along (Double Trouble), The Wonderful World of the Brothers Grimm, The Yellow Canary, The Brass Bottle, The New Interns, Ride the Wild Surf, 7 Faces of Dr. Lao, Quick Let's Get Married, The Amazing Dobermans, Harper Valley PTA, Chattanooga Choo Choo.
TELEVISION: *Series*: How to Marry a Millionaire, I Dream of Jeannie, Harper Valley P.T.A., A Brand New Life, Dallas. *Movies*: The Feminist and the Fuzz, A Howling in the Woods, The Woman Hunter, Guess Who's Sleeping in My Bed, The Stranger Within, Let's Switch, How to Break Up a Happy Divorce, Stonestreet: Who Killed the Centerfold Model?, The Girls in the Office, Condominium, Return of the Rebels, I Dream of Jeannie: 15 Years Later, The Stepford Children, The Secret Life of Kathy McCormick (also co-prod.), Your Mother Wears Combat Boots, Opposites Attract, Her Wicked Ways, Hell Hath No Fury, I Still Dream of Jeannie, Visions of Murder I & II, Eyes of Terror, Dean Man's Island (also co-prod.).

EDWARDS, ANTHONY

Actor. b. Santa Barbara, CA, July 19, 1962. Grandfather designed Walt Disney Studios in the 1930s and worked for Cecil B. De Mille as conceptual artist. Joined Santa Barbara YHouth Theatre; acted in 30 plays from age 12 to 17. At 16 worked professionally in TV commercials. 1980 attended Royal Acad. of Dramatic Arts, London, and studied drama at USC. On NY stage 1993 in Ten Below.
PICTURES: Fast Times at Ridgemont High (debut, 1982), Heart Like a Wheel, Revenge of the Nerds, The Sure Thing, Gotcha!, Top Gun, Summer Heat, Revenge of the Nerds II (cameo), Mr. North, Miracle Mile, How I Got Into College, Hawks, Downtown, Delta Heat, Pet Sematary II, The Client.
TELEVISION: *Series*: It Takes Two, Northern Exposure, ER (Emmy Award, 1998), Soul Man. *Movies*: The Killing of Randy Webster, High School U.S.A., Going for the Gold: The Bill Johnson Story, El Diablo, Hometown Boy Makes Good. *Specials*: Unpublished Letters, Sexual Healing.

EDWARDS, BLAKE

Director, Writer, Producer. r.n. William Blake McEdwards. b. Tulsa, OK, July 26, 1922. m. actress Julie Andrews. e. Beverly Hills H.S. Coast Guard during war. Film acting debut, Ten Gentlemen from West Point (1942).
RADIO: Johnny Dollar, Line-up; *writer-creator*: Richard Diamond.
PICTURES: *Writer*: Panhandle, Stampede, Sound Off, All Ashore, Cruising Down the River, Rainbow Round My Shoulder, Drive a Crooked Road, The Atomic Kid (story), My Sister Eileen, Operation Mad Ball, Notorious Landlady, Soldier in the Rain. *Producer*. Waterhole Branch *Director*: Bring Your Smile Along (also s.p.), He Laughed Last (also s.p.), Mister Cory (also s.p.), This Happy Feeling (also s.p.), The Perfect Furlough (also s.p.), Operation Petticoat, High Time, Breakfast at Tiffany's, Experiment in Terror, Days of Wine and Roses, The Pink Panther (also s.p.), A Shot in the Dark (also s.p., prod.), The Great Race (also s.p., prod.), What Did You Do in the War Daddy? (also s.p., prod.), Gunn (also prod.), The Party (also s.p., prod.), Darling Lili (also s.p., prod.), Wild Rovers (also s.p., prod.), The Carey Treatment (also s.p., prod.), The Tamarind Seed (also s.p.), The Return of the Pink Panther (also s.p., prod.), The Pink Panther Strikes Again (also s.p., prod.), Revenge of the Pink Panther (also s.p., prod.), "10" (also co-prod., s.p.), S.O.B. (also co-prod., s.p.), Victor/Victoria (also co-prod., s.p.), Trail of the Pink Panther (also co-prod., co-s.p.), The Curse of the Pink Panther (also co-prod., s.p.), The Man Who Loved Women (also prod., co-s.p.), Micki and Maude, A Fine Mess (also s.p.), That's Life (also co-prod.), Blind Date, Sunset (also s.p.), Skin Deep (also s.p.), Switch (also s.p.), Son of the Pink Panther (also s.p.).
TELEVISION: City Detective (prod., 1953), The Dick Powell Show (dir.), Creator: Dante's Inferno, Mr. Lucky, Justin Case (exec. prod., dir., writer), Peter Gunn (exec. prod., dir., writer), Julie (exec. prod., dir.). *Specials*: Julie! (prod., dir.), Julie on Sesame St. (exec. prod., dir.), Julie and Dick in Covent Garden (dir.).

EDWARDS, JAMES H.

Executive. President & CEO, Storey Theatres, Inc. b. Cedartown, GA, Aug. 14, 1927. e. Georgia State. U.S. Navy, 1948-50. With Ga. Theatre Co., 1950-1952; Storey Theatres, 1952-present. Formerly pres. & chmn., NATO of GA; formerly pres., Variety Club of Atlanta. Former dir. at large, Nat'l. NATO. Director, numerous theatre cos.

EDWARDS, RALPH

Producer, Emcee. b. Merino, CO, June 13, 1913. e. U. of California, Berkeley. Began career in radio in 1929 as writer-actor-prod.-announcer at station KROW, Oakland. Later joined CBS & NBC Radio in New York as announcer. Originated, produced and emceed Truth or Consequences, This Is Your Life and The Ralph Edwards Show for both radio & TV.
PICTURES: Seven Days Leave, Radio Stars on Parade, Bamboo Blonde, Beat the Band, I'll Cry Tomorrow, Manhattan Merry-go-round, Radio Stars of 1937.
TELEVISION: *Producer/Creator*: It Could Be You, Place the Face, About Faces, Funny Boners, End of the Rainbow, Who in the World, The Woody Woodbury Show, This is Your Life (specials for NBC; host). *Producers*: Wide Country, Name That Tune, Cross Wits, Knockout, Annabelle's Wish. *Producer* (with partner, Stu Billett): The People's Court, So You Think You Got Troubles?, Family Medical Center, Love Stories, Superior Court, Bzzz.

EGGAR, SAMANTHA

Actress. b. London, England,, March 5, 1939. e. student Webber-Douglas Dramatic Sch., London; Slade Sch. of Art.
PICTURES: The Wild and the Willing, Dr. Crippen, Doctor in Distress, Psyche '59, The Collector (Acad. Award nom.), Return From the Ashes, Walk Don't Run, Doctor Dolittle, The Molly Maguires, The Lady in the Car With Glasses and a Gun, The Walking Stick, The Grove, The Light at the Edge of the World, The Dead Are Alive, The Seven Percent Solution, The Uncanny, Welcome to Blood City, The Brood, The Exterminator, Demonoid, Why Shoot the Teacher?, Curtains, Hot Touch, Loner, Ragin' Cajun, Dark Horse, Inevitable Grace, The Phantom, Hercules.
TELEVISION: *Series*: Anna and the King. *Movies*: Double Indemnity, All The Kind Strangers, The Killer Who Wouldn't Die, Ziegfeld: the Man and His Women, The Hope Diamond, Love Among Thieves, A Ghost in Monte Carlo. A Case for Murder. *Mini-Series*: For the Term of His Natural Life, Davy Crockett, Great Escapes: Secrets of Lake Success. *Guest*: Columbo, Baretta, Love Story, Kojak, McMillan & Wife, Streets of San Francisco, Starsky and Hutch, Hart to Hart, Murder She Wrote, Finder of Lost Loves, George Burns Comedy Week, Lucas Tanner, Hotel, Fantasy Island, Magnum P.I., Stingray, Tales of the Unexpected, Heartbeat, Love Boat, 1st & Ten, Outlaws, Alfred Hitchcock Presents, Matlock, L.A. Law, Star Trek: The Next Generation. *Specials*: Man of Destiny, Hemingway Play.

EGOYAN, ATOM
Director, Writer, Producer, Editor, Actor, Cinematographer. b. Cairo, Egypt, July 19, 1960. Raised in Victoria, British Columbia, Canada. e. Univ. of Toronto. Made short films, one of which, Open House appeared on TV series Canadian Reflections.
PICTURES: *Various credits*: Howard in Particular, After Grad with Dad, Peep Show, Open House, Next of Kin, Men: A Passion Playground, Family Viewing, Speaking Parts, The Adjuster, Montreal Sextet, Calendar, Exotica, Curtis's Charm, A Portrait of Arshile, The Sweet Hereafter, Vinyl, Bach Cello Suite #4: Sarabande.
TELEVISION: *Movies*: In This Corner, Looking for Nothing, Gross Misconduct: The Life of Brian Spencer. *Series*: Alfred Hitchcock Presents, Twilight Zone, Friday the 13th.

EICHHORN, LISA
Actress. b. Reading, PA, Feb. 4, 1952. e. Queen's U. Kingston, Canada and Eng. for literature studies at Oxford. Studied at Royal Acad. of Dramatic Art.
THEATER: The Hasty Heart (debut, LA). NY: The Common Pursuit, The Summer Winds, The Speed of Darkness, Down the Road, Any Given Day.
PICTURES: Yanks, The Europeans, Why Would I Lie?, Cutter and Bone, Weather in the Streets, Wild Rose; Opposing Force, Moon 44, Grim Prairie Tales, The Vanishing, King of the Hill, A Modern Affair.
TELEVISION: *Series*: All My Children (1987). *Movies*: The Wall, Blind Justice, Devlin. *Mini-Series*: A Woman Named Jackie.

EIKENBERRY, JILL
Actress. b. New Haven, CT, Jan. 21, 1947. e. Yale U. Drama Sch. m. actor Michael Tucker.
THEATER: B'way: All Over Town, Watch on the Rhine, Onward Victoria, Summer Brave, Moonchildren. Off-B'way: Lemon Sky, Life Under Water, Uncommon Women and Others, Porch, The Primary English Class.
PICTURES: Between the Lines, The End of the World in Our Usual Bed in a Night Full of Rain, An Unmarried Woman, Butch and Sundance: The Early Days, Rich Kids, Hide in Plain Sight, Arthur, The Manhattan Project.
TELEVISION: *Movies*: The Deadliest Season, Orphan Train, Swan Song, Sessions, Kane & Abel, Assault and Matrimony, Family Sins, A Stoning in Fulham Country, My Boyfriend's Back, The Diane Martin Story, The Secret Life of Archie's Wife, An Inconvenient Woman, Living a Lie, A Town Torn Apart, Chantilly Lace, Parallel Lives, Without Consent, Rugged Gold, The Other Woman. *Series*: L.A. Law, The Best of Families (PBS). *Specials*: Uncommon Women & Others, Destined to Live (prod., host), A Family Again, On Hope.

EILBACHER, LISA
Actress. b. Dharan, Saudi Arabia, May 5, 1957. Moved to California at age 7; acted on TV as child.
PICTURES: The War Between Men and Women (debut, 1972), Run for the Roses (Thoroughbred), On the Right Track, An Officer and a Gentleman, Ten to Midnight, Beverly Hills Cop, Deadly Intent, Leviathan, Never Say Die, The Last Samurai.
TELEVISION: *Series*: The Texas Wheelers, The Hardy Boys Mysteries, Ryan's Four, Me and Mom. *Movies*: Bad Ronald, Panache, Spider Man, The Ordeal of Patty Hearst, Gone for Rent, To Race the Wind, This House Possessed, Monte Carlo, Deadly Deception, Joshua's Heart, Blind Man's Bluff, Deadly Matrimony, The Return of Hunter, Dazzle, 919 Fifth Avenue. *Mini-Series*: Wheels, The Winds of War. *Guest*: Wagon Train, Laredo, My Three Sons, Gunsmoke, Combat.

EISNER, MICHAEL D.
Executive. b. Mt. Kisco, NY, March 7, 1942. e. Denison U., B.A. Started career with programming dept. of CBS TV network. Joined ABC in 1966 as mgr. talent and specials. Dec., 1968 became dir. of program dev., east coast. 1968, named v.p., daytime programming, ABC-TV. 1975 made v.p., prog. planning and dev. 1976 named sr. v.p., prime time production and dev., ABC Entertainment. 1976, left ABC to join Paramount Pictures as pres. & chief operating officer. 1984, joined The Walt Disney Company as chmn. & CEO. Host of TV series, The Wonderful World of Disney, 1997.

EKBERG, ANITA
Actress. b. Malmo, Sweden, Sept. 29, 1931. Came to U.S. in 1951 as Miss Universe contestant. Worked as model before becoming actress appearing in small roles at Universal.
PICTURES: Mississippi Gambler, Abbott & Costello Go to Mars, Take Me to Town, The Golden Blade, Blood Alley, Artists and Models, Man in the Vault, War and Peace, Back from Eternity, Hollywood or Bust, Zarak, Pickup Alley, Valerie, Paris Holiday, The Man Inside, Screaming Mimi, Sign of the Gladiator, La Dolce Vita, The Dam on the Yellow River (Last Train to Shanghai), Little Girls and High Finance, Behind Locked Doors, The Last Judgment, The Mongols, Boccaccio '70, Call Me Bwana, 4 for Texas, L'Incastro, Who Wants to Sleep?, The Alphabet Murders, Way Way Out, How I Learned to Love Women, Woman Times Seven, The Glass Sphinx, The Cobra, Malenka the Vampire (Fangs of the Living Dead), If It's Tuesday This Must Be Belgium, The Clowns, Valley of the Widows, Killer Nun, Daisy Chain, Intervista, The Count.
TELEVISION: *Movies*: Gold of the Amazon Women, S*H*E.

EKLAND, BRITT
Actress. b. Stockholm, Sweden, Oct. 6, 1942. Was model before debuting in European films.
PICTURES: Short Is the Summer (debut, 1962), Il Commandante, After the Fox, The Double Man, The Bobo, The Night They Raided Minsky's, Stiletto, Cannibals, Machine Gun McCain, Tintomara, Percy, Get Carter, A Time for Loving, Endless Night, Baxter, Asylum, The Wicker Man, Ultimate Thrill, The Man With the Golden Gun, Royal Flash, Casanova & Co., High Velocity, Slavers, King Solomon's Treasure, The Monster Club, Satan's Mistress (Demon Rage), Hellhole, Fraternity Vacation, Marbella, Moon in Scorpio, Scandal, Beverly Hills Vamp, The Children.
TELEVISION: *England*: Carol for Another Christmas, Too Many Thieves, A Cold Peace. *USA: Guest*: Trials of O'Brien, McCloud, Six Million Dollar Man. *Movies*: Ring of Passion, The Great Wallendas, The Hostage Tower, Valley of the Dolls 1981, Dead Wrong.

ELAM, JACK
Actor. b. Miami, AZ, Nov. 13, 1916. e. Santa Monica Jr. Coll., Modesto Jr. Coll. Worked in Los Angeles as bookkeeper and theatre mgr.; civilian employee of Navy in W.W.II; Introduction to show business was as bookkeeper for Sam Goldwyn. Later worked as controller for other film producers. Given first acting job by prod. George Templeton in 1948; has since appeared in over 100 films.
PICTURES: Wild Weed (debut, 1949), Rawhide, Kansas City Confidential, Rancho Notorious, Ride Vaquero, Appointment in Honduras, The Moonlighter, Vera Cruz, Cattle Queen of Montana, The Far Country, Moonfleet, Kiss Me Deadly, Artists and Models, Gunfight at the OK Corral, Baby Face Nelson, Edge of Eternity, Girl in Lovers Lane, The Last Sunset, The Comancheros, The Rare Breed, The Way West, Firecreek, Never a Dull Moment, Once Upon a Time in the West, Support Your Local Sheriff, Rio Lobo, Dirty Dingus Magee, Support Your Local Gunfighter, The Wild Country, Hannie Caulder, Last Rebel, Pat Garrett and Billy the Kid, Hawmps, Grayeagle, Hot Lead Cold Feet, The Norsemen, The Villain, The Apple Dumpling Gang Rides Again, The Cannonball Run, Jinxed, Cannonball Run II, The Aurora Encounter, Big Bad John, Suburban Commando.
TELEVISION: *Series*: The Dakotas, Temple Houston, The Texas Wheelers, Struck by Lightning, Detective in the House, Easy Street. *Movies*: The Over-the-Hill Gang, The Daughters of Joshua Cabe, Black Beauty, Once Upon a Texas Train, Where the Hell's That Gold!!!?.

ELEFANTE, TOM
Executive. Began career as usher at Loews Riviera in Coral Gables, FL; progressed through ranks to asst. mgr., mgr. & Florida division mgr. 1972, joined Wometco Theatres as gen. mgr. 1975, returned to Loews Theatres as southeast div. mgr.; 1979, named natl. dir. of concessions, moving to h.o. in New York. 1987, appt. sr. v.p. & gen. mgr., Loews. Served as pres. and chmn. of NATO of Florida. 1990, then pres. of NATO of NY. Joined Warner Bros. Int'l Theatres as sr. v.p., 1992. Founded T.P. Consulting Co., 1997.

ELFAND, MARTIN
Executive. b. Los Angeles, CA, 1937. Was talent agent for ten years with top agencies; joined Artists Entertainment Complex in 1972. First film project as prod.: Kansas City Bomber, first venture of AEC, of which he was sr. v.p. In 1977 joined Warner Bros. as production chief.
PICTURES: *Prod.*: Dog Day Afternoon, It's My Turn, An Officer and a Gentleman, King David, Clara's Heart. *Exec. prod.*: Her Alibi, Talent for the Game.

ELFMAN, DANNY
Composer. b. Los Angeles, CA, May 29, 1953. Member of rock band Oingo Boingo, recorded songs for such films as The Tempest, Fast Times at Ridgemont High, 16 Candles, Beverly Hills Cop, Weird Science, Texas Chainsaw Massacre 2, Something Wild. Appeared in Hot Tomorrows, Back to School.
PICTURES: Forbidden Zone, Pee-wee's Big Adventure, Back to School, Wisdom, Summer School, Beetlejuice, Midnight Run, Big-Top Pee-wee, Hot to Trot, Scrooged, Batman, Nightbreed, Dick Tracy, Darkman, Edward Scissorhands, Pure Luck, Article 99, Batman Returns, Sommersby, The Nightmare Before Christmas (also vocalist), Black Beauty, Dolores Claiborne, To Die For, Dead Presidents, Mission: Impossible, The Frighteners, Mars Attacks!, Men in Black.
TELEVISION: *Series*: Pee-wee's Playhouse, Sledgehammer, Fast Times, Tales from the Crypt, The Simpsons, The Flash, Beetlejuice, segments of Amazing Stories (Mummy Dearest, Family Dog), Alfred Hitchcock Presents (The Jar).

ELG, TAINA
Actress, Dancer. b. Helsinki, Finland, March 9, 1930. Trained and performed with Natl. Opera of Finland. Attended Sadler's Wells Ballet Sch. Toured with Swedish Dance Theatre, then Marquis de Cuevas Ballet.
THEATER: Look to the Lilies, Where's Charley?, The Utter Glory of Morrissey Hall, Strider, Nine, O! Pioneers.
PICTURES: The Prodigal (debut, 1955), Diane, Gaby, Les Girls, Watusi, Imitation General, The 39 Steps, The Bacchae, Liebestraum, The Mirror Has Two Faces.
TELEVISION: *Movie*: The Great Wallendas. *Mini-Series*: Blood and Honor: Youth Under Hitler (narrator).

ELIAS, HAL
Executive. b. Brooklyn, NY, Dec. 23, 1899. Publicity dir., State Theatre, Denver; western exploitation mgr., MGM; adv. dept., pub. dept., MGM, Culver City studios; Head, MGM cartoon studio (Tom and Jerry); UPA Pictures, Inc., vice-pres. studio mgr.; Hollywood Museum; bd. dir., Academy of Motion Picture Arts & Sciences, 35 years; treasurer, AMPAS 1976-1979. Academy Oscar, 1979, for dedicated and distinguished service to AMPAS.

ELIZONDO, HECTOR
Actor. b. New York, NY, Dec. 22, 1936. m. actress Carolee Campbell. Studied with Ballet Arts Co. of Carnegie Hall and Actors Studio. Many stage credits in N.Y. and Boston.
THEATER: The Prisoner of Second Avenue, Dance of Death, Steambath (Obie Award), The Great White Hope, Sly Fox, The Price.
PICTURES: The Fat Black Pussycat, Valdez Is Coming, Born to Win, Pocket Money, Deadhead Miles, Stand Up and Be Counted, The Taking of Pelham One Two Three, Report to the Commissioner, Thieves, Cuba, American Gigolo, The Fan, Young Doctors in Love, The Flamingo Kid, Private Resort, Nothing in Common, Overboard, Beaches, Leviathan, Pretty Woman (Golden Globe nom.), Taking Care of Business, Necessary Roughness, Frankie and Johnny, Final Approach, Samantha, There Goes the Neighborhood, Being Human, Beverly Hills Cop III, Getting Even With Dad, Exit to Eden, Perfect Alibi, Dear God, Turbulence.
TELEVISION: Series: Popi (1976), Casablanca, Freebie and the Bean; A.K.A. Pablo (also dir.), Foley Sq, Down and Out in Bevery Hills, Fish Police (voice), Chicago Hope (Emmy Award, 1997). Guest: The Wendie Barrie Show (1947), The Impatient Heart, Kojack, the Jackie Gleason Show, All in the Family, The Pirates of Dark Water (voice), Tales of the Crypt. Movies: The Impatient Heart, Wanted: The Sundance Woman, Honeyboy, Women of San Quentin, Courage, Out of the Darkness, Addicted to His Love, Your Mother Wears Combat Boots, Forgotten Prisoners: The Amnesty Files, Finding the Way Home, Chains of Gold, The Burden of Proof. Mini-Series: The Dain Curse. Specials: Medal of Honor Rag, Mrs. Cage.

ELKINS, HILLARD
Producer. b. New York, NY, Oct. 18, 1929. e. NYU, B.A., 1951. Exec., William Morris Agy., 1949-51; exec. v.p., Gen. Artists Corp., 1952-53; pres., Hillard Elkins Mgmt., 1953-60; Elkins Prods. Intl. Corp., N.Y., 1960-71; Elkins Prods. Ltd., 1972-; Hillard Elkins Entertainment Corp., 1974; Media Mix Prods., Inc., 1979-82.
MEMBER: Academy of Motion Picture Arts & Sciences, Acad. of TV Arts & Sciences, Dramatists Guild, League of New York Theatres, American Fed. of TV & Radio Artists.
THEATER: Come On Strong, Golden Boy, Oh Calcutta!, The Rothschilds, A Doll's House, An Evening with Richard Nixon, Sizwe Banzi Is Dead, etc.
PICTURES: Alice's Restaurant, A New Leaf, Oh Calcutta!, A Doll's House, Richard Pryor Live in Concert, Sellers on Sellers, Inside.
TELEVISION: The Importance of Being Earnest, The Deadly Game, Princess Daisy, The Meeting (exec. prod.), Father & Son: Dangerous Relationsm A Father for Charlie, In His Father's Shoes.

ELKINS, KEN JOE
Broadcasting Executive. b. Prenter, WV, Oct. 12, 1937. e. Nebraska U., 1966-69. Eng. sta. KETV-TV, NE, 1960-67; asst. chief engr., 1967-70; ops. mgr., asst. nat. sales, gen. sales mgr., 1972-75; gen. mgr., 1975-80. Chief engr. sta. KOUB-TV, IA, 1970-71; gen mgr., 1871-72. Gen. mgr. sta. KSDK-TV, MO, 1980-81. V.P., CEO Pulitzer Broadcasting Co., St. Louis, 1981-84; pres., CEO, 1984-. Bd. Dirs.: Commerce Bank St. Louis; Maximum Svc. Telecasters, WA; Broadcast Music, Inc.; BJC Health Sys. Trustee, NE Broadcasters, 1979-80. Chmn., NBC Affiliate Bd. Govs. With USAF, 1957-61. Inducted into NE Broadcasters Hall of Fame, 1990. Mem.: Nat. Assn. Broadcasters; Found. Broadcasters Hall of Fame (bd. dirs., trustee 1990); TV Operators Caucus; Algonquin Club.

ELKINS, SAUL
Producer. b. New York, NY, June 22, 1907. e. City Coll. of New York, B.S., 1927. Radio writer, dir., prod. 1930-2; dir., prod. stock co. touring Latin America 1932-34; writer Fox Films, 20th Century-Fox; writer RKO, Columbia 1937-42; writer, dial-dir., dir. Warner Bros. 1943-7; prod. Warner Bros. since 1947. Member: AMPAS, Screen Writer's Guild. Exec. prod., Comprenetics, Inc. Dir., Pioneer Prods., 1982.
PICTURES: Younger Brothers, One Last Fling, Homicide, House Across the Street, Flaxy Martin, Barricade, Return of the Frontiersmen, This Side of the Law, Colt .45, Sugarfoot, Raton Pass, The Big Punch, Smart Girls Don't Talk, Embraceable You.

ELLIOTT, CHRIS
Actor, Writer. b. New York, NY, May 31, 1960. Father is comedian Bob Elliott. Was performer in improv. theatres, summer stock; also tour guide at Rockefeller Center. Became writer/performer for David Letterman starting in 1982. Author: Daddy's Boy: A Son's Shocking Account of Life With a Famous Father (1989).

PICTURES: Manhunter (debut, 1986), The Abyss, Hyperspace, Groundhog Day, CB4, Cabin Boy (also co-story), Kingpin, The Sky Is Falling, There's Something About Mary.
TELEVISION: Series: Late Night With David Letterman (also co-writer; 2 Emmy Awards for writing: 1984, 1985), Nick and Hillary, Get a Life (also creator, co-writer, prod.). Specials: Late Night With David Letterman Anniversary Specials (also co-writer; 2 Emmy Awards for writing: 1986, 1987), Chris Elliott's FDR: One-Man Show (also writer, prod.), The Naked Truth.

ELLIOTT, LANG
Producer, Director. b. Los Angeles, CA, Oct. 18, 1949. Began acting in films at an early age, influenced by his uncle, the late actor William Elliott (known as Wild Bill Elliott). Employed by, among others the McGowan Brothers. Turned to film production; co-founded distribution co., The International Picture Show Co., serving as exec. v.p. in chg. of financing, production & distribution. In 1976 formed TriStar Pictures, Inc. to finance and distribute product. In 1980 sold TriStar to Columbia, HBO and CBS. 1982, formed Lang Elliott Productions, Inc. Co-founded Longshot Enterprises with actor Tim Conway to prod. films and home videos, 1985. Videos include Dorf on Golf (the first made-for-home-video comedy), 'Scuse Me!, Dorf and the First Olympic Games. Formed Performance Pictures, Inc., in 1989, a prod. & distrib. company. Received Academy Award nom. for Soldier of Orange and The Magic of Lassie.
PICTURES: Prod: Ride the Hot Wind, Where Time Began, The Farmer, The Billion Dollar Hobo, They Went That-a-Way & That-a-Way, The Prize Fighter. Prod.-dir.: The Private Eyes, Cage, Cage II, and over 40 other pictures.
TELEVISION: Experiment in Love (prod.), Boys Will Be Boys (writer).

ELLIOTT, SAM
Actor. b. Sacramento, CA, Aug. 9, 1944. m. actress Katharine Ross. e. U. of Oregon.
PICTURES: Butch Cassidy and the Sundance Kid (debut in bit, 1969), The Games, Frogs, Molly and Lawless John, Lifeguard, The Legacy, Mask, Fatal Beauty, Shakedown, Road House, Prancer, Sibling Rivalry, Rush, Gettysburg, Tombstone.
TELEVISION: Movies: The Challenge, Assault on the Wayne, The Blue Knight, I Will Fight No More Forever, The Sacketts, Wild Times, Murder in Texas, Shadow Riders, Travis McGee, A Death in California. The Blue Lightning, Houston: The Legend of Texas, The Quick and the Dead, Conagher (also co-writer, exec. prod.), Fugitive Nights: Danger in the Desert, Buffalo Girls, The Ranger the Cook and a Hole in the Sky. Series: Mission: Impossible, The Yellow Rose. Mini-Series: Once and Eagle, Aspen (The Innocent and the Damned). Guest: Lancer, The FBI, Gunsmoke, Streets of San Francisco, Hawaii 5-0, Police Woman. Pilot: Evel Knievel.

ELWES, CARY
Actor. b. London, England, Oct. 26, 1962. e. Harrow. Studied for stage with Julie Bovasso at Sarah Lawrence, Bronxville, NY.
PICTURES: Another Country (debut 1984), Oxford Blues, The Bride, Lady Jane, The Princess Bride, Glory, Days of Thunder, Leather Jackets, Hot Shots!, Bram Stoker's Dracula, The Crush, Robin Hood: Men in Tights, Rudyard Kipling's The Jungle Book, Twister, Kiss the Girls, The Informant, Liar Liar, Quest for Camelot (voice).

EMMERICH, ROLAND
Director, Writer, Exec. Producer. b. Stuttgart, Germany, Nov. 10, 1955. Studied production design in film school in Munich. First film was student production, The Noah's Ark Principle, which opened the 1984 Berlin Film Festival and was sold to more than 20 countries. Formed Centropolis Film Productions. Prod. TV series, The Visitor, 1997.
PICTURES: Co-s.p./Dir.:Making Contact (a.k.a. Joey; dir. only), Ghost Chase, Eye of the Storm (prod. only), Moon 44, Universal Soldier, Stargate, Independence Day, Godzilla.

ENGEL, CHARLES F.
Executive. b. Los Angeles, CA, Aug. 30. e. Michigan State U., UCLA. Son of writer-prod. Samuel G. Engel. Pgm. devel., ABC-TV, 1964-68; v.p. Univ.-TV, 1972; sr. v.p., 1977; exec. v.p., 1980; pres., MCA Pay-TV Programming, 1981. ACE Award, 1988 for outstanding contribution to cable; v.p. Universal TV, exec. in chg. ABC Mystery Movie, 1989. Sr. v.p. 1992 in chg. Columbo, Murder She Wrote, SeaQuest, The Rockford Files. Founding member board of governors, the National Academy of Cable Programming. Member, Television Academy. Exec. v.p. of Programming Universal Television, 1997.
TELEVISION: The Aquarians (exec. prod.), Run a Crooked Mile (exec. prod.), Road Raiders (prod.), ABC Mystery Movie (exec. in chg. of prod.).

ENGELBERG, MORT
Producer. b. Memphis, TN. e. U. of Illinois, U. of Missouri. Taught journalism; worked as reporter for UPI, AP. Worked for US government, including USIA, Peace Corps., Office of Economic Opportunity; President's Task Force on War on Poverty. Left gov. service in 1967 to become film unit publicist, working on three films in Europe: Dirty Dozen, Far From the Madding Crowd, The Comedians. Returned to U.S.; appt. pub. mgr. for United Artists. Sent to Hollywood as asst. to Herb Jaffe, UA head of west coast prod., which post he assumed when Jaffe left. Left to join indep. prod., Ray Stark.
PICTURES: Smokey and the Bandit, Hot Stuff, The Villain, The Hunter, Smokey and the Bandit II, Smokey and the Bandit III, Nobody's Perfekt, The Heavenly Kid, The Big Easy, Maid to Order, Dudes, Three For the Road, Russkies, Pass the Ammo, Trading Hearts, Fright Night Part 2, Rented Lips, Remote Control.

ENGLANDER, MORRIS K.
Executive. b. New York, NY, July 5, 1934. e. Wharton Sch., U. of Pennsylvania. With General Cinema Corp. circuit before joining RKO Century Warner Theatres 1984 as exec. v.p., develp.; later co-vice chmn. of circuit. 1986, sr. real estate advisor, American Multi-Cinema. 1988: v.p. real estate Hoyts Cinemas Corp.; 1990 COO of Hoyts; pres. & COO of Hoyts. 1991.

ENGLUND, ROBERT
Actor. b. Glendale, CA, June 6, 1949. e. UCLA, RADA. First significant role was in the Cleveland stage production of Godspell, 1971.
PICTURES: Buster and Billie, Hustle, Stay Hungry, Death Trap (Eaten Alive), The Last of the Cowboys, St. Ives, A Star is Born, Big Wednesday, Bloodbrothers, The Fifth Floor, Dead and Buried, Galaxy of Terror, Don't Cry It's Only Thunder, A Nightmare on Elm Street, A Nightmare on Elm Street Part 2: Freddy's Revenge, Never Too Young to Die, A Nightmare on Elm Street 3: Dream Warriors, A Nightmare on Elm Street 4: The Dream Master, 976-EVIL (dir. only), A Nightmare on Elm Street: The Dream Child, Phantom of the Opera, The Adventures of Ford Fairlane, Danse Macabre, Freddy's Dead: The Final Nightmare, Eugenie, Wes Craven's New Nightmare, The Mangler, The Paper Route, Vampyre Wars, Killer Tongue, Regeneration, Wishmaster.
TELEVISION: Series: Downtown, V, Freddy's Nightmares, Nightmare Cafe. Specials and Movies: Hobson's Choice, Young Joe: The Forgotten Kennedy, The Ordeal of Patty Hearst, The Courage and the Passion, Mind Over Murder, Thou Shalt Not Kill, The Fighter, Journey's End, Starflight: The Plane That Couldn't Land, I Want to Live, Infidelity, A Perry Mason Mystery: The Case of the Lethal Lifestyle, Robin Cook's Mortal Fear, The Unspoken Truth. Mini-Series: V, North and South Book II. Host: Horror Hall of Fame, Sci-Fi Channel.

EPHRON, NORA
Writer, Director. b. New York, NY, May 19, 1941. e. Wellesley Col. Daughter of writers Henry and Phoebe Ephron. m. writer Nicholas Pileggi. Author: Heartburn, Crazy Salad, Scribble Scribble. Appeared in films Crimes and Misdemeanors, Husbands and Wives.
PICTURES: Writer: Silkwood, Heartburn, When Harry Met Sally... (also assoc. prod.), Cookie (also exec. prod.), My Blue Heaven (also exec. prod.), This is My Life (also dir.), Sleepless in Seattle (also dir.), Mixed Nuts (also dir.), Michael (also dir., prod., exec. prod.), You've Got Mail.
TELEVISION: Movie (writer): Perfect Gentlemen.

EPSTEIN, JULIUS J
Screenwriter. b. New York, NY, Aug. 22, 1909. e. Pennsylvania State U. Worked as publicist before going to Hollywood where began writing. Had long collaboration with twin brother, Philip G. Epstein. Under contract with Warner Bros. over 17 years.
PICTURES: In Caliente, Broadway Gondolier, Four Daughters, Daughters Courageous, Four Wives, Saturday's Children, No Time for Comedy, The Strawberry Blonde, The Bride Came C.O.D., The Man Who Came to Dinner, The Male Animal, Casablanca (Acad. Award, 1943), Arsenic and Old Lace, Mr. Skeffington (also co-prod.), Romanc on the High Seas, My Foolish Heart, Forever Female, The Last Time I Saw Paris, Young at Heart, The Tender Trap, Kiss Them for Me, Take a Giant Step (also prod.), Tall Story, Fanny, Light in the Piazza, Send Me No Flowers, Return From the Ashes, Any Wednesday (also prod.), Pete n' Tillie (also prod.), Jacqueline Susann's Once Is Not Enough, Cross of Iron, House Calls, Reuben Reuben (also co-prod.).

EPSTEIN, MEL
Producer. b. Dayton, OH, March 25, 1910; e. Ohio State U. Adv. & edit. depts. on newspapers; entered m.p. ind. as player in 1931; then asst. dir., unit prod. mgr., second unit & shorts dir.; U.S. Army Signal Corps (1st Lt.); apptd. Paramount prod., 1946. Now retired.
PICTURES: Whispering Smith, Hazard, Copper Canyon, Dear Brat, Branded, The Savage, Alaska Seas, Secret of the Incas.
TELEVISION: Broken Arrow, Men into Space, The Islanders, Asphalt Jungle, Rawhide, Long Hot Summer, The Monroes, Custer, Lancer (pilot), Lancer (unit mngr., series), Medical Center (series).

ERDMAN, RICHARD
Actor, Director. b. Enid, OK, June 1, 1925. e. Hollywood H.S.
PICTURES: Actor: Janie, Objective Burma, Time of Your Life, Four Days Leave, The Men, Cry Danger, Jumping Jacks, Happy Time, The Stooge, Stalag 17, The Power and the Prize, Saddle the Wind, Namu The Killer Whale. Director: Bleep, The Brothers O'Toole, Oscar In Limbo (also writer). Writer-Prod.: The Hillerman Project.
TELEVISION: Ray Bolger Show, Perry Mason, Police Story, Tab Hunter Show, Alice, Bionic Woman, One Day at a Time, Playhouse of Stars, Twilight Zone, The Lucy Show, Lou Grant, Cheers, Wings, Picket Fences. Movie: Jesse. Director: The Dick Van Dyke Show, Mooch (special). Writer-Prod.: More Than a Scarecrow.

ERICSON, JOHN
Actor. b. Detroit, MI, Sept. 25, 1926. e. American Acad. of Dramatic Arts. Appeared in summer stock; then Stalag 17 on Broadway.
PICTURES: Teresa (debut, 1951), Rhapsody, The Student Prince, Green Fire, Bad Day at Black Rock, The Return of Jack Slade, The Cruel Tower, Oregon Passage, Forty Guns, Day of the Bad Man, Pretty Boy Floyd, Under Ten Flags, Slave Queen of Babylon, 7 Faces of Dr. Lao, Operation Atlantis, The Money Jungle, The Destructors, Treasure of Pancho Villa, The Bamboo Saucer (Collision Course), Heads or Tails, Bedknobs and Broomsticks, Hustle Squad, Crash, Final Mission, Alien Zone, Project Saucer, Golden Triangle, Queens Are Wild, Hustler Squad, $10,000 Caper, Primary Target.
TELEVISION: Series: Honey West, General Hospital. Movies: The Bounty Man, Hog Wild, Hunter's Moon, House on the Rue Riviera, Tenafly. Mini-Series: Robert Kennedy and His Times, Space. Specials: Saturday's Children, Heritage of Anger, The Innocent Sleep. Guest: Marcus Welby, Mannix, Streets of San Francisco, Fantasy Island, Bonanza, Medical Center, Route 66, Murder She Wrote, Police Story, General Hospital, Air Wolf, Gunsmoke, Police Woman, The FBI, One Day at a Time, Magnum P.I.

ERMAN, JOHN
Director. b. Chicago, IL, Aug. 3, 1935. e. U. of California. Debut as TV director, Stoney Burke, 1962.
PICTURES: Making It, Ace Eli and Rodger of the Skies, Stella.
TELEVISION: Movies: Letters From Three Lovers, Green Eyes, Alexander the Other Side of Dawn, Just Me and You, My Old Man, Moviola (This Year's Blonde; Scarlett O'Hara War; The Silent Lovers), The Letter, Eleanor: First Lady of the World, Who Will Love My Children? (Emmy Award, 1983), Another Woman's Child, A Streetcar Named Desire, Right to Kill?, The Atlanta Child Murders, An Early Frost, The Two Mrs. Grenvilles (also sprv. prod.), When the Time Comes, The Attic: The Hiding of Anne Frank (also prod.), David (also sprv. prod.), The Last Best Year (also sprv. prod.), The Last to Go (also prod.), Our Sons, Carolina Skeletons, Breathing Lessons (also prod.), The Sunshine Boys (also prod.). Mini-Series: Roots: The Next Generations (co-dir.), Queen (also co-prod.), Scarlett (also prod.), The Boys Next Door (also prod.), Ellen Foster, (also prod.), Only Love.

ESBIN, JERRY
Executive. b. Brooklyn, NY, 1931. Started in mailroom at Columbia at 17 and worked for co. nearly 25 years. Then joined American Multi Cinema. Joined Paramount Pictures in 1975 as mgr. of branch operations; later named v.p., asst. sls. mgr. In 1980 named v.p., gen. sls. mgr. 1981, sr. v.p., domestic sls. & mktg. 1981, joined United Artists as sr. v.p., mktg. & dist.; 1982, named pres., MGM/UA m.p. dist. & mktg. div; 1983, sr. v.p., domestic dist., Tri-Star Pictures; 1985, promoted to exec. v.p.; 1989, joined Loews Theaters as sr. exec. v.p. and chief oper. officer, also in 1989 named pres. as well as chief operating officer, Loews Theater Management Corp.

ESMOND, CARL
Actor. b. Vienna, Austria, June 14, 1906. e. U. of Vienna. On stage Vienna, Berlin, London (Shakespeare, Shaw, German modern classics). Acted in many European films under the name Willy Eichberger. Originated part of Prince Albert in Victoria Regina (London). On screen in Brit. prod. incl. Blossom Time, Even Song, Invitation to the Waltz. To U.S. in 1938. Guest star on many live and filmed TV shows. US stage incl. The Woman I Love, Four Winds. Appeared in Oscar nom. docum. Resisting Enemy Interrogation.
PICTURES: Dawn Patrol, First Comes Courage, Little Men, Sergeant York, Panama Hattie, Seven Sweethearts, Address Unknown, Margin for Error, Master Race, Ministry of Fear, Experiment Perilous, Story of Dr. Wassell. The Catman of Paris, Smash-up, Story of a Woman, Casablanca, Climax, Slave Girl, Walk a Crooked Mile, The Navy Comes Through, Sundown, Lover Come Back, This Love of Ours, Without Love, Mystery Submarine, The Desert Hawk, The World in His Arms, Thunder in the Sun, From the Earth to the Moon, Brushfire, Kiss of Evil, Agent for H.A.R.M., Morituri.
TELEVISION: My Wicked Wicked Ways. Guest: The Man From Uncle, Lassie, The Big Valley, Treasury Agent, etc.

ESPOSITO, GIANCARLO
Actor. b. Copenhagen, Denmark, April 26, 1958. Made B'way debut as child in 1968 musical Maggie Flynn.
THEATER: *B'way:* Maggie Flynn, The Me Nobody Knows, Lost in the Stars, Seesaw, Merrily We Roll Along, Don't Get God Started, Sacrilege. *Off-B'way:* Zooman and the Sign (Theatre World Award, Obie Award), Keyboard, Who Loves the Dancer, House of Ramon Igleslas, Do Lord Remember Me, Balm in Gilead, Anchorman, Distant Fires, Trafficking in Broken Hearts.
PICTURES: Running, Taps, Trading Places, The Cotton Club, Desperately Seeking Susan, Maximum Overdrive, Sweet Lorraine, School Daze, Do the Right Thing, Mo'Better Blues, King of New York, Harley Davidson and the Marlboro Man, Night on Earth, Bob Roberts, Malcolm X, Amos & Andrew, Fresh, Smoke, The Keeper (co-prod. only), The Usual Suspects, Kla$h, Blue in the Face, The Keeper, Reckless, Loose Women, Nothing to Lose, The Maze, The People, Trouble on the Corner, Twilight, Phoenix.
TELEVISION: *Series:* Bakersfield P.D. *Movies:* The Gentleman Bandit, Go Tell It on the Mountain, Relentless: Mind of a Killer, The Tomorrow Man, Five Desperate Hours . *Special:* Roanok. *Guest:* Miami Vice, Spencer: For Hire, Legwork, NYPD Blue, Nash Bridges, Living Single, Chicago Hope.

ESSEX, DAVID
Actor, Singer, Composer. b. Plaistow, London, England, July 23, 1947. e. Shipman Sch., Custom House. Started as a singer-drummer in East London band. 1967: Joined touring Repertory Co. in The Fantasticks, Oh, Kay, etc. 1970: West End debut in Ten Years Hard, 1972: Jesus Christ in Godspell, Che in Evita; Lord Byron in Childe Byron, 1983-84: Fletcher Christian in own musical Mutiny! on album and stage. International recording artist. Variety Club of Great Britain show business personality of 1978. Many gold & silver disc intl. awards. 1989, Royal Variety performance. World concerts since 1974.
PICTURES: Assault, All Coppers Are..., That'll Be the Day, Stardust, Silver Dream Racer (also wrote score), Shogun Mayeda.
TELEVISION: Top of the Pops, Own Specials, The River (also composed music), BBC series. U.S.: Merv Griffin, Johnny Carson, Dinah Shore, American Bandstand, Midnight Special, Grammy Awards, Salute to The Beatles, Don Kirshner's Rock Concert, A.M. America, Phil Everly in Session, Paul Ryan Show, The David Essex Showcase.

ESTEVEZ, EMILIO
Actor, Director, Writer. b. New York, NY, May 12, 1962. Father is actor Martin Sheen; brother is actor Charlie Sheen. Made prof. debut at age 20 in TV movie starring his father, In the Custody of Strangers.
PICTURES: Tex (debut, 1982), The Outsiders, Nightmares, Repo Man, The Breakfast Club, St. Elmo's Fire, That Was Then This is Now (also s.p.), Maximum Overdrive, Wisdom (also dir., s.p.), Stakeout, Young Guns. Men at Work (also dir., s.p.), Young Guns II, Freejack, The Mighty Ducks, National Lampoon's Loaded Weapon 1, Another Stakeout, Judgment Night, D2: The Mighty Ducks, The Jerky Boys (co- exec. prod. only), The War at Home, Mighty Ducks 3.
TELEVISION: *Movies:* In the Custody of Strangers. Nightbreaker.

ESTRADA, ERIK
Actor. r.n. Enrique Estrada. m. actress Peggy Rowe. b. New York, NY, March 16, 1949. Began professional career in Mayor John Lindsay's Cultural Program, performing in public parks. Joined American Musical Dramatic Acad. for training. Feature film debut in The Cross and the Switchblade (1970).
PICTURES: The New Centurions, Airport '75, Midway, Trackdown, Where Is Parsifal?, Lightblast, The Repentant, Hour of the Assassin, The Lost Idol, A Show of Force, Night of the Wilding, Twisted Justice, Caged Fury, Guns, Spirits, Do or Die, The Divine Enforcer, Alien Seed, Night of the Wilding, National Lampoon's Loaded Weapon 1, The Last Riders, Gang Justice.
TELEVISION: *Series:* CHiPS. *Guest:* Hawaii Five-0, Six Million Dollar Man, Police Woman, Kojak, Medical Center, Hunter, Alfred Hitchcock Presents (1988), Cybill. *Movies:* Fire!, Honeyboy, The Dirty Dozen: The Fatal Mission, She Knows Too Much, Earth Angel.

ESZTERHAS, JOE
Writer. Author of novel Charlie Simpson's Apocalypse (nom. National Book Award, 1974), Nark!, and novelization of F.I.S.T.
PICTURES: F.I.S.T., Flashdance, Jagged Edge, Big Shots, Betrayed, Checking Out, Music Box (also co-exec. prod.), Basic Instinct, Nowhere to Run (co-sp., co-exec. prod.), Sliver (also co-exec. prod.), Jade (exec. prod. only), Hearts of Fire, Original Sin, Blaze of Glory.

ETTINGER, EDWIN D.
Publicist. b. New York, NY, 1921. Entered m.p. ind. as office boy, MGM; pub. rel. and publ. for industrial, comm. clients, 1946-52; joined Ettinger Co., pub. rel., 1952; pub. rel. dir., Disneyland Inc., 1955; marketing dir., Disneyland, 1955-65; v.p., M.C.A. Enterprises, Inc., 1965-66; Board chmn. & CEO, Recreation Environments, Inc., 1967-70; Board chmn. & CEO Recreations Inc., 1967-70; Pres., Ettinger, Inc., 1975-85; semi-retired in 1985.

ETTLINGER, JOHN A.
Producer, Director, Distributor. b. Chicago, IL, Oct. 14, 1924. e. Peddie Inst., Cheshire Acad. Signal Corps Photog. Center, 1942-45; with Paramount Theatres Corp., 1945-47; dir., KTLA, Paramount TV Prod., Inc., Los Angeles, 1948-50; radio-TV dir., Nat. C. Goldstone Agency, 1950-53; pres. Medallion TV Enterprises, Inc.; TV prod., View the Clue, Greenwich Village, High Road to Danger, Sur Demande, Star Route, Las Vegas Fights, Celebrity Billiards; Pres., KUDO-FM, Las Vegas.

EVANS, HARRY KENT
Executive. b. Long Beach, CA, July 16, 1935. Intl. representative, UAW, 1960-76. Exec. dir., International Photographers Guild, 1976-90. CEO of the ASC, 1990-94. Exec. VP, Meier Entertainment Group, Vancouver, BC, 1994-96. Exec. VP. Meier Worldwide Intermedia, 1996-.

EVANS, LINDA
Actress. b. Hartford, CT, Nov. 18, 1942. e. Hollywood H.S., L.A. TV commercials led to contract with MGM.
PICTURES: Twilight of Honor (debut, 1963), Those Calloways, Beach Blanket Bingo, The Klansman, Mitchell, Avalanche Express, Tom Horn.
TELEVISION: *Series:* The Big Valley, Hunter, Dynasty. *Movies:* Nakia, Nowhere to Run, Standing Tall, The Last Frontier, I'll Take Romance, The Reunion, Step Sister. *Mini-Series:* North & South Book II, Dazzle Bare Essence, The Gambler Returns: Luck of the Draw, Gambler: The Adventure Continues.

EVANS, RAY
Songwriter. b. Salamanca, NY, Feb. 4, 1915. e. Wharton Sch. of U. of Pennsylvania. Musician on cruise ships, radio writer spec. material. Hellzapoppin', Sons o' Fun. Member: exec. bd. Songwriters Guild of America, Dramatists Guild, West Coast advisory bd. ASCAP., bd., Myasthenia Gravis Fdn. CA chap., Songwriters Hall of Fame, Motion Picture Acad. Received star on Hollywood Blvd. Walk of Fame. Songs included on Great Composer Series, by Columbia Records.
SONGS: To Each His Own, Golden Earrings, Buttons and Bows (Acad. Award, 1948), Mona Lisa (Acad. Award, 1950), Whatever Will Be Will Be (Acad. Award, 1956), A Thousand Violins, I'll Always Love You, Dreamsville, Love Song from Houseboat, Tammy, Silver Bells, Dear Heart, Angel, Never Let Me Go, Almost in Your Arms, As I Love You, In the Arms of Love, Wish Me a Rainbow.
PICTURES: The Paleface, Sorrowful Jones, Fancy Pants, My Friend Irma, Aaron Slick From Punkin Crick, Son of the Paleface, My Friend Irma Goes West, The Night of Grizzly, Saddle the Wind, Isn't It Romantic, Capt. Carey U.S.A., Off Limits, Here Come the Girls, Red Garters, Man Who Knew Too Much, Stars Are Singing, Tammy, Houseboat, Blue Angel, A Private's Affair, All Hands on Deck, Dear Heart, The Third Day, What Did You Do in the War Daddy?, This Property Is Condemned.
BROADWAY MUSICALS: Oh Captain! Let It Ride!, Sugar Babies.
TELEVISION THEMES: Bonanza, Mr. Ed, Mr. Lucky, To Rome With Love.

EVANS, ROBERT
Producer. b. New York, NY, June 29, 1930. Son is actor Josh Evans. Radio actor at age 11; went on to appear in more than 300 radio prog. (incl. Let's Pretend, Archie Andrews, The Aldrich Family, Gangbusters) on major networks. Also appeared on early TV. At 20 joined brother, Charles, and Joseph Picone, as partner in women's clothing firm of Evan-Picone, Inc., 1952-67. In 1957 signed by Universal to play Irving Thalberg in Man of a Thousand Faces after recommendation by Norma Shearer, Thalberg's widow. Guest columnist NY Journal American, 1958. Independent prod. at 20th Century-Fox. 1966-76, with Paramount Pictures as head of prod., then exec. v.p. worldwide prod. (supervising Barefoot in the Park, Rosemary's Baby, Barbarella, Goodbye Columbus, Love Story, The Godfather I & II, The Great Gatsby, etc.). Resigned to become indep. prod. again; with exclusive contract with Paramount. *Autobiography:* The Kid Stays in the Picture (1994).
PICTURES: *Actor:* Man of a Thousand Faces, The Sun Also Rises, The Fiend Who Walked the West, The Best of Everything. *Producer:* Chinatown, Marathon Man, Black Sunday, Players, Urban Cowboy, Popeye, The Cotton Club, The Two Jakes, Sliver, Jade, The Phantom, The Saint, The Out of Towners.
TELEVISION: *Actor:* Elizabeth and Essex (1947), Young Widow Brown, The Right to Happiness. *Prod.:* Get High on Yourself.

EVERETT, CHAD
Actor. r.n. Raymond Lee Cramton. b. South Bend, IN, June 11, 1937. e. Wayne State U., Detroit. Signed by William T. Orr, head of TV prod. for Warner Bros. to 7-year contract. Appeared in many TV series as well as films. Next became contract player at MGM (1963-67). Received star on Hollywood Walk of Fame.
PICTURES: Claudelle Inglish (debut, 1961), The Chapman Report, Rome Adventure, Get Yourself a College Girl, The Singing Nun, Made in Paris, Johnny Tiger, The Last Challenge, Return of the Gunfighter, First to Fight, The Impossible Years, Firechasers, Airplane II: The Sequel, Fever Pitch, Jigsaw, Heroes Stand Alone, Official Denial, Hard to Forget.
TELEVISION: Series: The Dakotas, Medical Center, Hagen, The Rousters, McKenna, Dark Skies (narr. of pilot). Guest: Hawaiian Eye, 77 Sunset Strip, Surfside Six, Lawman, Bronco, The Lieutenant, Redigo, Route 66, Ironside, Hotel, Murder She Wrote, Shades of L.A., Cybil. Movies: Intruder, The Love Boat, Police Story, Thunderboat Row, Malibu, The French Atlantic Affair, Mistress in Paradise, Journey to the Unknown, In the Glitter Palace. Mini-Series: Centennial, McKenna, Star Command, When Time Expires.

EVERETT, RUPERT
Actor. b. Norfolk, England, 1959. e. Ampleforth Central School for Speech & Drama. Apprenticed with Glasgow's Citizen's Theatre. Originated role of Guy Bennett in Another Country on London stage in 1982 and made feature film debut in screen version in 1984. Author: Are You Working Darling?
PICTURES: Another Country, Real Life, Dance with a Stranger, Duet for One, Chronicle of a Death Foretold, The Right Hand Man, Hearts of Fire, The Gold-Rimmed Glasses, Jigsaw, The Comfort of Strangers, Inside Monkey Zetterland, Ready to Wear (Pret-a-Porter), The Madness of King George, Dunston Checks In, Cemetary Man, My Best Friend's Wedding, B. Monkey, The Next Best Thing.
TELEVISION: Arthur the King, The Far Pavilions, Princess Daisy.

EVIGAN, GREG
Actor. b. South Amboy, NJ, Oct. 14, 1953. Appeared on NY stage in Jesus Christ Superstar and Grease.
PICTURES: Stripped to Kill, DeepStar Six, House of the Damned.
TELEVISION: Series: A Year at the Top, B.J. and the Bear, Masquerade, My Two Dads, P.S. I Luv U, TekWar, Melrose Place, Pacific Palisades. Movies: B.J. and the Bear (pilot), Private Sessions, The Lady Forgets, Lies Before Kisses, TekWar, TekJustice, TekLab, TekLords, One of Her Own, Deadly Family Secrets, Nobody Lives Forever. Guest: One Day at a Time, Barnaby Jones, Murder She Wrote, New Mike Hammer, Matlock.

F

FABARES, SHELLEY
Actress. b. Los Angeles, CA, Jan. 19, 1944. r.n. Michele Marie Fabares. m. actor Mike Farrell. Earned gold record for 1962 single Johnny Angel.
PICTURES: Never Say Goodbye, Rock Pretty Baby, Marjorie Morningstar, Summer Love, Annette, Ride the Wild Surf, Girl Happy, Hold On!, Spinout, Clambake, A Time to Sing, Hot Pursuit, Love or Money.
TELEVISION: Series: Annie Oakley, The Donna Reed Show, The Little People (The Brian Keith Show), The Practice, Mary Hartman Mary Hartman, Forever Fernwood, Highcliffe Manor, One Day at a Time, Coach, Superman (voice). Guest: Twilight Zone, Mr. Novak, Love American Style, The Rookies, Marcus Welby, Hello Larry. Movies: U.M.C., Brian's Song, Two for the Money, Sky Heist, Pleasure Cove, Friendships Secrets & Lies, Donovan's Kid, The Great American Traffic Jam (Gridlock), Memorial Day, Run Till You Fall, Class Cruise, Deadly Relations, The Great Mom Swap, Dream Is a Wish Your Heart Makes: The Annette Funicello Story, A Nightmare Come True, Playing to Win: A Moment of Truth Movie.

FAHEY, JEFF
Actor. b. Olean, NY, Nov. 29, 1956. Family moved to Buffalo when he was 10 years old. Was member of Joffrey Ballet for 3 years. Appeared on B'way in Brigadoon (1980), tour of Oklahoma!, Paris prod. of West Side Story, and London prod. of Orphans.
PICTURES: Silverado (debut, 1985), Psycho III, Riot on 42nd Street, The Serpent of Death, Wrangler, Split Decisions, Backfire, Outback, True Blood, Out of Time, Last of the Finest, Impulse, White Hunter Black Heart, Body Parts, Iron Maze, The Lawnmower Man, Woman of Desire, Freefall, Wyatt Earp, Temptation, Quick, The Sweeper (also asst. prod.), Serpent's Liar, Eye of the Wolf, Darkman III: Die Darkman Die, When Justice Fails, Waiting for the Man, Operation Delta Force, Johnny 2.0, Catherine's Grove, Lethal Tender, The Underground (co-prod. only).
TELEVISION: Series: One Life to Live, The Marshal. Movies: Execution of Raymond Graham, Parker Kane, Curiosity Kills, Iran: Days of Crisis, Sketch Artist, In the Company of Darkness, The Hit List, Blindsided, Baree, Sketch Artist II: Hands That See, Virtual Seduction, Every Woman's Dream, On the Line.

FAIMAN, PETER
Director. b. Australia. Entered entertainment business through TV, involved early in production-direction of major variety series in Australia. Assoc. prod.-dir. of over 20 programs for The Paul Hogan Show and two Hogan specials filmed in England (1983). Developed Australia's most popular and longest-running national variety program, The Don Lane Show. Responsible for creative development of the TV Week Logie Awards on the Nine Network. For 4 years headed Special Projects Division of the Nine Network Australia. Resigned to establish own prod. co., Peter Faiman Prods. Pty Ltd. 1984. Made m.p. theatrical film debut as director of Crocodile Dundee, followed by Dutch.

FAIRBANKS, DOUGLAS, JR.
K.B.E., (Hon.) D.S.C., M.A., (Oxon), (Hon.) D.F.I., Westminster (Fulton, MO), (Hon.) LL.D (Denver). Actor, Producer, Executive. b. New York, NY, Dec. 9, 1909. e. Pasadena (CA) Polytech. Sch.; Harvard Mil. Acad., Los Angeles; Bovee and Collegiate Sch., N.Y.; was also tutored in Paris, London. Son of late Douglas Fairbanks. Began as screen actor 1923 in Stephen Steps Out; thereafter in more than 80 pictures. On U.S. stage from 1926. Formed own film prod. co. 1935; commissioned Lieut. (j.g.) USNR, 1940; Appt. Presidential envoy to certain South Amer. nations by Pres. Roosevelt. Helped org. British War Relief and was natl. chmn., Committee for CARE. W.A. White Committee to Defend America 1939-41. Promoted through ranks to Capt., USNR, Now retired. Awarded U.S. Silver Star, Combat Legion of Merit with "V" Attachment; Knight Commander of Order of British Empire, 1949. Distinguished Service Cross, Knight of Justice of Order of St. John of Jerusalem; French Legion of Honor, Croix de Guerre with Palm, etc. Chairman, American Relief for Korea. Entered TV film prod., 1952. Autobiographies: The Fairbanks Album (1975; with Richard Schickel), The Salad Days (1988), A Hell of a War (1993). FYI: republished in England, 1995.
THEATER: U.S.: Young Woodley, Saturday's Children, Present Laughter, Out on a Limb, Sleuth, The Pleasure of His Company (also U.K.), Ireland, Canada, Australia, Hong Kong), The Winding Journey, Moonlight in Silver, My Fair Lady, The Secretary Bird.
PICTURES: (since sound): The Forward Pass, The Careless Age, The Show of Shows, Party Girl, Loose Ankles, The Little Accident, The Dawn Patrol, Little Caesar, Outward Bound, One Night at Susie's, Chances, I Like Your Nerve, Union Depot, It's Tough to Be Famous, Love is a Racket, Parachute Jumper, Morning Glory, Life of Jimmy Dolan, The Narrow Corner, Captured, Catherine the Great, Success at Any Price, Mimi, The Amateur Gentleman (also prod.), Man of the Moment, Accused, When Thief Meets Thief, The Prisoner of Zenda, Joy of Living, Having Wonderful Time, The Rage of Paris, The Young in Heart, Gunga Din, The Sun Never Sets, Rulers of the Sea, Green Hell, Safari, Angels Over Broadway, The Corsican Brothers, Sinbad the Sailor, That Lady in Ermine, The Exile, The Fighting O'Flynn, State Secret, Mr. Drake's Duck, Another Man's Poison (prod. only), Chase a Crooked Shadow (prod. only), Ghost Story.
TELEVISION: Series: Douglas Fairbanks Presents (also prod.). Guest: The Rheingold Theatre (also prod.), The Chevy Show, Route 66, Dr. Kildare, The Love Boat, B.L. Stryker. Special: The Canterville Ghost (ABC Stage '67). Movies: The Crooked Hearts, The Hostage Tower.

FAIRBANKS, JERRY
Executive Producer. b. San Francisco, CA, Nov. 1, 1904. Cameraman, 1924-29; prod., shorts, Universal, 1929-34; prod., Popular Science, Unusual Occupations, Speaking of Animals Series, Para., 1935-49; Winner two Acad. Awards; set up film div., NBC, 1948; formed, NBC Newsreel, 1949; devel. Zoomar Lens and Multicam System; formed Jerry Fairbanks Prods., 1950.
PICTURES: The Last Wilderness, Down Liberty Road, With This Ring, Counterattack, Collision Course, Land of the Sea, Brink of Disaster, The Legend of Amaluk, North of the Yukon, Damage Report, The Boundless Seas.
TELEVISION: Public Prosecutor (first film series for TV); other series: Silver Theatre, Front Page Detective, Jackson and Jill, Hollywood Theatre, Crusader Rabbit.

FAIRCHILD, MORGAN
Actress. b. Dallas, TX, Feb. 3, 1950. e. Southern Methodist U.
PICTURES: Bullet for Pretty Boy, The Seduction, Pee-wee's Big Adventure, Red-Headed Stranger, Campus Man, Sleeping Beauty, Midnight Cop, Deadly Illusion, Phantom of the Mall, Body Chemistry 3: Point of Seduction, Freaked, Virgin Hunters, Naked Gun 33 1/3: The Final Insult.
TELEVISION: Series: Search for Tomorrow, Flamingo Road, Paper Dolls, Falcon Crest, Roseanne. Movies: The Initiation of Sarah, Murder in Music City, Concrete Cowboys, The Memory of Eva Ryker, Flamingo Road (pilot), The Dream Merchants, The Girl the Gold Watch and Dynamite, Honeyboy, The Zany Adventures of Robin Hood, Time Bomb, Street of Dreams, The Haunting of Sarah Harding, How to Murder a Millionare, Menu for Murder, Writer's Block. Perry Mason: The Case of the Skin-Deep Scandal, Based on an Untrue Story. Mini-Series: 79 Park Avenue, North and South Book II.

FAIRCHILD, WILLIAM
Writer, Director. b. Cornwall, England, 1918. e. Royal Naval Coll., Dartmouth. Early career Royal Navy.
AUTHOR: A Matter of Duty, The Swiss Arrangement, Astrology for Dogs, Astrology for Cats, Catsigns (U.S.), The Poppy Factory, No Man's Land (U.S.), Tierra de Nadie (Spain).
THEATER: Sound of Murder, Breaking Point, Poor Horace, The Pay-Off, The Flight of the Bumble B.
PICTURES: *Writer:* Morning Departure, Outcast of the Islands, The Gift Horse, The Net, Newspaper Story, Malta Story, The Seekers, Passage Home, Value For Money, John and Julie (also dir.), The Extra Day (also dir.), The Silent Enemy (also dir.), Star!, Embassy, The Darwin Adventure, Invitation to the Wedding, Bruno Rising, The Promise, Statues in a Garden. *Director only:* The Horsemasters (tv in U.S.).
TELEVISION: The Man with the Gun, No Man's Land, The Signal, Four Just Men, Some Other Love, Cunningham 5101, The Break, The Zoo Gang, Lady with a Past.

FALK, PETER
Actor. b. New York, NY, Sept. 16, 1927. e. New Sch. for Social Research, B.A., 1951; Syracuse U. M.F.A. Studied with Eva Le Gallienne and Sanford Meisner. Worked as efficiency expert for Budget Bureau State of CT.
THEATER: *Off-B'way:* Don Juan (debut, 1956), The Iceman Cometh, Comic Strip, Purple Dust, Bonds of Interest, The Lady's Not for Burning, Diary of a Scoundrel. *On Broadway:* Saint Joan, The Passion of Josef D., The Prisoner of Second Avenue. Regional: Light Up the Sky (L.A.), Glengarry Glen Ross (tour).
PICTURES: Wind Across the Everglades (debut, 1958), The Bloody Brood, Pretty Boy Floyd, The Secret of the Purple Reef, Murder Inc. (Acad. Award nom.), Pocketful of Miracles (Acad. Award nom.), Pressure Point, The Balcony, It's a Mad Mad Mad Mad World, Robin and the 7 Hoods, Italiano Brava Gente (Attack and Retreat), The Great Race, Penelope, Luv, Anzio, Castle Keep, Machine Gun McCann, Operation Snafu, Husbands, A Woman Under the Influence, Murder by Death, Mikey and Nicky, The Cheap Detective, The Brink's Job, Opening Night, The In-Laws, The Great Muppet Caper, All the Marbles, Big Trouble, Happy New Year, The Princess Bride, Wings of Desire, Vibes, Cookie, In the Spirit, Tune in Tomorrow, The Player, Faraway So Close!, Roommates.
TELEVISION: *Series:* The Trials of O'Brien, Columbo (1971-77; Emmy Awards: 1972, 1975, 1976), Columbo (1989, also co-exec. prod.; Emmy Award, 1990). *Guest:* Studio One, Kraft Theatre, Alcoa Theatre, N.T.A. Play of the Week, Armstrong Circle Theatre, Omnibus, Robert Montgomery Presents, Brenner, Deadline, Kraft Mystery Theatre, Rendezvous, Sunday Showcase, The Untouchables, Dick Powell Show (The Price of Tomatoes; Emmy Award, 1962), Danny Kaye Show, Edie Adams Show, Bob Hope Chrysler Theatre. *Movies:* Prescription: Murder, A Step Out of Line, Ransom for a Dead Man, Griffin and Phoenix: A Love Story, Columbo Goes to College, Caution: Murder Can Be Hazardous to Your Health, Columbo and the Murder of a Rock Star, Death Hits the Jackpot, Columbo: No Time to Die, Columbo: A Bird in the Hand (also exec. prod.), Columbo: It's All in the Game (also writer, exec. prod.), Columbo: Butterfly in Shades of Grey (also exec. prod.), Columbo: Undercover, Columbo: Strange Bedfellows (also exec. prod.). *Specials:* The Sacco-Vanzetti Story, The Million Dollar Incident, Brigadoon, A Hatful of Rain, Clue: Movies Murder and Mystery.

FARBER, BART
Executive. Joined United Artists Corp. in early 1960s when UA acquired ZIV TV Programs. Served as v.p. United Artists Television and United Artists Broadcasting. 1971 named v.p. in charge of legal affairs of the cos. 1978, named sr. v.p.—TV, video and special markets; indep. consultant, TV, Pay TV, home video. 1982, joined Cable Health Network as v.p., legal & business affairs; 1984, v.p., business & legal affairs, Lifetime Network; 1986, independent communications consultant.

FARENTINO, JAMES
Actor. b. Brooklyn, NY, Feb. 24, 1938. e. American Acad. of Dramatic Arts.
THEATER: *B'way:* Death of a Salesman, A Streetcar Named Desire (revival, 1973; Theatre World Award). *Off-B'way:* The Days and Nights of Bebe Fenstermaker, In the Summerhouse. *Regional:* One Flew Over the Cuckoo's Nest (Jos. Jefferson, Chas. MacArthur & Chicago Drama Critics League Awards), California Suite, The Best Man, The Big Knife, Good-Bye Charlie, A Thousand Clowns, Love Letters.
PICTURES: Psychomania (Violent Midnight), Engine Pulver, The War Lord, The Pad... And How to Use It (Golden Globe Award, 1966), The Ride to Hangman's Tree, Banning, Rosie!, Me Natalie, The Story of a Woman, The Final Countdown, Dead and Buried, Her Alibi, Bulletproof, Termination Man, Radio Silence.
TELEVISION: *Series:* The Lawyers (The Bold Ones), Cool Million, Dynasty, Blue Thunder, Mary Tyler Moore, Julie Andrews Show. *Guest:* Naked City, daytime soap operas, Laredo, Route 66, The Alfred Hitchcock Hour, Ben Casey, Twelve O'Clock High, Melrose Place, ER. *Special:* DOS Pasos USA. *Mini-Series:* Sins, Jesus of Nazareth (Emmy nom.), Dazzled, On Common Ground, Death of a Salesman, Vanished, Evita Peron, Secrets of the Sahara (Italy). *Movies:* Wings of Fire, The Whole World is Watching, The Sound of Anger, Longest Night, Family Rico,

Cool Million, The Elevator, Crossfire, Possessed, Silent Victory: Undercover Cop, The Kitty O'Neil Story, Son Rise: A Miracle of Love, That Secret Sunday, Something So Right (Emmy nom.), The Cradle Will Fall, License to Kill, A Summer to Remember, That Secret Sunday, Family Sins, Naked Lies, The Red Spider, Who Gets the Friends?, Picking Up the Pieces, In the Line of Duty: A Cop for the Killing, Miles From Nowhere, When No One Would Listen, One Woman's Courage, Honor Thy Father and Mother: The True Story of the Menendez Murders. *Pilot:* American Nuclear.

FARGAS, ANTONIO
Actor. b. Bronx, NY, Aug. 14, 1946. Studied acting at Negro Ensemble Co. and Actor's Studio.
THEATER: The Great White Hope, The Glass Menagerie, Mod Hamlet, Romeo and Juliet, The Slave, Toilet, The Amen Corner.
PICTURES: The Cool World (debut, 1964), Putney Swope, Pound, Believe in Me, Shaft, Cisco Pike, Across 110th Street, Cleopatra Jones, Busting, Foxy Brown, Conrack, The Gambler, Cornbread Earl and Me, Next Stop Greenwich Village, Car Wash, Pretty Baby, Up the Academy, Firestarter, Streetwalkin', Night of the Sharks, Shakedown, I'm Gonna Git You Sucka, The Borrower, Howling VI: The Freaks, Whore.
TELEVISION: *Series:* Starsky and Hutch, All My Children. *Movies:* Starsky and Hutch (pilot), Huckleberry Finn, Escape, Nurse, The Ambush Murders, A Good Sport, Florida Straits, Maid for Each Other, Percy and Thunder. *Guest:* Ironside, The Bill Cosby Show, Sanford and Son, Police Story, Kolchak The Night Stalker, Miami Vice, Kojak.

FARGO, JAMES
Director. b. Republic, WA, Aug. 14, 1938. e. U. of Washington, B.A.
PICTURES: The Enforcer, Caravans, Every Which Way But Loose, A Game for Vultures, Forced Vengeance, Born to Race, Voyage of the Rock Aliens, Riding the Edge (also actor).
TELEVISION: *Movies:* Gus Brown and Midnight Brewster, The Last Electric Knight, Hunter, Snoops, Sky High. *Series:* Tales of the Gold Monkey, Sidekicks.

FARINA, DENNIS
Actor. b. Chicago, IL, Feb. 29, 1944. Served 18 years with Chicago police before being introduced to producer-director Michael Mann who cast him in film Thief. Celebrity Chmn. of Natl. Law Enforcement Officers Memorial in Washington, D.C.
THEATER: A Prayer for My Daughter, Streamers, Tracers, Bleacher Bums, Some Men Need Help, The Time of Your Life.
PICTURES: Thief (debut, 1981), Jo Jo Dancer Your Life Is Calling, Manhunter, Midnight Run, Men of Respect, We're Talkin' Serious Money, Mac, Another Stakeout, Striking Distance, Romeo Is Bleeding, Little Big League, Get Shorty, Eddie, That Old Feeling.
TELEVISION: *Series:* Crime Story. *Mini-Series:* Drug Wars: Columbia. *Movies:* Six Against the Rock, Open Admissions, The Hillside Stranglers, People Like Us, Blind Faith, Cruel Doubt, The Disappearance of Nora, One Woman's Courage, The Corpse Had a Familiar Face, Bonanza: Under Attack, Out of Annie's Past. *Guest:* Miami Vice, Hunter, Tales from the Crypt. Special: The Killing Floor.

FARLEY, CHRIS
Actor. b. Madison, WI, 1960. e. Marquette Univ. Started with The Ark Improv. Theatre Group; performed comedy at Main Stage at Second City in Chicago where he met producer Lorne Michaels.
PICTURES: Coneheads (debut, 1993), Wayne's World 2, Airheads, Bill Madison (cameo), Tommy Boy, Black Sheep.
TELEVISION: *Series:* Saturday Night Live.
(d. Dec. 18, 1997)

FARNSWORTH, RICHARD
Actor. b. Los Angeles, CA, Sept. 1, 1920. Active as stuntman for 40 years before turning to acting.
PICTURES: Comes a Horseman, Tom Horn, Resurrection, The Legend of the Lone Ranger, Ruckus, Waltz Across Texas, The Grey Fox, The Natural, Rhinestone, Into the Night, Sylvester, Space Rage, The Two Jakes, Misery, Highway to Hell, The Getaway, Lassie.
TELEVISION: *Series:* Boys of Twilight. *Movies:* Strange New World, A Few Days in Weasel Creek, Travis McGee, Ghost Dancing, Anne of Green Gables, Chase, Wild Horses, Red Earth White Earth, Good Old Boy, The Fire Next Time, Best Friends for Life.

FARR, FELICIA
Actress. b. Westchester, NY, Oct. 4, 1932. e. Pennsylvania State Coll. m. Jack Lemmon. Stage debut: Picnic (Players Ring Theatre). In Memorandum for a Spy, 1965 tv movie.
PICTURES: Timetable, Jubal, Reprisal!, The First Texan, The Last Wagon, 3:10 to Yuma, Onionhead, Hell Bent for Leather, Kiss Me Stupid, The Venetian Affair, Kotch, Charley Varrick, That's Life!, The Player.

FARR, JAMIE
Actor. r.n. Jameel Joseph Farah. b. Toledo, OH, July 1, 1934. e. Columbia Coll. Trained for stage at Pasadena Playhouse. PICTURES: Blackboard Jungle (debut, 1955), The Greatest Story Ever Told, Ride Beyond Vengeance, Who's Minding the Mint?, With Six You Get Eggroll, The Gong Show Movie, Cannonball Run, Cannonball Run II, Happy Hour, Scrooged, Speed Zone, Curse II: The Bite.
TELEVISION: Series: The Chicago Teddy Bears, M*A*S*H (also dir. episodes), The Gong Show (panelist), The $1.98 Beauty Show (panelist), After M*A*S*H (also dir. episodes). Guest: Dear Phoebe, The Red Skelton Show, The Dick Van Dyke Show, The Danny Kaye Show, The Love Boat, The New Love American Style, Murder She Wrote. Movies: The Blue Knight, Amateur Night at the Dixie Bar and Grill, Murder Can Hurt You!, Return of the Rebels, For Love or Money, Run Till You Fall.

FARRELL, HENRY
Writer. Author of novels and screenplays
PICTURES: Whatever Happened to Baby Jane? Hush ... Hush Sweet Charlotte, What's the Matter with Helen?
TELEVISION: Movies: How Awful About Allan, The House That Would Not Die, The Eyes of Charles Sand.

FARRELL, MIKE
Actor, Producer. b. St. Paul, MN, Feb. 6, 1939. m. actress Shelley Fabares. Currently co-chair of Human Rights Watch in CA.; pres. of Death Penalty Focus; member of the adv. bd. of the Natl Coalition to Abolish the Death Penalty; member of the adv. bd. of the Cult Awareness Network; founding bd. member of Peace Studies, ATV, at Augusta Correctional Ctr in Virginia.
PICTURES: Captain Newman M.D., The Americanization of Emily, The Graduate, Targets. Prod.: Dominick and Eugene.
TELEVISION: Series: Days of Our Lives, The Interns, The Man and the City, M*A*S*H. Specials: JFK: One Man Show (PBS), The Best of Natl. Geographic Specials (host/narrator), Saving the Wildlife (co-host). Movies: The Longest Night, She Cried Murder!, The Questor Tapes, Live Again Die Again, McNaughton's Daughter, Battered, Sex and the Single Parent, Letters from Frank, Damien: The Leper Priest, Prime Suspect, Memorial Day (also prod.), Choices of the Heart, Private Sessions, Vanishing Act, A Deadly Silence, Price of the Bride, Incident at Dark River (also prod.), The Whereabouts of Jenny, Silent Motive (also prod.), Hart Attack, The Enemy Inside, Vows of Seduction, Twisted Path, Hart to Hart: Old Friends Never Die, Superman, Sins of the Mind. Director: Run Till You Fall. Guest: The Monroes.

FARROW, MIA
Actress. b. Los Angeles, CA, Feb. 9. 1945. r.n. Maria de Lourdes Villiers Farrow. d. of actress Maureen O'Sullivan and late dir. John Farrow. e. Marymount, Los Angeles, Cygnet House, London.
THEATER: The Importance of Being Earnest (debut, Madison Ave. Playhouse, NY, 1963); Royal Shakespeare Co. (Twelfth Night, A Midsummer Night's Dream, Ivanov, Three Sisters, The Seagull, A Doll's House), Mary Rose (London), Romantic Comedy (B'way debut, 1979).
PICTURES: Guns at Batasi (debut, 1964), A Dandy in Aspic, Rosemary's Baby, Secret Ceremony, John and Mary, See No Evil, The Public Eye, Dr. Popaul (High Heels), The Great Gatsby, Full Circle (The Haunting of Julia), Avalanche, A Wedding, Death on the Nile, Hurricane, A Midsummer Night's Sex Comedy, The Last Unicorn (voice), Zelig, Broadway Danny Rose, Supergirl, The Purple Rose of Cairo, Hannah and Her Sisters, Radio Days, September, Another Woman, New York Stories (Oedipus Wrecks), Crimes and Misde-meanors, Alice (Natl. Board of Review Award, 1990), Shadows and Fog, Husbands and Wives, Widow's Peak, Miami Rhapsody, Reckless.
TELEVISION: Series: Peyton Place. Specials: Johnny Belinda, Peter Pan. Movie: Goodbye Raggedy Ann.

FAWCETT, FARRAH
Actress. b. Corpus Christi, TX, Feb. 2, 1947. e. U. of Texas. Picked as one of the ten most beautiful girls while a freshman; went to Hollywood and signed by Screen Gems. Did films, TV shows, and made over 100 TV commercials. Off B'way debut: Extremities (1983).
PICTURES: Love Is a Funny Thing, Myra Breckinridge, Logan's Run, Somebody Killed Her Husband, Sunburn, Saturn 3, Cannonball Run, Extremities, See You in the Morning, Man of the House, The Apostle.
TELEVISION: Series: Charlie's Angels, Good Sports. Guest: Owen Marshall Counselor at Law, The Six Million Dollar Man, Rockford Files, Harry-O. Movies: Three's a Crowd, The Feminist and the Fuzz, The Great American Beauty Contest, The Girl Who Came Gift-Wrapped, Murder on Flight 502, Murder in Texas, The Burning Bed, Red Light Sting, Between Two Women, Nazi Hunter: The Beate Klarsfeld Story, Poor Little Rich Girl: The Barbara Hutton Story, Margaret Bourke-White, Small Sacrifices, Criminal Behavior, The Substitute Wife, Children of the Dust.

FAY, PATRICK J.
Director, Producer. b. June 7, 1916. e. Carnegie Tech. Dumont TV Network, 10 years. Director of over 100 Army training films; also dir. IBM Industrials.
AUTHOR: Melba, The Toast of Pithole, The Last Family Portrait in Oil, Coal Oil Johnny, French Kate, No Pardon in Heaven, An Ill Wind, Tighten Your G-String, As It Was in the Beginning (Television 50 Yrs. Ago).
PICTURES: Director for RCA, General Electric H.G. Peters Company, Bransby Films. Screenplays: Sanctuary, The Burning of New York City, Johnson's Island.
TELEVISION: Bishop Sheen, Broadway to Hollywood, Cavalcade of Stars, Manhattan Spotlight, Life is Worth Living, Front Row Center, Ilona Massey Show, Alec Templeton Show, Maggi McNellis Show, Key to Missing Persons, Kids and Company, Confession (also prod.), The Big Picture.

FEHR, RUDI
Editor, Executive. b. Berlin, Germany, July 6, 1911. m. Maris Wrixon, actress. Started career with Tobis-Klangfilm, Berlin. Joined Warner Bros. editorial department, 1936. Became producer, 1952; promoted to executive, 1956; Post Production Exec. Warner Bros.; WB title changed to dir. of editorial & post-prod. operations. Now retired; is consultant to industry.
PICTURES: Editor. Invisible Enemies, Honeymoon for Three, Desperate Journey, Watch on the Rhine, The Conspirators, Humoresque, Possessed, Key Largo, The Inspector General, House of Wax, Dial M for Murder, One From the Heart, Prizzi's Honor.

FEINGOLD, BEN
Executive. President, Columbia TriStar Home Video.

FEINSTEIN, ALAN
Actor. b. New York, NY, Sept. 8, 1941.
THEATER: NY: Malcolm, Zelda, A View from the Bridge (NY Drama Desk Award), As Is, A Streetcar Named Desire.
PICTURE: Looking for Mr. Goodbar.
TELEVISION: Series: Edge of Night, Love Of Life, Search for Tomorrow, Jigsaw John, The Runaways, The Family Tree, Berrenger's. Movies: Alexander: The Other Side of Dawn, Visions, The Hunted Lady, The Users, The Two Worlds of Jenny Logan, On Fire. Mini-Series: Masada.

FEITSHANS, BUZZ
Executive. b. Los Angeles, CA. e. USC. Started in film business as editor. Worked for 10 years at American-International as supvr. of prod. In 1975 formed A-Team Productions with John Milius. With Carolco Pictures: producer, 1981-6; exec. v.p. for mo. pic. production, member bd. dir. 1986-90. 1990\-, v.p. for Cinergi Prods.; 1994, pres. of Cinergi.
PICTURES: Producer: Dillinger, Act of Vengeance, Foxy Brown, Big Wednesday, Hardcore, 1941, Extreme Prejudice (exec. prod.), Conan the Barbarian, First Blood, Uncommon Valor, Rambo II, Red Dawn, Rambo III, Total Recall, Tombstone (exec. prod.), Color of Night, Shadow Conspiracy (exec. prod.).

FELDMAN, COREY
Actor. b. Reseda, CA, July 16, 1971. Has been performing since the age of 3 in over 100 commercials, television (Love Boat, Father Murphy, Foul Play, Mork and Mindy, Eight Is Enough, Alice, Gloria) and films.
PICTURES: Time After Time, The Fox and the Hound (voice), Friday the 13th—The Final Chapter, Gremlins, Friday the 13th—A New Beginning, The Goonies, Stand by Me, Lost Boys, License to Drive, The 'Burbs, Dream a Little Dream, Teenage Mutant Ninja Turtles (voice only), Rock 'n' Roll High School Forever, Edge of Honor, Meatballs 4, Round Trip to Heaven, Stepmonster, Blown Away, National Lampoon's Loaded Weapon 1, Lipstick Camera, National Lampoon's Last Resort, Maverick, Dream a Little Dream 2, A Dangerous Place, Evil Obsession, Tales From the Crypt: Bordello of Blood, Mr. Atlas, Born Bad, The Thief and the Stripper, She's Too Tall.
TELEVISION: Series: The Bad News Bears, Madame's Place. Movies: Willa, Father Figure, Kid with a Broken Halo, Still the Beaver, Out of the Blue, When the Whistle Blows, I'm a Big Girl Now, Exile, Legion. Specials: 15 & Getting Straight, How to Eat Like a Child.

FELDMAN, EDWARD S.
Producer. b. New York, NY, Sept. 5, 1929. e. Michigan State U. Trade press contact, newspaper and mag. contact, 20th Century Fox, 1950; dir. info. services, Dover Air Force Base. 1954-56; publ. coordinator, The World of Suzie Wong, 1960; joined Embassy, dir. of publicity, 1969; v.p. in chg., adv. & pub, 7 Arts Prods., 1962; v.p. exec. asst. to head prod. Warner-7 Arts Studio 1967; pres., m.p. dept., Filmways, 1970; Formed Edward S. Feldman Co., 1978.
PICTURES: Prod./exec. prod.: What's the Matter With Helen?, Fuzz, Save the Tiger, The Other Side of the Mountain, Two-Minute Warning, The Other Side of the Mountain Part 2, The Last Married Couple in America, Six Pack, The Sender, Hot Dog ... The Movie! (co-prod.), Witness, Explorers, The Golden Child, The Hitcher, Near Dark, Wired, Green Card, The Doctor, Honey I Blew Up the Kid, Forever Young, My Father the Hero, The Jungle Book, The Truman Show, 101 Dalmations.
TELEVISION: Exec. Prod.: Moon of the Wolf, My Father's House, Valentine, 300 Miles for Stephanie, Charles and Diana: A Royal Love Story, 21 Hours at Munich, King, Not in Front of the Children, Obsessed with a Married Woman.

FELDON, BARBARA
Actress. b. Pittsburgh, PA, Mar. 12, 1941. e. Carnegie Tech. Former fashion model, also appeared in many commercials. On NY stage in Past Tense, Cut the Ribbons.
PICTURES: Fitzwilly, Smile, No Deposit No Return.
TELEVISION: *Series*: Get Smart, The Marty Feldman Comedy Machine, The Dean Martin Comedy Hour (host), Special Edition (host), The 80's Woman (synd.; host), Get Smart (1995). *Movies*: Getting Away From It All, Playmates, What Are Best Friends For?, Let's Switch, A Guide for the Married Woman, Sooner or Later, A Vacation in Hell, Before and After, Children of Divorce, Get Smart Again!

FELDSHUH, TOVAH
Actress. b. New York, NY, Dec. 27, 1953. e. Sarah Lawrence Col., Univ. of MN. For humanitarian work received the Israel Peace Medal and the Eleanor Roosevelt Humanitarian Award.
THEATER: *NY*: Cyrano, Straws in the Wind, Three Sisters, Rodgers and Hart, Yentl (Theatre World Award), Sarava, The Mistress of the Inn, Springtime for Henry, She Stoops to Conquer, Lend Me a Tenor, A Fierce Attachment, Sarah and Abraham, Six Wives, Hello Muddah! Hello Fadduh!
PICTURES: White Lies, Nunzio, The Idolmaker, Cheaper to Keep Her, Daniel, Brewster's Millions, The Blue Iguana, A Day in October, Comfortably Numb.
TELEVISION: *Series*: As the World Turns, Mariah. *Movies*: Scream Pretty Peggy, The Amazing Howard Hughes, Terror Out of the Sky, The Triangle Factory Fire Scandal, Beggarman Thief, The Women's Room, Citizen Cohn, Sexual Considerations. *Specials*: Dosvedanya Mean Goodbye, Saying Kaddish. *Mini-Series*: Holocaust. Guest: LA Law, Law and Order, etc.

FELL, NORMAN
Actor. b. Philadelphia, PA, March 24, 1924. e. Temple U. Studied acting with Stella Adler. Member, Actors Studio. Professional debut at Circle-in-the-Square Theatre in N.Y. in Bonds of Interest. Summer Stock; appearances on TV; moved to Hollywood in 1958 to begin theatrical film career.
PICTURES: Pork Chop Hill, Ocean's Eleven, The Rat Race, Inherit the Wind, It's a Mad Mad Mad Mad World, The Graduate, Bullitt, If It's Tuesday This Must Be Belgium, Catch-22, The Stone Killer, Rabbit Test, The End, On the Right Track, Paternity, Stripped to Kill, C.H.U.D.II: Bud the Chud, The Boneyard, For the Boys, Hexed, Beachhouse, The Destiny of Marty Fine.
TELEVISION: Over 150 live plays from NY and some 200 shows filmed in Hollywood. *Series*: Joe and Mabel, 87th Precinct, Dan August, Needles and Pins, Three's Company, The Ropers, Teachers Only. *Guest*: Matt Houston, Crazy Like a Fox, Simon and Simon, It's Garry Shandling's Show, The Boys (pilot). *Mini-Series*: Rich Man Poor Man, Roots: The Next Generations. *Movies*: The Hanged Man, Three's a Crowd, The Heist, Thursday's Game, Death Stalk, Richie Brockelman, Moviola: This Year's Blonde, For the Love of It, Uncommon Valor, The Jessie Owens Story.

FELLMAN, DANIEL R.
Executive. b. Cleveland, OH, March 14, 1943. e. Rider Coll., B.S., 1964. Paramount Pictures, 1964-69; Loews Theatres, 1969-71; Cinema National Theatres, 1971-76; 1976-78, pres., American Theatre Mgmt. Joined Warner Bros. in 1978, named exec. v.p. Warner Bros. domestic distribution, Jan. 1993. President Variety Club Test 35, 1977-78. Bd. member, Will Rogers Foundation; Chairman, Foundation of Motion Picture Pioneers.

FELLMAN, NAT D.
Executive. b. New York, NY, Feb. 19, 1910. Started as office boy, Warner Bros. Pictures, 1928; transferred to Warner Bros. Theatres, asst. to chief booker; handled pool, partnership operations; head buyer, booker for Ohio zone, 1941; asst. to chief film buyer in New York, 1943; apptd. chief film buyer, 1952; exec. asst. to v.p. and gen. mgr., Stanley Warner Theatres, 1955; asst. gen. mgr., Stanley Warner Theatres, 1962; acting gen. mgr., Stanley Warner Theatres, July, 1964; Stanley Warner Theatres, v.p. and gen. mgr., 1965; v.p., NGC Theatre Corp. and division mgr. Fox Eastern Theatres, 1968; v.p. National General Corp., and pres., National General Theatres, 1969; 1974, formed Exhibitor Relations Co., operations consultant; sold it and retired in 1982. Served as vice pres., Variety Clubs International and NATO, Chmn., presidents' advisory comm.

FENADY, ANDREW J.
Producer, Writer. b. Toledo, OH, Oct. 4, 1928. e. U. of Toledo, 1946-50. Radio-prod.-actor-writer. *Novels*: The Man With Bogart's Face, The Secret of Sam Marlow, The Claws of the Eagle, The Summer of Jack London, Mulligan, Runaways.
PICTURES: Stakeout on Dope Street, The Young Captives, Ride Beyond Vengeance, Chisum, Terror in the Wax Museum, Arnold, The Man with Bogart's Face.
TELEVISION: *Series*: Confidential File, The Rebel, Branded, Hondo. *Movies*: The Woman Hunter, Voyage of the Yes, The Stranger, The Hanged Man, Black Noon, Sky Heist, Mayday 40,000 Ft., The Hostage Heart, Mask of Alexander, Masterpiece of Murder, Who Is Julia?, Jake Spanner—Private Eye, The Love She Sought, Yes Virginia There Is a Santa Claus, The Sea Wolf.

FENN, SHERILYN
Actress. b. Detroit, MI, Feb. 1, 1965.
PICTURES: The Wild Life (debut, 1984), Just One of the Guys, Out of Control, Thrashin', The Wraith, Zombie High, Two Moon Junction, Crime Zone, True Blood, Meridian: Kiss of the Beast, Wild at Heart, Backstreet Dreams, Ruby, Desire and Hell at Sunset Motel, Diary of a Hit Man, Of Mice and Men, Three of Hearts, Boxing Helena, Fatal Instinct, The Shadow Men, Lovelife, Johnny Hit and Run Pauline, Darkness Falls, Outside Ozona.
TELEVISION: *Series*: Twin Peaks, Rude Awakening. *Movies*: Silence of the Heart, Dillinger, Spring Awakening, Liz: The Elizabeth Taylor Story, Slave of Dreams, The Assassination File, The Don's Analyst, Nightmare Street. *Guest*: Cheers, 21 Jump Street, Heart of the City. *Specials*: Tales From the Hollywood Hills (A Table at Ciro's), Divided We Stand, A Family Again. *Mini-series*: A Season in Purgatory.

FERRARA, ABEL
Director, Writer. b. Bronx, NY, 1951. Moved to Peekskill, NY, as teenager where he made short films with future writer Nicholas St. John. Traveled to England, worked for the BBC. Returned to U.S. to attended SUNY/Purchase, making short Could This Be Love, which received some theatrical distribution. Has used the pseudonymn Jimmy Laine.
PICTURES: Driller Killer (also actor, s.p. songs), Ms. 45 (also actor), Fear City, China Girl (also songs), Cat Chaser, King of New York, Bad Lieutenant (also co-s.p.), Dangerous Game, Body Snatchers, The Addiction, The Funeral, The Blackout, New Rose Hotel.
TELEVISION: Miami Vice, Crime Story(pilot), Subway Stories: Tales from the Underground.

FERRARO, JOHN E.
Executive. b. Greenwich, CT, July 20, 1958. e. Emerson College, B.S. in Mass Communications, 1980. Joined Paramount Pictures Corp. 1980. 1983-84, story analyst, Paramount TV; 1984-85 supervisor, Drama Development; 1985-87 manager, Current Programs & Special Projects; 1987-88, dir. Drama Development. 1988, exec. dir., Acquisitions, Paramount Pictures; 1990, v.p., acquisitions; 1997, sr. v.p., acquisitions & co-productions.

FERRAZZA, CARL J.
Executive. b. Cleveland, OH, Aug. 29, 1920. e. Catholic U. of America, Washington, DC. Started career 1945: as asst. mgr. & mgr. for Loews Theatres. 1952, joined Cincinnati Theatre Co., first as mgr. for Keith's Theatre, Cincinnati, and after prom. dir. for circuit. 1963, field rep. for United Artists, covering midwest. 1968, UA prom. mgr., N.Y. 1975-83, dir. of field activities, MGM/UA; 1984, joined Orion Pictures Distributing Corp. as v.p. promotional and field activities.

FERRELL, CONCHATA
Actress. b. Charleston, WV, Mar. 28, 1943. e. Marshall Univ.
THEATER: *NY*: The Three Sisters, Hot L Baltimore, Battle of Angels, The Sea Horse (Theatre World, Obie & Vernon Rice Drama Desk Awards), Wine Untouched. *LA*: Getting Out, Picnic.
PICTURES: Deadly Hero, Network, Heartland, Where the River Runs Black, For Keeps?, Mystic Pizza, Edward Scissorhands, Family Prayers, True Romance, Samuari Cowboy, Heaven and Earth.
TELEVISION: *Series*: Hot L Baltimore, B.J. and the Bear, McClain's Law, E/R, Peaceable Kingdom, L. A. Law, Hearts Afire. *Movies*: The Girl Called Hatter Fox, A Death in Canaan, Who'll Save My Children?, Before and After, The Seduction of Miss Leona, Reunion, Rape and Marriage: The Rideout Case, Life of the Party: The Story of Beatrice, Emergency Room, Nadia, The Three Wishes of Billy Grier, North Beach and Rawhide, Samaritan: The Mitch Snyder Story, Eye on the Sparrow, Your Mother Wears Combat Boots, Goodbye Miss 4th of July, Opposites Attract, Deadly Intentions... Again?, Backfield in Motion. *Guest*: Good Times, Love Boat, Lou Grant, St. Elsewhere, Frank's Place, Murder She Wrote, Who's the Boss?, Matlock. *Specials*: The Great Gilly Hopkins, Portrait of a White Marriage, Runaway Ralph, Picnic.

FERRER, MEL
Actor, Producer, Director. r.n. Melchor Ferrer. b. Elberon, NJ, Aug. 25, 1917. e. Princeton U. During coll. and early career worked summers at Cape Cod Playhouse, Dennis, MA; then writer in Mexico, authored juvenile book, Tito's Hats; later ed. Stephen Daye Press, VT. Left publishing upon reaching leading-man status at Dennis; on B'way as dancer in You Never Know, Everywhere I Roam, others; also in Kind Lady, Cue For Passion; then to radio, serving apprenticeship in small towns; prod.-dir. for NBC Land of the Free, The Hit Parade, and Hildegarde program. Entered m.p. ind., 1945, when signed by Columbia as dial. dir.; then directed The Girl of the Limberlost; later, returned to Broadway, leading role, Strange Fruit; signed by David Selznick as producer-actor, on loan to John Ford as prod. asst. on The Fugitive; then to Howard Hughes-RKO for Vendetta.
THEATER: Kind Lady, Cue for Passion, Strange Fruit, Ondine, Gore Vidal's "The Best Man" (L.A., 1987), Cyrano (director).

PICTURES: *Actor*: Lost Boundaries (debut, 1949), Born to Be Bad, The Brave Bulls, Rancho Notorious, Scaramouche, Lili, Saadia, Knights of the Round Table, Oh Rosalinda!, Proibito (Forbidden), War and Peace, Paris Does Strange Things, The Sun Also Rises, The Vintage, Fraulein, The World the Flesh and the Devil, L'Homme a Femmes, The Hands of Orlac, Blood and Roses, Legge di Guerra, Devil and the 10 Commandments, The Longest Day, The Fall of the Roman Empire, Paris When It Sizzles (cameo), Sex and the Single Girl, El Greco (also prod.), El Senor de la Salle, The Black Pirate, The Girl From the Red Cabaret, Brannigan, The Tempter (The Antichrist), Death Trap (Eaten Alive), Hi-Riders, Pyjama Girl, Island of the Fish Men, The Norsemen, Yesterday's Tomorrow, The Visitor, The Fifth Floor, Nightmare City, Lili Marleen, Deadly Game, Screamers, Mad Dog Anderson. *Director*: The Girl of the Limberlost (debut, 1945), The Secret Fury, Vendetta (co-dir.), Green Mansions, Cabriola (Every Day Is a Holiday; also exec. prod., co-s.p.). *Producer*: Wait Until Dark, The Night Visitor, A Time for Loving, Embassy, W. TELEVISION: *Series*: Behind the Screen, Falcon Crest. *Movies*: One Shoe Makes It Murder, Seduced, Outrage, Dream West, Peter the Great, Christine Cromwell, A Thanksgiving Promise (prod.). *Special*: Mayerling.

FERRER, MIGUEL
Actor. b. Santa Monica, CA, Feb. 7, 1954. m. actress Leilani Sarelle. Son of actor Jose Ferrer and singer Rosemary Clooney. Began performing as a drummer. With actor Bill Mumy created comic book The Comet Man.
PICTURES: Heartbreaker (debut, 1983), Lovelines, Star Trek III: The Search for Spock, Flashpoint, Robocop, Deepstar Six, Valentino Returns, Revenge, The Guardian, Twin Peaks: Fire Walk With Me, Point of No Return, Hot Shots! Part Deux, Another Stakeout, It's All True (narrator), The Harvest, Blank Check.
TELEVISION: *Series*: Twin Peaks, Broken Badges, On the Air. *Guest*: Miami Vice, Hill Street Blues, Cagney & Lacey, Shannon's Deal. *Pilot*: Badlands 2005. *Mini-Series*: Drug Wars: The Camarena Story, The Stand. *Movies*: Downpayment on Murder, C.A.T. Squad, Guts & Glory: The Rise and Fall of Oliver North, Murder in High Places, In the Shadow of a Killer, Cruel Doubt, Scam, Royce, Incident at Deception Ridge, Jack Reed: Search for Justice, A Promise Kept: The Oksana Baiul Story, The Return of Hunter, In the Line of Duty: Hunt for Justice.

FIEDLER, JOHN
Executive. Launched m.p. career in 1975 working in commercials and industrial and ed. films. Joined Technicolor as sr. exec. in prod. svcs. in mktg. Joined Rastar 1980 as v.p., prod. dev. and asst. to Guy McElwaine, pres. & CEO. Joined Paramount as v.p. in prod.; then to Tri-Star Pictures in same post. Resigned to join Columbia Pictures as exec. v.p., worldwide prod., 1984, then pres. of prod. 1986. 1987, left to become independent prod. 1989 named pres. of prod., Rastar IndieProd.
PICTURES: *Producer*: The Beast, Tune in Tomorrow, Mortal Thoughts, Serial Mom, A Good Man in Africa, Radio Inside, I Love You—I Love You Not. *Exec. prod.*: Copycat.
TELEVISION: *Producer*: Beyond the Law.

FIELD, DAVID M.
Executive, Writer. b. Kansas City, MO, Apr. 22, 1944. e. Princeton U. Worked as reporter on city desk at Hartford (CT) Courant. In 1968 with NBC News in N.Y. and Washington, DC. Entered film school at U. of Southern California (L.A.) after which joined Columbia Pictures as west coast story editor. In 1973 went to ABC-TV Network as mgr., movies of the week. 1975, moved to 20th-Fox as v.p., creative affairs. Joined United Artists in 1978; named sr. v.p.—west coast production. Left in 1980 to become 20th-Fox exec. v.p. in chg. of worldwide production 1983, resigned to enter independent production deal with 20th-Fox. Consultant, Tri-Star Pictures. Wrote and produced Amazing Grace and Chuck, 1987.

FIELD, SALLY
Actress. b. Pasadena, CA, Nov. 6, 1946. m. Daughter of Paramount contract actress Maggie Field Mahoney. Stepdaughter of actor Jock Mahoney. e. Actor's Studio 1973-75. Acting classes at Columbia studios. Picked over 150 finalists to star as lead in TV series, Gidget, 1965.
PICTURES: The Way West (debut, 1967), Stay Hungry, Smokey and the Bandit, Heroes, The End, Hooper, Norma Rae (Academy Award, 1979), Beyond the Poseidon Adventure, Smokey and the Bandit II, Back Roads, Absence of Malice, Kiss Me Goodbye, Places in the Heart (Academy Award, 1984), Murphy's Romance (also exec. prod.), Surrender, Punchline (also prod.), Steel Magnolias, Not Without My Daughter, Soapdish, Dying Young (co-prod. only), Homeward Bound: The Incredible Journey (voice), Mrs. Doubtfire, Forrest Gump, Eye for an Eye, Homeward Bound II: Lost in San Francisco (voice). Merry Christmas George Bailey, From the Earth to the Moon.
TELEVISION: *Series*: Gidget, The Flying Nun, Alias Smith and Jones, The Girl With Something Extra. *Movies*: Maybe I'll Come Home in the Spring, Marriage Year One, Mongo's Back in Town, Home for the Holidays, Hitched, Bridger, Sybil (Emmy Award, 1977), The Christmas Tree (also prod., dir., co-s.p.). *Mini-Series*: A Woman of Independent Means (also co-exec. prod.). *Host*: Barbara Stanwyck: Fire and Desire. *Guest*: Hey Landlord, Marcus Welby M.D., Bracken's World. *Special*: All the Way Home.

FIELD, SHIRLEY-ANNE
Actress. b. London, Eng., June 27. Ent. films after repertory experience. Under contract to Ealing-M.G.M. 1958.
THEATER: The Lily White Boys, Kennedy's Children, Wait Until Dark, The Life and Death of Marilyn Monroe, How the Other Half Loves.
PICTURES: It's Never Too Late, The Silken Affair, The Good Companions, Horrors of the Black Museum, Upstairs and Downstairs, Beat Girl, The Entertainer, Man in the Moon, Once More With Feeling, Peeping Tom, Saturday Night and Sunday Morning, These Are the Damned, The War Lover, Kings of the Sun, Alfie, Doctor in Clover, Hell Is Empty, With Love in Mind, House of the Living Dead (Doctor Maniac), My Beautiful Laundrette, Getting It Right, The Rachel Papers, Shag, Hear My Song, At Risk, Carrington.
TELEVISION: *U.S.*: Bramwell, Santa Barbara, Anna Lees, Lady Chatterly.

FIELD, TED
Producer. r.n. Frederick W. Field. e. U. of Chicago, Pomona Coll. Started career as one of owners of Field Enterprises of Chicago; transferred to west coast, concentrating on movies and records. Founded Interscope Communications, diversified co., which develops and produces theatrical films; Interscope Records, 1990.
PICTURES: Revenge of the Nerds, Turk 182, Critical Condition, Outrageous Fortune, Three Men and a Baby, The Seventh Sign, Cocktail, Bill & Ted's Excellent Adventure (exec. prod.), Renegades (exec. prod.), Innocent Man, The First Power (exec. prod.), Bird on a Wire, Three Men and a Little Lady, Paradise, The Hand That Rocks the Cradle, The Cutting Edge, FernGully, The Gun in Betty Lou's Handbag, Out on a Limb, Jersey Girl, Holy Matrimony, Imaginary Crimes, Operation Dumbo Drop, The Tie That Binds, Jumanji, Mr. Holland's Opus, The Associate, Gridlock'd, The Associate.
TELEVISION: The Father Clements Story (co-exec. prod.). Everybody's Baby: The Rescue of Jessica McClure (co-exec. prod.), My Boyfriend's Back, A Mother's Courage: The Mary Thomas Story (co-exec. prod.), Crossing the Mob, Murder Ordained, Foreign Affairs (co-exec. prod.), A Part of the Family (co-exec. prod.), Body Language (co-exec. prod.).

FIELDS, ALAN
Executive. Spent five years with Madison Square Garden before joining Paramount Pictures. Career there included various positions: v.p. for pay-TV and Home Video TV. Spent two years at studio lot in L.A. as part of network TV organization. 1981, named bd. director for Paramount Pictures (U.K.) in London, serving as liaison to United Intl. Pictures and Cinema Intl. Corp., serving on operating committees of both. 1985, appt. v.p., Entertainment & Communications Group of Gulf & Western Industries, Inc., parent co. of Paramount; C.O.O., exec. v.p. Madison Square Garden Corp.

FIELDS, FREDDIE
Executive. b. Ferndale, NY, July 12, 1923. Vice-pres., member of bd. of directors, MCA-TV, MCA Canada Ltd., MCA Corp.; mem., Pres. Club, Wash., D.C.; pres., Freddie Fields Associates Ltd., 1960; founder pres., chief exec. officer Creative Management Assoc. Ltd. Agency, Chicago, Las Vegas, Miami, Paris, Los Angeles, N.Y., London, Rome, 1961. Was exclusive agent of Henry Fonda, Phil Silvers, Judy Garland, Paul Newman, Peter Sellers, Barbra Streisand, Steve McQueen, Woody Allen, Robert Redford, Mick Jagger, Liza Minnelli and others. In 1975 sold interest in CMA (now International Creative Mgt.) but continued as consultant. Produced for Paramount Pictures. 1977: Looking for Mr. Goodbar. American Gigolo, Citizen's Band; Victory. In 1983 named pres. and COO, MGM Film Co. and UA Pictures. Resigned 1985 to become independent producer for MGM/UA. Chairman, The Fields & Hellman Co; dir., Network Event Theater, Inc.; chairman, Net Programming Ltd.; dir., LA Sports and Entertainment Comm.
PICTURES: Fever Pitch. Poltergeist II, Crimes of the Heart, Millenium, Glory, The Year of Living Dangerously. *Exec. Prod.*: The Montel Williams Show.

FIENNES, RALPH
Actor. b. Suffolk, England, Dec. 22, 1962. e. Chelsea College of Art & Design, RADA. Stage work with the Royal Shakespeare Co. includes King Lear, Troilus and Cressida, Love's Labour's Lost. B'way debut in Hamlet (Tony & Theatre World Awards, 1995).
PICTURES: Wuthering Heights (tv in U.S.), The Baby of Macon, Schindler's List (Acad. Award nom.; Natl. Society of Film Critics, NY Film Critics & BAFTA Awards), Quiz Show, Strange Days, The English Patient, Oscar and Lucinda, The Avengers, Princee of Egypt, A Taste of Sunshine, Nemo.
TELEVISION: Prime Suspect, A Dangerous Man: Lawrence After Arabia, The Cormorant (theatrical release in U.S.).

FIERSTEIN, HARVEY
Actor, Writer. b. New York, NY, June 6, 1954. e. Pratt Inst.
THEATER: Actor: Andy Warhol's Pork, The Haunted Host, Pouf Positive. Actor-Writer: Torch Song Trilogy (NY & London; Tony Awards for best actor & play; Theatre World Award), Safe Sex. Writer: Spookhouse, La Cage Aux Folles (Tony Award), Legs Diamond.
PICTURES: Garbo Talks, The Times of Harvey Milk (narrator), Torch Song Trilogy (also s.p.), The Harvest, Mrs. Doubtfire, Bullets Over Broadway, Dr. Jekyll & Ms. Hyde, Independence Day.
TELEVISION: Movies: The Demon Murder Case (voice), Apology. Series: Daddy's Girls. Guest: Miami Vice, The Simpsons (voice), Cheers, Murder She Wrote. Specials: Tidy Endings, In the Shadow of Love.

FIGGIS, MIKE
Director, Writer, Musician. b. Kenya, 1949. At age 8 family moved to Newcastle, England. Studied music before performing with band Gas Boad; joined experimental theatre group The People Show in early 70's as musician. Began making indept. films including Redheugh, Slow Fade, Animals of the City. Made 1-hr. film The House for U.K.'s Channel 4.
PICTURES: Director: Stormy Monday (debut, 1988; also s.p., music), Internal Affairs (also music), Liebestraum (also s.p., music), Mr. Jones, Leaving Las Vegas (also s.p.; music; IFP Independent Spirit Award, 1996; Nat'l Society of Film Critics Award).

FINCH, JON
Actor. b. London, England, Mar. 2, 1943. Came to acting via backstage activities, working for five years as company manager and director.
PICTURES: The Vampire Lovers (debut, 1970), The Horror of Frankenstein, Sunday Bloody Sunday, L'affaire Martine Desclos, Macbeth, Frenzy, Lady Caroline Lamb, The Final Programme (The Last Days of Man on Earth), Diagnosis: Murder, Une Femme Fidele, The Man With the Green Cross, El Segundo Poder, Battle Flag, El Mister, Death on the Nile, La Sabina, Gary Cooper Which Art in Heaven, Breaking Glass, The Threat, Giro City (And Nothing But the Truth), Plaza Real, Streets of Yesterday, Game of Seduction, The Voice, Beautiful in the Kingdom, Mirror Mirror, Darklands, Lucan.
TELEVISION: The Martian Chronicles (U.S.), Peter and Paul, The Rainbow, Unexplained Laughter, Dangerous Curves, Maigret, Beautiful Lies, Make or Break, The Oddjob Man (series), Sherlock Homes, Counterstrike (series), Mary Queen of Scots, Riviera, White Men Are Cracking Up, A Love Renewed, Merlin of the Crystal Cave, Richard II, Henry IV, Much Ado About Nothing, South of the Border, Hammer House of Horrors, Ben Hall (series).

FINCHER, DAVID
Director. b. 1963. Ent. ind. at 18, working at Lucas' Industrial Light and Magic for 4 yrs; left to make TV commercials & dir. pop videos for Madonna, Paula Abdul & Aerosmith.
PICTURES: Return of the Jedi, Indiana Jones and the Temple of Doom, The Beat of the Live Drum, Alien 3, Se7en, The Game, Fight Club.

FINESHRIBER, WILLIAM H., JR.
Executive. b. Davenport, IA, Nov. 4, 1909. e. Princeton U., B.A., 1931. Pub., CBS, 1931-34; mgr. Carnegie Hall, N.Y., 1934-37; script writer, dir., music comm., dir. of music dept., CBS, 1937-40; dir. of short wave programs, CBS, 1940-43; gen. mgr. CBS program dept. 1943-49; v.p. in charge of programs MBS, 1949-51; exec. v.p. & dir., MBS, 1951-53; v.p. & gen. mgr. of networks, NBC, 1953-54; v.p. in charge of Radio Network, NBC, 1955; v.p. Television Programs of America, 1956; director International operations, Screen Gems, 1957; v.p., Motion Picture Assoc. of America and Motion Picture Export Assoc. of America, 1960; bd. of dir., NARTB: exec. comm., bd. of dir., R.A.B; v.p. Radio Pioneers. Author, Stendhal the Romantic Rationalist.

FINLAY, FRANK
Actor. C.B.E. b. Farnworth, Eng., Aug. 6, 1926. Rep. in Troon, 1951, Halifax and Sunderland, 1952-3, before winning Sir James Knott Scholarship to RADA. e. Studied acting at RADA. Appeared with Guildford Repertory Theatre Co. 1957. London stage debut: The Queen and the Welshman, 1957. Broadway debut, Epitaph for George Dillon, 1958.
THEATER: Work with Royal Court, Chichester Fest., National Theatre includes: Sergeant Musgrave's Dance, Chicken Soup with Barley, Roots, Platonov, Chips with Everything, Saint Joan, Hamlet, Othello, Saturday Sunday Monday, Plunder, Watch It Come Down, Weapons of Happiness, Tribute to a Lady, Filumena (and N.Y.), Amadeus, The Cherry Orchard, Mutiny, Beyond Reasonable Doubt, Black Angel, A Slight Hangover.
PICTURES: The Loneliness of the Long Distance Runner (debut, 1962), The Longest Day, Life for Ruth (Walk in the Shadow), Private Potter, Doctor in Distress, Underworld Informers, The Comedy Man, Agent 8 3/4 (Hot Enough for June), The Wild Affair, A Study in Terror, Othello (Acad. Award nom.), The Sandwich Man, The Jokers, The Deadly Bees,

Robbery, I'll Never Forget What's 'is Name, The Shoes of the Fisherman, Inspector Clouseau, Twisted Nerve, The Molly Maguires, Cromwell, The Body (narrator), Assault (The Devil's Garden), Gumshoe, Danny Jones, Sitting Target, Neither the Sea Nor the Sand, Shaft in Africa, The Three Musketeers, The Four Musketeers, The Wild Geese, Murder by Decree, Enigma, The Ploughman's Lunch, The Return of the Soldier, The Key, 1919, Lifeforce, The Return of the Musketeers (tv in U.S.), King of the Wind, Cthulhu Mansion.
TELEVISION: The Adventures of Don Quixote, Casanova, Candide, Julius Caesar, Les Miserables, This Happy Breed, The Lie, The Death of Adolph Hitler, Voltaire, The Merchant of Venice, Bouquet of Barbed Wire, 84 Charing Cross Road, Saturday Sunday Monday, Count Dracula, The Last Campaign, Thief of Bagdad, Betzi, Sakharov, A Christmas Carol, Arch of Triumph, The Burning Shore, In the Secret State, Verdict of Erebus, Mountain of Diamonds, Encounter, Stalin.

FINNEY, ALBERT
Actor. b. Salford, England, May 9, 1936. Studied for stage at Royal Acad. Dramatic Art making his West End debut 1958 in The Party. Appeared at Stratford-Upon-Avon 1959, playing title role in Coriolanus, etc.
THEATER: The Lily White Boys, Billy Liar, Luther (also NY), Much Ado About Nothing, Armstrong's Last Goodnight, Love for Love, Miss Julie, Black Comedy, A Flea in Her Ear, Joe Egg (NY), Alpha Beta, Krapp's Last Tape, Cromwell, Chez Nous, Hamlet, Tamburlaine, Uncle Vanya, Present Laughter. National Theatre, The Country Wife, The Cherry Orchard, Macbeth, The Biko Inquest, Sergeant Musgrave's Dance (also dir.), Orphans, Another Time (also Chicago), Reflected Glory.
PICTURES: The Entertainer (debut, 1960), Saturday Night and Sunday Morning, Tom Jones, The Victors, Night Must Fall (also co-prod.), Two for the Road, Charlie Bubbles (also dir.), The Picasso Summer (tv in U.K.), Scrooge, Gumshoe, Alpha Beta (tv in U.K.), Murder on the Orient Express, The Adventure of Sherlock Holmes' Smarter Brother (cameo), The Duellists, Wolfen, Looker, Loophole, Shoot the Moon, Annie, The Dresser, Under the Volcano, Orphans, Miller's Crossing, The Playboys, Rich in Love, The Browning Version, A Man of No Importance, The Run of the Country, Washington Square, Breakfast of Champions.
TELEVISION: The Claverdon Road Job, The Miser, Pope John Paul II, Endless Game, The Image, The Green Man, Joan of Arc: The Virgin Warrior.

FIORENTINO, LINDA
Actress. b. Philadelphia, PA, 1960. e. Rosmont Col. To New York, 1980, studied acting at Circle in the Square Theatre School.
PICTURES: Vision Quest (debut, 1985), Gotcha!, After Hours, The Modrens, Queens Logic, Shout, Chain of Desire, The Last Seduction, Bodily Harm, Jade, Unforgettable, Men in Black, Where the Money Is, Killer Kiss, Dogma, The Split.
TELEVISION: Movies: The Neon Empire, Acting on Impulse, The Desperate Trail.

FIRSTENBERG, JEAN
Director. The American Film Institute.

FIRTH, COLIN
Actor. b. Grayshott, Hampshire, Eng., Sept. 10, 1960. Studied acting at the Drama Centre at Chalk Farm. Author of A Month in the Country (screenplay), Making of Pride and Prejudice.
THEATRES: London: in Tartuffe, King Lear, Hamlet, Another Country, Doctor's Dilemma, The Lonely Road, Desire Under the Elms, The Caretaker, Chatsky.
PICTURES: Another Country, 1919, A Month in the Country, Apartment Zero, Valmont, Wings of Fame, The Hour of the Pig, The Pleasure Principle, Femme Fatale, Playmaker, The Advocate, Circle of Friends, The English Patient, Fever Pitch, A Thousand Acres, The World of Moss, Shakespeare in Love.
TELEVISION: Movies: Camille, Crown Court, Dutch Girls, Tumbledown, Hostages, Master of the Moor, The Deep Blue Sea, Pride and Prejudice, The Widowing of Mrs. Holroyd, Nostromo. Series: Lost Empires. Specials: Tales from the Hollywood Hills (Pat Hobby Teamed With Genius).

FIRTH, PETER
Actor. b. Bradford, Yorkshire, Oct. 27, 1953. Appeared in local TV children's show where casting director spotted him and got him role in series, The Flaxton Boys. Moved to London and worked in TV, first in children's show, later on dramas for BBC. Breakthrough role in Equus as National Theatre, 1973 which he repeated in film.
THEATER: Equus (Theatre World Award), Romeo and Juliet, Spring Awakening, Amadeus.
PICTURES: Diamonds on Wheels (debut, 1972; tv in U.S.), Brother Sun Sister Moon, Daniel and Maria, Equus (Acad. Award nom.), Joseph Andrews, Aces High, When You Comin' Back Red Ryder, Tess, Lifeforce, Letter to Brezhnev, Trouble in Paradise, White Elephant, A State of Emergency, Born of Fire, The Tree of Hands, Prisoner of Rio, Burndown, The Hunt for Red October, The Rescuers Down Under (voice), The Perfect Husband, White Angel, Shadowlands, An Awfully Big Adventure, The Garden of Redemption, Marco Polo, Amistad.

TELEVISION: *Series*: The Flaxon Boys, Home and Away, Country Matters. *Movies and specials*: Here Comes the Doubledeckers, Castlehaven, The Sullen Sisters, The Simple Life, The Magistrate, The Protectors, Black Beauty, Arthur, Her Majesty's Pleasure, the Picture of Dorian Gray, Lady of the Camillias, The Flip Side of Domenic Hide, Blood Royal, Northanger Abbey, The Way, The Truth: the Video, The Incident, Children Crossing, Prisoner of Honor, Married to Murder, The Laughter of God, Murder in Eden, Brighton Boy, The Broker's Man, Holding On.

FISCHER, JOSEPH A.
Executive. Executive v.p., MCA Motion Picture Group.

FISHBURNE, LAURENCE
Actor. b. Augusta, GA, July 30, 1961. Raised in Brooklyn. Landed role on daytime serial One Life to Live at age 11. On NY stage in Short Eyes, Two Trains Running (Tony and Theatre World Awards), Riff Raff (also wrote and directed).
PICTURES: Cornbread Earl and Me (debut, 1975), Fast Break, Apocalypse Now, Willie and Phil, Death Wish II, Rumble Fish, The Cotton Club, The Color Purple, Quicksilver, Band of the Hand, A Nightmare on Elm Street 3: Dream Warriors, Gardens of Stone, School Daze, Red Heat, King of New York, Cadence, Class Action, Boyz N the Hood, Deep Cover, What's Love Got to Do With It (Acad. Award nom.), Searching for Bobby Fischer, Higher Learning, Bad Company, Just Cause, Othello, Fled, Hoodlums (also exec. prod.), Event Horizon, The Matrix.
TELEVISION: *Series*: One Life to Live, Pee-wee's Playhouse. *Guest*: M*A*S*H, Trapper John, M.D., Spenser: For Hire, Tribeca (Emmy Award, 1993). *Movies*: A Rumor of War, I Take These Men, Decoration Day, The Tuskegee Airmen, Miss Ever's Boys, Always Outnumbered.

FISHER, AL
Executive. b. Brooklyn, NY. Entered m.p. industry as office boy, Fox Metropolitan Theatres; U.S. Army Provost Marshal General's Office, 1942-46; Universal Pictures, mgr., Park Avenue Theatre, N.Y. & Copley Plaza Theatre, Boston, 1946; Eagle Lion Film Co., mgr., Red Shoe's Bijou Theatre, N.Y., 1947; Stanley Kramer Prods., exploitation, Cyrano de Bergerac, 1951; press agent, 1951; prod., Bway show, Daphine, 1952; joined United Artists Corporation, 1952, named dir. of exploitation; now freelancing as producer's repr.

FISHER, CARRIE
Actress, Writer. b. Beverly Hills, CA, Oct. 21, 1956. e. London Central Sch. of Speech & Drama. Daughter of actress Debbie Reynolds and singer Eddie Fisher. On Broadway in the chorus of revival of Irene (1972; with mother); later in Censored Scenes from King Kong. *Author*: Postcards From the Edge (1987), Surrender the Pink (1990), Delusions of Grandma (1994).
PICTURES: Shampoo (debut, 1975), Star Wars, Mr. Mike's Mondo Video, The Empire Strikes Back, The Blues Brothers, Under the Rainbow, Return of the Jedi, Garbo Talks, The Man with One Red Shoe, Hannah and Her Sisters, Hollywood Vice Squad, Amazon Women on the Moon, Appointment with Death, The 'Burbs, Loverboy, She's Back, When Harry Met Sally..., Time Guardian, Postcards From the Edge (s.p. only), Sibling Rivalry, Drop Dead Fred, Soapdish, This Is My Life.
TELEVISION: *Movies*: Leave Yesterday Behind, Liberty, Sunday Drive, Sweet Revenge. *Specials*: Come Back Little Sheba, Classic Creatures: Return of the Jedi, Thumbelina (Faerie Tale Theatre), Paul Reiser: Out on a Whim, Two Daddies? (voice), Trying Times (Hunger Chic), Carrie Fisher: The Hollywood Family (also writer). *Guest*: Laverne and Shirley, George Burns' Comedy Week.

FISHER, EDDIE
Singer. b. Philadelphia, PA, Aug. 10, 1928. Daughter is actress Carrie Fisher. Band, nightclub, hotel singer; discovered by Eddie Cantor, 1949; U.S. Army, 1951-53; many hit records include Wish You Were Here, Lady of Spain and Oh My Papa; radio & TV shows, NBC.
PICTURES: Bundle of Joy, Butterfield 8, Nothing Lasts Forever.
TELEVISION: *Series*: Coke Time with Eddie Fisher (1953-57), The Eddie Fisher Show (1957-59).

FISHER, FRANCES
Actress. b. Milford-on-Sea, England, May 11. Father was intl. construction supervisor. Raised in Colombia, Canada, France, Brazil, Turkey. Made stage debut in Texas in Summer and Smoke.
THEATER: *NY*: Fool for Love, Desire Under the Elms, Cat on a Hot Tin Roof, The Hitch-Hikers, Orpheus Descending, A Midsummer Night's Dream, Jammed.
PICTURES: Can She Bake a Cherry Pie? (debut, 1983), Tough Guys Don't Dance, The Principal, Patty Hearst, Bum Rap, Heavy Petting, Pink Cadillac, Lost Angels, Welcome Home Roxy Carmichael, L.A. Story, Unforgiven, Babyfever, The Stars Fell on Henrietta, Waiting for Guffman, Female Perversion, Wild America, Titanic.
TELEVISION: *Series*: The Edge of Night (1976-81), The Guiding Light (1985), Strange Luck. *Movies*: Broken Vows, Devlin, Lucy & Desi: Before the Laughter, The Other Mother. *Pilots*: Elysian Fields. *Guest*: The Equalizer, Matlock, Newhart.

FISHER, GEORGE M.C.
Executive. b. Anna, IL. e. Univ. of IL, Brown Univ. Worked in research and devlop. at Bell Labs before joining Motorola in 1976, eventually becoming pres. & CEO in 1988. 1990, elected chmn. & CEO. Named chmn., pres. & CEO of Eastman Kodak Company, Dec. 1993.

FISHER, LUCY
Executive. b. Oct. 2, 1949. e. Harvard U., B.A. Exec. chg. creative affairs, MGM; v.p., creative affairs, 20th Century Fox; v.p., prod., Fox. 1980, head of prod., Zoetrope Studios; 1980-82, v.p., sr. prod. exec., Warner Bros.; 1983, sr. v.p. prod., WB. Joined Columbia TriStar in March, 1996 as vice chmn.

FISHER, THOMAS L.
Special Effects.
PICTURES: The Devil's Rain, City on Fire, First Blood, Legal Eagles, Desperate Hours, Terminator 2: Judgment Day, The Taking of Beverly Hills, Under Siege, On Deadly Ground, True Lies, Batman Forever, Titanic (Acad. Award, Best Visual Effects, 1997), Supernova.

FISK, JACK
Director. b. Ipava, IL. e. Cooper Union-Pa. Acad. of the Fine Arts. m. actress Sissy Spacek. Began in films as designer; turning to direction with Raggedy Man (1981).
PICTURES: *Director*: Raggedy Man, Violets Are Blue, Daddy's Dyin', ... Who's Got the Will? *Art Director*: Badlands, Phantom of the Paradise, Carrie, Days of Heaven, Heart Beat.

FITZGERALD, GERALDINE
Actress. b. Dublin, Ireland, Nov. 24, 1914. e. Dublin Art Sch. Mother of director Michael Lindsay-Hogg. On stage Gate Theat., Dublin; then in number of Brit. screen prod. including Turn of the Tide, Mill on the Floss. On N.Y. stage in Heartbreak House. Founded Everyman Street Theatre with Brother Jonathan Ringkamp.
THEATER: Sons and Soldiers, Portrait in Black, The Doctor's Dilemma, King Lear, Hide and Seek, A Long Day's Journey Into Night, (1971), Ah, Wilderness, The Shadow Box, A Touch of the Poet, Songs of the Streets (one woman show), Mass Appeal (dir. only), The Lunch Girls (dir.).
PICTURES: Blind Justice (debut, 1934), Open All Night, The Lad, The Aces of Spades, Three Witnesses, Lieutenant Daring RN, Turn of the Tide, Radio Parade of 1935, Bargain Basement (Department Store), Debt of Honor, Cafe Mascot, The Mill on the Floss, Wuthering Heights (U.S. debut, 1939; Acad. Award nom.), Dark Victory, A Child Is Born, 'Til We Meet Again, Flight from Destiny, Shining Victory, The Gay Sisters, Watch on the Rhine, Ladies Courageous, Wilson, The Strange Affair of Uncle Harry, Three Strangers, O.S.S., Nobody Lives Forever, So Evil My Love, The Late Edwina Black (The Obsessed), 10 North Frederick, The Fiercest Heart, The Pawnbroker, Rachel Rachel, The Last American Hero, Harry and Tonto, Cold Sweat, Echoes of a Summer, The Mango Tree, Bye Bye Monkey, Lovespell (Tristan and Isolde), Arthur, Blood Link, Easy Money, Poltergeist II, Arthur 2: On the Rocks.
TELEVISION: *Series*: Our Private World, The Best of Everything. *Movies*: Yesterday's Child, The Quinns, Dixie: Changing Habits, Do You Remember Love?, Circle of Violence, Night of Courage, Bump in the Night. *Mini-Series*: Kennedy. *Specials*: The Moon and Sixpence, Street Songs.

FITZGERALD, TARA
Actress. b. England, 1968. e. London's Drama Centre, 1990.
THEATER: *London*: Our Song. *NY*: Hamlet.
PICTURES: Hear My Song (debut, 1991), Sirens, A Man of No Importance, The Englishman Who Went Up a Hill But Came Down a Mountain, Brassed Off!
TELEVISION: The Black Candle, The Camomille Lawn, Anglo-Saxon Attitudes, Six Characters in Search of an Author, Fall From Grace, The Tenants of Wildfell Hall, The Woman in White, The Student Prince.

FLAGG, FANNIE
Actress, Writer. b. Birmingham, AL, Sept. 21, 1944. e. Univ. of AL. Studied acting at Pittsburgh Playhouse, Town & Gown Theatre. Had her own live 90 minute tv show in Birmingham. To NY where she wrote and appeared in revues for Upstairs at the Downstairs Club. *Comedy albums*: Rally 'Round the Flagg, My Husband Doesn't Know I'm Making This Phone Call. *Author*: Coming Attractions: A Wonderful Novel (Daisy Fay and the Miracle Man), Fried Green Tomatoes at the Whistle Stop Cafe, Fannie Flagg's Original Whistle Stop Cafe Cookbook.
THEATER: *B'way*: Patio Porch, Come Back to the Five and Dime Jimmy Dean Jimmy Dean, The Best Little Whorehouse in Texas. *Regional*: Private Lives, Gypsy, Mary Mary, Tobacco Road, Old Acquaintance, etc.
PICTURES: Five Easy Pieces (debut, 1970), Some of My Best Friends Are..., Stay Hungry, Grease, Rabbit Test, My Best Friend Is a Vampire, Fried Green Tomatoes (also co-s.p.; Acad. Award nom. for s.p.).
TELEVISION: *Series*: The New Dick Van Dyke Show, Match Game P.M., Liar's Club, Harper Valley P.T.A. *Movies*: The New Original Wonder Woman, Sex and the Married Woman. *Pilots*: Comedy News, Home Cookin'. *Producer*: Morning Show.

FLATTERY, THOMAS L.
Executive-Lawyer b. Detroit, MI, Nov. 14, 1922. e. U.S. Military Acad., West Point, B.S., 1944-47; UCLA, J.D., 1952-55; USC, LL.M. 1955-65. Radioplane Company, staff counsel and asst. contract admin. 1955-7. Gen'l counsel and asst. sec'y, McCulloch Corp., CA, 1957-64; sec. & corp. counsel, Technicolor, Inc., 1964-70; v.p., sec. & gen. counsel, Amcord, Inc. 1970-72; v.p., sec. & gen. counsel, Schick Inc., 1972-75; counsel asst. sec., C.F. Braun & Co., 1975-76; sr. v.p., sec. & gen. counsel PCC Technical Industries, Inc. 1976-86; v.p., gen. counsel & sec., G & H Technology, Inc. 1986.-93. Attorney at law, 1993.

FLAXMAN, JOHN P.
Producer. b. New York, NY, March 3, 1934. e. Dartmouth U., B.A. 1956. 1st Lt. U.S. Army, 1956-58. Ent. m.p. industry in executive training program, Columbia Pictures Corp., 1958-63; exec. story consultant, Profiles in Courage, 1964-65; head of Eastern Literary Dept., Universal Pictures, 1965; writer's agent, William Morris Agency, 1966; partner with Harold Prince in Media Productions, Inc. 1967; founded Flaxman Film Corp., 1975. President-Tricorn Productions 1977; pres. Filmworks Capital Corp., 1979-83; Becker/Flaxman & Associates, 1979-83; pres., Cine Communications, 1983-present. Producer Off-Broadway, Yours, Anne (1985). Co-prod. with NY Shakespeare Fest., The Petrified Prince.
PICTURES: Something for Everyone, Jacob Two-Two Meets the Hooded Fang.
TELEVISION: The Caine Mutiny Court-Martial (prod.).

FLEDER, GARY
Director.
PICTURES: Things to Do in Denver when You're Dead, Kiss the Girls, Thieves.
TELEVISION: Movies: Air Time (also prod.), The Companion. Series: Homicide: Life on the Street. Mini-series: From the Earth to the Moon.

FLEISCHER, RICHARD
Director. b. Brooklyn, NY, Dec. 8, 1916. e. Brown U., B.A.; Yale U., M.F.A. Son of animator Max Fleischer. Stage dir.; joined RKO Pathe 1942. Dir. and wrote This Is America shorts, prod./dir. Flicker Flashbacks. Author: Just Tell Me When to Cry.
PICTURES: Child of Divorce (debut, 1946), Banjo, Design for Death (also co-prod.); Academy Award for Best Feature-Length Documentary, 1948), So This Is New York, Bodyguard, Follow Me Quietly, Make Mine Laughs, The Clay Pigeon, Trapped, Armored Car Robbery, The Narrow Margin, The Happy Time, Arena, 20000 Leagues Under the Sea, Violent Saturday, Girl in the Red Velvet Swing, Bandido, Between Heaven and Hell, The Vikings, These Thousand Hills, Compulsion, Crack in the Mirror, The Big Gamble, Barabbas, Fantastic Voyage, Doctor Dolittle, The Boston Strangler, Che!, Tora! Tora! Tora!, 10 Rillington Place, The Last Run, See No Evil, The New Centurions, Soylent Green, The Don Is Dead, The Spikes Gang, Mr. Majestyk, Mandingo, The Incredible Sarah, Crossed Swords (The Prince and the Paupre), Ashanti, The Jazz Singer, Tough Enough, Amityville 3-D, Conan the Destroyer, Red Sonja, Million Dollar Mystery, Call From Space (Showcan).

FLEMING, JANET BLAIR
Executive. b. Ottawa, Canada, November 29, 1944. e. Carlton U., Ottawa, Canada, B.A. Secretary to Canada's Federal Minister of Transport 1967-72; 1973-77, asst. to Sandy Howard—business affairs; 1977, co-founder and v.p./sales & admin. of Producers Sales Organization; 1981, named sr. v.p., admin.; 1982, sr. v.p., acquisitions; 1983, exec. v.p., Skouras Pictures; 1985 promoted to pres., intl. div.; 1987-88 mgr. Lift Haven Inn, Sun Valley, ID; 1989-present, owner/partner Premiere Properties (prop. management, Sun Valley, ID).

FLEMING, RHONDA
Actress. r.n. Marilyn Louis. b. Los Angeles, CA, Aug. 10. m. Ted Mann (Mann Theatres). e. Beverly Hills H.S. Member, several charity orgs. Bd. of Dir. trustee of World Opportunities Intl. (Help the Children). Alzheimer Rsch., Childhelp USA, bd. of trustees of the UCLA Foundation. Opened Rhonda Fleming Mann Resource Center for Women with Cancer at UCLA Medical Center, 1994. Many awards incl. Woman of the Year Award from City of Hope 1986 & 1991; Woman of the World Award from Childhelp USA; Excellence in Media, Gold Angel Award; The Mannequins of Assistance of Southern California, Golden Eve Award. Stage incl. The Women (B'way), Kismet (LA), The Boyfriend (tour), one woman concerts.
PICTURES: Spellbound, Abiline Town, Spiral Staircase, Adventure Island, Out of the Past, A Connecticut Yankee in King Arthur's Court, The Great Lover, The Eagle and the Hawk, The Redhead and the Cowboy, The Last Outpost, Cry Danger, Crosswinds, Little Egypt, Hong Kong, Golden Hawk, Tropic Zone, Pony Express, Serpent of the Nile, Inferno, Those Redheads from Seattle, Jivaro, Yankee Pasha, Tennessee's Partner, While the City Sleeps, Killer Is Loose, Slightly Scarlet, Odongo, Queen of Babylon, Gunfight at the OK Corral, Buster Keaton Story, Gun Glory, Bullwhip, Home Before Dark, Alias Jesse James, The Big Circus, The Crowded Sky, The Patsy (cameo), Won Ton Ton The Dog Who Saved Hollywood, The Nude Bomb.
TELEVISION: Guest: Wagon Train, Police Woman, Love Boat, McMillian and Wife, Legends of the Screen, Road to Hollywood, Wildest West Show of Stars. Movies: The Last Hours Before Morning, Love for Rent, Waiting for the Wind.

FLEMYNG, ROBERT
Actor. b. Liverpool, England, Jan. 3, 1912. e. Halleybury Coll. Stage debut: Rope, 1931.
PICTURES: Head Over Heels (debut, 1937), Bond Street, The Guinea Pig, The Conspirators, The Blue Lamp, Blackmailed, The Magic Box, The Holly and the Ivy, Cast a Dark Shadow, Man Who Never Was, Funny Face, Let's Be Happy, Wisdom's Way, Blind Date, A Touch of Larceny, Radtus (Italian), The King's Breakfast, The Deadly Affair, The Spy with the Cold Nose, The Quiller Memorandum, Deathhead Avenger, Oh! What a Lovely War, Battle of Britain, Cause for Alarm, Young Winston, The Darwin Adventure, Travels with My Aunt, Golden Rendezvous, The Medusa Touch, The Four Feathers, The Thirty-Nine Steps, Paris By Night, Kafka, Shadowlands.
TELEVISION: appearances in England, U.S. inc.: Rainy Day, Playhouse 90, Wuthering Heights, Browning Version, After the Party, Boyd Q.C., They Made History, Somerset Maugham Show, Woman in White, The Datchet Diamonds, Probation Officer, Family Solicitor (series), Man of the World, Zero One, Compact (serial), Day by the Sea, The Living Room, Hawks and Doves, Vanity Fair, The Inside Man, The Doctor's Dilemma, The Persuaders, Major Lavender, Public Eye, Florence Nightingale, Edward VIII, Spy Trap, The Venturers' Loyalties, The Avengers, Crown Court, Enemy at the Door, Rebecca, Edward and Mrs. Simpson, The Ladykiller, Professionals, Fame Is the Spur, Crown Court, Spider's Webb, Executive Suite, Small World, Perfect Scoundrels, Short Story, The Vacillations of Poppy Crew, The Choir.

FLETCHER, LOUISE
Actress. b. Birmingham, AL, July 22, 1934. e. U. of North Carolina, B.A. Came to Hollywood at age 21; studied with Jeff Corey. Worked on TV shows (including Playhouse 90, Maverick). Gave up career to be a mother for 10 yrs.; returned to acting in 1973. Board of Directors: Deafness Research Foundation, 1980-. Honorary Degrees: Doctor of Humane Letters from Gallaudet U. and West Maryland Col. Advisory board: The Caption Center, The Nat'l Institute on Deafness and Other Communication Disorders.
PICTURES: Thieves Like Us, Russian Roulette, One Flew Over the Cuckoo's Nest (Academy Award, 1975), Exorcist II: The Heretic, The Cheap Detective, Natural Enemies, The Magician of Lublin, The Lucky Star, The Lady in Red, Strange Behavior, Mamma Dracula, Brainstorm, Strange Invaders, Firestarter, Once Upon a Time in America, Overnight Sensation, Invaders from Mars, The Boy Who Could Fly, Nobody's Fool, Flowers in the Attic, Two Moon Junction, Best of the Best, Shadow Zone, Blue Steel, Blind Vision, The Player, Georgino, Tollbooth, Return to Two Moon Junction, Virtuosity, High School High, 2 Days in the Valley, Mulholland Falls, Mojave Frankenstein, Edie and Pen, Gone Fishing, High School High, Girl Gets Moe, Heartless, Love Kills, Hollywood Salome.
TELEVISION: Series: Boys of Twilight, Deep Space Nine, Picket Fences, VR 5, Profiler. Movies: Can Ellen Be Saved?, Thou Shalt Not Commit Adultery, A Summer to Remember, Island, Second Serve, J. Edgar Hoover, The Karen Carpenter Story, Final Notice, Nightmare on the 13th Floor, In a Child's Name, The Fire Next Time, The Haunting of Seacliff Inn, Someone Else's Child, Stepford Husbands, Twisted Path, Breastmen, Married to a Stranger. Guest: Twilight Zone, Tales from the Crypt, Civil Wars, Dream On.

FLINN, JOHN C.
Publicist. b. Yonkers, NY, May 4, 1917. e. U. of California. p. late John C. Flinn, pioneer m.p. executive. In pub. dept. David O. Selznick, 1936-39; unit publicist, then head planter, Warner, 1936-46; joined Monogram as asst. to nat'l dir. & pub. head & pub. mgr. 1946; apptd. nat'l dir. of pub. & adv. of Allied Artists Pictures, 1951; apptd studio dir. adv. & pub., Columbia, 1959; v.p., Jim Mahoney & Assocs. (p.r. firm) 1971. Joined MGM West Coast publ. dept. as publ. coordinator, 1973; rejoined Columbia Pictures in 1974 as studio publ. dir.; 1979, promoted to dir. industry relations. Joined MGM/UA publ. staff, 1988 to work on m.p. academy campaign for Moonstruck. Engaged by Paramount 1988-89 to assist in Acad. Award campaigns. Retired.

FLOCKHART, CALISTA
Actress. b. Freeport, IL, Nov. 11, 1964. e. Rutgers College, NJ.
THEATER: B'way: The Glass Menagerie. Off B'way: The Loop, All for One, Sophistry, Wrong Turn at Lungfish, Beside Herself, Bovver Boys. Regional: The Three Sisters, Our Town, Death Takes a Holiday.
PICTURES: Quiz Show, Getting In, Naked in New York, Drunks, The Birdcage, Milk and Money, Telling Lies in America, A Midsummer's Night's Dream.
TELEVISION: Series: Ally McBeal (Golden Globe Award, 1998). Movie: Darrow. Guest: The Practice.

FLOREA, JOHN
Producer, Director, Writer. b. Alliance, OH, May 28, 1916. Served as photo journalist with Life magazine, 1940-50; assoc. editor Colliers magazine, 1950-53. Prod.-dir. with David Gerber 1979-84.
PICTURES: A Time to Every Purpose, The Astral Factor, The Invisible Strangler, Hot Child in the City.

TELEVISION: *Dir. several episodes*: Sea Hunt series, 1957-60; Bonanza, Outlaws, Outpost (pilot), The Virginian, Honey West, Daktari, Gentle Ben, Cowboy in Africa, High Chapparal, Flipper, Destry Rides Again, Not For Hire, Ironside, Highway Patrol, V, Target, Everglades, (also prod.), CHiPS, MacGyver. Prod.-dir. of film Islands of the Lost. With Ivon Tors Films. Nominated as one of the Top 10 directors in America by DGA for 1968 Mission Impossible episode. Dir. several Ironside episodes. Doc: Kammikazi, Attack Hawaiian Hospitality, Million Dollar Question, Marineland, Brink of Disaster. (Valley Freedom Award), Dangerous Report, (for CIA), The Runaways (Emmy Award), Down the Long Hills, Dark Canyon.

FLYNN, BEAU
Producer.
PICTURES: I.Q. (asst. prod.), Johns, Life During Wartime (exec. prod), The House of Yes, Dust & Stardust, Little City.

FLYNN, JOHN
Director, Writer. b. Chicago IL. e. George Washington U, Stanford, UCLA, B.A. (Eng.). Worked in mailroom at MCA then with p.r. firm. Began career as trainee script supvr. for dir. Robert Wise on West Side Story. Soon working as ass't. dir. on MGM-TV shows. Made dir. debut with The Sergeant, 1969.
PICTURES: The Jerusalem File, The Outfit (also s.p.), Rolling Thunder, Defiance, Touched, Best Seller, Lock Up, Brainscan.
TELEVISION: Marilyn—The Untold Story (dir.).

FOCH, NINA
Actress. b. Leyden, Holland, April 20, 1924. Daughter of Consuelo Flowerton, actress, & Dirk Foch, symphony orch. conductor. Adjunct Prof., USC, 1966-67; 1978-80, Adjunct professor, USC Cinema-TV grad. sch. 1986-; sr. faculty, American Film Inst,, 1974-77; bd. of Governors, Hollywood Acad. of Television Arts & Sciences, 1976-77; exec. Comm. Foreign Language Film Award, Acad. of Motion Picture Arts & Sciences, 1970-. Cochmn., exec. comm. Foreign Language Film Award 1983-.
PICTURES: The Return of the Vampire (debut, 1943), Nine Girls, Cry of the Werewolf, She's a Soldier Too, She's a Sweetheart, Shadows in the Night, I Love a Mystery, Prison Ship, Song to Remember, My Name is Julia Ross, Boston Blackie's Rendezvous, Escape in the Fog, The Guilt of Jane Ames, Johnny O'Clock, The Dark Past, Johnny Allegro, Undercover Man, St. Benny the Dip, An American in Paris, Young Man With Ideas, Scaramouche, Sombrero, Fast Company, Executive Suite (Acad. Award nom.), Four Guns to the Border, The Ten Commandments, Illegal, You're Never Too Young, Three Brave Men, Cash McCall, Spartacus, Such Good Friends, Salty, Mahogany, Jennifer, Rich and Famous, Skin Deep, Sliver, Morning Glory, It's My Party, 'Til There Was You, Kilronan, Hush, Reasonable Doubt.
TELEVISION: *Series*: Q.E.D. (panelist), It's News to Me (panelist), Shadow Chasers. *Movies*: Outback Bound, In the Arms of a Killer, The Sands of Time. *Mini-series*: War and Remembrance. *Special*: Tales of the City. Guest star, most major series incl. Studio One, Playhouse 90, US Steel Hour, L.A. Law, Dear John, Hunter; talk shows, specials.

FOGARTY, JACK V.
Executive, Producer, Writer. b. Los Angeles, CA. e. UCLA. Management, MGM, 1960-62; exec. prod. mgr., Cinerama, Inc., 1962-64; assoc. prod., The Best of Cinerama, 1963; est. own p.r. firm, 1965; pres., AstroScope, Inc., 1969-74.
TELEVISION: *Writer/prod.*: The Rookies, S.W.A.T., Charlie's Angels, Most Wanted, Barnaby Jones, A Man Called Sloane, Trapper John, T.J. Hooker, Crazy Like a Fox, The Equalizer, Jake and the Fatman, Murder She Wrote, Charlie's Angels (story edit.). *Exec.* Story consultant: Most Wanted, A Man Called Sloane, Sheriff Lobo, T.J. Hooker. *Producer*: T.J. Hooker, Jessie.

FOLEY, JAMES
Director. b. New York, NY. E. NYU, USC. While at USC directed two short films, Silent Night and November which brought him attention. Directed two Madonna videos: Live to Tell and Papa Don't Preach.
PICTURES: Reckless, At Close Range, Who's That Girl, After Dark My Sweet, Glengarry Glen Ross, A Day to Remember, Fear, Two Bits, The Chamber, Guns, The Corrupter.

FOLSEY, GEORGE, JR
Producer, Editor. b. Los Angeles, CA, Jan. 17, 1939. Son of late cinematographer George Folsey Sr. e. Pomona Coll., B.A., 1961. Chairman, Q Sound Labs, Canadian sound localization and Tech. Co., 1988-1992.
PICTURES: *Editor*: Glass Houses, Bone, Hammer, Black Caesar, Schlock, Trader Horn, Bucktown, J.D.'s Revenge, Norman... Is That You?, Tracks, The Chicken Chronicles, The Kentucky Fried Movie, National Lampoon's Animal House, Freedom Road, The Great Santini (addt'l editing), The Blues Brothers (also assoc. prod.), Bullet Proof. *Producer*: An American Werewolf in London, Twilight Zone—The Movie (assoc. prod.); Trading Places (exec. prod. & 2nd unit dir.), Into the Night (co-prod.), Spies Like Us (co-prod.), Clue (co-exec. prod.), Three Amigos, Coming to America (co-prod., co-editor), Greedy (co-exec. prod.), Grumpier Old Men.
VIDEO: Michael Jackson's Thriller (co-prod., editor).

FONDA, BRIDGET
Actress. b. Los Angeles, CA, Jan. 27, 1964. Daughter of actor Peter Fonda. Grew up in Los Angeles and Montana. e. NYU theater prog. Studied acting at Lee Strasberg Inst., and with Harold Guskin. Starred in grad. student film PPT. Workshop stage performances include Confession and Pastels.
PICTURES: Aria (Tristan and Isolde sequence; debut, 1987), You Can't Hurry Love, Light Years (voice), Scandal, Shag, Strapless, Frankenstein Unbound, The Godfather Part III, Drop Dead Fred (unbilled), Doc Hollywood, Leather Jackets, Out of the Rain, Iron Maze, Single White Female, Singles, Army of Darkness, Point of No Return, Bodies Rest and Motion, Little Buddha, It Could Happen to You, The Road to Wellville, Camilla, Rough Magic, Balto (voice), City Hall, Touch, Mr. Jealousy, South from Hell's Kitchen, The Road to Graceland, The Break-Up, A Simple Plan, Lake Placid.
TELEVISION: *Specials*: Jacob Have I Loved (Wonderworks), The Edge (The Professional Man). *Guest*: 21 Jump Street, In the Gloaming.

FONDA, JANE
Actress. b. New York, NY, Dec. 21, 1937. e. Emma Willard Sch., Troy, NY. Active in dramatics, Vassar. Father was late actor Henry Fonda. Brother is actor Peter Fonda. m. executive Ted Turner. Appeared with father in summer stock production, The Country Girl, Omaha, NB. Studied painting, languages, Paris. Art Students League, N.Y. Appeared in The Male Animal, Dennis, MA. Modeled, appeared on covers, Esquire, Vogue, The Ladies Home Journal, Glamour, and McCall's, 1959. Appeared in documentaries: Introduction to the Enemy, No Nukes.
THEATER: There Was A Little Girl (Theatre World Award), Invitation to a March, The Fun Couple, Strange Interlude.
PICTURES: Tall Story (debut, 1960), Walk on the Wild Side, The Chapman Report, Period of Adjustment, In the Cool of The Day, Sunday in New York, The Love Cage (Joy House), La Ronde (Circle of Love), Cat Ballou, The Chase, La Curee (The Game is Over), Any Wednesday, Hurry Sundown, Barefoot in the Park, Barbarella, Spirits of the Dead, They Shoot Horses Don't They? (Acad. Award nom.), Klute (Academy Award, 1971), F.T.A. (also prod.), Tout va Bien, Steelyard Blues, A Doll's House, The Bluebird, Fun With Dick and Jane, Julia (Acad. Award nom.), Coming Home (Academy Award, 1978), Comes a Horseman, California Suite, The China Syndrome (Acad. Award nom.), The Electric Horseman, Nine To Five, On Golden Pond (Acad. Award nom.), Rollover, Agnes of God, The Morning After (Acad. Award nom.), Leonard Part 6 (cameo), Old Gringo, Stanley and Iris.
TELEVISION: *Specials*: A String of Beads, Lily--Sold Out, The Helen Reddy Special, I Love Liberty, Tell Them I'm a Mermaid, Fonda on Fonda (host), A Century of Women (narrator). *Movie*: The Dollmaker (Emmy Award, 1984). *Series*: 9 to 5 (exec. prod. only).

FONDA, PETER
Actor, Director. b. New York, NY, Feb. 23, 1939. e. studied at U. of Omaha. Son of late actor Henry Fonda. Sister is actress Jane Fonda; daughter is actress Bridget Fonda.
PICTURES: Tammy and the Doctor (debut, 1963), The Victors, Lilith, The Young Lovers, The Wild Angels, The Trip, Spirits of the Dead, Easy Rider (also co-s.p., prod.), Idaho Transfer (dir.), The Last Movie, The Hired Hand (also dir.), Two People, Dirty Mary Crazy Larry, Open Season, Race With the Devil, 92 in the Shade, Killer Force, Fighting Mad, Futureworld, Outlaw Blues, High Ballin!, Wanda Nevada (also dir.), Cannonball Run (cameo), Split Image, Certain Fury, Dance of the Dwarfs, Mercenary Fighters, Jungle Heat, Diajobu My Friend, Peppermint Frieden, Spasm, The Rose Garden, Fatal Mission, Family Spirit, Reckless, South Beach, Bodies Rest & Motion, DeadFall, Molly & Gina, Love and a .45, Nadja, John Carpenter's Escape from L.A., Ulee's Gold (NY Film Crits. Circle Award, Golden Globe Award, Best Actor, 1997).
TELEVISION: *Movies*: A Reason to Live, The Hostage Tower, A Time of Indifference, Sound, Certain Honorable Men, Montana.

FONER, NAOMI
Writer, Producer. b. New York, NY. e. Barnard Col., Columbia U. m. dir. Stephen Gyllenhaal. Was media dir. of Eugene McCarthy's 1968 political campaign, then prod. asst. & researcher at PBS. 1968 joined Children's Television Workshop on staff of Sesame Street. Later helped develop series The Electric Company, 3-2-1 Contact. Creator and co-prod. of series The Best of Families. Wrote teleplay Blackout for PBS series Visions.
PICTURES: *Writer*: Violets Are Blue, Running on Empty (Golden Globe Award, Acad. Award nom.; also exec. prod.), A Dangerous Woman (also prod.), Losing Isaiah (also prod.).

FONTAINE, JOAN
Actress. b. Tokyo, Oct. 22, 1917. r.n. Joan de Beauvior de Havilland. e. American School in Japan. Sister is actress Olivia de Havilland. Started on stage in L.A., Santa Barbara and San Francisco in Kind Lady; then as Joan Fontaine in Call it a Day (L.A.), where she was spotted and signed to contract by prod. Jesse Lasky. Sold contract to RKO. On B'way in Tea and Sympathy (1954). *Author*: No Bed of Roses (1978) Appeared in The Lion in Winter at Vienna's English Speaking Theatre 1979.

PICTURES: No More Ladies (debut, 1935), Quality Street, You Can't Beat Love, Music for Madame, Maid's Night Out, A Damsel in Distress, Blonde Cheat, The Man Who Found Himself, The Duke of West Point, Sky Giant, Gunga Din, Man of Conquest, The Women, Rebecca (Acad. Award nom.), Suspicion (Academy Award, 1941), This Above All, The Constant Nymph (Acad. Award nom.), Jane Eyre, Frenchman's Creek, Affairs of Susan, From This Day Forward, Ivy, The Emperor Waltz, Letter From an Unknown Woman, Kiss the Blood Off My Hands, You Gotta Stay Happy, Born to Be Bad, September Affair, Darling How Could You?, Something to Live For, Othello (cameo), Ivanhoe, Decameron Nights, Flight to Tangier, The Bigamist, Casanova's Big Night, Serenade, Beyond a Reasonable Doubt, Island in the Sun, Until They Sail, A Certain Smile, Voyage to the Bottom of the Sea, Tender Is the Night, The Devil's Own.
TELEVISION: Crossings, Dark Mansions, Cannon, The Users, Bare Essence, Good King Wenceslas, etc.

FOOTE, HORTON
Writer. b. Wharton, TX, March 14, 1916. Actor before becoming playwright.
THEATER: Only the Heart, The Chase, The Trip to Bountiful, Traveling Lady, Courtship, 1918, The Widow Claire, The Habitation of Dragons, Lily Dale, Valentine's Day, Dividing the Estate, Talking Pictures, The Roads to Home, Night Seasons, The Young Man From Atlanta (Pulitzer prize), Cousins, The Death of Papa, Convicts, Roots In a Parched Ground, A Coffin In Egypt, Tomorrow, Getting Frankie Married and Afterwards, Laura Dennis, Vernon Early.
PICTURES: Storm Fear, To Kill a Mockingbird (Acad. Award, 1962), Baby the Rain Must Fall, The Chase, Hurry Sundown, Tomorrow, Tender Mercies (Acad. Award, 1983), 1918 (also co-prod.), The Trip to Bountiful (also co-prod.), On Valentine's Day, Convicts, Of Mice and Men.
TELEVISION: Only the Heart, Ludie Brooks, The Travelers, The Old Beginning, Trip to Bountiful, Young Lady of Property, Death of the Old Man, Flight, The Night of the Storm, The Roads to Home, Drugstore: Sunday Night, Member of the Family, Traveling Lady, Old Man (Emmy Award, 1997), Tomorrow, The Shape of the River, The Displaced Person, Barn Burning, The Habitation of Dragons.

FORBES, BRYAN
Actor, Writer, Producer, Director. b. Stratford (London), July 22, 1926. m. actress Nanette Newman. Former head of prod., man. dir., Associated British Prods. (EMI). Stage debut, The Corn Is Green (London), 1942; screen debut, The Small Back Room, 1948. Pres.: National Youth Theatre of Great Britain, 1985-; Pres.: Writers Guild of Great Britain, 1988-91.
AUTHOR: Short stories: Truth Lies Sleeping. Novels: The Distant Laughter, Familiar Strangers (U.S.: Stranger), The Rewrite Man, The Endless Game, A Song at Twilight (U.S.: A Spy at Twilight), The Twisted Playground, Partly Cloudy, Quicksand. Novelizations: The Slipper and the Rose, International Velvet. Non-Fiction: Ned's Girl (bio. of Dame Edith Evans) That Despicable Race (history of the British acting tradition). Autobiographies: Notes for a Life, A Divided Life.
THEATER: Director: Macbeth, Star Quality, Killing Jessica, The Living Room.
PICTURES: Actor: Tired Men, The Small Back Room All Over the Town, Dear Mr. Prohack, Green Grow The Rushes, The Million Pound Note (Man With a Million), An Inspector Calls, The Colditz Story, Passage Home, Appointment in London, Sea Devils, The Extra Day, Quatermass II, It's Great To be Young, Satellite in The Sky, The Baby and The Battleship, Yesterday's Enemy, The Guns of Navarone, A Shot in The Dark, Of Human Bondage, Restless Natives. Writer: The Cockleshell Heroes, The Black Tent, Danger Within, I Was Monty's Double (also actor), The League of Gentlemen (also actor), The Angry Silence (also prod., actor), Man in the Moon, Only Two Can Play, Station Six Sahara, Of Human Bondage (also actor), Hopscotch, Chaplin. Director-Writer: Whistle Down the Wind (dir. only), The L-Shaped Room (also actor), Seance on a Wet Afternoon (also prod.), King Rat, The Wrong Box, The Whisperers, Deadfall, The Madwoman of Chaillot (dir. only), The Raging Moon (Long Ago Tomorrow; also actor), The Stepford Wives (dir., actor), The Slipper and the Rose (also actor), International Velvet (also actor), Sunday Lovers (co-dir. only), Better Late Than Never (Menage a Trois), The Naked Face. Exec. Prod.: Hoffman, Forbush and the Penguins, The Railway Children, Peter Rabbit and the Tales of Beatrix Potter, The Go-Between, And Soon The Darkness, On The Buses, Dulcima.
TELEVISION: Actor: Johnnie Was a Hero, The Breadwinner, French Without Tears, Journey's End, The Gift, The Road, The Heiress, December Flower, First Amongst Equals. Writer/Dir.: I Caught Acting Like The Measles (documentary on the life of Dame Edith Evans) Goodbye Norma Jean and Other Things (documentary on the life of Elton John) Jessie, The Endless Game.

FORD, GLENN
Actor. r.n. Gwylin Ford. b. Quebec, Canada, May 1, 1916. Moved to Southern California as child. On stage with various West Coast theatre cos.; featured in The Children's Hour 1935; Broadway in Broom for a Bride, Soliloquy. Signed contract for film career with Columbia Pictures, 1939. Served in U.S. Marine Corps 1942-45.
PICTURES: Heaven With a Barbed Wire Fence (debut, 1940), My Son Is Guilty, Convicted Women, Men Without Souls, Babies for Sale, Blondie Play Cupid, The Lady in Question, So Ends Our Night, Texas, Go West Young Lady, The Adventures of Martin Eden, Flight Lieutenant, Destroyer, The Desperadoes, A Stolen Life, Gilda, Gallant Journey, Framed, The Mating of Millie, The Return of October, The Loves of Carmen, The Man from Colorado, Mr. Soft Touch, The Undercover Man, Lust for Gold, The Doctor and the Girl, The White Tower, Convicted, The Flying Missile, The Redhead and the Cowboy, Follow the Sun, The Secret of Convict Lake, Green Glove, Young Man with Ideas, Affair in Trinidad, Time Bomb (Terror on a Train), The Man from the Alamo, Plunder of the Sun, The Big Heat, Appointment in Honduras, Human Desire, The Americano, The Violent Men, Blackboard Jungle, Interrupted Melody, Trial, Ransom, The Fastest Gun Alive, Jubal, The Teahouse of the August Moon, 3:10 to Yuma, Don't Go Near the Water, Cowboy, The Sheepman, Imitation General, Torpedo Run, It Started With a Kiss, The Gazebo, Cimarron, Cry for Happy, Pocketful or Miracles, The Four Horsemen of The Apocalypse, Experiment in Terror, Love Is a Ball, The Courtship of Eddie's Father, Advance to the Rear, Fate Is the Hunter, Dear Heart, The Rounders, The Money Trap, Is Paris Burning?, Rage, A Time for Killing, The Last Challenge, Day of the Evil Gun, Heaven With a Gun, Smith!, Santee, Midway, Superman, The Visitor, Virus, Happy Birthday to Me, Border Shootout, Raw Nerve.
TELEVISION: Series: Cade's County, Friends of Man (narrator), The Family Holvak, When Havoc Struck (narrator). Movies: Brotherhood of the Bell, The Greatest Gift, Punch and Jody, The 3000 Mile Chase, Evening in Byzantium, The Sacketts, Beggarman Thief, The Gift, Final Verdict. Mini-Series: Once an Eagle.

FORD, HARRISON
Actor. b. Chicago, IL, July 13, 1942. e. Ripon Coll. Started acting in summer stock at Williams Bay, WI, in Damn Yankees, Little Mary Sunshine. Moved to L.A. where he acted in John Brown's Body. Signed by Columbia Studios under seven-year contract. Took break from acting to undertake carpentry work which included building Sergio Mendes' recording studio. Returned to acting in American Graffiti.
PICTURES: Dead Heat on a Merry-Go-Round (debut, 1966), Luv, A Time for Killing, Journey to Shiloh, Zabriskie Point, Getting Straight, American Graffiti, The Conversation, Star Wars, Heroes, Force 10 from Navarone, Hanover Street, The Frisco Kid, More American Graffiti (cameo), Apocalypse Now, The Empire Strikes Back, Raiders of the Lost Ark, Blade Runner, Return of the Jedi, Indiana Jones and the Temple of Doom, Witness (Acad. Award nom.), The Mosquito Coast, Frantic, Working Girl, Indiana Jones and the Last Crusade, Presumed Innocent, Regarding Henry, Patriot Games, The Fugitive, Jimmy Hollywood (cameo), Clear and Present Danger, Sabrina, The Devil's Own, Air Force One, Six Days Seven Nights.
TELEVISION: Movies: The Intruders, James A. Michener's Dynasty, The Possessed. Guest: The Virginian, Ironside, The FBI, Love American Style, Gunsmoke, The Young Indiana Jones Chronicles. Special: Trial of Lt. Calley.

FORD, MICHAEL
Set decorator, Sound, Actor.
PICTURES: Voyage to the Bottom of the Sea, Don't Worry We'll Think of a Title, Machismo-40 Graves for 40 Guns, The Empire Strikes Back, Raiders of the Lost Ark, Jinxed!, Return of the Jedi, Return of Oz, Empire of the Sun, The Living Daylights, Jaws: The Revenge, Back Street Jane, Licence to Kill, Kill Line, The Taking of Beverly Hills, Nostradamus, GoldenEye, Titanic (Acad. Award, Best Set. Decoration, 1997).
TELEVISION: Movies, actor: Giving Tongue, September.

FORLANI, CLAIR
Actress.
PICTURES: Gypsy Eyes, Police Academy: Mission to Moscow, Mallrats, The Rock, Garage Sale, Basquiat, Basil, The Last Time I Commited Suicide, Meet Joe Black, Elements.
TELEVISION: Mini-series: JFK: Reckless Youth. Guest: Press Gang.

FORMAN, SIR DENIS
O.B.E., M.A.: Executive. b. Moffat, Dumfriesshire, Scot., Oct. 13, 1917. e. Loretto Sch., Musselburgh, Pembroke Coll., Cambridge. Served in Argyll & Sutherland Highlanders, W.W.II. Entered film business 1946, production staff Central Office of Information, 1947; Chief Production Officer C.O.I. 1948; appointed dir. of the British Film Inst., 1949; joined Granada Television Ltd., 1955. Jnt. Mng. Dir., 1965 chmn., British Film Inst., bd. of Gov., 1971-73. Chmn. Granada T.V. 1975-87. Chmn. Novello & Co. 1972. Fellow, British Acad. Film & TV Arts, 1976. Dep. chmn. Granada Group, 1984-90, consultant, 1990-96. Deputy chmn. Royal Opera House, 1983-92.

FORMAN, JEROME A.

Executive. b. Hood River, Oregon, June 20, 1934. e. U Arizona. 1966, became gen. mgr. Forman and United Theatres of the Northwest. 1971, joined Pacific Theatres; 1972, appointed v.p. & gen. mgr.; 1978-87, exec. v.p.; 1987-present, pres. One of the original founders of the ShoWest Convention. Currently chmn. emeritus, NATO of Calif.; 1991, chmn. NATO. 1991 elected chmn. bd. of Will Rogers Memorial Fund. Board member of the Foundation of the Motion Picture Pioneers.

FORMAN, MILOS

Director. b. Caslav, Czechoslovakia, Feb. 18, 1932. Trained as writer at Czech Film Sch. and as director at Laterna Magika. Directed short films Audition (Competition), If There Were No Music. Won Int'l. attention with first feature length film Black Peter, 1963. Emigrated to U.S. after collapse of Dubcek govt. in Czechoslovakia, 1969. Appeared as actor in films Heartburn, New Year's Day.
PICTURES: Peter and Pavla/Black Peter (also co-s.p.; Czech Film Critics & Grand Prix Locarno Awards), Loves of a Blonde (also co- s.p.), The Firemen's Ball (also co-s.p.), Taking Off (U.S. debut, 1971), Visions of Eight (Decathalon segment), One Flew Over the Cuckoo's Nest (Academy Award, 1975), Hair, Ragtime, Amadeus (Acad. Award, 1984), Valmont, The People vs. Larry Flynt (Golden Globe Award, 1997).

FORREST, FREDERIC

Actor. b. Waxahachie, TX, Dec. 23, 1936. e. Texas Christian U., U. of Oklahoma, B.A. Studied with Sanford Meisner and Lee Strasberg. Began career off-off B'way at Caffe Cino in The Madness of Lady Bright then off-B'way in Futz, Massachusetts Trust and Tom Paine, all with La Mama Troupe under direction of Tom O'Horgan. Moved to Hollywood in 1970.
PICTURES: Futz (debut, 1969), When the Legends Die, The Don Is Dead, The Conversation, The Gravy Train, Permission to Kill, The Missouri Breaks, It Lives Again!, Apocalypse Now, The Rose (Acad. Award nom.), One From the Heart, Hammett, Valley Girl, The Stone Boy, Return, Where Are the Children?, Stacking, Tucker: The Man and His Dream, Valentino Returns, Music Box, The Two Jakes, Cat Chaser, Rain Without Thunder, Falling Down, Trauma, Chasers, One Night Stand.
TELEVISION: Movies: Larry, Promise Him Anything, Ruby and Oswald, Calamity Jane, Right to Kill?, The Deliberate Stranger, Quo Vadis, Little Girl Lost, Saigon: Year of the Cat (U.K.), Best Kept Secrets, Who Will Love My Children? A Shadow on the Sun, Margaret Bourke-White, Citizen Cohn, The Habitation of Dragons, Against the Wall. Mini-Series: Die Kinder.

FORREST, STEVE

Actor. b. Huntsville, TX, Sept. 29, 1925. r.n. William Forrest Andrews. Brother of late actor Dana Andrews. e. UCLA, 1950. Acted at La Jolla Playhouse; appeared on radio, TV; m.p. debut in Crash Dive billed as William Andrews.
PICTURES: Crash Dive (debut, 1942), The Ghost Ship, Geisha Girl, Sealed Cargo, Last of the Comanches, The Bad and the Beautiful (1st billing as Steve Forrest), Dream Wife, Battle Circus, The Clown, The Band Wagon, So Big, Take the High Ground, Phantom of the Rue Morgue, Prisoner of War, Rogue Cop, Bedevilled, The Living Idol, It Happened to Jane, Heller in Pink Tights, Five Branded Women, Flaming Star, The Second Time Around, The Longest Day, The Yellow Canary, Rascal, The Wild Country, The Late Liz, North Dallas Forty, Mommie Dearest, Sahara, Spies Like Us, Amazon Women on the Moon.
TELEVISION: Movies: The Hatfields and the McCoys, Wanted: The Sundance Women, The Last of the Mohicans, Testimony of Two Men, Maneaters are Loose, Hollywood Wives, Gunsmoke: Return to Dodge, Columbo: A Bird in the Hand. Series: The Baron, S.W.A.T., Dallas.

FORSTER, ROBERT

Actor. b. Rochester, NY, July 13, 1941. e. Heidelberg Coll., Alfred U., Rochester U., B.S.
THEATER: Mrs. Dally Has a Lover, A Streetcar Named Desire, The Glass Menagerie, 12 Angry Men, The Sea Horse, One Flew Over the Cuckoo's Nest, The Big Knife, In the Moonlight Eddie.
PICTURES: Reflections in a Golden Eye (debut, 1967), The Stalking Moon, Medium Cool, Justine, Cover Me Babe, Pieces of Dreams, Journey Through Rosebud, The Don is Dead, Stunts, Avalanche, The Black Hole, Lady in Red (unbilled), Crunch, Alligator, Vigilante, Walking the Edge, Hollywood Harry (also prod., dir.), The Delta Force, Committed, Esmeralda Bay, Heat from Another Sun, The Banker, Peacemaker, Diplomatic Immunity, 29th Street, In Between, Badge of Silence, Maniac Cop 3: Badge of Silence, South Beach, Cover Story, Body Chemistry 3: Point of Seduction, Demo U, American Perfekt, Jackie Brown, Outside Ozona, Kiss Toledo Goobye, Super Nova.
TELEVISION: Series: Banyon, Nakia, Once a Hero. Movies: Banyon, The Death Squad, Nakia, The City, Standing Tall, The Darker Side of Terror, Goliath Awaits, In the Shadow of a Killer, Sex Love and Cold Hard Cash. Pilots: Checkered Flag, Mickie & Frankie.

FORSYTH, BILL

Director. Writer. b. Glasgow, Scotland, July 29, 1946. At 16 joined film co. For next 10 years made industrial films, then documentaries. Joined Glasgow Youth Theater.
PICTURES: Director-Writer: That Sinking Feeling (debut, 1979; also prod.), Gregory's Girl, Local Hero, Comfort and Joy, Housekeeping, Breaking In, Rebecca's Daughters, Being Human.
TELEVISION: Andrina.

FORSYTHE, JOHN

Actor. b. Penn's Grove, NJ, Jan. 29, 1918. r.n. John Freund. Former commentator for Brooklyn Dodgers, prior to becoming actor. Debuted on tv in 1947.
THEATER: Mr. Roberts, All My Sons, Yellow Jack, Teahouse of the August Moon and others.
PICTURES: Destination Tokyo (debut, 1943), The Captive City, It Happens Every Thursday, The Glass Web, Escape From Fort Bravo, The Trouble With Harry, The Ambassador's Daughter, Everything But the Truth, Kitten With a Whip, Madame X, In Cold Blood, The Happy Ending, Topaze, Goodbye and Amen, And Justice for All, Scrooged, Hotel de Love.
TELEVISION: Series: Bachelor Father, The John Forsythe Show, To Rome With Love, Charlie's Angels (voice only), Dynasty, The Powers That Be. Movies: See How They Run, Shadow on the Land, Murder Once Removed, The Letters, Lisa—Bright and Dark, Cry Panic, Healers, Terror on the 40th Floor, The Deadly Tower, Amelia Earhart, Tail Gunner Joe, Never Con a Killer, Cruise Into Terror, With This Ring, The Users, A Time for Miracles, Sizzle, The Mysterious Two, On Fire, Opposites Attract, Dynasty: The Reunion. Guest: Studio One, Kraft Theatre, Robert Montgomery Presents, I Witness Video, Kings of the Court.

FORSYTHE, WILLIAM

Actor. b. Brooklyn, NY.
THEATER: A Streetcar Named Desire, A Hatful of Rain, Othello, Julius Caesar, 1776, Hair, Godspell, Vox Humana—#3, If You Don't Like It—You Can Leave.
PICTURES: King of the Mountain, Smokey Bites the Dust, The Man Who Wasn't There, Sons, Dead Bang, Torrents of Spring, Patty Hearst, Savage Dawn, Cloak and Dagger, The Lightship, Once Upon a Time in America, Raising Arizona, Extreme Prejudice, Weeds, Dick Tracy, Career Opportunities, Out for Justice, Stone Cold, The Waterdance, American Me, The Gun in Betty Lou's Handbag, Relentless 3, Direct Hit, Beyond Desire, The Immortals, Virtuosity, Don't Ask Too Much of love, Things to Do in Denver When You're Dead, The Substitute, The Rock, Palookaville, For Which He Stands, Firestorm, Hell's Kitchen.
TELEVISION: Series: The Untouchables (1993). Movies: The Miracle of Kathy Miller, The Long Hot Summer, Baja Oklahoma, Cruel Doubt, A Kiss to Die For, Bedroom Eyes, Willing to Kill: The Texas Cheerleader Story, Peacock Blues, Gotti. Guest: CHiPs, Fame, Hill Street Blues. Mini-Series: Blind Faith.

FORTE, FABIAN

Singer, Actor. b. Philadelphia, PA, Feb. 6, 1943. e. South Philadelphia H.S. At 14, signed contract with Chancellor Records. Studied with Carlo Menotti. Formerly billed simply as Fabian.
RECORDS: Turn Me Loose, Tiger, I'm a Man, Hound Dog Man, The Fabulous Fabian (gold album).
PICTURES: Hound Dog Man (debut, 1959), High Time, North to Alaska, Love in a Goldfish Bowl, Five Weeks in a Balloon, Mr. Hobbs Takes a Vacation, The Longest Day, Ride the Wild Surf, Dear Brigitte, Ten Little Indians, Fireball 500, Dr. Goldfoot and the Girl Bombs, Thunder Alley, Maryjane, The Wild Racers, The Devil's Eight, A Bullet for Pretty Boy, Lovin' Man, Little Laura and Big John, Disco Fever, Kiss Daddy Goodbye, Get Crazy.
TELEVISION: Movies: Getting Married, Katie: Portrait of a Centerfold, Crisis in Mid-Air. Guest: Bus Stop, Love American Style, Laverne & Shirley, The Love Boat.

FOSSEY, BRIGITTE

Actress. b. Tourcoing, France, Mar. 11, 1947. After debut at the age of 5 in Rene Clement's Forbidden Games (1952) returned to school, studying philosophy and translating. Rediscovered by director Jean-Gabriel Albicocco and cast in Le Grand Meaulnes (1967).
PICTURES: Forbidden Games (debut, 1952), The Happy Road, Le Grand Meaulnes (The Wanderer), Adieu l'Ami, M Comme Mathieu, Raphael ou le DeBauche, Going Places, La Brigade, The Blue Country, Femme Fetales, The Good and the Bad, The Man Who Loved Women, The Swiss Affair, Quintet, Mais ou et donc Orincar, The Triple Death of the Third Character, A Bad Son, The Party, Chanel Solitaire, A Bite of Living, Imperativ, The Party-2, Enigma, Au nom de tous les Meins, Scarlet Fever, A Strange Passion, A Case of Irresponsibility, The Future of Emily, The False Confidences, Cinema Paradiso.

FOSTER, CHRISTINE

Executive. r.n. Mary Christine Foster. b. Los Angeles, CA, March 19, 1943. e. Immaculate Heart Coll, B.A. 1967. UCLA MJ, 1968. Teacher while member of Immaculate Heart Community, 1962-65. Teacher, Pacific U., Tokyo, 1968; dir., research and dev. Metromedia Producers Corp., 1968-71; dir., dev. & prod. services, Wolper Org. 1971-76; mgr., film progs. NBC TV 1976-77; v.p. movies for TV & mini-series, Columbia Pictures TV, 1977-81; v.p. series programs, Columbia TV, 1981; v.p. prog. dev., Group W. Prods. 1981-87; v.p., The Agency, 1988-90; agent, Shapiro-Lichtman-Stein Talent Agency, 1990-. Member: exec. comm. Humanitas Awards, 1986-; exec. comm. Catholics in Media, 1993-; Activities Committee, Acad. of TV Arts & Sciences, 1989-91; L.A. Roman Catholic Archdiocesan Communications Comm., 1986-89; Women in Film, bd. of dirs., 1977-78; teacher UCLA Extension, 1987-. Foreign and domestic university and public group lecturer and speaker.

FOSTER, DAVID

Producer. b. New York, NY, Nov. 25, 1929. e. Dorsey H.S., U. of Southern California Sch. of Journalism. U.S. Army, 1952-54; entered public relations field in 1952 with Rogers, Cowan & Brenner; Jim Mahoney, 1956; Allan, Foster, Ingersoll & Weber, 1958; left field in 1968 to enter independent m.p. production. Was partner in Turman-Foster Co.
PICTURES: *Producer* (with Mitchell Brower): McCabe and Mrs. Miller, The Getaway. Produced (with Lawrence Turman): The Nickel Ride (exec. prod.), The Drowning Pool, The Legacy, Tribute (exec. prod.), Caveman, The Thing, Second Thoughts, Mass Appeal, The Mean Season, Short Circuit, Running Scared, Full Moon in Blue Water, Short Circuit II, Gleaming the Cube, The Getaway (1993), The River Wild, The Mask of Zorro.
TELEVISION: Jesse (co-exec. prod), Between Two Brothers, Surrogate Mother.

FOSTER, JODIE

Actress. r.n. Alicia Christian Foster. b. Los Angeles, CA, Nov. 19, 1962. e. Yale U. Started acting in commercials including famous Coppertone ad. Acting debut on Mayberry, R.F.D. TV series (1968). Followed with many TV appearances, from series to movies of the week.
PICTURES: Napoleon and Samantha (debut, 1972), Kansas City Bomber, Tom Sawyer, One Little Indian, Alice Doesn't Live Here Anymore, Taxi Driver (Acad. Award nom.), Echoes of a Summer, Bugsy Malone, Freaky Friday, The Little Girl Who Lives Down the Lane, Il Casotto (The Beach Hut), Moi fleur bleue (Stop Calling Me Baby!), Candleshoe, Foxes, Carny, O'Hara's Wife, The Hotel New Hampshire, Mesmerized (also co-prod.), Siesta, Five Corners, Stealing Home, The Accused (Academy Award, 1988), The Silence of the Lambs (Academy Award, 1991), Little Man Tate (also dir.), Shadows and Fog, Sommersby, Maverick, Nell (Acad. Award nom.; also co-prod.), Home for the Holidays (dir., co-prod. only), Hate, Contact, Flora Plum.
TELEVISION: *Series*: Bob & Carol & Ted & Alice, Paper Moon. *Guest*: The Courtship of Eddie's Father, Gunsmoke, Julia, Mayberry R.F.D., Ironside, My Three Sons. *Specials*: Alexander, Rookie of the Year, Menace on the Mountain, The Secret Life of T.K. Dearing, The Fisherman's Wife. *Movies*: Smile Jenny--You're Dead, The Blood of Others, Svengali, Backtrack.

FOSTER, JULIA

Actress. b. Lewes, Sussex, England, 1941. First acted with the Brighton Repertory Company, then two years with the Worthing, Harrogate and Richmond companies. 1956, TV debut as Ann Carson in Emergency Ward 10.
THEATER: The Country Wife, What the Butler Saw.
PICTURES: Term of Trial (debut, 1962), The Loneliness of the Long Distance Runner, Two Left Feet, The Small World of Sammy Lee, The System (The Gir Getters), The Bargee, One Way Pendulum, Alfie, Half a Sixpence, All Coppers Are..., The Great McGonagall.
TELEVISION: A Cosy Little Arrangement, The Planemakers, Love Story, Taxi, Consequences, They Throw It at You, Crime and Punishment, The Image, Henry VI Pt. 1 of 3, Cabbage Patch, The Tragedy of Richard III.

FOSTER, MEG

Actress. b. Reading, PA, May 14, 1948. e. N.Y. Neighborhood Playhouse.
PICTURES: Adam at 6 A.M. (debut, 1970), Thumb Tripping, Welcome to Arrow Beach (Tender Flesh), A Different Story, Once in Paris, Carny, Ticket to Heaven, The Osterman Weekend, The Emerald Forest, Masters of the Universe, The Wind, They Live, Leviathan, Relentless, Stepfather 2, Blind Fury, Tripwire, Jezebel's Kiss, Diplomatic Immunity, Dead One: Relentless II, Project Shadowchaser, Immortal Combat.
TELEVISION: *Movies*: The Death of Me Yet, Sunshine, Things In This Season, Promise Him Anything, James Dean, Sunshine Christmas, Guyana Tragedy, Legend of Sleepy Hollow, Desperate Intruder, Best Kept Secrets, Desperate, Back Stab, To Catch a Killer. *Series*: Sunshine, Cagney & Lacey. *Guest*: Here Come the Brides, Mod Squad, Men at Law, Hawaii Five-O, Murder She Wrote, Miami Vice. *Mini-Series*: Washington: Behind Closed Doors. *Special*: The Scarlet Letter.

FOWKES, RICHARD O.

Executive. b. Yonkers, NY, April 15, 1946. e. NYU, Geo. Washington U. Staff attorney for The Dramatists Guild, 1973-77; joined Paramount as assoc. counsel, 1977-80; moved to UA (NYC) as prod. attorney from 1980-82; returned to Paramount as v.p., legal & bus. affairs, MoPic division (LA) 1983; promoted to sr. v.p., bus. affairs & acquisitions, 1989; promoted to sr. v.p. in charge of bus. affairs, 1994.

FOWLER, HARRY

Actor. b. London, England, Dec. 10, 1926. e. West Central Sch., London. Stage debut, Nothing Up My Sleeve (London) 1950; Screen debut, 1941.
PICTURES: Demi-Paradise, Don't Take It to Heart, Champaigne Charlie, Painted Boats, Hue and Cry, Now Barabbas, The Dark Man, She Shall Have Murder, The Scarlet Thread, High Treason, The Last Page, I Believe in You, Pickwick Papers, Top of the Form, Angels One Five, Conflict of Wings (Fuss Over Feathers), A Day to Remember, Blue Peter, Home and Away, Booby Trap, Town on Trial, Lucky Jim, Birthday Present, Idle on Parade, Don't Panic Chaps, Heart of a Man, Crooks Anonymous, The Longest Day, Lawrence of Arabia, Flight from Singapore, The Golliwog, Ladies Who Do, Clash By Night, The Nanny, Life at the Top, Start the Revolution Without Me, The Prince and The Pauper, Fanny Hill, Chicago Joe and the Showgirl.
TELEVISION: Stalingrad, I Remember the Battle, Gideon's Way, That's for Me, Our Man at St. Mark's, Dixon of Dock Green, Dr. Finlay's Case Book, I Was There, Cruffs Dog Show, The Londoners, Jackanory, Get This, Movie Quiz, Get This (series), Going a Bundle, Ask a Silly Answer, London Scene, Flockton Flyer, Sun Trap, The Little World of Don Camillo, World's End, Minder, Dead Ernest, Morecambe Wise Show, Gossip, Entertainment Express, Fresh Fields, Supergram, A Roller Next Year, Harry's Kingdom, Body Contact, Davro's Sketch Pad, The Bill, In Sickness and in Health, Casualty, Leaves on the Line, Young Indiana Jones Chronicles, Southside Party, London Tonight.

FOX, EDWARD

Actor. b. London, England, April 13, 1937. Comes from theatrical family; father was agent for leading London actors; brother is actor James Fox.
PICTURES: The Mind Benders (debut, 1962), Morgan!, The Frozen Dead, The Long Duel, The Naked Runner, The Jokers, I'll Never Forget What's 'is Name, The Battle of Britain, Oh! What a Lovely War, Skullduggery, The Go-Between, The Day of The Jackal, A Doll's House, Galileo, The Squeeze, A Bridge Too Far, The Duellists, The Big Sleep, Force 10 from Navarone, The Cat and the Canary, Soldier of Orange, The Mirror Crack'd, Gandhi, Never Say Never Again, The Dresser, The Bounty, Wild Geese II, The Shooting Party, Return from the River Kwai, A Feast at Midnight, A Month by the Lake, Prince Valiant, Lost in Space.
TELEVISION: Edward and Mrs. Simpson, A Hazard of Hearts, Anastasia: The Mystery of Anna, Quartermaine's Terms, They Never Slept, Shaka Zulu, Robin Hood, The Crucifer of Blood, Forbidden Territory.

FOX, JAMES

Actor. b. London, England, May 19, 1939. Brother is actor Edward Fox. Ent. films as child actor in 1950 as William Fox. Left acting in 1973 to follow spiritual vocation. Returned to mainsteam films in 1982. B'way debut 1995 in Uncle Vanya.
PICTURES: The Miniver Story (debut, 1950; as William Fox), The Magnet, One Wild Oat, The Lavender Hill Mob, Timbuktu, The Queen's Guards, The Secret Partner, She Always Gets Their Man, What Every Woman Wants, The Loneliness of the Long-Distance Runner; Tamahine (1st film billed as James Fox), The Servant, Those Magnificent Men in Their Flying Machines, King Rat, The Chase, Thoroughly Modern Millie, Arabella, Duffy, Isadora, Performance, No Longer Alone, Runners, Greystoke: The Legend of Tarzan, A Passage to India, Pavlova, Absolute Beginners, The Whistle Blower, Comrades, High Season, The Mighty Quinn, Farewell to the King, The Boys in the Island, The Russia House, Patriot Games, Afraid of the Dark, The Remains of the Day, Anna Karenina, Up at the Villa, Shadow Run, Mickey Blue Eyes.
TELEVISION: The Door, Espionage, Love Is Old, Love Is New, Nancy Astor, Country, New World, Beryl Markham: A Shadow on the Sun, Sun Child, She's Been Away (BBC; shown theatrically in U.S.), Never Come Back, Slowly Slowly in the Wind, Patricia Highsmith Series, As You Like It, A Question of Attribution, Heart of Darkness, Fall from Grace, Hostage, Doomsday Gun, Headhunters, The Old Curiosity Shop, Fall From Grace, The Choir, Gulliver's Travels.

FOX, MICHAEL J.

Actor. b. Edmonton, Alberta, Canada, June 9, 1961. r.n. Michael Andrew Fox. m. actress Tracy Pollan. Appeared in Vancouver TV series Leo and Me, and on stage there in The Shadow Box. Moved to Los Angeles at age 18.

PICTURES: Midnight Madness (debut, 1980), The Class of 1984, Back to the Future, Teen Wolf, Light of Day, The Secret of My Success, Bright Lights Big City, Casualties of War, Back to the Future Part II, Back to the Future Part III, The Hard Way, Doc Hollywood, Homeward Bound: The Incredible Journey (voice), Life With Mikey, For Love or Money, Where the Rivers Flow North, Greedy, Coldblooded (also co-prod.), Blue in the Face, The American President, Homeward Bound II: Lost in San Francisco (voice), The Frighteners, Mars Attacks, Thirty Wishes.
TELEVISION: Series: Palmerstown U.S.A., Family Ties (3 Emmy Awards), Spin City (Golden Globe Award, 1998). Guest: Lou Grant, The Love Boat, Night Court, Trapper John M.D., Tales from the Crypt (The Trap; also dir.). Specials: Teachers Only, Time Travel: Fact Fiction and Fantasy, Dear America: Letters Home From Vietnam (reader), James Cagney: Top of the World (host). Movies: Letters From Frank, High School USA, Poison Ivy, Family Ties Vacation, Don't Drink the Water, I Am Your Child. Director: Brooklyn Bridge (episode).

FOX, RICHARD
Executive. b. New York, NY, Feb. 24, 1947. Joined Warner Bros. Intl. as mgt. trainee in October 1975, working in Australia and Japan. 1977, named gen. mgr. of Columbia-Warner Dist., New Zealand. Served as gen. mgr. of WB in Tokyo, 1978\-1981. Joined WB in L.A. as exec. asst. to Myron D. Karlin, pres. of WB Intl., 1981; appt. v.p., sls. 1982; 1983, promoted to exec. v.p. of intl. arm; 1985, named pres. of WB Intl., assuming post vacated by Karlin. 1992, promoted to exec. v.p., Intl. Theatrical Enterprises, WB.

FOX, RICHARD A.
Executive. b. Buffalo, NY, Jan 5, 1929. e. U. of Buffalo, 1950. Chmn., Fox Theatres Management Corp. Pres., Nat'l NATO 1984-86; chmn., Nat'l NATO 1986-1988.

FOX, VIVICA
Actress. b. July 30, 1964.
PICTURES: Born on the Fourth of July, Don't Be a Menace, Independence Day, Set It Off, Booty Call, Batman & Robin, Soul Food, Killing Mrs. Tingle, Why Do Fools Fall in Love?, Idle Hands.
TELEVISION: Series: The Young and the Restless, Generations, Out All Night, The Tuskegee Airmen, Arsenio. Guest: Who's the Boss, The Fresh Prince of Bel-Air, Beverly Hills 90210, Getting Personal.

FOXWELL, IVAN
Producer, Writer. b. London, Eng., Feb. 22, 1914. Entered m.p. ind. 1933 as technician with British & Dominions Film Corp., subsequently with Paramount British & London Films; Assoc. with Curtis Bernhardt in Paris 1937 becoming producer & collaborating on story, s.p. of Carefour, Le Train pour Venise, De Mayerling Sarajevo, others. WWII with BEF and AEF 1939-46. Returned to British films 1947. Director, Foxwell Film Prods. Ltd.
PICTURES: Producer: No Room at the Inn (also co-s.p.), Guilt Is My Shadow (also co-s.p.), Twenty-Four Hours of a Woman's Life, The Intruder (also co-s.p.), Manuela, A Touch of Larceny, Tiara Tahiti, The Quiller Memorandum, Decline and Fall (also s.p.).
TELEVISION: The Intruder (co-writer), The Colditz Story (prod.).

FOXWORTH, ROBERT
Actor. b. Houston, TX, Nov. 1, 1941. e. Carnegie-Mellon U. Began acting at age 10 at Houston Alley Theatre and stayed with stage part-time while completing formal education. Returned to theatre on full-time basis after graduation. Made TV debut in Sadbird, 1969.
THEATER: NY: Henry V, Terra Nova, The Crucible (Theatre World Award), Love Letters, Candida. Regional: Antony & Cleopatra, Uncle Vanya, Cyrano de Bergerac, Who's Afraid of Virginia Woolf?, Othello, Habeus Corpus, The Seagull, Macbeth.
PICTURES: Treasure of Matecumbe (debut, 1976), The Astral Factor, Airport '77, Damien: Omen II, Prophecy, The Black Marble, Beyond the Stars.
TELEVISION: Series: The Storefront Lawyers, Falcon Crest. Movies: The Devil's Daughter, Frankenstein, Mrs. Sundance, The Questor Tapes (pilot), The FBI Story: The FBI Vs. Alvin Karpis, James Dean, It Happened at Lakewood Manor, Death Moon, The Memory of Eva Ryker, Act of Love, Peter and Paul, The Return of the Desperado, Double Standard, Face to Face, The Price of the Bride, With Murder in Mind, For Love and Glory. Specials: Hogan's Goat, Another Part of the Forest.

FOXX, JAMIE
Actor. b. Terrell, TX, December 13, 1967.
PICTURES: Toys, The Truth About Cats & Dogs, The Great White Hype, Player's Club, Booty Call.
TELEVISION: Series: In Living Color, The Jamie Foxx Show (also prod.), C Bear and Jamal (voice).

FRAKER, WILLIAM A.
Cinematographer, Director. b. Los Angeles, CA, 1923. e. U. of Southern California Film Sch. Worked as camera operator with Conrad Hall; moved to TV before feature films. Photographed and co-prod. doc. Forbid Them Not.
PICTURES: Cinematographer: Games, The Fox, The President's Analyst, Fade In, Rosemary's Baby, Bullitt, Paint Your Wagon, Dusty and Sweets McGee, The Day of the Dolphin, Rancho Deluxe, Aloha Bobby and Rose, Lipstick, The Killer Inside Me, Gator, Exorcist II--The Heretic, Looking for Mr. Goodbar, American Hot Wax, Heaven Can Wait, Old Boyfriends, 1941, The Hollywood Knights, Divine Madness, Sharky's Machine, The Best Little Whorehouse in Texas, WarGames, Irreconcilable Differences, Protocol, Fever Pitch, Murphy's Romance, SpaceCamp, Burglar, Baby Boom, Chances Are, An Innocent Man, The Freshman, Memoirs of an Invisible Man, Honeymoon in Vegas, Tombstone (also co-assoc. prod.), Street Fighter, Father of the Bride II. Director: Monte Walsh, Reflection of Fear, Legend of the Lone Ranger.
TELEVISION: Stony Burke, Outer Limits, Ozzie and Harriet, Daktari, B.L. Stryker: The Dancer's Touch (dir.).

FRAKES, JONATHAN
Actor, Director. b. Bethlehem, PA, Aug. 19, 1952. m. Actress Gennie Francis.
PICTURES: Gargoyles: The Heroes Awaken (voice), Star Trek: Generations, Star Trek: First Contact (also dir.).
TELEVISION: Movies: Beach Patrol, The Night the City Screamed, Star Trek: The Next Generation, The Cover Girl and the Cop. Series: The Doctors, Bare Essence, Paper Dolls, Star Trek: The Next Generation (also dir.), Gargoyles (voice), University Hospital (dir. only), Gargoyles: The Goliath Chronicles (voice). Mini-series: Beulah Land, North & South, North & South II, Dream West, Nutcracker: Money—Madness & Murder, North & South III. Guest: Voyagers, Remington Steele, Highway to Heaven, Matlock, Married... With Children, The New Twilight Zone, Star Trek: Deep Space Nine (also dir.), Wings, Lois & Clark, Star Trek: Voyager (also dir.), Cybill.

FRANCIOSA, ANTHONY
Actor. b. New York, NY, Oct. 25, 1928. e. Ben Franklin h.s. in NY. Erwin Piscator's Dramatic Workshop (4-year scholarship). First stage part in YWCA play; joined Off-Broadway stage group; stock at Lake Tahoe, CA, Chicago and Boston.
THEATER: B'way: End as a Man, The Wedding Breakfast, A Hatful of Rain (Theatre World Award, Tony nom.), Rocket to the Moon, Grand Hotel. Tour: Love Letters.
PICTURES: A Face in the Crowd (debut, 1957), This Could Be The Night, A Hatful of Rain (Acad. Award nom.), Wild Is The Wind, The Long Hot Summer, The Naked Maja, Career, The Story on Page One, Go Naked in the World, Senilita (Carless), Period of Adjustment, Rio Conchos, The Pleasure Seekers, A Man Could Get Killed, Assault on a Queen, The Swinger, Fathom, In Enemy Country, The Sweet Ride, A Man Called Gannon, Ghost in the Noonday Sun, Across 110th Street, The Drowning Pool, Firepower, The World is Full of Married Men, Death Wish II, Julie Darling, Ghost in the Noonday Sun, Death Is in Fashion, Tenebrae, Help Me Dream, The Cricket, A Texas Legend, Backstreet Dreams, Death House, Brothers in Arms, Double Threat, City Hall.
TELEVISION: Series: Valentine's Day, The Name of the Game, Search, Matt Helm, Finder of Lost Loves. Movies: Fame is the Name of the Game, Deadly Hunt, Earth II, The Catcher, This is the West That Was, Matt Helm, Curse of the Black Widow, Side Show, Till Death Do Us Part, Ghost Writer. Mini-Series: Aspen, Wheels. Guest: Kraft Theatre, Philco Playhouse, Danger, Naked City, Arrest & Trial, Playhouse 90, etc Specials: A Lincoln Portrait, (narrator).

FRANCIS, ANNE
Actress b. Ossining, NY, Sept. 16, 1932. Child model; radio, TV shows as child & adult; on B'way in Lady in the Dark.
PICTURES: Summer Holiday (debut, 1948), So Young So Bad, Whistle at Eaton Falls, Elopement, Lydia Bailey, Dream Boat, A Lion Is in the Streets, Rocket Man, Susan Slept Here, Rogue Cop, Bad Day at Black Rock, Battle Cry, Blackboard Jungle, The Scarlet Coat, Forbidden Planet, The Rack, The Great American Pastime, The Hired Gun, Don't Go Near the Water, Crowded Sky, Girl of the Night, Satan Bug, Brainstorm, Funny Girl, Hook Line and Sinker, More Dead Than Alive, The Love God?, Impasse, Pancho Villa, Survival, Born Again, The High Fashion Murders, The Return, Little Vegas.
TELEVISION: Series: Honey West, My Three Sons, Dallas, Riptide. Guest: Partners in Crime, Crazy Like a Fox, Jake and the Fatman, Twilight Zone, Finder of Lost Loves, Golden Girls, Matlock, Murder She Wrote, Burke's Law. Movies: Wild Women, The Intruders, The Forgotten Man, Mongo's Back in Town, Fireball Forward, Haunts of the Very Rich, Cry Panic, FBI Vs. Alvin Karpis, The Last Survivors, A Girl Named Sooner, Banjo Hackett, Little Mo, The Rebels, Beggarman Thief, Detour to Terror, Rona Jaffe's Mazes and Monsters, Poor Little Rich Girl: The Barbara Hutton Story, Laguna Heat, My First Love, Love Can Be Murder, Fortune Hunter.

FRANCIS, ARLENE
Actress. r.n. Arlene Francis Kazanjian; b. Boston, MA, Oct. 20, 1908. e. Convent of Mount St. Vincent Acad., Riverdale, NY, Finch Finishing Sch., Theatre Guild Sch., NY. m. Martin Gabel, late actor. *Author:* That Certain Something (1960); Arlene Francis--A Memoir (1978).
THEATER: The Women (1937), Horse Eats Hat (Mercury Theater), Danton's Death, All That Glitters, Doughgirls, The Overtons, Once More With Feeling, Tchin-Tchin, Beekman Place, Mrs. Dally, Dinner at Eight, Kind Sir, Lion in Winter, Pal Joey, Who Killed Santa Claus?, Gigi, Social Security.
PICTURES: Murders in the Rue Morgue, Stage Door Canteen, All My Sons, One Two Three, The Thrill of It All, Fedora.
TELEVISION: Soldier Parade 1949-55, Blind Date, What's My Line; Home, Arlene Francis Show, Talent Patrol, etc.
RADIO: Arlene Francis Show, Emphasis, Monitor, Luncheon at Sardis.

FRANCIS, CONNIE
Singer. r.n. Constance Franconero. b. Newark, NJ, Dec. 12, 1938. Appeared, Star Time when 12 years old; won Arthur Godfrey's Talent Scout Show, 12 years old. Autobiography: Who's Sorry Now (1984). Regular on series The Jimmie Rodgers Show, 1959. Gold Records: Who's Sorry Now, My Happiness. Numerous vocalist awards.
PICTURES: Where the Boys Are, Follow the Boys, Looking For Love.

FRANCIS, FREDDIE
Producer, Director, Cinematographer. b. London, 1917. Joined Gaumont British Studios as apprentice to stills photographer; then clapper boy at B.I.P. Studios, Elstree; camera asst. at British Dominion. After W.W.II returned to Shepperton Studios to work for Korda and with Powell and Pressburger as cameraman.
PICTURES: *Director:* Two and Two Make Six (A Change of Heart/The Girl Swappers; debut, 1962), Paranoiac, Vengeance, The Evil of Frankenstein, Nightmare, Traitor's Gate, Hysteria, Dr. Terror's House of Horrors, The Skull, The Psychopath, The Deadly Bees, They Came from Beyond Space, Torture Garden, Dracula Has Risen from the Grave, Mumsy Nanny Sonny and Girly, Trog, Tales from the Crypt, The Creeping Flesh, Tales That Witness Madness, Son of Dracula, Craze, The Ghoul, Legend of the Werewolf, The Doctor and the Devils, Dark Tower. *Cinematographer:* Moby Dick (second unit photo., special effects), A Hill in Korea (Hell in Korea), Time Without Pity, Room at the Top, The Battle of the Sexes, Saturday Night and Sunday Morning, Sons and Lovers (Academy Award, 1960), The Innocents, Night Must Fall, The Elephant Man, The French Lieutenant's Woman, Dune, Memed My Hawk, Clara's Heart, Her Alibi, Brenda Starr, Glory (Academy Award, 1989), Man in the Moon, Cape Fear, School Ties, Princess Caraboo, Rainbow.
TELEVISION: *Movie:* A Life in the Theatre.

FRANCIS, KEVIN
Producer, Executive. b. London, England, 1949. Produced It's Life, Passport, Troubl with Canada, Persecution, The Ghoul, Legend of the Werewolf, etc. Executive produ. The Masks of Death, Murder Elite, A One-Way Ticket to Hollywood, etc. Exptn, prod. Film Technique Educational course for BFI. 1972-94, CEO Tyburn Prods. Ltd. 1994-present, Ar;ington Productions Ltd.

FRANKENHEIMER, JOHN
Director. b. Malba, NY, Feb. 19, 1930. e. Williams Coll. Actor, dir., summer stock; radio-TV actor, dir., Washington, DC; then joined CBS network in 1953. Theater: The Midnight Sun (1959).
PICTURES: The Young Stranger (debut, 1957), The Young Savages, Birdman of Alcatraz, All Fall Down, The Manchurian Candidate (also co-prod.), Seven Days in May, The Train, Seconds, Grand Prix, The Fixer, The Extraordinary Seaman, The Gypsy Moths, I Walk the Line, The Horsemen, The Impossible Object (Story of a Love Story), The Iceman Cometh, 99 and 44/100% Dead, French Connection II, Black Sunday, Prophecy, The Challenge, The Holcroft Covenant, 52 Pick-Up, Dead-Bang, The Fourth War, Year of the Gun, The Island of Dr. Moreau.
TELEVISION: *Series dir.:* I Remember Mama, You Are There, Danger, Climax, Studio One, Playhouse 90, Du Pont Show of the Month, Ford Startime, Sunday Showcase. *Specials:* The Comedian, For Whom the Bell Tolls, The Days of Wine and Roses, Old Man, The Turn of the Screw, The Browning Version, The Rainmaker. *Movies:* Against the Wall (Emmy Award, 1994), The Burning Season (Emmy Award, 1995; also co-prod.), George Wallace (Emmy Award, 1998). *Mini-Series:* Andersonville (Emmy Award, 1996).

FRANKLIN, BONNIE
Actress. b. Santa Monica, CA, Jan. 6, 1944. e. Smith College & UCLA.
THEATRE: *B'way.:* Applause (Theatre World Award, Tony nom. Outer Critics Circle award). *Off-B'way.:* Frankie and Johnny in the Claire de Lune, Grace & Glory, Dames at Sea, Your Own Thing.
TELEVISION: *Series:* One Day at a Time. *Movies:* The Law, A Guide for the Married Woman, Breaking Up Is Hard to Do, Portrait of a Rebel: Margaret Sanger, Your Place or Mine, Sister Margaret and Saturday Night Ladies, Shalom Sesame.

FRANKLIN, MICHAEL HAROLD
Executive. b. Los Angeles, CA, Dec. 25, 1923. e. U. of California, A.B., USC, LL.B. Admitted to CA bar, 1951; pvt. practice in L.A. 1951-52; atty. CBS, 1952-54; atty. Paramount, 1954-58; exec. dir. Writers Guild Am. West, Inc. 1958-78; natl exec. dir., Directors Guild of America 1978-. Mem. Am. Civil Liberties Union, Los Angeles Copyright Soc.

FRANKLIN, PAMELA
Actress. b. Tokyo, Japan, Feb. 4, 1950. Attended Elmshurst Ballet Sch., Camberley, Surrey.
PICTURES: The Innocents (debut, 1961), The Lion, The Third Secret, Flipper's New Adventure, The Nanny, Our Mother's House, The Prime of Miss Jean Brodie, The Night of the Following Day, And Soon the Darkness, Necromancy, Ace Eli and Rodger of the Skies, The Legend of Hell House, The Food of the Gods.
TELEVISION: *Movies:* The Horse Without a Head (theatrical in U.K.), See How They Run, David Copperfield (theatrical in U.K.), The Letters, Satan's School for Girls, Crossfire, Eleanor and Franklin.

FRANKLIN, RICHARD
Director, Producer, Writer. b. Melbourne, Australia, July 15, 1948. e. USC (Cinema, 1967).
PICTURES: *Director:* The True Story of Eskimo Nell (also co-prod., co-s.p.), Patrick (also co-prod., co-s.p.), The Blue Lagoon (co-prod. only), Road Games (also prod., co-s.p.), Psycho II, Cloak and Dagger, Into the Night (actor only), Link (also prod.), FX2, Hotel Sorrento (also prod.).
TELEVISION: *Pilots:* Beauty and the Beast, A Fine Romance. *Movie:* Running Delilah.

FRANKLIN, ROBERT A.
Executive. b. New York, NY, April 15. e. U. of Miami, B.B.A., 1958; Columbia Pacific U., M.B.A., 1979; Ph.D., 1980 majoring in marketing. Before entering film industry worked with House of Seagram, Canada Dry Corp., J. M. Mathes Adv. 1967, joined 20th Century-Fox as dir. of mkt. planning. Formed RP Marketing Intl. (entertainment consulting firm) in 1976 and World Research Systems (computer software marketer). 1981 joined MPAA; 1983, named v.p., admin. & info. services. 1986, named v.p. worldwide market research. Chmn., MPAA research comm.; member, AMA and ESOMAR.

FRANZ, ARTHUR
Actor. b. Perth Amboy, NJ, Feb. 29, 1920. e. Blue Ridge Coll., MD. U.S. Air Force. Radio, TV shows.
THEATER: A Streetcar Named Desire, Second Threshold.
PICTURES: Jungle Patrol (debut, 1948), Roseanna McCoy, The Red Light, The Doctor and the Girl, Sands of Iwo Jima, Red Stallion in the Rockies, Three Secrets, Tarnished, Abbott and Costello Meet the Invisible Man, Flight to Mars, Submarine Command, Strictly Dishonorable, The Sniper, Rainbow 'Round My Shoulder, The Member of the Wedding, Eight Iron Men, Invaders From Mars, Bad for Each Other, The Eddie Cantor Story, Flight Nurse, The Caine Mutiny, Steel Cage, Battle Taxi, New Orleans Uncensored, Bobby Ware Is Missing, Beyond a Reasonable Doubt, The Wild Party, Running Target, The Devil's Hairpin, Back From the Dead, The Unholy Wife, Hellcats of the Navy, The Young Lions, The Flame Barrier, Monster on the Campus, Atomic Submarine, The Carpetbaggers, Alvarez Kelly, Anzio, The Sweet Ride, The Human Factor, Sister of Death, That Championship Season.
TELEVISION: *Movies:* Murder or Mercy, Jennifer: A Woman's Story, Bogie.

FRANZ, DENNIS
Actor. b. Chicago, IL, Oct. 28, 1944. Started in Chicago Theatre.
PICTURES: Stony Island, Dressed to Kill, Blow Out, Psycho II, Body Double, A Fine Mess, The Package, Die Hard 2, The Player, American Buffalo.
TELEVISION: *Series:* Chicago Story, Bay City Blues, Hill Street Blues, Beverly Hills Buntz, Nasty Boys, N.Y.P.D. Blue (Emmy Award, 1994, 1996, 1997). *Movies:* Chicago Story (pilot), Deadly Messages, Kiss Shot, Moment of Truth: Caught in the Crossfire (also co-prod.), Texas Justice.

FRASER, BRENDAN
Actor. b. Indianapolis, IN, 1968. Raised in Holland, Switzerland, Canada. e. Actors' Conservatory, Cornish College of the Arts, Seattle. Member of Laughing Horse Summer Theatre in Ellensberg, WA.
THEATER: Waiting for Godot, Arms and the Man, Romeo and Juliet, A Midsummer Night's Dream, Moonchildren, Four Dogs and a Bone.
PICTURES: Dogfight (debut, 1991), Encino Man, School Ties, Twenty Bucks, Younger and Younger, With Honors, Airheads, The Scout, Now and Then, The Passion of Darkly Noon, Mrs. Winterbourne, George of the Jungle, Gods and Monsters.
TELEVSION: *Movie:* Guilty Until Proven Innocent. *Pilot:* My Old School.

FRAZIER, SHEILA E.
Actress, Producer. b. Bronx, NY, Nov. 13. e. Englewood, NJ.
Was exec. sect'y. and high-fashion model. Steered to acting
career by friend Richard Roundtree. Studied drama with N.Y.
Negro Ensemble Co. and New Federal Theatre, N.Y., also with
Bob Hickey at H.B. Studios, N.Y. Currently working as a TV pro-
ducer.
PICTURES: Super Fly (debut), Superfly T.N.T., The Super Cops,
California Suite, What Does It Take?, Three the Hard Way, The
Hitter, I'm Gonna Git You Sucker.
TELEVISION: *Movie*: Firehouse. *Mini-Series*: King. *Series*: The
Lazarus Syndrome.

FREARS, STEPHEN
Director. b. Leicester, Eng., June 20, 1941. e. Cambridge, B.A
in law. Joined Royal Court Theatre, working with Lindsay
Anderson on plays. Later assisted Karel Reisz on Morgan: A
Suitable Case for Treatment, Albert Finney on Charlie Bubbles,
and Lindsay Anderson on If ... Worked afterwards mostly in TV,
directing and producing. First directorial credit was 30-minute
film The Burning, 1967.
PICTURES: Gumshoe (dir. debut 1971), Bloody Kids, The Hit,
My Beautiful Laundrette, Prick Up Your Ears, Sammy and Rosie
Get Laid, Dangerous Liaisons, The Grifters, Hero (GB:
Accidental Hero), The Snapper, Mary Reilly, The Van.
TELEVISION: A Day Out (1971), England Their England, Match
of the Day, Sunset Across the Bay, Three Men in a Boat, Daft as
a Brush, Playthings, Early Struggles, Last Summer, 18 Months
to Balcomb Street, A Visit from Miss Protheroe, Abel's Will, Cold
Harbour, Song of Experience; series of six Alan Bennett plays;
Long Distance Information, Going Gently, Loving Walter, Saigon:
Year of the Cat, December Flower.

FREDERICKSON, H. GRAY, JR.
Producer. b. Oklahoma City, OK, July 21, 1937. e. U. of
Lausanne, Switzerland, 1958\-59; U. of Oklahoma. B.A., 1960.
Worked one yr. with Panero, Weidlinger & Salvatori Engineering
Co., Rome Italy. In 1979 named v.p. of feature films, Lorimar
Films.
PICTURES: Candy, Inspector Sterling, Gospel 70, An Italian in
America, The Man Who Wouldn't Die, The Good, the Bad and
the Ugly, Intrigue in Suez, How to Learn to Love Women, God's
Own Country, Wedding March, An American Wife, Natika, Echo
in the Village, Little Fauss and Big Halsey, Making It, The
Godfather (assoc. prod.), The Godfather Part II (co-prod;
Academy Award for Best Picture, 1974), Hit (exec. prod.),
Apocalypse Now (co.-prod.; Acad. Award nom.), One From the
Heart, The Outsiders, UHF, The Godfather Part III (co-prod.),
Ladybugs (exec. prod.), Bad Girls (story), Heaven's Prisoners.
TELEVISION: *Producer*. The Return of Mickey Spillane's Mike
Hammer, Houston Nights, Staying Afloat.

FREEDMAN, JERROLD
Director, Writer. b. Philadelphia, PA, Oct.29, 1942. e. Univ. of
PA. Novel: Against the Wind.
PICTURES: Kansas City Bomber, Borderline, Native Son.
TELEVISION: *Director-Writer*. Blood Sport, Betrayal, Some Kind
of Miracle, Legs, This Man Stands Alone. *Director*: The Streets
of L.A., The Boy Who Drank Too Much, Victims, The Seduction
of Gina, Best Kept Secrets, Seduced, Family Sins, Unholy
Matrimony, The Comeback, Night Walk, A Cold Night's Death,
The Last Angry Man, Goodnight Sweet Wife: A Murder in
Boston, Condition: Critical.

FREEMAN, AL, JR.
Actor. b. San Antonio, TX, March 21, 1934. e. LA City Coll.
THEATER: The Long Dream (1960), Kicks and Co., Tiger Tiger
Burning Bright, Trumpets of the Lord, Blues for Mister Charlie,
Conversation at Midnight, Look to the Lilies, Are You Now or
Have You Ever Been?, The Poison Tree.
PICTURES: Torpedo Run, Black Like Me, Dutchman, Finian's
Rainbow, The Detective, Castle Keep, The Lost Man, A Fable
(also dir.), Seven Hours to Judgement, Malcolm X.
TELEVISION: *Movies*: My Sweet Charlie, Assault at West Point.
Mini-Series: Roots: The Next Generations, King. *Series*: Hot L
Baltimore, One Life to Live (Emmy Award, 1979).

FREEMAN, JOEL
Producer. b. Newark, NJ, June 12, 1922. e. Upsala Coll. Began
career at MGM studios, 1941. Air Force Mot. Pic. Unit 1942-46.
Became assist. dir. at RKO, 1946. 1948 returned to MGM as
asst. dir.; later assoc. prod. 1956 entered indep. field as prod.
Supv. on various features and TV series. 1960 to Warner Bros.,
assoc. producing Sunrise at Campobello, The Music Man and
Act One. After such films as Camelot and Finian's Rainbow,
became studio exec. at Warners. Presently senior v.p. prod.,
New Century Entertainment Corp.
PICTURES: *Producer*: The Heart Is a Lonely Hunter, Shaft,
Trouble Man, Love at First Bite, Octagon, The Kindred, Soapdish
(co-prod.).

FREEMAN, KATHLEEN
Actress. b. Chicago, IL, Feb. 17, 1919.
PICTURES: Casbah (debut, 1948), The Saxon Charm, The
Naked City, Behind Locked Doors, Mr. Belvedere Goes to
College, The Reformer and the Redhead, A Life of Her Own,
The House by the River, Lonely Hearts Bandits, Appointment
With Danger, A Place in the Sun, The Company She Keeps, O.
Henry's Full House, Singin' in the Rain, Talk About a Stranger,
Love Is Better Than Ever, She's Back on Broadway, The Affairs
of Dobie Gillis, Half a Hero, Athena, Artists and Models, The Far
Country, The Midnight Story, Kiss Them for Me, Houseboat, The
Fly, The Missouri Traveler, The Buccaneer, North to Alaska, The
Ladies Man, The Errand Boy, Madison Avenue, The Nutty
Professor, The Disorderly Orderly, Mail Order Bride, The
Rounders, Marriage on the Rocks, Three on a Couch, Point
Blank, Hook Line and Sinker, The Good Guys and the Bad
Guys, Myra Breckinridge, The Ballad of Cable Hogue, Which
Way to the Front?, Support Your Local Gunfighter, Stand Up and
Be Counted, Where Does It Hurt?, Unholy Rollers, Your Three
Minutes Are Up, The Strongest Man in the World, The
Norsemen, The Blues Brothers, Heartbeeps, The Best of Times,
Malibu Bikini Shop, Dragnet, Innerspace, In the Mood, The
Willies, Gremlins 2: The New Batch, Joey Takes a Cab, Dutch,
FernGully ... The Last Rainforest (voice), Little Nemo:
Adventures in Slumberland (voice), Hocus Pocus, Naked Gun
33 1/3: The Final Insult, At First Sight.
TELEVISION: *Series*: Topper, Mayor of the Town, It's About
Time, Funny Face, Lotsa Luck. *Movies*: But I Don't Want to Get
Married!, Call Her Mom, Hitched, The Daughters of Joshua
Cabe Return, The Last Ride of the Dalton Gang.

FREEMAN, MORGAN
Actor. b. Memphis, TN, June 1, 1937. e. LA City Coll. Served in
Air Force 1955-59 before studying acting. Worked as dancer at
NY's 1964 World's Fair. Broadway debut in Hello Dolly! with
Pearl Bailey. Took over lead role in Purlie. Became known
nationally when he played Easy Reader on TV's The Electric
Company (1971-76).
THEATER: *NY*: Ostrich Feathers, The Nigger Lovers, Hello
Dolly!, Scuba Duba, Purlie, Cockfight, The Last Street Play, The
Mighty Gents (Drama Desk & Clarence Derwent Awards),
Coriolanus (Obie Award), Julius Caesar, Mother Courage, Buck,
Driving Miss Daisy (Obie Award), The Gospel at Colonus (Obie
Award), The Taming of the Shrew.
PICTURES: Who Says I Can't Ride a Rainbow? (debut, 1972),
Brubaker, Eyewitness, Death of a Prophet, Harry and Son,
Teachers, Marie, That Was Then...This Is Now, Street Smart (NY
& LA Film Critics & Natl. Board of Review Awards; Acad. Award
nom., 1987), Clean and Sober, Lean on Me, Johnny Handsome,
Glory, Driving Miss Daisy (Natl. Board of Review & Golden
Globe Awards; Acad. Award nom., 1989), The Bonfire of the
Vanities, Robin Hood: Prince of Thieves, The Power of One,
Unforgiven, Bopha (dir. only), The Shawshank Redemption
(Acad. Award nom.), Outbreak, Seven, Moll Flanders, Chain
Reaction, Hurricane (dir., prod., s.p., only), Kiss the Girls.
TELEVISION: *Movies*: Hollow Image, Attica, The Marva Collins
Story, The Atlanta Child Murders, Resting Place, Flight For Life,
Roll of Thunder Hear My Cry, Charlie Smith and the Fritter Tree,
Clinton and Nadine. *Series*: The Electric Company, Another
World (1982-4). *Specials* (narrator): The Civil War, Follow the
Drinking Gourd, The Promised Land.

FREEZER, HARLENE
Executive. Pres., New York Women in Film & Television.

FRESCO, ROBERT M.
Writer. b. Burbank, CA, Oct. 18, 1928. e. Los Angeles City Coll.
Newspaperman. Los Angeles, 1946-47; U.S. Army, 1948-49;
staff writer, Hakim Prod., 1950-51; various screenplays, 1951-
56.
PICTURES: Tarantula, They Came to Destroy the Earth,
Monolith.
TELEVISION: Scripts for Science Fiction Theatre, Highway
Patrol.

FREWER, MATT
Actor. b. Washington, D. C., Jan. 4, 1958. Raised in Victoria,
British Columbia. Studied drama at the Bristol Old Vic Theatre,
appearing in Romeo and Juliet, Macbeth, Waiting for Godot,
Deathtrap.
PICTURES: The Lords of Discipline (debut, 1983), Supergirl,
Spies Like Us, Ishtar, The Fourth Protocol, Far From Home,
Speed Zone, Honey I Shrunk the Kids, Short Time, The Taking
of Beverly Hills, Twenty Bucks, National Lampoon's Senior Trip,
Lawnmower Man II.
TELEVISION: *BBC*: Tender is the Night, Robin of Sherwood;
U.S. Series: Max Headroom, Doctor Doctor, Shaky Ground, The
Pink Panther (voice), Outer Limits. *Movie*: The Positively True
Adventures of the Alleged Texas Cheerleader-Murdering Mom,
The Day My Parents Ran Away, Kissinger and Nixon. *Mini-
Series*: The Stand. *Guest*: Miami Vice. Specials: Long Shadows,
In Search of Dr. Seuss.

FRICKER, BRENDA
Actress. b. Dublin, Ireland, Feb. 17, 1945. Appeared in short film The Woman Who Married Clark Gable. Theatre work includes appearances with the RSC, Royal Court Theatre, and The National Theatre.
PICTURES: Quatermass Conclusion, Bloody Kids, Our Exploits at West Poley, My Left Foot (Academy Award, best supporting actress, 1989), The Field, Utz, Home Alone 2: Lost in New York, So I Married an Axe Murderer, Angels in the Outfield, A Man of No Importance, Moll Flanders, A Time to Kill.
TELEVISION: Series: Casualty. Specials: Licking Hitler, The House of Bernarda Alba, The Ballroom Romance. Mini-Series: Brides of Christ, The Sound and the Silence, A Woman of Independent Means.

FRIEDBERG, A. ALAN
Executive. b. New York, NY, Apr. 13, 1932. e. Columbia Coll., B.A. 1952, Junior Phi Beta Kappa, Summa Cum Laude; Harvard Law School 1955. Past pres. and chmn. of bd. NATO, currently memb. of exec. committee. V.P. Foundation of Motion Picture Pioneers. 1990, named chmn. Loews Theatre Mgmt. Co. Exhib. consult., Sony Pictures Entertainment, 1992.

FRIEDKIN, JOHN
Executive. b. New York, NY, Dec. 9, 1926. e. Columbia Univ. Entered industry in New York as publicist for Columbia Pictures; spent eight years at Young & Rubicam adv. agency. Formed Sumner & Friedkin with Gabe Sumner as partner; left to join Rogers & Cowan, where named v.p. In 1967 resigned to join 20th-Fox, moving to California in 1972 when home offices were transferred. Appointed Fox v.p. worldwide publ. & promo. In 1979 joined Warner Bros. as v.p., adv. pub. for intl. div; 1988, joined Odyssey Distributors Ltd. as sr. v.p., intl. marketing. 1990, formed indept. marketing firm. 1995, rep. for Australia's Kennedy Miller Entertainment.

FRIEDKIN, WILLIAM
Director, Writer. b. Chicago, IL, Aug. 29, 1939. m. producer Sherry Lansing. Joined WGN-TV, 1957, worked for National Education TV, did TV documentaries before feature films. Dir. B'way play Duet for One.
PICTURES: Director: Good Times (debut, 1967), The Night They Raided Minsky's, The Birthday Party, The Boys in the Band, The French Connection (Academy Award, 1971), The Exorcist, Sorcerer (also prod.), The Brink's Job, Cruising (also s.p.), Deal of the Century, To Live and Die in L.A. (also co-s.p.), Rampage (also s.p.), The Guardian (also co-s.p.), Blue Chips, Jade.
TELEVISION: Movies: C.A.T. Squad (also exec. prod.), C.A.T. Squad: Python Wolf, Jailbreakers. Special: Barbra Streisand: Putting It Together. Series: Tales From the Crypt (On a Dead Man's Chest).

FRIEDMAN, JOSEPH
Executive. b. New York, NY. e. City Coll. of New York, 1940-42, NYU, 1946-47. U.S. Navy 3 yrs. Asst. to nat'l dir. field exploitation, Warner Bros. Pictures, 1946-58; nat'l exploitation mgr., Paramount 1958-60; exec. asst. to dir. of adv., publicity & exploitation, Para., 1961; dir. adv. & pub., Paramount 1964; v.p., Para., 1966; v.p. in charge of mktg., 1968; v.p., adv., and p.r., Avco Embassy, 1969; v.p., p.r. American Film Theatre, 1973; v.p., adv. and p.r., ITC, motion picture div., 1976, pres., Joseph Friedman Mktg. & Adv., Inc., 1977. Exec. dir. New Jersey M.P. & T.V. Commission, 1978; v.p. worldwide adv./pub. /promo., Edie & Ely Landau, Inc., 1980; exec. dir., NJ Motion Picture & Television Commission, 1981.

FRIEDMAN, PAUL
Executive. e. Princeton U. Woodrow Wilson Sch. of Public & Intl. Affairs, Columbia Sch. of Journalism. 1967, joined NBC News as newswriter in NY; 1970-75, served as reporter for WRC-TV in D.C., field prod. for The Huntley-Brinkley Report, sr. prod. for NBC Weekend Nightly News, exec. prod. of News 4 New York, sr. prod. NBC Nightly News; 1976-79, was exec. prod. of Today; 1982, joined ABC News as sr. prod. in London; there became dir. of news coverage for Europe, Africa, Middle East, while as operating the ABC News Bureaus in those areas; 1988-92, exec. prod. of World News Tonight With Peter Jennings; Jan. 1993 named exec. v.p. of ABC News.

FRIEDMAN, ROBERT L.
Executive. b. Bronx, NY, March 1, 1930. e. DeWitt Clinton H.S, Bronx. Started as radio announcer and commentator with Armed Forces Radio Service in Europe and U.S. sr. v.p., distrib. & mktg., United Artists Corp.; pres. domestic distribution, Columbia Pictures. 1984, named pres. AMC Entertainment Int'l Inc. 1992, named pres. of AMC Entertainment - the Motion Picture Group. On Century City bd. of dirs.; chmn. of Entertainment Industry Council. Member: M.P. Associates Foundation, Phila., pres. 2 yrs.; Variety Club (on board) M.P. Pioneers; (on board) area chmn. Distrib., chmn., Will Rogers Hospital Foundation, American Film Inst., Academy of M.P. Arts & Sciences. Member on DARE bd. of dirs.

FRIEDMAN, SEYMOUR MARK
Director. b. Detroit, MI, Aug. 17, 1917. e. Magdalene Coll., Cambridge, B.S. 1936; St. Mary's Hospital Medical Sch., London. Entered m.p. ind. as asst. film ed. 1937; 2nd asst. dir. 1938; 1st asst. dir. 1939, on budget pictures; entered U.S. Army 1942; returned to ind. 1946; dir. Columbia Pictures 1947. Vice president & executive production for Columbia Pictures Television, division of Columbia Pictures Industries, 1955. Member: Screen Directors Guild.
PICTURES: To the Ends of the Earth, Rusty's Birthday, Prison Warden, Her First Romance, Rookie Fireman, Son of Dr. Jekyll, Loan Shark, Flame of Calcutta, I'll Get You, Saint's Girl Friday, Khyber Patrol, African Manhunt, Secret of Treasure Mountain.

FRIELS, COLIN
Actor. b. Scotland, e. Australia Natl. Inst. of Dramatic Art. m. actress Judy Davis. First began acting with the State Theatre Co. of So. Australia and the Sydney Theatre Co. Theatre includes Sweet Bird of Youth and Hedda Gabler. TV includes special Stark.
PICTURES: Buddies, Monkey Grip, For the Term of His Natural Life, Kangaroo, Malcolm, High Tide, Ground Zero, Grievous Bodily Harm, Warm Nights on a Slow Moving Train, Darkman, Class Action, Dingo, A Good Man in Africa., Angel Baby, Back of Beyond.

FRIENDLY, FRED W.
Producer, Journalist, Writer, Educator. r.n. Fred Wachenheimer. b. New York, NY, October 30, 1915. e. Cheshire Acad., Nichols Junior Coll. U.S. Army, Information and Education Section 1941-45. Editor and correspondent for China, Burma and India for CBI Roundup 1941-45. President, CBS News 1964-66: Edward R. Murrow Professor of Broadcast Journalism, Columbia U., 1966-present; advisor on TV, Ford Foundation, 1966-; member: Mayor's Task Force on CATV and Telecommunications, NYC, 1968; teacher and director: Television Workshop, Columbia U. Sch. of Journalism. RADIO Producer-writer-narrator: Footprints in the Sand of Time, 1938; co-prod. Hear It Now, 1951. Ten George Foster Peabody Awards; DeWitt Carter Reddick Award, 1980; See It Now (35 major awards incl. Overseas Press Club, Page One Award, New York Newspaper Guild, National Headliners Club Award, 1954); CBS Reports (40 major awards). Honorary L.H.D. degrees: U. of Rhode Island, Grinnell U., Iowa U. Military: Legion of Merit medal, Soldier's Medal for heroism, 4 Battle Stars.
AUTHOR: See It Now (1955); Due to Circumstances Beyond Our Control (1967); The Good Guys, the Bad Guys and the First Amendment: Free Speech vs. Fairness in Broadcasting (1976), Minnesota Rag: The Dramatic Story of the Landmark Supreme Court Case that Gave New Meaning to Freedom of the Press (1981); The Constitution: That Delicate Balance (1984); The Presidency and the Constitution (1987).
(d. March 3, 1998)

FRIES, CHARLES W.
Executive, Producer. b. Cincinnati, OH. e. Ohio State U., B.S. Exec.-prod., Ziv Television; v.p., prod., Screen Gems; v.p., prod., Columbia Pictures; exec. v.p., prod. and exec. prod., Metromedia Prod. Corp., 1970-74; pres., exec. prod., Alpine Prods. and Charles Fries Prods. 1974-83; chmn. & pres., Fries Entertainment, 1984-1995; pres., Charles Fries Prods., 1996. Nat'l. treas., TV Academy; pres., Alliance TV Film Producers; exec. comm., MPPA. Chmn., Caucus of Producers, Writers and Directors, board of governors, secretary, Exec. committee & vice-chmn., American Film Institute. V.P. & dir. of the Center Theatre Group.
PICTURES: Prod.: Cat People, Flowers in the Attic, Troop Beverly Hills, Screamers.
TELEVISION: Movies: Toughlove, The Right of the People, Intimate Strangers, Bitter Harvest, A Rumor of War, Blood Vows: The Story of a Mafia Wife, The Alamo: 13 Days to Glory, Intimate Betrayal, Drop Out Mother, Crash Course, Supercarrier, Bridge to Silence, The Case of the Hillside Strangler, Deadly Web. Small Sacrifices, The Martian Chronicles. Specials: It's Howdy Doody Time: A 40 Year Celebration.

FRONTIERE, DOMINIC
Executive, Composer. b. New Haven, CT, June 17, 1931. e. Yale School of Music. Studied composing, arranging and conducting; concert accordionist, World's Champion Accordionist, 1943; An Hour with Dominic Frontiere, WNHC-TV, New Haven, 3 years, 1947; exec. vice-pres., musical dir., Daystar Prods. Composer or arranger over 75 films.
PICTURES: Giant, Gentlemen Prefer Blondes, Let's Make Love, High Noon, Meet Me in Las Vegas, 10,000 Bedrooms, Hit the Deck, Marriage-Go-Round, The Right Approach, One Foot in Hell, Hero's Island, Hang 'Em High, Popi, Barquero, Chisum, A for Alpha, Cancel My Reservation, Hammersmith is Out, Freebie and the Bean, Brannigan, The Gumball Rally, Cleopatra Jones and the Casino of Gold, The Stunt Man, Modern Problems, The Aviator.
TELEVISION: Composer-conductor: The New Breed, Stoney Burke, Bankamericard commercials (Venice Film Fest. Award for best use of original classical music for filmed TV commercials), Outer Limits, Branded, Iron Horse, Rat Patrol, Flying Nun, The Invaders, Name of the Game, That Girl, Twelve O'Clock High, Zig Zag, The Young Rebel, The Immortal, Fugitive, The Love War. Movie: Washington Behind Closed Doors.

FRUMKES, EDWARD E.
Executive. b. New York, May 1, 1958. e. George Washington University. BA intl finance, MBA intl marketing. Joined Columbia Pictures as Intl. Financial Analyst, then became mgr. special projects. Moved to London as Columbia's Dir., ad-pub., Europe, Africa, Middle East. Returned to NY as v.p. ad-pub. Joined Warner Bros. in 1988 as Dir., intl. thearical dist; v.p.; 1989; sr. v.p., 1992; exec. v.p., 1993; pres., WB Intl. theatrical dist., 1996.

FUCHS, FRED
Producer.
PICTURES: *Exec. Prod.*: Vietnam War Story: The Last Days, The Spirit of '76, The Godfather: Part III, The Secret Garden, Mary Shelley's Frankenstein, Don Juan DeMarco, Haunted, Jack, Buddy, The Rainmaker. Producer: New York Stories (segment 2), Tucker: The Man and His Dream, Bram Stoker's Dracula
TELEVISION: *Series*: Faerie Tale Theater. *Mini-Series*: The Odyssey. *Movies*: Dark Angel.

FUCHS, LEO L.
Independent producer. b. Vienna, June 14, 1929. Moved to U.S., 1939. e. Vienna and New York. U.S. Army cameraman 1951-53; int'l. mag. photographer until entered motion pictures as producer with Universal in Hollywood in 1961.
PICTURES: Gambit, A Fine Pair, Sunday Lovers, Just the Way You Are.

FUCHS, MICHAEL
Executive. b. New York, NY, March 9, 1946. e. Union Coll., NYU Law School (J.D. degree). Show business lawyer before joining Home Box Office in 1976, developing original and p.r. programming. Named chmn. and CEO of HBO in 1984. 1982-87, v.p. Time Inc. in NY; 1987-1995, exec. v.p. Time Inc.

FUEST, ROBERT
Director. b. London, 1927. Early career as painter, graphic designer. Ent. TV industry as designer with ABC-TV, 1958. 1962: directing doc., commercials. 1966: Wrote and dir. Just Like a Woman, 1967-68; dir. 7 episodes of The Avengers, 1969: wrote and directed 6 episodes of The Optimists.
PICTURES: And Soon the Darkness, Wuthering Heights, Doctor Phibes, Doctor Phibes Rides Again (also s.p.), The Final Programme (also s.p., design), The Devil's Rain, The Geller Effect (s.p. only), The New Avengers, The Gold Bug, Revenge of the Stepford Wives, The Big Stuffed Dog, Mystery on Fire Island, Aphrodite, Worlds Beyond, Cat's Eyes.

FULLER, SAMUEL
Director, Writer, Producer, Actor. b. Worcester, MA, Aug. 12, 1912. m. actress Christa Lang. Copy boy, N.Y. Journal; reporter, rewrite man, N.Y. Graphic, N.Y Journal, San Diego Sun; journeyman reporter many papers. Writer of many orig. s.p.; in U.S. Army, 16th Inf. 1st U.S. Inf. Div. 1942-45.
AUTHOR: Crown of India, 144 Piccadilly Street, Dead Pigeon on Beethoven Street, The Rifle, The Big Red One, The Dark Page, La Grande Melee (Battle Royal), Pecos Bill and the Soho Kid, Once Upon Samuel Fuller (Stories of America; interview book), Manhattan 1930.
PICTURES: *Director-Writer:* I Shot Jesse James, Baron of Arizona, The Steel Helmet (also prod.), Fixed Bayonets, Park Row (also prod.), Pickup On South Street, Hell and High Water, House of Bamboo, Run of the Arrow (also prod.), China Gate (also prod.), Forty Guns, Verboten!, The Crimson Kimono (also prod.), Underworld U.S.A. (also prod.), Merrill's Marauders, Shock Corridor (also prod.), The Naked Kiss (also prod.), Dead Pigeon on Beethoven Street, The Big Red One, White Dog (also actor), Thieves After Dark, Street of No Return (also actor, edit.), Tini Kling. Actor: The Last Movie, The American Friend, Scott Joplin, 1941, Hammett, State of Things, Slapstick of Another Kind, Return to Salem's Lot, Helsinki Napoli All Night Long, Sons, Somebody to Love, Tigrero: A Movie That Was Never Made, The Typewriter—the Rifle and the Movie Camera, The End of Violence (actor only).
(d. Oct. 31, 1997)

FUNT, ALLEN
Producer, Performer. b. New York, NY, Sept. 16, 1914. e. Cornell U. Best known as producer and creator of Candid Camera series which originated on radio in 1947 as Candid Microphone which inspired theatrical film shorts. TV version began in 1948 as Candid Mike, changed in 1949 to Candid Camera which played off and on until 1960 when became regular series on CBS, lasting until 1967. Revived briefly in early '70s and again in mid '80s in new format; then syndicated as The New Candid Camera. Joined in 1988 by son Peter Funt as host and prod. Specials: Candid Camera Christmas Special, Candid Camera: Eat! Eat! Eat!, Candid Camera on Wheels, Candid Camera's Vacation, Candid Camera Getting Physical, Candid Camera Goes to the Doctor, Candid Camera's Sporting Life. Produced and starred in film, What Do You Say to a Naked Lady?, Candid Camera's 50th Anniversary.

FURIE, SIDNEY J.
Director, Writer, Producer. b. Toronto, Canada, Feb. 28, 1933. Ent. TV and films 1954. Canadian features include: Dangerous Age, A Cool Sound from Hell. Also dir. many Hudson Bay TV series. To England 1960. 1961 appt. exec. dir. Galaworldfilm Productions, Ltd.
PICTURES: The Snake Woman, Doctor Blood's Coffin, Wonderful to Be Young, Night of Passion (also prod., s.p.), The Young Ones, The Leather Boys, Wonderful Life, The Ipcress File, The Appaloosa, The Naked Runner, The Lawyer, Little Fauss and Big Halsy, Lady Sings the Blues, Hit!, Sheila Levine Is Dead and Living in New York, Gable and Lombard, The Boys in Company C, The Entity, Purple Hearts (also prod., s.p.), Iron Eagle, Superman IV: The Quest For Peace, Iron Eagle II (also co-s.p.), The Taking of Beverly Hills, Ladybugs, Hollow Point, Iron Eagle IV, The Rage, Top of the World.

FURLONG, EDWARD
Actor. b. Glendale, CA, Aug. 2, 1977. Discovered by casting agent for Terminator 2, having no previous acting experience. Appeared in Aerosmith video Livin' on the Edge.
PICTURES: Terminator 2: Judgment Day (debut, 1991), Pet Sematary 2, American Heart, A Home of Our Own, Brainscan, Little Odessa, The Grass Harp, Before and After.

FURMAN, ROY L.
Attorney, Executive. b. New York, NY, April 19, 1939. e. Brooklyn Coll., A.B. 1960; Harvard U., L.L.B. 1963. Pres., Furman Selz. Chmn., Film Society of Lincoln Center.

FURST, AUSTIN O.
Executive. e. Lehigh U., B.S. in economics/marketing. Began career in mktg. dept., Proctor and Gamble; 1972, joined Time Inc. as dir., new subscription sales for Time magazine; later joined Time Inc.'s new magazine dev. staff for People magazine; named circulation mgr., People magazine, 1974; 1975 named pres., Time Inc.'s Computer Television Inc., a pay-per-view hotel operation and was responsible for successful turnaround and sale of co.; 1976, v.p., programming, Home Box Office; named exec. v.p. HBO, 1979; appointed pres. and CEO, Time-Life Films, Inc., 1980; 1981 established Vestron after acquiring home video rights to Time/Life Video Library; chmn. and CEO, Vestron, Inc.

G

GABOR, ZSA ZSA
Actress. r.n. Sari Gabor. b. Hungary, Feb. 6, 1918. e. Lausanne, Switzerland. Stage debut in Europe. *Author:* Zsa Zsa's Complete Guide to Men (1969), How to Get a Man How to Keep a Man and How to Get Rid of a Man (1971), One Lifetime is Not Enough (1991). As accomplished horsewoman has won many prizes in various intl. horse shows. Stage work incl. 40 Carats, Blithe Spirit.
PICTURES: Lovely to Look At, We're Not Married, Moulin Rouge, The Story of Three Loves, Lili, Three Ring Circus, The Most Wanted Man in the World, Death of a Scoundrel, Girl in the Kremlin, The Man Who Wouldn't Talk, Touch of Evil, Queen of Outer Space, Country Music Holiday, For the First Time, Pepe, Boys' Night Out, Picture Mommy Dead, Arrivederci Baby, Jack of Diamonds, Won Ton Ton the Dog Who Saved Hollywood, Frankenstein's Great Aunt Tillie, A Nightmare on Elm Street 3, The Naked Gun 2 1/2: The Smell of Fear, Happily Ever After (voice).

GAIL, MAX
Actor. b. Grosse Ile, MI, Apr. 5, 1943. e. William Coll. B.A. Economics, Univ. of Mich M.B.A.
THEATER: NY: The Babe, One Flew Over the Cuckoo's Nest (also S.F.). LA: Visions of Kerouac.
PICTURES: The Organization, Dirty Harry, D.C. Cab, Heart-breakers, Pontiac Moon, Mind Lies, Sodbusters, Ox and the Eye, Lords of Tanglewood.
TELEVISION: *Series*: Barney Miller, Whiz Kids, Normal Life. *Mini-Series*: Pearl. *Movies*: The Priest Killer, Like Mom Like Me, Desperate Women, The 11th Victim, The Aliens Are Coming, Fun and Games, Letting Go, The Other Lover, Killer in the Mirror, Intimate Strangers, Can You Feel Me Dancing?, Tonight's the Night, Man Against the Mob, The Outside Woman, Ride With the Wind, Robin Cook's Mortal Fear, Naomi & Winona: Love Can Build a Bridge, Secret Agent (prod.), Wrong Side of the Fence (prod.).

GALE, BOB
Writer, Producer. b. St. Louis, MO, May 25, 1951. e. USC Sch. of Cinema. Joined with friend Robert Zemeckis to write screenplays, starting with episode for TV series, McCloud. Also co-wrote story for The Nightstalker series. Turned to feature films, co-writing with Zemeckis script for I Wanna Hold Your Hand, on which Gale also acted as associate producer. Exec. prod. of CBS animated series Back to the Future. Wrote and directed interactive feature Mr. Payback.
PICTURES: I Wanna Hold Your Hand (co-s.p., co-assoc. prod.), 1941 (co-s.p.), Used Cars (prod., co-s.p.), Back to the Future (co-prod., s.p.), Back to the Future Part II (prod., co-s.p.), Back to the Future Part III (prod., s.p.), Trespass (co-exec. prod., co-s.p.), Tales From the Crypt: Bordello of Blood (co-s.p.).
TELEVISION: *Series*: Back to the Future (animated); exec. prod.), Tales From the Crypt (wrote, dir. House of Horror).

GALE, GEORGE

Executive. b. Budapest, Hungary, May 26, 1919. e. Sorbonne U., Paris, France. Feature editor, Budapest Ed., U.S. Army Pictorial Service. Feature and TV editor MGM, Hal Roach, Disney Studios; prod. and prod. exec. Ivan Tors; American National Enterprises, Inc. Producer and director. Supervised the production of over 30 features for tv syndication and numerous theatrical features. Member ACE and Academy of Motion Picture Arts and Sciences. Formed George Gale Productions, Inc. in 1976.

GALLAGHER, PETER

Actor. b. New York, NY, Aug. 19, 1955. e. Tufts Univ.
THEATER: *NY*: Hair (1977 revival), Grease, A Doll's Life (Theatre World Award), The Corn is Green, The Real Thing (Clarence Derwent Award), Long Day's Journey Into Night (Tony Award nom.; also London), Guys & Dolls. Also: Another Country, Pride & Prejudice (both Long Wharf), Pal Joey.
PICTURES: The Idolmaker (debut, 1980), Summer Lovers, Dream Child, My Little Girl, High Spirits, Sex Lies and Videotape, Tune in Tomorrow, Late for Dinner, The Cabinet of Dr. Ramirez, The Player, Bob Roberts, Watch It, Malice, Short Cuts, Mother's Boys, The Hudsucker Proxy, Mrs. Parker and the Vicious Circle, While You Were Sleeping, The Underneath, Cafe Society, The Last Dance, To Gillian on Her 37th Birthday, Watch that Man, Johnny Skidmarks.
TELEVISION: *Series*: Skag. *Movies*: Skag, Terrible Joe Moran, The Caine Mutiny Court-Martial, The Murder of Mary Phagan, I'll Be Home for Christmas, Love and Lies, An Inconvenient Woman, White Mile, Titanic, Path to Paradise, The Frightening Frammis, The Quiet Room, The Cabinet of Dr. Ramirez, Virtual Obsession, Host. *Specials*: The Big Knife, Long Day's Journey Into Night, Private Contentment, Guys & Dolls: Off the Record. *Mini-series*: Brave New World.

GALLIGAN, ZACH

Actor. b. New York, NY, Feb. 14, 1964. e. Columbia U.
PICTURES: Gremlins, Nothing Lasts Forever, Waxwork, Mortal Passions, Rising Storm, Gremlins II, Zandalee, Waxwork II: Lost in Time, Round Trip to Heaven, All Tied Up, Warlock: The Armageddon, Ice, Caroline at Midnight, The First to Go, Prince Valiant, Cupid.
TELEVISION: *Movies*: Jacobo Timerman: Prisoner Without a Name Cell Without a Number, Surviving, Psychic, For Love and Glory. *Specials*: The Prodigious Hickey, The Return of Hickey, The Beginning of the Firm, A Very Delicate Matter, The Hitchhiker: Toxic Shock. *Mini-Series*: Crossings. *Pilot*: Interns in Heat. *Guest*: Tales From the Crypt (Strung Along), Melrose Place, Extreme.

GAMBON, MICHAEL

Actor. b. Dublin, Ireland, Oct. 19, 1940. Ent. ind. 1966. Early experience in theatre. 1985-87 Acting at National Theatre and London's West End. 1988: in Harold Pinter's Mountain Language.
PICTURES: Othello, The Beast Must Die, Turtle Diary, Paris By Night, The Rachel Papers, A Dry White Season, The Cook the Thief His Wife and Her Lover, Mobsters, Toys, Clean Slate, The Browning Version, Squanto: A Warrior's Tale, A Man of No Importance, Midnight in St. Petersberg, Bullet to Beijing, The Innocent Sleep, Nothing Personal, Mary Reilly, The Wings of the Dove, The Gambler, Plunkett & MacLeane, Dancing at Lughnasa.
TELEVISION: Uncle Vanya, Ghosts, Oscar Wilde, The Holy Experiment, Absurd Person Singular, The Singing Detective (serial), The Heat of the Day, The Storyteller, Maigret Sets a Trap, Samson & Delilah.

GAMMON, JAMES

Actor. b. Newman, IL, Apr. 20. e. Boone H.S., Orlando, FL. Former television cameraman. First acting role was small part on Gunsmoke. Head of Los Angeles' Met Theatre for 10 years.
THEATER: The Dark at the Top of the Stairs (L.A. Critics Circle Award, best actor), Bus Stop (L.A. Drama Critics award, best director), Curse of the Starving Class (NY, L.A.), A Lie of the Mind (NY, L.A.).
PICTURES: Cool Hand Luke (debut, 1967), Journey to Shiloh, Macho Callahan, A Man Called Horse, Macon County Line, Black Oak Conspiracy, Urban Cowboy, Any Which Way You Can, Smithereens, Vision Quest, Sylvester, Silverado, Silver Bullet, Made in Heaven, Ironweed, The Milagro Beanfield War, Major League, Revenge, Coupe de Ville, I Love You to Death, Leaving Normal, Crisscross, The Painted Desert, Running Cool, Cabin Boy, Vegas Vice, Natural Born Killers, Wild Bill.
TELEVISION: *Series*: Bagdad Cafe. *Guest*: Bonanza, The Wild Wild West, Cagney & Lacey, The Equalizer, Crime Story, Midnight Caller. *Movies*: Kansas City Massacre, Rage, Women of San Quentin, M.A.D.D.: Mothers Against Drunk Drivers, Hell Town, The Long Hot Summer, Roe vs. Wade, Dead Aim, Conagher, Stranger at My Door, Men Don't Tell, Truman. *Mini-Series*: Lincoln.

GANIS, SIDNEY M.

Executive. b. New York, NY, Jan. 8, 1940. e. Brooklyn Coll. Staff writer, newspaper and wire service contact, 20th Century-Fox 1961-62; radio, TV contact and special projects, Columbia Pictures 1963-64. Joined Seven Arts Prod. 1965 as publicity mgr.; 1967, appt. prod. publicity mgr. Warner-7 Arts, Ass't prod., There Was a Crooked Man, 1969. Studio publicity dir., Cinema Center Films, 1970. Director of Ad-Pub for Mame, Warner Bros., 1973; Director of Advertising, Warner Bros., 1974; named WB v.p., worldwide adv. & pub., 1977; 1979, sr. v.p., Lucasfilm, Ltd.; 1982 Emmy winner, exec. prod., best documentary, The Making of Raiders of the Lost Ark. 1986, joined Paramount Pictures as pres., worldwide mktg; 1986, named pres., Paramount Motion Picture Group. 1988, elected trustee University Art Museum, Berkeley, CA. 1991, appointed exec. v.p., Sony Pictures Ent. Exec. v.p., pres. mktg. & distrib., Columbia Pictures, 1992. Elected to bd. of govs. AMPAS, 1992. Vice chmn., Columbia Pictures, 1994. Pres., worldwide mktg., Columbia TriStar. Pres. Out of the Blue... Ent., 1997.

GANZ, BRUNO

Actor. b. Zurich, Switzerland, March 22, 1941. Theatre debut in 1961. Founded the Berlin Theatre troupe, Schaubuehne, with Peter Stein in 1970.
THEATER: Hamlet (1967), Dans La Jungle Des Villes, Torquato Tasso, La Chevauchee Sur Le Lac de Constance, Peer Gynt.
PICTURES: Der Sanfte Lauf (1967), Sommergaste, The Marquise of O, Lumiere, The Wild Duck, The American Friend, The Lefthanded Woman, The Boys from Brazil, Black and White Like Day and Night, Knife in the Head, Nosferatu the Vampyre, Return of a Good Friend, 5% Risk, An Italian Woman, Polenta, La Provinciale, La Dame Aux Camelias, Der Erfinder, Etwas Wird Sichtbar, Circle of Deceit, Hande Hoch, Logik Der Gerfuhls, War and Peace, In the White City, System Ohne Schatten, Der Pendler, Wings of Desire, Bankomatt, Strapless, The Last Days of Chez Nous, Especially on Sunday, Faraway So Close!, Heller Tag, Lumiere & Company, Saint-Ex.
TELEVISION: Father and Son, Todliches Schweigen, Ein Richter In Angst, Tatort — Schattenwelt (German TV). *Mini-series*: Grande Fausto II.

GANZ, LOWELL

Writer, Producer, Director. b. New York, NY, Aug. 31, 1948. e. Queens Col. Worked as staff writer on tv series The Odd Couple. Met writing partner Babaloo Mandel at The Comedy Store in the early 1970s. Was co-creator Laverne & Shirley. First teamed with Mandel on script for 1982 comedy Night Shift.
PICTURES: *Writer*: Night Shift, Splash (Acad. Award nom.; also actor), Spies Likes Us, Gung Ho, Vibes, Parenthood (also actor), City Slickers, A League of Their Own (also actor), Mr. Saturday Night (also actor), Greedy (also actor), City Slickers II: The Legend of Curly's Gold, Forget Paris, Multiplicity, Father's Day, The Secret Life of Walter Mitty, Doctor Dolittle.
TELEVISION: *Writer-Exec. Prod* (series): The Odd Couple, Happy Days, Busting Loose, The Ted Knight Show, Makin' It, Joanie Loves Chachi, Gung Ho, Knight and Dave, Parenthood. *Producer*: Laverne & Shirley (also writer).

GANZ, TONY

Producer. b. New York, NY. e. studied film at Harvard U. Produced documentaries for PBS in N.Y. Moved to L.A. 1973 where in charge of dev., Charles Fries Productions. Then joined Ron Howard Productions 1980. Left to form own prod. co. with Deborah Blum.
PICTURES: Gung Ho, Clean and Sober, Vibes.
TELEVISION: *Series*: American Dream Machine, Maximum Security (exec. prod.). *Movies*: Bitter Harvest, Into Thin Air.

GARCIA, ANDY

Actor. b. Havana, Cuba, Apr. 12, 1956. r.n. Andres Arturo Garcia Menendez. Family moved to Miami Beach in 1961. e. Florida International U, Miami. Spent several years acting with regional theaters in Florida; also part of improv. group. Music producer of album: Cachao Master Sessions Vol. I (Grammy Award), Chachao Master Sessions Vol II (Grammy nom.).
PICTURES: The Mean Season, 8 Million Ways to Die, The Untouchables, Stand and Deliver, American Roulette, Black Rain, Internal Affairs, A Show of Force, The Godfather Part III (Acad. Award nom.), Dead Again, Hero, Jennifer Eight, Cachao... Como Su Ritmo No Hay Dos (Like His Rhythm There Is No Other; also dir., co-prod.), When a Man Loves a Woman, Steal Big Steal Little, Things to Do in Denver When You're Dead, Night Falls on Manhattan, The Disappearance of Federico Garcia Lorca, Hoods, Desperate Measures, Hoodlums, The Scalper (prod.).
TELEVISION: *Movie*: Clinton and Nadine.

GARDINER, PETER R.

Executive. b. Santa Monica, CA, Apr. 25, 1949. Independent still photographer and industrial filmmaker joined Paramount, 1973, in feature post-prod. 1979, joined Warner Bros. as asst. dir., corporate services. 1987, promoted to v.p., opns., WB corporate film-video services. 1993, promoted to v.p. Warner Bros. corp. film & video services.

167

GARDNER, ARTHUR
Producer. b. Marinette, WI, June 7. e. Marinette h.s. Entered m.p. ind. as actor, in orig. cast All Quiet on the Western Front, 1929. Juvenile leads in: Waterfront, Heart of the North, Assassin of Youth, Religious Racketeer; production, asst. dir. King Bros. 1941, then asst. prod. U.S. Air Force 1st Motion Picture Unit, 1943-45. Formed Levy-Gardner-Laven Prods. with Jules Levy, Arnold Laven, 1951.
PICTURES: (Asst. dir.): Paper Bullets, I Killed That Man, Rubber Racketeers, Klondike Fury, I Escaped From the Gestapo, Suspense; Asst. prod.: Gangster, Dude Goes West, Badmen of Tombstone, Gun Crazy, Mutiny, Southside 1-1000. Prod.: Without Warning, Vice Squad, Down Three Dark Streets, Return of Dracula, The Flame Barrier, The Vampire, The Monster that Challenged the World. Geronimo, The Glory Guys, Clambake, Scalphunters, Sam Whiskey, Underground, McKenzie Break, The Honkers, Hunting Party, Kansas City Bomber, White Lightning, McQ, Brannigan, Gator, Safari 3000.
TELEVISION: The Rifleman, Robert Taylor's Detectives, Law of the Plainsman, The Big Valley.

GARFIELD, ALLEN
Actor. b. Newark, NJ, Nov. 22, 1939. r.n. Allen Goorwitz. e. Upsala Col, Actors Studio. Worked as journalist for Newark Star Ledger and Sydney Morning Herald (Australia) prior to becoming an actor. Has also acted as Allen Goorwitz. Life Member of the Actors Studio, NYC.
PICTURES: Greetings, Putney Swope, Hi Mom!, The Owl and the Pussycat, Bananas, Believe in Me, Roommates, The Organization, Taking Off, Cry Uncle!, You've Got to Walk it Like You Talk It or You'll Lose That Beat, Get to Know Your Rabbit, The Candidate, Top of the Heap, Deadhead Miles, Slither, Busting, The Conversation, The Front Page, Nashville, Gable and Lombard, Mother Jugs & Speed, The Brink's Job, Skateboard, Paco, One-Trick Pony, The Stunt Man, Continental Divide, One from the Heart, The State of Things, The Black Stallion Returns, Get Crazy, Irreconcilable Differences, Teachers, The Cotton Club, Desert Bloom, Beverly Hills Cop II, Rich Boys, Let it Ride, Night Visitor, Dick Tracy, Club Fed, Until the End of the World, Jack and His Friends, Family Prayers, The Patriots, The Glass Shadow, Miracle Beach, Sketches of a Strangler, Destiny Turns on the Radio, Diabolique.
TELEVISION: Movies: Footsteps, The Marcus-Nelson Murders, The Virginia Hill Story, Serpico: The Deadly Game, The Million Dollar Rip-Off, Nowhere to Run, Ring of Passion, Leave 'Em Laughing, Citizen Cohn, Killer in the Mirror, Incident at Vichy, Judgment: The Trial of Julius and Ethel Rosenberg. Guest: Law and Order, Equal Justice, Eddie Dodd, Jack's Place, Taxi, etc.

GARFINKLE, LOUIS
Writer, Director, Producer. b. Seattle, WA, February 11, 1928. e. U. of California, U. of Washington, U. of Southern California (B.A., 1948). Writer KOMO, Seattle, 1945; Executive Research, Inc., 1948; writer, educ. doc. screenplays, Emerson Films, EBF. 1948-50; s.p. You Can Beat the A-Bomb (RKO), 1950; writer-dir. training films, info. films, Signal Photo, 1950-53; copy, Weinberg Adv., 1953; head of doc. research in TV, U. of California, Berkeley, 1954-55; staff, Sheilah Graham Show, 1955; formed Maxim Prod. Inc. with Albert Band, 1956. Co-creator Collaborator Interactive Computer Software to asst. in writing stories for screen & TV, 1990; formed Collaborator Systems Inc. with Cary Brown and Francis X. Feighan, 1991. Received Best Screenwriting Tool Award from Screen Writers Forum, 1991. Member: AMPAS, WGA West, ATAS, Dramatists Guild, Board of Advisers Filmic Writing Major, USC School of Cinema & TV.
PICTURES: Screenplay: The Young Guns (also story), I Bury the Living (also story, co-prod.), Face of Fire (also co-prod.), Hellbenders, A Minute to Pray A Second to Die, The Love Doctors (also story, prod.), Beautiful People, The Models (also story), The Doberman Gang (also story), Little Cigars (also story), The Deer Hunter (story collab.; Acad. Award nom.), Milena.
TELEVISION: Writer: 712 teleplays for Day in Court, Morning Court, Accused, 1959-66. Co-writer-creator: Direct Line (pilot), June Allyson Show, Threat of Evil, Death Valley Days, Crullers At Sundown, Captain Dick Mine, No. 3 Peanut Place (pilot).

GARFUNKEL, ART
Singer, Actor. b. New York, NY, Nov. 5, 1942. e. Columbia Coll. Began singing at age 4. Long partnership with Paul Simon began in grade school at 13 in Queens, NY; first big success in 1965 with hit single, Sound of Silence. Partnership dissolved in 1970. Winner of 4 Grammy Awards.
PICTURES: Catch-22 (debut, 1970), Carnal Knowledge, Bad Timing/A Sensual Obsession, Good to Go, Boxing Helena.

GARLAND, BEVERLY
Actress. b. Santa Cruz, CA, Oct. 17, 1930. r.n. Beverly Fessenden. e. Glendale Coll., 1945-47.
PICTURES: D.O.A., The Glass Web, Miami Story, Bittercreek, Two Guns and a Badge, Killer Leopard, The Rocket Man, Sudden Danger, Desperate Hours, Curucu: Beast of the Amazon, Gunslinger, Swamp Woman, The Steel Jungle, It Conquered the World, Not of This Earth, Naked Paradise, The Joker is Wild, Chicago Confidential, Badlands of Montana,

The Saga of Hemp Brown, Alligator People, Stark Fever, Twice Told Tales, Pretty Poison, The Mad Room, Where the Red Fern Grows, Airport 1975, Roller Boogie, It's My Turn, Death Falls, Haunted Symphony.
TELEVISION: Series: Mama Rosa, Pantomime Quiz, The Bing Crosby Show, My Three Sons, Scarecrow & Mrs. King, Decoy. Guest: Twilight Zone, Dr. Kildare, Medic (Emmy nom.), Magnum P.I., Remington Steele, Lois and Clark. Movies: Cutter's Trail, Say Goodbye Maggie Cole, Weekend Nun, Voyage of the Yes, Unwed Father, Healers, Day the Earth Moved, This Girl for Hire, The World's Oldest Living Bridesmaid, Finding the Way Home.

GARNER, JAMES
Actor. r.n. James Baumgarner. b. Norman, OK, April 7, 1928. e. Norman H.S. Joined Merchant Marine, U.S. Army, served in Korean War. Prod. Paul Gregory suggested acting career. Studied drama at N.Y. Berghof School. Toured with road companies; Warner Bros. studio contract followed.
PICTURES: Toward the Unknown (debut, 1956), The Girl He Left Behind, Shoot Out at Medicine Bend, Sayonara, Darby's Rangers, Up Periscope, Alias Jesse James (cameo), Cash McCall, The Children's Hour, Boys' Night Out, The Great Escape, The Thrill of It All, The Wheeler Dealers, Move Over Darling, The Americanization of Emily, 36 Hours, The Art of Love, Mister Buddwing, A Man Could Get Killed, Duel at Diablo, Grand Prix, Hour of the Gun, The Pink Jungle, How Sweet It Is, Support Your Local Sheriff, Marlowe, A Man Called Sledge, Support Your Local Gunfighter, Skin Game, They Only Kill Their Masters, One Little Indian, The Castaway Cowboy, Health, The Fan, Victor/Victoria, Tank, Murphy's Romance (Acad. Award nom.), Sunset, The Distinguished Gentleman, Fire in the Sky, Maverick, My Fellow Americans.
TELEVISION: Series: Maverick, Nichols, The Rockford Files, Bret Maverick, Man of the People. Movies: The Rockford Files (pilot), The New Maverick (pilot), The Long Summer of George Adams, The Glitter Dome, Heartsounds, Promise (also exec. prod.), Obsessive Love, My Name Is Bill W. (also exec. prod.), Decoration Day, Barbarians at the Gate, The Rockford Files: I Still Love L.A. (also co-exec. prod.), The Rockford Files: A Blessing in Disguise (also co-exec. prod.). Mini-Series: Space. Specials: Sixty Years of Seduction, Lily for President.

GAROFALO, JANEANE
Actress. b. Newton, NJ, Sept. 28, 1964. Created I Hate Myself Productions.
PICTURES: Late for Dinner, Reality Bites, Suspicious, I Shot a Man in Vegas, Bye Bye Love, Coldblooded, Now and Then, Kids in the Hall: Brian Candy, The Truth About Cats and Dogs, The Cable Guy, Larger than Life, Sweethearts, Touch, Romy and Michele's High School Reunion, Cop Land, The Matchmaker, Clay Pidgeons, Dog Park, Thick as Thieves, 200 Cigarettes, Half Baked, Permanent Midnight.
TELEVISION: Series: Saturday Night Live, The Larry Sanders Show, The Ben Stiller Show, TV Nation. Mini-series: Tales of the City. Guest: Law & Order, Seinfeld, Home Improvement, Space Ghost Coast to Coast, Ellen, NewsRadio, Dr. Katz—Professional Therapist.

GARR, TERI
Actress. b. Lakewood, OH, Dec. 11, 1949. Began career as dancer, performing S.F. Ballet at 13. Later appeared with L.S. Ballet and in original road show co. of West Side Story. Several film appearances as a dancer incl. Fun in Acapulco, Viva Las Vegas, What a Way to Go, Roustabout, etc. Did commercials; appeared in film Head written by a fellow acting student, Jack Nicholson. Career boosted by appearance on TV as semi-regular on The Sonny and Cher Show.
PICTURES: Maryjane, Head, The Moonshine War, The Conversation, Young Frankenstein, Won Ton Ton the Dog Who Saved Hollywood, Oh God!, Close Encounters of the Third Kind, Mr. Mike's Mondo Video, The Black Stallion, Witches' Brew, Honky Tonk Freeway, One from the Heart, The Escape Artist, Tootsie (Acad. Award nom.), The Sting II, The Black Stallion Returns, Mr. Mom, Firstborn, Miracles, After Hours, Full Moon in Blue Water, Out Cold, Let It Ride, Short Time, Waiting for the Light, The Player, Mom and Dad Save the World, Dumb & Dumber, Ready to Wear (Pret-a-Porter), Michael, A Simple Wish.
TELEVISION: Series regular: Shindig, The Ken Berry "Wow" Show, (1972), Burns and Schreiber Comedy Hour, Girl With Something Extra, The Sonny and Cher Comedy Hour, The Sonny Comedy Revue, Good and Evil, Good Advice, Women of the House. Movies: Law and Order, Doctor Franken, Prime Suspect, Winter of Our Discontent, To Catch a King, Intimate Strangers, Pack of Lies, A Quiet Little Neighborhood A Perfect Little Murder, Stranger in the Family, Deliver Them From Evil: The Taking of Alta View, Fugitive Nights: Danger in the Desert. Specials: The Frog Prince (Faerie Tale Theatre), Drive She Said (Trying Times), Paul Reiser: Out on a Whim, Mother Goose Rock 'n' Rhyme, The Whole Shebang, Aliens for Breakfast. Mini-Series: Fresno. Guest: Tales from the Crypt (The Trap), The Larry Sanders Show.

GARRETT, BETTY
Singer, Actress. b. St. Joseph, MO, May 23, 1919. e. scholarships: Annie Wright Seminary, Tacoma, WA; Neighborhood Playhouse, N.Y. Sang in night clubs, hotels, Broadway shows: Call Me Mister (Donaldson Award, 1946), Spoon River Anthology, A Girl Could Get Lucky, Meet Me in St. Louis (1989). Motion Picture Herald, Star of Tomorrow, 1949. Starred in one woman show, Betty Garrett and Other Songs, beginning in 1974 and touring through 1993 (Bay Area Critics & LA Drama Critics Awards); also in autobiographical show, No Dogs or Actors Allowed (Pasadena Playhouse, 1989), So There! (with Dale Gonyear; Pasadena Playhouse, 1993). Given Life Achievement Award by Los Angeles Drama Critics Circle, 1995. With Ron Rapaport author of Betty Garrett and Other Songs—A Life on Stage & Screen, 1998.
PICTURES: The Big City (debut, 1948), Words and Music, Take Me Out to the Ball Game, Neptune's Daughter, On the Town, My Sister Eileen, Shadow on the Window.
TELEVISION: Series: All in the Family, Laverne and Shirley. Guest: Love Boat, Black's Magic, Somerset Gardens, Murder She Wrote, Harts of the West, The Good Life. Movies: All the Way Home, Who's Happy Now, Golden Girls, Townies..

GARY, LORRAINE
Actress. b. New York, NY, Aug. 16, 1937. r.n. Lorraine Gottfried. m. executive Sidney J. Scheinberg. e. Columbia Univ.
PICTURES: Jaws, Car Wash, I Never Promised You a Rose Garden, Jaws 2, Just You and Me Kid, 1941, Jaws-The Revenge.
TELEVSION: Movies: The City, The Marcus-Nelson Murders, Partners in Crime, Pray for the Wildcats, Man on the Outside, Lanigan's Rabbi, Crash.

GASSMAN, VITTORIO
Actor. b. Genoa, Italy, Sept. 1, 1922. e. Acad. of Dramatic Art, Rome. Stage actor, 1943; m.p. debut, 1946.
PICTURES: Daniele Cortis, Mysterious Rider, Bitter Rice, Lure of Sila, The Outlaws, Anna, Streets of Sorrow; to U.S., Cry of the Hunted, Sombrero, The Glass Wall, Rhapsody, Girls Marked Danger, Mambo, War and Peace, World's Most Beautiful Woman, Tempest, The Love Specialist, The Great War, Let's Talk About Women, Il Successo, The Tiger, Woman Times Seven, Ghosts-Italian Style, Scent of a Woman, Viva Italia!, A Wedding, Quintet, Immortal Bachelor, The Nude Bomb, Sharky's Machine, Tempest, I Picari, The Family, The Sleazy Uncle, The House of the Lord, The Hateful Dead, To Forget Palermo, Los Alegres Picaro, Scheherzade, The Long Winter, Sleepers.

GATES, WILLIAM H.
Executive. b. 1957. Started computer programming at age 13. 1974, developed BASIC for the first microcomputer, MITS Altair. 1975, with Paul Allen formed Microsoft to develop software for personal computers. Chmn. & CEO of Microsoft Corp. leading provider of worldwide software for personal computers.

GATWARD, JAMES
Executive. b. London, England. Ent. Ind. 1957. Early career as freelance drama prod. dir. in Canada, USA, UK (with ITV & BBC). Prod. dir. various intern. co-productions in UK, Ceylond, Australia, Germany. Currently chief executive and Dep. chmn. TVS Television Ltd., chmn. Telso Communications Ltd., dir. of ITN, Channel Four, Super Channel, Oracle Teletext.

GAVIN, JOHN
Executive, Diplomat, Former Actor. b. Los Angeles, CA, April 8, 1932. m. actress Constance Towers. e. St. John's Military Acad., Villanova Prep at Ojai, Stanford Univ., Naval service: air intelligence officer in Korean War. Broadway stage debut: Seesaw, 1973. 1961-73 public service experience as spec. advisor to Secretary Gen. of OAS, performed gp. task work for Dept. of State and Exec. Office of the President. Pres. Screen Actors Guild, 1971-73. Named U.S. Ambassador to Mexico, 1981-86. Partner in Gavin & Dailey, a venture capital firm; Pres., Gamma Services Corp. (Intl. Consultants); dir., Atlantic Richfield Co., Dresser Industries, Pinkerton, Inc., The Hotchkiss and Wiley Funds, International Wire Group Co. Consultant to Dept. of State and serves pro-bono on several boards.
PICTURES: Behind the High Wall (debut, 1956), Four Girls in Town, Quantez, A Time to Love and a Time to Die, Imitation of Life, Psycho, Midnight Lace, Spartacus, A Breath of Scandal, Romanoff and Juliet, Tammy Tell Me True, Back Street, Thoroughly Modern Millie, The Madwoman of Chaillot, Pussycat Pussycat I Love You.
TELEVISION: Movies: Cutler's Trail, The New Adventures of Heidi, Sophia Loren: Her Own Story. Series: Destry, Convoy. Mini-Series: Doctors' Private Lives.

GAY, JOHN
Writer. b. Whittier, CA, April 1, 1924. e. LA City Coll.
PICTURES: Run Silent, Run Deep, Separate Tables, The Happy Thieves, Four Horsemen, The Courtship of Eddie's Father, The Hallelujah Trail, The Last Safari, The Power, No Way to Treat a Lady, Soldier Blue, Sometimes a Great Notion,

Hennessey, A Matter of Time.
TELEVISION: Amazing Howard Hughes, Kill Me If You Can, Captains Courageous, Red Badge of Courage, All My Darling Daughters, Les Miserables, Transplant, A Private Battle, A Tale of Two Cities, The Bunker, Berlin Tunnel 21, Stand By Your Man, Dial "M" For Murder, The Long Summer of George Adams, A Piano for Mrs. Cimino, The Hunchback of Notre Dame, Ivanhoe, Witness for the Prosecution, Samson and Delilah, Fatal Vision, Doubletake, Uncle Tom's Cabin, Outlaw, Six Against the Rock, Around the World in 80 Days, Blind Faith, Cruel Doubt.

GAYNOR, MITZI
Actress. r.n. Francisca Mitzi Von Gerber. b. Chicago, IL, Sept. 4, 1931. e. Powers Professional H.S., Hollywood. Studied ballet since age four; was in L.A. Light Opera prod. Roberta. Stage: Anything Goes (natl. co., 1989).
OPERA: Fortune Teller, Song of Norway, Louisiana Purchase, Naughty Marietta, The Great Waltz.
PICTURES: My Blue Heaven (debut, 1950), Take Care of My Little Girl, Golden Girl, We're Not Married, Bloodhounds of Broadway, The I Don't Care Girl, Down Among the Sheltering Palms, There's No Business Like Show Business, Three Young Texans, Anything Goes, The Birds and the Bees, The Joker Is Wild, Les Girls, South Pacific, Happy Anniversary, Surprise Package, For Love or Money.
TELEVISION: Specials: Mitzi, Mitzi's Second Special, The First Time, A Tribute to the American Housewife, Mitzi and a Hundred Guys, Roarin' in the 20s, Mitzi...Zings Into Spring, What's Hot What's Not.

GAZZARA, BEN
Actor. b. New York, NY, Aug. 28, 1930. e. Studied at CCNY 1947-49. Won scholarship to study with Erwin Piscator; joined Actor's Studio, where students improvised a play, End as a Man, which then was performed on Broadway with him in lead. Screen debut (1957) in film version of that play retitled The Strange One.
THEATER: Jezebel's Husband, End as a Man, Cat on a Hot Tin Roof, A Hatful of Rain, The Night Circus, Epitaph for George Dillon, Two for the Seesaw, Strange Interlude, Traveler Without Luggage, Hughie, Who's Afraid of Virginia Woolf, Dance of Death, Thornhill, Shimada.
PICTURES: The Strange One (debut, 1957), Anatomy of a Murder, The Passionate Thief, The Young Doctors, Convicts Four, Conquered City, A Rage to Live, The Bridge at Remagen, Husbands, The Neptune Factor, Capone, Killing of a Chinese Bookie, Voyage of the Damned, High Velocity, Opening Night, Saint Jack, Bloodline, They All Laughed, Inchon, Tales of Ordinary Madness, Road House, Quicker Than the Eye, Don Bosco, A Lovely Scandal, Girl from Trieste, Il Camorrista, Tattooed Memory, Beyond the Ocean (also dir., s.p.), Forever, Farmer & Chase, The Shadow Conspiracy, The Great Lebowski, The Spanish Prisoner, Buffalo 66, Illuminata, Happiness.
TELEVISION: Series: Arrest and Trial, Run for Your Life. Movies: When Michael Calls, Maneater, QB VII, The Death of Ritchie, A Question of Honor, An Early Frost, A Letter to Three Wives, Police Story: The Freeway Killings, Downpayment on Murder, People Like Us, Lies Before Kisses, Blindsided, Love Honor & Obey: The Last Mafia Marriage, Parallel Lives, Fatal Vows: The Alexandria O'Hara Story.

GEARY, ANTHONY
Actor. b. Coalville, UT, May 29, 1947. e. U. of Utah.
THEATRE: The Inspector General, The Glass Menagerie, The Wild Duck, Barabbas.
PICTURES: Blood Sabbath (debut, 1969), Johnny Got His Gun, Private Investigations, Disorderlies, Penitentiary III, You Can't Hurry Love, Pass the Ammo, Dangerous Love, It Takes Two, UHF, Night Life, Crack House, Night of the Warrior, Scorchers.
TELEVISION: Series: Bright Promise, General Hospital (1978-83; 1990-). Guest: The Young and the Restless, Osmond Family Holiday Special, Sunset Beat, Murder She Wrote, Hotel, All in the Family, Streets of San Francisco. Movies: Intimate Agony, Sins of the Past, The Imposter, Kicks, Perry Mason: The Case of the Murdered Madam, Do You Know the Muffin Man?

GEBHARDT, FRED
Producer, Writer, Exhibitor. b. Vienna, Austria, Mar. 16, 1925. e. Schotten Gymnasium, Vienna, UCLA, 1939. Usher Boyd Theatre, Bethlehem, PA; Mgr., Rivoli Thea. L.A., 1944; 18 yrs. mgr. many theatres. Fox West Coast, then Fine Arts Theatre. Writer, prod.: 12 To the Moon, The Phantom Planet; prod., Assignment Outer Space, Operation M; s.p., All But Glory, The Starmaker, Shed No Blood, Fortress in Heaven, Eternal Woman. Pres., Four Crown Prods., Inc.; recipient of Medal of Americanism, D.A.R., 1963; Honorary Lifetime Member, P.T.A., Young Man of The Year Award, 1956, 24 Showmanship Awards; Mem. Acad. M.P. Arts and Sciences, Ind. M.P. Prod. Assoc.
AUTHOR: Mental Disarmament, All But Glory, Starmaker, Shed No Blood, The Last of the Templars.

GEDRICK, JASON
Actor. b. Chicago, IL, Feb. 7, 1965.
PICTURES: Massive Retaliation (debut, 1984), The Zoo Gang, The Heavenly Kid, Iron Eagle, Stacking, Promised Land, Rooftops, Born on the Fourth of July, Backdraft, Crossing the Bridge.
TELEVISION: Series: Class of 96, Murder One.

GEESON, JUDY
Actress. b. Arundel, Sussex, England, Sept. 10, 1948. e. Corona Stage Sch. Began professional career on British TV, 1960.
THEATER: Othello, Titus Andronicus, Two Gentlemen of Verona, Section Nine, An Ideal Husband.
PICTURES: To Sir with Love, Berserk, Here We Go Round the Mulberry Bush, Prudence and the Pill, Hammerhead, Three into Two Won't Go, The Oblong Box, Two Gentlemen Sharing, The Executioner, Nightmare Hotel, 10 Rillington Place, Doomwatch, Fear in the Night, It's Not the Size That Counts, Brannigan, Diagnosis Murder, The Eagle Has Landed, Carry On England, Dominique, Horror Planet, The Plague Dogs (voice).
TELEVISION: Dance of Death, Lady Windermere's Fan, Room with a View, The Skin Game, Star Maidens, Poldark, She, The Coronation, Murder She Wrote, Astronomy (Triple Play II). Movie: The Secret Life of Kathy McCormick.

GEFFEN, DAVID
Executive, Producer. b. Brooklyn, NY, Feb. 21, 1943. Began in mailroom of William Morris Agency before becoming agent there and later at Ashley Famous. With Elliott Roberts founded own talent management co. for musicians. Founded Asylum Records, 1970. Pres. then chmn. Elektra-Asylum Records 1973-76. Sold co. to Warner Communications for whom he headed film prod. unit. Vice-chmn. Warner Bros. Pictures, 1975; exec. asst. to chmn., Warner Communications, 1977; Member music faculty Yale U., 1978. Formed Geffen Records 1980 and Geffen Film Co. Producer of Broadway shows Master Harold... and the Boys, Cats, Good, Dreamgirls, Social Security, Chess. 1990, sold record co. to MCA, Inc. With Steven Spielberg and Jeffrey Katzenberg formed Dreamworks entertainment company, 1995.
PICTURES: Personal Best, Risky Business, Lost in America, After Hours, Little Shop of Horrors, Beetlejuice (exec. prod.), Men Don't Leave, Defending Your Life, M. Butterfly, Interview With the Vampire.

GELBART, LARRY
Writer. b. Chicago, IL, Feb. 25, 1928. Began at age 16 writing for Danny Thomas on Fanny Brice Show. Followed by Duffy's Tavern, Bob Hope and Jack Paar radio shows. Author of Laughing Matters, 1998.
THEATER: The Conquering Hero, A Funny Thing Happened on the Way to the Forum (with Burt Shevlove; Tony Award, 1962), Sly Fox, Mastergate, City of Angels (Tony Award, 1990), Power Failure.
PICTURES: The Notorious Landlady, The Thrill of It All, The Wrong Box, Not With My Wife You Don't, The Chastity Belt, A Fine Pair, Oh God!, Movie Movie, Neighbors, Tootsie, Blame It on Rio.
TELEVISION: Series: Caesar's Hour, M*A*S*H (Emmy Award, 1974; also co-prod.), United States. Movie: Barbarians at the Gate (Cable Ace Award, 1993), Weapons of Mass Distraction. Special: Mastergate.

GELFAN, GREGORY
Executive. b. Los Angeles, CA, Aug. 7, 1950. Was entertainment atty. with Kaplan, Livingston et. al., and Weissmann, Wolff et. al. before joining Paramount Pictures in 1983 as dir. of business affairs. 1985, named v.p., business affairs, for M.P. Group of Paramount; 1989 promoted to sr. v.p. in chg. of business affairs. 1994, named exec. v.p. in chg. of business & legal affairs, 20th Century Fox.

GELLER, BRIAN L.
Executive. b. New York, NY, Feb. 3, 1948. e. Queens Coll. Entered industry with Columbia Pictures as sls. trainee in 1966, leaving in 1968 to go with American Intl. Pictures as asst. branch mgr. In 1969 joined Cinemation Industries as eastern div. sls. mgr.; 1978, left to become gen. sls. mr. of NMD Film Distributing Co. 1982, named dir. of dist., Mature Pictures Corp. 1983, gen. sls. mgr., Export Pix.; with Cinema Group as east. sls. mgr.; joined Scotti Brothers Pictures as national sales, mgr. Joined 20th Century Fox sls. dep't. Member of Motion Picture Bookers Club of N.Y.; Variety Tent 35, Motion Picture Pioneers.

GENDECE, BRIAN
Producer, Executive. b. St. Louis, MO, Dec. 3, 1956. e. Drury Coll., Springfield, MO. 1981-85, Director of Business Affairs, Weinstein/Skyfield Productions and Skyfield Management. 1986-87, dir. of business affairs, Cannon Films; 1987-89, dir. creative affairs, Cannon Films; 1989 co-pres., Sheer Entertainment; indie first look Epic Prods.; 1991 owner The Gendece Film Co.; 1991-93, prod./dir., 21st Century Film; 1993-96, dir. of mktg., Raleigh Film and Television Studios. 1997-98, pres., G & G Prods.
THEATER: Jack Klugman as Lyndon, The Bob Fosse Awards.
PICTURES: Runaway Train, Salsa, Rope Dancin', The Hunters, The American Samurai, Ceremony.
VIDEO: Bad Habits, Shape Up with Arnold, Laura Branigan's Your Love, How to Become a Teenage Ninja, L.A. Raiders' Wild Wild West, The Making of Crime and Punishment.

GEORGE, DAVID L.
Executive. Pres. Society of Motion Picture and Television Engineers.

GEORGE, GEORGE W.
Writer, Producer. b. New York, NY, Feb.8, 1920. e. Williams Coll. U.S. Navy, 1941-44; screen-writer since 1948. President, Jengo Enterprises, dev. theatrical and m.p. projects.
THEATER: Prod.: Dylan, Any Wednesday, Ben Franklin in Paris, The Great Indoors, Happily Never After, Night Watch, Via Galactica, Bedroom Farce, Program for Murder (also co-author).
PICTURES: Writer: Bodyguard, The Nevada, Woman on Pier 13, Peggy, Mystery Submarine, Red Mountain Experiment, Alcatraz, Fight Town, Smoke Signal, Desert Sands, Uranium Boom, Halliday Brand, Doc, The James Dean Story, The Two Little Bears. Prod.: The James Dean Story, A Matter of Innocence, Twisted Nerve, Hello-Goodbye, Night Watch, Rich Kids, My Dinner With Andre.
TELEVISION: Climax, Screen Gems, Loretta Young Show, The Rifleman, Peter Gunn, The Real McCoys, Adventures in Paradise, Hong Kong, Follow the Sun, Bonanza.

GEORGE, LOUIS
Executive. b. Karavas, Kyrenia, Cyprus, June 7, 1935. e. Kyrenia Business Acad., Cyprus (honored 1951). Emigrated to U.S. in 1952. After brief stint in Foreign Exchange Dept. of City National Bank, New York, served in U.S. Army, 1953-55. Entered industry in 1956 as theatre manager with Loew's Theatres in N.Y. metro area, managing Metropolitan, Triboro, New Rochelle, between 1958-66. 1966 joined MGM as dir. of intl. theatre dept. 1969 promoted to dir. of world-wide non-theatrical sales. 1972-74 served as regional dir. of MGM Far East operations. 1974 left MGM to establish Arista Films, Inc., an indep. prod./dist. co. Pres. & CEO, Arista Films, Inc. Also bd. member, American Film Marketing Assn., chmn. Copywright and Film Security Committee of the Assn.
PICTURES: Slaughterhouse Rock, Buying Time, Violent Zone (exec. prod.), Angels Brigade, Final Justice, Surf II, Crackdown.

GEORGE, SUSAN
Actress, Producer. b. Surrey, England, July 26, 1950. m. actor-prod. Simon MacCorkindale. e. Corona Acad.
PICTURES: Billion Dollar Brain, The Sorcerers, Up the Junction, The Strange Affair, The Looking Glass War, All Neat in Black Stockings, Twinky (Lola), Spring and Port Wine, Eye Witness (Sudden Terror), Die Screaming Marianne, Fright, Straw Dogs, Sonny and Jed, Dirty Mary Crazy Larry, Mandingo, Out of Season, A Small Town in Texas, Tintorera, Tomorrow Never Comes, Enter the Ninja, Venom, The House Where Evil Dwells, Jigsaw Man, Lightning: The White Stallion, Stealing Heaven (exec. prod. only), That Summer of White Roses (also exec. prod.), The House That Mary Bought (also exec. prod.).
TELEVISION: Swallows and Amazons, Adam's Apple, Weaver's Green, Compensation Alice, The Right Attitude, Dracula, Lamb to the Slaughter, Royal Jelly, Masquerade, Czechmate, Hotel, Blacke's Magic, Jack the Ripper, Castle of Adventure, Cluedo, Stay Lucky.

GERALD, HELEN
Actress. b. New York, NY, Aug. 13. e. U. of Southern California, 1948. Stage: Italian Teatro D'Arte, Les Miserables, The Civil Death, Feudalism.
PICTURES: The Gay Cavalier, The Trap, Tarzan and the Leopard Woman, Cigarette Girl, Meet Miss Bobby Socks, G.I. War Brides, Gentleman's Agreement, A Bell for Adano, Tomorrow Is Forever, Janie, Grand Prix, The Sandpiper, Make Mine Mink, Best of Everything.
TELEVISION: Robert Montgomery Presents, Frontiers of Faith, Valiant Lady, Kraft Theatre, Gangbusters, Adventures of The Falcon, Schlitz Playhouse of Stars, This Is the Answer, Man from U.N.C.L.E., Run for Your Life, Perry Mason.

GERARD, GIL
Actor. b. Little Rock, AK, Jan. 23, 1943. e. Arkansas State Teachers Coll. Appeared in over 400 TV commercials. On stage in I Do! I Do!, Music Man, Stalag 17, Applause, etc.
PICTURES: Some of My Best Friends Are (1971), Man on a Swing, Hooch (also co-prod.), Airport '77, Buck Rogers in the 25th Century, Soldier's Fortune, Ransom for Bruce.
TELEVISION: Series: The Doctors, Buck Rogers in the 25th Century, Nightingales, Sidekicks, E.A.R.T.H. Force, Fish Police, Code 3 (host). Movies: Ransom for Alice, Killing Stone, Help Wanted: Male, Not Just Another Affair, Hear No Evil, Johnny Blue (pilot), For Love or Money, Stormin' Home, International Airport, Final Notice, The Elite, Last Electric Knight.

GERARD, LILLIAN
Publicist, Writer b. New York, NY, Nov. 25, 1914. e. Baruch, CCNY, Columbia U. Publicity, Rialto Theatre, 1936; publicity-adv. Filmarte Theatre, 1938, Gerard Associates, 1938-47; V.P. and managing dir. of Paris Theatre, 1948-62; publicity-adv. dir., Rugoff Theatres, 1962. Film consultant to Times Films, Lopert Films, Landau Co., 1962-65. Adjunct Professor, Film, 1968-70, Columbia U., Sch. of the Arts, Special Projects Co-Ordinator, Museum of Modern Art, 1968-80. Now associated with Philip Gerard in Gerard Associates.

GERARD, PHILIP R.
Executive. b. New York, NY, Aug. 23, 1913. e. City Coll. of New York, B.B.A. 1935; Columbia U.. Publicity dir. Mayer-Burstyn 1936-39; Gerard Associates, 1939-41; in public relations U.S. War Dept. 1942-44; with MGM 1944-48; with Universal Pictures since 1948; Eastern pub. mgr., 1950-59; Eastern ad. and pub. dir., Dec. 1959-68; N.Y. Production Exec., 1968-76. As of Jan. 1, 1977 formed Gerard Associates, film consultants on marketing, production and acquisitions. N.Y.C. Board member of CSS/RSVP (Retired Seniors Volunteer Program); Community Service Society. Member: Visitor's Day Comm., New York Hospital; volunteer at the International Center.

GERBER, DAVID
Executive. b. Brooklyn, NY. e. U. of the Pacific. m. actress Laraine Stephens. Joined Batten, Barton, Durstine and Osborn ad agency in N.Y. as TV supvr. Left to become sr. v.p. of TV at General Artists Corp. 1956, named v.p. in chg. sales at 20th-Fox TV where sold and packaged over 50 prime-time series and specials. Entered indep. prod. with The Ghost and Mrs. Muir, followed by Nanny and the Professor. 1970 was exec. prod. of The Double Deckers, children's series made in England. 1972 joined Columbia Pictures Television as indep. prod.; 1974 was named exec. v.p. worldwide prod. for CPT. 1976 returned to indep. prod. 1985, joined MGM/UA TV broadcasting group in chg. world-wide prod. 1986 named president, MGM/UA Television. 1988-92, chmn & CEO, MGM/UA Television Prods. group.
TELEVISION: *Exec. prod.*: Cade's County, Police Story (Emmy, best dramatic series), Police Woman, The Lindbergh Kidnapping Case, Joe Forrester, The Quest and Gibbsville, To Kill a Cop, Power, Medical Story, Born Free, Beulah Land, The Night the City Screamed, Follow the North Star, Nothing Lasts Forever, Lady Blue, The Ghost and Mrs. Muir.

GERBER, MICHAEL H.
Executive. b. New York, NY, Feb. 6, 1944. e. St. Johns U., B.A., 1969; St. Johns U. School of Law, J.D., 1969. Atty. for Screen Gems, 1969-71; asst. secy. & asst. to gen. counsel, Columbia Pictures Industries, 1971-74; corporate counsel and secretary, Allied Artists Pictures, 1974, v.p. corporate affairs, Allied Artists, 1978; v.p., business affairs, Viacom Intl. 1980-86; 1986-89, sr. v.p.; 1989-93, pres., first run, intl. distrib. & acquisitions, Viacom Enterprises.

GERE, RICHARD
Actor. b. Philadelphia, PA, Aug. 29, 1949. e. U. of Massachusetts. Started acting in college; later joined Provincetown Playhouse and Seattle Repertory Theatre. Composed music for productions of these groups.
THEATER: *B'way*: Grease, Soon, Habeas Corpus, Bent (Theatre World Award), A Midsummer Night's Dream (Lincoln Center). *Off-B'way* in Killer's Head. *London*: Taming of the Shrew (with Young Vic).
PICTURES: Report to the Commissioner (debut, 1975), Baby Blue Marine, Looking for Mr. Goodbar, Days of Heaven, Bloodbrothers, Yanks, American Gigolo, An Officer and a Gentleman, Breathless, Beyond the Limit, The Cotton Club, King David, Power, No Mercy, Miles From Home, Internal Affairs, Pretty Woman, Rhapsody in August, Final Analysis (also co-exec. prod.), Sommersby (also co-exec. prod.), Mr. Jones (also co-exec. prod.), Intersection, First Knight, Primal Fear.
TELEVISION: *Movies*: Strike Force, And the Band Played On. *Guest*: Kojak. *Pilot*: D.H.P.

GERTZ, IRVING
Composer, Musical director. b. Providence, RI, May 19, 1915. e. Providence Coll. of Music, 1934-37. Assoc. with Providence Symph. Orch., comp. choral works for Catholic Choral Soc.; music dept., Columbia, 1939-41; U.S. Army, 1941-46; then comp. arranger, mus. dir. for many cos. incl. Columbia, Universal International, NBC, 20th Century Fox. Compositions: Leaves of Grass, Serenata for String Quartet, Divertimento for String Orchestra, Tableau for Orchestra.
PICTURES: Bandits of Corsica, Gun Belt, Long Wait, The Fiercest Heart, First Travelling Saleslady, Fluffy, Nobody's Perfect, Marines Let's Go!, It Came from Outer Space, The Man from Bitter Ridge, Posse from Hell, The Creature Walks Among Us, The Incredible Shrinking Man, Hell Bent for Leather, Seven Ways from Sundown, Francis Joins the WACS, Raw Edge, East of Sumatra, A Day of Fury, To Hell and Back, Cult of the Cobra, Plunder Road, Top Gun, Tombstone Express, The Alligator People, Khyber Patrol, The Wizard of Baghdad. Fluffy, Marines, Let's Go!
TELEVISION: *Orig. theme & scores*: America, The Golden Voyage, Across the Seven Seas, The Legend of Jesse James, Daniel Boone, Voyage to the Bottom of the Sea, Peyton Place, Land of the Giants, Lancer, Medical Center, Boutade for Wood-Wind Quartet, Salute to All Nations, A Village Fair, Liberty! Liberte! (for symphony orchestra).

GERTZ, JAMI
Actress. b. Chicago, IL, Oct. 28, 1965. e. NYU. Won a nation-wide talent search competition headed by Norman Lear to cast TV comedy series Square Pegs. Following series studied at NYU drama school. Los Angeles theater includes Out of Gas on Lovers' Leap and Come Back Little Sheba. On NY stage in Wrong Turn at Lungfish. Also appeared in the Julian Lennon music video Stick Around.
PICTURES: Endless Love (debut, 1981), On the Right Track, Alphabet City, Sixteen Candles, Mischief, Quicksilver, Crossroads, Solarbabies, The Lost Boys, Less Than Zero, Listen to Me, Renegades, Silence Like Glass, Don't Tell Her It's Me, Sibling Rivalry, Jersey Girls, Twister.
TELEVISION: *Series*: Square Pegs, Dreams, Sibs, ER. *Guest*: Diff'rent Strokes, The Facts of Life. *Movie*: This Can't Be Love.

GETTY, BALTHAZAR
Actor. b. California, Jan. 22, 1975. Spotted by talent agent while at Bel Air Prep School, winning lead role in remake of Lord of the Flies.
PICTURES: Lord of the Flies (debut, 1990), Young Guns II, My Heroes Have Always Been Cowboys, The Pope Must Die, December, Where the Day Takes You, Halfway House, Red Hot, Dead Beat, Natural Born Killers, Don't Do It, Terrified, Judge Dredd, City Scrapers, White Squall, Habitat, Lost Highway.
TELEVISION: *Special*: The Turn of the Screw.

GETTY, ESTELLE
Actress. b. New York, NY, July 25, 1923. e. attended New School for Social Research. Trained for stage with Gerald Russak and at Herbert Berghof Studios. Worked as comedienne on Borscht Belt circuit and as actress with Yiddish theatre. Founder Fresh Meadows Community theater. Also worked as acting teacher and coach and secretary. Author, If I Knew What I Know Now... So What? (1988).
THEATER: The Divorce of Judy and Jane (off-B'way debut, 1971), Widows and Children First, Table Settings, Demolition of Hannah Fay, Never Too Old, A Box of Tears, Hidden Corners, I Don't Know Why I'm Screaming, Under the Bridge There's a Lonely Place, Light Up the Sky, Pocketful of Posies, Fits and Starts, Torch Song Trilogy (off-B'way, B'way and tour, Drama Desk nom., 1982, Helen Hayes Award, best supp. performer in a touring show).
PICTURES: The Chosen, Tootsie, Protocol, Mask, Mannequin, Stop Or My Mom Will Shoot.
TELEVISION: *Series*: The Golden Girls (Golden Globe Award, Emmy Award, 1988), The Golden Palace, Empty Nest. *Movies*: No Man's Land, Victims for Victims: The Teresa Saldana Story, Copacabana. *Guest*: Cagney and Lacey, Nurse, Baker's Dozen, One of the Boys, Fantasy Island.

GETZ, JOHN
Actor. e. Univ Iowa, Amer. Conservatory Theatre (SF). Appeared on B'way in They're Playing Our Song, M. Butterfly. LA stage: Money & Friends.
PICTURES: Tattoo, Thief of Hearts, Blood Simple, The Fly, The Fly II, Born on the Fourth of July, Men at Work, Don't Tell Mom the Babysitter's Dead, Curly Sue, A Passion to Kill, Painted Hero, Mojave Moon.
TELEVISION: *Series*: Rafferty, Suzanne Pleshette is Maggie Briggs, MacGruder & Loud, Mariah. *Movies*: Killer Bees, A Woman Called Moses, Kent State, Rivkin: Bounty Hunter, Muggable Mary: Street Cop, Not in Front of the Children, Concrete Beat, The Execution, In My Daughter's Name, Betrayal of Trust, Untamed Love, Awake to Murder, The Late Shift. *Mini-Series*: Loose Change.

GHOSTLEY, ALICE
Actress. b. Eve, MO, Aug. 14, 1926. e. Univ. of OK.
THEATER: New Faces of 1952, Sandhog, Trouble in Tahiti, Maybe Tuesday, A Thurber Carnival, The Sign in Sidney Brustein's Window (Tony Award, 1965), Stop Thief Stop, Annie, The Beauty Part, Livin' The Life, Nunsense, Come Blow Your Horn, Bye Bye Birdie, Arsenic and Old Lace, Shangri-La.
PICTURES: New Faces (debut, 1954), To Kill a Mockingbird, My Six Loves, Ace Eli and Rodger of the Skies, Gator, Rabbit Test, Grease, Not for Publication, Viva Ace, The Flim Flam Man, With Six You Get Egg Roll, The Graduate, Blue Sunshine, Record City, The Wrong Guys, Odd Couple II.
TELEVISION: *Series*: The Jackie Gleason Show (1962-64), Captain Nice, The Jonathan Winters Show, Bewitched, Mayberry R.F.D., Nichols, The Julie Andrews Hour, Temperatures Rising, Small Wonder, Designing Women. *Movie*: Two on a Bench, Perry Mason: The Case of the Silenced Singer. *Specials*: Cinderella, Twelfth Night, Shangri-La, Everybody's Doin' It. *Guest*: Please Don't Eat the Daisies, Get Smart, Love American Style, Hogan's Heroes, The Odd Couple, What's Happening!, Good Times, Gimme a Break, The Golden Girls, The Client, Cybill, etc.

GIANNINI, GIANCARLO
Actor. b. Spezia, Italy, Aug. 1, 1942. Acquired degree in electronics but immediately after school enrolled at Acad. for Drama in Rome. Cast by Franco Zeffirelli as Romeo at age of 20. Subsequently appeared in a play also directed by Zeffirelli, Two Plus Two No Longer Make Four, written by Lina Wertmuller.
PICTURES: Rita la Zanzara, Arabella, Anzio, Fraulein Doktor, The Secret of Santa Vittoria, Love and Anarchy, The Seduction of Mimi, Swept Away by an Unusual Destiny in the Blue Sea of August, Seven Beauties, How Funny Can Sex Be?, A Night Full of Rain, The Innocent, Buone Notizie (also prod.), Revenge, Travels with Anita, Lili Marleen, Lovers and Liars, La Vita e Bella, Picone Sent Me, Immortal Bachelor, American Dreamer, Fever Pitch, Saving Grace, New York Stories (Life Without Zoe), I Picari, The Sleazy, Uncle, Snack Bar Budapest, Oh King, Blood Red, Brown Bread Sandwiches, Killing Time, Short Cut, Night Sun, Criminals, Once Upon a Crime, Giovanni Falcone, Colpo di Coda, Celluloide, A Walk in the Clouds, New York Crossing, Come Due Coccodrilli, La Frontiera, Broken Dreams, The Scirocco Room, The Last Target, Blood of a Poet, La Lupa, Heaven Before I Die, Lorca, Mimic, Vuoti o Perdere.
TELEVISION: Sins, Jacob, Nessuno Escluso, Voglia Di Volare, World Cup '98.

GIANNOLI, XAVIER
Director.
PICTURES: J'aime beaucoup ce que vous faites, Dialogue au sommet, L'Interview (Cannes Film Fest. Palme d'Or, 1998).

GIANOPULOUS, JIM
Executive. Pres., Fox International Theatrical Distribution, Twentieth Century Fox, Inc.

GIBBS, DAVID
Executive. b. 1944. Ent. motion picture industry 1961, Kodak research, worked as a photographer for Kodak 1963-66. Lectured at Harrow College of Technology and Kodak Photographic School until 1972. Left Kodak, 1975, after three years as a market specialist to join Filmatic Laboratories. Appt. asst. man. director, 1977, becoming chmn. and man. director, 1988. Member of RTS, SMPTE and IVCA. Past Chmn. BISFA 1988-90. Past president of the British Kinematograph, Sound and Television Society.

GIBBS, MARLA
Actress. b. Chicago, IL, June 14, 1931. e. Cortez Peters Business School, Chicago. Worked as receptionist, switchboard operator, travel consultant (1963-74) before co-starring as Florence Johnston on the Jeffersons (1974-85). Formed Marla Gibbs Enterprises, Los Angeles, 1978. Member of CA State Assembly, 1980. Image Award NAACP, 1979-83.
PICTURES: Black Belt Jones, Sweet Jesus, Preacher Man.
TELEVISION: Series: The Jeffersons, Checking In, 227. Movies: The Missing Are Deadly, Tell Me Where It Hurts, Nobody's Child. Mini-Series: The Moneychangers. Special: You Can't Take It With You.

GIBSON, DEREK
Executive. b. Huyton, England, July 7, 1945. e. Wigan Col. Head of Prod. at Astral Bellevue Pathe, 1979-80; v.p. Sandy Howard Prods.; Pres. Hemdale Film Group., 1982-present.
PICTURES: Prod./Exec.: Death Ship, Savage Harvest, Triumphs of a Man Called Horse, The Terminator, River's Edge, Platoon, Hoosiers, Salvador, At Close Range, Scenes from a Goldmine, Best Seller, War Party, Vampire's Kiss, Staying Together, Out Cold, Shag, Miracle Mile, Criminal Law, Hidden Agenda, Don't Tell Her It's Me, Bright Angel.

GIBSON, HENRY
Actor. b. Germantown, PA, Sept. 21, 1935. e. Catholic U. of America. Appeared as child actor with stock companies, 1943-57; B'way debut in My Mother My Father and Me, 1962.
PICTURES: The Nutty Professor, Kiss Me Stupid, The Outlaws Is Coming, Charlotte's Web (voice), The Long Goodbye, Nashville (Nat'l Soc. Film Critics Award, 1975), The Last Remake of Beau Geste, Kentucky Fried Movie, A Perfect Couple, The Blues Brothers, Tulips, Health, The Incredible Shrinking Woman, Monster in the Closet, Brenda Starr, Inner Space, Switching Channels, The 'Burbs, Night Visitor, Gremlins II, Tune in Tomorrow, Tom and Jerry: The Movie (voice), A Sailor's Tattoo, Biodome, Color of a Brisk and Leaping Day, Mother Night (voice), Asylum, A Stranger in the Kingdom.
TELEVISION: Series: Rowan and Martin's Laugh-In (1968-72). Movies: Evil Roy Slade, Every Man Needs One, The New Original Wonder Woman (pilot), Escape from Bogen County, The Night They Took Miss Beautiful, Amateur Night at the Dixie Bar & Grill, For the Love of It, Nashville Grab, Long Gone, Slow Burn, Return to Green Acres, Return to Witch Mountain. Mini-Series: Around the World in 80 Days.

GIBSON, MEL
Actor, Director. b. Peekskill, NY, Jan. 3, 1956. Emigrated in 1968 to Australia with family. Attended Nat'l Inst. of Dramatic Art in Sydney; in 2nd yr. was cast in his first film, Summer City. Graduated from NIDA, 1977. Joined South Australian Theatre Co. in 1978, appearing in Oedipus, Henry IV, Cedoona. Other plays include Romeo and Juliet, No Names No Pack Drill, On Our Selection, Waiting for Godot, Death of a Salesman.
PICTURES: Summer City (Coast of Terror; debut, 1977), Mad Max, Tim, Chain Reaction (unbilled), Attack Force Z, Gallipoli, The Road Warrior (Mad Max II), The Year of Living Dangerously, The Bounty, The River, Mrs. Soffel, Mad Max Beyond Thunderdome, Lethal Weapon, Tequila Sunrise, Lethal Weapon 2, Bird on a Wire, Air America, Hamlet, Lethal Weapon 3, Forever Young, The Man Without a Face (also dir.), Maverick, Braveheart (also dir., co-prod.; Academy Award, 1996; Golden Globe, 1996), Casper (cameo), Pocahontas (voice), Ransom, Conspiracy Theory, Lethal Weapon 4, Payback.
TELEVISION: Series: The Sullivans, The Oracle. Specials: The Ultimate Stuntman: A Tribute to Dar Robinson, Australia's Outback: The Vanishing Frontier (host). Guest host: Saturday Night Live.

GIELGUD, SIR JOHN
Actor. b. London, England, Apr. 14, 1904. e. Westminster Sch., Lady Benson's Sch. (dram.), London; Royal Acad. of Dramatic Art. Knighted, 1953. Autobiography: Early Stages (1983). Honorary degress: Oxford, London, St. Andrews, Brandeis (U.S), Assoc. Legion of Honor.
THEATER: Began stage career in Shakespearean roles; on London stage also in the Constant Nymph, The Good Companions, Dear Octopus, The Importance of Being Earnest, Dear Brutus, etc., various Shakespearean seasons, London & N.Y. 1988: The Best of Friends.
PICTURES: Who is the Man? (debut, 1924), The Clue of the New Pin; Insult (sound debut, 1932), The Good Companions, Secret Agent, The Prime Minister, Julius Caesar (1953), Romeo and Juliet, Richard III, Around the World in 80 Days, The Barretts of Wimpole Street, Saint Joan, Hamlet, Becket (Acad. Award nom.), To Die in Madrid (narrator), The Loved One, Chimes at Midnight (Falstaff), Sebastian, Assignment to Kill, The Charge of the Light Brigade, The Shoes of the Fisherman, Oh What a Lovely War, Julius Caesar (1971), Eagle in a Cage, Lost Horizon, Galileo, 11 Harrowhouse, Gold, Murder on the Orient Express, Aces High, Providence, Portrait of the Artist as a Young Man, Joseph Andrews, Murder by Decree, Caligula, The Human Factor, The Elephant Man, The Formula, Sphinx, Lion of the Desert, Arthur (Academy Award, best supporting actor, 1981), Chariots of Fire, Priest of Love, Gandhi, The Wicked Lady, Invitation to the Wedding, Scandalous, The Shooting Party, Plenty, Time After Time, Whistle Blower, Appointment With Death, Bluebeard Bluebeard, Arthur 2 on the Rocks, Getting It Right, Strike It Rich, Prospero's Books, Shining Through, The Power of One, First Knight, Haunted, Shine, The Leopard Son (narrator), Hamlet.
TELEVISION: Specials/Movies/Mini-Series: A Day by the Sea, The Browning Version, The Rehearsal, Great Acting, Ages of Man, Mayfly and th Frog, Cherry Orchard, Ivanov, From Chekhov With Love, St. Joan, Good King Charles' Golden Days, Conversation at Night, Hassan, Deliver Us from Evil, Heartbreak House, Brideshead Revisited, The Canterville Ghost, The Hunchback of Notre Dame, Inside the Third Reich, Marco Polo, The Scarlet and the Black, The Master of Ballantrae, Wagner, The Far Pavillions, Camille, Romance on the Orient Express, Funny You Don't Look 200, Oedipus the King, A Man For All Seasons, War and Remembrance, Summer Lease (Emmy Award, 1991), The Best of Friends, Inspector Alleyn: Hand in Glove, Leave All Fair, Ages of Man, John Gielgud: An Actor's Life, Lovejoy: The Lost Colony, Scarlett.

GILBERT, ARTHUR N.
Producer. b. Detroit, MI, Oct. 17, 1920. Lt., U.S.M.C., 1941-45. e. U. of Chicago, 1946. Special Agent, FBI, 1946-53; world sales dir., Gen. Motors, Cadillac Div., 1953-59; investments in mot. pictures and hotel chains, 1959-64; exec. prod., Mondo Hollywood, 1965; exec. prod. Jeannie-Wife Child, 1966; assoc. prod., The Golden Breed, 1967; commissioned rank of Colonel U.S.M.C., 1968; 1970-80, exec. prod. Jaguar Pictures Corp; Columbia, 1981-86; Indi Pic. Corp. Also account exec. and v.p. Pacific Western Tours. v.p., Great Basion Corp. Bev. Hills 1987-9; v.p., Lawrence 3-D TV 1990-present; v.p. Cougar Prods. Co. 1990-91. Producer in development at Jonte Prods. of Paris/London, 1992-94.
PICTURES: The Glory Stompers, Fire Grass, Cycle Savages, Bigfoot, Incredible Transplant, Balance of Evil.

GILBERT, BRUCE
Producer. b. Los Angeles, CA, March 28, 1947. e. U. of California. Pursued film interests at Berkeley's Pacific Film Archive; in summer involved in production in film dept. of San Francisco State U. Founded progressive pre-school in Bay Area. Became story editor in feature film division of Cine-Artists; involved in several projects, including Aloha, Bobby and Rose. Formally partnered with Jane Fonda in IPC Films, Inc., then pres., American Filmworks.
PICTURES: Coming Home (assoc. prod.), The China Syndrome (exec. prod.). Producer: Nine to Five, On Golden Pond, Rollover, The Morning After, Man Trouble, Jack the Bear.
TELEVISION: Series: Nine to Five (exec. prod.). Movies: The Dollmaker (exec. prod.), By Dawn's Early Light (writer, exec. prod.).

GILBERT, LEWIS
Producer, Writer, Director, Former Actor. b. London, England, Mar. 6, 1920. In RAF, W.W.II. Screen debut, 1932; asst. dir. (1930-39) with London Films, Assoc. British, Mayflower, RKO-Radio; from 1939-44 attached U.S. Air Corps Film Unit (asst. dir., Target for Today). In 1944 joined G.B.I. as writer and dir. In 1948, Gainsborough Pictures as writer, dir., 1949; Argyle Prod. 1950; under contract Nettlefold Films, Ltd. as dir.
PICTURES: *Actor*: Under One Roof, I Want to Get Married, Haunting Melody. Director: The Little Ballerina, Marry Me (s.p. only), Once a Sinner, Scarlet Thread, There Is Another Sun, Time Gentlemen Please, Emergency Call, Cosh Boy, Johnny on the Run, Albert R.N., The Good Die Young, The Sea Shall Not Have Them, Reach for the Sky, Cast a Dark Shadow, The Admirable Crichton, Carve Her Name with Pride, A Cry from the Street, Ferry to Hong Kong, Sink the Bismarck, Light Up the Sky, The Greengage Summer, H.M.S. Defiant, The Patriots, Spare the Rod, The Seventh Dawn, Alfie, You Only Live Twice, The Adventurers, Friends (also prod., story), Paul & Michelle (also prod., story), Operation Daybreak, Seven Nights in Japan, The Spy Who Loved Me, Moonraker, Educating Rita (also prod.), Not Quite Paradise, Shirley Valentine (also prod.), Stepping Out (also co-prod.), Haunted (also s.p.).

GILBERT, MELISSA
Actress. b. Los Angeles, CA, May 8, 1964. m. actor Bruce Boxleitner. Made debut at age of 3 in TV commercial. Comes from show business family: father, late comedian Paul Gilbert; mother, former dancer-actress Barbara Crane. Grandfather, Harry Crane created The Honeymooners. NY Off-B'way debut A Shayna Madel (1987; Outer Critics Circle & Theatre World Awards).
PICTURES: Sylvester (debut, 1985), Ice House.
TELEVISION: *Series*: Little House on the Prairie, Stand By Your Man, Sweet Justice. *Guest*: Gunsmoke, Emergency, Tenafly, The Hanna-Barbera Happy Hour, Love Boat. *Movies*: Christmas Miracle in Caulfield U.S.A., The Miracle Worker, Splendor in the Grass, Choices of the Heart, Choices, Penalty Phase, Family Secrets, Killer Instincts, Without Her Consent, Forbidden Nights, Blood Vows: The Story of a Mafia Wife, Joshua's Heart, Donor, The Lookalike, With a Vengeance, Family of Strangers, With Hostile Intent, Shattered Trust: The Shari Karney Story, House of Secrets, Dying to Remember, Babymaker: The Dr. Cecil Jacobson Story, Against Her Will: The Carrie Buck Story, Cries From the Heart, A Touch of Truth, Danielle Steel's Zoya, Seduction in a Small Town, Christmas in My Home Town, Childhood Sweetheart, Me & My Hormones (dir.).

GILER, DAVID
Producer, Writer, Director. b. New York, NY. Son of Bernie Giler, screen and TV writer. Began writing in teens; first work an episode for ABC series, The Gallant Men. Feature film career began as writer on Myra Breckenridge (1970).
PICTURES: *Writer*: The Parallax View, Fun with Dick and Jane, The Blackbird (also dir.), Southern Comfort (also prgd.). *Prod.*: Aliens (story), Rustlers' Rhapsody, Let It Ride, Alien³(ex. prod., also writer).
TELEVISION: *Writer*: The Kraft Theatre, Burke's Law, The Man from U.N.C.L.E., The Girl from U.N.C.L.E., Tales From the Crypt (exec. prod.).

GILLIAM, TERRY
Writer, Director, Actor, Animator. b. Minneapolis, MN, Nov. 22, 1940. e. Occidental Coll. Freelance writer and illustrator for various magazines and ad agencies before moving to London. Animator for BBC series Do Not Adjust Your Set, We Have Ways of Making You Laugh. Member, Monty Python's Flying Circus (1969-76). Books incl. numerous Monty Python publications. Honorary degrees: DFA Occidental Col. 1987, DFA Royal Col. of Art 1989.
PICTURES: And Now for Something Completely Different (animator, co-s.p., actor), Monty Python and the Holy Grail (co-dir., co-s.p., actor, animator), Jabberwocky (dir., co-s.p.), Life of Brian (actor, co-s.p., animator), The Do It Yourself Animation Film, Time Bandits (prod., dir., co-s.p.), Monty Python Live at the Hollywood Bowl (actor, co-s.p., animator, designer), The Miracle of Flight (animator, s.p.), Monty Python's The Meaning of Life (co-s.p., actor, animator), Spies Like Us (actor), Brazil (co-s.p., dir.), The Adventures of Baron Munchausen (dir., co-s.p.), The Fisher King (dir.), Twelve Monkeys (dir.).
TELEVISION: *Series*: Monty Python's Flying Circus (also animator, dir.), Do Not Adjust Your Set, We Have Ways of Making You Laugh, The Mart Feldman Comedy Machine, The Last Machine (1995).

GILMORE, WILLIAM S.
Producer. b. Los Angeles, CA, March 10, 1934. e. U. of California at Berkeley. Started career in film editing before becoming asst. dir. and prod. mgr. at Universal Studios, where worked on 20 feature films. Headed prod. for Mirisch Co. in Europe; then to Zanuck/Brown Co. as exec. in chg. prod. Sr. v.p./prod. of Filmways Pictures, supervising literary development, prod. and post-prod.

PICTURES: Jaws (prod. exec.), The Sugarland Express (prod. exec.), The Last Remake of Beau Geste, Defiance, Deadly Blessing, Tough Enough, Against All Odds, White Nights, Little Shop of Horrors, The Man in the Moon, The Player, A Few Good Men, Watch It, The Sandlot, Curse of the Starving Class, Fire Down Below.
TELEVISION: Just Me and You, One in a Million--The Ron Leflore Story, The Legend of Walks Far Woman, S.O.S. Titanic, Another Woman's Child, Women and Men, Women and Men 2.

GILROY, FRANK D.
Writer, Director. b. New York, NY, Oct. 13, 1925. e. Dartmouth; postgrad. Yale School of Drama. TV writer: Playhouse 90, US Steel Hour, Omnibus, Kraft Theatre, Lux Video Theater, Studio One. B'way playwright.
AUTHOR: *Plays*: Who'll Save the Plowboy? (Obie award, 1962), The Subject Was Roses (Pulitzer Prize & Tony Award, 1965), The Only Game in Town, Present Tense, The Next Contestant, Dreams of Glory, Real to Reel, Match Point, A Way with Words, The Housekeeper, Last Licks, Any Given Day. *Novels*: Private, Little Ego (with Ruth Gilroy), From Noon to 3. *Book*: I Wake Up Screening!: Everything You Need to Know About Making Independent Films Including a Thousand Reasons Not To (1993).
PICTURES: *Writer*: The Fastest Gun Alive, The Gallant Hours, The Subject Was Roses, The Only Game in Town. *Dir.-Writer*: Desperate Characters (also prod.), From Noon Till Three, Once in Paris, The Gig, The Luckiest Man in the World.
TELEVISION: *Writer-Dir.*: The Doorbell Rang, Turning Point of Jim Malloy, Money Plays.

GILULA, STEPHEN
Executive. b. Herrin, IL, Aug. 20, 1950. e. Stanford U. UA Theatre Circuit, film booker for San Francisco area, 1973; Century Cinema Circuit, film buyer, LA, 1974. Co-founder, Landmark Theatre Corp., 1974; serving as pres., 1982-present. Landmark became a subsidiary of Metromedia Intl. Group Inc., in 1996. Chmn. NATO of California/Nevada, 1991-present; also on bd. of dirs. of NATO, 1992-present.

GIMBEL, ROGER
Producer, Executive. b. March 11, 1925. e. Yale. Began tv prod. career as creative chief of RCA Victor TV, then became assoc. prod. of the Tonight Show for NBC; named head of prog. dev. of NBC daytime programming; then prod. of the 90-minute NBC Tonight Specials, including The Jack Paar Show and the Ernie Kovacs Show. Became prod. and co-packager of the Glen Campbell Goodtime Hour for CBS, 1969; v.p. in chg. of prod. for Tomorrow Entertainment, 1971. Formed his own prod. co., Roger Gimbel's Tomorrow Enterprises, Inc., 1975; prod. Minstrel Man. Became U.S. pres. of EMI-TV, 1976. Received special personal Emmy as exec. prod. of War of the Children, 1975. Produced 33 movies for TV under the EMI banner and won 18 Emmys. In 1984, EMI-TV became the Peregrine Producers Group, Inc., of which he was pres. & COO. 1987, spun off Roger Gimbel Prods. as an independent film co; 1988-89, pres./exec. prod., Carolco/Gimbel Productions, Inc. 1989-1996, pres. & exec. prod. of Roger Gimbel Prods Inc. in association with Multimedia Motion Pictures Inc. 1997, pres. & exec. prod. of Roger Gimbel Prods Inc for independent film production.
TELEVISION: *Movies/Specials*: The Autobiography of Miss Jane Pittman, Born Innocent, Birds of Prey, Brand New Life, Gargoyles, Glass House, In This House of Brede, I Heard the Owl Call My Name, I Love You Goodbye, Larry, Miles to Go Before I Sleep, Queen of the Stardust Ballroom, Tell Me Where It Hurts, The Man Who Could Talk to Kids, Things in Their Season, A War of Children (Emmy Award), The Amazing Howard Hughes, Deadman's Curve, Steel Cowboy, Betrayal, The Cracker Factory, Survival of Diana, Can You Hear the Laughter?, S.O.S. Titanic, Walks-Far Woman, Sophia Loren: Her Own Sotory, Manions of America, A Question of Honor, The Killing of Randy Webster, Broken Promise, A Piano for Mrs. Cimino, Deadly Encounter, Aurora, Rockabye, Blackout, Apology, Montana, Shattered Dreams, Chernobyl: The Final Warning, Desperate Rescue: The Cathy Mahone Story, Murder Between Friends, The Perfect Mother, etc.

GINNA, ROBERT EMMETT, JR.
Producer, Writer. b. New York, NY, Dec. 3, 1925. e. U. of Rochester, Harvard U., M.A. In U.S. Navy, WWII. Journalist for Life, Scientific American, Horizon, 1950-55; 1958-61, contributor to many magazines. Staff writer, producer, director NBC-TV, 1955-58; v.p., Sextant, Inc.; dir., Sextant Films Ltd., 1961-64. Founded Windward Productions, Inc., and Windward Film Productions, Ltd., 1965. Active in publishing 1974-82; sr. ed. People; ed. in chief, Little Brown; asst. mgr., Life. Resumed pres., Windward Prods, Inc., 1982; publishing consultant.
PICTURES: Young Cassidy (co-prod.), The Last Challenge (co-s.p.), Before Winter Comes (prod.), Brotherly Love (prod.).

GINNANE, ANTHONY I.
Executive, Producer. e. Melbourne U (law), 1976. 1977 formed joint venture with financier William Fayman for Australian film production and distribution. 1981 established company Film and General Holdings Inc. for locating film projects/financing.
PICTURES: *Producer or Exec. Prod:* Sympathy in Summer (debut, 1970; also dir.), Fantasm, Patrick, Snapshot, Thirst, Harlequin, Race for the Yankee Zephyr, Strange Behavior, Turkey Shoot, Prisoners, Second Tim Lucky, Mesmerized, Dark Age, Slate Wyn & Me, Initiation, High Tide, The Lighthorsemen, Time Guardian, Incident in Raven's Gate, The Everlasting Secret Family, The Dreaming, Grievous Bodily Harm, Boundaries of the Heart, Killer Instinct, Savage Justice, Outback, A Case of Honor, Siege of Firebase Gloria, Driving Force, Demonstone, Fatal Sky, No Contest, Screamers, Bonjour Timothy.

GINSBURG, LEWIS S.
Distributor, Importer, Prod. b. New York, NY, May 16, 1914. e. City Coll. of New York, 1931-32. Columbia U., 1932-33. Ent. film industry, tabulating dept., United Artists, 1933; sls. contract dept. 1934; asst. to eastern district mgr., 1938; slsmn., New Haven exch., 1939. Army, 1943. Ret. to U.S., then formed first buying & booking service in Connecticut, 1945-55; in chg., New England Screen Guild Exchanges, 1955; TV film distr., 1955; Formed & org. International Film Assoc., Vid-EX Film Distr. Corp., 1961. Prod., TV half-hour series; vice-pres. in chg., dist., Desilu Film Dist. C., 1962; organized Carl Releasing Co., 1963; Walter Reade-Sterling Inc., 1964-65; formed L.G. Films Corp.; contract and playdate mgr., 20th Fox, 1965-68. Cinerama Releasing Corp. Adm. Ass't to sales mgr., 1968-69; 20th Cent.-Fox. Nat'l sales coordinator, 1969-present. 1970, 20th Century-Fox, Asst. to the Sales Mgr. 1971, Transnational Pictures Corp., v.p. in chg. of dist., pres., Stellar IV Film Corp., 1972.

GIRARDOT, ANNIE
Actress. b. Paris, France, Oct. 25, 1931. Studied nursing. Studied acting at the Paris Conservatory, made her acting debut with the Comedie Franccaise. Has acted on the French stage and in reviews in the Latin Quarter.
PICTURES: Trezie a Table (debut, 1955), Speaking of Murder, Inspector Maigret, Love and the Frenchwoman, Rocco and His Brothers, Le Rendezvous, Crime Does Not Pay, Vice and Virtue, The Organizer, La Bonne Soupe (Careless Love), Male Companion, The Dirty Game, The Witches, Live for Life, Les Galoises Bleues, Dillinger Is Dead, The Seed of Man, Trois Chambres a Manhattan (Venice Film Fest. Award), The Story of a Woman, Love Is a Funny Thing, Shock!, Where THere's Smoke, Juliette et Juliette, The Slap, It Is Raining in Santiago, No Time for Breakfast (Cesar Award), Dear Inspector, The Skirt Chaser, Traffic Jam, Jupiter's Thigh, Five Days in June, La Vie Continue, Prisonniers, Comedie D'Amour, Girls With Guns, Les Miserables.

GISH, ANNABETH
Actress. b. Albuquerque, NM, Mar. 13, 1971. e. Duke U ('93). Started acting at age 8; appeared in several TV commercials in Iowa.
PICTURES: Desert Bloom, Hiding Out, Mystic Pizza, Shag, Coupe de Ville, Wyatt Earp, The Red Coat, Nixon, The Last Supper, Beautiful Girls, Steel.
TELEVISION: *Series:* Courthouse. *Movies:* Hero in the Family, When He's Not a Stranger, The Last to Go, Lady Against the Odds, Silent Cries. *Mini-Series:* Scarlett.

GIVENS, ROBIN
Actress. b. New York, NY, Nov. 27, 1964. e. Sarah Lawrence Col., Harvard Univ. Graduate Sch. of Arts & Sciences. While at college became model, made appearances on daytime dramas The Guiding Light and Loving.
PICTURES: A Rage in Harlem (debut, 1991), Boomerang, Foreign Student, Blankman.
TELEVISION: *Series:* Head of the Class, Angel Street, Courthouse, Sparks. *Movies:* Beverly Hills Madam, The Women of Brewster Place, The Penthouse, Dangerous Intentions.

GLASER, PAUL MICHAEL
Actor, Director. b. Cambridge, MA, March 25, 1943. e. Tulane U., Boston U., M.A. Did five seasons in summer stock before starting career in New York, making stage debut in Rockabye Hamlet in 1968. Appeared in numerous off-B'way plays and got early TV training as regular in daytime series, Love of Life and Love Is a Many Splendored Thing.
PICTURES: *Actor:* Fiddler on the Roof, Butterflies Are Free, Phobia. *Director:* Band of the Hand, The Running Man, The Cutting Edge, The Air Up There, Kazaam (also prod., story).
TELEVISION: *Series:* Starsky and Hutch. *Guest:* Kojak, Toma, The Streets of San Francisco, The Rockford Files, The Sixth Sense, The Waltons. *Movies:* Trapped Beneath the Sea, The Great Houdinis, Wait Till Your Mother Gets Home!, Princess Daisy, Jealousy, Attack on Fear, Single Bars Single Women, Amazons (dir. only).

GLASS, PHILIP
Composer, Actor, Writer. b. Baltimore, MD, Jan. 31, 1937.
PICTURES: Cenere, Chappaqua, Mark Di Suvero Sculptor, Four American Composers (also actor), Koyaanisqatsi, High Wire, Mishima: A Life in Four Chapters, Dead End Kids, Hamburger Hill, Einstein on the Beach: The Changing Image of Opera, The Thin Blue Line, Powaqqatsi, Le Chiesa, Mindwalk, Closet Land, Anima Mundi, Candyman, A Brief History of Time, Niki de Saint Phalle: Wer ist das Monster-du oder ich?, Jenipapo, Candyman: Farewell to the Flesh, The Secret Agent, Absence Stronger Than Presence, Bent, Kundun (LA Film Critics Award, Best Musical Score, 1997), The Truman Show (actor), Noyaqqatsi (also s.p.).

GLAZER, WILLIAM
Executive b. Cambridge, MA. e. State U. of New York, Entered m.p. ind. with Ralph Snider Theatres 1967-69; General Cinema Corp. 1969-71; Loews Theatres 1971-73; Joined Sack Theatres/USA Cinemas 1973 as Dist. mgr.; 1974 Exec. Asst. to Pres.; 1976 Gen. Mgr.; 1980 V.P. Gen. Mgr.; 1982-86 Exec. V.P. Joined Interstated Theatres 1987 (Pres.); Pax Theatres 1993-95. MP industry consultant, 1988-pres. Bd. of Dir. Member of SMPTE; NATO (Exec. Bd.); Theatre Owners of New England (Pres. and Chairman.)

GLEASON, LARRY
Executive. b. Boston, MA, Apr. 30, 1938. e. Boston Coll., M.A., 1960. Held various positions, western div., mgr., General Cinema Corp.; 1963-73; gen. mgr., Gulf States Theatres, New Orleans, 1973-74; pres., Mann Theatres, 1974-85; joined DeLaurentiis Entertainment Group as pres., mktg./dist., 1985. Named sr. v.p., Paramount Pictures Corp, theatrical exhibition group, 1989. Named pres. Paramount Pictures Corp. theatrical exhib. group, 1991. Joined MGM/UA as pres. of Worlwide Distrib., 1994. Foundation of Motion Picture Pioneers v.p. Member, Variety Club, Will Rogers Foundation.

GLEN, JOHN
Director. b. Sunbury on Thames, Eng., May 15, 1932. Entered industry in 1947. Second unit dir.: On Her Majesty's Secret Service, The Spy Who Loved Me, Wild Geese, Moonraker (also editor). Editor: The Sea Wolves.
PICTURES: For Your Eyes Only (dir. debut, 1981), Octopussy, A View to a Kill, The Living Daylights, Licence to Kill, Aces: Iron Eagle III, Christopher Columbus: The Discovery.
TELEVISION: *Series:* Space Precinct (7 episodes).

GLENN, CHARLES OWEN
Executive. b. Binghamton, NY, March 27, 1938. e. Syracuse U., B.A., U. of PA. Capt., U.S. Army, 1961-63. Asst. to dir. of adv., 20th Cent. Fox, 1966-67; asst. adv. mgr., Paramount, 1967-68; acct. spvsr. & exec., MGM record & m.p. div., 1968-69; nat'l adv. mgr., Paramount, 1969-70; nat'l dir. of adv., Paramount, 1970-71; v.p. adv.-pub.-prom., 1971-73; v.p. marketing, 1974; v.p. prod. mktg., 1975; joined American Intl. Pictures as v.p. in chg. of adv./creative affairs, 1979. 1980, when Filmways took AIP over he was named their v.p. in chg. worldwide adv./pub./promo.; joined MCA/Universal in 1982 as exec. v.p., adv.-promo.; 1984, appt. Orion Pictures adv.-pub.-promo. exec. v.p.; 1987, appt. Orion mktg. exec. v.p. 1989 recipient Outstanding Performance Award Leukemia Society of Amer. for completing NYC Marathon. 1993, pres. mktg., Bregman/Baer Prods. Featured actor in 1993 film Philadelphia. Member: Exec. comm. public relations branch, Academy of M.P. Arts & Sciences. Holder of NATO mktg. exec. of year (1983) award, Clio Award for U.S. adv. of Platoon; Variety Club, Motion Picture Pioneers, Screen Actors Guild.

GLENN, SCOTT
Actor. b. Pittsburgh, PA, Jan. 26, 1942. e. William & Mary Coll. Worked as U.S. Marine, newspaper reporter before going to New York to study drama at Actors Studio in 1968.
THEATER: *Off-B'way:* Zoo Story, Fortune in Men's Eyes, Long Day's Jack Street, Journey into Night. *B'way:* The Impossible Years, Burn This, Dark Picture.
PICTURES: The Baby Maker (debut, 1970), Angels Hard as They Come, Hex, Nashville, Fighting Mad, More American Graffiti, Apocalypse Now, Urban Cowboy, Cattle Annie and Little Britches, Personal Best, The Challenge, The Right Stuff, The Keep, The River, Wild Geese II, Silverado, Verne Miller, Man on Fire, Off Limits, Miss Firecracker, The Hunt for Red October, The Silence of the Lambs, My Heroes Have Always Been Cowboys, Backdraft, The Player, Night of the Running Man, Tall Tale, Reckless, Edie and Pen, Courage Under Fire, Carla's Song, Courage Under Fire, Edue & Pen, Absolute Power.
TELEVISION: *Movies:* Gargoyles, As Summers Die, Intrigue, The Outside Woman, Women & Men 2, Shadowhunter, Slaughter of the Innocents, Past Tense.

GLENNON, JAMES M.
Cinematographer. b. Burbank, CA, Aug. 29, 1942. e. UCLA. m. actress Charmaine Glennon. Focus Awards judge 1985-; bd. or dirs., UCLA Theatre Arts Alumni Assoc. 1985-. ASC - member of American Society of Cinematographers, AMPAS.
PICTURES: Return of the Jedi, El Norte, The Wild Life, Smooth Talk, Flight of the Navigator, Time of Destiny, A Show of Force, December, The Gift, Citizen Ruth, Best Men.
TELEVISION: Lemon Sky (American Playhouse), Laurel Ave, DEA (pilot), Bakersfield (pilot), Judicial Consent.

GLESS, SHARON
Actress. b. Los Angeles, CA, May 31, 1943. m. producer Barney Rosenzweig. London stage: Misery.
PICTURES: Airport 1975, The Star Chamber.
TELEVISION: *Series*: Marcus Welby M.D., Faraday and Co., Switch, Turnabout, House Calls, Cagney and Lacey (2 Emmy Awards, Golden Globe Award), The Trials of Rosie O'Neill (Golden Globe Award). *Mini-Series*: Centennial, The Immigrants, The Last Convertible. *Movies*: The Longest Night, All My Darling Daughters, My Darling Daughters' Anniversary, Richie Brockelman: Missing 24 Hours, The Flying Misfits, The Islander, Crash, Whisper in the Gloom (Disney), Hardhat and Legs, Moviola: The Scarlett O'Hara War, Revenge of the Stepford Wives, The Miracle of Kathy Miller, Hobson's Choice, The Sky's No Limit, Letting Go, The Outside Woman, Honor Thy Mother, Separated by Murder, Cagney & Lacey: The Return, Cagney & Lacey: Together Again, Cagney & Lacey: True Convictions, Cagney & Lacey: The View Through the Glass Ceiling, The Girl Next Door.

GLICK, PHYLLIS
Executive. b. New York, NY. e. Queens Coll. of C.U.N.Y. Began career with Otto-Windsor Associates, as casting director; left to be independent. 1979, joined ABC-TV as mgr. of comedy series development; promoted 1980 to director, involved with all comedy series developed for network. 1985, joined Paramount Pictures as exec. dir., production, for M.P. Group; 1989, co-exec. prod., Living Dolls.

GLOBUS, YORAM
Producer. b. Israel, Came to U.S. 1979. Has co-produced many films with cousin and former partner Menahem Golan. Sr. exec. v.p., Cannon Group; Pres. and CEO Cannon Entertainment and Cannon Films; 1989 named chmn. and C.E.O Cannon Entertainment and officer of Cannon Group Inc.; then co-pres. Pathe Communications Corp. and chmn. and C.E.O. Pathe Intl. Left MGM/Pathe in 1991.
PICTURES: All as producer or exec. prod. with Menahem Golan: Sallah; Trunk to Cairo; My Margo; What's Good for the Goose; Escape to the Sun; I Love You, Rosa; The House on Chelouch Street; The Four Deuces; Kazablan; Diamonds; God's Gun; Kid Vengeance, Operation Thunderbolt, The Uranium Conspiracy, Savage Weekend, The Magician of Lublin, The Apple, The Happy Hooker Goes to Hollywood, Dr. Heckyl and Mr. Hype, The Godsend, New Year's Evil, Schizoid, Seed of Innocence, Body and Soul, Death Wish II, Enter the Ninja, Hospital Massacre, The Last American Virgin, Championship Season, Treasure of Four Crowns, 10 to Midnight, Nana, I'm Almost Not Crazy..., John Cassavetes: The Man and His Work, The House of Long Shadows, Revenge of the Ninja, Hercules, The Wicked Lady, Sahara, The Ambassador, Bolero, Exterminator 2, The Naked Face, Missing in Action, Hot Resort, Love Streams, Breakin', Grace Quigley, Making the Grade, Ninja III-The Domination, Breakin' 2: Electric Boogaloo, Lifeforce, Over the Brooklyn Bridge, The Delta Force, The Assisi Underground, Hot Chili, The Berlin Affair, Missing in Action 2-The Beginning, Rappin', Thunder Alley, American Ninja, Mata Hari, Death Wish 3, King Solomon's Mines, Runaway Train, Fool for Love, Invasion U.S.A., Maria's Lovers, Murphy's Law, The Naked Cage, P.O.W.: The Escape, The Texas Chainsaw Massacre, Part 2, Invaders from Mars, 52 Pick-Up, Link, Firewalker, Dumb Dicks, The Nutcracker: The Motion Picture, Avenging Force, Hashigaon Hagadol, Journey to the Center of the Earth, Prom Queen, Salome, Otello, Cobra, America 3000, American Ninja 2: The Confrontation, Allan Quartermain and the Lost City of Gold, Assassination, Beauty and the Beast, Down Twisted, Duet for One, The Emperor's New Clothes, The Hanoi Hilton, The Barbarians, Dutch Treat, Masters of the Universe, Number One with a Bullet, Rumpelstiltskin, Street Smart, UnderCover, The Assault, Hansel and Gretel, Going Bananas, Snow White, Sleeping Beauty, Tough Guys Don't Dance, Shy People, Dancers, Red Riding Hood, King Lear, Braddock: Missing in Action III, Too Much, Die Papierene Brucke, Field of Honor, Barfly (exec. prod.), Surrender (exec. prod.), Death Wish 4: The Crackdown (exec. prod.), Gor (exec. prod.), Business as Usual (exec. prod.), Over the Top, Superman IV: The Quest for Peace. Prod.: Delta Force, Operation Crackdown, Manifesto, Stranglehold, Delta Force II, Cyborg, Step By Step. Exec. prod.: The Kitchen Toto, Doin' Time on Planet Earth, Kickboxer, Kinjite, A Man Called Sarge, The Rose Garden, The Secret of the Ice Cave.

GLOVER, CRISPIN
Actor. b. New York, NY, 1964. e. Mirman School. Trained for stage with Dan Mason and Peggy Feury. Stage debut, as Friedrich Von Trapp, The Sound of Music, Los Angeles, 1977. Wrote books, Rat Catching (1987), Oak Mot (1990), Concrete Inspection (1992), What It Is and How It Is Done (1995). Recorded album The Big Problem Does Not Equal the Solution- The Solution Equals Let it Be.
PICTURES: My Tutor, Racing with the Moon, Friday the 13th-The Final Chapter, Teachers, Back to the Future, At Close Range, River's Edge, Twister, Where the Heart Is, Wild at Heart, The Doors, Little Noises, Rubin and Ed, Thirty Door Key, What's Eating Gilbert Grape, Chasers, Even Cowgirls Get the Blues, Crime and Punishment, Dead Man, What Is It? (dir. and wrote), The People vs. Larry Flynt.
TELEVISION: *Movie*: High School U.S.A. *Special*: Hotel Room (Blackout).

GLOVER, DANNY
Actor. b. San Francisco, CA, July 22, 1947. e. San Francisco State U. Trained at Black Actors Workshop of American Conservatory Theatre. Appeared in many stage productions (Island, Macbeth, Sizwe Banzi Is Dead, etc.). On N.Y. stage in Suicide in B Flat, The Blood Knot, Master Harold... and the Boys (Theatre World Award).
PICTURES: Escape from Alcatraz (debut, 1979), Chu Chu and the Philly Flash, Out (Deadly Drifter), Iceman, Places in the Heart, Witness, Silverado, The Color Purple, Lethal Weapon, Bat-21, Lethal Weapon 2, To Sleep with Anger (also co-exec. prod.), Predator 2, Flight of the Intruder, A Rage in Harlem, Pure Luck, Grand Canyon, Lethal Weapon 3, Bopha!, The Saint of Fort Washington, Maverick (cameo), Angels in the Outfield, Operation Dumbo Drop, Gone Fishin'.
TELEVISION: *Mini-Series*: Chiefs, Lonesome Dove, Queen. *Movies*: Face of Rage, Mandela, Dead Man Out. *Series*: Storybook Classics (host), Civil War Journal (host). *Specials*: And the Children Shall Lead, How the Leopard Got Its Spots (narrator), A Place at the Table, A Raisin in the Sun, Override (dir. only), Shelley Duvall's Tall Tales and Legends: John Henry. *Guest*: Lou Grant, Palmerstown U.S.A., Gimme a Break, Hill Street Blues, Many Mansions.

GLOVER, JOHN
Actor. b. Kingston, NY, Aug. 7, 1944. e. Towson State Coll., Baltimore.
THEATER: On regional theatre circuit; Off-B'way in A Scent of Flowers, Subject to Fits, The House of Blue Leaves, The Selling of the President, Love! Valour! Compassion! (also B'way; Tony Award, 1995). With APA Phoenix Co. in Great God Brown (Drama Desk Award), The Visit, Don Juan, Chermin de Fer, Holiday. Other NY stage: The Importance of Being Earnest, Hamlet, Frankenstein, Whodunnit, Digby. L.A.: The Traveler (L.A. Drama Critics Award), Lips Together Teeth Apart.
PICTURES: Shamus, Annie Hall, Julia, Somebody Killed Her Husband, Last Embrace, Success, Melvin and Howard, The Mountain Men, The Incredible Shrinking Woman, A Little Sex, The Evil That Men Do, A Flash of Green, 52 Pick-Up, White Nights, Something Special, Masquerade, A Killing Affair, Rocket Gibraltar, The Chocolate War, Scrooged, Meet the Hollowheads, Gremlins 2: The New Batch, Robocop 2, Ed and His Dead Mother, Night of the Running Man, In the Mouth of Madness, Schemes, Automatics, Batman and Robin, Love! Valour! Compassion!.
TELEVISION: *Movies*: A Rage of Angels, The Face of Rage, Ernie Kovacs-Between the Laughter, An Early Frost (Emmy nom.), Apology, Moving Target, Hot Paint, Nutcracker: Money Madness and Murder (Emmy nom.), David, The Traveling Man (ACE nom.), Twist of Fate, Breaking Point, El Diablo, What Ever Happened to Baby Jane?, Dead on the Money, Drug Wars: The Cocaine Cartel, Grass Roots, Majority Rule, Assault at West Point. *Specials*: An Enemy of the People, Paul Reiser: Out on a Whim, Crime and Punishment (Emmy nom.). *Mini-Series*: Kennedy, George Washington. *Series*: South Beach. *Guest*: L.A. Law (Emmy nom.), Frasier (Emmy nom.)

GLYNN, CARLIN
Actress. b. Cleveland, OH, Feb. 19, 1940. m. actor-writer-dir. Peter Masterson. Daughter is actress Mary Stuart Masterson. e. Sophie Newcomb College, 1957-58. Studied acting with Stella Adler, Wynn Handman and Lee Strasberg in NY. Debut, Gigi, Alley Theatre, Houston, TX 1959. Adjunct professor at Columbia U film sch. Resource advisor at the Sundance Inst.
THEATRE: (NY debut, 1960) Waltz of The Toreadors, The Best Little Whorehouse in Texas (Tony, Eleanora Duse & Olivier Awards), Winterplay, Alterations, Pal Joey (Chicago; Jos. Jefferson Award), The Cover of Life, The Young Man From Atlanta (winner, Pulitzer Prize for Drama, 1995), Amazing Grace.
PICTURES: Three Days of the Condor, Continental Divide, Sixteen Candles, The Trip to Bountiful, Gardens of Stone, Blood Red, Night Game, Convicts, Blessing, Judy Berlin.
TELEVISION: *Series*: Mr. President. *Mini-Series*: A Woman Named Jackie.

GODARD, JEAN-LUC
Writer, Director. b. Paris, France, Dec. 3, 1930. e. Lycee Buffon, Paris. Journalist, film critic Cahiers du Cinema. Acted in and financed experimental film Quadrille by Jacques Rivette, 1951. 1954: dir. first short, Operation Beton, followed by Une Femme Coquette. 1956, was film editor. 1957: worked in publicity dept. 20th Century Fox.
PICTURES: *Director/Writer*: Breathless (A Bout de Souffle; feature debut, 1960), Le Petit Soldat, A Woman Is a Woman, My Life to Live, Les Carabiniers, Contempt, Band of Outsiders, The Married Woman, Alphaville, Pierrot le Fou, Masculine-Feminine, Made in USA, Two or Three Things I Know About Her, La Chinoise, Weekend, Sympathy for the Devil, Le Gai Savoir, Tout a Bien (co-dir.), Numero Deux, Every Man For Himself, First Name Carmen, Hail Mary, Aria (Armide segment), King Lear, Keep Up Your Right (also edit, actor), Nouvelle Vogue (New Wave), Helas Pour Moi (Oh Woe is Me). Germany Year, J.L.G. by J.L.G., The Kids Play Russian.

GOLAN, MENAHEM
Producer, Director, Writer. b. Tiberias, Israel, May 31, 1929. e. NYU. Studied theater dir. at Old Vic Theatre London, m.p. prod. at City Coll, NY. Co-founder and prod. with cousin Yoram Globus, Golan-Globus Prods., Israel, then L.A., 1962. Later Noah Films, Israel, 1963, Ameri-Euro Pictures Corp, before buying controlling share in Cannon Films, 1979. Sr. exec. v.p., Cannon Group; chmn. of bd., Cannon Entertainment and Cannon Films. 1988, dir. and sr. exec. v.p. Cannon Group, chmn. and head of creative affairs, Cannon Entertainment when it became div. of Giancarlo Parretti's Pathe Communications Corp. Resigned March, 1989 to form 21st Century Film Corp as chmn. and CEO.
PICTURES: *Director/co-writer*: Kasablan, Diamonds, Entebbe (Operation Thunderbolt), Teyve and His Seven Daughters, What's Good for the Goose? Lepke, The Magician of Lublin, The Goodsend, Happy Hooker Goes to Hollywood, Enter the Ninja. *Producer-Writer-Director*: Mack the Knife, Hanna's War. *Producer-Director*: The Uranium Conspiracy, Delta Force, Over the Brooklyn Bridge, Over the Top. *Producer/Exec. prod.*: Sallah, Runaway Train, Sallah, Fool For Love, Maria's Lovers, Cobra, Evil Angels, I Love You Rosa, Body and Soul, also: Deathwish II, The Last American Virgin, That Championship Season, House of Long Shadows, Revenge of the Ninja, Hercules, The Movie Tales (12 children's fairy tales films), The Wicked Lady, Cobra, Barfly (exec. prod.), Breakin', Missing in Action, Dancers (prod.), Surrender (exec. prod.), Death Wish 4: The Crackdown (exec. prod.), King Lear (prod.), Too Much (prod.), Powaqquatsi (exec. prod.), Mercenary Fighters (prod.), Doin' Time on Planet Earth (prod.), Manifesto (prod.), Kinjite (exec. prod.), Messenger of Death (prod.), Alien From L.A. (prod.), Hero and the Terror (exec. prod.), Haunted Summer (exec. prod.), A Cry in the Dark (exec. prod.), Delta Force-Operation Crackdown (prod.), A Man Called Sarge (exec. prod.), Stranglehold: Delta Force II (prod.), Cyborg (prod.), The Rose Garden (exec. prod.), Rope Dancing (exec. prod.), The Phantom of the Opera.

GOLCHAN, FREDERIC
Producer. b. Neuilly sur Seine, France, Nov. 20, 1955. e. UCLA Film School, HEC in Paris, NYU Bus.Sch. Journalist/photographer for various European magazines. Worked for American Express, 1979-80. Started indept. investment banking firm, 1980-84. Started own production co., 1985. Directed Victory of the Deaf. V.P. French Hollywood Circle
PICTURES: Flagrant Desire, Quick Change, Intersection, The Associate.
TELEVISION: Freedom Fighter, Home by Midnight, In The Deep Woods.

GOLD, ERNEST
Composer, Conductor. b. Vienna, Austria, July 13, 1921. e. State Acad. for Music and Performing Arts, Austria 1937-38; private study, 1939-49 in U.S. Worked as song writer 1939-42 and taught in private schools, 1942. Composed first score for Columbia Pictures, 1945. Musical dir., Santa Barbara Symphony, 1958-59. Taught at UCLA, 1973 and 1983-90 (adult ed.). Gold record for soundtrack of Exodus, 1968. Received star on Walk of Fame on Hollywood Blvd., 1975. Elected to bd. of govs., AMPAS, 1984.
PICTURES: Smooth as Silk, Wyoming, Witness for the Prosecution, The Pride and the Passion, Too Much Too Soon, On the Beach (Acad. Award nom.), Exodus (Academy Award, 1960), Inherit the Wind, The Last Sunset, Judgment at Nuremberg, Pressure Point, A Child Is Waiting, It's a Mad Mad Mad Mad World (Acad. Award nom.), Ship of Fools, The Secret of Santa Vittoria (Acad. Award nom.), The Wild McCullochs, Cross of Iron, Fun With Dick and Jane, Good Luck Miss Wyckoff, The Runner Stumbles, Tom Horn.
TELEVISION: Small Miracle, Wallenberg: a Hero's Story.

GOLDBERG, FRED
Executive. b. New York, NY, Aug. 26, 1921. e. Pace Col., Sch. of Mktg. & Advt. Expl. Paramount, 1946; asst. expl. mgr. trade contact, syndicate contact, NY newspaper contact promotion mgr., 1946-52; asst. publ. mgr. RKO, 1952; natl. publ. mgr., IFE, 1953; v.p. Norton and Condon, pub., 1953; returned to IFE Sept. 1954 as natl. pub. mgr.; head of NY office, Arthur Jacobs, then Blowitz-Maskel, 1956; exec. asst. to dir. pub., adv. UA Corp., 1958; exec. dir., adv., pub. exploitation, UA Corp., 1961; named v.p., 1962;

sr. v.p., 1972; sr. v.p., dir. of mrkt., 1977. Left in 1978 to be cons. with Diener, Hauser & Bates Agency. In 1979 joined Columbia Pics. as sr. v.p. in chg. of adv./pub. Left in 1981 to form new co. 1982, sr. v.p. mktg., Orion Pictures. Became teacher of M.P. Mktg. & Distrib. at Univ. of Miami's Sch. of Comm. Author: Motion Picture Marketing & Distribution.

GOLDBERG, LEONARD
Executive, Producer. b. Brooklyn, NY, Jan. 24, 1934. e. Wharton ch., U. of Pennsylvania. Began career in ABC-TV research dept.; moved to NBC-TV research div.; 1961 joined BBD&Q ad agency in charge of overall bdcst. coordinator. In 1963 rejoined ABC-TV as mgr. of program devel. 1964-66, v.p., Daytime programs. 1966 named VP in chg of network TV programming. Resigned in 1969 to join Screen Gems as VP in chg. of prod. Left for partnership with Aaron Spelling in Spelling/Goldberg Prods.; later produced TV and theatrical films under own banner, Mandy Prods. 1986, named pres., COO, 20th Century Fox. Resigned, 1989. Elected to the board of Spectradyne Inc.
PICTURES: *Prod.*: All Night Long, WarGames, Space Camp, Sleeping With the Enemy, The Distinguished Gentleman, Aspen Extreme, Double Jeopardy.
TELEVISION: *Series*: The Rookies, SWAT, Starsky and Hutch, Charlie's Angels, Family, Hart to Hart, T.J. Hooker, Fantasy Island, Paper Dolls, The Cavanaughs, Class of '96. *Movies*: Brian's Song, Little Ladies of the Night, The Legend of Valentino, The Boy in the Plastic Bubble, Something About Amelia, Alex: The Life of a Child, She Woke Up, and numerous others.

GOLDBERG, WHOOPI
Actress. b. New York, NY, Nov. 13, 1949. r.n. Caryn Johnson. e. Sch. for the Performing Arts. Began performing at age 8 in N.Y. with children's program at Hudson Guild and Helena Rubenstein Children's Theatre. Moved to San Diego, CA, 1974, and helped found San Diego Rep. Theatre appearing in Mother Courage, Getting Out. Member: Spontaneous Combustion (improv. group). Joined Blake St. Hawkeyes Theatre in Berkeley, partnering with David Schein. Went solo to create The Spook Show, working in San Francisco and later touring U.S. & Europe. 1983 performance caught attention of Mike Nichols which led to B'way show (for which she received a Theatre World Award) based on it and directed by him. Founding member of Comic Relief benefits. Theatrical film debut in The Color Purple (1985; Image Award NAACP, Golden Globe). Author of, Alice.
THEATER: small roles in B'way prods. of Pippin, Hair, Jesus Christ Superstar. Living on the Edge of Chaos (tour, 1988), A Funny Thing Happened on the Way to the Forum.
PICTURES: The Color Purple (debut, 1985; Acad. Award nom.), Jumpin' Jack Flash, Burglar, Fatal Beauty, The Telephone, Clara's Heart, Beverly Hills Brats (cameo), Homer and Eddie, Ghost (Academy Award, best supporting actress, 1990), The Long Walk Home, Soapdish, House Party 2 (cameo), The Player, Sister Act, Wisecracks, Sarafina!, The Magic World of Chuck Jones, National Lampoon's Loaded Weapon 1 (cameo), Made in America, Sister Act 2: Back in the Habit, Naked in New York (cameo), The Lion King (voice), The Little Rascals, Corrina Corrina, Star Trek: Generations, Theodore Rex, The Pagemaster (voice), Liberation (narrator), Boys on the Side, Moonlight and Valentino, The Celluloid Closet, Bogus, Eddie, The Associate, Ghosts of Mississippi, An Alan Smithee Film.
TELEVISION: *Series*: Star Trek: The Next Generation, Bagdad Cafe, The Whoopi Goldberg Show (synd. talk show). *Specials*: Whoopi Goldberg Direct From Broadway, Comic Relief, Carol Carl Whoopi and Robin, Scared Straight: 10 Years Later, Funny You Don't Look 200, Comedy Tonight (host), My Past is My Own (Schoolbreak Special), Free to Be... a Family, The Debbie Allen Special, Cool Like That Christmas (voice), 34th Annual Grammy Awards (host), A Gala for the President's at Ford's Theatre (host), The 66th Annual Academy Awards (host), The 68th Annual Academy Awards (host). *Guest*: Moonlighting (Emmy nom.), A Different World. *Movie*: Kiss Shot.

GOLDBLUM, JEFF
Actor. b. Pittsburgh, PA, Oct. 22, 1952. Studied at Sanford Meisner's Neighborhood Playhouse in New York. On B'way in Two Gentleman of Verona, The Moony Shapiro Songbook. Off-B'way: El Grande de Coca Cola, City Sugar, Twelfth Night.
PICTURES: Death Wish (debut, 1974), California Split, Nashville, Next Stop Greenwich Village, St. Ives, Special Delivery, The Sentinel, Annie Hall, Between the Lines, Remember My Name, Thank God It's Friday, Invasion of the Body Snatchers, Threshold, The Big Chill, The Right Stuff, The Adventures of Buckaroo Banzai, Into the Night, Silverado, Transylvania 6-5000, The Fly, Beyond Therapy, Vibes, Earth Girls Are Easy, Twisted Obsession, The Tall Guy, Mr. Frost, The Player, Deep Cover, The Favor the Watch and the Very Big Fish, Fathers and Sons, Jurassic Park, Hideaway, Nine Months, Powder, The Great White Hype, Independence Day, Mad Dog Time, The Lost World: Jurassic Park.
TELEVISION: *Movies*: The Legend of Sleepy Hollow, Rehearsal for Murder, Ernie Kovacs: Between the Laughter, The Double Helix (BBC), Framed, Lush Life. *Series*: Tenspeed and Brownshoe, Future Quest (host). *Guest*: The Blue Knight, It's Garry Shandling's Show.

GOLDEN, HERBERT L.
b. Philadelphia, PA, Feb. 12, 1914. e. Temple U., 1936, B.S. Reporter, rewrite man. asst. city ed., Philadelphia Record, 1933-38; joined Variety, 1938; on leave of absence, 1942-43, when asst. to John Hay Whitney and Francis Alstock, directors, M.P. Division, Coordinator of Inter-American Affairs (U.S.); in U.S. Navy, 1943-46; then returned to Variety. m.p. ed. Consultant on motion pictures, Good Housekeeping magazine McGraw-Hill Publications, American Yearbook. Ent. Ind. Div. Bankers Trust Co., NY, 1952; named v.p. 1954-56; v.p. & mem. of bd. United Artists Corp., 1958; member of board, MPAA, 1959; pres., Lexington Int., Inc. investments, 1962; mem. bd., chmn. exec. com., Perfect Photo Inc., 1962; 1965 sect. & mem. bd. Century Broadcasting Group; chmn. G & G Thea. Corp.; pres. Diversifax Corp., 1966; consult. Pathe Lab, 1967; Mem. bd. Childhood Prod. Inc., Music Makers Group, Inc., Cinecom Corp. pres., Vere/Swiss Corp., 1977; mem. bd., Coral Reef Publications, Inc., 1977. Returned to Bankers Trust, 1979, to head its Media Group (service to film and TV industries). Retired, 1992.

GOLDEN, JEROME B.
Executive, Attorney. b. New York, NY, Nov. 26, 1917. e. St. Lawrence U., LL.B., 1942. Member legal dept., Paramount Pictures, Inc., 1942-50; United Paramount Theatres, Inc., 1950-53; ABC, Inc., 1953; secy., ABC, 1958-86; v.p., ABC, 1959-86. Consultant.

GOLDEN, PAT
Casting Director, Director. b. Pittsburgh, PA, July 21, 1951. e. U Pittsburgh, Carnegie-Mellon U. Has directed plays for theatre incl. Homeboy at Perry St. Th. in NY. Was in casting dept. of NY Shakespeare Festival Public Th. Served as assoc. prod. on PBS series The Negro Ensemble Company's 20th Anniversary. Assoc. prod.: Hallelujah (PBS); dir.: House Party 2 documentary, My Secret Place (tv pilot).
PICTURES: Ragtime, Beat Street, Krush Groove, The Killing Fields, Blue Velvet, Platoon (Awarded Casting Society of America Award), Dear America, The Handmaid's Tale, House Party 2 (assoc. prod.), Voyager, Posse.

GOLDENSON, LEONARD H.
Executive. b. Scottsdale, PA, December 7, 1905. e. Harvard Coll., B.A., Harvard Law School, LL.B. Practiced law, NY; counsel in reorg. Paramount theatres in New England, 1933-37; 1937 apptd. asst. to v.p. Paramount in charge theat. operations; became head of theat. operations, 1938; elected pres. Paramount Theat. Service Corp., v.p. Paramount Pictures, 1938; dir. Paramount Pictures, 1942 (also pres. various Paramount theat. subsids) Pres., CEO & dir. United Paramount Theatres, Inc., 1950, and of American Broadcasting-Paramount Theatres, Inc., 1953, result of merger of ABC and United Paramount Theatres, Inc.; chmn. of bd. & CEO of ABC to 1986. Then chmn. of exec. comm. & dir. Capital Cities/ABC, Inc. 1972; mem., International Radio and TV Society, Natl. Acad. of TV Arts & Sciences, Broadcast Pioneers, Motion Picture Pioneers; founder/member of Hollywood Museum; grad. dir. of Advertising Council, Inc.; Trustee Emeritus Museum of TV & Radio; Hon. Chmn. Acad. of TV Arts & Sciences.

GOLDMAN, BO
Writer. b. New York, NY, Sept. 10, 1932. e. Princeton U., B.A., 1953. Wrote lyrics for B'way musical version of Pride and Prejudice entitled First Impressions (1959). Assoc. prod. & script editor for Playhouse 90 1958-60; writer-prod., NET Playhouse 1970-71, Theater in America 1972-74.
PICTURES: One Flew Over the Cuckoo's Nest (co-s.p.; WGA & Academy Awards, 1975), The Rose (co-s.p.), Melvin and Howard (NY Film Critics, WGA & Academy Awards, 1980), Shoot the Moon, Swing Shift (uncredited), Little Nikita (co-s.p.), Dick Tracy (uncredited), Scent of a Woman (Golden Globe Award, Acad. Award nom.), First Knight (co-s.p.), City Hall (co-s.p.).

GOLDMAN, EDMUND
Executive, Producer. b. Shanghai, China, Nov. 12, 1906. e. Shanghai and San Francisco. Entered ind. as asst. mgr., for Universal in Shanghai, 1935-36; named mgr. Columbia Pictures' Philippine office, 1937. 1951 named Far East. supvr. for Columbia, headquartering in Tokyo. 1953, co-founded Manson Intl. 1953-91 indep. m.p. dist., specializing in foreign mktg. representing indep. prods. and dist. Retired, 1991.
PICTURES: Surrender Hell (prod.), The Quick and the Dead (exec. prod.).

GOLDMAN, MICHAEL F.
Executive. b. Manila, Philippines, Sept. 28, 1939. e. UCLA, B.S. in acct., 1962 California C.P.A. certificate issued June, 1972. In 1962 incorporated Manson International, which was sold in 1986. Incorporated Quixote Prods., 1979. Also owner and sole proprietor Taurus Film co. of Hollywood, founded 1964. Co-founder and first chief financial officer of American Film Marketing Association, sponsor of First American Film Market in Los Angeles in 1981; v.p. of AFMA 1982 and 1983, President AFMA 1984 and 1985. Chmn. AFMA, 1992-3. AFMA bd. mbr., 1981-87, 1988-present; Co-founder, Cinema Consultants Group, 1988. Produced feature, Jessi's Girls in 1975. Founded Manson Interactive, 1995. Member A.M.P.A.S. since 1979. Director, Foundation of Motion Picture Pioneers.

GOLDMAN, MITCHELL
Executive. Pres., of Theatrical Distribution, New Line Distribution, Inc.

GOLDMAN, STEVE
Executive. e. Univ. of IL. 1980, joined Paramount as Midwest division mngr., Chicago. Then served in NY as v.p. Eastern regional mngr. 1983, to Hollywood office. 1985, exec. v.p., sls. & mktg. 1989, exec. v.p. 1992, pres. Paramount Domestic Television. 1995, named exec. v.p. of Paramount Television Group.

GOLDMAN, WILLIAM
Writer. b. Chicago, IL, Aug. 12, 1931. e. Oberlin College, B.A., Columbia U., M.A.
WRITER: The Temple of Gold, Your Turn to Curtsy—My Turn to Bow, Soldier in the Rain (filmed), Boys and Girls Together, No Way to Treat a Lady (filmed), The Thing of It Is, Father's Day, The Princess Bride (filmed), Marathon Man (filmed), Magic (filmed), Tinsel, Control, Heat (filmed), The Silent Gondoliers, The Color of Light, Brothers, Absolute Power(filmed), Four Screenplays, Five Screenplays, The Ghost & The Darkness. Non-fiction: The Season: A Candid Look at Broadway, Adventures in the Screen Trade, Wait Until Next Year (w/Mike Lupica), Hype and Glory.
PICTURES: Harper, Butch Cassidy and the Sundance Kid (Academy Award, 1969), The Hot Rock, The Stepford Wives, The Great Waldo Pepper, All the President's Men (Academy Award, 1976), Marathon Man (based on his novel), A Bridge Too Far, Magic (based on his novel), Mr. Horn, Heat (based on his novel), The Princess Bride (based on his novel), Misery, Memoirs of an Invisible Man (co-s.p.), Year of the Comet, Chaplin (co-s.p.), Maverick, The Ghost and the Darkness (based on his novel), Absolute Power (based.on his novel).

GOLDSMITH, JERRY
Composer. b. Los Angeles, CA, Feb. 10, 1929. e. Los Angeles City Coll. Studied piano with Jakob Gimpel and music composition, harmony, theory with Mario Castelnuovo-Tedesco. With CBS radio first with own show (Romance) and then moved on to others (Suspense). Began scoring for TV, including Climax, Playhouse 90, Studio One, Gunsmoke, etc. Emmy Awards for QB VIII, Masada, Babe, The Red Pony, Star Trek Voyager Theme.
PICTURES: Black Patch (debut, 1957), Lonely Are the Brave, Freud (Acad. Award nom.), The Stripper, The Prize, Seven Days in May, Lilies of the Field, In Harm's Way, Von Ryan's Express, Our Man Flint, A Patch of Blue (Acad. Award nom.), The Blue Max, Seconds, Stagecoach, The Sand Pebbles (Acad. Award nom.), In Like Flint, Planet of the Apes (Acad. Award nom.), The Ballad of Cable Hogue, Tora! Tora! Tora!, Patton (Acad. Award nom.), The Wild Rovers, The Other, Papillon (Acad. Award nom.), The Reincarnation of Peter Proud, Chinatown (Acad. Award nom.), Logan's Run, The Wind and the Lion (Acad. Award nom.), The Omen (Academy Award, 1976), Islands in the Stream, MacArthur, Coma, Damien: Omen II, The Boys From Brazil (Acad. Award nom.), The Great Train Robbery, Alien, Star Trek-The Motion Picture (Acad. Award nom.), The Final Conflict, Outland, Raggedy Man, The Secret of NIMH, Poltergeist (Acad. Award nom.), First Blood, Twilight Zone—The Movie, Psycho II, Under Fire (Acad. Award nom.), Gremlins, Legend (European ver.), Explorers, Rambo: First Blood II, Poltergeist II: The Other Side, Hoosiers (Acad. Award nom.), Extreme Prejudice, Innerspace, Lionheart, Rent-a-Cop, Rambo III, Criminal Law, The 'Burbs, Leviathan, Star Trek V: The Final Frontier, Total Recall, Gremlins 2: The New Batch (also cameo), The Russia House, Not Without My Daughter, Sleeping With the Enemy, Medicine Man, Basic Instinct (Acad. Award nom.), Mom and Dad Save the World, Mr. Baseball, Love Field, Forever Young, Matinee, The Vanishing, Dennis the Menace, Malice, Rudy, Six Degrees of Separation, Angie, Bad Girls, The Shadow, The River Wild, I.Q., Congo, First Knight, Powder, City Hall, Executive Decision, Powder, Chain Reaction, The Ghost and the Darkness, Star Trek: First Contact, Fierce Creatures, Air Force One, L.A. Confidential (Acad. Award nom.), Deep Rising, The Edge, U.S. Marshalls, Mulan.

GOLDSMITH, MARVIN F.
Executive. b. Brooklyn, NY. e. NY Inst. of Tech. Started as page at CBS, eventually becoming film editor. Was tv group supervisor with Batten Barton Durstine & Osborne. 1973, joined ABC as mgr. nighttime sales proposals; 1976-78, account exec. in sports sales, then v.p. prime time sales proposals, then v.p. Eastern Sales. 1986, promoted to sr. v.p., natl. sls. mngr.; 1989, became sr. v.p. gen. sls. mngr. 1992, promoted to pres., sls. & marketing, ABC Television Network.

GOLDSTEIN, MILTON
Executive. b. New York, NY, Aug. 1, 1926. e. NYU, 1949. In exec. capac., Paramount; foreign sales coord., The Ten Commandments, Psycho; v.p. foreign sales, Samuel Bronston org.; asst. to Pres., Paramount Int'l, special prods., 1964; Foreign sales mgr., 1966; v.p., world wide sales, 1967, Cinerama; Sr. v.p. Cinema Center Films, 1969; pres., Cinema Center Films, 1971; v.p. Theatrical Mktg. & Sales, Metromedia Producers Corp., 1973; in March, 1974, formed Boasberg-Goldstein, Inc., consultants in prod. and dist. of m.p.; 1975, named exec. vice pres., Avco Embassy Pictures; 1978, named exec. v.p. & chief operating officer, Melvin Simon Prods. 1980, named pres.; 1985, pres. Milt Goldstein Enterprises, Inc.; 1990, chairman and ceo, HKM Films. 1991, pres., Introvision movies.

GOLDSTONE, JAMES

Director. b. Los Angeles, CA. June 8, 1931. e. Dartmouth Coll., B.A., Bennington Coll., M.A. Film editor from 1950. Writer, story editor from 1957. Dir. starting from 1958. Visiting professor, Columbia Univ., 1996-97.

PICTURES: Jigsaw (debut, 1968), A Man Called Gannon, Winning, Brother John, Red Sky at Morning, The Gang That Couldn't Shoot Straight, They Only Kill Their Masters, Swashbuckler, Rollercoaster, When Time Ran Out.

TELEVISION: Pilots: Star Trek, Ironside, Iron Horse, The Senator, etc. Specials-Movies: A Clear and Present Danger (Emmy nom.), Eric (Virgin Islands Int'l. Film Fest. Gold Medal). Journey from Darkness (Christopher Award). Studs Lonigan (miniseries 1978), Kent State, (Emmy, best dir., special), Things in Their Season, Calamity Jane, The Sun Also Rises, Dreams of Gold, Earthstar Voyager.

GOLDTHWAIT, BOBCAT (BOB)

Comedian, Actor. b. Syracuse, NY, May 1, 1962. Performed with comedy troupe The Generic Comics in early 1980's. Album: Meat Bob.

PICTURES: Police Academy 2: Their First Assignment (debut, 1985), One Crazy Summer, Police Academy 3: Back in Training, Burglar, Police Academy 4: Citizens on Patrol, Hot to Trot, Scrooged, Shakes the Clown (also dir., s.p.), Freaked, Radioland Murders, Destiny Turns on the Radio, Hercules.

TELEVISION: Series: Capitol Critters (voice), Unhappily Ever After (voice). Specials: Bob Goldthwait: Don't Watch This Show, Share the Warmth, Is He Like That All the Time? (also dir., writer), Bob Saget: In the Dream Suite, Comic Relief, Medusa: Dare to be Truthful. Guest: Tales From the Crypt, Married... With Children, The Larry Sanders Show, E.R., Beavis and Butthead, Comic Relief, The John Laroquette Show.

GOLDWATER, CHARLES

Executive, Exhibitor. b. New Orleans, LA. e. Boston U., B.S. Broadcasting & Film. Began career with Walter Reade Organization as usher in 1971-74, promoted to manager. Sack Theatres/USA Cinemas 1974-88, began as manager, promoted to s.v.p. & general manager. National Amusements, exec. dir. Project Development, 1988-90. Loews/Sony Theatres, sr. v.p. & general manager, 1990-1995. Pres. & CEO, Cinamerica/Mann Theatres, 1995-1998. March, 1998 became Pres., CEO and Chairman, I Works Entertainment. NATO bd. of dir. 1987-present. Chmn. CARA/Product Committee, 1991-1996; Exec Comm.,1995-. General chmn. Showeast 1992-1995; chmn of the bd. Showeast, 1995-present. Bd. of directors, Motion Picture Pioneers, Will Rogers Organization. Past pres./chmn. of bd., Theatre Owners of New England. Past bd. of directors, Variety Clubs of New England & New York.

GOLDWYN, SAMUEL, JR.

Producer, Director. b. Los Angeles, CA, Sept. 7, 1926. e. U. of Virginia. Father of actor Tony Goldwyn. U.S. Army, 1944; following war writer, assoc. prod., J. Arthur Rank Org.; prod. Gathering Storm on London stage; returned to U.S., 1948; assoc. prod., Universal; recalled to Army service, 1951; prod., dir., Army documentary films including Alliance for Peace (Edinburgh Film Festival prize); prod. TV shows, Adventure series for CBS, 1952-53; prod. TV series, The Unexpected, 1954; pres., The Samuel Goldwyn Company, 1955-. Also established Samuel Goldwyn Home Entertainment, and Goldwyn Pavilion Cinemas.

PICTURES: Prod.: Man With the Gun, The Sharkfighters, The Proud Rebel, The Adventures of Huckleberry Finn, The Young Lovers (also dir.), Cotton Comes to Harlem, Come Back Charleston Blue, The Golden Seal, Mystic Pizza (exec. prod.), Stella, The Preacher's Wife.

TELEVISION: The Academy Awards, 1987, 1988; April Morning (co-exec. prod.).

GOLDWYN, TONY

Actor. b. Los Angeles, CA, May 20, 1960. e. Brandeis U., London Acad. of Music & Dramatic Art.

THEATER: Digby, The Foreigner, The Real Thing, Pride and Prejudice, The Sum of Us, Spike Heels, Inherit the Wind.

PICTURES: Friday the 13th Part VI: Jason Live (debut, 1986), Gaby-A True Story, Ghost, Kuffs, Traces of Red, The Pelican Brief, Reckless, The Substance of Fire, Nixon, The Substance of Fire, Kiss the Girls.

TELEVISION: Movies: Favorite Son, Dark Holiday, Iran: Days of Crisis, Taking the Heat, Love Matters, Doomsday Gun, The Last Word, The Boys Next Door, Truman. Mini-Series: A Woman of Independent Means. Special: The Last Mile. Guest: L.A. Law, Tales from the Crypt.

GOLINO, VALERIA

Actress. b. Naples, Italy, Oct. 22, 1966. Raised in Athens, Greece. Was model at age 14 before being discovered by dir. Lina Wertmuller for film debut.

PICTURES: A Joke of Destiny (debut, 1983), Blind Date, My Son Infinitely Beloved, Little Fires, Dumb Dicks, Storia d'Amore (Love Story), Last Summer in Tangiers, The Gold-Rimmed Glasses, Three Sisters, Big Top Pee-wee, Rain Man, Torrents of Spring, The King's Whore, Traces of an Amorous Life, Hot Shots!, The Indian Runner, Hot Shots! Part Deux, Clean Slate, Immortal Beloved, Leaving Las Vegas, Four Rooms, Escape From L.A., The Acrobats, Side Streets.

GONZALEZ-GONZALEZ, PEDRO

Actor. r.n. Ramiro Gonzalez-Gonzalez. b. Aguilares, TX, May 24, 1925. Comedian in San Antonio Mexican theatres.

PICTURES: Wings of the Hawk, Ring of Fear, Ricochet Romance, The High and the Mighty, Strange Lady in Town, Bengazi, I Died a Thousand Times, Bottom of the Bottle, The Sheepman, Gun the Man Down, Rio Bravo, The Young Land, The Adventures of Bullwhip Griffin, The Love Bug, The Love God, Hellfighters, Hook Line and Sinker, Chisum, Support Your Local Gunfighter, Zachariah, Six-Pack Annie, Won Ton Ton the Dog Who Saved Hollywood, Dreamer, Lust in the Dust, Uphill All the Way, Deception.

TELEVISION: Guest: O'Henry Playhouse, Felix the Fourth, Ann Southern Show, No Time for Sergeants, Gunsmoke, Perry Mason, The Monkees, Love American Style, Adam 12, Farmer's Daughter, Danny Kaye Show, National Velvet, Bachelor Father, Bonanza, The Fall Guy, Moonlighting, many others. Movies: Donor, Ghost Writer, Bates Motel (pilot).

GOOD, CHARLES E.

Executive. b. 1922. Joined Buena Vista in 1957 in Chicago office; progressed from salesman to branch mgr. and then district mgr. Later moved to Burbank as domestic sales mgr. in 1975; 1978, named v.p. & general sales mgr.; 1980, appointed pres., BV Distribution Co. Resigned presidency 1984; became BV consultant until retirement, 1987.

GOODALL, CAROLINE

Actress. b. London, England, Nov. 13, 1959. e. Natl Youth Theatre of Great Britain; Bristol Univ. On stage with Royal Court Theatre, Royal Natl. Theatre, Royal Shakespeare Co. Toured Australia in Richard III for RSC, 1986.

PICTURES: Every Time We Say Goodbye (debut, 1986), Hook, The Silver Brumby, The Webbers' 15 Minutes, Cliffhanger, Schindler's List, Disclosure, Hotel Sorrento, White Squall.

TELEVISION: Movies (Australia): Cassidy, Ring of Scorpio, The Great Air Race, Diamond Swords (Fr.). Mini-Series: After the War. Guest: Remington Steele, Tales of the Unexpected, Quantum Leap, The Commish, Rumpole of the Bailey, Poirot: Curse of the Western Star.

GOODING, CUBA, JR.

Actor. b. Bronx, NY, Sept. 2, 1968. Son of rhythm and blues vocalist Cuba Gooding. Raised in California. Prof. debut as dancer backing up Lionel Richie at 1984 Olympic Games. Recipient of NAACP Image Awards for Boyz in the Hood and tv movie Murder Without Motive. Voted by NATO/Showest as Newcomer of the Year, 1992.

PICTURES: Coming to America (debut, 1988), Sing, Boyz in the Hood, Hitz, Gladiator, A Few Good Men, Judgment Night, Lightning Jack, Outbreak, Losing Isaiah, Jerry Maguire (Acad. Award, 1996; Chicago Film Critics Award; Screen Actors Guild Award).

TELEVISION: Movies: Murder Without Motive: The Edmund Perry Story, Daybreak, The Tuskegee Airmen. Special: No Means No.

GOODMAN, DAVID Z.

Writer. e. Queens Coll., Yale School of Drama.

PICTURES: Lovers and Other Strangers, Straw Dogs, Farewell My Lovely, Logan's Run, Eyes of Laura Mars, Man Woman and Child (co.-s.p.).

GOODMAN, JOHN

Actor. b. Afton, MO, June 20, 1952. e. Southwest Missouri State U. Moved to NY in 1975 where he appeared on stage (incl. A Midsummer Night's Dream) and in commercials. On Broadway in Loose Ends, Big River. L.A. stage in Antony and Cleopatra.

PICTURES: Eddie Macon's Run (1983, debut), The Survivors, Revenge of the Nerds, C.H.U.D., Maria's Lovers, Sweet Dreams, True Stories, Raising Arizona, Burglar, The Big Easy, The Wrong Guys, Punchline, Everybody's All-American, Sea of Love, Always, Stella, Arachnophobia, King Ralph, Barton Fink, The Babe, Matinee, Born Yesterday, We're Back! A Dinosaur's Story (voice), The Flintstones, Pie in the Sky, Mother Night.

TELEVISION: Series: Roseanne. Movies: The Face of Rage, Heart of Steel, The Mystery of Moro Castle, Murder Ordained, Kingfish: A Story of Huey P. Long (also co-prod.), A Streetcar Named Desire. Mini-Series: Chiefs. Guest: The Equalizer, Moonlighting.

GOODRICH, ROBERT EMMETT

Executive. b. Grand Rapids, MI, June 27, 1940. e. U. of Michigan, B.A., 1962; J.D., 1964; NYU. LL.M, 1966. Pres. & Secty., Goodrich Quality Theaters, Inc. 1967-present, developed circuit from father's one theater to 177 screens at 22 locations in 11 Mich. cities, 4 Indiana cities, 4 Illinois cities. Owns and operates 6 FM/AM radio stations in Grand Rapids, MI, Muskegon, MI. Treasurer: NATO; Will Rogers Inst. advisory comm; bd. of dirs., Mich. Millers Mutual Insurance Co.; bd. of dirs., Western Migh. Branch ACLU. State of MI Bar Assn.

GOODWIN, RICHARD

Producer. b. Bombay, India, Sept. 13, 1934. e. Rugby. Entered film world by chance: while waiting to go to Cambridge U. took temporary job as tea boy at studio which led to 20-year-long association with producer Lord Brabourne.
PICTURES: *Prod. Mgr.*: The Sheriff of Fractured Jaw, Carve Her Name with Pride, The Grass Is Greener, Sink the Bismarck, HMS Defiant. *Prod.*: The Tales of Beatrix Potter. *Co-Prod.*: Murder on the Orient Express, Death on the Nile, The Mirror Crack'd, Evil Under the Sun, A Passage to India, Little Dorrit, Seven Years In Tiber (exec. prod.).

GOODWIN, RONALD

Composer, Arranger, Conductor. b. Plymouth, Eng., Feb. 17, 1925. e. Pinner County Grammar Sch. Early career: arranger for BBC dance orchestra; mus. dir., Parlophone Records; orchestra leader for radio, TV and records. Fut. m.p. ind., 1958. Many major film scores. Guest cond. R.P.O., B.S.O., Toronto Symph. Orch. New Zealand Symphony Orch., Sydney Symphony Orch. Royal Scottish Natl. Orch., BBC Scottish Symphony Orch., BBC Welsh Symphony Orch., BBC Radio Orch., BBC Concert Orch., London Philharmonic Orch., Gothenberg Symphony Orch., Norwegian Opera Orch. & Chorus, Halle Orchestra, Singapore Symphony Orch., Australian Pops Orch., Detroit Symphony Orchestra, Danish Radio Orchestra, Odense Symphony Orch., Norrkoping Symphony Orch.
PICTURES: Whirlpool, I'm All Right Jack, The Trials of Oscar Wilde, Johnny Nobody, Village of the Damned, Murder She Said, Follow the Boys, Murder at the Gallop, Children of the Damned, 633 Squadron, Murder Most Foul, Murder Ahoy, Operation Crossbow, The ABC Murders, Of Human Bondage, Those Magnificent Men in Their Flying Machines, The Trap, Mrs. Brown, You've Got a Lovely Daughter; Submarine X-1, Decline and Fall, Where Eagles Dare, Monte Carlo or Bust, Battle of Britain, The Executioner, The Selfish Giant, Frenzy, Diamonds on Wheels, The Little Mermaid, The Happy Prince, One of Our Dinosaurs Is Missing, Escape From the Dark, Born to Run, Beauty and the Beast, Candleshoe, Force Ten from Navarone, Spaceman and King Arthur, Clash of Loyalties, Valhalla.

GORDON, ALEX

Producer. b. London, Eng., Sept. 8, 1922. e. Canford Coll., Dorset, 1939. Writer, m.p. fan magazines, 1939-41; British Army, 1942-45; pub. dir. Renown Pictures Corp., 1946-47; P.R. and pub. rep. for Gene Autry, 1948-53; v.p. and prod. Golden State Productions, 1954-58; prod. Alex Gordon Prods., 1958-66; producer Twentieth Century-Fox Television, 1967-76; film archivist/preservationist, 1976-84; v.p., Gene Autry's Flying A Pictures, 1985.
PICTURES: Lawless Rider, Bride of the Monster, Apache Woman, Day the World Ended, Oklahoma Woman, Girls in Prison, The She-Creature, Runaway Daughters, Shake Rattle and Rock, Flesh and the Spur, Voodoo Woman, Dragstrip Girl, Motorcycle Gang, Jet Attack, Submarine Seahawk, Atomic Submarine, The Underwater City, The Bounty Killer, Requiem for a Gunfighter.
TELEVISION: Movie of the Year, Golden Century, Great Moments in Motion Pictures.

GORDON, BERT I.

Producer, Director, Writer. b. Kenosha, WI, Sept. 24, 1932. e. Univ. of WI. Started on tv as commercial prod.
PICTURES: *Dir./Prod.*: Serpent Island (debut, 1954), King Dinosaur, Beginning of the End, Cyclops (also s.p.), The Amazing Colossal Man (also co-s.p.), Attack of the Puppet People (also story), War of the Colossal Beast, The Spider, Tormented, The Boy and the Pirates, The Magic Sword (also story), Village of the Giants (also story), Picture Mommy Dead, How to Succeed With Sex (dir., also s.p.), The Big Bet, Necromancy (also s.p.), The Mad Bomber (also s.p.), The Police Connection (also s.p.), The Food of the Gods (also s.p.), Empire of the Ants (also s.p.), The Coming (also s.p.), Satan's Princess, Malediction.

GORDON, BRUCE

Executive. b. Sidney, Australia, Feb. 4, 1929. Began career in Australian entertainment industry 1952 with Tivoli Circuit, live theatre chain; acted as advance man, front-of-house mgr., adv. dir.; promoted to busn. mgr., 1958. Named Tivoli membr. bd. of management, 1960-62. Joined Desilu Studios in 1962, developing Far East territories; promoted 1968 when Paramount acquired Desilu to mng. dir. Para. Far East opns. Named to bd. of TV Corp., 1969, operator of Channel 9 TV stns. & co.'s theatres in Sydney, Melbourne. Dir. on bd. of Academy Investments, operator of Perth theatre chain; responsible for building Perth Entertainment Centre. Named pres., Paramount TV Intl. Services, Ltd., 1974, in New York office. 1981, pres. Intl. Television of Paramount Pictures.

GORDON, CHARLES

Executive, Producer. b. Belzoni, MS. Began career as a talent agent with William Morris Agency. Left to write and develop television programming creating and producing 5 pilots and 3 series. Left TV to enter motion picture production in partnership with brother Lawrence Gordon. President and chief operating officer, The Gordon Company.

PICTURES: *Exec. prod.*: Die Hard, Leviathan. *Co-prod.*: Night of the Creeps, The Wrong Guys, Field of Dreams, K-9, Lock Up, The Rocketeer, The Super, Unlawful Entry, Waterworld, Trojan War (prod.), Rocket Boys (prod.).
TELEVISION: *Writer-creator*: When the Whistle Blows. *Exec. prod.*: The Renegades, Just Our Luck (also creator), Our Family Honor (also creator).

GORDON, DON

Actor. r.n. Donald Walter Guadagno. b. Los Angeles, CA, Nov. 13, 1926. Served, U.S. Navy, 1941-45. Studied acting with Michael Chekhov. e. Columbia U. Theatre includes On an Open Roof, Stockade.
PICTURES: Bullitt, The Lollipop Cover (best actor, Chicago Film Fest.), W.U.S.A., The Last Movie, Papillon, The Gambler, Out of the Blue, The Final Conflict, The Beast Within, Lethal Weapon, Skin Deep, The Exorcist III, The Borrower.
TELEVISION: *Series*: The Blue Angels, Lucan, The Contender. *Guest*: The Defenders, Remington Steele, Charlie's Angels, Twilight Zone, Simon & Simon, Outer Limits, MacGyver, etc. *Movies*: Happiness is a Warm Clue, Street Killing, Confessions of a Married Man.

GORDON, JEROME

Executive, Exhibitor. b. Newport News, VA, Mar. 1, 1915. Began movie career at age 10 as usher in father's theatre. At age 18, owned and operated two theatres. Spent one year in theater decorating business in Philadelphia. Worked for Fox West Coast circuit in Los Angeles, 1937-40. Returned to VA and developed small theater circuit with brothers. Served as pres. of Virginia NATO for 4 yrs. 1975-, exec. dir., Virginia NATO; 1976-, exec. dir., Maryland & D.C. NATO. Coordinated Mid-Atlantic NATO convention from 1975 until it merged with ShowEast in 1989. Currently exec. dir., Mid-Atlantic NATO. 1978-86, spec. asst. to pres., NATO; coordinated campaigns to pass Anti-Blind Bidding Laws in individual states. Edited Regional Presidents' NATO Handbook. Member, bd. of dirs., NATO; chmn., NATO Membership Development Committee; secretary NATO, 1996-. Exec. Committee, ShowEast. Recipient of Distinguished Service Award, ShowEast, 1992; B.V. Sturdivant Award, NATO/ShowEast, 1992.

GORDON, KEITH

Actor, Director, Writer. b. Bronx, NY, Feb. 3, 1961.
THEATRE: A Traveling Companion, Richard III, Album, Back to Back The Buddy System, Third Street.
PICTURES: *Actor*: Jaws 2 (debut, 1978), All That Jazz, Home Movies, Dressed to Kill, Christine, The Legend of Billie Jean, Static (also co-s.p., co-prod.), Back to School, I Love Trouble. *Director-Writer*: The Chocolate War, A Midnight Clear. Mother Night (dir., prod.).
TELEVISION: *Mini-Series*: Studs Lonigan. *Movies*: Kent State, Single Bars Single Women, Combat High. *Special*: My Palikari (Amer. Playhouse). *Director*: Wild Palms, Homicide (1 episode), Fallen Angels: The Black Bargain.

GORDON, LAWRENCE

Producer, Executive. b. Yazoo City, MS, March 25, 1936. e. Tulane U. (business admin.). Assist. to prod. Aaron Spelling at Four Star Television, 1964. Writer and assoc. prod. on several Spelling shows. 1965, joined ABC-TV as head of west coast talent dev; 1966, TV and motion pictures exec. with Bob Banner Associates; 1968 joined AIP as v.p. in charge of project dev.; 1971 named v.p., Screen Gems (TV div. of Columbia Pictures) where he helped dev. Brian's Song and QB VII. Returned to AIP as v.p. worldwide prod. Formed Lawrence Gordon Prods. at Columbia Pictures; 1984-86, pres. and COO 20th Century Fox. Currently indep. prod. with 20th Century Fox. Producer of B'way musical Smile.
PICTURES: Dillinger (1973), Hard Times, Rolling Thunder, The Driver, The End, Hooper, The Warriors, Xanadu, Paternity, Jekyll and Hyde, Together Again, 48 Hours, Streets of Fire, Brewster's Millions, Lucas, Jumpin' Jack Flash, Predator, The Couch Trip, The Wrong Guys, Die Hard, Leviathan (exec. prod.), K-9, Field of Dreams, Lock Up, Family Business, Another 48 HRS, Die Hard 2, Predator 2, The Rocketeer, Used People, The Devil's Own, Boogie Nights, Event Horizon, Tomb Raider, Thieves, Mystery Men.
TELEVISION: *Co-creator and co-exec. prod.*: Dog and Cat, Matt Houston, Renegades, Just Our Luck, Our Family Honor, Timecop.

GORDON, RICHARD

Producer. b. London, Eng., Dec. 31, 1925. e. U. of London, 1943. Served in Brit. Royal Navy, 1944-46; ed. & writer on fan magazines & repr. independent American cos. 1946, with publicity dept. Assoc. Brit. Pathe 1947; org. export-import business for independent, British and American product; formed Gordon Films, Inc., 1949; formed Amalgamated prod., 1956; formed Grenadier Films, Ltd. 1971. 1992, prod. of A Tribute to Orson Welles.
PICTURES: The Counterfeit Plan, The Haunted Strangler, Fiend Without a Face, The Secret Man, First Man into Space, Corridors of Blood, Devil Doll, Curse of Simba, The Projected Man, Naked Evil, Island of Terror, Tales of the Bizarre, Tower of Evil, Horror Hospital, The Cat and the Canary, Inseminoid.

GORDON, STUART
Director, Writer. b. Chicago, IL, Aug. 11, 1947. e. Univ. of WI. Worked at commercial art studio prior to founding Broom Street Theater in Madison, WI. Later founder and prod. dir. of Organic Theater Co. in Madison, then Chicago, 1969-85. Was fight choreographer on 1976 film The Last Affair.
PICTURES: Director: Re-Animator (also co-s.p.), From Beyond (also co-s.p.), Dolls, Robot Jox (also wrote story), Honey I Shrunk the Kids (co-story only), The Pit and the Pendulum, Honey I Blew Up the Kid (exec. prod., co-story only), Fortress, Body Snatchers (co-s.p. only), Castle Freak (also co-story), Space Truckers (dir., prod., co-story).
TELEVISION: Director: Bleacher Bums (special), Daughter of Darkness (movie).

GORDY, BERRY
Executive. b. Detroit, MI, Nov. 28, 1929. Was working on auto assembly line in Detroit when decided to launch record co., Motown. In 1961 wrote song, Shop Around; recording by Smokey Robinson made it his first million dollar record. Expanded into music publishing, personal mgt., recording studios, film and TV, also backing stage shows. Former bd. chmn., Motown Industries. Chmn. The Gordy Co. Received Business Achievement Award, Interracial Council for Business Opportunity, 1967; Whitney M. Young Jr. Award, L.A. Urban League, 1980; Inducted into Rock and Roll Hall of Fame, 1988. Recipient of NARAS Trustee Award, 1991. Author of To Be Loved (1994). Member BMI, NAACP, A.M.P.A.S., DGI, NARAS.
PICTURES: Lady Sings the Blues (prod.), Bingo Long Traveling All-Stars and Motor Kings (exec. prod.), Mahogany (dir.), Almost Summer, The Last Dragon (exec. prod.).

GORE, MICHAEL
Composer, Producer. b. New York City, New York, March 5, 1951. e. Yale University and studied in Paris with composer Max Deustch. Began writing pop songs for his sister singer Lesley Gore; as a staff songwriter for Screen Gems-Columbia; and as a producer of classical recordings for CBS Records. Prod. for Philips Classics recording of The King and I (with Julie Andrews, Ben Kingsley). Wrote Whitney Houston's hit single All the Man That I Need.
PICTURES: Fame (2 Academy Awards for Best Score and Title Song, 1980), Terms of Endearment, Footloose, Pretty in Pink, Broadcast News, Defending Your Life, The Butcher's Wife, Mr. Wonderful.
TELEVISION: Generations (theme); Fame (theme).

GOROG, LASZLO
Writer. b. Hungary, Sept. 30, 1903. e. U. of Sciences, Budapest. Playwright, short story writer, asst. editor, Budapest, 1928-39.
PICTURES: Tales of Manhattan, The Affairs of Susan, She Wouldn't Say Yes, The Land Unknown, Mole People.
TELEVISION: 4 Star, Dupont, The Roaring Twenties, 77 Sunset Strip, Maverick, etc.

GORSHIN, FRANK
Actor. b. Pittsburgh, PA, Apr. 5, 1933. Also nightclub comic and impresionist. On B'way stage in Jimmy.
PICTURES: Hot Rod Girl, Dragstrip Girl, Invasion of the Saucer Men, Portland Exposse, Warlock, Bells Are Ringing, Studs Lonigan, Where the Boys Are, The Great Impostor, Ring of Fire, The George Raft Story, Sail a Crooked Ship, That Darn Cat, Ride Beyond Vengeance, Batman, Skidoo, Record City, Underground Aces, The Uppercrust, Hot Resort, Uphill All the Way, Hollywood Vice Squad, Midnight, Beverly Hills Bodysnatchers, Hail Caesar, The Meteor Man, Twelve Monkeys.
TELEVISION: Series: ABC Comedy Hour (The Kopycats), The Edge of Night. Movies: Sky Heist, Death on the Freeway, Goliath Awaits, A Masterpiece of Murder. Guest: Hennessey, The Detectives, Have Gun Will Travel, The Defenders, Naked City, The Munsters, Batman, Police Woman, SWAT, The Fall Guy, Murder She Wrote, etc.

GORTNER, MARJOE
Actor, Producer. b. Long Beach, CA, Jan. 14, 1944. Was child evangelist, whose career as such was basis for Oscar-winning documentary film, Marjoe. Acted in films and TV; later producer in 1978 for When You Comin' Back Red Ryder?
PICTURES: Earthquake, Bobbie Joe and the Outlaw, The Food of the Gods, Viva Knievel, Sidewinder One, Acapulco Gold, Starcrash, When You Comin' Back Red Ryder?, Mausoleum, Jungle Warriors, Hellhole, American Ninja III: Blood Hunt, Wild Bill.
TELEVISION: Movies: The Marcus-Nelson Murders, Pray for the Wildcats, The Gun and the Pulpit, Mayday at 40000 Feet. Guest: Police Story, Barnaby Jones, The A-Team. Series: Falcon Crest.

GOSSETT, LOUIS, JR.
Actor. b. Brooklyn, NY, May 27, 1936. e. NYU, B.S. Also nightclub singer during 1960s.
THEATER: Take a Giant Step (debut, 1953), The Desk Set, Lost in the Stars, A Raisin in the Sun, Golden Boy, The Blacks, Blood Knot, The Zulu and the Zayda, My Sweet Charlie, Carry Me Back to Morningside Heights, Murderous Angels (L.A. Drama Critics Award).

PICTURES: A Raisin in the Sun (debut, 1961), The Bushbaby, The Landlord, Skin Game, Travels With My Aunt, The Laughing Policeman, The White Dawn, The River Niger, J.D.'s Revenge, The Deep, The Choirboys, An Officer and a Gentleman (Academy Award, best supporting actor, 1982), Jaws 3-D, Finders Keepers, Enemy Mine, Iron Eagle, Firewalker, The Principal, Iron Eagle II, Toy Soldiers, The Punisher, Aces: Iron Eagle III, Diggstown, Monolith, Flashfire, Blue Chips (unbilled), A Good Man in Africa, Iron Eagle IV, Inside.
TELEVISION: Series: The Young Rebels, The Lazarus Syndrome, The Powers of Matthew Star, Gideon Oliver. Movies: Companions in Nightmare, It's Good to Be Alive, Sidekicks, Delancey Street, The Crisis Within, Don't Look Back, Little Ladies of the Night, To Kill a Cop, The Critical List, This Man Stands Alone, Sadat, The Guardian, A Gathering of Old Men, The Father Clements Story, Roots: The Gift, El Diablo, Sudie and Simpson, The Josephine Baker Story, Carolina Skeletons, Father & Son: Dangerous Relations (also co-exec. prod.), Ray Alexander: A Taste for Justice, A Father for Charlie (also co-exec. prod.), Curse of the Starving Class, Zooman, Ray Alexander: A Menu for Murder. Mini-Series: Roots (Emmy Award, 1977), Backstairs at the White House. Return to Lonesome Dove. Specials: Welcome Home, A Triple Play: Sam Found Out, Zora Is My Name, The Century Collection Presents Ben Vereen: His Roots, In His Father's Shoes (Emmy Award, 1998). Guest: The Mod Squad, Bill Cosby Show, Partridge Family, The Rookies, Love American Style, Police Story, Rockford Files, many others.

GOTTESMAN, STUART
Executive. b. New York, NY, June 11, 1949. Started career in mailroom of Warner Bros., 1972; later named promo. asst. to southwestern regional fieldman; promoted to that post which held for 10 years. 1987, named WB dir. field activities; 1990, appointed v.p. WB national field operations.

GOTTLIEB, CARL
Writer, Director, Actor. b. New York, NY, March 18. e. Syracuse U., B.S., 1960. Directed short film The Absent- Minded Waiter.
PICTURES: Actor: Maryjane, M*A*S*H, Up the Sandbox, Cannonball, The Sting II, Johnny Dangerously, The Committee, Into the Night, Clueless. Director: Caveman (also co-s.p.), Amazon Women on the Moon (co-dir.). Co-Writer: Jaws (also actor), Which Way Is Up?, Jaws II, The Jerk (also actor), Doctor Detroit, Jaws 3-D.
TELEVISION: Writer: Smothers Bros. Comedy Hour (Emmy Award, 1969), The Odd Couple, Flip Wilson, Bob Newhart Show, The Super, Crisis at Sun Valley, The Deadly Triangle. Director: Paul Reiser: Out on a Whim, Partners In Life, Campus Cops, Honey I Shrunk the Kids. Director-Co-creator: Leo & Liz in Beverly Hills. Co-creator: George Burns' Comedy Week.

GOTTLIEB, MEYER
Executive. Pres. & CEO, The Samuel Goldwyn Company.

GOUGH, MICHAEL
Actor. b. Malaya, Nov. 23, 1917. e. Rose Hill Sch., in Kent, England, and at Durham School. Studied at Old Vic School in London; first stage appearance in 1936 at Old Vic Theatre. N.Y. stage debut 1937 in Love of Women. London debut in 1938 in The Zeal of Thy House. Won 1979 Tony Award for Bedroom Farce.
PICTURES: Blanche Fury (debut, 1947), Anna Karenina, Saraband for Dead Lovers, The Small Back Room, The Man in the White Suit, Rob Roy, The Sword and the Rose, Richard III, Reach for the Sky, Horror of Dracula (Dracula), Horrors of the Black Museum, The Horse's Mouth, Konga, Candidate for Murder, I Like Money (Mr. Topaze), The Phantom of the Opera, Black Zoo, Dr. Terror's House of Horrors, The Skull, Berserk, They Came From Beyond Space, A Walk With Love and Death, Women in Love, Trog, Julius Caesar, The Go-Between, Savage Messiah, Legend of Hell House, Horror Hospital (Computer Killers), Galileo, The Boys from Brazil, Venom, The Dresser, Top Secret!, Oxford Blues, Out of Africa, Caravaggio, Memed My Hawk, The Fourth Protocol, The Serpent and the Rainbow, Batman, Strapless, Let Him Have It, Blackeyes, Batman Returns, Little Nemo (voice), The Age of Innocence, Wittgenstein, Uncovered, Batman Forever.
TELEVISION: The Search for the Nile, Six Wives of Henry VIII, QB VII, Shoulder to Shoulder, The Citadel, Smiley's People, Brideshead Revisited, Mistral's Daughter, Lace II, Inside the Third Reich, To the Lighthouse, Suez, Vincent the Dutchman, Heart Attack Hotel, After the War, The Shell Seekers, Children of the North, Dr. Who, Sleepers.

GOULD, ELLIOTT
Actor. r.n. Elliott Goldstein. b. Brooklyn, NY, August 29, 1938. e. Professional Children's Sch., NY 1955. Vaudeville: appeared at Palace Theater, 1950. Broadway debut in Rumple (1957). Son is actor Jason Gould.
THEATER: Say Darling, Irma La Douce, I Can Get It for You Wholesale, On the Town (London), Fantasticks (tour), Drat the Cat, Little Murders, Luv (tour), Hit the Deck (Jones Beach), Rumors, Breakfast With Les & Bess.

PICTURES: Quick Let's Get Married (debut, 1965), The Night They Raided Minsky's, Bob & Carol & Ted & Alice (Acad. Award nom.), M*A*S*H, Getting Straight, Move, I Love My Wife, Little Murders (also prod.), The Touch, The Long Goodbye, Busting, S*P*Y*S!, California Split, Who?, Nashville (cameo), Whiffs, I Will I Will... For Now, Harry and Walter Go to New York, Mean Johnny Barrows, A Bridge Too Far, Capricorn One, Matilda, The Silent Partner, Escape to Athena, The Muppet Movie, The Last Flight of Noah's Ark, The Lady Vanishes, Falling in Love Again, The Devil and Max Devlin, Dirty Tricks, The Naked Face, Over the Brooklyn Bridge, The Muppets Take Manhattan, Inside Out, My First 40 Years, Lethal Obsession (Der Joker), The Telephone, The Big Picture, Dangerous Love, Night Visitor, The Wounded King, The Lemon Sisters, Judgment, Dead Men Don't Die, Bugsy, Strawanser, The Player, Exchange Lifeguards, Wet and Wild Summer, Naked Gun 33 1/3: The Final Insult (cameo), White Man's Burden, The Glass Shield, Kicking and Screaming, A Boy Called Hate, Johns.
TELEVISION: Specials: Once Upon A Mattress, Come Blow Your Horn, Jack and the Beanstalk (Faerie Tale Theater), Paul Reiser: Out on a Whim, Prime Time, Out to Lunch, Casey at the Bat (Tall Tales & Legends), Guest: Twilight Zone, Electric Company, Saturday Night Live, George Burns Comedy Week, Ray Bradbury Theatre, The Hitchhiker, Friends. Movies: The Rules of Marriage, Vanishing Act, Conspiracy: The Trial of the Chicago 8, Stolen: One Husband, Somebody's Daughter, Bloodlines: Murder in the Family. Series: E/R, Together We Stand, Sessions (HBO).

GOULD, HAROLD
Actor. b. Schenectady, NY, Dec. 10, 1923. e. SUNY, Albany, B.A. Cornell U., M.A., Ph.D. Instructor of theatre and speech, 1953-56, Randolph Macon's Woman's Col., Lynchburg, VA. Asst. prof. drama and speech, 1956-60, Univ. of Calif., Riverside. Acted with Ashland, OR Shakespeare Fest. in 1958 and Mark Taper Forum (The Miser, Once in a Lifetime). Won Obie Award for Off-B'way debut in The Increased Difficulty of Concentration, 1969. ACE Award for Ray Bradbury Theatre. L.A. Drama Critics Award, 1994.
THEATER: The House of Blue Leaves, Fools, Grown Ups, Artist Descending a Staircase, I Never Sang for My Father, Freud (one man show), Love Letters, Incommunicado, King Lear (Utah Shakespearean Fest.), Mixed Emotions, Old Business, The Tempest (Utah Shakespearean Fest.), Substance of Five (San Diego Olde Globe).
PICTURES: Two for the Seesaw, The Couch, Harper, Inside Daisy Clover, Marnie, An American Dream, The Arrangement, The Lawyer, Mrs. Pollifax: Spy, Where Does It Hurt?, The Sting, The Front Page, Love and Death, The Big Bus, Silent Movie, The One and Only, Seems Like Old Times, Playing for Keeps, Romero, Flesh Suitcase, Killer.
TELEVISION: Series: Rhoda (Emmy nom.), Park Place, Foot in the Door, Under One Roof, Singer and Sons, Golden Girls, Feather and Father Gang. Movies: To Catch a Star, Moviola (Emmy nom.), Washington Behind Closed Doors, Aunt Mary, Better Late Than Never, King Crab, Have I Got a Christmas for You, Man in the Santa Claus Suit, I Never Sang For My Father, Get Smart Again!, Mrs. Delafield Wants to Marry (Emmy nom.), Love Bug II, Fox Hope. Special: The Sunset Gang. Guest: Police Story (Emmy nom.), Tales from the Hollywood Hills: The Closed Set, Ray Bradbury Theater (Emmy nom.).

GOULET, ROBERT
Singer, Actor. b. Lawrence, MA., Nov. 26, 1933. e. Edmonton; scholarship, Royal Conservatory of Music. Sang in choirs, appeared with numerous orchestras; disk jockey, CKUA, Edmonton; pub. rel., Rogo & Rove,Inc.
THEATER: NY: Camelot (as Lancelot; Theatre World Award), The Happy Time (Tony Award, 1968), Camelot (as King Arthur; 1993 revival). Regional: numerous tours including I Do I Do, Carousel, On a Clear Day You Can See Forever, Kiss Me Kate, South Pacific, The Fantasticks, Camelot (as King Arthur).
PICTURES: Gay Purr-ee (voice), Honeymoon Hotel, I'd Rather Be Rich, I Deal in Danger, Atlantic City, Beetlejuice, Scrooged, The Naked Gun 2 1/2: The Smell of Fear, Mr. Wrong.
TELEVISION: Series: Robert Goulet Show, Blue Light. Guest: The Ed Sullivan Show, Garry Moore, The Enchanted Nutcracker, Omnibus, The Broadway of Lerner and Loewe, Rainbow of Stars, Judy Garland Show, Bob Hope Show, The Bell Telephone Hour, Granada-TV special (U.K.), Jack Benny, Dean Martin, Andy Williams, Jack Paar, Red Skelton, Hollywood Palace, Patty Duke Show, The Big Valley, Mission: Impossible, Police Woman, Cannon, Murder She Wrote, Mr. Belvedere, Fantasy Island, Matt Houston, Glitter, WKRP in Cincinnati. Pilot: Make My Day. Specials: Brigadoon, Carousel, Kiss Me Kate. Movie: Based on an Untrue Story.

GOWDY, CURT
Sportscaster. b. Green River, WY, July 31, 1919. Basketball star at U. of Wyoming. All-Conference member; graduated U. of Wyoming. 1942. Officer in U.S. Air Force WWII, then became sportscaster. Voted Sportscaster of the Year, 1967, Nat'l Assn. of Sportswriters Broadcasters. Best Sportscaster, Fame, 1967. Did play-by-play telecasts for 16 World Series, 7 Super Bowls, 12 Rose Bowls, 8 Orange Bowls, 18 NCAA Final 4 college basketball championships. In 1970 was the first individual from the field of sports to receive the George Foster Peabody Award. Hosted the American Sportsman outdoor TV show on ABC for 20 years. (Received 8 Emmy Awards). Inducted into the Sportscasters Hall of Fame in 1981, the Fishing Hall of Fame in 1982, and the Baseball Hall of Fame in 1984, Pro Football Hall of Fame in 1992.

GRADE, LORD LEW
Executive. r.n. Louis Winogradsky. b. Tokmak, Russia, Dec. 25, 1906. Brother of Lord Bernard Delfont. Came to Eng. 1912. Was first a music hall dancer until 1934 when he became an agent with Joe Collins, founding Collins and Grade Co. Joint managing dir. Lew & Leslie Grade Ltd. theatrical agency until 1955; Chmn. & mng. dir., ITC Entertainment Ltd. 1958-82; chmn. & chief exec., Associated Communications Corp. Ltd., 1973-82; pres. ATV Network Ltd., 1977-82; chmn., Stoll Moss Theatres Ltd., 1969-82; chmn. & chief exec., Embassy Communications International Ltd., 1982-85; chmn. & chief exec., The Grade Co. 1985-; Dir. Euro Disney S.C.A. Paris 1988, v.p. British Olympic Assn. Fellow BAFTA, 1979, KCSS 1979. Chairman for Life Active–I.T.C., 1995. Consultant to Polygram Entertainment Group. Autobiography: Still Dancing (1988).
NY THEATER: Prod.: Merrily We Roll Along, Starlight Express, Sly Fox.
PICTURES: Prod.: The Cassandra Crossing, The Domino Principle, The Big Sleep, Escape to Athena, Raise the Titanic, Something to Believe In.
TELEVISION: Movies: Madame Sin, Destination Moonbase Alpha, Lady and the Highwayman, Duel of Hearts. Series: The Saint, The Return of the Saint, Root Into Europe (actor).

GRADE, MICHAEL
Executive. b. London, England, March 8, 1943. e. Stowe. Entered industry 1966. Early career as newspaper columnist, became an executive at London Weekend Television then Embassy Television in Hollywood. Joined BBC Television, 1983 as controller of BBC 1 and director of Programmes (TV), 1986. Joined Channel 4 as chief executive, 1988.

GRAFF, RICHARD B.
Executive. b. Milwaukee, WI, Nov. 9, 1924. e. U. of Illinois. Served U.S. Air Force; Universal Pictures 1946 to 1964 in Chicago, Detroit, Chicago and NY home office as asst. to genl. sales mgr.; 1964 joined National General in Los Angeles. 1967 became v.p. of general sales mgr. of National General Pictures, formed and operated company. 1968, exec. v.p. in charge of world-wide sales and marketing. 1968 made v.p. of parent company; v.p. general sales mgr. AIP in 1971; 1975, pres. Cine Artists Pictures; 1977, pres. Richard Graff Company Inc; 1983, pres. of domestic distribution, MGM/UA. 1987, pres., worldwide distribution, Weintraub Entertainment Group. 1990, pres. The Richard Graff Company, Inc.

GRAFF, TODD
Actor, Writer. b. New York, NY, Oct. 22, 1959. e. SUNY/Purchase.
THEATER: NY: Baby (Tony nom., Theatre World Award), Birds of Paradise. Author: The Grandma Plays, Sheila Levine.
PICTURES: Actor: Sweet Lorraine (also composed songs), Five Corners, Dominick & Eugene, The Abyss, An Innocent Man, Opportunity Knocks, City of Hope. Writer: Used People, The Vanishing (also co-prod.), Fly by Night (also actor), Angie (also co-prod., cameo), The Beautician and the Beast (prod. only).
TELEVISION: Special: Vietnam War Story.

GRAHAM, HEATHER
Actress. b. Milwaukee, WI. Jan. 29, 1970.
PICTURES: License to Drive, Twins, Drugstore Cowboy, I Love You to Death, Shout, Guilty as Charged, Twin Peaks: Fire Walk With Me, Diggstown, Six Degrees of Separation, Even Cowgirls Get the Blues, The Ballad of Little Jo, Mrs. Parker and the Vicious Circle, Don't Do It, Terrified, Desert Winds, Swingers, Entertaining Angels: The Dorothy Day Story, Two Girls and a Guy, Boogie Nights, Nowhere, Scream 2, Committed, Bofinger's Big Thing, Alien Love Triangle, Lost in Space.
TELEVISION: Movies: Student Exchange, O Pioneers!, Kiss and Tell. Series: Twin Peaks.

GRAMMER, KELSEY
Actor. b. St. Thomas, Virgin Islands, Feb. 20, 1955. e. Juilliard. Acting debut on tv in Another World. On B'way in Sunday in the Park With George. Supplied voice for Disney/Mickey Mouse short Runaway Brain.
PICTURE: Down Periscope.
TELEVISION: Series: Cheers, Frasier (5 Emmy Awards, 1994-98; Golden Globe, 1996), Fired Up (exec. prod. only). Guest: Simpsons (voice). Movies: Dance 'Til Dawn, Beyond Suspicion, The Innocent.

GRANATH, HERBERT A.
Executive. e. Fordham U. Started with ABC TV in sales, marketing and production. 1979, became v.p. of Capital Cities/ABC Video Enterprises Inc.; 1982-93, served as pres. of same; Oct. 1993, named pres. ABC Cable and International Broadcast Group, sr. v.p. Capital Cities/ABC Inc.

GRANET, BERT
Producer, Writer. b. New York, NY, July 10, 1910. e. Yale U. Sch. of Fine Arts (47 workshop). From 1936 author s.p. orig. & adapt. numerous pictures. Exec. prod.: Universal, 1967-69, CBS, Desilu Studios.
PICTURES: Quick Money, The Affairs of Annabel, Mr. Doodle Kicks Off, Laddie, A Girl a Guy and a Gob, My Favorite Wife, Bride by Mistake, Sing Your Way Home, Those Endearing Young Charms, The Locket, Do You Love Me?, The Marrying Kind, Berlin Express, The Torch, Scarface Mob.
TELEVISION: Desilu (1957-61), Twilight Zone (pilot), The Untouchables (pilot), Loretta Young Show (1955-56), Walter Winchell File 1956-57, Lucille Ball-Desi Arnaz Show 1957-60, Westinghouse Desilu Playhouse, The Great Adventure.

GRANGER, FARLEY
Actor. b. San Jose, CA, July 1, 1925. e. Hollywood. U.S. Armed Forces 1944-46. Joined Eva Le Gallienne's National Rep. Co. in 1960s (The Sea Gull, The Crucible, Ring Round the Moon).
PICTURES: The North Star (debut, 1943), The Purple Heart, Rope, Enchantment, The Live By Night, Roseanna McCoy, Side Street, Our Very Own, Edge of Doom, Strangers on a Train, Behave Yourself, I Want You, O. Henry's Full House, Hans Christian Andersen, Story of Three Loves, Small Town Girl, Senso, Naked Street, Girl in the Red Velvet Swing, Rogue's Gallery, Something Creeping in the Dark, They Call Me Trinity, Replica of a Crime, Amuk, The Slasher, The Redhead with the Translucent Skin, Kill Me My Love, Planet Venus, Night Flight From Moscow, Man Called Neon, Arnold, Savage Lady, The Co-ed Murders, Deathmask, The Prowler, The Imagemaker.
TELEVISION: Series: One Life to Live (1976-7), As the World Turns (1986-8). Movies: The Challengers, The Lives of Jenny Dolan, Widow, Black Beauty. Guest: Playhouse of Stars, U.S. Steel Hour, Producer's Showcase, Climax, Ford Theatre, Playhouse 90, 20th Century Fox Hour, Robert Montgomery Presents, Arthur Murray Dance Party, Wagon Train, Masquerade Party, Kojak, 6 Million Dollar Man, Ellery Queen.

GRANT, DAVID MARSHALL
Actor. b. Westport, CT, June 21, 1955. e. Yale School of Drama.
THEATER: NY: Sganarelle, Table Settings, The Tempest, Bent, The Survivor, Making Movies, Angels in America: Millenium Approaches/Perestroika, Three Sisters. Regional: Bent (also dir.), Once in a Lifetime, Lake Boat, Free and Clear, True West, The Wager, Rat in the Skull, Snakebit (author), The End of the Day.
PICTURES: French Postcards (debut, 1979), Happy Birthday Gemini, The End of August, American Flyers, The Big Town, Bat 21, Air America, Strictly Business, Forever Young, The Rock, The Chamber, Remembering Sex.
TELEVISION: Series: thirtysomething. Movies: Kent State, Legs, Sessions, Dallas: The Early Years, What She Doesn't Know, Citizen Cohn, Through the Eyes of a Killer. Special: A Doonesbury Special (voice). Pilot: Graham. Host: The Legend of Billy the Kid, Night Sins.

GRANT, HUGH
Actor. b. London, England, Sept. 9, 1960. e. New Coll., Oxford U. Acted with OUDS before landing role in Oxford Film Foundation's Privileged. Acted at Nottingham Playhouse and formed revue group, The Jockeys of Norfolk.
PICTURES: Privileged (debut, 1982), Maurice, White Mischief, The Lair of the White Worm, The Dawning, Remando al Viento (Rowing With the Wind), Bengali Night, Impromptu, Crossing the Line, The Remains of the Day, Night Train to Venice, Sirens, Four Weddings and a Funeral (BAFTA & Golden Globe Awards), Bitter Moon, The Englishman Who Went Up a Hill But Came Down a Mountain, Nine Months, An Awfully Big Adventure, Restoration, Sense and Sensibility, Extreme Measures (also prod.), The Nothing Hill Project, Mickey Blue-Eyes.
TELEVISION: Mini-Series: The Last Place on Earth. Series: The Demon Lover, Ladies in Charge. Movies/Specials: The Detective, Handel: Honour, Profit and Pleasure, Jenny's War, The Lady and the Highwayman, Champagne Charlie, 'Til We Meet Again, Our Sons (U.S.), The Changeling.

GRANT, LEE
Actress. r.n. Lyova Rosenthal. b. New York, NY, Oct. 31, 1931. m. producer Joseph Feury. Daughter is actress Dinah Manoff. At 4 was member of Metropolitan Opera Company; played princess in L'Orocolo. Member of the American Ballet at 11. e. Juilliard Sch. of Music, studied voice, violin and dance. At 18 with road co. Oklahoma as understudy. Acting debut: Joy to the World.
THEATER: acted in a series of one-acters at ANTA with Henry Fonda. Detective Story (Critics Circle Award, 1949), Lo and Behold, A Hole in the Head, Wedding Breakfast; road co. Two for the Seesaw, The Captains and the Kings; toured with Electra, Silk Stockings, St. Joan, Arms and the Man, The Maids (Obie Award), Prisoner of Second Avenue.
PICTURES: Detective Story (debut, 1951; Acad. Award nom.), Storm Fear, Middle of the Night, Affair of the Skin, The Balcony, Terror in the City, Divorce American Style, In the Heat of the Night, Valley of the Dolls, Buona Sera Mrs. Campbell, The Big Bounce, Marooned, The Landlord (Acad. Award nom.), There Was a Crooked Man, Plaza Suite, Portnoy's Complaint, The Internecine Project, Shampoo (Academy Award, best supporting actress, 1975), Voyage of the Damned (Acad. Award nom.), Airport '77, Damien: Omen II, The Swarm, The Mafu Cage, When You Comin' Back Red Ryder, Little Miss Marker, Charlie Chan and the Curse of the Dragon Queen, Visiting Hours, Teachers, The Big Town, Defending Your Life, Under Heat. Dir.: Tell Me a Riddle, Willmar Eight, Staying Together.
TELEVISION: Series: Search for Tomorrow (1953-4), Peyton Place (Emmy Award, 1965), Fay. Guest: Studio One, The Kraft Theatre, Slattery's People, The Fugitive, Ben Casey, The Nurses, The Defenders, East Side/West Side, One Day at a Time, Bob Hope Show (Emmy nom.). Movies: Night Slaves, The Love Song of Bernard Kempenski, BBC's The Respectful Prostitute, The Neon Ceiling (Emmy Award, 1971), Ransom for a Dead Man, Lt. Schuster's Wife, Partners in Crime, What Are Best Friends For?,

Perilous Voyage, The Spell, Million Dollar Face, For Ladies Only, Thou Shalt Not Kill, Bare Essence, Will There Really Be A Morning?, The Hijacking of the Achille Lauro, She Said No, Something to Live For: The Alison Gertz Story, In My Daughter's Name, Citizen Cohn. Mini-Series: Backstairs at the White House, Mussolini--The Untold Story. Special: Plaza Suite. Director: Nobody's Child, Shape of Things, When Women Kill, A Matter of Sex, Down and Out in America, No Place Like Home, Following Her Heart.

GRANT, RICHARD E.
Actor. b. Mbabane, Swaziland, May 5, 1957. e. Cape Town U., South Africa (combined English and drama course). Co-founded multi-racial Troupe Theatre Company with fellow former students and members of Athol Fugard and Yvonne Bryceland's Space Theatre, acting in and directing contemporary and classic plays. Moved to London 1982 where performed in fringe and rep. theater. Nominated most promising newcomer in Plays and Players, 1985, for Tramway Road.
PICTURES: Withnail and I, Hidden City, How to Get Ahead in Advertising, Killing Dad, Mountains of the Moon, Henry and June, Warlock, L.A. Story, Hudson Hawk, The Player, Bram Stoker's Dracula, Franz Kafka's It's A Wonderful Life (short), The Age of Innocence, Ready to Wear (Pret-a-Porter), Jack and Sarah, Twelfth Night.
TELEVISION: Series: Sweet Sixteen. Movies/Specials: Honest Decent and True, Lizzie's Pictures, Codename Kyril, Thieves in the Night (also released theatrically), Here Is the News, Suddenly Last Summer, Hard Times, Bed.

GRASGREEN, MARTIN
Executive. b. New York, NY, July 1, 1925. Entered m.p. ind. 1944, Columbia Pictures in contract dept. Promoted to travelling auditor 1947. Appt. office mgr. Omaha branch 1948; salesman Omaha, 1950. To Indianapolis, 1952, as city salesman; transferred to Cleveland as sales mgr., 1953. Left Columbia in 1960 to become 20th-Fox branch mgr. in Cleveland. Transferred to Philadelphia in 1965 as branch mgr.; transferred to NY in 1967 as Eastern dist. mgr. Resigned in 1970 to form Paragon Pictures, prod.-dist. co. 1975, formed Lanira Corp., representing producers for U.S. sales and dist. of films in U.S. Retired 1980.

GRASSHOFF, ALEX
Director. b. Boston, MA, Dec. 10, 1930. e. USC. 3 Acad. Award nominations for feature documentaries; Really Big Family; Journey to the Outer Limits; Young Americans (Acad. Award, 1968).
PICTURES: A Billion For Boris, J.D. and the Salt Flat Kid, The Last Dinosaur, The Jailbreakers.
TELEVISION: Series: The Rockford Files, Toma, Chips, Night Stalker, Barbary Coast, Movin' On. Specials: The Wave (Emmy Award), Future Shock (1973 Cannes Film Fest. Awards), Frank Sinatra, Family and Friends.

GRASSO, MARY ANN
Executive. b. Rome, NY, Nov. 3, 1952. e. U. of Calif., Riverside, B.A. art history, 1973; U. of Oregon, Eugene, Master of Library Science, 1974. Dir., Warner Research Collection, 1975-85; mgr., CBS-TV, docu-drama, 1985-88; Instructor 1980-88 UCLA Extension, American Film Institute. v.p. & exec. dir. National Association of Theater Owners, 1988-present. Theatre Arts instructor UCLA 1980-85. Amer. Film Inst., LA, 1985-88. Member: Acad. Motion Picture Arts & Sciences, Foundation of the Motion Picture Pioneers, American Society of Association Executives, Phi Beta Kappa. Woman of Achievement, BPOA Awarded 1984. TV credits: The Scarlet O'Hara Wars, This Year's Blonde, The Silent Lovers, A Bunnies Tale, Embassy. Member: NATO (VP), Business and Prof'l. Women's Assoc., AMPAS, Founder Motion Picture Pioneer, Habitat for Humanity.

GRAVES, PETER
Actor. r.n. Peter Aurness. b. Minneapolis, MN, March 18, 1926. e. U. of Minnesota. Brother of actor James Arness. Played with bands, radio announcer, while at school; U.S. Air Force 2 yrs.; summer stock appearances.
PICTURES: Rogue River (debut, 1950), Fort Defiance, Red Planet Mars, Stalag 17, East of Sumatra, Beneath the 12-Mile Reef, Killers From Space, The Raid, Black Tuesday, Wichita, Long Gray Line, Night of the Hunter, Naked Street, Fort Yuma, Court Martial of Billy Mitchell, It Conquered the World, The Beginning of the End, Death in Small Doses, Poor White Trash (Bayou), Wolf Larsen, A Rage to Live, Texas Across the River, Valley of Mystery, The Ballad of Josie, Sergeant Ryker, The Five Man Army, Sidecar Racers, Parts: The Clonus Horror, Survival Run, Airplane!, Savannah Smiles, Airplane II: The Sequel, Number One With a Bullet, Addams Family Values.
TELEVISION: Series: Fury, Whiplash, Court-Martial, Mission Impossible, New Mission: Impossible. Movies: A Call to Danger, The President's Plane is Missing, Scream of the Wolf, The Underground Man, Where Have All the People Gone?, Dead Man on the Run, SST-Death Flight, The Rebels, Death on the Freeway, The Memory of Eva Ryker, 300 Miles for Stephanie, If It's Tuesday It Still Must Be Belgium. Mini-Series: Winds of War, War and Remembrance. Host/narrator: Discover! The World of Science, Biography, Tarzan the Legacy of Edgar Rice Burroughs.

GRAVES, RUPERT
Actor. b. Weston-Super-Mare, England, June 30, 1963. Before film debut worked as a clown with the Delta travelling circus in England.
THEATER: The Killing of Mr. Toad, 'Tis Pity She's a Whore, St. Ursula's in Danger, Sufficient Carbohydrates, Amadeus, Torch Song Trilogy, Candida, Pitchfork Disney, History of Tom Jones, A Madhouse in Goa, A Midsummer Night's Dream, Design for Living.
PICTURES: A Room with a View, Maurice, A Handful of Dust, The Children, Where Angels Fear to Tread, Damage, The Madness of King George, The Innocent Sleep, Different for Girls, Mrs. Dalloway, Bent, The Revengers Comedies, Dreaming of Joseph Lees.
TELEVISION: Vice Versa, All for Love, A Life of Puccini, Fortunes of War, The Plot to Kill Hitler, The Sheltering Desert, Union Matters, Starting Out, Royal Celebration, Good and Bad at Games, Inspector Morse, Doomsday Gun.

GRAY, COLEEN
Actress. r.n. Doris Jensen. b. Staplehurst, NB, Oct. 23, 1922. e. Hamline U., B.A. summa cum laude, 1943, Actor's Lab. m. Fritz Zeiser. Member: Nat'l Collegiate Players, Kappa Phi, a capella choir, little theatres, 1943-44.
PICTURES: State Fair (debut, 1945), Kiss of Death, Nightmare Alley, Fury at Furnace Creek, Red River, Sleeping City, Riding High, Father Is a Bachelor, Apache Drums, Lucky Nick Cain, Models Inc., Kansas City Confidential, Sabre Jet, Arrow in the Dust, The Fake, The Vanquished, Las Vegas Shakedown, Twinkle in God's Eye, Tennessee's Partner, The Killing, Wild Dakotas, Death of a Scoundrel, Frontier Gambler, Black Whip, Star in the Dust, The Vampire, Hell's Five Hours, Copper Sky, Johnny Rocco, The Leech Woman, The Phantom Planet, Town Tamer, P.J., The Late Liz, Cry from the Mountain.
TELEVISION: Series: Window on Main Street, Days of Our Lives, (1966-67), Bright Promise (1968-72). Guest: Family Affair, Ironside, Bonanza, Judd for the Defense, Name of the Game, The FBI, The Bold Ones, World Premiere, Mannix, Sixth Sense, McCloud, Tales from the Dark Side. Movies: Ellery Queen: Don't Look Behind You, The Best Place to Be.

GRAY, DULCIE
C.B.E., F.L.S., F.R.S.A. Actress b. Malaya, Nov. 20, 1919. e. Webber Douglas Sch. Stage debut 1939, Aberdeen, Hay Fever, Author: Love Affair (play), 18 detective novels, book of short stories. 8 radio plays; co-author with husband Michael Denison, An Actor and His World; Butterflies on My Mind, The Glanville Women, Anna Starr; Mirror Image, Looking Forward Looking Back.
THEATER: Over 50 West End plays including Little Foxes, Brighton Rock, Dear Ruth, Rain on the Just, Candida, An Ideal Husband (1965, 1962, 1996 London & NY), Where Angels Fear to Tread, Heartbreak House, On Approval, Happy Family, No. 10, Out of the Question, Village Wooing, Wild Duck, At The End of the Day, The Pay Off, A Murder Has Been Announced, Bedroom Farce, A Coat of Varnish, School for Scandal, The Living Room, Tartuffe, Cavell, Pygmalion, The School Mistress (Chicester), Two of a Kind.
PICTURES: Two Thousand Women, A Man About the House, Mine Own Executioner, My Brother Jonathan, The Glass Mountain, They Were Sisters Wanted for Murder, The Franchise Affair, Angels One Five, There Was a Young Lady, A Man Could Get Killed, The Trail of the Pink Panther, The Curse of the Pink Panther, The Black Crow.
TELEVISION: Milestones, The Will, Crime Passionel, Art and Opportunity, Fish in the Family, The Governess, What the Public Wants, Lesson in Love, The Happy McBaines, Winter Cruise, The Letter, Tribute to Maugham, Virtue, Beautiful Forever, East Lynne, Unexpectedly Vacant, The Importance of Being Earnest, This Is Your Life (1977; and with Michael Denison, 1995), Crown Court, Making Faces, Read All About It, The Voysey Inheritance, Life After Death, The Pink Pearl, Britain in the Thirties, Rumpole (The Old Boy Net.), Cold Warrior, Hook, Line and Sinker, Howard's Way (series; 6 yrs.), Three Up, Two Down, The Time and the Place.

GRAY, LINDA
Actress. b. Santa Monica, CA, Sept. 12, 1940.
PICTURES: Under the Yum Yum Tree, Palm Springs Weekend, Dogs, Fun With Dick and Jane, Oscar.
TELEVISION: Series: Dallas, Models Inc. Guest: Touched By an Angel. Movies: The Big Ripoff, Murder in Peyton Place, The Grass is Always Greener Over the Septic Tank, Two Worlds of Jennie Logan, Haywire, The Wild and the Fire, Not in Front of the Children, The Entertainers, Highway Heartbreaker, Moment of Truth: Why My Daughter?, Bonanza: The Return, To My Daughter with Love, Accidental Meeting, Moment of Truth: Broken Pledges, When the Cradle Falls.

GRAY, SPALDING
Performance artist, Actor, Writer. b. Barrington, RI, June 5, 1941. Began career as actor in 1965 at Alley Theater, Housten, then off-B'way in Tom Paine at LaMama Co. In 1969 joined the Wooster Group, experimental performance group. Has written and performed autobiographical monologues (Three Places in Rhode Island, Sex and Death to the Age 14, Swimming to Cambodia, Monster in a Box, Gray's Anatomy) throughout U.S. Europe and Australia. Taught theater workshops for adults and children and is recipient of Guggenheim fellowship. Artist in resident Mark Taper Forum, 1986-87. B'way debut: Our Town (1988).

PICTURES: Actor: Almost You, The Killing Fields, Hard Choices, True Stories, Swimming to Cambodia (also s.p.), Stars and Bars, Clara's Heart, Beaches, Heavy Petting, Straight Talk, Monster in a Box (also s.p.), The Pickle, King of the Hill, Twenty Bucks, The Paper, Bad Company, Beyond Rangoon, Drunks, Diabolique, Gray's Anatomy, Bliss.
TELEVISION: Special: Terrors of Pleasure (HBO). Movies: The Image, To Save a Child, Zelda. Guest: The Nanny, Missing Links.

GRAY, THOMAS K.
Executive, producer. b. New York City, N.Y., July 1, 1945. e. U. of Arizona, B.A., post grad work at American Graduate School of Int'l Management, Phoenix. Began career as management trainee with United Atists film exchange in Spain, 1970, and year later became managing director, UA, Chile. Also managing director for UA, New Zealand, 1972; Columbia, 1973; South and East Africa, 1974. Joined Cinema Int'l Corp., London, as exec. assist. to co-chairman, 1974, and moved up to managing director of CIC/Warner, South Africa, 1976. Returned to UA as vice pres. Far East, Latin America, Africa and Australia, 1977. Joined Golden Communications Overseas Ltd., London, as vice pres. foreign sales, 1980. With Golden Harvest Films, Inc. since 1984 as sr. vice. pres., production. Executive in charge of prod. for Golden Harvest features: Flying, The Protector, China O'Brien, China O'Brien II, A Show of Force, Teenage Mutant Ninja Turtles, Best of Martial Arts (prod.), Teenage Mutant Ninja Turtles II: Secret of the Ooze (prod.), Teenage Mutant Ninja Turtles III. 1992, pres. and CEO of Rim Film Distribution Inc.

GRAYSON, KATHRYN
Actress, Singer. r.n. Zelma Hedrick. b. Winston-Salem, NC, Feb. 9, 1923. e. St. Louis schools.
THEATER: Camelot, Rosalinda, Merry Widow, Kiss Me Kate, Showboat.
PICTURES: Andy Hardy's Private Secretary (debut, 1941), The Vanishing Virginian, Rio Rita, Seven Sweethearts, Thousands Cheer; Anchors Aweigh, Ziegfeld Follies, Two Sisters from Boston, Till the Clouds Roll By, It Happened in Brooklyn, The Kissing Bandit, That Midnight Kiss, The Toast of New Orleans, Grounds for Marriage, Show Boat, Lovely to Look At, The Desert Song, So This Is Love, Kiss Me Kate, The Vagabond King.
TELEVISION: Guest: GE Theatre (Emmy nom.), Playhouse 90, Lux Playhouse, Murder She Wrote. Special: Die Fliedermaus.

GRAZER, BRIAN
Producer. b. Los Angeles, CA, July 12, 1951. e. U. of Southern California. Started as legal intern at Warner Bros.; later script reader for Brut/Faberge) & talent agent. Joined Edgar J. Scherick-Daniel Blatt Co.; then with Ron Howard as partner in Imagine Films Entertainment. Received NATO/ShoWest Producer of the Year Award, 1992.
PICTURES: Night Shift, Splash (also co-story), Real Genius, Spies Like Us, Armed and Dangerous (also co-story), Like Father Like Son, Vibes, The 'Burbs, Parenthood, Cry-Baby (co-exec. prod.), Kindergarten Cop, The Doors (co-exec. prod.), Closet Land (co-exec. prod.), Backdraft (exec. prod.), My Girl, Far and Away, Housesitter, Boomerang, CB4 (co-exec. prod.), Cop and a Half, For Love or Money, My Girl 2, Greedy, The Paper, The Cowboy Way, Apollo 13, Fear, Sgt. Bilko, The Nutty Professor, Ransom, Inventing the Abbotts, Liar Liar, Felicity, Fletch 3, Love for Hire, Bofinger's Big Things, Mercury Rising.
TELEVISION: Movies: Zuma Beach, Thou Shalt Not Commit Adultery, Splash Too. Series (executive prod.): Shadow Chasers, Take Five, Ohara, Parenthood, Felicity. Special: Poison (prod.), From Earth to the Moon, Hiller & Diller.

GREEN, ADOLPH
Writer, Actor. b. New York, NY, Dec. 2, 1915. m. actress-singer Phyllis Newman. Began career in the cabaret act The Revuers with partner Betty Comden and Judy Holliday (1944).
THEATER: Wrote book, sketches and/or lyrics for many Broadway shows including: On the Town (also actor), Billion Dollar Baby, Bonanza Bound! (also actor), Two on the Aisle, Wonderful Town (Tony Award for lyrics, 1953), Peter Pan (Mary Martin), Say Darling, Bells Are Ringing, A Party with Comden and Green (1959 & 1977), Do Re Mi, Subways Are For Sleeping, Fade Out Fade In, Halleulujah Baby (Tony Awards for lyrics & best musical, 1968), Applause (Tony Award for book, 1970), Lorelei: Or Gentlemen Still Prefer Blondes (new lyrics), By Bernstein (book), On the Twentieth Century (Tony Awards for book & lyrics, 1978), A Doll's Life, The Will Rogers Follies (Tony Award for lyrics, 1991).
PICTURES: Writer (with Betty Comden): Good News, On the Town, The Barkleys of Broadway, Take Me Out to the Ball Game (co-lyrics), Singin' in the Rain, The Band Wagon, It's Always Fair Weather, Auntie Mame, What a Way to Go. Actor: Greenwich Village, Simon, My Favorite Year, Lily in Love, Garbo Talks, I Want to Go Home.

GREEN, GUY
Director. b. Somerset, Eng. Nov. 5, 1913. Joined Film Advertising Co. as projectionist & camera asst. 1933; camera asst., Elstree Studios (BIP) 1935; started as camera operator on films including One of Our Aircraft Is Missing, In Which We Serve, This Happy Breed. 1944: Director of Photography; Dir of Allied Film Makers Ltd.
PICTURES: *Dir. of Photography:* The Way Ahead, Great Expectations (Acad. Award, 1947), Oliver Twist, Captain Horatio Hornblower, I Am a Camera. *Director:* River Beat (debut, 1954), Portrait of Alison, Tears for Simon, House of Secrets, The Snorkel, Desert Patrol (Sea of Sand), The Angry Silence, The Mark, Light in the Piazza, Diamond Head, A Patch of Blue (also co-exec. prod., s.p.), Pretty Polly (A Matter of Innocence), The Magus, A Walk in the Spring Rain (also co-exec. prod.), Luther, Once Is Not Enough, The Devil's Advocate.
TELEVISION: (U.S.) Incredible Journey of Dr. Meg Laurel; Isabel's Choice; Jennifer: A Woman's Story; Arthur Hailey's Strong Medicine, Jimmy B. and Andre, Inmates.

GREEN, JACK N.
Cinematographer. b. San Francisco. Started as camera operator for Bruce Surtees.
PICTURES: *Camera operator:* Fighting Mad, Firefox, Honky Tonk Man, Risky Business, Sudden Impact, Tightrope, Beverly Hills Cop, City Heat, Pale Rider, Ratboy. *Cinematographer:* Heartbreak Ridge, Like Father Like Son, The Dead Pool, Bird, Pink Cadillac, Race for Glory, White Hunter Black Heart, The Rookie, Deceived, Unforgiven, Rookie of the Year, A Perfect World, Bad Company, The Bridges of Madison County, The Net, The Amazing Panda Adventure, Twister, Speed 2: Cruise Control.

GREEN, JOSEPH
Executive, Producer, Director. b. Baltimore, MD, Jan. 28, 1938. e. U. of Maryland, B.A. Since 1970 has headed own distribution co. Joseph Green Pictures and released its library of 150 features to theatres, TV and cable.
PICTURES: The Brain that Wouldn't Die (dir., s.p.), The Perils of P.K. (assoc. prod., dir.), Psychedelic Generation (prod., dir., s.p.).

GREEN, MALCOLM C.
Theatre Executive. b. Boston, MA, Mar. 1, 1925. e. Harvard Coll. Began career as asst. mgr., Translux Theatre, Boston & Revere Theatre, Revere, MA. Treas., Interstate Theatres, 1959-64. Film Buyer, Interstate, 1959-72. Formed Theatre Management Services in 1972 with H. Rifkin and P. Lowe and Cinema Centers Corp. with Rifkin and Lowe families in 1973. Treas., Cinema Center, & pres., Theatre Mgmt. Services. Cinema Center grew to 116 theatres in 6 Northeast states, sold to Hoyts Cinemas Corp., 1986. Sr. v.p., Hoyts Cinemas Corp. 1986-89. Pres., Theatre Owners of New England, 1964-65; chmn bd., 1965-69; treas., 1970-84. Pres., NATO, 1986-88, Chmn Bd, 1988-90. Dir., Natl. Assoc. Theatre Owners. Chmn., NATO of New York State. Director, Vision Foundation. Dir., The Lyric Stage, Boston 1990-94; dir. & v.p., New Hampshire Music Festival, 1988-1996.

GREENAWAY, PETER
Director, Writer. b. Newport, Wales, Apr. 5, 1942. Trained as a painter, first exhibition was at Lord's Gallery in 1964. Started making short films and documentaries in 1966, including: A Walk Through H, The Falls, Act of God, Vertical Features Remake. Directorial feature debut in 1982. Author of numerous books including, 100 Objects to Represent the World, The Physical Self, Les Bruits des Nuages.
PICTURES: The Draughtsman's Contract, A Zed and Two Noughts, The Belly of an Architect, Drowning By Numbers, The Cook The Thief His Wife and Her Lover, Prospero's Books, The Baby of Macon, The Pillow Book.
TELEVISION: Death in the Seine, series of 9 Cantos from Dante's Inferno in collaboration with painter Tom Phillips, M Is for Man Music Mozart, Darwin.

GREENE, CLARENCE
Producer, Writer. b. New York, NY, 1918. e. St. John's U., L.L.B. Author of play Need a Lawyer. Formed Greene-Rouse prods. with Russell Rouse; Acad. Oscar co-orig. story Pillow Talk. Acad. award nom. co-orig. s.p. The Well. Two Writers Guild nominations. Writers Guild award outstanding teleplay, One Day in the Life of Ivan Denisovitch. Co-prod., writer TV series Tightrope.
PICTURES: *Prod., collab. s.p.:* The Town Went Wild, D.O.A., The Well, The Thief, Wicked Woman, New York Confidential, A House Is Not a Home, The Oscar. *Prod.:* Unidentified Flying Objects, The Gun Runners, Fastest Gun Alive, Thunder in the Sun, The Caper of the Golden Bulls, D.O.A. (story, 1988).

GREENE, DAVID
Director, Writer. b. Manchester, Eng., Feb. 22, 1921. Early career as actor. To U.S. with Shakespeare company early 1950's; remained to direct TV in Canada, New York and Hollywood.

PICTURES: The Shuttered Room, Sebastian, The Strange Affair, I Start Counting, Godspell, Gray Lady Down, Hard Country (prod., dir.).
TELEVISION: The Defenders. *Movies:* The People Next Door, Mdame Sin, Count of Monte Cristo, Friendly Fire, The Trial of Lee Harvey Oswald, A Vacation in Hell, The Choice, World War III, Rehearsal For Murder, Take Your Best Shot, Ghost Dancing, Prototype, Sweet Revenge, The Guardian, Fatal Vision (Emmy nom.), Guilty Conscience, This Child Is Mine, Vanishing Act, Miles to Go, Circle of Violence, The Betty Ford Story, After the Promise; Inherit the Wind, Liberace: Behind the Music, Red Earth, White Earth; The Penthouse (dir., exec. prod.), Small Sacrifices (Peabody Award), Honor Thy Mother.

GREENE, ELLEN
Actress, Singer. b. Brooklyn, NY, Feb. 22. e. Ryder Coll. After coll. joined musical road show. Appeared in cabaret act at The Brothers & Sisters Club and Reno Sweeney's, NY. Off-B'way debut, Rachel Lily Rosenbloom. B'way in the The Little Prince and The Aviator. With NY Shakespeare Fest. in In the Boom Boom Room, The Sorrows of Steven, The Threepenny Opera (Tony nom.). Film debut Next Stop, Greenwich Village (1976). Off B'way co-starred in musical Little Shop of Horrors 1982, repeated role in film. Also Off-B'way in Weird Romance. L.A. stage: David's Mother.
PICTURES: Next Stop Greenwich Village (debut, 1976), I'm Dancing as Fast as I Can, Little Shop of Horrors, Me and Him, Talk Radio, Pump Up the Volume, Stepping Out, Rock a Doodle (voice), Fathers and Sons, Naked Gun 33 1/3: The Final Insult, Wagons East!, The Professional, A Journal of Murder, Jaded, One Fine Day, States of Control.
TELEVISION: *Special:* Rock Follies. *Movie:* Glory Glory. *Mini-Series:* Seventh Avenue. *Pilot:* Road Show.

GREENE, GRAHAM
Actor. b. Six Nations Reserve, Ontario, Canada. Member of the Oneida tribe. First show business job as audio technician for several rock bands. Began acting in theater in England.
THEATER: Diary of a Crazy Boy, Coming Through Slaughter, Crackwalker, Jessica, Dry Lips Oughta Move to Kapuskasing.
PICTURES: Running Brave, Revolution, Powwow Highway, Dances With Wolves (Acad. Award nom.), Thunderheart, Clearcut, Savage Land, Rain Without Thunder, Benefit of the Doubt, Maverick, North, Camilla, Die Hard With a Vengeance, Sabotage, The Pathfinder, Dead Innocent, Song of Hiawatha, Wounded, The Education of the Little Tree.
TELEVISION: *U.S.: Series:* Northern Exposure. *Movies:* Unnatural Causes, The Last of His Tribe, Cooperstown, Huck and the King of Hearts, Rugged Gold, 500 Nations. *Guest:* Adderly, L.A. Law. *Canada: Series:* 9B, Spirit Bay. *Movies:* Murder Sees the Light, The Great Detective, Street Legal.

GREENFIELD, LEO
Executive. b. New York, NY, April 26, 1916. e. St. John's U, Coll. of Arts & Sciences. v.p., gen. sales mgr. Buena Vista, 1962; Columbia road show sales mgr. 1966; v.p.-gen. sales mgr., Cinerama Rel. Corp. 1966; pres.-gen. sales mgr., Warners, 1969; sr. v.p. worldwide distribution, MGM 1975; v.p. distribution & marketing, Marble Arch Productions, 1978; exec. v.p. Associated Film Distribution, 1979; pres., distribution, F/M, 1986; pres., dist., Kings Road Entertainment, 1987; pres., Greenlee Assoc., 1988.

GREENHUT, ROBERT
Producer. b. New York, NY. e. Univ. of Miami. Began career as prod. asst. on Arthur Hiller's The Tiger Makes Out, 1967. Worked as prod. manager and asst. director on such films as Pretty Poison, The Night They Raided Minsky's, Where's Poppa?, The Owl and the Pussycat, Husbands, Born to Win, Panic in Needle Park, The Last of the Red Hot Lovers. Received Crystal Apple from city of NY and Eastman Kodak Award for lifetime achievement.
PICTURES: *Prod./assoc. prod./exec. prod.:* Huckleberry Finn, Lenny, Dog Day Afternoon, The Front, Annie Hall, Interiors, Hair, Manhattan, Stardust Memories, Arthur, A Midsummer Night's Sex Comedy, The King of Comedy, Zelig, Broadway Danny Rose, The Purple Rose of Cairo, Hannah and Her Sisters, Heartburn, Radio Days, September, Big, Another Woman, Working Girl, New York Stories, Crimes and Misdemeanors, Quick Change, Postcards From the Edge, Alice, Regarding Henry, Shadows and Fog, A League of Their Own, Husbands and Wives, Manhattan Murder Mystery, Renaissance Man, Wolf, Bullets Over Broadway, Mighty Aphrodite, Everyone Says I Love You, The Preacher's Wife, Mom's On the Roof, With Friends Like These.
TELEVISION: *Movie:* Don't Drink the Water.

GREENSPAN, ALAN
Producer.
PICTURES: *Exec. Prod.:* Photographing Fairies, Donnie Brasco, Best Laid Plans.

GREENWALD, ROBERT
Director, Producer, Teacher. b. New York, NY, Aug. 28, 1948.
e. Antioch Coll., New School for Social Research. Teaches film
and theatre at NYU, New Lincoln, New School. Formed Robert
Greenwald Prods.
THEATER: A Sense of Humor, I Have a Dream, Me and
Bessie.
PICTURES: *Director:* Xanadu, Sweet Hearts Dance (also
exec. prod.), Hear No Evil, Breaking Up (also prod.).
TELEVISION: *Prod.:* The Desperate Miles, 21 Hours at
Munich, Delta Country USA, Escape From Bogen County,
Getting Married, Portrait of a Stripper, Miracle on Ice, The
Texas Rangers, The First Time. *Exec. prod.:* My Brother's Wife,
Hiroshima, Zelda, The Portrait, Daddy, Scattered Dreams,
Murder in New Hampshire, Death in Small Doses. *Director:*
Sharon: Portrait of a Mistress, In the Custody of Strangers,
The Burning Bed, Katie: Portrait of a Centerfold, Flatbed
Annie and Sweetpie: Lady Truckers, Shattered Spirits (also
exec. prod.), Forgotten Prisoners, A Woman of Independent
Means (also co-exec. prod.).

GREENWOOD, BRUCE
Actor. b. Noranda, Quebec, Canada, Aug. 14, 1956. e. Univ.
of British Columbia, London Sch. of Speech and Learning,
AADA. Worked in Canadian theater and as lead singer/gui-
tarist with blues/rock band in Vancouver before arriving in LA
in 1983.
PICTURES: Bear Island (debut, 1980), First Blood, Malibu
Bikini Shop, Another Chance, Wild Orchid, Passenger 57,
Exotica, Paint Cans, Dream Man, Father's Day.
TELEVISION: *Series:* Legmen, St. Elsewhere, Knots Landing,
Hardball, Nowhere Man, Sleepwalkers. *Movies:* Peyton Place:
The Next Generation, Destination: America, In the Line of
Duty: The FBI Murders, Perry Mason: The Case of the All-
Star Assassin, Spy, Summer Dreams: The Story of the Beach
Boys, The Great Pretender, Rio Diablo, Adrift, The Heart of a
Child, Bitter Vengeance, Treacherous Beauties, The
Companion, Servants of Twilight, Little Kidnappers, Twist of
Fate, Woman on the Run: The Lawrencia Bembenek Story,
Jazzle, The Judds: Love Can Build a Bridge. *Guest:*
Hitchhiker, Jake and the Fatman, Road to Avonlea.

GREER, JANE
Actress. b. Washington, DC, Sept. 9, 1924. r.n. Bettyjane
Greer. Orchestra singer; photograph as WAC on Life
Magazine cover won screen debut in Pan-Americana (as
Bettejane Greer).
PICTURES: Pan American (debut, 1945), Two O'Clock
Courage, George White's Scandals; Dick Tracy (1st film as
Jane Greer), Falcon's Alibi, Bamboo Blonde, Sunset Pass,
Sinbad the Sailor, They Won't Believe Me, Out of the Past,
Station West, Big Steal, You're in the Navy Now, The Company
She Keeps, You For Me, The Prisoner of Zenda, Desperate
Search, The Clown, Down Among the Sheltering Palms, Run
for the Sun, Man of a Thousand Faces, Where Love Has
Gone, Billie, The Outfit, Against All Odds, Just Between
Friends, Immediate Family.
TELEVISION: *Movie:* Louis L'Amour's The Shadow Riders.
Guest: Murder She Wrote, Twin Peaks.

GREGORY, JOHN R.
Executive, Producer, Writer. b. Brooklyn, NY, Nov. 19, 1918.
e. Grover Cleveland H.S., 1935, New Inst. of M.P. & Telev.,
1952; Sls., adv. dept. Fotoshop, Inc., N.Y., 1938-42; Spec.
Serv., Photo. instructor, chief projectionist, supv., war dept.
theatres, U.S. Army, 1942-46; sls. mgr.; J. L. Galef & Son, N.Y.;
1948-49, gen. mgr., Camera Corner Co.; 1949-58, pres.; City
Film Center, Inc., 1957; exec. v.p., Talent Guild of New York,
1958; pres., Teleview Prods., Inc., 1961; executive producer,
City Film Productions, 1970. Executive post-production supervisor, Jerry Liotta Films, 1977. Author of many articles in nat'l
publications dealing with m.p. practices and techniques; tech.
editor, Better Movie-Making magazine, 1962; editor, pub.,
National Directory of Movie-Making Information, 1963; assoc.
ed., Photographic Product News, 1964; contrib. editor, U.S.
Camera. M.P. columnist, contributing ed. Travel and Camera
magazine, 1969; Advisory panelist, Photo-methods (N.Y.),
1975. Consultant, Photographic Guidance Council, 1957,
assoc. Society of M.P. & Television-Engineers, 1952.

GREIST, KIM
Actress. b. Stamford, CT, May 12, 1958. e. New Sch. for Social
Research.
THEATER: Second Prize: Two Months in Leningrad, Twelfth Night
(NY Shakespeare Fest.).
PICTURES: C.H.U.D. (debut, 1984), Brazil, Manhunter, Throw
Momma from the Train, Punchline, Why Me?, Homeward Bound:
The Incredible Journey, Houseguest, Homeward Bound II: Lost in
San Francisco.
TELEVISION: *Guest:* Miami Vice, Tales From the Darkside,
Chicago Hope (recurring). *Movies:* Payoff, Duplicates, Roswell.

GREY, BRAD
Producer. e. SUNY Buffalo. Managed comedians and signed first
client, Bob Saget, while still an undergraduate; mngr., for Garry
Shandling, Dana Carvey, Dennis Miller. With manager, Bernie
Brillstein, formed the prod. co., Brillstein-Grey; later bought out
Brillstein's share, and currently runs the co.
PICTURES: The Burning, Opportunity Knocks, The Celluloid
Closet, Cat and Mouse, Happy Gilmore, The Cable Guy,
Bulletproof, Dirty Work.
TELEVISION: The Larry Sanders Show, Mr. Show, The Naked
Truth, The Steve Harvey Show, Just Shoot Me, Alright Already, C-
16: FBI.

GREY, JENNIFER
Actress. b. New York, NY, Mar. 26, 1960. Father is actor Joel
Grey. Appeared as dancer in Dr. Pepper commercial before
making NY stage debut in Off-B'way play Album. B'way in The
Twilight of the Golds.
PICTURES: Reckless (debut, 1984), Red Dawn, The Cotton
Club, American Flyers, Ferris Bueller's Day Off, Dirty Dancing,
Bloodhounds of Broadway, Stroke of Midnight (If the Shoe
Fits), Wind, Portraits of a Killer, Lover's Knot, Red Meat.
TELEVISION: *Movies:* Murder in Mississippi, Criminal Justice,
Eyes of a Witness, A Case for Murder, The West Side, Waltz,
Outrage, Since You've Been Gone.

GREY, JOEL
Actor, Singer, Dancer. b. Cleveland, OH, April 11, 1932. r.n. Joel
Katz. Father was performer Mickey Katz; daughter is actress
Jennifer Grey. e. Alexander Hamilton H.S., L.A. Acting debut at 9
years in On Borrowed Time at Cleveland Playhouse. Extensive
nightclub appearances before returning to theatre and TV.
Performed Silverlake in NY.
THEATER: *NY:* Come Blow Your Horn, Stop the World—I Want to Get
Off, Half a Sixpence, Harry: Noon and Night, Littlest Revue, Cabaret
(Tony Award, 1967), George M!, Goodtime Charley, The Grand Tour,
Cabaret (1987, B'way revival), Chicago. *Regional:* Herringbone.
PICTURES: About Face (debut, 1952), Calypso Heat Wave, Come
September, Cabaret (Academy Award, best supporting actor,
1972), Man on a Swing, Buffalo Bill and the Indians or Sitting Bull's
History Lesson, The Seven Percent Solution, Remo Williams: The
Adventure Begins..., Kafka, The Player, The Music of Chance, The
Fantasticks.
TELEVISION: *Specials:* Jack and the Beanstalk, George M!, The
Wizard of Oz in Concert. *Guest:* Maverick, December Bride,
Ironside, Night Gallery, The Burt Bacharach Show, The Tom
Jones Show, The Englebert Humperdinck Show, The Carol
Burnett Show, The Julie Andrews Hour, Dallas, Brooklyn Bridge,
Star Trek Voyager. *Movies:* Man on a String, Queenie.

GREY, VIRGINIA
Actress. b. Los Angeles, CA, March 22, 1917. Screen career
started 1927 with Uncle Tom's Cabin.
PICTURES: Misbehaving Ladies, Secrets, Dames, The Firebird, The
Great Ziegfeld, Rosalie, Test Pilot, The Hardys Ride High,
Hullaballoo, Blonde Inspiration, The Big Store, Grand Central Murder,
Idaho, Strangers in the Night, Blonde Ranson, Unconquered, Who
Killed Doc Robbin, The Bullfighter and the Lady, Highway 301,
Slaughter Trail, Desert Pursuit, Perilous Journey, Forty-Niners, Target
Earth, Eternal Sea, Last Command, Rose Tattoo, All That Heaven
Allows, Crime of Passion, Jeanne Eagles, The Restless Years, No
Name on the Bullet, Portrait in Black, Tammy Tell Me True, Back
Street, Bachelor In Paradise, Black Zoo, The Naked Kiss, Love Has
Many Faces, Madame X, Rosie, Airport.

GRIECO, RICHARD
Actor. b. Watertown, NY, 1966. Started with Elite Modeling
Agency. Studied acting at Warren Robertson Theatre Workshop
appearing in prods. of Orphans, Golden Boy. As musician
released album Waiting for the Sky to Fall.
PICTURES: Born to Ride, If Looks Could Kill, Mobsters, Tomcat:
Dangerous Desires, Bolt.
TELEVISION: *Series:* One Life to Live, 21 Jump Street,
Booker, Marker. *Movies:* Sin and Redemption, A Vow to Kill

GRIEM, HELMUT
Actor. b. Hamburg, Germany, 1940. e. Hamburg U.
PICTURES: The Girl From Hong Kong, The Damned, The
Mackenzie Break, Cabaret, Ludwig, Children of Rage, Desert
of the Tartars, Voyage of the Damned, Germany in Autumn,
The Glass Cell, Sgt. Steiner (Breakthrough), Berlin
Alexanderplatz, Malou, La Passante, The Second Victory.
TELEVISION: *Mini-Series:* Peter the Great.

GRIER, DAVID ALAN
Actor. b. Detroit, MI, June 30, 1955. e. U. of MI, Yale. Acted with Yale Rep.
THEATER: *NY:* A Soldier's Play, The First (Theatre World Award),
Richard III, Dreamgirls, The Merry Wives of Windsor.
PICTURES: Streamers (debut, 1983), A Soldier's Story, Beer,
From the Hip, Amazon Women on the Moon, Off Limits, I'm
Gonna Git You Sucka, Me and Him, Loose Cannons, Almost an
Angel, The Player, Boomerang, In the Army Now, Blankman,
Tales From the Hood, Jumanji.
TELEVISION: *Series:* All Is Forgiven, In Living Color, The Preston
Episodes (also co-exec. prod.).

GRIER, PAM
Actress. b. Winston-Salem, NC, 1949.
PICTURES: The Big Doll House, Big Bird Cage, Black Mama White Mama, Cool Breeze, Hit Man, Women in Cages, Coffy, Scream Blacula Scream, Twilight People, The Arena, Foxy Brown, Bucktown, Friday Foster, Sheba Baby, Drum, Greased Lightning, Fort Apache The Bronx, Tough Enough, Something Wicked This Way Comes, The Vindicator, On the Edge, Stand Alone, The Allnighter, Above the Law, The Package, Class of 1999, Bill & Ted's Bogus Journey, Posse, Original Gangstas, Mars Attacks, Jackie Brown.
TELEVISION: Mini-Series: Roots: The Next Generations. Movie: A Mother's Right: The Elizabeth Morgan Story. Guest: Miami Vice, Crime Story, Pacific Station, Frank's Place, The Cosby Show, Night Court, In Living Color, Sinbad Show, Fresh Prince of Bel Air.

GRIFFIN, MERV
Executive, Singer, Emcee. b. San Mateo, CA, July 6, 1925. e. U. of San Francisco, Stanford U. Host of The Merv Griffin Show, KFRC-Radio, 1945-48; vocalist, Freddy Martin's orch., 1948-52; recorded hit song I've Got a Lovely Bunch of Coconuts; contract Warner Bros., 1952-54; Prod. Finian's Rainbow, City Center, NY, 1955. Chairman, Merv Griffin Prods.
PICTURES: By the Light of the Silvery Moon, So This Is Love, Boy From Oklahoma, Phantom of the Rue Morgue, Hello Down There, Two Minute Warning, The Seduction of Joe Tynan, The Man With Two Brains, The Lonely Guy, Slapstick of Another Kind.
TELEVISION: Series: The Freddy Martin Show (vocalist), Summer Holiday, Morning Show, The Robert Q. Lewis Show, Keep Talking (emcee), Play Your Hunch (emcee), Saturday Prom, The Merv Griffin Show (1962-63), Talent Scouts, Word for Word, The Merv Griffin Show (1965-86; Emmy Award for writing, 2 Emmy Awards for hosting), Secrets Women Never Share (exec. prod., host, 1987). Creator: Jeopardy (Emmy Award, 1998), Wheel of Fortune.

GRIFFITH, ANDY
Actor. b. Mount Airy, NC, June 1, 1926. e. U. of North Carolina. Began career as standup comedian, monologist, recording artist (What It Was Was Football, 1954). TV acting debut in U.S. Steel Hour production of No Time for Sergeants, which he later played on Broadway and film.
THEATER: B'way: No Time for Sergeants (Theatre World Award), Destry Rides Again.
PICTURES: A Face in the Crowd (debut, 1957), No Time for Sergeants, Onionhead, The Second Time Around, Angel in My Pocket, Hearts of the West, Rustler's Rhapsody, Spy Hard.
TELEVISION: Series: The Andy Griffith Show, The Headmaster, The New Andy Griffith Show, Salvage One, Matlock. Movies: Strangers in 7A, Go Ask Alice, Pray for the Wildcats, Winter Kill, Savages, Street Killing, Girl in the Empty Grave, Deadly Games, Salvage, Murder in Texas, For Lovers Only, Murder in Coweta County, The Demon Murder Case, Fatal Vision, Crime of Innocence, Diary of a Perfect Murder, Return to Mayberry, Under the Influence, Matlock: The Vacation (also co-exec. prod.), The Gift of Love, Gramps. Mini-Series: Washington Behind Closed Doors, Centennial, From Here to Eternity, Roots: The Next Generations.

GRIFFITH, MELANIE
Actress. b. New York, NY, Aug. 9, 1957. m. Anotnio Banderas. Mother is actress Tippi Hedren. Moved to Los Angeles at 4. e. Catholic academies until Hollywood Prof. Sch., 1974. Did some modeling before being cast in Night Moves at 16. Studied acting with Stella Adler, Harry Mastrogeorge and Sandra Seacat.
PICTURES: The Harrad Experiment (debut, 1973), Smile, Night Moves, The Drowning Pool, One on One, Joyride, Underground Aces, Roar, Fear City, Body Double, Something Wild, Cherry 2000, The Milagro Beanfield War, Stormy Monday, Working Girl (Acad. Award nom.), In the Spirit, Pacific Heights, The Bonfire of the Vanities, Paradise, Shining Through, A Stranger Among Us, Born Yesterday, Milk Money, Nobody's Fool, Now and Then, Two Much, Mulholland Falls, Lolita, Crazy in Alabama, Celebrity, Another Day in Paradise, Shadow of a Doubt.
TELEVISION: Series: Carter Country. Mini-Series: Once an Eagle. Movies: Daddy I Don't Like It Like This, Steel Cowboy, The Star Maker, She's in the Army Now, Golden Gate, Women & Men: Stories of Seduction (Hills Like White Elephants), Buffalo Girls. Guest: Vega$, Miami Vice, Alfred Hitchcock Presents, Me and George.

GRILLO, BASIL F.
Executive. b. Angel's Camp, CA, Oct. 8, 1910. e. U. of California, Berkeley, A.B. Certified public accountant, exec. v.p., dir., Bing Crosby Ent., Inc., 1948-57; bus. mgr., Bing Crosby, 1945; co-organizer, dir., 3rd pres., & treas., Alliance of T.V. Film Producers, 1950-54; exec. prod., BCE, Inc., shows incl. Fireside Thea., Rebound, Royal Playhouse, The Chimps; dir., KCOP, Inc., 1957-60; dir. KFOX, Inc., 1958-62; pres., dir., Bing Crosby Prods., 1955-72; dir., Seven Leagues Ent., Inc., 1958; dir. Electrovision Prods., 1970, CEO, Bing Crosby Enterprises.

GRIMALDI, ALBERTO
Producer. b. Naples, Italy, Mar. 28, 1925. Studied law, serving as counsel to Italian film companies, before turning to production with Italian westerns starring Clint Eastwood and Lee Van Cleef. Is owner of P.E.A. (Produzioni Europee Associate, s.r.l.).
PICTURES: For a Few Dollars More, The Good the Bad and the Ugly, The Big Gundown, Three Steps in Delirium, A Quiet Place in the Country, The Mercenary, Satyricon, Burn!, The Decameron, Man of the East, The Canterbury Tales, Last Tango in Paris, Bawdy Tales, Arabian Nights, Salo or the 100 Days of Sodom, Burnt Offerings, Fellini's Casanova, 1900, Illustrious Corpses, Lovers and Liars, Hurricane Rosy, Ginger and Fred.

GRIMES, GARY
Actor. b. San Francisco, CA, June 2, 1955. Family moved to L.A. when he was nine. Made film debut at 15 in Summer of '42, 1971. Voted Star of Tomorrow in QP poll, 1971.
PICTURES: Summer of '42, The Culpepper Cattle Company, Cahill: U.S. Marshal, Class of '44, The Spikes Gang, Gus, Concrete Angels.
TELEVISION: Mini-Series: Once an Eagle.

GRIMES, TAMMY
Actress. b. Boston, MA, Jan. 30, 1934. Daughter is actress Amanda Plummer. e. Stephens Coll, The Neighborhood Playhouse. Recipient: Woman of Achievment Award (ADL), Mother of the Year Award, Mayor's Outstanding Contribution to the Arts Award (NYC). Member: bd. dirs. & v.p. of the Upper East-Side Historic Preservation District (NYC).
THEATER: Look After Lulu (Theatre World Award, 1959), Clerambard, The Littlest Revue, Stratford (Ont.) Shakespeare Fest., Bus Stop, The Cradle Will Rock, The Unsinkable Molly Brown (Tony Award, 1961), Rattle of a Simple Man, High Spirits, Private Lives (Tony Award, 1970), Trick, California Suite, 42nd Street, Tartuffe, A Month in the Country, The Guardsman, The Millionairess, Imaginary Invalid, The Importance of Being Earnest, Mademoiselle Columbe, Blythe Spirit, Waltz of the Toreadors, Molly, Taming of the Shrew, Orpheus Descending, Tammy Grimes: A Concert in Words and Music, A Little Night Music, Pygmalion.
PICTURES: Three Bites of the Apple (debut, 1967), Play It as It Lays, Somebody Killed Her Husband, The Runner Stumbles, Can't Stop the Music, The Last Unicorn (voice), The Stuff, No Big Deal, America, Mr. North, Slaves of New York, A Modern Affair.
TELEVISION: Specials: Omnibus, Hollywood Sings, Hour of Great Mysteries, Four Poster. Guest: St. Elsewhere, The Young Riders. Series: The Tammy Grimes Show. Movies: The Other Man, The Horror at 37,000 Feet, The Borrowers, You Can't Go Home Again, An Invasion of Privacy.

GRISSMER, JOHN
Executive, Producer, Director. b. Houston, TX, Aug. 28, 1933. e. Xavier U., B.S., 1955; Catholic U., M.F.A., dramatic writing, 1959. Taught drama courses, directed student productions at U. of CT & American U., Washington, DC. Produced and co-wrote House That Cried Murder, 1973; co-produced, wrote and directed Scalpel; directed Nightmare at Shadow Woods. Partner in P.J. Productions Co. & North Salem Prods., Inc. Guest Director, Xavier Univ. Theatre.

GRIZZARD, GEORGE
Actor. b. Roanoke Rapids, NC, April 1, 1928. e. U. of North Carolina, B.A., 1949. Has been member of Arena Stage, Washington, D.C., APA repertory company and Tyrone Guthrie resident company in Minneapolis.
THEATER: The Desperate Hours. (B'way debut, 1955), The Happiest Millionaire (Theatre World Award), The Disenchanted, Face of a Hero, Big Fish, Little Fish, Who's Afraid of Virginia Woolf?, The Glass Menagerie, You Know I Can't Hear You When the Water's Running, The Gingham Dog, Inquest, The Country Girl, The Creation of the World and Other Business, Crown Matrimonial, The Royal Family, California Suite, Man and Superman, Another Antiqone, Show Boat, A Delicate Balance (Tony Award, 1996).
PICTURES: From the Terrace, Advise and Consent, Warning Shot, Happy Birthday Wanda June, Comes a Horseman, Firepower, Seems Like Old Times, Wrong Is Right, Bachelor Party.
TELEVISION: Movies: Travis Logan D.A., Indict & Convict, The Stranger Within, Attack on Terror: The FBI vs. the Ku Klux Klan, The Lives of Jenny Dolan, The Night Rider, Attica, Not In Front of the Children, The Deliberate Stranger, Underseige, That Secret Sunday, International Airport, Embassy, The Shady Hill Kidnapping, Oldest Living Graduate (Emmy Award, 1980), Perry Mason: The Case of the Scandalous Scoundrel, David, Caroline?, Iran: Days of Crisis, Not in My Family, Triumph Over Disaster: The Hurricane Andrew Story, Suspicion of Innocence. Specials: Enemy of the People. Mini-Series: The Adams Chronicles, Robert Kennedy and His Times, Queen, Scarlett.

GRODIN, CHARLES
Actor, Director, Writer. b. Pittsburgh, PA, April 21, 1935. e. U. of Miami. After time with Pittsburgh Playhouse studied acting with Uta Hagen and Lee Strasberg; began directing career in New York 1965 as asst. to Gene Saks. Has appeared in some 75 plays all over the country. Has also written scripts, produced plays. Books: It Would Be So Nice If You Weren't Here, How I Get Through Life, We're Ready for You Mr. Grodin.
THEATER: Tchin-Tchin (B'way debut, 1962), Absence of a Cello, Same Time Next Year, It's a Glorious Day... And All That (dir., co-author), Lovers and Other Strangers (dir.), Thieves (prod., dir.), Unexpected Guests (prod., dir.), Price of Fame (also author), One of the All-Time Greats (author).
PICTURES: Sex and the College Girl (debut, 1964), Rosemary's Baby, Catch-22, The Heartbreak Kid, 11 Harrowhouse (also adapt.), King Kong, Thieves, Heaven Can Wait, Real Life, Sunburn, It's My Turn, Seems Like Old Times, The Incredible Shrinking Woman, The Great Muppet Caper, The Lonely Guy, The Woman in Red, Movers and Shakers (also s.p., co-prod.), Last Resort, Ishtar, The Couch Trip, You Can't Hurry Love, Midnight Run, Taking Care of Business, Beethoven, Dave, So I Married an Axe Murderer, Heart and Souls, Beethoven's 2nd, Clifford, It Runs in the Family (My Summer Story).
TELEVISION: Specials (writer): Candid Camera (also dir.), The Simon & Garfunkel Special, Paul Simon Special (also dir.; Emmy Award for writing, 1978). Specials (dir.): Acts of Love and Other Comedies, Paradise (also prod.). Actor: Guest: The Defenders, My Mother the Car, The FBI, Guns of Will Sonnett, The Big Valley. Specials: Grown Ups, Love Sex and Marriage (also writer), Charley's Aunt. Movies: Just Me and You, The Grass Is Always Greener Over the Septic Tank. Mini-Series: Fresno. Series: Charles Grodin (talk).

GROENING, MATT
Animator, Cartoonist. b. Portland, OR, Feb. 14, 1954. Moved to LA in mid 1980s, started drawing comic strip named "Life in Hell". In 1988 created The Simpsons, originally filler in The Tracy Ullman show, later TV series. Author of Kevin Newcombe (bio.). Guest on TV's, Space Ghost Coast to Coast.

GROSBARD, ULU
Director. b. Antwerp, Belgium. Jan. 9, 1929. e. U. of Chicago, B.A. 1950, M.A. 1952. Trained at Yale Sch. of Drama 1952-53. Asst. dir. to Eliza Kazan on Splendor in the Grass, 1961; asst. dir.: West Side Story, The Hustler, The Miracle Worker. Unit mgr.: The Pawnbroker.
THEATER: The Days and Nights of Beebee Fenstermaker, The Subject Was Roses, A View From the Bridge, The Investigation, That Summer—That Fall, The Price, American Buffalo, The Woods, The Wake of Jamie Foster, The Tenth Man.
PICTURES: The Subject Was Roses (debut, 1968), Who Is Harry Kellerman and Why Is He Saying Those Terrible Things About Me? (also co-prod.), Straight Time, True Confessions, Falling in Love, Georgia (also co-prod.), The Deep End of the Ocean.

GROSS, KENNETH H.
Executive. b. Columbus, OH, Feb. 12, 1949. e. New School for Social Research, U. of London. Conducted film seminars at New School and active in several indep. film projects. Published film criticism in various journals and magazines. Joined ABC Ent. 1971. Named supvr. of feature films for ABC-TV. Appt. mgr. of feature films, 1974. Promoted 1975 to program exec., ABC Ent. Prime Time/West Coast. Promoted to exec. prod., movies for TV, ABC Ent. 1976 in L.A.; 1978, with literary agency F.C.A. as partner in L.A.; 1979 prod. for Lorimar; then with Intl. Creative Mgt; 1982, formed own literary talent agency, The Literary Group; 1985, merged agency with Robinson-Weintraub & Assoc. to become Robinson-Weintraub-Gross & Assoc. 1993, founding partner of Paradigm, a talent and literary agency. 1997, formed Ken Gross Management, mgmt. and prod. co.

GROSS, MARY
Actress. b. Chicago, IL, March 25, 1953. Brother is actor Michael Gross. e. Loyola U. Is also student of the harp. In 1980 discovered by John Belushi who saw her perform as resident member of Chicago's Second City comedy troupe, where she won Chicago's Joseph Jefferson Award as best actress for the revue, Well, I'm Off to the Thirty Years War. First came to national attention as regular on Saturday Night Live, 1981-85.
PICTURES: Club Paradise, The Couch Trip, Casual Sex?, Big Business, Feds, Troop Beverly Hills, The Santa Clause.
TELEVISION: Series: Saturday Night Live, The People Next Door. Specials: Comic Relief I, The Second City 25th Anniversary Reunion.

GROSS, MICHAEL
Actor. b. Chicago, IL, June 21, 1947. m. casting dir. Elza Bergeron. Sister is actress Mary Gross. e. U. Illinois, B.A., Yale School of Drama, M.F.A.
THEATER: NY Shakespeare Fest. (Sganarelle, An Evening of Moliere Farces, Othello). Off-B'way: Endgame, No End of Blame (Obie Award), Put Them All Together, Geniuses, Territorial Rites. B'way: Bent, The Philadelphia Story. L.A. stage: Hedda Gabler, The Real Thing, Love Letters, Money & Friends.

PICTURES: Just Tell Me What You Want, Big Business, Tremors, Midnight Murders, Cool as Ice, Alan & Naomi, Tremors II: Aftershocks, Ground Control.
TELEVISION: Series: Family Ties. Movies: A Girl Named Sooner, FDR: The Last Year, Dream House, The Neighborhood, Little Gloria Happy at Last, Cook and Peary-The Race to the Pole, Summer Fantasy, Family Ties Vacation, A Letter to Three Wives, Right to Die, In the Line of Duty: The FBI Murders, A Connecticut Yankee in King Arthur's Court, Vestige of Honor, In the Line of Duty: Manhunt in the Dakotas, With a Vengeance, Snowbound: The Jim and Jennifer Stolpa Story, In the Line of Duty: The Price of Vengeance, Avalanche, Awake to Danger, Deceived by Trust.

GROSSBART, JACK
Producer. b. Newark, NJ, Apr. 18, 1948. e. Rutgers Univ. Was agent, 1975-80, then personal manager, Litke-Grossbart Mgmt., 1980-87. Became tv prod., Jack Grossbart Prods., 1987.
TELEVISION: Movies: Exec. prod./prod.: Shattered Vows, The Seduction of Gina, Rockabye, Killer in the Mirror, Something in Common, Dangerous Affection, Echoes in the Darkness, She Was Marked for Murder, The Preppie Murder, Joshua's Heart, Lies Before Kisses, Honor Bright, Last Wish, Something to Live For: The Alison Gertz Story, A Jury of One, Comrades of Summer, The Woman Who Loved Elvis, One of Her Own, Leave of Absence, Between Love & Honor, Rage Against Time: A Search for Sara, Unforgivable, Breaking Through. Series: Exec. prod.: Sydney, Cafe Americain.

GROSSBERG, JACK
Producer, Executive. b. Brooklyn, NY, June 5, 1927. Member: AMPAS.
PICTURES: Requiem for a Heavyweight, Pretty Poison, The Producers, Don't Drink the Water, Take the Money and Run, Bananas, Everything You Always Wanted To Know About Sex, Sleeper, A Delicate Balance, Luther, Rhinoceros, Leadbelly, King Kong, The Betsy, Fast Break, A Stranger is Watching, Brainstorm, Strange Brew, Touch and Go, The Experts, Little Monsters.

GROSSMAN, ERNIE
Executive. b. New York, NY, Sept. 19, 1924. Still dept., press-book edit., asst. field mgr., Warner Bros., 1940-58; Studio publicist, 1958-60; exploitation, promo. mgr. field dept., 1960-64; nat'l mgr., pub., exploit., promo.; 1964-67 exec. co-ord. advt., pub. & promo., Warner-7 Arts, 1967; WB nat'l supv. ad.-pub., 1970. exec. assist. to Richard Lederer, 1971-72; 1973 nat'l dir. of Pub. & Promotion, Warner Bros. Inc.; 1977, natl. dir. of adv.-pub.; 1980-85, natl. dir. promo. 1987, named south-west special events dir. Retired, 1994.

GRUEN, ROBERT
Executive. b. New York, NY, Apr. 2, 1913. e. Carnegie Mellon U., B.A. Stage designer, 1934-35; designer, 20th-Fox, 1936; prod. exec., National Screen Service Corp., 1936; head, Robert Gruen Associates, ind. design org., 1940; nat. pres. Industrial Designers Inst., 1954-55; dir. and v.p., National Screen Service Corp. since 1951; senior v.p. 1975-78; dir., NSS Corp., Continental Lithograph and NSS, Ltd., 1978-85. Retired 1985.

GRUENBERG, ANDY
Executive. b. Minneapolis, MN, March 10, 1950. e. University of Wisconsin. Held various sales positions with 20th Century Fox and Warner Bros. from 1976 to 1984. Joined Columbia Pictures as asst. general sales mgr. Lorimar Pictures s.v.p. and general sales mgr. 1985-89. Hemdale Prods. pres. of distribution, 1989-91. Joined MGM/UA in 1991, currently exec. v.p. of distribution.

GRUENBERG, LEONARD S.
Executive. b. Minneapolis, MN, Sept. 10, 1913. e. U. of Minnesota. Began as salesman Republic Pictures, Minneapolis, 1935; with RKO in same capacity, 1936; promoted to city sales mgr., St. Louis, 1937, then branch mgr., Salt Lake City, 1941; later that year apptd. Rocky Mt. Dist. Mgr. (hqts., Denver, CO); 1946 Metropolitan, div. mgr.; v.p. NTA, v.p. Cinemiracle Prods.; Pres., Chmn. of bd., Sigma III Corp., 1962. Chmn. of bd., Filmways, 1967. Chmn. of bd. Gamma III Dist. Co. & Chmn of bd. and Pres. Great Owl Corp., 1976. Member Variety Club, Sigma Alpha Mu Fraternity; Lieut. Civil Air Patrol, Lieut. Comdr., U.S.N.R.

GRUSIN, DAVID
Composer, Conductor, Performer. b. Littleton, CO, June 26, 1934. Directed music for the Andy Williams Show on TV for 7 yrs in the 1960s, where met Norman Lear and Bud Yorkin, producers of the series, who signed him to score their first feature film, Divorce, American Style (1967).
PICTURES: Waterhole No. 3, The Graduate, Candy, The Heart Is a Lonely Hunter, Winning, Where Were You When the Lights Went Out?, Generation, A Man Called Gannon, Tell Them Willie Boy Is Here, Adam at 6 A.M., Halls of Anger, The Gang That Couldn't Shoot Straight, The Pursuit of Happiness, Shoot Out, Fuzz, The Great Northfield Minnesota Raid, The Friends of Eddie Coyle, The Midnight Ride, W.W. and the Dixie Dancekings, The Yakuza, Three Days of the Condor, Murder By Death, The Front, Fire Sale, Mr. Billion, Bobby Deerfield, The Goodbye Girl, Heaven Can Wait, And Justice for All, The Champ, The Electric Horseman, My Bodyguard, Absence of Malice,

On Golden Pond, Reds, Author! Author!, Tootsie, Scandalous, Racing with the Moon, The Pope of Greenwich Village, The Little Drummer Girl, Falling in Love, Goonies, The Milagro Beanfield War (Acad. Award, 1988), Clara's Heart, Tequila Sunrise, A Dry White Season, Havana, The Bonfire of the Vanities, For the Boys, The Firm, Mulholland Falls, Selena, Hope Floats.
TELEVISION: *Movies*: Deadly Dream, Prescription: Murder, Scorpio Letters, Eric, The Family Rico, The Death Squad. *Series*: Maude, Good Times, Baretta, The Name of the Game, It Takes a Thief, The Girl From Uncle, St. Elsewhere, In the Gloaming.

GUBER, PETER
Producer. b. 1942. e. Syracuse U., B.A.; U. at Florence (Italy), S.S.P.; Sch. of Law, J.D., L.L.M. Recruited by Columbia Pictures as exec. asst. in 1968 while at NYU. Graduate Sch. of Business Adm. With Col. seven yrs. in key prod. exec. capacities, serving last three as studio chief. Formed own company, Peter Guber's Filmworks, which in 1976 was merged with his Casablanca Records to become Casablanca Record and Filmworks where he was co-owner & chmn. bd. 1980 formed Polygram Pictures later bringing in Jon Peters as partner. 1983 sold Polygram and formed Guber-Peters. 1988 merged co. with Burt Sugarman's Barris Industries to form Guber-Peters-Barris Entertainment Co. Co-chmn. & man. dir. 1989 took full control of co. with Sugarman's exit and addition of Australia's Frank Lowy as new partner. 1989 became CEO of Columbia Pictures Ent.; 1992 became chairman and CEo of Sony Pictures Ent. Awards: Producer of Year, NATO, 1979; NYU Albert Gallatin Fellowship; Syracuse U Ardent Award. Visiting prof., & chmn. producer's dept., UCLA Sch. of Theatre Arts. Member of NY, CA and Wash. DC Bars. *Books*: Inside the Deep, Above the Title.
PICTURES: The Deep (first under own banner), Midnight Express. Co-Prod. with Jon Peters: An American Werewolf in London, Missing, Flashdance (exec. prod.), D.C. Cab (exec. prod.), Endless Love, Vision Quest (exec. prod.), The Legend of Billie Jean, Head Office, Clan of the Cave Bear, Six Weeks (exec. prod.), The Pursuit of D.B. Cooper (exec. prod.), Clue (exec. prod.), The Color Purple (exec. prod.), The Witches of Eastwick (prod.), Innerspace (exec. prod.), Who's That Girl (exec. prod.), Gorillas in the Mist (exec. prod.), Caddyshack II, Rain Man (exec. prod.), Batman (prod.), Johnny Handsome, Tango and Cash (prod.), Batman Returns, This Boy's Life (exec. prod.), With Honors (exec. prod.).
TELEVISION: Mysteries of the Sea (doc. Emmy Award). *Exec. prod.*: Television and the Presidency, Double Platinum, Dreams (series). *Movies*: Stand By Your Man, The Toughest Man in the World (exec. prod.), Bay Coven, Oceanquest, Brotherhood of Justice, Nightmare at Bitter Creek, Finish Line.

GUEST, CHRISTOPHER
Actor, Writer, Composer, Director. b. New York, NY, Feb. 5, 1948. m. actress Jamie Lee Curtis. Brother is actor Nicholas Guest. Wrote the musical score and acted in National Lampoon's Lemmings off-B'way. On B'way in Room Service, Moonchildren.
PICTURES: The Hospital (debut, 1971), The Hot Rock, Death Wish, The Fortune, Girlfriends, The Last Word, The Long Riders, Heartbeeps, This Is Spinal Tap (also co-s.p.), Little Shop of Horrors, Beyond Therapy, The Princess Bride, Sticky Fingers, The Big Picture (dir. co-s.p., story), A Few Good Men, Waiting for Guffman (also dir.), Edwards and Hunt (also dir.).
TELEVISION: *Series*: Saturday Night Live (1984-5). *Movies*: It Happened One Christmas, Haywire, Million Dollar Infield, A Piano for Mrs. Cimino, Attack of the 50 Ft. Woman (dir.). *Specials*: The TV Show, The Chevy Chase Special (also writer), The Billion Dollar Bubble, Lily Tomlin (also writer, Emmy Award, 1976), A Nice Place to Visit (writer only), Spinal Tap Reunion (also co-writer). *Mini-Series*: Blind Ambition.

GUEST, LANCE
Actor. b. Saratoga, CA, July 21, 1960. e. UCLA.
PICTURES: Halloween II, I Ought To Be in Pictures, The Last Starfighter, Jaws-The Revenge, The Wizard of Loneliness, Plan B.
TELEVISION: *Series*: Lou Grant, Knots Landing, Life Goes On. *Guest*: St. Elsewhere. *Movies*: Confessions of a Married Man. *Specials*: One Too Many, My Father My Rival, The Roommate. *Mini-Series*: Favorite Son.

GUEST, VAL
Writer, Director, Producer. b. London, England, 1911. e. England and America. Journalist with Hollywood Reporter, Zit's Los Angeles Examiner and Walter Winchell. Debuted as dir. & writer of 1942 short film The Nose Has It.
PICTURES: *Director/Writer*: Miss London Ltd. (feature debut, 1943), Murder at the Windmill, Mass Pilgrim's Progress, The Body Said No, Mr. Drake's Duck, Happy Go Lovely, Another Man's Poison, Penny Princess, The Runaway Bus, Life With the Lyons, Dance Little Lady, Men of Sherwood Forest, Lyons in Paris, Break in the Circle, It's A Great Life, The Quatermass Experiment (The Creeping Unknown), They Can't Hang Me, The Weapon, It's a Wonderful World, Quatermass II (Enemy From Space), The Abominable Snowman, Carry on Admiral, The Camp on Blood Island, Up the Creek, Further Up the Creek, Yesterday's Enemy,

Expresso Bongo (also prod.), Life Is a Circus, Hell Is a City, Full Treatment (Stop Me Before I Kill; also prod.), The Day the Earth Caught Fire (also prod.), Jigsaw (also prod.), 80,000 Suspects (also prod.), The Beauty Jungle (Contest Girl; also co-prod.), Where the Spies Are (also co-prod.), Casino Royale (co-dir.), Assignment K, When Dinosaurs Ruled the Earth, Tomorrow, The Persuaders, Au Pair Girls, Confessions of a Window Cleaner, Killer Force (Diamond Mercenaries; dir. only), The Boys in Blue.
TELEVISION: Space 1999, The Persuaders, The Adventurer, The Shillingbury Blowers, The Band Played On, Sherlock Holmes & Dr. Watson, Shillingbury Tales, Dangerous Davies, The Last Detective, In Possession, Mark of the Devil, Child's Play, Scent of Fear.

GUILLAUME, ROBERT
Actor. b. St. Louis, MO, Nov. 30, 1937. e. St. Louis U., Washington U. Scholarship for musical fest. in Aspen, CO. Then apprenticed with Karamu Theatre where performed in operas and musicals. B'way plays and musicals include Fly Blackbird, Kwamina, Guys and Dolls, Purlie, Jacques Brel is Alive and Well and Living in Paris, Cyrano. In L.A. in Phantom of the Opera.
PICTURES: Super Fly T.N.T. (debut, 1973), Seems Like Old Times, Prince Jack, They Still Call Me Bruce, Wanted Dead or Alive, Lean On Me, Death Warrant, The Meteor Man, The Lion King (voice), First Kid, Spy Hard.
TELEVISION: *Series*: Soap (Emmy Award, 1979), Benson (Emmy Award, 1985), The Robert Guillaume Show, Saturdays, Pacific Station, Fish Police (voice), Happily Ever After... Fairytales for Every Child. *Guest*: Dinah, Mel and Susan Together, Rich Little's Washington Follies, Jim Nabors, All in the Family, Sanford and Son, The Jeffersons, Marcus Welby, M.D., Carol & Company, Sister Kate, A Different World. *Mini-Series*: North and South, Pandora's Clock. *Movies*: The Kid From Left Field, The Kid with the Broken Halo, You Must Remember This, The Kid with the 100 I.Q. (also exec. prod.), Perry Mason: The Case of the Scandalous Scoundrel, The Penthouse, Fire and Rain, Greyhounds, Children of the Dust, A Good Day to Die, Panic in the Skies!, Merry Christmas George Bailey, His Bodyguard. *Specials*: Purlie, 'S Wonderful 'S Marvellous 'S Gershwin, John Grin's Christmas, Martin Luther King: A Look Back A Look Forward, Living the Dream: A Tribute to Dr. Martin Luther King Jr. (host), The Debbie Allen Special, Carol & Company, Sister Kate, Story of a People (host), Mastergate, Cosmic Slop. *Pilot*: Driving Miss Daisy.

GUILLERMIN, JOHN
Director, Producer, Writer. b. London, England, Nov. 11, 1925. e. City of London Sch., Cambridge U. RAF pilot prior to entering film industry.
PICTURES: *Director*: Torment (debut, 1949; also co-prod., s.p.), Smart Alec, Two on the Tiles, Four Days, Song of Paris, Miss Robin Hood, Operation Diplomat (also co-s.p.), Adventure in the Hopfields, The Crowded Day, Dust and Gold, Thunderstorm, Town on Trial, The Whole Truth, I Was Monty's Double, Tarzan's Greatest Adventure (also co-s.p.), The Day They Robbed the Bank of England, Never Let Go (also co-story), Waltz of the Torreadors, Tarzan Goes to India (also co-s.p.), Guns at Batasi, Rapture, The Blue Max. P.J. (U.S. debut, 1968), House of Cards, The Bridge of Remagen, El Condor, Skyjacked, Shaft in Africa, The Towering Inferno, King Kong, Death on the Nile, Mr. Patman, Sheena, King Kong Lives, The Favorite.
TELEVISION: *Movie*: The Tracker.

GUINNESS, SIR ALEC
Actor. b. London, Eng., April 2, 1914. e. Pembroke Lodge, Southbourne & Roborough Sch., Eastbourne. Studied acting at Fay Compton Studio of Dramatic Art. Created C.B.E. 1955; Knighted 1959. C.H., 1994. Honorary degrees in literature: Oxford, 1977; Canterbury, 1991. Stage debut: London, 1934. First film appearance was extra in 1934 in Evensong. Special Academy Award, 1980, for services to film. Autobiography: Blessings in Disguise (1985). Also author of Blessings in Disguise, and My Name Escapes Me.
THEATER: Libel! (walk-on debut, 1934), Queer Cargo, Hamlet (1934), Noah, Romeo & Juliet (1935), The Seagull, Love's Labour's Lost, As You Like It, The Witch of Edmonton, Hamlet (1937), Twelfth Night (1937), Henry V, Richard III, School for Scandal, The Three Sisters, The Merchant of Venice (1937), The Doctor's Dilemma, Trelawny of the Wells, Hamlet (1938), Henry V, The Rivals, The Ascent of F.6, Romeo and Juliet (1939), Great Expectations (also adapt.), Cousin Muriel, The Tempest, Thunder Rock, Flare Path (B'way), Heart of Oak, The Brothers Karamozov, Vicious Circle, King Lear, An Inspector Calls, Cyrano de Bergerac, The Alchemist, Richard II, Saint Joan, The Government Inspector, Coriolanus, Twelfth Night (1948; also dir.), The Human Touch, The Cocktail Party (Edinburgh; B'way), Hamlet (1951; also dir.), Under the Sycamore Tree, All's Well That Ends Well, Richard III, The Prisoner, Hotel Paradiso, Ross, Exit the King, Dylan (B'way; Tony Award, 1964), Time Out of Mind, Voyage Round My Father, Habeas Corpus, A Family and a Fortune, Yahoo (also author), The Old Country, The Merchant of Venice (1984), A Walk in the Woods.

PICTURES: Great Expectations (debut, 1946), Oliver Twist, Kind Hearts and Coronets, A Run for Your Money, Last Holiday, The Mudlark, The Lavender Hill Mob (Acad. Award nom.), The Man in the White Suit, The Card (The Promoter), Malta Story, The Captain's Paradise, Father Brown (The Detective), To Paris With Love, The Prisoner, The Ladykillers, The Swan, The Bridge on the River Kwai (Academy Award, 1957), Barnacle Bill (All at Sea), The Horse's Mouth (also s.p.; Acad. Award nom. for s.p.), The Scapegoat (also co-prod.), Our Man in Havana, Tunes of Glory, A Majority of One, H.M.S. Defiant (Damn the Defiant!), Lawrence of Arabia, The Fall of the Roman Empire, Situation Hopeless But Not Serious, Doctor Zhivago, Hotel Paradiso, The Quiller Memorandum, The Comedians, Cromwell, Scrooge, Brother Sun Sister Moon, Hitler: The Last Ten Days, Murder by Death, Star Wars (Acad. Award nom.), The Empire Strikes Back, Raise the Titanic!, Lovesick, Return of the Jedi, A Passage to India, A Handful of Dust, Little Dorrit (Acad. Award nom.), Kafka.
TELEVISION: Movies/Specials/Mini-Series: The Wicked Scheme of Jebel Deeks, Twelfth Night, Conversation at Night, Solo, Little Gidding, The Gift of Friendship, Caesar and Cleopatra, Little Lord Fauntleroy, Tinker Tailor Soldier Spy (mini-series; BAFTA Award), Smiley's People (mini-series; BAFTA Award), Edwin, Monsignor Quixote, Tales From Hollywood, A Foreign Field, Eskimo Day.

GULAGER, CLU
Actor. b. Holdenville, OK, Nov. 16, 1928. Father, John Gulager, cowboy entertainer. e. Baylor U. Starred at school in original play, A Different Drummer, where spotted by prod. of TV's Omnibus; invited to New York to recreate role on TV.
PICTURES: The Killers, Winning, The Last Picture Show, Company of Killers, McQ, The Other Side of Midnight, A Force of One, Touched by Love, The Initiation, Lies, Into the Night, Prime Risk, The Return of the Living Dead, Hunter's Blood, The Hidden, Tapeheads, Uninvited, I'm Gonna Git You Sucka, Teen Vamp, My Heroes Have Always Been Cowboys, The Killing Device, Eddie Pressley, Puppet Master, Gunfighter.
TELEVISION: Series: The Tall Man, The Virginian, The Survivors, San Francisco International Airport, MacKenzies of Paradise Cove. Movies: San Francisco International, Glass House, Footsteps, Smile Jenny You're Dead, Houston We've Got a Problem, Hit Lady, Killer Who Wouldn't Die, Charlie Cobb: Nice Night for a Hanging, Ski Lift to Death, Sticking Together, A Question of Love, Willa, This Man Stands Alone, Kenny Rogers as The Gambler, Skyward, Living Proof: The Hank Williams Jr. Story, Bridge Across Time. Mini-Series: Once an Eagle, Black Beauty, King, North and South II, Space, Dan Turner Hollywood Detective, In the Line of Duty (Ambush in Waco).

GUMBEL, BRYANT
Announcer, News Show Host. b. New Orleans, LA, Sept. 29, 1948. e. Bates Coll. Started as writer for Black Sports Magazine, NY, 1971; sportscaster, then sports dir., KNBC, Los Angeles. Sports host NBC Sports NY 1975-82. Now host on Today Show, New York (Emmy Awards, 1976, 1977).
TELEVISION: Super Bowl games, '88 Olympics, Games People Play, The R.A.C.E, Public Eye With Bryant Gumbel.

GUMPERT, JON
Executive. e. Cornell U. Law Sch. Sr. v.p., business affairs, MGM/UA Entertainment; pres., World Film Services, Inc., indep. prod. co. in N.Y. 1985, named v.p., business affairs, Warner Bros; 1986 sr. v.p. Vista Films. Named sr. v.p. legal bus. affairs, Universal Pictures 1990. Named exec. v.p., legal business affairs, Universal Pictures, 1994. Group ex. v.p., Universal Pictures, 1996-.

GUNSBERG, SHELDON
Executive. b. Jersey City, NJ, Aug. 10, 1920. e. St. Peters Coll., New Jersey State Normal, NYU. With Night of Stars, Madison Sq. Garden, 1942; for. pub., 20th-Fox 1942; United Artists, 1945-47; Universal, roadshows. Rank product, asst. adv., pub. dir., 1947-54; v. pres., Walter Reade Theatres; exec. v.p., Walter Reade Org. 1962; Made chief operating officer, 1971; president, and Chief Executive Officer, 1973; chmn. & CEO. Member: Film Society of Lincoln Center: bd. of dirs. (1955-present), chmn., bldg. committee, Walter Reade Theatre (1986-92), exec. v.p. (1987-90). (d. June 18, 1998)

GUNTON, BOB
Actor. b. Santa Monica, CA, Nov. 15, 1945. e. UCal. Served in army during Vietnam War. Prof. acting debut at Cumberland County Playhouse in Tennesse U.S.A.
THEATER: Off-B'way: Who Am I? (debut, 1971), How I Got That Story (Obie Award), Tip Toes, The Death of Von Richtofen. B'way: Happy End (debut, 1977), Working, Evita (Drama Desk Award; Tony nom.), Passion, King of Hearts, Big River, Rozsa, Sweeney Todd (Drama Desk Award; Tony nom.).
PICTURES: Rollerover (debut, 1981), Static, Matewan, The Pick-Up Artist, Cookie, Born on the Fourth of July, Glory, JFK, Patriot Games, The Public Eye, Jennifer Eight, Demolition Man, The Shawshank Redemption, Dolores Claiborne, Ace Ventura: When Nature Calls, Broken Arrow, The Glimmer Man, Midnight in the Garden of Good and Evil.
TELEVISION: Series: Comedy Zone, Hot House, Courthouse. Movies: Lois Gibbs and the Love Canal, A Woman Named Jackie, Finnegan Begin Again, Ned Blessing, Dead Ahead: The Exxon Valdez Disaster, Murder in the Heartland, Sinatra, Ruby Ridge: An American Tragedy, Elvis Meets Nixon, Buffalo Soldiers. Mini-Series: Wild Palms.

GURIAN, PAUL R.
Executive, Producer. b. New Haven, CT, Oct.18, 1946. e. Lake Forest Coll., U. of Vienna, NYU. Started producing films in 1971 with Cats and Dogs, a dramatic short which won prizes at Chicago Int. Film Fest and Edinburgh Fest. In 1977 formed Gurian Entertainment Corp., to acquire film properties for production.
PICTURES: Cutter and Bone, Peggy Sue Got Married, The Seventh Sign (exec. prod.).
TELEVISION: The Garden Party (PBS program), Profile Ricardo Alegria (short), Bernice Bobs Her Hair (shown at 1977 N.Y. Film Festival)

GUTTENBERG, STEVE
Actor. b. Brooklyn, NY, Aug. 24, 1958. e. Sch. of Performing Arts, N.Y. Off-B'way in The Lion in Winter; studied under John Houseman at Juilliard; classes with Lee Strasberg and Uta Hagen. Moved to West Coast in 1976; landed first TV role in movie, Something for Joey. B'way debut 1991 in Prelude to a Kiss.
PICTURES: Rollercoaster, The Chicken Chronicles, The Boys from Brazil, Players, Can't Stop the Music, Diner, The Man Who Wasn't There, Police Academy, Police Academy 2: Their First Assignment, Cocoon, Bad Medicine, Police Academy 3: Back in Training, Short Circuit, The Bedroom Window, Police Academy 4: Citizens on Patrol (also prod. assoc.), Amazon Women on the Moon, Surrender, Three Men and a Baby, High Spirits, Cocoon: The Return, Don't Tell Her It's Me, Three Men and a Little Lady, The Big Green, Home for the Holidays, It Takes Two, Zeus and Roxanne, Casper, Airborne.
TELEVISION: Guest: Police Story, Doc. Series: Billy, No Soap Radio. Movies: Something for Joey, To Race the Wind, Miracle on Ice, The Day After. Specials: Gangs (co-prod.), Pecos Bill: King of the Cowboys.

GUY, JASMINE
Actress. b. March 10, 1964, Boston, MA. Toured with Grease!, 1996-97.
PICTURES: School Daze, Harlem Nights, Kla, America's Dream, Cats Don't Dance (voice), Perfect Crime.
TELEVISION: Movies: At Mother's Request, A Killer Among Us, Stomping at the Savoy. Series: A Different World. Mini-series: Alex Haley's Queen, A Century of Women. Guest: Melrose Place, Lois & Clark, Touched by an Angel, The Outer Limits.

GYLLENHAAL, STEPHEN
Director. b. Pennsylvania. e. Trinity Col, CT. Started career in NYC making industrial films. Directed short film Exit 10.m.. writer-producer Naomi Foner.
PICTURES: Waterland, A Dangerous Woman, Losing Isaiah, Piece of My Heart, Homegrown.
TELEVISION: Movies: The Abduction of Kari Swenson, Promised a Miracle, Leap of Faith, Family of Spies, A Killing in a Small Town, Paris Trout, Shattered Mind.

H

HAAS, LUKAS
Actor. b. West Hollywood, CA, Apr. 16, 1976. Kindergarten school principal told casting dir. about him which resulted in film debut in Testament. NY theater debut in Mike Nichols' Lincoln Center production of Waiting for Godot (1988). Appeared in AFI film The Doctor.
PICTURES: Testament (debut, 1983), Witness, Solarbabies, Lady in White, The Wizard of Loneliness, See You in the Morning, Music Box, Rambling Rose, Convicts, Alan and Naomi, Leap of Faith, Warrior Spirit, Boys, Johns, Palookaville, Mars Attacks!, Everyone Says I Love You, Boys, Mars Attacks!, Johns, In the Quiet Night, Breakfast of Champions.
TELEVISION: Movies: Love Thy Neighbor, Shattered Spirits, The Ryan White Story, The Perfect Tribute, Kiss and Tell, David and Lisa. Guest: Amazing Stories (Ghost Train), Twilight Zone, The Young Indiana Jones Chronicles. Pilot: Brothers-in-Law. Specials: A Place at the Table, My Dissident Mom, Peacemaker (Triple Play II).

HACK, SHELLEY
Actress. b. Greenwich, CT, July 6, 1952. e. Smith Coll. and U. of Sydney, Australia. Made modeling debut at 14 on cover of Glamour Magazine. Gained fame as Revlon's Charlie Girl on TV commercials.
PICTURES: Annie Hall, If Ever I See You Again, Time After Time, The King of Comedy, Troll, The Stepfather, Blind Fear, Me Myself and I, The Finishing Touch.
TELEVISION: Series: Charlie's Angels, Cutter to Houston, Jack and Mike. Movies: Death on the Freeway, Trackdown: Finding the Goodbar Killer, Found Money, Single Bars Single Women, Bridesmaids, Casualty of War, Taking Back My Life: The Nancy Ziegenmeyer Story, Not in My Family, The Case of the Wicked Wives, Falling From the Sky: Flight 174, Freefall, Frequent Flyer.

HACKER, CHARLES R.
Executive. b. Milwaukee, WI, Oct. 8, 1920. e. U. of Wisconsin. Thea. mgr., Fox Wisc. Amuse. Corp., 1940; served in U.S.A.F., 1943-45; rejoined Fox Wisconsin Amusement Corp.; joined Standard Theatres Management Corp. 1947, on special assignments; apptd. district mgr. of Milwaukee & Waukesha theatres 1948; joined Radio City Music Hall Corp. as administrative asst. July, 1948; mgr. of oper., 1952; asst. to the pres., Feb. 1957; v.p., Radio City Music Hall Corp., 1964; appointed executive vice president and chief operating officer, February 1, 1973. Pres., Landmark Pictures, May, 1979. Treas. Will Rogers Memorial Fund, 1978-95. Award: Quigley Silver Grand Award for Showmanship, 1947. Member: U.S. Small Business Admin. Region 1, Hartford Advisory Council 1983-93.

HACKETT, BUDDY
Actor. r.n. Leonard Hacker. b. Brooklyn, NY, Aug. 31, 1924. Prof. debut, borscht circuit.
THEATER: B'way: Call Me Mister, Lunatics and Lovers, I Had a Ball.
PICTURES: Walking My Baby Back Home (debut, 1953), Fireman Save My Child, God's Little Acre, Everything's Ducky, All Hands on Deck, The Music Man, The Wonderful World of the Brothers Grimm, It's a Mad Mad Mad Mad World, Muscle Beach Party, The Golden Head, The Good Guys and the Bad Guys (cameo), The Love Bug, Loose Shoes, Hey Babe!, Scrooged, The Little Mermaid (voice).
TELEVISION: Series: School House, Stanley, Jackie Gleason Show, Jack Paar Show, You Bet Your Life (1980), Fish Police (voice). Movie: Bud and Lou. Specials: Entertainment 55, Variety, The Mama Cass TV Program, Plimpton: Did You Hear the One About...?, Jack Frost (voice), Circus of the Stars, Buddy Hackett—Live and Uncensored.

HACKFORD, TAYLOR
Director, Producer. b. Santa Barbara, CA, Dec. 31, 1944. e. USC, B.A.. int'l. relations. Was Peace Corps volunteer in Bolivia 1968-69. Began career with KCET in Los Angeles 1970-77. As prod.-dir. won Oscar for short, Teenage Father, 1978. Theatrical film debut as dir. with The Idolmaker (1980).
PICTURES: Dir. &/or Prod.: The Idolmaker, An Officer and a Gentleman, Against All Odds, White Nights, Chuck Berry: Hail! Hail! Rock 'n' Roll, Everyone's All-American, Bound By Honor/Blood In Blood Out, Dolores Claiborne, The Devil's Advocate. Prod.: Rooftops, La Bamba, The Long Walk Home, Sweet Talker, Queens Logic, Defenseless, Mortal Thoughts, When We Were Kings.

HACKMAN, GENE
Actor. b. San Bernardino, CA, Jan. 30, 1930. First major broadway role in Any Wednesday. Other stage productions include: Poor Richard, Children from Their Games, A Rainy Day in Newark, The Natural Look, Death and the Maiden. Formed own production co., Chelly Ltd.
PICTURES: Mad Dog Coll (debut, 1961), Lilith, Hawaii, A Covenant With Death, Bonnie and Clyde (Acad. Award nom.), First to Fight, Banning, The Split, Riot, The Gypsy Moths, Downhill Racer, Marooned, I Never Sang for My Father (Acad. Award nom.), Doctors' Wives, The Hunting Party, The French Connection (Acad. Award, 1971), Cisco Pike, Prime Cut, The Poseidon Adventure, Scarecrow, The Conversation, Zandy's Bride, Young Frankenstein, Night Moves, Bite the Bullet, French Connection II, Lucky Lady, The Domino Principle, A Bridge Too Far, March or Die, Superman, All Night Long, Superman II, Reds, Eureka, Under Fire, Uncommon Valor, Misunderstood, Target, Twice in a Lifetime, Power, Hoosiers, Superman IV, No Way Out, Another Woman, Bat-21, Split Decisions, Full Moon in Blue Water, Mississippi Burning (Acad. Award nom.), The Package, Loose Cannons, Postcards From the Edge, Narrow Margin, Class Action, Company Business, Unforgiven (Acad. Award, Natl. Soc. of Film Critics, NY Film Critics, BAFTA, LA Film Critics & Golden Globe Awards, best supporting actor, 1992), The Firm, Geronimo: An American Legend, The Quick and the Dead, Crimson Tide, Get Shorty, Birdcage, Extreme Measures, The Chamber, Absolute Power, Antz (voice), Twilight, Enemy of the State.
TELEVISION: Guest: U.S. Steel Hour, The Defenders, Trials of O'Brien, Hawk, CBS Playhouse's My Father My Mother, The F.B.I., The Invaders, The Iron Horse. Movie: Shadow on the Land.

HADLOCK, CHANNING M.
Marketing. TV Executive. b. Mason City, IA. e. Duke U., U. of North Carolina. Newspaperman, Durham, NC Herald, war corr., Yank; NBC, Hollywood; television prod.-writer, Cunning-ham & Walsh Adv.; v.p. account supr. Chirug & Cairns Adv.; v.p. Marketing Innovations; dir. mktg. Paramount Pictures; mktg. svcs, Ogilvy & Mather; mktg. Time Life Books.

HAGERTY, JULIE
Actress. b. Cincinnati, OH, June 15, 1955. Studied drama for six years before leaving for NY where studied with William Hickey. Made acting debut in her brother Michael's theatre group in Greenwich Village called the Production Company.
THEATER: The Front Page (Lincoln Center), The House of Blue Leaves (Theatre World Award, 1986), Wild Life, Born Yesterday (Phil. Drama Guild), The Years, Three Men on a Horse, Wifey, A Cheever Evening, Raised in Captivity.

PICTURES: Airplane! (debut, 1980), A Midsummer Night's Sex Comedy, Airplane II: The Sequel, Lost in America, Goodbye New York, Bad Medicine, Beyond Therapy, Aria, Bloodhounds of Broadway, Rude Awakening, Reversal of Fortune, What About Bob?, Noises Off, The Wife, U Turn.
TELEVISION: Series: Princesses. Specials: The Visit (Trying Times). House of Blue Leaves, Necessary Parties. Movie: The Day the Women Got Even, London Suites.

HAGGAR, PAUL JOHN
Executive. b. Brooklyn, NY, Aug. 5, 1928. e. LA h.s. Veteran of over 40 yrs. with Paramount Pictures, working way up from studio mail room to become apprentice editor in 1953; promoted to asst. editor 1955; music editor, 1957. 1968, named head of postprod. for all films and TV made by Paramount. 1985, named sr. v.p., post-prod. for the Motion Picture Group.

HAGGARD, PIERS
Director. b. London, 1939. e. U. of Edinburgh. Son of actor Stephen Haggard; great grandnephew of author Rider Haggard. Began career in theatre in 1960 as asst. to artistic dir. at London's Royal Court. Named dir. of Glasgow Citizens' Theatre, 1962. 1963-65 worked with the National Theatre, where co-directed Hobson's Choice and The Dutch Courtesan. Has directed many prize winning TV commercials.
PICTURES: Wedding Night (debut, 1969; also co-s.p.), Blood on Satan's Claw (Satan's Skin), The Fiendish Plot of Dr. Fu Manchu, Venom, A Summer Story.
TELEVISION: Specials/Movies: A Triple Play: Sam Found Out (Liza Minnelli special), The Fulfillment of Mary Gray, Back Home, Quatermass Conclusion, Chester Cycle of Mystery Plays, Mrs. Reinhardt, Knockback, Visitors, Heartstones, I'll Take Romance, Four Eyes and Six-Guns, Eskimo Day, The Double (s.p.), Cold Enough for Snow. Series: Pennies from Heaven, Quatermass, Return to Treasure Island, Centrepoint, Space Precinct.

HAGMAN, LARRY
Actor. b. Fort Worth, TX, Sept. 21, 1931. e. Bard Coll. Son of late actress Mary Martin. First stage experience with Margo Jones Theatre in the Round in Dallas. Appeared in N.Y. in Taming of the Shrew; one year with London production of South Pacific. 1952-56 was in London with US Air Force where produced and directed show for servicemen. Returned to N.Y. for plays on and off B'way: God and Kate Murphy (Theatre World Award), The Nervous Set, The Warm Peninsula, The Beauty Part.
PICTURES: Ensign Pulver, Fail Safe, In Harm's Way, The Group, The Cavern, Up in the Cellar, Son of Blob (aka: Beware! The Blob; also dir.), Harry and Tonto, Stardust, Mother Jugs and Speed, The Big Bus, The Eagle Has Landed, Checkered Flag or Crash, Superman, S.O.B., Nixon, Primary Colors.
TELEVISION: Series: The Edge of Night, I Dream of Jeannie, The Good Life, Here We Go Again, Orleans, Dallas. Movies: Three's a Crowd, Vanished, A Howling in the Woods, Getting Away from It All, No Place to Run, The Alpha Caper, Blood Sport, What Are Best Friends For?, Sidekicks, Hurricane, Sarah T.-Portrait of a Teenage Alcoholic, The Big Rip-Off, Return of the World's Greatest Detective, Intimate Strangers, The President's Mistress, Last of the Good Guys, A Double Life, Deadly Encounter, Dallas: The Early Years, Staying Afloat, In the Heat of the Night: Who Was Geli Bendl? (dir. only), Dallas: War of the Ewings, Dallas: Who Killed J.R.?, Dallas: J.R. Returns. Special: Applause, Lone Star. Mini-series: The Third Twin, The Rhinemann Exchange.

HAHN, HELENE
Executive. b. New York, NY. e. Loyola U. Sch. of Law. Instructor of entertainment law at Loyola. Attorney for ABC before joining Paramount in 1977 in studio legal dept. 1979, moved to business affairs; promoted to dir. 1980, v.p., 1981; sr. v.p., 1983. Left in 1985 to join Walt Disney Pictures as sr. v.p., business & legal affairs for m.p. division. 1987, promoted to exec. v.p., Walt Disney Studios.

HAID, CHARLES
Actor, Director, Producer. b. San Francisco, CA, June 2, 1943. e. Carnegie Tech. Appeared on NY stage in Elizabeth the First. Co-produced Godspell. Prod. & dir. short film The Last Supper.
PICTURES: Actor: The Choirboys, Who'll Stop the Rain, Oliver's Story, House of God, Altered States, Square Dance (co-exec. prod. only), Cop, The Rescue, Nightbreed, Storyville. Director: Iron Will.
TELEVISION: Series: Kate McShane, Delvecchio, Hill Street Blues, Cop Rock (prod. only). Movies: The Execution of Private Slovik, Remember When, Things in Their Season, Kate McShane (pilot), Foster and Laurie, A Death in Canaan, The Bastard, Death Moon, Twirl, Divorce Wars, Children in the Crossfire (also co-prod.), Code of Vengeance, Six Against the Rock, Weekend War, The Great Escape II: The Untold Story, A Deadly Silence, Fire and Rain, Man Against the Mob: The Chinatown Murders, In the Line of Duty: A Cop for the Killing (also co-prod.), In the Line of Duty: Siege at Marion (dir. only), The Nightman (dir., prod. only), Cooperstown (also dir.), For Their Own Good, The Fire Next Time, Broken Trust.

HAIM, COREY
Actor. b. Toronto, Canada, Dec. 23, 1972. Performed in TV commercials at 10; signed as regular on children's show, The Edison Twins.
PICTURES: Firstborn (debut, 1984), Secret Admirer, Silver Bullet, Murphy's Romance, Lucas, The Lost Boys, License to Drive, Watchers, Dream a Little Dream, Fast Getaway (also assoc. prod.), Prayer of the Roller Boys, The Dream Machine, Oh What a Night, Blown Away, The Double-O Kid, National Lampoon's Last Resort, Fast Getaway 2, Dream a Little Dream 2, Life 101 (also assoc. prod.), Snowboard Academy, Fever Lake, Demolition High, Busted, Never Too Late, Tales From the Crypt: Bordello of Blood.
TELEVISION: Movies: A Time to Live, Just One of the Girls. Series: Roomies.

HAINES, RANDA
Director. b. Los Angeles, CA, Feb. 20, 1945. Raised in NYC. Studied acting with Lee Strasberg. e. School of Visual Arts. 1975 accepted into AFI's Directing Workshop for Women. Dir. & co-wrote short film August/September, which led to work as writer for series Family. Appeared in documentary Calling the Shots.
PICTURES: Children of a Lesser God, The Doctor, Wrestling Ernest Hemingway, A Family Thing (co-prod. only).
TELEVISION: Series: Family (writer), Hill Street Blues (dir. of 4 episodes), Alfred Hitchcock Presents (Bang You're Dead), Tales from the Crypt (Judy You're Not Yourself Today). Movie: Something About Amelia. Specials: Under This Sky, The Jilting of Granny Weatherall, Just Pals.

HALE, BARBARA
Actress. b. DeKalb, IL, Feb. 18, 1922. Was married to late actor Bill Williams. Son is actor William Katt. e. Chicago Acad. of Fine Arts. Beauty contest winner, Little Theatre actress. Screen debut, 1943.
PICTURES: Gildersleeve's Bad Day, The Seventh Victim, Higher and Higher, Belle of the Yukon, The Falcon Out West, Falcon in Hollywood, Heavenly Days, West of the Pecos, First Yank in Tokyo, Lady Luck, A Likely Story, Boy with Green Hair, The Clay Pigeon, Window, Jolson Sings Again, And Baby Makes Three, Emergency Wedding, Jackpot, Lorna Doone, First Time, Last of the Comanches, Seminole, Lone Hand, A Lion Is in the Streets, Unchained, Far Horizons, Houston Story, 7th Cavalry, Oklahoman, Slim Carter, Desert Hell, Buckskin, Airport, Soul Soldier, Giant Spider Invasion, Big Wednesday.
TELEVISION: Series: Perry Mason (Emmy Award, 1959). Movies: Flight of the Grey Wolf, Perry Mason Returns (1985) and 29 other Perry Mason's incl. The Case of the... Murdered Madam, Avenging Ace, Lady in the Lake, Scandalous Scoundrel, Lethal Lesson, Poisoned Pen, Fatal Fashion, Reckless Romeo.

HALEY, JR., JACK
Executive, Director. b. Los Angeles, CA, Oct.25, 1933. e. Loyola U. Son of late actor Jack Haley. 1959-67 Wolper Prods., 1967-73. sr. v.p. at Wolper before joining MGM. Named dir. of creative affairs. Left in 1974, to join 20th Century-Fox as pres. of TV div. and v.p., TV for 20th-Fox Film Corp. Winner of 2 Peabody Awards, best prod. at Int'l. TV Festival at Monte Carlo and 3 Silver Lion Awards at Venice Film Festival. Won Emmy for best dir. in music or variety shows for Movin' On with Nancy. Directed Academy Awards Show in 1970; prod. it in 1974 and 1979. Left Fox 1976 to be indep. prod.
PICTURES: Director: Norwood, The Love Machine, That's Entertainment (also prod, s.p.), Better Late Than Never (prod. only), That's Dancing (also co-prod., s.p.).
TELEVISION: The Incredible World of James Bond, The Legend of Marilyn Monroe, The Supremes, The Hidden World, Movin' with Nancy (Emmy Award, dir., 1968), With Love Sophia, Monte Carlo, Life Goes to War: Hollywood and the Homefront; Heroes of Rock n' Roll (exec. prod.), 51st Academy Awards (Emmy Award, 1979), Hollywood, the Golden Years (with David Wolper), Ripley's Believe It or Not, The Night They Saved Christmas, Cary Grant: A Celebration (exec. prod.).

HALL, ANTHONY MICHAEL
Actor. b. Boston, MA, Apr. 14, 1968.
PICTURES: Six Pack (debut, 1982), National Lampoon's Vacation, Sixteen Candles, The Breakfast Club, Weird Science, Out of Bounds, Johnny Be Good, Edward Scissorhands, A Gnome Named Norm, Into the Sun, Hail Caesar (also dir.), Six Degrees of Separation, Me and the Mob, The Grave, Exit in Red, Trojan War, Cold Night Into Dawn.
TELEVISION: Series: Saturday Night Live (1985-86). Mini-Series: Texas. Movies: Rascals and Robbers: The Secret Adventures of Tom Sawyer and Huck Finn, Running Out, A Bucket of Blood, Hijacked: Flight 285. Guest: NYPD Blue, Tales from the Crypt, Boys and Girls.

HALL, ARSENIO
Actor, Comedian. b. Cleveland, OH. Feb. 12, 1959. e. Kent State U. Became interested in magic at 7, which later led to own local TV special, The Magic of Christmas. Switched from advertising career to stand-up comedy, 1979. Discovered at Chicago nightclub by singer Nancy Wilson.
PICTURES: Amazon Women on the Moon (debut, 1987), Coming to America, Harlem Nights, Bopha! (exec. prod. only), Blankman.
TELEVISION: Series: The 1/2 Hour Comedy Hour (1983, co-host), Thicke of the Night, Motown Revue, The Late Show (1987, host), The Arsenio Hall Show, The Party Machine With Nia Peeples (prod. only), Arsenio. Special: Happy Birthday Elizabeth: A Celebration of Life.

HALL, CONRAD
Cinematographer. b. Papeete, Tahiti, June 21, 1926. Worked as camera operator with Robert Surtees, Ted McCord, Ernest Haller; moved to TV as dir. of photography before feature films.
PICTURES: Wild Seed, The Saboteur–Code Name: Morituri, Harper, The Professionals, Rogue's Gallery, Incubus, Divorce American Style, In Cold Blood, Cool Hand Luke, Hell in the Pacific, Butch Cassidy and the Sundance Kid (Academy Award, 1969), Tell Them Willie Boy Is Here, The Happy Ending, Fat City, Electra Glide in Blue, The Day of the Locust, Smile, Marathon Man, Black Widow, Tequila Sunrise, Class Action, Jennifer Eight, Searching for Bobby Fischer, Love Affair.
TELEVISION: Movie: It Happened One Christmas, Stoney Burke. Series: Outer Limits.

HALL, KURT C.
Executive. b. Burlington, VT. e. Univ. of VT. Served as dir. of financial reporting, dir. of finance, and v.p. & treas. of UA Entertainment before becoming v.p. & treas. of United Artists Theatre Circuit, 1990-91. Named exec. v.p. and CFO of United Artists Theatre Circuit, Inc.

HALL, HUNTZ (HENRY)
Actor. b. Boston, MA, Aug 15, 1920. In 1937 appeared in stage and screen production Dead End.
PICTURES: Dead End (debut, 1937), Crime School, Angels with Dirty Faces, They Made Me a Criminal, Hell's Kitchen, Muggs Rides Again, Live Wires, A Walk in the Sun, Jinx Money, Smuggler's Cove, Fighting Fools, Blues Busters, Bowery Battalion, Ghost Chasers, Crazy Over Horses, Let's Go Navy, Here Come the Marines, Hold That Line, Feudin' Fools, No Holds Barred, Private Eyes, Paris Playboys, Bowery Boys Meet the Monsters, Clipped Wings, Jungle Gents, Bowery to Bagdad, High Society, Spy Chasers, Jail Busters, Dig That Uranium, Up in Smoke, Second Fiddle to a Steel Guitar, Gentle Giant, The Phynx, Herbie Rides Again, The Manchu Eagle Murder Caper Mystery, Won Ton Ton the Dog Who Saved Hollywood, Valentino, Gas Pump Girls, The Escape Artist, Cyclone, Auntie Lee's Meat Pies.
TELEVISION: Series: The Chicago Teddy Bears. Movie: Escape, The Rating's Game. Guest: Barefoot in the Park, Diff'rent Strokes, Night Heat.

HALL, MONTY; O.C.
Actor. b. Winnipeg, Manitoba, Canada, Aug. 25, 1925. e. U. of Manitoba, B.S. Host of Keep Talking, 1958. Host of Let's Make a Deal, 1964-86. International chmn., Variety Clubs International. Appeared in tv movie The Courage & The Passion, 1978.

HALLSTROM, LASSE
Director. b. Stockholm, Sweden, 1946. m. actress Lena Olin. As teenager made 16mm film which was eventually screened on Swedish TV. Began professional career filming and editing inserts for Swedish tv. Directed program Shall We Dance? for Danish TV, followed by TV prod. on The Love Seeker, dir. of program Shall We Got to My or to Your Place or Each Go Home Alone?.
PICTURES: A Love and His Lass (debut, 1974), ABBA: The Movie, Father-to-Be, The Rooster, Happy We, The Children of Bullerby Village, More About the Children of Bullerby Village, My Life as a Dog (also co-s.p.; Acad. Award noms. for dir. & s.p.), Once Around (U.S. debut, 1991), What's Eating Gilbert Grape (also co-exec. prod.), Lumiere & Company, Something to Talk About, The Golden Hour, The Shipping News.

HALMI, ROBERT SR.
Producer. b. Budapest, Hungary, Jan 22, 1924. Originally writer-photographer under contract to Life Magazine.
PICTURES: Created documentaries for U.N. Features include: Hugo the Hippo, Visit to a Chief's Son, The One and Only, Brady's Escape, Cheetah, Mr. and Mrs. Bridge.
TELEVISION: Bold Journey (dir.-cin.), American Sportsman, The Oriental Sportsman, The Flying Doctor, The Outdoorsman, Julius Boros Series, Rexford, Who Needs Elephants, Calloway's Climb, Oberndorf Revisited, True Position, Wilson's Reward, Nurse, Buckley Sails, A Private Battle, My Old Man, Mr. Griffin and Me, When the Circus Came to Town, Best of Friends, Bush Doctor, Peking Encounter, Svengali, China Rose, Cook and Peary-The Race to the Pole, Terrible Joe Moran, Nairobi Affair, The Night They Saved Christmas, Spies, Lies and Naked Thighs. Exec. prod.: The Prize Pulitzer, Paradise, Bridesmaids, Face to Face, Margaret Bourke-White, The Incident, Josephine Baker Story, The Secret, An American Story, Call of the Wild, Blind Spot, Incident in a Small Town, Spoils of War, The Yearling, A Promise Kept: The Oksana Baiul Story, A Mother's Gift, Scarlett, Reunion, My Brother's Keeper, White Dwarf, Secrets, Bye Bye Birdie, Kidnapped, Gulliver's Travels (Emmy Award, 1996), Captains Courageous, Dead Man's Walk, The Oddysey, In Cold Blood, Mrs. Santa Claus, Forbidden Territory: Stanley's Search for Livingstone, A Christmas Memory, Mary and Tim, Moby Dick, Merlin, The Long Way Home.

HAMADY, RON
Producer. b. Flint, MI, June 16, 1947. e. U. of California, B.A. 1971. Co-founder of The Crystal Jukebox, record prod's., music mgmt. and music pub. co. Prod. 12 hit albums for Decca Records of England and London Records, U.S. Entered m.p. industry in 1975, producing Train Ride to Hollywood for Taylor-Laughlin dist. Co.
PICTURES: Fade to Black, Surf II, And God Created Woman (1987), Out Cold, Don't Tell Her It's Me, Meltdown.

HAMEL, VERONICA
Actress. b. Philadelphia, PA, Nov. 20, 1943. e. Temple U. Moved to NY and began a modelling career with Eileen Ford Agency. Off B'way debut: The Big Knife. Acted in dinner theater prods. Moved to L.A. 1975.
THEATER: B'way: Rumors. Off B'way: The Big Knife, The Ballad of Boris K.
PICTURES: Cannonball, Beyond the Poseidon Adventure, When Time Ran Out, A New Life, Taking Care of Business.
TELEVISION: Movies: The Gathering, Ski Lift to Death, The Gathering II, The Hustler of Muscle Beach, Valley of the Dolls, Sessions, Twist of Fate, She Said No, Stop at Nothing, Deadly Medicine (also co-exec. prod.), Baby Snatcher (also co-exec. prod.), The Disappearance of Nora, The Conviction of Kitty Dodds, Shadow of Obsession, A Child's Cry for Help, Intensive Care, Secrets, Here Come the Munsters, Blink of an Eye, Brother's Keeper. Mini-Series: 79 Park Avenue, Kane & Abel. Series: Hill Street Blues. Guest: Kojak, Rockford Files, Bob Newhart Show, Switch.

HAMILL, MARK
Actor. b. Oakland, CA, Sept. 25, 1951. While studying acting at LA City Col. made prof. debut in episode of The Bill Cosby Show, 1970. Featured in CD-ROM interactive game Wing Commander III.
THEATER: NY: The Elephant Man (B'way debut), Amadeus (also Natl. tour), Harrigan 'n' Hart, Room Service (off-B'way), The Nerd.
PICTURES: Star Wars (debut, 1977), Wizards (voice), Corvette Summer, The Empire Strikes Back, The Big Red One, The Night the Lights Went Out in Georgia, Britannia Hospital, Return of the Jedi, Slipstream, Midnight Ride, Black Magic Woman, Sleepwalkers (cameo), Time Runner, The Guyver, Batman: Mask of the Phantasm (voice), Village of the Damned.
TELEVISION: Series: General Hospital, The Texas Wheelers, Batman (voice). Movies: Sarah T.-Portrait of a Teenage Alcoholic, Eric, Delancey Street: The Crisis Within, Mallory: Circumstantial Evidence, The City, Earth Angel, Body Bags, Hollyrock-a-Bye Baby (voice). Guest: Room 222, The Partridge Family, Headmaster, Medical Center, Owen Marshall, The FBI, Streets of San Francisco, One Day at a Time, Manhunter, Hooperman, Alfred Hitchcock Presents, Amazing Stories, The Flash, seaQuest DSV. Specials: Get High on Yourself, Night of 100 Stars.

HAMILTON, GEORGE
Actor. b. Memphis, TN, Aug. 12, 1939. e. grammar, Hawthorne, CA; military sch., Gulfport, MS, N.Y. Hackley Prep Sch., FL, Palm Beach H.S. Won best actor award in Florida, high sch. contest.
PICTURES: Crime and Punishment USA (debut, 1959), Home From the Hill, All the Fine Young Cannibals, Where the Boys Are, Angel Baby, By Love Possessed, A Thunder of Drums, Light in the Piazza, Two Weeks in Another Town, Act One, The Victors, Looking for Love, Your Cheatin' Heart, Viva Maria, That Man George, Doctor You've Got to Be Kidding!, Jack of Diamonds, A Time for Killing, The Power, Togetherness, Evel Knievel (also co-p), Medusa (also exec. prod.), The Man Who Loved Cat Dancing, Once Is Not Enough, The Happy Hooker Goes to Washington, Love at First Bite (also co-exec. prod.), Sextette, From Hell to Victory, Zorro the Gay Blade (also co-prod.), The Godfather Part III, Doc Hollywood, Once Upon a Crime, Double Dragon, Amore!, Playback, Meet Wally Sparks, 8 Heads in a Duffel Bag.
TELEVISION: Mini-Series: Roots. Movies: Two Fathers' Justice, Monte Carlo, Poker Alice, Caution: Murder Can Be Hazardous to Your Health, The House on Sycamore Street, Two Fathers: Justice for the Innocent, Danielle Steel's Vanished, Rough Riders. Series: The Survivors, Paris 7000, Dynasty, Spies, The Bold & the Beautiful, The George and Alana Show (also prod.), The Guilt, Jenny. Guest: Rin Tin Tin, The Donna Reed Show, Dream On, The John Laroquette Show, The Bonnie Hunt Show, The Naked Truth. Special: The Veil.

HAMILTON, GUY
Director. b. Paris, France, Sept. 24, 1922. Ent. m.p. industry 1939 as apprentice at Victorine Studio, Nice; Royal Navy, 1940-45, in England asst. dir., Fallen Idol, Third Man, Outcast of the Islands, African Queen.
PICTURES: The Ringer, The Intruder, An Inspector Calls, Dragnet (actor only), Colditz Story, Manuela, The Devil's Disciple, A Touch of Larceny, The Best of Enemies, The Party's Over, Man in the Middle, Goldfinger, Funeral in Berlin, Battle of Britain, Diamonds Are Forever, Live and Let Die, The Man with the Golden Gun, Force Ten from Navarone, The Mirror Crack'd, Evil Under the Sun, Remo Williams, Try This One For Size.

HAMILTON, LINDA
Actress. b. Salisbury, MD, Sept. 26, 1956. Appeared on NY stage in Looice and Richard III.
PICTURES: Tag: The Assassination Game, Children of the Corn, The Stone Boy, The Terminator, Black Moon Rising, King Kong Lives!, Mr. Destiny, Terminator 2: Judgment Day, Silent Fall, The Shadow Conspiracy, Dante's Peak.
TELEVISION: Series: Secrets of Midland Heights, King's Crossing, Beauty and the Beast. Movies: Reunion, Rape and Marriage-The Rideout Case, Country Gold, Secrets of a Mother and Daughter, Secret Weapons, Club Med, Go Toward the Light, A Mother's Prayer. Guest: Hill Street Blues, Murder She Wrote.

HAMLIN, HARRY
Actor. b. Pasadena, CA, Oct. 30, 1951. e. U. of California, Yale U., 1974 in theatre, psychology. Awarded IT&T Fulbright Grant, 1977. 1974-1976 with the American Conservatory Theatre, San Francisco, then joined McCarter Theatre, Princeton (Hamlet, Faustus in Hell, Equus). B'way debut Awake and Sing! (1984). Also performed in Henry V, Smoke.
PICTURES: Movie Movie (debut, 1978), King of the Mountain, Clash of the Titans, Making Love, Blue Skies Again Maxie, Ebbtide, Save Me, The Celluloid Closet, Badge of Bertrayal, Allie & Me, Frogs for Snakes.
TELEVISION: Mini-series: Studs Lonigan, Master of the Game, Space, Favorite Son, Night Sins. Movies: Laguna Heat, Deceptions, Deadly Intentions... Again?, Deliver Them From Evil: The Taking of Alta View, Poisoned By Love: The Kern County Murders, In the Best of Families: Marriage Pride & Madness, Tom Clancy's Op Center, Her Deadly Rival. Series: L.A. Law, Ink.

HAMLISCH, MARVIN
Composer. b. New York, NY, June 2, 1944. e. Juilliard. Accompanist and straight man on tour with Groucho Marx 1974-75; debut as concert pianist 1975 with Minn. Orch. Scores of B'way shows: A Chorus Line (Tony Award & Pulitzer Prize); They're Playing Our Song, Smile, The Goodbye Girl. Composer of popular songs: Sunshine Lollipops and Rainbows, Nobody Does It Better. Winner 4 Grammy awards, 3 Oscars, 2 Emmys, 1 Tony, 3 Golden Globe awards. Autobiography, The Way I Was, 1992. Conductor for the Pittsburgh Symphony Orchestra, 1995-; Baltimore Symphony Orchestra, 1996-.
PICTURES: The Swimmer, Take the Money and Run, Bananas, Save the Tiger, Kotch, The Way We Were (2 Acad. Awards for orig. score and title song, 1973), The Sting (Acad. Award for music adapt., 1973), The Spy Who Loved Me, Same Time Next Year, Ice Castles, Chapter Two, Seems Like Old Times, Starting Over, Ordinary People, The Fan, Sophie's Choice, I Ought to Be in Pictures, Romantic Comedy, D.A.R.Y.L., Three Men and a Baby, Little Nikita, The January Man, The Experts, Frankie and Johnny, Open Season, The Mirror Has Two Faces.
TELEVISION: Series: Good Morning America (theme), Brooklyn Bridge. Movies: The Entertainer (also prod.), A Streetcar Named Desire, The Two Mrs. Grenvilles, Women & Men: Stories of Seduction, Switched at Birth, Seasons of the Heart.

HAMMOND, PETER
Actor, Writer, Director. b. London, England,, Nov.15, 1923. e. Harrow Sch. of Art. Stage debut: Landslide, Westminster Theatre. Screen debut: Holiday Camp. Dir./writer, 1959-61, tv plays.
PICTURES: The Huggetts, Helter Skelter, Fools Rush In, The Reluctant Widow, Fly Away Peter, The Adventurers, Operation Disaster, Come Back, Peter, Little Lambs Eat Ivy, Its Never Too Late, The Unknown, Morning Departure, Confession. Dir.: Spring and Port Wine.
TELEVISION: Series: William Tell, Robin Hood, The Buccaneers. Dir.: Avengers, 4 Armchair Theatres, Theatre 625, BBC classic serials Count of Monte Cristo, Three Musketeers, Hereward the Wake, Treasure Island, Lord Raingo, Cold Comfort Farm, The White Rabbit, Out of the Unknown, Holly Foot; Lukes Kingdom, Time to Think, Franklin's Farm, Sea Song, Shades of Greene, Our Mutual Friend, The House that Jack Built, The King of the Castle, The Black Knight, Kilvert's Diary, Turgenev's Liza, Wuthering Heights, Funnyman, Little World of Don Camillo, Rumpole of the Bailey, Bring on the Girls, Hallelujah Mary Plum, Aubrey Beardsley, The Happy Autumn Fields, The Combination, Tales of the Unexpected, The Glory Hole, The Hard Word, Shades of Darkness-The Maze, The Blue Dress.

HAMNER, EARL
Producer, Writer. b. Schuyler, VA, July 10, 1923. e. U. of Richmond 1940-43, Northwestern U.; U of Cincinnati, Coll. Conservatory of Music, B.F.A., 1958. With WLW, Cincinnati, as radio writer-prod.; joined NBC 1949 as writer; (The Georgia Gibbs Show, The Helen O'Connell Show); freelance 1961-71; writer, prod. Lorimar Prods. 1971-86; writer prod. Taft Entertainment 1986-; Pres. Amanda Prods.
PICTURES: Palm Springs Weekend, Spencer's Mountain, The Tamarind Seed, Charlotte's Web (adaptor), Where the Lilies Bloom.
TELEVISION: Exec. prod.: Series: The Waltons (creator, co-prod., narrator), Apple's Way (creator), The Young Pioneers (creator), Joshua's World, Falcon Crest, Boone (also creator), Morning Star/Evening Star (also narrator), Movies: The Homecoming: A Christmas Story (writer only), You Can't Get There From Here (writer only), A Wedding on Walton's Mountain, Mother's Day on Walton's Mountain, A Day of Thanks on Walton's Mountain (also actor), The Gift of Love--A Christmas Story (also writer).

HAMPSHIRE, SUSAN
O.B.E., 1995. Actress. b. London, England,, May 12, 1941.
THEATER: Expresso Bongo, Follow That Girl, Fairy Tales of New York, Ginger Man, Past Imperfect, She Stoops to Conquer, On Approval, The Sleeping Prince, A Doll's House, Taming of the Shrew, Peter Pan, Romeo & Jeanette, As You Like It, Miss Julie, The Circle, Arms and the Man, Man and Superman, Tribades, An Audience Called Edward, The Crucifer of Blood, Night and Day, The Revolt, House Guest, Blithe Spirit, Married Love, A Little Night Music, The King and I, Noel & Gertie, Relative Values, Susanna Andler, Black Chiffon.

PICTURES: The Three Lives of Thomasina, Night Must Fall, Wonderful Life, Paris Au Mois d'Aout, The Fighting Prince of Donegal, The Trygon Factor, Monte Carlo or Bust, Rogan, David Copperfield, A Room in Paris, Living Free, Time for Loving, Malpertius, Baffled, Neither the Sea nor the Sand, Roses and Green Peppers, David the King, Bang.
TELEVISION: Andromeda, The Forsyte Saga, Vanity Fair, Katy, The First Churchills; An Ideal Husband, The Lady Is a Liar, The Improbable Mr. Clayville, Dr. Jekyll and Mr. Hyde (musical), The Pallisers, Barchester Chronicles, Leaving, Leaving II, Going to Pot (I, II, and III), Don't Tell Father, The Grand I & II, Coming Home.

HAMPTON, JAMES
Actor. b. Oklahoma City, OK, July 9, 1936. e. N. Texas St. Univ.
PICTURES: Fade In, Soldier Blue, The Man Who Loved Cat Dancing, The Longest Yard, W.W. & The Dixie Dancekings, Hustle, Hawmps!, The Cat from Outer Space, Mackintosh & T.J., The China Syndrome, Hangar 18, Condorman, Teen Wolf, Teen Wolf Too, Police Academy 5, Pump Up the Volume, The Giant of Thunder Mountain.
TELEVISION: Series: F Troop, The Doris Day Show, Love—American Style, Mary, Maggie. Movies: Attack on Terror: The FBI Versus the Ku Klux Klan, Force Five, The Amazing Howard Hughes, Three on a Date, Thaddeus Rose and Eddie, Stand By Your Man, Through the Magic Pyramid, World War III, The Burning Bed. Mini-Series: Centennial.

HANCOCK, JOHN
Director. b. Kansas City, MO, Feb. 12, 1939. e. Harvard. Was musician and theatre dir. before turning to films. Dir. play A Man's a Man, NY 1962. Artistic dir. San Francisco Actors Workshop 1965-66, Pittsburgh Playhouse 1966-67. Obie for dir. Midsummer Night's Dream, NY 1968. Nominated for AA for short, Sticky My Fingers, Fleet My Feet.
PICTURES: Let's Scare Jessica to Death, Bang the Drum Slowly, Baby Blue Marine, California Dreaming, Weeds (also co-s.p.), Prancer, Steal the Sky.
TELEVISION: The Twilight Zone (1986), Hill Street Blues.

HAND, BETHLYN J.
Executive. b. Alton, IL. e. U. of Texas. Entered motion picture industry in 1966 as administrative assistant to president of Motion Picture Association of America, Inc. In 1975 became associate dir. of advertising administration of MPAA. In 1976 became dir. of advertising administration; in 1979 became; v.p.-west coast activities, board of directors, Los Angeles. S.P.C.A. 1981, appointed by Governor to Calif. Motion Picture Council 1983, elected vice chmn., California Motion Picture Council. 1990, named sr. v.p. MPAA.

HANDEL, LEO A.
Producer, Director. b. Vienna, Austria, Mar. 7, 1924. e. Univ. of Vienna (Ph.D. economics). Dir. audience research, MGM, 1942-51; organized Meteor Prod., 1951; organized Leo A. Handel Prod., for TV films, 1953; author, Hollywood Looks at Its Audience, also TV plays; pres., Handel Film Corp. Exec. prod. & v.p., Four Crown Prods., Inc. Prod.-writer-dir., feature film, The Case of Patty Smith, 1961; book, A Dog Named Duke, 1965.
TELEVISION: prod. TV series including Everyday Adventures, Magic of the Atom. exec. prod., Phantom Planet, Americana Series. Also produced numerous educational specials and videos.

HANKS, TOM
Actor. b. Concord, CA, July 9, 1956. m. actress Rita Wilson. Traveled around Northern CA. with family before settling in Oakland, CA. e. Chabot Jr. Col., California State U. Began career with Great Lakes Shakespeare Festival, Cleveland (3 seasons) and NY's Riverside Theater (Taming of the Shrew).
PICTURES: He Knows You're Alone (debut, 1980), Splash, Bachelor Party, The Man With One Red Shoe, Volunteers, The Money Pit, Nothing in Common, Every Time We Say Goodbye, Dragnet, Big (Acad. Award nom.), Punchline, The 'Burbs, Turner and Hooch, Joe Versus the Volcano, The Bonfire of the Vanities, Radio Flyer (unbilled), A League of Their Own, Sleepless in Seattle, Philadelphia (Academy Award, 1993; Golden Globe Award), Forrest Gump (Academy Award, 1994; Golden Globe Award), Apollo 13, Toy Story (voice), That Thing You Do! (also dir.), You've Got Mail.
TELEVISION: Series: Bosom Buddies. Guest: The Love Boat, Taxi, Happy Days, Family Ties, Saturday Night Live, Tales From the Crypt (None but the Lonely Heart; also dir.), Fallen Angels (I'll Be Waiting; also dir.), The Naked Truth. Movie: Rona Jaffe's Mazes and Monsters. Episode Dir.: A League of Their Own.

HANN-BYRD, ADAM
Actor.
PICTURES: Little Man Tate, Digger, Jumanji, Diabolique, The Ice Storm, Souvenir (voice), Halloween: H20.
TELEVISION: Guest: NYPD Blue.

HANNA, WILLIAM
Executive. b. Melrose, NM, July 14, 1910 e. Compton Coll. Studied engineering and journalism. Joined firm in CA as structural engineer; turned to cartooning with Leon Schlessinger's company in Hollywood. In 1937 hired by MGM as dir. and story man in cartoon dept. There met Joseph R. Barbera and created famous cartoon series Tom & Jerry, continuing to produce it from 1938 to 1957. Left MGM in 1957 to form Hanna-Barbera Productions to make cartoons for TV. Series have included Yogi Bear, Huckleberry Hound, The Flintstones, The Jetsons. Hanna-Barbera became a subsidiary of Taft Broadcasting Co. in 1968 with both men operating studio under long-term agreements with Taft (which became Great American Broadcasting, 1987). Received Governor's Award from Academy of Television Arts & Sciences, 1988.
PICTURES: Hey There It's Yogi Bear, A Man Called Flintstone, Charlotte's Web, C.H.O.M.P.S., Heidi's Song, Once Upon a Forest, The Flintstones (co-exec. prod. of live-action film; also cameo appearance).
TELEVISION: Series: The Huckleberry Hound Show (Emmy Award), Quick Draw McGraw, The Flintstones, The Jetsons, Jonny Quest, Top Cat, Scooby-Doo, Smurfs (2 Emmy Awards). Movies: I Yabba Dabba Do!, Hollyrock-a-Bye Baby.

HANNAH, DARYL
Actress. b. Chicago, IL, 1960. Niece of cinematographer Haskell Wexler. e. UCLA. Studied ballet with Maria Tallchief. Studied acting with Stella Adler.
PICTURES: The Fury (debut, 1978), The Final Terror, Hard Country, Blade Runner, Summer Lovers, Reckless, Splash, The Pope of Greenwich Village, Clan of the Cave Bear, Legal Eagles, Roxanne, Wall Street, High Spirits, Crimes and Misdemeanors, Steel Magnolias, Crazy People, At Play in the Fields of the Lord, Memoirs of an Invisible Man, Grumpy Old Men, The Little Rascals, The Tie That Binds, Two Much, Grumpier Old Men, The Real Blonde.
TELEVISION: Movies: Paper Dolls, Attack of the 50 Ft. Woman (also co-prod.).

HANNAH, JOHN
Actor. b. Kilbride, Scotland, UK, 1962. Was an apprentice electrician before entering mp industry.
PICTURES: Harbour Beat, Four Weddings and a Funeral, Madagascar Skin, The Innocent Sleep, The Final Cut, The James Gang, Sliding Doors, The Mummy.
TELEVISION: Movies: Paul Calf's Video Diary, Pauline Calf's Wedding Video, Truth or Dare, Romance and Rejection, Circles of Deceit: Kalon, The Love Bug. Series: Out of the Blue, McCallum. Guest: Taggart.

HANNEMANN, WALTER A.
Film editor. b. Atlanta, GA, May 2, 1914. e. USC, 1935. Editorial training, RKO 1936-40; edit. supvr., Universal, 1941-42; consultant 1970-75 national educational media. Bd. of govs., TV Academy (2 terms, 1960 & 1970); bd. of govs., AMPAS. 1970-86; board of dir., Motion Picture Film Editors, 1944-48, 1981-88, past v.p., American Cinema Editors.
PICTURES: Interval, The Revengers, Dream of Kings, Guns of the Magnificent Seven, Krakatoa: East of Java, The Bob Mathias Story, Pay or Die, Al Capone, (Amer. Cinema Editor's nom., 1959), Hell's Five Hours, Armoured Command, Only the Valiant, Time of Your Life, Kiss Tomorrow Goodbye, Blood on the Sun, Guest in the House, Texas Masquerade, Cannon for Cardoba, El Condor, Maurie, Lost in the Stars, Big Mo, Two Minute Warning (Acad. Award nom.) Smokey and the Bandit (Acad. Award nom.), The Other Side of the Mountain-Part II, The Visitor, The Villain, The Nude Bomb, Charlie Chan and the Curse of the Dragon Queen.
TELEVISION: Series: Death Valley Days, Reader's Digest, Rosemary Clooney Show, 77 Sunset Strip, June Allison Show, Stagecoach West, The Rifleman, Ben Casey, The New Breed, The Fugitive, Twelve O'Clock High, The Invaders, Storefront Lawyers, Hawaii Five-O, Streets of San Francisco, Cannon, Barnaby Jones, The F.B.I. on T.V., Caribe. Movies: The Abduction of Saine Anne, Intimate Strangers, The Day the Loving Stopped, The Man Who Broke a 1000 Chains, Sooner

HANSON, CURTIS
Director, Writer. b. Los Angeles, CA, Jan. 24, 1945. Editor of Cinema magazine before becoming screenwriter.
PICTURES: Writer: The Silent Partner, White Dog, Never Cry Wolf. Director: The Arousers (Sweet Kill), Little Dragons, The Bedroom Window (also s.p.), Bad Influence, The Hand That Rocks the Cradle, The River Wild, L.A. Confidential (also co-s.p., prod., Acad. Award, Best Adapted Screenplay, Chicago Film Crits. Award, LA Film Crits. Award, NY Film Crits. Award, Best Director, Best Screenplay, 1997), The Goonies (actor only).
TELEVISION: Movie: Killing at Hell's Gate, The Children of Times Square.

HARBACH, WILLIAM O.
Producer. b. Yonkers, NY, Oct. 12, 1919, e. Brown U. Father was lyricist Otto Harbach. Served with U.S. Coast Guard, 1940-45; actor, MGM, 1945-47; broadcast co-ordinator. NBC, 1947-49; stage mgr., 1949-50; dir., MGM, 1950-53
TELEVISION: Producer: Tonight, Steve Allen Show, Bing Crosby shows (also dir.), Milton Berle Special, Hollywood Palace, The Julie Andrews Show (Emmy Award, 1973), Shirley MacLaine's Gypsy in My Soul (Emmy Award, 1976), Bob Hope Specials.

HARBERT, TED
Executive. e. Boston Univ. 1976-77, prod. of new dept. at WHDH radio in Boston. Joined ABC, 1977 as feature film coordinator; 1979, named supervisor, feature film and late-night program planning, then assst. to v.p., program planning & scheduling; 1981, became dir. program planning & scheduling; 1984, promoted to v.p. program planning & scheduling; 1987, named v.p. motion pictures and scheduling, ABC Entertainment; 1988, v.p., prime time, ABC Entertainment; 1989, became exec. v.p., Prime Time, ABC Entertainment; 1993, promoted to pres. of ABC Entertainment.

HARDEN, MARCIA GAY
Actress. b. La Jolla, CA, Aug. 14, 1959.
Father was naval captain. Schooled in Athens, Munich, then returned to states attending Univ. of TX, NYU. Stage work in Washington D.C. in Crimes of the Heart, The Miss Firecracker Contest.
THEATER: Off-B'way: The Man Who Shot Lincoln (debut, 1989), Those the River Keeps, The Skin of Our Teeth, The Years, Simpatico. B'way: Angels in America: Millenium Approaches/ Perestroika (Theatre World Award; Tony nom.)
PICTURES: Miller's Crossing (debut, 1990), Late for Dinner, Used People, Crush, Safe Passage, The Spitfire Grill, The First Wives Club, Spy Hard, Desperate Measures, Absent Minded Professor, Meet Joe Black.
TELEVISION: Mini-Series: Sinatra. Movie: Fever, Path to Paradise.

HARDISON, KADEEM
Actor. b. Brooklyn, NY, July 24, 1966. Studied acting with Earl Hyman and at H.B.Studios.
PICTURES: Beat Street (debut, 1984), Rappin', School Daze, I'm Gonna Git You Sucka, Def by Temptation, White Men Can't Jump, Gunmen, Renaissance Man, Panther, Vampire in Brooklyn.
TELEVISION: Series: A Different World, Between Brothers. Specials: The Color of Friendship, Amazing Grace, Don't Touch, Go Tell It on the Mountain. Movie: Dream Date. Guest: The Cosby Show, Spenser for Hire.

HARE, DAVID
Writer, Director. b. St. Leonards, Sussex, England, June 5, 1947. e. Lancing Coll., Jesus Coll., Cambridge. After leaving univ. in 1968 formed Portable Theatre Company, experimental touring group. Hired by Royal Court Theater as literary manager, 1969. 1970, first full-length play, Slag, prod. at Hampstead Theatre Club. Resident dramatist, Royal Court (1970-71), and Nottingham Playhouse (1973). Assoc. dir., National Theatre. West End debut, Knuckle.
THEATER: Slag, The Great Exhibition, Brassneck, Knuckle, Fanshen, Teeth 'n' Smiles, Plenty, A Map of the World, Pravda, The Bay at Nice, Secret Rapture, Racing Demon, Murmuring Judges, Rules of the Game (new version of Pirandello Play), Brecht's The Absence of War, Skylight, Galileo, Mother Courage.
PICTURES: Writer: Plenty, Wetherby (also dir.), Paris by Night (also dir.), Strapless (also dir.), Damage.
TELEVISION: Writer: Licking Hitler (also dir.), Dreams of Leaving (also dir.), Saigon: Year of the Cat, Knuckle, Heading Home (also dir.).

HAREWOOD, DORIAN
Actor. b. Dayton, OH, Aug. 6, 1950. m. actress Ann McCurry. e. U. of Cincinnati.
THEATER: Jesus Christ Superstar (road co.), Two Gentlemen of Verona, Miss Moffat, Streamers, Over Here, Don't Call Back (Theatre World Award), The Mighty Gents, Kiss of the Spider Woman.
PICTURES: Sparkle (debut, 1976), Gray Lady Down, Looker, Tank, Against All Odds, The Falcon and the Snowman, Full Metal Jacket, Pacific Heights, Solar Crisis, The Pagemaster (voice), Sudden Death.
TELEVISION: Series: Strike Force, Trauma Center, Glitter, The Trials of Rosie O'Neill, Viper. Mini-Series: Roots: The Next Generations, Amerika. Movies: Foster and Laurie, Panic in Echo Park, Siege, An American Christmas Carol, High Ice, Beulah Land, The Ambush Murders, I Desire, The Jesse Owens Story, Guilty of Innocence, God Bless the Child, Kiss Shot, Polly, Polly-Comin' Home!, Getting Up and Going Home, Bermuda Grace, Shattered Image. Pilot: Half 'n' Half.

HARGREAVES, JOHN
Executive. b. Freckleton, Lancashire, England,, July 1921. Joined Gainsborough Pictures 1945. Transferred to Denham Studios 1946 and later Pinewood Studios. Joined Allied Film Makers 1960, then Salamander Film Productions as Bryan Forbes' financial controller and asst. prod. 1965. Joined EMI Film Prods. Ltd. as asst. man. dir. and prod. controller 1969-72. 1983-, U.K. dir. and production executive for Completion Bond Company, Inc. Cal. USA.
PICTURES: Don Quixote (prod.), The Slipper and the Rose (prod. asst.), International Velvet (assoc. prod.), The Awakening (prod. rep.), The Fiendish Plot of Dr. Fu Manchu (post-prod. exec.), Excalibur (prod. rep.), The Year of Living Dangerously, Carrington (financial consultant).

HARK, TSUI
Director, Producer. b. Vietnam, Jan. 2, 1951. e. University of Texas. Started filming 8mm movies at 13. Moved to Hong Kong in 1966, then in 1975 relocated to NY where he became editor for a local Chinese newspaper. Returned to Hong Kong in 1977 and made his directorial debut with The Butterfly Murders. In the 1990's played a major part in reviving "swordsfighting" and "kung-fu" movies.
PICTURES: Director: Dangerous Encounter, Hell Has No Door, All the Wrong Clues, Zu: Warriors From the Magic Mountain, Aces go Places III, Shanghai Blues, Working Class, Peking Opera Blues, A Better Tomorrow III, Once Upon A Time in China (also II, III, V), The Master, Green Snake, The Lovers, A Chinese Feast, Love In a Time of Twilight, Tri-Star, The Blade, Double Team. Co-director: Swordsman, The Banquet, Chess King, Twin Dragons. Producer: A Chinese Ghost Story (also II, III) A Better Tomorrow, I Love Maria, Deception, Gunmen, Diary of a Big Man, The Big Heat, The Killer, Spy Games, The Raid, The Wicked City, Swordsman II, Dragon Inn, The East is Red, Once Upon a Time in China (also IV), The Magic Crane, Burning Paradise, Shanghai Grand, Black Mask, Once Upon a Time in China & America, Chinese Ghost Story: The Tsui Hark Animation.

HARKINS, DANIEL E.
Executive, Exhibitor. b. Mesa, AZ, Feb. 6, 1953. e. Arizona State U. Joined Harkins Theatres in 1968. Acquired company in 1975. President and CEO Harkins Amusement Enterprises, Inc. National NATO bd. member. Pres., Arizona Theatre Assoc. V.P., Governor's Film Commission. Recipient of United Motion Picture Assoc. National Showman of the Year award 1976, 1980, 1981. Hollywood Reported Marketing Concept award, 1983. Box Office Showmandizer award, 1976, 1978. Phoenix Artistic Achievement award, 1989. American Institute of Architects award. 1996. Arizona Best awards, 1991-1995.

HARLIN, RENNY
Director. b. Helsinki, Finland, 1958. e. Univ. of Helsinki film school. Formed prod. co. The Forge with now ex-wife, actress Geena Davis.
PICTURES: Born American (debut, 1986), Arctic Heat (also s.p.), Prison, A Nightmare on Elm Street IV: The Dream Master, Die Hard 2, The Adventures of Ford Fairlane, Rambling Rose (prod. only), Cliffhanger, Speechless (co-prod. only), Cutthroat Island (also prod.), Exit Zero, The Long Kiss Goodnight (also prod.), Blast From the Past (prod. only).
TELEVISION: Movie: Mistrial.

HARMON, MARK
Actor. b. Burbank, CA, Sept. 2, 1951. Son of actress Elyse Knox and football star Tom Harmon. m. actress Pam Dawber. Brother of actresses Kelly and Kristin Harmon. On stage in Wrestlers, The Wager (both L.A.), Key Exchange (Toronto).
PICTURES: Comes a Horseman, Beyond the Poseidon Adventure, Let's Get Harry, Summer School, The Presidio, Stealing Home, Worth Winning, Till There Was You, Cold Heaven, Wyatt Earp, Magic in the Water, The Last Supper.
TELEVISION: Series: Sam, 240-Robert, Flamingo Road, St. Elsewhere, Reasonable Doubts, Charlie Grace. Movies: Eleanor and Franklin: The White House Years, Getting Married, Little Mo, Flamingo Road (pilot), The Dream Merchants, Goliath Awaits, Intimate Agony, The Deliberate Stranger, Prince of Bel Air, Sweet Bird of Youth, Dillinger, Fourth Story, Long Road Home, Shadow of a Doubt. Guest: Adam-12, Laverne & Shirley, Nancy Drew, Police Story, Moonlighting. Mini-Series: Centennial.

HARNELL, STEWART D.
Executive. b. New York, NY, Aug. 18, 1938. e. U. of Miami, UCLA, New School for Social Research. Entertainer with Youth Parade in Coral Gables, FL, 1948-55, performing for handicapped children, Variety Club, etc. as singer, dancer, musician. Had own bands, Teen Aces & Rhythm Rascals, 1950-56; performed on Cactus Jim TV show and Wood & Ivory, 1953-54, WTVJ, Miami. Catskills, Sand Lake, NY, 1954-55. Joined National Screen Service as exec. trainee in 1960 in Chicago; worked as booker & salesman. Transferred to NY home office, 1963; worked in special trailer production. Promoted to asst. gen. sls. mgr., 1964-66; New Orleans branch mgr., 1966-67; Atlanta division mgr., 1967-70. Formed own distribution co., 1970-77 Harnell Independent Productions. Resumed post as gen. sls. mgr. of NSS, New York, 1977-78; In 1986, founded Cinema Concepts. In 1995, founded Silver Screen Signs & Display, Inc. Chief barker of Variety Club of Atlanta, Tent 21, 1972, 1976, 1979, 1988, 1989, 1993, 1994. In 1986 formed Cinema Concepts Communications, film-video animation studio in Atlanta. Motion Picture Pioneers Bd. of Directors (1990-97).

HARPER, JESSICA
Actress. b. Chicago, IL, Oct. 10, 1949. m. prod. exec. Thomas E. Rothman. e. Sarah Lawrence Coll. Understudied on Broadway for Hair for one year. Appeared in summer stock and off-B'way shows (Richard Farina: Long Time Coming Longtime Gone, Doctor Selavy's Magic Theatre.)
PICTURES: Taking Off, Phantom of the Paradise, Love and Death, Inserts, Suspiria, The Evictors, Stardust Memories, Shock Treatment, Pennies from Heaven, My Favorite Year, The Imagemaker, Once Again, The Blue Iguana, Big Man on Campus, Mr. Wonderful, Safe.

TELEVISION: *Series*: Little Women, It's Garry Shandling's Show. *Mini-Series*: Studs Lonigan, Aspen (The Innocent and the Damned), When Dreams Come True. *Special*: The Garden Party. *Guest*: Tales From the Darkside, The Equalizer, Trying Times (Bedtime Story), Wiseguy, Chicago Hope.

HARPER, TESS
Actress. b. Mammoth Springs, AR, 1952. e. Southwest Missouri State Coll., Springfield. Worked in Houston, then Dallas in children's theater, dinner theater, and commercials.
PICTURES: Tender Mercies (debut, 1983), Amityville 3-D, Silkwood, Flashpoint, Crimes of the Heart (Acad. Award nom.), Ishtar, Far North, Her Alibi, Criminal Law, Daddy's Dyin'... Who's Got the Will?, My Heroes Have Always Been Cowboys, The Man in the Moon, My New Gun, Dirty Laundry.
TELEVISION: *Mini-Series*: Chiefs, Celebrity. *Movies*: Kentucky Woman, Starflight: The Plane That Couldn't Land, A Summer to Remember, Promises to Keep, Little Girl Lost, Unconquered, In the Line of Duty: Siege at Marion, Willing to Kill: The Texas Cheerleader Story, Death in Small Doses.

HARPER, VALERIE
Actress. b. Suffern, NY. Aug. 22, 1940. e. Hunter Coll, New Sch. for Social Research. Started as dancer in stage shows at Radio City Music Hall. First professional acting in summer stock in Conn.; actress with Second City Chicago 1964-69; Appeared on B'way. in Lil' Abner, Take Me Along, Wildcat, Subways Are for Sleeping, Something Different, Story Theatre, Metamorphosis. Won 3 Emmys for best performance in supporting role in comedy for portrayal of Rhoda on The Mary Tyler Moore Show and 1 for best leading actress on Rhoda. Off B'way, Death Defying Acts (1995-96).
PICTURES: Rock Rock Rock, Lil Abner, Freebie and the Bean, Chapter Two, The Last Married Couple in America, Blame It on Rio.
TELEVISION: *Series*: The Mary Tyler Show, Rhoda, Valerie, City, The Office, Mary & Rhoda. *Movies*: Thursday's Game, Night Terror, Fun and Games, The Shadow Box, The Day the Loving Stopped, Farrell for the People (pilot), Don't Go to Sleep, An Invasion of Privacy, Execution, Strange Voices, Drop Out Mother, The People Across the Lake, Stolen: One Husband, A Friend To Die For, The Great Mom Swap.

HARRINGTON, CURTIS
Director, Writer. b. Los Angeles, CA, Sept. 17, 1928. e. U. of Southern California, B.A. Exec. asst. to Jerry Wald, 1955-61 Associate prod. at 20th Cent. Fox.
PICTURES: Assoc. Prod.: Mardi Gras (also story), Hound Dog Man, Return to Peyton Place, The Stripper. Director: Night Tide (also s.p.), Queen of Blood (Planet of Blood; also s.p.), Games (also co-story), What's the Matter with Helen?, Who Slew Auntie Roo?, The Killing Kind, Ruby, Mata Hari.
TELEVISION: *Series episodes*: Hotel, Dynasty, The Colby's, Tales of the Unexpected, Twilight Zone, Baretta, Vega$, Glitter, Logan's Run. *Movies*: How Awful About Allan, The Cat Creature, Killer Bees, The Dead Don't Die, Devil Dog: The Hound of Hell.

HARRINGTON, PAT
Actor. b. New York, NY, Aug. 13, 1929. e. Fordham U. Served USAF as 1st Lt., 1952-54. Time salesman for NBC, 1954-58.
PICTURES: The Wheeler Dealers, Move Over Darling, Easy Come Easy Go, The President's Analyst, 2000 Years Later, The Candidate.
TELEVISION: *Series*: The Steve Allen Show, The Danny Thomas Show, The Jack Paar Show, Stump the Stars (host), Mr. Deeds Goes to Town, One Day at a Time (Emmy Award, 1984).

HARRIS, BARBARA
Actress. b. Evanston, IL, July 25, 1935. r.n. Sandra Markowitz. e. Wright Junior Coll., Chicago; Goodman Sch. of the Theatre; U. of Chicago. Joined acting troup, The Compass. Founding member, Second City Players, 1960. Came to NY where first role was in Oh Dad Poor Dad Mama's Hung You in the Closet and I'm Feeling So Sad (Theatre World Award), repeating role in film version.
THEATER: Mother Courage and Her Children, Dynamite Tonight, On a Clear Day You Can See Forever, The Apple Tree (Tony Award, 1967), Mahogany.
PICTURES: A Thousand Clowns (debut, 1965), Oh Dad Poor Dad Mama's Hung You in the Closet and I'm Feeling So Sad, Plaza Suite, Who Is Harry Kellerman and Why Is He Saying Those Terrible Things About Me? (Acad. Award nom.), The War Between Men and Women, The Manchu Eagle Murder Caper Mystery, Mixed Company, Nashville, Family Plot, Freaky Friday, Movie Movie, The North Avenue Irregulars, The Seduction of Joe Tynan, Second Hand Hearts, Peggy Sue Got Married, Nice Girls Don't Explode, Dirty Rotten Scoundrels.
TELEVISION: *Guest*: Alfred Hitchcock Presents, Naked City, The Defenders.

HARRIS, BURTT
Producer, Actor. Began career as actor; later worked with Elia Kazan as prod. asst. and asst. dir. on America America, Splendor in the Grass, and The Arrangement. Worked as second unit dir. and asst. dir. on many films as well as prod. and actor.
PICTURES: *Exec. prod./line prod./assoc. prod.*: The Wiz, Just Tell Me What You Want, Cruising, Prince of the City, The Verdict (also actor), Deathtrap, Garbo Talks, D.A.R.Y.L. (co-prod., actor), The Glass Menagerie, See No Evil Hear No Evil, Q & A (also actor), A Stranger Among Us (also actor), Drunks (also actor), The Last Good Time. *Assoc. prod.*: Little Murders, Gilda Live, Family Business. *Actor*: Splendor in the Grass, Fail Safe, The Taking of Pelham 1-2-3, The Wanderers, Undertow, Hudson Hawk, The Last Good Time. *Asst. dir.*: Illtown, Grace of My Heart, Affliction, The Devil's Advocate.
TELEVISION: *Movies*: Zoya.

HARRIS, ED
Actor. b. Tenafly, NJ, Nov. 28, 1950. m. actress Amy Madigan. Played football 2 years at Columbia U. prior to enrolling in acting classes at OK State U. Summer stock. Grad. CA Institute of the Arts, B.F.A, 1975. Worked in West Coast Theater.
THEATER: *NY*: Fool For Love (Off-B'way debut; Obie Award), Precious Sons (B'way debut; Theatre World Award), Simpatico, Taking Sides. *LA*: Scar.
PICTURES: Coma (debut, 1978), Borderline, Knightriders, Dream On, Creepshow, The Right Stuff, Under Fire, Swing Shift, Places in the Heart, Alamo Bay, A Flash of Green, Sweet Dreams, Code Name: Emerald, Walker, To Kill a Priest, Jacknife, The Abyss, State of Grace, Glengarry Glen Ross, The Firm, Needful Things, China Moon, Milk Money, Just Cause, Apollo 13, Eye for an Eye, Nixon, The Rock, Absolute Power.
TELEVISION: *Movies*: The Amazing Howard Hughes, The Seekers, The Aliens Are Coming (Alien Force), The Last Innocent Man, Paris Trout, Running Mates, Riders of the Purple Sage. *Mini-Series*: The Stand.

HARRIS, JAMES B.
Producer, Director, Writer. b. New York, NY, Aug. 3, 1928. e. Juilliard Sch. U.S. film export, 1947; Realart Pictures, 1948; formed Flamingo Films, 1949; formed Harris-Kubrick Productions, 1954. formed James B. Harris Prods., Inc., 1963.
PICTURES: *Producer*: The Killing, Paths of Glory, Lolita, The Bedford Incident (also dir.), Some Call It Loving (also dir., s.p.), Telefon, Fast-Walking (also dir., s.p.), Cop (also dir., s.p.), Boiling Point (dir., s.p.).

HARRIS, JULIE
Designer. b. London, England. e. Chelsea Arts Sch. Entered industry in 1945 designing for Gainsborough Studios. First film, Holiday Camp.
PICTURES: Greengage Summer, Naked Edge, The War Lover, Fast Lady, Chalk Garden, Psyche 59, A Hard Day's Night, Darling, Help!, The Wrong Box, Casino Royale, Deadfall, Prudence and the Pill, Decline and Fall, Goodbye Mr. Chips, Sherlock Holmes, Follow Me!, Live and Let Die, Rollerball, Slipper and The Rose, Dracula.
TELEVISION: Laura (with Lee Radziwill), Candleshoe, The Sailor's Return, Lost and Found, The Kingfisher, Arch of Triumph, Sign of Four, Hound of the Baskervilles, A Hazard of Hearts, A Perfect Hero.

HARRIS, JULIE
Actress. b. Grosse Pointe, MI, Dec. 2, 1925. e. Yale Drama Sch.
THEATER: Sundown Beach, Playboy of the Western World, Macbeth, Young and the Fair, Magnolia Alley, Monserrat, Member of the Wedding, I Am a Camera (Tony Award, 1952), Colombe, The Lark (Tony Award, 1956), A Shot in the Dark, Marathon 33, Ready When You Are, C.B., Break a Leg, Skyscraper, Voices, And Miss Reardon Drinks a Little, 40 Carats (Tony Award, 1969), The Last of Mrs. Lincoln (Tony Award, 1973), In Praise of Love, The Belle of Amherst (Tony Award, 1973), Driving Miss Daisy (Natl. co.), Lucifer's Child, Lettice & Lovage (tour), The Fiery Furnace (Off-B'way debut, 1993), The Glass Menagerie.
PICTURES: The Member of the Wedding (debut, 1952; Acad. Award nom.), East of Eden, I Am a Camera, The Truth About Women, The Poacher's Daughter, Requiem for a Heavyweight, The Haunting, Harper, You're a Big Boy Now, Reflections in a Golden Eye, The Split, The People Next Door, The Hiding Place, Voyage of the Damned, The Bell Jar, Nutcracker: The Motion Picture (voice), Gorillas in the Mist, Housesitter, The Dark Half, Carried Away.
TELEVISION: *Specials*: Little Moon of Alban (Emmy Award, 1959), Johnny Belinda, A Doll's House, Ethan Frome, The Good Fairy, The Lark, He Who Gets Slapped, The Heiress, Victoria Regina (Emmy Award, 1962), Pygmalion, Anastasia, The Holy Terror, The Power and The Glory, The Woman He Loved. *Movies*: The House on Greenapple Road, How Awful About Alan, Home for the Holidays, The Greatest Gift, The Gift, Too Good To Be True, The Christmas Wife, They've Taken Our Children: The Chowchilla Kidnapping, When Love Kills: The Seduction of John Hearn, One Christmas. *Series*: Thicker Than Water, The Family Holvak, Knots Landing. *Mini-Series*: Backstairs at the White House, Scarlett.

HARRIS, MEL

Actress. b. Bethlehem, PA, July 12, 1957. r.n. Mary Ellen Harris. e. Columbia. Career as successful model before turning to acting in 1984. NY theatre debut in Empty Hearts, 1992 (Theatre World Award).
PICTURES: Wanted: Dead or Alive, Cameron's Closet, K-9, Raising Cain, Desperate Motive (Distant Cousins), Suture, The Pagemaster.
TELEVISION: Series: thirtysomething, Something So Right. Guest: M*A*S*H, Alfred Hitchcock Presents, Rags to Riches, Heart of the City, The Wizard. Movies: Seduced, Harry's Hong Kong, Cross of Fire, My Brother's Wife, The Burden of Proof, Grass Roots, Child of Rage, With Hostile Intent, Desperate Journey: The Allison Wilcox Story, Ultimate Betrayal, The Spider and the Fly, The Women of Spring Break, Sharon's Secret.

HARRIS, NEIL PATRICK

Actor. b. Albuquerque, NM, June 15, 1973. While attending week-long theatre camp at New Mexico St. Univ. met writer Mark Medoff who suggested him for co-starring role in Clara's Heart.
THEATER: Luck Pluck and Virtue (Off-B'way debut, 1995).
PICTURES: Clara's Heart (debut, 1988), Purple People Eater, Hairspray.
TELEVISION: Series: Doogie Howser M.D., Capitol Critters (voice). Movies: Too Good to Be True, Home Fires Burning, Cold Sassy Tree, Stranger in the Family, A Family Torn Apart, Snowbound: The Jim and Jennifer Stolpa Story, Not Our Son, My Antonia, The Man in the Attic, Legacy of Sin: The William Coit Story. Guest: B. J. Stryker, Carol & Company, Roseanne, Quantum Leap, Murder She Wrote.

HARRIS, RICHARD

Actor. b. Limerick, Ireland, Oct. 1, 1930. Attended London Acad. of Music and Dramatic Arts. Prod.-dir. Winter Journey 1956. Prof. acting debut in Joan Littlewood's prod. of The Quare Fellow, Royal Stratford, 1956. Recorded hit song MacArthur's Park, 1968. Author of novel Honor Bound (1982) and poetry compilation: I in the Membership of My Days (1973).
THEATER: London: A View from the Bridge, Man Beast and Virtue, The Ginger Man. B'way: Camelot.
PICTURES: Alive and Kicking (debut, 1958), Shake Hands With the Devil, The Wreck of the Mary Deare, A Terrible Beauty (Night Fighters), The Long The Short and The Tall (Jungle Fighters), The Guns of Navarone, Mutiny on the Bounty, This Sporting Life (Acad. Award nom.), Red Desert, Major Dundee, The Heroes of Telemark, The Bible, Hawaii, Caprice, Camelot, The Molly Maguires, A Man Called Horse, Cromwell, The Hero (Bloomfield; also dir., s.p.), Man in the Wilderness, The Deadly Trackers, 99 and 44/100% Dead, Juggernaut, Echoes of a Summer (also co-exec. prod.), Robin and Marian, Return of a Man Called Horse (also co-exec. prod.), The Cassandra Crossing, Gulliver's Travels, Orca, Golden Rendezvous, The Wild Geese, Ravagers, The Last Word, Game for Vultures, Your Ticket Is No Longer Valid, Highpoint, Tarzan the Ape Man, Martin's Day, Triumphs of a Man Called Horse, Mack the Knife, The Field (Acad. Award nom.), Patriot Games, Unforgiven, Wrestling Ernest Hemingway, Silent Tongue, Savage Hearts, Cry the Beloved Country.
TELEVISION: Specials: Ricardo, The Iron Harp, The Snow Goose, Camelot. Movies: Maigret, The Return.

HARRIS, RICHARD A.

Editor.
PICTURES: The Bamboo Saucer, Downhill Racer, The Christian Licorice Store, Chandler, The Candidate, Catch My Soul, Smile, The Bad News Bears, Semi-Tough, The Bad News Bears Go to Japan, An Almost Perfect Affair, The Island, The Toy, The Survivors, Fletch, The Golden Child, Wildcats, The Couch Trip, Fletch Lives, L.A. Story, Terminator 2: Judgment Day, The Bodyguard, Last Action Hero, True Lies, Titanic (Acad. Award, 1997).
TELEVISION: Movies: Dracula, The Kansas City Massacre, Murder at the World Series, The Executioner's Song, Tiger Town, 14 Going on 30, My Boyfriend's Back, A Mother's Courage: The Mary Thomas Story, Indictment: The McMartin Trial.

HARRIS, ROBERT A.

Archivist, Producer. b. New York, NY, Dec. 27, 1945. e. NYU, Sch. of Commerce and Sch. of Arts, 1968. Worked as exec. trainee with 7 Arts assoc., NY while in school, 1960-68; worked in corp. communications, Pepsico, 1970-71; formed Center for Instructional Resources, SUNY Purchase, 1971-73; organized Images Film Archive, dist. of classic theatrical and non theat. films, 1974; pres., Images Video and Film Archive, 1985; formed Davnor Prods., pres., 1986; formed The Film Preserve, Ltd. pres. 1989-. 1975-80: restored Abel Gance films Beethoven, J'Accuse, Lucretia Borgia; 1974-79: worked with Kevin Brownlow to complete restoration of Abel Gance's Napoleon. Partnered with Francis Coppola/Zoetrope Studios to present Napoleon at Radio City Music Hall, 1981 and worldwide tour; 1986-89: reconstruction and restoration of David Lean's Lawrence of Arabia for Columbia Pictures, released 1989; The Grifters (prod.); restoration and reconstruction of Stanley Kubrick's Spartacus for Univ. Pictures, 1991; restoration of George Cukor's My Fair Lady for CBS Video, 1994, restoration in SuperVistaVision 70 of Alfred Hitchcock's Vertigo, 1996.

HARRIS, ROSEMARY

Actress. b. Ashby, Suffolk, Sept. 19, 1930. e. India and England. Early career, nursing; studied Royal Acad. of Dramatic Art, 1951-52.
THEATER: Climate of Eden (NY debut 1952), Seven Year Itch, Confidential Clerk (Paris Festival), and with Bristol Old Vic in The Crucible, Much Ado About Nothing, Merchant of Venice. With Old Vic, 1955-56; U.S. tour, 1956-57; U.S. stage, 1958-63. Chichester Festivals 1962 and 63; Nat'l Theatre 1963-64; You Can't Take It With You, 1965; The Lion in Winter (Tony Award, 1966), 1967, APA Repertory Co., Heartbreak House, The Royal Family, The New York Idea (Obie Award), Pack of Lies, Hay Fever, Lost in Yonkers, An Inspector Calls, A Delicate Balance.
PICTURES: Beau Brummell, The Shiralee, A Flea in Her Ear, The Boys from Brazil, The Ploughman's Lunch, Heartbreak House, Crossing Delancey, The Delinquents, The Bridge, Tom and Viv (Acad. Award nom.), Looking for Richard, Hamlet, World of Moses.
TELEVISION: Series: The Chisholms. Specials: Cradle of Willow (debut, 1951), Othello, The Prince and the Pauper, Twelfth Night, Wuthering Heights, Blithe Spirit, Profiles in Courage, To the Lighthouse, Strange Interlude, Tales From the Hollywood Hills: The Old Reliable, Notorious Woman (Emmy Award, 1976), Holocaust (Golden Globe Award), The Chisholms, The Camomile Lawn. Movie: The Little Riders.

HARRIS, TIMOTHY

Writer, Producer. b. Los Angeles, CA, July 21, 1946. e. Charterhouse, 1963-65; Peterhouse Coll., Cambridge, 1966-69, M.A. Honors Degree, Eng. lit. Author of novels, Knonski/McSmash, Kyd For Hire, Goodnight and Goodbye; author of novelizations, Steelyard Blues, Hit, Heatwave, American Gigolo.
PICTURES: Co-writer with Herschel Weingrod: Cheaper to Keep Her, Trading Places (BAFTA nom., orig. s.p.); NAACP Image Awards, best m.p. 1983), Brewster's Millions, My Stepmother is an Alien, Paint It Black, Twins (People's Choice Award, best comedy, 1988), Kindergarten Cop, Pure Luck. Co-Prod.: Falling Down, Space Jam (s.p. only).
TELEVISION: Street of Dreams (based on his novel Goodnight and Goodbye; also exec. prod.).

HARRISON, GEORGE

Singer, Composer, Producer. b. Liverpool, England, Feb. 25, 1943. Former member, The Beatles. Winner of 2 Grammys on own in addition to Beatles' group awards. Founder of Handmade Films.
PICTURES: Performer: A Hard Day's Night (debut, 1964), What's Happening! The Beatles in the U.S.A., The Beatles at Shea Stadium, Help!, The Magical Mystery Tour (also prod., dir., composer), Yellow Submarine (cameo), Let It Be, The Concert for Bangladesh (also prod.), The Compleat Beatles, Ready Steady Go—Volume 1, Ready Steady Go—Volume 2, Rolling Stone: The First 20 Years, It Was 20 Years Ago Today, Imagine: John Lennon. Exec. Prod.: Little Malcolm. Exec. Prod. (for Handmade Films): Life of Brian (also cameo), Time Bandits, Monty Python Live at the Hollywood Bowl, The Missionary, Privates on Parade, Scrubbers, Bullshot, A Private Function, Water (also cameo), Mona Lisa, Shanghai Surprise (also songs, cameo), Withnail and I, Five Corners, Bellman and True, The Lonely Passion of Judith Hearne, Track 29, How to Get Ahead in Advertising, Powwow Highway, Checking Out, Cold Dog Soup, Nuns on the Run, The Raggedy Rawney, Everest (composer only).
TELEVISION: All You Need Is Cash. Mini-series: The Beatles Anthology. Guest: Morecambe & Wise, Rutland Weekend Television, The Simpsons.

HARRISON, GREGORY

Actor, Producer, Director. b. Avalon, Catalina Island, CA, May 31, 1950. Started acting in school plays; then joined Army (1969-71). Studied at Estelle Harman Actors Workshop; later with Lee Strasberg and Stella Adler. Formed Catalina Productions with Franklin Levy, 1981.
THEATER: Child's Play, Carnal Knowledge, Picnic, The Hasty Heart, Love Letters, Festival, Billy Budd, The Subject Was Roses, The Promise, The Music Man, Paper Moon—The Musical.
PICTURES: Jim: the World's Greatest (debut, 1976), Fraternity Row, Razorback, North Shore (also 2nd unit dir.), Voice of a Stranger (also 2nd unit dir.), Cadillac Girls, It's My Party, Hard Evidence, Air Bud 2: Golden Retriever.
TELEVISION: Series: Logan's Run, Trapper John M.D. (also dir. 6 episodes), Falcon Crest, The Family Man, True Detectives, New York News. Guest: M*A*S*H, Barnaby Jones, Sisters. Movies (actor): The Gathering, Enola Gay, Trilogy in Terror, The Best Place To Be, The Women's Room, For Ladies Only (also co-prod.), The Fighter, Seduced (also exec. prod.), Oceans of Fire, Spot Marks the X (exec. prod. only), Hot Paint, Red River, Dangerous Pursuit, Angel of Death, Bare Essentials, Breaking the Silence, Duplicates, Split Images, Caught in the Act, The Tower (exec. prod. only), A Family Torn Apart, Lies of the Heart: The Story of Laurie Kellogg, Robin Cook's Mortal Fear, A Christmas Romance, A Dangerous Affair, When Secrets Kill. Mini-series: Centennial, Fresno, 500 Nations (narrator), Nothing Lasts Forever. Movies (exec. prod. only): Thursday's Child, Legs, Samson & Delilah.

HARROLD, KATHRYN
Actress. b. Tazewell, VA, Aug. 2, 1950. e. Mills Coll. Studied acting at Neighborhood Playhouse in N.Y., also with Uta Hagen. Appeared in Off-Off-B'way. plays for year; then joined experimental theatre group, Section Ten, touring East, performing and teaching at Connecticut Coll. and NYU. Cast in TV daytime serial, The Doctors.
PICTURES: Nightwing (debut, 1979), The Hunter, Modern Romance, The Pursuit of D.B. Cooper, Yes Gorgio, The Sender, Heartbreakers, Into the Night, Raw Deal, Someone to Love, The Companion.
TELEVISION: Movies: Son-Rise: A Miracle of Love, Vampire, The Women's Room, Bogie, An Uncommon Love, Women in White, Man Against the Mob, Dead Solid Perfect, Capital News, Rainbow Drive, Deadly Desire, The Companion, Rockford Files: The Crime & Punishment, Outrage. Series: The Doctors (1976-78), MacGruder and Loud, Bronx Zoo, I'll Fly Away, The Larry Sanders Show, Chicago Hope

HARRYHAUSEN, RAY
Special Effects Expert, Producer, Writer. b. Los Angeles, CA, June 29, 1920. e. Los Angeles City Coll. While at coll. made 16mm animated film, Evolution, which got him job as model animator for George Pal's Puppetoons in early '40s. Served in U.S. Signal Corps; then made series of filmed fairy tales with animated puppets for schools and churches. In 1946 worked on Mighty Joe Young as ass't. to Willis O'Brien. Designed and created special visual effects for The Beast from 20,000 Fathoms; then began evolving own model animation system called Dynarama. In 1952 joined forces with prod. Charles H. Schneer, using new process for first time in It Came from Beneath the Sea. Subsequently made many films with Schneer in Dynamation. Received Gordon E. Sawyer Award for Acad. of Motion Picture Arts & Sciences, 1992. Appeared in films Spies Like Us, Beverly Hills Cop III.
PICTURES: Mighty Joe Young, The Beast from 20000 Fathoms, It Came From Beneath the Sea, Earth Vs. the Flying Saucers, Animal World, Twenty Million Miles to Earth, 7th Voyage of Sinbad, The Three Worlds of Gulliver, Mysterious Island, Jason and the Argonauts, First Men in the Moon, One Million Years B.C., The Valley of Gwangi, The Golden Voyage of Sinbad, Sinbad and the Eye of the Tiger (also co-prod.), Clash of the Titans (also co. prod.).

HART, GARRETT S.
Executive. e. Univ. of MA, Amherst; Queens Col/CUNY. 1979, joined Paramount as mngr. then v.p. of research; 1982, became dir. of comedy develp. Served as sr. v.p., research for Lorimar-Telepictures Corp. before joining Universal 1987; 1990, became sr. v.p., current programs. 1993, named pres. of the network tv division of the Paramount Television Group.

HARTLEY, HAL
Director, Writer. b. Long Island, NY, 1959. e. SUNY/Purchase (film). Following graduation made 3 short movies: Kid, The Cartographer's Girlfriend, Dogs. For PBS made the shorts Theory of Achievement, Ambition, Surviving Desire; also NYC 3/94, Opera No. 1. Music videos: The Only Living Boy in New York (Everything But the Girl), From a Motel 6 (Yo La Tengo), Iris.
PICTURES: Director/Writer: The Unbelievable Truth (debut, 1990), Trust, Simple Men, Amateur, Flirt (also actor, editor), Henry Fool (Cannes Film Festival Award, Best Screenplay, 1998).

HARTLEY, MARIETTE
Actress. b. New York, NY, June 21, 1940. Student Carnegie Tech. Inst. 1956-57; studied with Eva Le Gallienne. Appeared with Shakespeare Festival, Stratford 1957-60. Co-host Today Show, 1980. Co-host on CBS Morning Show, 1987. Returned to stage in King John (NYSF in Central Park), 1989. Nominated for 6 Emmys for Best Actress. Received 3 Clio Awards, 1979, 1980, and 1981, for acting in commercials. Autobiography: Breaking the Silence.
THEATRE: The Sisters Rosensweig, Deathtrap, Sylvia.
PICTURES: Ride the High Country (debut, 1962), Drums of Africa, Marnie, Marooned, Barquero, The Return of Count Yorga, Skyjacked, The Magnificent Seven Ride!, Improper Channels, O'Hara's Wife, 1969, Encino Man, Snitch.
TELEVISION: Series: Peyton Place, The Hero, Good Night Beantown, WIOU. Guest: The Rockford Files, The Incredible Hulk (Emmy Award, 1979), Stone, Caroline in the City. Movies: Earth II, Sandcastles, Genesis II, Killer Who Wouldn't Die, Last Hurrah, M.A.D.D.: Mothers Against Drunk Drivers, Drop-Out Father, One Terrific Guy, Silence of the Heart, My Two Loves, Murder C.O.D., Diagnosis of Murder, The House on Sycamore Street, Child of Rage, Heaven & Hell: North and South Book III, Falling From the Sky!: Flight 174. Mini-Series: Passion and Paradise. Specials: The Halloween That Almost Wasn't, Wild About Animals (host).

HARTMAN BLACK, LISA
Actress. Houston, TX, June 1, 1956. m. musician Clint Black. Attended NYC's H.S. of Performing Arts prior to becoming a nightclub performer.
PICTURES: Deadly Blessing, Where the Boys Are.
TELEVISION: Series: Tabitha, Knots Landing, High Performance, 2000 Malibu Road. Movies: Murder at the World Series, Valentine Magic on Love Island, Where the Ladies Go, Gridlock, Jacqueline Susann's Valley of the Dolls 1981, Beverly Hills Cowgirl Blues, Full Exposure: The Sex Tapes Scandal, The Operation, The Take, Bare Essentials, Fire: Trapped on the 39th Floor, Not of This World, Red Wind, The Return of Eliot Ness, Without a Kiss Goodbye, Search for Grace, Dazzle, Someone Else's Child, Have You Seen My Son?, Out of Nowhere.

HARTMAN, PHIL
Actor. b. Branford, Ontario, Canada, Sept. 24, 1948. Raised in Connecticut and Los Angeles. e. Cal State Northridge (graphic design). Designed album covers before joining improv. comedy group the Groundlings.
PICTURES: Jumpin' Jack Flash, Three Amigos!, Blind Date, Fletch Lives, Quick Change, Coneheads, So I Married an Axe Murderer, Greedy, Houseguest, Sgt. Bilko, Jingle All the Way.
TELEVISION: Series: Six O'Clock Follies, Saturday Night Live, NewsRadio. Pilots: Top Ten, The Natural Snoop.
(d. May 28, 1998)

HARTZ, JIM
TV Newsman, Panelist. b. Tulsa, OK, Feb. 3, 1940. Pre-med student at U. of Tulsa, where received in spare time as reporter for radio station KRMG. 1963 left studies for career as newsman and joined KOTV in Tulsa. 1964 moved to NBC News in New York, acting as reporter and anchorman. 1974 became co-host of Today Show, joined Barbara Walters.

HARU, SUMI
Executive. 1st natl. v.p., Screen Actors Guild.

HARVEY, ANTHONY
Director, Editor. b. London, England,, June 3, 1931. Royal Acad. of Dramatic Art. Two yrs. as actor. Ent. m.p. ind. 1949 with Crown Film Unit.
PICTURES: Editor: Private's Progress, Brothers-in-Law, Man in a Cocked Hat (Carlton Brown of the F.O.), Alright Jack, The Angry Silence, The Millionairess, Lolita, The L-Shaped Room, Dr. Strangelove, The Spy Who Came In From the Cold, The Whisperers. Director: Dutchman (debut, 1966), The Lion in Winter, They Might Be Giants, Eagles' Wing, Players, The Abdication, Richard's Things, Grace Quigley.
TELEVISION: Movies: The Disappearance of Aimee, Svengali, The Patricia Neal Story, The Glass Menagerie, This Can't Be Love.

HARWOOD, RONALD
Writer. b. Cape Town, South Africa, 1934. e. Royal Acad. of Dramatic Art.
THEATER: The Dresser, Interpreters, J.J. Farr, Another Time, Reflected Glory, Poison Pen, Taking Sides.
PICTURES: Barber of Stamford Hill, Private Potter, High Wind in Jamaica, Arrivederci Baby, Diamonds for Breakfast, Sudden Terror (Eye Witness), One Day in the Life of Ivan Denisovich, Operation Daybreak (Price of Freedom), The Dresser (also prod.), The Doctor and the Devils, Tchin-Tchin, The Browning Version, Cry the Beloved Country.
TELEVISION: The Barber of Stamford Hill, Private Potter, Take a Fellow Like Me, The Lads, Convalescence, Guests of Honor, The Guests. Adapted several of the Tales of the Unexpected, The Deliberate Death of a Polish Priest, Mandela, Breakthrough at Rykjavik, Countdown to War, All the World's a Stage (series).

HASSANEIN, RICHARD C.
Executive. b. New York, NY, Aug. 13, 1951; e. Staunton Military Acad., 1966-70; American U., 1970-74. Booker/real estate dept. opns., United Artists Theater Circuit, 1974-77; joined United Film Distribution Co., 1977; 1978-88, pres. of UFD. 1988-91 served as pres., prod.s' rep., foreign & U.S. sls., of Myriad Enterprises. Joined Todd-AO Glen Glenn Studios in 1991 as v.p. of new bus. ventures. 1991 appointed exec. v.p. of Todd-AO Studios East, NY. 1993, elected to bd. of dirs. of Todd-AO Corp. 1995, appointed v.p. of Todd-AO Studios West, Los Angeles; 1996, pres. and COO of Todd-AO Studios West.

HASSANEIN, SALAH M.
Executive. b. Suez, Egypt, May 31, 1921. e. British Sch., Alexandria, Egypt. Nat'l Bank of Egypt, Cairo, 1939-42. Asst. division mgr. Middle East, 20th-Fox, Cairo, Egypt, 1942-44: U.S. armed forces, 1945-47; usher, asst. mgr., Rivoli Theatre, N.Y., 1947-48. Film buyer, booker, oper. v.p. U.A. Eastern Theas., 1948-59; pres. 1960; exec. v.p. U.A. Communications, Inc. 1960; v.p. United Artists Cable Corp., 1963. Exec. v.p., Todd-AO Corp., 1980. President, Warner Bros. International Theaters, 1988. President, Todd AO Corp., 1994.
PICTURES: Exec. prod.: Knightriders, Creepshow, Hello Again, Love or Money.

HASSELHOFF, DAVID
Actor. b. Baltimore, MD, July 17, 1952.
PICTURES: Starcrash, Starke Zeiten, Witchery, W.B. Blue and the Bean, The Final Alliance, Ring of the Musketeers.
TELEVISION: *Series*: The Young and the Restless, Knight Rider, Baywatch, Baywatch Nights. *Movies*: Griffin and Phoenix, Semi Tough, The Cartier Affair, Bridge Across Time, Perry Mason: The Case of the Lady in the Lake, Baywatch: Panic at Malibu Pier, Fire & Rain, Knight Rider 2000, Avalanche, Baywatch: Forbidden Paradise, Gridlock, Nick Fury, Baywatch: White Thunder at Glacier Bay.

HASTINGS, DON
Actor. b. Brooklyn, NY, Apr. 1, 1934. e. Professional Children's Sch., Lodge H.S. On B'way in I Remember Mama, Summer and Smoke, etc.; Natl. co. of Life With Father; on various radio shows. Also wrote scripts for tv series The Guiding Light.
TELEVISION: *Series*: Captain Video, The Edge of Night, As the World Turns (also writer).

HATFIELD, HURD
Actor. b. New York, NY, Dec. 7, 1918. e. Morristown prep, Horace Mann, Riverdale Acad., Bard Col., Chekhov Drama Sch., Devonshire, Eng.
THEATER: Lower Depths, Twelfth Night, Cricket on the Hearth, King Lear, Venus Observed, Camino Real, Love's Labor's Lost, Bullfight, Julius Caesar, The Count of Monte Cristo, Son Juan in Hell, Son of Whistler's Mother, Stuttgart.
PICTURES: Dragon Seed (debut, 1944), The Picture of Dorian Gray, Diary of a Chambermaid, The Beginning or the End?, The Unsuspected, The Checkered Coat, Joan of Arc, Chinatown at Midnight, Destination Murder, Tarzan and the Slave Girl, The Left-Handed Gun, King of Kings, El Cid, Harlow, Mickey One, The Boston Strangler, Von Richtofen and Brown, King David, Crimes of the Heart, Her Alibi.
TELEVISION: *Movies*: Thief, The Norliss Tapes, You Can't Go Home Again, Lies of the Twins. *Mini-Series*: The Word.

HATFIELD, TED
Executive. b. Wilton Junction, IA, Aug. 26, 1936. e. Hot Springs, AR. U.S. Army-NCO Academy, 1954. 1949-67 ABC Paramount Theatres, advanced from usher to district mgr. 1967-70 MGM asst. exploitation dir.; 1970-83, MGM national advertising coordinator; 1983-87, MGM/UA v.p., field operations. 1987-91, MGM/UA v.p., exhibitor relations. 1991-, Sony Pictures Releasing, v.p., exhib. rltns. Member: Motion Picture Pioneers, Western LA Council, Boy Scout Commissioner, Culver City Chamber of Commerce, past v.p./presidents award, Jaycees, Past State v.p., Advertising Federation, past state pres., Culver City Commissioner.

HAUER, RUTGER
Actor. b. Breukelen, Netherlands, Jan. 23, 1944. Stage actor in Amsterdam for six years.
PICTURES: Repelsteeltje (debut, 1973), Turkish Delight, Pusteblume, The Wilby Conspiracy, Keetje Tippel, Het Jaar van de Kreeft, Max Havelaar, Griechische Feigen, Soldier of Orange, Pastorale 1943, Femme Entre Chien et Loup, Mysteries (also co-prod.), Gripsta en de Gier, Spetters, Nighthawks, Chanel Solitaire, Blade Runner, Eureka, The Osterman Weekend, A Breed Apart, Ladyhawke, Flesh and Blood, The Hitcher, Wanted: Dead or Alive, The Legend of the Holy Drinker, Bloodhounds of Broadway, The Blood of Heroes, Blind Fury, Ocean Point, On a Moonlit Night, Past Midnight, Split Second, Buffy the Vampire Slayer, Arctic Blue, Beyond Forgiveness, Surviving the Game, Nostradamus, The Beans of Egypt Maine, Angel of Death.
TELEVISION: *Movies*: Escape from Sobibor, Inside The Third Reich, Deadlock, Blind Side, Voyage, Amelia Earhart: The Final Flight, Fatherland. *Series*: Floris (Netherlands TV). *Mini-Series*: Maketub: The Law of the Desert (Italy).

HAUG, WILLIAM F.
Executive. Pres. and CEO, Motion Picture and Television Fund.

HAUSER, WINGS
Actor. b. Hollywood, CA, 1947. Nickname derived from playing wing back on h.s. football team. Began studying acting in 1975.
PICTURES: First to Fight, Who'll Stop the Rain, Homework, Vice Squad, Deadly Force, Uncommon Valor (assoc. prod., story only), Night Shadows, A Soldier's Story, Jo Jo Dancer Your Life is Calling, 3:15, Tough Guys Don't Dance, Nightmare at Noon, The Wind, Hostage, Dead Man Walking, The Carpenter, The Siege of Firebase Gloria, No Safe Haven (also co-s.p.), Reason to Die, L.A. Bounty, Street Asylum, Pale Blood, Out of Sight Out of Mind, Nightmare at Noon, Living to Die, Exiled in America, Bedroom Eyes II, Wilding, The Killer's Edge, In Between, Frame Up, Cold Fire, Beastmaster 2: Through the Portal of Time, The Art of Dying, Mind Body & Soul, Frame-up III: The Cover Up, Watchers 3, Tales From the Hood, Victim of Desire, Life Among the Cannibals, Original Gangstas.
TELEVISION: *Series*: The Young and the Restless, The Last Precinct, Lightning Force, Command 5, Roseanne, Beverly Hills 90210. *Movies*: Hear No Evil, Ghost Dancing, Sweet Revenge, The Long Hot Summer, Perry Mason: The Case of the Scandalous Scoundrel, Highway Man, Bump In the Night. *Guest*: Murder She Wrote, China Beach, Hard Ball, The Young Riders, Space Rangers, Walker Texas Ranger, Jag.

HAUSMAN, MICHAEL
Producer. Former stockbroker and still photographer. Entered film industry as assoc. prod. and prod. mgr. on The Heartbreak Kid and Taking Off. Worked as head of prod. for Robert Stigwood on Saturday Night Fever.
PICTURES: I Never Promised You a Rose Garden, Alambrista!, Heartland, Rich Kids, One-Trick Pony, Ragtime (exec. prod., 1st asst. dir.), The Ballad of Gregorio Cortez, Silkwood, Amadeus (exec. prod.), Places in the Heart (exec. prod.), Desert Bloom, Flight of the Spruce Goose, No Mercy, House of Games, Things Change, Valmont, State of Grace, Homicide, Nobody's Fool, A Family Thing, Twilight.
TELEVISION: Lip Service (exec. prod.).

HAVERS, NIGEL
Actor. b. London, England,, Nov. 6, 1949. e. Leicester U., trained for stage at Arts Educational Trust. Father, Sir Michael Havers, was Attorney General of Britain. As child played Billy Owen on British radio series, Mrs. Dale's Diary. Records voice overs and books for the blind.
THEATER: Conduct Unbecoming, Richard II, Man and , Superman (RSC), Family Voices, Season's Greetings, The Importance of Being Earnest.
PICTURES: Pope Joan (debut, 1972), Full Circle, Who is Killing the Great Chefs of Europe?, Chariots of Fire, A Passage to India, Burke and Wills, The Whistle Blower, Empire of the Sun, Farewell to the King, Clichy Days.
TELEVISION: *Series*: A Horseman Riding By, Don't Wait Up. *Mini-Series*: The Glittering Prizes, Nicholas Nickleby, Pennies From Heaven, Winston Churchill: The Wilderness Years, Nancy Astor, The Little Princess, Death of the Heart, Naked Under Capricorn, Sleepers. *Movies*: The Charmer, Private War of Lucina Smith, Lie Down With Lions, The Burning Season. *Guest*: Thriller, Star Quality: Noel Coward Stories (Bon Voyage), A Question of Guilt, Aspects of Love, Upstairs Downstairs, Edward VII, Liz: The Elizabeth Taylor Story.

HAVOC, JUNE
Actress. r.n. Hovick. b. Seattle, WA, Nov. 8, 1916. Sister was late Gypsy Rose Lee. Made film bow at 2 yrs. old in Hal Roach/Harold Lloyd productions billed as Baby June. Danced with Anna Pavlova troupe, then entered vaudeville in own act. Later, joined Municipal Opera Company, St. Louis, and appeared in Shubert shows. Musical comedy debut: Forbidden Melody (1936). To Hollywood, 1942. Author: Early Havoc (1959), More Havoc (1980).
THEATER: Pal Joey, Sadie Thompson, Mexican Hayride, Dunnigan's Daughter, Dream Girl, Affairs of State, The Skin of Our Teeth, A Midsummer Night's Dream (Stratford, CT. American Shakespeare Fest., 1958), Tour for U.S. Dept. of St., 1961; wrote Marathon 33. The Ryan Girl, The Infernal Machine, The Beaux Strategem, A Warm Peninsula, Dinner at Eight, Habeas Corpus. An Unexpected Evening with June Havoc (one woman show, London 1985), The Gift (tour), Eleemosynary, The Old Lady's Guide to Survival, Do Not Go Gently.
PICTURES: Four Jacks and a Jill (debut, 1941), Powder Town, My Sister Eileen, Sing Your Worries Away, Hi Diddle Diddle, Hello Frisco Hello, No Time for Love, Casanova Burlesque, Timber Queen, Sweet and Low Down, Brewster's Millions, Intrigue, Gentleman's Agreement, When My Baby Smiles at Me, The Iron Curtain, The Story of Molly X, Red Hot and Blue, Chicago Deadline, Mother Didn't Tell Me, Once a Thief, Follow the Sun, Lady Possessed, Three for Jamie Dawn, The Private Files of J. Edgar Hoover, Can't Stop the Music, Return to Salem's Lot.
TELEVISION: Anna Christie, The Bear, Cakes and Ale, Daisy Mayme, The Untouchables, Willy, MacMillan & Wife, The Paper Chase, Murder She Wrote. *Series*: More Havoc (1964-65), Search for Tomorrow, General Hospital.

HAWKE, ETHAN
Actor. b. Austin, TX, Nov. 6, 1970. Attended NYU. Studied acting at McCarter Theatre in Princeton, NJ, the British Theatre Assn., Carnegie Mellon U. Stage debut in St. Joan. Co-founder of Malaparte Theatre Co. in NYC. Dir. & wrote short film Straight to One. Author of novel The Hottest State, 1996.
THEATER: NY: Casanova (Off-B'way debut, 1991), A Joke, The Seagull (B'way debut, 1992), Sophistry, Hesh, The Great Unwashed.
PICTURES: Explorers (debut, 1985), Dead Poets Society, Dad, White Fang, Mystery Date, A Midnight Clear, Waterland, Alive, Rich in Love, Reality Bites, White Fang 2: Myth of the White Wolf (cameo), Quiz Show (cameo), Floundering, Before Sunrise, Search and Destroy, Gattaca, The Velocity of Gary, Snow Falling on Cedars, The Newton Boys, Monterey Pop, Great Expectations.

HAWN, GOLDIE
Actress, Producer. b. Washington, DC, November 21, 1945. Started as professional dancer (performed in Can-Can at the N.Y. World's Fair, 1964), and made TV debut dancing on an Andy Griffith Special.

PICTURES: The One and Only Genuine Original Family Band (debut, 1968), Cactus Flower (Academy Award, best supporting actress, 1969), There's a Girl in My Soup, $ (Dollars), Butterflies Are Free, The Sugarland Express, The Girl From Petrovka, Shampoo, The Duchess and the Dirtwater Fox, Foul Play, Private Benjamin (Acad. Award nom.; also exec. prod.), Seems Like Old Times, Lovers and Liars (Travels With Anita), Best Friends, Swing Shift, Protocol (also exec. prod.), Wildcats (also exec. prod.), Overboard (also exec. prod.), Bird on a Wire, My Blue Heaven (co-exec. prod. only), Deceived, Crisscross (also co-exec. prod.), Housesitter, Death Becomes Her, Something to Talk About (exec. prod. only), The First Wives Club, Everyone Says I Love You, The Out-of-Towners, Chicago.
TELEVISION: Series: Good Morning World, Rowan & Martin's Laugh-In (1968-70). Specials: The Goldie Hawn Special, Goldie & Liza Together, Goldie and the Kids: Listen to Us.

HAWTHORNE, NIGEL
Actor. b. Coventry, England, Apr. 5, 1929. Extensive career on stage. Ent. TV ind. 1953. Films, 1957. Won 1991 Tony Award for best actor for Shadowlands; Olivier & Evening Standard Awards for The Madness of George III (Natl. Th.).
PICTURES: Young Winston, The Hiding Place, Watership Down (voice), History of the World Part 1, Plague Dogs (voice), Firefox, Gandhi, The Black Cauldron (voice), The Chain, Turtle Diary, Freddie as F.R.O.7 (voice), Demolition Man, The Madness of King George (Acad. Award nom.), BAFTA Award), Richard III, Inside, Twelfth Night, The Fragile Heart (BAFTA Award).
TELEVISION: Mapp and Lucia, The Knowledge, The Miser, The Critic, Barchester Chronicles, Marie Curie, Edward and Mrs. Simpson, Yes Minister, Yes Prime Minister (series), The Oz Trials, Flea-Bites, The Shawl, Relatively Speaking, Late Flowering Lust.

HAYEK, SALMA
Actress. b. Coatzacoalcos, Veracruz, Mexico, Sept. 22, 1968. Began her acting career in the 1980's in Mexican TV soap operas. Was first noticed in 1995 for her role in Desperado.
PICTURES: My Crazy Life, Midaq Alley, Desperado, Fair Game, Four Rooms, From Dusk Till Dawn, Fled, Fools Rush In, Follow Me Home, Breaking Up, The Velocity of Gary, Frida, Dogma, 54.
TELEVISION: Movies: Roadracers, The Hunchback. Series: Teresa, The Sinbad Show. Guest: Dream On, Nurses.

HAYES, ISAAC
Musician, Actor. b. Covington, TN, Aug. 20, 1942. Was session musician with Stax Records in Memphis, eventually working as composer, prod.. Debuted with solo album Presenting Isaac Hayes in 1968.
PICTURES: Music: Shaft (Academy Award for best song: Theme from Shaft, 1971), Shaft's Big Score. Actor: Wattstax, Save the Children, Three Tough Guys (also music), Truck Turner (also music), Escape From New York, I'm Gonna Git You Sucka, Guilty as Charged, Posse, Robin Hood: Men in Tights, It Could Happen to You, Flipper.
TELEVISION: Series theme: The Men.

HAYES, JOHN EDWARD
Broadcasting Executive. b. Niagara Falls, NY, Sept. 14, 1941. e. U. FL, BS broadcasting, 1963. State capitol bur. chief Sta. WTVJ-TV, FL, 1963-67. Exec. asst. FL, Dept. Comsumer Svcs., 1967-71. State capitol bur. chief Sta. WTVT-TV, Tallahassee, 1971-77. Asst. news dir. Sta. WTVT-TV, FL, 1977-79. News dir.: Sta. WBRC-TV, AL 1979-82; Sta. KNTV-TV, CA, 1982-83. V.p. gen. mgr. Sta. KLAS-TV, NV, 1983-87. Gen mgr. Sta. WIVB-TV, NY 1987-89. Pres. Jour. Broadcasting of Charlotte Co., 1989-92. V.p. TV Providence Jour. Co., 1992-. Recipient of: Nat. Headliners award Headliner Club, 1973; Emmy award TV Acad. Arts & Sci., 1982. Mem.: Nat. Assn. Broadcasters; TV Bur. Advertisers & NBC Affiliates.

HAYES, JOHN MICHAEL
Writer. b. Worcester, MA, May 11, 1919. e. U. of Massachusetts, 1941.
PICTURES: Red Ball Express, Thunder Bay, Torch Song, War Arrow, Rear Window, To Catch a Thief, The Trouble with Harry, It's a Dog's Life, The Man Who Knew Too Much, The Matchmaker, Peyton Place, But Not for Me, Butterfield 8, The Children's Hour, Where Love Has Gone, The Chalk Garden, Judith, Iron Will.
TELEVISION: Movie: Winter Kill, Nevada Smith, Pancho Barnes.

HAYES, PETER LIND
Actor. b. San Francisco, CA, June 25, 1915. m. Mary Healy. Was radio singer, actor, vaudeville, night clubs. Prod., Grace Hayes Lodge Review: on TV show with Mary Healy.
PICTURES: Million Dollar Legs, All Women Have Secrets, These Glamour Girls, Seventeen, Dancing on a Dime, Playmates, Seven Days Leave, The 5000 Fingers of Dr. T., Once You Kiss a Stranger.
(d. April 21, 1998)

HAYNES, TODD
Director, Writer, Producer, Editor, Actor.
PICTURES: Superstar: The Karen Carpenter Story, He Was Once, Poison (Sundance Film Fest. Grand Jury Prize, 1991), Swoon, Safe (Seattle Int'l. Film Fest. Amer. Indep. Award, 1995), Velvet Goldmine (Cannes Film Fest., Best Art. Contribution, 1998).
TELEVISION: Movies: Dottie Gets Spanked

HAYS, ROBERT
Actor. b. Bethesda, MD, July 24, 1947. e. Grossmont Coll., San Diego State U. Left school to join San Diego's Old Globe Theatre five years, appearing in such plays as The Glass Menagerie, The Man in the Glass Booth, Richard III.
PICTURES: Airplane! (debut, 1980), Take This Job and Shove It!, Utilities, Airplane II: The Sequel, Trenchcoat, Touched, Scandalous, Cat's Eye, Honeymoon Academy, Hot Chocolate, Homeward Bound: The Incredible Journey, Fifty Fifty, Raw Justice, Homeward Bound II: Lost in San Francisco.
TELEVISION: Series: Angie, Starman, FM, Cutters, Kelly Kelly. Movies: Young Pioneers, Young Pioneers' Christmas, Delta County U.S.A., The Initiation of Sarah, The Girl The Gold Watch and Everything, California Gold Rush, The Fall of the House of Usher, The Day the Bubble Burst, Murder by the Book, Running Against Time, No Dessert Dad 'Til You Mow the Lawn, Deadly Invasion: The Killer Bee Nightmare, Danielle Steel's Vanished. Mini-Series: Will Rogers: Champion of the People. Specials: Mr. Roberts, Partners. Guest: Love Boat, Harry O, Laverne and Shirley.

HAYSBERT, DENNIS
Actor. b. San Mateo, CA, June 2.
THEATER: Wedding Band, Yanks-3 Detroit-0 Top of the Seventh, Diplomacy, Othello, On the Death of, All Over Town, Blood Knot, No Place to Be Somebody, Jimmy Shine, The Time of Your Life, Ten Little Indians.
PICTURES: Major League, Navy SEALS, Mr. Baseball, Love Field, Suture, Major League 2, Amanda, Waiting to Exhale, Absolute Power, Heat, Prairie Fire.
TELEVISION: Series: Code Red, Off the Rack. Mini-Series: Queen. Movies: A Summer to Remember, Grambling's White Tiger, K-9000. Specials: The Upper Room, Hallelujah.

HEADLY, GLENNE
Actress. b. New London, CT, March 13, 1957. e. High Sch. of Performing Arts. Studied at HB Studios. In Chicago joined St. Nicholas New Works Ensemble. Won 3 Joseph Jefferson awards for work with Steppenwolf Ensemble in Say Goodnight Gracie, Miss Firecracker Contest, Balm in Gilead, Coyote Ugly, Loose Ends. Directed Canadian Gothic.
THEATER: NY: Balm in Gilead, Arms and the Man, Extremities, The Philanthropist (Theatre World Award).
PICTURES: Four Friends (debut, 1981), Dr. Detroit, Fandango, The Purple Rose of Cairo, Eleni, Making Mr. Right, Nadine, Stars and Bars, Dirty Rotten Scoundrels, Paperhouse, Dick Tracy, Mortal Thoughts, Getting Even With Dad, Mr. Holland's Opus, Sgt. Bilko, 2 Days in the Valley, Pronto, Breakfast of Champions, Base 2 (voice), X-Files.
TELEVISION: Movies: Say Goodnight Gracie, Seize the Day, Grand Isle, And the Band Played On. Mini-Series: Lonesome Dove (Emmy nom.). Guest: Frasier

HEALD, ANTHONY
Actor. b. New Rochelle, NY, Aug. 25, 1944. e. Michigan St. Univ.
THEATER: B'way: The Wake of Jamey Foster, The Marriage of Figaro, Anything Goes, A Small Family Business, Love! Valour! Compassion!, Inherit the Wind. Off-B'way: The Glass Menagerie, The Electra Myth, Inadmissible Evidence, Misalliance (Theatre World Award), The Caretaker, The Fox, The Philanthropist, Henry V, The Foreigner, Digby, Principia Scriptoriae, The Lisbon Traviata, Elliot Loves, Lips Together Teeth Apart, Pygmalion, Later Life, Love! Valour! Compassion! Regional: Quartermaine's Terms, J.B., Look Back in Anger, The Rose Tattoo, Bonjour la Bonjour, The Matchmaker.
PICTURES: Silkwood (debut, 1983), Teachers, Outrageous Fortune, Happy New Year, Orphans, Postcards From the Edge, The Silence of the Lambs, The Super, Whispers in the Dark, Searching for Bobby Fisher, The Ballad of Little Jo, The Pelican Brief, The Client, Kiss of Death, Bushwacked, A Time to Kill, Deep Rising.
TELEVISION: Movies: A Case of Deadly Force, Royce. Mini-Series: Fresno. Pilot: After Midnight. Special: Abby My Love. Guest: Hard Copy, Crime Story, Spenser for Hire, Miami Vice, Tales From the Darkside, Against the Law, Law and Order, Class of '96, Cheers, Murder She Wrote, Under Suspicion.

HEARD, JOHN
Actor. b. Washington, D.C., Mar. 7, 1947. e. Catholic U. Career began at Organic Theatre, starring in Chicago & N.Y. productions of Warp. Other stage roles include Streamers, G.R. Point (Theatre World Award), Othello, Split, The Glass Menagerie, Total Abandon, The Last Yankee.

PICTURES: Between the Lines (debut, 1977), First Love, On the Yard, Head Over Heels (Chilly Scenes of Winter), Heart Beat, Cutter and Bone (Cutter's Way), Cat People, Best Revenge, Violated, Heaven Help Us, Lies, C.H.U.D., Too Scared to Scream, After Hours, The Trip to Bountiful, The Telephone, The Milagro Beanfield War, The Seventh Sign, Big, Betrayed, Beaches, The Package, Home Alone, End of Innocence, Awakenings, Rambling Rose, Deceived, Mindwalk, Radio Flyer, Gladiator, Waterland, Home Alone 2: Lost in New York, In the Line of Fire, Me and Veronica, The Pelican Brief, Before and After, My Fellow Americans, 187, Executive Power, Men, Snake Eyes.
TELEVISION: Series: John Grisham's The Client. Specials: The Scarlet Letter, Edgar Allan Poe: Terror of the Soul. Mini-Series: Tender Is the Night. Movies: Will There Really Be a Morning?, Legs, Out on a Limb, Necessity, Cross of Fire, Dead Ahead: The Exxon Valdez Disaster, There Was a Little Boy, Spoils of War, Because Mommy Works.

HECHE, ANNE
Actress. b. Aurora, OH, May 25, 1969.
PICTURES: An Ambush of Ghosts, The Adventures of Huck Finn, A Simple Twist of Fate, Milk Money, I'll Do Anything, The Wild Side, Pie in the Sky, The Juror, Walking and Talking, Donnie Brasco, Volcano, Six Days Seven Nights, Wag the Dog, Force Majeure.
TELEVISION: Series: Another World. Movies: O Pioneers!, Against the Wall, Girls in Prison, Kingfish: A Story of Huey P. Long, If These Walls Could Talk, Subway Stories,. Guest: Murphy Brown.

HECKART, EILEEN
Actress. b. Columbia, OH, Mar. 29, 1919. e. Ohio State U., American Theatre Wing. m. Jack Yankee.Inducted into Theatre Hall of Fame, 1995. Awards: Foreign Press, and Donaldson, Oscar nom. and Film Daily Citation (Bad Seed), TV Sylvania for the Haven, Variety Poll of N.Y. and Drama Critics (Dark at The Top of the Stairs); Emmy (Save Me a Place at Forest Lawn). Also 5 Tony noms., 5 Emmy noms. Honorary Doctorates from: Ohio St. Univ., Sacred Heart, Niagara Univ.
THEATER: Voice of the Turtle, Brighten the Corner, They Knew What They Wanted, Hilda Crane, Picnic (Theatre World & Outer Critics Circle Awards), The Bad Seed, A View From the Bridge, Family Affair, Pal Joey, Invitation to a March, Everybody Loves Opal, The Dark at the Top of the Stairs, And Things That Go Bump in the Night, You Know I Can't Hear You When the Water's Running, Too True to Be Good, Barefoot in the Park, Butterflies Are Free, Veronica's Room, The Effect of Gamma Rays on Man in the Moon Marigolds, Eleemosynary, The Cemetery Club, Love Letters, Driving Miss Daisy.
PICTURES: Miracle in the Rain (debut, 1956), Somebody Up There Likes Me, The Bad Seed, Bus Stop, Hot Spell, Heller in Pink Tights, My Six Loves, Up the Down Staircase, No Way to Treat a Lady, The Tree, Butterflies Are Free (Academy Award, best supporting actress, 1972), Zandy's Bride, The Hiding Place, Burnt Offerings, Heartbreak Ridge, The First Wives' Club.
TELEVISION: Series: The Five Mrs. Buchanans. Guest: Kraft, Suspense, Philco Playhouse, The Web, Mary Tyler Moore, Annie McGuire, Love and War (Emmy Award, 1994), The Five Mrs. Buchanans, Murder One. Movies: The Victim, FBI Story: The FBI Versus Alvin Karpis, Sunshine Christmas, Suddenly Love, White Mama, FDR: The Last Year, The Big Black Pill, Games Mother Never Taught You, Seize the Day, Ultimate Betrayal, A Doll's House, Stuck with Each Other, Triumph Over Disaster: The Hurricane Andrew Story, Breathing Lessons, Ultimate Betrayal. Mini-Series: Backstairs at the Whitehouse.

HECKERLING, AMY
Director. b. New York, NY, May 7, 1954. e. Art & Design H.S., NYU, (film and TV), American Film Institute. Made shorts (Modern Times, High Finance, Getting It Over With), before turning to features.
PICTURES: Fast Times at Ridgemont High, Johnny Dangerously, Into the Night (actor only), National Lampoon's European Vacation, Look Who's Talking, Look Who's Talking Too, Look Who's Talking 3 (co-exec. prod. only), Clueless.
TELEVISION: George Burns Comedy Hour, Fast Times, They Came From Queens. Series: Clueless.

HEDAYA, DAN
Actor. b. Brooklyn, NY, July 24, 1940. e. Tufts Univ. Taught junior high school for seven yrs. before turning to acting. Joined NY Shakespeare Fest. in 1973.
THEATER: NY: Last Days of British Honduras, Golden Boy, Museum, The Basic Training of Pavlo Hummel, Conjuring an Event, Survivors, Henry V.
PICTURES: The Passover Plot (debut, 1976), The Seduction of Joe Tynan, Night of the Juggler, True Confessions, I'm Dancing As Fast As I Can, Endangered Species, The Hunger, The Adventures of Buckaroo Banzai, Blood Simple, Reckless, Tightrope, Commando, Wise Guys, Running Scared, Joe Vs. the Volcano, Pacific Heights, Tune in Tomorrow, The Addams Family, Boiling Point, Benny & Joon, Rookie of the Year, For Love or Money, Mr. Wonderful, Maverick, Search and Destroy, Clueless, Nixon, The Usual Suspects, To Die For, Marvin's Room, Freeway, Ransom, Daylight, In & Out, Alien: Resurrection, A Life Less Ordinary, A Civil Action.

TELEVISION: Series: The Tortellis, One of the Boys, ER. Movies: The Prince of Central Park, Death Penalty, The Dollmaker, Courage, Slow Burn, A Smoky Mountain Christmas, Betrayal of Trust, Reluctant Agent, The Whereabouts of Jenny, The Garden of Redemption. Guest: Hill Street Blues, Cheers, L.A. Law. Pilots: The Earthlings, The Flamingo Kid, The Rock. Special: Just Like Family, Mama's Boy, Veronica Clare, The Second Civil War.

HEDLUND, DENNIS
Executive. b. Hedley, TX, Sept. 3, 1946. e. U. of Texas, Austin, B.A., business admin., 1968. Captain U.S. Marine Corp, 1966-72. 1970-74, newscaster and disc jockey, KGNC Amarillo, TX; KOMA Oklahoma City, OK; WTIX New Orleans, LA; WFLA Tampa, FL. 1974-77, nat'l sales mgr., Ampex Corp., NY. 1977-80, v.p., Allied Artists Video Corp., NY. 1980-present, founder and pres., Kultur International Films Ltd., distributor of over 800 performing arts programs on home video. 1990, created White Star Entertainment, prod. of original programs for tv, and home video. marketer of over 400 non-theatrical home video titles. Recently acquired Duke USA, 1200 motorsports programs for tv and home video.
TELEVISION: Roger Miller: King of the Road, Jackie Mason: An Equal Opportunity Offender, Merle Haggard: A Portrait of a Proud Man, History of Talk Radio, George Jones: Golden Hits, Raised Catholic: Still Catholic After All These Fears.

HEDREN, TIPPI
Actress. r.n. Nathalie Hedren. b. Lafayette, MN, Jan. 18, 1935. Daughter is actress Melanie Griffith. Was hired by Alfred Hitchcock for leading role in The Birds after being spotted on a commercial on the Today Show. Author of The Cats of Shambala. Founder and pres. of The Roar Foundation. Founder of the Shambala preserve. Bd. member, The Wildlife Safari, The Elsa Wild Animal Appeal, The ASPCA, The American Heart Assoc., etc.
THEATRE: Black Comedy, A Hatful of Rain, Love Letters.
PICTURES: The Birds (debut, 1963), Marnie, A Countess From Hong Kong, The Man and the Albatross, Satan's Harvest, Tiger By the Tail, Mr. Kingstreet's War, The Harrad Experiment, Where the Wind Dies, Roar (also prod.), Foxfire Light, Deadly Spygames, Pacific Heights, In the Cold of the Night, Inevitable Grace, Theresa's Tattoo, Mind Lies, The Devil Inside, Citizen Ruth, I Woke Up Early the Day I Died, The Breakup.
TELEVISION: Series: The Bold and the Beautiful, Dream On. Guest: Run for Your Life, The Courtship of Eddie's Father, Alfred Hitchcock Presents (1985), Baby Boom, Hart to Hart, In the Heat of the Night, Hotel, Improv (guest host), Tales From the Darkside, Murder She Wrote, Capitol News, The Guardian, Heroes Die Hard, Our Time. Movies: Alfred Hitchcock Presents..., Through the Eyes of a Killer, Shadow of a Doubt, Perry Mason: The Case of the Skin-Deep Scandal, The Birds II: Land's End, Treacherous Beauties, Return to Green Acres, Kraft Suspense Theatre: The Trains of Silence, The Book of Virtues (voice), Freakazoid! (voice), Sixth Sense (short), Mulligans(short).Special: Inside The Birds.

HEFFNER, RICHARD D.
Executive. b. New York, NY, Aug. 5, 1925. e. Columbia U. Instrumental in acquisition of Channel 13 (WNET) as New York's educational tv station; served as its first gen. mngr. Previously had produced and moderated Man of the Year, The Open Mind, etc. for commercial and public TV. Served as dir. of public affairs programs for WNBC-TV in NY. Was also dir. of special projects for CBS TV Network and editorial consultant to CBS, Inc. Editorial Board. Was radio newsman for ABC. Exec. editor of From The Editor's Desk on WPIX-TV in NY. Taught history at U. of California at Berkeley, Sarah Lawrence Coll., Columbia U. and New School for Social Research, NY. Served as American specialist in communications for U.S. Dept. of State in Japan, Soviet Union, Germany, Yugoslavia, Israel, etc. Prof. of Communications and Public Policy at Rutgers U. 1974-94, chmn. of classification and rating admin. rating board. 1994-95, sr. fellow, Freedom Forum Media Studies Center at Columbia Univ.

HEFFRON, RICHARD T.
Director. b. Chicago, Oct. 6, 1930.
PICTURES: Fillmore, Newman's Law, Trackdown, Futureworld, Outlaw Blues, I the Jury, The French Revolution.
TELEVISION: The Morning After, Dick Van Dyke Special, I Will Fight No More Forever, Toma (pilot), Rockford Files (pilot), North and South (mini-series). Movies: The California Kid, Young Joe Kennedy, A Rumor of War, A Whale for the Killing, The Mystic Warrior, V: The Final Battle, Anatomy of an Illness, Convicted: A Mother's Story, Guilty of Innocence, Samaritan, Napoleon and Josephine: A Love Story, Broken Angel, Pancho Barnes, Tagget, Deadly Family Secrets, No Greater Love.

HEIDER, FREDERICK
Producer. b. Milwaukee, WI, Apr. 9, 1917. e. Notre Dame U., Goodman Theatre, Chicago. Actor in Globe Theatre, Orson Welles' Mercury Theatre.
TELEVISION & RADIO: Chesterfield Supper Club, Sammy Kaye's So You Want to Lead a Band, Frankie Carle Show, Jo Stafford Show, Paul Whiteman Goodyear Revue, Billy Daniels Show, Martha Wright Show, Earl Wrightson Show, Club Seven, Mindy Carson Show; Ted Mack Family Hour, Dr. I.Q., Miss America Pageant, Bishop Sheen's Life Is Worth Living, Voice of Firestone, Music for a Summer Night. Music for a Spring Night, The Bell Telephone Hour. Publisher, Television Quarterly, National Academy of Television Arts and Sciences. Became columnist, The Desert Sun, Palm Springs, CA.

HEILMAN, CLAUDE
Executive. b. Cologne, Germany, June 27, 1927. Early career in Europe in prod. and distribution. In U.S. joined Fox in Hollywood and NY; incl. mgmt. of Grauman's Chinese and other Fox theaters. Formed Vintage Prods. Inc., United Film Associates Intlo., Inter Road Shows. Currently pres./chief. exec. GEM Communications and Islandia Enterprises.
PICTURES: This Earth Is Mine, Odyssey of Justice Lee, The Adventures of Gulliver, Desamor, Sound General Quarters, Islandia.

HELGELAND, BRIAN
Writer, Director, Producer. b. Providence, RI, 1961.
PICTURES: *Writer*: A Nightmare on Elm Street 4: The Dream Master, 976-EVIL, Highway to Hell, Assassins, L.A. Confidential (also co-prod., Acad. Award, Best Adapted Screenplay, Chicago Film Crits. Award, LA Film Crits. Award, NY Film Crits. Circle Awards Best Screenplay, 1997), Conspiracy Theory, The Postman, Payback.
TELEVISION: *Series*: Tales from the Crypt (dir.).

HELGENBERGER, MARG
Actress. b. North Bend, NE, Nov. 16, 1958. e. Northwestern U. Came to NY where she landed first professional job as regular on daytime serial Ryan's Hope.
PICTURES: After Midnight (debut, 1989), Always, Crooked Hearts, Distant Cousins, The Cowboy Way, Bad Boys, Species, My Fellow Americans, Fire Down Below, Species II.
TELEVISION: *Series*: Ryan's Hope, Shell Game, China Beach (Emmy Award, 1990). *Movies*: Blind Vengeance, Death Dreams, The Hidden Room, Deadline (pilot), Through the Eyes of a Killer, The Tommyknockers, When Love Kills: The Seduction of John Hearn, Where Are My Children?, Red Eagle, Partners, Inflammable, Conundrum, Murder Live!, The Last Time I Commited Suicide, Gold Coast. *Special*: Fallen Angels. *Guest*: Spenser for Hire, thirtysomething, Tales From the Crypt, The Larry Sanders Show, ER. *Mini-series*: When Love Kills: The Seduction of John Hearn.

HELLER, FRANKLIN
Producer, Director. b. Dover, NJ, Sept. 15, 1911. e. Carnegie Inst. of Technology, B.A., 1934. Actor, 1934-36; stage mgr., Sam Harris-Max Gordon Prods., 1936-44; exec. prod., USO shows N.Y., 1944-45; prod. & dir., Paramount, 1945-47; dir., summer stock, 1947-48; prod. & dir., CBS TV, 1949-54; exec., prod. and dir. Goodson-Todman Prods., 1954-69; exec. prod. Protocol Prods., 1969-72 Literary Representative 1972. Dirs. Guild of America, Nat'l bd. 1965-77; Treas. 1965-69; Sec. 1970-73; Chr. Publications 1966-76. Retired.
TELEVISION: What's My Line?, Beat the Clock, The Front Page, The Web, Danger, To Tell the Truth, I've Got a Secret.

HELLER, PAUL M.
Producer. b. New York, NY, Sept. 25, 1927. e. Hunter Coll., Drexel Inst. of Technology. President, Intrepid Productions. Studied engineering until entry into U.S. Army as member of security agency, special branch of signal corps. Worked as set designer (Westport, East Hampton, Palm Beach) and in live TV and then on theatrical films. Produced the NY Experience and South Street Venture. Debut as film prod., David and Lisa, 1963. From 1964 to 1969 was president of MPO Pictures Inc. Joined Warner Bros. as prod. exec., 1970. Founded the Community Film Workshop Council for the American Film Institute. In 1972 founded Sequoia Pictures, Inc. with Fred Weintraub. Pres. of Paul Heller Prods. Inc. formed in 1978. Founded the Audrey Skirball-Kenis Theatre. Bd of dirs., the British Academy of Film and Television - Los Angeles, The Hearst Monument Foundation, The Geffen Theatre.
PICTURES: David and Lisa, The Eavesdropper, Secret Ceremony, Enter the Dragon, Truck Turner, Golden Needles, Dirty Knight's Work, Outlaw Blues, The Pack, The Promise, First Monday in October, Withnail and I, My Left Foot (exec. prod.), The Lunatic, Fatal Inheritance.
TELEVISION: Pygmalion, Falcon's Gold.

HELLMAN, JEROME
Producer. b. New York, NY, Sept. 4, 1928. e. NYU. Joined ad dept. of New York Times then went to William Morris Agency as apprentice. Made asst. in TV dept. Worked as agent for Jaffe Agency. After hiatus in Europe joined Ashley-Steiner Agency (later IFA) where clients included Franklin Schaffner, Sidney Lumet, George Roy Hill, John Frankenheimer. Functioned as TV prod., including Kaiser Aluminum Hour. Left to form own agency, Ziegler, Hellman and Ross. Switched to feature prod. with The World of Henry Orient in 1964.
PICTURES: The World of Henry Orient, A Fine Madness, Midnight Cowboy (Academy Award for Best Picture, 1969), The Day of the Locust, Coming Home, Promises in the Dark (also dir.), The Mosquito Coast.

HELLMAN, MONTE
Director, Editor. b. New York, NY, 1932. e. Stanford Univ., UCLA. Started by working for Roger Corman's company as dir., editor, 2nd Unit dir. Replaced deceased directors on the films The Greatest, Avalanche Express. Dialogue Director: St. Valentine's Day Massacre. Acted in The Christian Licorice Store, Someone to Love.

PICTURES: *Director*: Beast from Haunted Cave, Back Door to Hell, Flight to Fury (also story) , Ride in the Whirlwind (also edit., prod.), The Shooting (also edit., prod.), Two-Lane Blacktop (also edit.), Cockfighter, China 9 Liberty 37 (also prod.), Iguana (also s.p., edit.), Silent Night Deadly Night 3 (also story). *Editor*: The Wild Angels, The Long Ride Home, How to Make It, The Killer Elite. *Second Unit Director*: Last Woman on Earth, Ski Troop Attack, Creature from the Haunted Sea, The Terror. *Exec. Prod.*: Reservoir Dogs.

HELMOND, KATHERINE
Actress. b. Galveston, TX, July 5, 1934. Initial stage work with Houston Playhouse and Margo Jones Theatre, Dallas. Joined APA Theatre, NY, and Trinity Square Rep. Co., RI, Hartford Stage, CT and Phoenix Rep. NY. In 1950s opened summer stock theatre in the Catskills. Taught acting at American Musical and Dramatic Acad., Brown U. and Carnegie-Mellon U. 1983, accepted into AFI's Directing Workshop for Women. Directed Bankrupt.
THEATER: The Great God Brown, House of Blue Leaves (Clarence Derwent, NY and LA Drama Critics Awards, 1972), Mixed Emotions.
PICTURES: The Hindenberg, Baby Blue Marine, Family Plot, Time Bandits, Brazil, Shadey, Overboard, Lady in White, Inside Monkey Zetterland, Amore!, The Flight of the Dove, Fear & Loathing in Las Vegas.
TELEVISION: *Series*: Soap, Who's The Boss? (also episode dir), Benson (episode dir. only), Coach. *Movies*: Dr. Max, Larry, Locusts, The Autobiography of Miss Jane Pittman, The Legend of Lizzie Borden, The Family Nobody Wanted, Cage Without a Key, The First 36 Hours of Dr. Durant, James Dean, Wanted: The Sundance Woman, Little Ladies of the Night, Getting Married, Diary of a Teenage Hitchhiker, Scout's Honor, World War III, For Lovers Only, Rosie: The Rosemary Clooney Story, Meeting of the Minds, Save the Dog, When Will I Be Loved?, The Perfect Tribute, Deception: A Mother's Secret, Grass Roots, Liz: The Elizabeth Taylor Story, Steven Spielberg's Director's Chair, Ms. Scrooge. *Special*: Christmas Snow.

HEMINGWAY, MARIEL
Actress. b. Ketchum, ID, Nov. 22, 1961. Granddaughter of writer Ernest Hemingway. Sister of late actress-model Margaux Hemingway.
PICTURES: Lipstick (debut, 1976), Manhattan (Acad. Award nom.), Personal Best, Star 80, The Mean Season, Creator, Superman IV: The Quest for Peace, Sunset, The Suicide Club (also co-prod.), Delirious, Falling From Grace, Naked Gun 33 1/3: The Final Insult, Deceptions II: Edge of Deception, Bad Moon, Road Ends, Little Men, Deconstructing Harry, Drop-Dead, American Reel.
TELEVISION: *Series*: Civil Wars, Central Park West. *Movies*: I Want to Keep My Baby, Steal the Sky, Into the Badlands, Desperate Rescue: The Cathy Mahone Story, September, The Crying Child. *Mini-Series*: Amerika. *Guest*: Tales From the Crypt, Roseanne.

HEMMINGS, DAVID
Actor, Director. b. Guildford, England, Nov.18, 1941. Early career in opera. Ent. m.p. ind. 1956. Former co-partner in Hemdale Company.
THEATER: Adventures in the Skin Trade, Jeeves.
PICTURES: Five Clues to Fortune, Saint Joan, The Heart Within, In the Wake of a Stranger, No Trees in the Street, Men of Tomorrow, The Wind of Change, The Painted Smile (Murder Can Be Deadly), Some People, Play It Cool, Two Left Feet, West 11, Live It Up (Sing and Swing), The System (The Girl-Getters), Be My Guest, Dateline Diamonds, Eye of the Devil, Blow-Up, Camelot, The Charge of the Light Brigade, Only When I Larf, Barbarella, The Long Day's Dying, The Best House in London, Alfred the Great, The Walking Stick, Fragment of Fear, The Love Machine, Unman Wittering and Zigo, Voices, Juggernaut, Running Scared (dir.only), The 14 (dir. only), Mr. Quilp, Deep Red, Islands in the Stream, The Squeeze, The Disappearance, Blood Relatives, Crossed Swords, Power Play, Murder by Decree, Just a Gigolo (also dir.), Thirst, Beyond Reasonable Doubt, The Survivor (dir. only), Harlequin, Race to the Yankee Zephyr (dir., prod. only), Man Woman and Child, Prisoners (also exec. prod.), Coup D'Grat (also prod.), The Rainbow, Dark Horse (dir. only).
TELEVISION: Auto Stop, The Big Toe, Out of the Unknown, Beverly Hills Cowgirl Blues, Clouds of Glory, Davy Crockett: Rainbow in the Thunder (also dir.). *Director only*: Hardball, Magnum PI, A-Team, Airwolf, Murder She Wrote, In the Heat of the Night, Quantum Leap, The Turn of the Screw, Tales From the Crypt, Passport to Murder (movie). *Guest*: Northern Exposure, The Raven, Ned Blessing.

HEMSLEY, SHERMAN
Actor. b. Philadelphia, PA, Feb. 1, 1938. On NY stage in Purlie.
PICTURES: Love at First Bite, Stewardess School, Ghost Fever, Mr. Nanny, Home Angels, Casper: A Spirited Beginning, Sprung.
TELEVISION: *Series*: All in the Family, The Jeffersons, Amen, Dinosaurs (voice), Townsend Television, Goode Behavior. *Guest*: The Rich Little Show, Love Boat, E/R, 227, Family Matters, Lois & Clark, Fresh Prince of Bel Air, Sister Sister. *Movies*: Alice in Wonderland, Combat High, Camp Cucamonga.

HENDERSON, FLORENCE
Actress, Singer. b. Dale, IN, Feb. 14, 1934. e. AADA. Made B'way debut while teenager in musical Wish You Were Here.
THEATER: Oklahoma!, The Great Waltz, Fanny, The Sound of Music, The Girl Who Came to Supper, South Pacific. Tour: Annie Get Your Gun.
PICTURES: Song of Norway, Shakes the Clown, Naked Gun 33 1/3: The Final Insult, The Brady Bunch Movie.
TELEVISION: Series: Sing Along, The Jack Paar Show, Oldsmobile Music Theatre, The Brady Bunch, The Brady Bunch Hour, The Brady Brides, Florence Henderson's Home Cooking, The Bradys. Movies: The Love Boat (pilot), The Brady Girls Get Married, A Very Brady Christmas, Fudge-A-Mania. Guest: Car 54 Where Are You?, Garry Moore Show, Ed Sullivan Show, Medical Center, The Love Boat, Fantasy Island, It's Garry Shandling's Show, Police Squad, many others. Specials: Huck Finn, Little Women, An Evening With Richard Rodgers, etc.

HENDERSON, SKITCH
Music Director. r.n. Lyle Cedric Henderson. b. Birmingham, England, Jan. 27, 1918. e. U. of California. Began as pianist in dance bands, then theatre orchestras, films and radio on West Coast. Accompanist to Judy Garland on tour. Served, USAF, WW II. Music dir. radio, Bing Crosby. Toured with own dance band, 47-49. Music Dir. for NBC Network, Steve Allen Show, Tonight Show, Today Show, Street Scene (NY Opera). Guest conductor, symphony orchestras including NY Philharmonic, London Philharmonic. Founder and Music Dir., NY Pops Orchestra. Music Dir., Florida Orchestra Pops, Virginia Symphony Pops, Louisville Orchestra Pops. Grammy Award for RCA album NY Philharmonic with Leontyne Price and William Warfield, highlights from Porgy and Bess. Instrumental works: Skitch's Blues, Minuet on the Rocks, Skitch in Time, Come Thursday, Curacao. Scores: American Fantasy, Act One (film).

HENNER, MARILU
Actress. b. Chicago, IL, Apr. 6, 1952. e. U. of Chicago. Studied singing and dancing, appearing in musicals in Chicago and on Broadway in Over Here and Pal Joey. Autobiography: By All Means Keep on Moving (1994).
PICTURES: Between the Lines (debut, 1977), Blood Brothers, Hammett, The Man Who Loved Women, Cannonball Run II, Johnny Dangerously, Rustler's Rhapsody, Perfect, L.A. Story, Noises Off, Chasers, Grease, Social Security, Chicago.
TELEVISION: Series: Taxi, Evening Shade, Marilu. Movies: Dream House, Stark, Love with a Perfect Stranger, Ladykillers, Chains of Gold, Abandoned and Deceived (co-exec. prod. only), Fight for Justice, Grand Larceny, My Son Is Innocent, For the Future: The Irvine Fertility Scandal. Mini-series: Titanic.

HENNING, LINDA
Actress, Singer. b. Toluca Lake, CA, Sept. 16, 1944. Daughter of prod. Paul Henning. e. Cal State Northridge, UCLA. Member of California Artists Radio Theatre.
THEATER: Gypsy, Applause, Damn Yankees, I Do, I Do, Pajama Game, Sugar, Wonderful Town, Fiddler on the Roof, Sound of Music, Vanities, Born Yesterday, Mary, Mary, Bus Stop, etc.
PICTURES: Bye Bye Birdie, Mad About You.
TELEVISION: Series: Petticoat Junction, Sliders. Guest: Beverly Hillbillies, Happy Days, Mork & Mindy, Double Trouble, Barnaby Jones, The New Gidget, Hunter. Pilots: Kudzu, The Circle, Family. Movie: The Return of the Beverly Hillbillies.

HENNING, PAUL
Producer, Writer. b. Independence, MO, Sept. 16, 1911. e. Kansas City Sch. of Law, grad. 1932. Radio singer and disc jockey. Also acted, ran sound effects, sang, wrote scripts. To Chicago 1937-38, to write for Fibber McGee and Molly. To Hollywood as writer for Rudy Vallee, 1939. Wrote scripts for Burns and Allen 10 years, including transition radio to TV.
PICTURES: Writer: Lover Come Back, Bedtime Story, Dirty Rotten Scoundrels.
TELEVISION: Series (creator, writer, prod.): The Bob Cummings Show, The Beverly Hillbillies, Petticoat Junction, Green Acres (exec. prod.)

HENRIKSEN, LANCE
Actor. b. New York, NY, May 5, 1943. Appeared on B'way in The Basic Training of Pavo Hummel, Richard III.
PICTURES: It Ain't Easy (debut, 1972), Dog Day Afternoon, The Next Man, Mansion of the Doomed, Close Encounters of the Third Kind, Damien: Omen II, The Visitor, The Dark End of the Street, Prince of the City, Piranha II: The Spawning, Nightmares, The Right Stuff, Savage Dawn, The Terminator, Jagged Edge, Choke Canyon, Aliens, Near Dark, Deadly Intent, Pumpkinhead, Hit List, The Horror Show, Johnny Handsome, Survival Quest, The Last Samurai, Stone Cold, Comrades in Arms, Delta Heat, Alien³, Jennifer Eight, Excessive Force, The Outfit, Super Mario Bros., Hard Target, Man's Best Friend, No Escape, Color of Night, The Quick and the Dead, Powder.
TELEVISION: Series: Millenium. Guest: Scene of the Crime, Paul Reiser: Out on a Whim, Tales From the Crypt (Cutting Cards). Movies: Return to Earth, Question of Honor, Blood Feud, Reason for Living: The Jill Ireland Story, Wes Craven Presents Mind Ripper.

HENRY, BUCK
Actor, Writer. b. New York, NY, Dec. 9, 1930. r.n. Henry Zuckerman. e. Dartmouth Coll. Acted in Life with Father, (tour, 1948), Fortress of Glass, Bernardine, B'way; 1952-54, U.S. Army; No Time for Sergeants (Nat'l. Co.), The Premise, improvisational theatre, off-B'way.
PICTURES: Actor: The Secret War of Harry Frigg, Taking Off, The Man Who Fell to Earth, Old Boyfriends, Gloria, Eating Raoul, Aria, Dark Before Dawn, Rude Awakening, Tune in Tomorrow, Defending Your Life, The Player, The Linguini Incident, Short Cuts, Even Cowgirls Get the Blues, Grumpy Old Men Shotgun Freeway: Drives Through Lost L.A., The Real Blonde, Later Life, I'm Losing You. Actor-Writer: The Troublemaker, The Graduate, Is There Sex After Death?,Catch-22, Heaven Can Wait (also dir.), First Family (also dir.), To Die For. Writer: Candy, The Owl and the Pussycat, What's Up Doc?, The Day of the Dolphin, Protocol.
TELEVISION: Series: (writer) Garry Moore Show, Steve Allen Show (also performer), The Bean Show, That Was the Week That Was (also performer), Get Smart (co-creator, story ed.), Captain Nice (also exec. prod.), Alfred Hitchcock Presents (1985, also actor), Quark, The New Show (also performer), Falcon Crest (actor only), Trying Times: Hunger Chic (dir. only). Guest: Saturday Night Live, Murphy Brown. Movies: Keep the Change, Harrison Bergeron. Special: Mastergate.

HENRY, JUSTIN
Actor. b. Rye, NY, May 25, 1971. Debut at age 8 in Kramer vs. Kramer, 1979 for which he received an Academy Award nomination.
PICTURES: Kramer vs Kramer, Sixteen Candles, Martin's Day, Sweet Hearts Dance.
TELEVISION: Movies: Tiger Town, Andersonville.

HENSON, LISA
Executive. b. 1960. e. Harvard U. Father was performer-puppeteer-director Jim Henson. Joined Warner Bros., 1983, as exec. asst. to head of prod. 1985, named dir. of creative affairs. 1985, promoted to v.p., prod. 1992, became exec. v.p., production. 1993, named pres. of worldwide prod. of Columbia Pictures. 1994, named pres. of Columbia Pictures. Resigned in 1996 to form own production company.

HEPBURN, KATHARINE
Actress. b. Hartford, CT, May 12, 1907. Author: The Making of the African Queen (1987), Me: Stories of My Life (1991). Received a record 12 Academy Award nominations for acting.
THEATER: Death Takes a Holiday, The Warrior's Husband, The Lake, The Philadelphia Story, As You Like It, The Millionairess, The Merchant of Venice, The Taming of the Shrew, Measure for Measure, Coco, A Matter of Gravity, West Side Waltz.
PICTURES: A Bill of Divorcement (debut, 1932), Christopher Strong, Morning Glory (Academy Award, 1933). Little Women, Spitfire, The Little Minister, Break of Hearts, Alice Adams, Sylvia Scarlett, Mary of Scotland, A Woman Rebels, Quality Street, Stage Door, Bringing Up Baby, Holiday, The Philadelphia Story, Woman of the Year, Keeper of the Flame, Stage Door Canteen, Dragon Seed, Without Love, Undercurrent, The Sea of Grass, Song of Love, State of the Union, Adam's Rib, The African Queen, Pat and Mike, Summertime, The Iron Petticoat, The Rainmaker, The Desk Set, Suddenly Last Summer, Long Day's Journey Into Night, Guess Who's Coming to Dinner (Academy Award, 1967), The Lion in Winter (Academy Award, 1968), The Madwoman of Chaillot, The Trojan Women, A Delicate Balance, Rooster Cogburn, Olly Olly Oxen Free, On Golden Pond (Academy Award, 1981), Grace Quigley, Love Affair.
TELEVISION: Movies: The Glass Menagerie, Love Among the Ruins (Emmy Award, 1975), The Corn Is Green, Mrs. Delafield Wants To Marry, Laura Lansing Slept Here, The Man Upstairs, This Can't Be Love, One Christmas. Special: Katharine Hepburn: All About Me (host, co-writer).

HERALD, PETER
Executive. b. Berlin, Germany, Dec. 20, 1930. e. UCLA, B.A. US Gov't. film officer in Europe 8 years. In charge of continental European prod. operation for Walt Disney Prods., 6 years. Supervisory prod. manager, Columbia Pictures, 3 years. Corporate Prod. mgr. Universal 3 years.
PICTURES: Executive-, Co-, Assoc.-, Line Producer and/or Production Mgr.: Almost Angels, Magnificent Rebel, Miracle of the White Stallions, Emil and the Detectives, There Was a Crooked Man, Outrageous Fortune, National Lampoon's Class Reunion, Doctor Detroit, D. C. Cab; The Great Waltz, Foul Play, Nightwing. W. W. and the Dixie Dancekings, Mandingo, W. C. Fields and Me, Alex and the Gypsy, Silver Streak, Star Wars, Stick, Married to It, many others.

HEREK, STEPHEN
Director. b. San Antonio, TX, Nov. 10, 1958.
PICTURES: Critters (debut, 1986), Bill & Ted's Excellent Adventure, Don't Tell Mom the Babysitter's Dead, The Mighty Ducks, The Three Musketeers, Mr. Holland's Opus, 101 Dalmatians, Holy Man.

HERMAN, NORMAN
Producer, Director. b. Newark, NJ. e. Rutgers U., NYU. Was accountant in California; in 1955 switched to film ind., joining American Int'l Pictures. Headed AIP prod. dept. 4 years, incl. prod., post-prod., labor negotiations, supervising story dept., etc. Pres. of Century Plaza Prods. for 9 yrs. Sr. v.p./staff writer DEG, 1986-9; Pres. No. Carolina Studios, 1989-90.
PICTURES: Prod. except as noted: Sierra Stranger, Hot Rod Girl, Hot Rod Rumble, Crime Beneath Seas, Look in any Window (exec. prod. mgr.), Tokyo After Dark (also dir., s.p.), Everybody Loves It (dir.), Mondy Teeno (also dir. co-s.p.), Glory Stompers, Three in the Attic (assoc. prod.), Pretty Boy Floyd, Dunwich Horror, Three in the Cellar, Angel Unchained, Psych-Out, Sadismo (s.p.), Bloody Mama, Bunny O'Hare, Killers Three, Frogs (exec. prod.), Planet of Life (s.p.), Blacula, Dillinger (s.p.), Legend of Hell House, Dirty Mary Crazy Larry, Rolling Thunder, In God We Trust (exec. prod.).
TELEVISION: Writer. Robert Taylor Detective, Iron Horse, Invaders, Adam 12, Lancer. Dir.-Prod.: Hannibal Cobb, You Are the Judge.

HEROUX, CLAUDE
Producer. b. Montreal, Canada, Jan. 26, 1942. e. U. of Montreal. 1979, prod. v.p., Film Plan Intl., Montreal.
PICTURES: Valerie, L'Initiation, L'Amour Humain, Je t'aime, Echoes of a Summer, Jacques Brel Is Alive and Well and Living in Paris, Breaking Point,Born for Hell, Hog Wild, City of Fire, Dirty Tricks, Gas, Visiting Hours, Videodrome, The Funny Farm, Going Berserk, Of Unknown Origin, Covergirl.
TELEVISION: The Park is Mine, Popeye Doyle, Desjardins.

HERRMANN, EDWARD
Actor. b. Washington, DC, July 21, 1943. Raised in Grosse Pointe, MI. e. Bucknell U. Postgrad. Fulbright scholar, London Acad. Music and Dramatic Art 1968-69. Acted with Dallas Theater Center for 4 years.
THEATER: NY: The Basic Training of Pavlo Hummel, Moonchildren, Mrs. Warren's Profession (Tony Award, 1976), Journey's End, The Beach House, The Philadelphia Story, Plenty, Tom and Viv, Julius Caesar, Not About Heroes, Life Sentences. London: A Walk in the Woods. Regional: many prods. with Williamstown Playhouse; Harvey, Twelfth Night, Love Letters, Three Sisters, Life Sentences, Psychopathia Sexualis.
PICTURES: Lady Liberty, The Paper Chase, The Day of the Dolphin, The Great Gatsby, The Great Waldo Pepper, The Betsy, Brass Target, Take Down, The North Avenue Irregulars, Harry's War, Reds, Death Valley, A Little Sex, Annie, Mrs. Soffel, The Purple Rose of Cairo, The Man With One Red Shoe, Compromising Positions, The Lost Boys, Overboard, Big Business, Hero (unbilled), Born Yesterday, My Boyfriend's Back, Foreign Student, Richie Rich, Critical Care, Frank Lloyd Wright, A Civil Action, Better Living.
TELEVISION: Series: Beacon Hill, Our Century (host), The Practice. Guest: M*A*S*H, St. Elsewhere. Mini-Series: Freedom Road. Movies: Eleanor and Franklin, Eleanor and Franklin: The White House Years, A Love Affair: The Eleanor and Lou Gehrig Story, Portrait of a Stripper, The Gift of Life, Memorial Day, So Proudly We Hail, Sweet Poison, Fire in the Dark, The Face on the Milk Carton, Hostile Waters, The Soul of the Game, Pandora's Clock, Liberty! The American Revolution. Specials: Sorrows of Gin, The Private History of The Campaign That Failed, Murrow, Dear Liar, Concealed Enemies, The Return of Hickey, The Beginning of the Firm, Last Act is a Solo, The End of a Sentence, A Foreign Field.

HERSHEY, BARBARA
Actress. r.n. Barbara Herzstein. b. Los Angeles, CA, Feb. 5, 1948. e. Hollywood H.S. m. painter Stephen Douglas. Briefly, in the mid-1970's, acted under the name Barbara Seagull.
PICTURES: With You Get Eggroll (debut, 1968), Heaven With a Gun, Last Summer, The Liberation of L.B. Jones, The Baby Maker, The Pursuit of Happiness, Dealing, Boxcar Bertha, Angela (Love Comes Quietly), The Crazy World of Julius Vrooder, Diamonds, You and Me, The Last Hard Men, Dirty Knights' Work, The Stunt Man, Americana, Take This Job and Shove It, The Entity, The Right Stuff, The Natural, Hannah and Her Sisters, Hoosiers, Tin Men, Shy People (Cannes Film Fest. Award, 1987), A World Apart (Cannes Film Fest. Award, 1988), The Last Temptation of Christ, Beaches, Tune in Tomorrow, Defenseless, The Public Eye, Falling Down, Swing Kids, Splitting Heirs, A Dangerous Woman, Last of the Dogmen, Portrait of a Lady (LA Film Critics Award; Natl Society of Film Critics Award; , The Pallbearer.
TELEVISION: Series: The Monroes, From Here to Eternity. Guest: Gidget, The Farmer's Daughter, Run for Your Life, The Invaders, Daniel Boone, CBS Playhouse, Chrysler Theatre, Kung Fu, Alfred Hitchcock Presents (1985). Movies: Flood, In the Glitter Palace, Just a Little Inconvenience, Sunshine Christmas, Angel on My Shoulder, My Wicked Wicked Ways... The Legend of Errol Flynn, Passion Flower, A Killing in a Small Town (Emmy & Golden Globe Awards, 1990), Paris Trout, Stay the Night. Mini-Series: A Man Called Intrepid, Return to Lonesome Dove. Special: Working.

HERSKOVITZ, MARSHALL
Producer, Director, Writer. b. Philadelphia, PA, Feb. 23, 1952. e. Brandeis U., BA, 1973; American Film Inst., MFA. 1975. Worked as freelance writer, dir., and prod. on several TV shows. Received Humanitas Award, 1983 and Writers Guild award, 1984.
PICTURE: Jack the Bear (dir.), Legends of the Fall (co-prod.), Dangerous Beauty, Shakespeare in Love.
TELEVISION: Family (writer, dir.), White Shadow (writer), Special Bulletin (prod., writer, 2 Emmys for writing and dramatic special), thirtysomething (exec. prod., co-writer, dir; 2 Emmy awards for writing and dramatic series, 1988; also Humanitas Award and Directors Guild Award, 1988 & 1989, Peabody Award, 1989.), My So-Called Life, Relativity.

HERTZ, WILLIAM
Executive. b. Wishek, ND, Dec. 5, 1923. Began theatre career in 1939 with Minnesota Amusement in Minneapolis; 1946 joined Fox West Coast Theatres; theatre mgr., booking dept.; 1965 appointed Los Angeles first-run district mgr.; promoted to Pacific Coast Division Mgr., National General Corp., 1967; v.p. Southern Pacific Div. Mgr., National General Theatres, Inc. 1971. Joined Mann Theatres as dir. of marketing, public relations, 1973-.

HERZFELD, JOHN
Writer, Director, Actor, Producer.
PICTURES: Writer. Voices, Hard Feelings, Two of a Kind (also dir.), The Last Winter, Ha-Kala, 2 Days in the Valley, Turbulence.
TELEVISION: Movies: Lieutenant Schuster's Wife (actor only), Cannonball (actor only), Shattered Spirits (actor only), Cobra (actor only), On Fire (also actor), Daddy (also dir.), The Ryan White Story (also actor, dir.), The Preppie Murder (also dir.), Casualties of Love: The Long Island Lolita Story (also dir., prod.), Barbara Taylor Bradford's 'Remember,' (also dir.), Don King: Only in America (dir. only, Directors' Guild Award, 1998). Series: Tales from the Crypt (dir.)

HERZOG, WERNER
Director, Producer, Writer. r.n. Werner Stipetic. b. Sachrang, Germany, September 5, 1942. e. U. of Munich, Duquesne U., Pittsburgh. Wrote first s.p. 1957; 1961 worked nights in steel factory to raise money for films; 1966, worked for U.S. National Aeronautics and Space Admin.
PICTURES: Signs of Life (debut, 1968), Precautions Against Fanatics, Even Dwarfs Started Small (also composer), Fata Morgana, The Land of Silence and Darkness, Aguirre—Wrath of God, The Great Ecstasy of Woodcarver Steiner, The Mysery of Kasper Hauser, Nobody Wants to Play With Me, How Much Wood Would a Woodchuck Chuck, Heart of Glass, Stroszek, La Soufriere, Nosferatu: The Vampyre (also cameo), Woyzeck, Garlic Is As Good As Ten Mothers (actor), Werner Herzog Eats His Shoe (actor), Fitzcarraldo, Burden of Dreams (actor), Man of Flowers (actor), Tokyo-Ga (actor), Where the Green Ants Dream, Les Gauloises, Cobra Verde, Scream of Stone, Lessons in Darkness, Bride of the Orient (actor), It Isn't Easy Being God (actor), Echoes of a Somber Empire, Burning Heart (actor), Little Dieter Needs to Fly.
TELEVISION: Movies: Huie's Sermon, God's Angry Man, Chambre 666, The Dark Glow of the Mountains, Ballad of the Little Soldier, Herdsmen of the Sun, The Transformation of the World Into Music (actor), Death for Five Voices, and many others.

HESSEMAN, HOWARD
Actor. b. Salem, OR, Feb. 27, 1940. Started with the San Francisco group, The Committee and worked as a disc jockey in San Francisco in the late 1960s.
PICTURES: Petulia, Billy Jack, Steelyard Blues, Shampoo, The Sunshine Boys, Jackson County Jail, The Big Bus, The Other Side of Midnight, Silent Movie, Honky Tonk Freeway, Private Lessons, Loose Shoes, Doctor Detroit, This is Spinal Tap, Police Academy 2: Their First Assignment, Clue, My Chauffeur, Flight of the Navigator, Heat, Amazon Women on the Moon, Rubin and Ed, Little Miss Millions.
TELEVISION: Series: WKRP in Cincinnati, One Day at a Time, Head of the Class. Guest: Mary Hartman Mary Hartman, Fernwood 2night, George Burns Comedy Week. Movies: Hustling, The Blue Knight (pilot), Tail Gunner Joe, The Amazing Howard Hughes, Tarantulas: The Deadly Cargo, The Ghost on Flight 401, The Comedy Company, More Than Friends, Outside Chance, The Great American Traffic Jam, Victims, One Shoe Makes It Murder, Best Kept Secrets, The Diamond Trap, Call Me Anna, Murder in New Hampshire: The Pamela Smart Story, Quiet Killer, Lethal Exposure.

HESSLER, GORDON
Producer, Director. b. Berlin, Germany, 1930. e. Reading U., England. Dir., vice pres., Fordel Films, Inc., 1950-58; dir., St. John's Story (Edinborough Film Festival), March of Medicine Series, Dr. Albert Lasker Award; story edit., Alfred Hitchcock Presents 1960-62; assoc. prod., dir., Alfred Hitchcock Hour, 1962; prod., Alfred Hitchcock Hour; prod., dir., Universal TV 1964-66.
PICTURES: The Woman Who Wouldn't Die, The Last Shot You Hear, The Oblong Box, Scream and Scream Again, Cry of the Banshee, Murders of the Rue Morgue, Sinbad's Golden Voyage, Medusa, Embassy, Puzzle, Pray for Death, Rage of Honour, The Misfit Brigade, The Girl in a Swing (also s.p.), Out on Bail, Mayeda, Journey of Honor.

TELEVISION: *Series:* Alfred Hitchcock Presents (1960-62), Alfred Hitchcock Hour, Run for Your Life, Convoy, Bob Hope Chrysler Show, ABC Suspense Movies of the Week, ABC Movies of the Week, Lucas Tanner, Night Stalker, Amy Prentiss, Switch, Kung Fu, Sara, Hawaii Five-O, Blue Knight, Wonder Woman, Master, CHiPs, Tales of the Unexpected, Equilizer. *Pilots:* Tender Warriors.

HESTON, CHARLTON
Actor. b. Evanston, IL, Oct. 4, 1924. e. Northwestern U. Sch. of Speech. Radio, stage, TV experience. Following coll. served 8 yrs. 11th Air Force, Aleutians. After war, dir. and co-starred with wife at Thomas Wolfe Memorial Theatre, Asheville, NC in State of the Union, Glass Menagerie; member, Katharine Cornell's Co., during first year on Broadway; Anthony and Cleopatra, other Bway. plays, Leaf and Bough, Cockadoodle Doo; Studio One (TV): Macbeth, Taming of the Shrew, Of Human Bondage, Julius Caesar. Pres. Screen Actors Guild 1966-71; Member, Natl. Council on the Arts, 1967-72; Trustee: Los Angeles Center Theater Group, American Film Inst. 1971, chmn. 1981-; Received Jean Hersholt Humanitarian award, 1978. Pres., Nat'l Rifle Assoc., 1998-. *Autobiographies:* The Actor's Life (1978), In the Arena (1995).
RECENT THEATER: A Man for All Seasons, The Caine Mutiny (dir., in China).
PICTURES: Dark City (debut, 1950), The Greatest Show on Earth, The Savage, Ruby Gentry, The President's Lady, Pony Express, Arrowhead, Bad for Each Other, The Naked Jungle, The Secret of the Incas, The Far Horizons, Lucy Gallant, The Private War of Major Benson, The Ten Commandments, Three Violent People, Touch of Evil, The Big Country, The Buccaneer, Ben-Hur (Academy Award, 1959), The Wreck of the Mary Deare, El Cid, The Pigeon That Took Rome, 55 Days at Peking, Major Dundee, The Agony and the Ecstasy, The War Lord, The Greatest Story Ever Told, Khartoum, Counterpoint, Planet of the Apes, Will Penny, Number One, Beneath the Planet of the Apes, Julius Caesar, The Hawaiians, The Omega Man, Antony and Cleopatra (also dir.), Skyjacked, Soylent Green, The Three Musketeers, Airport 1975, Earthquake, The Four Musketeers, The Last Hard Men, Midway, Two Minute Warning, Crossed Swords (The Prince and the Pauper), Gray Lady Down, Mountain Men, The Awakening, Mother Lode (also dir.), Almost an Angel (cameo), Solar Crisis, Wayne's World 2 (cameo), Tombstone, True Lies, In the Mouth of Madness, Alaska, Hamlet.
TELEVISION: *Series:* The Colbys. *Mini-Series:* Chiefs. *Movies:* The Nairobi Affair, The Proud Men, A Man For All Seasons (also dir.), Original Sin, Treasure Island, The Little Kidnappers, The Crucifer of Blood, Crash Landing: The Rescue of Flight 232, The Avenging Angel, Texas (narrator). *Special:* Charlton Heston Presents the Bible (also writer).

HEYER, STEVEN
Executive. b. New York, NY, June 13, 1952. e. Cornell U., BS industrial relations, 1974; Stern Sch. of Business at NYU, MBA, 1976. Various positions with Booz, Allen & Hamilton, finally SVP/managing partner, 1976-92. Pres./COO Young & Rubicam Adv. Worldwide and exec. VP Young & Rubicam, Inc., 1992-94. Pres., Turner Broadcasting Sales Inc., 1994-98. Pres., worldwide sales/mktng./distribution/int'l. networks, Turner Broadcasting System, 1996-98. Pres/COO Turner Broadcasting System Inc., 1998-.

HEYMAN, JOHN
Producer. b. Germany, 1933. e. Oxford U. Started with Independent British Television creating,. writing and producing entertainment and documentary programs. Had 5 top-ten programs 1955-57. Expanded into personal management, forming International Artists, representing Elizabeth Taylor, Richard Burton, Richard Harris, Shirley Bassey, Laurence Harvey, Trevor Howard, among others. In 1963, formed World Film Services Ltd. to produce package and finance films and World Film Sales Ltd., the first major independent film sales co. Co-financed 250 major studio films 1969-91. In 1973, formed Genesis Project. In 1989 co-founded Island World and Islet. Island sold to Polygram, and in 1994, formed World Group of Companies Ltd., parent co. to World Production Ltd.
PICTURES: Privilege, Boom!, Secret Ceremony, Twinky, Bloomfield, The Go-Between (Grand Prix, Cannes 1971), Superstars, Hitler: The Last Ten Days, Black Gunn, Divorce His, Divorce Hers, The Hireling (Grand Prix, Cannes 1973), A Doll's House, Daniel, Beyond the Limit, The Dresser, A Passage to India (co-prod.), Martin's Day, Steaming, D.A.R.Y.L., Saturday Night Fever, Grease, Heaven Can Wait, Home Alone, Reds.

HICKS, CATHERINE
Actress. b. New York NY, Aug. 6, 1951. e. St. Mary's Notre Dame; Cornell U. (2 year classical acting prog.). On B'way. in Tribute, Present Laughter.
PICTURES: Death Valley, Better Late Than Never, Garbo Talks, The Razor's Edge, Fever Pitch, Peggy Sue Got Married, Star Trek IV: The Voyage Home, Like Father Like Son, Child's Play, She's Out of Control, Cognac, Liebestraum.
TELEVISION: *Series:* Ryan's Hope (1976-8), The Bad News Bears, Tucker's Witch, Seventh Heaven. *Movies:* Love for Rent, To Race the Wind, Marilyn- the Untold Story, Valley of the Dolls 1981, Happy Endings, Laguna Heat, Spy, Hi Honey I'm Dead, Redwood Curtain. *Pilot:* The Circle Game.

HICKS, SCOTT
Director, Writer, Producer. b. Australia, March 4, 1953.
PICTURES: *Director:* Down the Wind (also prodr.), Freedom, Call Me Mr. Brown (also writer), Sebastian and the Sparrow (also writer & prodr.), Shine (also writer; Golden Globe nom., Acad. Award nom), Snow Falling on Cedars, Arkansas.

HILL, ARTHUR
Actor. b. Melfort, Saskatchewan, Canada, Aug. 1, 1922. e. U. of British Columbia. Moved to England in 1948, spending ten years in varied stage & screen pursuits
THEATER: *B'way:* The Matchmaker, Home of the Brave, The Male Animal, Look Homeward Angel, All the Way Home, Who's Afraid of Virginia Woolf? (Tony Award, 1963), More Stately Mansions.
PICTURES: Miss Pilgrim's Progress, Scarlet Thread, Mr. Drake's Duck, A Day to Remember, Life With the Lyons, The Crowded Day, The Deep Blue Sea, Raising a Riot, The Young Doctors, The Ugly American, In the Cool of the Day, Moment to Moment, Harper, Petulia, The Chairman, Rabbit Run, The Pursuit of Happiness, The Andromeda Strain, The Killer Elite, Futureworld, A Bridge Too Far, A Little Romance, Butch and Sundance: The Early Days, The Champ, Dirty Tricks, Making Love, The Amateur, Something Wicked This Way Comes (narrator), One Magic Christmas.
TELEVISION: *Series:* Owen Marshall: Counselor-At-Law, Hagen, Glitter. *Movies:* The Other Man, Vanished, Ordeal, Owen Marshall: Counselor at Law (pilot; a.k.a. A Pattern of Morality), Death Be Not Proud, Judge Horton and the Scottsboro Boys, Tell Me My Name, The Ordeal of Dr. Mudd, Revenge of the Stepford Wives, The Return of Frank Cannon, Angel Dusted, Tomorrow's Child, Intimate Agony, Prototype, Love Leads the Way, Murder in Space, Churchill and the Generals, The Guardian, Perry Mason: The Case of the Notorious Nun.

HILL, BERNARD
Actor. b. Manchester, England,. Dec. 17, 1944. Joined amateur dramatic society in Manchester then studied drama at Manchester Art Coll. Joined Liverpool Everyman rep. co. West End debut as John Lennon in John, Paul, George, Ringo... and Burt. Also in Normal Service, Twelfth Night, Macbeth, Cherry Orchard, Gasping, A View From the Bridge.
PICTURES: Gandhi, The Bounty, The Chain, Restless Natives, No Surrender, Bellman and True, Drowning by Numbers, Shirley Valentine, Mountains of the Moon, Double X: The Name of the Game, Skallagrigg, Madagascar Skin, The Ghost and the Darkness, Titanic.
TELEVISION: I Claudius, Squaring the Circle, John Lennon: A Journey in the Life, New World, St. Luke's Gospel, Boys from the Blackstuff, Burston Rebellion.

HILL, DEBRA
Producer, Director, Writer. b. Philadelphia, PA. Career on feature films started with work as script supvr., asst. dir. and 2nd unit dir. of 13 pictures. Producer's debut with Halloween, 1980, for which also co-wrote script with dir. John Carpenter.
PICTURES: Halloween (also co-s.p.), The Fog (also co-s.p.), Escape from New York, Halloween II (and co-s.p.), Halloween III: Season of the Witch, The Dead Zone, Clue, Head Office, Adventures in Babysitting, Big Top Pee-wee, Heartbreak Hotel, Gross Anatomy, The Fisher King, Escape From L.A., Replacement Killers, Crazy in Alabama.
TELEVISION: Adventures in Babysitting (pilot, exec. prod.), Monsters (dir. episodes), Dream On (dir. episodes). *Movies:* El Diablo, Attack of the 50 Ft. Woman. *Rebel Highway Film Series:* Roadracers, Confessions of a Sorority Girl (also co-writer), Dragstrip Girl, Shake Rattle and Roll, The Cool and the Crazy, Runaway Daughters, Motocycle Gang, Drag Strip Girl, Reform School Girl, Jailbreakers (also co-writer), Girls in Prison.

HILL, GEORGE ROY
Director. b. Minneapolis, MN, Dec. 20, 1921. e. Yale U., Trinity Coll., Dublin. Started as actor, Irish theatres and U.S. Margaret Webster's Shakespeare Repertory Co., also off-B'way. Served as Marine pilot in WWII and Korean War. Wrote TV play, My Brother's Keeper, for Kraft Theatre, later rose to dir. with show.
THEATER: Look Homeward Angel (B'way debut, 1957), The Gang's All Here, Greenwillow, Period of Adjustment, Moon on a Rainbow Shawl (also prod.), Henry Sweet Henry.
PICTURES: Period of Adjustment (debut, 1962), Toys in the Attic, The World of Henry Orient, Hawaii, Thoroughly Modern Millie, Butch Cassidy and the Sundance Kid, Slaughterhouse Five, The Sting (Academy Award, 1973), The Great Waldo Pepper (also prod., story), Slap Shot, A Little Romance (also co-exec. prod.), The World According to Garp (also co-prod., cameo), The Little Drummer Girl, Funny Farm.
TELEVISION: *Writer-Dir.:* A Night to Remember, The Helen Morgan Story, Judgment at Nuremberg, Child of Our Time.

HILL, TERENCE
Actor, Director. r.n. Mario Girotti. b. Venice, March 29, 1939. Debuted as actor under his real name. First attracted attention as actor in Visconti's The Leopard, 1963. Gained fame in European-made westerns. Formed Paloma Films.

PICTURES: *as Mario Girotti:* Vacanze col Gangster (debut, 1951), Villa Borghese, Il Viale della speranza, La Vena d'oro, The Wide Blue Road, Mary Magdalene, Anna of Brooklyn, Hannibal, Pecado de amor, Carthage in Flames, Joseph and His Brethren, The Wonders of Aladdin, Seven Seas to Calais, The Leopard, Games of Desire, Last of the Renegades, Arizona Wildcat, Duell vor Sonnenuntergang, Ruf de Walder, Rampage at Apache Wells, Flaming Frontier, Whom the Gods Destroy, Blood River; *as Terence Hill:* The Crazy Kids of the War, Io non protesto io amo, Preparati la bara!, Rita in the West, God Forgives I Don't, Viva Django, Boot Hill, Ace High, Barbagia, Blackie the Pirate, Anger of the Wind, They Call Me Trinity, The True and the False, A Reason to Live a Reason to Die, Trinity Is Still My Name, Man of the East, Baron Blood, All the Way Boys!, My Name Is Nobody, The Two Missionaries, The Genius, Crime Busters, Mr. Billion, March or Die, Odds & Evens, I'm for the Hippopotamus, Super Fuzz, Watch Out We're Mad, Double Trouble, Don Camillo (also dir.), Miami Supercops, Renegade Luke (also exec. prod.), Go for It!, Lucky Luke (also dir.), The F(N)ight Before Christmas (also dir.), Botte di Natale, Troublemakers.

HILL, WALTER
Director, Writer, Producer. b. Long Beach, CA, Jan. 10, 1942. e. Michigan State U.; Mexico City College; U. of the Americas.
PICTURES: *Writer.* Hickey and Boggs, Thief Who Came to Dinner, The Getaway (1972), The Mackintosh Man, The Drowning Pool, Blue City (also prod.), Alien 3 (also prod.), The Getaway (1993; co-s.p.). *Writer/Dir.:* Hard Times, The Driver, The Warriors, Southern Comfort , 48 HRS, Streets of Fire (also exec. prod.), Red Heat (also prod.). *Director.* The Long Riders, Brewster's Millions, Crossroads, Extreme Prejudice, Johnny Handsome, Another 48 HRS, Trespass, Geronimo: An American Legend (also co-prod.), Wild Bill, Last Man Standing. *Other.* Alien (prod.), Aliens (exec. prod., story), Tales From the Crypt Presents Demon Knight (co-exec. prod.).
TELEVISION: *Series*: Dog and Cat (creator, writer), Tales From the Crypt (exec. prod.; also dir. & writer of episodes: The Man Who Was Death, Cutting Cards, Deadline (Cable ACE Award, Best Dir.).

HILLER, ARTHUR
Director. b. Edmonton, Alberta, Can., Nov. 22, 1923. e. U. of Alberta, U. of Toronto, U. of British Columbia. Worked for Canadian Broadcasting Corp. as dir. of live tv before moving to L.A. Pres. of DGA. 1993, became pres. of AMPAS. Appeared in Beverly Hills Cop III.
PICTURES: The Careless Years (debut, 1957), Miracle of the White Stallions, The Wheeler Dealers, The Americanization of Emily, Promise Her Anything, Penelope, Tobruk, The Tiger Makes Out, Popi, The Out-of-Towners, Love Story, Plaza Suite, The Hospital, Man of La Mancha, The Crazy World of Julius Vrooder (also co-prod.), The Man in the Glass Booth, W. C. Fields and Me, Silver Streak, Nightwing, The In-Laws (also co-prod.), Making Love, Author Author, Romantic Comedy, The Lonely Guy (also prod.), Teachers, Outrageous Fortune, See No Evil Hear No Evil, Taking Care of Business, The Babe, Married to It, Beverly Hills Cop III (actor only), Wild Bill: A Hollywood Maverick (actor only), Carpool, An Alan Smithee Film: Burn Hollywood Burn.
TELEVISION: Matinee Theatre, Playhouse 90, Climax, Alfred Hitchcock Presents, Gunsmoke, Ben Casey, Rte. 66, Naked City, The Dick Powell Show, Roswell (actor only), Frank Capra's American Dream (actor only).

HILLER, DAME WENDY
Actress. D.B.E., 1975, O.B.E., 1971, Hon. LLD, Manchester, 1984. b. Bramhall, Cheshire, Eng., Aug. 15, 1912. e. Winceby House Sch., Bexhill. On stage 1930, Manchester Repertory Theatre, England; then on British tour. London debut 1935 in Love On the Dole; to N.Y., same role 1936. m.p. debut in Lancashire Luck, 1937.
THEATER: First Gentleman, Cradle Song, Tess of the D'Urbervilles, Heiress (NY & London), Ann Veronica, Waters of the Moon, Night of the Ball, Old Vic Theatre, Wings of the Dove, Sacred Flame, Battle of Shrivings, Crown Matrimonial, John Gabriel Borkman, Waters of the Moon (revival), Aspern Papers (revival), The Importance of Being Earnest, Driving Miss Daisy.
PICTURES: Lancashire Luck (debut, 1937), Pygmalion, Major Barbara, I Know Where I'm Going, Outcast of the Islands, Single Handed (Sailor of the King), Something of Value, How to Murder a Rich Uncle, Separate Tables (Academy Award, best supporting actress, 1958) Sons and Lovers, Toys in the Attic, A Man For All Seasons, Murder on the Orient Express, Voyage of the Damned, The Cat and the Canary, The Elephant Man, Making Love, The Lonely Passion of Judith Hearne.
TELEVISION: The Curse of King Tut's Tomb, David Copperfield (theatrical in U.K.), Witness for the Prosecution, Anne of Green Gables-The Sequel, Peer Gynt, The Kingfisher, All Passion Spent, A Taste for Death, Ending Up, The Best of Friends, The Countess Alice.

HILLERMAN, JOHN
Actor. b. Denison, TX, Dec. 20, 1932. e. U. of Texas. While in U.S. Air Force joined community theatre group and went to New York after completing military service. Studied at American Theatre Wing, leading to summer stock and off-B'way.
PICTURES: The Last Picture Show, Lawman, The Carey Treatment, What's Up Doc?, Skyjacked, High Plains Drifter, The Outside Man, The Thief Who Came to Dinner, Paper Moon, Blazing Saddles, Chinatown, At Long Last Love, The Nickel Ride, The Day of the Locust, Lucky Lady, Audrey Rose, Sunburn, History of the World Part I, Up the Creek.
TELEVISION: *Series*: Ellery Queen, The Betty White Show, Magnum P.I. (Emmy Award, 1987), The Hogan Family. *Movies*: Sweet Sweet Rachel, The Great Man's Whiskers, The Law, Ellery Queen, The Invasion of Johnson County, Relentless, Kill Me If You Can, A Guide for the Married Woman, Betrayal, Marathon, The Murder That Wouldn't Die, Little Gloria... Happy at Last, Assault and Matrimony, Street of Dreams, Hands of a Murderer. *Mini-Series*: Around the World in 80 Days.

HILLMAN, WILLIAM BRYON
Writer, Director, Producer. b. Chicago, IL, Feb. 3, 1951. e. Oklahoma Military Acad., UCLA. Head of production at Intro-Media Prod.; Fairchild Ent.; Spectro Prod.; Double Eagle Ent. Corp; Excellent Films Inc.; Creative consultant for The Hit 'Em Corp. Presently head of SpectroMedia Ent.
AUTHOR: *Novels:* Silent Changes, The Combination, The Liar, Additives The Perfect Crime, Why Me, The Loner.
PICTURES: *Dir.-Writer.* His Name is Joey (also exec. prod.), Tis the Season (also co-prod.), Strangers (also co-prod.), Back on the Street (also co-prod.), Loner (also co-prod.), Fast & Furious, The Master, Lovelines (s.p. only), Double Exposure (also co-prod.), The Passage, Campus, The Photographer (also prod.), The Man From Clover Grove (also co-prod.), Thetus, The Trail Ride (also co-prod.), Betta Betta (also prod.), Ragin' Cajun (also co-prod.).
TELEVISION: Working Together (pilot writer), Disco-Theque Pilot (dir., writer), Everything Will Be Alright (writer), Money (dir., writer), RIPA (writer).

HINDERY, LEO JOSEPH , JR.
Media Co. Executive. b. Springfield, Ill, Oct. 31, 1947. e. Seattle U, BA 1969; Stanford U, MBA 1971. With US army, 1968-70. Asst. treas., Utah Internat, 1971-80. Treas. Natomas Co., 1980-82. Exec. v.p. fin. Jefferies & Co., 1982-83. Chief fin. officer A.G. Becker Paribas, 1983-85. Chief officer. planning & fin. Chronicle Pub. Co., 1985-88. Mng. gen. ptnr. Intermedia Ptnrs., 1988-. Bd. dirs.: Certus Fin. Corp.; Trustee Seattle U. Mem., Olympic club.

HINES, GREGORY
Actor, Dancer. b. NY, Feb. 14, 1946. Early career as junior member of family dancing act starting at age 2. Nightclub debut at 5 as Hines Kids with brother Maurice (later renamed Hines Brothers as teenagers) and joined by father as Hines, Hines and Dad. B'way debut at 8 in The Girl in Pink Tights. Continued dancing with brother until 1973. Formed and performed with jazz-rock band, Severance. Solo album, Gregory Hines (1988).
THEATER: The Last Minstral Show (closed out of town). B'way: Eubie (Theatre World Award), Comin' Uptown (Tony nom.), Sophisticated Ladies (Tony nom.), Twelfth Night, Jelly's Last Jam (Tony Award, 1992).
PICTURES: History of the World Part 1 (debut, 1981), Wolfen, Deal of the Century, The Muppets Take Manhattan, The Cotton Club (also choreog.), White Nights, Running Scared, Off Limits, Tap (also choreog.), Eve of Destruction, A Rage in Harlem, Renaissance Man, Waiting to Exhale, Mad Dog Time, The Preacher's Wife.
TELEVISION: *Movies*: White Lie, T Bone N Weasel, Dead Air, A Stranger in Town. *Guest*: The Tonight Show, Motown Returns to the Apollo, Saturday Night Live. *Series*: The Gregory Hines Show.

HINGLE, PAT
Actor. b. Miami, FL, July 19, 1924. e. U. of Texas, 1949. Studied at Herbert Berghof Studio, American Theatre Wing, Actor's Studio.
THEATER: End as a Man (N.Y. debut, 1953), The Rainmaker, Festival, Cat on a Hot Tin Roof, Girls of Summer, Dark at the Top of the Stairs, J.B., The Deadly Game, Macbeth and Troilus and Cressida (with American Shakespeare Festival, Stratford, CT), Strange Interlude, Blues for Mr. Charlie, A Girl Could Get Lucky, The Glass Menagerie, The Odd Couple, Johnny No-Trump, The Price, Child's Play, The Selling of the President, That Championship Season, The Lady from the Sea, A Life, Thomas Edison: Reflections of a Genius (one man show).
RADIO: Voice of America.
PICTURES: On the Waterfront (debut, 1954), The Strange One, No Down Payment, Splendor in the Grass, All the Way Home, The Ugly American, Invitation to a Gunfighter, Nevada Smith, Sol Madrid, Hang 'em High, Jigsaw, Norwood, Bloody Mama, WUSA, The Carey Treatment, One Little Indian, Running Wild, Nightmare Honeymoon, The Super Cops, The Gauntlet, When You Comin' Back Red Ryder?, Norma Rae, America: Lost and Found (narrator), Sudden Impact, Running Brave, Going Berserk, The Falcon and the Snowman, Brewster's Millions, Maximum Overdrive, Baby Boom, The Land Before Time (voice), Batman, The Grifters, Batman Returns, Lightning Jack, The Quick and the Dead, Batman Forever, Larger Than Life, Batman & Robin, A Thousand Acres.

TELEVISION: *Series*: Stone. *Guest*: Gunsmoke, MASH, Blue Skies, Matlock, Twilight Zone, The Untouchables, Trapper John M.D., Murder She Wrote, In the Heat of the Night, Cheers, Wings, American Gothic. *Movies*: The Ballad of Andy Crocker, A Clear and Present Danger, The City, Sweet Sweet Rachel, If Tomorrow Comes, Trouble Comes to Town, The Last Angry Man, The Secret Life of John Chapman, Escape from Bogen County, Sunshine Christmas, Tarantulas, Elvis, Stone (pilot), Disaster at the Coastliner, Wild Times, Of Mice and Men, Washington Mistress, The Fighter, Stranger on My Land, The Town Bully, Everybody's Baby: The Rescue of Jessica McClure, Not of This World, Gunsmoke: To the Last Man, Citizen Cohn, The Habitation of Dragons, Simple Justice, Against Her Will: The Carrie Buck Story, Truman. *Mini-Series*: War and Remembrance, The Kennedy's of Massachusetts, The Shining.

HINKLE, ROBERT
Actor, Producer, Director. b. Brownfield, TX, July 25, 1930. e. Texas Tech. U. Joined Rodeo Cowboys Association, 1950 and rodeoed professionally until 1953 when began acting career in Outlaw Treasure. Pres. Cinema Pictures, Inc.
PICTURES: *Actor*: Giant, All the Fine Young Cannibals, Hud, The First Texan, Dakota Incident, Gun the Man Down, The Oklahoman, First Traveling Saleslady, No Place to Land, Under Fire, Speed Crazy, The Gunfight at Dodge City, Broken Land, Law in Silver City, *Producer-Director*: Ole Rex, Born Hunter, Trauma, Something Can Be Done, Mr. Chat, Stuntman, Jumping Frog Jubilee, Mr. Chat-Mexico Safari, Trail Ride, Virginia City Cent., Texas Today, Texas Long Horns, Kentucky Thoroughbred Racing, Country Music, Guns of a Stranger.
TELEVISION: *Prod. & Dir.*: Test Pilot, Dial 111, Juvenile Squad, X13 Vertijet, Cellist Extraordinary, Sunday Challenge, The Drifter, Country Music Tribute, World of Horses, Country Music Videos.

HIRD, DAME THORA
Actress. b. Morecambe, Lancashire, England,, May28, 1911. e. The Nelson Sch., Morecambe.
PICTURES: (Screen debut, 1940) The Black Sheep of Whitehall; Street Corner, Turn the Key Softly, Personal Affair, The Great Game, Storks Don't Talk, Shop Soiled, For Better or Worse; Love Match, One Good Turn, Quatermass Experiment, Simon and Laura, Lost, Sailor Beware, Home and Away, Good Companions, The Entertainer, A Kind of Loving, Term of Trial, Bitter Harvest, Rattle of a Simple Man, Some Will Some Won't, The Nightcomers, Consuming Passions.
TELEVISION: The Winslow Boy, The Bachelor, What Happens to Love, The Witching Hour, So Many Children, The Queen Came By, Albert Hope, All Things Bright and Beautiful, Say Nothing, Meet the Wife, Who's a Good Boy Then? I AM! Dixon of Dock Green, Romeo and Juliet, The First Lady, Ours Is a Nice House, The Foxtrot, Seasons, She Stoops to Conquer, Villa Maroc, When We Are Married, In Loving Memory, Flesh and Blood, Your Songs of Praise Choice, Hallelujah, Happiness, That's the Main Thing, Intensive Care, In Loving Memory, Praise Be, Last of the Summer Wine, The Fall, Cream Cracker Under the Settee (Talking Heads), Perfect Scoundrels, Wide Eyed and Legless... It's a Girl, Pat & Margaret, Thora on the Broad 'n' Narrow... South Bank Show.

HIRSCH, JUDD
Actor. b. New York, NY, March 15, 1935. e. City Coll. of New York. Studied physics but turned to acting; studied at Amer. Acad. of Dramatic Arts., HB Studios. First acting job in 1962 in Crisis in the Old Sawmill in Estes, Colorado; then to Woodstock Playhouse, before returning to N.Y.C.
THEATER: *NY*: On the Necessity of Being Polygamous, Barefoot in the Park, Scuba Duba, Mystery Play, HotL Baltimore, King of the United States, Prodigal, Knock Knock, Chapter Two, Talley's Folly (Obie Award), I'm Not Rappaport (Tony Award), Conversations With My Father (Tony Award).
PICTURES: Serpico (debut, 1973), King of the Gypsies, Ordinary People (Acad. Award nom.), Without a Trace, The Goodbye People, Teachers, Running on Empty, Independence Day.
TELEVISION: *Series*: Delvecchio, Taxi (2 Emmy Awards: 1981, 1983), Detective in the House, Dear John, George & Leo. *Movies*: The Law, Fear on Trial, Legend of Valentino, The Keegans, Sooner or Later, Marriage is Alive and Well, Brotherly Love, First Steps, The Great Escape II: The Untold Story, She Said No, Betrayal of Trust, Color of Jusitce. *Special*: The Halloween That Almost Wasn't.

HIRSCHFIELD, ALAN J.
Executive. b. Oklahoma City, OK; Oct.10, 1935. e. U. of Oklahoma, B.A.; Harvard Business School, M.B.A. V.P., Allen & Co., 1959-66; Financial v.p. & dir. Warner/7 Arts, 1967-68; v.p. & dir., American Diversified Enterprises, 1969-73; pres. & chief exec. officer, Columbia Pictures Industries, 1973-78; consultant, Warner Communications, 1979, 1980-85, chmn. and chief exec. officer, 20th Century-Fox. Current: Co-CEO Data Broadcasting Corp. Dir., Cantel Inc., Chyron Corp.

HIRSHAN, LEONARD
Theatrical Agent. b. New York, NY, Dec.27, 1927. e. NYU. Joined William Morris Agency as agent trainee, New York, 1951. Agent legit theatre & TV dept. 1952-54. Sr. exec. agent M.P. dept., California office, 1955; sr. v.p., 1983; head of m.p. dept., west coast, 1986; named exec. v.p. and mem. bd. of dir., William Morris Agency, 1989; mem. bd. of dir., Center Theater Group, 1988; bd. governors Cedars-Sinai Hospital in L.A. 1987.

HIRSCHHORN, JOEL
Composer. b. Bronx, NY, Dec. 18, 1937. e. HS for the Performing Arts, Hunter Col.
PICTURES: *Songs* (with collaborator Al Kasha): The Fat Spy, The Cheyenne Social Club, The Poseidon Adventure (Academy Award for best song: The Morning After, 1972), The Towering Inferno (Acad. Award for best song: We May Never Love Like This Again, 1974), Freaky Friday, Pete's Dragon, Hot Lead Cold Feet, The North Avenue Irregulars, All Dogs Go to Heaven, Rescue Me, Hungry For You
TELEVISION: *Series*: Kids Inc., First and Ten, Getting in Touch, The Challengers. *Specials*: Kingdom Chums, A Precious Moments Christmas, The Magic Paintbrush, Caddie Woodlawn. *Movies*: Trapped Beneath the Sea, Someone I Touch, Charles Dickens' David Copperfield.

HITZIG, RUPERT
Producer, Director. b. New York, NY, Aug. 15, 1942. e. Harvard. At CBS as doc. writer-prod.-dir.; later moved into dramas and comedy. Alan King's partner in King-Hitzig Prods.
PICTURES: *Prod.*: Electra Glide in Blue, Happy Birthday Gemini, Cattle Annie and Little Britches, Wolfen (also 2nd unit dir.), Jaws 3-D, The Last Dragon, The Squeeze. *Dir.*: Night Visitor, Backstreet Dreams, The Legend of O.B. Taggart, Last Lives (dir.), Nowhere Land.
TELEVISION: Much Ado About Nothing, The Wonderful World of Jonathan Winters, Playboy After Dark, How to Pick Up Girls, Return to Earth, Saturday Night Live, Birds of Prey, Date My Dad, Save Our Streets, Snakes and Ladders (prod., dir.), annual comedy awards, television series and numerous specials.

HOBERMAN, DAVID
Executive. b. 1953. Started career as prod. exec. with TAT Communications for five years. 1982-85, worked as m.p. agent with Writers and Artists Agency and later at Ziegler Associates and ICM. 1985, named v.p. of prod. for Walt Disney Pictures based at studio. 1987, promoted to sr. v.p.; prod. 1988, named president, production. 1989, pres. Touchstone Pictures. 1994, appointed head of all motion pictures produced by Walt Disney. Resigned from Disney, 1995, to form Mandeville Films. Produced George of the Jungle, 1997. Produced The 6th Man, 1997.

HOCK, MORT
Executive. Blaine-Thompson Agency; A. E. Warner Bros., 1948; David Merrick B'way Prod., 1958; asst. adv. mgr., Paramount Pictures Corp., 1960; adv. mgr., United Artists Corp., 1962; dir. adv., UA Corp., 1964; adv. dir., Paramount, 1965; v.p. adv. & public rltns., Paramount, 1968-71; v.p., marketing, Rastar Prods., 1971; exec. v.p., Charles Schlaifer & Co., 1974; sr. v.p. entertainment div., DDB Needham Worldwide, 1983; exec. v.p. DDB, 1994.

HODGE, PATRICIA
Actress. b. Cleethorpes, Lincolnshire, England, Sept. 29, 1946. Studied at London Acad. of Music and Dramatic Arts.
THEATER: Popkiss, Two Gentlemen of Verona, Pippin, The Mitford Girls, Benefactors, Noel and Gertie, Separate Tables, The Prime of Miss Jean Brodie.
PICTURES: The Elephant Man, Betrayal, Sunset, Thieves in the Night, Diamond's Edge.
TELEVISION: The Naked Civil Servant, Rumpole of the Bailey, Edward and Mrs. Simpson, Holding the Fort, Jemima Shore Investigates, Hay Fever, Hotel Du Lac, The Life and Loves of a She-Devil, Exclusive Yarns, Let's Face the Music of..., Inspector Morse, The Shell Seekers, The Secret Life of Ian Fleming, The Heat of the Day, Rich Tea and Sympathy, The Cloning of Joanna May.

HOFFMAN, DUSTIN
Actor. b. Los Angeles, CA, Aug. 8, 1937. m. Lisa Hoffman. e. Los Angeles Conservatory of Music, Santa Monica Coll.; Pasadena Playhouse, 1958. Worked as an attendant at a psychiatric institution, a demonstrator in Macy's toy dept., and a waiter. First stage role 1960 in Yes Is for a Very Young Man at Sarah Lawrence Coll. Acted in summer stock, television and dir. at community theatre. Asst. dir. Off-B'way of A View From the Bridge. Recipient of the Golden Globe Cecil B. DeMille Award, 1997.
THEATER: *B'way and Off B'way*: A Cook for Mr. General (bit part, B'way debut), Harry Noon and Night, Journey of the Fifth Horse (Obie Award), Eh? (Vernon Rice & Theatre World Awards), Jimmy Shine, All Over Town (dir. only), Death of a Salesman (Drama Desk Award), The Merchant of Venice (also London).

PICTURES: The Tiger Makes Out (debut, 1967), Madigan's Millions, The Graduate, Midnight Cowboy, John and Mary, Little Big Man, Who Is Harry Kellerman and Why Is He Saying Those Terrible Things About Me?, Straw Dogs, Alfredo Alfredo, Papillon, Lenny, All the President's Men, Marathon Man, Straight Time, Agatha, Kramer vs. Kramer (Academy Award, 1979), Tootsie, Ishtar, Rain Man (Academy Award, 1988), Family Business, Dick Tracy, Billy Bathgate, Hook, Hero, Outbreak, American Buffalo, Sleepers, Mad City, Wag the Dog, Sphere, Cosm.
TELEVISION: Specials: Journey of the Fifth Horse, The Star Wagons, Free to Be You and Me, Bette Midler: Old Red Hair Is Back, Common Threads: Stories from the Quilt (narrator), The Earth Day Special. Movies: The Point (narrator), Death of a Salesman (Emmy Award, 1985). Guest: Naked City, The Defenders.

HOGAN, HULK
Actor. r.n. Terry Gene Bollea. b. Augusta, GA, Aug. 11, 1953. Former bodyguard then prof. wrestler using names Sterling Golden, Terry Boulder, then finally Hulk Hogan.
PICTURES: Rocky III (debut, 1982), No Holds Barred, Gremlins 2: The New Batch, Suburban Commado, Mr. Nanny, Santa with Muscles.
TELEVISION: Series: Hulk Hogan's Rock 'n' Wrestling (voice), Thunder in Paradise (also exec. prod.). Pilot: Goldie and the Bears. Guest: The A-Team, The Love Boat.

HOGAN, PAUL
Actor, Writer. b. Lightning Ridge, New South Ridge, Australia, Oct. 8, 1939. m. actress Linda Kozlowski. Worked as rigger before gaining fame on Australian TV as host of nightly current affairs show (A Current Affair) and The Paul Hogan Show. Shows now syndicated in 26 countries. In U.S. gained attention with commercials for Australian Tourist Commission. 1985, starred in dramatic role on Australian TV in series, Anzacs. Live one-man show, Paul Hogan's America, 1991.
PICTURES: Fatty Finn (debut, 1980), Crocodile Dundee (also co-s.p.), Crocodile Dundee II (also exec. prod., co-s.p.), Almost an Angel (also exec. prod., s.p.), Lightning Jack (also s.p., co-prod.), Flipper.
TELEVISION: Anzacs: The War Down Under.

HOLBROOK, HAL
Actor. b. Cleveland, OH, Feb. 17, 1925. m. actress Dixie Carter. e. Denison U., 1948. Summer stock 1947-53. Gained fame and several awards for performance as Mark Twain on stage in Mark Twain Tonight over a period of years throughout the US and abroad.
THEATER: Mark Twain Tonight (Tony Award, 1966), Do You Know the Milky Way?, Abe Lincoln in Illinois, American Shakespeare Fest., Lincoln Center Repertory (After the Fall, Marco Millions, Incident at Vichy, Tartuffe), The Glass Menagerie, The Apple Tree, I Never Sang For My Father, Man of La Mancha, Does a Tiger Wear a Necktie?, Lake of the Woods, Buried Inside Extra, The Country Girl, King Lear. Regional: Our Town, The Merchant of Venice, Uncle Vanya, Eye of God.
PICTURES: The Group (debut, 1966), Wild in the Streets, The People Next Door, The Great White Hope, They Only Kill Their Masters, Jonathan Livingston Seagull (voice), Magnum Force, The Girl From Petrovka, All the President's Men, Midway, Julia, Rituals (The Creeper), Capricorn One, Natural Enemies, The Fog, The Kidnapping of the President, Creepshow, The Star Chamber, Girls Night Out (The Scaremaker), Wall Street, The Unholy, Fletch Lives, The Firm, Carried Away.
TELEVISION: Series: The Bold Ones: The Senator (Emmy Award, 1971), Designing Women, Portrait of America (4 annual ACE Awards, 2 Emmy Awards, 1988, 1989), Evening Shade. Movies: Coronet Blue, The Whole World is Watching, A Clear and Present Danger, Travis Logan, Suddenly Single, Goodbye Raggedy Ann, That Certain Summer, Murder by Natural Causes, Legend of the Golden Gun, When Hell Was in Session, Off the Minnesota Strip, The Killing of Randy Webster, Under Siege, Behind Enemy Lines, Dress Gray, The Fortunate Pilgrim, Three Wishes for Billy Grier, Emma, Queen of the South Seas, Day One, Sorry Wrong Number, A Killing in a Small Town, Bonds of Love, A Perry Mason Mystery: The Case of the Lethal Lifestyle, A Perry Mason Mystery: The Case of the Grimacing Governor, A Perry Mason Mystery: The Case of the Jealous Jokester, She Stood Alone: The Tailhook Scandal. Specials: Mark Twain Tonight, Pueblo (Emmy Award, 1974), Sandburg's Lincoln (Emmy Award, 1976), Our Town, Plaza Suite, The Glass Menagerie, The Awakening Land, The Oath: 33 Hours in the Life of God, Omnibus. Mini-Series: North and South Books I & II, Celebrity, George Washington, Rockport Christmas.

HOLDRIDGE, LEE
Composer. b. Port-au-Prince, Haiti, March 3, 1944. e. Manhattan School of Music. Music arranger for Neil Diamond, 1969-73, with whom he collaborated on the score for Jonathan Livingston Seagull. Wrote score for B'way musical Into the Light (1986). With Alan Raph wrote score for the Joffrey Ballet's Trinity. One-act opera for L.A. Opera commission: Journey to Cordoba.

PICTURES: Jeremy, Jonathan Livingston Seagull, Forever Young Forever Free, Mustang Country, The Other Side of the Mountain—Part 2, The Pack, Moment By Moment, Oliver's Story, French Postcards, Tilt, American Pop, The Beastmaster, Mr. Mom, Micki and Maude, Splash, Sylvester, 16 Days of Glory, Transylvania 6-5000, The Men's Club, Big Business, Old Gringo, Pastime, Freefall, The Long Way Home.
TELEVISION: Series: One Life to Live, Hec Ramsey, Moonlighting, Beauty and the Beast, Bob. Movies: East of Eden, Fly Away Home, The Day the Loving Stopped, For Ladies Only, The Sharks, The Story Lady, One Against the Wind, In Love With an Older Woman, Running Out, Thursday's Child, Wizards and Warriors, The Mississippi, Legs, I Want to Live, Letting Go, Fatal Judgment, The Tenth Man, I'll Take Manhattan, Do You Know the Muffin Man?, Incident at Dark River, A Mother's Courage, In the Arms of a Killer, Face of a Stranger, Deadly Matrimony, Killer Rules, One Against the Wind, Call of the Wild, Torch Song, Barcelona '92: 16 Days of Glory, Jack Reed: Badge of Honor, Incident in a Small Town, The Yearling, Heidi, Texas, Buffalo Girls, The Tuskegee Airmen, Nothing Lasts Forever, Twilight of the Golds, Into Thin Air.

HOLLAND, AGNIESZKA
Director, Writer. b. Warsaw, Poland, Nov. 28, 1948. e. FAMU, Prague. m. dir. Laco Adamik. Studied filmmaking in Czechoslovakia. Worked in Poland with dir. Andrzej Wajda. Moved to Paris in 1981.
PICTURES: Dir./s.p.: Screen Tests, Provincial Actors, Bez Znieczulenia (s.p. only), A Woman Alone (co-s.p.), Danton (co-s.p.), Interrogation (actor only), A Love in Germany (co-s.p.), Angry Harvest (co-s.p.), Anna (only s.p., story), Les Possedes (only co-s.p.), La Amiga (only co-s.p.), To Kill a Priest (also co-s.p.), Korczak (s.p. only), Europa Europa, Olivier Olivier, Three Colors: Blue (s.p. only)The Secret Garden (dir. only), Total Eclipse (dir. only), Washington Square (dir. only).
TELEVISION: Movies: Evening With Abdon, The Children of Sunday, Something for Something, Lorenzaccio, The Trial, Largo Desolato. Series: Fallen Angels (dir. only).

HOLLAND, TODD
Director.
PICTURES: The Wizard, Krippendorf's Tribe.
TELEVISION: Series: Amazing Stories, Vietnam War Story, Max Headroom, Tales from the Crypt, Twin Peaks, Eerie Indiana, Bill & Ted's Excellent Adventures, The Larry Sanders Show (Emmy Award, 1998), My So-Called Life.

HOLLAND, TOM
Director, Writer. b. Highland, NY, July 11, 1945. e. Northwestern U. Started as actor, working at Bucks County Playhouse in PA and HB Studios in NY. Appeared on daytime serials Love of Life, Love is a Many-Splendored Thing. Turned to commercial prod. while attended UCLA law school, then took up screenwriting.
PICTURES: Writer: The Beast Within, The Class of 1984, Pyscho II (also actor), Scream for Help, Cloak and Dagger. Director: Fright Night (also s.p.), Fatal Beauty, Child's Play (also co-s.p.), The Temp, Stephen King's Thinner (also s.p.).
TELEVISION: Movie: The Stranger Within. Series: Tales From the Crypt (dir. 3 episodes: Love Come Hack to Me-also co-writer, Four-Sided Triangle-also co-writer, King of the Road). Mini-Series: Stephen King's The Langoliers (also writer, actor).

HOLLIMAN, EARL
Actor. b. Delhi, LA, Sept. 11, 1928. e. U. of Southern California, Pasadena Playhouse. Pres., Actors and Others for Animals.
THEATER: Camino Real (Mark Taper Forum), A Streetcar Named Desire (Ahmanson).
PICTURES: Scared Stiff, The Girls of Pleasure Island, Destination Gobi, East of Sumatra, Devil's Canyon, Tennessee Champ, The Bridges at Toko-Ri, Broken Lance, The Big Combo, I Died a Thousand Times, Forbidden Planet, Giant, The Burning Hills, The Rainmaker, Gunfight at the OK Corral, Trooper Hook, Don't Go Near the Water, Hot Spell, The Trap, Last Train From Gun Hill, Visit to a Small Planet, Armored Command, Summer and Smoke, The Sons of Katie Elder, A Covenant With Death, The Power, Anzio, The Biscuit Eater, Good Luck Miss Wyckoff, Sharky's Machine.
TELEVISION: Series: Hotel de Paree, Wide Country, Police Woman, P.S. I Luv You, Delta. Pilot: Twilight Zone. Movies: Tribes, Alias Smith and Jones, Cannon, The Desperate Mission, Trapped, Cry Panic, I Love You... Goodbye, Alexander: The Other Side of Down, The Solitary Man, Where the Ladies Go, Country Gold, Gunsmoke: Return to Dodge, American Harvest, P.S. I Luv You (pilot). Mini-Series: The Thorn Birds. Specials: The Dark Side of the Earth, The Return of Ansel Gibbs.

HOLLOWOOD, ANN
Costume Designer.
PICTURES: Nightbreed, The Second Jungle Book: Mowgli & Baloo.
TELEVISION: Movies: Tears in the Rain, The Old Man and the Sea. Mini-series: The Storyteller, The Storyteller: Greek Myths, Merlin (Emmy Award, 1998).

HOLLY, LAUREN
Actress. b. Bristol, PA, October 28, 1963.
PICTURES: Seven Minutes in Heaven, Band of the Hand, The Adventures of Ford Fairlane, Dragon: The Bruce Lee Story, Dumb & Dumber, Sabrina, Beautiful Girls,Down Periscope, Long Time Nothing New, Turbulence, A Smile Like Yours, Vig, No Looking Back.
TELEVISION: Series: All My Children, The Antagonists, Picket Fences. Movies: Archie: To Riverdale and Back Again, Fugitive Among Us, Dangerous Heart. Guest: Spenser For Hire.

HOLM, CELESTE
Actress. b. New York, NY, Apr. 29, 1919. e. Univ. Sch. for Girls, Chicago, Francis W. Parker, Chicago, Lyceae Victor Durui (Paris), U. of Chicago, UCLA. p. Theodor Holm and Jean Parke Holm. m. actor Wesley Addy.
THEATER: B'way: Gloriana, The Time of Your Life, 8 O'Clock Tuesday, Another Sun, Return of the Vagabond, My Fair Ladies, Papa Is All, All the Comforts of Home, The Damask Cheek, Oklahoma!, Bloomer Girl, She Stoops to Conquer, Affairs of State, Anna Christie, The King and I, Interlock, Third Best Sport, Invitation to a March, Mame, Candida, Habeas Corpus, The Utter Glory of Morrissey Hall, I Hate Hamlet. Off-B'way: A Month in the Country. Theatre-in-Concert for the U.S. State Department in 8 countries May-July 1966. Regional: Janet Flanner's Paris Was Yesterday. Natl. Tour: Mame (Sarah Siddons Award), Hay Fever, Road to Mecca, Cocktail Hour.
PICTURES: Three Little Girls in Blue (debut, 1946), Carnival in Costa Rica, Gentleman's Agreement (Academy Award, best supporting actress, 1947), Road House, The Snake Pit, Chicken Every Sunday, Come to the Stable (Acad. Award nom.), A Letter to Three Wives (voice), Everybody Does It, Champagne for Caesar, All About Eve (Acad. Award nom.), The Tender Trap, High Society, Bachelor Flat, Doctor You've Got To Be Kidding, Tom Sawyer, Bittersweet Love, The Private Files of J. Edgar Hoover, Three Men and a Baby.
TELEVISION: Specials: A Clearing in the Wood, Play of the Week, Cinderella, Nora's Christmas Gift. Mini-Series: Backstairs at the White House (Emmy nom.). Movies: Underground Man, Death Cruise, Love Boat II, Midnight Lace, The Shady Hill Kidnapping, This Girl for Hire, Murder by the Book, Polly, Polly-Comin' Home! Pilot: Road Show. Series: Honestly Celeste, Who Pays, Nancy, Jessie, Falcon Crest, Christine Cromwell, Loving, Promised Land. Guest: Love Boat, Trapper John M.D., Magnum P.I.
RADIO: People at the U.N., Theatre Guild on the Air, Mystery Theatre.

HOLM, IAN
C.B.E. Actor. b. Ilford, Essex, England, Sept. 12, 1931. r.n. Ian Holm Cuthbert. e. RADA. On British stage in Love Affair, Titus Andronicus, Henry IV, Ondine, Becket, The Homecoming (B'way: Tony Award, 1967), Henry V, Richard III, Romeo and Juliet, The Sea, etc.
PICTURES: The Bofors Gun (debut, 1968), A Midsummer Night's Dream, The Fixer, Oh! What a Lovely War, A Severed Head, Nicholas and Alexandra, Mary Queen of Scots, Young Winston, The Homecoming, Juggernaut, Robin and Marian, Shout at the Devil, March or Die, Alien, Chariots of Fire (Acad. Award nom.), Time Bandits, Return of the Soldier, Greystoke: The Legend of Tarzan Lord of the Apes, Dance With a Stranger, Wetherby, Dreamchild, Brazil, Laughterhouse, Another Woman, Henry V, Hamlet, Kafka, Naked Lunch, The Advocate, Mary Shelley's Frankenstein, The Madness of King George, Big Night, Night Falls On Manhattan, The Fifth Element, The Sweet Hereafter, A Life Less Ordinary.
TELEVISION: Mini-Series/Movies: Les Miserables, S.O.S. Titanic, Napoleon, We the Accused, All Quiet on the Western Front, Holocaust, Man in the Iron Mask, Jesus of Nazareth, Thief of Bagdad, Game Set and Match, A Season of Giants, The Borrowers. Specials: The Browning Version, Murder By the Book, Uncle Vanya, Tailor of Gloucester, The Lost Boys, The Last Romantics.

HOMEIER, SKIP
Actor. r.n. George Vincent Homeier. b. Chicago, IL, Oct. 5, 1930. e. UCLA. Started in radio, 1936-43; on B'way stage, Tomorrow the World, 1943-44 which led to film debut in adaptation of same (billed as Skippy Homeier).
PICTURES: Tomorrow the World (debut, 1944), Boys' Ranch, Mickey, Arthur Takes Over, The Big Cat, The Gunfighter, Halls of Montezuma, Fixed Bayonets, Sealed Cargo, Sailor Beware, Has Anybody Seem My Gal?, The Last Posse, The Lone Gun, Beachhead, Black Widow, Dawn at Socorro, Ten Wanted Men, The Road to Denver, At Gunpoint, Cry Vengeance, The Burning Hills, Between Heaven and Hell, Dakota Incident, No Road Back, Stranger at My Door, Thunder Over Arizona, The Tall T, Lure of the Swamp, Decision at Durango, Day of the Badman, Journey Into Darkness, The Punderers of Painted Flats, Commanche Station, Showdown, Bullet for a Badman, Stark Fear, The Ghost and Mr. Chicken, Dead Heat on a Merry-Go-Round, Tiger By the Tail, The Greatest.
TELEVISION: Series: Dan Raven, The Interns. Guest: Playhouse 90, Alcoa Hour, Kraft Theatre, Studio 1, Armstrong Circle Theatre, Alfred Hitchcock. Movies: The Challenge, Two for the Money, Voyage of the Yes, Helter Skelter, Overboard, The Wild Wild West Revisited. Mini-Series: Washington: Behind Closed Doors.

HOOKS, KEVIN
Actor, Director. b. Philadelphia, PA, Sept. 19, 1958. Son of actor-dir. Robert Hooks.
PICTURES: Sounder, Aaron Loves Angela, A Hero Ain't Nothin' But a Sandwich, Take Down, Innerspace, Strictly Business (also dir.), Passenger 57 (dir. only), Fled, Glory & Honor (also dir.), Black Dog (dir. only).
TELEVISION: Series: The White Shadow, He's the Mayor. Movies: Just an Old Sweet Song, The Greatest Thing That Almost Happened, Friendly Fire, Can You Hear the Laughter?-The Story of Freddie Prinze, Roots: The Gift (dir.), Murder Without Motive: The Edmund Perry Story (dir.). Mini-Series: Backstairs at the White House. Special: Home Sweet Homeless (dir.).

HOOKS, ROBERT
Actor, Director, Producer. b. Washington, D.C., April 18, 1937. Father of actor-dir. Kevin Hooks. Co-founder and exec. dir. Negro Ensemble Co. NY 1967-present. Founder DC Black Repertory Company, 1970-77. Co-star of TV series NYPD, 1967-69.
THEATER: B'way: A Raisin In the Sun (B'way debut, 1960), A Taste of Honey, Tiger Tiger Burning Bright, Arturo Ui, The Milktrain Doesn't Stop Here Anymore, Where's Daddy? (Theatre World Award for last two), Hallelujah, Baby?. Off B'way.: The Blacks, Dutchman, Happy Ending, Day of Absence, Henry V, Ballad for Bimshire, Kongi's Harvest. A Soldier's Play (Mark Taper Forum, LA). Co-prod. (with Gerald S. Krone): Song of the Lusitanian Bogey, Daddy Goodness, Ceremonies in Dark Old Men, Day of Absence, The Sty of the Blind Pig, The River Niger, The First Breeze of Summer.
PICTURES: Sweet Love Bitter, Hurry Sundown, The Last of the Mobile Hot-Shots, Trouble Man, Aaron Loves Angela, Airport '77, Fast-Walking, Star Trek III: The Search For Spock, Passenger 57, Posse, Fled, Glory and Honor, Free of Eden.
TELEVISION: Series: N.Y.P.D., Supercarrier, Seinfeld, Parenthood, Family Matters, Different World, Murder She Wrote. Pilots: The Cliff Dweller, Two for the Money, Down Home. Movies: Carter's Army, Vanished, The Cable Car Murder, Crosscurrent, Trapped, Ceremonies in Dark Old Men, Just an Old Sweet Song, The Killer Who Wouldn't Die, The Courage and the Passion, To Kill a Cop, A Woman Called Moses, Hollow Image, Madame X, The Oklahoma City Dolls, The Sophisticated Gents, Cassie and Co., Starflight:The Plane that Couldn't Land, Feel the Heat, Sister Sister, The Execution.

HOOL, LANCE
Producer, Director. b. Mexico City, Mex., May 11, 1948. e. Univ. of the Americas.
PICTURES: Producer: Cabo Blanco, Ten to Midnight, The Evil That Men Do, Missing in Action (also s.p.), Missing in Action 2 (dir.), Steel Dawn (also dir.), Options, Damned River, Pure Luck, The Air Up There, Gunmen, Road Flower, Flipper, McHale's Navy, One Man's Hero.
TELEVISION: The Tracker, Born To Run, Cover Girl Murders, Flashfire.

HOOPER, TOBE
Director. b. Austin, Texas, Jan. 25, 1943. e. Univ. of TX. Began film career making documentary and industrial films and commercials in Texas. Was asst. dir. of U. of Texas film program, continuing filmmaking while working with students. First feature film: documentary Peter Paul & Mary, followed by Eggshells. Directed Billy Idol video Dancing With Myself.
PICTURES: The Texas Chainsaw Massacre (also prod., co-s.p.), Eaten Alive (Death Trap), The Funhouse, Poltergeist, Lifeforce, Invaders from Mars, The Texas Chainsaw Massacre Part 2 (also co-prod., co- music), Spontaneous Combustion, Sleepwalkers (actor only), Night Terrors, The Mangler (also co-s.p.).
TELEVISION: Movie: I'm Dangerous Tonight. Mini-Series: Salem's Lot. Series episodes: Amazing Stories, Freddy's Nightmares (No More Mr. Nice Guy-1st episode), Equalizer (No Place Like Home), Tales from the Crypt (Dead Wait), Nowhere Man, Dark Skies. Pilots: Haunted Lives, Body Bags.

HOPE, BOB
Actor. r.n. Leslie Townes Hope. b. Eltham, England, May 29, 1903. To U.S. at age 4; raised in Cleveland, OH. Became American citizen in 1920. Was amateur boxer before appearing in vaudeville as comedian/song and dance man. Debuted on B'way 1933 in Roberta, followed by stage work in Ziegfeld Follies, Red Hot & Blue. Began film career 1934, appearing in 8 short films made in NY, before going to Hollywood for feature debut, 1938, signing contract with Paramount. Starred on radio, 1938-56; made countless trips overseas to entertain U.S. troops during wartime; lent name to Bob Hope Desert Classic golf tournament. Voted one of top ten Money-Making Stars in M.P. Herald-Fame Poll: 1941-47, 1949-53. Recipient: 5 special Academy Awards (1940, 1944, 1952, 1959, 1965); special Emmy Awards: Trustees Award (1959), Governors Award (1984); Kennedy Center Honors (1985); Presidential Medal of Freedom, and many other awards. Author (or-co-author): They Got Me Covered, I Never Left Home, So This Is Peace, Have Tux Will Travel, I Owe Russia $1,200, Five Women I Love: Obit Hope's Vietnam Story, The Last Christmas Show, The Road to Hollywood: My 40-Year Love Affair With the Movies, Confessions of a Hooker: My Lifelong Love Affair With Golf, Don't Shoot It's Only Me.

PICTURES: The Big Broadcast of 1938 (feature debut, 1938), College Swing, Give Me a Sailor, Thanks for the Memory, Never Say Die, Some Like It Hot, The Cat and the Canary, Road to Singapore, The Ghost Breakers, Road to Zanzibar, Caught in the Draft, Louisiana Purchase, My Favorite Blonde, Road to Morocco, Nothing But the Truth, They Got Me Covered, Star Spangled Rhythm, Let's Face It, Road to Utopia, The Princess and the Pirate, Monsieur Beaucaire, My Favorite Brunette, Where There's Life, Road to Rio, The Paleface, Casanova's Big Night, The Seven Little Foys, That Certain Feeling, The Iron Petticoat, Beau James, Paris Holiday (also prod., story), Alias Jesse James (also prod.), The Five Pennies (cameo), The Facts of Life, Bachelor in Paradise, The Road to Hong Kong, Call Me Bwana, A Global Affair, I'll Take Sweden, The Oscar (cameo), Boy Did I Get a Wrong Number!, Not With My Wife You Don't (cameo), Eight on the Lam, The Private Navy of Sgt. O'Farrell, How to Commit Marriage, Cancel My Reservation (also exec. prod.), The Muppet Movie (cameo), Spies Like Us (cameo).
TELEVISION: Series: Chesterfield Sound Off Time, Colgate Comedy Hour (rotating host), Bob Hope Presents the Chrysler Theatre (Emmy Award as exec. prod. and host, 1966). Movie: A Masterpiece of Murder. Many specials incl. prod. of Roberta, annual variety shows; also was frequent host of annual Academy Award telecast.

HOPE, HARRY
Producer, Director, Writer. b. May 26, 1926. e. UCLA, Etudes Universitaires Internationales, Ph.D. Entered m.p. industry as special effects man, Republic Studios, 1944; associate prod. Star Productions; formed Blue Bird Film Co. Has since produced, directed and written 33 feature films, including Like the Gull, 1967, which won creative classical film award as Asian Film Festival. Founded Western International and directed First Leisure Corp. as exec. v.p. until 1972. From then until present, pres. of Harry Hope Production. Among recent film credits: Smokey and the Judge, Sunset Cove, Doomsday Machine, Death Dimension, Thunderfist, Tarzana, The Mad Butcher, Death Blow, Pop's Oasis.

HOPE, TED
Producer. b. 1962.
PICTURES: Tiger Warsaw (assoc. prod.), The Unbelievable Truth, (1st asst. dir.), Theory of Achievement, Surviving Desire, Ambition, Pushing Hands (Tui Shou), I Was on Mars (also actor), Simple Men, The Wedding Banquet, Roy Cohn/Jack Smith, Eat Drink Man Woman, (assoc. prod.), Amateur, Safe (exec. prod.), The Brothers McMullen (exec. prod.), Flirt, Walking and Talking, She's the One, Little Cobras, Arresting Gena, The Myth of Fingerprints (exec. prod.), The Ice Storm, Office Killer, Love God, No Looking Back.
TELEVISION: Punch and Judy Get Divorced.

HOPKINS, SIR ANTHONY
C.B.E.: Actor. b. Port Talbot, South Wales, Dec. 31, 1937. Trained at Royal Acad. of Dramatic Art; Welsh Coll. of Music & Drama. Joined National Theatre, gaining fame on stage in England, then TV and films. Appeared in short The White Bus. Recordings: Under Milk Wood (1988), Shostakovich Symphony No. 13 Babi Yar (reciting Yevtushenko's poem, 1994). Dir. An Evening With Dylan Thomas, 1993. Received special award at Montreal Film Festival for Career Excellence, 1992; Evening Standard Film Awards Special Award for Body of Work, 1994; BAFTA Britannia Award for Outstanding Contribution to the International Film and TV Industry, 1995.
THEATER: Julius Caesar (debut, 1964), Juno and the Paycock, A Flea in Her Ear, The Three Sisters, Dance of Death, As You Like It, The Architect and the Emperor of Assyria, A Woman Killed With Kindness, Coriolanus, The Taming of the Shrew, Macbeth, Equus (NY, 1974-75; Outer Critics Circle, NY Drama Desk, US Authors & Celebrities Forum Awards), Equus (LA 1977, also dir.; LA Drama Critics Award), The Tempest, Old Times, The Lonely Road, Pravda (Variety Club Stage Actor Award, 1985; British Theatre Association Best Actor, Laurence Olivier & Observer Awards), King Lear, Antony and Cleopatra, M. Butterfly, August (also dir.).
PICTURES: The Lion in Winter (debut, 1967), The Looking Glass War, Hamlet, When Eight Bells Toll, Young Winston, A Doll's House, The Girl from Petrovka, Juggernaut, Audrey Rose, A Bridge Too Far, International Velvet, Magic, The Elephant Man, A Change of Seasons, The Bounty (Variety Club UK Film Actor Award, 1983), 84 Charing Cross Road (Moscow Film Fest. Award, 1987), The Good Father, The Dawning, A Chorus of Disapproval, Desperate Hours, The Silence of the Lambs (Academy Award, Natl. Board of Review, NY Film Critics, Boston Film Critics & BAFTA Awards, 1991), Freejack, One Man's War, Howards End, The Efficiency Expert (Spotswood), Bram Stoker's Dracula, Chaplin, The Remains of the Day (BAFTA, Variety Club UK Film Actor, LA Film Critics, Japan Critics Awards, 1993), The Trial, Shadowlands (Natl. Board of Review & LA Film Critics Award, 1993), The Road to Wellville, Legends of The Fall, The Innocent, August (also dir.), Nixon, Surviving Picasso, The Edge.

TELEVISION: A Heritage and Its History, Vanya, Hearts and Flowers, Decision to Burn, War & Peace, Cuculus Canorus, Lloyd George, QB VII, Find Me, A Childhood Friend, Possessions, All Creatures Great and Small, The Arcata Promise, Dark Victory, The Lindbergh Kidnapping Case (Emmy Award, 1976), Victory at Entebbe, Kean, Mayflower: The Pilgrim's Adventure, The Bunker (Emmy Award, 1981), Peter and Paul, Othello, Little Eyolf, The Hunchback of Notre Dame, A Married Man, Corridors of Power, Strangers and Brothers, Arch of Triumph, Mussolini and I / Mussolini: The Rise and Fall of Il Duce (ACE Award), Hollywood Wives, Guilty Conscience, Blunt, The Dawning, Across the Lake, Heartland, The Tenth Man, Great Expectations, One Man's War, To Be the Best, A Few Selected Exits, Big Cats.

HOPKINS, BO
Actor. b. Greenwood, SC, Feb. 2, 1942. Studied with Uta Hagen in N.Y. then with Desilu Playhouse training school in Hollywood. Parts in several prods. for that group won him an agent, an audition with dir. Sam Peckinpah and his first role in latter's The Wild Bunch.
PICTURES: The Wild Bunch (debut, 1969), Monte Walsh, The Moonshine War, The Culpepper Cattle Co., The Getaway, White Lightning, The Man Who Loved Cat Dancing, American Graffiti, The Nickel Ride, The Day of the Locust, Posse, The Killer Elite, A Small Town in Texas, Tentacles, Midnight Express, More American Graffiti, The Fifth Floor, Sweet Sixteen, Night Shadows, Trapper Country, What Comes Around, War, The Bounty Hunter, The Stalker, Nightmare at Noon, The Tenth Man, Big Bad John, Center of the Web, Inside Monkey Zetterland, The Ballad of Little Jo, Cheyenne Warrior, Radioland Murders, Riders in the Storm, The Feminine Touch.
TELEVISION: Series: Doc Elliott, The Rockford Files, Dynasty. Movies: The Runaway Barge, Kansas City Massacre, Charlie's Angels (pilot), The Invasion of Johnson County, Dawn: Portrait of a Teenage Runaway, Thaddeus Rose and Eddie, Crisis in Sun Valley, Plutonium Incident, A Smoky Mountain Christmas, Beggerman Thief, Down the Long Hills, Last Ride of the Dalton Gang, Casino, Rodeo Girl, Ghost Dancing, Blood Ties. Special: Wyatt Earp: Return to Tombstone.

HOPPER, DENNIS
Actor, Director. b. Dodge City, KS, May 17, 1936. e. San Diego, CA, public schools. Author: Out of the Sixties (1988; book of his photographs).
PICTURES: Rebel Without a Cause, I Died a Thousand Times, Giant, The Steel Jungle, The Story of Mankind, Gunfight at the OK Corral, From Hell to Texas, The Young Land, Key Witness, Night Tide, Tarzan and Jane Regained Sort Of, The Sons of Katie Elder, Queen of Blood, Cool Hand Luke, Glory Stompers, The Trip, Panic in the City, Hang 'Em High, True Grit, Easy Rider (also dir., co-s.p.), The Last Movie (also dir., s.p.), Kid Blue, James Dean-The First American Teenager, Bloodbath (The Sky Is Falling), Mad Dog Morgan, Tracks, The American Friend, Couleur Chair, The Sorcerer's Apprentices, L'Ordre et la Securite du Monde, Resurrection, Apocalypse Now, Out of the Blue (also dir.), King of the Mountain, Renacida, White Star, Human Highway, Rumble Fish, The Osterman Weekend, My Science Project, The Texas Chainsaw Massacre Part 2, Hoosiers (Acad. Award nom.), Blue Velvet, Black Widow, River's Edge, Straight to Hell, The Pick Up Artist, O.C. and Stiggs, Riders of the Storm, Blood Red, Colors (dir. only), Flashback, Chattachoochee, The Hot Spot (dir. only), Superstar: The Life and Times of Andy Warhol, The Indian Runner, Hearts of Darkness: A Filmmaker's Apocalypse, Midnight Heat, Eye of the Storm, Boiling Point, Super Mario Bros., True Romance, Red Rock West, Chasers (also dir.), Speed, Search and Destroy, Waterworld, Acts of Love, Basquiat, Carried Away.
TELEVISION: Movies: Wild Times, Stark, Paris Trout, Doublecrossed, Backtrack (also dir.), Nails, The Heart of Justice, Witch Hunt. Guest: Pursuit, Espionage, Medic, Loretta Young Show.

HORN, ALAN
Executive. b. New York, NY, Feb. 28, 1943. e. Union Coll., Harvard Business Sch. 1971, joined Tandem Prods., 1972; named v.p., business affairs, and of sister co., T.A.T. Communications, 1973; 1977, exec. v.p. & COO; pres., 1978. In 1983 named chmn. Embassy Communications. 1986 joined 20th Century Fox as pres., COO. Left Fox Sept. 1986. Co-founded Castle Rock Entertainment 1987; Chmn. & CEO after being acquired by Turner Broadcasting System Inc. in 1994.

HORNE, LENA
Singer, Actress. b. Brooklyn, NY, June 30, 1917. Radio with Noble Sissle, Charlie Barnet, other bands. Floor shows at Cotton Club, Cafe Society, Little Troc, etc. Started screen career 1942. Appeared in short subjects Harlem Hotshots, Boogie Woogie Dream. Autobiographies: In Person (1950), Lena (1965) Recipient Kennedy Center Honors for Lifetime contribution to the Arts, 1984. Spingarn Award, NAACP, 1983; Paul Robeson Award, Actors Equity Assn., 1985.
THEATER: Blackbirds, Dance With Your Gods, Jamaica, Pal Joey (L.A. Music Center), Lena Horne: The Lady and Her Music (Tony Award).

PICTURES: The Duke Is Tops (debut, 1938), Panama Hattie, Cabin in the Sky, Stormy Weather, I Dood It, Thousands Cheer, Broadway Rhythm, Swing Fever, Two Girls and a Sailor, Ziegfeld Follies, Till the Clouds Roll By, Words and Music, Duchess of Idaho, Meet Me in Las Vegas, Death of a Gunfighter, The Wiz, That's Entertainment III.
TELEVISION: Guest: Music '55, Perry Como Show, Here's to the Ladies, The Flip Wilson Show, Dean Martin Show, Sesame Street, Ed Sullivan Show, Sanford & Sons, Laugh-In, Hollywood Palace, The Cosby Show. Specials: The Lena Horne Show (1959), The Frank Sinatra Timex Show, Lena in Concert, Harry and Lena, The Tony & Lena Show, Lena Horne: The Lady and Her Music.

HORNER, JAMES
Composer. b. Los Angeles, CA, Aug. 14, 1953. e. Royal Col. of Music: London, USC, UCLA. Received Grammy Awards for the song Somewhere Out There (from the film An American Tail), and for instrumental composition from Glory.
PICTURES: The Lady in Red, Battle Beyond the Stars, Humanoids From the Deep, Deadly Blessing, The Hand, Wolfen, The Pursuit of D.B. Cooper, 48 HRS, Star Trek II: The Wrath of Khan, Something Wicked This Way Comes, Krull, Brainstorm, Testament, Gorky Park, The Dresser, Uncommon Valor, The Stone Boy, Star Trek III: The Search for Spock, Heaven Help Us, Cocoon, Volunteers, Journey of Natty Gann, Commando, Aliens, Where the River Runs Black, The Name of the Rose, An American Tail, P.K. and the Kid, Project X, Batteries Not Included, Willow, Red Heat, Vibes, Cocoon: The Return, The Land Before Time, Field of Dreams, Honey I Shrunk the Kids, Dad, Glory, I Love You to Death, Another 48 HRS., Once Around, My Heroes Have Always Been Cowboys, Class Action, The Rocketeer, An American Tail: Fievel Goes West, Thunderheart, Patriot Games, Unlawful Entry, Sneakers, Swing Kids, A Far Off Place, Jack the Bear, Once Upon a Forest, Searching for Bobby Fischer, The Man Without a Face, Bopha!, The Pelican Brief, Clear and Present Danger, Legends of the Fall, Braveheart, Casper, Apollo 13 (Acad. Award nom.), Jumanji, Courage Under Fire, Ransom, To Gillian on Her 37th Birthday, Titanic (Acad. Award, Best Dramatic Score, Best Orig. Song, Golden Globe Award, Best Orig. Score, Best Orig. Song, Chicago Film Crits. Award, Best Musical Score, 1997), The Devil's Own, Deep Impact, The Mask of Zorro, Mighty Joe Young.

HORSLEY, LEE
Actor. b. Muleshoe, TX, May 15, 1955. e. U. of No. Colorado. On stage in Mack and Mabel, West Side Story, Sound of Music, Oklahoma!, Forty Carats, 1776, Damn Yankees.
PICTURE: The Sword and the Sorcerer, Unlawful Passage.
TELEVISION: Series: Nero Wolfe, Matt Houston, Guns of Paradise, Bodies of Evidence, Hawkeye. Mini-series: Crossings, North and South Book II. Movies: The Wild Women of Chastity Gulch, Infidelity, When Dreams Come True, Thirteen at Dinner, Single Women Married Men, The Face of Fear, Danielle Steel's Palomino, French Silk, The Corpse Had a Familiar Face, Home Song, The Care and Handling of Roses, Nightmare Man. Documentary: Western Ranching Culture In Crisis, The Forest Wars.

HORTON, PETER
Actor. b. Bellevue, DC, Aug. 20, 1953. e. Univ. of CA, Santa Barbara. Stage work includes appearances with Lobero Rep. Co. Theatre in Santa Barbara, Butterflies Are Free in L.A.
PICTURES: Serial, Fade to Black, Split Image, Children of the Corn, Where the River Runs Black, Amazon Women on the Moon (also co-dir.), Sideout, Singles, The Cure (dir. only), The Baby-sitters Club, 2 Days in the Valley, Death Benefit.
TELEVISION: Series: Seven Brides for Seven Brothers, thirtysomething (also dir.), The Wonder Years (dir. only), Class of '96 (dir., actor). Pilot: Sawyer and Finn. Movies: She's Dressed to Kill, Miracle on Ice, Freedom, Choices of the Heart, Children of the Dark, Crazy Horse, One Too Many (dir. only), Murder Live!, Into Thin Air: Death on Everest. Special: The Gift. Guest: The White Shadow, St. Elsewhere.

HORTON, ROBERT
Actor. b. Los Angeles, CA, July 29, 1924. e. U. of Miami. UCLA, B.A. Cum Laude, 1949. Yale Grad School, 1949-50. With U.S. Coast Guard; many legit. plays; many radio & TV appearances. Star of Broadway musical 110 in the Shade.
PICTURES: A Walk in the Sun, The Tanks Are Coming, Return of the Texan, Pony Soldier, Apache War Smoke, Bright Road, The Story of Three Loves, Code Two, Arena, Prisoner of War, Men of the Fighting Lady, The Green Slime, The Dangerous Days of Kiowa Jones, The Spy Killer, Foreign Exchange.
TELEVISION: Series: Kings Row, Wagon Train, A Man Called Shenandoah, As the World Turns. Movie: Red River. Guest: Alfred Hitchcock Presents, Suspense, Houston Knights, Murder She Wrote.

HOSKINS, BOB
Actor. b. Bury St. Edmunds, Suffolk, England, Oct. 26, 1942. Porter and steeplejack before becoming actor at 25. Veteran of Royal Shakespeare Co. Appeared with Britain's National Theatre (Man Is Man, King Lear, Guys and Dolls, etc.)

PICTURES: The National Health (debut, 1973), Royal Flash, Inserts, Zulu Dawn, The Long Good Friday, Pink Floyd: The Wall, Beyond the Limit, Lassiter, The Cotton Club, Brazil, Sweet Liberty, Mona Lisa (Acad. Award nom.), A Prayer for the Dying, The Lonely Passion of Judith Hearne, Who Framed Roger Rabbit, The Raggedy Rawney (also dir., co-s.p.), Heart Condition, Mermaids, Shattered, The Inner Circle, The Favor the Watch and the Very Big Fish, Hook, Passed Away, Super Mario Bros., The Rainbow, The Secret Agent, Nixon, Balto (voice), Joseph Conrad's The Secret Agent, Michael.
TELEVISION: Villains on the High Road (debut, 1972), New Scotland Yard, On the Move, Rock Follies, In the Looking Glass, Napoleon, Flickers, Pennies from Heaven, Othello, Mussolini, The Dunera Boys, World War II: When Lions Roar, The Changeling.

HOUGH, JOHN
Director. b. London, England,, Nov. 21, 1941. Worked in British film prod. in various capacities; impressed execs. at EMI-MGM Studios, Elstree, London, so was given chance to direct The Avengers series for TV. Began theatrical films with Sudden Terror for prod. Irving Allen, 1971.
PICTURES: Sudden Terror, The Practice, Twins of Evil, Treasure Island, The Legend of Hell House, Dirty Mary Crazy Larry, Escape to Witch Mountain, Return From Witch Mountain, Brass Target, The Watcher in the Woods, The Incubus, Triumphs of a Man Called Horse, Biggles: Adventures in Time, American Gothic, Howling IV—The Original Nightmare.
TELEVISION: A Hazard of Hearts (also co-prod.), The Lady and the Highwayman (also prod.), A Ghost in Monte Carlo (also prod.), Duel of Hearts (also prod.), Distant Scream, Black Carrion, Check-Mate.

HOUNSOU, DJIMON
Actor. b. Benin, West Africa. Was model before he began acting.
PICTURES: Without You I'm Nothing, Unlawful Entry, Stargate, Amistad, Ill Gotten Gains, Deep Rising.

HOWARD, ARLISS
Actor. b. Independence, MO, 1955. e. Columbia Col., MO. m. actress Debra Winger.
THEATER: American Buffalo, Lie of the Mind.
PICTURES: The Prodigal, Sylvester, Door to Door, The Ladies Club, The Lightship, Full Metal Jacket, Plain Clothes, Tequila Sunrise, Men Don't Leave, For the Boys, Crisscross, The Sandlot, Wilder Napalm, Natural Born Killers, Wet, To Wong Foo—Thanks for Everything—Julie Newmar, Johns, Beyond the Call, The Lost World: Jurassic Park, Amistad.
TELEVISION: Movies: Hands of a Stranger, I Know My First Name is Steven, Somebody Has to Shoot the Picture, Iran: Days of Crisis, Till Death Us Do Part, Those Secrets, The Infiltrator, The Man Who Captured Eichmann, Old Man.

HOWARD, CLINT
Actor. b. Burbank, CA, Apr. 20, 1959. Brother is dir. Ron Howard; father is actor Rance Howard.
PICTURES: An Eye for an Eye, Gentle Giant, The Jungle Book (voice), Winnie the Pooh and the Blustery Day (voice), The Wild Country, The Grand Auto Theft, The Many Adventures of Winnie the Pooh (voice), Harper Valley P.T.A., Rock 'n' Roll High School, Evil Speak, Night Shift, Flip Out, Spalsh, Cocoon, Gung Ho, The Wraith, End of the Line, Freeway, B.O.R.N., An Innocent Man, Parenthood, Tango and Cash, Silent Night Deadly Night 4: Inititation, Disturbed, Backdraft, The Rocketeer, Silent Night Deadly Night 5: The Toy Maker, Voice of a Stranger, Far and Away, Ticks, Forced to Kill, Carnosaur, Leprechaun 2, The Paper, Bigfoot: The Unforgettable Encounter, Not Like Us, The Ice Cream Man, Fist of the North Star, Dillinger and Capone, Digital Man, Baby Face Nelson, Forget Paris, Apollo 13, Twisted Love, That Thing You Do!, Rattled, Barb Wire, Unhook the Stars, Santa with Muscles, The Protector, Austin Powers: International Man of Mystery, Telling You, Twilight.
TELEVISION: Series: The Andy Griffith Show, The Baileys of Balboa, Gentle Ben, Salty, The Cowboys, Gung Ho, Space Rangers. Movies: The Red Pony, Huckleberry Finn, The Death of Richie, Cotton Candy (also writer), Skyward, Little White Lies, Cheyenne Warrior, Sawbones, Humanoids from the Deep. Guest: The Streets of San Francisco, Happy Days, Star Trek, Night Gallery, Seinfeld, Star Trek: Deep Space Nine, Silk Stalkings, The Outer Limits, Gun.

HOWARD, JAMES NEWTON
Composer. m. actress Rosanna Arquette. Started as keyboard player for Elton John, before composing and producing for such artists as Cher, Diana Ross, Barbra Streisand, Chaka Khan, Randy Newman.
PICTURES: Tough Guys, Nobody's Fool, Head Office, Wildcats, 8 Million Ways to Die, Five Corners, Campus Man, Promised Land, Off Limits, Tap, Some Girls, Everybody's All-American, Major League, The Package, Marked for Death, Pretty Woman, Coupe de Ville, Flatliners, Three Men and a Little Lady, Dying Young, The Man in the Moon, My Girl, The Prince of Tides (Acad. Award nom.), Grand Canyon, Guilty by Suspicion, King Ralph, Dying Young, The Man in the Moon, Glengarry Glen Ross, Night and the City, American Heart, Diggstown, Alive, Falling Down, Dave,

The Fugitive (Acad. Award nom.), The Saint of Fort Washington, Intersection, Wyatt Earp, Junior (Acad. Award nom; Golden Globe nom.), Restoration, Just Cause, Outbreak, Eye for an Eye, The Juror, Primal Fear, The Trigger Effect, The Rich Man's Wife, Space Jam, One Fine Day (Acad. Award nom.), Dante's Peak, Liar Liar, Fathers' Day, My Best Friend's Wedding, The Devil's Advocate, The Postman, Snow Falling on Cedars, A Perfect Murder.
TELEVISION: *Movies*: The Image, Revealing Evidence: Stalking the Honolulu Stangler, Somebody Has to Shoot the Picture, Descending Angel, A Private Matter. *Series*: ER (Emmy nom.).

HOWARD, KEN
Actor. b. El Centro, CA, March 28, 1944. e. Yale Drama Sch. Left studies to do walk-on in B'way. musical, Promises Promises.
THEATER: Promises Promises, 1776 (Theatre World Award), Child's Play (Tony Award, 1970), Seesaw, 1600 Pennsylvania Avenue, The Norman Conquests, Equus, Rumors, Camping With Henry and Tom.PICTURES: Tell Me That You Love Me Junie Moon (debut, 1970), Such Good Friends, The Strange Vengeance of Rosalie, 1776, Second Thoughts, Oscar, Clear and Present Danger, The Net.
TELEVISION: *Series*: Adam's Rib, The Manhunter, The White Shadow, It's Not Easy, The Colbys, Dynasty, Dream Girl U.S.A., What Happened? (host). *Guest*: Bonanza, Medical Center. *Movies*: Manhunter, Superdome, Critical List, A Real American Hero, Damien: The Leper Priest, Victims, Rage of Angels, The Trial of George Armstrong Custer, He's Not Your Son, Rage of Angels: The Story Continues, Murder in New Hampshire: The Pamela Smart Story, Memories of Midnight, Hart to Hart Returns, Moment of Truth: To Walk Again, Tom Clancy's Op Center. *Specials*: Strange Interlude, The Man in the Brown Suit, Mastergate. *Mini-Series*: The Thorn Birds.

HOWARD, RON
Actor, Director, Producer. b. Duncan, OK, March 1, 1954. e. Univ. of So. Calif. Los Angeles Valley Col. Acting debut as Ronny Howard at age of 2 with parents, Rance and Jean Howard, in The Seven Year Itch at Baltimore's Hilltop Theatre. Two years later traveled to Vienna to appear in first film, The Journey. Brother is actor Clint Howard, also former child actor. Co-Chairman of Imagine Films Entertainment.
PICTURES: *Actor*: The Journey (debut, 1959), Door-to-Door Maniac, The Music Man, The Courtship of Eddie's Father, Village of the Giants, The Wild Country, American Graffiti, Happy Mother's Day... Love George, The Spikes Gang, Eat My Dust!, I'm a Fool, The Shootist, The First Nudie Musical (cameo), More American Graffiti, The Magical World of Chuck Jones. *Director*: Grand Theft Auto (dir. debut, 1977; also actor, co-s.p.),Night Shift, Splash, Cocoon, Gung Ho (also exec. prod.), Willow, Parenthood (also co-story), Backdraft, Far and Away (also co-story, co-story), The Paper, Apollo 13, Ransom. *Exec. prod/prod.:* Leo & Loree, No Man's Land, Vibes, Clean and Sober, Closet Land, Far and Away, The Chamber, Inventing the Abbotts.
TELEVISION: *Series*: The Andy Griffith Show, The Smith Family, Happy Days, Fonz and the Happy Days Gang (voice), Parenthood, Hiller & Diller (exec. prod), Felicity (prod.). *Movies*: The Migrants, Locusts, Huckleberry Finn, Cotton Candy (dir., co-writer), Act of Love, Bitter Harvest, Fire on the Mountain, When Your Lover Leaves (also co.exec. prod.), Through the Magic Pyramid (exec. prod., dir.), Splash Too, Skyward (co-exec. prod., dir.), Into Thin Air (exec. prod.), Return to Mayberry, Frank Capra's American Dream. *Mini-series*: From the Earth to the Moon.
Guest: Red Skelton Hour, Playhouse 90, Dennis the Menace, Many Loves of Dobie Gillis, Five Fingers, Twilight Zone, Dinah Shore Show, The Fugitive, Dr. Kildare, The Big Valley, I Spy, Danny Kaye Show, Gomer Pyle USMC, The Monroes, Love American Style, Gentle Ben, Gunsmoke; Disney TV films (incl. A Boy Called Nuthin', Smoke).

HOWARD, SANDY
Producer. b. Aug. 1, 1927. e. Florida So. Coll. Ent. m.p. ind. 1946.
PICTURES: Tarzan and the Trappers (dir. only), Perils of the Deep, Diary of a Bachelor (dir. only), Gamera the Invincible (dir. only), One Step to hell (also dir. & s.p.), Jack of Diamonds (s.p. only), A Man Called Horse, Man in the Wilderness, Together Brothers, Neptune Factor, The Devil's Rain (exec. prod.), Sky Riders, The Last Castle, Embryo, Magna I-Beyond the Barrier Reef, The Battle, Island of Dr. Moreau, City on Fire, Death Ship (exec. prod.), Avenging Angel, Vice Squad (s.p. only), Kidnapped, The Boys Next Door, Street Justice (exec. prod.), Nightstick, Dark Tower (exec. prod.), Truk Lagoon (exec. prod.).

HOWELL, C. THOMAS
Actor. b. Los Angeles, CA, Dec. 7, 1966. m. actress Rae Dawn Chong. Former junior rodeo circuit champion.
PICTURES: E.T.: The Extra Terrestrial (debut, 1982), The Outsiders, Tank, Grandview U.S.A., Red Dawn, Secret Admirer, The Hitcher, Soul Man, A Tiger's Tale, Young Toscanini, Side Out, Far Out Man, The Return of the Musketeers, Kid, Nickel and Dime, Breaking the Rules, First Force, That Night, Tattle Tale,

Streetwise, To Protect and Serve, Gettysburg, Jail Bate, Teresa's Tattoo, Power Play, Treacherous, Payback, Dangerous Indiscretion, Hourglass (also dir.), Baby Face Nelson, Mad Dogs and Englishmen, Pure Danger (also dir.), The Big Fall (also dir.), Sleeping Dogs, Last Lives, Dilemma, Burning Down the House, Felons, Death Do Us Part.
TELEVISION: *Series*: Little People (only 4 yrs. old), Two Marriages, Kindred: The Embraced. *Movies*: It Happened One Christmas, Into the Homeland, Curiosity Kills, Acting on Impulse, Dark Reflection, Suspect Device. *Guest*: Nightmare Classics (Eye of the Panther).

HOWELLS, URSULA
Actress. b. Sept. 17, 1922. e. St. Paul's Sch., London. Stage debut, 1939, at Dundee Repertory with Bird in Hand followed by several plays inc. Springtime for Henry in N.Y., 1951; m.p. debut in Flesh and Blood, 1950; TV debut in Case of the Frightened Lady for BBC, 1948.
PICTURES: Lolly Madonna XXX, Catch My Soul, Hardcore, Escape from New York, Vice Squad, Total Exposure, Twist of Fate, I Believe in You, The Weak and the Wicked, The Horse's Mouth, Track the Man Down, Handcuffs London, The Constant Husband, The Third Key, Keep It Clean, Account Rendered, The Sicilians, The Blood Suckers, Torture Garden, Assignment K, Girly, Crossplot, Time After Time, The Tichborne Claimant.
TELEVISION: *Movies*: King Lear, The Small Back Room, A Woman Comes Home, For Services Rendered, Mine Own Executioner, The Cocktail Party, Father Dear Father, A Murder is Announced, The Cold Room, Jewels. *Series*: The Forsyte Saga, The Many Wives of Patrick. *Mini-series*: Cousin Bette.

HUBBARD, STANLEY
Satellite Broadcast Executive. b. St. Paul, MN, May 28, 1933. B.A. Univ. MN 1955. With Hubbard Broadcasting from 1950, named president 1967, chmn. & CEO 1983. Chairman & CEO U.S. Satellite Broadcasting Corp. Bd. dir. Fingerhut Corp. Broadcasting & Cable Hall of Fame 1991, Dist. Service Award , NAB 1995.

HUBLEY, SEASON
Actress. b. New York, NY, Mar. 14, 1951. Studied acting with Herbert Berghoff.
THEATER: *LA*: Heat, Triplet Collection, Rhythm of Torn Stars.
PICTURES: The Oracle (Horse's Mouth), Track the Man Down, They Can't Hang Me, Keep It Clean, Long Arm (Third Key), Death and The Sky Above, Mumsy Nanny Sonny and Girly, Crossploit.
TELEVISION: *Series*: Kung Fu, Family, All My Children, *Pilots*: Lond and Davis in New York, Blues Skies, The City. *Movies/Specials*: She Lives, The Healers, Death Flight, Loose Change, Elvis, Mrs. R's Daughter, Three Wishes of Billy Grier, Under the Influence, Christmas Eve, Shakedown on Sunset Strip, Unspeakable Acts, Child of the Night, Steel Justice, Key to Rebecca, All I Could See From Where I Stood, Stepfather III, Caribbean Mystery, Black Carrion, Vestige of Honor, Humanoids From the Deep. *Guest*: The Partridge Family, The Rookies, Kojak, Twilight Zone, Alfred Hitchcock Presents, Twilight Zone, Hitchhiker.

HUDDLESTON, DAVID
Actor, Producer. b. Vinton, VA, Sept. 17, 1930. e. American Acad. of Dramatic Arts. Son is actor Michael Huddleston.
THEATER: A Man for All Seasons, Front Page, Everybody Loves Opal, Ten Little Indians, Silk Stockings, Fanny, Guys and Dolls, The Music Man, Desert Song, Mame. Broadway: The First, Death of a Salesman.
PICTURES: All the Way Home (debut, 1963), A Lovely Way to Die, Slaves, Norwood, Rio Lobo, Fools, Parade, Bad Company, Blazing Saddles, McQ, The World's Greatest Lover, Capricorn One, Gorp, Smokey and the Bandit II, The Act, Santa Claus, Frantic, Life With Mikey, Cultivating Charlie. Something to Talk About (unbilled), Joe's Apartment, The Big Lebowski.
TELEVISION: *Series*: Tenafly, Petrocelli, The Kallikaks, Hizzoner. *Movies*: Sarge: The Badge or the Cross, The Priest Killer, Suddenly Single, The Homecoming, Brian's Song, Tenafly (pilot), Brock's Last Case, Hawkins on Murder, Heatwave, The Gun and the Pulpit, The Oregon Trail, Shark Kill, Sherlock Holmes in New York, Kate Bliss and the Ticker Tape Kid, Oklahoma City Dolls, Family Reunion, Computerside, M.A.D.D.: Mothers Against Drunk Drivers, Finnegan Begin Again, Family Reunion, Spot Marks the X, The Tracker, Margaret Bourke-White, In a Child's Name. *Mini-Series*: Once an Eagle.

HUDSON, ERNIE
Actor. b. Benton Harbor, MI, Dec. 17, 1945. e. Wayne St. Univ., Yale Sch. of Drama. Former Actors Ensemble Theater while in Detroit. Professional stage debut in L.A. production of Daddy Goodness.
PICTURES: Leadbelly (debut, 1976), The Main Event, The Jazz Singer, Penitentiary II, Spacehunter: Adventures in the Forbidden Zone, Going Berserk, Ghostbusters, The Joy of Sex, Weeds, Leviathan, Ghostbusters II, The Hand That Rocks the Cradle, Sugar Hill, No Escape, The Crow, The Cowboy Way, Airheads, Speechless, The Basketball Diaries, Congo, The Substitute.
TELEVISION: *Series*: Highcliffe Manor, The Last Precinct, Broken Badges. *Mini-series*: Roots: The Next Generations, Wild Palms. *Movies*: White Mama, Dirty Dozen: The Fatal Mission, Love on the Run. *Guest*: Fantasy Island, Little House on the Praire, One Day at a Time, Diff'rent Strokes, St. Elsewhere.

HUDSON, HUGH
Producer, Director. b. England. e. Eton. Began career as head of casting dept. with ad agency in London; left for Paris to work as editor for small film co. Returned to London to form Cammell-Hudson-Brownjohn Film Co., production house., turning out award-winning documentaries (Tortoise and Hare, A is for Apple). 1970, joined Ridley Scott to make TV commercials. 1975, formed Hudson Films to produce.
PICTURES: *Director*: Chariots of Fire, Greystoke: The Legend of Tarzan Lord of the Apes (also prod.), Revolution, Lost Angels.

HUEY, WARD L. JR.,
Media Executive. b. Dallas, TX, Apr. 26, 1938. e. So. Meth. U, BA, 1960. With dept. prodn., sales svc. mgr., regional sales mgr., gen sales mgr. Sta. WFAA-TV, TX 1970-67; sta. mgr., 1972-75. V.p. gen. mgr. Belo Broadcasting Corp., 1975; vice chmn. bd. dirs., pres. broadcast div, A. H. Belo Corp., 1987-. Chmn. affiliate bd. govs. ABC-TV, 1981-82. Chmn. bd. TV Operators Caucus, 1989. Mem.: exec. com., So. Meth. U. Meadows Sch. Arts, 1986-; Goodwill Industries Dallas, 1978-79; State Fair Tex., 1992. Bd. Dirs.: Children's Med. Found., 1985-94; Dallas Found, 1993-. Mem.: Maximum Svc TV Assn. (vice chmn., 1988-94); TV Bur. ADvt. (bd. dirs., exec. com., 1984-88); Assn. Broadast Execs. Tex. (bd. dirs., 1977-78); Dallas Advt. league (bd. dirs 1975-76); Salesman Club Dallas (pres. 1992-93); Dallas Country Club.

HUGH KELLY, DANIEL
Actor. b. Hoboken, NJ, Aug. 10, 1949. Began acting with the National Players touring U.S. in such plays as Henry IV Part 1, Charlie's Aunt, School for Wives.
THEATER: Arena Stage (DC): An Enemy of the People, Once in a Lifetime, Long Day's Journey Into Night. Actors Theatre (Louisville): Much Ado About Nothing, The Best Man, The Taming of the Shrew, The Rainmaker. *Off-B'way*: Hunchback of Notre Dame, Miss Margarita's Way, Juno's Swans, Fishing, Short-Changed Revue. *B'way*: Born Yesterday, Cat on a Hot Tin Roof.
PICTURES: Cujo, Nowhere to Hide, Someone to Watch Over Me, The Good Son, Bad Company.
TELEVISION: *Series*: Chicago Story, Hardcastle and McCormick, Second Noah. *Movies*: Nutcracker, This Ice, Murder Ink, Night of Courage, Citizen Cohn, Moment of Truth: A Mother's Deception, A Child's Cry for Help, The Tuskegee Airmen, Never Say Never: The Deidre Hall Story, No Greater Love, Stranger in My Home, Five Desperate Hours, Bad As I Wanna Be: The Dennis Rodman Story.

HUGHES, BARNARD
Actor. b. Bedford Hills, NY, July 16, 1915. Winner of Emmy for role as Judge in Lou Grant series (1978) and Tony Award for Da (1978). Inducted into Theatre Hall of Fame (1993).
PICTURES: Midnight Cowboy, Where's Poppa?, Cold Turkey, The Pursuit of Happiness, The Hospital, Rage, Sisters, Deadhead Miles, Oh God!, First Monday in October, Tron, Best Friends, Maxie, Where Are the Children?, The Lost Boys, Da, Doc Hollywood, Sister Act 2: Back in the Habit, The Fantasticks, The Odd Couple II.
TELEVISION: *Series*: Doc, Mr. Merlin, The Cavanaughs, Blossom. *Movies*: Guilty or Innocent, The Sam Sheppard Murder Case, See How She Runs, The Caryl Chessman Story, Tell Me My Name, Look Homeward, Angel, Father Brown: Detective, Nova, Homeward Bound, The Sky's No Limit, A Caribbean Mystery, Night of Courage, A Hobo's Christmas, Day One, Home Fires Burning, Guts and Glory: The Rise and Fall of Oliver North, The Incident, Miracle Child, Trick of the Eye, Past the Bleachers. *Guest*: Homicide, The Marshal.

HUGHES, JOHN
Writer, Director, Producer. b. Detroit, MI, Feb. 18, 1950. e. Univ. of AZ. Editor of National Lampoon before writing film script of National Lampoon's Class Reunion (1982). Made directorial debut with Sixteen Candles in 1984 which also wrote. In 1985 entered into deal with Paramount Pictures to write, direct and produce films with his own production unit, The John Hughes Co.
PICTURES: *Writer*: National Lampoon's Class Reunion, National Lampoon's Vacation, Mr. Mom, Nate and Hayes, Sixteen Candles (also dir.), The Breakfast Club (also dir., co-prod.), National Lampoon's European Vacation, Weird Science (also dir.), Pretty in Pink (also co-exec. prod.). *Writer/Prod*: Ferris Bueller's Day Off (also dir.), Some Kind of Wonderful, Planes Trains & Automobiles (also dir.), She's Having a Baby (also dir.), The Great Outdoors (exec. prod., s.p.), Uncle Buck (also dir.), National Lampoon's Christmas Vacation, Home Alone, Career Opportunities (exec. prod., co-s.p.), Only the Lonely (co-prod. only), Dutch, Curly Sue (also dir.), Home Alone 2: Lost in New York, Dennis the Menace, Baby's Day Out, Miracle on 34th Street, 101 Dalmations, Reach the Rock, Flubber, Home Alone 3.

HUGHES, KATHLEEN
Actress. r.n. Betty von Gerkan; b. Hollywood, CA, Nov. 14, 1928. e. Los Angeles City Coll., UCLA. m. Stanley Rubin, prod., mother of 4, Michael played Baby Matthew on Peyton Place. Studied drama; under contract, 20th-Fox, 1948-51; starred in Seven Year Itch 1954, La Jolla Playhouse; signed by UI, 1952. Theatre includes You Can't Take It With You, An Evening With Tennessee Williams, The Bar Off Melrose.

PICTURES: Road House, Mother is a Freshman, Mr. Belvedere Goes to College, Take Care of My Little Girl, It Happens Every Spring, When Willie Comes Marching Home, My Blue Heaven, Mister 880, No Way Out, I'll See You in My Dreams, Thy Neighbor's Wife, For Men Only (The Tall Lie), Sally and Saint Anne, Golden Blade, It Came From Outer Space, Dawn at Socorro, Glass Web, Cult of the Cobra, Three Bad Sisters, Promise Her Anything, The President's Analyst, The Take, Pete and Tillie, Ironweed, The Couch Trip, Revenge.
TELEVISION: *Guest*: Bob Cummings Show, Hitchcock, 77 Sunset Strip, G.E. Theatre, Bachelor Father, Frank Sinatra Show, Ed Wynn Show, Alan Young Show, The Tall Man, Dante, Tightrope, Markham, I Dream of Jeannie, Peyton Place, Gomer Pyle, Kismet, Ghost and Mrs. Muir, Bracken's World, The Survivors, Julia, Here's Lucy, To Rome with Love, The Interns, The Man and the City, Mission Impossible, The Bold Ones, Lucas Tanner, Marcus Welby, Barnaby Jones, Medical Center, M.A.S.H., General Hospital, Quincy, Finder of Lost Loves, The Young and the Restless. *Movies*: Babe, Forbidden Love, The Spell, Portrait of an Escort, Capitol, Mirror, Mirror, And Your Name is Jonah.

HUGHES, KEN
Director, Writer. b. Liverpool, England,, 1922. Ent. ind. as sound engineer with BBC, 1940; Doc. films, Army training films. Wrote book and lyrics for stage musical Oscar. Member: Assn. Cine Technicians, Writers' Guild of Great Britain.
AUTHOR: High Wray, The Long Echo, An Enemy of the State. Scripts: The Matarese Circle, Tussy is Me, The Queen's Own, RatsHallo Berlin.
PICTURES: *Dir./Writer*: Wide Boy, The House Across the Lake, Black 13 (dir. only), The Brain Machine, Case of the Red Monkey, Confession (The Deadliest Sin), Timeslip (The Atomic Man), Joe Macbeth, Wicked as They Come, The Long Haul, Jazz Boat, In the Nick, The Trials of Oscar Wilde, The Small World of Sammy Lee, Of Human Bondage (dir. only), Arrivederci Baby (also prod.), Casino Royale (co-dir.), Chitty Chitty Bang Bang, Cromwell, The Internecine Project, Alfie Darling (Oh Alfie!), Sextette (dir. only), Night School.
TELEVISION: Eddie (Emmy Award for writing, 1959), Sammy (Brit. Acad. Award). *Serials*: Solo for Canary, Enemy of the State. *Series*: Lenin 1917 (The Fall of Eagles), The Haunting, The Voice, Oil Strike North, Colditz, Churchill (BBC).
AWARDS: Golden Globe, Emmy, British TV Acad. Award (Script Writer of Year), Avorias Festival Merit Award, British Writer's Guild Award, British Critics Award (best serial).

HUGHES, WENDY
Actress. b. Melbourne, Australia, July 29, 1952. Studied acting at National Institute of Dramatic Art, Sydney.
PICTURES: Petersen, Sidecar Racers, High Rolling, Newsfront, My Brilliant Career, Kostas, Lucinda Brayford, Touch and Go, Hoodwink, A Dangerous Summer, Partners, Duet for Four, Lonely Hearts, Careful He Might Hear You, My First Wife, Remember Me, An Indecent Obsession, Happy New Year, Echoes of Paradise, Warm Nights on a Slow Moving Train, Boundaries of the Heart, Luigi's Ladies (also co-s.p.), Wild Orchid II, Princess Caraboo, Lust & Revenge, Paradise Road.
TELEVISION: *Movies*: Coralie Landsdowne Says No, Puzzle, Promises to Keep, Can't Get Started, The Heist, Donor. *Mini-series*: Power Without Glory, Return to Eden, Amerika, A Woman Named Jackie, *Series*: Rush, Snowy River: The McGregor Saga, State Coroner. *Guest*: Star Trek: The Next Generation, Homicide: Life on the Street.

HUIZENGA, HARRY WAYNE
Entrepreneur, Entertainment Executive. b. Evergreen Park, IL, Dec 29, 1939. e. Calvin College, 1957-58. m. Martha Jean Pike, Apr. 17, 1972. Vice chmn., pres., chief operating officer Waste Mgmt. Inc., Oak Brook, IL, 1968-84; prin. Huizenga Holdings, Inc., Ft. Lauderdale, FL, 1984-; chmn., chief exec. officer Blockbuster Entertainment Corp., Ft. Lauderdale, 1987-1995; owner Florida Marlins, Miami, 1992-; co-owner Miami Dolphins, Joe Robbie Stadium. Mem. Florida Victory Com., 1988-89, Team Repub. Nat. com., Washington, 1988-90. Recipient Entrepenour of Yr. award Wharton Sch. U. Pa., 1989, Excalibur award Bus. Leader of Yr. News/Sun Sentinel, 1990, Silver Medallion Brotherhood award Broward Region Nat. Conf. Christians and Jews, 1990, Laureates award Jr. Achievement Broward and Palm Beach Counties, 1990, Jim Murphy Humanitarian Award The Emerald Soc., 1990, Entrepreneur of Yr. award Disting. Panel Judges Fla., 1990, Man of Yr. Billboard/Time Mag., 1990, Man of Yr. Juvenile Diabetes Found., 1990, Florida Free Enterpriser of Yr. award Fla. Coun. on Econ. Edn., 1990, commendation for youth restricted video State of Fla. Office of Gov., 1989, Hon. Mem. Appreciation award Bond Club Ft. Lauderdale, 1989, honored with endowed teaching chair Broward Community Coll., 1990. Mem. Lauderdale Yacht Club, Tournament Players Club, Coral Ridge Country Club, Fisher Island Club, Ocean Reef Club, Cat Cay Yacht Club, Linville Ridge Country Club. Avocations: golf, collecting antique cars. Sold Blockbuster Entertainment Corp. to Viacom, 1994. Retired.

HULCE, TOM
Actor. b. White Water, WI, Dec. 6, 1953. e. NC School of the Arts. Understudied and then co-starred in Equus on Broadway. Directorial stage debut Sleep Around Town. Appeared in IMAX film Wings of Courage. Recipient of Emmy Award, 1996.
THEATER: A Memory of Two Mondays, Julius Caesar, Candida, The Sea Gull, The Rise and Rise of Daniel Rocket, Eastern Standard, A Few Good Men (Tony nom.), Hamlet.
PICTURES: September 30, 1955 (debut, 1978), National Lampoon's Animal House, Those Lips Those Eyes, Amadeus (Acad. Award nom.), Echo Park, Slamdance, Dominick and Eugene, Parenthood, Shadowman, The Inner Circle, Fearless, Mary Shelley's Frankenstein, Wings of Courage, The Hunchback of Notre Dame (voice).
TELEVISION: Movies: Murder in Mississippi, Black Rainbow, The Heidi Chronicles. Mini-Series: The Adams Chronicles. Specials: Emily Emily, The Rise and Rise of Daniel Rocket, Song of Myself, Forget-Me-Not Lane, Tall Tales and Legends (John Henry).

HUNDT, REED
Federal Official. b. Ann Arbor, MI, March 3, 1948. B.A. Yale 1969, J.D. 1974. Served on various U.S. circuit courts 1975-80. Associate Latham & Watkins 1975, partner 1982. Named to FCC 1994 as Chairman. Resigned 1997.

HUNNICUT, GAYLE
Actress. b. Fort Worth, TX, February 6, 1943. e. UCLA, B.A., with honors, theater arts & English major. Early career, community theatres in Los Angeles.
THEATER: The Ride Across Lake Constance, Twelfth Night, The Tempest, Dog Days, The Admirable Crichton, A Woman of No Importance, Hedda Gabler, Peter Pan, Macbeth, Uncle Vanya, The Philadelphia Story, Miss Firecracker Contest, Exit The King, The Doctor's Dilemma, So Long on Lonely Street, The Big Knife, Edith Wharton at Home, The Little Foxes, Dangerous Corner.
PICTURES: The Wild Angels (debut, 1966), P.J., Eye of the Cat, Marlowe, Fragment of Fear, The Freelance, Voices, Running Scared, Legend of Hell House, Scorpio, L'Homme Sans Visage, The Spiral Staircase, The Sell Out, Strange Shadows in an Empty Room, Once in Paris, One Take Two, Fantomas, Privilege, Sherlock Holmes, Target, Dream Lover, Turnaround, Silence Like Glass.
TELEVISION: Series: Dallas (1989-91). Movies: The Smugglers, The Million Dollar Face, The Return of the Man From U.N.C.L.E., The First Olympics: Athens 1896. Specials: Man and Boy, The Golden Bowl, The Ambassadors, The Ripening Seed, Fall of Eagles, The Switch, Humboldt's Gift, The Life and Death of Dylan Thomas, Return of the Saint, The Lady Killers, Savage in the Orient, Strong Medicine. Mini-Series: A Man Called Intrepid, The Martian Chronicles, Dream West. Guest: Taxi.

HUNT, HELEN
Actress. b. Los Angeles, CA, June 15, 1963. Daughter of dir. Gordon Hunt.
THEATER: Been Taken, Our Town, The Taming of the Shrew, Methusalem.
PICTURES: Rollercoaster, Girls Just Want to Have Fun, Peggy Sue Got Married, Project X, Miles From Home, Trancers, Stealing Home, Next of Kin, The Waterdance, Only You, Bob Roberts, Mr. Saturday Night, Kiss of Death, Twister, As Good as It Gets (Acad. Award, Golden Globe Award, Best Actress, 1997).
TELEVISION: Series: Swiss Family Robinson, Amy Prentiss, The Fitzpatricks, It Takes Two, Mad About You (Emmy Award, 1996, 1997; Golden Globe Award, 1997). Movies: Pioneer Woman, All Together Now, Death Scream, The Spell, Transplant, Angel Dusted, Child Bride of Short Creek, The Miracle of Kathy Miller, Quarterback Princess, Bill: On His Own, Sweet Revenge, Incident at Dark River, Into the Badlands, Murder in New Hampshire: The Pamela Smart Story, In the Company of Darkness. Specials: Weekend, Land of Little Rain. Special: Sexual Healing. Guest: St. Elsewhere, Family, Mary Tyler Moore Show, The Hitchhiker.

HUNT, LINDA
Actress. b. Morristown, NJ, Apr. 2, 1945. e. Interlochen Arts Acad., MI, and Chicago's Goodman Theatre & Sch. of Drama. Narrated documentary Ecological Design: Inventing the Future.
THEATER: Long Wharf (New Haven):Hamlet, The Rose Tattoo, Ah Wilderness. NY: Mother Courage, End of the World (Tony nom.), A Metamorphosis in Miniature (Obie Award), Top Girls (Obie Award), Aunt Dan and Lemon, The Cherry Orchard. Regional: The Three Sisters.
PICTURES: Popeye (debut, 1980) The Year of Living Dangerously (Academy Award, best supporting actress, 1983), The Bostonians, Dune, Silverado, Eleni, Waiting for the Moon, She-Devil, Kindergarten Cop, If Looks Could Kill, Rain Without Thunder, Twenty Bucks, Younger and Younger, Ready to Wear (Pret-a-Porter), Pocahontas (voice), The Relic, Eat Your Heart Out, Amazon, Paul Monette: The Brink of Summer's End.
TELEVISION: Series: Space Rangers. Movie: The Room Upstairs. Specials: Ah Wilderness, The Room. Guest: Fame.

HUNT, MARSHA
Actress. b. Chicago, IL, Oct. 17, 1917.
THEATER: B'way: Joy to the World, Devils Disciple, Legend of Sarah, Borned in Texas, Tunnel of Love, The Paisley Convertible.
PICTURES: The Virginia Judge (debut, 1935), College Holiday, Easy to Take, Blossoms in the Dust, Panama Hattie, Joe Smith American, These Glamour Girls, Winter Carnival, Irene, Pride and Prejudice, Flight Command, The Affairs of Martha, Kid Glove Killer, Seven Sweethearts, Cheers for Miss Bishop, Trial of Mary Dugan, Thousands Cheer, The Human Comedy, None Shall Escape, Lost Angel, Cry Havoc, Bride by Mistake, Music for Millions, Valley of Decision, A Letter for Evie, Smash-Up, Carnegie Hall, The Inside Story, Raw Deal, Jigsaw, Take One False Step, Actors and Sin, Happy Time, No Place to Hide, Back from the Dead, Bombers B-52, Blue Denim, The Plunderers, Johnny Got His Gun.
TELEVISION: Series: Peck's Bad Girl. Guest: Philco, Studio One, Ford Theatre, Show of Shows, G.E. Theatre, Climax, Hitchcock, The Defenders, Twilight Zone, Cains Hundred, Gunsmoke, The Breaking Point, Outer Limits, Profiles in Courage, Ben Casey, Accidental Family, Run For Your Life, My Three Sons, The Outsiders, Name of the Game, Univ.'s 120, Ironside, Marcus Welby, M.D., Police Story, The Young Lawyers, Harry-O, The Mississippi, Hot Pursuit, Shadow Chaser, Matlock, Murder She Wrote, Star Trek: The Next Generation.

HUNT, PETER R.
Director, Editor. b. London, England,, March 11, 1928. e. Romford, England and Rome, Italy, London Sch. of Music. Actor English Rep. Entered film as camera asst. documentary, later asst film editor documentary, then asst editor features, London Films.
PICTURES: Editor: Stranger from Venus (Immediate Decision), Doublecross, A Hill in Korea, Secret Tent, Admirable Crichton, A Cry From the Streets, Next to No Time, Ferry to Hong Kong, Sink the Bismark!, There was a Crooked Man, The Greengage Summer (Loss of Innocence), On the Fiddle (Operation Snafu) H.M.S. Defiant (Damn the Defiant). Supervising editor/2nd Unit Director: Dr. No, Call Me Bwana, From Russia With Love, Goldfinger, The Ipcress File, Thunderball, You Only Live Twice. Assoc. Prod.: Chitty Chitty Bang Bang. Director: On Her Majesty's Secret Service, Gullivers Travels, Gold, Shout at the Devil, Death Hunt, Wild Geese II, Hyper Sapien, Assassination.
TELEVISION: Director: Series: The Persuaders, Shirley's World, The Pencil, Smart Alec Kill (Philip Marlowe). Movies: The Beasts Are in the Streets, Eyes of a Witness. Mini-Series: Last Days of Pompeii.

HUNT, PETER H.
Director. b. Pasadena, CA, Dec. 16, 1938. e. Hotchkiss, Yale U., Yale Drama Sch. m. actress Barbette Tweed. Dir. for Williamston Theatre since 1957. Lighting designer on B'way. (1963-69) Awards: Tony, Ace, Peabody (twice), N.Y. Drama Critics, London Drama Critics, Edgar Allan Poe, Christopher.
THEATER: 1776 (London & B'way.), Georgy (B'way.), Scratch (B'way.), Goodtime Charley (B'way.), Give 'Em Hell Harry, Magnificent Yankee (Kennedy Center). Tours: Bully, Three Penny Opera, Sherlock Holmes, Bus Stop.
PICTURES: 1776, Give 'Em Hell Harry.
TELEVISION: Specials: Adventures of Huckleberry Finn, Life on the Mississippi, A Private History of a Campaign That Failed, A New Start, Mysterious Stranger, Sherlock Holmes (cable), Bus Stop (cable). Movies: Flying High, Rendezvous Motel, When She Was Bad, Skeezer, The Parade, Sins of the Past, It Came Upon the Midnight Clear, Charley Hannah, Danielle Steel's Secrets, Sworn to Vengeance. Pilots: Adam's Rib, Hello Mother Goodbye, Ivan the Terrible, Quark, Mixed Nuts, Wilder and Wilder, The Main Event, Nuts and Bolts, The Good Witch of Laurel Canyon, Masquerade, Stir Crazy, The Wizard of Elm Street, Travelling Man, My Africa.

HUNT, WILLIE
Executive Producer. b. Van Nuys, CA, Oct. 1, 1941. e. Utah State U., B.A., 1963. m. writer Tim Considine. Started in industry as secretary at Warner Bros., 1965; named exec. secty. to Ted Ashley, WB, 1969; story analyst, WB, 1974; story editor, WB, 1975; named West Coast story editor for WB, 1978; joined MGM in 1979 as v.p., motion picture development. Moved to United Artists as v.p.-prod.; 1982. 1983 sr. v.p. of prod. at Rastar Prods.; 1984, indep. prod., Tri-Star; 1986, sr. v.p., Freddie Fields Prods. 1988: Loverboy (co-prod.) 1989, sr. v.p. Considine Prods. 1993, partner, Creative Entertainment Group.

HUNTER, HOLLY
Actress. b. Conyers, GA. March 20, 1958. e. studied acting, Carnegie-Mellon Univ. Appeared Off-B'way in Battery (1981) and Weekend Near Madison. Appeared in 5 Beth Henley plays: The Miss Firecracker Contest (Off-B'way), as a replacement in Crimes of the Heart (B'way) The Wake of Jamey Foster (B'way), Lucky Spot (Williamstown Theater Festival), and Control Freaks (L.A.; also co-prod.). Also: A Lie of the Mind (L.A.).

PICTURES: The Burning (debut, 1981), Swing Shift, Raising Arizona, Broadcast News (NY Film Critics, LA Film Critics and Natl. Board of Review Awards, Acad. Award nom., 1987), End of the Line, Miss Firecracker, Animal Behavior, Always, Once Around, The Firm (Acad. Award nom.), The Piano (Academy Award, Cannes Film Fest., LA Film Critics, NY Film Critics, Natl. Board of Review, Natl. Society of Film Critics & Golden Globe Awards, 1993), Home for the Holidays, Copycat, Crash.
TELEVISION: Movies: Svengali, An Uncommon Love, With Intent to Kill, A Gathering of Old Men, Roe vs. Wade (Emmy Award, 1989), Crazy in Love, The Positively True Adventures of the Alleged Texas Cheerleader-Murdering Mom (Emmy Award, 1993). Guest: Fame (pilot).

HUNTER, KIM
Actress. r.n. Janet Cole. b. Detroit, MI, Nov. 12, 1922. e. public schools. d. Donald and Grace Mabel (Lind) Cole. Studied acting with Charmine Lantaff Camine, 1938-40, Actors Studio; First stage appearance, 1939; played in stock, 1940-42; Broadway debut in A Streetcar Named Desire, 1947; frequent appearances in summer stock and repertory theater, 1940-; appeared Am. Shakespeare Festival, Stratford, CT, 1961. Autobiography-cookbook: Loose in the Kitchen (1975).
THEATER: NY: Darkness at Noon, The Chase, The Children's Hour (revival), The Tender Trap, Write Me a Murder, Weekend, The Penny Wars, The Women, The Cherry Orchard, To Grandmother's House We Go, When We Dead Awaken, Territorial Rites, Man and Superman, A Murder of Crows, Eye of the Beholder, An Ideal Husband. Tours: Two Blind Mice, They Knew What They Wanted, And Miss Reardon Drinks a Little, In Praise of Love, The Gin Game. Regional: The Glass Menagerie, The Lion in Winter, The Chalk Garden, Elizabeth the Queen, Semmelweiss, The Belle of Amherst, The Little Foxes, Another Part of the Forest, Ghosts, Death of a Salesman, Cat on a Hot Tin Roof, Life With Father, Sabrina Fair, Faulkner's Bicycle, Antique Pink, The Belle of Amherst, Painting Churches, A Delicate Balance, Jokers, Remembrance, The Gin Game, A Murder of Crows, Watch on the Rhine, Suddenly Last Summer, A Smaller Place, Open Window, The Cocktail Hour, The Belle of Amherst, Love Letters, Do Not Go Gentle, All The Way Home, Driving Miss Daisy, Greytop in Love.
PICTURES: The Seventh Victim (debut, 1943), Tender Comrade, When Strangers Marry (Betrayed), You Came Along, Stairway to Heaven (A Matter of Life and Death), A Canterbury Tale, A Streetcar Named Desire (Academy Award, best supporting actress, 1951), Anything Can Happen, Deadline: U.S.A., The Young Stranger, Bermuda Affair, Storm Center, Money Women and Guns, Lilith, Planet of the Apes, The Swimmer, Beneath the Planet of the Apes, Escape from the Planet of the Apes, Dark August, The Kindred, Two Evil Eyes, Midnight in the Garden of Good and Evil, A Price Below Rubies, A Smaller Place.
TELEVISION: Made TV debut on Actors Studio Program, 1948. Series: The Edge of Night (1979-80). Specials: Requiem for a Heavyweight, The Comedian (both on Playhouse 90); Give Us Barabbas, Stubby Pringle's Christmas, Project: U.F.O., Three Sovereigns for Sarah, Vivien Leigh: Scarlett and Beyond, Martin Luther King: The Dream and the Drum, Hurricane Andrew Project. Guest: Love American Style, Columbo, Cannon, Night Gallery, Mission Impossible, Marcus Welby, Hec Ramsey, Griff, Police Story, Ironside, Medical Center, Baretta, Gibbsville, The Oregon Trail, Scene of the Crime, Hunter, Murder She Wrote, Class of '96, Mad About You, L.A. Law, All My Children, As the World Turns. Movies: Dial Hot Line, In Search of America, The Magician (pilot), Unwed Father, Born Innocent, Bad Ronald, Ellery Queen (Too Many Suspects), The Dark Side of Innocence, The Golden Gate Murders, F.D.R.: The Last Year, Skokie, Private Sessions, Drop-Out Mother, Cross of Fire, Bloodlines: Murder in the Family, Hurricane Andrew. Mini-Series: Once an Eagle, Backstairs at the White House.

HUNTER, TAB
Actor. r.n. Arthur Gelien. b. New York, NY, July 11, 1931. Served with U.S. Coast Guard. Entered industry in 1948.
PICTURES: The Lawless (debut, 1950), Island of Desire, Gun Belt, Steel Lady, Return to Treasure Island, Track of the Cat, Battle Cry, Sea Chase, The Burning Hills, The Girl He Left Behind, Lafayette Escadrille, Gunman's Walk, Damn Yankees, That Kind of Woman, They Came to Cordura, The Pleasure of His Company, Operation Bikini, The Golden Arrow, Ride the Wild Surf, The Loved One, War Gods of the Deep, Birds Do It, Fickle Finger of Fate, Hostile Guns, The Arousers (Sweet Kill), Life and Times of Judge Roy Bean, Timber Tramp, Won Ton Ton the Dog Who Saved Hollywood, Polyester, Pandemonium, Grease 2, Lust in the Dust (also co-prod.), Cameron's Closet, Grotesque, Out of the Dark, Dark Horse (also story).
TELEVISION: Movies: San Francisco International, Katie: Portrait of a Centerfold. Series: The Tab Hunter Show, Mary Hartman Mary Hartman.

HUNTER, TIM
Director. e. Harvard, AFI.
PICTURES: Over the Edge (co-s.p.). Dir.: Tex (also s.p.), Sylvester, River's Edge, Paint It Black, The Saint of Fort Washington, The Maker .
TELEVISION: Movie: Lies of the Twins, People Next Door. Series: Homicide: Life on the Street, Chicago Hope, Nowhere Man.

HUPPERT, ISABELLE
Actress. b. Paris, France, March 16, 1955. e. Conservatoire National d'Art Dramatique.
PICTURES: Faustine and the Beautiful Summer (Growing Up; debut, 1971), Cesar and Rosalie, Going Places, Rosebud, The Rape of Innocence, The Judge and the Assassin, The Lacemaker, Violette (Cannes Fest. Award, 1977), The Bronte Sisters, Loulou, Heaven's Gate, Coup de Torchon, Every Man for Himself, The True Story of Camille, Wings of the Dove, Deep Water, Entre Nous, The Trout, Cactus, Signed Charlotte, The Bedroom Window, The Possessed, Story of Women (Venice Fest. Award, 1988), Milan Noir, Madame Bovary, Revenge of a Woman, Malina, Apres l'Amour (After Love), Amateur, The Separation, A Judgment in Stone, Love's Debris, The Elective Affinities, Les Palmes de M. Schultz, Rien ne va Plus.
TELEVISION: Gulliver's Travels (voice). Mini-series: Seobe.

HURD, GALE ANNE
Producer. b. Los Angeles, CA, Oct. 25, 1955. e. Stanford U., Phi Beta Kappa, 1977. Joined New World Pictures in 1977 as exec. asst. to pres. Roger Corman, then named dir. of advertising and pub. and moved into prod. management capacities on several New World films. Left in 1982 to form own co., Pacific Western Productions. Honored by NATO with special merit award for Aliens. Served as juror, U.S. Film Fest., Utah, 1988 and for 1989 Focus Student Film Awards. Member, Hollywood Women's Political Committee. Board of Trustees, AFI. The Amer. Film Inst. created Gale Anne Hurd production grants for Institute's Directing Workshop for Women. Bd. of dir. The Independent Feature Project/West.
PICTURES: Smokey Bites the Dust (co-prod. with Roger Corman, 1981), The Terminator (Grand Prix, Avoriaz Film Fest., France), Aliens (Hugo Award) Alien Nation (Saturn nom.), The Abyss, Downtown (exec. prod.), Tremors (exec. prod.), Terminator 2 (exec. prod.), The Waterdance, Raising Cain, No Escape, Safe Passage, The Relic, The Ghost and The Darkness, Dante's Peak, Switchback, Snake Eyes, Armageddon, Dead Man on Campus, Virus.
TELEVISION: Movies: Cast a Deadly Spell, Witch Hunt, Sugartime.

HURLOCK, ROGER W.
Pres. Hurlock Cine-World. b. Cambridge, MD, May 30, 1912. e. Baltimore City Coll. Ent. m.p. ind. as publicist, Hippodrome Theatre, Balt.; asst. mgr., Lessor-operator Imperial and Majestic Theatres, Balt., 1931-35; real estate, bldg., farming, Maryland and Alaska, 1936-58; elected bd. mem., Allied Artists, 1958; asst. to pres., 1961-63; chmn. budget comm., 1963; chmn. policy comm., 1964; c.p. exec. comm. member, 1964; v.p., chf. operating officer 1965; chmn. exec. comm., 1966; pres., 1967. pres., Hurlock Cine-World, 1969.

HURT, JOHN
Actor. b. Shirebrook, Derbyshire, Jan. 22, 1940. e. St. Martin's Sch. for Art, London, RADA.
THEATER: The Dwarfs, Little Malcolm and His Struggle Against the Eunuchs, Man and Superman, Belcher's Luck, Ride a Cock Horse, The Caretaker, Romeo and Juliet, Ruffian on the Streets, The Dumb Waiter, Travesties, The Arrest, The Seagull, The London Vertigo, A Month in the Country.
PICTURES: The Wild and the Willing (debut, 1962), This is My Street, A Man for All Seasons, The Sailor from Gibraltar, Before Winter Comes, Sinful Davey, In Search of Gregory, 10 Rillington Place, Mr. Forbush and the Penguins, The Pied Piper, Little Malcolm, The Naked Civil Servant, La Linea del Fiume, The Ghoul, East of Elephant Rock, The Disappearance, Midnight Express (Acad. Award nom.), Watership Down (voice), The Lord of the Rings (voice), The Shout, Alien, The Elephant Man (Acad. Award nom.), Heaven's Gate, History of the World Part I, Night Crossing, Partners, The Plague Dogs (voice), The Osterman Weekend, Champions, The Hit, Success Is the Best Revenge, 1984, After Darkness, The Black Cauldron (voice), Jake Speed, From the Hip, Spaceballs, Aria, Vincent (voice), White Mischief, Little Sweetheart, Poison Candy, Bengali Night, Scandal, Frankenstein Unbound, The Field, King Ralph, Romeo-Juliet, Resident Alien, Windprints, I Dreamt I Woke Up, Lapse of Memory, Dark at Noon or Eyes and Lies, Monolith, Hans Christian Andersen's Thumbelina (voice), Even Cowgirls Get the Blues, Crime and Punishment, Great Moments in Aviation, Second Best, Betrayal (voice), Rob Roy, Wild Bill, Two Nudes Bathing, Saigon Baby, Dead Man, Love & Death on Long Island, Contact, The Climb, Bandyta, If... Dog... Rabbit, Desert Blue, The Commissioner, All the Little Animals.
TELEVISION: Playboy of the Western World, A Tragedy of Two Ambitions, Green Julia, Nijinsky, Ten from the Twenties, The Peddler, The Naked Civil Servant, Spectre, Deadline, The Jim Henson Hour, King Lear, The Investigation: Inside a Terrorist Bombing, Six Characters in Search of an Author, Shades of Fear, Prisoners in Time. Mini-series: Crime and Punishment, I Claudius, The Storyteller, Red Fox.

HURT, MARY BETH
Actress. b. Marshalltown, IA, Sept. 26, 1946. m. writer-dir. Paul Schrader. e. U. of Iowa, NYU Sch. of Arts. Stage debut in 1973 with N.Y. Shakespeare Fest. (More Than You Deserve, Pericles, The Cherry Orchard).
THEATER: As You Like It (Central Park), 2 seasons with Phoenix Theater, Love For Love, Tralawny of the Wells, Secret Service, Boy Meets Girl, Father's Day, Crimes of the Heart, The Misanthrope, Benefactors, The Nest of the Wood Grouse, The Day Room, Othello, A Delicate Balance.
PICTURES: Interiors (debut, 1978), Head Over Heels (Chilly Scenes of Winter), A Change of Seasons, The World According to Garp, D.A.R.Y.L., Compromising Positions, Parents, Slaves of New York, Defenseless, Light Sleeper, My Boyfriend's Back, The Age of Innocence, Six Degrees of Separation, From the Journals of Jean Seberg, Alkali Iowa, Affliction, Boy's Life 2.
TELEVISION: Series: Nick and Hillary. Movies: Baby Girl Scott, Shimmer. Specials: The Five-Forty-Eight, Secret Service (NET Theatre). Guest: Kojak.

HURT, WILLIAM
Actor. b. Washington, DC, Mar. 20, 1950. Lived as child in South Pacific when father was dir. of Trust Territories for U.S. State Dept. e. Tufts as theology major, switched to drama in jr. year, Juilliard. Acted with Oregon Shakespearean Fest. Leading actor with New York's Circle Repertory Company (Theatre World Award), since 1976.
THEATER: NY: The Fifth of July, My Life (Obie Award), Ulysses in Traction, The Runner Stumbles, Hamlet, Childe Byron, Beside Herself. NY Shakespeare Festival: Henry V, A Midsummer's Night's Dream, Hurlyburly (off-B'way and B'way). Regional: Good (S.F.), Ivanov (Yale).
PICTURES: Altered States (debut, 1980), Eyewitness, Body Heat, The Big Chill, Gorky Park, Kiss of the Spider Woman (Academy Award, 1985), Children of a Lesser God, Broadcast News, A Time of Destiny, The Accidental Tourist, I Love You to Death, Alice, The Doctor, Until the End of the World, Mr. Wonderful, The Plague, Trial by Jury, Second Best, Smoke, Jane Eyre, Secrets Shared With a Stranger, Michael, Loved, Dark City, The Proposition, Lost in Space, One True Thing.
TELEVISION: Specials: Verna: USO Girl, Best of Families, All the Way Home, The Odyssey of John Dos Passos (voice).

HUSSEY, OLIVIA
Actress. b. Buenos Aires, Apr. 17, 1951. Attended Italia Conti Stage School, London. Began acting at age 8.
PICTURES: The Battle of the Villa Fiorita (debut, 1965), Cup Fever, All the Right Noises, Romeo and Juliet, Summertime Killer, Lost Horizon, Black Christmas, Death on the Nile, The Cat and the Canary, Virus, The Man With Bogart's Face, Escape 2000, Distortions, The Jeweler's Shop, The Undeclared War, Save Me, Ice Cream Man.
TELEVISION: Movies/Mini-Series: Jesus of Nazareth, The Pirate, The Bastard, Ivanhoe, Last Days of Pompeii, The Corsican Brothers, Psycho IV: The Beginning, Stephen King's IT, Save Me, Quest of the Delta Knights, H-Bomb, Dead Man's Island, Lonesome Dove, Shame, The Gardener. Guest: Murder She Wrote, Boy Meets World.

HUSTON, ANJELICA
Actress. b. Santa Monica, CA, July 8, 1951. Father is late writer-dir.-actor, John Huston. Brother is dir. Danny Huston. Raised in St. Clerans, Ireland. Studied acting at the Loft Studio and with Peggy Furey, Martin Landau. Appeared in 3-D Disney short Captain Eo.
PICTURES: A Walk With Love and Death (debut, 1969), Sinful Davey, Swashbuckler, The Last Tycoon, The Postman Always Rings Twice, Frances, The Ice Pirates, This is Spinal Tap, Prizzi's Honor (Academy Award, best supporting actress, 1985), Good to Go (Short Fuse), Gardens of Stone, The Dead, A Handful of Dust, Mr. North, Crimes and Misdemeanors, Enemies a Love Story (Acad. Award nom.), The Witches, The Grifters (Acad. Award nom.), The Addams Family, The Player, Manhattan Murder Mystery, Addams Family Values, The Perez Family, The Crossing Guard, Bastard Out of Carolina (dir.), Buffalo '66, Phoenix, Ever After: A Cinderella Story, The Mammy.
TELEVISION: Movies: The Cowboy and the Ballerina, Family Pictures, And the Band Played On. Specials: Faerie Tale Theatre, A Rose for Miss Emily. Mini-Series: Lonesome Dove, Buffalo Girls.

HUSTON, DANNY
Director. b. Rome, Italy, May 14, 1962. Youngest son of dir.-actor John Huston and actress Zoe Sallis. Brother of actress Anjelica and screenwriter Tony Huston. e. Overseas School, Rome; Intl branch of Milfield School in Exeter, London Film School. A constant visitor to his father's sets throughout the world, he began working on his father's films, beginning in Cuernavaca, Mexico as second-unit dir. on Under the Volcano. Directed TV doc. on Peru and on making of Santa Claus: The Movie; and TV features Bigfoot and Mr. Corbett's Ghost.
PICTURES: Mr. North (debut, 1988), Becoming Colette, The Maddening, Leaving Las Vegas (actor only), Ana Karenina (actor only).
TELEVISION: Movie: Ice Princess.

HUTCHINSON, LINDA TAYLOR
Executive. Pres. Association of Film Commissioners Intl.

HUTTE, ROBERT E.
Exhibitor. b. Escanaba, MI, Oct. 22, 1917. e. Wisc. Inst. of Technology. Mgr. insp. lab. Iowa Ord. Plant 1940-42, Army Artil. 1942, Entered business as exhibitor in Southern Iowa 1943; then theatre owner and manager there. Elected board of directors, Allied Theatre Owners of Iowa, Nebraska & Missouri 1948, 1950, 1952. Democratic candidate Iowa State Auditor 1960; Pres. Insurance Advisors, Des Moines, IA; pres Leisure Homes, Nursing Homes; pres., Leisure Homes of Texas; pres. Wodon & Romar Prods., Austin, TX 1970-75. Real estate broker & pres Leisure Mor, theatres in West TX; elected board of dir. National Independent Theatre Exhibitors 1979; Pres. Southwestern Indep. Theatre Exhibitors Assn. of TX, OK, AR, LA & NM; 1979 elected pres. Natl. Independent Theatre Exhibitors Assn. 1980-present. Lifetime member, Foundation of Motion Picture Pioneers.

HUTTON, BETTY
Actress. r.n. Betty June Thornburg. b. Battle Creek, MI, Feb. 26, 1921. Sister was singer-actress Marion Hutton. Was vocalist for Vincent Lopez orchestra earning nickname the Blonde Bombshell. Debuted on B'way 1940 in Two for the Show, followed by Panama Hattie. Signed by Paramount in 1941. Returned to stage in Fade Out Fade In, Annie.
PICTURES: The Fleet's In (debut, 1942), Star Spangled Rhythm, Happy Go Lucky, Let's Face It, The Miracle of Morgan's Creek, And the Angels Sing, Here Come the Waves, Incendiary Blonde, Duffy's Tavern, The Stork Club, Cross My Heart, The Perils of Pauline, Dream Girl, Red Hot and Blue, Annie Get Your Gun, Let's Dance, Sailor Beware (cameo), The Greatest Show on Earth, Somebody Loves Me, Spring Reunion.
TELEVISION: Series: The Betty Hutton Show (1959-60). Special: Satins and Spurs. Guest: Dinah Shore Chevy Show, Greatest Show on Earth, Burke's Law, Gunsmoke.

HUTTON, BRIAN, G.
Director. b. New York, NY, 1935. Started as bit player in films (incl. Fear Strikes Out, Gunfight at the O.K. Corral) before dir. for tv, then features.
PICTURES: The Wild Seed (debut, 1965), The Pad and How to Use It, Sol Madrid, Where Eagles Dare, Kelly's Heroes, X Y and Zee (Zee & Company), Night Watch, The First Deadly Sin, High Road to China, Hostile Takeover.
TELEVISION: Institute For Revenge.

HUTTON, LAUREN
Actress. r.n. Mary Hutton. b. Charleston, SC, Nov. 17, 1943. e. U. of South Florida, Sophie Newcombe Coll. As model featured on more covers than any other American. Stage debut at LA Public Theatre in Extremities.
PICTURES: Paper Lion (debut, 1968), Pieces of Dreams, Little Fauss and Big Halsy, Rocco Papaleo, The Gambler, Gator, Welcome to L.A., Viva Knievel!, A Wedding, American Gigolo, Paternity, Zorro the Gay Blade, Tout Feu tout Flamme (Hecate), Lassiter, Once Bitten, Flagrant Desire, Malone, Blue Blood, Bulldance (Forbidden Sun), Run For Your Life, Billions, Guilty as Charged, Missing Pieces, My Father the Hero.
TELEVISION: Mini-Series: The Rhinemann Exchange, Sins. Movies: Someone Is Watching Me, Institute for Revenge, Starflight, The Cradle Will Fall, Scandal Sheet, The Return of Mike Hammer, Time Stalker, Monte Carlo, Perfect People, Fear. Series: Paper Dolls, Falcon Crest, Lauren Hutton and... (talk show), Central Park West.

HUTTON, TIMOTHY
Actor. b. Malibu, CA, Aug. 16, 1960. Father was late actor Jim Hutton. Debut in bit part in father's film Never Too Late. Acted in high school plays; toured with father in Harvey during vacation. Directed Cars video Drive (1984).
THEATER: NY: Love Letters (B'way debut, 1989), Prelude to a Kiss, Babylon Gardens.
PICTURES: Never Too Late (debut, 1965), Ordinary People (Academy Award, best supporting actor, 1980; also Golden Globe & LA Film Critics Awards), Taps, Daniel, Iceman, The Falcon and the Snowman, Turk 182, Made in Heaven, A Time of Destiny, Betrayed (cameo), Everybody's All American, Torrents of Spring, Q&A, Strangers, The Temp, The Dark Half, French Kiss, Beautiful Girls, The Substance of Fire, City of Industry.
TELEVISION: Movies: Zuma Beach, Friendly Fire, The Best Place to Be, And Baby Makes Six, Young Love First Love, Father Figure, A Long Way Home, Zelda, The Last Word. Director: Amazing Stories (Grandpa's Ghost).

HUYCK, WILLARD
Writer, Director. e. U. of Southern California. Worked as reader for Larry Gordon, executive at American-International Pictures; named Gordon's asst., working on scene rewrites for AIP films. First screen credit on The Devil's Eight as co-writer with John Milius.
PICTURES: Writer: French Postcards (also dir.), Indiana Jones and the Temple of Doom, Best Defense (also dir.), Howard the Duck (also dir.), Radioland Murders, Mission: Impossible.
TELEVISION: A Father's Homecoming (co-exec. prod., co-s.p.), American River (co-exec. prod., co-s.p.).

HYAMS, JOSEPH
Advertising & Publicity Executive. b. New York, NY, Sept. 21, 1926. e. NYU Ent. industry, 1947. Various publicity posts, 20th Century-Fox, Columbia Pictures, 1947-55; eastern pub. mgr., Figaro Prods., 1955-56; West Coast pub. mgr., Hecht-Hill-Lancaster, 1955-58; pub. adv. dir., Batjac Prods. 1959-60 national adv. & pub. dir., Warner Bros.-7 Arts, 1960. v.p., world-wide pub., Warner Bros., Inc., 1970-87; appointed sr. v.p., special projects, 1987.

HYAMS, PETER
Director, Writer, Cinematographer. b. New York, NY, July 26, 1943. e. Hunter Coll., Syracuse U. Joined CBS news staff N.Y. and made anchor man. Filmed documentary on Vietnam in 1966. Left CBS in 1970 and joined Paramount in Hollywood as writer. Hired by ABC to direct TV features.
PICTURES: Writer: T.R. Baskin (also prod.), Telefon, The Hunter. Exec. Prod.: The Monster Squad. Director: Busting (dir. debut 1974; also s.p.), Our Time (also s.p.), Peeper, Capricorn One (also s.p.), Hanover Street (also s.p.), Outland (also s.p.), The Star Chamber (also s.p.), 2010 (also prod., s.p., photog.), Running Scared (also exec. prod., photog.), The Presidio (also photog.), Narrow Margin (also s.p., photog.), Stay Tuned (also photog.), Timecop (also photog.), Sudden Death (also photog.), The Relic (also photog.) .
TELEVISION: Movies (dir., writer): The Rolling Man, Goodnight My Love.

HYDE, TOMMY
Executive. r.n. Thomas L. b. Meridian, MS, June 29, 1916. e. Lakeland H.S., grad., 1935. Worked E.J. Sparks Theatres, 1932-41. Florida State Theatres, 1941-42. U.S. Navy, 1942-46. Florida State Theatres, 1946-47; city mgr. (Tallahassee). Talgar Theatres, 1947-58; v.p. and gen. mgr. Kent Theatres, 1958-86; vice-pres. Motion Picture Films, Inc.; pres., NATO of Florida, 1961-62; chmn. bd. 1963-70; 1987-, theatre consultant.

HYER, MARTHA
Actress. b. Fort Worth, TX, Aug. 10, 1924. e. Northwestern U., Pasadena Playhouse.
PICTURES: The Locket (debut, 1946), Thunder Mountain, Born to Kill, Woman on the Beach, The Velvet Touch, Gun Smugglers, The Judge Steps Out, Clay Pigeon, Roughshod, The Rustlers, The Lawless, Outcast of Black Mesa, Salt Lake Raiders, Frisco Tornado, Geisha Girl, The Kangaroo Kid, The Invisible Mr. Unmei, Wild Stallion, Yukon Gold, Abbott and Costello Go to Mars, So Big, Riders to the Stars, Scarlet Spear, Battle of Rogue River, Lucky Me, Down Three Dark Streets, Sabrina, Cry Vengeance, Wyoming Renegades, Kiss of Fire, Paris Follies of 1956, Francis in the Navy, Red Sundown, Showdown at Abilene, Battle Hymn, Kelly and Me, Mister Cory, The Delicate Delinquent, My Man Godfrey, Paris Holiday, Once Upon a Horse, Houseboat, Some Came Running (Acad. Award nom.), The Big Fisherman, The Best of Everything, Ice Palace, Desire in the Dust, Mistress of the World, The Right Approach, The Last Time I Saw Archie, Girl Named Tamiko, The Man from the Diner's Club, Wives and Lovers, Pyro, The Carpetbaggers, First Men in the Moon, Blood on the Arrow, Bikini Beach, The Sons of Katie Elder, The Chase, Night of the Grizzly, Picture Mommy Dead, War Italian Style, The Happening, Some May Live, Lo Scatenato (Catch as Catch Can), House of 1000 Dolls, Once You Kiss a Stranger, Crossplot, Day of the Wolves.
TELEVISION: Guest: Adventures of Wild Bill Hickock, Zane Greay Theatre, The Virginian, The Alfred Hitchcock Hour, Bewitched, The Young Lawyers.

HYLER, JOAN
Executive. Pres., Women In Film.

HYMAN, DICK
Composer. b. New York, NY, March 8, 1927.
PICTURES: Erased Off, French Quarter, Stardust Memories, Zelig, Broadway Danny Rose (also mus. supv.), The Purple Rose of Cairo, Moonstruck, Thelonious Monk: Straight—No Chaser, Radio Days (mus. supv.), The Lemon Sisters, Alan & Naomi, Mighty Aphrodite, Everyone Says I Love You.
TELEVISION: Bernice Bobs Her Hair, The Last Tenant, Natica Jackson, Ask Me Again.

I

IANNUCCI, SALVATORE J.
Executive. b. Brooklyn, NY, Sept. 24, 1927. e. NYU, B.A., 1949; Harvard Law School, J.D., 1952. 2 yrs. legal departments RCA and American Broadcasting Companies, Inc.; 14 yrs. with CBS Television Network: asst. dir. of bus. affairs, dir. of bus. affairs, v.p. of bus. affairs; 2 yrs. v.p. admin. National General Corp.; 2-1/2 yrs. pres. of Capital Records; 4-1/2 yrs. Corp. v.p. and dir. of Entertainment Div. of Playboy Enterprises, Inc.; 4 yrs. partner with Jones, Day Reavis & Pogue in Los Angeles office, handling entertainment legal work; Pres., Filmways Entertainment, and sr. v.p., Filmways, Inc.; exec. v.p., Embassy Communications; COO, Aaron Spelling Prods.; sr. partner Bushkin, Gaims, Gaines, & Jonas; pres. and chief operating officer, Brad Marks International; prod. of features, tv movies and infomercials.

IBBETSON, ARTHUR
Cinematographer. b. England, Sept. 8, 1922.
PICTURES: The Horse's Mouth, The Angry Silence, The League of Gentlemen, Tunes of Glory, Whistle Down the Wind, Lisa (The Inspector), Nine Hours to Rama, I Could Go on Singing, The Chalk Garden, A Countess from Hong Kong, Inspector Clouseau, Where Eagles Dare, The Walking Stick, Anne of the Thousand Days (Acad. Award nom.), The Railway Children, Willy Wonka and the Chocolate Factory, A Doll's House, 11 Harrow House, A Little Night Music, The Medusa Touch, The Prisoner of Zenda, Hopscotch, Nothing Personal (co-cin.), The Bounty, Santa Claus: The Movie.
TELEVISION: Frankenstein: the True Story, Little Lord Fauntleroy (Emmy Award), Brief Encounter, Babes in Toyland, Witness for the Prosecution, Master of the Game.

IBERT, LLOYD
Executive. Began career as mgng. editor, Independent Film Journal. 1973, joined Paramount Pictures pub. dept.; named sr. publicist. 1985, appointed dir., natl. pub. for M.P. Group.

ICE CUBE
Actor, Singer. r.n. O'Shea Jackson. b. Los Angeles, 1969. e. Phoenix Inst. of Tech. Debuted as rap performer with group N.W.A. Solo debut 1990 with album Amerikka's Most Wanted.
PICTURES: Boyz N the Hood (debut, 1991), Trespass, Higher Learning, Friday (also co-s.p., co-exec. prod.), The Glass Shield, Anaconda, Dangerous Ground (also exec. prod.), Players' Club, I Got the Hook-up.

ICE-T
Actor, Singer. r.n. Tracy Marrow. b. Newark, NJ. Raised in Los Angeles. Served 4 yrs. as ranger in U.S. army. Made debut as rap performer with 1982 single The Coldest Rap. Received Grammy Award 1990 for Back on the Block.
PICTURES: Breakin' (debut, 1984), Breakin' 2: Electric Boogaloo, New Jack City, Ricochet, Trespass, Who's the Man?, Surviving the Game, Tank Girl, Johnny Mnemonic, Below Utopia.
TELEVISION: Series: Players. Guest: New York Undercover.

IDLE, ERIC
Actor, Writer. b. South Shields, Co. Durham, Eng., March 29, 1943. e. Pembroke Coll., Cambridge, 1962-65. Pres. Cambridge's Footlights appearing at Edinburgh Fest. 1963-64. Member Monty Python's Flying Circus appearing on BBC, 1969-74.
THEATER: Oh What a Lovely War, Monty Python Live at the Hollywood Bowl, Monty Python Live, The Mikado (English Natl. Opera, 1986).
BOOKS: Hello Sailor, The Rutland Dirty Weekend Book, Pass the Bulter; as well as co-author of Monty Python books: Monty Python's Big Red Book, The Brand New Monty Python Book, Monty Python and the Holy Grail, The Complete Works of Shakespeare and Monty Python.
PICTURES: And Now for Something Completely Different (also co-s.p.), Monty Python and the Holy Grail (also co-s.p.), Monty Python's Life of Brian (also co-s.p.), Monty Python Live at the Hollywood Bowl (also co-s.p.), Monty Python's The Meaning of Life (also co-s.p.), Yellowbeard, National Lampoon's European Vacation, Transformers (voice), The Adventures of Baron Munchausen, Nuns on the Run, Too Much Sun, Missing Pieces, Mom & Dad Save the World, Splitting Heirs (also s.p., exec. prod.), Casper, The Wind and the Willows, Burn Hollywood Burn, Quest for Camelot.
TELEVISION: Isadora (debut, 1965), The Frost Report (writer), Do Not Adjust Your Set, Monty Python's Flying Circus, Rutland Weekend Television (series), All You Need is Cash (The Rutles), Faerie Tale Theater (The Frog Prince; dir., writer ACE Award, 1982; The Pied Piper), Saturday Night Live, The Mikado, Around the World in 80 Days, Nearly Departed (series).

IGER, ROBERT
Executive. b. New York, NY, 1951. e. Ithaca Col. Joined ABC in 1974 as studio supervisor. 1976 moved to ABC Sports. 1985, named v.p. in charge of program plan. & dev. as well as scheduling and rights acquisitions for all ABC Sports properties. 1987, named v.p. program. for ABC Sports and mgr. & dir. for ABC's Wide World of Sports; 1988, appt. exec. v.p., ABC Network Group. 1989 named pres., ABC Entertainment. 1992 became pres. of ABC TV Network Group.; 1993, sr. v.p. CC/ABC Inc., exec. v.p. of Capital Cities/ABC Inc. Sept., 1994, elected pres. & COO.

IMAMURA, SHOHEI
Director, Producer, Writer. b. Tokyo, Japan, Sept. 15, 1926. e. Waseda U. Joined Shochiku Ofuna Studio 1951 asst. dir., transferred Nikkatsu in 1954 as asst. dir., director Stolen Desire 1958 then 4 more films before refusing to work on any film distasteful to him; and wrote play later made into film directed by him in 1968; later turned to documentaries and from 1976 onward as independent; Ballad of Narayama awarded Golden Palm Prize, Cannes Festival, 1983.

PICTURES: *Director*: Bakumatsu Taiyoden (writer, asst. dir. only), Stolen Desire, Lights of Night, Endless Desire, Nianchan, Big Brother, Pigs and Battleships, Insect Woman, Intentions of Murder, The Pornographers, A Man Vanishes, The Profound Desire of the Gods, Human Evaporation, History of Postwar Japan, Karayuki-san—the Making of a Prostitue, Vengeance Is Mine, Why Not?, The Ballad of Narayama (also writer), Zegen, Black Rain (also writer), Unagi (The Eel, also writer; Palme d'Or).

IMI, TONY
Cinematographer. b. London, March 27, 1937. Ent. ind. 1959.
PICTURES: The Raging Moon, Dulcima, The Slipper and the Rose, International Velvet, Brass Target, Ffolkes, The Sea Wolves, Night Crossing, Nate and Hayes, Not Quite Jerusalem, Enemy Mine, Empire State, American Roulette, Buster, Options, Wired, Fire Birds, Pretty Hattie's Baby, Shopping, Downtime, Aimee and Jaguar.
TELEVISION: Queenie, The Return of Sherlock Holmes, Oceans of Fire, The Last Days of Frank and Jesse James, Reunion at Fairborough, A Christmas Carol, Sakharov, Princess Daisy, John Paul II, Little Gloria–Happy at Last, Inside the Third Reich, Dreams Don't Die, For Ladies Only, Nicholas Nickleby, A Tale of Two Cities, Babycakes, Old Man and the Sea, Fourth Story, The Last to Go, Our Sons, Carolina Skeletons, Child of Rage, Queen, Cobb's Law, For the Love of My Child: The Anissa Ayala Story, Blind Angel, Scarlett, The Sunshine Boys, The Turn of the Screw, Dalva, The Abduction, Desperate Justice.

IMMERMAN, WILLIAM J.
Producer, Attorney, Executive. b. New York, NY, Dec. 29, 1937. e. Univ. Wisconsin, BS, 1959; Stanford Law, J.D., 1963. 1963-65, served as deputy district attorney, LA County. 1965-72, assoc. counsel, v.p.-bus. affairs, American Intl. Pictures. 1972-77, v.p., business affairs, sr. v.p. feature film division 20th Century-Fox. 1977-1979, producer at Warner Bros. 1979-82, founder and chmn. of bd. of Cinema Group Inc. 1978-present, pres. Salem Productions. 1988-94, pres. Distribution Expense Co. 1988-present, pres., ImmKirk Financial Corp. 1988-89, spec. consultant to office of pres., Pathe Communications. 1989-90, vice chmn. Cannon Pictures. 1986-90, dir. Heritage Ent., Inc. 1991-present, v.p. The Crime Channel, 1983-93, of counsel to law firm of Barash and Hill. 1993-present, of Counsel to law firm of Kenoff and Machtinger (LA). 1990-present, Regional Adjudicator (Southwest). Member of AFMA Arbitration Panel. Member of AMPAS. Stage Productions: Berlin to Broadway (LA), The Knife Thrower's Assistant (LA, tour), The Wiz (B'way).
PICTURES: *Exec. prod.*: Highpoint, Southern Comfort, Hysterical, Mind Games, Take this Job and Shove It, Where the Red Ferns Grows Part II, The St. Tammany Miracle. *Prod.*: Primal Rage, Nightmare Beach (Welcome to Spring Break).

INDELLI, JOSEPH
Executive. e. Vanderbilt U., 1948. Began TV career at MGM/Chicago in sales, 1968-80, Regional Sales Mgr.; Pres., Columbia Pictures Television Dist., 1980-86; Pres., MTM Television Dist. Grp., 1986-89; Exec. VP, Orion Pictures Television, 1989-97.

INGALLS, DON
Producer, Writer. b. Humboldt, NE, July 29, 1928. e. George Washington U., 1948. Columnist, Washington Post; producer-writer, ATV England and Australia; writer-prod., Have Gun Will Travel, also prod. for TV: The Travels of Jamie McPheeters, The Virginian, Honey West, Serpico, Kingston: Confidential. Exec. story consultant The Sixth Sense; prod.: Fantasy Island, T.J. Hooker, Duel at Shiloh, Smile of the Dragon, In Preparation: Watchers on the Mountain, Hearts & Diamonds, Motherwit, Funny Man, Beaumaris.
PICTURES: Airport—1975, Who's Got the Body?
TELEVISION: *Writer*: Gunsmoke, Have Gun Will Travel, The Bold Ones, Marcus Welby M.D., Mod Squad, Star Trek, Honey West, Bonanza, The Sixth Sense, Then Came Bronson, Police Story, World Premier Movie, Shamus, Flood, Capt. America, The Initiation of Sarah, Blood Sport, Fantasy Island.

INGELS, MARTY
Actor, Former Comedian, Executive. b. Brooklyn, NY, Mar. 9, 1936. m actress-singer Shirley Jones. U.S. Infantry 1954-58. Ent. show business representing Army, Name That Tune. Stage: Sketchbook revue, Las Vegas. Pres., Celebrity Brokerage, packaging celebrity events and endorsements. Active in community affairs and charity funding.
PICTURES: The Ladies Man, Armored Command, The Horizontal Lieutenant, Wild and Wonderful, A Guide for the Married Man, If It's Tuesday It Must be Belgium, For Singles Only, Instant Karma, Round Numbers, The Opposite Sex, How to Live with Them, Cops and Roberts, Zork: Grand Inquisitor.
TELEVISION: *Series*: I'm Dickens... He's Fenster, The Phyllis Diller Show. *Guest*: Phil Silvers Show, Steve Allen, Jack Paar, Playboy Penthouse, Bell Telephone Hour, Manhunt, Ann Sothern Show, Peter Loves Mary, The Detectives, Joey Bishop Show, Hennessey, Dick Van Dyke Show, Burke's Law, Hollywood Palace, Family, Murder She Wrote.

INGSTER, BORIS
Writer, Director. b. 1913.
PICTURES: Writer: The Last Days of Pompeii, Dancing Pirate, Thin Ice, Happy Landing, Paris Underground, Something for the Birds, Abdullah's Harem, California, Cloak & Dagger, The Amazing Mrs. Holliday. Director: The Judge Steps Out, Southside 1-1000.
TELEVISION: Wagon Train, The Alaskans, The Roaring 20's, Travels of Jaimie McPheeters, The Man From U.N.C.L.E.

INMAN, ROBERT
Writer.
TELEVISION: *Movies*: Home Fires Burning, My Son Is Innocent, The Summer of Ben Tyler (also prod., Writers' Guild Award, 1998), Family Blessings.

INSDORF, ANNETTE
Film Professor, Critic, Translator, TV Host. b. Paris, France. e. 1963-68 studied voice, Juilliard Sch. of Music and performed as singer; Queens Coll. (summa cum laude), B.A. 1972; Yale U., M.A., 1973; Yale U., Ph.D., 1975. 1973: soloist in Leonard Bernstein's Mass (European premiere in Vienna and BBC/WNET TV). 1975-87: professor of film, Yale U. Author of Francois Truffaut (1979; updated 1989), Indelible Shadows: Film and the Holocaust (1983, updated 1989). Since 1979: frequent contributor to NY Times (Arts and Leisure), Los Angeles Times, San Francisco Chronicle, Film Comment, and Premiere. Named Chevalier dans l'ordre des arts et lettres by French Ministry of Culture, 1986. Since 1987, dir. of Undergrad. Film Studies, Columbia U., and prof. Graduate Film Div. 1990 named chmn. of Film Div. 1987: exec.-prod. Shoeshine (short film nom. for Oscar). 1989: exec. prod., Tom Abrams' Performance Pieces (named best fiction short, Cannes Fest).

IRONS, JEREMY
Actor. b. Isle of Wight, UK, Sept. 19, 1948. m. actress Sinead Cusack. e. Sherborne Sch., Dorset. Stage career began at Marlowe Theatre, Canterbury, where he was student asst. stage manager. Accepted at Bristol Old Vic Theatre Sch. for two-yr. course; then joined Bristol Old Vic Co. In London played in Godspell, Much Ado About Nothing, The Caretaker, Taming of the Shrew, Wild Oats, Rear Column, An Audience Called Edouard, etc. N.Y. stage debut, The Real Thing (Tony Award, 1984).
PICTURES: Nijinsky (debut, 1980), The French Lieutenant's Woman, Moonlighting, Betrayal, The Wild Duck, Swann in Love, The Mission, Dead Ringers, A Chorus of Disapproval, Danny the Champion of the World (tv in U.S.), Australia, Reversal of Fortune (Academy Award, 1990), Kafka, Waterland, Damage, M. Butterfly, The House of the Spirits, The Lion King (voice), Die Hard With a Vengeance, Lolita, The Man in the Iron Mask, Chinese Box.
TELEVISION: The Pallisers, Notorious Woman, Love for Lydia, Langrishe Go Down, Brideshead Revisited, The Captain's Doll, Autogeddon, Tales From Hollywood, The Dream of a Ridiculous Man.

IRONSIDE, MICHAEL
Actor. b. Toronto, Ontario, Canada, Feb. 12, 1950. e. Ontario Col. of Art.
PICTURES: Scanners, Visiting Hours, Spacehunter: Adventures in the Forbidden Zone, The Falcon and the Snowman, Jo Jo Dancer Your Life Is Calling, Top Gun, Extreme Prejudice, Nowhere to Hide, Hello Mary Lou: Prom Night II, Watchers, Total Recall, McBain, Highlander II: The Quickening, The Vagrant, Fortunes of War, The Killing Man, Free Willy, The Next Karate Kid, Major Payne, The Glass Shield.
TELEVISION: *Series*: V, ER, seaQuest DSV. *Movie*: Probable Cause (also co-exec. prod.).

IRVIN, JOHN
Director. b. Cheshire, England, May 7, 1940. In cutting rooms at Rank Organisation before making first film documentary, Gala Day, on grant from British Film Inst.; made other award-winning documentaries before turning to features.
PICTURES: The Dogs of War (debut, 1981), Ghost Story, Champions, Turtle Diary, Raw Deal, Hamburger Hill, Next of Kin, Eminent Domain, Widow's Peak, A Month by the Lake, City of Industry.
TELEVISION: The Nearly Man, Hard Times, Tinker Tailor Soldier Spy, Robin Hood (foreign theatrical), Crazy Horse.

IRVING, AMY
Actress. b. Palo Alto, CA, Sept. 10, 1953. e. American Conservatory Theatre, London Acad. of Dramatic Art. Daughter of late theatre dir. Jules Irving and actress Priscilla Pointer. m. director Bruno Barreto.
THEATER: *NY*: Amadeus, Heartbreak House, Road to Mecca, Broken Glass. *LA*: The Heidi Chronicles.
PICTURES: Carrie (debut, 1976), The Fury, Voices, Honeysuckle Rose, The Competition, Yentl (Acad. Award nom.), Micki and Maude, Rumpelstiltskin, Who Framed Roger Rabbit (voice), Crossing Delancey, Show of Force, An American Tail: Fievel Goes West (voice), Benefit of the Doubt, Kleptomania, Acts of Love (also co- exec. prod.), I'm Not Rappaport, Carried Away.
TELEVISION: *Movies*: James Dean, James A. Michener's Dynasty, Panache, Anastasia: The Mystery of Anna. Mini-*Series*: Once an Eagle, The Far Pavilions. *Specials*: I'm a Fool, Turn of the Screw, Heartbreak House, Twilight Zone: Rod Serling's Lost Classics: The Theater. *Guest*: The Rookies, Police Woman.

IRWIN, BILL
Actor. b. Santa Monica, CA, April 11, 1950.
THEATER: B'way: Accidental Death of an Anarchist, 5-6-7-8
Dance, Largely New York, Fool Moon. Off-B'way: The Regard of
Flight, The Courtroom, Not Quite New York, Waiting for Godot.
Regional: Scapin (also dir., adaptation).
PICTURES: Popeye (debut, 1980), A New Life, Eight Men Out, My
Blue Heaven, Scenes From a Mall, Hot Shots!, Stepping Out,
Silent Tongue, Manhattan by Numbers, Water Ride.
TELEVISION: Movies: Subway Stories: Tales from the
Underground. Specials: The Regard of Flight, Bette Midler—
Mondo Beyondo, The Paul Daniels Magic Show (BBC), The Last
Mile. Guest: Saturday Night Live, Tonight Show, Cosby Show,
Northern Exposure.

ISAACS, CHERYL BOONE
Executive. b. Springfield, MA. Entered m.p. industry 1977 as staff
publicist for Columbia Pictures. Worked five years after that for
Melvin Simon Prods., named v.p. Left to become dir. of adv./pub.
for The Ladd Co. 1984, named dir., pub. & promo., West Coast, for
Paramount Pictures. Promoted to vice pres., Worldwide Publicity,
Paramount, 1986; sr. v.p., Worldwide Publicity, Paramount, 1991;
exec. v.p., Worldwide Publicity, Paramount, 1994. Member
A.M.P.A.S. Board of Governors since 1988.

ISAACS, PHIL
Executive. b. New York, NY, May 20, 1922. e. City Coll. of New
York. In U.S. Navy, 1943-46. Joined Paramount Pictures in 1946
as bookers asst., N.Y. exch. Branch mgr. in Washington; then mgr.
Rocky Mt. div. In 1966 was Eastern-Southern sls. mgr.; 1967
joined Cinema Center Films as v.p. domestic dist. In 1972 named
v.p., marketing, for Tomorrow Entertainment; Joined Avco-
Embassy 1975 as v.p., gen. sls. mgr., named exec. v.p., 1977.
1978 joined General Cinema Corp. as v.p. 1980 v.p., gen. sls.
mgr., Orion Pictures. 1983, formed Phil Isaacs Co; 1988, v.p., general sales mgr., TWE Theatrical; 1989, appointed pres. Became
pres. South Gate Entertainment 1989.

ISRAEL, NEAL
Writer, Director, Producer.
PICTURES: Tunnelvision (exec. prod., s.p., actor), Cracking Up
(s.p., actor), Americathon (dir., s.p.), Police Academy (s.p.),
Bachelor Party (dir., s.p.), Johnny Dangerously (actor), Moving
Violations (dir., s.p.), Real Genius (s.p.), It's Alive III (s.p.), Buy
and Cell (co-s.p.), Look Who's Talking Too (co-prod., actor),
Spurting Blood (exec. prod., s.p.), All I Want for Christmas (co-
s.p.), Breaking the Rules (dir.), Surf Ninjas (dir., actor),
Tunnelvision (co-dir.),Three O'clock High (prod.).
TELEVISION: Lola Falana Special (writer), Mac Davis Show,
Ringo, Marie (prod.), Twilight Theatre (writer, prod.), Man of the
People (co-prod.), The Wonder Years (dir.), Hearts of the West
(dir.). Movies: The Cover Girl and the Cop (dir.), Woman With a
Past (co-exec. prod.), Combat High (dir.), Taking the Heat (co-
prod.), Dream Date (prod.), Bonnie and Clyde: The True Story (co-
prod.), A Quiet Little Neighborhood (co-prod.), Foster's Field Trip
(dir., writer), Family Reunion: A Relative Nightmare (dir., co-writer,
co-prod.), National Lampoon's Dad's Week Off (dir., writer), Nash
Bridges (dir.) Clueless (dir.).

ITAMI, JUZO
Director, Actor. b. Kyoto, Japan, 1933. m. actress Nobuko
Miyamoto. Son of Mansaku Itami, pioneering Japanese film
director. After successful stint as commercial artist, became
an actor as well as essayist (Listen, Women, a collection of
his work). Directing debut The Funeral (1984).
PICTURES: Actor: 55 Days at Peking, Lord Jim, I Am a Cat,
The Makioka Sisters, The Family Game. Director: The Funeral
(5 Japanese Acad. Awards), Tampopo, A Taxing Woman (8
Japanese Acad. Awards), A Taxing Woman's Return (dir.,
s.p.), Sweet Home (exec. prod. only), Tales of a Golden
Geisha, The Gangster's Moll.
(d. Dec. 20, 1997)

IVANEK, ZELJKO
Actor. b. Ljubljana, Yugoslavia, Aug. 15, 1957. Came to U.S. with
family in 1960 and returned to homeland before settling in Palo
Alto, CA, in 1967. Studied at Yale, majoring in theatre studies:
graduated in 1978. Also graduate of London Acad. of Music and
Dramatic Arts. Was member of Williamstown Theatre Festival,
appearing in Hay Fever, Charley's Aunt, Front Page. B'way debut
in The Survivor.
THEATER: B'way: The Survivor, Brighton Beach Memoirs, Loot,
Two Shakespearean Actors, The Glass Menagerie. Regional:
Master Harold... and the Boys (Yale Rep. premiere prod.), Hamlet
(Guthrie), Ivanov (Yale Rep.). Off B'way: Cloud 9, A Map of the
World, The Cherry Orchard.
PICTURES: Tex, The Sender, The Soldier, Mass Appeal, Rachel
River, School Ties.
TELEVISION: Movies: The Sun Also Rises, Echoes in the
Darkness, Aftermath: A Test of Love, Our Sons, My Brother's
Keeper, Truman. Special: All My Sons. Guest: Homicide: Life on
the Street.

IVANY, PETER
Executive. b. Melbourne, Australia, Aug. 23, 1954. e. Monash
U. Melbourne, B.A., M.B.A. Victoria Health Commission as
strategic planning analyst, 1978-80. Kodak Australia, estimat-
ing and planning analyst, 1980-81. Joined Hoyts Corporation
Pty Ltd. in 1981 as cinema mgr., then general mgr., Hoyts
Video; general mgr., corporate development, 1986-88.
Chairman and CEO Hoyts US Holdings, Inc. 1986 then CEO
to present.

IVEY, JUDITH
Actress. b. El Paso, TX, Sept. 4, 1951. m. ind. prod., Tim
Braine. e. Illinois State U. Stage debut in The Sea in Chicago,
1974.
THEATER: Bedroom Farce, The Goodbye People, Oh
Coward!, Design for Living, Piaf, Romeo and Juliet, Pastorale,
Two Small Bodies, Steaming (Tony & Drama Desk Awards),
Second Lady (off-B'way work she helped develop), Hurlyburly
(Tony & Drama Desk Awards), Precious Sons (Drama Desk
nom.), Blithe Spirit, Mrs. Dally Has a Lover, Park Your Car in
Harvard Yard (Tony nom.), The Moonshot Tape (Obie Award),
A Fair Country, A Madhouse in Goa. .
PICTURES: Harry and Son (debut, 1984), The Lonely Guy,
The Woman in Red, Compromising Positions, Brighton Beach
Memoirs, Hello Again, Sister Sister, Miles from Home, In
Country, Everybody Wins, Alice, Love Hurts, There Goes the
Neighborhood, Washington Square, The Devil's Advocate,
Without Limits, Mystery Alaska.
TELEVISION: Series: Down Home, Designing Women, The
Critic (voice), The Five Mrs. Buchanans, Buddies. Movies: The
Shady Hill Kidnapping, Dixie: Changing Habits, We Are the
Children, The Long Hot Summer, Jesse and the Bandit
Queen, Decoration Day, Her Final Fury: Betty Broderick—The
Last Chapter, On Promised Land, Almost Golden: The
Jessica Savitch Story, What the Deaf Man Saw. Special: Other
Mothers (Afterschool Special).

IVORY, JAMES
Director. b. Berkeley, CA, June 7, 1928. e. U. of Oregon,
B.F.A., 1951; U. of Southern California, M.A. (cinema) 1956.
First film Venice: Theme and Variations (doc. made as M.A.
thesis, 1957). Early work: The Sword and the Flute, The Delhi
Way. Formed Merchant Ivory Productions with prod. Ismail
Merchant and script writer Ruth Prawer Jhabvala. Received
D.W. Griffith Lifetime Achievement Award from DGA, 1995,
Commandeur Des Arts et Des Lettres, France 1996.
PICTURES: The Householder, Shakespeare Wallah (also co-
s.p.), The Guru (also co-s.p.), Bombay Talkie (also co-s.p.),
Savages, The Wild Party, Roseland, The Europeans (also
cameo), Quartet, Heat and Dust, The Bostonians, A Room
With a View, Maurice (also co-s.p.), Slaves of New York, Mr.
and Mrs. Bridge, Howards End, The Remains of the Day,
Jefferson in Paris, Surviving Picasso.
TELEVISION: Noon Wine (exec. prod.). Dir: Adventures of a
Brown Man in Search of Civilization, Autobiography of a
Princess (also released theatrically), Hullabaloo Over George
and Bonnie's Pictures, Jane Austen in Manhattan (also
released theatrically), The Five Forty Eight.

J

JACKSON, ANNE
Actress. b. Allegheny, PA, Sept. 3, 1926. e. Neighborhood
Playhouse, Actors Studio. Married to actor Eli Wallach. Stage
debut in The Cherry Orchard, 1944. Autobiography: Early Stages.
THEATER: Major Barbara, Middle of the Night, The Typist and the
Tiger, Luv, Waltz of the Toreadors, Twice Around the Park,
Summer and Smoke, Nest of the Woodgrouse, Marco Polo Sings
a Solo, The Mad Woman of Chaillot, Cafe Crown, Lost in Yonkers,
In Persons, The Flowering Peach, Love Letters.
PICTURES: So Young So Bad (debut, 1950), The Journey, Tall
Story, The Tiger Makes Out, How to Save a Marriage and Ruin
Your Life, The Secret Life of an American Wife, The Angel
Levine, Zig Zag, Lovers and Other Strangers, Dirty Dingus
Magee, Nasty Habits, The Bell Jar, The Shining, Sam's Son,
Funny About Love, Folks!
TELEVISION: Series: Everything's Relative. Special: 84 Charing
Cross Road. Movies: The Family Man, A Woman Called Golda,
Private Battle, Blinded By the Light, Leave 'em Laughing, Baby
M.

JACKSON, BRIAN
Actor, Film & Theatre Producer. b. Bolton, England, 1931. Early
career in photography then numerous stage performances incl.
Old Vic, Royal Shakespeare. Ent. film/TV industry 1958. Formed
Quintus Plays, 1965; formed Brian Jackson Productions 1966;
formed Hampden Gurney Studios Ltd. 1970. Co-produced The
Others 1967; presented The Button, 1969; co-produced the docu-
mentary film Village in Mayfair, 1970; 1971: Formed Brian Jackson
Films Ltd.; produced Yesterday, The Red Deer, The Story of
Tutankhamen.

THEATER: Mame, Drury Lane, Fallen Angels, In Praise of Love.
PICTURES: Incident in Karandi, Carry On Sergeant, Gorgo, Jack the Ripper, Taste of Fear, Heroes of Telemark, Only the Lonely, The Deadly Females, The Revenge of the Pink Panther, Deceptions, Shadow Chasers.
TELEVISION: Moon Fleet, Private Investigator, Life of Lord Lister, Z Cars, Vendetta, Sherlock Holmes, Mr. Rose, Hardy Heating International, Nearest & Dearest, The Persuaders, The Paradise Makers, The New Avengers, Smugglers Bay, The Tomorrow People, Secret Army, Last Visitor for Hugh Peters, Six Men of Dorset, Commercials: featured as the man from Delmonte for 5 years.

JACKSON, GLENDA
Actress. b. Birkenhead, England, May 9, 1936. Stage debut: Separate Tales (Worthing, England, 1957). 1964 joined Peter Brooks' Theatre of Cruelty which led to film debut. Became Member of Parliament, 1992.
THEATER: (Eng.): All Kinds of Men, Hammersmith, The Idiot, Alfie. Joined Royal Shakespeare Co in experimental Theatre of Cruelty season. Marat Sade (London, N.Y.), Three Sisters, The Maids, Hedda Gabler, The White Devil, Rose, Strange Interlude (N.Y.), Macbeth (N.Y.), Who's Afraid of Virginia Woolf? (L.A.).
PICTURES: The Persecution and Assassination of Jean-Paul Marat as Performed by the Inmates of the Asylum at Charenton Under the Direction of the Marquis de Sade (debut, 1967), Tell Me Lies, Negatives, Women in Love (Academy Award, 1970), The Music Lovers, Sunday Bloody Sunday, Mary Queen of Scots, The Boy Friend, Triple Echo, The Nelson Affair, A Touch of Class (Academy Award, 1973), The Maids, The Temptress, The Romantic Englishwoman, The Devil is a Woman, Hedda, The Incredible Sarah, Nasty Habits, House Calls, Stevie, The Class of Miss McMichael, Lost and Found, Health, Hopscotch, Giro City, The Return of the Soldier, Turtle Diary, Beyond Therapy, Business as Usual, Salome's Last Dance, The Rainbow, The Visit, King of the Wind.
TELEVISION: Movies: The Patricia Neal Story, Sakharov. Mini-Series: Elizabeth R (2 Emmy Awards, 1972). Special: Strange Interlude, A Murder of Quality, The House of Bernarda Alba, Secret Life of Sir Arnold Bax.

JACKSON, KATE
Actress. b. Birmingham, AL, Oct. 29, 1949. e. U. of Mississippi, Birmingham Southern U. Did summer stock before going to N.Y. to enter American Acad. of Dramatic Arts, appearing in Night Must Fall, The Constant Wife, Little Moon of Alban. Worked as model and became tour guide at NBC. First role on TV in Dark Shadows (series).
PICTURES: Night of Dark Shadows, Limbo, Thunder and Lightning, Dirty Tricks, Making Love, Loverboy.
TELEVISION: Movies: Satan's School for Girls, Killer Bees, Death Cruise, Death Scream, Charlie's Angels (pilot), Death at Love House, James at 15 (pilot), Topper, Inmates: A Love Story, Thin Ice, Listen to Your Heart, The Stranger Within, Quiet Killer, Homewrecker (voice), Adrift, Empty Cradle, Armed and Innocent, Justice in a Small Town. Series: Dark Shadows, The Rookies, Charlie's Angels, Scarecrow and Mrs. King, Baby Boom. Guest: The Jimmy Stewart Show.

JACKSON, MICHAEL
Singer, Composer. b. Gary, IN, Aug. 29, 1958. Musical recording artist with family group known as Jackson 5: all brothers, Jackie, Jermaine, Tito, Marlon, and Michael. Sister is singer Janet Jackson.
PICTURES: Save the Children, The Wiz, Moonwalker (also exec. prod., story).
TELEVISION: Series: The Jacksons (1976-77). Specials: Free to Be You and Me, Sandy in Disneyland, Motown on Showtime: Michael Jackson.

JACKSON, MICK
Director. b. Grays, England. e. Bristol Univ. Joined BBC as film editor, following post-grad work in film & tv. Produced and directed many documentaries for the BBC.
PICTURES: Chattahoochee, L.A. Story, The Bodyguard, Clean Slate, Volcano, Josiah's Canon.
TELEVISION: Documentaries: The Ascent of Man, Connections, The Age of Uncertainty. Movies/Specials: Threads, The Race for the Double Helix, Yuri Nosenko KGB (HBO), Indictment: The McMartin Trial. Mini-Series: A Very British Coup.

JACKSON, PETER
Director. b. New Zealand, Oct. 31, 1961.
PICTURES: Bad Taste, Meet the Feebles, Dead Alive, Heavenly Creatures, Forgotten Silver, The Frighteners, Contact (special effects only).

JACKSON, SAMUEL L.
Actor. b. 1949. e. Morehouse Col. m. actress LaTanya Richardson. Co-founder, member of the Just Us Theatre Co. in Atlanta.
THEATER: Negro Ensemble Company: Home, A Soldier's Story, Sally/Prince, Colored People's Time. NY Shakespeare Fest: Mother Courage, Spell No. 7, The Mighty Gents. Yale Rep: The Piano Lesson, Two Trains Running. Seattle Rep: Fences.

PICTURES: Ragtime (debut, 1981), Eddie Murphy Raw, School Daze, Coming to America, Do the Right Thing, Sea of Love, A Shock to the System, Def by Temptation, Betsy's Wedding, Mo' Better Blues, The Exorcist III, GoodFellas, Mob Justice, Jungle Fever (Cannes Film Fest. & NY Film Critics Awards, 1991), Strictly Business, Juice, White Sands, Patriot Games, Johnny Suede, Jumpin at the Boneyard, Fathers and Sons, National Lampoon's Loaded Weapon 1, Amos & Andrew, Menace II Society, Jurassic Park, True Romance, Hail Caesar, Fresh, The New Age, Pulp Fiction (Acad. Award nom.), Losing Isaiah, Kiss of Death, Die Hard With a Vengeance, Fluke (voice), The Great White Hype, A Time to Kill, The Long Kiss Goodnight, 187, Eve's Bayou (also prod.), Jackie Brown, The Red Violin, Sphere, OUt of Sight, The Negotiator, Training Day.
TELEVISION: Movies: Assault at West Point: The Court-Martial of Johnson Whittaker, Against the Wall.

JACOBI, DEREK
O.B.E. Actor. b. London, England, Oct. 22, 1938. e. Cambridge. On stage in Pericles, The Hollow Crown, Hobson's Choice, The Suicide, Breaking the Code (London, NY).
PICTURES: Othello (debut, 1965), Interlude, The Three Sisters, The Day of the Jackal, Blue Blood, The Odessa File, The Medusa Touch, The Human Factor, Enigma, The Secret of NIMH (voice), Little Dorrit, Henry V, Dead Again, Hamlet, Basil, Up at the Villa, Love Is the Devil.
TELEVISION: She Stoops to Conquer, Man of Straw, The Pallisers; I, Claudius; Philby, Burgess and MacLean, Hamlet. Movies: Othello, Three Sisters, Interlude, Charlotte, The Man Who Went Up in Smoke, The Hunchback of Notre Dame, Inside the Third Reich, The Secret Garden, The Tenth Man (Emmy Award). Series: Minder, Tales of the Unexpected, Mr. Pye, The Leper of St. Giles.

JACOBS, JOHN
Executive. b. New York, NY. e. Syracuse U.'s Newhouse Communications Sch. Full-service agency background, including 13 years with Grey Advertising agency, where handled Warner Bros. & Warner Home Video accts. Supvr. media on RCA, ABC-TV, Murdoch Publishing, Radio City Musical Hall, etc. Named v.p. & group media dir. for Grey. 1986, left to join Warner Bros. as v.p., media; then sr. v.p. worldwide media.

JACOBS, MICHAEL
Producer, Writer. b. New Brunswick, NJ. Studied at Neighborhood Playhouse in NY. Had first play, Cheaters, prod. on B'way when he was only 22 yrs. old, followed by Getting Along Famously.
PICTURE: 3:15 (writer only), Halloween 5 (writer only) Quiz Show.
TELEVISION: Series: Creator/prod.: Charles in Charge, No Soap Radio, Together We Stand, Singer and Songs, My Two Dads (also dir.), Dinosaurs, The Torkelsons (Almost Home), Boy Meets World, Where I Live, You Wish.

JACOBSEN, JOHN M.
Producer, Executive. b. Oslo, Norway, Dec. 27, 1944. Produced number of feature films incl. Pathfinder (Acad. Award nom.), Shipwrecked, Head Above Water. Pres., Norwegian Film and HTV Producers Assn.; Pres. AB Svensk Filmindustri Norwegian Operation. Produced Head Above Water, 1996.

JACOBY, FRANK DAVID
Director, Producer. b. New York, NY, July 15, 1925. e. Hunter Coll., Brooklyn Coll. m. Doris Storm, producer/director educational films, actress. 1949-52, NBC network tv dir.; 1952-56, B.B.D.O., Biow Co., tv prod./dir.; 1956-58 Metropolitan Educational TV Assn., dir. of prod.; 1958-65, United Nation, film prod./dir.; 1965 to present, pres., Jacoby/Storm Prods., Inc., Westport, CT—documentary, industrial, educational films and filmstrips. Clients include Xerox Corp., Random House, Publ., Lippincott Co., IBM, Heublein, G.E., and Pitney Bowes. Winner, Sherwood Award, Peabody Award. Member, Director's Guild of America; winner, Int'l TV & Film Festival, National Educational Film Festival, American Film Festival.

JACOBY, JOSEPH
Producer, Director, Writer. b. Brooklyn, NY, Sept. 22, 1942. e. NYU. Sch. of Arts and Sciences, majoring in m.p. As undergraduate worked part-time as prod. asst. on daytime network TV shows and as puppeteer for Bunin Puppets. 1964 joined Bil Baird Marionettes as full-time puppeteer, working also on Baird film commercials. Made feature m.p. debut as prod.-dir of Shame Shame Everybody Knows Her Name, 1968. Contributing essayist, NY Woman Magazine. Founder/Dir.-Prod., Children's Video Theatre starring The Bil Baird Marionettes. Adjunct professor, New School for Social Reserach, NY. Creator of tv series, Slugger's Corner, 1998.
PICTURES: Dir./Prod./Writer: Hurry Up or I'll Be 30, The Great Bank Hoax, Davy Jones' Locker.

JACOBY, SCOTT
Actor. b. Chicago, IL, Nov. 19, 1956.
PICTURES: The Little Girl Who Lives Down the Lane, Love and the Midnight Auto Supply, Our Winning Season, Return to Horror High, To Die For, To Die For II.
TELEVISION: Movies: No Place to Run, That Certain Summer (Emmy Award, 1973), The Man Who Could Talk to Kids, Bad Ronald, Smash-Up on Interstate 5, No Other Love, The Diary of Anne Frank. Mini-Series: 79 Park Avenue. Series: One Life to Live (1973-74). Guest: Medical Center, Marcus Welby M.D., The Golden Girls.

JAFFE, STANLEY R.
Producer. b. New York, NY, July, 31, 1940. Graduate of U. of Pennsylvania Wharton Sch. of Finance. Joined Seven Arts Associates, 1962; named exec. ass't to pres., 1964; later, head of East Coast TV programming. Produced Goodbye, Columbus, in 1968 for Paramount; then joined that company as exec. v.p., 1969. Named pres. of Paramount in 1970; resigned 1971 to form own prod. unit. Joined Columbia as exec. v.p. of global prod. in 1976, but resigned to be independent producer. Named pres. & COO of Paramount Communications in 1991-1994. Owner of Jaffilms LLC, 1994-.
PICTURES: Goodbye Columbus, A New Leaf, Bad Company, Man on a Swing, The Bad News Bears, Kramer vs. Kramer (Academy Award for Best Picture, 1979), Taps, Without a Trace (also dir.). Co-prod.(with Sherry Lansing): Racing with the Moon, Firstborn, Fatal Attraction, The Accused, Black Rain, School Ties.

JAFFE, STEVEN-CHARLES
Producer. b. Brooklyn, NY, 1954. e. U. of Southern California, cinema. First professional job as documentary prod. on John Huston's Fat City. Served as prod. asst. on The Wind and the Lion in Spain. Assoc. prod. on Demon Seed (written by brother Robert); served as location mgr. on Who'll Stop the Rain; assoc. prod. on Time After Time. On tv worked as 2nd unit dir. on The Day After.
PICTURES: Those Lips Those Eyes, Motel Hell (also co-s.p.), Scarab (dir.), Flesh + Blood (2nd unit. dir.), Near Dark, Plain Clothes (exec. prod.), The Fly II, Ghost (exec. prod., 2nd unit dir.), Company Business, Star Trek VI: The Undiscovered Country, Strange Days, The Informant.

JAGGER, MICK
Singer, Composer, Actor. b. Dartford, Kent, England, July 26, 1943. Lead singer with the Rolling Stones.
PICTURES: The Rolling Stones Rock and Roll Circus, Performance, Ned Kelly, Popcorn, Gimme Shelter, Sympathy for the Devil, Ladies and Gentlemen: The Rolling Stones, The London Rock 'n' Roll Show, Let's Spend the Night Together, At the Max, Freejack, Bent.
TELEVISION: Special: The Nightingale (Faerie Tale Theatre), History of Rock 'N' Roll Pt. 3, 5 and 6.

JAGGS, STEVE
Executive. b. London, England, June 29, 1946. Ent. motion picture industry, 1964. Gained experience in the film production and laboratory areas with Colour Film Service and Universal Laboratories. Joined Agfa-Gevaert Ltd., Motion Picture Division, 1976. Appt. sales manager, 1979; divisional manager, 1989. Joined Rank Organisation, 1992. Appoint. mng. dir. of Pinewood Studios, 1993.

JAGLOM, HENRY
Director, Writer, Editor, Actor. b. London, Eng., Jan. 26, 1943. Studied acting, writing and directing with Lee Strasberg and at Actors Studio. Did off-B'way. shows; went to West Coast where guest-starred in TV series (Gidget, The Flying Nun, etc.). Shot documentary film in Israel during Six Day War. Hired as edit consultant for Easy Rider by producer Bert Schneider. Acted in Psych Out, Drive He Said, The Last Movie, Thousand Plane Raid, Lili Aime Moi, The Other Side of the Wind (Orson Welles' unreleased last film). Wrote and dir. first feature, A Safe Place, in 1971. Created The Women's Film Co. (to prod. and distrib. motion pictures by women filmmakers), and Jagfilms Inc., Rainbow Film Company, and Rainbow Releasing. Presented Academy Award winning documentary Hearts and Minds, 1974.
PICTURES: Dir.-Writer-Prod.-Editor: A Safe Place, Tracks, Sitting Ducks (also actor), National Lampoon Goes to the Movies (co-dir. only), Can She Bake A Cherry Pie?, Always (also actor), Someone To Love (also actor), New Year's Day (also actor), Eating, Venice Venice (also actor), Babyfever, Last Summer in the Hamptons (dir., co-s.p., edit., actor), Deja Vu (dir., s.p., edit.).

JALBERT, JOE JAY
Executive. e. U. of Washington. Was ski captain in school and began film career as technical director on Downhill Racer, 1969, also cinematographer and double for Robert Redford. 1970, produced Impressions of Utah, documentary, with Redford. Won Emmy for cinematography on TV's Peggy Fleming Special. In 1970 formed Jalbert Productions, Inc., to make feature films, TV sports, specials, commercials, etc. Co. has prod. Winter Sportscast and 9 official films at Innsbruck Winter Olympics (1976), Lake Placid (1980), Sarajevo (1984). Albertville Winter Olympic Games official film, One Light One World, 1992. Ten years as the official film prod. for the U.S. ski team.

JAMES, BRION
Actor. b. Beaumont, CA, Feb. 20, 1945. e. Beaumont h.s., San Diego St. U., 1968. On stage in LA, San Diego, NY, as well as performing stand-up comedy at Comedy Store, The Improv.
THEATER: Long Day's Journey Into Night, Picnic, Basic Training Pavlo Hummell, Mother Courage, George Washington Slept Here, West Side Story, Spec, Lady Windermere's Fan.
PICTURES: Harry and Walter Go to New York (debut, 1975), Treasure of Matecumbe, Bound for Glory, Nickelodeon, Blue Sunshine, Black Sunday, Corvette Summer, Wholly Moses, The Postman Always Rings Twice, Southern Comfort, The Ballad of Gregorio Cortez, Blade Runner, 48 HRS, A Breed Apart, Silverado, Crimewave, Flesh $PL Blood, Enemy Mine, Armed and Dangerous, Steel Dawn, Dead Man Walking, Cherry 2000, Nightmare at Noon, The Wrong Guys, Red Heat, Red Scorpion, The Horror Show, Mom, Time of the Beast, Tango & Cash, Street Asylum, Savage Land, Another 48 HRS, The Player, Nemesis, Ultimate Desires, Brain Smasher—A Love Story, Nature of the Beast, Time Runner, Wishman, Future Shock, Striking Distance, Pterodactyl Women of Beverly Hills, The Soft Kill, Cyberjack, The Dark, Scanner Cop, Dominion, Cabin Boy, The Companion, Art Deco Detective, F.T.W., Radioland Murders, Steel Frontier, From the Edge, Hong Kong '97. Evil Obsession, Malevolence, Precious Find, The Killing Jar, Assault on Dome 4, American Strays, Bombshell, The Setting Son, The Gift, Brown's Requiem, The Underground, The 5th Element, Black Sea 213, A Place Called Truth, Heart of Stone, Snide & Prejudice, The Thief & the Stripper, In God's Hands.
TELEVISION: Movies: Flying High, Mrs. Sundance, Kiss Meets the Phantom of the Park, Trouble in High Timber Country, Killing at Hell's Gate, Hear No Evil, Precious Victims, Rio Diablo, Kenny Rogers as The Gambler: The Adventure Continues, Overkill: The Aileen Wuornos Story, Precious Victims, The Companion, Sketch Artist II: Hands That See, Terminal Virus, The Sentinel, Magnificent 7. Series: The Marshall. Guest: Rockford Files, Hunter, The Young Riders, Cagney & Lacey, Quincy, Little House on the Prairie, Dynasty, Amazing Stories, Tales from the Crypt, A-Team, Millennium, Walker Texas Ranger, Roots 74, Miami Vice, etc.

JAMES, CLIFTON
Actor. b. Portland, OR, May 29, 1925. e. U. of Oregon. Studied at Actors Studio. Made numerous appearances on stage and TV, as well as theatrical films.
THEATER: NY: B'way: J.B., All the Way Home, The Shadow Box, American Buffalo. Off-B'way: All the King's Men.
PICTURES: On The Waterfront, The Strange One, The Last Mile, Something Wild, Experiment in Terror, David and Lisa, Black Like Me, The Chase, The Happening, Cool Hand Luke, Will Penny, The Reivers, ...tick...tick...tick..., WUSA, The Biscuit Eater, The New Centurions, Kid Blue, Live and Let Die, The Iceman Cometh, Werewolf of Washington, The Last Detail, Bank Shot, Juggernaut, The Man with the Golden Gun, Rancho DeLuxe, Silver Streak, The Bad News Bears in Breaking Training, Superman II, Where Are the Children?, Whoops Apocalypse, Eight Men Out, The Bonfire of the Vanities.
TELEVISION: Series: City of Angels, Lewis and Clark. Movies: Runaway Barge, Friendly Persuasion, The Deadly Tower, Hart to Hart (pilot), Undercover With the KKK, Guyana Tragedy: The Story of Jim Jones, Carolina Skeletons, The John Vernon Story. Mini-Series: Captains and the Kings, Lone Star.

JAMES, FRANCESCA.
Actress, Director.
TELEVISION: Series: One Life to Live, All My Children (also dir., Emmy Awards, 1980, 1998), Loving (also dir.).

JAMES, POLLY
Writer. b. Ancon, Canal Zone. e. Smith Coll. Newspaper work, Panama; with trade mag., N.Y.; screenwriter since 1942.
PICTURES: Mrs. Parkington, The Raiders, Redhead from Wyoming, Quantrill's Raiders.

JAMESON, JERRY
Director. b. Hollywood, CA. Started as editorial asst.; then editor and supv. editor for Danny Thomas Prods. Turned to directing.
PICTURES: Dirt Gang, The Bat People, Brute Core, Airport '77, Raise the Titanic.
TELEVISION: Movies: Heatwave!, The Elevator, Hurricane, Terror on the 40th Floor, The Secret Night Caller, The Deadly Tower, The Lives of Jenny Dolan, The Call of the Wild, The Invasion of Johnson County, Superdome, A Fire in the Sky, High Noon--Part II, The Return of Will Kane, Stand By Your Man, Killing at Hell's Gate, Hotline, Starflight: The Plane That Couldn't Land, Cowboy, This Girl for Hire, Last of the Great Survivors, The Cowboy and the Ballerina, Stormin' Home, One Police Plaza, The Red Spider, Terror on Highway 91, Fire and Rain, Gunsmoke: The Last Ride.

JANKOWSKI, GENE F.
Executive. b. Buffalo, NY, May 21, 1934. e. Canisius Coll., B.S., Michigan State U., M.A. in radio, TV and film. Joined CBS radio network sls, 1961 as acct. exec.; eastern sls. mgr.; 1966; moved to CBS-TV as acct. exec. 1969; gen. sls. mgr. WCBS-TV, 1970; dir. sls, 1971; v.p. sls., CBS-TV Stations Divisions, 1973; v.p., finance & planning, 1974; v.p., controller, CBS Inc. 1976; v.p. adm., 1977;

exec. v.p. CBS/Broadcast Group, 1977; pres., CBS/Broadcast Group, 1977; chmn. CBS/Broadcast Group, 1988-89; chmn. Jankowski Communications Systems, Inc. 1989-. Member: pres., Intl. Council of National Acad. of Television Arts & Sciences; chmn. & trustee Amer. Film Institute; trustee, Catholic U. of Amer.; director, Georgetown U.; bd. of gov. American Red Cross; vice chmn., business comm. Metropolitan Museum of Art. Member, Library of Congress Film Preservation Board; adjunct prof. telecommunications, Michigan St. U.AWARDS: Received Distinguished Communications Medal from South Baptist Radio & Television Commission; honorary Doctorate of Humanities, Michigan State U.; Humanitarian Award, National Conference of Christians and Jews, etc.

JARMAN, CLAUDE, JR.
Actor. b. Nashville, TN, Sept. 27, 1934. e. MGM Sch. Received special Oscar for The Yearling. Exec. prod. of concert film Fillmore.
PICTURES: The Yearling (debut, 1946), High Barbaree, The Sun Comes Up, Intruder in the Dust, Roughshod, The Outriders, Inside Straight, Rio Grande, Hangman's Knot, Fair Wind to Java, The Great Locomotive Chase.
TELEVISION: *Mini-Series*: Centennial.

JARMUSCH, JIM
Director, Writer, Composer, Actor. b. Akron, OH, 1953. e. attended Columbia U., went to Paris in senior year. NYU Film Sch., studied with Nicholas Ray and became his teaching asst. Appeared as an actor in Red Italy and Fraulein Berlin. Composed scores for The State of Things and Reverse Angle. Wrote and directed New World using 30 minutes of leftover, unused film from another director. (Won International Critics Prize, Rotterdam Film Festival.) Expanded it into Stranger Than Paradise.
PICTURES: *Director-Writer*: Permanent Vacation (dir. debut, 1980; also prod., music, edit.), Stranger Than Paradise (also edit., Golden Leopard, Locarno Film Festival; Camera d'Or best new director, Cannes), Down by Law, Mystery Train (also actor) Night on Earth (also prod.), When Pigs Fly (prod. only), Coffee and Cigarettes (all II & III), Dead Man, Year of the Horse. *Actor*. American Autobahn, Straight to Hell, Running Out of Luck, Helsinki Napoli All Night Long, Candy Mountain, Leningrad Cowboys Go America, The Golden Boat, Iron Horsemen, In the Soup, Tigrero: A Film That Was Never Made, Blue in the Face, The Typewriter the Rifle & the Movie Camera, Cannes Man, Sling Blade, Divine Trash.

JARRE, MAURICE
Composer. b. Lyons, France, Sept. 13, 1924. Studied at Paris Cons. Was orchestra conductor for Jean Louis Barrault's theatre company four years. 1951 joined Jean Vilar's nat'l theatre co., composing for plays. Musical dir., French National Theatre for 12 years before scoring films. Also has written ballets (Masques de Femmes, Facheuse Rencontre, The Murdered Poet, Maldroros, The Hunchback of Notre Dame) and served as cond. with Royal Phil. Orch, London, Japan Phil. Orch, Osaka Symph. Orch., Quebec Symp. Orch, Central Orchestra of People's Republic of China.
PICTURES: La Tete contre les Murs (The Keepers; feature debut, 1959), Eyes Without a Face, Crack in the Mirror, The Big Gamble, Sundays and Cybele, The Longest Day, Lawrence of Arabia (Academy Award, 1962), To Die in Madrid, Behold a Pale Horse, The Train, The Collector, Is Paris Burning?, Weekend at Dunkirk, Doctor Zhivago (Academy Award, 1965), The Professionals, Grand Prix, Gambit, The Night of the Generals, Villa Rides!, Five Card Stud, Barbarella, Isadora, The Extraordinary Seaman, The Damned, Topaz, The Only Game in Town, El Condor, Ryan's Daughter, Plaza Suite, Red Sun, Pope Joan, The Life and Times of Judge Roy Bean, The Effect of Gamma Rays on Man-in-the-Moon Marigolds, The Mackintosh Man, Ash Wednesday, Island at the Top of the World, Mandingo, Posse, The Man Who Would Be King, Shout at the Devil, The Last Tycoon, Crossed Swords, Winter Kills, The Magician of Lublin, Resurrection, The American Success Company, The Black Marble, Taps, Firefox, Young Doctors in Love, Don't Cry It's Only Thunder, The Year of Living Dangerously, Dreamscape, A Passage to India (Academy Award, 1984), Top Secret!, Witness (BAFTA Award, 1985), Mad Max Beyond Thunderdome, Solarbabies, The Mosquito Coast, Tai-Pan, No Way Out, Fatal Attraction, Gaby--A True Story, Julia and Julia, Moon Over Parador, Gorillas in the Mist, Wildfire, Distant Thunder, Chances Are, Dead Poets Society (BAFTA Award, 1989), Prancer, Enemies a Love Story, Ghost, After Dark My Sweet, Jacob's Ladder, Almost an Angel, Only the Lonely, Fires Within, School Ties, Shadow of the Wolf, Mr. Jones, Fearless, A Walk in the Clouds (Golden Globe, 1996).

JARRICO, PAUL
Writer, Producer. b. Los Angeles, CA, Jan. 12, 1915. e. USC, 1936.
PICTURES: *Prod.*: Salt of the Earth. Writer: Beauty for the Asking, The Face Behind the Mask, Tom Dick and Harry (Acad. Award nom.), Thousands Cheer, Song of Russia, The Search, The White Tower, Not Wanted, The Day the Hot Line Got Hot, Messenger of Death.
TELEVISION: *Movies*: Call to Glory, Fortune Dane, Seaway, The Defenders.
(d. Oct. 28, 1997)

JARROTT, CHARLES
Director. b. London, England, June 16, 1927. Joined British Navy; wartime service in Far East. After military service turned to theatre as asst. stage mgr. with Arts Council touring co. 1949 joined Nottingham Repertory Theatre as stage dir. and juvenile acting lead. 1953 joined new co. formed to tour Canada; was leading man and became resident leading actor for Ottawa Theatre. 1955 moved to Toronto and made TV acting debut opposite Katharine Blake whom he later wed. 1957 dir. debut in TV for Canadian Bdcstg. Co. Became CBC resident dir. Moved to London to direct for Armchair Theatre for ABC-TV. Then became freelance dir., doing stage work, films, TV. Received BAFTA Best Director Award, 1962. Golden Globe Awards, 1969, 1987.
THEATER: The Duel, Galileo, The Basement, Tea Party, The Dutchman, etc.
PICTURES: Time to Remember (debut, 1962), Anne of the Thousand Days, Mary Queen of Scots, Lost Horizon, The Dove, The Littlest Horse Thieves, The Other Side of Midnight, The Last Flight of Noah's Ark, Condorman, The Amateur, The Boy in Blue, Morning Glory (co-s.p. only), The Secret Life of Algernon, Byron (s.p., dir.).
TELEVISION: *Series*: The Hot Potato Boys, Roll On, Bloomin' Death, Girl in a Birdcage, The Picture of Dorian Gray, Rain, The Rose Affair, Roman Gesture, Silent Song, The Male of the Species, The Young Elizabeth, A Case of Libel, Dr. Jekyll and Mr. Hyde. U.S. *Movies/Mini-Series*: A Married Man, Poor Little Rich Girl: The Barbara Hutton Story, The Woman He Loved, Till We Meet Again (mini-series), Night of the Fox (mini-series), Lucy & Desi: Before the Laughter, Changes, Yes Virginia There is a Santa Claus, Stranger in the Mirror, Jackie Collins' Lady Boss, Treacherous Beauties, Trade Winds, A Promise Kept: The Oksana Baiul Story (Emmy Award for dir.), At The Midnight Hour, The Christmas List.

JASON, RICK
Actor. b. New York, NY, May 21, 1923. e. American Acad. of Dramatic Arts. B'way debut in Now I Lfay Me Down To Sleep (Theatre World Award). Has acted in over 400 TV shows, beginning with Live TV (1945) and over 40 feature films.
PICTURES: Sombrero, Saracen Blade, This Is My Love, Lieutenant Wore Skirts, Wayward Bus, Partners, Illegally Yours.
TELEVISION: *Series*: The Case of the Dangerous Robin, Combat. *Mini-Series*: Around the World in 80 Days. *Movies*: The Monk, Who is the Black Dahlia?, The Best Place to Be.

JAYSTON, MICHAEL
Actor. b. Nottingham, England, Oct. 28, 1935. Member of Old Vic theatre Co. & Bristol Old Vic.
PICTURES: A Midsummer Night's Dream, Cromwell, Nicholas and Alexandra, The Public Eye (Follow Me), Alice's Adventures in Wonderland, The Nelson Affair, Tales That Witness Madness, The Homecoming, Craze, The Interneceine Project, Dominique, Zulu Dawn.
TELEVISION: She Fell Among Thieves, Tinker Tailor Soldier Spy.

JEFFREYS, ANNE
Actress. b. Goldsboro, NC, Jan. 26. m. actor Robert Sterling. Named by Theatre Arts Magazine as one of the 10 outstanding beauties of the stage. Trained for operatic career. Sang with NY's Municipal Opera Co. while supplementing income as a Powers model. Appeared as Tess Trueheart in Dick Tracy features.
THEATER: *B'way*: in Street Scene, Kiss Me Kate, Romance, Three Wishes for Jamie, Kismet. Stock: Camelot, King & I, Kismet, Song of Norway, Bells Are Ringing, Marriage Go Round, No Sex Please, We're British, Take Me Along, Carousel, Anniversary Waltz, Do I Hear a Waltz, Ninotchka, Pal Joey, Name of the Game, Destry Rides Again, The Merry Widow, Bitter Sweet, Desert Song, High Button Shoes, Sound of Music.
PICTURES: I Married an Angel, Billy the Kid, Trapped, Joan of Ozark, The Old Homestead, Tarzan's New York Adventure, X Marks the Spot, Yokel Boy, Catterbox, Man from Thunder River, Nevada, Step Lively, Dillinger, Sing Your Way Home, Those Endearing Young Charms, Zombies on Broadway, Dick Tracy Vs. Cueball, Genius at Work, Step By Step, Vacation in Reno, Trail Street, Riffraff, Return of the Bad Men, Boys' Night Out, Panic in the City, Southern Double Cross, Clifford.
TELEVISION: *Series*: Topper, Love That Jill, Bright Promise, Delphi Bureau, General Hospital, Finder of Lost Loves. *Guest*: Falcon Crest, Hotel, Murder She Wrote, L.A. Law, Baywatch. *Movies*: Beggarman Thief, A Message From Holly, American Movie Classics (host).

JEFFRIES, LIONEL
Actor, Director. b. Forest Hill, London, England, 1926. e. Queens Elizabeth's Grammar Sch, Wimbone Dorset. Ent. m.p. ind. 1952.
THEATER: Hello, Dolly!, See How They Run, Two Into One, Pygmalion (U.S.), The Wild Duck.
PICTURES: The Black Rider, The Colditz Story, No Smoking, Will Any Gentleman?, Windfall, All for Mary, Bhowani Junction, Eyewitness, Jumping for Joy, Lust for Life, Creeping Unknown (Quatermass Experiment), Baby and the Battleship, Decision Against Time, Doctor at Large, High Terrace, Hour of Decision, Up in the World, Behind the Mask, Blue Murder at St. Trinian's, Dunkirk, Girls at Sea, Law and Disorder, Orders to Kill, Revenge of Frankenstein, Up the Creek, Bobbikins, The Circle (The Vicious Circle), Idol on Parade, Nowhere to Go, The Nun's Story,

Jazzboat, Let's Get Married, Trials of Oscar Wilde, Please Turn Over, Tarzan the Magnificent, Two-Way Stretch, Fanny, The Hellions, Life is a Circus, Kill or Cure, Mrs. Gibbons' Boys, Operation Snatch, The Notorious Landlady, The Wrong Arm of the Law, Call Me Bwana, The Crimson Blade, First Men in the Moon, The Long Ships, Murder Ahoy, The Secret of My Success, The Truth About Spring, You Must Be Joking!, Arrivederci Baby!, The Spy With a Cold Nose, Oh Dad Poor Dad, Blast Off! (Rocket to the Moon), Camelot, Chitty Chitty Bang Bang, Sudden Terror, The Railway Children (dir., s.p. only), Lola (Twinky), Who Slew Auntie Roo?, The Amazing Mr. Blunden (dir., s.p. only), Baxter (dir. only), Royal Flash, Wombling Free (voice, also dir., s.p.), The Water Babies (dir. only), The Prisoner of Zenda, Better Late Than Never, A Chorus of Disapproval.
TELEVISION: Father Charlie, Tom Dick and Harriet, Cream in My Coffee, Minder, Danny: the Champion of the World, Jekyll and Hyde, Boon Morse, Ending Up, Look at It This Way, Bed.

JENKINS, DAN
Public Relations Consultant. b. Montclair, NJ, Dec. 5, 1916. e. U. of Virginia. 1938. U.S. Army, 1940-45; major, infantry. P.R. officer, Hq. Eighth Army. Mng. ed., Motion Picture Magazine, 1946-48; editor, Tele-Views Magazine, 1949-50; TV editor, columnist, Hollywood Reporter, 1950-53; Hollywood bureau chief, TV Guide, 1953-63; v.p., exec. dir. TV dept., Rogers, Cowan & Brenner, Inc., 1963-71. Formed Dan Jenkins Public Relations, Inc. 1971. Joined Charles A. Pomerantz Public Relations, Ltd. as v.p., 1975, while retaining own firm. Sr. associate, Porter, Novelli, Assocs., 1981. Mem. bd. trustees, Natl. Academy of TV Arts & Sciences; bd. gov., Hollywood chapter, Natl. Academy of TV Arts & Sciences, 1967-71. Rejoined Rogers & Cowan, 1983, v.p., TV dept. Retired, 1988.

JENKINS, GEORGE
Art Director. b. Baltimore, MD, Nov. 19, 1908. e. U. of Pennsylvania. Hollywood-New York art dir. since 1946; TV pictures for Four Star Playhouse and Revue productions; NBC-TV opera, Carmen; color dir., CBS-TV, 1954; NBC color spec. Annie Get Your Gun, 1957; TV music with Mary Martin, 1959. Professor, Motion Picture Design, UCLA, 1985-88.
THEATER: Mexican Hayride, I Remember Mama, Dark of the Moon, Lost in the Stars, Bell Book and Candle, The Bad Seed, The Happiest Millionaire, Two for the Seesaw, Ice Capades, Song of Norway, Paradise Island, Around the World in 80 Days, Mardi Gras, The Miracle Worker, Critic's Choice, A Thousand Clowns, Jennie, Generation, Wait Until Dark, Only Game in Town, Night Watch, Sly Fox.
PICTURES: The Best Years of Our Lives, The Secret Life of Walter Mitty, A Song Is Born, Rosanna McCoy, The Miracle Worker, Mickey One, Up the Down Staircase, Wait Until Dark, The Subject Was Roses, Klute, 1776, The Paper Chase, The Parallax View, Night Moves, Funny Lady, All the President's Men (Academy Award, 1976), Comes a Horseman, The China Syndrome (Acad. Award nom.), Starting Over, The Postman Always Rings Twice, Rollover, Sophie's Choice, Orphans, See You in the Morning, Presumed Innocent.
TELEVISION: Movie: The Dollmaker.

JENNINGS, PETER
TV News Anchor. b. Toronto, Canada, July 29, 1938. Son of Canadian broadcaster Charles Jennings. e. Carleton U.; Rider Coll. Worked as a bank teller and late night radio host in Canada. Started career as host of Club Thirteen, a Canadian American Bandstand-like dance prog., then as a newsman on CFJR (radio), Ottawa; then with CJOH-TV and CBC. Joined ABC in 1964 as NY corr.; 1965, anchor, Peter Jennings with the News; 1969, overseas assignments for ABC news; 1975, Washington correspondent and anchor for AM America; 1977, chief foreign corr.; 1978, foreign desk anchor, World News Tonight; 1983-, anchor, sr. editor, World News Tonight.

JENS, SALOME
Actress. b. Milwaukee, WI, May 8, 1935. e. Northwestern U. Member Actors Studio.
THEATER: The Disenchanted, Far Country, Night Life, Winter's Tale, Mary Stuart, Antony and Cleopatra, After the Fall, Moon For the Misbegotten, The Balcony.
PICTURES: Angel Baby (debut, 1961), The Fool Killer, Seconds, Me Natalie, Cloud Dancer, Harry's War, Just Between Friends, Coming Out Under Fire (narrator).
TELEVISION: Movies: In the Glitter Palace, Sharon: Portrait of a Mistress, The Golden Moment: An Olympic Love Story, A Killer in the Family, Playing with Fire, Uncommon Valor. Guest: Mary Hartman, Mary Hartman. Series: Falcon Crest. Mini-Series: From Here to Eternity.

JERGENS, ADELE
Actress. b. Brooklyn, NY, Nov. 26, 1917. Began career in musical shows during summer vacation at 15; won contest, New York's World Fair, as model; appeared on New York stage; night clubs, U.S. and abroad.
PICTURES: A Thousand and One Nights, She Wouldn't Say Yes, The Corpse Came C.O.D., Dwon to Earth, Woman From Tangier, The Fuller Brush Man, The Dark Past, Treasure of Monte Cristo, SLightly French, Edge of Doom, Side Street, Abbott and Costello Meet the Invisible Man, Sugarfoot, Try and Get Me, Show Boat, Somebody Loves Me, Aaron Slick from Punkin' Crick, Overland Pacific, Miami Story, Fireman Save My Child, Big Chase, Strange Lady in Town, The Cobweb, Girls in Prison, The Lonesome Trail, Treasure of Monte Cristo, Runaway Daughters, Fighting Trouble, The Day the World Ended.

JETER, MICHAEL
Actor. b. Lawrenceberg, TN, Aug. 20, 1952.e. Memphis State Univ.
THEATER: Alice, G.R. Point (Theatre World Award), Cloud 9, Greater Tuna, Once in a Lifetime, Zoo Story, Waiting for Godot, Only Kidding, The Boys Next Door, Grand Hotel (Tony Award, 1990).
PICTURES: Hair, Ragtime, Soup for One, Zelig, The Money Pit, Dead-Bang, Tango & Cash, Just Like in the Movies, Miller's Crossing, The Fisher King, Bank Robber, Sister Act 2: Back in the Habit, Drop Zone, Waterworld, Air Bud.
TELEVISION: Series: One Life to Live, Hothouse, Evening Shade (Emmy Award, 1992). Movies: My Old Man, Sentimental Journey, When Love Kills: The Seduction of John Hearn, Gypsy. Mini-Series: From Here to Eternity. Guest: Lou Grant, Designing Women.

JEWISON, NORMAN
Producer, Director. b. Toronto, Canada, July 21, 1926. e. Malvern Collegiate Inst., Toronto, 1940-44; Victoria Coll., U. of Toronto, 1946-50, B.A. Stage and TV actor 1950-52. Director, Canadian Broadcasting Corp 1953-58. Awarded 1988 Acad. of Canadian Cinema and Television Special Achievement Award. Made Companion Order of Canada, 1992.
PICTURES: Director: 40 Pounds of Trouble (debut, 1962), The Thrill of It All, Send Me No Flowers, The Art of Love, The Cincinnati Kid. Director-Producer: The Russians Are Coming the Russians Are Coming (Acad. Award nom. for picture), In the Heat of the Night (dir. only; Acad. Award nom.), The Thomas Crown Affair, Gaily Gaily, Fiddler on the Roof (Acad. Award nom. for dir. & picture), Jesus Christ Superstar (also co-s.p.), Rollerball, F.I.S.T., ... And Justice for All, Best Friends, A Soldier's Story (Acad. Award nom. for picture), Agnes of God, Moonstruck (Acad. Award noms. for dir. & picture), In Country, Other People's Money, Only You, Bogus. Producer: The Landlord, Billy Two Hats, The Dogs of War (exec. prod.), Iceman, The January Man.
TELEVISION: Exec. prod. of 8 episodes of The Judy Garland Show. Prod.-Dir.: Judy Garland specials, The Andy Williams Show. Dir. of Specials: Tonight with Harry Belafonte, The Broadway of Lerner and Loewe.

JHABVALA, RUTH PRAWER
Writer. b. Cologne, Germany, May 7, 1927. Emigrated with her family to England, 1939. e. Hendon County Sch., Queen Mary Coll., London U. (degree in English). m. architect C.S.H. Jhabvala, 1951 and moved to Delhi. Has written most of the screenplays for the films of Ismail Merchant and James Ivory.
AUTHOR: To Whom She Will, Esmond in India, The Nature of Passion, The Householder, Get Ready for Battle, Heat and Dust, In Search of Love and Beauty, Three Continents, Poet and Dancer, Shards of Memory.
PICTURES: The Householder (debut, 1963; based on her novel), Shakespeare Wallah (with Ivory), The Guru (with Ivory), Bombay Talkie (with Ivory), Roseland, The Europeans, Quartet, Heat and Dust (based on her own novel; BAFTA Award), The Bostonians, A Room with a View (Academy Award, 1986), Madame Sousatzka (co.-s.p. with John Schlesinger), Mr. and Mrs. Bridge (NY Film Critics Award), Howards End (Academy Award, 1992), The Remains of the Day, Jefferson in Paris, Surviving Picasso.
TELEVISION: Hullabaloo Over Georgie and Bonnie's Pictures, Autobiography of a Princess, Jane Austen in Manhattan.

JILLIAN, ANN
Actress. b. Cambridge, MA, Jan. 29, 1951. Began career at age 10 in Disney's Babes in Toyland; in film version of Gypsy at age 12. Broadway debut in musical, Sugar Babies, 1979. Formed own company: 9-J Productions, developing TV movies and series.
PICTURES: Babes in Toyland, Gypsy, Mr. Mom, Sammy the Way Out Seal.
TELEVISION: Series: Hazel, It's a Living, Jennifer Slept Here, Ann Jillian. Guest: Love Boat, Fantasy Island, Twilight Zone, Ben Casey, etc. Mini-Series: Ellis Island (Emmy & Golden Globe nom.), Alice in Wonderland, Malibu. Movies: Mae West (Emmy & Golden Globe nom.), Death Ride to Osaka, Killer in the Mirror, Convicted: A Mother's Story, Perry Mason: The Case of the Murdered Madam, The Ann Jillian Story (Golden Globe Award; Emmy nom.), Original Sin, This Wife for Hire, Little White Lies, Mario and the Mob, Labor of Love: The Arlette Schweitzer Story, Heart of a Child, The Disappearance of Vonnie, Fast Company, It's Him Or Us, My Son The Match Maker, The Care and Handling of Roses, I'll Be Home for Christmas.

JOANOU, PHIL
Director. b. La Canada, CA, Nov. 20, 1961. e. UCLA, USC. Student film The Last Chance Dance won him first professional job directing 2 episodes of tv's Amazing Stories (Santa 85, The Doll).
PICTURES: Three O'Clock High (debut, 1987), U2: Rattle and Hum (also edit., camera operator), State of Grace, Final Analysis, Heaven's Prisoners, Entropy.
TELEVISION: Mini-Series: Wild Palms (co-dir.). Series: Fallen Angels (Dead-End for Delia).

JOFFE, CHARLES H.
Executive. b. Brooklyn, NY, July 16, 1929. e. Syracuse U. Joined with Jack Rollins to set up management-production org., clients including Woody Allen, Ted Bessell, Billy Crystal, David Letterman, Tom Poston, Robin Williams.
PICTURES: Producer: Don't Drink the Water, Take the Money and Run, Everything You Always Wanted to Know About Sex but Were Afraid To Ask, Love and Death, Annie Hall (Academy Award for Best Picture, 1977), House of God. Exec. prod.: Play It Again Sam, Bananas, Sleeper, Manhattan, Interiors, Stardust Memories, Arthur, A Midsummer Nights' Sex Comedy, Zelig, Broadway Danny Rose, The Purple Rose of Cairo, Hannah and Her Sisters, Radio Days, September, Another Woman, New York Stories (Oedipus Wrecks), Crimes and Misdemeanors, Alice, Shadows and Fog, Husbands and Wives, Manhattan Murder Mystery, Bullets Over Broadway, Everyone Says I Love You (co-exec. prod.).
TELEVISION: Woody Allen specials. Star of the Family, Good Time Harry, Triplecross.

JOFFE, EDWARD
Producer, Director, Writer, Production Consultant. Worked in m.p., theatre, commercial radio and as journalist before ent. TV ind. in Britain as writer/prod with ATV. 1959-61 staff prod. Granada TV. 1962, dir., Traitor's Gate & Traveling Light for Robt Stigwood; prod. dir., numerous series for Grampian TV; 1967, dir. film The Price of a Record—Emmy finalist; 1967-68 films, Columba's Folk & So Many Partings ITV entries in Golden Harp Fest.; 1968, prod., dir. Tony Hancock Down Under in Australia, prod. dir. Up At The Cross; dir., This Is... Tom Jones; prod. dir., The Golden Shot; 1971, senior production lecturer, Thomson TV College; dir., films for U.S. for London Television Service; Evening Standard Commercials for Thames TV. Co. prod. dir.,ind. film Sound Scene, 1972-8, Contract prod. dir. Thames TV various series: Magpie, Today, Opportunity Knocks, The David Nixon Show, Seven Ages of Man, Problems, Finding Out; 1980 production consultant, CBC-TV; 1978-82, prod. dir. series Writers' Workshop, About Books; 1978, film, Places & Things (British Academy Award nom.) film, Who Do You Think You Are? (British Academy Award nom.), ITV's Japan Prize entry, Special Jury Award San Francisco Intl. Film Fest), 1981, Film Images, (British Academy Award nom.), Gold Plaque Chicago Intl. Film Fest.); The Protectors (medal winner Intl. Film & TV Festival, N.Y.). 1982-86: film Rainbow Coloured Disco Dancer. Various Series: Taste of China, Jobs Ltd., Spin-Offs, The Buzz. Doc.: War Games in Italy. 1989-95, devised, prod., dir. Video View for ITV Network; Co-prod. & dir. 2 series Sprockets; dir. Challenge. Dir. Screen Scene Prods, String of Pearls, PLC, String of Pearls 2 PLC. Companies produced mopics Double X, Little Devils - The Birth, To Catch a Yeti, Big Game, Shepherd on the Rock.

JOFFE, ROLAND
Director, Producer. b. London, England, Nov. 17, 1945. e. Lycee Francaise, Carmel Col. Manchester U., England. Worked in British theatre with the Young Vic, the National Theatre and the Old Vic. 1973 became youngest director at National Theatre. 1978, moved into directing TV for Granada TV, then Thames and B.B.C. before feature debut in 1984 with The Killing Fields.
PICTURES: Director: The Killing Fields (debut, 1984), The Mission, Fat Man and Little Boy (also co-s.p.), City of Joy (also co-prod.), The Scarlett Letter. Producer: Made in Bangkok, Super Mario Bros., Goodbye Lover.
TELEVISION: Documentaries: Rope, Ann, No Mama No. Plays: The Spongers, Tis Pity She's a Whore, The Legion Hall Bombing, United Kingdom (also co-wrote). Series: Coronation Street, Bill Brand, The Stars Look Down.

JOHNS, GLYNIS
Actress. b. Durban, South Africa, Oct. 5, 1923. e. in England. Daughter of Mervyn Johns, actor, and Alys Steele, pianist. On London stage from 1935 (Buckie's Bears, The Children's Hour, A Kiss for Cinderella, Quiet Week-End; Gertie, N.Y. stage, 1952; Major Barbara, N.Y., 1956-57.) Voted one of top ten British Money-making stars in Motion Picture Herald-Pathe poll, 1951-54.
THEATER: Too Good to Be True (NY), The King's Mare, Come as You Are, The Marquise (tour), A Little Night Music (NY; Tony Award), Cause Celebre, Harold and Maude (Canada, Hay Fever (U.K. tour), The Boy Friend (Toronto), The Circle (NY).
PICTURES: South Riding (debut, 1938), Murder in the Family, Prison Without Bars, On the Night of the Fire, Mr. Brigg's Family, Under Your Hat, The Prime Minister, 49th Parallel, Adventures of Tartu, Half-Way House, Perfect Strangers, This Man Is Mine, Frieda, An Ideal Husband, Miranda, Third Time Lucky, Dear Mr. Prohack, State Secret, Flesh and Blood, No Highway in the Sky, Appointment With Venus (Island Rescue), Encore, The Magic Box, The Card (The Promoter), The Sword and the Rose, Rob Roy the Highland Rogue, Personal Affair, The Weak and the Wicked, The Seekers (Land of Fury), The Beachcomber, Mad About Men, Court Jester, Josephine and Men, Loser Takes All,

All Mine to Give, Around the World in 80 Days, Another Time Another Place, Shake Hands with the Devil, The Sundowners, The Spider's Web, The Cabinet of Caligari, The Chapman Report, Papa's Delicate Condition, Mary Poppins, Dear Brigette, Don't Just Stand There, Lock Up Your Daughters, Under Milk Wood, Vault of Horror, Zelly and Me, Nukie, The Ref, While You Were Sleeping.
TELEVISION: Series: Glynis, Coming of Age. Guest: Dr. Kildare, Roaring Twenties, Naked City, The Defenders, Danny Kaye Show. Also: Noel Coward's Star Quality, Mrs. Amworth, All You Need Is Love, Across a Crowded Room, Little Gloria... Happy at Last, Skagg.

JOHNSON, ARTE
Actor. b. Chicago, IL, Jan. 20, 1934. e. Univ. of IL. To NY in 1950's where he landed role on B'way in Gentlemen Prefer Blondes. Also worked in nightclubs, summer stock, tv commercials. Gained fame on Rowan and Martin's Laugh-In in late 1960's. Much voice work on tv cartoons.
PICTURES: Miracle in the Rain, The Subterraneans, The Third Day, The President's Analyst, Love at First Bite, A Night at the Magic Castle, What Comes Around, Tax Season, Evil Spirits, Munchie, Second Chance, Captiva.
TELEVISION: Series: It's Always Jan, Sally, Hennesey, Don't Call Me Charlie, Rowan & Martin's Laugh-In (Emmy Award, 1969), Ben Vereen... Comin' at Ya!, The Gong Show (panelist), Games People Play, Glitter, General Hospital. Movies: Twice in a Lifetime, Bud and Lou, If Things Were Different, Detour to Terror, The Love Tapes, Condomimion, Making of a Male Model, Alice in Wonderland, Dan Turner—Hollywood Detective.

JOHNSON, DON
Actor. b. Flatt Creek, MO, Dec. 15, 1949. Worked at ACT (Amer. Conservatory Th.), San Francisco. On stage there in Your Own Thing. In L.A. in Fortune and Men's Eyes. Recording: Heartbeat (1986).
PICTURES: The Magic Garden of Stanley Sweetheart (debut, 1970), Zachariah, The Harrad Experiment, A Boy and His Dog, Return to Macon County, Soggy Bottom USA, Cease Fire, Sweet Hearts Dance, Dead-Bang, The Hot Spot, Harley Davidson and the Marlboro Man, Paradise, Born Yesterday, Guilty as Sin, Tin Cup, Goodbye Lover.
TELEVISION: Series: From Here to Eternity, Miami Vice, Nash Bridges (also prod.). Mini-Series: The Rebels, Beulah Land, The Long Hot Summer. Movies: First You Cry, Ski Lift to Death, Katie: Portrait of a Centerfold, Revenge of the Stepford Wives, Amateur Night at the Dixie Bar and Grill, Elvis and the Beauty Queen, The Two Lives of Carol Letner, In Pursuit of Honor. Special: Don Johnson's Heartbeat (music video, also exec. prod.). Guest: Kung Fu, The Bold Ones, Police Story.

JOHNSON, G. GRIFFITH
Executive. b. New York, NY, Aug. 15, 1912. e. Harvard U., 1934, A.M. 1936, Ph.D. 1938. U.S. Treasury Dept. 1936-39; Dept. of Comm., 1939-40; O.P.A. & predecessor agencies, 1940-46; consulting economist, 1946-47; dir., Econ. Stab. Div., Nat'l. Security Resources Bd., 1948-49; chief econ., U.S. Bur. of Budget, 1949-50; econ. advisor to Econ. Stab. Admin. 1950-52; Exec. v.p. MPEAA, 1965, MPAA, 1971; Asst. Sec'y of State for Economic Affairs, 1962-65; v.p. MPAA, 1953-62. Author of several books & articles.

JOHNSON, J. BOND
Producer, Executive. b. Fort Worth, TX, June 18, 1926. e. Texas Wesleyan Univ., B.S., 1947; Texas Christian U., M.Ed., 1948; Southern Methodist U., B.D., 1952; USC, Ph.D., 1967. Army Air Forces, WWII; public information officer, captain, U.S. Marine Corps, Korean War. Formerly member Marine Corps Reserve, Motion Picture Production Unit, Hollywood. Was Colonel, U.S. Army; now retired. Newspaper reporter, Fort Worth Star-Telegram, 1942-48; pres., West Coast News Service, 1960; pres., exec. prod., Bonjo Prods., Inc., 1960, President, chief executive officer, Cine-Media International, 1975 managing partner, Capra-Johnson Productions, Ltd., 1978.
PICTURES: Sands of Iwo Jima, Retreat Hell, Flying Leathernecks; photographed aerial portions, Jamboree 53, Norfleet, Devil at My Heels, Kingdom of the Spiders, Ordeal at Donner Pass, Place of the Dawn, Lies I Told Myself, Backstretch, Airs Above The Ground, The Jerusalem Concert, The Berkshire Terror, The Seventh Gate.
TELEVISION: Series: Creator, story consultant, tech. advisor, Whirlpool. Exec. producer, creator: On The Go (TV News-Sports), Coasties, Desert Rangers. Producer: Fandango.

JOHNSON, LAMONT
Director, Producer. b. Stockton, CA, Sept. 30, 1922. e. UCLA. 4 time winner of Director's Guild Award for TV work. Directed plays The Egg, Yes Is For a Very Young Man. Dir. two operas, L.A. Philharmonic, 1964; founder, dir., UCLA Professional Theatre Group.
PICTURES: A Covenant With Death (debut, 1967), Kona Coast, The McKenzie Break, A Gunfight, The Groundstar Conspiracy, You'll Like My Mother, The Last American Hero, Visit to a Chief's Son, Lipstick, One on One (also actor), Somebody Killed Her Husband, Cattle Annie and Little Britches, Spacehunter: Adventures in the Forbidden Zone.

TELEVISION: *Series:* The Defenders, Profiles in Courage, Twilight Zone. *Movies/Mini-Series:* Deadlock, My Sweet Charlie, That Certain Summer, The Execution of Pvt. Slovik, Fear on Trial, Off the Minnesota Strip, Crisis at Central High, Escape from Iran, Dangerous Company, Life of the Party: The Story of Beatrice, Ernie Kovacs: Between the Laughter, Wallenberg: A Hero's Story (also co-prod.; Emmy Award, 1985), Unnatural Causes, Gore Vidal's Lincoln (Emmy Award, 1988), The Kennedys of Massachusetts, Voices Within: The Lives of Truddi Chase, Crash Landing: The Rescue of Flight 232, The Broken Chain (also prod.).

JOHNSON, MARK
Producer. b. Washington, DC, Dec. 27, 1945. Moved to Spain at age 7, lived there for eleven years before returning to America. e. Univ. of VA, Univ. of IA. Joined Directors Guild training program receiving first credit on Next Stop Greenwich Village. Worked as prod. asst., then asst. dir. on High Anxiety, Movie Movie, The Brink's Job, and Escape From Alcatraz. Starting with Diner in 1982 served as executive prod. or prod. on all Barry Levinson films. With Levinson formed Baltimore Pictures in 1989.
PICTURES: Diner (exec. prod.). *Producer:* The Natural, Young Sherlock Holmes, Tin Men, Good Morning Vietnam, Rain Man (Academy Award for Best Picture of 1988), Avalon, Kafka (co-exec. prod.), Bugsy (L.A. Film Critics & Golden Globe Awards for Best Picture of 1991), Toys, Sniper, Wilder Napalm, A Perfect World, A Little Princess, Donnie Brasco, Mouse Hunt (exec. prod.), Home Fries, The Astronaut's Wife (exec. prod.), My Dog Skip (exec. prod.).

JOHNSON, RICHARD
Actor. b. Upminster, Essex, England, July 30, 1927. Studied at Royal Acad. of Dramatic Art. First stage appearance Opera House, Manchester, then with John Gielgud's repertory season, 1944. Served in Royal Navy 1945-48. Subsequent stage appearances incl. The Madwoman of Chaillot, The Lark. Visited Moscow with Peter Brook's production of Hamlet. Royal Shakespeare Thea.: Stratford, London, 1957-62. Royal Shakespeare Co. 1972-73. National Theatre, 1976-77. Founded United British Artists, 1983.
PICTURES: Captain Horatio Hornblower (debut, 1951), Calling Bulldog Drummond, Scotland Yard Inspector (Lady in the Fog), Saadia, Never So Few, Cairo, The Haunting, 80,000 Suspects, The Pumpkin Eater, The Amorous Adventures of Moll Flanders, Operation Crossbow, Khartoum, The Witch in Love, Deadlier Than the Male, The Rover, Danger Route, A Twist of Sand, Oedipus the King, Lady Hamilton, Some Girls Do, Julius Caesar, The Tyrant, The Beloved, Behind the Door, Hennessy, Night Child, The Cursed Medallion, Aces High, The Last Day of Spring, The Comeback, Zombie, The Monster Club, Screamers, What Waits Below, Lady Jane, Turtle Diary, Foreign Student, Diving In. Producer: Turtle Diary, Castaway, The Lonely Passion of Judith Hearne, The Secret Life of Ian Fleming, The Camomile Lawn, Duel of Hearts, Heavy Weather, Breaking the Code.
TELEVISION: The Flame is Love, Haywire, The Four Feathers, Portrait of a Rebel: Margaret Sanger, A Man For All Seasons, Voice of the Heart, The Crucifer of Blood, Duel of Hearts. Guest: Wagon Train, Lou Grant, Ironside, Knots Landing, That Girl, MacGyver, Police Story, Route 66, many others. Live TV incl. Lux Video Theatre, Front Row Center, Hallmark Hall of Fame.

JOHNSON, RUSSELL
Actor. b. Ashley, PA, Nov. 10, 1924. e. Girard Coll, Actors Laboratory, L.A. W.W.II, Army Air Corps. Author: Here on Gilligan's Isle (1993).
PICTURES: A Town of the 80's, Stand at Apache Landing, A Distant Trumpet, Ma & Pa Kettle at Waikiki, Rogue Cop, Loan Shark, Seminole, Tumbleweed, Blue Movies, It Came From Outer Space, Many Rivers to Cross, Law and Order, Black Tuesday, This Island Earth, Rock All Night, Attack of the Crab Monsters, The Space Children, For Men Only, The Greatest Story Ever Told, Hitchhike to Hell, MacArthur.
TELEVISION: *Series:* Black Saddle, Gilligan's Island. *Guest:* Studio One, Front Row Center, Playhouse 90, Lux Video Theatre, Mobile One, The Great Adventure Jane Powell Show, Climax, You Are There, Rawhide, Twilight Zone, Gunsmoke, Outer Limits, Cannon, Marcus Welby, That Girl, The FBI, Dallas, Fame, Dynasty, My Two Dads, Bosom Buddies, Buffalo Bill, Vanished, Harry Truman Biography, Truman vs. MacArthur, Knots Landing, Santa Barbara, Roseanne, many others. *Movie:* With a Vengeance.

JOHNSON, TOM
Sound.
PICTURES: Return of the Jedi, Indiana Jones and the Temple of Doom, Seize the Day, Howard the Duck, Dirty Rotten Scoundrels, Colors, The Couch Trip, Tucker: The Man and His Dream, The Karate Kid III, To Cross the Rubicon, The Five Heartbeats, Terminator II: Judgment Day, F/X2, Single White Female, Quiz Show, Forrest Gump, Nine Months, Strange Days, Stealing Beauty, Jack, One Fine Day, Titanic (Acad. Award, Best Sound, 1997), Beverly Hills Ninja, Contact, Wag the Dog.
TELEVISION: *Movies:* The Dreamer of Oz.

JOHNSON, VAN
Actor. b. Newport, RI, Aug. 25, 1916. Began in vaudeville; then on N.Y. stage New Faces of 1937, Eight Men of Manhattan, Too Many Girls, Pal Joey. Voted one of the top ten Money Making Stars in Motion Picture Herald-Fame Poll 1945-46. Stage includes The Music Man (London), La Cage aux Folles (NY) and numerous tours.
PICTURES: Too Many Girls (debut, 1940), Murder in the Big House, Somewhere I'll Find You, War Against Mrs. Hadley, Dr. Gillespie's New Assistant, The Human Comedy, Pilot No. 5, Dr. Gillespies's Criminal Case, Guy Named Joe, White Cliffs of Dover, Three Men in White, Two Girls and a Sailor, Thirty Seconds Over Tokyo, Between Two Women, Thrill of Romance, Weekend at the Waldorf, Easy to Wed, No Leave No Love, Till the Clouds Roll By, High Barbaree, Romance of Rosy Ridge, Bride Goes Wild, State of the Union, Command Decision, Mother is a Freshman, In the Good Old Summertime, Scene of the Crime, Battleground, Big Hangover, Duchess of Idaho, Three Guys Named Mike, Grounds for Marriage, Go For Broke, Too Young to Kiss, It's a Big Country, Invitation, When in Rome, Washington Story, Plymouth Adventure, Confidentially Connie, Remains to Be Seen, Easy to Love, Caine Mutiny, Siege at Red River, Men of the Fighting Lady, Brigadoon, Last Time I Saw Paris, End of the Affair, Bottom of the Bottle, Miracle in the Rain, 23 Paces to Baker Street, Slander, Kelly and Me, Action of the Tiger, The Last Blitzkreig, Subway in the Sky, Beyond This Place, Enemy General, Wives and Lovers, Divorce American Style, Yours Mine and Ours, Where Angels Go ... Trouble Follows, Company of Killers, Eagles Over London, The Kidnapping of the President, The Purple Rose of Cairo, Down There in the Jungle, Escape From Paradise, Three Days to a Kill.
TELEVISION: *Special:* Pied Piper of Hamelin. *Mini-Series:* Rich Man Poor Man, Black Beauty. *Movies:* Doomsday Flight, San Francisco International, Call Her Mom, The Girl on the Late Late Show, Superdome. *Guest:* I Love Lucy, G.E. Theatre, Batman, Love American Style, The Love Boat, Murder She Wrote.

JOHNSTON, MARGARET
Actress. b. Sydney, Australia, Aug. 10, 1918. e. Sydney U., Australia; RADA. London stage debut: Murder Without Crime.
THEATER: Ring of Truth, The Masterpiece, Lady Macbeth, Merchant of Venice, Measure for Measure, Othello.
PICTURES: The Prime Minister, The Rake's Progress (The Notorious Gentleman), A Man About the House, Portrait of Clare, The Magic Box, Knave of Hearts, Touch and Go, Burn With Burn (Night of the Eagle), The Nose on My Face, Girl in the Headlines (The Model Murder Case), Life at the Top, The Psychopath, Schizo, Sebastian.
TELEVISION: Always Juliet, Taming of the Shrew, Man with a Load of Mischief, Light of Heart, Autumn Crocus, Androcles and the Lion, Sulky Five, Windmill Near a Frontier, The Shrike, The Out of Towners, Looking for Garrow, The Typewriter, The Glass Menagerie, That's Where the Town's Going, The Vortex.

JOLIE, ANGELINA
Actress.
PICTURES: Cyborg 2: Glass Shadow, Hackers, Mojave Moon, Foxfire, Love Is All There Is, Playing God, Pushing Tin, Hell's Kitchen, Dancing About Architecture, Girl Interrupted, The Bone Collector.
TELEVISION: *Movies:* George Wallace (Golden Globe Award, 1998), Gia. *Mini-series:* True Women.

JOLLEY, STAN
Producer, Director, Production Designer, Art Director. b. New York, NY, May 17, 1926. e. U. of Southern California, col. of architecture. Son of actor I. Stanford Jolley. In Navy in W.W.II. Has acted in capacities listed for many feature films and TV series. One of orig. designers of Disneyland.
PICTURES: *Prod./Prod. Designer:* Knife for the Ladies. *Assoc. Prod./ Prod. Designer:* The Good Guys and the Bad Guys. *2nd Unit Dir.:* Superman. *Prod. Designer:* Dutch, The Good Mother, Witness (Acad. Award nom.), Taps, Caddyshack, Cattle Annie and Little Britches, Americathon (also second unit director), The Swarm, Drum, Framed, Dion Brothers, Mixed Company, Walking Tall, Terror in the Wax Museum, Night of the Lepus (also second unit director), War Between Men and Women, Law Man, The Phynx. *Art Director:* Young Billy Young, Ride Beyond Vengeance, Broken Saber, The Restless Ones, Mail Order Bride, Toby Tyler, The Grass Harp. *Assoc. Prod./Prod. designer & 2nd unit dir.:* Happily Ever After.
TELEVISION: *Movies: 2nd Unit Dir./Prod. Designer:* Swiss Family Robinson, Adventures of the Queen, Woman Hunter, Abduction of Carrie Swenson, Eagle One, No Man's Land, Last of the Great Survivors, Like Normal People, Rescue From Gilligan's Island, Flood, Voyage of the Yes, The Stranger, Punch & Jody, City Beneath the Sea, Women of San Quentin. *Mini-series:* Howards, The Amazing Mr. Hughes. *Series: Dir./Prod. Designer:* MacGyver, Today's FBI. *Assoc. Prod./Prod. Designer:* Jessie. *Prod. Designer:* Walking Tall, For Love and Honor. *Art Dir.:* Walt Disney Presents, Pete and Gladys, Gunsmoke, Mr. Ed, Branded, Voyage to the Bottom of the Sea, Land of the Giants, O'Hara Shane, Acapulco, The Racers, *Docu-drama:* Under Fire. *Pilots:* Get Smart, Some Like It Hot. *Cartoon:* Donald in Mathmagic Land. *Documentary:* Crisis in the Wetlands (prod./dir.).

JONAS, TONY
Executive. Pres., Warner Bros. Television.

JONES, AMY HOLDEN
Director, Writer. b. Philadelphia, PA, Sept. 17, 1953. m. cinematographer, Michael Chapman. e. Wellesley Coll., B.A., 1974; film and photography courses, Massachusetts Inst. of Technology. Winner, first place, Washington National Student Film Festival, 1973.
PICTURES: *Editor*: Hollywood Boulevard (debut, 1976), American Boy, Corvette Summer, Second Hand Hearts. *Director*: Slumber Party Massacre, Love Letters (also s.p.), Mystic Pizza (s.p. only), Maid to Order (also co-s.p.), Rich Man's Wife (also s.p.). *Writer*: Beethoven, Indecent Proposal, The Getaway, It Had to Be Steve (co-s.p.), The Relic (co-s.p.).
TELEVISION: *Pilot* (writer): Jack's Place.

JONES, CHUCK
Producer, Director, Writer, Animator. b. Spokane, WA, Sept. 21, 1912. e. Chouinard Art Inst. Dir., Warner Bros. Animation until 1962 where he created and directed Road Runner & Wile E. Coyote, Pepe le Pew; directed and helped create Bugs Bunny, Porky Pig, Daffy Duck etc. Created Snafu character, U.S. Armed Service. Later headed MGM Animation Dept. Lecturer at many Universities. Establisehd indept. co. Chuck Jones Enterprises. Academy Awards for best animated short subjects: For Scentimental Reasons (1950), The Dot and the Line (1965), best documentary short subject: So Much for So Little (1950). 1989, published Chuck Amuck: The Life and Times of an Animated Cartoonist. 1990, chmn. Chuck Jones Prods.; currently consultant and good-will representative to Warner Bros.
PICTURES: The Phantom Tollbooth, The Bugs Bunny/Road Runner Movie, The Magical World of Chuck Jones; created animated sequences for live-action features Stay Tuned, Mrs. Doubtfire.
TELEVISION: The Bugs Bunny Show (co-prod., writer, dir.). *Dir.*: How the Grinch Stole Christmas, Horton Hears a Who, Pogo. *Producer- Director-Writer*: The Cricket in Times Square, A Very Merry Cricket, Yankee Doodle Cricket, Rikki-Tikki-Tavi, The White Seal, Mowgli's Brothers, The Carnival of the Animals, A Connecticut Rabbit in King Arthur's Court, Raggedy Ann and Andy in The Great Santa Claus Caper, The Pumpkin Who Couldn't Smile, Daffy Duck's Thanks-for-Giving Special, Bugs Bunny's Bustin' Out All Over.

JONES, DAVID
Director, Producer. b. Poole, Eng., Feb. 19, 1934. e. Christ's Coll., Cambridge U., B.A., 1954, M.A., 1957. Immigrated to U.S. in 1979. Artistic controller, then assoc. dir., Royal Shakespeare Co., 1964-75; artistic dir, RSC at Aldwych Theatre 1975-78; artistic dir, Brooklyn Acad. of Music Theatre Co., NY 1979-81; prof. Yale Sch. of Drama, 1981.
THEATER: Sweeney Agonistes (debut, 1961); *U.S.*: Summerfolk, Loves Labour's Lost, Winter's Tale, Barbarians, Jungle of Cities.
PICTURES: Betrayal, Jacknife, The Trial.
TELEVISION: *Prod.*: Monitor 1958-64 (BBC series), Play of the Month, The Beaux' Stratagem, Langrishe Go Down, Ice Age. *Dir.*: Shakespeare series, BBC 1982-83, Devil's Disciple, The Christmas Wife, Sensibility and Sense, Is There Life Out There?

JONES, DEAN
Actor. b. Decatur, AL, Jan. 25, 1931. e. Asbury Coll., Wilmore, KY. Prof. debut as blues singer, New Orleans; U.S. Navy, 1950-54. Author: Under Running Laughter.
THEATER: There Was a Little Girl, Under the Yum-Yum Tree, Company, Into the Light, Show Boat.
PICTURES: Tea and Sympathy (debut, 1956), The Rack, The Opposite Sex, These Wilder Years, The Great American Pastime, Designing Woman, Ten Thousand Bedrooms, Jailhouse Rock, Until They Sail, Imitation General, Torpedo Run, Handle with Care, Night of the Quarter Moon, Never So Few, Under the Yum-Yum Tree, The New Interns, That Darn Cat, Two on a Guillotine, Any Wednesday, The Ugly Dachshund, Monkeys Go Home, Blackbeard's Ghost, The Horse in the Grey Flannel Suit, The Love Bug, $1,000,000 Duck, Snowball Express, Mr. Super Invisible, The Shaggy D.A., Herbie Goes to Monte Carlo, Born Again, Other People's Money, Beethoven, Clear and Present Danger, That Darn Cat II.
TELEVISION: *Series*: Ensign O'Toole, The Chicago Teddy Bears, What's It All About World?, Herbie the Love Bug, Beethoven (animated; voice). *Movies*: Guess Who's Sleeping in My Bed?, When Every Day Was the 4th of July, Long Days of Summer, Fire and Rain, The Great Man's Whiskers, Saved By the Bell: Hawaiian Style, The Computer Wore Tennis Shoes, The Love Bug Reunion. *Specials*: Journey to Mars, Out of Jerusalem.

JONES, GEMMA
Actress. b. London, Eng., Dec. 4, 1942. e. Royal Acad. of Dramatic Art.
THEATER: Baal, Alfie, The Cavern, The Pastime of M Robert, Portrait of a Queen, Next of Kin, The Marriage of Figaro, And A Nightingale Sang, reaking the Silence, Howards End, A Midsummer Night's Dream, The Homecoming, Mount Morgan, The Winter's Tale, etc.
PICTURES: The Devils, The Paper House, On the Black Hill, The Devils Feast of July, Sense and Sensibility, Wilde, The Winslow Boy, O.K. Garage.
TELEVISION: The Lie, The Way of the World, The Merchant of Venice, The Duchess of Duke Street (series), The Jim Henson Hour, Forget Me Not Lane,Call My Bluff, Dial M For Murder, The Way of the World, Churchill's People, The Cherry Orchard, The Lie, Man In A Sidecar, Shadows of Fear, Crimes of Passion, The Spoils of Poynton, The Duchess of Duke Street, The Importance of Being Earnest, Chelworth, After The Dance, Inspector Morse, The Storyteller, Sevises and Desires, Some Lie Some Die, Wycliffe, The Borrowers, Faith, Wilderness, Jane Eyre, The Phoenix and the Carpet, An Unsuitable Job for a Woman.

JONES, GLENN R.
Executive. Began career in law, representing cable TV cos. in acquisition efforts. Purchased his first cable TV system in 1967 which became part of Jones Intercable, Inc., founded 1970. Pres. and CEO of the corp. since its inception.

JONES, GRACE
Singer, Actress. b. Spanishtown, Jamaica, May 19, 1952. e. Syracuse U. Modelled and appeared in several Italian pictures before career as singer.
PICTURES: Conan the Destroyer, A View to a Kill, Vamp, Straight to Hell, Siesta, Boomerang.

JONES, HENRY
Actor. b. Philadelphia, PA, Aug. 1, 1912. e. St. Joseph's Coll. On stage in Hamlet, Henry IV, Time of Your Life, My Sister Eileen, The Solid Gold Cadillac, Bad Seed, Sunrise at Campobello (Tony Award, 1958), Advise and Consent.
PICTURES: This is the Army, Lady Says No, Taxi, The Bad Seed, The Girl He Left Behind, The Girl Can't Help It, Will Success Spoil Rock Hunter?, 3:10 to Yuma, Vertigo, Cash McCall, The Bramble Bush, Angel Baby, Never Too Late, The Champagne Murders, Stay Away Joe, Project X, Support Your Local Sheriff, Rascal, Angel in My Pocket, Butch Cassidy and the Sundance Kid, Rabbit Run, Dirty Dingus Magee, Skin Game, Support Your Local Gunfighter, Napoleon and Samantha, Pete 'n' Tillie, Tom Sawyer, The Outfit, Nine to Five, Deathtrap, Balboa, Caddo Lake, Nowhere to Run, Dick Tracy, Arachnophobia, The Grifters.
TELEVISION: *Series*: Honestly Celeste!, Channing, The Girl With Something Extra, Phyllis, Kate Loves a Mystery, Gun Shy, Code Name: Foxfire, I Married Dora. *Movies*: The Crucible, Something for a Lonely Man, The Movie Murderer, Love Hate Love, Who is the Black Dahlia?, Tail Gunner Joe, CaliforniaGold Rush, The Leftovers, Grass Roots. *Guest*: Lost in Space, We'll Get By, B.J. and the Bear, Falcon Crest.

JONES, JAMES EARL
Actor. b. Arkabutla, MS, Jan. 17, 1931. e. U. of Michigan. Son of actor Robert Earl Jones. Awarded Hon. Doctor of Fine Arts (Yale, Princeton)/ Medal for Spoken Language (Amer. Acad. and Inst. of Arts and Letter; Hon. Doctor of Humane Letters (Columbia Coll. & U. of Mich.).
THEATER: Moon on a Rainbow Shawl (Theatre World Award), The Cool World, Othello, Paul Robeson, Les Blancs, The Great White Hope (Tony Award, 1969), The Iceman Cometh, Of Mice and Men, A Lesson from Aloes, Master Harold ... and the Boys, Fences (Tony Award, 1986).
PICTURES: Dr. Strangelove, or: How I Learned to Stop Worrying and Love the Bomb (debut, 1964), The Comedians, King: A Filmed Record ... Montgomery to Memphis, End of the Road, The Great White Hope (Acad. Award nom.), Malcolm X (narrator), The Man, Claudine, Deadly Hero, Swashbuckler, The Bingo Long Travelling All-Stars and Motor Kings, The River Niger, The Greatest, Star Wars (voice), Exorcist II: The Heretic, The Last Remake of Beau Geste, A Piece of the Action, The Bushido Blade, The Empire Strikes Back (voice), Conan the Barbarian, Blood Tide (The Red Tide), Return of the Jedi (voice), City Limits, My Little Girl, Soul Man, Allan Quartermain and the Lost City of Gold, Gardens of Stone, Matewan, Pinocchio and the Emperor of the Night (voice), Coming to America, Three Fugitives, Field of Dreams, Best of the Best, The Hunt for Red October, Grim Prairie Tales, The Ambulance, True Identity, Convicts, Patriot Games, Sneakers, Sommersby, The Sandlot, The Meteor Man, Naked Gun 33 1/3: The Final Insult, Clean Slate, The Lion King (voice), Clear and Present Danger, Jefferson in Paris, Judge Dredd (voice), Cry the Beloved Country, Lone Star, A Family Thing.
TELEVISION: *Series*: As the World Turns, The Guiding Light, Paris, Me and Mom, Gabriel's Fire (Emmy Award, 1991), Pros & Cons, Under One Roof. *Movies*: The UFO Incident, Jesus of Nazareth, The Greatest Thing That Almost Happened, Guyana Tragedy—The Story of Jim Jones, Golden Moment: An Olympic Love Story, Philby, Burgess and MacLean, The Atlanta Child Murders, The Vegas Strip War, By Dawn's Early Light, Heat Wave (Emmy Award, 1991), Last Flight Out, The Last Elephant, Percy & Thunder, The Vernon Johns Story, Confessions: Two Faces of Evil. *Mini-Series*: Roots: The Next Generations. *Specials*: King Lear, Soldier Boy, Mathnet, Bailey's Bridge, Third and Oak: The Pool Hall, Teach 109, Hallelujah. Host: Black Omnibus, Vegetable Soup, Summer Show, Long Ago and Far Away.

JONES, JEFFREY

Actor. b. Buffalo, NY, Sept. 28, 1947. e. Lawrence U., Wisconsin. While pre-med student, performed in 1967 prod. of Hobson's Choice and was invited by Sir Tyrone Guthrie to join Guthrie Theatre in Minneapolis. After short time in South America, studied at London Acad. of Music and Dramatic Arts before joining Stratford Theater in Ontario. 1973-74 worked with Vancouver touring children's theater co. Playhouse Holiday. Moved to N.Y. where performed on stage.
THEATER: The Elephant Man (B'way debut), Trelawney of the Wells, Secret Service, Boy Meets Girl, Cloud Nine, Comedy of Errors, The Tempest, The Death of Von Richtoven, London Suite.
PICTURES: The Revolutionary, The Soldier, Easy Money, Amadeus, Transylvania 6-5000, Ferris Bueller's Day Off, Howard the Duck, The Hanoi Hilton, Beetlejuice, Without a Clue, Who Is Harry Crumb?, Valmont, The Hunt for Red October, Over Her Dead Body, Mom and Dad Save the World, Stay Tuned, Out on a Limb, Heaven and Earth (unbilled), Ed Wood, Houseguest, The Pest, The Crucible, Sante Fe, Flypaper, The Pest, The Devil's Advocate, There Is No Fish Food in Heaven, Ravenous.
TELEVISION: Mini-Series: George Washington: The Forging of a Nation, Fresno. Movies: Kenny Rogers as The Gambler III—The Legend Continues, The Avenging Angel. Guest: Amazing Stories, Twilight Zone, Remington Steele. Series: The People Next Door.

JONES, JENNIFER

Actress. r.n. Phyllis Isley. b. Tulsa, OK, Mar. 2, 1919. e. Northwestern U., American Acad. of Dramatic Arts. Daughter of Phil R., Flora Mae (Suber) Isley, exhib. m. industrialist Norton Simon. Son is actor Robert Walker Jr. Toured with parents stock company as child; in summer stock in East; little theat. East & West. Began screen career as Phyllis Isley. Pres., Norton Simon Museum.
PICTURES: Dick Tracy's G-Men (debut, 1939), The New Frontier, The Song of Bernadette (Academy Award, 1943; first film billed as Jennifer Jones), Since You Went Away, Love Letters, Cluny Brown, Duel in the Sun, Portrait of Jennie, We Were Strangers, Madame Bovary, Carrie, Wild Heart (Gone to Earth), Ruby Gentry, Indiscretion of an American Wife (Terminal Station), Beat the Devil, Love Is a Many-Splendored Thing, Good Morning Miss Dove, The Man in the Gray Flannel Suit, The Barretts of Wimpole Street, A Farewell to Arms, Tender Is the Night, The Idol, Angel Angel Down We Go (Cult of the Damned), The Towering Inferno.

JONES, KATHY

Executive. b. Aug. 27, 1949. Began career as acct. exec. for m.p. clients, Stan Levinson assoc., Dallas. Joined Paramount Pictures in 1977 as sr. publicist in field marketing then exec. dir., field mktg. Left to join Time-Life Films as v.p., domestic mktg., for m.p. div. Returned to Paramount 1981 as v.p., domestic pub. & promo. 1984, appt. sr. v.p., domestic pub. & promo. for Motion Picture Group, Paramount. Formed m.p. consultancy with Buffy Shutt, 1987. 1989, appt. exec. v.p., marketing, Columbia Pictures. 1991, appt. exec. v.p. marketing, TriStar Pictures.

JONES, QUINCY

Producer, Composer, Arranger, Recording Artist. b. Chicago, IL, March 14, 1933. e. Seattle U., Berklee Sch. Music, Boston Conservatory, Trumpeter and arranger for Lionel Hampton's orch. 1950-53, played with Dizzy Gillespie, Count Basie and arranged for orchs., singers-Frank Sinatra, Sarah Vaughn, Peggy Lee, Dinah Washington and led own orch. for European tours, and recordings. Prod. recordings for Michael Jackson, Tevin Campbell, Barbra Streisand, Donna Summer. Music dir. and v.p., Mercury Records 1961-64 before scoring films. Prod. & arranged We Are the World recording. Owns own Qwest Records record company. Received Jean Hersholt Humanitarian Award, 1995.
PICTURES: The Pawnbroker, Mirage, The Slender Thread, Made in Paris, Walk Don't Run, Banning, The Deadly Affair, In the Heat of the Night, In Cold Blood (Acad. Award nom.), Enter Laughing, A Dandy in Aspic, For Love of Ivy, The Hell With Heroes, The Split, Up Your Teddy Bear, Jocelyn, McKenna's Gold, The Italian Job, Bob & Carol & Ted & Alice, The Lost Man, Cactus Flower, John and Mary, The Last of the Mobile Hotshots, The Out-of-Towners, They Call Me Mister Tibbs, Brother John, $ (Dollars), The Anderson Tapes, Yao of the Jungle, The Hot Rock, The New Centurions, Come Back Charleston Blue, The Getaway, The Wiz (also cameo), The Color Purple (also co-prod.; Acad. Award nom.), Listen Up, Steel.
TELEVISION: Mini-Series: Roots (Emmy, 1977). Special: An American Reunion (exec. prod.). Series: Fresh Prince of Bel Air, In the House (prod.).

JONES, SAM J.

Actor. b. Chicago, IL, Aug. 12, 1954.
PICTURES: "10", Davinci's War, One Man Force, Night Rhythms, South Beach, Iron Fist, Where the Truth Lies, Evasive Action, Flash Gordon, Lady Dragon II, Last Breath, My Chauffeur, Under the Gun, Silent Assassins, Jane & the Lost City, White Fire, Trigon Factor, Driving Force, In Gold We Trust, Human Shields, Fists of Honor, Ballistic, American Strays, Texas Payback, Hard Vice, R.I.O.T., American Tigers, Baja Run, Earth Minus Zero.
TELEVISION: Series: Training Camp, Code Red, The Highwayman, Hollywood Safari. Movies: This Wife for Hire, Ray Alexander. Pilot: Hat Squad, Cobra, Thunder in Paradise,Stunts Unlimited, No Man's Land, The Spirit. Guest: Co-ed Fever, A-Team, Riptide, Hunter, Baywatch, Diagnosis Murder, Pacific Blue, and numerous others.

JONES, SHIRLEY

Actress. b. Smithton, PA, March 31, 1934. m. agent-prod. Marty Ingels. Mother of actors Shaun and Patrick Cassidy. Former Miss Pittsburgh. Natl. chair, Leukemia Foundation. Book: Shirley & Marty: An Unlikely Love Story (Wm. Morrow, 1990). Received hom. Doctor of Humane Letters degree from Point Park Col. 1991.
THEATER: Appeared with Pittsburgh Civic Light Opera in Lady in the Dark, Call Me Madam. B'way: South Pacific, Me and Juliet, Maggie Flynn.
PICTURES: Oklahoma! (debut, 1955), Carousel, April Love, Never Steal Anything Small, Bobbikins, Elmer Gantry (Academy Award, best supporting actress, 1960), Pepe, Two Rode Together, The Music Man, The Courtship of Eddie's Father, A Ticklish Affair, Dark Purpose, Bedtime Story, Fluffy, The Secret of My Success, The Happy Ending, El Golfo, Oddly Coupled, The Cheyenne Social Club, Beyond the Poseidon Adventure, Tank, There Were Times Dear, Jack L. Warner: The Last Mogul, Cops n' Roberts, Gideon's Webb
TELEVISION: Movies: Silent Night Lonely Night, But I Don't Want to Get Married, The Girls of Huntington House, The Family Nobody Wanted, Winner Take All, The Lives of Jenny Dolan, Yesterday's Child, Evening in Byzantium, Who'll Save Our Children? A Last Cry For Help, Children of An Lac, Intimates: A Love Story, Widow, Charlie, Dog's Best Friend. Series: The Partridge Family, Shirley, The Slap Maxwell Story. Guest: McMillan and Wife, The Love Boat, Hotel, Murder She Wrote, Empty Nest.

JONES, TERRY

Writer, Actor, Director. b. Colwyn Bay, North Wales, Feb. 1, 1942. Worked with various rep. groups before joining BBC script dept. Was member of Monty Python's Flying Circus.
PICTURES: Actor: And Now for Something Completely Different (also co-s.p.), Monty Python and the Holy Grail (also co-dir., co-s.p.), Monty Python's Life of Brian (also dir., co-s.p.), Monty Python's The Meaning of Life (also co-s.p., dir., music), Labyrinth (s.p. only), Personal Services (dir. only), Erik the Viking (also dir., s.p.), LA Story, The Wind and the Willows, Starship, Titanic.
TELEVISION: Late Night Lineup, The Late Show, A Series of Birds, Do Not Adjust Your Set, The Complete and Utter History of Britain, Monty Python's Flying Circus, Secrets, The Crusades (also dir., writer), So This Is Progress.

JONES, TOMMY LEE

Actor. b. San Saba, TX, Sept. 15, 1946. Worked in oil fields; graduated Harvard, where earned a degree, cum laude, in English. Broadway debut in A Patriot for Me; appeared on stage in Four in a Garden, Ulysses in Nighttown, Fortune and Men's Eyes.
PICTURES: Love Story (debut, 1970), Eliza's Horoscope, Jackson County Jail, Rolling Thunder, The Betsy, Eyes of Laura Mars, Coal Miner's Daughter, Back Roads, Nate and Hayes, The River Rat, Black Moon Rising, The Big Town, Stormy Monday, The Package, Firebirds, JFK (Acad. Award nom.), Under Siege, House of Cards, The Fugitive (Acad. Award, best supporting actor, 1993; LA Film Critics & Golden Globe Awards), Heaven and Earth, Blown Away, The Client, Natural Born Killers, Blue Sky, Cobb, Batman Forever, Men in Black, Volcano.
TELEVISION: Movies: Charlie's Angels (pilot), Smash-Up on Interstate 5, The Amazing Howard Hughes, The Executioner's Song (Emmy Award, 1983), Broken Vows, The Park is Mine, Yuri Nosenko: KGB, Gotham, Stranger on My Land, April Morning, The Good Old Boys (also dir., co-writer). Mini-Series: Lonesome Dove. Specials: The Rainmaker, Cat on a Hot Tin Roof.

JONES, TREVOR

Composer, conductor.
PICTURES: The Dollar Bottom, Brothers and Sisters, The Beneficiary, The Appointment, Excalibur, The Sender, The Dark Crystal, Nate and Hayes, Runaway Train, From an Immigrant's Diary, Labyrinth, Angel Heart, Sweet Lies, A Private Life, Mississippi Burning, Just Ask For Diamond, Dominick and Eugene, Sea of Love, Bad Influence, Arachnophobia, Ture Colors, CrissCross, Blame It on the Bellboy, Freejack, The Last of the Mohicans (Golden Globe nom.), In the Name of the Father, Cliffhanger, De Baby huilt, LochNess, Hideaway, Kiss of Death, Richard III, Brassed Off, Lawn Dogs, Roseanna's Grave, Talk of Angels, Desperate Measures, G.I. Jane, Plunkett & MacLeane, Analyse This, Dark Empire, The Mighty.
TELEVISION: Movies: Those Glory Glory Days, One of Ourselves, Aderyn Papur.. and Pigs Might Fly, Dr. Fischer of Geneva, A Private Life, Murder by Moonlight, By Dawn's Early Light, Chains of Gold, Guns... A Day In the Death of America, Death Train, Mini-series: Joni Jones, The Last Days of Pompeii, Jim Henson Presents the World of International Puppeteering, The Last Place on Earth, Gulliver's Travels, Merlin.

JORDAN, GLENN

Director, Producer, b. San Antonio, TX, April 5, 1936. e. Harvard, B.A.; Yale Drama Sch. Directed plays off-B'way and on tour.
PICTURES: Director: Only When I Laugh, The Buddy System, Mass Appea, Mary & Tim.
TELEVISION: Specials: Hogan's Goat, Paradise Lost, Benjamin Franklin (prod.; Emmy Award), Eccentricities of a Nightingale, The Oath, The Court Martial of Gen. George Armstrong Custer. Movies: Director: Frankenstein, The Picture of Dorian Gray, Shell Game, One of My Wives is Missing, The Displaced Person,

Delta County U.S.A., In the Matter of Karen Ann Quinlan, Sunshine Christmas, Les Miserables, Son Rise: A Miracle of Love, The Family Man, The , The Princess and the Cabbie, Lois Gibbs and the Love Canal, Heartsounds, Dress Grey (also prod.). *Series*: Family. *Dir./Prod.*: Women's Room, Promise (2 Emmy Awards), Something in Common, Echoes in the Darkness, Jesse, Home Fires Burning, Challenger, Sarah: Plain and Tall, Aftermath: A Test of Love, The Boys, O Pioneers!, Barbarians at the Gate (Emmy Award; co-exec. prod.), To Dance With the White Dog, Jane's House, My Brother's Keeper, A Streetcar Named Desire, Jake's Women, After Jimmy, A Christmas Memory.

JORDAN, HENRIETTA
Executive. b. New York, NY. Ent. m.p. ind. as ass't to exec. v.p. UPA Pictures, 1950. V.p. in charge of sales, Format Prods., Inc.; v.p. and assoc. prod., 1962-71. Assoc. prod. Levitow-Hanson Films, Inc., 1972. Prod., Image West, Ltd., 1975-84. Dir. sales., Cause & EFX, 1984-85. Dir. sales Modern Videofilm Braphics, 1986-88. Personal comm., Hank Jordan Enterprises, 1988-.

JORDAN, NEIL
Director, Writer. b. Sligo, Ireland, Feb. 25, 1950. e. University Coll, Dublin, B.A., 1972. Novels: The Past, Night in Tunisia, Dream of a Beast.
PICTURES: Traveller (s.p.), The Courier (co-exec. prod.). *Dir.-Writer*: Angel, The Company of Wolves, Mona Lisa (LA Film Critics Award for s.p., 1986), High Spirits, We're No Angels (dir. only), The Miracle, The Crying Game (Academy Award, WGA & NY Film Critics Awards for s.p., 1992), Interview With the Vampire, Michael Collins, The Butcher Boy.
TELEVISION: Mr. Solomon Wept (BBC), RTE (Ireland), Seduction, Tree, Miracles and Miss Langan.

JOSEPHSON, BARRY
Executive. Pres., of Worldwide production, Columbia Pictures.

JOSEPHSON, ERLAND
Actor, Director, Writer. b. Stockholm, Sweden, June 15, 1923. Acted in over 100 plays in Sweden. Joined Sweden's Royal Dramatic Theatre in 1956 replacing Ingmar Bergman as head of the theater, 1966-76. Closely associated with Bergman, with whom he staged plays in his late teens. Co-authored s.p. The Pleasure Garden and Now About These Women. Also has pub. poetry, six novels, and scripts for stage, screen and radio. American stage debut: The Cherry Orchard, 1988. In numerous movies on Swedish television.
PICTURES: It Rains on Our Love, To Joy (uncredited), Sceningang, Som man baddar, Brink of Life, The Magician, Hour of the Wolf, The Girls, Eva: Diary of Half Virgin, The Passion of Anna, Cries and Whispers, Scenes from a Marriage, Monismanien, Face to Face, A Look at Liv, Io ho paura, Beyond Good and Evil, Games of Love and Loneliness, I'm Afraid, Autumn Sonata, Die Erste Polka, To Forget Venice, One and One (also dir.), The Marmalade Revolution (also dir., s.p.), Karleken, Victor Sjostrom (voice), You Love Only Once, Montenegro, Sezona Mira u Parizu, Fanny and Alexander, Bella Donna, Nostalgia, House of the Yellow Carpet, After the Rehearsal, Angela's War, Bakom jalusin, Behind the Shutters, A Case of Irresponsibility, Dirty Story, Amorosa, The Flying Devils, Garibaldi, The General, The Last Mazurka, The Sacrifice, The Malady of Love, Saving Grace, Le Testament d'un poete juif assassine, Unbearable Lightness of Being, Directed by Andrei Tarkovsky, Hanussen, Good Evening Mr. Wallenberg, The Wicked, Meeting Venus, Prospero's Books, The Ox, The Accidental Golfer, Sofie, Holozan, The Dancer, Dreamplay, Ulysses' Gaze, Vendetta, Waiting for Sunset, Kristin Lavransdatter.

JOSEPHSON, MARVIN
Executive. b. Atlantic City, NJ, March 6, 1927. e. Cornell U., B.A., 1949; L.L.B. NYU, 1952. Lawyer at CBS Television 1952-55; founded company which today is ICM Holdings Inc. in 1955. ICM Holdings Inc. is the parent company of Intl. Creative Management Inc. and ICM Artists Ltd.

JOSIAH, JR., WALTER J.
Executive. b. New York, NY, Nov. 9, 1933. e. Fordham U., B.S., 1955; Harvard Law School, LL.B., 1962. U.S. Air Force, 1955-58, First Lt. and Pilot. Associate, Simpson Thacher & Bartlett, 1962-67. Legal staff, Paramount Pictures, 1967-69. Asst. resident counsel, 1969; chief resident counsel, 1970 and v.p. & chief resident counsel, 1971-82. ex.-v.p. & general counsel, Motion Picture Association of America, Inc., 1983-93. Professional Associations: Chmn., Committee 307, Authors Rights, 1981-82, Patent, Trademark & Copyright Law Section of the American Bar Assn.; Association of the Bar of the City of NY (Committee on Copyright and Literary Property, 1976-79, 1982-85, chmn. 1986-89): Copyright Society of the U.S.A.—Member of the Board of Trustees commencing 1981; v.p., from 1988; pres. beginning 1990; member, Motion Picture Academy of Arts and Sciences; Copyright Office Advisory Committee, 1981-82; National Sculpture Society advisor to the president; Advisory Board, Publication: Communications and the Law; Member, President's Club Executive Committee and Annual Fund Council, Fordham U.

JOURDAN, LOUIS
Actor, r.n. Louis Gendre. b. Marseille, France, June 19, 1921. Stage actor prior to m.p. On B'way in The Immoralist, Tonight in Samarkand, On a Clear Day You Can See Forever (Boston, previews), 13 Rue de l'Amour.
PICTURES: Le Corsaire (debut, 1940), Her First Affair, La Boheme, L'Arlesienne, La Belle, Adventure, Felicie Nanteuil, The Paradine Case, Letter from an Unknown Woman, No Minor Vices, Madame Bovary, Bird of Paradise, Anne of the Indies, The Happy Time, Decameron Nights, Three Coins in the Fountain, The Swan, Julie, The Bride is Much Too Beautiful, Dangerous Exile, Gigi, The Best of Everything, Can-Can, Leviathan, Streets of Montmartre, Story of the Count of Monte Cristo, Mathias Sandorf, The VIPs, Made in Paris, To Commit a Murder, A Flea in Her Ear, Young Rebel (Cervantes), The Silver Bears, Double Deal, Swamp Thing, Octopussy, The Return of Swamp Thing, Counterforce, Year of the Comet.
TELEVISION: *Series*: Paris Precinct, Romance Theatre (host). *Mini-Series*: The French Atlantic Affair, Dracula. *Movies*: Run a Crooked Mile, Fear No Evil, Ritual of Evil, The Great American Beauty Contest, The Count of Monte Cristo, The Man in the Iron Mask, The First Olympics-Athens, Beverly Hills Madam. *Guest*: Ford Theatre, The FBI, Name of the Game, Charlie's Angels.

JOY, ROBERT
Actor. b. Montreal, Canada, Aug. 17, 1951. e. Memorial Univ. of Newfoundland; Rhodes Scholar. Acted in regional and off-Broadway theatre. Off-B'way debut The Diary of Anne Frank (1978). Has composed music for stage, radio and film.
THEATER: NY Shakespeare Fest. (Found a Peanut, Lenny and the Heartbreakers, The Death of von Richtofen), Life and Limb, Fables for Friends, Welcome to the Moon, What I Did Last Summer, Lydie Breeze, Romeo and Juliet (La Jolla Playhouse; Drama-Logue Award), Hay Fever (B'way debut), Big River (premiere), The Nerd, Hyde in Hollywood, The Taming of the Shrew, Shimada, Goodnight Desdemona (Good Morning Juliet), Abe Lincoln in Illinois, No One Will Be Immune, June Moon.
PICTURES: Atlantic City, Ragtime, Ticket to Heaven, Threshold, Terminal Choice, Amityville 3-D, Desperately Seeking Susan, Joshua Then and Now, Adventure of Faustus Bidgood (also co-prod. music), Radio Days, Big Shots, The Suicide Club, She's Back!, Millenium, Longtime Companion, Shadows and Fog, The Dark Half, Death Wish 5: The Face of Death, I'll Do Anything, Henry & Verlin, Waterworld, A Modern Affair, Pharoah's Army, Dangerous Offender, Harriet the Spy, The Divine Ryans, Fallen.
TELEVISION: *Series*: One Life to Live, The High Life. *Guest*: The Equalizer, Moonlighting, Law and Order, The Marshal, New York Undercover, Wings. *Specials*: The Prodigious Hickey, The Return of Hickey, The Beginning of the Firm, Hyde in Hollywood. *Movies*: Escape from Iran: The Canadian Caper, Gregory K, Woman on the Run: The Lawrencia Bembenek Story, The High Life.

JUDD, ASHLEY
Actress. b. April 19, 1968. Mother and sister are country singers, Naomi and Wynona Judd.
PICTURES: Kuffs, Ruby in Paradise, The Passion of Darkly Noon, Smoke, A Time to Kill, Normal Life, The Locusts, Kiss the Girls, A Small Miracle, Eye of the Beholder.
TELEVISION: *Series*: Sisters. *Movies*: Till Death Us Do Part, Norma Jean and Marilyn. *Special*: Naomi & Wynona: Love Can Build a Bridge. *Guest*: Space Ghost Coast to Coast, Star Trek: The Next Generation.

JUDGE, MIKE
Animator, actor, director, producer. b. Ecuador, 1963.
PICTURES: Airheads (voice), Beavis & Butt-head Do America (also dir., prod., composer, voices), Beavis & Butt-head 2: Another Movie.
TELEVISION: *Series*: Beavis and Butt-head, (also dir., prod., composer, voices), King of the Hill (also prod., voices). Shorts: Frog Baseball (also voices, dir., prod., writer), Office Space (voice, composer, dir.).

JURADO, KATY
Actress. r.n. Maria Christina Jurado Garcia. b. Guadalajara, Mexico, Jan. 16, 1927. Appeared in numerous Mexican films beginning in 1943. Also m.p. columnist for Mexican publications.
PICTURES: No Maturas (debut, 1943), El Museo del Crimen, Rosa del Caribe, The Bullfighter and the Lady (U.S. debut, 1951), High Noon, San Antone, Arrowhead, Broken Lance (Acad. Award nom.), The Sword of Granada, The Racers, Trial, Trapeze, Man from Del Rio, Dragoon Wells Massacre, The Badlanders, One Eyed Jacks, Barabbas, Seduction of the South, Target for Killing, Smoky, A Covenant With Death, Stay Away Joe, Bridge in the Jungle, Pat Garrett and Billy the Kid, Once Upon a Scoundrel, The Children of Sanchez, Reasons of State, Under the Volcano, La Nueva Jerusalem.
TELEVISION: *Movies*: Any Second Now, A Little Game, Evita Peron, Lady Blue. *Series*: A.K.A. Pablo.

K

KAGAN, JEREMY

Director, Writer. b. Mt. Vernon, NY, Dec. 14, 1945. e. Harvard; NYU, MFA; student Amer. Film Inst. 1971. Film animator, 1968; multi-media show designer White House Conf. on Youth and Ed. Previously credited as Jeremy Paul Kagan.
PICTURES: Scott Joplin, Heroes, The Big Fix, The Chosen (Montreal World Film Fest. Prize, 1981), The Sting II, The Journey of Natty Gann (Gold Prize, Moscow Film Fest., 1987), Big Man on Campus, By the Sword.
TELEVISION: Series: Columbo, The Bold Ones, Chicago Hope (Emmy Award, 1996). Movies: Unwed Father, Judge Dee and the Monastery Murders, Katherine (also writer), Courage, Roswell (also co-prod., co-story). Specials: My Dad Lives in a Downtown Hotel, Conspiracy: The Trial of the Chicago 8 (also writer; ACE Award, 1988).

KAHN, MADELINE

Actress, Singer. b. Boston, MA., Sept. 29. e. Hofstra U. Broadway bow in New Faces of '68. Trained as opera singer and appeared in La Boheme, Showboat, Two by Two, Candide. Appeared in short film The Dove.
THEATER: Promenade, Two by Two, In the Boom Boom Room, On the Twentieth Century, Born Yesterday, The Sisters Rosensweig (Tony Award, 1993).
PICTURES: What's Up Doc? (debut, 1972), Paper Moon (Acad. Award nom.), From the Mixed-Up Files of Mrs. Basil E. Frankweiler (The Hideaways), Blazing Saddles (Acad. Award nom.), Young Frankenstein, At Long Last Love, The Adventures of Sherlock Holmes' Smarter Brother, Won Ton Ton the Dog Who Saved Hollywood, High Anxiety, The Cheap Detective, The Muppet Movie, Simon, Happy Birthday Gemini, Wholly Moses, First Family, History of the World—Part 1, Yellowbeard, Slapstick of Another Kind, City Heat, Clue, My Little Pony (voice), An American Tail (voice), Betsy's Wedding, Mixed Nuts, Nixon.
TELEVISION: Series: Comedy Tonight, Oh Madeline! (People's Choice award), Mr. President, New York News, Cosby. Specials: Harvey, The Perfect Guy (afterschool special, Emmy award), Celebrating Gershwin: The Jazz Age, Irving Berlin Gala, Stephen Sondheim Gala. Movie: For Richer For Poorer.

KAHN, MILTON

Publicist. b. Brooklyn, NY, May 3, 1934. e. Syracuse U., Ohio U., B.S.J. 1957. Formed Milton Kahn Associates, Inc. in 1958. Represented: Gregory Peck, Joan Crawford, Steve Allen, Glenn Ford, Lee Grant, Herb Alpert, Roger Corman, Robert Aldrich, Arthur Hiller, Chuck Norris, Bob Cousy, Gordie Howe, Michael Landon, Dean Hargrove, Bill Conti, etc. and New World Pictures (1970-83), Avco-Embassy, Vista Films, Roger Corman's Concorde (1983-), Electric Shadow Prods. Named Publicist of the Year by Book Pub. of So. CA, 1996.

KAHN, RICHARD

Executive. b. New Rochelle, NY, Aug. 19, 1929. e. Wharton Sch. of Finance and Commerce, U. of Pennsylvania, B.S., 1951; U.S. Navy, 3 yrs.; joined Buchanan & Co., 1954; ent. m.p. ind. as press-book writer, Columbia Pictures, 1955; exploitation mgr.; 1958; natl. coord. adv. and pub., 1963; natl. dir. of adv., pub. and exploitation, 1968; v.p., 1969; 1974 v.p. in chg. of special marketing projects; 1975; moved to MGM as v.p. in chg. of worldwide advertising, publicity and exploitation; 1978, named sr. v.p. in chg. worldwide mktg. & pres., MGM Intl. 1980, elected bd. of govs., Academy of M.P. Arts & Sciences. 1982, named exec. v.p. of adv., pub., promo. for MGM/UA; 1983, formed the Richard Kahn Co., dist. & mktg. consultancy, 1984-88. Faculty mem. Peter Stark m.p. producing prog., USC Sch. of Cinema & TV. Exec. chmn., Film Inf. Council. 1982-95 elected secretary Acad. of Motion Picture Arts & Sciences; elected v.p. 1983-87; elected pres. 1988.

KALB, MARVIN

TV news reporter. e. City Coll. of NY; Harvard, M.A., 1953, Russian Language Sch., Middlebury Coll. Worked for U.S. State Dept., American Embassy, Moscow; CBS News, 1957; writer, reporter-researcher. Where We Stand: reporter-assignment editor; Moscow Bureau Chief, 1960-63; first diplomatic corresp., Washington Bureau, 1963. Chief diplomatic corresp. CBS News and NBC News, moderator Meet the Press; Teacher and lecturer; first dir. Joan Shorenstein Barone Center on the Press, Politics and Public Policy at John F. Kennedy Sch. of Govt. of Harvard U., since 1987. Host of PBS series, Candidates '88. Author: Eastern Exposure, Kissinger, Dragon in the Kremlin, Roots of Involvement, The U.S. in Asia 1784-1971, Candidates '88 (with Hendrik Hertzberg).

KALISH, EDDIE

Executive. b. New York, NY, April 27, 1939. Reporter/reviewer, Variety, 1959-64; sr. publicist, Paramount Pictures, 1964-65; adv./pub./promo dir., Ken Greengras Personal Management, 1965-66; pub. dir., Harold Rand & Co., 1966-67; indept. publicist overseas, 1967-75; rejoined Paramount Pictures in 1975 as dir. of intl. mktg.; later named v.p.; 1978, named v.p., worldwide pub. & promo. 1979 appt. sr. v.p., worldwide mktg. 1980 joined United Artists as v.p. domestic mktg.; sr. v.p., adv., pub., promo. for MGM/UA 1981-82; became sr. v.p., worldwide mkt., PSO, 1982-1986. Now pres., Kalish/Davidson Marketing, Inc.

KAMBER, BERNARD M.

Executive. e. U. of Pennsylvania. New England exploitation rep. U.A. 1940; Army service 1941-43; dir. special events dept. U.A., 1943; asst. to Gradwell L. Sears, nat'l distrib. chmn. 6th War Loan Drive; dir. pub. 7th War Loan Drive, 1943-47; dir. pub. & prom. Eagle Lion Classics, 1951; org. Kamber Org., pub. rel. rep. for ind. prod. v.p. sales, adv. pub. Ivan Tors Prod. Greene-Rouse Prods. 1953; exec. asst. Hecht-Hill-Lancaster, chg. of N.Y. off., 1957; v.p. Hecht-Hill-Lancaster Companies, 1958; formed Cinex Distr. Corp., 1962; Pres. Cinex and Posfilm, Inc.; 1967, v.p. in chg. sls. Du Art Film Lab. Inc; 1975 joined Technicolor, Inc.

KAMEN, MICHAEL

Composer, conductor, arranger. b. New York, NY, 1948. Began career composing music for the Joffrey Ballet and the La Scala Opera Co. Wrote his first film score in 1970 for The Next Man. Has also written for David Bowie, Eric Clapton and the Eurythmics.
PICTURES: Scores: The Next Man (debut), Stunts, Between the Lines, Polyester, Venom, Pink Floyd—The Wall, Angelo My Love, The Dead Zone, Brazil, Lifeforce, Shoot for the Sun, Rita—Sue and Bob Too, Highlander, Mona Lisa, Shanghai Surprise, Suspect, Someone to Watch Over Me, Adventures in Babysitting, Lethal Weapon, The Raggedy Rawney, Crusoe, Action Jackson, Homeboy, Die Hard, Rooftops, For Queen and Country, The Adventures of Baron Munchausen, Road House, License to Kill, Dead-Bang, Lethal Weapon, Renegades, The Krays, Cold Dog Soup, Die Hard 2, Nothing But Trouble, Let Him Have It, Company Business, Robin Hood: Prince of Thieves (Acad. award nom., Golden Globe nom.), Hudson Hawk, The Last Boy Scout, Blue Ice, Shining Through, Lethal Weapon 3, Wilder Napalm, Splitting Hairs, Last Action Hero, The Three Musketeers, Stonewall, Mr Holland's Opus, Circle of Friends, Don Juan DeMarco, Die Hard: With a Vengeance, Jack, 101 Dalmations, Remember Me?, Inventing the Abbotts, Event Horizon, The Winter Guest, Lethal Weapon 4, The Avengers.
TELEVISION: Scores: Liza's Pioneer Diary, S*H*E, Amazing Stories, Edge of Darkness, Tales from the Crypt, The Heart Surgeon.

KANE, CAROL

Actress. b. Cleveland, OH, June 18, 1952. e. Professional Children's Sch., NY. Began professional acting career at age 14, touring, then on B'way in The Prime of Miss Jean Brodie.
THEATER: The Tempest, The Effect of Gamma Rays on Man-in-the-Moon Marigolds, Are You Now or Have You Ever Been? Arturo Ui, The Enchanted, The Tempest, Macbeth, Tales of the Vienna Woods, Frankie and Johnny in the Claire de Lune, Control Freaks.
PICTURES: Carnal Knowledge (debut, 1971), Desperate Characters, Wedding in White, The Last Detail, Dog Day Afternoon, Hester Street, Harry and Walter Go to New York, Annie Hall, Valentino, The World's Greatest Lover, The Mafu Cage, The Muppet Movie, When a Stranger Calls, Pandemonium, Norman Loves Rose, Over the Brooklyn Bridge, Racing With the Moon, The Secret Diary of Sigmund Freud, Transylvania 6-5000, Jumpin' Jack Flash, Ishtar, The Princess Bride, Sticky Fingers, License to Drive, Scrooged, Flashback, Joe Vs. the Volcano, My Blue Heaven, The Lemon Sisters, Ted and Venus, In the Soup, Addams Family Values, Even Cowgirls Get the Blues, Big Bully, The Pallbearer, Sunset Park.
TELEVISION: Series: Taxi (2 Emmy Awards: 1982, 1983), All Is Forgiven, American Dreamer. Movies: An Invasion of Privacy, Burning Rage, Drop Out Mother, Dad the Angel and Me, Freaky Friday. Specials: Faerie Tale Theatre, Paul Reiser: Out on a Whim, Tales From the Crypt (Judy, You're Not Yourself Today).

KANE, JOHN

Publicity Manager. b. New York, NY. e. Rutgers, B.A.; NYU, M.A. Publicist, Solters & Roskin, 1976-80. Unit publicist: Fame, Tender Mercies, Prince of the City, 1980-82. 1982-90, Home Box Office, unit publicist, manager. 1991, unit publ. for Ricochet, Arizona Dream.

KANE, STANLEY D.

Judge. b. Minneapolis, MN, Dec. 21, 1907. e. U of MN, B.A. (magna cum laude), 1930; M.A., 1931; MN Coll. of Law, LL.B., 1940. Instructor, U. of Minnesota, 1930-33. Exec. sec. Allied Theatre Owners of the Northwest, 1933-37; city attorney, 1940-60; exec. v.p. & gen. counsel, North Central Allied Independent Theatre Owners, 1946-63; dist. court judge, then sr. judge, Hennepin County, 1963-90.

KANER, MARK

Executive. Pres. of International Television, Fox, Inc.

KANEW, JEFF

Director.
PICTURES: Black Rodeo (also prod., edit.), Natural Enemies (also s.p., edit.), Eddie Macon's Run (also s.p., edit.), Revenge of the Nerds, Gotcha!, Tough Guys, Troop Beverly Hills, V. I. Warshawski.
TELEVISION: Alfred Hitchcock Presents (1985).

KANFER, MICHAEL
Special Effects.
PICTURES: Apollo 13, Titanic (Acad. Award, Best Visual Effects, 1997).

KANIN, FAY
Writer. b. New York, NY, May 9. e. Elmira Coll., U. of Southern California, 1937. m. Michael Kanin, writer. Contrib. fiction to mags., Writers Guild of Amer. pres. screen branch, 1971-73; Acad. Motion Picture Arts & Sciences 1983-88. also bd. mem. of latter. Co-chair, National Center for Film and Video Preservation; Bd. of trustees, Amer. Film Institute; Chair, Natl. Film Preservation Board.
THEATER: Goodbye My Fancy, His and Hers, Rashomon, The High Life, Grind (1985).
PICTURES: My Pal Gus, Rhapsody, The Opposite Sex, Teacher's Pet, Swordsman of Siena, The Right Approach.
TELEVISION: Heat of Anger, Tell Me Where It Hurts (Emmy Award, 1974), Hustling (also co-prod.), Friendly Fire (also co-prod., Emmy Award, San Francisco Film Fest. Award, Peabody Award), Heartsounds (Peabody Award; also co-prod.).

KANIN, GARSON
Director, Writer. b. Rochester, NY, Nov. 24, 1912. e. American Acad. of Dramatic Arts. Was married to actress Ruth Gordon (d: 8/28/85). m. actress Marian Seldes, 1990. Started as musician, actor, appearing in Spring Song, Little Ol' Boy, and others. Prod. assist. to George Abbott on plays Three Men on a Horse, Brother Rat, Room Service. 1937 joined Samuel Goldwyn's prod. staff; 1938, joined RKO, as prod.-dir. 1942, prod. for U.S. Office of Emergency Management. Joined armed forces, WWII. Documentary director: Fellow Americans, Ring of Steel, Night Shift, The True Glory (co-dir. with Carol Reed; Acad. Award, 1945), Salute to France (co-dir. with Jean Renoir). 1989, received Writers Guild Valentine Davies Award with brother Michael. Pres., Authors League of America.
AUTHOR: Remembering Mr. Maugham, Cast of Characters, Tracy and Hepburn, Hollywood, Blow Up a Storm, The Rat Race, A Thousand Summers, One Hell of an Actor, It Takes a Long Time to Become Young, Moviola, Smash, Together Again!, Cordelia.
THEATRE: Writer/Dir.: Born Yesterday, The Smile of the World, The Rat Race, The Live Wire, A Gift of Time, Do Re Mi, Come on Strong, Small War on Murray Hill, The Amazing Adele, The Good Soup, Dreyfus in Rehearsal, Happy Ending, Peccadillo. Dir.: Hitch Your Wagon, Too Many Heroes, The Rugged Path, Years Ago, How I Wonder, The Leading Lady, The Diary of Anne Frank, Into Thin Air, Hole in the Head, Sunday in New York, Funny Girl, I Was Dancing, A Very Rich Woman, We Have Always Lived in the Castle, Idiot's Delight, Ho! Ho! Ho!.
PICTURES: Dir.: A Man to Remember, Next Time I Marry, The Great Man Votes, Bachelor Mother, Tom Dick & Harry, My Favorite Wife, They Knew What They Wanted. Dir./Writer: Where It's At, Some Kind of a Nut. Writer: From This Day Forward, A Double Life, Adam's Rib, The Marrying Kind, Pat and Mike, It Should Happen To You, The Rat Race.
TELEVISION: Movie: Hardhat and Legs (co-writer). Series: Mr. Broadway.

KANTER, HAL
Writer, Director, Producer. b. Savannah, GA, Dec. 18, 1918. On B'way contributor to Hellzapoppin. Then began writing radio dramas before mil. service, WW II. Served as combat corresp. Armed Forces Radio; writer, Paramount, 1951-54; dir., RKO, 1956; writer, prod. for Lucille Ball Prods., 1979-80. Savannah Prods., 1982-86. Received Writers Guild Paddy Chayefsky Laurel Award, 1989. Writer (radio): Danny Kaye Show, Amos 'n Andy, Bing Crosby Show, Jack Paar, Beulah. Winner 3 Emmy Awards for writing, 1954, 1991, 1992; W.G.A.W. Valentine Davies award. Was member: bd. of dir., WGAW; bd. of govs. AMPAS; v.p. Writers Guild Foundation.
PICTURES: Writer. My Favorite Spy, Off Limits, Road to Bali, Casanova's Big Night, About Mrs. Leslie, Money from Home, Artists and Models, The Rose Tattoo, Loving You (also dir. only), Mardi Gras, Once Upon a Horse (also dir., prod.), Blue Hawaii, Pocketful of Miracles, Bachelor in Paradise, Move Over Darling, Dear Brigitte.
TELEVISION: Writer: Ed Wynn Show, George Gobel Show (also creator, prod.), Kraft Music Hall (also dir., prod.; 1958-59), Chrysler Theatre (also prod., dir.; 1966-67), Julia (also dir., prod., creator), Jimmy Stewart Show (also prod., dir., creator), All In The Family (exec. prod.: 1975-76), Chico & The Man (spv. prod., 1976-77), You Can't Take It With You. Specials (writer): AFI Life Achievement Awards for Henry Fonda & Alfred Hitchcock, 26 & 28 Annual Academy Awards and many others.

KANTER, JAY
Executive. b. Chicago, IL, Dec. 12, 1926. Entered industry with MCA, Inc., where was v.p. Left after more than 20 yrs. to become indep. prod., then pres. of First Artists Production Co., Ltd. 1975 joined 20th-Fox as v.p. prod.; 1976, named sr. v.p., worldwide prod. Named v.p., The Ladd Co., 1979. Joined MGM/UA Entertainment Co. as pres., worldwide prod., Motion Picture Division, 1984. 1985, named pres., worldwide prod., UA Corp.; then pres., production MGM Pictures Inc.; 1989, named chmn. of prod. of Pathe Entertainment Co. 1991, became COO & chmn. of prod., MGM-Pathe Commun. Co. (MGM Communi-cations, 1992). 1994-95, MGM consultant. March, 1995, independent prod.

KANTOR, IGO
Producer, Film Editor. b. Vienna, Austria, Aug. 18, 1930. e. UCLA, A.A. 1950; B.S., 1952; M.S., 1954. Foreign corres., Portugal magazine, FLAMA, 1949-57, music supvr., Screen Gems, Columbia 1954-63; post-prod. supvr., film ed., features, TV; assoc. prod., 1963-64; prod., exec., International Entertainment Corp., 1965; pres., Synchrofilm, Inc., post-production co. and Duque Films Inc., production co. 1968-74. 1975-present, produced and edited films. 1982, pres., Laurelwood Prods; 1988, pres. Major Arts Corp.
PICTURES: Assoc. Producer. Bye Bye Birdie, Under the Yum Yum Tree, Gidget Goes to Rome, A House Is Not a Home, Pattern for Murder, Willy. Producer: Assault on Agathon (also edit.), FTA, Dixie Dynamite (assoc. prod., edit.), Kingdom of the Spiders (also edit., music spvr.), The Dark (assoc. prod.), Good Luck Miss Wyckoff (prod. spvr.), Hardly Working, Kill and Kill Again, Mutant, Shaker Run, Act of Piracy, They Call Me Bruce Levy, Twirpy.
TELEVISION: From Hawaii with Love (1984), The Grand Tour, It's a Wonderful World (prod.-dir.), Nosotros Golden Eagle Awards (prod.), United We Stand (pre-Olympic special), Legends of the West With Jack Palance, Mom U.S.A., A Desperate Affair, Holiday Classics Cartoons (special).

KAPLAN, GABRIEL
Actor, Comedian. b. Brooklyn, NY, March 31, 1945. After high school worked as bellboy at Lakewood, NJ hotel, spending free time studying comedians doing routines. Put together a comedy act, landing engagements in small clubs and coffee houses all over U.S. Made several appearances on Tonight Show, Merv Griffin Show, Mike Douglas Show, etc. Has played Las Vegas clubs.
PICTURES: Fast Break, Tulips, Nobody's Perfekt.
TELEVISION: Series: Welcome Back Kotter, Gabriel Kaplan Presents the Future Stars, Lewis and Clark. Movie: Love Boat (pilot).

KAPLAN, JONATHAN
Director, Writer. b. Paris, Nov. 25, 1947. Son of composer Sol Kaplan. e. U. of Chicago, B.A.; NYU, M.F.A. Made short film Stanley Stanley. Member of tech. staff Fillmore East, NY 1969-71. New World Pictures' Roger Corman post-grad. sch. of filmmaking, Hollywood, 1971-73. As actor on B'way in Dark at the Top of the Stairs. Appeared in films: Cannonball, Hollywood Boulevard.
PICTURES: Director: Night Call Nurses, Student Teachers, The Slams, Truck Turner, White Line Fever (also co-s.p.), Mr. Billion, Over the Edge, Heart Like a Wheel, Project X, The Accused, Immediate Family, Unlawful Entry, Love Field, Bad Girls, Brokedown Palace.
TELEVISION: Movies: The 11th Victim, The Hustler of Muscle Beach, The Gentleman Bandit, Girls of the White Orchid, Reform School Girl, In Cold Blood. Series: Fallen Angels, ER.

KAPOOR, SHASHI
Actor. b. Calcutta, India, March 18, 1938. Son of late Prithviraj Kapoor, Indian film and stage actor. As child worked in Prithvi Theatre and in brother, Raj's films. Toured with father's co. at 18 and joined the Kendals' Shakespeareana Co. in India. Starred in over 200 Indian films as well as several Merchant-Ivory Prods.
PICTURES: Aag, Awara, Prem Patra, The Householder, Waqt, Shakespeare Wallah, A Matter of Innocence, Pretty Polly, Bombay Talkie, Sharmilee, Siddhartha, Roti Kapda Aur Makaan, Deewar, Kabhie Kabhie, Imaan Dharam, Trishul; Satyam, Shivam, Sundaram; Junoon (also prod.), Suhaag, Kaala Pathar, Shaan, Kalyug (also prod.), Do Aur do Paanch, 36 Chowringhee Lane (prod. only), Silsila, Bezubaan, Namak Halal, Heat and Dust, Door-desh, Utsav (also prod.), New Delhi Times, Abodh, Sammy and Rosie Get Laid, Ijaazat, The Deceivers, Nomads, Akayla, Ajooba (dir. only), In Custody, Side Streets.
TELEVISION: Movie: Gulliver's Travels.

KARDISH, LAURENCE
Curator, Dept. of Film, Museum of Modern Art. b. Ottawa, Ontario, Canada, Jan. 5, 1945. e. Carlton U. Ottawa, Canada, 1966, Honors B.A. in philosophy; Columbia U., Sch. of the Arts, 1968, M.F.A. in film, radio, and television. 1965-66: Canadian Film Inst., programmer for National Film Theatre, Ottawa; researched a history of Canadian filmmaking. 1965: founded first film society in Canada to exhibit Amer. avant-garde films (Carleton U. Cine Club); directed summer seminar on film, Carleton U., 1966. 1966-68: New American Cinema Group, Inc., NY, worked for the Film-Makers' Distribution Center. 1968: joined Dept. of Film, MOMA, made curator 1984. Since 1968 involved with Cineprobe prog. Since 1972 participated in selection of films for New Directors/New Films series; dir. exhibitions of surveys of national cinemas (Senegal, Scandinavia, French-speaking Canada) and retrospectives of ind. Amer. filmmakers (includ. Rudolph Burkhardt, Stan Brakhage, Shirley Clarke), The Lubitsch Touch, Columbia Pictures, Warner Bros., MGM, Universal, RKO, and directors. 1980: toured Europe with prog. of indep. Amer. films. Author: Reel Plastic Magic (1972); also essays and monographs. Dir.feature Slow Run (1968). On jury for Channel 13's Indep. Focus series and on Board of Advisors, Collective for Living Cinema, NY. 1982-82: bd. of dirs. of National Alliance of Media Arts Centers; 1987-89: on Jerome Foundation panel. 1986 on Camera d'Or jury, Cannes Film Fest.

KARLIN, FRED
Composer, Conductor. b. Chicago, IL, June 16, 1936. e. Amherst Coll., B.A. Composer and arranger for Benny Goodman. Won Academy Award for Best Song for For All We Know (from Lovers and Other Strangers) and Emmy for original music in The Autobiography of Miss Jane Pittman. 4 Acad. Award noms., 11 Emmy Award noms.; Image Award for score to Minstrel Man. Author: On the Track: A Guide to Contemporary Film Scoring (with Rayburn Wright), Listening to Movies. Creator and instructor of the ASCAP/Fred Karlin Film Scoring Workshop, since 1988.
PICTURES: Up the Down Staircase, Yours Mine and Ours, The Sterile Cuckoo (including music for song, Come Saturday Morning; Acad. Award nom.), The Stalking Moon, Westworld, Futureworld, Lovers and Other Strangers, Leadbelly, Loving Couples.
TELEVISION: The Autobiography of Miss Jane Pittman, The Awakening Land, The Plutonium Incident, Minstrel Man, Sophia Loren—Her Own Story, Green Eyes, Strangers: The Story of a Mother and Daughter, Calamity Jane, Ike: the War Years, Inside the Third Reich, Hollywood—The Gift of Laughter, Homeward Bound, Dream West, Hostage Flight, A Place to Call Home, Robert Kennedy and His Times, Dadah is Death, Bridge to Silence, The Secret, Film Music Masters: Jerry Goldsmith (prod. and dir.), Film Music Masters: Elmer Bernstein (prod. and dir.).

KARLIN, MYRON D.
Executive. b. Revere, MA, Sept. 21, 1918. e. UCLA. Joined m.p. business in 1946 as gen. mgr. for MGM in Ecuador. Two yrs. later assigned same spot for MGM in Venezuela. 1952-53 was gen. sales mgr. for MGM in Germany, after which managing dir. in Argentina, returning to Germany as mgr. dir. in 1956. Named mgn. dir. for United Artists in Italy. 1960-68 was pres. of Brunswick Int'l., while also serving as advisor to World Health Organization and UNESCO. 1969 was European mgr. for MGM and mgn. dir. in Italy. Joined Warner Bros. Int'l. in 1970 as v.p. of European dist. 1972 appt. v.p. in chg. of int'l. operations for WB; 1977, appt. pres., WB Intl. & exec. v.p., Warner Bros., Inc; 1985, named exec. v.p., intl. affairs, WB, Inc. Now pres. & COO, Motion Picture Export Assn. July, 1994, sr. consultant, Motion Picture assoc.

KARMAZIN, MEL
Executive. b. 1944. Station Mgr., CBS Radio, NY, 1960-70. VP and Gen'l Mgr. Metromedia Inc., 1970-81. Pres. Infinity Broadcast Corp., 1981-96. CEO Infinity Broadcast Corp., 1988-96. Chairman, CEO CBS Station Group, 1996-.

KARP, ALLEN
Executive. b. Toronto, Ontario, Canada, Sept. 18, 1940. e. Univ. of Toronto, bachelor of law degree, 1964; called to Ontario bar in 1966; masters of business law degree 1975, from Osgoode Hall Law School, York Univ. Upon graduation joined the law firm of Goodman & Carr, became a partner in 1970. Served as business lawyer and senior legal advisor, becoming dir. of Odeon Theatre Film circuit, 1977. 1986, named sr. exec. v.p. of Cineplex Odeon Corp; 1988, became pres. North American Theatres Division; 1989, pres. & COO; 1990, elected pres. & CEO. Chmn., CEO & dir., Cineplex Odeon Canada (Loews Cineplex Ent. Corp.), 1998-. On the bds. of Speedy Muffler King Inc., Alliance Communications Co. Member of the Canadian Civil Liverties Assn., New York City Partnership of CEO's.

KARRAS, ALEX
Actor. b. Gary, IN, July 15, 1935. e. Univ. of Iowa. As football player with Iowa State U., picked for All Amer. team. Received Outland Trophy, 1957. Former professional football player with Detroit Lions, 1958-62, and 1964-71. Sportswriter, Detroit Free Press, 1972-73. Also worked as prof. wrestler, salesman, steel worker and lecturer. m. actress Susan Clark. With her formed Georgian Bay Prods., 1979. Books: Even Big Guys Cry (with Herb Gluck, 1977), Alex Karras: My Life in Football Television and Movies (1979), Tuesday Night Football (1991).
PICTURES: Paper Lion (as himself; debut, 1968), Blazing Saddles, FM, Win Place or Steal, Jacob Two-Two Meets the Hooded Fang, When Time Ran Out, Nobody's Perfekt, Porky's, Victor/Victoria, Against All Odds.
TELEVISION: Commentator and host: Monday Night Football (1974-76). Mini-Series: Centennial. Movies: Hardcase, The 500-Pound Jerk, Babe, Mulligan's Stew, Mad Bull, Jimmy B. & Andre (also exec. prod.), Alcatraz: The Whole Shocking Story, Word of Honor (also exec. prod.), Maid in America (also exec. prod.), Fudge-a-Mania, Tracy Takes On.... Series: Webster (also co-prod.), The Tom Show.

KARTOZIAN, WILLIAM F.
Executive. b. San Francisco, CA, July 27, 1938. e. Stanford U., 1960; Harvard Law Sch., 1963. Deputy Attorney General State of CA, 1963-64; assoc. in law firm of Lillick, McHose Wheat Adams & Charles, San Francisco, 1964-65; corp. counsel and dir., Natl. Convenience Stores, Houston, 1965-67; v.p. and corp. counsel, UA Theatre Circuit, 1967-75; owner, Festival Enterprises, Inc., 1970-86; chmn. San Francisco Theatre Employers Assoc., 1973-76; Theatre Assoc. of CA, Inc., dir. 1972-86, v.p. 1974-75, pres. 1975-79, chmn. of bd. 1979-81; member, State of CA Industrial Welfare Comm. Amusement and Recreation Industries Wage Board, 1975-76; Natl Assoc. of Theatre Owners: dir. 1976-86, v.p. 1980-86, president 1988-present. Owner, Regency Enterprises, Inc., 1986-present; chmn. of bd., Lakeside Inn & Casino, Stateline, NV 1985-present. Member: Calif. Film Commission, 1988-present.

KARYO, TCHEKY
Actor. b. Istanbul, Turkey. Studied drama at the Cyrano Theatre and became a member of the Daniel Sorano Company, National Theatre of Strasbourg. Received the Jean Gabin Prize, 1986.
PICTURES: Vincent and Me, La Balance, The Return of Martin Guerre, All Night Long, La Java des ombres, The Outsider, Full Moon in Paris, Amour braque, L' Actor, États d'âme, Bleu comme l'enfer, L' Unique, Spirale, Sorceress, The Bear, Australia, La Fille des Collines, La Femme Nikita, Corps Perdus, Exposure, Isabelle Eberhardt, 1492: Conquest of Paradise, Sketch Artist, On Guard, Husbands and Lovers, And the Band Played On, The Black Angel, Nostradamus, Fear City: A Family-Style Comedy, Zadoc et le bonheur, GoldenEye, Operation Dumbo Drop, Bad Boys, Colpo di luna, Crying Freeman, Foreign Land, Albergo Roma, Gentle Into the Night, To Have and to Hold, Follow Your Heart, Les Mille merveilles de l'univers, Dobermann, Addicted to Love, Habitat, Que la lumière soit, World of Moss, Wing Commander.

KASDAN, LAWRENCE
Writer, Director, Producer. b. West Virginia, Jan. 14, 1949. e. U. of Michigan. Clio award-winning advertising copywriter, Detroit and LA before becoming screen writer. Became director with Body Heat (1981).
PICTURES: Dir./s.p./co-s.p.: The Empire Strikes Back, Raiders of the Lost Ark, Continental Divide, Body Heat, Return of the Jedi, The Big Chill (also co-exec. prod.), Into the Night (actor), Silverado (also prod), Cross My Heart (prod.), The Accidental Tourist (also co-prod.), Immediate Family (exec. prod.), I Love You to Death (also actor), Grand Canyon (also co-prod., actor), Jumpin at the Boneyard (exec. prod.), The Bodyguard (also co-prod.), Wyatt Earp (also co-prod.), French Kiss, Home Fires (prod.), Mumford.

KASLOFF, STEVE
Writer. b. New York, NY, Nov. 13, 1952. e. Pratt Institute, 1974, cum laude. Writer/supvr., Young & Rubicam, 1974-76; writer/sprv., Ally & Gargano, 1976; writer/supvr., Marsteller Inc., 1976-79; writer/creative supvr., Scali, McCabe, Sloves, 1979-82. hired as youngest v.p., Columbia Pictures, 1982; promoted to sr. v.p., creative dir., Columbia, 1983. Sr. v.p. creative dir., 20th Century Fox, 1992. Member, WGA. Winner of numerous Clio and Key Arts Awards and over 200 others for creative work (trailers, TV commercials, posters, etc.) on such films as Tootsie, Ghostbusters, Total Recall, Home Alone, Dances With Wolves, Terminator 2, Home Alone 2, Last Action Hero, Jurassic Park, Schindler's List, Dumb and Dumber, etc. Has directed stage productions, commercials & special teaser trailers. Screen-writing/Production deal with Columbia Pictures, 1988; 20th Century Fox Films, 1993-present.

KASSAR, MARIO
Executive, Producer. b. Lebanon, Oct. 10, 1951. At age of 18 formed own foreign distribution co. Kassar Films International, specializing in sale, dist. and exhibition of films in Asia and Europe. In 1976 became partners with Andrew Vajna who had own dist. co., forming Carolco. First prod. First Blood, followed by Rambo: First Blood Part II. Became sole chmn. of Carolco in 1989. Formed own production co. in 1996.
PICTURES: Exec. Prod.: Angel Heart, Extreme Prejudice, Rambo III, Red Heat, Iron Eagle II, Deep Star Six, Johnny Handsome, Mountains of the Moon, Total Recall, Air America, Jacob's Ladder, L.A. Story, The Doors, Terminator 2: Judgment Day, Rambling Rose, Basic Instinct, Universal Soldier, Light Sleeper, Chaplin, Cliffhanger, Heaven & Earth, Stargate, Last of the Dogmen, Showgirls, Cutthroat Island, Lolita (prod.), Icarus (prod.).

KASTNER, ELLIOTT
Producer. b. New York, NY, Jan. 7, 1933. e. U. of Miami, Columbia U. Was agent then v.p. with MCA, before becoming indep. prod., financing and personally producing 65 feature films in 25 yrs. Based in London, NY & LA.
PICTURES: Bus Riley's Back in Town, Harper, Kaleidoscope, The Bobo, Sweet November, Sol Madrid, Michael Kohlaas, Laughter in the Dark, Night of the Following Day, Where Eagles Dare, A Severed Head, Tam Lin, The Walking Stick, X Y and Zee (Zee & Company), The Nightcomers, Big Truck and Poor Clare, Face to the Wind, Fear Is the Key, The Long Goodbye, Cops and Robbers, Jeremy, 11 Harrowhouse, Spot, Rancho Deluxe, 92 in the Shade, Farewell My Lovely, Russian Roulette, Breakheart Pass, The Missouri Breaks, Swashbuckler, Equus, A Little Night Music, The Medusa Touch, The Big Sleep, Absolution, Goldengirl, Yesterday's Hero, Ffolkes, The First Deadly Sin, Death Valley, Man Woman and Child, Garbo Talks, Oxford Blues, Nomads, Heat, Angel Heart, Jack's Back, Spy Trap, Jack's Back, The Blob, White of the Eye, Zombie High, Never on Tuesday, Homeboy, A Chorus of Disapproval, The Last Party, Love is All There is.
TELEVISION: Movie: Frank and Jesse.

KATLEMAN, HARRIS L.
Executive. b. Omaha, NB, Aug. 19, 1928. e. UCLA. Joined MCA in 1949; 1952 transferred to NY as head of TV Packaging Dept. Left to join Goodson-Todman Prods. in 1955, where named v.p., 1956; exec. v.p., 1958; sr. exec. v.p. 1968. Was directly responsible for all programs prod. in L.A., including The Rebel, Branded, The Richard Boone Show, and Don Rickles Show, on which was exec. prod. Joined M-G-M in 1972 as v.p. of MGM-TV;

promoted following year to pres., MGM-TV and sr. v.p. of MGM, Inc. Resigned as pres., MGM-TV, 1977. Formed Bennett/Katleman Productions under contract to Columbia Pictures. Exec. prod.: From Here to Eternity, Salvage 1; 1980, named bd. chmn. 20th-Fox Television. Appointed pres. & CEO, Twentieth TV, 1982. Oversaw prod. of final years of M*A*S*H, as well as Mr. Belvedere, The Fall Guy, Trapper John M.D., L.A. Law, Hooperman, Anything But Love, Tracey Ullman Show, Alien Nation, The Simpsons, In Living Color. Resigned, 1992. Formed Shadow Hill Prods. under contract to Twentieth TV. Joined Mark Goodson Prods., 1993, as COO.

KATSELAS, MILTON GEORGE
Director, Writer, Teacher, Painter. b. Pittsburgh, PA, Feb. 22, 1933. e. drama dept., Carnegie Inst. of Technology (now Carnegie-Mellon U.). Acting teacher-owner, Beverly Hills Playhouse. Has exhibited paintings in several major solo exhibitions. Awards: 3 time recipient of the L.A. Drama Critics Circle Award, Drama Logue Best Director Award, NAACP and Tony Nominations for Best Director.
THEATER: B'way: The Rose Tattoo, Butterflies are Free, Camino Real. Off-B'way: Call Me By My Rightful Name, The Zoo Story.
PICTURES: Butterflies Are Free, 40 Carats, Report to the Commissioner, When You Comin' Back Red Ryder?
TELEVISION: Movies: The Rules of Marriage, Strangers—The Story of a Mother and Daughter.

KATT, WILLIAM
Actor. b. Los Angeles, CA, Feb. 16, 1955. Son of actors Barbara Hale and Bill Williams. e. Orange Coast Coll. Majored in music, playing piano and guitar. Acted with South Coast Repertory Theatre, later working in productions at the Ahmanson and Mark Taper Theatres in L.A. Phoenix Rep (N.Y.): Bonjour La Bonjour. Regional: Sarah and Abraham, Days of Wine and Roses.
PICTURES: Carrie (debut, 1976), First Love, Big Wednesday, Butch and Sundance: The Early Days, Baby, Rising Storm, House, White Ghost, Wedding Band, Naked Obsession, Double X: The Name of the Game, House IV: Home Deadly Home, Desperate Motive (Distant Cousins), Tollbooth, The Paperboy, Stranger by Night, Cyborg 3: The Recycler, Rattled, Devil's Food.
TELEVISION: Series: The Greatest American Hero, Top of the Hill, Good Sports, Models Inc.. Movies: Night Chase, The Daughters of Joshua Cabe, Can Ellen Be Saved?, Perry Mason Returns and several Perry Mason follow-ups (Case of the... Murdered Madam, Avenging Ace, Scandalous Scoundrel, Lady in the Lake, Notorious Nun, Shooting Star, Lost Love, Sinister Spirit), Swim Suit, Americanski Blues, Problem Child 3: Junior in Love, Piranha, Rough Riders. Specials: Pippin, The Rainmaker.

KATZ, GLORIA
Producer, Writer. e. UCLA. Film Sch. Joined Universal Pictures as editor, cutting educational films. Later joined forces with Willard Huyck, whom she had met at U.C.L.A. Pair signed by Francis Ford Coppola to write and direct for his newly created company, American Zoetrope.
PICTURES: Writer: American Graffiti, Lucky Lady, French Postcards (also prod.), Indiana Jones and the Temple of Doom, Best Defense (also prod.), Howard the Duck (also prod.), Radioland Murders.
TELEVISION: Co-Producer, Co-Writer: A Father's Homecoming, Mothers Daughters and Lovers.

KATZ, JAMES C.
Producer, Executive. b. New York, NY, March 17, 1939. e. Ohio St. U. Started in publicity dept. of United Artists, 1963, eventually serving as v.p. of publicity for UA, 1966-68. Publicity co-ord. on film Khartoum, 1964. To London, 1968 as unit publicist for The Charge of the Light Brigade, Joanna. Prod. & dir. for C.I.C. special shorts and documentaries. 1973-78, prod./dir. commercials for own company in London. 1980, pres. Universal Classics Dept.; 1984, v.p. prod, Universal Pictures. With Robert A. Harris worked on restoration of Spartacus, My Fair Lady.
PICTURES: Three Sisters (co-prod.), Lust in the Dust (exec. prod.), Nobody's Fool (prod.), Scenes From the Class Struggle in Beverly Hills (prod.).

KATZ, MARTY
Producer. b. Landsburg, West Germany, Sept. 2, 1947. e. UCLA, U. of Maryland. Served in Vietnam War as U.S. Army first lieut.; awarded Bronze Star as combat pictorial unit director. 1971, dir. of film prod., ABC Circle Films; 1976, exec. v.p., prod., Quinn Martin Prods; 1978-80, producer and consultant, Paramount Pictures' 1981-85, independent producer (Lost in America, Heart Like a Wheel). 1985, joined Walt Disney Prods. as sr. v.p., motion picture & TV prod. Named exec. v.p. motion picture and TV production, 1988-92. 1992-present, pres. Marty Katz Prods./Walt Disney Studios. Producer of Mr. Wrong.

KATZ, NORMAN B.
Executive. b. Scranton, PA, Aug. 23, 1919. e. Columbia U. In U.S. Army 1941-46 as intelligence officer, airborne forces. Entered m.p. industry in 1947 with Discina Films, Paris, France,

as prod. asst. Named exec. asst. to head of prod. in 1948. 1950 named v.p. Discina Int'l. Films and in 1952 exec. v.p. 1954 joined Associated Artists Prods. as foreign mgr.; named dir. of foreign operation in 1958. 1959 became dir. of foreign operations for United Artists Associated. 1961 joined 7 Arts Associated Corp. as v.p. in chg. of foreign optns.; 1964, named exec. v.p., 7 Arts Prods. Int'l.; 1967, exec. v.p. Warner Bros.-7 Arts Int'l. 1969 appt. exec. v.p. & CEO WB Int'l. & bd. mem. of WB Inc. 1974 named sr. v.p. int'l. div. of American Film Theatre. Pres. of Cinema Arts Assoc. Corp. 1979, exec. v.p. and bd. member, American Communications Industries and pres., CEO of ACI subsidiary, American Cinema; 1983, pres., The Norkat Co., Assoc. bd. chmn., CEO, American Film Mktg. Assoc., 1985-87; chmn. Amer. Film Export Assn. 1988-92.

KATZENBERG, JEFFREY
Executive. b. 1950. Entered motion picture industry in 1975 as asst. to Paramount Pictures chmn. and CEO Barry Diller in NY. In 1977, became exec. dir. of mktg.; later same year moved to west coast as v.p. of programming for Paramount TV. Promoted to v.p., feature production for Paramount Pictures 1978; 2 years later assumed role of sr. v.p. prod. of m.p. div; 1982, pres. of prod., m.p. and TV, Paramount Pictures. Left to join The Walt Disney Company, 1984; chairman of The Walt Disney Studios, 1984-94. With Steven Spielberg and David Geffen formed Dreamworks entertainment company, 1995.

KAUFMAN, HAL
Creative director, TV Writer, Producer. b. New York, NY, Dec. 16, 1924. e. U. of TX, 1943-44; U. of MI, 1944-47. Started career as petroleum geologist, Western Geophysical Co., 1947-48; TV writer-prod-dir., KDYL-TV, Salt Lake City, 1948-49; prog. dir., WLAV-TV, Grand Rapids, 1949-51; prod. mgr., WOOD-TV, Grand Rapids, 1951-54; TV writer-prod., Leo Burnett Company, Chicago, 1954-56; TV writer-prod., Gordon Best Company, Chicago, 1957-58; with Needham Louis & Brorby Inc.: 1959, sr. writer, TV/Radio creative dept.; 1962, v.p., asst. copy dir.; 1963, dir., tv, radio prod.; 1964, dir., broadcast design, production; assoc. creat. dir., asst. exec. v.p., Needham, Harper & Steers, Inc., 1965; creat. dir. L.A., 1966; sr. v.p. and mem. bd. of dir., 1966. 1969, creative & marketing consultant in Beverly Hills. 1970, exec. v.p., principle, Kaufman, Lansky Inc., Beverly Hills and San Diego; 1974 editor and publisher Z Magazine; program dir., Z Channel, Theta Cable TV. 1979, sr. v.p./adv. & p.r. & asst. to pres. & bd. chmn., World Airways, Inc. 1982, v.p., creative dir., Admarketing, Inc., Los Angeles. 1985, mktg. & adv. consultant copy dir., Teleflora, Inc.; pres. Hal Kaufman Inc., mktg. & adv. consultant; pres. Brochures on Video, library division, creators and prods. of promotional videos, distribs. religious videos to libraries; pres. Pious Publications, prods. and distribs. of religious videos. Member, Directors Guild of America, SAG, AFTRA. 1974.

KAUFMAN, LEONARD B.
Producer, Writer, Director. b. Newark, NJ, Aug. 31, 1927. e. NYU. In W.W.II served with Army Special Services writing and directing camp shows. Nat'l magazine writer, 1945-48; radio writer, including Errol Flynn Show, 1948-50; radio and TV writer, 1950-52. Headed own public relations firm: Kaufman, Schwartz, and Associates, 1952-64. Joined Ivan Tors Films as writer-prod., 1964. Films Corp., 1958.
PICTURES: Clarence the Cross-eyed Lion, Birds Do It (story).
TELEVISION: Daktari, Ivan Tors' Jambo, O'Hara U.S. Treasury (pilot feature and series). Producer: Hawaii-Five O, The New Sea Hunt, Scruples (mini-series), The Hawaiian (pilot), Writer: Knightrider, Dukes of Hazzard, Hawaii-Five O, Wet Heat (pilot), Hawaiian Heat, Island Sons (movie).

KAUFMAN, LLOYD
Executive. e. Yale Univ., 1969. From 1974-present, pres. of Troma, Inc.
PICTURES: The Girl Who Returned (prod., dir., s.p.), Cry Uncle (prod. mgr.), Joe (prod. asst.), Sugar Cookie (exec. prod., s.p.), Silent Night Bloody Night (assoc. prod.), Battle of Love's Return (dir., prod., s.p., actor), Big Gus What's the Fuss (dir., prod.), Sweet Savior (prod. mgr.), Mother's Day (assoc. prod.), Rocky (pre-prod. spvr.), Slow Dancing in the Big City (prod. spvr.), The Final Countdown (assoc. prod.), Squeeze Play (dir., prod.), Waitress (co-dir., prod.), Stuck on You (co-dir., co-prod., co-s.p.), The First Turn-On (co-dir., co-prod.), Screamplay (exec. prod.), When Nature Calls (assoc. prod.), The Toxic Avenger (co-dir., co-prod., co-s.p., story), Blood Hook (exec. prod.), Girl School Screams (exec. prod.), Class of Nuke 'Em High (co-dir., co-prod.), Lust for Freedom (exec. prod.), Monster in the Closet (exec. prod.), Troma's War (co-dir., co-prod., co-s.p., story), Toxic Avenger Part II (co-dir., co-prod., co-s.p., story), Fortress of Amerikkka (prod.), Toxic Avenger III: The Last Temptation of Toxie (co-dir., co-s.p., co-prod.), Class of Nuke 'Em High Part II: Subhumanoid Meltdown (co-s.p., co-prod., story), Sgt. Kabukiman N.Y.P.D. (co-dir., co-prod., co-s.p.), The Good the Bad and the Subhumanoid (co-s.p., co-prod., co-story).

KAUFMAN, PHILIP
Writer, Director, Producer. b. Chicago, IL, Oct. 23, 1936. e. U. of Chicago, Harvard Law Sch. Was teacher in Italy and Greece before turning to film medium.
PICTURES: *Co-Writer:* The Outlaw Josey Wales, Raiders of the Lost Ark. *Director:* Goldstein (co-dir., co-s.p., co-prod.), Fearless Frank (also s.p., prod.), The Great Northfield Minnesota Raid (also s.p., prod.), The White Dawn, Invasion of the Body Snatchers, The Wanderers (also co-s.p.), The Right Stuff (also s.p.), The Unbearable Lightness of Being (also co-s.p.), Henry & June (also co-s.p.), Rising Sun (also co-s.p.).

KAUFMAN, VICTOR
Executive. b. New York, NY, June 21, 1943. e. Queens Coll.; NYU Sch. of Law, J.D., 1967. Taught criminal law at UCLA before joining Wall St. law firm, Simpson Thacher & Bartlett. Joined Columbia Pictures as asst. general counsel, 1974. Named chief counsel, 1975; then made vice chmn. Columbia Pictures. Later exec. v.p. Columbia Pictures Industries and vice chmn. Columbia Pictures motion picture div. when conceived a new studio as a joint venture between Coca-Cola, Time Inc.'s Home Box Office and CBS, Inc. forming Tri-Star Pictures. Named chmn. and CEO Tri-Star, 1983. When Columbia Pictures and Tri-Star merged in late 1987, became pres. and CEO of new entity, Columbia Pictures Entertainment. In June 1988, dropped title of chmn. of Tri-Star. 1993 became head of Savoy Pictures.

KAUFMANN, CHRISTINE
Actress. b. Lansdorf, Graz, Austria, Jan. 11, 1945. e. school in Munich, Germany. Film debut as a dancer. Salto Mortale at 7 yrs of age.
PICTURES: The White Horse Inn, Salto Mortale, Der Klosterjager, Staatsanwaltin Corda, Rosenrosli (Little Rosie), Schweigende Engel (Silent Angel), Wenn die Alpenrosen Bluh'n, Ein Herz Schlagt fur Erika, Stimme der Sehnsucht, Witwer mit 5 Tochtern, Die Winzerin von Langenlois, Sag ja Muttil, First Love, Madchen in Uniform, Embezzled Heaven, Winter Vacation, Madchen von denen man spricht, Everybody Loves Peter, Toto Fabrizio e i Giovani D'oggi, Der Letzte Fubganger, The Last Days of Pompeii, Red Lips, Un Trono Para Cristy, A Man Named Rocca, Town Without Pity, Via Mala, The Phony American, Swordsman of Siena, Taras Bulba (U.S debut), Escape from East Berlin, Constantine the Great, Neunzig Minuten nach Mitternacht, Wild & Wonderful, Love Birds, The Death of Maria Malibran, Murder in the Rue Morgue, Willow Springs, Goodbye with Mums, Auf Biegen oder Brechen, Goldflocken, Rich and Respectable, Orgie des Todes, It Can only Get Worse, Day of the Idiots, Egon Schiele - Exzesse, Lili Marleen, Lola, Ziemlich weit Weg, The Wild Fifties, The Excluded, Pankow '95, The Swing, Bagdad Cafe, Hard to Be a God, Der Geschichtenerzahler, The Talking Grave, War of Neighbours.
TELEVISION: *Movies:* World on a Wire, Immobilien, Inflation im Paradies, Birkenhof & Kirchenau, Weihnachten mit Willy Wuff II - Eine Mama fur Lieschen, Ein Flotter Dreier. *Mini-series:* Wie ein Blitz, Lockruf des Goldes, Monaco Franze - Der Ewige Stenz.

KAURISMAKI, AKI
Director, Writer. b. Finland, April 4, 1957. Brother is filmmaker Mika Kaurismaki. First film credit was acting and writing his brother's The Liar in 1980. Directed short subjects: Rocky VI, Thru the Wire, Those Were the Days, These Boots. Served as writer on brother's features: Jackpot 2, The Worthless (also actor), The Clan: The Tale of the Frogs, Rosso.
PICTURES: *Director:* The Saimaa Gesture (co-dir., with Mika), Crime and Punishment, Calamari Union, Shadows in Paradise, Hamlet Goes Business, Ariel, Leningrad Cowboys Go America, The Match Factory Girl, I Hired a Contract Killer, La Vie de Boheme (The Bohemian Life), Leningrad Cowboys Meet Moses (also s.p., prod., edit.), Total Balalaika Show (also s.p.), Take Care of Your Scarf Tatiana (also s.p., prod., edit.), Drifting Clouds (also s.p.).

KAVNER, JULIE
Actress. b. Los Angeles, CA, Sept. 7, 1951. e. San Diego State U. Professional debut as Brenda Morgenstern on TV's Rhoda, 1974.
THEATER: Particular Friendships (Off-B'way), Two for the Seesaw (Jupiter, FLA), It Had to Be You (Canada).
PICTURES: National Lampoon Goes to the Movies, Bad Medicine, Hannah and Her Sisters, Radio Days, Surrender, New York Stories (Oedipus Wrecks), Awakenings, Alice, This Is My Life, Shadows and Fog, I'll Do Anything, Forget Paris.
TELEVISION: *Series:* Rhoda (Emmy Award, 1978), The Tracey Ullman Show, The Simpsons (voice). *Special:* The Girl Who Couldn't Lose (Afternoon Playbreak). *Movies:* Katherine, No Other Love, The Revenge of the Stepford Wives, Don't Drink the Water. *Pilot:* A Fine Romance. *Guest:* Lou Grant, Petrocelli, Taxi.

KAYLOR, ROBERT
Director. b. Plains, MT, Aug. 1, 1934. e. Art Center Sch. of Design. Received awards at Cannes, San Francisco and Dallas Film Festivals, Guggenheim Fellow, Amer. Film Inst.
PICTURES: Derby, Carny, Nobody's Perfect.

KAZAN, ELIA
Director. b. Constantinople, Turkey, Sept. 7, 1909. e. Williams Coll., Yale Dramatic Sch. With Group Theatre as apprentice & stage mgr.; on stage, 1934-41; plays include: Waiting for Lefty, Golden Boy, Gentle People, Five-Alarm, Lilliom. Author (novels): The Arrangement, The Assassins, The Understudy, Acts of Love, The Anatolian, A Life (autobiography, 1988), Beyond the Aegean (1994).
THEATER: *Director:* Skin of Our Teeth, All My Sons, Streetcar Named Desire, Death of a Salesman, Cat on a Hot Tin Roof (co-dir.), One Touch of Venus, Harriet, Jocobowsky and the Colonel, Tea and Sympathy, Dark at the Top of the Stairs, J.B., Sweet Bird of Youth, Lincoln Center Repertory Theatre (co-dir., prod.), After The Fall, But For Whom Charlie.
PICTURES: *Actor:* City for Conquest, Blues in the Night. *Director:* A Tree Grows in Brooklyn (debut, 1945), Boomerang!, The Sea of Grass, Gentleman's Agreement (Acad. Award, 1947), Pinky, Panic in the Streets, A Streetcar Named Desire, Viva Zapata!, Man on a Tightrope, On the Waterfront (Academy Award, 1954). *Producer/Director:* East of Eden, Baby Doll, A Face in the Crowd, Wild River, Splendor in the Grass, America America (also s.p.), The Arrangement (also s.p.), The Visitors, The Last Tycoon.

KAZAN, LAINIE
Singer, Actress. b. New York, NY, May 15, 1942. e. Hofstra U.
PICTURES: Dayton's Devils, Lady in Cement, Romance of a Horse Thief, One from the Heart, My Favorite Year, Lust in the Dust, The Delta Force, The Journey of Natty Gann, Harry and the Hendersons, Beaches, Eternity, 29th Street, I Don't Buy Kisses Anymore, The Cemetery Club.
TELEVISION: *Series:* The Dean Martin Summer Show, Tough Cookies, Karen's Song. *Pilot:* Family Business, The Lainie Kazan Show. *Movies:* A Love Affair: The Eleanor and Lou Gehrig Story, A Cry for Love, Sunset Limousine, The Jerk Too, Obsessive Love, Prince for a Day. *Guest:* Too Close for Comfort, Dick Van Dyke Show, Beverly Hills 90210, Tales From the Crypt, Faerie Tale Theatre (Pinocchio), Hotel, Johnny Carson Show, Dean Martin, Merv Griffin, Joan Rivers, Amazing Stories, Pat Sajak Show, The Famous Teddy Z, Murder She Wrote.

KAZANJIAN, HOWARD G.
Producer. b. Pasadena, CA, July 26, 1943. e. U. of Southern California Film Sch.; DGA Training Program.
PICTURES: *Asst. dir.:* Cool Hand Luke, Camelot, Finian's Rainbow, The Wild Bunch, The Great Bank Robbery, I Love You Alice B. Toklas, Christine, The Arrangement, The Girl From Petrovka, The Front Page, The Hindenberg, Family Plot. *Producer:* Rollercoaster (assoc. prod.) More American Graffiti, Raiders of the Lost Ark, Return of the Jedi, The Rookie, Demolition Man, One Dozen.
TELEVISION: The Making of More American Graffiti, The Making of Raiders of the Lost Ark (Emmy award), The Making of Return of the Jedi, Rattled, JAG.

KAZURINSKY, TIM
Actor, Writer. b. Johnstown, PA, March 3, 1950. Raised in Australia. Worked as copywriter for Chicago ad agency. Took acting class at Second City and quit job to become actor and head writer for Second City Comedy Troupe. Co-starred with John Candy in CTV/NBC's Big City Comedy, 1980. Joined cast of Saturday Night Live as writer-actor 1981-84.
PICTURES: *Actor:* My Bodyguard, Somewhere in Time, Continental Divide, Neighbors, Police Academy II: Their First Assignment, Police Academy III: Back in Training, About Last Night (also co-s.p.), Police Academy IV: Citizens on Patrol, For Keeps (s.p. only), Road to Ruin (also s.p.), Hot to Trot, Wedding Band, A Billion for Boris, Shakes the Clown, Plump Fiction.
TELEVISION: *Movies:* This Wife for Hire, Dinner at Eight, The Cherokee Kid (also s.p.).

KEACH, STACY
Actor, Director, Producer. b. Savannah, GA, June 2, 1942. Brother is actor James Keach. Began professional acting career in Joseph Papp's 1964 Central Park prod. of Hamlet.
THEATER: Long Day's Journey into Night (Obie Award), Macbird (Drama Desk & Obie Awards), Indians (Drama Desk Award & Tony nom.), Hamlet, Deathtrap, Hughie, Barnum, Cyrano de Bergerac, Peer Gynt, Henry IV Parts I & II, Idiot's Delight, Solitary Confinement, Richard III, The Kentucky Cycle (Helen Hayes Award), Steiglitz Loves O'Keefe.
PICTURES: The Heart Is a Lonely Hunter (debut, 1968), End of the Road, The Traveling Executioner, Brewster McCloud, Doc, The New Centurions, Fat City, Watched!, The Life and Times of Judge Roy Bean, Luther, The Gravy Train, The Killer Inside Me, Conduct Unbecoming, Street People, The Squeeze, The Duellists (narrator), Slave of the Cannibal God, The Great Battle, Gray Lady Down, Up in Smoke, The Ninth Configuration (Twinkle Twinkle Killer Kane), The Long Riders (also exec. prod., co-s.p.), Nice Dreams, Road Games, Butterfly, That Championship Season, Class of 1999, False Identity, Milena, Raw Justice, Batman: Mask of the Phantasm (voice), New Crime City, Escape from L.A., Prey of the Jaguar.

TELEVISION: *Series:* Caribe, Mickey Spillane's Mike Hammer, Case Closed (host). *Movies:* All the Kind Strangers, Caribe, The Blue and the Gray, Princess Daisy, Murder Me Murder You, More Than Murder, Wait Until Dark, Mistral's Daughter, Hemingway, Mickey Spillane's Mike Hammer: Murder Takes All, The Forgotten, Mission of the Shark, Revenge on the Highway, Rio Diablo, Body Bags, Against Their Will: Women in Prison, Texas, Amanda & the Alien. *Director:* Incident at Vichy, Six Characters in Search of an Author.

KEACH, SR., STACY
Executive. b. Chicago, IL, May 29, 1914. Father of actors, Stacy and James. e. Northwestern U., B.S. & M.A. Was instructor in theatre arts at Northwestern and Armstrong Coll. and dir. at Pasadena Playhouse before entering industry. For 4-1/2 yrs. was under contract at Universal Pictures; 3 yrs. at RKO; had own prod. on NBC, CBS. In 1946 began producing and directing industrial stage presentations for Union Oil Co. and from then on became full-time prod. of m.p. and stage industrial shows. In 1946 formed Stacy Keach Productions, of which is he pres. In addition to directing, producing and writing occasionally appears as actor in films (Cobb, etc.). Created radio show, Tales of the Texas Rangers, 1950-53. Played Clarence Birds Eye on TV commercials as well as other commercials. Voiceovers/ spokesman for many major American Cos. Autobiography: Stacy Keach, Go Home! (1996). Received Man of the Year Award from Pasadena Playhouse Alumni in 1995. Recipient of the Diamond Circle Award from the Pacific Pioneers Broadcasters Assoc., 1996.

KEATON, DIANE
Actress, Director. r.n. Diane Hall. b. Santa Ana, CA, Jan. 5, 1946. e. Santa Ana Coll. Appeared in summer stock and studied at Neighborhood Playhouse in N.Y. Made prof. debut in B'way prod. of Hair (1968); then co-starred with Woody Allen in Play It Again Sam, repeating role for film version. Off-B'way: The Primary English Class. Author: photography books: Reservations (co-ed.), Still Life. Directed 1982 short What Does Dorrie Want?
PICTURES: Lovers and Other Strangers (debut, 1970), The Godfather, Play It Again Sam, Sleeper, The Godfather Part II, Love and Death, I Will I Will... for Now, Harry and Walter Go to New York, Annie Hall (Acad. Award, 1977), Looking for Mr. Goodbar, Interiors, Manhattan, Reds, Shoot the Moon, The Little Drummer Girl, Mrs. Soffel, Crimes of the Heart, Radio Days, Heaven (dir. only), Baby Boom, The Good Mother, The Lemon Sisters (also prod.), The Godfather Part III, Father of the Bride, Manhattan Murder Mystery, Look Who's Talking Now (voice), Unstrung Heroes (dir. only), Father of the Bride 2, Marvin's Room, The First Wives Club, The Only Thrill, Northern Lights, Town and Country, The Other Sister, Hanging Up.
TELEVISION: *Movies:* Running Mates, Amelia Earhart: The Final Flight, Northern Lights. *Guest:* Love American Style, The FBI, Mannix. *Director:* The Girl With the Crazy Brother, Twin Peaks, Wildflower (movie).

KEATON, MICHAEL
Actor. r.n. Michael Douglas. b. Coraopolis, PA, Sept. 5, 1951. Speech major, Kent State U, 2 years. Drove cab and ice-cream truck, worked for PBS station in Pittsburgh and appeared in regional theatre prods. while performing in local coffeehouses. Became memb. of improvisational troupe Jerry Vale. Moved to L.A. where honed craft at Comedy Store and Second City Improv. Workshops as stand-up comic.
PICTURES: Night Shift (debut, 1982), Mr. Mom, Johnny Dangerously, Gung Ho, Touch and Go, The Squeeze, Beetlejuice, Clean and Sober, The Dream Team, Batman, Pacific Heights, One Good Cop, Batman Returns, Much Ado About Nothing, My Life, The Paper, Speechless, Multiplicity, Inventing the Abbotts (narrator), Jackie Brown, Frost, Desperate Measures.
TELEVISION: *Series:* All's Fair, Mary, The Mary Tyler Moore Hour, Working Stiffs, Report to Murphy. *Movie:* Roosevelt and Truman. *Special:* Frank Capra's American Dream.

KEEL, HOWARD
Actor. r.n. Harold Keel. b. Gillespie, IL, April 13, 1919. e. high school, Fallbrook, CA. Began career following George Walker scholarship award for singing, L.A.; appeared in plays, Pasadena Auditorium; concerts; won awards, Mississippi Valley and Chicago Musical Festivals. Stage debut: Carousel, 1945; followed by London prod. of Oklahoma! which led to contract with MGM.
THEATER: Carousel, Oklahoma!, Saratoga, No Strings, The Ambassador, Man of La Mancha.
PICTURES: The Small Voice (debut, 1948), Annie Get Your Gun, Pagan Love Song, Three Guys Named Mike, Show Boat, Texas Carnival, Callaway Went Thataway, Lovely to Look At, Desperate Search, I Love Melvin (cameo), Ride Vaquero!, Fast Company, Kiss Me Kate, Calamity Jane, Rose Marie, Seven Brides for Seven Brothers, Deep in My Heart, Jupiter's Darling, Kismet, Floods of Fear, The Big Fisherman, Armored Command, The Day of the Triffids, The Man From Button Willow (voice), Waco, Red Tomahawk, The War Wagon, Arizona Bushwhackers, That's Entertainment III.
TELEVISION: *Series:* Dallas. *Movie:* Hart to Hart: Home Is Where the Hart Is. *Guest:* Zane Grey Theatre, Bell Telephone Hour, Tales of Wells Fargo, Death Valley Days, Here's Lucy, Sonny and Cher, The Love Boat, etc. *Specials:* A Toast to Jerome Kern, Roberta, Music of Richard Rodgers.

KEESHAN, BOB
Performer. b. Lynbrook, NY, June 27, 1927. e. Fordham U. As network page boy became assistant to Howdy Doody's Bob Smith and originated role of Clarabelle the Clown; created children's programs Time for Fun, Tinker's Workshop, Mister Mayor, Captain Kangaroo (1955-85).

KEITEL, HARVEY
Actor. b. Brooklyn, NY, May 13, 1939. Served in U.S. Marine Corps. Studied with Frank Corsaro, Lee Strasberg, Stella Adler. Member of the Actors' Studio. Debuted in Martin Scorsese's student film Who's That Knocking at My Door?
THEATER: *NY:* Up to Thursday, Death of a Salesman, Hurlyburly, A Lie of the Mind.
PICTURES: Who's That Knocking at My Door? (debut, 1968), Mean Streets, Alice Doesn't Live Here Anymore, That's the Way of the World, Taxi Driver, Mother Jugs and Speed, Buffalo Bill and the Indians or: Sitting Bull's History Lesson, Welcome to L.A., The Duellists, Fingers, Blue Collar, Eagle's Wing, Deathwatch, Saturn 3, Bad Timing, The Border, Exposed, La Nuit de Varennes, Corrupt, Falling in Love, Knight of the Dragon (Star Knight), Camorra, Off Beat, Wise Guys, The Men's Club, The Investigation (The Inquiry), The Pick-Up Artist, The Last Temptation of Christ, The January Man, The Two Jakes, Mortal Thoughts, Thelma & Louise, Two Evil Eyes (The Black Cat), Bugsy (Acad. Award nom.), Sister Act, Reservoir Dogs (also co-prod.), Bad Lieutenant, Point of No Return, Rising Sun, The Piano, Dangerous Game, The Young Americans, Monkey Trouble, Pulp Fiction, Imaginary Crimes, Somebody to Love, Smoke, Clockers, Blue in the Face, Ulysses' Gaze, From Dusk Till Dawn, Head Above Water, Somebody to Love, City of Industry, Cop Land, Head Above Water.
TELEVISION: *Movie:* The Virginia Hill Story. *Special:* This Ain't Bebop (Amer. Playhouse).

KEITH, DAVID
Actor, Director. b. Knoxville, TN, May 8, 1954. e. U. of Tennessee, B.A., speech and theater. Appearance at Good-speed Opera House in musical led to role in CBS sitcom pilot, Co-Ed Fever.
PICTURES: The Rose (debut, 1979), The Great Santini, Brubaker, Back Roads, Take This Job and Shove It, An Officer and a Gentleman, Independence Day, The Lords of Discipline, Firestarter, The Curse (dir. only), White of the Eye, The Further Adventures of Tennessee Buck (also dir.), Heartbreak Hotel, The Two Jakes, Off and Running, Desperate Motive (Distant Cousins), Caged Fear, Raw Justice, Temptation, Major League II, Liar's Edge, Till the End of the Night, Born Wild, Gold Diggers: The Secret of Bear Mountain, Deadly Sins, The Indian in the Cupboard, A Family Thing, Invasion of Privacy, Judge & Jury, Red Blooded American Girl II, If... Dog... Rabbit.
TELEVISION: *Series:* Co-ed Fever, Flesh 'N' Blood, Strangers, High Incident, Local Heroes. *Movies:* Are You in the House Alone?, Friendly Fire, Gulag, Whose Child Is This?: The War for Baby Jessica, XXX's & OOO's (pilot), James Michener's Texas, If Looks Could Kill: From the Files of America's Most Wanted. *Mini-Series:* If Tomorrow Comes, Golden Moment: An Olympic Love Story, Guts and Glory: The Rise and Fall of Oliver North. Guest: Happy Days, Runaways.

KEITH, PENELOPE
O.B.E. Actress. b. Sutton, Surrey, Eng., 1939. London stage debut, The Wars of the Roses (RSC, 1964). Extensive theater work including The Norman Conquests, Donkey's Years, The Apple Cart, Hobson's Choice, Captain Brassbound's Conversion, Hay Fever.
PICTURES: Think Dirty (Every Home Should Have One), Take a Girl Like You, Penny Gold, Priest of Love.
TELEVISION: *Series:* Kate, The Good Life, To the Manor Born, Executive Stress. *Movies-Specials:* Private Lives, The Norman Conquests, Donkey's Years.

KELLER, MARTHE
Actress. b. Basel, Switzerland, 1945. e. Stanislavsky Sch., Munich. Joined a Heidelberg repertory group and Schiller Rep. in Berlin. Started acting in France and attracted attention of U.S. directors after appearing in Claude Lelouch's And Now My Love. Has acted in over 50 plays in French, German, Eng. & Italian.
PICTURES: Funeral in Berlin (debut, 1967), The Devil by the Tail, Give Her the Moon, La Vieille Fille, The Loser, Elle Court (Love in the Suburbs), And Now My Love, Down the Ancient Staircase, Le Guepier, Marathon Man, Black Sunday, Bobby Deerfield, Fedora, The Formula, Les Uns et les Autres, The Amateur, Wagner, Femmes de Personne, Joan Lui, I Come on Monday, Dark Eyes, Rouge Basier, The Artisan, Una Vittoria, Lapse of Memory, Mon Amie Max, According to Pereira, Nuits Blanches, K, Elles.
TELEVISION: Liberez mon Fils, Mein oder Dein, The Charthouse of Parma, Wagner, Die Frau des Reporters, La Ruelle de Clair de Lune, The Nightmare Years, Young Catherine, Turbulences, Im Kreis der Iris.

KELLERMAN, SALLY
Actress. b. Long Beach, CA, June 2, 1936. m. Jonathan Krane. e. Hollywood H.S. Studied acting in N.Y. at the Actors Studio and in Hollywood with Jeff Corey. Recorded album Roll With the Feeling. Has done voice-overs for many commercials.
THEATRE: Women Behind Bars, Holiday.
PICTURES: Reform School Girl (debut, 1959), Hands of a Stranger, The Third Day, The Boston Strangler, The April Fools, M*A*S*H (Acad. Award nom.), Brewster McCloud, Last of the Red Hot Lovers, Lost Horizon, Slither, Reflection of Fear, Rafferty and the Gold Dust Twins, The Big Bus, Welcome to L.A., The Mouse and His Child (voice), Magee and the Lady, A Little Romance, Serial, Head On (Fatal Attraction), Foxes, Loving Couples, Moving Violations, Lethal (KGB: The Secret War), Back to School, That's Life!, Meatballs III, Three For the Road, Someone to Love, You Can't Hurry Love, Paramedics (voice), All's Fair, Limit Up, The Secret of the Ice Cave, The Player, Doppelganger, Happily Ever After (voice), Younger and Younger, Ready to Wear (Pret-a-Porter).
TELEVISION: Mini-Series: Centennial. Movies: For Lovers Only, Dempsey, Secret Weapons, September Gun, Drop Dead Gorgeous, Boris and Natasha (also assoc. prod.). Specials: Big Blonde, Verna: USO Girl, Elena, Faerie Tale Theatre, Dr. Paradise. Guest: Mannix, It Takes a Thief, Chrysler Theatre.

KELLEY, DAVID E.
Producer, Writer.
PICTURES: Writer: From the Hip, To Gillian on Her 37th Birthday (also prod.), Lake Placid, Mystery Alaska (also prod.).
TELEVISION: Movies: Annie O (cam.). Series prod.: Doogie Howser M.D., Picket Fences, Chicago Hope, The Practice, Ally McBeal.

KELLEY, DeFOREST
Actor. b. Atlanta, GA, Jan. 20, 1920. e. Decatur Boys' H.S.
PICTURES: Fear in the Night (debut, 1947), Variety Girl, Canon City, The Men, House of Bamboo, Taxi, Illegal, The Man in the Gray Flannel Suit, Tension at Table Rock, Gunfight at the O.K. Corral, Raintree County, The Law and Jake Wade, Warlock, Where Love Has Gone, Marriage on the Rocks, Apache Uprising, Night of the Lepus, Star Trek: The Motion Picture, Star Trek II: The Wrath of Khan, Star Trek III: The Search for Spock, Star Trek IV: The Voyage Home, Star Trek V: The Final Frontier, Star Trek VI: The Undiscovered Country.
TELEVISION: Series: Star Trek. Guest: Gunsmoke, The Lineup, Matinee Theatre, The Web, Playhouse 90, Bonanza, Bat Masterson, The Deputy, Perry Mason, The Virginian, Room 222, and numerous others inlcuding Star Trek: The Next Generation.

KELLEY, SHEILA
Actress. b. Philadelphia, PA, Sept. 9, 1963.
PICTURES: Wish You Were Here, Hostile Witness, Staying Together, Some Girls, Breaking In, Mortal Passions, Where the Heart Is, Wild Blade, Soapdish, Pure Luck, Singles, Passion Fish, Passion to Kill, Mona Must Die, One Fine Day, Sante Fe.
TELEVISION: Series: L.A. Law, Sisters, Moving Story. Movie: Tonight's the Night, The Betty Ford Story, Terrorist on Trial: The United States vs. Salim Ajami, Fulfillment, The Chase, Deconstructing Sarah, The Secretary. Guest: Wings.

KELLOGG, PHILIP M.
Executive. b. Provo, WA, March 17, 1912. e. UCLA. Special feature writer for Hearst papers and magazines, 1933-34; MGM story dept., production dept., Universal, 1934-35; Warner Bros. film editor, 1935-41; Berg-Allenberg Agency, 1941-50; U.S. Naval Reserve officer, 1941-46; William Morris Agency, 1950-present, co-head of m.p. dept., dir. WMA, Ltd., London.

KELLY, FRANK
Executive. Was assoc. prod. of AM Los Angeles, then exec. prod./program dir. for KABC-TV prior to joining Paramount. 1983, named v.p. programming for Paramount domestic tv division; 1985, promoted to sr. v.p. 1989, became exec. v.p. programming. 1995, named pres. of creative affairs for domestic tv division of Paramount Television Group.

KELLY, MOIRA
Actress. b. 1969. e. Marymount Col. In addition to acting also trained as violinist, operatic soprano.
PICTURES: The Boy Who Cried Bitch (debut, 1991), Billy Bathgate, The Cutting Edge, Twin Peaks: Fire Walk With Me, Chaplin, With Honors, The Lion King (voice), Little Odessa, The Tie That Binds.
TELEVISION: Movies: Love Lies and Murder, Daybreak.

KELSEY, LINDA
Actress. b. Minneapolis, MN, July 28, 1946. e. U. of Minnesota, B.A.
TELEVISION: Series: Lou Grant, Day by Day, Sessions. Movies: The Picture of Dorian Gray, Something for Joey; Eleanor and Franklin: The White House Years, The Last of Mrs. Lincoln, A Perfect Match, Attack on Fear, His Mistress, Nutcracker, Baby Girl Scott, A Place to Be Loved, A Family Torn Apart, If Someone Had Known. Special: Home Sweet Homeless. Mini-Series: Captains and the Kings.

KEMENY, JOHN
Producer. b. Budapest, Hungary. Producer for National Film Board of Canada, 1957-69. Formed International Cinemedia Center, Ltd. in 1969 in Montreal, as partner.
PICTURES: Ladies and Gentlemen... Mr. Leonard Cohen, Don't Let the Angels Fall, Seven Times a Day, The Apprenticeship of Duddy Kravitz, White Line Fever, Shadow of the Hawk, Ice Castles, The Plouffe Family (exec. prod.), Quest for Fire (co-prod.), The Bad Boy, Murder in the Family (exec. prod.), The Wraith, The Boy in Blue, The Gate, Iron Eagle II, Gate II.
TELEVISION: Louisiana, The Blood of Others, Sword of Gideon (exec. prod.), The Park is Mine, Murderers Among Us: The Simon Wiesenthal Story (co-prod.), Red King White King, The Josephine Baker Story, The Teamster Boss: The Jackie Presser Story, Dead Silence.

KEMP, JEREMY
Actor. b. Chesterfield, England, Feb. 3, 1935. e. Abbottsholme Sch., Central Sch. of Speech and Drama. Service with Gordon Highlanders. Early career on stage incl. Old Vic Theatre Company, 1959-61. Recent theatre: Celebration, Incident at Vichy, Spoiled, The Caretaker. National Theatre, 1979-80.
PICTURES: Cleopatra (debut, 1963), Dr. Terror's House of Horrors, Face of a Stanger, Operation Crossbow (The Great Spy Mission), Cast a Giant Shadow, The Blue Max, Assignment K, Twist of Sand, The Strange Affair, Darling Lili, The Games, Sudden Terror (Eye Witness), Pope Joan, The Bellstone Fox, The Blockhouse, The Seven Percent Solution, East of Elephant Rock, Queen of Diamonds, A Bridge Too Far, The Thoroughbreds (Treasure Seekers), Leopard in the Snow, Caravans, The Prisoner of Zenda, The Return of the Soldier, Top Secret!, When the Whales Came, Angels and Insects, Four Weddings and a Funeral.
TELEVISION: Z Cars, The Lovers of Florence, The Last Reunion, Colditz, Brassneck, Rhinemann Exchange, Lisa, Goodbye, Henry VIII, St. Joan, The Winter's Tale, Unity, The Contract, Sadat, King Lear, Sherlock Holmes, George Washington, Peter the Great, The Winds of War, War and Remembrance, Slip-Up (The Great Paper Chase), Cop-out, Summers Lease, Prisoner of Honor, Duel of Hearts, The Magician, Conan: The Adventurer. Series: Star Trek: The Next Generation (guest).

KEMPER, VICTOR J.
Cinematographer. b. Newark, NJ, April 14, 1927. e. Seton Hall, B.S./Engineer. Channel 13, Newark 1949-54; Tech. supervisor EUE Screen Gems NY 1954-56; v.p. engineering General TV Network. Pres. VJK Prods.
PICTURES: Husbands, The Magic Garden of Stanley Sweetheart, They Might Be Giants, Who is Harry Kellerman?, The Hospital, The Candidate, Last of the Red Hot Lovers, Shamus, The Friends of Eddie Coyle, Gordon's War, The Hideaways, The Gambler, The Reincarnation of Peter Proud, Dog Day Afternoon, Stay Hungry, The Last Tycoon, Mikey and Nicky, Slapshot, Audrey Rose, Oh God!, The One and Only, Coma, Eyes of Laura Mars, Magic, Night of the Juggler, And Justice for All, The Jerk, The Final Countdown, Xanadu, The Four Seasons, Chu Chu and the Philly Flash, Partner, Author! Author!, National Lampoon's Vacation, Mr. Mom, The Lonely Guy, Cloak and Dagger, Secret Admirer, Pee-wee's Big Adventure, Clue, Bobo, Hot to Trot, Cohen and Tate, See No Evil, Hear No Evil, Crazy People, FX2, Another You, Married to It, Beethoven, Tommy Boy, Eddie, Jingle All the Way.

KENNEDY, BURT
Director, Writer. b. Muskegon, MI, Sept. 3, 1922. e. Ravenna H.S. U.S. Army 1942-46; awarded Silver Star, Bronze Star and Purple Heart with Oak Leaf Cluster. Began as writer of TV and film scripts, and was writer, producer and director of Combat series and many TV and theatrical westerns.
PICTURES: Writer: Seven Men From Now, Gun the Man Down, Man in the Vault, the Tall T, Fort Dobbs, Ride Lonesome, Yellowstone Kelly, Comanche Station, Six Black Horses, Stary Away Joe, The Littlest Horse Thiefs, White Hunter Black Heart. Director: The Canadians (debut, 1961; also s.p.), Mail Order Bride (also s.p.), The Rounders (also s.p.), The Money Trap, Return of the Seven, The War Wagon, Welcome to Hard Times (also s.p.), Support Your Local Sheriff, The Good Guys and the Bad Guys, Young Billy Young (also s.p.), Dirty Dingus Magee, Support Your Local Gunfighter (also exec. prod.), Hannie Caulder (also s.p. as Z.X. Jones), The Deserter, The Train Robbers (also s.p.), The Killer Inside Me, Wolf Lake (also s.p.), The Trouble with Spies (also prod., s.p.), Big Bad John (also s.p.), Suburban Commando.
TELEVISION: Series: Combat (prod., writer) The Rounders (also writer), How the West Was Won, The Yellow Rose, Simon & Simon, Magnum P.I. Mini-Series: The Rhinemann Exchange. Movies: Shoot out in a One-Dog Town, Side kicks (also prod.), All the Kind Strangers, Kate Bliss and the Ticker Tape Kid, The Wild Wild West Revisted, The Concrete Cowboys, More Wild Wild West, The Alamo-Thirteen Days to Glory, Down the Long Hills, Once Upon a Texas Train (also prod., writer), Where the Hell's That Gold?!!? (also prod., writer).

KENNEDY, GEORGE
Actor. b. New York, NY, Feb. 18, 1925. At 2 acted in touring co. of Bringing Up Father. At 7, disc jockey with his own radio show for children. Served in Army during WWII, earning two Bronze Stars and combat and service ribbons. In Army 16 years, became Capt. and Armed Forces Radio and TV officer. 1957, opened first Army Information Office, N.Y. Served as technical advisor to Phil Silvers's Sergeant Bilko TV series. Began acting in 1959 when discharged from Army.
PICTURES: The Little Shepard of Kingdom Come (debut, 1961), Lonely Are the Brave, The Man From the Diner's Club, Charade, Strait- Jacket, Island of the Blue Dolphins, McHale's Navy, Hush... Hush... Sweet Charlotte, Mirage, In Harm's Way, The Sons of Katie Elder, The Flight of the Phoenix, Shenandoah, Hurry Sundown, The Dirty Dozen, Cool Hand Luke (Acad. Award, best supporting actor, 1967), The Ballad of Josie, The Pink Jungle, Bandolero!, The Boston Strangler, The Legend of Lylah Claire, Guns of the Magnificent Seven, Gaily Gaily, The Good Guys and the Bad Guys, Airport, ... tick ... tick ... tick ..., Zigzag, Dirty Dingus Magee, Fool's Parade, Lost Horizon, Cahill: U.S. Marshal, Thunderbolt and Lightfoot, Airport 1975, Earthquake, The Human Factor, The Eiger Sanction, Airport '77, Ningen no Shomei (Proof of the Man), Mean Dog Blues, Death on the Nile, Brass Target, The Concorde—Airport '79, Death Ship, The Double McGuffin, Steel, Virus, Just Before Dawn, Modern Romance, A Rare Breed, Search and Destroy, Wacko, The Jupiter Menace, Bolero, Chattanooga Choo Choo, Hit and Run, Savage Dawn, The Delta Force, Radioactive Dreams, Creepshow 2, Born to Race, Demonwarp, Counterforce, Nightmare at Noon, Private Roads, Uninvited, The Terror Within, The Naked Gun: From the Files of Police Squad, Esmeralda Bay, Ministry of Vengeance, Brain Dead, Hangfire, The Naked Gun 2 1/2: The Smell of Fear, Driving Me Crazy, Distant Justice, Naked Gun 33 1/3: The Final Insult, Cats Don't Dance (voice), Dennis the Menace 2 .
TELEVISION: Series: The Blue Knight, Sarge, Counterattack: Crime in America, Dallas, Santo Bugito (voice). Guest: Sugarfoot, Cheyenne. Movies: See How They Run, Sarge: The Badge or the Cross, Priest Killer, A Great American Tragedy, Deliver Us From Evil, A Cry in the Wilderness, The Blue Knight, The Archer: Fugitive from the Empire, Jesse Owens Story, Liberty, International Airport, Kenny Rogers as the Gambler III, The Gunfighters, What Price Victory, Good Cops Bad Cops, Final Shot: The Hank Gathers Story, Dallas: J.R. Returns. Mini-Series: Backstairs at the White House.

KENNEDY, JAMES C.
Publishing & Media Executive. b. 1947. e. U. Denver, BBA, 1970. Prodn. asst. with Atlanta Newspapers, 1972-76, then exec. v.p. gen. mgr. 1976-79. Pres. Grand Junction newpapers, 1979-80. Pub. Grand Junction Daily Sentinel, 1980-85. V.p. Cox newspapers div. Cox Enterprises, Inc., 1985-86; exec. v.p. 1986-87; pres., COO, Exec. v.p., 1986-87; chmn., 1987-; chmn., CEO, Cox Ent. Inc., 1988-.

KENNEDY, JOSEPH W.
Executive. a.k.a. Scott Kennedy. b. New York, NY, Feb. 11, 1934. e. La Salle, NYU. Started as office boy at NBC in 1950, before studying acting in NY. Appeared on TV in The Defenders and The Naked City, in film Advise and Consent. Host of Scott Kennedy Luncheon radio show in 1964. Joined United Artists in Boston in 1967 as salesman. UA Chicago sls. mgr. 1969-72; Jacksonville branch mgr. 1972-78; southern div. mgr. 1978-79. 1980 named v.p. & asst. gen. sls. mgr. responsible for UA eastern sls. territories. 1983 joined Tri-Star Pictures as v.p. of southern div. mgr. Dallas.

KENNEDY, KATHLEEN
Producer. b. 1954. Raised in Weaverville and Redding in No. Calif. e. San Diego State U. Early TV experience on KCST, San Diego, working as camera operator, video editor, floor director and news production coordinator. Produced talk show, You're On. Left to enter m.p. industry as prod. asst. on Steven Spielberg's 1941. Founding member and pres. of Amblin Entertainment. 1992, with husband and partner Frank Marshall formed the Kennedy/Marshall Company.
PICTURES: Raiders of the Lost Ark (prod. assoc.), Poltergeist (assoc. prod.), E.T.: The Extra-Terrestrial (prod.), Twilight Zone: The Movie (co-assoc. prod.), Indiana Jones and the Temple of Doom (assoc. prod.). Exec. prod. (with Frank Marshall): Gremlins, The Goonies, Back to the Future, The Color Purple (prod.), Young Sherlock Holmes (co-prod.), An American Tail, Innerspace, Empire of the Sun, Batteries Not Included, Who Framed Roger Rabbit, The Land Before Time, Indiana Jones and the Last Crusade, (prod. exec.), Dad, Always (prod.), Joe Versus the Volcano, Gremlins II, Hook (co-prod.), Noises Off, Alive, A Far Off Place, Jurassic Park, Milk Money, The Bridges of Madison County, Congo, The Indian in the Cupboard, Twister. Exec. Prod: Schindler's List, A Dangerous Woman, The Flintstones, The Lost World: Jurassic Park.
TELEVISION: Amazing Stories (spv. prod.), You're On (prod.), Roger Rabbit & the Secrets of Toontown (exec. prod.).

KENNEY, H. WESLEY
Producer, Director. b. Dayton, OH, Jan. 3, 1926. e. Carnegie Inst. of Tech. Guest Instructor, UCLA; guest lecturer, Televisia: Mexico City.
THEATER: Dir. Ten Little Indians (Advent Th., L.A.), The Best Christmas Pageant Ever, Love Letters (WV State Theatre), Shadowlands (Tracey Roberts Theatre).
TELEVISION: Series: All in the Family (dir.), The Jefferson (pilot dir.), Days of Our Lives (exec. prod. 1979-81), Ladies Man (dir.), Filthy Rich (dir.), Flo (dir.), The Young and the Restless (exec. prod. 1981-86), General Hospital (exec. prod. 1986-89). Dir. Sopa Break. Infomercials (dir.): Elements of Beauty, Merle Norman Experience,

KENSIT, PATSY
Actress. b. London, England, March 4, 1968. Made film debut at the age of 4 in The Great Gatsby. Later appeared in commercials directed by Tony Scott and Adrian Lyne.
PICTURES: The Great Gatsby (debut, 1974), Alfie Darling, The Blue Bird, Hanover Street, Absolute Beginners, Lethal Weapon 2, A Chorus of Disapproval, Chicago Joe and the Showgirl, Timebomb, Twenty-One, Blue Tornado, Blame It on the Bellboy, Beltenebros, Kleptomania, The Turn of the Screw, Bitter Harvest, Angels and Insects, Grace of My Heart.
TELEVISION: BBC: Great Expectations, Silas Marner, Tycoon: The Story of a Woman, Adam Bede. U.S.: The Corsican Brothers, Fall from Grace, Love and Betrayal: The Mia Farrow Story, Human Bomb, The Last Don.

KENT, JEAN
Actress. r.n. Joan Summerfield. b. London, England, June 29, 1921. e. Marist Coll., Peekham, London. First stage appearance at 3; at age 10 played in parents' act; chorus girl at Windmill Theatre, London, 1935; 2 yrs. repertory before debuting on screen under real name.
PICTURES: The Rocks of Valpre (High Treason; debut, 1934), It's That Man Again (first film as Jean Kent, 1943), Fanny by Gaslight (Man of Evil), Champagne Charlie, 2000 Women, Madonna of the Seven Moons, The Wicked Lady, The Rake's Progress (The Notorious Gentleman), Caravan, The Magic Bow, The Man Within (The Smugglers), Good Time Girl, Bond Street, Sleeping Car to Trieste, Trottie True (Gay Lady), Her Favorite Husband, The Woman in Question, The Browning Version, The Big Frame (The Lost Hours), Before I Wake (Shadow of Fear), The Prince and the Showgirl, Bonjour Tristesse, Grip of the Strangler (The Haunted Strangler), Beyond This Place (Web of Evidence), Please Turn Over, Bluebeard's Ten Honeymoons, Shout at the Devil, The Saving of Aunt Esther.
TELEVISION: A Call on the Widow, The Lovebird, The Morning Star, November Voyage, Love Her to Death, The Lion and the Mouse, The Web, Sir Francis Drake series, Yvette, Emergency Ward 10, County Policy, Coach 7, Smile on the Face of the Tiger, No Hiding Place, Kipling, This Man Craig, The Killers, Vanity Fair, A Night with Mrs. Da Tanka, United serial: The Family of Fred, After Dark, Thicker than Water series, The Young Doctors, Brother and Sister, Up Pompei, Steptoe and Son, Doctor at Large, Family at War, K is for Killing, Night School, Tycoon series, Crossroads (series), Lyttons Diary, Lovejoy (series), Missing Persons, After Henry (series), Shrinks (series).

KENT, JOHN B.
Theatre executive, Attorney. b. Jacksonville, FL, Sept. 5, 1939. e. Yale U., U. of FL, Law Sch., NYU grad. sch. of law (L.L.M. in taxation, 1964). Partner in Kent Ridge & Crawford, P.A.; pres. & dir, Kent Investments, Inc. 1977-; dir., v.p. & gen. counsel, Kent Theatres, Inc. 1970-; dir. & v.p., Kent Enterprises, Inc. 1961-; dir. & v.p. Kent Cinemas Inc. 1993-. Was pres. of Kent Theatres Inc. 1967-70; resigned to devote full time to law practice. NATO dir. 1972 and Presidents' Advisory Cabinet, 1979-; v.p./dir. NATO of FL, 1968-. Member of Rotary Club ofJacksonville, Fla. Bar Ass'n., American Bar Ass'n.

KENYON, CURTIS
Writer. b. New York, NY, March 12, 1914.
PICTURES: Woman Who Dared, Lloyds of London, Wake Up and Live, Love and Hisses, She Knew All the Answers, Twin Beds, Seven Days' Leave, Thanks for Everything, Bathing Beauty, Fabulous Dorseys, Tulsa, Two Flags West, Mr. Ricco.
TELEVISION: Cavalcade of America, Fireside Theatre, Schlitz Playhouse, U.S. Steel Hour, 20th Century-Fox Hour. Series: Hawaii 5-O.

KERASOTES, GEORGE G.
Exhibitor. b. Springfield, IL. e. U. of IL, 1929-33; Lincoln Coll. of Law 1935-37. Past pres. & chmn., Kerasotes Theatres, 1935-85; Pres. & chmn., George Kerasotes Corp. & GKC Theatres, Inc., 1984-. Past pres. Theatre Owners of Illinois. Past pres. & chmn. Kerasotes Theatres, 1935-85. Past pres., Theatre Owners of America, 1959-60. Chmn. of board of TOA 1960-62; chmn. ACE Toll TV com.; bd. mem. NATO; treas., bd. of dirs., memebr, exec. comm., chmn., insurance comm. Director, St. Anthony's Hellenic Church, Hellenic Golf Classic. Director, Will Rogers Hospitals; Director, Pioneers. Robert W. Selig ShoWester of the Year, NATO, Las Vegas, 1992.

KERKORIAN, KIRK

Executive. b. Fresno, CA, June 6, 1917. e. Los Angeles public schools. Served as capt., transport command, RAF, 1942-44. Commercial air line pilot from 1940; founder Los Angeles Air Service (later Trans Intl. Airlines Corp.), 1948; Intl. Leisure Corp., 1968; controlling stockholder, Western Airlines, 1970; chief exec. officer, MGM, Inc., 1973-74; chmn. exec. com., vice-chmn. bd., 1974-1978. Stepped down from exec. positions while retaining financial interest in MGM/UA. Repurchased MGM in the summer of 1996.

KERNER, JORDAN

Producer. e. Stanford U, A.B. Political Science & Communications; U.C. Berkely, J.D.-M.B.A.. Bgean career in entertainment working for CBS affiliate KPIX-TV. Joined law firm of Ball, Hunt, Brown & Baerwitz. Talent & Program Negotiator for CBS. Worked for Universal Pictures & QM Prods., 1978-81. Joined ABC Entertainment as dir., Dramatic Series Development. Promoted to v.p., 1983. While at ABC, placed Moonlighting, MacGyver, Dynasty, Spencer for Hire, Call To Glory. Founded the Avnet/Kerner Co. in 1986 with Jordan Kerner. Currently dir., Allied Communications, Inc. Member, bd. of dirs., The Starbright Foundation, The Chrysalis Foundation. Member, President's Advisory Council for the City of Hope, Sen. Dianne Feinstein's California Cabinet, Planned Parenthood, Earth Communications Office, A.M.P.A.S., A.F.I. former gov., Academy of Television Arts & Sciences. Founder and former co-chmn., Committee for the Arts of the Beverly Hills Bar Asoc. Founder, COMM/ENT, the Journal of Communications & Entertainment Law.
PICTURES: Less Than Zero, Funny About Love, The Mighty Ducks, Fried Green Tomatoes, The War, The Three Musketeers, When A Man Loves A Woman, D2: The Mighty Ducks, Miami Rhapsody (exec. prod.), Up Close and Personal, Swiss Family Robinson, Dinner For Two at the El Cortez, To Live For, Friday Night Lights, Blaze of Glory, D3: The Mighty Ducks, Red Corner, George of the Jungle, Thirty Wishes, Inspector Gadget.
TELEVISION: Breaking Point, Do You Know the Muffin Man?, Heat Wave, Backfield in Motion, The Watchman, The Switch, For Their Own Good, The War, Love Can Build a Bridge, Side By Side, My First Love.

KERNS, JOANNA

Actress. b. San Francisco, CA, Feb. 12, 1953. r.n. Joanna de Varona. Former gymnast, became dancer, appeared on tv commercials. Sister is Olympic swimmer and tv commentator Donna de Varona. NY stage: Ulysses in Nighttown.
PICTURES: Coma, Cross My Heart, Street Justice, An American Summer.
TELEVISION: Series: The Four Seasons, Growing Pains (also wrote one episode). Guest: Three's Company, Magnum P.I., Hill Street Blues, Hunter, etc. Movies: The Million Dollar Rip-Off, Marriage Is Alive and Well, Mother's Day on Walton's Mountain, A Wedding on Walton's Mountain, A Day of Thanks on Walton's Mountain, The Return of Marcus Welby M.D., A Bunny's Tale, The Rape of Richard Beck, Stormin' Home, Mistress, Those She Left Behind, Like Mother Like Daughter, The Preppie Murder, Blind Faith, Captive, The Nightman, Not in My Family, The Man With 3 Wives, Shameful Secrets, No Dessert Dad 'Til You Mow the Lawn, Robin Cook's Mortal Fear, See Jane Run, Whose Daughter Is She?, Sisters and Other Strangers, Mother Knows Best, Morning Glory, Terror In the Family.

KERR, DEBORAH

Actress. b. Helensburgh, Scotland, Sept. 30, 1921; e. Phyllis Smale Ballet Sch. On stage 1939 in repertory before Brit. screen career began the following year. Voted Star of Tomorrow by Motion Picture Herald-Fame Poll, 1942. Voted one of top ten British money-making stars in Motion Picture Herald-Fame Poll, 1947. B'way debut in Tea and Sympathy, 1953. Received special Academy Award, 1994.
PICTURES: Major Barbara (debut, 1940), Love on the Dole, Penn of Pennsylvania, Hatter's Castle, The Day Will Dawn (The Avengers), The Life and Death of Colonel Blimp, Perfect Strangers (Vacation From Marriage), I See a Dark Stranger (The Adventuress), Black Narcissus (Acad. Award nom.), The Hucksters (U.S. debut), If Winter Comes, Edward My Son, Please Believe Me, King Solomon's Mines, Quo Vadis, The Prisoner of Zenda, Thunder in the East, Dream Wife, Julius Caesar, Young Bess, From Here to Eternity (Acad. Award nom.), End of the Affair, The King and I (Acad. Award nom.), The Proud and the Profane, Tea and Sympathy, Heaven Knows Mr. Allison (Acad. Award nom.), An Affair to Remember, Bonjour Tristesse, Separate Tables (Acad. Award nom.), The Journey, Count Your Blessings, Beloved Infidel, The Sundowners (Acad. Award nom.), The Grass Is Greener, The Innocents, The Naked Edge, The Chalk Garden, The Night of the Iguana, Marriage On the Rocks, Casino Royale, Eye of the Devil, Prudence and the Pill, The Gypsy Moths, The Arrangement, The Assam Garden.
TELEVISION: Movies: A Woman of Substance, Reunion at Fairborough, Hold the Dream, Witness for the Prosecution.

KERR, FRASER

Actor. b. Glasgow, Scotland, Feb. 25, 1931. Early career in repertory. Tours of Canada and America. Ent. TV 1956. Series incl. Emergency Ward 10, Dixon of Deck Green, Murder Bag. Many Shakespeare plays. Radio: BBC Drama Rep. Co., 39 Steps, The Ringer, The Bible, What Every Woman Knows, The Ruling Class.
THEATER & TELEVISION: Night Must Fall, Never a Cross Word, The Inside Man, On the Buses, Dr. Finlay's Casebook, Wicked Woman, Madelaine July, Doctor in the House, Counterstrike, Waggoner's Walk, Juno and the Paycock, Aquarius, Ev, Upstairs and Downstairs, Cover to Cover, Janine, Robert the Bruce, Caliph of Bagdad, Watch it, Sailor!, The Fosters, Weekend World, Doctor at Sea, Dads Army, Algernon Blackwood, Waiting for Sheila, Weekend Show, Mind Your Language, Yes, Minister, Dick Emery Show, Bottle Boys, The Hard Man, Brigadoon, Hair of the Dog.
PICTURES: What a Whopper, Carry on Regardless, Way of McEagle, Thomasina, Theatre of Death, Tom, Dick and Harriet, Granny Gets the Point, Nothing but the Night, The Lord of the Rings, Kidnapped, The Derelict, Bloomfield, Ace of Diamonds, Andy Robson, It's a Deal!, Howard's Way, One Step Beyond, The Trawler.
RECORD PRODUCER: Tales of Shakespeare Series, The Casket Letters of Mary Queen of Scots.

KERSHNER, IRVIN

Director. b. Philadelphia, PA, April 29, 1923. e. Tyler Sch. of Fine Arts of Temple U., 1946; Art Center Sch., U. of Southern California. Designer, photography, adv., documentary, architectural; doc. filmmaker, U.S.I.S., Middle East, 1950-52; dir., cameraman, TV doc., Confidential File, 1953-55; dir.-prod.-writer, Ophite Prod. Appeared as actor in film The Last Temptation of Christ.
PICTURES: Stakeout on Dope Street (debut, 1958; also co-s.p.), The Young Captives, The Hoodlum Priest, A Face in the Rain, The Luck of Ginger Coffey, A Fine Madness, The Flim-Flam Man, Loving, Up the Sandbox, S*P*Y*S, The Return of a Man Called Horse, Eyes of Laura Mars, The Empire Strikes Back, Never Say Never Again, Robocop 2, American Perkect (prod.).
TELEVISION: Series: The Rebel, Naked City, numerous pilots and other nat'l. shows. Movies: Raid on Entebbe (theatrical in Europe), The Traveling Man. Pilot: seaQuest dsv.

KERWIN, BRIAN

Actor. b. Chicago, IL, Oct. 25, 1949. e. USC.
THEATRE: NY: Emily (Theatre World Award), Lips Together Teeth Apart, Raised in Captivity. LA: Strange Snow (LA Drama Critics Award), Who's Afraid of Virginia Woolf?, A Loss of Roses, Torch Song Trilogy.
PICTURES: Hometown USA (debut, 1979), Nickel Mountain, Murphy's Romance, King Kong Lives, Torch Song Trilogy, S.P.O.O.K.s., Hard Promises, Love Field, Gold Diggers: The Secret of Bear Mountain, Getting Away With Murder, Jack, The Myth of Fingerprints, Mr. Jealousy, Flash.
TELEVISION: Series: The Young and the Restless (1976-77), The Misadventures of Sheriff Lobo, Angel Falls. Mini-Series: The Chisholms, The Blue and the Gray, Bluegrass. Movies: A Real American Hero, Power, Miss All-American Beauty, Intimate Agony, Wet Gold, The Greatest Thing That Almost Happened, Challenger, Switched at Birth, Against Her Will: An Incident in Baltimore, Abandoned and Deceived, It Came From Outer Space, Sins of Silence, Critical Choices, Volcano: Fire on the Mountain. Special: Natica Jackson (Tales of the Hollywood Hills). Guest: St. Elsewhere, The Love Boat, B.J. and the Bear, Roseanne, Murder She Wrote, Simon & Simon, Highway to Heaven.

KEYES, EVELYN

Actress. b. Port Arthur, TX, Nov. 20, 1919. e. high school. Began career as a dancer in night clubs.
AUTHOR: Novel: I Am a Billboard (1971). Autobiographies: Scarlett O'Hara's Younger Sister (1977), I'll Think About That Tomorrow (1991).
PICTURES: Artists and Models (debut, 1937), The Buccaneer, Men With Wings, Artists and Models Abroad, Sons of the Legion, Dangerous to Know, Paris Honeymoon, Union Pacific, Sudden Money, Gone with the Wind, Slightly Honorable, Before I Hang, Beyond Sacramento, The Lady in Question, The Face Behind the Mask, Here Comes Mr. Jordan, Ladies in Retirement, The Adventures of Martin Eden, Flight Lieutenant, There's Something About a Soldier, Dangerous Blondes, The Desperadoes, Nine Girls, Strange Affair, A Thousand and One Nights, The Jolson Story, Renegades, The Thrill of Brazil, The Mating of Millie, Johnny O'Clock, Enchantment, Mrs. Mike, Mr. Soft Touch, The Killer That Stalked New York, Smuggler's Island, The Iron Man, The Prowler, One Big Affair, Shoot First, 99 River Street, Hell's Half Acre, It Happend in Paris, Top of the World, The Seven Year Itch, Around the World in 80 Days, Across 110th Street, Return to Salem's Lot, Wicked Stepmother.
TELEVISION: Guest: Murder She Wrote.

KEYLOUN, MARK

Actor. b. Dec. 20, 1960. e. Georgetown U. Worked in New York theatre.
PICTURES: Those Lips Those Eyes, Sudden Impact, Forty-Deuce, Mike's Murder.
TELEVISION: Evergreen, War Stories: The Mine.

KHONDJI, DARIUS
Cinematographer.
PICTURES: Rive droite, rive gauche (first assistant camera-man), Le Tresor des chiennes, Delicatessen, Prague, Shadow of a Doubt, Before the Rain, Marie-Lousie ou la permission, City of Lost Children, Seven, Stealing Beauty, Evita (Academy Award nom.), Alien: Resurrection, Blue Vision.

KIAROSTAMI, ABBAS
Director, Producer, Writer, Editor. b. Teheran, Iran, June 22, 1940. Recipient of the 1997 UNESCO Fellini-Medal in Gold for achievement in film, freedom, peace & tolerance.
PICTURES: The Window, The Bread & Alley, The Breaktime, The Experience, The Traveller, So I Can, Two Solutions for One Problem, The Colours, Suit for Wedding, The Report (Gozaresh), Tribute to the Teachers, How to Make Use of Our Leisure Time?, Solution No. 1, First Case—Second Case, Dental Hygiene, Orderly or Unorderly, The Chorus, Fellow Citizen, Toothache, First Graders, Where is the Friend's Home, The Key, Homework, Close Up, And Life Goes on..., Journey to the Land of the Traveller, Under the Olive Trees, The Journey, Lumiere & Company, The White Balloon, The Taste of Cherry (Cannes Film Festival Palme d'Or, 1997).

KIDD, MICHAEL
Choreographer, Dancer, Actor. r.n. Milton Greenwald. b. Brooklyn, NY, Aug. 12, 1919. e. CCNY. Studied dance at School of the American Ballet. Was dancer with Lincoln Kirstein's Ballet Caravan, Eugene Loring's Dance Players, Ballet Theatre. Became stage choreographer starting in 1945. Recipient of the Academy Award for Career Achievement, 1997.
THEATER: B'way (choreographer): Finian's Rainbow (Tony Award, 1947), Love Life, Arms and the Girl, Guys and Dolls (Tony Award, 1951), Can-Can (Tony Award, 1954), Li'l Abner (Tony Award, 1957; also dir., prod.), Destry Rides Again (Tony Award, 1960; also dir.), Wildcat (also dir., co-prod.), Subways Are for Sleeping (also dir.), Here's Love, Ben Franklin in Paris, Skyscraper, The Rothschilds (also dir.). B'way (dir.): Cyrano, Good News, Pal Joey, The Music Man, The Goodbye Girl.
PICTURES: Choreographer: Where's Charley?, The Band Wagon, Knock on Wood, Seven Brides for Seven Brothers, Guys and Dolls, Merry Andrew (also dir.), Li'l Abner, Star!, Hello Dolly!, Movie Movie (also actor). Actor: It's Always Fair Weather, Smile, Skin Deep.
TELEVISION: Specials (choreographer): Baryshnikov in Hollywood, Academy Awards. Movie (actor): For the Love of It.

KIDDER, MARGOT
Actress. r.n. Margaret Kidder. b. Yellowknife, Canada, Oct. 17, 1948.
PICTURES: The Best Damned Fiddler From Calaboogie to Kaladar (debut, 1968), Gaily Gaily, Quackser Fortune Has a Cousin in the Bronx, Sisters, A Quiet Day in Belfast, The Gravy Train, Black Christmas, The Great Waldo Pepper, 92 in the Shade, The Reincarnation of Peter Proud, Superman, Mr. Mike's Mondo Video, The Amityville Horror, Willie and Phil, Superman II, Heartaches, Shoot the Sun Down, Some Kind of Hero, Trenchcoat, Superman III, Little Treasure, GoBots (voice), Superman IV: The Quest for Peace, Miss Right, Mob Story, White Room, Crime and Punishment, Maverick, Henry & Verlin, Beanstalk, The Pornographer, La Florida, Aaron Sent Me, Windrunner, Never Met Picasso, The Planet of Junior Brown .
TELEVISION: Series: Nichols, Shell Game. Movies: Suddenly Single, The Bounty Man, Honky Tonk, Louisiana, The Glitter Dome, Picking Up the Pieces, Vanishing Act, Body of Evidence, To Catch a Killer, One Woman's Courage, Bloodknot, Phantom 2040: The Ghost Who Walks, Young Ivanhoe, The Return of Alex Kelly. Specials: Bus Stop, Pygmalion. Guest: Murder She Wrote, Bostom Common. Director: White People, Love 40.

KIDMAN, NICOLE
Actress. b. Hawaii, June 20, 1967. m. actor Tom Cruise. Raised in Australia. Made acting debut at 14 in Australian film Bush Christmas. On Australian stage in Steel Magnolias (Sydney Theatre Critics Award for Best Newcomer).
PICTURES: Bush Christmas (debut, 1982), BMZ Bandits, Windrider, Dead Calm, Emerald City, Days of Thunder, Billy Bathgate, Far and Away, Flirting, Malice, My Life, Batman Forever, To Die For (Golden Globe, 1996), Portrait of a Lady, The Peacemaker, Practical Magic, Eyes Wide Shut.
TELEVISION: Mini-Series (Australia): Five-Mile Creek, Vietnam, Bangkok Hilton.

KIDRON, BEEBAN
Director. b. London, England. e. National Film School.
Made co-dir. debut with (Amanda Richardson) with documentary Carry Greenham Home (Chicago Film Fest. Hugo Award, 1983).
PICTURES: Antonia and Jane, Used People, Great Moments in Aviation, To Wong Foo—Thanks for Everything—Julie Newmar.
TELEVISION: The Global Gamble, Vroom, Oranges Are Not the Only Fruit.

KIEL, RICHARD
Actor. b. Detroit, MI, Sept. 13, 1939. Former nightclub bouncer.
PICTURES: The Phantom Planet (debut, 1961), Eegah!, House of the Damned, The Magic Sword, Roustabout, The Human Duplicators, Las Vegas Hillbillies, A Man Called Dagger, Skidoo, The Longest Yard, Flash and the Firecat, Silver Streak, The Spy Who Loved Me, Force 10 from Navarone, They Went Thataway and Thataway, Moonraker, The Humanoid, So Fine, Hysterical, Cannonball Run II, Pale Rider, Think Big, The Giant of Thunder Mountain (also co-s.p., co-exec. prod.).
TELEVISION: Series: The Barbary Coast, Van Dyke & Company. Movies: Now You See It Now You Don't, The Barbary Coast (pilot).

KIERZEK, TERRY
Executive. b. Chicago, IL, Feb. 15, 1951. e. U. of Il. Joined Paramount Pictures Domestic Distrib., as booker in Chicago, 1974. Promoted to Sales in 1976, Dallas, TX. Named branch mgr., Dallas/OK City, 1978. V.P., Eastern Division in Washington, D.C., 1982-84. V.P., Southern Division, Dallas, TX., 1984-86. V.P., Western Division, Los Angeles, 1986-89. Orion Pictures v.p., Western Division, Los Angeles, 1990-92. Joined National Film Service in 1993 as v.p., sales & mktg. Named exec. v.p., 1995. Appointed pres., National Film Service in 1996.

KILEY, RICHARD
Actor. b. Chicago, IL, March 31, 1922. e. Loyola U. Started prof. career on radio in Jack Armstrong, Tom Mix, Ma Perkins, etc.
THEATER: A Streetcar Named Desire (tour), Misalliance, Kismet, Time Limit, Redhead (Tony Award, 1959), No Strings, Man of LaMancha (Tony Award, 1966), Her First Roman, The Incomparable Max, Voices, Absurd Person Singular, All My Sons.
PICTURES: The Mob (debut, 1951), The Sniper, Eight Iron Men, Pick-Up on South Street, Blackboard Jungle, The Phenix City Story, Spanish Affair, Pendulum, The Little Prince, Looking for Mr. Goodbar, Endless Love, Howard the Duck (voice), Jurassic Park (voice), Phenomenon.
TELEVISION: Series: A Year in the Life (Emmy Award, 1988). Mini-Series: The Thorn Birds (Emmy Award, 1983), George Washington, If Tomorrow Comes, A.D. Movies: Night Gallery, Incident in San Francisco, Murder Once Removed, Jigsaw, Friendly Persuasion, The Macahans, Angel on My Shoulder, Golden Gate, Isabel's Choice, Pray TV, The Bad Seed, Do You Remember Love?, My First Love, The Final Days, Gunsmoke: The Last Apache, Separate But Equal, Absolute Strangers, The Cosby Mysteries, A Passion for Justice: The Hazel Brannon Smith Story, Secrets. Specials: Mastergate, 30 Years of National Geographic Specials (narrator). Guest: Picket Fences (Emmy Award, 1994).

KILMER, VAL
Actor. b. Los Angeles, CA, Dec. 31, 1959. e. Hollywood Professional Sch., Juilliard, NY. Appeared in IMAX film Wings of Courage.
THEATRE: NY: Electra and Orestes, How It All Began (also co-writer), Henry IV Part One, Slab Boys (B'way debut), 'Tis Pity She's a Whore. Also: As You Like It (Gutherie MN), Hamlet (Colorado Shakespeare Fest.).
PICTURES: Top Secret! (debut, 1984), Real Genius, Top Gun, Willow, Kill Me Again, The Doors, Thunderheart, True Romance, The Real McCoy, Tombstone, Batman Forever, Heat, The Island of Dr. Moreau, The Ghost and the Darkness, The Saint.
TELEVISION: Movies: Murders in the Rue Morgue, The Man Who Broke 1000 Chains, Gore Vidal's Billy the Kid.

KIMBLEY, DENNIS
Executive. Early career in Kodak Testing Dept. responsible for quality control motion picture films. Joined Marketing Division 1966. Chairman BKSTS FILM 75 and FILM 79 Conference Committee. President BKSTS 1976-78. Governor, London International Film School, 1983. Bd. member, British Board of Film Classification; dir. of Children's Film Unit.

KIMBROUGH, CHARLES
Actor. b. St. Paul, MN, May 23, 1936. e. Indiana U., Yale U.
THEATER: NY: All in Love (debut, 1961), Cop-Out (B'way debut, 1969), Company (Tony nom.), Candide, Love for Love, The Rules of the Game, Secret Service, Mr. Happiness, Same Time Next Year, Drinks Before Dinner, The Dining Room, Sunday in the Park With George, Hay Fever. Several prods. with Milwaukee Rep. Theatre (1966-73).
PICTURES: The Front (debut, 1976), The Seduction of Joe Tynan, Starting Over, It's My Turn, Switching Channels, The Good Mother, The Hunchback of Notre Dame (voice).
TELEVISION: Series: Murphy Brown (Emmy nom.). Movies: For Ladies Only, A Doctor's Story, Weekend War, Cast the First Stone. Pilot: The Recovery Room. Special: Sunday in the Park With George.

KIMMELMAN, KEN
Producer, Director, Animator. b. New York, NY. Aug. 6, 1940. e. School of Visual Arts. Has produced tv programs, political films, theatricals, TV commercials, and many films for Sesame Street. Consultant on the faculty of the Aesthetic Realism Roundation. Pres. of Imagery Film Ltd; prod. films for UN. Recipient of: National Emmy Award 1995 (The Heart Knows Better), Newark Black Film Festival's Paul Robeson Award; Atlanta Film Festival's Dir's. Choice Award; Cindy Award; ASIFA East's Best Children's Film Award. Taught and lectured at NYU, presently at School of Visual Arts, NY. Published numerous articles & letters.
TELEVISION: Director/Producer: People Are Trying to Put Opposites Together (documentary). Series: Doug (Emmy nom., 1992, 93), The Head, Daria, Mr. Hiccup.

KING, ALAN
Actor, Producer. r.n. Irwin Alan Kingberg. b. Brooklyn, NY, Dec. 26, 1927. Started as musician, stand-up comedian in Catskills, then nightclubs. Author: Anybody Who Owns His Own Home Deserves It, Help I'm a Prisoner in a Chinese Bakery.
THEATER: The Impossible Years, The Investigation, Dinner at Eight, The Lion in Winter, Something Different.
PICTURES: Actor: Hit the Deck (debut, 1955), Miracle in the Rain, The Girl He Left Behind, The Helen Morgan Story, On the Fiddle (Operation Snafu), Bye Bye Braverman, The Anderson Tapes, Just Tell Me What You Want, Prince of the City (cameo), Author! Author!, I the Jury, Lovesick, Cat's Eye, You Talkin' to Me?, Memories of Me (also co-prod.), Enemies a Love Story, The Bonfire of the Vanities, Night and the City, Casino. Producer: Happy Birthday Gemini, Cattle Annie and Little Britches (co-prod.), Wolfen (exec. prod.).
TELEVISION: Guest/Host: The Tonight Show, Kraft Music Hall. Prod-star NBC-TV specials: Comedy is King, On Location: An Evening With Alan King at Carnegie Hall, etc. Mini-Series: Seventh Avenue. Movies: Return to Earth (co-exec. prod. only), How to Pick Up Girls (also exec. prod.), Pleasure Palace, Dad the Angel and Me, The Infiltrator. Host: Alan King: Inside the Comic Mind (Comedy Central).

KING, ANDREA
Actress. r.n. Georgette Barry. b. Paris, France, Feb. 1, 1919. e. Edgewood H.S., Greenwich, CT. m. N.H. Willis, attorney. Started career on NY stage, following high school; in Growing Pains & Fly Away Home, Boy Meets Girl, Angel Street (Boston); Life with Father (Chicago); signed by Warner, 1943. Screen debut as Georgette McKee in The Ramparts We Watch, 1940.
PICTURES: Hotel Berlin, God is My Co-Pilot, The Very Thought of You, The Man I Love, The Beast With Five Fingers, Shadow of a Woman, Roughly Speaking, My Wild Irish Rose, Ride the Pink Horse, Mr. Peabody and the Mermaid, Song of Surrender, Southside 1-10001, I Was a Shoplifter, Dial 1119, The Lemon Drop Kid, Mark of the Renegade, World in His Arms, Red Planet Mars, Darby's Rangers, Band of Angels, Daddy's Gone A-Hunting, The Linguini Incident, The Color of Evening.
TELEVISION: Movie: Prescription Murder. Specials: Dream Girl, Officer and the Lady, Witness for the Prosecution. Guest: Fireside Theatre, Maya.

KING, LARRY
Talk Show Host, Writer. b. Brooklyn, NY, Nov. 19, 1933. Started as disc jockey on various Miami radio stations from 1958-64. Became host of radio talk show, broadcast from Miami before moving to Arlington, VA, in 1978. Show has run since then on Mutual Broadcasting System. Host of CNN tv talk show since 1985, Larry King Live. Starred in tv special Larry King Extra. Columnist for Miami Beach Sun-Reporter, Sporting News, USA Today. Appeared in films Ghostbusters, Eddie and the Cruisers II: Eddie Lives, The Exorcist III.
AUTHOR: Larry King by Larry King, Tell It to the King, Mr. King You're Having a Heart Attack, Tell Me More, How to Talk to Anyone Anytime Anywhere: The Secrets of Good Conversation.

KING, PERRY
Actor. b. Alliance, OH, April 30, 1948. e. Yale. Studied with John Houseman at Juilliard. B'way debut 1990 in A Few Good Men.
PICTURES: Slaughterhouse-Five (debut, 1972), The Possession of Joel Delaney, The Lords of Flatbush, Mandingo, The Wild Party, Lipstick, Andy Warhol's Bad, The Choirboys, A Different Story, Search and Destroy (Striking Back), Class of 1984, Killing Hour (The Clairvoyant), Switch, A Cry in the Night.
TELEVISION: Series: The Quest, Riptide, Almost Home, The Trouble With Larry. Guest: Medical Center, Hawaii Five-O, Apple's Way, Cannon. Mini-Series: Aspen, The Last Convertible, Captain and the Kings. Movies: Foster and Laurie, The Cracker Factory, Love's Savage Fury, City in Fear, Inmates: A Love Story, Golden Gate, Helen Keller: The Miracle Continues, Stranded, Perfect People, Shakedown on Sunset Strip, The Man Who Lived at the Ritz, Disaster at Silo 7, The Prize Pulitzer, Danielle Steel's Kaleidoscope, Only One Survived, Something to Live For, Sidney Sheldon's A Stranger in the Mirror, Jericho Fever, Good King Wenceslas, She Led Two Lives. Pilot: Half 'n' Half.

KING, PETER
Executive, Barrister-at-law. b. London, England, March 22, 1928. e. Marlborough, Oxford U. (MA, honors). Bd., Shipman & King Cinemas Ltd., 1956; borough councillor, 1959-61; chmn., London & Home counties branch, CEA, 1962-63; pres., CEA, 1964; mang. dir. Shipman & King Cinemas Ltd., 1959-68; chmn. & mang. dir. Paramount Pictures (U.K.) Ltd. Britain, 1968-70; mang. dir., EMI Cinemas and Leisure Ltd., 1970-74; chmn. & mang. dir. King Publications/pub. Screen Intl., 1974-89; pres., Screen Intl., 1989-90; chmn. & mang. dir., Rex Publications Ltd., 1990-; pub., Majesty, 1990-; pub. Preview.

KING, STEPHEN
Writer. b. Portland, ME, Sept. 21, 1947. e. Univ. of Maine at Orono (B.S.). Best-selling novelist specializing in thrillers many of which have been adapted to film by others. Movie adaptations: Carrie, The Shining, The Dead Zone, Christine, Cujo, Children of the Corn, Firestarter, Cat's Eye, Stand By Me (The Body), The Running Man, Pet Sematary, Misery, Apt Pupil, The Lawnmower Man, The Dark Half, Needful Things, The Shawshank Redemption, The Mangler, Dolores Claiborne. TV adaptations: Salem's Lot, IT, Sometimes They Come Back, The Tommyknockers, The Langoliers.
PICTURES: Knightriders (actor), Creepshow (s.p., actor), Children of the Corn (s.p.), Silver Bullet (s.p.), Maximum Overdrive (dir., s.p., actor), Creepshow II (actor), Pet Sematary (s.p., actor), Sleepwalkers (s.p., actor).
TELEVISION: Series: Golden Years (creator, writer). Mini-Series: The Stand (writer, actor), The Langoliers (actor).

KING, ZALMAN
Actor, Director, Writer. b. Trenton, NJ, 1941. r.n. Zalman King Lefkowitz. m. writer Patricia Knop.
PICTURES: Actor: The Ski Bum, You've Got to Walk It Like You Talk It or You'll Lose the Beat, Neither by Day Nor Night, Some Call It Loving, Trip with the Teacher, Sammy Somebody, The Passover Plot, Blue Sunshine, Tell Me a Riddle, Galaxy of Terror. Exec. Prod.: Roadie (also co-story), Endangered Species, Siesta. Prod./Writer: 9 1/2 Weeks. Director-Writer: Wildfire, Two Moon Junction, Wild Orchid, Wild Orchid II: Two Shades of Blue, Delta of Venus.
TELEVISION: Series: The Young Lawyers, Red Shoe Diaries (exec. prod., creator, dir. episodes). Guest: Alfred Hitchcock Presents, Land of the Giants, Gunsmoke, Adam 12, Charlie's Angels, etc. Movies: The Dangerous Days of Kiowa Jones, Stranger on the Run, The Young Lawyers (pilot), The Intruders, Smile Jenny You're Dead, Like Normal People, Lake Consequence (co-prod., co-writer).

KINGMAN, DONG
Fine Artist. b. Oakland, CA, March 31, 1911. e. Hong Kong 1916-1920. 1928, mem. motion picture co., Hong Kong branch; 1935; began to exhibit as fine artist in San Francisco; promotional, advertising or main title artwork for following films: World of Suzie Wong, Flower Drum Song, 55 Days of Peking, Circus World, King Rat, The Desperados, The Sand Pebbles, Lost Horizon. 1966-67, created 12 paintings for Universal Studio Tour for posters and promotion; 1968, cover painting for souvenir program for Ringling Bros.,Barnum and Bailey Circus; treasurer for Living Artist Production since 1954; Exec. V.P. 22nd-Century Films, Inc. since 1968, Prod. & dir. short, Hongkong Dong. Also short subject film Dong Kingman, filmed and directed by James Wong Howe. 1993 Chinese-American Arts Council exhibition of all motion picture work. 1996, created official poster for Olympic Games.

KINGSLEY, BEN
Actor. r.n. Krishna Banji. b. Snaiton, Yorkshire, England, Dec. 31, 1943. Started career with Salford Players, amateur co. in Manchester. Turned pro in 1966 and appeared on London stage at a Chichester Festival Theatre. 1967, joined Royal Shakespeare Co., appearing in A Midsummer Night's Dream, Tempest, Measure for Measure, Merry Wives of Windsor, Volpone, Cherry Orchard, Hamlet, Othello, Judgement. On NY stage in Kean. Played Squeers in Nicholas Nickleby in 1980 in London.
PICTURES: Fear Is the Key (debut, 1972), Gandhi (Acad. Award, 1982), Betrayal, Turtle Diary, Harem, Maurice, Testimony, Pascali's Island, Without a Clue, Bugsy (Acad. Award nom.), Sneakers, Dave, Searching for Bobby Fisher (Innocent Moves), Schindler's List, Death and the Maiden, Species, Twelfth Night, The Assignment, Photographing Fairies, Parting Shots.
TELEVISION: Movies/Specials: Silas Marner, Kean, Oxbridge Blues, Camille, Murderers Among Us: The Simon Wiesenthal Story, Joseph, Moses, Tale of Sweeney Todd.

KINGSLEY, WALTER
Executive. b. New York, NY, Oct. 20, 1923. e. Phillips Acad., Andover; Amherst Coll., B.A., 1947. Charter member Big Brothers of Los Angeles. WCOP, Boston, 1948-50; Ziv Television Programs, Inc., 1950-58; pres., Independent Television Corp. (ITC), 1958-62; member bd. dir Big Brothers of Amer.; pres. Kingsley Co., 1962-66; exec. v.p. Wolper Prods. Metromedia Prods. Corp., 1966-72; faculty, Inter-Racial Council of Business Opportunity, N.Y.; 1972-82, pres., Kingsley Company, Commercial Real Estate; 1983-present, special consultant, American Film Inst.; bd. mem.: Big Brothers/Big Sisters of America; Big Brothers of Greater Los Angeles.

KINOY, ERNEST
Writer. Started career in radio writing sci. fic. programs (X Minus One, Dimension X). Wrote for nearly all early dramatic shows, including Studio One, Philco Playhouse, Playhouse 90.
PICTURES: Brother John, Buck and the Preacher, Leadbelly, White Water Summer (co-s.p.).
TELEVISION: The Defenders (Emmy Award, 1964), Naked City, Dr. Kildare, Jacob and Joseph, David the King, Roots I & II, Victory at Entebbe, Skokie, Murrow, The President's Plane is Missing, Stones for Ibarra, Gore Vidal's Lincoln, The Fatal Shore, White Water Summer, Tad.

KINSKI, NASTASSJA
Actress. r.n. Nastassja Nakszynski. b. Berlin, Germany, Jan. 24, 1960. m. prod and talent agent, Ibrahim Moussa. Daughter of late actor Klaus Kinski.
PICTURE: Falsche Bewegung (The Wrong Move; debut, 1975), To the Devil a Daughter, Passion Flower Hotel, Stay as You Are, Tess, One From the Heart, Cat People, For Your Love Only, Exposed, The Moon in the Gutter, Unfaithfully Yours, The Hotel New Hampshire, Maria's Lovers, Paris Texas, Revolution, Symphony of Love, Harem, Malady of Love, Silent Night, Torrents of Spring, On a Moonlit Night, Magdalene, The Secret, Night Sun, Faraway So Close!, Crackerjack, Terminal Velocity, The Blonde, The Ring, One Night Stand, Little Boy Blue, Fathers' Day, Somebody is Waiting.

KIRBY, BRUNO
Actor. b. New York, NY, April 28, 1949. Also acted as B. Kirby Jr., and Bruce Kirby Jr. Father is actor Bruce Kirby. On B'way 1991 in Lost in Yonkers.
PICTURES: The Harrad Experiment (debut, 1973), Cinderella Liberty, Superdad, The Godfather Part 2, Baby Blue Marine, Between the Lines, Almost Summer, Where the Buffalo Roam, Borderline, Modern Romance, This Is Spinal Tap, Birdy, Flesh + Blood, Tin Men, Good Morning Vietnam, Bert Rigby You're a Fool, When Harry Met Sally ..., We're No Angels, The Freshman, City Slickers, Hoffa (unbilled), Golden Gate, The Basketball Diaries, Donnie Brasco.
TELEVISION: Series: The Super. Movies: All My Darling Daughters, A Summer Without Boys, Some Kind of Miracle, Million Dollar Infield. Specials: Run Don't Walk (Afterschool Special), The Trap, Mastergate. Guest: Room 222, Columbo, Kojak, Emergency, It's Garry Shandling's Show, Tales From the Crypt, The Larry Sanders Show, Fallen Angels (I'll Be Waiting).

KIRK (BUSH), PHYLLIS
Actress. r.n. Phyllis Kirkegaard. b. Syracuse, NY, Sept. 18, 1926. Perfume repr. model, Conover Agcy.; B'way debut in My Name Is Aquilon followed by Point of No Return. Worked as interviewer-host on all three major networks Executive with ICPR and Stone Associates. Joined CBS News in Los Angeles, 1978; 1988 named v.p. media relations Stone/Hallinan Associates.
PICTURES: Our Very Own (debut, 1950), A Life of Her Own, Two Weeks with Love, Mrs. O'Malley and Mr. Malone, Three Guys Named Mike, About Face, The Iron Mistress, Thunder Over the Plains, House of Wax, Crime Wave, River Beat, Canyon Crossroads, Johnny Concho, Back From Eternity, City After Midnight, The Sad Sack.
TELEVISION: Series: The Red Buttons Show, The Thin Man.

KIRKLAND, SALLY
Actress. b. NY, NY, Oct. 31, 1944. e. Actors Studio, studied acting with Uta Hagen and Lee Strasberg. Achieved notoriety in the 1960s for on-stage nudity (Sweet Eros, Futz), for work in experimental off-off B'way theater and as part of Andy Warhol's inner circle. Appeared as featured actress in over 25 films and countless avant-garde shows, before winning acclaim (and Acad. Award nom.) as the star of Anna (1987). 1983 founded Sally Kirkland Acting Workshop, a traveling transcendental meditation, yoga and theatrical seminar. Formed Artists Alliance Prods. with Mark and David Buntzman, 1988.
THEATER: The Love Nest, Futz, Tom Paine, Sweet Eros, Witness, One Night Stand of a Noisy Passenger, The Justice Box, Where Has Tommy Flowers Gone?, In the Boom Boom Room (L.A.), Drama-Logue's best actress award, 1981), Largo Desolato.
PICTURES: The Thirteen Most Beautiful Woman (1964), Blue Futz!, Coming Apart, Going Home, The Young Nurses, The Way We Were, Cinderella Liberty, The Sting, Candy Stripe Nurses, Big Bad Mama, Bite the Bullet, Crazy Mama, Breakheart Pass, A Star is Born, Pipe Dreams, Hometown U.S.A., Private Benjamin, The Incredible Shrinking Woman, Human Highway, Love Letters, Fatal Games, Talking Walls, Anna, Melanie Rose (High Stakes), Crack in the Mirror (White Hot), Paint It Black, Cold Feet, Best of the Best, Revenge, Bullseye, Two Evil Eyes, JFK, In the Heat of Passion, The Player, Blast 'Em, Primary Motive, Double Threat, Forever, Cheatin' Hearts (also co-exec. prod.).
TELEVISION: Movies: Kansas City Massacre, Death Scream, Stonestreet: Who Killed the Centerfold Model?, Georgia Peaches, Heat Wave, The Haunted. Double Jeopardy, The Woman Who Loved Elvis, Double Deception. Specials: Willow B—Women in Prison, Summer, Largo Desolato. Series: Falcon Crest. Guest: Roseanne.

KIRKWOOD, GENE
Producer. The Kirkwood Company.
PICTURES: Rocky, New York New York (assoc. prod.), Comes a Horseman, Uncle Joe Shannon, The Idolmaker, A Night in Heaven, Gorky Park, The Keep, The Pope of Greenwich Village, Ironweed, UHF (co-prod.), What Makes Sammy Run, Gia a Thing of Beauty, The Duke of Deception.

KIRKWOOD, PAT
Actress, Singer. r.n. Patricia Kirkwood. b. Pendleton, Manchester, England, Feb. 24, 1921. British stage debut 1936. US cabaret debut 1954. Autobiography The Time of My Life (1999). Recorded CD Miss Show Business (1999).
THEATRE: LONDON: Cinderella, Black Velvet, Top of the World, Lady Behave, Let's Face It, Happidrome, Starlight Roof, Roundabout, Ace of Clubs, Fancy Free, Peter Pan, Wonderful Town, Chrysanthemum, Pools Paradise, Villa Sleeps Four, Lock Up Your Daughters, The Constant Wife, The Rumpus, Hay Fever, Lady Frederick, A Chorus of Murder, Move Over Mrs. Markham, Pal Joey, The Cabinet Minister, An Evening with Pat Kirkwood, A Talent to Amuse, A Glamorous Night with Evelyn Laye and Friends, Glamorous Nights of Music, Noel/Cole-Let's Do It.
PICTURES: Save A Little Sunshine, Me and My Pal, Band Waggon, Come On George, Flight from Folly, No Leave No Love, Once A Sinner, Stars in Your Eyes, After the Ball, To See Such Fun.
TELEVISION: Starlight, Two of Everything, What's My Line?, The Pat Kirkwood Show, Our Marie, Pygmalion, The Great Little Tilley, From Me To You, Pat, Looks Familiar, Pebble Mill, Paul Merton's Palladium Story, This Is Your Life (subject).

KITT, EARTHA
Actress, Singer. b. Columbia, SC, Jan. 26, 1928. Professional career started as dancer in Katherine Dunham group; toured U.S., Mexico & Europe with group, then opened night club in Paris; in Orson Welles stage prod. of Faust (European tour). N.Y. night clubs before B'way debut in New Faces of 1952. Author: Thursday's Child, A Tart Is Not a Sweet, Alone with Me, Confessions of a Sex Kitten.
THEATRE: NY: New Faces of 1952, Shinbone Alley, Mrs. Patterson, The Skin of Our Teeth, The Owl and the Pussycat, Timbuktu.
PICTURES: New Faces (debut, 1954), The Mark of the Hawk (Accused), St. Louis Blues, Anna Lucasta, Saint of Devil's Island, Synanon, Uncle Tom's Cabin, Up the Chastity Belt, Friday Foster, The Last Resort, The Serpent Warriors, The Pink Chiquitas (voice), Master of Dragonard Hill, Erik the Viking, Ernest Scared Stupid, Boomerang, Fatal Instinct, Unzipped, Harriet the Spy, Ill Gotten Gains, I Woke Up Early the Day I Died, Kingdom of the Sun.
TELEVISION: Movies: Lt. Schuster's Wife, To Kill a Cop. Guest: Batman (as Catwoman), I Spy, Miami Vice.

KLEES, ROBERT E.
Executive. b. New York, NY, Feb. 21, 1927. e. Duke U., 1947-51. Univ. of CA Graduate Sch. of Mgt., 1973-75. U.S. Navy, 1944-46; Union Carbide Corp., 1951-57; Beckman Instruments Inc., 1957-69; International Biophysics Corp, 1969-73; sr. v.p., mktg., Deluxe Laboratories Inc., div. of 20th Century Fox, 1975-83. Retired member of AMPAS, ACE, AFI, ASC, SMPTE.

KLEIN, ALLEN
Producer. b. New Jersey, Dec. 18, 1931. e. Upsala. Pres. ABKCO Films, a division of ABKCO Music & Records, Inc.
PICTURES: Force of Impulse, Pity Me Not, Charlie is My Darling, Stranger in Town, Sympathy for the Devil, Mrs. Brown You've Got a Lovely Daughter, The Stranger Returns, The Silent Stranger, Come Together, Pearl & The Pole, Let It Be, Gimme Shelter, El Topo, Blind Man, The Concert for Bangladesh, The Holy Mountain, The Greek Tycoon, Personal Best, It Had to Be You, The Rolling Stones Rock and Roll Circus.

KLEIN, HAROLD J.
Executive. b. New York, NY, e. U. of West Virginia, New York Law Sch. Reviewer, sales staff. Showman's Trade Review; booker, Brandt Theatres; booker, later vice-pres., gen. mgr., JJ Theatres, 1941-59; account exec., exec. v.p., dir. of world-wide sales, ABC Films, Inc., N.Y., Pres., Klein Film Assn.; exec. v.p., Plitt Theatres, Inc. to Nov., 1985; pres., H.J.K. Film Associates, also acting consultant to P.E.G. (Plitt Entertainment Gp.). Retired.

KLEIN, MALCOLM C.
Executive. b. Los Angeles, CA, Nov. 22, 1927. e. UCLA, grad., 1948; U. of Denver. Prod. dir. management, KLAC-TV (KCOP), L.A., 1948-52; acct. exec., KABC-TV, 1952-56; asst. gen. sales mgr., KABC-TV, 1956-59; exec. v.p. gen. mgr., NTA Broadcasting, N.Y., 1959; v.p.; gen. mgr., RKO-General-KHJ-TV, 1960. Joined National General Corp. 1968, v.p. creative services and marketing; pres. National General TV Prods. Inc.; pres. NGC Broadcasting Corp. 1971, pres. Filmways TV Presentations. 1972, pres. Malcolm C. Klein & Assoc. mgmt. & mktg. consultants. 1973, gen'l. exec. Sterling Recreation Org. & Gen'l Mgr. Broadcast Division. 1976, pres., American Song Festival. Member of faculty, UCLA, USC. Exec. v.p., Telease Inc. & American Subscription Television. 1981, sr. v.p., mng. dir., STAR-TV (subscription TV). 1982, sr. v.p., InterAmerican Satellite TV Network. 1983, pres. Malcolm C. Klein & Assoc., management consultant. Exec. dir. programming, Interactive Network Inc; v.p., bus. development, Interactive Network Inc. 1995, exec. v.p., Vivid Travel Network. Consultant, Central European Media. Member of bd., Media Shower Inc.

KLEIN, ROBERT
Actor, Comedian. b. New York, NY, Feb. 8, 1942. e. Alfred U, Yale Drama School. Was member of Chicago's Second City comedy group. Comedy albums: Child of the '50s (Grammy nom.), Mind Over Matter, New Teeth, Let's Not Make Love.
THEATRE: *NY*: The Apple Tree, Morning Noon and Night, New Faces of 1968, They're Playing Our Song (Tony Award nom.), The Sisters Rosensweig.
PICTURES: The Landlord, The Owl and the Pussycat, Rivals, The Bell Jar, Hooper, Nobody's Perfekt, The Last Unicorn (voice), Tales from the Darkside—The Movie, Radioland Murders, Mixed Nuts, Jeffrey.
TELEVISION: *Series*: Comedy Tonight, Robert Klein Time, TV's Bloopers and Practical Jokes, Sisters. *Movies*: Your Place or Mine, Poison Ivy, This Wife for Hire. *Guest*: The Tonight Show, ABC Comedy Special, George Burns Comedy Week, Twilight Zone, Late Night With David Letterman. Also appeared in HBO comedy specials.

KLEINER, HARRY
Writer, Producer. b. Philadelphia, PA, Sept. 10, 1916. e. Temple U., B.S.; Yale U., M.F.A.
PICTURES: Fallen Angel, The Street With No Name, Red Skies of Mountain, Kangaroo, Miss Sadie Thompson, Salome, Carmen Jones, The Violent Men, The Garment Jungle (also prod.), Cry Tough (also prod.), The Rabbit Trap (prod. only), Ice Palace, Fever in the Blood, Fantastic Voyage, Bullitt, Le Mans, Extreme Prejudice, Red Heat.
TELEVISION: *Writer*: Rosenberg Trial.

KLEISER, RANDAL
Director, Producer. b. Lebanon, PA, July 20, 1946. e. U. of Southern California. For Disney Theme Parks dir. 70mm 3-D film Honey I Shrunk the Audience.
PICTURES: Street People (s.p.). *Director*: Grease, The Blue Lagoon, Summer Lovers (also s.p.), Grandview U.S.A., Flight of the Navigator, North Shore (exec. prod., co-story only), Big Top Pee-Wee, Getting It Right (also co-prod.), White Fang, Return to the Blue Lagoon (exec. prod. only), Honey I Blew Up the Kid, It's My Party, Shadow of Doubt.
TELEVISION: *Movies*: All Together Now, Dawn: Portrait of a Teenage Runaway, The Boy in the Plastic Bubble, The Gathering. *Series*: Marcus Welby, M.D., The Rookies, Starsky and Hutch, Family.

KLINE, FRED W.
Publicist. b. Oakland, CA, May 17, 1918. e. U. of California, Berkeley. M.P. pub. rel. since 1931; pres. & owner The Fred Kline Agency; pres. Kline Communications Corp.; Kline Communications Corp.; Fred W. Kline Prod., Inc.; Capitol News Service, Sacramento; L.A. News Bureau; Capitol Radio News Service, Inc.; Advisor, Calif. Film Commission. Member, Regional Filming Task Force Committee, Los Angeles City Council.

KLINE, KEVIN
Actor. b. St. Louis, MO, Oct. 24, 1947. m. actress Phoebe Cates. e. Indiana U, School of Music. Studied at Juilliard Drama Center (1970-72), and became founding member of John Houseman's The Acting Company, touring in classics, incl. The School for Scandal, She Stoops to Conquer, The Lower Depths, The Way of the World. Associate prod., NY Shakespeare Festival, 1993-1997.
THEATER: Understudied Raul Julia in Lincoln Center's The Threepenny Opera; The Three Sisters (B'way debut, 1973), On the Twentieth Century (Tony Award, 1978), Loose Ends, The Pirates of Penzance (Tony Award, 1981), Richard III, Henry V (Central Park), Arms and the Man, Hamlet, Much Ado About Nothing, Hamlet (1990, also dir.), Measure for Measure.
PICTURES: Sophie's Choice (debut, 1982), The Pirates of Penzance, The Big Chill, Silverado, Violets Are Blue, Cry Freedom, A Fish Called Wanda (Acad. Award for Best Supporting Actor, 1988), The January Man, I Love You to Death, Soapdish, Grand Canyon, Consenting Adults, Chaplin, Dave, George Balanchine's The Nutcracker (narrator), Princess Caraboo, French Kiss, Fierce Creatures, The Hunchback of Notre Dame (voice), The Ice Storm, In & Out, Looking for Richard, The Wild Wild West, A Midsummer Night's Dream.
TELEVISION: *Series*: Search For Tomorrow (1976-77). *Specials*: The Time of Your Life, Hamlet (also co-dir.).

KLUGMAN, JACK
Actor. b. Philadelphia, PA, April 27, 1922. e. Carnegie Tech. Much tv work in 1950's incl. Captain Video, Tom Corbett— Space Cadet, U.S. Steel Hour, Kraft Television Theatre, Playhouse 90.
THEATRE: *B'way*: Saint Joan, Stevedore, Mister Roberts, Gypsy, I'm Not Rappaport, Three Men on a Horse. *Tour/Stock*: The Odd Couple.
PICTURES: Timetable (debut, 1956), Twelve Angry Men, Cry Terror, The Scarface Mob, Days of Wine and Roses, I Could Go on Singing, The Yellow Canary, Act One, Hail Mafia, The Detective, The Split, Goodbye Columbus, Who Says I Can't Ride a Rainbow?, Two Minute Warning.
TELEVISION: *Series*: The Greatest Gift (daytime serial; 1954-55), Harris Against the World, The Odd Couple (2 Emmy Awards: 1971, 1973), Quincy M.E., You Again? *Guest*: The Defenders (Emmy Award, 1964), The Twilight Zone, The FBI, Ben Casey, 90 Bristol Court. *Movies*: Fame Is the Name of the Game, Poor Devil, The Underground Man, One of My Wives Is Missing, The Odd Couple: Together Again, Parallel Lives. *Mini-Series*: Around the World in 80 Days.

KNIGHT, SHIRLEY
Actress. b. Goessell, KS, July 5, 1936. e. Lake Forest Coll., D.F.A., 1978. Won 1976 Tony Award for Kennedy's Children; Joseph Jefferson Award for Landscape of the Body, 1977; New Jersey Drama Critics Awards for A Streetcar Named Desire, 1979.
PICTURES: Five Gates to Hell (debut, 1959), Ice Palace, The Dark at the Top of the Stairs (Acad. Award nom.) The Couch, Sweet Bird of Youth (Acad. Award nom.), House of Women, Flight from Ashiya, The Group, Dutchman (Venice Film Fest. Award), Petulia, The Counterfeit Killer, The Rain People, Juggernaut, Secrets, Beyond the Poseidon Adventure, Endless Love, The Sender, Prisoners, Color of Night, Stuart Saves His Family, Diabolique, Somebody Is Waiting, The Man Who Counted, As Good as It Gets, Little Boy Blue.
TELEVISION: *Movies*: The Outsider, Shadow Over Elveron, Friendly Persuasion, Medical Story, Return to Earth, 21 Hours at Munich, The Defection of Simas Kudirka, Champions: A Love Story, Playing for Time (Emmy nom.), Billionaire Boys Club, Bump in the Night, Shadow of a Doubt, To Save a Child, When Love Kills: The Seduction of John Hearn, A Mother's Revenge, Baby Brokers, The Yarn Princess, A Part of the Family, Children of the Dust, Indictment: The McMartin Trial (Emmy Award, 1995; Golden Glove Award, 1996), Ties That Bind, Tim, The Haunting of Patricia Johnson. *Specials*: The Country Girl, The Lie. *Guest*: The Equalizer (Emmy nom.), thirtysomething (Emmy Award), Law and Order (Emmy nom.), NYPD Blue (Emmy Award, 1995), Cybill, Outer Limits Tribute.

KNOTTS, DON
Actor. b. Morgantown, WV, July 21, 1924. e. WV U., U. of AZ. Drafted into U.S. Army where became part of show called Stars and Gripes, teamed with comedian Mickey Shaughnessy. After schooling resumed was offered teaching fellowship but went to New York to try acting instead. Started out in radio show Bobby Benson and the B Bar B's. Appeared on TV, leading to role in No Time for Sergeants on B'way; appeared in film version.
PICTURES: No Time for Sergeants (debut, 1958), Wake Me When It's Over, The Last Time I Saw Archie, It's a Mad Mad Mad Mad World, Move Over Darling, The Incredible Mr. Limpet, The Ghost and Mr. Chicken, The Reluctant Astronaut, The Shakiest Gun in the West, The Love God?, How to Frame a Figg (also co-story), The Apple Dumpling Gang, No Deposit No Return, Gus, Herbie Goes to Monte Carlo, Hot Lead and Cold Feet, The Apple Dumpling Gang Rides Again, The Prize Fighter, Ther Private Eyes, Cannonball Run II, Pinocchio and the Emperor of the Night (voice), Big Bully.
TELEVISION: *Series*: Search for Tomorrow (1953-55), The Steve Allen Show, The Andy Griffith Show (5 Emmy Awards: 1961, 1962, 1963, 1966, 1967), The Don Knotts Show, Three's Company, What a Country, Matlock. *Movies*: I Love a Mystery, Return to Mayberry.

KOCH, HOWARD W.
Producer, Director. b. New York, NY, April 11, 1916. Runner on Wall St. Began film career in Universal's contracts and playdate dept. in NY; asst. cutter, 20th-Fox; asst. dir., 20th-Fox, Eagle Lion, MGM; 2nd unit dir., freelance; In 1953, joined Aubrey Schenck Prod. forming Bel Air Prods., made films for U.A.; 1961-64, prod. Frank Sinatra Enterprises; v.p., chg. prod., Paramount Pictures Corp., 1964-66, Past pres. of the Academy of Motion Picture Arts and Sciences, 1977-79. 1977, elected to the National Board of Directors Guild of America for two year term. 1980 honored by NATO as prod. of year. 1985 Silver Medallion Award of Honor, Motion Picture Television Fund. Produced eight Academy Award shows, 1972-1983. Has had a 24 year relationship with Paramount as exec., prod., and dir. 1990, received Jean Hersholt Humanitarian Award, honored by Amer. Society of Cinematographers. 1991: Frank Capra Award from Directors Guild, Motion Picture Showmanship Award from the Publicists Guild; 1995: David O. Selznick Lifetime Achievement Award from the Producers Guild.
PICTURES: *Executive Producer*: Sergeants 3, The Manchurian Candidate, Come Blow Your Horn, X-15, Robin and the 7 Hoods, None But the Brave, The President's Analyst, For Those Who Think Young, Dragonslayer. *Producer*: War Paint, Beachhead, Yellow Tomahawk, Desert Sands, Fort Yuma, Frontier Scout, Ghost Town, Broken Star, Crimes Against Joe, Three Bad Sisters, Emergency Hospital, Rebel in Town, The Black Sheep, Pharaoh's Curse, Tomahawk Trail, Revolt at Fort Laramie, War Drums, Voodoo Island, Hellbound, The Dalton Girls, The Odd Couple, On a Clear Day You Can See Forever, Plaza Suite, Star Spangled Girl, Last of the Red Hot Lovers, Jacqueline Susann's Once Is Not Enough, Some Kind of Hero, Airplane II: The Sequel, Collision Course. A Howard W. Koch *Production*: A New Leaf, Airplane!, Ghost. *Director*: Jungle Heat, Shield for Murder, Big House USA, Fort Bowie, Violent Road, Untamed Youth, Born Reckless, Frankenstein 1970, Andy Hardy Comes Home, The Last Mile, Girl in Black Stockings, Badge 373 (also prod.), The Beautician & the Beast.
TELEVISION: *Director*: Miami Undercover, The Untouchables, Maverick, Cheyenne, Hawaiian Eye. *Mini-Series*: Prod.: The Pirate, Hollywood Wives, Crossings. *Movie*: The Odd Couple: Together Again (prod.). *Specials*: *Prod.*: Ol' Blue Eyes Is Back, Oscar's Best Actors (also dir.), Oscar's Best Movies (also dir.), Who Loves Ya Baby, On the Road with Bing (also dir.), The Stars Salute the Olympics.

KOCH, HOWARD W., JR.
Producer. b. Los Angeles, CA, Dec. 14, 1945. Was asst. dir. and in other industry posts before turning to production. Pres. & chief exec. off., Rastar (Peggy Sue Got Married, The Secret of My Success, Nothing in Common, Violets Are Blue, Amazing Chuck and Grace prod. under presidency); 1987, set up own prod. co. at De Laurentiis Entertainment Group. Oct. 1987: named president of the De Laurentiis Entertainment Group, Resigned April 1988 to produce independently.
PICTURES: Heaven Can Wait, The Other Side of Midnight, The Frisco Kid (exec. prod.). *Co-prod./prod.:* The Idolmaker, Gorky Park, Honky Tonk Freeway, The Keep, A Night in Heaven, The Pope of Greenwich Village, Rooftops, The Long Walk Home, Necessary Roughness, Wayne's World, The Temp, Sliver, Wayne's World 2, Losing Isaiah, Virtuosity, Primal Fear.

KOCH, JOANNE
Executive Director, The Film Society of Lincoln Center. b. NY, NY, Oct. 7, 1929. e. Goddard College, B.A. political science, 1950. Dept. of Film, Museum of Modern Art, as circulation asst., film researcher, motion picture stills archivist, 1950. Early 1960s, technical dir., film dept. MOMA, supervised the implementation of MOMA's film preservation program. 1967, asst. to publisher of Grove Press, active in preparation of Grove's case in I Am Curious Yellow censorship trial. Joined film div., Grove, first in distribution then as tech. dir. and prod. coord. 1971 joined Film Society of Lincoln Center as prog. dir. of Movies-in-the-Parks. 1971 made admin. dir. Exec. dir. of N.Y. Film Festival, Film Comment magazine, Film-in-Education, New Directors/New Films, annual Film Society Tribute and Walter Reade Theater at Lincoln Center.

KOENEKAMP, FRED J.
Cinematographer. b. Los Angeles, CA, Nov. 11, 1922. Father was special effects cinematographer Hans F. Koenekamp. Member of American Society of Cinematographers.
PICTURES: Doctor You've Got to Be Kidding, Sol Madrid, Stay Away Joe, Live a Little Love a Little, Heaven With a Gun, The Great Bank Robbery, Patton (Acad. Award nom.), Beyond the Valley of the Dolls, Flap, Skin Game, Billy Jack, Happy Birthday Wanda June, Stand Up and Be Counted, Kansas City Bomber, The Magnificent Seven Ride, Rage, Harry in Your Pocket, Papillon, Uptown Saturday Night, The Towering Inferno (Acad. Award, 1974), The Wild McCullochs, Doc Savage, Posse, Embryo, Fun With Dick and Jane, The Other Side of Midnight, Islands in the Streams (Acad. Award nom.), The Bad News Bears in Breaking Training, The Dominic Principle, White Line Fever, The Swarm, The Champ, The Amityville Horror, Love and Bullets, When Time Ran Out, The Hunter, First Family, First Monday in October, Carbon Copy, Yes Giorgio, It Came From Hollywood, Two of a Kind, The Adventures of Buckaroo Banzai: Across the 8th Dimension, Stewardess School, Listen to Me, Welcome Home, Flight of the Intruder.
TELEVISION: *Movies:* Disaster on the Coastline, Tales of the Gold Monkey, Money on the Side, Return of the Man from U.N.C.L.E., Summer Fantasies, Whiz Kids, Flight 90—Disaster on the Potomac, Obsessive Love, City Killer, Las Vegas Strip War, A Touch of Scandal, Not My Kid, Hard Time on Planet Earth (pilot), Return of the Shaggy Dog, Foreign Exchange, Splash Too, Hard Times, many others. *Series:* The Man From U.N.C.L.E. (Emmy nom.)

KOENIG, WALTER
Actor, Writer. b. Chicago, IL, Sept. 14, 1936. e. Grinnell Coll. (IA), U. of California. Performed in summer stock; after college enrolled at Neighborhood Playhouse, N.Y.; first acting job in TV's Day in Court. *Books:* Chekov's Enterprise, Buck Alice and the Actor Robot. Creator and writer of comic book series Raver.
PICTURES: Strange Lovers, The Deadly Honeymoon, Star Trek—The Motion Picture, Star Trek II: The Wrath of Khan, Star Trek III: The Search for Spock, Star Trek IV: The Voyage Home, Star Trek V: the Final Frontier, Moontrap, Star Trek VI: The Undiscovered Country, Star Trek: Generations, Drawing Down the Moon.
TELEVISION: *Series:* Star Trek. *Guest:* Colombo, Medical Center, Ironside, Mannix, Alfred Hitchcock Presents, Mr. Novak, Ben Casey, The Untouchables, Combat, Babylon V. *Movies:* The Questor Tapes, Goodbye Raggedy Ann. *Writer:* Family, The Class of '65, The Powers of Matthew Starr.

KOHN, HOWARD EDWARD, II
Executive. b. McKeesport, PA, Oct. 25, 1920. e. NYU. National dir. of adv., publicity, roadshow dept., United Artists; indep. prod., Hidden Fear, 1957; pres. Lioni-Warren-Kohn, Inc., 1958; national roadshow dir., Columbia Pictures, Porgy and Bess, 1959; World wide co-ordinator, national co-ordinator adv. & pub. for El Cid, 1961; named world wide co-ordinator adv., pub. all Samuel Bronston Productions, 1962; pres., Starpower Inc., 1968; exec. v.p., Avanti Films, 1970; v.p. Avariac Prods., 1971; pres., Blossom Films, 1973. Elected member of ASCAP, 1975. Pres., Avanti Associates, 1976. Pres. Channel Television Prods., Inc., 1985; pres. Search Television Prods. 1988. Pres. Avanti Music Co. 1991. Exec. v.p., Petard TV and Video Prods.

KOHNER, PANCHO
Producer. b. Los Angeles, CA, Jan. 7, 1939. e. U. of Southern California, U. of Mexico, Sorbonne.
PICTURES: The Bridge in the Jungle (also dir., s.p.), The Lie, Victoria (also s.p.), Mr. Sycamore (also dir., s.p.), St. Ives, The White Buffalo, Love and Bullets, Why Would I Lie?, 10 to Midnight, The Evil That Men Do, Murphy's Law, Assassination, Death Wish IV, Messenger of Death, Kinjite.

KOHNER, SUSAN
Actress, b. Los Angeles, CA. Nov. 11, 1936. m. designer & author John Weitz. Sons Paul and Christopher Weitz are screenwriters. Mother, Lupita Tovar, was one of Mexico's leading film actresses. Father was talent rep. Paul Kohner. e. U. of California, 1954-55. Received Golden Globe Awards, 1959 and 1960. Retired from acting in 1964. Co-chair, Juilliard Council, Juilliard Sch. NY.
THEATER: Love Me Little, He Who Gets Slapped, A Quiet Place, Rose Tatoo, Bus Stop, St. Joan, Sunday in New York, Take Her She's Mine, Pullman Car, Hiawatha, as well as summer stock.
PICTURES: To Hell and Back (debut, 1955), The Last Wagon, Trooper Hook, Dino, Imitation of Life (Acad. Award nom.), The Big Fisherman, The Gene Krupa Story, All the Fine Young Cannibals, By Love Possessed, Freud.
TELEVISION: Alcoa Hour, Schlitz Playhouse, Four Star Theatre, Matinee Theatre, Climax, Suspicion, Playhouse 90, Route 66, Dick Powell Theatre.

KONCHALOVSKY, ANDREI
Director, Writer. a.k.a. Mikhalkov Konchalovski. b. Moscow, Soviet Union, Aug. 20, 1937. Great grandfather: painter Sourikov; grandfather: painter Konchalovski; father is a writer; mother poet Natalia Konchalovskaia; brother is director Nikita Mikhalkov. e. as pianist Moscow Conservatoire, 1947-57; State Film Sch. (VGIK) under Mikhail Romm (1964). Dir. debut with 1961 short film The Boy and the Pigeon. Worked as scriptwriter during 1960s especially with Andrei Tarkovsky. 1962: asst. to Tarkovsky on Ivan's Childhood. In 1980, moved to US. In 1991, moved back to Russia.
THEATRE/OPERA: The Seagull (Theatre de L'Odeon, Paris), Eugene Onegin (La Scala, Milan), La Pique Dame (La Scala, Milan & Bastille Opera, Pairs).
PICTURES: *Writer:* The Steamroller and the Violin, Andrey Rublev, Tashkent City of Bread, The Song of Manshuk, The End of Chieftain. *Director:* The First Teacher (feature debut, 1965), Asya's Happiness, A Nest of Gentlefolk, Uncle Vanya, Romance for Lovers, Siberiade (Cannes Film Fest. Award, 1979), Maria's Lovers, Runaway Train, Duet for One, Shy People (also co-s.p.), Tango and Cash, Homer and Eddie, Ryaba, My Chicken (writer, dir.), The Inner Circle (also co-s.p.), Asia and the Hen with the Golden Eyes, Lumiere & Company..
TELEVISION: Split Cherry Terry (short). *Mini-series:* The Odyssey (Part I & II, Emmy Award, 1996).

KONIGSBERG, FRANK
Executive. b. Kew Gardens, NY, March 10, 1933. e. Yale, Yale Law Sch. Worked as lawyer at CBS for six years; moved to NBC 1960-65 in legal dept. as dir. prog. and talent administration. Left to package TV special for Artists Agency Rep. (later AFA) in Los Angeles; sr. v.p. of West Coast office seven years. Executive producer of many TV series, pilots, variety specials and made-for-TV movies. Formed own Konigsberg Company. Theatrical film debut as prod., Joy of Sex (1984).
TELEVISION: *Movies* (all exec. prod.): Pearl, Ellis Island, Bing Crosby: His Life and Legend, Dummy, Before and After, Guyana Tragedy, A Christmas Without Snow, The Pride of Jesse Hallam, Hard Case, Divorce Wars, Coming Out of the Ice, Onassis: The Richest Man in the World, Where the Hell's That Gold?!!?, Senior Prom, Babycakes. *Series* (exec. prod.): It's Not Easy, Breaking Away, Dorothy.

KOPELSON, ANNE
Producer. m. Producer, Arnold Kopelson.
PICTURES: *Exec. prod.:* Outbreak, Seven, Eraser, Murder at 1600, Mad City, Devil's Advocate, A Perfect Murder, U.S. Marshals.
TELEVISION: *Movies:* Past Tense.

KOPELSON, ARNOLD
Producer, Financier, Intl. Distributor. b. New York, NY, Feb. 14, 1935. e. New York Law Sch., J.D., 1959; NYU, B.S. 1956. Has executive-produced, produced, packaged, developed or distributed with wife, Anne Kopelson over 1400 films. Handled intl. dist. of Twice in a Lifetime, Salvador, Warlock, Triumph of the Spirit and prod. Platoon. Chmn. Arnold Kopelson Prods., Co-chmn. Inter-Ocean Film Sales, Ltd. Named NATO/ShoWest Producer of the Year, 1994.
PICTURES: *Exec. Prod.:* The Legacy, Lost and Found, Night of the Juggler, Dirty Tricks, Final Assignment, Gimme an "F", Fire Birds, Warlock. *Producer:* Foolin' Around, Platoon (Acad. Award for Best Picture, 1986), Triumph of the Spirit, Out for Justice, Falling Down, The Fugitive (Acad. Award nom.), Outbreak, Seven, Eraser, Murder at 1600, Mad City, The Devil's Advocate, A Perfect Murder, U.S. Marshals.
TELEVISION: *Movie:* Past Tense.

KOPLOVITZ, KAY
Executive. b. Milwaukee, WI, April 11, 1945. e. U. Wis., 1967, BA, Mich. State U., MA, Communications, 1968. Radio/TV prod., WTMJ-TV, Milwaukee 1967. Ed. Comm. Satellite Corp. 1968-72. Dir. Community Svcs. UA Columbia Cablevision 1973-75. VP, Exec. dir. UA Columbia Satellite Services, Inc. 1977-80. Founder, pres., CEO USA Network and Sci-Fi Channel 1980-1998. Member Nat'l Cable TV Assn. 1984-. Nat'l Acad. TV Arts and Scis. 1984-95. Women in Cable 1979-83.

KOPPEL, TED
TV News Correspondent, Anchor, Host. b. Lancashire, England, Feb. 8, 1940. To U.S. in 1953; became citizen, 1963. e. Syracuse U, Stanford U. Started as writer and news correspondent for WMCA radio in NYC. Joined ABC News in New York, 1963, serving as correspondent in Vietnam, 1967, 1969-71; Miami Bureau chief, 1968; Hong Kong Bureau chief, 1969-71; diplomatic correspondent, 1971-76, 1977-79. Anchor of NBC Saturday Night News, 1976-77. Host of Nightline, beginning in 1980. Author: The Wit and Wisdom of Adlai Stevenson, In the National Interest.
TELEVISION: Series: ABC News (1971-80), ABC Saturday Night News (1975-77); Nightline (1980-), 20/20 (1986). Host/anchor/writer of many ABC news specials.

KOPPLE, BARBARA
Director, Producer.
PICTURES: Dir.: Harlan County USA (also prod., Acad. Award, Best Doc., LA Film Crits. Special Award, 1976), American Dream (Acad. Award, Best Doc., 1990, Directors' Guild Award, 1992, Cannes Film Festival Grand Jury Prize, 1991), Beyond JFK: The Question of Conspiracy, Woodstock '94 (also prod.), Wild Man Blues. Prod.: Fallen Champ: The Mike Tyson Story (Directors' Guild Award, 1994).
TELEVISION: Movies, dir.: Keeping On. Series, dir.: Homicide: Life in the Street (Directors' Guild Award, 1998). Mini-series, dir.: A Century of Women.

KORMAN, HARVEY
Actor, Director. b. Chicago, IL, Feb. 15, 1927. e. Wright Junior Coll. Began dramatic studies at Chicago's Goodman Sch. of Drama at the Arts Inst. Acted in small roles in Broadway plays and did TV commercials until break came as comedian for Danny Kaye Show on TV. Staged comedy sketches for Steve Allen variety series in 1967. Became Carol Burnett's leading man on her show 1967-77. Directed two episodes of The New Dick Van Dyke Show.
PICTURES: Living Venus (debut, 1961), Gypsy, Lord Love a Duck, The Last of the Secret Agents?, The Man Called Flintstone (voice), Three Bites of the Apple, Don't Just Stand There, The April Fools, Blazing Saddles, Huckleberry Finn, High Anxiety, Americathon, Herbie Goes Bananas, First Family, History of the World Part I, Trail of the Pink Panther, Curse of the Pink Panther, The Longshot, Munchie, The Flintstones (voice), Radioland Murders, Dracula: Dead and Loving It.
TELEVISION: Series: The Danny Kaye Show, The Carol Burnett Show (4 Emmy Awards: 1969, 1971, 1972, 1974), The Tim Conway Show, Mama's Family, Leo and Liz in Beverly Hills, The Nutt House. Movies: Three's a Crowd, Suddenly Single, The Love Boat (pilot), Bud and Lou, The Invisible Woman, Carpool, Crash Course, Based on an Untrue Story. Special: The Carol Burnett Show: A Reunion (also co-exec. prod.).

KORMAN, LEWIS J.
Executive. b. 1945. Partner, Kaye, Scholer, Fierman, Hays & Handler 1978; founding partner, Gelberg & Abrams where pioneered dev. of public limited partnerships, Delphi Partners, to help finance Columbia Pictures' and Tri-Star Pictures' films. 1986, became consultant to Tri-Star involved in negotiations that led to acquisition of Loews Theatre Corp. that year. Joined Tri-Star, 1987, as sr. exec. v.p. 1988 appt. to additional post of COO and named dir. of Columbia Pictures Entertainment Inc.; 1989 also became chmn. Motion Picture Group. 1990, resigned his positions after Columbia sale to Sony. Co-founder, pres. & COO of Savoy Pictures Ent., Inc., 1992.

KORTY, JOHN
Director, Producer, Writer, Animator. b. Lafayette, IN, June 22, 1936. e. Antioch Coll, B.A. 1959. President, Korty Films. Documentary: Who Are the DeBolts? And Where Did They Get Nineteen Kids? (Acad. Award: 1977; Emmy & DGA Awards: 1978-79). Short Films: The Language of Faces (AFSC, 1961), Imogen Cunningham: Photographer (AFI grant, 1970), The Music School. Animation: Breaking the Habit (Oscar nom.), Twice Upon a Time. PICTURES: Crazy Quilt (1966), Funnyman, Riverrun, Alex and the Gypsy, Oliver's Story, Twice Upon a Time.
TELEVISION: Movies: The People, Go Ask Alice, Class of '63, The Autobiography of Miss Jane Pittman (Emmy & DGA Awards, 1974), Farewell to Manzanar (Humanitas, Christopher Awards), Forever, A Christmas Without Snow (also writer, prod.), The Haunting Passion, Second Sight: A Love Story, The Ewok Adventure, Resting Place, Baby Girl Scott, Eye on the Sparrow, Winnie, Cast the First Stone, A Son's Promise, Line of Fire: The Morris Dees Story, Long Road Home, Deadly Matrimony, They, Getting Out, Redwood Curtain, Scrooge, Oklahoma City: A Survivor's Story.

KOTCHEFF, TED
Director. r.n. William Theodore Kotcheff. b. Toronto, Canada, April 7, 1931. Ent. TV ind. 1952. After five years with Canadian Broadcasting Corp. joined ABC-TV in London, 1957.
THEATER: London: Progress the Park, Play with a Tiger, Luv, Maggie May, The Au Pair Man, Have You Any Dirty Washing, Mother Dear?
PICTURES: Tiara Tahiti (debut, 1963), Life at the Top, Two Gentlemen Sharing, Wake in Fright, Outback, Billy Two Hats, The Apprenticeship of Duddy Kravitz, Fun with Dick and Jane, Who Is Killing the Great Chefs of Europe?, North Dallas Forty (also co-s.p.), First Blood, Split Image (also prod.), Uncommon Valor (also exec. prod.), Joshua Then and Now, The Check is in the Mail (prod. only), Switching Channels, Winter People, Weekend at Bernie's (also actor), Folks!, The Shooter, The Populist.
TELEVISION: Movies: A Family of Cops, A Husband a Wife and a Lover, Borrowed Hearts, The Return of Alex Kelly. Specials: Of Mice and Men, Desperate Hours, The Human Voice.

KOTEAS, ELIAS
Actor. b. Montreal, Quebec, Canada, 1961. e. AADA.
PICTURES: One Magic Christmas, Some Kind of Wonderful, Gardens of Stone, Tucker: The Man and His Dream, Full Moon in Blue Water, Malarek, Blood Red, Friends Lovers and Lunatics, Teenage Mutant Ninja Turtles, Backstreet Dreams, Desperate Hours, Look Who's Talking Too, Almost an Angel, The Adjuster, Teenage Mutant Ninja Turtles III, Chain of Desire, Camilla, Exotica, The Prophecy, Hit Me, Crash, Gattaca, The Thin Red Line, Fallen, Apt Pupil.

KOTTO, YAPHET
Actor. b. New York, NY, Nov. 15, 1937. Has many stage credits, including starring roles on Broadway in The Great White Hope, The Zulu and the Zayda. Off-B'way: Blood Knot, Black Monday, In White America, A Good Place To Raise a Boy.
PICTURES: The Limit (also prod.), 4 for Texas, Nothing But a Man, 5 Card Stud, Thomas Crown Affair, The Liberation of L. B. Jones, Man and Boy, Across 110th Street, Bone, Live and Let Die, Truck Turner, Report to the Commissioner, Sharks' Treasure, Friday Foster, Drum, Monkey Hustle, Blue Collar, Alien, Brubaker, Fighting Back, Star Chamber, Eye of the Tiger, Warning Sign, Prettykill, The Running Man, Midnight Run, Nightmare of the Devil (also prod., dir.), Terminal Entry, Jigsaw, A Whisper to a Scream, Tripwire, Ministry of Vengeance, Hangfire, Freddy's Dead, Almost Blue, Intent to Kill, The Puppet Masters, Two If By Sea.
TELEVISION: Series: Homicide. Movies: Night Chase, Raid on Entebbe, Rage, Playing With Fire, The Park Is Mine, Women of San Quentin, Badge of the Assassin, Harem, Desperado, Perry Mason: The Case of the Scandalous Scoundrel, Prime Target, After the Shock, Chrome Soldiers, It's Nothing Personal, Extreme Justice, The American Clock, The Corpse Had a Familiar Face, Deadline for Murder: From the Files of Edna Buchanan. Guest: Alfred Hitchcock Presents.

KOVACS, LASZLO
Cinematographer. b. Hungary, May 14, 1933. Came to U.S. 1957; naturalized 1963. e. Acad. Drama and M.P. Arts, Budapest, MA 1956.
PICTURES: Hell's Angels on Wheels, Hell's Bloody Devils, Psych Out, The Savage Seven, Targets, A Man Called Dagger, Single Room Furnished, Easy Rider, That Cold Day in the Park, Getting Straight, Alex in Wonderland, Five Easy Pieces, The Last Movie, Marriage of a Young Stockbroker, The King of Marvin Gardens, Pocket Money, What's Up Doc?, Steelyard Blues, Paper Moon, Slither, A Reflection of Fear, Huckleberry Finn, For Pete's Sake, Freebie and the Bean, Shampoo, At Long Last Love, Baby Blue Marine, Nickelodeon, Close Encounters of the Third Kind (addl. photog. only), Harry and Walter Go to New York, New York New York, F.I.S.T., The Last Waltz, Paradise Alley, Butch and Sundance: The Early Days, The Runner Stumbles, Heart Beat, Inside Moves, The Legend of the Lone Ranger, Frances, The Toy, Crackers, Ghostbusters, Mask, Legal Eagles, Little Nikita, Say Anything, Shattered, Radio Flyer, Life With Mikey, Deception, The Next Karate Kid, The Scout, Free Willy 2: The Adventure Home, Copycat, Multiplicity, My Best Friend's Wedding, Frost.

KOZAK, HARLEY JANE
Actress. b. Wilkes-Barre, PA, Jan. 28, 1957. e. NYU's School of the Arts. Member of Nebraska Repertory Theatre.
PICTURES: House on Sorority Row, Clean and Sober, When Harry Met Sally..., Parenthood, Sideout, Arachnophobia, Necessary Roughness, The Taking of Beverly Hills, All I Want for Christmas, The Favor, Magic in the Water.
TELEVISION: Series: The Guiding Light, Santa Barbara, Texas, Harts of the West, Bringing Up Jack, You Wish. Guest: L.A. Law, Highway to Heaven. Movies: So Proudly We Hail, The Amy Fisher Story, The Android Affair, Dark Planet, Unforgivable, A Friend's Betrayal. Mini-series: Titanic.

KOZLOWSKI, LINDA
Actress. b. 1956. m. actor Paul Hogan. Began professional acting career soon after graduating from Juilliard Sch., N.Y., 1981. Stage debut in How It All Began at the Public Theatre. In regional theatre appeared in Requiem, Translations, Make and Break, as well as on Broadway and on tour with Dustin Hoffman in Death of a Salesman and the TV adaptation.
PICTURES: Crocodile Dundee, Crocodile Dundee II, Pass the Ammo, Helena, Almost an Angel, The Neighbor, Backstreet Justice, Zorn, Village of the Damned.
TELEVISION: Mini-Series: Favorite Son.

KRABBE, JEROEN
Actor. b. Amsterdam, The Netherlands, Dec. 5, 1944. Trained for stage at De Toneelschool, Acad. of Dramatic Art, Amsterdam, 1965. Also studied at painting at Acad. of Fine Arts, grad. 1981. Founded touring theater co. in the Netherlands and translated plays into Dutch. Also costume designer. As a painter, work has been widely exhibited (one-man show at Francis Kyle Galleries, London). Author: The Economy Cookbook. Theatre dir. debut, new stage adaptation of The Diary of Anne Frank, 1985 in Amsterdam.
PICTURES: Soldier of Orange, A Flight of Rainbirds, Spetters, The Fourth Man, Turtle Diary, Jumpin' Jack Flash, No Mercy, The Living Daylights, Shadow of Victory, A World Apart, Crossing Delancey, Shadowman, Scandal, The Punisher, Melancholia, Till There Was You, Kafka, The Prince of Tides, For a Lost Soldier, The Fugitive, King of the Hill, Immortal Beloved, Farinelli, Blood of a Poet, Business for Pleasure, Lorca, Dangerous Beauty, Left Luggage (dir. debut).
TELEVISION: Danton's Death (debut, 1966), William of Orange, World War III. Movies: One for the Dancer, Family of Spies, After the War, Secret Weapon, Robin Hood (theatrical in Europe), Murder East Murder West, Dynasty: The Reunion, Stalin. Mini-series: The Odyssey.

KRAMER, LARRY
Writer, Producer. b. Bridgeport, CT, June 25, 1935. e. Yale U., B.A. 1957. Ent. m.p. ind. 1958. Story edit. Columbia Pictures, N.Y. London 1960-65. Asst. to David Picker and Herb Jaffe, UA, 1965. Assoc. prod. and additional dialogue Here We Go Round the Mulberry Bush, 1968. Writ. prod. Women in Love (Acad. Award nom. for s.p., 1970). Lost Horizon, 1973 (s.p.). Novel: Faggots (1978). Theater: The Normal Heart (NY Shakespeare Festival and throughout the world), Just Say No, The Destiny of Me. Cofounder: Gay Men's Health Crisis, Inc. (community AIDS org.). Founder: ACT UP: AIDS Coalition to Unleash Power (AIDS activist and protest org.). Book of Essays: Reports from the Holocaust: The Story of an AIDS Activist (St. Martin's Press, 1995).

KRAMER, SIDNEY
Sales executive. b. New York, NY, Oct. 25, 1911. e. New York Law Sch., LL.B., City Coll. of New York. Gen. sales mgr., RKO Pathe, June 1953; dir. and v.p. Cellofilm Corp. 1941-56; foreign sales mgr., RKO Radio, 1954-59; v.p Cinemiracle Intl. 1960-61; v.p. T.P.E.A., 1960-61; foreign sls. mgr., Cinerama, Inc., 1962-65; exec. Commonwealth Theatres, Puerto Rico, Inc., 1965-68; exec. v.p. Cobian Jr. Enterprises Inc. 1968; m.p. consultant, exhibition, dist., foreign and Caribbean area, 1968-70; pres. Coqui Int'l Inc.; 1970-80; v.p. of UAPR, Inc., Puerto Rico, U.A. Communications, Inc. 1981-91. Retired.

KRAMER, STANLEY E.
Producer, Director. b. New York, NY, Sept. 29, 1913. e. NYU, B.Sc., 1933. Entered m.p. ind. via backlot jobs; with MGM research dept.; film cutter 3 yrs.; film ed.; m.p. & radio writer; served in US Signal Corps, 1st Lt. during WWII. Recipient of Irving G. Thalberg Award, 1961. Autobiography, A Mad Mad Mad Mad World, 1997.
PICTURES: Assoc. Prod.: So Ends Our Night, The Moon and Sixpence. Producer: So This Is New York, Champion, Home of the Brave, The Men, Cyrano de Bergerac, Death of a Salesman, High Noon, My Six Convicts, The Sniper, The Four Poster, The Happy Time, Eight Iron Men, The 5000 Fingers of Dr. T, The Wild One, The Juggler, Caine Mutiny, Pressure Point, A Child Is Waiting, Invitation to a Gunfighter. Dir./Prod.: Not as a Stranger (dir. debut, 1955), The Pride and the Passion, The Defiant Ones, On the Beach, Inherit the Wind, Judgment at Nuremberg, It's a Mad Mad Mad Mad World, Ship of Fools, Guess Who's Coming to Dinner, The Secret of Santa Vittoria, R.P.M., Bless the Beasts and Children, Oklahoma Crude, The Domino Principle, The Runner Stumbles.
TELEVISION: Guess Who's Coming to Dinner? (pilot), The Rosenberge: The Trial of Lt. Calley, The Trial of General Yamashito.

KRANE, JONATHAN
Executive. b. 1952. m. actress Sally Kellerman. e. St. Johns Coll. grad. with honors, 1972; Yale Law Sch., 1976. Joined Blake Edwards Entertainment in 1981, becoming pres. Formed talent management co. Management Company Entertainment Group representing clients such as John Travolta, Sally Kellerman, Kathryn Harrold, Sandra Bernhard, Howie Mandel, Drew Barrymore, others. Began producing vehicles for clients and transformed co. into production, distribution, management and finance co. Chairman and chief exec. officer, Management Company Entertainment Group (MCEG).

PICTURES: Exec. prod./prod.: Boardwalk, Honeymoon, Fly Away Home, The Man Who Loved Women, Micki & Maude, A Fine Mess, That's Life, The Chocolate War, The Experts, Fatal Charm, Boris and Natasha, Look Who's Talking, Chud II: Bud the Chud, Without You I'm Nothing (prod.), Look Who's Talking Too, Convicts, Cold Heaven, Breaking the Rules, Look Who's Talking Now, Face/Off.
TELEVISION: Prod.: Howie Mandel Life at Carnegie Hall, Howie Mandel: The North American Watusi Tour.

KRANTZ, STEVE
Executive. b. New York, NY, May 20, 1923. m. novelist Judith Krantz. e. Columbia U., B.A. Dir. progs., NBC, New York, 1953; dir. prog. dev., Screen Gems, N.Y., 1955; v.p., gen. mgr. Screen Gems, Canada, 1958; dir. int. sls., 1960; formed Steve Krantz Productions, Inc. 1964.
PICTURES: Producer: Fritz the Cat, Heavy Traffic, The Nine Lives of Fritz the Cat, Cooley High, Ruby, Which Way Is Up?, Jennifer. Swap Meet (also writer).
TELEVISION: Series: Steve Allen Show, Kate Smith Show, Hazel, Dennis the Menace, Winston Churchill—The Valiant Years, Marvel Super Heroes, Rocket Robin Hood. Mini-series: Princess Daisy, Sins, Mistral's Daughter, I'll Take Manhattan. Movies: Dadah is Death (exec. prod.), Till We Meet Again, Deadly Medicine, Deadly Matrimony, Torch Song, Jack Reed: Badge of Honor, House of Secrets, Children of the Dark, Dazzle.

KREIMAN, ROBERT T.
Executive. b. Kenosha, WI, Sept. 16, 1924. Served WWII, Capt Army Corps of Engineers-ETO. e. Stanford U.; U. of WI. Dir., sales training, mgr.; audio visual sales, Bell & Howell Co., 1949-58; v.p., Argus Cameras, Inc., 1958-61; v.p., gen. mgr., Commercial & Educ. Div., Technicolor 1961-69, v.p. gen. mgr., The Suburban Companies; 1969-71, pres. & CEO, Deluxe General, Inc. pres. & dir. of Movietonews, Inc.; bd. chmn. Keith Cole Photograph, Inc. 1972-78; bd. chmn., pres. & CEO, Pace International Corp., 1969-1993; past pres. of UCLA. Executive Program Ass'n. Fellow SMPTE, Member M.P. Academy; TV Academy; assoc. mem., American Society of Cinematographers.

KRESS, HAROLD F.
Film Editor, Director. b. Pittsburgh, PA, June 26, 1913. e. UCLA. Film ed., Command Decision, Madame Curie, Mrs. Miniver, The Yearling; crime shorts; 5-reel Army documentary short, Ward Care for Psychotic Patients. Member: Acad. of M.P. Arts and Sciences, Screen Directors Guild, Film Editors Guild.
PICTURES: Director: Painted Hills, No Questions Asked, Apache War Smoke. Editor: Ride Vaquero, Saadia, Rose Marie, Valley of the Kings, The Cobweb, The Prodigal, I'll Cry Tomorrow, The Teahouse of the August Moon, Silk Stockings, Until They Sail, Merry Andrew, Imitation General, The World the Flesh and the Devil, Count Your Blessings, Home from the Hill, How the West Was Won (Acad. Award, 1963), The Greatest Story Ever Told, Walk Don't Run, Alvarez Kelly, The Poseidon Adventure, The Iceman Cometh, 99 and 44/100% Dead, The Towering Inferno (Acad. Award, 1974).

KREUGER, KURT
Actor. b. St. Moritz, Switzerland, July 23, 1917. e. U. of Lausanne, Polytechnic. London. Came to U.S. 1937, partner in travel bureau: acted in Wharf Theat. group. Cape Cod, 1939; Broadway debut in Candle in the Wind with Helen Hayes, 1941.
PICTURES: The Moon Is Down, Edge of Darkness, The Strange Death of Adolph Hitler, Sahara, Mademoiselle Fifi, None Shall Escape, Escape in the Desert, Hotel Berlin, Paris Underground, The Spider, Dark Corner, Unfaithfully Yours, Spy Hunt, Fear, The Enemy Below, Legion of the Doomed, What Did You Do in the War Daddy?, The St. Valentine's Day Massacre.

KRIER, JOHN N.
Executive. b. Rock Island, IL. e. Augustana Coll. Joined A. H. Blank Theatres, Grad. Publix Theatres Manager Training Sch., 1930: managed theatres in Illinois, Iowa, Nebraska; joined Intermountain Theatres, Salt Lake City, 1937: appointed Purchasing Head, 1946: buyer-booker, 1952: v.p., gen. mgr., 1955: appt. v.p. gen mgr. ABC Theas., Arizona, 1968: appt. v.p. gen'l mgr. director Film Buying ABC Theatres of California & ABC Intermountain Theatres, Feb. 1972. Became consultant ABC Southern Theatres, 1974. Joined Exhibitors Relations Inc. as partner, 1978. Elected pres., 1982. Became owner, 1988.

KRIGE, ALICE
Actress. b. Upington, South Africa. Moved to London at 21 and studied at Central School of Speech and Drama. Professional debut on British TV: The Happy Autumn Fields. In London prod. of Forever Yours, Maylou. West End debut, Arms and the Man, 1981. Two seasons with Royal Shakespeare Co. at Stratford and London (The Tempest, King Lear, The Taming of the Shrew, Cyrano de Bergerac, Bond's Lear.), Venice Preserved at the Almeida, 1995.
PICTURES: Chariots of Fire (debut, 1981), Ghost Story, King David, Barfly, Haunted Summer, See You in the Morning, S.P.O.O.K.S., Sleepwalkers, Habitat, Institute Benjamenta, Amanda, Star Trek: First Contact, Twilight of the Icenymphs, The Commissioner.

TELEVISION: *Movies*: Wallenberg: A Hero's Story, Dream West, A Tale of Two Cities, Second Serve, Baja Oklahoma, Max and Helen, Iran: Days of Crisis, Ladykiller, Judgment Day: The John List Story, Double Deception, Jack Reed: Badge of Honor, Scarlet & Black, Sharpes Honour, Summer, Devil's Advocate, Donor Unknown, Joseph, Hidden in America, Like Father Like Son, Indefensible: The Truth About Edward Brannigan. *Mini-Series*: Ellis Island, Close Relations.

KRISTOFFERSON, KRIS
Actor, Singer. b. Brownsville, TX, June 22, 1936. e. Pomona Coll., Oxford U. (Rhodes Scholar). Joined U.S. Army briefly and taught English literature at West Point. Started writing songs (country music), hits have included Me and Bobby McGee, Why Me, Lord, Sunday Mornin' Comin' Down, etc.
PICTURES: The Last Movie (debut, 1971), Cisco Pike, Pat Garrett and Billy the Kid, Blume in Love, Bring Me the Head of Alfredo Garcia, Alice Doesn't Live Here Anymore, Vigilante Force, The Sailor Who Fell from Grace with the Sea, A Star Is Born, Semi-Tough, Convoy, Heaven's Gate, Rollover, Flashpoint, Songwriter, Trouble in Mind, Big Top Pee-wee, Millennium, Welcome Home, Original Intent, Night of the Cyclone, Sandino, No Place to Hide, Cheatin' Hearts, Lone Star, Fire Down Below.
TELEVISION: *Movies/Mini-Series*: Freedom Road, The Lost Honor of Kathryn Beck, The Last Days of Frank and Jesse James, Blood and Orchids, Stagecoach, The Tracker, Dead or Alive, Pair of Aces, Another Pair of Aces, Miracle in the Wilderness, Christmas in Connecticut, Troubleshooters: Trapped Beneath the Earth, Big Dreams & Broken Hearts: The Dottie West Story, Tad. *Mini-Series*: Amerika.

KRONICK, WILLIAM
Writer, Director. b. Amsterdam, NY. e. Columbia Coll., A.B. U.S. Navy photography; wrote, dir. featurette, A Bowl of Cherries.
PICTURES: Nights in White Satin (s.p.), Horowitz in Dublin (dir., s.p.), Flash Gordon and King Kong (2nd unit dir.).
TELEVISION: *Documentaries: Wrote, dir., prod.*: The Ultimate Stuntman: a Tribute to Dar Robinson, To the Ends of the Earth, Mysteries of the Great Pyramid; George Plimpton Specials; National Geographic, Ripley's Believe It or Not, The World's Greatest Stunts. *Prod.*: In Search of... Series. *Dir.*: (movie) The 500 Pound Jerk.

KRUEGER, RONALD P.
Executive. b. St. Louis, MO, Oct. 19, 1940. e. Westminister Coll., 1961. Began working in theatres as a teenager. Assumed presidency Wehrenberg Theatres, 1963. Member: NATO, bd. member; American Film Inst.; Motion Picture Pioneers; Demolay Legion of Honor; Mercantile Bank, bd. member; Big Game Hunters; World Presidents Org. Bd. trustees, Westminster Col. at Fulton, MO. Divan member. Moolah Temple Shrine. Past Master Tuscan Lodge 360 AF & AM. Scottish Rite 32 KCCH. Advisory bd. chmn., Salvation Army. Recipient of the NATO B.V. Sturdiviant award for Community Svc. Member & past pres. of Safari Club Intl.

KRUGER, HARDY
Actor, Writer. b. Berlin, Germany, April 12, 1928. Ent. m.p. ind. 1943; on stage since 1945. Starred in approx. 25 German films). Has published 11 books, novels, travelogues, etc.
PICTURES: The One That Got Away, Bachelor of Hearts, The Rest Is Silence (German film of Hamlet), Blind Date, Taxi Pour Tobrouk, Sundays and Cybele, Hatari! (U.S. debut, 1963), Le Gros Coup, Les Pianos Mecaniques (The Uninhibited), Le Chant du Monde, Flight of the Phoenix, The Defector, La Grande Sauterelle, Le Franciscain de Bourges, The Nun of Monza, The Secret of Santa Vittoria, The Battle of Neretva, The Red Tent, Night Hair Child, Death of a Stranger, Barry Lyndon, Paper Tiger, Un Solitaire, Potato Fritz, A Bridge Too Far, L'Autopsie d'un Monstre, The Wild Geese, Society Limited, Wrong Is Right, The Inside Man.
TELEVISION: *Mini-Series*: War and Remembrance. Series: Globetrotter (writer, prod; 1986).

KUBRICK, STANLEY
Director, Producer, Writer. b. Bronx, NY, July 26, 1928. e. Taft H.S. Staff photog. Look magazine; dir. cinematog. of short documentaries Day of the Fight, Flying Padre; dir., cinematog. of documentary The Seafarers. Received Luchino Visconti Award in Italy for contribution to the cinema, 1988.
PICTURES: *Director*: Fear and Desire (also prod., co-s.p., photog., edit.), Killer's Kiss (also co-prod., co-s.p., story, photog., edit.), The Killing (also s.p.), Paths of Glory (also co-s.p.), Spartacus, Lolita. *Director-Producer-Writer*: Dr. Strangelove, or: How I Learned to Stop Worrying and Love the Bomb, 2001: A Space Odyssey (also special photog. effects design. & dir.; Acad. Award for special effects, 1968), A Clockwork Orange, Barry Lyndon, The Shining, Full Metal Jacket, Eyes Wide Shut.

KUDROW, LISA
Actress. e. Vassar College, NY, B.S., in biology. Member of The Groundlings improvisational theatre group, 1989-.
PICTURES: L.A. on $5 a Day, The Unborn, Dance with Death, In the Heat of Passion, Unfaithful, Behind Closed Doors, The Crazysitter, Mother, Hacks, Romy and Michele's High School Reunion, Clockwatchers, Opposite of Sex, I Dream of Jeannie.
TELEVISION: *Series*: Bob, Mad About You, Friends (Emmy Award, 1998). *Guest*: Cheers, Newhart, Life Goes On, Coach, Flying Blind, Saturday Night Live, Hope & Gloria.

KUHN, THOMAS G.
Executive/Executive Producer. e. Northwestern U., B.A.; USC, M.B.A. KNBC-TV sales; NBC business affairs; dir. live night time progs. Warner Bros. TV, v.p. prod. TV *Exec. prod.*: Alice, The Awakening Land, Torn Between Two Lovers, The Jayne Mansfield Story, Long Way Home. Pres., RCA Video Prods. Pres., Lightyear Ent., 1987. *Exec. prod.*: Aria, The Return of Swamp Thing, Heaven, The Lemon Sisters, Stories to Remember. With partner Fred Weintraub: The JFK Assassination: The Jim Garrison Tapes, Trouble Bound, Gypsy Eyes, Backstreet Justice, Guinevere, Triplecross, Young Ivanhoe, Young Connecticut Yankee, Undertow, Playboy's Really Naked Truth, Iron Fist, Bruce Lee: Curse of the Dragon, Triplecross, The New Adventures of Robin Hood.

KULIK, SEYMOUR (BUZZ)
Producer, Director. b. New York, NY, 1923. Joined CBS-TV as prod.-dir., 1956; 1964: v.p. chg. West Coast Prods., Bob Banner Associates Inc., 1965; 1967 Prod-Dir. with Paramount Studios.
PICTURES: The Explosive Generation, The Yellow Canary, Warning Shot (also prod.), Villa Rides, Riot, To Find a Man, Shamus, The Hunter.
TELEVISION: *Series*: Lux Video Theatre, Kraft Theatre, You Are There, Climax, Playhouse 90, The Defenders, Dr. Kildare, Twilight Zone, Dick Powell Playhouse, Kentucky Jones (exec. prod.). Movies: Vanished, Owen Marshall—Counsellor at Law (A Pattern of Morality), Brian's Song (DGA Award), Incident on a Dark Street, Pioneer Woman, Remember When, Bad Ronald, Cage Without a Key, Matt Helm, Babe, The Lindbergh Kidnapping Case, Never Con a Killer, Kill Me If You Can, Ziegfeld: The Man and His Women, From Here to Eternity, Rage of Angels, George Washington (also sprv. prod.), Kane and Abel, Her Secret Life, Women of Valor, Too Young the Hero, Around the World in 80 Days, Jackie Collins' Lucky/Chances, Miles From Nowhere.

KUREISHI, HANIF
Writer. b. South London, Eng., Dec. 5, 1956. e. King's Coll. (philosophy). At 18, first play presented at Royal Court Theatre where he ushered before becoming writer in residence. Early in career, wrote pornography as Antonia French. Stage and TV plays include: The Mother Country, Outskirts, Borderline and adaptations (Mother Courage). The Rainbow Sign, With Your Tongue Down My Throat (novella) and short stories have been pub. Anglo-Pakistani writer's first s.p. My Beautiful Laundrette earned Acad. Award nom., 1986 and began creative relationship with dir. Stephen Frears.
PICTURES: My Beautiful Laundrette, Sammy and Rosie Get Laid, London Kills Me (also dir.).

KURI, EMILE
Set Decorator. b. Cuernavaca, Mex., June 11, 1907. e. Chaminade Coll., 1924-27. Career began with 50 Hopalong Cassidy episodes for Harry Sherman. Under contract to Selznick Intl., Liberty Films, and Walt Disney Prods. supv. all film and tv sets, and all decor for both Disneyland and Disney World.
PICTURES: 71 films incl.: The Silver Queen (Acad. Award nom.), I'll Be Seeing You, Spellbound, It's a Wonderful Life, Duel in the Sun, Paradine Case, The Heiress (Acad. Award, 1949), Fancy Pants, A Place in the Sun, Carrie (Acad. Award nom.), The War of the Worlds, Shane, The Actress, Executive Suite (Acad. Award nom.), 20,000 Leagues Under the Sea (Acad. Award, 1954), Old Yeller, The Absent-Minded Professor (Acad. Award nom.), The Parent Trap, Mary Poppins (Acad. Award nom.), Bedknobs & Broomsticks (Acad. Award nom.).
TELEVISION: 15 seasons of The Wonderful World of Disney (Emmy Award, 1963), The Academy Awards (1960-70).

KURI, JOHN A.
Producer, Writer. b. Los Angeles, CA, Feb. 16, 1945. Son of set decorator and Disneyland co-designer, Emile Kuri. Began 13 yr. employment with Disney at age 16 in construction and maintenance at Disneyland. Progressed through mgmt. in Park Operations. 1969 transferred to Disney Studios in set decorating. 1973 became art director. 1975 at 20th Century Fox as exec. asst. to prod. Irwin Allen. 1976, formed own co., wrote and prod. both television and motion picture projects. 1979 thru 1982 developed and prod. television in partnership with Ron Howard. 1988 thru 1990 as pres. of Sheffield Ent. developed master broadcasting plan for KCMY TV, Sacramento, CA. Published works: Determined to Live: An American Epic, Remember Wes.
PICTURES: Captive Hearts (prod., co-s.p. 2nd unit dir., co-lyrics.) *Set decorator*: Apple Dumpling Gang, Leadbelly, Report to the Commissioner, Castaway Cowboy, Superdad, Mad Mad Movie Makers.

TELEVISION: One More Mountain (prod., writer, 2nd unit dir.; Christopher Award, 1994), Conagher (prod.; Western Heritage Award from Cowboy Hall of Fame), O'Hara (co-creator of series), Airwolf (2nd unit prod., dir.), Skyward (prod., 2nd unit dir.; Golden Halo Award), Skyward Christmas (prod., 2nd unit dir.), Through the Magic Pyramid (assoc. prod., art dir.). Art dir.: The Plutonium Incident, Scared Straight Another Story, Young Love First Love, Marriage is Alive and Well, Little Shots, The Red Pony (and set decorator, Emmy nom., 1973). Set decorator: Michael O'Hara IV, The Mouse Factory (22 episodes).

KUROSAWA, AKIRA
Director, Writer. b. Japan. March 23, 1910. e. Attended Tokyo Acad. of Fine Arts, 1928. Asst. dir. to Kajiro Yamamoto, Photo-Chemical Laboratories (PCL Studios, later renamed Toho Films), 1936-43. Became dir., 1943. Founded Kurosawa Prods., 1960; Dir. Yonki Kai Prods., 1971. Autobiography: Something Like An Autobiography (1982).
PICTURES: *Director/Writer*: Sanshiro Sugata (debut, 1943), The Most Beautiful, The Men Who Tread on the Tiger's Tail, Sanshiro Sugata Part 2, No Regrets for Our Youth, Those Who Make Tomorrow (co- dir.), One Wonderful Sunday, Drunken Angel, The Quiet Duel, Stray Dog, Scandal, Rashomon, The Idiot, Ikiru, The Seven Samurai, I Live in Fear, Dersu Uzala. *Also co-prod or exec. prod.*: The Lower Depths, Throne of Blood, The Bad Sleep Well, The Hidden Fortress, Yojimbo (also s.p.), Sanjuro, High and Low, Red Beard, Dodes 'Ka-Den, Kagemusha, Ran, Runaway Train (adapt. from orig. s.p. only), Akira Kurosawa's Dreams, Rhapsody in August, Not Yet, Last Man Standing.
(d. Sept. 6, 1998)

KURTZ, GARY
Producer, Director. b. Los Angeles, CA, July 27, 1940. e. USC Cinema Sch. Began prof. career during college. Has worked as cameraman, soundman, editor, prod. supervisor and asst. dir. on documentaries and features. Worked on many low budget features for Roger Corman including: The Terror, Beach Ball, Track of the Vampire, Planet of Blood, The Shooting, Ride in the Whirlwind. Drafted into Marines. Spent 2 yrs. in photo field as cameraman, editor and still photo.
PICTURES: The Hostage (prod. spvr., ed.), Two-Lane Blacktop (line prod.), Chandler (line prod.), American Graffiti (co.-prod.); Star Wars (prod.), The Empire Strikes Back (prod.), The Dark Crystal (prod., 2nd unit dir.), Return to Oz (exec. prod.), Slipstream (prod.).

KURTZ, SWOOSIE
Actress. b. Omaha, NE. e. Studied at U. Southern Calif., London Acad. of Music and Dramatic Art.
THEATER: A History of the American Film (Drama Desk Award), Ah Wilderness (Tony nom.), Who's Afraid of Virginia Woolf? (with Mike Nichols and Elaine May), The Effect of Gamma Rays on Man-in-the Moon Marigolds, Fifth of July (Tony, Outer Critics Circle & Drama Desk Awards), House of Blue Leaves (Tony and Obie Awards), Uncommon Women and Others (Obie & Drama Desk Award), Hunting Cockroaches (Drama League nom.), Six Degrees of Separation, Lips Together Teeth Apart.
PICTURES: Slap Shot, First Love, Oliver's Story, The World According to Garp, Against All Odds, Wildcats, True Stories, Vice Versa, Bright Lights Big City, Dangerous Liaisons, Stanley and Iris, A Shock to the System, Reality Bites, Storybook, Citizen Ruth, Liar Liar.
TELEVISION: *Series*: As the World Turns (1971), Mary, Love Sidney (Emmy noms.), Sisters (Emmy & SAG noms), Suddenly Susan. *Movies*: Walking Through the Fire, Marriage Is Alive and Well, Mating Season, A Caribbean Mystery, Guilty Conscience, A Time to Live, Baja Oklahoma (Golden Globe nom.), The Image (Emmy & Cable ACE noms.), Terror on Track 9, The Positively True Adventures of the Alleged Texas Cheerleader-Murdering Mom, and The Band Played On (Emmy & Cable Ace noms.), One Christmas, Betrayed: A Story of Three Women, A Promise to Carolyn, Little Girls in Pretty Boxes. *Specials*: Uncommon Women, Fifth of July, House of Blue Leaves, The Visit (Trying Times). *Guest*: Kojak, Carol & Company (Emmy Award, 1990).

KURYS, DIANE
Director, Writer. b. Lyons, France, Dec. 3, 1948. In 1970 joined Jean-Louis Barrault's theatre group, acted for 8 years on stage, television and film. Adapted and translated staged plays. 1977, wrote screenplay for Dibolo Menthe (Peppermint Soda) which she also directed and co-prod. Film won Prix Louis Deluc, Best Picture. Co-prod. Alexandre Arcady's Coup de Sirocco and Le Grand Pardon.
PICTURES: *Dir./Writer*: Peppermint Soda (also co-prod.), Cocktail Molotov, Entre Nous, A Man in Love, C'est la vie, Apres L'amour, Six Days Six Nights.

KUSTURICA, EMIR
Director. b. Sarajevo, Yugoslavia, 1955. e. FAMU.
PICTURES: Do You Remember Dolly Bell? (debut, 1981; Golden Lion Award at Venice Film Fest.), When Father Was Away on Business (Golden Palme at Cannes Film Fest., 1985), Time of the Gypsies (also co-s.p.), Arizona Dream, Underground (Golden Palme at Cannes Film Fest., 1995), White Cat Black Cat.

KWAN, NANCY
Actress. b. Hong Kong, May 19, 1939. Trained as dancer at British Royal Ballet.
PICTURES: The World of Suzie Wong (debut, 1960), Flower Drum Song, The Main Attraction, Tamahine, Fate Is the Hunter, The Wild Affair, Honeymoon Hotel, Arrivederci Baby, Lt. Robin Crusoe USN, The Corrupt Ones, Nobody's Perfect, The Wrecking Crew, The Girl Who Knew Too Much, The McMasters, Girl From Peking, Supercock, The Pacific Connection, Project: Kill, Night Creature, Streets of Hong Kong, Angkor, Walking the Edge, Night Children, Cold Dog Soup, Dragon: The Bruce Lee Story, Mr. P's Dancing Sushi Bar.
TELEVISION: *Movies*: The Last Ninja, Blade in Hong Kong, Miracle Landing.

KWIT, NATHANIEL TROY, JR.
Executive. b. New York, NY, May 29, 1941. e. Cornell U., B.A.; NYU, M.B.A. 1964-68, American Broadcasting Co., Inc., exec. asst. to pres. of ABC Films. 1968-71, National Screen Service Corp., New York branch mgr., asst. genl. sls. mgr. 1971, founder, CEO Audience Marketing, Inc., later acquired by Viacom International as operating subsidiary. 1974 named v.p. marketing services, Warner Bros., Inc. 1979, named v.p. in charge video and special markets division, United Artists Corp.; 1981, named sr. v.p. in chg. UA television, video, special market div. Following acquisition of UA Corp. by MGM in 1981 promoted to pres., dist. & mktg. for MGM/UA Entertainment Co. 1983, pres. & CEO, United Satellite Communications, direct broadcast TV co. 1986, founder, pres. Palladium Entertainment, Inc.

L

LACHMAN, ED
Cinematographer. b. 1948. Son of a Morristown, NJ movie theater owner. e. Ohio U., BFA. Filmed documentaries Ornette: Made in America, Strippers, Huie's Sermon. Assisted Sven Nykvist on King of the Gypsies, Hurricane; Vittorio Storaro on Luna; Robby Muller on The American Friend and They All Laughed. Co-director of photography on Werner Herzog's La Soufriere and Stroszek and Wim Wenders' Lightning Over Water and A Tokyo Story.
PICTURES: Scalpel, Union City, Say Amen Somebody, Little Wars, Split Cherry Tree, Strippers, The Little Sister, Insignificance (American sequences) Desperately Seeking Susan, True Stories, Making Mr. Right, Chuck Berry: Hail Hail Rock 'n' Roll, Less Than Zero, El Dia Que Me Quieras, Mississippi Masala, Light Sleeper, London Kills Me, My New Gun, My Family/Mi Familia, Selena.
TELEVISION: Get Your Kicks on Route 66 (dir., cinematography, American Playhouse.), A Gathering of Old Men, Backtrack.

LACK, ANDREW
Executive. b. New York, NY, May 16, 1947. e. Sorbonne, Boston Univ. School of Fine Arts (BFA). Starting in 1976, worked at CBS as prod. for Who's Who, 60 Minutes, CBS Reports. 1981, named sr. prod. of CBS Reports and CBS News correspondent, 1983 became exec. prod. Exec. prod. and creator of Face to Face with Connie Chung, West 57th, Crossroads, Our Times With Bill Moyers. Exec. prod. of Street Stories, specials The 20th Anniversary of Watergate, Malcolm X. 1993, appointed pres. of NBC News.

LADD, JR., ALAN
Executive. b. Los Angeles, CA, Oct. 22, 1937. Son of late actor Alan Ladd. M. p. agent, Creative Mgmt. Associates, 1963-69.; m.p. prod., 1969-73. Joined 20th Century-Fox in 1973 in chg. of creative affairs in feature div.; promoted to v.p., prod., 1974; 1975, named sr. v.p. for worldwide prod.; 1976, promoted to pres. of 20th Century-Fox Pictures. Resigned & formed The Ladd Co., 1979. 1985, appt. pres. & COO, MGM/UA Ent. Film Corp; appt. chmn. of bd., CEO, MGM Pictures Inc.; 1986; resigned 1988. 1989, named co-chmn. Pathe Communications Corp. and chmn., CEO, Pathe Ent.; chmn., & CEO, MGM-Pathe Ent., 1989-92; chmn. & CEO MGM-Pathe Comm. Co., 1991-92; co-chmn. & co-CEO, MGM, 1992-93. Founded Ladd Pictures.
PICTURES: *Prod.*: Walking Stick, A Severed Head, Tam Lin, Villian, Zee and Co., Fear Is the Key, Braveheart (Acad. Award), The Phantom, A Very Brady Sequel. *Exec. prod.*: Nightcomers, Vice Versa, The Brady Bunch Movie.

LADD, CHERYL
Actress. r.n. Cheryl Stoppelmoor. b. Huron, S.D., July 12, 1951. Joined professional Music Shop Band while in high school; after graduation toured with group ending up in Los Angeles. Cast as voice of Melody character in animated Josie and the Pussycats. Studied acting with Milton Katselas. Did TV commercials, small parts in TV. Film debut 1972 in Jamaica Reef (aka Evil in the Deep, unreleased).
PICTURES: Purple Hearts, Now and Forever, Millennium, Lisa, Poison Ivy.

TELEVISION: *Series*: The Ken Berry "Wow" Show, Charlie's Angels, One West Waikiki. *Specials*: Ben Vereen... His Roots, General Electric's All-Star Anniversary, John Denver and the Ladies; The Cheryl Ladd Special, Looking Back: Souvenirs, Scenes From a Special. *Guest*: Police Woman, Happy Days, Switch, etc. *Movies*: Satan's School for Girls, When She Was Bad, Grace Kelly Story, Romance on the Orient Express, A Death in California, Crossings, Deadly Care, Bluegrass, Kentucky Woman, Jekyll & Hyde, The Fulfillment of Mary Gray, The Girl Who Came Between Them, Crash: The Mystery of Flight 1501, Danielle Steel's Changes, Locked Up: A Mother's Rage, Dead Before Dawn, Broken Promises: Taking Emily Back, Dancing With Danger, The Haunting of Lisa, Kiss & Tell, Tangled Web.

LADD, DAVID ALAN
Actor, Producer, Motion Picture Executive. b. Los Angeles, CA, Feb. 5, 1947. e. USC. Son of late actor Alan Ladd. On stage in The Glass Menagerie. Exec. v.p. motion picture prod. at Pathe Entertainment and Metro-Goldwyn-Mayer.
PICTURES: *Actor*: The Big Land, The Proud Rebel (Golden Globe Award), The Sad Horse, A Dog of Flanders, Raymie, Misty, R.P.M., Catlow, Deathline (Raw Meat), The Klansman, The Day of the Locust, Wild Geese. Producer: The Serpent and the Rainbow.
TELEVISION: *Guest*: Zane Gray Theatre, Wagon Train, Pursuit, Ben Casey, Gunsmoke, Love American Style (pilot), Kojak, Emergency, Tom Sawyer, Bonanza, Quest, Police Story, Medical Story, etc. *Producer*: When She Was Bad, ABC Variety specials.

LADD, DIANE
Actress. b. Meridian, MS. r.n. Diane Rose Lanier. Daughter is actress Laura Dern. e. St. Aloysius Acad.; trained for stage with Curt Conway and Frank Corsaro. Member of Actors Studio. Worked as model, singer and as Copacabana nightclub dancer. At 17 in touring co. of Hatful of Rain. NY debut: Orpheus Descending.
THEATER: Carry Me Back to Morningside Heights, One Night Stands of a Noisy Passenger. The Wall, The Goddess, The Fantastiks, Women Speak, Texas Trilogy; Lu Ann Hampton Laverty, Love Letters.
PICTURES: Wild Angels (debut, 1966), Rebel Rousers, The Reivers, Macho Calahan, WUSA, White Lightning, Chinatown, Alice Doesn't Live Here Anymore (Acad. Award nom.), Embryo, All Night Long, Sweetwater, The Reivers, Something Wicked This Way Comes, Black Widow, Plain Clothes, National Lampoon's Christmas Vacation, Wild at Heart (Acad. Award nom.), A Kiss Before Dying, Rambling Rose (Acad. Award nom.), The Cemetery Club, Forever, Carnosaur, Hold Me Thrill Me Kiss Me, Father Hood, Ghost of Mississippi, Primary Colors.
TELEVISION: *Movies*: The Devil's Daughter, Black Beauty, Thaddeus Rose and Eddie, Willa, Guyana Tragedy, Desperate Lives, Grace Kelly, Crime of Innocence, Bluegrass, Rock Hudson, The Lookalike, Shadow of a Doubt, Hush Little Baby, Mrs. Munck (also dir., writer). *Guest*: Hazel, Gunsmoke, City of Angels, The Love Boat, Dr. Quinn Medicine Woman (pilot), Grace Under Fire, Touched By An Angel. *Series*: The Secret Storm, Alice (Golden Globe Award). *Special*: The Gift.

LAFFERTY, PERRY
Executive. b. Davenport, IA, Oct. 3, 1920. e. Yale U. With CBS-TV as v.p., programs, Hollywood, 1965-76. Sr. v.p., programs and talent, west coast, for NBC Entertainment, 1979-85.
TELEVISION: Maybe Baby (exec. prod.), Murder C.O.D. (exec. prod.), An Early Frost (prod.).

LaGRAVENESE, RICHARD
Writer. b. Brooklyn, NY, Oct.30, 1959.
PICTURES: Rude Awakening, The Fisher King (also actor, Acad. Award nom.), The Ref (also prod.), A Little Princess, The Bridges of Madison County, Unstrung Heroes, The Mirror has Two Faces, The Kiss (also dir.), The Horse Whisperer, Defective Detective.

LAHTI, CHRISTINE
Actress. b. Birmingham, MI, April 4, 1950. m. dir. Thomas Schlamme. e. U. of Michigan. Trained for stage at Herbert Berghof Studios with Uta Hagen. TV commercials. As a mime, performed with Edinburgh Scotland's Travis Theatre. N.Y. stage debut in The Woods, 1978.
THEATER: The Zinger, Hooter (Playwrights Horizon), Loose Ends, Division St., The Woods (Theatre World Award), Scenes and Revelations, Present Laughter, The Lucky Spot, Summer and Smoke (LA), The Heidi Chronicles, Three Hotels.
PICTURES: ...And Justice For All (debut, 1979), Whose Life Is It Anyway?, Ladies and Gentlemen the Fabulous Stains, Swing Shift (Acad. Award nom.), Just Between Friends, Housekeeping, Stacking, Running on Empty, Miss Firecracker (cameo), Gross Anatomy, Funny About Love, The Doctor, Leaving Normal, Hideaway, Pie in the Sky, A Weekend in the Country, Lieberman In Love (short; Academy Award).
TELEVISION: *Series*: Chicago Hope (Golden Globe Award, Emmy Award, 1998). *Movies*: Dr. Scorpion, The Last Tenant, The Henderson Monster, The Executioner's Song, Love Lives On, Single Bars Single Women, No Place Like Home, Crazy From the Heart, The Fear Inside, The Good Fight, The Four Diamonds. *Mini-Series*: Amerika.

LAI, FRANCIS
Composer. b. France, April 26, 1932.
PICTURES: A Man and a Woman, I'll Never Forget What's 'is Name, The Bobo, Three Into Two Won't Go, Hello Goodbye, Hannibal Brooks, The Games, Mayerling, House of Cards, Rider on the Rain, Love Story (Academy Award, 1970), Le Petit Matin, Another Man, Another Chance, Wanted: Babysitter, Bilitis, The Good and the Bad, Widow's Nest, Cat and Mouse, The Body of My Enemy, Emmanuelle 2; The Forbidden Room, International Velvet, Oliver's Story, Passion Flower Hotel, Robert and Robert, The Small Timers, By the Blood Brothers, Beyond the Reef, Bolero, A Second Chance, Edith and Marcel, My New Partner, Marie, A Man and a Woman: 20 Years Later, Bernadette, Itinerary of a Spoiled Child., Der Aten (The Spirit), La Belle Histoire.
TELEVISION: The Berlin Affair, The Sex Symbol, Sins.

LAKE, RICKI
Actress. b. New York, NY, Sept. 21, 1968. e. Manhattan's Professional Children's School. Won role in Hairspray while attending Ithaca Col. Theatre in LA: A Girl's Guide to Chaos.
PICTURES: Hairspray (debut, 1988), Working Girl, Starlight: A Musical Movie, Cookie, Cry-Baby, Last Exit to Brooklyn, Where the Day Takes You, Inside Monkey Zetterland, Cabin Boy, Serial Mom, Skinner, Mrs. Winterbourne.
TELEVISION: *Series*: China Beach, Ricki Lake (synd. talk show). *Movies*: Babycakes, The Chase, Based on an Untrue Story.

LAM, RINGO
Director. e. York University, Toronto. Started training as an actor in 1973 but switched to production as asst. until 1976, then as TV dir. until 1978. In 1981 he returned to Hong Kong and two years later made his dir. debut with Esprit D'Amour.
PICTURES: The Other Side of a Gentleman, Cupid One, Aces Go Places IV: Mad Mission, City on Fire, Prison on Fire, School on Fire, Wild Search, Undeclared War, Touch and Go, Prison on Fire II, Full Contact, Twin Dragons, Burning Paradise (Rape of the Red Temple), The Adventurers, The Exchange, Full Alert.

LAMARR, HEDY
Actress. r.n. Hedwig Kiesler. b. Vienna, Austria, Nov. 9, 1915. Started in films as script girl, bit player before gaining fame for role in 1933 Czech prod. Ecstasy. To Hollywood, 1938. Autobiography: Ecstasy and Me (1966).
PICTURES: Ecstasy, Algiers (U.S. debut, 1938), Lady of the Tropics, I Take This Woman, Boom Town, Comrade X, Come Live With Me, Ziegfeld Girl, H. M. Pulham Esq., Tortilla Flat, Crossroads, White Cargo, The Heavenly Body, The Conspirators, Experiment Perilous, Her Highness and the Bellboy, The Strange Woman, Dishonored Lady, Let's Live a Little, Samson and Delilah, A Lady Without a Passport, Copper Canyon, My Favorite Spy, Love of 3 Queens, The Story of Mankind, The Female Animal.

LAMAS, LORENZO
Actor. b. Los Angeles, CA, Jan. 20, 1958. e. Santa Monica City Coll. Son of the late actor Fernando Lamas and actress Arlene Dahl. Studied at Tony Barr's Film Actors Workshop (Burbank Studios). Appeared on commercials for Diet Coke, BVD, Coors (Hispanic).
PICTURES: Grease, Tilt, Take Down, Body Rock, Snakeater, Night of the Warrior, Snakeater II, Final Impact, Snakeater III: His Law, Killing Streets, CIA Code Name: Alexa, CIA: Target Alexa, The Swordsman, Bounty Tracker, Final Round, C.I.A.: Target Alexa II, Bad Blood.
TELEVISION: *Series*: California Fever, Secrets of Midland Heights, Falcon Crest, Dancin' to the Hits (host), Renegade. *Guest*: The Love Boat, Switch, Sword of Justice, The Hitchhiker, Dear John. *Movies*: Detour to Terror, CIA: Code Name Alexa.

LAMBERT, CHRISTOPHER (also CHRISTOPHE)
Actor, Producer. b. New York , NY, Mar. 29, 1957; reared in Geneva; parents French. Studied at Paris Conservatoire Drama Academy.
PICTURES: La Bar du Telephone (debut, 1981), Putain d'Historie d'Amour, Legitime Violence, Greystoke: The Legend of Tarzan Lord of the Apes, Love Songs, Subway (Cesar Award), Highlander, I Love You, The Sicilian, Love Dream, To Kill a Priest, Un Plan d'Enfer, Why Me?, Highlander 2: The Quickening, Priceless Beauty, Knight Moves, Fortress, Gunmen, Road Flower, Highlander III: The Sorcerer, The Hunted, Nine Months (exec. prod. only), Mortal Kombat, North Star (also exec. prod.), When Saturday Comes (exec. prod. only).

LAMBERT, MARY
Director. b. Arkansas. e. attended U. of Denver, Rhode Island Sch. of Design where began making short films. Worked in variety of prod. jobs before moving to Los Angeles and directing TV commercials and music videos (includ. Madonna's Material Girl, Like a Virgin, Like a Prayer, others for Sting, Janet Jackson and Mick Jagger).
PICTURES: Siesta, Pet Sematary, Pet Sematary 2.
TELEVISION: *Movie*: Dragstrip Girl, Face of Evil, My Stepson My Lover, Clubland.

LAMBERT, VERITY
Producer. b. London, England, Nov. 27. Ent. TV 1961; prod. Dr. Who, Adam Adamant Lives, Detective, Somerset Maugham (all BBC series). Since 1971: (series), Budgie, Between The Wars. 1974: Appt. controller of Drama, Thames Television. 1979: Chief exec. Euston Films. 1983: Director of Production Thorn EMI Films Ltd. Relinquished her position as controller of Drama Thames Television and retained position as chief exec., Euston Films. Became indep. prod. developing projects for film and TV incl. BBC. Founded own company, Cinema Verity Ltd., 1985.
PICTURES: Link, Morons from Outer Space, Restless Natives, Dreamchild, Not for Publication, Clockwise, A Cry in the Dark.
TELEVISION: May to December, The Boys from the Bush, Sleepers, GBH, So Haunt Me, Comics, Coasting, Sam Saturday, Running Late, Class Act, She's Out, Heavy Weather.

LAMONT, PETER
Production designer.
PICTURES: Watch Your Stern, Night of the Eagle, This Sporting Life, On Her Majesty's Secret Service, Daimonds Are Forever, Sleuth, Live and Let Die, The Dove, The Main with the Golden Gun, Inside Out, Seven-Per-Cent Solution, The Spy Who Loved Me, The Boys from Brazil, Moonraker, For Your Eyes Only, Octopussy, Top Secret!, A View to a Kill, Aliens, The Living Daylights, Consuming Passions, Licence to Kill, Eve of Destruction, The Taking of Beverly Hills, True Lies, GoldenEye, Titanic (Acad. Award, Best Art Dir., LA Film Crits. Award, Best Prod. Design, 1997), Wing Commander, Bond 19.

LANDAU, JON
Producer. b. New York, NY.
PICTURES: Prod.: Campus Man (also unit prod. mgr.), Honey I Shrunk the Kids, Dick Tracy (also unit prod. mgr.), Titanic (Acad. Award, Best Pic., 1997), Mr. Hughes. Unit prod. mgr.: Manhunter, F/X, Making Mr. Right.

LANDAU, MARTIN
Actor. b. Brooklyn, NY, June 20, 1930. e. Pratt Inst., Art Students League, Was cartoon and staff artist on NY Daily News; studied at Actors Studio. Daughter is actress Juliet Landau. Recipient: Lifetime Achievement Awards from Houston Film Fest. and Charleston Film Fest. Spoken word recording, Harry Truman: The journey to Independence, 1997 (Grammy nom.).
THEATER: Middle of the Night, Uncle Vanya, Stalag 17, Wedding Breakfast, First Love, The Goat Song.
PICTURES: Pork Chop Hill (debut, 1959), North by Northwest, The Gazebo, Stagecoach to Dancer's Rock, Cleopatra, The Hallelujah Trail, The Greatest Story Ever Told, Decision at Midnight, Alien Attack, Nevada Smith, They Call Me Mister Tibbs, Situation Normal But All Fouled Up, A Town Called Hell, Black Gunn, Strange Shadows in an Empty Room, Meteor, Destination Moonbase Alpha, Without Warning, Trial By Terror, Cosmic Princess, Journey Through the Black Sun, The Last Word, The Return (The Alien's Return), Alone in the Dark, The Being, Access Code, Treasure Island, Run ... If You Can, Death Blow, W.A.R.: Women Against Rape, Sweet Revenge, Cyclone, Real Bullets, Empire State, Delta Fever, Tucker: The Man and His Dream (Acad. Award nom.), Crimes and Misdemeanors (Golden Globe Award, Acad. Award nom.), Paint It Black, Firehead, Tipperary, The Color of Evening, Mistress, Eye of the Stranger, Sliver, Intersection, Time Is Money, Ed Wood (Academy Award, best supporting actor, 1994; also Golden Globe, SAG, American Comedy, NY Film Critics, LA Film Critics, Natl. Society of Film Critics, Boston Film Critics, Chicago Film Critics & Texas Film Critics Awards), City Hall, Pinocchio, B.A.P.S., The Elevator, The X-Files, Rounders, The Joy Riders, Ed TV.
TELEVISION: Series: Mission Impossible (1966-69; 3 Emmy noms., Golden Globe Award), Space 1999. Movies: Welcome Home Johnny Bristol, Savage, The Death of Ocean View Park, Harlem Globetrotters on Gilligan's Island, Fall of the House of Usher, Max and Helen (ACE Award nom.), The Neon Empire, By Dawn's Early Light (ACE Award nom.), Something to Live For: The Alison Gertz Story, Legacy of Lies (ACE Award), 12:01, Joseph. Numerous guest appearances.

LANDES, MICHAEL
Executive, Producer.. b. Bronx, NY, Feb. 4, 1939. e. Fairleigh Dickinson, B.A., 1961; Rutgers, J.D., 1964; NYU, L.L.M., 1965. Bars passed: NJ 1965, NY 1966, US Supreme Ct. 1969. 17 years of corporate law and financing experience as sr. partner in law firm of Hahn and Hessen. Co-chmn of The ALMI Group formed, 1978. Co-chmn. & CEO of Almi Pictures Inc. formed, 1982. 1986, Almi sold its 97-screen RKO Century Warner Theatre chain to Cineplex Odeon. 1986, purchased Video Shack Inc. assets and formed RKO Warner Video, Inc.; Chmn since inception. 1988, became chmn, Damon Creations, Inc. which merged with Enro Holding Corp. and Enro Shirt Co. into Damon Creations. Sold Damon, 1988. Chmn./CEO, RKO Warner Intl. Ltd. a video franchisor and chmn./CEO of The Lexington Group Ltd., org. 1990. Member: World Presidents Organization (WPO). Chief Executives Organization (CEO); Association for a Better New York; bd. of dirs. Motion Picture Pioneers; Academy of Motion Picture Arts and Sciences; bd. of dirs. Periwinkle Theatre Productions.
PICTURES: Spaceship, The Big Score, I Am the Cheese, Rosebud Beach Hotel, Night Stalker, B. C. Roch, The Bostonians.

LANDIS, JOHN
Director, Producer, Writer, Actor. b. Chicago, IL, Aug. 3, 1950. Raised in Los Angeles. Started in mailroom at 20th Century-Fox, then worked in Europe as prod. asst. and stuntman before making first low-budget film, Schlock.
PICTURES: Director &/or Actor: Schlock (also writer), The Kentucky Fried Movie, National Lampoon's Animal House, The Blues Brothers (also co-s.p.), An American Werewolf in London (also s.p.), Trading Places, Twilight Zone—The Movie (sequence dir., also s.p., co-prod.), Into the Night, Spies Like Us, Clue (co-exec. prod., co-story only), Three Amigos!, Amazon Women on the Moon (sequence dir.; also co-exec. prod.), Coming to America, Oscar, Innocent Blood, Beverly Hills Cop III, The Stupids, Battle for the Planet of the Apes, Death Race 2000, 1941, The Muppets Take Manhattan, Spontaneous Combustion, Darkman, Diva Las Vegas, Voice of a Stranger, Sleepwalkers, Venice/Venice, The Silence of the Hams., Vampirella, Mad City.
TELEVISION: Series: Exec. prod.: Dream On (also. dir., actor), Topper (also dir.), Weird Science, Sliders, Campus Cops. Movie: Psycho IV (actor), Quicksilver Highway. Mini-series: The Stand. Specials: B.B. King Into the Night, Disneyland's 35th Anniversary Celebration. Videos: Thriller, Black or White (both for Michael Jackson).

LANDRES, PAUL
Director. b. New York, NY, Aug. 21, 1912. e. UCLA. Started as asst. film editor at Universal 1931. Editor 1937 to 1949 of many feature films. Director of feature films and TV since 1949. Under directorial contract to Warner Bros. 1961-62. Director of 22 feature films for theatrical release.
PICTURES: Oregon Passage, A Modern Marriage, Mark of the Vampire, Navy Bound, The Curse of Dracula, Miracle of the Hills, 54 Washington Street, Son of a Gunfighter, etc.
TELEVISION: Series: Bonanza, Daktari, The Rifleman, 77 Sunset Strip, Maverick Hawaiian Eye, The Plainsman, Readers Digest, Topper, Wyatt Earp, Blondie, and numerous others.

LANDSBERG, ALAN
Executive, Producer, Writer. b. New York, NY, May 10, 1933. e. NYU. Producer for NBC News Dept., 1951-59; producer-writer, CBS, 1959-60; exec. prod., Wolper Productions/ Metromedia Producers Corp., 1961-70; chairman, The Alan Landsburg Company, 1970-present.
PICTURES: Co-exec. prod.: Jaws 3-D, Porky's II: The Next Day.
TELEVISION: Exec. prod.: Biography, National Geographic Specials (1965-70): The Undersea World of Jacques Cousteau; In Search of..., That's Incredible. Movies: Adam, Fear on Trial, Parent Trap II, Adam: His Song Continues, The George McKenna Story, Long Gone, Strange Voices, Bluegrass, A Place at the Table, Too Young the Hero, A Stoning in Fulham County, High Risk, Destined to Live, Quiet Victory: The Charlie Wedemeyer Story, The Ryan White Story, Unspeakable Acts (co-exec. prod., writer), A Mother's Right: The Elizabeth Morgan Story (writer), The Hunter (writer).

LANE, DIANE
Actress. b. New York, NY, Jan. 2, 1965. Acted in stage classics (Medea, Electra, As You Like It) at La Mama Experimental Theatre Club, NY. Addtl. stage: The Cherry Orchard, Agamemnon, Runaways, Twelfth Night.
PICTURES: A Little Romance (debut, 1979), Touched by Love, National Lampoon Goes to the Movies, Cattle Annie and Little Britches, Six Pack, Ladies and Gentlemen the Fabulous Stains, The Outsiders, Rumble Fish, Streets of Fire, The Cotton Club, Big Town, Lady Beware, Priceless Beauty, Vital Signs, My New Gun, Chaplin, Knight Moves, Indian Summer, Judge Dredd, Wild Bill, Mad Dog Time, Jack, Murder at 1600, The Only Thrill.
TELEVISION: Movies: Child Bride of Short Creek, Miss All-American Beauty, Descending Angel, Oldest Living Confederate Widow Tells All. Special: Edith Wharton's Summer. Guest: Fallen Angels (Murder Obliquely). Mini-Series: Lonesome Dove.

LANE, NATHAN
Actor. r.n. Joseph Lane. b. Jersey City, NJ, Feb. 3, 1956. Received 1992 Obie Award for Sustained Excellence in Off-B'way Theatre.
THEATER: B'way: Present Laughter (Drama Desk nom.), Merlin, The Wind in the Willows, Some Americans Abroad, On Borrowed Time, Guys & Dolls (Drama Desk & Outer Critics Circle Awards; Tony nom.), Laughter on the 23rd Floor, Love! Valour! Compassion! (Drama Desk, Outer Critics Circle and Obie Awards; also Off-B'way), A Funny Thing Happened On The Way To The Forum (Tony Award). Off-B'way: A Midsummer Night's Dream, Measure for Measure, The Merry Wives of Windsor, She Stoops to Conquer, Claptrap, The Common Pursuit (Dramalogue Award), In a Pig's Valise, The Film Society, Uncounted Blessings, Hidden in This Picture, Love, The Lisbon Traviata (also L.A.; Drama Desk, Lucille Lortel, LA Drama Critics Circle & Dramalogue Awards), Bad Habits, Lips Together Teeth Apart (also L.A.).
PICTURES: Ironweed (debut, 1987), Joe Vs. the Volcano, The Lemon Sisters, He Said She Said, Frankie and Johnny, Life With Mikey, Addams Family Values, The Lion King (voice), Jeffrey (American Comedy Award nom.), The Birdcage (Golden Globe nom., American Comedy Award, SAG award)

247

TELEVISION: *Series*: One of the Boys. *Guest*: The Days and Nights of Molly Dodd, Miami Vice, Frasier (Emmy nom., American Comedy Award nom.). *Movies*: Hallmark Hall of Fame's The Boys Next Door, Timon and Pumba (Emmy Award). *Specials*: Alice in Wonderland, The Last Mile, Co-host 1995 Tony Awards, 1995 Kennedy Center Honors, Host 1996 Tony Awards (American Comedy Award nom.).

LANG, OTTO
Producer, Director. b. Tesanj, Austria (now Yugoslavia), Jan. 21, 1908. e. Salzburg, Austria. Four Academy Award nominations for Cinemascope Specials, Twentieth Century-Fox Film Corp.
PICTURES: *Dir.*: Search for Paradise. *Prod.*: Call Northside 777, Five Fingers, White Witch Doctor. *Assoc. prod*: Tora! Tora! Tora!
TELEVISION: Man from U.N.C.L.E., Daktari, Iron Horse, Cheyenne, Dick Powell Show, Zane Gray Theatre, Ann Sothern Show, Rifleman, Bat Masterson, Seahunt, The Deputy, Surfside 6, Hawaiian Eye. Prod. Twentieth Century Fox Hour. *Dir.*: Man and the Challenge, Aquanauts, World of Giants, The Legend of Cortez, Beethoven: Ordeal and Triumph, Saga of Western Man.

LANG, STEPHEN
Actor. b. Queens, NY, July 11, 1952. e. Swarthmore Col. Professional debut 1974 at Washington D.C.'s Folger Theatre.
THEATER: *NY*: Rosencrantz and Guildenstern Are Dead, Henry V, Bloomsday on Broadway, The Shadow of a Gun, Saint Joan, Hamlet, Johnny on the Spot, Death of a Salesman, Barbarians, The Winter's Tale, A Few Good Men, The Speed of Darkness.
PICTURES: Twice in a Lifetime (debut, 1985), Band of the Hand, Manhunter, Project X, Last Exit to Brooklyn, The Hard Way, Another You, Guilty As Sin, Gettysburg, Tombstone, Tall Tale, The Amazing Panda Adventure, The Shadow Conspiracy, An Occasional Hell, Fire Down Below, A Town Has Turned to Dust.
TELEVISION: *Series*: Crime Story. *Movies*: Death of a Salesman, Stone Pillow, Babe Ruth, Taking Back My Life: The Nancy Ziegenmeyer Story, Darkness Before Dawn, Murder Between Friends, A Season of Hope, The Possession of Michael D., The Phantoms, Strangers, Escape: Human Cargo. *Specials*: Anyone for Tennyson?, The Mother. *Guest*: Tribeca.

LANGE, HOPE
Actress. b. Redding Ridge, CT, Nov. 28, 1936. e. Reed Coll., Portland, OR; Barmore Jr. Coll., N.Y. Parents: John Lange, musician and Minnette Buddecke Lange, actress. Prof. stage debut in The Patriots on Broadway
THEATER: The Hot Corner (understudy), Same Time Next Year, The Supporting Cast.
PICTURES: Bus Stop (debut, 1956), The True Story of Jesse James, Peyton Place (Acad. Award nom.), The Young Lions, In Love and War, The Best of Everything, Wild in the Country, Pocketful of Miracles, Love Is a Ball, Jigsaw, Death Wish, I Am the Cheese, The Prodigal, A Nightmare on Elm Street Part 2, Blue Velvet, Tune in Tomorrow, Clear and Present Danger, Just Cause.
TELEVISION: *Series*: The Ghost and Mrs. Muir (2 Emmy Awards: 1969, 1970), The New Dick Van Dyke Show, Knight and Dave. *Movies*: Crowhaven Farm, That Certain Summer (Emmy nom.), The 500 Pound Jerk, I Love You— Goodbye, Fer-de-Lance, The Secret Night Caller, Love Boat II, Like Normal People, The Day Christ Died, Beulah Land, Pleasure Palace, Private Sessions, Dead Before Dawn, Cooperstown. Special: A Family Tree (Trying Times). *Mini-Series*: The Henry Ford Story: Man and the Machine, Message from Nam. Guest: Murder She Wrote.

LANGE, JESSICA
Actress. b. Cloquet, MN, Apr. 20, 1949. e. U. of Minnesota. Left to study mime 2 years under Etienne Decroux in Paris. Dancer, Opera Comique, Paris; model with Wilhelmina, NY. Worked in experimental theatre in New York. Broadway debut 1992 in A Streetcar Named Desire (Theatre World Award).
PICTURES: King Kong (debut, 1976), All That Jazz, How to Beat the High Cost of Living, The Postman Always Rings Twice, Frances, Tootsie (Academy Award, best supporting actress, 1982), Country (also co-prod.), Sweet Dreams, Crimes of the Heart, Far North, Everybody's All-American, Music Box, Men Don't Leave, Cape Fear, Night and the City, Blue Sky (Acad. Award, 1994), Losing Isaiah, Rob Roy, A Thousand Acres.
TELEVISION: *Special*: Cat on a Hot Tin Roof. *Movies*: O Pioneers!, A Streetcar Named Desire (Golden Globe, 1996).

LANGELLA, FRANK
Actor. b. Bayonne, NJ, Jan. 1, 1938. Studied acting at Syracuse U.; later in regional repertory, summer stock, and On- and Off-B'way. Joined Lincoln Ctr. Rep. Co., 1963.
THEATER: *NY*: The Immoralist (Off-B'way debut, 1963), Benito Cereno, The Old Glory (Obie Award), Good Day (Obie Award), The White Devil (Obie Award), Long Day's Journey Into Night, Yerma, Seascape (B'way debut, 1975; Tony Award), Dracula, A Cry of Players, Cyrano de Bergerac, The Tooth of the Crime, Ring Around the Moon, Amadeus, Passion, Design for Living, Sherlock's Last Case, The Tempest, Booth. *L.A.*: The Devils, Les Liaisons Dangereuses, My Fair Lady, Scenes From an Execution.

PICTURES: Diary of a Mad Housewife (debut, 1970), The Twelve Chairs, The Deadly Trap, The Wrath of God, Dracula, Those Lips Those Eyes, Sphinx, The Men's Club, Masters of the Universe, And God Created Woman, True Identity, 1492: Conquest of Paradise, Body of Evidence, Dave, Brainscan, Junior, Bad Company, Cutthroat Island, Eddie, Lolita, I'm Losing You, Small Soldiers, The Ninth Gate.
TELEVISION: *Specials*: Benito Cereno, The Good Day, The Ambassador, The Sea Gull, The American Woman: Portrait in Courage, Eccentricities of a Nightingale, Sherlock Holmes, Fortitude (Kurt Vonnegut's Monkey House). *Movies*: The Mark of Zorro, Liberty, Doomsday Gun.

LANGFORD, FRANCES
Singer, Actress. b. Lakeland, FL, April 4, 1913. e. Southern Coll. Stage experience in vaudeville, nightclubs, national radio programs.
PICTURES: Every Night at Eight, Collegiate, Broadway Melody of 1936, Palm Springs, Born to Dance, The Hit Parade, Hollywood Hotel, Dreaming Out Loud, Too Many Girls, The Hit Parade of 1941, All-American Coed, Mississippi Gambler, Yankee Doodle Dandy, Cowboy in Manhattan, This Is the Army, Never a Dull Moment, Career Girl, The Girl Rush, Dixie Jamboree, Radio Stars on Parade, Bamboo Blonde, Make Mine Laughs, People Are Funny, Deputy Marshall, Purple Heart Diary, The Glenn Miller Story.

LANGNER, PHILIP
Producer, b. New York, NY, Aug. 24, 1926. e. Yale U. President of The Theatre Guild and Theatre Guild Films, Inc. Producer the Westport Country Playhouse 1947-53. Joined The Theatre Guild 1954.
THEATER: The Matchmaker, Bells Are Ringing, The Tunnel of Love, Sunrise at Campobello, A Majority of One, The Unsinkable Molly Brown, A Passage to India, Seidman and Son, The Royal Hunt of the Sun, The Homecoming, Absurd Person Singular, Golda.
PICTURES: *Producer*: The Pawnbroker, Slaves, Born to Win. Associate Prod.: Judgment at Nuremberg, A Child Is Waiting.

LANSBURY, ANGELA
Actress. b. London, England, Oct. 16, 1925. Brothers are producers Bruce and Edgar Lansbury. e. South Hampstead Sch. for Girls, England; Acad. of Music, London; Feagin Dramatic Sch., N.Y. Mother was actress Moyna Macgill. To NY 1940 to study drama. Signed to contract by MGM, 1944. Exercise and lifestyle video: Positive Moves, 1988. Book: Positive Moves, 1990.
THEATER: *B'way*: Hotel Paradiso (NY debut, 1957), A Taste of Honey, Anyone Can Whistle, Mame (Tony Award, 1966), Dear World (Tony Award, 1969), Prettybelle (closed out of town), All Over, Gypsy (Tony Award, 1975), Hamlet, The King and I, Sweeney Todd: The Demon Barber of Fleet Street (Tony Award, 1979), A Little Family Business, Mame (1983 revival).
PICTURES: Gaslight (debut, 1944; Acad. Award nom.), National Velvet, The Picture of Dorian Gray (Acad. Award nom.), The Harvey Girls, The Hoodlum Saint, The Private Affairs of Bel Ami, Till the Clouds Roll By, If Winter Comes, Tenth Avenue Angel, State of the Union, The Three Musketeers, The Red Danube, Samson and Delilah, Kind Lady, Mutiny, Remains to Be Seen, The Purple Mask, A Lawless Street, The Court Jester, Please Murder Me, The Key Man (A Life at Stake), The Long Hot Summer, The Reluctant Debutante, The Summer of the 17th Doll (Season of Passion), The Dark at the Top of the Stairs, A Breath of Scandal, Blue Hawaii, All Fall Down, The Manchurian Candidate (Acad. Award nom.), In the Cool of the Day, The World of Henry Orient, Dear Heart, The Greatest Story Ever Told, Harlow, The Amorous Adventures of Moll Flanders, Mister Buddwing, Something for Everyone, Bedknobs and Broomsticks, Death on the Nile, The Lady Vanishes, The Mirror Crack'd, The Last Unicorn (voice), The Pirates of Penzance, The Company of Wolves, Beauty and the Beast (voice).
TELEVISION: *Special*: Sweeney Todd. *Movies*: Little Gloria... Happy at Last, The Gift of Love: A Christmas Story, The First Olympics: Athens 1896, A Talent for Murder, Lace, Rage of Angels: The Story Continues, Shootdown, The Shell Seekers, The Love She Sought, Mrs. 'arris Goes to Paris, Mrs. Santa Claus. *Series*: Pantomime Quiz, Murder She Wrote (also exec. prod.). *Guest*: Robert Montgomery Presents, Four Star Playhouse, Studio 57, Playhouse 90, GE Theatre, Fireside Theatre, Lux Video Theatre, Revlon Mirror Theatre, Ford Theatre, Schlitz Playhouse of the Stars, Stage 7, Front Row Center, Screen Directors Playhouse, Eleventh Hour, The Man from U.N.C.L.E., Climax, The Perry Como Show, The Julie Andrews Hour.

LANSBURY, BRUCE
Executive. b. London, England, Jan. 12, 1930. Brother of Angela and twin Edgar. e. UCLA. Mother was actress Moyna Macgill. Writer, prod. KABC-TV, Los Angeles, 1957-59; joined CBS-TV, 1959, was ass't. dir., program dev., program dev. and v.p., programs, New York; 1964-66, indep. prod.; Broadway stage: 1966-69 producer, Wild Wild West, CBS series; 1969-72, prod. Mission: Impossible, Paramount Movies of Week; now v.p., creative affairs, Paramount TV.
TELEVISION: Great Adventure (series; prod.), Wings of the Water (exec. prod.), Murder She Wrote.

LANSBURY, EDGAR
Producer, Director, Designer. b. London, England, Jan. 12, 1930. e. UCLA. Brother of Angela and Bruce Lansbury. Started career as scenic designer and art dir. 1955-60, art dir., CBS; 1962-63, exec. art dir. prod. for WNDT-TV, educational station.
THEATER: *Producer–B'way*: The Subject Was Roses, That Summer That Fall, Promenade, Waiting for Godot, Long Day's Journey into Night, Gospel, Gypsy, The Night That Made America Famous, American Buffalo, Amphigorey: The Musical, Any Given Day, In Circles, As Bees in Honey Drown, June Moon, etc. *Director*: Without Apologies, Advice From a Caterpillar, The Country Club.
PICTURES: *Producer*: The Subject Was Roses, Godspell, The Wild Party, Squirm, Blue Sunshine, He Knows You're Alone, The Clairvoyant.
TELEVISION: The Defenders (art. dir.), Summer Girl (exec. prod.), Wings of the Water (exec. prod.), A Stranger Waits.

LANSING, SHERRY LEE
Executive. b. Chicago, IL, July 31, 1944. e. Northwestern U. m. director William Friedkin. Taught math and English in L.A. city high schools, 1966-69. Acted in films (Loving, Rio Lobo) and numerous TV shows. Story Ed. Wagner Int'l. Prod. Co. 1972-74. Dir. West Coast Devel. 1974-75. Story Ed. Mgr. 1975-77, VP Creative Affairs 1977. VP Prod'n. Columbia Pictures 1977-80. Pres. 20th Century Fox Prod'n. 1980-82. Founded Jaffe-Lansing Prod'ns. w/ Stanley Jaffe 1982. Exec. Story Ed. Movies, Wagner Int'l. 1970-73. VP Prod'n. Heyday Prods 1973-75. Exec. Story Ed then VP Creative Affairs MGM Studios 1975-77. SVP Prod'n. Columbia Pictures 1977-80. Pres. 20th Century Fox Prods. 1980-83. Ind. producer Jaffe-Lansing Prods. 1983-91.
PICTURES: *Co-prod.*: Racing with the Moon, Firstborn, Fatal Attraction, The Accused, Black Rain, School Ties, Indecent Proposal (prod.).
TELEVISION: When the Time Comes (exec. prod.), Mistress.

LaPAGLIA, ANTHONY
Actor. b. Adelaide, Australia, 1959. Former teacher, moved to U.S. in 1984. Made Off-B'way debut in Bouncers, followed by On the Open Road. *B'way*: The Rose Tattoo (Theatre World Award).
PICTURES: Slaves of New York (debut, 1989), Dangerous Obsession (Mortal Sins), Betsy's Wedding, He Said/She Said, One Good Cop, 29th Street, Whispers in the Dark, Innocent Blood, So I Married an Axe Murderer, The Client, The Custodian, Mixed Nuts, Bulletproof Heart, Lucky Break, Empire Records, Nowhere Man, The Funeral, Brilliant Lies, The Garden of Redemption.
TELEVISION: *Movies*: Criminal Justice, Keeper of the City, Black Magic, Past Tense, Nitti: The Enforcer. *Series*: Murder One.

LARDNER, RING W., JR.
Writer. b. Chicago, IL, Aug. 19, 1915. p. writer-humorist Ring W. and Ellis A. e. Phillips Andover Acad, Princeton U. Was reporter on New York Daily Mirror. Publ. writer, Selznick International. 1947, member of "Hollywood 10." In collab. with Ian Hunter conceived and wrote under pseudonyms many episodes in 5 TV series while blacklisted. Uncredited writer of such films as A Breath of Scandal, The Cardinal. 1989, received Writers Guild Laurel Award. Author of novels: The Ecstacy of Owen Muir, All For Love, and memoir, The Lardners My Family Remembered. Also collab. on B'way musical Foxy. 1992, WGA Ian McLellan Hunter Memorial Award for Lifetime Achievement.
PICTURES: Woman of the Year (Academy Award, 1942), The Cross of Lorraine, Tomorrow the World, Forever Amber, Forbidden Street, Four Days Leave, Cloak and Dagger, The Cincinnati Kid, M*A*S*H (Academy Award, 1970), The Greatest.

LARKIN, JAMES J.
Executive. b. Brooklyn, NY, Nov. 2, 1925. e. Columbia U., 1947-52. U.S. Air Force, 1943-46; BOAC rep. to entertainment ind., 1948-60; pres., Transportation Counselors Inc., 1960-62; pres., Larkin Associates, Inc., 1962-65; exec. Radio N.Y. Worldwide, 1965-68; v.p. Grolier Educational Corp., 1968-69; v.p. Visual Informational Systems, 1969-73; pres., Business TV Services, Inc., 1973-; exec. prod., Madhouse Brigade, 1977-79; prod.-writer, All Those Beautiful Girls, 1979-80.

LARROQUETTE, JOHN
Actor. b. New Orleans, LA., Nov. 25, 1947. Disc jockey on FM radio during 1960s and early 70s. Acted on L.A. stage from 1973 (The Crucible, Enter Laughing, Endgame). Prof. debut, TV series Doctor's Hospital, 1976-78. Was narrator for film Texas Chainsaw Massacre.
PICTURES: Altered States, Heart Beat, Green Ice, Stripes, Cat People, Hysterical, Twilight Zone—The Movie, Choose Me, Meatballs II, Star Trek III: The Search for Spock, Summer Rental, Blind Date, Second Sight, Madhouse, Tune in Tomorrow, Richie Rich.
TELEVISION: *Series*: Doctor's Hospital, Baa Baa Black Sheep, Night Court (4 Emmy Awards, 1985-88), The John Larroquette Show. *Movies*: Bare Essence, The Last Ninja, Hot Paint, Convicted, One Special Victory (also co-exec. prod.), The Defenders. *Guest*: The Practice (Emmy Award, 1997).

LASSALLY, WALTER
Cinematographer. b. Berlin, Germany, Dec. 18, 1926. Entered indust. as clapper-boy at Riverside Studios. During 1950s allied himself with Britain's Free Cinema filmmakers working for Lindsay Anderson, Gavin Lambert, Tony Richardson and Karel Reisz.
PICTURES: A Girl in Black (feature debut, 1956), Beat Girl, A Taste of Honey, Electra, The Loneliness of the Long Distance Runner, Tom Jones, Zorba the Greek (Academy Award, 1964), The Day the Fish Came Out, Joanna, Oedipus the King, The Adding Machine, Three Into Two Won't Go, Something for Everyone, Twinky (Lola), Savages, Happy Mother's Day... Love George, To Kill a Clown, The Wild Party, Pleasantville, The Great Bank Hoax, The Woman Across the Way, Hullabaloo Over George and Bonnie's Pictures, Something Short of Paradise, The Blood of Hussain, Angel of Iron, Memoirs of a Survivor, Too Far to Go, Heat and Dust, Private School, The Bostonians, The Deceivers, Fragments of Isabella, The Perfect Murder, Ballad of the Sad Cafe, The Little Dolphins.
TELEVISION: Mrs. Delafield Wants to Marry, The Man Upstairs.

LASSER, LOUISE
Actress. b. New York, NY, April 11, 1939. e. Brandeis U., New School for Social Research. Appeared on stage before theatrical film debut in 1965 with What's New Pussycat? Won first Clio Award for best actress in a commercial.
THEATER: I Can Get it For You Wholesale, The Third Ear, Henry Sweet Henry, Lime Green/Khaki Blue, The Chinese, Marie & Bruce, A Coupla White Chicks Sitting Around Talking.
PICTURES: What's Up Tiger Lily? (voice), Take the Money and Run, Bananas, Such Good Friends, Everything You Always Wanted to Know About Sex, Slither, Simon, In God We Trust, Stardust Memories, Crimewave, Nightmare at Shadow Woods (Blood Rage), Surrender, Sing, Rude Awakening, Modern Love, Frankenhooker, The Night We Never Met.
TELEVISION: *Series*: Mary Hartman Mary Hartman, It's a Living. *Movies*: Coffee Tea or Me?, Isn't It Shocking?, Just Me and You (also writer), For Ladies Only. *Guest*: Bob Newhart Show, Mary Tyler Moor Show, Taxi, St. Elsewhere, Empty Nest, many others. Special: The Lie.

LASZLO ASC, ANDREW
Cinematographer. b. Papa, Hungary, Jan. 12, 1926. To U.S. in 1947, working as cameraman on tv before turning to feature films.
PICTURES: One Potato Two Potato, You're a Big Boy Now, The Night They Raided Minskys, Popi, The Out of Towners, Lovers and Other Strangers, The Owl and the Pussycat, Jennifer on My Mind, To Find a Man, The Effect of Gamma Rays on Man-in-the-Moon Marigolds, Class of '44, Countdown at Kusini, Thieves, Somebody Killed Her Husband, The Warriors, The Funhouse, Southern Comfort, I the Jury, First Blood, Streets of Fire, Thief of Hearts, Remo Williams: The Adventure Begins, Poltergeist II, Innerspace, Star Trek V: The Final Frontier, Ghost Dad, Newsies.
TELEVISION: *Documentaries*: High Adventure with Lowell Thomas, The Twentieth Century. *Series*: The Phil Silvers Show, Joe and Mabel, Mama, Brenner, Naked City, The Nurses, Doctors and Nurses, Coronet Blue. *Specials*: New York New York, The Beatles at Shea Stadium, Ed Sullivan Specials. *Movies and feature pilots*: The Happeners, The Cliffdwellers, Daphne, Teacher Teacher, Blue Water Gold, The Man Without a Country, The Unwanted, Spanner's Key, Thin Ice, Love is Forever. *Mini-series*: Washington Behind Closed Doors, The Dain Curse, Top of the Hill, Shogun, and numerous commericals.

LATSIS, PETER C.
Publicist. b. Chicago, IL, Mar. 9, 1919. e. Wright Jr. Coll., Chicago. Newspaper reporter, Chicago Herald-American, 1942-45; Army, 1943; joined Fox West Coast Theatres, Los Angeles, in theatre operations 1945; adv.-pub. dept. 1946; asst. dir. adv.-pub. 1955; press rep. National Theatres, 1958; press relations dir., National General Corp., 1963; home office special field pub. repr., American International Pictures, 1973; Filmways Pictures, 1980-82; Recipient of Publicists Guild's Robert Yeager Award, 1983. Member, Motion Picture Pioneers. Unit rep., Executive Bd. of Publicists Guild of America, 1993-95.

LATTANZI, MATT
Actor. m. actress-singer Olivia Newton-John.
PICTURES: Xanadu (1980), Rich and Famous, Grease 2, My Tutor, That's Life!, Roxanne, Blueberry Hill, Catch Me If You Can, Diving In.
TELEVISION: *Series*: Paradise Beach.

LATTUADA, ALBERTO
Director. b. Milan, Italy, 1914. Son of Felice Lattuada, musician, opera composer, and writer of scores of many of son's films. Studied architecture; founded the periodical Cominare. Later founded Italian Film Library of which he still pres. Also, pres., Cinema D'Essay, First screen work as scriptwriter and asst. dir. of two films, 1940.
PICTURES: Mill on the Po, Anna, The Overcoat, La Lupa, Love in the City, White Sister, Flesh Will Surrender, Without Pity, The She Wolf, Tempest, The Unexpected, Mafioso, The Mandrake, Matchless, The Betrayal, The Steppe, Oh Serafina, Stay as You Are.

LAUGHLIN, TOM
Actor, Producer, Director, Writer. b. Minneapolis, MN, 1938. e. U. of Indiana, U. of Minnesota where had athletic scholarships. m. actress Delores Taylor. Travelled around world, studying in Italy with Dr. Maria Montessori. Established, ran a Montessori school in Santa Monica for several yrs. Worked his way to Hollywood, where acted in bit parts until stardom came in Born Losers in 1967. Produced and starred in Billy Jack and The Trial of Billy Jack, also writing s.p. with wife under pseudonym Frank Christina. Heads own prod. co., Billy Jack Enterprises.
PICTURES: *Actor*: Tea and Sympathy, The Delinquents, South Pacific, Senior Prom, Lafayette Escadrille, Gidget, Battle of the Coral Sea, Tall Story, Born Losers, Callan, Brannigan, Voyage of the Damned, The Littlest Horse Thieves, The Big Sleep, The Legend of the Lone Ranger, Murder Elite, No Escape, Wild Bill: A Hollywood Maverick. *Actor-Dir.-Prod.-Writer*: The Proper Time, The Young Sinner, Born Losers, Billy Jack, The Trial of Billy Jack, The Master Gunfighter, Billy Jack Goes to Washington.
TELEVISION: *Movies*: The War That Never Ends, Zoya.

LAUNER, DALE
Writer. b. Cleveland, OH. E. Cal State Northridge. Son of actor John S. Launer.
PICTURES: Ruthless People, Blind Date, Dirty Rotten Scoundrels, My Cousin Vinny, Love Potion #9 (also dir.).

LAURENTS, ARTHUR
Writer, Director. b. New York, NY, July 14, 1917. e. Cornell U., B.A., 1937. First Professional writing as radio script writer in 1939. In Army 1941-45. Member of the Council of the Dramatists Guild; Theatre Hall of Fame.
THEATER: *Author*: Home of the Brave (Sidney Howard Award), Heartsong, The Bird Cage, The Time of the Cuckoo, A Clearing in the Woods, Invitation to a March, West Side Story, Gypsy, Hallelujah, Baby! (Tony Award), Scream, The Enclave, Running Time, Jolson Sings Again, The Radical Mystique. *Director*: Invitation to a March, I Can Get It for You Wholesale, La Cage aux Folles (Tony Award), Birds of Paradise. *Author-Director*: Anyone Can Whistle, Do I Hear a Waltz?, The Madwoman of Central Park West, Gypsy (revival), Nick and Nora.
PICTURES: *Writer*: The Snake Pit, Rope, Caught, Anna Lucasta, Anastasia, Bonjour Tristesse, The Way We Were (from his own novel), The Turning Point (also co-prod.; Golden Globe, Writer's Guild Award).

LAURIA, DAN
Actor. b. Brooklyn, NY, April 12, 1947. e. So Conn. St. Col., Univ. of Conn. Served in U.S. Marine Corps., 1970\-73.
PICTURES: Without a Trace, Stakeout, Another Stakeout, Excessive Force II: Force on Force.
TELEVISION: *Series*: Love of Life, One Life to Live, Hooperman, The Wonder Years. *Movies*: Johnny Brass, Johnny Bull, Doing Life, At Mother's Request, Angel in Green, David, Howard Beach: Making the Case for Murder, The Big One: The Great Los Angeles Earthquake, Overexposed, Dead and Alive, From the Files of Joseph Wambaugh: A Jury of One, In the Line of Duty: Ambush in Waco, In the Line of Duty: Hunt for Justice. *Guest*: Growing Pains, Mike Hammer, Moonlighting, Hill Street Blues, NYPD Blue, Chicago Hope, Party of Five. *Special*: Between Mother and Daughter.

LAURIE, PIPER
Actress. r.n. Rosetta Jacobs. b. Detroit, MI, Jan. 22, 1932. e. Los Angeles H.S. Acted in school plays, signed by U.I. in 1949.
THEATER: The Glass Menagerie (revival), Marco Polo Sings a Solo, The Innocents, Biography, Rosemary, The Alligators, The Last Flapper (tour), The Destiny of Me.
PICTURES: Louisa (debut, 1950), The Milkman, Francis Goes to the Races, The Prince Who Was a Thief, Son of Ali Baba, Has Anybody Seen My Gal, No Room for the Groom, Mississippi Gambler, Golden Blade, Dangerous Mission, Johnny Dark, Dawn at Socorro, Smoke Signal, Ain't Misbehavin', Kelly and Me, Until They Sail, The Hustler (Acad. Award nom.), Carrie (Acad. Award nom.), Ruby, The Boss's Son, Tim, Return to Oz, Children of a Lesser God (Acad. Award nom.), Distortions, Appointment with Death, Tiger Warsaw, Dream a Little Dream, Mother Mother, Other People's Money, Storyville, Rich in Love, Trauma, Wrestling Ernest Hemingway, The Crossing Guard, The Grass Harp.
TELEVISION: *Specials*: Days of Wine and Roses (Emmy nom.), The Road That Led Afar (Emmy nom.), The Deaf Heart (Emmy nom.), The Secret Life of Margaret Sanger. *Movies*: In the Matter of Karen Ann Quinlan, Rainbow, Skag, The Bunker (Emmy nom.), Mae West, Love Mary, Toughlove, Promise (Emmy Award, 1987), Go To the Light, Rising Son, Poisoned By Love: The Kern County Murders, Lies and Lullabies, Shadows of Desire, Fighting for My Daughter. *Series*: Skag, Twin Peaks (Golden Globe Award, Emmy nom.). *Mini-Series*: The Thorn Birds (Emmy nom.), Tender is the Night. *Guest*: St. Elsewhere (Emmy nom.)

LAUTER, ED
Actor. b. Long Beach, NY, Oct. 30, 1940.
PICTURES: The New Centurions, Hickey & Boggs, The Last American Hero, Executive Action, Lolly Madonna XXX, The Longest Yard, French Connection II, Breakheart Pass, Family Plot, King Kong, The Chicken Chronicles, Magic, The Amateur, Death Hunt, Timerider, The Big Score, Eureka, Lassiter, Cujo, Finders Keepers, Death Wish 3, Girls Just Want to Have Fun, Youngblood, 3:15, Raw Deal, Chief Zabu, Revenge of the Nerds II, Gleaming the Cube, Fat Man and Little Boy, Tennessee Waltz, School Ties, Wagons East!, Trial by Jury, Girl in the Cadillac, Digital Man, Crash, Rattled, Coyote Summer, Mulholland Falls, Top of the World, Allie & Me, The Day October Died.
TELEVISION: *Series*: B.J. and the Bear. *Movies*: Class of '63, The Migrants, The Godchild, Satan's Triangle, A Shadow in the Streets, Last Hours Before Morning, The Clone Master, The Jericho Mile, Love's Savage Fury, Undercover with the KKK, The Boy Who Drank Too Much, Guyana Tragedy—The Story of Jim Jones, Alcatraz:The Whole Shocking Story, In the Custody of Strangers, Rooster, The Seduction of Gina, Three Wishes of Billy Grier, The Last Days of Patton, The Thanksgiving Promise, Calendar Girl Cop Killer?: The Bambi Bembenek Story, Extreme Justice, The Return of Ironside, Secret Sins of the Father, Tuskegee Airmen, Ravenhawk, Under Wraps, Mercenary, A Bright Shining Lie.

LAVEN, ARNOLD
Director, Producer. b. Chicago, IL, Feb. 23, 1922.
PICTURES: Without Warning (debut, 1952), Vice Squad, Down Three Dark Streets, The Rack, The Monster That Challenged the World, Slaughter on Tenth Ave., Anna Lucasta, Geronimo (also prod.), The Glory Guys (also co-prod.), Clambake (co-prod. only), Rough Night in Jericho, Sam Whiskey (also co-prod.).
TELEVISION: Part creator and director TV pilots: The Rifleman, Robert Taylor's Detectives, The Plainsmen.

LAVIN, LINDA
Actress. b. Portland, ME, Oct. 15, 1937. e. Coll. of William & Mary. First professional job in chorus of Camden County (N.J.) Music Circus. Worked in plays both off and on Broadway before turning to TV, where guest-starred on such series as Family, Rhoda, Phyllis and Harry O.
THEATER: Oh Kay! (Off-B'way debut, 1960), A Family Affair (B'way debut), Revues: Wet Paint (Theatre World Award), The Game Is Up, The Mad Show, member acting co.: Eugene O'Neil Playwright's Unit, 1968; It's a Bird It's a Plane... It's Superman, Something Different, Little Murders (Outer Critics Circle & Sat. Review Awards), Cop Out, The Last of the Red Hot Lovers (Tony nom.), Story Theatre, Dynamite Tonight, Broadway Bound (Tony, Drama Desk, Outer Critics Circle & Helen Hayes Awards), Gypsy, The Sisters Rosensweig, Death Defying Acts.
PICTURES: The Muppets Take Manhattan, See You in the Morning, I Want to Go Home.
TELEVISION: *Series*: Barney Miller, Alice (2 Golden Globe Awards; 2 Emmy noms.), Room for Two (also co-exec. prod.). *Movies*: The Morning After, Like Mom and Me, The $5.20 an Hour Dream, A Matter of Life and Death (also exec. prod. & developed), Another Woman's Child, A Place to Call Home (also exec. prod. & developed), Lena: My Hundred Children, Room for Two, Stolen Moments, Secrets from the Rose Garden, A Dream Is a Wish Your Heart Makes, The Annette Funicello Story, The Ring, For the Children: The Irvine Fertility Scandal, Conrad Bloom, Best Friends for Life.

LAW, JOHN PHILLIP
Actor. b. Hollywood, CA, Sept. 7, 1937. e. Neighborhood Playhouse. B'way debut in Coming on Strong. Appeared at Lincoln Center in After the Fall, Marco Millions, The Changeling, and Tartuffe. Has made more than 50 films in more than 20 countries world wide.
PICTURES: High Infidelity, Three Nights of Love, The Russians Are Coming The Russians Are Coming the Russians Are Coming (U.S. debut), Hurry Sundown, Barbarella, Danger Diabolik, The Sergeant, Death Rides a Horse, Skidoo, Diary of a Telephone Operator, Von Richtofen and Brown, The Hawaiians, Michael Strogoff, The Love Machine, The Last Movie, The Golden Voyage of Sinbad, Stardust, Open Season, Your God My Hell, The Spiral Staircase, Dr. Justice, African Rage, Whisper in the Dark, Portrait of an Assassin, The Crystal Man, Death in November, Ring of Darkness, The Cassandra Crossing, Der Schimmelreiter, Attack Force Z, Tarzan the Ape Man, Night Train to Terror, The Tin Man, Rainy Day Friends (L.A. Bad), No Time to Die, American Commandos (Mr. Salvage), Johann Strauss, The Moon Under the Trees, Moon in Scorpio, Striker (Combat Force), The Overthrow, Mutiny in Space, Thunder Warrior III, A Case of Honor, Blood Delirium, Alienator, L.A. Heat, Gorilla, The Guest, Alaska Stories, Angel Eyes, Shining Blood, Marilyn Behind Bars, Day of the Pig, The Mountain of the Lord, Europa Mission.
TELEVISION: *Series*: The Young and the Restless (1989). *Movie*: The Best Place to Be, A Great Love Story (It.), Experiences (It.), The Fourth Man (Austrian), Little Women of Today (It.). *Guest*: The Love Boat, Murder She Wrote.

LAW, LINDSAY
Producer. e. NYU School of the Arts. Producer of specials for Warner Bros. Television, head of drama for WNET/New York and prod. for Theatre in America before becoming exec. prod. of American Playhouse. Advisory Board of Independent Feature Project/West, Sundance Film Festival.
PICTURES: *Exec. prod.*: On Valentine's Day, Smooth Talk, Native Son, In a Shallow Grave, Stand and Deliver, The Thin Blue Line, El Norte, The Wizard of Loneliness, Signs of Life, Bloodhounds of Broadway, Big Time, Eat a Bowl of Tea, Longtime Companion, Thousand Pieces of Gold, Straight Out of Brooklyn, Daughters of the Dust, Thank You and Goodnight, All the Vermeers in New York, Brother's Keeper, Ethan Frome, The Music of Chance, Golden Gate, I Shot Andy Warhol, Fast Cheap and Out of Control.
TELEVISION: *Prod.*: The Girls in Their Summer Dresses, The Time of Your Life, You Can't Take It With You, The Good Doctor, The Most Happy Fella, The Eccentricities of a Nightingale, Cyrano de Bergerac (assoc. prod.). *Prod. for American Playhouse*: Working, for Colored Girls Who Have Considered Suicide/When the Rainbow Is Enuf, Private Contentment, *Exec. prod.*: Concealed Enemies (Emmy Award, 1984), Land of Little Rain, Ask Me Again, The Diaries of Adam and Eve, A Walk in the Woods, Fires in the Mirror.

LAWRENCE, BARBARA
Actress. b. Carnegie, OK, Feb. 24, 1930. e. UCLA. Mother Berenice Lawrence. Child model; successful screen try-out, 1944; screen debut in Billy Rose Diamond Horse Shoe (1945).
PICTURES: Margie, Captain from Castile, You Were Meant for Me, Give My Regards to Broadway, Street with No Name, Unfaithfully Yours, Letter to Three Wives, Mother Is a Freshman, Thieves Highway, Two Tickets to Broadway, Here Come the Nelsons, The Star, Arena, Paris Model, Her 12 Men, Oklahoma, Man with the Gun, Joe Dakota, Kronos.

LAWRENCE, JOEY
Actor. b. Montgomery, PA, Apr. 20, 1976. e. USC.
PICTURES: Summer Rental, Oliver and Company (voice), Pulse, Radioland Murders, Tequila Body Shots.
TELEVISION: *Series*: Gimme a Break, Blossom, Brotherly Love. *Pilots*: Scamps, Little Shots. *Specials*: Andy Williams and the NBC Kids, Don't Touch, Alvin Goes Back to School, Umbrella Jack, Adventures in Babysitting, Disney's Countdown to Kids' Day, All That, Blossom in Paris, Kids' Choice Awards (host), etc. *Movies*: Chains of Gold, Prince for a Day, Brothers of the Frontier.

LAWRENCE, MARC
Actor. r.n. Max Goldsmith. b. New York, NY, Feb. 17, 1914. e. City Coll. of New York. On stage in The Tree (Eva La Galliene Rep. Theatre.), Sour Mountain, Waiting for Lefty, Golden Boy, View From the Bridge.
PICTURES: White Woman, Little Big Shot, Dr. Socrates, Road Gang, San Quentin, The Ox Bow Incident, I Am the Law, While New York Sleeps, Dillinger, Flame of Barbary Coast, Club Havana, Don't Fence Me In, The Virginian, Life with Blondie, Yankee Fakir, Captain from Castile, I Walk Alone, Calamity Jane and Sam Bass, The Asphalt Jungle, Hurricane Island, My Favorite Spy, Girls Marked Danger, Helen of Troy, Johnny Cool, Nightmare in the Sun, Savage Pampas, Johnny Tiger, Custer of the West, Nightmare in the Sun (dir. co- prod., co-story only), Krakatoa East of Java, The Kremlin Letter, Fraser: The Sensuous Lion, The Man With the Golden Gun, Marathon Man, A Piece of the Action, Foul Play, Goin' Cocoanuts, Hot Stuff, Night Train to Terror, The Big Easy, Ruby, Newsies, Marilyn I Love You.

LAWRENCE, MARTIN
Actor, Comedian. b. Frankfurt, Germany, 1965. Started as stand-up comic in Washington D.C.
PICTURES: Do the Right Thing (debut, 1989), House Party, Talkin' Dirty After Dark, House Party 2, Boomerang, You So Crazy (also exec. prod.), Bad Boys, Nothing to Lose.
TELEVISION: *Series*: What's Happening Now?, Kid 'n' Play (voice), Russell Simmons' Def Comedy Jam (host, prod. consultant), Martin (also creator, co-exec. prod.). *Pilots*: Hammer Slammer & Slade, A Little Bit Strange. *Guest*: Stand Up Spotlight, Yo! MTV Laffs, An Evening at the Improv.

LAWRENCE, STEVE
Actor. r.n. Sydney Leibowitz. b. Brooklyn, NY, July 8, 1935. m. singer Eydie Gorme. Singer in nightclubs and on TV.
THEATER: What Makes Sammy Run?, Golden Rainbow.
PICTURES: Stand Up and Be Counted, The Blues Brothers, The Lonely Guy, Blues Brothers 2000.
TELEVISION: *Specials*: Steve and Eydie Celebrate Irving Berlin (also co-exec. prod.), Emmy Award, 1979), many specials. *Series*: Tonight, The Steve Lawrence-Eydie Gorme Show (1958), The Steve Lawrence Show (1965), Foul-Ups Bleeps and Blunders (host). *Guest*: Police Story, Murder, She Wrote. *Movie*: Alice in Wonderland.

LAWRENCE, VICKI
Actress. b. Inglewood, CA, March 26, 1949. Singer and recording artist appearing with Young Americans (1965-67). Gained fame on The Carol Burnett Show as comedienne (1967-78), winning Emmy Award in 1976. Gold record for The Night the Lights Went Out in Georgia (1972). Author: *Vicki!: The True Life Adventures of Miss Fireball* (Simon & Schuster, 1995).
TELEVISION: *Movies*: Having Babies, Hart to Hart: Old Friends Never Die. *Series*: Carol Burnett Show, Jimmie Rodgers Show, Mama's Family. *Host*: Win Lose or Draw (1987-88), Vicki!, Fox After Breakfast (synd. talk shows).

LAWSON, SARAH
Actress. b. London, Eng., Aug. 6, 1928. e. Heron's Ghyll Sch., Sussex. Stage debut in Everyman (Edinburgh Festival) 1947.
PICTURES: The Browning Version (debut, 1951), The Night Won't Talk, Street Corner, Street Corner (Both Sides of the Law), Three Steps in the Dark, Meet Mr. Malcolm, You Know What Sailors Are, Blue Peter (Navy Heroes), It's Never Too Late, Links of Justice, Three Crooked Men, The Solitary Child, Night Without Pity, On the Run, The World Ten Times Over, Island of the Burning Doomed, The Devil's Bride (The Devil Rides Out), Battle of Britain, The Stud, The Dawning (prod.).
TELEVISION: Face to Face, River Line, Whole Truth, Lady From the Sea, Mrs. Moonlight, Silver Card, An Ideal Husband, Love and Money, Rendezvous, Invisible Man, Saber Buccaneers, White Hunter, Flying Doctor, On the Night of the Murder, Haven in Sunset, The Odd Man, Zero 1 (series), The Innocent Ceremony, Department S, The Marrying Kind, The Expert, The Persuaders, Trial, Starcast, The Midsummer of Colonel Blossum, Callen, Crime of Passion, Full House, Father Brown, Within These Walls These Walls Series, The Standard, The Purple Twilight, The Professionals, Bergerac, Cuffy, Lovejoy.

LAYBOURNE, GERALDINE
Executive. e. Vassar College, B.A.; U. Penn, M.S. Joined Nickelodeon in 1980. Was vice chmn., MTV Networks; pres., Nickelodeon/Nick at Nite. Bd. member Viacom exec. committee. Left Nickelodeon to join ABC as pres., Disney/ABC Cable Networks. Inducted into Broadcast and Cable Hall of Fame, 1996. Resigned ABC/Cable post in 1998 and started own network/cable/internet production company, Oxygen Media.

LAZARUS, PAUL N.
Executive. b. Brooklyn, NY, March 31, 1913. e. Cornell U., B.A., 1933. In U.S. Army, W.W. II. Entered m.p. ind. 1933 as gen. asst., press book dept., Warner Bros.; pres., AMPA, 1939-40. Joined Buchanan & Co., 1942 as m.p. account exec. To United Artists 1943 as dir. adv. & pub. Named asst. to pres., 1948; joined Columbia exec. staff, New York, 1950; elected v.p. Columbia, 1954-62; exec. v.p. Samuel Bronston Prods., 1962-64; v.p., chg. Motion Pictures, Subscription Television Inc., 1964; exec. officer and partner, Landau Releasing Organization, 1964-65; exec. v.p., member bd. of dir., Nat'l Screen Serv. Corp., 1965-75; lecturer and consultant, Film Studies Program, U. of CA at Santa Barbara, 1975-. Consultant to Kenya Film Corp., Nairobi, 1983. Director, Santa Barbara Intl. Film Festival, 1986-87. Chief of Staff, Santa Barbara Writers' Conference, 1976-. Vice-chmn. Santa Barbara County Film Council, 1989-92.

LAZARUS, PAUL N. III
Executive. b. New York, NY, May 25, 1938. e. Williams Coll., BA.; Yale Law Sch., L.L.B. Third generation film exec. Began career with Palomar Pictures Int'l. as exec. v.p.; joined ABC Pictures Corp. as v.p. in chg. of creative affairs. Mng. dir., CRM Productions, maker of educational films; v.p. for motion pictures. Marble Arch Productions; 1983, v.p. in chg. of prod., Home Box Office. 1985, Film Commissioner, New Mexico; 1987, Dir. of Film Program, U of Miami.
PICTURES: *Prod.*: Extreme Close-Up, Westworld, Futureworld, Capricorn One, Hanover Street, Barbarosa, Doubles.

LAZENBY, GEORGE
Actor. b. Gouburn, Australia, Sept. 5, 1939. Appeared in Australian and British tv commericals before being chosen to star as James Bond.
PICTURES: On Her Majesty's Secret Service (debut, 1969), Universal Soldier, Who Saw Her Die?, The Dragon Flies, Stoner, The Man From Hong Kong, The Kentucky Fried Movie, Death Dimension, The Falcon's Ultimatum, Saint Jack, L'ultimo Harem, Never Too Young to Die, Hell Hunters, Gettysburg.
TELEVISION: Is Anybody There?, Cover Girls, The Newman Shame, The Return of the Man From U.N.C.L.E.

LEACHMAN, CLORIS

Actress. b. Des Moines, IA, April 30, 1926. e. Northwestern U. Broadway stage, television, motion pictures.
PICTURES: Kiss Me Deadly (debut, 1955), The Rack, The Chapman Report, Butch Cassidy and the Sundance Kid, Lovers and Other Strangers, The People Next Door, W.U.S.A., The Steagle, The Last Picture Show (Acad. Award, best supporting actress, 1971), Dillinger, Charlie and the Angel, Happy Mother's Day... Love George, Daisy Miller, Young Frankenstein, Crazy Mama, High Anxiety, The Mouse and His Child (voice), The North Avenue Irregulars, The Muppet Movie, Scavenger Hunt, Foolin' Around, Yesterday, Herbie Goes Bananas, History of the World—Part I, My Little Pony (voice), Shadow Play, Walk Like a Man, Hansel and Gretel, Prancer, Texasville, Love Hurts, My Boyfriend's Back, The Beverly Hillbillies, A Troll in Central park (voice), Now and Then, Beavis and Butt-Head Do America (voice), Never Too Late, Gen 13, Iron Giant.
TELEVISION: Series: Hold It Please, Charlie Wild: Private Detective, Bob and Ray, Lassie, Mary Tyler Moore Show (Emmy Awards 1974, 1975), Phyllis (Golden Globe Award), The Facts of Life, The Nutt House, Walter & Emily. Movies: Silent Night Lonely Night, Suddenly Single, Haunts of the Very Rich, A Brand New Life (Emmy Award, 1973), Crime Club, Dying Room Only, The Migrants, Hitchhike!, Thursday's Game, Death Sentence, Someone I Touched, A Girl Named Sooner, Death Scream, The New Original Wonder Woman, The Love Boat (pilot), It Happened One Christmas, Long Journey Back, Willa, Mrs. R's Daughter, S.O.S. Titanic, The Acorn People, Advice to the Lovelorn, Miss All-American Beauty, Dixie: Changing Habits, Demon Murder Case, Ernie Kovacs: Between the Laughter, Deadly Intentions, Love Is Never Silent, Wedding Bell Blues, Danielle Steel's Fine Things, In Broad Daylight, A Little Piece of Heaven, Fade to Black, Without a Kiss Goodbye, Miracle Child, Double Double Toil and Trouble, Between Love and Honor, Annabella Wish. Specials: Oldest Living Graduate, Of Thee I Sing, Breakfast With Les and Bess, Screen Actors Guild 50th Anniversary Celebration (Emmy Award, 1984). Guest: Twilight Zone, Untouchables, Big Valley, That Girl, Marcus Welby, Night Gallery, Cher (Emmy Award, 1975), Love Boat, Promised Land (Emmy Award, 1997).

LEAR, NORMAN

Producer, Director, Writer. b. New Haven, CT, July 27, 1922. e. Emerson Coll. In public relations 1945-49. Began in TV as co-writer of weekly one-hour variety show, The Ford Star Revue in 1950. Followed as writer for Dean Martin and Jerry Lewis on the Colgate Comedy Hour and for the Martha Raye and George Gobel TV shows. With partner, Bud Yorkin, created and produced such specials as Another Evening with Fred Astaire, Henry Fonda and the Family, An Evening with Carol Channing, and The Many Sides of Don Rickles. In 1965 their company, Tandem Productions, also produced the original Andy Williams Show. Moved into motion pictures in 1963, writing and producing Come Blow Your Horn. Formed Act III Communications, 1987.
PICTURES: Come Blow Your Horn (co-prod., s.p.), Never Too Late (prod.), Divorce-American Style (prod., s.p.), The Night They Raided Minsky's (co-prod., co-s.p.), Start the Revolution Without Me (exec. prod.), Cold Turkey (dir., s.p., prod.), The Princess Bride (exec. prod.), Fried Green Tomatoes (co-exec. prod.).
TELEVISION: Creator-dir.: TV Guide Award Show (1962), Henry Fonda and the Family (1963), Andy Williams Specials, Robert Young and the Family. Exec. prod. and creator or developer: All in the Family (3 Emmy Awards), Maude, Good Times, Sanford and Son, The Jeffersons, Mary Hartman Mary Hartman, One Day at a Time, All's Fair, A Year at the Top, All that Glitters, Fernwood 2 Night, The Baxters, Palmerstown, I Love Liberty, Heartsounds, Sunday Dinner, The Powers That Be, 704 Hauser.

LEARNED, MICHAEL

Actress. b. Washington, DC, Apr. 9, 1939. Studied ballet and dramatics in school. Many stage credits include Under Milkwood, The Three Sisters, A God Slept Here, The Sisters Rosensweig, etc.; resident performances with Shakespeare festivals in Canada, Stratford, CT, and San Diego, CA. Gained fame on hit TV series, The Waltons, as the mother, Olivia.
PICTURES: Touched by Love, Shanghai Shadows (narrator), Power, Dragon: The Bruce Lee Story, Life During Wartime.
TELEVISION: Series: The Waltons (3 Emmy Awards: 1973, 1974, 1976), Nurse (Emmy Award, 1982), Hothouse, Living Dolls. Guest: Gunsmoke, Police Story, St. Elsewhere, Murder She Wrote, Who's the Boss?. Movies: Hurricane, It Couldn't Happen to a Nicer Guy, Widow, Little Mo, Nurse (pilot), Off the Minnesota Strip, A Christmas Without Snow, Mother's Day on Walton Mountain, The Parade, A Deadly Business, Mercy or Murder?, Roots: The Gift, Gunsmoke: The Last Apache, Aftermath: A Test of Love, Keeping Secrets, A Walton Thanksgiving Reunion, A Walton Wedding, A Father for Brittany. Specials: All My Sons, Picnic.

LEARY, DENIS

Actor. b. 1957. e. Emerson Coll., Boston. Performed with the New Voices Theater Company, Charlestown Working Theater. Debuted one-man stand-up show No Cure for Cancer at Edinburgh Intl. Arts Fest., then later in London, Off-B'way, and cable tv. Appeared in and dir. short film for Showtime, Thy Neighbor's Wife.
PICTURES: Strictly Business (debut), National Lampoon's Loaded Weapon 1, The Sandlot, Who's the Man?, Gunmen, Demolition Man, Judgment Night, The Ref, Operation Dumbo Drop, The Neon Bible, Two If by Sea (also co-s.p.), Suicide Kings.

LEAUD, JEAN-PIERRE

Actor. b. Paris, France, May 5, 1944. Parents were screenwriter Pierre Leaud and actress Jacqueline Pierreux. At 14 chosen to play Antoine Doinel in Truffaut's The 400 Blows and subsequent autobiographical films Love at 20, Stolen Kisses, Bed and Board, Love on the Run. Also closely identified with major films by Jean-Luc Godard.
PICTURES: The 400 Blows, Boulevard, The Testament of Orpheus, Love at Twenty, Masculine-Feminine, Made in USA, Le Depart, La Chinoise, Weekend, Stolen Kisses, Le Gai Savoir, Pigsty, The Oldest Profession, Bed and Board, Two English Girls, Last Tango in Paris, Day for Night, Lola's Lolos, Love on the Run, Rebelote, Detective, Just a Movie, Seen by... 20 Years After, Treasure Island, The Grandeur and Decadence of a Small-Time Filmmaker, With All Hands, Time to Aim, Jane B, par Agnes V.; 36 Fillete, La Femme de Paille (The Straw Woman), The Color of the Wind, Femme de Papier, Bunker Palace Hotel, Treasure Island, I Hired a Contract Killer, Paris at Dawn, The Birth of Love, Nobody Loves Me, The Seducer's Diary, A Hundred & One Nights, Irma Vep, Mon Homme, Pour Rire!, Elizabeth I.

LEDER, HERBERT JAY

Writer, Director, Producer. b. New York, NY, Aug. 15, 1922. e. B.A., Ph.D. Play Doctor on Broadway; Director TV dept., Benton and Bowles Adv. chg. all T.V. & Film production, 13 yrs. Sponsored Films: Child Molester, Bank Robber, Shoplifter, Untouchables.
PICTURES: Writer: Fiend Without a Face, Pretty Boy Floyd (also dir., co-prod.), Nine Miles to Noon (also dir., co-prod.), Aquarius Mission, Love Keeps No Score of Wrongs, The Frozen Dead (also dir., prod.), It (also dir., prod.), Candyman (also dir.), The Winners, The Way It Is, The Cool Crazies.

LEDER, MIMI

Director.
PICTURES: The Peacemaker, Deep Impact
TELEVISION: Nightingales, A Little Piece of Heaven, Woman With a Past, Marked for Murder, There Was a Little Boy, Rio Shannon, House of Secrets, Baby Brokers. Series: ER.

LEDERER, RICHARD

Executive. b. New York, NY, Sept. 22, 1916. e. U. of Virginia, B.S., 1938. Freelance writer, 1939-41; U.S. Army. Cryptanalyst, Signal Intell. Serv 1941-45; Adv. copywriter, Columbia Pictures, 1946-50; Adv. copywriter, Warner Bros., 1950-53; copy chief, Warner Bros., 1950-53; copy chief, Warner Bros., 1953-57; Asst. Nat'l Adv. mgr., Warner Bros. studios, 1957-59; Prod., theatrical, TV. Warner Bros. studios, 1959-60; Dir. of adv., publicity, Warner Bros. Pictures, 1960; v.p. Warner Bros. Pictures, 1963. V.P. production, Warner Bros. Studio, 1969-70; indep. prod. to 1971, when returned to WB as adv.-pub., v.p. Independent producer. 1980: Hollywood Knights. Joined Orion Pictures as v.p., adv. Resigned, 1984.

LEE, ANG

Director, Producer, Writer. b. Pingtung, Taiwan, Oct. 23, 1954.
PICTURES: Joe's Bed-Stuy Barbershop: We Cut Heads, Pushing Hands, The Wedding Banquet, Eat Drink Man Woman, Siao Yu, Sense and Sensibility, The Ice Storm, Ride with the Devil, Berlin Dances.

LEE, ANNA

Actress. M.B.E. r.n. Joan Boniface Winnifrith. b. Kent, England, Jan. 2, 1913. e. Central School of Speech Training and Dramatic Art, Royal Albert Hall. With London Repertory Theatre; toured in the Constant Nymph and Jane Eyre. In 1930s known as Britain's Glamour Girl. 1939 came to US to star in My Life With Caroline. Entertained troops with U.S.O. during WWII. 1950 moved to N.Y. to appear in live TV.
PICTURES: Ebb Tide (debut, 1932), Yes Mr. Brown, Say It With Music, Mayfair Girl, King's Cup, Chelsea Life, Mannequin, Faces, The Bermondsey Kid, Lucky Loser, The Camels Are Coming, Rolling in Money, Heat Wave, Passing of the Third Floor Back, First a Girl, The Man Who Changed His Mind, O.H.M.S. (You're in the Army Now), King Solomon's Mines, Non-Stop New York, The Four Just Men (The Secret Four), Return to Yesterday, Young Man's Fancy, Seven Sinners, My Life With Caroline, How Green Was My Valley, Flying Tigers, The Commandos Strike at Dawn, Hangmen Also Die, Flesh and Fantasy, Forever and a Day,

Summer Storm, Abroad With Two Yanks, Bedlam, G.I. War Brides, High Conquest, The Ghost and Mrs. Muir, Best Man Wins, Fort Apache, Prison Warden, Wyoming Mail, Boots Malone, Daniel Boone—Trail Blazer, Gideon of Scotland Yard, The Last Hurrah, The Horse Soldiers, Jet Over the Atlantic, This Eath Is Mine, The Big Night, The Crimson Kimono, Jack the Giant Killer, Two Rode Together, The Man Who Shot Liberty Valance, What Ever Happend to Baby Jane?, The Prize, The Unsinkable Molly Brown, For Those Who Think Young, The Sound of Music, Torn Curtain, Seven Women, Picture Mommy Dead, In Like Flint, Star!, Clash. TELEVISION: Guest on many major television shows from 1950-77. Series: General Hospital (1978-present). Movies: Eleanor and Franklin, The Night Rider, The Beasts are Loose, Scruples.

LEE, CHRISTOPHER
Actor. b. London, England, May 27, 1922. e. Wellington Coll. Served RAF 1940-46. Ent. m.p. ind. 1947. Autobiography: Tall, Dark and Gruesome (1977).
PICTURES: include: Corridor of Mirrors (debut, 1947), One Night With You, A Song for Tomorrow, Scott of the Antarctic, Hamlet, The Gay Lady, Capt. Horatio Hornblower, Valley of the Eagles, The Crimson Pirate, Babes in Bagdad, Moulin Rouge, Innocents of Paris, That Lady, The Warriors, Cockleshell Heroes, Storm Over the Nile, Port Afrique, Private's Progress, Beyond Mombasa, Battle of the River Plate, Night Ambush, She Played With Fire, The Traitors, Curse of Frankenstein, Bitter Victory, Truth About Women, Tale of Two Cities, Dracula, Man Who Could Cheat Death, The Mummy, Too Hot to Handle, Beat Girl, City of the Dead (Horror Hotel), Two Faces of Dr. Jekyll, The Terror of the Tongs, The Hands of Orlac, Taste of Fear, The Devil's Daffodil, Pirates of Blood River, Devil's Agent, Red Orchid, Valley of Fear, Katharsis, Faust '63, The Virgin of Nuremberg, The Whip and the Body, Carmilla, The Devil Ship Pirates, The Gorgon, The Sign of Satan, The House of Blood, Dr. Terror's House of Horrors, She, The Skull, The Mask of Fu Manchu, Dracula, Prince of Darkness, Rasputin, Theatre of Death, Circus of Fear, The Brides of Fu Manchu, Five Golden Dragons, Vengeance of Fu Manchu, Night of the Big Heat, The Pendulum, The Face of Eve, The Devil Rides Out, The Blood of Fu Manchu, The Crimson Altar, Dracula Has Risen from the Grave, The Oblong Box, De Sade 70, Scream and Scream Again, The Magic Christian, Julius Caesar, One More Time, Count Dracula, Bloody Judge, Taste the Blood of Dracula, The Private Life of Sherlock Holmes, El Umbragolo, Scars of Dracula, The House That Dripped Blood, I Monster, Hannie Caulder, Dracula A.D. 1972, Horror Express, Death Line (Raw Meat), Nothing But the Night (also co-exec. prod.), The Creeping Flesh, The Wicker Man, Poor Devil, Dark Places, Satanic Rites of Dracula, Eulalie Quitte les Champs, The Three Musketeers, Earthbound, The Man with the Golden Gun, The Four Musketeers, Killer Force, Diagnosis—Murder, Whispering Death, The Keeper, To the Devil a Daughter, Dracula and Son, Airport '77, Starship Invasions (Alien Encounters), The End of the World, Return from Witch Mountain, Caravans, The Passage, Arabian Adventure, Jaguar Lives, Circle of Iron (The Silent Flute), 1941, Bear Island, Serial, The Salamander, An Eye for an Eye, Safari 3000, House of Long Shadows, The Return of Captain Invincible, The Rosebud Beach Hotel, Roadtrip, Dark Mission, The Howling II: Your Sister is a Werewolf, Olympus Force, Jocks, Murder Story, Mio In the Land of Faraway, The Girl, The Return of the Musketeers, Honeymoon Academy, The French Revolution, Gremlins 2: The New Batch, Curse III: Blood Sacrifice, The Rainbow Thief, L'Avaro, Jackpot, Double Vision, Shogun Mayeda, Special Class, Journey of Honor, Cybereden, Funny Man, Police Academy: Mission to Moscow, A Feast at Midnight, The Stupids, Sorellina, Jinnah.
TELEVISION: The Disputation, Metier du Seigneur, Movies: Poor Devil, Harold Robbins' The Pirate, Captain America II, Once a Spy, Charles and Diana: A Royal Love Story, Far Pavilions, Shaka Zulu, Goliath Awaits, Massarati and the Brain, Around the World in 80 Days, Treasure Island, Young Indiana Jones, The Care of Time, Sherlock Holmes & The Leading Lady, Sherlock Holmes and the Incident at Victoria Falls, Death Train, The Tomorrow People, Tales of Mystery & Imagination, Moses, Ivanhoe.

LEE, JASON SCOTT
Actor. b. Los Angeles, CA, 1966. Raised in Hawaii. e. Fullerton Col., Organge County, CA.
PICTURES: Born in East L.A. (debut, 1987), Back to the Future II, Map of the Human Heart, Dragon: The Bruce Lee Story, Rapa Nui, Rudyard Kipling's The Jungle Book, Talos the Mummy, Soldier.
TELEVISION: Movie: Vestige of Honor. Special: American Eyes. Guest: Showtime's Hunger Series.

LEE, JOIE
Actress. b. 1968. e. Sarah Lawrence Col. Brother is director-writer Spike Lee. On NY stage in Mulebone. Appeared in short film Coffee and Cigarettes Part Two. Has also been billed as Joy Lee, Joie Susannah Lee.
PICTURES: She's Gotta Have It (debut, 1986), School Daze, Do the Right Thing, Bail Jumper, Mo' Better Blues, A Kiss Before Dying, Fathers and Sons, Crooklyn (also story, co-s.p., assoc. prod.), Losing Isaiah, Girl 6, Get on the Bus.

LEE, MICHELE
Actress. b. Los Angeles, CA, June 24, 1942. On Broadway in How to Succeed in Business Without Really Trying, Seesaw.
PICTURES: How to Succeed in Business Without Really Trying, The Love Bug, The Comic.
TELEVISION: Series: Knots Landing (also dir. several episodes). Movies: Dark Victory, Bud and Lou, Letter to Three Wives, Single Women Married Men (also exec. prod.), The Fatal Image, My Son Johnny, Broadway Bound, When No One Would Listen (also exec. prod.), Big Dreams & Broken Hearts: The Dottie West Story (also exec. prod.), Color Me Perfect (also dir., prod., co-s.p.).

LEE, PEGGY
Singer, Actress. r.n. Norma Egstrom. b. Jamestown, ND, May 26, 1920. Began career as night club vocalist in Fargo; became& radio singer, WDAY, then with bandleader Sev Olsen in Minneapolis, Will Osborne, Benny Goodman. Collabolrated with Dave Barbour on such songs as Manana, It's a Good Day, What More Can a Woman Do?, Fever, Johnny Guitar, So What's New. Also leading recording artist. PICTURES: Stage Door Canteen, Mr. Music, The Jazz Singer, Pete Kelly's Blues (Acad. Award nom.), Lady and the Tramp (voices, co- compser).
TELEVISION: Series: TV's Top Tunes, Songs for Sale. Guest: Jimmy Durante, Dean Martin, Ed Sullivan, many others.

LEE, SPIKE
Director, Producer, Writer, Actor. b. Atlanta, GA, Mar. 20, 1957. r.n. Shelton Jackson Lee. Son of jazz bass musician, composer Bill Lee. Sister is actress Joie Lee. e. Morehouse Coll B.A., Mass Comm., MFA NYU Film Sch. Completed 2 student features and hour-long thesis: Joe's Bed-Stuy Barbershop: We Cut Heads which won student Acad. Award from Acad. M.P. Arts & Sciences. Wrote, prod., dir., co-starred in indep. feature, She's Gotta Have It, budgeted at $175,000. Appeared in films Lonely in America, Hoop Dreams. Author of five books on his films. Director of numerous tv commercials for Nike, Levi's, ESPN and others. Director of over 35 music videos for Michael Jackson, Stevie Wonder, Miles Davis, and others.
PICTURES: Joe's Bed-Stuy Barbershop: We Cut Heads (co-prod., dir., s.p., editor). Dir.-Prod.-Writer-Actor: She's Gotta Have It (LA Film Critics Award for best new director, 1986), School Daze, Do the Right Thing (LA Film Critics Awards for best picture & dir., 1989), Mo' Better Blues, Jungle Fever, Malcolm X, Crooklyn, Clockers, Girl 6, Get On the Bus, 4 Little Girls, He Got Game, Summer of Sam. Executive Producer: Drop Squad also actor), New Jersey Drive, Tales From the Hood, Subway Stories: Tales from the Underground.
TELEVISION: Guest: The Debbie Allen's Special, Spike & Co. Do It A Capella.

LEEDS, MARTIN N.
Film-TV Executive. b. New York, NY, Apr. 6, 1916. e. NYU, B.S., 1936; J.D., 1938. Admitted NY Bar, 1938, CA Bar, 1948; dir. ind. rltns. Wabash Appliance Corp., 1943-44; ind. bus. rltns. cons. Davis & Gilbert, 1944-45; dir. ind. rltns. Flying Tiger Lines, 1947; dir. bus. affairs CBS TV div., 1947-53; exec. v.p. Desilu Productions, Inc., 1953-60; v.p. Motion Picture Center Studios, Inc.: memb. Industry comm. War Manpower Comm., 1943; chmn. Comm. to form Television Code of Ethics: U.S. Army 1941. Exec. v.p. in chg. of West Coast oper. & member of bd. of dir. Talent Associates—Paramount Ltd., Hollywood, 1962; TV production consultant; exec. v.p., Electronovision Prods. Inc., 1964; TV prod. & MP consultant, 1965; pres., CEO, memb. of bd., Beverly Hills Studios, Inc., 1969; sr. v.p., American Film Theatre; 1973; 1975, motion picture and TV attorney & consultant.

LEEWOOD, JACK
Producer. b. New York, NY. May 20, 1913. e. Upsala Coll., Newark U., NYU. 1926-31 with Gottesman-Stern circuit as usher, asst. and relief mgr.; 1931-43 Stanley-Warner, mgr. of Ritz, Capitol and Hollywood theatres 1943-47. Joined Warner Bros. field forces in Denver-Salt Lake; Seattle-Portland, 1947-48. Dir. pub. & adv. Screen Guild Prod.; 1948-52, Lippert Productions; prod. exec., 1953-56, Allied Artists; 1957-62 prod. 20th Cent. Fox; 1965-68, prod., Universal; 1976-78. Affiliated Theatre S.F. & HTN.; 1978-83. Hamner Prod.
PICTURES: Holiday Rhythm, Gunfire, Hi-Jacked, Roaring City, Danger Zone, Lost Continent, F.B.I. Girl, Pier 23, Train to Tombstone, I Shot Billy the Kid, Bandit Queen, Motor Patrol, Savage Drums, Three Desperate Men, Border Rangers, Western Pacific Agent, Thundering Jets, Lone Texan, Little Savage, Alligator People, 13 Fighting Men, Young Jesse James, Swingin' Along, We'll Bury You, 20,000 Eyes, Thunder Island, The Plainsman.
TELEVISION: Longest 100 Miles, Escape to Mindanao, Dallas Cowboys Cheerleaders, When Hell Was in Session, Fugitive Family, Dallas Cowboys Cheerleaders II, Million Dollar Face, Portrait of a Showgirl, Margin For Murder, Anatomy of an Illness, Malibu.

LEFFERTS, GEORGE
Producer, Writer, Director. b. Paterson, NJ. e. Univ. of MI. Dir., numerous award-winning TV series, films. Exec. prod.-Time-Life films prod./writer, Movie of the Week (NBC) Biog: Who's Who in America, Who's Who in the World. Exec. prod., Bing Crosby Productions, prod., NBC 10 yrs, Independent. Exec. prod. David Wolper prods. 4 Emmy Awards, 2 Golden Globe Awards, 2 New England Journalism Awards, 1 Cine Golden Eagle Award.
THEATER: Hey Everybody, The Boat.
PICTURES: The Stake, Mean Dog Blues, The Living End, The Boat, The Teenager.
TELEVISION: *Specials*: Teacher Teacher (Emmy Award, 1969), Benjamin Franklin (Emmy Award, 1975), Purex Specials for Women (Emmy Award, Producer's Guild Award; writer, prod. dir.), Our Group (writer), Jean Seberg Story. *Series*: Breaking Point (exec. prod.), The Bill Cosby Show, Studio One, Kraft Theatre, Chrysler Theatre, Sinatra Show, Lights Out, Alcoa, The Bold Ones, One Life to Live (WGA Award), Ryan's Hope (prod.). *Movies*: The Harness, She's Dressed to Kill, The Night They Took Miss Beautiful, Smithsonian Institution Specials (exec. prod.).

LEGATO, ROBERT
Special Effects, Director.
PICTURES: Interview with the Vampire, Apollo 13, Titanic (Acad. Award, Best Visual Effects, 1997).
TELEVISION: *Series*: Star Trek: The Next Generation (also dir.), Star Trek: Deep Space 9 (also dir.) *Movies*: Star Trek: Deep Space Nine-Emissary.

LEGRAND, MICHEL JEAN
Composer, Conductor. b. France, Feb. 24, 1932. Son of well-known arranger, composer and pianist, Raymond Legrand. At 11 Michel, a child prodigy, entered Paris Cons. and graduated nine years later with top honors in composition and as solo pianist. In late fifties turned to composing for films and has composed, orchestrated and conducted scores of more than 140 films.
PICTURES: Lola, Eva, Vivre Sa Vie, La Baie des Anges, The Umbrellas of Cherbourg, Banda a Part, Un Femme Mariee, Une Femme est une Femme, The Young Girls of Rochefort, Ice Station Zebra, The Thomas Crown Affair (Academy Award for best song: The Windmills of Your Mind, 1968), Pieces of Dreams, The Happy Ending, Picasso Summer, Wuthering Heights, The Go-Between, Summer of '42 (Academy Award, 1971), Lady Sings the Blues, The Nelson Affair, Breezy, The Three Musketeers, Sheila Levine, Gable and Lombard, Ode to Billy Joe, The Savage, The Other Side of Midnight, The Fabulous Adventures of the Legendary Baron Munchausen, The Roads of the South, The Hunter, The Mountain Men, Atlantic City, Falling in Love Again, Best Friends, A Love in Germany, Never Say Never Again, Yentl (Academy Award, 1983), Hell Train, Micki and Maude, Secret Places, Spirale, Parking, Switching Channels, Three Seats for the 26th Cinq jours en juin (dir. debut, s.p., music), Dingo, The Pickle, Ready to Wear (Pret-a-Porter).
TELEVISION: *Movies*: Brian's Song, The Jesse Owens Story, A Woman Called Golda, As Summers Die, Crossings, Sins, Promises to Keep, Not a Penny More Not a Penny Less, The Burning Shore, The Ring.

LE GROS, JAMES
Actor. b. Minneapolis, MN, Apr. 27, 1962.
THEATER: The Cherry Orchard, Galileo, Ceremony of Innocence, Table Settings, Curse of the Starving Class, American Buffalo, Bits and Bytes, Becoming Memories, Slab Boys.
PICTURES: Solarbabies, Near Dark, Fatal Beauty, Phantasm II, Drugstore Cowboy, Point Break, Blood & Concrete, The Rapture, Where the Day Takes You, Singles, My New Gun, Bad Girls, Floundering, Mrs. Parker and the Vicious Circle, Destiny Turns on the Radio, Panther, Safe, Living in Oblivion, Infinity, The Low Life, Boys, The Destiny of Marty Fine.
TELEVISION: *Movie*: Gun Crazy.

LEGUIZAMO, JOHN
Actor. b. Bogota, Colombia, July 22, 1964. Moved to Queens, NY at age 5. e. NYU. Appeared in award-winning student film Five Out of Six, while in school. Studied acting with Lee Strasberg and Wynn Handman. Made professional debut on Miami Vice on tv.
THEATER: A Midsummer Night's Dream, La Puta Vida, Parting Gestures, Mambo Mouth (also writer; Obie & Outer Critics Circle Awards), Spic-O-Rama (also writer; Drama Desk & Theatre World Awards).
PICTURES: Casualties of War, Revenge, Die Hard 2, Gentile Alouette, Street Hunter, Out for Justice, Hangin' With the Homeboys, Regarding Henry, Whispers in the Dark, Super Mario Bros., Night Owl, Carlito's Way, A Pyromaniac's Love Story, To Wong Foo—Thanks for Everything—Julie Newmar, Executive Decision, Spawn, Romeo and Juliet, The Pest.
TELEVISION: *Series*: House of Buggin'. *Specials*: Talent Pool Comedy Special (ACE Award), Mambo Mouth (also writer), Spic-O-Rama (also writer; 3 Cable ACE Awards).

LEHMAN, ERNEST
Writer, Producer, Director. b. New York, NY, 1923. e. City Coll. of New York. Began career as free-lance journalist and magazine fiction writer. First pub. books, The Comedian, The Sweet Smell of Success. First hardcover novel, The French Atlantic Affair followed by Farewell Performance, and first non-fiction book, Screening Sickness. Pres., WGAW, 1983-85.1987, 1988, 1990: Acad. Awards show (co-writer). The Ernest Lehman Collection is archived at the Humanities Research Center, Univ. of TX at Austin, and in part at USC Film Library and Margaret Herrick Library. Co-prod. of musical stage adaptation of Sweet Smell of Success. Laurel Award for Screen Achievement, WGAW, 1973. Five Best Screenplay Awards, WGAW.
PICTURES: *Writer*: Executive Suite, Sabrina (co-s.p.; Acad. Award nom.), The King and I, Somebody Up There Likes Me, Sweet Smell of Success (co-s.p.; based on his own novelette), North By Northwest (Acad. Award nom.), From the Terrace, West Side Story (Acad. Award nom.), The Prize, The Sound of Music, Who's Afraid of Virginia Woolf? (also prod.; 2 Acad. Award noms. for picture & s.p.), Hello Dolly! (also prod.; Acad. Award nom. for picture), Portnoy's Complaint (also dir., prod.), Family Plot, Black Sunday (co-s.p.).

LEHMANN, MICHAEL
Director. b. San Francisco, CA, March 30, 1957. e. U Cal, Berkeley, Columbia U. Started in industry supervising video systems used in the Francis Ford Coppola films One From the Heart, Rumble Fish, The Outsiders. Dir. short films for Saturday Night Live incl. Ed's Secret Life. Served as exec. prod. on Ed Wood.
PICTURES: Heathers (debut, 1989), Meet the Applegates, Hudson Hawk, Airheads, Ed Wood (exec. prod. only), The Truth About Cats and Dogs, My Giant.
TELEVISION: *Series*: The Larry Sanders Show, Homicide: Life on the Street.

LEHRER, JIM
News Anchor. b. Wichita, KS, 1934. e. Victoria Col., Univ. of MO. Served in US Marine Corps. 1959-66, reporter for Dallas Morning News, Dallas Times-Herald; 1968 became Times-Herald's city editor before moving into tv as exec. dir. of public affairs, host and editor of news program on KERA-TV in Dallas. To Washington where he became public affairs coord. for PBS, then corresp. for the Natl. Public Affairs Center for Television. 1973 first teamed with Robert MacNeil to cover Senate Watergate hearings. 1975, served as D.C. corresp. for the Robert MacNeil Report on PBS (showed was re-named The MacNeil/Lehrer Report in 1976). 1983, started The MacNeil/Lehrer NewsHour. 1995, became exec. editor and anchor of new version of series The NewsHour With Jim Lehrer.

LEIBMAN, RON
Actor. b. New York, NY, Oct. 11, 1937. m. actress Jessica Walter. e. Ohio Wesleyan U. Joined Actor's Studio in N.Y.; first professional appearance in summer theatre production of A View from the Bridge.
THEATER: The Premise, Dear Me, The Sky Is Falling, We Bombed in New Haven (Theatre World Award), Cop Out, Room Service, I Oughta Be in Pictures, The Deputy, Bicycle Ride to Nevada, Doubles, Rumors, Angels in America: Millenium Approaches (Tony & Drama Desk Awards).
PICTURES: Where's Poppa (debut, 1970), The Hot Rock, Slaughterhouse Five, Your Three Minutes Are Up, Super Cops, Won Ton Ton the Dog Who Saved Hollywood, Norma Rae, Up the Academy, Zorro the Gay Blade, Romantic Comedy, Phar Lap, Rhinestone, Door to Door, Seven Hours to Judgement, Night Falls on Manhattan.
TELEVISION: *Series*: Kaz (Emmy Award, 1979), Pacific Station, Central Park West. *Movies*: The Art of Crime, A Question of Guilt, Rivkin: Bounty Hunter, Many Happy Returns, Christmas Eve, Terrorist on Trial: The United States vs. Salim Ajami.

LEIDER, GERALD J.
Producer, Executive. b. Camden, NJ, May 28, 1931. e. Syracuse U., 1953; Bristol U., Eng., 1954, Fulbright Fellow-ship in drama. m. Susan Trustman. 1955 joined MCA, Inc., N.Y.; 1956-59 theatre producer in NY, London: Shinbone Alley, Garden District, and Sir John Gielgud's Ages of Man. 1960-61; director of special programs, CBS/TV; 1961-62, dir. of program sales, CBS-TV; 1962-69, v.p., v.p optns., Ashley Famous Agency, Inc.; 1969-74, pres. Warner Bros. TV, Burbank; 1975-76, exec. v.p. foreign prod. Warner Bros. Pictures, Rome; 1977-82, indept. prod. under Jerry Leider Prods.; 1982-87, pres., ITC Prods., Inc; named pres. and CEO, ITC Entertain-ment Group, 1987-91.
PICTURES: Wild Horse Hank, The Jazz Singer, Trenchcoat.
TELEVISION: *Movies*: And I Alone Survived, Willa, The Hostage Tower, The Scarlet and the Black, Secrets of a Married Man, The Haunting Passion, Letting Go, A Time to Live, The Girl Who Spelled Freedom, Unnatural Causes, Poor Little Rich Girl.

LEIGH, JANET
Actress. r.n. Jeanette Helen Morrison. b. Merced, CA, July 6, 1927. Mother of actresses Jamie Lee Curtis and Kelly Curtis. e. Coll. of Pacific, music. Author: There Really Was a Hollywood (autobiography, 1984), Behind the Scenes of Psycho (1995), House of Destiny (novel; 1995).
THEATER: includes: Murder Among Friends, Love Letters (with Van Johnson).
PICTURES: The Romance of Rosy Ridge (debut, 1947), If Winter Comes, Hills of Home, Words and Music, Act of Violence, Little Women, That Forsyte Woman, Red Danube, Doctor and the Girl, Holiday Affair, Two Tickets to Broadway, Strictly Dishonorable, Angels in the Outfield, It's a Big Country, Just This Once, Scaramouche, Fearless Fagan, Naked Spur, Confidentially Connie, Houdini, Walking My Baby Back Home, Prince Valiant, Living It Up, Black Shield of Falworth, Rogue Cop, My Sister Eileen, Pete Kelly's Blues, Safari, Jet Pilot, Touch of Evil, The Vikings, The Perfect Furlough, Who Was That Lady?, Psycho (Acad. Award nom.), Pepe, The Manchurian Candidate, Bye Bye Birdie, Wives and Lovers, Three on a Couch, Harper, An American Dream, Kid Rodelo, Grand Slam, Hello Down There, One Is a Lonely Number, Night of the Lepus, Boardwalk, The Fog, Other Realms.
TELEVISION: Movies: Honeymoon With a Stranger, House on Green Apple Road, The Monk, Deadly Dream, Mirror Mirror, Telethon, Murder at the World Series. Guest: Matt Houston, Starman, Murder She Wrote. Addtl.: Carriage from Britain, Murder in the First, Dear Deductible, Catch Me If You Can, One for My Baby, My Wives, Jane, The Chairman, Death's Head, This Is Maggie Mulligan, Tales of the Unexpected, On the Road.

LEIGH, JENNIFER JASON
Actress. b. Los Angeles, CA, Feb. 5, 1962. r.n. Jennifer Leigh Morrow. Daughter of late actor Vic Morrow and TV writer Barbara Turner. At age 14 debuted in Disney tv movie The Young Runaway. Won L.A. Valley Coll. best actress award for stage prod. The Shadow Box (1979).
PICTURES: Eyes of a Stranger (debut, 1981), Wrong Is Right, Fast Times at Ridgemont High, Easy Money, Grandview U.S.A., The Hitcher, Flesh + Blood, The Men's Club, Undercover, Sister Sister, Heart of Midnight, The Big Picture, Miami Blues (NY Film Critics Award, 1990), Last Exit to Brooklyn (NY Film Critics Award, 1990), Backdraft, Crooked Hearts, Rush, Single White Female, Short Cuts, The Hudsucker Proxy, Mrs. Parker and the Vicious Circle (Natl. Society of Film Critics & Chicago Film Critics Awards, 1994), Dolores Claiborne, Georgia (also co-prod.), Kansas City, A Thousand Acres, Washington Square, eXistenZ.
TELEVISION: Movies: The Young Runaway, Angel City, The Killing of Randy Webster, The Best Little Girl in the World, The First Time, Girls of the White Orchid, Buried Alive, The Love Letter, Thanks of a Grateful Nation.

LEIGH, MIKE
Director, Writer. b. Salford, England, Feb. 20, 1943. e. RADA, Camberwell Art Sch., Central Sch. of Arts & Crafts, London Film Sch. m. actress Alison Steadman. Began career in experimental theatre. Plays include Waste Paper Guards, The Box Play, Neena, Individual Fruit Pies, Down Here and Up There, Big Basil, Epilogue, Bleak Moments, A Rancid Pong, Wholesome Glory, The Jaws of Death, Dick Whittington and His Cat, Babies Grow Old, The Silent Majority, Abigail's Party, Ecstacy, Goose-Pimples, Smelling the Rat, Greek Tragedy, It's a Great Big Shame. Directed 1977 TV drama Abigail's Party. 1987 short: The Short and Curlies. Recipient of 1995 BAFTA Award for Outstanding British Contribution to Cinema.
PICTURES: Bleak Moments, Hard Labour, Nuts in May, The Kiss of Death, Who's Who, Grown-Ups, Home Sweet Home, Meantime, Four Days in July, High Hopes, Life Is Sweet, Naked, Secrets & Lies (Palme d'Or, Cannes 1996; LA Film Critics Award; BAFTA for Best Original S.P.), Career Girls.
TELEVISION: A Mug's Game, Plays for Britain.

LEIGH, SUZANNA
Actress. b. Reading, England, 1945. Studied at the Arts Educational Sch. and Webber Douglas Sch. 1965-66, under contract to Hal Wallis and Paramount.
PICTURES: Oscar Wilde, Bomb in High Street, Boeing Boeing, Paradise Hawaiian Style, The Deadly Bees, Deadlier Than the Male, The Lost Continent, Subterfuge, Lust for a Vampire (To Love a Vampire), Beware My Brethren, Son of Dracula.
TELEVISION: Series: Three Stars (France), One on an Island (West Indies). Special: The Plastic People. Guest: The Persuaders.

LEITCH, DONOVAN
Actor. Son of folksinger Donovan. Brother of actress Ione Skye. Acted in jr. high sch. musical then had bit part in PBS. show K.I.D.S.
PICTURES: And God Created Women (1988), The Blob, The In Crowd, Cutting Class, Glory, Gas Food Lodging, Dark Horse, I Shot Andy Warhol.
TELEVISION: Movie: For the Very First Time. Guest: Life Goes On.

LELAND, DAVID
Director, Writer, Actor. b. Cambridge, Eng., April 20, 1947. Began as actor at Nottingham Playhouse. Then joined newly formed company at Royal Court Theatre, London. Also appeared in films Time Bandits, The Missionary, and his own Personal Services (Peter Sellers Award for Comedy) and on TV in The Jewel in the Crown. As stage director specialized in complete seasons of new works at the Crucible in Sheffield and London venues. Wrote play Psy-Warriors.
PICTURES: Mona Lisa (co-s.p.), Personal Services (s.p.), Wish You Were Here (dir., s.p.; BAFTA Award for s.p.), Checking Out (dir.), The Big Man (dir.; a.k.a. Crossing the Line), Land Girls (co-s.p., dir.).
TELEVISION: Wrote Birth of a Nation, Flying Into the Wind, Rhino, Made in Britain, Beloved Enemy, Ligmalion, Psy-Warriors.

LELOUCH, CLAUDE
Director, Writer, Producer, Cinematographer, Editor. b. Paris, France, Oct. 30, 1937. Began m.p. career with short subjects, 1956; French military service, motion picture department, 1957-60; formed Films 13, 1960; publicity Films and Scopitones, 1961-62.
PICTURES: Le Propre de l'Homme (The Right of Man; debut, 1960; also s.p., prod., actor), L'amour avec des Si (Love With Ifs; aalso prod., s.p.), La Femme Spectacle (Night Women; also prod., photog.), Une Fille et des Fusils (To Be a Crook; also co-s.p., prod., edit.), Les Grands Moments (also co-prod.), A Man and A Woman (also co-s.p., story, prod., photog., edit.; Academy Awards for Best Foreign Language Film & Original Screenplay, 1966; also Acad. Award nom. for dir.), Live for Life (also co-s.p., co-photog., edit.), Farm From Vietnam (segment), 13 Jours en France (Grenoble; co-dir., co-s.p.), Life Love Death (also co-s.p.), Love Is a Funny Thing (also photog., co-s.p.), The Crook (also co- photog., co-s.p.), Smic Smac Smoc (also prod., s.p., photog., actor), Money Money Money (also s.p., prod., photog.), La Bonne Annee (Happy New Year; also prod., s.p., co-photog.), Visions of Eight (segment: The Losers), And Now My Love (also s.p., prod.), Marriage (also co-s.p.), Cat and Mouse (also s.p.), The Good and Bad (also s.p., photog.), Second Chance (also s.p., prod.), Another Man Another Chance (also s.p.), Robert and Robert (also s.p.), Adventure for Two, Bolero (also s.p., prod.), Edith and Marcel (also prod., s.p.), Vive la Vie (also prod., s.p., photog.), Partier Revenir (also prod., co-s.p.), A Man and a Woman: 20 Years Later (also prod., co-s.p.), Bandits (also prod., s.p.), Itinerary of a Spoiled Child (also co-prod., s.p.), There Were Days and Moons (also prod., co-s.p.), Les Miserables.
TELEVISION: Moliere (prod. only).

LE MAT, PAUL
Actor. b. Rahway, NJ, Sept. 22, 1945. Studied with Milton Katselas, Herbert Berghof Studio, A.C.T., San Francisco, Mitchel Ryan-Actor's Studio.
PICTURES: American Graffiti (debut, 1973), Aloha—Bobby and Rose, Citizens Band (Handle With Care), More American Graffiti, Melvin and Howard, Death Valley, Jimmy the Kid, Strange Invaders, P.K. and the Kid, Rock & Rule (voice), The Hanoi Hilton, Private Investigations, Puppet Master, Easy Wheels, Deuce Coupe, Grave Secrets, Veiled Threat, Wishman, Caroline at Midnight, Sensation, Deep Down, The Outfitters.
TELEVISION: Movies: Firehouse, The Gift of Life, The Night They Saved Christmas, The Burning Bed, Long Time Gone, Secret Witness, On Wings of Eagles, Into the Homeland, Blind Witness, In the Line of Duty: Siege at Marion, Woman With a Past. Series: Lonesome Dove.

LEMBERGER, KENNETH
Executive. Exec. v.p., Sony Pictures Entertainment, Inc.

LEMMON, JACK
Actor. b. Boston, MA. Feb. 8, 1925. r.n. John Uhler Lemmon III. e. Harvard U. m. actress Felicia Farr. Father of actor Chris Lemmon. Stage debut as a child; radio actor on soap operas; stock companies; U.S. Navy, W.W.II; many TV shows. Narrated film Stowaway in the Sky. Appeared in AFI short Wednesday. Albums: A Twist of Lemmon, Jack Lemmon Plays and Sings Music From Some Like It Hot. Recipient: American Film Institute Life Achievement Award (1988), Lincoln Center Tribute (1993).
THEATER: B'way: Room Service (debut, 1953), Face of a Hero, Tribute (also L.A., Denver), Long Day's Journey into Night (also London, Israel, D.C.). Off-B'way: Power of Darkness. L.A.: Idiot's Delight, Juno and the Paycock, A Sense of Humor (also Denver, S.F.). London: Veterans Day.

PICTURES: It Should Happen to You (debut, 1953), Phffft!, Three for the Show, Mister Roberts (Academy Award, best supporting actor, 1955), My Sister Eileen, You Can't Run Away from It, Fire Down Below, Operation Mad Ball, Cowboy, Bell Book and Candle, Some Like It Hot (Acad. Award nom.), It Happened to Jane, The Apartment (Acad. Award nom.), Pepe, The Wackiest Ship in the Army, The Notorious Landlady, Days of Wine and Roses (Acad. Award nom.), Irma La Douce, Under the Yum Yum Tree, Good Neighbor Sam, How to Murder Your Wife, The Great Race, The Fortune Cookie, Luv, The Odd Couple, The April Fools, The Out-of-Towners, Kotch (dir. debut; also cameo), The War Between Men and Women, Avanti!, Save the Tiger (Academy Award, 1973), The Front Page, The Prisoner of Second Avenue, Alex and the Gypsy, Airport '77, The China Syndrome (Cannes Film Fest. Award; Acad. Award nom., 1979), Tribute (Acad. Award nom.), Buddy Buddy, Missing (Cannes Film Fest. Award; Acad. Award nom., 1982), Mass Appeal, Macaroni, That's Life, Dad, JFK, The Player, Glengarry Glen Ross, Short Cuts, Grumpy Old Men, Getting Away With Murder, The Grass Harp, Grumpier Old Men, A Weekend in the Country, Hamlet, My Fellow Americans, Out to Sea, The Long Way Home.
TELEVISION: Series: That Wonderful Guy, Toni Twin Time (host), Ad Libbers, Heaven For Betsy, Alcoa Theatre. Guest on numerous dramatic shows: Studio One, Playhouse 90 (Face of a Hero), Kraft Theatre, The Web, Suspense, etc. Specials: The Day Lincoln Was Shot, 'S Wonderful 'S Marvelous 'S Gershwin, Get Happy, The Entertainer, Long Day's Journey into Night, The Wild West (narrator), A Life in the Theatre. Movies: The Murder of Mary Phagan, For Richer For Poorer, Twelve Angry Men, The Long Way Home.
RADIO: Serials: The Brighter Day, Road of Life.

LENFEST, H. F. "GERRY"
Executive. b. Jacksonville, FL. e. Mercersburg Academy, Washington and Lee U. and Columbia Law School. Served in US Navy, retired Captain. Practiced law in NYC before joining Triangle Publications., Inc. in Philadelphia as assoc. counsel in 1965. Became head of Triangle's Communications Div., 1970. Formed new co. in 1974 and bought two cable cos. from Triangle. Owns with his children Lenfest Communications, Inc. Subsidiaries incl. Suburban Cable, StarNet and Micronet.

LENO, JAY
Comedian, Actor. r.n. James Leno. b. New Rochelle, NY, April 28, 1950. e. Emerson College, B.A. speech therapy, 1973. Raised in Andover, MA. Worked as Rolls Royce auto mechanic and deliveryman while seeking work as stand-up comedian. Performed in comedy clubs throughout the U.S. and as opening act for Perry Como, Johnny Mathis, John Denver and Tom Jones. Guest on numerous talk shows and specials.
PICTURES: Fun With Dick and Jane, The Silver Bears, American Hot Wax, Americathon, Collision Course, What's Up Hideous Sun Demon? (voice), Dave, We're Back! (voice), Wayne's World 2, Major League 2, The Flintstones.
TELEVISION: Series: The Marilyn McCoo & Billy Davis Jr. Show, The Tonight Show (guest host: 1987-92; host: 1992-; Emmy Award, 1995). Specials: Jay Leno and the American Dream (also prod.), The Jay Leno Show, Our Planet Tonight, Jay Leno's Family Comedy Hour.

LENZ, KAY
Actress. b. Los Angeles, CA, March 4, 1953.
PICTURES: Breezy (debut, 1973), White Line Fever, The Great Scout and Cathouse Thursday, Moving Violation, Mean Dog Blues, The Passage, Fast-Walking, House, Stripped to Kill, Death Wish IV: The Crackdown, Headhunter, Physical Evidence, Fear, Streets, Falling From Grace.
TELEVISION: Series: Reasonable Doubts. Movies: The Weekend Nun, Lisa, Bright and Dark, A Summer Without Boys, Unwed Father, The Underground Man, The FBI Story: The FBI Versus Alvin Karpis, Journey from Darkness, Rich Man, Poor Man, The Initiation of Sarah, The Seeding of Sarah Burns, Sanctuary of Fear, The Hustler of Muscle Beach, Murder by Night, Heart in Hiding, How the West Was Won, Traveling Man, Escape, Hitler's Daughter, Against Their Will: Women in Prison, Trapped in Space, Shame II: The Secret. Guest: Midnight Caller (Emmy Award, 1989), Moonlighting, Hill St. Blues, Hotel, Cannon, McGyver, Cagney & Lacey, McCloud, Riptide, many others. Mini-Series: Rich Man Poor Man—Book II.

LEON, SOL
Executive. b. New York, NY, July 2, 1913. e. NYU, City Coll. of New York, Brooklyn Law Sch., B.B.L., master of law. Exec. v.p., William Morris Agency, L.A.

LEONARD, ROBERT SEAN
Actor. b. Westwood, NJ, Feb. 28, 1969. Raised in Ridgewood, NJ. Started acting at age 12 in local summer stock. Joined NY Shakespeare Festival at 15.
THEATER: Off-B'way: Coming of Age in Soho, Sally's Gone—She Left Her Name, The Beach House, When She Danced, Romeo and Juliet, Good Evening, The Great Unwashed. B'way: Brighton Beach Memoirs, Breaking the Code, The Speed of Darkness, Candida (Tony nom.), Philadelphia Here I Come!, Arcadia. Regional: Biloxi Blues (tour), Rocky and Diego, Long Day's Journey Into Night, King Lear, The Double Inconstancy.

PICTURES: The Manhattan Project (debut, 1986), My Best Friend Is a Vampire, Dead Poets Society, Mr. & Mrs. Bridge, Swing Kids, Married to It, Much Ado About Nothing, The Age of Innocence, Safe Passage, Killer: A Journal of Murder, I Love You—I Love You Not, Ground Control, Stand Off, The Last Days of Disco.
TELEVISION: Movies: My Two Loves, Bluffing It. Pilot: The Robert Klein Show, In the Gloaming.

LEONARD, SHELDON
Actor, Producer. r.n. Sheldon Leonard Bershad. b. New York, NY, Feb. 22, 1907. e. Syracuse U., B.A. Theatre mgr., Publix; N.Y. stage, 10 yrs.; sec., Directors Guild of America. 3 Emmy awards, Sylvania award, 4 TV Director of the Year nominations by D.G.A, Cinematographers Governors Award, D.G.A. Aldrich Award. Inducted into TV Hall of Fame, 1992.
PICTURES: Another Thin Man, Tall, Dark and Handsome, Private Nurse, Buy Me That Town, Week-End in Havana, Tortilla Flat, Rise and Shine, Street of Chance, Lucky Jordan, Hit the Ice, Uncertain Glory, To Have and Have Not, The Falcon in Hollywood, Why Girls Leave Home, Captain Kidd, Froniter Gal, Somewhere in the Night, Her Kind of Man, It's a Wonderful Life, The Gangster, If You Knew Susie, Sinbad the Sailor, My Dream Is Yours, Take One False Step, Iroquois Trail, Behave Yourself, Here Come the Nelsons, Young Man with Ideas, Stop You're Killing Me, Diamond Queen, Money from Home, Guys and Dolls, Pocketful of Miracles, The Brinks Job.
TELEVISION: Series (actor): The Duke, Make Room for Daddy/The Danny Thomas Show (also dir., prod.; Emmy Awards for dir.: 1956, 1961), Big Eddie. Series (exec. prod.): The Andy Griffith Show, The Dick Van Dyke Show, Gomer Pyler USMC, I Spy, My World and Welcome to It (Emmy Award, 1970). Movies: Top Secret (exec. prod., actor), The Islander (actor), I Spy Returns (co-exec. prod.). Dir.: Damon Runyon, G.E. Theatre, Electric Theatre, Jewelers' Showcase, Jimmy Durante Show.

LERNER, JOSEPH
Producer, Director, Writer. m. Geraldine Lerner. Actor on Broadway; radio actor & dir.; with RKO, Columbia and Republic as dir., dial. dir., writer, 2nd unit dir., test dir.; dir.-writer & head of special productions U.S. Army Signal Corps Photographic Center; writer of commercial and educational films 1946-47; v.p. in chg. of prod. Visual Arts Productions 1947; v.p. in chg. prod. Laurel Films 1949; Girl on the Run, comm. ind. films; dir., prod., writer, many TV commercials, documentaries 1967-73; pres., The Place for Film Making, Inc.; pres., Astracar Associates Ltd.; writer & line prod. for Gold Shield Prods; also lecturer and instructor at NYU, Wm. Patterson Coll., Broward Community Coll. (FL), College at Boca Raton. Member: Eastern Council of the Directors Guild of America. Trip the Light Fantastic, musical play in collaboration with song writer Dan Costello
TELEVISION: Dir./Prod.: Gangbusters, Grand Tour, Three Musketeers, United Nations Case Book. Dir./Prod./Writer. C-Man, Guilty Bystander, Mr. Universe, Dark of the Day, The Fight Never Ends, etc. Prod./Writer: Olympic Cavalcade, King of The Olympics, and many other documentaries.

LERNER, MICHAEL
Actor. b. Brooklyn, NY, June 22, 1941. e. Brooklyn Col., Univ. of CA, Berkeley. Prior to acting was professor of dramatic literature at San Francisco St. Col., 1968-69. Studied acting in London on Fullbright Scholarship. Was member of San Francisco's American Conservatory Theatre. On NY stage in Twelfth Night; L.A. stage in The Women of Trachis, Hurlyburly.
PICTURES: Alex in Wonderland (debut, 1970), The Candidate, Busting, Newman's Law, Hangup (Superdude), St. Ives, The Other Side of Midnight, Outlaw Blues, Goldengirl, Borderline, Coast to Coast, The Baltimore Bullet, The Postman Always Rings Twice, National Lampoon's Class Reunion, Threshold, Strange Invaders, Movers and Shakers, Anguish, Vibes, Eight Men Out, Harlem Nights, Any Man's Death, The Closer, Barton Fink (Acad. Award nom.), Newsies, Amos & Andrew, Blank Check, No Escape, Radioland Murders, The Road to Wellville, Girl in the Cadillac, A Pyromaniac's Love Story, The Beautician and the Beast.
TELEVISION: Series: Courthouse. Movies: Thief, Marriage Year One, What's a Nice Girl Like You...?, Magic Carpet, Firehouse (pilot), Reflections of Murder, The Rockford Files (pilot), The Death of Sammy (The Dream Makers), A Cry for Help, Starsky and Hutch (pilot), Sarah T: Portrait of a Teenage Alcoholic, Dark Victory, F. Scott Fitzgerald in Hollywood (The Screen Test), Scott Free, Killer on Board, A Love Affair: The Eleanor and Lou Gehrig Story, Vega$ (pilot), Ruby & Oswald, Hart to Hart (pilot), Moviola: This Year's Blonde, Gridlock (The Great American Traffic Jam), Blood Feud, Rita Hayworth: Love Goddess, The Execution, This Child is Mine, Betrayal of Trust (That Secret Sunday), Hands of a Stranger, King of Love, Framed, Omen IV: The Awakening, The Comrades of Summer. Special: The Missiles of October. Guest: Amazing Stories, Macgyver. Pilots: Grandpa Max, The Boys, I Gave at the Office.

LESLIE, ALEEN
Writer. b. Pittsburgh, PA, Feb. 5, 1908. e. Ohio State U. Contributor to magazines; columnist Pittsburgh Press; orig. & wrote radio series A Date with Judy 1941-50. B'way play Slightly Married, 1943; wrote, prod. Date with Judy, TV series; author, The Scent of the Roses, The Windfall.
PICTURES: Doctor Takes a Wife, Affectionately Yours, Henry Aldrich Plays Cupid, Stork Pays Off, Henry Aldrich Gets Glamour, It Comes Up Love, Rosie the Riveter, A Date With Judy, Father Was a Fullback, Father Is a Bachelor.

LESLIE, JOAN
Actress. r.n. Joan Brodell. b. Detroit, MI, January 26, 1925. e. St. Benedicts, Detroit; Our Lady of Lourdes, Toronto; St. Mary's Montreal; Immaculate Heart. H.S., L.A. Child performer on stage as part of The Three Brodels. Became model before going to Hollywood in 1936. Voted Star of Tomorrow, 1946. Now on bd. of dir., St. Anne's Maternity Home, Damon Runyon Foundation.
PICTURES: (as Joan Brodel): Camille (debut, 1937), Men with Wings, Nancy Drew—Reporter, Love Affair, Winter Carnival, Two Thoroughbreds, High School, Young as You Feel, Star Dust, Susan and God, Military Academy, Foreign Correspondent, Laddie. (as Joan Leslie): Thieves Fall Out, The Wagons Roll at Night, High Sierra, The Great Mr. Nobody, Sergeant York, The Hard Way, The Male Animal, Yankee Doodle Dandy, The Sky's the Limit, This Is the Army, Thank Your Lucky Stars, Hollywood Canteen, Rhapsody in Blue, Where Do We Go From Here?, Too Young to Know, Janie Gets Married, Cinderella Jones, Two Guys From Milwaukee, Repeat Performance, Northwest Stampede, Born To Be Bad, The Skipper Surprised His Wife, Man in the Saddle, Hellgate, Toughest Man in Arizona, The Woman They Almost Lynched, Flight Nurse, Hell's Outpost, Jubilee Trail, The Revolt of Mamie Stover.
TELEVISION: Guest: Ford Theatre, G.E. Theatre, Queen for a Day, Simon and Simon, Murder, She Wrote. Movies: Charley Hannah, The Keegans, Turn Back the Clock. Various commercials.

LESTER, MARK
Actor. b. Oxford, England, July 11, 1958. Ent. m.p. ind. 1963.
THEATER: The Murder Game, The Prince and the Pauper 1976.
PICTURES: Allez France (The Counterfeit Constable; debut, 1963), Spaceflight IC-1, Fahrenheit 451, Arrividerci Baby!, Our Mother's House, Oliver!, Run Wild Run Free, Sudden Terror (Eye Witness), Melody, Black Beauty, Who Slew Auntie Roo?, Redneck, Scalawag, Jungle Boy, Crossed Swords (The Prince and the Pauper).
TELEVISION: The Boy Who Stole the Elephants, Graduation Trip, Danza Alla Porto Gli Olmi (Italian Entry Berlin '75), Seen Dimly Before Dawn.

LESTER, MARK LESLIE
Director. b. Cleveland, OH, Nov. 26, 1949. e. U. of California, Northridge, B.A.
PICTURES: Director and/or Producer: Steel Arena (debut, 1973; also co-prod., s.p.), Truck Stop Women (also co-s.p.), Bobbie Jo and the Outlaw, Stunts, Roller Boogie, The Funhouse (co-exec. prod. only), The Class of 1984 (also co-exec. prod., co-s.p.), Firestarter, Commando, Armed and Dangerous, Class of 1999 (also story), Showdown in Little Tokyo, Night of the Running Man, The Ex, Public Enemy #1, Double Take, Misbegotten.
TELEVISION: Gold of the Amazon Women, Extreme Justice.

LESTER, RICHARD
Director. b. Philadelphia, PA, Jan. 19, 1932. e. Univ. of PA. Started as stagehand at tv studio before becoming dir. and music. dir. CBS-TV in Philadelphia, then CBC-TV, Toronto. To England in 1956 where he resumed work as tv dir. TV dir. The Goon Shows. Composed (with Reg. Owen) Sea War Series. Short Film: composer and dir., The Running Jumping and Standing Still Film. Directed sequences for Mondo Teeno/ Teenage Rebellion, Superman.
PICTURES: It's Trad Dad (debut, 1962; aka Ring-a-Ding Rhythm; also prod.), The Mouse on the Moon, A Hard Day's Night, The Knack... and How to Get It, Help!, A Funny Thing Happened on the Way to the Forum, How I Won the War (also prod.), Petulia, The Bed-Sitting Room (also co-prod.), The Three Musketeers, Juggernaut, The Four Musketeers, Royal Flash, Robin & Marian (also co-prod.), The Ritz, Butch and Sundance: The Early Days, Cuba, Superman II, Superman III, Finders Keepers (also exec. prod.), The Return of the Musketeers (tv in U.S.), Get Back.

LESTZ, EARL
Executive. Chmn. of the bd., Permanent Charities Committee of the Entertainment Industries.

LETTERMAN, DAVID
Performer, Writer. b. Indianapolis, IN, Apr. 12, 1947. e. Ball State U. Began career as weatherman and talk show host on Indianapolis TV before going to Hollywood. Cameo appearance in film Cabin Boy.
TELEVISION: Series Writer: Good Times, Paul Lynde Comedy Hour. Writer (specials): John Denver Special, Bob Hope Special. Series Performer: The Starland Vocal Band (also writer), Mary (1978), Tonight Show (guest host 1978-82), The David Letterman Show (Daytime Emmy Award for writing, 1981), Late Night with David Letterman (1982-93, on NBC; 4 Emmy Awards for Writing), Late Show With David Letterman (1993-, on CBS, 1997 Emmy Award). Guest performer: An NBC Family Christmas, The Larry Sanders Show.

LEVIN, GERALD M.
Executive. b. Philadelphia, PA, May 6, 1939. e. Haverford Col., Univ. of PA Law Sch. Attorney, 1963-67. Gen. mgr. & COO of Development Sources Corp., 1969. IBEC rep. in Tehran, Iran, 1971. Joined HBO in 1972 as v.p. of programming, then pres. & CEO, 1973-76; promoted to chmn. 1976. Became v.p. Time Inc., 1975; group v.p., video, 1979; exec. v.p. in 1984; on bd. of dirs., 1983-87. Named vice-chmn., Time Warner, 1989; COO, 1991; pres. & co-CEO of Time Warner, Inc., 1992; chmn. & CEO of Time Warner Inc., 1993.

LEVIN, MARC
Director, Writer, Actor, Producer.
PICTURES: The Last Party, Slam (Cannes Film Fest. Awards, Camera d'Or, Grand Jury Prize, 1998).

LEVIN, ROBERT B.
Executive. b. Chicago, IL, May 31, 1943. e. U. of Illinois, BS Journalism, 1965. Copywriter Sears Roebuck & Co. 1965-66, PR Natural Gas Pipeline Co. of Amer. 1966-69. Acct. Exec. Hurvis Binzer & Churchill 1969-70. McCann-Erickson 1975-82 Acct. Super. 1975-79, Mgmt. Super. Needham Harper Worldwide 1982-85. Pres. Mktg. WD Co. 1985-94, Chief Corp. Mktg. & Comm. 1994-95. Pres. Worldwide Mktg. Savoy Pictures 1995-96, Sony Pictures Entertainment, 1996-.

LEVINSON, ART
Producer. Began film career as office boy at Universal Studios where he entered training program and rapidly rose from asst. director to production manager on Harry and Tonto.
PICTURES: Shampoo, The Killing of a Chinese Bookie, Brothers, Audrey Rose, Breaking Away, Mr. Mom, The Money Pit, Mannequin, My Stepmother Is an Alien, Lethal Charm, Teenage Mutant Ninja Turtles III, Teachers, Stop or My Mom Will Shoot!, My Favorite Year, Racing with the Moon, Great Balls of Fire, Lethal Charm, A Family Torn Apart.
TELEVISION: The Kansas City Massacre, Billionaire Boys Club, Curacao (prod.), Fear Stalk, Shoot First: A Cop's Vengeance, Exclusive, A Family Torn Apart, The Yearling, The Great Mom Swap, True Crime. Mini-series: Return to Lonesome Dove.

LEVINSON, BARRY
Director, Producer, Writer, Actor. b. Baltimore, MD, Apr. 6, 1942. e. American Univ. Wrote and acted in L.A. comedy show leading to work on network tv incl. writing and performing on The Carol Burnett Show. Co-wrote film scripts with Mel Brooks, and then-wife Valerie Curtin. Appeared as actor in History of the World Part 1, Quiz Show.
PICTURES: Writer: Silent Movie (also actor), High Anxiety (also actor), ... And Justice for All (Acad. Award nom.), Inside Moves, Best Friends, Unfaithfully Yours. Director: Diner (also s.p.; Acad. Award nom. for s.p.), The Natural, Young Sherlock Holmes, Tin Men (also s.p.), Good Morning Vietnam, Rain Man (also actor; Acad. Award for Best Director, 1988), Avalon (also s.p.; WGA Award, Acad. Award nom. for s.p.), Bugsy (Acad. Award nom.), Toys (also co-s.p.), Jimmy Hollywood (also s.p., co-prod.), Disclosure (also co-prod.), Sleepers (also s.p., co-prod.), Donnie Brasco (prod. only), Wag the Dog (also co-prod.), Sphere (also co-prod.).
TELEVISION: Series: The Tim Conway Comedy Hour (writer), The Marty Feldman Comedy Machine (writer), The Carol Burnett Show (writer; Emmy Awards: 1974, 1975), Harry (exec. prod.), Homicide: Life on the Streets (dir., co-exec. prod.; Emmy Award for directing, 1993). Pilot: Diner (exec. prod., dir.), Oz (exec. prod.). Specials: Stopwatch 30 Minutes of Investigative Ticking (exec. prod.).

LEVINSON, NORM
Executive. b. New Haven, CT, Mar. 17, 1925. Started theatre business as usher for Loew's Theatres, 1940. U.S. Army, 1943-46. Returned Loew's Theatres managerial positions New Haven and Hartford, CT. MGM press representative, Minneapolis, Jacksonville, Atlanta, Dallas. General Manager, Trans-Texas Theatres, Dallas. President, Academy Theatres, Inc., Dallas. Promoted World Championship Boxing, Dallas and Johannesburg, South Africa. Executive Vice President, Cobb Theatres, Birmingham, Alabama; v.p.; world-wide mktg., Artists Releasing Corp., Encino, CA.; head film buyer, Chakeres Theatres, Ohio & Kentucky.

LEVY, BERNARD
Executive. b. Boca Raton, FL. e. Brooklyn Law Sch., L.L.B. Legal staff of Superintendent of Insurance of the state of New York in the rehabilitation and liquidation of guaranteed title and mortgage companies, 1934-36; private practice of law, 1936-46; legal staff, Paramount Pictures, Inc., 1946-50; legal staff, United Paramount Theatres, 1950-51; exec. asst. to Edward L. Hyman, v.p., ABC, Inc., in chg. of theatre administration, north, 1951-62; apptd. exec. liaison officer for southern motion picture theatres, ABC, Inc., 1962-64; exec. liaison officer, m.p. theas., ABC, Inc., 1965-72; v.p., ABC Theatre Division, 1973. Retired, 1976.

LEVY, BUD
Executive. b. Jackson Heights, NY, April 3, 1928. e. NYU. Member: Variety Clubs Int'l., M.P. Pioneers, President's Advisory Board-NATO. Director: NATO, TOP, CATO. Elected pres., Trans-Lux Corp., 1980; pres. Trans Lux Theatres, (a subsidiary of Cinamerica Theatres, later Crown Theatres), 1986-1991. Will Rogers Memorial Fund; chmn., Cara Committee for NATO; chmn. ShowEast; v.p. NATO; dir. Motion Picture Pioneers.

LEVY, DAVID
Executive, Producer, Writer. b. Philadelphia, PA, Jan. 2. e. Wharton Sch., U. of PA, B.S. in Eco., M.B.A., as v.p. & assoc. dir., Young & Rubicam. Inc., 1938-59, acquisitions for clients include: People's Choice, Kate Smith Hour, Wagon Train, Four Star Playhouse, What's My Line, Father Knows Best, Goodyear Playhouse, Life of Riley, Gunsmoke, Arthur Godfrey's Talent Scouts, I Married Joan, The Web, Treasury Men in Action, Person to Person, Maverick, etc. Prod. We the People, Manhattan at Midnight. Writer: Kate Smith radio series, Manhattan at Midnight, Reunion, Robert Montgomery Presents, Grand Central Station, CBS Radio Workshop, Alcoa/Goodyear. With War Finance div. of U.S. Treasury Dept. on detached duty from U.S. Navy, 1944-46. Was v.p. in chg. of network TV progs. & talent, NBC, 1959-61. Acquisitions for network include: Sing-a-Long With Mitch, Peter Pan, Bonanza, Dr. Kildare, Bob Newhart Show, Thriller, Car 54 Where Are You?, Loretta Young Show, Sunday Showcase, Alfred Hitchcock Presents, Dick Powell Show, Saturday Night at the Movies, Hazel, Klondike, Victory at Sea, Joey Bishop Show, Shirley Temple Show, etc. Created: Bat Masterson, The Addams Family, Americans, Outlaws, Pruitts of Southampton, Sarge, Hollywood Screen Test, Face the Music, etc. Developed: Double Life of Henry Phyffe, Name That Tune, You Asked for It, etc. Assigned as writer, training film section, photographic div., Bureau of Aeronautics, U.S. Navy, 1944. Novels: The Chameleons, The Gods of Foxcroft, Network Jungle, Potomac Jungle, as well as numerous TV plays and short stories. Currently creative consultant to Mark Goodson Prods. Pres., Wilshire Prods. Exec. dir., Caucus for Prods., Writers and Dirs.

LEVY, EUGENE
Actor, Writer, Director. b. Hamilton, Canada, Dec. 17, 1946. e. McMaster U. Acted with coll. ensemble theater. Film debut in Ivan Reitman's Cannibal Girls, 1970, before joining Toronto's Second City troupe which eventually led to his work as writer-performer on Second City Television's various programs, 1977-83. Canadian theater: Godspell (1971), The Owl and the Pussycat, Love Times Four.
PICTURES: Cannibal Girls, Running, Heavy Metal (voice), National Lampoon's Vacation, Strange Brew, Going Berserk, Splash, Armed and Dangerous, The Canadian Conspiracy, Club Paradise, Speed Zone, Father of the Bride, Once Upon a Crime (also dir.), Stay Tuned, I Love Trouble, Multiplicity.
TELEVISION: Series: Second City TV, SCTV Network 90, SCTV Network (Emmy Award as writer, 1983). Movies: Partners in Love, Sodbusters (dir., co-writer, co-exec. prod.), Harrison Bergeron.

LEVY, HERMAN M.
Attorney. b. New Haven, CT, Sept. 27, 1904. e. Yale, B.A., 1927, Yale Law Sch., LL.B., 1929; Phi Beta Kappa, was in legal dept. RCA Photophone; newspaper reporter; admitted to Connecticut bar, 1929. 1939 elected exec. secy. of MPTO of Connecticut. 1943 elected gen. counsel MPTOA. Gen. counsel, Theatre Owners of America, 1947-63. Pres., New Haven County Bar Assn., 1964; legislative agent, CT Assn. of Theatre Owners. Retired as legislative agent, 1981. Received Distinguished Service Award from ShowEast '93. Author: More Sinned Against, Natl. Bd. of Review Magazine, 1941. Proving the Death of a Non-Resident Alien, Conn. Bar Journal, 1950; Need for a System of Arbitration M.P. Ind., Arbitration Journal, 1950; reprint of Industry Case Digest, 20th Century-Fox vs. Boehm in the Journal (Screen Producers Guild); Book Review of Antitrust in the Motion Picture Industry, by Michael Conant (Univ. of Calif. Law Review).

LEVY, JULES
Producer. b. Los Angeles, CA, Feb. 12, 1923. e. USC. Started in prop-erty dept. of WB, 1941; first m.p. unit Army Air Force, Culver City, CA. PICTURES: The Vampire, Return of Dracula, Vice Squad, Without Warning, Down Three Dark Streets, Geronimo, The Glory Guys, Clambake, The Scalphunters, Sam Whiskey, The McKenzie Break, The Hunting Party, Kansas City Bomber, The Honkers, McQ, Branningan, White Lightning, Gator, Safari 3000. TELEVISION: Series: The Rifleman, Robert Taylor in The Detectives, Law of the Plainsman, The Big Valley.

LEVY, MICHAEL
Executive. b. Brooklyn, NY. e. Brown U. Started in industry in editorial dept. of trade-paper Variety; held posts in New York with ABC Motion Pictures and with Diener/Hauser/Bates Advertising. Worked for Lawrence Gordon Productions as exec. asst. to Gordon and as story editor. Joined 20th Century Fox in January, 1985, as dir. of creative affairs for studio. 1986, named v.p., pro-duction, m.p. div., Fox; appointed sr. v.p. production, 20th Century Fox, 1988; named pres., Silver Pictures, 1989.

LEVY, NORMAN
Executive. b. Bronx, NY, Jan. 3, 1935. e. City Coll. of New York. 1957 joined Universal Pictures, holding various sales positions; 1967, went to National General Pictures, ultimately being named v.p. and exec. asst. to pres.; 1974, Columbia Pictures, v.p., gen. sls. mgr. 1975 named Columbia exec. v.p. in chg. of domestic sls.; 1977, exec. v.p., mktg; 1978. pres., Columbia Pictures Domestic Distribution. 1980 joined 20th-Fox as pres. of Entertainment Group; 1981, vice-chmn., 20th Century-Fox Film Corp. Resigned 1985 to become chmn, ceo, New Century/Vista Film Co. 1991, chmn. and CEO, Creative Film Enterprises.

LEWELLEN, A. WAYNE
Executive. b. Dallas, TX, Feb. 16, 1944. e. U. of Texas. Joined Paramount Pictures 1973 as brch. mgr., Dallas-Oklahoma City territory; 1978, v.p. Southern div.; 1984, exec. v.p., gen. sls. mngr.; 1986, pres. domestic distrib.; 1993, pres. M.P. distrib.

LEWINE, JEFFREY G.
Executive. b. New York, NY, 1955. e. Syracuse U. Entered the industry while young, working as an usher, a ticker-take, a janitor, and eventually as a theatre manager while in high school and dur-ing summers in college. 1977, named general sl's. mng'r., of Cinema 5, responsible for marketing and distribution of notable Cinema 5 films such as Pumping Iron, Endless Summer, Swept Away and Monty Python and The Holy Grail; 1980, named v.p., managing company's theatre and distibution activities. 1981, became managing dir., Cinema Int'l. Corp., in Sydney, Australia; created a new division to manage merchandising and ancillary film sales which expanded to the Far East. 1987, returned to the U.S., and with his partners, the Edgar Bronfman family, acquired Cinemette, movie theatre circuit based in Pittsburgh; became pres. and CEO, of the renamed Cinema World; 1994, sold Cinema World to Carmike Cinemas, Inc. 1995-96, consultant to Coca-Cola USA in several divisions. 1997, founded JJL Consultants, Inc., agc'y. dealing with theatre and real estate negotiations. Nov. 1997, together with Warburg Pinctus Ventures, formed WestStar Cinemas to acquire Cinamerica Theatres which operates as Mann Theatres, and was named pres. and CEO of WestStar Cinemas. On Bd. of Dir's.: National Association of Theatre Owners, Will Rogers Memorial Foundation.

LEWIS, ARTHUR
Producer, Director, Writer. b. New York, NY, Sept. 15, 1918. e. USC, Yale U. Began career as writer and assoc. prod. on the Jones Family TV series. Five years in U.S. Army; returned to screenwriting before producing Three Wishes for Jamie on Broadway and producing and directing Guys and Dolls in London's West End. In mid-60s and 70s produced over 25 plays with Bernard Delfont in the West End of London.
PICTURES: Producer: Loot, Baxter, The Killer Elite, Brass Target.
TELEVISION: Brenner, The Asphalt Jungle, The Nurses. Movies: The Diary of Anne Frank, Splendor in the Grass.

LEWIS, EDWARD
Producer. b. Camden, NJ, Dec. 16, 1922. e. Bucknell U. Began entertainment career as script writer, then co-produced The Admiral Was a Lady and teamed with Marion Parsonnet to bring the Faye Emerson Show to TV. Subsequently prod. first Schlitz Playhouse and China Smith series. Was v.p. of Kirk Douglas' indep. prod. co., where was assoc. prod. and writer-prod. Collaborated with John Frankenheimer on 8 films.
PICTURES: Lizzie (assoc. prod.), The Careless Years (prod., s.p.), Spartacus, The Last Sunset, Lonely Are the Brave, The List of Adrian Messenger, Seconds, Grand Prix, The Fixer (exec. prod.), The Gypsy Moths (exec.), I Walk the Line (exec.), The Horsemen, The Iceman Cometh (exec.), Executive Action, Rhinoceros, Lost in the Stars, Missing (co-prod.), Crackers, The River, Brothers (prod., s.p.).
TELEVISION: Ishi: The Last of His Tribe (exec. prod.), The Thorn Birds (exec. prod.).

LEWIS, GEOFFREY
Actor. b. San Diego, CA, 1935. Father of actress Juliette Lewis, actors Lightfield & Peter Lewis.
PICTURES: Welcome Home Soldier Boys, The Culpepper Cattle Company, Bad Company, High Plains Drifter, Dillinger, Thunderbolt and Lightfoot, Macon County Line, The Great Waldo Pepper, Smile, The Wind and the Lion, Lucky Lady, The Return of a Man Called Horse, Every Which Way But Loose, Tilt, Human Experiments, Tom Horn, Broncho Billy, Heaven's Gate, Any Which Way You Can, Shoot the Sun Down, I the Jury, Ten to Midnight, Night of the Comet, Lust in the Dust, Stitches, Fletch Lives, Out of the Dark, Pink Cadillac, Catch Me If You Can, Disturbed, Double Impact, The Lawnmower Man, Point of No Return, Wishman, The Man Without a Face, Only the Strong, Army of One, Maverick.

TELEVISION: *Series*: Flo, Gun Shy. *Movies*: Moon of the Wolf, Honky Tonk, The Great Ice Rip-Off, Attack on Terror: The FBI Versus the Ku Klux Klan, The New Daughters of Joshua Cabe, The Great Houndinis, The Deadly Triangle, The Hunted Lady, When Every Day Was the Fourth of July, The Jericho Mile, Samurai, Salem's Lot, Belle Starr, The Shadow Riders, Life of the Party: The Story of Beatrice, The Return of the Man From U.N.C.L.E., Travis McGee, September Gun, Stormin' Home, Dallas: The Early Years, Day of Reckoning, Gambler V: Playing for Keeps, When the Dark Man Calls, Kansas. *Guest*: Mannix, Barnaby Jones, Starsky and Hutch, Streets of San Francisco, Police Woman, Little House on the Prairie, Laverne & Shirley, Lou Grant, Magnum P.I., Amazing Stories, Murder She Wrote, Paradise.

LEWIS, HAROLD G.
Executive. b. New York, NY, Sept. 18, 1938. e. Union Coll., 1960, electrical engineer. Joined ATA Trading Corp. in 1960 and has been pres. since 1977. Producer of feature animation. Importer and exporter for theatrical and TV features, documentaries, series, classics. Pres., ATA Trading Corp., and Favorite TV, Inc.

LEWIS, JERRY
Actor, Director, Writer, Producer. r.n. Joseph Levitch. b. Newark, NJ, Mar. 16, 1926. e. Irvington H.S. Parents Danny and Rae Lewis, prof. entertainers. Debut at 5 at a NY Borscht Circuit hotel singing Brother Can You Spare a Dime? 1946 formed comedy-team with Dean Martin at 500 Club, Atlantic City, NJ; then appeared on NBC tv, performed many theatres before being signed by Hal Wallis for m.p. debut. Voted Most Promising Male Star in Television in m.p. Daily's 2nd annual TV poll, 1950. Voted (as team) one of top ten money making stars in m.p. Herald-Fame poll: 1951-56 (including no. 1 position in 1952), voted as solo performer: 1957-59, 1961-64; named best comedy team in m.p. Daily's 16th annual radio poll, 1951-53. 1956 formed Jerry Lewis Prods. Inc., functioning as prod., dir., writer & star. National Chairman & bd. member, Muscular Dystrophy Association. Full professor USC; taught grad. film dir. Book: The Total Filmmaker (1971) based on classroom lectures. *Autobiography*: Jerry Lewis In Person (1982).
THEATER: Hellzapoppin (regional), Damn Yankees (B'way debut, 1995).
PICTURES: My Friend Irma (debut, 1949), My Friend Irma Goes West, At War With the Army, That's My Boy, Sailor Beware, Jumping Jacks, Scared Stiff, The Stooge, Road to Bali (cameo), The Caddy, Money From Home, Living It Up, Three Ring Circus, You're Never Too Young, Artists and Models, Pardners, Hollywood or Bust, The Delicate Delinquent (also prod.), The Sad Sack, Rock-a-Bye Baby, The Geisha Boy (also prod.), Don't Give Up the Ship, Li'l Abner (cameo), Visit to a Small Planet, Cinderfella (also prod.), The Bellboy (dir., prod., s.p.), The Ladies Man (also dir., prod., co-s.p.), The Errand Boy (also dir., co-s.p.), It's Only Money, The Nutty Professor (also dir., co-s.p.), Who's Minding the Store?, It's a Mad Mad Mad Mad World (cameo), The Patsy (also dir., co-s.p.), The Disorderly Orderly, Boeing-Boeing, The Family Jewels (also dir., prod., co-s.p.), Three on a Couch (also dir., prod.), Way... Way Out, The Big Mouth (also dir., prod., co-s.p.), Don't Raise the Bridge Lower the River, Hook Line and Sinker (also prod.), Which Way to the Front? (also dir., prod.), One More Time (dir. only), The Day the Clown Cried (also dir., co-s.p.), Hardly Working (also dir., co-s.p.), The King of Comedy, Smorgasbord (Cracking Up; also dir., co-s.p.), Slapstick of Another Kind, Cookie, Mr. Saturday Night (cameo), Arizona Dream, Funny Bones.
TELEVISION: *Movie*: Fight for Life. *Series*: Colgate Comedy Hour, The Jerry Lewis Show (1963), The Jerry Lewis Show (1967-69). *Guest*: Wiseguy (5 episodes).

LEWIS, JOSEPH H.
Director. b. New York, NY, Apr. 6, 1907. e. DeWitt Clinton H.S. Camera boy, MGM; then asst. film ed. in chge. film ed., Republic; dir. in chge. 2nd units; debuted as dir. at Universal; served in U.S. Signal Corps., WW II. Dir. musical numbers for The Jolson Story.
PICTURES: Navy Spy (co-dir. with Crane Wilbur; debut, 1937), Courage of the West, Singing Outlaw, The Spy Ring, Border Wolves, The Last Stand, Two-Fisted Rangers, The Return of Wild Bill, That Gang of Mine, The Invisible Ghost, Pride of the Bowery, Arizona Cyclone, Bombs Over Burma, The Silver Bullet, Secrets of a Co-Ed, The Boss of Hangtown Mesa, The Mad Doctor of Market Street, Minstrel Man, The Falcon in San Francisco, My Name is Julia Ross, So Dark the Night, The Swordsman, The Return of October, The Undercover Man, Gun Crazy, A Lady Without Passport, Retreat Hell!, Desperate Search, Cry of the Hunted, The Big Combo, A Lawless Street, The Seventh Cavalry, The Halliday Brand, Terror in a Texas Town.
TELEVISION: *Series*: The Rifleman, The Big Valley.

LEWIS, JULIETTE
Actress. b. California, June 21, 1973. Father is actor Geoffrey Lewis.
PICTURES: My Stepmother Is an Alien (debut, 1988), Meet the Hollowheads, National Lampoon's Christmas Vacation, Crooked Hearts, Cape Fear (Acad. Award nom.), Husbands and Wives, That Night, Kalifornia, What's Eating Gilbert Grape, Romeo Is Bleeding, Natural Born Killers, Mixed Nuts, The Basketball Diaries, Strange Days, From Dusk Till Dawn, The Evening Star, The Audition, From Dusk Til Dawn, Full Tilt Boogie, The Other Sister, Men.
TELEVISION: *Series*: Homefires, I Married Dora, A Family for Joe. *Movie*: Too Young to Die?

LEWIS, MICHAEL J.
Composer. b. Wales, 1939. First film score 1969, The Mad Woman of Chaillot, won Ivor Novello Award for best film score. 1973: first Broadway musical, Cyrano, Grammy nomination '74, Caesar and Cleopatra (T.V. '76), The Lion the Witch and the Wardrobe (Emmy, 1979).
PICTURES: The Man Who Haunted Himself, Julius Caesar. Upon This Rock, Unman Wittering and Zigo, Running Scared, Baxter, Theatre of Blood, 11 Harrowhouse, 92 in the Shade, Russian Roulette, The Stick-Up, The Medusa Touch, The Legacy, The Passage, The Unseen, ffolkes, Sphinx, Yes Giorgio, The Hound of the Baskervilles, On the Third Day, The Naked Face.

LEWIS, RICHARD
Comedian, Actor. b. Brooklyn, NY, June 29, 1949. e. Ohio St. Univ. (marketing degree). Was copywriter for adv. agency before becoming stand-up comic performing in nightclubs in NYC, Las Vegas, 1971.
PICTURES: The Wrong Guys (debut, 1988), That's Adequate, Once Upon a Crime, Robin Hood: Men in Tights, Wagons East!, Leaving Las Vegas, Drunks.
TELEVISION: *Series*: Harry, Anything But Love, Hiller & Diller. *Specials*: Richard Lewis: I'm in Pain, Richard Lewis: I'm Exhausted, Richard Lewis: I'm Doomed, Living Against the Odds (also writer). *Pilot*: King of the Building.

LI, GONG
Actress. b. Shenyang, Liaoning Province, China, Dec. 31, 1965.
PICTURES: Red Field, Red Sorghum, The Terracotta Warrior, Ju Dou, God of Gamblers III: Back to Shanghai, Raise the Red Lantern, The Story of Qiu Ju, Mary from Beijing, Farewell—My Concubine, Flirting Scholar, La Peintre, Semi-Gods and Semi-Devils, The Great Conqueror's Concubine, To Live, Shanghai Triad, Temptress Moon.

LIBERMAN, FRANK P.
Publicist. b. New York, NY, May 29, 1917. e. Cheshire Acad., CT, 1934; Lafayette Coll., Easton, PA, B.A. 1938. m. Patricia Harris, casting dir. Worked as copy boy, N.Y. Daily News, 1938-39. Began career as publicist at Warner Bros., home office as messenger, 1939, promoted to pressbooks dept., transferred to Warner's Chicago office as field exploitation man. U.S. Signal Corps., 1941, public relations officer, Army Pictorial Service, on temporary duty with War Dept., Bureau of Public Relations in Pentagon. Discharged as Capt., 1946. Rejoined Warner Bros. on coast 2 years, 1947, est. own public relations office, 1947. Owner, Frank Liberman and Associates, Inc.

LIBERTINI, RICHARD
Actor. b. Cambridge, MA, May 21. Original member of Second City troupe in Chicago. With MacIntyre Dixon appeared as the Stewed Prunes in cabaret performances.
THEATER: Three by Three (1961), Plays for Bleecker Street, The Cat's Pajamas, The Mad Show, . Bad Habits. Solo: The White House Murder Case, Don't Drink the Water, Paul Sill's Story Theatre, Ovid's Metamorphoses, The Primary English Class, Neopolitan Ghosts, Love's Labour's Lost, As You Like It.
PICTURES: The Night They Raided Minsky's, Don't Drink the Water, Catch-22, The Out-of-Towners, Lovers and Other Strangers, Lady Liberty, Fire Sale, Days of Heaven, The In-Laws, Popeye, Sharky's Machine, Soup for One, Best Friends, Deal of the Century, Going Berserk, Unfaithfully Yours, All of Me, Fletch, Big Trouble, Betrayed, Fletch Lives, Animal Behavior. Duck Tales: The Movie (voice), Lemon Sisters, Awakenings, The Bonfire of the Vanities, Cultivating Charlie, Nell.
TELEVISION: *Series*: Story Theatre, The Melba Moore-Clifton Davis Show, Soap, Family Man, The Fanelli Boys, Pacific Station. *Guest*: George Burns Comedy Week, Barney Miller, Bob Newhart. *Pilots*: Calling Dr. Storm, M.D., Fair Game. *Movies*: Three on a Date, Extreme Close-Up. *Specials*: Let's Celebrate, The Fourth Wise Man, Fame (Hallmark Hall of Fame), The Trial of Bernhard Goetz, Equal Justice, Murder She Wrote, Law and Order, L.A. Law.

LICCARDI, VINCENT G.
Executive. b. Brooklyn, NY. Started as messenger at Universal Pictures, asst. adv. mgr. on Around the World in 80 Days, asst. to exec. coord. of sales & adv. on Spartacus; National Dir. of Adv. & Publ., Continental; Nat. Dir. Adv. & Publ., Braintree Prod., adv. pub. mgr. Allied Artists, adv. mgr. Paramount, National Dir. Adv.-Pub., UMC Pictures, Screen-writer, Playboy to Priest, The Rivals, The Rivals-Part II, The Greatest Disaster of All Time, The Lady on the 9:40, All That Heaven Allows, All Mine to Love, Twice Over, Lightly!, Mr. Jim, The Reluctant Corpse.

LIEBERFARB, WARREN N.
Executive. e. Wharton Sch. of Commerce and Finance, U. of PA, B.S., economics; U. of Michigan. Started career in industry at Paramount Pictures as dir. of mktg. and exec. asst. to Stanley Jaffe, then pres. Later joined 20th-Fox as v.p., special market dist. (cable, pay-TV, non-theatrical). Joined Warner Bros. as v.p., exec. asst. to Ted Ashley, bd. chmn.; later named v.p., intl. adv.-pub. In 1979 joined Lorimar as v.p., of Lorimar Productions, Inc., the parent company, based in New York. Promoted to sr. v.p. 1982, named v.p. mktg., Warner Home Video; named pres., 1984.

LIEBERMAN, HAL
Executive. Pres. of production, Universal Pictures.

LIEBERMAN, ROBERT
Director, Producer. b. Buffalo, NY, July 16, 1947. e. Univ. of Buffalo. m. actress Marilu Henner. Moved to LA, became editor for Desort-Fisher commercial production house, which led to dir. tv ad spots. Formed own commercial company, Harmony Pictures.
PICTURES: Table for Five, All I Want for Christmas, Fire in the Sky, D3: The Mighty Ducks.
TELEVISION: Movies: Fighting Back: The Story of Rocky Blier, Will: G. Gordon Liddy, To Save a Child (also exec. prod.). Series: thirtysomething, Dream Street (pilot), The Young Riders (pilot), Gabriel's Fire (also exec. prod.), Pros and Cons (exec. consultant), Under Suspicion (also exec. prod.), Medicine Ball (also exec. prod.), Titanic.

LIEBERSON, SANFORD
Producer. b. Los Angeles, CA, 1936. Early career with William Morris Agency. 1961-62, agent in Rome for Grade Org. Returned to LA as Founding Member CMA agency then exec. in charge of European operations. 1979, named pres. of 20th-Fox Productions, which company he joined in 1977 as v.p. European production. Previously an independent producer forming Good Times. With David Putnam formed Visual Programming Systems to produce, acquire and consult in the Home Video area for CBS, Phillips, Time/Life, etc. As v.p. intl. prod. at Fox, spv. intl. release of such films as Star Wars, 1900, Alien, Chariots of Fire, Nine to Five, Quest for Fire. V.P. Intl. prod. for The Ladd Company. Outland, Body Heat, Blade Runner, The Right Stuff, Police Academy, etc. Chief of prod. at Goldcrest Harvest: Dance With a Stranger, Room With a View, Absolute Beginners, etc. Pres. intl. prod. MGM spv. Russia House, Thelma & Louise, Liebestraum, Not Without My Daughter, Criss Cross, etc. Currently head of prod. at the Natl. Film and Television School of Great Britain.
PICTURES: Producer: Melody, Pied Piper, Radio Wonderful, James Dean: First American Teenager, Bugsy Malone, Slade in Flame, Final Programme, Stardust, That'll Be the Day, Brother Can You Spare a Dime, Swastika, Double Headed Eagle, All This and World War II, Mahler, Lisztomania, Jabberwocky, Rita Sue and Bob Too, Stars and Bars, The Mighty Quinn, Performance.
TELEVISION: Movie: Frank & Jessie (exec. prod.).

LIGHT, JUDITH
Actress. b. Trenton, NJ, Feb. 9. e. Carnegie-Mellon Univ. (BFA). Toured with USO in prod. of Guys and Dolls during college. Acted with Milwaukee and Seattle rep. companies. Made B'way debut in 1975 prod. of A Doll's House with Liv Ullmann. Other stage work: A Streetcar Named Desire, As You Like It, Richard III. Landed role of Karen Wolek on daytime serial One Life to Live in 1977.
TELEVISION: Series: One Life to Live (2 Emmy Awards), Who's the Boss?, Phenom. Movies: Intimate Agony, Dangerous Affection, The Ryan White Story, My Boyfriend's Back, In Defense of a Married Man, Wife Mother Murderer, Men Don't Tell, Betrayal of Trust, Against Their Will: Women in Prison, Lady Killer, A Husband, A Wife and A Lover, Murder at My Door, A Step Toward Tomorrow, Too Close to Home. Guest: St. Elsewhere, Family Ties, Remington Steele.

LIGHTMAN, M. A.
Exhibitor. b. Nashville, TN, Apr. 21, 1915. e. Southwestern U., Vanderbilt U., 1936, B.A. Bd. chmn. Malco Theatres, Inc., Memphis, Tenn.

LINDBLOM, GUNNEL
Actress, Director. b. Gothenburg, Sweden, 1931. Discovered by Ingmar Bergman while studying at drama school of Gothenburg Municipal Theatre, 1950-53; she moved to Malmo, where he was director of the local Municipal Theatre. Under Bergman's direction she played in Easter, Peer Gynt, Faust, etc. between 1954-59. Later appeared in many Bergman films. Since 1968 has been on staff of Stockholm's Royal Dramatic Theatre, assisting Bergman and then beginning to direct on her own. Made film debut as director with Summer Paradise in 1977.
PICTURES: Actress: Love, Girl in the Rain, Song of the Scarlet Flower, The Seventh Seal, Wild Strawberries, The Virgin Spring, Winter Light, The Silence, My Love Is a Rose, Rapture, Loving Couples, Hunger, Woman of Darkness, The Girls, The Father, Brother Carl, Scenes From a Marriage, Misfire, Bakom Jalusin. Director: Summer Paradise (also co-s.p.), Sally and Freedom, Summer Nights on Planet Earth (also s.p.).

LINDEN, HAL
Actor. b. Bronx, NY, March 20, 1931. e. City Coll. of New York. Began career as saxophone player and singer, playing with bands of Sammy Kaye, Bobby Sherwood, etc. Drafted and performed in revues for Special Services. After discharge enrolled at N.Y.'s American Theatre Wing; appeared on B'way in Bells Are Ringing, replacing Sydney Chaplin.
THEATER: Wildcat, Something More, Subways Are for Sleeping, Ilya Darling, The Apple Tree, The Education of H*Y*M*A*N K*A*P*L*A*N, On a Clear Day You Can See Forever, Three Men on a Horse, The Pajama Game, The Rothschilds (Tony Award, 1971), I'm Not Rappaport, Unfinished Stories, The Sisters Rosensweig.
PICTURES: Bells Are Ringing, When You Comin' Back Red Ryder?, A New Life, Out to Sea.
TELEVISION: Series: Animals Animals Animals (host), Barney Miller, Blacke's Magic, F.Y.I. (Emmy Awards, 1983, 1984), Jack's Place, The Boys Are Back. Specials: I Do! I Do!, The Best of Everything. Movies: Mr. Inside/Mr. Outside, The Love Boat (pilot), How to Break Up a Happy Divorce, Father Figure, Starlight: The Plane That Couldn't Land, The Other Woman, My Wicked Wicked Ways: The Legend of Errol Flynn, The O'Connors, Dream Breakers, The Colony.

LINDHEIM, RICHARD D.
Executive. b. New York, NY, May 28, 1939. e. Univ. of Redlands, USC. Admin. Asst. Story Dept., CBS, 1962-64. Project Dir. Entertainment Testing ASI Mkt. Research, 1964-69. VP Prog. Research NBC 1969-78, VP Dramatic Prog. 1978-79, Prod. Universal TV 1979-81, VP Current Prog. 1981-85, SVP Series Prog. 1986-87. Exec. VP Creative Affairs 1987-91, Exec. VP Prog. Strategy MCA TV Group 1991-92. Exec. VP Paramount TV 1992-. Asst. Prof. CA State U. Sr. Lecturer, USC, UCLA. Author: Primetime Network TV Programming (w/ Richard Blum) 1987, Inside TV Producing 1991.

LINDO, DELROY
Actor. b. London, England, Nov. 18, 1952. Received NAACP Image Awards for film Malcolm X and play A Raisin in the Sun.
THEATER: B'way: Joe Turner's Come and Gone (Tony nom.), Master Harold and the Boys. Off-B'way: District Line, As You Like It, Romeo and Juliet, Spell #7, The Heliotrope Bouquet. Regional: Othello, Mrs. Ever's Boys, Cobb, A Raisin in the Sun, My Mark My Name, Union Boys, Macbeth, Black Branch, Home.
PICTURES: The Blood of Heroes (Salute to the Jugger; debut, 1990), Mountains of the Moon, Perfect Witness, The Hard Way, Bright Angel, Malcolm X, Bound by Honor, Mr. Jones, Behanzin, Crooklyn, Congo, Clockers, Get Shorty, Feeling Minnesota, Broken Arrow, Ransom.
TELEVISION: Guest: Going to Extremes, Against the Law, Hawk, Beauty and the Beast.

LINDSAY, ROBERT
Actor. b. Ilkeston, Derbyshire, Eng., Dec. 13, 1949. e. GLadstone Boys School, Ilkeston, Royal Acad. of Dramatic Art. With Manchester's Royal Exchange Theatre Co. (Hamlet, The Cherry Orchard, The Lower Depths). Also in Godspell, The Three Musketeers, Me and My Girl, (London—Olivier Award, NY—Tony, Theatre World & Drama Desk Awards, 1987), Becket (Olivier & Variety Club Awards), Cyrano de Bergerac.
PICTURES: That'll Be the Day (debut, 1974), Bert Rigby You're a Fool, Strike It Rich, Fierce Creatures.
TELEVISION: Series: Citizen Smith, Give Us A Break. Miniseries: Confessional. Specials: King Lear, G.B.H. (BAFTA Award), Genghis Cohn, Jake's Progress.

LINDSAY-HOGG, MICHAEL
Director. b. England, 1940. Mother is actress Geraldine Fitzgerald.
PICTURES: Let It Be, Nasty Habits, The Object of Beauty (also s.p.), Frankie Starlight.
TELEVISION: Brideshead Revisted (co-dir.), Master Harold ... and the Boys, As Is.

LINK, WILLIAM
Writer, Producer. b. Philadelphia, PA, Dec. 15, 1933. e. U. of Pennsylvania, B.S., 1956. With partner, late Richard Levinson, wrote and created numerous TV series and movies, specializing in detective-mystery genre. Books: Fineman, Stay Tuned: An Inside Look at the Making of Prime-Time Television, Off Camera. Stage incl.: Prescription Murder, Guilty Conscience, Merlin.
PICTURES: The Hindenberg, Rollercoaster.
TELEVISION: Series writer-creator: Mannix, Ellery Queen, Tenafly, Columbo (Emmy Award as writer, 1972), Murder She Wrote. Movies writer-prod.: That Certain Summer, My Sweet Charlie (Emmy Award as writer, 1970), The Judge and Jake Wyler, Savage (exec. prod., writer), The Execution of Private Slovik, The Gun, A Cry for Help (prod. only), The Storyteller, Murder by Natural Causes, Stone, Crisis at Central High, Rehearsal For Murder (also exec. prod.), Take Your Best Shot, Prototype (also exec. prod.), The Guardian (also exec. prod.), Guilty Conscience (also exec. prod.), Vanishing Act (also exec. prod.), The United States Vs. Salim Ajami, The Boys (also co-exec. prod.).

LINKLATER, RICHARD
Director, Writer, Producer. b. Houston, TX, 1961. Founded Austin Film Society, serving as artistic director. Filmed several super 8 films incl. feature It's Impossible to Learn to Plow by Reading Books.
PICTURES: Director/Writer: Slacker (also actor & prod.), Dazed and Confused (also co-prod.), The Underneath (actor only), Beavis & Butt-Head Do America (voice), Before Sunrise, Suburbia (dir. only), The Newton Boys.

LINKLETTER, ART
Emcee, Producer, Author. b. Moose Jaw, Saskatchewan, Canada, July 17, 1912. Raised in San Diego. e. San Diego State Coll. Radio prg. mgr., San Diego Exposition, 1935; radio pgm. mgr. S.F. World's Fair, 1937-39; freelance radio announcer and m.c. 1939-42; m.c. series People Are Funny starting in 1942. Author: The Secret World of Kids, 1959; Kids Say the Darndest Things, 1957; Linkletter Down Under, 1969; Yes You Can, 1979; Old Age Is Not For Sissies, 1988; Cavalcade of the Golden West; Cavalcade of America. Recorded albums: Howls, Boners & Shockers and We Love You, Call Collect (Grammy Award winner, 1966). Bd. of dir., MGM, 1979-88.

PICTURES: People Are Funny, Champagne for Caesar, The Snow Queen.
TELEVISION: *Series*: Art Linkletter's House Party, Life With Linkletter, People Are Funny (emcee), The Art Linkletter Show (emcee), Hollywood Talent Scouts. *Specials*: Inside Salute to Baseball (exec. prod., host), Art Linkletter's Secret World of Kids (host), Ford Startime, Young Man With A Band, Linkletters Spend Christmas in the Holy Land, Kid's Eye View of Washington. *Movies*: Zane Grey Theatre, G.E. Theatre, Wagon Train: Kid at the Stick.

LINN-BAKER, MARK
Actor, Director. b. St. Louis, MO, June 17, 1954. e. Yale Univ., Yale Sch. of Drama (M.F.A., 1979). Founding memb. American Repertory Th. in Cambridge, MA; founding prod./dir. NY Stage & Film Co. in NYC & Poughkeepsie. Co-founder of True Pictures, 1990.
THEATER: *B'way*: Doonesbury, Laughter on the 23rd Floor, A Funny Thing Happened On The Way To The Forum.
PICTURES: Manhattan (bit), The End of August, My Favorite Year, Me and Him (voice only), Noises Off, Me and Veronica (co-prod. only).
TELEVISION: *Series*: Comedy Zone, Perfect Strangers, Hangin' With Mr. Cooper (dir. only). *Movies*: Wedding Bell Blues, Bare Essentials. *Specials*: Doonesbury (voice of Kirby), The Ghost Writer (Amer. Playhouse), The Whole Shebang. *Director*: episodes of Family Matters, Family Man, Going Places.

LINSON, ART
Producer, Director. b. Chicago, IL, 1942. e. UCLA; LLD. UCLA, 1967. Was rock music manager with record prod. Lou Adler and ran own record co., Spin Dizzy records before turning to film production. Debuted as director also with Where the Buffalo Roam.
PICTURES: *Prod. &/or dir.*: Rafferty and the Gold Dust Twins (co.-prod.), Car Wash, American Hot Wax (also co-s.p.), Where the Buffalo Roam, Melvin and Howard, Fast Times at Ridgemont High (co-prod.), The Wild Life, The Untouchables, Scrooged (co-prod.), Casualties of War, We're No Angels, Dick Tracy (exec. prod.), Singles, Point of No Return, This Boy's Life , Heat, The Edge, Pushing Tin, Great Expectations.

LIOTTA, RAY
Actor. b. Newark, NJ, Dec. 18, 1955. e. Univ. of Miami. First prof. job on tv commercial, followed by continuing role on daytime serial, Another World.
PICTURES: Something Wild (debut, 1983), The Lonely Lady, Dominick and Eugene, Field of Dreams, GoodFellas, Article 99, Unlawful Entry, No Escape, Corrina Corrina, Operation Dumbo Drop, Unforgettable, Turbulence, Cop Land, Phoenix.
TELEVISION: *Series*: Another World, Casablanca, Our Family Honor. *Movies*: Harhat and Legs, Crazy Times, Women and Men 2: In Love There Are No Rules (Domestic Dilemma).

LIPPERT, ROBERT L., JR.
Producer, Exhibitor. b. Alameda, CA, Feb. 28, 1928. e. St Mary's Coll., 1946; all conference football 1947. Career began in theatre exhibition. Entered m.p. production in 1951. Film editor of 45 "b" features. Produced 9 pictures for Lippert Features and 20th Century Fox Films. Returned in 1966 to theatre exhibition. Became pres. of Affiliated, Lippert, Transcontinental theatrs (180 theatres nation-wide). Semi-retired as of 1994.

LIPSTONE, HOWARD H.
Executive. b. Chicago, IL, Apr. 28, 1928. e. UCLA, USC. Ass't to gen. mgr. at KLTA, 1950-55; program dir. at KABC-TV, 1955-65; exec. ass't to pres. at Selmur Prods., ABC subsidiary, 1965-69. Ivan Tors Films & Studios as exec. v.p., 1969-70; pres., Alan Landsburg Prods., 1970-1985; The Landsburg Co., 1985-. Co-exec. prod.: The Outer Space Connection, The Bermuda Triangle, Mysteries, The White Lions, Jaws 3-D.
TELEVISION: *Exec. in charge of prod.*: The Savage Bees, Ruby and Oswald, The Triangle Factory Fire Scandal, Strange Voices, A Place at the Table, Kate & Allie, Gimme a Break, A Stoning in Fulham County, The Ryan White Story, Quiet Victory, Unspeakable Acts, In Defense of a Married Man, Triumph of the Heart, Nightmare in Columbia County, A Mother's Right, The Elizabeth Morgan Story, The diamond Fleece, Terror in the Night, If Someone Had Known.

LIPTON, PEGGY
Actress. b. New York, NY, Aug. 30, 1947. Former model. Co-wrote song L.A. is My Lady (recorded by Frank Sinatra). Recorded album Peggy Lipton.
PICTURES: The Purple People Eater, Kinjite (Forbidden Subjects), Twin Peaks: Fire Walk With Me, Justice for Annie, The Postman.
TELEVISION: *Series*: The John Forsythe Show, The Mod Squad (Golden Globe Award, 1971), Twin Peaks, Angel Falls. *Movies*: The Return of the Mod Squad, Addicted to His Love, Fatal Charm, The Spider and the Fly, Deadly Vows.

LISI, VIRNA
Actress. r.n. Virna Pieralisi. b. Ancona, Italy, Nov. 8, 1936.
PICTURES: Desiderio e Sole, Violenza sul Lago, The Doll That Took the Town, Luna Nova, Vendicatta, La Rossa, Caterina Sforza, Il Mondo dei Miracoli, Duel of the Titans, Eva, Don't Tempt the Devil, The Black Tulip, The Shortest Day, How To Murder Your Wife, Casanova 70, The Possessed, A Virgin for a Prince, Kiss the Other Sheik, The Birds the Bees and the Italians, Made in Italy, La Bambole (The Dolls), Not With My Wife You Don't, Assault on a Queen, The 25th Hour, Anyone Can Play, The Girl and the General, Arabella, Better a Widow, The Girl Who Couldn't Say No, The Christmas Tree, The Secret of Santa Vittoria, If It's Tuesday This Must Be Belgium, Roma Bene, The Statue, Bluebeard, The Serpent, Ernesto, I Love N.Y., I Ragazzi di Via Panisperna, Beyond Good and Evil, Merry Christmas Happy New Year, Miss Right, Queen Margot (Cannes Film Fest. Award, 1994).
TELEVISION: *US*: Christopher Columbus.

LITHGOW, JOHN
Actor. b. Rochester, NY, Oct. 19, 1945. Father was prod. of Shakespeare Fests. in midwest. e. Harvard. Fulbright fellowship to study at London Acad. of Music and Dramatic Art. Interned in London with Royal Shakespeare Co. and Royal Court Theatre.
THEATER: *NY*: The Changing Room (Tony & Drama Desk Awards, 1973), My Fat Friend, Trelawney of the Wells, Comedians, Anna Christie, A Memory of Two Mondays, Once in a Lifetime, Spokesong, Bedroom Farce, Salt Lake City Skyline, Division Street (also LA), Kaufman at Large (also dir., writer), Beyond Therapy, Requiem for a Heavyweight (Drama Desk Award), The Front Page, M Butterfly. *Regional*: The Beggar's Opera, Pygmalion, Of Mice and Men, Troilus and Cressida, The Roar of the Greasepaint, What Price Glory?, The Lady's Not for Burning, Who's Afraid of Virginia Woolf? (LA Drama Critics Circle Award).
PICTURES: Dealing or The Berkeley-to-Boston Forty-Brick Lost-Bag Blues (debut, 1972), Obsession, The Big Fix, Rich Kids, All That Jazz, Blow Out, I'm Dancing as Fast as I Can, The World According to Garp (Acad. Award nom.), Twilight Zone—The Movie, Terms of Endearment (Acad. Award nom.), Footloose, The Adventures of Buckaroo Banzai: Across the Eighth Dimension, 2010, Santa Claus, The Manhattan Project, Mesmerized, Harry and the Hendersons, Distant Thunder, Out Cold, Memphis Belle, Ricochet, At Play in the Fields of the Lord, Raising Cain, Cliffhanger, The Pelican Brief, A Good Man in Africa, Princess Caraboo, Silent Fall, Hollow Point.
TELEVISION: *Series*: Third Rock From the Sun (Emmy Award, 1996, 1997; Golden Globe Award, 1997). *Guest*: Amazing Stories (Emmy Award, 1987), Saturday Night Live. *Movies*: Mom The Wolfman and Me, Not in Front of the Children, The Day After, The Glitter Dome, Resting Place, Baby Girl Scott, The Traveling Man, The Last Elephant (Ivory Hunters), The Boys, The Wrong Man, Love Cheat and Steal, World War II: When Lions Roared, Redwood Curtain, The Tuskegee Airmen. *Specials*: The Country Girl (TV debut, 1973), Secret Service, Big Blonde, The Oldest Living Graduate, Goldilocks and the Three Bears (Faerie Tale Theatre).

LITTLE, RICH
Actor. b. Ottawa, Canada, Nov. 26, 1938. Started as radio disc jockey, talk show host in Canada; then impressionist in night clubs.
PICTURES: Dirty Tricks, Happy Hour, Bebe's Kids (voice).
TELEVISION: *Series*: Love on a Rooftop, The John Davidson Show, ABC Comedy Hour (The Kopycats), The Julie Andrews Hour, The Rich Little Show, The New You Asked For It (host). *Specials*: The Rich Little Show, Rich Little's Christmas Carol (also writer), Rich Little's Washington Follies, The Rich Little Specials (HBO), Rich Little's Robin Hood, Come Laugh With Me, Night of 42 Stars, The Christmas Raccoons, Rich Little and Friends in New Orleans, etc.

LITTLEFIELD, WARREN
Executive. b. Montclair, NJ. e. American Univ. in DC, School of Government and Public Admin.; Hobart Col. (psych. degree). 1975-79, Westfall Prods., developing prime-time specials and movies before being promoted to v.p., develop. & prod. 1979, served as WB TV dir., comedy develop. Joined NBC 1979, as mngr. comedy develop. 1981, v.p. current comedy programs at NBC. 1985, sr. v.p. series specials & variety progs., NBC Entertainment; 1987, exec. v.p., Prime-Time progs. NBC Entertainment. 1990, named pres. NBC Entertainment.

LITTMAN, LYNNE
Director, Producer. b. New York, NY, June 26. e. Sarah Lawrence. B.A., 1962; Student the Sorbonne 1960-61. Researcher for CBS News 1965; assoc. prod. Natl. Educational TV 1964-68; dir. NIMH film series on drug abuse UCLA Media Center 1970; prod., dir. documentary films, news and pub. affairs series KCET Community TV, So. Calif. 1971-77; dir. WNET non-fiction film, Once a Daughter 1979; exec. v.p., movies-for-TV, ABC, 1980-81; Received Ford Fdn. Grant 1978 and numerous awards. Acad. Award film tribute to women, 1993.
PICTURES: In the Matter of Kenneth (doc.), Wanted-Operadoras (doc.), Till Death Do Us Part (doc.), Number Our Days (doc. short; Acad. Award 1977), Testament (co-prod., dir.), In Her Own Time (doc.).
TELEVISION: *Movies*: Cagney & Lacey, Marie Taquet, Freak City.

LITTO, GEORGE
Producer. b. Philadelphia, PA. e. Temple U. Joined William Morris Agency in New York and then became indep. literary agent. Opened own office in Hollywood, 1965. Packaged film and TV productions, including M*A*S*H, Hang 'Em High, Hawaii Five-O for TV prior to entering indep. prod.; 1981-82, chmn. bd. & CEO, Filmways; 1983-85 indep. prod. 20th Century Fox.
PICTURES: Thieves Like Us (exec. prod.), Drive-In (exec. prod.), Obsession (prod.), Over the Edge (prod.), Dressed To Kill (prod.). Blow Out (prod.), Kansas (prod.), Night Game (prod.).

LITVINOFF, SI
Producer, Executive. b. New York, NY, April 5. e. Adelphi Coll., A.B.; NYU Sch. of Law, LL.B. Theatrical lawyer, personal and business manager in New York until 1967 when left firm of Barovick, Konecky & Litvinoff to produce plays and films. June, 1987: sr. v.p. for production and dev., Hawkeye Entertainment, Inc.
THEATER: Leonard Bernstein's Theatre Songs, Cry of the Raindrop, Girl of the Golden West, Little Malcolm and His Struggle Against the Eunuchs, I and Albert (London).
PICTURES: The Queen, All the Right Noises, Walkabout, A Clockwork Orange (exec. prod.), Glastonbury Fayre (exec. in chg. prod.), The Man Who Fell to Earth (exec. prod.)
TELEVISION: Exec. prod.: 15th Annual Saturn Awards, Doobie Brothers Retrospective, Listen to the Music 1989.

LIVINGSTON, JAY
Composer, Lyricist. b. McDonald, PA, March 28, 1915. e. U. of PA, 1937, UCLA, 1964-65. Army, WWII. Accompanist and arranger for various NBC singers and singing groups 1940-42, NY; author music and special material for Olsen & Johnson, including various editions of Hellzapoppin', and Sons O'Fun; began composing m.p. songs, 1944. Under contract to Paramount, 1945-55; then freelanced. Cameo appearance in Sunset Boulevard. Writer of songs and special material for Bob Hope starting in 1945. Has written songs for over 100 pictures. Elected to Songwriters Hall of Fame, 1975. Received star on Hollywood Blvd. Walk of Fame, 1995.
SONGS INCLUDE: G'bye Now, Stuff Like That There, To Each His Own, Golden Earrings, Silver Bells, Buttons and Bows (Academy Award, 1949), Mona Lisa (Academy Award, 1951), Que Sera Sera/Whatever Will Be Will Be (Academy Award, 1957), Tammy (Acad. Award nom.), Almost In Your Arms (Acad. Award nom.), Dear Heart, (Acad. Award nom.), Wish Me a Rainbow, In the Arms of Love, Never Let Me Go, As I Love You, All the Time, Maybe September.
THEATER: B'way: Oh Captain!, Let It Ride, Sugar Babies (2 songs).
PICTURES: Monsieur Beaucaire, My Favorite Brunette, The Paleface, My Friend Irma, Sorrowful Jones, My Friend Irma Goes West, Streets of Laredo, Isn't It Romantic?, Fancy Pants, Here Comes the Groom, The Lemon-Drop Kid, Son of Paleface, The Stars Are Singing, Here Come the Girls, Somebody Loves Me, Aaron Slick from Punkin' Crick, Red Garters, The Man Who Knew Too Much, Houseboat, Tammy and the Bachelor, Dear Heart, The Night of the Grizzly, This Property Is Condemned, The Oscar, Never Too Late, Harlow, What Did You Do in the War Daddy?, Wait Until Dark.
TELEVISION: Series themes: Bonanza, Mister Ed.

LLOYD, CHRISTOPHER
Actor. b. Stamford, CT, Oct. 22, 1938. Studied at Neighborhood Playhouse, NY.
THEATER: NY: Kaspar (Drama Desk & Obie Awards, 1973), Happy End, Red White and Maddox. Regional: The Father, Hot L Baltimore, The Possessed, A Midsummer Night's Dream.
PICTURES: One Flew Over the Cuckoo's Nest (debut, 1975), Goin' South, Butch and Sundance: The Early Days, The Onion Field, The Lady in Red, Schizoid, The Black Marble, The Postman Always Rings Twice, The Legend of the Lone Ranger, National Lampoon Goes to the Movies, Mr. Mom, To Be or Not to Be, Star Trek III: The Search for Spock, The Adventures of Buckaroo Banzai Across the Eighth Dimension, Joy of Sex, Back to the Future, Clue, Legend of the White Horse, Miracles, Walk Like a Man, Who Framed Roger Rabbit, Track 29, Eight Men Out, The Dream Team, Back to the Future Part II, Why Me?, Back to the Future Part III, Duck Tales: The Movie (voice), White Dragon, Suburban Commando, The Addams Family, Dennis the Menace, Twenty Bucks, Addams Family Values, Angels in the Outfield, Camp Nowhere, Radioland Murders, The Pagemaster, Things to Do in Denver When You're Dead, Cadillac Ranch, Changing Habits, Anastasia, Tom Sawyer, It Came from the Sky, Dinner at Fred's, Convegence, Baby Geniuses.
TELEVISION: Series: Taxi (Emmy Awards: 1982, 1983), Back to the Future (voice for animated series), Deadly Games. Specials: Pilgrim Farewell, The Penny Elf, Tales From Hollywood Hills: Pat Hobby—Teamed With Genius, In Search of Dr. Seuss. Movies: Lacy and the Mississippi Queen, The Word, Stunt Seven, Money on the Side, September Gun, The Cowboy and the Ballerina, T Bone N Weasel, Dead Ahead: The Exxon Valdez Disaster. Guest: Barney Miller, Best of the West, Cheers, Amazing Stories, Avonlea (Emmy Award, 1992), Angels in the End Zone.

LLOYD, EMILY
Actress. b. North London, Eng., Sept. 29, 1970. r.n. Emily Lloyd Pack. Father is stage actor Roger Lloyd Pack, mother worked as Harold Pinter's secretary. Father's agent recommended that she audition for screenwriter David Leland's directorial debut Wish You Were Here when she was 15.
PICTURES: Wish You Were Here (Natl. Society of Film Critics & London Evening Standard Awards, 1987; BAFTA nom.), Cookie, In Country, Chicago Joe and the Showgirl, Scorchers, A River Runs Through It, Under the Hula Moon, When Saturday Comes.

LLOYD, EUAN
Producer. b. Rugby, Warwick, England, Dec. 6, 1923. e. Rugby. Entered m.p. ind. in 1939 as theatre manager, then pub. dir.; dir. of Publ. Rank, 1946; joined Associated British-Pathe, Ltd. in same capacity; 1952 asst. to prod., Warwick Film Prod. Ltd. v.p. Highroad Productions, 1962-64. Rep. Europe Goldwyn's Porgy & Bess 1959.
PICTURES: April in Portugal, Heart of Variety, Invitation to Monte Carlo, The Secret Ways, Genghis Khan, Poppy Is Also a Flower, Murderer's Row, Shalako, Catlow, The Man Called Noon, Paper Tiger, The Wild Geese, The Sea Wolves, Who Dares Wins, Wild Geese II, The Final Option.

LLOYD, NORMAN
Actor, Producer, Director. b. Jersey City, NJ, Nov. 8, 1914. e. NYU, 1932. Acted on B'way in: Noah, Liberty Jones, Everywhere I Roam, 1935-44; in various stock companies. Joined Orson Welles and John Houseman in the original company of Mercury Theatre, NY, 1937-38. Prod. asst. on films Arch of Triumph, The Red Pony. Produced film Up Above the World.
THEATER: With the Civic Repertory Theatre, 1932-33 and The Living Newspapers of The Federal Theatre, 1936: Triple a Plowed Under, Injunction Granted. Regional: Power, Medicine Show, Ask My Friend, Sandy, Volpone. American Shakespeare Festival: Measure for Measure, Taming of the Shrew (also dir.). With La Jolla Playhouse, 1948-1955: Village Green, King Lear, The Cocktail Party, The Lady's Not for Burning, Madame Will You Walk, The Golden Apple, Major Barbara, The Will & Bart Show, Quiet City.
PICTURES: Actor: Saboteur, Spellbound, The Southerner, A Walk in the Sun, A Letter for Evie, The Unseen, Green Years, The Beginning or The End, Limelight, Young Widow, No Minor Vices, The Black Book, Scene of the Crime, Calamity Jane and Sam Bass, Buccaneer's Girl, The Flame and the Arrow, He Ran All the Way, The Light Touch, Audrey Rose, FM, The Nude Bomb, Jaws of Satan, Dead Poets Society, Journey of Honor (Shogun Mayeda), The Age of Innocence.
TELEVISION: Assoc. prod./exec. prod.: The Alfred Hitchcock Show. Prod.-Dir.: The Alfred Hitchcock Hour, The Name of the Game, Hollywood Television Theater, Tales of the Unexpected, Omnibus (dir. of The Lincoln Films, 1952), Journey to the Unknown (series). Actor: St. Elsewhere (series), Harvest Home. Movies (prod.-dir.): The Smugglers, Companions in Nightmare, What's a Nice Girl Like You (prod.), The Bravos (prod.), Amityville: The Evil Escapes.

LOACH, KEN
Director, Writer. b. Nuneaton, England, June 17, 1936. e. Oxford (studied law). Served in Royal Air Force; then became actor. Began dir. career on British tv in early 1960's.
PICTURES: Poor Cow (debut, 1968; also co-s.p.), Kes (also co-s.p.), Family Life, Black Jack (also co-s.p.), Looks and Smiles (also co- s.p.), Fatherland (Singing the Blues in Red), Hidden Agenda, Riff- Raff, Raining Stones, Land and Freedom.
TELEVISION: Diary of a Young Man, 3 Clear Sundays, The End of Arthur's Marriage, Up the Junction, Coming Out Party, Cathy Come Home, In Two Minds, The Golden Vision, The Big Flame, In Black and White, After a Lifetime, The Rank and the File, Days of Hope, The Price of Coal, Auditions: The Gamekeeper, A Question of Leadership, Which Side Are You On.

LOBELL, MICHAEL
Producer. b. Brooklyn, NY, May 7, 1941. e. Michigan State U. on athletic baseball scholarship. Worked briefly in garment indust. Entered film industry in 1974 by buying Danish distribution rights to The Apprenticeship of Duddy Kravitz. Formed Lobell/ Bergman Prods. with Andrew Bergman.
PICTURES: Dreamer, Windows, So Fine, The Journey of Natty Gann, Chances Are, The Freshman, White Fang, Honeymoon in Vegas, Undercover Blues, Little Big League, It Could Happen to You, Striptease.

Lo BIANCO, TONY
Actor. b. New York, NY. Oct. 19, 1936. Performed on N.Y. stage as well as in films and TV. Former artistic dir. Triangle Theatre, NY.
THEATER: Yanks 3—Detroit 0—Top of the Seventh (Obie Award), The Office, The Rose Tattoo, A View From the Bridge (Outer Critics Circle Award), The Royal Hunt of the Sun, Hizzoner, Other People's Money (tour).

PICTURES: The Honeymoon Killers (debut, 1970), The French Connection, The Seven Ups, Demon (God Told Me To), F.I.S.T., Bloodbrothers, Separate Ways, City Heat, Too Scared to Scream (dir. only), Mean Frankie and Crazy Tony, La Romana, City of Hope, The Spiders Web, Boiling Point, The Ascent, The Last Home Run (dir. only), The Juror.
TELEVISION: Series: Love of Life, Jessie, Palace Guard. Guest: Police Story. Movies/Mini-Series: Mr. Inside Mr. Outside, The Story of Joseph and Jacob, Magee and the Lady (She'll Be Sweet), Jesus of Nazareth, Hidden Faces, Legend of the Black Hand, Lady Blue, Marco Polo, Welcome Home Bobby, Blood Ties, A Last Cry for Help, Marciano, Another Woman's Child, The Last Tenant, Goldenrod, Shadow in the Streets, Eugene O'Neill's A Glory of Ghosts, Police Story: The Freeway Killings, The Ann Jillian Story, Body of Evidence, Off Duty, True Blue, Perry Mason: The Case of the Poisoned Pen, Malcolm Takes a Shot, In the Shadow of a Killer, Stormy Weathers, Teamster Boss: The Jackie Presser Story, The First Circle, The Maharajah's Daughter, Tyson. Specials: Hizzoner (Emmy Award), A Glory of Ghosts. Director: Police Story, Kaz, Cliffhangers, When the Whistle Blows, The Duke.

LOCKE, SONDRA
Actress, Director. b. Shelbyville, TN, May 28, 1947. Autobiography: The Good the Bad and the Very Ugly, 1997.
PICTURES: The Heart Is a Lonely Hunter (debut, 1968; Acad. Award nom.), Cover Me Babe, Willard, A Reflection of Fear, The Second Coming of Suzanne, Death Game (The Seducers), The Outlaw Josey Wales, The Gauntlet, Every Which Way But Loose, Bronco Billy, Any Which Way You Can, Sudden Impact, Ratboy (also dir.), Impulse (dir. only), Do Me a Favor (dir.).
TELEVISION: Movies: Friendships, Secrets and Lies, Rosie: The Rosemary Clooney Story. Guest: Amazing Stories. Director: Death in Small Doses (movie).

LOCKHART, JUNE
Actress. b. New York, NY, June 25, 1925. p. actors, Gene and Kathleen Lockhart. B'way debut For Love or Money, 1947.
PICTURES: A Christmas Carol (debut, 1938), All This and Heaven Too, Adam Had Four Sons, Sergeant York, Miss Annie Rooney, Forever and a Day, White Cliffs of Dover, Meet Me in St. Louis, Son of Lassie, Keep Your Powder Dry, Easy to Wed, She-Wolf of London, Bury Me Dead, The Yearling, T-Men, It's a Joke Son, Time Limit, Butterfly, Deadly Games, Strange Invaders, Troll, Rented Lips, The Big Picture, Dead Women in Lingerie, Tis the Season, Sleep With Me.
TELEVISION: Series: Who Said That? (panelist), Lassie, Lost in Space, Petticoat Junction, General Hospital, Roseanne, Step By Step, Fired Up. Movies: But I Don't Want to Get Married, The Bait, Who is the Black Dahlia?, Curse of the Black Widow, The Gift of Love, Walking Through the Fire, The Night They Saved Christmas, Perfect People, A Whisper Kills, Danger Island. Mini-Series: Loose Change.

LOCKLEAR, HEATHER
Actress. b. Los Angeles, CA, Sept. 25, 1961. e. UCLA. Appeared in commercials while in college.
PICTURES: Firestarter (debut, 1984), The Return of Swamp Thing, The Big Slice, Illusions, Wayne's World 2, The First Wives Club, Money Talks, Double Tap.
TELEVISION: Series: Dynasty, T.J. Hooker, Fright Night Videos (host), Going Places, Melrose Place. Movies: Return of the Beverly Hillbillies, Twirl, City Killer, Blood Sport, Rich Men Single Women, Jury Duty: The Comedy, Her Wicked Ways, Dynasty: The Reunion, Body Language, Highway Heartbreaker, Fade to Black, Texas Justice. Specials: Battle of the Network Stars, Hollywood Starr, TV Guide 40th Anniversary Special (host). Guest: Fantasy Island, The Fall Guy, Matt Houston, Hotel, The Love Boat.

LOCKWOOD, GARY
Actor. r.n. John Gary Yusolfsky. b. Van Nuys, CA, Feb. 21, 1937. Began in Hollywood as stuntman.
PICTURES: Tall Story, Splendor in the Grass, Wild in the Country, The Magic Sword, It Happened at the World's Fair, Firecreek, 2001: A Space Odyssey, They Came to Rob Las Vegas, Model Shop, The Body, R.P.M., Stand Up and Be Counted, The Wild Pair, Night of the Scarecrow.
TELEVISION: Series: Follow the Sun, The Lieutenant. Movies: Earth II, Manhunter, The FBI Story: The FBI Versus Alvin Karpus—Public Enemy, The Ghost of Flight 401, The Incredible Journey of Dr. Meg Laurel, Top of the Hill, The Girl The Gold Watch & Dynamite, Emergency Room.

LOCKWOOD, ROGER
Executive. b. Middletown, CT, June 7, 1936. e. Ohio Wesleyan U. Sports writer for Akron Beacon Journal, 1960-62. On executive staff of Lockwood & Gordon Theatres; exec. v.p. SBC Theatres, 1969-73. 1974 asst. to exec. v.p., General Cinema Corp. 1975 formed Lockwood/Friedman Theatres, buying-booking and exhibition organization. Pres., Theatre Owners of New England, 1971-72; pres., Young NATO 1965-67; bd. of dir. NATO, 1962-1968. Board of dir. Tone, 1968-present; pres., Jimmy Fund, present; 1979-80, Variety Club of New England, pres. Director, Dana-Farber Cancer Institute, 1983-present. 1988, formed Lockwood/McKinnon Company Inc. operating theatres and Taco Bell Restaurants.

LOEKS, BARRIE LAWSON
Executive. b. Pittsburgh, PA. e. Univ. of MI, Univ. of MI Law Sch., 1979. Began career as associate in Grand Rapids, MI, law firm of Warner Norcross & Judd before serving for 7 yrs. as v.p. and gen. counsel of Jack Loeks Theatres; promoted to pres. of Loeks Michigan Theatre and Loeks-Star joint venture, 1988; Nov. 1992 named co-chmn., with husband Jim Loeks, of Sony Theatres, a Sony Retail Entertainment Co. Pres., Loeks Michigan, 1998-.

LOEKS, JIM
Executive. b. Grand Rapids, MI. e. Univ. of MI. Started as gen. mgr. of John Ball Concessions Inc, becoming chmn. of bd. and owner, 1976-91. 1978, elected v.p. of Jack Loeks Theatres Inc.; named pres. of chain in 1983. 1988, became chmn. & co-owner of Loeks Michigan Theatres Inc., also gen. partner & operating agent of Loeks-Star joint venture with Sony Pictures Entertainment. Nov., 1992 named co-chmn., with wife Barrie Lawson Loeks, of Sony Theatres.

LOEKS, JOHN D. Jr.
Executive. b. E. Grand Rapids, MI, Feb 24, 1945. e. Wheaton Coll., B.A. 1967; Wayne State U., J.D. 1970. Began own law practice in 1970 until 1990. President, Showspan Inc., 1982-present. President, Jack Loeks Theatres Inc., 1990-. Bd. member, Ausable Institute of Environmental Studies; 1988-present, bd. member, Grand Rapids Symphony Orchestra; 1992-present, bd. of dirs., NATO.

LOESCH, MARGARET
Executive. e. U. of S. MS, B.A; grad. work at U. of New Orleans. President, Fox Children's Network.

LOGAN, JEFF
Exhibitor. b. Mitchell, SD, Dec. 29, 1950. e. Dakota Wesleyan U. & U. of SD. Started working in family's Roxy Theatre at 9 yrs. old. Worked as announcer on KORN radio, 1969-70. Announcer, reporter & photographer, KUSD-TV, 1970-71. Relief anchor, KXON-TV, 1972-78. Took over management of family theatre. Built co. into present circuit, Logan Luxury Theatres. Member, bd. of trustess, Dakota Wesleyan U., 1990-present; bd. of trustees, Queen of Peace Hospital, 1991-1997. V.P., Variety Club of SD, 1994-96. Dir., NATO/North Central, 1980-90. V.P., VSDA of SD, 1989-present. Dir., NATO, 1997-present.

LOGGIA, ROBERT
Actor. b. New York, NY, Jan. 3, 1930. e. U. of Missouri, B.A. journalism, 1951. Studied with Stella Adler and at The Actors Studio. Broadway debut, the Man with the Golden Arm, 1955.
THEATER: Toys in the Attic, The Three Sisters, In the Boom Boom Room, Wedding Band.
PICTURES: Somebody Up There Likes Me (debut, 1956), The Garment Jungle, Cop Hater, The Lost Missile, Cattle King, The Greatest Story Ever Told, Che, First Love, Speed Trap, Revenge of the Pink Panther, The Ninth Configuration (Twinkle Twinkle Killer Kane), S.O.B., An Officer and a Gentleman, Trail of the Pink Panther, Psycho II, Curse of the Pink Panther, Scarface, Prizzi's Honor, Jagged Edge (Acad. Award nom.), Armed and Dangerous, That's Life, Over the Top, Hot Pursuit, The Believers, Gaby: A True Story, Big, Oliver & Company (voice), Relentless, S.P.O.O.K.S. (Code Name: Chaos), Triumph of the Spirit, Opportunity Knocks, The Marrying Man, Necessary Roughness, Gladiator, Innocent Blood, The Last Tattoo, Bad Girls, I Love Trouble, Man With a Gun, Independence Day, Lost Highway.
TELEVISION: Series: T.H.E. Cat, Emerald Point N.A.S., Mancuso FBI, Sunday Dinner. Specials: Miss Julie, The Nine Lives of Elfego Baca, Conspiracy: The Trial of the Chicago 8, Merry Christmas Baby. Movies: Mallory: Circumstantial Evidence, Street Killing, Scott Free, Raid on Entebbe, No Other Love, Casino, A Woman Called Golda, A Touch of Scandal, Streets of Justice, Intrigue, Dream Breakers (The O'Connors), Afterburn, Lifepod, Nurses on the Line: The Crash of Flight 7, White Mile, Jake Lassiter: Justice on the Bayou, Between Love and Honor, Mercy Mission: The Rescue of Flight 771, Right to Remain Silent. Mini-Series: Arthur Hailey's The Moneychangers, Echoes in the Darkness, Favorite Son, Wild Palms.

LOLLOBRIGIDA, GINA
Actress. b. Subiaco, Italy, July 4, 1927. e. Acad. of Fine Arts, Rome. Film debut (Italy) L'aguila nera, 1946. Published several volumes of her photography incl. Italia Mia, The Wonder of Innocence.
PICTURES: Pagliacci, The City Defends Itself, The White Line, Fanfan the Tulip, Times Gone By, Beat the Devil, Crossed Swords, The Great Game, Beauties of the Night, Wayward Wife, Bread Love and Dreams, Bread Love and Jealousy, Young Caruso, World's Most Beautiful Woman, Trapeze, Hunchback of Notre Dame, Solomon and Sheba, Never So Few, The Unfaithfuls, Fast and Sexy, Where the Hot Wind Blows, Go Naked in the World, Come September, Imperial Venus, Woman of Straw, That Splendid November, Hotel Paradiso, Buona Sera Mrs. Campbell, Plucked, The Private Navy of Sgt. O'Farrell, Bad Man's River, King Queen Knave, The Lonely Woman, Bambole.
TELEVISION: Movie: Deceptions. Series: Falcon Crest.

LOMITA, SOLOMON
Executive. b. New York, NY, April 23, 1937. Started industry career with United Artists Corp. as follows: adm., intl. dept., 1962; asst., intl. sales, same year. 1963, asst. intl. print mgr.; 1965, intl., print mgr. 1973 appt. dir. of film services. 1981, v.p., film services. 1985 named v.p., post-prod., Orion Pictures; 1989-92; then sr. v.p. post-prod.

LONDON, BARRY
Executive. Joined Paramount Pictures 1971 in L.A. branch office as booker; later salesman. 1973, sls. mgr., Kansas City-St. Louis; 1974, branch mgr. Transferred to San Francisco, first as branch mgr.; later as district mgr. 1977, eastern div. mgr. in Washington, DC, 1978-81, western div. mgr. 1981, named v.p., gen. sls. mgr. 1983, advanced to sr. v.p., domestic distrib.1984, named pres., domestic div., for Motion Picture Group of Paramount; 1985, named pres., marketing and domestic distrib.; 1988, named pres. worldwide distrib., Motion Picture Group. Producer, Barry London Co. Member: Variety Club NYC (VP, 1984-), Will Rogers Hospital Dist. Chmn., 1985-.

LONDON, JASON
Actor. b. San Diego, CA, 1973. Twin brother of actor Jeremy London. Raised in Oklahoma and Texas. Appeared in Aerosmith video Amazing.
PICTURES: The Man in the Moon (debut, 1991), December, Dazed and Confused, Safe Passage, To Wong Foo—Thanks for Everything—Julie Newmar, My Generation, Learning Curves, The Barefoot Executive, Fall Time, Countdown, Mixed Signals, Frontline, Broken Vessels.
TELEVISION: Movie: A Matter of Justice. Guest: I'll Fly Away, Tales From the Crypt, Friends Til the End.

LONDON, JERRY
Director. b. Los Angeles, CA, Jan 21, 1937. Apprentice film editor, Desilu Prods., 1955; film ed., Daniel Boone, 1962; staged plays in local theater workshops; editor, assoc. prod., then dir. Hogan's Heroes. Formed Jerry London Prods., 1984.
PICTURE: Rent-a-Cop (feature debut, 1988).
TELEVISION: Series: Mary Tyler Moore Show, Love American Style, The Bob Newhart Show, Marcus Welby, M.D., Kojak, The Six Million Dollar Man, Police Story, Rockford Files. Mini-series: Wheels, Shogun (DGA, best dir., special award), Chiefs (also sprv. prod.), Ellis Island (also sprv. prod.), If Tomorrow Comes, A Long Way From Home. Movies: Killdozer, McNaughton's Daughter, Cover Girls, Evening in Byzantium, Women in White, Father Figure, The Chicago Story, The Ordeal of Bill Carney (also prod.), The Gift of Life (also prod.), The Scarlet and the Black, Arthur Hailey's Hotel (also prod.), With Intent to Kill (exec. prod. only), Dark Mansions, Manhunt For Claude Dallas, Harry's Hong Kong, Family Sins (exec. prod. only), Macgruder and Loud (also prod.), Dadah Is Death (also prod.), Kiss Shot (also exec. prod.), The Haunting of Sarah Hardy (also exec. prod.), Vestige of Honor, A Season of Giants, Victim of Love, Grass Roots, Calendar Girl Cop Killer?: The Bambi Bembenek Story (also prod.), A Twist of the Knife, Labor of Love: The Arlette Schweitzer Story, A Mother's Gift.

LONDON, JULIE
Singer, Actress. r.n. Julie Peck. b. Santa Rosa, CA, Sept. 26, 1926. Launched as actress by agent Sue Carol (wife of Alan Ladd) who arranged screen test, followed by contract for 6 films. As singer has appeared in nightclubs and recorded.
PICTURES: Nabonga (Jungle Woman; debut, 1944), On Stage Everybody, Billy Rose's Diamond Horseshoe, Night in Paradise, The Red House, Tap Roots, Task Force, Return of the Frontiersman, The Fat Man, Fighting Chance, The Great Man, The Girl Can't Help It, Crime Against Joe, Drango, Saddle the Wind, Man of the West, Voice in the Mirror, A Question of Adultery, The Wonderful Country, Night of the Quarter Moon, The Third Voice, The George Raft Story.
TELEVISION: Series: Emergency. Guest: Perry Como Show, Steve Allen Show, Ed Sullivan Show. Movie: Emergency (pilot).

LONDON, MILTON H.
Executive. b. Detroit, MI, Jan. 12, 1916. e. U. of Michigan, B.A., 1937. Wayne U. Law Sch., 1938. U.S. Army 1943-46. Invented Ticograph system of positive admissions control for theatres, 1950; pres. Theatre Control Corp., 1950-62; secy-treas. Co-op. Theas. of Michigan Inc., 1956-63; exec. comm., Council of M.P. Organizations, 1957-66; dir. M.P. Investors, 1960-67; exec. dir. Allied States Assoc. of M.P. Exhib., 1961-66; exec. dir. National Assoc. of Theatre Owners, 1966-69; pres., NATO of Michigan, 1954-74; Chief Barker, Variety Club of Detroit, Tent No. 5. 1975-76; Life Patron and Lifeliner, Variety Clubs International; trustee, Variety Club Charity for Children; chmn., Variety Club Myoelectric Center; dir., Motion Picture Pioneers; dir., Will Rogers Inst.; trustee, Detroit Inst. for Children; pres., Metropolitan Adv. Co.; Intl. ambassador, Variety Clubs Int'l; Detroit News 1991 Michiganian of the Year.

LONE, JOHN
Actor. b. Hong Kong. Studied at Chin Ciu Academy of the Peking Opera in Hong Kong, Moved to LA where he studied acting at Pasadena's American Acad. of Dramatic Art, becoming member of the East-West Players.
THEATER: NY: F.O.B., The Dance and the Railroad (Obie Awards for both plays), Paper Angels (dir.), Sound and Beauty (also dir.).
PICTURES: Iceman (debut, 1984), Year of the Dragon, The Last Emperor, The Moderns, Echoes of Paradise, Shadow of China, Shanghai 1920, M. Butterfly, The Shadow, The Hunted.
TELEVISION: The Dance and the Railroad, Paper Angels (dir.).

LONG, SHELLEY
Actress. b. Ft. Wayne, IN, Aug. 23, 1949. e. Northwestern U. Was co-host, assoc. prod. of local tv show Sorting It Out.
PICTURES: A Small Circle of Friends (debut, 1980), Caveman, Night Shift, Losin' It, Irreconcilable Differences, The Money Pit, Outrageous Fortune, Hello Again, Troop Beverly Hills, Don't Tell Her It's Me, Frozen Assets, The Brady Bunch Movie, A Very Brady Sequel.
TELEVISION: Series: Cheers (Emmy Award, 1983), Good Advice. Movies: The Cracker Factory, Princess and the Cabbie, Promise of Love, Voices Within: The Lives of Truddi Chase, Fatal Memories, A Message From Holly, The Women of Spring Break, Freaky Friday. Special: Basic Values: Sex Shock & Censorship in the '90's.

LONGSTREET, STEPHEN
Writer, Painter. b. New York, NY, April 18, 1907. e. Rutgers U.; Parsons Coll.; Rand Sch., London, B.A. Humorist, cartoonist (New Yorker, Collier's, etc.) 1930-37; ed. Free World Theatre, radio plays; edit. film critic, Saturday Review of Literature, 1940, U.S. at War, Time 1942-43. On staff UCLA. Elected pres. Los Angeles Art Assoc. 1970. 1973, joined USC as prof. Film and book critic for Readers' Syndicate starting in 1970.
AUTHOR: Decade, Last Man Around the World, Chico Goes to the Wars, Pedlocks, Lion at Morning, Promoters, Sometimes I Wonder (with Hoagy Carmichael), Wind at My Back (with Pat O'Brien), Goodness Had Nothing to Do With It (with Mae West), The Young Men of Paris, The Wilder Shore, War Cries on Horseback, Yoshiwara, Geishas and Courtesans, Canvas Falcons, Men and Planes of World War I, We All Went to Paris. Chicago 1860-1919 (show business & society), Divorcing (a novel), The General (novel), All Star Cast (Hollywood), The Queen Bees, Our Father's House, Storyville to Harlem, Dictionary of Jazz, Dreams that Swallowed the World: The Movies, Jazz Solos (poems & images), My Three Nobel Prizes, Life With Faulkner/Hemingway/Lewis.
THEATER: High Button Shoes (book, revived in Jerome Robbins' Broadway, 1989).
PICTURES: The Gay Sisters, Golden Touch, Stallion Road, The Jolson Story, Silver River, Helen Morgan Story, The First Traveling Saleslady, Untamed Youth, The Crime, Uncle Harry, Rider on a Dead Horse, The Imposter.
TELEVISION: Casey Jones (series), Clipper Ship (Playhouse 90), Man Called X, The Sea, Press & Clergy, Viewpoint, Boy in the Model T, John Kennedy Young Man From Boston, Blue and the Grey.

LONSDALE, PAMELA
Producer and Executive Producer for Children's drama, Thames TV for 15 years. Now freelance. Prod. short feature film, Exploits at West Poley (for CFTF), Prod.:News at Twelve (Central TV comedy series). Exec. prod. for E.B.U.'s world drama exchange for 2 years. Winner British Acad. Award for Rainbow, 1975.
TELEVISION: Exploits at West Poley (prod.), Ace of Wands (series, dir., prod.).

LOPEZ, JENNIFER
Actress. b. Bronx, NY, July 24, 1970.
PICTURES: My Little Girl, My Family—Mi Familia, Money Train, Jack, Blood and Wine, Selena, Anaconda, U-Turn, Out of Sight.
TELEVISION: Movies: Nurses on the Line: The Crash of Flight 7. Series: Second Chances, Hotel Malibu.

LORD, JACK
Actor, Writer, Artist, Director, Producer. r.n. John Ryan. b. New York, NY, Dec. 30, 1930. e. NYU. (Chancellor Chase scholarship), B.S., Fine Arts, 1954. Studied at Sanford Meisner's Neighborhood Playhouse and with Lee Strasberg at the Actors Studio. Made film debut 1949 under his real name. Artist, represented in various museums worldwide. Received Fame Award as new male star, 1963. Awards: St. Gauden's Artist Award, G. Washington Honor Medal from Freedom Foundation at Valley Forge, Veterans Admin., Administrator's Award, East-West Center Distinguished Service Award. Author: Jack Lord's Hawaii...A Trip Through the Last Eden, 1971. Pres., Lord and Lady Enterprises, Inc. Appeared in Williamsburg documentary Story of a Patriot.
THEATER: B'way: Traveling Lady (Theatre World Award, 1959), Cat on a Hot Tin Roof.
PICTURES: The Red Menace (debut, 1949), Project X, Cry Murder, The Tattooed Stranger, The Court Martial of Billy Mitchell, Tip on a Dead Jockey, God's Little Acre, Man of the West, The Hangman, True Story of Lynn Stuart, Walk Like a Dragon, Dr. No, Ride to Hangman's Tree, The Counterfeit Killer, The Name of the Game Is Kill.

TELEVISION: *Series:* Stoney Burke (1962-63), Hawaii Five-O (1968-79; also dir. episodes), creator of Tramp Ship, McAdoo, Yankee Trader, The Hunter TV series. *Guest:* Man Against Crime (debut), Playhouse 90, Goodyear Playhouse, Studio One, U.S. Steel. Have Gun Will Travel (pilot), Untouchables, Naked City, Rawhide, Bonanza, The Americans, Route 66, Gunsmoke, Stagecoach West, Dr. Kildare, Greatest Show on Earth, Combat, Chrysler Theatre, 12 O'Clock High, The Loner, Laredo, The FBI, The Invaders, The Fugitive, The Virginian, Man from U.N.C.L.E., High Chaparral, Ironside. *Movies:* Doomsday Flight. *Director:* Death with Father, How to Steal a Masterpiece, Honor Is an Unmarked Grave, The Bells Toll at Noon, Top of the World, Why Won't Linda Die, Who Says Cops Don't Cry; episodes of Hawaii Five-O. *Special:* M Station: Hawaii (creator, dir., exec. prod.).
(d. Jan. 21, 1998)

LOREN, SOPHIA
Actress. b. Rome, Italy, Sept. 20, 1934. e. Naples. m. producer Carlo Ponti. *Autobiography:* Sophia: Living and Loving (with A.E. Hotchner, 1979).
PICTURES: Africa Beneath the Seas, Village of the Bells, Good People's Sunday, Neapolitan Carousel, Day in the District Court, Pilgrim of Love, Aida, Two Nights with Cleopatra, Our Times, Attila, Scourge of God, Gold of Naples, Too Bad She's Bad, Scandal in Sorrento, Miller's Beautiful Wife, Lucky to Be a Woman, Boy on a Dolphin (U.S. debut, 1957), The Pride and the Passion, Legend of the Lost, Desire Under the Elms, The Key, Houseboat, The Black Orchid, That Kind of Woman, Heller in Pink Tights, It Started in Naples, A Breath of Scandal, The Millionairess, Two Women (Academy Award, 1961), El Cid, Boccaccio 70, Madame Sans-Gene, Five Miles to Midnight, The Condemned of Altona, Yesterday Today and Tomorrow, The Fall of the Roman Empire, Marriage Italian Style, Operation Crossbow, Lady L, Judith, Arabesque, A Countess from Hong Kong, More than a Miracle, Ghosts—Italian Style, Sunflower, The Priest's Wife, Lady Liberty, White Sister, Man of La Mancha, The Voyage, The Verdict (Jury of One), The Cassandra Crossing, A Special Day, Angela, Brass Target, Firepower, Blood Feud (Revenge), Ready to Wear (Pret-a-Porter), Grumpier Old Men.
TELEVISION: *Movies/Specials:* Brief Encounter, Sophia Loren—Her Own Story, Softly Softly, Rivals of Sherlock Holmes, Fantasy Island, Aurora, Courage, Mario Puzo's The Fortunate Pilgrim.

LOUDON, DOROTHY
Actress. b. Boston, MA, Sept. 17, 1933.
THEATER: *B'way:* Nowhere to Go But Up (Theatre World Award), The Fig Leaves Are Falling, Sweet Potato, Three Men on a Horse, The Women, Annie (Tony Award, 1977), Ballroom, Sweeney Todd, West Side Waltz, Noises Off, Jerry's Girls, Comedy Tonight. *Off-B'way:* The Matchmaker. Regional: Driving Miss Daisy, Love Letters.
PICTURE: Garbo Talks.
TELEVISION: *Series:* It's a Business?, Laugh Line, The Garry Moore Show, Dorothy, The Thorns (sang opening song). *Specials:* Many appearances on the Tony Awards; also Carnegie Hall Salutes Stephen Sondheim.

LOUGHLIN, LORI
Actress. b. Long Island, NY, July 28, 1964. Started modeling at age 7 for catalogues, then tv commercials. First professional acting job at 18 as regular on daytime serial The Edge of Night.
THEATER: Grease.
PICTURES: Amityville 3-D (debut, 1983), The New Kids, Secret Admirer, Back to the Beach, The Night Before.
TELEVISION: *Series:* The Edge of Night, Full House, Hudson Street. *Movies:* North Beach and Rawhide, Brotherhood of Justice, A Place to Call Home, Doing Time on Maple Drive, A Stranger in the Mirror, Empty Cradle, One of Her Own, Abandoned and Deceived.

LOUIS-DREYFUS, JULIA
Actress. b. New York, NY, Jan. 13, 1961. e. Northwestern Univ. Member of Second City comedy troupe which resulted in casting on Saturday Night Live.
PICTURES: Troll (debut, 1986), Hannah and Her Sisters, Soul Man, National Lampoon's Christmas Vacation, Jack the Bear, North, Deconstructing Harry, Father's Day, A Bug's Life (voice).
TELEVISION: *Series:* Saturday Night Live (1982-85), Day by Day, Seinfeld (Golden Globe, 1994; Emmy Award, 1996). *Specials:* The Art of Being Nick, Spy Magazine's Hit List (host), Sesame Street's All-Star 25th Birthday. *Movies:* London Suite. *Guest:* Dinosaurs (voice), Dr Katz Professional Therapist.

LOUISE, TINA
Actress. r.n. Tina Blacker. b. New York, NY, Feb. 11. e. Miami U., N.Y. Neighborhood Playhouse, Actors Studio. Author, Sunday, 1997.
THEATER: Two's Company, The Fifth Season, John Murray Anderson's Almanac, Li'l Abner, Fade Out Fade In, Come Back to the 5 and Dime Jimmy Dean Jimmy Dean.

PICTURES: God's Little Acre (debut), The Trap, The Hangman, Day of the Outlaw, The Warrior Empress, Siege of Syracuse, Armored Command, For Those Who Think Young, The Wrecking Crew, The Good Guys and the Bad Guys, How to Commit Marriage, The Happy Ending, The Stepford Wives, Mean Dog Blues, Dogsday, Hellriders, Evils of the Night, O.C. and Stiggs, Dixie Lanes, The Pool, Johnny Suede.
TELEVISION: *Series:* Jan Murray Time, Gilligan's Island, Dallas, Rituals. *Guest:* Mannix, Ironside, Kung Fu, Police Story, Kojak, Roseanne. *Movies:* But I Don't Want to Get Married, A Call to Danger, Death Scream, Look What's Happened to Rosemary's Baby, Nightmare in Badham Country, SST—Death Flight, Friendships Secrets and Lies, The Day the Women Got Even, Advice to the Lovelorn, The Woman Who Cried Murder.

LOVITZ, JON
Actor, Comedian. b. Tarzana, CA, July 21, 1957. e. U. of California at Irvine. Studied acting at Film Actors Workshop. Took classes at the Groundlings, L.A. comedy improvisation studio, 1982. Performed with Groundling's Sunday Company, before joining main company in Chick Hazzard: Olympic Trials. Developed comedy character of pathological liar which he later performed when he became regular member of Saturday Night Live in 1985.
PICTURES: The Last Resort, Ratboy, Jumpin' Jack Flash, Three Amigos, Big, My Stepmother Is an Alien, The Brave Little Toaster (voice), Mr. Destiny, An American Tail: Fievel Goes West (voice), A League of Their Own, Mom and Dad Save the World, National Lampoon's Loaded Weapon 1, Coneheads, City Slickers II: The Legend of Curly's Gold, North, Trapped in Paradise, The Great White Hype, High School High, Happiness, The Wedding Singer.
TELEVISION: *Series:* Foley Square, Saturday Night Live (1985-90), The Critic (voice). *Special:* The Please Watch the Jon Lovitz Special. *Guest:* The Paper Chase.

LOWE, CHAD
Actor. b. Dayton, OH, Jan. 15, 1968. Brother is actor Rob Lowe. Stage debut in L.A. production of Blue Denim. On NY stage in Grotesque Love Songs.
PICTURES: Oxford Blues (debut, 1984), Apprentice to Murder, True Blood, Nobody's Perfect, Highway to Hell, Driven, Floating, Do Me a Favor, The Way We Are, Suicide: The Comedy.
TELEVISION: *Movies:* Silence of the Heart, There Must Be a Pony, April Morning, So Proudly We Hail, An Inconvenient Woman, Captive, Candles in the Dark, Fighting for My Daughter, In the Presence of Mine Enemies, Target Earth. *Series:* Spencer, Life Goes On (Emmy Award, 1993), Melrose Place. *Special:* No Means No (Emmy nom.).

LOWE, PHILIP L.
Executive. b. Brookline, MA, Apr. 17, 1917. e. Harvard. Army 1943-46. Checker, Loew's 1937-39; treasurer, Theatre Candy Co., 1941-58; Pres., ITT Sheraton Corp., 1969-70; Principal, Philip L. Lowe and Assoc.

LOWE, PHILIP M.
Executive. b. New Rochelle, NY, May 9, 1944. e. Deerfield Acad., Harvard Coll., cum laude in psychology, 1966; Columbia Business Sch., 1968. Work experience includes major marketing positions at General Foods, Gillette, Gray Advertising, and Estee Lauder Cosmetics before co-founding Cinema Centers Corp. and Theatre Management Services in Boston. Pres. of Lowe Group of Companies (cable television, broadcasting, hotels, real estate and management consulting). Past pres. and chmn. of the bd; National Association of Concessionaires (NAC); past director, National Association of Theater Owners (NATO). Professor of Marketing, Bentley Coll., Waltham, MA.; Contributing Editor; The Movie Business Book, Prentice-Hall, Inc. 1983.

LOWE, ROB
Actor. b. Charlottesville, VA, Mar. 17, 1964. Brother is Chad Lowe. Raised in Dayton, OH. Started acting as child appearing in commercials, local tv spots, summer stock. Family moved to California when he was 13 yrs. old. Job in Coca Cola commercial was followed by role on series A New Kind of Family. In 1992 made B'way debut in, A Little Hotel on the Side.
PICTURES: The Outsiders (debut, 1983), Class, The Hotel New Hampshire, Oxford Blues, St. Elmo's Fire, Youngblood, About Last Night..., Square Dance, Illegally Yours, Masquerade, Illegally Yours, Mulholland Falls, Bad Influence, Stroke of Midnight (If the Shoe Fits), Desert Shield, The Dark Backward, The Finest Hour, Wayne's World, Tommy Boy, For Hire, Contact.
TELEVISION: *Movies:* Thursday's Child, Frank and Jesse (also co-prod.), First Degree, Desert's Edge (s.p. dir.). *Series:* A New Kind of Family. *Mini-Series:* Stephen King's The Stand. *Specials:* A Matter of Time, Schoolboy Father, Suddenly Last Summer, On Dangerous Ground, Midnight Man.

LOWRY, DICK
Director. b. Oklahoma City, OK. e. U. of Oklahoma. Commercial photographer before being accepted by AFI. Dir. short film The Drought.
PICTURE: Smokey and the Bandit Part 3.
TELEVISION: *Mini-Series:* Dream West, Texas Justice, Dean Koontz's Mr. Murder. *Movies:* OHMS, Kenny Rogers as the Gambler, The Jayne Mansfield Story, Angel Dusted, Coward of the County, A Few Days in Weasel Creek, Rascals and Robbers: The Secret Adventures of Tom Sawyer and Huck Finn, Missing Children—A Mother's Story, Living Proof: The Hank Williams Jr. Story, Kenny Rogers as the Gambler—The Adventure Continues (also prod.), Off Sides (Pigs Vs. Freaks), Wet Gold, The Toughest Man in the World, Murder with Mirrors, American Harvest, Kenny Rogers as The Gambler III (also co-exec. prod.), Case Closed, In the Line of Duty: The FBI Murders, Unconquered (also prod.), Howard Beach: Making the Case For Murder, Miracle Landing (also prod.), Archie: To Riverdale and Back, In the Line of Duty: A Cop for the Killing (also prod.), In the Line of Duty: Manhunt in the Dakotas (also prod.), A Woman Scorned: The Betty Broderick Story (also co-prod.), In the Line of Duty: Ambush in Waco (also prod.), In the Line of Duty: The Price of Vengeance, One More Mountain, A Horse for Danny, In The Line of Duty: Hunt for Justice (also prod.), Forgotten Sins, Project Alf, In The Line of Duty: Smoke Jumpers (also prod.), Last Stand at Saber River, Blaze of Glory (also prod.).

LOWRY, HUNT
Producer. b. Oklahoma City, OK, Aug. 21, 1954. e. Rollins Coll., & Wake Forest. Abandoned plans to study medicine to enter film-making industry; first job for New World Pictures where he met Jon Davison, with whom was later to co-produce. Next made TV commercials as prod. asst. and then producer. Left to go freelance as commercials producer. 1980, appt. assoc. prod. to Davison on Airplane!
PICTURES: Humanoids from the Deep, Get Crazy, Top Secret!, Revenge, Career Opportunities, Only the Lonely, Last of the Mohicans, Striking Distance, My Life, First Knight, A Time to Kill.
TELEVISION: *Movies* (exec. prod.): Rascals and Robbers: The Secret Adventures of Tom Sawyer and Huckleberry Finn, Baja Oklahoma. *Movies* (prod.): His Mistress, Surviving, Wild Horses. *Mini-Series:* Dream West (prod.).

LUBCKE, HARRY R.
Registered Patent Agent. b. Alameda, CA, Aug. 25, 1905. e. U. of California, B.S., 1929. Holds numerous U.S. and foreign patents on television. In 1931: station W6XAO went on air on what is now television Channel No. 2 to become first station of kind in nation. Built Mt. Lee studios 1941 housing then largest TV stage. Pioneered present television standard of 525 line (Aug., 1940). 1942, television programs to promote war bond sale. 1942-46 dir. war research for which certificates of commendation were received from Army & Navy.

LUCAS, GEORGE
Producer, Director, Writer. b. Modesto, CA, May 14, 1944. e. USC, cinema. Made short film called THX-1138 and won National Student Film Festival Grand Prize, 1967. Signed contract with WB. Ass't. to Francis Ford Coppola on The Rain People, during which Lucas made 2-hr. documentary on filming of that feature entitled Filmmaker. Appeared as actor in film Beverly Hills Cop III. *Novel:* Shadow Moon (1995). Pres., Lucas Films, Industrial Light & Magic.
PICTURES: *Director/Writer:* THX-1138, American Graffiti, Star Wars. *Executive Producer:* More American Graffiti, The Empire Strikes Back (also story), Raiders of the Lost Ark (also co-story), Return of the Jedi (also co-s.p., story), Twice Upon a Time, Indiana Jones and the Temple of Doom (also story), Mishima, Labyrinth, Howard the Duck, Willow (also story), Tucker: The Man and His Dream, The Land Before Time, Indiana Jones and the Last Crusade (also co-story), Radioland Murders (also story), Indiana Jones and the Lost Continent.
TELEVISION: *Exec. Prod.:* The Ewok Adventure (movie), Ewoks: The Battle for Endor (movie); The Young Indiana Jones Chronicles (series).

LUCCHESI, GARY
Executive. b. San Francisco, CA, 1955. e. UCLA. Entered industry as a trainee with the William Morris Agency, 1977. Joined Tri-Star, 1983, as vice pres. of production, became sr. vice pres., 1985. Joined Paramount Pictures as exec. vice pres., April 1987; pres. of motion picture production division, 1987-92. Pres. of the Really Useful Film Company, Inc., 1994-present.
PICTURES: *Producer:* Jennifer Eight, Three Wishes, Virtuosity, Primal Fear, Gotti.

LUCCI, SUSAN
Actress. b. Scarsdale, NY, Feb. 23, 1948. e. Marymount Col. Was semifinalist in NY State Miss Universe Pageant. First professional job as "color girl" for CBS, sitting for cameras as new lighting system for color tv was developed. Had bit parts in films Me Natalie and Goodbye Columbus. Performed on 1983 album Love in the Afternoon.

PICTURES: Daddy You Kill Me, Young Doctors in Love (cameo).
TELEVISION: *Series:* All My Children (1970-). *Movies:* Invitation to Hell, Mafia Princess, Anastasia: The Story of Anna, Haunted By Her Past, Lady Mobster, The Bride in Black, The Woman Who Sinned, Double Edge, Between Love and Hate, French Silk, Seduced and Betrayed.

LUCKINBILL, LAURENCE
Actor. b. Fort Smith, AR, Nov. 21, 1934. m. actress Lucie Arnaz. e. U. of Arkansas, Catholic U. of America.
THEATER: NY: A Man for All Seasons, Arms and the Man, The Boys in the Band, Alpha Beta, The Shadow Box, Poor Murderer, Chapter Two, Past Tense.
PICTURES: The Boys in the Band, Such Good Friends, The Promise, Not for Publication, Cocktail, Messenger of Death, Star Trek V: The Final Frontier.
TELEVISION: *Series:* The Secret Storm, Where the Heart Is, The Delphi Bureau. *Movies:* The Delphi Bureau (pilot), Death Sentence, Panic on the 5:22, Winner Take All, The Lindbergh Kidnapping Case, The Mating Season, To Heal a Nation. *Mini-Series:* Ike. *Specials:* Lyndon Johnson (one-man show), Voices and Visions (narrator), The 5:48, Lucy & Desi: A Home Movie (co-exec. prod., co-dir., writer).

LUDDY, TOM
Producer. e. U. of California at Berkeley where he operated student film societies and rep. cinemas. Entered industry via Brandon Films. 1972, prog. dir. and curator of Pacific Film Archives. 1979, joined Zoetrope Studios as dir. of special projects where dev. and supervised revival of Gance's Napoleon and Our Hitler—A Film From Germany. Coordinated Koyaanis-qatsi, Every Man For Himself, Passion. A founder, Telluride Film Fest. Served on selection comm., N.Y. and pres. San Francisco Film Fest.
PICTURES: Mishima (co-prod.), Tough Guys Don't Dance (co-exec. prod.), Barfly, King Lear (assoc. prod.), Manifesto (exec. prod.), Powwaqatsi (assoc. prod.), Wait Until Spring Bandini, Wind, The Secret Garden (co-prod.), Mi Familia (exec. prod.)

LUDWIG, IRVING H.
Executive. b. Nov. 3. Rivoli Theatre, N.Y., mgr., theatre oper., Rugoff and Becker, 1938-39; opened first modern art type theatre, Greenwich Village, 1940. With Walt Disney Prod. in charge of theatre oper. on Fantasia, 1940-41; buyer-booker, Rugoff and Becker, 1942-45; film sales admin., Walt Disney Prod. home office, 1945-53; v.p. and domestic sales mgr., Buena Vista Dist. Co., 1953; pres. sales & mktg., 1959-80. Member of bd. of dirs.; Will Rogers Memorial Fund, Foundation of M.P. Pioneers; Motion Picture Club; Academy of M.P. Arts & Sciences.

LUEDTKE, KURT
Writer. b. Grand Rapids, MI, Sept. 29, 1938. e. Brown U., B.A., 1961. Reporter Grand Rapids Press 1961-62. Miami Herald, 1963-65; Detroit Free Press (reporter, asst. photography dir., asst. mgr. ed., asst. exec. ed., exec. ed. 1965-78.).
PICTURES: Absence of Malice, Out of Africa (Academy Award, 1985), Walls.

LUFT, LORNA
Actress, Singer. b. Hollywood, CA, Nov. 21, 1952. Daughter of actress-singer Judy Garland and producer Sid Luft. Has sung in nightclubs. Appeared on 1990 recording of Girl Crazy.
THEATER: *NY:* Judy Garland at Home at the Palace, Promises Promises, Snoopy, Extremities. *Tours:* They're Playing Our Song, Grease, Little Shop of Horrors, Jerry Herman's Broadway, The Unsinkable Molly Brown, Guys and Dolls.
PICTURES: I Could Go on Singing (extra, unbilled), Grease 2, Where the Boys Are.
TELEVISION: *Series:* Trapper John. *Movie:* Fear Stalk. *Guest:* Twilight Zone, Hooperman, Murder She Wrote, Tales from the Dark Side, The Cosby Show.

LUHRMANN, BAZ
Director. r.n.Baz Mark Luhrmann.
PICTURES: *Dir./Writer.:* Strictly Ballroom, Rome + Juliet (also prod., BAFTA Award, Best Direction, Best Adapted Screenplay, 1997). *Actor:* Winter of Our Dreams, The Dark Room.

LUKE, PETER
Writer, Director. b. England, Aug. 12, 1919. *Autobiography:* Sisyphus & Reilly.
THEATER: Hadrian VII, Bloomsbury.
TELEVISION: *Writer:* Small Fish Are Sweet, Pigs Ear with Flowers, Roll on Bloomin' Death, A Man on Her Back (with William Sansom), Devil a Monk Won't Be, Anach 'Cuan (also dir.), Black Sound—Deep Song (also dir.).

LUMET, SIDNEY
Director. b. Philadelphia, PA, June 25, 1924. e. Professional Children's Sch.; Columbia U. Child actor in plays: Dead End, George Washington Slept Here, My Heart's in the Highlands, and films: The 400 Million, One Third of a Nation. U.S. Armed Forces, WWII, 1942-46; dir. summer stock, 1947-49; taught acting, H.S. of Prof. Arts. Assoc. dir. CBS, 1950, dir. 1951. Appeared in documentary Listen Up: The Lives of Quincy Jones. Author: Making Movies (Alfred A. Knopf, 1995).

PICTURES: 12 Angry Men (debut, 1957), Stage Struck, That Kind of Woman, The Fugitive Kind, A View From the Bridge, Long Day's Journey Into Night, Fail-Safe, The Pawnbroker, The Hill, The Group, The Deadly Affair (also prod.), Bye Bye Braverman (also prod.), The Sea Gull (also prod.), The Appointment, The Last of the Mobile Hotshots (also prod.), King: A Filmed Record ... Montgomery to Memphis (co-dir., prod.), The Anderson Tapes, Child's Play, The Offence, Serpico, Lovin' Molly, Murder on the Orient Express, Dog Day Afternoon, Network, Equus, The Wiz, Just Tell Me What You Want (also co-prod.), Prince of the City (also co-s.p.), Deathtrap, The Verdict, Daniel (also co-exec. prod.), Garbo Talks, Power, The Morning After, Running on Empty, Family Business, Q & A (also s.p.), A Stranger Among Us, Guilty As Sin, Night Falls On Manhattan (also s.p.), Critical Care, Gloria.
TELEVISION: Series episodes: Mama, Danger, You Are There, Omnibus, Best of Broadway, Alcoa, Goodyear Playhouse, Kraft Television Theatre (Mooney's Kid Don't Cry, The Last of My Gold Watches, This Property is Condemned), Playhouse 90, Play of the Week (The Dybbuk, Rashomon, The Iceman Cometh—Emmy Award). Specials: The Sacco and Vanzetti Story, John Brown's Raid, Cry Vengeance.

LUNDGREN, DOLPH
Actor. b. Stockholm, Sweden, Nov. 3, 1959. e. Washington State U., won Fulbright to Massachusetts Inst. of Technology, Royal Inst. of Technology, Stockholm, M.S.C. Was doorman at Limelight disco in NY while studying acting. Full Contact Karate champion. Made workout video, Maximum Potential. On stage in Another Octopus.
PICTURES: A View to a Kill, Rocky IV, Masters of the Universe, Red Scorpion, The Punisher, I Come in Peace, Cover-Up, Showdown in Little Tokyo, Universal Soldier, Army of One, Pentathlon, Men of War, Johnny Mnemonic, The Shooter, The Algonquin Goodbye

LUPONE, PATTI
Actress. b. Northport, NY, Apr. 21, 1949. e. Juilliard.
THEATER: School for Scandal, Three Sisters, The Beggars Opera, The Robber Bridegroom, Meaure for Measure, Edward II, The Water Engine, Working, Evita (Tony Award, 1980), Oliver!, Anything Goes, Les Miserables (London), Sunset Boulevard (London), Master Class, The Old Neighborhood.
PICTURES: 1941, Fighting Back, Witness, Wise Guys, Driving Miss Daisy, Family Prayers, State and Maine, 24 Hour Woman.
TELEVISION: Series: Life Goes On. Movies: LBJ: The Early Years, The Water Engine, The Song Spinner, Her Last Chance.

LYDON, JAMES
Actor. b. Harrington Park, NJ, May 30, 1923; e. St. Johns Mil. Sch. On N.Y. stage in Prologue to Glory, Sing Out the News. For 20th Century Fox tv was assoc. prod. of series Anna and the King, Roll Out. Prod./Writer/Dir. of special The Incredible 20th Century. Dir. for Universal TV: 6 Million Dollar Man, Simon & Simon, Beggarman Thief.
PICTURES: Actor: Back Door to Heaven (debut, 1939), Two Thoroughbreds, Racing Luck, Tom Brown's Schooldays, Little Men, Naval Academy, Bowery Boy, Henry Aldrich for President, Cadets on Parade, The Mad Martindales, Star Spangled Rhythm, Henry Aldrich— Editor, Henry Aldrich Gets Glamour, Henry Aldrich Swings It, Henry Aldrich Haunts a House, Henry Aldrich Plays Cupid, Aerial Gunner, Henry Aldrich—Boy Scout, My Best Gal, The Town Went Wild, Henry Aldrich's Little Secret, When the Lights Go on Again, Out of the Night, Twice Blessed, The Affairs of Geraldine, Life With Father, Cynthia, Sweet Genevieve, The Time of Your Life, Out of the Storm, Joan of Arc, An Old-Fashioned Girl, Bad Boy, Miss Mink of 1949, Tucson, Gasoline Alley, Tarnished, When Willie Comes Marching Home, Destination Big House, Hot Rod, September Affair, The Magnificent Yankee, Island in the Sky, The Desperado, Battle Stations, Chain of Evidence, The Hypnotic Eye, I Passed for White, The Last Time I Saw Archie, Brainstorm, Death of a Gunfighter, Scandalous John, Bonnie's Kids, Vigilante Force. Assoc. Prod.: My Blood Runs Cold, An American Dream, A Covenant With Death, First to Fight, The Cool Ones, Chubasco, Countdown, Assignment to Kill, The Learning Tree.
TELEVISION: Guest: Frontier Circus (also assoc. prod.). Co-ordin. Prod.: Wagon Train, Alfred Hitchcock Hour. Assoc. Prod.: McHale's Navy, 77 Sunset Strip, Mr. Roberts. Series (actor): So This Is Hollywood, The First Hundred Years, Love That Jill. Movies: Ellery Queen, The New Daughters of Joshua Cabe, Peter Lundy and the Medicine Hat Stallion.

LYLES, A. C.
Producer. b. Jacksonville, FL. May 17, 1918. e. Andrew Jackson H.S. Paramount Publix's Florida Theatre, 1928; interviewed Hollywood celebrities, Jacksonville Journal, 1932; mail boy, Paramount Studios, Hollywood, 1937; publicity dept., 1938; hd. of adv., publ. dept., Pine-Thomas unit at Paramount, 1940; assoc. prod., The Mountain. President, A. C. Lyles Productions, Inc. (Paramount Pictures).
PICTURES: Short Cut to Hell, Raymie, The Young and the Brave, Law of the Lawless, Stage to Thunder Rock, Young Fury, Black Spurs, Hostile Guns, Arizona Bushwackers, Town Tamer, Apache Uprising, Johnny Reno, Waco, Red Tomahawk, Fort Utah, Buckskin, Rogue's Gallery, Night of the Lepus, The Last Day, Flight to Holocaust.
TELEVISION: Rawhide (series; assoc. prod.), A Christmas for Boomer, Here's Boomer (series), Dear Mr. President, Conversations With the Presidents.

LYNCH, DAVID
Director, Writer. b. Missoula, MT, Jan. 20, 1946. e. Pennsylvania Acad. of Fine Arts, where received an independent filmmaker grant from America Film Institute. Made 16mm film, The Grandmother. Accepted by Center for Advanced Film Studies in Los Angeles, 1970. Wrote and directed Eraserhead (with partial AFI financing). Acted in films Zelly & Me, Nadja (also exec. prod.).
PICTURES: Director-Writer: Eraserhead (also prod., edit., prod.-design, f/x), The Elephant Man, Dune, Blue Velvet, Wild at Heart, Twin Peaks: Fire Walk With Me (also co-exec. prod., actor), Crumb (presenter).
TELEVISION: Series: Twin Peaks (dir., exec. prod., writer), On the Air (exec. prod., dir., writer). Special: Hotel Room (co-dir., co-exec. prod.).

LYNCH, KELLY
Actress. b. Minneapolis, MN, 1959. Former model.
PICTURES: Osa, Bright Lights Big City, Cocktail, Road House, Warm Summer Rain, Drugstore Cowboy, Desperate Hours, Curly Sue, For Better and For Worse, Three of Hearts, Imaginary Crimes, The Beans of Egypt Maine, Virtuosity, White Man's Burden.
TELEVISION: Guest: Miami Vice, The Equalizer, Spenser for Hire, The Hitcher, The Edge (Black Pudding). Movie: Something in Common. Pilot: San Berdoo.

LYNCH, PAUL M.
Director.
PICTURES: Hard Part Begins, Blood and Guts, Prom Night, Cross Country, Flying, Blindside, Bullies.
TELEVISION: Series: Voyagers, Blacke's Magic, Murder She Wrote, In the Heat of the Night, Tour of Duty, Beauty and the Beast, Twilight Zone (1987), Moonlighting, Star Trek: The Next Generation, Dark Shadows, Tour of Duty, Top Cops, Mike Hammer, Hooperman, Bronx Zoo. Movies: Cameo By Night, Going to the Chapel, She Knows Too Much, Murder by Night, Drop Dead Gorgeous.

LYNCH, RICHARD
Actor. b. Brooklyn, NY. Trained with Lee Strasberg at Carnegie Hall. In 1970 became life time member of the Actors Studio, NY.
THEATRE: NY: The Devils (On and Off-B'way debut), The Basic Training of Pavlo Hummel, Lion in Winter, The Orphan, Arturo-U, The Lady From the Sea, One Night Stands of a Noisy Passenger, Action, Richard III, Live Like Pigs, The Man with the Flower in His Mouth, A View from the Bridge.
PICTURES: Scarecrow (debut, 1973), The Seven Ups, The Delta Fox, The Premonition, Steel, Open Season, The Formula, The Sword and the Sorcerer, Little Nikita, Savage Dawn, Invasion U.S.A., Cut and Run, Night Force, The Barbarians, Bad Dreams, The Ninth Configuration, Melanie Rose (High Stakes), Spirit, Aftershock, Return to Justice, One Man Force, The Forbidden Dance, October 32nd, Alligator II: The Mutation, Double Threat, H.P. Lovecraft's Necromonicon, Scanner Cop, Crime & Punishment.
TELEVISION: Series: Battlestar Gallactica, The Phoenix. Movies: Starsky and Hutch (pilot), Roger & Harry: The Mitera Target, Good Against Evil, Dog and Cat, Vampire, Alcatraz—The Whole Shocking Story, Sizzle, White Water Rebels, The Last Ninja.

LYNDON, VICTOR
Producer, Writer. b. London. e. St. Paul's. Ent. m.p. ind. 1942 as asst. dir., Gainsborough Pictures. Novel: Bermuda Blue (1984).
PICTURES: Prod. mgr.: The African Queen. Assoc. Prod.: Dr. Strangelove, Darling, 2001: A Space Odyssey. Prod.: Spare The Rod, Station Six—Sahara, The Optimists.

LYNE, ADRIAN
Director. b. Peterborough, England, March 4, 1941. Started as director of commercials.
PICTURES: Foxes, Flashdance, Nine 1/2 Weeks, Fatal Attraction, Jacob's Ladder, Indecent Proposal, Lolita.

LYNLEY, CAROL
Actress. b. New York, NY, Feb. 13, 1942. Was model as teenager.
PICTURES: The Light in the Forest (debut, 1958), Holiday for Lovers, Blue Denim, Hound-Dog Man, Return to Peyton Place, The Last Sunset, The Stripper, Under the Yum-Yum Tree, The Cardinal, The Pleasure Seekers, Shock Treatment, Harlow, Bunny Lake Is Missing, The Shuttered Room, Danger Route, Once You Kiss a Stranger, The Maltese Bippy, Norwood, Beware the Blob!, The Poseidon Adventure, Cotter, The Four Deuces, The Washington Affair, The Cat and the Canary, The Shape of Things to Come, Vigilante, Dark Tower, Blackout, Howling VI: The Freaks.
TELEVISION: Series: The Immortal. Movies: Shadow on the Land, The Smugglers, The Immortal, Weekend of Terror, The Cable Car Murder, The Night Stalker, The Elevator, Death Stalk, Willow B, Women in Prison, Flood, Fantasy Island, Having Babies II, Cops and Robin, The Beasts Are on the Streets.

LYNN, ANN
Actress. b. London, England, 1934. Ent. films and TV, 1958.
PICTURES: Johnny You're Wanted (debut, 1955), Moment of Indiscretion, Naked Fury, Piccadilly Third Stop, The Wind of Change, Strip Tease Murder, Strongroom, Flame in the Streets, HMS Defiant (Damn the Defiant), The Party's Over, Doctor in Distress, The Black Torment, The System (The Girl Getters), A Shot in the Dark, The Uncle, Four in the Morning, Separation, I'll Never Forget What's 'is Name, Baby Love, Hitler—The Last Ten Days, Screamtime.
TELEVISION: Specials/Movies: After The Show, All Summer Long, Trump Card, Man at the Top, The Expert, Hine, The Intruders, Too Far, King Lear, The Zoo Gang, Morning Tide, Estuary, Who Pays the Ferryman, The Professionals, Zeticula, Westway, The Perfect House, Minder, To the Sound of Guns, Crown Court, Just Good Friends, Starting Out, Paradise Park. Series: The Cheaters, The Other Side of the Underneath.

LYNN, JONATHAN
Director, Writer, Actor. b. Bath, England, Apr. 3, 1943. Was artistic dir. of Cambridge Theatre Company, 1976-81; Company Director of Natl. Theatre, 1987. Playwright: Pig of the Month. Books: A Proper Man, The Complete Yes Prime Minister, Mayday. Appeared as actor in Into the Night, Three Men and a Little Lady.
PICTURES: The Internecine Project (s.p.). Director: Clue (also s.p.), Nuns on the Run (also s.p.), My Cousin Vinny, The Distinguished Gentleman, Greedy (also actor), Sgt. Bilko, Trial and Error (also prod.).
TELEVISION: Doctor on the Go, My Name is Harry Worth, My Brother's Keeper, Yes Minister, Yes Prime Minister.

LYNTON, MICHAEL
Executive. Pres., Hollywood Pictures.

LYONS, S. DANIEL
Executive. b. Toronto, Canada, Sept., 9, 1955. e. Brandeis Univ., B.A. magna cum laude 1977. Univ. of Toronto, LL.B. 1981. 1985, joined Astral Films as a lawyer. Promoted to dir. of bus. affairs, then v.p., Dist. for the Astral Entertainment Group. 1997, became v.p., Dist & Mktg., Coscient/Astral Dist. Author of: Public Strategy and Motion Pictures, and Showman (play, Cubiculo Theatre, NY).

LYON, FRANCIS D. "PETE"
Director, Editor. b. Bowbells, ND, July 29, 1905. e. Hollywood H.S., UCLA. WWII: writer, prod., dir., OWI; assoc. with training, exploitation and information films. Maj. U.S. Army Signal Corps. Author: Twists of Fate: An Oscar Winner's International Career.
PICTURES: Editor: Things to Come (co-edit.), Knight Without Armour, Rembrandt, Intermezzo, Adam Had Four Sons, The Great Profile, Four Sons, Daytime Wife, Body and Soul (Academy Award, 1947), He Ran All the Way. Director: Crazylegs, The Bob Mathias Story (Christopher Award), The Great Locomotive Chase, Cult of the Cobra, The Oklahoman, Gunsight Ridge, Bailout at 43,000, Escort West, Cinerama South Seas Adventure (co-dir.), The Young and the Brave, Destination Inner Space, The Destructors, The Money Jungle, The Girl Who Knew Too Much. Producer: Tiger by the Tail.
TELEVISION: Series: Laramie, Perry Mason, Zane Grey Theatre, Bus Stop, M. Squad, Wells Fargo, Kraft Suspense Theatre, Death Valley Days, Follow the Sun, etc.

LYON, SUE
Actress. b. Davenport, IA, July 10, 1946. e. Hollywood Prof. Sch.
PICTURES: Lolita (debut, 1962), The Night of the Iguana, Seven Women, Tony Rome, The Flim Flam Man, Evel Knievel, Crash, End of the World, Alligator, Invisible Strangler.
TELEVISION: Movies: But I Don't Want to Get Married!, Smash-Up on Interstate 5, Don't Push—I'll Charge When I'm Ready.

M

MacARTHUR, JAMES
Actor. b. Los Angeles, CA, Dec. 8, 1937. e. Harvard. p. actress Helen Hayes, writer Charles MacArthur. Stage debut, summer stock; The Corn Is Green, Life with Father.
PICTURES: The Young Stranger (debut, 1957), The Light in the Forest, Third Man on the Mountain, Kidnapped, Swiss Family Robinson, The Interns, Spencer's Mountain, Cry of Battle, The Truth About Spring, The Battle of the Bulge, The Bedford Incident, Ride Beyond Vengeance, The Love-Ins, Hang 'em High, The Angry Breed.
TELEVISION: Series: Hawaii Five-O. Movies: Alcatraz—The Whole Shocking Story, The Night the Bridge Fell Down. Special: Willie and the Yank (Mosby's Marauders).

MACCHIO, RALPH
Actor. b. Long Island, NY, Nov. 4, 1962. Started in TV commercials at age 16 before winning role in series Eight Is Enough. Broadway debut in Cuba and His Teddy Bear, 1986; Off-B'way in Only Kidding.

PICTURES: Up the Academy (debut, 1980), The Outsiders, The Karate Kid, Teachers, Crossroads, The Karate Kid Part II, Distant Thunder, The Karate Kid Part III, Too Much Sun, My Cousin Vinny, Naked in New York.
TELEVISION: Series: Eight Is Enough. Movies: Journey to Survival, Dangerous Company, The Three Wishes of Billy Grier, The Last P.O.W.?: The Bobby Garwood Story.

MacCORKINDALE, SIMON
Actor, Producer, Director, Writer. b. Isle-of-Ely, England, Feb. 2, 1952. m. actress Susan George. On stage in Dark Lady of the Sonnets, Pygmalion, French Without Tears, etc.
PICTURES: Actor: Death on the Nile, Quatermass Conclusion, Cabolanco, Robbers of the Sacred Mountain, The Sword and the Sorcerer, Jaws 3-D, The Riddle of the Sands, Sincerely Violet. Producer: Stealing Heaven, That Summer of White Roses (also co-s.p.), The House That Mary Bought (also dir., co-s.p.).
TELEVISION: Specials: I Claudius, Romeo and Juliet, Quatermass. Movies: The Manions of America, Falcon's Gold, Jesus of Nazareth, Twist of Fate, Obsessive Love, No Greater Love, At The Midnight Hour, A Family of Cops, While My Pretty One Sleeps, The Sands of Eden. Mini-Series: Pursuit, The Way to Dusty Death. Series: Manimal, Falcon Crest, Counterstrike.

MacCURDY, JEAN
Executive. Began career in the Children's Prog. dept., NBC TV network. Joined Warner Bros. Cartoons in 1979, as dir. of Animation and Prog.; named v.p. & gen. mngr, WB Cartoons & served as prodn. exec., 1982. Named v.p., Children's Prog., 1983. Returned to WB Animation as v.p. & gen. mngr., 1988; named sr. v.p. & gen. mngr., 1991; became first pres., WB TV Animation, 1992-.

MacDOWELL, ANDIE
Actress. b. Gaffney, SC, April 21, 1958. r.n. Rose Anderson MacDowell. Started as model for Elite Agency in NY appearing for L'Ordeal Cosmetics, The Gap, Calvin Klein.
PICTURES: Greystoke: The Legend of Tarzan Lord of the Apes (debut, 1984), St. Elmo's Fire, Sex Lies and Videotape (L.A. Film Critics Award, 1989), Green Card, The Object of Beauty, Hudson Hawk, The Player, Groundhog Day, Short Cuts, Deception, Four Weddings and a Funeral, Bad Girls, Unstrung Heroes, Michael, Multiplicity, The End of Violence, Town and Country, Shadrach, The Scalper.
TELEVISION: Movie: Women and Men 2: In Love There Are No Rules (Domestic Dilemma). Mini-Series (Italy): Sahara's Secret.

MacGRAW, ALI
Actress. b. Pound Ridge, NY, April 1, 1939. e. Wellesley Coll. Son is actor Josh Evans. Editorial asst. Harper's Bazaar Mag.; asst. to photographer Melvin Sokolsky. Was top fashion model. Author: Moving Pictures (autobiography, 1991), Yoga Mind & Body (1995).
PICTURES: A Lovely Way to Die (debut, 1968). Goodbye Columbus, Love Story (Acad. Award nom.), The Getaway, Convoy, Players, Just Tell Me What You Want, Natural Causes, Glam.
TELEVISION: Mini-Series: The Winds of War. Movies: China Rose, Survive the Savage Sea, Gunsmoke: The Long Ride, The Hollywood Fashion Machine. Series: Dynasty.

MacLACHLAN, KYLE
Actor. b. Yakima, WA, Feb. 22, 1959. e. Univ. of WA. Acted in high school and college, then in summer stock. Joined Oregon Shakespeare Festival (Romeo and Juliet, Julius Caesar, Henry V). Cast as lead in Dune by dir. David Lynch in a nationwide search.
THEATRE: NY: Palace of Amateurs (Off-B'way).
PICTURES: Dune (debut, 1984), Blue Velvet, The Hidden, Don't Tell Her It's Me, The Doors, Twin Peaks: Fire Walk With Me, Where the Day Takes You, Rich in Love, The Trial, The Flintstones, Showgirls, Trigger Effect, Mad Dog Time, One Night Stand, Route 9.
TELEVISION: Series: Twin Peaks. Guest: Tales From the Crypt (Carrion Death). Movies: Dream Breakers, Against the Wall, Roswell, Windsor Protocol.

MacLAINE, SHIRLEY
Actress. b. Richmond, VA, April 24, 1934. r.n. Shirley MacLean Beaty. Brother is actor-prod. Warren Beatty. e. Washington and Lee H.S., Arlington, VA. Started as dancer; on B'way as understudy for Carol Haney in The Pajama Game, which resulted in contract with film prod. Hal Wallis. Prod., writer and co- dir. of Oscar-nominated film documentary: The Other Half of the Sky: A China Memoir. Returned to stage in Gypsy in My Soul, Shirley MacLaine on Broadway. Videos: Shirley MacLaine's Inner Workout, Relaxing Within.
AUTHOR: Don't Fall off the Mountain, You Can Get There from Here, Out on a Limb, Dancing in the Light, It's All In the Playing, Going Within, Dance While You Can, My Lucky Stars. Editor: McGovern: The Man and His Beliefs (1972).

PICTURES: The Trouble With Harry (debut, 1955), Artists and Models, Around the World in 80 Days, Hot Spell, The Matchmaker, The Sheepman, Some Came Running (Acad. Award nom.), Ask Any Girl, Career, Can-Can, The Apartment (Acad. Award nom.), Ocean's Eleven (cameo), All in a Night's Work, Two Loves, My Geisha, The Children's Hour, Two for the Seesaw, Irma La Douce (Acad. Award nom.), What a Way to Go!, John Goldfarb Please Come Home, The Yellow Rolls Royce, Gambit, Woman Times Seven, The Bliss of Mrs. Blossom, Sweet Charity, Two Mules for Sister Sara, Desperate Characters, The Possession of Joel Delaney, The Turning Point (Acad. Award nom.), Being There, Loving Couples, A Change of Seasons, Terms of Endearment (Acad. Award, 1983), Cannonball Run II, Madame Sousatzka, Steel Magnolias, Postcards From the Edge, Waiting for the Light, Defending Your Life (cameo), Used People, Wrestling Ernest Hemingway, Guarding Tess, Mrs. Winterbourne, The Celluloid Closet, Evening Star.
TELEVISION: Series: Shirley's World. Variety Specials: The Other Half of the Sky: A China Memoir (also prod., co-writer), If They Could See Me Now, Where Do We Go From Here?, Shirley MacLaine at the Lido, Every Little Movement (Emmy Award for co-writing, 1980), Illusions, The Shirley MacLaine Show. Movies: Out on a Limb (also co-writer), The West Side Waltz.

MacLEOD, GAVIN
Actor. b. Mt. Kisco, NY, Feb. 28, 1930. e. Ithaca Coll.
PICTURES: I Want to Live, Compulsion, Operation Petticoat, McHale's Navy, McHale's Navy Joins the Air Force, The Sand Pebbles, Deathwatch, The Party, Kelly's Heroes.
TELEVISION: Series: McHale's Navy, The Mary Tyler Moore Show, The Love Boat. Movies: The Intruders, Only with Married Men, Ransom for Alice, Murder Can Hurt You, Student Exchange, The Love Boat: The Valentine Voyage. Mini-Series: Scruples. Specials: Last Act Is a Solo, If I Die Before I Wake.

MacNAUGHTON, ROBERT
Actor. b. New York, NY, Dec. 19, 1966. Entered entertainment industry in 1979. Member Circle Rep. Co., NY.
THEATER: Critic's Choice, A Thousand Clowns, Camelot, The Diviners, The Adventures of Huckleberry Finn, Henry V, Tobacco Road, Master Harold... and the Boys, Tomorrow's Monday, Talley and Son.
PICTURES: E.T.: The Extra-Terrestrial, I Am the Cheese.
TELEVISION: Movies: Angel City, A Place to Call Home. Specials: Big Bend Country, The Electric Grandmother, Hear My Cry, Visitors.

MacNICOL PETER
Actor. b. Dallas, TX. e. U. of Minnesota.
THEATER: Manhattan Theatre Club: Crimes of the Heart. NY Shakespeare Fest: Found a Peanut, Rum and Coke, Twelfth Night, Richard II, Romeo & Juliet. Regional theatre includes Guthrie, Alaska Rep., Long Wharf, Dallas Theatre Center, Trinity Rep. B'way: Crimes of the Heart (Theatre World Award), The Nerd, Black Comedy/White Liars.
PICTURES: Dragonslayer (debut, 1981), Sophie's Choice, Heat, Ghostbusters II, American Blue Note, Hard Promises, Housesitter, Addams Family Values, Radioland Murders, Dracula: Dead and Loving It, Mojave Moon, Bean, Baby Geniuses.
TELEVISION: Movies: Johnny Bull, By Dawn's Early Light, Roswell. Guest: Faerie Tale Theatre, Days and Nights of Molly Dodd, Cheers. Series: Powers That Be, Chicago Hope, Abducted: A Father's Love, Silencing Mary.

MACY, WILLIAM H.
Actor. b. Miami, FL, March 13, 1950. e. Goddard Col.
THEATER: NY: The Man in 605 (debut, 1980), Twelfth Night, Beaurecrat, A Call From the East, The Dining Room, Speakeasy, Wild Life, Flirtations, Baby With the Bathwater, The Nice and the Nasty, Bodies Rest and Motion, Oh Hell!, Life During Wartime, Mr. Gogol and Mr. Preen, Oleanna, Our Town (B'way).
PICTURES: Without a Trace, The Last Dragon, Radio Days, House of Games, Things Change, Homicide, Shadows and Fog, Benny and Joon, Searching for Bobby Fischer, The Client, Oleanna, Murder in the First, Mr. Holland's Opus, Down Periscope, Fargo (Acad. Award nom.), Ghosts of Mississippi, Air Force One, A Civil Action.
TELEVISION: Movies: The Murder of Mary Phagan, Texan, A Murderous Affair, The Water Engine, Heart of Justice, A Private Matter, The Con. Guest: ER, Law and Order, Chicago Hope.

MADDEN, BILL
Executive. b. New York, NY, March 1, 1915. e. Boston U. Joined Metro-Goldwyn-Mayer as office boy, 1930; student salesman, 1938; asst. Eastern div. sales mgr., 1939; U.S. Navy, 1942-46; Boston sales rep., MGM, 1947-53; Philadelphia branch mgr., 1954-59; Midwest div. sales mgr., 1960-68; roadshow sales mgr., 1969; v.p., gen. sales mgr., 1969-74, MGM; corp., v.p. & gen. sls. mgr., MGM, 1974; retired from MGM, 1975; 1976-present, exec. consultant to motion picture industry; lecturer and instructor at UCLA. Member: AMPAS, Motion Picture Associates, American Film Institute. Motion Picture Pioneers.

MADDEN, DAVID
Executive, Producer, Director. b. Chicago, IL, July 25, 1955. e. Harvard U., 1976; UCLA, M.A., 1978. Joined 20th Century-Fox in 1978 as story analyst. Named story editor, 1980; exec. story editor, 1982. Appt. v.p., creative affairs for 20th-Fox Prods., 1983; v.p., prod., 20th Century-Fox Prods; 1984, v.p., prod., Paramount Pictures. 1987, joined Interscope Commun. as prod. 1996, Formed Cort Madden Co. at Paramount with Robert Cort
PICTURES: Producer: Renegades, Blind Fury (exec. prod.), The First Power, Eve of Destruction, Jersey Girls, The Hand That Rocks the Cradle, Holy Matrimony, Operation Dumbo Drop, The Tie That Binds, Separate Lives (dir only.) The Associate, Odd Couple II.
TELEVISION: Movies: A Part of the Family (dir., writer), Body Language (co-exec. prod.).

MADIGAN, AMY
Actress. b. Chicago, IL, Sept. 11, 1951. m. actor Ed Harris. For 10 years traveled country performing in bars and clubs with band. Then studied at Lee Strasberg Inst., L.A. NY Stage: The Lucky Spot (Theatre World Award), A Streetcar Named Desire.
PICTURES: Love Child (debut, 1982), Love Letters, Streets of Fire, Places in the Heart, Alamo Bay, Twice in a Lifetime (Acad. Award nom.), Nowhere To Hide, The Prince of Pennsylvania, Field of Dreams, Uncle Buck, The Dark Half, Female Perversions, Loved, With Friends Like These.
TELEVISION: Special: The Laundromat. Movies: Crazy Times, The Ambush Murders, Victims, Travis McGee, The Day After, Roe vs. Wade, Lucky Day, And Then There Was One, Riders of the Purple Sage, Big Guns Talk: The Story of the Western, A Bright Shining Lie..

MADONNA
Singer, Actress. r.n. Madonna Louise Veronica Ciccone. b. Pontiac, MI, Aug. 16, 1958. e. U. of Michigan. Gained fame as rock & recording star before professional acting debut in Desperately Seeking Susan, 1985. NY stage debut: Speed-the-Plow, 1988. Author: Sex (1992).
PICTURES: A Certain Sacrifice (debut, 1983), Vision Quest, Desperately Seeking Susan, Shanghai Surprise, Who's That Girl?, Bloodhounds of Broadway, Dick Tracy, Truth or Dare (also exec. prod.), Shadows and Fog, A League of Their Own, Body of Evidence, Dangerous Game, Blue in the Face, Four Rooms, Girl 6, Evita (Golden Globe Award, 1997).

MADSEN, MICHAEL
Actor. b. Chicago, IL, Sept. 25, 1958. Sister is actress Virginia Madsen. Started acting with Chicago's Steppenwolf Theatre appearing in such plays as Of Mice and Men, A Streetcar Named Desire. On B'way in A Streetcar Named Desire (1992).
PICTURES: WarGames (debut, 1983), Racing With the Moon, The Natural, The Killing Time, Shadows in the Storm, Blood Red, Kill Me Again, The End of Innocence, The Doors, Thelma & Louise, Straight Talk, Inside Edge, Reservoir Dogs, Trouble Bound, House in the Hills, Free Willy, Money for Nothing, Fixing the Shadow, The Getaway, Beyond the Law, Dead Connection, Wyatt Earp, Man With a Gun, Species, Free Willy 2: The Adventure Home, Mulholland Falls, Donnie Brasco.
TELEVISION: Movies: Our Family Honor, Montana, Baby Snatcher. Pilot: Diner.

MADSEN, VIRGINIA
Actress. b. Chicago, IL, Sept. 11, 1963. Mother is Emmy-winning Chicago filmmaker; brother is actor Michael Madsen. Studied with Chicago acting coach Ted Liss. Prof. debut, PBS, A Matter of Principle. Received Avoriaz & Saturn Awards for Best Actress for Candyman.
PICTURES: Class (debut, 1983), Electric Dreams, Dune, Creator, Fire With Fire, Modern Girls, Zombie High, Slam Dance, Mr. North, Hot to Trot, Heart of Dixie, The Hot Spot, Highlander 2: The Quickening, Candyman, Becoming Colette, Caroline at Midnight, Blue Tiger, The Prophecy, Ghosts of Mississippi, Suicide Kings, The Rainmaker, McClintocks Peach, The Florentine, Ballad of the Nightingale, Ambushed.
TELEVISION: Movies: Mussolini: The Untold Story, The Hearst and Davies Affair, Long Gone, Gotham, Third Degree Burn, Ironclads, Victim of Love, Love Kills, Linda, A Murderous Affair: The Carolyn Warmus Story, Bitter Revenge, Robert Ludlum's The Apocalypse Watch. Guest: The Hitchhiker.

MAGNOLI, ALBERT
Director, Writer, Editor.
PICTURES: Jazz (dir., editor, s.p.), Reckless (edit.), Purple Rain (dir., edit., s.p.), American Anthem (dir. only).
TELEVISION: Movie: Born to Run.

MAGNUSON, ANN
Actress, Writer, Performance Artist. b. Charleston, WV, Jan. 4, 1956. e. Denison U. Intern at Ensemble Studio Theatre when she came to NY in 1978. Ran Club 57, an East Village club, 1979. Has performed Off-B'way, in East Village clubs, downtown art spaces, on college campuses since 1980, and at Whitney Museum, Soguestu Hall (Tokyo), Walker Art Ctr. (Minn.), Lincoln Center, Serious Fun Festival, Joseph Papp's Public Theatre. Also performed with band Bongwater. Debut as solo recording artist on Geffen Records with The Luv Show, 1995.
PICTURES: Vortex, The Hunger, Perfect Strangers, Desperately Seeking Susan, Making Mr. Right, A Night in the Life of Jimmy Reardon, Sleepwalk, Mondo New York, Tequila Sunrise, Checking Out, Heavy Petting, Love at Large, Cabin Boy, Clear and Present Danger, Tank Girl, Before and After, Hugo Pool, Still Breathing, Levitation.
TELEVISION: Night Flight, Made for TV, Alive from Off Center (co-host), Vandemonium, Table at Ciro's (Tales From the Hollywood Hills), The Hidden Room, The Adventures of Pete and Pete. Guest: The John Laroquette Show, Caroline in the City, The Drew Carey Show. Series: Anything But Love, From the Earth to the Moon.

MAGUIRE, TOBEY
Actor. b. 1975.
PICTURES: This Boy's Life, S.F.W., Plane Fear, Duke of Groove, Empire Records, Se5duced by Madness, Joyride, The Ice Storm, Deconstructing Harry, To Live On, Pleasantville, Don's Plum, Fear and Loathing in Las Vegas.
TELEVISION: Movie: Spoils of War, A Child's Cry for Help. Series: Great Scott!. Guest: Roseanne, Walker Texas Ranger.

MAHARIS, GEORGE
Actor. b. Astoria, NY, Sept. 1, 1928. Studied at The Actors Studio.
PICTURES: Exodus (debut, 1960), Quick Before It Melts, Sylvia, The Satan Bug, A Covenant With Death, The Happening, The Desperadoes, Last Day of the War, The Land Raiders, The Sword and the Sorcerer, Doppelganger.
TELEVISION: Series: Search for Tomorrow, Route 66, Most Deadly Game. Guest: Naked City. Movies: Escape to Mindanao, The Monk, The Victim, Murder on Flight 502, Look What's Happened to Rosemary's Baby, SST—Death Flight, Return to Fantasy Island, Crash, A Small Rebellion. Mini-Series: Rich Man Poor Man. Special: A Death of Princes.

MAHONEY, JOHN
Actor. b. Manchester, England, June 20, 1940. Mem. of Stratford Children's Theatre from age 10\-13. Moved to U.S. at 19, taught Eng. at Western Illinois U. Then freelance ed. of medical manuscripts; assoc. ed., Quality Review Bulletin. At 35 quit medical book editing to become an actor. Studied acting, Chicago's St. Nicholas Theatre. Prof. debut, The Water Engine, 1977. Joined Steppenwolf Theatre Co., 1979. (The Hothouse, Taking Steps, Death of a Salesman). Chicago Film Crits. Special "Commitment to Chicago" Award, 1997.
THEATER: Orphans (Theatre World Award), The House of Blue Leaves (Tony & Clarence Derwent Awards), The Subject Was Roses.
PICTURES: Mission Hill, Code of Silence, The Manhattan Project, Streets of Gold, Tin Men, Suspect, Moonstruck, Frantic, Betrayed, Eight Men Out, Say Anything, Love Hurts, The Russia House, Barton Fink, Article 99, In the Line of Fire, Striking Distance, Reality Bites, The Hudsucker Proxy, The American President, Primal Fear, She's the One, Antz (voice), The Iron Giant (voice).
TELEVISION: Series: Lady Blue, H.E.L.P., The Human Factor, Frasier. Movies: The Killing Floor, Chicago Story, First Steps, Listen to Your Heart, Dance of the Phoenix, First Steps, Trapped in Silence, Favorite Son, The Image, Dinner at Eight, The 10 Million Dollar Getaway, The Secret Passion of Robert Clayton, Unnatural Pursuits. Special: The House of Blue Leaves.

MAJORS, LEE
Actor. r.n. Lee Yeary. b. Wyandotte, MI, April 23, 1939. Star athlete in high school; turned down offer from St. Louis Cardinals in final year at Eastern Kentucky State Coll. to pursue acting career. In L.A. got job as playground supervisor for park dept. while studying acting at MGM Studio. Debuted in films 1964 under his real name.
PICTURES: Strait-Jacket (debut, 1964), Will Penny, The Liberation of L. B. Jones, The Norsemen, Killer Fish, Steel, Agency, The Last Chase, Scrooged, Keaton's Cop, Trojan War.
TELEVISION: Series: The Big Valley, The Men From Shiloh, Owen Marshall-Counselor at Law, The Six Million Dollar Man, The Fall Guy, Tour of Duty, Raven. Pilot: Road Show (also exec. prod.). Movies: The Ballad of Andy Crocker, Weekend of Terror, The Gary Francis Powers Story, The Cowboy and the Ballerina, A Rocky Mountain Christmas, The Return of the Six Million Dollar Man and the Bionic Woman, Danger Down Under (exec. prod., actor), The Bionic Showdown: the Six Million Dollar Man and the Bionic Woman, Fire!, Trapped on the 37th Floor, The Cover Girl Murders, Bionic Ever After?, Lost Treasures of Dos Santos.

MAKEPEACE, CHRIS
Actor. b. Montreal, Canada, April 22, 1964. e. Jarvis Collegiate Institute. Trained for stage at Second City Workshop.
PICTURES: Meatballs (debut, 1979), My Bodyguard, The Last Chase, The Oasis, The Falcon and the Snowman, Vamp, Captive Hearts, Aloha Summer.

TELEVISION: Movies: The Terry Fox Story, The Mysterious Stranger, Mazes and Monsters, The Undergrads. Series: Going Great (host, 1982-84), Why On Earth?

MAKO
Actor. r.n. Makoto Iwamatsu. b. Kobe, Japan, Dec. 10, 1933. e. Pratt Inst.
THEATER: NY: Pacific Overtures (Tony nom.), Shimada. Regional: Rashomon.
PICTURES: The Ugly Dachshund, The Sand Pebbles (Acad. Award nom.), The Private Navy of Sgt. O'Farrell, The Great Bank Robbery, The Hawaiians, The Island at the Top of the World, Prisoners, The Killer Elite, The Big Brawl, The Bushido Blade, Under the Rainbow, An Eye for an Eye, Conan the Barbarian, The House Where Evil Dwells, Testament, Conan the Destroyer, Armed Response, P.O.W. The Escape, Silent Assassins, The Wash, Tucker: The Man and His Dream, An Unremarkable Life, Taking Care of Business, Pacific Heights, The Perfect Weapon, Sidekicks, Robocop 3, Rising Sun, Cultivating Charlie, A Dangerous Place, Highlander III: The Sorcerer.
TELEVISION: Series: Hawaiian Heat. Movies: The Challenge, If Tomorrow Comes, The Streets of San Francisco (pilot), Judge Dee and the Monastery Murders, Farewell to Manzanar, When Hell Was in Session, The Last Ninja, Girls of the White Orchid. Guest: McHale's Navy, Ensign O'Toole, 77 Sunset Strip, I Spy, F Troop, Hawaii Five-O.

MALDEN, KARL
Actor. r.n. Mladen Sekulovich. b. Gary, IN, March 22, 1914. e. Art Inst. of Chicago 1933-36; Goodman Theatre Sch. Elected pres., Acad. of Motion Picture Arts & Sciences, 1989.
THEATER: B'way: Golden Boy, Key Largo, Flight to West, Missouri Legend, Uncle Harry, Counterattack, Truckline Cafe, All My Sons, Streetcar Named Desire, Desperate Hours, Desire Under the Elms, The Egghead.
PICTURES: They Knew What They Wanted (debut, 1940), Winged Victory, 13 Rue Madeleine, Boomerang!, Kiss of Death, The Gunfighter, Where the Sidewalk Ends, Halls of Montezuma, A Streetcar Named Desire (Acad. Award, best supporting actor, 1951), The Sellout, Diplomatic Courier, Operation Secret, Ruby Gentry, I Confess, Take the High Ground, Phantom of the Rue Morgue, On the Waterfront (Acad. Award nom.), Baby Doll, Bombers B-52, Time Limit (dir. only), Fear Strikes Out, The Hanging Tree, One Eyed Jacks, Pollyanna, The Great Impostor, Parrish, All Fall Down, Birdman of Alcatraz, Gypsy, How the West Was Won, Come Fly With Me, Cheyenne Autumn, Dead Ringer, The Cincinnati Kid, Nevada Smith, Murderer's Row, Hotel, Blue, The Adventures of Bullwhip Griffin, Billion Dollar Brain, Hot Millions, Patton, Cat O'Nine Tails, Wild Rovers, Summertime Killer, Beyond the Poseidon Adventure, Meteor, The Sting II, Twilight Time, Billy Galvin, Nuts.
TELEVISION: Series: Streets of San Francisco, Skag. Movies: Captains Courageous, Word of Honor, With Intent to Kill, Alice in Wonderland, Fatal Vision (Emmy Award, 1985), My Father My Son, The Hijacking of the Achille Lauro, Call Me Anna, Absolute Strangers, Back to the Streets of San Francisco.

MALICK, TERRENCE
Wrtier, Director. b. Bartlesville, OK, November 30, 1943.
PICTURES: Writer: Deadhead Miles, Pocket Money, The Gravy Train. Writer, Director: Days of Heaven, Badlands (also prod.), The Thin Red Line, The Moviegoer. Producer: Endurance.
TELEVISION: Actor: Golden Fiddles, The Beast.

MALIN, AMIR JACOB
Executive. b. Tel-Aviv, Israel, March 22, 1954. e. Brandeis U., 1972-76; Boston U. Sch. of Law, 1976-79. Staff atty., WGBH-TV, Boston, 1979-81; pres. and co-CEO, Cinecom Entertainment Group Inc., 1982-92. Films acquired and distributed include Come Back to the Five and Dime Jimmy Dean Jimmy Dean, Metropolis, The Brother from Another Planet, Stop Making Sense, Coca-Cola Kid, A Room with a View, Swimming to Cambodia, Matewan, A Man in Love, Maurice, Miles From Home. Partner, October Films, Inc. Films acquired and distrib.: Life Is Sweet, Adam's Rib, The Living End, Tous les Matins du Monde (All the Mornings of the World), Ruby in Paradise, A Heart in Winter, Bad Behavior, Kika, Cronos, The Cement Garden, The Last Seduction, Search & Destroy, The Funeral, Breaking the Waves, Girlstown.
PICTURES: Exec. prod.: Swimming to Cambodia, Matewan, Miles From Home, Scenes from the Class Struggle in Beverly Hills, The Handmaid's Tale, Tune in Tomorrow.

MALKOVICH, JOHN
Actor, Producer, Director. b. Christopher, IL, Dec. 9, 1953. e. Illinois State U. Founding member Steppenwolf Ensemble in Chicago with group of college friends, 1976. Starred in Say Goodnight Gracie and True West (Obie Award) which then was brought to New York. NY Stage work includes Death of Salesman, Burn This, States of Shock. Dir.: Balm in Gilead, Arms and the Man, The Caretaker, Libra (also writer).

PICTURES: Places in the Heart (Acad. Award nom.), The Killing Fields, Eleni, Making Mr. Right, The Glass Menagerie, Empire of the Sun, Miles From Home, Dangerous Liaisons, The Accidental Tourist (co-exec. prod. only), The Sheltering Sky, Queens Logic, The Object of Beauty, Shadows and Fog, Of Mice and Men, Jennifer Eight, Alive, In the Line of Fire (Acad. Award nom.), The Convent, Beyond the Clouds, Mary Reilly, Mulholland Falls, Portrait of a Lady, Con Air.
TELEVISION: *Special*: Rocket to the Moon. *Movies*: Word of Honor, American Dream, Death of a Salesman (Emmy Award, 1986), Heart of Darkness.

MALLE, LOUIS
Director, Producer, Writer. b. Thumeries, France, Oct. 30, 1932. m. actress Candice Bergen. e. Sorbonne (Pol. Science). Studied filmmaking at Institut des Hautes Etudes Cinema-tographiques 1951-53. Started in film industry as assistant to Robert Bresson and cameraman to oceanographer Jacques Cousteau, 1954-55 then corres. for French TV in Algeria, Vietnam and Thailand 1962-64. Became internationally known with Les Amants (The Lovers) in 1958. Has also acted in films (A Very Private Affair, A Very Curious Girl, Milky Way, La Vie de Boheme).
PICTURES: Silent World (co-dir., photog. with J. Y. Cousteau), A Conedmned Man Escapes (prod. asst. to Bresson), Mon Oncle (photog. only). *Director*: Elevator to the Gallows (also s.p.), The Lovers (also s.p.), Calcutta (doc.; also s.p., photog., actor), Zazie in the Metro (also s.p.), A Very Private Affair (also s.p., actor), Vive Le Tour (doc.; also s.p., photog., actor), The Fire Within (also s.p.), Viva Maria (also prod., s.p.), The Thief of Paris (also prod., s.p.), Spirits of the Dead (co-dir.), Phantom India (doc.; also photog.), Murmur of the Heart (also s.p.; Acad. Award nom. for best s.p.), Humain Trop Humain (doc.; also prod., photog.), Place de la Republique (doc.; also prod., photog.), Lacombe Lucien (also prod., s.p.), Black Moon (also s.p.), Pretty Baby (also prod., story), Atlantic City (Acad. Award nom.), My Dinner With Andre, Crackers, Alamo Bay (also prod.), Au Revoir Les Enfants (Goodbye Children; also s.p., prod.), Golden Lion Award, Venice Film Fest., 1987), May Fools (Milou en Mai; also co-s.p.), Damage (also prod.), Vanya on 42nd Street.
TELEVISION: *Documentaries*: God's Country, And the Pursuit of Happiness.
(d. November 23, 1995)

MALMUTH, BRUCE
Director, Actor. b. Brooklyn, NY, Feb. 4, 1937. e. City Coll. of New York, Brooklyn Coll. Grad. studies in film, Columbia U. and U. of Southern California. Acted in and dir. college productions. Moved to California and obtained job as page at NBC. In Army assigned to special services as dir.; reassigned to New York. Upon release began 10-year Clio-winning career as dir. of TV commercials. Debut as dir. of features with Nighthawks, 1981. Founder, Los Angeles Aspiring Actors and Directors Workshop. Theatre incl.: Two Guys Second Wind (writer, dir., prod.), Thanksgiving Cries (writer, dir.).
PICTURES: *Director*: Nighthawks, The Man Who Wasn't There, Where Are the Children? (also actor), Hard to Kill, Pentathalon (also actor). *Actor*: The Karate Kid (also Part II), For Keeps?, Happy New Year, Lean on Me.
TELEVISION: Baseballs or Switchblades? (prod., writer, dir., Emmy Award), A Boy's Dream, Twilight Zone, Beauty and the Beast, Heartbreak Winner.

MALONE, DOROTHY
Actress. b. Chicago, IL, Jan. 30, 1925. e. Southern Methodist U., USC, AADA. Started as RKO starlet, 1943. Stage work incl. Little Me, Practice to Deceive.
PICTURES: The Big Sleep, Night and Day, One Sunday Afternoon, Two Guys From Texas, The Nevadan, The Bushwackers, Jack Slade, The Killer That Stalked New York, Scared Stiff, Torpedo Alley, The Lone Gun, Pushover, Security Risk, Private Hell 36, The Fast and the Furious, Young at Heart, Battle Cry, Sincerely Yours, Artists and Models, At Gunpoint, Five Guns West, Tall Man Riding, Pillars of the Sky, Tension at Table Rock, Written on the Wind (Acad. Award, best supporting actress, 1956), Man of a Thousand Faces, Quantez, The Tarnished Angels, Tip on a Dead Jockey, Too Much Toon Soon, Warlock, The Last Voyage, The Last Sunset, Beach Party, Fate is the Hunter (unbilled), Abduction, Golden Rendezvous, Good Luck Miss Wyckoff, Winter Kills, The Day Time Ended, The Being, Basic Instinct, Beverly Hills.
TELEVISION: *Series*: Peyton Place. *Guest*: Dick Powell Theatre, Loretta Young Show (twice hosted), Philip Morris Playhouse, Dr. Kildare, Bob Hope Show, Jack Benny Show, The Untouchables, Phyllis Diller Show, Ken Murray's Blackouts, Death Valley Days. *Movies*: The Pigeon, Little Ladies of the Night, Murder in Peyton Place, Katie: Portrait of a Centerfold, Condominium, Peyton Place: The Next Generation. *Mini-Series*: Rich Man Poor Man. *Specials*: Gertrude Stein Story, The Family That Prays Together.

MALONE, JOHN C.
Executive. b. Milford, CT, Mar. 7, 1941. e. Yale U. Pres. & CEO of Telecommunications Inc., 1973-present. With National Cable Television Association as: dir., 1974-77; treasurer, 1977-78; dir., 1980-94. Dir. of TCI; on bd. of dirs. for Turner Bordacasting, Cable Television Laboratories Inc. BET, Discovery.

MAMET, DAVID
Writer, Director. b. Chicago, IL, Nov. 30, 1947. e. Goddard Coll. Artist-in-residence, Goddard Coll. 1971-73. Artistic dir. St. Nicholas Theatre Co., Chicago, 1973-75. Co-founder Dinglefest Theatre; assoc. artistic dir., Goodman Theatre, Chicago. Appeared as actor in film Black Widow. Novel: The Village (1994).
THEATER: Lakefront, The Woods, American Buffalo, Sexual Perversity in Chicago, Duck Variations, Edmond, A Life in the Theatre, The Water Engine, Prairie du Chien, Glengarry Glen Ross (Pulitzer Prize, Tony Award, 1984), Speed-the-Plow, Sketches of War (benefit for homeless Vietnam Veterans), Oleanna, An Interview (Death Defying Acts), The Cryptogram.
PICTURES: *Writer*. The Postman Always Rings Twice, The Verdict, The Untouchables, House of Games (also dir.), Things Change (also dir.), We're No Angels, Homicide (also dir.), Hoffa, Vanya on 42nd Street (adaptation), Oleanna (also dir.), The Spanish Prisoner (dir.).
TELEVISION: Lip Service (exec. prod.), Hill Street Blues, A Life in the Theatre, Texan.

MANASSE, GEORGE
Producer. b. Florence, Italy, Jan. 1, 1938. e. U. of North Carolina.
PICTURES: *Prod.*: Who Killed Mary What's 'er Name?, Squirm, Blue Sunshine, He Knows You're Alone. Prod. Mgr.: Greetings, Joe, Fury on Wheels, Slow Dancing in the Big City, Tribute, Porky's II: The Next Day, Neighbors, Death Wish III, Torch Song Trilogy, Indecent Proposal, Coneheads, Lassie, Die Hard With a Vengeance, Eraser.
TELEVISION: *Line Prod.*: *Series*: American Playwright's Theatre (Arts & Ent.) The Saint in Manhattan (pilot), *Movie*: The Killing Floor, Vengeance: The Story of Tony Cimo. *Prod. Mgr.*: *Series*: St. Elsewhere, Annie McGuire. *Movies*: Sanctuary of Fear, Mr. Griffith and Me, Peking Encounter, When the Circus Came to Town, Murder, Inc. Muggable Mary, Running Out, Dropout Father, He's Hired, She's Fired, Intimate Strangers, Drop Out Mother, Vengeance: The Story of Tony Cimo, The Saint in Manhattan, The Diamond Trap, The Prize Pulitzer (also suprv. prod.), Orpheus Descending (also suprv. prod.), John and Yoko, Marilyn and Me, The Woman Who Sinned.

MANCIA, ADRIENNE
Curator, Dept. of Film, Museum of Modern Art. b. New York, NY. e. U. of Wisconsin. B.A.; Columbia U., M.A. Worked in film distribution industry in New York prior to joining Dept. of Film & Video, Museum of Modern Art, 1964; responsible for film exhibition since 1965. 1977, appointed curator. Restructured Museums' Auditorium Exhibition Prog., creating a balance between classic cinema and contemporary work. Initiated innovative programs such as Cineprobe and New Documentaries (formerly What's Happening?) Served on numerous int'l film juries. Co-founder New Directors/New Films. Chevalier de l'Ordre des Arts et des Lettres (France, 1985). Ufficiale dell Ordine al Merito della Repubblica Italiana, 1988.

MANCUSO, FRANK G.
Executive. b. Buffalo, NY, July 25, 1933. e. State U. of New York. Film buyer and operations supvr. for Basil Enterprises, theatre circuit, 1958-62. Joined Paramount as booker in Buffalo branch, 1962. Named sls. regr. for branch in 1964 and branch mgr. in 1967. 1970 appt. v.p./gen. sls. mgr., Paramount Pictures Canada, Ltd., becoming pres. in 1972. 1976 relocated with Paramount in U.S. as western div. mgr. in LA. 1977, appt. gen. sls. mgr. of NY, office; two months later promoted to v.p. domestic distribution; 1979, named exec. v.p., distrib. & mktg. 1983 made pres. of entire Paramount Motion Picture Group. 1984, appointed chmn. and CEO, Paramount Pictures; resigned 1991. Named Motion Picture Pioneers Man of the Year, 1987. Member of Board: AMPAS, M.P. Assoc. of America, Will Rogers Memorial Fund, Variety Clubs Intl., Sundance Institute, Amer. Film Institute, Museum of Broadcasting, Motion Picture Pioneers. Appointed Chmn. & CEO of MGM, 1993.

MANCUSO, JR., FRANK
Producer. b. Buffalo, NY, Oct. 9, 1958. Son of Frank G. Mancuso. e. Upsala Coll. Began with industry at age 14, booking short subjects in Canadian theatres. Worked in gross receipts dept. in Paramount corporate offices in New York and later with paralegal div. Initial prod. work as location asst. for Urban Cowboy in Houston, TX. Served as assoc. prod. of Friday the 13th Part II and prod. of Friday the 13th Part III in 3-D.
PICTURES: Off the Wall, The Man Who Wasn't There, April Fool's Day, Friday the 13th, Part IV: The Final Chapter; Friday the 13th—A New Beginning (exec. prod.), Friday the 13th, Part VII (exec. prod.); Back to the Beach; Permanent Record, Internal Affairs, He Said/She Said, Species, Fled, Hoodlum, Toby's Story, Species II, Ronin.
TELEVISION: Friday the 13th: The Series (exec. prod.), The Escape.

MANDEL, BABALOO
Writer. r.n. Marc Mandel. b. 1949. Started as comedy writer for Joan Rivers, among others. First teamed with Lowell Ganz on script for 1982 film Night Shift.
PICTURES: Night Shift, Splash (Acad. Award nom.; also actor), Spies Like Us, Gung Ho, Vibes, Parenthood, City Slickers, A League of Their Own, Mr. Saturday Night (also cameo), Greedy, City Slickers II: The Legend of Curly's Gold, Forget Paris, Multiplicity, Father's Day, The Secret LIfe of Walter Mitty, EdTV.
TELEVISION: Series co-writer: Laverne and Shirley, Busting Loose, Take Five (also co-creator). Series co-exec. prod.: Gung Ho, Knight and Daye, Parenthood.

MANDEL, LORING
Writer. b. Chicago, IL, May 5, 1928. e. U. of Wisconsin, B.S. 1949. Long career writing scripts for TV, dating back to 1955 when penned Shakedown Cruise. Governor, Natl. Acad. of TV Arts & Sciences 1964-68; Pres. Writers Guild of America East 1975-77; Natl. Chmn. 1977-79.
PICTURES: Countdown, Promises in the Dark, The Little Drummer Girl.
TELEVISION: Do Not Go Gentle Into That Good Night (Emmy, 1967), Breaking Up, Project Immortality (Sylvania Award, 1959), A House His Own, Trial of Chaplain Jensen, The Raider, etc.

MANDEL, ROBERT
Director. e. Columbia Univ.
PICTURES: Night at O'Rears (also prod.), Independence Day, F/X, Touch and Go, Big Shots, School Ties, The Substitute.
TELEVISION: Hard Time on Planet Earth.

MANDELL, ABE
Executive. b. Oct. 4, 1922. e. U. of Cincinnati. Entered broadcasting as actor on Cincinnati radio station prior to W.W.II. Served U.S. Army in Southwest Pacific, 1942-45. Formed indep. motion picture distribution co. in the Far East. Company, which became the largest indep. motion picture dist. in the Far East, also operated and owned motion picture theaters throughout the Phillipines and Indonesia, 1946-56; network-regional sales exec., Ziv Television, 1956-58; dir. foreign operations, Independent Television Corporation, 1958; v.p.-foreign oper., 1960; v.p.-sales and adm., 1961; exec. v.p., 1962; pres. 1965. 1976 corporate name changed from Independent Television Corp. to ITC Entertainment, Inc. President to 1983 of ITC Entertainment; with Robert Mandell heads New Frontier Prods.

MANDOKI, LUIS
Director. b. Mexico City, Mexico. e. San Francisco Art Institute, London Intl. Film School, London College's School of Film. Dir. short film Silent Music which won Intl. Amateur Film Fest. Award at 1976 Cannes Film Fest. Back in Mexico dir. shorts and documentaries for the Instituto Nacional Indignista Concaine, Centro de Produccionde Cortometraje. Won Ariel
PICTURES: Motel (debut, 1982), Gaby--A True Story, White Palace, Born Yesterday, When a Man Loves a Woman.

MANES, FRITZ
Producer. b. Oakland, CA, April 22, 1936. e. U.C., Berkeley, B.A. UCLA, 1956. Armed Service: 1951-54. U.S. Marines, Korea, Purple Heart. TV ad. exec. and stuntman before becoming exec. prod. on films for Clint Eastwood. Has formed own production co., Sundancer Prods. Membership, DGA, SAG.
PICTURES: In various capacities: The Outlaw Josey Wales, The Enforcer. Assoc. prod.: The Gauntlet, Every Which Way But Loose, Escape From Alcatraz, Bronco Billy. Prod.: Any Which Way You Can (Acad. of Country Music Tex Ritter award), Firefox (exec. prod.), Honky Tonk Man (exec. prod.), Tightrope (prod.), Sudden Impact (exec. prod.), City Heat (prod.), Pale Rider (exec. prod.), Ratboy (exec. prod.), Heartbreak Ridge (exec. prod., prod. mgr.), James Dean.

MANHEIM, CAMRYN
Actress. b. 1961.
PICTURES: The Bonfire of the Vanities, The Road to Wellville, David Searching, Jeffrey, Eraser, Romy and Michele's High School Reunion, Happiness, Wide Awake, Pleasant View Avenue.
TELEVISION: Movies: Deadley Whispers. Series: The Practice (Emmy Award, 1998).

MANKIEWICZ, DON M.
Writer. b. Berlin, Germany, Jan. 20, 1922. p. Herman J. Mankiewicz. e. Columbia, B.A., 1942; Columbia Law Sch. Served in U.S. Army, 1942-46; reporter, New Yorker magazine, 1946-48; author of novels See How They Run, Trial, It Only Hurts a Minute; magazine articles, short stories. President, Producers Guild of America, 1987; on Board of Directors, Writers Guild of America, 1992.
PICTURES: Trial, I Want to Live, (Acad. Award nom.), The Chapman Report, The Black Bird.
TELEVISION: Studio One, On Trial, One Step Beyond, Playhouse 90, Profiles in Courage. Exec. story consultant: Hart to Hart, Simon & Simon, Crazy Like a Fox, Adderly. Pilots: Ironside, Marcus Welby M.D., Sarge, Lanigan's Rabbi (collab.), Rosetti and Ryan (collab.).

MANKIEWICZ, TOM
Writer, Director. b. Los Angeles, CA, June 1, 1942. e. Yale U.
PICTURES: Writer: The Sweet Ride (debut), Diamonds Are Forever, Live and Let Die, The Man with the Golden Gun, Mother Jugs and Speed (also prod.), The Cassandra Crossing, The Eagle Has Landed, Ladyhawke. Exec. Prod.: Hot Pursuit. Creative consultant: Superman, Superman II. Director: Dragnet (also s.p.), Delirious.
TELEVISION: Pilot: Hart to Hart (writer, dir.). Movie: Taking the Heat (dir.), `Till Death Do Us Hart. Episode: Tales of the Crypt (dir.)

MANKOWITZ, WOLF
Writer, Producer. b. London, Nov. 7, 1924. Was journalist before ent. m.p. industry in 1952.
THEATRE: Expresso Bongo (from his story), Make Me An Offer, Belle, Pickwick, Passion Flower Hotel, Casanova's Last Stand, etc.
PICTURES: Make Me an Offer, A Kid for Two Farthings, The Bespoke Overcoat, Expresso Bongo, The Millionairess, The Long and the Short and the Tall, The Day the Earth Caught Fire, Waltz of the Toreadors, Where the Spies Are, Casino Royale (co-writer), The Assassination Bureau, Bloomfield, Black Beauty, Treasure Island, The Hebrew Lesson, The Hireling, Almonds and Raisins.
TELEVISION: The Killing Stones, A Cure for Tin Ear, The Battersea Miracle, Series: Conflict, Dickens of London.
(d. May 20, 1998)

MANN, ABBY
Writer. b. Philadelphia, PA, 1927. e. NYU. First gained fame on TV writing for Robert Montgomery Theatre, Playhouse 90, Studio One, Alcoa, Goodyear Theatre. Acad. Award for film adaptation of own teleplay Judgment at Nuremberg into theatrical film.
PICTURES: Judgment at Nuremberg, A Child Is Waiting, The Condemned of Altona, Ship of Fools (Acad. Award nom.), The Detective, Report to the Commissioner.
TELEVISION: Series: Kojak (creator), Skag, Medical Story. Movies: The Marcus-Nelson Murders (Emmy Award, 1973; also exec. prod.), Medical Story (also exec. prod.), The Atlanta Child Murders, King (Emmy nom.), Murderers Among Us: The Simon Wiesenthal Story (Emmy Award, 1989; co-writer, co-exec. prod.), Teamster Boss: The Jackie Presser Story (also co-exec. prod.), Indictment: The McMartin Trial (also co-exec. prod.; Emmy Award, 1995, Golden Globe Award).

MANN, DELBERT
Director, Producer. b. Lawrence, KS, Jan. 30, 1920. e. Vanderbilt U., Yale U. U.S. Air Force, 1942-45. Stage mgr., summer stock, dir. Columbia, S.C. Town Theatre, 1947-49. Asst. dir., NBC-TV, 1949; dir., NBC-TV, 1949-55. Past pres., Directors Guild of America.
THEATER: A Quiet Place, Speaking of Murder, Zelda, The Glass Menagerie, The Memoirs of Abraham Lincoln; opera: Wuthering Heights (NY City Center).
PICTURES: Marty (Acad. Award, 1955), The Bachelor Party, Desire Under the Elms, Separate Tables, Middle of the Night, The Dark at the Top of the Stairs, The Outsider, Lover Come Back, That Touch of Mink, A Gathering of Eagles, Dear Heart, Quick Before It Melts (also prod.), Mister Buddwing (also prod.), Fitzwilly, The Pink Jungle, Kidnapped, Birch Interval, Night Crossing.
TELEVISION: Philco-Goodyear TV Playhouse, Producer's Showcase, Omnibus, Playwrights '56, Playhouse 90, Ford Star Jubilee, Lights Out, Mary Kay and Johnny, The Little Show, Masterpiece Theatre, Ford Startime. Movies/Specials: Heidi, David Copperfield, No Place to Run, She Waits (also prod.), Jane Eyre, The Man Without a Country, A Girl Named Sooner, Francis Gary Powers: The True Story of the U-2 Spy Incident, Tell Me My Name, Breaking Up, Home to Stay, Love's Dark Ride, Thou Shalt Not Commit Adultery, All Quiet on the Western Front, Torn Between Two Lovers, To Find My Son, All the Way Home, The Member of the Wedding, The Gift of Love, Bronte, Love Leads the Way, A Death in California, The Last Days of Patton, The Ted Kennedy, Jr. Story, April Morning (also co-prod.), Ironclads, Against Her Will: An Incident in Baltimore (also prod.), Incident in a Small Town (also prod.), Lily in Winter.

MANN, MICHAEL
Director, Writer, Producer. b. Chicago, IL, Feb. 5, 1943. e. U. of Wisconsin, London Film Sch. Directed shorts, commercials and documentaries in England. Returned to U.S. in 1972. Wrote for prime-time TV (episodes of Starsky and Hutch, Police Story, created Vegas).
PICTURES: Exec. Prod.: Band of the Hand. Director-Writer: Thief (also exec. prod.), The Keep, Manhunter, The Last of the Mohicans (also co-prod.), Heat (also s.p.).
TELEVISION: The Jericho Mile (writer, dir.; DGA Award for dir., Emmy Award for writing, 1980), Miami Vice (exec. prod.), Crime Story (exec. prod.), L.A. Takedown (dir., writer, exec. prod.). Mini-Series: Drug Wars: The Camarena Story (exec. prod.; Emmy Award, 1990), Drug Wars: The Cocaine Cartel (exec. prod.).

MANNE, S. ANTHONY
Executive. b. New York, NY, July 19, 1940. e. Wharton School, Univ. of Pennsylvania, B.S. economics. Joined Columbia Pictures, 1963; intl. dept., 1964; asst. mgr., Brazil, 1968; mgr., Brazil, 1969-72. Joined JAD Films, 1976. V.p United Artists, Latin American supervisor, 1980. V.p. Columbia Pictures Intl., continental mgr., 1981; sr. v.p., sales manager, 1984; exec. v.p., Tri-Star Intl, 1987; exec. v.p., Columbia Tri-Star Film Dist. Intl., 1988-.

MANNING, MICHELLE
Executive. Began production career at Zoetrope Studios as prod. supervisor, then VP Production, Orion Pictures. Sr. VP Production, Viacom, Inc., 1991; promoted to Exec. VP, 1993. Pres. production, Paramount Motion Pictures, 1997.
PICTURES: Blue City (dir.), Another 48 Hours (musical dir.).
TELEVISION: Miami Vice (dir.), Friday the 13th (dir.).

MANOFF, DINAH
Actress. b. New York, NY, Jan. 25, 1958. e. CalArts. Daughter of actress-dir. Lee Grant and late writer Arnold Manoff. Prof. debut in PBS prod., The Great Cherub Knitwear Strike. Guest starred on Welcome Back Kotter.
THEATER: I Ought to Be in Pictures (Tony & Theatre World Awards, 1980), Gifted Children, Leader of the Pack, Alfred and Victoria: A Life (L.A. Theatre Center), Kingdom of Earth (TheatreWest).
PICTURES: Grease (debut, 1978), Ordinary People, I Ought to Be in Pictures, Child's Play, Staying Together, Bloodhounds of Broadway, Welcome Home Roxy Carmichael.
TELEVISION: Series: Soap, Empty Nest. Movies: Raid on Entebbe, Night Terror, The Possessed, For Ladies Only, A Matter of Sex, The Seduction of Gina, Flight No. 90: Disaster on the Potomac, Classified Love, Crossing the Mob, Backfire, Babies, Maid for Each Other (also co-exec. prod., co-story). Mini-Series: Celebrity.

MANSON, ARTHUR
Executive. b. Brooklyn, NY, Feb. 21, 1928. e. City Coll. of New York, grad. Inst. Film Technique, 1945. Editor, American Traveler, U.S. Army, 1946. Advance agent, co. mgr., Henry V, U.S., 1948-50; producer's publ. rep., Stanley Kramer Distributing Corp., Samuel Goldwyn Productions, 1951-52, dir. of adv. and publ., MGM Pictures of Canada, Ltd., 1952-53; publ. and adv. rep., Cinerama widescreen process, 1953-58; dir. worldwide ad-pub Cinerama 1958-60; adv. mgr., Columbia Pictures, 1961-62; nat'l dir. of adv., publ., Dino De Laurentiis, 1962-64; exec. asst. to v.p. adv. & pub., 20th Century-Fox, 1964-67; v.p., adv. & pub. Cinerama, Inc., and Cinerama Releasing Corp.; 1967-74; exec. v.p., sales & marketing, BCP, service of Cox Broadcasting Corp., 1974-75; v.p. worldwide marketing Warner Bros., 1976. 1977 formed own company, Cinemax Mkt. & Dist. Corp. and is pres. Chmn., NY events committee, AMPAS.

MANTEGNA, JOE
Actor. b. Chicago, IL, Nov. 13, 1947. e. Morton Jr. Coll., Goodman Sch. of Drama, 1967-69. Member: The Organic Theatre Company, Chicago (The Wonderful Ice Cream Suit, Cops, and 2 European tours with ensemble). Later member of Goodman Theater where he began long creative assoc. with playwright-dir. David Mamet (A Life in the Theatre, The Disappearance of the Jews). In national co. of Hair, Godspell, Lenny. B'way debut: Working. Narrated documentaries Crack U.S.A. and Death on the Job.
THEATER: Bleacher Bums (also conceived and co-author), Leonardo (L.A., co-author), Glengarry Glen Ross (Tony Award), Speed-the-Plow.
PICTURES: Who Stole My Wheels? (Towing), Second Thoughts, Compromising Positions, The Money Pit, Off Beat, Three Amigos, Critical Condition, House of Games, Weeds, Suspect, Things Change (Venice Film Fest. Award, 1988), Wait Until Spring Bandini, Alice, The Godfather Part III, Queens Logic, Homicide, Bugsy, Body of Evidence, Family Prayers, Searching for Bobby Fisher, Baby's Day Out, Airheads, For Better or Worse, Forget Paris, Up Close and Personal, Eye for an Eye, Thinner, Albino Alligator, Personal Unknowns, For Hire, Underworld, The Wonderful Ice Cream Suit, Jerry & Tom, Conundrum, Celebrity, Body And Soul/
TELEVISION: Series: Comedy Zone. Guest: Soap, Bosom Buddies, Archie Bunker's Place, Magnum P.I., Open All Night, Fallen Angels (The Quiet Room). Special: Bleacher Bums (Emmy Award). Movies: Elvis, Comrades of Summer, The Water Engine, State of Emergency, Above Suspicion, A Call to Remember, Face Down, Merry Christmas George Bailey, The Rat Pack. Mini-series: The Last Don, The Last Don II.

MANULIS, MARTIN
Producer, Director. b. New York, NY, May 30, 1915. e. Columbia Col., B.A. 1935. Lt. USN, 1941-45. Head of prod. John C. Wilson, 1941-49; mgr. dir., Westport Country Playhouse, 1945-50; dir. B'way plays; staff prod. & dir. CBS-TV, 1951-58; head prod. 20th-Fox Television. Now pres., Martin Manulis Prods. Ltd. 1987, artistic dir., Ahmanson Theatre, L.A.

THEATER: B'way/and on tour: Private Lives, Made in Heaven, The Philadelphia Story, Pride's Crossing, Laura, The Men We Marry, The Hasty Heart, The Show Off.
PICTURES: Producer: Days of Wine and Roses, Dear Heart, Luv, Duffy, The Out-of-Towners.
TELEVISION: Suspense, Studio One, Climax, Best of Broadway, Playhouse 90. Mini-Series: Chiefs, Space, The Day Christ Died, Grass Roots.

MARA, ADELE
Actress. r.n. Adelaida Delgado; b. Dearborn, MI, April 28, 1923. m. writer-prod. Roy Huggins. Singer, dancer with Xavier Cugat orchestra.
PICTURES: Navy Blues (feature debut, 1941), Shut My Big Mouth, Blondie Goes to College, Alias Boston Blackie, You Were Never Lovelier, Lucky Legs, Vengeance of the West, Reveille With Beverly, Riders of the Northwest Mounted, The Magnificent Rogue, Passkey to Danger, Traffic in Crime, Exposed, The Trespasser, Blackmail, Campus Honeymoon, Twilight on the Rio Grande, Robin Hood of Texas, Nighttime in Nevada, The Gallant Legion, Sands of Iwo Jima, Wake of the Red Witch, Rock Island Trail, California Passage, The Avengers, The Sea Hornet, Count The Hours, The Black Whip, Back from Eternity, Curse of the Faceless Man, The Big Circus.
TELEVISION: Series: Cool Million. Mini-Series: Wheels.

MARAIS, JEAN
Actor. b. Cherbourg, France, Dec. 11, 1913. e. Coll. St. Germain, Lycee Janson de Sailly, Lycee Condorcet. Painter; photog; stage actor; French Air Army; m.p. debut in Pavillon Brule.
PICTURES: Carmen, Eternal Return, Beauty and the Beast, Ruy Blas, Les Parents Terribles, Secret of Mayerling, Souvenir, Orpheus, Eagle with Two Heads, Inside a Girl's Dormitory, Royal Affairs in Versailles, Paris Does Strange Things, Le Capitan, Le Bossu, La Princesse de Cleves, Le Capitaine Fracasse, Honorable Stanilleu, Agent Secret, Patute, Fantomas, Le Gentleman de Cocody, Stealing Beauty.

MARBUT, ROBERT GORDON
Broadcast Executive. b. Athens, GA, April 11, 1935. Bachelor Industrial Engineering, Georgia Tech, 1957. M.B.A., Harvard, 1963. Copley Newspapers, 1963-91, named pres. & CEO 1971. Founder, chmn. & CEO Argyle communications, 1991.

MARCHAND, NANCY
Actress. b. Buffalo, NY, June 19, 1928. m. actor-dir. Paul Sparer. e. Carnegie Tech. Stage debut The Late George Apley (1946).
THEATER: The Taming of the Shrew (B'way debut, 1951), The Balcony (Obie Award, 1960), Morning's at Seven (Drama Desk & Outer Critics Circle Awards), Sister Mary Ignatius Explains It All to You, Taken in Marriage, The Plough and the Stars, Awake and Sing, The Cocktail Hour (Obie Award, 1990), The End of the Day, Black Comedy/White Liars. Was an original mem of APA-Phoenix Theater.
PICTURES: The Bachelor Party (debut, 1957), Ladybug Ladybug, Me Natalie, Tell Me That You Love Me Junie Moon, The Hospital, The Bostonians, From the Hip, The Naked Gun: From the Files of Police Squad, Jefferson in Paris, Sabrina, Dear God.
TELEVISION: Specials: Little Women, Marty, Kiss Kiss Dahlings, many others. Series: Beacon Hill, Adams Chronicles, Love of Life, Search for Tomorrow, Lou Grant (4 Emmy Awards: 1978, 1980, 1981, 1982). Movies: Some Kind of Miracle, Willa, Once Upon a Family, Killjoy, The Golden Moment—An Olympic Love Story, Sparkling Cyanide. Mini-Series: North and South Book II.

MARCOVICCI, ANDREA
Actress, Singer. b. New York, NY, Nov. 18, 1948. e. Bennett Col. Studied acting with Herbert Berghof. Acted on NY stage in The Wedding of Iphigenia, The Ambassadors, Nefertiti, Hamlet, Any Given Day. Frequent performer in night clubs.
PICTURES: The Front (debut, 1976), The Concorde: Airport 1979, The Hand, Spacehunter: Adventures in the Forbidden Zone, Kings and Desperate Men, The Stuff, Someone to Love, White Dragon, Jack the Bear.
TELEVISION: Series: Love Is a Many-Splendored Thing, Berrenger's, Trapper John M.D. Movies: Cry Rape!, Smile Jenny You're Dead, Some Kind of Miracle, A Vacation in Hell, Packin' It In, Sprague, Velvet, The Canterville Ghost, The Water Engine.

MARCUS, BEN
Executive. b. Poland, Aug. 10, 1911. Emigrated 1914. e. U. Minnesota. Opened first theatre 1935, acq'd. restaurants and hotels, formed Marcus Corp. at which he is pres. and COO. Holdings include Budgetel hotel chain, KFC restaurants, and 46 theatres.

MARCUS, JEFFREY A.
Executive. Began cable TV career selling cable door-to-door in college. Founded Marcus Communiations, Inc., in 1982 which merged in 1988 with Western Tele-Communications, Inc. to form WestMarc Communications, Inc. at which he served as Chairman and CEO. Created Marcus Cable Co. in 1990 by merging cable systems in Wisconsin, Texas, Delaware and Maryland and is currently Chairman and CEO of this continuously expanding company.

MARCUS, MICHAEL E.

Executive. b. Pittsburgh, PA, June 5, 1945. e. Penn State, 1963-67. Moved to LA where he started in industry in mailroom of General Artists Corp. Promoted to agent when co. merged with Creative Management Assocs. 1972 joined Bart/Levy Agency; 1980, became full partner and co-owner of Kohner/Levy/Marcus Agency. 1981, became sr. agent at Creative Artists Agency. 1993, named pres. & COO of MGM Pictures.

MARCUS. MORT

Executive. Pres., Buena Vista Television Production.

MARENSTEIN, HAROLD

Executive b. New York, NY, Nov. 30, 1916. e. City Coll. of New York, 1937. Shipping, picture checking service, Warner Bros., 1935-45; booking, Loew's Inc., 1945-48; booking, contracts, Selznick Rel. Org., 1948-51; contracts, Paramount, 1951-52; asst. sls. gr., International Rel. Org., 1952; asst. sls. mgr., Janus Films, 1961-64; sls. exec., Rizzoli Films, 1965; 1967, nat'l. sales dir., Continental Dist.; gen. sales mgr., Cinemation Industries, 1968; v.p.-sales, dir., Cinemation Industries, 1971; 1976, gen. sls. mgr., General National Films; 1980, gen. sls. mgr., Lima Productions. Now retired.

MARENZI, GARY

Executive. Pres., MGM/UA Communications Group.

MARGOLIN, STUART

Actor, Director, Writer. b. Davenport, IA, Jan. 31, 1940. Wrote play Sad Choices which was produced Off-B'way when he was only 20. PICTURES: The Gamblers, Kelly's Heroes, Limbo, Death Wish, The Big Bus, Futureworld, Days of Heaven, S.O.B., Class, Running Hot, A Fine Mess, Paramedics (dir. only), Iron Eagle II, Bye Bye Blues, Guilty By Suspicion, The Lay of the Land, Hi-Line. TELEVISION: Series: Occasional Wife, Love American Style, Nichols, The Rockford Files (Emmy Awards, 1979, 1980), Bret Maverick, Mr. Smith. Guest: Hey Landlord, He & She, The Monkees, M*A*S*H, Gunsmoke, The Mary Tyler Moore Show (also dir.), Rhoda, Magnum P.I., Hill Street Blues. Movies: The Intruders, The Ballad of Andy Crocker (writer, associate prod. only), A Summer Without Boys (voice), The Rockford Files (pilot), The California Kid, This is the West That Was, Lanigan's Rabbi, Perilous Voyage, A Killer in the Family, Three of a Kind, To Grandmother's House We Go, How the West Was Fun (dir. only), The Rockford Files: I Still Love L.A, The Rockford Files: A Blessing in Disguise. Director: Suddenly Love, A Shining Season, The Long Summer of George Adams, Double Double Toil and Trouble, Salt Water Moose (Dir's. Guild of America Award, 1997).

MARGULIES, JULIANNA

Actor. b. Spring Valley, NY, June 8, 1966. e. Sarah Lawrence College, BA.
PICTURES: Out of Justice, Paradise Road, Traveller, A Price Below Rubies, Newton Boys, Dinosaur.
TELEVISION: Series: ER (Emmy Award, 1995). Guest: The Larry Sanders Show, Homicide: Life on the Street, Murder She Wrote, Law & Order.

MARGULIES, STAN

Producer. b. New York, NY, Dec. 14, 1920. e. De Witt Clinton H.S., NYU, B.S., June, 1940. Army Air Force, May, 1942; p.r., Air Force and the Infantry, wrote service magazines, newspapers including Yank; spec. feature writer & asst. Sunday editor, Salt Lake City Tribune; publicist, RKO Studios, Hollywood, March, 1947; continued publicity work at CBS-Radio, 20th Century-Fox, Walt Disney Productions. Bryna Films, 1955; became vice-pres., 1958; also served exec. prod., TV series, Tales of the Vikings; prod. asst., Spartacus.
PICTURES: 40 Pounds of Trouble, Those Magnificent Men in Their Flying Machines, Don't Just Stand There, The Pink Jungle, If It's Tuesday This Must Be Belgium, I Love My Wife, Willy Wonka and the Chocolate Factory, One Is a Lonely Number, Visions of Eight.
TELEVISION: Movies: The 500 Pound Jerk, She Lives, The Morning After, Unwed Father, Men of the Dragon, I Will Fight No More Forever, Roots (Emmy Award, 1977), Roots: The Next Generations (Emmy Award, 1979), Moviola, Agatha Christie's Murder Is Easy, The Thorn Birds, Agatha Christie's A Caribbean Mystery, A Killer in the Family, Sparkling Cyanide, The Mystic Warrior, A Bunny's Tale, Out on a Limb, Broken Angel, Crossing to Freedom, Separate But Equal (Emmy Award, 1991).

MARILL, ALVIN H.

Writer. b. Brockton, MA, Jan. 10, 1934. e. Boston U., 1955. Dir. music programming, writer/prod., WNAC, Boston 1961-65; dir. music prog., WRFM, NY 1966-67; publicity writer, RCA Records 1967-72; sr. writer/editor, RCA Direct Marketing 1972-80; partner, TLK Direct Marketing 1977-80; mgr., A & R Administration, RCA Direct Marketing 1980-83; exec. editor, CBS TV (1984-88); editor, Carol Publ. Group (1988-94); v.p., Sandal Enterprises (1994-present). Television editor, Films in Review 1973-84. Writer/researcher: The Great Singers (record/tape collections). Jury member: 1983 Locarno Film Fest. Television Movie Hall of Fame.

AUTHOR: Samuel Goldwyn Presents, Robert Mitchum on the Screen, The Films of Anthony Quinn, The Films of Sidney Poitier, Katharine Hepburn: A Pictorial Study, Boris Karloff—A Pictorial Biography, Errol Flynn—A Pictorial Biography, The Complete Films of Edward G. Robinson, More Theatre: Stage to Screen to Television, Movies Made for Television 1964-96, The Films of Tyrone Power; Editor: Moe Howard & The 3 Stooges, The Films of Tommy Lee Jones, The Ultimate John Wayne Trivia Book. Assoc. editor: Leonard Maltin's Movie & Video Guide.

MARIN, CHEECH (RICHARD)

Actor, Writer. b. Los Angeles, CA, July 13, 1946. e. California State U, B.S. Teamed with Tommy Chong in improvisational group, City Works (Vancouver). Comedy recordings include Sleeping Beauty, Cheech and Chong Big Bama, Los Cochinos, The Wedding Album (Grammy Award), Get Out of My Room.
PICTURES: Up in Smoke (also co-s.p.), Cheech and Chong's Next Movie (also co-s.p.), Cheech and Chong's Nice Dreams (also co-s.p.), Things Are Tough All Over (also co-s.p.), It Came from Hollywood, Still Smokin' (also co-s.p.), Yellowbeard, Cheech and Chong's The Corsican Brothers (also co-s.p.), After Hours, Echo Park, Born in East L.A. (also s.p., dir.), Fatal Beauty, Oliver & Company (voice), Troop Beverly Hills (cameo), Ghostbusters II (cameo), Rude Awakening, Far Out Man, The Shrimp on the Barbie, FernGully... The Last Rainforest (voice), A Million to Juan, The Lion King (voice), Desperado, From Dusk Till Dawn, The Great White Hype, Tin Cup.
TELEVISION: Series: The Golden Palace, Nash Bridges. Movie: The Cisco Kid. Specials: Get Out of My Room (also dir., songs), Charlie Barnett—Terms of Enrollment.

MARK, LAURENCE M.

Producer, Executive. b. New York, NY. e. Wesleyan U., B.A.; NYU, M.A. Started career as trainee and publicist for United Artists; also asst. to prod. on Lenny, Smile, etc. Joined Paramount Pictures as mktg./prod. liaison dir. and then exec. dir., pub. for m.p. division in NY. Named v.p., prod./mktg. at Paramount Studio; 1980, v.p., west coast mktg.; 1982 promoted to post as v.p., prod. 1984 (projects incl. Trading Places, Terms of Endearment, Falling in Love, Lady Jane); joined 20th Century-Fox as exec. v.p., prod. (projects incl. The Fly, Broadcast News); 1986, established Laurence Mark Productions at Fox; 1989 moved headquarters to Walt Disney Studios.
THEATER: Brooklyn Laundry (L.A.), Big (N.Y.).
PICTURES: Producer/Exec. prod.: Black Widow, Working Girl , My Stepmother is an Alien, Cookie, Mr. Destiny, True Colors , One Good Cop, The Adventures of Huck Finn, Gunmen, Sister Act 2: Back in the Habit, Cutthroat Island, Tom & Huck, Jerry Maguire, Romy & Michele's High School Reunion, Deep Rising, As Good As It Gets, The Object of My Affection, Simon Birch.
TELEVISION: Exec. prod.: Sweet Bird of Youth, Oliver Twist.

MARKHAM, MONTE

Actor. b. Manatee, FL, June 21, 1938. e. U. of Georgia. Military service in Coast Guard after which joined resident theatre co. at Stephens College, MO, where he also taught acting. Joined Actor's Workshop Theatre, San Francisco, for three years. Made TV debut in Mission: Impossible episode. June, 1992 formed Perpetual Motion Films with Adam Friedman.
THEATER: B'way: Irene (Theatre World Award), Same Time Next Year.
PICTURES: Hour of the Gun, Guns of the Magnificent Seven, One Is a Lonely Number, Midway, Airport '77, Ginger in the Morning, Off the Wall, Jake Speed, Hot Pursuit, Defense Play (also dir.), Neon City (also dir.), At First Sight.
TELEVISION: Series: The Second Hundred Years, Mr. Deeds Goes to Town, The New Perry Mason, Dallas, Rituals, Baywatch (also dir. episodes), Melrose Place, Campus Cops. Movies: Death Takes a Holiday, The Astronaut, Visions, Hustling, Ellery Queen, Relentless, Drop-Out Father, Hotline, Baywatch: Panic at Malibu Pier. Host-narrator-prod.-dir.: Air Combat, Combat at Sea, Master of War, Epic Biographies, The Great Ships.

MARKLE, PETER

Director. b. Danville, PA, Sept. 24, 1946.
PICTURES: The Personals (also s.p., photog.), Hot Dog ... The Movie, Youngblood (also co-story, s.p.), Bat-21, Wagons East!, The Last Days of Frankie the Fly, A Night at the Roxbury.
TELEVISION: Movies: Desperate, Nightbreaker, Breaking Point, El Diablo, Through the Eyes of a Killer, Jake Lassiter: Justice on the Bayou, White Dwarf, Mob Justice. Series: Millenium.

MARKOWITZ, ROBERT

Director. b. Irvington, NJ, Feb. 7, 1935. e. Boston Univ. Mostly on TV before theatrical debut with Voices, 1979.
TELEVISION: Movies: Children of the Night, Phantom of the Opera, The Deadliest Season, The Storyteller, Kojak: The Belarus File, My Mother's Secret Life, Pray TV, A Long Way Home, Alex: The Life of a Child, Adam: His Song Continues, The Wall, A Cry for Help: The Tracey Thurman Story, Too Young to Die, A Dangerous Life, Decoration Day, Love Lies and Murder, Afterburn, Overexposed, Murder in the Heartland, Because Mommy Works, The Tuskegee Airmen. Special: Twilight Zone: Rod Serling's Lost Classics.

MARKS, ALFRED

O.B.E. Actor-Comedian. b. London, 1921. TV, own series, Alfred Marks Time with wife, comedienne Paddie O'Neil.
PICTURES: Desert Mice, There Was a Crooked Man, Weekend with Lulu, The Frightened City, She'll Have to Go, Scream and Scream Again, Our Miss Fred, Valentino, Sleeps Six.
TELEVISION: Blanding's Castle, Hobson's Choice, Paris 1900, The Memorandum.

MARKS, ARTHUR

Producer, Director, Writer, Film Executive. b. Los Angeles, CA, Aug. 2, 1927. At 19 began work at MGM Studios as production messenger. Became asst. dir. in 1950, youngest film member of Directors Guild of Amer., 1957. President and board member of Arthur Prod., Inc.
PICTURES: Togetherness (prod., dir., s.p.), Class of '74 (dir., s.p.), Bonnie's Kids (dir., s.p.), Roommates (dir., s.p.), Detroit 9000 (prod., dir.), The Centerfold Girls (prod., dir.), A Woman For All Men (exec. prod.), Wonder Woman (exec. prod.), The Candy Snatchers (exec. prod.), Bucktown (dir.), Friday Foster (prod., dir.), J.D.'s Revenge (prod., dir.), Monkey Hustle (prod., dir.).
Writer: Empress of the China Seas, Gold Stars, Mean Intentions, Hot Times, Starfire, There's A Killer in Philly.
TELEVISION: Series: Perry Mason series (1961-66; prod., also dir. of over 100 episodes); writer-dir. of numerous TV shows including: I Spy, Mannix, Starsky & Hutch, Dukes of Hazzard, Young Daniel Boone, My Friend Tony.

MARKS, RICHARD E.

Executive. e. UCLA; UCLA Sch. of Law. 1978-82, v.p., legal & business affairs for Ziegler/Diskant Literary Agency. Joined Paramount Pictures 1984 as sr. atty. for Network TV Div., as project atty. for Family Ties, Cheers, etc. 1985, named sr. atty. for M.P. Group for The Golden Child, Beverly Hills Cop II, etc.; 1987 joined Weintraub Ent. Group as v.p. business affairs; m.p. div. 1990; counsel for Disney projects such as The Rocketeer, Beauty and the Beast. 1991, joined Media Home Entertainment as sr. v.p. in charge of all business and legal affairs. 1994, joined the Kushner-Locke Company as sr. v.p., business affairs for feature division; currently exec. v.p., gen. counselor.

MARS, KENNETH

Actor. b. Chicago, IL, 1936.
PICTURES: The Producers, Butch Cassidy and the Sundance Kid, Desperate Characters, What's Up Doc?, The Parallax View, Young Frankenstein, Night Moves, The Apple Dumpling Gang Rides Again, Full Moon High, Yellowbeard, Protocol, Prince Jack, Beer, Fletch, Radio Days, For Keeps?, Illegally Yours, Rented Lips, Police Academy 6: City Under Siege, The Little Mermaid (voice), Shadows and Fog, We're Back (voice), The Land Before Time II: The Great Valley Adventure (voice), Thumbelina (voice), Land Before Time III, Rough Magic, Citizen Ruth.
TELEVISION: Series: He & She, The Don Knotts Show, Sha Na Na, The Carol Burnett Show (1979). Guest: Facts of Life, Murder She Wrote, The Twilight Zone, Garfield & Friends, Civil Wars, Tom, Star Trek Deep Space Nine, The Drew Carrey Show and many others. Movies: Second Chance, Guess Who's Sleeping in My Bed?, Someone I Touched, The New Original Wonder Woman, Before and After, The Rules of Marriage, Get Smart Again.

MARSH, JEAN

Actress, Writer. b. London, England, July 1, 1934. NY stage debut in Much Ado About Nothing, 1959. As a child appeared in films: Tales of Hoffman; as principal dancer in Where's Charley. Co-creator, co-author and starred as Rose, in Upstairs, Downstairs.
THEATER: B'way: Travesties, The Importance of Being Earnest, Too True to Be Good, My Fat Friend, Whose Life Is It Anyway?, Blithe Spirit.
PICTURES: Cleopatra, Unearthly Stranger, The Limbo Line, Frenzy, Dark Places, The Eagle Has Landed, The Changeling, Return to Oz, Willow.
TELEVISION: Upstairs Downstairs (Emmy Award, 1975), Nine to Five, The Grover Monster, A State Dinner with Queen Elizabeth II, Mad About the Boy: Noel Coward—A Celebration, Habeas Corpus, Uncle Vanya, Twelfth Night, Pygmalion, On the Rocks Theatre, The Corsican Brothers, Master of the Game, Danny, the Champion of the World, Act of Will, A Connecticut Yankee in King Arthur's Court.

MARSHALL, ALAN

Producer. b. London, England, Aug. 12, 1938. Co-founder Alan Parker Film Company, 1970. Formerly film editor. Received Michael Balcon Award, British Acad., Outstanding Contribution to Cinema, 1985.
PICTURES: Bugsy Malone, Midnight Express, Fame, Shoot the Moon, Pink Floyd: The Wall, Another Country (Cannes Film Fest. Award, 1984), Birdy (Special Jury Award, Cannes Film Fest., 1985), Angel Heart, Homeboy, Jacob's Ladder, Basic Instinct, Cliffhanger, Showgirls.
TELEVISION: No Hard Feelings, Our Cissy, Footsteps.

MARSHALL, E. G.

Actor. r.n. Everett G. Marshall. b. Owatonna, MN, June 18, 1910. e. Univ. of MN. Acting debut with Oxford Players, 1933.
THEATER: B'way: Jason, Jacobowsky and the Colonel, Skin of Our Teeth, Iceman Cometh, Woman Bites Dog, The Survivors, The Gambler, The Crucible, The Little Foxes.
PICTURES: The House on 92nd Street (debut, 1945), 13 Rue Madeleine, Call Northside 77, The Caine Mutiny, Pushover, Bamboo Prison, Broken Lance, The Silver Chalice, The Left Hand of God, The Scarlet Hour, The Mountain, 12 Angry Men, The Bachelor Party, Man on Fire, The Buccaneer, The Journey, Compulsion, Cash McCall, Town Without Pity, The Chase, The Bridge at Remagen, Tora! Tora! Tora!, The Pursuit of Happiness, Billy Jack Goes to Washington, Interiors, Superman II, Creepshow, Power, My Chauffeur, La Gran Fiesta, National Lampoon's Christmas Vacation, Two Evil Eyes (The Black Cat), Consenting Adults, Nixon.
TELEVISION: Series: The Defenders (2 Emmy Awards: 1962, 1963), The Bold Ones (The New Doctors), Chicago Hope. Movies: Collision Course, The Winter of Our Discontent, Under Siege, At Mother's Request, Emma, Queen of the South Seas, The Hijacking of the Achille Lauro, Ironclads, Stephen King's The Tommyknockers, Oldest Living Confederate Widow Tells All. (d. Aug. 24, 1998)

MARSHALL, FRANK

Producer, Director. b. 1954. Raised in Newport Beach, CA. Worked on first feature film in 1967 while still a student at UCLA. Protege of Peter Bogdanovich, working on his production crew and as asst. on Targets, location manager on The Last Picture Show, What's Up Doc?, assoc. prod. on Paper Moon, Daisy Miller, Nickelodeon, etc. Line prod. on Orson Welles' The Other Side of the Wind (unreleased) and Martin Scorsese's The Last Waltz. Worked with Walter Hill on The Driver (assoc. prod.) and The Warriors (exec. prod.). Began collaboration with Steven Spielberg as prod. for Raiders of the Lost Ark. 1992, with wife and partner Kathleen Kennedy formed The Kennedy/Marshall Company.
PICTURES: Raiders of the Lost Ark (prod.), Poltergeist (prod.), E.T.: The Extra-Terrestrial (prod. supvr.). Exec. Producer: Twilight Zone—The Movie, Indiana Jones and the Temple of Doom, Fandango, Gremlins, The Goonies, Back to the Future (also 2nd unit dir.), The Color Purple (prod.), Young Sherlock Holmes, An American Tail, Innerspace, The Money Pit (prod.), Empire of the Sun (prod.), Who Framed Roger Rabbit (prod., 2nd unit dir.), The Land Before Time, Indiana Jones and the Last Crusade, Dad, Back to the Future Part II, Always (prod.), Joe Versus the Volcano, Back to the Future Part III, Gremlins II, Arachnophobia (also dir.), Cape Fear, An American Tail: Fievel Goes West, Hook (co-prod.), Noises Off (prod.), Alive (also dir.), Swing Kids, A Far Off Place, We're Back, Milk Money, Congo (also dir.), The Indian in the Cupboard, The Thief of Always, Snow Falling on Cedars.
TELEVISION: Amazing Stories (series exec. prod.), Roger Rabbit and the Secrets of Toontown (exec. prod.), Alive: The Miracle of the Andes (exec. prod.).

MARSHALL, GARRY

Producer, Director, Writer, Actor. b. New York, NY, Nov. 13, 1934. r.n. Garry Marscharelli. Sister is dir.-actress Penny Marshall. e. Northwestern U. Copy boy and reporter for NY Daily News while writing comedy material for Phil Foster, Joey Bishop. Was drummer in his own jazz band and successful stand-up comedian and playwright. Turned Neil Simon's play The Odd Couple into long running TV series (1970). Partner with Jerry Belson many years. Playwright: The Roast (with Belson, 1980), Wrong Turn at Lungfish (with Lowell Ganz, 1992; also dir., actor). Autobiography: Wake Me When It's Funny (1995).
PICTURES: Writer-Producer: How Sweet It Is, The Grasshopper. Director: Young Doctors in Love (also exec. prod.), The Flamingo Kid (also co-s.p.), Nothing in Common, Overboard, Beaches, Pretty Woman, Frankie and Johnny (also co-prod.), Exit to Eden. Actor: Psych-Out, Mary Jane, The Escape Artist, Lost in America, Jumpin' Jack Flash, Soapdish, A League of Their Own, Hocus Pocus, Dear God.
TELEVISION: Series Writer: Jack Paar Show, Joey Bishop Show, Bill Dana Show, Danny Thomas Show, Lucy Show, Dick Van Dyke Show, I Spy, Sheriff Who??, Love, American Style. Series creator/exec. prod./writer: Hey Landlord! (also dir.), The Odd Couple, Barefoot in the Park, Me and the Chimp, The Little People (The Brian Keith Show), Happy Days, Laverne & Shirley, Angie. Series exec. prod./writer: Blansky's Beauties (also dir.), Who's Watching the Kids?, Mork and Mindy (also dir.), Joanie Loves Chachi. Series exec. prod.: The New Odd Couple, Nothing in Common. Series actor: A League of Their Own, Murphy Brown. Movie: Evil Roy Slade (co-prod., co-writer). Special: The Last Shot (actor).

MARSHALL, PENNY
Actress, Director. b. New York, NY, Oct. 15, 1942. Father: industrial filmmaker and Laverne and Shirley prod., Tony Marscharelli. Brother is prod.-dir. Garry Marshall. Daughter is actress Tracy Reiner. Dropped out of U. of New Mexico to teach dancing. Acted in summer stock and competed on The Original Amateur Hour before going to Hollywood to make TV debut in The Danny Thomas Hour (1967-68).
PICTURES: Actress: How Sweet It Is, The Savage Seven, The Grasshopper, 1941, Movers and Shakers, The Hard Way, Hocus Pocus, Odd Couple: Together Again, Get Shorty. Director: Jumpin' Jack Flash (debut, 1986), Big, Awakenings, A League of Their Own, Renaissance Man, The Preacher's Wife. Exec. Prod.: Calendar Girl.
TELEVISION: Series: The Bob Newhart Show, The Odd Couple, Friends and Lovers, Laverne and Shirley. Guest: Danny Thomas Hour, The Super, Happy Days, Saturday Night Live, Comedy Zone, Chico and the Man. Movies: The Feminist and the Fuzz, Evil Roy Slade, The Couple Takes a Wife, The Crooked Hearts, Love Thy Neighbor, Let's Switch, More Than Friends, Challenge of a Lifetime, The Odd Couple: Together Again. Specials: Lily for President, The Laverne and Shirley Reunion. Series Director: Laverne and Shirley, Working Stiffs, Tracey Ullman Show, A League of Their Own.

MARSHALL, PETER
Actor, TV Show Host. r.n. Pierre La Cock. b. Clarksburg, WV, March 30. Sister is actress Joanne Dru. Began career as NBC page in N.Y. Teamed with the late Tommy Noonan in comedy act for nightclubs, guesting on Ed Sullivan Show and other variety shows. In 1950, made Las Vegas stage debut and since has been headliner there and in Reno and Lake Tahoe. New York stage, in B'way musical Skyscraper. On London stage in H.M.S. Pinafore, Bye Bye Birdie. In La Cage aux Folles (national company and B'way), 42nd St. (Atlantic City), Rumors (natl. co.).
PICTURES: The Rookie, Swingin' Along (Double Trouble), Ensign Pulver, The Cavern, Americathon, Annie.
TELEVISION: Host: Two of the Most (local N.Y. show), The Hollywood Squares, NBC Action Playhouse, The Peter Marshall Variety Show, Mrs. America Pageant, Mrs. World; many guest appearances.

MARSHALL, MERYL
Executive. b. Los Angeles, CA, Oct. 16, 1949. e. UCLA, BA sociology, 1971. JD Loyola Marymound U., 1974. Deputy pub. defender, LA County, 1975-77. Partner, Markman & Markman, 1978-79. NBC: Sr. Atty., 1979-80. Dir. programs/contracts/bus. affairs, 1980; asst. gen'l counsel, 1980-82; VP, compliance/practices, 1982-87. VP prog. affairs, Group W Prods., 1987-92. Founder, Two Oceans Entertainment Grp., 1992. Pres., Acad. of TV Arts and Sciences, 1997-.

MARTEL, GENE
Producer, Director. b. New York, NY, June 19, 1906. e. City Coll. of New York , U. of Alabama, Sorbonne, Paris. Newspaperman, New York and Birmingham, AL; dancer, actor, choreographer, dir. Broadway; prod. dir., many documentaries; films for State Dept., others; dir. for Paramount Pictures. Joined Princess Pictures 1952 to make films in Europe; formed own co., Martel Productions Inc., 1956.
PICTURES: Check-mate, Double-Barrelled Miracle, The Lie, Double Profile, Sergeant and the Spy, Black Forest, Eight Witnesses, Fire One, Phantom Caravan, Doorway to Suspicion, Diplomatic Passport, Immediate Disaster.

MARTIN, ANDREA
Actress. b. Portland, ME, Jan. 15, 1947.
THEATRE: NY: My Favorite Year (Tony Award & Theatre World Award), The Merry Wives of Windsor.
PICTURES: Cannibal Girls, Soup for One, Club Paradise, Rude Awakening, Worth Winning, Too Much Sun, Stepping Out, All I Want for Christmas, Ted and Venus,. Bogus, Anastasia, Wag the Dog.
TELEVISION: Series: Second City TV, SCTV Network 90 (2 Emmy Awards for writing), The Martin Short Show, Life and Stuff, Damon. Special: In Search of Dr. Seuss. Movie: Harrison Bergeron.

MARTIN, DEWEY
Actor. b. Katemcy, TX, Dec. 8, 1923. e. U. of Georgia. U.S. Navy, WWII. In stock before film debut in 1949.
PICTURES: Knock on Any Door, Kansas Raiders, The Thing, The Big Sky, Tennessee Champ, Prisoner of War, Men of the Fighting Lady, Land of the Pharaohs, Desperate Hours, The Proud and Profane, 10,000 Bedrooms, Battle Ground, The Longest Day, Savage Sam, Seven Alone.
TELEVISION: G.E. Theatre, U.S. Steel, Playhouse 90, Playwrights 56, Daniel Boone, Doc Holliday, Wheeler and Murdoch, Outer Limits, Twilight Zone.

MARTIN, EDWIN DENNIS
Executive. b. Columbus, GA, Jan. 30, 1920. e. U. of Georgia, B.S., 1940. Past pres., Martin Theatre Cos.; past pres., TOA, International, past pres., Variety. Retired.

MARTIN, GARY
Executive. b. Santa Monica, CA, Aug, 14, 1944. e. CSU Northridge, 1962-65. V.P. of production, Columbia Pictures, 1984-86; exec. v.p., production, 1986-88. Pres. of production admin., Columbia Pictures and TriStar Pictures 1988-95, Columbia TriStar Motion Pictures, 1995-. Member, AMPAS., D.G.A. 1994, named pres. of prod. admn. for Columbia/TriStar.

MARTIN, MILLICENT
Actress, Singer. b. Romford, England, June 8, 1934. Toured U.S. in The Boy Friend, 1954-57.
THEATER: Expresso Bongo, The Crooked Mile, Our Man Crichton, Tonight at 8:30, The Beggar's Opera, Puss 'n Boots, Aladdin, Peter Pan, The Card, Absurd Person Singular, Aladdin, Side by Side by Sondheim, King of Hearts, Move Over Mrs. Markham, Noises Off, One Into Two, 42nd Street (N.Y. & L.A.), The Cemetery Club, Shirley Valentine, The Boyfriend, Noel, Follies, The Rivals, The Rise and Fall of Little Voice.
TELEVISION: Series: The Picadilly Palace, From a Bird's Eye View, Mainly Millicent, Millie, Dowtown. Also: Harry Moorings, Kiss Me Kate, London Palladium Color Show, Tom Jones, Englebert Humperdinck show, That Was the Week That Was, LA Law, Max Headroom, Newhart, Murphy Brown, Coach.
PICTURES: Libel, The Horsemasters (tv in U.S.), The Girl on the Boat, Nothing But the Best, Those Magnificent Men in Their Flying Machines, Alfie, Stop the World I Want To Get Off, Invasion Quartet.

MARTIN, PAMELA SUE
Actress. b. Westport, CT, Jan. 15, 1953. Did modelling and TV commercials before entering films.
PICTURES: To Find a Man, The Poseidon Adventure, Buster and Billie, Our Time, The Lady in Red, Torchlight (also assoc. prod. & s.p.), Flicks, A Cry in the Wild.
TELEVISION: Series: Nancy Drew Mysteries, Hardy Boys Mysteries, Dynasty, The Star Games (host). Movies: The Girls of Huntington House, The Gun and the Pulpit, Human Feelings, Bay Coven.

MARTIN, STEVE
Actor, Writer. b. Waco, TX, Aug. 14, 1945. e. Long Beach Col., UCLA. Raised in Southern California. Worked at Disneyland, teaching himself juggling, magic and the banjo. Became writer for various TV comedy shows, incl. Smothers Brothers Comedy Hour (Emmy Award for writing, 1968-69), Glen Campbell Show, Sonny & Cher. Co-writer for special Van Dyke and Company. Wrote and starred in Acad. Award nominated short The Absent-Minded Waiter. Author: Cruel Shoes (1980). Albums: Let's Get Small (Grammy Award, 1977), A Wild and Crazy Guy (Grammy Award, 1978), Comedy Is Not Pretty, The Steve Martin Brothers. Gold Record for single King Tut.
THEATER: Actor: Waiting for Godot (Off-B'way debut, 1988). Author: Picasso at the Lapin Agile (regional, 1993), WASP (Off-B'way).
PICTURES: Sgt. Pepper's Lonely Hearts Club Band (debut, 1978), The Kids Are Alright, The Muppet Movie, The Jerk (also co-s.p.), Pennies From Heaven, Dead Men Don't Wear Plaid (also co-s.p.), The Man With Two Brains (also co-s.p.), The Lonely Guy, All of Me (NY Film Critics & Natl. Board of Review Awards, 1984), Movers and Shakers, Three Amigos! (also co-s.p., exec. prod.), Little Shop of Horrors, Roxanne (also s.p., exec. prod.; Natl. Society of Film Critics & L.A. Film Critics Awards for actor, WGA Award for adapt. s.p., 1987), Planes Trains & Automobiles, Dirty Rotten Scoundrels, Parenthood, My Blue Heaven, L.A. Story (also s.p., co-exec. prod.), Father of the Bride, Grand Canyon, Housesitter, Leap of Faith, A Simple Twist of Fate (also s.p., exec. prod.), Mixed Nuts, Father of the Bride 2, Sgt. Bilko, The Spanish Prisoner.
TELEVISION: Series: Andy Williams Presents Ray Stevens, The Ken Berry "WOW" Show, Half the George Kirby Comedy Hour, The Sonny and Cher Comedy Hour, The Smothers Brothers Show (1975), The Johnny Cash Show. Guest: The Tonight Show, Cher, The Carol Burnett Show, Saturday Night Live, The Muppet Show, Steve Allen Comedy Hour. Specials: HBO On Location: Steve Martin, Steve Martin—A Wild and Crazy Guy, Comedy Is Not Pretty, All Commercials: A Steve Martin Special, Steve Martin's Best Show Ever, The Winds of Whoopie, Texas 150--A Celebration, The Smothers Brothers Comedy Hour 20th Reunion, Learned Pigs and Fireproof Women. Producer: Domestic Life (series). Pilot: Leo & Liz in Beverly Hills (writer, creator, co-prod., dir.). Movies: The Jerk Too (exec. prod. only), And the Band Played On.

MARTIN, TONY
Singer, Musician, Actor. b. Oakland, CA, Dec. 25, 1913. r.n. Alvin Morris. e. Oakland H.S., St. Mary's Coll. m. actress-dancer Cyd Charisse. Sang, played saxophone & clarinet in high school band, engaged by nearby theatres for vaudeville; with Five Red Peppers, jazz group at 14 yrs.; two yrs. later with band, Palace Hotel, San Francisco; radio debut Walter Winchell program, 1932; joined Tom Gerund's band, World's Fair Chicago, 1933; played night clubs. First starring radio show, Tune Up Time (singer & emcee); on Burns and Allen program; own show for Texaco, Carnation Contented Hour. Recordings: Begin the Beguine, Intermezzo, The Last Time I Saw Paris, I'll See You in My Dreams, Domino, September Song, For Every Man There's a Woman.
PICTURES: Pigskin Parade (debut, 1936), Banjo on My Knee, Sing Baby Sing, Follow the Fleet, Back to Nature, The Holy Terror, Sing and Be Happy, You Can't Have Everything, Life Begins in College, Ali Baba Goes to Town, Sally Irene and Mary, Kentucky Moonshine, Thanks for Everything, Up the River, Winner Take All, Music in My Heart, Ziegfeld Girl, The Big Store, Till the Clouds Roll By, Casbah, Two Tickets to Broadway, Here Come the Girls, Easy to Love, Deep in My Heart, Hit the Deck, Quincannon—Frontier Scout, Let's Be Happy, Dear Mr. Wonderful.

MASLANSKY, PAUL
Producer. b. New York, NY, Nov. 23, 1933. e. Washington and Lee U., 1954. Moved to Europe performing as jazz musician in Paris, 1959-60. Entered film business with documentary, Letter from Paris. Asst. to prods. Charles Shneer and Irving Allen in England, Italy and Yugoslavia, 1961-62. In charge of physical prod. in Europe for UA, 1965-67.
PICTURES: Castle of the Living Dead, Revenge of the Blood Beast, Sudden Terror (Eye Witness), Raw Meat, Deathline, Sister of Satan, Big Truck, Poor Claire, Deathline, Sugar Hill (also dir.), Race With the Devil, Hard Times, The Blue Bird, Circle of Iron, Damnation Alley (co-prod.), When You Comin' Back Red Ryder (co-prod.), Hot Stuff, The Villain, Scavenger Hunt, The Salamander, Ruckus, Love Child, Police Academy, Police Academy 2: Their First Assignment, Return to Oz, Police Academy 3: Back in Training, Police Academy 4: Citizens on Patrol, Police Academy 5: Assignment Miami Beach, For Better or Worse (exec. prod.), Police Academy 6: City Under Siege, Ski Patrol (exec. prod.), Honeymoon Academy (exec. prod.). The Russia House, Cop and a Half, Police Academy: Mission to Moscow, Fluke.
TELEVISION: Movie: The Gun and the Pulpit. Mini-Series: King.

MASON, JACKIE
Comedian, Actor. b. Sheboygan, WI June 9, 1934. e. City College. Was a rabbi before becoming stand-up comedian. Records include The World According to Me! Has lectureship in his name at Oxford Univ. in England.
THEATER: Enter Solly Gold (1965), A Teaspoon Every Four Hours (Amer. National Theatre & Academy Theatre), Sex-a-Poppin (revue, prod. only), The World According to Me! (one-man show, special Tony Award, 1987), Jackie Mason: Brand New, Politically Incorrect.
PICTURES: Operation Delilah (debut, 1966), The Stoolie (also prod.), The Jerk, History of the World Part I, Caddyshack II.
TELEVISION: Guest: Steve Allen, Ed Sullivan, Jack Paar, Garry Moore, Perry Como and Merv Griffin Shows. Johnny Carson, Arsenio Hall, Evening at the Improv, Late Night with David Letterman. Series: Chicken Soup, Jackie Mason (synd.). Specials: Jack Paar is Alive and Well!, The World According to Me! (ACE Award), Jackie Mason on Broadway (Emmy Award for Writing).

MASON, JOHN DUDLEY
Executive. b. Ashland, KY, Oct 29, 1949. e. Amherst Coll., B.A., cum laude, 1971; Claremont Graduate Sch. and University Center, M.A., 1973; Amos Tuck Sch. of Business Administration, Dartmouth Coll., M.B.A., 1978. Program officer, National Endowment for the Humanities, 1972-76; analyst (1978-79), asst. mgr. (1979-80), mgr. (1980) strategic planning, Consolidated Rail Corp.; Consultant, Frito-Lay, Division, PepsiCo (1980-82); mgr, corporate planning, Dun & Bradstreet Corp. (1982-86); finance dir., anti-piracy (1986-90), v.p. finance, anti-piracy (1990-92), Motion Picture Association of America, Inc. Chmn., New Century Artists' Mgmt., 1990-98. Chmn., Finance Comm. and mem., bd. of dir. Association de Gestion Int'l. Collective des Oeuvres Audiovisuelles (AGICOA) 1987-88. Dir., Instituto Venezolano de Representacion Cinematografica (INVERECI), Caracas, Venezuela (1988-92). Dir.: Foundation for the Protection of Film & Video Works (FVWP), Taipei, Taiwan (1987-92). Dir. sec. Korean Federation Against Copyright Theft, 1990-92; Dir., Japan & Intl. M.P. Copyright Assn., Tokyo, 1990-92; Trustee and Treasurer, Design Industries Foundation for AIDS, 1990-94. Mng. dir., B.L. Nickerson & Associates, 1997-present.

MASON, KENNETH M.
Executive. b. Rochester, NY; Sept. 21, 1917. e. Washington and Jefferson Coll. (BA, 1938); U. of Rochester, graduate work; Dr. of Laws (H), Washington & Jefferson Coll., 1989. Began career with Eastman Kodak Co. in Kodak Park cine processing dept. in 1935; transferred following year to film dev. dept., Kodak Research Lab. Later joined film planning dept., remaining there until entering U.S. Navy in 1943. Returned to Kodak in 1946 as staff engineer in Kodak Office motion picture film dept. 1950 appt. mgr. of Midwest Division, of M.P. Film Dept.; became gen. mgr., Midwest Division, m.p. products sales dept. in 1963; named sls. mgr. of NYC region in 1965; appt. regional sls. mgr., Pacific Southern Region, Hollywood, in 1970; 1974 appt. mgr., product programs and research, Motion Picture and Audiovisual Markets Division, Kodak Office; 1974 named gen. mgr. of that division. Elected asst. v.p. of co., 1974, then v.p., 1978. Retired 1982. Former chmn., Inter-Society Committee for the Enhancement of Theatrical Presentation. Member, Trustee emeritus, Board of Trustees of Washington and Jefferson Coll. (and former chmn); past pres. of Society of Motion Picture & Television Engineers and honorary member; honorary fellow of British Kinematograph Sound & Television Society; mem. of University Film & Video Assn., Motion Picture Academy, American Society of Cinematographers. Board of dir.: Univ. Film & Video Foundation.

MASON, MARSHA
Actress. b. St. Louis. April 3, 1942. e. Webster Coll. Came to N.Y. to continue dramatic studies and embark on theatre career. Member of American Conservatory Theatre, San Francisco.
THEATER: The Deer Park, Cactus Flower, The Indian Wants the Bronx, Happy Birthday Wanda June, King Richard III, Cactus Flower, Private Lives, You Can't Take It With You, Cyrano de Bergerac, A Doll's House, The Merchant of Venice, The Crucible, Twelfth Night, The Good Doctor, Old Times, The Big Love, Lake No Bottom. Escape from Happiness, Amazing Grace, Night of the Iguana. Director: Juno's Swans.
PICTURES: Hot Rod Hullabaloo (debut, 1966), Blume in Love, Cinderella Liberty (Acad. Award nom.), Audrey Rose, The Goodbye Girl (Acad. Award nom.), The Cheap Detective, Promises in the Dark, Murder by Death, Max Dugan Returns, Chapter Two (Acad. Award nom.), Only When I Laugh (Acad. Award nom.), Max Dugan Returns, Heartbreak Ridge, Stella, Drop Dead Fred, I Love Trouble, Nick of Time, 2 Days in the Valley.
TELEVISION: Series: Love of Life, Sibs, Frazier. Specials: Brewsie and Willie, The Good Doctor, Cyrano de Bergerac. Movies: Lois Gibbs and the Love Canal, Surviving, Trapped in Silence, The Image, Dinner at Eight, Broken Trust. Dir.: Little Miss Perfect.

MASON, PAMELA
Actress, Writer. b. Westgate. England. March 10, 1918. Stage debut, 1936, The Luck of the Devil, London; also playwright (in collab. with James Mason: Flying Blind, Made in Heaven), AUTHOR: This Little Hand, A Lady Possessed, The Blinds Are Down, Ignoramus, Marriage Is the First Step Toward Divorce, The Female Pleasure Hunt. Columnist for Movieline Magazine.
PICTURES: I Met a Murderer, They Were Sisters, The Upturned Glass, Pandora and the Flying Dutchman, Lady Possessed, Everything You Always Wanted to Know About Sex.
TELEVISION: Series (synd): The Pamela Mason Show, The Weaker Sex?.

MASSEN, OSA
Actress. b. Denmark, Copenhagen. Jan. 13, 1916.
PICTURES: Honeymoon in Bali, Honeymoon for Three, A Woman's Face, Accent on Love, You'll Never Get Rich, The Devil Pays Off, Iceland, Jack London, Cry of the Werewolf, Tokyo Rose, Strange Journey, Night Unto Night, Deadline at Dawn, Gentleman Misbehaves, Rocketship XM, Outcasts of the City.

MASSEY, ANNA
Actress. b. Sussex, England, Aug. 11, 1937. Daughter of late actor Raymond Massey. Brother is actor Daniel Massey. On London stage in The Reluctant Debutante (debut, 1958), The Prime of Jean Brodie, Slag, The Importance of Being Earnest, Spoiled, Doctor's Delimma, School for Scandal, With National Theatre, 1989.
PICTURES: Gideon of Scotland Yard, Peeping Tom, Bunny Lake Is Missing, DeSade, The Looking Glass War, David Copperfield (TV in U.S.), Frenzy, A Doll's House, Vault of Horror, A Little Romance, Sweet William, Another Country, The Chain, Five Days One Summer, Foreign Body, Mountains of the Moon, La Couleur du Vent, The Tall Guy, Killing Dad, Impromptu, Haunted.
TELEVISION: Remember the Germans, Wicked Woman, The Corn Is Green, Sakharov, Hotel Du Lac (BAFTA Award), A Hazard of Hearts, Around the World in 80 Days, Tears in the Rain, The Man from the Pru.

MASSEY, DANIEL
Actor. b. London, England, Oct. 10, 1933. e. Eaton and King's Colleges, Cambridge U. Father was late actor Raymond Massey. Sister is actress Anna Massey. On B'way in She Loves Me, Gigi. Recent London theatre incl. Follies, The Devil's Disciple.
PICTURES: In Which We Serve (debut, 1942), Girls at Sea, Upstairs and Downstairs, The Queen's Guard, Go to Blazes, The Entertainer, Operation Bullshine (Girls in Arms), The Amorous Adventures of Moll Flanders, The Jokers, Star! (Acad. Award nom.), Fragment of Fear, Mary Queen of Scots, Vault of Horror, The Incredible Sarah, The Devil's Advocate, Warlords of Atlantis, Bad Timing: A Sensual Obsession, The Cat and the Canary, Victory, Scandal, In the Name of the Father.
TELEVISION: Series: The Roads to Freedom. Mini-series: The Golden Bowl. Movies/Specials: Aren't We All (debut, 1958), Love with a Perfect Stranger, Intimate Contact, Inspector Morse, Look of Love, Bye Bye Columbus, Stalin, GBH.
(d. March 25, 1998)

MASTERS, BEN
Actor. b. Corvallis, OR, May 6, 1947. e. Univ. of Oregon.
THEATER: The Cherry Orchard, Waltz of the Toreadors, Plenty, Captain Brassbound's Conversion, The Boys in the Band, Eden Court, What the Butler Saw, The White Whore and the Bit Player, Key Exchange.
PICTURES: Mandingo, All That Jazz, Key Exchange, Dream Lover, Making Mr. Right.
TELEVISION: Series: Heartbeat. Guest: Barnaby Jones, Kojak. Movies: One of Our Own, The Shadow Box, The Neighborhood, Illusions, The Deliberate Stranger, Street of Dreams, Cruel Doubt, Running Mates, A Twist of the Knife, A Time to Heal, Lady Killer. Mini-Series: Loose Change, Celebrity, Noble House.

MASTERSON, MARY STUART
Actress. b. Los Angeles, CA, June 28, 1966. Daughter of writer-dir.-actor Peter Masterson and actress Carlin Glynn. e. Goddard Col. Made film debut at age 8 in The Stepford Wives (1975), which featured her father. Spent summer at Stage Door Manor in Catskills; two summers at Sundance Inst. Studied acting with Gary Swanson. Member of the Actor's Studio. Off-off B'way debut in Been Taken. Off-B'way debut in Lily Dale followed by The Lucky Spot (Manhattan Theatre Club). Regional: Moonlight and Valentines, Three Sisters.
PICTURES: The Stepford Wives (debut, 1975), Heaven Help Us, At Close Range, My Little Girl, Some Kind of Wonderful, Gardens of Stone, Mr. North, Chances Are, Immediate Family (Natl. Board of Review Award, 1989), Funny About Love, Fried Green Tomatoes, Mad at the Moon, Married to It, Benny & Joon, Bad Girls, Radioland Murders, Heaven's Prisoners, Bed of Roses, Dogtown, On the Second Day of Christmas, The Postman, Grapefruit Moon, The Florentine, Digging to China.
TELEVISION: Movie: Love Lives On, Lily Dale. Guest: Amazing Stories (Go to the Head of the Class).

MASTERSON, PETER
Actor, Writer, Director. r.n. Carlos Bee Masterson, Jr. b. Houston, TX, June 1, 1934. m. actress Carlin Glynn. Daughter is actress Mary Stuart Masterson. e. Rice U., Houston, BA. 1957. NY stage debut, Call Me By My Rightful Name, 1961.
THEATER: Marathon '33, Blues for Mr. Charlie, The Trial of Lee Harvey Oswald, The Great White Hope, That Championship Season, The Poison Tree, The Best Little Whorehouse in Texas (co-author, dir.), The Last of the Knucklemen (dir.).
PICTURES: Actor: Ambush Bay (debut, 1965), Counterpoint, In the Heat of the Night, Tomorrow, The Exorcist, Man on a Swing, The Stepford Wives, Gardens of Stone. Writer: The Best Little Whore House in Texas. Director: The Trip to Bountiful, Full Moon in Blue Water, Blood Red, Night Game, Convicts, The Only Thrill.
TELEVISION: Camera Three, Pueblo; The Quinns; A Question of Guilt.

MASTORAKIS, NICO
Writer, Director, Producer. b. Athens, Greece, 1941. Writer of novels and screenplays, including Fire Below Zero, and Keepers of the Secret (co-author). Pres. Omega Entertainment Ltd. since 1978.
PICTURES: Writer/dir./prod.: The Time Traveller, Blind Date, Sky High, The Zero Boys, The Wind, Terminal Exposure, Nightmare at Noon, Glitch, Ninja Academy, Hired to Kill, In the Cool of the Night, At Random. Prod.: The Greek Tycoon, Red Tide, Grandmother's House, Darkroom, Bloodstone (prod., co-s.p.).

MASTRANTONIO, MARY ELIZABETH
Actress. b. Oak Park, IL, Nov. 17, 1958. e. U. of Illinois 1976-78 where she trained for opera. m. dir. Pat O'Connor. Worked as singer & dancer for summer at Opryland Theme Park in Nashville. Came to NY as understudy and vacation replacement as Maria in West Side Story revival.
THEATER: NY: Copperfield (1981), Oh Brother, Amadeus, Sunday in the Park With George (Playwright's Horizons), The Human Comedy, Henry V, The Marriage of Figaro, Measure for Measure, The Knife, Twelfth Night.
PICTURES: Scarface (debut, 1983), The Color of Money (Acad. Award nom.), Slamdance, The January Man, The Abyss, Fools of Fortune, Class Action, Robin Hood: Prince of Thieves, White Sands, Consenting Adults, A Day to Remember, Three Wishes, Two Bits, World of Moses.
TELEVISION: Mini-Series: Mussolini: The Untold Story. Special: Uncle Vanya (BBC).

MASUR, RICHARD
Actor. b. New York, NY, Nov. 20, 1948. Directed Oscar-nominated short, Love Struck, 1987. Pres., Screen Actors Guild, 1995.
THEATRE: B'way: The Changing Room.
PICTURES: Whiffs (debut, 1975), Bittersweet Love, Semi-Tough, Who'll Stop the Rain, Hanover Street, Scavenger Hunt, Heaven's Gate, I'm Dancing as Fast as I Can, The Thing, Timerider, Risky Business, Under Fire, Nightmares, The Mean Season, My Science Project, Head Office, Heartburn, The Believers, Walker, Rent-a-Cop, Shoot to Kill, License to Drive, Far from Home, Flashback, Going Under, My Girl, Encino Man, The Man Without a Face, Six Degrees of Separation, My Girl 2, Forget Paris, Multiplicity, Fire Down Below.
TELEVISION: Series: Hot L Baltimore, One Day at a Time, Empire. Mini-Series: East of Eden. Movies: Having Babies, Betrayal, Mr. Horn, Walking Through the Fire, Fallen Angel, Money on the Side, An Invasion of Privacy, The Demon Murder Case, Adam, John Steinbeck's The Winter of Our Discontent, Flight #90: Disaster on the Potomac, The Burning Bed, Obsessed With a Married Woman, Wild Horses, Embassy, Adam: His Song Continues, Roses Are for the Rich, Cast the First Stone, When the Bough Breaks, Settle the Score, Always Remember I Love You, Stephen King's IT, The Story Lady, And the Band Played On, Search for Grace, My Brother's Keeper, The Face on the Milk Carton, Hiroshima, It Was Him or Us, Undue Influence. Director: Torn Between Two Fathers (After School Special, DGA nom.).

MATARAZZO, HEATHER
Actress. b. Nov. 10, 1982.
PICTURES: Welcome to the Dollhouse, Arresting Gena, The Devil's Advocate, The Deli, Hurricane Streets, 54, The Hairy Bird.
TELEVISION: Series: The Adventures of Pete & Pete, Roseanne. Guest: Townies, Roseanne, ER.

MATHESON, TIM
Actor. b. Los Angeles, CA, Dec. 31, 1947. e. California State U. Debut on TV at age 12 in Window on Main Street. At 19, contract player for Universal. 1985, turned to direction: St. Elsewhere episode and music videos. Set up own production co. at Burbank Studios 1985; acted off-B'way in True West. With partner Daniel Grodnick bought National Lampoon from founder Matty Simons, becoming exec. officer and chmn. 1989; resigned in 1991. Co-prod. film Blind Fury.
PICTURES: Divorce American Style (debut, 1967), Yours Mine and Ours, How to Commit Marriage, Magnum Force, Almost Summer, National Lampoon's Animal House, Dreamer, The Apple Dumpling Gang Rides Again, 1941, House of God, A Little Sex, To Be or Not To Be, Up the Creek, Impulse, Fletch, Speed Zone, Drop Dead Fred, Solar Crisis, Black Sheep.
TELEVISION: Movies: Owen Marshall: Counselor-at-Law, Lock Stock and Barrel, Hitched, Remember When, The Last Day, The Runaway Barge, The Quest, Mary White, Listen to Your Heart, Obsessed with a Married Woman, Blind Justice, Warm Hearts Cold Feet, Bay Coven, The Littlest Victims, Little White Lies, Buried Alive, Joshua's Heart, Stephen King's Sometimes They Come Back, The Woman Who Sinned, Quicksand: No Escape, Relentless: Mind of a Killer, Trial & Error, Dying to Love You, A Kiss to Die For, Robin Cook's Harmful Intent, Target of Suspicion, Breach of Conduct (dir., co-exec. prod. only), While Justice Sleeps, Fast Company. Series: Window on Main Street, Jonny Quest (voice), The Virginian, Bonanza, The Quest, Tucker's Witch, Just in Time (also co-exec. prod.), Charlie Hoover. Pilot: Nikki & Alexander. Special: Bus Stop.

MATHIS, SAMANTHA
Actress. b. New York, NY, 1971. Mother is actress Bibi Besch; grandmother was actress Gusti Huber. Began acting as teen landing role in tv pilot Aaron's Way at age 16.
PICTURES: The Bulldance (debut, 1988 in Yugoslav film), Pump Up the Volume, This Is My Life, FernGully ... The Last Rainforest (voice), Super Mario Bros., The Music of Chance, The Thing Called Love, Little Women, Jack and Sarah, How to Make an American Quilt, The American President, Broken Arrow.
TELEVISION: Series: Knightwatch. Movies: Cold Sassy Tree, To My Daughter, 83 Hours 'Til Dawn.

MATLIN, MARLEE
Actress. b. Morton Grove, IL, Aug. 24, 1965. e. John Hersey H.S., Chicago, public school with special education program for deaf; William Rainey Harper Coll., majoring in criminal justice. Performed at Children's Theatre of the Deaf in Des Plaines at age 8, playing many leading roles. As adult appeared in only one stage show. Theatrical film debut in Children of a Lesser God. Production company, Solo One Productions.
PICTURES: Children of a Lesser God (debut, 1986; Acad. Award, Golden Globe), Walker, The Player, The Linguini Incident, Hear No Evil, It's My Party, Snitch, Two Shades of Blue.
TELEVISION: Series: Reasonable Doubts, The Outer Limits, Picket Fences. Movies: Bridge to Silence, Against Her Will: The Carrie Buck Story, Dead Silence. Specials: Face the Hate, Meaning of Life, Free to Laugh, Creative Spirit, The Big Help, People In Motion (host). Guest: Sesame Street, Adventures in Wonderland, Picket Fences (Emmy Award nom.), Seinfeld (Emmy Award nom.).

MATTHAU, CHARLES
Director. b. New York, NY, Dec. 10, 1964. Son of actor Walter Matthau. e. U. of Southern California Film School. While at USC wrote and dir. The Duck Film, a silent comedy short (Golden Seal Award, London Amateur Film Fest. and C.I.N.E. Eagle Award.) Also dir. short, I Was a Teenage Fundraiser. President, The Matthau Company, organized 1990.
PICTURES: Doin' Time on Planet Earth. (nom. Saturn Award, best dir., Acad. of Science Fiction.), The Grass Harp (dir., prod.; Acad. of Family Films award, best dir., 1996)
TELEVISION: Movie: Mrs. Lambert Remembers Love (dir., prod.; Golden Eagle, Golden Medal & Houston Fest. Grand & Angel Awards, 1993).

MATTHAU, WALTER
Actor. b. New York, NY, Oct. 1, 1920. Served in Air Force WWII. Studied journalism at Columbia U. and acting at New Sch. for Social Research's dramatic workshop, 1946, then acted in summer stock.
THEATER: B'way: Anne of the Thousand Days (debut, 1948), Will Success Spoil Rock Hunter?, Once More With Feeling, Once There Was a Russian, A Shot in the Dark (Tony Award, 1962), The Odd Couple (Tony Award, 1965). LA: Juno and the Paycock.
PICTURES: The Kentuckian (debut, 1955), The Indian Fighter, Bigger Than Life, A Face in the Crowd, Slaughter on Tenth Avenue, King Creole, The Voice in the Mirror, Ride a Crooked Trial, Onionhead, Strangers When We Meet, The Gangster Story (also dir.), Lonely Are the Brave, Who's Got the Action?, Island of Love, Charade, Ensign Pulver, Fail Safe, Goodbye Charlie, Mirage, The Fortune Cookie (Acad. Award, best supporting actor, 1966), A Guide for the Married Man, The Odd Couple, The Secret Life of an American Wife, Candy, Cactus Flower, Hello Dolly!, A New Leaf, Plaza Suite, Kotch (Acad. Award nom.), Pete n' Tillie, Charley Varrick, The Laughing Policeman, Earthquake, The Taking of Pelham One Two Three, The Front Page, The Sunshine Boys (Acad. Award nom.), The Bad News Bears, Casey's Shadow, House Calls, California Suite, Little Miss Marker (also exec. prod.), Hopscotch, First Monday in October, Buddy Buddy, I Ought to Be in Pictures, The Survivors, Movers and Shakers, Pirates, The Couch Trip, Il Piccolo Diavolo (The Little Devil), JFK, Dennis the Menace, Grumpy Old Men, I.Q., The Grass Harp, I'm Not Rappaport, Grumpier Old Men, Out to Sea.
TELEVISION: Many assignments 1952-65 on Philco-Goodyear Playhouse, Studio One, Playhouse 90, Kraft Theatre, Awake and Sing, Insight. Series: Tallahassee 7000 (1961). Movies: The Incident, Mrs. Lambert Remembers Love, Against Her Will: An Incident in Baltimore, Incident in a Small Town. Special: The Stingiest Man in Town (voice).

MATURE, VICTOR
Actor. b. Louisville, KY, Jan. 29, 1913. Acted with Pasadena Playhouse before film debut. On B'way in Lady in the Dark; served with U.S. Coast Guard, WWII.
PICTURES: The Housekeeper's Daughter (debut, 1939), One Million B.C., Captain Caution, No No Nanette, I Wake Up Screaming, Shanghai Gesture, Song of the Islands, My Gal Sal, Footlight Serenade, Seven Days Leave, My Darling Clementine, Moss Rose, Kiss of Death, Fury at Furnace Creek, Cry of the City, Red Hot and Blue, Easy Living, Samson and Delilah, Wabash Avenue, I'll Get By (cameo), Stella, Gambling House, Las Vegas Story, Androcles and the Lion, Million Dollar Mermaid, Something for the Birds, Glory Brigade, Affair with a Stranger, The Robe, Veils of Bagdad, Dangerous Mission, Betrayed, Demetrius & the Gladiators, The Egyptian, Chief Crazy Horse, Violent Saturday, Last Frontier, The Sharkfighters, Safari, Zarak, The Long Haul, Pickup Alley, China Doll, Tank Force, The Bandit of Zhobe, Escort West, Big Circus, Timbuktu, Hannibal, The Tartars, After the Fox, Head, Every Little Crook and Nanny, Won Ton Ton the Dog Who Saved Hollywood, Firepower, The Screamer.
TELEVISION: Movie: Samson and Delilah.

MAURA, CARMEN
Actress. b. Madrid, Spain, Sept. 15, 1945. e. Madrid's Catholic Inst. Daughter of ophthalmologist; faced family disapproval and custody battle when she became an actress. After working as cabaret entertainer, translator (has degree in French), and occasional voiceover dubber, met aspiring dir. Pedro Almodovar when they were cast in stage prod. of Sartre's Dirty Hands and starred in several of his films. Hosted weekly Spanish tv talk show Esta Noche.
PICTURES: El Hombre Oculto (debut, 1970), El Love Feroz, The Petition, Paper Tigers, Que Hace una Chica Como tu en un Sitio Como Este?, Pepi Luci Bom ... And Other Girls on the Heap (1980), El Cid Cabreador, Dark Habits, What Have I Done to Deserve This?, Extramuros, Se Infiel y No Mires Con Quien, Matador, Law of Desire, Women on the Verge of a Nervous Breakdown, Baton Rouge, How to Be a Woman and Not Die Trying, Ay Carmela!, Chatarra, Between Heaven and Earth, The Anonymous Queen, Shadows in a Conflict, Louis the Child King, How to Be Miserable and Enjoy It, The Flowers of My Secret, Una Pareja de Tres, El Palomo cojo, Happiness Is in the Field, Tortilla y cinema, Alliance cherche doigt, Elles.

MAUREY, NICOLE
Actress. b. France, Dec. 20, 1926. Studied dancing; French films include Blondine, Pamela, Le Cavalier Noir, Journal D'Un Cure De Campagne, Les Compagnes de la Nuit; many television and stage appearances in France; U.S. film debut in Little Boy Lost (1953).
PICTURES: Little Boy Lost, The Secret of the Incas, The Bold and the Brave, The Weapon, The Constant Husband, The Scapegoat, Me and the Colonel, The Jayhawkers, House of the Seven Hawks, High Time, Day of the Triffids, Why Bother to Knock?, The Very Edge.
TELEVISION: U.S. and U.K.: Tomorrow We Will Love, Casablanca, The Billion Franc Mystery, Champion House, I Thought They Died Years Ago.

MAXWELL, LOIS
Actress. r.n. Lois Hooker. b. Canada, 1927. Started in U.S. films in late 1940's before working in Italy then Britain. Has done numerous Canadian films for tv.
PICTURES: That Hagen Girl, The Decision of Christopher Blake, The Big Punch, The Dark Past, Kazan, Domani e troppa Tardi (Tomorrow Is Too Late), La Grande Speranza (The Great Hope), Aida, Passport to Treason, Satellite in the Sky, Time Without Pity, Lolita, Dr. No, Come Fly With Me, The Haunting, From Russia With Love, Goldfinger, Thunderball, Operation Kid Brother, You Only Live Twice, On Her Majesty's Secret Service, Adventure in Rainbow Country, The Adventurers, Diamonds Are Forever, Live and Let Die, The Man With the Golden Gun, The Spy Who Loved Me, Moonraker, Mr. Patman, For Your Eyes Only, Octopussy, A View to a Kill, Martha Ruth and Eddie.

MAXWELL, RONALD F.
Director, Writer, Producer. b. Jan. 5, 1947. e. NYU Coll. of Arts & Sciences; NYU Sch. of the Arts, Inst. of Film & Television Graduate Sch., M.F.A., 1970. Prod., dir,. for PBS Theater-in-America (1974-78).
PICTURES: Director: The Guest, Little Darlings, The Night the Lights Went Out in Georgia, Kidco, Gettysburg (also co-s.p.), Joan of Arc: The Virgin Warrior.
TELEVISION: Director: Sea Marks (also prod.), Verna: USO Girl (also prod.), Parent Trap II.

MAY, ELAINE
Actress, Director, Writer. b. Philadelphia, PA, April 21, 1932. Daughter is actress Jeannie Berlin. Father was prod.-dir. Jack Berlin whose travelling theater she acted with from age 6 to 10. Repertory theatre in Chicago, 1954; comedy team with Mike Nichols starting in 1955. Appeared with improvisational theater group, The Compass, Chicago. Co-starred in An Evening with Mike Nichols and Elaine May.
THEATRE: Playwright: A Matter of Position, Not Enough Rope, Hot Line, Better Point of Valour, Mr. Gogol & Mr. Preen, Hotline (Death Defying Acts).
PICTURES: Luv (actress), Enter Laughing (actress), A New Leaf (actress, dir., s.p.), Such Good Friends (s.p. as Esther Dale), The Heartbreak Kid (dir.), Mikey and Nicky (dir., s.p.), Heaven Can Wait (co-s.p.), California Suite (actress), Ishtar (dir., s.p.), In the Spirit (actress), The Birdcage (s.p.).
TELEVISION: Series regular: Keep Talking (1958-59). Guest: Jack Paar, Omnibus, Dinah Shore Show, Perry Como, Laugh Lines.

MAY, JODHI
Actress. b. 1975.
PICTURES: A World Apart, Isabelle Eberhardt, Eminent Domain, The Last of the Mohicans, Sister My Sister, Second Best, The Scarlet Letter (voice), The Woodlanders, The Gambler.
TELEVISION: Max and Helen. Mini-series: Signs and Wonders.

MAYER, GERALD
Producer, Director. b. Montreal, Canada, 1919. Father was Jerry G. Mayer, mgr. MGM studio. e. Stanford U., journalism; corresp. for San Francisco Examiner; pres. Sigma Delta Chi, prof. journalism soc. Navy lieut., amphibious forces, WWII. Entered m.p. ind. in prod. dept. MGM studios; first dir. assignment Dial 1119 (1950).
PICTURES: Dial 1119, Inside Straight, The Sellout, Holiday for Sinners, Bright Road (Christopher Award for direction), The Marauders, African Drumbeat, The Man Inside (Canadian).
TELEVISION: Canadian Broadcasting Corp. (prod./dir., TV drama), prod. The Swiss Family Robinson (British-Canadian-West German TV series). Dir. for U.S. TV: One Last Ride (mini-series), Airwolf, Night Heat, Lou Grant, Eight Is Enough, Quincy, Logan's Run, Mannix, Mission Impossible, Police Surgeon, Cimarron Strip, Peyton Place, Judd for the Defense, Bonanza, The Fugitive, Chrysler Thea., Ben Casey, Slattery's People, Profiles in Courage, The Defenders, Gunsmoke, etc.

MAYER, MICHAEL F.
Attorney, Executive. b. White Plains, NY, Sept. 8, 1917. e. Harvard Coll., B.S., 1939; Yale Law Sch., L.L.B., 1942. Armed Forces 1942-46, Air Medal (1945). V.P., Kingsley International Pictures Corp., 1954-62. Exec. dir. and gen. counsel, Independent Film Importers and Distributors of America Inc. (IFIDA), 1959-67. Special Counsel, French Society of Authors, Composers and Publishers, 1961-72; British Performing Rights Society, 1962-67. Author: Foreign Films on American Screens (1966), Divorce and Annulment (1967), What You Should Know About Libel and Slander (1968), Rights of Privacy (1972), The Film Industries (1973, revised ed. pub. in 1978). Teacher of courses on Business Problems in Film, New School (1971-82). Secty. of Film Society of Lincoln Center, Inc. (1972-88).

MAYER, ROGER LAURANCE
Executive. b. New York, NY, April 21, 1926. e. Yale U., B.A. 1948; Yale Law Sch., L.L.B. and J.D. 1951. In 1952 was practicing attorney; joined Columbia Pictures that year as atty. and named general studio exec., 1957. Left in 1961 to join MGM Studio as asst. gen. mgr. With MGM as follows: v.p., operations, 1964; v.p., administration, 1975-84. Also exec. v.p., MGM Laboratories 1974-83. Named pres., MGM Laboratories and sr. v.p., studio admin.; MGM Entertainment Co. 1983-86; joined Turner Entertainment Co. as pres. and COO, 1986-present. Member of Los Angeles County Bar Assn., Calif. Bar Assn., Los Angeles Copyright Society, bd of govs., Acad. of Motion Picture Arts & Sciences. Trustee, chmn. Motion Picture & TV Fund.

MAYO, VIRGINIA
Actress. r.n. Virginia Jones. b. St. Louis, MO, Nov. 30, 1920. e. St. Louis dramatic school. With Billy Rose's Diamond Horseshoe; then N.Y. stage, Banjo Eyes.
PICTURES: Jack London (debut, 1943), Up in Arms, The Princess and the Pirate, Wonder Man, The Kid from Brooklyn, The Best Years of Our Lives, The Secret Life of Walter Mitty, Out of the Blue, A Song Is Born, Smart Girls Don't Talk, The Girl from Jones Beach, Flaxy Martin, Colorado Territory, Always Leave Them Laughing, White Heat, Red Light, Backfire, The Flame and the Arrow, West Point Story, Along the Great Divide, Captain Horatio Hornblower, Painting the Clouds with Sunshine, Starlift, She's Working Her Way Through College, Iron Mistress, She's Back on Broadway, South Sea Woman, Devil's Canyon, King Richard and the Crusaders, The Silver Chalice, Pearl of the South Pacific, Great Day in the Morning, The Proud Ones, Congo Crossing, The Big Land, The Story of Mankind, The Tall Stranger, Fort Dobbs, Westbound, Jet Over the Atlantic, Young Fury, Fort Utah, Castle of Evil, Won Ton Ton the Dog Who Saved Hollywood, French Quarter, Evil Spirits, Seven Days Ashore.

MAYRON, MELANIE
Actress, Director. b. Philadelphia, PA, Oct. 20, 1952. e. American Academy of Dramatic Arts, 1972. Debut Godspell (tour), NY stage debut: The Goodbye People, 1979. Gethsemane Springs, (Mark Taper Forum, 1976), Crossing Delancey, (1986, Jewish Rep. Theatre, NY). With Catlin Adams, co-prod., co-wrote short, Little Shiny Shoes.
PICTURES: Actress: Harry and Tonto (debut, 1974), Gable and Lombard, Car Wash, The Great Smokey Roadblock, You Light Up My Life, Girl Friends (Locarno Film Fest. Award) Heartbeeps, Missing, The Boss' Wife, Sticky Fingers (also co-s.p., co-prod), Checking Out, My Blue Heaven. Director: The Babysitters Club.
TELEVISION: Series: thirtysomething (Emmy Award, 1989). Movies: Playing For Time, Will There Really Be a Morning?, Hustling, The Best Little Girl in the World, Wallenberg: A Hero's Story, Ordeal in the Arctic, Other Women's Children. Guest: Rhoda. Specials: Lily Tomlin: Sold Out, Cinder Ella: A Modern Fairy Tale, Wanted: The Perfect Guy, Mad About You, Toothless, Something So Right. Director: Tribeca: Stepping Back (also writer), thirtysomething, Sirens, Moon Over Miami, Winnetka Road, Freaky Friday, Nash Bridges, New York Undercover, Arliss, The Larry Sanders Show.

MAYSLES, ALBERT
Director, Cinematographer. b. Boston, MA, Nov. 1926. e. Syracuse (B.A.). Boston U, M.A. Taught psychology there for 3 years. With late brother David (1932-87) pioneer in direct cinema documentary filmmaking, using a hand-held synchronous sound camera, no narration, to capture the drama of daily life, without need to invent stories. Entered filmmaking photographing Primary with D.A. Pennebaker, Richard Leacock and Robert Drew, 1960. Formed Maysles Films, Inc. 1962, making non-fiction feature films, commercials and corp. films.
PICTURES: Showman (1962), Salesman, What's Happening! The Beatles in the U.S.A., Meet Marlon Brando, Gimme Shelter, Christo's Valley Curtain, Grey Gardens, Running Fence, Vladimir Horowitz: The Last Romantic, Ozawa, Islands, Horowitz Plays Mozart, Fellow Passengers, Christo in Paris, Soldiers of Music: Rostropovitch Returns to Russia, Baroque Duet, Umbrellas.
TELEVISION: Vladimir Horowitz: The Last Romantic (Emmy Award, 1987), Soldiers of Music: Rostropovitch Returns to Russia (Emmy Award, 1991), Sports Illustrated: The Making of the Swimsuit Issue (co-dir.), Abortion: Desperate Choices (Emmy Award, 1992, Cable Ace Award), Letting Go: A Hospice Journey (Emmy Award, 1996), A Concept of Wills: The Making of the Getty Art Center.

MAZURSKY, PAUL
Producer, Director, Writer, Actor. b. Brooklyn, NY, April 25, 1930. e. Brooklyn Coll. Started acting in 1951 Off-B'way (Hello Out There, The Seagull, Major Barbara, Death of a Salesman, He Who Gets Slapped), TV and films. Was nightclub comic 1954-1960 and directed plays. Began association with Larry Tucker by producing, directing, writing and performing in Second City, semi-improvisational revue. For four years they wrote the Danny Kaye TV show and created and wrote the Monkees series. First theatrical film I Love You Alice B. Toklas, 1968, which he wrote and exec. produced with Tucker. Exec. prod. of film Taking Care of Business.
PICTURES: Dir.-Writer: Bob and Carol and Ted and Alice, Dir.-Prod.-Writer-Actor: Alex in Wonderland, Blume in Love, Harry and Tonto, Next Stop Greenwich Village (dir., prod., s.p. only), An Unmarried Woman, Willie and Phil, Tempest, Moscow on the Hudson, Down and Out in Beverly Hills, Moon Over Parador, Enemies: a Love Story, Scenes From a Mall, The Pickle, Faithful. Actor: Fear and Desire, Blackboard Jungle, Deathwatch, A Star Is Born, A Man a Woman and a Bank, History of the World Part 1, Into the Night, Punchline, Scenes From the Class Struggle in Beverly Hills, Man Trouble, Carlito's Way, Love Affair, Miami Rhapsody, Faithful, 2 Days in the Valley, Touch.
TELEVISION: Movies: Weapons of Mass Distruction.

MAZZELLO, JOSEPH
Actor. b. Rhineback, NY, Sept. 21, 1983. Made acting debut at age 5 in tv movie Unspeakable Acts.
PICTURES: Presumed Innocent (debut, 1990), Radio Flyer, Jurassic Park, Shadowlands, The River Wild, The Cure, Three Wishes, The Lost World: Jurassic Park, Star Kid, A Small Miracle.
TELEVISION: Movies: Unspeakable Acts, Desperate Choices: To Save My Child, A Father for Charlie.

McBRIDE, JIM
Director, Writer. b. New York, NY, Sept. 16, 1941. e. NYU. m. costume designer Tracy Tynan. Began in underground film scene in New York. First film: David Holzman's Diary, 1967, which won grand prize at Mannheim and Pesaro Film Festivals, and was named to the Library of Congress' list of important American films designated for preservation in 1991. Appeared as actor in film Last Embrace.
PICTURES: Director: David Holzman's Diary (also prod.), My Girlfriend's Wedding (also actor, s.p.), Glen and Randa (also s.p.), Hot Times (also s.p., actor), Breathless (also s.p.), The Big Easy, Great Balls of Fire (also co-s.p.), Uncovered (also co-s.p.).
TELEVISION: Series: The Wonder Years (3 episodes), Twilight Zone (The Once and Future King, 1986). Movies: Blood Ties, The Wrong Man, The Informant, Pronto, Dead by Midnight. Special: Fallen Angels (Fearless), Dead Before Midnight.

McCALL, JOAN
Writer, Actress. b. Grahn, KY. e. Berea Coll. Staff writer for Days of Our Lives, Another World, As the World Turns, under the pen name Joan Pommer; also Search for Tomorrow, Capitol, Santa Barbara, Divorce Court. Starred on B'way in Barefoot in the Park, The Star Spangled Girl, A Race of Hairy Men, and road companies of Barefoot in the Park, Any Wednesday, Star Spangled Girl, and Don't Drink the Water, Los Angeles co. of Jimmy Shine.
PICTURES: Grizzly, Act of Vengeance, The Devil Times Five. Screenwriter: Predator, Between Two Worlds, Timelapse, Heart Like a Wheel.

McCALLUM, DAVID
Actor. b. Glasgow, Scotland, Sept. 19, 1933. Early career in rep. theatres and dir. plays for Army. Entered industry in 1953.
PICTURES: The Secret Place (debut, 1957), Hell Drivers, Robbery Under Arms, Violent Playground, A Night to Remember, The Long and the Short and the Tall, Carolina, Jungle Street, Billy Budd, Freud, The Great Escape, The Greatest Story Ever Told, To Trap a Spy, The Spy With My Face, Around the World Under the Sea, One Spy Too Many, Three Bites of the Apple, Sol Madrid, Mosquito Squadron, The Kingfisher Caper, Dogs, King Solomon's Treasure, The Watcher in the Woods, Terminal Choice, The Wind, The Haunting of Morella, Hear My Song, Dirty Weekend, Healer.
TELEVISION: Series: The Man From U.N.C.L.E., Colditz (BBC, 1972-74), The Invisible Man, Sapphire and Steel (BBC), Trainer (BBC). Guest: Hitchcock, Murder She Wrote. Movies: Teacher Teacher, Hauser's Memory, Frankenstein: The True Story, Behind Enemy Lines, Freedom Fighters, She Waits, The Man Who Lived at the Ritz, The Return of Sam McCloud, Mother Love (BBC), Shattered Image.

McCAMBRIDGE, MERCEDES
Actress. b. Joliet, IL, March 17, 1918. e. Mundelein Coll., Chicago, B.A. Did some radio work while in college; opposite Orson Welles two seasons, on Ford Theatre, other air shows; New York stage in: Hope for the Best, (1945); Place of Our Own, Twilight Bar, Woman Bites Dog, The Young and Fair, Lost in Yonkers. Starred on own radio show, 1952. Member of National Inst. Alcohol Abuse and Alcoholism, Washington. Autobiography: The Two of Us.

PICTURES: All the King's Men (debut, 1949; Acad. Award, best supporting actress), Lightning Strikes Twice, Inside Straight, The Scarf, Johnny Guitar, Giant, A Farewell to Arms, Touch of Evil (unbilled), Suddenly Last Summer, Cimarron, Angel Baby, 99 Women, Like a Crow on a June Bug (Sixteen), The Exorcist (voice), Thieves, The Concorde—Airport '79, Echoes.
TELEVISION: Series: One Man's Family, Wire Service; also numerous guest appearances. Movies: Killer By Night, Two For the Money, The Girls of Huntington House, The President's Plane Is Missing, Who Is the Black Dahlia?, The Sacketts.

McCARTHY, ANDREW
Actor. b. Westfield, NJ, Nov. 29, 1962. Raised in Bernardsville, NJ. e. NYU. While at college won role in film Class. Studied acting at Circle-in-the-Square.
THEATER: B'way: The Boys of Winter. Off B'way: Bodies Rest and Motion, Life Under Water, Neptune's Hips, Mariens Kammer.
PICTURES: Class (debut, 1983), Heaven Help Us, St. Elmo's Fire, Pretty in Pink, Mannequin, Waiting for the Moon, Less Than Zero, Kansas, Fresh Horses, Weekend at Bernie's, Quiet Days in Clichy, Dr. M (Club Extinction), Year of the Gun, Only You, Weekend at Bernie's 2, The Joy Luck Club, Getting In (Student Body), Night of the Running Man, Mrs. Parker & the Vicious Circle, Dream Man, Dead Funny, Mulholland Falls, Things I Never Told You, White Dunes, Stag, I Woke Up Early the Day I Died, Folls Errand, A Breed Apart.
TELEVISION: Movie: The Courtyard. Specials: Dear Lola, Common Pursuit. Guest: Amazing Stories (Grandpa's Ghost), Tales From the Crypt (Loved to Death), A Father for Brittany.

McCARTHY, KEVIN
Actor. b. Seattle, WA, Feb. 15, 1914. Sister was late author Mary McCarthy. e. U. of Minnesota. Acted in sch. plays, stock; B'way debut in Abe Lincoln in Illinois. Served in U.S. Army.
THEATER: B'way: Flight to West, Winged Victory, Truckline Cafe, Joan of Lorraine, The Survivors, Death of a Salesman (London), Anna Christie, The Deep Blue Sea, Red Roses For Me, A Warm Body, Something About a Soldier, Love's Labour's Lost, Advise and Consent, The Day The Money Stopped, Two For the Seesaw, Cactus Flower, Alone Together, The Three Sisters, Happy Birthday Wanda June.
PICTURES: Death of a Salesman (debut, 1951; Acad. Award nom.), Drive a Crooked Road, The Gambler From Natchez, Stranger on Horseback, Annapolis Story, Nightmare, Invasion of the Body Snatchers, The Misfits, 40 Pounds of Trouble, A Gathering of Eagles, The Prize, The Best Man, An Affair of the Skin, Mirage, A Big Hand for the Little Lady, Three Sisters, Hotel, The Hell With Heroes, If He Hollers Let Him Go, Revenge in El Paso, Ace High, Kansas City Bomber, Alien Thunder (Dan Candy's Law), Order to Kill, Buffalo Bill and the Indians, Piranha, Invasion of the Body Snatchers (1978, cameo), Hero at Large, Those Lips Those Eyes, The Howling, My Tutor, Twilight Zone—The Movie, Hostage, innerspace, UHF, Fast Food, Dark Tower, Love or Money, The Sleeping Car, Eve of Destruction, Final Approach, The Distinguished Gentleman, Matinee, Greedy, Just Cause, Steal Big Steal Little, The Sister in Law.
TELEVISION: Active on TV since 1949. Movies: U.M.C., A Great American Tragedy, Exo-Man, Mary Jane Harper Cried Last Night, Flamingo Road, Portrait of an Escort, Rosie: The Story of Rosemary Clooney, Making of a Male Model, Invitation to Hell, Deadly Intentions, The Midnight Hour, A Masterpiece of Murder, Poor Little Rich Girl: The Barbara Hutton Story, The Long Journey Home, Once Upon a Texas Train, In the Heat of the Night, Channel 99, The Rose and the Jackal, Dead on the Money, Duplicates, The Sister-in-Law, Liz: The Elizabeth Taylor Story, Marlon Brando: The Wild One, The Second World War, Elvis Meets Nixon. Mini-series: Passion and Paradise. Series: The Colbys, The Survivors, Flamingo Road, Amanda's, Second Start. Guest: Dynasty. Pilot: Second Stage.

McCARTNEY PAUL
Singer, Musician. r.n. James Paul McCartney. b. Liverpool, England, June 18, 1942. Formerly with The Beatles, Wings.
PICTURES: Performer: A Hard Day's Night, (debut, 1964; also songs) Help! (also songs), Yellow Submarine (cameo; also songs), Let It Be (also songs; Acad. Award for best original song score, 1970), Rockshow (concert film), Give My Regards to Broad Street (also s.p., songs), Eat the Rich (cameo), Get Back (concert film) Songs for films: Live and Let Die (title song; Acad. Award nom.), Oh Heavenly Dog, Spies Like Us. Scores: The Family Way, Beyond the Limit.
TELEVISION: Specials: James Paul McCartney, Sgt. Pepper: It Was 20 Years Ago Today, Put It There, Paul McCartney Live in the New World, The Beatles Anthology.

McCLANAHAN, RUE
Actress. b. Healdton, OK, Feb. 21. e. U. of Tulsa (B.A. cum laude). Member: Actors Studio, NYC.
THEATER: On B'way in Sticks and Bones, Jimmy Shine, California Suite. Off-B'way: Who's Happy Now? (Obie Award, 1970), After Play. Vienna: Lettice and Lovage. London: Harvey.
PICTURES: Five Minutes to Love, Hollywood After Dark, How to Succeed With Girls, They Might Be Giants, The People Next Door, The Pursuit of Happiness, Modern Love, This World Then The Fireworks, Dear God, Starship Troopers, Out to Sea.

TELEVISION: Series: Maude, Mama's Family, The Golden Girls (Emmy Award, 1987), The Golden Palace, Apple Pie, Balckbird Hall. Movies: Having Babies III, Sgt. Matlovich Vs. the U.S. Air Force, Rainbow, Topper, The Great American Traffic Jam, Word of Honor, The Day the Bubble Burst, The Little Match Girl, Liberace, Take My Daughters Please, Let Me Hear You Whisper, To the Heroes, After the Shock, Children of the Bride, To My Daughter, The Dreamer of Oz, Baby of the Bride, Mother of the Bride (also co-exec. prod.), A Burning Passion: The Margaret Mitchell Story, Innocent Victims, A Christmas Love. Specials: The Wickedest Witch, The Man in the Brown Suit, Nunsense 2: The Sequel. Mini-Series: Message From Nam.

McCLORY, SEÁN
Actor. b. Dublin, Ireland, March 8, 1924. e. Jesuit Coll., Nat'l U. at Galway (medical sch.). With Gaelic Theatre, Galway; Abbey Theatre, Dublin. Brought to U.S. in 1946 under contract to RKO Pictures, then Warners, then Batjac (John Wayne's co.). Prod. and dir. numerous plays, member of the Directors Guild of America and author of drama, Moment of Truth; Pax: The Benedictions in China. Editor: The Jester: The Masques Club 50th Anniv. Mng. Editor: A.N.T.A. News (2 yrs). For past 4 years starred in 40 ninety-minute radio dramas for California Artists Radio Theatre and written some 90 min. shows for National Public Radio. Recipient, Irish American Partnership Special CA Achievement Award, 1998.
THEATER: Shining Hour, Juno and the Paycock, Anna Christie, Escape to Autumn, King of Friday's Men, Lady's Not for Burning, Billy Budd, Dial M for Murder, The Winslow Boy, Shadow of a Gunman (Dramalogue Award), Saint Joan, The Importance of Being Earnest, many others.
PICTURES: Roughshod, Beyond Glory, The Daughter of Rosie O'Grady, Anne of the Indies, Storm Warning, Lorna Doone, What Price Glory?, The Quiet Man, Rogue's March, Plunder of the Sun, Island in the Sky, Them, Ring of Fear, Man in the Attic, The Long Grey Lane, Diane, I Cover the Underworld, The King's Thief, Moonfleet, Guns of Fort Petticoat, Valley of the Dragons, Cheyenne Autumn, Follow Me Boys, The Gnome-Mobile, Bandolero, Day of the Wolves, Roller Boogie, In Search of Historic Jesus, My Chauffeur, The Dead.
TELEVISION: Series: The Californians (also dir. episodes), Kate McShane, Bring 'Em Back Alive, General Hospital. Mini-Series: The Captains and the Kings, Once an Eagle. Movies: Kate McShane (pilot), The New Daughters of Joshua Cabe, Young Harry Houdini. Guest: Matinee Theatre, Climax, Lost in Space, My Three Sons, Suspense, The Untouchables, Hitchcock, Thriller, Beverly Hillbillies, Bonanza, Gunsmoke, Mannix, Little House on the Prairie, Perry Mason, S.W.A.T., Fish, Columbo, How the West Was Won, Fantasy Island, Battlestar Galactica, Trapper John M.D., Blue Knight, Falcon Crest, Simon and Simon, Murder She Wrote.

McCLUGGAGE, KERRY
Executive. b. 1955. e. USC, Harvard U. 1978, programming asst. at Universal; 1979, dir. of current srs. programming; 1980, became v.p., Universal TV. 1982, sr. v.p. creative affairs. Served as v.p. of production, Universal Pictures and supv. prod. on series Miami Vice. 1987-991, pres. of Universal Television. 1991, joined Paramount as pres. of the Television Group. 1992, named chmn. of the Television Group of Paramount Pictures.

McCLURE, MARC
Actor. b. San Mateo, CA, March 31, 1957.
PICTURES: Freaky Friday, Coming Home, I Wanna Hold Your Hand, Superman, Superman II, Superman III, Supergirl, Back to the Future, Superman IV: The Quest for Peace, Amazon Women on the Moon, Perfect Match, Chances Are, After Midnight, Back to the Future Part III, Grim Prairie Tales, The Vagrant, Apollo 13, Sleepstalker.
TELEVISION: Series: California Fever. Movies: James at 15, Little White Lies. Guest: The Commish.

McCLURG, EDIE
Actress. b. Kansas City, MO, July 23, 1951. e. Syracuse Univ. Newswriter and documentary prod. for National Public Radio affiliate, KCUR-FM. Joined the Pitschel Players in LA in 1975; then became member of the Groundlings Improv Comedy Revue.
PICTURES: Carrie (debut, 1976), Cheech and Chong's Next Movie, Oh God Book II, Secret of NIMH (voice), Pandemonium, Cracking Up, Eating Raoul, Mr. Mom, The Corsican Brothers, Ferris Bueller's Day Off, Back to School, The Longshot, Planes Trains and Automobiles, She's Having a Baby, Elvira: Mistress of the Dark, The Little Mermaid (voice), Curly Sue, A River Runs Through It, Stepmonster, Airborne, Natural Born Killers, Under the Hula Moon, Carpool, Circuit Breaker, Casper: A Spirited Beginning, Flubber, Meeting Daddy, A Bug's Life.
TELEVISION: Series: Tony Orlando and Dawn, The Kallikaks, The Big Show, Harper Valley PTA, No Soap Radio, Madame's Place, Small Wonder, Toegther We Stand, Valerie (The Hogan Family), Drexell's Class, Life with Louie, Martin Mull's White POlitics in America. Specials: Cinderella (Faerie Tale Theatre), The Pee-wee Herman Show, Martin Mull's History of White People in America, Once Upon a Brothers Grimm, The Chevy Chase Show, A Home Run for Love. Guest: WKRP in Cincinnati, The Richard Pryor Show, The Jeffersons, Trapper John M.D., Alice, Diff'rent Strokes, The Incredible Hulk, Madame's Place, Picket Fences. Movies: Bill on His Own, Crash Course, Dance 'til Dawn, Menu for Murder. Voice Characterizations: The Snorks, The 13 Ghosts of Scooby Doo, The New Jetsons, Casper, Problem Child, Bobby's World of Monsters.

MCCONAUGHEY, MATTHEW
Actor.
PICTURES: Dazed and Confused, My Boyfriend's Back, Angels in the Outfield, The Return of the Texas Chainsaw Massacre, Boys on the Side, Scorpion Spring, Submission, Glory Daze, Larger Than Life, A Time to Kill, Lone Star, Amistad, Contact, Making Sandwiches, Newton Boys, South Beach, Last Flight of the Raven (prod. only), Johnny Diamond, Ed TV.

McCORMICK, PAT
Writer, Actor. b. July 17, 1934. Served as comedy writer for such performers as Jonathan Winters, Phyllis Diller.
PICTURES: *Actor:* Buffalo Bill and the Indians, Smokey and the Bandit, A Wedding, Hot Stuff, Scavenger Hunt, Smokey and the Bandit 2, History of the World Part 1, Under the Rainbow (also co-s.p.), Smokey and the Bandit 3, Bombs Away, Rented Lips, Scrooged, Beverly Hills Vamp.
TELEVISION: *Series* (as writer): Jack Paar Show, Tonight Show, etc. *Series* (as actor): The Don Rickles Show, The New Bill Cosby Show, Gun Shy. *Movies* (as actor): Mr. Horn, Rooster, The Jerk Too.

McCOWEN, ALEC
Actor. b. Tunbridge Wells, England, May 26, 1925. e. Royal Acad. of Dramatic Art. On stage in London in Hadrian the Seventh, among others. On B'way in Antony and Cleopatra, After the Rain, The Philanthropist, The Misanthrope, Equus, Someone Who'll Watch Over Me, etc.
PICTURES: The Cruel Sea, The Divided Heart, The Deep Blue Sea, The Good Companions, The Third Key (The Long Arm), Time Without Pity, Town on Trial, The Doctor's Dilemma, A Night to Remember, The One That Got Away, Silent Enemy, The Loneliness of the Long Distance Runner, In the Cool of the Day, The Devil's Own (The Witches), The Hawaiians, Frenzy, Travels with My Aunt, Stevie, Hanover Street, Never Say Never Again, The Assam Garden, Personal Services, Cry Freedom, Henry V, The Age of Innocence.

McCRANE, PAUL
Actor. b. Philadelphia, PA, Jan. 19, 1961. Stage debut at age 16 in NY Shakespeare Fest. prod. of Landscape of the Body.
THEATER: *NY:* Dispatches, Runaway, Split, The House of Blue Leaves, The Palace of Amateurs, Hooters, The Hostage, Curse of an Aching Heart
PICTURES: Rocky II (debut, 1979), Fame (also songwriter), The Hotel New Hampshire, Purple Hearts, Robocop, The Blob, The Shawshank Redemption.
TELEVISION: *Series:* Cop Rock, Under Suspicion. *Movies:* Baby Comes Home, We're Fighting Back, Money—Power—Murder, With Murder in Mind, The Portrait, Strapped, Zelda. *Mini-series:* North & South II.

McDERMOTT, DYLAN
Actor. b. Connecticut, Oct. 26, 1961. Raised in New York City. e. Fordham U., studied acting at Neighborhood Playhouse with Sanford Meisner.
THEATER: The Seagull, Golden Boy, The Glass Menagerie, Biloxi Blues (B'way), Floating Rhoda and the Glue Man.
PICTURES: Hamburger Hill, The Blue Iguana, Twister, Steel Magnolias, Where Sleeping Dogs Lie, Hardware, In the Line of Fire, The Cowboy Way, Miracle on 34th Street, Destiny Turns on the Radio, Home for the Holidays, 'Til There Was You.
TELEVISION: *Movies:* The Neon Empire, Into the Badlands, The Fear Inside. *Series:* The Practice

McDONNELL, MARY
Actress. b. Wilkes Bane, PA.
THEATER: *NY:* Buried Child, Savage in Limbo, All Night Long, Black Angel, A Weekend Near Madison, Three Ways Home, Still Life, The Heidi Chronicles, Summer and Smoke. *Regional:* National Athems, A Doll's House, A Midsummer Night's Dream, The Three Sisters.
PICTURES: Matewan, Tiger Warsaw, Dances With Wolves (Acad. Award nom.), Golden Globe Award), Grand Canyon, Sneakers, Passion Fish (Acad. Award nom.), Blue Chips, Mariette in Ecstasy, Independence Day.
TELEVISION: *Series:* E/R, High Society. Movies: Money on the Side, Courage, The American Clock. Special: O Pioneers!

McDORMAND, FRANCES
Actress. b. Illinois, 1958. Daughter of a Disciples of Christ preacher, traveled Bible Belt with family settling in PA at 8. e. Yale Drama School. Regional theater includes Twelfth Night, Mrs. Warren's Profession, The Three Sisters, All My Sons. Two seasons with O'Neill Playwrights Conference.
THEATER: Awake and Sing, Painting Churches, On the Verge, A Streetcar Named Desire (Tony nom.), The Sisters Rosensweig, The Swan.
PICTURES: Blood Simple, Raising Arizona, Mississippi Burning (Acad. Award nom.), Chattahoochee, Dark Man, Miller's Crossing (unbilled), Hidden Agenda, The Butcher's Wife, Passed Away, Short Cuts, Beyond Rangoon, Fargo (Acad. Award, 1996; Chicago Film Critics Award; Screen Actors Guild Award; Ind't Spirit Award), Lone Star, Primal Fear, Palookaville, Paradise Road.

TELEVISION
TELEVISION: *Series:* Leg Work. *Guest:* Twilight Zone, Spenser: For Hire, Hill St. Blues. *Movies:* Crazy in Love, The Good Old Boys.

McDOWALL, RODDY
Actor. b. London, England, Sept. 17, 1928. e. St. Joseph's, London. First appeared in British film Murder in the Family at age of 9. In 1940, was signed by 20th Century-Fox. Voted Star of Tomorrow, 1944. Named Screen Actors Guild representative on National Film Preservation Bd., 1989. Published four volumes of his photography: Double Exposure (& II, III, IV).
THEATER: *B'way:* Misalliance, Escapade, Doctor's Dilemma, No Time for Sergeants, Good as Gold, Compulsion, Handful of Fire, Look After Lulu, The Fighting Cock (Tony Award, 1960), Camelot, The Astrakhan Coat.
PICTURES: Murder in the Family (debut, 1938), I See Ice, John Halifax Gentleman, Convict 99, Scruffy, Yellow Sands, Hey Hey USA, Poison Pen, The Outsider, Dead Man's Shoes, Just Williams, His Brother's Keeper, Saloon Bar, You Will Remember, This England, Man Hunt (U.S. debut, 1941), How Green Was My Valley, Confirm or Deny, Son of Fury, On the Sunny Side, The Pied Piper, My Friend Flicka, Lassie Come Home, White Cliffs of Dover, The Keys of the Kingdom, Thunderhead Son of Flicka, Molly and Me, Holiday in Mexico, Macbeth, Rocky, Kidnapped, Tuna Clipper, Black Midnight, Killer Shark, Everybody's Dancin', Big Timber, Steel Fist, The Subterraneans, Midnight Lace, The Longest Day, Cleopatra, Shock Treatment, The Greatest Story Ever Told, That Darn Cat, The Loved One, The Third Day, Inside Daisy Clover, Lord Love a Duck, The Defector, It, The Adventures of Bullwhip Griffin, The Cool Ones, Planet of the Apes, Five Card Stud, Hello Down There, Midas Run, Angel Angel Down We Go (Cult of the Damned), Pretty Maids All in a Row, Escape from the Planet of the Apes, Bedknobs and Broomsticks, Corky (unbilled), Conquest of the Planet of the Apes, The Devil's Widow (Tam Lin; dir. only), Life and Times of Judge Roy Bean, The Poseidon Adventure, The Legend of Hell House, Arnold, Battle for the Planet of the Apes, Dirty Mary Crazy Larry, Funny Lady, Mean Johnny Barrows, Embryo, Sixth and Main, Rabbit Test, Laserblast, The Cat from Outer Space, Circle of Iron, Scavenger Hunt, The Black Hole (voice), Charlie Chan and the Curse of the Dragon Queen, Evil Under the Sun, Class of 1984, Fright Night, GoBots: Battle of the Rock Lords (voice), Dead of Winter, Overboard (also exec. prod.), Doin' Time on Planet Earth, The Big Picture, Destroyer, Fright Night Part 2, Cutting Class, Shakma, Going Under, The Color of Evening, Double Trouble, The Naked Target, Mirror Mirror 2, Angel 4: Undercover, Last Summer in the Hamptons, The Grass Harp, The Second Jungle Book: Mowgli and Baloo.
TELEVISION: *Series:* Planet of the Apes, Fantastic Journey, Tales of the Gold Monkey, Bridges to Cross. *Specials:* Stratford Shakespeare Festival, Heart of Darkness, He's for Me, Not Without Honor (Emmy Award, 1961), The Fatal Mistake, Camilla (Nightmare Classics). *Movies:* Night Gallery, Terror in the Sky, A Taste of Evil, What's a Nice Girl Like You...?, Miracle on 34th Street, The Elevator, Flood, Thief of Baghdad, The Immigrants, The Martian Chronicles, Hart to Hart (pilot), The Memory of Eva Ryker, Million Dollar Face, Mae West, This Girl for Hire, The Zany Adventures of Robin Hood, Alice in Wonderland, Earth Angel, An Inconvenient Woman, Deadly Game, The Sands of Time, Heads, Hart to Hart: Home Is Where the Hart Is. *Mini-Series:* The Rhinemann Exchange, Hollywood Wives, Around the World in 80 Days. *Guest:* Goodyear TV Playhouse, Ponds Theatre, Oldsmobile Music Theatre, Campbell Soundstage, Batman, The Invaders, Love American Style, Carol Burnett Show, George Burns Comedy Week, Love Boat, Matlock, Murder She Wrote, many others.
(d. Oct. 3, 1998)

McDOWELL, MALCOLM
Actor. b. Leeds, England, June 13, 1943. Was spearholder for the Royal Shakespeare Co. in season of 1965-66 when turned to TV and then to films. *NY stage:* Look Back in Anger (also on video), In Celebration, Another Time. *LA stage:* Hunting Cockroaches.
PICTURES: Poor Cow (debut, 1967), If..., Figures in a Landscape, The Raging Moon (Long Ago Tomorrow), A Clockwork Orange, O Lucky Man!, Royal Flash, Voyage of the Damned, Aces High, The Passage, Time After Time, Caligula, Cat People, Britannia Hospital, Blue Thunder, Cross Creek, Get Crazy, Sunset, Buy and Cell, The Caller, Class of 1999, Disturbed, In the Eye of the Snake, Moon 44, The Maestro, Schweitzer (The Light in the Jungle), Assassin of the Tsar, The Player, Happily Ever After (voice), Chain of Desire, East Wind, Night Train to Venice, Bopha!, Milk Money, Star Trek: Generations, Tank Girl, Kids of the Round Table, Where Truth Lies, Hugo Pool, Simpley.
TELEVISION: *Series:* Pearl. *Guest:* Faerie Tale Theatre (Little Red Riding Hood), Tales fromt the Crypt (Reluctant Vampire). *Movies:* Arthur the King, Gulag, Monte Carlo, Seasons of the Heart, The Man Who Wouldn't Die.

McELWAINE, GUY
Executive. b. Culver City, CA, June 29, 1936. Started career in pub. dept. of MGM, 1955; 1959, joined m.p. div. of Rogers and Cowen; 1964, formed own public relations firm; then joined CMA. Left to become sr. exec. v.p. in chg. worldwide m.p. production, Warner Bros., 1975. 1977 became sr. exec. v.p. in chg. worldwide m.p. activities and pres. of intl. film mktg. at Intl. Creative Management (ICM), formerly CMA. 1981, named pres. and CEO, Rastar Films. Left in 1982 to become pres., Columbia Pictures; given additional title of CEO, 1983. 1985 named chmn. and on board of Columbia Pictures Industries. Resigned, 1986. Joined Weintraub Entertainment Group as exec. v.p. and chmn., m.p. div. 1987-89; returned to ICM, 1989 as vice chmn.

McEVEETY, BERNARD
Director. Father was pioneer as unit mgr. at New York's Edison Studios; Brothers dir. Vincent and writer Joseph. Began career in 1953 at Paramount where he was asst. dir. for 6 yrs. Dir. debut on TV series, The Rebel.
PICTURES: Ride Beyond Vengeance, Brotherhood of Satan, Napoleon and Samantha, One Little Indian, The Bears and I.
TELEVISION: Numerous episodes of Bonanza, Gunsmoke, Combat and Cimarron Strip (also prod.), Centennial, Roughnecks, The Machans.

McEVEETY, VINCENT
Director. Brother is dir. Bernard McEveety. Joined Hal Roach Studios in 1954 as second asst. dir. Then to Republic for The Last Command. First Disney assignments: Davy Crockett shows and Mickey Mouse Club. Moved to Desilu as first asst. dir. on The Untouchables; made assoc. prod. with option to direct. Did segments of many series, including 34 Gunsmoke episodes.
PICTURES: Firecreek (debut, 1968), $1,000,000 Duck, The Biscuit Eater, Charley and the Angel, Superdad, The Strongest Man in the World, Gus, Treasure of Matecumbe, Herbie Goes to Monte Carlo, The Apple Dumpling Gang Rides Again, Herbie Goes Bananas, Amy.
TELEVISION: Blood Sport, Wonder Woman, High Flying Spy, Ask Max, Gunsmoke: Return to Dodge, Murder She Wrote, Simon and Simon (26 episodes); Columbo: Rest in Peace Mrs. Columbo.

McGAVIN, DARREN
Actor. b. Spokane, WA, May 7, 1922. e. Coll. of the Pacific. Studied acting at Neighborhood Playhouse, Actors Studio. Landed bit roles in films starting in 1945.
THEATER: Death of a Salesman, My Three Angels, The Rainmaker, The Lovers, The King and I, Dinner at Eight (revival), Captain Brassbound's Conversion (LA), The Night Hank Williams Died, Greetings.
PICTURES: A Song to Remember (debut, 1945), Kiss and Tell, Counter-Attack, She Wouldn't Say Yes, Fear, Queen for a Day, Summertime, The Man With the Golden Arm, The Court Martial of Billy Mitchell, Beau James, The Delicate Delinquent, The Case Against Brooklyn, Bullet for a Badman, The Great Sioux Massacre, Ride the High Wind, Mission Mars, Mrs. Polifax—Spy, Happy Mother's Day... Love George (Run Stranger Run; dir. only), No Deposit No Return, Airport '77, Hot Lead and Cold Feet, Zero to Sixty, Hangar 18, Firebird 2015 A.D., A Christmas Story, The Natural, Turk 182, Raw Deal, From the Hip, Dead Heat, Blood and Concrete: A Love Story, Billy Madison.
TELEVISION: Series: Crime Photographer, Mike Hammer, Riverboat, The Outsider, Kolchak: The Night Stalker, Small & Frye. Movies: The Outsider (pilot), The Challenge, The Challengers, Berlin Affair, Tribes, Banyon, The Death of Me Yet, Night Stalker, Something Evil, The Rookies, Say Goodbye Maggie Cole, The Night Strangler, The Six Million Dollar Man (pilot), Brink's: The Great Robbery, Law and Order, The Users, Love for Rent, Waikiki, Return of Marcus Welby M.D., My Wicked Wicked Ways, Inherit the Wind, The Diamond Trap, By Dawn's Early Light, The American Clock, Danielle Steel's A Perfect Stranger, Derby. Specials: Unclaimed Fortunes (host), Clara (ACE Award), Mastergate, Miracles and Other Wonders (host), The Secret Discovery of Noah's Ark (host). Mini-Series: Ike, The Martian Chronicles, Around the World in 80 Days. Guest: Goodyear TV Playhouse, Alfred Hitchcock Presents, Route 66, U.S. Steel Hour, The Defenders, Love American Style, The Name of the Game, Owen Marshall, Police Story, The Love Boat, Murphy Brown (Emmy Award, 1990), many others.

McGILLIS, KELLY
Actress. b. Newport Beach, CA, July 9, 1957. Studied acting at Pacific Conservatory of Performing Arts in Santa Maria, CA; Juilliard. While at latter, won role in film Reuben Reuben.
THEATER: D.C. Stage: The Merchant of Venice, Twelfth Night, Measure for Measure, Much Ado About Nothing. NY Stage: Hedda Gabler.
PICTURES: Reuben Reuben (debut, 1983), Witness, Top Gun, Once We Were Dreamers (Promised Land), Made in Heaven, The House on Carroll Street, The Accused, Winter People, Cat Chaser, Before and After Death, The Babe, North.
TELEVISION: Movies: Sweet Revenge, Private Sessions, Grand Isle (also prod.), Bonds of Love, In the Best of Families: Marriage Pride & Madness. Special: Out of Ireland (narrator).

McGINLEY, JOHN C.
Actor. b. New York, NY, Aug. 3, 1959. e. NYU (M.F.A.), 1984.
THEATRE: NY: Danny and the Deep Blue Sea, The Ballad of Soapy Smith, Jesse and the Games, Requiem for a Heavyweight, Love as We Know It, Talk Radio, Florida Crackers, Breast Men.
PICTURES: Sweet Liberty, Platoon, Wall Street, Shakedown, Talk Radio, Lost Angels, Fat Man and Little Boy, Born on the Fourth of July, Point Break, Highlander 2: The Quickening, Article 99, Little Noises, A Midnight Clear, Fathers and Sons, Hear No Evil, Watch It (also co-prod.), Car 54 Where Are You?, On Deadly Ground, Surviving the Game, Suffrin' Bastards (also co-s.p.), Wagons East!, Born to Be Wild, Captive (co-prod. only), Seven, Nixon, Johns, The Rock, Nothing to Lose, A.W.O.L., Three to Tango.
TELEVISION: Movies: Clinton & Nadine, Cruel Doubt, The Last Outlaw, The Return of Hunter, Intensity, The Pentagon Wars, Target Earth. Guest: Frasier.

McGOOHAN, PATRICK
Actor, Director. b. New York, March 19, 1928. Early career in repertory in Britain. London stage 1954 in Serious Charge; 1955, Orson Welles' Moby Dick. On B'way in Pack of Lies (1987).
PICTURES: The Dam Busters (debut, 1954), I Am a Camera, The Dark Avenger (The Warriors), Passage Home, Zarak, High Tide at Noon, Hell Drivers, The Gypsy and the Gentleman, Nor the Moon by Night (Elephant Gun), Two Living One Dead, All Night Long, Life for Ruth (Walk in the Shadow), The Quare Fellow, The Three Lives of Thomasina, Dr. Syn: Alias the Scarecrow (U.S. tv as: The Scarecrow of Romney Marsh), Ice Station Zebra, The Moonshine War, Mary—Queen of Scots, Catch My Soul (dir. only), Un Genio due Campari e un Pollo (The Genius), Porgi d'altra Guancia (Nobody's the Greatest), Silver Streak, Brass Target, Escape From Alcatraz, Scanners, Kings and Desperate Men, Finding Katie, Baby: Secret of the Lost Legend, Braveheart, The Phantom, A Time to Kill.
TELEVISION: Series: Danger Man (also dir. episodes), Secret Agent, The Prisoner (also creator, prod.), Rafferty. Movies/Specials: The Hard Way, Jamaica Inn, Of Pure Blood, The Man in the Iron Mask, Three Sovereigns for Sarah. Guest: Columbo (Emmy Awards: 1975, 1990; also dir. episodes).

McGOVERN, ELIZABETH
Actress. b. Evanston, IL, July 18, 1961. Family moved to Southern California when she was 10. Acted in high school in North Hollywood; performance in prod. of The Skin of Our Teeth won her agency represenation. Studied at American Conservatory Theatre, San Francisco and Juilliard Sch. of Dramatic Art. Open audition for Ordinary People resulted in her film debut. Appeared in IMAX film Wings of Courage.
THEATER: NY: To Be Young Gifted and Black (1981, debut), My Sister in This House (Theatre World, Obie Awards), Painting Churches, The Hitch-Hiker, A Map of the World, Aunt Dan and Lemon (L.A.), Two Gentlemen of Verona, A Midsummer Night's Dream (NY Shakespeare Fest.), Love Letters, Twelfth Night (Boston), Major Barbara (Alaska), Ring Around the Moon (D.C.), Maids of Honor, The Three Sisters, As You Like It.
PICTURES: Ordinary People (debut, 1980), Ragtime (Acad. Award nom.), Lovesick, Racing with the Moon, Once Upon a Time in America, Native Son, The Bedroom Window, She's Having a Baby, Johnny Handsome, The Handmaid's Tale, A Shock to the System, Tune in Tomorrow, King of the Hill, Me and Veronica, The Favor.
TELEVISION: Series: If Not for You. Movies: Women and Men: Stories of Seduction (The Man in the Brooks Brothers Shirt), Broken Trust. Specials: Ashenden, Tales From Hollywood, The Changeling (BBC).

McGRATH, JUDY
Executive. e. Cedar Crest Coll. President, MTV. Began at MTV as on-air promotions writer. Created Unplugged, MTV Books, MTV Online.

McGRATH, THOMAS J.
Producer, Attorney, Writer, Lecturer. b. New York, NY, Oct. 8, 1932. e. Washington Square Coll. of NYU, B.A., 1956; NYU Sch. of Law, LL.B., 1960. Served in Korea with U.S. Army, 1953-54. Has practiced law in N.Y. from 1960 to date. Became indep. prod. with Deadly Hero in 1976; Author, Carryover Basis Under The 1976 Tax Reform Act, published in 1977. Cobntributing author, Estate and Gift Tax After ERTA, 1982. Lecturer and writer: American Law Institute 1976-81; Practicing Law Institute, 1976-97. Dir., New York Philharmonic; Olloffson Corp.; Fast Food Development Corp. Pres.: American Austrian Foundation; Tanzania Wildlife Fund.

McGREGOR, CHARLES
Executive. b. Jersey City, NJ, April 1, 1927. e. NYU. 1958-69, co-founder, pres. and CEO, Banner Films, Inc. (World Wide TV Distribution); 1955-58, salesman and div. mgr., Flamingo Films (domestic TV Dist.); Professional mgr. ABC Music Publishing. 1951-53: Prod. and partner Telco Prods. and GM Productions (prods. of network and local shows). 1969-77: exec. v.p. in chg. of worldwide dist., WB-TV; 1977-89, pres. WB-TV Distribution; 1989, named exec. v.p., corp. projects, WB.

MCGREGOR, EWAN
Actor. b. Crieff, Scotland, UK, March 31, 1971. Formed Natural Nylon, prodn. co., with Johnny Lee Miller & Jude Law.
PICTURES: Being Human, Shallow Grave, Blue Juice, The Pillow Book, Trainspotting, Emma, Brassed Off, The Serpent's Kiss, Nightwatch, A Life Less Ordinary, Velvet Goldmine.
TELEVISION: *Movies*: Lipstick on Your Collar. *Mini-series*: Scarlet & Black, Karaoke. *Guest*: Tales from the Crypt, ER.

McGUIRE, DOROTHY
Actress. b. Omaha, NE, June 14, 1919. e. Ladywood convent, Indianapolis; Pine Manor, Wellesley, MA. Acting debut as teenager at Omaha Community Playhouse. Following summer stock and radio work, made B'way debut in 1938 as Martha Scott's understudy in Our Town. Came to Hollywood to repeat stage role in film version of Claudia.
THEATER: Our Town, My Dear Children, Swinging the Dream, Claudia, Legend of Lovers, Winesberg Ohio, Night of the Iguana (1976), Cause Celebre, Another Part of the Forest, I Never Sang for My Father.
PICTURES: Claudia (debut, 1943), A Tree Grows in Brooklyn, The Enchanted Cottage, The Spiral Staircase, Claudia and David, Till the End of Time, Gentleman's Agreement (Acad. Award nom.), Mother Didn't Tell Me, Mister 880, Callaway Went Thataway, I Want You, Invitation, Make Haste to Live, Three Coins in the Fountain, Trial, Friendly Persuasion, Old Yeller, The Remarkable Mr. Pennypacker, This Earth Is Mine, A Summer Place, The Dark at the Top of the Stairs, Swiss Family Robinson, Susan Slade, Summer Magic, The Greatest Story Ever Told, Flight of the Doves, Jonathan Livingston Seagull (voice).
TELEVISION: *Series*: Little Women. *Movies*: She Waits, The Runaways, Little Women, The Incredible Journey of Dr. Meg Laurel, Ghost Dancing, Amos, Between the Darkness and the Dawn, Caroline? *Mini-Series*: Rich Man Poor Man. *Specials*: The Philadelphia Story, To Each His Own, Another Part of the Forest, I Never Sang for My Father. *Guest*: The Love Boat, The Young & the Restless, Highway to Heaven, Fantasy Island, St. Elsewhere.

McGURK, CHRIS
Executive. Pres., The Walt Disney Motion Pictures Group.

McHATTIE, STEPHEN
Actor. b. Antigonish, Nova Scotia, Canada, Feb. 3, e. Acadia U. Trained for stage at American Acad. of Dramatic Arts.
THEATER: *NY*: The American Dream (debut, 1968), Pictures in the Hallway, Twelfth Night, Mourning Becomes Electra, The Iceman Cometh, Alive and Well in Argentina, The Winter Dancers, Casualties, The Three Sisters, The Misanthrope, Heartbreak House, Mensch Meier, Haven, Search and Destroy.
PICTURES: Von Richthofen and Brown (debut, 1970), The People Next Door, The Ultimate Warrior, Moving Violation, Tomorrow Never Comes, Death Valley, Best Revenge, Belizaire the Cajun, Salvation!, Call Me, Sticky Fingers, Caribe, Bloodhounds on Broadway, Erik, The Dark, Geronimo: An American Legend, Beverly Hills Cop III, Art Deco Detective.
TELEVISION: *Series*: Highcliffe Manor, Mariah, Scene of the Crime. *Mini-series*: Centennial. *Movies*: Search for the Gods, James Dean, Look What's Happened to Rosemary's Baby, Mary and Joseph: A Story of Faith, Roughnecks, Terror on Track 9, Jonathan Stone: Threat of Innocence, Deadlocked: Escape From Zone 14, Convict Cowboy.

McKEAN, MICHAEL
Actor, Writer. b. NYC, Oct. 17, 1947. e. NYU. Featured on L.A. radio show, The Credibility Gap.
THEATRE: Accomplice (Theatre World Award).
PICTURES: 1941, Used Cars, Young Doctors in Love, This is Spinal Tap (also co-s.p., co-wrote songs), D.A.R.Y.L., Clue, Jumpin' Jack Flash, Light of Day, Planes Trains and Automobiles, Short Circuit 2, Earth Girls Are Easy, The Big Picture (also co-s.p.), Hider in the House, Flashback, Book of Love, True Identity, Memoirs of an Invisible Man, Man Trouble, Coneheads, Airheads, Radioland Murders, Across the Moon, The Brady Bunch Movie, Edie and Pen, Jack.
TELEVISION: *Series*: Laverne & Shirley, Grand, Sessions, Saturday Night Live, Dream On. *Movies*: More Than Friends, Classified Love, Murder in High Places, MacShayne: The Final Roll of the Dice. *Specials*: Spinal Tap Reunion, The Laverne and Shirley Reunion.

McKELLEN, SIR IAN
Actor. b. Burnley, England, May 25, 1939. e. Cambridge. C.B.E. 1979, Knighted 1991.
THEATRE: *London*: A Scent of Flowers (debut, 1964), Trelawny of the Wells, A Lily in Little India, The Man of Destiny, Black Comedy, Dr. Faustus, Henceforward, Bent, Uncle Vanya, Hamlet, Macbeth, Romeo & Juliet, Richard III. B'way: The Promise, Amadeus (Tony Award, 1981), Ian McKellen Acting Shakespeare, Wild Honey (also London), Richard III (Brooklyn), A Knight Out. Assoc. Dir. Nat'l Theatre. Prof. of Contemporary Theatre, Oxford Univ., 1991.
PICTURES: Alfred the Great, Thank You All Very Much, A Touch of Love, Priest of Love, The Keep, Plenty, Zina, Scandal, Last Action Hero, The Ballad of Little Jo, Six Degrees of Separation, The Shadow, Jack & Sarah, Restoration, Thin Ice, Richard III (also co-s.p.), Apt Pupil.

TELEVISION: Hamlet, David Copperfield, The Scarlet Pimpernel, Hedda Gabler, Ian McKellen Acting Shakespeare, Every Good Boy Deserves Favor, Loving Walter, Windmills of the Gods, Macbeth, Othello, Countdown to War, And the Band Played On, Mister Shaw's Missing Millions, Tales of the City, Cold Comfort Farm, Rasputin (Golden Globe Award, 1997).

McKEON, DOUG
Actor. b. Pompton Plains, NJ, June 10, 1966.
THEATRE: Dandelion Wine, Truckload, Brighton Beach Memoirs, Death of a Buick, The Big Day.
PICTURES: Uncle Joe Shannon, On Golden Pond, Night Crossing, Mischief, Turnaround, Where the Red Fern Grows Part 2, The Empty Mirror.
TELEVISION: *Series*: Edge of Night, Big Shamus Little Shamus, Little Niagra. *Mini-Series*: Centennial, At Mother's Request, From the Earth to the Moon. *Movies*: Tell Me My Name, Daddy I Don't Like It Like This, The Comeback Kid, An Innocent Love, Desperate Lives, Silent Eye, Heart of a Champion: The Ray Mancini Story, Breaking Home Ties, Without Consent, Sub Down.

McKEON, NANCY
Actress. b. Westbury, NY, April 4, 1966.
PICTURE: Where the Day Takes You.
TELEVISION: *Series*: Stone, The Facts of Life, Can't Hurry Love. *Movies*: A Question of Love, The Facts of Life Goes to Paris, High School U.S.A., This Child Is Mine, Poison Ivy, Firefighter (also co-exec. prod.), The Facts of Life Down Under, Strange Voices (also co-exec. prod.), A Cry for Help: The Tracey Thurman Story, A Mother's Gift, Style and Substance, Just Right. *Specials*: Schoolboy Father, Scruffy (voice), Please Don't Hit Me Mom, Candid Kids (co-host).

McKERN, LEO
Actor. r.n. Reginald McKern. b. Sydney, New South Wales, Australia, March 16, 1920.
THEATER: She Stoops to Conquer, Hamlet, Merry Wives of Windsor, Cat on a Hot Tin Roof, A Man for All Seasons, Boswell for the Defence, Hobson's Choice.
PICTURES: Murder in the Cathedral, All For Mary, X the Unknown, Time Without Pity, A Tale of Two Cities, The Mouse That Roared, Yesterday's Enemy, Scent of Mystery, Jazz Boat, Mr. Topaze (I Like Money), The Day the Earth Caught Fire, Lisa (The Inspector), Doctor in Distress, A Jolly Bad Fellow, King and Country, Agent 8 3/4 (Hot Enough for June), Help!, The Amorous Adventures of Moll Flanders, A Man for All Seasons, Assignment K, Decline and Fall of a Bird Watcher, The Shoes of the Fisherman, Ryan's Daughter, Massacre in Rome, The Adventure of Sherlock Holmes' Smarter Brother, The Omen, Candleshoe, Damien: Omen II, The Last Tasmanian, The Blue Lagoon, The French Lieutenant's Woman, Ladyhawke, The Chain, Traveling North (Australian Film Award), Dave and Dad on Our Selection.
TELEVISION: King Lear, Murder with Mirrors, House on Garibaldi Street, Reilly: Ace of Spies, Rumpole of the Bailey, The Master Builder, The Last Romantics, A Foreign Field, Good King Wenceslas.

McLAGLEN, ANDREW V.
Director. b. London, England, July 28, 1920. Son of late actor Victor McLaglen. e. U. of Virginia, 1939-40. Asst. m.p. dir., 1944-54.
PICTURES: Gun the Man Down (debut, 1956), Man in the Vault, The Abductors, Freckles, The Little Shepherd of Kingdom Come, McLintock!, Shenandoah, The Rare Breed, The Way West, Monkeys Go Home!, The Ballad of Josie, The Devil's Brigade, Bandolero, Hellfighters, The Undefeated, Chisum, Fool's Parade (also prod.), Something Big (also prod.), One More Train to Rob, Cahill: U.S. Marshal, Mitchell, The Last Hard Men, The Wild Geese, Breakthrough (Sergeant Steiner), ffolkes (North Sea Hijack), The Sea Wolves, Sahara, Return to the River Kwai, Eye of the Widow.
TELEVISION: *Series*: Gunsmoke, Have Gun—Will Travel, Perry Mason, Rawhide, The Lineup, The Lieutenant. *Movies*: Log of the Black Pearl, Stowaway to the Moon, Banjo Hackett: Roamin' Free, Murder at the World Series, Louis L'Amour's The Shadow Riders, Travis McGee, The Dirty Dozen: The Next Mission. *Mini-Series*: The Blue and the Gray, On Wings of Eagles.

McLERIE, ALLYN ANN
Actress. b. Grand Mere, Quebec, Canada, Dec. 1, 1926. e. Prof. childrens school. m. actor-singer George Gaynes. e. high school, N.Y. Dancer since 15 in many B'way shows.
THEATER: One Touch of Venus, On the Town, Finian's Rainbow, Where's Charley?, Miss Liberty, Time Limit, South Pacific, Night of the Iguana, Julius Caesar, West Side Story, My Fair Lady, The Beast in Me, To Dorothy a Son.
PICTURES: Words and Music (debut 1948), Where's Charley?, Desert Song, Calamity Jane, Phantom of the Rue Morgue, Battle Cry, They Shoot Horses Don't They?, Monte Walsh, The Cowboys, Jeremiah Johnson, The Magnificent Seven Ride, The Way We Were, Cinderella Liberty, All the President's Men.
TELEVISION: *Series*: Tony Randall Show, Punky Brewster, Days and Nights of Molly Dodd. *Mini-Series*: The Thorn Birds, Beulah Land. *Specials*: Oldest Living Graduate, The Entertainer, Return Engagement, Shadow of a Gunman. *Guest*: WKRP in Cincinnati, Barney Miller, St. Elsewhere, Hart to Hart, Love Boat, Dynasty.

McMAHON, ED
Performer. b. Detroit, MI, March 6, 1923. e. Boston Coll.; Catholic U. of America, B.A., 1949. U.S. Marines, 1942-53. First job on TV was as the clown on Big Top, 1950-51. First joined Johnny Carson as his sidekick on daytime quiz show Who Do You Trust? in 1958.
THEATRE: stock; B'way: Impossible Years.
PICTURES: The Incident, Slaughter's Big Rip-Off, Fun with Dick and Jane, The Last Remake of Beau Geste (cameo), Butterfly, Full Moon High, Love Affair.
TELEVISION: Series: Big Top, Who Do You Trust?, The Tonight Show (1962-92), Missing Links (emcee), Snap Judgment (emcee), The Kraft Music Hall (host, 1968), Concentration (emcee), NBC Adventure Theatre (host), Whodunnit? (emcee), Star Search (host), TV's Bloopers and Practical Jokes (host). Movies: Star Marker, The Great American Traffic Jam (Gridlock), The Kid From Left Field. Specials: Macy's Thanksgiving Day Parade (host), Jerry Lewis Labor Day Telethon (co-host).

McMAHON, JOHN J.
Executive. b. Chicago, IL, 1932. e. Northwestern U. Served with U.S. Army in Korea, beginning career on WGN-TV, Chicago; associated with ZIV-United Artists TV Productions during 1950s; joined ABC in 1958; v.p. & gen. mgr., WXYTZ-TV, Detroit, then KABC-TV, Los Angeles, 1968; v.p., ABC, 1968-72; joined NBC in 1972 as v.p., programs, west coast, NBC-TV; president, Hollywood Radio & Television Society; board member, Permanent Charities Committee. 1980, named pres. of Carson Prods. (Johnny Carson's prod. co.).
TELEVISION: John & Yoko: A Love Story, If It's Tuesday It Still Must Be Belgium (exec. prod.), My Father My Son (exec. prod.), Passions, Brother of the Wind.

McMARTIN, JOHN
Actor. Warsaw, IN, e. Columbia U. Off-B'way debut: Little Mary Sunshine (1959: Theatre World Award).
THEATER: The Conquering Hero, Blood Sweat and Stanley Poole, Children from Their Games, A Rainy Day in Newark, Pleasures and Palaces (Detroit), Sweet Charity (Tony nom.), Follies, The Great God Brown (Drama Desk Award), Sondheim: A Musical Tribute, Forget-Me-Not-Lane (Mark Taper Forum), The Visit, Chemin de Fer, The Rules of the Game, A Little Family Business, Passion (Mark Taper), Solomon's Child, Julius Caesar, A Little Night Music (Ahmanson), Love for Love, Happy New Year, Don Juan (Drama Desk Award, Tony nom.), Artist Descending a Staircase, Henry IV (Kennedy Ctr.), Custer (Kennedy Ctr.), Money & Friends (L.A.), Show Boat (Tony nom.), High Society.
PICTURES: A Thousand Clowns, What's So Bad About Feeling Good?, Sweet Charity, All The President's Men, Thieves, Brubaker, Blow Out, Pennies From Heaven, Dream Lover, Legal Eagles, Native Son, Who's That Girl, A Shock to the System.
TELEVISION: Series: Falcon Crest, Beauty and the Beast. Guest: Cheers, Mary Tyler Moore Show, Murder She Wrote, Magnum P.I., The Golden Girls, Empty Nest, Law and Order, others. American Playhouse Specials: Edith Wharton Story, Rules of the Game, The Greatest Man in the World, Private Contentment, The Fatal Weakness, Concealed Enemies. Movies: Ritual of Evil, Fear on Trial, The Defection of Simas Kudirka, The Last Ninja, Murrow, Day One, Roots: The Gift, Separate But Equal, Citizen Cohn.

McNAMARA, WILLIAM
Actor. b. Dallas, TX, March 31, 1965. e. Columbia U. Joined Act I theatre group at Williamstown Theatre Festival, 1986; studied acting at Lee Strasberg Institute.
PICTURES: The Beat (debut, 1988), Stealing Home, Dream a Little Dream, Stella, Texasville, Terror at the Opera, Aspen Extreme, Surviving the Game, Chasers, Storybook, Girl in the Cadillac, Copycat, Dead Girl, The Brylcreem Boys, Sweet Jane, Something to Believe In, Stag, The Deli, Knockout, Implicated.
TELEVISION: Series: Island Son. Specials: Soldier Boys (Afterschool Special), Secret of the Sahara, The Edge (Indian Poker), It's Only Rock 'n' Roll (Afterschool Special). Movies: Wildflower (ACE Award nom.), Doing Time on Maple Drive, Honor Thy Mother, Sworn to Vengeance, Radio Inside, Liz: The Elizabeth Taylor Story, Natural Enemy. Pilot: The Wyatts.

McNAUGHTON, JOHN
Director. b. Chicago, IL, Jan. 13, 1950.
PICTURES: Henry: Portrait of a Serial Killer, The Borrower, Sex Drugs Rock & Roll, Mad Dog and Glory, Girls in Prison, Normal Life, Veeck as a Wreck, Condo Painting, Wild Things.

McNEELY, JOEL
Composer.
PICTURES: The Pick-Up Artist (add'l. music score), Iron Will (orchestration), You Talkin' to Me?, Samantha, Police Story III: Supercop, Squanto: A Warrior's Tale, Iron Will, Terminal Velocity, Radioland Murders, Gold Diggers: The Secret of Bear Mountain, Flipper, Virus, Vegas Vacation, Wild America, Air Force One (add'l.).
TELEVISION: Movies: Parent Trap III, Parent Trap Hawaiian Honemoon, Frankenstein: The College Years. Series: Tiny Toon Adventures, The Young Indiana Jones Chronicles.

McNICHOL, KRISTY
Actress. b. Los Angeles, CA, Sept. 11, 1962. Brother is actor Jimmy McNichol. Made debut at age of 7 performing in commercials. Given regular role in Apple's Way; began appearing on such series as Love American Style and The Bionic Woman. Attracted attention of Spelling-Goldberg Productions, who cast her as Buddy Lawrence in Family series, 1976-80.
PICTURES: The End (debut, 1978), Little Darlings, The Night the Lights Went Out in Georgia, Only When I Laugh, White Dog, The Pirate Movie, Just the Way You Are, Dream Lover, You Can't Hurry Love, Two Moon Junction, The Forgotten One.
TELEVISION: Series: Apple's Way, Family (2 Emmy Awards: 1977, 1979), Empty Nest. Movies: The Love Boat II, Like Mom Like Me, Summer of My German Soldier, My Old Man, Blinded by the Light, Love Mary, Women of Valor, Children of the Bride, Baby of the Bride, Mother of the Bride (also co-exec. prod.).

McRANEY, GERALD
Actor. b. Collins, MS, Aug. 19, 1948. m. actress Delta Burke. e. U. of Mississippi. Left school to become surveyor in oil fields after which joined acting company in New Orleans. Studied acting with Jeff Corey; landed guest role on TV series, Night Gallery.
PICTURES: Night of Bloody Horror, Keep Off My Grass, The Neverending Story, American Justice.
TELEVISION: Series: Simon & Simon, Major Dad (also exec. prod.), Home of the Brave, Promised Land. Guest: The Incredible Hulk, The Rockford Files, The Dukes of Hazzard, Eight Is Enough, How the West Was Won, Hawaii Five-O, Barnaby Jones, Gunsmoke, Designing Women. Movies: Roots II, The Jordan Chance, Women in White, Trial of Chaplain Jenson, The Law, The Haunting Passion, A Hobo's Christmas, Where the Hell's That Gold?!!?, The People Across the Lake, Dark of the Moon, Murder By Moonlight, Blind Vengeance, Vestige of Honor, Love and Curses... And All That Jazz (also dir., co-exec. prod.), Fatal Friendship, Scattered Dreams: The Kathryn Messenger Story, Armed and Innocent, Motorcycle Gang, Deadly Vows, Someone She Knows, Not Our Son, Simon & Simon: In Trouble Again, The Stranger Beside Me, Nothing Lasts Forever. Special: Fast Forward.

McSHANE, IAN
Actor. b. Blackburn, England, Sept. 29, 1942. e. RADA.
THEATRE: England: The House of Fred Ginger, The Easter Man, The Glass Menagerie, Rashomon, Next Time I'll Sing to You, Loot, The Big Knife, The Admirable Crichton. NY: The Promise. LA: Inadmissible Evidence, Betrayal, As You Like It.
PICTURES: The Wild and the Willing (debut, 1962), The Pleasure Girls, Gypsy Girl (Sky West and Crooked), If It's Tuesday This Must Be Belgium, The Battle of Britain, Freelance, Pussycat Pussycat I Love You, The Devil's Widow (Tam-Lin), Villain, Sitting Target, The Left Hand of Gemini, The Last of Sheila, Ransom, Journey Into Fear, The Fifth Musketeer, Yesterday's Hero, Cheaper to Keep Her, Exposed, Torchlight, Ordeal By Innocence, Too Scared to Scream.
TELEVISION: Wuthering Heights, The Pirate, Disraeli, The Letter, Marco Polo, Bare Essence, Grace Kelly, Evergreen, A.D., The Murders in the Rue Morgue, Grand Larceny, War and Remembrance, Chain Letter (pilot), The Great Escape II: the Untold Story, The Young Charlie Chaplin, Lovejoy, Sauce For Goose, Dick Francis Mysteries (Blood Sport), Perry Mason: The Case of the Desperate Deception, Columbo: Rest in Peace Mrs. Columbo, White Goods, Soul Survivors (prod.), Madson (prod.), Lovejoy (prod., dir.).

McTIERNAN, JOHN
Director. b. Albany, NY, Jan. 8, 1951. e. Juilliard (acting), SUNY/Old Westbury (filmmaking). m. prod. Donna Dubrow. First effort was film The Demon's Daughter, unreleased to date. Appeared in film Death of a Soldier.
PICTURES: Nomads (also s.p.), Predator, Die Hard, The Hunt for Red October, Medicine Man, Last Action Hero (also co-prod.), Die Hard With a Vengeance, The Thomas Crown Affair, Airframe, The 13th Warrior.

MEADOWS, JAYNE
Actress. b. Wu Chang, China, Sept. 27, 1924. m. performer Steve Allen. Sister of deceased actress Audrey Meadows. Parents were Episcopal missionaries. Came to U.S. in 1931. Studied acting with Stella Adler, Lee Strasberg, David Craig. Made B'way debut in 1941 in Spring Again.
THEATRE: NY: Once in a Lifetime (revival), The Gazebo, Spring Again, Another Love Story, Kiss Them for Me, Many Happy Returns, Odds on Mrs. Oakley. Regional: Lost in Yonkers, Love Letters, Cinderella, The Fourposter, Tonight at 8:30, Powerful Women in History (1 woman show).
PICTURES: Undercurrent (debut, 1946), Dark Delusion, Lady in the Lake, Luck of the Irish, Song of the Thin Man, David and Bathsheba, Enchantment, Norman Is That You?, The Fat Man, College Confidential, Da Capo (Finland), City Slickers (voice), City Slickers II: The Legend of Curly's Gold (voice), The Player, Casino.

TELEVISION: *Series*: Meeting of Minds, St. Elsewhere, Medical Center, I've Got a Secret, High Society, It's Not Easy, The Steve Allen Show, Art Linkletter Show, Steve Allen Comedy Hour, Steve Allen's Laugh Back. *Movies*: Alice in Wonderland, Alice Through the Looking Glass, Ten Speed and Brownshoe, Masterpiece of Murder, The Ratings Game, Miss All-American Beauty, The James Dean Story, Sex and the Married Woman, The Gossip Columnist, Parent Trap Hawaiian Honeymoon, Now You See It Now You Don't. *Guest*: Your Show of Shows, The Hollywood Palace, The Red Skelton Show, The Love Boat, Fantasy Island, The Paper Chase, Here's Lucy, Uncle Buck, Sisters, The Nanny, Murder She Wrote, and many others.

MEANEY, COLM
Actor. b. Ireland. Started acting as a teen, appearing at Gate Theatre in Dublin in play, The Hostage. Studied at Abbey Theatre then joined London's 7-84 Theatre Co., Half Moon Theatre Co., Belt and Braces touring co. On NY stage in Breaking the Code. Also acted with Great Lakes Fest. in Cleveland, OH, in Nicholas Nickelby.
PICTURES: The Dead, Dick Tracy, Die Hard 2, Come See the Paradise, The Commitments, The Last of the Mohicans, Under Siege, Far and Away, Into the West, The Snapper (Golden Globe nom.), The Road to Wellville, The Englishman Who Went Up a Hill But Came Down a Mountain, The Van, Last of the High Kings.
TELEVISION: *Series*: Star Trek: The Next Generation, Deep Space Nine. *Mini-Series*: Scarlett.

MEANEY, DONALD V.
Executive. b. Newark, NJ. e. Rutgers U. Sch. of Journalism. Worked as reporter for Plainfield (NJ) Courier-News, Newark Evening News. Became news dir. of radio station WCTC in New Brunswick, NJ; later for WNJR, Newark. Joined NBC in 1952 as news writer; two years later became nat'l TV news editor. Promoted to mgr., national news, 1960 and mrg., special news programs, 1961. Appt. dir. of news programs 1962 and gen. mgr., NBC News, 1965; v.p., news programming, NBC, 1967; v.p. news, Washington, 1974; mng. dir., affiliate & intl. liaison, 1979; sr. mng. editor, intl. liaison, 1984; retired from NBC, 1985. Now on faculty of American U. Sch. of Communications.

MEARA, ANNE
Actress, Writer. b. Brooklyn, NY Sept. 20, 1929. m. actor-writer Jerry Stiller. Son is actor-dir. Ben Stiller; daughter is actress Amy Stiller. e. Herbert Berghof Studio, 1953-54. Apprenticed in summer stock on Long Island and Woodstock NY, 1950-53. Acted with NY Shakespeare Fest. 1957 and 1988 (Romeo and Juliet). With husband joined St. Louis improv. theater The Compass, 1959 and Chicago's Medium Rare. They formed comedy act in 1962 appearing (34 times) on The Ed Sullivan Show and making the nightclub and comedy club circuit incl. The Village Gate, The Blue Angel, The Establishment. Formed own prod. company, writing, prod. and recording award-winning radio and TV commercials. With husband co-hosted video, So You Want to Be an Actor?
THEATER: A Month in the Country, Maedchen in Uniform, Ulysses in Nightown, The House of Blue Leaves, Spookhouse, Bosoms and Neglect, Eastern Standard, Anna Christie (Tony nom.), After-Play (also author, Outer Critics Circle Award, 1996).
PICTURES: The Out-of-Towners, Lovers and Other Strangers, Nasty Habits, The Boys From Brazil, Fame, The Perils of P.K., The Longshot, My Little Girl, Awakenings, Highway to Hell, Reality Bites, Heavyweights, Kiss of Death, An Open Window, The Daytrippers, Brass Ring (Southie), Fish in the Bathtub.
TELEVISION: Guest on numerous TV game and talk shows and variety shows. *Series*: The Greatest Gift (1954 soap opera), The Paul Lynde Show, The Corner Bar, Take Five with Stiller and Meara (1977-78; synd.), Kate McShane, Rhoda, Archie Bunker's Place, ALF, All My Children. *Movies*: Kate McShane (pilot), The Other Woman (co-writer), Jitters. *Specials*: The Sunset Gang, Avenue Z Afternoon.

MECHANIC, BILL
Executive. b. Detroit, MI. e. Michigan State U., B.A.; U. of Southern California, Ph.D. in film pending. Entered industry 1978 as dir. of programming for SelecTV; promoted to v.p., 1980. Joined Paramount 1982; 1984, to Disney as v.p., pay TV sls. 1985, named sr. v.p., video, of new Walt Disney video div.; 1987, named president, int'l theatrical distribution and worldwide video, Walt Disney. 1993, became pres,. 20th Century Fox; 1996, named chmn. & CEO, 20th Century Fox.

MEDAK, PETER
Director. b. Budapest, Hungary, Dec. 23, 1940. Appeared in film Beverly Hills Cop III.
THEATRE: Miss Julie. *Operas*: Salome, La Voix Humaine, Rigoletto.
PICTURES: Negatives, A Day in the Death of Joe Egg, The Ruling Class, Ghost in the Noonday Sun, The Odd Job, The Changeling, Zorro the Gay Blade, The Men's Club, The Krays, Let Him Have It, Romeo Is Bleeding, Pontiac Moon, Species 2.
TELEVISION: Third Girl from the Left, The Babysitter, The Dark Secret of Black Bayou, Mistress of Paradise, Cry for the Stranger, Faerie Tale Theatre, Twilight Zone, Nabokov, Crime Story, Mount Royal, La Voix Humaine, Tales From the Crypt, Homicide, The Kindred, Falls Road, Homicide, The Hunchback of Notre Dame.

MEDAVOY, MIKE
Executive. b. Shanghai, China, Jan. 21, 1941. e. UCLA, grad. 1963 with honors in history. Lived in China until 1947 when family moved to Chile. Came to U.S. in 1957. Started working in mail room at Universal Studios and became a casting dir., then went to work for Bill Robinson as an agent trainee. Two years later joined GAC and CMA where he was a v.p. in the m. p. dept. 1971 joined IFA as v.p. in charge of m. p. dept. Represented American and foreign creative talents, incl. Jane Fonda, Donald Sutherland, Michelangelo Antonioni, Jean-Louis Trintignant, Karel Reisz, Steven Spielberg, Robert Aldrich, George Cukor, John Milius, Terry Malick, Raquel Welch, Gene Wilder and Jeanne Moreau. While at IFA was involved in packaging The Sting, Young Frankenstein, Jaws and others, before joining United Artists Corp. in 1974, as sr. v.p. in chg. of West Coast prod. While at UA, was responsible for One Flew Over the Cuckoo's Nest, Annie Hall and Rocky among others. 1978 named exec. v.p., Orion Pictures Co. where he was responsible for Platoon, Amadeus, Dances With Wolves and Silence of the Lambs. (In 1982 Orion team took over Filmways, Inc.) 1990, apptd. chmn. Tri-Star Pictures, & mem. Columbia Pictures Bd. of Dir. Resigned in 1994. Became chmn. and CEO of Phoenix Pictures in 1995. Co-chmn., St. Petersburg Film Festival, 1994. Chmn. of the Jury, Tokyo Film Festival, 1994. Member of Filmex bd.; bd. of trustees, UCLA Foundation; chmn. advisory bd., College for Intl. Strategic Affairs at UCLA; steering comm. of Royce 270, UCLA; visiting comm., Boston Museum of Fine Arts; advisory bd., Tel Aviv U.; bd., Museum of Science & Industry; Co-Chmn.: Olympic Sports Federation, Music Center Unified Fund Campaign; founding bd. of governors, Sundance Inst. Recipient: Motion Picture Pioneer Award, 1993; Cannes Film Festival Award, 1998; UCLA Alumni Award for Excellence.

MEDOFF, MARK
Writer. e. U. of Miami, Stanford U. Honorary doctor of humane letters, Gallaudet Univ. Prof. & dramatist in residence, New Mexico St. Univ. Novel: Dreams of Long Lasting.
THEATER: When You Comin' Back Red Ryder? (Obie Award), Children of a Lesser God (Tony Award), The Wager, Kringle's Window.
PICTURES: Good Guys Wear Black, Children of a Lesser God (Acad. Award nom.), Clara's Heart, City of Joy, Homage (also prod.), Santa Fe, Mighty Joe Young.
TELEVISION: *Movie*: Apology, The Twilight of the Golds..

MEDWIN, MICHAEL
Actor, Writer, Producer. b. London, England, 1923. e. Institut Fischer, Switzerland. Stage debut 1940; m.p. acting debut in Root of All Evil, 1946. Acted with National Theatre 1977-78.
THEATRE: Spring and Port Wine, Joe Egg, Forget-me-not Lane, Chez Nous, Alpha Beta, Another Country, Crystal Clear, Interpreters, Orpheus, Noises Off.
PICTURES: *Actor*: My Sister and I, Mrs. Christopher, Gay One, Children of Chance, Operation Diamond, Black Memory, Just William's Luck, Ideal Husband, Picadilly Incident, Night Beat, Courtney's of Curzon Street, Call of the Blood, Anna Karenina, William Comes to Town, Woman Hater, Look Before You Love, Forbidden, For Them That Trespass, Queen of Spades, Trottie True, Boys in Brown, Trio, Long Dark Hall, Curtain Up, Street Corner (Both Sides of the Law), I Only Asked, Carry on Nurse, Wind Cannot Read, Heart of a Man, Crooks Anonymous, It's All Happening, Night Must Fall, I've Gotta Horse, 24 Hours To Kill, Scrooge, The Jigsaw Man. *Prod.*: Charlie Bubbles, If..., Spring and Port Wine, O Lucky Man! Gumshoe, Law and Disorder, Memoirs of a Survivor, Diamond's Edge.
TELEVISION: Granada's Army Game, Shoestring, The Love of Mike, Three Live Wires.

MEIER, JIM
Executive. b. Newport Beach, CA, Aug. 9, 1971.Pres., Meier Entertainment Group, Vancouver, BC, 1994-98. Dir., British Columbia Motion Picture Assoc., 1996-98. Member, Academy of Canadian Cinema and Television. Pres., CEO and Chairman, Meier Worldwide Intermedia, Inc., 1996-.

MELCHIOR, IB
Director, Writer. b. Copenhagen, Denmark, Sept. 17, 1917. Son of late singer Lauritz Melchior. e. Coll., Stenhus, Denmark, 1936; U. of Copenhagen, 1937. Actor. stage mgr., English Players, 1937-38; co-dir. 1938; actor in 21 stage prod. in Europe and U.S. on radio; set designer; stage man. dept., Radio City Music Hall, 1941-42; U.S. Military Intelligence, 1942-45; writer, dir., m.p. shorts for TV, 1947-48; TV actor, 1949-50; assoc. dir., CBS-TV, 1950; assoc. prod., G-L Enterprises, 1952-53; dir., Perry Como Show, 1951-54; dir. March of Medicine, 1955-56. Documentary writ. & dir., received Top Award by Nat'l. Comm. for Films for Safety, 1960. Golden Scroll Award, Acad. of Science Fiction, Best Writing, 1976; Hamlet Award, Shakespeare Society of America, excellence in playwriting, Hour of Vengeance, 1982.
AUTHOR: Order of Battle, Sleeper Agent, The Haigerloch Project, The Watchdogs of Abaddon, The Marcus Device, The Tombstone Cipher, Eva, V-3, Code Name: Grand Guignol, Steps & Stairways, Quest, Order of Battle: Hitler's Werewolves, Case by Case.

PICTURES: *Writer:* When Hell Broke Loose, Live Fast—Die Young, The Angry Red Planet (also dir.), The Case of Patty Smith (assoc. prod.), Reptilicus, Journey to the Seventh Planet, Robinson Crusoe on Mars, The Time Travellers (also dir.), Ambush Bay, Planet of the Vampires, Death Race 2000.

MELEDANDRI, CHRIS
Executive. Pres., Fox Family Films.

MELNICK, DANIEL
Executive. b. New York, NY, April 21, 1934. e. NYU. 1952-54, prod. The Children's Theatre at Circle in the Sq., NY. In 1954 was (youngest) staff prod. for CBS-TV; then exec. prod., East Side West Side and N.Y.P.D. Joined ABC-TV as v.p. in chg. of programming. Partner in Talent Associates. Joined MGM as v.p. in chg. of prod.; in 1974 named sr. v.p. & worldwide head of prod.; 1977 in charge of worldwide production, Columbia Pictures; named pres., 1978. Resigned to form independent production co., IndieProd. Company.
PICTURES: *Prod.:* Straw Dogs, That's Entertainment (exec. prod.), That's Entertainment Part 2, All That Jazz (exec. prod.), Altered States (exec. prod.), First Family, Making Love, Unfaithfully Yours (exec. prod.), Footloose (exec. prod.), Quicksilver, Roxanne, Punchline, Mountains of the Moon, Total Recall, Air America, L.A. Story.
TELEVISION: *Specials:* Death of a Salesman (prod.; Emmy Award, 1967), The Ages of Man (prod.; Emmy Award, 1966). *Exec. prod.:* East Side/West Side, N.Y.P.D., Get Smart, Chain Letter (pilot, exec. prod.). *Movie:* Get Smart Again! (exec. prod.).

MELNIKER, BENJAMIN
Producer, Attorney. b. Bayonne, NJ. e. Brooklyn Coll., LL.B., Fordham Law Sch. Loew's Theatres usher; private law practice. Employed by Legal Department MGM; v.p. & gen. counsel, 1954-69; exec. v.p., 1968-70; resigned from MGM, 1971; also member MGM bd. of dirs. and mem. MGM exec. com. Pres., & CEO of Jerry Lewis Cinemas, 1972. Prod. & exec. prod. motion pictures and television movies and series, 1974 to present. Adjunct assoc. prof., NY Law Sch., 1976-77. Former m.p. chmn. Anti-Defamation League, B'nai Brith. Mem. Amer., NY State bar assns., Bar Assn. of City NY, AMPAS.
PICTURES: Winter Kills. *Exec. prod:* Mitchell, Shoot, Batman, Batman Returns, Batman Forever, Batman & Robin. *Producer:* Swamp Thing, The Return of the Swamp Thing, Batman: Mask of the Phantasm.
TELEVISION: *Exec. prod.:*Three Sovereigns for Sarah, Television's Greatest Bits, Where On Earth Is Carmen Sandiego (Emmy Award), Little Orphan Annie's Very Animated Christmas , Swamp Thing, Harmful Intent, Fish Police, Dinosaucers.

MELVIN, MURRAY
Actor. b. London, England, 1932. On stage with Theatre Workshop.
PICTURES: The Criminal (debut, 1960), A Taste of Honey, HMS Defiant (Damn the Defiant), Sparrows Can't Sing, The Ceremony, Alfie, Kaleidoscope, Smashing Time, The Fixer, Start the Revolution Without Me, A Day in the Death of Joe Egg, The Devils, The Boy Friend, Ghost in the Noonday Sun, Barry Lyndon, The Bawdy Adventures of Tom Jones, Joseph Andrews, Comrades, Testimony, Little Dorrit, The Krays, Let Him Have It, Princess Caraboo.
TELEVISION: Little World of Don Camilllo, The Soldiers Tale, A Christmas Carol, This Office Life, Bulman, William Tell, Stuff of Madness, Sunday Pursuit, The Memorandum, The Stone of Montezuma, Surprises, England My England, The Village.

MENGES, CHRIS
Cinematographer, Director. b. Kington, England, Sept. 15, 1940.
PICTURES: *Cinematographer:* Kes, Gumshoe, The Empire Strikes Back (second unit), Local Hero, Comfort and Joy, The Killing Fields (Acad. Award, 1984), Marie, The Mission (Acad. Award, 1986), Singing the Blues in Red, Shy People, High Season, Michael Collins (LA Film Critics Award, 1997). *Director:* A World Apart, Crisscross, Second Best.
TELEVISION: World in Action, Opium Warlords, Opium Trail, East 103rd Street, etc.

MENKEN, ALAN
Composer. b. New York, NY, July 22, 1949. Raised in New Rochelle, NY. e. NYU. Began composing and performing at Lehman Engel Musical Theatre Workshop at BMI, where he met future partner, lyricist Howard Ashman. With Ashman made Off-B'way debut in 1979 with score of God Bless You Mr. Rosewater. Wrote music for workshop Battle of the Giants, and music and lyrics for Manhattan Theatre Club Prod. of Real Life Funnies. With Ashman wrote 1982 Off-B'way hit Little Shop of Horrors. Other theatre credits include: The Apprenticeship of Duddy Kravitz, Diamonds, Personals, Let Freedom Sing, Weird Romance, Beauty and the Beast, A Christmas Carol. Grammy Awards: The Little Mermaid (2), Beauty and the Beast (3), Aladdin (4), Pocahontas (1).
PICTURES: Little Shop of Horrors (Acad. Award nom. for song Mean Green Mother From Outer Space), The Little Mermaid (2 Acad. Awards: best song, Under the Sea, and music score,

1989), Rocky V (song), Beauty and the Beast (2 Acad. Awards: best song, title song, and music score, 1991), Newsies, Aladdin (2 Acad. Awards: for song, A Whole New World, and music score, 1992), Home Alone 2: Lost in New York (song), Life With Mikey, Pocahontas (Acad. Awards for Best Score & Best Original Song), The Hunchback of Notre Dame, Hercules.
TELEVISION: *Special:* Lincoln. *Movie:* Polly (song).

MERCHANT, ISMAIL
Producer, Director. b. Bombay, India, Dec. 25, 1936. e. St. Xavier's Coll., Bombay; NYU, M.A. business admin. Formed Merchant Ivory Prods., 1961 with James Ivory. First film, The Creation of Women (theatrical short, 1961, nom. for Acad. Award). Published 3 cook-books: Ismail Merchant's Indian Cuisine, Ismail Merchant's Passionate Meals, Ismail Merchant's Florence. Other books: Hullabaloo in Old Jeypore: The Making of The Deceivers (1989), The Proprietor: The Screenplay and Story Behind the Film.
PICTURES: *Producer:* The Householder, Shakespeare Wallah, The Guru, Bombay Talkie, Savages, Autobiography of a Princess, The Wild Party, Roseland, Hullabaloo Over Georgie and Bonnie's Pictures, The Europeans, Jane Austen in Manhattan, Quartet, Heat and Dust, The Bostonians, A Room With a View, Maurice, My Little Girl (exec. prod.), The Deceivers, Slaves of New York, The Perfect Murder (exec. prod.), Mr. and Mrs. Bridge, Ballad of the Sad Cafe, Howards End (BAFTA Award), The Remains of the Day, In Custody (dir. debut), Jefferson in Paris (also cameo), Feast of July (exec. prod.), The Proprietor (dir.).
TELEVISION: *Director:* Mahatma and the Mad Boy, Courtesans of Bombay.

MEREDITH, ANNE
Writer, Producer.
TELEVISION: Losing Chase, Bastard Out of Carolina (writer only, Writers' Guild Award, 1998).

MERRICK, DAVID
Producer. r.n. David Margulois. b. St. Louis, Nov. 27, 1911. e. Washington U. L.L.B.
THEATER: *B'way:* Fanny, The Matchmaker, Look Back in Anger, The Entertainer, Jamaica, The World of Suzie Wong, La Plume de Ma Tante, Epitaph for George Dillon, Destry Rides Again, Gypsy, Take Me Along, Irma La Douce, A Taste of Honey, Becket (Tony Award, 1961), Do Re Mi, Carnival, Sunday in New York, Ross, Subways Are For Sleeping, I Can Get It for You Wholesale, Stop the World—I Want to Get Off, Tchin Tchin, Oliver!, Luther (Tony Award, 1964), 110 in the Shade, Arturo Ui, One Flew Over the Cuckoo's Nest, The Milk Train Doesn't Stop Here Anymore, Hello Dolly! (Tony Award, 1964), Oh What a Lovely War, Pickwick, The Roar of the Greasepaint—The Smell of the Crowd, Inadmissible Evidence, Cactus Flower, Marat/Sade (Tony Award, 1966), Philadelphia Here I Come, Don't Drink the Water, I Do! I Do!, How Now Dow Jones, The Happy Time, Rosencrantz and Guildenstern Are Dead (Tony Award, 1968), 40 Carats, Promises Promises, Play It Again Sam, Child's Play, Four on a Garden, A Midsummer Night's Dream, The Philanthropist, Vivat Vivat Regina, Moonchildren, Sugar, Out Cry, Mack and Mabel, The Misanthrope, A Patriot for Me, Travesties, Very Good Eddie, Private Lives, 42nd Street (Tony Award, 1981), I Won't Dance, Loot, Oh Kay!, State Fair.
PICTURES: Child's Play (debut, 1972), The Great Gatsby, Semi-Tough, Rough Cut.

MERRILL, DINA
Actress. r.n. Nedenia Hutton. b. New York, NY, Dec. 29, 1928. Fashion model, 1944-46. A co-owner and vice-chmn., RKO Pictures, m.p. and TV prod. co.
THEATER: *Regional:* My Sister Eileen, Major Barbara, Misalliance, Othello, Twelfth Night, Loved, Surprise. *Off-B'way:* Importance of Being Earnest, Smile of the Cardboard Man, Suddenly Last Summer. *B'way:* Angel Street, Are You Now or Have You Ever Been?, On Your Toes.
PICTURES: The Desk Set (debut, 1957), A Nice Little Bank That Should Be Robbed, Don't Give Up the Ship, Operation Petticoat, The Sundowners, Butterfield 8, Twenty Plus Two, The Young Savages, The Courtship of Eddie's Father, I'll Take Sweden, Running Wild, The Meal (Deadly Encounter), The Greatest, A Wedding, Just Tell Me What You Want, Twisted, Caddyshack II, True Colors, The Player, Open Season, The Point of Betrayal, Milk & Money.
TELEVISION: *Debut:* Kate Smith Show 1956. *Guest:* Four Star Theatre, Playwrights `56, Climax!, Playhouse 90, Westinghouse Presents, The Investigators, Checkmate, The Rogues, Bob Hope Presents, To Tell the Truth, The Doctors, The Name of the Game, Hotel, Hawaii Five-O, Murder She Wrote, Something Wilder, The Nanny, Rosanne. *Series:* Hot Pursuit. *Mini-Series:* Roots: The Next Generations. *Movies:* The Sunshine Patriot, Seven in Darkness, The Lonely Profession, Mr. & Mrs. Bo Jo Jones, Family Flight, The Letters, Kingston: The Power Play, The Tenth Month, Repeat Performance, Turn Back the Clock, Fear, Brass Ring, Anne to the Infinite, Not in My Family, Something Borrowed Something Blue.

MERSON, MARC

Producer. b. New York, NY, Sept. 9, 1931. e. Swarthmore Coll. Entered Navy in 1953; assigned as publicist to Admiral's Staff of Sixth Fleet Command in the Mediterranean. Upon discharge joined trade paper Show Business as feature editor. Joined CBS-TV as asst. to casting dir.. Left after 3 yrs. to work for Ely Landau as casting dir., packager and sometime prod. of The Play of the Week on TV. Returned to CBS for 3-yr. stint doing specials and live programs. Left to organize Brownstone Productions as indep. prod. Partner with Alan Alda in Helix Productions to package and produce TV shows.
PICTURES: The Heart Is a Lonely Hunter, People Soup (short), Leadbelly, Doc Hollywood (exec. prod.).
TELEVISION: *Series*: Kaz, We'll Get By, Off the Rack, Jessica Novak, Waverly Wonders, Stage 67, Androcles and the Lion, Dummler and Son (pilot), The David Frost Revue (synd. series), We'll Get By. *Movie*: Rules of Marriage (spr. prod.).

MESSICK, DON

Actor. b. Buffalo, NY, Sept. 7, 1926. e. Nanticoke H.S., Maryland; Ramsay Street Sch. of Acting, Baltimore; American Theatre Wing, NY. Began performing as ventriloquist at age 13 in rural Maryland. Own radio show at 15 in Salisbury, MD (WBOC) for two years, writing and portraying all the characters in a one-man weekly comedy show. Worked in Hanna-Barbera cartoons since company began in 1957, voicing Ruff in their first series on NBC, 1958. *Voices*: Boo Boo Bear and Ranger Smith on Yogi Bear Show, Astro on The Jetsons, Scooby Doo and Scrappy Doo on Scooby Doo series, Papa Smurf and Azrael on Smurfs, Droopy on Droopy & Dripple, Dr. Benton Quest on Jonny Quest (all Hanna-Barbera Prods.); Hamton J. Pig on Tiny Toon Adventures (WB). Has done numerous national commercials.

MESTRES, RICARDO A. III

Executive. b. New York, NY, Jan. 23, 1958. e. Harvard U., A.B. 1980. Gained filmmaking experience during summers as prod. asst. on TV features. Joined Paramount Pictures as creative exec. 1981. Promoted to exec. dir. of production in 1982 and to v.p., prod. in 1984. Named v.p. of prod., Walt Disney Pictures, 1985. Promoted to sr. v.p., prod.,1986-88. Named pres. production, Touchstone Pictures, 1988-89. In 1989, became pres., Hollywood Pictures. Resigned, 1994. Co-founder Great Oaks Entertainment with John Hughes, 1995-1997. Principal Ricardo Mestres Productions. Disney Studios, 1997-present. Member, AMPAS.
PICTURES: *Prod.*: Jack, 101 Dalmatians, Flubber, Home Alone III.

METCALF, LAURIE

Actress. b. Edwardsville, IL, June 16, 1955. e. Illinois St. Univ. One of the original members of the Steppenwolf Theatre Company. On B'way in My Thing of Love.
THEATRE: Chicago: True West, Fifth of July. NY: Balm in Gilead (Obie & Theatre World Awards). LA: Wrong Turn at Lungfish.
PICTURES: Desperately Seeking Susan (debut, 1985), Making Mr. Right, Candy Mountain, Stars and Bars, Miles From Home, Uncle Buck, Internal Affairs, Pacific Heights, JFK, Mistress, A Dangerous Woman, Blink, Leaving Las Vegas, Dear God.
TELEVISION: *Series*: Roseanne (3 Emmy Awards: 1992-4). *Movie*: The Execution of Raymond Graham.

METZLER, JIM

Actor. b. Oneonta, NY, June 23, 1951. e. Dartmouth Coll.
PICTURES: Four Friends, Tex, River's Edge, Hot to Trot, Sundown: The Vampire in Retreat, 976-EVIL, Old Gringo, Circuitry Man, Delusion, One False Move, Waxwork II: Lost in Time, A Weekend with Barbara und Ingrid, Gypsy Eyes, C.I.A. Trackdown, Plughead Rewired: Circuitry Man II, Children of the Corn III: Urban Harvest, Cadillac Ranch, A Gun A Car A Blonde, L.A. Confidential, St Patrick's Day, Under the Influence, Phantom Town, Warm Texas Rain.
TELEVISION: *Series*: Cutter to Houston, The Best Times. *Mini-Series*: North and South, North and South Book II, On Wings of Eagles. *Movies*: Do You Remember Love, Princess Daisy, Christmas Star, The Alamo: 13 Days to Glory, The Little Match Girl, Murder By Night, Crash: The Mystery of Flight 1501, Love Kills, French Silk, Don't Look Back, Apollo II, Little Girls in Pretty Boxes, A Wing and a Prayer.

MEYER, BARRY M.

Executive. b. New York, NY, Nov. 28, 1943. With ABC-TV in legal and business affairs depts. before joining Warner Bros. TV in 1971 as dir. of business affairs. 1972, named v.p. of business affairs for Warner TV arm; promoted to exec. v.p. of div. 1978. 1984, named exec. v.p. of Warner Bros., Inc. 1994, named COO.

MEYER, NICHOLAS

Director, Writer. b. New York, NY, Dec. 24, 1945. e. U. of Iowa. Was unit publicist for Love Story, 1969. Story ed. Warner Bros. 1970-71.
AUTHOR: The Love Story Story, The Seven Percent Solution, Target Practice, The West End Horror, Black Orchid, Confession of a Homing Pigeon, The Canary Trainer.
PICTURES: The Seven Percent Solution (s.p.), Time After Time (s.p., dir.), Star Trek II: The Wrath of Khan (dir.), Volunteers (dir.), The Deceivers (dir.), Company Business (dir., s.p.) Star Trek VI: The Undiscovered Country (dir., co-s.p.), Sommersby (co-s.p.), Voices, The Informant.

TELEVISION: *Movies*: Judge Dee (writer), The Night That Panicked America (writer), The Day After (dir.).

MEYER, RON

Executive. b. 1945. Served in US Marine Corps. 1985, co-founded, with Mike Ovitz, Creative Artists talent agency, eventually serving as pres. 1995, appointed pres. & COO of MCA.

MEYER, RUSS

Producer, Director. b. Oakland, CA, March 21, 1922. In 1942 joined Army Signal Corps, learned m.p. photography and shot combat newsreels. Worked as photographer for Playboy Magazine. Pres., RM Films Intl. Inc. 3 vol. autobiography: A Clean Breast: The Life and Loves of Russ Meyer.
PICTURES: The Immoral Mr. Teas, Eve and the Handyman, Erotica, Wild Gals of the Naked West, Heavenly Bodies, Lorna, Motor Psycho, Fanny Hill, Mudhoney, Mondo Topless, Faster Pussycat Kill Kill, Finders Keepers Lovers Weepers, Goodmorning and Goodbye, Common Law Cabin, Vixen, Cherry Harry & Raquel, Beyond the Valley of the Dolls, The Seven Minutes, Black Snake, Supervixens, Up, Beneath the Valley of the Ultra Vixens, Amazon Women on the Moon (actor), Pandora Peaks, Europe In the Raw!, Melissa Mounds.

MEYERS, NANCY

Writer, Producer. b. Philadelphia, PA. e. American U., D.C. Began as story editor for Ray Stark. First teamed with Charles Shyer to write screenplay for Private Benjamin.
PICTURES: *Writer/Producer*: Private Benjamin (Acad. Award nom., Writers Guild Annual Award), Irreconcilable Differences, Baby Boom, Father of the Bride, I Love Trouble, Father of the Bride II.

MEYERS, ROBERT

Executive. b. Mount Vernon, NY, Oct. 3, 1934. e. NYU. Entered m.p. industry as exec. trainee in domestic div. of Columbia Pictures, 1956; sales and adv. 1956-60; transferred to sales dept. Columbia Pictures Int'l, NY: posts there included supervisor of int'l roadshows and exec. assistant. to continental mgr. Joined National General Pictures as v.p.-foreign sales, 1969. Created JAD Films International Inc. in Feb. 1974 for independent selling and packaging of films around the world. September, 1977, joined Lorimar Productions Inc. as sr. v.p. of Lorimar Distribution Intl. Became pres. in 1978. Joined Filmways Pictures in 1980, named pres. & COO. Pres. of American Film Mktg. Assn.; 1982, formed new co., R.M. Films International. Rejoined Lorimar 1985. as pres., Lorimar Motion Pictures, int'l distribution. 1988-92, pres., Orion Pictures Int'l. 1993-94, pres., Odyssey Entertainment. In 1995, joined Village Roadshow International as pres.

MICHAELS, JOEL B.

Producer. b. Buffalo, NY, Oct. 24, 1938. Studied acting with Stella Adler. Many co-prods. with Garth Drabinsky, Cineplex Corp. Pres. of Cineplex Odeon, 1986-90.
PICTURES: The Peace Killers, Your Three Minutes Are Up (prod. spvr.), Student Teachers (prod. spvr.), The Prisoners (assoc. prod.), Lepke (assoc. prod.), The Four Deuces (asso. prod.), Bittersweet Love, The Silent Partner, The Changeling, Tribute, The Amateur, Losin' It (exec. prod.), The Philadelphia Experiment, Black Moon Rising, Universal Soldier, Three of Hearts (exec. prod.), Stargate, Cutthroat Island (co-prod.), Last of the Dogmen, Lolita.

MICHAELS, LORNE

Writer, Producer. b. Toronto, Canada, Nov. 17, 1944. e. U. of Toronto, 1966. CEO, Broadway Video, since 1979. Named Broadcaster of the Year by the International Radio and Television Society, 1992.
THEATER: Gilda Radner Live From New York (prod., dir.).
PICTURES: *Producer*: Gilda Live (also co-s.p.), Nothing Lasts Forever, Three Amigos (also co-s.p.), Wayne's World, Coneheads, Wayne's World 2, Lassie, Tommy Boy, Stuart Saves His Family, Black Sheep.
TELEVISION: *Series*: Rowan and Martin's Laugh-In (writer, 1968-69), Saturday Night Live (creator, prod., writer: 1975-80, 4 Emmy Awards; 1985-), The New Show (prod.), The Kids in the Hall (series co-prod.), Late Night With Conan O'Brien (exec. prod.). *Specials*: Lily Tomlin Specials (writer, prod.: 1972-75, 2 Emmy Awards), Perry Como (writer, prod., 1974), Flip Wilson (writer, prod.), Beach Boys (writer, prod.), The Paul Simon Special (writer, prod., Emmy Award, 1978), The Rutles: All You Need Is Cash (writer, prod.), Steve Martin's Best Show Ever (prod.), Simon and Garfunkel: The Concert in the Park (exec. prod.), The Coneheads (exec. prod.), 1988 Emmy Awards (prod.), Coca-Cola Presents Live: The Hard Rock, On Location: Kids in the Hall (exec. prod.), The Rolling Stones: Steel Wheels Concert (exec. prod.), Paul Simon: Born at the Right Time in Central Park (exec. prod.).

MICHAELS, RICHARD

Director. b. Brooklyn, NY, Feb. 15, 1936. e. Cornell U. Script supervisor 1955-64 and associate prod. before starting directing career in 1968 with Bewitched (54 episodes; also assoc. prod.).

PICTURES: How Come Nobody's On Our Side?, Blue Skies Again. TELEVISION: *Series*: Love American Style, The Odd Couple, Delvecchio, Ellery Queen, Room 222. *Movies*: Once an Eagle (mini-series), Charlie Cobb, Having Babies II, Leave Yesterday Behind, My Husband Is Missing, ... And Your Name Is Jonah (winner, Christopher Award), Once Upon a Family, The Plutonium Incident, Scared Straight, Another Story (Scott Newman Drug Abuse Prevention Award), Homeward Bound (Banff Intl. TV Fest. Special Jury Award & Christopher Award), Berlin Tunnel 21, The Children Nobody Wanted, One Cooks, The Other Doesn't, Jessie (pilot), Silence of the Heart, Heart of a Champion: The Ray Mancini Story, Rockabye, Kay O'Brien (pilot), Leg Work (pilot), Red River (movie), Indiscreet, Love and Betrayal, Her Wicked Ways, Leona Helmsley: The Queen of Mean, Triumph of the Heart: The Ricky Bell Story, Backfield in Motion, Miss America: Behind the Crown, Father and Scout. *Mini-series*: Sadat, I'll Take Manhattan.

MICHEL, WERNER
Executive. e. U. of Berlin, U. of Paris, Ph.D., Sorbonne, 1931. Radio writer, dir., co-author two Broadway revues, 1938, 1940. Broadcast dir., Voice of America, 1942-46. Prod. & dir., CBS, 1946-48; asst. prog. dir., CBS, 1948-50. Prod. Ford TV Theatre, 1950-52 Prod. DuMont TV network, 1952-55. Dir. Electronicam TV-Film Prod., 1955-56. Prod. of Edge of Night, Procter and Gamble, 1956-57. V.P. & dir., TV-radio dept., Reach, McClinton Advertising, Inc., 1957-62. Consultant, TV Programming & Comm'l-Prod., N.W. Ayer & Son Inc. V.P. & dir., TV dept., SSCB Advertising, 1963. Program exec. at ABC-TV Hollywood, 1975. Sr. v.p. of creative affairs, 1980-82. Exec. v.p., Wrather Entertainment Intl., 1979. Returned to MGM-TV as sr. v.p., creative affairs, 1980-82. COO, Guber-Peters TV, 1982-84. Sr. v.p., corporate TV dept., Kenyon & Eckhart, & NY, 1984-86. Currently sr. v.p., sr. partner of TV dept., Bozell, Inc. NY.

MICHELL, KEITH
Actor. b. Adelaide, Australia, Dec. 1, 1926. Early career as art teacher, radio actor; toured Australia with Stratford Shakespearean Co. 1952-53; Stratford Memorial Theatre 1954-55, Old Vic Theatre 1956-57. Served as artistic dir., Chichester Festival Theatre, touring Australia.
THEATER: Irma la Douce, Art of Seduction, The First 400 Years, Robert & Elizabeth, Kain, The King's Mare, Man of La Mancha, Abelard & Heloise, Hamlet, Crucifer of Blood, On the Twentieth Century, Pete McGynty, Captain Beaky Christmas Show, On the Rocks, The Tempest, Amadeus, La Cage aux Folles, Portraits, The Bacarat Scandal, Henry VIII, Aspects of Love, Scrooge, Brazilian Blue, Caesar & Cleopatra.
PICTURES: True as a Turtle, Dangerous Exile, Gypsy and the Gentleman, The Hellfire Club, All Night Long, Seven Seas to Calais, Prudence and the Pill, House of Cards, Henry VIII and his Six Wives, Moments, The Deceivers.
TELEVISION: *U.K.*: Pygmalion, Act of Violence, Mayerling Affair, Wuthering Heights, The Bergonzi Hand, Ring Round The Moon, Spread of the Eagle, The Shifting Heart, Loyalties, Julius Caesar, Antony and Cleopatra, Kain, The Ideal Husband, The Six Wives of Henry VIII (series), Dear Love, Captain Beaky & His Band, Captain Beaky, Volume 2, The Gondoliers, The Pirates of Penzance, Ruddigore. *U.S.*: Story of the Marlboroughs, Jacob and Joseph, Story of David, The Tenth Month, The Day Christ Died, The Miracle, Murder She Wrote. *Australia*: *Series*: My Brother Tom, Captain James Cook.

MIDLER, BETTE
Actress, Singer. b. Honolulu, HI, Dec. 1, 1945. e. U. of Hawaii. Studied acting at Berghof Studios. Appeared on B'way in Fiddler on the Roof, Salvation; also in Tommy with Seattle Opera Co., 1971. Gained fame as singer-comic in nightclubs and cabarets. Has toured extensively with own stage shows: The Divine Miss M, Clams on the Half-Shell, Divine Madness, Art of Bust, Experience the Divine. Grammy Awards: The Divine Miss M, The Rose, Blueberry Pie (from In Harmony), Wind Beneath My Wings. *Author*: A View From a Broad, The Saga of Baby Divine. Special Tony Award, 1973.
PICTURES: Hawaii (debut, 1966), The Rose (Acad. Award nom.; 2 Golden Globe Awards), Divine Madness, Jinxed, Down and Out in Beverly Hills, Ruthless People, Outrageous Fortune, Big Business, Oliver & Company (voice), Beaches (also co-prod.), Stella, Scenes from a Mall, For the Boys (Acad. Award nom., Golden Globe Award; also co-prod.), Hocus Pocus, Get Shorty, First Wives Club, That Old Feeling, Isn't She Great.
TELEVISION: *Specials*: The Fabulous Bette Midler Show, Ol' Red Hair is Back (Emmy Award, 1978; also co-writer), Art or Bust (also prod., co-writer), Bette Midler's Mondo Beyondo (also creator, co-writer), Mud Will Be Flung Tonight, Bette Midler in Concert: Diva Las Vegas. *Movies*: Gypsy. *Guest*: Cher, The Tonight Show (Emmy Award, 1992).
RECORDINGS: The Divine Miss M, Bette Midler, Songs for the New Depression, Live at Last, The Rose, Thighs and Whispers, Divine Madness, No Frills, Mud Will Be Flung Tonight, Beaches, Some People's Lives, For the Boys, Experience the Divine, Bette of Roses.

MIFUNE, TOSHIRO
Actor. b. Tsingtao, China, April 1, 1920. e. Japanese schools. Served five years Japanese army. Joined Toho Studio 1946.
PICTURES: Snow Trail, Drunken Angel, Eagle of Pacific, Seven Samurai, I Live in Fear, Legend of Musashi, Throne of Blood, Riksha Man, Three Treasures, Last Gunfight, I Bombed Pearl Harbor, Rose in Mud, Rashomon, Yojimbo, Animus Trujano, Kiska, Red Beard, High and Low, Judo Saga, Grand Prix, Rebellion, Tunnel to the Sun, The Lost World of Sinbad, Admiral Yamamoto, Hell in the Pacific, Under the Banner of the Samurai, Red Sun, Paper Tiger, Midway, Winter Kills, 1941, The Challenge, Inchon, The Bushido Blade, Princess from the Moon, The Death of a Master, Journey of Honor, Shadow of the Wolf, Picture Bride.
TELEVISION: *US*: Shogun.
(d. Dec. 24, 1997)

MIGDEN, CHESTER L.
Executive. b. New York, NY, May 21, 1921; e. City Coll. of New York, B.A., 1941, Columbia U., J.D., 1947. Member New York Bar. Attorney for National Labor Relations Board 1947-51. Exec of Screen Actors Guild 1952-81. Nat'l exec. dir., 1973-81. Exec. dir., Assn. of Talent Agents, 1982-94. Arbitrator, consultant 1994-present.

MIKELL, GEORGE
Actor. b. Lithuania. In Australia 1950-56 acting with Old Vic Co. Ent. films 1955. TV 1957. To England 1957.
THEATER: Five Finger Exercise, Altona, The Millionairess, Love from a Stranger, Portrait of a Queen, Farewell, Judas, Flare Path.
PICTURES: The Guns of Navarone, The Password Is Courage, The Great Escape, Deadline for Diamonds, Where The Spies Are, The Spy Who Came in From the Cold, I Predoni Del Sahara (Italy), Sabina (Israel), The Double Man, Attack on the Iron Coast, Zeppelin, Young Winston, Scorpio, The Tamarind Seed, Sweeney Two, The Sea Wolves, Victory, Emerald, Kommissar Zufall (Germany).
TELEVISION: Counsel at Law, Six Eyes on a Stranger, The Mask of a Clown, Green Grows the Grass, Opportunity Taken, OSS Series, Espinage, The Danger Man, Strange Report, The Survivors, The Adventurer, Colditz, The Hanged Man, Quiller, Martin Hartwell, Flambards, Sweeney, The Secret Army, Sherlock Holmes, When the Boat Comes In, Brack Report, Bergerac, The Brief, Glass Babies (Australia), Hannay, Night of the Fox (mini-series), Secrets (Australia), Stark (Australia).

MILCH, DAVID
Producer, Consultant.
TELEVISION: *Movies*: Capital News. *Mini-series*: Murder One: Diary of a Serial Killer. *Series*: Capital News, NYPD Blue (Emmy Award, 1997), Murder One, Total Security, Brooklyn South.

MILCHAN, ARNON
Producer. b. Israel, Dec. 6, 1944. Began producing and financing films in Israel. Also prod. of stage plays including: Ipi Tombi, It's So Nice to be Civilized, and Amadeus in Paris starring Roman Polanski. Appeared in film Can She Bake a Cherry Pie?
PICTURES: Black Joy, The Medusa Touch, Dizengoff 99, The King of Comedy, Once Upon a Time in America (also actor), Brazil, Stripper (exec. prod.), Legend, Man on Fire, Who's Harry Crumb?, The War of the Roses, Big Man on Campus, Pretty Woman, Q & A, Guilty by Suspicion, JFK (exec. prod.), The Mambo Kings, Memoirs of an Invisible Man (exec. prod.), The Power of One, Under Siege, Sommersby, Falling Down (exec. prod.), Made in America, Free Willy (exec. prod.), That Night, Striking Distance, George Balanchine's The Nutcracker (exec. prod.), Six Degrees of Separation, Heaven and Earth, The Client, The New Age, Second Best, Boys on the Side, Copycat (co-prod.), Under Siege 2: Dark Territory, Free Willy 2: The Adventure Home, Heat, Bogus, Tin Cup (exec. prod.), A Time to Kill, The Mirror Has Two Faces, Murder at 1600, L.A. Confidential.
TELEVISION: *Mini-Series*: Masada. *Series*: John Grisham's The Client (exec. prod.), Michael Hayes.

MILES, CHRISTOPHER
Director. b. London, England, April 19, 1939. e. I.D.H.E.C., 1962. Sister is actress Sarah Miles. Studied film in Paris at the Institut des Hautes Etudes Cinematographiques.
PICTURES: The Six-Sided Triangle, Up Jumped a Swagman, The Virgin and the Gypsy, Time for Loving, The Maids (also co-s.p.), That Lucky Touch, Alternative 3 (also s.p.), Priest of Love (also prod.), The Marathon (also co-s.p.), Aphrodisias (also co-s.p.), Some Stones of No Value (also co-s.p.), Love In The Ancient World (also s.p.).

MILES, SARAH
Actress. b. Ingatestone, England, Dec. 31, 1941. e. RADA. Was married to late writer Robert Bolt. Brother is actor Christopher Miles. Appeared in short film Six-Sided Triangle.
THEATER: Dazzling, World War 2 1/2, Kelly's Eye, Vivat! Vivat Regina!

PICTURES: Term of Trial (debut, 1962), The Servant, The Ceremony, Those Magnificent Men in Their Flying Machines, I Was Right Here (Time Lost and Time Remembered), Blow-Up, Ryan's Daughter (Acad. Award nom.), Lady Caroline Lamb, The Man Who Loved Cat Dancing, The Hireling, Bride to Be (Pepita Jimenez), The Sailor Who Fell From Grace With the Sea, The Big Sleep, Priest of Love, Venom, Ordeal by Innocence, Steaming, Hope and Glory, White Mischief, The Silent Touch.
TELEVISION: Loving Walter (Walter and June), James Michener's Dynasty, Great Expectations, Harem, Queenie, A Ghost in Monte Carlo, Dandelion Dead, Ring Round the Moon, The Rehearsal.

MILES, SYLVIA
Actress. b. New York, NY, Sept. 9, 1934. Attended Pratt Inst., NYC. e. Washington Irving H.S., Actors Studio, Dramatic Workshop of the New School.
THEATER: Rosebloom, The Iceman Cometh, The Balcony, The Riot Act, Vieux Carre, Before Breakfast, The Night of the Iguana, Tea with Mommy and Jack, Ruthless.
PICTURES: Murder Inc. (debut, 1960), Parrish, Pie in the Sky, Violent Midnight, Terror in the City, Midnight Cowboy (Acad. Award nom.), The Last Movie, Who Killed Mary Whats'ername?, Heat, 92 in the Shade, Farewell My Lovely (Acad. Award nom.), The Great Scout and Cathouse Thursday, The Sentinel, Shalimar (Deadly Thief), Zero to Sixty, The Funhouse, Evil Under the Sun, No Big Deal, Critical Condition, Sleeping Beauty, Wall Street, Crossing Delancey, Spike of Bensonhurst, She-Devil, Denise Calls Up.
TELEVISION: Series: All My Children. Guest: Miami Vice, The Equalizer, Tonight Show, etc.

MILES, VERA
Actress. r.n. Vera Ralston. b. Boise City, OK, Aug. 23, 1929. e. public schools, Pratt and Wichita, KS.
PICTURES: Two Tickets to Broadway (debut, 1951), For Men Only, Rose Bowl Story, Charge at Feather River, So Big, Pride of the Blue Grass, Tarzan's Hidden Jungle, Wichita, The Searchers, 23 Paces to Baker Street, Autumn Leaves, Wrong Man, Beau James, Web of Evidence, FBI Story, Touch of Larceny, Five Branded Women, Psycho, Back Street, The Man Who Shot Liberty Valance, A Tiger Walks, Those Calloways, Follow Me Boys!, The Spirit Is Willing, Gentle Giant, Sergeant Ryker, Kona Coast, It Takes All Kinds, Hellfighters, Mission Batangas, The Wild Country, Molly and Lawless John, One Little Indian, The Castaway Cowboy, Twilight's Last Gleaming, Thoroughbred, Run for the Roses, Brainwaves, Psycho II, The Initiation, Into the Night.
TELEVISION: Movies: The Hanged Man, In Search of America, Cannon (pilot), Owen Marshall: Counselor at Law (pilot), A Howling in the Woods, Jigsaw, A Great American Tragedy, Baffled!, Runaway!, Live Again Die Again, Underground Man, The Strange and Deadly Occurence, NcNaughton's Daughter, Judge Horton and the Scottsboro Boys, Smash-up on Interstate 5, Fire!, And I Alone Survived, Roughnecks, Our Family Business, Rona Jaffe's Mazes and Monsters, Travis McGee, Helen Keller: The Miracle Continues, The Hijacking of the Achille Lauro. Guest: Climax, Pepsi Cola Playhouse, Schlitz Playhouse, Ford Theatre.

MILGRAM, HANK
Theatre Executive. b. Philadelphia, PA, April 20, 1926. e. U. of PA, Wharton Sch. Exec. v.p., Milgram Theatres. Variety Club Board member, past president and chairman of the board of Variety Club of Philadelphia; past Variety Club Intl. v.p.; President's council. Served for 12 yrs. as bd. member, Hahneman Univ. until 1993.

MILIUS, JOHN
Writer, Director. b. St. Louis, MO. April 11, 1944. e. Los Angeles City Coll., U. of Southern California (cinema course). While at latter, won National Student Film Festival Award. Started career as ass't. to Lawrence Gordon at AIP. Began writing screenplays, then became dir. with Dillinger (1973). Appeared in documentary Hearts of Darkness.
PICTURES: The Devil's Eight (co-s.p.), Evel Knievel (co-s.p.), The Life and Times of Judge Roy Bean (s.p.), Jeremiah Johnson (co-s.p.), Deadhead Miles (actor), Dillinger (dir. debut, 1973; also s.p.), Magnum Force (co-s.p.), The Wind and the Lion (dir., s.p.), Big Wednesday (dir., co-s.p., actor), Hardcore (exec. prod.), Apocalypse Now (s.p.), 1941 (exec. prod., co-story), Used Cars (co-exec. prod.), Conan the Barbarian (dir., co-s.p.), Uncommon Valor (co-prod.), Red Dawn (dir., co-s.p.), Extreme Prejudice (story), Farewell to the King (dir., s.p.), Flight of the Intruder (dir., co-s.p), Geronimo: An American Legend (co-s.p., story), Clear and Present Danger (co-s.p.), Rough Riders, Mexico.

MILKIS, EDWARD
Producer. b. Los Angeles, CA, July 16, 1931. e. U. of Southern California. Began career as asst. editor, ABC-TV, 1952; Disney, 1954; MGM, 1957; editor, MGM, 1960-65; assoc. prod., Star Trek, 1966-69; exec. in chg. post-prod., Paramount, 1969-72; formed Miller-Milkis Prods., 1972; Miller-Milkis-Boyett, 1979. Now heads Edward K. Milkis Prods.

PICTURES: Silver Streak, Foul Play, The Best Little Whorehouse in Texas.
TELEVISION: Petrocelli, Bosom Buddies (exec. prod.), Happy Days, Laverne and Shirley, Feel the Heat.

MILLAR, STUART
Producer, Director. b. New York, NY, 1929. e. Stanford U.; Sorbonne, Paris. Ent. industry working for Motion Picture Branch, State Dept., Germany. documentaries, Army Signal Corps, Long Island, Germany; journalist, International News Service, San Francisco; assoc. prod.-dir., The Desperate Hours; assoc. prod.-dir., Friendly Persuasion.
PICTURES: Producer: The Young Stranger, Stage Struck, Birdman of Alcatraz, I Could Go On Singing, The Young Doctors, Stolen Hours, The Best Man, Paper Lion, Little Big Man, When The Legends Die (also dir.), Rooster Cogburn (dir. only), Shoot the Moon (co-exec. prod.).
TELEVISION: Producer: Isabel's Choice, Vital Signs (also dir.), Killer Instinct, Dream Breaker (also dir.), Lady in a Corner.

MILLER, ANN
Actress. r.n. Lucille Ann Collier. b. Houston, TX, April 12, 1923. e. Albert Sidney Johnson H.S., Houston; Lawler Prof. Sch., Hollywood. Studied dance as child; played West Coast vaudeville theatres. Autobiography: Miller's High Life (1974), Tapping Into the Force.
THEATER: George White's Scandals, Mame, Sugar Babies.
PICTURES: Anne of Green Gables (debut, 1934), The Good Fairy, Devil on Horseback, New Faces of 1937, Life of the Party, Stage Door, Radio City Revels, Having Wonderful Time, Room Service, You Can't Take It with You, Tarnished Angel, Too Many Girls, Hit Parade of 1941, Melody Ranch, Time Out for Rhythm, Go West Young Lady, True to the Army, Priorities on Parade, Reveille with Beverly, What's Buzzin' Cousin?, Jam Session, Hey Rookie, Carolina Blues, Eadie Was a Lady, Eve Knew Her Apples, Thrill of Brazil, Easter Parade, The Kissing Bandit, On the Town, Watch the Birdie, Texas Carnival, Two Tickets to Broadway, Lovely To Look At, Small Town Girl, Kiss Me Kate, Deep in My Heart, Hit the Deck, The Opposite Sex, The Great American Pastime, Won Ton Ton the Dog Who Saved Hollywood, That's Entertainment III.
TELEVISION: Specials: Dames at Sea, Disney-MGM Special. Guest: Love American Style, The Love Boat.

MILLER, ARTHUR
Writer. b. New York, NY, Oct. 17, 1915. e. U. of Michigan. Plays include All My Sons, Death of a Salesman (Pulitzer Prize, 1949), The Crucible (Tony Award), A View from the Bridge, After the Fall, Incident at Vichy, The Price, Up From Paradise, Situation Normal, The American Clock, I Can't Remember Anything, Some Kind of Love Story, Clara, Broken Glass. Novel: Focus. Novella: Homely Girl. Autobiography: Time-bends (1987).
PICTURES: Film versions of plays: All My Sons, Death of a Salesman, The Crucible, A View From the Bridge. Original s.p.: The Misfits, Everybody Wins, The Crucible.
TELEVISION: Death of a Salesman (Emmy Award, 1967), Fame, After The Fall, Playing for Time (Emmy Award, 1981).

MILLER, BARRY
Actor. b. Los Angeles, CA, Feb. 6, 1958. New York stage debut, My Mother My Father and Me, 1980.
THEATER: Forty Deuce, The Tempest, Biloxi Blues (Tony, Theatre World, Outer Critics Circle and Drama Desk Awards, 1985), Crazy He Calls Me.
PICTURES: Lepke (debut, 1975), Saturday Night Fever, Voices, Fame, The Chosen, The Journey of Natty Gann, Peggy Sue Got Married, The Sicilian, The Last Temptation of Christ, Love at Large, The Pickle, Love Affair.
TELEVISION: Specials: The Roommate, Conspiracy: The Trial of the Chicago Eight. Series: Joe and Sons, Szyszynk, Equal Justice, The Practice (3 episodes). Guest: The Bill Cosby Show. Movies: Brock's Last Case, Having Babies, The Death of Richie.

MILLER, CHERYL
Actress. b. Sherman Oaks, CA, Feb. 4, 1942. e. UCLA, Los Angeles Conservatory of Music.
PICTURES: Casanova Brown, Marriage is a Private Affair, Unconquered, Cheaper by the Dozen, Fourteen Hours, Mr. 880, Executive Suite, The Next Voice You Hear, The Matchmaker, Blue Denim, North by Northwest, The Parent Trap, The Monkey's Uncle, Clarence the Cross-Eyed Lion, The Initiation, Doctor Death, Mr. Too Little.
TELEVISION: Series: Daktari, Bright Promise. Guest: Perry Mason, Bachelor Father, Flipper, Donna Reed, Leave It to Beaver, Farmer's Daughter, Wonderful World of Color, Moutain Man, Dobie Gillis, Bright Promise, Love American Style, Emergency, Cade's County. Movie: Gemini Man.

MILLER, DENNIS
Comedian, Actor. b. Pittsburgh, PA, Nov. 3, 1953. e. Point Park Coll., (journalism degree). Began as stand-up comic in local clubs, then moved to NY appearing at Catch a Rising Star and the Comic Strip. Back in Pittsburgh wrote essays for PM Magazine and hosted Saturday-morning series for teens, Punchline. Recording: The Off-White Album.

PICTURES: Madhouse, Disclosure, The Net, Tales From the Crypt: Bordello of Blood, Murder at 1600.
TELEVISION: *Series*: Saturday Night Live (1985-91), The Dennis Miller Show (talk), Dennis Miller Live (also writer; Emmy Award for writing, 1996). *Specials* (also exec. prod./writer): Mr. Miller Goes to Washington, Dennis Miller: Black and White, They Shoot HBO Specials Don't They?, MTV Video Awards (host, 1996), Dennis Miller: Citizen Arcane (also exec. prod./writer; Emmy Award, 1996, Writers' Guild Award, 1998).

MILLER, DENNIS
Executive. Exec. v.p., Sony Pictures Entertainment, Inc.

MILLER, DICK (RICHARD)
Actor, Writer. b. New York, NY, Dec. 25, 1928. e. City Coll. of New York, Columbia U. Grad. NYU. Theater Sch. of Dramatic Arts. Commercial artist, psychologist (Bellevue Mental Hygiene Clinic, Queens General Hosp. Psychiatric dept.) Served in U.S. Navy, WWII. Boxing champ, U.S. Navy. Semi-pro football. Broadway stage, radio disc jockey, The Dick Miller Show, WMCA, WOR-TV. Over 500 live shows. Did first live night talk show with Bobby Sherwood, Midnight Snack, CBS, 1950. Wrote, produced and directed radio and TV shows in NY in early 1950s. Wrote screenplays; T.N.T. Jackson, Which Way to the Front, Four Rode Out and others. Has appeared on many major TV series and was a regular on Fame (3 years) and The Flash.
PICTURES: Has appeared in over 150 features, including: Apache Woman, Oklahoma Woman, It Conquered the World, The Undead, Not of This Earth, The Gunslinger, War of the Satellites, Naked Paradise, Rock All Night, Sorority Girl, Carnival Rock, A Bucket of Blood, Little Shop of Horrors, Atlas, Capture That Capsule, Premature Burial, X—The Man With the X Ray Eyes, The Terror, Beach Ball, Ski Party, Wild Wild Winter, Wild Angels, Hell's Angels on Wheels, The Trip, St. Valentine's Day Masacre, A Time for Killing, The Dirty Dozen, Targets, The Legend of Lilah Clare, Wild Racers, Target Harry, Which Way to the Front (also co-s.p.), Night Call Nurses, The Grissom Gang, Ulzana's Raid, Executive Action, The Slams, Student Nurses, Big Bad Mama, Truck Turner, Capone, T.N.T. Jackson, The Fortune, White Line Fever, Crazy Mama, Moving Violation, Hustle, Cannonball, Vigilante Force, New York New York, Mr. Billion, Hollywood Boulevard, Grand Theft Auto, I Wanna Hold Your Hand, Piranha, Corvette Summer, Rock 'n' Roll High School, Lady in Red, Dr. Heckle and Mr. Hype, The Happy Hooker Goes Hollywood, Used Cars, The Howling, Heartbeeps, White Dog, Get Crazy, Lies, Heart Like a Wheel, All the Right Moves, Twilight Zone: The Movie, National Lampoon Goes to the Movies, Space Raiders, Swing Shift, Gremlins, The Terminator, Explorers, After Hours, Night of the Creeps, Project X, Armed Response, Chopping Mall, Amazon Women on the Moon, Innerspace, Angel III, The 'Burbs, Under the Boardwalk, Far From Home, Mob Boss, Gremlins 2: The New Batch, Unlawful Entry, Amityville 1992: It's About Time, Motorama, Matinee, Batman: Mask of the Phantasm (voice), Mona Must Die, Number One Fan, Tales From the Crypt Presents Demon Knight, Second Civil War, Small Soldiers.

MILLER, (DR.) GEORGE
Director, Producer. b. Chinchilla, Queensland, Australia, 1945. Practiced medicine in Sydney; quit to work on films with Byron Kennedy, who became longtime partner until his death in 1983. Early work: Violence in the Cinema Part One (short: dir., s.p.), Frieze—An Underground Film (doc.: editor only), Devil in Evening Dress (doc.: dir., s.p.). First worldwide success with Mad Max.
PICTURES: Mad Max (dir., s.p.), Chain Reaction (assoc. prod.), The Road Warrior (dir., co-s.p.), Twilight Zone—The Movie (dir. segment), Mad Max Beyond Thunderdome (co-dir., prod., co-s.p.), The Witches of Eastwick (dir.), The Year My Voice Broke (exec. prod.), Dead Calm (exec. prod.), Flirting (exec. prod.), Lorenzo's Oil (dir., co-s.p., co-prod.), Babe (co-s.p.).
TELEVISION: The Dismissal (mini-series; exec. prod., co-writer & dir. of first episode). Prod.: Bodyline, The Cowra Breakout. Exec. Prod.: Vietnam (mini-series), Dirtwater Dynasty, Sports Crazy.

MILLER, GEORGE
Director. b. Australia.
PICTURES: In Search of Anna (asst. dir.), The Man from Snowy River, The Aviator, The Never Ending Story II, Over the Hill, Frozen Assets, Gross Misconduct, Andre, Zeus and Roxanne.
TELEVISION: Cash and Company, Against the Wind, The Last Outlaw, All the Rivers Run.

MILLER, JAMES R.
Executive. Began m.p. industry career in 1971 in legal dept. of United Artists (N.Y.). Left to go with Paramount Pictures in legal dept.; then moved to Columbia in 1977 as sr. counsel; later assoc. gen. counsel. In 1979, named Warner Bros. v.p., studio business affairs; 1984, v.p. in chg. world-wide business affairs; 1987, sr. v.p.; 1989, exec. v.p. business and acquisition.

MILLER, JP
Writer. b. San Antonio, TX, Dec. 18, 1919. e. Rice U., 1937-41; Yale Drama Sch., 1946-47. U.S. Navy, Lieut., 1941-46; pub. poetry, short stories. Author of novels The Race for Home, Liv, The Skook.

THEATER: Days of Wine and Roses, The People Next Door, Privacy.
PICTURES: The Rabbit Trap, (story, s.p.) Days of Wine and Roses (story, s.p.) The Young Savages (co-author, s.p.) Behold a Pale Horse (s.p.) The People Next Door (story, s.p.).
TELEVISION: Philco TV Playhouse: Hide and Seek, Old Tasslefoot, The Rabbit Trap, The Pardon-me Boy; Playhouse 90, Days of Wine and Roses, CBS Playhouse, The People Next Door (Emmy Award, 1969), The Unwanted, The Lindbergh Kidnapping Case, Helter Skelter, Gauguin the Savage, I Know My First Name is Steven (story, co-s.p.).

MILLER, JASON
Writer, Actor. b. Scranton, PA, April 22, 1939. Entered regional playwriting contest during high school in Scranton, PA and since has moved back and forth between acting and writing. Wrote Nobody Hears a Broken Dream, That Championship Season (NY Drama Critics & Tony Awards, Pulitzer Prize, 1973). Acted on stage in Juno and the Paycock, Long Day's Journey Into Night.
PICTURES: *Actor*: The Exorcist (Acad. Award nom.), The Nickel Ride, The Ninth Configuration (Twinkle Twinkle Killer Kane), Monsignor, Toy Soldiers, Light of Day, The Exorcist III, Rudy. *Director-Writer*: That Championship Season, Small Kill, Rudy, Murdered Innocence, Mommy.
TELEVISION: *Movies*: A Home of Our Own, F. Scott Fitzgerald in Hollywood, Vampire, The Henderson Monster, Marilyn: The Untold Story, The Best Little Girl in the World, Deadly Care, A Mother's Courage: The Mary Thomas Story. *Mini-Series*: The Dain Curse.

MILLER, MAX B.
Executive. b. Los Angeles, Feb. 23, 1937. Father, Max Otto Miller, prod. silent features and shorts. Great grandfather was Brigham Young. e. Los Angeles Valley Coll., UCLA, Sherwood Oaks Coll. Writer of articles on cinema for American Cinematographer and other publications. Owns and manages Fotos Intl., entertainment photo agency with offices in 46 countries. Recipient of Golden Globe Award in 1976 for Youthquake, documentary feature. Also dir. of Films International (prod., Shoot Los Angeles) and pres. of MBM Prod., Inc. Active member of Hollywood Foreign Press Assn. (from 1974-82 bd member; twice chmn.), Independent Feature Project, Acad. of TV Arts & Sciences, L.A. Int'l, Film Exhibition, Soc. of M.P. & TV Engineers, Film Forum, Amer. Cinemateque.

MILLER, PENELOPE ANN
Actress. b. Los Angeles, CA, Jan. 13, 1964. Daughter of actor-filmmaker Mark Miller and journalist-yoga instructor Bea Ammidown. e. studied acting with Herbert Berghof.
THEATER: *NY*: The People From Work (1984), Biloxi Blues (B'way and LA), Moonchildren, Our Town (Tony nom.), On the Waterfront.
PICTURES: Adventures in Babysitting (1987, debut), Biloxi Blues, Big Top Pee-Wee, Miles From Home, Dead-Bang, Downtown, The Freshman, Awakenings, Kindergarten Cop, Other People's Money, Year of the Comet, The Gun in Betty Lou's Handbag, Chaplin, Carlito's Way, The Shadow, The Relic.
TELEVISION: *Series*: The Guiding Light, As the World Turns, The Popcorn Kid. *Guest*: Tales From the Darkside, Miami Vice, St. Elsewhere, Family Ties, The Facts of Life. *Specials*: Tales From the Hollywood Hills: The Closed Set, Our Town. *Movie*: Witchhunt.

MILLER, ROBERT ELLIS
Director. b. New York, NY, July 18, 1932. e. Harvard U. Worked on Broadway and TV before feature film debut with Any Wednesday (1966).
PICTURES: Any Wednesday (debut, 1966), Sweet November, The Heart Is a Lonely Hunter, The Buttercup Chain, The Big Truck, The Girl from Petrovka, The Baltimore Bullet, Reuben Reuben, Brenda Starr, Hawks, Bed and Breakfast.
TELEVISION: The Voice of Charlie Pont, The Other Lover, Madame X, Just an Old Sweet Song, Her Life as a Man, Ishi: Last of His Tribe, Intimate Strangers, Killer Rules, Point Man (pilot), A Walton Wedding.

MILLS, DONNA
Actress. b. Chicago, IL, Dec. 11, 1945. e. U. of Illinois. Left school to pursue career in theatre, beginning as dancer with stage companies around Chicago and touring. In NY became regular on soap opera, The Secret Storm. On B'way in Don't Drink the Water.
PICTURES: The Incident (debut, 1968), Play Misty for Me.
TELEVISION: *Series*: Love Is a Many Splendored Thing, The Good Life, Knots Landing. *Guest*: Lancer, Dan August. *Movies/Mini-Series*: Haunts of the Very Rich, Rolling Man, Night of Terror, The Bait, Live Again Die Again, Who is the Black Dahlia?, Beyond the Bermuda Triangle, Look What's Happened to Rosemary's Baby, Smash-Up on Interstate 5, Fire!, Curse of the Black Widow, The Hunted Lady, Superdome, Doctors' Private Lives, Hanging by a Thread, Waikiki, Bare Essence, He's Not Your Son, Woman on the Run, Outback Bound, The Lady Forgets, Intimate Encounters (also exec. prod.), The World's Oldest Living Bridesmaid (also exec. prod.), Runaway Father (also co-exec. prod.), False Arrest, In My Daughter's Name (also co-exec. prod.), The President's Child, Barbara Taylor Bradford's Remember, My Name Is Kate (also exec. prod.), Dangerous Intentions, Element of Truth (exec. prod.), Stepford Husbands.

MILLS, HAYLEY
Actress. b. London, England, April 18, 1946. Father is actor John Mills. Sister is actress Juliet Mills. e. Elmhurst Boarding Sch., Surrey, and Institute Alpine Vidamanette, Switz. Made m.p. debut in Tiger Bay 1959 with father; then signed Disney contract 1960. Received special Academy Award for her role in Pollyana.
THEATER: The Wild Duck, Peter Pan, Trelawney of the Wells, The Three Sisters, A Touch of Spring, The Importance of Being Earnest, Rebecca, The Summer Party, Hush & Hide, My Fat Friend, Tally's Folly, Dial M for Murder, The Secretary Bird, Toys in the Attic, The Kidnap Game, The King and I (Australian tour), Fallen Angels (U.K., Australia, New Zealand), Dead and Guilty.
PICTURES: Tiger Bay (debut, 1959), Pollyanna, The Parent Trap, Whistle Down the Wind, In Search of the Castaways, Summer Magic, The Chalk Garden, The Moonspinners, That Darn Cat, The Truth About Spring, Sky West and Crooked (Gypsy Girl), The Trouble With Angels, The Family Way, A Matter of Innocence (Pretty Polly), Twisted Nerve, Take a Girl Like You, Mr. Forbush and the Penguins (Cry of the Penguins), Endless Night, Deadly Strangers, Silhouettes, What Changed Charley Farthing, The Kingfisher Caper, Appointment with Death, After Midnight, A Troll in Central Park (voice).
TELEVISION: The Flame Trees of Thika (mini-series), Parent Trap (Parts II, III, IV, V), Amazing Stories, Illusion of Life, Good Morning Miss Bliss (series), Murder She Wrote, Back Home (series), Tales of the Unexpected, Deadly Strangers, Only a Scream Away, Walk of Life.

MILLS, SIR JOHN
Actor, Producer. b. Suffolk, England, February 22, 1908, m. Mary Hayley Bell. Father of actresses Hayley and Juliet Mills. Worked as clerk before becoming actor. One of top ten money-making Brit. stars in Motion Picture Herald-Fame Poll, 1945, 1947, 1949-50, 1954, 1956-58. Knighted, 1977. Recipient special award 1988, British Academy of Film and Television Arts. Autobiography: Up in the Clouds Gentlemen Please (1981).
THEATER: London: Good Companions, Great Expectations, Separate Tables, Goodbye Mr. Chips, Little Lies (also Toronto), The Petition, Pygmalion (NY), An Evening With John Mills.
PICTURES: The Midshipmaid (debut, 1932), Britannia of Billingsgate, The Ghost Camera, The River Wolves, A Political Party, The Lash, Those Were the Days, Blind Justice, Doctor's Orders, Regal Cavalcade, Born for Glory, Car of Dreams, Charing Cross Road, First Offence, Nine Days a Queen, OHMS (You're in the Army Now), The Green Cockatoo (Four Dark Hours), Goodbye Mr. Chipes, Old Bill and Son, Cottage to Let, The Black Sheep of Whitehall, The Big Blockade, The Young Mr. Pitt, In Which We Serve, We Dive at Dawn, This Happy Breed, Waterloo Road, The Way to the Stars, Great Expectations, So Well Remembered, The October Man, Scott of the Antarctic, The History of Mr. Polly, The Rocking Horse Winner (also prod.), Morning Departure (Operation Disaster), Mr. Denning Drives North, The Gentle Gunman, The Long Memory, Hobson's Choice, The End of the Affair, The Colditz Story, Above Us the Waves, Escapade, It's Great to Be Young, War and Peace, Around the World in 80 Days, Baby and the Battleship, Town on Trial, Vicious Circle, I Was Monty's Double, Dunkirk, Ice Cold in Alex, Summer of the 17th Doll (Season of Passion), Tiger Bay, Tunes of Glory, The Singer Not the Song, Swiss Family Robinson, Flame in the Streets, Tiara Tahiti, The Valiant, The Chalk Garden, The Truth About Spring, Operation Crossbow (The Great Spy Mission), King Rat, The Wrong Box, Sky West and Crooked (Gypsy Girl; dir., prod. only), The Family Way, Africa—Texas Style, Chuka, Emma Hamilton, La Morte non ha Sesso (A Black Veil For Lisa), Oh! What a Lovely War, Run Wild Run Free, Ryan's Daughter (Acad. Award, best supporting act, 1970), A Black Veil for Lisa, Adam's Woman, Dulcima, Oklahoma Crude, Young Winston, Lady Caroline Lamb, The Human Factor, Trial By Combat (Dirty Knight's Work), The Devil's Advocate, The Big Sleep, Zulu Dawn, The 39 Steps, Gandhi, Sahara, Who's That Girl, When the Wind Blows (voice), Deadly Advice.
TELEVISION: Masks of Death, Murder with Mirrors, Woman of Substance, Hold the Dream, Edge of the Wind, When the Wind Blows, Around the World in 80 Days, The Lady and the Highwayman, The True Story of Spit MacPhee, A Tale of Two Cities, Ending Up, Frankenstein, The Big Freeze.

MILLS, JULIET
Actress. b. London, England, Nov. 21, 1941. m. actor Maxwell Caulfield. Father is actor John Mills. Mother is writer Mary Hayley Bell. Sister is actress Hayley Mills. Made stage debut at 14 in Alice Through the Looking Glass. Also toured with Fallen Angels with sister; 1995, The Cherry Orchard, in Canada. Also in 1995, the Molière Comedies and Time of My Life; in 1996, It Could Be Any One of Us..
PICTURES: So Well Remembered, The History of Mr. Polly, No My Darling Daughter, Twice Round the Daffodils, Nurse on Wheels, Carry on Jack, The Rare Breed, Oh! What a Lovely War, Avanti!, Beyond the Door, The Man With the Green Cross, Primevals.
TELEVISION: Series: Nanny and the Professor. Movies: Wings of Fire, The Challengers, Letters from Three Lovers, Alexander: The Other Side of Dawn, The Cracker Factory, Barnaby and Me (Australia), Columbo: No Time to Die, A Stranger in the Mirror. Mini-Series: QB VII (Emmy Award, 1975), Once an Eagle. Guest: Hotel, Dynasty, The Love Boat. Special: She Stoops to Conquer.

MILNER, MARTIN
Actor. b. Detroit, MI, Dec. 28, 1927. e. USC. Army 1952-54, directed 20 training films.
PICTURES: Life With Father (debut, 1947), Sands of Iwo Jima, The Halls of Montezuma, Our Very Own, Operation Pacific, I Want You, The Captive City, Battle Zone, Mr. Roberts, Pete Kelly's Blues, On the Threshold of Space, Gunfight at the O.K. Corral, Sweet Smell of Success, Marjorie Morningstar, Too Much Too Soon, Compulsion, 13 Ghosts, Valley of the Dolls.
TELEVISION: Series: The Stu Erwin Show, The Life of Riley, Route 66, Adam-12, Swiss Family Robinson. Movies: Emergency!, Runaway!, Hurricane, Swiss Family Robinson (pilot), Flood, SST—Death Flight, Black Beauty, Little Mo, Crisis in Mid-Air, The Seekers, The Ordeal of Bill Carney, Nashville Beat. Mini-Series: The Last Convertible.

MIMIEUX, YVETTE
Actress. b. Los Angeles, CA, Jan. 8, 1942. e. Vine Street Sch., Le Conte Jr. H.S., Los Angeles, Los Ninos Heroes de Chapultepec, Mexico City, Hollywood H.S., CA. Appeared with a theatrical group, Theatre Events; Concerts: Persephone, Oakland Orchestra, 1965, N.Y. Philharmonic, Lincoln Center, L.A. Philharmonic, Hollywood Bowl.
THEATER: I Am a Camera (1963), The Owl and the Pussycat.
PICTURES: Platinum High School (debut, 1960), The Time Machine, Where the Boys Are, The Four Horsemen of the Apocalypse, Light in the Piazza, The Wonderful World of the Brothers Grimm, Diamond Head, Toys in the Attic, Joy in the Morning, The Reward, Monkeys Go Home, The Caper of the Golden Bulls, Dark of the Sun, The Picasso Summer, Three in the Attic, The Delta Factor, Skyjacked, The Neptune Factor, Journey Into Fear, Jackson County Jail, The Black Hole, Mystique (Circle of Power), Lady Boss.
TELEVISION: Series: The Most Deadly Game, Berrenger's. Movies: Death Takes A Holiday, Black Noon, Hit Lady (also-writer), The Legend of Valentino, Snowbeast, Ransom for Alice, Devil Dog: The Hound of Hell, Outside Chance, Disaster on the Coastliner, Forbidden Love, Night Partners, Obsessive Love (also co-prod., co-writer), Perry Mason: The Case of the Desperate Deception.

MINER, STEVE
Director. b. Chicago, IL, June 18, 1951. e. Dean Junior Col. Began career as prod. asst. on Last House on the Left (1970). Launched a NY-based editorial service, and dir., prod., edited sport, educational and indust. films.
PICTURES: Here Come the Tigers! (co-prod.), Manny's Orphans (co-prod., s.p.), Friday the 13th (assoc. prod.). Director: Friday the 13th Part 2 (also prod.), Friday the 13th Part 3, Soul Man, House, Warlock (also prod.), Wild Hearts Can't Be Broken, Forever Young, My Father the Hero, Big Bully, Halloween: The Revenge of Laurie Strode.
TELEVISION: Series: The Wonder Years (sprv. prod., dir., DGA Award for pilot), Chicago Hope, The Practice, Dawson's Creek. Pilots: B-Men, Elvis, Laurie Hill, Against the Grain.

MINGHELLA, ANTHONY
Director, Writer. b. Ryde, Isle of Wight, UK, Jan. 6, 1954.
PICTURES: Truly Madly Deeply, Mr Wonderful (writer only), The English Patient (Acad. award., Golden Globe nom.).
TELEVISION: Writer: Jim Henson's The Storyteller, Living With Dinosaurs.

MINNELLI, LIZA
Actress, Singer. b. Los Angeles, CA, March 12, 1946. p. actress-singer Judy Garland & dir. Vincente Minnelli. e. attended sch. in CA, Switzerland, and the Sorbonne. Left to tour as lead in The Diary of Anne Frank, The Fantastiks, Carnival and The Pajama Game. In concert with mother, London Palladium 1964. In concert Carnegie Hall, 1979, 1987, 1993. Film debut as child in mother's film In the Good Old Summertime (1949). Recordings incl. Liza with a Z, The Singer, Live at the Winter Garden, Tropical Nights, Live at Carnegie Hall, Liza Minnelli at Carnegie Hall, Results, Live at Radio City Music Hall, The Day After That.
THEATER: Best Foot Forward (off-B'way debut, 1963, Theatre World Award), Flora The Red Menace (Tony Award, 1965), Liza at the Winter Garden (special Tony Award, 1974), Chicago, The Act (Tony Award, 1978), Are You Now or Have You Ever Been?, The Rink (Tony nom.).
PICTURES: In the Good Old Summertime, Journey Back to Oz (voice; 1964, released in U.S. in 1974), Charlie Bubbles, The Sterile Cuckoo (Acad. Award nom.), Tell Me That You Love Me Junie Moon, Cabaret (Acad. Award; also British Acad. & Golden Globe Awards, 1972), That's Entertainment!, Lucky Lady, Silent Movie, A Matter of Time, New York New York, Arthur, The Muppets Take Manhattan, That's Dancing!, Rent-a-Cop, Arthur 2 on the Rocks, Stepping Out.
TELEVISION: Specials: Judy and Liza at the London Palladium, The Dangerous Christmas of Red Riding Hood, Liza, Liza with a Z (Emmy Award, 1972). Goldie and Liza Together, Baryshnikov on Broadway, Liza in London, Faerie Tale Theater (Princess and the Pea), A Triple Play: Sam Found Out, Frank Sammy and Liza: The Ultimate Event, Liza Minnelli Live From Radio City Music Hall. Movies: A Time to Live (Golden Globe Award), Parallel Lives, The West Side Waltz.

MIOU-MIOU
Actress r.n. Sylvette Herry. b. Paris, France, Feb. 22, 1950. First job as apprentice in upholstery workshop. In 1968, helped to create Montparnasse cafe-theatre, Cafe de la Gare, with comedian Coluche. Returned to stage in Marguerite Duras' La Musica, 1985.
PICTURES: La Cavale (debut, 1971), Themroc, Quelques Messieurs Trop Tranquilles, Elle Court, Elle Court La Banlieue, Les Granges Brulees, The Mad Adventures of Rabbi Jacob, Going Places, Un Genie Deux Associes une Cloche, D'Amour et D'Eau Fraiche, Victory March, F... comme Fairbanks, On Aura Tout Vu, Jonah Who Will Be 25 in the Year 2000, Dites-lui Que Je l'aime, Les Routes du Sud, Le Grand Embouteillage, Memoirs of a French Whore, Au Revoir...a Lundi, La Femme Flic (Lady Cop), Est-ce Bien Raisonnable?, La Geule du Loup, Josepha, Guy De Maupassant, Coup de Foudre (Entre Nous), Canicule, Le Vol du Sphinx, Blanche et Marie, Menage, The Revolving Doors, La Lectrice, Milou in May, La Totale, Le Bal des Casse-Pieds, Tango, Montparnasse-Pondichery, Germinal.

MIRISCH, DAVID
Executive. b. Gettysburg, PA, July 24, 1935. e. Ripon Coll. United Artists Corp., 1960-63. Former exec. with Braverman-Mirisch, adv. public rel. firm. Pres. of David Mirisch Ent., intl prom. firm. Also member of Mirisch Film Co, which has produced Hawaii, West Side Story, Fiddler on the Roof, The Great Escape, The Pink Panther, Some Like it Hot, In the Heat of the Night and The Magnificent Seven.

MIRISCH, MARVIN E.
Executive. b. New York, NY, March 19, 1918. e. CCNY, B.A., 1940. Print dept., contract dept., asst. booker, NY exch.; head booker, Grand National Pictures, Inc., 1936-40; officer, gen. mgr. vending concession operation 800 theatres, Midwest, Theatres Candy Co., Inc., Milwaukee, Wisc., 1941-52; exec., corporate officer in chg., indep. prod. negotiations, other management functions, Allied Artists Pictures, Inc., 1953-57; chmn. of bd., CEO in chg. of all business affairs, admin. & financing, distr. liaison, The Mirisch Company, Inc., 1957 to present. Member of Board of Governors and former v.p., AMPAS. Member Motion Pictures Pioneers. Past president of AMPAS Foundation.
PICTURES: *Exec. prod.*: Dracula, Romantic Comedy.

MIRISCH, WALTER
Producer. b. New York, NY, Nov. 8, 1921. e. U. of Wisconsin, B.A., 1942; Harvard Grad. Sch. of Business Admin., 1943. In m.p. indust. with Skouras Theatres Corp., 1938-40; Oriental Theatre Corp., 1940-42. 1945 with Monogram/Allied Artists; apptd. exec. prod. Allied Artists, 1951 (spv. such films as The Big Combo, The Phoenix City Story, Invasion of the Body Snatchers, Friendly Persuasion, Love in the Afternoon); established The Mirisch Company, supervising such films as Some Like It Hot, The Horse Soldiers, The Apartment, West Side Story, Irma La Douce, The Great Escape, The Pink Panther, A Shot in the Dark, The Fortune Cookie, The Russians Are Coming the Russians Are Coming, Fiddler on the Roof; 1960-61 Pres. of Screen Prod. Guild; 1962, mem. bd. dir., MPAA; bd. Gvnrs., AMPAS, 1964, 1972; 1967, pres., Center Thea. Group of L.A.; named pres. and exec. head of prod., The Mirisch Corporation, 1969; pres., Permanent Charities Committee 1962-63; pres., AMPAS, 1973-77. Recipient: Irving Thalberg Award 1978, Jean Hersholt Humanitarian Award 1984, Honorary Doctor of Humanities, Univ. of WI 1989, UCLA Medal 1989.
PICTURES: *Producer or Exec. Producer*: Fall Guy, I Wouldn't Be in Your Shoes, Bomba on Panther Island, Bomba the Jungle Boy, Bomba and the Hidden City, County Fair, The Lost Volcano, Cavalry Scout, Elephant Stampede, Flight to Mars, The Lion Hunters, Rodeo, African Treasure, Wild Stallion, The Rose Bowl Story, Flat Top, Bomba and the Jungle Girl, Hiawatha, Safari Drums, The Maze, The Golden Idol, Killer Leopard, The Warriors, Annapolis Story, Lord of the Jungle, Wichita, The First Texan, The Oklahoman, The Tall Stranger, Fort Massacre, Man of the West, Cast a Long Shadow, Gunfight at Dodge City, The Man in the Net, The Magnificent Seven, By Love Possessed, Two for the Seesaw, Toys in the Attic, In the Heat of the Night (Acad. Award for Best Picture, 1967), Sinful Davey, Some Kind of a Nut, Halls of Anger, The Hawaiians, They Call Me Mister Tibbs, The Organization, Scorpio, Mr. Majestyk, Midway, Gray Lady Down, Same Time Next Year, The Prisoner of Zenda, Dracula, Romantic Comedy.
TELEVISION: *Movies* (exec. prod.): Desperado, Return of Desperado, Desperado: Avalanche at Devil's Ridge, Desperado: The Outlaw Wars, Desperado: Badlands Justice, Troubleshooters: Trapped Beneath the Earth, Lily In Winter, A Case for Life.

MIRREN, HELEN
Actress. b. London, England, 1946.
THEATER: Troilus and Cressida, 2 Gentlemen of Verona, Hamlet, Miss Julie, Macbeth, Teeth 'n' Smiles, The Seagull, Bed Before Yesterday, Henry VI, Measure for Measure, The Duchess of Malfi, Faith Healer, Antony and Cleopatra, Roaring Girl, Extremities, Madame Bovary, Two Way Mirror, Sex Please We're Italian!, Woman in Mind (LA), A Month in the Country (also B'way).
PICTURES: A Midsummer's Night Dream (debut, 1968), Age of Consent, Savage Messiah, O Lucky Man!, Hamlet, Caligula, Hussy, The Fiendish Plot of Dr. Fu Manchu, Excalibur, The Long Good Friday, Cal, 2010, White Nights, Heavenly Pursuits, The Mosquito Coast, Pascali's Island, When the Whales Came, The Cook The Thief His Wife and Her Lover, The Comfort of Strangers, Where Angels Fear to Tread, Dr. Bethune, The Gift, The Hawk, Prince of Jutland, The Madness of King George (Acad. Award nom.; Cannes Film Fest. Award), Losing Chase, (Golden Globe Award, 1997), Some Mother's Son.
TELEVISION: Miss Julie, The Applecart, The Little Minister, The Changeling, Blue Remembered Hills, As You Like It, A Midsummer Night's Dream, Mrs. Reinhart, After the Party, Cymbeline, Coming Through, Cause Celebre, Red King White Knight, Prime Suspect (BAFTA Award), Prime Suspect 2, Prime Suspect 3 (Emmy Award, 1996).

MISCHER, DON
Producer, Director. b. San Antonio, TX, March 5, 1941. e. U. of TX, B.A. 1963, M.A. 1965. Pres., Don Mischer Productions. Founded Don Mischer Productions, 1978. Recipient of 12 Emmy Awards, 9 Directors Guild Awards, 3 NAACP Image Awards, Peabody Award.
TELEVISION: *Producer*: Opening and closing ceremonies of the 1996 Centennial Olympics Games (Emmy Award, 1997), Michael Jackson's Super Bowl XXVII Halftime Show, The Kennedy Center Honors (Emmy Awards, 1981, 1987, 1994, 1996), Tony Awards (3 yrs; Emmy Awards, 1987, 1989), Carnegie Hall 100th Anniversary, Gregory Hines Tap Dance in America, Opening of EuroDisney, The Muppets Celebrate Jim Henson, AFI Salutes to Billy Wilder and Gene Kelly, Irving Berlin's 100th Birthday (Emmy Award, 1988), Baryshnikov by Tharp, Motown 25: Yesterday Today Forever (Emmy Award, 1983), Motown Returns to the Apollo (Emmy Award, 1985), Grand Reopening of Carnegie Hall, specials with Goldie Hawn, Liza Minnelli, Bob Hope, Robin Williams, Pointer Sisters. Also: The Great American Dream Machine, Donohue and Kids: Project Peacock (Emmy Award, 1981), The Presidential Inaugural, 6 Barbara Walters Specials, Ain't Misbehavin', It's Garry Shandling's Show.

MITCHELL, LEE ROY
Executive. Pres., CEO Cinemark USA, Dallas, TX.

MOCIUK, YAR W.
Executive. b. Ukraine, Jan. 26, 1927. e. CCNY; World U.; Peoples U. of Americas, Puerto Rico. Expert in field of m.p. care and repair; holds U.S. patent for method and apparatus for treating m.p. film. Has also been film prod. and dir.. Founder and pres. of CM Films Service, Inc. until 1973. Now chmn. of bd. and pres. of Filmtreat International Corp. Member: M.P. & TV Engineers; Univ. Film Assn. Pres., Ukrainian Cinema Assn. of America.

MODINE, MATTHEW
Actor. b. Loma Linda, CA, March 22, 1959. Raised in Utah. Studied acting with Stella Adler. Stage work incl. Our Town, Tea and Sympathy, The Brick and the Rose.
PICTURES: Baby It's You (debut, 1983), Private School, Streamers, The Hotel New Hampshire, Mrs. Soffel, Birdy, Vision Quest, Full Metal Jacket, Orphans, Married to the Mob, La Partita (The Gamble), Gross Anatomy, Pacific Heights, Memphis Belle, Wind, Equinox, Short Cuts, The Browning Version, Bye Bye Love, Fluke, Cutthroat Island., The Real Blonde, The Blackout, The Maker, If...Dog...Rabbit.
TELEVISION: *Movies*: And the Band Played On, Jacob, What the Deaf Man Heard. *Specials*: Amy and the Angel, Eugene O'Neill: Journey Into Greatness. *Series*: Texas (daytime serial).

MOFFAT, DONALD
Actor. b. Plymouth, England, Dec. 26, 1930. Studied acting Royal Academy of Dramatic Art, 1952-54. London stage debut Macbeth, 1954. With Old Vic before Broadway debut in Under Milkwood, 1957. Worked with APA-Phoenix Theatre Co. and as actor and dir. of numerous B'way and regional productions.
THEATER: The Bald Soprano, Jack, Ivanov, Much Ado About Nothing, The Tumbler, Duel of Angels, A Passage to India, The Affair, The Taming of the Shrew, The Caretaker, Man and Superman, War and Peace, You Can't Take It With You, Right You Are... If You Think You Are, School for Scandal, The Wild Duck, The Cherry Orchard, Cock-a-Doodle Dandy, Hamlet, Chemin de Fer, Father's Day, Forget-Me-Not-Lane, Terra Nova, The Kitchen, Waiting for Godot, Painting Churches, Play Memory, Passion Play, The Iceman Cometh, Uncommon Ground, Love Letters, As You Like It, The Heiress.
PICTURES: Pursuit of the Graf Spee (The Battle of the River Plate; debut, 1957), Rachel Rachel, The Trial of the Catonsville Nine, R.P.M., The Great Northfield Minnesota Raid, Showdown, The Terminal Man, Earthquake, Land of No Return (Snowman), Promises in the Dark, Health, On the Nickel, Popeye, The Thing, The Right Stuff, Alamo Bay, The Best of Times, Monster in the Closet, The Unbearable Lightness of Being, Far North, Music Box, The Bonfire of the Vanities, Class Action, Regarding Henry, Housesitter, Clear and Present Danger, Trapped in Paradise.

TELEVISION: *Series*: The New Land, Logan's Run. *Guest*: Camera Three (1958), You Can't Have Everything (U.S. Steel Hour), Murder, She Wrote, Dallas. *Specials*: Forget-Me-Not Lane, Tartuffe, Waiting for Godot. *Movies*: Devil and Miss Sarah, Call of the Wild, Eleanor and Franklin: The White House Years, Exo-Man, Mary White, Sergeant Matlovich vs. the U.S. Air Force, The Word, The Gift of Love, Strangers: The Story of a Mother and Daughter, Ebony Ivory and Jade, Mrs. R's Daughter, The Long Days of Summer, Jacqueline Bouvier Kennedy, Who Will Love My Children?, Through Naked Eyes, License to Kill, Cross of Fire, A Son's Promise, Kaleidoscope, The Great Pretender, Babe Ruth, Columbo: No Time to Die, Teamster Boss: The Jackie Presser Story, Majority Rule, Love Cheat and Steal, Is There Life Out There? *Mini-Series*: Tales of the City.

MOGER, STANLEY H.
Executive. b. Boston, MA, Nov. 13, 1936. e. Colby Coll., Waterville, ME, B.A., 1958. Announcer/TV personality/WVDA and WORL (Boston) 1953-54; WGHM (Skowhegan) 1955-56; WTWO-TV (Bangor) 1955; WMHB (Waterville) 1956-57; WTVL (Waterville) 1957-58; unit pub. dir., Jaguar Prods., 1958-59; US Army reserve, 1958-64, with calls to active duty in 1958-59, 1961-62. Account exec., NBC Films/California National Productions, Chicago 1959-60; asst. sales mgr., Midwest, RCA/NBC Medical Radio System, 1960; acct. exec. Hollingbery Co., Chicago, 1960-63; and NY 1963-66; acct. exec., Storer TV Sales, 1966-69; co-founded SFM, 1969. 1978, named pres., SFM Entertainment which was responsible for the revival of Walt Disney's Mickey Mouse Club, The Adventures of Rin-Tin-Tin; Mobil Showcase Network, SFM Holiday Network. Pres.: SFM Entertainment, Inc. Exec. prod.: Television-Annual, 1978-79: Your New Day with Vidal Sassoon, The Origins Game, Believe You Can and You Can, Walt Disney Presents Sport Goofy (series), The World of Tomorrow, March of Time ... on the March (England), Sports Pros and Cons, Unclaimed Fortunes, Sea World Summer Night Magic, America's Dance Honors, Allen & Rossi's 25th Anniversary Special, Paris '89 Celebration, U.S. Sports Academy Awards, K-Nite Color Radio, Into the Night With Brad Garrett (ABC-TV), Family Film Awards (CBS), Sea World/Busch Gardens Annual Specials (CBS and Nickelodeon), Everybody Rides the Carousel (Lifetime), Gift of the Magi (Lifetime), Zoobilee Zoo (PBS), Pillar of Fire (History Channel), AFI Life Achievement Awards (CBS, ABC, NBC, Fox), AFI's 100 Years...100 Movies (CBS & TNT), The Journey Inside (Sci-Fi), Open Book (A&E), Indomitable Teddy Roosevelt (ABC), Ray Harryhausen Chronicles (AMC), Crusade in Europe (History/A&E), Visions of Light (PBS/Encore), Alice Through the Looking Glass (Disney), Witness to the Execution (HBO/Cinemax.)

MOKAE, ZAKES
Actor. b. Johannesburg, South Africa, Aug. 5, 1935. e. RADA. Came to US in 1969. Has appeared in many plays written by Athol Fugard incl. Master Harold...and the Boys, Blood Knot.
PICTURES: The Comedians, The Island, Roar, Cry Freedom, The Serpent and the Rainbow, A Dry White Season, Gross Anatomy, Dad, A Rage in Harlem, The Doctor, Body Parts, Dust Devil, Outbreak, Waterworld, Vampire in Brooklyn, Krippendorf's Tribe.
TELEVISION: *Special*: Master Harold... and the Boys. *Movies*: One in a Million: The Ron LeFlore Story, Parker Kane, Percy & Thunder, Slaughter of the Innocents, Rise & Walk: The Dennis Byrd Story.

MOL, GRETCHEN
Actress. e. William Esper Studio.
PICTURES: The Funeral, Girl 6, Donnie Brasco, The Last Time I Committed Suicide, The Deli, Rounders, The 13th Floor, Music From Another Room, Celebrity, Cherry Pink.
TELEVISION: *Movie*: Calm at Sunset Calm at Dawn, Subway Stories, Tales from the Underground. *Mini-series*: Dead Man's Walk

MOLEN, GERALD R.
Producer. Unit prod. mngr. on The Postman Always Rings Twice, Tootsie, Let's Spend the Night Together, A Soldier's Story, The Color Purple. Assoc. prod. on Batteries Not Included. Co-prod. on Rain Man. Joined Amblin Entertainment to oversee prod. of feature film projects.
PICTURES: *Exec. Producer*: Bright Lights Big City, Days of Thunder, A Far Off Place, The Flintstones, The Little Rascals, Little Giants, Casper, Twister, The Trigger Effect. *Producer*: Hook, Jurassic Park, Schindler's List (Acad. Award for Best Picture, 1993), The Lost World.

MOLINA, ALFRED
Actor. b. London, England, May 24, 1953. e. Guildhall Sch. of Music and Drama. Began acting with the National Youth Theatre. Worked as stand-up comic for street theatre group. Joined Royal Shakespeare Co., 1977.
THEATER: Frozen Assets, The Steve Biko Inquest, Dingo, Bandits, Taming of the Shrew, Happy End, Serious Money, Speed-the-Plow, Accidental Death of an Anarchist (Plays and Players' Most Promising New Actor Award), The Night of the Iguana, Molly Sweeney (off-B'way).

PICTURES: Raiders of the Lost Ark (debut, 1981), Meantime, Number One, Ladyhawke, Eleni, Water, Letter to Brezhnev, Prick Up Your Ears, Manifesto, Not Without My Daughter, Enchanted April, American Friends, The Trial, When Pigs Fly, Cabin Boy, White Fang 2: Myth of the White Wolf, Maverick, Hideaway, The Perez Family, The Steal, Species, Before and After, Dead Man, Scorpion Spring, Anna Karenina, Boogie Nights, The Man Who Knew Too Little, The Treat, Meteor, The Odd Couple II.
TELEVISION: The Losers, Anyone for Dennis, Joni Jones, Cats' Eyes, Blat, Casualty, Virtuoso, Apocolyptic Butterflies, The Accountant, Drowning in the Shallow End, El C.I.D., Ashenden, Hancock, A Polish Practice, Year in Provence, Requiem Apache, Nervous Energy.

MOLL, RICHARD
Actor. b. Pasadena, CA, Jan. 13, 1943.
PICTURES: Caveman, The Sword and the Sorcerer, Metal-storm: The Destruction of Jared-Syn, The Dungeonmaster, House, Wicked Stepmother, Think Big, Driving Me Crazy, National Lampoon's Loaded Weapon 1, Sidekicks, The Flintstones, Storybook, Galaxis, The Glass Cage, The Secret Agent Club, The Perils of Being Walter Wood, Jingle All the Way,.Ghost Central Station
TELEVISION: *Series*: Night Court. *Movies*: The Jericho Mile, The Archer: Fugitive from the Empire, Combat High, Dream Date, Class Cruise, Summertime Switch, The Ransom of Red Chief. *Specials*: Reach for the Sun, The Last Halloween, Words Up! *Guest*: Remington Steele, Facts of Life, Sledge Hammer, My Two Dads, Highlander, Weird Science, Married...With Children.

MONASH, PAUL
Producer, Writer. b. New York, NY, June 14, 1917. e. U. of WI, Columbia U. Was in U.S. Army Signal Corps and Merchant Marine; newspaper reporter, high school teacher, and civilian employee of U.S. gov't. in Europe. Wrote two novels: How Brave We Live, The Ambassadors. Entered industry writing TV scripts for Playhouse 90, Studio One, Theatre Guild of the Air, Climax, etc. Authored two-part teleplay which launched The Untouchables. 1958 won Emmy award for The Lonely Wizard (Schlitz Playhouse of Stars), dramatization of life of German-born electrical inventor Charles Steinmetz. Made m.p. debut as exec. prod. of Butch Cassidy and the Sundance Kid, 1969.
PICTURES: *Exec. Prod.*: Butch Cassidy and the Sundance Kid. *Producer*: Slaughterhouse-Five, The Friends of Eddie Coyle (also s.p.), The Front Page, Carrie, Big Trouble in Little China.
TELEVISION: *Series*: Peyton Place (exec. prod.). *Movies* (exec. prod.): The Trial of Chaplain Jensen, The Day the Loving Stopped, Child Bride of Short Creek, Killer Rules (writer), Stalin (writer), Kingfish: A Story of Huey P. Long (writer).

MONICELLI, MARIO
Director. b. Rome, Italy, May 15, 1915. Ent. m.p. industry in production; later co-authored, collab., comedies.
PICTURES: The Tailor's Maid (also s.p.), Big Deal on Madonna Street (also s.p.), The Great War, The Passionate Thief, Boccaccio '70 (dir. segment; cut for U.S. release), The Organizer (also s.p.), Casanova '70 (also s.p.), Girl With a Pistol, The Queens, Lady Liberty (Mortadella), Romanzo Popolare (also s.p.), My Friends, Caro Michele, Signore e Signori Buonanotte (also s.p.), The New Monsters, Hurricane Rosy, Sono Fotogencio, Lovers and Liars (Travels With Anita; also s.p.), Il Marchese del Grillo (also s.p.), Amici Miei Atto (All My Friends 2; also s.p.), Bertoldo Bertoldino e Cacasenna (also s.p.), The Two Lives of Mattia Pascal (also s.p.), Let's Hope It's a Girl (also s.p.), The Rogues (also co-s.p.), The Obscure Illness (also s.p.), Looking for Paradise.

MONKHOUSE, BOB
Comedian, Writer. b. Beckenham, Kent, England, June 1, 1928. e. Dulwich Coll. Debut 1948 while serving in RAF, own radio comedy series 1949-83 (winters), own TV series, BBC 1952-56, ITV 1956-83, BBC 1983-90, ITV 1990-. Major cabaret attraction. Voted Comedian of the Year, 1987. After-Dinner Speaker of the Year, 1989.
THEATER: The Boys from Syracuse, Come Blow Your Horn; The Gulls, several West End revues.
PICTURES: Carry On Sergeant, Weekend with Lulu, Dentist in the Chair, She'll Have to Go, The Bliss of Mr. Blossom
TELEVISION: *Series*: What's My Line?; Who Do You Trust?, Mad Movies, Quick on the Draw, Bob Monkhouse Comedy Hour, The Golden Shot, Celebrity Squares, I'm Bob He's Dickie!, Family Fortunes, Bob Monkhouse Tonight (1983-86), Bob's Full House (1984-90), Bob Says Opportunity Knocks (1987-89), $64,000 Question (1990-ongoing).

MONKS, JOHN, JR.
Writer, Actor, Producer, Director. b. Brooklyn, NY, June 25, 1910. e. Virginia Military Inst., A.B. Actor, stock, B'way, radio, m.p. U.S. Marines, 1942; commissioned Major, 1945. Co-author of Brother Rat. Wrote book A Ribbon and a Star.
PICTURES: *Writer*: Brother Rat, Brother Rat and a Baby, Strike Up the Band, The House on 92nd Street, 13 Rue Madeleine, Wild Harvest, Dial 1119, The West Point Story, People Against O'Hara, Where's Charley, So This Is Love, Knock on Any Door, No Man Is an Island.

TELEVISION: Climax (The Gioconda Smile, A Box of Chocolates), 20th Century-Fox Hour (Miracle on 34th St.), Gen. Electric Theatre: (Emily), CBS Special: High Tor, SWAT. *Creator serial:* Paradise Bay.

MONTAGNE, EDWARD J.
Producer, Director. b. Brooklyn, NY, May 20, 1912. e. Loyola U., Univ. of Notre Dame. RKO Pathe, 1942; U.S. Army, 1942-46; prod. many cos. after army. Exec. prod. of film-CBS-N.Y. Prod. & head of programming, Wm. Esty Adv. Co., 1950; Program consultant, William Esty Co.; v.p. Universal TV prod. & dir.
PICTURES: Tattooed Stranger, The Man with My Face, McHale's Navy, McHale's Navy Joins the Air Force, P.J., The Reluctant Astronaut, I am in My Pocket.
TELEVISION: Man Against Crime, Cavalier Theatre, The Vaughn Monroe Show, The Hunter, I Spy, McHale's Navy, Phil Silvers Show. TV *Movies:* Ellery Queen: A Very Missing Person, Short Walk to Daylight, Hurricane, Terror on the 40th Floor, Francis Gary Powers, Million Dollar Ripoff, Crash of Flight 401, High Noon—Part 2.

MONTALBAN, RICARDO
Actor. b. Mexico City, Mex., Nov. 25, 1920. Appeared in Mexican pictures 1941-45. On B'way in Her Cardboard Lover with Tallulah Bankhead. Later in Jamaica, The King and I, Don Juan in Hell. Autobiography: Reflections: A Life in Two Worlds (1980).
PICTURES: Fiesta (U.S. debut, 1947), On an Island With You, The Kissing Bandit, Neptune's Daughter, Battleground, Border Incident, Mystery Street, Right Cross, Two Weeks with Love, Across the Wide Missouri, Mark of the Renegade, My Man and I, Sombrero, Latin Lovers, The Saracen Blade, The Courtesans of Babylon (Queen of Babylon), Sombra Verde, A Life in the Balance, Untouched, The Son of the Sheik, Three for Jamie Dawn, Sayonara, Let No Man Write My Epitaph, The Black Buccaneer, Hemingway's Adventures of a Young Man, The Reluctant Saint, Love Is a Ball, Cheyenne Autumn, The Money Trap, Madame X, The Singing Nun, Sol Madrid, Blue, Sweet Charity, The Deserter, Escape From the Planet of the Apes, Conquest of the Planet of the Apes, The Train Robbers, Joe Panther, Won Ton Ton the Dog Who Saved Hollywood, Star Trek II: The Wrath of Khan, Cannonball Run II, The Naked Gun: From the Files of Police Squad.
TELEVISION: *Series:* Fantasy Island, The Colbys, Heaven Help Us. *Guest:* How the West Was Won Part II (Emmy Award, 1978). *Movies:* The Longest Hundred Miles, The Pigeon, Black Water Gold, The Aquarians, Sarge: The Badge or the Cross, Face of Fear, Desperate Mission, Fireball Foreward, Wonder Woman, The Mark of Zorro, McNaughton's Daughter, Fantasy Island (pilot), Captains Courageous, Return to Fantasy Island.

MONTGOMERY, GEORGE
Actor. r.n. George Montgomery Letz. b. Brady, MT, Aug. 29, 1916. e. U. of MT. Armed Services, WWII. Was champion heavyweight boxer. Debuted in films as extra, stuntman, then bit player billed as George Letz.
PICTURES: Singing Vagabond (debut, 1935), Springtime in the Rockies, The Lone Ranger, Rough Riders' Round-up, Frontier Pony Express, Man of Conquest, Star Dust, Jennie, Cisco Kid and the Lady, Charter Pilot, Hi-Yo Silver, Young People, The Riders of the Purple Sage, Cadet Girl, Accent on Love, The Cowboy and the Blonde, The Last of the Duanes, Ten Gentlemen from West Point, Roxie Hart, Orchestra Wives, China Girl, Coney Island, Bomber's Moon, Three Little Girls in Blue, The Brasher Doubloon, Lulu Belle, The Girl from Manhattan, Belle Starr's Daughter, Dakota Lil, Davy Crockett Indian Scout, The Iroquois Trail, The Texas Rangers, Cripple Creek, Jack McCall Desperado, Gun Belt, Fort Ti, The Pathfinder, The Battle of Rogue River, Seminole Uprising, Robber's Roost, Masterson of Kansas, Huk!, Canyon River, Street of Sinners, Pawnee, Gun Duel in Durango, Black Patch, Last of the Badmen, Toughest Gun in Tombstone, Badman's Country, Man from God's Country, Samar (also dir., s.p., prod.), Guerillas in Pink Lace (also dir., s.p., prod.), Satan's Harvest (also dir.), Proscrito del rio Colorado, Battle of the Bulge, Hell of Borneo (also dir., s.p., prod.), Hallucination Generation, Hostile Guns, The Daredevil, Wild Wind.
TELEVISION: *Series:* Cimarron City.

MOODY, RON
Actor. r.n. Ronald Moodnick. b. London, England, Jan. 8, 1924. e. London Sch. of Economics. *Novels:* The Devil You Don't, Very Very Slightly Imperfect, Off The Cuff, The Amazon Box.
THEATER: *London:* Intimacy at Eight (debut, 1952), For Adults Only, Candide, Oliver! (also NY revival: Theatre World Award), Joey Joey (Bristol; also writer, composer, lyricist), Peter Pan, Hamlet, The Clandestine Marriage, The Showman (also writer), Sherlock Holmes—The Musical. *Author:* Saturnalia, Move Along Sideways.
PICTURES: Davy (debut, 1958), Follow a Star, Make Mine Mink, Five Golden Hours, The Mouse on the Moon, A Pair of Briefs, Summer Holiday, Ladies Who Do, Murder Most Foul, San Ferry Ann, The Sandwich Man, Oliver! (Acad. Award nom.), The Twelve Chairs, Flight of the Doves, Dogpound Shuffle, Dominique, Unidentified Flying Oddball, Wrong Is Right, Where Is Parsifal?, A Kid in King Arthur's Court.

TELEVISION: *Series:* Nobody's Perfect, Tales of the Gold Monkey. *Mini-Series:* The Word. *Movies:* David Copperfield (theatrical in U.K.), Dial M for Murder (U.S.), The Caucasian Chalk Circle, Hideaway. *Specials:* Portrait of Petulia, Bing Crosby's Merrie Olde Christmas, Winter's Tale, Othello, Other Side of London, Baden Powell, Lights Camera Action, Last of the Summer Wine.

MOONJEAN, HANK
Producer, Director. Began as asst. dir. at MGM. Later turned to producing.
PICTURES: *Assoc. Prod.:* The Great Gatsby, WUSA, The Secret Life of An American Wife, Child's Play, Welcome to Hard Times, The Singing Nun. *Exec. Prod.:* The Fortune, The End. *Producer:* Hooper, Smokey and the Bandit II, The Incredible Shrinking Woman, Paternity, Sharky's Machine, Stroker Ace, Stealing Home, Dangerous Liaisons.

MOORE, CONSTANCE
Actress. b. Sioux City, IA, Jan. 18, 1922. Sang on radio: Lockheed program, Jurgen's Show. Screen debut 1938. TV shows, nightclubs. N.Y. Stage: The Boys from Syracuse, By Jupiter, Annie Get Your Gun, Bells Are Ringing, Affairs of State.
PICTURES: Prison Break, A Letter of Introduction, You Can't Cheat an Honest Man, I Wanted Wings, Take a Letter Darling, Show Business, Atlantic City, Delightfully Dangerous, Earl Carroll Vanities, In Old Sacramento, Hit Parade of 1947, Spree.

MOORE, DAN
Costume Designer.
PICTURES: Southern Comfort, Rocky III, Brewster's Millions, Blue City, Crossroads, Punchline, Red Heat, She's Out of Control, Johnny Handsome, Another 48 Hrs., Necessary Roughness, Trespass, Geronimo: An American Legend, Wild Bill, This World Then the Fireworks, Last Man Standing, Broken Arrow.
TELEVISION: *Movies:* Twisted Desire, The Cherokee Kid, The Second Civil War, 12 Angry Men. *Series:* The Magnificent Seven (Emmy Award, 1998).

MOORE, DEMI
Actress. b. Roswell, NM, Nov. 11, 1962. r.n. Demetria Guynes. m. actor Bruce Willis. Began modeling at age 16. *Off-B'way debut:* The Early Girl, 1987 (Theatre World Award).
PICTURES: Choices (debut, 1981), Parasite, Young Doctors in Love, Blame It on Rio, No Small Affair, St. Elmo's Fire, About Last Night, One Crazy Summer, Wisdom, The Seventh Sign, We're No Angels, Ghost, Nothing But Trouble, Mortal Thoughts (also co-prod.), The Butcher's Wife, A Few Good Men, Indecent Proposal, A Century of Cinema, Disclosure, The Scarlett Letter, Now and Then (also co-prod.), The Juror, The Hunchback of Notre Dame (voice), Striptease, Destination Anywhere, G.I. Jane (also prod.), Austin Powers (prod. only), Deconstructing Harry, Passion of Mind, Airframe.
TELEVISION: *Series:* General Hospital. *Guest:* Kaz, Vega$, Moonlighting, Tales from the Crypt (Dead Right). *Specials:* Bedrooms, The New Homeowner's Guide to Happiness. *Movies:* If These Walls Could Speak.

MOORE, DICKIE
Actor. b. Los Angeles, CA, Sept. 12, 1925. m. actress Jane Powell. Began picture career when only 11 months old, playing John Barrymore as a baby in The Beloved Rogue. Appeared in numerous radio, television and stage prods. In NY and L.A. and over 100 films; appeared in several Our Gang shorts. Co-author and star, RKO short subject, The Boy and the Eagle (Acad. Award nom.). Author: Opportunities in Acting, Twinkle Twinkle Little Star (But Don't Have Sex or Take the Car), 1984. Now public relations executive.
PICTURES: Passion Flower, The Squaw Man, Manhattan Parade, Million Dollar Legs, Blonde Venus, So Big, Gabriel Over the White House, Oliver Twist, Cradle Song, This Side of Heaven, Upper World, Little Men, Peter Ibbetson, So Red the Rose, The Story of Louis Pasteur, The Life of Emile Zola, The Arkansas Traveler, The Under-Pup, The Blue Bird, A Dispatch From Reuters, Sergeant York, Adventures of Martin Eden, Miss Annie Rooney, Heaven Can Wait, The Happy Land, The Eve of St. Mark, Youth Runs Wild, Out of the Past, Killer Shark, 16 Fathoms Deep, Eight Iron Men, The Member of the Wedding.

MOORE, DUDLEY
Actor, Writer, Musician. b. Dagenham, Essex, England, April 19, 1935. e. Oxford, graduating in 1958. Toured British Isles with jazz group before joining Peter Cook, Jonathan Miller and Alan Bennett in creating hit revue, Beyond the Fringe, in U.K. and N.Y. Appeared later with Peter Cook on B'way in Good Evening. Composed film scores: Inadmissible Evidence, Staircase.

PICTURES: The Wrong Box (debut, 1966), Bedazzled (also composer), 30 is a Dangerous Age Cynthia (also co-s.p., composer), Monte Carlo or Bust (Those Daring Young Men in Their Jaunty Jalopies), The Bed Sitting Room, Alice's Adventures in Wonderland, The Hound of the Baskervilles, Foul Play, "10", Wholly Moses, Arthur (Acad. Award nom.), Six Weeks, Lovesick, Romantic Comedy, Unfaithfully Yours, Best Defense, Micki and Maude, Santa Claus, Like Father Like Son, Arthur 2 On the Rocks (also exec. prod.), The Adventures of Milo and Otis (narrator), Crazy People, Blame It on the Bellboy, The Pickle, A Weekend in the Country.
TELEVISION: Series: Dudley, Daddy's Girls. Movie: Parallel Lives.

MOORE, ELLIS
Consultant. b. New York, NY, May 12, 1924. e. Washington and Lee U., 1941-43. Newspaperman in AK, TN, 1946-52. Joined NBC 1952; mgr. of bus. pub., 1953; dir., press dept., 1954; dir., press & publicity, 1959; vice-pres., 1961; pub. rel. dept., Standard Oil Co. (N.J.), 1963-66; v.p. press relations, ABC-TV Network, 1966-68; v.p. public relations ABC-TV Network, 1968-70; v.p. public relations, ABC, 1970, v.p. public relations, ABC, Inc., 1972; v.p. corporate relations, ABC, Inc., 1979; v.p., public affairs, ABC, Inc., 1982-85. P.R. consultant, 1985. Retired, 1992.

MOORE, JULIANNE
Actress. b. 1961. e. Boston Univ. Sch. for the Arts.
THEATRE: Off-B'way: Serious Money, Ice Cream/Hot Fudge, The Road to Nirvana, Hamlet, The Father.
PICTURES: Tales From the Darkside (debut, 1990), The Hand That Rocks the Cradle, Body of Evidence, Benny & Joon, The Fugitive, Short Cuts, Vanya on 42nd Street, Roommates, Safe, Nine Months, Assassins, Surviving Picasso, The Lost World: Jurassic Park, The Myth of Fingerprints, Boogie Nights (LA Film Crits. Award, Best Supporting Actress, 1997), The Big Lebowski.
TELEVISION: Series: As the World Turns (Emmy Award). Movies: I'll Take Manhattan, The Last to Go, Cast a Deadly Spell.

MOORE, MARY TYLER
Actress. b. Brooklyn. NY, Dec. 29, 1936. Began as professional dancer and got first break as teenager in commercials (notably the elf in Hotpoint appliance ads); then small roles in series Bachelor Father, Steve Canyon, and finally as the switchboard oper. in series Richard Diamond Private Detective (though only her legs were seen). Chairman of Bd., MTM Enterprises, Inc, which she founded with then-husband Grant Tinker.
THEATER: B'way: Breakfast at Tiffany's (debut), Whose Life Is It Anyway? (special Tony Award, 1980), Sweet Sue.
PICTURES: X-15 (debut, 1961), Thoroughly Modern Millie, Don't Just Stand There, What's So Bad About Feeling Good?, Change of Habit, Ordinary People (Acad. Award nom.), Six Weeks, Just Between Friends, Flirting With Disaster, Reno Fins Her Mom, Keys to Tulsa.
TELEVISION: Series: Richard Diamond—Private Detective, The Dick Van Dyke Show (2 Emmy Awards: 1964, 1966), The Mary Tyler Moore Show (1970-77; 4 Emmy Awards: 1973, 1974 (2), 1976), Mary (1978), The Mary Tyler Moore Hour (1979), Mary (1985-86), Annie McGuire, New York News, Mary & Rhoda. Guest: Bachelor Father, Steve Canyon, 77 Sunset Strip, Hawaiian Eye, Love American Style, Rhoda. Movies: Run a Crooked Mile, First You Cry, Heartsounds, Finnegan Begin Again, Gore Vidal's Lincoln, The Last Best Year, Thanksgiving Day, Stolen Babies (Emmy Award, 1993), Forbidden Memories, Payback, Three Cats from Miami and Other Pet Practicioners (host). Specials: Dick Van Dyke and the Other Woman, How to Survive the 70's, How to Raise a Drugfree Child.

MOORE, MICHAEL
Director, Writer. b. Davison, MI, 1954. e. Univ. of MI. Was editor of The Michigan Voice and Mother Jones magazine, commentator on radio show All Things Considered, before gaining fame with first film Roger & Me. Established Center for Alternative Media to support indept. filmmakers.
PICTURES: Dir./Prod./Writer/Actor: Roger & Me (debut, 1989), Canadian Bacon, The Big One.
TELEVISION: Series: TV Nation (dir., exec. prod., writer, host). Special: Pets and Meat: The Return to Flint.

MOORE, ROGER
Actor. b. London, England, Oct. 14, 1927. e. art school, London; Royal Acad. of Dramatic Art. Had bit parts in British films Vacation From Marriage, Caesar and Cleopatra, Piccadilly Incident, Gay Lady. Appointed Special Ambassador for UNICEF, 1991.
THEATER: Mr. Roberts, I Capture the Castle, Little Hut, others. B'way: A Pin to See the Peepshow.
PICTURES: The Last Time I Saw Paris, Interrupted Melody, The King's Thief, Diane, The Miracle, Gold of the Seven Saints, The Sins of Rachel Cade, Rape of the Sabines, Crossplot, The Man Who Haunted Himself, Live and Let Die, Gold, The Man With the Golden Gun, That Lucky Touch, Street People, Shout at the Devil, The Spy Who Loved Me, The Wild Geese, Escape To Athena, Moonraker, ffolkes (North Sea Hijack), The Sea Wolves, Sunday Lovers, For Your Eyes Only, The Cannonball Run, Octopussy, The Curse of the Pink Panther, The Naked Face, A View to a Kill, The Magic Snowman (voice), Fire Ice and Dynamite, Bed and Breakfast, Bullseye!, The Quest.
TELEVISION: Series: The Alaskans, Maverick, The Saint, The Persuaders. Movies: Sherlock Holmes in New York, The Man Who Wouldn't Die (also co-exec. prod.).

MOORE, TERRY
Actress. r.n. Helen Koford. b. Los Angeles, CA, Jan. 7, 1929. Mother was Luella Bickmore, actress. Photographer's model as a child; acted on radio; with Pasadena Playhouse 1940. Voted Star of Tomorrow: 1958. Author: The Beauty and the Billionaire (1984). Formed Moore/Rivers Productions, 1988 with partner-manager Jerry Rivers. Has also acted as Helen Koford, Judy Ford, and Jan Ford.
PICTURES: Maryland (debut as Helen Koford, 1940), The Howards of Virginia, On the Sunny Side (billed as Judy Ford), A-Haunting We Hill Go, My Gal Sal, True to Life, Date With Destiny, Gaslight, Since You Went Away, Son of Lassie, Sweet and Low Down, Shadowed, Summer Holiday, Devil on Wheels, The Return of October (1st billing as Terry Moore), Mighty Joe Young, The Great Ruppert, He's a Cockeyed Wonder, Gambling House, The Barefoot Mailman, Two of a Kind, Sunny Side of the Street, Come Back Little Sheba (Acad. Award nom.), Man on a Tightrope, Beneath the 12-Mile Reef, King of the Khyber Rifles, Daddy Long Legs, Shack Out on 101, Postmark for Danger (Portrait of Alison), Between Heaven and Hell, Peyton Place, Bernardine, A Private's Affair, Cast a Long Shadow, Why Must I Die?, Platinum High School, City of Fear, Black Spurs, Town Tamer, Waco, A Man Called Dagger, Daredevil, Death Dimension (Black Eliminator), Double Exposure, Hellhole, W.A.R., Beverly Hills Brats (also co-prod., co-story), Mighty Joe Young.
TELEVISION: Series: Empire. Movies: Quarantined, Smash-Up on Interstate 5, Jake Spanner: Private Eye, Marilyn and Me.

MOORE, THOMAS W.
Executive. e. U. of Missouri. Naval aviator, USNR, 1940-45. Adv. dept., The Star, Meridian, MS; v.p., adv. mgr., Forest Lawn Memorial Park; account exec., CBS-TV Film Sales, Los Angeles; gen. sales mgr., CBS-TV Film Sales, 1956; v.p. in chg. programming & talent, 1958; pres., ABC-TV Network, 1962; chmn. bd., Ticketron, 1968; pres., Tomorrow Entertainment, Inc. 1971; chmn., 1981.

MORALES, ESAI
Actor. b. Brooklyn, NY, 1963. e. NY's High School for the Performing Arts. NY stage debut at age 17 in NY Shakespeare Fest. prod. of The Tempest, 1981.
THEATRE: Short Eyes, Tamer of Horses, El Mermano, Salome.
PICTURES: Forty Deuce (debut, 1982), Bad Boys, L.A. Bad, Rainy Day Friends, La Bamba, The Principal, Bloodhounds of Broadway, Naked Tango, Amazon, Freejack, In the Army Now, Rapa Nui, My Family/Mi Familia, Scorpion Spring.
TELEVISION: Mini-Series: On Wings of Eagles. Movies: The Burning Season, Deadlocked: Escape From Zone 14. Special: The Great Love Experiment. Guest: The Equalizer, Miami Vice.

MORANIS, RICK
Actor, Writer. b. Toronto, Canada, April 18, 1954. Began career as part-time radio engineer while still in high school. Hosted own comedy show on radio then performed in Toronto cabarets and nightclubs and on TV. Joined satirical TV series SCTV during its 3rd season on CBC, for which he won Emmy for writing when broadcast in U.S. Created characters of the McKenzie Brothers with Dave Thomas and won Grammy nom. for McKenzie Brothers album. With Thomas co-wrote, co-directed and starred in film debut Strange Brew, 1983. Supplied voice for cartoon series Rick Moranis in Gravedale High.
PICTURES: Strange Brew (debut, 1983; also co-dir., co-s.p.), Streets of Fire, Ghostbusters, The Wild Life, Brewster's Millions, Head Office, Club Paradise, Little Shop of Horrors, Spaceballs, Ghostbusters II, Honey I Shrunk the Kids, Parenthood, My Blue Heaven, L.A. Story, Honey I Blew Up the Kid, Splitting Heirs, The Flintstones, Little Giants, Big Bully.

MOREAU, JEANNE
Actress. b. Paris, France, Jan. 23, 1928. e. Nat'l Conservatory of Dramatic Art. Stage debut with Comedie Francaise, acting there until 1952 when she joined the Theatre Nationale Populaire. Directorial debut: La Lumiere (film), 1976. Recipient of 1995 BAFTA Film Craft Fellowship Award.
THEATER: A Month in the Country, La Machine Infernale, Pygmalion, Cat on a Hot Tin Roof.
PICTURES: The She-Wolves, Elevator to the Scaffold, The Lovers, Le Dialogue Des Carmelites, Les Liaisons Dangereuses, Moderato Cantabile, La Notte, Jules and Jim, A Woman is a Woman, Eva, The Trial, Bay of Angels, The Victors, Le Feu Follet, Diary of a Chambermaid, The Yellow Rolls-Royce, The Train, Mata Hari, Viva Maria, Mademoiselle, Chimes at Midnight, Sailor From Gibraltar, The Bride Wore Black, The Immortal Story, Great Catherine, Monte Walsh, Alex in Wonderland, The Little Theatre of Jean Renoir, Louise, The Last Tycoon, French Provincial, La Lumiere (also dir., s.p.), Mr. Klein, The Adolescent (dir., s.p. only), Plein Sud, Querelle, The Trout, Le Miracle, La Femme Nikita, The Suspended Step of the Stork, La Femme Farde, Until the End of the World, Alberto Express, The Lover (voice), Map of the Human Heart, Anna Karamazova, The Summer House, See You Tomorrow, My Name Is Victor, The Old Lady Who Walks in the Sea, Beyond the Clouds, I Love You I Love You Not, The Proprietor.
TELEVISION: A Foreign Field (BBC).

MORENO, RITA

Actress. r.n. Rosa Dolores Alvario. b. Humacao, Puerto Rico, Dec. 11, 1931. Spanish dancer since childhood; night club entertainer. Has won all 4 major show business awards: Oscar, Tony, 2 Emmys and Grammy (for Best Recording for Children: The Electric Company, 1972).
THEATER: Skydrift (debut, 1945), The Sign in Sidney Brustein's Window, Gantry, Last of the Red Hot Lovers, The National Health (Long Wharf, CT), The Ritz (Tony Award, 1975), Wally's Cafe, The Odd Couple (female version), Sunset Boulevard (London).
PICTURES: So Young So Bad (debut, 1950, as Rosita Moreno), Pagan Love Song, The Toast of New Orleans, Singin' in the Rain, The Ring, Cattle Town, Ma and Pa Kettle on Vacation, Latin Lovers, Fort Vengeance, Jivaro, El Alamein, Yellow Tomahawk, Garden of Evil, Untamed, Seven Cities of Gold, Lieutenant Wore Skirts, The King and I, The Vagabond King, The Deerslayer, This Rebel Breed, Summer and Smoke, West Side Story (Acad. Award, best supporting actress, 1961), Cry of Battle, The Night of the Following Day, Marlowe, Popi, Carnal Knowledge, The Ritz, The Boss' Son, Happy Birthday Gemini, The Four Seasons, Life in the Food Chain (Age Isn't Everything), The Italian Movie, Blackout, I Like It Like That, Angus.
TELEVISION: *Series*: The Electric Company, Nine to Five, B.L. Styker, Top of the Heap, The Cosby Mysteries. *Movies*: Evita Peron, Anatomy of a Seduction, Portrait of a Showgirl. *Guest*: The Muppet Show (Emmy Award, 1977), The Rockford Files (Emmy Award, 1978). *Special*: Tales From the Hollywood Hills: The Golden Land.

MORGAN, ANDRE

Producer. b. Morocco, 1952. e. U. of Kansas. Golden Harvest Films prod., 1972-84. Exec. v.p., Golden Communications 1976-84. Formed Ruddy-Morgan Organization with Albert S. Ruddy, 1984.
PICTURES: Enter the Dragon, The Amsterdam Kill, The Boys in Company C, Cannonball Run II, High Road to China, Lassiter, Farewell to the King, Speed Zone, Impulse, Ladybugs, Bad Girls, The Scout, Heaven's Prisoners.
TELEVISION: *Series*: Walker Texas Ranger. *Movies*: Miracle in the Wilderness, Staying Afloat.

MORGAN, DEBBI

Actress. b. Dunn, NC, Sept. 20, 1956.
PICTURES: Cry Uncle! (debut, 1971), Mandingo, Monkey Hustle, Dirty Mary, Eve's Bayou (Chicago Crits. Award, Best Supporting Actress, 1997), Asunder.
TELEVISION: *Movies*: Love's Savage Fury, The Jesse Owens Story, Guilty of Innocence: The Lenell Geter Story, Perry Mason: The Case of the Fatal Framing. *Mini-series*: Roots: The Next Generations. *Series*: General Hospital, Behind the Screen, All My Children, Generations, Loving, The City, Port Charles.

MORGAN, HARRY

Actor. r.n. Harry Bratsburg. b. Detroit, MI, April 10, 1915. e. U. of Chicago. Previously acted as Henry Morgan.
THEATER: Gentle People, My Heart's in the Highlands, Thunder Rock, Night Music, Night Before Christmas.
PICTURES: To the Shores of Tripoli (debut, 1942), The Loves of Edgar Allen Poe, Crash Dive, Orchestra Wives, The Ox-Bow Incident, Happy Land, Wing and a Prayer, A Bell for Adano, Dragonwyck, From This Day Forward, The Gangster, All My Sons, The Big Clock, Moonrise, Yellow Sky, Madame Bovary, The Saxon Charm, Dark City, Appointment with Danger, The Highwayman, When I Grow Up, The Well, The Blue Veil, Bend of the River, Scandal Sheet, My Six Convicts, Boots Malone, High Noon, What Price Glory, Stop You're Killing Me, Arena, Torch Song, Thunder Bay, The Glenn Miller Story, About Mrs. Leslie, Forty-Niners, The Far Country, Not as a Stranger, Backlash, Strategic Air Command, The Teahouse of the August Moon, Inherit the Wind, The Mountain Road, How the West Was Won, John Goldfarb Please Come Home, What Did You Do in the War Daddy?, Frankie and Johnny, The Flim Flam Man, Support Your Local Sheriff, Viva Max!, The Barefoot Executive, Support Your Local Gunfighter, Scandalous John, Snowball Express, Charlie and the Angel, The Apple Dumpling Gang, The Greatest, The Shootist, The Cat From Outer Space, The Apple Dumpling Gang Rides Again, Dragnet.
TELEVISION: *Series*: December Bride, Pete and Gladys, The Richard Boone Show, Kentucky Jones, Dragnet, The D.A., Hec Ramsey, M*A*S*H (Emmy Award, 1980), After M*A*S*H, Blacke's Magic, You Can't Take It With You. *Movies*: Dragnet (pilot), But I Don't Want to Get Married!, The Feminist and the Fuzz, Ellery Queen: Don't Look Behind You, Hec Ramsey (pilot), Sidekicks, The Last Day (narrator), Exo-Man, The Magnificent Magnet of Santa Mesa, Maneaters Are Loose!, Murder at the Mardi Gras, The Bastard, Kate Bliss and the Ticker Tape Kid, The Wild Wild West Revisited, Better Late Than Never, Roughnecks, Scout's Honor, More Wild Wild West, Rivkin: Bounty Hunter, Agatha Christie's Sparkling Cyanide, The Incident, Against Her Will: An Incident in Baltimore, Incident in a Small Town. *Mini-Series*: Backstairs at the White House, Roots: The Next Generations.

MORGAN, MICHELE

Actress. r.n. Simone Roussel. b. Paris, France, Feb. 29, 1920. e. Dieppe, dramatic school, Paris. Won starring role at 17 opposite Charles Boyer in Gribouille (The Lady in Question). Made several pictures abroad; to U.S. 1941. Recent theatre includes Les Monstres Sacres. *Autobiography*: With Those Eyes (1977).
PICTURES: Gribouille, Port of Sahadows, Joan of Paris (U.S. debut, 1942), The Heart of a Nation, Two Tickets to London, Higher and Higher, Passage to Marseilles, The Chase, La Symphonie Pastorale, The Fallen Idol, Fabiola, Souvenir, The Naked Heart (Maria Chapdelaine), The Moment of Truth, Daughters of Destiny, The Proud and the Beautiful, Napoleon, Grand Maneuver, Marguerite de la Nuit, Marie Antoinette, There's Always a Price Tag, The Mirror Has Two Faces, Maxime, Love on the Riviera, Three Faces of Sin, Crime Does Not Pay, Landru (Bluebeard), Web of Fear, Lost Command, Benjamin, Cat and Mouse, Robert et Robert, A Man and a Woman: 20 Years Later, Everybody's Fine.

MORIARTY, CATHY

Actress. b. Bronx, NY, Nov. 29, 1960. Raised in Yonkers, NY.
PICTURES: Raging Bull (debut, 1980; Acad. Award nom.), Neighbors, White of the Eye, Burndown, Kindergarten Cop, Soapdish, The Mambo Kings, The Gun in Betty Lou's Handbag, Matinee, Another Stakeout, Me and the Kid, Pontiac Moon, Forget Paris, Casper, Foxfire, Opposite Corners, Cop Land, Hugo Pool.
TELEVISION: *Series*: Bless This House. *Movie*: Another Midnight Run. *Guest*: Tales from the Crypt (ACE Award).

MORIARTY, MICHAEL

Actor. b. Detroit, MI, April 5, 1941. e. Dartmouth. Studied at London Acad. of Music and Dramatic Arts. Appeared with New York Shakespeare Festival, Charles Street Playhouse (Boston), Alley Theatre (Houston) and Tyrone Guthrie Theatre (Minneapolis). B'way debut in The Trial of the Catonsville Nine.
THEATER: Find Your Way Home (Tony & Theatre World Awards, 1974), Richard III, Long Day's Journey Into Night, Henry V, GR Point, Whose Life Is It Anyway (Kennedy Center), The Ballad of Dexter Creed, Uncle Vanya, The Caine Mutiny Court-Martial, My Fair Lady.
PICTURES: Glory Boy (debut, 1971), Hickey and Boggs, Bang the Drum Slowly, The Last Detail, Shoot It Black Shoot It Blue, Report to the Commissioner, Who'll Stop the Rain, Q, Blood Link, Odd Birds, Pale Rider, The Stuff, Troll, The Hanoi Hilton, It's Alive III: Island of the Alive, Return to Salem's Lot, Dark Tower, Full Fathom Five, The Secret of the Ice Cave, Courage Under Fire.
TELEVISION: *Series*: Law and Order. *Movies*: A Summer Without Boys, The Glass Menagerie (Emmy Award, 1974), The Deadliest Season, The Winds of Kitty Hawk, Too Far to Go (also distributed theatrically), Windmills of the Gods, Frank Nitti: Enforcer, Tailspin: Behind the Korean Airline Tragedy, Born Too Soon, Children of the Dust. *Mini-Series*: Holocaust (Emmy Award, 1978). *Guest*: The Equalizer.

MORITA, NORIYUKI "PAT"

Actor. b. Isleton, CA, June 28, 1932. Began show business career as comedian in nightclubs for such stars as Ella Fitzgerald, Johnny Mathis, Diana Ross and the Supremes, Glen Campbell, etc. Worked in saloons, coffee houses, and dinner theatres before becoming headliner in Las Vegas showrooms, Playboy Clubs, Carnegie Hall, etc. Guest on most TV talk, variety shows and series: M*A*S*H, Love Boat, Magnum, P.I. etc.
PICTURES: Thoroughly Modern Millie, Every Little Crook and Nanny, Cancel My Reservation, Where Does It Hurt?, Midway, When Time Ran Out, Full Moon High, Savannah Smiles, Jimmy the Kid, The Karate Kid (Acad. Award nom.), Night Patrol, Slapstick of Another Kind, The Karate Kid Part II, Captive Hearts, Collision Course, The Karate Kid Part III, Do Or Die, Lena's Holiday, Honeymoon in Vegas, Miracle Beach, Even Cowgirls Get the Blues, The Next Karate Kid, American Ninja 5.
TELEVISION: *Series*: The Queen and I, Sanford and Son, Happy Days, Mr. T and Tina, Blansky's Beauties, Ohara, The Karate Kid (voice for animated series). *Movies*: Evil Roy Slade, A Very Missing Person, Brock's Last Case, Punch and Jody, Farewell to Manzanar, Human Feelings, For the Love of It, The Vegas Strip Wars, Amos, Babes in Toyland, Hiroshima: Out of the Ashes, Greyhounds, Hart to Hart: Secrets of the Hart.

MORITZ, MILTON I

Executive. b. Pittsburgh, PA, April 27, 1933. e. Woodbury Coll., grad. 1955. Owned, operated theatres in L.A., 1953-55; U.S. Navy 1955-57; American International Pictures asst. gen. sls. mgr., 1957; nat'l. dir. of adv. and publ. 1958; v.p. and bd. mem. of American International Pictures, 1967; pres. of Variety Club of So. Cal, Tent 25, 1975-76; 1975, named sr. v.p.; in 1980, formed own co., The Milton I. Moritz Co., Inc., Inc., mktg. & dist. consultant. 1987-94, joined Pacific Theatres as v.p. in chg. of adv., p.r. & promotions. 1995, reactivated the Milton I. Moritz Co., Inc.

MORRICONE, ENNIO
Composer, Arranger. b. Rome, Italy, Nov. 10, 1928. Studied with Goffredo Petrassi at the Acad. of Santa Cecilia in Rome. Began career composing chamber music and symphonies as well as music for radio, TV and theater. Wrote for popular performers including Gianni Morandi. Early film scores for light comedies. Gained recognition for assoc. with Italian westerns of Sergio Leone (under name of Dan Davio).
PICTURES: Il Federal (1961, debut), A Fistful of Dollars, The Good the Bad and the Ugly, El Greco, Fists in the Pocket, Battle of Algiers, Matcheless, Theorem, Once Upon a Time in the West, Investigation of a Citizen, Fraulein Doktor, Burn, The Bird with the Crystal Plumage, Cat O'Nine Tails, The Red Tent, Four Flies in Grey Velvet, The Decameron, The Black Belly of the Tarantula, Bluebeard, The Serpent, Blood in the Streets, Eye of the Cat, The Human Factor, Murder on the Bridge, Sunday Woman, The Inheritance, Partner, Orca, Exorcist II: The Heretic, 1900, Days of Heaven, La Cage aux Folles, Bloodline, Stay as You Are, The Humanoid, The Meadow, A Time to Die, Travels With Anita (Lovers and Liars), When You Comin' Back Red Ryder?, Almost Human, La Cage aux Folles II, The Island, Tragedy of a Ridiculous Man, Windows, Butterfly, So Fine, White Dog, Copkiller, Nana, The Thing, Treasure of the Four Crowns, Sahara, Once Upon a Time in America, Thieves After Dark, The Cage, La Cage aux Folles III, The Forester's Sons, The Red Sonja, Repentier, The Mission, The Venetian Woman, The Untouchables, Quartiere (Neighborhood), Rampage, Frantic, A Time of Destiny, Casualties of War, Cinema Paradiso, State of Grace, Hamlet, Bugsy, City of Joy, The Bachelor, In the Line of Fire, Wolf, Love Affair, Disclosure, Lolita.
TELEVISION: U.S.: Marco Polo, Moses—The Lawgiver, Scarlet and the Black, C.A.T. Squad, The Endless Game, Octopus 4, Abraham.

MORRIS, ERROL
Director, Writer. b. Hewlett, NY, 1948. e. Univ. of WI, Univ. of CA/Berkeley.
PICTURES: Gates of Heaven, Vernon Florida, The Thin Blue Line, The Dark Wind, A Brief History of Time, Fast Cheap & Out Of Control.

MORRIS, GARRETT
Actor. b. New Orleans, LA, Feb. 1, 1937. e. Dillard Univ., Juilliard Sch. of Music, Manhattan Sch. of Music. Was singer and arranger for Harry Belafonte Folk Singers and B'way actor before achieving fame as original cast member of Saturday Night Live.
THEATER: Porgy and Bess, I'm Solomon, Show Boat, Hallelujah Baby!, The Basic Training of Pavlo Hummel, Finian's Rainbow, The Great White Hope, Ain't Supposed to Die a Natural Death, The Unvarnished Truth.
PICTURES: Where's Poppa? (debut, 1970), The Anderson Tapes, Cooley High, Car Wash, How to Beat the High Cost of Living, The Census Taker, The Stuff, Critical Condition, The Underachievers, Dance to Win, Motorama, Children of the Night, Almost Blue, Coneheads, Black Rose of Harlem, Black Scorpion II: Aftershock, Santa with Muscles.
TELEVISION: Series: Roll Out, Saturday Night Live (1975-80), It's Your Move, Hunter, Martin, Cleghorne!, The Jamie Foxx Show. Movies: The Invisible Woman, Earth Angel, Maid for Each Other, Black Scorpion. Guest: Scarecrow and Mrs. King, Love Boat, Married With Children, Murder She Wrote, The Jeffersons.

MORRIS, HOWARD
Actor, Director, Writer. b. New York, NY, Sept. 4, 1919. e. NYU. U.S. Army, 4 yrs.
THEATER: Hamlet, Call Me Mister, John Loves Mary, Gentlemen Prefer Blondes, Finian's Rainbow.
PICTURES: Director: Who's Minding the Mint?, With Six You Get Egg Roll, Don't Drink the Water, Goin' Cocoanuts. Actor: Boys' Night Out, 40 Pounds of Trouble, The Nutty Professor, Fluffy, Way... Way Out, High Anxiety, History of the World Part 1, Splash, Transylvania Twist, Life Stinks.
TELEVISION: Series: Your Show of Shows (also writer), Caesar's Hour. Movies: The Munster's Revenge, Portrait of a Showgirl, Return to Mayberry. Voices: Jetsons, Flintstones, Mr. Magoo. Producer: The Corner Bar. Director: Dick Van Dyke Show, Get Smart, Andy Griffith Show (also frequent guest); also many commericals.

MORRIS, JOHN
Composer, Conductor, Arranger. b. Elizabeth, NJ. e. Juilliard Sch. Music 1946-48, U. of Washington. 1947, New Sch. Social Research 1946-49. Member: ASCAP, Acad. of M.P. Arts & Sciences, American Federation of Musicians.
THEATER: Composer: B'way: My Mother My Father and Me, A Doll's House, Camino Real, A Time For Singing (musical), Take One Step, Young Andy Jackson, 15 Shakespeare plays for NY Shakespeare Fest. & Amer. Shakespeare Fest, Stratford CT. Musical supervisor, conductor, dance music arranger: Mack and Mabel, Much Ado About Nothing, Bells Are Ringing, Bye Bye Birdie and 23 other B'way musicals. Off-B'way: Hair.

PICTURES: The Producers, The Twelve Chairs, Blazing Saddles (Acad. Award nom.), Bank Shot, Young Frankenstein, The Adventure of Sherlock Holmes' Smarter Brother, Silent Movie, The Last Remake of Beau Geste, The World's Greatest Lover, High Anxiety, The In-Laws, In God We Trust, The Elephant Man (Acad. Award nom.), History of the World Part 1, Table for Five, Yellowbeard, To Be or Not to Be, The Woman in Red, Johnny Dangerously, The Doctor and the Devils, Clue, Haunted Honeymoon, Dirty Dancing, Spaceballs, Ironweed, The Wash, Second Sight, Stella, Life Stinks.
TELEVISION: Composer: Fresno, Katherine Anne Porter, Ghost Dancing, The Firm, The Mating Season, Splendor in the Grass, The Electric Grandmother, The Scarlet Letter, Georgia O'Keeffe, The Adams Chronicles, The Franken Project, The Tap Dance Kid (Emmy Award, 1986), Make Believe Marriage, The Desperate Hours, The Skirts of Happy Chance, Infancy and Childhood, The Fig Tree, The Little Match Girl, Favorite Son, The Last Best Year, The Last to Go, The Sunset Gang, Our Sons, When Lions Roared, Scarlett. Themes: ABC After School Special, Making Things Grow, The French Chef, Coach. Musical sprv., conductor, arranger Specials: Anne Bancroft Special (Emmy Award), S'Wonderful S'Marvelous S'Gershwin (Emmy Award), Hallmark Christmas specials.
RECORDINGS: Wildcat, All-American, Bells Are Ringing, First Impressions, Bye Bye Birdie, Kwamina, Baker Street, Rodgers and Hart, George Gershwin Vols. 1 & 2, Jerome Kern, Lyrics of Ira Gershwin, Cole Porter, others.

MORRIS, OSWALD
Cinematographer. b. London, England, Nov. 22, 1915. Left school at 16 to work for two years as camera dept. helper at studios. Was lensman for cameraman Ronald Neame who gave Morris first job as cameraman; in 1949, when Neame directed The Golden Salamander, he made Morris dir. of photography.
PICTURES: The Golden Salamander, The Card, The Man Who Never Was, Moulin Rouge, Beat the Devil, Moby Dick, Heaven Knows Mr. Allison, A Farewell to Arms, The Roots of Heaven, The Key, The Guns of Navarone, Lolita, Term of Trial, Of Human Bondage, The Pumpkin Eater (BFA Award, 1964), Mister Moses, The Hill (BFA Award, 1965), The Spy Who Came in from the Cold, Life at the Top, Stop the World- -I Want to Get Off, The Taming of the Shrew, Reflections in a Golden Eye, Oliver!, Gooodbye Mr. Chips, Scrooge, Fiddler on the Roof (Acad. Award, 1971), Sleuth, Lady Caroline Lamb, The Mackintosh Man, The Odessa File, The Man Who Would Be King, The Seven Per Cent Solution, Equus, The Wiz, Just Tell Me What You Want, The Great Muppet Caper, The Dark Crystal.
TELEVISION: Dracula (1974).

MORRISSEY, PAUL
Writer, Director, Photographer. b. New York, NY, 1938. e. Fordham U. 2nd lt. in Army. A writer, cameraman and dir. in indt. film prod. prior to becoming Andy Warhol's mgr. in all areas except painting. Discovered and managed The Velvet Underground and Nico. Founded Interview magazine. Story, casting, dir. & photog. for Warhol Productions' Chelsea Girls, Four Stars, Bike Boy, I A Man, Lonesome Cowboys, Blue Movie, and San Diego Surf.
PICTURES: writer/photog./edit./dir.: Flesh, Trash, Heat, L'Amour, Women in Revolt. writer/dir.: Flesh For Frankenstein, Blood for Dracula, The Hound of the Baskervilles, Madame Wang's, Forty Deuce, Mixed Blood, Beethoven's Nephew, Spike of Bensonhurst.

MORROW, ROB
Actor. b. New Rochelle, NY, Sept. 21, 1962.
THEATRE: NY: The Substance of Fire, Aven'U Boys, The Chosen, Scandal (workshop), Soulful Scream of a Chosen Son, The Boys of Winter, Slam, Third Secret.
PICTURES: Private Resort, Quiz Show, The Last Dance, Mother, Magic, Labor Pains, The Day Lincoln Was Shot, Only Love.
TELEVISION: Series: Tattinger's, Northern Exposure. Guest: Spenser: For Hire, Everything's Relative, Fame.

MORSE, DAVID
Actor. b. Beverly, MA, Oct. 11, 1953.
THEATRE: B'way: On the Waterfront.
PICTURES: Inside Moves, Desperate Hours, The Indian Runner, The Good Son, The Getaway, The Crossing Guard, Twelve Monkeys, The Rock, Contact, The Legend of Pig Eye, A.W.O.L., The Negotiator, The Green Mile.
TELEVISION: Series: St. Elsewhere, Big Wave Dave's, Friday the 13th (dir. only). Movies: Shattered Vows, When Dreams Come True, Prototype, Downpayment on Murder, Six Against the Rock, Winnie, Brotherhood of the Rose, Cross of Fire, A Cry in the Wild: The Taking of Peggy Ann, Dead Ahead: The Exxon Valdez Disaster, Miracle on Interstate 880, Tecumseh: The Last Warrior. Mini-Series: Stephen King's The Langoliers. Guest: Nurse. Special: A Place at the Table.

MORSE, ROBERT
Actor. b. Newton, MA, May 18, 1931. Served U.S. Navy. Studied with American Theatre Wing, New York. Following radio work, appeared on B'way stage in The Matchmaker, 1956.

THEATER: *B'way*: The Matchmaker, Say Darling (Theatre World Award), Take Me Along, How to Succeed in Business Without Really Trying (Tony Award, 1962), Sugar, So Long 174th Street, Tru (Tony Award, 1990).
PICTURES: The Proud and the Profane (debut, 1956), The Matchmaker, The Cardinal, Honeymoon Hotel, Quick Before It Melts, The Loved One, Oh Dad Poor Dad Mama's Hung You in the Closet and I'm Feeling So Sad, How to Succeed in Business Without Really Trying, A Guide for the Married Man, Where Were You When the Lights Went Out?, The Boatniks, Hunk, The Emperor's New Clothes.
TELEVISION: *Series*: The Secret Storm (1954), That's Life, All My Children, Pound Puppies (voice). *Specials*: The Stingiest Man in Town (voice), Kennedy Center Tonight—Broadway to Washington, Tru (Emmy Award, 1993). *Movie*: The Calendar Girl Murders, Here Come the Munsters. *Mini-Series*: Wild Palms. *Guest*: Masquerade, Alfred Hitchcock Presents, Naked City, Love American Style, Twilight Zone, Murder She Wrote.

MORTENSEN, VIGGO
Actor. b. 1959.
PICTURES: Witness, Salvation!, Prison, Fresh Horses, Tripwire, Leatherface: Texas Chainsaw Massacre III, Young Guns II, The Reflecting Skin, The Indian Runner, The Young Americans, Ruby Cairo, Ewangelia wedlug Harry'ego, Carlito's Way, Boiling Point, Floundering, Desert Lunch, The Crew, American Yakuza, The Passion of Darkly Noon, Gimlet, Crimson Tide, The Prophecy, Albino Alligator, The Portrait of a Lady, Daylight, La Pistola de mi herm ano, G. I. Jane, Blouse Man, A Perfect Murder.
TELEVISION: *Movie*: Vanishing Point. *Mini-series*: George Washington.

MORTON, ARTHUR
Composer, Arranger. b. Duluth, MN, Aug. 8, 1908. e. U. of MN, 1929.
PICTURES: Night Life of the Gods, Princess O'Hara, Riding on Air, Fit for a King, Turnabout, Walking Hills, The Nevadan, Rogues of Sherwood Forest, Father is a Bachelor, Never Trust a Gambler, Harlem Globetrotters, Big Heat, Pushover, He Laughed Last. Orchesrtal Arrangements: Laura, From Here to Eternity, Jolson Story, Salome, Born Yesterday, The Long Gray Line, Man from Laramine, My Sister Eileen, Picnic, Strangers When We Meet, That Touch of Mink, Diamond Head, Toys in the Attic, Von Ryan's Express, In Harm's Way, What a Way to Go, The New Interns, Our Man Flint, Planet of the Apes, Patton, Tora Tora Tora, Papillon, Chinatown, Logan's Run, The Omen, MacArthur, The Boys from Brazil, Magic, Superman, Alien, Star Trek: The Motion Picture, Poltergeist, First Blood, Gremlins, Rambo: First Blood Part II, Hoosiers, The 'Burbs, Star Trek V: The Final Frontier, Total Recall, Medicine Man, Gladiator, Mr. Baseball, Forever Young, The Vanishing, Rudy, Angie, The Shadow, The River Wild, many others.
TELEVISION: Black Saddle, Laramie, Bus Stop, Follow the Sun, My Three Sons, Peyton Place, Medical Center, Daniel Boone, Lancers, National Geographic, Say Goodbye, How to Stay Alive, Hooray For Hollywood, The Waltons, Apple's Way, Masada, Medical Story.

MORTON, JOE
Actor. b. New York, NY, Oct. 18, 1947. e. Hofstra U.
THEATRE: *NY*: Hair, Raisin (Theatre World Award), Oh Brother, Honky Tonk Nights, A Midsummer Night's Dream, King John, Cheapside, Electra, A Winter's Tale, Oedipus Rex, Julius Caesar, The Tempest. Dir.: Heliotrope Bouquet.
PICTURES: ...And Justice for All, The Brother From Another Planet, Trouble in Mind, Zelly and Me, The Good Mother, Tap, Terminator 2: Judgment Day, City of Hope, Of Mice and Men, Forever Young, The Inkwell, Speed, The Walking Dead, Lone Star, Executive Decision.
TELEVISION: *Series*: Grady, Equal Justice, Tribeca (also dir.), Under One Roof, New York News. *Movies*: The Challenger, Terrorist on Trial: The United States vs. Salim Ajami, Howard Beach: Making a Case for Murder, Death Penalty, Legacy of Lies, In the Shadow of Evil. *Special*: The File of Jill Hatch. *Guest*: A Different World, Hawk, Homicide: Life on the Street.

MOSK, RICHARD M.
Executive. b. Los Angeles, CA, May 18, 1939. e. Stanford U, Harvard Law School. Admitted to California Bar, 1964. Principal in firm of Sanders Barnet Goldman Simons & Mosk, a prof. corp. Named chmn. of the movie industry's voluntary rating system, the Classification & Rating Administration, June 1994; co-chmn, 1997-. Judge, Iran-U.S. Claims Tribunal.

MOSLEY, ROGER E.
Actor. b. Los Angeles, CA. Planned career in broadcasting but turned to acting, first appearing in small roles on TV in: Night Gallery, Baretta, Kojak, Cannon, Switch.
PICTURES: The New Centurions (debut, 1972), Hit Man, Terminal Island, Stay Hungry, Leadbelly, The Greatest, Semi-Tough, Steel, Heart Condition, Unlawful Entry.
TELEVISION: *Series*: Magnum P.I., You Take the Kids. *Guest*: Baretta, Kojak, Cannon, Switch. *Movies*: Cruise Into Terror, I Know Why the Caged Bird Sings, The Jericho Mile, Attica. *Mini-Series*: Roots: The Next Generations.

MOSS, FRANK L.
Writer, Producer. b. New York, NY, Aug. 25, 1913. e. Duke U., Columbia U. Reporter, drama & film critic, N.Y. U.S. Army Air Force, 1942-46. Instructor, UCLA, 1985-86 on advanced screen-play writing. 1987-88, private tutoring on screenplay and TV writing. For military made 22 Air Force training films, 17 documentaries. Author: The Hack.
THEATER: *Author*: Glamour Girl, Call To Arms (collab), So Goes the Nation (collab), Some People's Children, American Pastoral, City on a Hill.
PICTURES: To Have and Have Not, The Unvanquished, Whiphand, Caribbean, Sangaree, Papago Wells, The Half Breed, Sweetheart of Sigma Chi.
TELEVISION: *Writer*: Telephone Hour, Four Star Playhouse, Winston Churchill's Valiant Years, Route 66, Wagon Train, Laramie, Wild Wild West, The Texan, G.E. Theater, Wire Service, U.S. Marshall, M-Squad, Stoney Burke, Tales of the Texas Rangers, T.V. Reader's Digest, Sheriff of Cochise, Whirlybirds, Line-Up, Wyatt Earp, Rin Tin Tin, Walter Winchell File, Daniel Boone, Man Who Never Was, Felony Squad, Richard Diamond, Lassie, Like the Rich People, Hired Mother, Shenandoah, Counterspy, White Hunter, Hondo, Northwest Mounted Police, Casey Jones, Cowboy in Africa. *Pilots*: Outer Limits, Grand Jury, The Texam, Bush Pilot, Lafitte, Cortez. *Prod./Story Ed.*: Screen Televideo, Sovereign Prod., Wire Service, T.V. Reader's Digest, Wyatt Earp.

MOSS, IRWIN
Executive. e. Syracuse U., Harvard Law Sch. Member NY State Bar. Began industry career as dir. of package negotiations for CBS-TV; 1970-80, exec. v.p. & natl. head of business affairs for I.C.M.; 1978-80, sr. v.p., NBC Entertainment; 1980, pres., Marble Arch TV. 1982, joined Paramount Pictures as sr. v.p. for motion picture div. 1984, exec. v.p., L. Taffner Ltd.

MOSTEL, JOSH
Actor, Director. b. New York, NY, Dec. 21, 1946. Father was late actor Zero Mostel. m. prod. Peggy Rajski. e. Brandeis U., B.A. 1970. Part of The Proposition, a Boston improvisational comedy group. Stage debut: The Homecoming (Provincetown Playhouse, MA).
THEATER: *Actor*: Unlikely Heroes, The Proposition, An American Millionaire, A Texas Trilogy, Gemini, Men in the Kitchen, The Dog Play, The Boys Next Door, A Perfect Diamond, Threepenny Opera, My Favorite Year, The Flowering Peach. *Director*: Ferocious Kisses, Love As We Know It, Misconceptions, Red Diaper Baby.
PICTURES: Going Home (debut, 1971), The King of Marvin Gardens, Jesus Christ Superstar, Harry and Tonto, Deadly Hero, Fighting Back, Sophie's Choice, Star 80, Almost You, The Brother from Another Planet, Windy City, Compromising Positions, The Money Pit, Stoogemania, Radio Days, Matewan, Wall Street, Heavy Petting, Animal Behavior, City Slickers, Naked Tango, Little Man Tate, City of Hope, Searching for Bobby Fischer, The Chase, City Slickers II: The Legend of Curly's Gold, Billy Madison, The Basketball Diaries, The Maddening.
TELEVISION: *Series*: Delta House, At Ease, Murphy's Law. *Mini-Series*: Seventh Avenue. *Special*: The Boy Who Loved Trolls (PBS). *Co-writer*: Media Probes: The Language Show.

MOUND, FRED
Executive. b. St. Louis, MO, April 10, 1932. e. St. Louis U., Quincy Coll. 1946-52, assoc. with father, Charles Mound, at Park Theatre in Valley Park, Mo.; 1952-53, Universal Pictures (St. Louis); 1953, booker, UA, St. Louis; 1955 promoted to salesman in Kansas City; 1957, salesman, St. Louis; 1962, Indianapolis branch mgr. 1967 named UA regional mgr., Dallas and in 1970 became S.W. div. mgr; 1976-77, asst. gen. sls. mgr. for Southern, N.W. and S.W. div. operating out of Dallas. 1977 appt. v.p., asst. gen. sls. mgr. of UA; 1978, appt. v.p. gen sls. mgr. for AFD Pictures in Los Angeles; 1981, v.p. asst. gen. sls. mgr. for Universal; 1984, sr. v.p., gen. sls. mgr., Universal Pictures Distribution; named exec. v.p. 1988. Foundation of Motion Picture Pioneers v.p., 1989. Appointed pres. Universal distrib., 1990.

MOUNT, THOM
Executive. b. Durham, NC, May 26, 1948. e. Bard Coll.; CA Institute of the Arts, MFA. Started career with Roger Corman and as asst. to prod., Danny Selznick at MGM. Moved to Universal under prod. exec. Ned Tanen. At 26, named pres. and head of prod. at Universal. During 8-year tenure, was responsible for dev. and prod. of more than 140 films (including Smokey and the Bandit, Animal House, others).
THEATER: Open Admissions (co-prod.), Death and the Maiden.
PICTURES: Pirates (exec. prod.), My Man Adam, Can't Buy Me Love, Frantic, Bull Durham (co-prod.), Stealing Home, Tequila Sunrise, Roger Corman's Frankenstein Unbound, The Indian Runner (exec. prod.), Death and the Maiden, Natural Born Killers, Night Falls on Manhattan (prod.).
TELEVISION: Son of the Morning Star, Open Admissions.

MOYERS, BILL
TV Correspondent. b. Hugo, OK, June 5, 1934. e. U. of Texas; Southwestern Baptist Theological Sem. Aide to Lyndon B. Johnson; assoc. dir., Peace Corps, 1961-62, and deputy dir., 1963. Spec. asst. to Pres. Johnson, 1963-65 and press secty., 1965-67. Editor and chief corr., CBS Reports. Bill Moyers Journal on PBS. Established Public Affairs TV, Inc., 1986.

MUDD, ROGER
Newscaster. b. Washington, DC, Feb. 9, 1928. e. Washington & Lee U., U. of North Carolina. Reporter for Richmond News-Leader, 1953; news. dir., WRNL, 1954; WTOP, Washington, 1956; joined CBS News 1961 as Congressional correspondent (2 Emmy Awards). 1977, Natl. Aff. corr.; 1978, corr., CBS Reports; 1980-87: NBC News as chief Washington corr., chief political corr., co-anchor; 1987 joined The MacNeil/Lehrer News Hour as special correspondent; essayist, and chief congressional correspondent. 1992 became contributing correspondent.

MUELLER-STAHL, ARMIN
Actor. b. Tilsit, East Prussia, Dec. 17, 1930. Moved to West Germany in 1980. e. Berlin Conservatory. Studied violin before turning to acting. Author: Verordneter Sonntag (Lost Sunday), Drehtage, Nuterwegs Nach Hause (On the Way Home).
PICTURES: Naked Among the Wolves, The Third, Jacob the Liar, The Flight, Lite Trap, Lola, Wings of Night, Veronika Voss, A Cop's Sunday, A Love in Germany, Thousand Eyes, Trauma, Colonel Redl, L'Homme blesse, God Doesn't Believe in Us Anymore, Angry Harvest, The Blind Director, Following the Fuhrer, Momo, The Jungle Mission, Lethal Obsession, Midnight Cop, Music Box, Das Spinnenetz, Just for Kicks, Avalon, Bronstein's Children, Kafka, The Power of One, Night on Earth, Utz, The House of the Spirits, Holy Matrimony, The Last Good Time, A Pyromaniac's Love Story, Taxandria, Shine, Theodore Rex, Peacemaker, The Game, Commissioner.
TELEVISION: Mini-Series: Amerika.

MUHL, EDWARD E.
Executive, Producer. b. Richmond, IN, Feb. 17, 1907. Gen. mgr., Universal 1948-53; v.p., studio in charge of prod. 1953-68. Consultant, Alcor Prods., Ft. Smith, AR, 1985-90. Co-author, consultant, s.p., Soldier: Other Side of Glory, 1991-92.

MUIR, E. ROGER
Producer. b. Canada, Dec. 16, 1918. e. U. of Minnesota. Partner Minn. Advertising Services Co.; Photographer, Great Northern Railway; motion picture prod. Army Signal corps; NBC TV prod., Howdy Doody; exec. prod., Concentration. Now pres. Nicholson-Muir Prods, TV program packager, U.S. Spin-Off, Pay Cards, Canada Pay Cards, Headline Hunters, Definition, Celebrity Dominoes; co-creator Newlywed Game, exec. prod. I Am Joe's Heart, I Am Joe's Lung, I Am Joe's Spine, I Am Joe's Stomach, The New Howdy Doody Show, Supermates, Second Honeymoon, Groaner, Generation Jury, Shopping Game, Guess What, I Am Joe's Kidney, I Am Joe's Liver, It's Howdy Doody Time: A 40 Year Celebration. Retired 1993.

MULDAUR, DIANA
Actress. b. New York, NY, Aug. 19, 1943. e. Sweet Briar Coll. Began on New York stage then turned to films and TV, appearing on numerous major network shows.
PICTURES: The Swimmer (debut, 1968), Number One, The Lawyer, One More Train to Rob, The Other, McQ, Chosen Survivors, Beyond Reason.
TELEVISION: Series: The Secret Storm, The Survivors, McCloud, Born Free, The Tony Randall Show, Hizzoner, Fitz and Bones, A Year in the Life, L.A. Law, Star Trek: The Next Generation. Movies: McCloud: Who Killed Miss U.S.A.?, Call to Danger, Ordeal, Planet Earth, Charlie's Angels (pilot), Pine Canyon is Burning, Deadly Triangle, Black Beauty, To Kill a Cop, Maneaters Are Loose!, The Word, The Miracle Worker, The Return of Frank Cannon, Terror at Alcatraz, The Return of Sam McCloud.

MULGREW, KATE
Actress. b. Dubuque, IA, April 29, 1955. e. NYU. Stage work includes stints with American Shakespeare Festival, NY Shakespeare Festival, Seattle Rep. Theatre, Mark Taper Forum (LA). B'way: Black Comedy.
PICTURES: Lovespell, A Stranger Is Watching, Remo Williams: The Adventure Begins, Throw Momma from the Train, Camp Nowhere, Round Numbers, Lovespell.
TELEVISION: Series: Ryan's Hope (1975-77), Kate Columbo (Kate Loves a Mystery), Heartbeat, Man of the People, Star Trek: Voyager. Movies: The Word, Jennifer: A Woman's Story, A Time for Miracles, The Manions of America, Roses Are for the Rich, Roots: The Gift, Danielle Steel's Daddy, Fatal Friendship, For Love and Glory.

MULHERN, MATT
Actor. b. Philadelphia, PA, July 21, 1960. e. Rutgers Univ.
THEATRE: NY: Biloxi Blues, Wasted, The Night Hank Williams Died.
PICTURES: One Crazy Summer, Extreme Prejudice, Biloxi Blues, Junior, Infinity, The Sunchaser, Walking the Waterline.
TELEVISION: Series: Major Dad. Movie: Gunsmoke: To the Last Man, Terror in the Night, A Burning Passion: The Margaret Mitchell Story.

MULHOLLAND, ROBERT E.
Executive. b. 1933. e. Northwestern U. Joined NBC News as newswriter in Chicago in 1962. 1964 made midwestern field prod. for Huntley-Brinkley Report. 1964 moved to London as European prod. for NBC News; 1965, named Washington prod. of Huntley-Brinkley Report. Transferred to L.A. in 1967 to be dir. of news, west coast. Named exec. prod. of NBC Nightly News.

1973 appt. v.p., NBC news.; 1974 exec. v.p. of NBC News. 1977 appt. pres. of NBC Television Network; also elected to board of directors; 1981, pres. & CEO. Resigned, 1984. Dir. Television Info. Office, NYC 1985-87. Prof. Northwestern U. 1988-.

MULL, MARTIN
Actor. b. Chicago, IL, Aug. 18, 1943. e. Rhode Island Sch. of Design. Started as humorist, making recordings for Warner Bros., Capricorn, ABC Records, etc.
PICTURES: FM (debut, 1978), My Bodyguard, Serial, Take This Job and Shove It, Flicks, Mr. Mom, Bad Manners, Clue, O.C. and Stiggs, Home Is Where the Hart Is, Rented Lips (also s.p., exec. prod.), Cutting Class, Ski Patrol, Far Out Man, Think Big, Ted and Venus, The Player, Miracle Beach, Mrs. Doubtfire, Mr. Write, Edie and Pen.
TELEVISION: Series: Mary Hartman Mary Hartman, Fernwood 2-Night, America 2-Night, Domestic Life, His and Hers, Roseanne, The Jackie Thomas Show, Family Dog (voice). Specials: The History of White People in America (also prod.), Candid Camera Christmas Special (1987), Portrait of a White Marriage, The Whole Shebang. Movies: Sunset Limousine, California Girls, The Day My Parents Ran Away, How the West Was Fun.

MULLAN, PETER
Actor.
PICTURES: The Big Man, Shallow Grave, Ruffian Hearts, Good Day for the Bad Guys, Braveheart, Trainspotting, Fairy Tale: A True Story, My Name Is Joe (Cannes Film Fest. Award, Best Actor, 1998).
TELEVISION: Movies: Bogwoman, Nightlife.

MULLER, ROBBY
Cinematographer. b. Netherlands, April 4, 1940. e. Dutch Film Acad. Asst. cameraman in Holland before moving to Germany where he shot 9 films for Wim Wenders.
PICTURES: Alabama: 2000 Light Years, Summer in the City, Jonathan, Carlos, The Goalkeeper's Fear of the Penalty Kick, The Scarlet Letter, Die Reise Nach Wien, Kings of the Road, Alice in the Cities, Perahim Die Zweite Chance, Wrong Move, The American Friend, Mysteries, The Glass Cell, Opname, Saint Jack, Honeysuckle Rose, A Cop's Sunday, They All Laughed, Body Rock, Repo Man, Paris Texas, To Live and Die in L.A., The Longshot, Down By Law, Tricheurs, The Believers, Barfly, Il Piccolo Diavolo (The Little Devil), Mystery Train, Korczak, Until the End of the World, When Pigs Fly, The Ditvoorst Domains (actor only), Mad Dog and Glory, Breaking the Waves (NY Society of Film Critics Award and Natl Society of Film Critics Awards, 1997), Dead Man (NY Society of Film Critics Awards, 1997), Last Call, Beyond the Clouds, The Tango Lesson.

MULLIGAN, RICHARD
Actor. b. New York, NY Nov. 13, 1932
THEATER: Nobody Loves an Albatross, All the Way Home, Never Too Late, Mating Dance, Hogan's Goat, Thieves, etc.
PICTURES: Love With the Proper Stranger (debut, 1963), One Potato Two Potato, The Group, The undefeated, Little Big Man, Irish Whiskey Rebeliion, From the Mixed-Up Files of Mrs. Basil E. Frankweiler, The Big Bus, Scavenger Hunt, S.O.B., Trail of the Pink Panther, Meatballs Part II, Teachers, Micki and Maude, Doin' Time, The Heavenly Kid, A Fine Mess, Quicksilver, Oliver & Company (voice).
TELEVISION: Movies: Having Babies III, Malibu, Jealousy, Poler Alice, Gore Vidal's Lincoln, Guess Who's Coming for Christmas? Series: The Hero, Diana, Soap (Emmy Award, 1980), Reggie, Empty Nest (Emmy Award 1989, Golden Globe), London Suite, Dog's Best Friend.

MULLIGAN, ROBERT
Director. b. Bronx, NY. Aug. 23, 1925. e. Fordham U. Served in Navy during WWII. After working as copyboy for NY Times joined CBS in mailroom. Eventually became TV dir. before moving into features.
PICTURES: Fear Strikes Out (debut, 1957), The Rat Race, The Great Imposter, Come September, The Spiral Road, To Kill a Mockingbird, Love With the Proper Stranger, Baby the Rain Must Fall, Inside Daisy Clover, Up the Down Staircase, The Stalking Moon, The Pursuit of Happiness, Summer of `42, The Other, The Nickel Ride, Bloodbrothers, Same Time Next Year, Kiss Me Goodbye, Clara's Heart, The Man in the Moon.
TELEVISION: The Moon and the Sixpence (Emmy Award, 1960), Billy Budd, Ah Wilderness, A Tale of Two Cities, The Bridge of San Luis Rey, Playhouse 90, Philco-Goodyear, Suspense, Studio One, Hallmark Hall of Fame.

MULRONEY, DERMOT
Actor. b. Alexandria, VA, Oct. 31, 1963. e. Northwestern Univ.
PICTURES: Sunset, Young Guns, Survival Quest, Staying Together, Longtime Companion, Career Opportunities, Bright Angel, Where the Day Takes You, Samantha, Point of No Return, The Thing Called Love, Silent Tongue, Bad Girls, Angels in the Outfield, There Goes My Baby, Living in Oblivion, Copycat, How to Make an American Quilt, Kansas City, Trigger Effect.
TELEVISION: Movies: Sin of Innocence, Daddy, Unconquered, Long Gone, The Heart of Justice, Family Pictures, The Last Outlaw. Special: Toma: The Drug Knot.

MUMY, BILL
Actor. r.n. Charles William Mumy Jr. b. El Centro, CA, Feb. 1, 1954. Began acting as Billy Mumy at age 6. Played with band America in 1970's, also with bands Bill Mumy & The Igloos, and The Jenerators. Has made 8 albums with Barnes & Barnes. With actor Miguel Ferrer, wrote comic books Comet Man and Trip to the Acid Dog. Has also written stories for Star Trek, The Hulk, and Spiderman comic books, and Lost in Space comic published by Innovation. Wrote music for Disney's Adventures in Wonderland series (Emmy nom.)
PICTURES: Tammy Tell Me True, Palm Springs Weekend, A Ticklish Affair, A Child is Waiting, Dear Brigitte, Rascal, Bless the Beasts and Children, Papillon, Twilight Zone—The Movie, Hard to Hold, Captain America, Double Trouble, Three Wishes, The Fantasy Worlds of Irwin Allen.
TELEVISION: Series: Lost in Space, Sunshine. Movies: Sunshine, The Rockford Files (pilot), Sunshine Christmas. Guest: The Twilight Zone, Alfred Hitchcock Presents, Bewitched, The Virginian, I Dream of Jeannie, The Adventures of Ozzie and Harriet, Ben Casey, The Red Skelton Show, Lancer, Here Come the Brides, Riverboat, Have Gun Will Travel, Matlock, Me and Mom, The Flash, Superboy, Babylon 5. Pilots: The Two of Us, Archie, Space Family Robinson. Host: Inside Space (SciFi Channel).

MURDOCH, RUPERT
Executive. b. Australia, March 11, 1931. Son of Sir Keith Murdoch, head of The Melbourne Herald and leading figure in Australian journalism. e. Oxford U., England. Spent two years on Fleet St. before returning home to take over family paper, The Adelaide News. Acquired more Australian papers and in 1969, expanded to Britain, buying The News of the World. Moved to U.S. in 1973, buying San Antonio Express and News. Conglomerate in 1985 included New York Post, New York Magazine, The Star, The Times of London, The Boston Herald, The Chicago Sun-Times along with TV stations, book publishing companies, airline, oil and gas companies, etc. 1985, made deal to buy 20th Century-Fox Film Corp. from owner Martin Davis. Sold the NY Post, 1988 to conform with FCC regulations. Purchased Triangle Publications 1988 (including TV Guide).

MUREN, DENNIS E.
Visual Effects Creator and Director. b. Glendale, CA, Nov. 1, 1946. AA Pasadena CC, 1966. Studied at UCLA. Freelance special effects 1968-75. Cameraman Cascade 1975-76. Dir. of photography, visual effects Industrial Light Magic 1976-80. AMPAS Scientific/Technical Award, 1981. Member ASC, AMPAS.
PICTURES: Star Wars, Close Encounters of the Third Kind, The Empire Strikes Back (Acad. Award), Dragonslayer, E.T., the Extraterrestrial (Acad. Award), Return of the Jedi (Acad. Award, BAFTA Award), Indiana Jones and the Temple of Doom (Acad. Award, BAFTA award), Young Sherlock Holmes, Captain Eo (short feature), Star Tours (short feature), Innerspace (Acad. Award), Empire of the Sun, Willow, Ghostbusters II, The Abyss (Acad. Award), Terminator 2 (Acad. Award, BAFTA award), Jurassic Park (Acad. Award, BAFTA award), Casper, The Lost World: Jurassic Park.
TELEVISION: Battlestar Galactica, Caravan of Courage (Emmy award).

MURPHY, BEN
Actor. b. Jonesboro, AR, March 6, 1942. e. U. of Illinois. Degree in drama from Pasadena Playhouse. Acted in campus productions and toured in summer stock. Film debut with small role in The Graduate, 1967.
PICTURES: Yours Mine and Ours, The Thousand Plane Raid, Sidecar Racers, Time Walker.
TELEVISION: Movies: The Letters, Wild Bill Hickock, Bridger, Heat Wave, Runaway, This Is the West That Was, Gemini Man, Hospital Fire, The Cradle Will Fall, Stark: Mirror Image. Series: The Name of the Game, Alias Smith and Jones, Griff, Gemini Man, The Chisholms, Lottery!, Berrenger's, The Dirty Dozen. Mini-Series: The Winds of War.

MURPHY, EDDIE
Actor. b. Brooklyn, NY, April 3, 1961. e. Roosevelt High Sch. Wrote and performed own comedy routines at youth centers and local bars at age 15. Worked on comedy club circuit; at 19 joined TV's Saturday Night Live as writer and performer. Recordings: Eddie Murphy, Eddie Murphy: Comedian, How Could It Be?, Love's Alright. Voted Top-Money Making Star of 1988 on Quigley Poll, NATO/ShoWest Star of the Decade, for 1980's.
PICTURES: 48 HRS. (debut, 1982), Trading Places, Best Defense, Beverly Hills Cop, The Golden Child, Beverly Hills Cop II, Eddie Murphy Raw (also s.p., exec. prod.), Coming to America (also story), Harlem Nights (also dir., s.p, exec. prod.), Another 48 HRS., Boomerang (also story), The Distinguished Gentleman, Beverly Hills Cop III, Vampire in Brooklyn (also co-prod.), The Nutty Professor (also co-exec. prod.; Nat'l Society of Film Critics Award, 1997), Metro.
TELEVISION: Series: Saturday Night Live (1981-84). Pilots (exec. prod.): What's Alan Watching? (also cameo), Coming to America. Movie (exec. prod.): The Kid Who Loved Christmas.

MURPHY, LAWRENCE P.
Executive. Exec. v.p. of strategic planning & development, The Walt Disney Company.

MURPHY, MICHAEL
Actor. b. Los Angeles, CA, May 5, 1938. e. U. of Arizona. m. actress Wendy Crewson. Taught English and Drama in L.A. city school system, 1962-64. N.Y. stage debut as dir. of Rat's Nest, 1978.
PICTURES: Double Trouble (debut, 1967), Countdown, The Legend of Lylah Clare, The Arrangement, That Cold Day in the Park, M*A*S*H, Count Yorga: Vampire, Brewster McCloud, McCabe and Mrs. Miller, What's Up Doc?, The Thief Who Came to Dinner, Phase IV, Nashville, The Front, An Unmarried Woman, The Great Bank Hoax, The Class of Miss MacMichael, Manhattan, The Year of Living Dangerously, Strange Behavior, Cloak and Dagger, Salvador, Mesmerized, Shocker, Folks!, Batman Returns, Clean Slate, Bad Company, Kansas City.
TELEVISION: Series: Two Marriages, Hard Copy. Guest: Saints and Sinners, Ben Casey, Dr. Kildare, Bonanza, Combat. Movies: The Autobiography of Miss Jane Pittman, The Caine Mutiny Court-Martial, Tailspin: Behind the Korean Airlines Tragedy. Specials: John Cheever's Oh Youth and Beauty, Tanner '88.

MURPHY, THOMAS S.
Executive. e. Cornell Univ (B.S.M.E.), Harvard U. Grad. Sch. of Bus. Admin. (M.B.A.). Joined Capital Cities at its inception in 1954. Named a dir. in 1957, then pres. in 1964. Chmn. & CEO of Capital Cities, 1966-90. Company named Capital Cities/ABC Inc. in 1986 after acquistion of American Broadcasting Companies Inc. 1990-94, chmn. of bd. Resumed position of chmn. & CEO in Feb., 1994.

MURRAY, BARBARA
Actress. b. London, England, Sept. 27, 1929. Stage debut in Variety, 1946.
PICTURES: Badger's Green (debut, 1948), Passport to Pimlico, Don't Ever Leave Me, Boys in Brown, Poets Pub, Tony Draws a Horse, Dark Man, Frightened Man, Mystery Junction, Another Man's Poison, Hot Ice, Street Corner (Both Sides of the Law), Meet Mr. Lucifer, Doctor at Large, Campbell's Kingdom, A Cry from the Streets, Girls in Arms, A Dandy in Aspic, Tales From the Crypt.
TELEVISION: Series: The Power Game, The Bretts.

MURRAY, BILL
Actor. b. Wilmette, IL, Sept. 21, 1950. e. attended Regis Coll. Was pre-med student; left to join brother, Brian Doyle-Murray, in Second City the Chicago improvisational troupe. Appeared with brother on radio in National Lampoon Radio Hour, and in off-B'way revue, National Lampoon Show. Also on radio provided voice of Johnny Storm the Human Torch on Marvel Comics' Fantastic Four. Hired by ABC for Saturday Night Live with Howard Cosell; then by NBC for Saturday Night Live, 1977.
PICTURES: Jungle Burger (debut, 1975), Meatballs, Mr. Mike's Mondo Video, Where the Buffalo Roam, Loose Shoes (Coming Attractions), Caddyshack, Stripes, Tootsie, Ghostbusters, The Razor's Edge (also co-s.p.), Nothing Lasts Forever, Little Shop of Horrors, Scrooged, Ghostbusters II, Quick Change (also co-dir., co-prod.), What About Bob?, Groundhog Day, Mad Dog and Glory, Ed Wood, Space Jam, Larger Than Life, Kingpin, The Man Who Knew Too Little, With Friends Like These, Veeck As in Wreck, Rushmore, Wild Things, The Cradle Will Rock.
TELEVISION: Series: Saturday Night Live (1977-80; also writer; Emmy Award for writing 1977). Pilot: The TV TV Show. Movie: All You Need Is Cash. Specials: It's Not Easy Being Me—The Rodney Dangerfield Show, Steve Martin's Best Show Ever, Second City—25 Years in Revue.

MURRAY, DON
Actor, Director, Writer. b. Hollywood, CA, July 31, 1929. e. AADA. Mother was a Ziegfeld Girl, father was dance dir. for Fox Studio.
THEATER: B'way: Insect Comedy, The Rose Tattoo, The Skin of Our Teeth, The Hot Corner, Smith (musical), The Norman Conquests, Same Time Next Year. National tours: California Suite, Chicago.
PICTURES: Bus Stop (debut, 1956; Acad. Award nom.), The Bachelor Party, A Hatful of Rain, From Hell to Texas, These Thousand Hills, Shake Hands With the Devil, One Foot in Hell, The Hoodlum Priest (also co-prod., co-s.p. as Don Deer), Advise and Consent, Escape From East Berlin, One Man's Way, Baby the Rain Must Fall, Kid Rodelo, The Plainsman, Sweet Love Bitter, The Viking Queen, Childish Things (Confession of Tom Harris; also prod., co-s.p.), The Cross and the Switchblade (dir., co-s.p. only), Happy Birthday Wanda June, Conquest of the Planet of the Apes, Cotter, Call Me by My Rightful Name (also prod., co-s.p.), Deadly Hero, Damien (dir., s.p. only), Endless Love, I Am the Cheese, Radioactive Dreams, Peggy Sue Got Married, Scorpion, Made in Heaven, Ghosts Can't Do It.

TELEVISION: *Series*: Made in America (panelist), The Outcasts, Knots Landing, Brand New Life, Sons and Daughters. *Movies*: The Borgia Stick, Daughter of the Mind, The Intruders, The Girl on the Late Late Show, The Sex Symbol, A Girl Named Sooner, Rainbow, Crisis in Mid-Air, If Things Were Different, The Boy Who Drank to Much, Fugitive Family, Return of the Rebels, Thursday's Child, Quarterback Princess, License to Kill, A Touch of Scandal, Something in Common, Stillwatch, The Stepford Children, Mistress, Brand New Life. *Specials*: For I Have Loved Strangers (also writer), Hasty Heart, Billy Budd, Winterset, Alas Babylon, Justin Morgan Had a Horse, My Dad Isn't Crazy Is He?, Montana Crossroads (Emmy nom.)

MURRAY, JAN
Comedian, Actor. b. Bronx, NY, Oct. 4, 1917. Started as comedian, nightclub performer, continuing on radio, tv.
THEATER: A Funny Thing Happened on the Way to the Forum, Guys and Dolls, Silk Stockings, Bye Bye Birdie, A Thousand Clowns, Come Blow Your Horn, The Odd Couple, Make a Million, Don't Drink the Water, Critic's Choice, You Know I Can't Hear You When the Water Is Running.
PICTURES: Who Killed Teddy Bear? (debut, 1965), Tarzan and the Great River, The Busy Body, A Man Called Dagger, Which Way to the Front?, History of the World Part I, Fear City.
TELEVISION: *Series (emcee/host)*: Songs for Sale, Go Lucky, Sing It Again, Blind Date, Dollar a Second (also creator, prod.), Jan Murray Time, Treasure Hunt (also creator, prod.), Charge Account (also creator, prod.), Chain Letter. *Guest*: Zane Grey Theatre, Dr., Kildare, Burke's Law, The Lucy Show, Love American Style, Mannix, Ellery Queen, Hardcastle and McCormick. *Movies*: Roll Freddy Roll, Banjo Hackett: Roamin' Free, The Dream Merchants.

MUSANTE, TONY
Actor. b. Bridgeport, CT, June 30. e. Oberlin Coll. B.A. Directed local theatre, then appeared off-Broadway, in regional theater, and on Dupont Show of the Month (Ride With Terror).
THEATER: *B'way*: The Lady From Dubuque, P.S. Your Cat Is Dead, 27 Wagons Full of Cotton, Memory of Two Mondays. *Off-B'way*: Grand Magic, Cassatt, A Gun Play, Benito Cereno, L'Histoire du Soldat, Match-Play, The Zoo Story, The Pinter Plays (The Collection), Kiss Mama, The Balcony, Snow Orchid, The Flip Side, Frankie and Johnny in the Claire de Lune. *Regional*: The Big Knife, A Streetcar Named Desire, The Taming of the Shrew, Widows, The Archbishop's Ceiling, Dancing in the Endzone, Two Brothers, Souvenir, APA Shakespeare Rep., Wait Until Dark, Anthony Rose, Mount Allegro, Double Play, Falling Man, Breaking Legs, Love Letters, The Sisters, Italian Funerals and Other Festive Occasions.
PICTURES: Once a Thief, The Incident, The Detective, The Mercenary, The Bird with the Crystal Plumage, The Grissom Gang, The Last Run, Anonymous Venetian, Collector's Item, The Repenter, The Pisciotta Case, Goodbye and Amen, Break Up, Nocturne, The Pope of Greenwich Village, One Night at Dinner, Appointment in Trieste, Devil's Hill, The Deep End of the Ocean.
TELEVISION: *Series*: Toma, Oz. *Guest*: Chrysler Theatre, Alfred Hitchcock Hour, N.Y.P.D., The Fugitive, Trials of O'Brien, Police Story, Medical Story, Thomas Gottschallk's Late Night TV, Loving, Acapulco H.E.A.T., Nothing Sacred. *Movies*: Rearview Mirror, The Court Martial of Lt. William Calley, Desperate Miles, The Quality of Mercy, Nowhere to Hide, My Husband is Missing, The Story of Esther, High Ice, Last Waltz on a Tightrope, Weekend (Amer. Playhouse), Nutcracker: Money Madness & Murder, Breaking Up Is Hard To Do, The Baron, The Seventh Scroll, Deep Family Secrets.

MYERS, JULIAN F.
Public Relations Executive. b. Detroit, MI, Feb. 22, 1918. e. Wayne U., 1935-37, USC, 1937-39. Distribution, Loew's Detroit, 1941-42; asst. story editor, idea man, Columbia, 1942-46; publicist, 20th Century-Fox, 1948-62; public relations, Julian F. Myers, Inc., 1962; pres., Myers Studios, Inc., 1966; pres., New Horizons Broadcasting Corp., 1968-69; sr. publicist American Intl. Pictures, 1970-80. Pres., Hollywood Press Club; former member Variety Club; Academy of Motion Pictures Arts & Sciences; Board of Governors Film Industry Workshops, Inc. 1977, 1979, western v.p.; Publicists Guild; Recipient of Publicists Guild's Robert Yeager Award. First male member Hollywood Women's Press Club. Co-founder HANDS (Hollywood Answering Needs of Disaster Survivors). Member, M.P. Pioneers. Winner, 1980 Publicists Guild Les Mason Award. Instructor in publicity, UCLA, 1979-present, and at Loyola Marymount U, 1991-present. Filmways Pictures, pub. dept., 1980-81. Exec. v.p., worldwide m.p. and TV pub./mktg., Hanson & Schwam Public Relations 1981-91. Author of Myersystem and Myerscope guides. Member: USC Cinema & TV Alumni Assn., West Coast P.R. Will Rogers Inst., Acad. TV Arts Sciences; p.r. coord. comm., Academy of Motion Picture Arts & Sciences. Bd. of dirs., Show Biz Expo. Publicist, Prods. Guild of America. Pres. Julian Myers Public Relations, nominated MoPic Showmanship of the Year, Publicists Guild of America, 1993. Columnist, Drama-Logue Magazine. Special Award of Merit, Publicists Guild of America, 1998. Member, Women in Film.

MYERS, PETER S.
Executive. b. Toronto, Ont., Canada, May 13, 1923. e. U. of Toronto. Toronto branch mgr., 20th Century-Fox, 1948; mng. dir., Canada, 1951; gen. sales mgr. in charge of domestic distrib., US & Canada, 1968; sr. v.p., 20th-Fox Ent.; pres., 20th-Fox Classics, 1983; pres., Hemdale Releasing Corp., 1986; pres. & CEO, Four Seasons Entertainment, 1989.

MYERS, STANLEY
Composer. b. London, England, 1939.
PICTURES: Kaleidoscope (debut, 1966), Ulysses, No Way to Treat a Lady, Michael Kohlhaas, Otley, Two Gentlemen Sharing, Take a Girl Like You, Tropic of Cancer, The Walking Stick, Long Ago Tomorrow, A Severed Head, Tam Lin, King Queen Knave, Sitting Target, Summer Lightning, X Y & Zee, The Blockhouse, The Apprenticeship of Duddy Kravitz, Caravan to Vaccares, Little Malcolm, The Wilby Conspiracy, Coup de Grace, The Greek Tycoon, The Deer Hunter, The Class of Miss MacMichael, A Portrait of the Artist as a Young Man, The Secret Policeman's Other Ball, Yesterday's Hero, Watcher in the Woods, Absolution, The Incubus, Lady Chatterly's Lover, Eureka, Moonlighting, Blind Date, Beyond the Limit, The Next One, Success is the Best Revenge, The Chain, Dreamchild, Insignificance, The Lightship, The Wind, Castaway, My Beautiful Laundrette, Prick Up Your Ears, Wish You Were Here, The Second Victory, Taffin, Track 29, Stars and Bars, Trading Hearts, Sammy and Rosie Get Laid, Scenes From the Class Struggle in Beverly Hills, Torrents of Spring.
TELEVISION: *Series* (U.K.): Widows (parts 1 & 2), Nancy Astor, Diana. *Series* (U.S.): The Martian Chronicles, Florence Nightingale. *Movies*: Strong Medicine, Smart Money, Baja Oklahoma, Monte Carlo.

MYERSON, BERNARD
Executive. b. New York, NY, March 25, 1918. Entered m.p. ind. with Fabian Theatres, 1938-63; last position as exec. v.p.; joined Loew's Theatres as v.p., 1963; exec. v.p. and board member, Loew's Corp.; pres. Loew's Theatres, 1971. Chmn. & pres., Loews Theatre Management Corp., 1985, presently retired. Member of Executive Committee Greater N.Y. Chapter, National Foundation of March of Dimes; Honorary chmn., bd. mem., & former pres., Will Rogers Memorial Fund; exec. comm., bd., National Assn. Theatre Owners; bd. member & former pres., Motion Picture Pioneers; treas. Variety Intl.; member bd. of dirs., Burke Rehabilitation Center; member, N.Y.S. Governor's Council on M.P. & T.V. Development; vice-chmn., adv. bd. of Tisch Sch. of Arts, NYU.

N

NABORS, JIM
Actor. b. Sylacauga, AL, June 12, 1932. Discovered performing in an L.A. nightclub in early 1960's by Andy Griffith, who asked him to appear on his series. Developed a second career as a singer. Between 1966-72 had 12 albums on best selling charts.
PICTURES: The Best Little Whorehouse in Texas, Stroker Ace, Cannonball Run II.
TELEVISION: *Series*: The Andy Griffith Show, Gomer Pyle USMC, The Jim Nabors Hour, The Lost Saucer, The Jim Nabors Show (synd. talk show). *Movie*: Return to Mayberry.

NADER, GEORGE
Actor. b. Pasadena, CA, Oct. 19, 1921. e. Occidental Coll., B.A.; Pasadena Playhouse, B.T.A. Served in U.S. Navy. Wrote novel: Chrome (Putnam).
PICTURES: Monsoon (debut, 1953), Memory of Love, Robot Monster, Rustlers on Horseback, Overland Telegraph, Carnival Story, Miss Robin Crusoe, Sins of Jezebel, Phone Call from a Stranger, Four Guns to the Border, Six Bridges to Cross, Lady Godiva, The Second Greatest Sex, Away All Boats, Appointment With a Shadow, Congo Crossing, The Unguarded Moment, Four Girls in Town, Man Afraid, The Female Animal, Flood Tide, Joe Butterfly, Nowhere to Go, The Secret Mark of D'Artagnan, The Great Space Adventure, Zigzag, The Human Duplicators, House of a Thousand Dolls, The Million Eyes of Sumuru, Alarm on 83rd Street, Murder at Midnight, Count-Down for Manhattan, Dynamite in Green Silk, The Check and an Icy Smile, Murder Club from Brooklyn, Death in Red Jaguar, End Station of the Damned, Beyond Atlantis.
TELEVISION: *Series*: Ellery Queen, Man and the Challenge, Shannon. *Guest*: Letter to Loretta, Fireside Theatre, Chevron Theatre, Alfred Hitchcock, Andy Griffith Show, etc. *Movie*: Nakia.

NAIFY, MARSHALL
Executive. Chairman, Todd-AO/Glenn Studios.

NAIFY, ROBERT
Executive. b. Sacramento, CA. e. Attended Stanford U. Worked for United California Theatres starting in 1946 in various capacities including: theatre manager, purchasing agent, film buyer, general manager and president. 1963 became exec. v.p. United Artists Communications; 1971 became pres. & CEO until 1987. Currently president, Todd-AO Corporation.

NAIR, MIRA
Director, Producer. b. Bhubaneshwar, India, October 15, 1957. e. Irish Catholic Missionary School in India, Delhi U., Harvard U. A course in documentary filmmaking at Harvard led to directing 4 non-fiction films including India Cabaret (1985) and Children of Desired Sex.
PICTURES: *Director-Producer*. Salaam Bombay! (Cannes Film Fest. Camera d'Or/Prix du Publique; Acad. Award nom.), Mississippi Masala (also s.p.), The Perez Family, Kama Sutra: A Tale of Love.

NALLE, BILLY
Theatre Concert Organist, Composer. b. Fort Myers, FL, Apr. 24, 1921. Postgrad, Juilliard Sch. Over 5,000 major telecasts from NY; now artist emeritus, Wichita Theatre Organization, Inc. RCA, Telarc, Reader's Digest & WTO Records Artist. Now residing in Fort Myers, FL.

NAMATH, JOE
Actor. b. Beaver Falls, PA, May 31, 1943. e. U. of Alabama. Former professional football star.
PICTURES: Norwood (debut, 1970), C.C. & Company (Chrome Hearts), The Last Rebel, Avalanche Express, Chattanooga Choo Choo, Going Under.
TELEVISION: *Series*: The Waverly Wonders. *Host*: Monday Night Football (1985). *Movie*: Marriage Is Alive and Well. *Guest*: Here's Lucy, The Brady Bunch, The Love Boat, Kate and Allie.

NARDINO, GARY
Executive. b. Garfield, NJ, Aug. 26, 1935. e. Seton Hall U. Awarded honorary degree of Doctor of Laws. Entered industry in 1959 as agent, representing Lorimar Prods. and Talent Associates, among others. Named sr. v.p. of ICM's New York TV dept; then v.p. of William Morris Agency, heading N.Y. TV dept. Pres. of Paramount TV Production Division, 1977-83. Pres. of Gary Nardino Prods., Inc., formed 1983, to dev. and produce theatrical feature and TV programming; 1988-90, chmn. & CEO, Orion Television Entertainment.
PICTURES: Star Trek III: The Search for Spock (exec. prod.), Fire with Fire (prod.).
TELEVISION: *Exec. prod.*: Pacific Blue, Time Trax, Brothers, At Your Service, Joanna.
(d. Jan. 31, 1998)

NARIZZANO, SILVIO
Producer, Director. b. Montreal, Canada, Feb. 8, 1927. e. U. of Bishop's, Lennoxville, Quebec, B.A. Was active as actor-director in Canadian theatre before going to England for TV and theatrical film work.
PICTURES: *Director*: Under Ten Flags (co-dir.), Die! Die! My Darling! (Fanatic), Georgy Girl, Blue, Loot, Redneck (also prod.), The Sky Is Falling, Why Shoot the Teacher?, The Class of Miss MacMichael, Choices, Double Play. *Producer*: Negatives, Fade-In.
TELEVISION: The Babysitter, Poet Game, The Little Farm, Come Back Little Sheba, Staying On, Young Shoulders, The Body in the Library. *Series*: Miss Marple.

NASH, N. RICHARD
Writer. b. Philadelphia, PA, June 8, 1913.
AUTHOR: Cry Macho, East Wind, Rain, The Last Magic, Aphrodite's Cave, Radiance, Behold the Man, The Wildwood.
THEATER: *B'way*: Second Best Bed, The Young and Fair, See the Jaguar, The Rainmaker, Girls of Summer, Handful of Fire, Wildcat, 110 in the Shade, Fire, The Happy Time, Echoes, Wildfire, The Torch, Magic, The Bluebird of Happiness, The Loss of D-Natural, Breaking the Tie, Come As You Are, Everybody Smile, Life Anonymous, The Green Clown.
PICTURES: Nora Prentiss, Welcome Stranger, The Vicious Years, The Rainmaker, Dear Wife, Porgy and Bess, Sainted Sisters, Dragonfly.
TELEVISION: Many TV plays for Television Playhouse, U.S. Steel, General Electric.

NATHANSON, MICHAEL
Executive. Began his career at NBC Sports, NY. In 1977 moved to LA and worked as prod. asst. on The Deep, Sinbad the Eye of the Tiger. 1980-85, v.p., prod., MGM, United Artists, Warner Bros. 1987, exec. v.p., prod., Columbia Pictures; 1989-94, pres. of Worldwide Prod. at Columbia Pictures; projects included: Awakenings, The Prince of Tides, Boyz N the Hood, A River Runs Through It, A League of Their Own, In the Line of Fire, Groundhog Day, Bram Stoker's Dracula, and others. 1994-97, chmn. & CEO, Regency Productions; produced: A Time to Kill, Tin Cup, Natural Born Killers, Heat, Copy Cat. 1997-, pres. & CEO, MGM Pictures; produced: Species 2, Dirty Work.

NAUGHTON, DAVID
Actor, Singer. b. Hartford, CT, Feb. 13, 1951. Brother is actor James Naughton. e. U. of Pennsylvania, B.A. Studied at London Acad. of Music and Dramatic Arts. Numerous TV commercials, including music for Dr. Pepper. On B'way in Hamlet, Da, Poor Little Lambs.
PICTURES: Midnight Madness (debut, 1980), An American Werewolf in London, Separate Ways, Hot Dog... The Movie, Not for Publication, The Boy in Blue, Separate Vacations, Kidnapped,

Quite By Chance, Beanstalk, The Sleeping Car, Overexposed, Wild Cactus, Desert Steel, Amityville: A New Generation, Beanstalk, Ice Cream Man, Urban Safari.
TELEVISION: *Series*: Makin' It, At Ease, My Sister Sam, Temporary Insanity, The Belles of Bleeker St., Those Two. *Movies*: I Desire, Getting Physical, Goddess of Love. *Guest*: Twilight Zone, Murder She Wrote, Touched By An Angel, Seinfeld, Cybil, Melrose Place.

NAUGHTON, JAMES
Actor. b. Middletown, CT, Dec. 6, 1945. Father of actors Greg Naughton and Keira Naughton. e. Brown U., A.B., 1967; Yale U., M.F.A., drama, 1970.
THEATER: *NY*: I Love My Wife (B'way debut, 1977), Long Day's Journey Into Night (Theatre World, Drama Desk and New York Critics Circle Awards, 1971), Whose Life Is It Anyway?, Losing Time, Drinks Before Dinner, City of Angels (Tony & Drama Desk Awards, 1990), Four Baboons Adoring the Sun. Regional: Who's Afraid of Virginia Woolf? (Long Wharf), The Glass Menagerie (Long Wharf), Hamlet (Long Wharf), Julius Caesar (Amer. Shakespeare Festival), 8 seasons at Williamstown Theatre Festival, Chicago (B'way, 1996-97).
PICTURES: The Paper Chase (debut, 1973), Second Wind, A Stranger is Watching, Cat's Eye, The Glass Menagerie, The Good Mother, First Kid.
TELEVISION: *Special*: Look Homeward Angel (1972). *Series*: Faraday and Company, Planet of the Apes, Making the Grade, Trauma Center, Raising Miranda, The Cosby Mysteries. *Movies*: F. Scott Fitzgerald and the Last of the Belles, The Last 36 Hours of Dr. Durant, The Bunker, My Body My Child, Parole, The Last of the Great Survivors, Between Darkness and the Dawn, Sin of Innocence, Traveling Man, Antigone, The Cosby Mysteries (pilot), The Birds II: Land's End, Cagney & Lacey: The Return, Cagney & Lacey: Together Again, Raising Caines.

NEAL, PATRICIA
Actress. b. Packard, KY, Jan. 20, 1926. e. Northwestern U. Worker as doctor's asst., cashier, hostess, model, jewelry store clerk prior to prof. career as actress. In summer stock before B'way debut in The Voice of the Turtle, 1946. Autobiography: As I Am (with Richard DeNeut, 1988).
THEATER: *NY*: The Voice of the Turtle, Another Part of the Forest (Tony, Donaldson & Drama Critic Awards), The Children's Hour, Roomful of Roses, The Miracle Worker. *England*: Suddenly Last Summer.
PICTURES: John Loves Mary (debut 1949), The Fountainhead, It's a Great Feeling, The Hasty Heart, Bright Leaf, Three Secrets, The Breaking Point, Raton Pass, Operation Pacific, The Day the Earth Stood Still, Weekend With Father, Diplomatic Courier, Washington Story, Something for the Birds, Stranger From Venus (Immediate Disaster), Your Woman, A Face in the Crowd, Breakfast at Tiffany's, Hud (Academy Award, BFA Award, 1963), Psyche '59, In Harm's Way (BFA Award, 1965), The Subject Was Roses (Acad. Award nom.), The Night Digger, Baxter, Happy Mother's Day Love George (Run Stranger Run), "B" Must Die, The Passage, Ghost Story, An Unremarkable Life.
TELEVISION: *Movies*: The Homecoming, Things in Their Season, Eric, Tail Gunner Joe, A Love Affair: The Eleanor and Lou Gehrig Story, The Bastard, All Quiet on the Western Front, Shattered Vows, Love Leads the Way, Caroline?, A Mother's Right: The Elizabeth Morgan Story, Heidi. *Guest*: Little House on the Prairie, Murder She Wrote. *BBC*: Days & Nights of Beebee Finstermaker, The Country Girl, Clash By Night, The Royal Family.

NEAME, RONALD
C.B.E. Cinematographer, Producer, Director. b. Hendon, Eng. April 23, 1911. e. U. Coll. Sch., London. p. Elwin Neame, London photog., & Ivy Close, m.p. actress. Entered m.p. ind. 1928; asst. cameraman on first full-length Brit. sound film, Blackmail, dir. by Alfred Hitchcock, 1929; became chief cameraman & lighting expert, 1934; in 1945 joint assoc. prod., Noel Coward Prods.
PICTURES: *Cinematographer*: Girls Will Be Boys (co-cine.), Happy (co-cine.), Elizabeth of England, Honours Easy (co-cine.), Invitation to the Waltz (co-cine.), Joy Ride, Music Hath Charms, The Crimes of Stephen Hawke, The Improper Dutchess, A Star Fell From Heaven, Against the Tide, Brief Ecstasy, Feather Your Nest, Keep Fit, Weekend Millionaire, Gaunt Stranger, The Phantom Strikes, The Crime of Peter Frame, Dangerous Secrets, I See Ice (co-cine.), Penny Paradise, Who Goes Next? Cheers Boys Cheer, Sweeney Todd: The Demon Barber of Fleet Street, Let's Be Famous, Trouble Brewing, The Ware Case, It's In the Air (co-cine.), Let George Do It, Return to Yesterday, Saloon Bar, Four Just Men, Major Barbara, A Yank in the R.A.F. (Brit. flying sequence), One of Our Aircraft is Missing, In Which We Serve, This Happy Breed, Blithe Spirit, Brief Encounter, Great Expectations (also co-s.p.), Oliver Twist (also co-s.p.), A Young Man's Fancy, Passionate Friends. *Director*: Take My Life, Golden Salamander (also co-s.p.), The Card (The Promoter; also prod.), Man With a Million (The Million Pound Note), The Man Who Never Was, The Seventh Sin, Windom's Way, The Horse's Mouth, Tunes of Glory, Escape from Zahrain, I Could Go on Singing, The Chalk Garden, Mister Moses, Gambit, A Man Could Get Killed (co-dir.), Prudence and the Pill (co-dir.), The Prime of Miss Jean Brodie, Scrooge, The Poseidon Adventure, The Odessa File, Meteor, Hopscotch, First Monday in October, Foreign Body, The Magic Balloon.

NEEDHAM, HAL
Director, Writer. b. Memphis, TN, March 6, 1931. e. Student public schools. Served with Paratroopers, U.S. Army 1951-54. Founder Stunts Unlimited, Los Angeles, 1970; stuntman Stunts Unlimited, 1956-65; dir. and stunt coordinator second unit, 1965-75. Chmn. of bd., Camera Platforms International, Inc. 1985. Owner Budweiser Rocket Car (fastest car in the world). Member Screen Actors Guild, AFTRA, Writers Guild of America, Directors Guild of America.
PICTURES: Dir.: Smokey and the Bandit (debut, 1977; also co-story), Hooper, The Villain, Smokey and the Bandit II, The Cannonball Run, Megaforce (also co-s.p.), Stroker Ace (also co-s.p.), Cannonball Run II (also co-s.p.), RAD, Body Slam.
TELEVISION: Series: Hal Needham's Wild World of Stunts (synd. series; also writer, star). Movie: Death Car on the Freeway. Pilot: Stunts Unlimited (pilot). Episode: B.L. Stryker.

NEESON, LIAM
Actor. b. Ballymena, Northern Ireland, June 7, 1952. m. actress Natasha Richardson. Former amateur boxer. Was driving a fork lift truck for a brewery when he joined the Lyric Player's Theatre in Belfast. Made prof. debut in The Risen (1976) and stayed with rep. co. 2 years. Moved to Dublin as freelance actor before joining the Abbey Theatre.
THEATER: The Informer (Dublin Theatre Fest.), Translations (National Theatre, London). NY theatre debut 1992 in Anna Christie (Theatre World Award).
PICTURES: Excalibur (debut, 1981), Krull, The Bounty, Lamb, The Innocent, The Mission, Duet For One, A Prayer for the Dying, Suspect, Satisfaction, The Dead Pool, The Good Mother, High Spirits, Next of Kin, Dark Man, Crossing the Line (The Big Man), Shining Through, Under Suspicion, Husbands and Wives, Leap of Faith, Ethan Frome, Deception, Schindler's List (Acad. Award nom.), Nell, Rob Roy, Before and After, Michael Collins, A Leap of Faith (voice), Alaska: Spirit of the Wild (voice), Ambrose Chapel, Everest (narrator), Star Wars: Episode I.
TELEVISION: Merlin and the Sword, Across the Water (BBC), Ellis Island, A Woman of Substance, Sweet As You Are, The Great War.

NEILL, SAM
Actor. r.n. Nigel Neill. b. Northern Ireland, Sept. 14, 1947. Raised in New Zealand. e. U. of Canterbury. In repertory before joining N.Z. National Film Unit, acting and directing documentaries and shorts. 1992, awarded the O.B.E. for his services to acting. Co-directed, co-wrote and appeared in New Zealand documentary Cinema of Unease: A Personal Journey by Sam Neill.
PICTURES: Sleeping Dogs (debut, 1977), The Journalist, My Brilliant Career, Just Out of Reach, Attack Force Z, The Final Conflict, Possession, Enigma, Le Sang des Autres, Robbery Under Arms, Plenty, For Love Alone, The Good Wife, A Cry in the Dark (Australian Film Inst. Award), Dead Calm, The French Revolution, The Hunt for Red October, Until the End of the World, Hostage, Memoirs of an Invisible Man, Death in Brunswick, Jurassic Park, The Piano, Sirens, Rudyard Kipling's The Jungle Book, In the Mouth of Madness, Country Life, Restoration, Victory, Event Horizon, The Revengers' Comedies, The Horse Whisperer.
TELEVISION: The Sullivans, Young Ramsay, Lucinda Brayford, The Country Girls. Mini-Series: Kane and Abel, Reilly Ace of Spies, Amerika, Merlin. Movies: From a Far Country: Pope John Paul II, Ivanhoe, The Blood of Others, Arthur Hailey's Strong Medicine, Leap of Faith, Fever, One Against the Wind, The Sinking of the Rainbow Warrior, Family Pictures.

NELLIGAN, KATE
Actress. r.n. Patricia Colleen Nelligan. b. London, Ontario, Canada, March 16, 1951.
THEATER: Barefoot in the Park, A Streetcar Named Desire, Playboy of the Western World, Private Lives, Plenty, Serious Money, Spoils of War, Bad Habits.
PICTURES: The Romantic Englishwoman (debut, 1975), Dracula, Mr. Patman, Eye of the Needle, Without a Trace, The Mystery of Henry Moore, Eleni, Frankie and Johnny (BAFTA Award), The Prince of Tides (Acad. Award nom.), Shadows and Fog, Fatal Instinct, Wolf, Margaret's Museum, How to Make an American Quilt, Up Close and Personal, U.S. Marshals, Stolen Moments.
TELEVISION: Movies/Specials: The Onedin Line, The Lady of the Camelias, Therese Raquin, Count of Monte Cristo, Victims, Kojak: The Price of Justice, Love and Hate: The Story of Colin and Joann Thatcher, Three Hotels, Terror Strikes the Class Reunion, Diamond Fleece, Liar Liar, Shattered Trust: The Shari Karney Story, Spoils of War, Million Dollar Babies, Captive Heart: The James Mink Story.

NELSON, BARRY
Actor. r.n. Robert Neilson. b. Oakland, CA, Apr. 16, 1920. e. U. of California. London stage in No Time for Sergeants, 1957.
THEATER: B'way: Light Up the Sky, The Rat Race, The Moon Is Blue, Mary Mary, Cactus Flower, Everything in the Garden, Seascape, The Norman Conquests, The Act, 42nd Street.

PICTURES: Shadow of the Thin Man, Johnny Eager, Dr. Kildare's Victory, Rio Rita, Eyes in the Night, Bataan, The Human Comedy, A Guy Named Joe, Winged Victory, The Beginning or the End, Undercover Maisie, The Man With My Face, The First Traveling Saleslady, Mary Mary, Airport, Pete 'n' Tillie, The Shining, Island Claws.
TELEVISION: Series: The Hunter, My Favorite Husband. Mini-Series: Washington: Behind Closed Doors. Movies: The Borgia Stick, Seven in Darkness, Climb an Angry Mountain. Guest: Suspense, Alfred Hitchcock Presents, Longstreet, Taxi, Magnum P.I., Murder She Wrote.

NELSON, CRAIG T.
Actor. b. Spokane, WA, April 4, 1946. Began career as writer/performer on Lohman and Barkley Show in Los Angeles. Teamed with Barry Levinson as a comedy writer. Wrote for Tim Conway Show, Alan King TV special; guest appearances on talk shows and Mary Tyler Moore Show. Produced series of 52 half-hour films on American artists, American Still. Returned to L.A. in 1978 and acting career.
PICTURES: And Justice for All (debut, 1979), Where the Buffalo Roam, Private Benjamin, Stir Crazy, The Formula, Poltergeist, Man Woman and Child, All the Right Moves, The Osterman Weekend, Silkwood, The Killing Fields, Poltergeist II, Red Riding Hood, Action Jackson, Rachel River, Me and Him, Troop Beverly Hills, Turner & Hooch, I'm Not Rappaport, Ghosts of Mississippi.
TELEVISION: Series: Call to Glory, Coach (Emmy Award, 1992).Guest: Wonder Woman, Charlie's Angels, How the West Was Won. Movies: Diary of a Teenage Hitchhiker, Rage, Promise of Love, Inmates: A Love Story, Chicago Story, Paper Dolls, Alex: The Life of a Child, The Ted Kennedy Jr. Story, Murderers Among Us: The Simon Wiesenthal Story, Extreme Close-Up, The Josephine Baker Story, The Switch, The Fire Next Time, Ride With the Wind (also co-writer), Probable Cause, Take Me Home Again. Mini-Series: Drug Wars: The Camarena Story.

NELSON, DAVID
Actor. b. New York, NY, Oct. 24, 1936. e. Hollywood H.S., U. of Southern California. Son of Ozzie Nelson and Harriet Hilliard Nelson; brother of late Rick Nelson.
PICTURES: Here Comes the Nelsons, Peyton Place, The Remarkable Mr. Pennypacker, Day of the Outlaw, The Big Circus, "30," The Big Show, No Drums No Bugles, Cry-Baby. Director: A Rare Breed, The Last Plane Out.
TELEVISION: Series: The Adventures of Ozzie and Harriet (also dir. episodes). Movies: Smash-Up on Interstate 5, High School U.S.A. Guest: Hondo, The Love Boat. Dir.: Easy To Be Free (special), OK Crackerby (series).

NELSON, GENE
Dancer, Actor, Director, Choreographer. r.n. Gene Berg. b. Seattle, WA, March 24, 1920. e. Santa Monica, CA, H.S. Began dancing and ice skating in school; joined Sonja Henie Hollywood Ice Revue, featured in It Happens on Ice in NY; served in WWII. Joined Hollywood group prod. stage musical, Lend an Ear; to Warner for Daughter of Rosie O'Grady (1950). Prof. of Theatre Arts at San Francisco State U. School of Creative Arts, 1989-90.
THEATER: B'way: Actor: Lend an Ear, Follies, The Music Music, Good News. Director: Follies, Elephant Man, Oklahoma!, Stepping Out.
PICTURES: Actor: This Is the Army (debut, 1943), I Wonder Who's Kissing Her Now, Gentleman's Agreement, Apartment For Peggy, The Daughter of Rosie O'Grady, Tea for Two, Starlift, The West Point Story, Lullaby of Broadway, Painting the Clouds With Sunshine, She's Working Her Way Through College, She's Back on Broadway, Three Sailors and a Girl, Crime Wave, So This Is Paris, Oklahoma!, The Way Out (Dial 999), The Atomic Man (Timeslip), 20,000 Eyes, The Purple Hills, Thunder Island, S.O.B. Director: The Hand of Death, Hootenany Hoot, Your Cheatin' Heart, Kissin' Cousins, Harum Scarum, The Cool Ones (also s.p.).
TELEVISION: Series Director: Mod Squad, I Dream of Jeannie, FBI, 12 O'Clock High, Hawaii Five-O, Farmer's Daughter, Donna Reed Show, Burke's Law, Felony Squad, Laredo, The Rifleman, The Wackiest Ship, Iron Horse, FBI, The Rookies, Quincy, Operation Petticoat. Movies (Director): Wake Me When the War is Over (also co-prod.), The Letters. Movies (Actor): Family Flight, A Brand New Life.

NELSON, JUDD
Actor. b. Portland, ME, Nov. 28, 1959. e. Haverford/Bryn Mawr Coll. Studied acting at Stella Adler Conservatory. NY theatre includes Carnal Knowledge.
PICTURES: Making the Grade (debut, 1984), Fandango, The Breakfast Club, St. Elmo's Fire, Blue City, Transformers (voice), From the Hip, Relentless, Far Out Man, New Jack City, The Dark Backward, Primary Motive, Entangled, Conflict of Interest, Caroline at Midnight, Hail Caesar, Every Breath (also s.p.), Flinch, Circumstances Unknown, Blackwater Trail, Steel.
TELEVISION: Series: Suddenly Susan. Guest: Moonlighting. Movies: Billionaire Boys Club, Hiroshima: Out of the Ashes, Conflict of Interest, Blindfold: Acts of Obsession.

NELSON, LORI
Actress. r.n. Dixie Kay Nelson. b. Santa Fe, NM, Aug. 15, 1933. e. Canoga Park H.S. Started as child actress, photographer's model before film debut in 1952.
THEATER: The Pleasure of His Company, Who Was That Lady I Saw You With, Affairs of Mildred Wilde, Sweet Bird of Youth, Picnic, 'Night Mother.
PICTURES: Ma and Pa Kettle at the Fair (debut, 1952), Bend of the River, Francis Goes to West Point, All I Desire, All-American, Walking My Baby Back Home, Tumbleweed, Underwater, Destry, Revenge of the Creature, I Died a Thousand Times, Sincerely Yours, Mohawk, Day the World Ended, Pardners, Hot Rod Girl, Ma and Pa Kettle at Waikiki, Gambling Man, Untamed Youth.
TELEVISION: Series: How to Marry a Millionaire. Guest: Wagon Train, Laramie, Family Affair, The Texan, Wanted Dead or Alive, Sam Spade, G.E. Theatre, Riverboat, Sugarfoot, The Young and the Restless, Climax, The Millionaire, Wells Fargo, etc. Special: The Pied Piper of Hamelin.

NELSON, TRACY
Actress, Singer, Dancer. b. Santa Monica, CA, Oct., 1963. e. Bard Coll. Daughter of late singer-actor Rick Nelson. Sister of singers Matthew & Gunnar Nelson. Studied acting in England.
THEATER: Grease (Nat'l touring co. & B'way).
PICTURES: Yours Mine and Ours (debut, 1968), Maria's Lovers, Down and Out in Beverly Hills, Chapters.
TELEVISION: Series: Square Pegs, Glitter, Father Dowling Mysteries, A League of Their Own, Melrose Place, The Man from Snowy River. Movies: Katie's Secret, Tonight's the Night, If It's Tuesday It Still Must Be Belgium, Fatal Confessions, For Hope, In the Shadow of Evil, Pleasures, Highway Heartbreaker, Ray Alexander: Murder in Mind, Ray Alexander: A Taste for Justice, No Child of Mine. Guest: The Adventures of Ozzie and Harriet, Hotel, Family Ties, The Love Boat.

NELSON, WILLIE
Composer, Singer, Actor. b. Abbott, TX, April 30, 1933. Worked as salesman, announcer, host of country music shows on local Texas stations; bass player with Ray Price's band. Started writing songs in the 60's; performing in the 70's.
PICTURES: The Electric Horseman (debut, 1979), Honeysuckle Rose, Thief, Barbarosa, Hell's Angels Forever, Songwriter, Red-Headed Stranger (also prod.), Walking After Midnight, Gone Fishin'.
TELEVISION: Movies: The Last Days of Frank and Jesse James, Stagecoach, Coming Out of the Ice, Baja Oklahoma, Once Upon a Texas Train, Where the Hell's That Gold?!!?, Pair of Aces, Another Pair of Aces, Wild Texas Wind, Big Dreams & Broken Hearts: The Dottie West Story. Special: Willie Nelson—Texas Style (also prod.).

NEMEC, CORIN
Actor. r.n. Joseph Charles Nemec IV. b. Little Rock, AR, Nov. 5, 1971. Began acting in commercials at age 13.
PICTURES: Tucker: The Man and His Dream, Solar Crisis, Drop Zone, Operation Dumbo Drop, The War at Home, Mojave Moon, Quality Time, The First to Go, Goodbye America, Legacy, Foreign Correspondents.
TELEVISION: Series: Parker Lewis Can't Lose. Movies: I Know My First Name is Steven (Emmy nom.), For the Very First Time, My Son Johnny, The Lifeforce Experiment, Summer of Fear, Blade Squad, Silencing May. Mini-Series: The Stand. Pilot: What's Alan Watching? Guest: Webster, Sidekicks.

NERO, FRANCO
Actor. r.n. Franceso Spartanero. b. Parma, Italy, Nov. 23, 1942. e. Univ. La Bocconi, Milan. m. Vanessa Redgrave.
PICTURES: Celestina (Made at Your Service; debut, 1964), The Deadly Diaphanoids, I Knew Her Well, Wild Wild Planet, The Third Eyes, The Bible, The Tramplers, Django, The Avenger (Texas Addio), Hired Killer, The Brute and the Beast, Mafia, Camelot, L'uomo l'Orgoglio la Vendetta, Island of Crime, The Mercenary, The Day of the Owl, A Quiet Place in the Country, The Battle of Neretva, Detective Belli, Sardinia: Ramsom, Companeros, Tristana, The Virgin and the Gypsy, Drop Out!, Confessions of a Police Commissioner, Killer From Yuma, Redneck, The Monk, The Vacation, Pope Joan, Deaf Smith and Johnny Ears, The Fifth Day of Peace, The Aquarian, High Crime, Blood Brothers (I Guappi), Cry Onion, The Anonymous Avenger, Challenge to White Fang, Death Drive, Violent Breed, Submission, The Last Days of Mussolini, Force Ten From Navarone, The Man With Bogart's Face, The Visitor, Shark Hunter, Blue-Eyed Bandit, Danzig Roses, Day of the Cobra, The Falcon, The Salamander, Sahara Cross, Enter the Ninja, Mexico in Flames, Querelle, Wagner, Sweet Country, The Girl, Garibaldi the General, Race to Danger, Marathon, Django Strikes Again, Top Line, Silent Night, Young Toscanini, The Betrothed, The Magistrate, Heart of Victory, The Repenter, The Forester's Sons, Die Hard 2, Brothers and Sisters, Crimson Down, Oro, Deep Blue, The Lucona Affair, Babylon Complot, A Breath of Life, Jonathan of the Bears, Conflict of Interest, The Dragon's Ring, Talk of Angels, The Innocent Sleep, The King and Me.

TELEVISION: Mini-series: The Last Days of Pompeii, Desideria, The Return of Sandokan, Bella Mafia, Painted Lady. Movies: The Legend of Valentino, 21 Hours at Munich, The Pirate, Young Catherine, David, The Versace Murder, Das Babylon Komplott, Il Deserto di fuoco.

NESMITH, MICHAEL
Musician, Producer. r.n. Robert Michael Nesmith. b. Houston, TX, Dec. 30, 1942. Original member of The Monkees, later became producer of videos and films. Chmn. & CEO Pacific Arts Publishing video company. Won Grammy award for music video Elephant Parts. Exec. prod. & performer in video Dr. Duck's Super Secret All-Purpose Sauce.
PICTURES: Actor: Head, Burglar (cameo), Heart and Soul. Exec. Prod.: Timerider (also co-s.p.), Repo Man, Square Dance, Tapeheads.
TELEVISION: Series: The Monkees, Michael Nesmith in Television Parts (also prod.). Special: 33-1/3 Revolutions Per Monkee.

NETTER, DOUGLAS
Executive, Producer. b. Seattle, WA. 1955-57, gen. mgr. Todd A.O.; 1958-60, Sam Goldwyn Productions; 1961-67, formed own co. representing producers; 1968-69, Jalem Productions; 1969-75, exec. v.p. MGM. Films: Mr. Ricco (prod.), The Wild Geese (co-prod.).
TELEVISION: Louis L'Amour's The Sacketts (prod.), The Buffalo Soldiers (exec. prod.), Wild Times (prod.), Roughnecks (exec. prod.), Cherokee Trail (exec. prod.), Five Mile Creek (exec. prod.; Australian based TV series for Disney Channel), Captain Power and the Soldiers of the Future (exec. prod.), Stealth F22 (exec. prod.), Babylon 5 (exec. prod.).

NETTLETON, LOIS
Actress. b. Oak Park, IL, 1931. e. Studied at Goodman Theatre, Chicago and Actors Studio. Replaced Kim Hunter in Darkness at Noon on B'way. Emmy Award: Performer Best Daytime Drama Spec., The American Woman: Portraits in Courage (1977). Also Emmy: Religious Program, Insight (1983).
THEATER: Cat on a Hot Tin Roof, Silent Night, Lonely Night, God and Kate Murphy, The Wayward Stork, The Rainmaker, A Streetcar Named Desire.
PICTURES: A Face in the Crowd (debut, 1957), Period of Adjustment, Come Fly with Me, Mail Order Bride, Valley of Mystery, Bamboo Saucer, The Good Guys and the Bad Guys, Dirty Dingus Magee, The Sidelong Glances of a Pigeon Kicker, The Honkers, The Man in the Glass Booth, Echoes of a Summer, Deadly Blessing, Butterfly, Soggy Bottom U.S.A., The Best Little Whorehouse in Texas.
TELEVISION: Series: Accidental Family, You Can't Take It With You. Guest: Medical Center, Barnaby Jones, Alfred Hitchcock, All That Glitters, In the Heat of the Night. Movies: Any Second Now, Weekend of Terror, The Forgotten Man, Terror in the Sky, Women in Chains, Fear on Trial, Tourist, Brass, Manhunt for Claude Dallas. Mini-Series: Washington: Behind Closed Doors, Centennial. Specials: Rendezvous, Meet Me in St. Louis, Traveler's Rest.

NEUFELD, MACE
Producer. b. New York, NY, July 13, 1928. e. Yale Col. Started as professional photographer, before becoming prod. asst. at Dumont Television Network. Wrote musical material for performers incl. Sammy Davis Jr., Dorothy Loudon, Ritz Brothers, etc., and theme for Heckle and Jeckle animated series. In 1951, formed independent TV prod. and personal mgmt. co. For TV produced programs for Dick Van Dyke, Elaine May and Mike Nichols. Formed independent production co. with Nichols and Buck Henry. In 1980, created Neufeld-Davis Prods. with Marvin Davis. Formed Neufeld/Rehme Prods. with Robert G. Rehme in 1989; Mace Neufeld Prods., 1997. On B'way, prod. Flying Karamazov Brothers show. Voted Producer of the Year by NATO/ShoWest, 1992.
PICTURES: The Omen, Damien: Omen II, The Frisco Kid, The Funhouse, The Aviator, Transylvania 6-5000, No Way Out, The Hunt for Red October, Flight of the Intruder, Necessary Roughness, Patriot Games, Gettysburg, Beverly Hills Cop III, Clear and Present Danger, The Saint, The General's Daughter, Lost in Space.
TELEVISION: Movies/Miniseries: East of Eden, Angel on My Shoulder, American Dream, Cagney and Lacey (pilot), A Death in California, White Hot. Specials: The Magic Planet, The Flying Karamazov Brothers, Blind Faith, A Woman Undone, Escape—Human Cargo.

NEUWIRTH, BEBE
Actress. b. Newark, NJ, Dec. 31. e. Juilliard. Started as chorus dancer.
THEATER: NY: Little Me, Dancin', Upstairs at O'Neal, The Road to Hollywood, Sweet Charity (Tony Award, 1986), Showing Off, Damn Yankees. Tour: A Chorus Line. Regional: Just So, Kicks (also choreog.), Chicago. London: Kiss of the Spider Woman.
PICTURES: Say Anything... (debut, 1989), Green Card, Bugsy, Paint Job, Malice, Jumanji, All Dogs Go to Heaven (voice), The Associate.
TELEVISION: Series: Cheers (2 Emmy Awards). Movies: Without Her Consent, Unspeakable Acts. Mini-Series: Wild Palms. Guest: Frasier.

NEWELL, MIKE
Director. b. St. Albans, England, March 28, 1942. e. Cambridge U. Took directorial training course at Granada Television.
PICTURES: The Awakening (debut, 1980), Bad Blood, Dance With a Stranger, The Good Father, Amazing Grace and Chuck, Common Ground, Enchanted April, Into the West, Four Weddings and a Funeral, An Awfully Big Adventure, Donnie Brasco, Photographing Fairies (exec. prod.), Pushing Tin, Best Laid Plan (exec. prod.).
TELEVISION: Baa Baa Black Sheep, Silver Wedding, Jill and Jack, Ready When You Are Mr. McGill, Lost Your Tongue, Mr. & Mrs. Bureaucrat, Just Your Luck, The Man in the Iron Mask, The Gift of Friendship, Destiny, Tales Out of School, Birth of a Nation, Blood Feud.

NEWHART, BOB
Actor, Comedian. b. Chicago, IL, Sept. 5, 1929. e. Loyola U. In Army 2 yrs., then law school; left to become copywriter and accountant. Acted with theatrical stock co. in Oak Park; hired for TV man-in-street show in Chicago. Recorded hit comedy album for Warner Bros., The Button-Down Mind of Bob Newhart (Grammy Award, 1960), followed by two more successful albums. Did series of nightclub engagements and then acquired own TV variety series in 1961. Grand Marshall: Tournament of Roses Parde, 1991. Inducted into TV Hall of Fame, 1993.
PICTURES: Hell Is for Heroes (debut, 1962), Hot Millions, Catch-22, On a Clear Day You Can See Forever, Cold Turkey, The Rescuers (voice), Little Miss Marker, First Family, The Rescuers Down Under (voice), In & Out.
TELEVISION: Series: The Bob Newhart Show (1961-62, variety), The Entertainers, The Bob Newhart Show (1972-78, sitcom), Newhart, Bob, George & Leo. Movies: Thursday's Game, Marathon, The Entertainers.

NEWLAND, JOHN
Actor, Director. b. Cincinnati, OH, Nov. 23, 1917. Began as a singer-dancer in vaudeville and on B'way; many TV appearances, especially as host of One Step Beyond. Actor, dir., Robert Montgomery Show, My Lover, My Son. Turned to full-time dir. and prod. in the 1960's.
PICTURES: T-Men, Nora Prentiss, Gentleman's Agreement, Let's Live a Little, Homicide for Three, The Challenge, 13 Lead Soldiers, Bulldog Drummond, That Night!, The Violators, The Spy With My Face, Hush-a-Bye Murder, Purgatory, My Lover My Son.
TELEVISION: Movies: The Gold Diggers, Crawlspace, The Deadly Hunt (also prod.), The Legend of Hillbilly John, Don't Be Afraid of the Dark, A Sensitive Passionate Man, Overboard, The Suicide's Wife, The Five of Me (exec. prod.), The Execution (exec. prod.), Arch of Triumph (prod.), Timestalkers (prod.), Too Good to Be True (prod.). Series: One Man's Family, Alfred Hitchcock Presents, Bachelor Father, Naked City, Robert Montgomery Presents, Alcoa Presents: One Step Beyond (host), Daniel Boone, Star Trek, Route 66, Dr. Kildare, Man from U.N.C.L.E., The Young Lawyers, Police Woman, Harry O, Executive Suite, The Next Step Beyond (host, prod.), Fantasy Island. Guest: Philco TV Playhouse, Eye Witness, Schlitz Playhouse of Stars, Loretta Young Show, Thriller.

NEWLEY, ANTHONY
Actor, Writer, Composer, Singer. b. Hackney, Eng., Sept. 24, 1931. Recipient of Male Singer of the Year Award, Las Vegas, 1972; Elected to Songwriters Hall of Fame, 1989. Gold records for composing Goldfinger, Candy Man, What Kind of Fool Am I?
THEATER: West End stage: Cranks (also dir., writer), Stop The World—I Want to Get Off (also composer with Leslie Bricusse, dir., writer; also NY), The Roar of the Greasepaint—The Smell of the Crowd (also composer with Bricusse, writer, dir.; also NY), The Good Old Bad Old Days (also composer with Bricusse, writer, dir.), Royalty Follies (also dir., writer), The World's Not Entirely to Blame, It's a Funny Old World We Live In. Regional: Chaplin, Once Upon a Song. British tour: Scrooge (1992-96).
PICTURES: Adventures of Dusty Bates (debut, 1946), Little Ballerina, The Guinea Pig, Vice Versa, Oliver Twist, Vote for Huggett, Don't Ever Leave Me, A Boy a Girl and a Bike, Golden Salamander, Madeleine, Highly Dangerous, Those People Next Door, Top of the Form, The Weak and the Wicked, Up to His Neck, Blue Peter, The Cockleshell Heroes, Battle of the River Plate, Above Us the Waves, Port Afrique, The Last Man to Hang, Fire Down Below, How to Murder a Rich Uncle, Good Companions, X the Unknown, High Flight, No Time to Die (Tank Force), The Man Inside, The Bandit of Zhobe, The Lady Is a Square, Idle on Parade, Killers of Kilimanjaro, Let's Get Married, Jazz Boat, In the Nick, The Small World of Sammy Lee, Play It Cool, Stop the World I Want to Get Off (songs only), Doctor Dolittle, Sweet November, Can Hieronymus Merkin Ever Forget Mercy Humppe and Find True Happiness? (also dir., s.p., songs), Willie Wonka and the Chocolate Factory (songs only), Summertree (dir. only), Mr. Quilp (also music), It Seemed Like a Good Idea at the Time, The Garbage Pail Kids Movie.

TELEVISION: Specials: Sunday Night Palladium, Saturday Spectaculars, Anthony Newley Special (London). Guest: The Johnny Darling Show, Hollywood Squares, Merv Griffin Show, The Tonight Show, Limited Partners, Fame, Magnum P.I., Alfred Hitchcock Theatre, Murder She Wrote, Simon & Simon. Movies: Malibu, Alice in Wonderland, Blade in Hong Kong, Stagecoach, Coins in a Fountain, Polly Comin' Home, Boris and Natasha, Anna Lee: Dupe. Series (BBC): Sammy, The Strange World of Gurney Slade, The Anthony Newley Show (1972).

NEWMAN, ALFRED S.
Executive. b. Brooklyn, NY, Nov. 16. e. NYU. Public relations work for Equitable Life Insurance, Trans World Airlines prior to joining Columbia Pictures in 1968 as writer in publicity dept.; named New York publicity mgr., 1970; national publicity mgr., 1972; joined MGM as East adv.-pub. dir., 1972; named director of adv., pub. and promotion, 1974; named v.p., worldwide adv., pub., promo., 1978; v.p., pub.-promo., MGM/UA, 1981. With 20th Century-Fox as v.p. adv.-pub.-promo. for TV & corporate, 1984-85; joined Rogers & Cowan as sr. v.p. & head of corporate entertainment, 1985; named exec. v.p., 1987; Oct. 1988 named pres. and CEO. Sterling Entertainment Co. and exec. v.p. worldwide marketing of parent co. MCEG; formed Newman & Associates, 1989; joined Hill and Knowl Entertainment as founding mng. dir., 1990. Re-opened Newman and Assocs., 1991.

NEWMAN, BARRY
Actor. b. Boston, MA, Nov. 7, 1938. e. Brandeis U.
PICTURES: Pretty Boy Floyd (debut, 1960), The Moving Finger, The Lawyer, Vanishing Point, The Salzburg Connection, Fear is the Key, City on Fire, Amy.
TELEVISION: Series: Petrocelli, Nightingales. Movies: Night Games, Sex and the Married Woman, King Crab, Fantasies, Having It All, Second Sight: A Love Story, Fatal Vision, My Two Loves, The Mirror Crack'd (BBC).

NEWMAN, DAVID
Composer. b. Los Angeles, CA, Mar. 11, 1954. e. USC (masters degree). Son of late composer Alfred Newman. Cousin of composer Randy Newman. Music director at Robert Redford's Sundance Institute.
PICTURES: Critters, Vendetta, The Kindred, My Demon Lover, Malone, Dragnet, Throw Momma from the Train, Pass the Ammo, Bill & Ted's Excellent Adventure, Disorganized Crime, The Brave Little Toaster, Heathers, Little Monsters, Gross Anatomy, The War of the Roses, Madhouse, Fire Birds, The Freshman, DuckTales: The Movie, Mr. Destiny, Meet the Applegates, The Marrying Man, Talent for the Game, Don't Tell Mom the Babysitter's Dead, Bill & Ted's Bogus Journey, Rover Dangerfield, Paradise, Other People's Money, The Runestone, The Mighty Ducks, Hoffa, The Sandlot, Coneheads, The Air Up There, My Father the Hero, The Flintstones, The Cowboy Way, Tommy Boy, Operation Dumbo Drop, The Phantom, Mathilda, The Nutty Professor, Out to Sea.

NEWMAN, DAVID
Writer. b. New York, NY, Feb. 4, 1937. e. U. of Michigan, M.S., 1959. Was writer-editor at Esquire Magazine where he met Robert Benton, an art director, and formed writing partnership. All early credits co-written with Benton; later ones with Leslie Newman and others.
THEATER: It's a Bird... It's a Plane... It's Superman (libretto), Oh! Calcutta (one sketch).
PICTURES: Bonnie and Clyde, There Was a Crooked Man, What's Up Doc?, Bad Company, Superman, Superman II, Jinxed, Still of the Night (co-story), Superman III, Sheena, Santa Claus, Moonwalker.

NEWMAN, EDWIN
News Correspondent. b. New York, NY, Jan. 25, 1919. Joined NBC News in 1952, based in N.Y. since 1961. Reports news on NBC-TV and often assigned to anchor instant specials. Has been substitute host on Today, appeared on Meet the Press and has reported NBC News documentaries. Series host: Edwin Newman Reporting, The Nation's Future, What's Happening to America, Comment, Speaking Freely, Television (PBS series).

NEWMAN, JOSEPH M.
Producer, Director, Writer. b. Logan, UT, Aug. 7, 1909. Started as office boy MGM, 1925; jobs in production dept. to 1931; asst. to George Hill, Ernst Lubitsch, etc., 1931-37; asstd. in organization of MGM British studios 1937; dir. short subjects 1938; dir. Crime Does Not Pay series 1938-42; Major in U.S. Army Signal Corps 1942-46; dir. 32 Army Pictorial Service Pictures. TV work includes Alfred Hitchcock Presents, Twilight Zone. Member of AMPAS, SDG Masons.
PICTURES: Northwest Rangers, Abandoned, Jungle Patrol, Great Dan Pitch, 711 Ocean Drive, Lucky Nick Cain, The Guy Who Came Back, Love Nest, Red Skies of Montana, Outcasts of Poker Flat, Pony Soldier, Dangerous Crossing, Human Jungle, Kiss of Fire, This Island Earth, Flight to Hong Kong, Fort Massacre, The Big Circus, Tarzan the Ape Man, King of the Roaring Twenties, Twenty Plus Two, The George Raft Story, Thunder of Drums.

NEWMAN, LARAINE
Actress. b. Los Angeles, CA, Mar. 2, 1952. Founding member of comedy troupe the Groundlings.
THEATER: *B'way*: Fifth of July.
PICTURES: Tunnelvision (debut, 1976), American Hot Wax, Wholly Moses!, Stardust Memories (unbilled), Perfect, Sesame Street Presents Follow That Bird (voice), Invaders from Mars, Problem Child 2, Witchboard II, Coneheads, The Flintstones, Jingle All the Way.
TELEVISION: *Series*: Manhattan Transfer, Saturday Night Live, Bone Chillers. *Guest*: George Burns Comedy Week, St. Elsewhere, Laverne & Shirley, Alfred Hitchcock Presents, Amazing Stories, Faerie Tale Theatre (The Little Mermaid), Twilight Zone, Dream On, Likely Suspects, Friends, Chicago Hope, Third Rock From the Sun. *Specials*: Steve Martin's Best Show Ever, The Lily Tomlin Special, Bob Ray Jane Laraine & Gilda. *Movies*: Her Life as a Man, This Wife for Hire. *Voice*: Pinky and the Brain, Sylvester & Tweetie, The Tick, Rapunzel, Superman, Wonder Woman.

NEWMAN, NANETTE
Actress, Writer. b. Northampton, Eng., 1934. m. prod.-dir.-writer Bryan Forbes. Ent. films in 1946 and TV in 1951.
AUTHOR: God Bless Love, That Dog, Reflections, The Root Children, Amy Rainbow, Pigalev, Archie, Christmas Cookbook, Summer Cookbook, Small Beginnings, Bad Baby, Entertaining with Nanette Newman and Her Daughters, Charlie the Noisy Caterpillar, Sharing, The Pig Who Never Was, ABC, 123, Cooking for Friends, Spider the Horrible Cat, There's a Bear in the Bath, Karmic Mothers (Teleplay), There's a Bear in the Classroom, The Importance of Being Ernest, The Earwig, Take 3 Cooks.
PICTURES: The Personal Affair, The League of Gentlemen, The Rebel, Twice Around the Daffodils, The L-Shaped Room, The Wrong Arm of the Law, Of Human Bondage, Seance on a Wet Afternoon, The Wrong Box, The Whisperers, Deadfall, The Madwoman of Chaillot, Captain Nemo and the Underwater City, The Raging Moon (Long Ago Tomorrow), The Stepford Wives, It's a 2'2" Above the Ground World (The Love Ban), Man at the Top, International Velvet, Restless Natives, The Mystery of Edwin Drood.
TELEVISION: The Glorious Days, The Wedding Veil, Broken Honeymoon, At Home, Trial by Candlelight, Diary of Samuel Pepys, Faces in the Dark, Balzac (BBC), Fun Food Factory, TV series, Stay with Me Till Morning, Let There Be Love (series), West Country Tales, Jessie, Late Expectations (series), Ideal Cooks (presenter), The Endless Game.

NEWMAN, PAUL
Actor, Director, Producer. b. Cleveland, OH, Jan. 26, 1925. m. actress Joanne Woodward. e. Kenyon Coll., Yale Sch. of Drama, The Actors Studio. Formed First Artists Prod. Co., Ltd. 1969 with Sidney Poitier, Steve McQueen and Barbra Streisand. Appeared in documentaries: King: A Filmed Record... Memphis to Montgomery, Hello Actors Studio. Recipient of special Academy Award, 1986; Jean Hersholt Humanitarian Award, 1994.
THEATER: *B'way*: Picnic, The Desperate Hours, Sweet Bird of Youth, Baby Want a Kiss.
PICTURES: The Silver Chalice (debut, 1954), The Rack, Somebody Up There Likes Me, The Helen Morgan Story, Until They Sail, The Long Hot Summer, The Left-Handed Gun, Cat on a Hot Tin Roof, Rally 'Round the Flag Boys!, The Young Philadelphians, From the Terrace, Exodus, The Hustler, Paris Blues, Sweet Bird of Youth, Hemingway's Adventures of a Young Man, Hud, A New Kind of Love, The Prize, What a Way to Go!, The Outrage, Harper, Lady L, Torn Curtain, Hombre, Cool Hand Luke, The Secret War of Harry Frigg, Rachel Rachel (dir. prod. only), Winning, Butch Cassidy and the Sundance Kid, WUSA (also prod.), Sometimes a Great Notion (also dir.), Pocket Money, The Life and Times of Judge Roy Bean, The Effect of Gamma Rays on Man-in-the-Moon Marigolds (dir., prod. only), The Mackintosh Man, The Sting, The Towering Inferno, The Drowning Pool, Buffalo Bill and the Indians or Sitting Bull's History Lesson, Silent Movie, Slap Shot, Quintet, When Time Ran Out..., Fort Apache the Bronx, Absence of Malice, The Verdict, Harry and Son (also dir., co-s.p., co-prod.), The Color of Money (Academy Award, 1986), The Glass Menagerie (dir. only), Fat Man & Little Boy, Blaze, Mr. and Mrs. Bridge, The Hudsucker Proxy, Nobody's Fool.
TELEVISION: *Guest* (on 1950's anthology series): The Web (Bell of Damon, One for the Road), Goodyear TV Playhouse (Guilty is the Stranger), Danger (Knife in the Dark), Appointment With Adventure (Five in Judgment), Philco TV Playhouse (Death of Billy the Kid), Producers Showcase (Our Town), Kaiser Aluminum Hour (The Army Game, Rag Jungle), U.S. Steel Hour (Bang the Drum Slowly), Playhouse 90 (The 80-Yard Run). *Movie* (dir. only): The Shadow Box.

NEWMAN, RANDY
Composer, Singer. b. Los Angeles, CA, Nov. 28, 1943. Nephew of musicians Lionel and Alfred Newman. Studied music at UCLA. Debut album: Randy Newman Creates Something New Under the Sun. Songs include Short People, I Think It's Gonna Rain Today, I Love L.A. Was music director on film Performance. Began writing songs and scores for films in 1971 with The Pursuit of Happiness. Composed opera, Faust.

PICTURES: Pursuit of Happiness, Cold Turkey, Ragtime, The Natural, Three Amigos (also co-wrote s.p.), Parenthood, Avalon, Awakenings, The Paper, Maverick, James and the Giant Peach, The Quest, Michael, Cat's Don't Dance, Pleasantville, A Bug's Life.

NEWMAN, SYDNEY
Producer, Writer. O. C., F.R.S.A., F.R.T.S. for Canadian Film Development Corp. b. Toronto, Canada, Apr. 1, 1917. Studied painting, drawing, commercial art at Central Tech. Sch. To Hollywood in 1938. Joined National Film Board of Canada under John Grierson. Prod. over 300 shorts. Later became exec. prod. all Canadian government cinema films, 1947-52; Canadian Broadcasting Corp., 1952, as dir. outside broadcasts, features and documentaries. Later became drama sup. and prod. General Motors Theatre. Joined ABC-TV in England, 1958 as sup. of drama and prod. of Armchair Theatre: Head of Drama Group, TV, BBC, 1963. Commissioned and prod. first TV plays by Arthur Hailey, Harold Pinter, Mordecai Richler, Alun Owen, Angus Wilson, Peter Luke. Devised, created Dr. Who (1962) and The Avengers (1959). Fellow of Society of Film & TV Arts, 1968; Fellow of Royal Television Society, 1990. Prod. Associated British Pictures. SFTA award 1968; Zeta award, Writers Guild, Gt. Btn., 1970. 1970, special advisor, ch. dir., Broadcast Programmes branch, Canadian Radio & TV Commission, Ottawa. 1970, appt. Canadian Govt. Film Commissioner and chmn., National Film Board of Canada; Trustee, National Arts Centre, Ottawa; bd. mem., Canadian Broadcasting Corporation, Canadian Film Development Corp. Recognition Award from S.M.P.T.E. (USA), Canadian Picture Pioneers Special Award. Special Advisor on Film to the Secretary of State for Canada, 1975-77; pres., Sydney Newman Enterprises. 1981, made officer of the Order of Canada. Left Canadian Film Develop. Corp. 1983. At present Creative Consultant to film & tv producers. (d. Dec. 30, 1997)

NEWMAR, JULIE
Actress. r.n. Julie Newmeyer. b. Hollywood, CA, Aug. 16, 1933. e. UCLA. Studied acting with Lee Strasberg at the Actor's Studio. Holds patent for special panty hose design. Appeared in George Michael video Too Funky.
THEATER: *NY*: Silk Stockings, Li'l Abner, The Marriage-Go-Round (Tony Award, 1959). *Other*: In the Boom Boom Room (L.A.), Damn Yankees, Irma La Douce, Guys and Dolls, Dames at Sea, Stop the World, The Women.
PICTURES: Just for You (debut, 1952), Seven Brides for Seven Brothers, The Rookie, Li'l Abner, The Marriage-Go-Round, For Love or Money, McKenna's Gold, The Maltese Bippy, Hysterical, Streetwalkin', Body Beat, Nudity Required, Ghosts Can't Do It, Oblivion, To Wong Foo—Thanks for Everything—Julie Newmar.
TELEVISION: *Series*: My Living Doll, Batman (frequent guest; as Catwoman). *Movies*: McCloud: Who Killed Miss U.S.A.?, The Feminist and the Fuzz, A Very Missing Person, Terraces. *Guest*: Omnibus, Route 66, Jonathan Winters Show, Beverly Hillbillies, The Monkees, Love American Style, Love Boat, Half Nelson, Fantasy Island, Hart to Hart, Buck Rogers.

NEWTON-JOHN, OLIVIA
Actress, Singer. b. Cambridge, Eng. Sept. 26, 1948. m. actor Matt Lattanzi. Brought up in Melbourne, Australia, where won first talent contest at 15, winning trip to England. Stayed there 2 yrs. performing as part of duo with Australian girl singer Pat Carroll (Farrar) in cabarets and on TV. Started recording; several hit records. Became a regular guest on TV series, It's Cliff Richard. Gained world-wide prominence as singer, winning several Grammys and other music awards. 1983 opened Koala Blue, U.S. Clothing Stores featuring Australian style clothes and goods.
PICTURES: Tomorrow (debut, 1970), Grease, Xanadu, Two of a Kind.
TELEVISION: *Specials*: Olivia Newton-John: Let's Get Physical, Standing Room Only: Olivia Newton-John, Olivia Newton-John in Australia, Christmas in Washington. *Movies*: A Mom for Christmas, A Christmas Romance.

NEY, RICHARD
Actor, Writer, Producer, Financier. b. New York, NY, Nov. 12, 1917. e. Columbia U., B.A., 1940. Acted in RCA TV demonstration, New York World's Fair; on stage in Life with Father. Was Naval Officer in WWII. Financial advisor consultant, Richard Ney and Associates; financial advisor, lecturer; author, The Wall Street Jungle, The Wall Street Gang, Making it in the Market.
PICTURES: Mrs. Miniver, The War Against Mrs. Hadley, The Late George Apley, Ivy, Joan of Arc, The Fan, Secret of St. Ives, Lovable Cheat, Babes in Bagdad, Miss Italia, Sergeant and The Spy, Midnight Lace, The Premature Burial.

NICHOLAS, DENISE
Actress, Writer. b. Detroit, MI, July 12, 1946. e. USC.
THEATER: Performances with the Free Southern Theatre, The Negro Ensemble Company, Crossroads Theatre Co., New Federal Theatre, Los Angeles Theatre Company, Media Forum. PICTURES: Ghost Dad, Capricorn One, A Piece of the Action, Let's Do It Again, Blacula, The Soul of Nigger Charley, Marvin and Tige.

TELEVISION: *Series*: Room 222, Baby I'm Back, In the Heat of the Night (also wrote 6 episodes). *Movies*: incl. The Sophisticated Gents, On Thin Ice, Mother's Day, Ring of Passion, In the Heat of the Night. *Guest*: The Cosby Show, A Different World, Benson, Magnum P.I., The Paper Chase, Police Story, Living Single, many others.
AUTHOR: Buses (one act play), Augustine, Myrtle, Marty and Me (short story, Essence Magazine), various published articles and poetry.

NICHOLS, FRED R.
Executive. Chairman, CEO and President, TCA Cable TV, Inc.

NICHOLS, MIKE
Director, Producer, Performer. r.n. Michael Igor Peschkowsky. b. Berlin, Germany, Nov. 6, 1931. m. news correspondent Diane Sawyer. e. U. of Chicago. Member of Compass Players; later teamed with Elaine May in night clubs.
THEATER: *Director*: Barefoot in the Park (Tony Award), The Knack, Luv (Tony Award), The Odd Couple, The Apple Tree, The Little Foxes, Plaza Suite (Tony Award), Uncle Vanya, The Prisoner of 2nd Avenue (Tony Award), Streamers, Comedians, The Gin Game, Drinks Before Dinner, Annie (prod. only; Tony Award), The Real Thing (2 Tony Awards), Hurlyburly, Social Security, Waiting for Godot, Elliot Loves, Death and the Maiden.
PICTURES: *Director*: Who's Afraid of Virginia Woolf? (debut, 1966), The Graduate (Academy Award, 1967), Catch-22, Carnal Knowledge, The Day of the Dolphin, The Fortune, Gilda Live, Silkwood (also co-prod.), The Longshot (exec. prod. only), Heartburn, Biloxi Blues, Working Girl, Postcards From the Edge, Regarding Henry, The Remains of the Day (co-prod. only), Wolf, The Birdcage, Primary Colors.
TELEVISION: *Specials*: B'way, An Evening with Mike Nichols and Elaine May. *Exec. prod.*: Family, The Thorns.

NICHOLS, NICHELLE
Actress. b. Robbins, IL, 1936. Started singing and dancing with Duke Ellington and his band at age 16. Was appointee to the bd. of dirs. of the National Space Institute in the 1970's; recruited women and minority astronauts for Space Shuttle Program. Received NASA's distinguished Public Service Award. Member of the bd. of govs. of the National Space Society. One of the original founders of KWANZA Foundation. Awarded star on Hollywood Walk of Fame (1992). *Autobiography*: Beyond (1994). Novels: Saturn's Child (1995), Saturna's Quest (1996).
THEATER: Horowitz and Mrs. Washington, Reflections (one woman show). Nominated for Sarah Siddons Award for performances in Kicks and Company, The Blacks.
PICTURES: Porgy and Bess, Mr. Buddwing, Made in Paris, Truck Turner, Star Trek: The Motion Picture, Star Trek II: The Wrath of Khan, Star Trek III: The Search for Spock, Star Trek IV: The Voyage Home, Star Trek V: The Final Frontier, Star Trek VI: The Undiscovered Country.
TELEVISION: *Series*: Star Trek. *Guest*: The Lieutenant, Tarzan. *Special*: Antony and Cleopatra.

NICHOLSON, JACK
Actor, Producer, Director, Writer. b. Neptune, NJ, April 22, 1937. Began career in cartoon department of MGM. Made acting debut in Hollywood stage production of Tea and Sympathy. Made directing debut with Drive, He Said (1971). Has received 10 Academy Award nominations for acting. Recipient of American Film Institute's Life Achievement Award, 1994.
PICTURES: Cry Baby Killer (debut, 1958), Too Soon to Love, Little Shop of Horrors, Studs Lonigan, The Wild Ride, The Broken Land, The Raven, The Terror, Thunder Island (co-s.p. only), Back Door to Hell, Flight to Fury (also s.p.), Ensign Pulver, Ride in the Whirlwind (also co-prod., s.p.), The Shooting (also co-prod., s.p.), St. Valentine's Day Massacre, Rebel Rousers, Hell's Angels on Wheels, The Trip (s.p. only), Head (also co-prod., co-s.p.), Psych-Out, Easy Rider, On a Clear Day You Can See Forever, Five Easy Pieces, Carnal Knowledge, Drive He Said (dir., co-prod., co-s.p. only), A Safe Place, The King of Marvin Gardens, The Last Detail, Chinatown, Tommy, The Passenger, The Fortune, One Flew Over the Cuckoo's Nest (Academy Award, 1975), The Missouri Breaks, The Last Tycoon, Goin' South (also dir.), The Shining, The Postman Always Rings Twice, Reds, The Border, Terms of Endearment (Academy Award, best supporting actor, 1983), Prizzi's Honor, Heartburn, The Witches of Eastwick, Broadcast News, Ironweed, Batman, The Two Jakes (also dir.), Man Trouble, A Few Good Men, Hoffa, Wolf, The Crossing Guard, Mars Attacks!, The Evening Star, As Good As It Gets (Acad. Award, Golden Globe Award, Best Actor, 1997).
TELEVISION: *Guest*: Tales of Wells Fargo, Cheyenne, Hawaiian Eye, Dr. Kildare, Andy Griffith Show, Guns of Will Sonnett.

NICHOLSON, WILLIAM
Writer. b. England, 1948. e. Cambridge U. Was graduate trainee at BBC, becoming prod./dir./writer of over 40 documentaries.
THEATER: Shadowlands, Map of the Heart.
PICTURES: Sarafina!, Shadowlands (Acad. Award nom.), Nell, First Knight, Firelight (also dir.), Gray Owl.
TELEVISION: *Exec. Prod.*: Everyman, Global Report, Lovelaw. *Writer*: Martin Luther, New World, Life Story, The Vision, Shadowlands, Sweet as You Are, The Race for the Double Helix, The March, A Private Matter, Crime of the Century.

NICKSAY, DAVID
Executive, Producer. e. Mass., Hampshire Coll. Entered industry through Directors Guild of America's training program, apprenticing on Rich Man Poor Man and rising to second asst. dir. on Oh, God. Producer of many TV projects and theatrical films with Edgar Scherick prod. co. In 1986, joined Paramount Pictures as v.p., prod., for M.P. Group. Assoc. prod., prod. mgr.: I'm Dancing as Fast as I Can. Became sr. v.p., prod. Paramount, M.P. Group, 1987; resigned 1989 to become pres. and head of prod. at Morgan Creek Prods. Mem. of bd.
PICTURES: The One & Only, When I am King, Mrs. Soffel, Lucas, Young Guns II, Pacific Heights, Robin Hood:Prince of Thieves, Freejak, White Sands, Big Top Pee-Wee, Summer School, Coming to America, The Untouchables, Scrooged, Star Trek V: The Final Frontier, Major League, We're No Angels, Harlem Nights, The Two Jakes, Stay Tuned, Addams Family Values, Up Close and Personal, Flubber, The Negotiator.
TELEVISION: Call to Glory (pilot), Little Gloria Happy at Last.

NICOL, ALEX
Actor, Director. b. Ossining, NY, Jan. 20, 1919. e. Fagin Sch. of Dramatic Arts, Actor's Studio. U.S. Cavalry.
THEATER: Forward the Heart, Sundown Beach, Hamlet, Richard II, South Pacific, Mr. Roberts, Cat on a Hot Tin Roof.
PICTURES: The Sleeping City, Tomahawk, Target Unknown, Air Cadet, Raging Tide, Meet Danny Wilson, Red Ball Express, Because of You, Redhead From Wyoming, Lone Hand, Law and Order, Champ for a Day, Black Glove, Heat Wave, About Mrs. Leslie, Dawn at Socorro, Strategic Air Command, Man from Laramie, Great Day in the Morning, The Gilded Cage, Sincerely Yours, Five Branded Women, Via Margutta, Under 10 Flags, Gunfighters at Casa Grande, The Screaming Skull (dir.), Then There Were Three (dir.), The Brutal Land, Bloody Mama, Homer, Point of Terror (dir.), The Night God Screamed, A-P-E.

NIELSEN, LESLIE
Actor. b. Regina, Sask., Canada, Feb. 11, 1926. e. Victoria H.S., Edmonton. Disc jockey, announcer for Canadian radio station; studied at Lorne Greene's Acad. of Radio Arts, Toronto and at Neighborhood Playhouse; N.Y. radio actor summer stock. Toured country in one-man show, Darrow, 1979. *Author*: The Naked Truth (1993), Leslie Nielsen's Stupid Little Golf Book (1995).
PICTURES: Ransom (debut, 1956), Forbidden Planet, The Vagabond King, The Opposite Sex, Hot Summer Night, Tammy and the Bachelor, The Sheepman, Night Train To Paris, Harlow, Dark Intruder, Beau Geste, The Plainsman, Gunfight in Abilene, The Reluctant Astronaut, Rosie!, Counterpoint, Dayton's Devils, How to Commit Marriage, Change of Mind, Four Rode Out, The Resurrection of Zachary Wheeler, The Poseidon Adventure, And Millions Will Die, Day of the Animals, Viva Knievel!, The Amsterdam Kill, City on Fire, Airplane!, Prom Night, The Creature Wasn't Nice, Wrong Is Right, Creepshow, The Patriot, Soul Man, Nightstick, Nuts, Home Is Where the Hart Is, The Naked Gun: From the Files of Police Squad!, Dangerous Curves, Repossessed, The Naked Gun 2 1/2: The Smell of Fear, All I Want for Christmas, Surf Ninjas, Naked Gun 33 1/3: The Final Insult, Dracula: Dead and Loving It, Spy Hard (also co-exec. prod.).
TELEVISION: *Series*: The New Breed, Peyton Place, The Protectors, Bracken's World, The Explorers (host), Police Squad, Shaping Up. *Guest*: Studio One, Kraft, Philco Playhouse, Robert Montgomery Presents, Pulitzer Prize Playhouse, Suspense, Danger, Justice, Man Behind the Badge, Ben Casey, Walt Disney (Swamp Fox), Wild Wild West, The Virginian, The Loner. *Special*: Death of a Salesman. *Movies*: See How They Run, Shadow Over Elveron, Hawaii Five-O (pilot), Companions in Nightmare, Trial Run, Deadlock, Night Slaves, The Aquarians, Hauser's Memory, Incident in San Francisco, They Call It Murder, Snatched, The Letters, The Return of Charlie Chan (Happiness Is a Warm Clue), Can Ellen Be Saved?, Brink's: The Great Robbery, Little Mo, Institute for Revenge, OHMS, The Night the Bridge Fell Down, Cave-In!, Reckless Disregard, Blade in Hong Kong, Fatal Confession: A Father Dowling Mystery, Chance of a Lifetime. *Mini-Series*: Backstairs at the White House.

NIMOY, LEONARD
Actor, Director. b. Boston, MA, Mar. 26, 1931. e. Boston Col. Joined Pasadena Playhouse. Along with active career in films, TV and stage, has been writer and photographer. Author of three books on photography and poetry, as well as autobiography, I Am Not Spock. Has also been speaker on college lecture circuit. Created comic book Primortals.
THEATER: Full Circle, Equus, Sherlock Holmes, Vincent (also dir., writer; one-man show), Love Letters.
PICTURES: Queen for a Day, Rhubarb, Francis Goes to West Point, Them!, Satan's Satellite's (edited from serial Zombies of the Stratosphere), The Brain Eaters, The Balcony, Catlow, Invasion of the Body Snatchers, Star Trek—The Motion Picture, Star Trek II: The Wrath of Khan, Star Trek III: The Search for Spock (also dir.), Transformers: The Movie (voice),

Star Trek IV: The Voyage Home (also. dir., co-story), Three Men and a Baby (dir. only), The Good Mother (dir. only), Star Trek V: The Final Frontier, Funny About Love (dir. only), Star Trek VI: The Undiscovered Country (also exec. prod., co-story), Holy Matrimony (dir. only), The Pagemaster (voice), Jellies & Other Ocean Drifters (voice), Carpati: 50 Miles, 50 Years (voice), A Life Apart: Hasidism in America (voice), Sinbad: Beyond the Veil of Mists.
TELEVISION: *Series*: Star Trek, Mission: Impossible, In Search Of... (host), Outer Limits. *Movies*: Assault on the Wayne, Baffled, The Alpha Caper, The Missing Are Deadly, The Sun Also Rises, A Woman Called Golda, Never Forget (also co-prod.), Bonanza: Under Attack, David, Alien Voices, Brave New World. *Mini-Series*: Marco Polo. *Guest*: Bonanza, Twilight Zone, Perry Mason, Laramie, Wagon Train, Man From U.N.C.L.E., The Virginian, Get Smart, Night Gallery, Columbo, T.J. Hooker, Star Trek: The Next Generation, The Simpsons (voice). *Special*: Seapower: A Global Journey (narrator). *Episode Dir.*: Deadly Games.

NIVEN, DAVID, JR.
Executive. b. London, England, Dec. 15, 1942. e. Univ. of Grenoble; London Sch. of Economics. Joined William Morris Agency in Beverly Hills in 1963. Transferred same yr. to New York; over next five yrs. worked for agency's European offices in Rome, Madrid and London. 1968-72, Columbia Pictures' U.K. office as v.p. of production; 1972-76, mng. dir. and v.p. of Paramount Pictures in U.K. 1976 became indep. prod. West Coast corresp. & interviewer for Inside Edition. Appeared as actor in films Lisa, Cool Surface, and on tv series, America's Most Wanted. 1993, became chmn. of R.A.D.D. (Recording-Artists Against Drunk Driving)
PICTURES: *Producer*: The Eagle Has Landed, Escape to Athena, Monsignor, Better Late Than Never, Kidco, That's Dancing!, Pyscho Cop II, Girl With the Hungry Eyes, Cool Surface (also actor), Blue Flame.
TELEVISION: The Night They Saved Christmas (exec. prod., s.p.), Cary Grant: A Celebration, Minnelli on Minnelli, The Wonderful Wizard of Oz. Panelist: To Tell the Truth (1991-92).

NIX, WILLIAM PATTERSON
Executive. b. Philadelphia, PA, April 10, 1948. e. Georgetown U., A.B., 1970; Antioch, M.A., 1971; Hofstra U. Sch. of Law, J.D., 1976; NYU Sch. of Law, LL.M., 1979. Formerly., v.p., Cartier, Frankfurt, Garbus, Klein & Selz, P.C., Entertainment & Media co. V.P. bus. affairs, NBA Properties Inc., NY. Prior to that, was sr. v.p. of both the Motion Picture Association of America and Motion Picture Export Assoc. of America. Chmn. of MPAA committee on copyright and literary property matters, and COO of film industry's intellectual property protection division (1976-91). Lifetime member, AMPAS.

NIXON, AGNES
Writer, Producer. b. Nashville, TN, Dec. 10, 1927. e. Northwestern Sch. of Speech, Catholic U. Landed 1st job writing radio serial dialogue (Woman in White, 1948-51), three days after graduating from college. Became a freelance writer for TV dramatic series. Guest writer, New York Times 1968-72, and TV Guide. Trustee, Television Conference Inst., 1979-82. Received National Acad. of Television Arts & Sciences' Trustee Award, 1981; Junior Diabetic Assn. Super Achiever Award, 1982; Communicator Award for American Women in Radio and Television, 1984. Gold Plate Award, American Acad. Achievement, 1993; inducted into TV Hall of Fame, 1993. Popular Culture Lifetime Achievement Award, 1995; Public Service Award, Johns Hopkins Hospital, 1995. Humanitarian Award, National Osteoporosis Foundation, 1996. Member, Int'l Radio & TV Society; Nat'l Acad. of TV Arts & Sciences; bd. of Harvard Foundation; The Friars Club.
TELEVISION: *Series writer*: Studio One, Philco Playhouse, Robert Montgomery Presents, Somerset Maugham Theatre, Armstrong Circle Theatre, Hallmark Hall of Fame, My True Story, Cameo Theatre, Search For Tomorrow, As The World Turns, Guiding Light, Another World. *Series creator-producer*: One Life to Live, All My Children, Loving. *Mini-Series*: The Manions of America.

NIXON, CYNTHIA
Actress. b. New York, NY, April 9, 1966. e. Barnard Coll. Started stage career at age 14.
THEATER: *B'way*: The Philadelphia Story (Theatre World Award), Hurlyburly, The Real Thing, The Heidi Chronicles, Angels in America: Millenium Aproaches/Perestroika, Indiscretions. *Off-B'way*: Moonchildren, Romeo and Juliet, The Balcony Scene, Servy N Bernice 4-Ever, On the Bum, The Illusion, The Scarlet Letter.
PICTURES: Little Darlings (debut, 1980), Tattoo, Prince of the City, I Am the Cheese, Amadeus, The Manhattan Project, Let It Ride, Addams Family Values, The Pelican Brief, Baby's Day Out, Marvin's Room.
TELEVISION: *Movies*: The Murder of Mary Phagan, The Love She Sought, Love Lies and Murder, Face of a Stranger. *Specials*: The Fifth of July, Kiss Kiss Dahlings, Tanner '88. *Guest*: The Equalizer, Gideon Oliver, Murder She Wrote.

NOIRET, PHILIPPE
Actor. b. Lille, France, Oct. 1, 1930. e. Centre Dramatique de l'Ouest. Company member of Theatre National Populaire 1951-63; nightclub entertainer before film debut in Agnes Varda's short, La Pointe Court. B'way debut Lorenzaccio (1958).
PICTURES: Gigi (debut, 1948), Olivia, Agence Matrimoniale, La Pointe Courte, Ravissante, Zazie dans le Metro, The Billionaire, Crime Does Not Pay, Therese Desqueyroux, Cyrano and D'Artagnan, None But the Lonely Spy, Death Where Is Thy Victory?, Monsieur, Les Copains, Lady L, La Vie de Chateau, Tender Scoundrel, The Night of the Generals, Woman Times Seven, The Assassination Bureau, Mr. Freedom, Justine, Topaz, Clerambard, Give Her the Moon, A Room in Paris, Murphy's War, A Time for Loving, Five-Leaf Clover, The Assassination, Sweet Deception, Poil de Carotte, The French Conspiracy, The Serpent, The Day of the Jackel, La Grande Bouffe, Let Joy Reign Supreme, The Old Gun, The Judge and the Assassin, A Woman at Her Window, Purple Taxi, Dear Inspector, Due Pezzi di Pane, Who Is Killing the Great Chefs of Europe?, Death Watch, Street of the Crane's Foot, A Week's Vacation, Heads or Tails, Three Brothers, Kill Birgitt Haas, Coup de Torchon, L'Etoile du Nord, Amici, Miei, Atto 2, L'Africain, A Friend of Vincents, Le Grand Carnival, Fort Saganne, Les Ripoux, Souvenirs, Next Summer, The Gold-Rimmed Glasses, No Downing Allowed, My New Partner, 'Round Midnight, Let's Hope It's a Girl, The 4th Power, The Thrill of Genius, The Secret Wife, Twist Again in Moscow, Masks, The Family Chouans!, IL Frullo del Passero, Young Toscanini, The Return of the Musketeers, Moments of Love, Cinema Paradiso, Life and Nothing But, Palermo Connection, My New Partner 2, Uranus, I Don't Kiss, The Two of Us, Especially on Sunday, The Postman, Grosse Fatigue, D'Artagnan's Daughter, The King of Paris, Marianna Ucria, Le Grand ducs, Fantome avec Chauffeur, Soleil, Les Palmes de M. Schutz, On Guard.

NOLTE, NICK
Actor. b. Omaha, NB, Feb. 8, 1941. Attended 5 colleges in 4 yrs. on football scholarships, including Pasadena City Coll. and Phoenix City Coll. Joined Actors Inner Circle at Phoenix and appeared in Orpheus Descending, After the Fall, Requiem For a Nun. Did stock in Colorado. In 1968, joined Old Log Theatre in Minneapolis and after 3 yrs. left for New York, appearing at Cafe La Mama. Went to L.A. and did plays The Last Pad and Picnic, as well as several guest spots on TV series before big break in mini-series, Rich Man Poor Man as Tom Jordache.
PICTURES: Return to Macon County (debut, 1975), The Deep, Who'll Stop the Rain, North Dallas Forty, Heart Beat, Cannery Row, 48 HRS., Under Fire, Teachers, Grace Quigley, Down and Out in Beverly Hills, Extreme Prejudice, Weeds, Three Fugitives, New York Stories (Life Lessons), Farewell to the King, Everybody Wins, Q&A, Another 48 HRS, Cape Fear, The Prince of Tides (Golden Globe Award, Acad. Award nom.), The Player, Lorenzo's Oil, I'll Do Anything, Blue Chips, I Love Trouble, Jefferson in Paris, Mulholland Falls, Nightwatch, Mother Night, Afterglow, Affliction, U-Turn, Thin Red Line, Breakfast of Champions.
TELEVISION: *Mini-Series*: Rich Man Poor Man. *Movies*: Winter Kill (pilot), The California Kid, Death Sentence, The Runaway Barge. *Guest*: Medical Center, Streets of San Francisco, The Rookies.

NOONAN, TOM
Actor, Writer. b. Greenwich, CT, Apr. 12, 1951. e. Yale.
THEATER: Buried Child (Off-B'way debut, 1978), Invitational Farmyard, The Breakers, Five of Us, Spookhouse, What Happened Was (also writer), Wifey (also writer).
PICTURES: Heaven's Gate, Wolfen, Eddie Macon's Run, Easy Money, The Man With One Red Shoe, F/X, Manhunter, The Monster Squad, Mystery Train, Robocop 2, Last Action Hero, What Happened Was (also dir., s.p.), The Wife (also composer, s.p., & dir.). Heat, Phoenix, The Astronaut's Wife.
TELEVISION: *Mini-series*: Monsters, North & South II. *Movies*: Rage, Red Wind (s.p.), The 10 Million Dollar Getaway, Heaven & Hell: North & South Book III. *Guest*: X-Files.

NORMAN, BARRY
Writer/presenter. b. London. Early career as show business editor London Daily Mail; humorous columnist for The Guardian. Entered TV as writer, presenter FILM 1972-81 and 1983-93. 1982, presenter Omnibus. Writer/host: The Hollywood Greats and Talking Pictures. Radio work incl.: Going Places, The News Quiz, Breakaway, The Chip Shop.
AUTHOR: The Hollywood Greats, Movie Greats, Film Greats, Talking Pictures, 100 Best Films of the Century. Novels: A Series of Defeats, Have a Nice Day, Sticky Wicket, The Bird Dog Tapes.
PICTURES: Blues for the Avatar (dir.).

NORRIS, CHUCK
Actor. r.n. Carlos Ray. b. Ryan, OK, Mar. 10, 1940. World middle weight karate champion 1968-74. Owner of LA karate schools which led to film career.
PICTURES: The Wrecking Crew (debut, 1969), Slaughter in San Francisco, Return of the Dragon, The Student Teachers, Breaker! Breaker!, Good Guys Wear Black, Game of Death, A Force of One, The Octagon, An Eye for an Eye, Silent Rage, Forced Vengeance, Lone Wolf McQuade, Missing in Action, Missing in Action 2, Code of Silence, Invasion U.S.A. (also co-s.p.), Delta Force, Firewalker, Braddock: Missing in Action III (also co-s.p.), Hero and the Terror, Delta Force II, The Hitman, Sidekicks (also co-exec. prod.), Hellbound, Top Dog.
TELEVISION: Series: Chuck Norris's Karate Kommandos (animated series, voice), Walker: Texas Ranger (also co-exec. prod.). Special: The Ultimate Stuntman: A Tribute to Dar Robinson (host), Wind in the Wire.

NORTH, SHEREE
Actress. r.n. Dawn Bethel. b. Los Angeles, CA, Jan. 17, 1933. e. Hollywood H.S. Amateur dancer with USO at 11; prof. debut at 13; many TV appearances
THEATER: B'way: Hazel Flagg (Drama Desk Award, Critics' Award), I Can Get It For You Wholesale. Other: Madwoman of Chaillot, ... And to My Daughter, Stepping Out, California Dogfight, 6 Rms. Riv Vue, Turnstyle, Thursday Is a Good Night, Dutchman, Private Lives, Irma La Douce, Bye Bye Birdie, Your Own Thing, Can-Can, Two for the Seesaw, Breaking Up the Act, etc. Also directed and produced several productions.
PICTURES: Excuse My Dust, Here Come the Girls, Living It Up, How to Be Very Very Popular, The Lieutenant Wore Skirts, The Best Things in Life Are Free, Way to the Gold, No Down Payment, In Love and War, Mardi Gras, Destination Inner Space, Madigan, The Gypsy Moths, The Trouble With Girls, Lawman, The Organization, Charley Varick, The Outfit, Breakout, The Shootist, Telefon, Rabbit Test, Telefon, Cold Dog Soup, Defenseless.
TELEVISION: Series: Big Eddie, I'm a Big Girl Now, Bay City Blues. Guest: Hawaii 5-0, Kojak, Family, Archie Bunker's Place, Murder She Wrote, Golden Girls, Matlock, Seinfeld, Hunter, Magnum P.I., many others. Movies: Then Came Bronson (pilot), Vanished, Rolling Man, Trouble Comes to Town, Snatched, Maneater, Key West, Winter Kill, A Shadow in the Streets, Most Wanted, The Night They Took Miss Beautiful, A Real American Hero, Amateur Night at the Dixie Bar and Grill, Women in White, Portrait of a Stripper, Marilyn: The Untold Story, Legs, Scorned and Swindled, Jake Spanner—Private Eye, Dead on the Money.

NOSSECK, NOEL
Director, Producer. b. Los Angeles, CA, Dec. 10, 1943. Began as editor with David Wolper Prods; made documentaries; turned to features.
PICTURES: Director: Best Friends (also prod.), Youngblood, Dreamer, King of the Mountain.
TELEVISION: Movies: Return of the Rebels, The First Time, Night Partners, Summer Fantasies, Different Affair, Stark, A Mirror Image, Roman Holiday, Full Exposure: The Sex Tapes Scandal, Follow Your Heart, Opposites Attract, A Mother's Justice, Without a Kiss Goodbye, Born Too Soon, French Silk, Sister in Law, Down Out and Dangerous. Pilots: Aaron's Way, Half 'n Half, Fair Game, Heaven Help Us.

NOURI, MICHAEL
Actor. b. Washington, DC, Dec. 9, 1945. e. Avon Old Farms, Rollins Coll., Emerson Coll. Studied for theatre with Larry Moss and Lee Strasberg. New York stage debut in Forty Carats, 1969.
THEATER: Forty Carats, Victor/Victoria.
PICTURES: Goodbye Columbus (debut, 1969), Flashdance, Gobots (voice), The Imagemaker, The Hidden, Chameleon, Fatal Sky, Total Exposure, Black Ice, Fortunes of War, To the Limit.
TELEVISION: Series: Beacon Hill, Search for Tomorrow, The Curse of Dracula, The Gangster Chronicles, Bay City Blues, Downtown, Love and War. Movies: Contract on Cherry Street, Fun and Games, Secrets of a Mother and Daughter, Spraggue, Between Two Women, Rage of Angels: The Story Continues, Quiet Victory: the Charlie Wedemeyer Story, Shattered Dreams, Danielle Steel's Changes, In the Arms of a Killer, Psychic, Exclusive, The Sands of Time, The Hidden 2, Eyes of Terror, Between Love and Honor. Mini-Series: The Last Convertible.

NOVAK, KIM
Actress. r.n. Marilyn Novak. b. Chicago, IL, Feb, 13, 1933. e. Wright Junior Coll., Los Angeles City Coll. Started as model, named World's Favorite Actress, Brussels World's Fair.
PICTURES: The French Line (debut, 1954), Pushover, Phffft!, Five Against the House, Son of Sinbad, Picnic, The Man with the Golden Arm, The Eddy Duchin Story, Jeanne Eagles, Pal Joey, Vertigo, Bell Book and Candle, Middle of the Night, Pepe, Strangers When We Meet, The Notorious Landlady, Boys'

Night Out, Of Human Bondage, Kiss Me Stupid, The Amorous Adventures of Moll Flanders, The Legend of Lylah Clare, The Great Bank Robbery, Tales That Witness Madness, The White Buffalo, The Mirror Crack'd, Just a Gigolo, The Children, Liebestraum.
TELEVISION: Series: Falcon Crest. Guest: Alfred Hitchcock Presents (1985). Movies: Third Girl From the Left, Satan's Triangle, Malibu.

NOVELLO, DON
Writer, Comedian, Actor. b. Ashtabula, OH, Jan. 1, 1943. e. U. of Dayton, B.A., 1964. Best known as Father Guido Sarducci on Saturday Night Live. Was advertising copy writer before writing and performing on The Smothers Brothers Comedy Hour (1975). Writer for Van Dyke and Company, and writer-performer on Saturday Night Live 1978-80. Producer: SCTV Comedy Network (1982) and performer-writer on B'way in Gilda Radner—Live From New York (1979), as well as filmed version (Gilda Live!). Recordings: Live at St. Douglas Convent, Breakfast in Heaven. Author: The Lazlo Letters: The Amazing Real-Life Actual Correspondence of Lazlo Toth, American!, The Blade, Citizen Lazlo.
PICTURES: Gilda Live!, Head Office, Tucker: The Man and His Dream, New York Stories (Life Without Zoe), The Godfather Part III, Casper (cameo), One Night Stand, Jack.
TELEVISION: Cable specials: Fr. Guido Sarducci Goes to College, The Vatican Inquirer—The Pope Tour.

NOYCE, PHILLIP
Director. b. Griffith, New South Wales, Australia, April 29, 1950. Began making films at school and university. Made first short film at age 15, Better to Reign in Hell. In 1980, became part-time mgr., Sydney Filmmaker's Co-operative and in 1973 was selected for Australian Nat'l Film School in Sydney, for year-long training prog. which resulted in shorts, Good Afternoon, Caravan Park, Castor and Pollux, God Knows Why But It Works, and 60-minute film Backroads.
PICTURES: Backroads (also prod., s.p.), Newsfront (also s.p.; Australian Acad. Awards for best dir. & s.p., 1978), Heatwave (also co-s.p.), Echoes of Paradise, Dead Calm, Blind Fury, Patriot Games, Sliver (also cameo), Clear and Present Danger, The Saint, The Bone Collector, Blast Off (also s.p.).
TELEVISION: Mini-Series: Dismissal, Cowra Breakout. Episodes: The Hitchhiker, Nightmare Cafe.

NUNN, BILL
Actor. b. Pittsburgh, PA. Teamed with friend Al Cooper as member of comedy team Nunn and Cooper in nightclubs, 1980-83. On stage with various theatrical companies including the Alliance, the Academy, Theatrical Oufit, Just Us Theatre.
THEATER: T-Bone and Weasel, Split Second, Home, A Lesson From Aloes, A Soldier's Play, Macbeth, The River Niger, Fences.
PICTURES: School Daze, Do the Right Thing, Def by Temptation, Cadillac Man, Mo' Better Blues, New Jack City, Regarding Henry, Sister Act, National Lampoon's Loaded Weapon 1, The Last Seduction, Canadian Bacon, Things to Do in Denver When You're Dead, Candyman 2, Money Train, Mr. & Mrs. Loving, BulletProof, Extreme Measures, Kiss the Girls, Mad City, He Got Game.
TELEVISION: Movies: The Littlest Victims, The Affair, Carriers, Quicksilver Highway, Ellen Foster, Always Outnumbered. Specials: Native Strangers, Dangerous Heart, War Stories, A Yankee in King Arthur's Court. Guest: Fallen Angels.

NYKVIST, SVEN
Cinematographer. b. Moheda, Sweden, Dec. 3, 1922. e. Stockholm Photog. Sch. Asst. cameraman 1941-44. Became internationally known by photographing most of Ingmar Bergman's pictures. Recipient of American Society of Cinematographers Life Achievement Award, 1996.
PICTURES: Sawdust and Tinsel, The Virgin Spring, Winter Light, Karin Mansdotter, The Silence, Loving Couples, Persona, Hour of the Wolf, Cries and Whispers (Academy Award, 1973), The Dove, Black Moon, Scenes from a Marriage, The Magic Flute, Face to Face, One Day in the Life of Ivan Denisovich, The Tenant, The Serpents' Egg, Pretty Baby, Autumn Sonata, King of the Gypsies, Hurricane, Starting Over, Willie and Phil, From the Life of the Marionettes, The Postman Always Rings Twice, Cannery Row, Fanny and Alexander (Academy Award, 1983), Swann in Love, The Tragedy of Carmen, After the Rehearsal, Agnes of God, Dream Lover, The Sacrifice, The Unbearable Lightness of Being, Katinka, Another Woman, New York Stories (Oedipus Wrecks), Crimes and Misdemeanors, The Ox (dir., co-s.p. only), Chaplin, Sleepless in Seattle, What's Eating Gilbert Grape, With Honors, Kirsten Lavrandatter, Only You, Mixed Nuts, Something to Talk About, Confession.
TELEVISION: Movie: Nobody's Child.

O

O'BRIAN, HUGH
Actor. r.n. Hugh C. Krampe. b. Rochester, NY, Apr. 19, 1925. Raised in Chicago. e. Kemper Military Sch., U. of Cincinnati, UCLA. U.S. Marine Corps, where at age 18 he served as youngest drill instructor in Marine Corps history. Actor in stock cos. before film career. Founder, chmn. development: Hugh O'Brian Youth Foundation, 1958; Nat'l Chmn., Cystic Fibrosis Research Foundation 1969-74; Co-founder and pres. Thalians 1955-58; Founder Hugh O'Brian Annual Acting Awards at UCLA, 1962.
THEATER: B'way: Destry Rides Again, First Love, Guys and Dolls, Cactus Flower, The Decision. Regional: The Music Man, Rainmaker, Plaza Suite, On 20th Century, Stalag 17, Thousand Clowns, etc.
PICTURES: Young Lovers (debut, 1949), Never Fear, Rocketship X-M, The Return of Jesse James, Vengeance Valley, Fighting Coast Guard, Little Big Horn, On the Loose, The Cimarron Kid, Red Ball Express, The Battle at Apache Pass, Sally and Saint Anne, Son of Ali Baba, The Raiders, The Lawless Breed, Meet Me at the Fair, Seminole, Man from the Alamo, Back to God's Country, The Stand at Apache River, Saskatchewan, Fireman Save My Child, Drums Across the River, Broken Lance, There's No Business Like Show Business, White Feather, The Twinkle in God's Eye, Brass Legend, The Fiend Who Walked the West, Alias Jesse James, Come Fly with Me, Love Has Many Faces, In Harm's Way, Ten Little Indians, Ambush Bay, Africa--Texas Style!, Killer Force, The Shootist, Game of Death, Doin' Time on Planet Earth, Twins.
TELEVISION: Series: The Life and Legend of Wyatt Earp, Search. Specials: Dial M for Murder, A Punt a Pass and a Prayer, Going Home, Engagement Ring, Invitation to a Gunfighter, Reunion, Chain of Command, It's a Man's World, Wyatt Earp: Return to Tombstone. Movies: Wild Women, Harpy, Probe (Search), Murder on Flight 502, Benny & Barney: Las Vegas Undercover, Fantasy Island, Murder at the World Series, Cruise Into Terror, The Seekers, Gunsmoke: The Last Apache, The Gambler Returns: Luck of the Draw.

O'BRIEN, CONAN
Performer, Writer. b. Brookline, MA, Apr. 18, 1963. e. Harvard. Served two years as pres. of Harvard Lampoon before landing work as tv writer for The Simpsons, Saturday Night Live (Emmy Award, 1989). Prod. of pilot Lookwell. Series: Not Necessarily the News, NBC's Late Night With Conan O'Brien (Emmy nom., 1996).

O'BRIEN, MARGARET
Actress. r.n. Angela Maxine O'Brien. Los Angeles, CA, Jan. 15, 1938. Screen debut at 3 in Babes on Broadway (1941). Awarded special Academy Award as best child actress, 1944. Voted one of ten best money-making stars in Motion Picture Herald-Fame Poll 1945-46.
PICTURES: Babes on Broadway (debut, 1941), Journey for Margaret, Dr. Gillespie's Criminal Case, Lost Angel, Thousands Cheer, Madame Curie, Jane Eyre, The Canterville Ghost, Meet Me in St. Louis, Music for Millions, Our Vines Have Tender Grapes, Bad Bascomb, Three Wise Fools, Unfinished Dance, Tenth Avenue Angel, The Big City, The Secret Garden, Little Women, Her First Romance, Two Persons Eyes (Jap.), Agente S3S Operazione Uranio (It.), Glory, Heller in Pink Tights, Anabelle Lee, Diabolic Wedding, Amy, Sunset After Dark.
TELEVISION: Movies: Death in Space, Split Second to an Epitaph, Testimony of Two Men. Guest: Robert Montgomery Presents, Lux Video Theatre, Playhouse 90, Wagon Train, Studio One, U.S. Steel Hour, Dr. Kildare, Love American Style, Marcus Welby M.D.

O'BRIEN, VIRGINIA
Actress. b. Los Angeles, CA, Apr. 18, 1919. e. North Hollywood h.s. Singer, comedienne with a distinctive dead-pan delivery. On stage in Meet the People. 1990, performed at London Palladium.
PICTURES: Hullabaloo (debut, 1940), The Big Store, Lady Be Good, Ringside Maisie, Ship Ahoy, Panama Hattie, DuBarry Was a Lady, As Thousands Cheer, Meet the People, Two Girls and a Sailor, The Harvey Girls, Ziegfeld Follies, Till Clouds Roll By, The Showoff, Merton of the Movies, Francis in the Navy, Gus.

OBST, LYNDA
Producer. b. New York, NY, Apr. 14, 1950. e. Pomona Col., Columbia Univ. Former editor for New York Times Magazine, 1976-79; then exec. at Polygram Pictures, 1979-81; Geffen Films, 1981-83, co-prod. at Paramount, 1983-85; prod. for Walt Disney, 1986, before moving over to Columbia. Co-Author: Dirty Dreams (with Carol Wolper).
PICTURES: Flashdance (assoc. prod.). Producer: Adventures in Babysitting, Heartbreak Hotel, The Fisher King, This Is My Life, Bad Girls, One Fine Day, Hope Floats. Exec. Prod.: Sleepless in Seattle.
AUTHOR: Hello, He Lied and Other Truths From the Hollywood Trenches.

OCHS, MILLARD L.
Executive. e. U. of Akron. Beginning in July 1946, worked as an usher, projectionist and concession manager and later as cinema manager for his father Lee A. Ochs, while in college. After graduation, became city mng'r. for RKO Stanley Warner Theatre,

Cincinnati, OH; followed by district mng'r. for AMC, covering SW territoris of AR and S. CA. 1985, while with AMC, transferred to England and began developing the multiplex concept at Milton Keynes; over next three years, AMC opened eight locations in England, then sold their interest to Univ./Paramount Studio Joint Venture of United Cinema Int'l.; stayed on with UCI until June 1993. Joined WB Int'l. Theatres as exec. v.p.; July 1994, promoted to pres. and began working with Ira Stiegler, v.p., architecture & planning, to introduce the Looney Tune Themed lobby. Awards: Exhibitor of the Year, Cinema Expo in Amsterdam, June 1996; co-recipient, Exhibitor of the Year, ShoWest, March 1998.

O'CONNELL, JACK
Producer, Director, Writer. b. Boston, MA. e. Princeton U., Harvard Business Sch. After being a creative group head in all media and doing 500 tv commercials entered feature films working with Fellini on La Dolce Vita, then asst. dir. to Antonioni on L'Avventura.
PICTURES: Writer/Prod./Dir.: Greenwich Village Story, Revolution, Christa (aka Swedish Flygirls), Up the Girls Means Three Cheers for Them All, The Hippie Revolution.

O'CONNOR, CARROLL
Actor. b. New York, NY, Aug. 2, 1924. e. University Coll., Dublin; U. of Montana. Three years with Dublin's Gate Theatre, then N.Y.
THEATER: NY: Ulysses in Nighttown, Playboy of the Western World, The Big Knife, Brothers (also dir.), Home Front. Author: Ladies of Hanover Tower.
PICTURES: A Fever in the Blood (debut, 1961), Parrish, By Love Possessed, Lad: A Dog, Belle Sommers, Lonely Are the Brave, Cleopatra, In Harm's Way, What Did You Do in the War Daddy?, Hawaii, Not With My Wife You Don't, Warning Shot, Point Blank, Waterhole No. 3, The Devil's Brigade, For Love of Ivy, Death of a Gunfighter, Marlowe, Kelly's Heroes, Doctors' Wives, Law and Disorder.
TELEVISION: Series: All in the Family (4 Emmy Awards: 1972, 1977, 1978, 1979; later retitled Archie Bunker's Place), In the Heat of the Night (Emmy Award, 1989). Guest: U.S. Steel Hour, Armstrong Circle Theatre, Kraft Theatre, The Untouchables, Dr. Kildare, East Side/West Side, Gunsmoke, Wild Wild West, Party of Five, Mad About You, etc. Special: Of Thee I Sing. Movies: Fear No Evil, The Last Hurrah (also writer), Brass, Convicted, The Father Clements Story, In the Heat of the Night: A Matter of Justice (also co-exec. prod.), In the Heat of the Night: Who Was Geli Bendl? (also co-exec. prod.), In the Heat of the Night: By Duty Bound (also co-exec. prod.), In the Heat of the Night: Grow Old With Me (also co-exec. prod.).

O'CONNOR, DONALD
Actor. b. Chicago, IL, Aug. 28, 1925. In vaudeville with family and Sons o' Fun (Syracuse, N.Y.) before screen debut 1938 in Sing You Sinners; return to vaudeville 1940-41, then resumed screen career with What's Cookin'?, 1942. Entered armed services, 1943. Voted Star of Tomorrow, 1943; best TV performer by M.P. Daily poll, 1953.
PICTURES: Sing You Sinners (debut, 1938), Sons of the Legion, Men With Wings, Tom Sawyer—Private Detective, Unmarried, Death of a Champion, Million Dollar Legs, Night Work, On Your Toes, Beau Geste, Private Buckaroo, Give Out Sisters, Get Hep to Love, When Johnny Comes Marching Home, Strictly in the Groove, It Comes Up Love, Mr. Big, Top Man, Chip Off the Old Block, Patrick the Great, Follow the Boys, The Merry Monahans, Bowery to Broadway, This Is the Life, Something in the Wind, Are You With It?, Feudin' Fussin' and a-Fightin', Yes Sir That's My Baby, Francis, Curtain Call at Cactus Creek, The Milkman, Double Crossbones, Francis Goes to the Races, Singin' in the Rain, Francis Goes to West Point, I Love Melvin, Call Me Madam, Francis Covers the Big Town, Walking My Baby Back Home, Francis Joins the WACS, There's No Business Like Show Business, Francis in the Navy, Anything Goes, The Buster Keaton Story, Cry for Happy, The Wonders of Aladdin, That Funny Feeling, That's Entertainment, Ragtime, Pandemonium, A Time to Remember, Toys.
TELEVISION: Series: The Colgate Comedy Hour (host: 1951-54; Emmy Award, 1954), The Donald O'Connor Texaco Show (1954-55), The Donald O'Connor Show (synd., 1968). Movies: Alice in Wonderland, Bandit and the Silver Angel. Guest: Dinah Shore, Hollywood Palace, Carol Burnett, Julie Andrews, Ellery Queen, The Love Boat, Highway to Heaven, Tales From the Crypt. Specials: The Red Mill, Hollywood Melody, Olympus 7-0000.

O'CONNOR, GLYNNIS
Actress. b. New York, NY, Nov. 19, 1955. Daughter of ABC News prod. Daniel O'Connor and actress Lenka Peterson. e. State U., NY at Purchase. Stage includes Domestic Issues (Circle Rep., NY, 1983), The Taming of the Shrew (Great Lakes Shakespeare Fest.), The Seagull (Mirror Rep.).
PICTURES: Jeremy (debut, 1973), Baby Blue Marine, Ode to Billy Joe, Kid Vengeance, California Dreaming, Those Lips Those Eyes, Night Crossing, Melanie, Johnny Dangerously.
TELEVISION: Series: Sons and Daughters. Mini-series: Black Beauty. Movies: The Chisholms, Someone I Touched, All Together Now, The Boy in the Plastic Bubble, Little Mo, My Kidnapper, My Love, The Fighter, Love Leads the Way, Why Me?, Sins of the Father, The Deliberate Stranger, To Heal a Nation, Death in Small Doses, Past the Bleachers.

O'CONNOR, KEVIN J.
Actor. b. 1964. e. DePaul Univ.'s Goodman Sch. of Drama. On stage in Colorado Catechism (NY), El Salvador (Chicago).
PICTURES: One More Saturday Night, Peggy Sue Got Married, Candy Mountain, The Moderns, Signs of Life, Steel Magnolias, Love at Large, F/X 2, Hero, Equinox, No Escape, Color of Night, Virtuosity, Lord of Illusions, Canadian Bacon, Hit Me, Amistad, Gods & Monsters, Chicago Cab, Deep Rising.
TELEVISION: Movie: The Caine Mutiny Court Martial, The Love Bug. Special: Tanner 88. Guest: Birdland. Series: Tanner 88, Birdland. Guest: Law & Order, Birdland.

O'CONNOR, PAT
Director. b. Ardmore, Ireland. 1943. After working in London at odd jobs (putting corks in wine bottles, paving roads), came to U.S. e. UCLA, B.A. Studied film and TV at Ryerson Institute in Toronto. 1970, trainee prod., dir. with Radio Telefis Eireann. 1970-78 prod. and dir. over 45 TV features and current affairs documentaries. (The Four Roads, The Shankhill, Kiltyclogher, One of Ourselves, Night in Ginitia) A Ballroom of Romance won BAFTA Award (1981).
PICTURES: Cal (debut, 1984), A Month in the Country, Stars and Bars, The January Man, Fools of Fortune, Circle of Friends, Sacred Hearts, Inventing the Abbotts.
TELEVISION: Movie: Zelda.

O'DONNELL, CHRIS
Actor. b. Winetka, IL, 1970.
PICTURES: Men Don't Leave (debut, 1990), Fried Green Tomatoes, School Ties, Scent of a Woman, The Three Musketeers, Blue Sky, Circle of Friends, Mad Love, Batman Forever, The Chamber, In Love and War, Batman & Robin.

O'DONNELL, ROSIE
Actress. b. Commack, NY, 1961. e. Dickinson Col., Boston Univ. Stand-up comic first gaining attention on series Star Search.
THEATER: Grease! (B'way debut, 1994).
PICTURES: A League of Their Own, Sleepless in Seattle, Another Stakeout, Car 54 Where Are You?, I'll Do Anything, The Flintstones, Exit to Eden, Now and Then, Beautiful Girls, Harriet the Spy.
TELEVISION: Series: Gimme a Break, Stand-Up Spotlight (host, exec. prod.), Stand by Your Man, The Rosie O'Donnell Show (host; Emmy, 1997-98).

O'HARA, CATHERINE
Actress, Writer, Director. b. Toronto, Canada, Mar. 4, 1954. Professional debut in 1974 with Toronto's Second City. Co-founder of SCTV in 1976 (Emmy and Canadian Nellie Awards for writing).
PICTURES: Nothing Personal, Rock & Rule (voice), After Hours, Heartburn, Beetlejuice, Dick Tracy, Betsy's Wedding, Home Alone, Little Vegas, There Goes the Neighborhood, Home Alone 2: Lost in New York, The Nightmare Before Christmas (voice), The Paper, Wyatt Earp, A Simple Twist of Fate, Tall Tale, Last of the High Kings.
TELEVISION: Series: SCTV, Steve Allen Comedy Hour, SCTV Network 90. Guest: Trying Times (Get a Job), Comic Relief, Dream On (also dir.).

O'HARA, GERRY
Director, Writer. b. Boston-Lincs, England 1924. e. St. Mary's Catholic Sch., Boston. Junior Reporter Boston Guardian. Entered industry in 1942 with documentaries and propaganda subjects.
PICTURES: Director: That Kind of Girl (debut, 1963), Game for Three Lovers, Pleasure Girls (also s.p.), Maroc 7, Love in Amsterdam, All the Right Noises (also s.p.), Leopard in the Snow, The Bitch, Fanny Hill, The Mummy Lives (also co-s.p.). Writer: Ten Little Indians, Havoc in Chase County, Phantom of the Opera, De Sade's Nightmare, Sherlock Holmes and the Affair in Transylvania, Catherine the Great.
TELEVISION: The Avengers, Man in a Suitcase, Journey into the Unknown, The Professionals (story editor, writer), Special Squad (story consultant), Cats Eyes (exec. story editor), Operation Julie (writer; mini-series), Sherlock Holmes & The Leading Lady, Sherlock Holmes & The Incident at Victoria Falls (co-writer).

O'HARA, MAUREEN
Actress. r.n. Maureen FitzSimons. b. Dublin. Aug. 17, 1921. Abbey Sch. of Acting. Won numerous prizes for elocution. Under contract to Erich Pommer-Charles Laughton. Co-starred, Abbey & Repertory Theatre.
PICTURES: Kicking the Moon Around (debut, 1938), My Irish Molly, Jamaica Inn, The Hunchback of Notre Dame, A Bill of Divorcement, Dance Girl Dance, They Met in Argentina, How Green Was My Valley, To the Shores of Tripoli, Ten Gentlemen From West Point, The Black Swan, The Immortal Sergeant, This Land Is Mine, The Fallen Sparrow, Buffalo Bill, The Spanish Main, Sentimental Journey, Do You Love Me?, Miracle on 34th Street, Sinbad the Sailor, The Homestretch, The Foxes of Harrow, Sitting Pretty, Woman's Secret, Forbidden Street,

Father Was a Fullback, Bagdad, Comanche Territory, Tripoli, Rio Grande, At Sword's Point, Flame of Araby, The Quiet Man, Kangaroo, Against All Flags, The Redhead From Wyoming, War Arrow, Fire Over Africa, The Magnificent Matador, Lady Godiva, Long Gray Line, Lisbon, Everything But the Truth, Wings of Eagles, Our Man in Havana, The Parent Trap, The Deadly Companions, Mr. Hobbs Takes a Vacation, McLintock!, Spencer's Mountain, The Battle of the Villa Fiorita, The Rare Breed, How Do I Love Thee?, Big Jake, Only the Lonely.
TELEVISION: Movie: The Red Pony, The Christmas Box. Specials: Mrs. Miniver, Scarlet Pimpernel, Spellbound, High Button Shoes, Who's Afraid of Mother Goose.

O'HERLIHY, DAN
Actor. b. Wexford, Ireland, May 1, 1919. e. National U. of Ireland (Bachelor of Architecture). Actor with Abbey Theatre, Dublin Gate, Longford Prod.; announcer on Radio Eireann; on Broadway in The Ivy Green.
PICTURES: Odd Man Out (debut, 1946), Kidnapped, Larceny, Macbeth, Iroquois Trail, The Blue Veil, The Desert Fox, The Highwayman, Soldiers Three, At Swords Point, Invasion U.S.A., Operation Secret, Actors and Sin, Sword of Venus, The Adventures of Robinson Crusoe (Acad. Award nom.), The Black Shield of Falworth, Bengal Brigade, The Purple Mask, The Virgin Queen, City After Midnight, Home Before Dark, Imitation of Life, The Young Land, Night Fighters (A Terrible Beauty), One Foot in Hell, The Cabinet of Caligari, Fail-Safe, The Big Cube, 100 Rifles, Waterloo, The Carey Treatment, The Tamarind Seed, MacArthur, Halloween III: The Season of the Witch, The Last Starfighter, The Whoopee Boys, Robocop, The Dead, Robocop 2.
TELEVISION: Series: The Travels of Jamie McPheeters, The Long Hot Summer, Hunter's Moon, Whiz Kids, Man Called Sloane, Twin Peaks. Mini-series: QB VII, Jennie: Lady Randolph Churchill, Nancy Astor. Movies: The People, Deadly Game, Woman on the Run, Good Against Evil, Love Cheat and Steal. Guest: The Equalizer, L.A. Law, Murder She Wrote, Ray Bradbury Theatre, Father Dowling. BBC: Colditz, The Secret Servant, Artemis, The Last Day, Jennie, Nancy Astor, The Rat Pack.

OHLMEYER, DONALD W., JR.
Executive, Producer, Director. b. New Orleans, LA, Feb. 3, 1945. e. U. of Notre Dame, B.A. (Communications), 1967. Producer and director at both ABC and NBC. Formed Ohlmeyer Communications Company, 1982 (diversified prod. and dist. of entertainment and sports prog.). Assoc. dir., ABC Sports, NY 1967-70; director, ABC Sports, 1971-72 (dir. 1972 Olympic Games); prod.: ABC Sports, NY 1972-77 (prod. and dir. 1976 Winter and Summer Olympics; prod. ABC's Monday Night Football, 1972-76); exec. prod.: NBC Sports, NY 1977-82 (exec. prod., 1980 Olympics, The World Series, The Super Bowl). Special Bulletin (exec. prod.), John Denver's Christmas in Aspen (exec. prod.). Chmn. and CEO, Ohlmeyer Communications Co., LA, 1982-present. 1993, named pres. NBC West Coast. Recipient of 14 Emmy Awards, Humanitas Prize, Award for Excellence, National Film Board. Member, Directors Guild of America.
TELEVISION: Specials: Heroes of Desert Storm (dir.), Disney's Christmas on Ice (dir.), Crimes of the Century (prod.). Series: Lifestories (dir./exec. prod.), Fast Copy (prod.). Movies: Cold Sassy Tree (exec. prod.), Crazy in Love (exec. prod.), Right to Die (exec. prod.).

O'KEEFE, MICHAEL
Actor. b. Larchmont, NY, April 24, 1955. e. NYU, AADA. m. singer Bonnie Raitt. Co-founder, Colonnades Theatre Lab, NY.
THEATER: B'way: Mass Appeal (Theatre World Award), Fifth of July. Off-B'way: Killdere (NYSF), Moliere in Spite of Himself, Christmas on Mars, Short Eyes. Regional: Streamers, A Few Good Men (tour).
PICTURES: Gray Lady Down (debut, 1978), The Great Santini (Acad. Award nom.), Caddyshack, Split Image, Nate and Hayes, Finders Keepers, The Slugger's Wife, Ironweed, Out of the Rain, Me and Veronica, Nina Takes a Lover, Three Lovers, Edie and Pen, Ghosts of Mississippi.
TELEVISION: Series: Against the Law, Roseanne. Movies: The Lindbergh Kidnapping Case, Friendly Persuasion, Panache, The Dark Secret of Harvest Home, A Rumor of War, Unholy Matrimony, Bridge to Silence, Disaster at Silo 7, Too Young to Die?, In the Best Interest of the Child, Fear, Incident at Deception Ridge, The People Next Door.

OLDKNOW, WILLIAM H.
Executive. b. Atlanta, GA, Sept. 3, 1924. e. U.S.C. Served in USNR from 1943-46. Pres., Sero Development Co., (formerly Sero Amusement Co.) 1947-present (drive-in theatres, shopping centers, and commercial real-estate). Sole proprietor, Starlight Drive-in Theatre, Atlanta, GA. Chmn. and pres., De Anza Land & Leisure Corp.

OLDMAN, GARY
Actor. r.n. Leonard Gary Oldman. b. New Cross, South London, England, March 21, 1958. Won scholarship to Rose Bruford Drama College (B.A. Theatre Arts) after studying with Greenwich Young People's Theatre. Acted with Theatre Royal, York and joined touring theatre co. Then in 1980 appeared with Glasgow Citizens Theatre in Massacre at Paris, Chinchilla,

Desperado Corner, A Waste of Time (also touring Europe and South America). Received Evening Standard Film Award for Best Newcomer for Sid and Nancy, 1986.
THEATER: *London*: Minnesota Moon, Summit Conference, Rat in the Skull, Women Beware Women, The War Plays, Real Dreams, The Desert Air, Serious Money (Royal Shakespeare Co.), The Pope's Wedding (Time Out's Fringe Award, best newcomer 1985-86; British Theatre Assc. Drama Mag. Award, Best Actor 1985).
PICTURES: Sid and Nancy (debut, 1986), Prick Up Your Ears, Track 29, We Think the World of You, Criminal Law, Chattahoochee, State of Grace, Rosencrantz and Guildenstern Are Dead, Exile, Before and After Death, JFK, Bram Stoker's Dracula, True Romance, Romeo Is Bleeding, The Professional, Immortal Beloved, Murder in the First, Dead Presidents, The Scarlet Letter, Basquiat, Air Force One, Nil by Mouth (s.p., dir., prod. only, BAFTA Award, Outstanding Brit. Film, Best Orig. Screenplay, 1997), Lost in Space, Quest for Camelot (voice), The Thin Red Line.
TELEVISION: Remembrance, Meantime, Honest Decent and True, Rat in the Skull, The Firm, Heading Home, Fallen Angels.

OLIN, KEN
Actor, Director. b. Chicago, IL, July 30, 1954. e. Univ. of PA. m. actress Patricia Wettig. Studied acting with Warren Robertson and Stella Adler. Made Off-B'way debut in Taxi Tales, 1978.
PICTURES: Ghost Story, Queen's Logic, White Fang 2: Myth of the White Wolf (dir.), 'Til There Was You.
TELEVISION: *Series*: The Bay City Blues, Hill Street Blues, Falcon Crest, thirtysomething (also dir.). *Movies* (actor): Women at West Point, Flight 90: Disaster on the Potomac, There Must Be a Pony, Tonight's the Night, Cop Killer, A Stoning in Fulham County, Goodnight Sweet Wife: A Murder in Boston, Telling Secrets, Nothing But the Truth. *Movies (director)*: The Broken Cord, Doing Time on Maple Drive, In Pursuit of Honor. *Guest*: Murder She Wrote, Hotel, The Hitchhiker.

OLIN, LENA
Actress. b. Stockholm, Sweden, 1955. Member of the Royal Dramatic Theatre in Stockholm. Daughter of actor-director Stig Olin. m. director Lasse Hallstrom.
THEATER: *NY*: Miss Julie.
PICTURES: The Adventures of Picasso, Karleken, Fanny and Alexander, Grasanklingar, After the Rehearsal, A Matter of Life and Death, Friends, The Unbearable Lightness of Being, S/Y Joy (Gladjen), Enemies a Love Story (Acad. Award nom.), Havana, Mr. Jones, Romeo Is Bleeding, The Night and the Moment, Night Falls on Manhattan.

OLMI, ERMANNO
Director, Writer, Producer, Editor. b. Bergamo, Italy, July 24, 1931. e. Accademia d'Arte Drammatica, Milan. Worked as a clerk for an electric company Edisonvolta 1949-52, until 1952 when he began directing theatrical and cinematic activities sponsored by co. 1952-61, directed or supervised over 40 short 16mm and 35mm documentary films. 1959 first feature film, semi-doc. Time Stood Still. With other friends and Tullio Kezich formed prod. co., 22 December S.P.A., 1961. 1982, Helped found Hypothesis Cinema, a sch. for aspiring dirs.
PICTURES: *Director/Writer*: Time Stood Still (debut, 1959), The Sound of Trumpets, The Fiances (also prod.), And There Came a Man (A Man Named John), One Fine Day (also edit.), The Tree of the Wood Clogs (Cannes Film Fest. Award, 1978; also photog., edit.), Camminacammina (also photog., edit., design), Milano '83 (also photog., edit.), Long Live the Lady (also co-photog., edit.), Legend of the Holy Drinker (also edit.), Il Segreto Del Bosco Vecchio. Documenaries: Artigiani Veneti, Lungo Il Fiume, The Secret of the Old Woods.
TELEVISION: The Scavengers (also photog.), During the Summer (also photog., edit.), The Circumstance (also photog., edit.), Genesis: The Creation & the Flood.

OLMOS, EDWARD JAMES
Actor. b. East Los Angeles, CA, February 24, 1947. e. East Los Angeles City Coll., CA State U. m. actress Lorraine Bracco. Started as rock singer with group Eddie James and the Pacific Ocean. By the early 1970s acted in small roles on Kojak and Hawaii Five-O. 1978 starred in Luis Valdez's musical drama Zoot Suit at Mark Taper Forum (L.A. Drama Critics Circle Award, 1978), later on B'way (Theatre World Award, Tony nom.), and in film version. Formed YOY Productions with director Robert Young. Numerous awards for humanitarian work.
PICTURES: Aloha Bobby and Rose (debut, 1975), Alambrista!, Virus, Wolfen, Zoot Suit, Blade Runner, The Ballad of Gregorio Cortez (also assoc. prod., composer and music adaptor), Saving Grace, Stand and Deliver (Acad. Award nom.; also co-prod.), Triumph of the Spirit, Talent for the Game, American Me (also dir., co-prod.), A Million to Juan, Mirage, My Family/Mi Familia, Roosters, Caught, Selena, The Wonderful Ice Cream Suit.
TELEVISION: *Movies*: Evening in Byzantium, 300 Miles for Stephanie, Menendez: A Killing in Beverly Hills, The Burning Season. *Specials*: Sequin, Y.E.S. Inc. *Series*: Miami Vice (Golden Globe & Emmy Awards, 1985; also dir. episodes). *Mini-series*: Mario Puzo's The Fortunate Pilgrim.

O'LOUGHLIN, GERALD STUART
Actor. b. New York, NY, Dec. 23, 1921. e. Blair Acad., Lafayette Col., U. of Rochester, Neighborhood Playhouse. U.S. Marine, WWII.
THEATER: *B'way*: Streetcar (ANTA series), Shadow of a Gunman, Dark at the Top of the Stairs, A Touch of the Poet, Cook for Mr. General, One Flew Over the Cuckoo's Nest, Calculated Risk, Lovers and Other Strangers. *Off-B'way*: Who'll Save the Plowboy (Obie Award), Harry Noon and Night, Machinal.
PICTURES: Lovers and Lollipops, Cop Hater, A Hatful of Rain, Ensign Pulver, A Fine Madness, In Cold Blood, Ice Station Zebra, Desperate Characters, The Organization, The Valachi Papers, Twilight's Last Gleaming, Frances, Crimes of Passion, City Heat, Quicksilver. Audio narration, The Secret Kingdom.
TELEVISION: *Movies*: The D.A.: Murder One, Murder at the World Series, Something for Joey, A Love Affair: The Eleanor and Lou Gehrig Story, Crash of Flight 401, Detour to Terror, Pleasure Palace, A Matter of Life and Death, Under Siege, Perry Mason: The Case of the Notorious Nun, Child's Cry, In the Arms of a Killer, The Crime of the Century. *Mini-Series*: Wheels, Roots: The Next Generations, Blind Ambition, Women in White, The Blue and the Gray. *Series*: The Storefront Lawyers (Men at Law), The Rookies, Automan, Our House. *Guest*: Alcoa Premiere, Philco-Goodyear, Suspense, The Defenders, Ben Casey, Dr. Kildare, 12 O'Clock High, Going My Way, Naked City, Gunsmoke, Green Hornet, Mission Impossible, Mannix, Judd For The Defense, Hawaii 5-0, Cannon, Room 222, Charlie's Angels, M*A*S*H, Trapper John M.D., Fame, T.J. Hooker, Murder She Wrote, Highway to Heaven, Dirty Dancing, Eual Justice, ER, and many others.

OLSON, DALE C.
Executive. b. Fargo, ND, Feb. 20, 1934. e. Portland State Coll., OR. Owner, Dale C. Olson & Associates; formerly sn. v.p. & pres., m.p. div., Rogers & Cowan public relations. Journalist on Oregonian newspaper, West Coast editor, Boxoffice Magazine, 1958-60; critic and reporter, Daily Variety, 1960-66; dir. of publ., Mirisch Corp., 1966-68; Rogers & Cowan, 1968-85. Past pres., Hollywood Press Club, awarded Bob Yaeger and Les Mason award by Publicists Guild; v.p. Diamond Circle, City of Hope; delegate for U.S. to Manila International Film Festival. Chmn. public rltns. coordin. committee & member nat'l bd. of trustees, A.M.P.A.S., 1989-91. Chmn. Western Council, Actors Fund of America, 1991. On Nat'l Bd. of Trustees, 1992-present.

OLSON, JAMES
Actor. b. Evanston, IL, Oct. 8, 1930. e. Northwestern U.
THEATER: *NY*: The Young and the Beautiful, Romulus, The Chinese Prime Minister, J.B., Slapstick Tragedy, Three Sisters, Sin of Pat Muldoon, Winter's Tale, Of Love Remembered, Twelve Dreams.
PICTURES: The Sharkfighters, The Strange One, Rachel Rachel, Moon Zero Two, The Andromeda Strain, The Groundstar Conspiracy, The Mafu Cage, Ragtime, Amityville II: The Possession, Commando, Rachel River.
TELEVISION: *Movies*: Paper Man, Incident on a Dark Street, Manhunter, A Tree Grows in Brooklyn, The Sex Symbol, The Family Nobody Wanted, Someone I Touched, Man on the Outside, Strange New World, Law and Order, The Spell, Moviola: The Silent Years, Cave-In!, The Parade. *Specials*: Missiles of October, Vince Lombardi Story, Court-Martial of Geoge Armstrong Custer.

OLSON, NANCY
Actress. b. Milwaukee, WI, July 14, 1929. e. U. of Wisconsin, UCLA. No prof. experience prior to films.
PICTURES: Canadian Pacific (debut, 1949), Sunset Boulevard (Acad. Award nom.), Union Station, Mr. Music, Submarine Command, Force of Arms, Big Jim McLain, So Big, The Boy From Oklahoma, Battle Cry, Pollyanna, The Absent-Minded Professor, Son of Flubber, Smith!, Snowball Express, Airport 1975, Making Love.
TELEVISION: *Series*: Kingston: Confidential, Paper Dolls. *Special*: High Tor.

O'NEAL, RON
Actor. b. Utica, NY, Sept. 1, 1937. e. Ohio State U. Spent 9 yrs. at Karamu House in Cleveland (inter-racial theatre) from 1957 to 1966, acting in 40 plays. 1967-68 spent in N.Y. teaching acting in Harlem. Appeared in all-black revue 1968, The Best of Broadway, then in summer stock. Acted off-B'way in American Pastorale and The Mummer's Play. 1970 joined the Public Theatre. Break came with No Place To Be Somebody, which won him the Obie, Clarence Derwent, Drama Desk and Theatre World Awards.
THEATER: Tiny Alice, The Dream of Monkey Mountain.
PICTURES: Move (debut, 1970), The Organization, Super Fly, Super Fly TNT (also dir., co-story), The Master Gunfighter, Brothers, A Force of One, When a Stranger Calls, The Final Countdown, St. Helens, Red Dawn, Mercenary Fighters, Hero and the Terror, Up Against the Wall (also dir.), Death House.
TELEVISION: *Series*: Bring 'em Back Alive, The Equalizer. *Mini-Series*: North and South. *Movies*: Freedom Road, Brave New World, Guyana Tragedy: The Story of Jim Jones, Sophisticated Gents, Playing with Fire, North Beach and Rawhide, As Summers Die.

O'NEAL, RYAN
Actor. r.n. Patrick Ryan O'Neal. b. Los Angeles, CA, April 20, 1941. Parents, screenwriter-novelist, Charles O'Neal, and actress Patricia Callaghan. Daughter is actress Tatum O'Neal; son is actor Griffin O'Neal. Boxer, L.A. Golden Gloves, 1956-57. Began career as stand-in, stunt man, then actor in Tales of the Vikings series, in Germany, 1959; freelanced in Hollywood.
PICTURES: The Big Bounce (debut, 1969), The Games, Love Story (Acad. Award nom.), Wild Rovers, What's Up Doc?, Paper Moon, The Thief Who Came to Dinner, Barry Lyndon, Nickelodeon, A Bridge Too Far, The Driver, Oliver's Story, The Main Event, So Fine, Green Ice, Partners, Irreconcilable Differences, Fever Pitch, Tough Guys Don't Dance, Chances Are, Faithful.
TELEVISION: Series: Empire, Peyton Place, Good Sports. Movies: Love Hate Love, Small Sacrifices, The Man Upstairs. Special: Liza Minnelli: A Triple Play. Guest: Dobie Gillis, Bachelor Father, Leave It to Beaver, My Three Sons, Perry Mason, The Larry Sanders Show. Pilot: 1775.

O'NEAL, TATUM
Actress. b. Los Angeles, CA, Nov. 5, 1963. p. actors Ryan O'Neal and Joanna Moore. NY stage debut 1992 in A Terrible Beauty, followed by Adroscoggin Fugue.
PICTURES: Paper Moon (debut, 1973; Academy Award, best supporting actress), The Bad News Bears, Nickelodeon, International Velvet, Little Darlings, Circle of Two, Certain Fury, Little Noises, Basquiat.
TELEVISION: Movie: Woman on the Run: The Lawrencia Bembenek Story. Special: 15 and Getting Straight. Guest: Cher, Faerie Tale Theatre (Goldilocks and the Three Bears).

O'NEIL, THOMAS F.
Executive. b. Kansas City, MO, Apr. 18, 1915. e. Holy Cross Coll., 1933-37. Employed by General Tire and Rubber Co., 1937-41; U.S. Coast Guard, 1941-46; v.p., dir., Yankee Network, Boston, 1948-51; pres. chmn. of bd. RKO General, Inc., 1952. Arranged purchase RKO Radio by General Teleradio, Inc. from Howard Hughes, July, 1955; chairman of the Board, RKO General, Inc., dir., General Tire & Rubber Co.
(d. March 14, 1998)

O'NEILL, ED
Actor. b. Youngstown, OH, Apr. 12, 1946. e. Ohio Univ., Youngstown State. Taught social studies in Youngstown prior to becoming an actor. Made NY stage debut Off-Off-B'way in Requiem for a Heavyweight at SoHo Rep. Theatre. B'way debut in Knockout.
PICTURES: Deliverance, Cruising, The Dogs of War, Disorganized Crime, K-9, The Adventures of Ford Fairlane, Sibling Rivalry, Dutch, Wayne's World, Wayne's World 2, Blue Chips, Little Giants, Prefontaine.
TELEVISION: Series: Married... With Children. Pilot: Farrell for the People. Movies: When Your Lover Leaves, The Day the Women Got Even, Popeye Doyle, A Winner Never Quits, Right to Die, Police School, The Whereabouts of Jenny, W.E.I.R.D. World.

O'NEILL, JENNIFER
Actress. b. Rio de Janeiro, Brazil, Feb. 20, 1949. e. Dalton Sch. Model before entering films. Spokeswoman: CoverGirl cosmetics. Pres., Point of View Productions and Management.
PICTURES: Rio Lobo, Summer of '42, Such Good Friends, The Carey Treatment, Glass Houses, Lady Ice, The Reincarnation of Peter Proud, Whiffs, Caravans, The Psychic, The Innocent, A Force of One, Cloud Dancer, Steel, Scanners, Committed, I Love N.Y., Love is Like That, Invasion of Privacy, The Gentle People, Discretion Assured, The Corporate Ladder.
TELEVISION: Series: Bare Essence, Cover Up. Movies: Love's Savage Fury, The Other Victim, An Invasion of Privacy, Chase, Perry Mason: The Case of the Shooting Star, The Red Spider, Glory Days, Full Exposure: The Sex Tapes Scandal, Personals, Perfect Family, The Cover Girl Murders, Frame-up, Jonathan Stone: Threat of Innocence, Silver Strand. Mini-Series: A.D.

ONTKEAN, MICHAEL
Actor. b. Vancouver, British Columbia, Canada, Jan. 24, 1946. e. U. of New Hampshire. Son of Leonard and Muriel Cooper Ontkean, actors. Acting debut at 4 with father's rep. theater. Child actor with Stratford Shakespeare Fest., CBC and Natl Film Bd. Attended coll. 4 years on hockey scholarship. Has performed with Public Theatre, NY, Willamstown Theatre Fest., Mark Taper Lab, The Kitchen, Soho.
PICTURES: The Peace Killers (debut, 1971), Pick Up on 101, Necromancy, Hot Summer Week, Slap Shot, Voices, Willie and Phil, Making Love, Just the Way You Are, The Allnighter, Maid to Order, Clara's Heart, Street Justice, Cold Front, Bye Bye Blues, Postcards From the Edge, Bayou Boy, The Toy Factory, Summer, Access All Areas, Le Sang des Autres, Cutting Loose, Square Deal, Rapture.
TELEVISION: Series: The Rookies, Twin Peaks. Movies: The Rookies (pilot), The Blood of Others, Kids Don't Tell, The Right of the People, Twin Peaks (pilot), Defense of a Married Man, In a Child's Name, Legacy of Lies, Whose Child Is This? The War for Baby Jessica, Vendetta 2: The New Mafia, Danielle Steel's Family Album, The Man Next Door, Man From the South.

OPHULS, MARCEL
Director, Writer. r.n. Hans Marcel Oppenheimer. b. Frankfurt-am-Main, Germany, Nov. 1, 1927. Son of German director Max Ophuls. e. Occidental Coll., U. of California, Berkeley, Sorbonne (philosophy). Family moved to France, 1932, then to Hollywood, 1941. Military service with Occupation forces in Japan, 1946; performed with theater unit, Tokyo. 1951 began working in French film industry as asst. dir., using name Marcel Wall. Asst. dir. on Moulin Rouge, Act of Love, Marianne de ma Jeunesse, Lola Montes. 1956-59, radio and TV story ed., West Germany. Later worked for French TV as reporter and dir. news mag. features. Dir. & wrote short film Henri Matisse. 1968 doc. dir. for German TV. 1975-78 staff prod. CBS News, then ABC News. MacArthur Fellowship 1991. Member of AMPAS.
PICTURES: Director/Writer: Love at 20 (dir. segment), Banana Peel, Fire at Will, Munich or Peace in Our Time, The Sorrow and the Pity (also prod.; Natl. Soc. of Film Critics, NY Film Critics & Prix de Dinard Awards, 1970), The Harvest at Mai Lai, A Sense of Loss, The Memory of Justice, Hotel Terminus--The Life and Times of Klaus Barbie (also prod.; Academy Award, Berlin Peace Prize, Cannes Jury Prize, 1988), The Troubles We've Seen (also prod., Intl. Film Critics Prize, 1994).
TELEVISION: America Revisited, Two Whole Days, November Days.

OPOTOWSKY, STAN
Executive. b. New Orleans, LA, Apr. 13, 1923. e. Tulane U. Served in U.S. Marine Corps as combat corr. and later joined United Press, working in New Orleans, Denver, and New York. Published own weekly newspaper in Mississippi before returning to N.Y. to join New York Post as mgr. editor and traveling natl. corr. Is also cinematographer and film editor. Joined ABC News as TV assignment editor; named asst. assignment mgr. 1974 named dir. of operations for ABC News TV Documen-taries. 1975 named dir. of TV News Coverage, ABC News.
TELEVISION: Author: The Big Picture, The Longs of Louisiana, The Kennedy Government, Men Behind Bars.

O'QUINN, TERRY
Actor. b. Michigan.
THEATER: B'way: Foxfire, Curse of an Aching Heart. Off-B'way: Richard III, Groves of Academy, Total Abandon. Regional: Streamers, Measure for Measure, The Front Page.
PICTURES: Heaven's Gate, Without a Trace, All the Right Moves, Places in the Heart, Mrs. Soffel, Mischief, Silver Bullet, SpaceCamp, The Stepfather, Black Widow, Young Guns, Pin, Stepfather 2, Blind Fury, The Rocketeer, Prisoners of the Sun, Company Business, The Cutting Edge, Amityville: A New Generation, Tombstone, Lipstick Camera.
TELEVISION: Movies: FDR: The Final Year, Prisoner Without a Name Cell Without a Number, Right to Kill, Unfinished Business, An Early Frost, Stranger on My Land, Women of Valor, When the Time Comes, Perry Mason: The Case of the Desperate Deception, Son of the Morning Star, The Last to Go, Deliver Them From Evil: The Taking of Alta View, Trial: The Price of Passion, Sexual Advances, Wild Card, The Good Fight, Born Too Soon, Visions of Murder, Heart of a Child, Don't Talk to Strangers, Justice in a Small Town, A Friend to Die For, Ray Alexander: A Menu for Murder.

ORBACH, JERRY
Actor. b. Bronx, NY, Oct. 20, 1935. e. U. of Illinois, Northwestern U. Trained for stage with Herbert Berghof and Lee Strasberg. N.Y. stage debut in Threepenny Opera, 1955.
THEATER: The Fantasticks (original cast, 1960), Carnival, The Cradle Will Rock, Guys and Dolls, Scuba Duba, Promises Promises (Tony Award, 1969), 6 Rms Riv Vu, Chicago, 42nd Street.
PICTURES: Cop Hater, Mad Dog Coll, John Goldfarb Please Come Home, The Gang That Couldn't Shoot Straight, A Fan's Notes, Foreplay (The President's Woman), The Sentinel, Underground Aces, Prince of the City, Brewster's Millions, F/X, The Imagemaker, Dirty Dancing, Someone to Watch Over Me, Crimes and Misdemeanors, Last Exit to Brooklyn, I Love N.Y., A Gnome Named Norm, California Casanova, Dead Women in Lingerie, Out for Justice, Toy Soldiers (unbilled), Delusion, Delirious, Beauty and the Beast (voice), Straight Talk, Universal Soldier, Mr. Saturday Night, The Cemetery Club.
TELEVISION: Series: The Law and Harry McGraw, Law and Order. Guest: Shari Lewis Show, Jack Paar, Bob Hope Presents, Love American Style, Murder She Wrote, Kojak, Golden Girls, Hunter. Movies: An Invasion of Privacy, Out on a Limb, Love Among Thieves, In Defense of a Married Man, Broadway Bound, Quiet Killer. Mini-Series: Dream West.

ORMOND, JULIA
Actress. b. England, 1965. Studied acting at Webber Douglas Acad., London.
THEATER: The Rehearsal, Wuthering Heights, Arms and the Man, The Crucible, Faith Hope and Charity (London Drama Critics Award, 1989).
PICTURES: The Baby of Macon, Nostradamus, Legends of the Fall, First Knight, Captives, Sabrina.
TELEVISION: Mini-Series: Traffik. Movies: Young Catherine, Stalin.

ORTEGA, KENNY
Director, Choreographer. b. Palo Alto, CA. e. American Conserv. Theatre, Canada Coll. Started acting at age 13. Earned several scholarships to dance academies in San Francisco Bay area. Regional theatre roles in Oliver, Hair, The Last Sweet Days of Isaac, before staging shows for rock band The Tubes. First major tv job choreographing Cher special. Directed/choreographed concerts and/or music videos for such performers as Michael Jackson, Kiss, Elton John, Cher, Rod Stewart, Diana Ross, Madonna, Billy Joel, Oingo Boingo, Miami Sound Machine, Pointer Sisters, Toto. Artistic dir. and choreographer, 1996 Centennial Olympic Games opening and closing ceremonies.
PICTURES: *Director/Choreographer.* Newsies, Hocus Pocus, Ferris Bueller's Day Off. *Choreographer.* Quest for Camelot, To Wong Foo–Thanks for Everything–Julie Newmar, Dirty Dancing, Road House, Shag, The Great Outdoors, Lost Boys, Pretty in Pink, Salsa, God Created Woman, One from the Heart, St. Elmo's Fire, Xanadu, The Rose.
TELEVISION: *Series Director.* Dirty Dancing (also choreog.), Hull Street High, Chicago Hope (also choreog.), Fame L.A., McKenna, Second Noah. *Choreographer.* American Music Awards, Academy Awards, NAACP Awards, 1996 Olympics, Mickey's 60th Birthday, Totally Mine, America Picks the #1 Hit, Nosotros Awards, Good Time Rock 'n' Roll, Jump. *Specials Choreographer.* Olivia Newton-John, Cher, The Pointer Sisters, Neil Diamond, Smokey Robinson, Cheryl Ladd.

O'SHEA, MILO
Actor. b. Dublin, Ireland, June 2, 1926. Member of Dublin Gate Theatre Co., 1944, before screen career.
THEATER: *NY:* Staircase, Dear World, The Comedians, A Touch of the Poet, Waiting For Godot (Brooklyn Acad. of Music), Mass Appeal, My Fair Lady, Corpse!, Meet Me in St. Louis, Remembrance (Off-B'way), Philadelphia Here I Come!, Alive Alive Oh! (alo co-writer), Mrs. Warren's Profession. *London:* Treasure Hunt, Glory Be, Hans Andersen, Corpse, Can-Can.
PICTURES: Carry on Cabby, Never Put It in Writing, Ulysses, Romeo and Juliet, Barbarella, The Adding Machine, The Angel Levine, Paddy, Sacco and Vanzetti, Loot, Theatre of Blood, Digby: The Biggest Dog in the World, It's Not the Size That Counts, Arabian Adventure, The Pilot, The Verdict, The Purple Rose of Cairo, The Dream Team, Opportunity Knocks, Only the Lonely, The Playboys, Rooney, Never Put It In Writing, The Butcher Boy.
TELEVISION: *Series:* Once a Hero, Frasier. *Mini-Series:* QB VII, Ellis Island, The Best of Families. *Movies/Specials:* Two By Forsythe, Peter Lundy and the Medicine Hat Stallion, Portrait of a Rebel: Margaret Sanger, And No One Could Save Her, A Times for Miracles, Broken Vows, Angel in Green, Murder in the Heartland. *Guest:* The Golden Girls, Cheers, Who's the Boss, Beauty and the Beast, St. Elsewhere.

OSHIMA, NAGISA
Director, Writer. b. Kyoto, Japan, March 31, 1932. e. U. of Kyoto (law), 1954. Joined Shochiku Ofuna Studios in 1954 as asst. dir.; 1956 wrote film criticism and became editor-in-chief of film revue Eiga hihyo; 1959 promoted to director. 1962-65 worked exclusively in TV; 1962-64 made documentaries in Korea and Vietnam; 1975 formed Oshima Prods. 1976, his book of Realm of the Senses seized by police. With editor, prosecuted for obscenity, acquitted. Pres. of Directors Guild of Japan, 1980-present.
PICTURES: *Dir./Writer.* A Town of Love and Hope (debut, 1959), Cruel Story of Youth, The Sun's Burial, Night and Fog in Japan, The Catch (dir. only), The Christian Rebel, A Child's First Adventure, I'm Here Bellett, The Pleasures of the Flesh, Violence at Noon (dir. only), Band of Ninja (also co-prod.), Sing a Song of Sex (also co- prod.), Japanese Summer: Double Suicide (also co-prod.), Death By Hanging, Three Resurrected Drunkards (A Sinner in Paradise), Diary of a Shinjuku Thief, Boy (dir. only), He Died After the War, The Ceremony, Dear Summer Sister, In the Realm of the Senses, Phantom Love, Empire of Passion (Phantom Love; also co-prod.), Merry Christmas Mr. Lawrence, Max My Love.

OSMOND, DONNY
Singer, TV Host. b. Ogden, UT, Dec. 9, 1957. Seventh of 9 children, he was fifth member of family to become professional singer. (Four brothers: Alan, Wayne, Merrill and Jay, were original members of Osmond Bros., who originally sang barbershop quartet.) Made debut at 4 on Andy Williams Show. Has had 12 gold albums. Was co-host with sister of Donny & Marie on TV.
THEATER: Little Johnny Jones, Joseph and the Amazing Technicolor Dreamcoat.
PICTURE: Goin' Coconuts, Mulan (voice).
TELEVISION: *Series:* The Andy Williams Show, Donny and Marie. *Movie:* The Wild Women of Chastity Gulch. *Guest:* The Jerry Lewis Show, Here's Lucy, The Love Boat.

OSMOND, MARIE
Singer, TV Host. b. Ogden, UT, Oct. 13, 1959. Began career at age of 3 on Andy Williams Show. Her first album, Paper Roses went gold. Appeared with brother Donny in feature film Goin' Coconuts.
TELEVISION: *Series:* Donny and Marie, Marie, Ripley's Believe It or Not (co-host), Maybe This Time. *Movies:* Gift of Love, I Married Wyatt Earp, Side By Side.

O'STEEN, SAM
Editor, Director. b. Nov. 6, 1923. Entered m.p. industry 1956 as asst. to editor George Tomassini on The Wrong Man. Became full editor in 1963 on Youngblood Hawke. Directorial debut with TV film A Brand New Life, 1972.
PICTURES: Youngblood Hawke, Kisses for My President, Robin and the 7 Hoods, Marriage on the Rocks, None But the Brave, Who's Afraid of Virginia Woolf?, Cool Hand Luke, The Graduate, Rosemary's Baby, The Sterile Cuckoo (spv. edit.), Catch-22, Carnal Knowledge, Portnoy's Complaint, The Day of the Dolphin, Chinatown, Sparkle (dir.), Straight Time, Hurricane, Amityville II: The Possession, Silkwood, Heartburn, Nadine, Biloxi Blues, Frantic, Working Girl, A Dry White Season (co-edit.), Postcards from the Edge, Regarding Henry, Wolf.
TELEVISION: *Director.* A Brand New Life, I Love You Goodbye, Queen of the Stardust Ballroom (DGA Award), High Risk, Look What's Happened to Rosemary's Baby, The Best Little Girl in the World, Kids Don't Tell.

O'SULLIVAN, KEVIN P.
Executive. b. New York, NY, April 13, 1928. e. Queens Coll., Flushing, NY. Associated with television 40 yrs., initially as a talent; later as businessman. Won first prize in Arthur Godfrey Talent Scouts competition in 1948. 1950-55 professional singer, actor on TV, in theatre, night clubs. 1955-57 on radio-TV promotion staff, Ronson Corp. 1958-61, salesman, Television Programs of America. 1961-67 dir. of program services, Harrington, Righter and Parsons. 1967 joined ABC Films, domestic sales div. as v.p. & gen. sales mgr. 1969 named v.p., gen. mgr. then pres., ABC Films, Inc.; 1970 made pres., ABC Int'l. TV, while retaining position as pres., ABC Films. 1973 became pres., COO, Worldvision Enterprises, Inc., co. formed to succeed ABC Films when FCC stopped networks from TV program dist. Elected chmn. & CEO, Worldvision, 1982. Named pres., Great American Broadcasting Group, 1987. Resigned, 1988. Named pres., Kenmare Prods. Inc., 1988.

O'SULLIVAN, MAUREEN
Actress. b. Boyle, Ireland, May 17, 1911. Daughter is actress Mia Farrow. e. convents in Dublin, London; finishing sch., Paris. Discovered by dir. Frank Borzage; came to Hollywood in 1930 under contract to Fox.
THEATER: Never Too Late, The Front Page, No Sex Please, We're British, Mornings at Seven; regional theatre.
PICTURES: Song of My Heart (debut, 1930), Just Imagine, The Princess and the Plumber, A Connecticut Yankee, Skyline, The Big Shot, Tarzan the Ape Man, The Silver Lining, Skyscraper Souls, Strange Interlude, Payment Deferred, Tugboat Annie, Stage Mother, The Barretts of Wimpole Street, The Thin Man, Tarzan and His Mate, Hide-Out, David Copperfield, West Point of the Air, The Flame Within, Woman Wanted, Anna Karenina, Cardinal Richelieu, The Bishop Misbehaves, Tarzan Escapes, The Voice of Bugle Ann, The Devil Doll, A Day at the Races, The Emperor's Candlesticks, Between Two Women, My Dear Miss Aldrich, A Yank at Oxford, Hold That Kiss, Port of Seven Seas, The Crowd Roars, Spring Madness, Let Us Live, Tarzan Finds a Son, Sporting Blood, Pride and Prejudice, Maisie Was a Lady, Tarzan's Secret Treasure, Tarzan's New York Adventure, The Big Clock, Where Danger Lives, Bonzo Goes to College, All I Desire, Mission Over Korea, Duffy of San Quentin, The Steel Cage, The Tall T, Wild Heritage, Never Too Late, The Phynx, Too Scared to Scream, Hannah and Her Sisters, Peggy Sue Got Married, Stranded.
TELEVISION: *Movies:* The Crooked Hearts, The Great Houdinis, With Murder in Mind, The Habitation of Dragons, Hart to Hart: Home is Where the Hart Is. *Guest:* Pros & Cons, many others. *Special:* Good Old Boy (Wonderworks).
(d. June 22, 1998).

O'TOOLE, ANNETTE
Actress. b. Houston, TX, April 1, 1953. e. UCLA.
PICTURES: Smile (debut, 1975), One on One, King of the Gypsies, Foolin' Around, Cat People, 48 HRS, Superman III, Cross My Heart, Love at Large, Andre (voice), Imaginary Crimes.
TELEVISION: *Movies:* The Girl Most Likely To..., The Entertainer, The War Between the Tates, Love For Rent, Stand By Your Man, Copacabana, Arthur Hailey's Strong Medicine, Broken Vows, Stephen King's IT, The Dreamer of Oz, White Lies, Kiss of a Killer, Love Matters, A Mother's Revenge, My Brother's Keeper. *Mini-Series:* The Kennedys of Massachusetts. *Specials:* Vanities, Best Legs in the Eighth Grade, Secret World of the Very Young, Unpublished Letters, On Hope.

O'TOOLE, PETER
Actor. b. Connemara, Ireland, Aug. 2, 1932. Studied at Royal Acad. of Dramatic Art. Early career with Bristol Old Vic. Partner with Jules Buck, Keep Films, Ltd. Autobiography: Loitering With Intent (1993).
THEATER: *London:* Major Barbara, Oh My Papa, The Long the Short and the Tall, Baal, Hamlet, Ride a Cock Horse, Macbeth, Man and Superman, Jeffrey Bernard is Unwell, Our Song. 1960, with the Stratford-on-Avon Company (The Taming of the Shrew, Merchant of Venice, etc). *Dublin:* Arms and the Man, Waiting for Godot. *Toronto:* Present Laughter, Uncle Vanya. B'way debut 1987: Pygmalion.

PICTURES: Kidnapped (debut, 1959), The Savage Innocents, The Day They Robbed the Bank of England, Lawrence of Arabia, Becket, Lord Jim, What's New Pussycat?, The Bible, How to Steal a Million, The Night of the Generals, Casino Royale (cameo), Great Catherine, The Lion in Winter, Goodbye Mr. Chips, Brotherly Love (Country Dance), Murphy's War, Under Milk Wood, The Ruling Class, Man of La Mancha, Rosebud, Man Friday, Foxtrot, Caligula, Power Play, Zulu Dawn, The Stunt Man, My Favorite Year, Supergirl, Creator, Club Paradise, The Last Emperor, High Spirits, On a Moonlit Night, Helena, Wings of Fame, The Nutcracker Prince (voice), The Rainbow Thief, Isabelle Eberhardt, King Ralph, Rebecca's Daughters, The Seventh Coin. TELEVISION: Movies: Rogue Male (BBC), Svengali, Kim, Crossing to Freedom, Heaven & Hell: North and South Book III. Specials: Present Laughter, Pygmalion, The Dark Angel. Series: Strumpet City (BBC). Mini-Series: Masada.

OTWELL, RONNIE RAY
Theatre Executive. b. Carrollton, GA, Aug. 13, 1929. e. Georgia Inst. of Technology. Entered industry as mgr., Bremen Theatre, GA, 1950; dir. pub., adv., Martin Theatres, Columbus, GA, 1950-63; v.p., dir. Martin Theatres of Ga., Inc., 1963, Martin Theatres of Ala., Inc., 1963; dir. Martin Theatres of Columbus, 1963; sr. v.p., Martin Theatres Companies, 1971.

OVERALL, PARK
Actress. b. Nashville, TN, March 15, 1957. Attended British boarding school, earned teaching degree, before turning to acting.
THEATER: NY: Biloxi Blues, Wild Blue, Only You, Loose Ends, Something About Baseball, Marathon '88.
PICTURES: Body Passion, Biloxi Blues, Mississippi Burning, Talk Radio (voice), Lost Angels, Kindergarten Cop, The Vanishing, House of Cards, Undercover Blues.
TELEVISION: Series: Empty Nest. Movies: Luck of the Draw: The Gambler Returns, Overkill: The Aileen Wuornos Story, Precious Victims, The Good Old Boys. Pilot: The Line.

OVITZ, MICHAEL
Talent Agent, Executive. b. Chicago, IL, Dec. 14, 1946. e. UCLA, 1968. Started as trainee at William Morris Agency before becoming agent, 1969-75. Co-founder of Creative Artists Agency, 1975; became chmn. and chief stock holder. 1995 named pres. The Walt Disney Company; resigned from The Walt Disney Company, 1996.

OWEN, BILL
Actor. r.n. Bill Rowbotham. b. Acton, Eng., Mar. 14, 1914.
PICTURES: The Way to the Stars (debut, 1945), School for Secrets, Daybreak, Dancing With Crime, Easy Money, When the Bough Breaks, My Brother's Keeper, Martha, Parlor Trick, The Roundabout, Trottie True, Once a Jolly Swagman, A Day to Remember, You See What I Mean, Square Ring, Rainbow Jacket, Ship That Died of Shame, Not so Dusty, Davy, Carve Her Name with Pride, Carry on Sergeant, Carry on Nurse, Night Apart, Shakedown, Hell Fire Club, Carry on Regardless, Carry on Cabby!, Secret of Blood Island, Georgy Girl, Headline Hunters, O Lucky Man!, Kadoyng, In Celebration, When The Screaming Stopped, Comeback, Laughter House.
TELEVISION: Series: Last of the Summer Wine.

OWENSBY, EARL
Producer, Actor. b. North Carolina, 1935. Set up his own studio in Shelby, NC. Built new studio in Gaffney, SC, 1985.
PICTURES: Challenge, Dark Sunday, Buckstone County Prison, Frank Challenge—Manhunter, Death Driver, Wolfman, Seabo, Day of Judgment, Living Legend, Lady Grey, Rottweiler, Last Game, Hyperspace, Hit the Road Running, Rutherford County Line.

OXENBERG, CATHERINE
Actress. b. NY, NY, Sept. 21, 1961. Daughter of the exiled Princess Elizabeth of Yugoslavia, raised among intl. jet set with Richard Burton acting as her tutor. Modeled before making TV debut in The Royal Romance of Charles and Diana (1982).
PICTURES: The Lair of the White Worm, The Return of the Musketeers.
TELEVISION: Series: Dynasty, Acapulco H.E.A.T. Movies: The Royal Romance of Charles and Diana, Roman Holiday, Swimsuit, Trenchcoat in Paradise, Ring of Scorpio, K-9000, Charles & Diana: Unhappily Ever After, Rubdown, Treacherous Beauties.

OZ, FRANK
Puppeteer, Director, Performer. b. Hereford, England, May 25, 1944. r.n. Frank Oznowicz. Gained fame as creator and performer of various characters on Sesame Street and the Muppet Show (Fozzie Bear, Miss Piggy, Animal, Cookie Monster, Grover and Bert). V.P., Jim Henson Prods.
PICTURES: Performer: The Muppet Movie, The Blues Brothers, The Empire Strikes Back, The Great Muppet Caper (also prod.), An American Werewolf in London, The Dark Crystal (also co-dir.), Return of the Jedi, Trading Places, The Muppets Take Manhattan (also dir., co-s.p.), Spies Like Us, Labyrinth, Innocent Blood, The Muppet Christmas Carol (also exec. prod.), Muppet Treasure Island (voice). Director only:

Little Shop of Horrors, Dirty Rotten Scoundrels, What About Bob?, Housesitter, The Indian in the Cupboard, In & Out.
TELEVISION: Series: Sesame Street (3 Emmy Awards), The Muppet Show (Emmy Award, 1978), Saturday Night Live; various variety shows.

P

PAAR, JACK
Actor. b. Canton, OH, May 1, 1918. Radio announcer in Cleveland, Buffalo; served in U.S. Armed Forces, WWII; entertained in Pacific zone with 28th Special Service Div. On radio with own show, then quiz show Take It or Leave It. First host of The Tonight Show; various specials.
AUTHOR: I Kid You Not, My Sabre Is Bent, Three on a Toothbrush, P.S. Jack Paar.
PICTURES: Variety Time (debut, 1948), Easy Living, Walk Softly Stranger, Footlight Varieties, Love Nest, Down Among the Sheltering Palms.
TELEVISION: Series: Up to Paar (emcee, 1952), Bank on the Stars (emcee, 1953), The Jack Paar Show (1954), The Morning Show (1954), The Tonight Show (retitled The Jack Paar Show: 1957-62), The Jack Paar Program (1962-65), ABC Late Night (1973). Specials: Jack Paar Diary, Jack Paar Remembers, Jack Paar Is Alive and Well (also prod.), He Kids You Not.

PACINO, AL
Actor. b. New York, NY, April 25, 1940. e. High Sch. for the Performing Arts, NY; Actors Studio, 1966; HB Studios, NY. Gained attention as stage actor initially at Charles Playhouse, Boston (Why Is a Crooked Letter, The Peace Creeps, Arturo Ui). Served as artistic dir. (with Ellen Burstyn), Actors Studio (1982-84).
THEATER: NY: The Indian Wants the Bronx (Obie Award), Does a Tiger Wear a Necktie? (Tony & Theatre World Awards, 1969), The Local Stigmatic, Camino Real, The Connection, Hello Out There, Tiger at the Gates, The Basic Training of Pavlo Hummel (Tony Award, 1977), Richard III, American Buffalo, Julius Caesar, Chinese Coffee, Salome, Hughie (also dir.).
PICTURES: Me Natalie (debut, 1969), The Panic in Needle Park, The Godfather, Scarecrow, Serpico, The Godfather Part II, Dog Day Afternoon, Bobby Deerfield, ... And Justice for All, Cruising, Author! Author!, Scarface, Revolution, Sea of Love, Dick Tracy, The Godfather Part III, Frankie and Johnny, Glengarry Glen Ross, Scent of a Woman (Acad. Award, 1992), Carlito's Way, A Day to Remember, City Hall, Heat, Two Bits, Looking for Richard (also dir.), Donnie Brasco, Devil's Advocate.

PACULA, JOANNA
Actress. b. Tomaszowau, Poland, Jan. 2, 1957. Member of Polish National Theatre School. Modeled in Poland, France, then U.S. where she moved in early 1980's.
PICTURES: Gorky Park, Not Quite Paradise, Death Before Dishonor, The Kiss, Sweet Lies, Options, Marked for Death, Husbands and Lovers, Tombstone.
TELEVISION: Series: E.A.R.T.H. Force. Movies: Escape From Sobribor, Breaking Point, Not Like Us.

PAGE, ANTHONY
Director. b. Bangalore, India, Sept. 21, 1935. e. Oxford. Stage work includes Inadmissible Evidence, Waiting for Godot, A Patriot for Me, Look Back in Anger, Uncle Vanya, Mrs. Warren's Profession, Alpha Beta, Heartbreak House, Absolute Hell, etc.
PICTURES: Inadmissible Evidence (debut, 1968), Alpha Beta, I Never Promised You a Rose Garden, Absolution, The Lady Vanishes.
TELEVISION: Specials: Pueblo, The Missiles of October, The Parachute, Sheppey. Movies: Collision Course, F. Scott Fitzgerald in Hollywood, FDR—The Last Year, The Patricia Neal Story, Bill, Johnny Belinda, Grace Kelly, Bill—On His Own, Murder: By Reason of Insanity, Forbidden, Monte Carlo, Second Serve, Pack of Lies, Scandal in a Small Town, The Nightmare Years, Chernobyl: The Final Warning, Absolute Hell, Guests of the Emperor, Middlemarch.

PAGE, PATTI
Performer, Recording Artist. r.n. Clara Ann Fowler. b. Claremore, OK, Nov. 8, 1927. e. U. of Tulsa. Staff performer, radio stat. KTUL, Tulsa; Top recording star of the 1950's and 60's (The Tennessee Waltz, Cross Over the Bridge, How Much is That Doggie in the Window?, etc.). Appeared on CBS radio show. Author of Once Upon a Dream.
PICTURES: Elmer Gantry (debut, 1960), Dondi, Boys' Night Out.
TELEVISION: Series host: Music Hall, Scott Music Hall, The Patti Page Show, The Big Record, The Patti Page Olds Show. Guest: Appointment With Adventure, U.S. Steel Hour, Bachelor Father, etc.

PAGET, DEBRA
Actress. r.n. Debrahlee Griffin. b. Denver, CO, Aug. 19, 1933. e. Hollywood Prof. Sch. , also studied drama & dancing privately. Stage debut in Merry Wives of Windsor, 1946; in Jeanne D'Arc little theatre prod.

PICTURES: Cry of the City (debut, 1948), It Happens Every Spring, House of Strangers, Broken Arrow, Fourteen Hours, Bird of Paradise, Anne of the Indies, Belles on Their Toes, Les Miserables, Stars & Stripes Forever, Prince Valiant, Demetrius & the Gladiators, Princess of the Nile, Gambler from Natchez, White Feather, Seven Angry Men, Last Hunt, The Ten Commandments, Love Me Tender, The River's Edge, Omar Khayyam, From the Earth to the Moon, Why Must I Die?, Cleopatra's Daughter, Journey to the Lost City, The Most Dangerous Man Alive, Tales of Terror, The Haunted Palace.
TELEVISION: Guest: Steve Allen, Colgate Comedy Hour, Climax, Wagon Train, Rawhide, etc.

PAGETT, NICOLA
Actress. b. Cairo, Egypt, June 15, 1945. r.n. Nicola Scott. e. Royal Acad. of Dramatic Art. Appeared with Citizen's Rep. Theatre, Glasgow.
THEATER: Cornelia (debut, 1964, Worthing, U.K.), A Boston Story (London debut, 1968), A Midsummer Night's Dream, Widowers' Houses, The Misanthrope, A Voyage 'Round My Father, The Ride Across Lake Constance, Ghosts, The Seagull, Hamlet, The Marriage of Figaro, A Family and a Fortune, Gaslight, Yahoo, Old Times (L.A.).
PICTURES: Anne of the Thousand Days, There's a Girl in My Soup, Operation Daybreak, Oliver's Story, Privates on Parade.
TELEVISION: Series: Upstairs Downstairs. Movies: Frankenstein: The True Story, The Sweeney, Aren't We All, A Woman of Substance (mini-series), Anna Karenina.

PAIGE, JANIS
Actress r.n. Donna Mae Jaden. b. Tacoma, WA, Sept. 16, 1923. Sang with Tacoma Opera Co. Star of Tomorrow, 1947. Album: Let's Fall in Love. Owns and operates Ipanema, Janeiro, Rio-Cali, and Dindi Music Cos.
THEATER: Pajama Game, Remains to Be Seen, Here's Love, Mame, Alone Together.
PICTURES: Hollywood Canteen (debut, 1944), Of Human Bondage, Two Gals and a Guy, The Time the Place and the Girl, Two Guys from Milwaukee, Her Kind of Man, Cheyenne, Love and Learn, Always Together, Wallflower, Winter Meeting, One Sunday Afternoon, Romance on the High Seas, House Across the Street, The Younger Brothers, Mr. Universe, Fugitive Lady, Two Guys and a Gal, Silk Stockings, Please Don't Eat the Daisies, Bachelor in Paradise, The Caretakers, Welcome to Hard Times, Love at the Top, The Dark Road (It.), Follow the Boys (Fr.), Natural Causes.
TELEVISION: Special: Roberta (1958 and 1969). Series: It's Always Jan, Lanigan's Rabbi, Gun Shy, Baby Makes Five, Trapper John M.D., Capitol, General Hospital, Santa Barbara. Guest: Plymouth Playhouse, Alcoa Premiere, Columbo, Banacek, Flamingo Road, St. Elsewhere. Movies: The Turning Point of Jim Malloy, Return of Joe Forrester, Lanigan's Rabbi (pilot), Valentine Magic on Love Island, Angel on My Shoulder, The Other Woman, No Man's Land.

PAINE, CHARLES F.
Executive. b. Cushing, TX, Dec. 23, 1920. e. Stephen F. Austin U. Pres. Tercar Theatre Company; pres., NATO of Texas, 1972-73. NATO board member, 1973 to present; Motion Picture Pioneers member; Variety Club of Texas member.

PAKULA, ALAN J.
Producer, Director. b. New York, NY, April 7, 1928. e. Yale U., B.A., 1948. Worked in Leland Hayward's office; asst. administrator, Warner Bros. cartoon dept, Prod. apprentice, MGM, 1950; prod. asst., Paramount 1951; prod. Paramount, 1955. Own prod. co., Pakula-Mulligan Prod. Stage prod. and m.p. dir. prod. 1988 received Eastman Award for Continued Excellence in M.P. Won London Film Critics Award for best dir. for Klute.
THEATER: Comes a Day, Laurette, There Must Be a Pony.
PICTURES: Producer: Fear Strikes Out, To Kill a Mockingbird, Love With the Proper Stranger, Baby the Rain Must Fall, Inside Daisy Clover, Up the Down Staircase, The Stalking Moon. Director: The Sterile Cuckoo, Klute (also prod.), Love and Pain and the Whole Damn Thing (also prod.), The Parallax View (also prod.), All the President's Men (NY Film Critics Award, 1976), Comes a Horseman, Starting Over (also prod.), Rollover, Sophie's Choice (also prod., s.p.), Dream Lover (also prod.), Orphans (also prod.), See You in the Morning (also prod., s.p.), Presumed Innocent, Consenting Adults (also prod.), The Pelican Brief (also prod., co-s.p.), The Devil's Own.

PALANCE, JACK
Actor. b. Lattimer, PA, Feb. 18, 1920. e. U. of North Carolina. Professional fighter; U.S. Air Corps.
THEATER: The Big Two, Temporary Island, The Vigil, A Streetcar Named Desire, Darkness at Head.
PICTURES: Panic in the Streets (debut, 1950), Halls of Montezuma, Sudden Fear (Acad. Award nom.), Shane (Acad. Award nom.), Flight to Tangier, Arrowhead, Second Chance, Man in the Attic, Sign of the Pagan, Silver Chalice, Kiss of Fire,

Big Knife, I Died a Thousand Times, Attack!, Lonely Man, House of Numbers, The Man Inside, Ten Seconds to Hell, Battle of Austerlitz, Sword of the Conqueror, The Mongols, Barabbas, Warriors Five, Contempt, Once a Thief, The Professionals, Torture Garden, Kill a Dragon, The Mercenary, Deadly Sanctuary, They Came to Rob Las Vegas, The Desperados, Che, Legion of the Damned, A Bullet for Rommel, The McMasters, Monte Walsh, Companeros, The Horsemen, Chato's Land, Oklahoma Crude, Craze, The Four Deuces, The Great Adventure, The Sensuous Nurse, Portrait of a Hitman, One Man Jury, Angel's Brigade, The Shape of Things to Come, Cocaine Cowboys, Hawk the Slayer, Without Warning, Alone in the Dark, Gor, Bagdad Cafe, Young Guns, Outlaw of Gor, Batman, Tango and Cash, City Slickers (Acad. Award, best supporting actor, 1991), Solar Crisis, Cops and Robbersons, City Slickers II: The Legend of Curly's Gold, The Swan Princess (voice).
TELEVISION: Specials: Requiem for a Heavyweight (Emmy Award, 1957), Dr. Jekyll and Mr. Hyde, Twilight Zone: Rod Serling's Lost Classics: Where the Dead Are. Movies: Dracula, The Godchild, The Hatfields and the McCoys, Bronk (pilot), Last Ride of the Dalton Gang, The Ivory Ape, Golden Moment: An Olympic Love Story, Keep the Change, Buffalo Girls. Series: The Greatest Show on Earth, Bronk, Ripley's Believe It or Not (host).

PALCY, EUZHAN
Director. b. Martinique, 1957. e. Earned a degree in French lit., Sorbonne and a film degree from Vaugirard School in Paris. Began career working as TV writer and dir. in Martinique. Also made 2 children's records. In Paris worked as film editor, screenwriter and dir. of shorts. She received grant from French gov. to make 1st feature Sugar Cane Alley which cost $800,000 and won Silver Lion Prize at Venice Film Fest., 1983.
PICTURES: Sugar Cane Alley (also writer), A Dry White Season (also co-s.p.), Simeon (also writer), Aime Cesaire: A Voice for History, Wings Against the Wind (also story).

PALIN, MICHAEL
Actor, Writer. b. Sheffield, Yorkshire, England, May 5, 1943. e. Oxford. Performed there in Pinter's The Birthday Party and in revue Hang Your Head Down and Die (also in West End prod., 1964). At Oxford met Terry Jones; began writing comedy together, incl. TV series The Frost Report. Became member of Monty Python's Flying Circus. On stage with troupe both in London and on B'way.
PICTURES: And Now for Something Completely Different (also co-s.p.), Monty Python and the Holy Grail (also co-s.p.), Jabberwocky, Life of Brian (also co-s.p.), Time Bandits, The Secret Policeman's Other Ball, Monty Python Live at the Hollywood Bowl (also co-s.p.), The Missionary (also prod., s.p.), Monty Python's The Meaning of Life (also co-music, co-s.p.), A Private Function, Brazil, A Fish Called Wanda, American Friends (also co-s.p.), Fierce Creatures, The Wind In The Willows (voice).
TELEVISION: Do Not Adjust Your Set, The Frost Report, Monty Python's Flying Circus, Marty Feldman Comedy Machine, How To Irritate People, Pythons in Deutschland, Secrets, Ripping Yarns, Around the World in 80 Days, GBH, Pole to Pole.

PALMER, BETSY
Actress. b. East Chicago, IN, Nov. 1, 1929. e. DePaul U. Studied at Neighborhood Playhouse, HB Studio with Uta Hagen. On Broadway in The Grand Prize, South Pacific, Affair of Honor, Cactus Flower, Roar Like a Dove, Eccentricities of a Nightingale, Same Time Next Year and many regional prods.
PICTURES: Mister Roberts, The Long Gray Line, Queen Bee, The Tin Star, The Last Angry Man, Friday the 13th, Friday the 13th Part 2.
TELEVISION: All major live shows such as Studio One, U.S. Steel Hour, Kraft Theatre. Series: Masquerade Party (panelist), What's It For? (panelist), I've Got a Secret (panelist, 11 years), No. 96 (series), Candid Camera (host), The Today Show (host), Wifeline (host). Guest: As the World Turns, Murder She Wrote, Out of This World, Charles in Charge, Knots Landing, Newhart, Love Boat. Movies: Isabel's Choice, Windmills of the Gods, Goddess of Love, Still Not Quite Human, Columbo: Death Hits the Jackpot.

PALMER, GREGG
Actor. r.n. Palmer Lee. b. San Francisco, CA, Jan. 25, 1927. e. U. of Utah. U.S. Air Force, 1945-46; radio announcer, disc jockey; then to Hollywood.
PICTURES: Cimarron Kid, Battle at Apache Pass, Son of Ali Baba, Red Ball Express, Francis Goes to West Point, Sally and St. Anne, The Raiders, Back at the Front, The Redhead From Wyoming, Column South, Veils of Bagdad, Golden Blade, The All American, Taza Son of Cochise, Magnificent Obsession, Playgirl, To Hell and Back, Creature Walks Among Us, Hilda Crane, Zombies of Mora Tau, Revolt of Fort Laramie, Rebel Set, Commacheros, Quick Gun, Prize, It Happened Every Thursday, Female Animal, Thundering Jets, Forty Pounds of Trouble, Night Hunt, The Undefeated, Chisum, Rio Lobo, Big Jake, Providencia (It.), Ci Risiamo Vero Providencia (It-Sp), Cat Man, The Sad Horse, Most Dangerous Man Alive, Cutter's Trail, Mongo's Back in Town, The Shootist, The Man With Bogart's Face, Scream.

TELEVISION (has appeared in over 400 TV programs): *Series*: Run Buddy Run. *Guest* appearances incl: Wagon Train, Loretta Young, Wyatt Earp, Have Gun Will Travel, Sea Hunt, Roaring 20's, Mannix, The High Chaparral, Cannon, Baretta, Gunsmoke, etc.). *Movies*: Mongo's Back in Town, Go West Young Girl, Hostage Heart, How the West Was Won, True Grit, Beggarman Thief, The Blue and the Gray (mini-series).

PALMER, PATRICK J.
Producer. b. Los Angeles, CA, Dec. 28, 1936. Began career with 10-year apprenticeship at Mirisch Company, involved in making of West Side Story, Seven Days in May, The Fortune Cookie, etc. 1966, began association with Norman Jewison, serving as assoc. prod. on The Landlord, Fiddler on the Roof, Jesus Christ Superstar, Rollerball, etc. 1972, prod., with Jewison, Billy Two Hats; exec. prod. on The Dogs of War.
PICTURES: *Co-prod.*: And Justice for All, Best Friends, Iceman, A Soldier's Story, Agnes of God, Children of a Lesser God, Moonstruck, Stanley & Iris, Mermaids, Paradise (also writer), Made in America, Milk Money (exec. prod.), Iron Will (prod.), Don Juan Demarco.

PALMINTERI, CHAZZ
Actor, Writer. b. Bronx, NY, May 15, 1951. e. Bronx Comm. Coll. NY stage in The Guys in the Truck (B'way), The King's Men, 22 Years, The Flatbush Faithful, A Bronx Tale (which he also wrote).
PICTURES: The Last Dragon (debut, 1985), Oscar, Innocent Blood, There Goes the Neighborhood, A Bronx Tale (also s.p.), Bullets Over Broadway (Acad. Award nom.), The Perez Family, The Usual Suspects, Faithful (also s.p.), Jade, Mulholland Falls, Diabolique.
TELEVISION: *Movie:* The Last Word.

PALTROW, BRUCE
Director, Producer, Writer. b. New York, NY, Nov. 26, 1943. e. Tulane U., B.F.A. m. actress Blythe Danner. Daughter is actress Gwyneth Paltrow. Has also produced stage plays.
PICTURE: A Little Sex (co-prod., dir.).
TELEVISION: *Movies*: Shirts and Skins (co-prod., writer), Ed McBain's 87th Precinct (dir.). *Series*: The White Shadow (creat. dir.), St. Elsewhere (exec. prod.-dir.), Tattinger's (exec. prod., dir., co-writer), Nick & Hillary (exec. prod.).

PALTROW, GWYNETH
Actress. b. Los Angeles, CA. p. actress Blythe Danner. prod. Bruce Paltrow. Family moved to NY when she was 11.
THEATER: *Williamstown*: Picnic, The Adventures of Huck Finn, Sweet Bye and Bye, The Seagull.
PICTURES: Shout (debut, 1991), Hook, Malice, Flesh and Bone, Mrs. Parker and the Vicious Circle, Jefferson in Paris, Moonlight and Valentino, Seven, The Pallbearer, Sydney, Emma, Hush, Out of the Past, Sliding Door, Out of the Past, Great Expectations, A Perfect Murder, Shakespeare in Love, The Talented Mr. Ripley.
TELEVISION: *Movie:* Cruel Doubt.

PANAMA, CHARLES A. (CHUCK)
Publicist, b. Chicago, IL, Feb. 2, 1925. e. Northwestern U., Beloit Coll., UCLA. Publicist, Los Angeles Jr. Chamber of Commerce; So. Calif. sports ed., Los Angeles bureau, INS; publicist, 20th Century-Fox Studios; adv.-pub. dir., Arcola Pics.; opened L.A. office, John Springer Associates; v.p. Jerry Pam & Assoc.; account exec., Rogers, Cowan & Brenner, Inc.; dir. m.p. div., Jim Mahoney & Assoc.; v.p. Guttman & Pam, Ltd.; asst. pub. dir., Twentieth TV. Owner, pres. Chuck Panama P.R.; winner 1990 Les Mason Award and 1993 Robert Yeager Award, Publicists Guild of America.

PANAMA, NORMAN
Writer, Producer, Director. b. Chicago, IL, April 21, 1914. Co-authored The Glass Bed (novel), and plays: A Talent for Murder, The Bats of Portobello.
PICTURES: *Co-Writer:* My Favorite Blonde, Happy Go Lucky, Star-Spangled Rhythm, Thank Your Lucky Stars, And the Angels Sing, Duffy's Tavern, Road to Utopia (Acad. Award nom.), Our Hearts Were Growing Up, Monsieur Beaucaire, It Had to Be You, Mr. Blandings Builds His Dream House, Return of October, White Christmas, Li'l Abner, The Facts of Life. *Co-Dir./Co-Writer* (with Melvin Frank): The Reformer and the Redhead, Strictly Dishonorable, Callaway Went Thataway, Above and Beyond, Knock on Wood (Acad. Award nom. for s.p.), The Court Jester. *Dir./Writer.* The Road to Hong Kong, Not With My Wife You Don't, How to Commit Marriage, I Will I Will... for Now.
TELEVISION: *Dir.*: Barnaby and Me, The Stewardesses, Li'l Abner, Mrs. Katz and Katz (pilot), How Come You Never See Dr. Jekyll and Mr. Hyde Together?, Coffee Tea or Me.

PANKIN, STUART
Actor. b. Philadelphia, PA, April 8, 1946. e. Dickinson Coll., Columbia U. Stage debut 1968 in The War of the Roses.
THEATER: *NY*: Timon of Athens, Tale of Cymbeline, Mary Stuart, The Crucible, Twelfth Night, Glorious Age, Wings, Gorky, Joseph and the Amazing Technicolor Dreamcoat, Three Sisters, The Inspector General.

PICTURES: Scavenger Hunt, Hangar 18, The Hollywood Knights, An Eye for an Eye, Earthbound, Irreconcilable Differences, The Dirt Bike Kid, Fatal Attraction, Love at Stake, Second Sight, That's Adequate, Arachnophobia, Mannequin 2 on the Move, The Vagrant, I Love Trouble, The Silence of the Hams, Squanto: A Warrior's Tale, Congo, Striptease, Honey We Shrunk Ourselves.
TELEVISION: *Series*: The San Pedro Beach Bums, No Soap Radio, Not Necessarily the News (ACE Award), Nearly Departed, Dinosaurs (voice). *Movies*: Valentine Magic on Love Island, Father & Scout, Down Out and Dangerous. *Pilots*: Car Wash, Wonderful World of Philip Malley. *Guest*: Night Court, Crazy Like a Fox, Golden Girls, Stingray, Family Ties, It's Garry Shandling's Show, Hooperman, Barney Miller. *Special*: Stuart Pankin (also co-exec. prod., co-writer).

PANTOLIANO, JOE
Actor. b. Jersey City, NJ, Sept. 12, 1954.
THEATER: *NY*: The Kitchen, The Off Season, The Death Star, Visions of Kerouac. *Regional*: One Flew Over the Cuckoo's Nest, Skaters, Brothers, Italian American Reconciliation (Dramalogue Award), Orphans (Dramalogue Award, Drama Critic Circle nomination), Pvt. Wars.
PICTURES: The Idolmaker, Monsignor, Risky Business, Eddie and the Cruisers, The Mean Season, The Goonies, Running Scared, La Bamba, The Squeeze, Amazon Women on the Moon, Empire of the Sun, The In Crowd, Midnight Run, Downtown, The Last of the Finest, Short Time, Zandalee, Used People, Three of Hearts, Goin' to Mexico, The Fugitive, Calendar Girl, Me and the Kid, Teresa's Tattoo, Baby's Day Out, Bad Boys, Congo, Steal Big Steal Little, Bound, The Immortals.
TELEVISION: *Series*: Free Country, The Fanelli Boys. *Mini-Series*: Robert F. Kennedy: His Life and Times, From Here to Eternity. *Guest*: Tales from the Crypt (ACE Award nomination), Amazing Stories, L.A. Law, The Hitchhiker. *Movies*: More Than Friends, Alcatraz: The Whole Shocking Story, Nightbreaker, Destination America, El Diablo, One Special Victory, Through the Eyes of a Killer, The Last (also co-assoc. prod.).

PAPAS, IRENE
Actress. b. Chiliomodion, Greece, Sept. 3, 1926. Entered dramatic school at 12. At 16 sang and danced in variety shows before debuting in Greek films, 1950. 1958 appeared with Greek Popular Theatre in Athens. Received Salonika Film Fest. Awards for the films Antigone, Electra.
THEATER: The Idiot, Journey's End, The Merchant of Venice, Inherit the Wind, That Summer, That Fall, Iphigenia in Aulis.
PICTURES: Lost Angels (debut, 1950), Dead City, The Unfaithful, Atilla the Hun, Theodora the Slave Empress, Whirlpool, Tribute to a Bad Man, Antigone, The Guns of Navarone, Electra, The Moon-Spinners, Zorba the Greek, We Still Kill the Old Way, The Desperate Ones, The Brotherhood, Anne of the Thousand Days, Z, A Dream of Kings, The Trojan Women, Roma Bene, Bambina, Mohammed: Messenger of God, Iphigenia, Bloodline, (Christ Stopped at) Eboli, Lion of the Desert, Erendira, Into the Night, The Assisi Underground, Sweet Country, High Season, Chronicle of a Death Foretold, Island, Drums of Fire, Banquet, Zoe, Up Down and Sideways.
TELEVISION: Moses the Lawgiver.

PAQUIN, ANNA
Actress. b. Winnipeg, Manitoba, Canada, July 24, 1982.
PICTURES: The Piano (Acad. Award, 1994; Golden Globe nom.), Fly Away Home, Jane Eyre, Amistad, Over the Moon, Hurly-burly, Begin the Beguine.
TELEVISION: *Movie:* The Member of the Wedding.

PARE, MICHAEL
Actor. b. Brooklyn, NY, Oct. 9, 1959. e. Culinary Inst. of America, Hyde Park, NY. Worked as chef and model before being discovered by ABC talent agent.
PICTURES: Eddie and the Cruisers (debut, 1983), Streets of Fire, The Philadelphia Experiment, Under Cover (Aust.), Space Rage, Instant Justice, The Women's Club, World Gone Wild, Eddie and the Cruisers II: Eddie Lives, Moon 44, Dragon Fight, Concrete War, The Closer, Into the Sun, Midnight Heat, First Light, Point of Impact, Village of the Damned, Bad Moon.
TELEVISION: *Series*: The Greatest American Hero, Houston Knights. *Movie:* Crazy Times.

PARISH, JAMES ROBERT
Film Historian, Executive. b. Cambridge, MA, April 21, 1944. e. U. of PA (BA, Phi Beta Kappa); U. of PA Law School (LLB). Member of NY Bar. Founder Entertainment Copyright Research Co., Inc. 1968-69, film reporter, Motion Picture Daily, weekly Variety. 1969-70, entertainment publicist, Harold Rand & Co. (NY). Currently marketing consultant in direct marketing industry, contributor to arts sections of major national newspapers and entertainment trade papers, and series editor of show business books.

AUTHOR: Hollywood's Great Musicals, Prostitution in Hollywood Films, Ghosts & Angels in Hollywood Films, Hollywood Songsters, Prison Pictures From Hollywood, Hollywood Baby Boomers, The Great Detective Pictures, The Great Cop Pictures, The Great Science Fiction Pictures II, Complete Actors TV Credits (1948-88), The Great Combat Pictures, Black Action Pictures From Hollywood, The Great Detective Pictures, The Great Western Pictures II: The Great Gangster Pictures II: The Great Spy Pictures II, Actors TV Credits, The Best of MGM, The Forties Gals, The Great American Movies Book, Hollywood Happiness, The Funsters, Hollywood on Hollywood, The Hollywood Beauties, Elvis!, The Great Science Fiction Pictures, The Child Stars, The Jeannette MacDonald Story, Great Movie Heroes, Liza!, The RKO Gals, Vincent Price Unmasked, The George Raft File, The Emmy Awards, Hollywood Death Book, Gays & Lesbians in Mainstream Cinema, Hollywood Celebrity Death Book (updated), Let's Talk: America's Favorite TV Talk Show Hosts, Today's Black Hollywood, Pirates and Seafaring Swashbucklers, Rosie: Rosie O'Donnell's Story, The Unofficial 'Murder She Wrote' Casebook, Whoopi Goldberg, among others.

PARKER, ALAN
Director, Writer. b. Islington, London, England, Feb. 14, 1944. Worked way up in advertising industry from mail room to top writer and dir. of nearly 500 TV commercials between 1969-78. Appointed chmn. of British Film Institute, 1997.
PICTURES: Melody (s.p., 1968). Director: No Hard Feelings (also s.p.), Our Cissy (also s.p.), Footsteps (also s.p.), Bugsy Malone (also s.p.; Brit. Acad. Award for best s.p.), Midnight Express (Brit. Acad. Award), Fame, Shoot the Moon, Pink Floyd—The Wall, Birdy, Angel Heart, Mississippi Burning, Come and See the Paradise (also s.p.), The Commitments (also cameo; BAFTA Award for best dir., 1991), The Road to Wellville (also s.p., co-prod.), Evita (also prod., s.p.).
TELEVISION: The Evacuees (Brit. Acad. Award).

PARKER, COREY
Actor. b. New York, NY, July 8, 1965. e. NYU.
THEATER: NY: Meeting the Winter Bike Rider (Off-B'way debut, 1984), Been Taken, The Bloodletters, The Semi-Formal.
PICTURES: Scream for Help (debut, 1984), Friday the 13th Part V: A New Beginning, Something Special, Nine 1/2 Weeks, Biloxi Blues, How I Got Into College, Big Man on Campus, White Palace, Flesh Suitcase, Mr. & Mrs. Loving, Fool's Paradise, Scream 2.
TELEVISION: Series: Eddie Dodd, Flying Blind, Blue Skies, The Love Boat: The Next Wave. Movies: Courage, At Mother's Request, Liz: The Elizabeth Taylor Story, A Mother's Prayer, Encino Woman. Specials: Don't Touch, Teen Father, The Lost Language of Cranes. Pilot: Sons of Gunz. Guest: The Bronx Zoo, thirtysomething.

PARKER, ELEANOR
Actress. b. Cedarville, OH, June 26, 1922. In Cleveland play group; in summer stock Martha's Vineyard; at Pasadena Community Playhouse.
PICTURES: They Died With Their Boots On (debut, 1941), Buses Roar, Mysterious Doctor, Mission to Moscow, Between Two Worlds, The Very Thought of You, Crime By Night, Hollywood Canteen, Last Ride, Pride of the Marines, Never Say Goodbye, Of Human Bondage, Escape Me Never, Woman in White, Voice of the Turtle, It's a Great Feeling, Chain Lightning, Caged (Acad. Award nom.), Three Secrets, Valentino, Millionaire for Christy, Detective Story (Acad. Award nom.), Scaramouche, Above and Beyond, Escape from Fort Bravo, Naked Jungle, Valley of the Kings, Many Rivers to Cross, Interrupted Melody (Acad. Award nom.), Man with the Golden Arm, King and Four Queens, Lizzie, Seventh Sin, A Hole in the Head, Home from the Hill, Return to Peyton Place, Madison Avenue, Panic Button, The Sound of Music, The Oscar, An American Dream, Warning Shot, Tiger and the Pussycat, Eye of the Cat, Sunburn.
TELEVISION: Series: Bracken's World. Movies: Maybe I'll Come Home in the Spring, Vanished, Home for the Holidays, The Great American Beauty Contest, Fantasy Island (pilot), The Bastard, She's Dressed to Kill, Once Upon a Spy, Madame X, Dead on the Money. Pilot: Guess Who's Coming to Dinner. Special: Hans Brinker. Guest: Buick Electra Playhouse, Kraft Suspense Theatre, The Man from U.N.C.L.E., Vega$, Hawaii 5-0, The Love Boat, Hotel, Murder She Wrote, etc.

PARKER, FESS
Actor. b. Fort Worth, TX, Aug. 16, 1924. e. USC. U.S. Navy, 1943-46; national co., Mr. Roberts, 1951.
PICTURES: Untamed Frontier (debut, 1952), No Room for the Groom, Springfield Rifle, Thunder Over the Plains, Island in the Sky, The Kid From Left Field, Take Me to Town, Them!, Battle Cry, Davy Crockett—King of the Wild Frontier (from Disney TV show), Davy Crockett and the River Pirates (from TV show), The Great Locomotive Chase, Westward Ho! the Wagons, Old Yeller, The Light in the Forest, The Hangman, Alias Jesse James (cameo), The Jayhawkers, Hell Is for Heroes, Smoky.

TELEVISION: Series: Mr. Smith Goes to Washington, Daniel Boone. Guest: Jonathan Winters, Walt Disney presents (Davy Crockett), Playhouse 90 (Turn Left at Mount Everest), Ed Sullivan, Danny Kaye Show, Phyllis Diller, Joey Bishop, Dean Martin, Red Skelton, Glen Campbell, Andy Williams, Vicki Lawrence. Movie: Climb an Angry Mountain.

PARKER, JAMESON
Actor. b. Baltimore, MD, Nov. 18, 1947. e. Beloit Coll. Professional stage debut in Washington Theatre Club production, Caligula. Acted with Arena Stage in DC; worked in dinner theatres and summer stock. Moved to N.Y., working in TV commercials and acted in play, Equus (Coconut Grove Playhouse).
PICTURES: The Bell Jar (debut, 1979), A Small Circle of Friends, White Dog, American Justice (also prod.), Jackals, Prince of Darkness, Curse of the Crystal Eye.
TELEVISION: Series: Somerset, One Life to Live, Simon and Simon. Movies: Women at West Point, Anatomy of a Seduction, The Gathering Part II, The Promise of Love, Callie and Son, A Caribbean Mystery, Who Is Julia?, Spy, She Says She's Innocent, Dead Before Dawn, Simon & Simon: In Trouble Again, Have You Seen My Son?, Dead Man's Island; Something Borrowed, Something Blue.

PARKER, MARY-LOUISE
Actress. b. Ft. Jackson, SC, Aug. 2, 1964. e. Bard Coll. 1990, received Clarence Derwent Award for her work in the theatre.
THEATER: B'way: Prelude to a Kiss (Theatre World Award). Off-B'way: Hayfever, The Girl in Pink, Babylon Gardens, Throwing Your Voice, Four Dogs and a Bone, Communicating Doors. Regional: The Importance of Being Earnest, Up in Saratoga, The Miser, Hay Fever, The Night of the Iguana, The Age of Pie.
PICTURES: Signs of Life (debut, 1989), Longtime Companion, Grand Canyon, Fried Green Tomatoes, Mr. Wonderful, Naked in New York, The Client, Bullets Over Broadway, Boys on the Side, Reckless, The Portrait of a Lady, Murder in Mind, The Maker, Let the Devil Wear Black, Goodbye Cover.
TELEVISION: Movies: Too Young the Hero, A Place for Annie.

PARKER, SARAH JESSICA
Actress. b. Nelsonville, OH, March 25, 1965. Was dancer with Cincinnati Ballet and American Ballet Theatre. Professional debut at age 8 in TV special The Little Match Girl.
THEATER: NY: The Innocents, By Strouse, Annie (title role for 2 yrs.), To Gillian on Her 37th Birthday, The Heidi Chronicles, The Substance of Fire, Sylvia, How To Succeed In Business Without Really Trying, Once Upon A Mattress.
PICTURES: Rich Kids (debut, 1979), Somewhere Tomorrow, Footloose, Firstborn, Girls Just Want to Have Fun, Flight of the Navigator, L.A. Story, Honeymoon in Vegas, Hocus Pocus, Striking Distance, Ed Wood, Miami Rhapsody, If Lucy Fell, The Substance of Fire, First Wives Club, Extreme Measures, Mars Attacks!, 'Til There Was You.
TELEVISION: Series: Square Pegs, A Year in the Life, Equal Justice. Specials: The Almost Royal Family, Life Under Water. Movies: My Body My Child, Going for the Gold: The Bill Johnson Story, A Year in the Life, The Room Upstairs, Dadah Is Death, Twist of Fate, The Ryan White Story, In the Best Interest of the Children, The Sunshine Boys.

PARKER, SUZY
Actress. r.n. Cecelia Parker. b. San Antonio, TX, Oct. 28, 1933. m. actor Bradford Dillman. e. schools in NY, FL. Began career at 17 as fashion model; becoming the highest paid fashion model and cover girl in U.S.; went to Paris under contract to fashion magazine; film debut as model in Funny Face (1957); signed by 20th-Fox prod. chief Buddy Adler for part opposite Cary Grant in Kiss Them for Me.
PICTURES: Funny Face, Kiss Them For Me, Ten North Frederick, The Best of Everything, Circle of Deception, The Interns, Flight From Ashiya, Chamber of Horrors.

PARKES, WALTER F.
Producer, Writer. b. Bakersfield, CA. e. Yale, Stanford Univ. 1978 prod. & dir. documentary The California Reich which was nominated for Acad. Award.
PICTURES: WarGames (s.p.; Acad. Award nom.). Exec. Prod.: Volunteers, Project X, True Believer, Awakenings (Acad. Award nom.), Sneakers (also co-s.p.), Little Giants; To Wong Foo, Thanks for Everything, Julie Newmar; How to Make an American Quilt, Twister, The Trigger Effect, Amistad, Men In Black, The Peacemaker, Deep Impact, Small Soldiers, The Mask of Zorro.
TELEVISION: Series: Eddie Dodd (prod., writer). Pilot: Birdland (prod., writer).

PARKINS, BARBARA
Actress. b. Vancouver, British Columbia, Canada, May 22, 1942.
PICTURES: Valley of the Dolls, The Kremlin Letter, The Mephisto Waltz, Puppet on a Chain, Asylum, Shout at the Devil, Bear Island, Breakfast in Paris.

TELEVISION: *Series*: Peyton Place, Scene of the Crime. *Mini-Series*: Captains and the Kings. *Movies*: A Taste of Evil, Snatched, Law of the Land, Testimony of Two Men, Young Joe: The Forgotten Kennedy, Ziegfield: The Man and His Women, The Critical List, The Manions of America, Uncommon Valor, To Catch a King, Calendar Girl Murders, Peyton Place: The Next Generation, Jennie: Lady Randolph Churchill. *Guest*: G.E. Theatre, My Three Sons, Dr. Kildare, Gibbsville, Hotel, The Love Boat, Murder She Wrote. *Special*: Jennie.

PARKS, GORDON
Director, Writer, Photographer, Composer, Poet, Photojournalist. b. Fort Scott, KS, Nov. 30, 1912. From the age of 15 worked as piano player, bus boy, dining car waiter and prof. basketball player in MN before taking up photography in late 1930's. Awarded 1st Julius Rosenwald Fellowship in photog., 1942. Worked with Roy Stryker at Farm Security Admin., WWII Office of War Info. correspondent. Photo-journalist, Life Mag., 1949-68, editorial dir. (and founder): Essence Magazine 1970-73. Film debut 1961 with doc. Flavio (dir. and writer), followed by Diary of a Harlem Family (doc.; Emmy Award). Winner of numerous awards including NAACP's Spingarn Medal and Kansas Governor's Medal of Honor, Nat'l Medal of Arts, 1988. Recipient of 23 honorary degrees in lit., fine arts, humane letters. Member of NAACP, AMPAS, PEN American Center, AFI, etc.
AUTHOR: The Learning Tree, A Choice of Weapons, A Poet and His Camera, Whispers of Intimate Things, In Love, Born Black, Moments Without Proper Names, Flavio, To Smile in Autumn, Shannon, Voices in the Mirror, Irias In Silence, Glimpses Toward Infinity.
PICTURES: The Learning Tree (Library of Congress Nat'l Film Registry Classics honor, 1989), Shaft, Shaft's Big Score, Super Cops, Leadbelly.
TELEVISION: The Odyssey of Solomon Northup, Moments Without Proper Names, Martin.

PARKS, MICHAEL
Actor. b. Corona, CA, April 4, 1938.
PICTURES: Wild Seed (debut, 1964), Bus Riley's Back in Town, The Bible, The Idol, The Happening, The Last Hard Men, Sidewinder One, ffolkes, Hard Country, Savannah Smiles, Spiker, Club Life, The Return of Josey Wales (also dir.), Spiker, Arizona Heat, Nightmare Beach, Prime Suspect, The Hitman, Storyville, Death Wish 5: The Face of Death, Stranger by Night.
TELEVISION: *Series*: Then Came Bronson, The Colbys, Twin Peaks. *Movies*: Can Ellen Be Saved?, Savage Bees, Chase, Dangerous Affection, Gore Vidal's Billy the Kid, The China Lake Murders, Hart to Hart: Secrets of the Hart.

PARKS, VAN DYKE
Composer, actor. Albums include: Song Cycle, Discover America, Clang of the Yankee Reaper, Jump!, Tokyo Rose, Orange Crate Art (with Brian Wilson).
PICTURES: The Swan, A Gift for Heidi (actor only), Goin' South, Popeye (actor only), Loose Shoes (actor only), Sesame Street Presents Follow That Bird, Club Paradies, The Brave Little Toaster (songs), Vibes (actor only), Casual Sex?, The Two Jakes (actor only), He Said She Said (actor only), Out on a Limb, Wild Bill, Bastard Out of Carolina, Private Parts, Shadrach.
TELEVISION: *Movies*: Mother Goose Rock 'n' Rhyme (actor only), One Christmas, Next Door, The Summer of Ben Tyler, Oliver Twist. *Series*: Bonino (actor only).

PARRETTI, GIANCARLO
Executive. b. Orvieto, Italy, Oct. 23, 1941. Hotelier in Sicily in the late 1970's. Managing dir. of Naples newspaper Diario, until 1981. 1987, purchased Cannon Group, renaming it Pathe Communications. 1990, company acquired MGM/UA, Communications. Resigned 1991.

PARSONS, ESTELLE
Actress. b. Marblehead, MA, Nov. 20, 1927. e. Connecticut Coll. for Women, Bachelor's degree in political science. Attended Boston U. Law Sch. Helped harvest crops in England with the Women's Land Army. Was active in politics; worked for the Committee for the Nation's Health in Wash. and the Republican Finance Committee in Boston. Was elected to public office in Marblehead, Mass. Joined NBC-TV's Today Show as prod. asst.; then writer, feature prod. and commentator. Appeared in two Julius Monk revues, Jerry Herman's Nightcap.
THEATER: Happy Hunting, Whoop Up, Beg Borrow or Steal, Mrs. Dally Has a Lover (Theater World Award), Next Time I'll Sing to You (Obie Award), In the Summer House (Obie Award), Ready When You Are C.B., Malcolm, The Seven Descents of Myrtle, ...And Miss Reardon Drinks a Little, The Norman Conquests, Ladies of the Alamo, Miss Margarida's Way, Pirates of Penzance, The Unguided Missile, Threepenny Opera, Lincoln Center Repertory Theatre, Mahagonny, Forgiving Typhoid Mary, Shimada, The Shadow Box, Twice Removed, Grace & Glorie.

PICTURES: Ladybug Ladybug (debut, 1963), Bonnie and Clyde (Acad. Award, best supporting actress, 1967), Rachel Rachel (Acad. Award nom.), Don't Drink the Water, Watermelon Man, I Walk the Line, I Never Sang for My Father, Two People, For Pete's Sake, Foreplay (The President's Woman), Dick Tracy, The Lemon Sisters, Boys on the Side, That Darn Cat, Looking for Richard.
TELEVISION: *Mini-Series*: Backstairs at the White House. *Special*: The Front Page. *Movies*: Terror on the Beach, The Gun and the Pulpit, The UFO Incident, The Gentleman Bandit, Open Admissions, A Private Matter, The American Clock. *Series*: Roseanne. *Guest*: All in the Family.

PARTON, DOLLY
Singer, Composer, Actress. b. Sevierville, TN, Jan. 19, 1946. Gained fame as country music singer, composer and radio and TV personality. Co-partner with Sandy Gallin, Sandollar Prods. *Author*: My Life and Other Unfinished Business (autobiography), Coat of Many Colors.
PICTURES: Nine to Five (debut, 1980; also wrote & sang title song), The Best Little Whorehouse in Texas (also wrote addtl. songs), Rhinestone (also songs), Steel Magnolias, Straight Talk (also songs), The Beverly Hillbillies.
TELEVISION: *Series*: Dolly (1976), Dolly (1987-88). *Guest*: Porter Wagoner Show, Cass Walker Program, Bill Anderson Show, Wilbur Bros. Show. *Specials*: Kenny Dolly & Willie: Something Inside So Strong, A Tennessee Mountain Thanksgiving. *Movies*: A Smoky Mountain Christmas (also songs), Wild Texas Wind (also co-writer, co-prod.), Big Dreams & Broken Hearts: The Dottie West Story.

PASDAR, ADRIAN
Actor. b. 1965 Pittsfield, MA. e. Univ. of Central FL. Studied acting with People's Light and Theatre Co., Lee Strasberg Institute.
THEATER: *Regional*: The Glass Menagerie, Shadow Box, Hotters, Sorry Wrong Number, Cold Foot, Monkey's Paw.
PICTURES: Top Gun (debut, 1986), Streets of Gold, Solarbabies, Near Dark, Made in USA, Cookie, Vital Signs, Torn Apart, Just Like a Woman, The Pompatus of Love, Ties to Rachel, Wounded, A Brother's Kiss.
TELEVISION: *Series*: Profit, Feds. *Movies*: The Lost Capone, A Mother's Gift, Touched by Evil, Love in Antother Town, The Perfect Getaway. *Mini-Series*: House of Frankenstein. *Special*: Big Time.

PASETTA, MARTY
Producer-Director. b. June 16, 1932. e. U. Santa Clara.
TELEVISION: AFI Salutes to Fred Astaire, John Huston, Lillian Gish, Alfred Hitchcock and Jimmy Stewart, Gene Kelly Special, Elvis Aloha From Hawaii, Oscar (17), Emmy (2) and Grammy (8) Award Shows, A Country Christmas (1978-81), The Monte Carlo Show, Texaco Star Theatre-Opening Night, Burnett Discovers Domingo, Disneyland's 30th Anniversary Celebration, 15 Years of Cerebral Palsy Telethons, A Night at the Moulin Rouge, Soap Opera Awards, An All-Star Celebration Honoring Martin Luther King, Disneyland's Summer Vacation Party, Disney's Captain EO Grand Opening, 15th Anniversary of Disney World; Beach Boys... 25 Years Together, Super Night at the Superbowl, 20th Anniversary of Caesars Palace, Paris by Night with George Burns, I Call You Friend Papal Spacebridge '87, Walt Disney World's Celebrity Circus, Las Vegas: An All-Star 75th Anniversary, Julio Iglesias—Sold Out, The Ice Capades with Kirk Cameron, American All-Star Tribute Honoring Elizabeth Taylor.

PASOLINI, UBERTO
Producer.
PICTURES: The Killing Fields, The Frog Prince, The Mission, Meeting Venus, Palookaville, The Full Monty (BAFTA Award, Outstanding Brit. Film, 1997).
TELEVISION: *Movies*: A Dangerous Man: Lawrence After Arabia.

PASSER, IVAN
Director, Writer. b. Prague, Czechoslovakia, July 10, 1933. e. Film Faculty of Acad. of Musical Arts, Prague. 1961, asst. dir. to Milos Forman on Audition which led to scripting for Forman. 1969, moved to U.S., worked in NY as longshoreman while studying Eng. U.S. dir. debut: Born to Win, 1971.
PICTURES: *Writer*: Loves of a Blonde, A Boring Afternoon, Fireman's Ball. *Director*: Intimate Lighting (also s.p.), Born to Win, Law and Disorder, Crime and Passion, The Silver Bears, Cutter and Bone, Creator, Haunted Summer.
TELEVISION: *U.S.*: Faerie Tale Theatre. *Movies*: Fourth Story, Stalin, While Justice Sleeps, Kidnapped.

PASTER, GARY M.
Executive. b. St. Louis, MO, July 4, 1943. e. U. of MO, B.A.; UCLA, USC Graduate Sch. of Business. 1970, joined Burbank Studios as asst. to pres.; treas.; 1976 v.p., admin. and chmn. of the exec. comm.; 1977 pres. Member: AMPAS, LA Film Dev. Council, Hollywood Radio & T.V. Society, Acad. of Television Arts and Sciences. Advisory bd., Kaufman Astoria Studios, N.Y.

PASTORELLI, ROBERT
Actor. b. New Brunswick, NJ, June 21, 1954.
TELEVISION: I Married a Centerfold, California Girls, Hands of a Stranger, Outrageous Fortune, Beverly Hills Cop II, Memories of Me, Lady Mobster, Dances with Wolves, Painted Heart, Folks!, Fern Gully: The Last Rainforest, Striking Distance, Sister Act 2: Back in the Habit, Robin Cook's Harmful Intent, The Yam Princess, The West Side Waltz, Eraser, Michael, A Simple Wish. *Series*: Murphy Brown, Double Rush, Cracker. *Guest*: Tucker's Witch, Hill Street Blues, MacGyver, Batman.

PATINKIN, MANDY
Actor. b. Chicago, IL, Nov. 30, 1952. r.n. Mandel Patinkin. e. U. of Kansas, Juilliard Sch. (Drama Div.; 1972-74). m. actress Kathryn Grody. In regional theatre before coming to New York where played with Shakespeare Festival Public Theater (Trelawny of the Wells, Hamlet, Rebel Women). Recordings: Mandy Patinkin, Dress Casual, Experiment.
THEATER: Savages, The Shadow Box (B'way debut), Evita (Tony Award, 1980), Henry IV, Part I (Central Park), Sunday in the Park With George (Tony nom.), The Knife, Follies in Concert, A Winter's Tale, Mandy Patinkin: Dress Casual (solo concert), The Secret Garden, Falsettos.
PICTURES: The Big Fix (debut, 1978), Last Embrace, French Postcards, Night of the Juggler, Ragtime, Daniel, Yentl, Maxie, The Princess Bride, The House on Carroll Street, Alien Nation, Dick Tracy, True Colors, Impromptu, The Doctor, The Music of Chance, Life With Mikey (cameo), Squanto: A Warrior's Tale.
TELEVISION: *Series*: Chicago Hope (Emmy Award, 1995). *Guest*: That Thing on ABC, That 2nd Thing on ABC, Taxi, Sparrow, Streets of Gold, Midnight Special. *Movie*: Charleston.

PATRIC, JASON
Actor. b. Queens, NY, June 17, 1966. Son of playwright-actor Jason Miller. Grandson of performer Jackie Gleason. Began professional career with Vermont's Champlain Shakespeare Festival.
THEATER: *NY*: Beirut. *LA*: Out of Gas on Lovers' Leap.
PICTURES: Solarbabies (debut, 1986), The Lost Boys, The Beast, Denial, After Dark My Sweet, Roger Corman's Frankenstein Unbound, Rush, Geronimo: An American Legend, The Journey of August King, Sleepers, Speed 2: Cruise Control.
TELEVISION: *Movie*: Tough Love. *Special*: Teach 109.

PATRICK, C.L., Sr.
Theatre Executive. b. Honaker, VA, Dec. 6, 1918. Former pres. of Fuqua Industries which owned Martin Theatres and Gulf States Theatres. Prior to this was pres. and chairman of Martin Theatres. Presently chairman of board Carmike Cinemas, Inc.; v.p. Variety International; dir., Will Rogers Institute; Motion Picture Pioneer of 1976; Recipient of: Sherrill Corwin Award, 1984; Salah Hassanein Humanitarian Award, ShowEast '88; Show South's Exhibitor of the Decade Award, 1990.

PATRICK, MICHAEL W.
Executive. b. Columbus, GA, May 17, 1950. e. Columbus Coll., B.S., 1972. Pres., CEO, Carmike Cinemas. 1989. Board of dir., Columbus Bank and Trust Co. Member: exec. comm., Will Rogers Institute; Variety Int'l; Motion Picture Pioneers.

PATRICK, ROBERT
Actor. b. Marietta, GA. 1959.
PICTURES: Eye of the Eagle, Equalizer 2000, Killer Instinct, Hollywood Boulevard II, Future Hunters, Die Hard 2, Terminator 2: Judgment Day, Double Dragon, Body Shot, Fire in the Sky, Zero Tolerance, Hong Kong 97, The Cool Surface, Last Gasp, Decoy, Terminator 2: 3-D, Asylum, Striptease, The Only Thrill, Hacks, Rosewood, Cop Land, Ravager (prod. only), Very Bad Things, Winter, Counter Force, A Breed Apart, Texas Blood Money, The Faculty.
TELEVISION: *Movies*: Resident Alien, Body Language. *Series*: Real Adventures of Jonny Quest. *Guest*: The Outer Limits.

PATTON, WILL
Actor. b. Charleston, SC, June 14, 1954. e. NC School of the Arts, 1975.
THEATER: *NY*: Tourists and Refugees #2 (La Mama E.T.C., Obie Award), Fool For Love (Obie Award), Goose and Tomtom (Public Theatre), A Lie of the Mind.
PICTURES: King Blank, Silkwood, Variety, Desperately Seeking Susan, After Hours, Chinese Boxes, Belizaire the Cajun, No Way Out, Stars and Bars, Wildfire, Signs of Life, Everybody Wins, A Shock to the System, The Rapture, Cold Heaven, In the Soup, The Paint Job, Romeo Is Bleeding, Natural Causes, Midnight Edition, Tollbooth, The Client, The Puppet Masters, Copycat, Johns, Inventing the Abbotts, The Postman, O.K. Garage, I Woke Up Early the Day I Died, Breakfast of Champions, Armageddon.
TELEVISION: *Movies*: Kent State, Dillinger, A Gathering of Old Men, The Deadly Desire, In the Deep Woods, A Child Lost Forever, Taking the Heat, Judicial Consent. *Series*: Ryan's Hope, Search For Tomorrow.

PAULEY, JANE
TV Host, Journalist. b. Indianapolis, IN, Oct. 31, 1950. m. Doonesbury creator Garry Trudeau. e. Indiana U. Involved in Indiana state politics before joining WISH-TV, Indianapolis, as reporter. Co-anchored midday news reports and anchored weekend news reports. Co-anchor of nightly news at WMAQ-TV, NBC station in Chicago. Joined Today Show in October, 1976, as featured regular, prior to which had made guest appearances on that program; co-host until 1990. Began own series Real Life With Jane Pauley in 1991.

PAVAN, MARISA
Actress, r.n. Marisa Pierangeli. b. Cagliari, Sardinia, Italy, June 19, 1932. e. Torquato Tasso Coll. Twin sister of late actress Pier Angeli. Came to U.S. 1950.
PICTURES: What Price Glory? (debut, 1952), Down Three Dark Streets, Drum Beat, The Rose Tattoo (Acad. Award nom.), Diane, The Man in the Gray Flannel Suit, The Midnight Story, John Paul Jones, Solomon and Sheba, A Slightly Pregnant Man.

PAVLIK, JOHN M.
Executive. b. Melrose, IA, Dec. 3, 1939. e. U. of Minnesota, B.A., 1963. Reporter, Racine (WI) Journal-Times, San Bernardino (CA) Sun-Telegram, 1963-66; writer, News Bureau, Pacific Telephone, Los Angeles, 1966-68; asst. dir. of publ. rltns., Association of Motion Picture and Television Producers, 1968-72; dir. of PR, 1972-78; v.p., 1978-79; special consultant, California Motion Picture Council, 1974-79; member, exec. council, Los Angeles Film Dev. Committee, v.p., 1977-78; exec. admin., Academy of Motion Picture Arts and Sciences, 1979-82; member, bd. of dir., Permanent Charities Comm. of the Entertainment Industries, 1979-84; member, bd. of dir., Hollywood Chamber of Commerce, 1979-85; exec. dir., M.P. & TV Fund, 1982-88; consultant, 1988-89; member, advisory board, Assn. of Film Commissioners Int'l, 1988-91; dir. of endowment dev., Academy Foundation, 1989-92; dir. of communications, AAMPA, 1992-present.

PAXSON, LOWELL W.
Executive. b. Rochester, NY. e. Syracuse U. As teenager worked in radio in Rochester and became announcer while in college. Purchased first broadcast entity, WACK radio in Newark NY, 1954. Began selling merchandise on a Florida AM station in 1977. Conceived and founded Home Shopping Network, 1982. Est. Silver King Communications, 1986. Sold interest in HSN and Silver King in 1990 and bought WCRJ radio in Florida, start of Paxson Communications Corp. Sold radio interests in 1997 and acquired The Travel Channel, which has since been sold to Discovery Communications, Inc. Launched PAX TV, the seventh US TV network, in 1998. CEO and Chairman, Paxson Communications Corp.

PAXTON, BILL
Actor. b. Fort Worth, TX, May 17, 1955. e. NYU. First professional job as set dresser for film Big Bad Mamma. Studied acting in NYC with Stella Adler. Dir. short films Fish Heads, Scoop (also s.p.)
PICTURES: Stripes, The Lords of Discipline, Mortuary, Streets of Fire, Impulse, The Terminator, Weird Science, Commando, Aliens, Near Dark, Pass the Ammo, Slipstream, Next of Kin, Back to Back, Brain Dead, The Last of the Finest, Navy SEALS, Predator 2, The Dark Backward, One False Move, The Vagrant, Trespass, Indian Summer, Boxing Helena, Future Shock, Monolith, Tombstone, True Lies, Apollo 13, The Last Supper, Twister, The Evening Star, Titanic, Traveller, A Simple Plan, Mighty Joe Young.
TELEVISION: *Mini-Series*: Fresno. *Movies*: Deadly Lessons, The Atlanta Child Murders, An Early Frost, Frank and Jesse, A Bright Shining Lie. *Guest*: Miami Vice.

PAY, WILLIAM
UK Manager Quigley Publishing Co., Inc. b. London, England. Joined London office Quigley Publications. Served in RAF, 1941-46; rejoined Quigley; dir. Burnup Service Ltd., 1951; London news ed., Quigley Pub., 1955; dir., Quigley Pub. Ltd., 1961; appt. mgr. dir., 1963; mgr. dir., Burnup Company. Appt. Sec. British Kinematograph Sound & TV Society. Conference Co-ordinator biennial Intern. Film & TV Technology Conferences in U.K., 1975-87.

PAYMER, DAVID
Actor. b. Long Island, NY, Aug. 30, 1954. e. Univ. of Mich. First professional job with natl. company of Grease, which he later appeared in on B'way. Has also taught acting at UCLA and the Film Actor's Workshop, performed stand-up comedy and served as staff writer on The New Leave It to Beaver Show.
PICTURES: The In-Laws (debut, 1979), Airplane II: The Sequel, Best Defense, Irreconcilable Differences, Perfect, Howard the Duck, No Way Out, Crazy People, City Slickers, Mr. Saturday Night (Acad. Award nom.), Searching for Bobby Fischer, Heart and Souls, City Slickers II: The Legend of Curly's Gold, Quiz Show, City Hall, The American President, Unforgettable, Nixon, Get Shorty, The Sixth Man, Amistad, The Long Way Home (voice), Gang Related, Mighty Joe Young, Mumford, Payback, Outside Ozona.

TELEVISION: *Series:* The Commish. *Guest:* Cagney & Lacy, The Paper Chase, Taxi, Cheers, L.A. Law, Hill Street Blues, Moonlighting, Murphy Brown. *Movies:* Grace Kelly, Pleasure, Cagney & Lacey: The Return, Cagney & Lacey: Together Again, Crime of the Century. *Special:* In Search of Dr. Seuss.

PAYNTER, ROBERT
Cinematographer. b. London, England, March 12, 1928. e. Mercer Sch. First job in industry at 15 years as camera trainee with Government Film Dept.
PICTURES: Hannibal Brooks (debut, 1969), The Games, Lawman, The Nightcomers, Chato's Land, The Mechanic, Scorpio, The Big Sleep, Superman, Firepower, The Final Conflict, Superman II, An American Werewolf in London, Superman III, Trading Places, The Muppets Take Manhattan, Into the Night, National Lampoon's European Vacation, Spies Like Us, Little Shop of Horrors, When the Whales Came, Strike It Rich, Get Back.

PAYS, AMANDA
Actress. b. Berkshire, England, June 6, 1959. m. actor Corbin Bernsen. Began as a model. Studied French, art and pottery at Hammersmith Polytechnic. Acting debut: Cold Room (HBO).
PICTURES: Oxford Blues, The Kindred, Off Limits, Leviathan, Exposure, Solitaire for Two.
TELEVISION: *Series:* Max Headroom, The Flash. *Mini-Series:* A.D. *Movies:* 13 at Dinner, The Pretenders, Parker Kane, Dead on the Money, The Thorn Birds: The Lost Years.

PAYSON, MARTIN D.
Executive. b. Brooklyn, NY, Jan. 4, 1936. e. Cornell U., NYU Sch. of Law, LLB, 1961. Practiced law privately before joining Warner Communications, Inc. as v.p. 1970. Later named exec. v.p., gen. counsel. 1987, appt. to 3-member office of pres., WCI. Was vice chmn. Time Warner Inc., until Dec. 1992. Retired.

PEAKER, E. J.
Actress, Singer, Dancer. r.n. Edra Jeanne Peaker. b. Tulsa, OK, Feb. 22. e. U. of New Mexico, U. of Vienna, Austria. Stage debut Bye, Bye Birdie
PICTURES: Hello Dolly! (debut, 1969), All American Boy, Private Roads, The Four Deuces, Graduation Day, Fire in the Night, I Can't Lose, Out of This World.
TELEVISION: *Series:* That's Life. *Guest:* The Flying Nun, That Girl, Love American Style, Odd Couple, Police Woman, Rockford Files, Get Christie Love, Houston Knights, Hunter, Quincy, Charlie's Angels, Six Million Dollar Man. *Movies:* There's a Crowd, Getting Away From It All, Broken Promises (assoc. prod., writer).

PEARCE, CHRISTOPHER
Producer. b. Dursley, Eng, Nov. 19, 1943. Entered industry as gen. mgr. American Zoetrope. From 1982 to 1985 served as exec. in chg. of prod. for Cannon Films Inc. overseeing prod. on 150 films incl. That Championship Season, Runaway Train, Fool For Love and Barfly. 1987 became sr. v.p. and COO Cannon Group. Has since become pres. & CEO Cannon Pictures. TV movie: Coming Out of the Ice.

PEARCE, CRAIG
Actor.
PICTURES: I Can't Get Started, Vicious!, Strictly Ballroom (s.p. only), Mad Bomber in Love, The Seventh Floor, Romeo + Juliet (BAFTA Award, Best Adapted Screenplay, 1997).

PEARCE, RICHARD
Director, Cinematographer. b. San Diego, CA, Jan. 25, 1943. e. Yale U., B.A. degree in Eng. lit., 1965. New School for Social Research, M.A. degree in political economics. Worked with Don Pennebaker and Richard Leacock on documentaries. Photographed Emile de Antonio's America Is Hard to See. In 1970 went to Chile where he dir., photographed and edited Campeamento, an award-winning documentary.
PICTURES: As photographer (Acad. Award winning documentaries): Woodstock, Marjoe, Interviews With My Lai Veterans, Hearts and Minds. *Director:* Heartland (debut, 1979), Threshold, Country, No Mercy, The Long Walk Home, Leap of Faith, A Family Thing.
TELEVISION: The Gardener's Son, Siege, No Other Love, Sessions, Dead Man Out, The Final Days.

PECK, GREGORY
Actor, Producer. r.n. Eldred Gregory Peck. b. La Jolla, CA, April 5, 1916. e. U. of California; Neighborhood Playhouse Sch. of Dramatics. Father of actors Tony and Cecilia Peck. On dramatic stage (The Doctor's Dilemma, The Male Animal, Once in a Lifetime, The Play's the Thing, You Can't Take It With You, The Morning Star, The Willow and I, Sons and Soldiers, etc.). Voted one of ten best Money-Making Stars Motion Picture Herald-Fame Poll, 1947, 1952. Co-prod. and starred in Big Country, for his company, Anthony Productions; prod. the Trial of the Catonsville Nine, The Dove (St. George Productions). Pres., Acad. M.P. Arts and Sciences, 1967-70. Founding mem., bd. mem. and chmn. American Film Inst. Recipient, Jean Hersholt Humanitarian Award, 1986. AFI Life Achievement Award, 1989. Voice of Florenz Ziegfeld in 1991 B'way musical The Will Rogers Follies.

PICTURES: Days of Glory (debut, 1944), The Keys of the Kingdom, The Valley of Decision, Spellbound, The Yearling, Duel in the Sun, The Macomber Affair, Gentleman's Agreement, The Paradine Case, Yellow Sky, The Great Sinner, Twelve O'Clock High, The Gunfighter, Only the Valiant, David and Bathsheba, Captain Horatio Hornblower, The World in His Arms, The Snows of Kilimanjaro, Roman Holiday, Night People, Man With a Million, The Purple Plain, The Man in the Gray Flannel Suit, Moby Dick, Designing Woman, The Bravados, The Big Country (also co-prod.), Pork Chop Hill (also prod.), Beloved Infidel, On the Beach, Guns of Navarone, To Kill a Mockingbird (Acad. Award, 1962), Cape Fear (also prod.), How the West Was Won, Captain Newman M.D., Behold a Pale Horse (also prod.), John F. Kennedy: Years of Lightning—Day of Drums (narrator), Mirage, Arabesque, MacKenna's Gold, Stalking Moon, The Chairman, Marooned, I Walk the Line, Shootout, Billy Two Hats, The Omen, MacArthur (also prod.), The Boys from Brazil (also prod.), The Sea Wolves (also prod.), Amazing Grace and Chuck, Old Gringo, Other People's Money, Cape Fear (1991).
TELEVISION: *Mini-series:* The Blue and the Gray. *Movies:* The Scarlet and the Black (also prod.), The Portrait. *Special:* We the People 200: The Constitutional Gala, The First 50 Years.

PEDAS, JIM
Executive. b. Youngstown, OH. e. Thiel College. Opened Circle Theatre in Washington, D.C. in 1957 with brother Ted. 1984 formed Circle Releasing, serving as Secretary/ Treasurer; Circle Films, serving as v.p. See Ted Pedas entry.

PEDAS, TED
Executive. b. Farrell, PA, May 6, 1931. e. Youngstown St. Univ., Wharton Sch. of Business at Univ. of Pa., Geo. Washington Univ. 1957, with brother Jim, opened Circle Theatre in Washington D.C. one of the first repertory houses. Circle/Showcase group of m.p. theatres expanded to over 80 quality screens before being sold in 1988. 1973-78, served on board of Cinema 5 in NY. 1984, Circle Releasing formed to distribute films with Ted serving as president. Releases include Blood Simple, The Navigator and the Killer. Circle Films has produced the Coen Brothers' Raising Arizona, Miller's Crossing, Barton Fink and Caught.

PEERCE, LARRY
Director. b. Bronx, NY. Father was late singer Jan Peerce.
PICTURES: One Potato Two Potato, The Big T.N.T. Show, The Incident, Goodbye Columbus, The Sporting Club, A Separate Peace, Ash Wednesday, The Other Side of the Mountain, Two Minute Warning, The Other Side of the Mountain—Part II, The Bell Jar (also exec. prod.), Why Would I Lie?, Love Child, Hard to Hold, Wired.
TELEVISION: *Movies:* A Stranger Who Looks Like Me, Love Lives On, I Take These Men, The Fifth Missile, Prison for Children, Queenie, Elvis and Me, The Neon Empire, The Court-Martial of Jackie Robinson, Child of Rage, Poisoned by Love: The Kern County Murders, Heaven & Hell: North and South Book III, A Burning Passion: The Margaret Mitchell Story, In Pursuit of Honor (co-exec. prod. only), An Element of Truth, The Abduction, Love-Struck.

PEÑA, ELIZABETH
Actress. b. N.J., Sept. 23, 1961 of cuban parents. Moved to New York City in 1969 where she attended NY High School for Performing Arts. Off-B'way in Blood Wedding, Antigone, Romeo & Juliet, Act One & Only, Italian American Reconciliation, and many others.
PICTURES: El Super, Times Square, They All Laughed, Fat Chance, Crossover Dreams, Down and Out in Beverly Hills, La Bamba, Batteries Not Included, Vibes, Blue Steel, Jacob's Ladder, The Waterdance, Across the Moon, Free Willy 2: The Adventure Home, Dead Funny, Lone Star (Ind't Spirit Award, 1997), Strangeland, The Pass, Rush Hour.
TELEVISION: *Series:* Tough Cookies, I Married Dora, Shannon's Deal. *Movies:* Fugitive Among Us, Roommates, It Came From Outer Space, Contagious, Second Civil War. *Miniseries:* Drug War, The Camarena Story, The Invaders, Aldrich Ames: America Betrayed.

PENDLETON, AUSTIN
Actor. b. Warren, OH, March 27, 1940. e. Yale Univ. Started acting with Williamstown Theatre Festival. Teaches acting at the Herbert Berghof Studio. Named artistic dir. of NY's Circle Rep. Theatre, 1995.
THEATER: *Actor:* Oh Dad Poor Dad Mama's Hung You in the Closet and I'm Feeling So Sad, Fiddler on the Roof, The Little Foxes, The Last Sweet Days of Isaac (NY Drama Critics & Outer Critics Circle Awards), Educating Rita, Doubles, The Sorrows of Frederick, Grand Hotel, Hamlet, Sophistry. *Director:* The Runner Stumbles, Say Goodnight Gracie, John Gabriel Borkman, The Little Foxes. *Author:* Booth, Uncle Bob.

PICTURES: Skidoo (debut, 1968), Catch-22, What's Up Doc?, Every Little Crook and Nanny, The Thief Who Came to Dinner, The Front Page, The Great Smokey Roadblock (The Last of the Cowboys), The Muppet Movie, Starting Over, Simon, First Family, My Man Adam, Off Beat, Short Circuit, Hello Again, Mr. & Mrs. Bridge, The Ballad of the Sad Cafe, True Identity, My Cousin Vinny, Charlie's Ear, Rain Without Thunder, My Boyfriend's Back, Searching for Bobby Fischer, Mr. Nanny, Greedy, Guarding Tess, Dangerous Minds, Two Much, Home for the Holidays, Sgt. Bilko, Trial and Error.
TELEVISION: *Movie*: Don't Drink the Water. *Guest*: Miami Vice, The Equalizer.

PENN, ARTHUR
Director. b. Philadelphia, PA, Sept. 27, 1922. e. Black Mountain Coll., Asheville, NC; U. of Perugia, U. of Florence in Italy. Began as TV dir. in 1953, twice winner of Sylvania Award. Appeared in 1994 film Naked in New York.
THEATER: Two for the Seesaw, Miracle Worker (Tony Award, 1960), Toys in the Attic, All the Way Home, Golden Boy, Wait Until Dark, Sly Fox, Monday After the Miracle, Hunting Cockroaches.
PICTURES: The Left-Handed Gun (debut, 1958), The Miracle Worker (Acad. Award nom.), Mickey One (also prod.), The Chase, Bonnie and Clyde (Acad. Award nom.), Alice's Restaurant (Acad. Award nom.; also co-s.p.), Little Big Man, Visions of Eight (dir. segment: The Highest), Night Moves, The Missouri Breaks, Four Friends (also co-prod.), Target, Dead of Winter, Penn and Teller Get Killed (also prod.), Inside.
TELEVISION: *Movie*: The Portrait.

PENN, CHRISTOPHER
Actor. b. Malibu, CA. Son of dir. Leo Penn and actress Eileen Ryan. Brother of actor Sean Penn and musician Michael Penn. Studied acting with Peggy Feury.
PICTURES: Rumble Fish (debut, 1983), All the Right Moves, Footloose, The Wild Life, Pale Rider, At Close Range, Made in USA, Return From the River Kwai, Best of the Best, Mobsters, Leather Jackets, Reservoir Dogs, Best of the Best 2, The Pickle, The Music of Chance, True Romance, Short Cuts, Josh and S.A.M., Beethoven's 2nd, Imaginary Crimes, Fist of the Northstar, Under the Hula Moon, To Wong Foo–Thanks for Everything–Julie Newmar, Sacred Cargo, Mulholland Falls, The Boys Club, The Funeral.
TELEVISION: *Guest*: Magnum P.I., The Young Riders, North Beach, Rawhide, Chicago Hope.

PENN, ROBIN WRIGHT
Actress. b. Dallas, TX, 1966. m. actor Sean Penn. Was model at age 14 before making acting debut on tv series The Yellow Rose.
PICTURES: Hollywood Vice Squad (debut, 1986), The Princess Bride, Denial, State of Grace, The Playboys, Toys, Forrest Gump, The Crossing Guard, Moll Flanders, Loved, She's So Lovely, Message In a Bottle, Hurly-burly.
TELEVISION: *Series*: Santa Barbara. *Pilot*: Home.

PENN, SEAN
Actor, Director, Writer. b. Burbank, CA, Aug. 17, 1960. Son of actor-dir. Leo Penn and actress Eileen Ryan. Brother of actor Christopher Penn and musician Michael Penn. m. actress Robin Wright. e. Santa Monica H.S. Served as apprentice for two years at Group Repertory Theatre, L.A. Acted in: Terrible Jim Fitch, Earthworms, The Girl on the Via Flaminia, etc. First prof. appearance as guest star on TV's Barnaby Jones. On B'way in Heartland, Slab Boys. Also in Hurlyburly (Westwood Playhouse, LA), Goose & Tom Tom (Lincoln Center Theater). Directed, The Kindness of Women (Santa Monica Pink Theater); exec. prod., Remembrance (Santa Monica Playhouse).
PICTURES: *Actor*: Taps (debut, 1981), Fast Times at Ridgemont High, Bad Boys, Crackers, Racing with the Moon, Falcon and the Snowman, At Close Range, Shanghai Surprise, Colors, Judgment in Berlin, Casualties of War, We're No Angels, State of Grace, Carlito's Way, Dead Man Walking, She's So Lovely (also exec. prod.; Cannes Film Festival Award, 1997), Loved (also prod.), U-Turn (also prod.), The Game, Hurlyburly, Thin Red Line. *Dir./Writer*: The Indian Runner, The Crossing Guard (also co-prod.).
TELEVISION: *Movie*: The Killing of Randy Webster. *Guest*: Barnaby Jones. *Special*: Dear America (reader).

PENNEBAKER, D.A.
Director. b. Evanston, IL, July 15, 1925. r.n. Donn Alan Pennebaker. e. Yale U. Studied engineering, set up own electronics firm. Worked in advertising, before writing and directing documentaries, as well as experimental films. 1958 joined Richard Leacock, Willard Van Dyke and Shirley Clarke in equipment-sharing film co-op, Filmakers. 1960 joined Robert Drew operating out of Time Life with Leacock, Albert Maysles and others. Set up Leacock Pennebaker with Leacock and made several films that were blown up from 16mm to 35mm and released in theatres. Currently works with co-dir. and wife Chris Hegedus and son Frazer Pennebaker, continuing to film unscripted dramas of real events in cinema verite style. Dir. music videos for Suzanne Vega, Victoria Williams, Branford Marsalis, Randy Newman, etc.

PICTURES: Daybreak Express (1956), Opening in Moscow, Primary, David, Jane, Crisis, The Chair, On the Pole, Mr. Pearson, Don't Look Back, Monterey Pop, Beyond the Law, One P.M., Sweet Toronto, Maidstone, Ziggy Stardust and the Spiders From Mars, On the Pole, Town Bloody Hall, The Energy War, Dance Black America, Rockaby, Delorean, Happy Come Home, Depeche Mode, The Music Tells You, The War Room.

PEPLOE, MARK
Writer. b. Kenya. Sister is writer Clare Peploe. Raised in England and Italy. e. Magdalen Col., Oxford. Became researcher for documentary dept. of the BBC; then worked as research, writer and dir. for series Creative Persons.
PICTURES: The Pied Piper, The Passenger, The Babysitter, High Season, The Last Emperor (Acad. Award, 1987), The Sheltering Sky, Afraid of the Dark (also dir.), Little Buddha, Victory.

PERAKOS, SPERIE P.
Executive. b. New Britain, CT, Nov. 12, 1920. e. Cheshire Acad., Yale U. Harvard Law Sch. Student mgr., Stanley-Warner Theatres, 1939-40; Perakos Theatres 1940 to present; Capt., U.S.A. Intelligence with 35 inf. division. Fellow, Pierson Coll., Yale, 1946-present; Yale Alumni Bd., 1949 to present; Yale Alumni Film Bd. 1952 to 1980; member Alumni Council for Yale Drama Sch.; past pres. Yale Club of New Britain, Conn.; dir. of Films & Filmings Seminars, Pierson Coll., Yale; prod. Antigone, 1964; pres. Norma Film Prod., Inc., 1962 to present. Past pres. and chmn. Yale's Peabody Museum Associates. Pres., Perakos Theatres, Conn. Theatre Associates, Inc. Pres., Connecticut Association of Theatre Owners, Secretary, ShowEast. Member, Exec. Board of Natl' Assn. of Theatre Owners, C.A.R.A.

PERENCHIO, ANDREW J.
Executive. b. Fresno, CA, Dec. 20, 1930. e. U. of California. Vice pres., Music Corp. of America, 1958-62; General Artists Corp., 1962-64; pres., owner, Chartwell Artists, Ltd., theatrical agency, Los Angeles, 1964; pres. & CEO, Tandem Productions, Inc., and TAT Communications Co., 1973-83, then became principal with Norman Lear in Embassy Communications. Held post of pres. & CEO of Embassy Pictures.

PEREZ, ROSIE
Actress. b. Brooklyn, 1964. Attended sch. in L.A. where she became a dancer on Soul Train; then choreographer for music videos and stage shows for such performers as Bobby Brown, The Boys, Diana Ross, LL Cool J, etc. Acting debut in Do the Right Thing.
PICTURES: Do the Right Thing (also choreog.; debut, 1989), White Men Can't Jump, Night on Earth, Untamed Heart, Fearless (Acad. Award nom.), It Could Happen to You, Somebody to Love, A Brother's Kiss.
TELEVISION: *Movie*: Criminal Justice. *Series*: In Living Color (choreographer). *Specials*: Rosie Perez Presents Society's Ride (exec. prod.), In a New Light: Sex Unplugged (co-host).

PERKINS, ELIZABETH
Actress. b. Forest Hills, Queens, NY, Nov. 18, 1960. Grew up in Vermont. After high school moved to Chicago to study at Goodman School of Drama. Two months after moving to NY in 1984, landed a role in the national touring co. of Brighton Beach Memoirs, later performing part on Broadway. Acted with Playwright's Horizon, NY Ensemble Theater, Shakespeare in the Park and Steppenwolf Theatre Co. Appeared in short film Teach 109.
PICTURES: About Last Night... (debut, 1986), From the Hip, Big, Sweet Hearts Dance, Love at Large, Avalon, Enid Is Sleeping (Over Her Dead Body), He Said She Said, The Doctor, Indian Summer, The Flintstones, Miracle on 34th Street, Moonlight and Valentino, Lesser Prophets, I'm Losing You, Crazy in Alabama.
TELEVISION: *Movie*: For Their Own Good, Cloned. *Mini-series*: The Rescuers: Two Women.

PERKINS, MILLIE
Actress. b. Passaic, NJ, May 12, 1938. Was model when chosen by dir. George Stevens for starring role in The Diary of Anne Frank.
PICTURES: The Diary of Anne Frank (debut, 1959), Wild in the Country, Dulcinea, Ensign Pulver, Ride in the Whirlwind, The Shooting, Wild in the Streets, Cockfighter, Lady Cocoa, The Witch Who Came From the Sea, Table for Five, At Close Range, Jake Speed, Slam Dance, Wall Street, Necronomicon, Two Moon Junction, The Pistol, Bodily Harm, The Chamber.
TELEVISION: *Series*: Knots Landing, Elvis. *Guest*: U.S. Steel Hour, Breaking Point, Murder She Wrote, Our House, Jessie, Hart to Hart, Glitter, Wagon Train, thirtysomething, Touched By An Angel. *Movies*: A.D., The Thanksgiving Promise, Penalty Phase, Anatomy of an Illness, Shattered Vows, License to Kill, Strange Voices, Broken Angel, Best Intentions, The Other Love, Haunting Passion, A Gun in the House, Model Mother, Macbeth (cable tv), Call Me Anna, 72 Hours, Murder of Innocence, The Writing on the Wall, God, The Universe and Hot Fudge Sundaes, The Bounty Hunter: Miles To Go Before I Sleep, The Summer of Ben Tyler, Harvest of Fire.

PERKINS, ROWLAND
Executive. Vice-President, Creative Services, William Morris Agency, 1952–75. Founding President, Creative Artists Agency, 1975–95. Established The Rowland Perkins Company (a.k.a. Double Eagle Entertainment) in 1994 to develop and produce feature, network and cable films; television series and sepcials; Broadway shows, etc.

PERLMAN, RHEA
Actress. b. Brooklyn, NY, March 31, 1948. e. Hunter Coll. m. actor-dir. Danny DeVito. Co-founder Colonnades Theatre Lab., NY and New Street prod. co with Danny DeVito.
PICTURES: Love Child, My Little Pony (voice), Enid is Sleeping (Over Her Dead Body), Ted & Venus, Class Act, There Goes the Neighborhood, Canadian Bacon, Sunset Park, Matilda.
TELEVISION: Series: Cheers (4 Emmy Awards: 1984, 1985, 1986, 1989), Pearl (co-exec. prod.). Movies: I Want to Keep My Baby!, Stalk the Wild Child, Having Babies II, Intimate Strangers, Mary Jane Harper Cried Last Night, Like Normal People, Drop-out Father, The Ratings Game, Dangerous Affection, A Family Again, To Grandmother's House We Go, A Place to Be Loved, Spoils of War. Specials: Funny You Don't Look 200, Two Daddies (voice), The Last Halloween.

PERLMAN, RON
Actor. b. New York, NY, April 13, 1950. While in high school, part of comedy team that played clubs. e. City U. of NY, U. of Minnesota, M.F.A. Joined Classic Stage Company, NY, for 2 years.
THEATER: NY: The Architect and the Emperor of Assyria (also toured Europe), American Heroes, The Resistible Rise of Arturo Ui, Tiebele and Her Demon, La Tragedie de Carmen, A Few Good Men.
PICTURES: Quest for Fire, The Ice Pirates, The Name of the Rose, Sleepwalkers, The Adventures of Huck Finn, Double Exposure, Romeo Is Bleeding, Crime and Punishment, Cronos, Fluke, The City of Lost Children, The Last Summer, The Island of Dr. Moreau.
TELEVISION: Series: Beauty and the Beast. Movies: A Stoning in Fulham County, Blind Man's Bluff, Original Sins.

PERLMUTTER, DAVID M.
Producer. b. Toronto, Canada, 1934. e. U. of Toronto. Pres., Quadrant Films Ltd.
PICTURES: The Neptune Factor, Sunday in the Country, It Seemed Like a Good Idea at the Time, Love at First Sight, Find the Lady, Blood and Guts, The Third Walker, Two Solitudes, Fast Company, Double Negative, Nothing Personal, Misdeal, Love.

PERMUT, DAVID A.
Producer. b. New York, NY, March 23, 1954. In 1974, became pres., Diversified Artists Intl.; 1975, pres., Theatre Television Corp.; 1979, formed Permut Presentations, Inc., of which is pres. Production deals with Columbia Pictures (1979), Lorimar Productions (1981), Universal (1985), United Artists (1986), and New Line Cinema (1991).
PICTURES: Give 'Em Hell Harry, Fighting Back (exec. prod.), Blind Date, Richard Pryor—Live in Concert (exec. prod.), Dragnet, The Marrying Man, 29th Street, Captain Ron, Consenting Adults, The Temp, Three of Hearts, Surviving the Game, Trapped in Paradise, Eddie, Face/Off, Chippendales.
TELEVISION: Mistress (sprv. prod.), Love Leads the Way (exec. prod.), Triumph of the Heart: The Ricky Bell Story (prod.), Breaking the Silence (prod.).

PERREAU, GIGI
Actress. r.n. Ghislaine Perreau. b. Los Angeles, CA, Feb. 6, 1941. e. Immaculate Heart H.S. & College. Many stage and TV guest appearances. Now teaching and directing. Among first 50 stars to be honored with star on Hollywood Walk of Fame.
PICTURES: Madame Currie (debut, 1943), Abigail, Dear Heart, Dark Waters, San Diego I Love You, Two Girls and a Sailor, The Master Race, The Seventh Cross, Mr. Skeffington, Yoland and the Thief, Voice of the Whistler, God Is My Co-Pilot, To Each His Own, Alias Mr. Twilight, High Barbaree, Song of Love, Green Dolphin Street, Family Honeymoon, Enchantment, Sainted Sisters, Roseanna McCoy, Song of Surrender, My Foolish Heart, Shadow on the Wall, For Heaven's Sake, Never a Dull Moment, Reunion in Reno, The Lady Pays Off, Weekend with Father, Has Anybody Seen My Gal, Bonzo Goes to College, There's Always Tomorrow, The Man in the Gray Flannel Suit, Dance With Me Henry, Wild Heritage, The Cool and the Crazy, Girls' Town, Tammy Tell Me True, Look in Any Window, Journey to the Center of Time, Hell on Wheels, The Sleepless.
TELEVISION: Series: The Betty Hutton Show, Follow the Sun. Guest: Alfred Hitchcock Presents, Perry Mason, The Rifleman, The Brady Bunch, and many others.

PERRINE, VALERIE
Actress. b. Galveston, TX, Sept. 3 1943. e. U. of Arizona. Was showgirl in Las Vegas before discovered by agent Robert Walker who got her contract with Universal Pictures.
PICTURES: Slaughterhouse 5 (debut, 1972), The Last American Hero, Lenny (NY Film Critics & Cannes Film Fest. Awards; Acad. Award nom.), W. C. Fields & Me, Mr. Billion, Superman, The Magician of Lublin, The Electric Horseman, Can't Stop the Music, Superman II, Agency, The Border, Water, Maid to Order, Reflections in a Dark Sky, Bright Angel, Boiling Point, Girl in the Cadillac, The Break, My Girlfriend's Boyfirend, Curtain Call, 54.
TELEVISION: Movies: The Couple Takes a Wife, Ziegfeld: The Man and His Women, Marian Rose White, Malibu, When Your Lover Leaves, Sweet Bird of Youth, Un Casa a Roma, The Burning Shore. Series: Leo and Liz in Beverly Hills. Special: Steambath.

PERRY, LUKE
Actor. r.n. Coy Luther Perry III. b. Mansfield, OH, Oct. 11, 1966. r.n. Coy Luther Perry III. To LA then NY as teen to become actor, landing role on daytime serial Loving.
PICTURES: Terminal Bliss (debut, 1992), Scorchers, Buffy the Vampire Slayer, At Home With the Webbers (cameo), 8 Seconds, From the Edge, Christmas Vacation, Normal Life, American Strays, Lifebreath, The Fifth Element, Last Breath, Indiscreet, The Florentine.
TELEVISION: Movies: Riot. Series: Loving, Another World, Beverly Hills 90210.

PERRY, SIMON
Producer, Writer. b. Farnham, England, Aug. 5, 1943. e. Cambridge Univ., 1965. Ent. ind. 1974. Early career in stage and television production. Prod. mini-budget feature Knots; prod. dir. Eclipse. Served on bureau staff of Variety. Ran the National Film Development Fund for two years. 1982 set up Umbrella Films to produce Another Time Another Place, Loose Connections, Nineteen Eighty Four, Hotel Du Paradis, Nanou, White Mischief, The Playboys, Innocent Lies. Chief exec. of British Screen Finance since 1991.

PERSKY, LESTER
Executive. b. New York, NY, July 6, 1927. e. Brooklyn Coll. Officer in U.S. Merchant Marine, 1946-48. Founder and pres. of own adv. agency. 1951-1964. Theatrical stage prod., 1966-69. 1973, creative dir. and co-owner Persky Bright Org. (owner-financier of numerous motion pictures for private investment group). Films: Last Detail, Golden Voyage of Sinbad, For Pete's Sake, California Split, The Man Who Would Be King, The Front, Shampoo, Hard Times, Taxi Driver, Missouri Breaks, Funny Lady, Gator, Bound for Glory, Sinbad and the Eye of the Tiger. Lester Persky Productions, Inc.
PICTURES: Producer: Fortune and Men's Eyes, Equus, Hair, Yanks.
TELEVISION: Mini-Series: Poor Little Rich Girl (Golden Globe Award, 1987), A Woman Named Jackie (Emmy Award, 1992), Liz: The Elizabeth Taylor Story.

PERSOFF, NEHEMIAH
Actor. b. Jerusalem, Israel, Aug. 2, 1919. e. Hebrew Technical Inst., 1934-37. Electrician, 1937-39; signal maint., N.Y. subway, 1939-41. Studied acting with Stella Adler and the Actors Studio. L.A. Critics Award 1971 for Sholem-Sholem Alecheim, and The Dybbuk. Has had exhibitions of his watercolor paintings in California, Florida; on permanent exhibit in Cambria, Ca.
THEATER: Sundown Beach, Galileo, Richard III, King Lear, Peter Pan, Peer Gynt, Tiger At the Gates, Colombe, Flahooly, Montserrat, Only in America. Tour: Fiddler on the Roof, Man of La Mancha, Oliver, Death of a Salesman (Stratford, Ont.), Peter Pan, I'm Not Rappaport, Sholem Aleichem (Drama Log & Bay Area Critics Circle Awards).
PICTURES: On the Waterfront, The Wild Party, The Harder They Fall, The Wrong Man, Men in War, This Angry Age, The Badlanders, Never Steal Anything Small, Al Capone, Some Like It Hot, Green Mansions, The Big Show, The Comancheros, The Hook, A Global Affair, Fate Is the Hunter, The Greatest Story Ever Told, The Power, The Money Jungle, Panic in the City, Mafia, The People Next Door, Mrs. Pollifax—Spy, Red Sky at Morning, Psychic Killer, Voyage of the Damned, In Search of Historic Jesus, Yentl, An American Tail (voice), The Last Temptation of Christ, Twins, Day of the Outlaw, The Dispossessed, An American Tail: Fievel Goes West (voice), An American Tail III (voice).
TELEVISION: Guest: Playhouse 90, Philco-Goodyear Show, Kraft, For Whom the Bells Tolls (Sylvania Award, 1958), Producers Showcase, Danger, You Are There, Untouchables, Route 66, Naked City, Wagon Train, Rawhide, Gunsmoke, Thriller, Hitchcock, Bus Stop, Mission Impossible, Henderson Monster, Rebels, Twilight Zone, Five Fingers, Mr. Lucky, The Wild Wild West, I Spy, Hawaii 5-0, Columbo, Barney Miller, L.A. Law, Star Trek, Law and Order, Reasonable Doubts. Movies: Sadat, Adderly, The French Atlantic Affair, Sex Symbol, Stranger Within.

PESCI, JOE
Actor. b. Newark, NJ, Feb. 9, 1943. Raised in Belleville, NJ. First show business job as child on TV's Star Time Kids. Worked as mason's laborer, restaurant owner, prior to becoming actor.
PICTURES: Death Collector, Raging Bull, I'm Dancing as Fast as I Can, Dear Mr. Wonderful (Ruby's Dream), Easy Money, Eureka, Once Upon a Time in America, Man on Fire, Moonwalker, Lethal Weapon 2, Betsy's Wedding, Goodfellas (Acad. Award, best supporting actor, 1990), Home Alone, The Super, JFK, My Cousin Vinny, Tuti Dentro, Lethal Weapon 3, The Public Eye, Home Alone 2: Lost in New York, A Bronx Tale, Jimmy Hollywood, With Honors, Casino, 8 Heads in a Duffel Bag, Gone Fishing.
TELEVISION: *Series*: Half Nelson. *Movies*: Half Nelson (pilot), Backtrack. *Guest*: Tales From the Crypt (Split Personality).

PETERS, BERNADETTE
Actress. r.n. Bernadette Lazzara. b. New York, NY, Feb. 28, 1948. e. Quintano Sch. for Young Professionals, NY. Professional debut at age 5 on TV's Horn & Hardart Children's Hour, followed by Juvenile Jury and Name That Tune. Stage debut with N.Y. City Center production of The Most Happy Fella (1959).
THEATER: Gypsy (1961), This is Goggle, Riverwind, The Penny Friend, Curley McDimple, Johnny No-Trump, George M! (Theatre World Award), Dames at Sea (Drama Desk Award), La Strada, W.C. & Me, On the Town (1971 revival), Tartuffe, Mack and Mabel, Sally and Marsha, Sunday in the Park With George, Song and Dance (Tony, Drama Desk & Drama League Awards), Into the Woods, The Goodbye Girl.
PICTURES: Ace Eli and Rodger of the Skies (debut, 1973), The Longest Yard, W.C. Fields & Me, Vigilante Force, Silent Movie, The Jerk, Tulips, Pennies from Heaven, Heartbeeps, Annie, Slaves of New York, Pink Cadillac, Alice, Impromptu.
TELEVISION: *Series*: All's Fair. *Mini-Series*: The Martian Chronicles. *Specials*: George M, They Said It with Music, Party at Annapolis, Rich Thin and Beautiful (host), Faerie Tale Theatre, The Last Mile. *Pilot*: The Owl and the Pussycat. *Movies*: The Islander, David, Fall from Grace, The Last Best Year.

PETERS, BROCK
Actor. r.n. Brock Fisher. b. Harlem, NY, July 2, 1927. e. CCNY, U. of Chicago. Had numerous featured roles on and off B'way. in road and stock cos., nightclubs, TV. Toured with DePaur Infantry Chorus as bass soloist, 1947-50. Appeared in short film From These Roots.
THEATER: Porgy and Bess (debut, 1943), Anna Lucasta, My Darlin' Aida, Mister Johnson, King of the Dark Chamber, Othello, Kwamina, The Great White Hope (tour), Lost in the Stars, Driving Miss Daisy (Natl. Co.).
PICTURES: Carmen Jones (debut, 1954), Porgy and Bess, To Kill a Mockingbird, Heavens Above, The L-Shaped Room, The Pawnbroker, Major Dundee, The Incident, P.J., The Daring Game, Ace High, The MacMasters, Black Girl, Soylent Green, Slaughter's Big Rip-off, Lost in the Stars, Million Dollar Dixie Deliverance, Framed, Two-Minute Warning, Star Trek IV: The Voyage Home, Star Trek VI: The Undiscovered Country, Alligator II: The Mutation, The Importance of Being Earnest.
TELEVISION: Arthur Godfrey's Talent Scouts (debut, 1953), *Series*: The Young and the Restless. *Guest*: Eleventh Hour, It Takes a Thief, Mannix, Mod Squad. *Mini-series*: Seventh Avenue, Black Beauty, Roots: The Next Generations. *Movies*: Welcome Home Johnny Bristol, SST: Death Flight, The Incredible Journey of Doctor Meg Laurel, The Adventures of Huckleberry Finn, Agatha Christie's Caribbean Mystery, To Heal a Nation, Broken Angel, The Big One: The Great Los Angeles Earthquake, Highway Heartbreakers, The Secret. *Specials*: Challenge of the Go Bots (voice), Living the Dream: A Tribute to Dr. Martin Luther King. *Co-prod.*: This Far By Faith.

PETERS, JANICE C.
Executive. e. Wayne State U., BS, and Stanford U., masters in mgmt. Began in local/long distance telecom. field. Became pres., CEO, U S WEST NewVector Group, a cellular comm. co., and pres. of wireless ops., U S WEST MediaOne before becoming managing dir. of One 2 One, a cellular comm. co. in the UK in 1996. Currently pres. and CEO of MediaOne, broadband svcs. under MediaOne Group.

PETERS, JON
Producer. b. Van Nuys, CA, 1947. Started hair-styling business; built it into multimillion-dollar firm before turning film producer. Formed Jon Peters Organization. 1980, joined with Peter Guber and Neil Bogart to form The Boardwalk Co. (dissolved 1981). Later Guber-Peters-Barris Company. 1989, became co-chairman of Columbia Pictures. Resigned, 1991.
PICTURES: A Star Is Born, Eyes of Laura Mars, The Main Event, Die Laughing, Caddyshack. *Co-Prod./Co-Exec. Prod. with Peter Guber*: An American Werewolf in London, Missing, Six Weeks, Flashdance, D.C. Cab, Vision Quest, Legend of Billie Jean, Clue, The Color Purple, Head Office, The Clan of the Cave Bear, Youngblood, The Witches of Eastwick, Innerspace, Who's That Girl, Gorillas in the Mist, Caddyshack II, Rain Man, Batman, Tango and Cash, The Bonfire of the Vanities, Batman Returns, This Boy's Life, With Honors, Money Train. *Also: Prod.*: My Fellow Americans (prod.), Rosewood.
TELEVISION: *Movies*: Bay Coven (co-exec. prod.), Nightmare at Bitter Creek (exec. prod.).

PETERSEN, PAUL
Actor. b. Glendale, CA, Sept. 23, 1945. e. Valley Coll. Original Disney Mouseketeer (TV). Recorded hit songs She Can't Find Her Keys, and My Dad in 1962. In the late 1960's turned to writing beginning with a Marcus Welby script followed by paperback novels in 1970's. Author of book about Disney empire, Walt Mickey and Me (1977), and co-author of It's a Wonderful Life Trivia Book (1992). President and founder of A Minor Consideration, a support foundation for former kid actors with a current membership of 150 movie, tv and sports stars spanning the past 70 years.
PICTURES: Houseboat, This Could Be the Night, The Happiest Millionaire, Journey to Shiloh, A Time for Killing.
TELEVISION: *Series*: The Donna Reed Show. *Guest*: Playhouse 90, Lux Video Theatre, GE Theatre, The Virginian, Ford Theatre, Valentine's Day, Shindig. *Movies*: Something for a Lonely Man, Gidget Grows Up, Scout's Honor.

PETERSEN, WILLIAM
Actor. b. Chicago, IL, 1953. e. Idaho State U. Active in Chicago theatre; helped to found Ix, an ensemble acting group now called the Remains Theatre. Acted in Moby Dick, In the Belly of the Beast, A Streetcar Named Desire, etc. 1986, formed company with prod. Cynthia Chvatal called High Horse Prods.
THEATER: *NY*: To Live and Die in L.A., Manhunter, Amazing Grace and Chuck, Cousins, Young Guns II, Hard Promises (also co-prod.), Passed Away, Fear.
TELEVISION: *Movies*: Long Gone (HBO), Keep the Change (also co-prod.), Curacao. *Mini-Series*: The Kennedys of Massachusetts, Return to Lonesome Dove, The Beast.

PETERSEN, WOLFGANG
Director, Writer. b. Emden, Germany, March 14, 1941. Career as asst. stage dir. at Ernst Deutsch Theatre in Hamburg before entering 4 year program at the German Film & TV Academy wher he directed for television and later theatrical films.
PICTURES: One of Us Two, Black and White Like Day and Night (also s.p.), The Consequence (also s.p.), Das Boot (The Boat; also s.p.; Acad. Award nom. for dir.), The Neverending Story (also s.p.), Enemy Mine, Shattered (also s.p., co-prod.), In the Line of Fire (also co-exec.prod.), Outbreak (also co-prod.), Air Force One (also prod.).
TELEVISION: I Will Kill You Wolf (dir. debut 1970), Tatort (series), Smog (Prix Futura Award, 1975), For Your Love Only (also released theatrically), Scene of the Crime (series).

PETERSON, S. DEAN
Executive. b. Toronto, Canada, December 18, 1923. e. Victoria Coll., U. of Toronto. WWII service RCNVR; 1946 TV newsreel cameraman NBC; founded own prod. co. in 1947; incorporated Dordean Realty Limited to acquire new studios 1950; formed Peterson Productions Limited in 1957 to make TV commercials and sponsored theatrical shorts; formed Studio City Limited in 1965 to produce TV series and features acquiring an additional studio complex and backlot in Kleinberg, Ontario; 1972 formed SDP Communications Ltd. to package M.P. and TV; 1970 incorporated Intermedia Financial Services Limited to provide specialized financing and consultation to companies in M.P. and TV industries. Past-President Canadian Film and Television Production Assn.; mbr. Variety Club, Tent 28; Canadian Society of Cinematographers; Directors Guild of America, Directors Guild of Canada, SMPTE.

PETERSON, RICHARD W.
Executive. b. Denver, CO, June 15, 1949. e. Col. Sch. of Broadcasting, Harper Coll. Joined Kennedy Theatres, Chicago, 1966. 1968 went with Great States Theatres (now Cineplex Odeon), Chicago. Was city mgr. of Crocker and Grove Theatres, Elgin, IL. 1973 joined American Automated Theatres, Oklahoma City, as dir. of adv., pub. Promoted to dir. of U.S. theatre operations. Worked for American International Pictures, Dallas, TX. Then moved to Dal Art Film Exchange and B & B Theatres as general mgr.; 1987 took over 7 screens from McLendon and formed own co., Peterson Theatres, Inc, now operating 17 screens.

PETIT, HENRI-DOMINIQUE
Executive. b. Baden-Baden, Germany. e. Ecole Superieure de Physique et Chimie de Paris, Univ. of Paris. Joined Kodak 1975 as asst. mgr. of the Purchasing Division, Kodak Pathe, France. 1980, asst., then mgr. of Kodak Pathe Photofinishing Lab (1981). 1984, became bus. mgr. Business Information Systems and Corporate Accounts, Kodak Pathe. 1987, named bus. mgr. of Photofinishing Systems Division. 1989, appointed gen. mgr. and v.p. Motion Picture and Television Imaging, Europe/Africa/Middle East Region. Dec., 1992, named v.p. and gen. mgr. Motion Picture and Television Imaging.

PETRIE, DANIEL
Director. b. Glace Bay, Nova Scotia, Nov. 26, 1920. e. St. Francis Xavier U., Nova Scotia; Columbia U., MA, 1945; postgrad. Northwestern U. Broadway actor 1945-46. TV dir. from 1950. Son Daniel Petrie Jr. is a screenwriter; son Donald Petrie is a dir.
THEATER: Shadow of My Enemy, Who'll Save the Plowboy?, Mornin' Sun, Monopoly, The Cherry Orchard, Volpone, A Lesson from Aloes.

PICTURES: The Bramble Bush (debut, 1960), A Raisin in the Sun, The Main Attraction, Stolen Hours, The Idol, The Spy With a Cold Nose, The Neptune Factor, Buster and Billie, Lifeguard, The Betsy, Resurrection, Fort Apache The Bronx, Six Pack, The Bay Boy (also s.p.; Genie Award), Square Dance (also prod.), Rocket Gibraltar, Cocoon: The Return, Lassie, The Associate.
TELEVISION: *Movies*: Silent Night Lonely Night, A Howling in the Woods, A Stranger in Town, Moon of the Wolf, Trouble Comes to Town, Mousey, Returning Home, Eleanor and Franklin (Emmy Award, 1976), Sybil, Eleanor and Franklin: The White House Years (Emmy Award, 1977), Harry Truman, Plain Speaking (Emmy nom.), The Dollmaker (Emmy nom.), The Execution of Raymond Graham (Emmy nom.), Half a Lifetime, My Name is Bill W. (also prod.; Emmy nom.), Mark Twain and Me (also prod., Emmy Award), A Town Torn Apart (also prod., Emmy nom.), Kissinger and Nixon, Calm at Sunset.

PETRIE, DONALD
Director. b. New York, NY. Son of dir. Daniel Petrie. Moved to LA as teenager, becoming tv actor. Attended American Film Inst. dir. program, where he made short film The Expert. Was then hired to dir. Mister Magic esisode of Amazing Stories.
PICTURES: Mystic Pizza (debut, 1988), Opportunity Knocks, Grumpy Old Men, The Favor, Richie Rich, The Associate, My Favorite Martian.
TELEVISION: *Series episodes*: MacGyver, The Equalizer, L.A. Law, Players. *Special*: Have You Tried Talking to Patty?

PETROU, DAVID MICHAEL
Writer, Producer, Public Relations Executive. b. Washington, DC, Nov. 3, 1949. e. U. of Maryland, B.A.; Georgetown U., M.A. Publicity assoc., Psychiatric Institutes of America, Washington, DC, 1971; assoc. dir. of publicity & film liaison, Random House, 1974; guest lecturer, screen writing & film production, The American University Consortium, Washington, DC, spring, 1980; Woodrow Wilson Fellowship, 1971. Entered industry in 1975. Joined Salkind Organization in chg. of literary projects. Worked in numerous production capacities on Crossed Swords, Superman, Superman II. 1977, exec. in chg. of literary development, Salkind. Wrote Crossed Swords (1978) and The Making of Superman. Co-authored screenplay, Shoot to Kill. 1978-79, promotional dev. on Time after Time for Warner Bros.; 1980-83, dir., special projects Joseph Kennedy Foundation. 1983-84, sr. edit. for entertainment, Regardie's Magazine; 1984-86, sr. exec., p.r. div., Abramson Associates; 1986-88, sr. v.p., Eisner, Held & Petrou, Inc., p.r. agency; 1988-present, pres. & COO, Eisner Petrou & Associates Inc. Baltimore-Wash., marketing communications agency. 1992, named chmn. of American Film Institute's Second Decade Council.

PETTET, JOANNA
Actress. b. London, England, Nov. 16, 1944. Raised in Canada. Studied acting at Neighborhood Playhouse in NY.
PICTURES: The Group (debut, 1966), The Night of the Generals, Casino Royale, Robbery, Blue, The Best House in London, Welcome to Arrow Beach (Tender Flesh), The Evil, An Eye for an Eye, Double Exposure, Sweet Country, Terror in Paradise.
TELEVISION: *Series*: Knots Landing. *Mini-Series*: Captains and the Kings. *Movies*: Footsteps, The Delphi Bureau, The Weekend Nun, Pioneer Woman, A Cry in the Wilderness, The Desperate Miles, The Hancocks, The Dark Side of Innocence, Sex and the Married Woman, Cry of the Innocent, The Return of Frank Cannon.

PETTY, LORI
Actress. b. Chattanooga, TN, 1965. Worked as graphic artist before turning to acting.
PICTURES: Cadillac Man, Point Break, A League of Their Own, Free Willy, Poetic Justice, In the Army Now, Tank Girl, The Glass Shield.
TELEVISION: *Series*: The Thorns, Booker, Lush Life.

PEYSER, JOHN
Producer, Director. b. New York, NY, Aug. 10, 1916. e. Colgate U., 1938. In TV ind. since 1939, with Psychological Warfare Div., ETO., W.W.II; pres. Peyser/Vance Productions, Woodland Hills, CA.
PICTURES: The Open Door, Kashmiri Run, Four Rode Out, Massacre Harbor.
TELEVISION: *Director*: Hawaii Five-O, Mannix, Movin On, Swiss Family Robinson, Bronk, Combat, Untouchables, Rat Patrol, Honeymoon with a Stranger.

PFEIFFER, MICHELLE
Actress. b. Santa Ana, CA, April 29, 1957. Sister of actress Deedee Pfeiffer. While attending jr. coll. and working as supermarket checkout clerk, won Miss Orange County beauty contest. Began taking acting classes in L.A. Stage debut in L.A. prod. of A Playground in the Fall. NY Theatre debut 1989 in Twelfth Night (Central Park).

PICTURES: The Hollywood Nights (debut, 1980), Falling in Love Again, Charlie Chan and the Curse of the Dragon Queen, Grease 2, Scarface, Into the Night, Ladyhawke, Sweet Liberty, The Witches of Eastwick, Amazon Women on the Moon, Married to the Mob, Tequila Sunrise, Dangerous Liaisons (Acad. Award nom.), The Fabulous Baker Boys (NY, LA & & Natl. Society of Film Critics Awards; Acad. Award nom.), The Russia House, Frankie and Johnny, Batman Returns, Love Field (Acad. Award nom.), The Age of Innocence, Wolf, Dangerous Minds, Up Close and Personal, To Gillian On Her 37th Birthday, One Fine Day (also exec. prod.), A Thousand Acres, A Midsummer Night's Dream, The Deep End of the Ocean (also prod.), Prince of Egypt (voice), Star Quality.
TELEVISION: *Series*: Delta House, B.A.D. Cats. *Movies*: The Solitary Man, Callie and Son, Splendor in the Grass, The Children Nobody Wanted. *Specials*: One Too Many, Tales from the Hollywood Hills (Natica Jackson). *Guest*: Fantasy Island.

PHILLIPS, JULIA
Producer. b. Brooklyn, NY, April 7, 1944. e. Mt. Holyoke Coll. Production asst. at McCall's Magazine; later became textbook copywriter for Macmillan; story editor, Paramount; creative exec., First Artists Prods., NY. In 1970 with former husband, Michael Phillips and actor Tony Bill formed Bill/Phillips Productions to develop film projects. Author of You'll Never Eat Lunch in This Town Again (Random House, 1991).
PICTURES: Steelyard Blues, The Sting (Acad. Award for Best Picture, 1973), Taxi Driver, The Big Bus, Close Encounters of the Third Kind, The Beat (co-prod.).

PHILLIPS, LESLIE
Actor, Producer. b. London, England, April 20, 1924. Early career as child actor. Ent. m.p. ind. 1935.
PICTURES: A Lassie From Lancashire (debut, 1935), The Citadel, Rhythm Serenade, Train of Events, The Woman With No Name (Her Paneled Door), Pool of London, The Galloping Major, Breaking the Sound Barrier, The Fake, The Limping Man, Time Bomb (Terror on a Train), The Price of Greed, Value for Money, The Gamma People, As Long as They're Happy, The Big Money, Brothers in Law, The Barretts of Wimpole Street, Just My Luck, Les Girls, The Smallest Show on Earth, High Flight, I Was Monte's Double, The Man Who Liked Funerals, The Angry Hills, Carry on Nurse, Ferdinand of Naples, This Other Eden, Carry on Teacher, Please Turn Over, The Navy Lark, Doctor in Love, Watch Your Stern, No Kidding (Beware of Children), Carry on Constable, Inn for Trouble, Raising the Wind, In the Doghouse, Very Important Persons, Crooks Anonymous, The Longest Day, The Fast Lady, Father Came Too, Doctor in Clover, You Must Be Joking, Maroc 7, Some Will Some Won't, Doctor in Trouble, The Magnificent 7 Deadly Sins, Not Now Darling, Don't Just Lie There Say Something!, Spanish Fly, Not Now Comrade, Out of Africa, Empire of the Sun, Scandal, Mountains of the Moon, King Ralph, Carry on Columbus, August, Caught In The Act.
TELEVISION: Our Man at St. Marks, Impasse, The Gong Game, Time and Motion Man, Reluctant Debutante, A Very Fine Line, The Suit, The Culture Vultures (series), Edward Woodward Show, Casanova 74 (series), Redundant—or the Wife's Revenge, You'll Never See Me Again, Mr. Palfrey of Westminister, Monte Carlo, Rumpole, Summers Lease, Chancer, Comic Strip, Who Bombed Birmingham, Life After Life, Thacker, Chancer II, The Oz Trial, Lovejoy, Boon, The Changeling, Bermuda Grace, Royal Celebration, Honey for Tea, House of Windsor, Two Golden Balls, Love on a Branch Line, Vanity Dies Hard, Edgar Wallace (Germany), Canterville Ghost, Woof, The Bill, The Pale Horse.

PHILLIPS, LOU DIAMOND
Actor. b. Philippines, Feb. 17, 1962. Raised in Corpus Christi, TX. e. U. of Texas, Arlington (BFA drama). Studied film technique with Adam Roarke, becoming asst. instructor with the Film Actor's Lab, 1983-86. Regional theater includes: A Hatful of Rain, Whose Life Is It Anyway?, P.S. Your Cat Is Dead, The Lady's Not for Burning, Doctor Faustus, Hamlet.
THEATER: *NY*: The King and I (Bdwy. debut, Tony nom.)
PICTURES: Angel Alley, Interface, Trespasses (also co-s.p.), Harley, La Bamba, Stand and Deliver, Young Guns, Dakota (also assoc. prod.), Disorganized Crime, Renegades, The First Power, A Show of Force, Young Guns II, Ambition (also s.p.), The Dark Wind, Shadow of the Wolf, Dangerous Touch (also dir.), Teresa's Tattoo, Sioux City (also dir.), Undertow, Boulevard, Courage Under Fire.
TELEVISION: *Movies*: Time Bomb, The Three Kings, Extreme Justice, The Wharf Rat. *Specials*: Avenue Z Afternoon, Wind in the Wire. *Guest*: Dallas, Miami Vice.

PHILLIPS, MICHAEL
Producer. b. Brooklyn, NY, June 29, 1943. e. Dartmouth Coll., B.A., 1965. NYU, Law Sch. J.D., 1968. Indep. m.p. prod. 1971.
PICTURES: Steelyard Blues, The Sting (Acad. Award for Best Picture, 1973), Taxi Driver (Golden Palm Award at Cannes), The Big Bus, Close Encounters of the Third Kind, Heartbeeps, Cannery Row, The Flamingo Kid, Don't Tell Mom the Babysitter's Dead, Mom and Dad Save the World, Eyes of an Angel, The Companion.
TELEVISION: *Movie*: Jane's House.

PHILLIPS, MICHELLE
Actress. b. Long Beach, CA, June 4, 1944. r.n. Holly Michelle Gilliam. Daughter is actress-singer Chynna Phillips. Former member of The Mamas and the Papas. Co-wrote hit single California Dreamin'. Author: California Dreamin': The Story of The Mamas and The Papas (1986).
PICTURES: Monterey Pop, The Last Movie, Dillinger, Valentino, Sidney Sheldon's Bloodline, The Man With Bogart's Face, Savage Harvest, American Anthem, Let It Ride, Scissors, Army of One, Keep on Running.
TELEVISION: *Series*: Hotel, Knots Landing, Second Chances. *Mini-Series*: Aspen, The French Atlantic Affair. *Movies*: The Death Squad, The California Kid, The Users, Moonlight, Mickey Spillane's Mike Hammer: Murder Me Murder You, Secrets of a Married Man, Stark: Mirror Image, Assault and Matrimony, Trenchcoat in Paradise, Rubdown, Paint Me a Murder, Covenant. *Guest*: Owen Marshall, Matt Houston, The Fall Guy, Murder She Wrote, T.J. Hooker, Hotel, Fantasy Island, Love Boat, Burke's Law, Robin's Hood, Lois & Clark, Herman's Head, many others.

PHILLIPS, SIAN
Actress. b. Bettws, Wales. e. Univ. of Wales. Studied acting at RADA. London stage debut 1957 in title role in Hedda. Has made numerous recordings including Pal Joey, Gigi, A Little Night Music, Remember Mama.
THEATER: Saint Joan, The Three Sisters, Taming of the Shrew, Duchess of Malfi, Lizard on the Rock, Gentle Jack, The Night of the Iguana, Ride a Cock Horse, Man and Superman, The Burglar, The Cardinal of Spain, Alpha Beta, Spinechiller, A Woman of No Importance, You Never Can Tell, Dear Liar, Pal Joey (SWET nom.), Major Barbara, Gigi, Paris Match, Painting Churches, Vanilla, Ghosts (Artist of the Year nom.), Marlene, A Little Night Music (Olivier nom.), Snow Spider, many others. B'way debut 1994 in An Inspector Calls.
PICTURES: Becket, Young Cassidy, Laughter in the Dark, Goodbye Mr. Chips (NY Film Critics & Critics Circle Awards, 1969), Murphy's War, Under Milk Wood, Clash of the Titans, Dune, The Doctor and the Devils, Valmont, The Age of Innocence, A Painful Case, House of America.
TELEVISION: *Mini-Series*: Shoulder to Shoulder, How Green Was My Valley (BAFTA Award), I Claudius (BAFTA & Royal TV Society Awards), Crime and Punishment, Tinker Tailor Soldier Spy, Vanity Fair. *Movies*: Ewoks: The Battle for Endor–Dark River, The Two Mrs. Grenvilles, Out of Time, Dark River. *Specials*: Off to Philadelphia in the Morning, Sean O'Casey, How Many Miles to Babylon?, Lady Windermere's Fan, Language and Landscape, Heartbreak House, Don Juan in Hell, Summer Silence, Shadow of the Noose, Snow Spider, The Quiet Man, The Sex Game, A Mind To Kill, Ivanhoe, Chestnut Soldier (BAFTA nom.).

PHOENIX, JOAQUIN
Actor. b. Puerto Rico, Oct. 28, 1974. Brother of the late River Phoenix.
PICTURES: SpaceCamp, Russkies, Parenthood, To Die For, Inventing the Abbotts, U Turn, Force Majeure, Clay Pigeons, 8 Millimeter, The Yards.
TELEVISION: *Movie*: Secret Witness. *Series*: Morningstar/Eveningstar.

PIALAT, MAURICE
Director, Writer. b. Cunlhat, Puy de Dome, France, Aug. 21, 1925. Worked as a painter and sometime actor before turning to film in 1952. Made a number of short films including L'Amour Existe (award winner Venice Film Fest., 1960). Worked in television before feature debut in 1967.
PICTURES: *Dir./Writer*. L'Enfance Nue (Naked Childhood; Prix Jean Vigo Award), We Will Not Grow Old Together, La Gueule Ouverte (also prod.), Passe ton Bac d'Abord (Graduate First), Loulou, A Nos Amours (also actor; Prix Louis Delluc Award), Police, Under Satan's Sun (also actor; Golden Palm Award, Cannes Festival), Van Gogh, Le Garcu, Bastard Brood (actor only), Les Auto-Stoppeuses.
TELEVISION: Janine, Maitre Galip, La Maison des Bois.

PICARDO, ROBERT
Actor. b. Philadelphia, PA, Oct. 27, 1953. e. Yale. Studied acting at Circle in the Square Theater School.
THEATER: *NY*: Sexual Perversity in Chicago, Gemini, Tribute.
PICTURES: The Howling, Star 80, Oh God You Devil, Explorers, Legend, Back to School, Munchies, Innerspace, Amazon Women on the Moon, Jack's Back, Dead Heat, The 'Burbs, 976-EVIL, Loverboy, Total Recall, Gremlins II, Samantha, Motorama, Matinee, Wagons East!, The Pagemaster (voice), Menno's Mind, Star Trek: First Contact, Small Soldiers.
TELEVISION: *Series*: China Beach, The Wonder Years, Star Trek: Voyager. *Movies*: The Dream Merchants, The Violation of Sarah McDavid, Lois Gibbs and the Love Canal, Dixie: Changing Habits, The Other Woman, Runaway Daughters, White Mile, Out There, The Second Civil War.

PICCOLI, MICHEL
Actor. b. Paris, France, Dec. 27, 1925. r.n. Jacques Piccoli. Since his film debut in The Sorcerer in 1945 has had impressive career on the French stage and in films working for major French dirs. Renoir, Bunuel, Melville, Resnais, Clouzot, Godard as well as Hitchcock. Until 1957 was mgr. of Theatre Babylone in Paris. Formed prod. co. Films 66. Produced: Themroc (1972); La Faille; Les Enfants Gates.
PICTURES: The Sorcerer, Le Point du Jour, French Can Can, The Witches of Salem, Le Bal des Espiona, Gina, Le Doulos, Contempt, Diary of a Chambermaid, Lady L, La Guerre Est Finie, The Young Girls of Rochefort, Un Homme de Trop, Belle de Jour, La Chamade, Dillinger Is Dead, L'Invasion, The Milky Way, Topaz, The Things of Life, Ten Days' Wonder, The Discreet Charm of the Bourgeoisie, Themroc, Wedding in Blood, La Grande Bouffe, The Last Woman, Leonor, 7 Deaths by Prescription, The Weak Spot, F For Fairbanks, Mado, Todo Modo, Rene the Cane, Spoiled Children, Strauberg Is Here, The Fire's Share, Little Girl in Blue Velvet, The Savage State, The Sugar, The Bit Between the Teeth, La Divorcement, Leap into the Void, The Price for Survival, Atlantic City, The Prodigal Daughter, Beyond the Door, The Eyes The Mouth, Passion, A Room in Town, Will the High Salaried Workers Please Raise Their Hands!!!, The General of the Dead Army, La Passante, The Prize of Peril, Adieu Bonaparte, Dangerous Moves, Danger in the House, Long Live Life!, Success Is the Best Revenge, The Sailor 512, Departure, Return, Mon Beau-Frere a Tue Ma Soeur, The Nonentity, The Prude, Bad Blood, Undiscovered Country, Blanc de Chine, Le Peuple Singe (narrator), The French Revolution, May Fools, La Belle Noiseuse, The Children Thief, Archipelago, Punctured Life, Martha and I, Traveling Companion.

PICERNI, PAUL
Actor. b. New York, NY, Dec. 1, 1922. e. Loyola U., Los Angeles. U.S. Air Force 1943-46; head of drama dept. Mt. St. Mary's Coll., 1949-50.
PICTURES: Saddle Tramp, Breakthrough, Operation Pacific, The Tanks Are Coming, Force of Arms, I Was a Communist for the FBI, Mara Maru, Operation Secret, The Desert Song, She's Back on Broadway, House of Wax, The System, Shanghai Story, To Hell and Back, Bobby Ware Is Missing, Miracle in the Rain, Omar Khayyam, The Brothers Rico, Marjorie Morningstar, The Young Philadelphians, Strangers When We Meet, The Young Marrieds, The Scarface Mob, The Scalphunters, Che!, Airport, Kotch, Beyond the Poseidon Adventure.
TELEVISION: *Series*: The Untouchables. *Guest*: Philco Playhouse, Climax, Lux, Loretta Young Show, Desilu, Kojak, Mannix, Police Story, Lucy Special, Quincy, Alice, Trapper John M.D., Vegas, Fall Guy, Capitol, Hardcastle and McCormick, Matt Houston, Simon and Simon.

PICKER, DAVID V.
Executive. b. New York, NY, May 14, 1931. e. Dartmouth Coll., B.A., 1953. Father Eugene Picker, exec. Loew's Theatres. Ent. industry in 1956 as adv. pub. & exploitation liaison with sls. dept., United Artists Corp.; exec. v.p. U.A. Records; asst. to Max Youngstein, v.p.; v.p. U.A.; first v.p. UA; pres. 1969. Resigned 1973 to form own production co. 1976 joined Paramount Pictures as pres. of m.p. div.; v.p., Lorimar Productions; independent; 1987, pres. & COO, Columbia Pictures. Resigned.
PICTURES: Juggernaut, Lenny, Smile, Royal Flash, Won Ton Ton the Dog Who Saved Hollywood, The One and Only, Oliver's Story, Bloodline (prod.), The Jerk (prod.), Dead Men Don't Wear Plaid (prod.), The Man with Two Brains, Beat Street (prod.), The Appointments of Dennis Jennings (short, prod.), Stella (exec. prod.), Traces of Red, Leap of Faith, Matinee, The Saint of Fort Washington, The Crucible.

PICKMAN, JEROME
Executive. b. New York, NY, Aug. 24, 1916. e. St. John's U.; Brooklyn Law Sch. of St. Lawrence U., LL.B. Reporter N.Y. newspapers; U.S. Army World War II; Ad-pub exec. 20th-Fox, 1945-46; v.p., dir., adv. & pub., later v.p. domestic gen. sls. mgr., Paramount Pictures; sr. sls. exec. Columbia Pictures; pres. Motion Picture Div. of Walter Reade Org.; pres., Levitt-Pickman Film Corp.; sr. v.p., domestic distribution, Lorimar Productions; pres., Pickman Film Corp.; Cineworld Enterprises Corp.; pres. Scotti Bros. Pictures Distribution, 1986. Consultant, various entertainment entities, legal and financial individuals and organizations.

PIERCE, DAVID HYDE
Actor. b. Albany, NY, April 3, 1959. e. Yale U.
PICTURES: Bright Lights Big City, Crossing Delancey, Rocket Gibraltar, The Fisher King, Little Man Tate, Sleepless in Seattle, Addams Family Values, Wolf, Nixon.
TELEVISION: *Series*: The Powers That Be, Frasier (Emmy Award, 1995, 1997; Emmy nom., 1996). *Guest*: Dream On, Crime Story, Spenser: For Hire, The OUter Limits.
THEATER: *Off-B'way*: Summer, That's It Folks, Donuts, Hamlet, The Moderati, The Cherry Orchard, Zero Positive, Much About Nothing, Elliot Loves. *B'way*: Beyond Therapy, The Heidi Chronicles. *Regional*: work with Long Wharf, Guthrie, Goodman, Doolittle Theatres.

PIERCE, FREDERICK S.

Executive. b. New York, NY, April 8, 1933. e. Bernard Baruch Sch. of B.A., City Coll. of New York. Served with U.S. Combat Engineers in Korean War. Associated with Benj. Harrow & Son, CAP, before joining ABC in 1956. Served as analyst in TV research dep.; prom. to supvr. of audience measurements, 1957, named mgr. next year. 1961 made dir. of research; 1962 dir. of research, sales dev. Named dir. of sales planning, sales devel. 1962; elec. v.p., 1964 and made nat. dir. of sales for TV. 1968 named v.p., planning; 1970 named asst. to pres.; 1972, named v.p, in chg. ABC TV planning and devel. and asst. to pres. ABC TV, 1973. Named sr. v.p., ABC TV, 1974. Elected pres., ABC Television Division, 1974. Pres. & COO, ABC, Inc., 1983. Formed Frederick Pierce Co. and also Pierce/Silverman Co. with Fred Silverman, 1989.

PIERSON, FRANK

Producer, Director, Writer. b. Chappaqua, NY, May 12, 1925. e. Harvard U. Was correspondent for Time magazine before entering show business as story editor of TV series, Have Gun, Will Travel. Later served as both prod. and dir. for show. Developed a number of properties for Screen Gems before writing theatrical screenplays.
PICTURES: Writer: Cat Ballou, The Happening, Cool Hand Luke, The Anderson Tapes, Dog Day Afternoon (Acad. Award, 1975), In Country, Presumed Innocent. Director-Writer: The Looking Glass War, A Star Is Born, King of the Gypsies.
TELEVISION: Series: Nichols (prod.), Alfred Hitchcock Presents (1985; dir.) Movies: The Neon Ceiling (dir.), Haywire (co-writer), Somebody Has to Shoot the Picture (dir.; ACE Award, 1990), Citizen Cohn (dir.), Lakota Woman: Siege at Wounded Knee (dir.), Truman.

PIGOTT-SMITH, TIM

Actor. b. Rugby, England, May 13, 1946. e. U. of Bristol, B.A., Bristol Old Vic Theatre Sch., 1969. Acted with Bristol Old Vic, Royal Shakespeare Co. Artistic Director of Compass Theatre, 1989-93.
THEATER: Actor: As You Like It, Major Barbara, Hamlet, School for Scandal, Sherlock Holmes (B'way debut, 1974), Benefactors, Entertaining Strangers, The Winter's Tale, Antony and Cleopatra, Cymbeline, The Tempest, Jane Eyre, The Picture of Dorian Gray, Retreat. Director: Company, Royal Hunt of the Sun, Playing the Wife, Hamlet, The Letter, Retreat, Mary Stuart.
PICTURES: Aces High (debut, 1975), Man in a Fog, Sweet William, Richard's Things, Joseph Andrews, Clash of the Titans, Lucky Village, Victory, State of Emergency, The Remains of the Day.
TELEVISION: Dr. Who (debut, 1970). Mini-series: Winston Churchill: The Wilderness Years, The Jewel in the Crown. Movies: Eustace and Hilda, The Lost Boys, I Remember Nelson, Measure for Measure, Henry IV, Day Christ Died, The Hunchback of Notre Dame, Fame Is the Spur, Glittering Prizes, Dead Man's Folly, The Case of Sherlock Holmes (host), Life Story, Hannah, The True Adventures of Christopher Columbus, The Chief, Bullion Boys, The Shadowy Third, Calcutta Chronicles.

PIKE, CORNELIA M.

Executive. b. Holyoke, MA, 1933. e. Boston U. Sch. of Commun., BS Magna Cum Laude. Asst. Promotion & Publicity Dir. WNAC/WNAC-TV 1954-56, Boston, MA. Women's Dir./On-air personality: WKNE Keene, NH 1957-60; WSMN Nashua, NH 1963-67; WHOB, Nashua, NH 1967-68. Mngr. Trade Winds Interior Design, Boston, MA 1979-81. Sls. Mngr./VP Pike Productions, Inc. 1981 to present. Company produces and markets trailers to exhibitors in U.S., UK, Germany, Australia and New Zealand. Alpha Epsilon Rho, Natl. Bdcstg. Soc. 1st VP, Variety Club of New England. Bd. dirs., Variety Club of New England. Life Patron, Variety Clubs International.

PIKE, JOHN S.

Executive. b. Cleveland, OH, Oct. 26, 1946. e. Univ. of Miami. Joined Paramount Pictures as v.p., video programming; promoted to sr. v.p., video prog. 1984, named sr. v.p., current network programming; 1985, promoted to exec. v.p., Paramount Network TV. Appt. pres., Network TV and Intl. co-production, 1991.

PINCHOT, BRONSON

Actor. b. New York, NY, May 20, 1959. e. Yale U. Grew up in Pasadena. Studied acting at Yale. On NY stage in Poor Little Lambs, Zoya's Apartment.
PICTURES: Risky Business (debut, 1983), Beverly Hills Cop, The Flamingo Kid, Hot Resort, After Hours, Second Sight, Blame It on the Bellboy, True Romance, Beverly Hills Cop III, It's My Party, Courage Under Fire.
TELEVISION: Series: Sara, Perfect Strangers, The Trouble With Larry, Meego. Movie: Jury Duty—The Comedy. Mini-Series: Stephen King's The Langoliers.

PINKETT, JADA

Actress. b. Baltimore, MD, Sept. 18, 1971. m. actor Will Smith.
PICTURES: Menace II Society, A Low Down Dirty Shame, Jason's Lyric, The Inkwell, Tales from the Crypt Presents: Demon Knight, The Nutty Professor, Set It Off, Scream 2, Force Majeure, Love For Hire (writer only), Woo.
TELEVISION: Series: A Different World. Movie: If These Walls Could Talk. Guest: 21 Jump Street.

PINSKER, ALLEN

Executive. b. New York, NY, Jan. 23, 1930. e. NYU. Mgr., Hempstead Theatre, 1950. 1954 joined Island Theatre Circuit as booker-buyer; named head buyer 1958. 1968 joined United Artists Eastern Theatres as film buyer; head buyer, 1969, v.p., 1970. Named v.p. United Artists Theatre Circuit, 1972. 1973 named UAET exec. v.p., member bd., 1974. Appt. pres. & COO, UA Communications, Inc., theatre division, 1987. 1987, named pres. and CEO, United Artists Theatre Circuit, Inc. and exec. v.p., United Artists Communications, Inc.; 1988, became member, bd. dir. United Artists Comm. Inc.

PINTER, HAROLD

Writer, Director, Actor. b. London, England, Oct. 10, 1930. Began career as actor then turned to writing and direction.
THEATER: The Dumb Waiter, Slight Ache, The Room, The Birthday Party, The Caretaker, The Homecoming, The Collection, Landscape, Silence, Old Times, No Man's Land, The Hothouse, Betrayal, One for the Road, Mountain Language, Party Time, Moonlight.
PICTURES: Writer: The Caretaker (The Guest), The Servant (also actor), The Pumpkin Eater, The Quiller Memorandum, Accident (also actor), The Birthday Party, The Go-Between, The Homecoming, Butley (dir. only), The Last Tycoon, The French Lieutenant's Woman, Betrayal, Turtle Diary (also actor), The Handmaid's Tale, Reunion, The Comfort of Strangers, The Trial.
TELEVISION: A Night Out, Night School, The Lover, Tea Party, The Basement, Langrishe Go Down, Heat of the Day.

PISANO, A. ROBERT

Executive. e. San Jose St. Univ., Boalt Hall School of Law at Univ. of CA, Berkeley. Was partner at law firm of O'Melveny & Myers prior to entering m.p. industry. 1985-91, exec. v.p. of Paramount Pictures serving as gen. counsel, member of office of chmn.; 1993, named exec. v.p. of MGM responsible for all business and legal affairs, home video and pay tv. In 1997, became Vice Chairman, with overall responsibility for business operations of MGM.

PISCOPO, JOE

Actor, Comedian. b. Passaic, NJ, June 17, 1951. Stage appearances in regional and dinner theaters in South and Northeast. Worked as stand-up comic at the Improvisation and the Comic Strip clubs, NY 1976-80. Author: The Piscopo Tapes. Television debut as regular on Saturday Night Live, 1980.
PICTURES: American Tickler or the Winner of 10 Academy Awards (1976), King Kong, Johnny Dangerously, Wise Guys, Dead Heat, Sidekicks, Huck and the King of Hearts, Two Bits & Pepper, Captain Nuke and the Bomber Boys, Open Season.
TELEVISION: Series: Saturday Night Live (1980-84). Guest: Comic Relief. Special: The Joe Piscopo Special (HBO). Movie: Huck and the King of Hearts.

PISIER, MARIE-FRANCE

Actress. b. Dalat, Indochina, May 10, 1944. Began appearing in French films at age 17. Returned to school at Univ. of Paris for degrees in law and political science; continued to work in films.
PICTURES: Qui ose nous Accuser? (debut, 1961), Love at Twenty (Truffaut episode), La Mort d'un Tueur, Les Yeux cernes, Trans-Europe Express, Stolen Kisses, Celine and Julie Go Boating, French Provincial, Cousin Cousine, Serail, Barocco, The Other Side of Midnight, Love on the Run, Les Apprentis Sourciers, The Bronte Sisters, French Postcards, La Banquiere, Chanel Solitaire, Der Zauberberg (The Magic Mountain), Miss Right, Hot Touch, The Prize of Peril, The Silent Ocean, L'Ami de Vincent, Les Nanas, Parking, Blue Note, Why is My Mother in My Bed?
TELEVISION: U.S.: French Atlantic Affair, Scruples.

PITT, BRAD

Actor. b. Shawnee, OK, Dec. 18, 1963. r.n. William Bradley Pitt. Raised in Springfield, MO. Studied journalism at Univ. of MO at Columbia. Moved to L.A. to attend art school, instead studied acting with Roy London. Appeared in short film Contact.
PICTURES: Cutting Class (debut, 1989), Happy Together, Across the Tracks, Thelma & Louise, Cool World, Johnny Suede, A River Runs Through It, Kalifornia, True Romance, The Favor, Interview With the Vampire. Legends of the Fall, Seven, Twelve Monkeys (Golden Globe, 1996), Sleepers, The Devil's Own, Seven Years In Tibet, Meet Joe Black, Fight Club, Ambrose Chapel.
TELEVISION: Series: Another World, Glory Days. Movies: A Stoning in Fulham County, Too Young to Die, The Image. Guest: Dallas, Growing Pains, Head of the Class, Tales From the Crypt.

PIVEN, JEREMY
Actor. b. New York, NY. Raised in Chicago where parents ran Piven Theater Workshop. e. Drake Univ. Studied acting at Eugene O'Neill Theater Center, Natl. Theater of Great Britain, NYU. Eventually joined Chicago's Second City comedy troupe. Co-founded Chicago's New Criminals Theatre Company, 1988.
THEATER: Fear & Loathing in Las Vegas, Peacekeeper, Methusalen, Knuckle, Macbeth.
PICTURES: Lucas, One Crazy Summer, Say Anything, White Palace, The Grifters, Pay Dirt, The Player, Bob Roberts, Singles, Judgment Night, Twenty Bucks, Car 54 Where Are You?, Twogether, PCU, Miami Rhapsody, Dr. Jekyll and Ms. Hyde, Heat, Grosse Pointe Blank, Very Bad Things, Music From Another Room, Phoenix.
TELEVISION: Series: Carol and Company, The Larry Sanders Show, Pride and Joy. Pilots: Heads Will Roll, Ready or Not. Movie: Don King: Only in America.

PLACE, MARY KAY
Actress, Writer. b. Tulsa, OK, Sept. 23, 1947. e. U. of Tulsa. Worked in production jobs and as Tim Conway's asst. for his TV show also as sect. for Norman Lear on Maude before starting to write for TV series (Mary Tyler Moore Show, Phyllis, Maude, M*A*S*H, etc.).
PICTURES: Bound For Glory (debut, 1976), New York New York, More American Graffiti, Starting Over, Private Benjamin, Modern Problems, Waltz Across Texas, The Big Chill, Smooth Talk, A New Life, Bright Angel, Captain Ron, Samantha, Teresa's Tattoo, Manny and Lo, Precious, Citizen Ruth.
TELEVISION: Series: Mary Hartman Mary Hartman (Emmy Award, 1977). Guest: All in the Family, Mary Tyler Moore Show, Fernwood 2-Night, Tonight Show, Saturday Night Live (host), thirtysomething. Movies: The Girl Who Spelled Freedom, Act of Love, For Love or Money, Out on the Edge, Just My Imagination, Telling Secrets, In the Line of Duty: The Pride of Vengeance. Specials: John Denver Special, Martin Mull's History of White People in America I & II, Portrait of a White Marriage, The Gift, Tales of the City, Leslie's Folly.

PLATT, OLIVER
Actor. b. 1962. Raised in Asia, Africa and Washington DC. e. Tufts Univ.
THEATER: Off-B'way: The Tempest, Moon Over Miami, Sparks in the Park, Urban Blight, Ubu, Elliot Loves.
PICTURES: Married to the Mob (debut, 1988), Working Girl, Crusoe, Flatliners, Postcards From the Edge, Beethoven, Diggstown, The Temp, Indecent Proposal, Benny & Joon, The Three Musketeers, Tall Tale, Funny Bones, Executive Decision, A Time to Kill, Dangerous Beauty.
TELEVISION: Movie: The Infiltrator.

PLESHETTE, SUZANNE
Actress. b. New York, NY. e. H.S. for the Performing Arts, Finch Coll., Syracuse U. Broadway debut, Compulsion.
THEATER: The Cold Wind and the Warm, The Golden Fleecing, The Miracle Worker, Compulsion, Two for the Seesaw, Special Occasions.
PICTURES: The Geisha Boy (debut, 1958), Rome Adventure, 40 Pounds of Trouble, The Birds, Wall of Noise, A Distant Trumpet, Fate Is the Hunter, Youngblood Hawke, A Rage to Live, The Ugly Dachshund, Nevada Smith, Mister Buddwing, The Adventures of Bullwhip Griffin, Blackbeard's Ghost, The Power, If It's Tuesday This Must Be Belgium, Suppose They Gave a War and Nobody Came, Target Harry (How to Make It), Support Your Local Gunfighter, The Shaggy D.A., Hot Stuff, Oh God! Book II, Lion King II.
TELEVISION: Series: The Bob Newhart Show, Suzanne Pleshette Is Maggie Briggs, Bridges to Cross, Nightingales, The Boys Are Back., The Single Guy. Movies: Wings of Fire, Along Came a Spider, Hunters Are for Killing, River of Gold, In Broad Daylight, Law and Order, Richie Brockelman: Missing 24 Hours, Kate Bliss and the Ticker Tape Kid, Flesh and Blood, For Love or Money, Fantasies, If Things Were Different, Help Wanted— Male, Dixie Changing Habits, Starmaker, One Cooks, The Other Doesn't, Legend of Valentino, Kojak The Belarus File, A Stranger Waits, Alone in the Neon Jungle, Leona Helmsley: The Queen of Mean, Battling for Baby, A Twist of the Knife. Special: Where Are They Now.

PLESKOW, ERIC
Executive. b., Vienna, Austria, April 24, 1924. Served as film officer, U.S. War dept., 1946-48; entered industry in 1948 as asst. gen. mgr., Motion Picture Export Association, Germany; 1950-51, continental rep. for Sol Lesser Prods.; joined United Artists in 1951 as Far East Sales Mgr.; named mgr., S. Africa, 1952; mgr., Germany, 1953-58; exec. asst. to continental mgr., 1958-59; asst. continental mgr., 1959-60; continental mgr., 1960-62; v.p. in charge of foreign distrib., 1962; exec. v.p. & CEO, Jan., 1973; pres. & CEO, Oct. , 1973. Resigned in 1978 to become pres. and CEO of Orion Pictures Co.; 1982, became pres. & CEO, Orion Pictures Corp; appointed chmn. of bd. 1991. Resigned 1992. Partner, Pleskow/Spikings Partnership, Beverly Hills, 1992-present. Prod., Beyond Rangoon.

PLIMPTON, MARTHA
Actress. b. New York, NY, Nov. 16, 1970. Daughter of actors Shelley Plimpton and Keith Carradine. Acting debut in film work-shop of Elizabeth Swados's musical Runaways. At 11 gained recognition as model in Richard Avedon's commercials for Calvin Klein jeans. Also on stage in The Hagadah, Pericles, The Heidi Chronicles, Robbers, subUrbia, The Great Unwashed.
PICTURES: Rollover (debut 1981, in bit role), The River Rat, The Goonies, The Mosquito Coast, Shy People, Stars and Bars, Running on Empty, Another Woman, Parenthood, Stanley and Iris, Silence Like Glass, Samantha, Inside Monkey Zetterland, Josh and S.A.M., My Life's in Turnaround, Mrs. Parker and the Vicious Circle, The Beans of Egypt Maine, Last Summer in the Hamptons, Beautiful Girls, I Shot Andy Warhol, I'm Not Rappaport, Eye of God.
TELEVISION: Movies: Daybreak, Chantilly Lace.

PLOWRIGHT, JOAN
C.B.E. Actress. b. Scunthrope, Brigg, Lincolnshire, England, Oct. 28, 1929. m. late actor, Lord Laurence Olivier. Trained for stage at Laban Art of Movement Studio, 1949-50; Old Vic Theatre Sch. 1950-52; with Michel St. Denis, Glen Byam Shaw and George Devine. London stage debut The Duenna, 1954. Broadway debut The Entertainer, 1958. Won Tony Award in 1961 for A Taste of Honey. With Bristol Old Vic Rep., Royal Court, National Theatre in numerous classics and contemporary plays.
RECENT THEATER: Saturday Sunday Monday, The Seagull, The Bed Before Yesterday, Filumena, Enjoy, Who's Afraid of Virginia Woolf?, Cavell, The Cherry Orchard, The Way of the World, Mrs. Warren's Profession, Time and the Conways, If We Are Women.
PICTURES: Moby Dick (debut, 1956), Time Without Pity, The Entertainer, Uncle Vanya, Three Sisters, Equus, Brimstone and Treacle, Britannia Hospital, Wagner (tv in U.S.), Revolution, The Dressmaker, Drowning By Numbers, I Love You to Death, Avalon, Enchanted April (Acad. Award nom.), Last Action Hero, Dennis the Menace, A Pin for the Butterfly, The Summer House, Widow's Peak, A Pyromaniac's Love Story, Hotel Sorrento, The Scarlett Letter, Jane Eyre, Mr. Wrong, Surviving Picasso, 101 Dalmatians.
TELEVISION: Odd Man In, Secret Agent, School for Scandal, The Diary of Anne Frank, Twelfth Night, Merchant of Venice, Daphne Laureola, Saturday Sunday Monday, The Divider, Conquest of the South Pole, A Nightingale Sang, House of Bernarda Alba, Stalin, On Promised Land, A Place for Annie, The Return of the Native. Pilot: Driving Miss Daisy (U.S.).

PLUMMER, AMANDA
Actress. b. New York, NY, March 23, 1957. e. Middlebury Coll. Daughter of actors Christopher Plummer and Tammy Grimes.
THEATER: Artichokes, A Month in the Country, A Taste of Honey (Theatre World Award), Agnes of God (Tony Award, 1982), The Glass Menagerie, A Lie of the Mind, Life Under Water, You Never Can Tell, Pygmalion, The Milk Train Doesn't Stop Here Anymore.
PICTURES: Cattle Annie and Little Britches (debut, 1981), The World According to Garp, Daniel, The Hotel New Hampshire, Static, The Courtship, Made in Heaven, Prisoners of Inertia, Joe Versus the Volcano, California Casanova, The Fisher King, Freejack, So I Married an Axe Murderer, Needful Things, Nostradamus, Pulp Fiction, Pax, Butterfly Kiss, The Propechy, Drunks, Freeway, A Simple Wish.
TELEVISION: Movies: The Dollmaker, The Unforgivable Secret, Riders to the Sea, Miss Rose White (Emmy Award, 1992), The Sands of Time, Last Light, Whose Child Is This? The War for Baby Jessica. Guest: Outer Limits (Emmy Award, 1996). Specials: Gryphon, The Courtship. Pilot: True Blue.

PLUMMER, CHRISTOPHER
Actor. b. Toronto, Canada, Dec. 13, 1927. Daughter is actress Amanda Plummer. Stage & radio career began in Canada (French & English).
THEATER: toured U.S. in The Constant Wife; B'way debut in The Starcross Story, 1953. B'way: The Dark is Light Enough, Home Is the Hero, J.B., The Lark, The Good Doctor, Cyrano (Tony Award, 1974), Othello (Tony nom.), Macbeth, No Man's Land. London: leading actor, Royal Shakespeare Theatre, 1961-62, Becket (Evening Standard Award), Natl. Theatre, 1969-70. Canada: leading actor, Stratford Festival (6 yrs.).
PICTURES: Stage Struck (debut, 1958), Wind Across the Everglades, The Fall of the Roman Empire, The Sound of Music, Inside Daisy Clover, The Night of the Generals, Triple Cross, Oedipus the King, The High Commissioner (Nobody Runs Forever), The Battle of Britain, The Royal Hunt of the Sun, Lock Up Your Daughters, Waterloo, The Pyx, The Return of the Pink Panther, Conduct Unbecoming, The Man Who Would Be King, The Spiral Staircase, Aces High, Assassination at Sarajevo (The Day That Shook the World), The Assignment, The Disappearance, International Velvet, Murder by Decree, The Silent Partner, Hanover Street, Starcrash, RIEL, Highpoint, Somewhere in Time, Eyewitness, Being Different (narrator), The Amateur, Dreamscape, Ordeal by Innocence, Lily in Love, The Boy in Blue, The Boss' Wife, An American Tail (voice), Dragnet,

Souvenir, Light Years (voice), Nosferatu in Venice, I Love N.Y., Shadow Dancing, Mindfield, Kingsgate, Red-Blooded American Girl, Where the Heart Is, Don't Tell Mom the Babysitter's Dead, Star Trek VI: The Undiscovered Country, Firehead, Rock-a-Doodle (voice), Money, Liar's Edge, Impolite, Malcolm X, Wolf, Dolores Claiborne, Twelve Monkeys.
TELEVISION: *Series*: Counterstrike. *Movies/Specials*: Hamlet at Elsinore (Emmy nom.), Don Juan in Hell (BBC), Little Moon of Alban, Prince and the Pauper, Jesus of Nazareth, Steiglitz and O'Keefe, Oedipus Rex, Omnibus, After the Fall, The Moneychangers (Emmy Award, 1977), Desperate Voyage, The Shadow Box, When the Circus Came to Town, Dial M for Murder, Little Gloria—Happy at Last, The Scarlet and the Black, The Thorn Birds, The Velveteen Rabbit, Crossings, A Hazard of Hearts, A Ghost in Monte Carlo, Young Catherine, Danielle Steel's Secrets, Stranger in the Mirror, Liar's Edge, Madeline (narrator; Emmy Award, 1994), Harrison Bergeron.

PODELL, ALBERT N.
Attorney. b. New York, NY, Feb. 25, 1937. e. Cornell U., U. of Chicago, NYU Sch. of Law. Non-fiction ed., Playboy magazine, 1959-60; dir. of photog. and m.p. reviewer Argosy magazine, 1961-64; Author: Who Needs a Road? (Bobbs-Merrill, 1967; re-published, Wolfenden, 1998), mng. ed., The Players Magazine, 1965-66; acct. exec. on 20th Century-Fox at Diener, Hauser, Greenthal, 1966-68; natl. advt. mgr., Cinema Center Films, 1969; acct. supervisor and creative dir. on Columbia Pictures at Charles Schlaifer, 1969-72; creator & dir. of Annual Motion Picture Advertising Awards sponsored by Cinema Lodge, B'nai B'rith. Attorney specializing in litigation, matrimonial law, rep. of performers and producers (1976-present). Pres., 1990-95 Jean Cocteau Rep. Th. Chmn. of Trustees; 1980-90, Assn. for Development of Dramatic Arts. Pres., Far Above Films. Dir. & writer: A Class Above, The Class on the Cutting Edge, Lift the Chorus, This Is Christmas.

PODHORZER, MUNIO
Executive. b. Berlin, Germany, Sept. 18, 1911. e. Jahn-Realgymnasium, U. of Berlin Medical Sch. U.S. Army, 1943-47; pres. United Film Enterprises, Inc.; formerly secy.-treas. 86th St. Casino Theatre, N.Y.; former v.p. Atlantic Pictures Corp.; former pres. Casino Films, Inc.; former pres. Film Development Corp.; former rep. Export-Union of the German Film Ind.; former U.S. rep. Franco-London Film, Paris; former pres., Venus Productions Corp.; former U.S. rep. Atlas Int'l Film GmbH, Munich; former U.S. rep. Bavaria Atelier Gesellschaft U.S.; past rep. Israfilm Ltd., Tel-Aviv; past rep. Tigon British Film Prod., London; past rep. Elias Querejeta, P.C., Madrid; past rep. Equiluz Films, Madrid; past rep. Airport Cine, Haiti; Les Films Du Capricorne, Paris; Schongerlims, German; Profilmes, Spain; Ligno, Spain; Films D'Alma, France; Intra Films, Italy. Member: Variety Club, Cinema Lodge, B'nai B'rith, Past Board of Governors IFIDA; past pres. CID Agents Assoc. Former gen. foreign sales mgr.; theatrical division of National Telefilm Associates; past rep. Barcino Films, S.A. Spain; Eagle Films Ltd., UK; Les Films Jacques Leitienne, France; Nero Film Classics, USA; Schongerlims, Germany; Profilmes, S.A. Spain; VIP Ltd., Israel. Presently representing Atlas Film & AV, Germany; KFM Films, Inc. U.S.A.; Compagnie France Film, Canada; Cia. Iberoamerican de TV, S.A. Spain; Israel. Co-chmn., entertainment div., United Jewish Appeal, Federation of Jewish Philanthropies, 1981-83.

PODHORZER, NATHAN
Executive. b. Brody, Poland, Nov. 27, 1919. e. City Coll. of New York, Rutgers U., U. of Southern California. U.S. Army, 1942-46; documentary film prod., Israel, 1946-57; CEO, United Film Enterprises, Inc. U.S. purchasing agent: Atlas Air, Atlas Film & Medien (Germany), Co. France Film (Canada).

POE, STEPHEN
Executive. Began career as lawyer with Rutan & Tucker; 1976, joined 20th Century-Fox as prod. counsel; later v.p., business affairs. Turned to producing in 1982, first in association with Frank Mancuso Jr. Productions. 1986, acted as consultant and indep. prod. counsel for United Artists Pictures. 1987, joined CBS/Fox Video as sr. v.p. of acquisitions and programming.

POITIER, SIDNEY
Actor, Director. b. Miami, FL, Feb. 20, 1927. Raised in the Bahamas. m. actress Joanna Shimkus. e. Miami, FL. On stage with Amer. Negro Theatre in Days of Our Youth. Appeared in Army Signal Corps documentary From Whence Cometh My Help. Formed First Artists Prod. Co. Ltd., 1969, with Paul Newman and Barbra Streisand. *Autobiography*: This Life (1980). Recipient 1992 AFI Life Achievement Award.
THEATER: Strivers Road, You Can't Take It With You, Anna Lucasta (B'way debut, 1948), Lysistrata, Freight, A Raisin in the Sun.
PICTURES: No Way Out (debut 1950), Cry the Beloved Country, Red Ball Express, Go Man Go, Blackboard Jungle, Goodbye My Lady, Edge of the City, Something of Value, Band of Angels,

Mark of the Hawk, The Defiant Ones, Virgin Island, Porgy and Bess, All the Young Men, A Raisin in the Sun, Paris Blues, Pressure Point, Lilies of the Field (Acad. Award, 1963), The Long Ships, The Greatest Story Ever Told, The Bedford Incident, The Slender Thread, A Patch of Blue, Duel at Diablo, To Sir With Love, In the Heat of the Night, Guess Who's Coming to Dinner, For Love of Ivy, The Lost Man, They Call Me Mister Tibbs, Brother John, The Organization, Buck and the Preacher (also dir.), A Warm December (also dir.), Uptown Saturday Night (also dir.), The Wilby Conspiracy, Let's Do It Again (also dir.), A Piece of the Action (also dir.), Stir Crazy (dir. only), Hanky Panky (dir. only), Fast Forward (dir. only), Shoot To Kill, Little Nikita, Ghost Dad (dir. only), Sneakers, The Jackal.
TELEVISION: *Movies*: Separate But Equal, Children of the Dust, To Sir With Love II, Mandela and de Klerk, Free of Eden. *Guest*: Philco TV Playhouse, ABC Stage '67.

POLANSKI, ROMAN
Director, Writer. b. Paris, France, Aug. 18, 1933. m. actress Emmanuelle Seigner. Lived in Poland from age of three. Early career, art school in Cracow; Polish Natl. Film Acad., Lodz 1954-59. Radio Actor 1945-47; on stage 1947-53; asst. dir., Kamera film prod. group 1959-61. Co-founder Cadre Films, 1964. Wrote, dir. and acted in short films: Two Men and a Wardrobe, When Angels Fall, The Fat and the Lean, Mammals. On stage as actor in Amadeus (and dir., Warsaw & Paris), Metamorphosis (Paris, 1988). *Autobiography*: Roman (1984).
PICTURES: *Dir./Writer*: Knife in the Water (feature debut, 1962), Repulsion, Cul-de-Sac, The Fearless Vampire Killers or: Pardon Me But Your Teeth Are in My Neck (also actor), Rosemary's Baby, A Day at the Beach (s.p. only), Weekend of a Champion (prod. only), Macbeth (also prod.), What? (a.k.a. Che?; also actor), Chinatown (dir. & actor only), The Tenant (also actor), Tess, Pirates, Frantic, Bitter Moon, Death and the Maiden. *Actor only*: The Generation, The Magic Christian, Andy Warhol's Dracula, Back in the U.S.S.R., A Pure Formality, Grosse Fatigue.

POLEDOURIS, BASIL
Composer. b. Kansas City, MO, Aug. 21, 1945. e. Long Beach St. Univ., USC. While at USC composed music for short films by John Milius and Randal Kleiser. Became first American Film Institute intern.
PICTURES: Big Wednesday, Tintorera, Dolphin, The Blue Lagoon, Conan the Barbarian, Summer Lovers, House of God, Conan the Destroyer, Making the Grade, Red Dawn, Protocol, Flesh and Blood, Iron Eagle, Robocop, No Man's Land, Cherry 2000, Spellbinder, Split Decisions, Farewell to the King, Wired, The Hunt for Red October, Quigley Down Under, Flight of the Intruder, White Fang, Return to the Blue Lagoon, Harley Davidson & the Marlboro Man, Wind, Hot Shots Part Deux, Free Willy, Robocop 3, On Deadly Ground, Serial Mom, Lassie, The Jungle Book, Under Siege 2: Dark Territory, Free Willy 2: The Adventure Home, It's My Party, Celtic Pride, Breakdown, Starship Troopers, Les Miserables.
TELEVISION: *Mini-Series*: Amerika, Lonesome Dove (Emmy Award, 1989). *Movies*: Congratulations It's a Boy, A Whale for the Killing, Fire on the Mountain, Amazons, Single Women Single Bars, Prison for Children, Misfits of Science, Island Sons, Intrigue, L.A. Takedown, Nasty Boys, Ned Blessing, Lone Justice, Danielle Steel's Zoya.

POLL, MARTIN H.
Producer. b. New York, NY, Nov. 24, 1926. e. Wharton Sch., U. of Pennsylvania. Pres. Gold Medal Studios (1956-61).
PICTURES: A Face in the Crowd, Middle of the Night, The Goddess, Butterfield 8, Love Is a Ball, Sylvia, The Lion in Winter, The Appointment, The Magic Garden of Stanley Sweetheart, The Man Who Loved Cat Dancing, Night Watch, Love and Death (exec. prod.); The Man Who Would Be King, The Sailor Who Fell From Grace with the Sea, Somebody Killed Her Husband, Nighthawks, Gimme an F, Haunted Summer, My Heroes Have Always Been Cowboys.
TELEVISION: *Series*: Car 54 Where Are You? *Movies*: Arthur the King, Stunt Seven. *Mini-Series*: A Town Called Alice, The Dain Curse, Diana: Her True Story.

POLLACK, SYDNEY
Director, Producer. b. South Bend, IN, July 1, 1934. m. Claire Griswold. e. Neighborhood Playhouse. Assistant to Sanford Meisner at Neighborhood Playhouse. Appeared as actor on B'way in A Stone for Danny Fisher, The Dark is Light Enough. Dir. debut in 1960. Dir. play at UCLA, P.S. 193. Prepared the American version of The Leopard.
PICTURES: *Director*: The Slender Thread (debut, 1965), This Property Is Condemned, The Scalphunters, Castle Keep, They Shoot Horses Don't They? (also prod.), Jeremiah Johnson, The Way We Were (also prod.), The Yakuza (also prod.), Three Days of the Condor, Bobby Deerfield (also prod.), The Electric Horseman, Asence of Malice (also prod.), Tootsie (also prod., actor), Out of Africa (also prod.; Acad. Awards for Best Picture & dir., 1985), Havana (also prod.), The Firm, Sabrina (also prod.). *Producer*: Songwriter, Bright Lights Big City, The Fabulous Baker Boys, Presumed Innocent. *Exec. Producer*: Honeysuckle Rose, White Palace, King Ralph, Dead Again, Leaving Normal, Searching for Bobby Fischer, Flesh and Bone, Sense and Sensibility. *Actor*: War Hunt, The Player, Death Becomes Her, Husbands and Wives.

TELEVISION: *As actor.* Playhouse 90 (several segments), Shotgun Slade. *Dir.:* Ben Casey (15 episodes), The Game (Bob Hope-Chrysler Theatre; Emmy Award), Two is the Number. *Co-prod.* (movie): A Private Matter. *Exec. prod.* (series): Fallen Angels.

POLLAK, KEVIN
Actor. b. San Francisco, CA, Oct. 30, 1958. Started doing stand-up comedy in the San Francisco Bay area, then continued in L.A. clubs.
PICTURES: Million Dollar Mystery (debut, 1987), Willow, Avalon, L.A. Story, Another You, Ricochet, A Few Good Men, The Opposite Sex and How to Live With Them, Indian Summer, Wayne's World 2, Grumpy Old Men, Reality Bites, Clean Slate, Miami Rhapsody, The Usual Suspects, Canadian Bacon, Casino, Nowhere Man, Chameleon, House Arrest, Grumpier Old Men, That Thing You Do!, National Lampoon's The Don's Analyst, Truth or Consequences N.M., Outside Ozona.
TELEVISION: *Series:* Coming of Age, Morton and Hayes. *Specials:* One Night Stand (also prod., writer), Stop With the Kicking (also prod., writer), The Seven Deadly Sins (also writer, dir.). *Movie:* Ruby Bridges. *Mini-series:* From the Earth to the Moon.

POLLAN, TRACY
Actress. b. New York, NY, June 22, 1960. m. actor Michael J. Fox.
THEATER: *B'way:* Jake's Women.
PICTURES: Promised Land, Bright Lights Big City, A Stranger Among Us.
TELEVISION: *Series:* Family Ties. *Movies:* For Lovers Only, Sessions, Trackdown: Finding the Goodbar Killer, A Good Sport, Dying to Love You, Children of the Dark.

POLLARD, MICHAEL J.
Actor. r.n. Michael J. Pollack. b. Passaic, NJ, May 30, 1939. e. Montclair Academy, Actors Studio.
THEATER: Comes a Day, Loss of Roses, Enter Laughing, Bye Bye Birdie, Leda Had a Little Swan, Our Town.
PICTURES: Adventures of a Young Man (debut, 1962), The Stripper, Summer Magic, The Russians Are Coming the Russians Are Coming, The Wild Angels, Caprice, Enter Laughing, Bonnie and Clyde (Acad. Award nom.), Jigsaw, Hannibal Brooks, Little Fauss and Big Halsy, The Legend of Frenchie King (Petroleum Girls), Dirty Little Billy, Between the Lines, Melvin and Howard, Heated Vengeance, America, The Patriot, The American Way (Riders of the Storm), Roxanne, Scrooged, Fast Food, Season of Fear, Next of Kin, Tango and Cash, Night Visitor, Sleepaway Camp 3, Why Me?, Dick Tracy, I Come in Peace, Joey Takes a Cab, The Art of Dying, Another You, Enid Is Sleeping (Over Her Dead Body), Split Second, The Arrival, Heartstopper, Arizona Dream, Motorama, Skeeter.
TELEVISION: *Series:* Leo and Liz in Beverly Hills. *Guest:* Alfred Hitchcock Presents (Anniversary Gift), Going My Way, Route 66, Here's Lucy, Mr. Novak, Honey West, I Spy, Lost in Space, Dobie Gillis, Get Christie Love, Star Trek, Simon & Simon, The Fall Guy, Gunsmoke, Guns of Paradise, The Young Riders, Nasty Boys. *Movies:* The Smugglers, Stuck With Each Other, Working Trash.

POLLEXFEN, JACK
Producer, Director, Writer. b. San Diego, CA, June 10, 1918. e. Los Angeles City Coll. Newspaperman, magazine writer, playwright: prod. for RKO, United Artists, Columbia, Allied Artists.
PICTURES: Son of Sinbad, At Swords Point, Secret of Convict Lake, Desert Hawk, Lady in the Iron Mask, Dragon's Gold, Problem Girls, Captive Women, Captain Kidd and the Slave Girl, Neanderthal Man, Captain John Smith and Pocahontas, Return to Treasure Island, Sword of Venus, Daughter of Dr. Jekyll, Monstrosity, Son of Dr. Jekyll, Mr. Big, Man from Planet X, Indestructible Man, Port Sinister, Treasure of Monte Cristo, Bulldog Drummond, Grey City.

POLLOCK, DALE
Producer. b. Cleveland, OH, May 18, 1950. e. Brandeis U., B.A. anthropology, San Jose State, M.S., mass communication. Began journalistic career in Santa Cruz in early '70s, serving as reporter and film critic for Daily Variety, 1977-80. Joined Los Angeles Times as film writer, winning paper's Award for Sustained Excellence in 1984. 1985 left to take post with The Geffen Film Co. as executive in chg. creative development. Joined A&M Films as v.p. in chg. prod., 1986. Became pres., 1989. Author: Skywalking (about George Lucas).
PICTURES: The Beast (exec. prod.), The Mighty Quinn (exec. prod.). *Producer:* House of Cards, Worth Winning, Blaze, Crooked Hearts, A Midnight Clear, A Home of Our Own, S.F.W., Mrs. Winterbourne.

POLLOCK, THOMAS
Executive. b. 1943. In 1971, after 3 years as business mgr. for American Film Institute's film marketing wing, formed law firm Pollock Bloom, and Dekom with young filmmakers such as George Lucas and Matthew Robbins as clients. Served as chmn. Filmex, 1973-81. 1986, named chmn. MCA's Universal motion picture group., now vice chmn., MCA, Inc.

POLONSKY, ABRAHAM
Writer, Director. b. New York, NY, Dec. 5, 1910. e. CCNY, B.A.; Columbia Law Sch. Taught at City Coll. 1932 until war. Blacklisted from 1951-66.
AUTHOR: The Enemy Sea, The Discoverers, The World Above, The Season of Fear, Zenia's Way.
PICTURES: *Writer:* Golden Earrings, Body and Soul (also story), Force of Evil (also dir.), I Can Get It for You Wholesale, Odds Against Tomorrow, Madigan, Tell Them Willie Boy is Here (also dir.), Romance of a Horse Thief, Avalanche Express, Monsignor.

PONTECORVO, GILLO
Director. b. Pisa, Italy, Nov. 19, 1919. Younger brother of Prof. Bruno Pontecorvo, Harwell scientist who defected in 1950. Former photo-journalist. Worked as asst. dir., directed documentary shorts before feature debut in 1957.
PICTURES: Die Windrose (Giovanna episode), La Grande Strada Azzurra (The Long Blue Road; also co-s.p.), Kapo (also co-s.p.), The Battle of Algiers (also story; Acad. Award noms. as dir. & writer), Queimada! (Burn; also co-story), Ogro (The Tunnel; also co-s.p.).

PONTI, CARLO
Producer. b. Milan, Italy, Dec. 11, 1913. m. actress Sophia Loren. e. U. of Milan, 1934. Prod. first picture in Milan, Little Old World; prod. Lux Film Rome; prod. first of a series of famous Toto pictures, Toto Housebunting.
PICTURES: A Dog's Life, The Knight Has Arrived, Musolino, The Outlaw, Romanticism, Sensuality, The White Slave, Europe 1951, Toto in Color, The Three Corsairs, The Gold of Naples, Ulysses, The Woman of the River, An American of Rome, Attila, La Strada, War and Peace, The Last Lover, The Black Orchid, That Kind of Woman, A Breath of Scandal, Heller in Pink Tights, Two Women, Boccaccio '70, Bluebeard, The Condemned of Altona, Marriage Italian Style, Casanova '70, Operation Crossbow, Doctor Zhivago, Lady L, Blow Up, More Than a Miracle, The Girl and the General, Sunflower, The Best House in London, Zabriskie Point, The Priest's Wife, Lady Liberty, White Sister, What?, Andy Warhol's Frankenstein, The Passenger, The Cassandra Crossing, A Special Day, Saturday Sunday Monday.
TELEVISION: Mario Puzo's The Fortunate Pilgrim (exec. prod.).

POP, IGGY
Musician, Actor. b. MI, April 21, 1947. r.n. James Osterberg. Has recorded 16 albums with band the Stooges and solo.
PICTURES: *Actor:* Cry Baby, Hardware (voice only), Dead Man, The Crow: City of Angels. *Songs:* Rock 'N' Rule. *Score:* The Brave.

PORTMAN, NATALIE
Actress. b. Jerusalem, Israel, June 9, 1981. e. Stagedoor Manor Performing Arts Camp. B'way debut in The Diary of Anne Frank, 1997.
PICTURES: The Professional, Heat, Everyone Says I Love You, Beautiful Girls, Mars Attacks!, South Beach, Prince of Egypt (voice), The Little Black Book, Anywhere But Here, Star Wars: Episode I.

PORTMAN, RACHEL
Composer. b. Haslemere, England, Dec. 11, 1960.
PICTURES: Privileged, First Love, Last Day of Summer, Sharma and Beyond, 90 Degrees South, High Hopes, Oranges Are Not the Only Fruit, Life Is Sweet, Antonia and Jane, Where Angels Fear to Tread, Used People, Rebecca's Daughters, The Joy Luck Club, Great Moments in Aviation, Friends, Ethan Frome, Benny & Joon, War of the Buttons, Only You, Sirens, The Road to Wellville, To Wong Foo—Thanks for Everything! Julie Newmar, A Pyromaniac's Love Story, Smoke, The Adventures of Pinocchio, Emma (Acad. Award, 1996), Palookaville, Marvin's Room, Home Fries, Beauty and the Beast: The Enchanted Christmas, Addicted to love, Mulan, Beloved.
TELEVISION: *Movies:* Reflections, Four Days in July, Good as Gold, The Short and Curlies, 1914 All Out, Sometime in August, Loving Hazel, Young Charlie Chaplin, The Woman in Black, Precious Bane, Monster Maker, Living with Dinosaurs, The Widowmaker, Shoot to Kill, Flea Bites, The Cloning of Joanna May. *Mini-series:* A Little Princess, Jim Henson's The Storyteller, Jim Henson's The Storyteller: Greek Myths.

POSEY, PARKER
Actress. b. Laurel, MS, Nov. 8, 1968. e. NC School of the Arts; SUNY Purchase.
PICTURES: Joey Breaker, Dazed and Confused, Coneheads, Mixed Nuts, Dead Connection, Amateur, Sleep with Me, Frisk, Drunks, Party Girl, Kicking and Screaming, The Doom Generation, Flirt, Waiting for Guffman, The Daytrippers, Basquiat, Henry Fool, Dinner at Fred's, SubUrbia, Clockwatchers, The House of Yes, The Misadventures of Margaret, Cross Country, What Rats Don't Do, You've Got Mail.
TELEVISION: *Series:* As The World Turns. *Mini-series:* Tales of the City, More Tales of the City.

POST, TED
Producer, Director. b. Brooklyn, NY, March 31, 1918. Dir. many stage plays; dir. CBS-TV Repertoire Thea.; Prod.-dir., NBC-TV Coney Island of the Mind. Directed Everyone Can Make Music.
PICTURES: The Peacemaker (debut, 1956), The Legend of Tom Dooley, Hang 'em High, Beneath The Planet of the Apes, The Baby, The Harrad Experiment, Magnum Force, Whiffs, Good Guys Wear Black, Go Tell the Spartans, Nightkill, The Human Shield.
TELEVISION: Series: Studio One, Ford Theatre, Playhouse of Stars, Alcoa Theatre, Gunsmoke, Rawhide, Twilight Zone, Wagon Train, Combat, Peyton Place, Alcoa, Defenders, Route 66, Baretta, Columbo. Movies: Night Slaves, Dr. Cook's Garden, Yuma, Five Desperate Women, Do Not Fold Spindle or Mutilate, The Bravos, Sandcastles, Girls in the Office, Diary of a Hitchhiker, Stagecoach. Pilots: Cagney & Lacey, Beyond Westworld, Steve Canyon, Perry Mason. Mini-series: Rich Man, Poor Man II (episode 3).

POSTER, STEVEN
Cinematographer. A.S.C. b. Chicago, IL, March 1, 1944. e. L.A. Art Center Coll. Started as commercial cinematographer before moving into feature films. 2nd unit work includes: Close Encounters of the Third Kind, Blade Runner. 2nd v.p., American Society of Cinematographers.
PICTURES: Blood Beach, Dead and Buried, Spring Break, Strange Brew, Testament, The New Kids, The Heavenly Kid, Blue City, The Boy Who Could Fly, Aloha Summer, Someone to Watch Over Me, Big Top Pee-wee, Next of Kin, Opportunity Knocks, Rocky V, Life Stinks, The Cemetery Club, Once You Meet a Stranger, A Midwife's Tale, Boy's Life 2, Rocket Man.
TELEVISION: Movies: The Grass is Always Greener, The Night Rider, The Beggarman Thief, Coward of the County, Mysterious Two, The Cradle Will Fall, I'll Take Manhattan, Class of '65, Courage, Shanghai La Plaza, Roswell, The Color of Justice.

POSTLETHWAITE, PETE
Actor. b. Lancashire, England. Feb. 16, 1946.
THEATER: RSC: Every Man and His Humour, A Midsummer Night's Dream, MacBeth, King Lear, The Taming of the Shrew.
PICTURES: The Duellists, A Private Function, Distant Voices Still Lives, The Dressmaker, To Kill a Priest, Hamlet, Alien³, The Last of the Mohicans, Waterland, In the Name of the Father (Acad. Award nom.), Anchoress, The Usual Suspects, James and the Giant Peach (voice), Dragonheart, When Saturday Comes.
TELEVISION: The Muscle Market, A Child From the South, Treasure Island (theatrical in U.K.), Martin Chuzzlewit.

POSTON, TOM
Actor. b. Columbus, OH, Oct. 17, 1927. Made B'way debut 1947 in Cyrano de Bergerac.
PICTURES: City That Never Sleeps (debut, 1953), Zotz!, The Old Dark House, Soldier in the Rain, Cold Turkey, The Happy Hooker, Rabbit Test, Up the Academy, Carbon Copy, Krippendorf's Tribe.
TELEVISION: Movies: The Girl The Gold Watch and Everything, Save the Dog!, A Quiet Little Neighborhood A Perfect Little Murder. Series: The Steve Allen Show (Emmy Award, 1959), Pantomime Quiz, To Tell the Truth, On the Rocks, We've Got Each Other, Mork and Mindy, Newhart, Grace Under Fire. Guest: Goodyear Playhouse, Phil Silvers Show, Password, The Defenders, Fame, The Love Boat, Dream On, etc.

POTTS, ANNIE
Actress. b. Nashville, TN, Oct. 28, 1952. e. Stephens Coll., MO, BFA. Amateur stage debut at 12 in Heidi. Then in summer stock; on road in Charley's Aunt, 1976. Serves on auxilliary bd. of MADD (Mothers Against Drunk Driving). Ambassador for Women for the Amer. Arthritis Fdn.
PICTURES: Corvette Summer (debut, 1978), King of the Gypsies, Heartaches, Ghostbusters, Crimes of Passion, Pretty in Pink, Jumpin' Jack Flash, Pass the Ammo, Who's Harry Crumb?, Ghostbusters II, Texasville, Breaking the Rules, Toy Story (voice).
TELEVISION: Movies: Black Market Baby, Flatbed Annie and Sweetie Pie, Cowboy, It Came Upon the Midnight Clear, Why Me?, Her Deadly Rival. Series: Goodtime Girls, Designing Women, Love & War, Dangerous Minds, Over the Top. Guest: Remington Steele, Magnum P.I., Twilight Zone.

POUND, LESLIE
Executive. b. London, England, Nov. 3, 1926. Entered industry in 1943 as reporter on British trade paper, The Cinema. Now, Screen International. Following military service in India and Singapore returned to work for that publication until 1952 when joined Paramount pub. office in London on the The Greatest Show on Earth. Named dir. of adv./pub. in U.K. for Paramount. 1958, retained Paramount position when Cinema Int'l Corp. was formed. 1977, joined Lew Grade in ITC Entertainment as world-wide dir. of pub./adv. 1977, int'l pub. chief for Embassy Pictures in Los Angeles. 1982, named Paramount Pictures v.p., int'l mktg. for motion picture div., N.Y. 1983. Relocated to L.A. with mktg. div. as sr. v.p. Returned to London, 1993 as sr. v.p. International markets for Paramount Pictures.

POWELL, JANE
Actress, Singer. r.n. Suzanne Burce. b. Portland, OR, April 1, 1929. m. pub. relations exec. Dick Moore. Had own radio program over KOIN, Portland; singer on nat'l networks; Star of Tomorrow, 1948. Autobiography: The Girl Next Door ... and How She Grew (1988). Video: Jane Powell's Fight Back With Fitness.
THEATER: Irene (B'way, 1974). After-Play (off-B'way, 1996). Toured nationally with South Pacific, Peter Pan, My Fair Lady, The Unsinkable Molly Brown, I Do I Do, Same Time Next Year, Chapter Two.
PICTURES: Song of the Open Road (debut, 1944), Delightfully Dangerous, Holiday in Mexico, Three Daring Daughters, A Date With Judy, Luxury Liner, Nancy Goes to Rio, Two Weeks With Love, Royal Wedding, Rich Young and Pretty, Small Town Girl, Three Sailors and a Girl, Seven Brides for Seven Brothers, Athena, Deep in My Heart, Hit the Deck, The Girl Most Likely, The Female Animal, Enchanted Island.
TELEVISION: Specials: Ruggles of Red Gap, Give My Regards to Broadway, Meet Me in St. Louis, Jane Powell Show. Series: Alcoa Theatre, Loving, As the World Turns. Guest: The Love Boat, Growing Pains, Murder She Wrote, others. Movies: The Letters, Mayday at 40,000 Feet, The Making of Seven Brides for Seven Brothers. Host: The Movie Musicals.

POWELL, MICHAEL
Executive. b. Birmingham, AL, March 23, 1963. e. College of William and Mary, AB, government, 1985. Georgetown U. Law Center, JD, 1993. US Army officer, 1985-88. Policy adviser to Sec'y of Defense, Defense Dept., 1988-90. Law clerk for Harry Edwards, chief judge, US Court of Appeals, 1993-94. Associate, O'Melveny & Myers, 1994-96. Chief of staff, Justice Dept. antitrust div., 1996-97. Commissioner of the FCC, 1997- .

POWELL, ROBERT
Actor. b. Salford, England, June 1, 1944. e. Manchester U. Stage work includes Tovarich.
PICTURES: Robbery (debut, 1967), Far From the Madding Crowd, Joanna, The Italian Job, Walk a Crooked Path, Secrets, Running Scared, Asylum, The Asphyx (Horror of Death), Mahler, Tommy, Oltre il Bene e il Male (Beyond Good and Evil), Cocktails for Three, The Thirty-Nine Steps, The Dilessi Affair, Harlequin (Dark Forces), Jane Austin in Manhattan, The Survivor, Imperative (Venice Film Fest. Award), The Jigsaw Man, What Waits Below, D'Annunio and I Down There in the Jungle, Romeo-Juliet (voice), The Sign of Command, Once on Chunuk Bar.
TELEVISION: Series: Doomwatch, Hannay, The First Circle. Mini-series: Jesus of Nazareth. Movies/Specials: Shelley, Jude the Obscure, Mrs. Warren's Profession, Mr. Rolls & Mr. Royce, Looking for Clancy, The Four Feathers, The Hunchback of Notre Dame, Pygmalion, Frankenstein, Shaka Zulu, Merlin of the Crystal Cave, The Golden Years.

POWERS, MALA
Actress. r.n. Mary Ellen Powers. b. San Francisco, CA, Dec. 20, 1931. p. George and Dell Powers, latter, dramatic coach. e. Studied acting with Michael Chekhov. e. UCLA. Pasadena Playhouse in For Keeps, 1946, followed by Distant Isle; Actor's Lab, Hollywood; did considerable radio, theatre and tv work. Writer, narrator Children's Story, and Dial A Story (1979). Author: Follow the Star (1980), Follow the Year (1984). Teaches Michael Chekhov technique of acting.
PICTURES: Tough as They Come (debut, 1942), Outrage, Edge of Doom, Cyrano de Bergerac, Rose of Cimarron, City Beneath the Sea, City That Never Sleeps, Geraldine, The Yellow Mountain, Rage at Dawn, Bengazi, Tammy and the Bachelor, The Storm Rider, Death in Small Doses, The Colossus of New York, Sierra Baron, The Unknown Terror, Man on the Prowl, Flight of the Lost Balloon, Rogue's Gallery, Doomsday, Daddy's Gone-A-Hunting, Six Tickets to Hell.
TELEVISION: Series: Hazel, The Man and the City. Guest: Daniel Boone.

POWERS, C. F. (MIKE) JR.
Executive. b. San Francisco, CA, March 6, 1923. e. Park Coll., MO, Columbia U., N.Y., graduated U. of Oregon. Entered film business with P.R.C. in Portland, OR, 1947. Became Eagle Lion branch mgr. in Portland, 1950, and then United Artists. Moved to Seattle, WA as branch mgr. of 20th Century Fox, 1960. Was then western division mgr. for 20th Century Fox until 1967, then western division mgr. for Cinerama until 1973. Became exec. v.p., head film buyer for Robert L. Lippert Theatres, Transcontinental Theatres and Affiliated Theatres until 1978. Western div. mgr. Orion Pictures, 1982-4. Mike Powers Ent. (a buying and booking combine and indept. film distrib.). 1984-86 Western district mgr. Embassy Pictures. Became western division mgr. for Filmways Pictures. Past president of Catholic Entertainment Guild of Northern Calif.; past pres. of Variety Club Tent 32, San Francisco. Currently m.p. consultant to U.S. Federal Govt.

POWERS, STEFANIE
Actress. r.n. Stefania Federkiewicz. b. Hollywood, CA, Nov. 2, 1942. After graduation from Hollywood High signed by Columbia Studios. PICTURES: Tammy Tell Me True (debut, 1962), Experiment in Terror, The Young Sinner, The Interns, If a Man Answers, McClintock!, Palm Springs Weekend, The New Interns, Love Has Many Faces, Die Die My Darling (Fanatic), Stagecoach, Warning Shot, The Boatniks, Crescendo, The Magnificent 7 Ride, Herbie Rides Again, Gone With the West, It Seemed Like a Good Idea at the Time, Escape to Athena, Invisible Stranger (The Astral Factor).
TELEVISION: Series: The Girl From U.N.C.L.E., Feather and Father Gang, Hart to Hart. Mini-series: Washington: Behind Closed Doors, Hollywood Wives. Movies: Five Desperate Women, Paper Man, Sweet Sweet Rachel, Hardcase, No Place to Run, Shootout in a One-Dog Town, Skyway to Death, Sky Heist, Return to Earth, Family Secrets (also prod.), A Death in Canaan, Nowhere to Run, Mistral's Daughter, Deceptions, At Mother's Request, Beryl Markham: A Shadow on the Sun (also co-prod.), She Was Marked for Murder, Love and Betrayal, When Will I Be Loved?, The Burden of Proof, Survive the Night, Hart to Hart Returns (also co-prod.), Hart to Hart: Home is Where the Hart Is, Hart to Hart: Crimes of the Hart (also co-prod.), Hart to Hart: Old Friends Never Die, The Good Ride, Good King Wenceslas, Hart to Hart: Secrets of the Hart, Hart to Hart: Til Death Do Us Hart.

PRENTISS, PAULA
Actress. r.n. Paula Ragusa. b. San Antonio, TX, March 4, 1939. m. actor-dir. Richard Benjamin. e. Northwestern U., Bachelor degree in drama, 1959. On stage in As You Like It, Arf!, The Norman Conquests, Love Letters, Secrets, Demons (Amer. Rep. Theatre, Cambridge, MA), Angel's Share (Tiffany Theater, L.A.). PICTURES: Where the Boys Are (debut, 1960), The Honeymoon Machine, Bachelor in Paradise, The Horizontal Lieutenant, Follow the Boys, Man's Favorite Sport?, The World of Henry Orient, Looking for Love, In Harm's Way, What's New Pussycat?, Catch-22, Move, Born to Win, Last of the Red Hot Lovers, Crazy Joe, The Parallax View, The Stepford Wives, The Black Marble, Saturday the 14th, Buddy Buddy, Mrs. Winterbourne.
TELEVISION: Series: He & She, Burke's Law. Movies: The Couple Takes a Wife, Having Babies II, No Room to Run (Australian), Friendships Secrets and Lies, Top of the Hill, Packin' It In, M.A.D.D.: Mothers Against Drunk Drivers.

PRESLE, MICHELINE
Actress. r.n. Micheline Chassagne. b. Paris, France, Aug. 22, 1922. e. Raymond Rouleau Dram. Sch. m.p. debut in Je Chante; on stage in Colinette. Am. Stram Gram, Spectacle des Allies; to U.S., 1945; Flea in Her Ear, Magic Circus, Who's Afraid of Virginia Woolf? (tour), Gigi, Nuit de Valognes, Boomerang, Adriana Mont, etc.
PICTURES: Jeunes Filles en Detresse, L'Histoire de Rire, La Nuit Fantastique, Felicie Nanteuil, Seul Amour, Faibalas, Boule de Suif, Jeux Sont Faix, Diable au Corps, Under My Skin, Some Kind of News, An American Guerilla in the Philippines, Adventures of Captain Fabian, Sins of Pompeii, House of Ricordi, Archipelago of Love, Thieves After Dark, Le Chien, At the Top of the Stairs, Le Jour de Rois. Fine Weather, But Storms Due Towards Evening, Confidences, Alouette, Je te plumerai, I Want to Go Home.
TELEVISION: The Blood of Others.

PRESLEY, PRISCILLA
Actress. b. Brooklyn, NY, May 24, 1945. Raised in Connecticut. e. Wiesbaden, West Germany where met and married Elvis Presley (1967-73). Studied acting with Milton Katselas, dance at Steven Peck Theatre Art School and karate at Chuck Norris Karate School. Formed a business, Bis and Beau, marketing exclusive dress designs. Became TV spokesperson for beauty products. PICTURES: The Naked Gun: From the Files of Police Squad! (debut, 1988), The Adventures of Ford Fairlane, The Naked Gun 2 1/2: The Smell of Fear, Naked Gun 33 1/3: The Final Insult.
TELEVISION: Series: Those Amazing Animals (host, 1980-81), Dallas. Movies: Love is Forever, Elvis and Me (prod. only).

PRESSMAN, EDWARD R.
Producer. b. New York, NY. e. Fieldston Sch.; grad., Stanford U.; studied at London Sch. of Economics. Began career with film short, Girl, in collaboration with dir. Paul Williams in London. They formed Pressman-Williams Enterprises.
PICTURES: Prod. or Exec. prod.: Out of It, The Revolutionary, Dealing: or the Berkeley to Boston Forty Brick, Lost Bag Blues, Sisters, Badlands, Phantom of the Paradise, Despair, Paradise Alley, Old Boyfriends, Heartbeat, The Hand, Conan the Barbarian, Das Boot, The Pirates of Penzance, Crimewave, Plenty, Half Moon Street, True Stories, Good Morning Babylon, Masters of the Universe, Walker, Wall Street, Cherry 2000, Paris By Night, Talk Radio, Martians Go Home, Blue Steel, Reversal of Fortune, To Sleep with Anger, Waiting for the Light, Homicide, Year of the Gun, Iron Maze (co-exec. prod.), Storyville, Bad Lieutenant, Hoffa, Dream Lover, The Crow, Street Fighter, Judge Dredd, City Hall, The Island of Dr. Moreau, The Crow: City of Angels, The Winter Guest, Two Girls and a Guy, The Blackout, The Crow: World of Gods and Monsters, American Psycho.

PRESSMAN, LAWRENCE
Actor. b. Cynthiana, KY, July 10, 1939. e. Kentucky Northwestern U. On B'way in Man in the Glass Booth, Play It Again, Sam, etc.
PICTURES: The Man in the Glass Booth, The Crazy World of Julius Vrooder, Hellstrom Chronicle, Shaft, Making It, Walk Proud, Nine to Five, Some Kind of Hero, The Hanoi Hilton, The Waterdance, The Maker, Trial & Error, Mighty Joe Young, My Giant.
TELEVISION: Series: Mulligan's Stew, Doogie Howser M.D., Law and Order, N.Y.P.D. Blue, The Late Shift. Movies: Cannon, The Snoop Sisters, The Marcus-Nelson Murder, Winter Kill, The First 36 Hours of Dr. Durant, Rich Man, Poor Man, Man from Atlantis, The Trial of Lee Harvey Oswald, The Gathering, Like Mom, Like Me, Blind Ambition, Little Girl Lost, Breaking Point, White Hot: The Mysterious Murder of Thelma Todd.

PRESSMAN, MICHAEL
Director, Producer. b. New York, NY, July 1, 1950. e. California Inst. of Arts. Comes from show business family; was actor in college.
PICTURES: Director: The Great Texas Dynamite Chase, The Bad News Bears Breaking Training, Boulevard Nights, Those Lips Those Eyes (also prod.), Some Kind of Hero, Doctor Detroit, Teenage Mutant Ninja Turtles II: The Secret of the Ooze, To Gillian On Her 37th Birthday.
TELEVISION: Movies: Like Mom, Like Me, The Imposter, The Christmas Gift, Final Jeopardy, Private Sessions, Haunted by Her Past, To Heal a Nation, Shootdown, The Revenge of Al Capone, Incident at Dark River, Man Against the Mob (also co-prod.), Joshua's Heart, Quicksand: No Escape. Series: The Practice.

PRESTON, FRANCES W.
Executive. Joined Broadcast Music Inc. in 1958. Pres. & CEO BMI, 1986-present.

PRESTON, KELLY
Actress. b. Honolulu, HI, Oct. 13, 1962. e. UCLA, USC. m. actor John Travolta.
PICTURES: Metalstorm: The Destruction of Jared-Syn (debut, 1983), Christine, Mischief, Secret Admirer, SpaceCamp, 52 Pick-Up, Amazon Women on the Moon, A Tiger's Tale, Love at Stake, Spellbinder, Twins, The Experts, Run, Only You, Love Is a Gun, Cheyenne Warrior, Waiting to Exhale, From Dusk Till Dawn, Citizen Ruth, Addicted to Love, Jerry Maguire, Nothing to Lose, Jack Frost, Holy Man.
TELEVISION: Series: For Love and Honor, Capitol. Movies: The Perfect Bride, The American Clock, Mrs. Munck. Guest: Quincy, Blue Thunder, Riptide.

PREVIN, ANDRE
Composer, Conductor. b. Berlin, Germany, April 6, 1929. Composed and conducted over 50 m.p. scores. Music dir., Pittsburgh Symphony Orchestra, & conductor emeritus of London Symphony Orchestra. Music dir., Royal Philharmonic Orch., 1985-89. Guest conductor of most major symphony orchestras in U.S. and Europe. Music dir., Pittsburgh Symphony 1972-81. Conductor, London Symphony, 1968-78. Conductor Emeritus London Symphony, 1992-present. Received Knighthood of British Empire in 1996.
PICTURES: Three Little Words, Cause for Alarm, It's Always Fair Weather, Bad Day at Black Rock, Invitation to the Dance, Catered Affair, Designing Woman, Silk Stockings, Gigi (Acad. Award, 1958), Porgy and Bess (Acad. Award, 1959), The Subterraneans, Bells Are Ringing, Pepe, Elmer Gantry, The Four Horsemen of the Apocalypse, One Two Three, Two for the Seesaw, Long Day's Journey Into Night, Irma LaDouce (Acad. Award, 1963), My Fair Lady (Acad. Award, 1964), Goodbye Charlie, Inside Daisy Clover, The Fortune Cookie, Thoroughly Modern Millie, Valley of the Dolls, Paint Your Wagon, The Music Lovers, Jesus Christ Superstar, Rollerball, One Trick Pony.

PRICE, FRANK
Executive. b. Decatur, IL, May 17, 1930. e. Michigan State U. following naval service. Joined CBS in N.Y. in 1951 as story editor and writer. Moved to Hollywood in 1953, serving as story editor first at Columbia and then NBC (Matinee Theatre). In 1958 joined Universal as an assoc. prod. and writer. In 1961 named exec. prod. of The Virginian TV series. Appt. exec. prod. of Ironside; later did It Takes a Thief and several World Premiere movies. 1964 named v.p. of Universal TV; 1971, sr. v.p.; 1974, pres. Also v.p., MCA, Inc. 1978 left to join Columbia as pres. of new company unit, Columbia Pictures Productions. In 1979 named chmn. & CEO of Columbia Pictures. In 1983 joined Universal: named chmn., motion picture group, pres. of Universal Pictures, and v.p. of MCA. In 1987 formed Price Entertainment Inc. as chmn. & CEO to produce movies and create TV shows for dist. through Columbia Pictures Entertainment. 1990, integrated Price Entertainment Inc., into Columbia and was named chairman. Resigned, 1991. Prod. tv movie, The Tuskegee Airmen; prod. film, Zeus and Roxanne, 1997.

PRICE, RICHARD
Writer. b. Bronx, NY, Oct. 12, 1949. e. Cornell Univ., Columbia Univ.
AUTHOR: The Wanderers, Bloodbrothers, Ladies' Man, The Breaks, Clockers.
PICTURES: *Cameos:* The Wanderers, The Paper. *Writer:* The Color of Money (Acad. Award nom.; also cameo), Streets of Gold, New York Stories (Life Lessons; also cameo), Sea of Love, Night and the City (also cameo), Mad Dog and Glory (also exec. prod., cameo), Ethan Frome (exec. prod. only), Kiss of Death (also co-prod., cameo), Clockers (also co-prod.), Ransom (also cameo).

PRIES, RALPH W.
Executive. b. Atlanta, GA, August 31, 1919. Graduated Georgia Inst. of Technology. V.P., MEDIQ, Inc.; pres. MEDIQ/ PRN Life Support Services, Inc.; past pres., Odgen Food Service Corp.; exec. comm. and bd., Firstrust Savings Bank and chmn. of audit comm.; Boards of St. Christopher's Hospital for Children, Moss Rehabilitation Hospital, United Hospital Corp., Philadelphia Heart Instit. Former intl pres., Variety Clubs Intl.; previously on bd. of Hahnemann U. and Hosp., chmn. of bd. Likoff Cardiovascular Instit., pres. Main Line Reform Temple, Wynnewood, PA.

PRIESTLEY, JASON
Actor. b. Vancouver, Canada, Aug. 28, 1969. First screen appearance was as baby in 1969 film That Cold Day in the Park, in which his mother had bit part. Child actor in many Canadian TV commercials. First major U.S. acting job in 1986 TV movie Nobody's Child. Moved to L.A. in 1987. Theatre includes The Addict, The Breakfast Club.
TELEVISION: *Series:* Sister Kate, Beverly Hills 90210 (also co-prod.). *Movies:* Stacie (Canada), Nobody's Child, Teen Angel & Teen Angel Returns (Disney TV). *Guest:* Danger Bay (Canada), MacGyver, 21 Jump Street, Adventures of Beans Baxter, Quantum Leap.
PICTURES: The Boy Who Could Fly, Nowhere to Run, Watchers, Calendar Girl, Tombstone, Coldblooded.

PRIMUS, BARRY
Actor. b. New York, NY, Feb. 16, 1938. e. Bennington Coll., City Coll. of NY.
THEATER: The King and the Duke, The Nervous Set, Henry IV, Parts I and II, Creating the World, Teibele and the Demon, Lincoln Center Rep. (The Changling, After the Fall).
PICTURES: The Brotherhood, Puzzle of a Downfall Child, Been Down So Long It Looks Like Up to Me, Von Richtofen and Brown, Boxcar Bertha, The Gravy Train, New York New York, Avalanche, Autopsy, The Rose, Heartland, Night Games, Absence of Malice, The River, Down and Out in Beverly Hills, Jake Speed, SpaceCamp, Talking Walls, The Stranger, Big Business, Cannibal Women in the Avocado Jungle of Death, Torn Apart, Guilty by Suspicion, Mistress (dir., s.p. only), Night and the City.
TELEVISION: *Series:* Cagney and Lacey. *Mini-Series:* Washington Behind Closed Doors. *Movies:* Big Rose, Roger & Harry: The Mitera Target, Portrait of a Showgirl, Paper Dolls, I Want to Live, Heart of Steel, Brotherly Love, The Women of Spring Break. *Guest:* Law and Order.

PRINCE
Singer, Actor. r.n. Prince Rogers Nelson. b. Minneapolis, MN, June 7, 1958. Rock star and recording artist.
PICTURES: Purple Rain (also wrote songs; Acad. Award for best orig. song score, 1984), Under the Cherry Moon (also dir., s.p., songs), Sign O' the Times (also dir., songs), Batman (songs only), Graffiti Bridge (also dir., s.p., songs).

PRINCE, HAROLD
Director. b. New York, NY, Jan. 30, 1928. e. U. of Pennsylvania. Worked as stage mgr. for George Abbott on three shows, later co-produced and/or directed the following: The Pajama Game (Tony Award), Damn Yankees (Tony Award), New Girl In Town, West Side Story, A Swim in the Sea, Fiorello! (Tony Award, Pulitzer Prize), Tenderloin, A Call on Kurpin, Take Her She's Mine, A Funny Thing Happened on the Way to the Forum (Tony Award), She Loves Me, The Matchmaker (revival), Fiddler on the Roof, Poor Bitos, Baker Street, Flora, The Red Menace, Superman, Cabaret (Tony Award), Zorba, Company, Follies, The Great God Brown, The Visit, Love for Love (the last three all revivals), A Little Night Music (Tony Award), Candide (Tony Award), Pacific Overtures, Side by Side by Sondheim, Some of My Best Friends, On the Twentieth Century, Evita (also London), Sweeney Todd (Tony Award 1979; also London), Merrily We Roll Along, A Doll's Life, Play Memory, End of the World, Diamonds, Grind, Roza, Cabaret (revival), Phantom of the Opera (Tony Award, 1988; also London), Grandchild of Kings (dir. & adapt.), Kiss of the Spider Woman (Tony Award, 1993), Show Boat (Tony Award, 1995); and also directed the operas Ashmadel, Silverlake, Sweeney Todd, Candide and Don Giovanni for N.Y. City Opera, Girl of Golden West for Chicago Lyric Opera Co. and San Francisco Opera; Willie Stark for Houston Grand Opera; Madama Butterfly for Chicago Lyric Opera and Turandot for Vienna State Opera and Faust for Metropolitan Opera.
AUTHOR: Contradictions: Notes on Twenty-Six Years in the Theatre (1974).
PICTURES: *Co-producer:* The Pajama Game, Damn Yankees. *Director:* Something for Everyone, A Little Night Music.

PRINCIPAL, VICTORIA
Actress. b. Fukuoka, Japan, Jan 3, 1950. Father was in U.S. air force. Went to New York to become model; studied acting privately with Jean Scott at Royal Acad. of Dramatic Art in London before moving to Hollywood. Worked as talent agent in the mid-1970's.
PICTURES: The Life and Times of Judge Roy Bean (debut, 1972), The Naked Ape, Earthquake, I Will I Will... for Now, Vigilante Force.
TELEVISION: *Series:* Dallas. *Guest:* Fantasy Island (pilot), Love Story, Love American Style, Greatest Heroes of the Bible. *Movies:* The Night They Stole Miss Beautiful, The Pleasure Palace, Last Hours Before Morning, Not Just Another Affair, Mistress, Naked Lie (also exec. prod.), Blind Witness (also exec. prod.), Sparks: The Price of Passion (also exec. prod.), Don't Touch My Daughter (also exec. prod.), The Burden of Proof, Seduction: Three Tales From the Inner Sanctum (also co-exec. prod.), Midnight's Child (exec. prod. only), Beyond Obsession, River of Rage: The Taking of Maggie Keene, Dancing in the Dark, The Abduction.

PRINE, ANDREW
Actor. b. Jennings, FL, Feb. 14, 1936. e. U. of Miami. m. actress Heather Lowe. Mem. Actors Studio. On stage in Look Homeward, Angel, A Distant Bell, Mrs. Patterson, Borak. Ahmanson Theatre, LA: Long Day's Journey into Night, The Caine Mutiny. South Coast Rep.: Goodbye Freddy.
PICTURES: The Miracle Worker, Advance to the Rear, Texas Across the River, Bandolero!, The Devil's Brigade, This Savage Land, Generation, Chisum, Riding Tall, Simon: King of the Witches, Barn of the Naked Dead (Terror Circus), One Little Indian, The Centerfold Girls, Grizzly, The Town That Dreaded Sundown, Winds of Autumn, High Flying Lowe, The Evil, Amityville II: The Possession, Playing with Fire, Eliminators, Chill Factor, The Big One, Life on the Edge, Double Exposure, Gettysburg, Inferno, Dark Dancer, Gathering Evidence, Without Evidence.
TELEVISION: *Series:* The Wide Country, The Road West, W.E.B., Dallas, Room for Two, Weird Science. *Movies:* And the Children Shall Lead, Roughing It, Callie & Son, The Deputies, Another Part of the Forest, Night Slaves, Split Second to an Epitaph, Along Came a Spider, Night Slaves, Wonder Woman, Law of the Land, Tail Gunner Joe, Last of the Mohicans, A Small Killing, Mind over Murder, M-Station Hawaii, Christmas Miracle in Caulfield, Young Abe Lincoln, U.S.A., Donner Pass: The Road to Survival, Mission of the Shark, Scattered Dreams: The Kathryn Messenger Story, The Avenging Angel. *Mini-Series:* V: The Final Battle.

PROCHNOW, JURGEN
Actor. b. Berlin, Germany, June 10, 1941. Studied acting at the Folkwang-Schule. In provinical theatre before making tv debut on the series Harbour at the Rhine River, 1970.
PICTURES: Zoff (debut, 1971), Zartlichkeit der Wolfe, The Lost Honor of Katharina Blum, The Consequence, Einer von uns beiden, Das Boot (The Boat; Berlin Film Fest. Award), The Keep, Dune, Der Bulle und das Madchen, Killing Cars, Terminus, Beverly Hills Cop II, Devil's Paradise, The Seventh Sign, A Dry White Season, The Fourth War, The Man Inside, Twin Peaks: Fire Walk With Me, Body of Evidence, In the Mouth of Madness, Judge Dredd, The Replacement Killers.
TELEVISION: Forbidden, Murder by Reason of Insanity, Danielle Steel's Jewels, The Lucona Affair, Love Is Forever, Robin Hood, The Fire Next Time.

PROSKY, ROBERT
Actor. b. Philadelphia, PA, Dec. 13, 1930. Won TV amateur talent search contest, leading to scholarship with American Theatre Wing. 23-year veteran with Washington's Arena stage. Taught acting and appeared in over 150 plays
THEATER: Death of a Salesman, Galileo, The Caucasian Chalk Circle, You Can't Take it With You, Our Town, The Price (Helen Hayes Award). *B'way:* Moonchildren, A View from the Bridge, Pale Horse Pale Rider, Arms and the Man, Glengarry Glen Ross (Tony nom.), A Walk in the Woods (Tony nom.). *Off-B'way:* Camping With Henry and Tom. Tours incl.: Our Town, Inherit the Wind, A Walk in the Woods (Soviet Union), After the Fall (Hong Kong).
PICTURES: Thief, Hanky Panky, Monsignor, The Lords of Discipline, Christine, The Keep, The Natural, Outrageous Fortune, Big Shots, Broadcast News, The Great Outdoors, Things Change, Loose Cannons, Gremlins II: The New Batch, Funny About Love, Green Card, Life in the Food Chain (Age Isn't Everything), Far and Away, Hoffa, Last Action Hero, Rudy, Mrs. Doubtfire, Miracle on 34th Street, The Scarlet Letter, Dead Man Walking, Mad City.
TELEVISION: *Series:* Hill Street Blues, Lifestories (host), Veronica's Closet. *Movies:* World War III, The Ordeal of Bill Carny, Lou Grant, The Adams Chronicles, Old Dogs, Into Thin Air, The Murder of Mary Phagan, Home Fires Burning, From the Dead of Night, Heist, Dangerous Pursuit, Johnny Ryan, Against the Mob, A Green Journey, The Love She Sought, Double Edge, Life on the High Wire, Teamster Boss: The Jackie Presser Story, The Lake. *Guest:* Coach.

PROVINE, DOROTHY
Actress. b. Deadwood, SD, Jan. 20, 1937. e. U. of Washington. Retired from films in 1969.
PICTURES: The Bonnie Parker Story (debut, 1958), Live Fast Die Young, Riot in Juvenile Prison, The 30 Foot Bride of Candy Rock, Wall of Noise, It's a Mad Mad Mad Mad World, Good Neighbor Sam, The Great Race, That Darn Cat, One Spy Too Many, Kiss the Girls and Make Them Die, Who's Minding the Mint?, Never a Dull Moment.
TELEVISION: Series: The Alaskans, The Roaring 20's. Movie: The Sound of Anger.

PRYCE, JONATHAN
Actor. b. North Wales, June 1, 1947. e. Royal Acad. of Dramatic Art. Actor and artistic dir. of Liverpool Everyman Theatre Co.
THEATER: London: Comedians, Taming of the Shrew, Antony and Cleopatra, Tally's Folly, Hamlet (Olivier Award), The Caretaker, Macbeth, The Seagull, Uncle Vanya, Miss Saigon (Olivier & Variety Club Awards), Oliver! NY: Comedians (Tony & Theatre World Awards, 1977), Accidental Death of an Anarchist, Miss Saigon (Tony & Drama Desk Awards, 1991).
PICTURES: Voyage of the Damned (debut, 1976), Breaking Glass, Loophole, The Ploughman's Lunch, Something Wicked This Way Comes, The Doctor and the Devils, Brazil, Haunted Honeymoon, Jumpin' Jack Flash, Man on Fire, Consuming Passions, The Adventures of Baron Munchausen, The Rachel Papers, Freddie as F.R.O. 7 (voice), Glengarry Glen Ross, The Age of Innocence, A Business Affair, Great Moments in Aviation, A Troll in Central Park (voice), Deadly Advice, Shopping, Carrington (Cannes Film Fest. Award, 1995), Evita, Tomorrow Never Dies.
TELEVISION: Comedians, Playthings, Partisans, For Tea on Sunday, Timon of Athens, Praying Mantis, Murder Is Easy, Daft as a Brush, Martin Luther Heretic, The Caretaker, Glad Day, The Man From the Pru, Roger Doesn't Live Here Anymore, Selling Hitler, Whose Line is It Anyway?, Mr. Wroes Virgins, Barbarians at the Gate, Thicker Than Water, David.

PRYOR, RICHARD
Actor. b. Peoria, IL, Dec. 1, 1940. At age 7 played drums with professionals. Made NY debut as standup comic in 1963, leading to appearances on TV (Johnny Carson, Merv Griffin, Ed Sullivan). Co-wrote TV scripts for Lily Tomlin (Emmy Award, 1974) and Flip Wilson. Won Grammy Awards for albums That Nigger's Crazy, Is It Something I Said?, Bicentennial Nigger. Autobiography: Pryor Convictions and Other Life Sentences (1995).
PICTURES: The Busy Body (debut, 1967), The Green Berets, Wild in the Streets, The Phynx, You've Got to Walk It Like You Talk It Or You'll Lose That Beat, Dynamite Chicken, Lady Sings the Blues, Hit!, Wattstax, The Mack, Some Call It Loving, Blazing Saddles (co-s.p. only), Uptown Saturday Night, Adios Amigo, The Bingo Long Traveling All-Stars and Motor Kings, Car Wash, Silver Streak, Greased Lightning, Which Way Is Up?, Blue Collar, The Wiz, California Suite, Richard Pryor—Live in Concert (also prod., s.p.), The Muppet Movie, Richard Pryor Is Back Live in Concert (also s.p.), Wholly Moses, In God We Trust, Stir Crazy, Bustin' Loose (also co-prod., co-s.p.), Richard Pryor Live on the Sunset Strip (also prod., s.p.), Some Kind of Hero, The Toy, Superman III, Richard Pryor Here and Now (also dir., s.p.), Brewster's Millions, Jo Jo Dancer Your Life Is Calling (also dir., prod., s.p.), Critical Condition, Moving, See No Evil Hear No Evil, Harlem Nights, Another You, A Century of Cinema, Mad Dog Time, Lost Highway.
TELEVISION: Series: The Richard Pryor Show (1977), Pryor's Place. Guest: Wild Wild West, The Partridge Family, The Mod Squad, Chicago Hope. Movies: The Young Lawyers, Carter's Army.

PRYOR, THOMAS M.
Journalist. b. New York, NY, May 22, 1912. Joined NY Times, 1929; m.p. dept. 1931 as reporter, editor, asst. film critic; Hollywood bureau chief, corres., NY Times, 1951-59; editor, Daily Variety, 1959-88; 1988-90. Consultant to Variety & Daily Variety. 1990, retired.

PTAK, JOHN
Agent. b. San Diego, CA. Graduated UCLA film department, 1968. Theatre mgr. and booker for Walter Reade Organization and Laemmle Theatres, 1966-1969. Admin. exec. at American Film Institute's Center for Advanced Studies, 1969-1971. International Famous Agency (ICM), 1971-1975, William Morris Agency, 1976-91, Creative Artists Agency, 1991-. Represents motion picture and television talent. Co-chmn., Center for Film & Video Preservation at AFI. Member, National film Preservation Board. Bd. of dir., National Film Preservation Foundation, Motion Picture & Television Fund Foundation.

PULLMAN, BILL
Actor. b. Hornell, NY, Dec. 17, 1953. e. SUNY at Oneonta, Univ. of Mass. at Amherst.
THEATER: NY: Dramathon '84, Curse of the Starving Class. LA: All My Sons, Barabbas, Nanawatai, Demon Wine, Control Freaks.

PICTURES: Ruthless People (debut, 1986), Spaceballs, The Serpent and the Rainbow, Rocket Gibraltar, The Accidental Tourist, Cold Feet, Brain Dead, Sibling Rivalry, Bright Angel, Going Under, Newsies, A League of Their Own, Singles, Nervous Ticks, Sommersby, Sleepless in Seattle, Malice, Mr. Jones, The Favor, Wyatt Earp, While You Were Sleeping, Casper, Mr. Wrong, Independence Day.
TELEVISION: Movies: Home Fires Burning, Crazy in Love, The Last Seduction (also released theatrically).

PURCELL, PATRICK B.
Executive. b. Dublin, Ireland, March 16, 1943. e. Fordham U., M.B.A., 1973. In pub. & acct., England, 1969-69; acct., Associated Hosp. Service, N.Y., 1968-70; joined Paramount Pictures, 1970; v.p., fin., 1980-83; exec. v.p. chief fin. & admin. officer 1983-.

PURL, LINDA
Actress. b. Greenwich, CT, Sept. 2, 1955. Moved to Japan at age 2. Appeared in Japanese theatre, TV. e. Toho Geino Academy. Back to US in 1971.
THEATER: Deborah (New Haven, NYC), Hedda Gabler, The Real Thing (Mark Taper), The Merchant of Venice (Old Globe Theatre), Romeo & Juliet, Doll's House, Hallelujah Hallelujah (NYC), Three Penny Opera, Nora, All the Way Home, The Road to Mecca, Long Wharf, Beyond Therapy.
PICTURES: Jory, Crazy Mama, W.C. Fields & Me, Leo and Loree, The High Country, Visiting Hours, Viper, Natural Causes.
TELEVISION: Series: The Secret Storm, Beacon Hill, Happy Days, Matlock, Under Cover, Young Pioneers, Robin's Hoods. Movies: Eleanor and Franklin, Little Ladies of the Night, Testimony of Two Men, A Last Cry for Help, Women at West Point, Like Normal People, The Flame is Love, The Night the City Screamed, The Adventures of Nellie Bly, The Last Days of Pompeii, The Manions of America, Addicted to His Love, Spies Lies and Naked Thighs, Before the Storm, Spy Games, Danielle Steel's Secrets, Body Language, Accidental Meeting, Incident at Deception Ridge, Absolute Truth.

PUTTNAM, LORD DAVID
CBE: Hon. LL.D Bristol 1983; Hon. D. Litt, Leicester 1986. Hon. Litt. D., Leeds 1992. Knighted, 1995. Producer. b. London, England 1941. e. Michenden Sch. In advertising before joining VPS/Goodtimes Prod. Co. Dir. of Britain's National Film Finance Corp. (1980-85); Also served on Cinema Films Council and governing council of the British Acad. of Film & Television Arts. Officier dans L'Ordre des Arts et des Lettres, 1986. Chmn. National Film and Television Soc., 1988. Past Pres., Council for the Protection of Rural England; Fellow, Royal Soc. of Arts; Fellow, Royal Geographical Soc., Hon. Fellow, The Chartered Society of Designers. appt. Chmn. & CEO, Columbia Pictures. Resigned 1987. Received Eastman 2nd Century Award, 1988. 1988 formed a joint venture for his Enigma Productions Ltd. with Warner Bros., Fujisankei Comm. Gp. of Japan, British Satellite Broadcasting & Country Nat West to prod. 4 films. Appt. chmn. ITEL intl. TV dist. agency, 1989. Dir., Anglia Television Group and Survival Anglia. V.P., BAFTA. Founding pres., Atelier du Cinema Europeen. Member, European Commission's 'Think Tank' for audio-visual policy.
PICTURES: Melody, The Pied Piper, That'll Be The Day, Stardust, Mahler, Bugsy Malone, The Duellists, Midnight Express, Foxes, Chariots of Fire (Acad. Award for Best Picture, 1981), Local Hero, Cal, The Killing Fields, The Mission, Defence of the Realm, Memphis Belle, Meeting Venus, Being Human, War of the Buttons, Le Confessional. Co-produced documentaries: Swastika, James Dean—The First American Teenager, Double-Headed Eagle, Brother Can You Spare a Dime?
TELEVISION: P'Tang Yang Kipperbang, Experience Preferred, Secrets, Those Glory Glory Days, Sharma and Beyond, Winter Flight, Josephine Baker, Without Warning: The James Brady Story, A Dangerous Man: Lawrence After Arabia, The Burning Season.

Q

QUAID, DENNIS
Actor. b. Houston, TX Apr. 9, 1954. Brother is actor Randy Quaid. m. actress Meg Ryan. e. U. of Houston. Appeared in Houston stage productions before leaving for Hollywood. On N.Y. stage with his brother in True West, 1984. Performer with rock band The Electrics; wrote songs for films The Night the Lights Went Out in Georgia, Tough Enough, The Big Easy. Formed Summers/Quaid Productions with producer Cathleen Summers, 1989.
PICTURES: Crazy Mama (debut, 1975), I Never Promised You a Rose Garden, September 30, 1955, Our Winning Season, Seniors, G.O.R.P., Breaking Away, The Long Riders, All Night Long, Caveman, The Night the Lights Went Out in Georgia, Tough Enough, Jaws 3-D, The Right Stuff, Dreamscape, Enemy Mine, The Big Easy, Innerspace, Suspect, D.O.A., Everybody's All-American, Great Balls of Fire, Postcards From the Edge, Come See the Paradise, Wilder Napalm, Undercover Blues, Flesh & Bone, Wyatt Earp, Hideaway (co-prod. only), Something to Talk About, Dragonheart.
TELEVISION: Movies: Are You in the House Alone?, Amateur Night at the Dixie Bar and Grill, Bill, Johnny Belinda, Bill: On His Own.

QUAID, RANDY

Actor. b. Houston, TX, Oct. 1, 1950. Brother is actor Dennis Quaid. Discovered by Peter Bogdanovich while still jr. at Drama Dept. at U. of Houston and cast in his Targets and The Last Picture Show, 1971. Off-B'way debut: True West (1983).
PICTURES: Targets (debut, 1968), The Last Picture Show, What's Up Doc?, Paper Moon, Lolly-Madonna XXX, The Last Detail (Acad. Award nom.), The Apprenticeship of Duddy Kravitz, Breakout, The Missouri Breaks, Bound for Glory, The Choirboys, Midnight Express, Three Warriors, Foxes, The Long Riders, Heartbeeps, National Lampoon's Vacation, The Wild Life, The Slugger's Wife, Fool for Love, The Wraith, Sweet Country, No Man's Land, Moving, Caddyshack II, Parents, Bloodhounds of Broadway, Out Cold, National Lampoon's Christmas Vacation, Martians Go Home!, Days of Thunder, Quick Change, Cold Dog Soup, Texasville, Freaked, The Paper, Major League 2, Bye Bye Love, The Last Dance, Independence Day, Kingpin, Vegas Vacation, P.U.N.K.S., Bug Buster, Hard Rain.
TELEVISION: Movies: Getting Away From It All, The Great Niagara, The Last Ride of the Dalton Gang, To Race the Wind, Guyana Tragedy: The Story of Jim Jones, Of Mice and Men, Inside the Third Reich, Cowboy, A Streetcar Named Desire, LBJ: The Early Years, Dead Solid Perfect, Evil in Clear River, Frankenstein, Roommates, Next Door, Ed McBain's 87th Precinct, Purgatory West of the Pecos. Series: Saturday Night Live (1985-86), Davis Rules, Gun. Special: Dear America (reader).

QUIGLEY, MARTIN, JR.

Educator, Writer. b. Chicago, IL, Nov. 24, 1917. e. A.B. Georgetown U.; M.A., Ed. D., Columbia U. M.P. Herald, Oct. 1939; spcl. ed. rep., M.P. Herald & M.P. Daily, May, 1941. U.S. Office of Coordination of Info., 1942; U.S. Office of Strategic Svc's., Special Intelligence Div., Eire & Italy, 1943-45. Assoc. ed., Quigley Pub., Oct. 1945; ed. M.P. Herald, July, 1949; also edit. dir. of all Quigley Pub., 1956; pres. Quigley Pub. Co., 1964. Author: Great Gaels, 1944; Roman Notes, 1946; Magic Shadows—The Story of the Origin of Motion Pictures, 1948; Gov't. Relations of Five Universities, 1975; Peace Without Hiroshima, 1991; First Century of Film, 1995. Editor: New Screen Techniques, 1953; m.p. tech. section, Encyclopaedia Brit., 1956. Co-author: Catholic Action in Practice, 1963; Films in America, 1929-69, 1970. Pres., QWS, Inc., ed. cons., 1975-81. Adjunct prof. of higher ed., Baruch College Univ. City of N.Y. 1977-89; Teachers College, Columbia Univ., 1990. Village of Larchmont, N.Y., trustee, 1977-79; mayor, 1980-84. Bd. of trustees, American Bible Society, 1984-; Religious Ed. Ass'n., treasurer, 1975-80 & chairperson, 1981-84; Laymen's Nat'l. Bible Ass'n., chmn. ed. com., 1983-93; Will Rogers Institute, chmn. Health ed. com., 1980-97; dir., William J. Donovan Memorial Foundation, 1995-.

QUIGLEY, WILLIAM J.

Executive. b. New York, NY, July 6, 1951. e. Wesleyan U., B.A., 1973; Columbia U., M.S., 1983. From 1973 to 1974 was advt. circulation mgr. for Quigley Publishing Co. Taught school in Kenya in 1974; returned to U.S. to join Grey Advt. as media planner. 1975 joined Walter Reade Organization as asst. film buyer; promoted to head film buyer in 1977. Named v.p., 1982. In 1986 joined Vestron, Inc. as sr. v.p. to establish Vestron Pictures. Named pres., Vestron Pictures, 1987-89. In 1990 joined Fair Lanes Entertainment, Inc. as v.p. mktg. 1993, joined United Artists Theatre as sr. v.p., marketing & new business. 1997, pres. Entertainment Express; partner, Spellbound Pictures.
PICTURES: Exec. prod.: Steel Dawn, The Dead, Salome's Last Dance, The Unholy, Waxwork, Burning Secret, The Lair of the White Worm, Paint It Black, The Rainbow, Twister.

QUINLAN, KATHLEEN

Actress. b. Pasadena, CA, Nov. 19, 1954. Played small role in film, One Is a Lonely Number, while in high school.
THEATER: Taken in Marriage (NY Public Theatre; Theatre World Award), Uncommon Women and Others, Accent on Youth (Long Wharf, CT), Les Liaisons Dangereuses.
PICTURES: One Is a Lonely Number (debut, 1972), American Graffiti, Lifeguard, Airport '77, I Never Promised You a Rose Garden, The Promise, The Runner Stumbles, Sunday Lovers, Hanky Panky, Independence Day, Twilight Zone—The Movie, The Last Winter, Warning Sign, Wild Thing, Man Outside, Sunset, Clara's Heart, The Doors, Trial by Jury, Apollo 13, Zeus and Roxanne, Breakdown, Event Horizon.
TELEVISION: Movies: Can Ellen Be Saved?, Lucas Tanner (pilot), Where Have All the People Gone?, The Missing Are Deadly, The Abduction of St. Anne, Turning Point of Jim Malloy, Little Ladies of the Night, She's in the Army Now, When She Says No, Blackout, Children of the Night, Dreams Lost Dreams Found, Trapped, The Operation, Strays, An American Story, Stolen Babies, Last Light, Perfect Alibi.

QUINN, AIDAN

Actor. b. Chicago, IL, March 8, 1959. Raised in Rockwell, IL, also spent time in Ireland as a boy and following high sch. graduation. Returned to Chicago at 19, worked as tar roofer before debuting on Chicago stage in The Man in 605, followed by Scheherazade, The Irish Hebrew Lesson, Hamlet.

THEATER: Fool for Love (off-B'way debut), A Lie of the Mind, A Streetcar Named Desire (Theatre World Award).
PICTURES: Reckless (debut, 1984), Desperately Seeking Susan, The Mission, Stakeout, Crusoe, The Handmaid's Tale, The Lemon Sisters, Avalon, At Play in the Fields of the Lord, The Playboys, Benny & Joon, Blink, Mary Shelley's Frankenstein, Legends of the Fall, The Stars Fell on Henrietta, Haunted, Looking for Richard, Michael Collins, Commandments, The Assignment.
TELEVISION: Special: All My Sons. Movies: An Early Frost, Perfect Witness, Lies of the Twins, A Private Matter.

QUINN, ANTHONY

Actor. b. Chihuahua, Mexico, Apr. 21, 1915. Came to U.S. as child. Brief stage work before bit roles in films. Autobiographies: The Original Sin (1972), One Man Tango (1995).
THEATER: B'way: A Streetcar Named Desire, Beckett, Zorba.
PICTURES: Parole (debut, 1936), Daughter of Shanghai, Last Train From Madrid, Partners in Crime, The Plainsman, Swing High Swing Low, Waikiki Wedding, The Buccaneer (1938), Bulldog Drummond in Africa, Dangerous to Know, Hunted Men, King of Alcatraz, Tip-Off Girls, Island of Lost Men, King of Chinatown, Television Spy, Union Pacific, City for Conquest, Emergency Squad, Ghost Breakers, Parole Fixer, Road to Singapore, Blood and Sand, Bullets for O'Hara, Knockout, Manpower, The Perfect Snob, Texas Rangers Ride Again, They Died With Their Boots On, Thieves Fall Out, The Black Swan, Larceny Inc., Road to Morocco, Guadalcanal Diary, The Ox-Bow Incident, Buffalo Bill, Irish Eyes Are Smiling, Roger Touhy Gangster, Ladies of Washington, China Sky, Back to Bataan, Where Do We Go From Here?, California, Imperfect Lady, Sinbad the Sailor, Black Gold, Tycoon, The Brave Bulls, Mask of the Avenger, Viva Zapata! (Academy Award for Best Supporting Actor, 1952), The Brigand, The World in His Arms, Against All Flags, Ride Vaquero, City Beneath the Sea, Seminole, Blowing Wild, East of Sumatra, Long Wait, Magnificent Matador, Ulysses, Naked Street, Seven Cities of Gold, La Strada, Attila the Hun, Lust for Life (Academy Award for Best Supporting Actor, 1956), Wild Party, Man from Del Rio, The Hunchback of Notre Dame, Ride Back, The River's Edge, Wild is the Wind, The Buccaneer (1958; dir. only), Hot Spell, Black Orchid, Last Train From Gun Hill, Warlock, Portrait in Black, Heller in Pink Tights, Savage Innocents, The Guns of Navarone, Barabbas, Requiem for a Heavyweight, Lawrence of Arabia, Behold a Pale Horse, The Visit, Zorba the Greek (also assoc. prod.), High Wind in Jamaica, Marco the Magnificent, Lost Command, The 25th Hour, The Happening, Guns for San Sebastian, The Rover, The Magus, Shoes of the Fisherman, The Secret of Santa Vittoria, A Dream of Kings, A Walk in the Spring Rain, R.P.M., Flap, Across 110th Street (also exec. prod.), Deaf Smith and Johnny Ears, The Don Is Dead, The Destructors, The Inheritance, The Con Artists, Mohammad: Messenger of God, The Greek Tycoon, Caravans, The Passage, Lion of the Desert, High Risk, The Salamander, A Man of Passion, Stradivarius, Revenge, Ghosts Can't Do It, A Star for Two, Only the Lonely, Jungle Fever, Mobsters, Last Action Hero, Somebody to Love, A Walk in the Clouds, Il Sindaco Di Rione Sanita, The Seven Servants.
TELEVISION: Much dramatic work in the early 1950s. Series: The City, American Playwrights Theater (host). Movies: Jesus of Nazareth, Treasure Island (Italian TV), Onassis: The Richest Man in the World, The Old Man and the Sea, This Can't Be Love, Hercules and the Amazon Women, Hercules and the Lost Kingdom, Hercules and the Circle of Fire, Gotti.

R

RABE, DAVID WILLIAM

Writer. b. Dubuque, IA, March 10, 1940. m. actress Jill Clayburgh. e. Loras Coll.
THEATER: The Basic Training of Pavlo Hummel (Obie Award, 1971), Sticks and Bones (Tony Award, 1971), The Orphan, In the Boom Boom Room, Streamers, Hurly-burly, Those the River Keeps.
PICTURES: I'm Dancing As Fast As I Can (also exec. prod.), Streamers, Casualties of War, State of Grace, The Firm, Hurly-burly.
TELEVISION: Special: Sticks and Bones.

RABINOVITZ, JASON

Executive. b. Boston, MA, e. Harvard Coll., B.A. where elected to Phi Beta Kappa. Following WWII service as military intelligence captain with paratroops, took M.B.A. at Harvard Business Sch., 1948. Started in industry in 1949 as asst. to secty.-treas., United Paramount Theatres. Asst. controller, ABC, 1953; adm. v.p., ABC-TV, 1956; joined MGM as asst. treas., 1957; named MGM-TV gen. mgr., dir. of business & financial affairs, 1958; treas. & CFO, MGM, Inc., 1963; financial v.p. & CFO, 1967. 1971, named exec. v.p. & dir. Encyclopedia Britannica Education Corp.; sr. v.p., American Film Theatre, 1974-75. Rejoined MGM as v.p./exec. asst. to the pres., 1976. Elected v.p. finance, 1977; promoted to sr. v.p., finance & corporate admin., MGM Film Co. & UA Communications, Inc. Resigned, 1984. Now film & TV consultant and indep. prod. Dir., Pacific Rim Entertainment, 1993-95.

RADFORD, MICHAEL
Director, Writer. b. New Dehli, India, Feb. 24, 1946. e. Oxford U. Worked briefly as a teacher before beginning work as documentary filmmaker.
PICTURES: *Director & Writer*: Another Time Another Place, Nineteen Eight-Four (1984), White Mischief, Il Postino (Academy Award nom., Directors Guild Award nom.), The Swedish Cavalier. *Director*: Delta of Venus, The Elixir, Tania, B. Monkey.
TELEVISION: *Series*: Homicide: Life on the Street.

RADIN, PAUL
Producer. b. New York, NY, Sept. 15, 1913. e. NYU. After college went in adv. Became v.p. in chg. of m.p. div. of Buchanan & Co. During WWII posted in Middle East as film chief for Office of War Information for that area. On return to U.S. assigned by Buchanan to ad campaign for Howard Hughes' The Outlaw. Turned to talent mgr., joining the Sam Jaffe Agency. Then joined Ashley-Famous Agency. Became exec. prod. for Yul Brynner's indep. prod. co. based in Switzerland, with whom made such films as The Journey, Once More with Feeling, Surprise Package.
PICTURES: Born Free, Living Free, Phase IV, The Blue Bird, The Ghost and the Darkness.
TELEVISION: The Incredible Journey of Dr. Meg Laurel, The Ordeal of Dr. Mudd, Crime of Innocence. *Series*: Born Free, The Wizard.

RADNITZ, ROBERT B.
Producer. b. Great Neck, NY, Aug. 9, 1924. e. U. of VA. Taught 2 years at U. of VA, then became reader for Harold Clurman; wrote several RKO This Is America scripts, then to Broadway where co-prod. The Frogs of Spring; prod. The Young and the Beautiful; to Hollywood working at United Artists, then as story consultant to Buddy Adler, head of prod., 20th Century-Fox, 1957-58. V.P., Producer Guild of America, 1982, 1984, 1985; bd. member, Producers Branch, AMPAS, last 4 yrs. First producer with retrospective at Museum of Modern Art, and first producer honored by joint resolution of both houses of Congress for his work, 1973. Pres. Robert B. Radnitz Productions, Ltd.
PICTURES: *Producer*: A Dog of Flanders (debut, 1960; first U.S. film to win Golden Lion Award at Venice Film Fest.), Misty, Island of the Blue Dolphins, And Now Miguel, My Side of the Mountain, The Little Ark, Sounder (Acad. Award nom.), Where the Lilies Bloom, Birch Interval, Sounder 2, A Hero Ain't Nothin' But a Sandwich, Cross Creek.
TELEVISION: Mary White (Emmy & Christopher Awards), Never Forget (ACE Award nom.).

RAFELSON, BOB
Producer, Director, Writer. b. New York, NY, Feb. 21, 1933. e. Dartmouth, B.A. (philosophy). Left NY in teens to ride in rodeos in AZ. Worked on cruise ship, then played drums and bass with jazz combos in Acapulco. 1953 won Frost Natl. Playwriting competition. Dir. his award-winning play at Hanover Experimental Theatre, N.H. After Army Service did program promotion for a radio station, was advisor for Shochiku Films, Japan, then hired by David Susskind to read scripts for Talent Assocs. Writerassoc. prod., DuPont Show of the Month and Play of the Week (also script sprv.). Joined Screen Gems in California, developing program ideas for Jackie Cooper, then head of TV prod. arm of Columbia. Later formed BBS Productions with Burt Schneider and Steve Blauner. Appeared as actor in 1985 film Always.
PICTURES: *Co-Prod.* only: Easy Rider, The Last Picture Show, Drive He Said. *Director*: Head (debut, 1968; also co-prod., co-s.p.), Five Easy Pieces (also co-prod., co-story; Acad. Award noms. for picture & writing), The King of Marvin Gardens (also prod., co-s.p.), Stay Hungry (also co-prod., co-s.p.), The Postman Always Rings Twice (also co-prod.), Black Widow, Mountains of the Moon (also co-s.p.), Man Trouble, Blood and Wine, Wet (also s.p.), Tales of Erotica, Always (actor only), Leaving Las Vegas.
TELEVISION: *Series*: The Monkees (1966-68, creator, writer, dir.; Emmy Award, 1967), Adapted 34 prods., Play of the Week. *Dir. music video*: All Night Long, with Lionel Ritchie.

RAFFERTY, FRANCES
Actress. b. Sioux City, IA, June 26, 1922. e. U. of California, premedical student UCLA. TV series, December Bride, Pete and Gladys.
PICTURES: Seven Sweethearts, Private Miss Jones, Girl Crazy, War Against Mrs. Hadley, Thousands Cheer, Dragon Seed, Honest Thief, Mrs. Parkington, Barbary Coast Gent, Hidden Eye, Abbott and Costello in Hollywood, Adventures of Don Coyote, Money Madness, Lady at Midnight, Old Fashioned Girl, Rodeo, Shanghai Story, Wings of Chance.

RAFFIN, DEBORAH
Actress. b. Los Angeles, CA, March 13, 1953. m. producer Michael Viner. Mother is actress Trudy Marshall. e. Valley Coll. Was active fashion model before turning to acting when discovered by Ted Witzer. Author: Sharing Christmas (Vols. I & II). Debut in 40 Carats (1973). Publisher Dove Books On Tape. Head of Dove Films, prod. co.

PICTURES: 40 Carats (debut, 1973), The Dove, Once Is Not Enough, God Told Me To (Demon), Assault on Paradise (Maniac!), The Sentinel, Touched by Love, Dance of the Dwarfs (Jungle Heat), Death Wish 3, Claudia, Scanners II, Wilde, Family Blessings.
TELEVISION: *Series*: Foul Play. *Movies*: A Nightmare in Badham County, Ski Lift to Death, How to Pick Up Girls, Willa, Mind Over Murder, Haywire, For the Love of It, Killing at Hell's Gate, For Lovers Only, Running Out, Sparkling Cyanide, Threesome, The Sands of Time, Morning Glory (also co-s.p.), A Perry Mason Mystery: The Case of the Grimacing Governor, Home Song, Unwed Father. *Mini-Series*: The Last Convertible, James Clavell's Noble House, Windmills of the Gods (also co-prod.). *Guest*: B.L. Stryker.

RAGLAND, ROBERT O.
Composer. b. Chicago, IL, July 3, 1931. e. Northwestern U., American Conservatory of Music, Vienna Acad. of Music. Professional pianist at Chicago nightclubs. In U.S. Navy; on discharge joined Dorsey Bros. Orchestra as arranger. On sls. staff at NBC-TV, Chicago. 1970, moved to Hollywood to become composer for movies; has scored 67 feature films plus many TV movies and series segments. Has also written some 45 original songs.
PICTURES: The Touch of Melissa, The Yin and Yang of Mr. Go, The Thing with Two Heads, Project: Kill, Abby, Seven Alone, The Eyes of Dr. Chaney, Return to Macon County, The Daring Dobermans, Shark's Treasure, Grizzly, Pony Express Rider, Mansion of the Doomed, Mountain Family Robinson, Only Once in a Lifetime, Jaguar Lives, The Glove, Lovely But Deadly, "Q", The Day of the Assassin, A Time To Die, The Winged Serpent, Trial by Terror, The Guardian, Ten to Midnight, Dirty Rebel, Hysterical, Brainwaves, Where's Willie?, The Supernaturals, Nightstick, Pretty Kill, Deep Space, Messenger of Death, The Fifth Monkey, No Place to Hide, The Buffalo Soldiers, The Raffle, Morty, Crime and Punishment, The Fear, Evil Obsession, Warhead, Top of the World, Plato's Run, Motel Blue.
TELEVISION: Photoplay's Stars of Tomorrow, Wonder Woman, Barnaby Jones, Streets of San Francisco, High Ice, The Girl on the Edge of Town, The Guardian, etc.

RAILSBACK, STEVE
Actor. b. Dallas, TX, 1948. Studied with Lee Strasberg. On stage in Orpheus Descending, This Property Is Condemned, Cherry Orchard, Skin of Our Teeth, etc.
PICTURES: The Visitors, Cockfighter, Angela, The Stunt Man, Deadly Games, Turkey Shoot, The Golden Seal, Torchlight, Lifeforce, Armed and Dangerous, Blue Monkey, The Wind, Distortions, Deadly Intent, Alligator II: The Mutation, AfterShock, Private Wars, Forever, Calendar Girl, Nukie, Save Me.
TELEVISION: *Movies*: Helter Skelter, Good Cops Bad Cops, The Forgotten, Spearfield's Daughter, Sunstroke, Bonds of Love, Separated by Murder. *Mini-Series*: From Here to Eternity.

RAIMI, SAM
Director, Writer, Producer, Actor. b. Royal Oak, MI, Oct. 23, 1959. e. Michigan St. Univ. Formed Renaissance Pictures, Inc.
PICTURES: *Dir./Writer*: The Evil Dead, Crimewave, Evil Dead II, Darkman, Army of Darkness, The Quick and the Dead (dir. only). *Co-Producer*: Hard Target, Timecop. *Actor*: Spies Like Us, Thou Shalt Not Kill... Except, Maniac Cop, Miller's Crossing, Innocent Blood, Indian Summer, Intruder, The Hudsucker Proxy (also co-writer), The Flintstones, Galaxis (actor), The Quick and the Dead (dir.), Darkman III (exec. prod.), A Simple Plan (dir.), The Lamia (dir.).
TELEVISION: *Movies*: Journey to the Center of the Earth (actor), Mantis (prod., writer), Body Bags (actor), The Stand (actor). *Series*: American Gothic (exec. prod.), Xena: Warrior Princess (exec. prod.), Hercules: The Legendary Journeys (exec. prod.), American Gothic (exec. prod.), Spy Game (exec. prod.) *Mini-Series*: The Shining (actor).

RAJSKI, PEGGY
Producer. b. Stevens Point, WI. e. Univ. of Wisconsin. m. actor Josh Mostel. Began film career as prod. manager on John Sayles film Lianna, before becoming producer. Prod. of Bruce Springsteen music videos, incl. Glory Days which won American Video Award. Received 1994 Academy Award for short film Trevor.
PICTURES: The Brother From Another Planet, Matewan, Eight Men Out, The Grifters, Little Man Tate, Used People, Home for the Holidays, Boy's Life 2.

RAKSIN, DAVID
Composer. b. Philadelphia, PA, Aug. 4, 1912. e. U. of Pennsylvania, studied music with Isadore Freed and Arnold Schoenberg. Composer for films, ballet, dramatic and musical comedy, stage, radio and TV, symphony orchestra and chamber ensembles. Arranger of music of Chaplin film, Modern Times; pres. Composers and Lyricists Guild of America, 1962-70; animated films include Madeline and The Unicorn in the Garden (UPA). Professor of Music and Urban Semester, U. of Southern California. Coolidge Commission from the Library of Congress: Oedipus Memneitai (Oedipus Remembers) for bass/baritone, 6-part chorus and chamber orchestra premiered there under dir. of composer, Oct. 1986. Pres., Society for the Preservation of Film Music, 1992. Recipient of ASCAP Golden Score Award for Career Achievement, 1992. Elected to ASCAP bd. of dirs., 1995.

PICTURES: Laura, Secret Life of Walter Mitty, Smoky, Force of Evil, Across the Wide Missouri, Carrie, Bad and the Beautiful, Apache, Suddenly, Big Combo, Jubal, Hilda Crane, Separate Tables, Al Capone, Night Tide, Too-Late Blues, Best of the Bolshoi (music for visual interludes), Two Weeks in Another Town, The Redeemer, Invitation to a Gunfighter, Sylvia, A Big Hand for the Little Lady, Will Penny, Glass Houses, What's the Matter With Helen?

TELEVISION: Series: Five Fingers, Life With Father, Father of the Bride, Ben Casey, Breaking Point. Specials: Journey, Tender is the Night, Prayer of the Ages, Report from America, The Olympics (CBC), The Day After, Lady in a Corner.

RALPH, SHERYL LEE
Actress. b. Waterbury, CT, Dec. 30, 1956. e. Rutgers U. Studied with Negro Ensemble Company in NYC.
THEATER: NY: Reggae, Dreamgirls. LA: Identical Twins From Baltimore.
PICTURES: A Piece of the Action (debut, 1977), Oliver and Company (voice), The Mighty Quinn, Skin Deep, To Sleep With Anger, Mistress, The Distinguished Gentleman, Sister Act 2: Back in the Habit, The Flintstones, White Man's Burden, Bogus.
TELEVISION: Series: Code Name: Foxfire, Search for Tomorrow, It's a Living, Designing Women, George. Movies: The Neighborhood, Sister Margaret and the Saturday Night Ladies, Luck of the Draw: The Gambler Returns, No Child of Mine. Specials: Happy Birthday Hollywood, Voices That Care, Story of a People: The Black Road to Hollywood (host).

RAMIS, HAROLD
Writer, Director, Actor, Producer. b. Chicago, IL, Nov. 21, 1944. e. Washington U., St. Louis. Assoc. ed. Playboy Mag. 1968-70; writer, actor, Second City, Chicago 1970-73; National Lampoon Radio Show, 1974-75. Recipient of Chicago Film Critics "Commitment to Chicago" Award, 1997.
PICTURES: National Lampoon's Animal House (co-s.p.), Meatballs (co-s.p.), Caddyshack (co-s.p., dir.), Stripes (co-s.p., actor), Heavy Metal (voice), National Lampoon's Vacation (dir.), Ghostbusters (co-s.p., actor), Back to School (co-s.p., exec. prod.), Club Paradise (co-s.p., dir.), Armed and Dangerous (exec. prod., co-s.p.), Baby Boom (actor), Caddyshack II (co-s.p.), Stealing Home (actor), Ghostbusters II (co-s.p., actor), Rover Dangerfield (co-story), Groundhog Day (dir., co-s.p., co-prod., actor), Airheads (actor), Love Affair (actor), Stuart Saves His Family (dir.), Multiplicity (dir., co-prod.), As Good As It Gets (actor), Run for Your Wife (dir., prod.), Ghostbusters III (actor, dir., s.p.), Bedazzled (dir.), Analyze This (dir.).
TELEVISION: Series: SCTV (head writer, performer, 1976-78), Rodney Dangerfield Show (head writer, prod.). Special: Will Rogers—Look Back and Laugh (exec. prod.).

RAMPLING, CHARLOTTE
Actress. b. Sturmer, England, Feb. 5, 1946. e. Jeanne D'Arc Academie pour Jeune Filles, Versailles; St. Hilda's, Bushey, England.
PICTURES: The Knack... and How to Get It (debut, 1965), Rotten to the Core, Georgy Girl, The Long Duel, Sequestro di Persona (Island of Crime), The Damned, Target: Harry (How to Make It), Three, The Ski Bum, Corky, Addio Fratello Crrudele (Tis Pity She's a Whore), Asylum, The Night Porter, Giordano Bruno, Zardoz, Caravan to Vaccares, La Chair de l'orchidee, Farewell My Lovely, Foxtrot (The Other Side of Paradise), Yuppi-Du, Orca, Purple Taxi, Stardust Memories, The Verdict, Viva La Vie, Tristesse et Beaute, On ne Meurt que deux Fois (He Died With His Eyes Open), Angel Heart, Mascara, D.O.A., Max My Love, Rebus, Paris By Night, Helmut Newton: Frames from the Edge (doc.), Hammers Over the Anvil, Time is Money, Invasion of Privacy, Asphalt Tango.
TELEVISION: BBC Series: The Six Wives of Henry VIII, The Superlative Seven, The Avengers. Movies: Sherlock Holmes in New York, Mystery of Cader Iscom, The Fantasists, What's in it for Henry, Zinotchka, Infidelities, La Femme Abandonnee, Radetzky March, Murder In Mind, Samson Le Maqnifique, La Dernière Fête.

RAND, HAROLD
Executive. b. New York, NY, Aug. 25, 1928. e. Long Island U., B.S., 1948-50; CCNY, 1945-46. U.S. Army 1946-48; ent. m.p. ind. 1950, pub. dept. 20th-Fox; variety of posts incl. writer, trade press, newspaper contacts; joined Walt Disney's Buena Vista pub. mgr., 1957; pub. mgr. Paramount Pictures, 1959; formed own pub. rel. firm, 1961; dir. of pub. Embassy Picture Corp. 1962; dir. of world pub. 20th Century Fox 1962; resigned 1963; dir. of adv. & pub., Landau Co., 1963; dir. world pub., Embassy Pictures, 1964; est. Harold Rand & Co., Inc., 1966, pres. of p.r. & mktg. firm. Appt. mktg., dir., Kaufman Astoria Studios, 1984; elected v.p., 1985.

RANDALL, TONY
Actor. r.n. Leonard Rosenberg. b. Tulsa, OK, Feb. 26, 1920. e. Northwestern U. Prof. N.Y. debut as actor in Circle of Chalk; U.S. Army 1942-46; radio actor on many shows. Founder/Artistic Director of National Actors Theatre in NYC, 1991.

THEATER: Candida, The Corn is Green, Antony & Cleopatra, Caesar & Cleopatra, Inherit the Wind, Oh Men! Oh Women!, Oh Captain, The Sea Gull, The Master Builder, M. Butterfly, A Little Hotel on the Side, Three Men on a Horse, The Government Inspector, The Odd Couple (tour).
PICTURES: Oh Men! Oh Women! (debut, 1957), Will Success Spoil Rock Hunter?, No Down Payment, The Mating Game, Pillow Talk, The Adventures of Huckleberry Finn, Let's Make Love, Lover Come Back, Boys' Night Out, Island of Love, The Brass Bottle, 7 Faces of Dr. Lao, Send Me No Flowers, Fluffy, The Alphabet Murders, Bang Bang You're Dead, Hello Down There, Everything You Always Wanted to Know About Sex* But Were Afraid to Ask, Scavenger Hunt, Foolin' Around, The King of Comedy, My Little Pony (voice), It Had to Be You, That's Adequate, Gremlins 2: The New Batch (voice), Fatal Instinct.
TELEVISION: Series: One Man's Family, Mr. Peepers, The Odd Couple (Emmy Award, 1975), The Tony Randall Show, Love Sidney. Guest: TV Playhouse, Max Liebman Spectaculars, Sid Caesar, Dinah Shore, Playhouse 90, Walt Disney World Celebrity Circus. Movies: Kate Bliss and the Ticker Tape Kid, Sidney Shorr: A Girl's Best Friend, Off Sides, Hitler's SS: Portrait in Evil, Sunday Drive, Save the Dog!, The Odd Couple: Together Again.

RANSOHOFF, MARTIN
Executive. b. New Orleans, LA, 1927. e. Colgate U., 1949. Adv., Young & Rubicam, 1948-49; slsmn, writer, dir., Caravel Films 1951; formed own co., Filmways, 1952; industrial films, commercials; formed Filmways TV Prods., Filmways, Inc., Filmways of Calif.; bd. chmn. Filmways, Inc. Resigned from Filmways in 1972 and formed Martin Ransohoff Prods., Inc, independent m. p. and tv prod. co.
PICTURES: Boys' Night Out, The Wheeler Dealers, The Americanization of Emily, The Loved One, The Sandpiper, The Cincinnati Kid, The Fearless Vampire Killers, Don't Make Waves, Ice Station Zebra, Castle Keep, Hamlet (exec. prod.), Catch-22, The Moonshine War, King Lear, See No Evil, 10 Rillington Place, Fuzz, Save The Tiger, The White Dawn, Silver Streak (exec. prod.), Nightwing, The Wanderers, The Mountain Men, A Change of Seasons, American Pop, Hanky Panky, Class, Jagged Edge, The Big Town, Switching Channels, Physical Evidence, Welcome Home, Guilty as Sin, Turbulence (prod.).
TELEVISION: Series: Mister Ed, The Beverly Hillbillies, Petticoat Junction, Green Acres, The Addams Family.

RAPAPORT, MICHAEL
Actor. b. New York, NY, 1970. Started as stand-up comic appearing at Improv in LA before becoming actor.
PICTURES: Zebrahead, Point of No Return, Poetic Justice, Money for Nothing, True Romance, The Scout, Higher Learning, The Basketball Diaries, Kiss of Death, Mighty Aphrodite, The Pallbearer, A Brother's Kiss, Metro.

RAPHAEL, FREDERIC
Writer. b. Chicago, IL, Aug. 14, 1931. e. Charterhouse, St. John's Coll., Cambridge.
AUTHOR: The Earlsdon Way, The Limits of Love, A Wild Surmise, The Graduate Wife, The Trouble With England, Lindmann, Orchestra and Beginners, Like Men Betrayed, Who Were You With Last Night?, April June and November, Richard's Things, California Time, The Glittering Prizes, Sleeps Six & Other Stories, Oxbridge Blues & Other Stories, Heaven & Earth, Think of England and other stories, After the War, A Double Life, The Latin Lover and other stories, Old Scores. Biographies: Somerset Maugham and His World, Byron. Translations: (with Kenneth McLeish), Poems of Catullus The Oresteia. Essays: Cracks in the Ice, Of Gods and Men, La Putain du roi, Eyes Wide Shut.
THEATER: From the Greek (1979), An Early Life.
PICTURES: Nothing But the Best, Darling (Academy Award, 1965), Two for the Road, Far from the Madding Crowd, A Severed Head, Daisy Miller, Richard's Things, Women and Men: Stories of Seduction, Women and Men 2: In Love There Are No Rules.
TELEVISION: The Glittering Prizes (Royal TV Society Writer Award 1976), Rogue Male, School Play, Something's Wrong, Best of Friends, Richard's Things, Oxbridge Blues (ACE Award, best writer), After the War, Byrow, The Man in the Brooks Brothers Shirt (also dir.; ACE Award best picture).

RAPHEL, DAVID
Executive. b. Boulogne-Seine, France, Jan. 9, 1925. e. university in France. Entered m.p. ind. as asst. to sales mgr. in France, 20th-Fox, 1950-51; asst. mgr. in Italy, 1951-54; mgr. in Holland, 1954-57; asst. to European mgr. in Paris, 1957-59; European mgr. for TV activities in Paris, 1959-61; Continental mgr. in Paris, 1961-64, transferred to NY as v.p. in chg. of intl. sales, 1964; named pres., 20th Century-Fox International, 1973. 1975, also appointed sr. v.p., worldwide marketing, feature film division, for 20th-Fox, (L.A.). 1976, joined ICM, appointed dir. general of ICM (Europe) headquartered in Paris. 1979 elected pres. ICM (L.A.). 1980, formed Cambridge Film Group Ltd.

RAPPER, IRVING
Director. b. London, Eng., Jan. 16, 1904. Stage prod. London: Five Star Final, Grand Hotel. NY: The Animal Kingdom, The Firebird, The Late Christopher Bean.

PICTURES: Shining Victory (debut, 1941), One Foot in Heaven, The Gay Sisters, Now Voyager, The Adventures of Mark Twain, Rhapsody in Blue, The Corn Is Green, Deception, The Voice of the Turtle, Anna Lucasta, The Glass Menagerie, Another Man's Poison, Forever Female, Bad for Each Other, The Brave One, Strange Intruder, Marjorie Morningstar, The Miracle, Joseph and His Brethren, Pontius Pilate, The Christine Jorgensen Story, Born Again, Justus.

RAPPOPORT, GERALD J.
Executive, Film Producer. b. New York, NY, Aug. 25, 1925. e. NYU. U.S. Marine Corps. Pres., Major Artists Representatives Corp., 1954-58; dir. of Coast Sound Services, Hollywood; 1959-61, pres., International Film Exchange Ltd.; 1960-91, CEO of IFEX Int'l; 1991-94, pres. CIFEX Corporation, 1995-present.

RASHAD, PHYLICIA
Actress-singer. b. Houston, TX, June 19, 1948. m. sportscaster Ahmad Rashad. Sister of Debbie Allen. e. Howard U., B.F.A., magna cum laude, 1970. NY School of Ballet. Acted under maiden name of Phylicia Ayers-Allen. Recording, Josephine Superstar (1979). Conceived (with Michael Peters) and appeared in revue Phylicia Rashad & Co. in 1989 in Las Vegas.
THEATER: Ain't Supposed to Die a Natural Death, The Duplex, The Cherry Orchard, The Wiz, Weep Not For Me, Zooman and the Sign, In an Upstate Motel, Zora, Dreamgirls, Sons and Fathers of Sons, Puppetplay, A Raisin in the Sun, Into the Woods, Jelly's Last Jam.
PICTURE: Once Upon A Time...When We Were Colored.
TELEVISION: Series: One Life to Live, The Cosby Show (People's Choice Award, NAACP Image Award, Emmy nom.), Cosby. Movies: Uncle Tom's Cabin, False Witness, Polly, Polly—Comin' Home!, Jailbirds, David's Mother, The Possession of Michael D. Specials: Nell Carter—Never Too Old to Dream, Superstars and Their Moms, Our Kids and the Best of Everything, The Debbie Allen Special, Hallelujah.

RATHER, DAN
News Correspondent, Anchor. b. Wharton, TX, Oct. 31, 1931. e. Sam Houston State Teachers Coll., BA journalism, 1953. Instructor there for 1 year. Graduate e.: U. of Houston Law School, S. Texas School of Law. Worked for UPI and Houston Chronicle. Radio: KSAM, Huntsville, KTRH, Houston. Joined CBS News in 1962 as chief of southwest bureau in Dallas. Transferred to overseas burs. (including chief of London Bureau 1965-66), then Vietnam before returning as White House corr. 1966. White House Correspondent, 1964-74. Covered top news events, from Democratic and Republican national conventions to President Nixon's trip to Europe (1970) and to Peking and Moscow (1972). Anchored CBS Reports, 1974-75. Presently co-editor of 60 minutes (since 1975) and anchors Dan Rather Reporting on CBS Radio Network (since 1977). Anchor for 48 Hours, 1988. Winner of numerous awards, including 5 Emmys. Anchorman on CBS-TV Evening News, 1981-. Books: The Palace Guard (1974); The Camera Never Blinks (1977); I Remember (1991); The Camera Never Blinks Twice (1994); Mark Sullivan's Our Times (editor, 1995).

RAUCHER, HERMAN
Writer. b. Apr. 13, 1928. e. NYU. Author of novels Watermelon Man, Summer of '42 and Ode to Billy Joe, adapted to films by him. Other novels inc. A Glimpse of Tiger, There Should Have Been Castles, Maynard's House.
PICTURES: Sweet November, Can Hieronymous Merkin Ever Forget Mercy Humppe and Find True Happiness?, Watermelon Man, Summer of '42, Class of '44, Ode to Billy Joe, The Other Side of Midnight.
TELEVISION: Studio One, Alcoa Hour, Goodyear Playhouse, Matinee Theatre, Remember When? (movie).

RAVETCH, IRVING
Writer, Producer. b. Newark, NJ, Nov. 14, 1920. e. UCLA. m. Harriet Frank, with whom he often collaborated.
PICTURES: Writer: Living in a Big Way, The Outriders, Vengeance Valley, Ten Wanted Men, The Long Hot Summer, The Sound and the Fury, Home from the Hill, The Dark at the Top of the Stairs, Hud (also co-prod.), Hombre (also co-prod.), The Reivers (also prod.), House of Cards (as James P. Bonner), The Cowboys, Conrack, Norma Rae, Murphy's Romance, Stanley and Iris.

RAYBURN, GENE
Performer. b. Christopher, IL, Dec. 22, 1917. e. Knox Coll., Galesburg, IL. NBC guide; with many radio stations in Baltimore, Philadelphia, NY; US Army Air Force, 1942-45; Rayburn and Finch Show, WNEW, NY, 1945-52; Gene Rayburn Show, NBC radio; TV shows: Many appearances as host-humorist on game shows, variety shows, drama shows. Also acted in summer stock; AFTRA, past pres. NY local; trustee on H&R Board for over 25 years.
THEATER: B'way: Bye Bye Birdie, Come Blow Your Horn.
TELEVISION: Series: The Name's the Same, Tonight (second banana), Make the Connection, The Steve Allen Show, The Steve Lawrence-Eydie Gorme Show (announcer), The Match Games, Dough Re Mi, The Sky's the Limit, Choose Up Sides, Tic Tac Dough, Play Your Hunch, Snap Judgment, Amateur's Guide to Love, Break the Bank. Guest: The Love Boat, Fantasy Island.

RAYMOND, PAULA
Actress. r.n. Paula Ramona Wright, b. San Francisco, CA., Nov. 23, 1925. e. San Francisco Jr. Coll. 1942. Started career in little theatre groups, concerts, recitals, San Francisco; leading stage roles in Ah! Wilderness, Peter Pan, etc.; also sang lead coloratura rules in Madame Butterfly, Aidia, Rigoletto, Faust, etc.; ballerina with S.F. Opera Ballet; classical pianist; model, Meade-Maddick Photographers.
PICTURES: Racing Luck (debut, 1948), Rusty Leads the Way, Blondie's Secret, East Side West Side, Challenge of the Range, Adam's Rib, Devil's Doorway, Sons of New Mexico, Duchess of Idaho, Crisis, Grounds For Marriage, Inside Straight, The Tall Target, Texas Carnival, The Sellout, Bandits of Corsica, City That Never Sleeps, The Beast from 20,000 Fathoms, The Human Jungle, King Richard & the Crusaders, The Gun That Won the West, Hand of Death, The Flight That Disappeared, The Spy With My Face, Blood of Dracula's Castle, Five Bloody Graves, Mind Twister.
TELEVISION: Guest: Perry Mason, 77 Sunset Strip, Wyatt Earp, Man from U.N.C.L.E., Maverick, The Untouchables, Bachelor Father, Bat Masterson, Temple Houston, Peter Gunn, many others.

RAYNOR, LYNN S.
Producer, Production Executive. b. Chicago, IL, Feb. 11, 1940. Produced West Coast premiere of The Balcony by Genet, The Crawling Arnold Review by Feiffer. Joined Television Enterprises, 1965; Commonwealth United, 1968 as business affairs exec. later prod. spvr. 1972 opened London branch of the Vidtronics Co. 1974, formed Paragon Entertainment & RAH Records. 1980-95, prod. of TV Movies and Mini-Series. Prod. & editor of 12 minute tv vignettes, A Hall of Fame Story.
PICTURE: Freejack.
TELEVISION: Special: Waiting for Godot. Movies: Marilyn: The Untold Story, The Execution, A Winner Never Quits, On Wings of Eagles, Stranger in My Bed, Hands of a Stranger, The High Price of Passion, The Kennedys of Massachusetts, Common Ground, Face of Love, The Rape of Doctor Willis, Quiet Killer, Love Honor & Obey: The Last Mafia Marriage, Tony & Nancy: The Inside Story, Tecumseh: The Last Warrior, It Was Him Or Us, The Lover Letter, Glory & Honor. Series: Camp Wilderness. Mini-Series: True Women. Pilot: Murphy's Law.

REA, STEPHEN
Actor. b. Belfast, Northern Ireland, Oct. 31, 1948. e. Queens Univ. (BA in English Lit.). Started acting at Abbey Theatre in Dublin. Formed the Field Day Theatre Co. in 1980 in Londonderry, acting in or directing most of their productions. Also acted with Royal Natl. Theatre.
THEATER: Playboy of the Western World, Comedians, High Society, Endgame, Freedom of the City, Someone Who'll Watch Over Me (also B'way; Theatre World Award, Tony nom.).
PICTURES: Danny Boy (Angel), Loose Connections, The Company of Wolves, The Doctor and the Devils, The House, Life Is Sweet, The Crying Game (Acad. Award nom.), Bad Behavior, Angie, Princess Caraboo, Ready to Wear (Pret-a-Porter), Between the Devil and the Deep Blue Sea, Interview With A Vampire, All Men Are Mortal, ,Trojan Eddie, Michael Collins, A Further Gesture, Last of the High Kings, Hacks, Fever Pitch, Double Top, This Is My Father, Still Crazy, The Butcher Boy, Blue Vision.
TELEVISION: Shadow of a Gunman, Fugitive, I Didn't Know You Cared, Professional Foul, The Seagull, Out of Town Boys, Calbe Williams, Joyce in June, The House, Four Days in July, Shergar, Scout, Lost Belongings, The Big Gamble, Not With a Bang, Saint Oscar, Hedda Gabler, Citizen X, Crime of the Century.

REAGAN, RONALD
Actor, Politician. b. Tampico, IL, Feb. 6, 1911. e. high school, Eureka Coll. m. former actress Nancy Davis. Wrote weekly sports column for a Des Moines, IA newspaper; broadcast sporting events. Signed as actor by Warner Bros. in 1937. In WWII 1942-45, capt., USAAF. Actor until 1966. Served as Governor, California, 1967-74. Businessman and rancher. Elected President of the United States, 1980. Re-elected, 1984. Autobiography: Where's the Rest of Me? (1965).
PICTURES: Love Is On the Air (debut, 1937), Hollywood Hotel, Sergeant Murphy, Swing Your Lady, Brother Rat, Going Places, Accidents Will Happen, Cowboy from Brooklyn, Boy Meets Girl, Girls on Probation, Dark Victory, Naughty but Nice, Hell's Kitchen, Code of the Secret Service, Smashing the Money Ring, Angels Wash Their Faces, Brother Rat and a Baby, Murder in the Air, Tugboat Annie Sails Again, Knute Rockne—All American, Santa Fe Trail, Angel From Texas, Nine Lives Are Not Enough, The Bad Man, International Squadron, Million Dollar Baby, Kings Row, Juke Girl, Desperate Journey, This Is the Army, Stallion Road, That Hagen Girl, The Voice of the Turtle, Night Unto Night, John Loves Mary, The Girl From Jones Beach, It's a Great Feeling (cameo), The Hasty Heart, Louisa, Storm Warning, The Last Outpost, Bedtime for Bonzo, Hong Kong, She's Working Her Way Through College, The Winning Team, Tropic Zone, Law & Order, Prisoner of War, Cattle Queen of Montana, Tennessee's Partner, Hellcats of the Navy, The Young Doctors (narrator), The Killers.
TELEVISION: Series: The Orchid Award (emcee), General Electric Theater (host, frequent star), Death Valley Days (host). Guest: Ford Theratre, Schlitz Playhouse of Stars, Lux Video Theatre, Startime.

REARDON, BARRY
Executive. b. Hartford, CT, Mar. 8, 1931. e. Holy Cross Col., Trinity Col. Began industry career with Paramount Pictures; named v.p.; left to join General Cinema Theatres Corp. as sr. v.p. Now with Warner Bros. as pres. of domestic distribution co.

REASON, REX
Actor. b. Berlin, Germany, Nov. 30, 1928. e. Hoover H.S., Glendale, CA. Worked at various jobs; studied dramatics at Pasadena Playhouse.
PICTURES: Storm Over Tibet, Salome, Mission Over Korea, Taza Son of Cochise, This Island Earth, Smoke Signal, Lady Godiva, Kiss of Fire, Creature Walks Among Us, Raw Edge, The Rawhide Trail, Under Fire, Thundering Jets, The Sad Horse, Yankee Pasha, Band of Angels, Miracle of the Hills.
TELEVISION: Series: Man Without a Gun, Roaring Twenties.

REDDY, HELEN
Singer. b. Melbourne, Australia, Oct. 25, 1942. Parents were producer-writer-actor Max Reddy and actress Stella Lamond. e. in Australia. Began career at age four as singer and had appeared in hundreds of stage and radio roles with parents by age of 15. Came to New York in 1966, subsequently played nightclubs, appeared on TV. First single hit record: I Don't Know How To Love Him (Capitol). Grammy Award, 1973, as best female singer of year for I Am Woman. Most Played Artist by the music operators of America: American Music Award 1974; Los Angeles Times Woman of the Year (1975); No. 1 Female Vocalist in 1975 and 1976; Record World, Cash Box and Billboard; named one of the Most Exciting Women in the World by International Bachelor's Society, 1976. Heads prod. co. Helen Reddy, Inc.
THEATER: B'way: Blood Brothers.
PICTURES: Airport 1975 (debut), Pete's Dragon.
TELEVISION: Series: The Helen Reddy Show (Summer, 1973), Permanent host of Midnight Special. Appearances: David Frost Show, Flip Wilson Show, Mike Douglas Show, Tonight Show, Mac Davis Show, Merv Griffin Show (guest host), Sesame Street, Live in Australia (host, 1988); Muppet Show, Home for Easter.

REDFORD, ROBERT
Actor, Director, Producer. b. Santa Monica, CA, Aug. 18, 1937. r.n. Charles Robert Redford. Attended U. of Colorado; left to travel in Europe, 1957. Attended Pratt Inst. and American Acad. of Dramatic Arts. Founded Sundance Film Institute, Park City, Utah, workshop for young filmmakers.
THEATER: B'way: Tall Story (walk on), The Highest Tree, Sunday in New York (Theatre World Award), Barefoot in the Park.
PICTURES: Actor: War Hunt (debut, 1962), Situation Hopeless But Not Serious, Inside Daisy Clover, The Chase, This Property Is Condemned, Barefoot in the Park, Downhill Racer (also exec. prod.), Butch Cassidy and the Sundance Kid, Tell Them Willie Boy is Here, Little Fauss and Big Halsy, The Hot Rock, The Candidate (also co-exec. prod.), Jeremiah Johnson, The Way We Were, The Sting (Acad. Award nom.), The Great Gatsby, The Great Waldo Pepper, Three Days of the Condor, All The President's Men (also exec. prod.), A Bridge Too Far, The Electric Horseman, Brubaker, The Natural, Out of Africa, Legal Eagles, Havana, Sneakers, Indecent Proposal, Up Close and Personal, Anthem. Exec. Producer: Promised Land, Some Girls, Yosemite: The Fate of Heaven (also narrator), The Dark Wind, Incident at Oglala (also narrator), Strawberry & Chocolate (presenter). Director: Ordinary People (Acad. Award, 1980), The Milagro Beanfield War (also co-prod.), A River Runs Through It (also prod., narrator), Quiz Show (also prod.); NY Film Critics Award for Best Picture; Acad. Award noms. for picture & dir.).
TELEVISION: Guest: Maverick, Playhouse 90, Play of the Week (The Iceman Cometh), Alfred Hitchcock Presents, Route 66, Twilight Zone, Dr. Kildare, The Untouchables, The Virginian, The Defenders.

REDGRAVE, CORIN
Actor. b. London, England, July 16, 1939. e. Cambridge. p. late Sir Michael Redgrave and Rachel Kempson. Brother of Vanessa and Lynn Redgrave.
THEATER: On stage with England Stage Co.: A Midsummer Night's Dream, Chips with Everything. RSC: Lady Windermere's Fan, Julius Caesar, Comedy of Errors, Antony and Cleopatra. Young Vic: Rosmersholm.
PICTURES: A Man for All Seasons, The Deadly Affair, Charge of the Light Brigade, The Magus, Oh What a Lovely War, When Eight Bells Toll, Serail, Excalibur, Eureka, Between Wars, The Fool, In the Name of the Father, Four Weddings and a Funeral, Persuasion.
TELEVISION: I Berlioz, Measure for Measure, Persuasion, Henry IV, Circle of Deceit.

REDGRAVE, LYNN
Actress. b. London, England, Mar. 8, 1943. Sister of Vanessa and Corin Redgrave. p. late Sir Michael Redgrave and Rachel Kempson. m. dir.-actor-manager John Clark. Ent. m.p. and TV industries, 1962.

THEATER: NY: Black Comedy (B'way debut), My Fat Friend (1974), Mrs. Warren's Profession, Knock Knock, Misalliance, St. Joan, Twelfth Night (Amer. Shakespeare Fest), Sister Mary Ignatius Explains It All For You, Aren't We All?, Sweet Sue, A Little Hotel on the Side, The Master Builder, Shakespeare for My Father (also writer). LA: Les Liaisons Dangereuses.
PICTURES: Tom Jones (debut, 1963), Girl With Green Eyes, Georgy Girl (Acad. Award nom.), The Deadly Affair, Smashing Time, The Virgin Soldiers, Last of the Mobile Hot-Shots, Los Guerilleros (Killer From Yuma), Viva la Muerta—Tua! (Don't Turn the Other Cheek), Every Little Crook and Nanny, Everything You Always Wanted to Know About Sex* But Were Afraid to Ask, The National Health, The Happy Hooker, The Big Bus, Sunday Lovers, Morgan Stewart's Coming Home, Midnight, Getting It Right, Shine.
TELEVISION: BBC: Pretty Polly, Ain't Afraid to Dance, The End of the Tunnel, I Am Osango, What's Wrong with Humpty Dumpty, Egg On the Face of the Tiger, Blank Pages, A Midsummer Night's Dream, Pygmalion, William, Vienna 1900, Daft as a Brush, Not For Women Only, Calling the Shots. United States: Co-host: A.M. America. Movies: Turn of the Screw, Sooner or Later, Beggarman Thief, Gauguin the Savage, Seduction of Miss Leona, Rehearsal for Murder, The Bad Seed, My Two Loves, Jury Duty: The Comedy, What Ever Happened to Baby Jane? Mini-Series: Centennial. Series: House Calls, Teachers Only, Chicken Soup. Guest: The Muppet Show, Walking on Air, Candid Camera Christmas Special, Woman Alone, Tales From the Hollywood Hills: The Old Reliable, Death of a Son.

REDGRAVE, VANESSA
O.B.E. Actress. b. London, England, Jan. 30, 1937. p. Sir Michael Redgrave and Rachel Kempson. Sister of Lynn and Corin Redgrave. Mother of actresses Joely and Natasha Richardson. Early career with Royal Shakespeare Company. Appeared in documentary Tonight Let's All Make Love in London. Autobiography, 1994.
THEATER: Daniel Deronda, Cato Street, The Threepenny Opera, Twelfth Night, As You Like It, The Taming of the Shrew, Cymbeline, The Sea Gull, The Prime of Miss Jean Brodie, Antony & Cleopatra, Design for Living, Macbeth, Lady from the Sea, The Aspern Papers, Ghosts, Anthony and Cleopatra, Tomorrow Was War, A Touch of the Poet, Orpheus Descending, Madhouse in Goa, The Three Sisters, When She Danced, Maybe, Heartbreak House, Vita & Virginia.
PICTURES: Behind the Mask (debut, 1958), Morgan!: A Suitable Case for Treatment (Acad. Award nom.), A Man for All Seasons, Blow-Up, The Sailor From Gibraltar, Red and Blue, Camelot, The Charge of the Light Brigade, Isadora (Acad. Award nom.), Oh! What a Lovely War, The Sea Gull, A Quiet Place in the Country, Drop Out, The Trojan Women, La Vacanza, The Devils, Mary—Queen of Scots (Acad. Award nom.), Murder on the Orient Express, Out of Season, The Seven Percent Solution, Julia (Acad. Award, best supporting actress, 1977), Agatha, Yanks, Bear Island, The Bostonians (Acad. Award nom.), Steaming, Wetherby, Prick Up Your Ears, Consuming Passions, Comrades, The Ballad of the Sad Cafe, Romeo-Juliet (voice), Howards End (Acad. Award nom.), Breath of Life, Sparrow, The House of the Spirits, Crime and Punishment, Mother's Boys, Great Moments in Aviation, Little Odessa, A Month by the Lake, Mrs. Dalloway.
TELEVISION: Movies/Specials: A Farewell to Arms, Katherine Mansfield, Playing for Time (Emmy Award, 1981), My Body My Child, Wagner (theatrical in Europe), Three Sovereigns for Sarah, Peter the Great, Second Serve, A Man For All Seasons, Orpheus Descending, Young Catherine, What Ever Happened to Baby Jane?, They, Down Came a Blackbird. Guest: Faerie Tale Theatre (Snow White and the 7 Dwarfs).

REDSTONE, EDWARD S.
Exhibitor. b. Boston, MA, May 8, 1928. e. Colgate U., B.A., 1949; Harvard Grad. Sch. of Bus. Admin., M.B.A., 1952. v.p., treas.; Northeast Drive-In Theatre Corp.; v.p.; Theatre Owners of New England, 1962; chmn., advis. coms., mem. bd. dirs., TOA; gen. conven. chmn., joint convention TOA & NAC, 1962; pres. National Assn. of Concessionaires, 1963; chief barker. Variety Club of New England, 1963; pres., Theatre Owners of New England; gen. chmn., 35th annual reg. convention.

REDSTONE, SUMNER M.
Executive, Attorney; b. Boston, MA, May 27, 1923. e. Harvard, B.A., 1944, LLB., 1947. Served to 1st Lt. AUS, 1943-45. Admitted to MA Bar 1947; U.S. Ct. Appeals 1st Circuit 1948, 8th Circuit 1950, 9th Circuit 1948; D.C. 1951; U.S. Supreme Ct. 1952; law sec. U.S. Ct. Appeals for 9th Circuit 1947-48; instr. U. San Francisco Law Sch. and Labor Management Sch., 1947; special asst. to U.S. Atty. General, 1948-51; partner firm Ford Bergson Adams Borkland & Redstone, Washington, D.C. 1951-54; exec. v.p. Northeast Drive-In Theatre Corp., 1954-68; pres. Northeast Theatre Corp.; chmn. bd., pres. & CEO, National Amusements, Inc.; chmn. bd., Viacom Int'l, Inc., 1987; asst. pres. Theatre Owners of America, 1960-63; pres. 1964-65; bd. chmn,

National Assoc. of Theatre Owners, 1965-66. Member: Presidential Advisory Committee John F. Kennedy Center for the Performing Arts; chmn. Jimmy Fund, Boston 1960; chmn., met. div. Combined Jewish Philanthropies 1963; sponsor Boston Museum of Science; Trustee Children's Cancer Research Foundation; Art Lending Library; bd. of dirs. of TV Acad. of Arts and Sciences Fund; bd. dirs. Boston Arts Festival; v.p., exec. committee Will Rogers Memorial Fund; bd. overseers Dana Farber Cancer Institute; corp. New England Medical Center; Motion Picture Pioneers; bd. mem. John F. Kennedy Library Foundation; 1984-85; 1985-86 State Crusade Chairman American Cancer Society; Board of Overseers Boston Museum of Fine Arts; Professor, Boston U. Law Sch. 1982-83, 1985-86; Boston Latin School's Graduate of the Year, 1989; Acquired Viacom in 1987 which purchased Paramount Communications in 1993. Member of exec. committe of the National Assoc. of Theatre Owners. Member, exec. bd., Combined Jewish Philanthropies. Judge on Kennedy Library Foundation. Founding trustee, American Cancer Society. Visiting professor, Brandies University; lecturer, Harvard Law School.
AWARDS: (Entertainment related) include: Communicator of the Year B'nai B'rith Communications, Cinema Lodge 1980; Man of the Year, Entertainment Industries div.; UJA-Federation, NY, 1988; Variety of New England Humanitarian Award, 1989; Motion Picture Pioneers Pioneer of the Year, 1991; Golden Plate Award American Acad. Achievement 32nd Annual Salute to Excellence Program; 1994, Man of the Year Award from MIP-COM, the Int'l Film and Programme Market for TV Video Cable and Satellite; 1995, Variety Club International Humanitarian Award; Hall of Fame Award, Broadcast & Cable Magazine, 1995; Honoree 7th Annual Fundraiser, Montefiore Medical Center; Expeditioner's Award, New York City Outward Bound Center, 1996; Patron of the Arts Award, Songwriter's Hall of Fame, 1996; Vision 21 Award and Doctor of Humane Letter, New York Institute of Technology, 1996;

REED, OLIVER
Actor. b. Wimbledon, England, Feb. 13, 1938. Nephew of late British dir. Sir Carol Reed. Dropped out of school in teens and worked as bouncer, boxer, taxi driver before first break on BBC-TV series The Golden Spur. Film debut as extra in Value for Money.
PICTURES: Value for Money (debut, 1955), Hello London, The Square Peg, The Captain's Table, Beat Girl (Wild for Kicks), The League of Gentlemen, The Angry Silence, The Two Faces of Dr. Jekyll (House of Fright), Sword of Sherwood Forest, His and Hers, No Love for Johnnie, The Bulldog Breed, The Rebel (Call Me Genius), Curse of the Werewolf, The Pirates of Blood River, Captain Clegg (Night Creatures), These Are the Damned, The Party's Over, The Scarlet Blade, Paranoic, The System (The Girl-Getters), The Brigand of Kandahar, The Trap, The Jokers, The Shuttered Room, I'll Never Forget What's 'is Name, Oliver!, The Assassination Bureau, Hannibal Brooks, Women in Love, Take a Girl Like You, The Lady in the Car with Glasses and a Gun, The Hunting Party, The Devils, Z.P.G., Sitting Target, Triple Echo, One Russian Summer, Dirty Weekend, Revolver (Blood in the Streets), Blue Blood, The Three Musketeers, Tommy, The Four Musketeers, Lisztomania (cameo), Ten Little Indians, Royal Flash, Sell Out, Blood in the Streets, Burnt Offerings, The Great Scout and Cathouse Thursday, Assault on Paradise (Ransom), Tomorrow Never Comes, Crossed Swords (The Prince and the Pauper), The Big Sleep, The Class of Miss MacMichael, Touch of the Sun, Dr. Heckyl & Mr. Hype, The Brood, Lion of the Desert, Condorman, Venom, The Great Question, Spasms, The Sting II, 99 Women, Two of a Kind, Black Arrow, Gor, Captive, Castaway, Dragonard, Fair Trade, The Return of the Musketeers, Hold My Hand I'm Dying, Fire With Fire, The Misfit Brigade, Rage to Kill, Skeleton Coast, Damnation Express, Captive Rage, The Adventures of Baron Munchausen, The Fall of the House of Usher, Master of Dragonard Hill, Outlaws, The Pit and the Pendulum, Panama, Severed Ties, Funny Bones, The Bruce, Parting Shots, Marco Polo.
TELEVISION: The Lady and the Highwayman, Treasure Island, A Ghost in Monte Carlo, Prisoner of Honor, Army, Return to Lonesome Dove.

REED, PAMELA
Actress. b. Tacoma, WA, Apr. 2, 1953. Ran day-care center and worked with Head Start children before studying drama at U. of Washington. Worked on Trans-Alaska pipeline. Off-Broadway showcases.
THEATER: Curse of the Starving Class (Off-B'way debut, 1978), All's Well That Ends Well (Central Park), Getting Out (Drama Desk Award), Aunt Dan and Lemon, Fools, The November People (Broadway debut), Sorrows of Stephen, Mrs. Warren's Profession, Getting Through the Night, Best Little Whorehouse in Texas, Fen, Standing on My Knees, Elektra.
PICTURES: The Long Riders (debut, 1980), Melvin and Howard, Eyewitness, Young Doctors in Love, The Right Stuff, The Goodbye People, The Best of Times, Clan of the Cave Bear, Rachel River, Chattahoochee, Cadillac Man, Kindergarten Cop, Passed Away, Bob Roberts, Junior, Santa Fe, Bean.

TELEVISION: *Series*: The Andros Targets (TV debut, 1977), Grand, Family Album, The Home Court. *Movies*: Inmates—A Love Story, I Want To Live, Heart of Steel, Scandal Sheet, Caroline?, Woman With a Past, Born Too Soon, Deadly Whispers, The Man Next Door, Critical Choices, Carriers. *Special*: Tanner '88. *Mini-Series*: Hemingway. *Guest*: L.A. Law, The Simpsons (voice).

REES, ROGER
Actor. b. Aberystwyth, Wales, May 5, 1944. e. Camberwell Sch. of Art, Slade Sch. of Fine Art. Stage debut Hindle Wakes (Wimbledon, U.K., 1964). With Royal Shakespeare Co. from 1967. Starred in the title role The Adventures of Nicholas Nickleby (London and NY, Tony Award), also on stage in Hapgood (London, L.A.), Indiscretions (NY). Off-B'way in The End of the Day. Assoc. dir. Bristol Old Vic Theatre Co., 1986-present. Playwright with Eric Elice of Double Double and Elephant Manse.
PICTURES: Star 80 (debut, 1983), Keine Storung Bitte, Mountains of the Moon, If Looks Could Kill, Stop! Or My Mom Will Shoot, Robin Hood: Men in Tights, Sudden Manhattan.
TELEVISION: *Movies*: A Christmas Carol (released theatrically in Europe), Place of Peace, Under Western Eyes, Bouquet of Barbed Wire, Saigon: The Year of the Cat, Imaginary Friends, The Adventures of Nicolas Nickleby, The Comedy of Errors, Macbeth, The Voysey Inheritance, The Ebony Tower, The Finding, The Return of Sam McCloud, Charles & Diana: Unhappily Ever After, The Tower, The Possession of Michael D. *Series*: Cheers, Singles, M.A.N.T.I.S.

REESE, DELLA
Actress, Singer. b. Detroit, MI, July 6, 1932. r.n. Deloreese Patricia Early. e. Wayne St. Univ. As teen toured with Mahalia Jackson. Began recording in 1950's. Hit songs include Don't You Know.
PICTURES: Let's Rock!, Psychic Killer, Harlem Nights, The Distinguished Gentleman, A Thin Line Between Love and Hate.
TELEVISION: *Series*: The Della Reese Show, Chico and the Man, It Takes Two, Charlie & Company, The Royal Family, Touched by an Angel. *Guest*: The Ed Sullivan Show, Sanford and Son, The Rookies, McCloud, Welcome Back Kotter, The Love Boat, Night Court, The A-Team. *Movies*: The Voyage of the Yes, Twice in a Lifetime, The Return of Joe Forrester, Nightmare in Badham County. *Mini-Series*: Roots: The Next Generations.

REEVE, CHRISTOPHER
Actor. b. New York, NY, Sept. 25, 1952. e. Cornell U., B.A.; graduate work at Juilliard. Stage debut at McCarter Theatre in Princeton at age 9. B'way debut with Katharine Hepburn in A Matter of Gravity.
THEATER: *NY*: A Matter of Gravity, My Life, Fifth of July, The Marriage of Figaro, A Winter's Tale, Love Letters. *LA*: Summer and Smoke. *Williamstown*: The Front Page, Mesmer, Richard Corey, Royal Family, The Seagull, The Greeks, Holiday, Camino Real, John Brown's Body, Death Takes a Holiday, The Guardsman. *Regional*: The Irregular Verb to Love, Beggar's Opera, Troilus and Cressida, The Love Cure. *London debut*: The Aspern Papers.
PICTURES: Gray Lady Down (debut, 1978), Superman, Somewhere in Time, Superman II, Deathtrap, Monsignor, Superman III, The Bostonians, The Aviator, Street Smart, Superman IV: The Quest for Peace (also co-story), Switching Channels, Noises Off, Morning Glory, The Remains of the Day, Above Suspicion, Speechless, Village of the Damned.
TELEVISION: *Series*: Love of Life. *Mini-Series*: Kidnapped. *Movies*: Anna Karenina, The Great Escape II: The Untold Story, The Rose and the Jackal, Bump in the Night, Death Dreams, Mortal Sins, Nightmare in the Daylight, The Sea Wolf, Black Fox. *Specials*: Faerie Tale Theatre (Sleeping Beauty), The Last Ferry Home, Earth and the American Dream. *Guest*: Tales From the Crypt.

REEVES, KEANU
Actor. b. Beirut, Lebanon, Sept. 2, 1964. Lived in Australia and NY before family settled in Toronto. e. Toronto's High School for the Performing Arts, then continued training at Second City Workshop. Made Coca-Cola commercial at 16. At 18 studied at Hedgerow Theatre in PA for summer. Professional debut on Hanging In, CBC local Toronto TV show. Toronto stage debut in Wolf Boy; later on stage in Romeo and Juliet, Hamlet.
PICTURES: Youngblood (debut, 1986), River's Edge, The Night Before, Permanent Record, The Prince of Pennsylvania, Dangerous Liaisons, Bill and Ted's Excellent Adventure, Parenthood, I Love You to Death, Tune in Tomorrow, Point Break, Bill and Ted's Bogus Journey, My Own Private Idaho, Bram Stoker's Dracula, Much Ado About Nothing, Freaked (cameo), Even Cowgirls Get the Blues, Little Buddha, Speed, Johnny Mnemonic, A Walk in the Clouds, Chain Reaction, Feeling Minnesota.
TELEVISION: *Movies*: Act of Vengeance, Under the Influence, Brotherhood of Justice, Babes In Toyland. *Specials*: I Wish I Were Eighteen Again, Life Under Water. *Guest*: The Tracey Ullman Show.

REEVES, STEVE
Actor. b. Glasgow, MT, Jan. 21, 1926. Delivered newspapers before winning body building titles Mr. Pacific, Mr. America, Mr. World, Mr. Universe. On stage in Kismet, The Vamp, Wish You Were Here.
PICTURES: Athena (debut, 1954), The Hidden Face, Jail Bait, Hercules, Hercules Unchained, Goliath and the Barbarians, The White Warrior, The Giant of Marathon, Morgan the Pirate, Thief of Baghdad, The Last Days of Pompeii, Duel of the Titans, The Trojan Horse, The Avenger (The Last Glories of Troy), The Slave (Son of Spartacus), The Shortest Day, Sandokan the Great, A Long Ride From Hell.

REGNIER, NATACHA
Actress. b. in Belgium.
PICTURES: The Motorcycle Girl, Le nid tombe de l'oiseau, Dis-moi oiu..., Cecile mon enfant, Encore, La Mouette, The Dreamlife of Angels (Cannes Film Fest. Award, Best Actress, 1998).

REHME, ROBERT G.
Executive. b. Cincinnati, OH, May 5, 1935. e. U. of Cincinnati. 1953, mgr., RKO Theatres, Inc., Cincinnati; 1961, adv. mgr., Cincinnati Theatre Co.; 1966, dir. of field adv., United Artists Pictures; 1969, named dir. of pub. and field adv./promotion, Paramount Pictures; 1972, pres., BR Theatres and v.p., April Fools Films, gen. mgr. Tri-State Theatre Service; 1976, v.p. & gen. sls. mgr., New World Pictures; 1978, joined Avco Embassy Pictures as sr. v.p. & COO, then named exec. v.p.; 1979, named pres., Avco Embassy Pictures, Inc.; 1981, joined Universal Pictures as pres. of distrib. & marketing; 1982, named pres. of Universal Pictures; 1983, joined New World Pictures as co-chmn. & CEO; elected pres., Academy Foundation, 1988; pres. Foundation of Motion Picture Pioneers, 1989; 1st v.p., AMPAS; 1989, partner, Neufeld/Rehme prods. at Paramount; 1992, pres. of Academy of Motion Picture Arts & Sciences.
PICTURES: Flight of the Intruder, Necessary Roughness, Patriot Games, Gettysburg, Beverly Hills Cop III, Clear and Present Danger, Woman Undone, Blind Faith, Lost in Space, Black Dog, Joan of Arc: The Virgin Warrior, The General's Daughter.
TELEVISION: Movies: Gridock, For the Children: The Irvine Fertility Scandal, Escape, Human Cargo. Series: Lightning Force.

REID, TIM
Actor. b. Norfolk, CA, Dec. 19, 1944. m. actress Daphne Maxwell. Started as half of comedy team of Tim and Tom in 1969, before becoming solo stand-up comedian. Published photo/poetry collection As I Feel It, 1982.
PICTURES: Dead Bang, The Fourth War. Prod, dir. Once Upon A Time...When We Were Colored.
TELEVISION: Series: Easy Does It... Starring Frankie Avalon, The Marilyn McCoo and Billy Davis Jr. Show, The Richard Pryor Show, WKRP in Cincinnati, Teachers Only, Simon and Simon, Frank's Place (also co-exec. prod.), Snoops (also co-exec. prod.), Sister Sister, Save Our Streets. Guest: That's My Mama, Rhoda, What's Happening, Matlock. Movies: Perry Mason: The Case of the Silenced Singer, Stephen King's IT, Race to Freedom: The Underground Railroad (also co-exec. prod.), Simon & Simon: In Trouble Again. Special: Mastergate.

REILLY, CHARLES NELSON
Actor, Director. b. New York, NY, Jan. 13. 1931. e. U. of CT. On Broadway mostly in comedy roles before turning to TV and films. Recently directed stage plays.
THEATER: As actor: Bye Bye Birdie (debut), How to Succeed in Business Without Really Trying (Tony Award, 1962), Hello Dolly!, Skyscraper, God's Favorite. Acted in 22 off-B'way plays. Founded musical comedy dept. HB Studios. Conceived and dir.: The Belle of Amherst, Paul Robeson, The Nerd (dir.). Resident dir.: Burt Reynolds' Jupiter Theatre.
PICTURES: A Face in the Crowd, Two Tickets to Paris, The Tiger Makes Out, Cannonball Run II, Body Slam, All Dogs Go to Heaven (voice), Rock-a-Doodle (voice), A Troll in Central Park (voice).
TELEVISION: Series: The Steve Lawrence Show, The Ghost and Mrs. Muir, Dean Martin Presents The Golddiggers, Liddsville, Arnie, It Pays to Be Ignorant (1973-74), Match Game P.M., Sweethearts (game show host). Guest: Tonight Show (guest host), Dean Martin Show. Movies: Call Her Mom, The Three Kings, Bandit, Bandit Goes Country. Special: Wind in the Wire.

REILLY, MICHAEL
Executive. Pres., Variety Clubs International.

REINAUER, RICHARD
Executive. b. Chicago, IL, April 28, 1926. e. U. of Illinois, grad. 1952. Prod., dir., freelance, 1952-59; bus. mgr., asst. prod., Showcase Theatre Evanston, 1952; prod., dir., NBC, Chicago, 1953-55; film dir., Kling Studios, 1956; broadcast supervisor. Foote Cone & Belding, 1956-59; dir., radio, TV & m.p., American Medical Assoc., 1959-64; pres., Communications Counselors,

1963-64; exec. dir., TV Arts & Sciences Foundation, 1964; pres., Acad. of TV Arts & Sciences, Chicago Chapter, 1970-72; assoc. prod. & asst. dir. Wild Kingdom & asst. to pres., Don Meier Prods., 1965-1988. Member: Illinois Nature Preserve Commission. Lifetime member: Acad. of TV Arts & Sciences, Pres. Pinewood Prods. Film Co. Communications consultant and advisor.

REINER, CARL
Actor, Director, Writer, Producer. b. New York, NY, March 20, 1922. Son is actor-director-writer Rob Reiner. Comedian on B'way: Call Me Mr., Inside U.S.A., Alive and Kicking. Author (novels): Enter Laughing, All Kinds of Love, Continue Laughing. Playwright: Something Different.
PICTURES: Actor only: Happy Anniversary, Gidget Goes Hawaiian, It's a Mad Mad Mad Mad World, The Russians Are Coming the Russians Are Coming, Don't Worry We'll Think of a Title, A Guide for the Married Man, Generation, The End, The Spirit of '76. Writer-Actor: The Gazebo, The Thrill of It All (also co-prod.), The Art of Love. Director: Enter Laughing (also co-s.p.), The Comic (also s.p., actor), Where's Poppa?, Oh God! (also actor), The One and Only, The Jerk (also actor), Dead Men Don't Wear Plaid (also co-s.p., actor), The Man With Two Brains (also co-s.p.), All of Me, Summer Rental, Summer School (also actor), Bert Rigby You're a Fool (also s.p.), Sibling Rivalry, Fatal Instinct (also actor), That Old Feeling.
TELEVISION: Series: The Fashion Story, The Fifty-Fourth Street Revue, Eddie Condon's Floor Show, Your Show of Shows (also writer), Droodles (panelist), Caesar's Hour (also writer; 2 Emmy Awards for supporting actor, 1956, 1957), Sid Caesar Invites You, Keep Talking, Dinah Shore Chevy Show (writer), Take a Good Look (panelist), The Dick Van Dyke Show (also creator-prod.-dir.-writer; 5 Emmy Awards: writing: 1962, 1963, 1964, producing: 1965, 1966), Art Linkletter Show, The Celebrity Game (host), The New Dick Van Dyke Show (creator-prod.-writer), Good Heavens (also exec. prod.), Sunday Best (host). Movies: Medical Story, Skokie. Guest: Comedy Spot, Judy Garland Show, Burke's Law, That Girl, Night Gallery, Faerie Tale Theatre (Pinocchio), It's Garry Shandling's Show, Mad About You (Emmy Award, 1995). Special: The Sid Caesar-Imogene Coca-Carl Reiner-Howard Morris Special (Emmy Award for writing, 1967).
RECORDINGS: Carl Reiner and Mel Brooks, The 2000 Year Old Man, The 2001 Year Old Man, 2013 Year Old Man, Continue Laughing, A Connecticut Yankee in King Arthur's Court, Miracle on 34th Street, Jack and the Beanstalk, Aesop's Fables, The Prince and the Pauper.

REINER, ROB
Actor, Director, Writer. b. New York, NY, March 6, 1947. Father is actor-writer-director-producer Carl Reiner. Worked as actor with regional theatres and improvisational comedy troupes. Wrote for the Smothers Brothers Comedy Hour. Breakthrough as actor came in 1971 when signed by Norman Lear for All in the Family. Directorial debut with This Is Spinal Tap, 1984. Co-founder of Castle Rock Entertainment.
PICTURES: Actor: Enter Laughing, Halls of Anger, Where's Poppa?, Summertree, Fire Sale, Throw Momma From the Train, Postcards From the Edge, The Spirit of '76, Sleepless in Seattle, Bullets Over Broadway, Mixed Nuts, Bye Bye Love. Director: This is Spinal Tap (also actor, co-s.p.), The Sure Thing, Stand by Me, The Princess Bride. Dir./Co-Prod.: When Harry Met Sally..., Misery, A Few Good Men (Acad. Award nom. for best picture; DGA nom.), North, The American President, Ghosts of Mississippi.
TELEVISION: Series: All in the Family (2 Emmy Awards: 1974, 1978), Free Country (also co-writer), Morton & Hayes (also co-creator, co-exec. prod.). Movies: Thursday's Game, More Than Friends (also co-writer, co-exec. prod.), Million Dollar Infield (also co-prod., co-writer). Guest: Gomer Pyle, Batman, Beverly Hillbillies, Room 222, Partridge Family, Odd Couple, It's Garry Shandling's Show. Special: But... Seriously (exec. prod.).

REINHOLD, JUDGE
Actor. b. Wilmington, DE, May 21, 1957. r.n. Edward Ernest Reinhold Jr. e. Mary Washington Coll., North Carolina Sch. of Arts. Acted in regional theatres including Burt Reynolds dinner theater in FL before signed to TV contract at Paramount.
PICTURES: Running Scared (debut, 1979), Stripes, Pandemonium, Fast Times at Ridgemont High, Lords of Discipline, Roadhouse 66, Gremlins, Beverly Hills Cop, Head Office, Off Beat, Ruthless People, Beverly Hills Cop II, Vice Versa, Rosalie Goes Shopping, Daddy's Dyin', Enid is Sleeping (Over Her Dead Body), Zandalee, Near Misses, Baby on Board, Bank Robber, Beverly Hills Cop III, The Santa Clause.
TELEVISION: Series: Secret Service Guy. Movies: Survival of Dana, A Matter of Sex, Promised a Miracle, Black Magic, Four Eyes and Six-Guns, Dad the Angel and Me, As Good as Dead, The Wharf Rat. Guest: Seinfeld. Specials: A Step Too Slow, The Willmar Eight, The Parallax Garden.

REISENBACH, SANFORD E.
Executive. e. NYU. Associated with Grey Advertising for 20 years; exec. v.p. and pres./founder of Grey's Leisure & Entertainment division in N.Y. In August, 1979, joined Warner Bros. as exec. v.p. of worldwide adv. & pub.; named pres. worldwide adv. & pub., 1985. Appt. corporate exec. of marketing and planning, Warner Bros., 1989.

REISER, PAUL
Actor. b. New York, NY, Mar. 30, 1957. e. SUNY/Binghamton. Started performing as a stand-up comic in such clubs as Catch a Rising Star, the Improv, and the Comic Strip. Author: Couplehood (1994).
PICTURES: Diner (debut, 1982), Beverly Hills Cop, Aliens, Beverly Hills Cop II, Cross My Heart, Crazy People, The Marrying Man, Mr. Write, Bye Bye Love.
TELEVISION: Series: My Two Dads, Mad About You. Special: Paul Reiser—Out on a Whim. Guest: The Tonight Show, Late Night With David Letterman. Movies: Sunset Limousine, The Tower. Pilots: Diner, Just Married.

REISNER, ALLEN
Director. b. New York, NY.
PICTURES: The Day They Gave the Babies Away, St. Louis Blues, All Mine to Give.
TELEVISION: Movies/Specials: Captain and the Kings, Mary Jane Harper Cried Last Night, Your Money or Your Wife, To Die in Paris, The Clift, Skag, They're Playing Our Song, The Gentleman From Seventh Avenue, Escape of Pierre Mendes-France, Deliverance of Sister Cecelia, The Sound of Silence. Series: Murder She Wrote, Twilight Zone, Hardcastle & McCormick, Airwolf, The Mississippi, Hawaii Five-O, Blacke's Magic, Law and Harry McGraw, Playhouse 90, Studio One, Climax, United States Steel Hour, Suspense, Danger, etc.

REISS, JEFFREY C.
Executive. b. Brooklyn, NY, April 14, 1942. e. Washington U., St. Louis, B.A., 1963. Consultant at NYU and Manhattanville Coll. and instructor at Brooklyn Coll. before entering industry. Agent in literary dept. for General Artists Corp., 1966. Supervised development in NY of Tandem Prods. for Norman Lear, 1968. Produced off-B'way plays 1968-70. Dir. of program acquistion devel. for Cartridge TV, Inc. (mfg. of first home video cassette players-recorders), 1970-73. Joined ABC Entertainment as director of network feature films, 1973-75. Founder and pres., Showtime Pay TV Network, 1976-80. Co-founder, pres. & CEO, Cable Health Network, 1981-83. 1983, named vice chmn. & CEO, Lifetime Cable Network following Cable Health Network merger with Daytime. Chmn. of the board, pres. & CEO, Reiss Media Enterprises, Inc. 1984. Founder & chmn. of board, Request Television (pay-per-view svc.), 1985.

REISS, STUART A.
Set Decorator. b. Chicago, IL, July 15, 1921. e. L.A. High Sch., 1939. Property man, 20th-Fox, 1939-42; U.S. Army Air Corps, 1942-45; joined 20th-Fox as set decorator in 1945. Worked on over 30 tv shows and over 100 motion pictures, receiving 6 Academy Award noms. and 2 Oscars.
PICTURES: Titanic, How to Marry a Millionaire, Hell and High Water, There's No Business Like Show Business, Soldier of Fortune, The Seven Year Itch, Man in the Grey Flannel Suit, Teen Age Rebel, The Diary of Anne Frank (Academy Award, 1959), What a Way to Go, Fantastic Voyage (Academy Award, 1966), Doctor Doolittle, Oh God!, The Swarm, Beyond the Poseidon Adventure, Carbon Copy, All the Marbles, The Man Who Loved Women, Micki and Maude, A Fine Mess.

REITMAN, IVAN
Director, Producer. b. Komarmo, Czechoslovakia, Oct. 26, 1946. Moved to Canada at age 4. e. McMaster U. Attended National Film Board's Summer Institute directing three short films including Orientation (1968) which received theatrical distribution. Produced Canadian TV show in 1970s with Dan Aykroyd as announcer.
THEATER: Prod.: The National Lampoon Show, The Magic Show, Merlin (also dir.).
PICTURES: Dir./Prod.: Foxy Lady (debut, 1971; also edit., music), Cannibal Girls, Meatballs (dir. only), Stripes, Ghostbusters, Legal Eagles (also co-story), Twins, Ghostbusters II, Kindergarten Cop, Dave, Junior, Father's Day, Six Days Seven Nights. Prod. only: Columbus of Sex, They Came From Within (Shivers), Death Weekend, Rabid (co-exec. prod.), Blackout, National Lampoon's Animal House, Heavy Metal, Spacehunter: Adventures in the Forbidden Zone (exec. prod.), Big Shots (exec. prod.), Casual Sex? (exec. prod.), Feds (exec. prod.), Stop! Or My Mom Will Shoot, Beethoven (exec. prod.), Beethoven's 2nd (exec. prod.), Space Jam, Commandments (exec. prod.), Private Parts, Ghostbusters III.
TELEVISION: Series: Delta House.

RELPH, MICHAEL
Producer, Director, Writer, Designer. 1942, became art dir. Ealing Studios then assoc. prod. to Michael Balcon on The Captive Heart, Frieda, Kind Hearts and Coronets, Saraband (also designed: Oscar nom.). 1948 appt. producer and formed prod/dir. partnership Basil Dearden (until 1972). 1971-76, Governor, Brit. Film Institute. Chairman BFI Prod. Board. Chairman Film Prod. Assoc. of G.B.; member Films Council.
PICTURES: For Ealing: The Blue Lamp (BFA Award, 1950), I Believe in You, The Gentle Gunman, The Square Ring, The Rainbow Jacket, Out of the Clouds, The Ship That Died of Shame, Davy, The Smallest Show on Earth (for Brit. Lion), Violent Playground (for Rank), Rockets Galore (Island Fling), Sapphire (BFA Award, 1959). 1960 Founder Dir. Allied Film Makers: Prod. The League of Gentlemen, Man in the Moon (co-s.p.), Victim, Life For Ruth (Walk in the Shadow). Also produced: Secret Partner, All Night Long, The Mind Benders, A Place To Go (s.p.), Woman of Straw (co-s.p.), Masquerade (co-s.p.), The Assassination Bureau (prod., s.p., designer), The Man Who Haunted Himself (prod., co-s.p.). 1978, exec. in chg. prod., Kendon Films, Ltd. Exec. prod., Scum, 1982. Co-prod., An Unsuitable Job for a Woman. 1984, exec. prod.: Treasure Houses of Britain; TV series, prod., Heavenly Pursuits, 1985-86; Gospel According to Vic (U.S.). Prod. Consultant: Torrents of Spring.

RELPH, SIMON
Producer. b. London, Eng., April 13, 1940. Entered industry 1961.
PICTURES: Reds (exec. prod.), The Return of the Soldier, Privates on Parade, The Ploughman's Lunch, Secret Places, Laughterhouse (exec. prod.), Wetherby, Comrades, Enchanted April (exec. prod.), Damage (coprod.), The Secret Rapture, Camilla, Look Me In The Eye, Blue Juice, The Slab Boys, The Land Girls.

RELYEA, ROBERT E.
Producer, Executive. b. Santa Monica, CA, May 3, 1930. e. UCLA, B.S., 1952. In Army 1953-55. Entered industry in 1955; asst. dir. on The Magnificent Seven and West Side Story; assoc. prod. and 2nd unit dir. on The Great Escape; partnered with Steve McQueen as exec. prod. on Bullitt and The Reivers. 1979-82, exec. v.p. with Melvin Simon Prods. Served as exec. v.p. in chg. world wide prod., Keith Barish Prods. 1983-85. Served as sr. v.p. prod., Lorimar Prods. 1985-90. Named sr. v.p. features prod. management, Paramount Pictures Motion Picture Gp., 1989.
PICTURES: Exec. Prod.: Bullitt, The Reivers, Day of the Dolphin. Prod.: Love at First Bite, My Bodyguard, Porky's, Blame It On Rio (assoc. prod.), Last Action Hero (co-prod.). Actor: Seven.

REMAR, JAMES
Actor. b. Boston, MA, Dec. 31, 1953. Studied acting at NY's Neighborhood Playhouse and with Stella Adler. Appeared on NY stage in Yo-Yo, Early Dark, Bent, California Dog Fight.
PICTURES: On the Yard (debut, 1979), The Warriors, Cruising, The Long Riders, Windwalker, Partners, 48 HRS, The Cotton Club, The Clan of the Cave Bear, Band of the Hand, Quiet Cool, Rent-a-Cop, The Dream Team, Drugstore Cowboy, Tales from the Darkside, Silence Like Glass, White Fang, Fatal Instinct, Blink, Renaissance Man, Miracle on 34th Street, Boys on the Side, Session Man (Academy Award, Best Action Short, 1991), Across the Moon, Judge Dredd (unbilled), The Quest, The Phantom, Robo-Warriors, Tale From The Darkside: The Movie, Wild Bill, Exquisite Tenderness (The Surgeon), The Phantom, Born Bad, Mortal Kombat Annihilation.
TELEVISION: Movies: The Mystic Warrior, Desperado, Deadlock, Brotherhood of the Gun, Fatal Charm, Indecency, Night Vision. Guest: Hill Street Blues, Miami Vice, The Equalizer, The Hitchhiker, Tales From The Crypt, Total Security.

REMBUSCH, MICHAEL J.
Executive. b. Indianapolis, IN, April 8, 1950. e. Ball State U. Son of Trueman T. Rembusch. Began working for father's circuit, Syndicate Theatres, Inc., in 1967. From 1970-80, managed various theatres in circuit. 1980-85, v.p., operations. 1985-90, acquired Heaston circuit (Indianapolis). Became pres., Syndicate Theatres, Inc. 1987-90, chmn, Indiana Film Commission. 1992 to present, pres., Theatre Owners of Indiana.

REMBUSCH, TRUEMAN T.
Exhibitor. b. Shelbyville, IN, July 27, 1909. f. Frank J. Rembusch, pioneer exhibitor. Inventor & manufacturer Glass Mirror Screen. e. U. of Notre Dame Sch. of Commerce, 1928. m. Mary Agnes Finneran. Ent. m.p. ind., 1928, servicing sound equip., father's circuit; became mgr., 1932; elect. bd. of dir., Allied Theatre Owners of Ind., 1936-45, pres. 1945-51, 1952-53;

dir. chmn. Allied TV Committee, 1945-50; pres. Allied States Assn., 1950-51; 1952, named by Allied as one of triumvirate heading COMPO; 1953, named by Gov. of Indiana as dir. State Fair Board; elected chmn. Joint Com. on Toll TV, 1954; currently pres. Syndicate Theatres, Inc., Franklin, Ind; member, Notre Dame Club of Indianapolis (Man of Yr., 1950); BPOE, 4th Degree K of C, Meridian Hills Country Club, Marco Island Country Club. American Radio Relay League (amateur & commerce, licenses); OX5 Aviation Pioneers; awarded patent, recording 7 counting device, 1951; dir. Theatre Owners of Indiana; dir. to NATO; dir. NATO member ad hoc comm; 1972 chair., NATO Statistical Committee; 1976, NITE Award service to Independent Exhibition.

REMSEN, BERT
Actor. b. Glen Cove, NY, Feb. 25, 1925. e. Ithaca Coll.
PICTURES: Pork Chop Hill, Kid Galahad, Moon Pilot, Brewster McCloud, Thieves Like us, Baby Blue Marine, McCabe and Mrs. Miller, Sweet Hostage, California Split, Nashville, Tarantulas, Buffalo Bill and the Indians, A Wedding, The Rose, Uncle Joe Shannon, Carny, Borderline, Second Hand Hearts, Joni, Inside Moves, Looking to Get Out, The Sting II, Lies, Independence Day, Code of Silence, Stand Alone, Eye of the Tiger, South of Reno, Remote Control, Vietnam Texas, Miss Firecracker, Daddy's Dyin'...Who's Got the Will?, Dick Tracy, Only the Lonely, Evil Spirits, The Player, The Bodyguard, Jack the Bear, Army of One, Maverick.
TELEVISION: Series: Gibbsville, It's a Living, Dallas. Movies: Who Is Julia?, The Awakening Land, Burning Rage, Crazy Times, Hobson's Choice, If Tomorrow Comes, Love For Rent, Mothers Against Drunk Driving, Little Ladies of the Night, Memorial Day, Maid for Each Other, There Was a Little Boy, In the Shadows Someone's Watching, Rise and Walk: The Dennis Byrd Story. Guest: Matlock, Jake and the Fatman. Mini-Series: Space.

RENO, JEAN
Actor. r.n. Juan Moreno b. Casablanca, Morocco July 30, 1948. To France in early 1970's to serve in French military. Began acting in Paris with theatre workshop, then established his own travelling acting company.
PICTURES: Claire de Femme, Le Dernier Combat, Subway, Signes Exterieurs de Richesse, Notre Histoire, I Love You, The Big Blue, La Femme Nikita, L'homme au Masque d'Or, L'Operation Corned Beef, Loulou Graffiti, The Professional (Leon), French Kiss, The Visitors (also s.p.), Beyond the Clouds, Mission Impossible, Le Jaguar, Witch Way Love, Roseanna's Grave, Ronin, Le Couloirs du Temps, Godzilla, Tripwire.

RESNAIS, ALAIN
Director. b. Cannes, France, June 3, 1922. Began career as asst. dir. to Nicole Vedres on compilation of film for Paris 1900. During '50s worked as asst. editor and editor; experimented with making his own 16mm films. Directed or co-dir. several short films: Van Gogh, Gauguin, Guernica, The Statues Also Die, Night and Fog, etc.
PICTURES: Hiroshima Mon Amour (feature debut, 1959), Last Year at Marienbad, Muriel, La Guerre Est Finie (The War Is Over), Je t'Aime Je t'Aime (also co-s.p.), Stavisky, Providence, Mon Oncle d'Amerique, Life Is a Bed of Roses, L'Amour a Mort (Love Unto Death), Melo (also s.p.), I Want to Go Home, Smoking/No Smoking, Same Old Song.

RESNICK, JOEL H.
Executive. b. New York, NY, April 28, 1936. e. U. of PA, B.A., 1958; NY Law Sch. 1961, admitted to NY State Bar. 1962 received Masters of Law degree in taxation; 1961-66 served as associate with NY law firm, Phillips Nizer Benjamin Krim & Ballon; Was in-house counsel to United Artists Corp. 1967, joined UA as spec. asst. to the sr. v.p. & gen. mgr.; 1970, moved to American Multi-Cinema, Inc., Kansas City, as asst. to pres.; 1972, named v.p. in chg. development; 1976, promoted to v.p. in chg. film development; 1977, named exec. v.p.; 1983, elected exec. v.p. & dir., AMC Entertainment; 1984, appt. to office of pres. as chmn. & CEO, film mktg.; 1986, resigned to join Orion Pictures Distribution Corp. as pres.; has served as co-chmn. NATO trade practices comm. since 1979. 1982 elected pres., NATO; 1984, became chmn. NATO bd.; 1989, v.p. Foundation of Motion Picture Pioneers; 1990, resigned from Orion; pres., GKC Theatres, Springfield, IL, 1991-92; Cinemark Theatres, Intl. Development, 1994-.

REUBENS, PAUL (PEE-WEE HERMAN)
Actor, Writer. r.n. Paul Rubenfeld. Professional name Paul Reubens. b. Peekskill, NY, Aug. 27, 1952. Raised in Sarasota, FL. e. Boston U., California Inst. of the Arts (1976). Pee-wee character made debut, 1978 at Groundlings, improvisational theater, Los Angeles which gave birth to The Pee-wee Herman Show, a live show which gave 5 months of sold-out performances at the L.A. rock club, Roxy, and was later taped for HBO special. Guest appearances on Late Night With David Letterman, The Gong Show, 227, Tonight Show, Mork & Mindy, Joan Rivers' The Late Show, and The Dating Game.

PICTURES: Midnight Madness, The Blues Brothers, Cheech & Chong's Next Movie, Cheech and Chong's Nice Dreams, Pandemonium, Meatballs Part II, Pee-wee's Big Adventure (also co-s.p.), Flight of the Navigator (voice), Back to the Beach, Big Top Pee-wee (also co-s.p., co-prod.), Batman Returns, Buffy the Vampire Slayer, Tim Burton's The Nightmare Before Christmas (voice), Dunston Checks In, Matilda, Buddy, Doctor Doolittle (voice).
TELEVISION: Series: Pee-wee's Playhouse (also creator, co-dir., co-writer, exec. prod.; 12 Emmy Awards). Specials: Pinocchio (Faerie Tale Theatre), Pee-wee Herman Show, Pee-wee's Playhouse Christmas Special (also exec. prod., co-dir. co-writer). Guest: Murphy Brown.

REVELL, GRAEME
Composer.
PICTURES: Spontaneous Combustion, Dead Calm, Till There Was You, Child's Play 2, Love Crimes, Until the End of the Crime, Traces of Red, Deadly, The People Under the Stairs, The Hand That Rocks the Cradle, Hear No Evil, Ghost in the Machine, The Crush, Body of Evidence, Boxing Helena, Hard Target, Street Fighter, S.F.W., No Escape, The Crow, Killer: A Journal of Murder, The Basketball Diaries, Tank Girl, Mighty Morphin Power Rangers: The Movie, The Tie That Binds, Strange Days, From Dusk Till Dawn, Race the Sun, The Craft, Fled, The Crow: City of Angels, Chinese Box, The Saint, Spawn, Suicide Kings, Lulu on the Bridge, The Big Hit, The Negotiator, Phoenix.

REVILL, CLIVE
Actor. r.n. Selsby. b. Wellington, New Zealand, Apr. 18, 1930. e. Rongotal Coll., Victoria U.
THEATER: Irma La Douce, The Mikado, Oliver, Marat/Sade, Jew of Malta, Sherry, Chichester Season, The Incomparable Max, Sherlock Holmes, Lolita, Pirates of Penzance, Mystery of Edwin Drood, My Fair Lady, Bandido.
PICTURES: Reach for the Sky, The Headless Ghost, Bunny Lake Is Missing, Once Upon a Tractor, Modesty Blaise, A Fine Madness, Kaleidoscope, The Double Man, Fathom, Italian Secret Service, Nobody Runs Forever, Shoes of the Fisherman, Assassination Bureau, The Private Life of Sherlock Holmes, The Buttercup Chain, A Severed Head, Boulevard de Rhum, Avanti!, Escape to the Sun, Ghost in the Noonday Sun, The Legend of Hell House, The Little Prince, The Black Windmill, One of Our Dinosaurs Is Missing, Galileo, Matilda, Zorro the Gay Blade, Transformers (voice), Rumpelstiltskin, The Emperor's New Clothes, Mack the Knife, CHUD II: Bud the Chud, Frog Prince, Let Him Have It, Robin Hood: Men in Tights, Crime and Punishment, Arabian Knight (voice), The Wacky Adventures of Dr. Boris and Nurse Shirley, Dracula—Dead and Loving It!, Possums.
TELEVISION: Chicken Soup with Barley, Volpone, Bam Pow Zapp, Candida, Platonov, A Bit of Vision, Mill Hill, The Piano Player, Hopcroft in Europe, A Sprig of Broome, Ben Franklin in Paris, Pinocchio, The Great Houdini, Show Business Hall of Fame, Feather and Father, Winner Take All, The New Avengers, Licking Hitler, Columbo, Centennial, A Man Called Sloane, Nobody's Perfect, Marya, Moviola, Diary of Anne Frank, Mikado, The Sorcerer, Wizards & Warriors, George Washington, Murder She Wrote, Faerie Tale Theatre, Twilight Zone, Newhart, Hunter, Star Trek, The Sea Wolf, Babylon 5, Fortune Hunter, The Preston Episodes (series), Murphy Brown.

REYNOLDS, BURT
Actor, Director. b. Waycross, GA, Feb. 11, 1936. Former Florida State U. football star; TV and film stunt performer. Won fame as actor on TV in series Riverboat. Founded the Burt Reynolds Dinner Theater in Jupiter, FL, 1979. Autobiography: My Life (1994).
THEATER: Mister Roberts (NY City Center), Look We've Come Through (B'way debut, 1956), The Rainmaker.
PICTURES: Angel Baby (debut, 1961), Armored Command, Operation CIA, Navajo Joe, Fade In, Impasse, Shark, Sam Whiskey, 100 Rifles, Skullduggery, Fuzz, Deliverance, Everything You Always Wanted To Know About Sex, Shamus, White Lightning, The Man Who Loved Cat Dancing, The Longest Yard, W.W. & The Dixie Dancekings, At Long Last Love, Hustle, Lucky Lady, Gator (also dir.), Silent Movie, Nickelodeon, Smokey and the Bandit, Semi-Tough, The End (also dir.), Hooper, Starting Over, Rough Cut, Smokey and the Bandit II, Cannonball Run, Paternity, Sharky's Machine (also dir.), The Best Little Whorehouse in Texas, Best Friends, Stroker Ace, Smokey and the Bandit III (cameo), The Man Who Loved Women, Cannonball Run II, City Heat, Stick (also dir.), Uphill All the Way (cameo), Heat, Malone, Rent-a-Cop, Switching Channels, Physical Evidence, Breaking In, All Dogs Go to Heaven (voice), Modern Love, The Player (cameo), Cop and a Half, The Maddening, Devil Inside, Meet Wally Sparks, Striptease, Mad Dog Time, Citizen Ruth, Boogie Nights (Golden Globe Award, Chicago Film Crits. Award, LA Film Crits. Award, NY Film Circle Crits. Award, Best Supporting Actor, 1997).
TELEVISION: Series: Riverboat, Gunsmoke, Hawk, Dan August, Out of This World (voice), B.L. Stryker (also co-exec. prod.), Evening Shade (Emmy Award, 1991). Movies: Hunters Are for Killing, Run Simon Run, The Man Upstairs (co-exec. prod. only), The Man From Left Field (also dir.). Host: The Story of Hollywood. Special: Wind in the Wire. Dir.: Alfred Hitchcock Presents (1985).

REYNOLDS, DEBBIE
Actress. r.n. Mary Frances Reynolds. b. El Paso, TX, April 1, 1932. Daughter is actress Carrie Fisher. e. Burbank & John Burroughs H.S., Burbank, CA. With Burbank Youth Symphony during h.s.; beauty contest winner (Miss Burbank) 1948; signed by Warner Bros.; on stage in Personal Appearances, Blis-Hayden Theater. Voted Star of Tomorrow, 1952. Autobiography: Debbie: My Life (1988).
THEATER: B'way: Irene, Woman of the Year.
PICTURES: June Bride (debut, 1948), The Daughter of Rosie O'Grady, Three Little Words, Two Weeks With Love, Mr. Imperium, Singin' in the Rain, Skirts Ahoy, I Love Melvin, Give a Girl a Break, The Affairs of Dobie Gillis, Susan Slept Here, Athena, Hit the Deck, The Tender Trap, The Catered Affair, Bundle of Joy, Tammy and the Bachelor, This Happy Feeling, The Mating Game, Say One for Me, It Started with a Kiss, The Gazebo, The Rat Race, Pepe (cameo), The Pleasure of His Company, The Second Time Around, How the West Was Won, My Six Loves, Mary Mary, Goodbye Charlie, The Unsinkable Molly Brown (Acad. Award nom.), The Singing Nun, Divorce American Style, How Sweet It Is, What's the Matter with Helen?, Charlotte's Web (voice), That's Entertainment!, The Bodyguard (cameo), Heaven and Earth, That's Entertainment III, Mother, In & Out.
TELEVISION: Series: The Debbie Reynolds Show, Aloha Paradise. Movies: Sadie and Son, Perry Mason: The Case of the Musical Murders, Battling for Baby. Special: Jack Paar Is Alive and Well.

REYNOLDS, GENE
Actor, Executive, Producer. b. Cleveland, OH, April 4, 1925. Acted from 1936-55. Currently pres. Director's Guild of America, Inc.
PICTURES: Actor: Thank You, Jeeves; Sins of Man, Thunder Trail, In Old Chicago, The Californian, Of Human Hearts, Love Finds Andy Hardy, The Crowd Roars, Boys Town, The Spirit of Culver, The Flying Irishman, Bad Little Angel, They Shall Have Music, Santa Fe Trail, The Mortal Storm, Gallant Sons, The Blue Bird; Edison, the Man; Andy Hardy's Private Secretary, Adventure in Washington, The Penalty, The Tuttles of Tahiti, Junior G-men of the Air, Eagle Squadron, Jungle Patrol, The Big Cat, Slattery's Hurricane, 99 River Street, The Country Girl, The Bridges at Toko-Ri, Down Three Dark Streets.
TELEVISION: Director: Series: Wanted: Dead or Alive, My Three Sons, Hogan's Heroes, F Troop, The Ghost and Mrs. Muir, M*A*S*H (also exec. prod.), Lou Grant (also exec. prod), Christy, Touched by and Angel. Movies: In Defense of Kids, Doing Life (also exec. prod.), The Whereabouts of Jenny (also prod.).

REYNOLDS, KEVIN
Director, Writer. b. 1950. e. Texas Marine Acad., Trinity Univ., Baylor Univ. (law degree), USC film school. Student film Proof led to offer to do expanded feature version subsequently retitled Fandango.
PICTURES: Red Dawn (co-s.p.). Director: Fandango (dir. debut, 1985; also s.p.), The Beast, Robin Hood: Prince of Thieves, Rapa Nui (also s.p.), Waterworld, 187.

REYNOLDS, SHELDON
Writer, Producer, Director. b. Philadelphia, PA, 1923. e. NYU. Radio-TV writer; programs include My Silent Partner, Robert Q. Lewis Show, We the People, Danger, Adventures of Sherlock Holmes (prod., dir., writer), Dick and the Duchess (prod., dir., writer), Foreign Intrigue (dir., prod., writer). TV Special: Sophia Loren's Rome (dir., writer). Movies: Foreign Intrigue (dir., prod., s.p.), Assignment to Kill (dir., s.p.).

REYNOLDS, STUART
Producer. b. Chicago, IL, March 22, 1907. e. Chicago law schools. Adv. exec., Lord and Thomas, BBDO. General Mills; sales exec. Don Lee-Mutual; formed Stuart Reynolds Prod., TV films. Now motion picture & TV program consultant.
TELEVISION: General Electric Theatre, Cavalcade of America, Your Jeweler's Showcase, Wild Bill Hickok. Producer and world-wide distributor of educational/training films; Eye of the Beholder.

REZNOR, TRENT
Composer. r.n. Michael Trent Reznor. b. Mercer, PA, May 17, 1965. Head of Nothing Records, a division of Interscope Records. Creator of the industrial/punk/rock band Nine Inch Nails. Composed music and sounds for id Software's computergame QUAKE.
PICTURES: Light of Day (actor), Seven, Natural Born Killers, Lost Highway.

RHAMES, VING
Actor. e. Juilliard Sch. of Drama.
THEATER: B'way: The Boys of Winter. Off-B'way: Map of the World, Short Eyes, Richard III, Ascension Day. Europe: Ajax.
PICTURES: Native Son, Patty Hearst, Casualties of War, Jacob's Ladder, The Long Walk Home, Flight of the Intruder, Homicide, The People Under the Stairs, Stop! Or My Mom Will Shoot, Bound by Honor, Dave, The Saint of Fort Washington,

Pulp Fiction, Drop Squad, Kiss of Death, Mission: Impossible, Striptease, Rosewood, Con Air, Dangerous Ground, The Split, Out of Sight, Sonny Liston, Mission: Impossible 2, Duets, Bringing Out the Dead, Entrapment.
TELEVISION: Series: Another World, Men, ER. Movies: Go Tell It on the Mountain, Rising Son, When You Remember Me, Iran: Days of Crisis, Terror on Track 9, Ed McBain's 87th Precinct: Lightning, Deadly Whispers, Don King: Only in America (Golden Globe Award, 1998). Guest: Miami Vice, Spenser: For Hire, Tour of Duty, Crime Story.

RHODES, CYNTHIA
Actress, Dancer. b. Nashville, TN, Nov. 21, 1956. m. singer Richard Marx. Appeared on many TV specials, inc. Opryland USA, Music Hall America.
PICTURES: Xanadu, One From the Heart, Flashdance, Staying Alive, Runaway, Dirty Dancing, Curse of the Crystal Eye.

RHYS-DAVIES, JOHN
Actor. b. Salisbury, England, 1944. Grew up in Wales and East Africa. Began acting at Truro School in Cornwall at 15. e. U. of East Angelia where he founded school's dramatic society. Worked as teacher before studying at Royal Academy of Dramatic Art, 1969. Appeared in 23 Shakespearean plays.
PICTURES: The Black Windmill, Sphinx, Raiders of the Lost Ark, Victor/Victoria, Sahara, Sword of the Valiant, Best Revenge, King Solomon's Mines, In the Shadow of Kilimanjaro, Firewalker, The Living Daylights, Waxwork, Rising Storm, Indiana Jones and the Last Crusade, Young Toscanini, Journey of Honor, Unnameable II, The Seventh Coin, The Great White Hype.
TELEVISION: Mini-series: Shogun, James Clavell's Noble House, Riley, Ace of Spies, I, Claudius, War and Remembrance. Movies: The Little Match Girl, Sadat, Kim, The Naked Civil Servant, The Trial of the Incredible Hulk, Goddess of Love, The Gifted One, Great Expectations, Desperado, Secret Weapon, Before the Storm, Spy Games, Perry Mason: The Case of the Fatal Framing. Series: Under Cover, The Untouchables, Archaeology, Sliders.

RICCI, CHRISTINA
Actress. b. Santa Monica, CA, 1980. Raised in Long Island, NY, and Montclair, NJ. Started professional acting career in commercials.
PICTURES: Mermaids (debut, 1990), The Hard Way, The Addams Family, The Cemetery Club, Addams Family Values, Casper, Gold Diggers: The Secret of Bear Mountain, Now and Then, Last of the High Kings, The Ice Storm, That Darn Cat, Souvenir, I Woke Up Early the Day I Died, Buffalo 66, 200 Cigarettes, The Opposite of Sex, Fear and Loathing in Las Vegas, Pecker.

RICH, JOHN
Producer, Director. b. Rockaway Beach, NY, e. U. of Michigan, B.A., Phi Beta Kappa, 1948; M.A. 1949; Sesquicentennial Award, 1967; bd. of dir., Screen Dir. Guild of America, 1954-1960; v.p. 1958-1960, Founder-Trustee, Producers-Directors Pension Plan, chmn. of bd. 1965, 1968, 1970; treasurer, Directors Guild of America, 1966-67; v.p. 1967-72. Awards: Directors Guild Award, Most Outstanding Directorial Achievement, 1971. Christopher award: Henry Fonda as Clarence Darrow, 1975. NAACP Image Award, 1974; 2 Golden Globe Awards: All in the Family, 1972-73. DGA Robert B. Aldrich Award for 1992.
PICTURES: Director: Wives and Lovers, The New Interns, Roustabout, Boeing-Boeing, Easy Come Easy Go.
TELEVISION: Director: Academy Awards, The Dick Van Dyke Show, All in the Family (also prod.), Mr. Sunshine, Dear John, MacGyver, The Good Life.

RICH, LEE
Producer, Executive. b. Cleveland, OH, Dec. 10, 1926. e. Ohio U. Adv. exec.; resigned as sr. v.p., Benton & Bowles, to become producer for Mirisch-Rich TV, 1965 (Rat Patrol, Hey Landlord). Resigned 1967 to join Leo Burnett Agency. Left to form Lorimar Productions in 1969 and served as pres. until 1986 when left to join MGM/UA Communications as chmn. & CEO. Resigned 1988; signed 3-year deal with Warner Bros. setting up Lee Rich Prods. Twice named Television Showman of the Year by Publishers' Guild of America.
PICTURES: Producer: The Sporting Club, Just Cause, The Amazing Panda Adventure, Big Bully. Executive Producer: The Man, The Choirboys, Who Is Killing the Great Chefs of Europe?, The Big Red One, Hard to Kill, Innocent Blood, Passenger 57, Just Cause, The Amazine Panda Adventure, Big Bully, Desperate Measures, Gloria.
TELEVISION: Exec. Prod.: Series: The Waltons (Emmy Award, 1973), Dallas, Knots Landing, Against the Grain. Mini-series: The Blue Knight, Helter Skelter, Studs Lonigan. Movies: Do Not Fold Spindle or Mutilate, The Homecoming: A Christmas Story,

The Crooked Hearts, Pursuit, The Girls of Huntington House, Dying Room Only, Don't Be Afraid of the Dark, A Dream for Christmas, The Stranger Within, Bad Ronald, The Runaway Barge, Runaways, Returning Home, Eric, Conspiracy of Terror, Widow, Green Eyes, Killer on Board, Desperate Women, Long Journey Back, Mary and Joseph: A Story of Faith, Mr. Horn, Some Kind of Miracle, Young Love, First Love, A Man Called Intrepid, Flamingo Road, Marriage Is Alive and Well, A Perfect Match, Reward, Skag, Killjoy, A Matter of Life and Death, Our Family Business, Mother's Day on Walton's Mountain, This is Kate Bennett, Two of a Kind, A Wedding on Walton's Mountain, A Day of Thanks on Walton's Mountain, Secret of Midland Heights, Face of Fear, Killer Rules.

RICHARD, SIR CLIFF
O.B.E. Singer, Actor. r.n. Harry Webb. b. India, Oct. 14, 1940. Ent. show business 1958 in TV series Oh Boy. Other TV includes Sunday Night at the London Palladium, several Cliff Richard Shows; top British Singer, 1960-71. Voted top box-office star of Great Britain, 1962-63, 1963-64. Twice rep. U.K. in Eurovision Song Contest. Innumerable platinum, gold and silver discs. 1989 became first UK artist to release 100 singles; voted top male vocalist of the 80's by UK Indept. TV viewers. Has made numerous videos. Knighted, 1995.
THEATER: Aladdin, Five Finger Exercise, The Potting Shed, Time.
PICTURES: Serious Charge (debut, 1959), Expresso Bongo, The Young Ones (Wonderful to Be Young), Summer Holiday, Wonderful Life (Swingers' Paradise), Finder's Keepers, Two a Penny, Take Me High (Hot Property).

RICHARDS, BEAH
Actress. b. Vicksburg, MS. e. Dillard U. On B'way in The Miracle Worker, A Raisin in the Sun, The Amen Corner (Theatre World Award), etc.
PICTURES: Take a Giant Step, The Miracle Worker, Gone Are the Days, In the Heat of the Night, Hurry Sundown, Guess Who's Coming to Dinner, The Great White Hope, Mahogany, Homer and Eddie, Drugstore Cowboy.
TELEVISION: Series: The Bill Cosby Show (1970), Sanford and Son, Frank's Place (Emmy Award, 1988), Hearts Afire. Movies: Footsteps, Outrage, A Dream for Christmas, Just an Old Sweet Song, Ring of Passion, Roots II—The Next Generation, A Christmas Without Snow, One Special Victory, Out of Darkness.

RICHARDS, DICK
Director, Producer, Writer. b. New York, NY, July 9, 1934. In U.S. Army as photo-journalist; work appeared in Life, Look, Time, Esquire, etc. Won over 100 int'l. awards, for commercials and photographic art work.
PICTURES: Director: The Culpepper Cattle Co. (also story), Rafferty and the Gold Dust Twins, Farewell My Lovely, March or Die (also co- prod., co-story), Death Valley, Tootsie (co-prod. only), Man Woman and Child, Heat.

RICHARDS, MICHAEL
Actor. b. Culver City, July 14, 1950. e. California Inst. of Arts. Work as stand-up comedian led to appearances on tv including regular stint on series Fridays. Acted on stage with San Diego Rep. Co.
THEATER: LA: The American Clock, Wild Oats.
PICTURES: Young Doctors in Love, Transylvania 6-5000, Whoops Apocalypse, UHF, Problem Child, Coneheads, So I Married an Axe Murderer, Airheads, Unstrung Heroes, Trial and Error.
TELEVISION: Series: Fridays, Marblehead Manor, Seinfeld (2 Emmy Awards: 1993, 1994, 1997).

RICHARDSON, JOELY
Actress. b. London, Eng., January 9, 1965. Daughter of actress Vanessa Redgrave and director Tony Richardson, sister of actress Natasha Richardson. e. Lycee, St. Paul's Girl's School, London; Pinellas Park H.S. (Florida), The Thacher Sch. (Ojai, CA), Royal Acad. of Dramatic Art. London stage: Steel Magnolias, Beauty and the Beast (Old Vic); also at Liverpool Playhouse, RSC.
PICTURES: Wetherby (debut, 1985 with mother), Drowning By Numbers, About That Strange Girl, King Ralph, Shining Through, Rebecca's Daughters, I'll Do Anything, Sister My Sister, Hollow Reed, Lochness, 101 Dalmations, Event Horizon.
TELEVISION: Body Contact, Behaving Badly, Available Light, Heading Home, Lady Chatterly.

RICHARDSON, MIRANDA
Actress. b. Southport, England, 1958. Studied acting at the drama program at Bristol's Old Vic Theatre School. Began acting on stage, 1979. Appeared in Moving, at the Queen's Theatre and continued in All My Sons, Who's Afraid of Virginia Woolf?, The Life of Einstein in provincial theatres. Also A Lie of the Mind (London), The Changeling, Mountain Language.
PICTURES: Dance With a Stranger (debut, 1985), The Innocent, Empire of the Sun, Eat the Rich, Twisted Obsession, The Bachelor, Enchanted April, The Crying Game, Damage (BAFTA Award; Acad. Award nom.), Tom and Viv, Century, The Night and the Moment, Kansas City, The Evening Star, The Apostle.

TELEVISION: The Hard Word, Sorrel and Son, A Woman of Substance, After Pilkington, Underworld, Death of the Heart, The Black Adder (series), Die Kinder (mini-series), Sweet as You Are (Royal TV Society Award), Fatherland (Golden Globe Award).

RICHARDSON, NATASHA
Actress. b. London, England, May 11, 1963. m. actor Liam Neeson. Daughter of actress Vanessa Redgrave and director Tony Richardson; sister is actress Joely Richardson. e. Central Sch. of Speech and Drama. Appeared at the Leeds Playhouse in On the Razzle, Top Girls, Charley's Aunt. Performed A Midsummer Night's Dream and Hamlet with the Young Vic. 1985 starred with mother in The Seagull (London), also starred in the musical High Society. Won London Theatre Critics Most Promising Newcomer award, 1986. NY stage debut 1992 in Anna Christie.
PICTURES: Every Picture Tells a Story (debut, 1984). Gothic, A Month in the Country, Patty Hearst, Fat Man and Little Boy, The Handmaid's Tale, The Comfort of Strangers, The Favor the Watch and the Very Big Fish, Widow's Peak, Nell, The Parent Trap.
TELEVISION: Ellis Island (mini-series), In a Secret State, The Copper Beeches (epis. of Sherlock Holmes), Ghosts, Past Midnight, Suddenly Last Summer, Hostages, Zelda, Tales From the Crypt (guest).

RICHARDSON, PATRICIA
Actress. b. Bethesda, MD, Feb. 23, 1951. e. Southern Methodist Univ.
THEATER: NY: Gypsy, Loose Ends, The Wake of Jamie Foster, The Collected Works of Billy the Kid, The Frequency, Vanities, The Miss Firecracker Contest, The Coroner's Plot, Fables for Friends. Regional: The Killing of Sister George, King Lear, The Philadelphia Story, Fifth of July, About Face.
PICTURES: Gas, C.H.U.D., You Better Watch Out, Lost Angels, In Country, Ulee's Gold.
TELEVISION: Series: Double Trouble, Eisenhower and Lutz, FM, Home Improvement, Storytime (PBS). Movies: Hands of a Stranger, Parent Trap III, Sophie and the Moonhanger, Undue Influence. Guest: Love Sidney, Kate and Allie, The Cosby Show, Quantum Leap.

RICHMAN, PETER MARK
Actor. b. Philadelphia, PA, April 16, 1927. e. Philadelphia Coll. of Pharmacy & Science with Bachelor of Science Degree in Pharmacy. Previously acted as Mark Richman. Member of Actors Studio since 1954.
THEATER: B'way: End as a Man, Masquerade, A Hatful of Rain. Off B'way: The Dybbuk, The Zoo Story, 4 Faces (also author). Regional: Blithe Spirit, The Night of the Iguana, 12 Angry Men, Babes in Toyland, Funny Girl, The Best Man, Equus, The Rainmaker, 4 Faces (Drama-Logue Best Performance Award, 1995).
PICTURES: Friendly Persuasion, The Strange One, The Black Orchid, Dark Intruder, Agent for H.A.R.M., For Singles Only, Friday 13th Part VIII—Jason Takes Manahattan, The Naked Gun 2 1/2: The Smell of Fear, Judgment Day (Manila).
TELEVISION: Series: Longstreet, Dynasty, Cain's Hundred, My Secret Summer (Berlin). Movies: House on Greenapple Road, Yuma, Mallory: Circumstantial Evidence, The Islander, The Psi Factor, Dempsey, Blind Ambition, City Killer, Bonanza: The Next Generation. Guest: Three's Company, Murder She Wrote, Star Trek: The Next Generation, Matlock, Beverly Hills 90210, Nothing Sacred and over 500 guest roles.

RICHMOND, TED
Producer. b. Norfolk, VA, June 10, 1912. e. MIT. Entered m.p. ind. as publicity dir., RKO Theatres; later mgr. Albany dist.; publ. dir. Fabian circuit, NY, Paramount upper NY state theats.; Grand Nat'l Pictures. Author Grand Nat'l series Trigger Pal, Six Gun Rhythm. Formed T. H. Richmond Prods., Inc., 1941. Formed Copa Prod. with Tyrone Power, 1954. Formed Ted Richmond Prod. Inc. for MGM release, 1959. Reactivated Copa Prod. Ltd., England, 1960.
PICTURES: Hit the Hay, The Milkman, Kansas Raiders, Shakedown, Smuggler's Island, Strange Door, Cimarron Kid, Bronco Buster, Has Anybody Seen My Gal, No Room for the Groom, Weekend with Father, The Mississippi Gambler, Desert Legion, Column South, Bonzo Goes to College, Forbidden, Walking My Baby Back Home, Francis Joins the Wacs, Bengal Brigade, Count Three and Pray, Nightfall, Abandon Ship, Solomon and Sheba, Charlemagne, Bachelor in Paradise, Advance to the Rear, Pancho Villa, Return of the 7, Red Sun, Papillon (exec. prod.), The Fifth Musketeer.

RICHTER, W. D.
Writer, Director. b. New Britain, CT, Dec. 7, 1945. e. Dartmouth Coll. B.A.; U. of Southern California Film Sch., grad. study.
PICTURES: Writer: Slither, Peeper, Nickelodeon, Invasion of the Body Snatchers, Dracula, Brubaker, All Night Long, Big Trouble in Little China, Needful Things, Home for the Holidays. Prod.-Dir.: Adventures of Buckaroo Banzai Across the Eighth Dimension, Late for Dinner.

RICKERT, JOHN F.
Executive. b. Kansas City, MO, Oct. 29, 1924. e. USC. Joined Universal Pictures in 1951; left in 1957 to start independent productions. 1960-68 handled indep. roadshow distribution (4-walling). 1969 formed Cineworld Corporation, natl. dist. co., of which he is pres. 1975-76 did tax shelter financing for 13 films. Currently involved in distribution, production packaging and intl. co-production as pres. of Coproducers Corp. Produced Mistress of the Apes.

RICKLES, DON
Actor, Comedian. b. New York, NY, May 8, 1926. e. AADA.
PICTURES: Run Silent Run Deep, Rabbit Trap, The Rat Race, X: The Man With the X-Ray Eyes, Muscle Beach Party, Bikini Beach, Beach Blanket Bingo, Enter Laughing, The Money Jungle, Where It's At, Kelly's Heroes, Keaton's Cop, Innocent Blood, Casino, Toy Story (voice), Little Redux Riding Hood (voice), Dennis the Menace 2, Quest for Camelot (voice), Dirty Work, Toy Story 2 (voice).
TELEVISION: Series: The Don Rickles Show (1968), The Don Rickles Show (1972), C.P.O. Sharkey, Foul-Ups Bleeps and Blunders, Daddy Dearest. Movie: For the Love of It. Guest: The Big Show, F Troop, Laugh-In, Kraft Music Hall, Dean Martin's Celebrity Roasts, Tales From the Crypt, many others.

RICKMAN, ALAN
Actor. b. London, England. Began as graphic designer before studying acting at RADA. Joined the Royal Shakespeare Co. where he starred in Les Liaisons Dangereuses; received Tony Award nomination for 1987 NY production.
THEATER: Commitments, The Last Elephant, The Grass Widow, Lucky Chance, The Seagull, As You Like It, Troilus and Cressida, Tango At the End of Winter, Hamlet.
PICTURES: Die Hard (debut, 1988), The January Man, Quigley Down Under, Closet Land, Truly Madly Deeply, Robin Hood: Prince of Thieves (BAFTA Award, 1991), Close My Eyes, Bob Roberts, Mesmer, An Awfully Big Adventure, Sense and Sensibility, Michael Collins, The Winter Guest (dir.).
TELEVISION: Series: The Barchester Chronicles (BBC). Specials: Romeo and Juliet. Guest: Fallen Angels (Murder Obliquely). Movie: Rasputin (Emmy, 1996, 1997; Golden Globe, Screen Actors Guild Awards 1996), Revolutionary Witness, Spirit of Man.

RICOTTA, FRANK
Executive. Pres., Technicolor, Inc., Association of Cimena & Video Laboratories, Inc.

RIEGERT, PETER
Actor. b. New York, NY, Apr. 11, 1947. e. U. of Buffalo, B.A. Brief stints as 8th grade English teacher, social worker, and aide de camp to politician Bella Abzug 1970, before turned actor, off-off B'way. Appeared with improvisational comedy group War Babies. Film debut in short, A Director Talks About His Film.
THEATER: Dance with me (B'way debut), Minnie's Boys (as Chico Marx), Sexual Perversity in Chicago, Isn't it Romantic?, La Brea Tarpits, A Rosen By Any Other Name, The Nerd, Mountain Language/The Birthday Party, The Road to Nirvana.
PICTURES: National Lampoon's Animal House, Americathon, Head Over Heels, National Lampoon Goes to the Movies, Local Hero, City Girl, A Man in Love, Le Grand Carnaval, The Stranger, Crossing Delancey, That's Adequate, The Passport, A Shock to the System, The Object of Beauty, Beyond the Ocean, Oscar, The Runestone, Passed Away, Utz, The Mask, White Man's Burden, Coldblooded, Pie in the Sky.
TELEVISION: Specials: Concealed Enemies, The Hit List, W. Eugene Smith: Photography Made Difficult. Mini-Series: Ellis Island. Movies: News at Eleven, Barbarians at the Gate, Gypsy, The Infiltrator, Element of Truth. Series: The Middle Ages.

RIFKIN, MONROE M.
Executive. e. New York U., BA Finance. Began career with Amer. TV and Communications Corp. as CEO, 1968-82, and Chairman, 1974-82. Bd. member, Nat'l. Cable TV Assoc., 1968-84, and as Chairman, 1983-84. Founder, dir. and Chairman of Rifkin & Associates.

RIFKIN, RON
Actor. b. New York, NY, Oct. 31, 1939. e. NYU.
THEATER: B'way: Come Blow Your Horn, The Goodbye People, The Tenth Man. Off-B'way: Rosebloom, The Art of Dining, Temple, The Substance of Fire.
PICTURES: The Devil's 8 (debut, 1969), Flareup, Silent Running, The Sunshine Boys, The Big Fix, The Sting II, Husbands and Wives, Manhattan Murder Mystery, Wolf, Last Summer in the Hamptons, The Substance of Fire, I'm Not Rappaport, L.A. Confidential, The Negotiator.
TELEVISION: Series: Adam's Rib, When Things Were Rotten, Husbands Wives & Lovers, One Day at a Time, Falcon Crest, Leaving L.A. Mini-Series: The Winds of War. Movie: Norma Jean & Marilyn

RIGG, DIANA
C.B.E. (1987). Actress. b. Doncaster, England, July 20, 1938. With the Royal Shakespeare Co. at Aldwych Theatre, 1962-64. Recent London stage: Follies, Medea (also B'way).
PICTURES: A Midsummer's Night Dream (debut, 1968), The Assassination Bureau, On Her Majesty's Secret Service, Julius Caesar, The Hospital, Theatre of Blood, A Little Night Music, The Great Muppet Caper, Evil Under the Sun, Snow White, A Good Man in Africa.
TELEVISION: Series: The Avengers, Diana, Mystery (host). Movies: In This House of Brede, Witness for the Prosecution, A Hazard of Hearts, Mother Love, Mrs. 'arris Goes to Paris, Running Delilah, Genghis Cohn, Danielle Steel's Zoya, The Haunting of Helen Walker. Specials: King Lear, Bleak House, Rebecca (Emmy, 1997).

RINGWALD, MOLLY
Actress. b. Sacramento, CA, Feb. 16, 1968. Daughter of jazz musician Bob Ringwald; began performing at age 4 with his Great Pacific Jazz Band at 6 and recorded album, Molly Sings. Professional debut at 5 in stage play, The Glass Harp. Appeared in bit on TV's New Mickey Mouse Club, a West Coast stage production of Annie and in TV series, The Facts of Life, Off-B'way debut: Lily Dale (Theatre World Award, 1986).
PICTURES: Tempest (debut, 1982), P.K. and the Kid, Spacehunter: Adventures in the Forbidden Zone, Sixteen Candles, The Breakfast Club, Pretty in Pink, The Pick-Up Artist, For Keeps?, King Lear, Fresh Horses, Strike It Rich, Betsy's Wedding, Face the Music, Seven Sundays, Malicious, Baja, Bastard Brood, Office Killer, Requiem for Murder, Killing Mrs. Tingle.
TELEVISION: Series: The Facts of Life, Townies. Movies: Packin' It In, Surviving, Women and Men: Stories of Seduction (Dust Before Fireworks), Something to Live For: The Alison Gertz Story, Since You've Been Gone. Mini-Series: The Stand.

RISHER, SARA
Executive. Chairperson of production, New Line Productions, Inc.
PICTURES: Co-prod./assoc. prod.: Polyester, A Nightmare on Elm Street, Quiet Cool, Critters, A Nightmare on Elm Street 3: Dream Warriors, My Demon Lover. Exec. prod.: A Nightmare on Elm Street 4: The Dream Master, A Nightmare on Elm Street 5: The Dream Child, Book of Love, Pump Up the Volume, Wide Sargasso Sea, Surf Ninjas, Blink, A Nightmare on Elm Street 7 (also actress), In Love & War, Last Man Standing, The Deep Blue.

RISSIEN, EDWARD L.
Executive. b. Des Moines, IA. e. Grinnell Coll., Stanford U., B.A., 1949. Army Air Force, WWII. B'way stage, mgr., 1950-53; v.p., Mark Stevens Prods., 1954-56; prod., v.p., Four Star, 1958-60; prog. exec., ABC-TV, 1960-62; v.p., Bing Crosby Prods., 1963-66; v.p., Filmways TV Prods.; assoc. prod., Columbia, 1968-69; indept. prod., 1970; prod., WB, 1971; exec. v.p., Playboy Prods., 1972-80; consultant & indept. prod., 1981-82; sr. consultant, cable, Playboy Prods., 1982-85; pres., Playboy Programs, 1985-88; bd. of dirs.: Heritage Entertainment, Inc. 1985-88; indept. prod., 1989-present. Theatre producer in London: The School of Night.
PICTURES: Snow Job (prod.), Castle Keep (prod. exec.), The Crazy World of Julius Vrooder (prod.), Saint Jack (exec. prod.).
TELEVISION: Movies (exec. prod.): Minstrel Man, A Whale for the Killing, The Death of Ocean View Park, Big Bob Johnson, The Great Niagara, Third Girl from the Left, A Summer Without Boys.

RISSNER, DANTON
Executive. b. Brooklyn, NY, March 27, 1940. e. Florida So. Col. Began as agent with Ashley Famous (later Intl. Famous), 1967-69. 1969 joined Warner Bros. as v.p., chg. European prod.; 1970, moved to United Artists as v.p., chg. European prod.; 1973, named v.p. in chg. East Coast & European prod. for UA; 1975-78, v.p. in chg. of world-wide prod.; 1981, exec. v.p., 20th Century-Fox.; 1984, joined UA as sr. v.p., motion pictures.
PICTURES: Prod.: Up the Academy, A Summer Story.
TELEVISION: Backfire (prod.).

RITCHIE, MICHAEL
Director. b. Waukesha, WI, Nov. 28, 1938. e. Harvard U. where he directed first production of Arthur Kopit's play, Oh Dad Poor Dad Mama's Hung You in the Closet and I'm Feeling So Sad. Professional career began as ass't. to Robert Saudek on Ford Foundation's Omnibus TV series. Later became assoc. prod. and then dir. on Saudek's Profiles in Courage series; dir. assignments on tv series. Appeared as actor in film Innocent Blood.
PICTURES: Downhill Racer (debut, 1969), Prime Cut, The Candidate, Smile (also prod., lyricist), The Bad News Bears, Semi-Tough, An Almost Perfect Affair (also co-s.p.), The Island, Divine Madness (also prod.), The Survivors, Fletch, Wildcats, The Golden Child, The Couch Trip, Fletch Lives, Diggstown, Cops and Robbersons, The Scout, The Fantasticks, A Simple Wish.
TELEVISION: Series: Profiles in Courage (also prod.), The Man from U.N.C.L.E., Run for Your Life, Dr. Kildare, The Big Valley, Felony Squad, The Outsider (pilot), The Sound of Anger. Movie: The Positively True Adventures of the Alleged Texas Cheerleader-Murdering Mom, Comfort Texas.

RITTER, JOHN
Actor. b. Burbank, CA, Sept. 17, 1948. Father was late Tex Ritter, country-western star. Attended Hollywood H.S. Began acting at USC in 1968. Appeared with college cast at Edinburgh Festival; later with Eva Marie Saint in Desire Under the Elms.
PICTURES: The Barefoot Executive (debut, 1971), Scandalous John, The Other, The Stone Killer, Nickelodeon, Americathon, Hero at Large, Wholly Moses, They All Laughed, Real Men, Skin Deep, Problem Child, Problem Child II, Noises Off, Stay Tuned, North, Slingblade. Montana.
TELEVISION: Movies: The Night That Panicked America, Leave Yesterday Behind, The Comeback Kid, Pray TV, In Love With an Older Woman, Sunset Limousine, Love Thy Neighbor, Letting Go, Unnatural Causes, A Smoky Mountain Christmas, The Last Fling, Prison for Children, Tricks of the Trade, My Brother's Wife, Stephen King's IT, The Dreamer of Oz, The Summer My Father Grew Up, Danielle Steel's Heartbeat, The Only Way Out, Gramps, The Colony, Unforgivable. Series: The Waltons, Three's Company (Emmy Award, 1984), Three's a Crowd, Hooper-man, Have Faith (exec. prod.), Anything But Love (exec. prod., also guest), Fish Police (voice), Hearts Afire, Buffy the Vampire (guest).

RIVERA, CHITA
Actress, Dancer. b. Washington, DC, Jan. 23, 1933. r.n. Concita del Rivero. Trained for stage at American School of Ballet.
THEATER: Call Me Madam (1952), Guys and Dolls, Can-Can, Shoestring Revue, Seventh Heaven, Mr. Wonderful, Shinbone Alley, West Side Story, Bye Bye Birdie, Bajour, Sondheim: A Musical Tribute, Chicago, Hey Look Me Over, Merlin, The Rink (Tony Award, 1984), Jerry's Girls, Kiss of the Spider Woman (Tony Award, 1993).
PICTURE: Sweet Charity (1969).
TELEVISION: Series: The New Dick Van Dyke Show. Specials: Kennedy Center Tonight—Broadway to Washington!, Pippin, Toller Cranston's Strawberry Ice, TV Academy Hall of Fame, 1985. Movies: The Marcus-Nelson Murders, Mayflower Madam.

RIVERA, GERALDO
Journalist. b. New York, NY, July 4, 1943. e. U. of Arizona, Brooklyn Law Sch., 1969, Columbia Sch. of Journalism. Started legal career 1st as lawyer with Harlem Assertion of Rights Community Action for Legal Services 1968-70. Switched to journalism, joined WABC-TV, New York, 1970. Made several TV documentaries on such subjects as institutions for retarded, drug addiction, migrant workers, etc. Chmn.: One-to-One Foundation, Maravilla Foundation. Winner 3 national and 4 local Emmys, George Peabody Award, 2 Robert F. Kennedy Awards. Appeared in film The Bonfire of the Vanities.
TELEVISION: Series: Good Morning America (contributor), Good Night America, 20/20, The Geraldo Rivera Show, Now It Can Be Told, Rivera Live. Specials: The Mystery of Al Capone's Vault, American Vice: The Doping of a Nation, Innocence Lost: The Erosion of American Childhood, Sons of Scarface: The New Mafia, Murder: Live From Death Row, Devil Worship: Exposing Satan's Underground. Movie: Perry Mason: The Case of the Reckless Romeo.

RIVERS, JOAN
Actress, Writer, Director. r.n. Joan Molinsky. b. New York, NY, June 8, 1933. e. Barnard Coll. (Phi Beta Kappa). Formerly fashion coordinator for Bond clothing stores. Performed comedy act in nightclubs, then with Second City 1961-62; TV debut: Johnny Carson Show, 1965; nat'l syndicated columnist, Chicago Tribune 1973-76; Hadassah Woman of the Year, 1983; Jimmy Award for Best Comedian 1981; Chair., National Cystic Fibrosis Foundation. 1978 created TV series Husbands Wives and Lovers.
AUTHOR: Having a Baby Can Be a Scream (1974), Can We Talk? (1983), The Life and Hard Times of Heidi Abramowitz (1984), Enter Talking (1986), Still Talking (1990).
THEATER: B'way: Fun City (also co-writer), Broadway Bound, Sally Marr... and Her Escorts (also co-writer).
PICTURES: The Swimmer, Rabbit Test (also dir., s.p.), The Muppets Take Manhattan, Spaceballs (voice), Serial Mom.
TELEVISION: Series: The Tonight Show (regular substitute guest host: 1983-86), The Late Show (host), The New Hollywood Squares, The Joan Rivers Show (morning talk show). Movies: How to Murder a Millionaire, Tears and Laughter: The Joan and Melissa Rivers Story.

ROBARDS, JASON
Actor. b. Chicago, IL, July 26, 1922. Served in Navy during WWII. Studied acting at Acad. of Dramatic Arts. Began with Children's World Theatre (1947), then stock radio parts, asst. stage mgr. and actor in Stalag 17, The Chase, D'Oyly Carte Opera Co., Stratford Ontario Shakespeare Fest. American Gothic, Circle in the Square.
THEATER: The Iceman Cometh (Obie Award, 1956), Long Day's Journey into Night (Theatre World Award), The Disenchanted (Tony Award, 1959), Toys in the Attic, Big Fish Little Fish, A Thousand Clowns, After the Fall, But for Whom Charlie, Hughie, The Devils, We Bombed in New Haven, The Country Girl, A Moon for the Misbegotten, Long Day's Journey Into Night (Brooklyn Acad. of Music, 1975; B'way, 1988), A Touch of the Poet, O'Neill and Carlotta, You Can't Take It With You, Ah Wilderness, A Month of Sundays, Established Price (Long Wharf), Love Letters, Park Your Car in Harvard Yard, No Man's Land.

PICTURES: The Journey (debut, 1959), By Love Possessed, Tender Is the Night, Long Day's Journey Into Night, Act One, A Thousand Clowns, A Big Hand for the Little Lady, Any Wednesday, Divorce American Style, The St. Valentine's Day Massacre, Hour of the Gun, The Night They Raided Minsky's, (Loves of) Isadora, Once Upon a Time in the West, Operation Snafu, The Ballad of Cable Hogue, Tora! Tora!, Fools, Julius Caesar, Johnny Got His Gun, Murders in the Rue Morgue, The War Between Men and Women, Pat Garrett and Billy the Kid, A Boy and His Dog, Mr. Sycamore, All the President's Men (Academy Award, best supporting actor, 1976), Julia (Academy Award, best supporting actor, 1977), Comes a Horseman, Hurricane, Raise the Titanic!, Caboblanco, Melvin and Howard, Legend of the Lone Ranger, Burden of Dreams, Max Dugan Returns, Something Wicked This Way Comes, Square Dance, Bright Lights Big City, The Good Mother, Dream a Little Dream, Parenthood, Quick Change, Reunion, Storyville, The Adventures of Huck Finn, The Trial, Philadelphia, The Paper, Little Big League, Crimson Tide, A Thousand Acres.
TELEVISION: Specials: Abe Lincoln in Illinois, The Iceman Cometh, A Doll's House, Noon Wine, Belle of 14th Street, The House Without a Christmas Tree, For Whom the Bell Tolls, You Can't Take It With You, Hughie. Mini-Series: Washington: Behind Closed Doors. Movies: A Christmas to Remember, Haywire, F.D.R.: The Last Year, The Atlanta Child Murders, The Day After, Sakharov, Johnny Bull, The Long Hot Summer, Laguna Heat, Norman Rockwell's Breaking Home Ties, Inherit the Wind (Emmy Award, 1988), The Christmas Wife, The Perfect Tribute, Chernobyl: The Final Warning, An Inconvenient Woman, Black Rainbow, Mark Twain & Me, Heidi, The Enemy Within, My Antonia. Guest: Studio One, Philco Playhouse, Hallmark.

ROBARDS, SAM
Actor. b. New York, NY, December 16. m. actress Suzy Amis. Son of actors Jason Robards and Lauren Bacall. e. National Theater Institute and studied with Uta Hagen at H.B. Studios.
THEATER: Off-B'way: Album, Flux, Taking Steps, Moonchildren. Kennedy Center: Idiot's Delight and regional theater.
PICTURES: Tempest, Not Quite Paradise, Fandango, Bright Lights Big City, Bird, Casualties of War, The Ballad of Little Jo, Mrs. Parker and the Vicious Circle, Donor Unknown, Beautiful Girls, Dinner and Driving.
TELEVISION: Series: Movin' Right Along (PBS), TV 101, Get a Life!, Maximum Bob. Movies: Jacobo Timerman: Prisoner Without a Name Cell Without a Number, Into Thin Air, Pancho Barnes, The Man Who Captured Eichmann.

ROBBINS, MATTHEW
Writer, Director. e. U. of Southern California Sch. of Cinema. Wrote early scripts in collaboration with Hal Barwood, Robbins branching out into directing also with Corvette Summer in 1978.
PICTURES: Writer: The Sugarland Express, The Bingo Long Traveling All-Stars and Motor Kings, Corvette Summer (also dir.), Dragonslayer (also dir.), Warning Sign, Batteries Not Included (also dir.), Bingo (dir. only), Mimic (also story).

ROBBINS, RICHARD
Composer. b. Boston, MA, Dec. 4, 1940. Bachelor of Music and Graduate Studies at New England Conservatory of Music. Received Frank Huntington Beebe Fellowship to Austria where he studied musicology, chamber music. Later became dir. of Mannes College of Music Preparatory School, N.Y. Has worked closely with James Ivory and Ismail Merchant. Also dir. doc. films Sweet Sounds, Street Musicians of Bombay. Awards: Best Score, Venice Film Festival for Maurice; Best Score, BFI Anthony Asquith Award for A Room With a View. Acad. Award nom. for Howards End and The Remains of the Day.
PICTURES: The Europeans (supr. score), Jane Austen in Manhattan, Quartet, Heat and Dust, The Bostonians, A Room with a View, Maurice, Sweet Lorraine, My Little Girl, Slaves of New York, Mr. & Mrs. Bridge, The Ballad of the Sad Cafe, Howards End, The Remains of the Day, Jefferson in Paris, Surviving Picasso, The Proprietor.
TELEVISION: Love and Other Sorrows, In The Gloaming.

ROBBINS, TIM
Actor, Director. b. West Covina, CA, Oct. 16, 1958. Son of Greenwich Village folksinger, worked as actor while in high school. e. NYU. Transferred to UCLA theatre program appearing in guest roles on tv. 1981, co-founder and artistic dir., The Actors Gang, in L.A.; dir. them in and co-authored Alagazam: After the Dog Wars, Violence: The Misadventures of Spike Spangle—Farmer, Carnage: A Comedy (also prod. in NY).
PICTURES: Toy Soldiers (debut, 1984), No Small Affair, Fraternity Vacation, The Sure Thing, Top Gun, Howard the Duck, Five Corners, Bull Durham, Tapeheads, Miss Firecracker, Twister (cameo), Erik the Viking, Cadillac Man, Jacob's Ladder, Jungle Fever, The Player (Cannes Film Fest. Award, 1992), Bob Roberts (also dir., s.p., co-wrote songs), Short Cuts, The Hudsucker Proxy, The Shawshank Redemption, Ready to Wear (Pret-a-Porter), I.Q., Dead Man Walking (dir.), Nothing to Lose, The Moviegoer, Arlington Road, The Cradle Will Rock (dir.).
TELEVISION: Movies: Quarterback Princess, Malice in Wonderland. Guest: Hardcastle and McCormick, St. Elsewhere, Hill Street Blues.

ROBERTS, BRIAN L.
Executive. b. Philadelphia, PA. e. Wharton School at U. of Penn. Joined Comcast Corp. a major cable TV and cell. tele. network operating co., in 1982. Several mgt. positions, incl. exec. VP of ops., before becoming president in 1990. He also serves as a director of Comcast.

ROBERTS, CURTIS
Producer. b. Dover, England. e. Cambridge U. Child actor. England, Germany; numerous pictures for Rank Org.; prod. England, on Broadway in Gertie, Island Visit; co-prod. on Broadway, Horses in Midstream, Golden Apple, Tonight or Never; tour and NY The Journey. Recipient: Lawrence J. Quirk Photoplay Award 1990. Now pres., CGC Films, Munich.
AUTHOR: History of Summer Theatre, The History of Vaudeville, Other Side of the Coin, History of Music (Popular) 1900-70, History of English Music Halls, Latta, Then There Were Some, I Live to Love, Gabor the Merrier, I Live to Love II.
THEATER: Tours: Blithe Spirit, Showboat, Kiss Me Kate, Generation, The Camel Bell, Farewell Party, Twentieth Century, Great Sebastians, Goodbye Charlie, Time of the Cuckoo, Under Papa's Picture, Everybody's Gal, Divorce Me Darling, Gingerbread Lady, September Song, Same Time Next Year, Funny Girl, Pal Joey, South Pacific, It Girl, Fanny, Breaking Up the Act, Good, Good Friends, Together, I Remember Mama, Applause Too.
PICTURES: An Actress in Love, La Die, Hypocrite, Jet Over the Atlantic, The Vixen, Farewell Party, Polly's Return, Rain Before Seven, Halloween, Malaga, My Dear Children, Norma, The Lion's Consort, Whispers, Golden Idol, London Belongs To Me, The Ann Moriss Story.
TELEVISION: Rendezvous, Deadly Species, Top Secret, The Ilona Massey Show, When In Rome, Ethan Frome, Black Chiffon, Illusion in Java (mini-series), Diamonds Don't Burn (mini-series), BBC Specials: My Family Right Or Wrong, The Psychopathic Dog.

ROBERTS, ERIC
Actor. b. Biloxi, MS, April 18, 1956. Father founded Actors and Writers Workshop in Atlanta, 1963. Sister is actress Julia Roberts. Began appearing in stage prods. at age 5. Studied at American Acad. of Dramatic Arts. Stage debut in Rebel Women.
THEATER: Mass Appeal, The Glass Menagerie (Hartford Stage Co.), A Streetcar Named Desire (Princeton's McCarter Theater), Alms for the Middle Class (Long Wharf), Burn This (B'way debut; Theatre World Award).
PICTURES: King of the Gypsies (debut, 1978), Raggedy Man, Star 80, The Pope of Greenwich Village, The Coca Cola Kid, Runaway Train (Acad. Award nom.), Golden Globe nom.), Nobody's Fool, Rude Awakening, Blood Red, Best of the Best, The Ambulance, Lonely Hearts, Final Analysis, Best of the Best 2, By the Sword, Freefall, Babyfever, Love Is a Gun, The Specialist, Nature of the Beast, The Grave, Heaven's Prisoners, It's My Party, From the Edge, The Immortals, Power 98, The Cable Guy, American Strays, TNT, The Shadow Men, Making Sandwiches, Most Wanted, Two Shades of Blue, The Prophecy II, La Cucaracha, Facade, Death Valley.
TELEVISION: Series: Another World, C-16: FBI. Specials: Miss Lonelyhearts, Dear America: Letters Home from Vietnam (reader). Movies: Pauls' Case, Slow Burn, To Heal a Nation, The Lost Capone, Descending Angel, Vendetta: Secrets of a Mafia Bride, Fugitive Among Us, Love Honor & Obey: The Last Mafia Marriage, Voyage, Love Cheat and Steal, Saved by the Light, The Odyssey, Dr. Who, Dark Angel, In Cold Blood, Purgatory West of the Pecos.

ROBERTS, JULIA
Actress. b. Smyrna, GA, Oct. 28, 1967. Brother is actor Eric Roberts. Parents ran theater workshop in Atlanta. Moved to NY to study acting; modeled for the Click Agency before making prof. debut in brother's film Blood Red.
PICTURES: Blood Red (debut, 1986), Satisfaction, Mystic Pizza, Steel Magnolias (Acad. Award nom.), Pretty Woman (Acad. Award nom.), Flatliners, Sleeping With the Enemy, Dying Young, Hook, The Player, The Pelican Brief, I Love Trouble, Ready to Wear (Pret-a-Porter), Something to Talk About, Mary Reilly, Michael Collins, Everyone Says I Love You, My Best Friend's Wedding, Conspiracy Theory, Tracks, The Notting Hill Project, The Moviegoer, The Women (also prod.), Good Night Moon (also prod.).
TELEVISION: Movie: Baja Oklahoma. Guest: Crime Story, Friends.

ROBERTS, PERNELL
Actor. b. Waycross, GA, May 18, 1930. e. U. of Maryland. Left college to begin working with summer stock companies, joining Arena Stage in Washington, DC in 1950. 1952 began appearing off-B'way (where he won a Drama Desk Award for Macbeth, 1957); made B'way debut in 1958 in Tonight in Samarkand.
PICTURES: Desire Under the Elms (debut, 1958), The Sheepman, Ride Lonesome, The Errand Boy (cameo), Four Rode Out, The Magic of Lassie.

TELEVISION: Series: Bonanza, Trapper John M.D., FBI: The Untold Stories (host). Movies: The Silent Gun, San Francisco International, The Bravos, Adventures of Nick Carter, Assignment: Munich, Dead Man on the Run, The Deadly Tower, The Lives of Jenny Dolan, Charlie Cobb: Nice Night for a Hanging, The Immigrants, The Night Rider, Hot Rod, High Noon Part II: The Return of Will Kane, Incident at Crestridge, Desperado, Perry Mason: The Case of the Sudden Death Payoff, Perry Mason: The Case of the All-Star Assassin, Donor. Mini-Series: Captains and the Kings, Centennial, Around the World in 80 Days.

ROBERTS, RALPH J.
Executive. b. Philadelphia, PA. e. Wharton School at U. of Penn. Served 4-year tour of duty in US Navy. Began career in 1950's as acct. exec., Aitken Kynett Advertising Agency. VP, Muzak Corp. Exec. VP, dir. of advertising and later pres. and CEO of Pioneer Industries, a men's accessory co. Pres. and Chairman, Comcast Corp., a cable TV and cell. tele. network operating co. Chairman only since 1989.

ROBERTS, TONY
Actor. b. New York, NY, Oct. 22, 1939. e. Northwestern U.
THEATER: B'way: How Now Dow Jones, Don't Drink the Water, Play It Again Sam, Promises Promises, Barefoot in the Park, Absurd Person Singular, Sugar, Murder at the Howard Johnson's, They're Playing Our Song, Doubles, Arsenic and Old Lace, Jerome Robbins' Broadway, The Seagull, The Sisters Rosensweig, Victor/Victoria. Off-B'way: The Cradle Will Rock, The Good Parts, Four Dogs and a Bone. NY City Opera: Brigadoon, South Pacific. Dir: One of the All-Time Greats (Off-B'way).
PICTURES: Million Dollar Duck, Star Spangled Girl, Play It Again Sam, Serpico, The Taking of Pelham One Two Three, Lovers Like Us (Le Sauvage), Annie Hall, Just Tell Me What You Want, Stardust Memories, A Midsummer Night's Sex Comedy, Amityville 3-D, Key Exchange, Hannah and Her Sisters, Radio Days, 18 Again, Popcorn, Switch.
TELEVISION: Series: Rosetti and Ryan, The Four Seasons, The Lucie Arnaz Show, The Thorns. Movies: The Lindbergh Kidnapping Case, Girls in the Office, If Things Were Different, Seize the Day, Messiah on Mott Street, A Question of Honor, A Different Affair, Our Sons, Not in My Family, The American Clock, A Perry Mason Mystery: The Case of the Jealous Jokester. Guest: The Defenders, Phyllis, Storefront Lawyers, MacMillan, Trapper John M.D., Love American Style, Love Boat, Hotel.

ROBERTS, WILLIAM
Writer, Producer. b. Los Angeles, CA. e. U. of Southern California.
PICTURES: You For Me, Fast Company, Easy To Love, Her Twelve Men, The Private War of Major Benson, The Sheepman, The Mating Game, The Magnificent Seven, The Wonderful World of the Brothers Grimm, Come Fly with Me, The Devil's Brigade, The Bridge At Remagen, One More Train to Rob, Red Sun, The Last American Hero, Posse, The Legend of the Lone Ranger, Ten to Midnight, Major Payne.
TELEVISION: Donna Reed Show (creator), Life With Father.

ROBERTSON, CLIFF
Actor, Writer, Director. b. La Jolla, CA, Sept. 9, 1925.
THEATER: Mr. Roberts, Late Love, The Lady and the Tiger, Ghosts of 87 (one-man show). B'way: The Wisteria Tree, Orpheus Descending (Theatre World Award), Love Letters.
PICTURES: Picnic (debut, 1955), Autumn Leaves, The Girl Most Likely, The Naked and the Dead, Gidget, Battle of the Coral Sea, As the Sea Rages, All in a Night's Work, Underworld USA, The Big Show, The Interns, My Six Loves, PT 109, Sunday in New York, The Best Man, 633 Squadron, Love Has Many Faces, Masquerade, Up From the Beach, The Honey Pot, The Devil's Brigade, Charly (Academy Award, 1968), Too Late the Hero, J.W. Coop (also dir., s.p.), The Great Northfield Minnesota Raid, Ace Eli and Rodger of the Skies, Man on a Swing, Out of Season, Three Days of the Condor, Shoot, Obsession, Dominique, Fraternity Row (narrator), Class, Brainstorm, Star 80, Shaker Run, Malone, Wild Hearts Can't Be Broken, Wind, Renaissance Man, Dazzle, The Sunset Boys, Escape From L.A.
TELEVISION: Series: Falcon Crest. Guest: Philco-Goodyear, Studio One, Robert Montgomery Presents, The Game (Emmy Award, 1966), Batman. Movies: Man Without a Country, My Father's House, Washington: Behind Closed Doors, Dreams of Gold, Key to Rebecca, Henry Ford—The Man and the Machine, Dead Reckoning, Dazzle, The Last Best Days, Assignment Berlin. Special: Days of Wine and Roses (Playhouse 90). Also spokesman for AT&T.

ROBERTSON, DALE
Actor, Producer. r.n. Dayle Robertson. b. Harrah, OK, July 14, 1923. e. Oklahoma Military Coll. Prof. prizefighter; U.S. Army, 1942-45. Film debut as bit player. Voted Star of Tomorrow, M.P. Herald Fame Poll, 1951.

PICTURES: The Boy With Green Hair (debut, 1948), Flamingo Road, Fighting Man of the Plains, Caribou Trail, Two Flags West, Call Me Mister, Take Care of My Little Girl, Golden Girl, Lydia Bailey, Return of the Texan, The Outcasts of Poker Flat, O. Henry's Full House, The Farmer Takes a Wife, Devil's Canyon, The Silver Whip, City of Bad Men, The Gambler from Natchez, Sitting Bull, Son of Sinbad, Day of Fury, Dakota Incident, Hell Canyon Outlaws, Fast and Sexy, Law of the Lawless, Blood on the Arrow, Coast of Skeletons, The One-Eyed Soldier.
TELEVISION: Series: Tales of Wells Fargo, The Iron Horse, Death Valley Days, Dynasty, Dallas, J.J. Starbuck. Movies: Scalplock, Melvin Purvis: G-Man, Kansas City Massacre, Last Ride of the Dalton Gang. Guest: The Love Boat, Matt Houston, Murder She Wrote.

ROBERTSON, TIMOTHY B.
Executive. e. Univ of VA, Gordon-Conwell Thelogical Seminary, Columbia Univ. Manager of WXNE-TV in Boston, 1980-82; supervisor of Christian Broadcasting Network's tv facility; 1982-90, in charge of Middle East Television after purchase by CBN. Became President & CEO of International Family Entertainment Inc., holdings include The Family Channel, Fit TV, United Family Communications.

ROBINSON, BRUCE
Actor, Director, Writer. b. Kent, England, 1946. e. Central School of Speech and Drama. As actor appeared in 12 films but began writing novels and screenplays long before he gave up acting in 1975.
PICTURES: Actor: Romeo and Juliet (debut), The Story of Adele H. (last film as actor). Writer: The Killing Fields (Acad. Award nom.), Fat Man and Little Boy. Director-Writer: Withnail and I, How to Get Ahead in Advertising, Jennifer Eight.

ROBINSON, JAMES G.
Executive, Producer. e. Univ. of Maryland. Was prof. photographer and business entrepreneur prior to entering m.p. industry as co-prod. of The Stone Boy, and exec. prod. of Where the River Runs Black, Streets of Gold. Founded Morgan Creek Prods. in 1988, Morgan Creek Intl. in 1989, Morgan Creek Music Group in 1990, Morgan Creek Theatres and Morgan Creek International Theatres in 1992. Chairman and CEO of Morgan Creek.
PICTURES: Exec. Prod. for Morgan Creek: Young Guns, Skin Deep, Renegades, Enemies a Love Story, Nightbreed, Coupe de Ville, Young Guns II, The Exorcist III, Pacific Heights, Robin Hood: Prince of Thieves, Freejack, White Sands, The Last of the Mohicans, True Romance. Prod. for Morgan Creek: Stay Tuned, The Crush, Ace Ventura: Pet Detective, Major League II, Chasers, Trial by Jury, Silent Fall, Imaginary Crimes, A Walk in the Clouds, Big Bully, Ace Ventura: When Nature Calls, Two If By Sea, Diabolique, Bad Moon, Wild America, Incognito, Major League: Back to the Minors.

ROBINSON, PHIL ALDEN
Director, Writer. b. Long Beach, NY, Mar. 1, 1950. e. Union Coll., Schenectady. Write and directed training films for Air Force, before writing two episodes for series Trapper John M.D.
PICTURES: Rhinestone (co-s.p.), All of Me (s.p., assoc. prod.). Dir./Writer: In the Mood, Field of Dreams, Sneakers.
TELEVISION: Series: Trapper John M.D. (writer), The George Burns Comedy Week (dir.)

ROCCO, ALEX
Actor. b. Cambridge, MA, Feb. 29, 1936.
PICTURES: Motor Psycho, St. Valentine's Day Massacre, Blood Mania, The Godfather, Slither, Detroit 9000, Friends of Eddie Coyle, The Outside Man, Stanley, Freebie and the Bean, Three the Hard Way, Rafferty and the Gold Dust Twins, Hearts of the West, Fire Sale, House Calls, Rabbit Test, Voices, Herbie Goes Bananas, The Stunt Man, Nobody's Perfekt, The Entity, Cannonball Run II, Stick, Gotcha!, P.K. and the Kid, Return to Horror High, Dream a Little Dream, Wired, The Pope Must Die, That Thing You Do, Just-Write, Dead of Night.
TELEVISION: Over 400 television shows incl: Series: Three for the Road, The Famous Teddy Z (Emmy Award, 1990), Sibs, The George Carlin Show. Movies: Hustling, The Blue Knight, A Question of Guilt, The Grass is Always Greener Over the Septic Tank, Badge of the Assassin, Rock 'n' Roll Mom, The First Time, A Quiet Little Neighborhood A Perfect Little Murder, An Inconvenient Woman, Boris & Natasha, Love Honor & Obey: The Last Mafia Marriage, Robin Cook's Harmful Intent. Mini-Series: 79 Park Avenue.

ROCK, CHRIS
Actor, comedian. b. Brooklyn, NY, Feb. 7, 1966.
PICTURES: Beverly Hills Cop II, I'm Gonna Git You Sucka, New Jack City, Boomerang, CB4 (also writer, co-prod.), The Immortals, Panther, Sgt. Bilko, Beverly Hills Ninja, Dogma, Doctor Dolittle (voice), Lethal Weapon 4.
TELEVISION: Series: Saturday Night Live, In Living Color, The Chris Rock Show. Guest: Miami Vice, The Fresh Prince of Bel-Air, Homicide: Life on the Street, King of the Hill.

RODDAM, FRANC
Director. b. Stockton, England, Apr. 29, 1946. Studied at London Film Sch. Spent two years as adv. copywriter/prod. with Ogilvy, Benson, Mather before joining BBC as documentary filmmaker. Founder of Union Pictures 1991.
PICTURES: Quadrophenia (also co-s.p.), The Lords of Discipline, Rain Forest (s.p. only), The Bride, Aria (sequence), War Party (also co-exec. prod.), K2.
TELEVISION: Director: The Family, Mini, Dummy. Creator: Aufwiedersehen Pet, Making Out, Masterchief, Harry.

RODRIGUEZ, ROBERT
Director, Writer, Producer, Editor. e. Univ. of TX. While in college created comic strip Los Hooligans. Made several short films including Bedhead which won several festival awards.
PICTURES: Director/Writer: El Mariachi (feature debut, 1993; also co-prod., story, photog., editor, sound), Desperado (also prod., editor), Four Rooms (segment), From Dusk Till Dawn (dir.), The Faculty.
TELEVISION: Movie (dir./writer): Roadracers.

ROEG, NICOLAS
Director, Cameraman. b. London, England. Aug. 15, 1928. m. actress Theresa Russell. Entered film industry through cutting rooms of MGM's British Studios, dubbing French films into English. Moved into prod. as clapper boy and part of photographer Freddie Young's crew at Marylebone Studios London, 1947. Next became camera operator (Trials of Oscar Wilde, The Sundowners). Had first experience as cameraman on TV series (Police Dog and Ghost Squad). Debut as director on Performance, co-directed with Donald Cammell. First solo dir. film, Walkabout.
PICTURES: Cameraman: The Miniver Story, The Trial of Oscar Wilde, The Sundowners, Lawrence of Arabia, Jazz Boat, Information Received, The Great Van Robbery. Dir. of Photography: The Caretaker, Dr. Crippen, Nothing But the Best, Masque of the Red Death, A Funny Thing Happened on the Way to the Forum, Fahrenheit 451, Far from the Madding Crowd, The Girl-Getters, Petulia. Director-Cameraman: Performance (co.-dir.), Walkabout. Director: Don't Look Now, The Man Who Fell To Earth, Bad Timing, Eureka, Insignificance, Castaway, Aria (sequence, also co-s.p.), Track 29, The Witches, Without You I'm Nothing (exec. prod. only), Cold Heaven.
TELEVISION: Movies: Sweet Bird of Youth, Heart of Darkness.

ROËVES, MAURICE
Actor, Director, Writer. b. Sunderland, England, Mar. 19, 1937. Ent. industry, 1964. Played Macduff to Alec Guinness's Macbeth, London stage. Early films: Ulysses, Oh! What a Lovely War, Young Winston, The Eagle Has Landed, Who Dares Wins. Dir. many stage plays.
THEATER: The Killing of Michael Malloy (Best Leading Actor Award, 1994).
PICTURES: Hidden Agenda, Last of the Mohicans, Judge Dredd.
TELEVISION: In USA and UK incl.: Scobie (series), The Gambler, Allergy, Magnum P.I., Remington Steele, Escape to Victoria, Inside the Third Reich, Journal of Bridgitte Hitler, Tutti Frutti, Unreported Incident, Bookie, North & South Part II, 919 Fifth Ave., Moses (mini-series), Hillborough, David.

ROGERS, CHARLES (BUDDY)
Actor. b. Olathe, KS, Aug. 13, 1904. e. U. of Kansas, and was trained for screen in Paramount Picture Sch. In armed services WWII. 1945 named v.p. & treas. Comet Prods., Inc. Assoc. prod. Sleep My Love, 1950, pres. PRB, Inc., prod. radio, video shows.
PICTURES: Fascinating Youth, So's Your Old Man, Wings, My Best Girl, Get Your Man, Abie's Irish Rose, The Lawyer's Secret, Road to Reno, Working Girls, This Reckless Age, Best of Enemies, Take a Chance, Dance Band, Old Man Rhythm, One in a Million, Let's Make a Night of It, This Way Please, Golden Hoofs, Mexican Spitfire's Baby, Sing for Your Supper, Mexican Spitfire at Sea, Mexican Spitfire Sees a Ghost, Don't Trust Your Husband, The Parson and the Outlaw, many others.

ROGERS, FRED
Television Host, Producer. b. Latrobe, PA, March 20, 1928. e. Rollins Coll., B.A., music composition, 1951; Pittsburgh Theol. Seminary, M. Div. 1962. 1951 served as asst. prod. of NBC-TV's The Voice of Firestone and NBC-TV Opera Theatre. Later promoted to network floor dir., supervising Your Lucky Strike Hit Parade, Kate Smith Hour, etc. 1953, joined WQED-TV in Pittsburgh, educational TV station, to handle programming. 1954 started Children's Corner series, writing, producing and performing; it ran 7 years. 1963 was ordained minister of Presbyterian Church, dedicated to working with children and families through media. Same year introduced Mister Rogers on Canadian Broadcasting Corp. of 15-min. daily program. Ran for one year—was similar in content to present half-hour program, Mister Rogers' Neighborhood. 1964 programs were incorporated into larger, half-hour format on ABC affiliate in Pittsburgh.

1966, 100 programs acquired by Eastern Educational Network, broadcast in Pittsburgh, and seen for first time in other cities (and on some cable services) with underwriting by Sears & Roebuck Foundation. Mister Rogers' Neighborhood in its present format began on Feb. 19, 1968 on NET (now PBS). Program now carried over 300 PBS stations. Author of numerous fiction books for children and non-fiction books for adults; and albums and videos released by Family Communication. Also prod. 20 part PBS series Old Friends New Friends, interview/documentary format for adults, 1978-9. Produced Fred Rogers' Heroes (adult special for PBS). Recipient of 2 Emmy Awards, 2 Peabody Awards and over 25 honorary degrees from colleges and universities.

ROGERS, KENNY
Singer, Actor, Songwriter. b. Crockett, TX, Aug. 21, 1938. Country and western singer. Member Bobby Doyle Trio, Christy Minstrels, 1966-67; The First Edition 1967-76. On screen in Six Pack (1982).
TELEVISION: Series: McShane (NBC Friday Night Mystery). Movies: The Dream Makers, Kenny Rogers as The Gambler, Coward of the County, Kenny Rogers as the Gambler: The Adventure Continues, Wild Horses; Kenny Rogers as The Gambler Part III: The Legend Continues, Christmas in America, The Gambler Returns: Luck of the Draw, Real West, Rio Diablo, MacShayne: The Final Roll of the Dice, Gambler IV: Playing for Keeps, Big Dreams & Broken Hearts: The Dottie West Story. Specials: Kenny, Dolly & Willie: Something Inside So Strong, and numerous others. Guest: Dr. Quinn, Medicine Woman.

ROGERS, LAWRENCE H., II
Executive. b. Trenton, NJ, Sept. 6, 1921. e. Princeton U. 1942, U.S. Army, 1942-1946; with WSAZ, Huntington, WV, as radio & tv, v.p. & gen. mgr., 1949-55; WSAZ, Inc., pres., 1955-59; Taft Broadcasting Co., v.p., 1959-63; Taft Broadcasting Co., pres., 1963-76; cert., Harvard Business Sch., 1963; vice chmn., Hanna-Barbera Prods., LA, and Cinemobile Systems, Hollywood. Director Cincinnati Financial Corporation, 1963-94. Chmn., Cincinnati Branch, Federal Reserve Bank of Cleveland, 1974-80. Pres., Omega communications, 1979-84; Director Cine Artists International, Hollywood; Theater Development Fund, NY. Director of Cardinal Group of Mutual Funds, 1970-present. Author: Business of Broadcasting, 1964; Orlando Shoot-Out, 1990.

ROGERS, MIMI
Actress. b. Coral Gables, FL, Jan. 27, 1959.
PICTURES: Blue Skies Again (debut, 1983), Gung Ho, Street Smart, Someone to Watch Over Me, The Mighty Quinn, Hider in the House, Desperate Hours, The Doors, The Rapture, The Palermo Connection, The Player, White Sands, Dark Horse, Monkey Trouble, Far From Home: The Adventures of Yellow Dog, Bulletproof Heart, Reflections in the Dark, The Mirror Has Two Faces, Lost In Space, Austin Powers International Man of Mystery.
TELEVISION: Series: The Rousters, Paper Dolls. Episodes: Magnum, P.I., Hart to Hart, Quincy, M.E., Hill Street Blues, Tales From the Crypt. Movies: Divorce Wars, Hear No Evil, You Ruined My Life, Fourth Story, Deadlock, Ladykiller, Bloodlines: Murder in the Family, A Kiss to Die For, Weapons of Mass Distraction, Full Body Massage, Tricks.

ROGERS, PETER
Executive. b. Rochester, Eng., Feb. 20, 1916. e. Kings Sch., Rochester. Journalist and in theatre and BBC; joined G. W. H. Productions 1941 as script writer; with Gainsborough Studios; asst. scenario ed. to Muriel Box; assoc. prod.; personal asst. to Sydney Box 1949.
PICTURES: Dear Murderer, Holiday Camp, When the Bough Breaks, Here Come the Huggetts, Huggetts Abroad, Vote for Huggett, It's Not Cricket, Marry Me, Don't Ever Leave Me, Appointment with Venus (Island Rescue), The Clouded Yellow, The Dog and the Diamonds (Children's Film Found), Up to His Neck, You Know What Sailors Are, Cash on Delivery, To Dorothy A Son, Gay Dog, Circus Friends, Passionate Stranger, After the Ball, Time Lock, My Friend Charles, Chain of Events, Carry on Sergeant, Flying Scott, Cat Girl, Solitary Child, Carry On Teacher, Carry On Nurse, Carry On Constable, Please Turn Over, Watch Your Stern, The Tommy Steele Story, The Duke Wore Jeans, No Kidding, Carry On Regardless, Raising the Wind, Twice Around the Daffodils, Carry on Cruising, The Iron Maiden, Nurse on Wheels, Carry on Cabby, This Is My Street, Carry On Jack, Carry on Spying, Carry on Cleo, The Big Job, Carry on Cowboy, Carry on Screaming, Don't Lose Your Head, Follow that Camel, Carry on Doctor, Carry on Up the Khyber, Carry on Camping, Carry on Assault, Carry on Henry, Quest, Revenge, Carry on At Your Convenience, All Coppers Are..., Carry on Matron, Carry on Abroad, Bless This House, Carry on Girls, Carry on Dick, Carry on Behind, Carry on England, The Best of Carry On, Carry on Emmanuelle, Carry on Columbus.
TELEVISION: Ivanhoe (series), Carry on Laughing, Carry on Laughing, What a Carry On, Laugh With the Carry On's.

ROGERS, ROY
Actor. r.n. Leonard Slye. b. Cincinnati, OH Nov. 5, 1911. m. actress-singer Dale Evans. Radio singer. Changed named to Dick Wesson and formed singing group Sons of the Pioneers, with which he made his film debut. Voted No. 1 Money-Making Western Star in M.P. Herald-Fame, 1943-54 inclusive; also voted one of ten best money-making stars in 1945, 1946. Acting & prod. TV films, 1952 with wife, Dale Evans; one-hour spectaculars, Chevy Show, 1959-60; contracted for several TV specials and for nationwide appearances with Roy Rogers touring show in Canada & U.S., 1962; state fairs, rodeos since 1962; TV series; Happy Trails with Roy and Dale (cable). Star of 86 feature films and 104 TV episodes.
PICTURES: Way Up Thar (debut, 1935, as Dick Wesson), Rhythm on the Range, Under Western Stars (1st billing as Roy Rogers), The Old Barn Dance, Billy the Kid Returns, Come On Rangers, Rough Riders, Round-Up, Frontier, Pony Express, Southward Ho!, In Old Caliente, Wall Street Cowboy, Heart of the Golden West, Sunset Serenade, Pals of the Golden West, Son of Paleface, Alias Jesse James (cameo), MacIntosh and T.J.
TELEVISION: Series: The Roy Rogers Show, The Roy Rogers & Dale Evans Show.
(d. July 6, 1998)

ROGERS, THOMAS C.
Executive. e. Columbia Law School, Wesleyan Univ. 1981-86, sr. counsel, U.S. House of Representatives Subcommittee on Telecommunications, Consumer Protection and Finance; Joined NBC in 1987 as v.p., policy and planning and business development. 1988 became pres. of NBC Cable and Business Development. 1992, also named exec. v.p. of NBC.

ROGERS, WAYNE
Actor. b. Birmingham, AL, April 7, 1933. e. Princeton U. After graduation entered the army for three yrs.; studied at Sanford's Meisner's Neighborhood Playhouse and with Martha Graham. Currently gen. partner of Balanced Value Fund, an investment firm; founder, mem on advisory bd., of Plaza Bank of Commerce. Chmn., Easter Seals. Member: Executive Committee of the Arthritis Foundation; Juvenile Diabetes Foundation; Trustees of the Webb School; Kenan Institute of Private Enterprise. Affiliate, School of Business Adm. of the U of NC. Spokesperson, J.B. Oxford & Co.
PICTURES: Odds Against Tomorrow (debut, 1959), The Glory Guys, Chamber of Horrors, Cool Hand Luke, WUSA, Pocket Money, Once in Paris, The Gig, The Killing Time, Ghosts of Mississippi.
TELEVISION: Series: Edge of Night, Stagecoach West, M*A*S*H, City of the Angels, House Calls, High Risk (host). Movies: Lamp Unto My Feet, Attack on Terror: The FBI Versus the Ku Klux Klan, Making Babies II, It Happened One Christmas, The Top of the Hill, Chiefs, He's Fired She's Hired, The Lady from Yesterday, American Harvest, Drop-Out Mother, One Terrific Guy, Bluegrass, Passion and Paradise, Miracle Landing, The Goodbye Bird. Guest: The Fugitive, The Invaders, Gunsmoke, The F.B.I., Gomer Pyle. Mini-Series: Chiefs. Exec. prod.: Perfect Witness, Age-Old Friends, The Charlie Rose Special, AMC Hollywood Report (also host), Money Plays.

ROHRBECK, JOHN H.
Executive. e. Univ. of WA. 1967, account exec. for NBC Spot Sales in San Francisco, then NY. 1969-78, with KNBC-TV in mngmt. and sales, became station manager in 1976. 1978-84, v.p. & gen. mngr. WRC-TV in Washington DC. Became pres. & gen. mngr. of KNBC-TV in 1984. Named pres. of NBC Television Stations, 1991. Also in charge of network's daytime programming 1992-95.

ROHMER, ERIC
Director. Writer. r.n. Jean Maurice Scherer. b. Nancy, France, April 4, 1920. Professor of literature. Film critic for La Gazette du Cinema and its successor Cahiers du Cinema which he edited, 1957-63. With Claude Chabrol wrote book on Alfred Hitchcock as a Catholic moralist, 1957. 1959 directorial debut, Le Signe du Lion. 1962 began a series of 6 Moral Tales; from 1980 with The Aviator's Wife began another series of 7 films called Comedies and Proverbs. Staged Catherine de Heilbronn in Nanterre, 1979.
PICTURES: Short films: Presentation ou Charlotte et Son Steack (1961), La Boulangere de Monceau, Veronique et Son Cancre, Nadja a Paris, Place de L'etoile, Une Etudiante d'aujourd'hui, Fermiere a Montfaucon. Feature films (dir. & s.p.): Le Signe du Lion (The Sign of Leo; debut, 1959), La Carriere de Suzanne, Six in Paris (episode), La Collectionneuse, My Night at Maude's, Claire's Knee, Chloe in the Afternoon, The Marquise of O, Perceval, The Aviator's Wife, Le Beau Mariage, Pauline at the Beach, Full Moon in Paris, Summer, Boyfriends and Girlfriends, Four Adventures of Reinette and Mirabelle (also prod.), A Tale of Springtime, A Tale of Winter, The Tree, The Mayor and the Mediatheque, Citizen Langlois (actor), Rendezvous in Paris, A Summer's Tale; An Autumn Tale.
TELEVISION: Carl Dreyer, Le Celluloid et le Marbre, Ville Nouvelle, Catherine de Heilbronn. Between 1964-69 directed series of documentaries for French TV: Les Cabinets et Physique du XVIII siecle, Les Metamorphoses du Paysage Industriel, Don Quichotte, Edgar Poe, Pascal, Louis Lumiere, etc.

ROIZMAN, OWEN
Cinematographer. b. Brooklyn, NY, Sept. 22, 1936. e. Gettysburg Col.
PICTURES: The French Connection, The Gang That Couldn't Shoot Straight, Play It Again Sam, The Heartbreak Kid, The Exorcist, The Taking of Pelham 1-2-3, The Stepford Wives, Independence, Three Days of the Condor, The Return of the Man Called Horse, Network, Straight Time, Sgt. Pepper's Lonely Hearts Club Band, The Electric Horseman, The Black Marble, True Confessions, Absence of Malice, Taps, Tootsie, Vision Quest, I Love You to Death, Havana, The Addams Family, Grand Canyon, Wyatt Earp, French Kiss.

ROLLE, ESTHER
Actress. b. Pompano Beach, FL, Nov. 8, 1922. e. New School for Social Research. An original member of Negro Ensemble Co. in NY. Has appeared both off and on B'way (in The Blacks, Amen Corner, Blues for Mister Charlie, Don't Play Us Cheap, Member of the Wedding) and in several TV series.
PICTURES: Nothing But a Man, Cleopatra Jones, P.K. and the Kid, The Mighty Quinn, Driving Miss Daisy, House of Cards, How to Make an American Quilt, Rosewood.
TELEVISION: Guest: N.Y.P.D., Like It Is, Darkroom, The Winners, The Grand Baby. Series: One Life to Live, Maude, Good Times. Movies: I Know Why the Caged Bird Sings, Summer of My German Soldier (Emmy Award, 1979), A Raisin in the Sun, Age-Old Friends, The Kid Who Loved Christmas, To Dance With the White Dog. Mini-Series: Scarlett.

ROLLINS, JACK
Producer. b. 1914. Co-founder of talent management firm Rollins, Joffe, Mora and Brezner Inc. handling careers of Woody Allen, Nichols and May, Robin Williams, Robert Klein, David Letterman, Dick Cavett, Billy Crystal.
PICTURES: Co-prod./exec. prod. with Charles Joffe: Take the Money and Run, Bananas, Everything You Always Wanted to Know About Sex, Sleeper, Love and Death, The Front, Annie Hall (Acad. Award for Best Picture, 1977), Interiors, Manhattan, Stardust Memories, Zelig, Broadway Danny Rose (also actor), The Purple Rose of Cairo, Hannah and Her Sisters, Radio Days, September, Another Woman, New York Stories (Oedipus Wrecks), Crimes and Misdemeanors, Alice, Shadows and Fog, Husbands and Wives, Manhattan Murder Mystery, Bullets Over Broadway, Mighty Aphrodite, Everyone Says I Love You, Deconstructing Harry.
TELEVISION: Prod./exec. prod.: The Dick Cavett Show, Late Night With David Letterman.

ROMAN, LAWRENCE
Writer. b. Jersey City, NJ, May 30, 1921. e. UCLA, 1943.
THEATER: Author: Under the Yum Yum Tree, P.S. I Love You, Alone Together, Buying Out, Crystal, Crystal Chandelier (prod. in Stockbridge, Mass), Coulda Woulda Shoulda (premiered in Berlin, Germany), Moving Mountains (premiered in Berlin as Grapes and Raisins).
PICTURES: Drums Across the River, Vice Squad, Naked Alibi, One Desire, Man from Bitter Ridge, Kiss Before Dying, Slaughter on Tenth Avenue, Under the Yum Yum Tree, The Swinger, Paper Lion, Red Sun, A Warm December, McQ.
TELEVISION: Movies: Anatomy of an Illness, Badge of the Assassin, Three Wishes for Jamie, Final Verdict, The Ernest Green Story (Peabody Award).

ROMAN, RUTH
Actress. b. Boston, MA, Dec. 23, 1924. p. professionals. e. Girls H.S., Boston; Bishop Lee Dramatic Sch. Started career with little theatre groups: New Eng. Repertory Co., Elizabeth Peabody Players. Chicago Theatre includes Night of the Iguana, Two for the Season (Sarah Siddons Award). Screen debut in Universal serial, Queen of the Jungle.
PICTURES: Good Sam, Belle Starr's Daughter, The Window, Champion, Barricade, Beyond the Forest, Always Leave Them Laughing, Colt .45, Three Secrets, Dallas, Strangers on a Train, Tomorrow is Another Day, Invitation, Lightning Strikes Twice, Starlift, Mara Maru, Young Man With Ideas, Blowing Wild, Far Country, Shanghai Story, Tanganyika, Down Three Dark Streets, Joe Macbeth, Bottom of the Bottle, Great Day in the Morning, Rebel in Town, Five Steps to Danger, Bitter Victory, Desert Desperadoes, Look in Any Window, Miracle of the Cowards (Spanish), Love Has Many Faces, Impulse, The Killing Kind, The Baby, Day of the Animals, Echoes.
TELEVISION: Series: The Long Hot Summer, Knots Landing. Guest: Naked City, Route 66, The Defenders, Breaking Point, Eleventh Hour, Producers Showcase, Dr. Kildare, Murder She Wrote, Cannon, Ironside. Movies: The Old Man Who Cried Wolf, Incident in San Francisco, Go Ask Alice, Punch and Jody, The Sacketts.

ROMERO, GEORGE A.
Director, Writer, Editor. b. New York, NY, 1940. e. Carnegie-Mellon Univ.
PICTURES: Dir./Writer/Cameraman: Night of the Living Dead (debut, 1968), There's Always Vanilla (The Affair), The Crazies (Code Name: Trixie), Jack's Wife (Hungry Wives; also edit.). Director-Writer: Martin (also edit., actor), Dawn of the Dead (dir. only), Knightriders, Creepshow (dir., co-edit. only), Day of the Dead (also edit.), Monkey Shines, Night of the Living Dead (s.p., co-exec. prod. only), Two Evil Eyes (The Facts in the Case of M. Valdemar), The Dark Half (also exec. prod.).
TELEVISION: Tales from the Dark Side (exec. prod., writer).

RONA, JEFF
Composer. b. March 3, 1957.
PICTURES: Composer: Lipstick Camera, White Squall, Do Me a Favor. Additional Music: Toys, The Net, Assassins, The Fan, Black Cat Run.
TELEVISION: Movies: Toys, Death in Small Doses. Series: Homicide: Life on the Street, Chicago Hope, Profiler, High Incident, Gun, Teen Angel, Sleepwalkers.

ROOKER, MICHAEL
Actor. b. Jasper, AL, 1955. e. Goodman School of Drama. Studied Japanese martial art of Aikido prior to establishing himself in Chicago theatre, where he appeared in Union Boys, The Crack Walker and Moon Children.
PICTURES: Streets of Fire (debut, 1984), Light of Day, Rent-a-Cop, Eight Men Out, Mississippi Burning, Sea of Love, Music Box, Henry: Portrait of a Serial Killer, Days of Thunder, JFK, The Dark Half, Cliffhanger, Tombstone, The Hard Truth, Mallrats, The Trigger Effect, Rosewood, Liar, The Replacement Killers.
TELEVISION: Movies: Afterburn, Johnny & Clyde.

ROONEY, ANDREW A
Writer, Producer. b. Albany, NY, Jan. 14, 1919. e. Colgate U. Started career as writer at MGM 1946-7, then for Arthur Godfrey, Garry Moore; wrote and produced documentaries, including Black History: Lost Stolen or Strayed (Emmy Award, 1969), An Essay on War, An Essay on Bridges, In Praise of New York City, Mr. Rooney Goes to Washington, etc. Commentator, 60 Minutes (CBS), 1978-present. Newspaper columnist for Tribune Syndicate, 1979-present.
AUTHOR: Air Gunner, The Story of the Stars and Stripes, Conqueror's Peace, A Few Minutes With Andy Rooney, And More Any Rooney, Pieces of My Mind, Sweet and Sour, The Fortunes of War, Not That You Asked, Word for Word, My War.

ROONEY, MICKEY
Actor. r.n. Joe Yule, Jr. b. Brooklyn, NY, Sept. 23, 1920. Son of Joe Yule & Nell Carter, vaudeville performers. U.S. Army, WWII. In vaudeville as child with parents and others before m.p. debut and after; from age of 5 to 12 (1926-33) created screen version of Fontaine Fox newspaper comic character Mickey McGuire in series of short subjects (also billed as Mickey McGuire). Adopted name of Mickey Rooney, returned to vaudeville, then resumed screen career in features. Special Academy Award 1940 for Andy Hardy characterization; voted among first ten Money-Making Stars in M.P. Herald-Fame Poll: 1938-43. Autobiographies: i.e. (1965), Life is Too Short (1991). Novel: The Search for Sonny Skies (1994). Received honorary Academy Award, 1983.
THEATER: B'way: Sugar Babies, The Will Rogers Follies. Regional: W.C., Lend Me a Tenor.
PICTURES: Orchids and Ermine (feature debut, 1927), Emma, The Beast of the City, Sin's Pay Day, High Speed, Officer Thirteen, Fast Companions, My Pal the King, The Big Cage, The Life of Jimmy Dolan, The Big Chance, Broadway to Hollywood, The World Changes, The Chief, Beloved, I Like It That Way, Love Birds, Half a Sinner, The Lost Jungle, Manhattan Melodrama, Upperworld, Hide-Out, Chained, Blind Date, Death on the Diamond, The County Chairman, Reckless, The Healer, A Midsummer Night's Dream, Ah Wilderness, Riff-Raff, Little Lord Fauntleroy, The Devil is a Sissy, Down the Stretch, Captains Courageous, Slave Ship, A Family Affair, Hoosier Schoolboy, Live Love and Learn, Thoroughbreds Don't Cry, You're Only Young Once, Love is a Headache, Judge Hardy's Children, Hold That Kiss, Lord Jeff, Love Finds Andy Hardy, Boys Town, Stablemates, Out West With the Hardys, The Adventures of Huckleberry Finn, The Hardys Ride High, Andy Hardy Gets Spring Fever, Babes in Arms (Acad. Award nom.), Judge Hardy and Son, Young Tom Edison, Andy Hardy Meets Debutante, Strike Up the Band, Andy Hardy's Private Secretary, Men of Boy's Town, Life Begins for Andy Hardy, Babes on Broadway, The Courtship of Andy Hardy, A Yank at Eton, Andy Hardy's Double Life, The Human Comedy (Acad. Award nom.), Girl Crazy, Thousands Cheer, Andy Hardy's Blonde Trouble, National Velvet, Love Laughs at Andy Hardy, Killer McCoy, Summer Holiday, Words and Music, The Big Wheel, Quicksand, He's a Cockeyed Wonder, The Fireball, My Outlaw Brother, The Strip, Sound Off, All Ashore, Off Limits, A Slight Case of Larceny,

Drive a Crooked Road, The Atomic Kid (also prod.), The Bridges at Toko-Ri, The Twinkle in God's Eye, Francis in the Haunted House, The Bold and the Brave (Acad. Award nom.), Magnificent Roughnecks, Operation Mad Ball, Baby Face Nelson, Andy Hardy Comes Home, A Nice Little Bank That Should Be Robbed, The Last Mile, The Big Operator, Platinum High School, The Private Lives of Adam and Eve (also co-dir.), Breakfast at Tiffany's, King of the Roaring Twenties, Requiem for a Heavyweight, Everything's Ducky, It's a Mad Mad Mad Mad World, Secret Invasion, 24 Hours to Kill, The Devil in Love, Ambush Bay, How to Stuff a Wild Bikini, The Extraordinary Seaman, Skidoo, The Comic, 80 Steps to Jonah, The Cockeyed Cowboys of Calico County, Hollywood Blue, B.J. Lang Presents (The Manipulator), Richard, Pulp, The Godmothers (also s.p., music), Ace of Hearts, Thunder County, That's Entertainment, Journey Back to Oz (voice), From Hong Kong With Love, Rachel's Man, Find the Lady, The Domino Principle, Pete's Dragon, The Magic of Lassie, The Black Stallion (Acad. Award nom.), Arabian Adventure, The Fox and the Hound (voice), The Emperor of Peru, The Black Stallion Returns, The Care Bears Movie (voice), Lightning the White Stallion, Erik the Viking, My Heroes Have Always Been Cowboys, Sweet Justice, The Legend of Wolf Mountain, Little Nemo (voice), Silent Night Deadly Night 5: The Toymaker, The Milky Life (La Vida Lactea), Revenge of the Red Baron, That's Entertainment III, Animals (And the Tollkeeper).
TELEVISION: *Series:* Hey Mickey, One of the Boys, The Black Stallion. *Many specials including:* Playhouse 90, Pinocchio, Eddie, Somebody's Waiting, The Dick Powell Theater. *Movies:* Evil Roy Slade, My Kidnapper My Love, Leave 'Em Laughing, Bill (Emmy Award, 1982), Senior Trip, Bill: On His Own, It Came Upon the Midnight Clear, Bluegrass, Home for Christmas, The Gambler Returns: Luck of the Draw. *Many guest appearances including:* The Golden Girls, The Judy Garland Show, Naked City, Wagon Train, Twilight Zone, The Lucy Show, Hollywood Squares, Night Gallery, The Love Boat.

ROONEY, PAT E.
Producer. e. Santa Monica College, Marquette U., Denver U., UCLA. Was Captain in U.S. Army. Entertainer Far East Command Forces, Korean War. In 1960, joined CBS Films, producing TV series and pilot films. 1962 formed Pat Rooney Prods. with Del E. Webb and Jerry Buss. Has worked as independent producer for MGM, Paramount, Universal, 20th Century Fox, Warber Bros, Goldwyn. 1993 partnered with John Veitch (former pres. of Columbia Pictures).
PICTURES: Dime With A Halo, Danger Pass, Caged, Law of the Lawless, Requiem for a Gunfighter, Bounty Killer, Young Once, Hell's Angels, Fools, Christmas Couple, Black Eye, Deadman's Curve, Deadly Attack, Secret Ceremony, Kings Row, Devil Planes, Gentlemen of the Night, Kapo Women, Lillies of the Field, Light Fingers, Poison Ivy, Nylon Noose, A Love Story, Gattling Gun.

ROOS, FRED
Producer. b. Santa Monica, CA, May 22, 1934. e. UCLA, B.A. Directed documentary films for Armed Forces Radio and Television Network. Worked briefly as agent for MCA and story editor for Robert Lippert Productions. Worked as casting dir. in 1960s and served as casting dir. on The Godfather, beginning longtime association with filmmakers Francis Coppola and George Lucas.
PICTURES: The Conversation, The Godfather Part II, Apocalypse Now, The Black Stallion, The Escape Artist (exec. prod.), The Black Stallion Returns, Hammett, One From the Heart, The Outsiders, Rumble Fish, The Cotton Club, Seven Minutes in Heaven, Peggy Sue Got Married (special consultant), Barfly, Gardens of Stone (exec. prod.), Tucker: The Man and His Dream, New York Stories (Life Without Zoe), Wait Until Spring Bandini, The Godfather Part III, Hearts of Darkness: A Filmmaker's Apocalypse (exec. prod.), The Secret Garden, Radioland Murders, Jack (spec. consultant), The Rainmaker (exec. consultant).
TELEVISION: *Series:* The Outsiders (exec. prod.). *Movie:* Montana.

ROSE, ALEX
Producer. r.n. Alexandra Rose. b. Jan. 20, 1946. e. U. of WI, BS. Started in m.p. distribution with Medford Films. Later became asst. sls. mgr. for New World Pictures.
PICTURES: *Co-prod.:* Drive-In, I Wanna Hold Your Hand, Big Wednesday, Norma Rae, Nothing in Common (solo prod.), Overboard (co-prod.), Quigley Down Under, Frankie and Johnny.
TELEVISION: Nothing in Common (co-exec. prod. with Garry Marshall), *Pilots:* Norma Rae, Just Us Kids.

ROSE, CHARLIE
Talk Show Host. b. Henderson, NC, Jan. 5, 1942. e. Duke Univ. (history, law). Was exec. prod. for Bill Moyers' Journal, 1975.
TELEVISION: *Series (host/anchor):* A.M. Chicago, The Charlie Rose Show (NBC, 1979, 1981), CBS News Nightwatch, E.D.J. Entertainment Daily Journal (Personalities), Charlie Rose (synd; also exec. prod., editor). *Specials:* Public Debate With Charlie Rose, In Concert at the United Nations (host).

ROSE, REGINALD
Writer. b. New York, NY, Dec. 10, 1920. e. City Coll. of New York. Worked as clerk, publicist, Warner Bros.; adv. acct. exec., copy chief; U.S. Air Force, WWII; first TV play, Bus to Nowhere, 1951; since then numerous TV plays, Studio One, Playhouse 90. Creator of The Defenders, other programs.
PICTURES: Crime in the Streets, 12 Angry Men, Dino, Man of the West, The Man in the Net, Baxter, Somebody Killed Her Husband, The Wild Geese, The Sea Wolves, Whose Life Is It Anyway?, Wild Geese II, The Final Option.
TELEVISION: Dear Friends, Thunder on Sycamore Street, Tragedy in a Temporary Town, My Two Loves, The Rules of Marriage, Studs Lonigan, Escape from Sobibor.

ROSE, STEPHEN
Executive. Entered m.p. industry in 1964 with Columbia Pictures; named adv. dir. 1970 joined Cinema V Distributing, Inc. as dir. of adv.; left in 1971 to take post at Cinemation Industries, where was named v.p. and bd. member. 1975 joined Paramount Pictures as dir. of adv.; promoted to v.p./adv. 1979 formed Barrich Prods. with Gordon Weaver. 1982, rejoined Paramount as v.p., mktg; 1983, named v.p. of mktg. for Paramount; sr. v.p., mktg., 1983. Resigned in 1984 to form Barrich Marketing with Gordon Weaver.

ROSEANNE
Actress. b. Salt Lake City, UT, Nov. 3, 1952. Started performing in bars; prod. showcase for women performers, Take Back the Mike at U. of Boulder. 1983 won Denver Laff-Off. Moved to Los Angeles where performed at The Comedy Store, and showcased on TV special Funny and The Tonight Show. Has previously performed under the names Roseanne Barr, Roseanne Arnold. *Autobiographies:* My Life as a Woman (1989), My Lives (1994).
PICTURES: She-Devil (debut, 1989), Look Who's Talking Too (voice), Freddy's Dead, Even Cowgirls Get the Blues, Blue in the Face.
TELEVISION: *Series:* Roseanne (also co-exec. prod.; Peabody & Golden Globe Awards for Best Series; Emmy Award for Best Actress, 1993), The Jackie Thomas Show (co-exec. prod, guest), Tom (co-exec. prod.). *Specials:* Fast Copy, Rodney Dangerfield—It's Not Easy Bein' Me, Live From Minneapolis: Roseanne, Roseanne Arnold: Live From Trump Castle. *Movies:* Backfield in Motion, The Woman Who Loved Elvis (also co-exec. prod.), I Am Your Child.

ROSEN, ROBERT L.
Producer. b. Palm Springs, CA, Jan. 7, 1937. e. U. of Southern Calif.
PICTURES: *Exec. prod.:* French Connection II, Black Sunday, Prophecy, Going Ape, The Challenge, Courage (also dir.), Porky's Revenge, World Gone Wild, Dead-Bang (exec. prod.), Year of the Gun, Spy Hard, Mr. Magoo, Wrongfully Accused. *Exec. in chg. of prod.:* Little Big Man, Le Mans, The Reivers, Rio Lobo, Big Jake, Scrooge, Fourth War (Line Producer).
TELEVISION: Gilligan's Island, Hawaii Five-O, Have Gun Will Travel.

ROSENBERG, FRANK P.
Producer, Writer. b. New York, NY, Nov. 22, 1913. e. Columbia U., NYU. Joined Columbia 1929; writer m.p. novelizations & radio dramatizations; 1933, conceived and wrote script for first-ever ship-to-shore CBS network broadcast for Lady for a Day; exploit. mgr.; 1941; apptd. national dir. adv., royalty, exploitation, Columbia Pictures, 1944. Pub. dir. M.P. Victory Loan, 1945; dir. pub. Columbia Pictures Studios, Hollywood, 1946. Resigned 1947 to enter production.
PICTURES: Man-Eater of Kumaon, Where the Sidewalk Ends, The Secret of Convict Lake, Return of the Texan, The Farmer Takes a Wife, King of the Khyber Rifles, Illegal, Miracle in the Rain, The Girl He Left Behind, One-Eyed Jacks, Critic's Choice, Madigan, The Steagle, The Reincarnation of Peter Proud, Gray Lady Down.
TELEVISION: Exec. prod. and prod. for Schlitz Playhouse programs during 1957-58; prod., The Troubleshooters; exec. prod., Arrest and Trial, 1963-64; exec. prod. Kraft Suspense Theatre, 1964-65; v.p. MCA Universal 1964-69; co-exec. prod., CBS tv movie Family of Strangers, 1993.

ROSENBERG, GRANT E.
Executive. b. San Francisco, CA, 1952. e. Univ. of Cal. at Davis. Started career in research dept., NBC; 1977, joined Paramount in research and later in development; 1984, v.p., dramatic dev.; then sr. v.p., dev., for TV group, Paramount. 1985, named sr. v.p., network TV for Walt Disney Pictures; 1988, named pres., Lee Rich Productions, TV div., and exec. prod. of Molloy TV series. 1990, writer, prod., Paramount TV. Series: MacGyver (writer), Star Trek: The Next Generation (writer), Time Trax (exec. prod., creator), Lois & Clark (writer, prod.). Writer, prod. for Warner Bros. TV.

ROSENBERG, RICHARD K.
Executive, Attorney. b. Paterson, NJ, Apr. 4, 1942. e. Indiana Univ. Corporation & intl. entertainment attorney for major corps. and celebrities. Formed RKR Entertainment Group in 1977 with subsidiaries RKR Releasing, RKR Artists and RKR Productions. Subsequently consolidated into RKR Pictures Inc. Author: Negotiating Motion Picture Contracts. Films include Alice Sweet Alice (Holy Terror), Hell's Angels Forever, Mother Lode, Best Revenge, The Wild Duck, Primary Motive, Fatal Past, Dutchman's Creek. V.p.; Cinetel Films, 1991-93. Exec. v.p. and bd. mem., Jones Entertainment Group Ltd., 1995.

ROSENBERG, RICK
Producer. b. Los Angeles, CA. e. Los Angeles City Coll., UCLA. Started career in mail room of Columbia Pictures, then asst. to prod. Jerry Bresler on Major Dundee and Love Has Many Faces. Asst. to Col. v.p., Arthur Kramer. Was assoc. prod. on The Reivers and in 1970 prod. first feature, Adam at Six A.M., with Bob Christiansen, with whom co-prod. all credits listed below.
PICTURES: Adam at Six A.M., Hide in Plain Sight.
TELEVISION: Suddenly Single, The Glass House, A Brand New Life, The Man Who Could Talk to Kids, The Autobiography of Miss Jane Pittman, I Love You... Goodbye, Queen of the Stardust Ballroom, Born Innocent, A Death in Canaan, Strangers, Robert Kennedy and His Times, Kids Don't Tell, As Summers Die, Gore Vidal's Lincoln, Red Earth White Earth, Heist, A House of Secrets and Lies, The Last Hit, Heart of Darkness, Tad, Kingfish: A Story of Huey P. Long, Redwood Curtain.

ROSENBERG, STUART
Director, Producer. b. New York, NY, Aug. 11, 1927. e. NYU.
PICTURES: Murder, Inc. (co-dir.; debut, 1960), Question 7, Cool Hand Luke, The April Fools, Move (also co-exec. prod.), WUSA (also co-exec. prod.), Pocket Money, The Laughing Policeman (also prod.), The Drowning Pool, Voyage of the Damned, The Amityville Horror, Love and Bullets, Brubaker, The Pope of Greenwich Village, Let's Get Harry (under pseudonym Allan Smithee), My Heroes Have Always Been Cowboys.
TELEVISION: Numerous episodes of such series as The Untouchables, Naked City, The Defenders (Emmy Award, 1963), Espionage, Chrysler Theatre, Twilight Zone, Alfred Hitchcock Theater.

ROSENFELT, FRANK E.
Executive. b. Peabody, MA, Nov. 15, 1921. e. Cornell U., B.S.; Cornell Law Sch., L.L.B. Served as atty. for RKO Radio Pictures, before joining MGM in 1955 as member of legal dept. Appt. secty. in 1966. Named v.p., gen. counsel in 1969 and pres. in 1973. 1974-81, CEO, bd. chmn. & CEO, MGM; now vice chmn., MGM/UA Communications Co. Member: Bd. of Governors, Academy of M.P. Arts & Sciences for 9 years. Retired from MGM/UA in Aug. 1990, now consultant to MGM-Pathe Commun. Co.

ROSENFELT, SCOTT
Producer, Director. b. Easton, PA, Dec. 20, 1955. e. NYU.
PICTURES: Producer: Teen Wolf, Extremities, Russkies, Mystic Pizza, Big Man on Campus (co-prod.), Home Alone, Family Prayers (dir.), Smoke Signals.
TELEVISION: Movie: T-Bone N Weasel.

ROSENFIELD, JONAS, JR.
Executive. b. Dallas, TX, June 29, 1915. e. U. of Miami, A.B. In U.S. Navy, WWII. Warner Bros. advertising copy dept., 1936-40; adv. mgr. Walt Disney, 1941; a founder & pres. N.Y. Screen Publicists Guild; adv. mngr. & dir., 20th Cent.-Fox, 1941-1950; v.p. Italian Films Export, 1950-55; v.p. in chg. adv. pub. expl. Columbia Pictures, 1955-63; v.p. worldwide adv., publ. and pro-motion, 20th Century-Fox, 1963-77; film mktg. consultant, 1977-78; lecturer in mktg., USC, 1978-79; v.p. in chg. of worldwide mktg., Melvin Simon Prods., 1979-1981; Filmways Pictures as exec. v.p., worldwide adv./pub., promo. 1982; lecturer adjunct, USC Sch. of Cinema & TV, 1982-84; pres. American Film Marketing Association, 1983 to present.

ROSENMAN, HOWARD
Producer. b. Brooklyn, NY, Feb. 1, 1945. e. Brooklyn Col. Asst. to Sir Michael Benthall on B'way show; prod., Benton & Bowles Agency; ABC-TV; RSO Prods. Co-pres., Sandollar Prods.; cur-rently pres. Brillstein-Grey Motion Pictures.
PICTURES: Sparkle, The Main Event, Resurrection, Lost Angels, Gross Anatomy, True Identity, Father of the Bride, Shining Through, Straight Talk, A Stranger Among Us, Buffy the Vampire Slayer, The Celluloid Closet.
TELEVISION: Movies: Isn't It Shocking? Altogether Now, Death Scream, Virginia Hill, Killer Bees. Specials: Common Threads: Stories from the Quilt (co-exec. prod.), Tidy Endings.

ROSENMAN, LEONARD
Composer. b. New York, NY, Sept. 7, 1924.
PICTURES: East of Eden, Cobweb, Rebel Without a Cause, Edge of the City, The Savage Eye, The Chapman Report, Fantastic Voyage, Hellfighters, Beneath the Planet of the Apes, Barry Lyndon (Academy Award, 1975), Birch Interval, Race With the Devil, Bound For Glory (Academy Award, 1976), A Man Called Horse, The Car, September 30, 1955, The Enemy of the People, The Lord of the Rings, Promises in the Dark, Prophecy, Hide in Plain Sight, The Jazz Singer, Making Love, Miss Lonely Hearts, Cross Creek, Heart of the Stag, Star Trek IV: The Voyage Home, Robocop 2, Ambition, The Color of Evening, Mrs. Munck, Levitation.
TELEVISION: Movies/Mini-Series: Sybil (Emmy Award), Friendly Fire (Emmy Award), City in Fear, Murder in Texas, Vanished, The Wall, Miss Lonelyhearts, Celebrity, The Return of Marcus Welby MD, Heartsounds, First Steps, Promised a Miracle, Keeper of the City, The Face on the Milk Carton.

ROSENSTEIN, GERTRUDE
Director. b. New York, NY. e. Barnard Coll., B.A., Neighborhood Playhouse. Exec. asst. to George Balanchine & Lincoln Kirstein, N.Y.C. Ballet. Assoc. with Gian Carlo Menotti, Festival of Two Worlds, Spoleto, Italy. Assoc. dir., NBC Opera Theatre, Emmy Awards, Kennedy Memorial Mass. TV staff dir., NBC. Now free-lance director, news programs, election coverages, music and dance programs, commercials. Governor, NY Television Academy. Member, Emmy Awards Committee.

ROSENTHAL, BUD
Executive. b. Brooklyn, NY, Mar. 21, 1934. e. Brooklyn Coll., B.A., 1954, NYU. US Army, 1954-56; college correspondent, NY Times. Entered m.p. ind. as assoc. editor, Independent Film Journal, 1957-59. Publicist, Columbia Pictures, 1959-61. Natl. publ mgr., Columbia Pictures, 1962-67. Publ. dir. for Anderson Tapes, Such Good Friends, The Blue Bird; Story edit. and cast-ing dir., Otto Preminger's Sigma Productions, 1972-75. Assoc. prod., Broadway play, Full Circle. Warner Bros. worldwide mtg. coordinator, Superman, Superman II, Superman III, Batman, Space Jam. Project coordinator, Time Warner Earth Day Special, Warner Bros. Studio Rededication, Celebration of Tradition. International mktg. consultant, 1976-present.
PICTURES: Something for Everyone (asst. prod.), Rosebud (assoc. prod.). Int'l mktg. co-ord. on films: Ghostbusters, Labyrinth, Tune in Tomorrow, Boyz 'N the Hood, Addams Family, Bugsy, Batman Returns, A Few Good Men, Last Action Hero, Jumanji.

ROSENTHAL, JANE
Executive. b. Denver, CO. e. NYU. 1976-84, dir. of film for TV at CBS; 1984-87, v.p. prod. Disney; 1987-88, v.p. of TV & Mini-Series, Warners TV; 1988-93, co-founder, Tribeca Prods., Tribeca Film Center; 1993-present, pres. of Tribeca Prods.; 1992-93, exec. prod. of series Tribeca. Producer of films Thunderheart, Faithful, Night and the City, Bronx Tale, Marvin's Room, Wag the Dog, Analyze This, Entropy, Flawless, Rocky and Bullwinkle.

ROSENTHAL, RICK
Director. b. New York, NY, June 15, 1949. e. Harvard, B.A. cum laude, 1971. Launched career as filmmaker-in-residence with New Hampshire TV Network. Moved to Los Angeles to study at American Film Institute where filmed Moonface, 1973.
PICTURES: Halloween II (debut, 1981), Bad Boys, American Dreamer, Russkies, Distant Thunder.
TELEVISION: Movies: Fire on the Mountain, Code of Vengeance, Secrets of Midland Heights, Nasty Boys, Devlin, Birds II, The Land's End. Series: Life Goes On, Witches of Eastwick, The Practice, Feds, Early Edition, Dellaventura.

ROSENZWEIG, BARNEY
Producer. b. Los Angeles, CA, Dec. 23, 1937. e. USC, 1959. m. actress Sharon Gless.
PICTURES: Morituri (assoc. prod.), Do Not Disturb (assoc. prod.), Caprice (assoc. prod.), Who Fears the Devil (prod.).
TELEVISION: Prod.: Daniel Boone (series), Men of the Dragon, One of My Wives Is Missing, Charlie's Angels (series), Angel on My Shoulder, American Dream (pilot), John Steinbeck's East of Eden (mini-series; Golden Globe Award). Exec. prod.: Modesty Blaise (pilot), This Girl for Hire (movie), Cagney and Lacey (series; 2 Emmy Awards: 1985, 1986), The Trials of Rosie O'Neill (series), Christy (movie, series), Cagney & Lacey: The Return (movie), Cagney & Lacey: Together Again (movie), Cagney & Lacey: The View Through the Glass Ceiling (movie), Cagney & Lacey: True Convictions (movie).

ROSS, DIANA
Singer, Actress. b. Detroit, MI, Mar. 26, 1944. Formed musical group at age 14 with two friends, Mary Wilson and Florence Ballard. In 1960 they auditioned for Berry Gordy, head of Motown Record Corp. and were hired to sing backgrounds on records for Motown acts. After completing high school, the trio was named the Supremes and went on tour with Motor Town Revue. Over period of 10 yrs. Supremes had 15 consecutive hit records and once had five consecutive records in the number one spot on charts. In 1969 Diana Ross went on her own, appearing on TV and in nightclubs. Memoirs: Secrets of a Sparrow (1993).

PICTURES: Lady Sings the Blues (debut as actress, 1972; Acad. Award nom.), Mahogany, The Wiz.
TELEVISION: *Movie*: Out of Darkness (also co-exec. prod.). *Specials*: Diana! (also exec. prod. & writer), Motown 25: Yesterday Today Forever, Motown Returns to the Apollo, Diana's World Tour.

ROSS, HERBERT
Director. b. New York, NY, May 13, 1927. m. Lee Radziwill. e. studied dance with Doris Humphrey, Helene Platova, Caird Leslie. Trained for stage with Herbert Berghof, 1946-50. As B'way dancer in Laffing Room Only, Beggars Holiday, Bloomer Girl, Look Ma I'm Dancing, Inside U.S.A., and with the American Ballet Theatre. Resident choreographer 1958-59 ABT for Caprichos, Concerto in D, The Maids, Tristan, Thief Who Loved a Ghost. Ent. m.p. ind. as choreographer for Carmen Jones, The Young Ones, Summer Holiday (also dir. musical sequences), Inside Daisy Clover, Dr. Doolittle, Funny Girl (also dir. musical numbers), La Bohème on film Soapdish.
THEATER/OPERA: *B'way Choreographer-Director*. A Tree Grows in Brooklyn, The Gay Life, I Can Get It For You Wholesale, Tovarich, Anyone Can Whistle, Do I Hear a Waltz, On a Clear Day You Can See Forever, The Apple Tree, Finian's Rainbow, Wonderful Town. *Dir.*: Chapter Two, I Ought To Be in Pictures, Follies in Concert, Anyone Can Whistle (fundraiser for GMHC; Grammy nom.), La Bohème (L.A. & Dallas).
PICTURES: Goodbye Mr. Chips (debut, 1969), The Owl and the Pussycat, T.R. Baskin, Play It Again Sam, The Last of Sheila (also prod.), Funny Lady, The Sunshine Boys, The Seven Percent Solution (also prod.), The Turning Point (also prod.), The Goodbye Girl, California Suite, Nijinsky (also prod.), Pennies from Heaven (also prod.), I Ought to Be in Pictures (also prod.), Max Dugan Returns (also prod.), Footloose, Protocol (also prod.), The Secret of My Success (also prod.), Dancers (also prod.), Steel Magnolias, My Blue Heaven (also prod.), True Colors (also prod.), Undercover Blues (also exec. prod.), Boys on the Side (also prod.).
TELEVISION: *Choreographer: Series*: Milton Berle Show (1952-57), Martha Raye Show, Bell Telephone Hour (also prod., dir.). *Specials*: Wonderful Town (also dir.), Meet Me in St. Louis, Jerome Kern Special, Bea Lillie and Cyril Ritchard Show (dir.), The Fantastiks, The Fred Astaire Special (1968, dir.).

ROSS, KATHARINE
Actress. b. Los Angeles, CA, Jan. 29, 1943. m. actor Sam Elliott. e. Santa Rosa Coll. Joined the San Francisco Workshop, appeared in The Devil's Disciple, The Balcony. TV debut, 1962 in Sam Benedict segment.
PICTURES: Shenandoah (debut, 1965), Mister Buddwing, The Singing Nun, Games, The Graduate (Golden Globe Award, Acad. Award nom.), Hellfighters, Butch Cassidy and the Sundance Kid, Tell Them Willie Boy is Here, Fools, Get to Know Your Rabbit, They Only Kill Their Masters, The Stepford Wives, Voyage of the Damned, The Betsy, The Swarm, The Legacy, The Final Countdown, Wrong Is Right, Daddy's Deadly Darling, Red-Headed Stranger.
TELEVISION: *Movies*: The Longest Hundred Miles, Wanted: The Sundance Woman, Murder by Natural Causes, Rodeo Girl, Murder in Texas, Marian Rose White, Shadow Riders, Travis McGee, Secrets of a Mother and Daughter, Conagher (also co-script). *Guest*: Ben Casey, The Bob Hope-Chrysler Theatre, The Virginian, Wagon Train, Kraft Mystery Theatre, The Lieutenant, The Road West. *Series*: The Colbys.

ROSS, KENNETH
Writer. b. London, Sept. 16, 1941. Entered m.p. industry 1970.
THEATER: The Raft, Under The Skin, Mr. Kilt & The Great I Am.
PICTURES: Brother Sun Sister Moon, Slag, The Reckless Years (also orig. story), Abelard & Heloise, The Day of the Jackal (So. Cal. M.P. Council Award; nom. for Writers' Guild, SFTA, and Golden Globes), The Devil's Lieutenant, The Odessa File (nom. for Writers' Guild Award), Quest (also orig. story), Black Sunday (Edgar Allen Poe Award, Mystery Writers of America, 1977), The Fourth War, Epiphany (also orig. story).
TELEVISION: The Roundelay, The Messenger.

ROSSELLINI, ISABELLA
Actress. b. Rome, Italy, June 18, 1952. Daughter of actress Ingrid Bergman and director Roberto Rossellini. Came to America in 1972. Worked as translator for Italian News Bureau. Taught Italian at New Sch. for Social Research. Worked 3 years on second unit assignments for journalist Gianni Mina and as NY corresp. for Ital. TV series, The Other Sunday. Model for Vogue, Harper's Bazaar, Italian Elle, Lancome Cosmetics.
PICTURES: A Matter of Time (debut 1976; with her mother), The Meadow, Il Papa'Occhio, White Nights, Blue Velvet, Tough Guys Don't Dance, Siesta, Red Riding Hood, Zelly and Me, Cousins, Les Dames Galantes, The Siege of Venice, Wild at Heart, Death Becomes Her, The Pickle, Fearless, Wyatt Earp, Immortal Beloved, The Innocent, Big Night.
TELEVISION: *Movies*: The Last Elephant, Lies of the Twins, The Crime of the Century. *Guest*: The Tracey Ullman Show. *Specials*: The Gift, Fallen Angels (The Frightening Frammis). *Guest*: Tales From the Crypt (You Murderer).

ROSSO, LEWIS, T.
Executive. b. Hoboken, NJ, Feb. 3, 1909. Ent. m.p. ind. 1930; prod. & mgt. for Consolidated Film Ind., 1930-44; Republic producer, 1944-50; prod. mgr., 1950-55; asst. sec'y & asst. treas., 1959; exec. asst. to exec. prod. mgr., 20th Century-Fox Films, 1960; plant mgr., Samuel Goldwyn Studios, 1961-71; exec. admin. asst. plant mgr., The Burbank Studios, 1972-88.

ROSSOVICH, RICK
Actor. b. Palo Alto, CA, August 28, 1957. e. Calif. St. Univ. Sacramento (art history). Studied acting with coach Vincent Chase.
PICTURES: The Lords of Discipline (debut, 1983), Losin' It, Streets of Fire, The Terminator, Fast Forward, Warning Sign, Top Gun, Let's Get Harry, The Morning After, Roxanne, Paint It Black, The Witching Hour, Spellbinder, Navy SEALS, Cognac, Tropical Heat, New Crime City, Cover Me, Black Scorpion II, Truth or Consequences N.M., Telling You, Cross Country.
TELEVISION: *Series*: MacGruder and Loud, Sons and Daughters, ER. *Guest*: Tales from the Crypt (The Switch), Pacific Blue. *Special*: 14 Going On 30. *Movies*: Deadly Lessons, The Gambler Returns: Luck of the Draw, Black Scorpion, Fatally Yours, Legend of the Lost Tomb.

ROTH, BOBBY
Director, Writer, Producer.
PICTURES: The Boss' Son, Circle of Power, Independence Day, Heartbreakers, The Man Inside, Amanda.
TELEVISION: *Episodes*: Miami Vice, The Insiders, Crime Story. *Movies*: Tonight's the Night, The Man Who Fell to Earth, Dead Solid Perfect (dir., co-s.p.), Baja Oklahoma (dir., co-s.p.), The Man Inside, Rainbow Drive, Keeper of the City, The Switch, Judgement Day: The John List Story, Ride With the Wind, Nowhere to Hide, Love Can Build a Bridge, In the Line of Duty: Kidnapped, Tell Me No Secrets, Inheritance, The Devil's Child.

ROTH, JOE
Executive, Producer, Director. b. New York, NY, 1948. Began career working as prod. assistant on commercials and feature films in San Francisco. Also ran the lights for improv group Pitchel Players. Moved with them to Los Angeles, and prod. their shows incl. the $250,000 film Tunnelvision. 1987, co-founder of independent film prod. co. Morgan Creek Productions. 1989, left to become chmn. of newly-formed Fox Film Corp., the theatrical film unit of 20th Century Fox Film Corp. Also named head of News Corp. unit. Resigned from Fox, 1993. Pres. & founder, Caravan Pictures, 1993. 1994, became chmn. Walt Disney Motion Pictures Group.
PICTURES: *Producer*: Tunnelvision, Cracking Up, Americathon, Our Winning Season, The Final Terror, The Stone Boy, Where the River Runs Black, Bachelor Party, Off Beat, Streets of Gold (also dir. debut), Tall Tale, Angels in the Outfield. *Exec. prod.*: Revenge of the Nerds II: Nerds in Paradise (also dir.), Young Guns, Dead Ringers, Skin Deep, Major League, Renegades, Enemies a Love Story, Pacific Heights, The Three Musketeers, Angie, I Love Trouble, Angels in the Outfield, A Low Down Dirty Shame, Houseguest, Tall Tale, While You Were Sleeping, Before and After. *Dir.*: Coupe de Ville.

ROTH, PAUL A.
Executive. b. Asheville, NC, March 28, 1930. e. U. of North Carolina, A.B. political science, 1948-51; George Washington U. Law Sch., 1951-52. U.S. Army 1952-55. Dist. Mgr. Valley Enterprises, Inc. 1955-56; v.p. Roth Enterprises, Inc. 1956-65; pres. Roth Enterprises, Inc. 1965-present; pres., Valley Lanes Inc. 1975-present; v.p., CAPA Ltd. 1976-87; pres., Thrashers Ocean Fries, 1987-present; dir. Riggs Bank of Maryland, 1984-93; pres. NATO of Virginia 1971-73; chmn. bd. NATO of Virginia, 1973-75; member National NATO Board, 1971-present; exec. comm. NATO of VA & MD, 1965-present; Variety Club Tent 11 Board Member 1959-65; pres. National NATO, 1973-75; chmn. National NATO bd. dir. 1975-77. Chmn., NATO Government Relations Committee, 1988-1996. member Foundation Motion Picture Pioneers, 1973-present; member & advisory committee, Will Rogers Hospital, 1973-present; trustee American Film Institute, 1973-75; Recipient: NATO Mid-Atlantic Exhibitor of the Year (1990), S.M. Hassanein Humanitarian Award at ShowEast (1991), ShoWester Award (1993).

ROTH, RICHARD A.
Producer. b. Beverly Hills, CA, 1943. e. Stanford U. Law Sch. Worked for L.A. law firm before beginning film career as lawyer and literary agent for Ziegler-Ross Agency. In 1970 left to develop s.p. Summer of '42 with Herman Raucher.
PICTURES: Summer of '42, Our Time, The Adventures of Sherlock Holmes' Smarter Brother, Julia, Outland, In Country, Havana.

ROTH, TIM
Actor. b. London, England, 1961. Started acting with various fringe theatre groups such as Glasgow Citizen's Theatre, The Oval House, and the Royal Court. Also on London stage in Metamorphosis.

PICTURES: The Hit, A World Apart, The Cook the Thief His Wife and Her Lover, Vincent & Theo, Rosencrantz and Guildenstern Are Dead, Jumpin at the Boneyard, Reservoir Dogs, Backsliding, Bodies Rest and Motion, Pulp Fiction, Rob Roy (BAFTA Award, 1995), Little Odessa, Captives, Hoodlums, Four Rooms, Everyone Say I Love You, Liar, Animals (And the Tollkeeper).
TELEVISION: *Specials/Movies* (BBC): Meantime, Made in Britain, Metamorphosis, Knuckle, Yellow Backs, King of the Ghetto, The Common Pursuit, Murder in the Heartland (U.S.), Heart of Darkness.

ROTHMAN, THOMAS E.
Executive. b. Baltimore, MD, Nov. 21, 1954. m. actress Jessica Harper. e. Brown U., B.A. 1976; Columbia Law Sch., J.D. 1980. Worked as law clerk with Second Circuit Court of Appeals 1981-82 before becoming partner at entertainment law firm, Frankfurt Garbus Klein & Selz 1982-87; 1987 joined Columbia Pictures as exec. v.p. and asst. to pres., named exec. prod. v.p. Left in 1989 to join Samuel Goldwyn Co. as pres. of worldwide production. Currently pres. of Fox Searchlight Films.
PICTURES: *Co-prod.:* Down By Law, Candy Mountain. *Exec. Prod.:* The Program.

ROTUNNO, GIUSEPPE
Cinematographer. b. Rome, Italy, March 19, 1923. Gained fame as leading cinematographer of Italian films working with Federico Fellini. Later moved to Hollywood.
PICTURES: Tosca, Monte Carlo Story, White Nights, The Naked Maja, On the Beach, Fast and Sexy, The Angel Wore Red, Five Branded Women, Rocco and His Brothers, Boccaccio '70, The Leopard, The Organizer, Juliet of the Spirits, The Bible, Anizo, Candy, Spirits of the Dead, Fellini Satyricon, The Secret of Santa Vittoria, Carnal Knowledge, Fellini's Roma, Man of La Mancha, Amarcord, Love and Anarchy, Fellini's Casanova, All Screwed Up, End of the World in Our Usual Bed in a Night Full of Rain, Orchestra Rehearsal, All That Jazz, City of Women, Popeye, Rollover, Five Days One Summer, And the Ship Sails On, American Dreamer, Desire, Nothing Left to Do But Cry, The Red Sonja, Hotel Colonial, Julia and Julia, Rent-a-Cop, Rebus, Haunted Summer, The Adventures of Baron Munchausen, Regarding Henry, Once Upon a Crime, Wolf, The Night the Moment, Sabrina, La Sindrome di Stendhal.
TELEVISION: The Scarlet and the Black.

ROUNDTREE, RICHARD
Actor. b. New Rochelle, NY, July 9, 1942. e. Southern Illinos U. Former model; Ebony Magazine Fashion Fair; joined workshop of Negro Ensemble Company, appeared in Kongi's Harvest, Man Better Man, Mau Mau Room; played lead role in Philadelphia road company of The Great White Hope before film debut.
PICTURES: What Do You Say to a Naked Lady? (debut, 1970), Shaft, Embassy, Charley One-Eye, Shaft's Big Score, Embassy, Shaft in Africa, Earthquake, Diamonds, Man Friday, Portrait of a Hitman, Escape to Athena, Game for Vultures, An Eye for an Eye, Inchon, Q (The Winged Serpent), One Down Two to Go, The Big Score, Young Warriors, Killpoint, City Heat, Opposing Force, Jocks, Maniac Cop, Homer and Eddie, Angel III: The Final Chapter, The Party Line, Getting Even, American Cops, The Banker, Night Visitor, Crack House, Bad Jim, Lost Memories, Body of Influence, Deadly Rivals, Amityville: A New Generation, Gypsy Angels, Mind Twister, Seven, Once Upon A Time...When We Were Colored, Theodore Rex, Original Gangstas, George of the Jungle, Steel.
TELEVISION: *Series:* Shaft, Outlaws, Cop Files (host), 413 Hope St. *Movies:* Firehouse, The Fifth Missile, Christmas in Connecticut, Bonanza: The Return, Shadows of Desire, Bonanza: Under Attack. *Mini-Series:* Roots, A.D.

ROURKE, MICKEY
Actor. b. Schenectady, NY, Sept. 1956. Moved to Miami as a boy. Fought as an amateur boxer 4 years in Miami. Studied acting with Sandra Seacat while working as a nightclub bouncer, a sidewalk pretzel vendor and other odd jobs. Moved to LA, 1978. Debut: TV movie City in Fear (1978).
PICTURES: 1941 (debut, 1979), Fade to Black, Heaven's Gate, Body Heat, Diner (Natl. Society of Film Critics Award, 1982), Rumblefish, Eureka, The Pope of Greenwich Village, Year of the Dragon, 9-1/2 Weeks, Angel Heart, A Prayer for the Dying, Barfly, Homeboy (also wrote orig. story), Francesco, Johnny Handsome, Wild Orchid, Desperate Hours, Harley Davidson and the Marlboro Man, White Sands, F.T.W., Fall Time, Double Team, Another 9-1/2 Weeks, The Rainmaker, Buffalo 66.
TELEVISION: *Movies:* City in Fear, Rape and Marriage: The Rideout Case, Act of Love, The Last Outlaw.

ROUSSELOT, PHILIPPE
Cinematographer. b. Meurthe-et-Moselle, France, 1945. e. Vaugirard Film Sch., Paris. Worked as camera assistant to Nestor Almendros on My Night at Maud's, Claire's Knee, Love in the Afternoon.

PICTURES: The Guinea Pig Couple, Adom ou le sang d'Abel, Paradiso, Pauline et l'ordinateur, Peppermint Soda, For Clemence, Cocktail Molotov, La Provinciale, A Girl From Lorraine, Diva (Cesar, Natl. Society of Film Critics, and Moscow Awards), The Jaws of the Wolf, The Moon in the Gutter, Thieves After Dark, The Emerald Forest, Therese (Cesar Award), Hope and Glory, Dangerous Liaisons, The Bear, We're No Angels, Too Beautiful for You, Henry and June, A River Runs Through It (Academy Award, 1992), Sommersby, Interview With the Vampire, Queen Margot, Mary Reilly, The People vs. Larry Flynt.

ROWE, ROY
Exhibitor. b. Burgaw, May 29, 1905. e. U. of NC. Eng. instructor, private bus. coll., 1926-29; Publix Sch. for Mgrs., NY, 1930-31; mgr. theatres, Spartanburg, SC; Greensboro & Raleigh, NC; Warner Theatre, Pittsburgh, PA, 1931-34; city mgr. for Warner Theatres, Washington, PA, 1934-35; opened own theatres in NC 1935; member NC Senate, 1937, 1941, 1945, 1949, 1957, 1965; 1935-75, House of Rep., 1943; Major, Civil Air Patrol, WWII; pres. Carolina Aero Club, 1943-44; chmn. NC Aeronautics Comm., 1941-49; dir. Theatre Owners No. & So. Carolina 1943-45; pres., Theatre Owners of SC & NC 1944-45; pres., Assn. of Governing Boards of State Univs., 1964; Rowe Insurance Agency, 1967-69; Mem. Exec. Bd., U. of NC Trustees, 1969. Principal Clerk, NC Senate 1969-75. Owner-operator Rowe Amusement Co., Burgaw, NC. Retired.

ROWLANDS, GENA
Actress. r.n. Virginia Cathryn Rowlands. b. Cambria, WI, June 19, 1934. e. U. of Wisconsin. Son is actor Nicholas Cassavetes. Came to New York to attend American Acad. of Dramatic Arts, where she met and married John Cassavetes. Made B'way debut as understudy and then succeeded to role of The Girl in The Seven Year Itch. Launched as star with part in The Middle of the Night, which she played 18 mos.
PICTURES: The High Cost of Loving (debut, 1958), Lonely Are the Brave, The Spiral Road, A Child Is Waiting, Tony Rome, Faces, Machine Gun McCain, Minnie and Moskowitz, A Woman Under the Influence (Acad. Award nom.), Two Minute Warning, The Brink's Job, Opening Night, Gloria (Acad. Award nom.), Tempest, Love Streams, Light of Day, Another Woman, Once Around, Ted and Venus, Night on Earth, The Neon Bible, Something to Talk About, Unhook The Stars.
TELEVISION: *Movies:* A Question of Love, Strangers: The Story of a Mother & Daughter, Thursday's Child, An Early Frost, The Betty Ford Story (Emmy Award, 1987), Montana, Face of a Stranger (Emmy Award, 1992), Crazy in Love, Silent Cries, Parallel Lives. *Guest:* The Philco TV Playhouse, Studio One, Alfred Hitchcock Presents, Dr. Kildare, Bonanza, The Kraft Mystery Theatre, Columbo. *Series:* Top Secret USA, 87th Precinct, Peyton Place.

ROWLEY, JOHN H.
Executive. b. San Angelo, TX, Oct. 6, 1917. e. U. of TX, 1935-39. Past pres., NATO of Texas; past Int'l Chief banker, Variety Clubs Int'l; past pres., TOA. Currently exec. dir. NATO of TX.

RUBEN, JOSEPH
Director. b. Briarcliff, NY, 1951. e. U. of Michigan, majoring in theater and film; Brandeis U., B.A. Interest in film began in high sch. Bought a Super-8 camera and filmed his first movie, a teenage love story. First feature, The Sister-in-Law, a low budget feature which he wrote and dir. in 1975.
PICTURES: *Dir./Writer.* The Sister-in-Law (also prod.), The Pom-Pom Girls (also prod.), Joy Ride, Our Winning Season. *Dir.:* G.O.R.P., Dreamscape (also co-s.p.), The Stepfather, True Believer, Sleeping With the Enemy, The Good Son, Money Train, Force Majeure.
TELEVISION: Breaking Away (pilot), Eddie Dodd.

RUBIN, STANLEY
Producer, Writer. b. New York, NY, Oct. 8, 1917; ed. UCLA, 1933-37. Phi Beta Kappa. Writer for radio, magazines, pictures, 1937-41; U.S. Army Air Force, 1942-45; writer, prod., owner, Your Show Time, Story Theatre TV series; winner of 1st Emmy awarded to filmed series: The Necklace, 1949. Producer, RKO, 20th-Fox, U.I., MGM, Paramount, Rastar.
PICTURES: The Narrow Margin, My Pal Gus, Destination Gobi, River of No Return, Destry, Francis in the Navy, Behind the High Wall, Rawhide Years, The Girl Most Likely, Promise Her Anything, The President's Analyst, Revenge, White Hunter Black Heart (co-prod.).
TELEVISION: G.E. Theatre, Ghost and Mrs. Muir, Bracken's World, The Man and the City, Executive Suite. *Movies:* Babe (co-prod.; Golden Globe Award), And Your Name is Jonah, Don't Look Back: The Story of Satchel Page (Image Award), Escape From Iran: The Canadian Caper (exec. prod.).

RUBINEK, SAUL
Actor. b. Fohrenwold, Germany, July 2, 1948. Family moved to Canada when he was a baby. Acting debut at age 8 with local theatre groups. Founding member of the Toronto Free Stage Theatre.

PICTURES: Nothing Personal, Highpoint, Agency, Death Ship, Ticket to Heaven, Soup for One, Young Doctors in Love, By Design, Against All Odds, Martin's Day, Sweet Liberty, Taking Care, Wall Street, Obsessed, The Outside Chance of Maximillian Glick, The Bonfire of the Vanities, Man Trouble, Unforgiven, The Quarrel, True Romance, Undercover Blues, Death Wish V, Getting Even With Dad, I Love Trouble, Open Season, Nixon.
TELEVISION: Concealed Enemies, The Terry Fox Story, Clown White, Interrogation in Budapest, Woman on the Run, And the Band Played On, The Android Affair.

RUBINSTEIN, JOHN
Actor, Composer, Director. b. Los Angeles, CA, December 8, 1946. Son of concert pianist Arthur Rubinstein and dancer-writer Aniela Rubinstein. e. UCLA.
THEATER: Pippin (NY debut, 1972; Theatre World Award), Picture (Mark Taper, LA), Children of a Lesser God (Tony Award, Drama Desk, L.A. Drama Critics Awards, 1980), Fools, The Caine Mutiny Court-Martial, M. Butterfly, Kiss of the Spider Woman, Love Letters, Hurlyburly, Getting Away With Murder, Camelot, Ragtime, On A Clear Day You Can See Forever, Counsellor-at-Law (also dir; Drama-Logue, Ovation, L.A. Drama Critics Awards, 1995), Into the Woods (also dir.), Merrily We Roll Along, Streamers, The Tempest, Candida, Arms and the Man, Three Hotels, Broken Glass, Sight Unseen. Director: The Rover, Les Liaisons Dangereuses, Phantasie, Nightingale, The Old Boy, She Loves Me.
PICTURES: Journey to Shiloh (debut, 1968), The Trouble With Girls, Getting Straight, The Wild Pack, Zachariah, The Car, The Boys From Brazil, In Search of Historic Jesus, Daniel, Someone to Watch Over Me, Another Stakeout, Mercy, Kid Cop.
TELEVISION: Series: Family, Crazy Like a Fox. Guest: The Virginian, Ironside, Dragnet, Room 222, The Psychiatrist, The Mary Tyler Moore Show, Cannon, The Mod Squad, Nichols, Hawaii Five-O, Barnaby Jones, Policewoman, Barbary Coast, The Rookies, The Streets of San Francisco, Harry O, Vegas, The Class of '65, Movin' On, Stop the Presses, Wonder Woman, Lou Grant, Fantasy Island, The Quest, Quincy, Trapper John M.D., The Love Boat, Father Dowling, The Paper Chase, Murder She Wrote, Against the Grain, Frasier, Jake and the Fatman, Hotel, Matlock, Highway to Heaven, NYPD Blue, Lois and Clark, Party of Five, Diagnosis Murder, Star Trek: Voyager, Early Edition, E.R., Robocop. Special: Triple Play—Sam Found Out. Movies: The Marriage Proposal, God Bless the Children, A Howling in the Woods, Something Evil, All Together Now, The Gift of the Magi, Roots: The Next Generations, Just Make Me an Offer, The French Atlantic Affair, Corey: For the People, Happily Ever After, Moviola, Skokie, The Mr. and Ms. Mysteries, Killjoy, Freedom to Speak, Someone's Killing the High Fashion Models; I Take These Men, M.A.D.D.: Mothers Against Drunk Driving, Liberace, Voices Within: The Lives of Truddi Chase, In My Daughter's Name, The American Clock, Perry Mason, Norma and Marilyn, Sleepwalker. Director: A Matter of Conscience, Summer Stories: The Mall, High Tide.
SCORES: Films: Paddy, Jeremiah Johnson, The Candidate, Kid Blue, The Killer Inside Me. Television: All Together Now, Emily, Emily, Stalk the Wild Child, Champions: A Love Story, To Race the Wind, The Ordeal of Patty Hearst, Amber Waves, Johnny Belinda, Secrets of a Mother and Daughter, Choices of the Heart, The Dollmaker, Family (Emmy nom.), The Fitzpatricks, The Mackenzies of Paradise Cove, The New Land, For Heaven's Sake, The Lazarus Syndrome, The City Killer, China Beach, A Walton Wedding.

RUBINSTEIN, RICHARD P.
Producer, Executive. b. New York, NY, June 15, 1947. e. American U. B.S. 1969, Columbia U. MBA 1971. Pres. & CEO, New Amsterdam Entertainment, Inc.
PICTURES: Martin, Dawn Of The Dead, Knightriders, Creepshow, Day Of The Dead, Creepshow 2, Pet Sematary, Tales From the Darkside: The Movie, Stephen King's The Night Flier.
TELEVISION: Exec. Prod.: Series: Tales From the Darkside, Monsters, Stephen King's Golden Years. Mini-Series: Stephen King's The Stand. Movies: The Vernon Johns Story, Precious Victims.

RUDDY, ALBERT S.
Producer. b. Montreal, Canada, March 28, 1934. e. U. of Southern California, B.S. in design, Sch. of Architecture, 1956. Exec. prod. of 1991 TV movie Miracle in the Wilderness.
PICTURES: The Wild Seed, Little Fauss & Big Halsey, Making It, The Godfather, The Longest Yard, Coonskin, Matilda, The Cannonball Run, Megaforce, Lassiter, Cannonball Run II, Farewell to the King, Paramedics, Speed Zone, Impulse, Ladybugs, Bad Girls, The Scout, Heaven's Prisoners.
TELEVISION: Series: Walker—Texas Ranger. Movies: Miracle in the Wilderness, Staying Afloat.

RUDIE, EVELYN
Actress, Singer, Songwriter. r.n. Evelyn Rudie Bernauer, b. Hollywood, Calif. March 28. e. Hollywood H.S., UCLA. At 19, after childstar career in TV and films, stage debut at Gallery Theatre in Hollywood as songwriter, musical dir., choreographer and star performer: Ostrogoths and King of the Schnorrers. Currently producer, artistic dir., Santa Monica Playhouse; founder of own repertoire co. Received Emmy Nomination for first TV leading role, Eloise, Playhouse 90, 1956. Filmdom's Famous Fives critics award, 1958. Star on Hollywood's Walk of Fame.
PICTURES: Daddy Long Legs (debut, 1955). The Wings of Eagles, Gift of Love, Bye Bye Birdie.
TELEVISION: Hostess with the Mostess, Playhouse 90, Dinah Shore, Red Skelton Show, George Gobel Show, Omnibus, Matinee Theatre, Hitchcock Presents, Gale Storm Show, Jack Paar, Wagon Train, G.E. Theatre, 77 Sunset Strip, etc.

RUDIN, SCOTT
Executive. b. New York, NY, July 14, 1958. Began career as prod. asst. on B'way for producers Kermit Bloomgarden, Robert Whitehead; then casting director. 1984, became producer for 20th Century Fox; named exec. v.p. prod.; 1986, appt. pres. prod., 20th-Fox. Resigned 1987 becoming independent producer.
PICTURES: Prod.: I'm Dancing as Fast as I Can, Reckless, Mrs. Soffel, Flatliners (exec. prod.), Pacific Heights, Regarding Henry, Little Man Tate, The Addams Family, White Sands, Sister Act, Jennifer Eight, Life With Mikey, The Firm, Searching for Bobby Fisher, Addams Family Values, Sister Act 2: Back in the Habit, Nobody's Fool, I.Q., Clueless, Sabrina, Up Close and Personal, Marvin's Room, In & Out.
TELEVISION: Little Gloria... Happy at Last (exec. prod.).

RUDNER, RITA
Actress, Writer. b. Miami, FL, 1956. m. producer Martin Bergman. Was stage dancer then stand-up comic. Author: Naked Beneath My Clothes, Rita Rudner's Guide to Men.
THEATER: Annie (B'way), Promises Promises, Follies, Mack and Mabel.
PICTURES: The Wrong Guys (debut, 1988), Gleaming the Cube, That's Adequate, Peter's Friends (also co-s.p.), A Weekend in the Country (also s.p.).
TELEVISION: Series: George Schlatter's Funny People (co-host). Specials: Women of the Night, One Night Stand: Rita Rudner, Rita Rudner: Born to Be Mild, The Rita Rudner Comedy Specials (also writer), Comic Relief, Rita Rudner: Married Without Children.

RUDOLPH, ALAN
Director, Writer. b. Los Angeles, CA, Dec. 18, 1943. Son of Oscar Rudolph, TV director of '50s and '60s. Made his screen debut in his father's The Rocket Man (1954). Began in industry doing odd jobs in Hollywood studios. 1969 accepted for Directors Guild assistant director's training program. Worked with Robert Altman as asst. dir. on California Split, The Long Goodbye and Nashville and co-writer on Buffalo Bill and the Indians.
PICTURES: Director: Welcome to L.A. (debut, 1977; also s.p.), Remember My Name (also s.p.), Roadie (also story), Endangered Species (also co-s.p.), Return Engagement, Songwriter, Choose Me (also s.p.), Trouble in Mind (also s.p.), Made in Heaven, The Moderns (also co-s.p.), Love at Large (also s.p.), Mortal Thoughts, The Player (actor only), Equinox (also s.p.), Mrs. Parker and the Vicious Circle (also co-s.p.), Afterglow.

RUEHL, MERCEDES
Actress. b. Queens, NY, 1950. Raised in Silver Spring, MD. e. College of New Rochelle, B.A. English lit. Worked for years in regional theater, mostly in classics.
THEATER: B'way: I'm Not Rappaport, Lost in Yonkers (Tony Award, 1991), The Shadow Box, The Rose Tattoo. Off-B'way: American Notes, The Marriage of Bette and Boo (Obie Award), Coming of Age in Soho, Other People's Money.
PICTURES: The Warriors (debut, 1979), Four Friends, Heartburn, Radio Days, 84 Charing Cross Road, The Secret of My Success, Leader of the Band, Big, Married to the Mob, Slaves of New York, Crazy People, Another You, The Fisher King (Acad. Award, best supporting actress, 1991), Lost in Yonkers, Last Action Hero, For Roseanna.
TELEVISION: Movie: Indictment: The McMartin Trial. Series: Frasier. Pilot: Late Bloomer. Guest: Our Family Honor. Special: On Hope.

RUGOLO, PETE
Composer, Arranger. b. Sicily, Italy, Dec. 25, 1915. To U.S., 1919. e. San Francisco State Coll., Mills Coll., Oakland. Armed Forces, 1942-46; pianist, arr. for many orch. including Stan Kenton. Conductor and arrang. for Nat King Cole, Peggy Lee, Harry Belafonte, many others. Received 3 Emmy Awards.
PICTURES: The Strip, Skirts Ahoy, Glory Alley, Latin Lovers, Easy to Love, Jack the Ripper, Foxtrot, Buddy Buddy, Chu Chu and the Philly Flash.
TELEVISION: Richard Diamond, The Thin Man, Thriller, The Fugitive, Run for Your Life, The Bold Ones, Leave It to Beaver, more than 25 movies.

RUIZ-ANCHIA, JUAN

Cinematographer. b. Bilbao, Spain, 1949. e. Escuela Official de Cinematografica, 1972. Worked on such Spanish prods. as 19/19, Cornica del Alba, Odd and Even, Soldier of Metal. Moved to L.A. Granted 2 yr. fellowship at American Film Inst. from which he graduated in 1981. First U.S. prod. was Reborn, 1982.
PICTURES: The Stone Boy, That Was Then This Is Now, Maria's Lovers, At Close Range, Where the River Runs Black, House of Games, Surrender, The Seventh Sign, Things Change, Lost Angels, The Last of the Finest, Dying Young, Naked Tango, Liebstraum, Glengarry Glen Ross, A Far Off Place, Mr. Jones, The Jungle Book, Two Bits, The Adventures of Pinocchio, Lorca.

RULE, JANICE

Actress. b. Cincinnati, OH, Aug. 15, 1931. e. Wheaton & Glenbard H.S., Glen Ellyn, IL. Received Phd in Clinical & Research Psychoanalysis, 1983. Dancer 4 yrs. in Chicago & New York nightclubs; stage experience in It's Great To Be Alive, as understudy of Bambi Lynn.
THEATER: Miss Liberty, Picnic (B'way debut, 1953), The Happiest Girl in the World.
PICTURES: Goodbye My Fancy (debut, 1951), Starlift, Holiday for Sinners, Rogue's March, A Woman's Devotion, Gun for a Coward, Bell Book and Candle, The Subterraneans, Invitation to a Gunfighter, The Chase, Alvarez Kelly, Welcome to Hard Times, The Swimmer, The Ambushers, Doctors' Wives, Gumshoe, Kid Blue, 3 Women, Missing, Rainy Day Friends, American Flyers.
TELEVISION: Movies: Shadow on the Land, Trial Run, The Devil and Miss Sarah, The Word.

RUSH, BARBARA

Actress. b. Denver, CO, Jan. 4, 1927. e. U. of CA. First stage appearance at age of ten, Loberto Theatre, Santa Barbara, CA, in fantasy, Golden Ball; won acting award in college for characterization of Birdie (The Little Foxes); scholarship, Pasadena Playhouse Theatre Arts Coll.
THEATER: A Woman of Independent Means, 40 Carats, Same Time Next Year, Steel Magnolias, The Golden Age.
PICTURES: Molly (debut, 1950), The First Legion, Quebec, When Worlds Collide, Flaming Feather, Prince of Pirates, It Came From Outer Space, Taza—Son of Cochise, The Magnificent Obsession, The Black Shield of Falworth, Captain Lightfoot, Kiss of Fire, World in My Corner, Bigger Than Life, Flight to Hong Kong, Oh Men! Oh Women!, No Down Payment, The Young Lions, Harry Black and the Tiger, The Young Philadelphians, The Bramble Bush, Strangers When We Meet, Come Blow Your Horn, Robin and the 7 Hoods, Hombre, The Man, Superdad, Can't Stop the Music, Summer Lovers.
TELEVISION: Series: Saints and Sinners, Peyton Place, The New Dick Van Dyke Show, Flamingo Road, 7th Heaven. Movies: Suddenly Single, Cutter, Eyes of Charles Sand, Moon of the Wolf, Crime Club, The Last Day, Death on the Freeway, The Seekers, Flamingo Road (pilot), The Night the Bridge Fell Down.

RUSH, GEOFFREY

Actor. b. Toowomba, Queensland, Australia, 1951. In tv series, Mercury.
PICTURES: Hoodwink, Starstruck, Twelfth Night, Dad and Dave: On Our Selection, Call Me Sal, Shine (Acad. Award, 1996; Golden Globe), Children of the Revolution, Les Miserables, A Little Bit of Soul.

RUSH, HERMAN

Executive. b. Philadelphia, PA, June 20, 1929. e. Temple U., Sales mgr., Official Films Inc., 1952-57. Headed Flamingo Telefilms, Inc. 1957-60; 1960-71, pres., tv div. of Creative Mgt. Assoc.; pres., Herman Rush Assoc. Inc., 1971-77; 1977-78 chmn. bd., Rush-Flaherty Agency, Inc.; 1970 headed Marble Arch TV; 1980 named pres., Columbia TV; 1984, pres. of newly formed Columbia Pictures TV Group; 1986, chmn. of newly formed Coca-Cola Telecommunications, Inc.; 1988, chmn., Rush Entertainment Group; 1989, became creative consultant for CBN Producers Group; 1992, Katz/Rush Ent., partner; co-founder, dir. of Transactional Media, Informercial and Transactional Program Production Co.; 1993-94 exec. prod. Willard Scott's New Original Amateur Hour; 1994-95, exec. prod. Susan Powter Show; exec. prod. of The Montel Williams Show.

RUSH, RICHARD

Director, Producer, Writer. b. New York, NY, 1930.
PICTURES: Director: Too Soon To Love (also prod., s.p.), Of Love and Desire (also prod., s.p.), A Man Called Dagger, Fickle Finger of Fate, Thunder Alley, Hell's Angels on Wheels, Psych-Out (also s.p.), Savage Seven, Getting Straight (also prod.), Freebie and the Bean (also prod.), The Stunt Man (also prod., s.p.; Acad. Award nom. for best dir., s.p.), Air America (co-s.p.), Color of Night.

RUSSELL, CHUCK

Director. Asst. dir., and line prod. on many low-budget films for Roger Corman and Sunn Classics, including Death Race 2000.
PICTURES: Dreamscape (co-s.p., line prod.), Back to School (prod.), Nightmare on Elm Street III (dir., co-s.p.), The Blob (dir., co-s.p.), The Mask, Eraser.

RUSSELL, JANE

Actress. r.n. Ernestine Jane Russell. b. Bemidji, MN, June 21, 1921. e. Max Reinhardt's Theatrical Workshop & Mme. Ouspenskaya. Photographer's model.
PICTURES: The Outlaw (debut, 1943), Young Widow, The Paleface, His Kind of Woman, Double Dynamite, Macao, Son of Paleface, Montana Belle, Las Vegas Story, Road to Bali (cameo), Gentlemen Prefer Blondes, The French Line, Underwater, Gentlemen Marry Brunettes, Foxfire, Tall Men, Hot Blood, The Revolt of Mamie Stover, The Fuzzy Pink Nightgown, Fate Is the Hunter, Waco, Johnny Reno, Born Losers, Darker Than Amber.
TELEVISION: Series: Yellow Rose.

RUSSELL, KEN

Director, Producer, Writer. b. Southampton, England, July 3, 1927. e. Walthamstow Art Sch. Early career as dancer, actor, stills photographer, TV documentary film-maker. Ent. TV ind. 1959. Made 33 documentaries for BBC-TV. Also made numerous pop videos.
PICTURES: French Dressing, Billion Dollar Brain, Women in Love, The Music Lovers (also prod.), The Devils (also prod., s.p.), The Boy Friend (also prod., s.p.), Savage Messiah (also prod.), Mahler (also s.p.), Tommy (also prod., s.p.), Lisztomania (also s.p.), Valentino, Altered States, Crimes of Passion, Gothic, Aria (sequence), Salome's Last Dance (also s.p., actor), The Lair of the White Worm (also prod., s.p.), The Rainbow (also prod., co-s.p.), The Russia House (actor only), Whore (also s.p.), Mindbender.
TELEVISION: The Secret Life of Sir Arnold Box, Lady Chatterly's Lover, Portrait of a Soviet Composer, Elgar, A House in Bayswater, Always on Sunday, The Debussy Film, Isadora Duncan, Dantes Inferno, Song of Summer—Delius, Dance of the Seven Veils. HBO: Dust Before Fireworks, Prisoner of Honor.

RUSSELL, KURT

Actor. b. Springfield, MA, March 17, 1951. Son of former baseball player-turned-actor Bing Russell (deputy sheriff on Bonanza). At 12 got lead in tv series The Travels of Jamie McPheeters (1963-64). Starred as child in many Disney shows and films. Professional baseball player 1971-73. Host, Kurt Russell Celebrity Shoot Out, 4-day fishing tournament.
PICTURES: It Happened at the World's Fair (debut, 1963), Follow Me Boys, The One and Only Genuine Original Family Band, The Horse in the Grey Flannel Suit, The Computer Wore Tennis Shoes, The Barefoot Executive, Fools' Parade, Now You See Him Now You Don't, Charley and the Angel, Superdad, The Strongest Man in the World, Used Cars, Escape from New York, The Fox and The Hound (voice), The Thing, Silkwood, Swing Shift, The Mean Season, The Best of Times, Big Trouble in Little China, Overboard, Tequila Sunrise, Winter People, Tango and Cash, Backdraft, Unlawful Entry, Captain Ron, Tombstone, StarGate, Executive Decision, Escape From L.A., Breakdown, Soldier.
TELEVISION: Series: The Travels of Jamie McPheeters, The New Land, The Quest. Movies: Search for the Gods, The Deadly Tower, The Quest (pilot), Christmas Miracle in Caulfield U.S.A., Elvis, Amber Waves. Guest: The Fugitive, Daniel Boone, Gilligan's Island, Lost in Space, The F.B.I., Love American Style, Gunsmoke, Hawaii Five-O.

RUSSELL, THERESA

Actress. r.n. Theresa Paup. b. San Diego, CA, Mar. 20, 1957. m. dir.-cinematographer Nicolas Roeg. e. Burbank H.S. Began modeling career at 12. Studied at Actors' Studio in Hollywood.
PICTURES: The Last Tycoon (debut, 1976), Straight Time, Bad Timing/A Sensual Obsession, Eureka, The Razor's Edge, Insignificance, Black Widow, Aria, Track 29, Physical Evidence, Impulse, Whore, Kafka, Cold Heaven, The Grotesque, Trade Off, The Spy Within, EroticTales II, Wild Things, Running Woman.
TELEVISION: Mini-Series: Blind Ambition. Movie: Thicker Than Water, Flight of the Dove, The Trade Off, The Proposition, Woman's Guide to Adultery, Hotel Paradise, When You Meet a Stranger, Public Enemy.

RUSSO, JAMES

Actor. b. New York, NY, Apr. 23, 1953. e. NYU, where he wrote and starred in prize-winning short film Candy Store.
THEATER: NY: Welcome to Andromeda, Deathwatch, Marat/Sade, Extremities (Theatre World Award).
PICTURES: A Strange Is Watching (debut, 1982), Fast Times at Ridgemont High, Vortex, Exposed, Once Upon a Time in America, Beverly Hills Cop, The Cotton Club, Extremities, China Girl, The Blue Iguana, Freeway, We're No Angels, State of Grace, A Kiss Before Dying, My Own Private Idaho, Cold Heaven, Dangerous Game, Bad Girls, Donnie Brasco, The Postman, Felons.
TELEVISION: Movie: The Secretary.

RUSSO, RENE

Actress. b. California, 1955. Raised in Burbank. Worked as top fashion model for Eileen Ford Agency prior to acting.
PICTURES: Major League (debut, 1989), Mr. Destiny, One Good Cop, Freejack, Lethal Weapon 3, In the Line of Fire, Outbreak, Get Shorty, Tin Cup, Ransom, Buddy.
TELEVISION: Series: Sable.

RUTHERFORD, ANN
Actress. b. Toronto, Canada, Nov. 2, 1920. Trained by mother (cousin of Richard Mansfield); with parents in stock as child; later on Los Angeles radio programs. Screen debut, 1935.
PICTURES: Waterfront Lady (debut, 1935), Judge Hardy's Children, Of Human Hearts, A Christmas Carol, You're Only Young Once, Dramatic School, Love Finds Andy Hardy, Out West With the Hardys, The Hardys Ride High, Four Girls in White, Dancing Co-Ed, Andy Hardy Gets Spring Fever, Gone With the Wind, These Glamour Girls, Judge Hardy and Son, Wyoming, Pride and Prejudice, The Ghost Comes Home, Andy Hardy Meets Debutante, Washington Melodrama, Life Begins for Andy Hardy, Badlands of Dakota, Andy Hardy's Private Secretary, Whistling in the Dark, Orchestra Wives, The Courtship of Andy Hardy, Whistling in Dixie, Andy Hardy's Double Life, This Time for Keeps, Happy Land, Whistling in Brooklyn, Bermuda Mystery, Two O'Clock Courage, Bedside Manner, The Madonna's Secret, Murder in the Music Hall, Inside Job, The Secret Life of Walter Mitty, Operation Haylift, Adventures of Don Juan, They Only Kill Their Masters, Won Ton Ton the Dog Who Saved Hollywood.

RYAN, ARTHUR N.
Executive. Joined Paramount in N.Y. in 1967 as asst. treas; later made dir. of admin. and business affairs, exec. asst. to Robert Evans and asst. scty. 1970 appt. v.p.-prod. adm. 1975 named sr. v.p. handling all prod. operations for Paramount's m.p. and TV divisions; 1976, asst. to the chmn. & CEO; chmn. & pres. Magicam, Inc.; chmn. Fortune General Corp.; chmn. Paramount Communications; co-chmn. of scholarship comm. of AMPAS; trustee of Univ. Film Study Center in Boston; joined Technicolor in 1976 as pres., COO & dir.; vice chmn., 1983-85; chmn. & CEO, 1985-; chmn. Technicolor Audio-Visual Systems International, Inc.; dir. Technicolor S.P.A.; dir. Technicolor, Film Intl.; and chmn. of exec. committee, Technicolor Graphics Services, Inc.; dir., Technicolor, Inc.; chmn., Technicolor Fotografica, S.A.; chmn. Technicolor Film Intl. Service Company, Inc.; dir. & deputy chmn. Technicolor Ltd.; chmn. & dir., The Vidtronics Company, Inc.; chmn. & CEO, Compact Video, Inc., 1984-; dir, Four Star Int'l., 1983-; dir., MacAndrews & Forbes, Inc. 1985-; Permanent charities committee of the Entertainment Industry; Hollywood Canteen Foundations. Vice-chmn. & dir., Calif. Inst. of Arts. Trustee: Motion Picture & Television Fund. 1985 named chmn., Technicolor.

RYAN, JOHN
Actor. b. New York, NY, July 30, 1936. e. City Coll. of NY.
THEATER: NY: Duet for Three, Sgt. Musgrave's Dance, Yerma, Nobody Hears a Broken Drum, The Love Suicide at Schofield Barracks, The Silent Partner, Twelve Angry Men, Medea.
PICTURES: The Tiger Makes Out (debut, 1967), A Lovely Way to Die, What's So Bad About Feeling Good?, Five Easy Pieces, The King of Marvin Gardens, The Legend of Nigger Charley, Cops and Robbers, Dillinger, Shamus, It's Alive, The Missouri Breaks, Futureworld, It Lives Again, The Last Flight of Noah's Ark, On the Nickel, The Postman Always Rings Twice, The Escape Artist, Breathless, The Right Stuff, The Cotton Club, Runaway Train, Avenging Force, Death Wish 4: The Crackdown, Delta Force II, Fatal Beauty, Three O'Clock High, Rent-a-Cop, Paramedics, City of Shadows, Best of the Best, White Sands, Hoffa, Star Time, Young Goodman Brown, Batman: Mask of the Phantasm (voice), Tall Tale, Bound.
TELEVISION: Series: Archer. Guest: M*A*S*H, Kojak, Starsky & Hutch, Matt Helm, Matt Houston, Miami Vice. Movies: Target Risk, Death Scream, Kill Me If You Can, A Killing Affair, Houston: The Legend of Texas, Blood River, Shooting Stars.

RYAN, MEG
Actress. b. Bethel, CT, Nov. 19, 1961. e. NYU. m. actor Dennis Quaid. Supported herself, while studying journalism at NYU, by making commercials. Auditioned for and won first prof. role as Candice Bergen's daughter in film Rich and Famous.
PICTURES: Rich and Famous (debut, 1981), Amityville 3-D, Top Gun, Armed and Dangerous, Innerspace, Promised Land, D.O.A., The Presidio, When Harry Met Sally, Joe Versus the Volcano, The Doors, Prelude to a Kiss, Sleepless in Seattle, Flesh & Bone, When a Man Loves a Woman, I.Q., French Kiss, Restoration, Courage Under Fire, Addicted to Love.
TELEVISION: Series: One of the Boys, As the World Turns (1982-84), Wild Side (Disney TV).

RYAN, MITCHELL
Actor. b. Louisville, KY, Jan. 11, 1928. Entered acting following service in Navy during Korean War. Was New York stage actor working off-B'way for Ted Mann and Joseph Papp; on B'way in Wait Until Dark. Member of Arena Stage group in Washington.
PICTURES: Monte Walsh, The Hunting Party, My Old Man's Place, High Plains Drifter, The Friends of Eddie Coyle, ElectraGlide in Blue, Magnum Force, Labyrinth, Winter People.
TELEVISION: Series: Chase, Executive Suite, Having Babies, The Chisholms, Dark Shadows, High Performance, King Crossings. Movies: Angel City, The Five of Me, Death of a Centerfold—The Dorothy Stratten Story, Uncommon Valor, Medea, Kenny Rogers as the Gambler—The Adventure Continues, Robert Kennedy & His Times, Fatal Vision, Favorite Son, The Ryan White Story, Margaret Bourke-White.

RYDELL, MARK
Director, Producer, Actor. b. New York, NY March 23, 1934. e. Juilliard Sch. of Music. Studied acting with Sanford Meisner of NY Neighborhood Playhouse. Became member of Actors Studio. Was leading actor for six years on daytime CBS serial, As The World Turns. Made Broadway debut in Seagulls over Sorrento and film debut in Crime in the Streets. Went to Hollywood as TV director (Ben Casey, I Spy, Gunsmoke, etc.). Partner with Sydney Pollack in Sanford Prods., film, TV prod. co. Formed own production co., Concourse Productions.
PICTURES: Director: The Fox (debut, 1968), The Reivers, The Cowboys (also prod.), Cinderella Liberty (also prod.), Harry and Walter Go To New York, The Rose, On Golden Pond, The River, Man in the Moon (prod. only), For the Boys (also exec. prod.), Intersection (also co-prod.), Crime of the Century. Actor: Crime in the Streets, The Long Goodbye, Punchline, Havana.

RYDER, WINONA
Actress. b. Winona, MN, Oct. 29, 1971. r.n. Winona Horowitz. Grew up in San Francisco. At 7, moved with family to Northern CA commune. At 13 discovered by talent scout during a performance at San Francisco's American Conservatory theatre, where she was studying, and given screen test.
PICTURES: Lucas (debut, 1986), Square Dance, Beetlejuice, 1969, Heathers, Great Balls of Fire, Welcome Home Roxy Carmichael, Edward Scissorhands, Mermaids, Night on Earth, Bram Stoker's Dracula, The Age of Innocence (Golden Globe Award; Acad. Award nom.), Reality Bites, The House of the Spirits, Little Women (Acad. Award nom.), How to Make an American Quilt, Boys, Looking for Richard, The Crucible, Alien: Resurrection, Just to Be Together, Celebrity.

RYDSTROM, GARY
Sound.
PICTURES: Indiana Jones and the Temple of Doom, Cocoon, Luxo Jr., Red's Dream, Spaceballs, Tin Toy, Cocoon: The Return, Willow, Colors, Knickknack, Ghostbusters II, Always, Romero, The Hot Spot, Rush, Luxo Jr. in 'Surprise' and 'Light & Heavy,' Backdraft, Terminator 2: Judgment Day, F/X2, A River Runs Through It, Single White Female, Mrs. Doubtfire, Meteor Man, Jurassic Park, Quiz Show, Baby's Day Out, Casper, Strange Days, Toy Story, Jumanji, James and the Giant Peach, Mission: Impossible, Sleepers, Titanic (Acad. Award, Best Sound, 1997), Hercules, The Lost World: Jurassic Park, The Horse Whisperer, Saving Private Ryan, Star Wars: Episode I -- The Phantom Menace.

S

SACKHEIM, WILLIAM B.
Producer, Writer. b. Gloversville, NY, Oct. 31, 1921. e. UCLA.
PICTURES: The Art of Love, The In-Laws (co-prod.), The Competition, First Blood (co-s.p.), The Survivors (prod.), No Small Affair (prod.), The Hard Way (prod.), Pacific Heights (prod.), White Sands (prod.).
TELEVISION: The Law (Emmy Award, Peabody Award, 1975), Gideon Oliver (series, exec. prod.), Almost Grown (exec. prod.), The Antagonists (exec. prod.), The Human Factor (exec. prod.), The Harness (prod.), The Neon Ceiling (prod.), The Senator (exec. prod.).

SACKS, SAMUEL
Attorney, Agent. b. New York, NY, March 29, 1908. e. CCNY, St. John's Law Sch., LL.B., 1930. Admitted Calif. Bar, 1943; priv. law practice, NY 1931-42; attorney, William Morris Agency, Inc., 1942; head of west coast TV business affairs, 1948-75; bd. of dir., Alliance of Television Film Producers, 1956-60; LA Copyright Society Treasurer, Beverly Hills Bar Assn., LA Bar Assn., American Bar Assn.; Academy of TV Arts & Sciences; Hollywood Radio & TV Society; counsel, entertainment field, Simon & Sheridan, 1975-89, Los Angeles Citizens' Olympic Committee; arbitrator for Screen Actors Guild, Assn. of Talent Agents and American Arbitration Assn.; bd. of dirs., Friars Club, 1991-95; Counsel for the Caucus for Producers, Writers & Directors, 1975-95.

SADLER, WILLIAM
Actor. b. Buffalo, NY, April 13, 1950. e. SUNY, Cornell U. Made stage debut in title role in Hamlet for Colorado Shakespeare Fest. Also acted with La Jolla Playhouse, Yale Rep.
THEATER: NY: Ivanov (Off-B'way debut, 1975), Limbo Tales (Obie Award), Chinese Viewing Pavilion, Lennon, Necessary Ends, Hannah, Biloxi Blues (B'way debut, 1985; Clarence Derwent & Dramalogue Awards). Regional: Journey's End, A Mad World My Masters, Romeo and Juliet, Night Must Fall, etc.
PICTURES: Hanky Panky, Off Beat, Project X, K-9, Hard to Kill, Die Hard 2, The Hot Spot, Bill & Ted's Bogus Journey, Rush, Trespass, Freaked, The Shawshank Redemption, Tales From the Crypt Presents Demon Knight, Solo.
TELEVISION: Series: Private Eye. Movies: The Great Walendas, Charlie and the Great Balloon Race, Face of Fear, The Last to Go, Bermuda Grace. Guest: Hooperman, Roseanne, Dear John, Gideon Oliver, The Equalizer, In the Heat of the Night, Tales From the Crypt, Murphy Brown.

SAFER, MORLEY
News Correspondent. b. Toronto, Ont., 1931. e. U. of Western Ontario. Started as corresp. and prod. with Canadian Broadcasting Corp. Joined CBS News London Bureau 1964, chief of Saigon Bureau, 1965. Chief of CBS London bureau 1967-70. Joined 60 Minutes as co-editor in Dec., 1970.

SAFFLE, M. W. "BUD"
Executive. b. Spokane, WA, June 29, 1923. e. U. of Washington. In service 1943-46. Started in m.p. business as booker, 1948. Entire career with Saffle Theatre Service as buyer-booker; named pres. in 1970. Also pres. of Grays Harbor Theatres, Inc., operating theatres in Aberdeen, WA. Also operates drive-in in Centralia, WA. On bd. of NATO of WA for 15 yrs; pres. of same for 2 terms and secty.-treas. 6 yrs. Elected to National NATO bd. in 1972. Founder of Variety Tent 46, serving as chief barker three times.

SAGANSKY, JEFF
Executive. b. 1953. Joined CBS 1976 in bdcst. finance; 1977, NBC, assoc. in pgm. development.; 1977, mgr. film pgms.; 1978, dir. dramatic dev.; 1978, v.p., dev. David Gerber Co.; 1981, returned to NBC as series dev. v.p.; 1983, sr. v.p. series programming; 1985, joined Tri-Star Pictures as pres. of production; 1989 promoted to president of Tri-Star, later that year joined CBS as entertainment division president. Resigned, 1994.

SAGEBRECHT, MARIANNE
Actress. b. Starnberg, Germany, Aug. 27, 1945. In 1977 conceived revue Opera Curiosa, followed by stage role in Adele Spitzeder.
PICTURES: Die Schaukel (debut, 1983), Sugarbaby, Crazy Boys, Bagdad Cafe, Moon Over Parador, The War of the Roses, Rosalie Goes Shopping, Martha and I, The Milky Life, Dust Devil, Mr. Bluesman, Il Piccolo lord, Erotique, Mona Must Die, All Men Are Mortal, Lorenz Im Land Der Lugner, The Ogre, Soleil, Johnny, Left Luggage, Asterix et Obelix.
TELEVISION: Movies: Herr Kischott, Eine Mutter Kampft un Ihren Sohn, My Lord, Und Plotzlich War Alles Anders, Frau Nach Mab Eine.

SAGET, BOB
Actor. b. Philadelphia, PA, May 17, 1956. Started as stand-up comedian.
PICTURE: Critical Condition.
TELEVISION: Series: Full House, America's Funniest Home Videos (host). Movie: Father and Scout (also co-exec. prod.).

SAINT, EVA MARIE
Actress. b. Newark, NJ, July 4, 1924. e. Bowling Green State U., Ohio, Actors Studio. Radio, tv actress; on Broadway in Trip to Bountiful before film debut.
THEATER: Trip to Bountiful, The Rainmaker, Desire Under the Elms, The Lincoln Mask, Summer and Smoke, Candida, Winesburg Ohio, First Monday in October, Duet for One, The Country Girl, Death of a Salesman, Love Letters, The Fatal Weakness, On The Divide.
PICTURES: On the Waterfront (debut, 1954; Acad. Award, best supporting actress), That Certain Feeling, Raintree County, Hatful of Rain, North by Northwest, Exodus, All Fall Down, 36 Hours, The Sandpiper, The Russians Are Coming the Russians Are Coming, Grand Prix, The Stalking Moon, Loving, Cancel My Reservation, Nothing in Common, Mariette in Ecstasy.
TELEVISION: Movies: Carol for Another Christmas, The Macahans, A Christmas to Remember, When Hell Was in Session, Fatal Weakness, Curse of King Tut's Tomb, Best Little Girl in the World, Splendor in the Grass, Malibu, Jane Doe, Love Leads the Way, Fatal Vision, The Last Days of Patton, A Year in the Life, Norman Rockwell's Breaking Ties, I'll Be Home for Christmas, Voyage of Terror: The Achille Lauro Affair, People Like Us (Emmy Award, 1991), Danielle Steel's Palomino, Kiss of a Killer, My Antonia, After Jimmy, Titanic. Series: Campus Hoopla, One Man's Family, Moonlighting. Special: Our Town, First Woman President, Primary Colors: The Story of Corita.

SAINT JAMES, SUSAN
Actress. b. Los Angeles, CA, Aug. 14, 1946. r.n. Susan Miller. e. Connecticut Coll. for Women. Was model for 2 years; then signed to contract by Universal Pictures.
PICTURES: P.J., Where Angels Go... Trouble Follows, What's So Bad About Feeling Good?, Jigsaw, Outlaw Blues, Love at First Bite, How to Beat the High Cost of Living, Carbon Copy, Don't Cry It's Only Thunder.
TELEVISION: Series: The Name of the Game (Emmy Award, 1969), McMillan & Wife, Kate and Allie. Movies: Fame Is the Name of the Game, Alias Smith and Jones, Once Upon a Dead Man, Magic Carpet, Scott Free, Night Cries, Desperate Women, The Girls in the Office, Sex and the Single Parent, S.O.S. Titanic, The Kid from Nowhere, I Take These Men. Special: A Very Special Christmas Party.

SAJAK, PAT
TV Host. b. Chicago, IL, Oct. 26, 1946. e. Columbia Coll., Chicago. Broadcasting career began as newscaster for Chicago radio station. 1968 drafted into Army, where served 4 years as disc jockey for Armed Forces Radio in Saigon, Vietnam. Moved to Nashville, where continued radio career while also working as weatherman and host of public affairs prog. for local TV station. 1977 moved to LA to become nightly weatherman on KNBC. Took over as host of daytime edition of Wheel of Fortune and later the syndicated nighttime edition (4 Emmy nom.; Emmy, 1997). 1989, The Pat Sajak Show.
PICTURE: Airplane II: The Sequel.
TELEVISION: Host: The Thanksgiving Day Parade, The Rose Parade.

SAKS, GENE
Director, Actor. b. New York, NY, Nov. 8, 1921. e. Cornell U. Attended dramatic workshop, New School for Social Research. Active in off-Broadway in 1948-49, forming cooperative theatre group at Cherry Lane Theatre. Joined Actor's Studio, followed by touring and stock. Also appeared in live TV dramas (Philco Playhouse, Producer's Showcase). Directed many Broadway plays before turning to film direction with Barefoot in the Park (1967) President of SSDC.
THEATER: B'way: Director: Enter Laughing, Nobody Loves an Albatross, Generation, Half a Sixpence, Mame, A Mother's Kisses, Sheep on the Runway, How the Other Half Loves, Same Time Next Year, California Suite, I Love My Wife (Tony Award), Brighton Beach Memoirs (Tony Award), Biloxi Blues (Tony Award), The Odd Couple (1985), Broadway Bound, Rumors, Lost in Yonkers, Jake's Women. Actor: Middle of the Night, Howie, The Tenth Man, A Shot in the Dark, A Thousand Clowns.
PICTURES: Director: Barefoot in the Park, The Odd Couple, Cactus Flower, Last of the Red Hot Lovers, Mame, Brighton Beach Memoirs, Tchin-Tchin, A Fine Romance. Actor: A Thousand Clowns, Prisoner of Second Avenue, The One and Only, Lovesick, The Goodbye People, Nobody's Fool, I.Q., Deconstructing Harry.
TELEVISION: Movie: Bye Bye Birdie. Guest: Law & Order.

SALANT, RICHARD S.
Executive. b. New York, NY, April 14, 1914. e. Harvard Coll. A.B., 1931-35; Harvard Law Sch., 1935-38. Atty. Gen.'s Com. on Admin. Procedure, 1939-41; Office of Solicitor Gen., U.S. Dept. of Justice, 1941-43; U.S. Naval Res., 1943-46; assoc., Roseman, Goldmark, Colin & Kave, 1946-48; then partner, 1948-51; pres. CBS news div., 1961-64; v.p. special asst. to pres. CBS, Inc., 1951-61, 1964-66; pres., CBS news div., 1966; mem. bd. of dir., CBS, Inc. 1964-69; vice chmn., NBC bd., 1979-81; sr. adviser, 1981-83; pres. CEO, National News Council, 1983-84. Retired.

SALDANA, THERESA
Actress. b. Brooklyn, NY, Aug. 20, 1954. Following attack by stalker founded advocacy group Victims for Victims. Author: Beyond Survival, 1986.
PICTURES: Nunzio, I Wanna Hold Your Hand, Defiance, Raging Bull, Double Revenge, Angel Town.
TELEVISION: Series: The Commish, All My Children. Movies: Sophia Loren: Her Own Story, Victims for Victims: The Theresa Saldana Story, Confessions of a Crime, The Highwayman, Shameful Secrets, She Woke Up Pregnant.

SALEH, ANGELIKA T.
Executive. Chmn., Angelika Films, Inc.

SALEM, KARIO
Actor, Writer.
PICTURES: Underground Aces, Triumph of the Spirit, 1492: Conquest of Paradise, Killing Zoe, Savage.
TELEVISION: Movies: Under the Influence, The Red Spider, Shooter, Liberace, Kojak: Ariana, Jericho Fever, Without Warning, Mr. Stitch, Divas (writer), Don King: Only in America (writer, Emmy Award, 1998), The Rat Pack (writer). Mini-series: Centennial. Series: Heart of the City,

SALES, SOUPY
Comedian. r.n. Milton Hines. b. Franklinton, NC, Jan. 8, 1926. Was radio DJ before debuting with his own children show in Detroit, 1953. Program was picked up by ABC in 1955. Continued to perform on radio over the years.
PICTURES: Birds Do It, And God Spoke.
TELEVISION: Series: Soupy Sales (1955), Lunch With Soupy Sales, The Soupy Sales Show (1962), The Soupy Sales Show (1965-67), What's My Line (panelist), The Soupy Sales Show (1978-79), Sha Na Na. Guest: The Rebel, The Real McCoys, Route 66, The Beverly Hillbillies, Love American Style, The Love Boat, Wings.

SALHANY, LUCIE
Executive. e. Kent State U., Kent, OH. Began career 1967 WKBF-TV, Cleveland, OH. Prog. mgr., WLVI-TV, Boston, 1975. VP, TV and cable prog., Taft Broadcasting Co., 1979-85. Pres. & CEO, Paramount Domestic TV, 1985. Chairman, 20th TV, 1991. Chairman, Fox Broadcasting Co., 1993. Pres., UPN, 1995.

SALKIND, ILYA
Producer. b. Mexico City, 1947. e. U. of London. Father is producer, Alexander Salkind. First film job as production runner on The Life of Cervantes for father. Was assoc. prod. on Light at the Edge of the World.
PICTURES: The Three Musketeers, The Four Musketeers, Superman, Superman II (exec. prod.), Supergirl (exec. prod.), Superman III (exec. prod.), Christopher Columbus: The Discovery.
TELEVISION: Superboy (exec. prod.).

SALKOW, SIDNEY
Director, Writer. b. New York, NY, June 16, 1911. e. City Coll. of New York, B.A.; Harvard Law Sch. Master of Fine Arts, USC. Stage dir. & prod. asst. number N.Y. dram. prods. (Dir. Bloodstream, Black Tower, etc.) and mgr. summer theatre. From 1933 variously dialogue dir., assoc. dir., writer & dir. numerous pictures Paramount, Universal, Republic, Columbia, etc.; dir. number of pictures in Lone Wolf series (for Columbia), Tillie the Toiler, Flight Lieutenant, etc. In armed service, WWII. Head of film dept., CSUN, emeritus prof. Headed prod. for FF Prod. in Rome, 1967-71.
PICTURES: Murder With Pictures (prod. only), Rhythm on the Range (prod. only), Girl Overboard, Four Days' Wonder, Exclusive (prod. only), That's My Story, Behind the Mike, Storm Over Bengal, The Night Hawk, Prison Nurse (prod. only), Come On Leathernecks! (prod. only), The Zero Hour, Woman Doctor, Street of Missing Men, She Married a Cop, Flight at Midnight, Fighting Thoroughbreds, The Lone Wolf Strikes, The Lone Wolf Meets a Lady, Girl from God's Country, Street of Missing Women, Tillie the Toiler, The Lone Wolf Takes a Chance (also prod.), The Lone Wolf Keeps a Date (also prod.), Time Out for Rhythm, Flight Lieutenant, The Adventures of Martin Eden, City Without Men, Faithful in My Fashion, Millie's Daughter, Bulldog Drummond at Bay, Sword of the Avenger (also prod.), Fugitive Lady, The Admiral Was a Lady (prod. only), Shadow of the Eagle, Golden Hawk, Scarlet Angel, Prince of Pirates, Jack McCall Desperado, Raiders of the 7 Seas (also prod.), The Pathfinder, Sitting Bull, Robbers' Roost, Las Vegas Shakedown, Toughest Man Alive, Gun Brothers, Duel in Durango, Chicago Confidential, Iron Sheriff, The Big Night, Twice-Told Tales, The Last Man on Earth, The Quick Gun, Blood on the Arrow, Great Sioux Massacre, The Murder Game, Martin Eden.
TELEVISION: Creator/prod./dir.: This Is Alice (for Desilu), Lassie, Fury, Wells Fargo, The Addams Family.

SALOMON, MIKAEL
Cinematographer, Director. b. Copenhagen, Denmark, Feb. 24, 1945.
PICTURES: Europe: The Dreamers, Z.P.G., Three From Haparanda, The Five, Me and My Kid Brothers, The Owlfarm Brothers, Five on the Run, Magic in Town, 24 Hours With Ilse, Why?, Bedside Freeway, My Sister's Children Goes Astray, Around the World, Tumult, Welcome to the Club, Violets Are Blue, Tintomare, Tell It Like It Is Boys, Cop, Elvis Elvis, Hearts Are Trump, The Marksman, The Flying Devils, Peter von Scholten, The Baron, Once a Cop..., Early Spring, The Wolf at the Door. U.S.: Zelly and Me, Torch Song Trilogy, Stealing Heaven, The Abyss (Acad. Award nom.), Always, Arachnophobia, Backdraft, Far and Away, A Far Off Place (dir. only), Congo (2nd unit dir.), Judge Dredd (trailer dir.), Hard Rain (dir. only).
TELEVISION: Movie: The Man Who Broke 1,000 Chains (ACE Award). Series: Space Rangers (dir.). Also commercials for Mitsubishi, Nescafe, Converse, Mazda, etc.

SALZBURG, JOSEPH S.
Producer, Editor. b. New York, NY, July 27, 1917. Film librarian, then rose to v.p. in chg. of prod., Pictorial Films, 1935-42; civilian chief film ed. U.S. Army Signal Corps Photo Center, 1942-44; U.S. Army Air Forces, 1944-46; prod. mgr., Pictorial Films, 1946-50; prod. mgr. Associated Artists Prod., then M.P. for TV, 1950-51; org. m.p. prod. & edit. service for theatrical, non-theatrical & TV films 1951-56; prod. mgr., dir. of films oper., official Films. 1956-59; prod. sup. tech. dir. Lynn Romero Prod. features and TV; assoc. prod. Lynn Romero Prod. TV series, Counterthrust 1959-60; v.p., sec'y, B.L. Coleman Assoc., Inc. & Newspix, Inc. 1961; pres. National Production Assoc., Inc. 1960-1962, chief of production, UPI Newsfilm, 1963-66. Prod./account exec. Fred A. Niles Comm. Center, 1966. Appt. v.p., F.A. Niles Communications Centers Inc., NY., 1969. 1979 appointed in addition exec. producer & gen. mgr., F. A. Niles Communication centers Inc., N.Y. studio. 1989, elected mem. bd. dir., Florida Motion Pictures & Television Assn., Palm Beach area chap.; 1989 professor m.p. & TV prod. course at Palm Beach Comm. Coll.: Breaking into TV and Movie Making in South Florida.

SAMMS, EMMA
Actress. b. London, England, Aug. 28, 1960. Former fashion model. Has worked as commercial photographer for such magazines as Ritz, Metro, and Architectural Digest. Co-founder of charitable org. the Starlight Foundation.
PICTURES: Arabian Adventure (debut, 1979), The Shrimp on the Barbie, Delirious.
TELEVISION: Series: General Hospital, Dynasty, The Colbys. Movies: Goliath Awaits, Agatha Christie's Murder in Three Acts, The Lady and the Highwayman, A Connecticut Yankee in King Arthur's Court, Bejeweled, Shadow of a Stranger, Robin Cook's Harmful Intent, Treacherous Beauties. Guest: Hotel, The New Mike Hammer, Murder She Wrote, Newhart, My Two Dads.

SAMPSON, LEONARD E.
Exhibitor. b. New York, NY, Oct. 9, 1918. e. City Coll. of New York, B.B.A., 1939. Entered m.p. industry as stagehand helper and usher, Skouras Park Plaza, Bronx 1932-36; asst. mgr. Gramercy Park, 1937-38; mgr., 5th Avenue Playhouse, 1939-41; mgr., Ascot Bronx, 1941-42. In Army 1942-46. On return entered into partnership with cousin Robert C. Spodick in Lincoln, a New Haven art house. Organized Nutmeg Theatres in 1952 in assn. with Norman Bialek, operating 6 art and conventional theatres in Conn., mainly in Westport and Norwalk. Sold Nutmeg in 1968 to Robert Smerling (became Loews Theatres, now Sony Theatres). Built Groton, CT, Cinemas I & II in 1970 and Norwich, CT, Cinema I & II, 1976 and acquired Village Cinemas I, II & III, Mystic, in association with Spodick and William Rosen. Operated as Gemini Theatre Circuit. Acquired Westerly Cinema I, II & III, 1982. Sold Gemini Theatre Circuit to Hoyts Theatres, 1987. Retains partnership with Spodick in New Haven's York Sq., until 1996 when he became an inactive partner due to illness.

SAMUELSON, DAVID W.
F.R.P.S., F.B.K.S., B.S.C.: Executive. b. London, England, July 6, 1924. Son of early producer G.B. Samuelson. Joined ind. 1941 with British Movietone News. Later film cameraman, 1947. Left Movietone 1960 to join family company, Samuelson Film Service Ltd. Dir., Samuelson Group Plc, 1958-84. Past president British Kinematograph Sound & TV Soc., Past Chmn, British Board of Film Classification, London Intl. Film Sch. Author: Hands On Manual for Cinematographer, Motion Picture Camera and Lighting Equipment, Motion Picture Camera Techniques, Motion Picture Camera Data, Samuelson Manual of Cinematography, Panaflex User's Manual and Cinematographers Computer Program. Currently consultant on technology film making, author, lecturer. Won Acad. Award for Engineering, 1980 and Acad. Award for Tech. Achievement, 1987.

SAMUELSON, PETER GEORGE WYLIE
Producer. b. London, England, October 16, 1951. e. Cambridge U., M.A., English literature. Early career as interpreter, production assistant, then prod. mgr. 1975, Return of the Pink Panther. 1979-85, exec. v.p., Interscope Communications, Inc. 1982-present, Intl. Pres., Starlight Foundation. 1986-present, pres., Film Associates, Inc. 1985-90 chmn., Samuelson Group, Inc. 1990-present, partner, Samuelson Prods. of Los Angeles and London.
PICTURES: Speed Merchants, High Velocity, One by One, Return of the Pink Panther, Santa Fe, A Man a Woman and a Bank, Revenge of the Nerds, Turk 182, Tom and Viv, Playmaker, Dog's Best Friend, Wilde.

SAMUELSON, SIR SYDNEY
C.B.E., B.S.C., Hon. F.B.K.S., Executive. b. London, England, Dec. 7, 1925. e. Irene Avenue Council Sch., Lancing, Sussex. Early career as cinema projectionist, 1939-42; Gaumont British News, 1942-43; Royal Air Force, 1943-47; asst. cameraman, cameraman, director/cameraman until 1960; founded Samuelson Film Service, 1954; Trustee and chmn. board of management, British Acad. of Film and Television Arts (chmn. of Council 1973-76). Member (Pres. 1983-86; Trustee: 1982-89) Cinema and Television Benevolent Fund. Member of Executive, Cinema & Television Veterans (pres. 1980-81); assoc. member, American Society of Cinematographers. Hon. Tech. Adviser, Royal Naval Film Corp. Hon. member, Guild of British Camera Technicians, 1986 (now BECTU); Member, British Society of Cinematographers (governor, 1969-79; 1st vice pres., 1976-77), Hon. Mem. for Life, Assn. of Cinema & Television Technicians, 1990. Appointed first British Film Commissioner by U.K. government, 1991. Recipient of two British Academy Awards: Michael Balcon (1985), Fellowship (1993). Received knighthood for services to British Film Industry, 1995. Lifetime Honorary Fellowship, British Kinematograph, Sound & Television Society, 1995.

SANDA, DOMINIQUE
Actress. b. Paris, France, March 11, 1951. r.n. Dominique Varaigne. e. Saint Vincent de Paul, Paris. Was a popular model for women's magazines when cast by Robert Bresson as the tragic heroine in his Dostoyevsky adaptation Un Femme Douce (1968).
THEATER: Madame Klein, Les Liaisons Dangereuses, Un Mari Ideal, Carte Blanche de Dominique Sanda.

PICTURES: Un Femme Douce, First Love, The Conformist, The Garden of the Finzi-Contini, La Notte Dei Fiori, Sans Mobile Apparent, Impossible Object, Steppenwolf, Conversation Piece, 1900, L'Heritage, Le Berceau de Cristal, Damnation Alley, Au Dela du Bien et du Mal, Beyond Good and Evil, The Song of Roland, Utopia, The Navire Night, Travels on the Sly, Caboblanco, A Room in Town, Dust of the Empire, The Way to Bresson, The Sailor 512, Corps et Biens, Les Mendiants, On a Moonlit Night, Warrior and Prisoners, Je Ne Vous Derangerai Plus, Moi La Pire De Toutes, Le Voyage, Emile Rosen, Henri Le Vert.
TELEVISION: The Sealed Train, La Naissance Du Jour, Il Decimo Clandestino, Voglia Di Vivere, Achille Lauro, Warburg, Comme Par Hazard, Non Siamo Soli, Albert Savarus, Der Lange Weg des Lukas B, The Lucona Affair, Nobody's Children, Brennendes Herz, Joseph.

SANDERS, JAY O.
Actor. b. Austin, TX, April 16, 1953. e. SUNY/Purchase. First professional theatre experience with NY Shakespeare-in-the-Park prods. of Henry V and Measure for Measure. Appeared in Abel's Sister for England's Royal Court Theatre.
THEATER: NY: Loose Ends, The Caine Mutiny Court-Martial, Buried Child, In Trousers, Geniuses, The Incredibly Famous Willy Powers, Heaven on Earth, Girls Girls Girls, King John, Saint Joan, Three Birds Alighting on a Field.
PICTURES: Starting Over (debut, 1979), Hanky Panky, Eddie Macon's Run, Cross Creek, Tucker: The Man and His Dream, The Prince of Pennsylvania, Glory, Just Like in the Movies, Mr. Destiny, V.I. Warshawski, Defenseless, Meeting Venus, JFK, Angels in the Outfield, Kiss of Death, Down Came a Blackbird, The Big Green, Three Wishes, Kiss the Girls, Daylight, The Matchmaker, For Richer or Poorer, Wrestling With Alligators, The Odd Couple II.
TELEVISION: Series: Aftermash, Crime Story, Lonesome Dove. Movies: The Day Christ Died, Living Proof: The Hank Williams Jr. Story, A Doctor's Story, Cold Sassy Tree, Hostages, State of Emergency, Nobody's Children, Rio Shannon, The Prosecutors. Special: The Revolt of Mother. Guest: Roseanne, The Young Riders, Spenser: For Hire, A Man Called Hawk, Kate and Allie, Miami Vice, Northern Exposure, NY Undercover, The Outer Limits, Nothing Sacred.

SANDERS, TERRY BARRETT
Producer, Director, Writer. b. New York, NY, Dec. 20, 1931. e. UCLA, 1951; Co-prod., photographed, A Time Out of War, 1954. Academy Award best two-reel subject, and won first prize Venice Film Festival, etc.; co-wrote The Day Lincoln Was Shot, CBS-TV; s.p. The Naked and the Dead; prod. Crime and Punishment—USA., prod., co-dir. War Hunt; prod. and dir. Portrait of Zubin Mehta for U.S.I.A. Assoc. dean, Film Sch., California Inst. of the Arts. Prod.-Dir.: Four Stones for Kanemitsu (Acad. Award nom.). Prod.-Dir.-Writer: Rose Kennedy: A Life to Remember (Acad. Award nom.) Professor, UCLA. Pres., American Film Foundation.
PICTURES: Maya Lin: A Strong Clear Vision (prod., Acad. Award), Never Give Up: The 20th Century Odyssey of Herbert Zipper (prod., dir., Acad. Award nom.).
TELEVISION: Prod./dir.: Hollywood and the Stars, The Legend of Marilyn Monroe, National Geographic Society specials, The Kids from Fame, Film Bios Kennedy Center Honors, Slow Fires, Lillian Gish: The Actor's Life for Me (Emmy Award).

SANDRICH, JAY
Director. b. Los Angeles, CA, Feb. 24, 1932. e. UCLA.
TELEVISION: Special: The Lily Tomlin Show (DGA Award, 1975). Movies: The Crooked Hearts, What Are Best Friends For?, For Richer For Poorer. Series: The Mary Tyler Moore Show (Emmy Awards: 1971, 1973), Soap, Phyllis (pilot), Tony Randall Show (pilot), Bob Newhart Show (pilot), Benson (pilot), Golden Girls (pilot; DGA Award, 1985), Empty Nest (pilot), The Cosby Show (Emmy Awards: 1985, 1986; DGA Award 1985).
PICTURE: Seems Like Old Times, Neil Simon's London Suite.

SANDS, JULIAN
Actor. b. Yorkshire, England, 1958. e. Central School of Speech and Drama, London 1979. Formed small theater co. that played in schools and youth clubs. Professional debut in Derek Jarman's short, Broken English and one-line part in Privates on Parade. Then opposite Anthony Hopkins in British TV series A Married Man (1981).
PICTURES: Privates on Parade (debut, 1982), Oxford Blues, The Killing Fields, After Darkness, The Doctor and the Devils, A Room with a View, Gothic, Siesta, Vibes, Wherever You Are, Manika: The Girl Who Lived Twice, Arachnophobia, Warlock, Night Sun, Impromptu, Naked Lunch, Wicked, Husbands and Lovers, Tale of a Vampire, Boxing Helena, Warlock: The Armageddon, Black Water, The Browning Version, Leaving Las Vegas.
TELEVISION: Series: A Married Man. Movies: Romance on the Orient Express, Harem, The Room, Murder By Moonlight, Grand Isle, Crazy in Love, Witch Hunt, The Great Elephant Escape.

SANDS, TOMMY
Singer. b. Chicago, IL, Aug. 27, 1937. e. Schools there and Houston, TX, Greenwood, LA. Father, Benny Sands, concert pianist. Started career as guitar player, singer when 5, at KWKH station, Shreveport. One of pioneers of rock music. First manager was Col. Tom Parker. Acting debut: Kraft TV show The Singin' Idol; recording contract won him million record sales of Teen Age Crush.
PICTURES: Sing Boy Sing, Mardi Gras, Love in a Goldfish Bowl, Babes in Toyland, The Longest Day, Ensign Pulver, None But the Brave, The Violent Ones.

SANFORD, ISABEL
Actress. b. New York, NY, Aug. 29, 1929. e. Textile H.S., Evander Childs H.S. Began acting in elementary school and continued through high school. Joined American Negro Theatre in the 1930's (then The Star Players) which disbanded in W.W.II. Later associated with YWCA project and off-B'way plays. B'way debut in The Amen Corner.
PICTURES: Guess Who's Coming to Dinner, The Young Runaways, Pendulum, The Comic, Stand Up and Be Counted, The New Centurions, Love at First Bite, South Beach, Original Gangstas.
TELEVISION: Series: All in the Family, The Jeffersons (Emmy Award, 1981). Movie: The Great Man's Whiskers. Guest: Fresh Prince of Bel Air, Roseanne, Hangin' With Mr. Cooper, Living Single, In the House, Fresh Prince of Bel Air, Lois & Clark, Cybill.

SAN GIACOMO, LAURA
Actress. b. New Jersey, 1962. e. Carnegie Melon Univ. m. actor Cameron Dye. Appeared Off-B'way in North Shore Fish, Beirut, The Love Talker, Italian American Reconciliation, Wrong Turn at Lungfish, Three Sisters.
PICTURES: Sex Lies and Videotape (debut, 1989), Pretty Woman, Vital Signs, Quigley Down Under, Once Around, Under Suspicion, Where the Day Takes You, Nina Takes a Lover, Stuart Saves His Family, Suicide Kings, Eat Your Heart Out, The Apocalypse, With Friends Like These, Mom's on the Roof.
TELEVISION: Series: Just Shoot Me. Movie: For Their Own Good, The Right to Remain Silent. Mini-Series: Stephen King's The Stand. Guest: The Equalizer, Crime Story.

SANSOM, LESTER A.
Producer. b. Salt Lake City, UT, April 24, 1910. e. U. of Utah. Radio singer under name of Jack Allen, 1930; ent. m.p. ind. in editorial dept., Fox Film Corp., 1931; served in U.S. Navy as head of film library, Washington, DC, 1942-45; head of edit. dept. & post-prod., Allied Artists, from 1953; assoc. prod. Skabenga; prod., co-writer, Battle Flame; assoc. prod. Hell to Eternity, exec. prod. The Thin Red Line, prod. Crack in the World; prod. Bikini Paradise, Battle of the Bulge, Custer of the West, Co-prod., Krakatoa—East of Java; exec. prod. 12+1.

SAPERSTEIN, DAVID
Writer, Director. b. Brooklyn, NY. e. Bronx H.S. of Science, CCNY, Film Institute, Chemical Engineering. 1960-80 wrote, prod. and dir. documentary films, TV commercials. Also wrote lyrics and managed rhythm and blues and rock 'n roll groups. Assoc. Professor NYU Graduate Film & TV, Manhattan Marymount College. Has directed various music videos.Wrote libretto and lyrics for Blue Planet Blue, Clowns and Cocoon: The Musical.
AUTHOR: Cocoon, Metamorphosis, Red Devil, Funerama, Fatal Reunion, Dark Again.
PICTURES: Cocoon (story), Killing Affair (dir., s.p.), Personal Choice (dir., s.p.), Fatal Reunion (s.p.), Queen of America (s.p.), Torch, Sara Deri, Hearts & Diamonds, Vets, Do Not Disturb, Point of Honor, Snatched, Jack in the Box, Schoolhouse, Roberto: The Roberto Clemente Story, Roamers, Joshua's Golden Band, Beyond the Stars (dir., s.p.), Bab's Labs (s.p.), Fighting Back (s.p.), Silyan (s.p.).
TELEVISION: The Vintage Years (pilot), Dance of the Athletes (dir., writer), Rodeo—A Matter of Style (dir., writer), Mama Sings, The Corky Project, OB/GYN (pilot), Reppies (prod.).

SAPERSTEIN, HENRY G.
Executive. b. Chicago, IL, June 2, 1918. e. U. of Chicago. Theatre owner, Chicago, 1943-45; pres. Television Personalities, Inc., 1955-67, Mister Magoo, Dick Tracy, TV shows, 1960-62; 1960-67 Glen Films, Inc.; prod., All-Star Golf, 1958-62; prod. Championship Bowling, 1958-60; prod. Ding Dong School, 1959-60; pres. owner, UPA Pictures, Inc. Prod.: Mr. Magoo, Dick Tracy cartoon series, Mr. Magoo's Christmas Carol, T.N.T. Show, Turnon, Tune In Drop Out. Pres. Screen Entertainment Co., Benedict Pictures Corp., United Prod. of America; pres. H. G. Saperstein & Associates. Producer: The Vaudeville Thing, Tchaikovsky Competition, Gerald McBoing Boing Show.
PICTURES: Producer: Gay Purr-ee, What's Up Tiger Lily?, T-A-M-I, Swan Lake, Monster Zero, War of the Gargantuas, Hell in the Pacific, Mr. Magoo (exec. prod.).
(d. June 24, 1998)

SARA, MIA
Actress. b. Brooklyn, NY, 1968. Started doing TV commercials; landed role in soap opera, All My Children.
PICTURES: Legend (debut, 1986), Ferris Bueller's Day Off, The Long Lost Friend, Apprentice to Murder, A Row of Crows, Imagination, Any Man's Death, Shadows in the Storm, A Stranger Among Us, By the Sword, Timecop, The Pompatus of Love, The Maddening, Undertow, Bullet to Beijing, Black Day Blue Night.
TELEVISION: *Movies*: Queenie, Till We Meet Again, Daughter of Darkness, Blindsided, Call of the Wild, The Set Up. *Special*: Big Time. *Guest*: Alfred Hitchcock Presents. *Mini-series*: 20,000 Leagues Under the Sea.

SARAFIAN, RICHARD C.
Director. b. New York, NY. April 28, 1935. Studied medicine and law before entering film industry with director Robert Altman making industrial documentaries.
PICTURES: Andy (debut, 1965), Run Wild Run Free, Ballad of a Badman, Fragment of Fear, Man in the Wilderness, Vanishing Point, Lolly Madonna XXX, The Man Who Loved Cat Dancing, The Next Man (also prod.), Sunburn, The Bear, Songwriter (actor only), Street Justice (also actor), Crisis 2050, Truk Lagoon.
TELEVISION: Gunsmoke, Bonanza, Guns of Will Sonnet, I Spy Wild, Wild West; Maverick, Twilight Zone, Gangster Chronicles. *Movies*: Shadow on the Land, Disaster on the Coastline, Splendor in the Grass, A Killing Affair, Liberty, Golden Moment—An Olympic Love Story. *As Actor*: Foley Square, Long Time Gone, Miami Hustle.

SARANDON, CHRIS
Actor. b. Beckley, WV, July 24, 1942. e. U. of West Virginia. Mem. Catholic U.'s National Players touring U.S. in Shakespeare and Moliere. Acted with Washington, D.C. improvisational theater co. and Long Wharf. B'way debut, The Rothschilds.
THEATER: Two Gentlemen of Verona, Censored Scenes from King Kong, Marco Polo Sings a Solo, The Devil's Disciple, The Soldier's Tale, The Woods, Nick & Nora.
PICTURES: Dog Day Afternoon (debut, 1975; Acad. Award nom.), Lipstick, The Sentinel, Cuba, The Osterman Weekend, Protocol, Fright Night, Collision Course, The Princess Bride, Child's Play, Slaves of New York, Forced March, Whispers, The Resurrected, Dark Tide, The Nightmare Before Christmas (voice), Just Cause, Tales From the Crypt: Bordello of Blood, Edie and Pen, Road Ends, Little Men, American Perfekt, Great Sex.
TELEVISION: *Series*: The Guiding Light. *Movies*: Thursday's Game, You Can't Go Home Again, The Day Christ Died, A Tale of Two Cities, This Child Is Mine, Broken Promises, Liberty, Mayflower Madam, Tailspin: Behind the Korean Airliner Tragedy, The Stranger Within, A Murderous Affair: The Carolyn Warmus Story, David's Mother, When the Dark Man Calls, No Greater Love.

SARANDON, SUSAN
Actress. r.n. Susan Abigail Tomaling. b. New York, NY, Oct. 4, 1946. e. Catholic U. Raised in Metuchen, New Jersey. Returned to New York to pursue acting, first signing with Ford Model Agency.
THEATER: *NY*: An Evening with Richard Nixon and..., A Coupla White Chicks Sitting Around Talking, Extremities.
PICTURES: Joe (debut, 1970), Lady Liberty, Lovin' Molly, The Front Page, The Great Waldo Pepper, The Rocky Horror Picture Show, Dragonfly (One Summer Love), Checkered Flag or Crash, The Last of the Cowboys (The Great Smokey Roadblock; also co-prod.), The Other Side of Midnight, Pretty Baby, King of the Gypsies, Something Short of Paradise, Loving Couples, Atlantic City (Acad. Award nom.), Tempest, The Hunger, The Buddy System, Compromising Positions, The Witches of Eastwick, Bull Durham, Sweet Hearts Dance, The January Man, A Dry White Season, Through the Wire (narrator), White Palace, Thelma & Louise (Acad. Award nom.), The Player, Light Sleeper, Bob Roberts, Lorenzo's Oil (Acad. Award nom.), The Client (Acad. Award nom.), Little Women, Safe Passage, The Celluloid Closet, Dead Man Walking (Acad. Award), James and the Giant Peach (voice), Father Roy: Inside the School of Assassins, 187: Documented, Illuminata, Twilight, Good Night Moon.
TELEVISION: *Series*: Search For Tomorrow. *Guest*: Calucci's Dept, Owen Marshall: Counsellor at Law. *Specials*: Rimers of Eldritch, June Moon, Who Am I This Time?, One Woman One Vote (narrator). *Mini-Series*: A.D. *Movies*: F. Scott Fitzgerald & the Last of the Belles, Mussolini: Decline and Fall of Il Duce, Women of Valor.

SARDI, JAN
Writer.
PICTURES: Moving Out, Street Hero, Ground Zero, Breakaway, Secrets, Shine.
TEIEVISION: Mission Impossible, Phoenix, The Feds, The Man From Snowy River, Halifax f.p.

SARGENT ALVIN
Writer. b. Philadelphia, PA, April 12, 1927. Began career as writer for TV, then turned to theatrical films.
PICTURES: Gambit (co-s.p.), The Stalking Moon, The Sterile Cuckoo, I Walk the Line, The Effect of Gamma Rays on Man-in-the-Moon Marigolds, Paper Moon (Acad. Award nom.), Love and Pain (and the Whole Damn Thing), Julia (Acad. Award, 1977), Bobby Deerfield, Straight Time (co-s.p.), Ordinary People (Acad. Award, 1980), Nuts (co-s.p.), Dominick and Eugene (co-s.p.), White Palace (co-s.p.), What About Bob? (co-story), Other People's Money, Hero (co-story), Bogus.
TELEVISION: *Movies*: Footsteps, The Impatient Heart. *Series*: The Naked City, Route 66, Ben Casey, Alfred Hitchcock Presents, The Nurses, Mr. Novak, Empire.

SARGENT, JOSEPH
Director. r.n. Giuseppe Danielle Sargente. b. Jersey City, NJ, July 25, 1925. e. studied theatre, New Sch. for Social Research 1946-49.
PICTURES: One Spy Too Many, The Hell With Heroes, Colossus: The Forbin Project, White Lightning, The Taking of Pelham One Two Three, MacArthur, Goldengirl, Coast to Coast, Nightmares, Jaws—The Revenge (also prod.).
TELEVISION: *Special*: The Spy in the Green Hat. *Mini-series*: The Manions of America, James Mitchener's Space. *Movies*: The Sunshine Patriot, The Immortal (pilot), The Man, Tribes, The Marcus-Nelson Murders (Emmy Award, 1973), Maybe I'll Come Home in the Spring (also prod.), The Man Who Died Twice, The Night That Panicked America, Sunshine (also prod.), Friendly Persuasion, Amber Waves, Hustling, Freedom, Tomorrow's Child, Memorial Day, Terrible Joe Moran, Choices of the Heart (also prod.), Space, Love Is Never Silent (Emmy Award, 1986), Passion Flower, Of Pure Blood, There Must Be a Pony, The Karen Carpenter Story, Day One, The Incident, Caroline? (Emmy Award, 1990), The Last Elephant, Never Forget, Miss Rose White (Emmy Award, 1992), Somebody's Daughter (also prod.), Skylark (also prod.), Abraham, World War II: When Lions Roared, My Antonia.

SARLUI, ED
Executive. b. Amsterdam, The Netherlands, Nov. 10, 1925. Owner, Peruvian Films, S.A.; pres., Radio Films of Peru, S.A.; pres. Bryant Films Educatoriana, S.A.; partner, United Producers de Colombia Ltd.; pres. Royal Film N.V.; pres., United Producers de Centroamerica, S.A.; pres. United Producers de Mexico, S.A.; pres., United Producers Int'l, Inc., Continental Motion Pictures, Inc. 1988, formed Cinema Corp. of America with Moshe Diamant and Elliott Kastner. Co-chmn. Epic Prods. Inc.
PICTURES: *Exec. prod.*: Full Moon in Blue Water, High Spirits, Teen Witch, Courage Mountain, Night Game.

SARNOFF, THOMAS W.
Executive. b. New York, NY, Feb. 23, 1927. e. Phillips Acad., Andover, MA, 1939-43, Princeton U., 1943-45, Stanford U. grad. 1948, B.S. in E.E.; Grad Sch. of Bus. Admin. 1948-49. Sgt., U.S. Army Signal Corps, 1945-46; prod. & sales, ABC-TV, Hollywood, 1949-50; prod. dept. MGM, 1951-52; asst. to dir. of finance and oper., NBC, 1952-54; dir. of prod. and bus. affairs, 1954-57; v.p., prod. and bus. affairs, 1957-60; v.p. adm. west coast, 1960-62; v.p. west coast, 1962; exec. v.p. 1965-77; bd. of dir., NBC prods 1961-77; bd of dir. Hope Enterprises 1960-75; dir. NABCAT, Inc. 1967-75; dir. Valley County Cable TV, Inc. 1969-75; Pres. NBC Entertainment Corp. 1972-77; pres. Sarnoff International Enterprises Inc. 1977-81; pres., Sarnoff Entertainment Corp., 1981-; pres., Venturetainment Corp. 1986-; past pres. Research Foundation at St. Joseph Hospital of Burbank; past pres. Permanent Charities of the Entertainment Ind.; past ch. bd. of trustees, National Acad. of TV Arts and Sciences. Pres. Acad. of TV Arts & Sciences Foundation 1990-.

SARRAZIN, MICHAEL
Actor. r.n. Jacques Michel Andre Sarrazin. b. Quebec, Canada, May 22, 1940. Began acting at 17 on CBC TV; signed by Universal, 1965.
PICTURES: Gunfight in Abilene (debut, 1967), The Flim-Flam Man, The Sweet Ride, Journey to Shiloh, A Man Called Gannon, Eye of the Cat, In Search of Gregory, They Shoot Horses Don't They?, The Pursuit of Happiness, Sometimes a Great Notion, Believe in Me, The Groundstar Conspiracy, Harry in Your Pocket, For Pete's Sake, The Reincarnation of Peter Proud, The Loves and Times of Scaramouche, The Gumball Rally, Caravans, Double Negative, The Seduction, Fighting Back, Joshua Then and Now, Captive Hearts, Mascara, Keeping Track, Malarek, Lena's Holiday, Bullet to Beijing.
TELEVISION: *Movies*: The Doomsday Flight, Frankenstein: The True Story, Beulah Land, Passion and Paradise. *Guest*: Chrysler Theatre, The Virginian, World Premiere.

SAUL, OSCAR
Writer. b. Brooklyn, NY, Dec. 26, 1912. e. Brooklyn Coll. 1932. Co-author play, Medicine Show; m.p. ed., U.S. Public Health Svce; numerous radio and TV plays. Wrote novel The Dark Side of Love.

PICTURES: Once Upon a Time, Strange Affair, Road House, Lady Gambles, Once More My Darling, Woman in Hiding, Secret of Convict Lake, A Streetcar Named Desire, Thunder on the Hill, Affair in Trinidad, Let's Do It Again (prod.), Helen Morgan Story, Joker is Wild, The Naked Maja, The Second Time Around, Major Dundee, The Silencers, Man and Boy.
TELEVISION: A Streetcar Named Desire, many others.

SAUNDERS, DAVID
Executive. Pres., Triumph Films, Inc.
PICTURES: *Exec. prod.*: Hellraiser, High Spirits, Bat *21 (co-prod.), Wild Orchid, Wild Orchid II: Two Shades of Blue, The Assignment, Masterminds, In God's Hands, Baby Geniuses.
TELEVISION: *Series*: Red Shoe Diaries. *Movies*: Red Shoe Diaries, Red Shoes Diaries 3: Another Woman's Lipstick.

SAUNDERS, WILLIAM
Executive. b. London, England, Jan. 4, 1923. e. left Upton House Central Sch. at 16. Served in British Eighth Army, 1941-47. Entered industry in 1947 as salesman with 20th Century Fox Film Co. in London; sales mgr., Anglo-Amalgamated Film Co., London, 1951-61; with Motion Picture Producers Assoc. of Amer. as sales dir. in Lagos, Nigeria, dist. Amer. feature films to West African countries, 1962-64; joined 20th Century Fox TV Intl., Paris as v.p. European TV sales, 1964-83; 20th Century TV Intl., Los Angeles as sr. v.p., 1983; named exec. v.p. 1987 and pres., 1988. Retired.

SAURA, CARLOS
Director. b. Huesca, Spain, January 4, 1932. e. educated as engineer. Worked as professional photographer from 1949. Studied at Instituto de Investigaciones y Experiencias Cinematograficos, Madrid, 1952-57 where he then taught from 1957-64 until being dismissed for political reasons. 1957-58 dir. shorts La tarde del domingo and Cuenca.
PICTURES: *Director &/or Writer*: Los Golfos (The Urchins), Lament for a Bandit, La Caza (The Hunt), Peppermint Frappe, Stress es Tres Tres, La Madriguera (The Honeycomb), The Garden of Delights, Anna and the Wolves, Cousin Angelica (Cannes Fest. jury prize, 1974), Cria! (Cannes Fest. jury prize, 1976), Elisa Vide Mia, Los ojos Vendados (Blindfold), Mama Turns 100, Hurry Hurry (Golden Bear, Berlin Fest., 1981), Blood Wedding, Dulces Horas (Sweet Hours), Antonieta, Carmen, Los Zancos (The Stilts), El Amor Brujo (Love the Magician), El Dorado, The Dark Night, Ay Carmela!, Sevillanas, Outrage, Flamenco, Taxi, Tango, Pajarico, Esa luz!.

SAVAGE, DAVID
Executive Producer, Advertising Executive, b. New York, NY, March 17, 1929. e. Rochester Inst. of Technology. In research development & testing div., Eastman Kodak Co., 2 yrs.; adv. mgr. asst. nat'l sales mgr., Official Films; org., film dept. mgr. WCBS-TV; dir. of films procurement, CBS; mgr. of film procurement, NBC; mgr. planning, merchandising, Recorded Tape Dept., RCA Records; promo. mgr., special products mktg. RCA Records Div.; program and marketing chmn. RCA SelectaVision group; v.p., operations, Wunderman, Rilotto, & Kline, 1970; pres., Response Industries, Inc., (direct response adv. agency), 1973 which became affiliate of McCann Erickson, and was sr. v.p. of McCann Erickson Pres., Mattel Direct Marketing, 1982; v.p. and man. dir., Foote Cene Belding, subsid. Knipp-Taylor USA, 1985.

SAVAGE, FRED
Actor. b. Highland Park, IL, July 9, 1976. e. Stanford Univ. While in kindergarten auditioned for commercial at local community center. Didn't get the job but called back by same dir. for two more tests. Chosen for Pac-Man vitamin ad which led to 27 on-camera TV commercials and 36 voice-over radio spots.
PICTURES: The Boy Who Could Fly, The Princess Bride, Vice Versa, Little Monsters, The Wizard.
TELEVISION: *Series*: Morningstar/Eveningstar, The Wonder Years, Working. *Movies*: Convicted: A Mother's Story, Run Till You Fall, When You Remember Me, Christmas on Division Street, No One Would Tell. *Special*: Runaway Ralph. *Guest*: The Twilight Zone, Seinfeld, The Outer Limits.

SAVAGE, JOHN
Actor. r.n. John Youngs. b. Old Bethpage, Long Island, NY, Aug. 25, 1949. Studied at American Acad. of Dramatic Arts. In Manhattan organized Children's Theatre Group which performed in public housing. Won Drama Desk Award for performance in One Flew Over the Cuckoo's Nest (Chicago & LA).
THEATER: Fiddler on the Roof, Ari, Siamese Connections, The Hostage, American Buffalo, Of Mice and Men.
PICTURES: Bad Company (debut, 1972), Steelyard Blues, The Killing Kind, The Sister in Law (also composed score), The Deer Hunter, Hair, The Onion Field, Inside Moves, Cattle Annie and Little Britches, The Amateur, Brady's Escape, Maria's Lovers, Salvador, Beauty and the Beast, Hotel Colonial, Soldier's Revenge, The Beat, Caribe, Do the Right Thing, Point of View, Any Man's Death, The Godfather Part III, Hunting, Primary Motive, My Forgotten Man, C.I.A. II: Target Alexa, Red Scorpion 2, Killing Obsession, Carnosaur 2, From the Edge, The Dangerous, Centurion Force, The Crossing Guard, White Squall, Where Truth Lies, American Strays, Little Boy Blue, The Mouse, Club Vampire, Burning Down the House, Amnesia, Hostile Intent, The Thin Red Line, Message in a Bottle.

TELEVISION: *Series*: Gibbsville. *Movies*: All the Kind Strangers, Eric (also wrote and performed songs), The Turning Point of Jim Malloy, Coming Out of the Ice, The Tender Age (The Little Sister), Silent Witness, The Nairobi Affair, Desperate, The Burning Shore, Daybreak, Shattered Image, Tom Clancy's Op Center, Before Women Had Wings. *Special*: Date Rape (Afterschool Special). *Guest*: Tales From the Crypt, Birdland, X Files, Walker Texas Ranger, The Outer Limits.

SAVOCA, NANCY
Director. e. NYU film sch. m. prod.-writer Richard Guay. While in school directed and wrote short films Renata and Bad Timing. Received Haig P. Manoogian Award for filmmaking at 1984 NYU Student Film Festival. Made feature debut with True Love which won Grand Jury Prize at 1989 United States Film Festival.
PICTURES: True Love (also co-s.p.), Dogfight, Household Saints (also co-s.p.), 24-Hour Woman.

SAWYER, DIANE
News Correspondent, Anchor. b. Glasgow, KY, Dec. 22, 1945. m. director Mike Nichols. e. Wellesley Coll. Studied law before deciding on career in TV. Former Junior Miss winner and weather reporter on a Louisville TV station before arriving in Washington, 1970. Worked for Nixon Administration in press office from 1970-74; assisted Nixon in writing memoirs, 1975-78. Joined CBS News as reporter in Washington bureau in 1978; named correspondent in 1980. Served as CBS State Dept. correspondent 1980-81. Joined Charles Kuralt as co-anchor of the weekday editions of CBS Morning News in 1981; 1984-89 correspondent on 60 Minutes; 1989, signed by ABC News as co-anchor of Primetime Live news prog. with Sam Donaldson. 1994, co-anchor of Turning Point.

SAXON, JOHN
Actor. r.n. Carmine Orrico. b. Brooklyn, NY, Aug. 5, 1936.
PICTURES: Running Wild (debut, 1955), The Unguarded Moment, Rock Pretty Baby, Summer Love, The Reluctant Debutante, This Happy Feeling, The Restless Years, The Big Fisherman, Cry Tough, Portrait in Black, The Unforgiven, The Plunderers, Posse from Hell, Mr. Hobbs Takes a Vacation, War Hunt, Evil Eye, The Cardinal, The Ravagers, The Cavern, The Appaloosa, Queen of Blood, Night Caller From Outer Space, For Singles Only, Death of a Gunfighter, Company of Killers, Joe Kidd, Enter The Dragon, Black Christmas, Mitchell, The Swiss Conspiracy, Strange Shadows in an Empty Room, Moonshine County Express, Shalimar, The Bees, The Glove, The Electric Horseman, Battle Beyond the Stars, Beyond Evil, Blood Beach, Cannibal in the Streets, Wrong Is Right, The Big Score, Nightmare on Elm Street, Prisioners of the Lost Universe, Fever Pitch, Nightmare on Elm Street 3: Dream Warriors, Criminal Act, Death House (also dir.), My Mom's a Werewolf, Aftershock, Blood Salvage, Hellmaster, Crossing the Line, Maximum Force, No Escape No Return, Jonathan of the Bears, Killing Obsession, Beverly Hills Cop III, Wes Craven's New Nightmare.
TELEVISION: *Series*: The Bold Ones (The New Doctors), Falcon Crest. *Movies*: The Doomsday Flight, Winchester 73, Istanbul Express, The Intruders, Snatched, Linda, Can Ellen Be Saved?, Planet Earth, Crossfire, Strange New World, Raid on Entebbe, The Immigrants, Golden Gate, Rooster, Prisoners of the Lost Universe, Payoff, Blackmail, Genghis Khan, Liz: The Elizabeth Taylor Story.

SAYLES, JOHN
Writer, Director, Editor, Actor. b. Schnectady, NY, Sept. 28, 1950. e. Williams Coll., B.S. psychology, 1972. Wrote two novels: Pride of the Bimbos, 1975 and Union Dues, 1978; also The Anarchist's Convention, collection of short stories and, Thinking in Pictures: The Making of the Movie Matewan (1987). Wrote and directed plays off-B'way (New Hope for the Dead, Turnbuckle). Directed Bruce Springsteen music videos (Born in the U.S.A., I'm on Fire, Glory Days). Recipient of MacArthur Foundation Grant for genius.
PICTURES: Piranha (s.p., co-story, actor), Lady in Red (s.p.), Battle Beyond the Stars (story, s.p.), Return of the Secaucus Seven (dir., s.p., actor, edit.), Alligator (s.p., story), The Howling (co-s.p., actor), The Challenge (co-s.p.), Lianna (dir., s.p., actor, edit.), Baby It's You (dir., s.p.), The Brother from Another Planet (dir., s.p., edit., actor), Enormous Changes at the Last Minute (co-s.p.), The Clan of the Cave Bear (s.p.), Hard Choices (actor), Something Wild (actor), Wild Thing (s.p.), Matewan (dir., s.p., actor), Eight Men Out (dir., s.p., actor), Breaking In (s.p.), Little Vegas (actor), City of Hope (dir., s.p., edit.), Straight Talk (actor), Malcolm X (actor), Passion Fish (dir., s.p., edit.), Matinee (actor), My Life's in Turnaround (actor), The Secret of Roan Inish (dir., s.p., edit.), Lone Star (dir., s.p.), Men With Guns (dir., s.p., edit.), Mimic.
TELEVISION: *Movies*: A Perfect Match, Unnatural Causes (actor, writer), Shannon's Deal (writer, creative consult.). *Special*: Mountain View (Alive From Off Center).

SCACCHI, GRETA
Actress. b. Milan, Italy, Feb. 18, 1960. e. England and Australia. Acted in Bristol Old Vic Theatre in England.
PICTURES: Das Zweiter Gesicht, Heat and Dust, The Coca Cola Kid, Burke & Wills, Defence of the Realm, A Man in Love, Good Morning Babylon, White Mischief, Paura e Amore (Fear and Love), Woman in the Moon, Presumed Innocent, Fires Within, Shattered, The Player, Turtle Beach, Desire, The Browning Version, Jefferson in Paris, Country Life, Cosi.
TELEVISION: Mini-Series: Waterfront (Australia). Movies: Ebony Tower, Dr. Fischer of Geneva, Camille, Rasputin (Emmy Award, 1996).

SCARWID, DIANA
Actress. b. Savannah, GA. e. St. Vincent's Acad. (Savannah), American Acad. of Dramatic Arts, Pace U., 1975. Member of National Shakespeare Conservatory (Woodstock, NY) and worked in regional theatres before moving to Hollywood 1976.
PICTURES: Pretty Baby (debut, 1978), Honeysuckle Rose, Inside Moves (Acad. Award nom.), Mommie Dearest, Rumble Fish, Strange Invaders, Silkwood, The Ladies Club, Psycho III, Extremities, Heat, Brenda Starr, Gold Diggers: The Secret of Bear Mountain, The Cure, The Neon Bible, Bastard Out of Carolina.
TELEVISION: Mini-Series: Studs Lonigan. Movies: In the Glitter Palace, The Possessed, Forever, Battered, Guyana Tragedy: The Story of Jim Jones, Desperate Lives, Thou Shalt Not Kill, A Bunny's Tale, After the Promise, Night of the Hunter, Simple Justice, Labor of Love: The Arlette Schweitzer Story, JFK: Reckless Youth, Truman. Series: The Outer Limits.

SCHAEFER, CARL
Media Consultant, Publicist. b. Cleveland, OH, Sept. 2, 1908. e. UCLA. Contr. to mag., including Vanity Fair, Hollywood Citizen-News, 1931-35; Warner Bros., 1935.; Huesped de Honor, Mexico, 1943; OSS WWII, 1944-45; Int'l Comt. AMPS, chmn. 1966-67; Italian Order of Merit, 1957; Chevalier de l'ordre de la Couronne, Belgium, 1963. Pres., Foreign Trade Assn. of Southern Calif.; 1954; chmn. of bd., 1955; British-American C. of C., Dir., 1962; Chevalier French Legion d'Honneur, 1955; Comm. Hollywood Museum; dir., intl. relations, Warner Bros. Seven Arts Int'l Corp., 1960; formed own firm, Carl Schaefer Enterprises, 1971. Dir. pub. rel., British-American Chamber of Commerce, 1971; dir. pub. rel. for Iota Intl. Pictures, 1971; dir. pub. rel. Lyric Films Intl., 1971; bureau chief (Hollywood) Movie/TV Marketing, 1971; man. dir., Intl. Festival Advisory Council, 1971; dir. pub. rel. & adv. Francis Lederer Enterprises Inc. (American National Acad. of Performing Arts, and Canoga Mission Gallery) 1974; West Coast rep. Angelika Films of N.Y. 1974, Hwd. rep Korwitz/Geiger Products. 1975-; Hwd. corresp. Movie News, S'pore, & Femina, Hong Kong, 1974-; member Westn. Publications Assn. 1975-; field rep. Birch Records 1975; Hollywood rep Antena Magazine, Buenos Aires; dir. pub. rel., Style Magazine. Coordinator Hollywood Reporter Annual Key Art Awards; coordinator Hollywood Reporter Annual Marketing Concept Awards; exec. comm. & historian ShoWest; Mem: National Panel of Consumer Arbitrators, 1985; Hollywood Corr., Gold Coast Times of Australia, 1986-87. Winner 1990 Key Art Award. Member: AMPAS, awarded certif. of Appreciation, 1962; charter member, Publicists Guild of America; pres. Pacific Intercollegiate Press Assn., while UCLA Daily Bruin Editor, 1930-31. Poetry anthologies, 1995-96, National Library of Poetry.

SCHAFFEL, ROBERT
Producer. b. Washington, DC, March 2, 1944. Partner with Jon Voight in Voight-Schaffel Prods. Now heads Robert Schaffel Prods.
PICTURES: Gordon's War, Sunnyside, Lookin' to Get Out, Table for Five, American Anthem, Distant Thunder, Jacknife, Diggstown, Pontiac Moon.

SCHATZBERG, JERRY
Director. b. New York, NY, June 26, 1927. e. student U. of Miami, 1947-48. Early career in photography as asst. to Bill Helburn 1954-56. Freelance still photographer and TV commercials dir. 1956-69. Contrib. photographs to several mags. incl. Life.
PICTURES: Puzzle of a Downfall Child (debut, 1970), The Panic in Needle Park, Scarecrow, Sweet Revenge (also prod.), The Seduction of Joe Tynan, Honeysuckle Rose, Misunderstood, No Small Affair, Street Smart, Reunion.
TELEVISION: Movie: Clinton and Nadine.

SCHEIDER, ROY
Actor. b. Orange, NJ, Nov. 10, 1932. e. Franklin and Marshall Coll. where he twice won the Theresa Helburn Acting Award. First professional acting in 1961 NY Shakespeare Festival prod. of Romeo and Juliet. Became member of Lincoln Center Repertory Co. and acted with Boston Arts Festival, American Shakespeare Festival, Arena Stage (Wash., DC) and American Repertory Co. Appeared in documentary In Our Hands.
THEATER: Richard III, Stephen D, Sergeant Musgrave's Dance, The Alchemist, Betrayal.

PICTURES: Curse of the Living Corpse (debut, 1964), Paper Lion, Star!, Stiletto, Loving, Puzzle of a Downfall Child, Klute, The French Connection (Acad. Award nom.), The Outside Man, The French Conspiracy, The Seven Ups, Sheila Levine is Dead and Living in New York, Jaws, Marathon Man, Sorcerer, Jaws 2, Last Embrace, All That Jazz (Acad. Award nom.), Still of the Night, Blue Thunder, 2010, Mishima (narrator), The Men's Club, 52 Pickup, Cohen and Tate, Listen to Me, Night Game, The Fourth War, The Russia House, Naked Lunch, Romeo Is Bleeding, Covert Assassin.
TELEVISION: Movies: Assignment Munich, Jacobo Timerman: Prisoner Without a Name Cell Without a Number, Tiger Town, Somebody Has to Shoot the Picture, Wild Justice. Series: seaQuest DSV. Guest: Hallmark Hall of Fame, Studio One, N.Y.P.D. Special: Portrait of the Soviet Union (host).

SCHEINMAN, ANDREW
Producer. b. 1948. e. Univ. of VA, law degree. Professional tennis player before entering film business as producer of three Charlton Heston films. Became one of 5 founding partners of Castle Rock Entertainment.
PICTURES: Prod/Exec. Prod.: The Mountain Man, The Awakening, Modern Romance, Mother Lode, The Sure Thing, Stand By Me, The Princess Bride, When Harry Met Sally..., Misery, A Few Good Men, North (also co-s.p.). Director: Little Big League.
TELEVISION: Series: Seinfeld (exec. prod.)

SCHELL, MARIA
Actress. b. Vienna, Austria, Jan. 5, 1926. Brother is actor Maximilian Schell. Made debut as teenager in Swiss film, Steinbruch (Quarry). Subsequently appeared in many British and American films.
PICTURES: Quarry (debut, 1941), Angel with the Trumpet, The Affairs of Dr. Holl, The Magic Box, Angelika, So Little Time, The Heart of the Matter, Der Traumende Mund (Dreaming Lips), The Last Bridge (Cannes Film Fest. Award, 1954), Angelika, The Rats, Napoleon, Gervaise (Venice Film Fest. Award, 1956), Liebe (Love), Rose Bernd, Le Notti Bianche (White Nights), Une Vie (End of Desire), The Brothers Karamazov, The Hanging Tree, Der Schinderhanners (Duel in the Forest), As the Sea Rages, Cimarron, The Mark, Only a Woman, La Assassin connait la Musique, Rendezvous in Trieste, Who Has Seen the Wind?, 99 Women, Devil By the Tail, Night of the Blood Monster, Lust in the Sun, The Odessa File, Voyage of the Damned, Folies Bourgeoises (The Twist), Superman, Just a Gigolo, 1919.
TELEVISION: U.S.: Heidi, Christmas Lilies of the Field, Inside the Third Reich, Martian Chronicles, Samson and Delilah.

SCHELL, MAXIMILIAN
Actor, Director. b. Vienna, Dec. 8, 1930. Sister is actress Maria Schell. e. Switzerland. Stage debut 1952. B'way debut in Interlock.
PICTURES: Children Mother and the General (debut, 1955), The Young Lions (U.S. debut, 1958), Judgment at Nuremberg (Acad. Award, 1961), Five Finger Exercise, The Reluctant Saint, The Condemned of Altona, Topkapi, Return from the Ashes, The Deadly Affair, Counterpoint, The Desperate Ones, The Castle (also prod.), Krakatoa—East of Java, Simon Bolivar, First Love (also dir., co-s.p., co-prod.), Trotta (also dir., s.p.), Pope Joan, Paulina 1880, The Pedestrian (also dir., prod., s.p.), The Odessa File, The Man in the Glass Booth, End of the Game (also dir., co-prod., co-s.p.), St. Ives, The Day That Shook the World, A Bridge Too Far, Cross of Iron, Julia, Players, Avalanche Express, Together?, The Black Hole, Tales From the Vienna Woods (also prod., s.p.), The Chosen, Les Iles, Morgen in Alabama, Marlene (dir., s.p., interviewer), The Rose Garden, The Freshman, Labyrinth, An American Place, A Far Off Place, Little Odessa.
TELEVISION: Judgment at Nuremberg (Playhouse 90), The Fifth Column, The Diary of Anne Frank, Turn The Key Deftly, Phantom of the Opera, Heidi, The Assisi Underground, Peter the Great (mini-series), Young Catherine, Stalin, Miss Rose White, Candles in the Dark (also dir.).

SCHENCK, AUBREY
Producer. b. Brooklyn, NY, Aug. 26, 1908. e. Cornell U., NYU. With law firm of O'Brien, Driscoll & Raftery; buyer & attorney for Natl. Theatres, 1936; prod for 20th Century-Fox 1945; exec. prod. Eagle Lion 1946; contract prod. Universal Internatl. 1948; Aubrey Schenck Productions, Inc.
PICTURES: Shock, Johnny Comes Flying Home, Strange Triangle, Repeat Performance, T-Men, Mickey, It's a Joke Son, Trapped, Port of New York, Wyoming Man, Undercover Girl, Fat Man, Target Unknown; formed own co. to prod. War Paint, Beachhead. Also: Yellow Tomahawk, Shield for Murder, Big House, U.S.A., Crime Against Joe, Emergency Hospital, Ghost Town, Broken Star, Rebels in Town, Pharaoh's Curse, Three Bad Sisters, Fort Yuma, Desert Sands, Quincannon, Frontier Scout, Black Sleep, Hot Cars, War Drums, Voodoo Island, Revolt at Fort Laramie, Tomahawk Trail, Untamed Youth, Girl in Black Stockings, Bop Girl Goes Calypso, Up Periscope, Violent Road, Reckless, Frankenstein 1970, Wild Harvest, Robinson Crusoe On Mars, Don't Worry, Ambush Bay, Kill a Dragon, Impasse, More Dead Than Alive, Barquero, Daughters of Satan.
TELEVISION: Miami Undercover, series.

SCHEPISI, FRED
Producer, Director, Writer. b. Melbourne, Australia, Dec. 26, 1939. e. Assumption Col., Marist Bros. Juniorate, Marcellin Col. Assessed student films at Melbourne's Swinburne Inst. of Tech.; worked on gov. sponsored experimental Film Fund; made TV commercials. Founded The Film House prod. co. Dir. short film The Party.
PICTURES: Director: Libido (co-dir.), Barbarosa, Iceman, Plenty, Roxanne, A Cry in the Dark (also co-s.p.; Australian Film Inst. Award for best dir. & s.p.), Fierce Creatures. Dir./Prod.: The Devil's Playground (also s.p.), The Chant of Jimmie Blacksmith (also s.p.), The Russia House, Mr. Baseball, Six Degrees of Separation, I.Q. Producer: That Eye the Sky (exec.)

SCHERICK, EDGAR J
Executive, Producer. b. New York, NY, Oct. 16, 1924. e. Harvard U.; elected to Phi Beta Kappa. Asst. dir. of radio and TV; assoc. media dir. and dir. of sports special events, Dancer-Fitzgerald-Sample ad agency, NY during 1950s. Introduced Wide World of Sports on TV through his co., Sports Programs, Inc. Was v.p. in chg. of network programming at ABC-TV. Pres. of Palomar Pictures Int'l. Now independent producer.
PICTURES: For Love of Ivy, The Birthday Party, Take the Money and Run, They Shoot Horses Don't They?, The Killing of Sister George, Ring of Bright Water, Jenny, Sleuth, The Heartbreak Kid, Law and Disorder, The Stepford Wives, I Never Promised You a Rose Garden, The Taking of Pelham One Two Three, American Success Company, I'm Dancing As Fast As I Can, Shoot the Moon, White Dog, He Makes Me Feel Like Dancin' (Acad. Award, 1983), Reckless, Mrs. Soffel.
TELEVISION: The Man Who Wanted to Live Forever, The Silence, Circle of Children, Raid on Entebbe, Panic in Echo Park, Zuma Beach, An American Christmas Carol, The Seduction of Miss Leona, Revenge of the Stepford Wives, Hitler's SS, The High Price of Passion, The Stepford Children, Unholy Matrimony, Little Gloria... Happy at Last, On Wings of Eagles, Hands of a Stranger, Home Fires, He Makes Me Feel Like Dancin' (Emmy Award, 1983), Stranger on My Land (exec. prod.), And the Band Played On, The Kennedys of Massachusetts, Satin's Touch (exec. prod.), Phantom of the Opera, The Secret Life of Ian Fleming, Tyson.

SCHIAVELLI, VINCENT
Actor. b. Brooklyn, NY. e. NYU. On Stage in Hunting Cockroaches, Alphabetical Order, Angel City.
PICTURES: Taking Off, The Great Gatsby, For Pete's Sake, One Flew Over the Cuckoo' Nest, The Happy Hooker, Next Stop Greenwich Village, An Unmarried Woman, The Frisco Kid, Butch and Sundance: The Early Days, Seed of Innocence, The Return, American Pop (voice), Chu Chu and the Philly Flash, Night Shift, Fast Times at Ridgemont High, Kidco, The Adventures of Buckaroo Banzai Across the 8th Dimension, Amadeus, Better Off Dead, Valmont, Homer and Eddie, Cold Feet, Ghost, Waiting for the Light, Playroom, Penny Ante, Mister Frost, Ted and Venus, Another You, Miracle Beach, Batman Returns, Lurking Fear, Cultivating Charlie, Lod of Illusions, A Little Princess, Ninjas Knuckle Up, Two Much, The People vs. Larry Flynt, Back to Back, The Beautician and the Beast, Tomorrow Never Dies.
TELEVISION: Series: The Corner Bar, Taxi, Fast Times. Movies: Rescue from Gilligan's Island, White Mama, Escape, The Ratings Game, Bride of Boogedy, Escape to Witch Mountain, The Whipping Boy. Guest: Moonlighting, Shell Game, Star Trek: The Next Generation, Batman: The Animated Series (voice), Knots Landing, Eerie Indiana, The X-Files, TBS Dinner & A Movie.
AUTHOR: Papa Andrea's Sicilian Table, Bruculinu America.

SCHIFRIN, LALO
Composer, b. Buenos Aires, Argentina, June 21, 1932. Father was conductor of Teatro Colon in B.A. for 30 years. Schifrin studied with Juan Carlos Paz in Arg. and later Paris Cons. Returned to homeland and wrote for stage, modern dance, TV. Became interested in jazz and joined Dizzie Gillespie's band in 1962 as pianist and composer. Settled in L.A. Pres. Young Musicians Fed. Music; dir. and conductor, Paris Philharmonic 1987.
PICTURES: El Jefe, Rhino!, Joy House/Les Felins, Once A Thief, Gone With the Wave, Dark Intruder, The Cincinnati Kid, Way...Way Out!, The Liquidator, I Deal in Danger, Blindfold, Who's Minding the Mint?, The Venetian Affair, Sullivan's Empire, The President's Analyst, Murderer's Row, Cool Hand Luke (Acad. Award nom.), Sol Madrid, Hell in the Pacific, The Fox (Acad. Award nom.), Coogan's Bluff, Bullitt, The Bortherhood/The Heroin Gang, The Eye of the Cat, Che!, W.U.S.A., Pussycat Pussycat I love You, Kelly's Heroes, Imago, I Love My Wife, THX-1138, Pretty Maids All in a Row, Mrs. Pollifax–Spy, The Hellstrom Chronicle, Dirty Harry, The Christian Licorice Store, The Beguiled, The Wrath of God, Rage, Prime Cut, Joe Kidd, The Neptune Factor, Magnum Force, Hit!, Harry in Your Pocket, Enter the Dragon, Charlie Varrick, Man On a Swing, Golden Needles, The Master Gunfighter, The Four Musketeers, Voyage of the Damned (Acad. Award nom.), St. Ives, Special Delivery, The Sky Riders, Return From Witch Mountain, Telefon, Rollercoaster, The Eagle Has Landed, The Day of the Animals, Nunzio, The Manitou, The Cat From Outer Space, Love and Bullets, Escape to Athena, Boulevard Nights,

The Concorde: Airport '79, The Amityville Horror, When Time Ran Out, Serial, The Nude Bomb, The Competition (Acad. Award nom.), Brubaker, The Big Brawl, The Seduction, La Pelle, Loophole, Caveman, Buddy Buddy, Las Viernes de la Etertnidad, Fast-Walking, The Class of 1984, A Stranger Is Watching, Amytiville II–The Possession, Airplane II–The Sequel, Sudden Impact, The Sting II, The Osterman Weekend, Dr. Detroit, Tank, The New Kids, The Mean Season, The Ladies Club, Black Moon Rising, The Fourth Protocol, The Silence at Bethany, Little Sweetheart, The Dead Pool, Berlin Blues, Return to the River Kwai, Fridays to Eternity, Naked Tango, FX 2, The Beverly Hillbillies, Rice Beans & Ketchuo, Scoprion Spring, Mission: Impossible, Tango, Something to Believe In, Money Talks.
TELEVISION: Theme, Episode, Movie & Miniseries scores: Mission Impossible, Mannix, Medical Center, T.H.E. Cat, Planet of the Apes, Starsky and Hutch, Bronk, Braddock, The Blue Light, Dr. Kildare, 90 Bristol Court, The Young Lawyers, The Black Cloak, The Cliff Dwellers, Ben Casey, I.F.M., Johnny Comes Home, Delancy Street, Foster and Laurie, Egan, How I Spent My Summer Vacation, The World of Jacques Cousteau, Three for Danger, Brenda Starr, Good Against Evil, The Chicago Story, The Victims, Starflight One, Princess Diasy, Sprague, House Detective, Command 5, Glitter, A.D., Hollywood Wives, Terror at London Bridge, Private Sessions, The Equalizer, Beverly Hills Madam, Out on a Limb, Hunter, The Doomsday Flight, Jericho, The Highest Fall of All, Maryk, The Nativity, Quest, Petrocelli, The President's Mistress, Pay the Piper, The Rise and Fall of the Third Reich, The Hidden World of Insects, The Way-Out Men, Sullivan Country, The Aquarians, Shipwreck, Sam Sheppard, Sixth Sense, Memo From Purgatory, Kraft Suspense Theatre, The Virginians, Wagon Train, Private Eye, Shakedown on the Sunset Strip, Earthstar Voyager, Neon Empire, Little White Lies, Face to Face, Original Sins, Berlin Blues, El Quixote, A Woman Named Jackie, Danger Theater.

SCHILLER, FRED
Playwright, Screen & TV Writer. b. Vienna, Austria, Jan. 6, 1924. e. Columbia Univ. (B.A.). Awarded: New York Literary Prize for McCall magazine story Ten Men and a Prayer. Member of Dramatists' Guild and Writer's Guild of America. Formerly chief corresp. European Newspaper Feature Services. Honored by the U. of Wyoming and the American Heritage Center for literary achievements with a special Fred Schiller Collection for their library. Awarded the Honor Silver Cross by Austrian Govt., for literary achievements and for furthering cultural relations between Austria and U.S. Screen plays for pictures by MGM, Columbia, RKO, Republic, Harry Sokal Productions.
THEATER: Come On Up (U.S. key citiies , London), Anything Can Happen (London), Demandez Vicky (Paris), Finder Please Return (L.A., San Francisco, Madrid, Vienna), Finder Bitte Melden (Berlin, Baden-Baden, Vienna), The Love Trap.
TELEVISION: Wrote some 53 TV plays incl. The Inca of Perusalem, Demandez Vicky! for Paris and Finder Bitte Melden! for Austria.

SCHILLER, LAWRENCE J.
Producer, Director. b. New York, NY, Dec. 28, 1936. Photojournalist with Life Magazine & Saturday Evening Post, 1958-70; collaborated on numerous books including three by Norman Mailer: The Executioner's Song, Marilyn, and The Faith of Graffiti; also Muhammad Ali (with Wilfrid Sheed), Minamata (with Eugene Smith).
PICTURES: The Man Who Skied Down Everest (editorial concept & direction), Butch Cassidy & the Sundance Kid (conceived and executed special still montages & titles); The American Dreamer (prod., dir.)
TELEVISION: Prod.: Hey I'm Alive (also dir.), The Trial of Lee Harvey Oswald, The Winds of Kitty Hawk, Marilyn, The Untold Story, An Act of Love, Child Bride of Short Creek, The Executioner's Song (also dir.), Peter the Great, Margaret Bourke-White (also dir.).

SCHINE, G. DAVID
Executive. b. Gloversville, NY, Sept. 11, 1927. e. Harvard U., Pres., gen. mgr. Schine Hotels 1950-63. Film exhibitor until 1966 in New York, Ohio, Kentucky, Maryland, Delaware, and West Virginia. Exec. prod. of French Connection, 1971. Writer, prod., dir. of That's Action!, 1977. Chief Exec. officer of Schine Productions (production) and Epic Productions (distribution), Visual Sciences, Inc., High Resolution Sciences, Inc., and Studio Television Services, Inc.

SCHLAIFER, CHARLES
Executive. b. Omaha, NB, July 1, 1909. Reporter Daily News, World-Herald (Omaha). 1930 appt. adv. mngr. Paramount theatres, then Publix theatres in Omaha; then mngr. of Tri-State circuit, NE, Iowa; 1936-42 mng. dir. United Artists Theatres, San Francisco; advisor, nat'l adv., United Artists prods.; 1942 appt. adv. mgr. 20th Cent.-Fox; 1944, named asst. dir. adv., publicity, & exploitation; 1945-49, v.p. & dir. of advertising, pub., exploitation and radio; 1949, resigned to establish own adv. agency becoming pres., Charles Schlaifer & Co., Inc.; chmn. advertising advisory council, MPAA; revised m.p. adv. code; permanent chmn. first MPAA public relations committee.

SCHLATTER, GEORGE
Producer, Director, Writer. b. Birmingham, AL, Dec. 31, 1932. m. former actress Jolene Brand. e. Pepperdine U. on football scholarship. First industry job was MCA agent in band and act dept. Then gen. mgr. and show producer Ciro's nightclub (where he met Dick Martin and Dan Rowan). Produced shows at Frontier Hotel and Silver Slipper, Las Vegas. Sang 2 seasons St. Louis Municipal Opera Co.
TELEVISION: *Created*: Laugh-In, Real People (3 Emmys, 27 nominations). *Specials with*: Goldie Hawn, Robin Williams, Shirley MacLaine, Doris Day, John Denver, Frank Sinatra, Jackie Gleason, Danny Thomas, Bob Hope, Milton Berle, Danny Kaye, George Burns, Dinah Shore, Lucille Ball, Goldie & Liza Together, Salute to Lady Liberty, Las Vegas 75th Anniversary, Speak Up America, Real Kids, Best of Times, Look At Us, Shape of Things, Magic or Miracle, Grammy Awards (first 5 years: also writer), series with Dinah Shore, Judy Garland, Bill Cosby, Steve Lawrence; also ABC American Comedy Awards (3 years), George Schlatter's Comedy Club, George Schlatter's Funny People, Beverly Hills 75th Anniversary, Humor and the Presidency, Frank Liza & Sammy... The Ultimate Event, Comedy Hall of Fame, She TV (series), Sinatra's 75th Birthday, The Best Is Yet to Come, Muhammad Ali's 50th Birthday, Welcome Home America, Laugh-In 25th Anniversary Reunion.

SCHLESINGER, JOHN
Director, Producer. b. London, England, Feb. 16, 1926. e. Oxford U., BBC dir. 1958-60: Wrote and dir. Terminus for British Transport Films (Golden Lion, best doc., Venice); The Class. Some episodes The Valiant Years series. Appeared as actor in films: Sailor of the King (1953), Pursuit of the Graf Spee, Brothers in Law, The Divided Heart, The Last Man to Hang, Fifty Years of Action (DGA doc.). Assoc. dir., National Theatre, London 1973-89. Recipient of 1995 BAFTA Fellowship.
THEATER: No Why (RSC), Timon of Athens (RSC), Days in the Trees (RSC), I and Albert, Heartbreak House (NT), Julius Caesar (NT), True West (NT).
PICTURES: A Kind of Loving (Berlin Golden Bear Award, 1961), Billy Liar, Darling (NY Film Critics Award), Far From the Madding Crowd, Midnight Cowboy (Acad. Award, 1969), Sunday Bloody Sunday, Visions of Eight (sequence), The Day of the Locust, Marathon Man, Yanks, Honky Tonk Freeway, The Falcon and the Snowman (also co-prod.), The Believers (also co-prod.), Madame Sousatzka (also co-s.p.), Pacific Heights (also cameo), The Innocent, Eye for an Eye.
TELEVISION: Separate Tables, An Englishman Abroad (BAFTA Award), The Lost Language of Cranes (actor only), A Question of Attribution (BAFTA Award), Cold Comfort Farm.
OPERA: Les Contes d'Hoffmann (Royal Opera House 1981; SWET award), Der Rosenkavalier, Un Ballo in Maschera (Salzburg Fest., 1989).

SCHLONDORFF, VOLKER
Director. b. Wiesbaden, Germany, March 31, 1939. m. dir.-actress Margarethe von Trotta. Studied in France, acquiring degree in political science in Paris. Studied at French Intl. Film Sch. (IDHEC) before becoming asst. to Jean-Pierre Melville, Alain Resnais, and Louis Malle.
PICTURES: Young Torless (debut, 1966; also s.p.), A Degree of Murder (also s.p.), Michael Kohlhass, Baal, The Sudden Fortune of the Poor People of Kombach, Die Moral der Ruth Halbfass, A Free Woman, The Lost Honor of Katharina Blum (also s.p.), Coup de Grace, The Tin Drum (also s.p.), Valeska Gert (also s.p.), Circle of Deceit, Swann in Love (also s.p.), The Handmaid's Tale, Voyager (also co-s.p.).
TELEVISION: Death of a Salesman, A Gathering of Old Men.

SCHLOSSBERG, JULIAN
Producer, Distributor, Director, Radio TV Host. b. New York, NY, Jan. 26, 1942. e. N.Y. Joined ABC-TV network 1964 as asst. acct. rep.; named act. rep. 1965; 1966, joined Walter Reade Organization as asst. v.p. chg. of TV; 1969, moved to WRO Theatre Div.; 1970, joined faculty of School of Visual Arts; 1971 named v.p. of WRO Theatres; 1976, joined Paramount Pictures as v.p. in charge of feature film acquisition. Since 1978 pres. & owner of Castle Hill Productions; 1974, prod. & moderated An Evening with Joseph E. Levine at Town Hall, N.Y.; 1974-1980, host of radio show Movie Talk on WMCA (N.Y.), WMEX (Boston), WICE (Providence); 1982-83 host of syndicated TV show, Julian Schlossbergs' Movie Talk; producers' rep. for Elia Kazan, Dustin Hoffman, Elaine May, George C. Scott. Responsible for restored version of Orson Welles' Othello, re-released in 1992.
THEATER: It Had To Be You, An Evening with Nichols and May, Rainbow Room N.Y., Mr. Gogol and Mr. Preen, Damn Yankees, Vita & Virginia, Death Defying Acts, Moscow Stations, Below the Belt, Cakewalk.
PICTURES: Going Hollywood: The War Years, Hollywood Uncensored, Hollywood Ghost Stories, No Nukes, Going Hollywood: The 30's, 10 From Your Show of Shows, In the Spirit, Bad Girls, Widow's Peak.
TELEVISION: Steve Allen's Golden Age of Comedy; All the Best, Steve Allen, Sex & Justice: The Anita Hill/Clarence Thomas Hearings, Slapstick Too, Elia Kazan: A Director's Journey (Emmy nom.), Nichols & May: Take Two.

SCHLOSSER, HERBERT S.
Executive. b. Atlantic City, NJ, April 21, 1926. e. Princeton U., Yale Law Sch. Joined law firm of Phillips, Nizer, Benjamin, Krim & Ballon, 1954; attorney, California National Productions (subsidiary of National Broadcasting Company) 1957; v.p. & gen. mgr., 1960; joined NBC-TV as director, talent & program admin., 1961; v.p., talent & program admin., 1962; v.p. programs, west coast, 1966-72; exec. v.p., NBC-TV, 1972; pres., 1973; pres. & COO, 1974-76; pres. & CEO, 1977-78; exec. v.p. RCA, 1978-85; sr. advisor, broadcasting & entertainment, Schroder Wertheim & Co., 1986.

SCHMIDT, WOLF
Producer, Distributor. b. Freiburg/Br., Germany, June 30, 1937. Came to U.S. 1962 as freelance journalist. Started producing in 1969, distributing independently since 1972. Now pres. Big Bearing Licensing Corp.
PICTURES: *Prod./Exec. Prod.*: Ski Fever, Stamping Ground, Young Hannah, Things Fall Apart, The Passover Plot, Run for the Roses, Ghost Fever, Defense Play, Riding the Edge, The Fourth War, Neon City, Extreme Justice, Silent Hunter.

SCHMOELLER, DAVID
Writer, Director. b. Louisville, KY, Dec. 8, 1947. e. Universidad de Las Americas, 1967-69, studied film and theater under Luis Bunuel and Alejandro Jodorowsky; U. of TX, B.A., M.A., 1969-74. Wrote and directed 7 short films while studying at college; won 27 intl. awards. In Hollywood spent 6 months working as intern to Peter Hyams on film, Capricorn One. Now heads own co., The Schmoeller Corp.
AUTHOR: The Seduction.
PICTURES: Tourist Trap (debut as dir.), The Seduction (dir., s.p.), Crawlspace (dir., s.p.). *Writer*: The Day Time Ended, The Peeper, Last Chance Romance, Thrill Palace, Warriors of the Wind (Eng. adaptation), Ghost Town (story). *Director*: Catacombs, Puppet Master, The Arrival, Netherworld, Catch the Wind (also s.p.).
TELEVISION: James at 15 (writer), Kid Flicks (cable; writer, prod.), Silk Stalkings (dir.), Renegades (dir.).

SCHNEER, CHARLES H.
Producer, b. Norfolk, VA, May 5, 1920. e. Columbia Coll. pres., Morningside Prods. Inc. & Pictures Corp.; 1956. Founded Andor Films 1974. Chmn. Acad. of MP Arts & Sciences, London Screening Committee.
PICTURES: *Prod.*: The 3 Worlds of Gulliver, The 7th Voyage of Sinbad, I Aim at the Stars, Face of a Fugitive, Good Day for a Hanging, Battle of the Coral Sea, Tarawa Beachhead, Mysterious Island, Jason and the Argonauts, First Men In The Moon, Half A Sixpence, Land Raiders, Valley of Gwangi, The Executioner, The Golden Voyage of Sinbad, Sinbad & The Eye of the Tiger, Clash of the Titans.

SCHNEIDER, DICK
Producer, Director. b. Cazadero, CA, March 7. e. Univ. of the Pacific, Stockton, CA. US Navy, WWII. Has received 9 Emmy Awards.
TELEVISION: Dough Re Mi, Wide Wide World, Colgate Comedy Hour, Beatrice Lillie, Jackie Gleason, Henry Morgan Show, Kate Smith Show, Big Story, Treasury Men in Action, Doorway to Danger, Today Show, Home, Tonight Show, General Mills Circus, Princess Margaret's Wedding, Paris Summit Conference, Eleanor Roosevelt Specials, Something Special 61, At This Very Moment, Inauguration, Gemini, Papal Mass for all networks at Yankee Stadium, Orange Bowl, Jr. Miss Pageant, College Queen (Emmy Award), New Communication, Big Sur, Dream House, Who What or Where, Stars and Stripes, Post Parade, Salute to Sir Lew, NBC Star Salute, Rose Parade, UCP Telethons, Macy's Parade, People's Choice, Jeopardy, Photo Finish.

SCHNEIDER, JOHN
Actor. b. Mount Kisco, NY, April 8, 1954. Active in drama club in high school in Atlanta. Worked as fashion model and played guitar singing own compositions in various Atlanta clubs. Active in local community theatre. Summer stock in New Hampshire. B'way debut 1991 in Grand Hotel.
PICTURES: Smokey and the Bandit, Million Dollar Dixie Deliverance, Eddie Macon's Run, The Curse, Cocaine Wars, Speed Zone, Ministry of Vengeance.
TELEVISION: *Series*: Dukes of Hazzard, Grand Slam, Second Chances, Heaven Help Us. *Specials*: John Schneider—Back Home, Wild Jack. *Movies*: Dream House, Happy Endings, Stagecoach, Christmas Comes to Willow Creek, Outback Bound, Gus Brown and Midnight Brewster, Highway Heartbreaker, Desperate Journey: The Allison Wilcox Story, Texas.

SCHNEIDER, PETER
Executive. President, Walt Disney Feature Animation; pres., Waly Disney Theatrical Productions.

SCHNEIER, FREDERICK
Executive. b. New York, NY, May 31, 1927; e. NYU, 1951, bus. admin.; NYU Grad. Sch., M.B.A., 1953. Dir. sls. planning, Mutual Broadcasting System, 1947-53; media research dir., RKO Teleradio, 1953-55; RKO Teleradio Advisory Comm., 1955-56; exec. staff RKO Teleradio & dir., marketing services, 1956-58; exec. vice-pres., Showcorporation, 1958-71; v.p. TV programming, RKO General, 1972-1973; v.p., Hemdale Leisure Corp., 1973-79; Viacom Enterprises v.p., feature films, 1979; sr. v.p., program acquisitions & motion pictures, 1980-83; sr. v.p., acquisitions, Showtime/The Movie Channel, 1983-85; sr. v.p. program acquisitions, program enterprises, 1985-87; exec. v.p., programming; 1987-89; pres. & CEO, Viacom Pictures Inc., 1989-92; pres. & CEO, FSA Film Enterprises.

SCHOEFFLING, MICHAEL
Actor. b. Philadelphia, PA. e. Temple Univ.
PICTURES: Sixteen Candles (debut, 1984), Vision Quest, Sylvester, Bellizaire the Cajun, Let's Get Harry, Slaves of New York, Longtime Companion, Mermaids, Wild Hearts Can't Be Broken.

SCHOENFELD, LESTER
Executive. b. Brooklyn, NY, Dec. 6, 1916. e. CCNY, 1934-38. Asst. mgr., Randforce Amusement, 1936-38; mgr., Rugoff & Becker circuit, 1938-47; mgr., Golden & Ambassador Theatres, 1948; print & sales dept., Film Classics, 1948-50; chg. of theatrical, non-theatrical & TV dist., Brit. Info. Serv.; est. Lester A. Schoenfeld Films, 1958; Schoenfeld Films Distributing Corp., 1960.

SCHORR, DANIEL
Radio, Television News Correspondent. b. New York, NY, Aug. 31, 1916. e. City Coll. of New York. Started with various news services and newspapers. Joined CBS in 1953 as Washington correspondent; 1955, reopened CBS bureau in Moscow; 1958-60, roving assignment; 1960-1966, chief German Bureau; 1966-76, Washington Bureau; 1979, Public Radio and TV; 1980, sr. Washington correspondent for Cable News Network; 1985, sr. news analyst, National Public Radio.

SCHRADER, PAUL
Writer, Director. b. Grand Rapids, MI, July 22, 1946. m. actress Mary Beth Hurt. e. Calvin Coll. (theology & philosophy); Columbia U., UCLA, M.A., cinema. Served as film critic for L.A. Free Press and Cinema 1970-72. Former professor at Columbia U.
PICTURES: Writer &/or Director: The Yakuza (co-s.p.), Taxi Driver, Rolling Thunder, Obsession, Blue Collar (co-s.p., dir.). Hardcore, Old Boyfriends (co-s.p., exec. prod.), American Gigolo, Raging Bull (co-s.p.), Cat People, Mishima (co-s.p.), The Mosquito Coast, Light of Day, The Last Temptation of Christ, Patty Hearst, The Comfort of Strangers, Light Sleeper, City Hall (co-s.p.), Touch, Affliction.
TELEVISION: Movie: Witch Hunt (dir.), The Hollywood Fashion Machine (act. only).

SCHRODER, RICK
Actor. b. Staten Island, NY, April 13, 1970. Started modelling while only four months; did many TV commercials before theatrical film debut in The Champ, at age eight.
PICTURES: The Champ, The Last Flight of Noah's Ark, The Earthling, Apt Pupil, Across the Tracks, There Goes My Baby, Crimson Tide.
TELEVISION: Series: Silver Spoons. Movies: Little Lord Fauntleroy, Something So Right, Two Kinds of Love, A Reason to Live, Too Young the Hero, Terror on Highway 91, Out on the Edge, A Son's Promise, The Stranger Within, Blood River, My Son Johnny, Miles From Nowhere, Call of the Wild, To My Daughter with Love, Texas. Mini-Series: Lonesome Dove, Return to Lonesome Dove.

SCHROEDER, BARBET
Producer, Director. b. Teheran, Iran, Aug. 26, 1941. Critic for Cahiers du Cinema and L'Air de Paris, 1958-63. 1963: asst. to Jean-Luc Godard on Les Carabiniers. 1964: formed own prod. co. Les Films du Losange. As actor only: Paris vu par, La Boulangere de Monceau Roberte, Celline and Julie Go Boating, Beverly Hills Cop III, La Reine Margot, Mars Attacks!
PICTURES: Producer: La Boulangere de Monceau (26 mins.), La Carriere de Suzanne (52 mins.), Mediterrannee, Paris Vu Par, La Collectionneuse, Tu Imagines Robinson, My Night at Maud's, Claire's Knee, Chloe in the Afternoon, Out One (co-prod.), The Mother and the Whore (co-prod.), Celine and Julie Go Boating, Flocons D'Or, The Marquise of O, Roulette Chinoise (co-prod.), The American Friend (co-prod.), Le Passe-Montagne, The Rites of Death, Perceval Le Gallois, Le Navire Night, Le Pont du Nord, Mauvaise Conduite, Une Sale Historie. Director & Producer: More (1969), Sing-Sing (doc.), La Vallee, General Idi Amin Dada (doc.), Maitresse, Koko a Talking Gorilla (doc.), Charles Bukowski Tapes (doc.), Tricheurs, Barfly, Reversal of Fortune, Single White Female, Kiss of Death, Before and After, Desperate Measures.

SCHUCK, JOHN
Actor. b. Boston, MA, Feb. 4, 1940. e. Denison (BA). Cabaret act: An Evening With John Schuck.
THEATER: B'way: Annie. Off-B'way: The Streets of NY, The Shrike. London: The Caine Mutiny. Regional incl. Long Day's Journey Into Night, As You Like It.
PICTURES: M*A*S*H, The Moonshine War, Brewster McCloud, McCabe and Mrs. Miller, Hammersmith Is Out, Blade, Thieves Like Us, Butch and Sundance: The Early Days, Just You and Me Kid, Earthbound, Finders Keepers, Star Trek VI: The Voyage Home, Outrageous Fortune, The New Adventures of Pippi Longstocking, My Mom's a Werewolf, Second Sight, Dick Tracy, Star Trek IV: The Undiscovered Country, Holy Matrimony, Pontiac Moon, Tales From the Crypt Presents Demon Knight.
TELEVISION: Series: McMillan and Wife, Holmes and Yoyo, Turnabout, The New Odd Couple, The Munsters Today. Mini-Series: Roots. Movies: Once Upon a Dead Man, Hunter, Till Death Us Do Part. Guest: Murder She Wrote, Time Trax, Deep Space Nine, many others.

SCHULBERG, BUDD WILSON
Writer. b. New York, NY, March 27, 1914. son of B. P. Schulberg, prod. e. Dartmouth Coll. Publicist, Paramount Pictures, 1931; writer for screen from 1932. Armed services WWII. Syndicated newspaper columnist: The Schulberg Report.
AUTHOR: Novels: What Makes Sammy Run?, The Disenchanted, The Harder They Fall, On the Waterfront, Some Faces in the Crowd, Everything That Moves, Sanctuary V, Love Action Laughter and Other Sad Tales. Non-fiction books: Writers in America, Moving Pictures: Memories of a Hollywood Prince, Swan Watch, Loser and Still Champion: Muhammad Ali, Sparring With Hemingway and Other Legends of the Fight Game. Short stories: Some Faces In the Crowd, Love, Action, Laughter and Other Sad Tales
THEATER: The Disenchanted (with Harvey Breit, 1958), What Makes Sammy Run? (book for musical), On the Waterfront (with Stan Silverman).
PICTURES: A Star is Born (additional dial.), Nothing Sacred (add. dial.), Little Orphan Annie (co-s.p.), Winter Carnival (co-s.p. with F. Scott Fitzgerald), Weekend for Three (orig. and co-s.p.), City Without Men (co-story), Government Girl (adapt.). Original s.p.: On the Waterfront (Acad. Award, & Writers Guild Award, 1954), A Face In the Crowd, Wind Across the Everglades, Joe Louis: For All Time (doc., Cine Golden Eagle Award, 1985).
TELEVISION: Teleplays: What Makes Sammy Run?, Paso Doble, The Pharmacist's Mate, Memory In White, The Legend That Walks Like A Man, A Question of Honor, A Table at Ciro's.

SCHULMAN, JOHN A.
Executive. b. Washington, D.C., June 13, 1946. e. Yale U., 1968; law degree from Boalt Hall, U. of California, Berkeley, 1972. Founding partner in Beverly Hills law firm, Weissmann, Wolff, Bergman, Coleman & Schulman in 1981 after nine years with firm of Kaplan, Livingston, Goodwin, Berkowitz & Selvin. Joined Warner Bros. 1984 as v.p. & gen. counsel; 1989 sr. v.p. and gen. counsel; 1991, exec. v.p. and gen. counsel.

SCHULMAN, TOM
Screenwriter. e. Vanderbilt U, BA.
PICTURES: Dead Poets Society (Acad. Award, 1989), What About Bob?, Honey I Shrunk the Kids, Second Sight, Medicine Man, Indecent Proposal (exec. prod.)

SCHULTZ, DWIGHT
Actor. b. Baltimore, MD, Nov. 24, 1947. e. Townson St. Univ. Acted with Williamstown Theatre Fest. prior to NY stage work, incl. The Crucifer of Blood, The Water Engine, Night and Day.
PICTURES: The Fan, Alone in the Dark, Fat Man and Little Boy, The Long Walk Home, The Temp.
TELEVISION: Series: The A-Team, Star Trek: The Next Generation. Movies: Child of Rage, When Your Lover Leaves, Perry Mason: The Case of the Sinister Spirit, Perry Mason: The Case of the Musical Murder, A Woman With a Past, The Last Wish, A Killer Among Us, Victim of Love: The Shannon Mohr Story, Menendez: A Killing in Beverly Hills.

SCHULTZ, MICHAEL
Director, Producer. b. Milwaukee, WI, Nov. 10, 1938. e. U. of Wisconsin, Marquette U.
THEATER: The Song of the Lusitainian Bogey, Kongi's Harvest, Does a Tiger Wear a Necktie?, Operation Sidewinder, What the Winesellers Buy, The Cherry Orchard, Mulebone, Dream on Monkey Mountain.
PICTURES: Director: Together for Days, Honeybaby Honeybaby, Cooley High, Car Wash, Greased Lightning, Which Way Is Up?, Sgt. Pepper's Lonely Hearts Club Band, Scavenger Hunt, Carbon Copy, The Last Dragon, Krush Groove (also prod.), Disorderlies (also co-prod.), Livin' Large.
TELEVISION: Specials: To Be Young Gifted and Black, Ceremonies in Dark Old Men, For Us the Living, Fade Out: The Erosion of Black Images in the Media (documentary), Hollywood Follies, Travels With Father. Series: The Young Indiana Jones Chronicles, Picket Fences, Chicago Hope, Sisters. Pilot: Shock Treatment. Movies: Benny's Place, The Jerk Too, Timestalkers, Rock 'n' Roll Mom, Tarzan in Manhattan, Jury Duty, Dayo.

SCHUMACHER, JOEL
Director, Writer. b. New York, NY, Aug. 29, 1939. Worked as design and display artist for Henri Bendel dept. store NY while attending Parson's Sch. of Design. As fashion designer opened own boutique, Paraphernalia. Joined Revlon as designer of clothing and packaging before entering m.p. indus. as costume designer on Play It As It Lays, Sleeper, The Last of Sheila, Blume in Love, Prisoner of 2nd Avenue, Interiors.
PICTURES: *Writer*: Car Wash, Sparkle, The Wiz. *Director*: The Incredible Shrinking Woman (debut, 1981), D.C. Cab (also s.p.), St. Elmo's Fire (also s.p.), The Lost Boys, Cousins, Flatliners, Dying Young, Falling Down, The Client, Batman Forever, A Time to Kill, Batman & Robin.
TELEVISION: *Director*: *Movies*: The Virginia Hill Story (also writer), Amateur Night at the Dixie Bar & Grill (also writer). *Music video*: Devil Inside for rock group INXS (dir.). *Series*: 2000 Malibu Drive. *Exec. Prod.*: Slow Burn.

SCHUMACHER, MARTHA
Producer. a.k.a Martha De Laurentiis. m. Dino De Laurentiis, producer.
PICTURES: Firestarter (assoc. prod.), Silver Bullet, Cat's Eye, King Kong Lives, Raw Deal, Maximum Overdrive, The Bedroom Window, Desperate Hours (exec. prod.). As Martha De Laurentiis: Once Upon a Crime (exec. prod.), Temptation (exec. prod.), Slave of Dreams, Unforgettable, Breakdown

SCHWAB, SHELLY
Executive. Station mgr., WAGA-TV, Atlanta; various sls. & mgr. posts with CBS. Joined MCA, 1978, becoming exec. v.p., MCA-TV. 1986, appt. pres., MCA TV Enterprises, 1989 appt. pres. MCA TV.

SCHWARTZ, BERNARD
Producer. Brought to Hollywood by the late Howard Hughes to watch his film interests; Schwartz teamed with atty. Greg Bautzer to package movie deals for clients. Re-cut number of Buster Keaton's silent movies into documentary anthologies (The Golden Age of Comedy, When Comedy Was King, etc.). Subsequently made TV series, One Step Beyond, followed by The Wackiest Ship in the Army, Miss Teen International specials, etc. Named pres. Joseph M. Schenck Enterprises, for which he made Journey to the Center of the Earth, Eye of the Cat, A Cold Wind in August, I Passed for White, The Shattered Room, Trackdown. Presently partnered with Alan Silverman.
PICTURES: Coal Miner's Daughter (prod.), Road Games (exec. prod.) Psycho II (exec. prod.), St. Elmo's Fire (co-exec. prod.).
TELEVISION: Elvis and Me (co-exec. prod.).

SCHWARY, RONALD L.
Producer. b. Oregon, May 23, 1944. e. U. of Southern California. Started as movie extra before becoming asst. dir.; served as assoc. prod. on The Electric Horseman.
PICTURES: Ordinary People (Acad. Award for Best Picture, 1980), Absence of Malice, Tootsie, A Soldier's Story, Batteries Not Included, Havana, Scent of a Woman, Cops and Robbersons, Sabrina, The Mirror Has Two Faces (co-exec. prod.).
TELEVISION: Tour of Duty.

SCHWARZENEGGER, ARNOLD
Actor. b. Graz, Austria, July 30, 1947. m. NBC reporter Maria Shriver. e. U. Wisconsin, B.A. Bodybuilding Titles: Junior Mr. Europe (at age 18), Mr. Universe (3 time winner), Mr. Olympia (7 times), Mr. Europe, Mr. World. Special Olympics weightlifting Coach (1989), Prison Weightlifting Rehabilitation Prog. Awards: Sportsman of the Year (1977, Assn. Physical Fitness Ctrs.), Golden Globe (best newcomer, 1977), ShoWest '85 Intl. Star, ShoWest Career Achievement Award, NATO Male Star of Yr. (1987).
AUTHOR: Arnold: The Education of a Bodybuilder, Arnold's Bodyshaping for Women, Arnold's Bodybuilding for Men, The Encyclopedia of Modern Bodybuilding, Arnold's Fitness for Kids (3 Vols.).
PICTURES: Hercules in New York (a.k.a. Hercules Goes Bananas; debut, 1970; billed as Arnold Strong), The Long Goodbye, Stay Hungry, Pumping Iron, The Villain, Scavenger Hunt, Conan the Barbarian, Conan the Destroyer, The Terminator, Red Sonja, Commando, Raw Deal, Predator, The Running Man, Red Heat, Twins, Total Recall, Kindergarten Cop, Terminator 2: Judgment Day, Beretta's Island (cameo), Dave (cameo), Last Action Hero (also exec. prod.), True Lies, Junior, Eraser, Jingle All the.Way, Batman and Robin.
TELEVISION: *Movie*: The Jayne Mansfield Story. *Special*: A Very Special Christmas Party (host). *Guest*: Streets of San Francisco. *Director*: Tales from the Crypt (The Switch), Christmas in Connecticut (movie).

SCHYGULLA, HANNA
Actress. b. Kattowitz, Germany, Dec. 25, 1943. Worked with Rainer Werner Fassbinder in Munich's Action Theater; a founder of the ``anti-theatre'' group. Made film debut in 1968 short Der Brautigam die Komodiantin und der Zuhalter (The Bridegroom, the Comedienne and the Pimp).

PICTURES: Love Is Colder Than Death (feature debut, 1969), Gods of the Plague, Beware of a Holy Whore, The Merchant of Four Seasons, The Bitter Tears of Petra Von Kant, House by the Sea, Jail Bait, Effi Briest, The Marriage of Maria Braun, Berlin Alexanderplatz, Lili Marleen, The Night of Varennes, Passion, A Labor of Love, A Love in Germany, The Delta Force, The Future Is a Woman, Forever Lulu, Miss Arizona, The Summer of Ms. Forbes, Dead Again.
TELEVISION: *U.S.*: Rio das Mortes, Peter the Great, Barnum, Casanova.

SCIORRA, ANNABELLA
Actress. b. New York, NY, 1964. As teen studied acting at HB Studio; then AADA. Founded The Brass Ring Theatre Co. Won role of Sophia Loren's daughter in mini-series Fortunate Pilgrim.
THEATER: Orpheus Descending, Bus Stop, Three Sisters, Snow Angel, Cries and Shouts, Trip Back Down, Love and Junk, Stay With Me, Those the River Keeps.
PICTURES: True Love (debut, 1989), Internal Affairs, Cadillac Man, Reversal of Fortune, The Hard Way, Jungle Fever, The Hand That Rocks the Cradle, Whispers in the Dark, The Night We Never Met, Mr. Wonderful, Romeo is Bleeding, The Cure, The Addiction, The Innocent Sleep, The Funeral, Cop Land, Little City.
TELEVISION: *Mini-Series*: The Fortunate Pilgrim. *Movie*: Prison Stories: Women on the Inside.

SCOFIELD, PAUL
Actor. b. Hurstpierpoint, England, Jan. 21, 1922.
THEATER: ADventure Story, Ring Round the Moon, Richard II, The Way of the World, Venice Preserved, Time Remembered, Hamlet, Power and the Glory, Family Reunion, Espresso Bongo, A Man For All Seasons (also B'way: Tony Award, 1962), Coriolanus, Don Armando, King Lear, Timon, Troilus, Pericles, Henry V, MacBeth, Staircase, The Government Inspector, Hotel In Amsterdam, Uncle Vanya, The Captain of Kopernik, Rules of the Game, Savages, The Tempest, Volpone, Madras House, The Family, Amadeus, Othello, Don Quixote, A Midsummer Night's Dream, I'm Not Rappaport, Heartbreak Housem, John Gabriel Borkman.
PICTURES: That Lady (debut, 1955), Carve Her Name With Pride, The Train, A Man for All Seasons (Acad. Award, 1966), Tell Me Lies, King Lear, Bartleby, Scorpio, A Delicate Balance, 1919, When the Whales Came, Henry V, Hamlet, Utz, Quiz Show, London (narrator), The Crucible (BAFTA Award, 1997).
TELEVISION: *Movies*: Anna Karenina, The Attic: The Hiding of Anne Frank. *Specials*: The Male of the Species (Emmy Award, 1969), The Ambassadors, The Potting Shed, Martin Chuzzlewit, Little Riders, The Crucible.

SCOGGINS, TRACY
Actress. b. Galveston, TX, Nov. 13, 1959. Studied acting at H.B. Studies, Wynn Handman Studios. Appeared on stage in L.A. in The Sicilian Bachelor.
PICTURES: Some Kind of Hero, Toy Soldier, In Dangerous Company, The Gumshoe Kid, Watchers II, Time Bomb, Silhouette, Ultimate Desires, Alien Intruder, Demonic Toys, Dead On.
TELEVISION: *Series*: Renegades, Hawaiian Heat, The Colbys, Lois & Clark: The New Adventures of Superman. *Movies*: Twirl, Jury Duty, Dan Turner: Hollywood Detective, Jake Lassiter: Justice on the Bayou. *Pilots*: The Naturals, High Life, Unauthorized Biographies. *Guest*: Hotel, Crazy Like a Fox, Dallas, Magnum P.I., The Fall Guy, Mike Hammer, The Heights.

SCOLA, ETTORE
Director, Writer. b. Trevico, Italy, May 10, 1931. e. U. of Rome. Began career in 1947 as journalist; 1950, wrote for radio shows. Then made first film as script writer 1954; debut as directorwriter, 1964. Has written 50 other scripts for other directors.
PICTURES: *Dir/Writer*: Let's Talk about Women (debut, 1964), La Congiuntura, Thrilling (segment: Il Vittimista), The Devil in Love, Will Your Heroes Find Their Friends Who Disappeared so Mysteriously in Africa?, Inspector Pepe, The Pizza Triangle, Rocco Papaleo, The Greatest Evening of My Life, We All Loved Each Other So Much, Down and Dirty, Signore e Signori Buonanotte (segment), A Special Day, Viva Italia! (segment), The Terrace, Passion d'Amore, La Nuit de Varennes, Le Bal, Macaroni, The Family, Splendor, What Time is It?, Le Capitain Fracassa, Mario Maria and Mario, Romanzo di un Giovane Povero

SCOLARI, PETER
Actor. b. New Rochelle, NY, Sept. 12, 1954.
PICTURES: The Rosebud Beach Hotel, Corporate Affairs, Ticks, Camp Nowhere, That Thing You Do!.
TELEVISION: *Series*: Goodtime Girls, Bosom Buddies, Baby Makes Five, Newhart, Family Album, Dweebs. *Movies*: Carpool, Amazon, Fatal Confession, The Ryan White Story. *Guest*: Remington Steele, The Love Boat, Family Ties, The New Mike Hammer, Trying Times (Death and Taxes), Fallen Angels (I'll Be Waiting).

SCORSESE, MARTIN
Writer, Director, Editor, Actor. b. New York, NY, Nov. 17, 1942. Began career while film arts student at NYU, doing shorts What's A Nice Girl Like You Doing in a Place Like This? (dir., s.p.), It's Not Just You Murray and The Big Shave. Other short films: Street Scenes, Italianamerican, American Boy, Mirror Mirror, Somewhere Down the Crazy River. Dir. 2 commercials for Armani. Currently campaigning for the preservation and restoration of historic films. Recipient of the American Film Institute Life Achievement Award, ,1997.
THEATER: The Act.
PICTURES: Editor: Woodstock, Medicine Ball Caravan, Unholy Rollers, Elvis on Tour. Producer: The Grifters, Mad Dog and Glory, Naked in New York (exec. prod.), Clockers. Actor: Cannonball, 'Round Midnight, Akira Kurosawa's Dreams, Guilty by Suspicion, Quiz Show, Search and Destroy (also co-exec. prod.). Director: Who's That Knocking at My Door? (also s.p., assoc. prod., actor), Boxcar Bertha (also actor), Mean Streets (also co-s.p., actor), Alice Doesn't Live Here Anymore, Taxi Driver (also actor), New York New York, The Last Waltz (also cameo), Raging Bull, The King of Comedy (also actor), After Hours (also cameo), The Color of Money, The Last Temptation of Christ, New York Stories (Life Lessons; also cameo), GoodFellas (also co-s.p., cameo), Cape Fear, The Age of Innocence (also co-s.p., cameo), Casino (also co-s.p.).
TELEVISION: Series episode: Amazing Stories (dir.). Special: A Personal Journey With Martin Scorsese Through American Movies (dir. writer).

SCOTT, CAMPBELL
Actor. b. New York, NY, July 19, 1962. e. Lawrence Univ. Son of George C. Scott and Colleen Dewhurst. Studied with Geraldine Page and Stella Adler.
THEATER: NY: The Last Outpost, The Real Thing, Copperhead, The Queen and the Rebels, Hay Fever, A Man For All Seasons, Long Day's Journey Into Night, Measure for Measure, Pericles, On the Bum. Regional: Romeo and Juliet, Our Town, Gilette, School for Wives, Hamlet.
PICTURES: Five Corners (debut, 1988), From Hollywood to Deadwood, Longtime Companion, The Sheltering Sky, Dying Young, Dead Again, Singles, Mrs. Parker and the Vicious Circle, The Innocent, The Daytrippers, Big Night (also co-dir.), The Spanish Prisoner.
TELEVISION: Mini-Series: The Kennedys of Massachusetts. Guest: Family Ties, L.A. Law. Movie: The Perfect Tribute.

SCOTT, DEBORAH LYNN
Costume Designer.
PICTURES: The Private Eyes, Don't Answer the Phone!, E.T. the Extra-Terrestrial, Never Cty Wolf, Back to the Future, Armed and Dangerous, Blue City, About Last Night..., Who's That Girl?, Life Is Sweet, Coupe de Ville, Hear My Song, Defending Your Life, Eve of Destruction, Blame It on the Bellboy, Hoffa, Jack the Bear, Sliver, Legends of the Fall, Sister My Sister, Persuasion, Funny Bones, Jack and Sarah, The Indian in the Cupboard, Othello, Heat, Looking for Richard, To Gillian on Her 37th Birthday, Titanic (Acad. Award, 1997), The Wild Wild West.
TELEVISION: Movies: Dancing Queen.

SCOTT, GEORGE C.
Actor, Director. b. Wise, VA, Oct. 18, 1927. m. actress Trish VanDevere. Son is actor Campbell Scott. Served 4 years Marine Corps. e. U. of Missouri, appeared in varsity productions, summer stock, Shakespeare.
THEATER: Off-B'way: Richard III (Theatre World Award), As You Like It, Children of Darkness, General Seeger, Merchant of Venice, Desire Under the Elms, Antony and Cleopatra, Wrong Turn at Lungfish (also L.A.), Inherit the Wind (Tony nom.). B'way: Comes a Day, The Andersonville Trial, The Wall, The Little Foxes, Plaza Suite, Uncle Vanya, All God's Chillun Got Wings (dir.), Death of a Salesman (also dir.), Sly Fox, Present Laughter (also dir.), The Boys in Autumn, On Borrowed Time (also dir.).
PICTURES: The Hanging Tree (debut, 1959), Anatomy of a Murder, The Hustler, The List of Adrian Messenger, Dr. Strangelove: Or How I Learned to Stop Worrying and Love the Bomb, The Yellow Rolls Royce, The Bible, Not With My Wife You Don't, The Flim-Flam Man, Petulia, This Savage Land, Patton (Acad. Award, 1970), They Might Be Giants, The Last Run, The Hospital, The New Centurions, Rage (also dir.), Oklahoma Crude, The Day of the Dolphin, Bank Shot, The Savage Is Loose (also dir., prod.), The Hindenburg, Islands in the Stream, Crossed Swords, Movie Movie, Hardcore, The Changeling, The Formula, Taps, Firestarter, The Exorcist III, The Rescuers Down Under (voice), Malice, Angus, Country Justice, Gloria.
TELEVISION: Series: East Side West Side, Mr. President, Traps. Movies: Jane Eyre, Fear on Trial, Oliver Twist, China Rose, A Christmas Carol, Choices, The Last Days of Patton, The Murders in the Rue Morgue, Pals, The Ryan White Story, Descending Angel, Finding the Way Home, Curacao, The Whipping Boy, In the Heat of the Night: A Matter of Justice, Tyson, Titanic, 12 Angry Men (Emmy Award, 1998). Mini-Series: Mussolini--The Untold Story. Guest: DuPont Show of the Month, Playhouse 90, Hallmark Hall of Fame, Kraft Theatre, Omnibus, Armstrong Theatre, Play of the Week, NBC Sunday Showcase, Dow Hour of Great Mysteries, Esso Theatre. Specials: Power and the Glory, The Brass Bottle, The Savage Land, The Crucible, The Price (Emmy Award, 1971), Beauty and the Beast, The Andersonville Trial (dir.).

SCOTT, MARTHA
Actress. b. Jamesport, MO, September 22, 1914. e. U. of Michigan. In little theatres over U.S.; summer stock NY; on radio with Orson Welles; Broadway debut Our Town (1938), film debut in film adaptation of same. Became theater producer in 1968 with Henry Fonda and Alfred De Liagre at Kennedy Center and on B'way (Time of Your Life, First Monday in October).
THEATER: Our Town, Soldier's Wife, The Voice of the Turtle, The Number, The Male Animal, The Remarkable Mr. Pennypacker, Forty-Second Cousin, The Crucible.
PICTURES: Our Town (debut, 1940; Acad. Award nom.), The Howards of Virginia, Cheers for Miss Bishop, They Dare Not Love, One Foot in Heaven, In Old Oklahoma (The War of the Wildcats), Hi Diddle Diddle, So Well Remembered, Strange Bargain, When I Grow Up, The Desperate Hours, The Ten Commandments, Eighteen and Anxious, Sayonara, Ben-Hur, Charlotte's Web (voice), Airport 1975, The Turning Point, Doin' Time on Planet Earth.
TELEVISION: Movies: The Devil's Daughter, Thursday's Game, The Abduction of Saint Anne, Medical Story, Charleston, Father Figure, Summer Girl, Adam, Adam: His Song Continues, Love and Betrayal, Daughter of the Streets. Mini-Series: The Word, Beulah Land. Guest: Murder She Wrote, Hotel, A Girl's Life (pilot).

SCOTT, RIDLEY
Director, Producer. b. South Shields, Northumberland, England, Nov. 30, 1937. Brother is director Tony Scott. e. Royal College of Art, London. Joined newly formed Film Sch. First film: Boy on Bicycle (short). Won design scholarship in NY. Returned to London and joined BBC as set designer (Z-Cars, The Informer series). Directed almost 3,000 commercials in 18 years. Formed Percy Main Prods. Also mng. dir. of Ridley Scott Assocs.Exec. Prod. film Monkey Trouble, prod. of The Browning Version.
PICTURES: Director: The Duellists (debut, 1978), Alien, Blade Runner, Legend, Someone to Watch Over Me (also exec. prod.), Black Rain, Thelma & Louise (also prod.), 1492: Conquest of Paradise (also prod.), White Squall (also exec. prod.), G.I. Jane (also prod.), G.I. Jane.

SCOTT, TONY
Director. b. Newcastle, England. Began career in TV commercials, being partnered with his brother Ridley in prod. co. Winner of numerous Clios, Gold & Silver Lions, and other awards. Entered m.p. industry 1972, directing half-hr. film, One of the Missing, for British Film Inst. and Loving Memory, 1-hr. feature for Albert Finney.
PICTURES: The Hunger (debut, 1983), Top Gun, Beverly Hills Cop II, Revenge, Days of Thunder, The Last Boy Scout, True Romance, Crimson Tide, The Fan.

SCOTT-THOMAS, KRISTIN
Actress. b. Redruth, Cornwall, England. Lived in France since 18. e. Central School of Speech and Drama, London; Ecole Nationale des Arts et Technique de Theatre, Paris. Stage debut in La Lune Declinante Sur 4 Ou 5 Personnes Qui Danse. Other theater work in Paris.
PICTURES: Djomel et Juliette, L'Agent Troube, La Meridienne, Under the Cherry Moon, A Handful of Dust, Force Majeure, Bille en tete, Autobus/In the Eyes of the World, The Governor's Party, The Bachelor, Bitter Moon, Somebody to Love, Four Weddings and a Funeral, An Unforgettable Summer, Mayday, The Confessional, Angels and Insects, Les Milles, Richard III, The Pompatus of Love, Portraits Chinois, Mission: Impossible, Microcosmos: Le Peuple de L'Herbe, The English Patient, Amour et Confusions.
TELEVISION: L'Ami D'Enfance de Maigret, Blockhaus, Chameleon/La Tricheuse (Aust.), Sentimental Journey (Germany), The Tenth Man, The Endless Game, Framed, The Secret Life of Ian Fleming, Titmuss Regained, Look at it This Way, Weep No More My Lady, Body & Soul, La Belle Epoque, Gulliver's Travels.

SCULLY, JOE
Talent Executive, Casting Director, Producer, Writer. b. Kearny, NJ, March 1, 1926. e. Goodman Memorial Theatre of the Art Inst. of Chicago, 1946. m. Penelope Gillette. Acted until 1951. CBS-TV, NY. Casting Dir., Danger, You Are There, Omnibus, The Web, 1951-56. Wrote The Little Woman for CBS Danger Anthology Series, 1954. 1956-60, CBS-TV, Associate Prod., Studio One, Dupont Show of the Month, Playhouse 90; 1962-64, Writer for CBS Repertoire Workshop anthology series; 1963-64, CBS Stations div. KNXT, prod., Repertoire Workshop; 1965-70 casting dir., 20th Century-Fox Films; 1970-74, indept. casting dir.; 1974-75 Universal TV, casting dir. Member, AMPAS since 1975; NBC-TV Manager, Casting & Talent; 1978, re-established Joe Scully Casting, indept. service to the industry. Founding member, CSA, 1982; 1983, casting dir., Walt Disney Pictures. 1991 published story in Emmy Magazine: Have You Ever... You Know? Conducted AMPAS Seminar, 'The Casting Process in Motion Pictures.'
PICTURES: Hello Dolly, In Like Flint, Valley of the Dolls, Planet of the Apes, The Flim-Flam Man, Sounder, Lady Sings the Blues, Play It as It Lays, The Stone Killer, Parallax View, Lifeguard, Man in the Glass Booth, Middle Age Crazy, Death Wish II, Frankenweenie (short), North of Chiang Mai, Chained in Paradiso (video).

TELEVISION: *Series*: Peyton Place, Bonanza, Room 222, Nichols, Snoop Sisters, Columbo, Switch, McMillan & Wife, Tales of the Unexpected, Gone Are the Days (Disney Channel). *Pilots*: Julia, The Ghost and Mrs. Muir, The Bill Cosby Show. *Movies*: Thief, Missiles of October, Gone Are the Days, Earth II. Australian: Flair (mini-series), Ebb Tide (movie).

SEAGAL, STEVEN
Actor, Director, Producer, Writer. b. Lansing, MI, April 10, 1952. Became skilled at martial arts at an early age, studying Aikido. Lived in Japan for 15 yrs. where he opened a martial arts academy. Opened similar academy upon his return to U.S. in Los Angeles. Was martial arts choreographer/coordinator on film The Challenge.
PICTURES: Above the Law (debut, 1988; also co-prod., co-story), Hard to Kill, Marked for Death (also co-prod.), Out for Justice (also co-prod.), Under Siege (also co-prod.), On Deadly Ground (also dir., co-prod.). Under Siege 2: Dark Territory (also co- prod.), Executive Decision, The Glimmer Man, Fire Down Below (also prod.).

SEAGROVE, JENNY
Actress. b. Kuala Lumpur, Malaysia. e. Bristol Old Vic. Theatre Sch. Stage debut 1979. Early TV: The Brack Report, The Woman in White, Diana. Recent stage: Jane Eyre, King Lear, Present Laughter, The Miracle Worker, Dead Guilty.
PICTURES: Moonlighting, Local Hero, Nate and Hayes, Appointment With Death, A Chorus of Disapproval, The Guardian, Bullseye!, Miss Beatty's Children.
TELEVISION: A Woman of Substance, Hold The Dream, In Like Flynn, Killer, Lucy Walker, Magic Moments, Some Other Spring, The Betrothed, Deadly Game, The Sign of Four, The Incident at Victoria Falls, A Shocking Accident.

SECOMBE, SIR HARRY
C.B.E.: Singer, Comedian, Actor. b. Swansea, Wales, Sept. 8, 1921. Awarded, C.B.E., 1963. Awarded Knight Bachelor, 1991.
AUTHOR: Twice Brightly, Goon for Lunch, Katy and the Nurgla, Welsh Fargo, Goon Abroad, The Harry Secombe Diet Book, Harry Secombe's Highway, The Highway Companion. Autobiography: Arias and Raspberries.
THEATER: *London*: Pickwick (also NY), The Four Musketeers, The Plumber's Progress, Pickwick (revival: Chichester Fest., Sadlers Wells Theatre, natl. tour, 1993-95).
PICTURES: Hocus Pocus (debut, 1948), Helter Skelter, London Entertains, Penny Points to Paradise, Forces' Sweetheart, Down Among the Z Men, Svengali, Davy, Jet Storm, Oliver!, The Bed Sitting Room, Song of Norway, Rhubarb, Doctor in Trouble, The Magnificent Seven Deadly Sins, Sunstruck.
TELEVISION: Numerous appearances, incl. own *series*: Secombe and Friends, The Harry Secombe Show, Secombe with Music. Also special version, Pickwick. Presenter of Tyne Tees TV's Highway 1983-93; Presenter of BBC-TV Songs of Praise, 1995-96.

SEDGWICK, KYRA
Actress. b. New York, NY, Aug. 19, 1965. e. USC. m. actor Kevin Bacon.
THEATER: *NY*: Time Was, Dakota's Belly Wyoming, Ah Wilderness (Theatre World Award), Maids of Honor. *LA*: Oleanna.
PICTURES: War and Love, Tai-Pan, Kansas, Born on the Fourth of July, Mr. & Mrs. Bridge, Pyrates, Singles, Heart & Souls, Murder in the First, Something to Talk About, The Low Life, Losing Chase, Phenomenon, Montana, Critical Care.
TELEVISION: *Movies*: The Man Who Broke 1000 Chains, Women & Men II (In Love There Are No Rules), Miss Rose White, Family Pictures, The Wide Net. *Series*: Another World. *Guest*: Amazing Stories. *Specials*: Cinder Ella: A Modern Fairy Tale, The Wide Net, Lemon Sky.

SEGAL, GEORGE
Actor. b. New York, NY, Feb. 13, 1934. e. Columbia U., B.A., 1955. Worked as janitor, ticket-taker, soft-drink salesman, usher and under-study at NY's Circle in the Square theatre. Acting debut: Downtown Theatre's revival of Don Juan. Formed a night-club singing act with Patricia Scott. Record album of ragtime songs and banjo music: The Yama Yama Man. *Dir. debut*: Bucks County Playhouse prod. Scuba Duba.
THEATER: The Iceman Cometh (1956 revival), Antony and Cleopatra N.Y. Shakespeare Festival, Leave It to Jane, The Premise (satiric improv revue), Gideon, Rattle of a Simple Man, The Knack, Requiem for a Heavyweight, The Fourth Wall (regional).
PICTURES: The Young Doctors (debut, 1961), The Longest Day, Act One, The New Interns, Invitation to a Gunfighter, Ship of Fools, King Rat, Lost Command, Who's Afraid of Virginia Woolf? (Acad. Award nom.), The Quiller Memorandum, The St. Valentine's Day Massacre, Bye Bye Braverman, No Way to Treat a Lady, The Southern Star, The Bridge at Remagen, The Girl Who Couldn't Say No, Loving, The Owl and the Pussycat, Where's Poppa?, Born to Win, The Hot Rock, A Touch of Class,

Blume in Love, The Terminal Man, California Split, Russian Roulette, The Black Bird, The Duchess and the Dirtwater Fox, Fun with Dick and Jane, Rollercoaster, Who Is Killing the Great Chefs of Europe?, Lost and Found, The Last Married Couple in America, Carbon Copy, Killing 'em Softly, Stick, All's Fair, Look Who's Talking, The Clearing, For the Boys, Look Who's Talking Now, Army of One, Direct Hit, Deep Down, Flirting With Disaster, The Cable Guy, The Feminine Touch, The Mirror Has Two Faces.
TELEVISION: *Series*: Take Five, Murphy's Law, High Tide. *Specials*: Death of a Salesman, Of Mice and Men, The Desperate Hours. *Guest*: The Nurses, Naked City, Alfred Hitchcock Presents. *Movies*: Trackdown: Finding the Goodbar Killer, The Cold Room, The Zany Adventures of Robin Hood, Not My Kid, Many Happy Returns, Endless Game, Taking the Heat, Following Her Heart.

SEGAL, MAURICE
Publicist. b. New York, NY, July 22, 1921. e. CCNY, 1937-41. Entered m.p. ind., adv. dept., 20th Fox, 1941-42; U.S. Army 1942-46; feature writer, publ. dept., 20th Fox, 1946; asst. to dir., adv., publ., Century Circuit, 1947; press book dept., Paramount, 1949; trade press rep. 1950; trade press rep. RKO Radio, 1952; resigned to join Richard Condon-Kay Norton, publicists, 1953; adv., pub. dept., U-I. 1954; asst. pub. mgr., United Artists 1957; Hollywood publ. coordinator, 1958; exec. in chg. of M.P. press dept., Universal City Studios, 1966; West Coast adv.-publ. dir., National Gen. Pictures, 1971; pres., Maurice E. Segal Co., 1974; dir., West Coast operations, Charles Schlaifer & Co., 1976; v.p., Max Youngstein Enterprises, 1979; exec. v.p., Taft Intl. Pictures, 1980; pres. Maurice E. Segal Co., 1982; pres. The Segal Company, 1987.

SEIDELMAN, ARTHUR ALLAN
Director, Producer, Writer. b. New York, NY, October 11. e. Whittier Coll., B.A.; UCLA, M.A. Former staff member, Repertory Theatre of Lincoln Center and Phoenix Theatre, NY.
THEATER: *Dir.: LA*: The Sisters, Gypsy Princess, The Beautiful People, Five Finger Exercise, The Purification, etc. *Dir.: NY*: Awakening of Spring, Hamp, Ceremony of Innocence, The Justice Box, Billy, Vieux Carre, The World of My America, Awake and Sing, The Four Seasons, Inherit the Wind, The Most Happy Fella, as well as numerous regional prods. and national tours.
PICTURES: Hercules in New York, Children of Rage (dir., s.p.), Echoes, The Caller, Rescue Me.
TELEVISION: *Director*: Family, Magnum, P.I., Murder She Wrote, Hill Street Blues, Trapper John M.D., Paper Chase, Knots Landing, Bay City Blues, Capitol News, WIOU, L.A. Law, FBI: The Untold Stories, Sweet Justice, Heaven Help Us, Amazing Grace. *Movies*: Which Mother is Mine? A Special Gift, Schoolboy Father, A Matter of Time, I Think I'm Having a Baby, Sin of Innocence, Kate's Secret, Ceremony of Innocence, Poker Alice, The People Across the Lake, Addicted to His Love, Kate's Secret, A Friendship in Vienna, A Place at the Table, An Enemy Among Us, Glory Years, Strange Voices, A Taste of Honey, Look Away, False Witness, The Kid Who Loved Christmas, Body Language, Trapped in Space, Dying to Remember, Wing and a Prayer, Harvest of Fire, I Love Liberty, The Summer of Ben Tyler, Deep Family Secrets.

SEIDELMAN, SUSAN
Director. b. near Philadelphia, PA, Dec.11, 1952. e. Drexel Univ. B.A. Worked at a UHF television station in Phila., NYU film school M.F.A. Debut: 28-min. student film And You Act Like One Too. Then dir. Deficit (short, funded by AFI), and Yours Truly, Andrea G. Stern.
PICTURES: Smithereens (dir., prod., co-s.p.; 1st Amer. indep. feature accepted into competition at Cannes Film Fest., 1982), Desperately Seeking Susan, Making Mr. Right, Cookie (also exec. prod.), She-Devil, The Dutch Master (short, Acad. Award nom.).
TELEVISION: Sex and the City, Confessions of a Suburban Girl (BBC; also writer, actress), The Barefoot Executive.

SEINFELD, JERRY
Comedian, Actor. b. Brooklyn, NY, April 29, 1954. e. Queens Col. Stand-up comic; guested on such shows as The Tonight Show, Late Night With David Letterman. Received American Comedy Award for funniest male comedy stand-up, 1988. Author: Seinlanguage (1993).
TELEVISION: *Series*: Benson, Seinfeld (also co-creator, writer). *Pilot*: The Seinfeld Chronicles. *Specials*: Jerry Seinfeld—Stand-Up Confidential (also writer), Abott and Costello Meet Jerry Seinfeld (host).

SELBY, DAVID
Actor. b. Morganstown, WV. Feb. 5, 1941. e. West Virginia U. Acted in outdoor dramas in home state and did regional theatre elsewhere. Was asst. instructor in lit. at Southern Illinois U.
PICTURES: Night of Dark Shadows, Up the Sandbox, Super Cops, Rich Kids, Raise the Titanic, Rich and Famous, Dying Young, Intersection, Headless Body in Topless Bar.

TELEVISION: *Series*: Dark Shadows, Flamingo Road, Falcon Crest. *Mini-Series*: Washington: Behind Closed Doors. *Movies*: Telethon, The Night Rider, Love for Rent, Doctor Franken, King of the Olympics: The Lives and Loves of Avery Brundage, Grave Secrets: The Legacy of Hilltop Drive, Lady Boss. *Guest*: Kojak, Doogie Howser M.D.

SELF, WILLIAM
Producer. b. Dayton, OH, June 21, 1921. e. U. of Chicago, 1943. Prod.-dir., Schlitz Playhouse of Stars, 1952-56; prod., The Frank Sinatra Show, 1957; exec. prod., CBS-TV, The Twilight Zone, Hotel De Paree; 1960-61 exec. prod., 20th Century-Fox TV: Hong Kong, Adventures in Paradise, Bus Stop, Follow The Sun, Margie; v.p. in chg. of prod., 20th Century-Fox TV, 1962; exec. v.p., 1964; pres., Fox TV 1969; v.p. 20th Century Fox Film Corp., 1969; pres. of William Self Productions, Inc., partner, Frankovich/Self Productions; 1975; v.p., programs, Hollywood CBS TV Network, 1976; 1977, v.p. motion pictures for tv and miniseries, CBS TV; 1982, pres., CBS Theatrical Films; 1985, pres., William Self Prods. in association with CBS Prods; 1990, pres. Self Productions, Inc.
TELEVISION: *Movies* (exec. prod.): The Tenth Man (also prod.), Sarah Plain & Tall, Skylark.

SELIG, ROBERT WILLIAM
Exhibitor. b. Cripple Creek, CO, Feb., 1910. e. U. of Denver, 1932, B.A.; doctorate, 1959. 1932 joined advertising sales div., 20th Century Fox, Denver. Founding mem. Theatre Owners of Amer. and NATO. Consultant, Pacific Theatres. Lifetime Trustee, U. of Denver. Member Kappa Sigma, Omicron Delta Kappa, Beta Gamma Sigma; Nat'l Methodist Church Foundation; Past Pres., Theatre Association of California and CEO NATO of CA; board of directors Los Angeles Chamber of Commerce; founder NATO/ShoWest Conventions. Received NATO Sherrill C. Corwin Award, 1989.

SELLECCA, CONNIE
Actress. b. Bronx, NY, May 25, 1955. m. anchor-host John Tesh. TELEVISION: *Series*: Flying High, Beyond Westworld, The Greatest American Hero, Hotel, P.S. I Luv U, Second Chances. *Movies*: The Bermuda Depths (debut, 1978), Flying High (pilot), Captain America II, She's Dressed to Kill, The Last Fling, International Airport, Downpayment on Murder, Brotherhood of the Rose, Turn Back the Clock, Miracle Landing, People Like Us, A House of Secrets and Lies (also co-exec. prod.), Passport to Murder, She Led Two Lives, A Dangerous Affair. *Specials*: The Celebrity Football Classic, Celebrity Challenge of the Sexes, Circus of the Stars.

SELLECK, TOM
Actor. b. Detroit, MI, Jan. 29, 1945. e. U. of Southern California. Grew up in Southern California, appearing in several commercials before being signed to 20th Century Fox. First acting job was on tv series Lancer.
PICTURES: Myra Breckenridge (debut, 1970), Midway, The Washington Affair, Coma, High Road to China, Lassiter, Runaway, Three Men and a Baby, Her Alibi, An Innocent Man, Quigley Down Under, Three Men and a Little Lady, Folks!, Christopher Columbus: The Discovery, Mr. Baseball, In & Out.
TELEVISION: *Series*: Magnum P.I. (Emmy Award, 1984; also Golden Globe & People's Choice Awards). *Movies*: Most Wanted, Superdome, Returning Home, The Sacketts, The Concrete Cowboys, Divorce Wars, Louis L'Amour's The Shadow Riders, Broken Trust, Ruby Jean and Joe, Last Stand at Saber River, Memoir of the 1997 Cowboy, Hall of Fame Heritage Award. *Exec. prod.*: Magnum P.I., B.L. Stryker (series), Revealing Evidence, The Silver Fox. *Guest*: The Young and the Restless, The Rockford Files, Friends

SELTZER, DAVID
Writer, Director. b. Highland Park, IL, 1940. m. flutist Eugenia Zukerman. e. Northwestern U. School for Film and Television. Moved to NY where worked on TV game show I've Got a Secret. Made short My Trip to New York. 1966 moved to LA to write for David Wolper's Incredible World of Animals. Then dir. and prod. Wolper documentaries. Worked as ghostwriter on film Willy Wonka and the Chocolate Factory.
PICTURES: *Writer*: The Hellstrom Chronicle, One Is a Lonely Number, The Omen, Damien: The Omen Part II, The Other Side of the Mountain, Six Weeks, Table for Five, Lucas (also dir.), Punchline (also dir.), Bird on a Wire, Shining Through (also dir., co-exec. prod.).
TELEVISION: National Geographic Specials (prod., dir., writer), William Holden in Unconquered Worlds (prod., dir., writer), The Underworld World of Jacques Cousteau. Movies (writer): The Story of Eric, Green Eyes, My Father's House, Larry.

SELTZER, WALTER
Executive. b. Philadelphia, PA, Nov. 7, 1914. e. U. of PA. Publicity Asst. for Warner Bros. Theatres, Philadelphia; Fox West Coast Theatres; with MGM 1936-39; Warner Bros., 1939-40; Columbia, 1940-41. Enlisted U.S. Marine Corps., 1941-44. Publ. dir., Hal Wallis, 1945-54; v.p. in chg. adv & pub., Hecht-Lancaster Orgn., 1954-56; assoc. prod., The Boss; partner, Glass-Seltzer, pub. rel. firm; v.p. & exec. prod, Pennebaker Production; 1982, v.p., M.P. & TV Fund; pres., WSP Inc. Bd. of trustees, v.p. 1980-87 of Motion Picture and TV Fund.

PICTURES: One-Eyed Jacks, Shake Hands With the Devil, Paris Blues, The Naked Edge, Man in the Middle, Wild Seed, War Lord, Beau Geste, Will Penny, Number One, Darker Than Amber, The Omega Man, Skyjacked, Soylent Green, The Cay, The Last Hard Men.

SEMEL, TERRY
Executive. b. New York, NY, Feb. 24, 1943. e. Long Island Univ., B.S. Accounting 1964. Warner Bros. sales trainee 1966. Branch mgr., Cleveland, Los Angeles. V.P. Domestic sls. mgr. for CBS, 1971-73. Buena Vista as v.p., gen. sls. mgr., 1973-5. 1975 went to Warner Bros. as pres. domestic sls. 1978 named exec. v.p. and COO WB Inc. Named pres., Warner Bros. & COO, 1980. Named Pioneer of the Year by Foundation of Motion Picture Pioneers, 1990.

SEMLER, DEAN
Cinematographer. b. Australia. Served as 2nd unit dir. and cameraman on the mini-series Lonesome Dove, Son of the Morningstar.
PICTURES: The Earthling, The Coca Cola Kid, The Road Warrior, Hoodwink, Kitty and the Bagman, Razorback, Mad Max Beyond Thunderdome, The Coca-Cola Kid, Going Sane, The Lighthorsemen, Cocktail, Young Guns, Farewell to the King, K-9, Dead Calm, Impulse, Young Guns II, Dances With Wolves (Acad. Award, 1990), City Slickers, The Power of One, Super Mario Bros., Last Action Hero, The Three Musketeers, The Cowboy Way, Waterworld, Gone Fishin', Firestorm, The Patriot.

SEMPLE, LORENZO, JR.
Writer.
THEATER: The Golden Fleecing (filmed as The Honeymoon Machine).
PICTURES: Fathom, Pretty Poison, Daddy's Gone A-Hunting (co-s.p.), The Sporting Club, The Marriage of a Young Stockbroker, Papillon (co-s.p.), Super Cops, The Parallax View (co-s.p.), The Drowning Pool (co-s.p.), Three Days of the Condor (co-s.p.), King Kong, Hurricane (and exec. prod.), Flash Gordon, Never Say Never Again, Sheena (co-s.p.), Never Too Young to Die.
TELEVISION: *Series*: Batman (1966). *Movie*: Rearview Mirror.

SENDREY, ALBERT
Music Composer, Arranger, Conductor. b. Chicago, IL, Dec. 26, 1921. e. Trinity Coll. Music, London, USC, Paris, & Leipzig Conservatories. Composer, arr., orch. for many plays, films and TV. On stage was pianist/conductor for Lauritz Melchior, Kathryn Grayson, Ray Bolger, Danny Kaye, Tony Martin, Buddy Ebsen. Numerous B'way productions, including Mary Martin's Peter Pan, Ginger Rogers' Pink Jungle and Yul Brynner's Penelope.
PICTURES: *Orchestrations*: The Yearling, Three Musketeers, Father's Little Dividend, Duchess of Idaho, Royal Wedding, Easy to Love, Great Caruso, An American in Paris, Brigadoon, Guys and Dolls, Meet Me in Las Vegas, High Society, Raintree County, Ride the High Country, Hallelujah Trail, The Hook, The Comancheros, Nevada Smith, The Oscar, Thoroughly Modern Millie, Hello Down There, Private Navy of Sgt. O'Farrell, Bad Day at Black Rock (with Andre Previn), Undercurrent, Sea of GRass (with H. Stothart).
TELEVISION: *Comp. music*: Laramie, Wagon Train, Ben Casey, Wolper Documentaries, Americans Abroad, J. F. Kennedy Anthology, Young Man from Boston, High Chaparral, The Monroes, Ken Murray's Hollywood.

SARGENT, HERB
Executive. Pres., Writer Guild of America East, Inc. Prod. radio program, NPR's Backfire; s.p., Bye Bye Branerman; writer, prod. for many comedy shows.

SERNA, ASSUMPTA
Actress. b. Barcelona, Spain, Sept. 16, 1957. Abandoned plans to be a lawyer, making stage debut 1978 with anti- Franco theatre company.
PICTURES: Sweet Hours (debut, 1980), The Hunting Ground, Crime of Cuenca, Revolt of the Birds, Circle of Passions, Tin Soldier, Secret Garden, Extramuros, The Old Music, Lola, Matador, Ballad of Dogs, Lucky Ravi, La Brute, La Nuite de L'Ocean, What Belongs to Caesar, Neon Man, Wild Orchid, I the Worst of All, Rossini Rossini, Adelaide, Chain of Desire, Cracked Nut, Fencing Master, Green Henry, Nostradamus, Shortcut to Paradise, Belle al Bar, The Shooter, Como un Relampago, The Craft, Stolen Moments.
TELEVISION: Valentina, First Brigade, Falcon Crest, Fur Elise, Drug Wars, Revolver, Sharpe, Day of Reckoning, Les Derniers Jours de la Victime.

SEWELL, RUFUS
Actor. b. Twickenham, England, Oct. 29, 1967. e. London's Central School of Speech and Drama.
THEATER: *London*: (stage debut) Making It Better, Arcadia. *B'way*: (debut) Translations.
PICTURES: Twenty-One, Dirty Weekend, A Man of No Importance, Victory, Cold Comfort Farm, Carrington, Hamlet, The Woodlanders, Illuminata, Dark City, Dangerous Beauty, Martha Meet Frank Daniel and Laurence.
TELEVISION: *Movie*: The Last Romantics. *Mini-series*: Middlemarch.

SEYMOUR, JANE
Actress. r.n. Joyce Frankenberg. b. Hillingdon, England, Feb. 15, 1951. Dancer with London Festival Ballet at 13. On B'way in Amadeus (1980). British Repertory including Canterbury, Harrogate, Sussex, Windsor.
PICTURES: Oh! What a Lovely War (debut, 1968), The Only Way, Young Winston, Live and Let Die, Sinbad and the Eye of the Tiger, Battlestar Galactica, Oh Heavenly Dog, Somewhere in Time, Lassiter, Head Office, The Tunnel, The French Revolution, Keys to Freedom.
TELEVISION: Series: The Onedine Line, Dr. Quinn: Medicine Woman (Golden Globe, 1996). Movies/Mini-Series: Here Come the Double Deckers, Frankenstein: The True Story, Captains and the Kings, Benny and Barney: Las Vegas Undercover, Seventh Avenue, Killer on Board, Our Mutual Friend, The Four Feathers, The Awakening Land, Love's Dark Ride, The Hanged Man, Dallas Cowboys Cheerleaders, The Story of David, McCloud, East of Eden, The Scarlet Pimpernal, Phantom of the Opera, The Haunting Passion, Dark Mirror, The Sun Also Rises, Obsessed with a Married Woman, Jamaica Inn, Crossings, War and Remembrance, The Woman He Loved, Onassis: The Richest Man in the World (Emmy Award, 1988), Jack the Ripper, Angel of Death, I Remember You, Memories of Midnight, Are You Lonesome Tonight?, Matters of the Heart, Sunstroke (also exec. prod.), Heidi, Praying Mantis (also co-exec. prod.), A Passion for Justice: The Hazel Brannon Smith Story (also co-exec. prod.), The Absolute Truth. Host: The Heart of Healing.

SHABER, DAVID
Screenwriter. b. Cleveland, OH. e. Western Reserve U., Yale U., Taught at Allegheny Coll. and Smith Coll. in speech and drama dept. Prof. of screenwriting Columbia Univ. Film School. Contributor to Cosmopolitan, Life, Esquire; had several short stories in O'Henry prize collections. Also wrote dramas (Shake Hands with the Clown, The Youngest Shall Ask, Bunker Reveries, etc.). First screenplay was Such Good Friends for Otto Preminger.
PICTURES: The Last Embrace, The Warriors, Those Lips, Those Eyes, Night Hawks, Rollover, The Hunt for Red October (uncredited), Flight of the Intruder.

SHAFER, MARTIN
Executive. Pres., Castle Rock Pictures, a division of Castle Rock Entertainment.

SHAGAN, STEVE
Writer. b. New York, NY. Oct. 25, 1927. Apprenticed in little theatres, film lab chores, stagehand jobs. Wrote, produced and directed film short, One Every Second; moved to Hollywood in 1959. Was IATSE technician, working as grip, stagehand, electrician to support film writing. Also did freelance advertising and publicity; produced Tarzan TV show. In 1968 began writing and producing two-hour films for TV.
AUTHOR: Save the Tiger, City of Angels, The Formula, The Circle, The Discovery, Vendetta, Pillars of Fire, A Cast of Thousands.
PICTURES: Writer: Save the Tiger (also prod.; Acad. Award nom., WGA Award, 1973), W.W. and the Dixie Dancekings (exec. prod.), Hustle, Voyage of the Damned (co.-s.p.; Acad. Award nom.), Nightwing (co-s.p.), The Formula (also prod.), The Sicilian, Primal Fear (co-s.p.).
TELEVISION: Writer-producer: River of Mystery, Spanish Portrait, Sole Survivor, A Step Out of Line, House on Garibaldi Street (exec. prod.), John Gotti.

SHAIMAN, MARC
Composer, Arranger. b. Newark, NJ, Oct. 22, 1959. Began career at 16 as vocal arranger for Bette Midler; became her Musical Director and Co-producer as well as writing special material for The Divine Miss M! Wrote music for Saturday Night Live; co-wrote musical material for Billy Crystal for the Academy Awards (Emmy Award for "Oscar Medleys"). Prod. and arranger for several Harry Connick, Jr. albums. Received Grammy noms. for "When Harry Met Sally" and "We Are In Love". Appeared on stage in Harlem Nocturne.
PICTURES: Divine Madness (music dir., arranger), The Cotton Club (music sprv., arranger), Broadcast News (cameo), Big Business (music sprv., arranger), Beaches (arranger), When Harry Met Sally... (music spvr.), Misery (music), Scenes From a Mall (music, adapt., cameo), City Slickers (music), Hot Shots (cameo), For the Boys (music sprv., arranger, co-composer), The Addams Family (music, cameo, co-wrote song "Mamuschka"), Sister Act (music, adapt.), Mr. Saturday Night (music, cameo), A Few Good Men (music), Life With Mikey (music spvr.), Sleepless in Seattle (musical spvr., co-wrote song "With a Wink and a Smile"; Acad. Award nom.), Hocus Pocus (music prod.), Heart and Souls (music, cameo), For Love or Money (co-composer), Addams Family Values (music), Sister Act 2: Back in the Habit (music, adaptations), That's Entertainment III (music spvr.), City Slickers II: The Legend of Curly's Gold (music), North (music, cameo), The American President (Acad. Award nom.), Speechless, Stuart Saves His Family, Forget Paris, The First Wives Club (Acad. Award nom.), Ghosts of Mississippi, Mother, George of the Jungle, In & Out.

SHALIT, GENE
Critic. b. New York, NY, 1932. e. U. of Illinois. Started as freelance writer; joined NBC Radio Network, working on Monitor, 1968. Has been book and film critic, sports and general columnist. Since 1973 has been featured regular on NBC Today Show. Edits newsletter Shalit's Sampler.

SHANDLING, GARRY
Actor, Comedian, Writer, Producer. b. Chicago, IL, Nov. 29, 1949. e. Univ. of AZ. Moved to LA where he became writer for such sitcoms as Sandford & Son, Welcome Back Kotter, Three's Company. Became stand-up comedian in nightclubs which led to appearances on The Tonight Show.
PICTURES: The Night We Never Met (debut, 1993), Love Affair, Mixed Nuts.
TELEVISION: Series: It's Garry Shandling's Show (also exec. prod., writer; ACE Awards for Best Series & Actor), The Larry Sanders Show (also co-exec. prod., co-creator, co-writer, Emmy Award, 1998). Specials: Garry Shandling—Alone in Las Vegas (also writer, prod.), It's Garry Shandling's Show—25th Anniversary Special (also exec. prod., writer), Grammy Awards (host), Garry Shandling: Stand-Up (also writer). Guest: Tonight Show (also frequent guest host), Late Night With David Letterman.

SHANLEY, JOHN PATRICK
Writer, Director. b. New York, NY, 1950. e. NYU. Cameo appearance in 1988 film Crossing Delancey. Dir. and wrote short I am Angry.
THEATER: Writer: Rockaway, Welcome to the Moon, Danny and the Deep Blue Sea, Savage in Limbo, Dreamer Examines His Pillow. Writer-Dir.: Italian-American Reconciliation, Beggars in the House of Plenty, Four Dogs and a Bone.
PICTURES: Writer: Moonstruck (Acad. Award & Writers Guild Award, 1987), Five Corners (also assoc. prod.), The January Man, Joe Versus the Volcano (also dir.), Alive, We're Back!, Congo.

SHAPIRO, ROBERT W.
Producer. b. Brooklyn, NY, March 1, 1938. e. USC. Joined William Morris Agency, Inc., 1958; dir. and head of motion picture dept., William Morris Agency (UK) Ltd., 1969; mng. dir., 1970; 1974 v.p., head int'l. m.p. dept.; 1977 joined Warner Bros. as exec. v.p. in chg. of worldwide production; 1981, named WB pres., theatrical production div. Resigned 1983 to produce pictures.
PICTURES: Pee-Wee's Big Adventure, Empire of the Sun (exec. prod.), Arthur 2 On the Rocks, There Goes My Baby, Black Beauty, Dr. Jekyll and Ms. Hyde, An Alan Smithee Film: Burn Hollywood Burn (actor only), Somewhere in the City (actor only).
TELEVISION: Movie: The Summer My Father Grew Up, Do You Know the Muffin Man.

SHARE, MICHAEL
Executive. Began career with Paramount Pictures 1974 as booker in Indianapolis; 1975-76 appt. salesman; 1976-77 sls. mgr. in Philadelphia; 1977, Cincinnati branch mgr.; 1980, Chicago branch mgr.; 1985, promoted to v.p., eastern div., Paramount.

SHARIF, OMAR
Actor. r.n. Michel Shahoub. b. Alexandria, Egypt, April 10, 1932. e. Victoria Coll., Cairo.; pres. of College Dramatic Society. Starred in 21 Egyptian (billed as Omar el Cherif or Omar Cherif) and two French films prior to English-language debut in Lawrence of Arabia. Left Egypt 1964. Champion contract bridge player. 1983 made rare stage appearance in The Sleeping Prince (Chichester, then West End).
PICTURES: The Blazing Sun (debut, 1954), Our Happy Days, La Chatelane du Liban, Goha, The Mameluks, Lawrence of Arabia (Acad. Award nom.), The Fall of the Roman Empire, Behold a Pale Horse, Marco the Magnificent, Genghis Khan, The Yellow Rolls-Royce, Doctor Zhivago, The Poppy Is Also a Flower, The Night of the Generals, More Than a Miracle, Funny Girl, Mackenna's Gold, The Appointment, Mayerling, Che!, The Last Valley, The Horsemen, The Burglars, The Right to Love (Brainwashed), The Tamarind Seed, The Mysterious Island of Captain Nemo, Juggernaut, Funny Lady, Crime and Passion, The Pink Panther Strikes Again (cameo), Ashanti, Bloodline, The Baltimore Bullet, Oh Heavenly Dog, Green Ice, Chanel Solitaire, Top Secret!, The Possessed, Paradise Calling, The Blue Pyramids, Keys to Freedom, Novice, Mountains of the Moon, Michelangelo and Me, Drums of Fire, Le Guignol, The Puppet, The Rainbow Thief, Journey of Love, Mother, 588 Rue Paradis.
TELEVISION: S*H*E, Pleasure Palace, The Far Pavilions, Peter the Great, Harem, Anastasia, Grand Larceny, Omar Sharif Returns to Egypt, The Mysteries of the Pyramids Live (host), Memories of Midnight, Mrs. 'arris Goes to Paris, Lie Down with Lions.

SHARP, ALAN
Writer. b. Glasgow, Scotland.
PICTURES: The Hired Hand, Ulzana's Raid, Billy Two Hats, Night Moves, The Osterman Weekend, Little Treasure (also dir.), Freeway, Cat Chaser (co-s.p.).
TELEVISION: Coming Out of the Ice.

SHATNER, WILLIAM
Actor. b. Montreal, Quebec, March 22, 1931. e. McGill U. Toured Canada in various stock, repertory companies before U.S. tv debut in 1956. Author: TekWar, TekLords, TekLab, Tek Vengeance, TekSecret, Believe, Star Trek Memories (co-author with Chris Kreski), Star Trek Movie Memories (co-author with Kreski), The Return, Man O'War.
THEATER: NY: Tamburlaine the Great, The World of Susie Wong (Theatre World Award), A Shot in the Dark, L'Idiote.
PICTURES: The Brothers Karamazov (debut, 1958), Judgment at Nuremberg, The Explosive Generation, The Intruder, The Outrage, Incubus, White Comanche, Impulse, Big Bad Mama, The Devil's Rain, Kingdom of the Spiders, Land of No Return, Star Trek—The Motion Picture, The Kidnapping of the President, Visiting Hours, Star Trek II: The Wrath of Khan, Airplane II: The Sequel, Star Trek III: The Search for Spock, Star Trek IV: The Voyage Home, Star Trek V: The Final Frontier (also dir., orig. story), Bill & Ted's Bogus Journey (cameo), Star Trek VI: The Undiscovered Country, National Lampoon's Loaded Weapon 1, Star Trek: Generations.
TELEVISION: Series: For the People, Star Trek, Barbary Coast, T.J. Hooker, Rescue 911 (host), TekWar: The Series (also dir., co-exec. prod.). Movies: Sole Survivor, Vanished, Owen Marshall: Counselor at Law (pilot), The People, The Hound of the Baskervilles, Incident on a Dark Street, Go Ask Alice, The Horror at 37000 Feet, Pioneer Woman, Indict and Convict, Pray for the Wildcats, Barbary Coast (pilot), Perilous Voyage, The Bastard, Little Women, Crash, Disaster on the Coastliner, The Baby Sitter, Secrets of a Married Man, North Beach and Rawhide, Broken Angel, Family of Strangers, Columbo: Butterfly in Shades of Grey, TekWar (also dir., co-exec. prod.), TekLab, TekWar: TekJustice, Janek: A Silent Betrayal. Special: TekWar: TekPower, TekMoney, Ashes of Money. Mini-Series: Testimony of Two Men.

SHAVELSON, MELVILLE
Writer, Director. b. Brooklyn, NY, April 1, 1917. e. Cornell U., 1937, A.B. Radio writer: We The People, Bicycle Party, 1937, Bob Hope Show, 1938-43, then screen writer; apptd. prod., Warner Bros, 1951. Conceived for TV: Make Room for Daddy, My World and Welcome To It. Author: book, How To Make a Jewish Movie, Lualda, The Great Houdinis, The Eleventh Commandment, Ike, Don't Shoot It's Only Me. Pres., Writers Guild of America, West, 1969-71, 1979-81, 1985-87; Pres., Writers Guild Foundation 1978-96.
PICTURES: Writer. The Princess and the Pirate, Wonder Man, The Kid From Brooklyn, Sorrowful Jones, It's a Great Feeling, The Daughter of Rosie O'Grady, Always Leave Them Laughing, Where There's Life, On Moonlight Bay, Double Dynamite, I'll See You in My Dreams, Room for One More (The Easy Way), April in Paris, Trouble Along the Way, Living It Up. Director-Writer. The Seven Little Foys (dir. debut, 1955), Beau James, Houseboat, It Started in Naples, The Five Pennies, On the Double, The Pigeon That Took Rome (also prod.), A New Kind of Love (also prod.), Cast a Giant Shadow (also prod.), Yours Mine and Ours, The War Between Men and Women, Mixed Company.
TELEVISION: Movies: The Legend of Valentino, The Great Houdinis, Ike, The Other Woman, Deceptions. Specials: Academy Awards, 1988, 1990 (writer).

SHAVER, HELEN
Actress. b. St. Thomas, Ontario, Canada, Feb. 24, 1951. e. Banff Sch. of Fine Arts, Alberta. Worked on stage and screen in Canada before coming to Los Angeles 1978.
THEATER: Tamara, Are You Lookin'? Ghost on Fire, A Doll's House, The Master Builder, The Hostage, Jake's Women (B'way debut; Theatre World Award).
PICTURES: Christina, Shoot, Starship Invasions, Outrageous!, High-Ballin', The Amityville Horror, In Praise of Older Women, Who Has Seen the Wind, Gas, Harry Tracy, The Osterman Weekend, Best Defense, Desert Hearts, The Color of Money, The Believers, The Land Before Time (voice), Walking After Midnight, Innocent Victim (Tree of Hands), Zebrahead, That Night, Dr. Bethune, Morning Glory, Change of Heart, Open Season, Born to Be Wild.
TELEVISION: Series: United States, Jessica Novak, WIOU. Movies: Lovey: Circle of Children II, Between Two Brothers, Many Happy Returns, The Park is Mine, Countdown To Looking Glass, No Blame, B.L. Stryker: The Dancer's Touch, Pair of Aces, Columbo: Rest in Peace Mrs. Columbo, Survive the Night, Poisoned By Love: The Kern County Murders, Trial & Error, The Forget-Me-Not Murders, Ride With the Wind, Without Consent, Janek: A Silent Betrayal. Guest: Ray Bradbury Theatre, Amazing Stories.

SHAW, MICHAEL M. (JOHN)
Executive. b. Ashland, KY, Jan. 10, 1945. e. Eastern KY Univ., Univ. of KY, Univ of MS. 1968-69, asst. booker, 20th Century Fox, Denver; 1969, head booker, Fox; 1970, salesman, Paramount Pictures, S.F.; 1970-71, head booker, sales Paramount L.A.; 1971-73, booker, Commonwealth Theatres; 1973, booker, McLendon theatres, Dallas; 1973-78, div. mngr. Mulberry Square Prods., Dallas; 1978-79, branch mngr. Filmways Pictures, Dallas; 1980-82, owner, Sequoyah Cinema Svc., Denver; 1983-87, head film buyer, Presidio Theatres, Austin; 1987-88, head film buyer, Santikos Theatres, San Antonio; 1988-present, pres./CEO, Film Booking Office Corp., Movieline Int'l, Dallas. Member: Motion Picture Pioneers, Variety Club.

SHAW, STAN
Actor. b. Chicago, IL, July 14, 1952. On stage received NAACP Image Award for West Coast premiere of Home, 1982.
PICTURES: The Bingo Long Travelling All-Stars and Motor Kings, Rocky, The Boys in Company C, The Great Santini, Tough Enough, Runaway, The Monster Squad, Harlem Nights, Fried Green Tomatoes, Body of Evidence, Rising Sun, Houseugest, Cutthroat Island, Daylight.
TELEVISION: Series: The Mississippi. Mini-Series: Roots: The Next Generations. Movies: Call to Glory, Maximum Security, The Gladiator, The Billionaire Boys Club, The Three Kings, The Court-Martial of Jackie Robinson, Lifepod. Guest: Starsky and Hutch, Wiseguy, Murder She Wrote, Hill Street Blues, Matlock.

SHAWN, WALLACE
Playwright, Actor. b. New York, NY, Nov. 12, 1943. Son of former New Yorker editor William Shawn. e. Harvard; Oxford U. Taught English in India on a Fulbright scholarship 1965-66. English, Latin and drama teacher, NY 1968-70.
THEATER: Writer: Our Late Night (1975, Obie Award), The Mandrake (translation, also actor), A Thought in Three Parts, Marie and Bruce, The Hotel Play, Aunt Dan and Lemon (also actor), The Fever (Obie Award, 1991; also actor). Opera: The Music Teacher (with Allen Shawn). Actor: The Master and Margarita, Chinchilla, Wifey.
PICTURES: Manhattan (debut, 1979), Starting Over, All That Jazz, Strong Medicine, Simon, Atlantic City, My Dinner With Andre (also co-s.p.), A Little Sex, Lovesick, The First Time, Deal of the Century, Strange Invaders, Saigon—Year of the Cat, Crackers, The Hotel New Hampshire, The Bostonians, Micki and Maude, Heaven Help Us, Head Office, The Bedroom Window, Radio Days, Prick Up Your Ears, Nice Girls Don't Explode, The Princess Bride, The Moderns, She's Out of Control, Scenes From the Class Struggle in Beverly Hills, We're No Angels, Shadows and Fog, Mom and Dad Save the World, Nickel and Dime, The Cemetery Club, Un-Becoming Age, The Meteor Man, Vanya on 42nd Street, Mrs. Parker and the Vicious Circle, A Goofy Movie (voice), Clueless, Canadian Bacon, Toy Story (voice), The Wife, House Arrest, All Dogs Go to Heaven II (voice).

SHAYE, ROBERT
Executive. b. Detroit, MI, March 4, 1939. e. U. of Michigan, B.B.A.; Columbia U. Law. At 15 wrote, prod. dir. training film for father's supermarket staff. Later won first prize in Society of Cinematologists' Rosenthal Competition (best m.p. by American dir. under 25). Wrote, prod., dir., edited short films, trailers and TV commercials, including award-winning shorts, Image and On Fighting Witches (prod., dir.). Founded New Line Cinema 1967. Chmn. & CEO, New Line Cinema.
PICTURES: Prod./exec. prod.: Stunts, XTRO, Alone in the Dark, The First Time, Polyester, Critters, Quiet Cool, My Demon Lover, A Nightmare on Elm Street (also parts 2,3,4,5,6), The Hidden, Stranded, Critters 2, Hairspray, Heart Condition, Book of Love (dir.), Wes Craven's New Nightmare (also actor).
TELEVISION: Freddy's Nightmare: the Series (exec. prod.).

SHEA, JOHN
Actor. b. Conway, NH, April 14, 1949. Raised in MA. e. Bates Coll., ME, B.A. 1970; Yale Drama School, M.F.A. 1973. Worked as asst. dir. Chelsea Theater; taught part-time at Pratt Inst.
THEATER: Yentl (debut 1975, Off-B'way and B'way; Theatre World Award), Sorrows of Stephen, Long Day's Journey Into Night (Joseph Jefferson Award nom.), The Master and Margarita, Romeo and Juliet (Circle in the Sq.), American Days (Drama Desk Award), The Dining Room, End of the World (B'way), The Normal Heart (London, 1987), Animal Kingdom, Rosmersholm (La Mama), Impossible Spy (China's Golden Panda Award).
PICTURES: Hussy, Missing, Windy City (Best Actor Montreal Film Festival), A New Life, Unsettled Land, Honeymoon, Stealing Home, Freejack, Honey I Blew Up the Kid, A Weekend in the Country, Brass Ring (also dir., co-writer).
TELEVISION: Series: WIOU, Lois and Clark. Movies: The Nativity, Family Reunion, Coast to Coast (BBC), Hitler's S.S.: Portrait in Evil, A Case of Deadly Force, The Impossible Spy, Magic Moments, Baby M (Emmy Award), Do You Know the Muffin Man, Small Sacrifices, Notorious, Ladykiller, Justice in a Small Town, See Jane Run, Forgotten Sins, The Dining Room. Mini-Series: The Last Convertible, Kennedy, The Apocalypse Watch. Special: Leslie's Folly.

SHEAFF, DONALD J.
Executive. b. Oct. 23, 1925. e. U.of California at L.A., 1948; Pierce Coll., 1957. Served 4 yrs. during W.W.II in Navy Air Corps in South Pacific. 1946, joined Technicolor Motion Picture Div. in supervisory capacity; 1957, lab. supervisor, Lookout Mountain Air Force Station, handling Top Secret film for Air Force and Atomic Energy Commission; est. and org. the installation of Vandenberg Air Force Base Lab. facilities, which Technicolor designed; 1961 joined Panacolor Corp.; 1963, joined Pacific Title and Art Studio in charge of color control for special effects and titles; returned to Technicolor Corp. app't. Plant Mgr. of TV div., 1966; v.p. & gen. mngr. of the TV div., 1973; appt v.p. & gen. mgr., Motion Picture Division, 1976; mgr., special visual effects, Universal City Studios. Member: SMPTE, Nat'l Academy of Television Arts & Sciences. Has conducted scientific seminars for SMPTE.

SHEARER, HARRY
Writer, Actor. b. Los Angeles, CA, Dec. 23, 1943. e. UCLA (pol. science); grad. work in urban gov., Harvard. At 7 appeared on The Jack Benny Show. Worked as freelance journalist for Newsweek, L.A. Times and publ. articles in New West, L.A. Magazine and Film Comment. Also taught h.s. Eng. and social studies and worked in CA State Legislature in Sacramento. Founding mem. The Credibility Gap, co-wrote, co-prod. and performed on comedy group's albums (A Great Gift Idea, The Bronze Age of Radio). Co-wrote, co-prod. Albert Brooks' album A Star is Bought. Performed with group Spinal Tap. Host of Le Show, L.A. radio prog. Writer-cast mem. Saturday Night Live (1979-80 & 1984-85).
THEATER: Accomplice (Pasadena Playhouse).
PICTURES: Actor. Abbott and Costello Go to Mars (debut, as child, 1953), Cracking Up, Real Life (also co-s.p.), Animalympics (voice), The Fish That Saved Pittsburgh, Serial, One-Trick Pony, The Right Stuff, This is Spinal Tap (also co-s.p.), Plain Clothes, My Stepmother is an Alien (voice), Oscar, Pure Luck, Blood & Concrete, The Fisher King, A League of Their Own, Wayne's World 2, I'll Do Anything, Speechless, Thrill Ride: The Science of Fun.
TELEVISION: Series: Fernwood 2-Night (creative consultant), The Simpsons (voice), Harry Shearer's News Quiz. Specials: Likely Stories, It's Just TV, Paul Shaffer: Viva Shaf Vegas, Comedy Hour, Portrait of a White Marriage (also dir.), The Magic of Live, Spinal Tap Reunion (also co-writer).

SHEEDY, ALLY
Actress. r.n. Alexandra Sheedy. b. New York, NY, June 13, 1962. e. USC. m. actor David Lansbury. Daughter of literary agent Charlotte Sheedy. As child performed with American Ballet Theatre. At age 12 wrote children's book, She Was Nice to Mice; later wrote pieces for NY Times, Village Voice, Ms. Published book of poetry: Yesterday I Saw the Sun. Began acting in TV commercials at 15. Chicago Theatre in Wrong Turn at Lungfish; NY stage debut in Advice from a Caterpillar.
PICTURES: Bad Boys (debut, 1983), WarGames, Oxford Blues, The Breakfast Club, St. Elmo's Fire, Twice in a Lifetime, Blue City, Short Circuit, Maid to Order, Heart of Dixie, Betsy's Wedding, Only the Lonely, Home Alone 2: Lost in New York (cameo), Tattletale, The Pickle, Man's Best Friend, One Night Stand, High Art.
TELEVISION: Movies: The Best Little Girl in the World, The Violation of Sarah McDavid, The Day the Loving Stopped, Splendor in the Grass, Deadly Lessons, We Are the Children, Fear, The Lost Capone, Lethal Exposure, Chantilly Lace, Ultimate Betrayal, Parallel Lives, The Haunting of Seacliff Inn, The Tin Soldier. Guest: Hill Street Blues, St. Elsewhere.

SHEEN, CHARLIE
Actor. r.n. Carlos Irwin Estevez. b. Los Angeles, Sept. 3, 1965. Father is actor Martin Sheen. Brother of actors Emilio, Ramon and Renee Estevez. Made debut as extra in TV movie, The Execution of Private Slovik (starring father) and as extra in Apocalypse Now (also starring father).
PICTURES: Grizzly II—The Predator, Red Dawn, The Boys Next Door, Lucas, Ferris Bueller's Day Off, The Wraith, Platoon, Wisdom, Three for the Road, No Man's Land, Wall Street, Never on Tuesday, Young Guns, Eight Men Out, Major League, Beverly Hills Brats, Courage Mountain, Navy Seals, Men at Work, The Rookie, Cadence, Hot Shots!, National Lampoon's Loaded Weapon 1 (cameo), Hot Shots Part Deux!, DeadFall, The Three Musketeers, The Chase (also co-exec. prod.), Major League 2, Beyond the Law, Terminal Velocity, The Shadow Conspiracy, All Dogs Go to Heaven II (voice), The Arrival, Money Talks.
TELEVISION: Movies: Silence of the Heart, Backtrack.

SHEEN, MARTIN
Actor. r.n. Ramon Estevez. b. Dayton, OH, Aug. 3, 1940. Father of actors Emilio Estevez, Charlie Sheen, Ramon Estevez and Renee Estevez. Wrote play as Ramon G. Estevez) Down the Morning Line (prod. Public Theatre, 1969). Emmy Award as dir., exec. prod. Babies Having Babies (1986).

THEATER: The Connection (debut, 1959 with the Living Theater), Women of Trachis, Many Loves, In the Jungle of Cities, Never Live Over a Pretzel Factory, The Subject Was Roses, The Wicked Crooks, Hamlet, Romeo and Juliet, Hello Goodbye, The Happiness Cage, Death of a Salesman (with George C. Scott), Julius Caesar, The Crucible.
PICTURES: The Incident (debut, 1967), The Subject Was Roses, Catch-22, No Drums No Bugles, Rage, Pickup on 101, Badlands, The Legend of Earl Durrand, The Cassandra Crossing, The Little Girl Who Lives Down the Lane, Apocalypse Now, Eagle's Wing, The Final Countdown, Loophole, Gandhi, That Championship Season, Enigma, Man Woman and Child, The Dead Zone, Firestarter, The Believers, Siesta, Wall Street, Walking After Midnight, Da (also co-exec. prod.), Judgment in Berlin (also exec. prod.), Beverly Hills Brats, Cold Front, Beyond the Stars, The Maid, Cadence (also dir.), JFK (narrator), Hear No Evil, Hot Shots Part Deux (cameo), Gettysburg, Trigger Fast, Hits!, Fortunes of War, Sacred Cargo, The Break, Dillinger & Capone, Captain Nuke and the Bomber Boys, Ghost Brigade, The Cradle Will Rock, Dead Presidents, Dorothy Day, Gospa, The American President, The War At Home, Spawn.
TELEVISION: Series: As the World Turns. Movies: Then Came Bronson, Mongo's Back in Town, Welcome Home Johnny Bristol, That Certain Summer, Letters for Three Lovers, Pursuit, Catholics, Message to My Daughter, The Execution of Private Slovik, The California Kid, The Missiles of October, The Story of Pretty Boy Floyd, Sweet Hostage, The Guardian, The Last Survivors, Blind Ambition, The Long Road Home (Emmy Award, 1981), In the Custody of Strangers, Choices of the Heart, The Atlanta Child Murders, Consenting Adult, Shattered Spirits, News at Eleven, Out of the Darkness, Samaritan, Conspiracy: The Trial of the Chicago 8, No Means No (exec. prod. only), Nightbreaker (also exec. prod.), Guilty Until Proven Innocent, The Water Engine (voice), The Last P.O.W.?: The Bobby Garwood Story, A Matter of Justice, One of Her Own, Roswell. Mini-Series: Kennedy, Queen. Guest: Tales From the Crypt, Murphy Brown (Emmy Award, 1994). Narrator: Eyewitness (PBS).

SHEFFER, CRAIG
Actor. b. York, PA, 1960. e. East Stroudsberg Univ., PA. Started career in tv commercials; in soap opera, One Life to Live. On NY stage in Fresh Horses, G.R. Point, Torch Song Trilogy (B'way & Off-B'way). Starred in IMAX film Wings of Courage.
PICTURES: That Was Then This Is Now (debut, 1985), Fire with Fire, Some Kind of Wonderful, Voyage of the Rock Aliens, Split Decisions, Nightbreed, Instant Karma (also exec. prod.), Blue Desert, Eye of the Storm, A River Runs Through It, Fire in the Sky, The Program, Sleep With Me, Roadflower, The Grave, Head Above Water.
TELEVISION: Series: The Hamptons. Movies: Babycakes, In Pursuit of Honor, The Desperate Trail.

SHEFFIELD, JOHN
Actor. b. Pasadena, CA, April 11, 1931. e. UCLA. Stage debut at 7 in On Borrowed Time. Created screen role of Tarzan's son in Tarzan Finds a Son, followed by 7 other entries in Tarzan series, and role of Bomba in Bomba series.
PICTURES: Babes in Arms, Tarzan Finds a Son, Lucky Cisco Kid, Little Orvie, Knute Rockne—All-American, Million Dollar Baby, Tarzan's Secret Treasure, Tarzan's New York Adventure, Tarzan Triumphs, Tarzan's Desert Mystery, Tarzan and the Amazons, Tarzan and the Leopard Woman, Tarzan and the Huntress, Roughly Speaking, Bomba the Jungle Boy, Bomba on Panther Island, Lost Volcano, Bomba and the Hidden City, The Lion Huntress, Bomba and the Elephant Stampede, African Treasure, Bomba and the Jungle Girl, Safari Drums, The Golden Idol, Killer Leopard, Lord of the Jungle.
TELEVISION: Series: Bantu the Zebra Boy.

SHEINBERG, SIDNEY JAY
Executive. b. Corpus Christi, TX, Jan. 14, 1935. e. Columbia Coll., A.B. 1955; LL.B., 1958. Admitted to Calif. bar, 1958; assoc. in law U. of California Sch. of Law, Los Angeles, 1958-59; joined MCA, Inc, 1959; pres., TV div., 1971-74; exec. v.p., parent co., 1969-73. Named MCA pres. & chief oper. off., 1973. Resigned from position 1995 to form company The Bubble Factory to produce films for MCA. 1997, prod. films: The Pest, A Simple Wish.

SHELDON, DAVID
Producer, Director, Writer. b. New York, NY. e. Yale U. Sch. of Drama, M.F.A.; Principia Coll., B.A.; Actors Studio, directors unit. 1972-74 was exec. at American Int'l Pictures supervising development and production of 18 films include: Futureworld, Walking Tall, Dillinger, Sisters, Macon County Line, Reincarnation of Peter Proud, Slaughter, Dr. Phibes. Prod./Dir., The Gateway Playhouse in NY where dir. over 50 plays and musicals. Started the Sheldon/Post Company in 1991 with Ira Post. Exec. prod./writer of Secret of a Small Town.
PICTURES: Prod./Dir.: Grizzly Adams and The Legend of Dark Mountain. Producer: Just Before Dawn, Abby, Day of the Animals, The Manitou. Director: Lovely But Deadly. Writer: The Predator. Prod./Writer: Grizzly, Sheba Baby, The Evil, Project: Kill.

SHELDON, JAMES
Director. r.n. Schleifer. b. New York, NY. Nov. 12. e. U. of NC. Page boy, NBC; announcer-writer-dir., NBC Internat'l Div.; staff dir., ABC radio; staff prod. dir., Young & Rubicam; free lance prod. dir. of many programs live tape and film, N.Y. and Hollywood.
TELEVISION: Series (prod./ dir.): Mr. Peepers, Armstrong Circle Theatre, Robert Montgomery Presents, Schlitz Playhouse, West Point, Zane Grey Theatre, The Millionaire, Desilu Playhouse, Perry Mason, Twilight Zone, Route 66, Naked City, The Virginian, Alfred Hitchcock Presents, Fugitive, Espionage, Defenders, Nurses, Bing Crosby Show, Family Affair, Wonderful World of Disney, Man From UNCLE, Felony Squad, That Girl, Ironside, My World and Welcome To It, To Rome With Love, Owen Marshall, Room 222, Apple's Way, Love American Style, McMillan and Wife, Sanford and Son, Ellery Queen, Rich Man, Poor Man II, Family, MASH, Switch, Loveboat, Sheriff Lobo, Knots Landing, The Waltons, 240-Robert, Nurse, Dukes of Hazard, Todays F.B.I., McLain's Law, 7 Brides for 7 Brothers, Lottery, Partners in Crime, Jessie, Santa Barbara, Half Nelson, Stir Crazy, The Equalizer, Sledge Hammer, Cagney & Lacey. Movies: Gidget Grows Up, With This Ring, The Gossip Columnist.

SHELDON, SIDNEY
Writer, Director, Producer, Novelist. b. Chicago, IL, Feb. 11, 1917. e. Northwestern U.
AUTHOR: The Naked Face, The Other Side of Midnight, A Stranger in the Mirror, Bloodline, Rage of Angels, Master of the Game, If Tomorrow Comes, Windmills of the Gods, The Sands of Time, Memories of Midnight, The Doomsday Conspiracy, The Stars Shine Down, Nothing Lasts Forever, Morning Noon & Night, The Best Laid Plans, Tell Me Your Dreams.
THEATER: Redhead (Tony Award, 1959). Alice in Arms, Jackpot, Dream With Music, Merry Widow (revision), Roman Candle.
PICTURES: Writer: The Bachelor and the Bobbysoxer (Acad. Award, 1947), Easter Parade, Annie Get Your Gun, Three Guys Named Mike, Dream Wife (also dir.), Remains to Be Seen, You're Never Too Young, Pardners, The Buster Keaton Story (also prod., dir.), The Birds and the Bees, Gambling Daughters, Dangerous Lady, Bill Rose's Jumbo. Novels made into films: The Naked Face, The Other Side of Midnight, Bloodline.
TELEVISION: Series: Patty Duke Show (creator), I Dream of Jeannie (creator, prod.), Nancy (creator, prod.), Hart to Hart (creator). Novels made into Mini-Series/Movies: Rage of Angels, Master of the Game, Windmills of the Gods, If Tomorrow Comes, Memories of Midnight, The Sands of Time, Stranger in the Mirror, Nothing Lasts Forever.

SHELLEY, CAROLE
Actress. b. London, England, Aug. 16, 1939. e. Arts Educational Sch., RADA.
THEATER: NY: The Odd Couple (debut, 1965), The Astrakhan Coat, Loot, Sweet Potato, Little Murders, Hay Fever, Absurd Person Singular (Tony nom.), The Norman Conquests, The Elephant Man (Tony Award, 1979), Twelve Dreams (Obie Award), The Misanthrope, Noises Off, Stepping Out (Tony nom.), What the Butler Saw, The Miser, Maggie and Misha, The Destiny of Me, Later Life, London Suite, Show Boat. London: Simon and Laura (debut, 1955), New Cranks, Boeing-Boeing, Mary Mary, Lettice and Lovage. Also appearances with Shaw Festival, Stratford Fest., Amer. Shakespeare Fest., etc.
PICTURES: Give Us this Day (debut, 1949), Cure for Love, It's Great to Be Young, Carry on Regardless, Carry on Cabby, The Odd Couple, The Boston Strangler, The Aristocats (voice), Robin Hood (voice), The Super, Little Noises, Quiz Show, The Road to Wellville.
TELEVISION: Series: The Odd Couple. Specials: Coconut Downs, Gabby, A Salute to Noel Coward. Movie: Devlin. Guest: Brian Rix, Dickie Henderson Show, The Avengers.

SHELTON, RON
Writer, Director, Producer. b. Whittier, CA, Sept. 15, 1945. e. Westmont Coll., Santa Barbara, CA, 1967; U of Arizona, Tucson, AZ, 1974. For 5 years played second base for Baltimore Orioles farm team. Cleaned bars and dressed mannequins to support his art: painting and sculpture. A script he wrote, A Player to Be Named Later (which he later filmed himself as Bull Durham), attracted attention of dir. Roger Spottiswoode who directed his first two scripts.
PICTURES: The Pursuit of D. B. Cooper (assoc. prod.), Open Season (exec. prod.). Writer: Under Fire (also 2nd unit dir.), The Best of Times (also 2nd unit dir.), Bull Durham (also dir.), Blaze (also dir.), White Men Can't Jump (also dir.), Blue Chips (also co-exec. prod.), Cobb (also dir.), The Great White Hype (co-s.p.), Tin Cup (also prod., s.p.).

SHENSON, WALTER
Producer. b. San Francisco, CA. e. Stanford U., Calif.; Ent. m.p. ind. 1941; studio exec., writing, prod., prom. shorts, trailers, Columbia; sup. publ., expl., London, Columbia European production, 1955.
PICTURES: Prod.: The Mouse That Roared, A Matter of Who, The Mouse on the Moon, A Hard Day's Night, Help!, 30 Is a Dangerous Age Cynthia, Don't Raise the Bridge Lower the River, A Talent for Loving, Welcome to the Club (also dir.), The Chicken Chronicles, Reuben Reuben, Echo Park, Ruby Jean and Joe.

SHEPARD, SAM
Writer, Actor. r.n. Samuel Shepard Rogers. b. Fort Sheridan, IL, Nov. 5, 1943. Raised in California, Montana and South Dakota. Worked as stable hand, sheep shearer, orange picker in CA, a car wrecker in MA and musician with rock group Holy Modal Rounders. Lived near San Francisco, where, in addition to writing, ran a drama workshop at the U. of California at Davis. Recipient of Brandeis U. Creative Arts Citation, 1976, and American Acad. of Arts and Letters Award, 1975.
THEATER: Playwright: Icarus' Mother, Red Cross (triple bill—Obie Award, 1966), La Turista (Obie Award, 1967), Forensic and the Navigators, Melodrama Play, Tooth of Crime (Obie Award, 1973), Back Dog Beast Bait, Operation Sidewinder, 4-H Club, The Unseen Hand, Mad Dog Blues, Shaved Splits, Rock Garden, Curse of the Starving Class (Obie Award, 1978), Buried Child (Obie Award & Pulitzer Prize, 1979), True West, Fool For Love, A Lie of the Mind, Simpatico.
PICTURES: Actor: Renaldo and Clara (debut, 1978), Days of Heaven, Resurrection, Raggedy Man, Frances, The Right Stuff (Acad. Award nom.), Country, Fool for Love, Crimes of the Heart, Baby Boom, Steel Magnolias, Bright Angel, Defenseless, Voyager, Thunderheart, The Pelican Brief, Safe Passage, The Only Thrill. Writer: Me and My Brother (co-s.p.), Zabriskie Point (co-s.p.), Oh Calcutta! (contributor), Renaldo and Clara (co-s.p.), Paris Texas, Fool for Love, Far North (also dir.), Silent Tongue (also dir.).
TELEVISION: Special: Fourteen Hundred Thousand Blue Bitch (BBC). Movie: The Good Old Boys.

SHEPHERD, CYBILL
Actress, Singer. b. Memphis, TN, Feb. 18, 1950. e. Hunter Coll., NYU, USC. Was fashion model (won Model of the Year title, 1968) before acting debut in 1971. Debut record album, Cybill Does It... To Cole Porter, 1974, followed by Stan Getz: Mad About the Boy, Vanilla, Somewhere Down the Road.
PICTURES: The Last Picture Show (debut, 1971), The Heartbreak Kid, Daisy Miller, At Long Last Love, Taxi Driver, Special Delivery, Silver Bears, The Lady Vanishes, The Return, Chances Are, Texasville, Alice, Once Upon a Crime, Married to It.
TELEVISION: Series: The Yellow Rose, Moonlighting, Cybill (also co-exec. prod.; Golden Globe, 1996). Movies: A Guide for the Married Woman, Secrets of a Married Man, Seduced, The Long Hot Summer, Which Way Home, Memphis (also co-writer, co-exec. prod.), Stormy Weathers, Telling Secrets, There Was a Little Boy, Baby Brokers, For the Love of My Daughter, While Justice Sleeps, The Last Word.

SHEPHERD, RICHARD
Producer. b. Kansas City, MO, June 4, 1927. e. Stanford U. In U.S. Naval Reserve, 1944-45. Entered entertainment field as exec. with MCA, 1948, functioning in radio, TV, and m.p. fields until 1956, with time out for U.S. Army, 1950-52. 1956 became head of talent for Columbia Pictures. 1962 joined CMA talent agency on its founding, becoming exec. v.p. in chg. of m.p. div.; 1972-74, exec. v.p. for prod. Warner Bros.; 1974 became indept. prod.; 1976 named MGM sr. vp. & worldwide head of theatrical prod. 1985 to present, partner in The Artists Agency.
PICTURES: Twelve Angry Men, The Hanging Tree, The Fugitive Kind, Breakfast at Tiffany's, Alex and the Gypsy, Robin and Marian, Volunteers, The Hunger.

SHER, LOUIS K.
Executive. b. Columbus, OH, Feb. 25, 1914. e. Ohio State U., 1933. Exec., Stone's Grills Co., 1934-37; owned & operated, Sher Vending Co., 1937-43. U.S. Army, 1943-46. V.p., Sons Bars & Grills, 1947-54; org. & pres. Art Theatre Guild, 1954; opened art theatres for first time in many cities, org. opera film series, film classic series and similar motion picture activities in many cities; org., Film Festival at Antioch Coll., 1960; pioneer in fighting obscenity laws in Ohio; operates 4 theatres in midwest and western states. Co-producer of the musical broadway production Shenandoah and American Dance Machine. Produced film, Deathmask.

SHERAK, THOMAS
Executive. b. Brooklyn, NY June 22, 1945. e. New York Community Coll., mktg. degree. 1967-69, US Army, Specialist E5 Sgt.; 1970, began career in m.p. industry, Paramount Pictures sls. dept.; 1974, R/C Theatres, booking dept.; 1977, joined General Cinema Theatres as district film buyer; 1978, promoted to v.p., films; 1982, promoted to v.p. head film buyer; 1983, joined 20th Century Fox as pres., domestic dist. & mktg.; 1985, pres., domestic dist.; 1986, president, domestic dist. & marketing. 1990-present, exec. v.p., 20th Century Fox.

SHERIDAN, JAMEY
Actor. b. Pasadena, CA, July 12, 1951. e. Univ. of CA, Santa Barbara.
THEATER: Off-B'way: Just a Little Bit Less Than Normal, The Arbor, One Wedding Two Rooms Three Friends. B'way: The Man Who Came to Dinner, Hamlet, Biloxi Blues, All My Sons (Tony nom.), Long Day's Journey Into Night, Ah Wilderness, The Shadow Box. Regional: Major Barbara, Loose Ends, Deathtrap, Homesteaders.

PICTURES: Jumpin' Jack Flash (debut, 1986), The House on Carroll Street, Distant Thunder, Stanley & Iris, Quick Change, Talent for the Game, All I Want for Christmas, A Stranger Among Us, Whispers in the Dark, White Squall.
TELEVISION: Series: Shannon's Deal, Chicago Hope. Movies: One Police Plaza, Shannon's Deal (pilot), A Mother's Courage: The Mary Thomas Story, Murder in High Places, My Breast, Spring Awakening, Killer Rules. Mini-Series: The Stand. Guest: The Doctors, Another World, St. Elsewhere, Spenser: For Hire, Picket Fences, The Equalizer.

SHERIDAN, JIM
Director, Writer. b. Dublin, Ireland, 1949. e. Univ Col. in Dublin, NYU Inst. of Films & TV. Started as director-writer at Lyric Theatre in Belfast and Abbey Theatre in Dublin; also at Project Arts Theatre (1976-80), NY Irish Arts Center (1982-87) as artistic director. Founded Children's Theatre Company in Dublin.
PICTURES: Dir.-Writer: My Left Foot, The Field, Into the West (s.p. only), In the Name of the Father.
THEATER: Writer: Mobile Homes, Spike in the First World War (Edinburgh Festival Fringe Award for best play, 1983).

SHERIDAN, NICOLLETTE
Actress. b. Worthing, Sussex, England, Nov. 21, 1963. Moved to LA in 1973. Became model in NYC before turning to acting.
PICTURES: The Sure Thing (debut, 1985), Noises Off, Spy Hard.
TELEVISION: Series: Paper Dolls, Knots Landing. Movies: Dark Mansions, Agatha Christie's Dead Man's Folly, Jackie Collins' Lucky/Chances, Deceptions, A Time to Heal, Shadows of Desire, Robin Cook's Virus.

SHERMAN, RICHARD M.
Composer, Lyricist, Screenwriter. b. New York, NY, June 12, 1928. e. Bard Coll., B.A., 1949. Info. & Educ. Br., U.S. Army, 1953-55. Songwriter, composer, Walt Disney Prods 1960-71, then freelance. With partner-brother Robert has won, 9 Acad. Award nom., 2 Grammys, 17 gold and platinum albums, 1st Prize, Moscow Film Fest. (for Tom Sawyer) and a star on Hollywood Walk of Fame. Have written over 500 pub. and recorded songs. Also wrote score for B'way musical Over Here (1974) and songs for Disney Theme Parks.
SONGS: Things I Might Have Been, Tall Paul, Christmas in New Orleans, Mad Passionate Love, Midnight Oil, The Ugly Bug Ball, You're Sixteen, That Darn Cat, The Wonderful Thing About Tiggers, It's a Small World, A Spoonful of Sugar, Supercalifragilistic, Feed the Birds, Let's Go Fly a Kite, Age of Not Believing, When You're Loved, Pineapple Princess, Let's Get Together, Maggie's Theme, Chim Chim Cheree (Acad. Award, 1964), Chitty Chitty Bang Bang, Hushabye Mountain, Winnie the Pooh, Fortuosity, Slipper and the Rose Waltz, many others. Comedy Album: Smash Flops.
PICTURES: Nightmare, The Cruel Tower, The Absent Minded Professor, The Parent Trap, Big Red, In Search of the Castaways, Moon Pilot, Bon Voyage, Legend of Lobo, Summer Magic, Miracle of the White Stallions, The Sword in the Stone, The Misadventures of Merlin Jones, Mary Poppins (2 Acad. Awards for song & score, 1964), Those Calloways, The Monkey's Uncle, That Darn Cat, Follow Me Boys!, Winnie the Pooh, Monkeys Go Home!, Chitty Chitty Bang Bang, The Gnome-Mobile, The Jungle Book, The Happiest Millionaire, The One and Only Genuine Original Family Band, The Aristocats, Bedknobs & Broomsticks, Snoopy Come Home, Charlotte's Web, Beverly Hills Cop III, The Mighty Kong. Songs & S.P.: Tom Sawyer, The Slipper and the Rose, The Magic of Lassie, Huckleberry Finn, Little Nemo: Adventures in Slumberland.
TELEVISION: Wonderful World of Color, Bell Telephone Hour, Welcome to Pooh Corner, The Enchanted Musical Playhouse, The Timberwood Tales, Goldilocks, Harry Anderson's Sideshow.

SHERMAN, ROBERT B.
Composer, Lyricist, Screenwriter. b. New York, NY, Dec. 19, 1925. e. Bard Coll., B.A., 1949. U.S. Army, WWII, 1943-45 (purple heart). Songwriter, 1952-60; pres., Music World Corp., 1958; songwriter, composer, Walt Disney, 1971, then freelance. Hon. Phd., Lincoln Col, 1990. With partner-brother Richard Sherman, has won, 9 Acad. Award nom., 2 Grammys, 17 gold and platinum albums, 1st Prize, Moscow Film Fest. (for Tom Sawyer) and a star on Hollywood Walk of Fame. Have written over 500 pub. and recorded songs. Also wrote score for B'way musical Over Here (1974) and songs for Disney Theme Parks. (see Richard M. Sherman for co-writing credits.)

SHERMAN, SAMUEL M.
Producer, Director, Writer. b. New York, NY. e. CCNY, B.A. Entered m.p. ind. as writer, cameraman, film ed., neg. & sound cutter; nat'l mag. ed., Westerns Magazine 1959; pres., Signature Films; prod., dir., TV pilot, The Three Mesquiteers, 1960; prod., Pulse Pounding Perils, 1961; helped create, ed., dir., Screen Thrills Illustrated; exec. prod., Screen Thrills; v.p., Golden Age Films, 1962; prod., Joe Franklin's Silent Screen, 1963; NY rep., Victor Adamson Prods.; NY rep., Tal prods.; Hlywd.; adv. & pub. Hemisphere Pictures; prod., writer, Chaplin's Art of Comedy,

The Strongman; prod., Hollywood's Greatest Stuntman; story adapt., Fiend With the Electronic Brain; tech. consul., Hal Roach Studios, Music from the Land; 1968, NY rep. East West Pict. of Hollywood. 1968, N.Y. rep., Al Adamson Prods. of Hollywood; Ed.-in-chief, bk., The Strongman; pres., Independent-International Pictures Corp. (and tv div.); pres., Producers Commercial Productions, Inc. Chmn. of Creditors' Committee, Allied Artists Television Corp.; pres., Technovision Inc.; pres., Super Video, Inc.
PICTURES: Assoc. prod.: Horror of the Blood Monsters, Blood of Ghastly Horror. Prod., s.p.: Brain of Blood. Prod. supervisor: Dracula vs. Frankenstein. Exec. prod.: Angels, Wild Women, The Naughty Stewardesses (prod., s.p.), Girls For Rent, The Dynamite Brothers, Blazing Stewardesses (prod., s.p.), Cinderella 2000, Team-Mates (also story), Raiders of the Living Dead (dir., s.p.).

SHERMAN, VINCENT
Director. b. Vienna, GA, July 16, 1906. e. Oglethorpe U. B.A. Writer, actor, dialogue dir., then prod. dir.
PICTURES: The Return of Doctor X (debut, 1939), Saturday's Children, The Man Who Talked Too Much, Underground, Flight from Destiny, The Hard Way, All Through the Night, Old Acquaintance, In Our Time, Mr. Skeffington, Pillow to Post, Janie Gets Married, Nora Prentiss, The Unfaithful, Adventures of Don Juan, The Hasty Heart, The Damned Don't Cry, Harriet Craig, Goodbye My Fancy, Lone Star, Affair in Trinidad, Difendo il mio Amore, The Garment Jungle, The Naked Earth, The Young Philadelphians, Ice Palace, A Fever in the Blood, The Second Time Around, Cervantes (The Young Rebel).
TELEVISION: 35 episodes of Medical Center, Westside Medical, Baretta, Waltons, Doctors Hospital, Trapper John, Movies: The Last Hurrah, Women at West Point, The Yeagers (pilot), Bogey, The Dream Merchants, Trouble in High Timber Country, High Hopes—The Capra Years.

SHERRIN, NED
Producer, Director, Writer. b. Low Ham, Somerset, England, Feb. 18, 1931. Early career writing plays and musical plays. Prod., dir., ATV Birmingham, 1955-57; prod., Midlands Affairs, Paper Talk, etc. Joined BBC-TV 1957 and produced many TV talk programs. Novels: (with Caryl Brahms) Cindy-Ella or I Gotta Shoe (also prod. as stage play), Rappell 1910, Benbow Was His Name.
AUTHOR: Autobiography: A Small Thing Like a Earthquake. Anthology: Cutting Edge Theatrical Anecdotes. 1995, edit. of Oxford Dictionary of Humorous Quotations. Novel: Scratch an Actor. Diaries: Serrin's Year: 1995.
PICTURES: Prod.: The Virgin Soldiers (with Leslie Gilliat), Every Home Should Have One, Up Pompeii, Girl Stroke Boy (co-author with Caryl Brahms), Up the Chastity Belt, Rentadick, The Garnet Saga, Up the Front, The National Health, The Cobblers of Umbridge (dir. with Ian Wilson). Actor: Orlando.
TELEVISION: England: Prod.: Ask Me Another, Henry Hall Show, Laugh Line, Parasol. Assoc. prod.: Tonight series, Little Beggars. Prod., creator: That Was The Week That Was. Prod., dir.: Benbow Was His Name (co-author), Take a Sapphire (co-author), The Long Garden Party, The Long Cocktail Party. ABC of Britain revue, Not So Much a Programme—More a Way of Life. Appearances inc.: Your Witness, Quiz of The Week, Terra Firma, Who Said That, The Rather Reassuring Programme, Song by Song, Loose Ends Radio 4.

SHERWOOD, MADELEINE
Actress. b. Montreal, Canada, Nov. 13, 1922. e. Yale Drama Sch. Trained with Montreal Rep. and Actors Studio. Has dir. prods. at Actors Studio and regional theaters, as well as 2 AFI films Goodnight Sweet Prince and Sunday.
THEATER: The Crucible, Sweet Bird of Youth, Cat on a Hot Tin Roof, Invitation to a March, The Garden of Sweets, Camelot, Hey You, Light Man!, Brecht on Brecht, Night of the Iguana, Arturo Ui, Do I Hear a Waltz?, Inadmissible Evidence, All Over, Older People, Getting Out, The Suicide, Eclipse, Miss Edwina.
PICTURES: Baby Doll, Cat on a Hot Tin Roof, Parrish, Sweet Bird of Youth, The 91st Day, Hurry Sundown, Pendulum, Wicked Wicked, The Changeling, Resurrection, Teachers, An Unremarkable Life, Silence Like Glass.
TELEVISION: Series: The Flying Nun. Mini-Series: Rich Man Poor Man. Movies: The Manhunter, Nobody's Child, Palace Guard; many guest appearances.

SHIELDS, BROOKE
Actress. b. New York, NY, May 31, 1965. e. Princeton U. Honors in French Lit. Discovered at age 11 months by photographer Francesco Scavullo to pose in Ivory Soap ads.
THEATER: Off-B'way: The Eden Cinema; B'way debut 1994 in Grease! (Theatre World Award).
PICTURES: Alice Sweet Alice (Holy Terror/Communion; debut 1977), Pretty Baby, King of the Gypsies, Tilt, Wanda Nevada, Just You and Me Kid, The Blue Lagoon, Endless Love, Sahara, The Muppets Take Manhattan (cameo), Speed Zone (cameo), Back Street Dreams, Brenda Starr, An American Love (It.), The Seventh Floor, Freeway.
TELEVISION: Movies: The Prince of Central Park, West Gold, The Diamond Trap, I Can Make You Love Me: The Stalking of Laura Black; Nothing Lasts Forever; numerous specials. Guest: Friends. Series: Suddenly Susan.

SHIELDS, WILLIAM A.
Executive. b. New York, NY, 1946. e. El Camino Coll., California State Coll. at LA. Entered the motion picture industry in 1966 with Pacific Theatres, then MGM sales dept., L.A. and Denver, 1970; New World Pictures, 1972; 20th Century-Fox, Washington, 1973; NY district manager, 20th Century-Fox, 1973-75; joined Mann Theatres Corp. of California as head booker in 1975; gen. sls. mgr., Far West Films, 1977-79; joined Avco Embassy as Western div. mgr., promoted to asst. gen. sls. mgr., 1980; promoted to v.p.-gen. sls. mgr., 1981; 1983 joined New World Pictures as exec. v.p., worldwide mktg. & acquisitions; promoted to pres., worldwide sls. & mktg., 1985; 1987, pres. CEO, New World Intl.; 1989, joined Trans Atlantic Pictures as pres., CEO when company purchased assets of New World's feature film division. Sold ownership in Trans Atlantic and formed G.E.L. Prod. & Distrib., 1992. Exec. prod. Au Pair (1991); exec. in charge of prod. Death Ring (1992). Exec. prod. of Uninvited. Past chmn., American Film Mktg. Assn. (1987-91). Presently chmn. American Film Export Assn.

SHIFF, RICHARD
Executive. b. New York, NY, March 3, 1942. e. Queens College, B.A., M.A., Brooklyn Col., P.D. Joined Warner Bros. as sales analyst, 1977. 1979 named dist. coordinator; 1980, asst. dir. sls. admin. 1982, promoted to post, dir. sls. admin. 1987, v.p., theatrical sls. operations.

SHIRE, DAVID
Composer. b. Buffalo, NY, July 3, 1937. m. actress Didi Conn. e. Yale U., 1959, B.A. Composer of theater scores: The Sap of Life, Urban Blight, Starting Here Starting Now, Baby, Closer Than Ever, Big. Emmy noms. Raid on Entebbe, The Defection of Simas Kudirka, Do You Remember Love? and The Kennedys of Massachusetts. Grammy Awards for Saturday Night Fever.
PICTURES: One More Train to Rob, Summertree, Drive, He Said; Skin Game, To Find a Man, Showdown, Two People, Steelyard Blues (adapt.), Class of '44, The Conversation, The Taking of Pelham 1-2-3, The Fortune, Farewell My Lovely, The Hindenberg, All the President's Men, The Big Bus, Harry and Walter Go to New York, Saturday Night Fever (adapt. & add. music), Straight Time, The Promise (Acad. Award nom.), Old Boyfriends, Norma Rae (Acad. Award for best song, It Goes Like It Goes, 1979), Only When I Laugh, The Night the Lights Went Out in Georgia, Paternity, The World According to Garp, Max Dugan Returns, Oh God You Devil, 2010, Fast Break, Return to Oz, Short Circuit, 'night Mother, Vice Versa, Monkey Shines, Bed and Breakfast, One Night Stand.
TELEVISION: Series themes: Sarge, McCloud, The Practice, Sirota's Court, Joe & Sons, Lucas Tanner, Alice, Tales of the Unexpected, Brewster Place, Room for Two. Movies: Priest Killer, McCloud, Harpy, Three Faces of Love, Killer Bees, Tell Me Where It Hurts, The Defection of Simus Kudirka, Three for the Road, Amelia Earhart, Something for Joey, Raid on Entebbe, The Storyteller, Promise, Mayflower Madam, Echoes in the Darkness, Jesse, God Bless the Child, Common Ground, The Clinic, Convicted, The Women of Brewster Place, I Know My First Name is Steven, The Kennedys of Massachusetts (miniseries), The Great Los Angeles Earthquake, The Boys, Sarah: Plain and Tall, Always Remember I Love You, Paris Trout, Four Eyes, Broadway Bound, Bed of Lies, Last Wish, Alison, Habitation of Dragons, Lily in Winter, Reunion, Serving in Silence, My Brother's Keeper, My Antonia, The Heidi Chronicles, The Man Who Wouldn't Die, Tecumseh: The Last Warrior, Almost Golden: The Jessica Savitch Story, many others.

SHIRE, TALIA
Actress. r.n. Talia Coppola. b. New York, NY, April 25, 1946. Raised on road by her father, arranger-conductor Carmine Coppola, who toured with Broadway musicals. After 2 yrs. at Yale Sch. of Drama she moved to L.A. where appeared in many theatrical productions. Brother is dir. Francis Ford Coppola. Started in films as Talia Coppola.
PICTURES: The Wild Racers, The Dunwich Horror, Gas-s-s-s, The Christian Licorice Store, The Outside Man, The Godfather, The Godfather Part II (Acad. Award nom.), Rocky (Acad. Award nom.), Old Boyfriends, Prophecy, Rocky II, Windows, Rocky III, Rocky IV, RAD, Lionheart (co-prod.), New York Stories (Life Without Zoe), Rocky V, The Godfather III, Bed and Breakfast, Cold Heaven, DeadFall, One Night Stand (dir. only), She's So Lovely, Lured Innocence.
TELEVISION: Mini-Series: Rich Man Poor Man. Movies: Foster and Laurie, Kill Me If You Can, Daddy I Don't Like It Like This, For Richer For Poorer, Chantilly Lace, Born Into Exile. Special: Please God I'm Only 17.

SHIVAS, MARK
Producer. e. Oxford.
PICTURES: Producer: Richard's Things, Moonlighting, A Private Function, The Witches. Exec. Prod.: Bad Blood, Truly Madly Deeply, Enchanted April, The Grass Arena, Memento Mori, The Snapper, Priest, An Awfully Big Adventure, Jude, The Van, Small Faces.

TELEVISION: Presenter of Cinema. Producer: The Six Wives of Henry VIII, Casanova, The Edwardians, The Evacuees, The Glittering Prizes, Abide With Me, Rogue Male, 84 Charing Cross Road, The Three Hostages, She Fell Among Thieves, Professional Foul, Telford's Change, On Giant's Shoulders, The Price, What If it's Raining?, The Storytellers. Exec. prod.: Regeneration.

SHORE, HOWARD
Composer, Musician. b. Oct., 18, 1994, Toronto, Ontario, Canada. Began career as musical director for Saturday Night Live, 1975.
PICTURES: I Miss You Hugs and Kisses, The Brood, Scanners, Gilda Live (actor), Videodrome, The Fly, Nothing Lasts Forever, After Hours, Fire with Fire, The Fly, Heaven, Belizaire the Cajun, Nadine, Moving, Big, Dead Ringers, Signs of Life, She-Devil, The Local Stigmatic, An Innocent Man, The Lemon Sisters, Made in Milan, Postcards From the Edge (musical numbers sprv.), The Silence of the Lambs, A Kiss Before Dying, Naked Lunch, Prelude to a Kiss, Single White Female, Sliver, Guilty as Sin, M. Butterfly, Mrs. Doubtfire, Philadelphia, Ed Wood, The Truth About Cats & Dogs, Striptease, Looking for Richard, Crash, That Thing You Do!, The Game, Cop Land, eXistenZ, Chinese Coffee.
TELEVISION: Saturday Night Live, Coca-Cola Presents Live: The Hard Rock, Late Night with Conan O'Brien.

SHORE, PAULY
Actor. b. Los Angeles, CA, 1968. Son of comedian Sammy Shore and nightclub owner Mitzi Shore. Worked as stand-up comedian at mother's club, The Comedy Store.
PICTURES: For Keeps? (debut, 1988), 18 Again!, Lost Angels, Phantom of the Mall, Wedding Band, Encino Man, Class Act, Son-in-Law, In the Army Now, Jury Duty, Bio-Dome.
TELEVISION: Series: Totally Pauly, Totally Different Pauly. Special: Pauly Does Dallas. Movie: Home By Midnight. Guest: 21 Jump Street, Married... with Children.

SHORT, MARTIN
Actor, Comedian, Writer. b. Toronto, Can., March 26, 1950. e. McMaster U. Trained as social worker but instead performed on stage in Godspell as well as in revues and cabarets in Toronto, 1973-78, including a stint as a member of the Toronto unit of the Second City comedy troupe, 1977-78. Created such characters as Ed Grimley, Jackie Rogers Jr. B'way debut 1993 in The Goodbye Girl (Theatre World Award; Tony nom.).
PICTURES: Lost and Found, The Outsider, Three Amigos!, Innerspace, Cross My Heart, Three Fugitives, The Big Picture, Pure Luck, Father of the Bride, Captain Ron, Clifford, The Pebble and the Penguin (voice), Father of the Bride Part 2, An Indian in the City, Mars Attacks!, Jungle 2 Jungle, A Simple Wish, Mumford, Akbar's Adventure Tours, Prince of Egypt (voice).
TELEVISION: Series: The Associates, I'm a Big Girl Now, SCTV Network (Emmy Award for writing, 1983), Saturday Night Live (1985- 86), The Completely Mental Misadventures of Ed Grimley (cartoon series), The Martin Short Show (also exec. prod., writer). Specials: All's Well That Ends Well, Really Weird Tales, Martin Short's Concert for the North Americas (SHO), Martin Short Goes Hollywood (HBO), The Show Formerly Known as the Martin Short Show (also exec. prod., co-writer). Movies: The Family Man, Sunset Limousine, Money for Nothing (BBC). Mini-Series: Merlin.

SHORT, THOMAS C.
Executive. International Pres., International Alliance of Theatrical Stage Employees, Moving Picture Technicians, Artists and Allied Crafts of the United States and Canada AFL-CIO, CLC.

SHOWALTER, MAX
Actor, Composer. r.n. Casey Adams. b. Caldwell, KS, June 2, 1917. e. Caldwell H.S.; Pasadena Playhouse. Composed background music for films: Vicki, Return of Jack Slade, B'way Harrigan 'n Hart (composer), Touch of the Child (lyricist-composer). Recordings incl. The Brementown Musicians, The Gold Dog (as narrator, composer, pianist and singer). On bd. of trustees: Eugene O'Neill Theatre Center, Natl. Theatre of the Deaf, Ivorytown Playhouse, Shoreline Alliance for the Arts. Gov's Bd.: Commission for the Arts.
THEATER: B'way: Knights of Song, Very Warm for May, My Sister Eileen, Showboat, John Loves Mary, Make Mine Manhattan, Lend an Ear, Hello Dolly!, The Grass Harp.
PICTURES: Always Leave Them Laughing (debut, 1949), With a Song in My Heart, What Price Glory?, My Wife's Best Friend, Niagara, Destination Gobi, Dangerous Crossing, Vicki, Night People, Naked Alibi, The Indestructible Man, The Return of Jack Slade, Never Say Goodbye, Bus Stop, Dragoon Wells Massacre, Down Three Dark Streets, Designing Woman, Female Animal, The Monster That Challenged the World, Voice In the Mirror, The Naked and the Dead, It Happened to Jane, Elmer Gantry, Return to Peyton Place, Summer and Smoke, The Music Man, Bon Voyage, My Six Loves, Move Over Darling, Sex and the Single Girl, Fate Is the Hunter, How to Murder Your Wife, Lord Love a Duck, A Talent for Loving, The Moonshine War, The Anderson Tapes, 10, Racing with the Moon, Sixteen Candles.

SHUE, ELISABETH
Actress. b. South Orange, NJ, Oct. 6, 1963. e. Harvard. Brother is actor Andrew Shue.
PICTURES: The Karate Kid (debut, 1984), Adventures in Babysitting, Link, Cocktail, Back to the Future Part II, Back to the Future Part III, The Marrying Man, Soapdish, Twenty Bucks, The Underneath, Leaving Las Vegas (Chicago Film Critics Award; Nat'l Film Critics Award; LA Film Critics Award), Trigger Effect, The Saint, Radio Inside, Palmetto, Deconstructing Harry, Cousine Bette (LA Film Critics Award).
TELEVISION: Series: Call to Glory. Movies: Charles and Diana, Double Switch, Hale the Hero, Blind Justice.

SHULER-DONNER, LAUREN
Producer. b. Cleveland, OH. B.S. in film & bdcstg., Boston U. Began filmmaking career as ed. of educational films then camera-woman in TV prod., assoc. prod., story editor, creative affairs exec.; TV movie: Amateur Night at the Dixie Bar and Grill (prod.). Assoc. prod. on film Thank God It's Friday. Cameo in film Maverick.
PICTURES: Mr. Mom, Ladyhawke, St. Elmo's Fire, Pretty in Pink, Three Fugitives, The Favor, Radio Flyer, Dave, Free Willy, Free Willy 2: The Adventure Home, Assassins, Volcano, Free Willy 3, Bulworth, You've Got Mail, On Any Sunday, X-Men.

SHULL, RICHARD B.
Actor. b. Evanston, IL, Feb. 24, 1929. e. State U. of Iowa. B.A. drama, 1950., Kemper Mil. Sch. AA Humanities, 1986. U.S. Army, 1953. Armed Forces Korea Network. 1953-56, exec. asst. prod. Gordon W. Pollock Prods.; 1954-56 stage mgr. Hyde Park Playhouse; other prod. jobs and freelance stage mgr. and dir. 1950-70. NY stage debut in Wake Up Darling (1956), also in Minnie's Boys, Goodtime Charley (Tony nom.; Drama Desk nom.), The Marriage of Bette and Boo (Obie Award), One of the All-Time Greats, Ain't Broadway Grand, Victor Victoria.
PICTURES: The Anderson Tapes (debut, 1971), B.S. I Love You, Such Good Friends, Hail to the Chief, Slither, Sssss, Cockfighter, The Fortune, The Black Bird, Hearts of the West, The Big Bus, The Pack, Dreamer, Wholly Moses, Heartbeeps, Spring Break, Lovesick, Unfaithfully Yours, Splash, Garbo Talks, Tune in Tomorrow, Housesitter, For Love or Money, Trapped in Paradise, Cafe Society, Private Parts.
TELEVISION: Series: Diana, Holmes & Yoyo. Guest: Your Hit Parade (1950), Rockford Files, Good Times, Love American Style, Hart to Hart, Lou Grant. Movies: Ziegfeld: A Man and His Women, Studs Lonigan, Will There Really Be a Morning? The Boy Who Loved Trolls, Keeping the Faith, Seize the Day.

SHURPIN, SOL
Executive. b. New York, NY, Feb. 22, 1914. e. Pace Inst., 1936. Law stenog., 1932-33; Joe Hornstein, Inc., 1933-41; National Theatre Supply, 1941-48; purchased interest in Raytone Screen Corp., became v.p., 1948; pres., Raytone, 1952; pres., Technikote Corp., which succeeded Raytone Screen, 1956-present; sole owner, Technikote Corp., 1962.

SHUTT, BUFFY
Executive. e. Sarah Lawrence Col. Joined Paramount 1973 as sect. with N.Y. pub. staff; 1975, natl. mag. contact. 1978, named dir. of pub.; later exec. dir. of pub. Promoted 1980 to v.p., pub. & promo. Resigned to join Time-Life Films as v.p. east coast prod; returned to Paramount in 1981 as sr. v.p. & asst. to pres. of Motion Picture Group. 1983, appointed pres. of mktg. 1986, resigned. Formed Shutt-Jones Communications, 1987, marketing consultancy with Kathy Jones. 1989, pres. of marketing, Columbia Pictures & TriStar Pictures. 1991, pres. of marketing, TriStar Pictures. 1994, pres. of marketing, Universal Pictures.

SHYER, CHARLES
Director, Writer. b. Los Angeles, CA. e. UCLA. Was asst. dir. and prod. mgr. before becoming head writer for tv series The Odd Couple. First teamed with Nancy Meyers on Private Benjamin.
PICTURES: Writer: Smokey and the Bandit, House Calls, Goin' South, Private Benjamin (Acad. Award nom.; also prod.), The Parent Trap (also prod.). Director-Writer: Irreconcilable Differences, Baby Boom, Father of the Bride, I Love Trouble, Father of the Bride Part II.

SIDARIS, ANDY
Producer, Director, Writer. b. Chicago, IL, Feb. 20, 1932. e. Southern Methodist U., B.A., radio-TV. Began television career in 1950 in Dallas, TX as a director at station WFAA-TV; now pres., The Sidaris Company. Won 8 Emmy Awards.
PICTURES: Dir.: Stacey, The Racing Scene, M*A*S*H (football sequences), Seven (also prod.). Dir.-Writer: Malibu Express (also prod.), Hard Ticket to Hawaii, Picasso Trigger, Savage Beach, Guns, Do or Die, Hard Hunted, Fit to Kill, Day of the Warrior, Return to Savage Beach. Exec. Prod.: Enemy Gold, The Dallas Connection.
TELEVISION: Dir.: The Racers/Mario Andretti/Joe Leonard/Al Unser, ABC's Championship Auto Racing, ABC's NCAA Game of the Week, 1968 Summer Olympics: 1968 (Mexico City), 1972 (Munich), 1976 (Montreal), 1984 (L.A.), Winter Olympics: 1964 (Innsbruck), 1968 (Grenoble), 1976 (Innsbruck), 1980 (Lake Placid), 1988 (Calgary), Wide World of Sports, The Racers/Craig and Lee Breedlove, The Burt Reynolds Late Show, Kojak episode, Nancy Drew episodes.

SIDNEY, GEORGE
Director, Producer. b. New York, NY, Oct. 4, 1916. Son of L. K. Sidney, veteran showman and v.p. MGM, and Hazel Mooney, actress. From 1932 at MGM as test, second unit and short subjects dir. Won Academy Awards for shorts: Quicker 'n' a Wink (Pete Smith speciality), Of Pups and Puzzles (Passing Parade). In 1941 made feature dir. debut, MGM. Pres., Director's Guild of America, 16 yrs; spec. presidential assignment to Atomic Energy Commission and U.S. Air Force; 1961-66, pres., Hanna-Barbera Productions; Doctorate of Science Hanneman Medical University and Hospital. Member ASCAP. Pres., Directors, Inc., since 1969; v.p.; v.p., D.W. Griffith Foundation; life mem., ACTT (England) and DGA. Directed U.N. special, Who Has Seen the Wind? Awarded Gold Medal for service to D.G.A. 1959, Doctorate from Collegio Barcelona 1989, Life Membership in D.G.A.
PICTURES: Free and Easy (debut, 1941), Pacific Rendezvous, Pilot No. 5, Thousands Cheer, Bathing Beauty, Anchors Aweigh, The Harvey Girls, Holiday in Mexico, Cass Timberlane, The Three Musketeers, The Red Danube, Key to the City, Annie Get Your Gun, Show Boat, Scaramouche, Young Bess, Kiss Me Kate, Jupiter's Darling, The Eddy Duchin Story, Jeanne Eagels (also prod.), Pal Joey, Who Was That Lady? (also prod.), Pepe (also prod.), Bye Bye Birdie, A Ticklish Affair, Viva Las Vegas (also co-prod.), The Swinger (also prod.), Half a Sixpence (also co-prod.).

SIDNEY, SYLVIA
Actress. b. New York, NY, Aug. 8, 1910. r.n. Sophia Kosow. e. Theatre Guild Sch. Prof. stage debut at age 16. NY debut 1927.
THEATER: Nice Women, Crossroads, Bad Girl, The Gentle People, Auntie Mame, Joan of Lorraine, Angel Street, Enter Laughing, Vieux Carre.
PICTURES: Broadway Nights (debut, 1927), Thru Different Eyes, City Streets, Ladies of the Big House, Confessions of a Co-Ed, An American Tragedy, Street Scene, The Miracle Man, Merrily We Go to Hell, Make Me a Star (cameo), Madame Butterfly, Pick-Up, Jennie Gerhardt, Good Dame, Thirty Day Princess, Behold My Wife, Accent on Youth, Mary Burns—Fugitive, The Trail of the Lonesome Pine, Fury, Sabotage (A Woman Alone), You Only Live Once, Dead End, You and Me, One Third of a Nation, The Wagons Roll at Night, Blood on the Sun, Mr. Ace, The Searching Wind, Love From a Stranger, Les Miserables, Violent Saturday, Behind the High Wall, Summer Wishes Winter Dreams (Acad. Award nom.), Gold Told Me To (Demons), I Never Promised You a Rose Garden, Damien: Omen II, Corrupt, Hammett, Beetlejuice, Used People, Mars Attacks!.
TELEVISION: Movies: Do Not Fold Spindle or Mutilate, Death at Love House, Raid on Entebbe, The Gossip Columnist, FDR—The Last Year, The Shadow Box, A Small Killing, Come Along With Me, Having It All, Finnegan Begin Again, An Early Frost, Pals. Specials: Andre's Mother, The Witching of Ben Wagner. Guest: thirtysomething.

SIEMASZKO, CASEY
Actor. b. Chicago, IL, March 17, 1961. r.n. Kazimierz Siemaszko. e. Goodman Theatre School of Drama, Chicago.
PICTURES: Class (debut, 1983), Secret Admirer, Back to the Future, Stand By Me, Gardens of Stone, Three O'Clock High, Biloxi Blues, Young Guns, Breaking In, Back to the Future Part II, Of Mice and Men, Teresa's Tattoo, My Life's in Turnaround, Milk Money, The Phantom, Bliss.
TELEVISION: Movie: Miracle of the Heart: A Boys Town Story, The Chase, Children Remember the Holocaust, Black Scorpion, Rose Hill, Mistrial. Mini-series: Storm of the Century.

SIGHVATSSON, SIGURJON (JONI)
Producer. b. Reykjavik, Iceland, June 15, 1952. e. Iceland Community Col, Univ. of Iceland. Came to U.S. in 1978. Also attended USC. Was film and music video prod. for Blue-Ice Prods. Founder and chairperson with Steve Golin of Propaganda Films.
PICTURE: Assoc. Prod: Hard Rock Zombies, American Drive-In. Producer: Private Investigations, The Blue Iguana, Kill Me Again, Fear Anxiety and Depression, Daddy's Dyin'... Who's Got the Will?, Wild at Heart, Truth or Dare, Ruby, A Stranger Among Us, Candyman, Kalifornia, Red Rock West, S.F.W., Lord of Illusions, Canadian Bacon, 'Til There Was You (exec. prod.), The Real Blonde (exec. prod.).
TELEVISION: Movie: Memphis. Specials: Rock the Vote, Education First, Tales of the City. Series: Twin Peaks.

SIKKING, JAMES B.
Actor. b. Los Angeles, CA, March 5, 1934. e. UCLA, B.A. Theatre includes Waltz of the Toreadors, Plaza Suite, Damn Yankees, The Big Knife.
PICTURES: The Magnificent Seven, Von Ryan's Express, Chandler, The New Centurions, The Electric Horseman, Capricorn One, Ordinary People, Outland, The Star Chamber, Up the Creek, Star Trek III—The Search for Spock, Morons from Outer Space, Soul Man, Narrow Margin, Final Approach.

TELEVISION: *Series*: General Hospital, Turnabout, Hill Street Blues, Doogie Howser, M.D., Brooklyn South. *Movies*: The Jesse Owens Story, First Steps, Bay Coven, Brotherhood of the Rose, Too Good to be True, Desperado: Badlands Justice, Doing Time on Maple Drive, Jake Lassiter: Justice on the Bayou, In Pursuit of Honor, Tyson. *Mini-Series*: Around the World in 80 Days. *Specials*: Tales from the Hollywood Hills (Golden Land), Ollie Hopnoodle's Haven of Bliss.

SILVA, HENRY
Actor. b. Brooklyn, NY, 1928. Studied acting with Group Theatre, Actors Studio.
PICTURES: Viva Zapata!, Crowded Paradise, A Hatful of Rain, The Law and Jake Wade, The Bravados, Green Mansions, Cinderfella, Ocean's Eleven, Sergeants 3, The Manchurian Candidate, A Gathering of Eagles, Johnny Cool, The Secret Invasion, Hail Mafia, The Return of Mr. Moto, The Reward, The Hills Ran Red, The Plainsman, Matchless, Never a Dull Moment, The Animals, Man and Boy, The Italian Connection, The Kidnap of Mary Lou, Shoot, Thirst, Buck Rogers in the 25th Century, Love and Bullets, Virus, Alligator, Sharky's Machine, Wrong Is Right, Megaforce, Cannonball Run II, Lust in the Dust, Code of Silence, Alan Quartermain and the Lost City of Gold, Amazon Women on the Moon, Above the Law, Bulletproof, Dick Tracy, Fists of Steel, Trained to Kill, Possessed by the Night.
TELEVISION: *Movies*: Black Noon, Drive Hard Drive Fast, Contract on Cherry Street, Happy. *Series*: Buck Rogers in the 25th Century.

SILVER, CASEY
Executive. Chmn., Universal Pictures, Inc. Began career in motion picture industry as a screenwriter. Was asst. to dir. Adrian Lyne on Flashdance. Became dir. of devt. and prod. for Simpson-Bruckheimer Prods. V.P., prod., TriStar Pictures. Sr. v.p., prod., TriStar. Joined Universal Pictures as exec. v.p., prod., 1987. Became pres. of prod. in January, 1989; pres., Universal Pictures, June, 1994. Appointed chmn., Universal Pictures, November, 1995. Responsible for leadership of prod., mktg., dist., and home video.

SILVER, JOAN MICKLIN
Writer, Director. b. Omaha, NB, May 24, 1935. m. producer Raphael Silver. Daughter is dir. Marisa Silver. e. Sarah Lawrence Coll. Began career as writer for educational films. Original s.p., Limbo, purchased by Universal Pictures. In 1972 Learning Corp. of Am. commissioned her to write and direct a 30-min. film, The Immigrant Experience. Also wrote and directed two children's films for same co; dir. & wrote short film Bernice Bobs Her Hair. First feature was Hester Street, which she wrote and directed.
THEATER: *Director*: Album, Maybe I'm Doing It Wrong, A ... My Name is Alice, A ... My Name is Still Alice (co-conceived & co-dir. with Julianne Boyd).
PICTURES: *Director*: Hester Street (also s.p.), Between the Lines, On the Yard (prod.), Head Over Heels (also s.p.; retitled Chilly Scenes of Winter), Crossing Delancey, Loverboy, Big Girls Don't Cry... They Get Even, A Fish In the Bathtub.
TELEVISION: Finnegan Begin Again (dir.), The Nightingale: Faerie Tale Theatre (writer), Parole Board (Prison Stories: Women on the Inside), A Private Matter (dir.), In the Presence of Mine Enemies.

SILVER, JOEL
Producer. b. South Orange, NJ, July 14, 1952. e. NYU. Made first film, a short called Ten Pin Alley; moved to Los Angeles with job as asst. to Lawrence Gordon. Named pres., Lawrence Gordon Prods.; developed with Gordon and produced and marketed Hooper, The End, The Driver, The Warriors (also assoc. prod.). At Universal Pictures as prod. v.p.; supervising Smokey and the Bandit II. Honored 1990 as NATO/Showest's Producer of the Year. Appeared in 1988 film Who Framed Roger Rabbit.
PICTURES: Xanadu (co-prod.), Jekyll & Hyde ... Together Again (exec. prod.), 48 HRS., Streets of Fire, Brewster's Millions, Weird Science, Commando, Jumpin' Jack Flash, Lethal Weapon, Predator, Action Jackson, Die Hard, Road House, Lethal Weapon 2, The Adventures of Ford Fairlane, Die Hard 2, Predator 2, Hudson Hawk, Ricochet, The Last Boy Scout, Lethal Weapon 3, Demoliton Man, The Hudsucker Proxy, Richie Rich, Tales From the Crypt Presents Demon Knight (co-exec. prod.), Fair Game, Assassins, Executive Decision, Conspiracy Theory, Father's Day, Conspiracy Theory, Matrix, Lethal Weapon 4.
TELEVISION: Tales from the Crypt (exec. prod. & prod.; also dir. episode), Two Fisted Tales, Parker Can, W.E.I.R.D. World (co-exec. prod.).

SILVER, LEON J.
Executive. b. Boston, MA, March 25, 1918. e. USC, 1935-39. Independent prod. of short subjects, 1939; story analyst, Paramount, 1940, film writer, U.S. Army Pictorial Service, 1941-45; freelance writer, 1946; film writer. prod., U.S. Public Health Service, 1946-51; asst. chief, foreign film prod., U.S. Dept. of State, 1951-54; acting chief, domestic film prod., U.S. Information Agency, 1955; division chief, Worldwide Documentary Film & Television Product, U.S. Information Agency, 1968; 1978-79, sr. advisor IV, film production. Coordinator of TV & film, all Fed Govt. Agencies Private Industry under Exec. Office, pres. of U.S. 1980. Resigned, 1980. Now TV network writer-producer-novelist.

SILVER, MARISA
Director. b. New York, NY, April 23, 1960. Daughter of director Joan Micklin Silver and prod.-dir. Raphael Silver. e. Harvard U. where she directed short Dexter T. and edited doc. Light Coming Through: a Portrait of Maud Morgan.
PICTURES: Old Enough, Permanent Record, Vital Signs, He Said/She Said (co-dir.), Indecency.
TELEVISION: *Co-dir.*: A Community of Praise (an episode of PBS series Middletown, 1982).

SILVER, RAPHAEL D.
Producer. b. Cleveland, OH, 1930. e. Harvard Coll. and Harvard Graduate Sch. of Business Adm. Is pres. of Middex Devel. Corp. 1973 formed Midwest Film Productions to produce Hester Street, written and directed by Joan Micklin Silver. Also distributed film independently. Also produced Between the Lines. Exec. prod. of Crossing Delancey. Directed On the Yard, A Walk on the Moon; writer/prod. A Fish in the Bathtub. Currently pres. Silverfilm Prods. Inc.

SILVER, RON
Actor, Director. b. New York, NY, July 2, 1946. e. U. of Buffalo, St. John's U., Taiwan, M.A. Trained for stage at Herbert Berghof Studios and Actors Studio. N.Y. stage debut in Kasper and Public Insult, 1971. Elected pres. of Actors Equity Assn., 1991.
THEATER: El Grande de Coca Cola, Lotta, More Than You Deserve, Angel City (Mark Taper, LA), Hurlyburly, Social Security, Hunting Cockroaches, Speed-the-Plow (Tony & Drama Desk Award), Gorilla (Chicago, Jefferson Award nom.; N.YU. & L.A., Dramalogue Award), Friends, And, Broken Glass.
PICTURES: Tunnelvision, Welcome to L.A., Semi-Tough, Silent Rage, Best Friends, The Entity, Lovesick, Silkwood, Garbo Talks, Oh God! You Devil, Goodbye People, Eat and Run, Enemies A Love Story, Blue Steel, Reversal of Fortune, Mr. Saturday Night, Married to It, Timecop, Danger Zone, Deadly Takeover, Girl 6, The Arrival, Rhapsody in Bloom, Black & White.
TELEVISION: *Series*: Mac Davis Show, Rhoda, Dear Detective, The Stockard Channing Show, Baker's Dozen, Chicago Hope. *Movies*: The Return of the World's Greatest Detective, Murder at the Mardi Gras, Betrayal, Word of Honor, Billionaire Boys Club, Fellow Traveler, Forgotten Prisoners: The Amnesty Files, Live Wire, Blindside, Lifepod (also dir.), Almost Golden: The Jessica Savitch Story, Billionaire Boys Club (Emmy nom.), Shadow zone, The Undead, Express, The Beneficiary. *Mini-Series*: A Zoman of Independent Means. *Guest*: Trying Times (Drive He Said), Hill Street Blues. *Special*: Loyalty and Betrayal: The Story of the American Mob (narrator).

SILVERMAN, FRED
Producer. b. New York, NY, Sept., 1937. e. Syracuse U., Ohio State U., master's in TV and theatre arts. Joined WGN-TV, indep. sta. in Chicago. Came to NY for exec. post at WPIX-TV, where stayed only six weeks. CBS-TV hired him as dir. of daytime programs. Named v.p., programs 1970. 1975 left CBS to become pres., ABC Entertainment. 1978, named pres. and CEO of NBC. Now Pres., The Fred Silverman Company, Los Angeles.
TELEVISION: *Prod./exec. prod.*: *Series*: Perry Mason Movies, Matlock, In the Heat of the Night, Jake and the Fatman, Father Dowling Mysteries, Diagnosis Murder, Bonechillers, Bedtime Stories. *Movies*: Gramps, My Very Best Friend, Journey to Mars.

SILVERMAN, JONATHAN
Actor. b. Los Angeles, CA, Aug. 5, 1966. e. USC, NYU.
THEATER: *NY*: Brighton Beach Memoirs, Biloxi Blues, Broadway Bound. *LA*: The Illusion (Dramalogue Award), Pay or Play (Dramalogue Award), Sticks and Stones (Dramalogue Award).
PICTURES: Brighton Beach Memoirs (debut, 1986), Caddyshack II, Stealing Home, Weekend at Bernie's, Class Action, Breaking the Rules, Life in the Food Chain (Age Isn't Everything), Little Sister, Weekend at Bernie's II, Little Big League, Teresa's Tattoo, French Exit, At First Sight.
TELEVISION: *Series*: Gimme a Break, The Single Guy. *Movies*: Challenge of a Lifetime, Traveling Man, For Richer For Poorer, Broadway Bound, 12:01, Sketch Artist II: Hands That See.

SILVERSTEIN, ELLIOT
Director. b. Boston, MA, Aug. 3, 1937. e. Boston Coll., Yale U. Started career on television.
PICTURES: Cat Ballou, The Happening, A Man Called Horse, Deadly Honeymoon, The Car (also co-prod.), Flashfire.
TELEVISION: *Pilot*: Belle Sommers (debut, 1962). *Movies*: Betrayed by Innocence, Night of Courage, Fight for Life, Rich Men Single Women. *Series*: Tales From the Crypt.

SILVERSTEIN, MAURICE
Executive. b. Syracuse, NY, March 1, 1912. Booker, salesman, MGM domestic dep't; International Dep't, MGM; supervisor Southeast Asia Hdqts. Singapore, MGM, 1938-42; OWI chief, film distribution for Europe, hdqts. London, during WWII; asst. sales supervisor, Far East, MGM; regional director, Latin America, 1947; liaison exec. to handle independent productions MGM, 1956; v.p., MGM International, 1957; first v.p., 1958; pres., MGM International, 1963; v.p., parent company, Metro-Goldwyn-Mayer Inc. in charge of foreign production, 1970; Silverstein Int'l Corp., pres.

SILVERSTONE, ALICIA
Actress. b. California, 1977. Made stage debut at Met Theater in Los Angeles in Carol's Eve. Starred in three Aerosmith videos including Cryin'. Formed own production co., First Kiss Prods.
PICTURES: The Crush (debut, 1993), The Babysitter, True Crime, Le Nouveau Monde, Hideaway, Clueless, Excess Baggage (also prod.), Batman & Robin, Excess Baggage.
TELEVISION: Movies: Torch Song, Shattered Dreams, The Cool and the Crazy. Guest: The Wonder Years.

SILVESTRI, ALAN
Composer.
PICTURES: The Doberman Gang, The Amazing Dobermans, The Fifth Floor, Romancing the Stone, Summer Rental, Fandango, Cat's Eye, Back to the Future, No Mercy, Flight of the Navigator, American Anthem, The Delta Force, The Clan of the Cave Bear, Overboard, Critical Condition, Predator, Outrageous Fortune, My Stepmother Is an Alien, Mac and Me, Who Framed Roger Rabbit, She's Out of Control, The Abyss, Back to the Future Part II, Downtown, Back to the Future Part III, Young Guns II, Predator 2, Father of the Bride, Dutch, Back to the Future... The Ride, Soapdish, Shattered (also orchestration), Ricochet, FernGully: The Last Rainforest, Stop! Or My Mom Will Shoot, The Bodyguard, Sidekicks, Death Becomes Her, Judgment Night, In Search of the Obelisk, Grumpy Old Men, Super Mario Bros., Cop & 1/2, Richie Rich, Clean Slate, Forrest Gump (Acad. Award nom.), Golden Globe nom.), Blown Away, The Quick and the Dead, The Perez Family, Judge Dredd, Father of the Bride Part II, Grumpier Old Men, Sgt. Bilko, Eraser, The Long Kiss Goodnight, Fools Rush In, Volcano, Contact, Mouse Hunt, The Odd Couple II, Holy Man.
TELEVISION: Starsky and Hutch, CHiPs, Airwolf, Tales From the Crypt.

SIMMONS, ANTHONY
Director, Writer. b. London, England. e. Grad. from the LSE with LL.B. Practiced briefly as a barrister before entering the industry as writer/director of documentaries, then commercials and feature films. Awards: Grand Prix (shorts), Venice, Grand Prix, Locarno; 2 Int. Emmys, various Intl. Awards for commercials. Publications: The Optimists of Nine Elms, A Little Space for Issie Brown.
PICTURES: Sunday By the Sea, Bow Bells, Time Without Pity (co- prod.), Four in the Morning, The Optimists, Black Joy, Little Sweetheart, Poison Candy.
TELEVISION: On Giant's Shoulders, Supergran and the Magic Ray, Harry Carpenter Never Said It Was Like This, Life After Death, Day After the Fair, Inspector Morse, Van de Valk, Inspector Frost, The Good Guys, 99-1.

SIMMONS, JEAN
Actress. b. London, England, Jan. 31, 1929. e. Aida Foster Sch., London. Screen debut 1944 at age 14. Voted one of top ten British money-making stars in M.P. Herald-Fame Poll, 1950-51. London stage: A Little Night Music. Awards: Cannes Film Festival Homage 1988, Italian Outstanding Film Achievement Award 1989, French Govt. Commandeur de L'Ordre des Arts des Lettres. 1990.
PICTURES: Give Us the Moon (debut, 1944), Mr. Emmanuèl, Meet Sexton Blake, Kiss the Bride Goodbye, Sports Day, Caesar and Cleopatra, Way to the Stars, Great Expectations, Hungry Hill, Black Narcissus, Uncle Silas, The Women In the Hall, Hamlet (Acad. Award nom.), Blue Lagoon, Adam and Evelyne, Trio, So Long at the Fair, Cage of Gold, The Clouded Yellow, Androcles and the Lion (U.S. film debut, 1953), Angel Face, Young Bess, Affair with a Stranger, The Actress, The Robe, She Couldn't Say No, A Bullet Is Waiting, The Egyptian, Desiree, Footsteps in the Fog, Guys and Dolls, Hilda Crane, This Could Be the Night, Until They Sail, The Big Country, Home Before Dark, This Earth Is Mine, Elmer Gantry, Spartacus, The Grass Is Greener, All the Way Home, Life at the Top, Mister Buddwing, Rough Night in Jericho, Divorce American Style, The Happy Ending (Acad. Award nom.), Say Hello to Yesterday, Mr. Sycamore, Dominique, Going Undercover, The Dawning, How to Make an American Quilt.
TELEVISION: Movies & Specials: Heidi, Beggarman Thief, The Easter Promise, The Home Front, Golden Gate, Jacqueline Susann's Valley of the Dolls 1981, A Small Killing, Inherit the Wind, Great Expectations, Sensibility and Sense, The Laker Girls, Perry Mason: The Case of Lost Love, People Like Us, December Flower. Mini-Series: The Dain Curse, The Thorn Birds (Emmy Award, 1983), North and South Book II. Series: Dark Shadows (1991).

SIMMONS, MATTY
Producer. b. Oct. 3. As bd. chmn., National Lampoon, Inc. produced National Lampoon Radio Hour, National Lampoon Lemmings, National Lampoon Show. Resigned from National Lampoon Inc. 1989. Now heads Matty Simmons Productions.
PICTURES: National Lampoon's Animal House, National Lampoon's Vacation, National Lampoon Goes to the Movies, National Lampoon's Class Reunion, National Lampoon's European Vacation, National Lampoon's Christmas Vacation (exec. prod.), Vegas Vacation (exec. prod.).
TELEVISION: National Lampoon's Disco Beavers, National Lampoon's Class of '86 (exec. prod.), Delta House.

SIMON, MELVIN
Executive. b. New York, NY, Oct. 21, 1926. e. City Coll.of New York, B.B.A., 1949; graduate work at Indiana U. Law Sch. Owner and operator, in partnership with two brothers, of over 110 shopping centers in U.S. 1978 formed Melvin Simon Productions, privately owned corp., to finance films. Dissolved Co. in 1983.
PICTURES: Exec. Prod.: Dominique, Love at First Bite, When a Stranger Calls, The Runner Stumbles, Scavenger Hunt, Cloud Dancer, The Stunt Man, My Bodyguard, Zorro the Gay Blade, Chu Chu and the Philly Flash, Porky's, Porky's II—The Next Day, Uforia, Wolf Lake, Porky's Revenge.

SIMON, NEIL
Playwright, Screenwriter, Producer. b. Bronx, NY, July 4, 1927. e. NYU. U.S. Army Air Force, 1945-46. Wrote comedy for radio with brother, Danny, (Robert Q. Lewis Show and for Goodman Ace), also TV scripts for Sid Caesar, Red Buttons, Jackie Gleason, Phil Silvers, Garry Moore, Tallulah Bankhead Show. With Danny contributed to B'way revues Catch a Star (1955), and New Faces of 1956. Adapted most of own plays to screen.
THEATER: Playwright: Come Blow Your Horn, Little Me, Barefoot in the Park, The Odd Couple (Tony Award, 1965), Sweet Charity, The Star Spangled Girl, Plaza Suite, Promises Promises, Last of the Red Hot Lovers, The Gingerbread Lady, The Prisoner of Second Avenue, The Sunshine Boys, The Good Doctor, God's Favorite, California Suite, Chapter Two, They're Playing Our Song, I Ought to Be in Pictures, Fools, Little Me (revised version), Brighton Beach Memoirs, Biloxi Blues (Tony Award, 1985), The Odd Couple (female version), Broadway Bound, Rumors, Lost in Yonkers (Pulitzer Prize, Tony Award, 1991), Jake's Women, The Goodbye Girl (musical), Laughter on the 23rd Floor, London Suite (Off-B'way), The Out-of-Towners, The Odd Couple II.
PICTURES: After the Fox, Barefoot in the Park (also assoc. prod.), The Odd Couple, The Out-of-Towners, Plaza Suite, Last of the Red Hot Lovers, The Heartbreak Kid, The Prisoner of Second Avenue, The Sunshine Boys, Murder by Death, The Goodbye Girl, The Cheap Detective, California Suite, Chapter Two, Seems Like Old Times, Only When I Laugh (also co-prod.), I Ought to Be in Pictures (also co-prod.), Max Dugan Returns (also co-prod.), The Lonely Guy (adaptation), The Slugger's Wife, Brighton Beach Memoirs, Biloxi Blues (also co-prod.), The Marrying Man, Lost in Yonkers.
TELEVISION: Specials: The Trouble With People, Plaza Suite. Movie: Broadway Bound, Jake's Women.

SIMON, PAUL
Singer, Composer, Actor. b. Newark, NJ, Oct. 13, 1941. e. Queens Coll., BA, postgrad. Brooklyn Law Sch. Teamed with Art Garfunkel in 1964, writing and performing own songs; they parted in 1970. Reunited for concert in New York, 1982, which was televised on HBO. Songs: With Garfunkel incl.: Mrs. Robinson (Grammy Award), The Boxer, Bridge Over Troubled Water (Grammy Award).
PICTURES: The Graduate (songs), Annie Hall (actor), One Trick Pony (s.p., actor, composer)
TELEVISION: Specials: The Fred Astaire Show, The Paul Simon Special (Emmy Award), Home Box Office Presents Paul Simon, Graceland: The African Concert, Mother Goose Rock 'n' Rhyme, Paul Simon's Concert in the Park. Guest: Sesame Street.
ALBUMS: with Garfunkel: Wednesday Morning 3 a.m., Sounds of Silence, Parsley, Sage, Rosemary and Thyme, The Graduate (Grammy Award), Bookends, Bridge Over Troubled Water (Grammy Award), Simon & Garfunkel's Greatest Hits, Concert in the Park. Solo: Paul Simon, There Goes Rhymin' Simon, Live Rhymin', Still Crazy After All These Years (Grammy Award), Greatest Hits, One Trick Pony, Hearts and Bones, Graceland (Grammy Award), Negotiations and Love Songs, The Rhythm of the Saints, Paul Simon's Concert in the Park.

SIMON, SIMONE
Actress. b. April 23, 1911, Marseilles, France. Played in many films in Europe, among them Les Beaux Jours, La Bete Humaine, and Lac aux Dames. On stage in Toi C'est Moi, and others.
PICTURES: Girl's Dormitory (U.S. debut, 1936), Ladies in Love, Seventh Heaven, All That Money Can Buy, Cat People, Tahiti Honey, Johnny Doesn't Live Here Any More, The Curse of the Cat People, Mademoiselle Fifi, Petrus, Temptation Harbor, La Ronde, Olivia (Pit of Loneliness), Le Plaisir (House of Pleasure), Double Destin, The Extra Day, La Femme en Bleu.

SIMPSON, GARRY
Producer, Director, Executive. b. Camden, MI, Feb. 16, 1914. e. Stanford U. Major shows with NBC-TV: Jimmy Durante Show, Armstrong Circle Theatre, Campbell Soundstage, Comedy Hour, Ford Festival, Chevrolet Tele-Theater, Ed Wynn Show, The World of Mr. Sweeney, Philco TV Playhouse, Wide Wide World, Ballet Theatre. Dir. of programming, Vermont State PBS Network and writer-prod. of documentary films. Awards: Peabody, NY Film & TV Fest., Chicago Film Fest., & 3 Emmys.

SIMPSON, O.J.
Actor. b. San Francisco, CA, July 9, 1947. r.n. Orenthal James Simpson. e. U. of Southern California. Was star collegiate and professional football player and winner of Heisman Trophy. Began sportscasting in 1969.
PICTURES: The Klansman (debut, 1974), The Towering Inferno, Killer Force, The Cassandra Crossing, Capricorn One, Firepower, Hambone & Hillie, The Naked Gun: From the Files of Police Squad, The Naked Gun 2 1/2: The Smell of Fear, Naked Gun 33 1/3: The Final Insult.
TELEVISION: Mini-Series: Roots. Movies: A Killing Affair, Goldie and the Boxer (also exec. prod.), Detour to Terror (also exec. prod.), Goldie and the Boxer Go to Hollywood (also exec. prod.), Cocaine and Blue Eyes (also exec. prod.), Student Exchange. Prod.: High Five (pilot), Superbowl Saturday Night (host & co-prod.). Series: First and Ten (HBO), NFL Live (co-host).

SIMS, JOAN
Actress. b. Laindon, England, May 9, 1930. e. Trained at RADA. Early career in repertory and West End Theatre.
PICTURES: Dry Rot, Off the Record, No Time for Tears, Just My Luck, The Naked Truth, The Captain's Table, Passport to Shame, Emergency Ward 10, Most of the Carry On' films, Doctor in Love, Watch Your Stern, Twice Round the Daffodils, The Iron Maiden, Nurse on Wheels, Doctor in Clover, Doctor in Trouble, The Garnett Saga, Not Now Darling, Don't Just Lie There Say Something, Love Among the Ruins, One of Our Dinosaurs Is Missing, Till Death Us Do Part, The Way of the World, Deceptions, The Fool, My Good Friend, As Time Goes By, The Canterville Ghost.
TELEVISION: Over 100 shows incl. Stanley Baxter Show, Dick Emery Show, Carry on Shows, Love Among the Ruins, Born and Bred, Worzel Gummidge, Ladykillers, Crown Court, Cockles, Fairly Secret Army, Tickle on the Tum, Miss Marple: A Murder Is Announced, Hay Fever, In Loving Memory, Drummonds, Farrington of the F.O., Dr. Who, On the Up (3 series), Boys From the Bush, Simon & the Witch, Children's TV, Boys From the Bush, Tender Loving Care, Canterville Ghost, My Good Friend, Smokescreen, As Time Goes By, Just William, Henrietta Wainthrop Investigates.

SINATRA, FRANK
Actor, Singer. b. Hoboken, NJ, Dec. 12, 1915. Sportswriter; then singer on radio various NY stations; joined Harry James orchestra, later Tommy Dorsey. Children: singer-actress Nancy Sinatra, singer-conductor Frank Sinatra Jr., producer Tina Sinatra. On screen as a band vocalist in Las Vegas Nights, Ship Ahoy, Reveille with Beverly. Special Academy Award 1945 for acting in The House I Live In, short subject on tolerance. Received Jean Hersholt Humanitarian Award, 1971.
PICTURES: Las Vegas Nights (debut, 1941), Ship Ahoy, Reveille With Beverly, Higher and Higher (acting debut, 1943), Step Lively, Anchors Aweigh, Till the Clouds Roll By, It Happened in Brooklyn, The Miracle of the Bells, The Kissing Bandit, Take Me Out to the Ball Game, On the Town, Double Dynamite, Meet Danny Wilson, From Here to Eternity (Acad. Award, best supporting actor, 1953), Suddenly, Young at Heart, Not as a Stranger, The Tender Trap, Guys and Dolls, The Man With the Golden Arm, Meet Me in Las Vegas (cameo), Johnny Concho (also prod.), High Society, Around the World in 80 Days, The Pride and the Passion, The Joker Is Wild, Pal Joey, Kings Go Forth, Some Came Running, A Hole in the Head, Never So Few, Can-Can, Ocean's Eleven, Pepe (cameo), The Devil at 4 O'Clock, Sergeants 3 (also prod.), The Road to Hong Kong (cameo), The Manchurian Candidate, Come Blow Your Horn, The List of Adrian Messenger, 4 for Texas, Robin and the 7 Hoods (also prod.), None But the Brave (also dir., prod.), Von Ryan's Express, Marriage on the Rocks, Cast a Giant Shadow, The Oscar (cameo), Assault on a Queen, The Naked Runner, Tony Rome, The Detective, Lady in Cement, Dirty Dingus Magee, That's Entertainment!, The First Deadly Sin (also exec. prod.), Cannonball Run II (cameo), Listen Up: The Lives of Quincy Jones.
TELEVISION: Series: The Frank Sinatra Show (1950-52; 1957-58); numerous specials, and guest appearances, incl. Club Oasis, Anything Goes (1954), Hollywood Palace, Our Town (1955), Frank Sinatra: A Man and His Music (Emmy Award, 1965), Francis Albert Sinatra Does His Thing, Ol' Blue Eyes Is Back, Magnum P.I., Frank Liza & Sammy: The Ultimate Event, Sinatra: Concert for the Americas. Movies: Contract on Cherry Street, Young at Heart. (d. May 14, 1998)

SINBAD
Actor. r.n. David Adkins. b. Benton Harbor, MI, Nov. 10, 1956. e. Univ. of Denver. Served in Air Force before becoming stand-up comic. Career was subsquently launched by appearances on tv series Star Search.
PICTURES: Necessary Roughness (debut, 1991), Coneheads, The Meteor Man, Houseguest, First Kid (also co-exec. prod.), Jingle All the Way, Homeward Bound II: Lost in San Francisco, First Kid, Jingle All the Way, Good Burger.
TELEVISION: Series: The Redd Foxx Show, A Different World, It's Showtime at the Apollo (host), The Sinbad Show (also exec. prod.). Specials: Sinbad: Brain Damaged, Afros and Bellbottoms, Take No Prisoners, Sinbad and Friends All the Way Live... Almost (also writer), Aliens for Breakfast. Guest: The Cosby Show, Saturday Night Live.

SINCLAIR, MADGE
Actress. b. Kingston, Jamaica, April 28, 1938. e. Shortwood Women's College. Worked in Jamaica as a teacher and in the insurance business before moving to NY. Chairwoman, Madge Walters Sinclair Inc., Caribbean Child Life Foundation. Awards: NAACP Image Award, 1981 and 1983, best actress in dramatic series, Trapper John M.D.; Drama-Logue Critics Award, 1986, Boseman & Lena; Mother of the Year Award, 1984. L.A. area Emmy Award, Look Away. Member: bd. of dir., Lost Angeles Theatre Center.
THEATER: Kumaliza (NYSF, debut, 1969), Iphigenia (NYSF, NY and with Young Vic, London), Mod Donna, Ti-Jean and His Brothers, Blood, Division Street (Mark Taper Forum), Boesman & Lena (LA Theatre Center), Tartuffe (L.A. Theatre Center), Stars in the Morning (LATC), Piano (LATC), Jacques and His Master (LATC), Trinity (New Federal Theatre).
PICTURES: Conrack (debut, 1974), Cornbread Earl & Me, Leadbelly, I Will I Will... For Now, Convoy, Uncle Joe Shannon, Star Trek IV: The Voyage Home, Coming to America, The Lion King (voice).
TELEVISION: Series: Grandpa Goes to Washington, Trapper John M.D., O'Hara, Gabriel's Fire (Emmy Award, 1991; revamped as Pros & Cons), Me and the Boys. Guest: Madigan, Medical Center, The Waltons, Joe Forester, Doctor's Hospital, Executive Suite, Medical Story, Serpico, The White Shadow, All in the Family, Homeroom, Midnight Caller, Roseanne. Mini-Series: Roots, The Orchid House (Britain), Queen. Movies: I Love, You, Goodbye, One in a Million: The Ron LeFlore Story, I Know Why the Caged Bird Sings, High Ice, Jimmy B and Andre, Guyana Tragedy: The Story of Jim Jones, Victims, Look Away: The Emancipation of Mary Todd Lincoln, Divided We Stand, Jonathan: The Boy Nobody Wanted, The Man With 3 Wives. Special: A Century of Women.

SINDEN, DONALD
Actor. b. Plymouth, England, Oct. 9, 1923. Stage debut 1942 in fit-up shows; London stage includes There's a Girl in My Soup, The Relapse, Not Now Darling, King Lear, Othello, Present Laughter, Uncle Vanya, The School for Scandal, Two Into One, The Scarlet Pimpernel, Oscar Wilde, Major Barbara, Out of Order, Venus Observed, She Stoops to Conquer, Hamlet, That Good Night. B'way: London Assurance, Habeas Corpus. TV debut 1948.
PICTURES: Portrait From Life (The Girl in the Painting; debut, 1948), The Cruel Sea, Mogambo, A Day to Remember, You Know What Sailors Are, Doctor in the House, The Beachcomber, Mad About Men, An Alligator Named Daisy, Black Tent, Eyewitness, Tiger in the Smoke, Doctor at Large, Rockets Galore (Mad Little Island), The Captain's Table, Operation Bullshine, Your Money or Your Wife, The Siege of Sydney Street, Twice Around the Daffodils, Mix Me a Person, Decline and Fall, Villain, Rentadick, The Island at the Top of the World, That Lucky Touch, The Children, The Canterville Ghost.
TELEVISION: Bullet in the Ballet, Road to Rome, Dinner With the Family, Odd Man In, Love from Italy, The Frog, The Glove, The Mystery of Edwin Drood, The Happy Ones, The Comedy of Errors, The Wars of the Roses, The Red House, Blackmail, A Bachelor Gray, Our Man at St. Marks (3 series), The Wind in the Tall Paper Chimney, A Woman Above Reproach, Call My Bluff, Relatively Speaking, Father Dear Father, The 19th Hole, Seven Days in the Life of Andrew Pelham (serial), The Assyrian Rejuvenator, The Organization (serial), The Confederacy of Wives, Tell It to the Chancellor, The Rivals, Two's Company (4 series), All's Well That Ends Well, Never the Twain (11 series), Cuts.

SINGER, LORI
Actress. b. Corpus Christi, TX, Nov. 6, 1962. Brother is actor Marc Singer; father was symphony conductor Jacques Singer. Concert cellist while in teens. Won starring role in TV series Fame (1981).
PICTURES: Footloose (debut, 1984), The Falcon and The Snowman, The Man with One Red Shoe, Trouble in Mind, Summer Heat, Made in U.S.A., Warlock, Equinox, Sunset Grill, Short Cuts (Golden Globe Award), F.T.W.
TELEVISION: Series: Fame, VR5. Movies: Born Beautiful, Storm and Sorrow, Inspired by Bach. Special: Sensibility and Sense.

SINGER, MARC
Actor. b. Vancouver, B.C., Canada, Jan. 29. Brother of actress Lori Singer. Son of symphony conductor Jacques Singer. Trained in summer stock and regional theatre.
PICTURES: Go Tell the Spartans, If You Could See What I Hear, The Beastmaster, Born to Race, A Man Called Sarge, Watchers II, Body Chemistry, Dead Space, In the Cold of the Night, Beastmaster 2, Sweet Justice, The Berlin Conspiracy, Alien Intruder, Beastmaster 3.
TELEVISION: Series: The Contender, V, Dallas. Mini-Series: 79 Park Avenue, Roots: The Next Generation. Movies: Things in Their Season, Journey from Darkness, Something for Joey, Never Con a Killer, Sergeant Matlovich vs. the U.S. Air Force, The Two Worlds of Jennie Logan, For Ladies Only, Paper Dolls, V, Her Life as a Man, V—The Final Battle, Deadly Game, The Sea Wolf.

SINGLETON, JOHN
Director, Writer. b. Los Angeles, CA, Jan. 6, 1968. Entered USC's Filmic Writing Program, where he received a Robert Riskin Writing Award and two Jack Nicholson Writing Awards. With debut feature Boyz N the Hood (1991) he became the first African-American and youngest person ever to be nominated for an Academy Award for Best Director. Appeared in film Beverly Hills Cop III.
PICTURES: Director-Writer: Boyz N the Hood (Acad. Award noms. for dir. & s.p.), Poetic Justice (also co-prod.), Higher Learning (also co-prod.), Rosewood.

SINGLETON, PENNY
Actress. r.n. Dorothy McNulty. b. Philadelphia, PA, September 15, 1908. e. Columbia U. First Broadway success came as top comedienne in Good News., exec. pres. AGVA.
PICTURES: Outside of Paradise, Swing Your Lady, Men Are Such Fools, Boy Meets Girl, Mr. Chump, Mad Miss Manton, Garden of the Moon, Secrets of an Actress, Hard to Get, 28 films in Blondie series (from Blondie, 1938, to Blondie's Hero, 1950), Rocket Busters, Go West Young Lady, Footlight Glamor, Young Widow, The Best Man, Jetsons: The Movie (voice).
TELEVISION: Series: The Jetsons (voice).

SINISE, GARY
Actor, Director. b. 1955. Co-founder and artistic dir. of Chicago's Steppenwolf Theatre Company, 1974.
THEATER: NY: Balm in Gilead, True West, The Caretaker, The Grapes of Wrath. Chicago: Of Mice and Men, Getting Out. Director: True West (Obie Award), Orphans, Buried Child.
PICTURES: Miles From Home (dir. only), A Midnight Clear, Of Mice and Men (also dir., co-prod.), Jack the Bear, Forrest Gump (Acad. Award nom.), The Quick and the Dead, Apollo 13, Albino Alligator, Ransom., Snake Eyes, Bruno
TELEVISION: Mini-Series: The Stand. Movies: Family Secrets, My Name is Bill W, The Final Days, Truman (Golden Globe Award), George Wallace (Emmy Award, 1998). Director: Crime Story, thirtysomething, China Beach.

SIODMAK, CURT
Director, Writer. b. Dresden, Germany, Aug. 10, 1902. e. U. of Zurich. Engineer, newspaper reporter, writer in Berlin; novelist, including F.P.1 Does Not Answer, adapt. 1932 for Ufa. Originals and screenplays in France and England including France (Le Bal), Transatlantic Tunnel, GB.
PICTURES: Writer: Her Jungle Love (co-story), The Invisible Man Returns, Black Friday, The Ape, Aloma of the South Sea (co-story), The Wolf Man, Invisible Agent, Frankenstein Meets the Wolf Man, I Walked With a Zombie, Son of Dracula (co-story), The Mantrap, House of Frankenstein (story), The Climax, Shady Lady, The Beast with Five Fingers, Berlin Express (story), Tarzan's Magic Fountain, Four Days Leave, Bride of the Gorilla (also dir.), The Magnetic Monster (also dir.), Curucu—Beast of the Amazon (also dir.), Love Slaves of the Amazon (also dir., prod.), Riders to the Stars, Creature with the Atom Brain, Earth vs. the Flying Saucers.

SIZEMORE, TOM
Actor. b. Detroit, MI. e. Wayne St. Univ., Temple Univ.Stage incl. The Land of the Astronauts in NYC and D.C.
PICTURES: Lock Up, Rude Awakening, Penn and Teller Get Killed, Born on the Fourth of July, Blue Steel, Flight of the Intruder, Guilty by Suspicion, Harley Davidson and the Marlboro Man, A Matter of Degrees, Passenger 57, Watch It, Heart and Souls, True Romance, Striking Distance, Wyatt Earp, Natural Born Killers, Devil in a Blue Dress, Strange Days, Heat, The Relic.

SKASE, CHRISTOPHER
Executive. b. Australia, 1946. Began career as reporter for Fairfax publication, Australian Financial Review. In 1970s set up investment company with about $20,000. Revived Australian TV Seven network in Melbourne and then in U.S. bought Hal Roach Studios and NY based prod.-dist. Robert Halmi which he merged into Qintex Entertainment. Qintex Entertainment produced TV mini-series Lonesome Dove.

SKERRITT, TOM
Actor. b. Detroit, MI, Aug. 25, 1933. e. Wayne State U., UCLA. Model for Guess? jeans ads.
PICTURES: War Hunt (debut, 1962), One Man's Way, Those Calloways, M*A*S*H, Wild Rovers, Fuzz, Harold and Maude, Run Joe Run, Big Bad Mama, Thieves Like Us, The Devil's Rain, La Madonna, The Turning Point, Up in Smoke, Ice Castles, Alien, Savage Harvest, The Silence of the North, A Dangerous Summer (The Burning Man), Fighting Back, The Dead Zone, Top Gun, Opposing Force (Hell Camp), SpaceCamp, Wisdom, Maid to Order, The Big Town, Poltergeist III, Steel Magnolias, Big Man on Campus, Honor Bound, The Rookie, Wild Orchid II: Two Shades of Blue, Poison Ivy, Singles, A River Runs Through It, Knight Moves, Contact, Not Like You.

TELEVISION: Series: Ryan's Four, Cheers, Picket Fences (Emmy Award, 1993). Movies: The Bird Men, The Last Day, Maneaters Are Loose!, The Calendar Girl Murders, Miles to Go, Parent Trap II, A Touch of Scandal, Poker Alice, Moving Target, Nightmare at Bitter Creek, The Heist, Red King White Knight, The China Lake Murders, Child of the Night, In Sickness and in Health, Getting Up and Going Home. Director: A Question of Sex (Afterschool Special), Picket Fences (3 episodes), Divided by Hate.

SKLAR, MARTY
Executive. Pres., Walt Disney Imagineering.

SKOLIMOWSKI, JERZY
Director, Writer. b. Lodz, Poland, May 5, 1938. e. Warsaw U., State Superior Film Sch., Lodz, Poland. Scriptwriter for Wajda's Innocent Sorcerers (also actor), Polanski's Knife in the Water and Lomnicki's Poslizg. Author: Somewhere Close to Oneself, Somebody Got Drowned.
PICTURES: Director-Writer. Identification Marks—None (also actor, edit., art dir.), Walkover (also actor, edit.), Barrier, The Departure, Hands Up (also actor), Dialogue, The Adventures of Gerard, Deep End, King Queen Knave (dir. only), The Shout, Circle of Deceit (actor only), Moonlighting (also prod., actor), Success Is the Best Revenge, The Lightship, White Nights (actor), Big Shots (actor), Torrents of Spring (also actor), 30 Door Key (also co-s.p., prod.), The Hollow Men (prod.).

SKYE, IONE
Actress. r.n. Ione Skye Leitch. b. London, England, Sept. 4, 1971. Daughter of folksinger Donovan (Leitch) and sister of actor Donovan Leitch. m. singer-actor Adam Horovitz. Raised in San Francisco, Connecticut, Los Angeles. Fashion photo of her in magazine led to audition for film River's Edge.
PICTURES: River's Edge (debut, 1987 as Ione Skye Leitch), Stranded, A Night in the Life of Jimmy Reardon, Say Anything..., The Rachel Papers, Mindwalk, Samantha, Guncrazy, Carmilla, Wayne's World, The Color of Evening, Gas Food Lodging, Four Rooms, The Size of Watermelons, One Night Stand, Dream for an Insomniac, Went to Coney Island on a Mission from God...Be Back by Five.
TELEVISION: Series: Covington Cross. Movies: Napoleon and Josephine, Girls in Prison. Specials: It's Called the Sugar Plum, Nightmare Classics (Carmilla).

SLATER, CHRISTIAN
Actor. b. New York, NY, Aug. 18, 1969. Mother is NY casting dir. Mary Jo Slater; father Los Angeles stage actor Michael Hawkins. Made prof. debut at 9 in The Music Man starring Dick Van Dyke, natl. tour, then on B'way Also on B'way in Macbeth, A Christmas Carol, David Copperfield and Merlin. Off-B'way in Landscape of the Body, Between Daylight and Boonville, Somewhere's Better. Also summer theatre. Directed 1992 L.A. prod. of The Laughter Epidemic.
PICTURES: The Legend of Billie Jean (debut, 1985), Twisted, The Name of the Rose, Tucker: The Man and His Dream, Gleaming the Cube, Heathers, The Wizard, Tales from the Dark Side: The Movie, Beyond the Stars (Personal Choice), Young Guns II, Pump Up the Volume, Robin Hood: Prince of Thieves, Mobsters, Star Trek VI: The Undiscovered Country (cameo), Kuffs, FernGully... The Last Rainforest (voice), Where the Day Takes You, Untamed Heart, True Romance, Jimmy Hollywood, Interview With the Vampire, Murder in the First, Broken Arrow, Bed of Roses, Julian Po, Very Bad Things, Hard Rain.
TELEVISION: Series: One Life to Live, Ryan's Hope. Specials: Sherlock Holmes, Pardon Me for Living, The Haunted Mansion Mystery, Cry Wolf, The Edge (Professional Man). Movies: Living Proof: The Hank Williams Jr. Story, Desperate For Love.

SLATER, HELEN
Actress. b. New York, NY, Dec. 19, 1963. Off-B'way: Responsible Parties, Almost Romance.
PICTURES: Supergirl (debut, 1984), The Legend of Billie Jean, Ruthless People, The Secret of My Success, Sticky Fingers, Happy Together, City Slickers, A House in the Hills, Betrayal of the Dove, Lassie, The Steal, The Long Way Home (voice).
TELEVISION: Series: Capital News. Movies: 12:01, Chantilly Lace, Parallel Lives, Toothless, Best Friend for Life.

SLATZER, ROBERT FRANKLIN
Writer, Director, Producer. b. Marion, OH, April 4, 1927. e. Ohio State U., UCLA, 1947. Radio news commentator sports-caster, wrote radio serials; adv. dir., Brush-Moore Newspapers; feature writer, Scripps-Howard Newspapers; adv. exec., The Columbus Dispatch; syn. columnist, NY Journal-American; wrote guest columns for Dorothy Kilgallen; author of western short stories and novels; wrote, dir., prod. industrial films, docs., sports specials and commercials; 1949-51, writer for Grand National Studios Prods, Monogram Pictures, Republic Studios, Eagle-Lion Films; 1951, publicist, Hope Enterprises; pub. dir. Paramount Pictures; 1952, personal mgr. to Marilyn Monroe, Ken Maynard, James Craig, Gail Russell and other stars; 1953, story editor and assoc. prod., Joe Palooka Productions; 1953-54, staff writer Universal Studios, RKO Radio Pictures, MGM,

Columbia and Paramount; 1958, formed Robert F. Slatzer Productions; 1960, exec. in chg. of prod., Jaguar Pictures Corp.; 1963-65, pres., Slatzer Oil & Gas Co.; 1966-67, bd. dir., United Mining & Milling Corp.; 1970-74, exec., Columbia Pictures Corp.; 1974, resumed producing and financing features and television films; 1976, honored as Fellow, Mark Twain Inst.
AUTHOR: *Novels*: Desert Empire, Rose of the Range, Rio, Rawhide Range, The Cowboy and the Heiress, Daphne, Campaign Girl, Scarlet, The Dance Studio Hucksters, Born to be Wild, Single Room Furnished, The West is Still Wild, Gusher, The Young Wildcats. *Biographies*: The Life and Curious Death of Marilyn Monroe, The Life and Legend of Ken Maynard, Who Killed Thelma Todd?, The Duke of Thieves, Bing Crosby—The Hollow Man, Duke: The Life and Times of John Wayne, The Marilyn Files.
PICTURES: White Gold, The Obsessed, Mike and the Heiress, Under Texas Skies, They Came To Kill, Trail of the Mounties, Jungle Goddess, Montana Desperado, Pride of the Blue, Green Grass of Wyoming, The Naked Jungle, Warpaint, Broken Lance, Elephant Walk, South of Death Valley, The Big Gusher, Arctic Flight, The Hellcats, Bigfoot, John Wayne's No Substitute for Victory', Joniko-Eskimo Boy, Operation North Slope, Claws, Don't Go West, Mulefeathers, The Unfinished, Single Room Furnished, Viva Zapata, Inchon.
TELEVISION: The Great Outdoors, Adventures of White Arrow, Let's Go Boating, The Joe Palooka Story, Amos & Andy, I Am the Law, Files of Jeffrey Jones, Fireside Theatre, The Unser Story, Year of Opportunity, The Big Ones, Ken Maynard's West, Where are They Now?, The Groovy Seven, The Untouchables, The Detectives, Wild Wild West, Wagon Train, Playhouse 90, Highway Patrol, David Frost Special, Today Show, ABC News, 20/20, Inside Edition, The Reporters, Current Affair, The Geraldo Show, Hard Copy, Larry King Show, Marilyn and Me, The Marilyn Files.

SLAVIN, GEORGE
Writer. b. Newark, NJ, March 2, 1916. e. Bucknell U., drama, Yale U. Has written over 300 TV episodes & pilots. WGA TV Award. Collected work at U. Wyoming. Received Stanford U, Maxwell Anderson Playwriting Award.
PICTURES: Intrigue, Woman on Pier 13, The Nevadan, Mystery Submarine, Peggy, Red Mountain, City of Bad Men, Weekend with Father, Thunder Bay, Rocket Man, Smoke Signal, Uranium Boom, Desert Sands, The Halliday Brand, Son of Robin Hood, Big House USA, Fighting Stallions.

SLOAN, JOHN R.
Producer. e. Merchiston Castle School, Edinburg, 1932-39; asst. dir. and prod. man. Warners, London, Hollywood; 1939-46, Army.
PICTURES: Sea Devils, The End of the Affair, Port Afrique, Abandon Ship, The Safecracker, Beyond this Place, The Killers of Kilimanjaro, Johnny Nobody, The Reluctant Saint, The Running Man, The Last Command, To Sir With Love, Fragment of Fear, Dad's Army, Lord Jim, No Sex Please, We're British, The Odessa File, High-Ballin', Force 10 From Navarone, The Children's Story.

SLOCOMBE, DOUGLAS
Cinematographer. b. England, Feb. 10, 1913. Former journalist. Filmed the invasion of Poland and Holland. Under contract to Ealing Studios 17 years.
PICTURES: Dead of Night, The Captive Heart, Hue and Cry, The Loves of Joanna Godden, It Always Rains on Sunday, Saraband for Dead Lovers, Kind Hearts and Coronets, Cage of Gold, The Lavender Hill Mob, Mandy, The Man in the White Suit, The Titfield Thunderbolt, Man in the Sky, Ludwig II, Lease on Life, The Smallest Show on Earth, Tread Softly, Stranger, Circus of Horrors, The Young Ones, The Mark, The L-Shaped Room, Freud, The Servant (BAFTA Award), Guns at Batashi, A High Wind in Jamaica, The Blue Max, Promise Her Anything, The Vampire Killers, Fathom, Robbery, Boom, The Lion in Winter, The Italian Job, The Music Lovers, Murphy's War, The Buttercup Chain, Travels With My Aunt (Acad. Award nom.), Jesus Christ Superstar, The Great Gatsby, Rollerball, Hedda, The Sailor Who Fell From Grace With the Sea, Nasty Habits, Julia (Acad. Award nom.), Close Encounters of the Third Kind (co-photog.), Caravans, Lost and Found, The Lady Vanishes, Nijinsky, Raiders of the Lost Ark (Acad. Award nom.), The Pirates of Penzance, Never Say Never Again, Indiana Jones and the Temple of Doom, Water, Lady Jane, Indiana Jones and the Last Crusade.
TELEVISION: Movie: Love Among the Ruins.

SMART, JEAN
Actress. b. Seattle, WA, Sept. 13, 1951. e. Univ. of WA. Member of Oregon Shakespeare Fest, 1975-77; also with Hartford Stage Co., Pittsburgh Public Theatre Co., Intiman Theatre Co.
THEATER: *Regional*: Equus, Much Ado About Nothing, A Moon for the Misbegotten, Terra Nova, Cat's Play, Saint Joan, A History of the American Film, Last Summer at Bluefish Cove (LA Drama Critics Circle, Dramalogue & LA Drama Desk Awards), Mrs. California, Strange Snow. *NY*: Last Summer at Bluefish Cove, Piaf (B'way debut, 1981).

PICTURES: Flashpoint (debut, 1984), Protocol, Fire With Fire, Project X, Mistress, Homeward Bound: The Incredible Journey, The Brady Bunch Movie, Edie & Pen, The Odd Couple II.
TELEVISION: *Series*: Reggie, Teachers Only, Designing Women, High Society, Hey Arnold, Style and Substance. *Movies*: Single Bars Single Women, A Fight for Jenny, A Seduction in Travis County, A Stranger in Town (also co-prod.), The Yarn Princess, The Yearling, A Stranger in Town, Undue Influence. *Specials*: Piaf, Maximum Security, Royal Match, A Palce at the Table.

SMITH, CHARLES MARTIN
Actor, Director. b. Los Angeles, CA, Oct. 30, 1953. e. California State U. Father is animation artist Frank Smith.
PICTURES: The Culpepper Cattle Company (debut, 1972), Fuzz, The Spikes Gang, American Graffiti, Pat Garrett and Billy the Kid, Rafferty and the Gold Dust Twins, No Deposit No Return, The Hazing, The Buddy Holly Story, More American Graffiti, Herbie Goes Bananas, Never Cry Wolf (also co-wrote narration), Starman, Trick or Treat (also dir.), The Untouchables, The Experts, The Hot Spot, Deep Cover, Fifty-Fifty (also dir.), I Love Trouble, Perfect Alibi, Speechless, He Ain't Heavy.
TELEVISION: *Series*: Speed Buggy (voice). *Guest*: The Brady Bunch, Monte Nash, Baretta, Streets of San Francisco, Petrocelli, The Rookies, Grizzly Adams, Twilight Zone, Ray Bradbury Theatre, Outer Limits, L.A. Law, Picket Fences, Northern Exposure, Tales From the Crypt. *Movies*: Go Ask Alice, Law of the Land, Cotton Candy, Boris and Natasha (also dir.), And the Band Played On, Roswell. *Special*: Partners. *Mini-Series*: Streets of Laredo.

SMITH, DAVID R.
Archivist. b. Pasadena, CA, Oct. 13, 1940. e. Pasadena City Coll., A.A., 1960; U. of California, Berkeley, B.A. 1962, MLS 1963. Writer of numerous historical articles. Worked as librarian at Library of Congress, 1963-65 and as reference librarian, UCLA 1965-70 before becoming archivist for The Walt Disney Co. 1970-present. Exec. dir., The Manuscript Society, 1980-; member, Society of CA Archivists, Intl. Animated Film Society (ASIFA), Fellow of the Manuscript Society, 1993. Received service award, ASIFA, and award of distinction, Manuscript Soc, 1983. Co-Author: The Ultimate Disney Trivia Book (1992), Book 2 (1994), Disney A to Z: The Official Encyclopedia (1996), Book 3 (1997).

SMITH, HOWARD K.
News commentator. b. Ferriday, LA, May 12, 1914. e. Tulane U., 1936; Heidelberg U., Germany; Oxford U., Rhodes scholarship. United Press, London, 1939; United Press Bureau, Copenhagen; United Press, Berlin, 1940; joined CBS News, Berlin corr., 1941. Reported on occupied Europe from Switzerland to 1944; covered Nuremberg trials, 1946; ret. to U.S., moderator, commentator or reporter, CBS Reports, Face the Nation, Eyewitness to History, The Great Challenge, numerous news specials (Emmy Award, 1960 for The Population Explosion). Sunday night news analysis. CBS News Washington corr., 1957; chief corr. & mgr., Washington Bureau, 1961; joined, ABC News, Jan. 1962. News and comment, ABC news. Anchorman and commentator, ABC Evening News. Author: Last Train from Berlin, 1942, The State of Europe, 1949. Washington, D.C.—The Story of Our Nation's Capital, 1967, Events Leading Up to My Death —The Life of a 10th Century Reporter, 1996.

SMITH, HY
Executive. b. New York, NY, June 3, 1934. e. Baruch Sch., CCNY, B.B.A. Joined Paramount Pictures 1967, foreign ad.-pub coordinator; 1969, joined United Artists as foreign ad.-pub mgr.; named intl. ad.-pub dir., 1970; named v.p., intl. adv.-pub. 1976; v.p. worldwide adv., publ. & promo., 1978; 1981, named first v.p., adv./pub./promo; 1982, joined Rastar Films as v.p., intl. project director for Annie; 1983, joined United Intl. Pictures as sr. v.p., adv/pub, based in London. 1984, named sr. v.p., mktg. 1995, promoted to exec. v.p., mktg.

SMITH, JACLYN
Actress. b. Houston, TX, Oct. 26, 1947. Started acting while in high school and studied drama and psychology at Trinity U. in San Antonio. Appeared in many commercials as model.
PICTURES: The Adventurers, Bootleggers, Nightkill, Deja Vu.
TELEVISION: *Series*: Charlie's Angels, Christine Cromwell. *Guest*: McCloud, Get Christy Love, The Rookies. *Movies*: Probe (Switch), Charlie's Angels (pilot), Escape From Bogen County, The Users, Jacqueline Bouvier Kennedy, Rage of Angels, The Night They Saved Christmas, Sentimental Journey, Florence Nightingale, Rage of Angels: The Story Continues, Windmills of the Gods, The Bourne Identity, Settle the Score, Danielle Steel's Kaleidoscope, Lies Before Kisses, The Rape of Dr. Willis, In the Arms of a Killer, Nightmare in the Daylight, Love Can Be Murder, Cries Unheard: The Donna Yalich Story, Danielle Steel's Family Album.

SMITH, JAN
Eexecutive. Vice President, Disney Publishing & Mouseworks.

SMITH, JOSEPH P.
Executive. b. Brooklyn, NY, March 28, 1921. e. Columbia U. Started career Wall Street; joined RKO Radio Pictures, served in sales and managerial posts; exec. v.p., Lippert Productions, Hollywood; v.p., Telepictures, Inc.; formed and pres., Cinema-Vue Corp.; pres., Pathe Pictures, Inc., Pathe News, Inc.

SMITH, KURTWOOD
Actor. b. New Lisbon, WI, July 3, 1943. e. B.A. San Jose (1966), M.F.A. Stanford (1969). Starred in Oscar-nominated short 12:01 P.M. THEATER: Plymouth Rock, The Price, Faces by Chekhov, Familiar Faces, Enemy of the People, The Debutante Ball (all in Calif.), The Lucky Spot (Williamston), Signature (Poughkeepsie), Hamlet, Taming of the Shrew, and over 20 other Shakespeare productions in CA.
PICTURES: Roadie (debut, 1980), Zoot Suit, Going Berserk, Staying Alive, Flashpoint, Robocop, Rambo III, True Believer, Dead Poets Society, Heart of Dixie, Quick Change, Oscar, Company Business, Star Trek VI: The Undiscovered Country, Shadows and Fog, The Crush, Heart and Souls, Fortress, Boxing Helena, Under Siege 2: Dark Territory, Last of the Dogmen, To Die For, Broken Arrow, A Time to Kill, Citizen Ruth, Precious, Shelter, Prefontaine.
TELEVISION: Series: The Renegades, The New Adventures of Beans Baxter, Big Wave Dave's. Movies: Murder in Texas, Missing Pieces, The Midnight Hour, International Airport, Deadly Messages, The Christmas Gift, Doorways, While Justice Sleeps. Mini-Series: North and South Book II, The Nightmare Years (Ace Award nom.). Guest: Stir Crazy, Stingray, Newhart, 21 Jump Street, It's Garry Shandling's Show, The Famous Teddy Z, Picket Fences.

SMITH, LANE
Actor. b. Memphis, TN, April 29.
THEATER: NY: Visions of Kerouac, Brechtesgarten, Glengarry Glen Ross (Drama Desk Award).
PICTURES: Network, Honeysuckle Rose, Prince of the City, Frances, Purple Hearts, Red Dawn, Places in the Heart, Weeds, Prison, Race for Glory, Air America, My Cousin Vinny, The Mighty Ducks, The Distinguished Gentleman, Son-in-Law, The Scout, Lost & Found.
TELEVISION: Series: V, Kay O'Brien, Good Sports, Good and Evil. Mini-Series: Chiefs, From the Earth to the Moon. Movies: A Death in Canaan, Crash, The Solitary Man, Disaster on the Coastliner, City in Fear, Gideon's Trumpet, A Rumor of War, The Georgia Peaches, Mark I Love You, Dark Night of the Scarecrow, Prime Suspect, Thou Shalt Not Kill, Special Bulletin, Something About Amelia, Dress Gray, The Final Days, False Arrest, Duplicates, Alien Nation: The Udara Legacy. Specials: Displaced Person, Member of the Wedding.

SMITH, DAME MAGGIE
D.B.E. C.B.E. Actress. b. Ilford, England, Dec. 28, 1934. Early career Oxford Playhouse. With the Old Vic 1959-60. Also with Stratford Ontario Shakespeare Fest. 1975-78, & 1980. Received C.B.E. 1970; D.B.E., 1990.
THEATER: Twelfth Night (debut, 1952), Cakes and Ale, New Faces of 1956 (NY debut, as comedienne), Share My Lettuce, The Stepmother, What Every Woman Knows, Rhinoceros, The Rehearsal, The Private Ear, The Public Eye, Mary Mary, The Recruiting Officer, Othello, The Master Builder, Hay Fever, Much Ado About Nothing, Black Comedy, Miss Julie, Trelawney of the Wells, The Beaux Stratagem, The Three Sisters, Hedda Gabler, Design for Living (L.A.), Private Lives (London & NY), Slap, Peter Pan, As You Like It, Macbeth, Night and Day (London & NY), Virginia, Way of the World, Lettice and Lovage (London & NY, Tony Award), The Importance of Being Earnest, Three Tall Women.
PICTURES: Nowhere to Go (debut, 1958), Go to Blazes, The V.I.P.s, The Pumpkin Eater, Young Cassidy, Othello, The Honey Pot, Hot Millions, The Prime of Miss Jean Brodie (Acad. Award, BAFTA Award, 1969), Oh! What a Lovely War, Travels With My Aunt, Love and Pain and the Whole Damn Thing, Murder by Death, Death on the Nile, California Suite (Acad. Award, best supporting actress, 1978), Clash of the Titans, Quartet, Evil Under the Sun, The Missionary, Better Late Than Never, A Private Function (BAFTA Award, 1985), Lily in Love, A Room with a View, The Lonely Passion of Judith Hearne, Romeo-Juliet (voice), Hook, Sister Act, The Secret Garden, Sister Act 2: Back in the Habit, Richard III, Washington Square.
TELEVISION: Much Ado About Nothing, Man and Superman, On Approval, Home and Beauty, Mrs. Silly, Bed Among the Lentils, Memento Mori, Suddenly Last Summer.

SMITH, ROGER
Actor, Producer. b. South Gate, CA, Dec. 18, 1932. m. actress-performer Ann Margret. e. U. of Arizona. Started career at age 7, one of the Meglin Kiddies, appearing at the Mayan Theater, Wilshire, Ebell. Sings, composes, American folk songs. Producer: Ann-Margret cabaret and theater shows.

PICTURES: No Time to Be Young, Crash Landing, Operation Madball, Man of a Thousand Faces, Never Steal Anything Small, Auntie Mame, Rogues Gallery.
TELEVISION: The Horace Heidt Show, Ted Mack Original Amateur Hour, 77 Sunset Strip (series), writer, ABC-TV. Co-prod.: Homestead.

SMITH, WILL
Actor, Singer. b. Philadelphia, PA, Sept. 25, 1968. Teamed with musician Jeff Townes as rap duo D.J. Jazzy Jeff & the Fresh Prince. Albums: Rock the House, He's the DJ I'm the Rapper, And in This Corner, Homebase. Recipient of 2 Grammy Awards.
PICTURES: Where the Day Takes You (debut, 1992), Made in America, Six Degress of Separation, Bad Boys, Independence Day, Men in Black, Enemy of the State.
TELEVISION: Series: Fresh Prince of Bel Air (also co-exec. prod.).

SMITH, WILLIAM
Actor. b. Columbia, MO, March 24, 1932. e. Syracuse, U., BA; UCLA, MA.
PICTURES: Darker Than Amber, C.C. and Company, The Losers, Run, Angel, Run, Blood and Guts, Seven, Fast Company, No Knife, Twilight's Last Gleaming, The Frisco Kid, Any Which Way You Can, Rumble Fish, Red Dawn, Eye of the Tiger, Commando Squad, Moon in Scorpio, Hell Comes to Frogtown, Maniac Cop, Red Nights, Nam, B.O.R.N., Action U.S.A., Deadly Breed, Evil Altar, Jungle Assault, L.A. Vice, Slow Burn, Terror in Beverly Hills, Hell on the Battleground, Forgotten Heroes, Instant Karma, Empire of Ash, Emperor of the Bronx, Rock n' Roll Cops, Broken Vessels.
TELEVISION: Mini-Series: Rich Man Poor Man. Series: Laredo, Rich Man Poor Man: Book II. Series: Laredo, Rich Man Poor Man: Book II, Hawaii 5-0, Wildside. Movies: The Over-the-Hill Gang, Crowhaven Farm, The Rockford Files (pilot), The Sex Symbol, Death Among Friends, Manhunter, The Rebels, Wild Times, The Jerk Too.

SMITROVICH, BILL
Actor. b. Bridgeport, CT, May 16, 1947. e. Univ. of Bridgeport, Smith Col. Studied acting at Actors and Directors Lab.
THEATER: B'way: The American Clock. Off-B'way: Never Say Die, Frankie and Johnny in the Claire de Lune, Seks. Regional: Requeim for a Heavyweight, Food from Trash, Of Mice and Men, The Love Suicide at Schofield Barracks.
PICTURES: A Little Sex, Without a Trace, Splash, Maria's Lovers, Key Exchange, Silver Bullet, Band of the Hand, Manhunter, A Killing Affair, Her Alibi, Renegades, Crazy People, Bodily Harm, The Phantom, The Trigger Effect, Independence Day, Air Force One.
TELEVISION: Series: Crime Story, Life Goes On. Guest: Miami Vice, Millenium, L.A. Medical. Movies: Born Beautiful, Muggable Mary, Gregory K, Labor of Love: The Arlette Schweitzer Story, Children of the Dark, Texas Justice.

SMITS, JIMMY
Actor. b. New York, NY, July 9, 1955. e. Brooklyn Coll., B.A.; Cornell U., M.F.A. Worked as community organizer before acting with NY Shakespeare Fest. Public Theater.
THEATER: Hamlet (NY Shakespeare Fest., 1983), Little Victories, Buck, The Ballad of Soapy Smith, Death and the Maiden.
PICTURES: Running Scared (debut, 1986), The Believers, Old Gringo, Vital Signs, Fires Within, Switch, Gross Misconduct, My Family/Mi Familia, Marshal Law, Murder in Mind.
TELEVISION: Series: L.A. Law (Emmy Award, 1990), NYPD Blue (Golden Globe, 1996). Pilot: Miami Vice. Movies: Rockabye, The Highwayman, Dangerous Affection, Glitz, The Broken Cord, The Tommyknockers, The Cisco Kid, Solomon and Sheba, The Last Word. Specials: The Other Side of the Border (narrator), Happily Ever After Fairy Tales: Cinderella, Hispanic Americans: The New Frontier (host), The Story of the Western.

SMOTHERS BROTHERS
Comedians, Singers.
SMOTHERS, DICK: b. New York, NY, Nov. 20, 1939. e. San Jose State College. Films: The Silver Bears (debut, 1978), Casino.
SMOTHERS, TOM: b. New York, NY, Feb. 2, 1937. e. San Jose State College. In films Get to Know Your Rabbit, The Silver Bears, There Goes the Bride, Serial, Pandemonium.
Began career as coffeehouse folk singers with a bit of comic banter mixed in. After success at some of hipper West Coast clubs, appeared on Jack Paar's Tonight Show, The Jack Benny Show and as regulars on Steve Allen's show, 1961. 1962-65 had a series of popular albums. After starring in a situation comedy show, they hosted their own variety program. On B'way in musical I Love My Wife. Both appeared in film Speed Zone.
TELEVISION: Series: The Steve Allen Show (1961), The Smothers Brothers Show (1965-66), The Smothers Brothers Comedy Hour (1967-69), The Smothers Brothers Show (1970), The Smothers Brothers Show (1975), Fitz and Bones, The Smothers Brothers Comedy Hour. Specials: The Smothers Brothers Reunion.

SNELL, PETER R. E.
Producer. b. Nov. 17, 1941. Entered industry 1967. Appt. head of prod. and man. dir. British Lion 1973. Joined Robert Stigwood group 1975. Returned to indep. prod., 1978; Hennessy. Appt. chief exec., Britannic Film & Television Ltd. 1985, purchased British Lion Film Prods., Ltd. from Thorn/EMI 1986-87. 1988: chmn. and chief executive British Lion.
PICTURES: Prod.: Winters Tale, Some May Live, A Month in the Country, Carnaby 68, Subterfuge, Julius Caesar, Goodbye Gemini, Antony and Cleopatra, The Wicker Man, Hennessy, Bear Island, Mother Lode, Lady Jane, Turtle Diary, A Prayer for the Dying.
TELEVISION: Exec. Prod.: A Man For All Seasons, Tears in the Rain, Treasure Island, The Crucifer of Blood. Prod.: Death Train, Nightwatch.

SNIDER, STACEY
Executive. Co-President of production, Universal Pictures.

SNIPES, WESLEY
Actor. b. Bronx, NY, July 31, 1962. e. SUNY/Purchase. Performed with puppet theatre group called Struttin Street Stuff before landing NY stage work. Appeared in Michael Jackson video Bad.
PICTURES: Wildcats (debut, 1986), Streets of Gold, Critical Condition, Major League, Mo' Better Blues, King of New York, New Jack City, Jungle Fever, White Men Can't Jump, The Waterdance, Passenger 57, Boiling Point, Rising Sun, Demolition Man, Sugar Hill, Drop Zone, To Wong Foo—Thanks for Everything—Julie Newmar, Money Train, Waiting to Exhale, The Fan, Murder at 1600.
TELEVISION: Series: H.E.L.P. Special: Vietnam War Stories (ACE Award, 1989). Guest: Miami Vice.
THEATER: B'way: The Boys of Winter, Death and the King's Horsemen, Execution of Justice.

SNODGRESS, CARRIE
Actress. b. Chicago, IL, Oct 27, 1945. e. Northern Illinois U. and M.A. degree from the Goodman Theatre. Plays include All Way Home, Oh What a Lovely War, Caesar and Cleopatra and Tartuffe (Sarah Siddons Award, 1966), The Price, Vanities, The Curse of the Starving Class.
PICTURES: Rabbit Run (debut, 1970), Diary of a Mad Housewife (Acad. Award nom.), The Fury, The Attic, Homework, Trick or Treats, A Night in Heaven, Pale Rider, Rainy Day Friends, Murphy's Law, Blueberry Hill, The Chill Factor, Nowhere to Run, Across the Tracks, The Ballad of Little Jo, 8 Seconds, Blue Sky, White Man's Burden.
TELEVISION: Movies: The Whole World Is Watching, Silent Night Lonely Night, The Impatient Heart, Love's Dark Ride, Fast Friends, The Solitary Man, Nadia, The Rose and the Jackal, Woman With a Past, Rise & Walk: The Dennis Byrd Story. Guest: The Outsider, The Virginian, Judd for the Defense, Medical Center, Marcus Welby, M.D.

SNOW, MARK
Composer. b. Brooklyn, NY, 1946. e. Juilliard School of Music, 1968. As co-founder and member of New York Rock 'n' Roll Ensemble, appeared with the Boston Pops, at Carnegie Hall concerts and on the college circuit in the 1960s and 1970s.
PICTURES: Skateboard, Something Short of Paradise, High Risk, Jake Speed, Born to Be Wild.
TELEVISION: Series: The Rookies, Starsky and Hutch, The Gemini Man, Family, The San Pedro Beach Bums, The Love Boat, The Next Step Beyond, Vega$, Hart to Hart, When the Whistle Blows, Dynasty, Falcon Crest, Strike Force, Cagney and Lacey, T.J. Hooker, The Family Tree, Lottery!, Double Trouble, Crazy Like a Fox, Hometown, The X-Files, Millenium, La Femme Nikita. Miniseries: Blood and Orchids, Night Sins. Movies: The Boy in the Plastic Bubble, Overboard, The Return of the Mod Squad, Angel City, Games Mother Never Taught You, John Steinbeck's Winter of Our Discontent, Packin' It In, I Married a Centerfold, Something About Amelia, Challenge of a Lifetime, California Girls, I Dream Of Jeannie: Fifteen Years Later, Not My Kid, The Lady From Yesterday, Beverly Hills Cowgirl Blues, Acceptable Risks, News at Eleven, The Girl Who Spelled Freedom (Emmy nom.), Murder By the Book, A Hobo's Christmas, The Father Clements Story, Still Crazy Like a Fox, Cracked Up, Roman Holiday, Pals, Murder Ordained, Louis L'Amour's Down the Long Hills, The Saint, The Return of Ben Casey, Bluegrass, Alone in the Neon Jungle, Those She Left Behind, Stuck With Each Other, Settle the Score, Archie: To Riverdale and Back Again, Child of the Night, Dead Reckoning, Follow Your Heart, The Girl Who Came Between Them, The Little Kidnappers, Miracle Landing, When He's Not a Stranger, Opposites Attract, Crash: The Mystery of Flight 1501, In the Line of Duty, The Marla Hanson Story, A Woman Scorned: The Betty Broderick Story, Highway Heartbreaker, Deliver Them From Evil: The Taking of Alta View, An American Story, Telling Secrets, The Man With 3 Wives, Born Too Soon, In the Line of Duty: Ambush in Waco, Precious Victims, Scattered Dreams: The Kathryn Messenger Story, In the Line of Duty: The Price of Heaven, Murder Between Friends, Moment of Truth: Cradle of Conspiracy, Substitute Wife, Down Out and Dangerous, Cloned, The Day Lincoln Was Shot, The X-Files: Fight the Future. Specials: Day-to-Day Affairs, Vietnam War Story.

SNYDER, BRUCE M.
Executive. b. New York, NY, July 1, 1946. e. Queens Coll. Began entertainment career with Paramount Pictures as a booker in San Francisco, 1968-69. Paramount sales, NY 1969-76. Became eastern div. mgr., 20th century Fox, 1976-80. New York sales mgr., American Cinema Releasing, 1980-82. Eastern div. mgr., Embassy Pictures, 1982-83. Eastern div. mgr., TriStar Pictures, 1984-85. General sales mgr., 20th Century Fox, 1985-89. Pres., domestic distribution, 20th Century Fox, 1989-present.

SNYDER, TOM
Newscaster, Host. b. Milwaukee, WI, May 12, 1936. e. Marquette U. First job in news dept. of WRIT, Milwaukee. Subsequently with WSAV-TV, Savannah; WAII-TV, Atlanta; KTLA-TV, Los Angeles; and KYW-TV, Philadelphia, before moving to KNBC in L.A. in 1970 as anchorman for weeknight newscast. Named host of NBC-TV's Tomorrow program in 1973 (Emmy Award), moved to NY in 1974, as anchorman of one-hour segment of NewsCenter 4. 1975, inaugurated the NBC News Update, one-minute weeknight prime time news spot. Host for Tomorrow talk show, Tom Snyder Show (ABC Radio), The Late Late Show With Tom Snyder.

SOADY, WILLIAM C.
Executive. b. Toronto, Canada, Oct. 7, 1943. Career with Universal Pictures started in 1970 when named Toronto branch mgr.; promoted to v.p. & gen. sls. mgr. of Universal Film (Canada) in 1971. Promoted to v.p. & gen. sls. mgr., Universal Pictures, 1981, in NY relocating to L.A. later that year. 1983 named pres. of Universal Pictures Distribution, new domestic dist. div. of Universal; resigned, 1988. Named exec. v.p. distrib., Tri-Star Pictures, 1988; pres. of distrib., 1992. Named pres. & CEO of Showscan Entertainment Inc. in 1994. Became pres. of distrib. for Polygram Films in 1997.

SOAMES, RICHARD
Executive. b. London, England, June 6, 1936. Joined Film Finances Ltd. 1972; Appt. director Film Finances Ltd., 1977: Appt. man. dir. 1979. Appt. pres. Film Finances Canada Ltd. 1982: Appt. pres., Film Finances Inc. Also formed Doric Prods. Inc.
PICTURES: The Boss's Wife, The Principal, Honey I Shrunk the Kids, Tap.

SODERBERGH, STEVEN
Director, Writer, Editor. b. Atlanta, GA, Jan. 14, 1963. First major professional job was directing concert film for rock group Yes for Grammy-nominated video, 1986.
PICTURES: Director-Editor: Sex Lies and Videotape (debut, 1989; also s.p.; Cannes Fest. Palme d'Or Award; Acad. Award nom. for s.p.), Kafka, King of the Hill (also s.p.), The Underneath (also s.p.), Schizopolis (also actor), Gray's Anatomy, Out of Sight. Producer: Suture (exec. prod.), The Day Trippers, Pleasantville.
TELEVISION: Series: Fallen Angels (The Quiet Room).

SOKOLOW, DIANE
Executive. b. New York, NY. e. Temple U. m. Mel Sokolow. 1975, v.p., East Coast operations, for Lorimar; with Warner Bros. 1977-81; served as v.p. of East Coast production. Left to form The Sokolow Co. with husband, Mel, to produce films. 1982, returned to WB as v.p., East Coast prod. 1984, joined Motown Prods. as exec. v.p.; producer, MGM-UA 1986-87. Currently S.V.P., East Coast Production, Phoenix Pictures.
PICTURE: My Son's Brother (co-prod.).
TELEVISION: Exec. Prod.: Miles from Nowhere, Trial: The Price of Passion, Lady Against the Odds, Fallen Champ, Silent Cries.

SOLO, ROBERT H.
Producer. b. Waterbury, CT, Dec. 4, 1932. e. U. of Connecticut, BA. Early career as agent with Ashley-Famous; later production as exec. asst. to Jack Warner and Walter MacEwen at Warner Bros. 1971, named WB v.p., foreign production 1974, named exec. v.p., prod. at Burbank Studio. Now indep. prod.
PICTURES: Scrooge, The Devils (co-prod.), Invasion of the Body Snatchers, The Awakening, I the Jury, Bad Boys, Colors, Above the Law (exec. prod.), Winter People, Blue Sky, Car 54 Where Are You?, Body Snatchers.

SOLONDZ, TODD
Director, Producer, Writer. b. Newark, NJ. e. NYU Film Sch. After first feature film release, left filmmaking to teach English as a Second Language. Returned with Welcome to the Dollhouse.
PICTURES: Feelings (NYU short), Babysitter (NYU short), Schatt's Last Shot (NYU short), Fear Anxiety and Depression, Married to the Mob (actor only), Welcome to the Dollhouse (Jury Prize, Sundance Film Fest.), Happiness. Actor: As Good as It Gets.
TELEVISION: How I Became a Leading Artistic Figure in New York City's East Village Cultural Landscape (short for Saturday Night Live).

SOLT, ANDREW W.
Producer, Writer, Director. b. London, England, December 13, 1947. e. UCLA.
PICTURES: Imagine: John Lennon, This is Elvis, It Came From Hollywood.
TELEVISION: Honeymooners' Reunion, The Muppets... A Celebration of 30 Years, Cousteau's Mississippi, Happy Birthday Donald Duck, America Censored, Remembering Marilyn, Great Moments in Disney Animation, ET & Friends, Disney's DTV, Heroes of Rock 'n Roll, Bob Hope's Christmas Tours, Disney Goes To The Oscars, Cousteau: Oasis In Space (series), Cousteau: Odyssey, Best of the Ed Sullivan Show (4 specials), The History of Rock 'n' Roll, Sesame Street's 25th Birthday Special, Grammy's Greatest Moments, TV Guide's 40th Anniversary Special, 25x5: The Continuing Adventures of the Rolling Stones, Andy Griffith Show Reunion, Cousteau: Search for Atlantis I&II, All My Children 25th Anniversary Special, Hunt for Amazing Treasure, Great Moments in Disney Animation.

SOMERS, SUZANNE
Actress. r.n. Suzanne Mahoney. b. San Bruno, CA, Oct. 16, 1946. e. Lone Mountain Sch., San Francisco Coll. for Women. Pursued modeling career; worked as regular on Mantrap, syndicated talk show. Did summer stock and theatrical films. Author: Touch Me Again, Keeping Secrets, Some People Live More Than Others, Wednesday's Children: Adult Survivors of Abuse Speak Out.
PICTURES: Bullitt (debut, 1968), Daddy's Gone A-Hunting, Fools, American Graffiti, Magnum Force, Yesterday's Hero, Nothing Personal, Serial Mom.
TELEVISION: Series: Three's Company, She's the Sheriff, Step by Step, The Suzanne Somers Show (talk). Guest: One Day at a Time, Lotsa Luck, The Rockford Files, Starsky & Hutch, The Rich Little Show, Battle of the Network Stars, Love Boat. Movies: Sky Heist, It Happened at Lakewood Manor (Ants), Happily Ever After, Zuma Beach, Rich Men Single Women, Keeping Secrets (also exec. prod.), Exclusive (also co-exec. prod), Seduced by Evil. Mini-Series: Hollywood Wives. Specials: Us Against the World, Suzanne, Suzanne Somers Presents: Showtime's Triple Crown of Comedy, Disney's Totally Minnie.

SOMMER, ELKE
Actress. r.n. Elke Schletz. b. Berlin, Germany, Nov. 5, 1940. Entered films in Germany, 1958.
PICTURES: Das Totenschiff (debut, 1958), Lampenfieber, The Day It Rained, Heaven and Cupid, Love the Italian Way, Why Bother to Knock? (English-language debut, 1961), Daniela by Night, Violent Ecstasy, Auf Wiedersehen, Cafe Oriental, Bahia de Palma, The Victors, Island of Desire, The Prize, Frontier Hellcat, Le Bambole (The Dolls), A Shot in the Dark, The Art of Love, The Money Trap, The Corrupt Ones, The Oscar, Boy Did I Get a Wrong Number, The Venetian Affair, Deadlier Than the Male, The Wicked Dreams of Paula Schultz, The Invincible Six, They Came to Rob Las Vegas, The Wrecking Crew, Baron Blood, Zeppelin, Percy, It's Not the Size That Counts (Percy's Progress), Ten Little Indians, The Swiss Conspiracy, Carry on Behind, House of Exorcism (Lisa and the Devil), Das Netz, The Astral Factor (Invisible Strangler), Thoroughbreds, I Miss You—Hugs and Kisses, The Prisoner of Zenda, A Nightingale Sang in Berkeley Square, The Double McGuffin, Exit Sunset Blvd., The Man in Pyjamas, Lily in Love, Death Stone, Himmelsheim, Neat and Tidy, Severed Ties.
TELEVISION: Movies: Probe, Stunt Seven, The Top of the Hill, Inside the Third Reich, Jenny's War, Anastasia: The Mystery of Anya. Mini-Series: Peter the Great.

SOMMER, JOSEF
Actor. b. Greifswald, Germany, June 26, 1934. Raised in North Carolina. e. Carnegie-Mellon U. Studied at American Shakespeare Festival in Stratford, CT, 1962-64. US Army, 1958-60. NY stage debut in Othello, 1970.
PICTURES: Dirty Harry (debut, 1971), Man on a Swing, The Front, Close Encounters of the Third Kind, Oliver's Story, Hide in Plain Sight, Absence of Malice, Reds, Rollover, Hanky Panky, Still of the Night, Sophie's Choice (narrator), Independence Day, Silkwood, Iceman, Witness, D.A.R.Y.L., Target, The Rosary Murders, Chances Are, Dracula's Widow, Forced March, Bloodhounds of Broadway, Shadows and Fog, The Mighty Ducks, Malice, Cultivating Charlie, Nobody's Fool, Strange Days, Moonlight & Valentino, The Chamber, The Proposition.
TELEVISION: Series: Hothouse, Under Cover. Specials: Morning Becomes Electra, The Scarlet Letter, Saigon. Movies: Too Far to Go, Doctor Franken, The Henderson Monster, Sparkling Cyanide, The Betty Ford Story, A Special Friendship, Bridge to Silence, The Bionic Showdown: The Six Million Dollar Man and the Bionic Woman, Money Power Murder, Spy Games, An American Story, Citizen Cohn, Hostages, The Enemy Within, Don't Drink the Water, The Minutes, Kansas, Letter to My Killer, Hidden in America, Mistrial, The Widenet. Mini-Series: The Kennedys of Massachusetts, A Woman Named Jackie.

SONDHEIM, STEPHEN
Composer, Lyricist. b. New York, NY, March 22, 1930. e. Williams Coll. Writer for Topper TV series, 1953. Wrote incidental music for The Girls of Summer (1956), Invitation to a March (1961), Twigs (1971). Winner of 6 Grammy Awards: Cast Albums 1970, 1973, 1979, 1984, 1988 and song of the year 1975. Named Visiting Prof. of Contemporary Theater, Oxford U. 1990.
THEATER: Lyrics only: West Side Story, Gypsy, Do I Hear a Waltz? Music and lyrics: A Funny Thing Happened on the Way to the Forum, Anyone Can Whistle, Company (Tony Award, 1971), Follies (Tony Award, 1972), A Little Night Music (Tony Award, 1973), The Frogs, Candide (new lyrics for revival), Pacific Overtures, Sweeney Todd, (Tony Award, 1979), Merrily We Roll Along, Sunday in the Park with George (Pulitzer Prize, 1985), Into the Woods (Tony Award, 1988), Assassins, Passion (Tony Award, 1994). Theater anthologies of his songs: Side By Side By Sondheim; Marry Me a Little, You're Gonna Love Tomorrow, Putting It Together.Play: Getting Away With Murder.
PICTURES: West Side Story (lyrics), Gypsy (lyrics), A Funny Thing Happened on the Way to the Forum (music, lyrics), The Last of Sheila (s.p.), Stavisky (score), A Little Night Music (music, lyrics), Reds (score), Dick Tracy (music, lyrics; Acad. Award for best song: Sooner or Later, 1990).
TELEVISION: Special: Evening Primrose (music, lyrics; ABC Stage '67).

SONNENFELD, BARRY
Director, Cinematographer. b. 1953. Received Emmy Award for photography on series Out of Step.
PICTURES: Cinematographer: Blood Simple (debut, 1984), Compromising Positions, Raising Arizona, Three O'Clock High, Throw Momma From the Train, Big, When Harry Met Sally..., Miller's Crossing, Misery. Director: The Addams Family (debut, 1991), For Love or Money (also co-prod.), Addams Family Values (also cameo), Get Shorty (also exec. prod.), Men in Black., The Wild Wild West.
TELEVISION: Movies: Doubletake, Welcome Home Bobby, Classified Love..

SORVINO, MIRA
Actress. b. Tenafly, NJ, 1968. Father is actor Paul Sorvino. e. Harvard U., A.B., 1990.
PICTURES: Amongst Friends (also assoc. prod.), Quiz Show, Parallel Lives, Barcelona, Tarantella, Sweet Nothing, Mighty Aphrodite (Acad. Award, Golden Globe), The Dutch Master (short), The Second Greatest Story Ever Told (short), Blue in the Face, Tales of Erotica, New York Cop, Beautiful Girls, Woody Allen Fall Project, Romy and Michele's High School Reunion, The Replacement Killers, Mimic, The Replacement Killers, Too Tired to Die, Lulu on the Bridge, Free Money, At First Sight, Joan of Arc: The Virgin Warrior.
TELEVISION: Movies: Norma Jean and Marilyn, Jake's Women. Series: Swans Crossing. Mini-series: The Buccaneers.

SORVINO, PAUL
Actor. b. New York, NY, 1939. Daughter is actress Mira Sorvino.
THEATER: Bajour, An American Millionaire, The Mating Dance, King Lear, That Championship Season, Marlon Brando Sat Right Here.
PICTURES: Where's Poppa? (debut, 1970), The Panic in Needle Park, Made for Each Other, A Touch of Class, The Day of the Dolphin, The Gambler, Shoot It Black Shoot It Blue, I Will I Will... For Now, Oh God, Bloodbrothers, Slow Dancing in the Big City, The Brink's Job, Lost and Found, Cruising, Reds, I The Jury, That Championship Season, Off the Wall, Very Close Quarters, Turk 182, The Stuff, A Fine Mess, Vasectomy, Dick Tracy, GoodFellas, The Rocketeer, Life in the Food Chain (Age Isn't Everything), The Firm, Nixon, Romeo and Juliet, Money Talks.
TELEVISION: Series: We'll Get By, Bert D'Angelo: Superstar, The Oldest Rookie, Law and Order. Mini-Series: Seventh Avenue, Chiefs. Movies: Tell Me Where It Hurts, It Couldn't Happen to a Nicer Guy, Dummy, A Question of Honor, My Mother's Secret Life, With Intent to Kill, Surviving, Don't Touch My Daughter, The Case of the Wicked Wives, Parallel Lives, Without Consent. Guest: Moonlighting, Murder She Wrote. Special: The Last Mile.

SOTHERN, ANN
Actress. r.n. Harriet Lake. b. Valley City, ND, Jan. 22, 1909. e. Washington U. p. Annette Yde-Lake, opera singer. In m.p. since 1927. Star of 10 Maisie movies in series from 1939-47. Has recently become noted painter.
PICTURES: Broadway Nights (debut in bit part, 1927), Hearts in Exile, The Show of Shows, Hold Everything, Whoopee, Doughboys, Broadway Through a Keyhole, Let's Fall in Love, Melody in Spring, The Party's Over, The Hellcat, Blind Date, Kid Millions, Folies Bergere, Eight Bells, Hooray for Love, The Girl Friend, Grand Exit, You May Be Next, Hell Ship Morgan, Don't Gamble With Love, My American Wife, Walking on Air, The Smartest Girl in Town, Dangerous Number, Fifty Roads to Town,

There Goes My Girl, Super Sleuth, Danger: Love at Work, There Goes the Groom, She's Got Everything, Trade Winds, Hotel For Women, Maisie (and subsequent series of 9 other films), Fast and Furious, Joe and Ethel Turp Call on the President, Brother Orchid, Dulcy, Lady Be Good, Panama Hattie, Cry Havoc, Thousands Cheer, Three Hearts for Julia, April Showers, Words and Music, The Judge Steps Out, A Letter to Three Wives, Shadow on the Wall, Nancy Goes to Rio, The Blue Gardenia, Lady in a Cage, The Best Man, Sylvia, Chubasco, The Killing Kind, Golden Needles, Crazy Mama, The Manitou, The Little Dragons, The Whales of August (Acad. Award. nom).
TELEVISION: Series: Private Secretary, The Ann Sothern Show, My Mother The Car (voice of the car). Movies: The Outsider, Congratulations It's a Boy, A Death of Innocence, The Weekend Nun, The Great Man's Whiskers, A Letter to Three Wives. Mini-Series: Captains and the Kings.

SOUL, DAVID
Actor. r.n. David Solberg. b. Chicago, IL, Aug. 28, 1943.
PICTURES: Johnny Got His Gun, Magnum Force, Dog Pound Shuffle, The Hanoi Hilton, Appointment with Death, Pentathalon.
TELEVISION: Series: Here Come the Brides, Owen Marshall-Counselor at Law, Starsky and Hutch, Casablanca, Yellow Rose, Unsub. Movies: The Disappearance of Flight 412, Starsky and Hutch (pilot), Little Ladies of the Night, Salem's Lot, Swan Song (also co-prod.), Rage, Homeward Bound, The Manions of America, World War III, Through Naked Eyes, The Fifth Missile, Harry's Hong Kong, In the Line of Duty: The FBI Murders, Prime Target, So Proudly We Hail, Bride in Black, A Cry in the Wild, The Taking of Peggy Ann, Perry Mason: The Case of the Fatal Framing, Grave Secrets: The Legacy of Hilltop Drive.

SPACEK, SISSY
Actress. r.n. Mary Elizabeth Spacek. b. Quitman, TX, Dec. 25, 1949. m. director Jack Fisk. Cousin of actor Rip Torn. Attended acting classes in New York under Lee Strasberg. Had bit role in Andy Warhol's Trash. Worked as set decorator on films Death Game, Phantom of the Paradise.
PICTURES: Prime Cut (debut, 1972), Ginger in the Morning, Badlands, Carrie, Welcome to L.A., 3 Women, Heart Beat, Coal Miner's Daughter (Acad. Award, 1980), Raggedy Man, Missing, The Man With Two Brains (voice), The River, Marie, Violets Are Blue, 'night Mother, Crimes of the Heart, The Long Walk Home, JFK, Hard Promises, Trading Mom, The Grass Harp, Affliction, Blast from the Past.
TELEVISION: Movies: The Girls of Huntington House, The Migrants, Katherine, A Private Matter, The Good Old Boys, If These Walls Could Talk. Special: Verna: USO Girl. Guest: The Rookies, The Waltons.

SPACEY, KEVIN
Actor. b. South Orange, NJ, July 26, 1959. Raised in southern CA. e. L.A. Valley Coll., appearing in stage productions as well as stand-up comedy clubs, before attending Juilliard Sch. of Drama. Has appeared in numerous regional and repertory productions including Kennedy Center (The Seagull), Williamstown Theatre Fest. and Seattle Rep. Theatre, and with New York Shakespeare Fest.
THEATER: Henry IV Part I, The Robbers, Barbarians, Ghosts, Hurlyburly, Long Day's Journey into Night, National Anthems, Lost in Yonkers (Tony Award, 1991), Playland.
PICTURES: Heartburn (debut, 1986), Rocket Gibraltar, Working Girl, See No Evil Hear No Evil, Dad, A Show of Force, Henry and June, Glengarry Glen Ross, Consenting Adults, Iron Will, The Ref, Outbreak, Swimming With Sharks (also co-prod.), The Usual Suspects (Acad. Award, Chicago Film Critics Award), Seven, Albino Alligator (dir.), A Time to Kill, Looking for Richard, L.A. Confidential, Midnight in the Garden of Good and Evil, Hurly-burly, The Negotiator, A Bug's Life.
TELEVISION: Specials: Long Day's Journey into Night, Darrow, Steve McQueen: The King of Cool. Movies: The Murder of Mary Phagan, Fall from Grace, When You Remember Me, Doomsday Gun. Series: Wiseguy, Tribeca. Guest: L.A. Law.

SPADE, DAVID
Actor. b. Birmingham, MI. Raised in Scottsdale, AZ. Performed stand-up comedy in clubs and colleges which led to debut on Saturday Night Live in 1990. Prod., s.p., story, act. film, Lost & Found, 1997.
PICTURES: Light Sleeper (debut, 1982), Coneheads, Reality Bites, P.C.U., Tommy Boy, Black Sheep, 8 Heads in a Duffel Bag.
TELEVISION: Series: Saturday Night Live, Just Shoot Me.

SPADER, JAMES
Actor. b. Boston, MA, Feb. 7, 1960. e. Phillips Academy. Studied acting at Michael Chekhov Studio.
PICTURES: Endless Love (debut, 1981), The New Kids, Tuff Turf, Pretty in Pink, Mannequin, Baby Boom, Less Than Zero, Wall Street, Jack's Back, The Rachel Papers, Sex Lies and Videotape (Cannes Fest. Award, 1989), Bad Influence, White Palace, True Colors, Storyville, Bob Roberts, The Music of Chance, Dream Lover, Wolf, Stargate, 2 Days in the Valley, Crash, Critical Care, Curtain Call, Supernova.
TELEVISION: Series: The Family Tree. Movies: Cocaine: One Man's Seduction, A Killer in the Family, Starcrossed, Family Secrets, Keys to Tulsa.

SPANO, VINCENT
Actor. b. New York, NY, Oct. 18, 1962. While attending Stuyvesant H.S. made stage debut at 14 in The Shadow Box (Long Wharf and B'way).
THEATER: The Shadow Box, Balm in Gilead.
PICTURES: Over the Edge (debut, 1979), The Double McGuffin, The Black Stallion Returns, Baby It's You, Rumblefish, Alphabet City, Maria's Lovers, Creator, Good Morning Babylon, And God Created Woman, 1753: Venetian Red, High Frequency (Aquarium), Oscar, City of Hope, Alive, Indian Summer, The Ascent, The Tie That Binds, A Brooklyn State of Mind, The Unknown Cyclist.
TELEVISION: Series: Search for Tomorrow. Movies: The Gentleman Bandit, Senior Trip, Blood Ties, Afterburn.

SPEARS, JR., HAROLD T.
Executive. b. Atlanta, GA, June 21, 1929. e. U. of Georgia, 1951. With Floyd Theatres, Lakeland, FL, since 1953; now pres. Pres., Sun South Theatres, Inc., 1996.

SPECKTOR, FREDERICK
Executive. b. Los Angeles, CA, April 24, 1933. e. USC, UCLA. M.P. agent, Ashley Famous Agency, 1962-64; Artists Agency Corp., 1964-68; exec. M.P. dept., William Morris Agency, 1968-78; exec. Creative Artists Agency, 1978-present. Trustees Council, Education First, bd. of dirs., Amer. Jewish Committee. Bd. of dirs. for the ACLU and Center for Gun-Violence Prevention.

SPELLING, AARON
Executive. b. Dallas, TX, April 22, 1928. e. SMU. Daughter is actress Tori Spelling. Was actor/writer before becoming producer at Four Star in 1957. Won Harvard Award for Best Original One-act Play. Producer of series and tv movies: 1967, formed Thomas/Spelling Productions; 1969, formed his own co., Aaron Spelling Productions; 1972, partnered with Leonard Goldberg. Chairman/CEO Spelling TV, Inc. Produced so far over 111 movies for television. Winston Churchill Medal of Wisdom, 1988. Special People's Choice Award, 1992.
PICTURES: Mr. Mom (exec. prod.), Surrender, Three O'Clock High (exec. prod.), Cross My Heart (co-exec. prod.), Satisfaction (co-prod.), Loose Cannons, Soapdish.
TELEVISION: Series: The Mod Squad, The Rookies, Charlie's Angels, Fantasy Island, Starsky and Hutch, Hart to Hart, T.J. Hooker, Family, The Love Boat, Vega$, Dynasty, Matt Houston, Hotel, The Colbys, Life with Lucy, Nightingales, HeartBeat, Beverly Hills 90210, The Heights, Melrose Place, The Round Table, Winnetka Road, 7th Heaven. Movies (exec. prod./prod.): The Over-the-Hill Gang, Wake When the War Is Over, The Monk, The Pigeon, The Ballad of Andy Crocker, Say Goodbye Maggie Cole, Rolling Man, Shooting Stars, Dark Mirror, Making of a Male Model, The Three Kings, Nightingales, Day One (Emmy Award, 1989), Rich Men Single Women, The Love Boat: The Valentine Voyage, Jailbirds, Back to the Streets of San Francisco, Grass Roots, Terror on Track 9, A Stranger in the Mirror, And the Band Played On (Emmy Award, 1994), Jane's House, Green Dolphin Beat, many others.

SPENGLER, PIERRE
Producer. b. Paris, France, 1947. Went on stage at 15; returned to language studies at Alliance Franccaise. Entered film industry as production runner and office boy. Teamed for first time with friend Ilya Salkind on The Light at the Edge of the World, produced by Alexander Salkind.
PICTURES: Bluebeard, The Three Musketeers, The Four Musketeers, Crossed Swords, Superman, Superman II, Superman III, Santa Claus: The Movie, The Return of the Musketeers (tv in U.S.).

SPHEERIS, PENELOPE
Director. b. New Orleans, LA, 1945. e. UCLA. Film Sch., MFA.
PICTURES: Real Life (prod. only). Director: The Decline of Western Civilization (also prod., s.p.), Suburbia (also s.p.), The Boys Next Door, Summer Camp Nightmare (s.p. only), Hollywood Vice Squad, Dudes, The Decline of Western Civilization-Part II: The Metal Years, Wedding Band (actress only), Wayne's World, The Beverly Hillbillies, The Little Rascals, Black Sheep, The Decline of Western Civilization Part III, Senseless.
TELEVISION: Saturday Night Live (prod. only), Danger Theatre (co-creator, dir., co-writer). Movie: Prison Stories: Women on the Inside (New Chicks), Applewood 911 (dir.).

SPIEGEL, LARRY
Producer, Writer, Director. b. Brooklyn, NY. e. Ohio U. With CBS-TV; Benton & Bowles; Wells, Rich, Green; BBDO. Now heads Appledown Films, Inc.
PICTURES: Hail (s.p.), Book of Numbers (s.p.), Death Game (prod.), Stunts (prod.), Spree (dir., s.p.), Phobia (prod.), Remo Williams: The Adventure Begins (prod.), Dove Against Death (prod.), The Sunchaser (prod.).
TELEVISION: ABC Afterschool Specials, Bear That Slept Through Christmas (writer), Never Fool With A Gypsy Ikon (writer), Planet of The Apes (animated; writer), Jan Stephenson Golf Video (prod.), Remo Williams (pilot ABC; prod.).

SPIELBERG, STEVEN
Director, Producer. b. Cincinnati, OH, Dec. 18, 1947. e. California State Coll. m. actress Kate Capshaw. Made home movies as child; completed first film with story and actors at 12 yrs. old in Phoenix. At 13 won film contest for 40-min. war movie, Escape to Nowhere. At 16 made 140-min. film, Firelight. At California State Coll. made five films. First professional work, Amblin', 20 min. short which led to signing contract with Universal Pictures at age 20. Formed own co. Amblin Entertainment, headquartered at Universal Studios. Received Irving G. Thalberg Memorial Award, 1987; American Film Institute Life Achievement Award, 1995. Parterned with David Geffen and Jeffrey Katzenberg formed film company DreamWorks, 1995.
PICTURES: *Director.* The Sugarland Express (debut, 1974; also story), Jaws, Close Encounters of The Third Kind (also s.p.; Acad. Award nom. for dir.), 1941, Raiders of the Lost Ark (Acad. Award nom.), E.T. The Extra-Terrestrial (also co-prod.; Acad. Award noms. for dir. & picture), Twilight Zone—The Movie (sequence dir.; also exec. prod.), Indiana Jones and the Temple of Doom, The Color Purple (also co-prod.; Acad. Award nom. for picture), Empire of the Sun (also co-prod.), Indiana Jones and the Last Crusade, Always (also co-prod.), Hook, Jurassic Park, Schindler's List (also co-prod.; Acad. Awards for Best Director & Picture, 1993; DGA, Golden Globe & Natl. Society of Film Critics Awards for director; NY Film Critics, LA Film Critics, Natl. Board of Review. Natl. Society of Film Critics & Golden Globe Awards for picture), The Lost World. *Co-exec. prod.:* I Wanna Hold Your Hand, Used Cars, Continental Divide (exec. prod.), Poltergeist (co-prod., co-s.p.), Gremlins (also cameo), The Goonies (also story), Back to the Future, Young Sherlock Holmes, The Money Pit, An American Tail, Innerspace, Batteries Not Included, Who Framed Roger Rabbit, The Land Before Time, Dad, Back to the Future Part II, Joe Versus the Volcano, Back to the Future Part III, Gremlins 2: The New Batch, Arachnophobia, Cape Fear, An American Tail: Fievel Goes West (co-prod.), We're Back!: A Dinosaur's Story, The Flintstones, The Little Rascals, Casper (co-prod.), The Bridges of Madison County (co-prod.), Men in Black (exec. prod.). *Actor only:* The Blues Brothers, Listen Up: The Lives of Quincy Jones, The Martian Chronicles, Deep Impact, Mask of Zorro, Saving Pirate Ryan.
TELEVISION: *Series episodes* (dir.): Columbo, Owen Marshall: Counsellor-at-Law, The Pyschiatrist, Toonsylvania. *Movies* (dir.): Night Gallery (episode dir.), Duel, Something Evil, Savage. *Exec. prod.:* Amazing Stories (series; also dir. of 2 episodes), Tiny Toon Adventures (series; Emmy Award, 1991), Class of '61 (movie), Family Dog (series), seaQuest DSV (series), Pinky and the Brain (series).

SPIKINGS, BARRY
Executive. b. Boston, England, Nov. 23, 1939. Ent. m.p. ind. 1973. Joint man. dir. British Lion Films Ltd., 1975. Appt. jnt. man. dir. EMI Films Ltd., 1977. 1979, appt. chmn. & chief exec., EMI Film & Theatre Corp.; chmn. & chief exec, EMI Films, Ltd., chmn. EMI Cinemas, Ltd.; chmn., Elstree Studios, Ltd.; chmn. EMI-TV Programs, Inc., 1980; appt. chmn. chief exec., EMI Films Group, 1982; 1985 Barry Spikings Productions Inc. (U.S.A.); 1985 became director Galactic Films Inc. (with Lord Anthony Rufus Issacs); 1986, acquired Embassy Home Entertainment from Coca Cola Co., renamed Nelson Entertainment Inc., appointed pres. and COO. 1992, Pleskow/Spikings Partnership, film prod. and distrib. partnership with Eric Pleskow.
PICTURES: *Prod.:* Conduct Unbecoming, The Man Who Fell to Earth, The Deer Hunter, Texasville, Beyond Rangoon. *Exec. prod.:* Convoy.

SPINELLA, STEPHEN
Actor.
THEATER: Angels in America: Millenium Approaches (Tony award), Angels in America: Perestroika (Tony award).
PICTURES: Tarantella, Virtuosity, Faithful, The Unknown Cyclist, Love! Valour! Compassion!, The Jackal, Ravenous, Out of the Past (voice), Great Expectations.

SPINER, BRENT
Actor. b. Houston, TX. Recorded solo album Ol' Yellow Eyes Is Back.
THEATER: *NY:* The Seagull, The Three Musketeers, Sunday in the Park With George, Big River.
PICTURES: Stardust Memories, The Miss Firecracker Contest, Corrina Corrina, Star Trek: Generations, Independence Day, Phenomenon, Star Trek: First Contact, Out to Sea.
TELEVISION: *Series:* Star Trek: The Next Generation.

SPINETTI, VICTOR
Actor. b. South Wales, Sept. 2, 1933. e. Monmouth School. Entered industry in 1955. Appeared on Broadway in Oh! What a Lovely War winning 1965 Tony and Theatre World Awards.
THEATER: *London:* Expresso Bongo, Candide, Make Me an Offer, Oh What a Lovely War (also B'way), The Odd Couple, Cat Among the Pigeons, etc.

PICTURES: A Hard Day's Night, The Wild Affair, Help!, The Taming of the Shrew, The Biggest Bundle of Them All, Can Hieronymous Merkin Ever Forget Mercy Humppe and Find True Happiness?, Under Milk Wood, The Little Prince, The Return of the Pink Panther, Under the Cherry Moon, The Krays, The Princess and the Goblin (voice).
TELEVISION: The Magical Mystery Tour, Vincent Van Gogh, Paradise Club, The Attic.

SPINOTTI, DANTE
Cinematographer. b. Tolmezzo, Italy, Aug. 22, 1943.
PICTURES: La Disubbidienza, Cinderella '80, Hearts and Armour, Sogno di una notte di meza estate, Softly Softly, Cosi parlo Bellavista, The Berlin Affair, The Dark Side of Love, Manhunter, Crimes of the Heart, Choke Canyon, From the Hip, The Legend of the Holy Drinker (actor), Illegally Yours, Fair Game, Beaches, Torrents of Spring, A Violent Life, The Comfort of Strangers, True Colors, Hudson Hawk, Frankie and Johnny, The Last of the Mohicans, The Secret of the Old Woods, The End Is Known, Blink, Nell, The Quick and the Dead, The Star Maker, Heat, The Mirror Has Two Faces, L.A. Confidential (LA Film Crits. Award, Best Cinematography, 1997), Goodbye Lover, Man of the People.
TELEVISION: Basileus Quartet.

SPIRA, STEVEN S.
Executive. b. New York, NY, March 25, 1955. e. City Coll. of New York; Benjamin Cardozo Sch. of Law. Associated 10 years with N.Y. law firm, Monasch Chazen & Stream. 1984, joined 20th Century Fox as sr. counsel; 1985, to Warner Bros. Now exec. v.p., theatrical business affairs, Warner Bros.

SPODICK, ROBERT C.
Exhibitor. b. New York, NY, Dec. 3, 1919. e. CCNY, 1940; ent. NYC m.p. ind. as errand boy Skouras Park Plaza, Bronx 1932-33; reel boy, asst. mgr., Loew's Theatres; mgr., Little Carnegie and other art theatres; exploitation man, United Artists. Acquired Lincoln, New Haven art house in 1945 in partnership with cousin Leonard E. Sampson; developed Nutmeg Theatre circuit, which was sold in 1968 to Robert Smerling. Beginning in 1970, built Groton, CT., Cinemas I and II; Norwich Cinemas I and II, Mystic Village Cinemas I, II and III, and Westerley Triple Cinemas in RI as Gemini Cinema Circuit in partnership with Sampson and William Rosen. Gemini sold to Interstate Theatres, 1986. With Sampson presently operates York Square I & II and The New Lincoln in New Haven. Pres., Allied of CT, 1962-64; Pres. NATO of Conn. 1968-73. Past Chmn. Exec. Comm., CT Ass'n of Theatre Owners, and still active member of Board of Directors in 1997.

SPOTTISWOODE, ROGER
Director. b. England. Film editor of TV commercials and documentaries before turning to direction.
PICTURES: *Editor:* Straw Dogs, The Getaway, Pat Garrett and Billy the Kid, Hard Times, The Gambler; Who'll Stop the Rain? (assoc. prod.), Baby: Secret of the Lost Legend (exec. prod.). Director: Terror Train (debut, 1980), The Pursuit of D.B. Cooper, Under Fire, The Best of Times, Shoot to Kill, Turner & Hooch, Air America, Stop Or My Mom Will Shoot.
TELEVISION: *Movies:* The Renegades, The Last Innocent Man, Third Degree Burn, And the Band Played On, Hiroshima. *Special:* Time Flies When You're Alive.

SPRADLIN, G.D.
Actor. b. Daylight Township, Garvin County, OK, Aug. 31, 1920. e. Univ. of Oklahoma-doctor of Juris Prudence (1948). Started career as lawyer, became Independent Oil Producer. Active in local politics before turning to acting. Joined Oklahoma Repertory Theatre in 1964.
PICTURES: Will Penny (debut, 1968), Number One, Zabriskie Point, Monte Walsh, Tora! Tora! Tora!, The Hunting Party, The Godfather Part II, MacArthur, One on One, North Dallas Forty, Apocalypse Now, The Formula, Wrong Is Right, The Lords of Discipline, Tank, The War of the Roses, Clifford, Ed Wood, Canadian Bacon.
TELEVISION: *Series:* Rich Man Poor Man Book II. *Mini-Series:* Space, Dream West, Nutcracker: Money Madness and Murder, Robert Kennedy and His Times, War and Remembrance. *Movies:* Dial Hot Line, Sam Hill: Who Killed the Mysterious Mr. Foster?, Oregon Trail, Maneaters Are Loose!, And I Alone Survived, Jayne Mansfield Story, Resting Place, Shoot First: A Cop's Vengeance, Telling Secrets.

SPRINGER, PAUL D.
Executive. e. Brooklyn Law Sch. Served as assoc. for NY law firm, Johnson and Tannebaum. Later with legal dept. of Columbia Pictures. 1970, joined Paramount Pictures N.Y. legal dept. 1970; promoted to v.p. Theatrical Distrib. Counsel, 1979; promoted to sr. v.p., chief resident counsel, 1987; promoted to sr. v.p., asst. general counsel responsible for all legal functions for Paramount's distribution and marketing depts. Mem., NY and California Bars.

SPRINGFIELD, RICK
Actor, Singer, Songwriter. b. Sydney, Australia, Aug. 23, 1949.
PICTURES: Battlestar Galactica, Hard to Hold (act., addl. music).
TELEVISION: *Series*: General Hospital, Human Target, High Tide. *Specials*: An Evening at the Improv, Countdown '81. *Movies*: Nick Knight, Dead Reckoning, In the Shadows Someone's Watching.

SQUIRES, BUDDY
Cinematographer.
PICTURES: Brooklyn Bridge (also prod.), Huey Long, The Statue of Liberty (Acad. Award nom.), The Donner Party, High Lonesome: The Story of Bluegrass Music, Out of the Past, Frank Lloyd Wright.
TELEVISION: *Mini-series*: The Civil War, Baseball, The West, Lewis & Clark, The Irish in America: Long Journey Home.

STACK, ROBERT
Actor. b. Los Angeles, CA, Jan. 13, 1919. e. U. of Southern California. In U.S. Armed Forces (Navy), W.W.II. Studied acting at Henry Duffy School of Theatre 6 mo. then signed a contract with Universal. National skeet champion at age 16. Autobiography: Straight Shooting (1980).
PICTURES: First Love (debut, 1939), When the Daltons Rode, The Mortal Storm, A Little Bit of Heaven, Nice Girl?, Badlands of Dakota, To Be or Not To Be, Eagle Squadron, Men of Texas, Fighter Squadron, A Date With Judy, Miss Tatlock's Millions, Mr. Music, The Bullfighter and the Lady, My Outlaw Brother, Bwana Devil, War Paint, Conquest of Cochise, Sabre Jet, The Iron Glove, The High and the Mighty, House of Bamboo, Good Morning Miss Dove, Great Day in the Morning, Written on the Wind (Acad. Award nom.), The Gift of Love, The Tarnished Angels, John Paul Jones, The Last Voyage, The Caretakers, Is Paris Burning?, The Corrupt Ones, Action Man, Story of a Woman, A Second Wind, 1941, Airplane!, Uncommon Valor, Big Trouble, Transformers (voice), Plain Clothes, Caddyshack II, Dangerous Curves, Joe Versus the Volcano, Beavis and Butt-Head Do America.
TELEVISION: *Series*: The Untouchables (Emmy Award, 1960), The Name of the Game, Most Wanted, Strike Force, Unsolved Mysteries (host), Final Appeal (host). *Guest*: Playhouse 90 (Panic Button). *Movies*: The Strange and Deadly Occurance, Adventures of the Queen, Murder on Flight 502, Most Wanted (pilot), Undercover With the KKK (narrator), Midas Valley, Perry Mason: The Case of the Sinister Spirit, The Return of Eliot Ness. *Mini-Series*: George Washington, Hollywood Wives.

STAHL, AL
Executive. b. July 3, 1916. Syndicated newspaper cartoonist; asst. animator, Max Fleischer, gag ed. Terrytoons; U.S. Signal Corps; opened own studios, 1946; pres., Animated Prod.; prod. live and animated commercials; member of bd. NTFC. Developed and built first animation camera and stand, 1950. Designed and produced opening animation for The Honeymooners, The Electric Company, Saturday Night Live. Produced over 5,000 tv spots. Prod. 50 min. documentary War and Pieces for U.S. Army Commandy of War in the Gulf, 1991.

STAHL, NICK
Actor. b. Dallas, TX, 1980. Started acting at age 4.
PICTURES: The Man Without a Face (debut, 1993), Safe Passage, Tall Tale, Eye of God, The Thin Red Line.
TELEVISION: *Movies*: Stranger at My Door, Woman With a Past, Incident in a Small Town, My Son Is Innocent.

STALLONE, SYLVESTER
Actor, Writer, Director. b. New York, NY, July 6, 1946. After high school taught at American Coll. of Switzerland instructing children of career diplomats, young royalty, etc. Returned to U.S. in 1967 and studied drama at U. of Miami, 1969. Came to New York to seek acting career, taking part-time jobs, including usher for Walter Reade Theatres. Then turned to writing, selling several TV scripts.
PICTURES: Party at Kitty and Studs (debut, 1970), Bananas, Rebel (A Man Called Rainbo), The Lords of Flatbush (also co-s.p.), The Prisoner of 2nd Avenue, Capone, Death Race 2000, Farewell My Lovely, Cannonball, Rocky (also s.p.; Acad. Award noms. for actor & s.p.), F.I.S.T. (also co-s.p.), Paradise Alley (also s.p., dir.), Rocky II (also s.p., dir.), Nighthawks, Victory, Rocky III (also s.p., dir.), First Blood (also co-s.p.), Staying Alive (cameo; also dir., prod., co-s.p.), Rhinestone (also co-s.p.), Rambo: First Blood Part II (also co-s.p.), Rocky IV (also dir., s.p.), Cobra (also s.p.), Over the Top (also co-s.p.), Rambo III (also co-s.p.), Lock Up, Tango and Cash, Rocky V (also s.p.), Oscar, Stop Or My Mom Will Shoot, Cliffhanger (also co-s.p.), Demolition Man, The Specialist, Judge Dredd, Assassins, Daylight, Cop Land.
TELEVISION: *Guest*: Kojak, Police Story, Dream On.

STAMOS, JOHN
Actor. b. Cypress, CA, Aug. 19, 1963. Landed role of Blackie Parrish on daytime serial General Hospital in 1982. Has toured with his own band John Stamos and the Bad Boyz.

THEATER: *B'way*: How to Succeed in Business Without Really Trying.
PICTURES: Never Too Young to Die, Born to Ride, Private Parts.
TELEVISION: *Series*: General Hospital, Dreams, You Again?, Full House. *Movies*: Daughter of the Streets, Captive, The Disappearance of Christina, Fatal Vows: The Alexandra O'Hara Story, A Match Made in Heaven.

STAMP, TERENCE
Actor. b. London, England, July 23, 1938. Stage experience including Alfie on Broadway. Recent stage: Dracula, The Lady from the Sea, Airborne Symphony. *Autobiography*: Coming Attractions (1988).
PICTURES: Billy Budd (debut 1962; Acad. Award nom.), Term of Trial, The Collector (Cannes Film Fest. Award, 1965), Modesty Blaise, Far from the Madding Crowd, Poor Cow, Blue, Teorema, Spirits of the Dead, The Mind of Mr. Soames, A Season in Hell, Hu-Man, The Divine Nymph, Strip-Tease, Superman, Meetings with Remarkable Men, Together?, Superman II, Monster Island, Death in the Vatican, The Hit, The Company of Wolves, Link, Legal Eagles, The Sicilian, Wall Street, Young Guns, Alien Nation, Stranger in the House (also dir., co-s.p.), Genuine Risk, Beltenebros, The Real McCoy, The Adventures of Priscilla-- Queen of the Desert, Mindbender.
TELEVISION: *Movie*: The Thief of Bagdad.

STANFILL, DENNIS C.
Executive. b. Centerville, TN, April 1, 1927. e. Lawrenceburg H.S.; U.S. Naval Acad., B.S.; 1949; Oxford U. (Rhodes Scholar), M.A., 1953; U. of South Carolina, L.H.D. (hon.). Corporate finance specialist, Lehman Brothers 1959-65; v.p. finance, Times Mirror Company, Los Angeles, 1965-69; exec. v.p. finance, 20th Century-Fox Film Corp., 1969-71, pres., 1971, chmn. bd./CEO, 1971-81; pres., Stanfill, Bowen & Co., venture capital firm, 1981-90; chmn. bd./CEO, AME, Inc., 1990-92; co-chmn. bd./co-CEO, MGM, 1992-93. Sr. advisor to Credit Lyonnais, 1993-95. Private Investments, 1995-.

STANG, ARNOLD
Performer, b. Chelsea, MA, Sept. 28, 1927. Radio, 1935-50; on B'way, in five plays and in m.p. and short subjects; guest appearances on TV shows. Much voice-over cartoon work. Starred in 36 shorts.
TELEVISION: *Series*: School House, Henry Morgan Show, Doc Corkle, Top Cat (voice), Broadside. *Guest*: Captain Video, Milton Berle, Danny Thomas, Perry Como, Ed Sullivan, Red Skelton, Frank Sinatra, Wagon Train, Jack Benny, Johnny Carson, December Bride, Playhouse 90, Batman, Bonanza, Bob Hope, Danny Kaye, Jackie Gleason, Emergency, Feeling Good, Chico & the Man, Super Jaws & Catfish, Busting Loose, Flying High, Robert Klein Specials, Tales from the Dark Side, True Blue, Cosby Show.
PICTURES: Seven Days Leave, My Sister Eileen, Let's Go Steady, They Got Me Covered, So This is New York, Double for Della, Return of Marco Polo, Spirit of '76, The Man with the Golden Arm, Dondi, The Wonderful World of the Brothers Grimm, It's a Mad Mad Mad Mad World, Pinocchio in Outer Space (voice), Alakazam the Great (voice), Hello Down There, Skidoo, The Aristocats (voice), Raggedy Ann & Andy (voice), Gang That Couldn't Shoot Straight, That's Life, Hercules in New York, Ghost Dad, Dennis the Menace, At The Cottonwood.

STANLEY, KIM
Actress. r.n. Patricia Reid. b. Tularosa, NM, Feb. 11, 1925. e. U. of NM. Began stage acting in college and later in stock. Worked as model in NY while training with Elia Kazan and Lee Strasberg at Actors Studio. In late 1960s and 1970s taught drama, Coll. of Santa Fe, NM.
THEATER: The Dog, Beneath the Skin (NY debut, 1948), Him, Yes Is For a Very Young Man, Montserrat, The House of Bernarda Alba, The Chase, Picnic (NY Drama Critics Award, 1953), The Traveling Lady, The Great Dreamer, Bus Stop, A Clearing in the Woods, A Touch of the Poet, A Far Country, Natural Affection, The Three Sisters.
PICTURES: The Goddess (debut, 1958), Seance on a Wet Afternoon (Acad. Award nom.), The Three Sisters, Frances (Acad. Award nom.), The Right Stuff.
TELEVISION: *Specials*: Clash by Night, The Travelling Lady, Cat on a Hot Tin Roof (Emmy Award, 1985). *Movie*: U.M.C. *Guest*: Ben Casey (A Cardinal Act of Mercy; Emmy Award, 1963).

STANTON, HARRY DEAN
Actor. b. West Irvine, KY, July 14, 1926. Acting debut at Pasadena Playhouse. Billed in early film appearances as Dean Stanton.
PICTURES: Revolt at Fort Laramie (debut, 1957), Tomahawk Trail, The Proud Rebel, Pork Chop Hill, The Adventures of Huckleberry Finn, A Dog's Best Friend, Hero's Island, The Man From the Diner's Club, Ride in the Whirlwind, The Hostage, A Time for Killing, Rebel Rousers, Cool Hand Luke, Day of the Evil Gun, The Miniskirt Mob, Kelly's Heroes, Cisco Pike, Two-Lane Blacktop, Face to the Wind (Cry for Me Billy), Pat Garrett and Billy the Kid, Dillinger, Where the Lilies Bloom, Cockfighter,

Zandy's Bride, The Godfather Part II, Rafferty and the Gold Dust Twins, Rancho Deluxe, Farewell My Lovely, 92 in the Shade, Win Place or Steal, The Missouri Breaks, Straight Time, Renaldo and Clara, Alien, The Rose, Wise Blood, Death Watch, The Black Marble, Private Benjamin, Escape From New York, One From the Heart, Young Doctors in Love, Christine, Repo Man, Red Dawn, The Bear, Paris Texas, The Care Bears Movie (voice), One Magic Christmas, Fool for Love, UFOria, Pretty in Pink, Slamdance, Stars and Bars, Mr. North, The Last Temptation of Christ, Dream a Little Dream, Twister, The Fourth War, Stranger in the House, Wild at Heart, Man Trouble, Twin Peaks: Fire Walk With Me, Blue Tiger, Never Talk to Strangers, Down Periscope, She's So Lovely, Fire Down Below.
TELEVISION: Movies: Flatbed Annie & Sweetpie: Lady Truckers, I Want to Live, Payoff, Hostages, Against the Wall. Special: Hotel Room (Tricks).

STAPLETON, JEAN
Actress. r.n. Jeanne Murray. b. New York, NY. e. Wadleigh H.S. Summer stock in NH, ME, MA, and PA. Broadway debut in the Summer House (1954). Chair, Advisory bd., Women's Research and Education Inst. (Wash., D.C.); bd.: Eleanor Roosevelt Val-kill, Hyde Park; trustee: Actors Fund of America.
THEATER: Harvey, Damn Yankees, Bells Are Ringing, Juno, Rhinoceros, Funny Girl, Arsenic and Old Lace (B'way and tour), Mountain Language/The Birthday Party (Obie Award), The Learned Ladies, Bon Appetit, The Roads to Home, Night Seasons, Morning's at Seven, You Can't Take It With You, The Show-Off, The Mystery of Edwin Drood (natl. tour). and extensive regional work at the Totem Pole Playhouse, Fayetteville, PA, Pocono Playhouse, Mountain Home Pa; Peterborough Playhouse, N.H. and others. Operatic debut with Baltimore Opera Co. in Candide, then The Italian Lesson and Bon Appetit. Cinderella, NY City Opera. Starred in San Jose Civic Light Opera Co.'s Sweeney Todd. Off B'way in The Entertainer. The Matchmaker, A.C.T. San Francisco.
PICTURES: Damn Yankees (debut, 1958), Bells Are Ringing, Something Wild, Up the Down Staircase, Cold Turkey, Klute, The Buddy System, Michael.
TELEVISION: Series: All in the Family (3 Emmy Awards: 1971, 1972, 1978), Bagdad Cafe, Mrs. Piggle-Wiggle. Movies: Tail Gunner Joe, Aunt Mary, Angel Dusted, Isabel's Choice, Eleanor: First Lady of the World (Emmy nom.), A Matter of Sex, Dead Man's Folly, Fire in the Dark, The Habitation of Dragons, Ghost Mom, Lily Dale. Specials: You Can't Take It With You, Grown-Ups (ACE nom.), Jack and the Beanstalk and Cinderella (Faerie Tale Theatre), Something's Afoot, Let Me Hear You Whisper, Mother Goose Rock 'n' Rhyme, Parallax Garden.

STAPLETON, MAUREEN
Actress. b. Troy, NY, June 21, 1925. e. Siena Col. Worked as a model and waitress while studying acting with Herbert Berghof in NY. Became member of Actors Studio. Broadway debut, 1946, in The Playboy of the Western World. Autobiography: A Hell of a Life (1995).
THEATER: NY: Antony and Cleopatra, Detective Story, The Bird Cage, The Rose Tattoo (Tony Award, 1951), The Emperor's Clothes, The Crucible, Richard III, The Seagull, 27 Wagons Full of Cotton, Orpheus Descending, The Cold Wind and the Warm, Toys in the Attic, The Glass Menagerie (1965 & 1975), Plaza Suite, Norman Is That You?, The Gingerbread Lady (Tony Award, 1971), The Country Girl, The Secret Affairs of Mildred Wild, The Gin Game, The Little Foxes. LA: Juno and the Paycock.
PICTURES: Lonelyhearts (debut, 1958; Acad. Award nom.), The Fugitive Kind, A View From the Bridge, Bye Bye Birdie, Airport (Acad. Award nom.), Plaza Suite, Interiors (Acad. Award nom.), Lost and Found, The Runner Stumbles, The Fan, On the Right Track, Reds (Acad. Award, best supporting actress, 1981), Johnny Dangerously, The Cosmic Eye (voice), Cocoon, The Money Pit, Heartburn, Sweet Lorraine, Made in Heaven, Nuts, Doin' Time on Planet Earth (cameo), Cocoon: The Return, Passed Away, Trading Mom, The Last Good Time.
TELEVISION: Series: What Happened? (panelist, 1952), The Thorns. Specials: For Whom the Bell Tolls, Among the Paths to Eden (Emmy Award, 1968).Movies: Tell Me Where It Hurts, Queen of the Stardust Ballroom, Cat on a Hot Tin Roof, The Gathering, Letters From Frank, The Gathering Part II, The Electric Grandmother, Little Gloria--Happy at Last, Family Secrets, Sentimental Journey, Private Sessions, Liberace: Behind the Music, Last Wish, Miss Rose White.

STARGER, MARTIN
Producer, Executive. b. New York, NY, May 8, 1932. e. CCNY. Served in U.S. Army Signal Corp., where prod. training films. Joined BBDO, starting in TV prod. dept.; later made v.p. & assoc. dir. of TV. Joined ABC in 1966, as v.p. of programs, ABC-TV, East Coast. 1968, promoted to v.p. and natl prog. dir; 1969 named v.p. in chg. progr.; named pres., ABC Entertainment, 1972; 1975 formed & became pres. of Marstar Productions Inc., M.P. & TV prod. co.; 1978 formed Marble Arch Productions, of which he was pres. Formed Full/Starger Co. with Elton Rule, 1988.
PICTURES: Exec. prod./Producer: Nashville, The Domino Principle, Movie/Movie, The Muppet Movie, Raise the Titanic, Saturn 3, The Great Muppet Caper, Hard Country, The Legend of the Lone Ranger, On Golden Pond, Sophie's Choice, Barbarosa, Mask.

TELEVISION:
TELEVISION: Friendly Fire (Emmy Award, 1979), Escape from Sobibor, Consenting Adult, Earth Star Voyager, Marcus Welby M.D., A Holiday Affair, The Return of Marcus Welby M.D., The Elephant Man, All Quiet on the Western Front.

STARK, RAY
Producer. e. Rutgers U. Began career after WWII as agent handling Red Ryder radio scripts, and later literary works for such writers as Costain, Marquand and Hecht. Publicity writer, Warner Bros. Joined Famous Artists Agency, where he represented such personalities as Marilyn Monroe, Kirk Douglas and Richard Burton; in 1957, resigned exec. position to form Seven Arts Prods. with Eliot Hyman, serving as exec. v.p. and head of production until 1966, when he left to take on personal production projects. Founded Rastar Prods. and Ray Stark Prods. Received Irving Thalberg Award from Acad. of M.P. Arts and Sciences 1980. TV production: Barbarians at the Gate (Emmy Award).
PICTURES: The World of Susie Wong, The Night of the Iguana, This Property Is Condemned, Oh Dad Poor Dad Mama's Hung You in the Closet and I'm Feeling So Sad, Reflections in a Golden Eye, Funny Girl, The Owl and the Pussycat, Fat City, The Way We Were, Summer Wishes Winter Dreams, For Pete's Sake, Funny Lady, The Sunshine Boys, Robin and Marian, Murder by Death, The Goodbye Girl, Casey's Shadow, The Cheap Detective, California Suite, The Electric Horseman, Chapter Two, Seems Like Old Times, Annie, The Slugger's Wife, Nothing in Common, Brighton Beach Memoirs, Biloxi Blues, Steel Magnolias, Revenge, Lost in Yonkers, Harriet the Spy, To Gillian on Her 37th Birthday, Random Hearts.

STARR, MIKE
Actor. b. Queens, NY. e. Hofstra Univ. Theatre debut with Manhattan Punchline.
THEATER: NY: Requiem for a Heavyweight, The Guys in the Truck, Map of the World, Vesper's Ever.
PICTURES: Bushido Blade, Cruising, The Natural, The Last Dragon, Cat's Eye, The Money Pit, Violets Are Blue, Off-Beat, Collision Course, Five Corners, Funny Farm, Lean on Me, Blue Steel, Uncle Buck, Last Exit to Brooklyn, Miller's Crossing, GoodFellas, Billy Bathgate, Freejack, The Bodyguard, Mac, Mad Dog and Glory, Son of the Pink Panther, Cabin Boy, On Deadly Ground, The Hudsucker Proxy, Blown Away, Baby's Day Out, Trial by Jury, Ed Wood, Radioland Murders, Dumb & Dumber, A Pyromaniac's Love Story, Clockers, Two If By Sea, James & the Giant Peach, Blood & Wine, Hoodlum, The Deli, Frogs for Snakes.
TELEVISION: Series: Hardball. Mini-series: The Last Don. Movies: The Frank Nitti Story, Hot Paint, Stone Pillow, Path to Paradise. Guest: Kojak, Hawk, The Equalizer, Crime Story, Spenser: For Hire.

STARR, RINGO
O.B.E. Singer, Musician, Songwriter, Actor. r.n. Richard Starkey. b. Liverpool, England, July 7, 1940. m. actress Barbara Bach. Former member of The Beatles.
PICTURES: A Hard Day's Night (debut, 1964), Help!, Yellow Submarine (cameo), Candy, The Magic Christian, Let It Be, 200 Motels, Blindman, The Concert for Bangladesh, Lisztomania, The Last Waltz, Sextette, The Kids Are Alright, Caveman, Give My Regards to Broad Street, Water (cameo), Walking After Midnight.
TELEVISION: Movies: Princess Daisy, Alice in Wonderland. Series: Shining Time Station.

STEADMAN, ALISON
Actress. b. Liverpool, England, Aug. 26, 1946. m. director Mike Leigh. Studied acting with East 15 Acting School.
THEATER: The Prime of Miss Jean Brodie, Hamlet, Wholesome Glory, The Pope's Wedding, The Anchor, The King, Abigail's Party, Joking Apart, Unlce Vanya, The Rise and Fall of Little Voice, Othello, The Plotters of Cabbage Patch Corner.
PICTURES: Kipperbang (debut, 1982), Champions, Number One, A Private Function, Clockwise, Stormy Monday, The Misadventures of Mr. Wilt, Shirley Valentine, Life Is Sweet, Blame It on the Bellboy.
TELEVISION: Virtuoso, The Singing Detective, The Finding, Hard Labour, Nuts in May, Throught the Night, Pasmore.

STEEL, DAWN
Executive. b. New York, NY, Aug. 19, 1946. m. producer Charles Roven. e. marketing student, Boston U. 1964-65, NYU 1966-67; sportswriter, Major League Baseball Digest and NFL/NY 1968-69; 1969-75, editor of Penthouse Magazine; Pres. Oh Dawn! merchandising co. 1979-80, v.p. merchandising Paramount Pictures; 1978-79, merchandising consult.; Playboy NYC; 1980-83, v.p. prod. Paramount Pictures. Joined Columbia Pictures 1987 as president (first woman studio pres.), resigned 1990. Formed Steel Pictures for the Walt Disney Co., 1990. Prod. for Disney: Honey I Blew Up the Kid, Cool Runnings, Sister Act 2. Prod. for New Line: Angus. Recipient of Crystal Award (1989). Author: They Can Kill You... But They Can't Eat You (1993). Member: AMPAS, Amer. Film Inst. (bd. 1988-90), NOW Legal Defense Fund; 1993-present, member of dean's advisory bd. at UCLA Sch. of Theatre, Film & TV.
(d. Dec. 20, 1997)

STEELE, BARBARA
Actress. b. Trenton Wirrall, England, Dec. 29, 1937. Studied to be painter prior to joining rep. cos. in 1957.
PICTURES: Bachelor of Hearts (debut, 1958), Sapphire, Your Money or Your Wife, Black Sunday, The Pit and the Pendulum, Revenge of the Mercenaries, The Horrible Dr. Hitchcock, 8 1/2, Danse Macabre (Castle of Blood), The Ghost, The Hours of Love, White Voices, Nightmare Castle, The Maniacs, Terror Creatures From the Grave, The She Beast, Young Torless, Crimson Cult, They Came From Within, Caged Heat, I Never Promised You a Rose Garden, Piranha, Pretty Baby, The Silent Scream.

STEELE, TOMMY
Performer. r.n. Tommy Hicks. b. London, Dec. 17, 1936. Early career Merchant Navy. 1956 first gained fame as successful pop singer. First TV and film appearances, 1957. Composed and sang title song for The Shiralee.
THEATER: Half a Sixpence, Hans Andersen, Singin' in the Rain, Some Like It Hot.
PICTURES: Kill Me Tomorrow (debut, 1957), The Tommy Steele Story (Rock Around the World), The Duke Wore Jeans, Tommy the Toreador, Light Up the Sky, It's All Happening (The Dream Maker), The Happiest Millionaire, Half a Sixpence, Finian's Rainbow, Where's Jack?
TELEVISION: Tommy Steele Spectaculars, Richard Whittington Esquire (Rediffusion), Ed Sullivan Show, Gene Kelly in NY NY, Perry Como Show, Twelfth Night, The Tommy Steele Hour, Tommy Steele in Search of Charlie Chaplin, Tommy Steele and a Show, Quincy's Quest.

STEENBURGEN, MARY
Actress. b. Newport, AR, Feb. 8, 1953. Graduated from Neighborhood Playhouse. Received honorary doctorate degrees from Univ. of Ark. at Little Rock and Hendrix Col. in Conway, AR. On B'way stage 1993 in Candida.
PICTURES: Goin' South (debut, 1978), Time After Time, Melvin and Howard (Acad. Award, best supporting actress, 1980), Ragtime, A Midsummer Night's Sex Comedy, Cross Creek, Romantic Comedy, One Magic Christmas, Dead of Winter, End of the Line (also exec. prod.), The Whales of August, Miss Firecracker, Parenthood, Back to the Future Part III, The Long Walk Home (narrator), The Butcher's Wife, What's Eating Gilbert Grape, Philadelphia, Clifford, It Runs in the Family (My Summer Story), Pontiac Moon, My Family/Mi Familia, Powder, The Grass Harp, Nixon.
TELEVISION: Series: Ink (also co-exec. prod.). Mini-Series: Tender Is the Night. Specials: Faerie Tale Theatre (Little Red Riding Hood), The Gift. Movie: The Attic: The Hiding of Anne Frank, Gulliver's Travels, About Sarah. Series: Back to the Future (voice for animated series), Ink.

STEIGER, ROD
Actor. b. Westhampton, NY, April 14, 1925. e. Westside H.S., Newark, NJ. Served in U.S. Navy, then employed in Civil Service; studied acting at N.Y. Theatre Wing Dramatic Workshop Actors' Studio; numerous TV plays; on Broadway in ANTA prod. of Night Music.
PICTURES: Teresa (debut, 1951), On the Waterfront, The Big Knife, Oklahoma!, The Court Martial of Billy Mitchell, Jubal, The Harder They Fall, Back From Eternity, Run of the Arrow, The Unholy Wife, Across the Bridge, Cry Terror, Al Capone, Seven Thieves, The Mark, World in My Pocket, 13 West Street, Convicts 4, The Longest Day, Hands Over the City, Time of Indifference, The Pawnbroker, The Loved One, Dr. Zhivago, And There Came a Man (A Man Called John), In the Heat of the Night (Acad. Award, 1967), The Girl and the General, No Way to Treat a Lady, The Sergeant, The Illustrated Man, Three Into Two Won't Go, Waterloo, Happy Birthday Wanda June, Duck You Sucker! (A Fistful of Dynamite), The Heroes, Lolly Madonna XXX, Lucky Luciano, Mussolini: Dead or Alive (The Last Days of Mussolini), Hennessey, Dirty Hands, W.C. Fields and Me, Wolf Lake, F.I.S.T., Breakthrough (Sgt. Steiner), The Amityville Horror, Love and Bullets, Klondike Fever, The Lucky Star, Lion of the Desert, Cattle Annie and Little Britches, The Chosen, The Magic Mountain, Portrait of a Hitman (Jim Buck), The Naked Face, The Kindred, Catch the Heat, American Gothic, The January Man, Men of Respect, The Ballad of the Sad Cafe, Midnight Murders, Guilty as Charged, That Summer of White Roses, The Player, The Neighbor, The Last Tattoo, Black Water, The Specialist, Mars Attacks!, Animals (And the Tollkeeper).
TELEVISION: Many appearances in 1950s live TV including Marty. Movies: Jesus of Nazareth, Cook & Perry: The Race to the Pole, Sword of Gideon, Desperado: Avalanche at Devil's Ridge, Passion and Paradise, In the Line of Duty: Manhunt in the Dakotas, Sinatra, Tom Clancy's Op Center, Choices of the Heart: The Margaret Sanger Story, In Pursuit of Honor, Columbo: Strange Bedfellows. Mini-Series: Hollywood Wives. Special: Tales of the City.

STEINBERG, DAVID
Actor, Writer, Director. b. Winnipeg, Canada, Aug. 9, 1942. e. U. of Chicago; Hebrew Theological Coll. Member Second City troupe; comedian at comedy clubs: Mr. Kelly's Hungry i, Bitter End. Starred in London and B'way stage prods. B'way includes Little Murders, Carry Me Back to Morningside Heights.
PICTURES: Actor: The Lost Man, The End, Something Short of Paradise, The Best of the Big Laff Off, The Tommy Chong Roast. Director: Paternity, Going Berserk (also co.-s.p.), Cats Don't Dance (exec. prod. only), The Wrong Guy, Kids in the Hall: Brain Candy (exec. prod. only) .
TELEVISION: Series: Music Scene (writer, co-host), Tonight Show (guest host), David Steinberg Show, Good Grief (exec. prod.). Special: Second City: 25 Years in Revue. Director: Newhart, The Popcorn Kid, Golden Girls, One Big Family, Faerie Tale Theatre, Richard Belzer Special, Baby on Board, Annie McGuire, Seinfeld, Mad About You, Evening Shade, Designing Women, Friends, Good Grief, and many commercials.

STEINBERG, HERB
Executive. b. New York, NY, July 3, 1921. e. City Coll. of New York, 1937-41. Capt. U.S. Army, 1942-46; pub. PRC, 1946, Eagle Lion, 1946-49, Paramount 1949; pub. mgr. 1951; expl. mgr., 1954; studio adv. & pub. dir., 1958; exec. chg. of spec. proj., press dept., Universal City Studio, 1963; v.p., Universal Studio Tours, 1971; 1974 v.p., MCA Recreation Services. Appt. to California Tourism Commission, Calif. Tourism Hall of Fame, 1984; consultant, MCA, Inc., 1987; bd. trustees, Motion Picture & TV Fund, 1987; bd. of trustees Hollywood Canteen Foundation, 1988; Communications dir. Alliance of Motion Picture & Television Producers.

STEINMAN, MONTE
Executive. b. New York, NY, May 18, 1955. e. Wharton Sch. of Univ. of PA. Joined Paramount Pictures 1980 as sr. financial analyst. Series of promotions followed, culminating in appt. as dir. of financial planning of Gulf & Western's Entertainment and Communications Group, 1984. 1985, named exec. dir., financial planning. 1990, joined Viacom Intl., as mgr. financial planning. 1993, dir. financial planning, MTV Networks. 1994, v.p. finance at MTV Networks.

STEMBLER, JOHN H.
Executive. b. Miami, FL, Feb. 18, 1913. e. U. of FL Law Sch., 1937. Asst. U.S. att., South. dist. of FL, 1941; U.S. Air Force, 1941-45; pres. Georgia Theatre Co., 1957; named chmn., 1983; NATO member exec. comm. and past pres.; Major Gen. USAF (Ret); past bd. chmn., National Bank of Georgia.

STEMBLER, WILLIAM J.
Executive. b. Atlanta, GA, Nov. 29, 1946. e. Westminster Sch., 1964; U. of FL, 1968; U. of GA Law Sch., 1971. 1st. lt. U.S. Army, 1971; capt., U.S. Army Reserve; resigned 1976. Enforcement atty., SEC, Atlanta office, 1972-73; joined Georgia Theatre Co., 1973; pres. 1983-86; joined United Artists Communications, Inc., 1986, as v.p.; Incorporated Value Cinemas 1988 and Georgia Theatre Co. II in 1991 as its chmn. & pres. Bd. of dir., & vice chmn., NATO; member, NATO OF GA & past-pres., 1983-85; Rotary Club of Atlanta, pres. 1991-92.

STERLING, JAN
Actress. r.n. Jane Sterling Adriance. b. New Yor, NY, April 3, 1923. e. private tutors; Fay Compton Sch. of Dramatic Art, London. N.Y. stage debut: Bachelor Born.
THEATER: Panama Hattie, Present Laughter, John Loves Mary, Two Blind Mice, Front Page, Over 21, Born Yesterday, The November People.
PICTURES: Johnny Belinda (debut, 1948), Appointment with Danger, Mystery Street, Caged, Union Station, The Skipper Surprised His Wife, The Big Carnival (Ace in the Hole), The Mating Season, Rhubarb, Flesh and Fury, Sky Full of Moon, Pony Express, The Vanquished, Split Second, Alaska Seas, The High and the Mighty (Acad. Award nom.), Return From the Sea, Human Jungle, Women's Prison, Female on the Beach, Man with the Gun, 1984, The Harder They Fall, Slaughter on Tenth Avenue, Kathy O', The Female Animal, High School Confidential, Love in a Goldfish Bowl, The Incident, The Angry Breed, The Minx, First Monday in October.
TELEVISION: Series: You're in the Picture (panelist, 1961), Made in America, The Guiding Light (1969-70). Mini-Series: Backstairs at the White House. Movies: Having Babies, Dangerous Company, My Kidnapper My Love.

STERLING, ROBERT
Actor. r.n. William Sterling Hart. b. Newcastle, PA, Nov. 13, 1917. e. U. of Pittsburgh. m. Anne Jeffreys, actress. Daughter is actress Tisha Sterling. Fountain pen salesman, day laborer, clerk, industrial branch credit mgr., clothing salesman on West Coast; served as pilot-instructor U.S. Army Corps. 3 yrs.

PICTURES: The Amazing Mr. Williams (debut, 1939), Blondie Brings Up Baby, Blondie Meets the Boss, Only Angels Have Wings, Manhattan Heartbeat, Yesterday's Heroes, Gay Caballero, Penalty, I'll Wait for You, Get-Away, Ringside Maisie, Two-Faced Woman, Dr. Kildare's Victory, Johnny Eager, This Time for Keeps, Somewhere I'll Find You, Secret Heart, Roughshod, Bunco Squad, Sundowners, Show Boat, Column South, Voyage to the Bottom of the Sea, Return to Peyton Place, A Global Affair.
TELEVISION: Series: Topper, Love That Jill, Ichabod and Me. Movies: Letters from Three Lovers, Beggarman, Thief.

STERN, DANIEL
Actor, Director. b. Bethesda, MD, Aug. 28, 1957. e. H.B. Studios. Appeared in 1984 short film Frankenweenie.
PICTURES: Breaking Away (debut, 1979), Starting Over, A Small Circle of Friends, Stardust Memories, It's My Turn, One-Trick Pony, Honky Tonk Freeway, I'm Dancing As Fast As I Can, Diner, Blue Thunder, Get Crazy, C.H.U.D., Key Exchange, The Boss' Wife, Hannah and Her Sisters, Born in East L.A., D.O.A., The Milagro Beanfield War, Leviathan, Little Monsters, Friends Lovers and Lunatics, Coupe de Ville, My Blue Heaven, Home Alone, City Slickers, Home Alone 2: Lost in New York, Rookie of the Year (also dir.), City Slickers II: The Legend of Curly's Gold, Bushwhacked (also exec. prod.), Celtic Pride, Very Bad Things.
TELEVISION: Movies: Samson and Delilah, Weekend War, The Court-Martial of Jackie Robinson, Big Guns Talk: The Story of the Western. Series: Hometown, The Wonder Years (narrator; also episode dir.).

STERN, EDDIE
Film buyer. b. New York, NY, Jan. 13, 1917. e. Columbia Sch. of Journalism. Head film buyer and booker, specializing in art theatres, for Rugoff and Becker, NY; Captain, USAF; joined Wometco Ent. in 1952 as asst. to film buyer; v.p. motion picture theatre film buying and booking, Wometco Enterprises, Inc. Retired from Wometco 1985. 1985-96, film buying and booking, Theatres of Nassau, Ltd. Retired in 1996.

STERN, EZRA E.
Attorney. b. New York, NY, March 22, 1908. e. Southwestern U. 1930, LL.B. pres., Wilshire Bar Assn. Former legal counsel for So. Calif. Theatre Owners Assn. Member: Calif. State Bar; member, Int'l Variety Clubs; former chief barker, Variety Club So. Calif. Tent 25; pres., Variety Int'l Boys' Club; board of dir., Los Angeles Metropolitan Recreation & Youth Services Council; bd. of trustees, Welfare Planning Council, Los Angeles Region; former mem. Los Angeles Area Council, Boys' Club of America; pres., Variety International Boys' Club 1976-77 and 1979-80. Member bd., Will Rogers Inst., M.P. Pioneers. 1984, honored by Variety Boys and Girls Club as founder of youth recreational facility.

STERN, STEWART
Writer. b. New York, NY, March 22, 1922. e. Ethical Culture Sch., 1927-40; U. of Iowa, 1940-43. Rifle Squad Leader, S/Sgt. 106th Inf. Div., 1943-45; actor, asst. stage mgr., The French Touch, B'way, 1945-46; dialogue dir. Eagle-Lion Studios, 1946-48. 1948 to date: screenwriter.
TELEVISION: Crip, And Crown Thy Good, Thunder of Silence, Heart of Darkness, A Christmas to Remember, Sybil (Emmy Award, 1977).
PICTURES: Teresa, Rebel Without a Cause, The Rack, The James Dean Story, The Outsider, The Ugly American, Rachel Rachel, The Last Movie, Summer Wishes Winter Dreams.

STERNHAGEN, FRANCES
Actress. b. Washington, DC, Jan. 13, 1930. e. Vassar Coll., drama dept.; Perry-Mansfield School of Theatre. Studied with Sanford Meisner at Neighborhood Playhouse, NY. Was teacher at Milton Acad. in MA. Acted with Arena Stage, Washington, DC, 1953-54.
THEATER: Thieves Carnival (off-B'way debut, 1955), The Skin of Our Teeth, The Carefree Tree, The Admirable Bashville, Ulysses in Night Town, Viva Madison Avenue!, Red Eye of Love, Misalliance, Great Day in the Morning, The Right Honorable Gentleman, The Displaced Person, The Cocktail Party, Cock-a-Doodle Dandy, Playboy of the Western World, The Sign in Sidney Brustein's Window, Enemies, The Good Doctor (Tony Award, 1974), Equus, Angel, On Golden Pond, The Father, Grownups, Summer, You Can't Take It With You, Home Front, Driving Miss Daisy, Remembrance, A Perfect Ganesh, The Heiress (Tony Award, 1995), Long Day's Journey Into Night.
PICTURES: Up the Down Staircase (debut, 1967), The Tiger Makes Out, The Hospital, Two People, Fedora, Starting Over, Outland, Independence Day, Romantic Comedy, Bright Lights Big City, See You in the Morning, Communion, Sibling Rivalry, Misery, Doc Hollywood, Raising Cain, Curtain Call, Landfall.
TELEVISION: Series: Love of Life, Doctors, Golden Years, Under One Roof, The Road Home. Movies: Who'll Save Our Children?, Mother and Daughter: The Loving War, Prototype, Follow Your Heart, She Woke Up, Labor of Love: The Arlette Schweitzer Story, Reunion. Guest: Cheers, Tales From the Crypt, Outer Limits, The Con, To Live Again.

STEUER, ROBERT B.
Executive. b. New Orleans, LA, Nov. 18, 1937. e. U. of Illinois, & 1955-57; Tulane U., 1957-59, B.B.A. Booker-Southern D.I. circuit, New Orleans, 1959; assoc., prod., Poor White Trash; 1960; v.p. Cinema Dist. America, 1961; co-prod., Flesh Eaters, Common Law Wife, Flack Black Pussy Cat; partner, gen. mgr., radio station WTVF, Mobile, 1963; dir. special projects, American Intl. Pictures, 1967; so. div. sls. mgr., AIP, 1971; v.p. asst. gen. sls. mgr., AIP, 1974; partner, United Producers Organization, producing Screamers, 1977; v.p., sls., Ely Landau Org., 1979; v.p., gen. sls. mgr., Film Ventures Intl., 1981; exec. v.p. world-wide mktg., 1983; pres., FVI, 1986-89. 1987, exec. v.p. world-wide mktg. Film Ventures Intl; 1987-88 exec. prod. Operation: Take No Prisoners, Most Dangerous Women Alive, Tunnels, Criminal Act, Au Pair; 1989 sales consultant, 20th Century Fox, 1990-present, prods. rep.; When the Wales Came, China Cry, Twogether, Sweet and Short, Taxi to Soweto, and worldwide mktg., distrib. and sls. consultant to entertainment industry. Films incl. Bound and Gagged: A Love Story, Skin Art, Yankee Zulu.

STEVENS, ANDREW
Actor, Director, Writer, Producer. b. Memphis, TN, June 10, 1955. Mother is actress Stella Stevens. e. Antioch U., L.A., B.A. (psychology). L.A. stage includes Journey's End, Mass Appeal, Leader of the Pack, Billy Budd (also prod.), P.S. Your Cat is Dead, Bouncers (L.A. Drama Circle Critics Award). Pres., CEO Royal Oaks Entertainment Intl. Film Distributors.
PICTURES: Actor: Shampoo, Day of the Animals, Massacre at Central High, Las Vegas Lady, Vigilante Force, The Boys in Company C, The Fury, Death Hunt, The Seduction, Ten to Midnight, Scared Stiff, Tusks, Fine Gold, Deadly Innocents, Down the Drain, Eyewitness to Murder, The Ranch, The Terror Within, Blood Chase, Counterforce, The Terror Within II (also dir., s.p.), Red Blooded American Girl, Night Eyes (also s.p., prod.), Munchie, Double Threat, Night Eyes II (also s.p., prod.), Deadly Rivals, Night Eyes III (also s.p., dir.), Body Chemistry III (also prod.), Scorned (also dir.), Illicit Dreams (also dir.), Victim of Desire (prod. only), The Skateboard Kid 2 (also dir.), Body Chemistry 4 (prod. only), Hard Bounty (prod. only), Grid Runners (dir. only), Munchie Strikes Back. Producers: Victim of Desire, Body Chemistry 4, Starhunter, Cyber Zone, Masseuse, Virtual Desire, Alone in the Woods, Invisible Mom, Innocence Betrayed, Illicit Dreams 2, Over the Wire, Terminal Rush, Flash Frame (also dir.)
TELEVISION: Series: Oregon Trail, Code Red, Emerald Point N.A.S., Dallas. Mini-Series: Hollywood Wives, Once an Eagle. Movies: Beggarman Thief, The Rebels, The Bastard, The Last Survivors, The Oregon Trail, Secrets, Topper (also prod.), Women at Westpoint, Code Red, Miracle on Ice, Journey's End, Forbidden Love, Murder in Malibu (Columbo). Special: Werewolf of Woodstock. Guest: Adam-12, Apple's Way, The Quest, Police Story, Shazam, Hotel, Westside Medical, Murder She Wrote, Love Boat. Director: Swamp Thing (3 episodes), Silk Stalkings (2 episodes), General Hospital (3 eps), Walker—Texas Ranger, Marker.

STEVENS, CONNIE
Actress. r.n. Concetta Ann Ingolia. b. Brooklyn, NY, August 8, 1938. e. Sacred Heart Acad., Hollywood Professional Sch. Began career as winner of several talent contests in Hollywood; prof. debut, Hollywood Repertory Theatre's prod. Finian's Rainbow; B'way in Star Spangled Girl (Theatre World Award); recordings include: Kookie Kookie Lend Me Your Comb, 16 Reasons, What Did You Wanna Make Me Cry For, From Me to You, They're Jealous of Me, A Girl Never Knows.
PICTURES: Eighteen and Anxious (debut, 1957), Young and Dangerous, Dragstrip Riot, Rock-a-Bye Baby, The Party Crashers, Parrish, Susan Slade, Palm Springs Weekend, Two on a Guillotine, Never Too Late, Way ... Way Out, The Grissom Gang, The Last Generation, Scorchy, Sgt. Pepper's Lonely Hearts Club Band (cameo), Grease 2, Back to the Beach, Tapeheads, Love Is All There Is.
TELEVISION: Movies: Mister Jerico, Call Her Mom, Playmates, Every Man Needs One, The Sex Symbol, Love's Savage Fury, Scruples, Bring Me the Head of Dobie Gillis, Race with Destiny: The James Dean Story. Series: Hawaiian Eye, Wendy and Me, Kraft Music Halls Presents The Des O'Connor Show, Starting from Scratch.

STEVENS, CRAIG
Actor. r.n. Gail Shikles. b. Liberty, MO, July 8, 1918. Was married to late actress Alexis Smith. e. U. of Kansas. Played in coll. dramatics.
PICTURES: Affectionately Yours (debut, 1941), Law of the Tropics, Dive Bomber, Steel Against the Sky, Secret Enemies, Spy Ship, The Hidden Hand, Hollywood Canteen, Since You Went Away, The Doughgirls, God Is My Co-Pilot, Roughly Speaking, Too Young to Know, Humoresque, The Man I Love, That Way With Women, Love and Learn, Night Unto Night, The Lady Takes a Sailor, Where the Sidewalk Ends, Blues Busters, The Lady From Texas, Drums in the Deep South, Phone Call from a Stranger, Murder Without Tears, Abbott and Costello Meet Dr. Jekyll Mr. Hyde, The French Line, Duel on the Mississippi, The Deadly Mantis, Buchanan Rides Alone, Gunn, S.O.B., La Truite (The Trout).

TELEVISION: *Guest*: Lux Video Theatre, Four Star Playhouse, Loretta Young Show, Schlitz Playhouse, Dinah Shore, Ernie Ford Shows, Chevy Show, Summer on Ice, The Millionaire, The Bold Ones. *Series*: Peter Gunn (1958-61), Man of the World (ATV England), Mr. Broadway, The Invisible Man, Dallas. *Movies*: The Killer Bees; The Cabot Connection, The Home Front, Supercarrier, Marcus Welby, M.D.-A Holiday Affair. *Mini-Series*: Rich Man Poor Man.
THEATER: Here's Love, King of Hearts, Plain and Fancy, Critics Choice, Mary Mary, Cactus Flower (natl. co.), My Fair Lady.

STEVENS, FISHER
Actor. b. Chicago, IL, Nov. 27, 1963. e. NYU. Artistic Director of Naked Angels Theatre Co. in NYC.
THEATER: *NY*: Torch Song Trilogy (Off-B'way & B'way), Brighton Beach Memoirs, A Perfect Ganesh, Carousel.
PICTURES: The Burning, Baby It's You, The Brother From Another Planet, The Flamingo Kid, My Science Project, Short Circuit, The Boss's Wife, Short Circuit 2, Point of View, Reversal of Fortune, The Marrying Man, Mystery Date, Bob Roberts, Hero, When the Party's Over, Super Mario Bros., Nina Takes a Lover, Only You, Hackers, Cold Fever, Four Days in September.
TELEVISION: *Series*: Key West, Early Edition. *Guest*: Columbo. *Special*: It's Called the Sugar Plum, The Right to Remain Silent.

STEVENS, GEORGE, JR.
Director, Writer, Producer. b. Los Angeles, CA, April 3, 1932. Son of late director George Stevens. e. Occidental Coll., 1949-53, B.A. 1st Lieut. U.S. Air Force; TV dir., Alfred Hitchcock Presents, Peter Gunn, 1957-61; prod. asst. Giant Productions, 1953-54; prod. asst. Mark VII, Ltd., 1956-57; dir. M.P. Service, U.S. Information Agency 1962-67; chmn., U.S. deleg. to Film Festivals at Cannes (1962, 1964), Venice (1962, 1963), Moscow (1963); Founding director, American Film Institute, 1967-79; co-chmn., American Film Institute, 1979 to present.
PICTURES: The Diary of Anne Frank (assoc. prod.), The Greatest Story Ever Told (assoc. prod.), John F. Kennedy: Years of Lightning Day of Drums (prod.), America at the Movies (prod.), George Stevens: A Filmmaker's Journey (dir., s.p., prod.; 1988 WGA Award for TV broadcast).
TELEVISION: *Specials*: American Film Institute's Salutes (exec. prod./writer, 1973-; received 1975 Emmy Award as exec. prod. of The American Film Institue Salute to James Cagney), The Stars Salute America's Greatest Movies (exec. prod.), The Kennedy Center Honors (prod./writer, 1978-; Emmy Awards: 1984, 1986, 1989, 1996), America Entertains Vice Premier Deng (prod./writer), Christmas in Washington, (exec. prod./writer, 1982-), The Murder of Mary Phagan (co-writer, prod., 1988; Emmy Award for prod.; also Christopher & Peabody Awards), Separate But Equal (dir., writer, co-exec. prod.; Emmy Award for exec. prod.; also Christopher Award, Ohio State Award, Paul Selvin Award by the Writers Guild of America), George Stevens: D-Day to Berlin, The Kennedy Center Honors (co. prod., co-writer; Emmy Award, 1996).

STEVENS, STELLA
Actress, Director. b. Yazoo City, MS, Oct. 1, 1938. r.n. Estelle Eggleston. Mother of actor Andrew Stevens. e. Attended Memphis State U. Modeled in Memphis when she was discovered by talent scouts. Was briefly a term contract actress at 20th Century-Fox, later under exclusive contract to Paramount, then Columbia. *Director*: The American Heroine (feature length doc.), The Ranch (feature comedy). Creator/owner of Sexy Fragrances.
PICTURES: Say One For Me (debut, 1959), The Blue Angel, Li'l Abner, Man Trap, Girls! Girls! Girls!, Too Late Blues, The Nutty Professor, The Courtship of Eddie's Father, Advance to the Rear, Synanon, The Secret of My Success, The Silencers, Rage, Where Angels Go Trouble Follows, How to Save a Marriage and Ruin Your Life, Sol Madrid, The Mad Room, The Ballad of Cable Hogue, A Town Called Hell, Slaughter, Stand Up & Be Counted, The Poseidon Adventure, Arnold, Cleopatra Jones and the Casino of Gold, Las Vegas Lady, Nickelodeon, The Manitou, Wacko, Chained Heat, The Longshot, Monster in the Closet, Down the Drain, Last Call, The Terror Within II, Eye of the Stranger, The Guest, Exiled in America, The Nutty Nut, Hard Drive, Molly & Gina, Body Chemistry 3: Point of Seduction, Illicit Dreams, The Granny.
TELEVISION: *Series*: Ben Casey, Flamingo Road, Santa Barbara. *Guest*: Bob Hope Bing Crosby Special, Frontier Circus, Johnny Ringo, Alfred Hitchcock, Love Boat, Highway to Heaven, Murder She Wrote, Martin Mull's White America, A Table at Ciros, In the Heat of the Night, Hotel, Night Court, Newhart, Dangerous Curves, The Commish, Burke's Law. *Movies*: In Broad Daylight, In Cold Blood, Climb an Angry Mountain, Linda, The Day The Earth Moved, Honky Tonk, New Original Wonder Woman (pilot), Kiss Me Kill Me, Wanted: The Sundance Woman, Charlie Cobb (pilot), The Night They Took Miss Beautiful, Murder in Peyton Place, The Jordan Chance, Cruise into Terror, New Love Boat (pilot), Friendship Secrets and Lies, Hart to Hart (pilot), The French Atlantic Affair, The Pendragon Affair (Eddie Capra Mystery pilot), Make Me an Offer, Children of Divorce, Twirl, Amazons, Women of San Quentin, No Man's Land, A Masterpiece of Murder, Fatal Confessions (Father Dowling pilot), Man Against The Mob, Jake Spanner: Private Eye. *Special*: Attack of the 5'2" Woman, The Christmas List, Reunion in Hazzard.

STEVENSON, CYNTHIA
Actress. b. Oakland, CA, Aug. 2, 1963. Raised in Washington, Vancouver.
THEATER: Ladies Room.
PICTURES: The Player, The Gun in Betty Lou's Handbag, Watch It, Forget Paris, Home for the Holidays, Live Nude Girls.
TELEVISION: *Series*: My Talk Show, Bob, Hope and Gloria. *Movie*: Double Your Pleasure. *Guest*: Empty Nest, Cheers, Dream On.

STEVENSON, JULIET
Actress. b. England, Oct. 30, 1956. e. RADA.
THEATER: Other Worlds, Measure for Measure, Breaking the Silence, Troilus and Cressida, As You Like It, Les Liaisons Dangereuses, Yerma, Hedda Gabler, On the Verge, Burn This, Death and the Maiden, Scenes From an Execution (LA), The Duchess of Malfi.
PICTURES: Drowning by Numbers (debut, 1988), Ladder of Swords, Truly Madly Deeply, The Trial, The Secret Rapture, Emma.
TELEVISION: The Mallens (TV debut), Maybury, Bazaar and Rummage, Life Story, Stanley, Out of Love, Antigone, Oedipus at Colonus, Living With Dinosaurs, Amy, The March, A Doll's House, The Politician's Wife.

STEVENSON, PARKER
Actor. b. Philadelphia, PA, June 4, 1952. e. Princeton U. m. actress Kirstie Alley. Began professional acting career by starring in film, A Separate Peace, while high school senior, having attracted attention through work on TV commercials.
PICTURES: A Separate Peace (debut, 1972), Our Time, Lifeguard, Stroker Ace, Stitches, Official Denial.
TELEVISION: *Series*: Hardy Boys Mysteries, Falcon Crest, Probe, Baywatch, Melrose Place. *Guest*: The Streets of San Francisco, Gunsmoke. *Mini-Series*: North & South Book II, All the Rivers Run. *Movies*: This House Possessed, Shooting Stars, That Secret Sunday, Baywatch: Panic at Malibu Pier, The Cover Girl and the Cop, Are You Lonesome Tonight?, Nighttide, Shadow of a Stranger, Official Denial, Not of This Earth.

STEWART, DOUGLAS DAY
Writer, Director.
PICTURES: *Writer*: The Blue Lagoon, An Officer and a Gentleman, The Scarlet Letter. *Director-Writer*: Thief of Hearts, Listen to Me, The Visionary (dir. only).
TELEVISION: *Writer*: Boy in the Plastic Bubble, The Man Who Could Talk to Kids, Murder or Mercy, Silver Strand.

STEWART, JAMES L.
Executive. e. U. of Southern California, B.A. in cinema-TV and M.B.A. in finance. Worked for two years in sales for CBS Radio Network-West Coast. Spent four years with MGM in promotion and marketing. With Walt Disney Prods. for 12 years, functioning in marketing, management and administrative activities; named v.p.-corp. relations & admin. asst. to pres. 1978 joined in formation of Aurora Pictures, as exec. v.p., secty., & COO.
PICTURES: *Exec. prod.*: Why Would I Lie?, The Secret of NIMH, Eddie and the Cruisers, Heart Like a Wheel, East of the Sun, West of the Moon, Maxie.

STEWART, MARILYN
Marketing & Public Relations Executive. b. New York, NY. e. Hunter Coll. Entered ind. as scty. then asst. to MGM dir. of adv. Left to become prom.-pub. dir. for Verve/Folkways Records; duties also included ar and talent scouting. In 1966 joined 20th-Fox as radio/tv pub. coordinator. In 1969 went to Para. Pictures as mag. pub. coordinator; 1970 named worldwide dir. of pub. for Para., including creation of overall mkt. concepts, becoming 1st woman to be appt. to that position at major co. Campaigns included Love Story and The Godfather. 1972 opened own consulting office specializing in m.p. marketing and p.r. Headquarters in NY; repr. in L.A. Has represented The Lords of Flatbush, Bang the Drum Slowly, The Kids Are Alright, Autumn Sonata, The Tin Drum, A Cry in the Dark, The Russia House, Filmex, Michael Moriarty, Arthur Hiller, Fred Schepisi, Volker Schlondorff, Hemdale Pictures, Lucasfilm.

STEWART, PATRICK
Actor. b. Mirfield, England, July 13, 1940. Trained at Bristol Old Vic Theatre School. Made professional stage debut 1959 in Treasure Island with Lincoln Rep. Co. at the Theatre Royal in Lincoln.
THEATER: *NY*: A Midsummer Night's Dream, A Christmas Carol, The Tempest. Numerous London theatre credits incl.: The Investigation, Henry V, The Caretaker, Body and Soul, Who's Afraid of Virginia Woolf?, Yonadab. Associate artist with Royal Shakespeare Co. since 1967; many appearances with them incl. Antony and Cleopatra for which he received the Olivier Award for Best Supporting Actor in 1979.
PICTURES: Hennessy, Hedda, Excalibur, The Plague Dogs (voice), Races, Dune, Lifeforce, Code Name: Emerald, Wild Geese II, The Doctor and the Devils, Lady Jane, L.A. Story, Robin Hood: Men in Tights, Gunmen, Star Trek: Generations, The Pagemaster (voice), Liberation (narrator), Jeffrey, Star Trek: First Contact, Conspiracy Theory, Masterminds.

TELEVISION: *Series*: Eleventh Hour (BBC), Maybury (BBC), Star Trek: The Next Generation (U.S.). *Mini-Series*: I Claudius, Smiley's People. *Movies*: Little Lord Fauntleroy, Pope John Paul II, Death Train. *Special*: In Search of Dr. Seuss. *BBC Specials*: Oedipus Rex, Miss Julie, Hamlet, The Devil's Disciple, Fall of Eagles, The Artist's Story, Love Girl and the Innocent, Conrad, A Walk With Destiny, Alfred the Great, The Madness, When the Actors Come, Tolstoy: A Question of Faith, The Anatomist, The Mozart Inquest.

STIERS, DAVID OGDEN
Actor. b. Peoria, IL, Oct. 31, 1942. Guest conductor: 50 American orchestras incl. Chicago, San Diego, Dallas, Utah, and Chamber Orchestra of Baltimore. Resident conductor of Yaquina Chamber Orchestra in Oregon.
THEATER: *NY*: The Magic Show, Ulysses in Nighttown, The Three Sisters, Beggar's Opera, Measure for Measure.
PICTURES: Drive He Said, THX 1138, Oh God!, The Cheap Detective, Magic, Harry's War, The Man With One Red Shoe, Better Off Dead, Creator, Another Woman, The Accidental Tourist, Doc Hollywood, Beauty and the Beast (voice), Shadows and Fog, Iron Will, Bad Company, Pocahontas (voice), Steal Big Steal Little, Mighty Aphrodite, Meet Wally Sparks, The Hunchback of Notre Dame (voice).
TELEVISION: *Series*: Doc, M*A*S*H. *Movies*: Charlie's Angels (pilot), A Circle of Children, A Love Affair: The Eleanor and Lou Gehrig Story, Sgt. Matlovich Vs. the U.S. Air Force, Breaking Up is Hard to Do, Damien: The Leper Priest, The Day the Bubble Burst, Anatomy of an Illness, The First Olympics: Athens 1896, The Bad Seed, 5 Perry Mason Movies (Shooting Star, Lost Love, Sinister Spirit, Avenging Ace, Lady in the Lake), Mrs. Delafield Wants to Marry, The Alamo: 13 Days to Glory, The Kissing Place, Final Notice, The Final Days, How to Murder a Millionaire, Wife Mother Murderer, The Last of His Tribe, Without a Kiss Goodbye. *Specials*: The Oldest Living Graduate, The Innocents Abroad, Mastergate. *Mini-Series*: North and South (also Book II).

STILLER, BEN
Actor, Director. b. New York, NY, 1966. Son of performers Jerry Stiller and Anne Meara. e. UCLA. Made short film parody of The Color of Money, called The Hustler of Money which landed him work on Saturday Night Live. Acting debut in 1985 B'way revival of The House of Blue Leaves.
PICTURES: Hot Pursuit, Empire of the Sun, Fresh Horses, Next of Kin, That's Adequate, Stella, Highway to Hell, Reality Bites (also dir.), Heavyweights, Get Shorty, Flirting With Disaster, The Cable Guy (also dir.).
TELEVISION: *Series*: Saturday Night Live (also writer), The Ben Stiller Show (also creator, dir., writer; Emmy Award as writer). *Specials*: House of Blue Leaves, Colin Quinn Back in Brooklyn (dir., writer). *Movie*: Working Trash.

STILLER, JERRY
Actor. b. New York, NY, June 8, 1929. m. actress Anne Meara. Son is actor Ben Stiller, daughter is acress Amy Stiller. With partner Meara gained recognition as comedy team in nightclubs, theatres and on tv, most notably The Ed Sullivan Show. Video with Meara, So You Want to Be An Actor?
THEATER: *B'way*: The Ritz, Passione, Hurlyburly, Three Men on a Horse, What's Wrong With This Picture?, The Three Sisters.
PICTURES: The Taking of Pelham One Two Three, Airport 1975, The Ritz, Nasty Habits, Those Lips Those Eyes, Hot Pursuit, Nadine, Hairspray, That's Adequate, Little Vegas, Highway to Hell, The Pickle, Heavyweights, The Fish in the Bathtub.
TELEVISION: *Movies*: Madame X, The Other Woman, Seize the Day. Series: The Paul Lynde Show, Joe and Sons, Take Five With Stiller and Meara (synd), Tattingers, Seinfeld. *Guest*: L.A. Law, In the Heat of the Night, Homicide, Murder She Wrote, Touched By an Angel.

STING
Musician, Actor. r.n. Gordon Matthew Sumner. b. Newcastle-Upon-Tyne, England, Oct. 2, 1951. e. Warwick U. A schoolteacher before helping form rock group, The Police as songwriter, singer and bass player. B'way debut, Threepenny Opera, 1989.
PICTURES: Quadrophenia, Radio On, The Great Rock 'n' Roll Swindle, The Secret Policeman's Other Ball, Brimstone and Treacle, Dune, The Bride, Plenty, Bring on the Night, Julia and Julia, Stormy Monday, The Adventures of Baron Munchausen, Resident Alien, The Music Tells You, The Grotesque.

ST. JOHN, JILL
Actress. r.n. Jill Oppenheim. b. Los Angeles, CA, Aug. 19, 1940. m. actor Robert Wagner. On radio series One Man's family. Television debut, A Christmas Carol, 1948.
PICTURES: Summer Love, The Remarkable Mr. Pennypacker, Holiday for Lovers, The Lost World, The Roman Spring of Mrs. Stone, Tender Is the Night, Come Blow Your Horn, Who's Minding the Store?, Who's Been Sleeping in My Bed?, Honeymoon Hotel, The Liquidator, The Oscar, Banning, Tony Rome, Eight on the Lam, The King's Pirate, Diamonds Are Forever, Sitting Target, The Concrete Jungle, The Act, The Player.

TELEVISION: *Series*: Emerald Point. *Movies*: Fame Is the Name of the Game, How I Spent My Summer Vacation, The Spy Killer, Foreign Exchange, Brenda Starr, Telethon, Hart to Hart (pilot), Rooster. *Guest*: Dupont Theatre, Fireside Theatre, Batman, The Love Boat. *Mini-Series*: Around the World in 80 Days.

STOCKWELL, DEAN
Actor. b. Hollywood, CA, March 5, 1935. p. Harry and Betty Veronica Stockwell. Brother is actor Guy Stockwell. e. Long Island public schools and Martin Milmore, Boston. On stage in Theatre Guild prod. Innocent Voyage. Appeared on radio in Death Valley Days and Dr. Christian. Named in 1949 M.P. Herald-Fame Stars of Tomorrow poll; 1976 retired to Santa Monica as a licensed real estate broker but soon returned to acting.
PICTURES: Anchors Aweigh (debut, 1945), The Valley of Decision, Abbott and Costello in Hollywood, The Green Years, Home Sweet Homicide, The Mighty McGurk, The Arnelo Affair, The Romance of Rosy Ridge, Song of the Thin Man, Gentleman's Agreement, Deep Waters, The Boy With Green Hair, Down to the Sea in Ships, The Secret Garden, The Happy Years, Kim, Stars in My Crown, Kim, Cattle Drive, Gun for a Coward, The Careless Years, Compulsion, Sons and Lovers, Long Day's Journey Into Night, Rapture, Psych-Out, The Dunwich Horror, The Last Movie, The Loners, The Werewolf of Washington, Win Place or Steal (The Big Payoff), Won Ton Ton The Dog Who Saved Hollywood, Stick Fighter (South Pacific Connection), Tracks, She Came to the Valley, Alsino and the Condor, Sandino, Human Highway (also co-dir., s.p.), Wrong Is Right, To Kill a Stranger, Paris Texas, Dune, The Legend of Billie Jean, To Live and Die in L.A., Blue Velvet, Gardens of Stone, Beverly Hills Cop II, Banzai Runner, The Blue Iguana, Tucker: The Man and His Dream, Married to the Mob (Acad. Award nom.), Palais Royale, Limit Up, Buying Time, Time Guardian, The Player, Chasers, Mr. Wrong, Air Force One, McHale's Navy.
TELEVISION: *Series*: Quantum Leap. *Guest*: Miami Vice, Hart to Hart, Simon and Simon, The A-Team, Wagon Train, Twilight Zone, Playhouse 90, Bonanza, Hallmark Hall of Fame, Hunter, Police Story, Greatest Show on Earth. *Movies*: Paper Man, The Failing of Raymond, The Adventures of Nick Carter, The Return of Joe Forrester, Three for the Road, A Killing Affair, Born to Be Sold, Sweet Smell of Death (U.K.), The Gambler III: The Legend Continues, Son of the Morning Star, Backtrack, Shame, Fatal Memories, Bonanza: The Return, In the Line of Duty: The Price of Vengeance, Justice in a Small Town, The Innocent, Madonna: Innocence Lost, Deadline for Murder: From the Files of Edna Buchanan, Stephen King's The Langoliers. *Pilot*: Caught in the Act.

STODDARD, BRANDON
Executive. b. Brideport, CT, March 31, 1937. e. Yale U., BS Amer. Studies, 1958. Columbia Law Sch. Was program ass't at Batton, Barton, Durstine and Osborn before joining Grey Advertising, 1962, where was successively prog. ops. supvr., dir. daytime prog., VP TV/radio prog. Joined ABC in 1970; named v.p. daytime programs for ABC Entertainment, 1972; v.p. children's programs, 1973. Named v.p., motion pictures for TV, 1974; 1976 named v.p., dramatic progs. and m.p. for TV; 1979, named pres., ABC Motion Pictures; 1985 appt. pres., ABC Entertainment. Resigned 1989 to head ABC Prods. unit to create and prod. series and movies for ABC and other networks. Resigned that position, 1995.

STOLNITZ, ART
Executive. b. Rochester, NY, March 13, 1928. e. U. of Tennessee, LL.B., 1952. U.S. Navy Air Force. Legal dept., William Morris Agency, 1953, dir. business affairs, ZIV, 1959; dir. new program development, ZIV-United Artists, 1960; literary agent, MCA, 1961; dir. business affairs, Selmur Productions, Selmur Pictures, 1963; v.p. ABC Pictures, 1969; v.p. Metromedia Producers Corporation, 1970, executive v.p. Metromedia Producers Corporation; 1975 exec. v.p. and prod. Charles Fries Prods. 1976, prod. Edgar J. Scherick Productions; 1976-77 prod., Grizzly Adams (TV); 1977; v.p. business affairs, Warner Bros.-TV; 1980, sr. v.p., business affairs; 1990, exec. v.p. business & financial affairs, Lorimar; 1993, exec. v.p. business and financial affairs, Warner Bros. TV.

STOLOFF, VICTOR
Producer, Writer, Director, Editor. b. March 17, 1913. e. French Law U. Ac. Fines Arts. Prod. dir. writer of award winning documentaries (Warner Bros. release); Prod. dir. writer first U.S. film made in Italy, When in Rome; contract writer, dir. to Sidney Buchman, Columbia.
PICTURES: *Writer*: Volcano, The Sinner, Shark Reef, Journey Around the World. Of Love and Desire (also prod.), Intimacy (also prod., dir.), The Washington Affair (prod., dir.), The 300 Year Weekend (also dir.).
TELEVISION: Ford Theatre, Lloyd Bridges series, National Velvet, High Adventure with Lowell Thomas, *Prod.*: Hawaii Five-O. *Created* Woman of Russia (dir., writer), Audience (exec. prod., dir.).

STOLTZ, ERIC
Actor. b. Los Angeles, CA, 1961. Moved to American Samoa at age 3; family returned to California when he was 8. Spent 2 years at U. of Southern California in theatre arts; left to study with Stella Adler and later William Traylor and Peggy Feury.
THEATRE: Off-B'way: The Widow Claire, The American Plan, Down the Road, The Importance of Being Earnest. B'way: Our Town (B'way debut; Theatre World Award, Tony nom. & Drama Desk nom., 1988), Two Shakespearean Actors, Three Sisters. Regional: Tobacco Road, You're a Good Man Charlie Brown, Working (all with an American Rep. Co. in Scotland), Arms and the Man, Glass Menagerie (Williamstown Theater Festival).
PICTURES: Fast Times at Ridgemont High (debut, 1982), Surf II, Running Hot, The Wild Life, The New Kids, Mask, Code Name: Emerald, Some Kind of Wonderful, Lionheart, Sister Sister, Haunted Summer, Manifesto, The Fly II, Say Anything, Memphis Belle, The Waterdance, Singles (cameo), Bodies Rest & Motion (also co-prod.), Naked in New York, Killing Zoe, Sleep With Me (also prod.), Pulp Fiction, Little Women, Rob Roy, Fluke, The Prophecy, Kicking and Screaming, Grace of My Heart, 2 Days in the Valley, Inside, Anaconda, Mr. Jealousy (also prod.), The Passion of Ayn Rand, Hi-Life.
TELEVISION: Movies: The Grass Is Always Greener Over the Septic Tank, The Seekers, The Violation of Sarah McDavid, Paper Dolls, Thursday's Child, A Killer in the Family, Money, The Heart of Justice, Foreign Affairs, Roommates, Keys to Tulsa. Specials: Things Are Looking Up, Sensibility and Sense, Our Town. Guest: Mad About You, Homicide. Series: ER.

STONE, ANDREW L.
Director, Producer, Writer. b. Oakland, CA, July 16, 1902. e. U. of CA. Ent. ind. 1918 at Universal San Francisco exch.; later author, prod., dir. series of pictures for Paramount; prod., dir. for Sono-Art; 1932-36 org. and oper. Race Night company. Formed Andrew Stone Prods., 1943. Co-prod. with wife Virginia beginning in 1958.
PICTURES: Dir.: Dreary House (debut, 1928; also prod.), Hell's Headquarters, The Girl Said No (also prod., story), Stolen Heaven (also prod., story), Say It in French (also prod.), The Great Victor Herbert (also prod., co-story), There's Magic in Music (also prod., co-story), Stormy Weather, Hi Diddle Diddle (also prod.), Sensations of 1945 (also prod., co-s.p.), Bedside Manner (also prod.), The Bachelor's Daughters (also prod., s.p.), Fun on a Weekend (also prod., s.p.), Highway 301 (also s.p.), Confidence Girl (also prod., story, s.p.), The Steel Trap (also story, s.p.), Blueprint for Murder (also story, s.p.), The Night Holds Terror (also prod., story), Julie (also s.p.). Dir./Co-Prod./Writer: Cry Terror, The Decks Ran Red, The Last Voyage, Ring of Fire, The Password Is Courage, Never Put It in Writing, The Secret of My Success, Song of Norway, The Great Waltz.

STONE, AUBREY
Executive. b. Charlotte, NC, Jan. 14, 1964. e. U. of NC-Chapel Hill. Joined Consolidated Theatres Inc. in 1987. Helped to found a new motion picture exhibition company, Consolidated Theatres/The Stone Group, 1990. V.P., Consolidated Theatres/The Stone Group, 1990-95. Assumed role of v.p./general mgr. in 1996. Bd. of dir., NATO of NC & SC, 1991-present; pres., NATO of NC & SC, 1995-96. Bd of dir., National NATO, 1995-present; chmn., Programs & Services Committee, National NATO, present.

STONE, BURTON
Executive. b. Feb. 16, 1928; e. Florida Southern Coll. Was film ed., Hollywood Film Co. 1953-61; serv. mgr., sales mgr. and gen. mgr., Consolidated Film Inds., 1953-61; nat'l sales mgr., Movielab, 1961-63; pres., Allservice Film Laboratories, 1963-64; v.p. Technicolor, Inc., 1964-70. Pres., Precision Film Labs., 1965-76. Pres., Deluxe Laboratories, Inc., a wholly-owned subsidiary of 20th Century Fox, 1976-91. 1991, pres. Deluxe color, a sub of the Rank Org. Member: Board of directors, Will Rogers Foundation and Motion Picture Pioneers; member Acad. of Motion Picture Arts & Sciences, American Society of Cinematographers; awarded fellowship in Society of Motion Picture & Television Engineers; past pres., Association of Cinema & Video Laboratories; awarded fellowship in British Kinematograph, Sound & Television Society.

STONE, DEE WALLACE
Actress. r.n. Deanna Bowers. b. Kansas City, MO, Dec. 14, 1948. m. actor Christopher Stone. e. U. of Kansas, theater and education. Taught high school English. Came to NY to audition for Hal Prince and spent 2 years working in commercials and industrial shows. First break in Police Story episode.
PICTURES: The Stepford Wives (debut, 1975), The Hills Have Eyes, 10, The Howling, E.T. the Extra-Terrestrial, Jimmy the Kid, Cujo, Critters, Secret Admirer, Club Life, Shadow Play, The White Dragon, Alligator II: The Mutation, Popcorn, Rescue Me, Frighteners.

TELEVISION: Series: Together We Stand, Lassie, High Sierra Search and Rescue. Movies: The Sky's No Limit, Young Love First Love, The Secret War of Jackie's Girls, Child Bride of Short Creek, The Five of Me, A Whale for the Killing, Skeezer, Wait Til Your Mother Gets Home, Happy, I Take These Men, Hostage Flight, Sin of Innocence, Addicted to His Love, Stranger on My Land. Terror in the Sky, The Christmas Visitor, I'm Dangerous Tonight, Prophet of Evil: The Ervil LeBaron Story, Witness to the Execution, Search and Rescue, Moment of Truth: Cradle of Conspiracy, Huck and the King of Hearts. Guest: CHiPs.

STONE, MARIANNE
Actress. b. London, England. Studied Royal Acad. of Dramatic Art, West End debut in The Kingmaker, 1946.
PICTURES: Brighton Rock, Seven Days to Noon, The Clouded Yellow, Wrong Arm of the Law, Heavens Above, Stolen Hours, Nothing But the Best, Curse of the Mummy's Tomb, Hysteria, The Beauty Jungle, A Hard Day's Night, Rattle of a Simple Man, Echo of Diana, Act of Murder, Catch Us If You Can, You Must Be Joking, The Countess from Hong Kong, The Wrong Box, To Sir With Love, The Bliss of Mrs. Blossom, Here We Go Round the Mulberry Bush, Carry on Doctor, The Twisted Nerve, The Best House in London, Oh! What a Lovely War; The Raging Moon, There's a Girl in My Soup, All the Right Noises, Assault, Carry On at Your Convenience, All Coppers Are..., Carry on Girls, Penny Gold, The Vault of Horror, Percy's Progress, Confessions of a Window Cleaner, Carry on Dick, That Lucky Touch, Sarah, Carry on Behind, Confessions From a Holiday Camp, The Chiffy Kids, What's Up Superdoc?; The Class of Miss McMichael, The Human Factor, Dangerous Davies, Funny Money, Terry on the Fence, Carry on Laughing, The Wicked Lady, Deja Vu.
TELEVISION: Maigret, Bootsie and Snudge, Jimmy Edwards Show, Wayne and Schuster Show, Roy Hudd Show, Harry Worth Show, Steptoe and Son, Informer, Love Story, Father Dear Father, Bless This House, The Man Outside, Crown Court, Public Eye, Miss Nightingale, She, Little Lord Fauntleroy, The Secret Army (2 series), Shillingbury Tale, The Bright Side (series), Tickets for the Titanic (series), The Balance of Nature, Always, Hammer House of Mystery & Suspense, The Nineteenth Hole, In Possession.

STONE, OLIVER
Director, Writer. b. New York, NY, Sept. 15, 1946. e. Yale U., NYU, B.F.A., 1971. Teacher in Cholon, Vietnam 1965-66. U.S. Infantry specialist 4th Class. 1967-68 in Vietnam (Purple Heart, Bronze Star with Oak Leaf Cluster honors).
PICTURES: Sugar Cookies (assoc. prod.), Seizure (dir., s.p., co-editor, 1974), Midnight Express (s.p.; Acad. Award, 1978), The Hand (dir., s.p., cameo), Conan the Barbarian (co-s.p.), Scarface (s.p.), Year of the Dragon (co-s.p.), Salvador (dir., co-s.p., co-prod.), 8 Million Ways to Die (co-s.p.), Platoon (dir., s.p., cameo; Acad. Award & DGA Award for Best Director, 1986), Wall Street (dir., co-s.p., cameo), Talk Radio (dir., co-s.p.), Born on the Fourth of July (dir., co-s.p., cameo; Acad. Award & DGA Award for Best Director, 1989), Blue Steel (co-prod.), Reversal of Fortune (co-prod.), The Doors (dir., co-s.p., cameo), Iron Maze (co-exec. prod.), JFK (dir., co-prod., co-s.p.), South Central (co-exec. prod.), Zebrahead (co-exec. prod.), Dave (actor), The Joy Luck Club (co-exec. prod.), Heaven and Earth (dir., co-prod., s.p.), Natural Born Killers (dir., co-prod., co-s.p.), The New Age (exec. prod.), Nixon (dir., co-s.p., co-prod.; Chicago Film Critics Award), Killer: A Journal of Murder (co-exec. prod.), The People vs. Larry Flynt (prod.), Evita (co-prod.), Savior (prod.), Scud: The Disposable Assassin (prod.), On Any Given Sunday (dir., prod.), Chains (exec. prod.), The Art of War (prod.), The Corrupter (prod.).
TELEVISION: Mini-Series: Wild Palms (co-exec. prod.). Movie: Indictment: The McMartin Trial (co-exec. prod.), Frank Capra's American Dream.

STONE, PETER
Writer. b. Los Angeles, CA, Feb. 27, 1930. Son of film prod. John Stone and screenwriter Hilda Hess Stone. e. Bard Col., B.A. 1951; Yale U, M.F.A., 1953. Won Mystery Writers of America Award for Charade, Christopher Award for 1776.
THEATER: Kean, Skyscraper, 1776 (Tony and NY Drama Critics Circle Awards, 1969), Two By Two, Sugar, Full Circle, Woman of the Year (Tony Award, 1981), My One and Only, Will Rogers Follies (Tony, Grammy and NY Drama Critics Circle Awards, 1991), Titanic.
PICTURES: Charade, Father Goose (Acad. Award, 1964), Mirage, Arabesque, The Secret War of Harry Frigg, Jigsaw, Sweet Charity, Skin Game, The Taking of Pelham One Two Three, 1776, The Silver Bears, Who Is Killing the Great Chefs of Europe?, Why Would I Lie?, Grand Larceny, Just Cause.
TELEVISION: Movies: Studio One, Brenner, Witness, Asphalt Jungle, The Defenders (Emmy Award, 1962). Androcles and the Lion, Baby on Board, The Taking of Pelham One Two Three. Series: Adam's Rib, Ivan the Terrible.

STONE, SHARON
Actress. b. Meadville, PA, March 10, 1958. e. Edinboro St. Univ. Started as model, appearing in several TV commercials.
PICTURES: Stardust Memories (debut, 1980), Deadly Blessing, Bolero, Irreconcilable Differences, King Soloman's Mines, Allan Quartermain and the Lost City of Gold, Cold Steel, Police Academy 4: Citizens on Patrol, Action Jackson, Above the Law, Blood and Sand, Beyond the Stars (Personal Choice), Total Recall, He Said/She Said, Scissors, Year of the Gun, Basic Instinct, Diary of a Hit Man, Where Sleeping Dogs Lie, Sliver, Last Action Hero (cameo), Intersection, The Specialist, The Quick and the Dead (also co- prod.), Casino (Golden Globe Award), The Last Dance, Diabolique, The Mighty, Sphere, Gloria, Antz.
TELEVISION: Series: Bay City Blues. Mini-Series: War and Remembrance. Movies: Not Just Another Affair, The Calendar Girl Murders, The Vegas Strip Wars, Tears in the Rain. Pilots: Mr. & Mrs. Ryan, Badlands 2005. Guest: T.J. Hooker, Magnu P.I., Roseanne, Big Guns Talk: The Story of the Western.

STOPPARD, TOM
Writer, Director. b. Zlin, Czechoslovakia, July 3, 1937. r.n. Tomas Straussler. Playwright whose works include Rosencrantz and Guildenstern Are Dead, Jumpers, Travesties, The Real Thing, Hapgood, Arcadia.
PICTURES: The Romantic Englishwoman, Despair, The Human Factor, Squaring the Circle, Brazil, Empire of the Sun, The Russia House, Rosencrantz and Guildenstern Are Dead (also dir.), Billy Bathgate, Fifteen Minute Hamlet, Shakespeare in Love, Enigma.
TELEVISION: Movies: Three Men in a Boat, The Dog It Was That Died, Poodle Springs.

STORARO, VITTORIO
Cinematographer. b. Rome, Italy, June 24, 1940. Trained at Rome's Centro Sperimentale Cinematografia and began filming short films. His work as Bernardo Bertolucci's regular cine- matographer won him an international reputation and award- winning work in Europe and America, including 3 Academy Awards.
PICTURES: Giovinezza Giovinezza (Youthful Youthful), The Gallery Murders, The Conformist, The Spider's Stratagem, The Fifth Cord, Malice, 'Tis Pity She's a Whore, Last Tango in Paris, Giordano Bruno, Footprints, The Driver's Seat, 1900, Submission, Agatha, Apocalypse Now (Acad. Award, 1979), La Luna, Reds (Acad. Award, 1981), One From the Heart, Wagner, Ladyhawke, Captain Eo, Ishtar, The Last Emperor (Acad. Award, 1987), Tucker: The Man and His Dream, New York Stories (Life Without Zoe), Dick Tracy, The Sheltering Sky, Tosca, Little Buddha, Roma! Imago Urbis, Flamenco, Taxi, Tango (Canne Film Fest. Award, Tech. Prize, 1998), Bulworth.

STOREY, FREDERICK
Executive. b. Columbus, GA, Nov. 12, 1909. e. Georgia Tech. Adv. staff Atlanta Journal, 1933-38; adv. staff C. P. Clark Adv. Agcy., 1938; partner 1940; U.S. Navy, 1941-46; staff Georgia Theatre Co., 1946; v.p. 1947-52. Founded Storey Theatres Inc., Atlanta, GA; 1952, now bd. chmn. emeritus (formerly pres.) of Georgia State Theatres; dir. numerous theatre cos.; v.p. dir., Motion Picture Theatre Owners of Georgia, Dist. Alumnus award, Georgia Tech, 1979.

STORKE, WILLIAM F.
Producer. b. Rochester, NY, Aug. 12, 1927. e. UCLA, B.A. 1948. In Navy, WWII. First position with NBC Hollywood guest relations staff, 1948. Moved to continuity advance dept. as comm. edi- tor. Prom. to asst. mgr, comm. spvr. before joining NBC West Coast sales dept., 1953. Transferred to N.Y. as prog. acct. exec., 1955; named administrator, participating prog. sales, 1957. Named dir., participating program sales, 1959. Named dir., pro- gram adm., NBC-TV, 1964; then elected v.p., program adm.; 1967 named v.p., programs, East Coast; 1968, appt. v.p., special programs, NBC-TV Network; 1979, pres., Claridge Group, Ltd.; exec. v.p. Entertainment Partners, Inc., N.Y., 1982-. Pres., Storke Enterprises Inc. 1988-
TELEVISION: Producer: Oliver Twist, To Catch A King, A Christmas Carol, The Last Days of Patton, A Special Friendship, The Ted Kennedy Jr. Story, Buck James (series, exec. prod.), Old Man and the Sea, Hands of a Murderer (Sherlock Holmes).

STORM, GALE
Actress. r.n. Josephine Cottle. b. Bloomington, TX, April 5, 1922. Won Gateway to Hollywood talent contest while still in high school, in 1939. Also launched successful recording career. Autobiography: I Ain't Down Yet (1981).
PICTURES: Tom Brown's Schooldays (debut, 1939), Smart Alecks, Foreign Agent, Nearly Eighteen, Where Are Your Children?, Revenge of the Zombies, The Right to Live, Sunbonnet Sue, Swing Parade of 1946, It Happened on Fifth Avenue, The Dude Goes West, Stampede, The Kid From Texas, Abandoned, Between Midnight and Dawn, Underworld Story, Curtain Call at Cactus Creek, Al Jennings of Oklahoma, Texas Rangers, Woman of the North Country.
TELEVISION: Series: My Little Margie, The Gale Storm Show.

STOSSEL, JOHN
News Correspondent. b. 1947. e. Princeton U. Started as pro- ducer-reporter with KGW-TV in Portland, OR. Joined WCBS-TV in New York as investigative reporter and consumer editor, win- ning 15 local Emmy Awards. 1981 joined ABC-TV, appearing on Good Morning America and 20/20 as consumer editor. Also pro- vides twice-weekly consumer reports on ABC Radio Information Network. Author: Shopping Smart (1982).

STOWE, MADELEINE
Actress. b. Los Angeles, CA, Aug. 18, 1958. e. USC. m. actor Brian Benben. Began acting at the Solari Theatre in Beverly Hills where she appeared in The Tenth Man.
PICTURES: Stakeout (debut, 1987), Tropical Snow, Worth Winning, Revenge, The Two Jakes, Closet Land, China Moon, Unlawful Entry, The Last of the Mohicans, Another Stakeout, Short Cuts, Blink, Bad Girls, Twelve Monkeys, The Proposition.
TELEVISION: Series: The Gangster Chronicles. Movies: The Nativity, The Deerslayer, Amazons, Blood and Orchids. Mini- Series: Beulah Land.

STRAIGHT, BEATRICE
Actress. b. Old Westbury, NY, Aug. 2, 1914. Trained in classics; won Tony award early in career for best actress in Arthur Miller's The Crucible.
THEATER: NY: King Lear, Twelfth Night, The Possessed, Land of Fame, Eastward in Eden, The Heiress (B'way & on tour), The Crucible (Tony Award), Phedra, Everything in the Garden, Ghosts, All My Sons. Regional: A Streetcar Named Desire, The Lion in Winter, Old Times.
PICTURES: Phone Call from a Stranger (debut, 1952), Patterns, The Nun's Story, Garden Party, Network (Acad. Award, best sup- porting actress, 1976), The Promise, Bloodline, The Formula, Endless Love, Poltergeist, Two of a Kind, Power.
TELEVISION: Series: Beacon Hill, King's Crossing, Jack and Mike. Mini-Series: The Dain Curse, Robert Kennedy and His Times. Specials: The Borrowers, Faerie Tale Theatre (The Princess and the Pea). Movies: Killer on Board, Under Siege, Run Till You Fall, Chiller, People Like Us.

STRASBERG, SUSAN
Actress. b. New York, NY, May 22, 1938. e. NY. p. late Lee Strasberg, stage dir. & dir. of Actors Studio, and Paula Miller, actress. Off-B'way stage debut in Maya; followed by The Duchess and the Smugs, Romeo and Juliet, The Diary of Anne Frank (B'way; Theatre World Award), Time Remembered, Zeffirelli's Lady of the Camillias, Shadow of a Gunman, Agnes of God (tour). Author: Bittersweet. Also teaches acting.
PICTURES: The Cobweb (debut, 1955), Picnic, Stage Struck, Scream of Fear, Adventures of a Young Man, The High Bright Sun (McGuire Go Home!), The Trip, Psych-Out, Chubasco, The Name of the Game Is Kill, The Brotherhood, So Evil My Sister, Legend of Hillbilly John, And Millions Will Die, Rollercoaster, The Manitou, In Praise of Older Women, Sweet 16, The Delta Force, Bloody Birthday, Prime Suspect, The Runnin' Kind, Schweitzer, The Cherry Orchard.
TELEVISION: Movies: Marcus Welby M.D. (A Matter of Humanities), Hauser's Memory, Mr. & Mrs. Bo Jo Jones, SST- Death Flight, Beggarman, Thief, The Immigrants, Toma (pilot), Frankenstein, Rona Jaffe's Mazes and Monsters. Series: The Marriage, Toma. Guest: Murder She Wrote, Cagney and Lacy.

STRATHAIRN, DAVID
Actor. b. San Francisco, CA, 1949. e. Williams Col.
THEATER: Einstein and the Polar Bear, Blue Plate Special, Fen, I'm Not Rappaport, Salonika, A Lie of the Mind, The Birthday Party, Danton's Death, Mountain Language, L'Atelier, A Moon for the Misbegotten, Temptation.
PICTURES: Return of the Secaucus 7, Lovesick, Silkwood, Iceman, The Brother from Another Planet, When Nature Calls, Enormous Changes at the Last Minute, At Close Range, Matewan, Stars and Bars, Dominick and Eugene, Call Me, Eight Men Out, The Feud, Memphis Belle, City of Hope, Big Girls Don't Cry... They Get Even, A League of Their Own, Bob Roberts, Sneakers, Passion Fish, Lost in Yonkers, The Firm, A Dangerous Woman, The River Wild, Losing Isaiah, Dolores Claiborne, Mother Night.
TELEVISION: Series: The Days and Nights of Molly Dodd. Movies: Day One, Son of the Morning Star, Heat Wave, Judgment, Without Warning: The James Brady Story, O Pioneers!, The American Clock. Guest: Miami Vice, The Equalizer.

STRAUSS, PETER
Actor. b. Croton-on-Hudson, NY., Feb. 20, 1947. e. Northwestern U. Spotted at N.U. by talent agent and sent to Hollywood. On stage at Mark Taper Theatre in Dance Next Door, The Dirty Man.
PICTURES: Hail Hero! (debut, 1969), Soldier Blue, The Trial of the Catonsville Nine, The Last Tycoon, Spacehunter: Adventures in the Forbidden Zone, Nick of Time.

TELEVISION: *Series*: Moloney. *Movies*: The Man Without a Country, Attack on Terror: The FBI Versus the Ku Klux Klan, Young Joe: The Forgotten Kennedy, The Jericho Mile (Emmy Award, 1979), Angel on My Shoulder, Heart of Steel, Under Siege, A Whale for the Killing, Penalty Phase, Proud Men, Brotherhood of the Rose, Peter Gunn, 83 Hours Till Dawn, Flight of Black Angel, Fugitive Among Us, Trial: The Price of Passion, Men Don't Tell, Thicker Than Blood: The Larry McLinden Story, The Yearling, Reunion, Texas Justice. *Mini-Series*: Rich Man Poor Man, Masada, Kane & Abel, Tender Is The Night.

STRAUSS, PETER E.

Executive. b. Oct. 7, 1940. e. Oberlin Coll., London Sch. of Economics, Columbia U. Sch. of Law, L.L.B., 1965. Vice pres., University Dormitory Dev. Co., 1965-68; v.p., Allart Cinema 16, 1968-69; v.p. prod., Allied Artists Pictures Corp., 1970; 1978-80, exec. v.p. Rastar Films; left to become independent as pres., Panache Prods., 1980-86. 1987, pres. & CEO of The Movie Group.
PICTURE: *Producer*: Best of the Best, Cadence, By the Sword, Best of the Best II, Best of the Best III.

STREEP, MERYL

Actress. r.n. Mary Louise Streep. b. Summit, NJ, June 22, 1949. e. Vassar. Acted for a season with traveling theater co. in VT. Awarded scholarship to Yale Drama School, 1972. NY stage debut: Trelawny of the Wells (1975) with New York Shakespeare Fest. Appeared in 1984 documentary In Our Hands.
THEATER: *Off-B'way*: 27 Wagons Full of Cotton (Theatre World Award), A Memory of Two Mondays, Secret Service, Henry V, (NY Shakespeare Fest.), Measure for Measure (NYSF), The Cherry Orchard, Happy End (B'way debut, 1977), The Taming of the Shrew (NYSF), Taken in Marriage, Alice in Concert, Isn't It Romantic?
PICTURES: Julia (debut, 1977), The Deer Hunter, Manhattan, The Seduction of Joe Tynan, Kramer vs. Kramer (Acad. Award, best supporting actress, 1979), The French Lieutenant's Woman, Still of the Night, Sophie's Choice (Acad. Award, 1982), Silkwood, Falling in Love, Plenty, Out of Africa, Heartburn, Ironweed, A Cry in the Dark, She-Devil, Postcards From the Edge, Defending Your Life, Death Becomes Her, The House of the Spirits, The River Wild, The Bridges of Madison County, Before and After, Marvin's Room, One True Thing, Antz, Dancing at Lughnasa.
TELEVISION: *Mini-Series*: Holocaust (Emmy Award, 1978). *Movies*: The Deadliest Season. *Specials* (PBS): Secret Service, Uncommon Women and Others, Age 7 in America (host), First Do No Harm.

STREISAND, BARBRA

Singer, Actress, Director, Producer. b. New York, NY, April 24, 1942. e. Erasmus H.S., Brooklyn. Son is actor Jason Gould. Appeared as singer in NY night clubs. NY stage debut: Another Evening with Harry Stoones (1961), followed by Pins and Needles. On Broadway in I Can Get It For You Wholesale, Funny Girl. Performed song Prisoner for 1978 film Eyes of Laura Mars. Appeared in 1990 documentary Listen Up.
PICTURES: Funny Girl (debut; Acad. Award, 1968), Hello Dolly!, On a Clear Day You Can See Forever, The Owl and the Pussycat, What's Up Doc?, Up the Sandbox, The Way We Were (Acad. Award nom.), For Pete's Sake, Funny Lady, A Star Is Born (also co-composer, exec. prod.; Acad. Award for best song: Evergreen, 1976), The Main Event (also co-prod.), All Night Long, Yentl (also dir., prod., co- s.p.), Nuts (also prod., co-composer), The Prince of Tides (also dir., co-prod.; Acad. Award nom. for picture), The Mirror Has Two Faces (also dir.).
TELEVISION: *Specials*: My Name Is Barbra (Emmy Award, 1965), Color Me Barbra, The Belle of 14th Street, A Happening in Central Park, Barbra Streisand… And Other Musical Instruments, Putting It Together, One Voice, Barbra Streisand: The Concert (also co-prod.; 2 Emmy Awards, 1995). *Movie*: Serving in Silence: The Margarethe Cammermeyer Story (co-exec. prod. only). *Guest*: Ed Sullivan, Merv Griffin, Judy Garland Show, Saturday Night Live, Late Show With David Letterman.

STRICK, WESLEY

Writer. b. New York, NY, Feb. 11, 1954. e. UC at Berkeley, 1975. Was rock critic for magazines Rolling Stone, Cream, Circus.
PICTURES: True Believer, Arachnophobia, Cape Fear, Final Analysis, Batman Returns, Wolf, The Tie That Binds (dir.), The Saint (s.p.), Return to Paradise.
TELEVISION: *Series*: Eddie Dodd (pilot).

STRICKLAND, GAIL

Actress. b. Birmingham, AL, May 18. e. Florida St. Univ. NY Theatre includes Status Quo Vadis, I Won't Dance.
PICTURES: The Drowning Pool, Bittersweet Love, Bound for Glory, One on One, Who'll Stop the Rain, Norma Rae, Lies, Oxford Blues, Protocol, The Man in the Moon, Three of Hearts, When a Man Loves a Woman, How to Make an American Quilt, The American President.

TELEVISION: *Series*: The Insiders, What a Country, Heartbeat. *Movies*: Ellery Queen, My Father's House, The Dark Side of Innocence, The Gathering, A Love Affair: The Eleanor and Lou Gehrig Story, The President's Mistress, Ski Lift to Death, Letters from Frank, King Crab, Rape and Marriage: The Rideout Case, A Matter of Life and Death, My Body My Child, Eleanor: First Lady of the World, Life of the Party: The Story of Beatrice, Starlight: The Plane That Couldn't Land, The Burden of Proof, Silent Cries, Spies, Barbara Taylor Bradford's Remember, A Mother's Prayer.

STRICKLYN, RAY

Actor. b. Houston, TX, October 8, 1928. e. U. of Houston. Official U.S. representative at Edinburgh Int'l Festival (1988); and Israel Intl. Festival (1989).
THEATER: The Climate of Eden (B'way debut; Theatre World Award). Tour: Stalag 17. Off-B'way: The Grass Harp, Confessions of a Nightingale (also LA, tour; LA Drama Critics, LA Weekly, Dramalogue, Oscar Wilde Awards). LA: Vieux Carre, Compulsion, The Caretaker, Naomi Court, Bus Stop.
PICTURES: The Proud and the Profane, Crime in the Streets, Somebody Up There Likes Me, The Catered Affair, The Last Wagon, Return of Dracula, 10 North Frederick, The Remarkable Mr. Pennypacker, The Big Fisherman, Young Jesse James, The Plunderers, The Lost World, Track of Thunder, Arizona Raiders, Dogpound Shuffle.
TELEVISION: *Movies*: Jealousy, Danielle Steel's Secrets, Hart to Hart Returns.

STRINGER, HOWARD

Executive. b. Cardiff, Wales. Feb. 19, 1942. e. Oxford U., B.A., M.A., modern history/international relations. Received Army Commendation Medal for meritorious achievement for service in Vietnam (1965-67). Joined CBS, 1965, at WCBS-TV, NY, rising from assoc. prod., prod. to exec. prod. of documentary broadcasts. Served as prod., dir. and writer of CBS Reports: The Palestinians (Overseas Press Club of America, Writers Guild Awards, 1974); The Rockefellers (Emmy Award, 1973). Won 9 Emmy Awards as exec. prod., prod., writer or dir: CBS Reports: The Boston Goes to China; CBS Reports: The Defense of the United States; CBS Evening News with Dan Rather: The Beirut Bombing; The Countdown Against Cancer; The Black Family. Exec. prod., CBS Reports; exec. prod., CBS Evening News with Dan Rather, 1981-84. Appointed exec. vice pres., CBS News Division, 1984; pres., CBS News, 1986; pres., CBS/Broadcast Group, 1988. Chmn. & CEO, Tele-TV 1995. Pres., Sony Corporation of America.

STRITCH, ELAINE

Actress. b. Detroit, MI, Feb. 2, 1926. e. studied acting with Erwin Piscator at the New Sch. for Social Research. Major career on stage. B'way debut 1946 in Loco.
THEATER: *NY*: Made in Heaven, Angel in the Wings, Call Me Madam, Pal Joey, On Your Toes, Bus Stop, Goldilocks, Sail Away, Who's Afraid of Virginia Woolf?, Wonderful Town, Company, Show Boat, A Delicate Balance (Tony Award nom.). *London*: Gingerbread Lady, Small Craft Warnings, Company.
PICTURES: The Scarlet Hour (debut, 1955), Three Violent People, A Farewell to Arms, The Perfect Furlough, Who Killed Teddy Bear?, Sidelong Glances of a Pigeon Kicker, The Spiral Staircase, Providence, September, Cocoon: The Return, Cadillac Man, Out to Sea.
TELEVISION: *Series*: Growing Paynes (1948), Pantomine Quiz (regular, 1953-55, 1958), My Sister Eileen, The Trials of O'Brien, Two's Company (London), Nobody's Perfect (London; also adapt.) The Ellen Burstyn Show. *Specials*: Company: the Making of the Album, Kennedy Center Tonight, Follies in Concert, Sensibility and Sense. Movies: The Secret Life of Archie's Wife, An Inconvenient Woman, Chance of a Lifetime. *Guest*: Law & Order (Emmy Award, 1993).

STROCK, HERBERT L.

Producer, Writer, Director, Film editor. b. Boston, MA, Jan. 13, 1918. e. USC, A.B., M.A. in cinema. Prof. of cinema, USC, 1941. Started career, publicity leg man, Jimmy Fidler, Hollywood columnist; editorial dept., MGM, 1941-47; pres., IMPPRO, Inc., 1955-59; assoc. prod.-supv. film ed., U.A.; director: AIP, Warner Bros. independent, Phoenix Films. Pres., Herbert L. Strock Prods. Lecturer at American Film Institute.
PICTURES: Storm Over Tibet, Magnetic Monster, Riders to the Stars, The Glass Wall. *Director*: Gog, Battle Taxi, Donovan's Brain, Rider on a Dead Horse, Devil's Messenger, Brother on the Run, One Hour of Hell, Witches Brew, Blood of Dracula, I Was a Teenage Frankenstein, The Crawling Hand; Soul Brothers Die Hard, Monstroids. *Writer-film editor*, Hurray for Betty Boop (cartoon). *Sound Effects editor* on Katy Caterpillar (cartoon feature). *Editor*: Night Screams, Detour. *Post-prod. spvr.*: King Kung Fu, Sidewalk Motel. *Co-director*: Deadly Presence. *Editor*: Snooze You Lose, Gramma's Gold, Distance, Fish Outta Water. *Prod/edit.*: The Visitors, Statistically Speaking.

TELEVISION: Highway Patrol, Harbor Command, Men of Annapolis, I Led Three Lives, The Veil, Dragnet, 77 Sunset Strip, Maverick, Cheyenne, Bronco, Sugarfoot, Colt 45, Science Fiction Thea., Seahunt, Corliss Archer, Bonanza, Hallmark Hall of Fame, The Small Miracle, Hans Brinker, The Inventing of America (specials); What Will We Say to a Hungry World (telethon), They Search for Survival (special), Flipper (series). *Documentaries*: Atlantis, Legends, UFO Journals, UFO Syndrome, Legend of the Lochness Monster, China-Mao to Now, El-Papa—Journey to Tibet. *Editor*: Peace Corps' Partnership in Health. *L.A. Dept. of Water & Power*: Water You Can Trust. Olympic Comm. Your Olympic Legacy—AAF.

STROLLER, LOUIS A.
Producer. b. Brooklyn, NY, April 3, 1942. e. Nicholas Coll. of Business Admin., BBA, 1963. Entered film business in 1963 doing a variety of jobs in local NY studios, and TV commercials. Unit manager on The Producers. Moved to L.A. in 1970s. First asst. dir. Charley, Take the Money and Run, Lovers and Other Strangers, They Might Be Giants, Man on a Swing, 92 in the Shade. Prod. mgr.: Mortadella, Sisters, Sweet Revenge, The Eyes of Laura Mars, Telefon. *Assoc. prod.*: Badlands, Carrie. The Seduction of Joe Tynan.
PICTURES: *Exec. prod. or prod.*: Simon, The Four Seasons, Venom, Eddie Macon's Run, Scarface, Sweet Liberty, Real Men, A New Life, Sea of Love, Betsy's Wedding, Back in the U.S.S.R., The Real McCoy, Carlito's Way, The Shadow, The Rock, Nothing to Lose.
TELEVISION: Half a Lifetime (exec. prod.; nom. 4 ACE Awards), Blue Ice.

STRONG, JOHN
Producer, Director, Writer, Actor. b. New York, NY, Dec. 3. e. U. of Miami, Cornell U., B.S., architectural engineering. Began acting in small role in film Duel in the Sun; on B'way in Annie Get Your Gun and understudy for James Dean in Immoralist. Appeared in many radio and TV serials, regular on Captain Video and the Video Ranger, later under contract as actor to Universal and Warner Bros. Member, Writers Guild America West, Directors Guild of America, Producers Guild of America, Dramatists Guild. Pres., Cinevent Corp.
PICTURES: Perilous Journey (exec. prod., s.p.), Eddie & the Cruisers (sprv. prod.), Heart Like a Wheel (sprv. prod.), For Your Eyes Only (s.p.), The Earthling (prod.), The Mountain Men (actor, prod.), Savage Streets (prod.), Steel Justice (prod.), Knights of the City (prod.), Garbage Pail Kids (sprv. prod.), Cop (sprv. prod.), Wild Thing (sprv. prod.), Summer Heat (sprv. prod.), Teen Wolf II (sprv. prod.), Atlantic Entertainment (sprv. prod.), Show of Force (prod., s.p.), Prime Directive (prod., s.p.), Sinapore Sling (prod., s.p.), Willie Sutton Story (prod.), Bandit Queen (prod.), Fatal Charm (exec. prod.), Colors of Love (prod.), Black Ice (dir., s.p.).
TELEVISION: The John Strong Show (host, exec. prod.), The Nurse (special, writer), McCloud (prod., writer), The Thrill of the Fall (prod.), Search (prod., writer, 2nd unit dir.), Outer Limits (exec. chg. prod.), Name of the Game (exec. chg. prod.), I Spy (writer), Love American Style (writer), All in the Family (writer), Changes (prod., dir., writer), Charlie's Angels (writer), Hawaii Five O' (writer).

STROUD, DON
Actor. b. Honolulu, Hawaii, Sept. 1, 1943. e. Kaimuki h.s. Was surfing champion, ranked 4th in the world.
PICTURES: Games, Madigan, Journey to Shiloh, What's So Bad About Feeling Good?, Coogan's Bluff, Bloody Mama, Explosion, Angel Unchained, Tick Tick Tick, Von Richtofen and Brown, Joe Kidd, Slaughter's Big Rip-Off, Scalawag, Murph the Surf, The Killer Inside Me, The House by the Lake, The Choirboys, The Buddy Holly Story, The Amityville Horror, The Night the Lights Went Out in Georgia, Search and Destroy, Sweet Sixteen, Armed and Dangerous, Licence to Kill, Down the Drain, The Divine Enforcer, King of the Kickboxers, Cartel, Mob Boss, Street Wars, Frogtown, Deady Avenger, Danger Sign, Carnosaur II, Of Unknown Origin, Sudden Death, Dillinger and Capone, Twisted Justice, Two to Tango, Ghost Ship, Precious Find, Wild America, Perdita Durango.
TELEVISION: *Series*: Kate Loves a Mystery, Mike Hammer, The New Gidget, Dragnet. *Pilot*: Barefoot in Paradise. *Movies*: Split Second to an Epitaph, Something for a Lonely Man, DA: Conspiracy to Kill, Deadly Dream, Daughters of Joshua Cabe, Rolling Man, The Elevator, Return of Joe Forrester, High Risk, Katie: Portrait of a Centerfold, Out on a Limb, I Want to Live, Manhunters, Murder Me Murder You, The Alien Within, Sawbones, Barefoot in Paradise. *Special*: Hatful of Rain. *Guest*: Murder She Wrote, Quantum Leap, The FBI, Gunsmoke, Baywatch, Starsky and Hutch, The Mod Squad, Marcus Welby, Babylon 5, Walker: Texas Ranger, Nash-Bridges, many others.

STRUTHERS, SALLY
Actress. b. Portland, OR, July 28, 1948. First tv appearance was as dancer on a Herb Alpert special. Appeared on Broadway stage in Wally's Cafe.
PICTURES: The Phynx, Five Easy Pieces, The Getaway.

TELEVISION: *Series*: The Summer Smothers (1970), The Tim Conway Comedy Hour, All in the Family (Emmy Awards: 1972, 1979), Pebbles and Bamm-Bamm (voice), Flintstones Comedy Hour (voice), Gloria, 9 to 5, Dinosaurs (voice). *Movies*: The Great Houdinis, Aloha Means Goodbye, Hey I'm Alive, Intimate Strangers, My Husband is Missing, And Your Name is Jonah, A Gun in the House, A Deadly Silence, In the Best Interests of the Children.

STUBBS, IMOGEN
Actress. b. Newcastle-upon-Tyne, England, Feb. 2, 1961. Brought up in West London on sailing barge on the Thames. Grandmother was playwright Esther McCracken. e. Exeter Coll. First class degree at Oxford U. in English. Joined Oxford U. Dramatic Society appearing in revues and at Edinburgh Festival in play called Poison. Trained for stage at Royal Acad. of Dramatic Art. Prof. stage debut in Cabaret and The Boyfriend, in Ipswich. Acted with Royal Shakespeare Co. in The Two Noble Kinsmen, The Rover (promising newcomer critics award), Richard II, Othello, Heartbreak House, St. Joan, Uncle Vanya.
PICTURES: Privileged, A Summer Story, Nanou, Erik the Viking, True Colors, A Pin for the Butterfly, Sandra C'est la Vie, Jack & Sarah, Sense and Sensibility, Twelfth Night.
TELEVISION: The Browning Version, Deadline, The Rainbow, Fellow Traveller, After the Dance, Relatively Speaking, Othello, Anna Lee, Mother Time.

STULBERG, GORDON
Executive. b. Toronto, Canada, Dec. 17, 1927. e. U. of Toronto, B.A., Cornell Law Sch., LL.B. Was assoc. & member, Pacht, Ross, Warne & Bernhard; ent. m.p. ind. as exec. asst. to v.p., Columbia Pictures Corp., 1956-60; v.p. & chief studio admin. off., 1960-67; pres. of Cinema Center Films (div. of CBS) 1967-71; pres. 20th Century-Fox, 1971-75; 1980, named pres. & COO, PolyGram Pictures. Member of NY, Calif. bars, Chairman, American Interactive Media (Polygram subsidiary).

SUGAR, LARRY
Executive. b. Phoenix, AZ, May 26, 1945. m. Bonnie Sugar. e. Cheshire Acad., 1962; CSUN, B.A., 1967; U. of Southern Calif., J.D., 1971. Writer and co-author, Calif. Primary Reading Program, 1967-68. Joined Warner Bros. as dir., legal and corp. affairs, 1971-74; 20th Century Fox legal staff, 1974-77; co-owner with Bonnie Sugar, Serendipity Prods., 1977-81; named pres., intl., Lorimar Prods. 1981-84; exec. v.p., distribution, CBS 1984-85; exec. v.p. worldwide distribution, Weintraub Entertainment Group 1987-89; formed Sugar Entertainment, chmn., 1989-1991; pres. intl., Republic Pictures, Inc. 1991-93; pres. Larry Sugar Entertainment, 1993-.
PICTURES: *Exec. prod.*: Slapstick, Steel Dawn, Options, Damned River, Fatal Sky, Graveyard Shift, Shattered, Dark Horse, Family Prayers, The Plague, Boxing Helena. *Prod.*: With Deadly Intent, Annie O, Robin of Locksley, Ronnie & Julie.
TELEVISION: *Movies*: The Prisoner of Zenda Inc., The Halfback of Notre Dame, Dead Man's Gun.

SUGARMAN, BURT
Producer. b. Beverly Hills, CA, Jan. 4. e. U. of Southern California. Chmn. & CEO, GIANT GROUP, LTD., diversified co. traded on NYSE.
PICTURES: Kiss Me Goodbye, Extremities, Children of a Lesser God, Crimes of the Heart.
TELEVISION: Midnight Special, Switched on Symphony, The Mancini Generation, Johnny Mann's Stand Up and Cheer, etc.

SULLIVAN, REV. PATRICK J.
S.J., S.T.D.: Provost, Graduate Center at Tarrytown, Fordham U. b. New York, NY, March 25, 1920. e. Regis H.S.: Georgetown U., A.B., 1943; Woodstock Coll., M.A., 1944; Fordham U., 1945-47; S.T.L. Weston Coll., 1947-51; S.T.D. Gregorian U. (Rome), 1952-54. Prof. of Theology, Woodstock Coll., 1954-57; Consultor, Pontifical Commission for Social Communications, 1968-82; Exec. Dir., U.S. Catholic Conference, Film & Broadcasting Office, 1965-80; Fordham Univ. Grad Sch. of Business, Assoc. Dean 1982-83, Dean 1983-85.

SUMMERS, GARY
Sound.
PICTURES: Star Wars, The Empire Strikes Back, Raiders of the Lost Ark, Return of the Jedi, Indiana Jones and the Temple of Doom, Cocoon, Captain Eo, Howard the Duck, Spaceballs, Always, Indiana Jones and the Last Crusade, Defenseless, The Cross the Rubicon, Rush, The Five Heartbeats, Terminator 2: Judgment Day, F/X2, The Addams Family, House of Cards, Jurassic Park, Miracle on 34th Street, Casper, Toy Story, Special Effects: Anything Can Happen, Titanic (Acad. Award, Best Sound, 1997), The Lost World: Jurassic Park.
TELEVISION: *Series*: Fame L.A.

SUNSHINE, ROBERT HOWARD
Publisher. b. Brooklyn, NY, Jan. 17, 1946. e. U. of RI; Brooklyn Law Sch., 1971. Admitted to NY State Bar, 1971. President of Pubsun Corp., owner of Film Journal International (formerly Film Journal). Publisher of Film Journal International. Exec. dir., International Theatre Equipment Association, 1979-present; sec. and exec. dir. Foundation of the Motion Picture Pioneers, 1975-present; exec. dir., Natl. Assoc. of Theatre Owners of NY State, 1985-present; Producer of Variety Telethon, 1985-present; coordinator and producer, Show East Convention; coordinator and prod., Cinema Expo Intl., Amsterdam, Holland; coordinator and producer, CineAsia, Singapore.

SURTEES, BRUCE
Cinematographer. b. Carmel, CA, Aug. 3, 1944. Son of cinematographer Robert L. Surtees.
PICTURES: The Beguiled, Play Misty for Me, Dirty Harry, The Great Northfield Minnesota Raid, Conquest of the Planet of the Apes, Joe Kidd, The Outfit, High Plains Drifter, Blume in Love, Lenny (Acad. Award nom.), Night Moves, Leadbelly, The Outlaw Josey Wales, The Shootist, Three Warriors, Sparkle, Big Wednesday, Movie Movie (segment: Baxter's Beauties of 1933), Dreamer, Escape from Alcatraz, Ladies and Gentlemen the Fabulous Stains, White Dog, Firefox, Inchon, Honkytonk Man, Bad Boys, Risky Business, Sudden Impact, Tightrope, Beverly Hills Cop, Pale Rider, Psycho III, Out of Bounds, Ratboy, Back to the Beach, License to Drive, Men Don't Leave, Run, The Super, The Crush, That Night. Corrina Corrina, The Stars Fell on Henrietta, The Substitute, Isn't It Romantic.

SUSCHITZKY, PETER
Cinematographer. Spent long time in Latin America as documentary cinematographer. Later made commercials in France, England and U.S. First feature was It Happened Here, 1962.
PICTURES: Over 30 features including: A Midsummer Night's Dream, Charlie Bubbles, Leo the Last, Privilege, That'll Be the Day, Lisztomania, The Rocky Horror Picture Show, All Creatures Great and Small (TV in U.S.), Valentino, The Empire Strikes Back, Krull, Falling in Love, In Extremis, Dead Ringers, Where the Heart Is, Naked Lunch, The Public Eye, The Vanishing, M. Butterfly, Immortal Beloved, Crash, Mars Attacks, The Man in the Iron Mask, eXistenZ.

SUTHERLAND, DONALD
Actor. b. St. John, New Brunswick, Canada, July 17, 1935. Son is actor Kiefer Sutherland. e. U. of Toronto, B.A., 1956. At 14 became a radio announcer and disc jockey. Worked in a mine in Finland. Theatre includes: The Male Animal (debut), The Tempest (Hart House Theatre, U. of Toronto), Two years at London Acad. of Music and Dramatic Art. Spent a year and a half with the Perth Repertory Theatre in Scotland, then repertory at Nottingham, Chesterfield, Bromley and Sheffield.
THEATER: August for the People (London debut), On a Clear Day You Can See Canterbury, The Shewing Up of Blanco Posnet, The Spoon River Anthology, Lolita (B'way debut, 1981).
PICTURES: Castle of the Living Dead (debut, 1964), The World Ten Times Over, Dr. Terror's House of Horrors, Die Die My Darling (Fanatic), The Bedford Incident, Promise Her Anything, The Dirty Dozen, Billion Dollar Brain, Sebastian, Oedipus the King, Interlude, Joanna, The Split, M*A*S*H, Start the Revolution Without Me, Act of the Heart, Kelly's Heroes, Alex in Wonderland, Little Murders, Klute, Johnny Got His Gun, F.T.A. (also co-prod., co-dir., co-s.p.), Steelyard Blues (also exec. prod.), Lady Ice, Alien Thunder (Dan Candy's Law), Don't Look Now, S*P*Y*S, The Day of the Locust, End of the Game (cameo), Fellini's Casanova, The Eagle Has Landed, 1900, The Disappearance, The Kentucky Fried Movie, National Lampoon's Animal House, Invasion of the Body Snatchers, The Great Train Robbery, Murder by Decree, Bear Island, A Man a Woman and a Bank, Nothing Personal, Ordinary People, Blood Relatives, Gas, Eye of the Needle, Threshold, Max Dugan Returns, Crackers, Ordeal by Innocence, Heaven Help Us, Revolution, Wolf at the Door, The Rosary Murders, The Trouble With Spies, Apprentice to Murder, Lost Angels, Lock Up, A Dry White Season, Eminent Domain, Backdraft, Buster's Bedroom, JFK, Scream of Stone, Buffy the Vampire Slayer, Shadow of the Wolf, Benefit of the Doubt, Dr. Bethune (Bethune: The Making of a Hero), Younger and Younger, Six Degrees of Separation, Robert A. Heinlein's The Puppet Masters, Disclosure, Outbreak, Hollow Point, The Shadow Conspiracy, A Time to Kill, The Assignment, Free Money, Fallen, Without Limits, Virus, Toscano, Instinct.
TELEVISION: Specials: (British) Marching to the Sea, The Death of Bessie Smith, Hamlet at Elsinore, Gideon's Way, The Champions, Bethune (Canada), Give Me Your Answer True, The Prize (narrator), People of the Forest: The Chimps of Gombe (narrator). Guest: The Saint, The Avengers. Movies: The Sunshine Patriot, The Winter of Our Discontent, Quicksand: No Escape, The Railway Station Man, The Lifeforce Experiment, Oldest Living Confederate Widow Tells All, Citizen X (Emmy Award, 1995; Golden Globe Award 1995), Natural Enemy. Series: Great Books (narrator).

SUTHERLAND, KIEFER
Actor. b. London, England, CA, Dec. 18, 1966. Son of actor Donald Sutherland and actress Shirley Douglas. Moved to Los Angeles at age 4, then to Toronto at 8. Debut with L.A. Odyssey Theater at age 9 in Throne of Straw. Worked in local Toronto theater workshops before landing starring role in The Bay Boy (1984) for which he won Canadian Genie Award.
PICTURES: Max Dugan Returns (debut, 1983), The Bay Boy, At Close Range, Stand By Me, Crazy Moon, The Lost Boys, The Killing Time, Promised Land, Bright Lights Big City, Young Guns 1969, Renegades, Flashback, Chicago Joe and the Showgirl, Flatliners, Young Guns II, The Nutcracker Prince (voice), Article 99, Twin Peaks: Fire Walk With Me, A Few Good Men, The Vanishing, The Three Musketeers, The Cowboy Way, Teresa's Tattoo, Eye for an Eye, Freeway, A Time To Kill, Truth or Consequences—N.M. (also dir.), Dark City.
TELEVISION: Movies: Trapped in Silence, Brotherhood of Justice, Last Light (also dir.), Dark Reflection (co-exec. prod. only). Guest: Amazing Stories (The Mission).

SUTTON, JAMES T.
Executive. b. California, Sept. 13. e. Columbia U. Film inspector, U.S. government; overseas m.p. service, WW II; co-owner, gen. mgr., Hal Davis Studios; hd. TV commercial div., Allan Sandler Films; Academy Art Pictures; pres., chmn. of bd., exec. prod., Royal Russian Studios, Inc., western hemisphere div.; pres. exec. prod. Gold Lion Prods., Inc.; pres. exec. prod. James T. Sutton-John L. Carpenter Prods.; pres., exec. dir., Airax Corp.; pres. of Skyax (div. of Airax).

SUZMAN, JANET
Actress. b. Johannesburg, South Africa, Feb. 9, 1939. e. Kingsmead Coll., U. of Witwaterstrand. Trained at L.A.M.D.A. London stage debut in The Comedy of Errors. Recent theater: Another Time, Hippolytos, The Sisters Rosensweig. Director: Othello for Market Theatre and Channel 4 (TV), Death of a Salesman, A Dream of People, The Deep Blue Sea.
PICTURES: Nicholas and Alexandra (Acad. Award nom.), A Day in the Death of Joe Egg, The Black Windmill, Nijinsky, Priest of Love, The Draughtsman's Contract, And the Ship Sails On, A Dry White Season, Nuns on the Run, Leon the Pig Farmer.
TELEVISION: Specials/Movies: The Three Sisters, Hedda Gabler, The House on Garibaldi Street, The Zany Adventures of Robin Hood, Miss Nightingale, Macbeth, Mountbatten—Last Viceroy of India (series), The Singing Detective (series), Clayhanger (series), The Miser, Revolutionary Witness, Saint Joan, Twelfth Night, Master Class on Shakespearean Comedy, Inspector Morse, The Ruth Rendell Mysteries.

SVENSON, BO
Actor. b. Goteborg, Sweden, Feb. 13, 1941. e. UCLA, 1970-74. U.S. Marine Corps 1959-65.
PICTURES: Maurie (debut, 1973), The Great Waldo Pepper, Part 2: Walking Tall, Breaking Point, Special Delivery, Portrait of a Hitman, Final Chapter: Walking Tall, Our Man in Mecca, The Inglorious Bastard, North Dallas Forty, Virus, Night Warning, Thunder Warrior, Deadly Impact, Wizards of the Lost Kingdom, The Manhunt, The Delta Force, Choke Canyon, Heartbreak Ridge, War Bus 2, Silent Hero, Thunder Warrior II, White Phantom, Deep Space, Justice Done, The Train, Soda Cracker, Curse II: The Bite, Captain Henkel, Running Combat, Steel Frontier, Private Obsession, Speed 2: Cruise Control.
TELEVISION: Series: Here Come the Brides, Walking Tall. Movies: The Bravos, Frankenstein, You'll Never See Me Again, Hitched, Target Risk, Snowbeast, Gold of the Amazon Women, Jealousy, Dirty Dozen: The Deadly Mission, 3 Days to Kill, Heartless.

SWAIM, BOB
Director, Writer. b. Evanston, IL, Nov. 2, 1943. e. Calif. State U, B.A.; L'Ecole Nationale de la Cinematographie, Paris, BTS 1969. American director who has often worked in France. Began career making shorts: Le Journal de M Bonnafous, Self Portrait of a Pornographer, Vive les Jacques. Received Cesar award French Acad. M.P., 1982; Chevalier des Arts et des Lettres 1985.
PICTURES: La Nuit de Saint-Germain-des-Pres (1977), La Balance, Spies Like Us, (actor), Half Moon Street, Masquerade, Atlantide, Da Costa, Parfum de Meurte, Femme de Passions, The Climb.
TELEVISION: Series: Rainbow Drive (actor), Frauen in Angst (s.p.), Target of Suspicion (actor, dir., cam.).

SWANSON, DENNIS
Executive. e. Univ. of IL. B.A. in journalism, 1961, M.S. in communications/political science, 1966. 1966-67, news prod. & assignment mngr. for WGN radio & tv in Chicago; 1968-70, assign. edit. & field prod. for NBC news at WMAQ TV in Chicago; 1971-74, sportscaster and prod. WMAQ; worked for TVN in Chicago and served as company's NY dir. of news division; 1976, became exec. prod. of KABC-TV in LA; 1981, appointed station mngr. KABC-TV; 1983, v.p. & gen. mngr. WLS-TV, Chicago; 1985, named pres. of ABC Owned TV Stations; 1986, became pres. of ABC Sports; 1990, pres., ABC Daytime and ABC Children's Programming.

SWANSON, KRISTY
Actress. b. Mission Viejo, CA, Dec. 12, 1969. Signed with modeling agency at age 9, appearing in over 30 commercials. Acting debut at 13 on Disney series Dreamfinders.
PICTURES: Pretty in Pink, Ferris Bueller's Day Off, Deadly Friend, Flowers in the Attic, Diving In, Mannequin Two on the Move, Hot Shots, Highway to Hell, Buffy the Vampire Slayer, The Program, The Chase, Getting In (Student Body), Higher Learning, The Phantom, Marshal Law, Lover Girl, 8 Heads in a Duffel Bag, Tinseltown, Supreme Sanction, Past Imperfect, Meeting Daddy.
TELEVISION: *Series*: Dreamfinders, Knots Landing, Nightingales. *Movies*: Miracle of the Heart: A Boys Town Story, Not Quite Human, Bad to the Bone.

SWAYZE, PATRICK
Actor, Dancer. b. Houston, TX. Aug. 18, 1952. e. San Jacinto Col. m. actress-dancer Lisa Niemi. Son of choreographer Patsy Swayze (Urban Cowboy). Brother is actor Don Swayze. Began as dancer appearing in Disney on Parade on tour as Prince Charming. Songwriter and singer with 6 bands. Studied dance at Harkness and Joffrey Ballet Schs. On B'way as dancer in Goodtime Charley, Grease. Co-author of play Without a Word.
PICTURES: Skatetown USA (debut, 1979), The Outsiders, Uncommon Valor, Red Dawn, Grandview USA (also choreographer), Youngblood, Dirty Dancing (also co-wrote and sang She's Like the Wind), Steel Dawn, Tiger Warsaw, Road House, Next of Kin, Ghost, Point Break, City of Joy, Father Hood, Tall Tale, To Wong Foo—Thanks for Everything—Julie Newmar, Three Wishes.
TELEVISION: *Mini-Series*: North and South: Books I and II. *Movies*: The Comeback Kid, Return of the Rebels, The Renegades (pilot), Off Sides. *Series*: Renegades. *Guest*: M*A*S*H, Amazing Stories.

SWEENEY, ANNE
Executive. e. College of New Rochelle, BA, and Harvard U., Ed. M. Began career at Nickelodeon/Nick at Nite in 1981, finally becoming SVP of Prog. Enterprises. Joined Fox, 1993, as Chairman and CEO of FX Networks. Exec. VP of Disney/ABC Cable Networks, 1996; Appointed Pres., 1998.

SWEENEY, D. B.
Actor. r.n. Daniel Bernard Sweeney. b. Shoreham, NY, 1961. e. NYU, 1984 B.F.A.
THEATER: *NY*: The Caine Mutiny Court-Martial (B'way), The Seagull: The Hamptons: 1990, Distant Fires (L.A.), among others.
PICTURES: Power (debut, 1986), Fire With Fire, Gardens of Stone, No Man's Land, Eight Men Out, Memphis Belle, Blue Desert, Sons, Leather Jackets, Heaven Is a Playground, The Cutting Edge, A Day in October, Hear No Evil, Fire in the Sky, Roommates.
TELEVISION: *Series*: Strange Luck, C-16: FBI. *Mini-Series*: Lonesome Dove. *Movies*: Out of the Darkness, Miss Rose White.

SWERLING, JO
Writer. b. Russia, April 8, 1897. Newspaper & mag. writer; author vaude. sketches; co-author plays, The Kibitzer, Guys and Dolls (Tony Award, 1951).
PICTURES: The Kibitzer, Platinum Blonde, Washington Merry-Go-Round, Dirigible, Man's Castle, Whole Town's Talking, No Greater Glory, Pennies from Heaven, Double Wedding, Made for Each Other, The Westerner, Confirm or Deny, Blood and Sand, Pride of the Yankees, Lady Takes a Chance, Crash Dive, Lifeboat, Leave Her to Heaven, Thunder in the East.
TELEVISION: The Lord Don't Play Favorites.

SWERLING, JO, JR.
Executive, Producer. b. Los Angeles, CA, June 18, 1931. e. UCLA, 1948-51; California Maritime Acad., 1951-54. Son of writer Jo Swerling. Active duty US Navy 1954-56. Joined Revue Prods./Universal Television, 1957-81, as prod. coordinator, assoc. prod., prod., assoc. exec. prod., exec. prod., writer, director, actor; currently sr. v.p. and supervising prod., The Cannell Studios.
TELEVISION: *Series*: Kraft Suspense Theater (prod.), Run for Your Life (prod., writer, Emmy, nom.), The Rockford Files (prod., writer), Cool Million (prod.), Alias Smith & Jones (assoc. exec. prod.), Baretta (prod., Emmy nom.), City of Angels (exec. prod.), Toma (exec. prod.), Jigsaw (prod.), The Bold Ones (prod., writer), Lawyers (prod., writer). *Mini-series*: Captains and the Kings (prod., Emmy nom.), Aspen (prod.), The Last Convertible (exec. prod., dir.). *Movies* (prod.): This Is the West That Was, The Whole World Is Watching, The Invasion of Johnson County, The Outsider, Do You Take This Stranger, Burn the Town Down, The Three-Thousand Mile Chase, How to Steal an Airplane. *Supervising prod.*, Stephen J. Cannell Productions: The Greatest American Hero, Quest, The A-Team, Hardcastle & McCormick, Riptide, The Last Precinct, Hunter, Stingray, Wiseguy, 21 Jump Street, J.J. Starbuck, Sonny Spoon, The Rousters, Unsub, Booker, Top of the Hill, Broken Badges, Dead End Brattigan, The Hat Squad, Traps, Profit.

SWIFT, LELA
Director.
TELEVISION: Studio One, Suspense, The Web, Justice, DuPont Show of the Week, Purex Specials For Women (Emmy Award) Dark Shadows, Norman Corwin Presents, ABC Late Night 90 min. Specials, ABC Daytime 90 min. Play Break, Ryan's Hope (Emmy Awards: 1977, 1979, 1980; Montior Awards: 1985, 1989), The Rope (A & E).

SWINK, ROBERT E.
Film Editor. b. Rocky Ford, CO, June 3, 1918. Joined editorial dept., RKO Radio, 1936; appt. film ed., 1941. In U.S. Army Signal Corps, 1944-45; supv. editor, Fox studio. Edited numerous productions.
PICTURES: Detective Story, Carrie, Roman Holiday, Desperate Hours, Friendly Persuasion, The Big Country, The Diary of Anne Frank, The Young Doctors, The Children's Hour, The Best Man, The Collector, How to Steal a Million, The Flim Flam Man, Funny Girl, The Liberation of L.B. Jones, The Cowboys, Skyjacked, Lady Ice, Papillion, Three the Hard Way, Rooster Cogburn, Midway, Islands in the Stream, Gray Lady Down, The Boys From Brazil, The In-Laws, Going in Style, Sphinx, Welcome Home.

SWIT, LORETTA
Actress. b. Passaic, NJ, Nov. 4, 1939. Stage debut in Any Wednesday. Toured in Mame for year. Arrived in Hollywood in 1971 and began TV career.
THEATER: Same Time Next Year, The Mystery of Edwin Drood (B'way), Shirley Valentine (Sarah Siddons Award).
PICTURES: Stand Up and Be Counted (debut, 1972), Freebie and the Bean, Race with the Devil, S.O.B., Beer, Whoops Apocalypse, Lords of Tanglewood.
TELEVISION: *Series*: M*A*S*H (Emmy Awards, 1980, 1982; also Genii, Silver Satellite & People's Choice Awards), Those Incredible Animals (host). *Guest*: Perry Como Show, Mac Davis, Dolly Parton, Bobby Vinton, etc. *Movies*: Hostage Heart, Shirts/Skins, The Last Day, Coffeeville, Valentine, Mirror Mirror, Friendships Secrets and Lies, Cagney & Lacey, Games Mother Never Taught You, Friendships Secrets & Lies, First Affair, The Execution, Dreams of Gold: The Mel Fisher Story, Hell Hath No Fury, A Killer Among Friends. *Specials*: 14 Going on 30, Best Christmas Pageant Ever, Texaco Salute to Broadway, It's a Bird It's a Plane It's Superman, Miracle at Moreaux, My Dad Can't Be Crazy Can He?, A Matter of Principal.

SWOPE, HERBERT BAYARD, JR.
Director, Producer, Commentator. b. New York, NY. e. Horace Mann Sch., Princeton U. U.S. Navy, 1941-46; joined CBS-TV as remote stunt dir., 1946 directing many firsts in sportscasting; winner, Variety Show Management Award for sports coverage & citation by Amer. TV Society, 1948; joined NBC as dir., 1949; prod. dir., 1951; winner, 1952 Sylvania TV Award Outstanding Achievement in Dir. Technique; became exec. prod., NBC-TV in charge of Wide Wide World; film prod., 18th Century-Fox; 1960-62, exec. prod. 20th-Fox TV; 1970-72 exec. at N.Y. Off-Track Betting Corp. 1973-74; v.p., Walter Reade Organization, Inc.; 1975-76 producer-host, This Was TV, Growth of a Giant; 1976 to present commentator-interviewer, Swope's Scope, (radio—WSBR-AM)); Critic's Views (TV: WTVJ, Ch. 5); Column: Now and Then (Palm Beach Pictorial).
THEATER: *Dir./Co-Prod.*: Step on a Crack, Fragile Fox, Fair Game for Lovers.
PICTURES: *Producer*: Hilda Crane, Three Brave Men, True Story of Jesse James, The Bravados, The Fiend Who Walked the West.
TELEVISION: *Prod/Dir.*: Lights Out, The Clock, The Black Robe, Robert Montgomery Presents, Arsenic and Old Lace, Climax, Many Loves of Dobie Gillis, Five Fingers.

SYKES, ERIC
O.B.E.: Writer, Comedian, Actor. b. Oldham, England, May 4, 1923. Early career as actor; 1948 wrote first three series, BBC's Educating Archie TV comedy series for Frankie Howerd, Max Bygraves, Harry Secombe. BBC panel show member. Sykes Versus TV, The Frankie Howerd Series. Longterm contract with ATV 1956. Own BBC series 1958-78, Sykes and A... *Specials*: Silent Movies for TV, The Plank (also dir. & s.p.), If You Go Down Into the Woods Today, Rhubarb, It's Your Move, Mr. H Is Late, 19th Hole, The Big Freeze.
THEATER: Big Bad Mouse (tour: 1966-9 in America, Rhodesia, Australia, Canada), One Man Show (1982), Time and Time Again, Run for Your Wife, Two Into One, The 19th Hole, several pantomimes.
PICTURES: Watch Your Stern, Very Important Person, Invasion Quartet, Village of Daughters, Kill or Cure, Heavens Above, The Bargee, One Way Pendulum, Those Magnificent Men in Their Flying Machines, Rotten to the Core, The Liquidator, The Spy With The Cold Nose, Shalako, Monte Carlo or Bust, Theatre of Blood, Boys in Blue, Gabrielle and the Doodleman, Absolute Beginners, Splitting Heirs.

SYLBERT, ANTHEA
Executive. b. New York, NY, Oct. 6, 1939. e. Barnard Coll., B.A.; Parsons Sch. of Design, M.A. Early career in costume design with range of B'way (The Real Thing), off-B'way and m.p. credits (Rosemary's Baby, John & Mary, Carnal Knowledge, A New Leaf, The Heartbreak Kid, The Cowboys, Bad Company, Shampoo, The Fortune, The Last Tycoon, F.I.S.T.). Two Acad. award. nominations for costume designs for Julia and Chinatown. Joined Warner Bros. in 1977, as v.p., special projects, acting as liaison between creative execs., prod. dept., and creative talent producing films for company. 1978, named v.p., prod. (projects included One Trick Pony, Personal Best, etc.). 1980 appointed v.p. prod., for United Artists, working on Jinxed, Still of the Night, Yentl, etc. 1982 become indept. prod. in partnership with Goldie Hawn (Hawn/Sylbert Movie Co.) producing Swing Shift, Protocol, Wildcats, Overboard, My Blue Heaven, Deceived, Crisscross, Something to Talk About. TV Movie: Truman, Hope.

SYMES, JOHN
Executive. e. Univ. of CA at Berkeley. Started at Paramount in tech. opts. dept. of Paramount's domestic tv distrib. div., then became mngr. of videotape opts., dir. of opts. Became sr. v.p. current programs for Paramount Network tv, then exec. v.p. creative affairs for same. Jan. 1994, became pres. of MGM Worldwide TV.

SYMS, SYLVIA
Actress. b. London, June 1, 1934. e. Convent and Grammar Sch.
PICTURES: My Teenage Daughter (debut, 1956), No Time For Tears, The Birthday Present, Woman in a Dressing Gown, Ice Cold in Alex (Desert Attack), The Moonraker, Bachelor of Hearts, No Trees in the Street, Ferry to Hong Kong, Expresso Bongo, Conspiracy of Hearts, The Virgins of Rome, The World of Suzie Wong, Flame in the Streets, Victim, The Quare Fellow, The Punch and Judy Man, The World Ten Times Over, East of Sudan, Operation Crossbow, The Big Job, Hostile Witness, Danger Route, Run Wild Run Free, The Desperados, Asylum, The Tamarind Seed, Give Us Tomorrow, There Goes the Bride, Absolute Beginners, A Chorus of Disapproval, Shirley Valentine, Shining Through, Dirty Weekend, Staggered, The House of Angelo, Food of Love.
TELEVISION: Something to Declare, Bat Out of Hell, Department in Terror, Friends and Romans, Strange Report, Half-hour Story, The Root of All Evil, The Bridesmaid, Clutterbuck, Movie Quiz, My Good Woman, Looks Familiar, Love and Marriage, The Truth About Verity, I'm Bob, He's Dickie, Blankety Blank, The Story of Nancy Astor, Give Us a Clue, Sykes, Crown Court, A Murder Is Announced, Murder at Lynch Cross, Rockcliffes Follies, Dr. Who, Countdown, Ruth Rendell Mystery, May to December, Intimate Contact, Thatcher: The Final Days, Natural Lies, Mulberry, Peak Practice, Half the Picture, Master of the Moor, Original Sin. Series: The Human Jungle, The Saint, The Baron, Mini-series: The Glass Virgin.

SZABO, ISTVAN
Director. b. Budapest, Hungary, Feb. 18, 1938. e. Academy of Theatre and Film Art, Budapest, 1961. Debut Koncert (short, diploma film) 1961. Short films: Variations on a Theme, You, Piety, Why I Love It, City Map. Appeared in film Tusztortenet (Stand Off).
PICTURES: Age of Illusions (feature debut, 1964), Father, A Film About Love, 25 Fireman's Street, Premiere, Tales of Budapest, The Hungarians, Confidence (Silver Bear Award, Berlin Fest.), The Green Bird, Mephisto (Hungarian Film Critics Award; Acad. Award, Best Foreign Film, 1982), Bali, Colonel Redl, Hanussen (also co-s.p.), Opera Europa, Meeting Venus, Dear Emma—Sweet Bobe, Offenbach Titkai.

SZWARC, JEANNOT
Director. b. Paris, France, Nov. 21, 1939.
PICTURES: Extreme Close-Up, Bug, Jaws II, Somewhere in Time, Enigma, Supergirl, Santa Claus, Honor Bound.
TELEVISION: Series: Ironside, To Catch a Thief, Kojak, Columbo, Night Gallery, Crime Club, True Life Stories, Twilight Zone (1986). Movies: Night of Terror, The Weekend Nun, The Devil's Daughter, You'll Never See Me Again, The Small Miracle, Lisa: Bright and Dark, A Summer Without Boys, Crime Club, Code Name: Diamond Head, Murders in the Rue Morgue, The Rockford Files: A Blessing in Disguise.

T

MR. T
Actor. r.n. Lawrence Tero. b. Chicago, IL, May 21, 1953. Professional bodyguard when hired by Sylvester Stallone in 1980 to play prizefighter in Rocky III.
PICTURES: Penitentiary II, Rocky III, D.C. Cab, Freaked, The Magic of the Golden Bear: Goldy III.
TELEVISION: Series: The A Team, T & T. Movie: The Toughest Man in the World. Guest: Silver Spoons.

TAFFNER DONALD L.
Executive. b. New York, NY. e. St. Johns U. William Morris Agency, 1950-59; Paramount Pictures. 1959-63; D. L. Taffner Ltd., 1963-present.
TELEVISION: Prod.: Three's Company, Too Close For Comfort.

TAGAWA, CARY-HIROYUKI
Actor.
PICTURES: Armed Response, The Last Emperor, Spellbinder, Twins, The Last Warrior, License to Kill, Showdown in Little Tokyo, The Perfect Weapon, Kickboxer 2: The Road Back, Raven: Return of the Black Dragons, American Me, Nemesis, Rising Sun, Natural Causes, The Dangerous, Soldier Boyz, Picture Pride, Mortal Kombat, White Tiger, Provocateur, Danger Zone, The Phantom, Top of the World, American Dragons, Vampires.
TELEVISION: Movies: Star Trek: The Next Generation - Encounter at Farpoint, L.A. Takedown, Murder in Paradise, Vestige of Honor, Not of This World, Mission of the Shark: The Saga of the U.S.S Indianapolis, Raven: Return of the Black Dragons, Day of Reckoning. Series: Nash Bridges.

TAIT, CATHERINE
Executive. Exec. dir., The Independent Feature Project.

TAKEI, GEORGE
Actor. b. Los Angeles, CA, April 20, 1937. e. U. of California, UCLA. Professional debut in Playhouse 90 production while training at Desilu Workshop in Hollywood. Gained fame as Sulu in Star Trek TV series. Author: Mirror Friend Mirror Foe (novel), To the Stars (autobiography; 1994).
PICTURES: Ice Palace, A Majority of One, Hell to Eternity, PT 109, Red Line 7000, An American Dream, Walk Don't Run, The Green Berets, Star Trek: The Motion Picture, Star Trek II: The Wrath of Khan, Star Trek III: The Search for Spock, Star Trek IV: The Voyage Home, Star Trek V: The Final Frontier, Return From the River Kwai, Prisoners of the Sun, Star Trek VI: The Undiscovered Country, Live by the Fist, Oblivion, Chongbal, Oblivion 2: Backlash, Star Trek: Starfleet Academy, Mulan (voice), Bug Buster.
TELEVISION: Series: Star Trek. Movies: Kissinger and Nixon, Space Cases, Star Trek Voyager. Guest: Perry Mason, Alcoa Premiere, Mr. Novak, The Wackiest Ship in the Army, I Spy, Magnum PI, Trapper John M.D., Miami Vice, Murder She Wrote, McGyver, Hawaiian Eye, Californian, Hawaii Five-O, My Three Sons, John Forsythe Show, Death Valley Days, Theatre in America, Game Night, Kung Fu: The Legend Continues, The Simpsons.

TAMBLYN, RUSS
Actor b. Los Angeles, CA, Dec. 30, 1934. e. No. Hollywood H.S. West Coast radio shows; on stage with little theater group; song-and-dance act in Los Angeles clubs, veterans hospitals.
PICTURES: The Boy with Green Hair, Reign of Terror, Samson and Delilah, Gun Crazy, Kid from Cleveland, The Vicious Years, Captain Carey U.S.A., Father of the Bride, As Young As You Feel, Father's Little Dividend, Cave of Outlaws, Winning Team, Retreat Hell, Take the High Ground, Seven Brides for Seven Brothers, Deep in My Heart, Many Rivers to Cross, Hit the Deck, Last Hunt, Fastest Gun Alive, The Young Guns, Don't Go Near the Water, Peyton Place (Acad. Award nom.), High School Confidential, Tom Thumb, Cimarron, West Side Story, Wonderful World of the Brothers Grimm, How the West Was Won, Follow the Boys, The Haunting, Long Ships, Son of a Gunfighter, War of the Gargantuas, Scream Free, Dracula Vs. Frankenstein, Satan's Sadists, The Female Bunch, The Last Movie, Win Place or Steal, Murder Gang, Human Highway, Aftershock, Commando Squad, Cyclone, Necromancer, B.O.R.N., Phantom Empire, Bloodscream, Wizards of the Demon Sword, Desert Steel, Cabin Boy, Attack of the 60 Ft. Centerfold, Johnny Mysto: The Boy Wizard, Little Miss Magic, Invisible Dad, Ghost Dog.
TELEVISION: Series: Twin Peaks. Guest: The Walter Winchell Show, ABC's Wide World of Entertainment, The Ed Sullivan Show, Gunsmoke, Name of the Game, Tarzan, Rags to Riches, Channing, Iron Horse, Perry Como Show, Love American Style, Grizzly Adams, Fame, Running Mates, Greatest Show on Earth, Burke's Law, Cade's County, The Quest, Quantum Leap, Babylon 5, Invisible Mom, Nash Bridges. Specials: The Making of Seven Brides for Seven Brothers.

TAMBOR, JEFFREY
Actor. b. San Francisco, CA, July 8, 1944. e. San Francisco St. (BA), Wayne St. (MA). Acted with Seattle Rep., Actors Theatre of Louisville, Loeb Drama Ctr. (Harvard), Milwaukee Rep. Theatre, Acad. Festival Theatre (Chicago), Old Globe Theatre in San Diego, South Coast Rep. Theatre. B'way in Measure for Measure, Sly Fox.
PICTURES: And Justice for All, Saturday the 14th, Mr. Mom, The Man Who Wasn't There, No Small Affair, Three O'Clock High, Lisa, City Slickers, Life Stinks, Pastime, Article 99, Brenda Starr, Crossing the Bridge, At Home with the Webbers, Face Dancer, Under Pressure, A House in the Hills, Radioland Murders, Heavyweights, Big Bully, Learning Curves, Bad with Numbers, Big Bully, Meet Joe Black, Killing Mrs. Tingle, Doctor Dolittle, There's Something About Mary.

TELEVISION: *Series*: The Ropers, Hill Street Blues, 9 to 5, Mr. Sunshine, Max Headroom, Studio 5-B, American Dreamer, The Larry Sanders Show, Me and George, The Lionhearts. *Movies*: Alcatraz: The Whole Shocking Story, A Gun in the House, The Star Maker, Take Your Best Shot, Cocaine: One Man's Seduction, Sadat, The Awakening of Candra, The Three Wishes of Billy Grier, The Burden of Proof, Honey Let's Kill the Neighbors, Another Midnight Run, The Man Who Captured Eichmann, Weapons of Mass Destruction. *Mini-Series*: Robert Kennedy & His Times. *Guest*: Three's Company, M*A*S*H, Barney Miller, Tales From the Crypt, The Golden Globe, Empty Nest, Doogie Howser M.D., Equal Justice, Murder She Wrote.

TANEN, NED
Executive. b. Los Angeles, CA, 1931. e. UCLA, law degree. Joined MCA, Inc. 1954; appt. v.p. in 1968. Brought Uni Records, since absorbed by MCA Records, to best-seller status with such artists as Neil Diamond, Elton John, Olivia Newton-John. First became active in theatrical film prod. in 1972. 1975 began overseeing feature prod. for Universal. 1976 named pres. of Universal Theatrical Motion Pictures, established as div. of Universal City Studios. Left in 1982 to become independent producer. 1985, joined Paramount Pictures as pres. of Motion Picture Group. Resigned 1988 to continue as sr. advisor at Paramount. Producer: Guarding Tess, Cops and Robbersons.

TANKERSLEY, ROBERT K.
Executive. b. Decatur, IL, July 31, 1927. In U.S. Navy, 1945-46; Marine Corps, 1949-55. With Natl. Theatre Supply as salesman in Denver 13 yrs. 1959-87, pres. Western Service & Supply, Denver, theatre equip. co.; 1987-present, mgr., Tankersley Enterprises theatre equip. Also was CEO of Theatre Operators, Inc., Bozeman, Mont. Member: Theatre Equipment Assn. (past pres.), National NATO Presidents Advisory Council; Rocky Mt. Motion Picture Assn. (past pres.), SMPTE, Motion Picture Pioneers, past chief barker, Variety Club Tent #37. Colorado, Wyoming NATO (past pres.) chmn.-elect Exhibitors West.

TAPLIN, JONATHAN
Producer. b. Cleveland, OH, July 18, 1947. e. Princeton U.
PICTURES: Mean Streets, The Last Waltz, Carny (exec. prod.), Grandview U.S.A. (co-exec. prod.), Under Fire, Baby, My Science Project, Until the End of the World, K2, To Die For (exec. prod.), Rough Magic (exec. prod.).
TELEVISION: Shelly Duvall's Faerie Tale Theatre (6 episodes), 1968: The 25th Anniversary, The Native Americans, The Prize, *Mini-series*: Cadillac Desert (exec. prod.).

TAPS, JONIE
Producer. Executive. Columbia Studio. Member of Friars Club, Hillcrest Country Club.
PICTURES: *Produced*: When You're Smiling, Sunny Side of Street, Sound Off, Rainbow Round My Shoulder, All Ashore, Cruisin' Down the River, Drive a Crooked Road, The Eddy Duchin Story, Three for the Show, Bring Your Smile Along, He Laughed Last, Shadow on the Window.

TARADASH, DANIEL
Writer, Director. b. Louisville, KY, Jan. 29, 1913. e. Harvard Coll., A.B., 1933; Harvard Law Sch., LL.B., 1936. Passed NY Bar, 1937; won nationwide playwriting contest, 1938; U.S. Army WWII. Pres. Screen Writers Branch, WGA, 1955-56; v.p.; Writers Guild of America, West 1956-59; mem. Writers Guild Council, 1954-65; mem., bd. of govnrs. Motion Picture Acad. Arts & Sciences, 1964-74, 1990-93; v.p. 1968-70 and pres. 1970-73. Trustee, Producers-Writers Guild Pension plan 1960-73. chmn., 1965. Mem. Bd. of Trustees of American Film Institute 1967-69. WGA's Valentine Davies Award, 1971. Pres., Academy M.P. Arts & Sciences, 1970-73, mem. bd. trustees, Entertainment Hall of Fame Foundation. Mem., Public Media General Programs panel for the National Foundation for the Arts, 1975-85, 1992; Pres. Writers Guild of America, West, 1977-79. Natl. chmn., Writers Guild of America, 1979-81. WGA's Morgan Cox Award, 1988. WGA's Edmund H. North Founders Award 1991. Festival to present Taradash Screenwriting Award 1992-; USC retrospective and tribute, 1992. Writer of TV special Bogie. Recipient of the Writers Guild of America West Laurel Award, 1996.
PICTURES: Golden Boy, A Little Bit of Heaven, Knock on Any Door, Rancho Notorious, Don't Bother to Knock, From Here to Eternity (Academy Award 1953), Desiree, Storm Center (also dir., co-story), Picnic, Bell Book and Candle, The Saboteur Code Name—Morituri, Hawaii, Castle Keep, Doctors' Wives, The Other Side of Midnight.

TARANTINO, QUENTIN
Writer, Director, Actor, Producer. b. Knoxville, TN, March 27, 1963. Graduate of Sundance Institute Director's Workshop and Lab. With producer Lawrence Bender, formed production co. A Band Apart.
PICTURES: Past Midnight (assoc. prod., co-s.p.), Reservoir Dogs (dir., s.p., actor), True Romance (s.p.), Killing Zoe (co-exec. prod.), Natural Born Killers (story), Sleep With Me (actor),

Pulp Fiction (dir., s.p., co-story, actor; Cannes Film Fest. Award for Best Film; LA Film Critics, NY Film Critics, Natl. Soc. of Film Critics, Chicago Film Critics & Independent Spirit Awards for dir. & s.p.; Academy Award & Golden Globe for s.p.; Natl. Bd. of Review Award for dir., 1994), Destiny Turns on the Radio (actor), Somebody to Love (actor), Desperado (actor), Four Rooms (co-s.p., co-exec. prod.), From Dusk Till Dawn (s.p., actor, co-exec. prod.), Girl 6 (actor), Curdled (exec. prod.), God Said, Ha, Full Tilt Boogie, Jackie Brown.
TELEVISION: *Guest*: The Golden Girls, All-American Girl. *Dir*: E/R (1 episode).

TARNOFF, JOHN B.
Producer. b. New York, NY, Mar. 3, 1952. e. UCLA, motion pictures & TV, 1973-74; Amherst Coll., B.A., 1969-73. Named field exec. with Taylor-Laughlin Distribution (company arm of Billy Jack Enterprises) 1974; left in 1975 to be literary agent with Bart/Levy, Inc.; later with Michael Levy & Associates, Paul Kohner/Michael Levy Agency; Headed TV dept., Kohner/Levy, 1979. Joined MGM as production exec., 1979; v.p., development, 1979-80; sr. v.p. production & devel., 1981-82; exec. v.p., Kings Road Prods., 1983-84; v.p., prod., Orion Pictures Corp., 1985; exec. prod., Out of Bounds, Columbia Pictures, 1986; v.p., prod., De Laurentiis Entertainment Group, 1987. Head of production, DeLaurentiis Entertainment, Australia, 1987-88. Exec. v.p. production, Village Roadshow Pictures, 1988-. Exec. prod.: The Delinquents, Blood Oath. 1990-93, personal mngr., Addis-Wechsler & Assoc. 1994, New Line Cinema/Overseas Film Group; prod., Nature of the Beast. 1995, founder, Newspeak Media Inc. 1996, founder, Personality Factory, Inc. 1998, exec. prod. Big Brother, cd-rom adventure based on Orwell's 1984; writer/designer, WarGames, cd-rom.

TARSES, JAMIE
Executive. b. Pittsburgh, PA. e. Williams Coll. Prior to joining NBC, worked as a casting director for Lorimar Productions. Joined NBC in Sept. 1987 as Mgr., Creative Affairs for NBC Productions. In Dec. 1987, named Mgr., Current Comedy Programs, NBC Entertainment and was NBC's Program Exec. for such series as Cheers, Amen, 227 and A Different World. In 1988, named Mgr., Comedy Development. In Feb. 1989, promoted to Director, Comedy Development, NBC Entertainment. Was directly involved in the development of Friends, NewsRadio, Caroline in the City, Mad About You, Frasier and several other NBC programs. In Aug. 1994, was named to supervise one of NBC's two programming teams before being promoted in 1995 to S.V.P., Primetime Series. In June of 1996, joined ABC Entertainment as President.

TARSES, JAY
Producer, Writer, Actor. b. Baltimore, MD, July 3, 1939. e. Williams Coll., Ithaca Coll., BFA theatre. Wrote and acted with little-theater co. in Pittsburgh, drove a truck in NY for Allen Funt's Candid Camera and worked in advertising and promotion for Armstrong Cork Co. in Lancaster, PA where he met Tom Patchett. Formed Patchett and Tarses, stand-up comedy team played coffeehouse circuit in the late 1960s. Later twosome became TV writing team and joined writing staff of Carol Burnett Show winning Emmy in 1972.
PICTURES: *Co-s.p. with Patchett*: Up the Academy, The Great Muppet Caper, The Muppets Take Manhattan.
TELEVISION: *Series*: *Actor*: Make Your Own Kind of Music, Open All Night, The Duck Factory, The Days and Nights of Molly Dodd. *Specials*: *With Tom Patchett*: The Bob Newhart Show (exec. prod., writer), The Tony Randall Show (exec. prod., writer), We've Got Each Other (creator, exec. prod., writer), Mary (prod.), Open All Night (creator, prod., writer), Buffalo Bill (creator, exec. prod., writer). *Solo*: The Days and Nights of Molly Dodd (creator, prod., writer), The "Slap" Maxwell Story (creator, prod., writer), Smoldering Lust (creator, prod., writer), Public Morals (co-creator, exec. prod., writer). *Pilots*: The Chopped Liver Brothers (exec. prod., writer), The Faculty (exec. prod., dir., writer), Baltimore (creator, prod., writer), Harvey Berger: Salesman (co-creator, prod., writer), Jackass Junior High (creator, prod., writer).

TARTIKOFF, BRANDON
Executive. b. New York, NY, Jan. 13, 1949. e. Yale U. Started TV career in 1971 in promo. dept. of ABC affiliates in New Haven, CT. Joined promo. staff at ABC affiliate in Chicago. In 1976 went to New York, with ABC-TV as mgr., dramatic development; moved to NBC Entertainment in Sept., 1977, as dir., comedy programs. In 1978 appt. v.p., programs, West Coast, NBC Entertainment; 1980, named pres. of that division. Pres. NBC Entertainment since 1980. Also heads own prod. co., NBC Productions. 1990, appointed chairman of NBC Entertainment Group. 1991, appointed chmn. of Paramount Pictures. Resigned from Paramount, Oct. 1992. Became chmn. of New World Entertainment, 1994. *Co-exec. prod. tv movie* Tom Clancy's Op Center.
PICTURES: Square Dance, Satisfaction.
(d. August 27, 1997)

TAVERNIER, BERTRAND
Director, Writer. b. Lyon, France, April 25, 1941. After 2 yrs. of law study, quit to become film critic for Cahiers du Cinema and Cinema 60. Asst. to dir. Jean-Pierre Melville on Leon Morin Priest (1961), also worked as film publicist. Wrote film scripts and a book on the Western and a history of American cinema. Partner for 6 yrs. with Pierre Rissient in film promotion company, during which time he studied all aspects of film-making. 1963: directed episode of Les Baisers. Pres., Lumiere Inst., Lyon. Book: 50 Years of American Cinema, Qu'est ce Qu'on Attend?, Amis Americains.
PICTURES: Director-Co-writer: The Clockmaker (L'Horloger de Saint-Paul), Let Joy Reign Supreme (Que La Fête Commence), The Judge and the Assassin (Le Judge et l'Assassin), Spoiled Children (also co-prod.), Deathwatch. Dir./Co-Writer/Prod.: A Week's Vacation, Clean Slate (Coup de Torchon; 11 César nom., Oscar nom.), Mississippi Blues (co-dir. with Robert Parrish), A Sunday in the Country (Un Dimanche a la Campagne; Best Direction Cannes, New york Critics Prize), 'Round Midnight, Beatrice (dir. co-prod. only), Life and Nothing But, Daddy Nostalgia, The Undeclared War (co-dir. with Patrick Rutman), L627, La Fille de D'Artagnan, L'Appat, Capitaine Conan.
TELEVISION: Phillippe Soupault, October Country (co-dir. with Robert Parrish), Lyon, le regard interieur.

TAVIANI, PAOLO and VITTORIO
Directors, Writers. b. San Miniato, Pisa, Italy, (Paolo: Nov. 8, 1931; Vittorio: Sept. 20, 1929); e. Univ. of Pisa (Paolo: liberal arts; Vittorio: law). The two brothers always work in collaboration from script preparation through shooting and editing. 1950: With Valentino Orsini ran cine-club at Pisa. 1954: In collab. with Caesare Zavattini directed short about Nazi massacre at San Miniato. 1954-59: with Orsini made series of short documentaries (Curatorne e Montanara; Carlo Pisacane; Ville della Brianza; Lavatori della pietra; Pitori in cita; I Pazzi della domenica; Moravia, Cabunara). Worked as assistant to Rosellini, Luciano Emmer and Raymond Pellegrini. 1960: collaborated on an episode of Italy Is Not a Poor Country.
PICTURES (all by both): A Man for Burning (debut, 1962; co-dir. with Valentino Orsini), Matrimonial Outlaws (co-dir. with Orsini), The Subversives, Under the Sign of Scorpio, Saint Michael Had a Rooster, Allonsanfan, Padre Padrone (Cannes Film Fest.: Grand Prix & Critics International Prize, 1977), The Meadow, The Night of the Shooting Stars (1981, Best Director Award, Natl. Society of Film Critics; Special Jury Prize, Cannes), Kaos, Good Morning Babylon, The Sun Also Shines at Night, Fiorile.

TAYLOR, DELORES
Actress, Writer, Producer. b. Winner, SD, Sept. 27, 1939. e. U. of South Dakota, studying commercial art. m. Tom Laughlin. First TV experience was heading art dept. at RCA wholesale center in Milwaukee. Established first Montessori School in U.S. in Santa Monica for several yrs., with husband. Made feature film debut as actress in Billy Jack in 1971. Wrote s.p. with husband for that and sequels, The Trial of Billy Jack, Billy Jack Goes to Washington, under pseudonym Teresa Christina.
PICTURES: Exec. Prod., Writer: Proper Time, Young Sinners, Born Losers, The Master Gunfighter. Exec. Prod., Writer, Actress: Billy Jack, Trial of Billy Jack, Billy Jack Goes to Washington, Return of Billy Jack.

TAYLOR, DON
Actor, Director. b. Freeport, PA, Dec. 13, 1920. e. Pennsylvania State U. Appeared in Army Air Corps' Winged Victory on stage & screen.
PICTURES: Actor: The Human Comedy, Girl Crazy, Thousands Cheer, Swing Shift Maisie, Salute to the Marines, Winged Victory, The Red Dragon, Song of the Thing Man, The Naked City, For the Love of Mary, Battleground, Ambush, Father of the Bride, Target Unknown, Father's Little Dividend, Submarine Command, Flying Leathernecks, The Blue Veil, Japanese War Bride, Stalag 17, The Girls of Pleasure Island, Destination Gobi, Johnny Dark, Men of Sherwood Forest, I'll Cry Tomorrow, The Bold and the Brave, Lost Slaves of the Amazon, Ride the High Iron, The Savage Guns. Director: Everything's Ducky (debut, 1961), Ride the Wild Surf, Jack of Diamonds, Five Man Army, Escape From the Planet of the Apes, Tom Sawyer, Echoes of a Summer, The Great Scout and Cathouse Thursday, The Island of Dr. Moreau, Damien—Omen II, The Final Countdown.
TELEVISION: Movies (director): Something for a Lonely Man, Wild Women, Heat of Anger, Night Games, Honky Tonk, The Manhunter, Circle of Children, The Gift, The Promise of Love, Broken Promise, Red Flag: The Ultimate Game, Drop Out Father, Listen to Your Heart, September Gun, My Wicked Wicked Ways: The Legend of Errol Flynn, Secret Weapons, Going for the Gold: The Bill Johnson Story, Classified Love, Ghost of a Chance, The Diamond Trap.

TAYLOR, ELIZABETH
Actress. b. London, Eng., Feb. 27, 1932. e. Bryon House, London. When 3 years old danced before Princess Elizabeth, Margaret Rose. Came to U.S. at outbreak of WWII. Author: World Enough and Time (with Richard Burton; 1964), Elizabeth Taylor (1965), Elizabeth Takes Off (1988). Initiated Ben Gurion U.—Elizabeth Taylor Fund for Children of the Negev, 1982. Co-founded American Foundation for AIDS Research, 1985. Named Comdr. Arts & Letters (France) 1985, Legion of Honor, 1987. Established the Elizabeth Taylor AIDS Foundation in 1991. Developed various perfume products: Elizabeth Taylor's Passion, Passion Body Riches, Passion for Men, White Diamonds, Diamonds and Emeralds, Diamonds and Sapphires, Diamond and Rubies; 1993 launched Elizabeth Taylor Fashion Jewelry Collection. Recipient of AFI Life Achievement Award (1993), Jean Hersholt Humanitarian Award (1993).
THEATER: B'way: The Little Foxes (also London), Private Lives.
PICTURES: There's One Born Every Minute (debut, 1942), Lassie Come Home, Jane Eyre, White Cliffs of Dover, National Velvet, Courage of Lassie, Life with Father, Cynthia, A Date With Judy, Julia Misbehaves, Little Women, Conspirator, The Big Hangover, Father of the Bride, Father's Little Dividend, A Place in the Sun, Callaway Went Thataway (cameo), Love Is Better Than Ever, Ivanhoe, The Girl Who Had Everything, Rhapsody, Elephant Walk, Beau Brummel, The Last Time I Saw Paris, Giant, Raintree County, Cat on a Hot Tin Roof, Suddenly Last Summer, Scent of Mystery (cameo), Butterfield 8 (Academy Award, 1960), Cleopatra, The V.I.P.s, The Sandpiper, Who's Afraid of Virginia Woolf? (Academy Award, 1966), The Taming of the Shrew, Doctor Faustus, Reflections in a Golden Eye, The Comedians, Boom!, Secret Ceremony, The Only Game in Town, X Y and Zee (Zee and Company), Under Milk Wood, Hammersmith Is Out, Night Watch, Ash Wednesday, That's Entertainment!, The Driver's Seat, The Blue Bird, A Little Night Music, Winter Kills (cameo), The Mirror Crack'd, Genocide (narrator), Young Toscanini, The Flintstones, The Visit.
TELEVISION: Movies: Divorce His/Divorce Hers, Victory at Entebbe, Return Engagement, Between Friends, Malice in Wonderland, There Must Be a Pony, Poker Alice, Sweet Bird of Youth. Mini-Series: North and South. Guest: Here's Lucy (1970 with Richard Burton), General Hospital (1981), All My Children (1983), Hotel. Specials: Elizabeth Taylor in London, America's All-Star Salute to Elizabeth Taylor.

TAYLOR, LILI
Actress. b. Chicago, 1967.
THEATER: NY: What Did He See, Aven U Boys. Regional: Mud, The Love Talker, Fun. Director: Collateral Damage.
PICTURES: Mystic Pizza (debut, 1988), Say Anything, Born on the Fourth of July, Bright Angel, Dogfight, Watch It, Household Saints, Short Cuts, Rudy, Arizona Dream, Mrs. Parker and the Vicious Circle, Ready to Wear (Pret-a-Porter), The Addiction, Cold Fever, Four Rooms, Things I Never Told You, I Shot Andy Warhol, Girl's Town, Ransom, Kicked in the Head, O.K. Garage, The Imposters, Spring Forward, A Slipping.
TELEVISION: Movies: Subway Stories: Tales from the Underground.

TAYLOR, MESHACH
Actor. b. Boston, MA, Apr. 11. e. Florida A & M Univ. Hosted Chicago TV show Black Life.
THEATER: Streamers, Sizwe Banzi is Dead, The Island, Native Son, Wonderful Ice Cream Suit, Bloody Bess, Sirens of Titan, Night Feast, Huckleberry Finn, Cops.
PICTURES: Damien: Omen II, The Howling, The Beast Within, Explorers, Warning Sign, One More Saturday Night, From the Hip, Mannequin, The Allnighter, House of Games, Welcome to Oblivion, Mannequin 2 on the Move, Class Act.
TELEVISION: Series: Buffalo Bill, Designing Women, Dave's World. Guest: Lou Grant, Barney Miller, Melba, Golden Girls, M*A*S*H, The White Shadow, What's Happening Now, ALF. Movies: An Innocent Man, How to Murder a Millionaire, Double Double Toil and Trouble, Virtual Seduction. Specials: Huckleberry Finn, The Rec Room.

TAYLOR, RENEE
Actress, Writer. b. New York, NY, March 19, 1935. Wife of actor Joseph Bologna, with whom she collaborates in writing. Their B'way plays include Lovers and Other Strangers, It Had to Be You. Stage actress: One of the All-Time Greats.
PICTURES: Actress: The Errand Boy, The Detective, The Producers, A New Leaf, Lovers and Other Strangers (also s.p.), Made for Each Other (also s.p.), Last of the Red Hot Lovers, Lovesick, It Had to Be You (also co-dir., co-s.p.), That's Adequate, White Palace, End of Innocence, Delirious, All I Want for Christmas, Forever.
TELEVISION: Writer: Acts of Love... and Other Comedies (Emmy Award, 1973), Paradise, Calucci's Department, The American Dream Machine, Bedrooms (Writers Guild Award, 1984), etc. Actress: Series regular: The Jack Paar Show, Mary Hartman Mary Hartman, Daddy Dearest, The Nanny. Movie: Woman of the Year (also co-writer).

TAYLOR, ROD
Actor. b. Sydney, Australia, Jan. 11, 1930. e. East Sydney Fine Arts Coll. Started out as artist then turned to acting on stage. Formed own company, Rodler, Inc., for TV-film production.
PICTURES: The Sturt Expedition (debut, 1951), King of the Coral Sea, Long John Silver, Top Gun, The Virgin Queen, Hell on Frisco Bay, World Without End, The Rack, Giant, The Catered Affair, Raintree County, Step Down to Terror, Separate Tables, Ask Any Girl, The Time Machine, Seven Seas to Calais, 101 Dalmatians (voice), The Birds, A Gathering of Eagles, The V.I.Ps, Sunday in New York, Fate is the Hunter, 36 Hours, Young Cassidy, Do Not Disturb, The Glass Bottom Boat, The Liquidator, Hotel, Chuka (also prod.), Dark of the Sun, High Commissioner (Nobody Runs Forever), The Hell with Heroes, Zabriskie Point, Darker Than Amber, The Man Who Had Power Over Women, The Heroes, The Train Robbers, Trader Horn, The Deadly Trackers, Hell River, Blondy, Picture Show Man, A Time To Die, On the Run, Close Enemy, Open Season, Point of Betrayal, Welcome to Woop-Woop.
TELEVISION: Movies: Powerkeg, Family Flight, The Oregon Trail, Cry of the Innocent, Jacqueline Bouvier Kennedy, Charles and Diana: A Royal Love Story, Outlaws, Danielle Steel's Palomino, Grass Roots. Series: Hong Kong, Bearcats, Masquerade, The Oregon Trail, Outlaws, Falcon Crest.

TAYLOR, RONNIE
Director of Photography. b. London, England, 1924. Ent. m.p. ind. 1941 at Gainsborough Studios
PICTURES: Tommy, The Silent Flute, Circle of Iron, Savage Harvest, Gandhi, High Road to China, The Hound of the Baskervilles, The Champions, Master of the Game (UK shoot), A Chorus Line, Foreign Body, Cry Freedom, Opera (Italy), The Experts, Sea of Love, Popcorn, The Rainbow Thief, Jewels, Age of Treason, The Steal, The Good King.

TAYLOR, JOHN RUSSELL
Writer, Critic. b. Dover, England, June 19, 1935. e. Cambridge U., B.A., 1956. Editor: Times Educational Supplement, London, 1959-60; film critic, The Times, London, 1962-73; art critic, 1978-; editor, Films and Filming, 1983-; prof., division of Cinema, USC, 1972-78. Member: London Film and TV Press Guild, London Critics Circle, NY Society of Cinematologists.
BOOKS: Joseph L. Mankiewicz: An Index, The Angry Theatre, Anatomy of a Television Play, Cinema Eye Cinema Ear, Shakespeare: A Celebration (cont.), New English Dramatists 8 (ed. & intr.), The Hollywood Musical, The Second Wave: Hollywood Dramatists for the 70s, Masterworks of the British Cinema, Directors and Directions: Peter Shaffer, Hitch, Cukor's Hollywood, Impressionism, Strangers in Paradise, Ingrid Bergman, Alec Guinness: A Celebration, Vivien Leigh, Hollywood 1940s, Portraits of the British Cinema.

TAYLOR-YOUNG, LEIGH
Actress. b. Washington, DC, Jan. 25, 1945. e. Northwestern U. B'way debut 1966 in Three Bags Full. Additional stage: The Beckett Plays (Off-B'way, LA), Knives, Sleeping Dogs.
PICTURES: I Love You Alice B. Toklas (debut, 1968), The Games, The Big Bounce, The Adventurers, The Buttercup Chain, The Horsemen, The Gang That Couldn't Shoot Straight, Soylent Green, Can't Stop the Music, Looker, Secret Admirer, Jagged Edge, Honeymoon Academy, Accidents.
TELEVISION: Series: Peyton Place, The Devlin Connection, The Hamptons, Dallas, Picket Fences (Emmy Award, 1994). Movies: Marathon, Napoleon and Josephine: A Love Story, Perry Mason: The Case of the Sinister Spirit, Who Gets the Friends, Bonnie and McCloud, Moment of Truth: Murder or Memory? Guest: Civil Wars, The Young Riders, Alfred Hitchcock Presents, Spenser for Hire, Evening Shade. Pilots: Ghostwriter, Houston Knights.

TEAGUE, LEWIS
Director. b. 1941. e. NYU. Editor and/or 2nd unit dir. on such films as Cockfighter, Crazy Mama, Death Race 2000, Avalanche, Fast Charlie: The Moonbeam Rider, The Big Red One.
PICTURES: Dirty O'Neil (co-dir.), Lady in Red (also editor), Alligator, Fighting Back, Cujo, Cat's Eye, The Jewel of the Nile, Collision Course, Navy SEALS, Fortune Hunter.
TELEVISION: Series episodes: Alfred Hitchcock Presents, Daredevils, Shannon's Deal. Movies: T Bone N Weasel, Tom Clancy's Op Center, Time Traxx, Saved by the Light, Profiler, Justice League of America, The Reunion: Dukes of Hazzard.

TELLER, IRA
Executive. b. New York, NY, July 3, 1940. e. City Coll. of New York, & 1957-61; NYU Graduate Sch. of Arts, 1961-62. Publicist, Pressbook Dept., 20th Century Fox., 1961-62; asst. to adv. mgr., Embassy Pictures Corp., 1962-63; asst. adv. mgr., Columbia Pictures Corp., 1963; adv. mgr., Columbia Pictures Corp., 1964, 1964-65; asst. to chmn. of bd., Diener, Hauser, Greenhalt Agy., 1966; adv. mgr., 20th Century-Fox, 1966-67; 1967, adv. dir. 20th Cent.-Fox.; dir. of adv., Nat'l General Pictures Corp., 1969; eastern dir., adv.-pub., 1972; national dir., adv-pub., 1973; Bryanston Distributors, Inc. v.p. adv.-pub., 1974; Cine Artists Pictures Corp. v.p. adv-pub., 1975; Lorimar Productions, v.p., adv.-marketing, 1976-77; 1977-present, pres. Ira Teller and Company, Inc.; This Is It Productions, prod.

TEMPLE, JULIEN
Director. b. London, England, Nov. 26, 1953. e. Cambridge, London's National Film School. Dir. many rock videos.
PICTURES: The Great Rock 'n' Roll Swindle (debut, 1979), The Secret Policeman's Other Ball, Undercover (also s.p.), Running Out of Luck (also s.p.), Absolute Beginners, Aria (segment: Rigoletto), Earth Girls Are Easy, Rolling Stones: At the Max (creative consultant), Bullet, Catching Fire.

TEMPLE (BLACK), SHIRLEY
Actress, Diplomat. b. Santa Monica, CA, April 23, 1928. In 1932 screen debut, Red Haired Alibi. In 1933 To the Last Man; then leading figure in series of Educational shorts called Baby Burlesque and Frolics of Youth, until breakthrough role in Stand Up and Cheer, 1934, which resulted in career as child and teen star. Voted one of ten best Money-Making Stars in Motion Picture Herald-Fame Poll, 1934-39. As an adult, turned her attention to government and international issues. Republican candidate for U.S. House of Representatives, 1967. Rep. to 24th General Assembly of U.N. (1969-70). Special asst. to chmn., President's Council on the Environment (1970-72). U.S. Ambassador to Ghana (1974-76). Chief of Protocol, White House (1976-77); member of U.S. delegation on African Refugee problems, Geneva, 1981; 1987 made 1st honorary U.S. Foreign Service Rep. for State Dept.; 1989, appt. Ambassador to Czechoslovakia. Autobiography: Child Star (1988).
PICTURES: The Red-Haired Alibi (feature debut, 1932), To the Last Man, Out All Night, Mandalay, Carolina, Stand Up and Cheer, Baby Take a Bow, Now and Forever, Bright Eyes, Now I'll Tell, Change of Heart, Little Miss Marker, The Little Colonel, Our Little Girl, Curly Top, The Littlest Rebel, Captain January, Poor Little Rich Girl, Dimples, Stowaway, Wee Willie Winkle, Heidi, Rebecca of Sunnybrook Farm, Little Miss Broadway, Just Around the Corner, Little Princess, Susannah of the Mounties, The Blue Bird, Young People, Kathleen, Miss Annie Rooney. Since You Went Away, I'll Be Seeing You, Kiss and Tell, That Hagen Girl, Honeymoon, Bachelor and the Bobby-Soxer, Fort Apache, Mr. Belvedere Goes to College, Adventure in Baltimore, Story of Seabiscuit, Kiss for Corliss.
TELEVISION: Series: Shirley Temple's Storybook (host, performer).

TENNANT, VICTORIA
Actress. b. London, England, Sept. 30, 1953. e. Central Sch. of Speech & Drama. Daughter of ballerina Irina Baronova and talent agent Cecil Tennant.
THEATER: Love Letters (Steppenwolf), Getting Married (NY), Taming of the Shrew (NY).
PICTURES: The Ragman's Daughter, Strangers Kiss, All of Me, The Holocraft Covenant, Best Seller, Flowers in the Attic, Fool's Mate, The Handmaid's Tale, L.A. Story, Whispers, The Plague.
TELEVISION: Mini-Series: Voice of the Heart, Winds of War, Chiefs, War and Remembrance, Act of Will, The Man from Snowy River. Movies: Maigret, Dempsey, Under Siege.

TETZLAFF, TED
Director. b. Los Angeles, CA, June 3, 1903. Joined camera dept. Fox Studios, became first cameraman; dir., 1940; served in U.S. Air Corps as a Major, WWII.
PICTURES: Cameraman: Enchanted Cottage, Notorious. Dir.: World Premiere, Riffraff, Fighting Father Dunne, Window, Johnny Allegro, Dangerous Profession, Gambling House, White Tower, Under the Gun, Treasure of Lost Canyon, Terror on a Train, Son of Sinbad, Seven Wonders of the World, The Young Land.

TEWKESBURY, JOAN
Writer, Director. b. Redlands, CA, April 8, 1936. e. USC. Student American Sch. Dance 1947-54. Was ostrich and understudy in Mary Martin's Peter Pan. Directed and choreographed Theatre prods. in L.A., London, Edinburgh Festival, Scotland. Taught dance and theory, American Sch. of Dance 1959-64; taught in theatre arts depts. of two universities: USC, Immaculate Heart. Became script supvr. for Robert Altman on McCabe & Mrs. Miller. Off-B'way: Cowboy Jack Street (writer, dir.). Teacher in film dept. UCLA. Sundance advisor, 1992-93: directors lab-writers lab. American Musical Theatre Festival in Philadelphia. Chippy (dir.), Jammed (Edinburgh Festival; writer, dir.). Dance Card (Oregon Ballter Theatre; writer, dir., co-choreo.)
PICTURES: Thieves Like Us (co.-s.p.), Nashville, (s.p.), Old Boyfriends (dir.), Hampstead Center (doc. of Anna Freud, writer, dir.), A Night in Heaven (s.p.), The Player (actress).
TELEVISION: Series: Director: Alfred Hitchcock Presents (also writer), Elysian Fields (pilot; also writer, exec. prod.), Almost Grown, Shannon's Deal (also writer), Nothing Sacred. Movies: Director/Writer: The Acorn People, The Tenth Month, Cold Sassy Tree, Sudie and Simpson, Wild Texas Wind, The Stranger, On Promised Land, Scattering Dad.

THALHIMER, JR., MORTON G.
Former Theatre Executive. b. Richmond, VA, June 27, 1924. e. Dartmouth Coll., 1948, B.A.; U. of Virginia, 1959. Naval aviator in WWII. Joined Century Theatres as trainee 1948; Jamestown Amusement, 1949-50. Past pres. Neighborhood Theatre, Inc. 1967-86. Charter member of Theatre Owners of America; past member and v.p. of NATO, served on finance comm. and Trade Practice comm. bd. member and past president of NATO of VA, 1973-75. Mem. Variety Club Int'l., Tent 11; patron life member, Variety Club of Israel, Tent 51.

THAXTER, PHYLLIS
Actress. b. Portland, ME, Nov. 20, 1919. e. St. Genevieve Sch., Montreal. Daughter is actress Skye Aubrey.
PICTURES: Thirty Seconds Over Tokyo (debut, 1944), Bewitched, Weekend at the Waldorf, Sea of Grass, Living in a Big Way, Tenth Avenue Angel, Sign of the Ram, Blood on the Moon, Act of Violence, No Man of Her Own, The Breaking Point, Fort Worth, Jim Thorpe_All American, Come Fill the Cup, She's Working Her Way Through College, Springfield Rifle, Operation Secret, Women's Prison, Man Afraid, The World of Henry Orient, Superman.
TELEVISION: *Movies:* Incident in San Francisco, The Longest Night, Three Sovereigns for Sarah. *Mini-Series:* Once an Eagle. *Guest:* Wagon Train, Alfred Hitchcock, Twilight Zone, Purex Specials For Women, Playhouse 90, The Fugitive, The Defenders, Murder She Wrote.

THEODORAKIS, MIKIS
Composer. b. Greece, 1925.
PICTURES: Eva, Night Ambush, Shadow of the Cat, Phaedra, Five Miles to Midnight, Zorba the Greek, The Day the Fish Came Out, The Trojan Women, State of Siege, Serpico, Iphigenia.

THEWLIS, DAVID
Actor. b. Blackpool, England, 1962. e. Guildhall School of Music and Drama, The Barbicon, London. First prof. job in breakfast food commercial.
PICTURES: Little Dorrit, Resurrected, Life Is Sweet, Afraid of the Dark, Damage, The Trial, Naked (Cannes Film Fest., NY Film Critics & Natl. Soc. of Film Critics Awards, 1993), Black Beauty, Restoration,Total Eclipse, Dragonheart, James and the Giant Peach (voice), The Island of Dr. Moreau, Seven Years in Tibet, American Perfekt, Divorcing Jack, The Big Lebowski, Great Sex.
TELEVISION: Only Fools and Horses, The Singing Detective, Filipino Dreamgirls, Prime Suspect, Dandelion Dead.

THIGPEN, LYNNE
Actress, Singer. b. Joliet, IL, Dec. 22, 1948.
THEATER: *NY:* Godspell, The Magic Show, But Never Jam Today, Tintypes, And I Ain't Finished Yet, Full Hookup, Balm in Gilead, A Month of Sundays, Fences, Boesman & Lena, An American Daughter (B'way).
PICTURES: Godspell (debut, 1973), The Warriors, Tootsie, Streets of Fire, Sweet Liberty, Hello Again, Running on Empty, Lean on Me, Impulse, Article 99, Bob Roberts, The Paper, Naked in New York, Blankman, Just Cause.
TELEVISION: *Series:* Love Sidney, The News is the News, FM, All My Children, Where in the World is Carmen Sandiego? *Pilot:* Pottsville. *Guest:* The Equalizer, Gimme a Break, L.A. Law, Days and Nights of Molly Dodd, Roseanne, Frank's Place, The Cosby Show, Dear John, thirtysomething, Preston Episodes. *Movies:* Fear Stalk, Separate But Equal, A Mother's Instinct, Boys Next Door, Cagney & Lacey. *Pilot:* For the People, Those Two, A Mother Instinct, The Boys Next Door, Chance of a Lifetime.

THINNES, ROY
Actor. b. Chicago, IL, April 6, 1938. Made tv debut as teen on DuPont Theatre, 1957.
PICTURES: Journey to the Far Side of the Sun, Charlie One-Eye, Airport 75, The Hindenburg, Rush Week.
TELEVISION: *Series:* General Hospital (1963-65), The Long Hot Summer, The Invaders, The Psychiatrist, From Here to Eternity, One Life to Live, Falcon Crest, Dark Shadows. *Movies:* The Other Man, The Psychiatrist: God Bless the Children, Black Noon, The Horror at 37000 Feet, The Norliss Tales, Satan's School for Girls, Death Race, The Manhunter, Secrets, Code Name: Diamond Head, Sizzle, The Return of the Mod Squad, Freedom, Dark Holiday, Blue Bayou, The Hand in the Glove, An Inconvenient Woman, Lady Against the Odds, Stormy Weathers, The Indians. *Mini-Series:* From Here to Eternity, Scruples.

THOMAS, BETTY
Director, Actress. b. St. Louis, MO, July 27, 1949. e. Ohio U, Chicago Art Inst., Roosevelt U. Former member of Chicago's Second City improv group.
PICTURES: *Actress:* Tunnelvision, Chesty Anderson—U.S. Navy, Loose Shoes, Used Cars, Homework, Troop Beverly Hills, Jackson County Jail. *Director:* Only You, The Brady Bunch Movie, Private Parts.
TELEVISION: *Series:* Hill Street Blues (Emmy Award, 1985). *Movies:* Outside Chance, Nashville Grab, When Your Lover Leaves, Prison. Director (series): Doogie Howser M.D., Dream On (Emmy Award, 1993), Hooperman, Mancuso FBI, Arresting Behavior, Couples. *Movie:* My Breast. *Specials:* The Late Shift (Dir's Guild of America Award, 1997).

THOMAS, DAVE
Actor, Writer, Director. b. St. Catherines, Ontario, Canada, May 20, 1949. e. McMaster Univ.
PICTURES: Stripes (debut, 1981), Strange Brew (also co-dir., co-s.p.), My Man Adam, Sesame Street Presents Follow That Bird, Love at Stake, Nightflyers, Moving, The Experts (dir. only), Cold Sweat, Coneheads.
TELEVISION: *Series (actor/writer):* Second City TV, SCTV Network The New Show, The Dave Thomas Comedy Show (also exec. prod., dir.), Maniac Mansion, Grace Under Fire (actor only). *Movies:* Home to Stay, Just Me and You, The Canadian Conspiracy, Boris and Natasha, Ghost Mom (writer). *Pilot:* From Cleveland. *Specials:* Twilight Theatre, Martin Short Concert for the North, Dave Thomas: The Incredible Time Travels of Henry Osgood (also dir., exec. prod., writer), Andrea Martin: Together Again, Inside America's Totally Unsolved Lifestyles (also exec. prod., writer).

THOMAS, HARRY E.
Exhibitor. b. Monroe, LA, May 22, 1920. e. Louisiana State U., 1938-41. Psychological Branch of Army Air Force, 1942-46. Past pres., secy., and treas. of NATO of MS. Dir. of Design & Const. & Sec. Gulf State Theatres Inc. Retired 1978.

THOMAS, HENRY
Actor. b. San Antonio, TX, Sept. 8, 1971. Made film debut at the age of 9 in Raggedy Man, 1981. On stage in Artichoke, The Guardsman.
PICTURES: Raggedy Man (debut, 1981), E.T. The Extra-Terrestrial, Misunderstood, Cloak and Dagger, The Quest, Murder One, Valmont, Fire in the Sky, Legends of the Fall.
TELEVISION: *Movies:* Psycho IV: The Beginning, A Taste for Killing, Curse of the Starving Class, Indictment: The McMartin Trial. *Special:* The Steeler and the Pittsburgh Kid.

THOMAS, JAY
Actor. b. New Orleans, LA, July 12, 1948. Started as stand-up comedian before pursuing acting career in NY. Appeared on NY stage with Playwrights Horizons and Off-B'way in Isn't It Romantic? Also morning disc jockey on L.A. radio station KPWR-FM.
PICTURES: C.H.U.D., The Gig, Straight Talk, Mr. Holland's Opus, A Smile Like Yours, Dirty Laundry, A Smile Like Yours, The Adventures of Ragtime.
TELEVISION: *Movies:* Miracle Landing, A Husband A Wife A Lover, Deserts Edge, Killing Mr. Griffin. *Series:* Mork & Mindy, Cheers, Married People, Love & War. *Guest:* Murphy Brown (Emmy Award, 1991).

THOMAS, JEREMY
Producer. b. London, Eng., July 26, 1949. e. Millfield School. Son of dir. Ralph Thomas (Doctor comedies) and nephew of dir. Gerald Thomas (Carry On... comedies). Entered industry 1969. Worked as film edit. on Brother Can You Spare a Dime, 1974. Received Evening Standard Special Award for Outstanding Contribution to Cinema in 1990, BAFTA's Michael Balcon Award in 1991. Appointed chmn. of British Film Institute, 1992.
PICTURES: Mad Dog Morgan, The Shout, The Great Rock 'n' Roll Swindle, Bad Timing: A Sensual Obsession, Eureka, Merry Christmas Mr. Lawrence, The Hit, Insignificance, The Last Emperor (Academy Award, 1987), Everybody Wins, The Sheltering Sky, Let Him Have It (exec. prod.), Naked Lunch, Little Buddha, Stealing Beauty, Blood and Wine, The Brave, All the Little Animals (dir.).

THOMAS, LEO J.
Executive. b. Grand Rapids, MN. e. Univ. of MI, Univ. of IL. Started as research chemist in 1961 at Color Photog. Division of the Kodak Research Labs. 1967-70, head of Color Physics and Engingeering Lab; 1970-72, asst. head of Color Photog. Division; 1972-74, tech. asst. to dir. of the Research Labs; 1974, appointed sec. of Technical Affairs Committe. 1977, named dir. of Research Laboratories; later that year became v.p. of the company; 1978 elected sr. v.p. 1984, appointed gen. mgr. Life Sciences. 1988, v.p. Sterling Drug; 1989, gen. mgr. of Health Group; 1989, v.p. of Health Group; 1991, pres. of Imaging Group; 1994, exec. v.p. Eastman Kodak Company.

THOMAS, MARLO
Actress. b. Detroit, MI, Nov. 21, 1938. Daughter of late Danny Thomas. m. Phil Donahue. Brother is TV producer Tony Thomas. e. U. of Southern California. Started career with small TV roles, summer stock. Appeared in London stage prod. of Barefoot in the Park. Most Promising Newcomer Awards from both Fame and Photoplay for series That Girl. Conceived book, record and TV special Free to Be You and Me (Emmy Award, 1974).
THEATER: *NY:* Thieves, Social Security, The Shadow Box.Regional: Six Degrees of Separation.
PICTURES: Jenny, Thieves, In the Spirit, The Real Blonde, Starfucker.

TELEVISION: *Series*: The Joey Bishop Show, That Girl. *Specials*: Acts of Love and Other Comedies, Free To Be You and Me (also prod.; Emmy Award, 1974), The Body Human: Facts for Girls (Emmy Award, 1981), Love Sex... and Marriage (also exec. prod.), Free to Be a Family (host, exec. prod.; Emmy Award, 1989). *Movies*: It Happened One Christmas (also co-prod.), The Lost Honor of Kathryn Beck (also exec. prod.), Consenting Adult, Nobody's Child (Emmy Award, 1986), Leap of Faith (co-exec. prod. only), Held Hostage: The Sis and Jerry Levin Story, Ultimate Betrayal, Reunion (also exec-prod.). *Guest*: Dobie Gillis, Zane Grey Theatre, Thriller.

THOMAS, PHILIP MICHAEL
Actor. b. Columbus, OH, May 26, 1949. e. Oakwood Coll.
PICTURES: Black Fist, Sparkle, Death Drug, The Wizard of Speed and Time.
TELEVISION: *Series*: Miami Vice. *Movies*: Toma, The Beasts Are on the Streets, This Man Stands Alone, Valentine, A Fight for Jenny, False Witness. *Special*: Disney's Totally Minnie, The Debbie Allen Special.

THOMAS, RALPH
Director. b. Hull, Yorkshire, England, Aug. 10, 1915. e. Tellisford Coll., Clifton and University Coll., London. Journalist in early career, entered m.p. ind. 1932 as film ed.; service with 9th Lancers, 1939-45; then film director.
PICTURES: Helter Skelter, Once Upon a Dream, Traveller's Joy, The Clouded Yellow, Appointment With Venus (Island Rescue), The Assassin (The Venetian Bird), A Day to Remember, Doctor in the House, Mad about Men, Above Us the Waves, Doctor at Sea, The Iron Petticoat, Checkpoint, Doctor at Large, Campbell's Kingdom, A Tale of Two Cities, The Wind Cannot Read, The 39 Steps, Upstairs and Downstairs, Conspiracy of Hearts, Doctor in Love, No Love for Johnnie, No My Darling Daughter, A Pair of Briefs, The Wild and the Willing, Doctor in Distress, Hot Enough for June (Agent 8 3/4), The High Bright Sun (McGuire Go Home!), Doctor in Clover, Deadlier Than the Male, Nobody Runs Forever (The High Commissioner), Some Girls Do, Doctor in Trouble, Percy, Quest for Love, The Love Ban, Percy's Progress (It's Not the Size That Counts), A Nightingale Sang in Berkeley Square, Pop Pirates.

THOMAS, RICHARD
Actor. b. New York, NY, June 13, 1951. e. Columbia U. Made TV debut at age 7 on Hallmark Hall of Fame special The Christmas Tree. That same year appeard on Brodawy in Sunrise at Campobello.
THEATER: Sunrise at Campobello, Everything in the Garden, Fifth of July, The Front Page, Love Letters, Square One, The Lisbon Traviata, Danton's Death, Richard II, Richard III.
PICTURES: Winning (debut, 1969), Last Summer, Red Sky at Morning, The Todd Killings, You'll Like My Mother, September 30, 1955, Battle Beyond the Stars.
TELEVISION: *Series*: One Two Three Go, As the World Turns, The Waltons (Emmy Award, 1973). *Guest*: Great Ghost Tales, Bonanza, Love American Style, Medical Center, Marcus Welby M.D., The F.B.I., Tales From the Crypt (Mute Witness to Murder), The Outer Limits. *Movies*: Homecoming, The Red Badge of Courage, The Silence, Getting Married, No Other Love, All Quiet on the Western Front, To Find My Son, Berlin Tunnel 21, Johnny Belinda, Living Proof: The Hank Williams Jr. Story, Hobson's Choice, The Master of Ballantrae, Final Jeopardy, Glory Glory, Go To the Light, Common Ground, Stephen King's IT, Mission of the Shark, Yes Virginia There Is a Santa Claus, Crash Landing: The Rescue of Flight 232, I Can Make You Love Me: The Stalking of Laura Black, Precious Victims, Linda, A Walton Thanksgiving Reunion, Death in Small Doses, A Walton Wedding, Down Out and Dangerous. *Specials*: A Doll's House, Give Us Barabbas, HMS Pinafore, Barefoot in the Park, Fifth of July, Andre's Mother.

THOMAS, ROBERT G.
Producer, Director. b. Glen Ridge, NJ, July 21, 1943. e. U. of Bridgeport, Fairleigh Dickinson U. Prod. educational radio programs, 1962, WPKN-FM. Asst. stage mgr. Meadowbrook Dinner Theatre, 1963; 1964, began career as TV cameraman for NY stations. Worked both full-time and freelance for major TV and video tape studios. 1968, started Bob Thomas Productions, producing business/sales films and TV commercials. Has 8 awards from natl. film festivals; nominated for 5 Emmys for TV series called The Jersey Side he produced for WOR-TV. Inventor of Futurevision 2000 multi-imaging video system for conventions and exhibits and museums (American Museum of Natural History: Hall of Human Biology to be shown over 15 years). Inventor and pres. of Video Mail Marketing Inc., low cost, light weight paper board video cassettes for the direct mail video marketing industry. *Shorts*: Valley Forge with Bob Hope, New Jersey—200 Years, Road-Eo '77.
TELEVISION: The Jersey Side (talk/entertainment), Jersey People (weekly talk/entertainment prog.), Movies '89 (synd. film preview series).

THOMAS, ROBERT J. (BOB)
Columnist, Associated Press, Hollywood. b. San Diego, CA, Jan. 26, 1922. p. George H. Thomas, publicist. e. UCLA. Joined Associated Press staff, Los Angeles, 1943; corr. Fresno, 1944; Hollywood since 1944. Writer mag. articles; appearances, radio; orig. story Big Mike.
AUTHOR: The Art of Animation, King Cohn, Thalberg, Selznick, Winchell—Secret Boss of California, The Heart of Hollywood, Howard—The Amazing Mr. Hughes, Weekend '33, Marlon—Portrait of the Rebel as an Artist, Walt Disney—An American Original, Bud and Lou—The Abbott and Costello Story, The Road to Hollywood (with Bob Hope), The One and Only Bing, Joan Crawford, Golden Boy: The Secret Life of William Holden, Astaire: The Man the Dancer, I Got Rhythm— The Ethel Merman Story, Liberace, Clown Prince of Hollywood (Jack L. Warner), Disney's Art of Animation.

THOMOPOULOS, ANTHONY D.
Executive. b. Mt. Vernon, NY, Feb. 7, 1938. e. Georgetown U. Began career in broadcasting at NBC, 1959, starting as mailroom clerk and moving to radio division in prod. & admin. Shortly named to post in int'l division sales, involved with programming for stations and in dev. TV systems for other nations. Joined Four Star Entertainment Corp. as dir. of foreign sales, 1964; named v.p., 1965; exec. v.p., 1969; 1970 joined RCA SelectaVision Div. as dir. of programming; 1971 joined Tomorrow Entertainment as v.p.; 1973 joined ABC as v.p., prime-time programs in N.Y.; 1974, named v.p., prime-time TV creative operations, ABC Entertainment; 1975 named v.p. of special programs, ABC Entertainment; 1976 made v.p., ABC-TV, assisting pres. Frederick S. Pierce in supervising all activities of the division; 1978 named pres. of ABC Entertainment; 1983 promoted to pres., ABC Broadcast Group in chg. all TV & radio operations; 1986-88, pres. & COO, United Artists Corp.; independent prod. with Columbia, 1989. Formed Thomopoulos Productions in 1989. Pres., Amblin Television, 1991-95. Responsible for the original placement of E.R. in addition to several other series on network television.

THOMPSON, CAROLINE
Writer. b. Washington, DC, Apr. 23, 1956. e. Amherst Col., Harvard. Started as free-lance journalist. Wrote novel First Born, which led to screenwriting.
PICTURES: Edward Scissorhands (also assoc. prod.), The Addams Family, Homeward Bound: The Incredible Journey, The Secret Garden (also assoc. prod.), The Nightmare Before Christmas, Black Beauty (also dir.), Buddy (also dir.).

THOMPSON, EMMA
Actress. b. London, England, Apr. 15, 1959. e. Cambridge Univ. Daughter of actors Eric Thompson and Phyllida Law. Acted with the Footlights at the Edinburgh Fringe. At Cambridge co-wrote, co-produced, co-directed and co-starred in school's first all-female revue Woman's Hour, as well as solo show Short Vehicle.
THEATER: *London*: Me and My Girl, Look Back in Anger. Renaissance Theatre Company (World Tour): A Midsummer Night's Dream, King Lear.
PICTURES: Henry V, The Tall Guy, Impromptu, Dead Again, Howards End (Academy Award, BAFTA, NY Film Critics, LA Film Critics, Golden Globe, Nat'l Society of Film Critics & Nat'l Board of Review Awards for Best Actress of 1992), Peter's Friends, Much Ado About Nothing, The Remains of the Day (Acad. Award nom.), In the Name of the Father (Academy Award nom.), My Father the Hero (unbilled), Junior, Carrington, Sense and Sensibility (also s.p.; BAFTA Award, 1995; Academy Award, 1996; Writers Guild Award, 1996; Golden Globe Award, 1996), The Winter Guest, Judas Kiss, Primary Colors.
TELEVISION: *Series*: Thompson (also writer). *Mini-Series*: Tutti Frutti, Fortunes of War (BAFTA Best Actress award). *Specials*: The Emma Thompson Special, The Winslow Boy, Look Back in Anger, Knuckle, The Blue Boy, Hospital. *Guest*: Cheers.

THOMPSON, FRED (DALTON)
Actor. b. Sheffield, AL, Aug. 19, 1942. Raised in TN. e. Memphis St. U., Vanderbilt U, studying law. Was Federal prosecutor before going to DC to serve as minority counsel on the Senate Select Committee on Presidential Campaign Activies, which involved investigation of the Watergate scandal. Hired to serve as consultant on film Marie, then was asked to play himself in the movie, resulting in acting career. 1994 elected to U.S. senate as Republican representative from Tennessee. *Author*: At That Point in Time (1975).
PICTURES: Marie (debut, 1985), No Way Out, Feds, Fat Man and Little Boy, The Hunt for Red October, Days of Thunder, Die Hard 2, Flight of the Intruder, Class Action, Necessary Roughness, Curly Sue, Cape Fear, Thunderheart, White Sands, Aces: Iron Eagle III, Born Yesterday, In the Line of Fire, Baby's Day Out.
TELEVISION: *Movies*: Bed of Lies, Keep the Change, Stay the Night, Day-O, Barbarians at the Gate.

THOMPSON, J. LEE
Director, Writer, Producer. b. Bristol, England, 1914. On Brit. stage as actor with Nottingham Rep. Co.; *Playwright*: Murder Without Crime, Cousin Simon, Curious Dr. Robson (collab.) Thousands of Summers, Human Touch. To films, 1934 as actor, then writer, before turning to directing.
PICTURES: *Writer*: The Middle Watch, For Them That Trespass. *Director*: Murder Without Crime (dir. debut, 1950; also story, s.p.), The Yellow Balloon (also s.p.), The Weak and the Wicked (also co-s.p.), For Better or Worse (also s.p.), As Long as They're Happy, An Alligator Named Daisy, Yield to the Night, The Good Companions (also co-prod.), Woman in the Dressing Gown (also co-prod.), Ice Cold in Alex (Desert Attack), No Trees in the Street (also co-exec. prod.), Northwest Frontier (Flame Over India), Tiger Bay, I Aim at the Stars, The Guns of Navarone, Cape Fear, Taras Bulba, Kings of the Sun, What a Way to Go!, John Goldfarb Please Come Home (also co-exec. prod.), Return From the Ashes (also prod.), Eye of the Devil, Mackenna's Gold, Before Winter Comes, The Chairman, Country Dance (Brotherly Love), Conquest of the Planet of the Apes, Battle for the Planet of the Apes, Huckleberry Finn, The Reincarnation of Peter Proud, St. Ives, The White Buffalo, The Greek Tycoon, The Passage, Caboblanco, Happy Birthday to Me, 10 to Midnight, The Evil That Men Do, The Ambassador, King Solomon's Mines, Murphy's Law, Firewalker, Death Wish IV: The Crackdown, Messenger of Death, Kinjite.
TELEVISION: A Great American Tragedy, The Blue Knight, Widow.

THOMPSON, JACK
Actor. r.n. John Payne. b. Sydney, Australia, Aug. 31, 1940. e. Queensland U. Joined drama workshop at school; first part was in TV soap opera as continuing character. 1988, appt. to bd. of Australian Film Finance Corp. Formed Pan Film Enterprises.
PICTURES: The Savage Wild, Outback (Wake in Fright), Libido, Petersen, A Sunday Too Far Away, Caddie, Scobie Malone, Mad Dog Morgan, The Chant of Jimmie Blacksmith, The Journalist, Breaker Morant, The Earthling, The Club, The Man From Snowy River, Bad Blood, Merry Christmas Mr. Lawrence, Flesh + Blood, Burke & Willis, Ground Zero, Waterfront, Turtle Beach, Wind, A Far Off Place, Deception, The Sum of Us, The Last Dance, Excess Baggage, Midnight in the Garden of Good and Evil.
TELEVISION: The Last Frontier, A Woman Called Golda, Waterfront, The Letter, Beryl Markham: A Shadow on the Sun, Paradise, Last Frontier, Wreck of the Stinson, A Woman of Independent Means, Thornbirds: The Missing Years.

THOMPSON, LEA
Actress. b. Rochester, MN, May 31, 1961. m. director Howard Deutch. Danced professionally since age of 14; won scholarship to Pennsylvania Ballet Co., American Ballet Theatre, San Francisco Ballet. Gave up that career for acting, appearing in several commercials for Burger King. *L.A. stage*: Bus Stop, The Illusion.
PICTURES: Jaws 3-D (debut, 1983), All the Right Moves, Red Dawn, The Wild Life, Back to the Future, Howard the Duck, Some Kind of Wonderful, Casual Sex?, Going Undercover, The Wizard of Loneliness, Back to the Future Part II, Back to the Future Part III, Article 99, Dennis the Menace, The Beverly Hillbillies, The Little Rascals, The Unknown Cyclist, Right to Remain Silent, A Will of Their Own.
TELEVISION: *Series*: Caroline in the City. *Movies*: Nightbreaker, Montana, Stolen Babies, The Substitute Wife, The Unspoken Truth. *Guest*: Tales From the Crypt.

THOMPSON, PATRICIA
Publisher, Editor. b. Portsmouth, UK, June 28, 1927. Co-found. Ontario Film Institute and Theatre, Ontario Science Center, 1969; co-ordinator, 1970-72. Co-ordinator, Stratford International Film Festival. Exec. dir., Canadian Film Awards (Genie Awards), 1977-78. Edit., Canadian Film Digest Yearbook, 1977-85. Short Film programmer for Cineplex cinemas. Columnist and contributor, Cinema Canada, 1983-89. Contributor, Kinema (Jour. for Film and Audiovisual Media), 1996-. Pub., edit., Film Canada Yearbook. Can. edit., Intl. M.P. Almanac and Intl. TV & Video Almanac, Quigley Pub. Awarded Queen's Silver Jubilee Medal, for svc's. to arts/film in Can., 1977.

THOMPSON, SADA
Actress. b. Des Moines, IA, Sept. 27, 1929. e. Carnegie Inst. of Technology, Pittsburgh. First N.Y. stage appearance in Under Milk Wood. B'way incl. The Effect of Gamma Rays (Obie, Drama Desk, Variety Poll), Twigs (Tony Award, 1972), Saturday, Sunday, Monday. Recent theater: Real Estate, Any Given Day.
PICTURES: Pursuit of Happiness, Desperate Characters.
TELEVISION: *Specials*: Sandburg's Lincoln, Our Town, The Skin of Our Teeth, Andre's Mother, Painting Churches. *Movies*: The Entertainer, Princess Daisy, My Two Loves, Fatal Confession: A Father Dowling Mystery, Home Fires Burning, Fear Stalk, Indictment: The McMartin Trial. *Series*: Family (Emmy Award, 1978). *Mini-Series*: Queen.

THORNTON, BILLY BOB
Actor, Director, Writer. b. Hot Springs, AR, Aug. 5, 1955.
PICTURES: *Actor*: Hubter's Blood, South of Reno, Babes Ahoy, One False Move, For the Boys, Trouble Bound, Chopper Chicks in Zombietown, Tombstone, Some Folks Call It a Sling Blade, Bound by Honor, On Deadly Ground, Floundering, Stars Fell on Henrietta, Dead Man, The Winner, Sling Blade (also dir., s.p.; Acad. Award, for best adapt. s.p.; 1996; Chicago Film Critics Award for best actor; Ind't Spirit Awards), U-Turn, A Thousand Miles, A Simple Plan, Primary Colors, Homegrown, The Apostle, A Gun A Car A Blonde, Armageddon, A Simple Plan, Texas Starkers. *Writer*: One False Move, Some Folks Call It a Sling Blade, A Family Thing.
TELEVISION: *Movies*: The 1,000 Chains (actor), Don't Look Back (actor., writer). *Series*: The Outsiders (actor), Hearts Afire (actor). *Guest*: Matlock, Ellen.

THULIN, INGRID
Actress, Director. b. Solleftea, Sweden, Jan. 27, 1929. m. Harry Schein. Made acting debut at 18 at the Municipal Theatre in Norrkoping. Studied at Stockholm's Royal Dramatic Theatre. Worked with Malmo and Stockholm repertory. Appeared on Swedish stage in nearly 50 plays including Gigi, Peer Gynt, Two for the Seesaw, Twelfth Night, Miss Julie. Has directed plays and films in Stockholm. N.Y. stage debut, 1967: Of Love Remembered. Author: Somebody I Knew (1993).
PICTURES: Where the Wind Blows, Love Will Conqueror, Jack of Hearts, Foreign Intrigue, Wild Strawberries, Brink of Life (Cannes Film Fest. Award), The Magician, The Judge, The Four Horsemen of the Apocalypse, Winter Light, The Silence, Games of Desire, Return From the Ashes, La Guerre est Finie, Night Games, Adelaide, Hour of the Wolf, I a Virgin, The Ritual, The Damned, Cries and Whispers, A Handful of Love, La Cage, Moses, Madame Kitty, The Cassandra Crossing, Broken Sky, At the Rehearsal, Control, House of Smiles, Rabbit Face.

THURMAN, UMA
Actress. b. Boston, MA, Apr. 29, 1970. Named after a Hindu deity. Raised in Woodstock, NY and Amherst, MA where father taught Asian studies. Father's work took family to India where they lived three years. e. Professional Children's School, NY. Worked as model while still in high school.
PICTURES: Kiss Daddy Good Night (debut, 1988), Johnny Be Good, Dangerous Liaisons, The Adventures of Baron Munchausen, Where the Heart Is, Henry and June, Final Analysis, Jennifer Eight, Mad Dog and Glory, Even Cowgirls Get the Blues, Pulp Fiction (Acad. Award nom.), A Month by the Lake, The Truth About Cats and Dogs, Beautiful Girls, Batman and Robin, Gattaca.
TELEVISION: *Movie*: Robin Hood.

THURSTON, DONALD A.
Executive. b. Gloucester, MA, April 2, 1930. Began career in broadcasting in 1949. Former Chmn., National Assoc. of Broadcasters. Past Pres., Massachusetts Broadcasters Assoc. Former Commissioner of Massachusetts Cable TV Commission. Currently Dir. and former Chmn. of Broadcast Capital Fund, Inc. a venture capital co. that assists minorities in the acquisition of broadcast properties. Pres. Berkshire Broadcasting Co. Inc. Director and Chmn., Broadcast Music, Inc. Received Honorary Doctor of Humanities from North Adams State College (1977), Doctor of Humane Letters, Emerson college (1995). Recipient of the Distinguished Service Award of the National Association of Broadcasters.

TICOTIN, RACHEL
Actress. b. Bronx, NY, Nov. 1, 1958. Began career as dancer with the Ballet Hispanico of New York before becoming a production assist. on such films as The Wanderers, Dressed to Kill and Raging Bull.
PICTURES: King of the Gypsies, Fort Apache: The Bronx, Critical Condition, Total Recall, One Good Cop, FX2, Falling Down, Natural Born Killers, Don Juan DeMarco, Steal Big Steal Little, Turbulence, Con-Air, The Day October Died.
TELEVISION: *Series*: For Love and Honor, Ohara, Crime and Punishment. *Movies*: Love Mary, Rockabye, When the Bough Breaks, Spies Lies and Naked Thighs, Prison Stories: Women on the Inside, Keep the Change, From the Files of Joseph Wambaugh: A Jury of One, Thicker Than Blood: The Larry McLinden Story, Deconstructing Sarah, The Wharf Rat, First Time Felon.

TIERNEY, LAWRENCE
Actor. b. Brooklyn, NY, Mar. 15, 1919. Brother of actor Scott Brady. e. Manhattan Coll. Track athlete (natl. championship Cross Country Team, N.Y. Athletic Club). Stage actor before screen debut 1943.

PICTURES: The Ghost Ship (debut, 1943), Government Girl, Gildersleeve on Broadway, The Falcon Out West, Youth Runs Wild, Back to Bataan, Dillinger, Mama Loves Papa, Those Endearing Young Charms, Badman's Territory, Step By Step, San Quentin, The Devil Thumbs a Ride, Born to Kill, Bodyguard, Kill or Be Killed, Shakedown, The Hoodlum, The Bushwhackers, Best of the Bad Men, The Greatest Show on Earth, The Steel Cage, Female Jungle, Singing in the Dark, A Child Is Waiting, Custer of the West, Such Good Friends, Abduction, Andy Warhol's Bad, The Kirlian Witness, Never Pick Up a Stranger (Bloodrage), Gloria, Arthur, Rosemary's Killer, Midnight, Prizzi's Honor, Stephen King's Silver Bullet, Murphy's Law, Tough Guys Don't Dance, The Offspring (From a Whisper to a Scream), The Horror Show, Wizards of the Demon Sword, Why Me?, City of Hope, The Runestone, Reservoir Dogs, A Kiss Goodnight, Junior, Fatal Passion, Ben Johnson: Third Cowboy on the Right, 2 Days in the Valley, American Hero, Southie, Armageddon.
TELEVISION: Movies: Terrible Joe Moran, Dillinger. Guest: Hill Street Blues, Star Trek: The Next Generation, Tales From the Dark Side, Hunter.

TIFFIN, PAMELA
Actress. r.n. Pamela Wonso. b. Oklahoma City, OK, Oct. 13, 1942. e. Hunter Coll., Columbia U., Loyola U, Rome Center. Studied acting with Stella Adler and Harold Clurman. Started modeling as a teenager.
THEATER: Dinner at Eight (Theatre World Award), Uncle Vanya.
PICTURES: Summer and Smoke (debut, 1961), One Two Three, State Fair, Come Fly with Me, For Those Who Think Young, The Lively Set, The Pleasure Seekers, Kiss the Other Sheik, The Hallelujah Trail, Harper, Paranoia, Viva Max!, The Godson, Giornata Nera per l'Ariete, Deaf Smith and Johnny Ears, Puntto e a Capo, Evil Fingers.

TIGHE, KEVIN
Actor. b. Los Angeles, CA, Aug. 13, 1944. e. Cal. State, B.A. in psychology; USC M.F.A. in performing arts. Served in U.S. Army, 1967-69. Received N.E.A. Director's Fellowship, Seattle Rep. Theatre, 1988-89.
PICTURES: The Graduate (debut, 1967), Matewan, Eight Men Out, K-9, Lost Angels, Road House, Another 48 HRS, Bright Angel, City of Hope, Newsies, School Ties, A Man in Uniform (Genie Award), Geronimo: An American Legend, What's Eating Gilbert Grape, Scorpion Spring, Jade, Race the Sun, The Wentonicawa Flash, Mumford.
TELEVISION: Series: Emergency, Murder One. Guest: Tales From the Crypt (Cutting Cards). Movies: Better Off Dead, Betrayal of Trust, The Avenging Angel, Winchell.

TILLY, JENNIFER
Actress. b. Harbour City, CA, 1958. Sister is actress Meg Tilly.
THEATER: One Shoe Off (Off-B'way debut, 1993; Theatre World Award).
PICTURES: No Small Affair, Moving Violations, Inside Out, He's My Girl, Johnny Be Good, Rented Lips, High Spirits, Far From Home, Let It Ride, The Fabulous Baker Boys, Made in America, The Getaway, Bullets Over Broadway (Acad. Award nom.), Man With a Gun, Embrace of the Vampire, House Arrest, The Pompatus of Love, Bound, Bird of Prey, Edie and Pen, American Strays, Liar Liar.
TELEVISION: Series: Shaping Up. Movie: Heads.

TILLY, MEG
Actress. b. Long Beach, CA, Feb. 14, 1960. Sister is actress Jennifer Tilly. Began acting and dancing in community theatrical prods. while in high school. To New York at 16; appeared on TV in Hill Street Blues. Author: Singing Songs (1994).
PICTURES: Fame (debut, 1980), Tex, Psycho II, One Dark Night, The Big Chill, Impulse, Agnes of God (Acad. Award nom.), Off Beat, Masquerade, The Girl in a Swing, Valmont, The Two Jakes, Leaving Normal, Body Snatchers, Sleep with Me.
TELEVISION: Series: Winnetka Road. Specials: The Trouble With Grandpa, Camilla (Nightmare Classics). Movies: In the Best Interest of the Child, Trick of the Eye. Guest: Fallen Angels (Dead-End for Delia).

TINKER, GRANT A.
Executive. b. Stamford, CT., Jan. 11, 1926. e. Dartmouth Coll., 1947. Joined NBC radio prog. dept. 1949. In 1954 with McCann-Erickson ad agency, TV dept. In 1958, Benton & Bowles Ad Agency, TV dept.; 1961-66 with NBC, v.p., programs, West Coast; v.p. in chg. of programming, NY, 1966-67; joined Universal Television as v.p., 1968-69; 20th-Fox, v.p., 1969-70. Became pres. MTM Enterprises, Inc. 1970. Named NBC bd. chmn. & CEO, 1981-86. Received ATAS Governor's Award in 1987. Formed indep. prod. co. G.T.G. Entertainment, 1988.

TINKER, MARK
Director, Producer.
TELEVISION: Movies: Private Eye, Capital News, N.Y.P.D. Mounted, Babe Ruth, Bonanza: Under Attack. Series: L.A. Law, NYPD Blue, Chicago Hope, ER, Brooklyn South (prod., Emmy Award, 1998).

TISCH, LAURENCE A.
Executive. b. Brooklyn, NY, March 5, 1923. e. NYU, 1941; U. of Pennsylvania Wharton Sch., 1942; Harvard Law Sch., 1946. Pres. Tisch Hotels, Inc., 1950-59; pres. Americana Hotel, Inc., Miami Beach, 1956-59; Chmn. of bd. and co-chief executive officer of Loews Corp since 1960. Also chmn. of bd. of CNA Financial Corp since 1947. President and chief executive officer and chmn. of board, CBS since 1986.

TISCH, PRESTON ROBERT
Executive. b. Brooklyn, NY, April 29, 1926. e. Bucknell U., Lewisberg, PA, 1943-44; U. of Michigan, B.A., 1948. Pres. Loew's Corporation. Postmaster General of the US. 1986-1988. March, 1988 returned to Loews Corp. as president and co-chief executive. Elected member of bd. CBS Inc. 1988, 1994, position changed to co-chmn. & co-CEO of Loews Corp.

TISCH, STEVE
Producer. b. Lakewood, NJ, 1949. e. Tufts U. Son of Preston Tisch. Worked during school breaks for John Avildsen and Fred Weintraub. Signed upon graduation as exec. asst. to Peter Guber, then prod. head at Columbia Pictures. Entered producer ranks with Outlaw Blues, 1977, collaborating with Jon Avnet with whom formed Tisch/Avnet Prods. Alliance with Phoenix Entertainment 1988.
PICTURES: Outlaw Blues, Almost Summer, Coast to Coast, Risky Business, Deal of the Century, Soul Man, Big Business, Hot to Trot, Heart of Dixie, Heart Condition, Bad Influence, Forrest Gump (Academy Award for Best Picture, 1994), Corrina Corrina, The Long Kiss Goodnight (exec. prod.), Dear God, Wild America (exec. prod.), American History X, The Postman, Nico the Unicorn.
TELEVISION: Homeward Bound, No Other Love, Prime Suspect, Something So Right, Calendar Girl Murders, The Burning Bed (exec. prod.), Call to Glory (series), Triple Cross, Silence of the Heart, In Love and War (sole prod.), Evil in Clear River, Dirty Dancing (series), Out on the Edge (exec. prod.), Judgment (exec. prod.), Lies of the Heart, The Vidiots (pilot), Victim of Love, Keep the Change, Afterburn (exec. prod.), Freshman Dorm (pilot & series), The People Next Door.

TOBACK, JAMES
Writer, Producer, Director. b. New York, NY, Nov. 23, 1944. e. Harvard U. Taught literature at City Coll. of New York; contributed articles and criticism to Harper's, Esquire, Commentary, etc. Wrote book Jim, on actor-athlete Jim Brown (1971). First screenplay, The Gambler, filmed in 1974.
PICTURES: Writer: The Gambler, Fingers (also dir.), Love and Money (also dir., prod.), Exposed (also dir., prod.), The Pick-Up Artist (also dir.), The Big Bang (also dir., actor), Alice (actor), Bugsy (also actor).

TOBOLOWSKY, STEPHEN
Actor. b. Dallas, TX, May 30, 1951. e. Southern Methodist Univ.
THEATER: Actor: Whose Life Is It Anyway?, Crimes of the Heart, Godspell, Three Sisters, The Glass Menagerie, Barabass, The Wake of Jamey Foster, The Wild Duck, No Scratch, The Miss Firecracker Contest, The Importance of Being Earnest, Purlie, Whispers in the Wind. Director: The Miss Firecracker Contest, The Lucky Spot, The Bridgehead (Dramalogue Award), The Secret Rapture (Dramalogue Award), Our Town, The Debutante Ball.
PICTURES: Swing Shift, True Stories (co-s.p.), Nobody's Fool, Spaceballs, Mississippi Burning, Checking Out, Two Idiots in Hollywood (dir. & s.p.), Great Balls of Fire!, In Country, Breaking In, Bird on a Wire, Funny About Love, Welcome Home Roxy Carmichael, The Grifters, Thelma & Louise, Memoirs of an Invisible Man, Basic Instinct, Roadside Prophets, Single White Female, Sneakers, Where the Day Takes You, Sneakers, Hero, Groundhog Day, The Pickle, Calendar Girl, Josh and S.A.M., My Father the Hero, Radioland Murders, Murder in the First, Dr. Jekyll and Ms. Hyde, Power 98, The Glimmer Man, The Curse of the Inferno, Boys Life III, Mr. Magoo, The Operator, Black Dog, One Man Hero.
TELEVISION: Movies: Last Flight Out, Marla Hanson Story, Perry Mason: The Case of the Maligned Mobster, Tagget, Deadlock, Deadly Medicine, When Love Kills: The Seduction of John Hearn, Night Visitors. Series: Against the Grain, Blue Skies, A Whole New Ballgame, Dweebs. Guest: Crazy Like a Fox, Designing Women, L.A. Law, Days and Nights of Molly Dodd, Seinfeld, Picket Fences, Chicago Hope, Hearts of the West, Baby Talk, Knots Landing, Falcon Crest.

TODD, BEVERLY
Actress, Director, Producer. b. Chicago, IL, July 11.
THEATER: NY: Carry Me Back to Morningside Heights, Black Visions. Producer: A Tribute to Ella Fitzgerald. Director: I Need a Man, Sneaky.
PICTURES: The Lost Man, They Call Me Mister Tibbs!, Brother John, Vice Squad, Homework, The Ladies Club, Happy Hour, Baby Boom, Moving, Clara's Heart, Lean on Me, The Surgeon.

TELEVISION: *Series*: Love of Life, Having Babies, The Redd Foxx Show. *Mini-Series*: Roots. *Movies*: Deadlock, The Ghost of Flight 401, Having Babies II, The Jericho Mile, Don't Look Back, A Touch of Scandal, A Different Affair. *Guest*: Magnum P.I., The Robert Guillaume Show, Falcon Crest, Quincy M.E., Hill Street Blues, Family, Benson, Lou Grant, A Different World, Good News, Sparks. *Special*: A Laugh a Tear: The Story of Black Humor in America (prod.), Don't Hit Me Mom (Afterschool Special), The Class of '61.

TODD, RICHARD
O.B.E. Actor. b. Dublin, Ireland, June 11, 1919. e. Shrewsbury. In repertory, 1937; founder-member, Dundee Repertory Theatre, 1939; distinguished war service, 1939-46; Dundee Repertory, 1946-48; screen debut, 1948; For Them That Trespass, 1948. 1970 Founder-Director Triumph Theatre Productions. Published autobiography, 1986, Volume II, 1989. Awarded O.B.E., 1993.
THEATER: An Ideal Husband, Dear Octopus. Co-founder, Triumph Theatre Prods., Ltd. plays since 1970: Roar Like a Dove, Grass Is Greener, The Marquise (U.S.) Sleuth (England and Australia). Murder by Numbers, The Hollow Crown (with RSC), Equus. On Approval, Quadrille, This Happy Breed, The Business of Murder (London), Intent to Kill, The Woman in Black, Beyond Reasonable Doubt, Sweet Revenge, Brideshead Revisited.
PICTURES: For Them That Trespass (debut, 1948), The Hasty Heart, Interrupted Journey, Stage Fright, Portrait of Clare, Lightning Strikes Twice (U.S.), Flesh and Blood, Story of Robin Hood, 24 Hours of a Woman's Life, The Venetian Bird, Sword and the Rose, Rob Roy, Les Secrets d'Alcove (Fr.), A Man Called Peter (U.S.), The Virgin Queen (U.S.), Dam Busters, D-Day the Sixth of June (U.S.), Marie Antoinette (Fr.), Yangtse Incident, Saint Joan, Chase a Crooked Shadow, The Naked Earth, Intent to Kill, Danger Within, Never Let Go, The Long the Short and the Tall, Don't Bother to Knock (also exec. prod.), The Hellions, The Longest Day, Crime Does Not Pay (Fr.), The Boys, The Very Edge, Death Drums Along the River, Battle of the Villa Fiorita, Operation Crossbow, Coast of Skeletons, The Love-Ins, Subterfuge, Dorian Gray, Asylum, The Sky is Falling, Number One of the Secret Service, The Big Sleep, House of the Long Shadows.
TELEVISION: Wuthering Heights, Carrington V.C., The Brighton Mesmerists, Beautiful Lies, The Boy Dominic, Murder She Wrote, Virtual Murder.

TOKOFSKY, JERRY H.
Executive. b. New York, NY, Apr. 14, 1936. e. NYU, B.S., journalism, 1956; New York Law, 1959. Entered William Morris Agency while at NYU 1953, working in night club dept. to live TV. Moved to Beverly Hills office, 1959. Entered m.p. div. WMA, 1960. Joined Columbia Pictures, as Prod. V.P., 1963-70. Joined Paramount Pictures 1970 as prod. v.p. To MGM as prod. v.p., 1971. Producer & Exec. V.P., Zupnik Enterprises, Inc. until 1992.
PICTURES: *Producer*: Where's Poppa, Born to Win, Paternity, Dreamscape, Fear City, Wildfire, Glengarry Glen Ross.

TOLAN, PETER
Producer, Writer.
PICTURES: Alice (actor), My Fellow Americans, Analyze This.
TELEVISION: *Series*: Murphy Brown (Emmy Award, 1992), The Larry Sanders Show (Emmy Award, 1998), Style and Substance.

TOLKAN, JAMES
Actor. b. Calumet, MI, June 20, 1931. e. Univ. of Iowa. Trained with Stella Adler.
THEATER: *NY*: Abe Lincoln in Illinois, Once in a Lifetime, Three Sisters, The Cannibals, Mary Stuart, The Silent Partner, 42 Seconds from Broadway, Full Circle, Macbeth, Dream of a Blacklisted Actor, Jungle of Cities, Wings.
PICTURES: Stiletto, They Might Be Giants, The Friends of Eddie Coyle, Serpico, Love and Death, The Amityville Horror, Wolfen, Prince of the City, Author! Author!, Hanky Panky, Nightmares (voice), WarGames, Iceman, The River, Turk 182!, Flanagan, Back to the Future, Off Beat, Top Gun, Armed and Dangerous, Masters of the Universe, Made in Heaven, Viper, Split Decisions, True Blood, Second Sight, Back to the Future Part II, Family Business, Opportunity Knocks, Back to the Future Part III, Dick Tracy, Hangfire, Problem Child 2, Driving Me Crazy, Boiling Point, Love in Ambush.
TELEVISION: *Series*: Mary, The Hat Squad, Cobra. *Movies*: Little Spies, Leap of Faith, Weekend War, The Case of the Hillside Stranglers, Sketch Artist, Beyond Betrayal, Sketch Artist II: Hands That See. *Guest*: Remington Steele, Miami Vice, The Equalizer, Tales From the Crypt.

TOLKIN, MICHAEL
Writer, Director, Producer. b. New York, NY, Oct. 17, 1950. e. Middlebury Col, VT. Started as writer for LA Times, Village Voice, before becoming story editor on tv series Delta House. Novels: The Player (1988), Among the Dead (1992).
PICTURES: *Writer*: Gleaming the Cube, The Rapture (also dir.), The Player (also co-prod.; actor; WGA Award, Acad. Award nom.), Deep Cover (also story), The New Age (also dir.), Deep Impact, 20 Billion.
TELEVISION: *Movie*: The Burning Season (co-writer).

TOMEI, MARISA
Actress. b. Brooklyn, NY, Dec. 4, 1964. e. Boston U.
THEATER: Beirut (L.A.). *NY*: Daughters (Theatre World Award), The Comedy of Errors, What the Butler Saw, Slavs!
PICTURES: The Flamingo Kid (debut, 1984), Playing for Keeps, Oscar, Zandalee, My Cousin Vinny (Academy Award, best supporting actress, 1992), Chaplin, Untamed Heart, Equinox, The Paper, Only You, The Perez Family, Four Rooms, A Brother's Kiss, Unhook the Stars, Welcome to Sarajevo, The Women, The Slums of Beverly Hills, Only Love.
TELEVISION: *Series*: As the World Turns, A Different World. *Guest*: Seinfeld. *Movie*: Parker Kane, Since You've Been Gone.

TOMLIN, LILY
Actress. r.n. Mary Jean Tomlin. b. Detroit, MI, Sept. 1, 1939. e. Wayne State U. (studied pre-med). Studied mime with Paul Curtis. Started inventing characters for comedy sketches in college, used them in cafe and night club dates in Detroit. 1965 went to NY performing skits on coffee-house circuit, landed job on The Garry Moore Show. Moved to L.A. where she appeared on The Music Scene. 1969, first appeared on Laugh-In TV series, gaining national attention with such characters as telephone operator Ernestine and child Edith Ann.
THEATER: Appearing Nitely (special Tony Award, 1977), The Search for Signs of Intelligent Life in the Universe (1985, on B'way and on tour; Tony Award).
PICTURES: Nashville (debut, 1975; NY Film Critics Award; Acad Award nom.), The Late Show, Moment by Moment, Nine to Five, The Incredible Shrinking Woman, All of Me, Big Business, The Search for Signs of Intelligent Life in the Universe, Shadows and Fog, The Player, Short Cuts, The Beverly Hillbillies, Blue in the Face, Getting Away With Murder, The Celluloid Closet (narrator), Flirting With Disaster, Krippendorf's Tribe.
TELEVISION: *Series*: The Music Scene (host, 1969), Rowan and Martin's Laugh-In (1969-73), Magic School Bus (voice for animated series; Emmy Award), Murphy Brown. *Specials*: Lily (Emmy Award as writer, 1974), Lily Tomlin (Emmy Award as writer, 1976), The Paul Simon Special (Emmy Award as writer, 1978), Lily: Sold Out! (also exec. prod.; Emmy Award as exec. prod., 1981), The Muppets Go to the Movies, Lily for President?, Live—and in Person, Funny You Don't Look 200, Free to Be... a Family, Edith Ann: A Few Pieces of the Puzzle (voice, exec. prod.), Edith Ann: Homeless Go Home (voice, exec. prod.), Edith Ann's Christmas: Just Say Noel (voice, exec. prod; Peabody Award). *Movie*: And the Band Played On. *Guest*: Homicide.
RECORDS: This Is a Recording (Grammy Award, 1971), Modern Scream, And That's the Truth, Lily Tomlin On Stage.

TOPOL
Actor. b. Tel-Aviv, Israel, Sept. 9, 1935. r.n. Chaim Topol.
THEATER: Fiddler on the Roof (London, 1967, 1994-95 also U.K. tour; NY 1989: Tony nom.; Canada & Japan tour) Chicester Fest. Theatre: Caucasian Chalk Circle, Romanov and Juliet, Othello, View From the Bridge.
PICTURES: Sallah, Cast a Giant Shadow, Before Winter Comes, A Talent for Loving, Fiddler on the Roof (Acad. Award nom.), Follow Me (The Public Eye), Galileo, Flash Gordon, For Your Eyes Only, Ervinka, A Dime Novel.
TELEVISION: *Movies*: House on Garibaldi Street, Queenie. *Mini-Series*: The Winds of War, War and Remembrance. *Series* (BBC): It's Topol, Topol's Israel.

TORME, MEL
Singer, Actor. b. Chicago, IL, Sept. 13, 1925. Singing debut at age of 4; won radio audition 1933; on radio; composed song Lament to Love; with Chico Marx's orchestra as drummer, arranger & vocalist 1942; served in U.S. Army, WWII; org. vocal group Meltones; many recordings; night club and concert appearances. *Author*: The Other Side of the Rainbow: With Judy Garland on the Dawn Patrol (1970), It Wasn't All Velvet (1988), My Singing Teachers: Reflections on Singing Popular Music (1994).
PICTURES: Higher and Higher (debut, 1943), Pardon My Rhythm, Let's Go Steady, Janie Gets Married, Junior Miss, Night and Day, Good News, Words and Music, Duchess of Idaho, The Big Operator, Girls Town, Walk Like a Dragon, The Patsy, A Man Called Adam, The Land of No Return (Snowman), Daffy Duck's Quackbusters (voice), The Naked Gun 2 1/2: The Smell of Fear.
TELEVISION: Series: TV's Top Tunes, The Judy Garland Show (musical advisor, frequent guest), It Was a Very Good Year (host). *Movie*: Pray TV. *Guest*: Night Court.

TORN, RIP
Actor. r.n. Elmore Torn, Jr. b. Temple, TX, Feb. 6, 1931. e. Texas A & M U., U. of TX. Served in army. Signed as understudy for lead in Cat on a Hot Tin Roof on Broadway.
THEATER: Orpheus Descending, Sweet Bird of Youth (Theatre World Award), Daughter of Silence, Macbeth, Desire Under the Elms, Strange Interlude, Blues For Mr. Charlie, The Kitchen, The Deer Park (Obie Award), The Beard, The Cuban Thing, Dream of a Blacklisted Actor, The Dance of Death, Anna Christie.

PICTURES: Baby Doll (debut, 1956), A Face in the Crowd, Time Limit, Pork Chop Hill, King of Kings, Hero's Island, Sweet Bird of Youth, Critic's Choice, The Cincinnati Kid, One Spy Too Many, You're a Big Boy Now, Beach Red, Sol Madrid, Beyond the Law, Coming Apart, Tropic of Cancer, Maidstone, Slaughter, Payday, Crazy Joe, Birch Interval, The Man Who Fell to Earth, Nasty Habits, The Private Files of J. Edgar Hoover, Coma, The Seduction of Joe Tynan, Heartland, One Trick Pony, First Family, A Stranger is Watching, The Beastmaster, Jinxed, Airplane II: The Sequel, Cross Creek (Acad. Award nom.), Misunderstood, Songwriter, Flashpoint, City Heat, Summer Rental, Beer, Extreme Prejudice, Nadine, The Telephone (also dir.), Cold Feet, Hit List, Blind Curve, The Hunt for Red October, Defending Your Life, Silence Like Glass, Beautiful Dreamers, Hard Promises, Robocop 3, Dolly Dearest, Where the Rivers Flow North, Canadian Bacon, How to Make an American Quilt, Down Periscope.
TELEVISION: Series: The Larry Sanders Show (Emmy Awatd, 1996). Movies: The President's Plane Is Missing, Attack on Terror: The FBI vs. the Ku Klux Klan, Betrayal, Steel Cowboy, A Shining Season, Sophia Loren—Her Own Story, Rape and Marriage—The Rideout Case, Laguna Heat, When She Says No, The Execution, The Atlanta Child Murders, Manhunt for Claude Dallas, J. Edgar Hoover, The King of Love, April Morning, Sweet Bird of Youth, Pair of Aces, By Dawn's Early Light, Another Pair of Aces, My Son Johnny, Death Hits the Jackpot, T Bone N Weasel, A Mother's Right: The Elizabeth Morgan Story, Dead Ahead: The Exxon Valdez Disaster, She Stood Alone: The Tailhook Scandal, Letter to My Killer. Mini-Series: Blind Ambition, The Blue and the Gray, Heaven & Hell: North and South Book III, Heart of a Child.

TORNATORE, GIUSEPPE
Director. b. Bagheria, Sicily, Italy, 1956. Made directorial debut at age 16 with short film Il Carretto. 1978- 85, served as pres. of the CLTC filmmaking cooperative.
PICTURES: The Professor (debut, 1986), Cinema Paradiso, Everybody's Fine, The Blue Dog (segment), Especially on Sunday (segment), A Pure Formality.
TELEVISION: Portrait of a Thief, Metting With Francesco Rosi, Sicilian Writers and Films, Il Diario di Guttuso, Ethnic Minorities in Sicily (Salerno Film Fest. Prize), A Hundred Days in Palermo (also writer, 2nd unit dir.).

TOTTER, AUDREY
Actress. b. Joliet, IL, Dec. 20, 1918. In many stage plays. On radio 1939-44.
THEATER: Copperhead, Stage Door, Late Christopher Bean, My Sister Eileen.
PICTURES: Main Street After Dark (debut, 1944), Her Highness and the Bellboy, Dangerous Partners, The Sailor Takes a Wife, Adventure, The Hidden Eye, The Secret Heart, The Postman Always Rings Twice, Cockeyed Miracle, Lady in the Lake, Beginning or the End, Unsuspected, High Wall, The Saxon Charm, Alias Nick Beal, Any Number Can Play, Tension, The Set-Up, Under the Gun, The Blue Veil, Sellout, F.B.I. Girl, Assignment-Paris, My Pal Gus, Woman They Almost Lynched, Cruisin' Down the River, Man in the Dark, Mission Over Korea, Champ for a Day, Massacre Canyon, Women's Prison, A Bullet for Joey, Vanishing American, Ghost Diver, Jet Attack, Man or Gun, The Carpetbaggers, Harlow, Chubasco, The Apple Dumpling Gang Rides Again.
TELEVISION: Series: Cimarron City, Our Man Higgins, Medical Center (1972-76). Movies: The Outsider, U.M.C., The Nativity, The Great Cash Giveaway, City Killer. Guest: Murder, She Wrote.

TOWERS, CONSTANCE
Actress. b. Whitefish, MT, May 20, 1934. m. John Gavin, actor and former U.S. Ambassador to Mexico. e. Juilliard Sch. of Music. Stage work on Broadway and tour. In Concert with John Raitt, 1998.
THEATER: B'way: Ari, Anya, Engagement Baby, The King and I (1977-79 opp. Yul Brynner), Showboat. Regional: Steel Magnolias, Follies, Sound of Music, I Do I Do, Mame, 110 In the Shade, Carousel, Oklahoma, Dumas & Son, Guys & Dolls, Oh Coward.
PICTURES: Bring Your Smile Along, Horse Soldiers, Sergeant Rutledge, Fate Is the Hunter, Shock Corridor, Naked Kiss, Sylvester, Fast Forward, Nutty Nut, The Next Karate Kid, The Relic, A Perfect Murder.
TELEVISION: Series: Love Is a Many Splendored Thing, VTV, Capitol, 2000 Malibu Road, General Hospital. Mini-Series: On Wings of Eagles, Sands of Time. Guest: Home Show, The Loner, Murder, She Wrote, Hour Mag, MacGyver, Designing Women, Midnight Caller, Matlock, Baywatch, Prince of Bel Air, Thunder in Paradise, L.A. Law, Civil Wars, Frasier, Robin's Nest, Caroline In the City, The Young & the Restless.

TOWERS, HARRY ALAN
Executive, Producer. b. London, England, 1920.
PICTURES: Sanders of the River (also s.p.), Code Seven Victim Five (also s.p.), City of Fear, Mozambique, Coast of Skeletons, Sandy the Seal, 24 Hours to Kill, The Face of Fu Manchu, Ten Little Indians, Marrakesh, Circus of Fear, The Brides of Fu Manchu, Sumuru, Five Golden Dragons, The Vengeance of Fu Manchu, Jules Verne's Rocket to the Moon, House of a Thousand Dolls, The Face of Eve, Blood of Fu Manchu, 99 Women, Girl From Rio, Marquis de Sade's Justine, Castle of Fu Manchu, Venus in Furs, Philosophy in the Boudoir, Eugenie, Dorian Gray, Count Dracula, The Bloody Judge, Black Beauty, Night Hair Child, The Call of the Wild, Treasure Island, White Fang, Death in Persepolis, Ten Little Indians, End of Innocence, Black Cobra, Black Velvet—White Silk, Night of The High Tide, King Solomon's Treasure, Shape of Things to Come, Klondike Fever, Fanny Hill, Frank and I, Black Venus, Christmas, Black Arrow, Pompeii, Love Circles, Lightning—The White Stallion, Gor, Outlaw of Gor, Dragonard, Skeleton Coast, Master of Dragonard Hill, Nam, Fire With Fire, Jekyll and Hyde, River of Death, Cobra Strike, The Howling IV: The Original Nightmare, Skeleton Coast, Edge of Sanity, Ten Little Indians, Platoon Leader, Captive Rage, American Ninja III: Blood Hunt, The Fall of the House of Usher, Edgar Allan Poe's Buried Alive, Phantom of the Opera, Oddball Hall, Terror of Manhattan, The Lost World, Return to the Lost World, Black Museum, Golden Years of Sherlock Holmes, The Mangler, Midnight in St. Petersburg, Bullet to Beijing (The Return of Harry Palmer), Cry the Beloved Country, China Bill, She, Stanley & Livingstone, The Zodiac Conspiracy.

TOWNE, ROBERT
Writer, Director, Producer. b. Los Angeles, CA, 1936. Raised in San Pedro. Was member of Warren Beatty's production staff on Bonnie and Clyde and contributed to that screenplay. Also uncredited, wrote Pacino-Brando garden scene in The Godfather; script doctor on Marathon Man, The Missouri Breaks and others.
PICTURES: Writer: The Last Woman on Earth (as Edward Wain), The Tomb of Ligeia, Villa Rides, The Last Detail, Chinatown (Academy Award, 1974), Shampoo (co-s.p.), The Yazuka (co-s.p.), Personal Best (also dir., prod.), Greystoke: The Legend of Tarzan (s.p., uncredited), Tequila Sunrise (also dir.), Days of Thunder, The Two Jakes, The Firm (co-s.p.), Love Affair (co-s.p.), Mission: Impossible (co-s.p.), Without Limits.

TOWNSEND, ROBERT
Actor, Producer, Director, Writer. b. Chicago, IL, Feb. 6, 1957. e.Illinois State U., Hunter Coll. Veteran of Experimental Black Actors Guild and Second City. TV commercials; stand-up comedy at NY Improvisation; taped Evening at the Improv.
PICTURES: Actor: Cooley High (debut, 1974), Willie and Phil, Streets of Fire, A Soldier's Story, American Flyers, Odd Jobs, Ratboy, Hollywood Shuffle (also prod., dir., co-s.p.), Eddie Murphy Raw (dir. only), The Mighty Quinn, That's Adequate, The Five Heartbeats (also dir., exec. prod., co-s.p.), The Meteor Man (also dir., s.p., co-prod.), B.A.P.S. (dir. only).
TELEVISION: Series: Another Page (PBS series), Townsend Television, The Parent 'Hood (also co-creator, exec. prod.). Specials: Robert Townsend and His Partners in Crime, Take No Prisoners: Robert Townsend and His Partners in Crime II (HBO). Movies: Women at West Point, Senior Trip!, In Love With an Older Woman.

TRAMBUKIS, WILLIAM J.
Executive. b. Providence, R.I., July 26, 1926. e. Mt. Pleasant Bus. Col. Began career as usher with Loew's in Providence, RI, 1941. Served 1943-46 with Navy Seabees. Recipient of Quigley Awards. Managed/supervised Loew's Theatres in several New England cities, Harrisburg, PA, Syracuse, Rochester, Buffalo, NY, Washington, DC, Richmond, Norfolk, VA, Toronto, Canada, Atlanta, GA. Appt. Loew's NorthEastern Division mgr. 1964, Loew's gen. mgr. 1975: v.p. in 1976; sr. v.p., 1985. Retired, 1987.

TRAVANTI, DANIEL J.
Actor. b. Kenosha, WI, March 7, 1940. e. U. of Wisconsin (B.A.), Loyola Marymount Univ. (M.A.), Yale Sch. of Drama. Woodrow Wilson fellow, 1961. Formerly acted as Dan Travanty. On stage in Twigs, Othello, I Never Sang for My Father, Only Kidding, The Taming of the Shrew, Les Liaisons Dangereuses, A Touch of the Poet, Antony & Cleopatra, A Touch of the Poet.
PICTURES: St. Ives, Midnight Crossing, Millenium, Megaville, Weep No More My Lady, Just Cause, Siao Yu, Who Killed Teddy Bear.
TELEVISION: Series: General Hospital, Hill Street Blues (Emmy Awards, 1981, 1982; Golden Globe Award, 1981), Missing Persons. Movies: The Love War, Adam, Aurora, Murrow, Adam: His Song Continues, I Never Sang for My Father, Fellow Traveler, Howard Beach: Making the Case for Murder, Tagget, Eyes of a Witness, The Christmas Stallion, In the Shadows Someone's Watching, My Name is Kate, Wasp Woman, A Case of Libel, To Sir With Love II.

TRAVIS, NANCY

Actress. b. New York, NY, Sept. 21, 1961. Raised in Baltimore, MD, and Farmingham, MA. e. NYU. Attended Circle-in-the-Square Theatre school. Acted with NY Amer. Jewish Theatre before landing role in touring prod. of Brighton Beach Memoirs.
THEATER: NY: It's Hard to Be a Jew, The Signal Season of Dummy Hoy, I'm Not Rappaport (B'way). Tour: Brighton Beach Memoirs. *La Jolla Playhouse*: My Children My Africa, Three Sisters.
PICTURES: Three Men and a Baby (debut, 1987), Married to the Mob, Eight Men Out, Internal Affairs, Loose Cannons, Air America, Three Men and a Little Lady, Passed Away, Chaplin, The Vanishing, So I Married an Axe Murderer, Greedy, Destiny Turns on the Radio, Fluke, Bogus.
TELEVISION: *Series*: Almost Perfect. *Movies*: Malice in Wonderland, Harem, I'll Be Home for Christmas, Body Language. *Special*: High School Narc (ABC Afterschool Special).

TRAVOLTA, JOHN

Actor. b. Englewood, NJ, Feb. 18, 1954. m. actress Kelly Preston. First stage role in Who Will Save the Plowboy? Did off-B'way prod. of Rain; then on Broadway in Grease (also on tour for 10 months), Over Here (with the Andrew Sisters). Author of Staying Fit, 1984.
PICTURES: The Devil's Rain (debut, 1975), Carrie, Saturday Night Fever (Acad. Award nom.), Grease, Moment by Moment, Urban Cowboy, Blow Out, Staying Alive, Two of a Kind, Perfect, The Experts, Look Who's Talking, Look Who's Talking Too, Shout, Eyes of an Angel, Look Who's Talking Now, Pulp Fiction (Acad. Award nom.), White Man's Burden, Get Shorty (Golden Globe winner), Broken Arrow, Phenomenon, Michael, Face/Off, She's So Lovely (also exec. prod.).
TELEVISION: *Series*: Welcome Back Kotter. *Movies*: The Boy in the Plastic Bubble, Chains of Gold, Boris & Natasha (cameo). *Special*: The Dumb Waiter. *Guest*: Emergency, Owen Marshall--Counselor at Law, The Rookies, Medical Center.

TREBOT, JEAN-PIERRE

Executive. Exec. dir., The Friars Club.

TREMAYNE, LES

Actor. b. London, England, Apr. 16, 1913. e. Northwestern U., Chicago Art Inst., Columbia U., UCLA. First professional appearance in British mp., 1916, with mother; stock, little theatres, vaudeville, 1925-40; entered radio field, 1930. Blue ribbon award for best perf. of the month for A Man Called Peter; dir. Hollywood Rep. Theatre, 1957; pres. Hollywood Actors' Council, 1951-58; chmn. Actors Div. workshop com. Acad. TV Arts & Sciences; Mem.: The Workshop Comm. of the Hollywood M.P. & TV Museum Comm. One of 17 founding members, Pacific Pioneer Broadcasters; Life member, Actor's Fund; charter/founding mem. AFTRA, Chicago local. (delegate to most conventions since 1938). mem. Local, L.A. and Natl. AFTRA bds.
THEATER: Woman in My House, Errand of Mercy, You Are There, One Man's Family, Heartbeat Theatre, The First Nighter (lead 7 yrs.); on Broadway in Heads or Tails, Detective Story.
PICTURES: The Racket, Blue Veil, Francis Goes to West Point, It Grows on Trees, I Love Melvin, Under the Red Sea, Dream Wife, War of the Worlds, Susan Slept Here, Lieutenant Wore Skirts, Unguarded Moment, Everything But the Truth, Monolith Monsters, Perfect Furlough, North by Northwest, Say One for Me, The Gallant Hours, The Angry Red Planet, The Story of Ruth, The Fortune Cookie, Daffy Duck's Movie: Fantastic Island (voice), Starchaser (voice), Rainbow Brite and the Star Stealer.
TELEVISION: Lux Video Theatre, 20th Century-Fox Hour, Navy Log, One Man's Family, Meet Mille, The Millionaire, The Whistler, Truth or Consequences, NBC Matinee, The Girl, O'Henry series, Rin Tin Tin, Bachelor Father, The Texan, Adventures of Ellery Queen, Court of Last Resort, Rifleman, State Trooper, Rescue 8, June Allyson-Dupont Show, Wagon Train, M Squad, Hitchcock Presents, Mr. Ed., Perry Mason.

TREVOR, CLAIRE

Actress. b. New York, NY, Mar. 8, 1910. e. American Acad. of Dramatic Arts; Columbia U. On Broadway in Party's Over, Whistling in the Dark, Big Two. On radio in Big Town for 4 yrs.
PICTURES: Life in the Raw (debut, 1933), The Last Trail, Mad Game, Jimmy and Sally, Hold That Girl, Baby Take a Bow, Elinore Norton, Wild Gold, Dante's Inferno, Spring Tonic, Navy Wife, Black Sleep, Human Cargo, My Marriage, The Song and Dance Man, To Mary—With Love, 15 Maiden Lane, Career Woman, Star for a Night, One Mile From Heaven, Time Out for Romance, Second Honeymoon, Big Town Girl, Dead End (Acad. Award nom.), King of Gamblers, The Amazing Dr. Clitterhouse, Walking Down Broadway, Valley of the Giants, Two of a Kind, I Stole a Million, Stagecoach, Allegheny Uprising, Dark Command, Texas, Honky Tonk, Street of Chance, The Adventures of Martin Eden, Crossroads, Woman of the Town, The Desperadoes, Good Luck Mr. Yates, Murder My Sweet, Johnny Angel, Crack-Up, The Bachelor's Daughters, Born to Kill, Raw Deal, The Babe Ruth Story, The Velvet Touch, Key Largo (Academy Award, best supporting actress, 1948), The Lucky Stiff, Borderline, Best of the Bad Men, Hard Fast and Beautiful, Hoodlum Empire, My Man and I, Stop You're Killing Me, The Stranger Wore a Gun, The High and the Mighty (Acad. Award nom.), Man Without a Star, Lucy Gallant, The Mountain, Marjorie Morningstar, Two Weeks in Another Town, The Stripper, How to Murder Your Wife, The Capetown Affair, Kiss Me Goodbye.

TELEVISION: Specials/Movies

TELEVISION: *Specials/Movies*: If You Knew Elizabeth, Dodsworth (Emmy Award, 1957), No Sad Songs for Me, Ladies in Retirement, Breaking Home Ties. *Guest*: Alfred Hitchcock Presents, The Untouchables, Love Boat, Murder She Wrote.

TREXLER, CHARLES B.

Exhibitor. b. Wadesboro, NC, Feb. 8, 1916. 1937-48 was practicing CPA except for 2 yrs. in U.S. Army in WWII. Joined Stewart & Everett Theatres in 1948 as controller. 1953 named gen. mgr.; 1954, exec. v.p., treas.; 1962 named pres.; 1983, named bd. chmn.; former bd. chmn., NATO of North and South Carolina; v.p. & bd. mem., National NATO.

TRIKONIS, GUS

Director. b. New York, NY. Started career in chorus of West Side Story on B'way. Turned to directing, making low-budget weekenders (films shot in 12 days only on weekends).
PICTURES: *Actor*: West Side Story, Pajama Party, The Unsinkable Molly Brown, The Sand Pebbles, The Hell Cats, St. Valentine's Day Massacre, *Director*: Five the Hard Way, The Swinging Mermaids, Supercock (also actor), The Student Body, Nashville Girl, Moonshine County Express, The Evil, Touched by Love, Take This Job and Shove It.
TELEVISION: *Movies*: The Darker Side of Terror, She's Dressed To Kill, Flamingo Road (pilot), Elvis and the Beauty Queen, Twirl, Miss All-American Beauty, Dempsey, First Affair, Dempsey, Dance of the Dwarfs, Midas Valley, Malice in Wonderland, Love on the Run, Open Admissions, Unknown Subject, The Great Pretender, Insel der Furcht. *Mini-Series*: The Last Convertible (co-dir.). *Episode*: Twilight Zone (1985). *Series*: Burke's Law, Hercules: The Legendary Journeys, Baywatch Nights, The Sentinel.

TRINTIGNANT, JEAN-LOUIS

Actor. b. Piolenc, France, Dec. 11, 1930. m. Nadine Marquand, director. Theatre debut: 1951, To Each According to His Hunger. Then Mary Stuart, Macbeth (at the Comedie de Saint-Etienne). 1955 screen debut.
PICTURES: Si Tous Les Gars du Monde, La Loi des Rues, And God Created Woman, Club de Femmes, Les Liaisons Dangereuses, L'Estate Violente, Austerlitz, La Millieme Fenetre, Pleins Feux sur L'Assasin, Coeur Battant, L'Atlantide, The Game of Truth, Horace 62, Les Sept Peches Capitaux (7 Capital Sins), Le Combat dans L'Ile, The Easy Life, Il Successo, Nutty Naughty Chateau, Les Pas Perdus, La Bonne Occase, Mata-Hari, Meurtre a L'Italienne, La Longue Marche, Un Jour a Paris, Is Paris Burning?, The Sleeping Car Murders, A Man and a Woman, Enigma, Safari Diamants, Trans-Europ-Express, Mon Amour, Mon Amour, Un Homme a Abattre, La Morte Ha Fatto L'Uovo, Les Biches, Grand Silence, Z, Ma Nuit Chez Maud (My Night at Maud's), The Conformist, The Crook, Without Apparent Motive, The Outside Man, The French Conspiracy, Simon the Swiss, Agression, Les Violons du Bal, The Sunday Woman, Under Fire, La Nuit de Varennes, Long Live Life!, Next Summer, Departure, Return, The Man With the Silver Eyes, Femme Je Personne, Confidentially Yours, A Man and a Woman: 20 Years Later, La Vallee Fantome; Rendezvous, Bunker Palace Hotel, Three Colors: Red, The City of Lost Children, Fiesta, Un homme est tombe dans la rue, L'Insoumise, Les Bidochon, C'est jamais loin, Self-Made Hero, Tykho Moon, Those Who Love Me Can Take the Train.

TRIPP, STEVEN L.

Executive. b. Worthington, MN, Sept. 29, 1958. e. St. Cloud State U. Managed local hometown theatres from 1978-82, then promoted to operation mgr., Tentelino Enterprises Circuit. Became general mgr. after Tentelino was purchased by Lakes & Rivers Cinemas in 1989. 1994-present, general mgr. and film buyer. Formed Midwest Theatres Corp. dba Cinemagic Theatres in 1996. Currently serving as Pres. & COO.

TRIPPLEHORN, JEANNE

Actress. b. Tulsa, OK, 1964. e. Julliard Sch. of Drama. On stage at NY's Public Theatre in The Big Funk, 'Tis Pity She's a Whore.
PICTURES: Basic Instinct (debut, 1992), The Night We Never Met, The Firm, Waterworld.
TELEVISION: *Movie*: The Perfect Tribute.

TRUMBULL, DOUGLAS

Director, Cinematographer. b. Los Angeles, CA, Apr. 8, 1942. Inventor Showscan Film process. Produced and directed Universal Studios attraction Back to the Future: The Ride; Luxor Las Vegas attractions. Director: Showscan short films New Magic, Let's Go, Big Ball, Leonardo's Dream, Night of the Dreams, Chevy Collector. Former Vice Chmn., The Imax Corp. Currently Pres. & CEO, Entertainment Design Workshop.
PICTURES: *Cinematographer*: 2001: A Space Odyssey, Silent Running (also dir.), The Andromeda Strain, Close Encounters of the Third Kind, Star Trek: The Motion Picture, Blade Runner, Brainstorm (also dir., prod.).

TUBB, BARRY

Actor. b. Snyder, TX, 1963. Former rodeo star. Studied acting at Amer. Conservatory Theatre in SF.
THEATER: Sweet Sue (B'way), The Authentic Life of Billy the Kid.

PICTURES: Mask, The Legend of Billie Jean, Top Gun, Valentino Returns, Warm Summer Rain, Guilty By Suspicion.
TELEVISION: *Series*: Bay City Blues. *Guest*: Hill Street Blues. *Movies*: Consenting Adult, The Billionaire Boys Club, Without Her Consent. *Mini-Series*: Lonesome Dove, Return to Lonesome Dove.

TUCCI, STANLEY
Actor. b. Peekskill, NY. e. SUNY.
THEATER: *B'way*: The Misanthrope, Brighton Beach Memoirs, The Iceman Cometh. Moon Over Miami, Scapin, Dalliance, Balm in Gilead.
PICTURES: Who's That Girl, Monkey Shines, Slaves of New York, Fear Anxiety and Depression, The Feud, Quick Change, Men of Respect, Billy Bathgate, Beethoven, Prelude to a Kiss, The Public Eye, In the Soup, Undercover Blues, The Pelican Brief, It Should Happen to You, Mrs. Parker and the Vicious Circle, Kiss of Death, A Modern Affair, Big Night (also co-dir; Ind't Spirit Awards, 1997.).
TELEVISION: *Series*: The Street, Wiseguy, Murder One. *Guest*: Miami Vice, The Equalizer, thirtysomething, Equal Justice.

TUCKER, MELVILLE
Executive. b. New York, NY, Mar. 4, 1916. e. Princeton U. Asst. purchasing agent Consolidated Laboratories, N.Y., 1934-36; sound effects & picture ed., Republic Productions, Inc. 1936-8; then asst. production mgr. & first asst. dir., 1938-42; served in U.S. Army 1942-46; asst. prod. Republic 1946; assoc. producer, 1947-52; prod., Universal 1952-54; prod. exec. v.p., Universal, 1955-70; production exec. U-I, 1954-71; became prod.Verdon Prods., 1971.
PICTURES: *Prod.*: The Missourians, Thunder in God's Country, Rodeo King and the Senorita, Utah Wagon Train, Drums Across the River, Black Shield of Falworth, A Warm December, Uptown Saturday Night, Let's Do It Again, A Piece of the Action. *Exec. prod.*: Stir Crazy, Hanky Panky, Fast Forward.

TUCKER, MICHAEL
Actor. b. Baltimore, MD, Feb. 6, 1944. m. actress Jill Eikenberry. e. Carnegie Tech. Drama Sch. Worked in regional theater (Long Wharf, Washington's Arena Stage, Milwaukee Rep.) and with the NY Shakespeare Festival in Trelawney of the Wells, Comedy of Errors, Measure for Measure, The Merry Wives of Windsor. Also prod. revival of El Grande de Coca Cola (1986).
THEATER: Moonchildren, Modigliani, The Goodbye People, The Rivals, Mother Courage, Waiting for Godot, Oh What a Lovely War, I'm Not Rappaport (American Place Theatre).
PICTURES: A Night Full of Rain (debut, 1977), An Unmarried Woman, Eyes of Laura Mars, Diner, The Goodbye People, The Purple Rose of Cairo, Radio Days, Tin Men, Checking Out, For Love or Money, D2: The Mighty Ducks.
TELEVISION: *Series*: L.A. Law. *Movies*: Concealed Enemies, Vampire, Assault and Matrimony, Day One, Spy, Too Young to Die?, Casey's Gift: For Love of a Child, The Secret Life of Archie's Wife, In the Nick of Time, A Town Torn Apart. *Specials*: Love Sex... and Marriage, A Family Again, On Hope. *Guest*: Hill Street Blues.

TUCKERMAN, DAVID R.
Executive. b. Perth Amboy, NJ, Nov. 9, 1946. e. Monmouth Coll., F.L.U. 1967-70; B.S.B.A. Entered industry with A.I.T. Theatres, 1967; gen. mgr., Music Makers Theatres, 1973; v.p., Leigh Group, MMT, head film buyer, 1976; sr. v.p., MMT, 1980; Loews Film Buyer, 1986; Loews (now Sony) v.p. film, 1993. Member: SMPTE, Variety Int., MPBC, AFI, Motion Picture Pioneers.

TUGGLE, RICHARD
Director, Writer. b. Coral Gables, FL, Aug. 8, 1948. e. U. Virginia, B.A. 1970. Wrote screenplays before directorial debut with Tightrope, 1984.
PICTURES: Escape from Alcatraz (s.p.), Tightrope (dir., s.p.), Out of Bounds (dir.).

TUNE, TOMMY
Actor, Director, Choreographer, Dancer. b. Wichita Falls, TX, Feb. 28, 1939. e. Univ of Texas at Austin. Began professional career dancing in chorus of B'way shows (Baker Street, A Joyful Noise, How Now Dow Jones, etc.). Recipient of 9 Tony Awards.
THEATER: *Performer*: Seesaw, My One and Only, Bye Bye Birdie (tour), Tommy Tune Tonite! (B'way & tour). *Director and/or choreographer*: The Club, Cloud 9, The Best Little Whorehouse in Texas, Nine, A Day in Hollywood/A Night in the Ukraine, Stepping Out, My One and Only, Grand Hotel, The Will Rogers Follies.
PICTURES: Hello Dolly!, The Boy Friend.
TELEVISION: *Series*: Dean Martin Presents the Goldiggers, The Bold and the Beautiful, also numerous specials, Tony Award Shows.

TURMAN, LAWRENCE
Producer. b. Los Angeles, CA, Nov. 28, 1926. e. UCLA. In textile business 5 years, then joined Kurt Frings Agency; left in 1960 to form Millar-Turman Prods.
PICTURES: *Prod.*: The Young Doctors, I Could Go on Singing, The Best Man. Formed own prod. co., Lawrence Turman, Inc., to make The Flim-Flam Man, The Graduate, Pretty Poison (exec. prod.), The Great White Hope, The Marriage of a Young Stockbroker (also dir.), The Nickel Ride (exec. prod.), The Drowning Pool, First Love, Heroes, Walk Proud, Tribute,

Caveman, The Thing, Second Thoughts (also dir.), Mass Appeal, The Mean Season, Short Circuit, Running Scared, Short Circuit 2, Full Moon in Blue Water, Gleaming the Cube, The Getaway, The River Wild.
TELEVISION: *Co-prod. with David Foster*: The Gift of Love, News at Eleven, Between Two Brothers. *Prod.*: The Morning After, She Lives, Unwed Father. *Co-exec. prod.*: Jesse.

TURNER, JANINE
Actress. r.n. Janine Gauntt. b. Lincoln, NE, Dec. 6, 1962. Raised in Texas. Studied dance, joined Forth Worth Ballet. Started modeling at age 15 in NYC, enrolled in Professional Children's School. First major acting job was on series Dallas. On stage in Full Moon and High Tide in the Ladies Room.
PICTURES: Young Doctors in Love, Knights of the City, Tai-Pan, Monkey Shines, Steel Magnolias, The Ambulance, Cliffhanger, The Curse of the Inferno, Leave It to Beaver.
TELEVISION: *Movies*: Stolen Women Captured Hearts, Circle of Deceit. *Series*: Behind the Screen, General Hospital (1982-83), Another World (1986-87), Northern Exposure. *Guest*: The Love Boat, The A-Team, Mike Hammer.

TURNER, KATHLEEN
Actress. b. Springfield, MO, June 19, 1954. e. U. of Maryland, SMSU.
THEATER: *B'way*: Gemini, Cat on a Hot Tin Roof (Theatre World Award), Indiscretions. *Regional*: Camille (Long Wharf), A Midsummer Night's Dream (DC), Toyer (DC).
PICTURES: Body Heat (debut, 1981), The Man With Two Brains, Romancing the Stone, Crimes of Passion, A Breed Apart, Prizzi's Honor, The Jewel of the Nile, Peggy Sue Got Married (Acad. Award nom.), Julia and Julia, Switching Channels, Who Framed Roger Rabbit (voice), The Accidental Tourist, The War of the Roses, V.I. Warshawski, House of Cards, Undercover Blues, Serial Mom, Naked in New York, Moonlight & Valentino, A Simple Wish, Legalese, Baby Geniuses, The Virgin Suicides.
TELEVISION: *Series*: The Doctors. *Movies*: Friends at Last, Love in the Ancient World. *Special*: Dear America: Letters Home From Vietnam (reader). *Director*: Leslie's Folly.

TURNER, TED
Executive. r.n. Robert Edward Turner. b. Cincinnati, OH., Nov. 19, 1938. e. Brown U. m. actress Jane Fonda. Began career in Savannah in family's outdoor adv. business, selling space on billboards. Inherited co. in 1963 and in 1970 entered broadcasting with purchase of a failing TV station in Atlanta which he turned into WTBS, a "superstation" which in 1994 reached 95% of U.S. homes equipped with cable. 1980, established CNN a 24-hr. cable news service. Purchased MGM film library. Co-owner of two professional sports teams in Atlanta: Braves (baseball) and Hawks (basketball). Started Headline News, 1982; CNN International 1985; Turner Network Television 1988; Sportsouth, 1990; Cartoon Network in 1992; acquired Castle Rock Entertainment, 1993; merger with New Line Cinema, 1994; started Turner Classic Movies, 1994; CNNfn Financial Network, 1995.

TURNER, TINA
Singer, Actress. r.n. Annie Mae Bullock. b. Brownsville, TX, Nov. 26, 1939. Previously married to Ike Turner and appeared with him on road in Ike and Tina Turner Revue. Many hit records. *Autobiography*: I Tina.
PICTURES: Gimme Shelter, Taking Off, Soul to Soul, Tommy, Sound of the City, Mad Max Beyond Thunderdome, What's Love Got to Do With It (vocals), Last Action Hero.
TELEVISION: S*pecial*: Tina—Live From Rio.

TURTURRO, JOHN
Actor. b. Brooklyn, NY, Feb. 28, 1957. e. SUNY/New Paltz; Yale Drama School, 1983. m. actress Katherine Borowitz. Worked in regional theater and off-B'way.
THEATER: Danny and the Deep Blue Sea (Obie & Theatre World Awards, 1985), Men Without Dates, Tooth of the Crime, La Puta Viva, Chaos and Hard Times, The Bald Soprano, Of Mice and Men, The Resistible Rise of Arturo Ui, Death of a Salesman (B'way debut, 1984).
PICTURES: Raging Bull (debut, 1980), Exterminator II, The Flamingo Kid, Desperately Seeking Susan, To Live and Die in L.A., Hannah and Her Sisters, Gung Ho, Off Beat, The Color of Money, The Sicilian, Five Corners, Do the Right Thing, Mo' Better Blues, State of Grace, Miller's Crossing, Men of Respect, Jungle Fever, Barton Fink (Cannes Film Fest. Award), Brain Donors, Mac (also dir., co-s.p.), Fearless, Being Human, Quiz Show, Search and Destroy, Clockers, Unstrung Heroes, Grace of My Hear, Box of Moonlight, Girl 6, The Search for One-eye Johnny, Lesser Prophets, Animals, O.K. Garage, Illuminata, The Big Lebowski, He Got Game, Rounders, The Cradle Will Rock.
TELEVISION: *Mini-Series*: The Fortunate Pilgrim. *Movie*: Backtrack.

TUSHINGHAM, RITA
Actress. b. Liverpool, England, March 14, 1942. Student at Liverpool Playhouse.
THEATER: The Giveaway, Lorna and Ted, Mistress of Novices, The Undiscovered Country, Mysteries.

PICTURES: A Taste of Honey (debut, 1961; BFA Award), The Leather Boys, A Place to Go, Girl With Green Eyes, The Knack... and How to Get It, Doctor Zhivago, The Trap, Smashing Time, Diamonds for Breakfast, The Guru, The Bed Sitting Room, Straight on Till Morning, The Case of Laura C., Where Do You Go From Here?, Situation, Instant Coffee, The Human Factor, Rachel's Man, The Slum Boy, The Black Journal, Bread Butter and Jam, Mysteries, Felix Krull, Spaghetti Thing, Dream to Believe, Flying, Seeing Red, The Housekeeper, Resurrected, Dante and Beatrice in Liverpool, Hard Days Hard Nights, Paper Marriage, Desert Lunch, An Awfully Big Adventure, The Boy From Mercury, Under the Sun, Swing.
TELEVISION: U.S.: Green Eyes, Bread, Sunday Pursuit, Gutt Ein Journalist, Hamburg Poison.

TUTIN, DOROTHY
Actress. b. London, Eng., Apr. 8, 1930. e. St. Catherine's Sch. Bramley, Guildford (Surrey). Stage debut in The Thistle & the Rose, 1949.
THEATER: Much Ado About Nothing, The Living Room, I Am a Camera, The Lark, Wild Duck, Juliet, Ophelia, Viola, Portia, Cressida, Rosalind, The Devils, Once More With Feeling, The Cherry Orchard, Victoria Regina-Portrait of a Queen, Old Times, Peter Pan, What Every Woman Knows, Month in the Country, Macbeth, Antony and Cleopatra, Undiscovered Country, Reflections, After the Lions, Ballerina, A Kind of Alaska, Are You Sitting Comfortably?, Chalk Garden, Brighton Beach Memoirs, Thursday's Ladies, The Browning Version, A Little Night Music, Henry VIII, Party Time, The Seagull, Getting Married.
PICTURES: The Importance of Being Earnest, The Beggar's Opera, A Tale of Two Cities, Cromwell, Savage Messiah, The Shooting Party, The Great Kandinsky.
TELEVISION: Living Room, Victoria Regina, Invitation to a Voyage, Antigone, Colombe, Carrington V.C., The Hollow Crown, Scent of Fear, From Chekhov With Love, The Queen and the Welshman, Flotsam and Jetsam, Mother & Son, South Riding, Willow Cabins, Ghosts, Sister Dora, The Double Dealer, The Combination, La Ronde, Tales of the Unexpected, 10 Downing Street, Life After Death, King Lear, Murder with Mirrors, Great Moments in Aviation, Dancing Queen, Landscape, The Father, The Demon Lover, Robin Hood, All Creatures Great and Small, A Kind of Alaska, The Bill, Lease of Death, Anglo-Saxon Attitudes, The Great Kandinsky, Indian Summer. Mini-series: The Six Wives of Henry VIII, Vienna 1900, Body and Soul, Scarlett, Jake's Progress.

TWAINE, MICHAEL
Actor, Director. b. New York, NY, Nov. 1, 1939. e. Ohio State U. Served U.S. Army. While studying with Lee Strasberg, worked as private detective, school teacher. Made stage debut City Center, 1956, in Mr. Roberts. Became village coffee house and club comedian 1968 to 1972.
PICTURES: Marriage Italian Style (voice), American Soap, Blood Bath, F.I.S.T., Cheap Shots, Platoon (voice), Billy Bathgate (voice).
TELEVISION: The Silent Drum, Starsky & Hutch, Wonder Woman, Streets of San Francisco, Soap, Lou Grant, Diff'rent Strokes, Nurse, Stalk the Wild Child, The Courage and the Passion, Eischied, America's Most Wanted, Beyond the Universe.

TWIGGY
Actress. r.n. Leslie Hornby. b. London, England, Sept. 19, 1949. m. actor Leigh Lawson. At 17 regarded as world's leading high fashion model. Made m.p. debut in The Boy Friend, 1971. Starred in many London West End Shows, including Cinderella and Captain Beaky Presents. 1983: on Broadway in musical, My One and Only.
PICTURES: The Boyfriend (debut, 1971), W, There Goes the Bride, The Blues Brothers, The Doctor and the Devils, Club Paradise, Madame Sousatzka, Istanbul.
TELEVISION: Series: Twiggy, Twiggy and Friends, Juke Box (U.S.), Princesses (U.S.). Specials: Pygmalion, Sun Child, Young Charlie Chaplin. Movies: The Diamond Trap, Body Bags.

TYLER, LIV
Actress. b. July, 1977. Daughter of fashion model Bebe Buell and musician Steven Tyler. Began as a model at age 14.
PICTURES: Silent Fall (debut), Empire Records, Heavy, Stealing Beauty, That Thing You Do!, Inventing the Abbotts, U-Turn, Plunkett & MacLeane, Eugene Onegin, Armageddon, The Little Black Book.

TYRRELL, SUSAN
Actress. b. San Francisco, CA, 1946. Made first prof. appearance with Art Carney in summer theatre tour prod. of Time Out for Ginger. Worked in off-B'way prods. and as waitress in coffee house before attracting attention in Lincoln Center Repertory Co. prods. of A Cry of Players, The Time of Your Life, Camino Real.
THEATER: The Knack, Futz, Father's Day, A Coupla White Chicks Sitting Around Talking, The Rotten Life.

PICTURES: Shoot Out (debut, 1971), The Steagle, Been Down So Long It Looks Like Up to Me, Shoot Out, Fat City (Acad. Award nom.), Catch My Soul, Zandy's Bride, The Killer Inside Me, Islands in the Stream, Andy Warhol's Bad, I Never Promised You a Rose Garden, Another Man Another Chance, September 30, 1955, Racquet, Loose Shoes, Forbidden Zone, Subway Riders, Night Warning, Fast-Walking, Liar's Moon, Tales of Ordinary Madness, Fire and Ice (voice), Angel, The Killers, Avenging Angel, Flesh and Blood, The Chipmunk Adventure (voice), The Offspring, Big Top Pee-Wee, Tapeheads, The Underachievers, Far From Home, Cry-Baby, Motorama, Powder.
TELEVISION: Series: Open All Night. Movies: Lady of the House, Midnight Lace, Jealousy, Thompson's Last Run, Poker Alice, The Christmas Star, Windmills of the Gods. Mini-Series: If Tomorrow Comes.

TYSON, CICELY
Actress. b. New York, NY, Dec. 19, 1933. e. NYU. Studied at Actor's Studio. Former secretary and model. Co-founder, Dance Theatre of Harlem.
THEATER: The Blacks, Moon on a Rainbow Shawl, Tiger Tiger Burning Bright, The Corn Is Green.
PICTURES: A Man Called Adam (debut, 1966), The Comedians, The Heart Is a Lonely Hunter, Sounder (Acad. Award nom.), The Blue Bird, The River Niger, A Hero Ain't Nothin' But a Sandwich, The Concorde—Airport '79, Bustin' Loose, Fried Green Tomatoes, The Grass Harp.
TELEVISION: Series: East Side West Side, The Guiding Light, Sweet Justice. Movies: Marriage: Year One, The Autobiography of Miss Jane Pittman (Emmy Award, 1974), Just An Old Sweet Song, Wilma, A Woman Called Moses, The Marva Collins Story, Benny's Place, Playing with Fire, Acceptable Risks, Samaritan: The Mitch Snyder Story, The Women of Brewster Place, Heat Wave, The Kid Who Loved Christmas, Duplicates, When No One Would Listen, House of Secrets, Oldest Living Confederate Widow Tells All (Emmy Award, 1994), Mama Flora's Family. Guest: B.L. Stryker. Special: Without Borders (host). Mini-Series: Roots. Pilot: Clippers.

U

UGGAMS, LESLIE
Singer. b. New York, NY, May 25, 1943. e. Professional Children's Sch., grad., 1960. Juilliard Sch. of Music. Beg. singing career age 5. TV debut as Ethel Waters' niece on Beulah. Also on Johnny Olsen's TV kids at age 7, Your Show of Shows as singer, 1953; Recording artist for Columbia Records, Atlantic, Motown Wrote The Leslie Uggams Beauty Book (1962).
THEATER: Hallelujah Baby (Tony & Theatre World Awards, 1968), Her First Roman, Blues in the Night, Jerry's Girls, Anything Goes (natl. co. & Bdwy), Stringbean (Dallas), Into the Woods (Long Beach, CA).
PICTURES: Two Weeks in Another Town, Poor Pretty Eddie, Black Girl, Heartbreak Motel, Skyjacked, Sugar Hill.
TELEVISION: Series: Sing Along With Mitch, The Leslie Uggams Show (1969), Fantasy (Emmy Award, 1984). Guest: Beulah (1949), Kids and Company, Milton Berle Show, Name That Tune, Jack Paar Show, Garry Moore. Mini-Series: Roots, Backstairs at the White House. Movie: Sizzle. Specials: The Book of Lists (co-host). Fantasy (Emmy Award, 1983, host), I Love Men, 'S Wonderful, 'S Marvelous, 'S Gershwin, Sinatra and Friends, Placido Domingo Steppin' Out With the Ladies, Jerry Herman Tribute, Rooms for Improvement.
RADIO: Peter Lind Hayes-Mary Healy Show, Milton Berle, Arthur Godfrey, Star Time.

ULANO, MARK
Sound.
PICTURES: Think Me Nothing, Hospital Massacre, Time Walker, Cujo, Lovelines, Once Bitten, Sweet Hearts Dance, Desperado, Rough Magic, The Winner, From Dusk Till Dawn, Titanic (Acad. Award, Best Sound Mixing, 1997), The Pest, Austin Powers: International Man of Mystery, Jackie Brown.
TELEVISION: Movies: High School U.S.A., The Parade, The Cartier Affair, A Time to Triumph, Shattered Spirits, Lena: My 100 Children, Dance 'Til Dawn, Shadow of a Doubt, Empty Cradle. Series: The Trials of Rosie O'Neill, Significant Others. Mini-series: Drug Wars: The Camarena Story.

ULLMAN, TRACEY
Actress, Comedian, Singer. b. Hackbridge, England, Dec. 29, 1959. m. British TV prod. Allan McKeown. e. won a performance sch. scholarship at 12. Attended the Italia Conti School for 4 years. Soon after appeared on British TV and onstage in Grease and The Rocky Horror Picture Show. Also performed in improvisational play Four in a Million (1981) at the Royal Court Theatre, London (London Theatre Critics Award). Recorded gold-selling album You Broke My Heart in Seventeen Places. Appeared in music video They Don't Know. U.S. TV debut, The Tracey Ullman Show (debuted April, 1987).
THEATRE: NY: The Taming of the Shrew, The Big Love.

PICTURES: Give My Regards to Broad Street, Plenty, Jumpin' Jack Flash, I Love You to Death, Happily Ever After (voice), Robin Hood: Men in Tights, Household Saints, Bullets Over Broadway, Ready to Wear (Pret-a-Porter).
TELEVISION: *Series*: Three of a Kind (BBC), The Tracey Ullman Show (Emmy Awards, 1989, 1990),. *Specials*: The Best of the Tracey Ullman Show (Emmy Award, 1990),, Tracey Ullman—A Class Act. *Guest*: Love & War (Emmy Award, 1993), Tracey Ullman: Takes on New York (Emmy Award, 1994) Tracey Takes On... (Emmy, Cable Ace Awards, 1997)

ULLMANN, LIV
Actress. b. Tokyo, Japan, of Norwegian parents, Dec. 16, 1939. Accompanied parents to Canada when WWII began and later returned to Norway. Was catapulted to fame in a succession of Swedish films directed by Ingmar Bergman. *Author*: Changing, Choices. Ambassador for UNICEF since 1980. Youngest person to date to receive the Order of St. Olav from the King of Norway. Recipient of 11 honorary doctorates.
THEATER: *U.S.*: A Doll's House, Anna Christie, I Remember Mama (musical), Ghosts, Old Times.
PICTURES: Fjols til Fjells (debut, 1957), The Wayward Girl, Tonny, Kort ar Sommaren, De Kalte Ham Skarven, Persona, Hour of the Wolf, Shame, The Passion of Anna, The Night Visitor, Cold Sweat, The Emigrants, Pope Joan, Cries and Whispers, Lost Horizon, Forty Carats, The New Land, Scenes From a Marriage, Zandy's Bride, The Abdication, Leonor, Face to Face, Couleur Chair, A Bridge Too Far, The Serpent's Egg, Autumn Sonata, Players (cameo), Richard's Things, The Wild Duck, Bay Boy, Dangerous Moves, Let's Hope It's a Girl, Gaby—A True Story. Moscow Adieu (Donatello Award, 1987), A Time of Indifference, La Amiga, The Rose Garden, Mindwalk, The Ox, The Long Shadow, Sophie (dir., co-s.p. only), Kristin Lavrandsdatter (dir., s.p. only).
TELEVISION: Lady From the Sea, Jacobo Timerman: Prisoner Without a Name Cell Without a Number.

ULRICH, SKEET
Actor. r.n. Bryan Ray Ulrich. b. New York, NY, Jan. 20, 1969.
PICTURES: Albino Alligator, Last Dance, The Craft, Boys, Scream, Touch, Old Friends, As Good As It Gets, Newton Boys, To Live On, Sweetheart of the Song Tra Bong.

UNDERWOOD, BLAIR
Actor. b. Tacoma, WA, Aug. 25, 1964. e. Carnegie-Mellon Univ. NY stage: Measure for Measure.
PICTURES: Krush Groove, Posse, Just Cause, Set It Off, The Eighth Day.
TELEVISION: *Series*: One Life to Live, Downtown, L.A. Law, High Incident. *Movies*: The Cover Girl and the Cop, Heat Wave, Murder in Mississippi, Father & Son: Dangerous Relations (also assoc. prod.), Soul of the Game, Mistrial. *Guest*: Scarecrow and Mrs. King, The Cosby Show, Knight Rider, 21 Jump Street.

UNDERWOOD, RON
Director. b. Glendale, CA, Nov. 6, 1953. e. USC, American Film Institute.
PICTURES: Tremors (also co-story), City Slickers, Heart and Souls, Speechless, Mighty Joe Young.
TELEVISION: The Mouse and the Motorcycle (Peabody Award), Runaway Ralph (Emmy nom.).

UNGER, ANTHONY B.
Executive, Producer. b. New York, NY, Oct. 19, 1940. e. Duke U., USC. Prod. ass't Third Man, TV series, 1961. v.p. Unger Productions, Inc., 1964; v.p. Landau-Unger Co., Inc., 1965; v.p. Commonwealth United Entertainment in London, 1968; pres., Unger Prods. Inc., 1978-present.
PICTURES: The Desperate Ones. The Madwoman of Chaillot. The Battle of Neretva, The Magic Christian, Julius Caesar, The Devil's Widow, Don't Look Now, Force Ten From Navarone, The Unseen, Silent Rage, The Dark Side of Hollywood (doc., prod.).

UNGER, STEPHEN A.
Executive. b. New York, NY, May 31, 1946. e. NYU, Grad. Film and Television Instit. Started as independent prod. and dist. of theatrical and TV films. 1978, joined Universal Pictures Intl. Sales as foreign sls. mgr.; named v.p. Universal Theatrical Motion Pictures in 1979, responsible for licensing theatrical or TV features not handled by U.I.P. in territories outside U.S. & Canada and worldwide acquisitions; 1980 joined CBS Theatrical Films as intl. v.p., sls.; 1982-88, pres., Unger Intl. Distributors, Inc.; 1988 joined Korn/Ferry Intl. as exec. v.p., worldwide entertainment div. Promoted to mng. dir., 1989-91. Joined Spencer Stuart Exec. Search Consultants as mng. dir., Worldwide Ent. Div. 1991.

URBANSKI, DOUGLAS
Producer.
PICTURES: Nil By Mouth (BAFTA Award, Outstanding Brit. Film, 1997).

URICH, ROBERT
Actor. b. Toronto, OH, Dec. 19, 1946. e. Florida State U., B.A., radio and TV communications; Michigan State U., M.A. Communications Mgmt. Appeared in university plays. Was sales account executive at WGN Radio, Chicago, before turning to stage acting (Ivanhoe Theatre, Chicago).
PICTURES: Magnum Force, Endangered Species, The Ice Pirates, Turk 182.
TELEVISION: *Series*: Bob & Carol & Ted & Alice, S.W.A.T., Soap, Tabitha, Vega$, Gavilan, Spenser For Hire, American Dreamer, Crossroads, National Geographic Explorers (host), It Had to Be You, Lazarus Man, Boatworks, The Love Boat: The Next Wave. *Guest*: The FBI, Gunsmoke, Kung Fu, Marcus Welby MD, The Love Boat. *Movies*: Killdozer, Vega$ (pilot), Leave Yesterday Behind, When She Was Bad, Fighting Back, Killing at Hell's Gate, Take Your Best Shot, Princess Daisy, Invitation to Hell, His Mistress, Scandal Sheet, Young Again, April Morning, The Comeback, She Knows Too Much, Murder By Night, Night Walk, Blind Faith, Spooner, A Quiet Little Neighborhood A Perfect Little Murder, Stranger at My Door, And Then She Was Gone, Survive the Savage Sea, Blind Man's Bluff (also co-prod.), Double Edge, Revolver, Deadly Relations, Spenser: Ceremony (also co-exec. prod.), Spenser: Pale Kings and Princes (also co-exec. prod.), Danielle Steel's A Perfect Stranger, Spenser: The Judas Goat, A Horse for Danny, She Stood Alone: The Tailhook Scandal, Captains Courageous, Final Descent. *Mini-Series*: Mistral's Daughter, Amerika, Lonesome Dove.

URMAN, MARK
Executive. b. New York, NY, Nov. 24, 1952. e. Union Coll., 1973; NYU, cinema, 1973-74. m. story analyst Deborah Davis. 1973, apprentice publicist, Universal Pictures; 1973-82, United Artists intl. dept. as assoc. publicist, sr. publicist and ultimately asst. to v.p. worldwide ad-pub.; 1982-84, dir., publicity and marketing, Triumph Films (Columbia/Gaumont); 1985-86, exec. dir. East Coast pub., Columbia Pictures; 1986-89, v.p. East Coast pub., Columbia Pictures. Joined Dennis Davidson Associates as v.p., 1989; promoted to sr.v.p., 1991. Member: Motion Picture Academy.

USLAN, MICHAEL E.
Producer, Writer. b. Bayonne, NJ, June 2, 1951. e. Indiana U., A.B., M.S., J.D. Wrote 12 books, including Dick Clark's 1st 25 Years of Rock 'n' Roll; 1976-80 atty. with United Artists; writer of syndicated comic strip Terry and the Pirates; produced with Benjamin Melniker.
PICTURES: Swamp Thing (prod.), The Return of Swamp Thing (prod.), Batman (exec. prod.), Batman Returns (exec. prod.), Batman: The Animated Movie (prod.), Batman Forever (exec. prod.), Batman & Robin (exec. prod.).
TELEVISION: Three Sovereigns for Sarah (exec. prod.), Dinosaucers (exec. prod., creator, writer), Swamp Thing (exec. prod. for both live-action and animated series), Fish Police (exec. prod.), South Korea cultural segments NBC Summer Olympics 1988 (exec. prod.), Television's Greatest Bits (prod., creator, writer), 1st National Trivia Quiz (prod., writer), Where On Earth Is Carmen Sandiego? (animated, exec. prod.; Emmy Award), Robin Cook's Harmful Intent (exec. prod.; writer); remakes of The Kiss, The Sneeze, The Great Train Robbery, The Barbershop, Streetcar Chivalry, Smashing a Jersey Mosquito (prod., dir.).

USTINOV, SIR PETER
Actor, Writer, Director. b. London, Eng., Apr. 16, 1921. e. Westminster Sch. In Brit. Army, W.W.II. On Brit. stage from 1937. Screen debut 1941 in Brit. picture Mein Kampf, My Crimes. Awards: 3 Emmy Awards (Specials: Life of Samuel Johnson, Barefoot in Athens, A Storm in Summer); Grammy Award for Peter and the Wolf; NY Critics Award and Donaldson Award for best foreign play (The Love of Four Colonels); British Critics Award (Romanoff and Juliet). Chancellor, Durham Univ., 1992. Received Britannia Award from BAFTA, 1992; Critics Circle Award, 1993; German Cultural Award, 1994; German Bambi, 1994; Rudolph Valentino Award, 1995.
THEATER: Romanoff and Juliet, N.Y., London; and 17 other plays. Dir., acted, Photo Finish; wrote, Life In My Hands, The Unknown Soldier and His Wife, Half Way Up The Tree, King Lear, Beethoven's Tenth, An Evening With Peter Ustinov.
PICTURES: *Actor*: The Goose Steps Out, One of Our Aircraft Is Missing, The Way Ahead (co-s.p.), School for Secrets (wrote, dir. & co-prod. only) Vice Versa (dir., s.p. only), Private Angelo (also adapt., dir., co-prod.), Odette, Quo Vadis (Acad. Award nom.), The Magic Box, Hotel Sahara, The Egyptian, Beau Brummell, We're No Angels, Lola Montez, The Spies, The Man Who Wagged His Tail, School for Scoundrels (adapt. only), The Sundowners, Spartacus (Academy Award, best supporting actor, 1960), Romanoff and Juliet (also prod., s.p.), Billy Budd (also prod., dir., s.p.), Topkapi (Academy Award, best supporting actor, 1964), John Goldfarb Please Come Home, Lady L. (also dir., s.p.), The Comedians, Blackbeard's Ghost, Hot Millions, Viva Max. Hammersmith Is Out (also dir.), Robin Hood (voice), One of Our Dinosaurs Is Missing, Logan's Run, Treasure of Matecumbe, Purple Taxi, The Last Remake of Beau Geste, Doppio Delitto, Death on the Nile, Ashanti, Charlie Chan and the Curse of the Dragon Queen, Grendel Grendel Grendel (voice), The Great Muppet Caper, Evil Under the Sun, Memed My Hawk (also dir., s.p.), Appointment with Death, Lorenzo's Oil, The Phoenix and the Magic Carpet.

RECENT TV: The Well Tempered Bach, 13 at Dinner, Deadman's Folly, Peter Ustinov's Russia, World Challenge, Murder in Three Acts, The Secret Identity of Jack the Ripper (host), Around the World in 80 Days, The Mozart Mystique, Ustinov on the Orient Express, Ustinov Meets Pavarotti, Inside the Vatican, The Old Curiosity Shop, Haydn Gala, An Evening With Sir Peter Ustinov, Paths of the Gods.

V

VACCARO, BRENDA
Actress. b. Brooklyn, NY, Nov. 18, 1939. e. Thomas Jefferson H.S., Dallas; studied two yrs. at Neighborhood Playhouse in N.Y. Was waitress and model before landing first B'way role in Everybody Loves Opal. Toured in Tunnel of Love and returned to N.Y. for role in The Affair.
THEATER: Everybody Loves Opal (Theatre World Award), Tunnel of Love (tour), The Affair, Children From Their Games, Cactus Flower (Tony Award, 1965), The Natural Look, How Now Dow Jones (Tony nom.), The Goodbye People (Tony nom.), Father's Day, The Odd Couple, Jake's Women.
PICTURES: Where It's At (debut, 1969), Midnight Cowboy, I Love My Wife, Summertree, Going Home, Once Is Not Enough (Acad. Award nom., Golden Globe Award), Airport '77, House by the Lake (Death Weekend), Capricorn One, Fast Charlie the Moonbeam Rider, The First Deadly Sin, Zorro the Gay Blade, Supergirl, Water, Cookie, Heart of Midnight, Masque of the Red Death, Ten Little Indians, Lethal Games, Love Affair.
TELEVISION: Series: Sara, Dear Detective, Paper Dolls. Guest: The F.B.I., The Name of the Game, The Helen Reddy Show, The Shape of Things (Emmy Award, 1974), The Golden Girls, Columbo, Murder She Wrote, Flesh & Blood, Golden Girls (Emmy nom.), Civil Wars, Red Shoe Diaries, Friends, Johnny Bravo (voice). Movies: Travis Logan D.A., What's a Nice Girl Like You...?, Honor Thy Father, Sunshine, The Big Ripoff, Guyana Tragedy, The Pride of Jesse Hallam, The Star Maker, A Long Way Home, Deceptions, Julius and Ethel Rosenberg: Stolen: One Husband, Red Shoes Diaries, Following Her Heart, When Husbands Cheat.

VADIM, ROGER
Director, Writer. b. Paris, Jan. 26, 1928. r.n. Roger Vadim Plemiannikow. m. actress Marie-Christine Barrault. Appeared in films Rich and Famous, Into the Night.
PICTURES: Futures Vedettes (s.p.). Writer-Director: And God Created Woman, No Sun in Venice, The Night Heaven Fell, Les Liaisons Dangereuses, Blood and Roses, Please Not Now!, Seven Capital Sins (Pride segment), Love on a Pillow, Vice and Virtue (also prod.), Nutty Naughty Chateau, La Ronde (Circle of Love), The Game is Over (also prod.), Spirits of the Dead (Metzengerstein segment), Barbarella, Pretty Maids All in a Row, Helle, Ms. Don Juan, Night Games, Hot Touch, Surprise Party, Come Back, And God Created Woman (1988), The Mad Lover.
TELEVISION: Beauty and the Beast (Faerie Tale Theatre).

VAJNA, ANDREW
Executive. b. Budapest, Hungary, Aug. 1, 1944. e. UCLA. Launched career with purchase of m.p. theaters in Far East. Founded Panasia Film Ltd. in Hong Kong. Exhibitor and dist. of feature films since 1970. Formed Carolco Service, Inc. (foreign sls. org.), with Mario Kassar 1976. Founder and Pres., American Film Mkt. Assn., 1982. Resigned from Carolco, 1989; formed independent production co., Cinergi Prods., 1989.
PICTURES: Exec. Prod.: The Deadly China Doll, The Silent Partner, The Changeling, Victory, The Amateur, First Blood, Superstition, Rambo: First Blood Part II, Angel Heart, Extreme Prejudice, Rambo III, Red Heat, Iron Eagle II, Deepstar Six, Johnny Handsome, Music Box, Mountains of the Moon, Total Recall, Air America, Narrow Margin, Jacob's Ladder, Medicine Man, Tombstone, Renaissance Man, Color of Night, Die Hard With a Vengeance, Judge Dredd, The Scarlet Letter, The Shadow Conspiracy, Nixon, Evita.

VALENTI, JACK J.
Executive. b. Sept. 5, 1921. e. U. of Houston, B.A., 1946; Harvard U., M.B.A., bus. admin., 1948. Air force pilot in European theatre, W.W.II; adv. and pub. rel. exec. in Houston; special asst. and advisor to Pres. Lyndon B. Johnson, 1963-66, elected pres., Motion Picture Association of America, MPEA and AMPTP, since June, 1966. Named Motion Picture Pioneer of the Year, 1988.

VALENTINE, DEAN
Executive. b. Romania, 1954. e. U. of Chicago, English major, honors grad. Began career in journalism at Time, Life and The Saturday Review. Dir., comedy programming, NBC. 1988, joined Walt Disney Television as dir., of TV dev't; 1990, sr. v.p.; appt'd. pres. of WD Television and WD Television Animation. 1997, appointed COO, United Paramount Networks.

VALENTINE, KAREN
Actress. b. Sebastopol, CA, May 25, 1947.
PICTURES: Forever Young Forever Free, Hot Lead and Cold Feet, The North Avenue Irregulars.
TELEVISION: Series: Room 222 (Emmy Award, 1970), Karen, Our Time (host). Guest: My Friend Tony, Hollywood Squares, Laugh-In, The Bold Ones, Sonny and Cher, Mike Hammer, Murder, She Wrote. Movies: Gidget Grows Up, The Daughters of Joshua Cabe, Coffee Tea or Me?, The Girl Who Came Gift-Wrapped, The Love Boat (pilot), Having Babies, Murder at the World Series, Return to Fantasy Island, Go West Young Girl, Muggable Mary: Street Cop, Money on the Side, Skeezer, Illusions, Jane Doe, Children in the Crossfire, He's Fired She's Hired, A Fighting Choice, Perfect People. Special: The Emancipation of Lizzie Stern (Afterschool Special).

VALLI, ALIDA
Actress. r.n. Alida von Altenburger. b. Pola, Italy, May 31, 1921. e. M.P. Acad., Rome (dramatics); m. Oscar de Mejo, pianist-composer. In Italian m.p.; won Venice Film Festival Award in Piccolo Mondo Antico (Little Old World); to U.S. in 1947, billed simply as Valli.
PICTURES: Vita Ricomincia, Giovanna; The Paradine Case, The Miracle of the Bells, The Third Man, Walk Softly Stranger, The White Tower, Lovers of Toledo, We the Women, Senso, The Stranger's Hand, The Night Heaven Fell, This Angry Age (The Sea Wall), The Horror Chamber of Dr. Faustus, The Long Absence, The Happy Thieves, The Castilian, Ophelia, Oedipus Rex, The Spider's Stratagem, Tender Dracula, La Jeu de Solitaire, The Cassandra Crossing, Suspiria, 1900, The Tempter, Luna, Inferno, Le Jupon Rouge, A Notre Regrettable Epoux, A Month by the Lake.

VALLONE, RAF
Actor. b. Turin, Italy, Feb. 17, 1916. e. U. of Turin. Former newspaper writer. Directed operas Norma, La Traviata, Adrianna in NY, San Francisco and Houston.
PICTURES: Bitter Rice (debut, 1949), Vendetta, Under the Olive Tree, Anna, Path of Hope, White Line, Rome 11 O'Clock, Strange Deception, Anita Garibaldi, Daughters of Destiny, Teresa Raquin, Riviera, The Secret Invasion. Two Women, El Cid, Phaedra, A View From the Bridge, The Cardinal, Harlow, Nevada Smith, Kiss the Girls and Make Them Die, The Desperate Ones, The Secret Invasion, The Italian Job, The Kremlin Letter, Cannon for Cordoba, A Gunfight, Summertime Killer, Rosebud, The Human Factor, That Lucky Touch, The Other Side of Midnight, The Devil's Advocate, The Greek Tycoon, An Almost Perfect Affair, A Time to Die, Lion of the Desert, The Godfather Part III.
TELEVISION: Fame (Hallmark Hall of Fame), Honor Thy Father, Catholics, The Scarlet and the Black, Christopher Columbus, Goya.

VAN ARK, JOAN
Actress. b. New York, NY. m. NBC news reporter John Marshall. e. Yale U of Drama. Began career in touring co., then on Broadway and in London in Barefoot in the Park. Also appeared on B'way with the APA-Phoenix Rep. Co. in the 1970s. As a runner has competed in 12 marathons, incl. Boston Marathon. On TV also created voices for animated series Spiderwoman, Thundarr and Dingbat, Dumb and Dumber, Santo Bugito and the Creeps and special Cyrano de Bergerac. Estee Lauder spokesperson.
THEATER: School for Wives (Tony Award nom.; Theatre World Award), The Rules of the Game (Theatre World Award). L.A.: Cyrano de Bergerac, Ring Around the Moon, Chemin de Fer, As You Like It (L.A. Drama Critics Award). Williamstown Theatre Fest.: Night of the Iguana, The Legend of Oedipus, Little Night Music. Off-B'way & L.A.: Love Letters, Three Tall Women.
PICTURES: Frogs, Dedication Day (dir. only).
TELEVISION: Series: Temperatures Rising, We've Got Each Other, Dallas, Knots Landing. Guest: The F.B.I., The Girl with Something Extra, Quark, Dallas, Quincy, Rockford Files, Rhoda. Co-host: Miss USA and Miss Universe Pageants, Battle of the Network Stars, Macy's Thanksgiving Parade, Tournament of Roses parade. Movies: The Judge and Jake Wyler, Big Rose, Testimony of Two Men, Shell Game, The Last Dinosaur, Red Flag—The Ultimate Game, Glitter, Shakedown on the Sunset Strip, My First Love, Always Remember I Love You, The Grand Central Murders, Tainted Blood, In the Shadows Someone's Watching (also co-exec. prod.), Moment of Truth: A Mother's Deception, When the Dark Man Calls, Loyal Opposition: Terror in the White House. Special: Boys Will Be Boys (also dir.). Miniseries: Knots Landing: Back to the Cul-de-Sac.

VANCE, COURTNEY B.
Actor. b. Detroit, MI, Mar. 12, 1960. e. Harvard (B.A.), Yale Drama Sch. (M.A.).
THEATER: B'way: Fences (Theatre World & Clarence Derwent Awards; Tony nom.), Six Degrees of Separation (Tony nom.). Off-B'way: My Children My Africa (Obie Award), Romeo and Juliet, Temptation. Regional: A Lesson From Aloes, Rosencrantz and Guildenstern Are Dead, Hamlet, Butterfly, Jazz Wives Jazz Lives, Geronimo Jones.
PICTURES: Hamburger Hill, The Hunt for Red October, The Adventures of Huck Finn, Holy Matrimony, Panther, Dangerous Moves, The Last Supper, The Preacher's Wife.
TELEVISION: Movies: Percy and Thunder, Race to Freedom, Tuskegee Airmen, The Affair, Black Tuesday.

VAN DAMME, JEAN-CLAUDE
Actor. b. Brussels, Belgium, Apr. 1, 1961. r.n. Jean-Claude Van Varenberg. Former European karate champion, began studying martial arts at 11 yrs. old. Won the European Professional Karate Association's middleweight championship. As teen established the California Gym in Brussels; also worked as a model before coming to U.S. in 1981. Resumed career teaching martial arts before landing first film role.
PICTURES: No Retreat No Surrender, Bloodsport, Black Eagle, Cyborg, Kickboxer (also co-story), Death Warrant, Lionheart (also co-s.p., story), Double Impact (also co-prod., co-s.p., co-story, fight choreog.), Universal Soldier, Nowhere to Run, Last Action Hero (cameo), Hard Target, Timecop, Street Fighter, Sudden Death, The Quest (also dir. & story), Maximum Risk, Double Team, Legionnaire, Knock Off, Inferno, Abominable.

VAN DEVERE, TRISH
Actress. b. Englewood Cliffs, NJ, March 9, 1945. e. Ohio Wesleyan U. m. actor George C. Scott. On B'way in Sly Fox, Tricks of the Trade, etc.
PICTURES: The Landlord (debut, 1970), Where's Poppa?, The Last Run, One Is a Lonely Number, Harry in Your Pocket, The Day of the Dolphin, The Savage Is Loose, Movie Movie, The Changeling, The Hearse, Uphill All the Way, Hollywood Vice Squad, Messenger of Death.
TELEVISION: Movies: Stalk the Wild Child, Beauty and the Beast, Sharon: Portrait of a Mistress, Mayflower—The Pilgrim's Adventure, All God's Children, Haunted, Curacao.

VAN DOREN, MAMIE
Actress. r.n. Joan Lucille Olander. b. Rowena, SD, Feb. 6, 1933. e. Los Angeles H.S. Secy. law firm, L.A.; prof. debut as singer with Ted Fio Rita orch.; debuted in films as Joan Olander.
THEATER: Stock: Once in a Lifetime, Boy Meets Girl, Come Back Little Sheba.
PICTURES: His Kind of Woman (debut, 1951), Forbidden, The All-American, Yankee Pasha, Francis Joins the WACs, Ain't Misbehavin', The Second Greatest Sex, Running Wild, Star in the Dust, Untamed Youth, The Girl in Black Stockings, Teacher's Pet, Guns Girls and Gangsters, High School Confidential, The Beat Generation, The Big Operator, Born Reckless, Girls' Town, The Private Lives of Adam and Eve, Sex Kittens Go to College, College Confidential, Vice Raid, The Sheriff Was a Lady, The Candidate, Three Nuts in Search of a Bolt, The Navy vs. the Night Monsters, Las Vegas Hillbillies, You've Got to Be Smart, Voyage to the Planet of the Prehistoric Women, The Arizona Kid, Boarding School (Free Ride).

VAN DYKE, DICK
Actor. b. West Plains, MO, Dec., 13, 1925. Brother is actor Jerry Van Dyke. Son is actor Barry Van Dyke. Served in USAF, WWII. After discharge from service, opened advertising agency in Danville, IL. Teamed with friend in nightclub act called Eric and Van, The Merry Mutes, and for 4 yrs. toured country doing a routine in which they pantomimed and lip-synched to records. 1953 hosted local TV show in Atlanta, then New Orleans. 1955 to NY as host of CBS Morning show.
THEATER: NY: The Girls Against the Boys (Theatre World Award), Bye Bye Birdie (Tony Award, 1961), The Music Man (revival).
PICTURES: Bye Bye Birdie (debut, 1963), What a Way to Go!, Mary Poppins, The Art of Love, Lt. Robin Crusoe USN, Divorce American Style, Fitzwilly, Chitty Chitty Bang Bang, Some Kind of a Nut, The Comic, Cold Turkey, The Runner Stumbles, Dick Tracy.
TELEVISION: Series: The Morning Show (host), CBS Cartoon Theatre (host), The Chevy Showroom, Pantomine Quiz, Laugh Line (emcee), The Dick Van Dyke Show (3 Emmy Awards: 1964, 1965, 1966), The New Dick Van Dyke Show, Van Dyke and Company (Emmy Award, 1977), The Carol Burnett Show, The Van Dyke Show, Diagnosis Murder. Guest: Jake and the Fat Man, Highway to Heaven, Matlock. Movies: The Morning After, Wrong Way Kid, Drop-Out Father, Found Money, The Country Girl, Ghost of a Chance, Keys to the Kingdom, Daughters of Privilege, The House on Sycamore Street, A Twist of the Knife. Pilot: Harry's Battles. Specials: The Dick Van Dyke Special, Dick Van Dyke and the Other Woman, Julie and Dick in Covent Garden, The Confessions of Dick Van Dyke, CBS Library: The Wrong Way Kid (Emmy Award, 1984), Breakfast With Les and Bess, The Town Santa Forgot (narrator), The People's Choice Awards (host).

VAN DYKE, JERRY
Actor. b. Danville, IL, July 27, 1931. Brother is actor Dick Van Dyke. Served in U.S. Air Force before becoming standup comic, banjo player in nightclubs. Guested on The Dick Van Dyke Show, playing Van Dyke's brother.
PICTURES: The Courtship of Eddie's Father (debut, 1963), McLintock!, Palm Springs Weekend, Love and Kisses, Angel in My Pocket, W.A.R.: Women Against Rape, Run If You Can, Annabelle's Wish.
TELEVISION: Series: Picture This, The Judy Garland Show, My Mother the Car, Accidental Family, Headmaster, 13 Queens Boulevard, Coach, You Wish, Teen Angel. Mini-Series: Fresno. Movie: To Grandmother's House We Go. Pilots: My Boy Googie, You're Only Young Twice, Merry Christmas, George Bailey.

VANGELIS
Composer, Conductor. Full name: Vangelis Papathanassiou. b. Greece, March 23, 1943. Began composing as child, performing own compositions at 6. Left Greece for Paris by late 1960s. Composed and recorded his symphonic poem Faire que Ton Reve Soit Plus Long que la Nuit, and album Terra. Collaborated with filmmaker Frederic Rossif for whom composed La Cantique des Creatures. Moved to London then to Greece in 1989. Formed band Formynx in Greece; then Aphrodite's Child in Paris.
PICTURES: Chariots of Fire (Academy Award, 1981), Antarctica, Missing, Blade Runner, The Year of Living Dangerously, The Bounty, Wonders of Life, Wild and Beautiful, Nosferatu in Venice, Francesco, 1492: Conquest of Paradise, Bitter Moon, Cavafy.

VANOCUR, SANDER
News Commentator. b. Cleveland, OH, Jan. 8, 1928. e. Northwestern U. Began career as journalist on London staff of Manchester Guardian 1954-5; City staff, NY Times 1956-57. Joined NBC in 1957, hosting First Tuesday series. Resigned in 1971 to be correspondent of the National Public Affairs Center for PBS. TV Critic for Washington Post, 1975-7. In 1977 joined ABC News as v.p., special reporting units 1977-80. Chief overview corr. ABC news, 1980-81; sr. corr. 1981-present. Anchor: Business World.

VAN PALLANDT, NINA
Actress. b. Copenhagen, Denmark, July 15, 1932. e. USC. Returned to Denmark where she was married to Baron Frederik Van Pallandt with whom she appeared as folk singer throughout Europe, as well as making 3 films with him; went on world tour together before divorcing. Has appeared in New York as singer.
PICTURES: The Long Goodbye, Assault on Agathon, A Wedding, Quintet, American Gigolo, Cloud Dancer, Cutter and Bone, Asi Como Habian Sido, The Sword and the Sorcerer, Jungle Warriors, Time Out, O.C. and Stiggs.
TELEVISION: Movie: Guilty or Innocent: The Sam Shepherd Murder Case.

VAN PATTEN, DICK
Actor. b. New York, NY, Dec. 9, 1928. Sister is actress Joyce Van Patten. Father of actors James and Vincent Van Patten. Began career as child actor with B'way debut at 7 yrs., playing son of Melvyn Douglas in Tapestry in Gray.
THEATER: The Lady Who Came to Stay, O Mistress Mine, On Borrowed Time, Ah, Wilderness, Watch on the Rhine, The Skin of Our Teeth, Kiss and Tell, Mister Roberts, Thieves.
PICTURES: Reg'lar Fellers (debut, 1941), Psychomania, Charly, Zachariah, Making It, Joe Kidd, Soylent Green, Dirty Little Billy, Westworld, Superdad, The Strongest Man in the World, Gus, Treasure of Matecumbe, The Shaggy D.A., Freaky Friday, High Anxiety, Spaceballs, The New Adventures of Pippi Longstocking, Robin Hood: Men in Tights, A Dangerous Place, Demolition High, Love Is All There Is.
TELEVISION: Series: Mama, The Partners, The New Dick Van Dyke Show, When Things Were Rotten, Eight Is Enough, WIOU. Guest: Arnie, The Rookies, Cannon, Banyon, The Little People, The Streets of San Francisco, Hotel, Growing Pains, Love Boat, Murder She Wrote. Specials: Jay Leno's Family Comedy Hour, A Mouse A Mystery and Me, 14 Going On 30. Movies: Hec Ramsey (pilot), The Crooked Hearts, The Love Boat (pilot), With This Ring, Diary of a Hitchhiker, Eight Is Enough Reunion, Going to the Chapel, An Eight Is Enough Wedding, Jake Spanner—Private Eye, The Odd Couple: Together Again, The Gift of Love.

VAN PATTEN, JOYCE
Actress. b. New York, NY, March 9, 1935. Brother is actor Dick Van Patten. Mother of actress Talia Balsam.
THEATER: NY: Spoon River Anthology, Same Time Next Year, The Supporting Cast, The Seagull, I Ought to Be in Pictures, Brighton Beach Memoirs, Murder at the Howard Johnson's, Rumors, Jake's Women.
PICTURES: Reg'lar Fellers (debut, 1941), Fourteen Hours, The Goddess, I Love You Alice B. Toklas, Making It, Something Big, Thumb Tripping, The Manchu Eagle Murder Caper Mystery, Mame, The Bad News Bears, Mikey and Nicky, The Falcon and the Snowman, St. Elmo's Fire, Billy Galvin, Blind Date, Trust Me, Monkey Shines.
TELEVISION: Series: The Danny Kaye Show, The Good Guys, The Don Rickles Show, Mary Tyler Moore Hour, Unhappily Ever After. Guest: Brooklyn Bridge. Movies: But I Don't Want to Get Married!, Winter Kill, The Stranger Within, Let's Switch, Winner Take All, To Kill a Cop, Murder at the Mardi Gras, The Comedy Company, Eleanor: First Lady of the World, Another Woman's Child, The Demon Murder Case, In Defense of Kids, Malice in Wonderland, Under the Influence, The Haunted, Maid for Each Other. Mini-Series: The Martian Chronicles. Special: Bus Stop.

VAN PEEBLES, MARIO
Actor, Director, Producer, Writer. b. Mexico D.F., Mexico, Jan. 15, 1957. Father is filmmaker Melvin Van Peebles. e. Columbia U., B.A. economics, 1980. Studied acting with Stella Adler 1983. Served as budget analyst for NY Mayor Ed Koch and later worked as a Ford model. Directed music videos for Kid Creole and the Coconuts, Nighttrain (also prod., cameo) and for film Identity Crisis. Appeared as child in father's film Sweet Sweetback's Baadasssss Song. Dir., prod., wrote and starred in short, Juliet. Exec. prod. of soundtracks for Posse and Gunmen.

THEATER: Waltz of the Stork (B'way debut, 1984), Take Me Along, The Legend of Deadwood Dick, Champeen, Friday the 13th.
PICTURES: The Cotton Club, Delivery Boys, Exterminator II, 3:15, Rappin' (also wrote and performed 5 songs), South Bronx Heroes, Heartbreak Ridge (also songs), Last Resort, Jaws: the Revenge, Hot Shot, Identity Crisis (also s.p.), New Jack City (also dir.), Posse (also dir.), Gunmen, Highlander: The Sorcerer, Panther (also dir., prod.), Jaws IV: The Revenge, Solo, Los Locos (also s.p., prod., exec. prod.).
TELEVISION: Series: Sonny Spoon. Guest: L.A. Law, One Life to Live, The Cosby Show, The Pat Sajack Show (guest host), In Living Color, Living Single, Outer Limits: Bodies of Evidence. Movies: The Cable Car Murder, Sophisticated Gents, Children of the Night (Bronze Halo Award), The Facts of Life Down Under, The Child Saver, Blue Bayou, Triumph of the Heart: The Ricky Bell Story, Stompin' at the Savoy, In the Line of Duty: Street War, Crosscurrents: Cable Car Murder, Full Eclipse. Specials: American Masters: A Glory of Ghosts (Emperor Jones, All God's Chillun), Third & Oak: The Pool Hall (CBS play), Strangers: Leave, Gang In Blue, Riot, Stag, Gang In Blue (also. co-direct, co-prod.). Director: Sonny Spoon, 21 Jump Street, Top of the Hill, Wise Guy, Malcolm Takes a Shot (DGA nom.), Gabriel's Fire, Missing Persons.

VAN PEEBLES, MELVIN
Producer, Director, Writer, Composer, Editor, Actor. b. Chicago, IL, Aug. 21, 1932. e. Ohio Wesleyan U., 1953. Father of actor Mario Van Peebles. Was portrait painter in Mexico, cable car driver in San Francisco; journalist in Paris and (in 1970s) options trader on Wall Street. Dir. Funky Beat music video.
AUTHOR: Books: The Big Heart, A Bear for the FBI, Le Chinois de XIV, La Permission (Story of a Three Day Pass) La Fete a Harlem, The True American, Sweet Sweetback's Baadasssss Song, Just an Old Sweet Song, Bold Money, No Identity Crisis (co-author with Mario Van Peebles), Panther.
THEATER: B'way (writer, prod., dir.): Ain't Supposed to Die a Natural Death, Don't Play Us Cheap, Waltz of the Stork (also actor). Off-B'way: Champeen, Waltz of the Stork, Kickin the Science.
PICTURES: The Story of a Three-Day Pass (dir., s.p., music), Watermelon Man (dir., music), Sweet Sweetback's Baadasssss Song (prod., dir., s.p., edit., music, actor), Don't Play Us Cheap (prod., dir., s.p., edit., music), Greased Lightning (co-s.p.), America (actor), O.C. and Stiggs (actor), Jaws: The Revenge (actor), Identity Crisis (prod., dir., co-edit., actor), True Identity (actor), Boomerang (actor), Posse (actor), Last Action Hero (actor), Terminal Velocity (actor), Fist of the North Star (actor), Panther (s.p., actor, prod., co-edit.).
TELEVISION: Writer: Down Home, Just an Old Sweet Song, The Day They Came to Arrest the Book (Emmy Award). Actor: Taking Care of Terrific, Sophisticated Gents, Sonny Spoons (series). Director: Nipsey Russell at Harrah's, Vroom Vroom Vroom (also writer; German TV).
ALBUMS: Composer: Brer Soul, Watermelon Man, Sweet Sweetback's Baadasssss Song, As Serious as a Heart Attack, Don't Play Us Cheap, Ain't Suppose to Die a Natural Death, What the #*!% You Mean I Can't Sing, Ghetto Gothic.

VAN PRAAG, WILLIAM
Executive, Producer, Director, Writer, Editor, Advertising Consultant. b. New York, NY, Sept. 13, 1924. e. CREI, Columbia U. U.S. Army, 1942. Paramount, 1945; Brandt Bros. Prods., 1946; NBC, 1947; v.p. Television Features, 1948; devlpd. vidicon system in m.p. prod.; 1949; Started, pres., Van Praag Prod. Inc. 1951; formed Ernst-Van Praag, Inc. 1971, a communications and marketing counseling firm (NY, Brussels, Tokyo); pres., International Film, TV and A-V Producers Assn, 1969; creator of Van-O-Vision. Winner of commercial, short subject and feature theatrical awards. Author of Color Your Picture, Primer of Creative Editing, and Van Praag's Magic Eye. Past pres., Film Producer's Assn, mem. DGA, SAG, 771 IATSE, National Academy of TV Arts and Sciences, International Radio and TV Executive Society and Soc. of MP and TV Engineers.

VAN SANT, GUS
Director, Writer. b. Louisville, KY, 1952. Raised in Darien, CT, then moved to Oregon at age 17. e. Rhode Island Sch. of Design, where he studied painting. Went to L.A. in 1976, becoming prod. asst. to dir. Ken Shapiro. Made first low-budget film, Alice in Hollywood, which was never released. Later made commercials for NY ad agency before returning to filmmaking.
PICTURES: Mala Noche, Drugstore Cowboy (Natl. Soc. of Film Critics Awards for best dir. & s.p.; NY Film Critics & L.A. Film Critics Award for s.p.), My Own Private Idaho, Even Cowgirls Get the Blues, To Die For, Ballad of the Skeletons, Good Will Hunting, Psycho.

VARNEY, JIM
Actor. b. Lexington, KY, June 15, 1949. Studied acting at the Barter Theatre. Performed as stand-up comedian in NY and LA. Appeared in dinner theatre productions of Death of a Salesman, Camelot, Guys and Dolls, etc. During 1970's starred as Sgt. Glory in long running series of TV commercials. Became famous with character of Ernest P. Worrell in TV commercials beginning in 1980.

PICTURES: Ernest Goes to Camp, Ernest Saves Christmas, Fast Food, Ernest Goes to Jail, Ernest Scared Stupid, Wilder Napalm, The Beverly Hillbillies, Ernest Rides Again, Ernest Goes to School, Toy Story (voice), The Expert, Snowboard Academy, 3 Ninjas.
TELEVISION: Series: The Johnny Cash Show (1976), Operation Petticoat, Pink Lady, Tom T.'s Pop Goes the Country, The Rousters, Hey Vern It's Ernest (Emmy Award, 1989). Guest: Fernwood 2-Night, Alice, America 2-Nite, Roseanne. Pilot: Operation Petticoat.

VAUGHN, ROBERT
Actor. b. New York, NY, Nov. 22, 1932. e. L.A. State coll., B.S. and M.A. Theatre Arts 1956; USC, Ph.D. Communications, 1970. Gained fame as Napoleon Solo in The Man From U.N.C.L.E. TV series. Author: Only Victims, 1972.
PICTURES: The Ten Commandments (debut, 1956), Hell's Crossroads, No Time to Be Young, Teenage Caveman, Unwed Mother, Good Day for a Hanging, The Young Philadelphians (Acad. Award nom.), The Magnificent Seven, The Big Show, The Caretakers, To Trap a Spy, The Spy With My Face, One Spy Too Many, The Glass Bottom Boat (cameo), The Venetian Affair, How to Steal the World, Bullitt, The Bridge at Remagen, If It's Tuesday This Must Be Belgium (cameo), The Mind of Mr. Soames, Julius Caesar, The Statue, Clay Pigeon, The Towering Inferno, The Babysitter, Lucifer Complex, Demon Seed (voice), Starship Invasions, Brass Target, Good Luck Miss Wycoff, Hangar 18, Sweet Dirty Tony, Battle Beyond the Stars, Virus, S.O.B., Superman III, Black Moon Rising, The Delta Force, Rampage, Nightstick, Hour of the Assassin, Skeleton Coast, River of Death, Captive Rage, Nobody's Perfect, Fair Trade, Edgar Allan Poe's Buried Alive, That's Adequate, Blind Vision, C.H.U.D. II: Bud the Chud, Transylvania Twist, Going Under, Twilight Blue, Joe's Apartment.
TELEVISION: Series: The Lieutenant, The Man From U.N.C.L.E., The Protectors, Emerald Point N.A.S., The A-Team, Danger Theatre, As the World Turns. Mini-Series: Captains and the Kings, Washington: Behind Closed Doors (Emmy Award, 1978), Centennial, Backstairs at the White House, The Blue and the Gray, Evergreen. Movies: The Woman Hunter, Kiss Me Kill Me, The Islander, The Rebels, Mirror Mirror, Doctor Franken, The Gossip Columnist, City in Fear, Fantasies, The Day the Bubble Burst, A Question of Honor, Inside the Third Reich, Intimate Agony, The Return of the Man From U.N.C.L.E., International Airport, Murrow, Prince of Bel Air, Desperado, Perry Mason: The Case of the Defiant Daughter, Dark Avenger, Dancing in the Dark. BBC: One of Our Spies is Missing, The Spy in the Green Hat, The Karate Killers.

VAUGHN, VINCE
Actor. b. Minneapolis, MN, March 28, 1970.
PICTURES: Rudy, At Risk, Swingers, Just Your Luck, The Locusts, The Lost World: Jurassic Park, Force Majeure, Clay Pigeons, A Cool Dry Place, The Gelfin, Psycho.
TELEVISION: Guest: Doogie Howser M.D., China Beach, 21 Jump Street.

VEL JOHNSON, REGINALD
Actor. b. Queens, NY, Aug. 16, 1952. e. Long Island Inst. of Music and Arts, NYU.
THEATER: NY: But Never Jam Today, Inacent Black, World of Ben Caldwell, Staggerlee.
PICTURES: Wolfen (debut, 1981), Ghostbusters, The Cotton Club, Remo Williams, Armed and Dangerous, Crocodile Dundee, Die Hard, Turner & Hooch, Die Hard 2, Posse.
TELEVISION: Series: Perfect Strangers, Family Matters. Movies: Quiet Victory: The Charlie Wedemeyer Story, The Bride in Black, Jury Duty: The Comedy, Grass Roots, One of Her Own.

VENORA, DIANE
Actress. b. Hartford, CT, 1952. e. Juilliard Sch. (BFA degree). Member of Juilliard's Acting Company, Circle Repertory Co. and the Ensemble Studio Theatre.
THEATER: A Midsummer Night's Dream, Hamlet (New York Shakespeare Festival), Uncle Vanya (at La Mama), Messiah (Manhattan Theatre Club), Penguin Toquet, Tomorrow's Monday (Circle Rep), Largo Desolato, School for Scandal, The Seagull, A Man for All Seasons (Roundabout Theatre Co.), Peer Gynt (Williamstown Fest.), The Winter's Tale, Hamlet (NYSF).
PICTURES: All That Jazz, Wolfen, Terminal Choice, The Cotton Club, F/X, Ironweed, Bird (NY Film Critics Award, 1988; Golden Globe nom.), Heat, Three Wishes, Surviving Picasso, The Subsitute, Romeo and Juliet, The Jackal.
TELEVISION: Mini-Series: A.D. Movie: Cook and Peary: The Race to the Pole. Specials: Getting There, Rehearsing Hamlet, Hamlet. Guest: Law and Order. Series: Thunder Alley, Chicago Hope.

VERDON, GWEN
Actress, Dancer, Choreographer. b. Culver City, CA, Jan. 13, 1925. Married to late dir.-choreographer Bob Fosse. Studied dancing with her mother, E. Belcher, Carmelita Marrachi, and Jack Cole.
THEATER: Bonanza Bound!, Magdalena (asst. choreographer to Jack Cole), Alive and Kicking, Can-Can (Donaldson & Tony Awards, 1954), Damn Yankees (Tony Award, 1956), New Girl in Town (Tony Award, 1958), Redhead (Tony Award, 1959), Sweet Charity, Children! Children!, Milliken's Breakfast Show, Damn Yankees (revival Westbury), Chicago, Dancin' (asst. choreogra-

pher, prod. sprv. road co.), Sing Happy (tribute to Kander and Ebb), Parade of Stars Playing the Palace (Actors' Fund benefit), Night of 100 Stars II (1985).
PICTURES: On the Riviera (debut, 1951), David and Bathsheba, The Mississippi Gambler, Meet Me After the Show, The Merry Widow, The I Don't Care Girl, Farmer Takes a Wife, Damn Yankees, The Cotton Club, Cocoon, Nadine, Cocoon: The Return, Alice, Marvin's Room.
TELEVISION: Movies: Legs, The Jerk Too, Oldest Living Confederate Widow Tells All, Best Friends for Life. Special: Steam Heat. Guest: M*A*S*H, Fame, All My Children, Magnum P.I., The Equalizer, All is Forgiven, Dear John, Dream On, Homicide, many others.

VEREEN, BEN
Singer, Dancer, Actor. b. Miami, FL, Oct. 10, 1946. e. High School of Performing Arts.
THEATER: NY: Hair, Sweet Charity, Jesus Christ Superstar (Theatre World Award), Pippin (Tony Award, 1973), Grind.
PICTURES: Sweet Charity, Gasss, Funny Lady, All That Jazz, The Zoo Gang, Buy and Cell, Friend to Friend, Once Upon a Forest (voice).
TELEVISION: Movies: Louis Armstrong—Chicago Style, The Jesse Owens Story, Lost in London, Intruders. Mini-Series: Roots, Ellis Island, A.D. Series: Ben Vereen... Comin' at Ya, Ten Speed and Brown Shoe, Webster, Zoobilee Zoo, You Write the Songs (host), J.J. Starbuck, Silk Stalkings. Specials: Ben Vereen—His Roots, Uptown— A Tribute to the Apollo Theatre.

VERHOEVEN, PAUL
Director. b. Amsterdam, The Netherlands, July 18, 1938. e. U. of Leiden, Ph.D., (mathematics and physics) where he began making films.
PICTURES: Business Is Business, Turkish Delight, Keetje Tippel (Cathy Tippel), Soldier of Orange, Spetters, The Fourth Man, Flesh + Blood, Robocop, Total Recall, Basic Instinct, Showgirls, Starship Troopers.

VERNON, ANNE
Actress. r.n. Edith Antoinette Alexandrine Vignaud. b. Paris, Jan. 7, 1924. e. Ecole des Beaux Arts, Paris. Worked for French designer; screen debut in French films; toured with French theatre group; first starring role, Le Mannequin Assassine 1948. Wrote French cookbooks. Was subject of 1980 French TV film detailing her paintings, Les Peintres Enchanteurs.
PICTURES: Edouar et Caroline, Terror on a Train, Ainsi Finit La Nuit, A Warning to Wantons, Patto Col Diavolo, A Tale of Five Cities, Shakedown, Song of Paris, The Umbrellas of Cherbourg, General Della Rovere, La Rue L'Estrapade, Love Lottery, Therese and Isabelle.

VERNON, JOHN
Actor. b. Montreal, Canada, Feb. 24, 1932. r.n. Adolphus Raymondus Vernon Agopowicz. e. Banff Sch. of Fine Arts, Royal Acad. of Dramatic Art. Worked on London stage and radio. First film work as voice of Big Brother in 1984 (1956). Daughter is actress Kate Vernon.
PICTURES: 1984 (voice; debut, 1956), Nobody Waved Goodbye, Point Blank, Justine, Topaz, Tell Them Willie Boy is Here, One More Train to Rob, Dirty Harry, Fear Is the Key, Charley Varrick, W (I Want Her Dead), The Black Windmill, Brannigan, Sweet Movie, The Outlaw Josey Wales, Angela, A Special Day, The Uncanny, Golden Rendezvous, National Lampoon's Animal House, It Rained All Night the Day I Left, Crunch, Fantastica, Herbie Goes Bananas, Heavy Metal (voice), Airplane II: The Sequel, Chained Heat, Curtains, Savage Streets, Jungle Warriors, Fraternity Vacation, Doin' Time, Double Exposure (Terminal Exposure), Ernest Goes to Camp, Blue Monkey, Nightstick, Border Heat, Deadly Stranger, Dixie Lanes, Killer Klowns From Outer Space, Bail-Out, I'm Gonna Git You Sucka, Office Party, War Bus Commando, Mob Story, The Naked Truth.
TELEVISION: Series: Tugboat Annie (Canadian TV), Wojeck (Canadian TV), Delta House, Hail to the Chief. Movies: Trial Run, Escape, Cool Million, Hunter, The Questor Tapes, Mousey, The Virginia Hill Story, The Imposter, Swiss Family Robinson, The Barbary Coast, Matt Helm, Mary Jane Harper Cried Last Night, The Sacketts, The Blood of Others, Two Men (Can.), The Woman Who Sinned, The Fire Next Time, The Forget-Me-Not Murders. Mini-Series: The Blue and the Gray, Louisiana (Fr.). Pilots: B-Men, War of the Worlds. Guest: Tarzan, Kung Fu, Faerie Tale Theatre (Little Red Riding Hood), The Greatest American Hero, Fall Guy, Alfred Hitchcock Presents, Knight Rider, Tales From the Crypt, etc.

VERONA, STEPHEN
Director, Producer, Writer. b. Illinois, Sept. 11, 1940. e. Sch. of Visual Arts. Directed and wrote some 300 commercials (over 50 award-winners) before turning to feature films in 1972, which he wrote as well. Also dir. award-winning short subjects (featuring Barbra Streisand, The Beatles, Simon and Garfunkle and The Lovin' Spoonful). Also prod., dir. of Angela Lansbury's Positive Moves video. Is an artist whose works have been exhibited at numerous CA and NY galleries. Dir. Acad. Award nom. short subject, The Rehearsal, 1971.

PICTURES: Director: The Lords of Flatbush (prod., co-dir., co-s.p.), Pipe Dreams (also prod., s.p.), Boardwalk (also co-s.p.), Talking Walls (also s.p.).
TELEVISION: Class of 1966 (prod. designer, ani. dir.), Diff'rent Strokes, The Music People, Sesame Street, Take a Giant Step, Double Exposure, Flatbush Avenue (pilot, prod., co-s.p.).

VETTER, RICHARD
Executive. b. San Diego, CA, Feb. 24, 1928. e. Pepperdine Coll., B.A., 1950; San Diego State Coll., M.A., 1953; UCLA, Ph.D., 1959. U.S. Navy: aerial phot., 1946-48, reserve instr., San Diego County Schools, 1951-54; asst. prof., audio-vis. commun., U.C.L.A., 1960-63. Inventor, co-dev., Dimension 150 Widescreen Process. 1957-63: formed D-150 Inc., 1963; exec. v.p. mem.: SMPTE, Technical & Scientific Awards Committee, AMPAS.

VICTOR, JAMES
Actor. r.n. Lincoln Rafael Peralta Diaz. b. Santiago, Dominican Republic, July 27, 1939. e. Haaren H.S., N.Y. Studied at Actors Studio West. Member of Academy of Mo. Pic. Arts & Sciences, Actors Branch. Recipient of Cleo Award, 1975, for Mug Shot; Golden Eagle Award, 1981, for consistent outstanding performances in motion pictures.
THEATER: Bullfight, Ceremony for an Assassinated Blackman, Latina (Drama-Logue Critics Award, 1980), The Man in the Glass Booth, The M.C. (Drama-Logue Critics, and Cesar best actor awards, 1985), I Gave You a Calendar (Drama-Logue Critics Award, 1983), I Don't Have To Show You No Stinking Badges (Drama-Logue Critics Award, 1986), The Rooster and the Egg, One Hour Without Television, The Red Devil Battery Sign.
PICTURES: Fuzz, Rolling Thunder, Boulevard Nights, Defiance, Losin' It, Borderline; Stand and Deliver, Gunfighter's Moon.
TELEVISION: Series: Viva Valdez, Condo, I Married Dora, Angelica Mi Vida, The New Zorro, Murder She Wrote. Many appearances on specials. Movies: Robert Kennedy and His Times, Twin Detectives, Remington Steel, The Streets of L.A., I Desire, Second Serve, Grand Slam, Falcon Crest. Mini-Series: Streets of Laredo.

VIGODA, ABE
Actor. b. New York, NYU, Feb. 24, 1921.
PICTURES: The Godfather, The Don Is Dead, Newman's Law, The Cheap Detective, Vasectomy - A Delicate Matter, Plain Clothes, Look Who's Talking, Prancer, Joe vs. the Volcano, Sugar Hill, Jury Duty, Good Burger.
TELEVISION: Series: Dark Shadow, Barney Miller, Fish, One Life to Live. Movies: The Devil's Daughter, Tomaa, Having Babies, How to Pick Up Girls, Death Car on the Freeway. Guest: Mannix, Kojak, The Rookies, B.J. and the Bear, B.K. Stryker.

VINCENT, JR., FRANCIS T
Executive. b. Waterbury, CT, May 29, 1938. e. Williams Coll. B.A., 1960; Yale Law Sch. LL.B., 1963. Bar, CT 1963; NY, 1964; D.C. 1969. 1969-78, partner in law firm of Caplin & Drysdale, specializing in corporate banking and securities matters; 1978, assoc. dir. of, Division of Corporation Finance of Securities & Exchange Commission; exec. v.p. of the Coca-Cola Company and pres. & CEO of its entertainment business sector. Also chmn. & CEO of Columbia Pictures Industries, Inc.; appt. pres. CEO, 1978; mem. bd. of dir. of The Coca-Cola Bottling Co. of NY. 1987-88; rejoined law firm of Caplin & Drysdale, Washington, D.C., 1988. Trustee of Williams Coll. & The Hotchkiss Sch.

VINCENT, JAN-MICHAEL
Actor. b. Denver, CO, July 15, 1945. e. Ventura City (CA) Coll. as art major. Joined National Guard. Discovered by agent Dick Clayton. Hired by Robert Conrad to appear in his film, Los Bandidos. Signed to 6-mo. contract by Universal, for which made U.S. debut in Journey to Shiloh. Then did pilot TV movie for 20th-Fox based on Hardy Boys series of book. Originally called self Michael Vincent; changed after The Undefeated.
PICTURES: Los Bandidos (debut, 1967), Journey to Shiloh, The Undefeated, Going Home, The Mechanic, The World's Greatest Athlete, Buster and Billie, Bite the Bullet, White Line Fever, Baby Blue Marine, Vigilante Force, Shadow of the Hawk, Damnation Alley, Big Wednesday, Hooper, Defiance, Hard Country, The Return, The Last Plane Out, Born in East L.A., Enemy Territory, Hit List, Deadly Embrace, Demonstone, Hangfire, Raw Nerve, Alienator, Haunting Fear, Gold of the Samurai, The Divine Enforcer, Beyond the Call of Duty, Sins of Desire, Hidden Obsession, Xtro II, Deadly Avenger, Midnight Witness, Ice Cream Man, Abducted II: The Reunion.
TELEVISION: Series: Dangerous Island (Banana Splits Hour), The Survivors, Airwolf. Movies: Tribes, The Catcher, Sandcastles, Deliver Us From Evil, Six Against the Rock, Tarzan in Manhattan. Mini-Series: The Winds of War. Guest: Lassie, Bonanza.

VINCENT, KATHARINE
Actress. r.n. Ella Vincenti. b. St. Louis, MO, May 28, 1918.
THEATER: B'way: Love or Bust, Could She Tell?, Banners of 1939, Czarina Smith.
PICTURES: Peptipa's Waltz, Error in Her Ways, Stars and Stripes on Tour, Skin Deep, The Hungry, Voodoo Village, Welcome to Genoa, Unknown Betrayal, The Hooker, Study by M. Atget.
TELEVISION: The Untouchables, Moses the Lawgiver, Dolce Far Niente (mini-series, Roma).

VINER, MICHAEL
Producer, Writer. b. 1945. m. actress Deborah Raffin. e. Harvard U., Georgetown U. Served as aide to Robert Kennedy; was legman for political columnist Jack Anderson. Settled in Hollywood, where worked for prod. Aaron Rosenberg, first as prod. asst. on three Frank Sinatra films; then asst. prod. on Joaquin Murietta. In music industry was record producer, manager, executive, eventually heading own division, at MGM. Debut as writer-producer in 1976 with TV special, Special of the Stars. Theatrical film debut as prod.-co-writer of Touched by Love, 1980. Television: Windmills of the Gods (exec. prod.). *Exec. Prod.*: Rainbow Drive; *Prod.*: Memories of Midnight. *President*: Dove Audio.

VITALE, RUTH
Executive. e. Tufts U., B.A.; Boston U., M.S. Prior to motion picture career, worked in advertising and media. Senior v.p., Vestron Pictures then s.v.p. of feature production at United Artists and management at Constantin Film Development before joining New Line. Joined New Line as exec. v.p. of worldwide acquisitions. Currently pres., Fine Line Features, a wholly owned division of New Line Cinema.

VITTI, MONICA
Actress. r.n. Maria Luisa Ceciarelli. b. Rome, Italy, Nov. 3, 1933. Started acting in plays as teen, studying at Rome's Natl. Acad. of Dramatic Arts.
PICTURES: Ridere Ridere Ridere (debut, 1955), Smart Girls, L'Avventura, La Notte, L'Eclipse, Dragees du Poivre (Sweet and Sour), Three Fables of Love, The Nutty Naughty Chateau, Alta Infidelitata (High Infidelity), The Red Desert, Le Bambole (The Dolls), Il Disco Volante, Le Fate (The Queens), Modesty Blaise, The Chastity Belt (On My Way to the Crusades I Met a Girl Who...), Girl with a Pistol, La Femme Ecarlate, The Pizza Triangle, The Pacifist, Teresa la Ladra, Tosca, The Phantom of Liberty, Midnight Pleasures, My Loves, Duck in Orange Sauce, An Almost Perfect Affair, The Mystery of Oberwald, Tigers in Lipstick, The Flirt (also s.p.), When Veronica Calls, Secret Scandal (also dir., co- s.p.).

VOGEL, DAVID E.
Executive. President of Walt Disney Pictures.

VOIGHT, JON
Actor. b. Yonkers, NY. Dec. 29, 1938. e. Archbishop Stepinac H.S., White Plains, NY; Catholic U. of Amer., D.C. (B.F.A.) 1960; studied acting at the Neighborhood Playhouse and in private classes with Stanford Meisner, four yrs.
THEATER: *B'way*: The Sound of Music (debut, 1959), That Summer That Fall (Theatre World Award), The Seagull. *Off-B'way*: A View From the Bridge (1964 revival). *Regional*: Romeo & Juliet, A Streetcar Named Desire, Hamlet.
PICTURES: Hour of the Gun (debut, 1967), Fearless Frank, Midnight Cowboy, Out of It, Catch-22, The Revolutionary, Deliverance, All-American Boy, Conrack, The Odessa File, End of the Game, Coming Home (Acad. Award, 1978), The Champ, Lookin' To Get Out (also co-s.p., prod.), Table for Five (also prod.), Runaway Train, Desert Bloom, Eternity, Heat, Rosewood, U-Turn, Mission Impossible, Anaconda, The Rainmaker.
TELEVISION: *Movies*: Chernobyl: The Final Warning, The Last of His Tribe, The Tin Soldier (also dir.), Convict Cowboy. *Mini-Series*: Return to Lonesome Dove. *Special*: The Dwarf (Public Broadcast Lab). *Guest*: Gunsmoke, Naked City, The Defenders, Coronet Blue, NYPD.

VON SYDOW, MAX
Actor. b. Lund, Sweden, April 10, 1929. Theatrical debut in a Cathedral Sch. of Lund prod. of The Nobel Prize. Served in the Swedish Quartermaster Corps two yrs. Studied at Royal Dramatic Theatre Sch. in Stockholm. Tour in municipal theatres. Has appeared on stage in Stockholm, London (The Tempest, 1988), Paris and Helsinki in Faust, The Legend and The Misanthrope. 1954 won Sweden's Royal Foundation Cultural Award. Appeared on B'way in Duet for One.
PICTURES: Bara en Mor (Only a Mother; debut, 1949), Miss Julie, Ingen Mans Kvinna, Ratten att Alska, The Seventh Seal, Prasten i Uddarbo, Wild Strawberries, Brink of Life, Spion 503, The Magician, The Virgin Spring, Brollopsdagen, Through a Glass Darkly, Nils Holgerssons Underbara Resa, Alskarinnen, Winter Light, 4x4, The Greatest Story Ever Told (English-language debut, 1965), The Reward, Hawaii, The Quiller Memorandum, Hour of the Wolf, Here Is Your Life, Svarta Palmkronor, Shame, Made in Sweden, The Kremlin Letter, The Passion of Anna, The Night Visitor, The Touch, The Emigrants, Appelbriget, Embassy, The New Land, The Exorcist, Steppenwolf, Egg! Egg!, Illustrious Corpses, Three Days of the Condor, The Ultimate Warrior, Foxtrot (The Other Side of Paradise), Cuore di Cane, Voyage of the Damned, Les Desert des Tartares, Exorcist II: The Heretic, March or Die, Brass Target, Gran Bolitto, Hurricane, Deathwatch, Venetian Lies, Flash Gordon, Victory, She Dances Alone (voice), Conan the Barbarian, Flight of the Eagle, Strange Brew, Never Say Never Again, Target Eagle, Dreamscape, Dune, Code Name: Emerald,

Hannah and Her Sisters, Duet for One, The Second Victory, Wolf at the Door, Pelle the Conqueror (Acad. Award nom.), Katinka (dir.), Cellini: A Violent Life, Awakenings, A Kiss Before Dying, Until the End of the World, Zentropa (narrator), The Bachelor, The Best Intentions, The Ox, Father, Grandfather's Journey, Needful Things, The Silent Touch, Time Is Money, The Atlantic (narrator), Judge Dredd, Needful Things, Jerusalem, Hamsun.
TELEVISION: *Movies/Mini-Series*: Samson and Delilah, Christopher Columbus, Kojak: The Belarus File, Brotherhood of the Rose, Hiroshima: Out of the Ashes, Red King White Knight, Radetzky March, Citizen X, A Que Punto E La Notte, Uncle Vanya, Confessions, Hostile Waters, Fantasma Per Caso, Salomone, La Principessa E Il Povero.

VON TRIER, LARS
Director, Writer, Editor, Actor. r.n. Lars Trier. b. Copenhagen, Denmark, April 30, 1956. e. Danish Film Institute. Attracted international attention with Forbrydelsens Element (The Element of Crime). Is woring on a film project taking a 3 minute shoit every year from different locations all over Europe for a period of 33 years; begun in 1991, the premiere is expected in the year 2024.
PICTURES: *Director*: Orchidegartneren (1976), Menthe la bienheureuse, Den Sidste detalje, Befrielsesbilleder (also s.p.), The Element of Crime (also actor, s.p.), Epidemic (also actor, s.p., edit.), Medea (also s.p.), Un Monde de Difference (actor only), Zentropa (a.k.a. Europa; also actor, s.p.), The Kingdom (orig. for Danish TV; also s.p.), Breaking the Waves (also s.p.; Grand Jury Prize, Cannes, 1996).

VON TROTTA, MARGARETHE
Director, Writer. b. Berlin, Germany, Feb. 21, 1942. e. Studied German and Latin literature in Munich and Paris. Studied acting in Munich and began career as actress. 1970 began collaborating on Schlondorff's films as well as acting in them.
PICTURES: *Actress*: Hands Up!, Madchen zwischen Nacht und Morgen, Schrage Vogel, Brandstifter, Gotter der Pest, Baal, Drucker, Der Amerikanische Soldat, Gods of the Plague, Why Does Herr R. Run Amok?, The Sudden Wealth of the Poor People of Kombach (also co-s.p.), Beware the Holy Whore, Die Moral der Ruth Halbfass, Free Woman (also co-s.p.), Desaster, Ubernachtung in Tirol, Die Atlantikschwimmer, Bierkampf, Coup de Grace (also co-s.p.). *Dir./ Co-s.p.*: The Lost Honor of Katharina Blum (co-dir., co-s.p., with Schlondorff), The Second Awakening of Christa Klages, Sisters or the Balance of Happiness, Circle of Deceit, Marianne and Julianne, Friends & Husbands, Unerreichbare Nahe, Rosa Luxemburg, Felix, Paura e Amore (Three Sisters), The African Woman, The Long Silence, The Promise.

VON ZERNECK, FRANK
Producer. b. New York, NY, Nov. 3, 1940. e. Hofstra Coll., 1962. Has produced plays in New York, Los Angeles and on national tour. Partner, von Zerneck/Sertner Films. Devised Portrait film genre for TV movies: Portrait of a Stripper, Portrait of a Mistress, Portrait of a Centerfold, etc. Past chmn. of California Theatre Council; former officer of League of Resident theatres; member of League of New York Theatres & Producers; Producers Guild of America; chmn's council, the Caucus for Producers, Writers and Directors; Board of Directors, Allied Communications, Inc. Museum of Radio & Television in NYC, Hollywood Television & Radio Society, Acad. of TV Arts & Sciences, Natl. Acad. of Cable Programming. Received American Film Institute Charles Fries Producer of the Year Award.
PICTURE: God's Lonely Man, Living In Oblivion.
TELEVISION: 21 Hours at Munich, Dress Gray, Miracle on Ice, Combat Night, Queenie, In the Custody of Strangers, The First Time, Baby Sister, Policewoman Centerfold, Obsessive Love, Invitation to Hell, Romance on the Orient Express, Hostage Flight. *Exec. prod.*: The Proud Men, Man Against the Mob, To Heal a Nation, Lady Mobster, Maybe Baby, Full Exposure: the Sex Tapes Scandal, Gore Vidal's Billy the Kid, Too Young to Die, The Great Los Angeles Earthquake, The Court-Martial of Jackie Robinson, White Hot: The Mysterious Murder of Thelma Todd, Survive the Savage Sea, Opposites Attract, Menu for Murder, Battling for Baby, Woman With a Past, Jackie Collins' Lady Boss, Danger Island, The Broken Chain, Beyond Suspicion, French Silk, The Corpse Had a Familiar Face, Robin Cook's Mortal Fear, Take Me Home Again, The Other Woman, Seduced and Betrayed, Robin Cook's Virus, The West Side Waltz, Crazy Horse, Robin Cook's Terminal, She Said No, Terror In the Family, My Son Is Innocent, Tornado!, Border Music, No One Would Tell, Robin Cook's Invasion, Nightscream, Mother Knows Best, Dying To Belong, Holiday In Your Heart, Virtual Obsession, Still Holding on: The Legend of Cadillac Jack, Two Came Back, Murder Live!.

W

WADLEIGH, MICHAEL
Director. b. Akron, OH, Sept. 24, 1941. e. Ohio State U., B.S., B.A., M.A., Columbia Medical Sch.
PICTURES: Woodstock (dir.), Wolfen (dir., co-s.p.), Out of Order, The Village at the End of the Universe (dir., s.p.).

WAGGONER, LYLE
Actor. b. Kansas City, KS, April 13, 1935. e. Washington U., St. Louis. Was salesman before becoming actor with road co. prod. of Li'l Abner. Formed own sales-promo co. to finance trip to CA for acting career in 1965. Did commercials, then signed by 20th-Fox for new-talent school.
PICTURES: Love Me Deadly, Journey to the Center of Time, Catalina Caper, Surf II, Murder Weapon, Dead Women in Lingerie, Gypsy Angels.
TELEVISION: Series: The Carol Burnett Show, The Jimmie Rodgers Show, It's Your Bet (host), Wonder Woman. Movies: Letters from Three Lovers, The New Original Wonder Woman, The Love Boat II, The Gossip Columnist, Gridlock.

WAGNER, JANE
Writer, Director, Producer. b. Morristown, TN, Feb. 26, 1935. e. attended Sch. of Visual Arts, NY. Worked as designer for Kimberly Clark, created Teach Me Read Me sheets for Fieldcrest.
THEATER: B'way: Appearing Nitely (dir., co-writer), The Search for Signs of Intelligent Life in the Universe (dir., writer; NY Drama Desk Award & Special NY Drama Critics Award), both starring Lily Tomlin.
PICTURES: Moment by Moment (s.p., dir.), The Incredible Shrinking Woman (s.p., exec. prod.), The Search for Signs of Intelligent Life in the Universe (s.p.; exec. prod.).
TELEVISION: Specials: Exec. prod./writer: J.T. (Peabody Award), Lily (prod., co-writer; Emmy & WGA Awards, 1974), Lily Tomlin (also prod.; Emmy Award for writing, 1976), People (also prod.), Lily—Sold Out (co-writer; Emmy Award for producing, 1981), Lily for President? (co-writer), The Edith Ann Show , Edith Ann: A Few Pieces of the Puzzle, Edith Ann: Homeless Go Home, Edith Ann's Christmas: Just Say Noel (Peabody Award).

WAGNER, LINDSAY
Actress. b. Los Angeles, CA, June 22, 1949. Appeared in school plays in Portland, OR; studied singing and worked professionally with rock group. In 1968 went to L.A. Signed to Universal contract in 1971.
PICTURES: Two People, The Paper Chase, Second Wind, Nighthawks, High Risk, Martin's Day, Ricochet, Frog and Wombat, The Fourth Horseman.
TELEVISION: Series: The Bionic Woman (Emmy Award, 1977), Jessie, Peaceable Kingdom. Guest: The F.B.I., Owen Marshall: Counselor at Law, Night Gallery, The Bold Ones, Marcus Welby M.D., The Six Million Dollar Man. Movies: The Rockford Files (pilot), The Incredible Journey of Dr. Meg Laurel, The Two Worlds of Jennie Logan, Callie and Son, Memories Never Die, I Want to Live, Princess Daisy, Two Kinds of Love, Passions, This Child Is Mine, Child's Cry, Convicted, Young Again, Stranger in My Bed, The Return of the Six Million Dollar Man and the Bionic Woman, Student Exchange, Evil in Clear River, The Taking of Flight 847, Nightmare at Bitter Creek, From the Dead of Night, The Bionic Showdown: The Six-Million Dollar Man and the Bionic Woman, Shattered Dreams, Babies, Fire in the Dark, She Woke Up, Treacherous Crossing, To Be the Best, A Message From Holly, Nurses on the Line: The Crash of Flight 7, Danielle Steel's Once in a Lifetime, Bionic Ever After?, Fighting for My Daughter, Their, Second Chance, Contagious, Sins of Silence, A Mother's Instinct.

WAGNER, RAYMOND JAMES
Producer. b. College Point, NY, Nov. 3, 1925. e. Middlebury Coll., Williams Coll. Joined Young & Rubicam, Inc., as radio-TV commercial head in Hollywood, 1950-59. Head of pilot devt., Universal Studios, 1960-65. V.P. of prod. (features) for MGM, 1972-79. Presently indt. prod.
PICTURES: Prod.: Petulia, Loving (exec. prod.), Code of Silence, Rent-a-Cop, Hero and the Terror, Turner and Hooch, Run, Fifty Fifty.

WAGNER, ROBERT
Actor. b. Detroit, MI, Feb. 10, 1930. e. Saint Monica's H.S. m. actress Jill St. John. Signed to contract with 20th Century-Fox, 1950.
PICTURES: The Happy Years (debut, 1950), The Halls of Montezuma, The Frogmen, Let's Make It Legal, With a Song in My Heart, What Price Glory?, Stars and Stripes Forever, The Silver Whip, Titanic, Beneath the 12-Mile Reef, Prince Valiant, Broken Lance, White Feather, A Kiss Before Dying, The Mountain, Between Heaven and Hell, The True Story of Jesse James, Stopover Tokyo, The Hunters, In Love and War, Say One for Me, All the Fine Young Cannibals, Sail a Crooked Ship, The Longest Day, The War Lover, The Condemned of Altona, The Pink Panther, Harper, Banning, The Biggest Bundle of Them All, Don't Just Stand There, Winning, The Towering Inferno, Midway, The Concorde—Airport '79, Trail of the Pink Panther, Curse of the Pink Panther, I Am the Cheese, Delirious, The Player, Dragon: The Bruce Lee Story, Austin Powers.
TELEVISION: Series: It Takes A Thief, Colditz (UK), Switch, Hart to Hart, Lime Street. Movies: How I Spent My Summer Vacation, City Beneath the Sea, The Cable Car Murder, Killer by Night, Madame Sin (also exec. prod.), Streets of San Francisco (pilot), The Affair, The Abduction of St. Anne, Switch (pilot), Death at Love House, Cat on a Hot Tin Roof, The Critical List, Hart to Hart (pilot), To Catch a King, There Must Be a Pony, Love Among Thieves, Windmills of the Gods, Indiscreet, This Gun for Hire,

False Arrest, Daniel Steel's Jewels, Deep Trouble, Hart to Hart Returns (also co-exec. prod.), Hart to Hart: Home is Where the Hart Is, Hart to Hart: Crimes of the Hart, Hart to Hart: Old Friends Never Die, Parallel Lives, Hart to Hart: Secrets of the Heart. Mini-Series: Pearl, Around the World in 80 Days, Heaven & Hell: North and South Book III.

WAHL, KEN
Actor, Producer. b. Chicago, IL, Feb. 14, 1957. No acting experience when cast in The Wanderers in 1978.
PICTURES: The Wanderers (debut, 1979), Fort Apache The Bronx, Race to the Yankee Zephyr, Jinxed, The Soldier, Purple Hearts, The Omega Syndrome, The Taking of Beverly Hills (also co-exec. prod.), The Favor, Back in the U.S.A.
TELEVISION: Movies: The Dirty Dozen: The Next Mission, The Gladiator, Search for Grace, Wise Guy. Series: Double Dare, Wiseguy.

WAITE, RALPH
Actor. b. White Plains, NY, June 22, 1929. e. Bucknell U.; Yale U. Social worker, publicity dir., assistant editor and minister before turning to acting. Founder of the Los Angeles Actors Theatre.
THEATER: B'way: Hogan's Goat, The Watering Place, Trial of Lee Harvey Oswald. Off-B'way: The Destiny of Me, The Young Man From Atlanta. Regional: Hometown Heroes.
PICTURES: Cool Hand Luke, A Lovely Way to Die, Last Summer, Five Easy Pieces, Lawman, The Grissom Gang, The Sporting Club, The Pursuit of Happiness, Chato's Land, The Magnificent Seven Ride, Trouble Man, Kid Blue, The Stone Killer, On the Nickel (also dir., prod., s.p.), Crash and Burn, The Bodyguard, Cliffhanger, Sioux City, Homeward Bound II: Lost in San Francisco.
TELEVISION: Series: The Waltons, The Mississippi. Movies: The Secret Life of John Chapman, The Borgia Stick, Red Alert, Ohms, Angel City, The Gentleman Bandit, A Wedding on Waltons Mountain, Mother's Day on Waltons Mountain, A Day for Thanks on Waltons Mountain, A Good Sport, Crime of Innocence, Red Earth White Earth, A Walton Thanksgiving Reunion, Sin and Redemption, A Season of Hope, A Walton Wedding. Mini-Series: Roots.

WAITE, RIC
Cinematographer. b. Sheboygan, WI, July 10, 1933. e. Univ. of CO. Photographed more than 40 movies-of-the-week for TV, 1979-83.
PICTURES: The Other Side of the Mountain (debut, 1975), Defiance, On the Nickel, The Long Riders, The Border, Tex, 48 Hrs., Class, Uncommon Valor, Footloose, Red Dawn, Volunteers, Summer Rental, Brewster's Millions, Cobra, Adventures in Babysitting, The Great Outdoors, Marked for Death, Out for Justice, Rapid Fire, On Deadly Ground, Last Stand at Saber River, Truth or Consequences—N.M.
TELEVISION: Nakia, The November Plan, Captains and the Kings (Emmy Award, 1977), Tail Gunner Joe (Emmy nom.), Huey P. Long (Emmy nom.), The Initiation of Sarah, And Baby Makes Six, Revenge of the Stepford Wives, Baby Comes Home, Dempsey, Police Story: Burnout, Scam, Last Light, Andersonville, Money Plays, Hope, Andersonville (Emmy nom.), Last Stand at Saber River.

WAITS, TOM
Singer, Composer, Actor. b. Pomona, CA, Dec. 7, 1949. Recorded numerous albums and received Acad. Award nom. for his song score of One from the Heart. Composed songs for On the Nickel, Streetwise, Paradise Alley, Wolfen, American Heart, Dead Man Walking, Night on Earth (score). Featured songs in Smoke and Things to Do in Denver When You're Dead. Has starred in Chicago's Steppenwolf Theatre Co.'s Frank's Wild Years (also co-wrote, wrote the music) and Los Angeles Theatre Co.'s Demon Wine. Wrote songs and music for opera The Black Rider (1990). Co-wrote songs and music for opera Alice by Robert Wilson. Received Grammy Award for album, Bone Machine, 1992.
PICTURES: As actor: Paradise Alley, Poetry in Motion, The Outsiders, Rumble Fish, The Cotton Club, Down by Law (also music), Ironweed, Candy Mountain, Big Time (also co-s.p.), Cold Feet, Bearskin, Night On Earth (music only), The Two Jakes, Queens Logic, The Fisher King, At Play in the Fields of the Lord, Bram Stoker's Dracula, Short Cuts.

WAJDA, ANDRZEJ
Director, Writer. b. Suwalki, Poland, March 6, 1926. e. Fine Arts Academy, Krakow, Poland, 1945-48; High School of Cinematography, Lodz, Poland, 1950-52. 1940-43, worked as asst. in restoration of church paintings. 1942, joined Polish gov. in exile's A.K. (Home Army Resistance) against German occupation. 1950-52, directed shorts (While You Sleep; The Bad Boy, The Pottery of Ilzecka) as part of film school degree; 1954, asst. dir. to Aleksander Ford on 5 Boys from Barska Street. 1981, concentrated on theatrical projects in Poland and film prods. with non-Polish studios. 1983, gov. dissolved his Studio X film prod. group. 1984, gov. demanded Wajda's resignation as head of filmmakers' assoc. in order to continue org.'s existence. 1989, appt. artistic dir. of Teatr Powszechny, official Warsaw theater. Also leader of the Cultural Comm. of the Citizen's Committee. 1989, elected senator. Short films: While You Sleep, The Bad Boy, The Pottery of Ilza, I Go to the Sun.

PICTURES: *Dir.-Writer:* A Generation (debut, 1957), Kanal, Ashes and Diamonds, Lotna, Innocent Sorcerers, Samson, Siberian Lady Macbeth (Fury Is a Woman), Love at 20 (Warsaw Poland episode), Ashes, Gates to Paradise, Everything for Sale, Hunting Flies, Landscape After the Battle, The Wedding, Promised Land, Shadow Line, Man of Marble, Without Anesthetic, The Girls From Wilko, The Orchestra Conductor, Man of Iron (Golden Palm Award, Cannes, 1981), Danton, A Love in Germany, Chronicle of Love Affairs, The Possessed, Korczak.
TELEVISION: Roly-Poly, The Birch Wood, Pilate and the Others, The Dead Class, November Night, Crime and Punishment.

WALD, MALVIN
Writer, Producer. b. New York, NY, Aug. 8, 1917. e. Brooklyn Coll., B.A., J.D. Woodland U. Coll. of Law; grad. work Columbia U., NYU, USC. Newspaper reporter, editor, publicist, social worker, radio actor. Screenplays and original stories for Columbia, 20th-Fox, UA, MGM, WB. U.S. Air Force tech. sgt., wrote 30 doc. films for film unit. Exec. prod., 20th Century Fox tv doc. unit, 1963-64. Writer-prod. U.S.I.A., 1964-65. Writer-prod., Ivan Tors Films, 1965-69. Prof., USC Sch. of Cinema, TV, 1956-96. Bd. of dir., Writer's Guild of America; 1983-85, Trustee, Writers Guild Foundation. Edit. bd. WGA Journal, 1996; editorial bd., Creative Screenwriting, 1996. Acad. of Motion Picture Arts and Sciences, co-author of book, Three Major Screenplays. Contributor to books, American Screenwriters, The Search for Reality, Close-Ups, Henry Miller: A Book of Tributes, Tales From the Casting Couch. Published s.p., Naked City. Consultant, Natl. Endowment for Humanities and Corp. for Public Broadcasting. Visiting professor, Southern Illinois Univ., Univ of PA. Pre-selection judge, Focus writing awards. Media & prod. consultant, Apache Mountain Spirit (PBS). Playwright, ANTA-West, Actors Alley, Rep. Theatre. Co-author, L.A. Press Club 40th Anniversary Show, 1987. Mag. articles published in Film Comment, Journal of Popular Film & TV, Journal of Writers Guild of America, American Heritage, Creative Screenwriting, Directors Guild Magazine, Hollywood: Then and Now, Writers Digest, Producers Guild Magazine, 1991-. Shorts: An Answer, Employees Only (Acad. Award nom.), Boy Who Owned a Melephant (Venice Children's Film Fest. gold medal), Unarmed in Africa, The Policeman, James Weldon Johnson, Me an Alcoholic?, Problem Solving, Managerial Control, UFO—Fact or Fiction? Was admitted to Producers Guild Hall of Fame, 1996.
PICTURES: The Naked City (Acad. Award nom., best story), Behind Locked Doors, The Dark Past, Ten Gentlemen from West Point, The Powers Girl, Two in a Taxi, Undercover Man, Outrage, On the Loose, Battle Taxi, Man on Fire, Al Capone, Venus in Furs, In Search of Historic Jesus, Legend of Sleepy Hollow, Mysteries From Beyond Earth.
TELEVISION: Many credits including Playhouse 90, Marilyn Monroe, Hollywood: The Golden Years, The Rafer Johnson Story, D-Day, Project: Man in Space, Tales of Hans Christian Andersen, John F. Kennedy, Biography of A Rookie, Alcoa-Goodyear Hour, Climax, Shirley Temple Storybook, Life of Riley, Peter Gunn, Perry Mason, Dobie Gillis, Combat, Moonport (U.S.I.A.; prod., writer), Daktari, (assoc. prod.) Primus, California Tomorrow (prod.), Mod Squad, Untamed World, Around the World of Mike Todd, The Billie Jean King Show, Life and Times of Grizzly Adams, Mark Twain's America, Greatest Heroes of the Bible, Littlest Hobo, Rich Little's You Asked For It, Hugh Hefner's Bunny Memories, Hollywood Commandores, Visiting with Huell Howser.

WALKEN, CHRISTOPHER
Actor. b. Astoria, NY, Mar. 31, 1943. Began career in off-B'way play J.B. billed as Ronnie Walken. Appeared in Madonna video Bad Girl.
THEATER: *NY:* Best Foot Forward (Clarence Derwent Award), Kid Champion (Obie Award), High Spirits (B'way debut, 1964), The Lion in Winter (Clarence Derwent Award), The Rose Tattoo (Theatre World Award), Hurlyburly (B'way), Him (also author). NY Shakespeare Festival: Coriolanus, Othello.
PICTURES: The Anderson Tapes (debut, 1971), The Happiness Cage, Next Stop Greenwich Village, The Sentinel, Annie Hall, Roseland, The Deer Hunter (Academy Award, best supporting actor, 1978), Last Embrace, Heaven's Gate, The Dogs of War, Shoot the Sun Down, Pennies from Heaven, Brainstorm, The Dead Zone, A View to a Kill, At Close Range, Deadline, The Milagro Beanfield War, Biloxi Blues, Puss in Boots, Homeboy, Communion, King of New York, The Comfort of Strangers, McBain, All-American Murder, Batman Returns, Mistress, Le Grand Pardon, Day of Atonement, True Romance, Wayne's World 2, A Business Affair, Pulp Fiction, Search and Destroy, The Prophecy, The Addiction, Wild Side, Things to Do in Denver When You're Dead, Nick of Time, The Funeral, Last Man Standing, Touch, Excess Baggage, Suicide Kings.
TELEVISION: *Movies:* Sarah: Plain and Tall, Skylark, Scam. *Special:* Who Am I This Time? *Guest:* Saturday Night Live.

WALKER, E. CARDON
Executive. b. Rexburg, ID, Jan. 9, 1916. e. UCLA, B.A. 1938. Four years officer, U.S. Navy. Started with Walt Disney Productions, camera, story, unit dir. short subjects, budget control, 1938; headed adv. & pub.; 1950; v.p. in chg. of adv. & sales, 1956; member bd. of dir. & exec. comm., 1960; v.p., mkt., 1965; exec. v.p. operations, 1967; exec. v.p. and COO, 1968; pres., 1971; pres. and CEO, 1976; named bd. chmn. & CEO, 1980; chmn. of exec. committee, 1983-84. Remains a bd. member.

WALKER, KATHRYN
Actress. b. Philadelphia, PA, Jan. 9. e. Wells Coll., Harvard. m. singer-songwriter James Taylor. Studied acting at London Acad. of Music and Dramatic Art on Fulbright Fellowship. Stage roles include part in Private Lives with Elizabeth Taylor and Richard Burton, and Wild Honey with Ian McKellen.
PICTURES: Slap Shot, Rich Kids, Neighbors, D.A.R.Y.L., Dangerous Game, Emma and Elvis.
TELEVISION: *Series:* Beacon Hill. *Movies:* The Winds of Kitty Hawk, Too Far to Go, FDR: The Last Year, A Whale for the Killing, Family Reunion, Special Bulletin, The Murder of Mary Phagan. *Mini-Series:* The Adams Chronicles (Emmy Award, 1976).

WALKER, SHIRLEY
Composer.
PICTURES: *Composer:* The End of August, Touched, Violated, Ghoulies, The Dungeonmaster, Batman (mus. conductor only), Immediate Family (mus. conductor only), Strike It Rich, Chicago Joe and the Showgirl, Nightbreed, Days of Thunder, Born to Ride, Memoirs of an Invisible Man, A League of Their Own (mus. conductor only), Batman: Mask of the Phantasm, It Came from Outer Space II, John Carpenter's Escape from L.A., Turbulence (also mus. conductor). *Orchestration:* The Accused, Black Rain, Arachnophobia, Defending Your Life, The Butcher's Wife, Backdraft (also mus. conductor), Johnny Mnemonic (also mus. conductor).
TELEVISION: *Movie:* The Flash, Majority Rule, Rasputin, (mus. conductor), The Garbage Picking Field Goal, Kicking Philadelphia Phenomenon. *Series:* The Flash, Batman: The Animated Series, Space: Above and Beyond, Superman, Spawn. *Mini-series:* Asteroid.

WALLACE, MIKE
TV Commentator, Interviewer. b. Brookline, MA, May 9, 1918. e. U. of Michigan, 1939. Night Beat, WABD, N.Y., 1956; The Mike Wallace Interview, ABC, 1956-58; newspaper col., Mike Wallace Asks, N.Y. Post, 1957-58; News Beat, WNTA-TV, 1959-61; The Mike Wallace Interview, WNTA-TV, 1959-61; Biography, 1962; correspondent, CBS News, 1963, CBS Radio; Personal Closeup, Mike Wallace at Large; Co-editor, 60 Minutes (Emmy Awards, 1971, 1972, 1973), CBS News, Host, 20th Century, 1994.

WALLACH, ELI
Actor. b. Brooklyn, NY, Dec. 7, 1915. e. U. of TX. m. actress Anne Jackson. Capt. in Medical Admin. Corps during WWII. After college acting, appeared in summer stock. Charter member of the Actors Studio.
THEATER: Skydrift (B'way debut, 1945), Antony & Cleopatra, The Rose Tattoo (Tony Award, 1951), Mademoiselle Colombe, Camino Real, The Teahouse of August Moon (also London), Major Barbara, Rhinoceros, Luv, Twice Around the Park, Cafe Crown, The Price, In Persons (Off-B'way), The Flowering Peach, Visiting Mr. Green.
PICTURES: Baby Doll (debut, 1956; BFA Award), The Line Up, The Magnificent Seven, Seven Thieves, The Misfits, Hemingway's Adventures of A Young Man, How the West Was Won, The Victors, Act One, The Moonspinners, Kisses for My President, Lord Jim, Genghis Khan, How to Steal a Million, The Good the Bad and the Ugly, The Tiger Makes Out, How to Save a Marriage and Ruin Your Life, MacKenna's Gold, A Lovely Way to Die, Ace High, The Brain, Zigzag, The People Next Door, The Angle Levine, The Adventures of Gerard, Romance of a Horse Thief, Cinderella Liberty, Crazy Joe, Stateline Motel, Don't Turn the Other Cheek, The Sentinel, Nasty Habits, The Deep, The Domino Principle, Girlfriends, Movie Movie, Circle of Iron, Firepower, Winter Kills, The Hunter, The Salamander, Sam's Son, Tough Guys, Nuts, Funny, The Two Jakes, The Godfather Part III, Article 99, Mistress, Night and the City, Two Much, The Associate.
TELEVISION: *Series:* Our Family Honor. *Guest:* Studio One, Philco Playhouse, Playhouse 90, The Poppy Is Also a Flower (Emmy Award, 1967), Law & Order. *Movies:* Cold Night's Death, Indict and Convict, Seventh Avenue, The Pirate, Fugitive Family, Pride of Jesse Halam, Skokie, The Wall, Anatomy of an Illness, Murder: By Reason of Insanity, Something in Common, Executioner's Song, Christopher Columbus, Embassy, The Impossible Spy, Vendetta: Secrets of a Mafia Bride, Legacy of Lies, Teamster Boss: The Jackie Presser Story, Vendetta 2: The New Mafia.

WALLACH, GEORGE
Producer, Writer, Director. b. New York, NY, Sept. 25, 1918. e. SUNY-Westbury. Actor in theater & radio 1936-45. U.S. Navy 1942-45. Supvr. radio-TV Div. of American Theatrical Wing, 1946-48. Dir., WNEW, 1946-48. Prod./dir., Wendy Barrie Show, 1948-49. Prod.-dir. for WNBC-WNBT, 1950; dir., news, spec. events WNBT-WNBC, 1951-52; prod. mgr., NBC Film Div. 1953-56, appt. TV officer, U.S.I.A., 1957. Film-TV officer American Embassy, Bonn, Germany, 1961; Film-TV officer American Embassy, Tehran, Iran, 1965-66. MoPix Prod. Officer, JUSPAO, American Embassy, Saigon, 1966. Prod., dir.,writer, Greece Today, 1967-68. Exec. prod.,dir., George Wallach Productions, spec. doc., travel, and industrial films. Chmn., Film-TV Dept., N.Y. Institute of Photography, 1968-75. Prof. film-TV-radio, Brooklyn Coll., 1975-80. Dir., special projects, Directors Guild of America 1978-88. Presently: intl. rep. for Denver Film Festival; U.S. Contact for Moscow Film Festival; U.S. prod. for A Native of Beijing in NY, a series of 20 1 hr. programs for Beijing TV.

PICTURES: It Happened in Havana, Bwana Devil (assoc. prod., prod. mgr.).
TELEVISION: *NBC producer*: Inner Sanctum, The Falcon, His Honor Homer Bell, Watch the World. *Dir.*: Wanted.

WALLMAN, KATHLEEN
Attorney. e. Catholic U. of America, BA; Georgetown U, MS, JD. Clerked for various judges on the U.S. Court of Appeals, District of Columbia & Federal Circuits, 1984-86. Became assoc., Arnold & Porter, 1987-92; partner, 1992-94. In 1994, became Deputy Chief, FCC Cable Services Bureau. Chief, FCC Common Carrier Bureau, 1994-95. Deputy Counsel to the President, 1995-97. Deputy Asst. to the Pres. for Economic Policy/Chief of Staff, National Economic Council, 1997.

WALSH, DYLAN
Actor. Raised in Africa, Indonesia, India, Washington D.C. e. Univ. of VA. On D.C. stage with Arena Stage and Studio Theatre, Heritage Rep. Co. Appearing in A Midsummer Night's Dream, Curse of the Starving Class, Romeo & Juliet, Death of a Salesman.
PICTURES: Where the Heart Is, Betsy's Wedding, Arctic Blue, Nobody's Fool, Congo, Eden, Changing Habits, Men.
TELEVISION: *Series*: Gabriel's Fire, Brooklyn South. *Guest*: Kate and Allie. *Movies*: Telling Secrets, Radio Inside.

WALSH, J.T.
Actor. b. San Francisco, CA. Did not begin acting until age 30, when he quit job in sales to join off-B'way theater co.
THEATER: Glengarry Glen Ross (Drama Desk Award), Rose, Last Licks, Richard III, Macbeth, Half a Lifetime, The American Clock.
PICTURES: Eddie Macon's Run, Hard Choices, Power, Hannah and Her Sisters, Tin Men, House of Games, Good Morning Vietnam, Things Change, Tequila Sunrise, Wired, The Big Picture, Dad, Crazy People, Why Me?, Narrow Margin, Misery, The Grifters, The Russia House, Backdraft, Defenseless, True Identity, Iron Maze, A Few Good Men, Hoffa, Sniper, National Lampoon's Loaded Weapon 1, Red Rock West, Needful Things, Morning Glory, Blue Chips, The Client, Miracle on 34th Street, Outbreak, The Low Life, Nixon, Executive Decision, The Babysitter, Black Day Blue Night, Breakdown.
TELEVISION: *Movies*: Little Gloria: Happy at Last, Jacobo Timerman: Prisoner Without a Name Cell Without a Number, Right to Kill, Tough Cookies, Windmills of the Gods, In the Shadow of a Killer, The American Clock, The Last Seduction, Against Their Will: Women in Prison, Crime of the Century. *Special*: Partners.
(d. Feb. 27, 1998)

WALSH, M. EMMET
Actor. r.n. Michael Emmet Walsh. b. Ogdensburg, NY, Mar. 22, 1935. e. Clarkson Col. (B.B.A., 1958), American Academy of Dramatic Arts (1959-61).
THEATER: *B'way*: Does the Tiger Wear a Necktie?, That Championship Season. *Off-B'way*: Shepherds of the Shelf, The Old Glory, The Outside Man, Death of the Well Loved Boy, Three From Column 'A', Are You Now or Have You Ever Been, Marathon '93. Extensive summer stock and regional theatre.
PICTURES: End of the Road, Midnight Cowboy, Alice's Restaurant, Stiletto, Loving, They Might Be Giants, The Traveling Executioner, Little Big Man, Escape from the Planet of the Apes, Get to Know Your Rabbit, The Gambler, The Prisoner of 2nd Avenue, What's Up Doc?, Kid Blue, The Fish That Saved Pittsburgh, Serpico, Mikey and Nicky, Cold Turkey, At Long Last Love, Nickelodeon, Bound for Glory, Airport '77, Slap Shot, Straight Time, The Jerk, Raise the Titanic, Brubaker, Ordinary People, Reds, Back Roads, Fast-Walking, The Escape Artist, Cannery Row, Blade Runner, Silkwood, Blood Simple, Scandalous, (Raw) Courage, Grandview USA, The Pope of Greenwich Village, Back to School, Critters, Missing in Action, Fletch, Wildcats, The Best of Times, Raising Arizona, Harry and the Hendersons, The Milagro Beanfield War, No Man's Land, Sunset, War Party, Clean and Sober, Catch Me If You Can, Thunderground, Sundown: The Vampire in Retreat, Chattahoochee, Red Scorpion, The Mighty Quinn, Narrow Margin, Killer Image, The Naked Truth, White Sands, Equinox, Wilder Napalm, The Music of Chance, Bitter Harvest, Cops and Robbersons, Relative Fear, The Glass Shield, Probable Cause, Dead Badge, Camp Nowhere, Panther, Free Willy 2: The Adventure Home, Criminal Hearts, Portraits of a Killer, Albino Alligator, The Killing Jar, A Time to Kill, Romeo & Juliet, Retroactive, Carrot Top—Chairman of the Board, My Best Friend's Wedding, Legal Tender, Twilight, Me and Will, Iron Giant, Jack of Hearts.
TELEVISION: *Series*: The Sandy Duncan Show, Dear Detective, Unsub. *Movies*: Sarah T.—Portrait of a Teenage Alcoholic, Crime Club, Invasion of Johnson County, Red Alert, Superdome, A Question of Guilt, No Other Love, The Gift, Skag, City in Fear, High Noon Part II, Hellinger's Law, Night Partners, The Deliberate Stranger, Resting Place, Broken Vows, Hero in the Family, The Abduction of Kari Swenson, Murder Ordained, Brotherhood of the Rose, Love and Lies, Fourth Story, Wild Card, Four Eyes and Six-Guns, From the Mixed-Up Files of Mrs. Basil E. Frankweiler, The Lottery, Dogs. *Mini-Series*: The French-Atlantic Affair, East of Eden. *Guest*: Julia, Amy Prentiss, The Jimmy Stewart Show, Bonanza, All in the Family, Rockford Files, Baretta, The Waltons, Nichols, Starsky & Hutch, Amazing Stories, Twilight Zone, The Flash, Jackie Thomas Show, Tales From the Crypt, Home Improvement, The Outer Limits, many others. *Pilot*: Silver Fox.

WALSTON, RAY
Actor. b. New Orleans, LA, Nov. 2, 1918. Stage debut in Houston, 1936. To NY where he appeared on stage in South Pacific, The Front Page, Me and Juliet, Damn Yankees (Tony Award, 1956).
PICTURES: Kiss Them For Me (debut, 1957), South Pacific, Damn Yankees, Say One for Me, Tall Story, The Apartment, Portrait in Black, Convicts Four, Wives and Lovers, Who's Minding the Store?, Kiss Me Stupid, Caprice, Paint Your Wagon, The Sting, Silver Streak, The Happy Hooker Goes to Washington, Popeye, Galaxy of Terror, Fast Times at Ridgemont High, O'Hara's Wife, Private School, Johnny Dangerously, RAD, From the Hip, O.C. and Stiggs, A Man of Passion, Blood Relations, Saturday the 14th Strikes Back, Paramedics, Ski Patrol, Blood Salvage, Popcorn, The Player, Of Mice and Men, House Arrest.
TELEVISION: *Series*: My Favorite Martian, Stop Susan Williams (Cliffhangers), Silver Spoons, Fast Times, Picket Fences (Emmy Awards, 1995 & 1996). *Guest*: You Are There, Producers Showcase, There Shall Be No Night, Studio One, Playhouse 90, On Madeline, Crash Course. *Movies*: Institute for Revenge, The Kid With the Broken Halo, The Fall of the House of Usher, This Girl for Hire, The Jerk Too, Amos, Red River, I Know My First Name Is Steven, One Special Victory. *Mini-Series*: Stephen King's The Stand.

WALTER, JESSICA
Actress. b. Brooklyn, NY, Jan. 31, 1944. m. actor Ron Leibman. e. H.S. of the Performing Arts. Studied at Bucks County Playhouse and Neighborhood Playhouse. Many TV performances plus lead in series, For the People. Broadway debut in Advise and Consent, 1961. Also, Photo Finish (Clarence Derwent Award), Night Life, A Severed Head, Rumors.
PICTURES: Lilith (debut, 1964), The Group, Grand Prix, Bye Bye Braverman, Number One, Play Misty for Me, Goldengirl, Going Ape, Spring Fever, The Flamingo Kid, Tapeheads, Ghost in the Machine.
TELEVISION: *Series*: For the People, Love of Life, Amy Prentiss (Emmy Award, 1975), Bare Essence, Aaron's Way, Dinosaurs (voice), The Round Table, One Life to Live. *Movies*: The Immortal (pilot), Three's a Crowd, They Call It Murder, Women in Chains, Home for the Holidays, Hurricane, Having Babies, Victory at Entebbe, Black Market Baby, Wild and Wooly, Dr. Strange, Secrets of Three Hungry Wives, Vampire, She's Dressed to Kill, Miracle on Ice, Scruples, Thursday's Child, The Return of Marcus Welby M.D., The Execution, Killer in the Mirror, Leave of Absence, Mother Knows Best, Doomsday Rock. *Mini-Series*: Wheels.

WALTER, TRACEY
Actor. b. Jersey City, NJ, Nov. 25.
PICTURES: Goin' South, Blue Collar, Hardcore, The Hunter, The Hand, Raggedy Man, Honkytonk Man, Timerider, Rumble Fish, Conan the Destroyer, Repo Man, At Close Range, Something Wild, Malone, Mortuary Academy, Married to the Mob, Under the Boardwalk, Out of the Dark, Batman, Homer and Eddie, Young Guns II, The Two Jakes, Pacific Heights, The Silence of the Lambs, City Slickers, Delusion, Amos and Andrew, Philadelphia, Mona Must Die, Destiny Turns on the Radio, Wild America, Road to Ruin, Dorothy Day, Junior, Amanda, Larger Than Life, Matilda, Desperate Measures, Playing God, Kiss the Girls, Beloved.
TELEVISION: *Series*: Best of the West, On the Air, Nash Bridges. *Movies*: Ride With the Wind, In the Line of Duty: Kidnapped, Buffalo Girls, Bill On His Own, Mad Bull, Out of this World, Tell Me No Secrets, The Devil's Child.

WALTERS, BARBARA
Broadcast Journalist. b. Boston, MA, Sept. 25, 1931. e. Sarah Lawrence Coll. Daughter of Latin Quarter nightclub impressario Lou Walters. Began working in TV after graduation. Joined the Today Show in 1961 as writer-researcher, making occasional on-camera appearances. In 1963, became full-time on camera. In April, 1974, named permanent co-host. Also hosted own synd. prog., Not for Women Only. In 1976, joined ABC-TV Evening News, (host, 1976-78), correspondent World News Tonight (1978); corresp. 20/20 (1979-present). Host of The Barbara Walters Specials (1979-present). Author: How to Talk with Practically Anybody About Practically Anything (1970). Recipient of numerous awards including Emmy, Media, Peabody. Named one of women most admired by American People in 1982 & -84 Gallup Polls. Inducted into the Television Academy Hall of Fame, 1990. 1994, co-anchor of Turning Point.

WALTERS, JULIE
Actress. b. Birmingham, England, Feb. 22, 1950. Trained for 2 years to be a nurse before studying drama at Manchester Polytechnic, followed by year at Granada's Stables Theatre. Joined Everyman Theatre, Liverpool. Also toured Dockland pubs with songs, dance and imitations.
THEATER: Breezeblock Park, Funny Perculiar, The Glad Hand, Good Fun, Educating Rita, Jumpers, Fool for Love, When I Was a Girl I Used to Scream and Shout, Frankie and Johnnie in the Claire de Lune, Macbeth, Having a Ball, The Rose Tattoo, Jumpers, Fool for Love, When I Was a Girl I Used to Scream and Shout, Frankie and Johnny.
PICTURES: Educating Rita (debut, 1983; Acad. Award nom.), She'll Be Wearing Pink Pyjamas, Car Trouble, Personal Services, Prick Up Your Ears, Buster, Mack the Knife, Killing Dad, Stepping Out, Wide Eyed and Legless, The Summer House, The Wedding Gift, Just Like a Woman, Sister My Sister.

TELEVISION: Unfair Exchanges, Talent, Nearly a Happy Ending, Family Man, Happy Since I Met You, The Secret Diary of Adrian Mole (series), Wood and Walters (series), Say Something Happened, Intensive Care, The Boys from the Black Stuff, Talking Heads, Victoria Wood As Seen on TV (series & special), The Birthday Party, Her Big Chance, Nearly a Happy Ending, Julie Walters & Friends (special), GBH (series), The All-Day Breakfast Show (special).

WANG, WAYNE
Director. b. Hong Kong, 1949. e. came to U.S. to study photography at College of Arts and Crafts, Oakland, CA. m. actress Cora Miao. With a Master's Degree in film and television, returned to Hong Kong. Worked on TV comedy series. First dir. work, as asst. dir. for Chinese sequences of Golden Needle. First film was A Man, A Woman and a Killer. Won grant from AFI and National Endowment for the Arts, used to finance Chan is Missing (1982) which cost $22,000.
PICTURES: Chan is Missing (also s.p., editor, prod.), Dim Sum: A Little Bit of Heart (also prod., story), Slam Dance, Eat a Bowl of Tea, Life is Cheap... But Toilet Paper is Expensive (also exec. prod., story), The Joy Luck Club, Smoke, Blue in the Face (also co-s.p.).

WARD, DAVID S.
Writer, Director. b. Providence, RI, Oct. 24, 1947. Raised in Cleveland. e. Pomona Col. (BA), UCLA (MFA).
PICTURES: Writer: Steelyard Blues, The Sting (Academy Award, 1973), Cannery Row (also dir.), The Milagro Beanfield War (co-s.p.), Major League (also dir.), King Ralph (also dir.), Sleepless in Seattle (co-s.p.; Acad. Award nom.), The Program (also dir.), Major League 2 (dir.). Director: Major League II, Down Periscope.

WARD, FRED
Actor. b. San Diego, CA, 1943. Raised in Louisiana and Texas. Studied at Herbert Berghof Studio. Moved to Rome to work in experimental theatre. Returned to U.S. to appear on San Fransico stage with Sam Shepard's Magic Theatre in Inacoma and Angel City. Additional stage work in The Glass Menagerie, One Flew Over the Cuckoo's Nest, Domino Courts, Simpatico.
PICTURES: Escape From Alcatraz (debut, 1979), Tilt, Carny, Southern Comfort, Timerider, The Right Stuff, Silkwood, Uncommon Valor, Swing Shift, Uforia, Secret Admirer, Remo Williams: The Adventure Begins, Off Limits, Big Business, The Prince of Pennsylvania, Tremors, Miami Blues (also co-exec. prod.), Henry and June, Thunderheart, The Player, Bob Roberts, The Dark Wind, Equinox, Short Cuts, Naked Gun 33 1/3: The Final Insult, Two Small Bodies, The Blue Villa, Chain Reaction.
TELEVISION: Movies: Belle Starr, Noon Wine, Florida Straits, Cast a Deadly Spell, Backtrack, Four Eyes and Six-Guns. Special: Noon Wine (Amer. Playhouse), First Do No Harm.

WARD, RACHEL
Actress. b. London, 1957. m. actor Bryan Brown. Top fashion and TV commercial model before becoming actress. Studied acting with Stella Adler and Robert Modica. On stage in Sydney in A Doll's House, Hopping to Byzantium.
PICTURES: Night School (debut, 1981), The Final Terror, Sharky's Machine, Dead Men Don't Wear Plaid, Against All Odds, The Good Wife, Hotel Colonial, How to Get Ahead in Advertising, After Dark My Sweet, Christopher Columbus: The Discovery, Wide Sargasso Sea, The Ascent.
TELEVISION: Mini-Series: The Thorn Birds, Shadow of the Cobra (U.K.). Movies: Christmas Lillies of the Field, Fortress, And the Sea Will Tell, Black Magic, Double Jeopardy.

WARD, SELA
Actress. b. Meridian, MS, July 11, 1956.
PICTURES: The Man Who Loved Women, Rustler's Rhapsody, Nothing in Common, Steel Justice, Hello Again, The Fugitive, My Fellow Americans.
TELEVISION: Series: Emerald Point N.A.S., Sisters (Emmy Award, 1994). Movies: Almost Golden: The Jessica Savitch Story (Cable Ace Award, 1996), The Haunting of Sarah Hardy, Bridesmaids, Killer Rules, Double Jeopardy.

WARD, SIMON
Actor. b. London, England, Oct. 19, 1941. Ent. ind. 1964.
PICTURES: If... (debut, 1969), Frankenstein Must Be Destroyed, I Start Counting, Quest for Love, Young Winston, Hitler—The Last Ten Days, The Three Musketeers, The Four Musketeers, Deadly Strangers, Aces High, Children of Rage, Battle Flag, The Chosen, Dominique, Zulu Dawn, La Sabina, The Monster Club, L'Etincelle, Supergirl, Leave All Fair, Double X, Wuthering Heights.
TELEVISION: Spoiled, Chips with Everything, The Corsican Brothers, All Creatures Great and Small, Dracula, Valley Forge, The Last Giraffe (Raising Daisy Rothschild), Around the World in 80 Days.

WARD, VINCENT
Director, Writer. b. New Zealand, 1956. e. Ilam Sch. of Art. At 21 dir. & co-wrote short film A State of Siege (Hugo Award, Chicago Film Fest.)
PICTURES: In Spring One Plants Alone (Silver Hugo, Chicago Film Fest.), Vigil (Grand Prix Awards, Madrid & Prades Film Fests), The Navigator (Australian Film Awards for Best Picture & Director), Alien^3 (story only), Map of the Human Heart, Leaving Las Vegas (actor only), The Shot (actor only), One Night Stand (actor only), What Dreams May Come.

WARDEN, JACK
Actor. b. Newark, NJ, Sept. 18, 1920. r.n. Jack Warden Lebzelter. Started with Margo Jones theatre in Dallas (rep. co.).
THEATER: B'way: Golden Boy, Sing Me No Lullaby, Very Special Baby, Cages (Obie Award), A View from the Bridge, The Man in the Glass Booth, The Body Beautiful. Repertory: Twelfth Night, She Stoops to Conquer, The Importance of Being Earnest, Summer and Smoke, The Taming of the Shrew, etc.
PICTURES: You're in the Navy Now (U.S.S. Teakettle; debut, 1951), The Frogmen, The Man With My Face, Red Ball Express, From Here to Eternity, Edge of the City, 12 Angry Men, The Bachelor Party, Darby's Rangers, Run Silent Run Deep, The Sound and the Fury, That Kind of Woman, Wake Men When It's Over, Escape From Zahrain, Donovan's Reef, The Thin Red Line, Blindfold, Bye Bye Braverman, The Sporting Club, Summertree, Who Is Harry Kellerman?, Welcome to the Club, Billy Two Hats, The Man Who Loved Cat Dancing, The Apprenticeship of Duddy Kravitz, Shampoo (Acad. Award nom.), All the President's Men, The White Buffalo, Heaven Can Wait (Acad. Award nom.), Death on the Nile, The Champ, Dreamer, Beyond the Poseidon Adventure, And Justice for All, Being There, Used Cars, The Great Muppet Caper, Chu Chu and the Philly Flash, Carbon Copy, So Fine, The Verdict, Crackers, The Aviator, September, The Presidio, Everybody Wins, Problem Child, Problem Child 2, Passed Away, Night and the City, Toys, Guilty As Sin, Bullets Over Broadway, While You Were Sleeping, Things to Do in Denver When You're Dead, Mighty Aphrodite, Ed.
TELEVISION: Series: Mr. Peepers, Norby, The Asphalt Jungle, The Wackiest Ship in the Army, N.Y.P.D., Jigsaw John, The Bad News Bears, Crazy Like a Fox. Guest: Philco Goodyear Producer's Showcase, Kraft. Movies: The Face of Fear, Brian's Song (Emmy Award, 1972), What's a Nice Girl Like You...?, Man on a String, Lt. Schuster's Wife, Remember When, The Godchild, Journey From Darkness, They Only Come Out at Night, Raid on Entebbe, Topper, A Private Battle, Hobson's Choice, Helen Keller: The Miracle Continues, Hoover vs. The Kennedys, The Three Kings, Dead Solid Perfect, Judgment, Problem Child 3: Junior in Love. Mini-Series: Robert Kennedy and His Times, A.D.

WARNER, DAVID
Actor. b. Manchester, England, July 29, 1941. e. Royal Acad. of Dramatic Art. Made London stage debut in Tony Richardson's version of A Midsummer Night's Dream (1962). Four seasons with Royal Shakespeare Co. Theater includes Afore Night Comes, The Tempest, The Wars of the Roses, The Government Inspector, Twelfth Night, I Claudius.
PICTURES: Tom Jones (debut, 1963), Morgan!, The Deadly Affair, A King's Story (voice), Work Is a Four Letter Word, A Midsummer's Night Dream, The Bofors Gun, The Fixer, The Seagull, Michael Kolhaus, The Ballad of Cable Hogue, Perfect Friday, Straw Dogs, A Doll's House, From Beyond the Grave, Little Malcolm (and His Struggle Against the Eunuch), Mr. Quilp, The Omen, Providence, The Disappearance, Cross of Iron, Silver Bears, Nightwing, The Concorde—Airport '79, Time After Time, The 39 Steps, The Island, The French Lieutenant's Woman, Time Bandits, Tron, The Man With Two Brains, The Company of Wolves, Hansel and Gretel, My Best Friend Is a Vampire, Waxworks, Mr. North, Silent Night, Office Party, Hanna's War, Pulse Pounders, Keys to Freedom, Star Trek V: The Final Frontier, S.P.O.O.K.S., Tripwire, Mortal Passions, Teenage Mutant Ninja Turtles II: The Secret of the Ooze, Star Trek VI: The Undiscovered Country, Blue Tornado, Drive, Unnameable II, Dark at Noon, In the Mouth of Madness.
TELEVISION: Movies: S.O.S. Titantic, Desperado, A Christmas Carol, Hitler's SS—Portrait in Evil, Perry Mason: The Case of the Poisoned Pen, The Secret Life of Ian Fleming, Cast a Deadly Spell, The House on Sycamore Street, Perry Mason: The Case of the Skin-Deep Scandal, John Carpenter Presents Body Bags, Danielle Steel's Zoya. Mini-Series: Holocaust, Masada (Emmy Award, 1981), Marco Polo, Wild Palms. Specials: Love's Labour's Lost, Uncle Vanya.

WARNER, JULIE
Actress. b. New York, NY. e. Brown Univ., B.A. in Theatre Arts.
PICTURES: Doc Hollywood (debut, 1991), Mr. Saturday Night, Indian Summer, The Puppet Masters, Tommy Boy, White Lies, Wedding Bell Blues.
TELEVISION: Series: Pride and Joy. Guest: Star Trek: The Next Generation, 21 Jump Street, The Outsiders.

WARNER, MALCOLM-JAMAL
Actor. b. Jersey City, NJ, Aug. 18, 1970. Raised in Los Angeles. Was 13 years old when signed to play Bill Cosby's son on The Cosby Show.
THEATER: Three Ways Home (off-B'way debut, 1988).
PICTURE: Drop Zone (debut, 1994), Restaurant.
TELEVISION: Series: The Cosby Show (also dir. episode), Here and Now, Magic School Bus (voice), Malcolm & Eddie. Movies: The Father Clements Story, Mother's Day, Tyson. Special: Kids Killing Kids (host).

WARREN, GENE
Executive. b. Denver, CO, Aug. 12, 1916. Pres. of Excelsior Prods., prod. co. specializing in special effects and animation. Has headed 2 other cos. of similar nature over past 20 years, functioning at various times as prod., dir., studio prod. head and writer. Prod., dir., of following shorts: The Tool Box, Suzy Snowflake, Santa and the

Three Dwarfs, Land of the Midnight Sun and these documentaries/training films: Mariner I, Mariner III, Apollo, U.S. Navy titles. Special effects on theatrical features incl: Black Sunday, tom thumb, The Time Machine (Academy Award, 1960), The Wonderful World of the Brothers Grimm, 7 Faces of Dr. Lao, The Power, Legend of Hillybilly John. TV series include: The Man from Atlantis, Land of the Lost, Star Trek, Outer Limits, Twilight Zone, Mission Impossible. *TV Movie:* Satan's School for Girls.

WARREN, JENNIFER
Actress, Producer. b. New York, NY, Aug. 12, 1941. e. U. of Wisconsin, Madison, B.A. Graduate work at Wesleyan U. Studied acting with Uta Hagen at HB Studios. As part of AFI Women's Directing Workshop, directed Point of Departure, short film which received Cine Golden Eagle and Aspen Film Festival Awards. Formed Tiger Rose Productions, indep. film-TV prod. co., 1988. Exec. prod., You Don't Have to Die (Acad. Award, doc. short, 1989). Dir., The Beans of Egypt Maine, 1994. Recipient of 2 Spirit Awards.
THEATER: Scuba Duba (off-B'way debut, 1967), 6 RMS RIV VU (Theatre World Award), Harvey, P.S., Your Cat Is Dead, B'way: Saint Joan, Volpone, Henry V (Guthrie Theatre).
PICTURES: Night Moves (debut, 1975), Slapshot, Another Man Another Chance, Ice Castles, Fatal Beauty.
TELEVISION: *Series:* Paper Dolls. *Pilots:* Double Dare, Knights of the Kitchen Table. *Guest:* Kojak. *Movies:* Banjo Hackett: Roamin' Free, Shark Kill, First You Cry, Steel Cowboy, Champions: A Love Story, Angel City, The Choice, The Intruder Within, Freedom, Paper Dolls (pilot), Confessions of a Married Man, Amazons, Full Exposure: The Sex Tape Scandal. *Mini-Series:* Celebrity.

WARREN, LESLEY ANN
Actress. b. New York, NY, Aug. 16, 1946. Studied acting under Lee Strasberg. Big break came in Rodgers and Hammerstein's 1964 tv prod. of Cinderella, where she was seen by Disney scout. Broadway debut in 110 in the Shade (1963, Theatre World Award), followed by Drat! The Cat! Appeared in Aerosmith video Janie's Got a Gun.
PICTURES: The Happiest Millionaire (debut, 1967), The One and Only Genuine Original Family Band, Pickup on 101, Harry and Walter Go to New York, Victor/Victoria (Acad. Award nom.), A Night in Heaven, Songwriter (Golden Globe nom.), Choose Me, Race to the Yankee Zephyr, Clue, Burglar, Cop, Worth Winning, Life Stinks, Pure Country, Color of Night, Bird of Prey, Natural Enemy, The First Man, 79 Park Avenue (Golden Globe winner).
TELEVISION: *Series:* Mission: Impossible. *Mini-Series:* 79 Park Avenue, Pearl, Evergreen, Family of Spies, Joseph. *Movies:* Seven in Darkness, Love Hate Love, Assignment Munich, The Daughters of Joshua Cabe, The Letters, The Legend of Valentino, Betrayal, Portrait of a Stripper, Beulah Land, Portrait of a Showgirl, A Fight for Jenny, Apology, Baja Oklahoma (Ace Award nom.), A Seduction in Travis County, In Sickness and in Health, Willing to Kill: The Texas Cheerleader Story, A Mother's Revenge, Family of Spies (Emmy nom.), Murderous Intent, 27 Wagons Full of Cotton. *Specials:* The Saga of Sonora, It's a Bird It's a Plane It's Superman, A Special Eddie Rabbit, The Dancing Princess, 27 Wagons Full of Cotton (Ace Award nom.), Willie Nelson: Big Six-O.

WARRICK, RUTH
Actress. b. St. Joseph, MO, June 29, 1916. Started as radio singer. Autobiography: The Confessions of Phoebe Tyler (1980).
PICTURES: Citizen Kane (debut, 1941), Obliging Young Lady, The Corsican Brothers, Journey Into Fear, Forever and a Day, Perilous Holiday, The Iron Major, Secret Command, Mr. Winkle Goes to War, Guest in the House, China Sky, Song of the South, Driftwood, Daisy Kenyon, Arch of Triumph, The Great Dan Patch, Make Believe Ballroom, Three Husbands, Let's Dance, One Too Many, Roogie's Bump, Ride Beyond Vengeance, The Great Bank Robbery, Deathmask, The Returning, The Battle Over Citizen Kane.
TELEVISION: *Movie:* Peyton Place—The Next Generation. *Series:* Peyton Place, All My Children. *Guest:* Studio One, Robert Montgomery Presents, Lux Star Playhouse. *Special:* Sometimes I Don't Love My Mother.

WARZEL, PETER C.
Executive. b. Buffalo, NY, May 31, 1952. e. Univ. of Rochester, Canisius Col. Joined Tele-Communications Inc., 1982, also serving as v.p. of industrial relations at Community Tele-Communications Inc., a TCI subsidiary. 1988, became sr. v.p. of United Artists Entertainment Co.; 1990, promoted to pres. & CEO of United Artists Theatre Circuit. 1992, was party to management buy-out of UATC as pres. & COO.

WASHBURN, DERIC
Writer. b. Buffalo, NY. e.Harvard U., English lit. Has written number of plays, including The Love Nest and Ginger Anne.
PICTURES: Silent Running (co-s.p.), The Deer Hunter (co-s.p.), The Border, Extreme Prejudice.

WASHINGTON, DENZEL
Actor. b. Mt. Vernon, NY, Dec. 28, 1954. e. Fordham U., B.A., journalism. Studied acting with American Conservatory Theatre, San Francisco.

THEATER: When the Chickens Come Home to Roost (Audelco Award), Coriolanus, Spell #7, The Mighty Gents, Ceremonies in Dark Old Men, A Soldier's Play, Checkmates, Richard III.
PICTURES: Carbon Copy (debut, 1981), A Soldier's Story, Power, Cry Freedom (Acad. Award nom.), The Mighty Quinn, For Queen and Country, Glory (Academy Award, best supporting actor, 1989; Golden Globe Award), Heart Condition, Mo' Better Blues, Ricochet, Mississippi Masala, Malcolm X (NY Film Critics Award; Acad. Award nom.), Much Ado About Nothing, Philadelphia, The Pelican Brief, Crimson Tide, Virtuosity, Devil in a Blue Dress, Courage Under Fire, The Preacher's Wife.
TELEVISION: *Movies:* Wilma, Flesh and Blood, License to Kill, The George McKenna Story. *Series:* St. Elsewhere.

WASSERMAN, DALE
Writer, Producer. b. Rhinelander, WI, Nov. 2, 1917. Stage: lighting designer, dir., prod.; dir. for. attractions, S. Hurok; began writing, 1954. Founding member & trustee of O'Neill Theatre Centre; artistic dir. Midwest Playwrights Laboratory; member, Acad. M.P. Arts & Sciences; awards include Emmy, Tony, Critics Circle (Broadway), Outer Circle; Writers Guild.
PICTURES: Cleopatra, The Vikings, The Sea and the Shadow, Quick Before It Melts, Mister Buddwing, A Walk with Love and Death, Man of La Mancha.
TELEVISION: The Fog, The Citadel, The Power and the Glory, Engineer of Death, The Lincoln Murder Case, I Don Quixote, Elisha and the Long Knives, and others.PLAYS: Livin' the Life, 998, One Flew Over the Cuckoo's Nest, The Pencil of God, Man of La Mancha, Play With Fire, Shakespeare and the Indians, Mountain High, Western Star, Green.

WASSERMAN, LEW
Executive. b. Cleveland, OH, March 15, 1913. Natl. dir. advertising and pub., Music Corporation of Amer. 1936-38; v.p. 1938-39; v.p. motion picture div. 1940; chmn. of the bd., CEO, MCA, Inc., Universal City, CA. Named chmn. emeritus of MCA in 1995. Received Jean Hersholt Humanitarian Award, 1973; awarded Presidential Medal of Freedom, 1995.

WASSON, CRAIG
Actor. b. Ontario, OR, March 15, 1954. Also musician/songwriter.
THEATER: Godspell, All God's Chillun Got Wings, Death of a Salesman (also wrote incidental music), Jock, Children of Eden, M. Butterfly, Skin of Our Teeth, The Sisters (Pasadena Playhouse), etc. Wrote incidental music for prod. of The Glass Menagerie and Death of a Salesman.
PICTURES: Rollercoaster, The Boys in Company C (also wrote and performed song Here I Am), Go Tell the Spartans, The Outsider, Carny, Schizoid, Ghost Story, Four Friends, Second Thoughts (also wrote and performed music), Body Double, The Men's Club, A Nightmare on Elm Street 3, The Trackers, Midnight Fear (co-s.p.), Malcolm X, Bum Rap (also wrote and performed music), Velocity Trap, The Debt, Father, The Image Maker, The Outfitters.
TELEVISION: *Series:* Phyllis (also wrote and performed orig. songs), Skag, One Life to Live, The Tomorrow Man. *Guest:* M*A*S*H, Baa Baa Black Sheep, Rockford Files, Hart to Hart, L.A. Law, Kung Fu: The Legend Continues, Dr. Quinn Medicine Woman, Murder She Wrote, Walker Texas Ranger, Deep Space Nine, Dangerous minds, Profiler, The Practice, Touched By an Angel. *Movies:* The Silence, Mrs. R's Daughter, Skag, Thornwell, Why Me?, Strapped, Trapped in Space, The Calvin Mire Story, The Becky Bell Story, Sister in Law, Harvest of Fire, Deep Family Secrets, Seed. *Specials:* A More Perfect Union, Innocents Abroad.

WATANABE, GEDDE
Actor. b. Ogden, UT, June 26. Trained for stage at American Conservatory Theatre, San Francisco. Appeared with N.Y. Shakespeare Fest. Shakespeare in the Park series and with Pan Asian Repertory Theatre, N.Y.
THEATER: Pacific Overtures (debut, as Tree Boy, B'way and on tour, 1976), Bullet Headed Birds, Poor Little Lambs, Dispatches, Music Lesson, Good Person.
PICTURES: Sixteen Candles (debut, 1984), Gremlins, Volunteers, Gung Ho, Vamp, UHF, Boys on the Side, That Thing You Do, Nick and Jane, Booty Call, Mulan (voice).
TELEVISION: *Series:* Gung Ho, E.R.. *Movie:* Miss America: Behind the Crown.

WATERHOUSE, KEITH
Writer. b. Leeds, England, Feb. 6, 1929. Early career as journalist, novelist. Author: There is a Happy Land, Billy Liar, Jubb, The Bucket Shop. Ent. m.p. ind. 1960.
PICTURES: *Writer* (with Willis Hall): Whistle Down the Wind, A Kind of Loving, Billy Liar, Man in the Middle, Pretty Polly, Lock Up Your Daughters, The Valiant, West Eleven.
TELEVISION: *Series:* Inside George Webley, Queenie's Castle, Budgie, Billy Liar, There is a Happy Land, Charters and Caldicott.

WATERS, JOHN
Director, Writer. b. Baltimore, MD, April 22, 1946. First short film Hag in a Black Leather Jacket (1964) shot in Baltimore, as are most of his films. Other shorts include Roman Candles, Eat Your Makeup. Feature debut, Mondo Trasho. Appeared as actor in films Something Wild, Homer and Eddie. On tv in Homicide: Life on the Streets.
PICTURES: Director/Writer/Prod.: Mondo Trasho (also photo., edit.), Multiple Maniacs (also ed., sound), Pink Flamingos (also photo., edit.), Female Trouble (also photo.), Desperate Living, Polyester, Hairspray (also co-prod., actor), Cry-Baby, Serial Mom, Divine Trash (also actor), Anthem (also actor).
TELEVISION: Guest: The Simpsons.

WATERSTON, SAM
Actor. b. Cambridge, MA, Nov. 15, 1940. e. Yale U. Spent jr. year at Sorbonne in Paris as part of the Amer. Actors' Workshop run by American dir. John Berry. Broadway debut in Oh Dad Poor Dad ... (1963). Film debut, The Plastic Dome of Norma Jean (made 1965; unreleased). TV debut Pound (Camera Three). Has worked in New York Shakespeare Festival prods. since As You Like It (1963).
THEATER: N.Y. Shakespeare Festival: As You Like It, Ergo, Henry IV (Part I & II), Cymbeline, Hamlet, Much Ado About Nothing, The Tempest. Off-B'way: The Knack, La Turista, Waiting for Godot, The Three Sisters. B'way: The Paisley Convertible, Halfway Up the Tree, Indian, Hay Fever, The Trial of Cantonsville Nine, A Meeting by the River, Much Ado About Nothing (Drama Desk and Obie Awards), A Doll's House, Lunch Hour, Benefactors, A Walk in the Woods, Abe Lincoln in Illinois.
PICTURES: Fitzwilly, Three, Generation, Cover Me Babe, Mahoney's Estate, Who Killed Mary What's 'er Name?, Savages, The Great Gatsby, Journey Into Fear, Rancho Deluxe, Sweet Revenge, Capricorn One, Interiors, Eagle's Wing, Sweet William, Hopscotch, Heaven's Gate, The Killing Fields, Warning Sign, Hannah and Her Sisters, Just Between Friends, A Certain Desire, The Devil's Paradise, September, Welcome Home, Crimes and Misdemeanors, The Man in the Moon, Mindwalk, A Captive in the Land, Serial Mom, The Journey of August King (also co-prod.), The Proprietor, The Shadow Conspiracy.
TELEVISION: Specials: Pound, Robert Lowell, The Good Lieutenant, Much Ado About Nothing, Oppenheimer, A Walk in the Woods. Movies: The Glass Menagerie, Reflections of Murder, Friendly Fire, Games Mother Never Taught You, In Defense of Kids, Dempsey, Finnegan Begin Again, Love Lives On, The Fifth Missile, The Room Upstairs, Terrorist on Trial: The United States vs. Salim Ajami, Gore Vidal's Lincoln, Lantern Hill, The Shell Seekers, Assault at West Point: The Court-Martial of Johnson Whittaker, David's Mother, The Enemy Within. Mini-Series: The Nightmare Years, The Civil War (voice), Thomas Jefferson, Lewis & Clark. Series: Q.E.D., I'll Fly Away. Guest: Amazing Stories.

WATKIN, DAVID
Director of Photography. b. Margate, England, March 23, 1925. Entered British documentary ind. in Jan., 1948. With British Transport Films as asst. cameraman, 1950 -55; as cameraman, 1955 -61. Feature film debut The Knack beginning long creative relationship with director Richard Lester.
PICTURES: The Knack... and How to Get It (debut, 1965), Help!, Marat/Sade, How I Won the War, The Charge of the Light Brigade, The Bed-Sitting Room, Catch-22, The Devils, The Boyfriend, The Homecoming, A Delicate Balance, The Three Musketeers, The Four Musketeers, Mahogany, To the Devil a Daughter, Robin and Marian, Joseph Andrews, Hanover Street, Cuba, That Summer, Endless Love, Chariots of Fire, Yentl, The Hotel New Hampshire, Return to Oz, White Nights, Out of Africa (Academy Award, 1985), Moonstruck, Sky Bandits, Masquerade, The Good Mother, Last Rites, Journey to the Center of the Earth, Memphis Belle, Hamlet, The Object of Beauty, Used People, This Boy's Life, Bopha!, Milk Money.

WATROS, CYNTHIA
Actress. b. Sept. 2, 1968.
PICTURES: Cafe Society, His and Hers.
TELEVISION: Series: Guiding Light (Emmy Award, 1998), Another World. Guest: Spin City.

WATSON, EMILY
Actor. b. London, England, 1966.
PICTURES: Breaking the Waves (Acad. Award nom., 1997; Golden Globe nom.; NY Society of Film Critics Award; Nat'l Society of Film Critics Award;), Mill on the Floss, Metroland, The Boxer.

WAX, MORTON DENNIS
Public Relations Executive. b. New York, NY, March 13, 1932. e. Brooklyn Coll., 1952. President of Morton Dennis Wax & Assoc., Inc., p.r. and marketing firm servicing int'l creative marketplace, established 1956. Recent PR & Marketing for foreign films: Hungarian Fairy Tale, December Bride, Eden Valley. Contrib. writer to Box Office Magazine, Film Journal. Recent articles: Creativity (Advertising Age), Rolling Stone's Marketing Through Music, Words & Music, Campaign Magazine, Songwriters Guild of America National Edition. As sect. of VPA, conceptualized int'l Monitor Award, an annual event, currently under auspices of ITS. Public relations counsel to London Int'l Advertising Awards. Member of The Public Relations Society of America, Nat'l Academy of TV Arts & Sciences, Nat'l Acadrmy of Recording Arts & Sciences, Publishers Publicity Association. Morton Dennis Wax & Assocs. in NY was awarded the first EPM Entertainment Marketing Cause Event Award for creating, developing and promoting a nat'l fund raising campaign to combat homelessness, called Brother Can You Spare a Dime Day.

WAYANS, DAMON
Actor, Writer, Producer. b. New York, NY, Sept. 4, 1960. Brother is comedian-actor Keenen Ivory Wayans. Started as stand up comedian.
PICTURES: Beverly Hills Cop (debut, 1984), Hollywood Shuffle, Roxanne, Colors, Punchline, I'm Gonna Git You Sucka, Earth Girls Are Easy, Look Who's Talking Too (voice), The Last Boy Scout, Mo' Money (also s.p., co-exec. prod.), Last Action Hero (cameo), Blankman (also co-s.p., exec. prod.), Major Payne (also co-s.p., co-exec. prod.), The Great White Hype, Bulletproof.
TELEVISION: Series: Saturday Night Live (1985 -6), In Living Color (also writer), 413 Hope St., (also prod.), Damon. Special: The Last Stand? (HBO).

WAYANS, KEENEN IVORY
Actor, Director, Writer. b. NYC, June 8, 1958. e. Tuskegee Inst. Began as stand-up comic at The Improv in NYC and L.A. Brother is comedian-actor Damon Wayans.
PICTURES: Star 80 (debut, 1983), Hollywood Shuffle (also co-s.p.), Eddie Murphy Raw (co-prod., co-s.p. only), I'm Gonna Git You Sucka (also dir., s.p.), The Five Heartbeats (co-s.p. only), A Low Down Dirty Shame (also dir., s.p.), The Glimmer Man, America's Most Wanted (also s.p., exec. prod.).
TELEVISION: Series: For Love and Honor, In Living Color (also exec. prod. & writer; Emmy Award 1990), Keenen Ivory Wayans Show (also exec. prod., writer). Guest: Benson, Cheers, CHiPS, A Different World. Special: Partners in Crime (also co-writer).

WAYLAND, LEN
Actor. b. California, Dec. 28. e. Junior Coll., Modesto, CA. Wrote, prod. weekly radio series 1939-41, KPAS, KTRB, Calif. Service, radar navigator, 1941-45; theatre, Tobacco Road, 1946; 1973, formed Len Wayland Prods. for prod. of theatrical pictures and TV series. 1976-77: prod./dir.: Don't Let It Bother You. 1978, prod., dir., You're not there yet, for own co.
THEATER: A Streetcar Named Desire (B'way, tour), Heaven Can Wait, My Name Is Legion, Love of Four Colonels, Stalag 17, A Man For All Seasons.
TELEVISION: A Time to Live (serial), First Love, Armstrong Circle Theatre, Justice, Sgt. Bilko, Kraft Theatre; Dr. Weaver, From These Roots. Profiles in Courage, Dr. Kildare, Gunsmoke, Slattery's People, Ben Casey, A Noise in the World, Love Is a Many Splendored Thing; Dragnet, Outsider; Ironside, Name of the Game, The Bold Ones, Daniel Boone, The Virginian, Project U.F.O., Sam (series), The Blue and the Gray, Hunter, A-Team, Dallas, Amy on the Lips, Generations (serial).

WAYNE, JOEL
Executive. Began career with Grey Advertising; in 17 years won many awards (60 Clios, 25 N.Y. Art Director Club Awards, etc.). Was exec. v.p. & creative dir. of agency when left in 1979 to join Warner Bros. as v.p., creative adv. 1987, named sr. v.p., worldwide creative adv., then exec. v.p. worldwide creative adv. & publicity.

WAYNE, MICHAEL A.
Executive. r.n. Michael A. Morrison. b. Los Angeles, CA, Nov. 23, 1934. Father was late actor John Wayne. e. Loyola H.S.; Loyola U., B.B.A. Asst. dir., various companies, 1955-56; asst. dir., Revue Prods., 1956-57; pres. Batjac Prods, and Romina Prods., 1961.
PICTURES: Asst. to producer: China Doll, Escort West, The Alamo (asst. to prod.). Prod.: McLintock!, Cast Giant Shadow (co- prod.), The Green Berets, Chisum (exec. prod.), Big Jake, The Train Robbers, Cahill: U.S. Marshal, McQ (exec. prod.), Brannigan (exec. prod.).

WAYNE, PATRICK
Actor. b. Los Angeles, July 15, 1939. e. Loyola U, 1961, BS in biology. Father was late actor John Wayne. Made film debut at age 11 in Rio Grande with father.
PICTURES: The Long Gray Line, Mister Roberts, The Searchers, The Alamo, The Comancheros, McClintock, Donovan's Reef, Cheyenne Autumn, Shenandoah, An Eye for an Eye, The Green Berets, The Deserter, Big Jake, The Gatling Gun, Beyond Atlantis, The Bears and I, Mustang Country, Sinbad and the Eye of the Tiger, The People Time Forgot, Rustler's Rhapsody, Young Guns, Her Alibi, Blind Vengeance, Chill Factor.
TELEVISION: Series: The Rounders, Shirley. Movies: Sole Survivor, Yesterday's Child, Flight to Holocaust, The Last Hurrah, Three on a Date. Guest: Frank's Place.

WEATHERS, CARL
Actor. b. New Orleans, LA, Jan. 14, 1948. e. San Diego State Univ.
PICTURES: Bucktown (debut, 1975), Friday Foster, Rocky, Close Encounters of the Third Kind, Semi-Tough, Force Ten From Navarone, Rocky II, Death Hunt, Rocky III, Rocky IV, Predator, Action Jackson, Hurricane Smith, Happy Gilmore.
TELEVISION: Series: Fortune Dane, Tour of Duty, Street Justice, In the Heat of the Night. Movies: The Hostage Heart, The Bermuda Depths, Breaker, Dangerous Passion, In the Heat of the Night: A Matter of Justice, In the Heat of the Night: Who Was Geli Bendl?, In the Heat of the Night: By Duty Bound, Tom Clancy's Op Center, In the Heat of the Night: Grow Old With Me, The Defiant Ones, Shadow Warriors, Shadow Warriors II. Director: Silk Stalkings (7 episodes), Renegade (1 episode).

WEAVER, DENNIS
Actor, Director. b. Joplin, MO, June 4, 1925. e. U. of Oklahoma, B.A., fine arts, 1948.
PICTURES: Horizons West (debut, 1952), The Raiders, The Redhead From Wyoming, The Lawless Breed, Mississippi Gambler, Law and Order, It Happens Every Thursday, Column South, The Man From the Alamo, The Golden Blade, The Nebraskan, War Arrow, Dangerous Mission, Dragnet, Ten Wanted Men, The Bridges at Toko-Ri, Seven Angry Men, Chief Crazy Horse, Storm Fear, Touch of Evil, The Gallant Hours, Duel at Diablo, Way... Way Out, Gentle Giant, Mission Batangas, A Man Called Sledge, What's the Matter With Helen?, Walking After Midnight.
TELEVISION: Series: Gunsmoke (Emmy Award, 1959), Kentucky Jones, Gentle Ben, McCloud, Stone, Emerald Point NAS, Buck James, Lonesome Dove. Movies: McCloud: Who Killed Miss USA?, The Forgotten Man, Duel, Rolling Man, Female Artillery, The Great Man's Whiskers, Terror on the Beach, Intimate Strangers, The Islander, Ishi: The Last of His Tribe, The Ordeal of Patty Hearst, Stone (pilot), Amber Waves, The Ordeal of Dr. Mudd, The Day the Loving Stopped, Don't Go to Sleep, Cocaine: One Man's Seduction, Bluffing It, Disaster at Silo 7, The Return of Sam McCloud (also co-exec. prod.), Greyhounds. Mini-Series: Centennial, Pearl. Special: Mastergate.

WEAVER, FRITZ
Actor. b. Pittsburgh, PA, Jan. 19, 1926. e. U. of Chicago.
THEATER: The Chalk Garden (Theatre World Award), Miss Lonelyhearts, All American, A Shot in the Dark, Baker Street, Child's Play (Tony, 1970), The Price, The Crucible, The Professional, etc.
PICTURES: Fail Safe (debut, 1964), The Guns of August (narrator), The Maltese Bippy, A Walk in the Spring Rain, Company of Killers, The Day of the Dolphin, Marathon Man, Demon Seed, Black Sunday, The Big Fix, Jaws of Satan, Creepshow, Power.
TELEVISION: Movies: The Borgia Stick, Berlin Affair, Heat of Anger, The Snoop Sisters, Hunter, The Legend of Lizzie Borden, Captains Courageous, The Hearst and Davies Affair, A Death in California, My Name is Bill W, Ironclads, Citizen Cohn, Blind Spot. Mini-Series: Holocaust, The Martian Chronicles, Dream West, I'll Take Manhattan.

WEAVER, SIGOURNEY
Actress. r.n. Susan Weaver. b. New York, NY, Oct. 8, 1949. e. Stanford U., Yale U. Daughter of Sylvester (Pat) Weaver, former NBC pres. Mother, actress Elizabeth Inglis (one-time contract player for Warner Bros.). After college formed working partnership with fellow student Christopher Durang for off-B'way improv. productions. First professional appearance on stage in 1974 in The Constant Wife with Ingrid Bergman. Formed Goat Cay Prods.
THEATER: Off-Off-B'way: The Nature and Purpose of the Universe. Off-B'way: Titanic/Das Lusitania Songspiel (also co-writer), Gemini, Marco Polo Sings a Solo, New Jerusalem, The Merchant of Venice, Beyond Therapy. B'way: Hurlyburly.
PICTURES: Madman (Israeli; debut, 1976), Annie Hall, Alien, Eyewitness, The Year of Living Dangerously, Deal of the Century, Ghostbusters, One Woman or Two, Aliens (Acad. Award nom.), Half Moon Street, Gorillas in the Mist (Acad. Award nom.), Working Girl (Acad. Award nom.), Ghostbusters II, Alien 3 (also co-prod.), 1492: Conquest of Paradise, Dave, Death and the Maiden, Jeffrey, Copycat, The Ice Storm (BAFTA Award, Best Supporting Actress, 1997).
TELEVISION: Series: The Best of Families (PBS), Somerset. Special: The Sorrows of Gin.

WEAVER, SYLVESTER L., JR.
Executive. b. Los Angeles, CA, Dec. 21, 1908. e. Dartmouth Coll. Daughter is actress Sigourney Weaver. CBS, Don Lee Network, 1932-35; Young & Rubicam adv. agency, 1935-38; adv. mgr., American Tobacco Co., 1938-47; v.p. Young & Rubicam, 1947-49; joined NBC as v.p., chg. TV, 1949; appt'd v.p. chg. NBC Radio & TV networks, 1952; vice-chmn. bd., NBC, 1953; pres.,

NBC, 1953; bd. chmn., 1955; as head of NBC during TV's formative years, Weaver is credited as the father of TV talk/service program, founding both Tonight and Today shows, also innovated the rotating multi-star anthology series, the Wide Wide World series and concept of TV "special;" Own firm, 430 Park Avenue., N.Y., 1956; chmn. of bd. McCann-Erickson Corp. (Intl.), 1959; pres., Subscription TV, Inc. Comm. Consultant in Los Angeles, CA and President, Weaver Productions, Inc. On magazine series Television: Inside and Out (1981-82). Author: The Best Seat in the House (1994). Awards: Emmy Trustees' and Governor's Award (1967) and Governor's Award (1983), TV Hall of Fame (1984), NAB Hall of Fame (1986), Dartmouth Lifetime Achievement Award, 1993.

WEBB, CHLOE
Actress. b. New York, NY. e. Boston Conservatory of Music and Drama. On stage with Boston Shakespeare Co., Goodman Theatre in Chicago and Mark Taper Forum, L.A., improv. groups Imagination Theatre Co., Paul Sills Theatre.
THEATER: Forbidden Broadway (Off-B'way and L.A.), Addiction, Family Album, The Model Apartment (LA Critics Circle & Dramalogue Awards), House of Blue Leaves (Dramlogue Award), School Talk, A Midsummer Night's Dream.
PICTURES: Sid and Nancy (debut, 1986; Natl. Society of Film Critics Award), Twins, Heart Condition, The Belly of an Architect, Queens Logic, A Dangerous Woman, Love Affair, She's So Lovely, The Newton Boys.
TELEVISION: Series: Thicke of the Night. Special: Who Am I This Time? Movies: Lucky Day, Silent Cries. Mini-Series: Tales of the City. Guest: Remington Steele, China Beach (pilot).

WEBER, STEVEN
Actor. e. Purchase Col. Acted with Mirror Rep. Co. Off-B'way.
THEATER: NY: Paradise Lost, The Real Thing (B'way debut, 1985), Something About Baseball. Regional: Made in Bangkok, Come Back Little Sheba, Naked at the Coast, Death of a Salesman.
PICTURES: The Flamingo Kid, Flanagan, Hamburger Hill, Les Anges, Single White Female, The Temp, Jeffrey, Dracula: Dead and Loving It, I Woke Up Early the Day I Died, The Breakup, Sour Grapes, At First Sight.
TELEVISION: Series: Wings. Mini-Series: The Kennedys of Massachusetts, The Shining. Movies: In the Company of Darkness, In the Line of Duty: The Undercover Murders, Deception: A Mother's Secret, Betrayed by Love. Special: Pudd'nhead Wilson.

WEDGEWORTH, ANN
Actress. b. Abilene, TX, Jan. 21, 1935. e. U. of Texas. On stage in Thieves, Blues for Mr. Charlie, Chapter Two (Tony Award, 1978), etc.
PICTURES: Andy, Bang the Drum Slowly, Scarecrow, The Catamount Killing, Law and Disorder, Dragonfly (One Summer Love), Birch Interval, Thieves, Handle With Care, No Small Affair, Sweet Dreams, The Men's Club, Made in Heaven, A Tiger's Tale, Far North, Miss Firecracker, Steel Magnolias, Green Card, Hard Promises, Love and a .45, The Whole Wide World.
TELEVISION: Series: The Edge of Night, Another World, Somerset, Three's Company, Filthy Rich, Evening Shade. Movies: The War Between the Tates, Bogie, Elvis and the Beauty Queen, Killjoy, Right to Kill?, A Stranger Waits, Cooperstown, A Burning Passion: The Margaret Mitchell Story, Fight for Justice: The Nancy Conn Story. Pilot: Harlan & Merleen.

WEILER, GERALD E.
Producer. b. Mannheim, Germany, May 8, 1928. e. Harvard, 1946-48; Columbia, B.S., 1949-51; New York U. Grad. Sch., 1951-53. Writer, WHN, N.Y. writer, sports ed., news ed., Telenews Prod., Inc., 1948-52; asst. to prod., Richard de Rochemont, Vavin, Inc., 1952; U.S. Army, 1953-55; v.p., Vavin Inc. 1955-73; President, Weiler Communications Inc. 1973. Winner, NY "Lotto" Lottery, 1988; retired 1989.

WEILL, CLAUDIA
Director. b. New York, NY 1947. e. Radcliffe, B.A., 1969. Teacher of acting, Cornish Institute, 1983; guest lecturer on film directing, NYU and Columbia U. Winner of Donatello Award, best director, 1979; Mademoiselle Woman of the Year, 1974; AFI Independent Filmmakers Grant, 1973. Worked as prod. asst. on doc., Revolution.
THEATER: An Evening for Merlin Finch (debut, 1975, Williamstown), Stillife, Found a Peanut, The Longest Walk.
PICTURES: Doc. shorts: This Is the Home of Mrs. Levant Grahame, Roaches' Serenade, Joyce at 34. Director: The Other Half of the Sky—A China Memoir (also photog., edit.), Girlfriends (also prod., story), It's My Turn.
TELEVISION: Series: The 51st State, Sesame Street, Joyce at 34, The Great Love Experiment, thirtysomething, My So-Called Life, Chicago Hope. Movie: A Child Lost Forever, Critical Choices.

WEINBLATT, MIKE
Executive. b. Perth Amboy, NJ, June 10, 1929. e. Syracuse U. Served in Army as counter-intelligence agent, mostly in Japan, 1952-53. Joined NBC in 1957; has headed two major TV network functions—talent/program admin. & sls.; joined network business affairs dept. in 1958 as mgr., business affairs, facilities operations; rose to post of director, pricing & financial services before moving to sales in 1962, as mgr., participating program sales; named v.p., eastern sales, NBC-TV, 1968; named v.p., talent & program admin., 1968; promoted to v.p. sales, 1973; 1975 named sr. v.p., sales; later became exec. v.p.; appointed exec. v.p. & gen. mgr. of NBC TV network, 1977; appointed Pres., NBC Entertainment, 1978; 1980, joined Showtime/Movie Channel as pres. & COO; 1984, pres., Multi Media Entertainment; 1990, chmn. Weinblatt Communications Co. Inc. 1991, mng. dir. Interequity Capital Corp.

WEINGROD, HERSCHEL
Writer, Producer. b. Milwaukee, WI, Oct. 30, 1947. e. U. of Wisconsin, 1965-69; London Film Sch., 1969-71.
PICTURES: Co-writer with Timothy Harris: Cheaper to Keep Her, Trading Places (BAFTA nom.), Brewster's Millions, My Stepmother Is An Alien, Paint It Black, Twins, Kindergarten Cop, Pure Luck, Falling Down (prod. only), Space Jam (co-s.p.).
TELEVISION: Street of Dreams (exec. prod.).

WEINSTEIN, BOB
Executive. With brother Harvey founded distribution company Miramax Films in 1979. Company branched into feature production in 1989 with film Scandal. Serves as Miramax co-chairman.
PICTURES: Light Years (Bob: prod., Harvey: co-s.p. version). Co-Executive Producers: Scandal, The Lemon Sisters, Hardware, A Rage in Harlem, The Miracle, Crossing the Line, The Night We Never Met, Benefit of the Doubt, True Romance, Into the West, Mother's Boys, Pulp Fiction, Ready to Wear (Pret-a-Porter), The Englishman Who Went Up a Hill But Came Down a Mountain, Smoke, The Crossing Guard, The Journey of August King, Last of the High Kings, Addicted to Love, Air Bud, Cop Land, The English Patient, Scream .

WEINSTEIN, HARVEY
Executive. With brother Bob founded distribution company Miramax Films in 1979. Company branched into feature production in 1989 with film Scandal. Serves as Miramax co-chairman. (For list of films see Bob Weinstein).

WEINSTEIN, PAULA
Producer. b. Nov. 19, 1945. e. Columbia U. Daughter of late prod. Hannah Weinstein. Raised in Europe. Partnered with Gareth Wigan in WW Productions at Warner Brothers. Started as theatrical agent with William Morris and ICM. With Warner Brothers, 1976-78 as production v.p.; left to go to 20th Century-Fox in same capacity; named Fox sr. v.p., worldwide prod; 1980, appointed v.p., prod., the Ladd Company; 1981, joined United Artists as pres., m.p. div.; 1983, began own prod. company at Columbia Pictures, also serving as a consultant for Columbia; 1987, joined MGM as exec. consultant; With late husband Mark Rosenberg formed Spring Creek Prods.
PICTURES: Prod.: A Dry White Season, The Fabulous Baker Boys, Fearless, Flesh and Bone, With Honors, Something to Talk About, The Incredible Mr. Limpet, Analyze This.
TELEVISION: Movies: The Rose and the Jackal, Citizen Cohn, Truman (Emmy Award, 1996), The Cherokee Kid, First-time Felon, Cloned.

WEINTRAUB, FRED
Executive, Producer. b. Bronx, NY, April 27, 1928. e. U. of PA, Wharton Sch. of Bus. Owner of The Bitter End Coffeehouse to 1971. Personal management, Campus Coffee House Entertain-ment Circuit; TV Production Hootenanny, Popendipity; syndicated TV show host: From The Bitter End; motion picture prod.; v.p., creative services, Warner Bros. 1969; exec. in chg. Woodstock; prod. motion pictures, Weintraub-Heller Productions, 1974; then Fred Weintraub Productions, which became Weintraub/Kuhn Prods. in 1990.
PICTURES: Enter the Dragon, Rage, Black Belt Jones, Truck Turner, Golden Needles, Animal Stars, Hot Potato, The Ultimate Warrior, Dirty Knights Work, Those Cuckoo Crazy Animals, Crash, Outlaw Blues, The Pack, The Promise, Tom Horn, Battle Creek Brawl, Force Five, High Road to China, Out of Control, Gymkata, Princess Academy, Born to Ride.
TELEVISION: My Father My Son (prod.), Triplecross. Produced: Trouble Bound, Dead Wrong, JFK Assassination (doc.), The Bruce Lee Story (doc.), The New Adventures of Robin Hood.

WEINTRAUB, JERRY
Producer. b. New York, NY, Sept. 26, 1937. m. former singer Jayne Morgan. Sole owner and chmn. of Management Three, representing entertainment personalities, including John Denver, John Davidson, Frank Sinatra, Neil Diamond, etc. Also involved with Intercontinental Broadcasting Systems, Inc. (cable programming) and Jerry Weintraub/Armand Hammer Prods. (production co.). 1985, named United Artists Corp. chmn. Resigned, 1986. 1987: formed Weintraub Entertainment Group.

PICTURES: Nashville, Oh God!, Cruising, All Night Long, Diner, The Karate Kid, The Karate Kid Part II, The Karate Kid Part III, Pure Country, The Firm (actor), The Next Karate Kid, The Specialist.

WEINTRAUB, SY
Executive. b. New York, NY, 1923. e. U. of Missouri, B.A., journalism, 1947; graduate of American Theater Wing. Started career in 1949 forming with associates a TV syndication co., Flamingo Films, Inc., which merged with Associated Artists to form Motion Pictures for Television, Inc., largest syndicator at that time. Originated Superman and Grand Ol' Opry series for TV. 1958, bought Sol Lesser Prods., owners of film rights for Tarzan, and began producing and distributing Tarzan films through Banner Productions, Inc. Also formerly chmn. of bd. of Panavision, Inc.; bd. mem. and pres. of National General Television Corp., and pres. of KMGM-TV in Minneapolis. In 1978, named chmn. of Columbia Pictures Industries' new Film Entertainment Group, also joining office of the chief executive of CPI.

WEIR, PETER
Director, Writer. b. Sydney, Australia, Aug. 21, 1944. e. attended Scots Coll. and Sydney U. Briefly worked selling real estate, traveled to England 1965. Entered Australian TV industry as stagehand 1967 while prod. amateur revues. Dir. shorts: Count Vim's Last Exercise, The Life and Times of Reverend Buck Shotte, Homeside, Incredible Floridas, What Ever Happened to Green Valley? 1967-73.
PICTURES: Director: Three to Go (debut, 1970; segment: Michael), The Cars That Ate Paris (also s.p., co-story; a.k.a. The Cars That Eat People), Picnic at Hanging Rock, The Last Wave (also s.p.), The Plumber (also s.p.; tv in Australia), Gallipoli (also story), The Year of Living Dangerously (also co-s.p.), Witness, The Mosquito Coast, Dead Poets Society, Green Card (also prod., s.p.), Fearless.

WEIS, DON
Director, Writer, Producer. b. Milwaukee, WI, May 13, 1922. e. USC. Started as dialogue dir. on such films as Body and Soul, The Red Pony, Champion, Home of the Brave, The Men.
PICTURES: Bannerline (debut, 1951), It's a Big Country (segment), Just This Once, You for Me, I Love Melvin, Remains to Be Seen, A Slight Case of Larceny, Half a Hero, The Affairs of Dobie Gillis, The Adventures of Haji Baba, Ride the High Iron, The Gene Krupa Story, Critic's Choice, Looking for Love, Pajama Party, Billie (also prod.), The King's Pirate, Did You Hear the One About the Traveling Saleslady?, Zero to Sixty.
TELEVISION: Dear Phoebe, The Longest Hundred Miles, It Takes a Thief, Ironside, M*A*S*H., Happy Days, Planet of the Apes, Bronk, Petrocelli, The Magician, Mannix, Night Stalker, Barbary Coast, Courtship of Eddie's Father, Starsky & Hutch, Hawaii Five-O, Chips, Charlie's Angels, Love Boat, Fantasy Island, Remington Steele, Hill St. Blues, Murphy's Law.

WEISS, STEVEN ALAN
Executive. b. Glendale, CA, Oct. 19, 1944. e. Los Angeles City Coll., A.A., 1964; USC, M.S., 1966; Northwestern U., B.S., 1967; LaSalle Extension U., J.D., 1970. U.S. Navy-San Diego, Great Lakes, Vallejo & Treasure Island, 1966-67; shipyard liaison officer, Pearl Harbor Naval Shipyard, U.S. Navy, 1967-70; gen. mgr., Adrian Weiss Prods., 1970-74; organized Weiss Global Enterprises with Adrian Weiss 1974 for production, acquisition & distribution of films. Purchased with Tom J. Corradine and Adrian Weiss from the Benedict E. Bogeaus Estate nine features, 1974. Sec./Treas. of Film Investment Corp. & Weiss Global Enterprises which own, control or have dist. rights to over 300 features, many TV series, documentaries, etc. CFO/COO Flo-Fowes, a full service telecommunications corp., 1992-present. Member of the Nat'l Assn. of TV Program Executive Int'l, National Cable TV Assn., American Film Institute.

WEISSMAN, MURRAY
Executive. b. New York, NY, Dec. 23. e. U. of Southern California. Asst. dir. of press info., CBS, 1960-66; mgr., TV press dept., Universal Studio, 1966-68; executive in charge of m.p. press dept., Universal Studios & asst. secy., Universal Pictures, 1968-76; marketing exec., Columbia Pictures, 1976-77; vice pres. of advertising & publicity, Lorimar Productions, 1977; vice pres., ICPR Public Relations Company, 1978-81; now principal, Weissman/Delson Communications.

WEISWASSER, STEPHEN A.
Executive. e. Wayne St. Univ., John Hopkins Univ., Harvard Law School. Partner at Wilmer Cutler & Pickering law firm until he joined Capital Cities/ABC in 1986 as sr. v.p. Aug. 1993 became pres. of Capital Cities/ABC Multimedia Group until Oct. 1995. Nov. 1995, became pres. & CEO of Americast.

WEITZNER, DAVID
Executive. b. New York, NY, Nov. 13, 1938. e. Michigan State U. Entered industry in 1960 as member Columbia Pictures adv. dep't; later with Donahue and Coe as ass't exec. and Loew's Theatres adv. dep't; later with Embassy Pictures, adv. mgr.; dir. of adv. and exploitation for Palomar Pictures Corp.; v.p. in charge of adv., pub., and exploitation for ABC Pictures Corp.; v.p., entertainment/leisure div., Grey Advertising; v.p., worldwide adv., 20th Century Fox; exec. v.p. adv./pub./promo., Universal Pictures; exec. v.p., mktg. & dist., Embassy Pictures; 1985, joined 20th Century-Fox Films as pres. of mktg. 1987, pres., mktg., Weintraub Entertainment Group; 1988 joined MCA/Universal as pres. worldwide marketing, MCA Recreation Services.

WELCH, RAQUEL
Actress. r.n. Raquel Tejada. b. Chicago, IL, Sept. 5, 1940. e. La Jolla H.S. Theatre arts scholarship San Diego State Coll. Worked as model before landing bit parts in films. Broadway debut, Woman of the Year, 1981.
PICTURES: A House Is Not a Home (debut, 1964), Roustabout, Do Not Disturb, A Swingin' Summer, Fantastic Voyage, Shoot Loud Louder... I Don't Understand, One Million Years B.C., Fathom, The Oldest Profession, Bedazzled, The Biggest Bundle of Them All, Le Fate (The Queens), Bandolero, Lady in Cement, 100 Rifles, Flare Up, The Magic Christian, Myra Breckinridge, Restless, Hannie Caulder, Kansas City Bomber, Fuzz, Bluebeard, The Last of Sheila, The Three Musketeers, The Four Musketeers, The Wild Party, Mother Jugs and Speed, Crossed Swords, L'Animal, Naked Gun 33 1/3: The Final Insult.
TELEVISION: Specials: Really Raquel, Raquel. Movies: The Legend of Walks Far Woman, Right to Die, Scandal in a Small Town, Trouble in Paradise, Tainted Blood, Judith Krantz's Torch Song, Hollyrock-a-Bye Baby (voice). Guest: Cher, The Muppet Show, Saturday Night Live.

WELD, TUESDAY
Actress. r.n. Susan Weld. b. New York, NY, Aug. 27, 1943. m. violinist Pinchas Zuckerman. e. Hollywood Professional Sch. Began modeling at 4 yrs.
PICTURES: Rock Rock Rock (debut, 1956), Rally 'Round the Flag Boys! The Five Pennies, Because They're Young, High Time, Sex Kittens Go to College, The Private Lives of Adam and Eve, Return to Peyton Place, Wild in the Country, Bachelor Flat, Soldier in the Rain, I'll Take Sweden, The Cincinnati Kid, Lord Love a Duck, Pretty Poison, I Walk the Line, A Safe Place, Play It As It Lays, Looking for Mr. Goodbar (Acad. Award nom.), Who'll Stop the Rain, Serial, Thief, Author! Author!, Once Upon a Time in America, Heartbreak Hotel, Falling Down.
TELEVISION: Series: The Many Loves of Dobie Gillis (1959-60). Movies: Reflections of Murder, F. Scott Fitzgerald in Hollywood, A Question of Guilt, Mother and Daughter: The Loving War, Madame X, The Winter of Our Discontent, Scorned and Swindled, Something in Common, Circle of Violence. Special: The Rainmaker.

WELLER, PETER
Actor. b. Stevens Point, WI, June 24, 1947. Acting since 10 years old. e. North Texas State U. Studied at American Acad. of Dramatic Arts with Uta Hagen. Member, Actor's Studio.
THEATER: Sticks and Bones (moved up from understudy, B'way debut), Full Circle, Summer Brave, Macbeth, The Wool-Gatherer, Rebel Women, Streamers, The Woods, Serenading Louie, Daddy Wolf.
PICTURES: Butch and Sundance: The Early Years (debut, 1979), Just Tell Me What You Want, Shoot the Moon, Of Unknown Origin, The Adventures of Buckaroo Banzai Across the 8th Dimension, Firstborn, Robocop, Shakedown, A Killing Affair, Leviathan, The Tunnel, Robocop 2, Cat Chaser, Naked Lunch, Fifty Fifty, Sunset Grill, The New Age, Screamers, Mighty Aphrodite, Beyond the Clouds, Top of the World.
TELEVISION: Movies: The Man Without a Country, The Silence, Kentucky Woman, Two Kinds of Love, Apology, Women & Men: Stories of Seduction (Dust Before Fireworks), Rainbow Drive, The Substitute Wife, The Road to Ruin, Decoy, Michael Hayes (dir.), Gold Coast (dir.). Guest: Lou Grant, Exit 10. Special: Partners (also dir., co-writer).

WENDERS, WIM
Director, Writer. b. Dusseldorf, Germany, August 14, 1945. Studied film 1967-70 at Filmhochschule in Munich. Worked as film critic 1968-70 for Filmkritik and Die Suddeutsche Zeitung. 1967 made first short films (Schauplatze) and three others before first feature, Summer in the City.
PICTURES: Director-Writer: Summer in the City (debut, 1970; also prod., actor), The Scarlet Letter, The Goalie's Anxiety at the Penalty Kick, Alice in the Cities, Wrong Move (dir. only), Kings of the Road (also prod.), The American Friend, Lightning Over Water (also actor), Chambre 66 (dir., actor), Hammett (dir. only), The State of Things, Paris Texas (dir. only), I Played It for You (dir., actor only), Tokyo-Ga (also edit.), Wings of Desire (also prod.), Notebooks on Cities and Clothes (also photog.), Until the End of the World, Faraway So Close! (also prod.), Lisbon Story, Beyond the Clouds (co-dir. & co-s.p. with Michelangelo Antonioni) Actor only: Long Shot, King Kong's Faust, Helsinki Napoli All Night Long, Motion and Emotion.

WENDKOS, PAUL
Director. b. Philadelphia, PA, Sept. 20, 1926. e. Temple U., Columbia, the New School.
PICTURES: The Burglar, Tarawa Beachhead, Gidget, Face of a Fugitive, Battle of the Coral Sea, Because They're Young, Angel Baby, Gidget Goes to Rome, Miles to Terror, Guns of the Magnificent Seven, Cannon for Cordova, The Mephisto Waltz, Special Delivery.
TELEVISION: Hawaii 5-0 (pilot), Fear No Evil, The Brotherhood of the Bell, Travis Logan D.A., A Tattered Web, A Little Game, A Death of Innocence, The Delphi Bureau, Haunts of the Very Rich, Footsteps, The Strangers in 7-A, Honor Thy Father, Terror on the Beach, The Underground Man, The Legend of Lizzie Borden, Death Among Friends, The Death of Ritchie, Secrets, Good Against Evil, Harold Robbins' 79 Park Avenue, A Woman Called Moses, The Ordeal of Patty Hearst, Act of Violence, Ordeal of Doctor Mudd, A Cry for Love, The Five of Me, Golden Gate, Farrell for the People, Cocaine: One Man's Seduction, Intimate Agony, The Awakening of Candra, Celebrity, Scorned and Swindled, The Execution, The Bad Seed, Picking Up the Pieces, Rage of Angels: The Story Continues, Sister Margaret and the Saturday Night Ladies, Six Against the Rock, Right to Die, The Taking of Flight 847: The Uli Derickson Story, The Great Escape II: The Untold Story (co-dir.), From the Dead of Night, Cross of Fire, Blind Faith, Good Cops Bad Cops, The Chase, White Hot: The Murder of Thelma Todd, Guilty Until Proven Innocent, The Trail, Bloodlines.

WENDT, GEORGE
Actor. b. Chicago, IL, Oct. 17, 1948. e. Rockhurst Col. Joined Second City's acting troupe in 1973. Appeared in NBC pilot Nothing but Comedy.
PICTURES: My Bodyguard, Somewhere in Time, Airplane II: The Sequel, Jekyll & Hyde Together Again, The Woman in Red, Dreamscape, Thief of Hearts, No Small Affair, Fletch, House, Gung Ho, Plain Clothes, Guilty by Suspicion, Forever Young, The Little Rascals, Man of the House.
TELEVISION: Series: Making the Grade, Cheers, The George Wendt Show. Guest: Alice, Soap, Taxi, Hart to Hart, Saturday Night Live, Seinfeld. Movies: Oblomov (BBC), The Ratings Game, Hostage for a Day, Columbo: Strange Bedfellows, Shame II: The Secret, Bye Bye Birdie.

WERNER, PETER
Producer, Director. b. New York, NY, Jan. 17, 1947. e. Dartmouth Coll., AFI. Received Academy Award for short subject, In the Region of Ice, 1976.
PICTURES: Don't Cry It's Only Thunder, No Man's Land.
TELEVISION: Movies: Director: Battered, William Faulkner's Barn Burning, Sins of the Father, Aunt Mary, No Man's Land, Women in Song, No Man's Land, LBJ: The Early Years. Men (exec. prod.; dir.; Emmy nom.), The Image (Ace Award), Hiroshima: Out of the Ashes (D.G.A. nom.), The Good Policeman, Doorways, Middle Ages (co-exec. prod.), Substitute Wife, The Four Diamonds, The Unspoken Truth, Inflammable, Almost Golden: The Jessica Savitch Story (D.G.A. nom.), For the Love of Zachary, On the Edge of Innocence, House of Frankenstein, Parallels. Series: Moonlighting (Emmy & D.G.A. nom.), Outlaws (pilot), The Wonder Years, D.E.A. (pilot), Ned Blessing (pilot), Nash Bridges (pilot).

WERTHEIMER, THOMAS
Executive. b. 1938. e. Princeton U., B.A. 1960; Columbia U., LLB, 1963. V.p. business affairs subs. ABC 1964-72; joined MCA Inc, 1972; v.p. Universal TV dir.; corp. v.p. 1974 -83; exec. v.p. 1983-; chmn., MCA Television and Home Entertainment Groups. Consultant, 1996-present

WERTMULLER, LINA
Director, Writer. b. Rome, Italy, Aug. 14, 1928. m. sculptor-set designer Enrico Job. e. Acad. of Theatre, Rome, 1951. Began working in theatre in 1951; Prod.-dir. avant-garde plays in Italy 1951-52; member puppet troupe 1952-62; actress, stage mgr., set designer, publicity writer, for theater, radio & TV, 1952-62. Began film career as asst. to Fellini on 8 1/2 in 1962. Following year wrote and directed first film, The Lizards. Had big TV success with series called Gian Burasca and then returned to theatre for a time. 1988, named Special Commissioner of Centro Sperimentale di Cinematografia. Was the first woman to be nominated for an Academy Award for Best Director (Seven Beauties, 1976).
PICTURES: Director-Writer: The Lizards (dir. debut, 1963), Let's Talk About Men, The Seduction of Mimi (Cannes Film Fest Award, 1972), Love and Anarchy, All Screwed Up, Swept Away... By an Unusual Destiny in the Blue Sea of August, Seven Beauties (Acad. Award noms. for dir. & s.p., 1976), The End of the World in Our Usual Bed in a Night Full of Rain, Blood Feud, A Joke of Destiny (Lying in Wait Around the Corner Like a Bandit), A Complex Plot About Women, Sotto Sotto (Softly Softly), Summer Night With Greek Profile Almond Eyes and a Scent of Basil, The Tenth One in Hiding, On a Moonlit Night, Saturday Sunday Monday, Ciao Professore!
TELEVISION: Rita the Mosquito, Il Decimo Clandestino (Cannes Fest. Award).

WEST, ADAM
Actor. b. Walla Walla, WA, Sept. 19, 1929. r.n. William West Anderson. e. Whitman Col. (B.A.), Stanford Univ. Created classic Batman role. Appeared in interactive short film Ride for Your Life, and CD-ROM The Golden Nugget.
PICTURES: The Young Philadelphians, Geronimo, Soldier in the Rain, Tammy and the Doctor, Robinson Crusoe on Mars, The Outlaws Is Coming!, Mara of the Wilderness, Batman, The Girl Who Knew Too Much, Marriage of a Young Stockbroker, The Specialist, Hell River, Hooper, The Happy Hooker Goes to Hollywood, Blonde Ambition, One Dark Night, Young Lady Chatterly, Hell Raiders, Zombie Nightmare, Doin' Time on Planet Earth, Mad About You, John Travis: Solar Survivor, Maxim Xul, Night of the Kickfighter, The New Age, Not This Part of the World, Bigger Than Watermelon, An American Vampire Story.
TELEVISION: Series: The Detectives, Batman, The Last Precinct, Danger Theatre, The Clinic. Movies: The Eyes of Charles Sands, For the Love of It, I Take These Men, Nevada Smith, Poor Devil, The Last Precinct. Guest: Hawaiian Eye, 77 Sunset Strip, Bonanza, The Outer Limits, Petticoat Junction, Bewitched, The Big Valley, Love American Style, Night Gallery, Mannix, Alice, Murder She Wrote, Hope and Gloria, Lois and Clark, Burke's Law, The Simpsons (voice), The Critic (voice), Batman (animated series; voice), Politically Incorrect, Weird Science, Rugrats (voice), Animaniacs (voice), Murphy Brown, Pauly Shore Show, Wayans Brothers, MTV's Singled Out. Pilots: Lookwell, 1775, Reel Life, Doc Holliday, Burnett, Johnny Cinderella, Alexander the Great.

WEST, TIMOTHY
Actor. b. Yorkshire, England, Oct. 20, 1934. m. actress Prunella Scales. e. John Lyon Sch. Harow. Ent. ind. 1960. Began acting 1956 after two years as recording engineer. Worked in regional repertory, London's West End and for Royal Shakespeare Company. Dec., 1979 appointed artistic controller of Old Vic. Has directed extensively in the theatre.
PICTURES: Twisted Nerve, The Looking Glass War, Nicholas and Alexandra, The Day of the Jackal, Hedda, Joseph Andrews, The Devil's Advocate, Agatha, The Thirty Nine Steps, Rough Cut, Cry Freedom, Consuming Passions.
TELEVISION: Edward VII, Hard Times, Crime and Punishment, Henry VIII, Churchill and the Generals, Brass, The Monocled Mutineer, The Good Doctor Bodkin Adams, What the Butler Saw, Harry's Kingdom, The Train, When We Are Married, Breakthrough at Reykjavik, Strife, A Shadow on the Sun, The Contractor, Blore, m.p., Survival of the Fittest, Oliver Twist, Why Lockerbie, Framed, Smokescreen, Eleven Men Against Eleven, Cuts, The Place of the Dead.

WESTON, JAY
Producer. b. New York, NY, March 9, 1929. e. New York U. Operated own pub. agency before moving into film prod. In 1965 launched Weston Production; sold orig. s.p., The War Horses, to Embassy Pictures; acquired and marketed other properties. Became prod. story exec. for Palomar-ABC Pictures in 1967.
THEATER: Does a Tiger Wear a Necktie? (co-prod.).
PICTURES: For Love of Ivy (co-prod.), Lady Sings the Blues (co-prod.), W.C. Fields and Me, Chu Chu and the Philly Flash, Night of the Juggler, Buddy Buddy, Side Out.
TELEVISION: Laguna Heat (exec. prod.).

WETTIG, PATRICIA
Actress. b. Cincinnati, OH, Dec. 4, 1951. m. actor Ken Olin. e. Temple Univ. Studied at Neighborhood Playhouse. Began acting career with NY's Circle Repertory Company appearing in The Wool Gatherer, The Diviners and A Tale Told. Other theatre work includes The Dining Room, Talking With (LA), Threads, Innocent Thoughts, My Mother Said I Never Should.
PICTURES: Guilty by Suspicion, City Slickers, Veronica & Me, City Slickers II: The Legend of Curly's Gold.
TELEVISION: Series: St. Elsewhere, thirtysomething (2 Emmy Awards), Courthouse. Movies: Silent Motive, Taking Back My Life: The Nancy Ziegenmeyer Story, Parallel Lives, Nothing But the Truth, Kansas. Mini-Series: Stephen King's The Langoliers.

WEXLER, HASKELL
Cinematographer, Director. b. Chicago, IL June 2, 1922. Photographed educational and industrial films before features. Documentaries as cinematographer include: The Living City, The Savage Eye, T. for Tumbleweed, Stakeout on Dope Street, Brazil—A Report on Torture, Interviews With Mai Lai Veterans, Interview—Chile's President Allende, Introduction to the Enemy. Elected by AMPAS to Bd. of Governors, Cinematographers Branch. 1991, elected by AMPAS to bd. of govs., Cinematographers Branch; 1993, received lifetime achievement award from American Society of Cinematographers.
PICTURES: Studs Lonigan, Five Bold Women, The Hoodlum Priest, Angel Baby, A Face in the Rain, America America, The Best Man, The Bus (also dir., prod.), The Loved One (also co-prod.), Who's Afraid of Virginia Woolf? (Academy Award,

1966), In the Heat of the Night, The Thomas Crown Affair, Medium Cool (also dir., co-prod., s.p.), Trial of Catonsville Nine, American Graffiti, One Flew Over the Cuckoo's Nest, Bound for Glory (Academy Award, 1976), Coming Home, Days of Heaven (addit. photog.), No Nukes (also co-dir.), Second Hand Hearts, Richard Pryor: Live on the Sunset Strip, Lookin' to Get Out, The Man Who Loved Women, Matewan (Oscar nom.), Colors, Latino (dir., writer only), Three Fugitives, Blaze (Oscar nom.), Through the Wire, Other People's Money, Rolling Stones at the MAX, The Babe, The Secret of Roan Inish, Canadian Bacon, The Sixth Sun: Mayan Uprising in Chiapas, Mulholland Falls, Rich Man's Wife, IMAX: Mexico, Stakeout on Dope Street.
TELEVISION: Steve McQueen: The King of Cool.

WHALEY, FRANK
Actor. b. Syracuse, NY, July 20, 1963. e. SUNY, Albany. With his brother formed rock band the Niagaras. Member of Malaparte Theatre Co. in NY.
THEATER: NY: Tigers Wild (debut, 1986), Face Divided, The Indian Wants the Bronx, The Years, Good Evening, Hesh, The Great Unwashed.
PICTURES: Ironweed (debut, 1987), Field of Dreams, Little Monsters, Born on the Fourth of July, The Freshman, Cold Dog Soup, The Doors, Career Opportunities, JFK, Back in the U.S.S.R., A Midnight Clear, Hoffa, Swing Kids, Pulp Fiction, I.Q., Swimming With Sharks, Homage, Cafe Society, Broken Arrow, Retroactive, Glam, When Trumpets Fade, Went to Coney Island on a Mission from God... Be Back By Five.
TELEVISION: Specials: Soldier Boys, Seasonal Differences. Movies: Unconquered, Flying Blind, Fatal Deception: Mrs. Lee Harvey Oswald, To Dance With the White Dog, The Desperate Trail, Dead Man's Gun. Pilot: Flipside. Guest: Spenser: For Hire, The Equalizer.

WHALLEY-KILMER, JOANNE
Actress. b. Manchester, England, Aug. 25, 1964. Began stage career while in teens including season of Edward Bond plays at Royal Court Theatre (Olivier Award nom.) and The Three Sisters, The Lulu Plays. NY: What the Butler Saw (Theatre World Award).
PICTURES: Dance with a Stranger, No Surrender, The Good Father, Willow, To Kill a Priest, Scandal, Kill Me Again, Navy SEALS, Crossing the Line, Shattered, Storyville, Mother's Boys, The Secret Rapture, Trial by Jury, A Good Man in Africa, The Man Who Knew Too Little.
TELEVISION: The Singing Detective, A Quiet Life, Edge of Darkness, A Christmas Carol, Save Your Kisses, Will You Love Me Tomorrow, Scarlett.

WHEATON, WIL
Actor. r.n. Richard William Wheaton III. b. Burbank, CA, July 29, 1972. Began acting in commercials at age 7. Graduated L.A. Professional H.S., June, 1990.
PICTURES: The Secret of NIMH (voice), The Buddy System, Hambone and Hillie, The Last Starfighter, Stand by Me, The Curse, Toy Soldiers, December, The Liars' Club, Pie in the Sky.
TELEVISION: Series: Star Trek: The Next Generation. Pilots: Long Time Gone, 13 Thirteenth Avenue, The Man Who Fell to Earth. Movies: A Long Way Home (debut, 1981), The Defiant Ones, Young Harry Houdini, The Last Prostitute. Specials: The Shooting, My Dad Can't Be Crazy Can He?, Lifestories (A Deadly Secret). Guest: St. Elsewhere, Family Ties, Tales From the Crypt, Outer Limits.

WHITAKER, FOREST
Actor, Director. b. Longview, TX, July 15, 1961. Raised in Los Angeles. e. Pomona Col., studying music; USC, studying opera and drama. Prof. debut in prod. of The Beggar's Opera.
THEATER: Swan, Romeo and Juliet, Hamlet, Ring Around the Moon, Craig's Wife, Whose Life Is It Anyway?, The Greeks (all at Drama Studio London); School Talk (LA), Patchwork Shakespeare (CA Youth Theatre), The Beggar's Opera, Jesus Christ Superstar. Dir.: Look Back in Anger, Drums Across the Realm.
PICTURES: Tag: The Assassination Game (debut, 1982), Fast Times at Ridgemont High, Vision Quest, The Color of Money, Platoon, Stakeout, Good Morning Vietnam, Bloodsport, Bird (Cannes Film Fest. Award, 1988), Johnny Handsome, Downtown, Rage in Harlem (also co-prod.), Article 99, Diary of a Hit Man, Consenting Adults, The Crying Game, Bank Robber, Body Snatchers, Blown Away, Jason's Lyric, Ready to Wear (Pret-a-Porter), Smoke, Species, Waiting to Exhale (dir.only), Phenomenon.
TELEVISION: Movies: Hands of a Stranger, Criminal Justice, Last Light, Strapped (dir. only), Lush Life, The Enemy Within. Guest: Amazing Stories, Hill Street Blues, Cagney and Lacey, Trapper John M.D., The Fall Guy, Different Strokes. Mini-Series: North and South Parts I & II.

WHITE, BETTY

Actress. b. Oak Park, IL, Jan. 17, 1924. Graduated from Beverly Hills H.S. Performed on radio beginning in early 1940's on such shows as Blondie, The Great Gildersleeve, This Is Your FBI. Became local L.A. tv personality in early 1950's prior to starring in her first series to be seen nationwide, Life With Elizabeth, in 1953. Was married to late tv host Allen Ludden. Inducted into Academy of Television Arts & Sciences Hall of Fame, 1994. Recipient of Comedy Lifetime Achievement Award.
AUTHOR: Betty White's Pet Love (1983), Betty White In Person (1987), The Leading Lady: Dinah's Story (1991), Here We Go Again: My Life in Television (1995).
PICTURE: Advise and Consent, The Flood.
TELEVISION: Series: Life With Elizabeth, Make the Connection (panelist), Date With the Angels, The Betty White Show (1958), The Jack Paar Show, The Pet Set, The Mary Tyler Moore Show (2 Emmy Awards: 1975, 1976), Match Game P.M. (panelist), Liar's Club (panelist), The Betty White Show (1977-78), Just Men (host; Emmy Award, 1983), Mama's Family, The Golden Girls (Emmy Award, 1986), The Golden Palace, Bob, Maybe This Time. Movies: Vanished, With This Ring, The Best Place to Be, Before and After, The Gossip Columnist, Chance of a Lifetime. Host: Macy's Thanksgiving Parade for 10 yrs, Tournament of Roses Parade (20 yrs.). Guest: The Millionaire, U.S. Steel Hour, Petticoat Junction, The Odd Couple, Sonny and Cher, The Love Boat, Hotel, Matlock, The John Laroquette Show (Emmy Award, 1996), Suddenly Susan, many others.

WHITE, LEONARD

Executive. Chairman & CEO, Orion Pictures Corporation.

WHITE, ROY B.

Executive, Exhibitor. b. Cincinnati, OH, July 30, 1926. e. U. of Cincinnati. U.S. Air Force during WWII; sales department of 20th Century-Fox, 1949-52; began in exhibition, 1952; past pres., Mid-States Theatres; chmn. R. M. White Management, Inc.; past president, National Association of Theatre Owners, past Chairman of the Board, NATO, Board of Trustees—American Film Inst.; bd.of dirs. NATO of Ohio, Motion Picture Pioneers Foundation; Will Rogers Hospital, Nat'l. Endowment for Arts.

WHITELAW, BILLIE

C.B.E., D.Litt.: Actress. b. Coventry, England, June 6, 1932. Acted on radio and television since childhood. Winner of the TV Actress of the Year and 1972, Guild Award, Best Actress, 1960. British Acad. Award 1969; U.S. National Society of Film Critics Award best supp. actress, 1968. Evening News, Best Film Actress, 1977; best actress Sony Radio Award 1987, 1989. 1988 Evening Standard Award for Best Actress.
THEATER: England Our England (revue), Progress to the Park, A Touch of the Poet, Othello; 3 yrs. with Natl. Theatre of Great Britain; Trelawney of the Wells, After Haggerty, Not I, Alphabetical Order, Footfalls, Molly, The Greeks, Happy Days, Passion Play, Rockaby (also in N.Y. and Adelaide Festival), Tales from Hollywood, Who's Afraid of Virginia Woolf?
PICTURES: The Fake (debut, 1953), Companions in Crime, The Sleeping Tiger, Room in the House, Small Hotel, Miracle in Soho, Gideon of Scotland Yard, Carve Her Name With Pride, Bobbikins, Mania, Hell Is a City, Make Mine Mink, No Love for Johnnie, Mr. Topaze (I Like Money), Payroll, The Devil's Agent, The Comedy Man, Charlies Bubbles, The Adding Machine, Twisted Nerve, Start the Revolution Without Me, Leo the Last, Eagle in a Cage, Gumshoe, Frenzy, Night Watch, The Omen, Leopard in the Snow, The Water Babies, An Unsuitable Job for a Woman, The Dark Crystal (voice), Tangier, Slayground, Shadey, The Chain, Murder Elite, Maurice, The Dressmaker, Joyriders, The Krays, Freddie as F.R.O.7 (voice), Deadly Advice.
TELEVISION: Over 100 leading roles including: No Trains to Lime Street, Lady of the Camelias, Resurrection, Beyond the Horizon, Anna Christie, You and Me, A World of Time, Dr. Jekyll and Mr. Hyde, Poet Game, Sextet (8 plays for BBC), Wessex Tales, The Fifty Pound Note, Supernatural (2 plays), Four plays by Samuel Beckett, Eustace and Hilda, The Oresteia of Aeschylus, The Haunted Man, Private Schultz, Jamaica Inn, Happy Days, Camille, Imaginary Friends, The Secret Garden, The Picnic, A Tale of Two Cities, The Fifteen Streets, Three Beckett plays, Lorna Doone, Duel of Love, A Murder of Quality, The Cloning of Joanna May, The Entertainer, Firm Friends, Skallagrigg.

WHITEMORE, HUGH

Writer. b. England, 1936. Studied acting at Royal Acad. of Dramatic Art. Has since written for television, film, theatre.
THEATER: Stevie, Pack of Lies, Breaking the Code, The Best of Friends, It's Ralph.
PICTURES: All Neat in Black Stockings, All Creatures Great and Small, Stevie, The Return of the Soldier, 84 Charing Cross Road, Utz, Jane Eyre.
TELEVISION: Cider With Rosie (Writers' Guild Award 1971), Elizabeth R (Emmy Award, 1971), Country Matters (Writers' Guild Award, 1972), Dummy (RAT—Prix Italia, 1979), Rebecca, All For Love, A Dedicated Man, Down at the Hydro, A Bit of Singing and Dancing, Concealed Enemies (Emmy & Neil Simon Awards, 1984), Pack of Lies, The Final Days, The Best of Friends, The Turn of the Screw.

WHITMAN, STUART

Actor. b. San Francisco, CA., Feb. 1, 1928. Army Corp. of Engineers (1945-1948), at Fort Lewis, WA; while in army, competed as light heavyweight boxer. Studied drama under G.I. Bill at Ben Bard Drama Sch. and L.A. City Coll. Performed in Heaven Can Wait and became member of Michael Chekhov Stage Society and Arthur Kennedy Group. Entered films in early 1950's. TV debut on 26 episodes of Highway Patrol.
PICTURES: When Worlds Collide, The Day The Earth Stood Still, Rhapsody, Seven Men From Now, War Drums, Johnny Trouble, Darby's Rangers, Ten North Frederick, The Decks Ran Red, China Doll, The Sound and the Fury, These Thousand Hills, Hound Dog Man, The Story of Ruth, Murder Inc., Francis of Assisi, The Fiercest Heart, The Mark (Acad. Award nom.), The Comancheros, Convicts 4, The Longest Day, The Day and the Hour (Fr./It.), Shock Treatment, Rio Conchos, Those Magnificent Men In Their Flying Machines, Sands of the Kalahari, Signpost to Murder, An American Dream, The Invincible Six, The Last Escape, Captain Apache (US/Sp.), Night Of The Lepus, Welcome To Arrow Beach (Tender Flesh), Crazy Mama, Call Him Mr. Shatter, Assault on Paradise (Maniac/Ransom), Mean Johnny Barrows, Las Vegas Lady, Eaten Alive!, Tony Saitta/Tough Tony (It.), Strange Shadows In An Empty Room, Ruby, The White Buffalo; Delta Fox, Thoroughbred (Run for the Roses), Oil (It. as Red Adair), La Murjer de la Tierra Caliente (Sp./It.); Guyana: Cult of the Damned, Cuba Crossing, Jamaican Gold, The Monster Club, Demonoid, Butterfly, Treasure of The Amazon, John Travis: Solar Survivor, Deadly Reactor, Moving Target, Mob Boss, Private Wars, Trail by Jury, Improper Conduct, Land of Milk and Honey.
TELEVISION: Series: Cimarron Strip, Shaunessy (pilot). Guest: The Crowd Pleaser (Alcoa-Goodyear), Highway Patrol, Dr. Christian, Hangman's Noose (Zane Grey), Walker Texas Ranger, Adventures of Brisco County Jr., Time Trax, Courthouse. Mini-Series: The Last Convertible, Hemingway. Movies: The Man Who Wanted to Live Forever, City Beneath the Sea, Revenge, The Woman Hunter, The Man Who Died Twice, Cat Creature, Go West Young Girl, The Pirate, Women in White, The Seekers, Condominium, Stillwatch, Once Upon a Texas Train, Wounded Heart.

WHITMORE, JAMES

Actor. r.n. James Allen Whitmore, Jr. b. White Plains, NY, Oct. 1, 1921. e. Yale U. In Yale Drama Sch. players; co-founder Yale radio station, 1942; U.S. Marine Corps, W.W.II; in USO, in American Wing Theatre school, in stock. Broadway debut in Command Decision, 1947.
THEATER: Give 'em Hell Harry, Will Rogers USA, Almost an Eagle.
PICTURES: The Undercover Man (debut, 1949), Battleground (Acad. Award nom.), The Asphalt Jungle, The Next Voice You Hear, Mrs. O'Malley and Mr. Malone, The Outriders, Please Believe Me, Across the Wide Missouri, It's a Big Country, Because You're Mine, Above and Beyond, The Girl Who Had Everything, All the Brothers Were Valiant, Kiss Me Kate, The Command, Them!, Battle Cry, The McConnell Story, The Last Frontier (Savage Wilderness), Oklahoma!, Crime in the Streets, The Eddie Duchin Story, The Deep Six, Face of Fire, Who Was That Lady?, Black Like Me, Chuka, Waterhole No. 3, Nobody's Perfect, Planet of the Apes, Madigan, The Split, Guns of the Magnificent Seven, Tora! Tora! Tora!, Chato's Land, The Harrad Experiment, Where the Red Fern Grows, Give 'em Hell Harry (Acad. Award nom.), The Serpent's Egg, Bully, The First Deadly Sin, The Adventures of Mark Twain (voice), Nuts, Old Explorers, The Shawshank Redemption, The Relic.
TELEVISION: Series: The Law and Mr. Jones, My Friend Tony, Temperature's Rising. Movies: The Challenge, If Tomorrow Comes, I Will Fight No More Forever, Rage, Mark I Love You, Glory! Glory!, Sky High. Mini-Series: The Word, Celebrity, Favorite Son. Special: All My Sons.

WHITTON, MARGARET

Actress. b. Baltimore, MD, Nov. 30, 1950. Raised in Haddonfield, NJ. Has written articles for Village Voice, The National.
THEATER: NY: Nourish the Beast (Off-B'way debut, 1973), Another Language, The Art of Dining, Chinchilla, Othello, One Tiger to a Hill, Henry IV Part 1, Don Juan, Steaming, Aunt Dan and Lemon, Ice Cream/Hot Fudge. Regional: Hamlet, Camille, Time and the Conways, The House of Blue Leaves.
PICTURES: National Lampoon Goes to the Movies (debut, 1981), Love Child, The Best of Times, 9-1/2 Weeks, The Secret of My Success, Ironweed, Major League, Little Monsters, Big Girl Don't Cry... They Get Even, The Man Without a Face, Major League 2, Trial by Jury.
TELEVISION: Series: Search for Tomorrow, Hometown, A Fine Romance, Good and Evil. Special: Motherlove. Movies: The Summer My Father Grew Up, Menendez: A Killing in Beverly Hills.

WIDMARK, RICHARD
Actor. b. Sunrise, MN, Dec. 26, 1914. e. Lake Forest U. Was
drama instructor, 1936, before going to NY where he acted on
many radio dramas, then stage.
PICTURES: Kiss of Death (debut, 1947), Road House, Street
With No Name, Yellow Sky, Down to the Sea in Ships, Slattery's
Hurricane, Night and the City, Panic in the Streets, No Way Out,
Halls of Montezuma, The Frogmen, Red Skies of Montana,
Don't Bother to Knock, O. Henry's Full House, My Pal Gus,
Destination Gobi, Pickup on South Street, Take the High
Ground, Garden of Evil, Hell & High Water, Broken Lance, Prize
of Gold, The Cobweb, Backlash, Run for the Sun, The Last
Wagon, Saint Joan, Time Limit, The Law and Jake Wade, The
Tunnel of Love, The Trap, Warlock, The Alamo, The Secret Ways,
Two Rode Together, Judgment at Nuremberg, How the West
Was Won, Flight from Ashiya, The Long Ships, Cheyenne
Autumn, The Bedford Incident, Alvarez Kelly, The Way West,
Madigan, Death of a Gunfighter, A Talent for Loving, The
Moonshine War, When The Legends Die, Murder on the Orient
Express, The Sell Out, To the Devil a Daughter, Twilight's Last
Gleaming, The Domino Principle, Rollercoaster, Coma, The
Swarm, Dinero Maldito, Bear Island, National Lampoon Goes to
the Movies, Hanky Panky, Who Dares Wins, The Final Option,
Against All Odds, True Colors.
TELEVISION: Series: Madigan. Movies: Vanished, Brock's Last
Case, The Last Day, Mr. Horn, All God's Children, A Whale for
the Killing, Blackout, A Gathering of Old Men, Once Upon a
Texas Train, Cold Sassy Tree. Special: Benjamin Franklin.

WIESEN, BERNARD
Producer, Director, Writer, Executive. b. New York, NY. e. City
Coll. of New York, B.A.; Pasadena Playhouse Coll. of Theatre,
Master of Theatre Arts; Dramatic Workshop of New School.
THEATER: First Monday in October (B'way, co. prod).
PICTURES: Producer-Director: Fear No More. Asst. Dir.: The
King and I, The Left Hand of God, The Rains of Ranchipur, To
Catch a Thief, The Trouble with Harry.
TELEVISION: Director: How to Marry a Millionaire, Valentine's
Day. Assoc. Producer: Valentine's Day, Three on an Island,
Cap'n Ahab, Sally and Sam. Assoc. Prod.: Daniel Boone.
Producer/Director: Julia, Co-Producer-Director: The Jimmy
Stewart Show. Prod. Exec.: Executive Suite (pilot). Exec.
Paramount TV, director of current programming. Writer: Love 4
Love, The Grand Turk.

WIEST, DIANNE
Actress. b. Kansas City, MO, March 28, 1948. e. U. of Maryland.
Studied ballet but abandoned it for theatre. Did regional theatre
work (Yale Repertory, Arena Stage), performed with NY
Shakespeare Festival, toured with American Shakespeare Co.
THEATER: Regional: Arena Stage (DC): Heartbreak House, Our
Town, The Dybbuk, Inherit the Wind. Yale Rep.: Hedda Gabler, A
Doll's House. NY: Ashes (NY debut, 1977, at Public Theatre),
Agamemnon, Leave It to Beaver Is Dead, The Art of Dining
(Obie & Theatre World Awards), Bonjour La Bonjour,
Frankenstein (B'way), Three Sisters, Othello, Beyond Therapy,
Other Places, Serenading Louie (Obie Award), After the Fall,
Not About Heroes (dir.; also at Williamstown Fest.), Hunting
Cockroaches, Square One, In the Summer House, Blue Light,
The Shawl (Off B'way), One Flea Spare (NY Public Theatre).
PICTURES: It's My Turn (debut, 1980), I'm Dancing as Fast as I
Can, Independence Day, Footloose, Falling in Love, The Purple
Rose of Cairo, Hannah and Her Sisters (Acad. Award, support-
ing actress, 1986), Radio Days, The Lost Boys, September,
Bright Lights Big City, Parenthood (Acad. Award nom.), Cookie,
Edward Scissorhands, Little Man Tate, Cops and Robbersons,
The Scout, Bullets Over Broadway (Academy Award, best sup-
porting actress, 1994; also Golden Globe, NY Film Critics, LA
Film Critics, Natl. Bd. of Review Awards), Drunks, The Birdcage,
The Associate, Practical Magic, The Horse Whisperer, Portofino.
TELEVISION: Specials: Zalman or the Madness of God, Out of
Our Father's House. Movies: The Wall, The Face of Rage. Guest:
Avonlea (Emmy Award, 1997)

WIGAN, GARETH
Executive. b. London, England, Dec. 2, 1931. e. Oxford. Agent,
MCA London; 1957; John Redway & Associates, 1960; co-
founder, agent Gregson & Wigan Ltd., 1961; co-founder, agent
London Intl., 1968; independent prod., 1970; v.p., creative
affairs, 20th Century Fox, 1975; v.p., prod., Fox, 1976; v.p., The
Ladd Co., 1979 -83. Company W.W. Prods. Currently exec. pro-
duction consultant, Columbia Pictures.
PICTURES: Unman Wittering & Zigo, Running Scared.

WIHTOL, ARN S.
Executive. b. Millville, NJ, Sept. 4, 1944. e. San Jose State. Exec.
v.p., international sales, Pacific International Enterprises.
PICTURES: Production Exec., Co-Writer: Mystery Mansion. Casting,
Controller: Dream Chasers. Producer's asst.: Sacred Ground.

WIKLUND, LENNART
Executive. Pres., CEO AB Svensk Filmindustri, Stockholm,
Sweden 1984-96. Exec. VP Bonnier Group (Svensk's parent),
1996-.

WILBY, JAMES
Actor. b. Rangoon, Burma, Feb. 20, 1958. Lived a nomadic
childhood moving from Burma to Ceylon, then Jamaica and
finally England. e. Durham U. Trained at Royal Acad. of Dramatic
Art where he played Shakespearean roles and landed a part in
Oxford Film Foundation's Privileged (1982). West End stage
debut Another Country. Also acted in regional theater. 1988: The
Common Pursuit.
PICTURES: Privileged (debut, 1982), Dreamchild, Maurice, A
Handful of Dust, A Summer Story, Immaculate Conception,
Howards End, The Chess Game, Une Partie d'Echec,
Regeneration: Tom's Midnight Garden.
TELEVISION: Dutch Girls, A Tale of Two Cities, Mother Love, Tell
Me That You Love Me, Adam Bede, Lady Chatterly, You Me and
It, Crocodile Shoes, Treasure Seekers, Original Sin, Witness
Against Hitler, The Woman in White.

WILDE, ARTHUR L.
Publicist. b. San Francisco, CA, May 27. S.F. Daily News;
Matson Lines; pub. dept., Warner Bros., 1936; photo editor at
Columbia Pictures, RKO Pictures, Universal Pictures; dir.
exploitation, CBS; pub. dir., Hal Wallis Prod.; pub. dept.,
Paramount; pub., Hecht-Hill-Lancaster; v.p., Arthur Jacobs, pub-
lic rel.; Blowitz-Maskell Publicity Agency; pub. dir., C. V. Whitney
Pictures; gen. v.p., 1958; owner, pub.-ad. agency, The Arthur L.
Wilde Co., 1961-65; freelance publicist, 1965-66; pub. rel. con-
sultant, Marineland of Florida 1965; unit publicity dir., United
Artists, National General, Paramount, 1966-69; freelance publicity, 1971; unit publicist, MGM, Paramount, United Artists, 1972-
74; staff position; Features Publicity at Paramount Pictures,
1973. Freelance unit publicist again in 1976 at Universal,
Paramount and Lorimar Productions. 1978-79, Columbia
Pictures & Universal Studios; 1980, Marble Arch. Prods. &
Northstar Intl. Pictures; 1981, studio pub. mgr. 20th Century-Fox;
recently staff unit publicist for 20th-Fox; 1984-89; currently freelance unit publicist for feature films.

WILDER, BILLY
Director, Writer, Producer. r.n. Samuel Wilder. b. Austria, June
22, 1906. Newspaperman in Vienna and Berlin; then author of
screen story People on Sunday (debut, 1929) followed by 10
other German films. including Emil and the Detectives (s.p.). Co-
dir. French film Mauvaise Graine with Alexander Esway (also
story), marking debut as director, 1933. To Hollywood 1934.
Head of Film Section, Psych. Warfare Div., U.S. Army, 1945,
American Zone, Germany. Recipient: American Film Institute
Life Achievement Award, 1987; Irving Thalberg Memorial Award,
1988.
PICTURES: U.S.: Co-Writer: Adorable (co-story), Music in the
Air, Lottery Lover, Champagne Waltz (co-story), Bluebeard's
Eighth Wife, Midnight, Ninotchka, What a Life, Rhythm on the
River (co-story), Arise My Love, Ball of Fire, Hold Back the
Dawn. Director/Co-Writer: The Major and the Minor (U.S. dir.
debut, 1942), Five Graves to Cairo, Double Indemnity, The Lost
Weekend (Academy Awards for Best Director and Adapted
Screenplay, 1945), The Emperor Waltz, A Foreign Affair, Sunset
Boulevard (Academy Award for Best Original Story &
Screenplay, 1950). Director-Co-Writer-Producer: Ace in the Hole
(The Big Carnival), Stalag 17, Sabrina, The Seven Year Itch (dir.
& co-s.p. only), The Spirit of St. Louis, Love in the Afternoon,
Witness for the Prosecution (dir. & co-s.p. only), Some Like It
Hot, The Apartment (Academy Awards for Best Picture, Director
and Original Story & Screenplay, 1960), One Two Three, Irma La
Douce, Kiss Me Stupid, The Fortune Cookie, The Private Life of
Sherlock Holmes, Avanti!, The Front Page (dir. & co-s.p. only),
Fedora, Buddy Buddy (dir. & co-s.p. only).

WILDER, GENE
Actor, Director, Writer. r.n. Jerry Silberman. b. Milwaukee, WI,
June 11, 1935. e. U. of Iowa. Joined Bristol Old Vic company in
England, became champion fencer; in NY, worked as chauffeur,
fencing instructor, etc. before NY off-B'way debut in Roots. Co-
founder of Gilda's Club, a cancer support center in Manhattan.
THEATER: B'way: The Complacent Lover, Mother Courage, Luv,
One Flew Over the Cuckoo's Nest.
PICTURES: Bonnie and Clyde (debut, 1967), The Producers
(Acad. Award nom.), Start the Revolution Without Me, Quackser
Fortune Has a Cousin in the Bronx, Willy Wonka and the
Chocolate Factory, Everything You Always Wanted to Know
About Sex* But Were Afraid to Ask, Rhinoceros, Blazing
Saddles, The Little Prince, Young Frankenstein (also co-s.p.),
The Adventure of Sherlock Holmes' Smarter Brother (also dir.,
s.p.), Silver Streak, The World's Greatest Lover (also dir., s.p.,
prod.), The Frisco Kid, Stir Crazy, Sunday Lovers (also dir. &
s.p.: episode: Skippy), Hanky Panky, The Woman in Red (also
dir., s.p.), Haunted Honeymoon (also dir., s.p., prod.), See No
Evil Hear No Evil (also co-s.p.), Funny About Love, Another You.
TELEVISION: Series: Something Wilder. Specials: The Man
Who Refused to Die, Death of a Salesman (1966), The
Scarecrow, Acts of Love—And Other Comedies, Annie and the
Hoods, The Trouble With People, Marlo Thomas Special. Movie:
Thursday's Game.

WILKINSON, TOM
Actor.
PICTURES: A Pocketful of Rye, Wetherby, Sylvia, Sharma and Beyond, Paper Mask, In the Name of the Father, Priest, All Things Bright and Beautiful, Business Affair, Sense and Sensibility, The Ghost and the Darkness, Wilde, Smilla's Sense of Snow, The Full Monty (BAFTA Award, Best Supporting Actor, 1997), Oscar and Lucinda, The Governess, Rush Hour, Shakespeare in Love, Father Damien.
TELEVISION: *Movies*: Sakharov, Shake Hands Forever, The Woman He Loved, The Attic: The Hiding of Anne Frank, First and Last, Prime Suspect, Resnick: Lonely Hearts, Eskimo Day, Crossing the Floor, Cold Enough for Snow. *Mini-series*: Spyship, Martin Chuzzlewit.

WILLENBORG, GREGORY H.
Producer. b. Miami, FL, Feb. 18, 1959. e. Geroge Washington U., B.B.A. 1981; UCLA M.B.A. Marketing & Strategic Planning 1983. During grad. school, worked at the political fundraising firm of Lynn, Bryan & Associates. In 1983, he formed Willenborg & Associates, a consulting grp. specializing in marketing and fundraising. Raised 25 million for the Bob Hope Cultural Center in Palm Desert, CA.
TELEVISION: America's Hope Awards (creator), America's Dance Awards (creator), America's Hope Award Honoring Bob Hope, America's All-Star Tribute to Elizabeth Taylor, Ray Charles: 50 Years in Music, An All-Star Tribute to Oprah Winfrey, Jerry Herman's Broadway at the Hollywood Bowl.

WILLIAMS, ANDY
Singer, Performer. b. Wall Lake, IA, Dec. 3, 1927. Sang as teen with brothers, performing on radio in Des Moines, Chicago, and Los Angeles. William Brothers were back up singers on Bing Crosby's hit recording of Swinging on a Star. Andy dubbed singing voice of Lauren Bacall in To Have and Have Not. Went solo after group disbanded in early 1950's.
PICTURES: Something to Sing About, I'd Rather Be Rich.
TELEVISION: *Series*: The College Bowl, Tonight (with Steve Allen; 1954-57), The Andy Williams and June Valli Show, The Chevy Showroom, The Andy Williams Show (1958), The Andy Williams Show (1962-67, 1969-71), The Andy Williams Show (synd.: 1976-77). *Specials*: Love Andy, Kaleidoscope Company, Magic Lantern Show Company, The NBC Kids Search for Santa, The NBC Kids Easter in Rome, many Christmas specials.

WILLIAMS, BERT
Executive, Actor. b. Newark, NJ, April 12, 1922. e. USC. Navy, 1942-45. Summer Stock, 1940-41; world's prof. diving champion, 1945-48; star diver, Larry Crosby, Buster Crabbe, Johnny Weismuller, Dutch Smith Shows, 1945-48; writer, asst. prod., Martin Mooney Prods., PRC, Goldwyn Studios; pres., Bert Prods., Bert Williams Motion Picture Producers and Distributors, Inc. Member, MP Academy of Fine Arts & TV Academy of Arts & Science. Masters Outdoor & Indoor National Diving, 1985-87, 89, 90. 1989 World Masters Diving Champion; 1990 & 1994 World Games Diving Champion.
THEATER: Cat on a Hot Tin Roof, Hamlet, Run From The Hunter, Sugar and Spice, Hope Is a Thing Called Feathers, 69 Below, Tribute.
PICTURES: *Actor*: Fort Apache, Rio Grande, American Bandito, Angel Baby; The Nest of the Cuckoo Birds (also prod., dir.), Around the World Under the Sea, Deathwatch 28 (s.p.), Gambit, No Secret, This Must be the Last Day of Summer, Twenty Eight Watched (dir.), Adventure To Treasure Reef (prod., dir.), Knife Fighters (s.p.), Black Freedom; A Crime of Sex, The Masters (prod., dir.), Crazy Joe, Serpico, Lady Ice, The Klansman, Report to the Commissioner, Tracks, All the President's Men, From Noon Till Three, While Buffalo, Shark Bait (s.p.), The Big Bus, Wanda Nevada, Cuba Crossing, Sunnyside, Cuba, The Last Resort, The All Night Treasure Hunt. Tom Horn, Kill Castro, Midnight Madness, The All-American Hustler, 10 to Midnight, Police Academy 2, One More Werewolf Picture, Silent Scream, Murphy's Law, Cobra, Assassinations, Penitentiary III, Messenger of Death, Death Under the Rock, Innocent Blood, Public Access, Tropic of Desire, Duel at Pueblo Solo, Project Eliminators, No Secret, The Usual Suspects.
TELEVISION: Flipper, Sea Hunt, Final Judgment, Project Eliminator, Speargun, Gentle Ben, The Law (pilot) and Police Story (actor), Get Christy Love, General Hospital, Columbo, Brenner for the People, Mayday 40,000 Feet, Jigsaw John (Blue Knight episode), Police Woman, Chips, Mobil One, Street Killing, East of Eden, Report for Emily, Brett Maverick, Today's F.B.I., The Judge, Fifth St. Gym (also prod., dir., s.p.; pilot), Helter Skelter, The Green Eyed Bear, The Amazing Howard Hughes, Mike Douglas Show, Johnny Carson Show, Tales from the Dark Side, The Last Car, This Is the Life, Deadly Intentions, Divorce Court, Man Who Broke 1000 Chains, Nightmare Classics (Eye of the Panther), Man from Atlantis, Land's End.

WILLIAMS, BILLY DEE
Actor. b. New York, NY, April 6, 1937. e. National Acad. of Fine Arts and Design. Studied acting with Paul Mann and Sidney Poitier at actor's workshop in Harlem. Was child actor in the Firebrand of Florence with Lotte Lenya; Broadway adult debut in The Cool World in 1961.
THEATER: A Taste of Honey, Hallelujah Baby, I Have a Dream, Fences.
PICTURES: The Last Angry Man (debut, 1959), The Out-of-Towners, The Final Comedown, Lady Sings the Blues, Hit!, The Take, Mahogany, The Bingo Long Travelling All-Stars and Motor Kings, Scott Joplin, The Empire Strikes Back, Nighthawks, Return of the Jedi, Marvin and Tige, Fear City, Number One with a Bullet, Deadly Illusion, Batman, The Pit and the Pendulum, Driving Me Crazy, Giant Steps, Alien Intruder.
TELEVISION: *Series*: The Guiding Light, Double Dare. *Mini-Series*: Chiefs. *Movies*: Carter's Army, Brian's Song, The Glass House, Christmas Lilies of the Field, Children of Divorce, The Hostage Tower, The Imposter, Courage, Oceans of Fire, The Right of the People, Dangerous Passion, The Jacksons: An American Dream, Marked for Murder, Percy & Thunder, Heaven & Hell: North and South Book III, Falling for You. *Guest*: The F.B.I., The Interns, Mission Impossible, Mod Squad, Dynasty, In Living Color.

WILLIAMS, CARA
Actress. r.n. Bernice Kamiat. b. Brooklyn, NY, June 29, 1925. e. Hollywood Professional Sch. Ent. ind., 20th Century Fox, child actress.
PICTURES: The Happy Land (debut, 1943), Something for the Boys, In the Meantime Darling, Boomerang!, Don Juan Quilligan, Sitting Pretty, The Saxon Charm, Knock on Any Door, The Girl Next Door, Monte Carlo Baby, The Great Diamond Robbery, Meet Me in Las Vegas, The Helen Morgan Story, Never Steal Anything Small, The Defiant Ones (Acad. Award nom.), The Man from the Diners' Club, Doctors' Wives, The White Buffalo.
TELEVISION: *Series*: Pete and Gladys, The Cara Williams Show, Rhoda. *Guest*: Alfred Hitchcock Presents, Desilu Playhouse, The Jackie Gleason Show, Henry Fonda Special.

WILLIAMS, CARL W.
Executive. b. Decatur, IL, March 9, 1927. e. Illinois State Normal U., B.S., 1949; UCLA, M.A., 1950. dir. adv. photo., Clark Equipment Co., 1951-54; film dir., WKAR-TV, E. Lansing, MI, 1954-56; Prod., dir., Capital Films, E. Lansing, MI, 1957; dir., A-V Laboratory, U.C.L.A., 1957-63; co-dev. Dimension 150 Widescreen process, 1957; formed D-150 Inc., 1963; Filbert Co., 1970, v.p., 1977; v.p., Cinema Equipment Sales of Calif., Inc., 1986; pres. 1992. Member: AMPAS, SMPTE, AFI.

WILLIAMS, CINDY
Actress. b. Van Nuys, CA., Aug. 22, 1947. e. Los Angeles City Coll. Appeared in high school and college plays; first prof. role in Roger Corman's film Gas-s-s-s. Made TV debut in Room 222 and had recurring role.
PICTURES: Gas-s-s-s (debut, 1970), Beware! the Blob, Drive He Said, The Christian Licorice Store, Travels With My Aunt, American Graffiti, The Conversation, Mr. Ricco, The First Nudie Musical, More American Graffiti, UFOria, Rude Awakening, Big Man on Campus, Bingo!, Father of the Bride II (co-prod. only), Meet Wally Sparks.
TELEVISION: *Series*: The Funny Side, Laverne and Shirley, Normal Life, Getting By. *Guest*: Barefoot in the Park, My World and Welcome to It, Love American Style, Nanny and the Professor, Getting Together, Lois and Clark. *Movies*: The Migrants, Helped Wanted: Kids, Save the Dog, Tricks of the Trade, The Leftovers, Perry Mason: The Case of the Poisoned Pen, Menu for Murder (Murder at the PTA Luncheon), Earth Angel, Escape From Terror: The Teresa Stamper Story, The Stepford Husbands. *Special*: The Laverne and Shirley Reunion. *Pilot*: Steel Magnolias, The Neighbors.

WILLIAMS, CLARENCE, III
Actor. b. New York, NY, Aug. 21, 1939. B'way stage: Slow Dance on the Killing Ground (Tony nom.; Theatre World Award), The Great Indoors, Night and Day.
PICTURES: Rituals, The End, Judgment, Road to Galveston, Purple Rain, 52 Pick-Up, Tough Guys Don't Dance, I'm Gonna Git You Sucka, My Heroes Have Always Been Cowboys, Deep Cover, Dead Fall, Sugar Hill, Tales From the Hood, The Immortals.
TELEVISION: *Series*: The Mod Squad. *Guest*: The Nasty Boys, Crazy Love, Miami Vice, Twin Peaks, Uptown Undercover, Cosby Mysteries. *Movies*: The Return of the Mod Squad, Against the Wall.

WILLIAMS, ELMO
Film Editor, Director, Producer. b. Oklahoma City, OK, Apr. 30, 1913. Film editor 1933-39, with British & Dominion Studio, England. Since then with RKO-Radio as film editor for numerous major productions; mgr., dir., 20th Century Fox Prod. Ltd. v.p., worldwide production, 20th Century-Fox Film 1971. President Ibex Films. Exec. v.p., Gaylord Prods., 1979; promoted to pres., worldwide prods.
PICTURES: High Noon (edit; Academy Award, 1952), Tall Texan (dir., edit.), The Cowboy (prod., dir., edit.), 20,000 Leagues Under the Sea (edit.), Apache Kid (dir.), The Vikings (2nd unit dir., film ed.), The Big Gamble (2nd Unit dir.), The Longest Day (assoc. prod.), Zorba the Greek (exec. prod.), Those Magnificent Men in Their Flying Machines (exec. prod.), The Blue Max (exec. prod.), Tora! Tora! Tora! (prod.), Sidewinder One (edit.), Caravans (edit.), Man Woman and Child (prod.).
TELEVISION: Tales of the Vikings (co-prod., dir.).

WILLIAMS, ESTHER
Actress, Swimmer. b. Los Angeles, CA, Aug. 8, 1923. e. USC. Swimmer at San Francisco World's Fair Aquacade; professional model. Signed to movie contract by MGM. Voted one of Top Ten Money-Making Stars in M.P. Herald-Fame poll, 1950.
PICTURES: Andy Hardy's Double Life (debut, 1942), A Guy Named Joe, Bathing Beauty, Thrill of a Romance, Ziegfeld Follies, The Hoodlum Saint, Easy to Wed, Fiesta, This Time for Keeps, On an Island With You, Take Me Out to the Ball Game, Neptune's Daughter, Pagan Love Song, Duchess of Idaho, Texas Carnival, Callaway Went Thataway (cameo), Skirts Ahoy!, Million Dollar Mermaid, Dangerous When Wet, Easy to Love, Jupiter's Darling, The Unguarded Moment, Raw Wind in Eden, The Big Show, The Magic Fountain, That's Entertainment III.
TELEVISION: Specials: Esther Williams in Cypress Gardens, Live From New York, Esther Williams Aqua Spectacular.

WILLIAMS, JO BETH
Actress. b. Houston, TX, Dec. 6, 1948. m. director John Pasquin. e. Brown U. One of Glamour Magazine's top 10 college girls, 1969-70. Acted with rep. companies in Rhode Island, Philadelphia, Boston, Washington, DC, etc. Spent over two years in New York-based day-time serials, Somerset and The Guiding Light.
THEATER: Ladyhouse Blues (1979), A Coupla White Chicks Sitting Around Talking, Gardenia.
PICTURES: Kramer vs. Kramer (debut, 1979), Stir Crazy, The Dogs of War, Poltergeist, Endangered Species, The Big Chill, American Dreamer, Teachers, Desert Bloom, Poltergeist II, Memories of Me, Welcome Home, Switch, Dutch, Stop Or My Mom Will Shoot, Me Myself & I, Wyatt Earp, Jungle 2 Jungle, Little City, It Came From the Sky.
TELEVISION: Movies: Fun and Games, The Big Black Pill, Feasting with Panthers, Jabberwocky, The Day After, Adam, Kids Don't Tell, Adam: His Song Continues, Murder Ordained, Baby M, My Name is Bill W, Child of the Night, Bump in the Night (co-exec. prod. only), Victim of Love, Jonathan: The Boy Nobody Wanted, Sex Love and Cold Hard Cash, Chantilly Lace, Final Appeal, Parallel Lives, Voices From Within, A Season of Hope. Series: Fish Police (voice), John Grisham's The Client.

WILLIAMS, JOHN
Composer. b. New York, NY, Feb. 8, 1932. e. UCLA, Juilliard Sch. Worked as session musician in '50s; began career as film composer in late '50s. Considerable experience as musical director and conductor as well as composer. Since 1977 conductor of Boston Pops.
PICTURES: I Passed for White, Because They're Young, The Secret Ways, Bachelor Flat, Diamond Head, Gidget Goes to Rome, The Killers, None But the Brave, John Goldfarb Please Come Home, The Rare Breed, How to Steal a Million, The Plainsman, Not with My Wife You Don't, Penelope, A Guide for the Married Man, Fitzwilly, Valley of the Dolls, Daddy's Gone A-Hunting, Goodbye Mr. Chips (music supvr. & dir.), The Reivers, Fiddler on the Roof (musc. dir.; Acad. Award, 1971). The Cowboys, Images, Pete 'n' Tillie, The Poseidon Adventure, Tom Sawyer (musc. supvr.), The Long Goodbye, The Man Who Loved Cat Dancing, The Paper Chase, Cinderella Liberty, Conrack, The Sugarland Express, Earthquake, The Towering Inferno, The Eiger Sanction, Jaws (Acad. Award, 1975), Family Plot, The Missouri Breaks, Midway, Black Sunday, Star Wars (Acad. Award, 1977), Raggedy Ann & Andy, Close Encounters of the Third Kind, The Fury, Jaws II, Superman, Meteor, Quintet, Dracula, 1941, The Empire Strikes Back, Raiders of the Lost Ark, Heartbeeps, E.T.: The Extra-Terrestrial (Acad. Award, 1982), Yes Giorgio, Monsignor, Return of the Jedi, Indiana Jones and the Temple of Doom, The River, SpaceCamp, The Witches of Eastwick, Empire of the Sun, The Accidental Tourist, Indiana Jones and the Last Crusade, Born on the Fourth of July, Always, Stanley & Iris, Presumed Innocent, Home Alone, Hook, JFK, Far and Away, Home Alone 2: Lost in New York, Jurassic Park, Schindler's List (Acad. Award, 1993), Sabrina., The Lost World, Seven Years In Tibet.

TELEVISION: Once Upon a Savage Night, Jane Eyre (Emmy Award), Sergeant Ryker, Heidi (Emmy Award), The Ewok Adventure. Series themes: Checkmate, Alcoa Premiere, Wide Country, Lost in Space, The Time Tunnel, NBC News Theme, Amazing Stories.

WILLIAMS, KENNETH S.
Executive. b. Tulsa, OK, Dec. 31, 1955. e. Harvard Coll., B.A. 1978; Columbia U., M.S. 1985. Began as team leader of Chase Manhattan's motion picture lending group 1978-81. Joined Sony Pictures Entertainment in Jan. 1982 as dir. of corporate finance, was promoted to assistant treas. Oct. 1982. He became treas. in Feb. 1984 and named a v.p. in Nov. 1984. Served as v.p. & treas. of both Columbia Pictures Industries, Inc. and the Entertainment Business Sector of the Coca-Cola Co. (Sony Pictures previous parent co.), 1986-87. 1987-90, corporate v.p. & treas. of Sony Pictures Entertainment and was then promoted to s.v.p., Corporate Operations. Was named exec. v.p. of Sony Picture Entertainment in Aug. 1995. Named pres. of Digital Division of Sony Pictures in Jan. 1997.

WILLIAMS, PAUL
Actor, Composer. b. Omaha, NE, Sept. 19, 1940. Began career at studios as set painter and stunt parachutist. Bit and character parts in commercials followed. Became song writer, collaborating briefly with Biff Rose and later with Roger Nichols, with whom wrote several best-sellers, including We've Only Just Begun, Rainy Days and Mondays, Just an Old-Fashioned Love Song.
PICTURES: Actor: The Loved One (debut, 1965), The Chase, Watermelon Man, Battle for the Planet of the Apes, Phantom of the Paradise (also songs), Smokey and the Bandit, The Cheap Detective, The Muppet Movie (also songs), Stone Cold Dead, Smokey and the Bandit II, Smokey and the Bandit 3, Zombie High, The Chill Factor, The Doors, Solar Crisis (voice), A Million to Juan, Headless Body in Topless Bar. Songs for Films: Cinderella Liberty, Bugsy Malone (also vocals), Lifeguard, A Star Is Born (co-composer; Academy Award for best song: Evergreen, 1976), One on One, The End, Agatha, Ishtar, The Muppet Christmas Carol, Headless Body in Topless Bar.
TELEVISION: Series: Sugar Time! (songs, music spvr.). Movies (actor): Flight to Holocaust, The Wild Wild West Revisited, Rooster, The Night They Saved Christmas, People Like Us, Hart to Hart Returns.

WILLIAMS, PAUL
Director. b. New York, NY, Nov. 12, 1943. e. Harvard (Phi Beta Kappa, 1965). First gained attention as director of film short, Girl, which won Golden Eagle award, made in collaboration with producer Edward R. Pressman, with whom he formed Pressman-Williams Enterprises which prod. Badlands, Phantom of the Paradise, etc. Now with Fulcrum Productions. In Rose Against the Odds, tv movie.
PICTURES: Out of It (also s.p.), The Revolutionary, Dealing: or the Berkeley-to-Boston Forty-Brick Lost-Bag-Blues (also s.p.), Nunzio, Miss Right (also story), The November Men (also actor), Mirage (also actor), Men (prod.).

WILLIAMS, RICHARD
Producer, Painter, Film Animator. b. March, 1933, Toronto, Canada. Entered industry in 1955. Founded Richard Williams Animation Ltd. in 1962, having entered films by producing The Little Island (1st Prize, Venice Film Festival) in 1955. His company produces TV commercials for England, America, France and Germany, entertainment shorts and animated films. Designed animated feature titles/sequences for What's New Pussycat?, A Funny Thing Happened On The Way To The Forum, Casino Royale, The Charge of the Light Brigade, A Christmas Carol (Academy Award for best animated short, 1972), Who Framed Roger Rabbit (dir. of animation), Arabian Knight (dir., prod., co-s.p.). Awards: at Festivals at Venice, Edinburgh, Mannheim, Montreal, Trieste, Melbourne, West Germany, New York, Locarno, Vancouver, Philadelphia, Zagreb, Hollywood, Cork, Los Angeles. 1989, Academy Award, BAFTA Award, AMPAS Award, special effects, also Special Achievement Awards for work over 30 years, esp. Roger Rabbit by both BAFTA and AMPAS.

WILLIAMS, ROBIN
Actor, Comedian. b. Chicago, IL, July 21, 1951. e. Claremont Men's Coll. (CA), Coll. of Marin (CA), studying acting at latter. Continued studies at Juilliard with John Houseman in New York augmenting income as a street mime. As San Francisco club performer appeared at Holy City Zoo, Intersection, The Great American Music Hall and The Boardinghouse. In Los Angeles performed as stand-up comedian at The Comedy Store, Improvisation, and The Ice House. First TV appearance on 1977 Richard Pryor series followed by The Great American Laugh Off. Guest on Happy Days as extraterrestrial Mork from Ork, led to own series.

PICTURES: Can I Do It...Til I Need Glasses? (debut, 1977), Popeye, The World According to Garp, The Survivors, Moscow on the Hudson, The Best of Times, Club Paradise, Good Morning Vietnam (Acad. Award nom.), The Adventures of Baron Munchausen, Dead Poets Society (Acad. Award nom.), Cadillac Man, Awakenings, Dead Again, The Fisher King (Acad. Award nom.), Hook, Shakes the Clown, FernGully... The Last Rainforest (voice), Aladdin (voice), Toys, Mrs. Doubtfire (also co-prod.), Being Human, Nine Months, To Wong Foo—Thanks for Everything—Julie Newmar, Jumanji, Birdcage, Jack, Hamlet, Good Will Hunting (Acad. Award, Best Supporting Actor, 1997), Flubber, What Dreams May Come.
TELEVISION: Series: The Richard Pryor Show (1977), Laugh-In (1977-78 revival; later aired as series in 1979), Mork and Mindy, Shakespeare: The Animated Tales (host). Guest: America Tonight, Ninety Minutes Live, The Alan Hamel Show. Specials: An Evening With Robin Williams, E.T. & Friends, Faerie Tale Theatre (The Frog Prince), Carol Carl Whoopi and Robin (Emmy Award, 1987), Free To Be... a Family, Dear America: Letters Home from Vietnam (reader), ABC Presents a Royal Gala (Emmy Award, 1988), In Search of Dr. Seuss. Movie: Seize the Day.

WILLIAMS, ROGER
Pianist, Concert, Film, TV Personality. b. Omaha, NE, Oct. 1, 1924. e. Drake U., Idaho State Coll. Hon. Ph.D. Midland and Wagner Colls. Served U.S. Navy WWII. Appeared as guest artist in number of films. Public debut on TV's Arthur Godfrey Talent Scouts and Chance of a Lifetime. Other TV appearances include Ed Sullivan, Hollywood Palace, Kraft Summer Series, Celanese Special. Recorded 75 Albums, Kapp (now MCA) Records, with sales over 15 million albums.

WILLIAMS, TREAT
Actor. r.n. Richard Williams. b. Rowayton, CT, Dec. 1, 1952. e. Franklin and Marshall Coll. Landed role on B'way in musical, Over Here! also played leading role in Grease on B'way.
THEATER: Over Here, Bus Stop (Equity Library Theatre), Once in a Lifetime, The Pirates of Penzance, Some Men Need Help, Oh Hell, Oleanna.
PICTURES: Deadly Hero (debut, 1976), The Ritz, The Eagle Has Landed, Hair, 1941, Why Would I Lie?, Prince of the City, The Pursuit of D. B. Cooper, Once Upon a Time in America, Flashpoint, Smooth Talk, The Men's Club, Dead Heat, Sweet Lies, Heart of Dixie, Night of the Sharks, Russicum, Beyond the Ocean, Where the Rivers Flow North, Hand Gun, Things to Do in Denver When You're Dead, Mulholland Falls, The Phantom, The Devil's Own.
TELEVISION: Movies: Dempsey, A Streetcar Named Desire, J. Edgar Hoover, Echoes in the Darkness, Third Degree Burn, Max and Helen, Final Verdict, Till Death Us Do Part, The Water Engine, Deadly Matrimony, Bonds of Love (also co-exec. prod), Parallel Lives, In the Shadow of Evil. Mini-Series: Drug Wars: The Camarena Story. Specials: The Little Mermaid (Faerie Tale Theatre), Some Men Need Help, Texan (also dir.), Edgar Allan Poe: Terror of the Soul. Series: Eddie Dodd, Good Advice. Guest: Tales From the Crypt.

WILLIAMS-JONES, MICHAEL
Executive. b. England, June 3, 1947. Joined United Artists as trainee, 1967; territorial mgr., South Africa, 1969; territorial mgr., Brazil, 1971; territorial mgr., England, 1976; appt. v.p., continental European mgr., 1978; sr. v.p. foreign mgr., 1979; 1982 joined United Intl. Pictures as sr. v.p. intl. sls., based in London. 1984, named pres. UIP motion picture group; 1986, named pres. & CEO. In Dec. 96, retired from UIP to create own production co., Merlin Angelsey U.K. Ltd.

WILLIAMSON, FRED
Actor, Director, Producer, Writer. b. Gary, IN, March 5, 1937. e. Northwestern U. Spent 10 yrs. playing pro football before turning to acting.
PICTURES: M*A*S*H (debut, 1970), Tell Me That You Love Me Junie Moon, Fist of Fear Touch of Death, Taxi Killer (prod.), The Legend of Nigger Charlie, Hammer, That Man Bolt, The Soul of Nigger Charlie, Hell Up in Harlem, Black Caesar, Three Tough Guys, Three Days to a Kill (also dir., s.p.), Justice Done (also dir.), Soda Cracker (also dir., prod.), Three the Hard Way, Crazy Joe, Black Eye, `Boss Nigger, Death Journey (also dir., prod.), Bucktown, The Black Bounty Killer (also prod.), Adios Amigo (also dir., prod., s.p.), Take a Hard Ride, Mean Johnny Barrows (also dir., prod.), Joshua, No Way Back (also dir., prod., s.p.), Quel Maledetto Treno Blindato, Mr. Mean (also dir., prod.), Hell's Heroes, Blind Rage, Express to Terror, Fist of Fear Touch of Death, Vigilante, Warriors of the Wasteland, One Down Two to Go (also dir., prod.), The Last Fight (also dir., s.p.), Warriors of the Year 2072, The Big Score (also dir.), 1990: The Bronx Warriors, Warrior of the Lost World, White Fire, Deadly Impact, Foxtrap (also dir., prod.), Delta Force Commando, The Black Cobra, Deadly Intent, Taxi Killer (prod. only), The Kill Reflex (also dir.), Detective Malone, Steele's Law (also dir.), Critical Action (also dir.), Delta Force Commando II: Priority Red One, South Beach (also dir., prod.), Silent Hunter (also dir.), From Dusk Till Dawn, Original Gangstas (also prod.), Full Tilt Boogie.

TELEVISION: Series: Julia, Monday Night Football, Half Nelson, Fast Track. Guest: Police Story, The Rookies, Lou Grant. Movies: Deadlock, 3 Days to a Kill. Mini-series: Wheels

WILLIAMSON, NICOL
Actor. b. Hamilton, Scotland, Sept. 14, 1938. Has played many classical roles with Royal Shakespeare Co., including Macbeth, Malvolio, and Coriolanus. Starred on Broadway in Inadmissible Evidence, Rex (musical debut), Macbeth, I Hate Hamlet. London: Jack.
PICTURES: Inadmissible Evidence (debut, 1968), The Bofors Gun, Laughter in the Dark, The Reckoning, Hamlet, The Jerusalem File, The Monk, The Wilby Conspiracy, Robin and Marian, The Seven Percent Solution, The Goodbye Girl (cameo), The Cheap Detective, The Human Factor, Excalibur, Venom, I'm Dancing as Fast as I Can, Return to Oz, Black Widow, The Exorcist III, Apt Pupil, The Advocate.
TELEVISION: Movies: Sakharov, Passion Flower. Mini-Series: Lord Mountbatten, The Word, Christopher Columbus. Specials: Of Mice and Men, Macbeth, I Know What I Meant.

WILLIAMSON, PATRICK
Executive. b. England, Oct. 1929. Joined Columbia Pictures London office 1944—career spanned advertising & publicity responsibilities until 1967 when appt. managing dir. Columbia Great Britain; also mng. dir. on formation of Columbia-Warner; promoted to exec. position in Columbia's home office, NY, 1973, and pres. of intl. optns. 1974; v.p., Coca-Cola Export Corp., 1983; exec. v.p. Columbia Pictures Industries, 1985; director, CPI, 1985; exec. v.p., Coca-Cola Entertainment Business Sector, 1987; promoted to special asst. to pres. & CEO of Coca-Cola Entertainment Business Sector, 1987; served on boards of Tri-Star Pictures, RCA/Columbia Home Video, RCA/Columbia Int'l. Video; 1987, named pres. Triumph Releasing Corp., a unit of Columbia Pictures Entertainment; Consultant to Sony Pictures Entertainment, 1989. 1994, dir. & co-founder, Sports Alliance Intl. TV.

WILLIS, BRUCE
Actor. b. Germany, March 19, 1955. m. actress Demi Moore. Moved to New Jersey when he was 2. After graduating high school, worked at DuPont plant in neighboring town. First entertainment work was as harmonica player in band called Loose Goose. Formed Night Owl Promotions and attended Montclair State Coll. NJ, where he acted in Cat on a Hot Tin Roof. NY stage debut: Heaven and Earth. Member of Barbara Contardi's First Amendment Comedy Theatre; supplemented acting work by doing Levi's 501 jeans commercials and as bartender in NY nightclub, Kamikaze. Appeared as extra in film The First Deadly Sin.
THEATER: Fool for Love.
PICTURES: Blind Date, Sunset, Die Hard, In Country, Look Who's Talking (voice), That's Adequate, Die Hard 2, Look Who's Talking Too (voice), The Bonfire of the Vanities, Mortal Thoughts, Hudson Hawk (also co-story), Billy Bathgate, The Last Boy Scout, The Player, Death Becomes Her, National Lampoon's Loaded Weapon 1 (cameo), Striking Distance, North, Color of Night, Pulp Fiction, Nobody's Fool, Die Hard With a Vengeance, Twelve Monkeys, Last Man Standing, Mercury Rising, Armageddon.
TELEVISION: Series: Moonlighting (Emmy Award, 1987). Guest: Hart to Hart, Miami Vice, Twilight Zone. Special: Bruce Willis: The Return of Bruno (also writer, prod.).

WILLIS, GORDON
Cinematographer. Acted two summers in stock at Gloucester, MA, where also did stage settings and scenery. Photographer in Air Force; then cameraman, making documentaries. In TV did commercials and documentaries.
PICTURES: End of the Road, Loving, The Landlord, The People Next Door, Little Murders, Klute, The Godfather, Bad Company, Up the Sandbox, The Paper Chase, The Parallax View, The Godfather Part II, The Drowning Pool, All the President's Men, Annie Hall, Interiors, September 30, 1955, Comes a Horseman, Manhattan, Stardust Memories, Pennies from Heaven, A Midsummer Night's Sex Comedy, Zelig, Broadway Danny Rose, The Purple Rose of Cairo, Perfect, The Money Pit, The Pick-Up Artist, Bright Lights Big City, Presumed Innocent, The Godfather Part III, Malice, The Devil's Own. Director: Windows (1980; debut).
TELEVISION: Movie: The Lost Honor of Kathryn Beck.

WILSON, ELIZABETH
Actress. b. Grand Rapids, MI, April 4, 1921.
THEATER: B'way: Picnic (debut, 1953), The Desk Set, The Tunnel of Love, Little Murders, Big Fish Little Fish, Sheep on the Runway, Sticks and Bones (Tony Award, 1972), Uncle Vanya, Morning's at Seven, Ah! Wilderness, The Importance of Being Earnest, You Can't Take It With You, A Delicate Balance. Off-B'way: Sheep on the Runway, Token in Marriage (Drama Desk Award), Three Penny Opera, Salonika, Ante Room, Eh?, All's Well That Ends Well. Tour: The Cocktail Hour.

PICTURES: Picnic (debut, 1955), Patterns, The Goddess, The Tunnel of Love, Happy Anniversary, A Child is Waiting, The Birds, The Tiger Makes Out, The Graduate, Jenny, Catch-22, Little Murders, Day of the Dolphin, Man on a Swing, The Happy Hooker, The Prisoner of Second Avenue, Nine to Five, The Incredible Shrinking Woman, Grace Quigley, Where Are the Children?, The Believers, Regarding Henry, The Addams Family, Quiz Show, Nobody's Fool.
TELEVISION: Series: East Side West Side, Doc, Morningstar/ Eveningstar, Delta. Movies: Miles to Go Before I Sleep, Once Upon a Family, Million Dollar Infield, Sanctuary of Fear, Morning's at Seven, Nutcracker: Money Madness and Murder (Emmy nom.), Conspiracy of Love, Skylark, In the Best of Families: Marriage Pride & Madness, Bitter Blood, In the Best Families, Spring Awakening, Journey to Mars. Mini-Series: Queen, Scarlett, Promised Land, Delaventure. Specials: Patterns, Happy Endings, You Can't Take It With You. Guest: U.S. Steel Hour, Maude, All in the Family, Love Sidney, Murder She Wrote, The Boys Next Door.

WILSON, FLIP
Performer. r.n. Clerow Wilson. b. Newark, NJ, Dec. 8, 1933. Left school at 16 to join Air Force; played clubs in FL & Bahamas until 1965 when made guest appearance on NBC.
PICTURES: Uptown Saturday Night, Skatetown USA, The Fish That Saved Pittsburgh.
TELEVISION: Series: The Flip Wilson Show (Emmy Award for writing, 1971), People Are Funny (1984, host), Charlie & Co. Guest: That's Life, Sammy and Company, Love American Style, Here's Lucy, The Six Million Dollar Man, 227, etc. Specials: Flip Wilson Special (1969), Clerow Wilson and the Miracle of P.S. 114, Clerow Wilson's Great Escape, Pinocchio, Zora is My Name.

WILSON, HUGH
Producer, Director, Writer. b. Miami, FL, Aug. 21, 1943. e. Univ. of FL., 1965. Gained fame for creating, writing, producing and directing TV series, WKRP in Cincinnati, Frank's Place and The Famous Teddy Z. Feature film dir. debut with Police Academy (1984).
PICTURES: Director &/or Writer: Stroker Ace, Rough Riders, Police Academy, Rustler's Rhapsody, Burglar, Guarding Tess (also voice), Down Periscope (co-s.p.), Blast From the Past, The First Wives Club.

WILSON, ROYCE
Executive. b. Rison, AR, Feb. 19, 1957. e. U. of Arkansas, BS/BA, 1980. Sales mgr., Viacom: 1980-83. Sales mgr., KATV Little Rock, 1983-84. VP (southwest), Paramount TV, 1984-87. East. reg. mgr., 1987-90. SVP, syndication, Columbia TriStar Domestic TV, 1990-94. Founder, MaXaM, 1994-96. Pres., Eyemark Entertainment, CBS Entertainment Division, CBS, Inc., 1996-.

WILSON, SCOTT
Actor. b. Atlanta, GA, 1942. Was college athlete on basketball scholarship when injured and had to leave school. Moved to L.A. and enrolled in local acting class.
PICTURES: In the Heat of the Night (debut, 1967), In Cold Blood, The Gypsy Moths, Castle Keep, The Grissom Gang, The New Centurions, Lolly Madonna XXX, The Great Gatsby, Twinkle Twinkle Killer Kane (The Ninth Configuration), The Right Stuff, The Aviator, On the Line, A Year of the Quiet Sun, Blue City, Malone, Johnny Handsome, The Exorcist III, Young Guns II, Femme Fatale, Pure Luck, Flesh and Bone, Geronimo: An American Legend, Tall Tale, Judge Dredd, The Grass Harp, Dead Man Walking, Shiloh, G.I. Jane, Our God's Brother, Clay Pigeons, Pride.
TELEVISION: Movies: Jesse, Elvis and the Colonel, Soul Survivors, California Quartet, Tracker.

WINANS, CHARLES A.
Executive. Exec. dir., National Association of Concessionaires.

WINCER, SIMON
Director. b. Australia. Directed over 200 hours of dramatic programs for Australian TV, including Cash and Company, Tandarra, Ryan, Against the Wind, The Sullivans, etc. Exec. prod. of The Man from Snowy River, then the top-grossing theatrical film in Australia.
PICTURES: Snapshot (The Day After Halloween), Harlequin, Phar Lap, D.A.R.Y.L., The Lighthorsemen (also co.-prod.), Quigley Down Under, Harley Davidson and the Marlboro Man, Free Willy, Lightning Jack (also co-prod.), Operation Dumbo Drop, The Phantom, Flash.
TELEVISION: Movies: The Last Frontier, Bluegrass, Lonesome Dove (Emmy Award, 1989), The Girl Who Spelled Freedom. Series: Homicide (prod.) Matlock Police, The Box, Cash & Company, Young Ramsey, The Young Indiana Jones Chronicles. Escape: Human Cargo. Mini-series: Against the Wind.

WINCHELL, PAUL
Actor, Ventriloquist. b. New York, NY, Dec. 21, 1922. e. Sch. of Industrial Arts. At 13 won first prize Major Bowes Radio Amateur Hour; signed by Ted Weems; created dummies Jerry Mahoney and Knucklehead Smiff. On radio as host of his own show in 1940's. In the news in 1975 as inventor of an artificial heart.
PICTURES: Stop! Look! and Laugh! (actor), Winnie the Pooh and the Blustery Day (short; voice), The Aristocats (voice), Which Way to the Front? (actor), Winnie the Pooh and Tigger Too (short; voice), The Fox and the Hound (voice).
TELEVISION: Series: The Bigelow Show, The Paul Winchell-Jerry Mahoney Spiedel Show (also prod., writer), Jerry Mahoney's Club House (also writer), What's My Name?, Circus Time (ringmaster), Toyland Express (also prod.), The Paul Winchell Show (1957-60), Banana Splits Adventure Hour (voice), Runaround. Voices for series: The Wacky Races, Cartoonsville, Dastardly and Mutley, Help It's the Hair Bear Bunch, Goober and the Ghost Chaser, The Oddball Couple, Clue Club, The C.B. Bears, Wheelie and the Chopper, Heathcliff and Marmaduke Show, The Smurfs, Winnie the Pooh Hour, various Dr. Seuss specials, Smurf specials. Movie: The Treasure Chest. Guest: Pat Boone Show, Polly Bergen Show, The Lineup, Candid Camera, The Beverly Hillbillies, 77 Sunset Strip, Donna Reed Show, Perry Mason, Dick Van Dyke Show, Lucy Show, Love American Style, Brady Bunch, many others.

WINCOTT, MICHAEL
Actor. b. Canada, Jan. 6, 1959. Studied acting at Juilliard. NY stage incl. Talk Radio, States of Shock.
PICTURES: Wild Horse Hank (debut, 1979), Circle of Two, Ticket to Heaven, Curtains, The Sicilian, Talk Radio, Suffering Bastards, Bloodhounds of Broaway, Born on the Fourth of July, The Doors, Robin Hood: Prince of Thieves, 1492: Conquest of Paradise, The Three Musketeers, Romeo Is Bleeding, The Crow, Panther, Strange Days, Dead Man, Basquiat, Alien: Resurrection, Metro, Gunshy.
TELEVISION: Movies: Tragedy of Flight 103: The Inside Story. Guest: Miami Vice, Crime Story, The Equalizer. Special: High School Narc.

WINDOM, WILLIAM
Actor. b. New York, NY, Sept. 28, 1923.
PICTURES: To Kill a Mockingbird (debut, 1962), Cattle King, For Love or Money, One Man's Way, The Americanization of Emily, Hour of the Gun, The Detective, The Gypsy Moths, The Angry Breed, Brewster McCloud, Fool's Parade, Escape From the Planet of the Apes, The Mephisto Waltz, The Man, Now You See Him Now You Don't, Echoes of a Summer, Mean Dog Blues, Separate Ways, Last Plane Out, Grandview U.S.A., Prince Jack, Space Rage, Funland, Pinocchio and the Emperor of the Night (voice), Planes Trains and Automobiles, She's Having a Baby, Sommersby, Miracle on 34th Street.
TELEVISION: Series: The Farmer's Daughter, My World and Welcome to It (Emmy Award, 1970), The Girl With Something Extra, Brothers and Sisters, Murder She Wrote, Parenthood. Movies: Prescription: Murder, U.M.C., The House on Greenapple Road, Assault on the Wayne, Escape, A Taste of Evil, Marriage: Year One, The Homecoming, Second Chance, A Great American Tragedy, Pursuit, The Girls of Huntington House, The Day the Earth Moved, The Abduction of St. Anne, Journey from Darkness, Guilty or Innocent: The Sam Sheppard Murder Case, Bridger, Richie Brockelman: Missing 24 Hours, Hunters of the Reef, Portrait of a Rebel: Margaret Sanger, Leave 'Em Laughing, Side Show, Desperate Lives, The Rules of Marriage, Why Me?, Off Sides, Velvet, Surviving, There Must Be a Pony, Dennis the Menace, Chance of a Lifetime, Attack of the 50 Ft. Woman. Mini-Series: Once an Eagle, Seventh Avenue, Blind Ambition. Guest: Robert Montgomery Presents, Ben Casey, Lucy Show, The FBI, Gunsmoke, Partridge Family, That Girl, The Rookies, Streets of San Francisco, Barney Miller, Kojak, Police Woman, Love Boat, St. Elsewhere, Newhart, Night Gallery, Twilight Zone, Star Trek, many others.

WINDSOR, MARIE
Actress. r.n. Emily Marie Bertelsen. b. Marysvale, UT, Dec. 11, 1919. Winner of beauty contests, including Queen of Covered Wagon Days. Worked as telephone girl, dancing teacher. Trained for acting by Maria Ouspenskaya. Won Look Mag. Award, best supporting actress, 1957.
PICTURES: All-American Co-Ed (debut, 1941), Song of the Thin Man, Unfinished Dance, On an Island With You, Three Musketeers, Kissing Bandit, Force of Evil, Oupost in Morocco, Fighting Kentuckian, Beautiful Blonde From Bashful Bend, Frenchie, Dakota Lil, Little Big Horn, Two Dollar Bettor, Hurricane Island, The Narrow Margin, Japanese War Bride, The Jungle, The Sniper, The Tall Texan, The City That Never Sleeps, The Eddie Cantor Story, Trouble Along the Way, Cat Women of the Moon, Hell's Half Acre, The Bounty Hunter, No Man's Woman, Abbott & Costello Meet the Mummy, Swamp Women, Two Gun Lady, The Killing, The Unholy Wife, The Story of Mankind, Girl in Black Stockings, Parson and the Outlaw, Island Woman, Paradise Alley, The Day Mars Invaded Earth, Critics Choice, Mail Order Bride, Bedtime Story,

Chamber of Horrors, Support Your Local Gunfighter, The Good Guys and the Bad Guys, One More Train To Rob, Cahill U.S. Marshall, The Outfit, Hearts of the West, Freaky Friday, Lovely But Deadly.
TELEVISION: *Series*: Supercarrier. *Movies*: Wild Women, Manhunter, Salem's Lot, J.O.E. and the Colonel.

WINFIELD, PAUL
Actor. b. Los Angeles, CA, May 22, 1940. e. attended U. of Portland 1957-59, Stanford U., L.A. City Coll, and UCLA. Inducted in Black Filmmakers Hall of Fame.
THEATER: Regional work at Dallas Theatre Center (A Lesson From Aloes), Goodman Theatre (Enemy of the People), Stanford Repertory Theatre and Inner City Cultural Center, L.A.; At Lincoln Center in The Latent Heterosexual, and Richard III. B'way: Checkmates, Othello, Merry Wives of Windsor.
PICTURES: The Lost Man (debut, 1969), R.P.M., Brother John, Sounder (Acad. Award nom.), Trouble Man, Gordon's War, Conrack, Huckleberry Finn, Hustle, Twilight's Last Gleaming, The Greatest, Damnation Alley, A Hero Ain't Nothin' But a Sandwich, High Velocity, Carbon Copy, Star Trek II—The Wrath of Khan, White Dog, On the Run, Mike's Murder, The Terminator, Blue City, Death Before Dishonor, Big Shots, The Serpent and the Rainbow, Presumed Innocent, Cliffhanger, Dennis the Menace, Original Gangstas, Mars Attacks!.
TELEVISION: *Series*: Julia, The Charmings, Wiseguy, 227, Built to Last. *Movies*: The Horror at 37,000 Feet, It's Good to Be Alive (The Fight), Green Eyes, Angel City, Key Tortuga, The Sophisticated Gents, Dreams Don't Die, Sister Sister, For Us the Living, Go Tell It on the Mountain, Under Siege, The Roy Campanella Story, Guilty of Innocence, Women of Brewster Place, Roots: The Gift, Back to Hannibal, Breathing Lessons, Tyson. *Mini-Series*: King, Backstairs at the White House, The Blue and the Gray, Roots: The Next Generations, Queen, Scarlett.

WINFREY, OPRAH
TV Talk Show Hostess, Actress, Producer. b. Kosciusko, MS, Jan. 29, 1954. e. Tennessee State U. Started as radio reporter then TV news reporter-anchor in Nashville. Moved to Baltimore in same capacity, later co-hosting successful morning talk show. Left for Chicago to host own show AM Chicago which became top-rated in only a month; expanded to national syndication in 1986. Formed own production co., Harpo Productions, Inc. in 1986 which assumed ownership and prod. of The Oprah Winfrey Show in 1988. Named Broadcaster of the Year by Intl. Radio and TV Soc., 1988. Purchased Chicago movie and TV production facility, 1988; renamed Harpo Studios. National Daytime Emmy Award, 1987, Outstanding Talk/Service Program Host.
PICTURES: The Color Purple (debut, 1985; Acad. Award nom.), Native Son, Throw Momma From the Train (cameo), Listen Up: The Lives of Quincy Jones, Beloved.
TELEVISION: *Movies*: The Women of Brewster Place (actress, co-exec. prod.), Overexposed (co-prod. only), There Are No Children Here, Lincoln (voice), Before Women Had Wings, About Us: The Dignity of Children. *Series*: The Oprah Winfrey Show (many Emmy Awards), Brewster Place (also exec. prod.). *Special*: Pee-wee's Playhouse Christmas Special. *Mini-series*: The Wedding.

WINGER, DEBRA
Actress. b. Cleveland, OH, May 16, 1955. e. California State U. Began career on TV series Wonder Woman.
PICTURES: Slumber Party '57 (debut, 1977), Thank God It's Friday, French Postcards, Urban Cowboy, Cannery Row, An Officer and a Gentleman (Acad. Award nom.), Terms of Endearment (Acad. Award nom.), Mike's Murder, Legal Eagles, Black Widow, Made in Heaven, Betrayed, Everybody Wins, The Sheltering Sky, Leap of Faith, Wilder Napalm, A Dangerous Woman, Shadowlands (Acad. Award nom.), Forget Paris.
TELEVISION: *Movie*: Special Olympics. *Guest*: Wonder Woman, James at 16.

WINITSKY, ALEX
Producer. b. New York, NY, Dec. 27, 1924. e. NYU, BS, LLB, JD. In partnership as attorneys in L.A. for 20 years with Arlene Sellers before they turned to financing and later production of films.
PICTURES: *Co-prod. with Sellers*: End of the Game, The White Dawn, The Seven-Per-Cent Solution, Cross of Iron, Silver Bears, The Lady Vanishes, Cuba, Blue Skies Again, Irreconcilable Differences, Scandalous, Swing Shift, Bad Medicine, Stanley & Iris, Circle of Friends.
TELEVISION: Ford—The Man and the Machine.

WINKLER, HENRY
Actor, Producer, Director. b. New York, NY, Oct. 30, 1945. e. Emerson Coll., Yale Sch. of Drama, MA. Appeared with Yale Repertory Co.; returned to N.Y. to work in radio. Did 30 TV commercials before starring in The Great American Dream Machine and Masquerade on TV. Formed Fairdinkum Productions with Ann Daniel.

PICTURES: *Actor*: Crazy Joe (debut, 1974), The Lords of Flatbush, Heroes, The One and Only, Night Shift, Scream, The Waterboy. *Exec. Prod*: The Sure Thing, Sightings 6 Years, Dead Man's Gun. *Director*: Memories of Me, Cop and a Half.
TELEVISION: *Series* (actor): Happy Days, Monty. *Series (prod.)*: Ryans Four (co-prod.), Mr. Sunshine (co-exec. prod.), McGyver, A Life Apart. *Guest*: The Mary Tyler Moore Show, The Bob Newhart Show, The Paul Sand Show, Rhoda, Laverne & Shirley, The Larry Sanders Show. *Specials*: Henry Winkler Meets William Shakespeare, America Salutes Richard Rodgers, A Family Again (exec. prod.), Two Daddies (voice, exec. prod.). *Movies*: Katherine, An American Christmas Carol, Absolute Strangers, The Only Way Out, Truman Capote's One Christmas, A Child Is Missing. *Director*: A Smoky Mountain Christmas (movie), All the Kids Do It (also actor, exec. prod.; Emmy Award as exec. prod., 1985). *Exec. prod.*: Who Are the DeBolts and Where Did They Get 19 Kids?, Scandal Sheet, When Your Lover Leaves, Starflight, Second Start, Morning Glory (pilot), MacGyver: Lost Treasure of Atlantis, MacGyver: Trail to Doomsday.

WINKLER, IRWIN
Producer, Director. b. New York, NY, May 28, 1934. e. NYU.
PICTURES: *Producer*: Double Trouble, Blue, The Split, They Shoot Horses Don't They?, The Strawberry Statement, Leo the Last, Believe in Me, The Gang That Couldn't Shoot Straight, The Mechanic, The New Centurions, Up the Sandbox, Busting, S*P*Y*S, The Gambler, Breakout, Peeper, Rocky (Academy Award for Best Picture, 1976), Nickelodeon, New York New York, Valentino, Comes a Horseman, Uncle Joe Shannon, Rocky II, Raging Bull, True Confessions, Rocky III, Author! Author!, The Right Stuff, Rocky IV, Revolution, 'Round Midnight, Betrayed, Music Box, GoodFellas, Rocky V, The Juror, At First Sight (also writer, dir.). *Director*: Guilty by Suspicion (also s.p.), Night and the City, The Net (also co-s.p., co-prod.).

WINNER, MICHAEL
Producer, Director, Writer. b. London, England, Oct. 30, 1935. e. Cambridge U. Ent. m.p. ind. as columnist, dir., Drummer Films. *Presenter*: Michael Winner's True Crimes. *Actor*: For the Greater Good, Decadence, Calliope, Kenny Everett Show, The Full Wax, Birds of a Feather.
PICTURES: *Writer*: Man With A Gun. *Dir.-Writer*: Haunted England (also prod.), Shoot to Kill, Swiss Holiday, Climb Up the Wall, Out of the Shadow, Some Like It Cool, Girls Girls Girls, It's Magic, Behave Yourself, The Cool Mikado, You Must Be Joking, West 11 (dir. only). *Dir./Prod.*: The System (The Girl-Getters), I'll Never Forget What's 'is Name, The Jokers, Hannibal Brooks (also s.p.), The Games, Lawman, The Nightcomers, Chato's Land, The Mechanic (dir. only), Scorpio (also s.p.), The Stone Killer, Death Wish, Won Ton Ton the Dog Who Saved Hollywood, The Sentinel (also s.p.), The Big Sleep (also s.p.), Firepower (also s.p.), Death Wish II, The Wicked Lady (also s.p.), Scream for Help, Death Wish III (dir. only), Appointment With Death (also s.p.), A Chorus of Disapproval (also s.p.), Bullseye (also s.p.), Dirty Weekend (also s.p.).
TELEVISION: *Series*: White Hunter, Dick and the Duchess.

WINNINGHAM, MARE
Actress. r.n. Mary Megan Winningham. b. Phoenix, AZ, May 16, 1959. TV debut at age 16 as a singer on The Gong Show. Debut solo album What Might Be released in 1992.
PICTURES: One-Trick Pony, Threshold, St. Elmo's Fire, Nobody's Fool, Made in Heaven, Shy People, Miracle Mile, Turner and Hooch, Hard Promises, Teresa's Tattoo, Wyatt Earp, The War, Georgia (Indep. Spirit Award, Best Supporting Actress, 1996), The Deliverance of Elaine, Bad Day on the Block.
TELEVISION: *Mini-Series*: The Thorn Birds, Studs Lonigan. *Movies*: Special Olympics, The Death of Ocean View Park, Amber Waves (Emmy Award, 1980), Off the Minnesota Strip, The Women's Room, Freedom, A Few Days in Weasel Creek, Missing Children: A Mother's Story, Helen Keller: The Miracle Continues, Single Bars Single Women, Love Is Never Silent, Who is Julia, A Winner Never Quits, Eye on the Sparrow, God Bless the Child, Love and Lies, Crossing to Freedom, Fatal Exposure, She Stood Alone, Those Secrets, Intruders, Better Off Dead, Betrayed by Love, Letter to My Killer, The Boys Next Door, George Wallace (Emmy Award, 1998), Little Girl Fly Away, Everything That Rises.

WINSLET, KATE
Actress. b. Reading, England, Oct. 5, 1975. Began studying drama at age 11.
THEATER: *U.K. Regional*: Adrian Mole, Peter Pan, What the Butler Saw, A Game of Soldiers.
PICTURES: Heavenly Creatures, Sense and Sensibility (BAFTA, Screen Actors Guild Awards, Academy Award nom. 1996), A Kid In King Arthur's ourt, Jude, Hamlet, Titanic.
TELEVISION: *Series*: Casualty, Dark Season, Get Back.

WINSTON, STAN
Makeup and Special Effects Artist. b. 1946. e. UofVA. Started in business in 1970 as apprentice to Robert Schiffer at makeup dept. of Walt Disney Studios. Established Stan Winston Studio in Van Nuys, CA.
PICTURES: W.C. Fields and Me, The Wiz, Dead and Buried, Heart Beeps, The Thing, The Entity, Something Wicked This Way Comes, The Terminator, Starman, Invaders From Mars, Aliens (Academy Award for Visual Effects, 1986), Predator, The Monster Squad, Alien Nation, Pumpkinhead (dir. debut), Leviathan, Predator 2, Edward Scissorhands, Terminator 2: Judgment Day (2 Academy Awards: Visual Effects and Makeup, 1991), A Gnome Named Gnorm (dir.), Batman Returns, Jurassic Park (Academy Award for Visual Effects, 1993), Interview With the Vampire, Tank Girl, Congo, Ghosts.
TELEVISION: Movies: Gargoyles (Emmy Award for Makeup, 1972), The Autobiography of Miss Jane Pittman (Emmy Award for Makeup, 1974), Roots. Specials: Masquerade, Pinocchio, An Evening With Diana Ross.

WINTER, ALEX
Actor. b. London, England, July 17, 1965. e. NYU. At age 4 began studying dance. Played opposite Vincent Price in St. Louis Opera production of Oliver! Co-founder of Stern-Winter Prods. Produced videos for Red Hot Chili Peppers, Human Radio, Ice Cube, etc. Co-directed TV special Hard Rock Cafe Presents: Save the Planet.
THEATER: B'way: The King and I (1977 revival), Peter Pan (1979 revival). Off-B'way: Close of Play.
PICTURES: Death Wish III, The Lost Boys, Haunted Summer, Bill & Ted's Excellent Adventure, Rosalie Goes Shopping, Bill & Ted's Bogus Journey, Freaked (also co-dir., co-s.p., co-prod.).
TELEVISION: Movie: Gaugin the Savage. Series: Idiot Box (also co-creator, co-dir., co-writer).

WINTERS, DAVID
Choreographer, Actor, Director. b. London, April 5, 1939. Acted in both Broadway and m.p. version of West Side Story (as A-rab). Directed and acted in number of TV shows. Pres., A.I.P. Distribution, A.I.P. Productions and A.I.P. Home Video, 1989, formed Pyramid Distributors.
PICTURES: Choreographer: Viva Las Vegas, Billie, Send Me No Flowers, Bus Riley's Back In Town, Tickle Me, Pajama Party, Girl Happy, The Swinger, Made in Paris, Easy Come, Easy Go, The Island of Doctor Moreau, Roller Boogie, A Star is Born, Blame It on the Night. Director: Welcome to My Nightmare, Racquet, The Last Horror Show, The Last Horror Film (also prod., s.p., act.), Thrashin', Rage to Kill, The Mission... Kill, Space Mutiny (also prod.), Code Name Vengeance. Producer: Young Lady Chatterley, Future Force, Raw Nerve, Operation Warzone, Raw Justice, Good Cop Bad Cop, The Dangerous, Codename: Silencer. Actor: Rock Rock Rock, West Side Story, The Crazy-Quilt.
TELEVISION: Choreographer: Series: Hullabaloo, Shindig, Donny and Marie Osmond, The Big Show, and Steve Allen Show. Specials starring: Joey Heatherton, Nancy Sinatra, Diana Ross, Raquel Welch, Ann Margret, Lucille Ball. Movies: Firehead, Raw Nerve, Center of the Web, Double Vision.

WINTERS, DEBORAH
Actress. b. Los Angeles, CA. e. Professional Children's Sch., New York; began studying acting at Stella Adler's with Pearl Pearson. at age 13 and Lee Strasberg at 16. Acting debut at age 5 in TV commercials. Casting dir.: Aloha Summer (asst.), Breakdancers From Mars (assoc. prod., casting dir.), Into the Spider's Web, The Hidden Jungle, Haunted, Broken Spur, Behind the Mask (also assoc. prod.).
PICTURES: Me Natalie, Hail Hero!, The People Next Door, Kotch, Class of '44, Blue Sunshine, The Lamp, The Outing.
TELEVISION: Special: Six Characters in Search of an Author. Guest: Matt Houston, Medical Center. Movies: Lottery, Gemini Man. Tarantulas: The Deadly Cargo, Little Girl Lost, Space City. Mini-Series: The Winds of War.

WINTERS, JONATHAN
Actor. b. Dayton, OH, Nov. 11, 1925. e. Kenyon Coll.; Dayton Art Inst., B.F.A. Disc jockey, Dayton and Columbus stations; night club comedian performing at Blue Angel and Ruban Bleu (NY), Black Orchid (Chicago), Flamingo, Sands, Riviera (Las Vegas), then on B'way in John Murray Anderson's Almanac. Author: Mouse Breath, Conformity and Other Social Ills, Winters Tales, Hang Ups (book on his paintings). Recorded 7 comedy albums. Won Grammy Award for "Crank Calls" comedy album, 1996.
PICTURES: Alakazam the Great! (voice), It's a Mad Mad Mad Mad World, The Loved One, The Russians Are Coming the Russians Are Coming, Penelope, Oh Dad Poor Dad Mama's Hung You in the Closet and I'm Feeling So Sad, Eight on the Lam, Viva Max, The Fish That Saved Pittsburgh, The Longshot, Say Yes, Moon Over Parador, The Flintstones, The Shadow, Arabian Knight (voice).

TELEVISION: Series: And Here's the Show, NBC Comedy Hour, The Jonathan Winters Show (1956-57), Masquerade Party (panelist), The Andy Williams Show, The Jonathan Winters Show (1967-69), Hot Dog, The Wacky World of Jonathan Winters, Mork and Mindy, Hee Haw, The Smurfs (voice of Papa Smurf), The Completely Mental Misadventures of Ed Grimley (voices), Davis Rules (Emmy Award, 1991), Fish Police (voice). Guest: Steve Allen Show, Garry Moore Show, Jack Paar, Omnibus, Twilght Zone, Bob Hope specials, Tonight Show, Hollywood Squares, many others. Specials: The Jonathan Winters Special, The Jonathan Winters Show (1964, 1965), Jonathan Winters Presents 200 Years of American Humor, 'Tis the Season to Be Smurfy (voice). Movies: Now You See It—Now You Don't, More Wild Wild West.

WINTERS, SHELLEY
Actress. r.n. Shirley Schrift. b. St. Louis, MO, Aug. 18, 1922. e. Wayne U. Clerked in 5 & 10 cent store; in vaudeville, chorus girl in night clubs; NY stage (Conquest, Night Before Christmas, Meet the People, Rosalinda, A Hatful of Rain, Girls of Summer, Minnie's Boys, One Night Stand of a Noisy Passenger. (Off-B'way). Autobiographies: Shelley Also Known as Shirley (1981), Shelley II: The Middle of My Century (1989).
PICTURES: What a Woman! (debut, 1943), Nine Girls, Sailor's Holiday, Knickerbocker Holiday, Cover Girl, A Double Life, Cry of the City, Larceny, Take One False Step, Johnny Stool Pigeon, The Great Gatsby, South Sea Sinner, Winchester '73, Frenchie, A Place in the Sun, He Ran All the Way, Behave Yourself, The Raging Tide, Phone Call From a Stranger, Meet Danny Wilson, Untamed Frontier, My Man and I, Tennessee Champ, Executive Suite, Saskatchewan, Playgirl, To Dorothy a Son (Cash on Delivery), Mambo, Night of the Hunter, I Am a Camera, Big Knife, Treasure of Pancho Villa, I Died a Thousand Times, The Diary of Anne Frank (Academy Award, best supporting actress, 1959), Odds Against Tomorrow, Let No Man Write My Epitaph, Young Savages, Lolita, Chapman Report, The Balcony, Wives and Lovers, Time of Indifference, A House Is Not a Home, A Patch of Blue (Academy Award, best supporting actress, 1965), The Greatest Story Ever Told, Harper, Alfie, Enter Laughing, The Scalphunters, Wild in the Streets, Buona Sera Mrs. Campbell, The Mad Room, How Do I Love Thee?, Bloody Mama, Flap, What's the Matter with Helen?, Who Slew Auntie Roo?, The Poseidon Adventure, Cleopatra Jones, Something to Hide, Blume in Love, Diamonds, Journey Into Fear, That Lucky Touch, Next Stop Greenwich Village, The Tenant, Tentacles, Pete's Dragon, King of the Gypsies, The Magician of Lublin, The Visitors, City on Fire, S.O.B., Over the Brooklyn Bridge, Ellie, Witchfire (also assoc. prod.), Deja Vu, Very Close Quarters, The Delta Force, The Order of Things, Purple People Eater, An Unremarkable Life, Touch of a Stranger, Stepping Out, Weep No More My Lady, The Pickle, The Silence of the Hams, Heavy, Jury Duty, Portrait of a Lady.
TELEVISION: Special: Bob Hope Chrysler Theatre: Two Is the Number (Emmy Award, 1964). Movies: Revenge, A Death of Innocence, The Adventures of Nick Carter, The Devil's Daughter, Big Rose, The Sex Symbol, The Initiation of Sarah, Elvis, Alice in Wonderland, Mrs. Munck. Mini-Series: The French Atlantic Affair.

WINTMAN, MELVIN R.
Theatre Executive, b. Chelsea, MA. e. U. of Massachusetts, Northeastern U., J.D. Major, infantry, AUS, W.W.II. Attorney. Now consultant & dir., General Cinema Corp.; formerly exec. v.p., GCC and pres., GCC Theatres, Inc., Boston. Dir. Will Rogers Memorial Fund. Former pres. Theatre Owners of New England (1969-70); past dir. NATO (1969-70); treas., Nat'l Assoc. of Concessionaires (1960).

WISDOM, NORMAN
O.B.E. Actor, Singer, Comedian. b. London, England, Feb. 4, 1915. Awarded Order of the British Empire (O.B.E.), 1995. Many London West End stage shows including royal command performances. N.Y. B'way shows include Walking Happy and Not Now Darling.
PICTURES: A Date With a Dream (debut, 1948), Meet Mr. Lucifer, Trouble in Store, One Good Turn, As Long as They're Happy, Man of the Moment, Up in the World, Just My Luck, The Square Peg, Follow a Star, There Was a Crooked Man, The Bulldog Breed, The Girl on the Boat, On the Beat, A Stitch in Time, The Early Bird, Press for Time, The Sandwich Man, The Night They Raided Minsky's, What's Good for the Goose, Double X.
TELEVISION: Androcles and the Lion.

WISE, ROBERT
Director, Producer. b. Winchester, IN, Sept. 10, 1914. e. Franklin Coll., Franklin, IN. Ent. m.p. ind. in cutting dept. RKO, 1933; sound cutter, asst. edit.; film edit., 1938; edited Citizen Kane, Magnificent Ambersons; 1944, became dir.; to 20th Century-Fox, 1949; ass'n Mirisch Co. independent prod. 1959; assn. MGM independent prod., 1962; assn. 20th Century Fox Independent Prod. 1963. Partner, Filmakers Group, The Tripar Group. Amer. Film Inst. Life Achievement Award, 1998.

PICTURES: Curse of the Cat People (debut as co-dir., 1944), Mademoiselle Fifi, The Body Snatcher, A Game of Death, Criminal Court, Born to Kill, Mystery in Mexico, Blood on the Moon, The Set-Up, Three Secrets, Two Flags West, The House on Telegraph Hill, The Day the Earth Stood Still, The Captive City, Something for the Birds, Destination Gobi, The Desert Rats, So Big, Executive Suite, Helen of Troy, Tribute to a Bad Man, Somebody Up There Likes Me, Until They Sail, This Could Be the Night, Run Silent Run Deep, I Want to Live!, Odds Against Tomorrow (also prod.), West Side Story (co-dir., prod.; Acad. Awards for Best Picture & Director, 1961), Two For the Seesaw, The Haunting (also prod), The Sound of Music (also prod.; Acad. Awards for Best Picture & Director, 1965), The Sand Pebbles (also prod.), Star! (also prod.), The Andromeda Strain (also prod.), Two People (also prod.), The Hindenburg (also prod.), Audrey Rose, Star Trek: The Motion Picture, Wisdom (exec. prod. only), Rooftops.

WISEMAN, FREDERICK
Documentary Filmmaker, Producer, Director & Editor. b. Boston, MA, Jan. 1, 1930. e. Williams College, B.A., 1951; Yale Law Sch., L.L.B., 1954. Member: MA Bar. Private law practice, Paris, 1956-57. Lecturer-in-Law, Boston U. Law Sch., 1959-61; Russell Sage Fndn. Fellowship, Harvard U., 1961-62; research assoc., Brandeis U., dept. of sociology, 1962-66; visiting lecturer at numerous universities. Author: Psychiatry and Law: Use and Abuse of Psychiatry in a Murder Case (American Journal of Psychiatry, Oct. 1961). Co-author: Implementation (section of report of President's Comm. on Law Enforcement and Administration of Justice). Fellow, Amer. Acad. of Arts & Sciences, 1991; John D. and Catherine T. MacArthur Foundation Fellowship, 1982-87; John Simon Guggenheim Memorial Foundation Fellowship, 1980-81. Films are distributed through his Zipporah Films, located in Cambridge, MA. Awards include 3 Emmys, Peabody Award, Intl. Documentary Assn. Career Achievement Award, 3 Columbia Dupont Awards for Excellence in Broadcast Journalism, among others.
PICTURES: Titicut Follies, High School, Law and Order, Hospital, Basic Training, Essene, Juvenile Court, Primate, Welfare, Meat, Canal Zone, Sinai Field Mission, Manoeuvre, Model, Seraphita's Diary, The Store, Racetrack, Deaf, Blind, Multi-Handicapped, Adjustment and Work, Missile, Near Death, Central Park, Aspen, Zoo, High School II, Ballet, La Comedie Francaise, Public Housing.

WISEMAN, JOSEPH
Actor. b. Montreal, Canada, May 15, 1918.
THEATER: King Lear, Golden Boy, The Diary of Anne Frank, Uncle Vanya, The Last Analysis, Enemies, Detective Story, Three Sisters, Tenth Man, Incident at Vickey, Marco Williams, Unfinished Stories, many others.
PICTURES: Detective Story (debut, 1951), Viva Zapata, Les Miserables, Champ for a Day, The Silver Chalice, The Prodigal, Three Brave Men, The Garment Jungle, The Unforgiven, Happy Thieves, Dr. No, Bye Bye Braverman, The Counterfeit Killer, The Night They Raided Minsky's, Stiletto, Lawman, The Valachi Papers, The Apprenticeship of Duddy Kravitz, Journey Into Fear, The Betsy, Buck Rogers in the 25th Century, Jaguar Lives.
TELEVISION: Mini-Series: QB VII, Masada, Rage of Angels. Movies: Pursuit, Murder at the World Series, Seize the Day, Lady Mobster, Ghost Writer. Series: Crime Story.

WITHERS, GOOGIE
Actress. b. Karachi, India, Mar. 12, 1917. Trained as a dancer under Italia Conti, Helena Lehmiski & Buddy Bradley; stage debut Victoria Palace in Windmill Man, 1929. Best Actress Award, Deep Blue Sea, 1954. Began screen career at 18. TV also. Theatrical tours Australia, Sun Award, Best Actress, 1974. Awarded officer of the Order of Australia (A.O.) 1980. U.S. ACE Cable award, best actress for Time After Time, 1988.
THEATER: Britain: Winter Journey, Deep Blue Sea, Hamlet, Much Ado About Nothing. Australia: Plaza Suite, Relatively Speaking, Beckman Place, Woman in a Dressing Gown, The Constant Wife, First Four Hundred Years, Roar Like a Dove, The Cherry Orchard, An Ideal Husband. London: Getting Married, Exit the King. New York: The Complaisant Lover. Chichester Festival Theatre and Haymarket, London, in The Circle, The Kingfisher, Importance of Being Earnest, The Cherry Orchard, Dandy Dick, The Kingfisher (Australia and Middle East), Time and the Conways (Chichester), School for Scandal (London), Stardust (UK tour). 1986: The Chalk Garden, Hay Fever, Ring Round the Moon, The Cocktail Hour (UK, Australian tour), High Spirits (Aus. tour), On Golden Pond (UK tour).
PICTURES: Haunted Honeymoon, Jeannie, One of Our Aircraft Is Missing, On Approval, Dead of Night, It Always Rains on Sunday, Miranda, Traveler's Joy, Night and the City, White Corridors, Lady Godiva Rides Again, Derby Day, Devil on Horseback, Safe Harbor, Nickel Queen, Country Life, Shine.
TELEVISION: Series: Within These Walls, Time After Time, Movies: Hotel Du Lac, Northanger Abbey, Ending Up.

WITHERS, JANE
Actress. b. Atlanta, GA, April 12, 1927. By 1934 attracted attention as child player on screen, after radio appearance in Los Angeles and experimental pictures parts, in 1934 in Fox production Bright Eyes, Ginger; thereafter to 1942 featured or starred in numerous 20th-Fox prod. Voted Money-Making Star M.P. Herald-Fame Poll, 1937, 1938. Starred as Josephine the Plumber in Comet tv commercials. TV Movie: All Together Now.
PICTURES: Handle With Care (debut, 1932), Bright Eyes, Ginger, This Is the Life, The Farmer Takes a Wife, Paddy O'Day, Pepper, Gentle Julia, Little Miss Nobody, Can This Be Dixie?, Wild and Woolly, The Holy Terror, Checkers, Angel's Holiday, Forty-Five Fathers, Always in Trouble, Rascals, Keep Smiling, Arizona Wildcat, Pack Up Your Troubles, Chicken Family Wagon, Boy Friend, Shooting High, High School, Youth Will Be Served, The Girl From Avenue A, Golden Hoofs, A Very Young Lady, Her First Beau, Small Town Deb, Young America, The Mad Martindales, Johnny Doughboy, The North Star, My Best Gal, Faces in the Fog, The Affairs of Geraldine, Danger Street, Giant, The Right Approach, Captain Newman M.D.

WITT, PAUL JUNGER
Producer. b. New York, NY, Mar. 20, 1941. e. Univ. of VA. Was assoc. prod., prod. and dir. for Screen Gems, starting in 1965; prod. for Spelling-Goldberg Prods., 1972; Prod.-exec. prod. for Danny Thomas Prods., 1973. With Tony Thomas became co-founder, exec. prod. of Witt/Thomas Prods., 1975.
PICTURES: Firstborn, Dead Poets Society, Final Analysis, Mixed Nuts.
TELEVISION: Series: Here Come the Brides, The Partridge Family, The Rookies, Soap, Benson, It's a Living, I'm a Big Girl Now, It Takes Two, Condo, Hail to the Chief, The Golden Girls (Emmy Awards: 1986, 1987), Beauty and the Beast, Empty Nest, Blossom, Good and Evil, Herman's Head, Nurses, Woops, Golden Palace, The John Larroquette Show, Brotherly Love, Minor Adjustments, Common Law, Pearl. Movies: Brian's Song (Emmy Award: 1972), No Place to Run, Home for the Holidays, A Cold Night's Death, The Letters, Blood Sport, Remember When, The Gun and the Pulpit, Satan's Triangle, Griffin and Phoenix, High Risk, Trouble in High Timber Country, Radiant City.

WOLF, DICK
Producer, Writer. b. New York, NY, Dec. 20, 1946. e. Univ. of PA. Started in advertising winning three Clio Awards for excellence.
PICTURES: Prod./Writer: Skateboard, Gas, No Man's Land, Masquerade (exec. prod., writer, actor), School Ties (story only).
TELEVISION: Series (exec. prod.): Miami Vice (also writer), Gideon Oliver (also writer), Christine Cromwell (also creator), Nasty Boys (also creator, writer), H.E.L.P. (also creator, writer), Law and Order (also creator, writer), Mann and Machine (also writer), The Human Factor, Crime and Punishment (also creator), South Beach (also creator), New York Undercover (also creator), The Wright Verdicts (also creator), FEDS (creator), Players (prod.).

WOLF, EMANUEL L.
Executive. b. Brooklyn, NY, Mar. 27, 1927. e. Syracuse U., B.A., 1950; Maxwell Sch., Syracuse U., M.A. 1952; Maxwell Scholar in Public Admin.-Economics; Chi Eta Sigma (Econ. Hon.). 1952-55. Management consultant, exec. office of Secretary of Navy & Dept. of Interior, Wash, DC, 1956; pres. E.L. Wolf Assocs., Washington, DC, 1961-65; Kalvex, Inc., treas: 1962, dir.: 1963, pres./chmn. of bd.: 1966; dir. Allied Artists Pictures Corp., 1965; chmn. of bd. Vitabath, Inc., Lexington Instruments, Pharmaceutical Savings Plan, Inc. (also pres.) Syracuse U.; corp. advisory bd., American Committee for the Weizmann Institute of Science (Bd. of Directors); pres. & chmn. of bd., Allied Artists Pictures Corp: 1976: pres., bd. chmn. & CEO, Allied Artists Industries Inc.; a company formed by Merger of Allied Artists Pictures Corp., Kalvex Inc. and PSP, Inc. 1985, formed indep. prod. co., Emanuel L. Wolf Prods.; 1986-90, pres. & chmn. of bd., Today Home Entertainment. 1991-present. Emanuel L. Wolf Prods., Inc. Chmn., Allied Artists Entertainment Group. Member, AMPAS.

WOLF, THOMAS HOWARD
TV News Exec. b. New York, NY, April 22, 1916. e. Princeton U., B.A., magna cum laude, 1937. Time & Life Mag. 1937-39; 1937-39 NEA (Scripps-Howard) 1940-46; European mgr., NEA, 1942-46. War correspondent, (ETO, MTO) NBC radio correspondent, Paris, 1944-45; co-owner, pres., Information Prod., Inc. founded 1951; co-owner, chmn. Butterfield & Wolf, Inc. founded 1955; prod. CBS series Tomorrow, 1960; exec. prod., CBS daily live Calendar Show, 1961-62; sr. prod., ABC News Report, 1963; exec. prod., ABC Scope, 1964-66. v.p. dir. of TV Documentaries, 1966; v.p., dir. of TV Public Affairs, 1974; dir. TV Cultural Affairs, 1976. Pres., Wolf Communications, Inc., 1981-; consultant Smithsonian Institution, 1981-88.
TELEVISION: ABC News Reports, ABC Scope, Now, Issues and Answers, Directions, Make a Wish, Animals Animals Animals.

WOLFSON, RICHARD
Executive. b. New York, NY, Jan. 7, 1923. e. Harvard Coll., Yale Law Sch., 1945-47, law clerk to Justice Wiley Rutledge, U.S. Supreme Court. Law instructor at NYU Law Sch.; 1952, joined Wometco Ent. as counsel and asst. to pres.; named v.p. and dir. in 1959 and sr. v.p. in 1962; named exec. v.p. and general counsel in 1973; named chmn., exec. comm., 1976; retired from Wometco 1982.

WOLPER, DAVID L.
Producer. b. New York, NY, Jan. 11, 1928. m. Gloria Diane Hill. e. Drake U., U. of Southern California. Treas., Flamingo Films, 1948; merged with Associated Artist to form M.P. for TV, Inc., acting as v.p. in chg. of West Coast oper., 1950; v.p. reactivated Flamingo Films, 1954; also pres. Harris-Wolper Pictures, Inc.; pres. Wolper Prod. 1958; pres. Dawn Prod.; v.p. bd. dir. Metromedia, 1965; pres. Wolper Pictures Ltd. 1967; ch. of bd. Wolper Prod., Inc., 1967; pres. Wolper Pictures, 1968; pres. Wolper Productions, 1970; pres. & chmn. of bd. of dir. The Wolper Organization, Inc., 1971; consultant to Warner Bros. & Warner Communications. Pres., David L. Wolper Prods., Inc. 1977. Received Jean Hersholt Humanitarian Award, 1985; Intl. Documentary Assn. Career Achievement Award, 1988. Also received French Natl. Legion of Honor Medal, Lifetime Achievement Award from Producers Guild, Charles de Gaulle Centennial Medal. Shows have won 52 Emmys, 5 Peabody Awards and 7 Golden Globes.
PICTURES: Four Days in November, If It's Tuesday This Must Be Belgium, One Is a Lonely Number, The Hellstrom Chronicle, Willy Wonka and the Chocolate Factory, I Love My Wife, Visions of Eight, Birds Do It Bees Do It, This Is Elvis, The Man Who Saw Tomorrow, Imagine: John Lennon, Murder in the First, Surviving Picasso, L.A. Confidential.
TELEVISION: Specials: The Race For Space, The Making of the President (1960, 1964, 1968), National Geographic Society Specials (1965-68, 1971-75), The Rise and Fall of the Third Reich, The Undersea World of Jacques Cousteau (1967-68), George Plimpton specials (1970-72), American Heritage specials (1973-74), Primal Man specials (1973-75), Judgment specials (1974), Smithsonian Specials, Sandburg's Lincoln, The Man Who Saw Tomorrow, Opening & Closing Ceremonies: Olympic Games 1984, Liberty Weekend 1986, A Celebration of Tradition for Warner Bros, Here's Looking at You Warner Bros., Golf—The Greatest Game. Series: Story of..., Biography, Hollywood and the Stars, Men in Crisis, The March of Time (1965-66); Appointment With Destiny, Get Christie Love, Chico and the Man, Welcome Back Kotter, Casablanca, Golf: Heroes of the Game. Movies: Say Goodbye, The 500 Pound Jerk, I Will Fight No More Forever, Victory at Entebbe, Agatha Christie's Murder Is Easy, What Price Victory, Roots: The Gift, When You Remember Me, The Betty Ford Story, Dillinger, The Plot to Kill Hitler, Murder in Mississippi, Bed of Lies, The Flood: Who Will Save Our Children?, Fatal Deception: Mrs. Lee Harvey Oswald, Without Warning, Prince For a Day. Mini-Series: Roots (Emmy Award, 1977), Roots: The Next Generations, (Emmy Award, 1979), Moviola (This Year's Blonde, The Scarlett O'Hara War, The Silent Lovers), The Thorn Birds, North & South, North & South Book II: Love & War, North & South Book III: Heaven & Hell, Napoleon & Josephine: A Love Story, Queen, The Thorn Birds: The Missing Years.

WONG, KAR-WAI
Director. b. Shanghai, 1959. e. B.A. in graphic design, Hong Kong, 1980.
PICTURES: Prod.: The Eagle Shooting Heroes, Fallen Angels (also dir., s.p.), First Love: A Litter on the Breeze, Happy Together (also dir. s.p.). Dir.: As Tears Go By (also s.p.), The True Story of Ah Fei (also s.p.), Let's Go Slam Dunk, Ashes of Time (also s.p.), Hong Kong Express (also s.p.). Writer: Intellectual Trio, The Final Test, The Final Victory, The Haunted Copshop, Dragon and Tiger Fight, The Haunted Copshop II, Saviour of Souls, Beijing Summer.

WONG, VICTOR
Actor. b. San Francisco, CA. e. UC Berkeley, poli. sci. & journalism; U of Chicago; San Francisco Art Institute. Was reporter in San Francisco's Chinatown, 1968-75, before working on stage at Joseph Papp's Public Theatre.
PICTURES: Dim Sum: A Little Bit of Heart, Year of the Dragon, Big Trouble in Little China, Shanghai Surprise, The Golden Child, Bloodsport, Prince of Darkness, The Last Emperor, Eat a Bowl of Tea, Tremors, Life Is Cheap... But Toilet Paper Is Expensive, 3 Ninjas, The Joy Luck Club, The Ice Runner, 3 Ninjas Kick Back, 3 Ninjas Knuckle Up, The Stars Fell on Henrietta, Jade, Seven Years in Tibet, 3 Ninjas: High Noon at Mega Mountain.
TELEVISION: Series: Search for Tomorrow. Movies/Specials: Night Song, Fortune Cookie, Paper Angel, Mild Bunch, Search, China Nights.

WOO, JOHN
Director. r.n. Yusen Wu. b. Guangzhou, China, 1948. e. Matteo Ricci Col, Hong Kong. Started making experimental 16 mm films in 1967. Joined film industry in 1969 as prod. asst. for Cathay Film Co., then asst. dir. 1971 joined Shaw Brothers working as asst. dir. to Zhang Che.
PICTURES: The Young Dragons (debut, 1973), The Dragon Tamers, Countdown in Kung Fu, Princess Chang Ping, From Riches to Rags, Money Crazy, Follow the Star, Last Hurrah for Chivalry, To Hell With the Devil, Laughing Times, Plain Jane to the Rescue, Sunset Warriors (Heroes Shed No Tears), The Time You Need a Friend, Run Tiger Run, A Better Tomorrow, A Better Tomorrow II, Just Heroes, The Killer, Bullet in the Head, Once a Thief, Hard Boiled, Hard Target (U.S. debut, 1993), Cinema of Vengeance (act. only), Broken Arrow, Face/Off, The Big Hit (exec. prod. only), The Replacement Killers (exec. prod. only), King's Ransom, Mission: Impossible 2, The Last Word (prod.).
TELEVISION: Movie: John Woo's Once a Thief (prod.), Black Jack (also prod.).

WOOD, ELIJAH
Actor. b. Cedar Rapids, IA, Jan. 28, 1981. Started in commercial modeling. Landed first acting job in Paula Abdul video Forever Your Girl.
PICTURES: Back to the Future Part II (debut, 1989), Internal Affairs, Avalon, Paradise, Radio Flyer, Forever Young, The Adventures of Huck Finn, The Good Son, North, The War, Flipper, The Ice Storm.
TELEVISION: Movies: Child of the Night, Day-O.

WOODARD, ALFRE
Actress. b. Tulsa, OK, Nov. 8, 1953. e. Boston U., B.A. Soon after graduation landed role in Washington, D.C. Arena Stage theater in Horatio, and Saved.
THEATER: A Christmas Carol, Bugs Guns, Leander Stillwell, For Colored Girls Who Have Considered Suicide/When the Rainbow Is Enuf, A Map of the World, A Winter's Tale, Two By South.
PICTURES: Remember My Name, Health, Cross Creek (Acad. Award nom.), Extremities, Scrooged, Miss Firecracker, Grand Canyon, The Gun in Betty Lou's Handbag, Passion Fish, Rich in Love, Heart and Souls, Blue Chips, Crooklyn, How to Make an American Quilt, Primal Fear, Star Trek: First Contact, Follow Me Home, Mumford, Down in the Delta, Dinosaur, Brown Sugar.
TELEVISION: Series: Tucker's Witch, Sara, St. Elsewhere. Guest: Palmerstown USA, What Really Happened to the Class of '65?, Hill Street Blues (Emmy Award, 1984), L.A. Law (Emmy Award, 1987). Mini-series: Cadillac Desert. Movies: Freedom Road, Sophisticated Gents, Go Tell It on the Mountain, Sweet Revenge, Unnatural Causes, The Killing Floor, Mandela, A Mother's Courage: The Mary Thomas Story, Blue Bayou, Race to Freedom: The Underground Railroad, The Piano Lesson, Member of the Wedding, Miss Evers' Boys (Golden Globe Award, 1998). Specials: For Colored Girls Who Haved Considered Suicide/When the Rainbow Is Enuf, Trial of the Moke, Words by Heart, Aliens for Breakfast.

WOODS, DONALD
Actor. b. Brandon, Manitoba, Canada, Dec. 2, 1906. e. UC Berkeley. Appeared in WB shorts Song of a Nation, and Star in the Night (Oscar winner, 1945).
THEATER: Holiday, Charley's Aunt, Dracula, Strange Interlude, Two for the Seesaw, Rosmersholm, One by One, Soldier, You Can't Take It With You, Twelfth Night, Assassination 1865, Perfect Gentleman, Kansas City Repertory.
PICTURES: A Tale of Two Cities, Story of Louis Pasteur, Anthony Adverse, Forgotten Girls, Love Honor and Oh Baby, I Was a Prisoner on Devil's Island, Watch on the Rhine, Bridge of San Luis Rey, Wonder Man, Roughly Speaking, Barbary Pirate, 13 Ghosts, Kissin' Cousins, Moment to Moment; many other films.
TELEVISION: G.E. Theatre, Wind from the South, Wagon Train, Thrillers, Sunset Strip, Ben Casey, Laramie, The Rebel, The Law and Mr. Jones, The Roaring 20's, Wild Wild West, Bonanza. Series: Tammy.
(d. March 5, 1998)

WOODS, JAMES
Actor. b. Vernal UT, Apr. 18, 1947. e. Massachusetts Inst. of Technology (appeared in 36 plays at MIT, Harvard and Theatre Co. of Boston). Left college to pursue acting career in New York.
THEATER: Borstal Boy (B'way debut, 1970), followed by Conduct Unbecoming (off-B'way, Obie Award), Saved, Trial of the Catonsville Nine, Moonchildren (Theatre World Award), Green Julia (off-B'way), Finishing Touches.

PICTURES: The Visitors (debut, 1971), Hickey and Boggs, The Way We Were, The Gambler, Distance, Night Moves, Alex and the Gypsy, The Choirboys, The Onion Field, The Black Marble, Eyewitness, Fast-Walking, Split Image, Videodrome, Against All Odds, Once Upon a Time in America, Cat's Eye, Joshua Then and Now, Salvador (Acad. Award nom.; Indept. Film Project Spirit Award, 1986), Best Seller, Cop (also co-prod.), The Boost, True Believer, Immediate Family, The Hard Way, Straight Talk, Diggstown, Chaplin, The Getaway, The Specialist, For Better or Worse, Casino, Nixon, Killer: A Journal of Murder, Ghosts of Mississippi, Hercules (voice), Contact, Another Day in Paradise, Vampires, The Virgin Suicides, True Crime, On Any Sunday, The General's Daughter.
TELEVISION: Movies: Footsteps, A Great American Tragedy, Foster and Laurie, F. Scott Fitzgerald in Hollywood, The Disappearance of Aimee, Raid on Entebbe, Billion Dollar Bubble, The Gift of Love, The Incredible Journey of Dr. Meg Laurel, And Your Name Is Jonah, Badge of the Assassin, Promise (Emmy & Golden Globe Awards, 1987), In Love and War, My Name is Bill W. (Emmy Award, 1989), Women & Men: Stories of Seduction (Hills Like White Elephants), The Boys, Citizen Cohn, Jane's House, Next Door, Curse of the Starving Class, Indictment: The McMartin Trial, The Summer of Ben Tyler. Specials: All the Way Home, Crimes of Passion (host), Wildfire (host), Mobs and Mobsters (host), Fallen Angels, A Salute to Martin Scorcese, America's Endangered Species: Don't Say Goodbye (narrator). Mini-series: Holocaust. Guest: Kojak, Rockford Files, Streets of San Francisco, The Rookies, Police Story, Saturday Night Live, Dream On, The Simpsons (voice).

WOODWARD, EDWARD
O.B.E.: Actor, Singer. b. Croydon, England, June 1, 1930. e. Royal Acad. of Dramatic Art. As singer has recorded 11 LPs. 2 Gold Discs. Television Actor of the Year, 1969-70; also Sun Award, Best Actor, 1970-72. Has received 15 national & international awards.
THEATER: With Royal Shakespeare Company, 1958-59; Cyrano, 20 West End plays and musicals, including The Art of Living, The Little Doctor, A Rattle of a Simple Man (West End/B'way), The High Bid, The Male of the Species, High Spirits (B'way musical), The Best Laid Plans, On Approval, The Wolf, Richard III, The Assassin.
PICTURES: Where There's a Will (debut, 1955), Becket, File on the Golden Goose, Incense for the Damned, Young Winston, Sitting Target, Hunted, Wicker Man, Callan, Stand Up Virgin Soldiers, Breaker Morant, The Appointment, The Final Option (Who Dares Wins), Champions, King David, Mister Johnson, Deadly Advice.
TELEVISION: Series: Callan, Nice Work, The Equalizer (4 Emmy noms.), Golden Globe Award), Over My Dead Body, In Suspicious Cirumstances. Movies/Specials: Sword of Honour, Bassplayer and Blonde (mini-series), Saturday, Sunday, Monday, Rod of Iron, The Trial of Lady Chatterly, Wet Job–Callan Special, Churchill: The Wilderness Years, Blunt Instrument, Killer Contract, Arthur the King, Uncle Tom's Cabin, A Christmas Carol, Codename: Kyril, Hunted, The Man in the Brown Suit, Hands of a Murderer, World War II, Suspicious Circumstances, The Shamrock Conspiracy, Common as Muck, Harrison, Gulliver's Travels.

WOODWARD, JOANNE
Actress. b. Thomasville, GA, Feb. 27, 1930. m. Paul Newman. e. Louisiana State U. Studied at Neighborhood Playhouse Dramatic Sch. and the Actors Studio. Appeared in many TV dramatic shows.
THEATER: Picnic, The Lovers, Baby Want a Kiss, Candida, The Glass Menagerie (Williamstown, The Long Wharf), Golden Boy (dir., the Blue Light Theatre Company).
PICTURES: Count Three and Pray (debut, 1955), A Kiss Before Dying, Three Faces of Eve (Academy Award, 1957), No Down Payment, The Long Hot Summer, Rally 'Round the Flag Boys, The Sound and the Fury, The Fugitive Kind, From the Terrace, Paris Blues, The Stripper, A New Kind of Love, Signpost to Murder, A Big Hand for the Little Lady, A Fine Madness, Rachel Rachel (Acad. Award nom.), Winning, WUSA, They Might Be Giants, The Effect of Gamma Rays on Man-in-the-Moon Marigolds, Summer Wishes Winter Dreams (Acad. Award nom.), The Drowning Pool, The End, Harry and Son, The Glass Menagerie, Mr. and Mrs. Bridge (Acad. Award nom.), The Age of Innocence (narrator), Philadelphia.
TELEVISION: Specials: Broadway's Dreamers: The Legacy of The Group Theater (host, co-prod.; Emmy Award, 1990), Family Thanksgiving Special (dir. only). Movies: Sybil, Come Back Little Sheba, See How She Runs (Emmy Award, 1978), A Christmas to Remember, The Streets of L.A., The Shadow Box, Crisis at Central High, Passions, Do You Remember Love? (Emmy Award, 1985), Foreign Affairs, Blind Spot (also co-prod.).

WOOLDRIDGE, SUSAN
Actress. b. London, England. e. Central Sch. of Speech & Drama/Ecole/Jacques LeCoq. Paris. Ent. ind. 1971.
THEATER: Macbeth, School for Scandal, Merchant of Venice, The Cherry Orchard, Look Back in Anger, 'night Mother, Map of the Heart.
PICTURES: The Shout, Butley, Loyalties, Hope and Glory, How to Get Ahead in Advertising, Bye Bye Blues, Twenty-One, Afraid of the Dark, Just Like a Woman, The Hummingbird Tree.
TELEVISION: The Naked Civil Servant, John McNab, The Racing Game, The Jewel in the Crown, The Last Place on Earth, Hay Fever, Time and the Conways, Dead Man's Folly, The Devil's Disciple, The Dark Room, Pastoralcare, The Small Assassin, A Fine Romance, Ticket to Ride, Changing Step, Pied Piper, Crimestrike, Broke, Miss Pym's Day Out, An Unwanted Woman, The Humming Bird Tree, Inspector Alleyn Mysteries, Tracey Ullman Show, Bad Company, Under the Hammer, All Quiet on the Preston Front, Wycliffe, The Writing Game. Guest: The Ray Bradbury Theatre.

WOOLF, SIR JOHN
Knighted 1975. Producer. b. England, 1913. e. Institut Montana, Switzerland. Awarded U.S. Bronze star for service in WWII. Asst. dir. Army Kinematography, War Office 1944-45; Founder and chmn. Romulus Films Ltd, since 1948. Man dir. since 1967; chmn. since 1982 of British & American Film Holdings Plc; dir. First Leisure Corp. Plc since 1982. Co-founder and exec. dir., Anglia TV Group PLC, 1958-83. Member: Cinematograph Films Council, 1969-79; bd. of gov., Services Sound & Vision Corp (formerly Services Kinema Corp.) 1974-83; exec. council and trustee, Cinema and Television Benevolent Fund; Freeman, City of London, 1982; FRSA 1978. Received special awards for contribution to British film indust. from Cinematograph Exhibitors Assoc. 1969. and Variety Club of GB, 1974.
PICTURES: Prod. by Romulus Gp.: The African Queen, Pandora and the Flying Dutchman, Moulin Rouge, Beat the Devil, I Am a Camera, Carrington VC, The Bespoke Overcoat (short; Acad. Award, BAFTA Award), Story of Ester Costello, Room at the Top (BAFTA Award, best film, 1958), Wrong Arm of the Law, The L-Shaped Room, Term of Trial, Life at the Top, Oliver! (Acad. Award, Golden Globe, best film, 1968), Day of the Jackal, The Odessa File.
TELEVISION: Prod. for Anglia TV incl.: 100 Tales of the Unexpected, Miss Morrison's Ghosts, The Kingfisher, Edwin, Love Song.

WOPAT, TOM
Actor. b. Lodi, WI, Sept. 9, 1951. e. U. of Wisconsin. Left school to travel for two years with rock group as lead singer and guitarist. Spent two summers at Barn Theater in MI. Came to New York; Off-B'way in A Bistro Car on the CNR. On B'way in I Love My Wife, City of Angels, Guys and Dolls.
TELEVISION: Series: The Dukes of Hazzard, Blue Skies, A Peaceable Kingdom, Cybill, Prime Time Country (host). Movies: Christmas Comes to Willow Creek, Burning Rage, Just My Imagination, Contagious, The Dukes of Hazzard: Reunion!, Meteorites.

WORKMAN, CHUCK
Director, Writer, Producer. b. Philadelphia, PA. June 5. e. Rutgers U., B.A.; Cornell U. Pres., International Documentary Assoc. 1987-88; Member: Directors Guild of America, National Board. Lecturer, U. of Southern California. Pres. Calliope Films, Inc. Winner Clio Award, 1969, 1970. Acad. Award, 1987; ShowEast Achievement Award, 1996; Cable Ace Award, 1996.
THEATER: Bruno's Ghost (1981, writer, dir.), Diplomacy (writer, dir.), The Man Who Wore White Shoes (writer), Bloomers (writer).
PICTURES: Monday's Child (1967, editor), Traitors of San Angel (editor), The Money (dir., s.p.), Protocol (dir., media sequences), Stoogemania (dir., co-s.p.), Precious Images (Acad. Award, Best Live Action Short, 1986; Gold Hugo Award, Cannes Film Fest., N.Y. Film Fest.), Words (Best Short, Houston Fest., N.Y. Film Fest., 1988), Pieces of Silver, Superstar (dir.-prod.), The First 100 Years (dir., prod.).
DOCUMENTARIES: The Making of the Deep (prod., dir., writer), The Director and the Image (CINE Golden Eagle Award, 1980), The Game, The Best Show in Town (CINE Golden Eagle), And the Winner Is..., The Keeper of the Light.

WORONOV, MARY
Actress. b. Brooklyn, NY, Dec. 8, 1946. e. Cornell. On NY stage in In the Boom Boom Room (Theatre World Award).

PICTURES: The Chelsea Girls, Kemek: It's Controlling Your Mind, Sugar Cookies, Seizure, Cover Girl Models, Death Race 2000, Cannonball, Jackson County Jail, Hollywood Boulevard, Bad Georgia Road, Mr. Billion, The One and Only, The Lady in Red, Rock 'n' Roll High School, National Lampoon Goes to the Movies, Angel of H.E.A.T., Heartbeeps, Eating Raoul, Get Crazy, Night of the Comet, Hellhole, My Man Adam, Nomads, Movie House Massacre, Chopping Mall, Terrorvision, Black Widow, Scenes From the Class Struggle in Beverly Hills, Let It Ride, Mortuary Academy, Dick Tracy, Watchers II, Warlock, Club Fed, Where Sleeping Dogs Lie, Motorama, Good Girls Don't, Hell-Rollers, Grief.
TELEVISION: Movies: In the Glitter Palace, Challenge of a Lifetime, Acting on Impulse.

WORTH, IRENE
Actress. r.n. Hattie Abrams. b. Nebraska, June 23, 1916. e. UCLA. Formerly a teacher. B'way debut in The Two Mrs. Carrolls, after which went to London where made her home. Appeared with Old Vic and Royal Shakespeare Co.; returned to U.S. to appear on B'way in the Cocktail Party.
THEATER: Hotel Paradiso, Mary Stuart, The Potting Shed, Toys in the Attic, Tiny Alice (Tony Award, 1965), Sweet Bird of Youth (Tony Award, 1976), Cherry Orchard, Old Times Happy Days, Coriolanus (NY Shakespeare Fest), Lost in Yonkers (Tony Award, 1991).
PICTURES: One Night With You, Secret People, Orders to Kill (British Acad. Award, best actress), The Scapegoat, Seven Seas to Calais, King Lear, Nicholas and Alexander, Rich Kids, Eyewitness, Deathtrap, Fast Forward, Lost in Yonkers, Eugene Onegin.
TELEVISION: The Lady from the Sea, The Duchess of Malfi, The Way of the World, Prince Orestes, Forbidden, The Big Knife, The Shell Seekers. Guest: Remember WENN.

WORTH, MARVIN
Producer, Writer. b. Brooklyn, NY. Jazz promoter and manager before starting to write special material for Alan King, Buddy Hackett, Joey Bishop, Lenny Bruce and many others.
THEATER: Lenny (prod.).
PICTURES: Writer: Boys' Night Out, Three on a Couch, Promise Her Anything. Producer: Diabolique, Where's Poppa?, Malcolm X (documentary), Lenny, Fire Sale, The Rose, Up the Academy, Soup for One, Unfaithfully Yours, Rhinestone, Falling in Love, Less Than Zero, Patty Hearst, Running Mates, See No Evil, Hear No Evil, Flashback, Malcolm X, Norma Jean and Marilyn.
TELEVISION: Steve Allen Show, Jackie Gleason, Ray Bolger's Washington Square, Chevy Shows, General Motors' 50th Anniversary Show, Milton Berle Show, Colgate Comedy Hour, Martha Raye Show, Polly Bergen Show, Ann Sothern Show, Judy Garland Show, Get Smart, others.
(d. April 22, 1998)

WOWCHUK, HARRY N.
Actor, Writer, Photographer, Producer, Executive. b. Philadelphia, PA. Oct. 16, 1948. e. Santa Monica City Coll., UCLA, theater arts, 1970. Started film career as actor, stunt-driver-photographer. T.V. and commercial credits include: TV Guide, Seal Test, Camel Cigarettes, Miller High Life, American Motors, Camera V, AW Rootbeer. Former exec. v.p. International Cinema, in chg. of prod. and distribution; V.P. J. Newport Film Productions; pres., United West Productions.
PICTURES: The Lost Dutchman, Las Vegas Lady, This Is a Hijack, Tidal Wave, Tunnel Vision, Incredible 2-Headed Transplant, Jud, Bad Charleston Charlie, Some Call It Loving, Summer School Teachers, Five Minutes of Freedom, Pushing Up Daisies, Money-Marbles-Chalk, The Models, Love Swedish Style, Up-Down-Up, Sunday's Child, Soul Brothers, Freedom Riders, Perilous Journey, Claws of Death, Georgia Peaches.

WOWCHUK, NICHOLAS
Executive, Producer, Writer, Editor, Financier. b. Philadelphia, PA. e. St. Basil's Coll., UCLA. Founder-publisher: All-American Athlete Magazine, Sports and Health Digest, The Spectator. Former sports writer: Phila. Evening Public Ledger; Phila. Daily Record; Phila. Inquirer. Founder & bd. chmn.: Mutual Realty Investment Co.; Mutual Mortgage Co., Beverly Hills, CA. President: Mutual General Films, Bev. Hills, CA; Abbey Theatrical Films, NY; Mutual Film Distribution Co.; Mutual Recording & Broadcasting Enterprises.
PICTURES: Exec. Prod.: Perilous Journey, The Incredible 2-Headed Transplant, Pushing Up Daisies, Money-Marbles-Chalk, Five Minutes of Freedom, The Campaign, Claws of Death. Prod.: Scorpion's Web, Pursuit, Brave Men, Sea of Despair, Cossacks in Battle, The Straight White Line, Tilt, Rooster, To Live... You Gotta Win.

WRAY, FAY
Actress. b. Alberta, Canada, Sept. 15, 1907. On stage in Pilgrimage Play, Hollywood, 1923; m.p. debut in Gasoline Love; thereafter in many m.p. for Paramount to 1930; then in films for various Hollywood and Brit. prod. Autobiography: On the Other Hand (1989).
PICTURES: Streets of Sin, The Wedding March, The Four Feathers, The Texan, Dirigible, Doctor X, The Most Dangerous Game, The Vampire Bat, The Mystery of the Wax Museum, King Kong, The Bowery, Madame Spy, The Affairs of Cellini, The Clairvoyant, They Met in a Taxi, Murder in Greenwich Village, The Jury's Secret, Smashing the Spy Ring, Navy Secrets, Wildcat Bus, Adam Had Four Sons, Melody for Three, Not a Ladies' Man, Small Town Girl, Treasure of the Golden Condor, Queen Bee, The Cobweb, Hell on Frisco Bay, Crime of Passion, Rock Pretty Baby, Tammy and the Bachelor, Summer Love, Dragstrip Riot, Frank Capra's American Dream.
TELEVISION: Series: Pride of the Family. Movie: Gideon's Trumpet.

WRIGHT, AMY
Actress. b. Chicago, IL, Apr. 15, 1950. e. Beloit Col. Studied acting with Uta Hagen; 1976, joined Rip Torn's Sanctuary Theatre. B'way in Fifth of July, Noises Off, Mrs. Klein.
PICTURES: Not a Pretty Picture, Girlfriends, The Deer Hunter, Breaking Away, The Amityville Horror, Heartland, Wise Blood, Stardust Memories, Inside Moves, Off Beat, The Telephone, Crossing Delancey, The Accidental Tourist, Miss Firecracker, Daddy's Dyin', Deceived, Love Hurts, Hard Promises, Josh and S.A.M., Tom and Huck.
TELEVISION: Movies: Trapped in Silence, Settle the Score, To Dance With the White Dog. Special: Largo Desolato. Pilot: A Fine Romance.

WRIGHT, ROBERT C.
Executive. b. Hempstead, NY, April 23, 1943. e. Coll. Holy Cross, B.A. history, 1965; U. of Virginia, LLB 1968. Mem. NY, VA, MA, NJ Bar. 1969, joined General Electric; lawyer in plastics div. Later moved into product & sls. management in plastics div. 1980, moved to Cox Cable as pres. Returned to GE 1983 heading small appliances div.; moved to GE Financial Services & GE Credit Corp. as pres., which posts he held when named head of NBC following purchase of NBC's parent RCA by GE. Pres. and CEO, National Broadcasting Co. (NBC), 1986-. Humanitarian Award from Foundation Fighting Blindness, 1995.

WRIGHT, TERESA
Actress. b. New York, NY, Oct. 27, 1918. e. Columbia H.S., Maplewood, NJ, 1938.
THEATER: Tours: Mary Mary, Tchin-Tchin, The Effect of Gamma Rays on Man-in-the-Moon Marigolds, Noel Coward in Two Keys, The Master Builder. Regional: Long Day's Journey into Night, You Can't Take It With You, All The Way Home, Wings. NY: Life with Father, Dark at the Top of the Stairs, I Never Sang for My Father, Death of a Salesman, Ah Wilderness!, Morning's at Seven (also London), On Borrowed Time.
PICTURES: The Little Foxes (debut, 1941), Pride of the Yankees, Mrs. Miniver (Academy Award, best supporting actress, 1942), Shadow of a Doubt, Casanova Brown, The Best Years of Our Lives, The Trouble With Women, Pursued, Imperfect Lady, Enchantment, The Capture, The Men, Something to Live For, California Conquest, Steel Trap, Count the Hours, The Actress, Track of the Cat, The Search for Bridey Murphy, Escapade in Japan, The Restless Years, Hail Hero, The Happy Ending, Roseland, Somewhere in Time, The Good Mother, The Red Coat, The Rainmaker.
TELEVISION: Specials: The Margaret Bourke-White Story, The Miracle Worker, The Golden Honeymoon, The Fig Tree, A Century of Women. Movies: Crawlspace, The Elevator, Flood, Bill—On His Own, Perry Mason: The Case of the Desperate Deception, Lethal Innocence, Diamonds on the Silver Screen. Mini-series: A Century of Women. Guest: The U.S. Steel Hour, Climax, The Alcoa Hour, Playhouse 90, Picket Fences.

WUHL, ROBERT
Actor, Writer. b. Union, NJ, Oct. 9, 1951. e. Univ. of Houston. Worked as stand-up comedian and joke writer. Was story editor on series Police Squad! Appeared in 1988 Academy Award winning short Ray's Male Heterosexual Dance Hall.
PICTURES: The Hollywood Knights (debut, 1980), Flashdance, Good Morning Vietnam, Bull Durham, Batman, Blaze, Wedding Band, Mistress, A Kiss Goodnight, Blue Chips, Cobb, Dr. Jekyll and Ms. Hyde, Open Season (also dir., s.p.).
TELEVISION: Series: Arliss. Pilots: Rockhopper, Sniff. Guest: Tales from the Crypt, Moonlighting, L.A. Law, Falcon Crest. Specials: The Big Bang (also dir.), Comic Relief IV, The Earth Day Special, The Real Deal. Movie: Percy & Thunder. Writer: Police Squad, Sledge Hammer, Grammy Awards (1987-89), Academy Awards (Emmy Award, 1991).

WYATT, JANE
Actress. b. Campgaw, NJ, Aug. 12, 1910. e. Miss Chapin's Sch., Barnard Coll. m. Edgar B. Ward. Joined Apprentice Sch., Berkshire Playhouse, Stockbridge, Mass. Understudied in Tradewinds and The Vinegar Tree. Appeared in Give Me Yesterday and the Tadpole. In 1933 succeeded Margaret Sullavan in Dinner at Eight.
THEATER: The Autumn Garden (NY), The Bishop Misbehaves, Conquest, Eveningsong, The Mad Hopes, Hope for the Best, The Joyous Season For Services Rendered, Driving Miss Daisy, Love Letters.
PICTURES: One More River (debut, 1934), Great Expectations, We're Only Human, The Luckiest Girl in the World, Lost Horizon, The Girl From God's Country, Kisses for Breakfast, Hurricane Smith, Weekend for Three, Army Surgeon, The Navy Comes Through, The Kansan, Buckskin Frontier, None But the Lonely Heart, Strange Conquest, The Bachelor's Daughters, Boomerang!, Gentleman's Agreement, Pitfall, No Minor Vices, Bad Boy, Canadian Pacific, Task Force, House By the River, Our Very Own, My Blue Heaven, The Man Who Cheated Himself, Criminal Lawyer, Interlude, Two Little Bears, Never Too Late, Treasure of Matecumbe, Star Trek IV: The Voyage Home.
TELEVISION: Series: Father Knows Best (1954-59; 3 Emmy Awards: 1957, 1958, 1959), Confidential For Women. Guest: Bob Hope Chrysler Theater, The Virginian, Wagon Train, U.S. Steel Hour, Bell Telephone Hour, My Father My Mother, Barefoot in the Park, The Ghost and Mrs. Muir, Here Come the Brides, Love American Style, Fantasy Island, Love Boat. Movies: Katherine, Tom Sawyer, Father Knows Best Reunion, A Love Affair, Amelia Earhart, Superdome, The Nativity, The Millionaire, Missing Children—A Mother's Story, Legacy of the Hollywood Blacklist, Amityville: The Evil Escapes, Neighbors, Ladies of the Corridor, Star Trek, Frank Capra's American Dream.

WYMAN, JANE
Actress. r.n. Sarah Jane Fulks. b. St. Joseph, MO, Jan. 5, 1917. e. Univ. of MO. Started in show business as radio singer calling herself Jane Durrell. Debuted in films as bit player using her real name. Voted one of top ten money-making stars in M.P. Herald-Fame poll, 1954.
PICTURES: Cain and Mabel, Golddiggers of 1937, My Man Godfrey, King of Burlesque, Smart Blonde, Stage Struck, King and the Chorus Girl, Ready Willing and Able, Slim, The Singing Marine, Public Wedding, Mr. Dodd Takes the Air, The Crowd Roars, Brother Rat, Wide Open Faces, The Spy Ring, He Couldn't Say No, Fools for Scandal, Kid Nightingale, Tail Spin, Private Detective, Kid from Kokomo, Torchy Plays With Dynamite, Brother Rat and a Baby, An Angel From Texas, Gambling on the High Seas, Tugboat Annie Sails Again, My Love Came Back, The Body Disappears, Honeymoon for Three, Bad Men of Missouri, You're in the Army Now, Larceny, Inc., My Favorite Spy, Footlight Serenade, Princess O'Rourke, Doughgirls, Make Your Own Bed, Crime by Night, Hollywood Canteen, Lost Weekend, One More Tomorrow, Night and Day, The Yearling, Cheyenne, Magic Town, Johnny Belinda (Academy Award, 1948), A Kiss in the Dark, The Lady Takes a Sailor, It's a Great Feeling, Stage Fright, The Glass Menagerie, Three Guys Named Mike, Here Comes the Groom, Blue Veil, Starlift, Just for You, Story of Will Rogers, Let's Do It Again, So Big, Magnificent Obsession, Lucy Gallant, All That Heaven Allows, Miracle in the Rain, Holiday for Lovers, Pollyanna, Bon Voyage!, How to Commit Marriage, Wild Bill: A Hollywood Maverick.
TELEVISION: Series: Fireside Theatre (The Jane Wyman Show), Summer Playhouse, Falcon Crest. Movies: The Failing of Raymond, The Incredible Journey of Dr. Meg Laurel.

WYMAN, THOMAS H.
Executive. b. 1931. Joined CBS, Inc. in 1980 as pres. & chief exec. Then chmn until 1986. William H. Donaldson Faculty Fellow at Yale School of Mgmt., 1987. Prior career as chief exec. of Green Giant Co.; became v. chmn. to 1988, of Pillsbury Co. when it acquired Green Giant in 1979. Chairman of Bd., Amherst College. Trustee, Ford Foundation.

WYNN, TRACY KEENAN
Writer. b. Hollywood, CA, Feb. 28, 1945. e. UCLA Theatre Arts Dept., BA in film/TV division, 1967. Fourth generation in show business: son of actor Keenan Wynn, grandson of Ed Wynn, great-grandson of Frank Keenan, Irish Shakespearean actor who made B'way debut in 1880.
PICTURES: The Longest Yard, The Drowning Pool (co-s.p.), The Deep (co. s.p.).
TELEVISION: Movies: The Glass House, Tribes (also assoc. prod.: Emmy & WGA Awards, 1971), The Autobiography of Miss Jane Pittman (Emmy Award & WGA Awards, 1974), Hit Lady (dir. only), Quest, Bloody Friday (also co-prod.), Capone in Jail, Carolina Skeletons.

XYZ

YABLANS, FRANK
Executive. b. Brooklyn, NY, Aug. 27, 1935. Entered m.p. ind. as Warner Bros. booker, 1957. Warner Bros. salesman in N.Y., Boston, Milwaukee, Chicago, 1957-59. Milwaukee br. mgr. Buena Vista, 1959-66. Midwest sales mgr., Sigma III, 1966. Eastern sales mgr., 1967, sales v.p. 1968. V.P. general sales mgr., Paramount Pic. Corp., 1969; v.p.-dist., 1970; sr. v.p.-mkt., 1970; exec. v.p., 1971; named pres. 1971. 1975, became an indep. prod. for his company, Frank Yablans Presentations Inc. 1983, MGM/UA Entertainment Co. as bd. chmn. & CEO. Held titles of bd. chmn. & CEO with both MGM and UA Corp when resigned, 1985. Same year teamed with PSO Delphi to form Northstar Entertainment Co.; 1986, non-exclusive deal with Empire Entertainment; 1988, non-exclusive 3-year deal with Columbia Pictures; 1989, pres. Epic Prods., pres., CEO Nova Intl. Films Inc.
PICTURES: Producer: Silver Streak (exec. prod.), The Other Side of Midnight, The Fury, North Dallas Forty (also co-s.p.), Mommie Dearest (also co-s.p.), Monsignor (co.-prod), Star Chamber, Kidco, Buy and Cell, Lisa, Congo (exec. prod.).

YABLANS, IRWIN
Executive. b. Brooklyn, NY, July 25, 1934. Began career in industry at WB in 1956 after two-yr. stint with U.S. Army in Germany. Held m.p. sales posts in Washington, DC, Albany, Detroit, Milwaukee and Portland. In 1962 joined Paramount as L.A. mgr.; in 1964 made western sales mgr. In 1972 entered production as assoc. prod. on Howard W. Koch's Badge 373. Pres. of Compass Int'l. Pictures. Exec. v.p., low budget films, Lorimar Productions. Resigned June, 1984. In 1985 named chmn., Orion Pictures Distributing Corp. 1988: named chmn. and CEO of newly formed Epic Pictures.
PICTURES: The Education of Sonny Carson. Exec. prod.: Halloween, Roller Boogie (also story), Fade To Black (also story), Seduction (prod.), Halloween II, Halloween III: Season of the Witch, Parasite, Tank, Hell Night, Prison Arena, Why Me?, Men at Work.

YATES, PETER
Producer, Director. b. Ewshoot, England, July 24, 1929. e. Royal Acad. of Dramatic Art. Entered m.p. ind. as studio mgr. and dubbing asst. with De Lane Lea. Asst. dir.: The Entertainer, The Guns of Navarone, A Taste of Honey, The Roman Spring of Mrs. Stone. Stage dir.: The American Dream, The Death of Bessie Smith, Passing Game, Interpreters. Received Acad. Award noms. for Best Director/Picture (Producer): Breaking Away, The Dresser.
PICTURES: Summer Holiday, One Way Pendulum, Robbery (also co-s.p.), Bullitt, John and Mary, Murphy's War, The Hot Rock, The Friends of Eddie Coyle, For Pete's Sake, Mother Jugs and Speed (also prod.), The Deep, Breaking Away (also prod.), Eyewitness (also prod.), Krull, The Dresser (also prod.), Eleni, Suspect, The House on Carroll Street (also prod.), An Innocent Man, Year of the Comet (also co-prod.), Needful Things (exec. prod. only), Roommates, The Run of the Country (also co-prod.).
TELEVISION: Series: Danger Man (Secret Agent), The Saint.

YELLEN, LINDA
Producer, Director, Writer. b. New York, NY, July 13. e. Barnard Coll., B.A.; Columbia U., M.F.A., Ph.D. Lecturer Barnard Coll., Yale U.; asst. professor, City U. of N.Y. Member: exec. council, DGA.
THEATER: Chantilly Lace (dir., prod., writer), Parallel Lives (dir., prod. writer).
PICTURES: The End of Summer (dir., prod., s.p.), Looking Up (prod., dir.), Prospera, Come Out Come Out, Everybody Wins (prod.).
TELEVISION: Movies: Mayflower: The Pilgrims' Adventure (prod.), Playing for Time (exec. prod.; Emmy, Peabody & Christopher Awards, 1980), Hardhat and Legs (prod.), The Royal Romance of Charles and Diana (exec. prod., co-writer), Prisoner Without a Name Cell Without a Number (prod., dir., co-writer; Peabody & WGA Awards), Liberace: Behind the Music (exec. prod.), Sweet Bird of Youth (exec. prod.), Rebound (dir., co-writer).

YORDAN, PHILIP
Writer. b. Chicago, IL, April 1, 1914. e. U. of Illinois, B.A., Kent Coll. of Law, LL.D. Was attorney, then author, prod., playwright (Anna Lucasta). Began screen writing 1942 with collab. s.p. Syncopation.
PICTURES: Syncopation, The Unknown Guest, Johnny Doesn't Live Here Anymore, When Strangers Marry, Dillinger, Whistle Stop, Suspense, The Chase, Reign of Terror, Bad Men of Tombstone, Anna Lucasta, House of Strangers, Edge of Doom, Drums in the Deep South, Detective Story, Mutiny, Mara Maru,

Man Crazy, Houdini, Blowing Wild, The Naked Jungle, Broken Lance, Johnny Guitar, Joe MacBeth, Conquest of Space, The Big Combo, Man from Laramie, The Last Frontier, The Harder They Fall, No Down Payment, Gun Glory, Four Boys and a Gun, Men in War, The Fiend Who Walked the West, The Bravados, God's Little Acre, Day of the Outlaw, The Bramble Bush, Studs Lonigan, King of Kings, El Cid, The Day of the Triffids, 55 Days at Peking, Fall of the Roman Empire, Circus World, Battle of the Bulge, Royal Hunt of the Sun, Captain Apache, Bad Man's River, Night Train to Terror, Fort Saganne, Bloody Wednesday, Cry Wilderness, The Unholy.

YORK, MICHAEL

Actor. r.n. Michael York-Johnson. b. Fulmer, England, March 27, 1942. Early career with Oxford U. Dramatic Society and National Youth Theatre; later Dundee Repertory, National Theatre. Chmn., California Youth Theatre. 1992 *Autobiography*: Accidentally on Purpose (Simon & Schuster).
THEATER: Any Just Cause, Hamlet, Ring Round the Moon (Los Angeles), Cyrano de Bergerac, Ira Gershwin At 100. *B'way*: Outcry, Bent, The Little Prince and the Aviator, Whisper in the Mind, The Crucible, Someone Who'll Watch Over Me, Nora.
PICTURES: The Taming of the Shrew, Accident, Red and Blue, Smashing Time, Romeo and Juliet, The Strange Affair, The Guru, Alfred the Great, Justine, Something for Everyone, Zeppelin, La Poudre D'Escampette, Cabaret, England Made Me, Lost Horizon, The Three Musketeers, Murder on the Orient Express, The Four Musketeers, Conduct Unbecoming, Logan's Run, Seven Nights in Japan, The Last Remake of Beau Geste, The Island of Dr. Moreau, Fedora, The Riddle of the Sands (also assoc. prod.), Final Assignment, The White Lions, The Weather in the Streets, Success Is the Best Revenge, Dawn, Lethal Obsession (Der Joker), The Return of the Musketeers, Phantom of Death, The Secret of the Sahara, Midnight Cop, The Wanderer, The Long Shadow, Wide Sargasso Sea, Rochade, Discretion Assured, The Shadow of a Kiss, Gospa, Goodbye America, Austin Powers, Dark Planet.
TELEVISION: *Specials*: The Forsyte Saga, Rebel in the Grave, Jesus of Nazareth, True Patriot, Much Ado About Nothing. *Series*: Knots Landing. *Guest*: Seaquest, The Naked Truth, Babylon 5, Sliders. *Movies*: Great Expectations, A Man Called Intrepid, The Phantom of the Opera, The Master of Ballantrae, Space, For Those I Loved, The Far Country, Dark Mansions, Sword of Gideon, Four Minute Mile, The Lady and the Highwayman, The Heat of the Day, Till We Meet Again, Night of the Fox, A Duel of Love, The Road to Avonlea, Charles Dickens' David Copperfield (voice), Fall from Grace, Tek War: Tek Lab, September, A Young Connecticut Yankee in King Arthur's Court, Not of This Earth, The Out of Towner, Danielle Steel's The Ring, True Women. *Host*: The Hunt for Stolen War Treasure, The Magic Paint Brush, Gardens of the World.

YORK, SUSANNAH

Actress. b. London, England, Jan. 9, 1941. Ent. tv 1959; m.p. ,1960. Author: In Search of Unicorns, Lark's Castle.
THEATER: A Cheap Bunch of Flowers, Wings of the Dove, Singular Life of Albert Nobbs, Man and Superman, Mrs. Warren's Profession, Peter Pan, The Maids, Private Lives, The Importance of Being Earnest, Hedda Gabler (N.Y.), Agnes of God, The Human Voice, Penthesilea, Fatal Attraction, The Apple Cart, Private Treason, Lyric for a Tango, The Glass Menagerie, A Streetcar Named Desire, September Tide. Produced The Big One, a variety show for peace, 1984.
PICTURES: Tunes of Glory (debut, 1960), There Was a Crooked Man, Greengage Summer (Loss of Innocence), Freud, Tom Jones, The Seventh Dawn, Sands of the Kalahari, Kaleidoscope, A Man for All Seasons, Sebastian, Duffy, The Killing of Sister George, Oh What a Lovely War, The Battle of Britain, Lock Up Your Daughters, They Shoot Horses Don't They? (Acad. Award nom.), Brotherly Love (Country Dance), Zee & Co. (X Y & Zee), Happy Birthday Wanda June, Images, The Maids, Gold, Conduct Unbecoming, That Lucky Touch, Sky Riders, The Silent Partner, Superman, The Shout, Falling in Love Again, The Awakening, Superman II, Loophole, Yellowbeard, Land of Faraway, Superman IV (voice), Prettykill, Bluebeard Bluebeard, A Summer Story, American Roulette, Diamond's Edge, Melancholia, En Hanfull Tio, Fate, Pretty Princess.
TELEVISION: *Movies*: The Crucible, The Rebel and the Soldier, The First Gentleman, The Richest Man in the World, Slaughter of St. Teresa's Day, Kiss On A Grass Green Pillow, Fallen Angels, Prince Regent, Second Chance, Betjeman's Briton, We'll Meet Again, Jane Eyre, A Christmas Carol, Star Quality, Macho, Return Journey, After the War, The Man From the Pru, The Haunting of the New, Devices and Desires, Boon, Little Women, Illusions. *Series*: Trainer.

YORKIN, BUD

Producer, Director. r.n. Alan Yorkin. b. Washington, PA, Feb. 22, 1926. e. Carnegie Tech., Columbia U. U.S. Navy, 1942-45. Began career in tv in NBC's engineering dept. Moved into prod., first as stage mgr., then assoc. dir. of Colgate Comedy Hour (Martin and Lewis) and dir. of Dinah Shore Show. Formed Tandem Productions with Norman Lear; 1974 formed own production co.
PICTURES: Come Blow Your Horn (dir., co-prod., adapt.), Never Too Late (dir.), Divorce American Style (dir.), The Night They Raided Minsky's (exec. prod.), Inspector Clouseau (dir.), Start the Revolution Without Me (prod., dir.), Cold Turkey (exec. prod.), Thief Who Came to Dinner (prod., dir.), Deal of the Century (prod.), Twice in a Lifetime (prod., dir.), Arthur 2 on the Rocks (dir.), Love Hurts (prod., dir.), For the Boys (actor), Intersection (co-prod.).
TELEVISION: *Series dir*: Songs at Twilight, Martin & Lewis Show, Abbott and Costello Show, Spike Jones Show, Tony Martin Show (also prod., writer), George Gobel Show, The Ford Show Starring Tennesse Ernie Ford (also prod.). *Specials (dir.)*: An Evening with Fred Astaire (Emmy Award, 1959), Another Evening with Fred Astaire, The Jack Benny Hour Specials (Emmy Award, 1960), Henry Fonda and the Family, We Love You Madly with Duke Ellington, TV Guide Awards Show, Bobby Darin and Friends, Danny Kaye Special, Where It's At with Dick Cavett, Many Sides of Don Rickles, Robert Young and the Family, owner. *Series co-prod.*: All In The Family, Sanford and Son, Maude, Good Times, What's Happening!, Carter Country, Diff'rent Strokes, Archie Bunker's Place.

YOUNG, ALAN

Actor. r.n. Angus Young. b. North Shield, Northumberland, England, Nov. 19, 1919. First acted as monologist for 13 years in Canada; radio comedian 10 yrs. in Canada and U.S. Served in Canadian Navy as sub-lt. 1942-44. Wrote, dir. and acted in comedy broadcasts. Author: Mister Ed and Me (1995).
PICTURES: Margie (debut, 1946), Chicken Every Sunday, Mr. Belvedere Goes to College, Aaron Slick from Punkin Crick, Androcles and the Lion, Gentlemen Marry Brunettes, Tom Thumb, The Time Machine, Baker's Hawk, The Cat from Outer Space, The Great Mouse Detective (voice), Duck Tales: The Movie (voice), Beverly Hills Cop III.
TELEVISION: *Series*: The Alan Young Show (Emmy Award, 1950), Saturday Night Revue, Mr. Ed, Coming of Age. *Movies*: Earth Angel, Hart to Hart: Home is Where the Hart Is.

YOUNG, BURT

Actor, Writer. b. New York, NY, April 30, 1940. Worked at variety of jobs (boxer, trucker, etc.) before turning to acting and joining Actor's Studio. Appeared in off-B'way plays which led to Hollywood career. On B'way in Cuba and His Teddy Bear.
PICTURES: The Gang that Couldn't Shoot Straight, Carnival of Blood, Across 110th Street, Cinderella Liberty, Chinatown, The Gambler, Murph the Surf, You Can't Steal Love, The Killer Elite, Rocky (Acad. Award nom.), Harry & Walter Go to New York, Twilight's Last Gleaming, The Choirboys, Uncle Joe Shannon (s.p. only), Convoy, Uncle Joe Shannon (also s.p.), Rocky II, Blood Beach, ...All the Marbles, Rocky III, Lookin' To Get Out, Amityville II: The Possession, Over the Brooklyn Bridge, Once Upon a Time in America, The Pope of Greenwich Village, Rocky IV, Back to School, Bandini, Going Overboard, Blood Red, Beverly Hills Brats, Last Exit to Brooklyn, Medium Rare, Betsy's Wedding, Wait Until Spring Bandini, Diving In, Backstreet Dreams, Rocky V, Bright Angel, Red American, Club Fed, Excessive Force, North Star, Red Blooded American Girl II, The Undertaker's Wedding, She's So Lovely, Kicked in the Head, Heaven Before I Die, Firehouse, The Deli, The Mouse, Mickey Blue-Eyes.
TELEVISION: *Series*: Roomies. *Guest*: M*A*S*H, The Rockford Files, Miami Vice, The Equalizer, Alfred Hitchcock Presents, Tales From the Crypt, Miami Vice, The Equilizer, Law & Order, Walker Texas Ranger, The Outer Limits, Law & Order. *Movies*: The Great Niagara, Hustling, Serpico: The Deadly Game, Woman of the Year, Daddy I Don't Like It Like This (also s.p.), Murder Can Hurt You, A Summer to Remember, Vendetta: Secrets of a Mafia Bride, Double Deception, Vendetta 2: The New Mafia, Before Women Had Wings, Greener Fields. *Mini-series*: The Maharaja's Daughter, Crocodile Shoes, The Last Don.

YOUNG, CHRIS

Actor. b. Chambersburg, PA, April 28, 1971. Stage debut in college production of Pippin, followed by On Golden Pond.
PICTURES: The Great Outdoors (debut, 1988), Book of Love, December, The Runestone, Warlock: The Armageddon, PCU, Deep Down.
TELEVISION: *Series*: Max Headroom, Falcon Crest, Live-In, Married People. *Pilot*: Jake's Journey. *Movies*: Dance 'Til Dawn, Breaking the Silence, MacShayne: The Final Roll of the Dice, Runaway Daughters. *Special*: Square One. *Guest*: Crime & Punishment.

YOUNG, FREDDIE
O.B.E. Cinematographer. r.n. Frederick Young. b. England, 1902. Entered British film industry in 1917. Gaumont Studio Shepherd's Bush, London as lab asst. First picture as chief cameraman, 1927 then chief cameraman to Herbert Wilcox British & Dominions Studios Elstree Herts. Army capt. Army Film prod. group directing training films 3 yrs. Invalided out. Signed with MGM British 15 yrs. Also credited as F.A. Young. BAFTA Fellowship 1972, Prix D'Honeur (Lawrence of Arabia) O.B.E. 1970.
PICTURES: Victory 1918, A Peep Behind the Scenes, The Speckled Band, Goodnight Vienna, The Loves of Robert Burns, The King of Paris, White Cargo (first British talkie), Rookery Nook, A Cuckoo in the Nest, Canaries Sometimes Sing, A Night Like This, Plunder, Thark, On Approval, Mischief, Return of the Rat, The Happy Ending, Yes Mr. Brown, This'll Make You Whistle, That's a Good Girl, Nell Gwynne, Peg of Old Drury, The Little Damozel, Bitter Sweet, The Queen's Affair, Sport of Kings, A Warm Corner, The W Plan, Victoria the Great, Sixty Glorious Years, Goodbye Mr. Chips, Nurse Edith Cavell, The 49th Parallel, Contraband, Busman's Honeymoon, The Young Mr. Pitt, Caesar and Cleopatra, Escape, So Well Remembered, Edward My Son, The Conspirator, The Winslow Boy, Calling Bulldog Drummond, Ivanhoe, Knights of the Round Table, Invitation to the Dance, Bhowani Junction, The Barretts of Wimpole Street, The Little Hut, Indiscreet, I Accuse, Inn of the Sixth Happiness, Solomon and Sheba, Betrayed, Island in the Sun, Treasure Island, Lust for Life, Macbeth, Greengage Summer, Lawrence of Arabia (Acad. Award, 1962), The Seventh Dawn, Lord Jim, The Deadly Affair, Rotten to the Core, Doctor Zhivago (Acad. Award, 1965), You Only Live Twice, The Battle of Britain, Sinful Davey, Ryan's Daughter (Acad. Award, 1970), Nicholas and Alexandra, The Asphyx, Luther, The Tamarind Seed, Permission to Kill, The Blue Bird, Seven Nights in Japan, Stevie, Bloodline, Rough Cut, Richard's Things, Sword of the Valiant, Invitation to the Wedding.
TELEVISION: Great Expectations, The Man in the Iron Mask, Macbeth (Emmy Award, 1960), Ike: The War Years, Arthur's Hollowed Ground (dir.).

YOUNG, IRWIN
Executive. b. New York, NY. e. Perkiomen Sch., Lehigh U., B.S., 1950. Pres., Du Art Film Laboratories, Inc.

YOUNG, IRWIN W.
Executive. President of the Film Society of Lincoln Center.

YOUNG, KAREN
Actress. b. Pequonnock, NJ, Sept. 29, 1958. Trained at Image Theatre/Studio in NYC.
THEATER: A Lie of the Mind, 3 Acts of Recognition, Five of Us, Mud People.
PICTURES: Deep in the Heart (debut, 1983), Almost You, Birdy, 9-1/2 Weeks, Heat, Jaws the Revenge, Torch Song Trilogy, Criminal Law, Night Game, The Boy Who Cried Bitch, Hoffa, The Wife, Daylight, Pants on Fire, Pleasant View Avenue.
TELEVISION: Movies: The Execution of Raymond Graham, The 10 Million Dollar Getaway, The Summer My Father Grew Up, Drug Wars: The Cocaine Cartel, On the Edge of Innocence. Guest: The Equilizer.

YOUNG, LORETTA
Actress. r.n. Gretchen Young. b. Salt Lake City, UT, Jan. 6, 1913. e. Ramona Convent, Alhambra, CA, Immaculate Heart Coll. Hollywood. Family moved to Hollywood when she was 3 yrs. old; began acting as child. After small part in Naughty But Nice, lead in Laugh Clown, Laugh. Played in almost 100 films. Autobiography: The Things I Had to Learn (1962).
PICTURES: Laugh Clown Laugh (debut, 1928), Loose Ankles, The Squall, Kismet, I Like Your Nerve, The Devil to Pay, Platinum Blonde, The Hatchet Man, Big Business Girl, Life Beings, Zoo in Budapest, Life of Jimmy Dolan, Midnight Mary, Heroes for Sale, The Devil's in Love, She Had to Say Yes, A Man's Castle, The House of Rothschild, Bulldog Drummond Strikes Back, Born to Be Bad, Caravan, The White Parade, Clive of India, Call of the Wild, Shanghai, The Crusades, The Unguarded Hour, Private Number, Ramona, Ladies in Love, Love is News, Cafe Metropolis, Wife Doctor and Nurse, Second Honeymoon, Four Men and a Prayer, Suez, Kentucky, Three Blind Mice, Wife Husband and Friend, The Story of Alexander Graham Bell, Eternally Yours, The Doctor Takes a Wife, He Stayed for Breakfast, Lady from Cheyenne, The Men in Her Life, Bedtime Story, A Night to Remember, China, Ladies Courageous, And Now Tomorrow, Along Came Jones, The Stranger, The Perfect Marriage, The Farmer's Daughter (Acad. Award, 1947), The Bishop's Wife, Rachel and the Stranger, The Accused, Mother Is a Freshman, Come to the Stable, Key to the City, Cause for Alarm, Half Angel, Paula, Because of You, It Happens Every Thursday.
TELEVISION: Series: The Loretta Young Show (1953-61; 3 Emmy Awards: 1954, 1956, 1959), The New Loretta Young Show (1962-63). Movies: Christmas Eve, Lady in a Corner.

YOUNG, ROBERT
Actor. b. Chicago, IL, Feb. 22, 1907. Acted at Pasadena Playhouse which led to film roles.
PICTURES: Black Camel (debut, 1931), The Sin of Madelon Claudet, Strange Interlude, The Kid From Spain, Today We Live, Men Must Fight, Hell Below, Tugboat Annie, Saturday's Millions, The Right to Romance, Carolina, Lazy River, The House of Rothchild, Spitfire, Paris Interlude, Whom the Gods Destroy, Death on the Diamond, The Band Plays On, Vagabond Lady, Calm Yourself, Red Salute, Remember Last Night?, West Point of the Air, The Bride Comes Home, It's Love Again, Secret Agent, 3 Wise Guys, The Bride Walks Out, Sworn Enemy, The Longest Night, Stowaway, Dangerous Number, Married Before Breakfast, The Emperor's Candlesticks, I Met Him in Paris, The Bride Wore Red, Navy Blue and Gold, Paradise for Three, Josette, The Toy Wife, Three Comrades, Rich Man Poor Girl, Shining Hour, Bridal Suite, Honolulu, Miracles For Sale, Maisie, Northwest Passage, The Mortal Storm, Florian, Western Union, Sporting Blood, Dr. Kildare's Crisis, The Trial of Mary Dugan, Lady Be Good, Married Bachelor, H.M. Pulham Esq., Joe Smith American, Cairo, Journey for Margaret, Slightly Dangerous, Claudia, Sweet Rosie O'Grady, The Canterville Ghost, The Enchanted Cottage, Those Endearing Young Charms, The Searching Wind, Claudia and David, Lady Luck, They Won't Believe Me, Crossfire, Relentless, Sitting Pretty, Adventure in Baltimore, That Forsyte Woman, Bride for Sale, And Baby Makes Three, The Second Woman, The Half-Breed, Goodbye My Fancy, Secret of the Incas.
TELEVISION: Series: Father Knows Best (2 Emmy Awards: 1956, 1957), Window on Main Street, Marcus Welby M.D. (Emmy Award, 1970). Movies: Marcus Welby M.D. (pilot; a.k.a. A Matter of Humanities), Vanished, All My Darling Daughters, My Darling Daughters' Anniversary, Little Women, The Return of Marcus Welby M.D., Marcus Welby M.D.: A Holiday Affair. (d. July 6, 1998)

YOUNG, ROBERT M.
Director. b. New York, NY, Nov. 22, 1924. e. Harvard.
PICTURES: Nothing But a Man (prod., co-s.p.), The Plot Against Harry (co-prod., photog.), Short Eyes, Rich Kids, One-Trick Pony, The Ballad of Gregorio Cortez (also s.p. adapt.), Alambrista! (also s.p., photog.), Extremities, Saving Grace, Dominick and Eugene, Triumph of the Spirit, Talent for the Game, American Me (co-prod. only), Children of Fate (exec. dir. & exec. prod. only), Roosters, Caught.
TELEVISION: Specials: Sit-In, Angola—Journey to a War (Peabody Award), The Inferno (Cortile Cascino; also prod., writer, edit.), Anatomy of a Hospital, The Eskimo: Fight for Life (Emmy Award, 1971). Movie: Solomon and Sheba.

YOUNG, SEAN
Actress. r.n. Mary Sean Young. b. Louisville, KY, Nov. 20, 1959. e. Interlochen Arts Acad., MI, studied dance, voice, flute and writing. After graduating, moved to N.Y., worked as receptionist, model for 6 months and signed with ICM. Shortly after signing with ICM debuted in Jane Austen in Manhattan. On L.A. Stage in Stardust.
PICTURES: Jane Austen in Manhattan (debut, 1980), Stripes, Blade Runner, Young Doctors in Love, Dune, Baby: The Secret of the Lost Legend, No Way Out, Wall Street, The Boost, Cousins, Fire Birds, A Kiss Before Dying, Love Crimes, Once Upon a Crime, Hold Me Thrill Me Kiss Me, Forever, Fatal Instinct, Ace Ventura: Pet Detective, Even Cowgirls Get the Blues, Mirage, Dr. Jekyll and Ms. Hyde, The Proprietor.
TELEVISION: Special: Under the Biltmore Clock. Mini-Series: Tender Is the Night. Movies: Blood and Orchids, The Sketch Artist, Blue Ice, Witness to the Execution, Model by Day, Evil Has a Face, Everything to Gain.

YULIN, HARRIS
Actor. b. Los Angeles, Nov. 5, 1937. On B'way in Watch on the Rhine, A Lesson from Aloes, etc. Founder of the Los Angeles Classic Theatre.
THEATER: The Little Foxes, Who's Afraid of Virginia Woolf?, Becket, The Entertainer, The Doctor's Dilemma, Night of the Iguana, School for Wives, Uncle Vanya, Tempest, Timon of Athens, The Seagull, Next Time I'll Sing to You (NY debut), Look Back in Anger, A Midsummer Night's Dream, King John, Hamlet, Julius Caesar, Tartuffe, Approaching Zanzibar, Henry V, The Visit (B'way), Arms and the Man, It's a Mad Mad World, Arts and Leisure, Diary of Anne Frank, The Visit. Director: Baba Goya, The Front Page, The Guardsman, Sheba, The Man Who Came to Dinner, Guns of Carrar, Cuba Si, Candida, Don Juan in Hell, Jitta's Atonement, As You Like It, The Rehearsal, After the Fall, Winterplay, Last Meeting of the Knights of the White Magnolia.
PICTURES: End of the Road, Doc, The Midnight Man, Night Moves, Steel, Scarface, The Believers, Fatal Beauty, Candy Mountain, Bad Dreams, Judgement in Berlin, Another Woman, Ghostbusters II, Narrow Margin, Final Analysis, There Goes the Neighborhood, Clear and Present Danger, Stuart Saves His Family, The Baby-sitters Club, Looking for Richard, Multiplicity, Loch Ness, Bean.

TELEVISION: *Specials/Movies*: The Thirteenth Day—The Story of Esther, When Every Day Was the Fourth of July, Missiles of October, Conspiracy: Trial of the Chicago Seven, Last Ride of the Dalton Gang, Robert Kennedy and His Times, Tailspin: Behind the Korean Airlines Tragedy, Face of a Stranger, The Last Hit, Incident at Vichy, How the West Was Won, Truman. *Series*: WIOU, Frasier.

YUN-FAT, CHOW
Actor. b. May 18, 1955, Nam Nga Island, Hong Kong.
PICTURES: Massage Girls, Heroic Cops, Miss O, See-Bar, Patrol Horse, Woo Yuet's Story, Blood Money, Shanghai Beach, Shanghai Beach 2, The Head Hunter, Flower City, Love in a Fallen City, The Occupant, Waiting for Daybreak, Woman, Witch from Nepal, The Story of Rose, The Phantom Bride, The Seventh Curse, A Better Tomorrow, A Hearty Response, 100 Ways to Murder Your Wife, You Will I Will, Dream Lovers, Lunatic's True Story, Love Unto Waste, The Missed Date, Blacklist, A Better Tomorrow II, Heroic Hero, Scared Stiff, City on Fire, An Autumn's Tale, Dragon and Tiger Fight, Drifter Love, Prison Turbulence, The Romancing Star, Goodbye My Friend, Legend of Yu Ta Fu, City War, Tiger Goes on the Beat, The Greatest Lover, Diary of a Big Man, Fractured Follies, The Eighth Happiness, All About Ah-Long, A Better Tomorrow III, Brotherhood, The Inside Story, The Fun The Luck and the Tycoon, God of Chambers, The Killer, Wild Search, Once a Thief, Black Vengeance, Prison on Fire II, Full Contact, Now You See Love Now You Don't, Hard-Boiled, All for the Winner, Treasure Hunt, God of Gamblers Returns, The Peach Hotel, The Killer, The Replacement Killers, King's Ransom, The Corruptor.
TELEVISION: *Movies*: The Reincarnation.

ZAENTZ, SAUL
Producer. b. Passaic, NJ. Recipient of the Irving R. Thalberg Award, 1997.
PICTURES: One Flew Over the Cuckoo's Nest (Acad. Award: Best Picture, 1975), Three Warriors, The Lord of the Rings, Amadeus (Acad. Award: Best Picture, 1984), The Mosquito Coast (exec. prod.), The Unbearable Lightness of Being, At Play in the Fields of the Lord, The English Patient (Acad. Award: Best Picture, 1996).

ZAILLIAN, STEVEN
Writer. Director. b. 1951.
PICTURES: The Falcon and the Snowman, Awakenings, Jack the Bear, Searching for Bobby Fischer (also dir.), Schindler's List (Acad. Award, 1993; WGA & Golden Globe Awards), Clear and Present Danger (co-s.p.), Mission: Impossible (co-s.p.), Amistad, A Civil Action.

ZANE, BILLY
Actor. b. Chicago, IL, 1966. Sister is actress Lisa Zane. Studied acting at American School in Switzerland. To Hollywood in 1984 landing small role in Back to the Future. On stage in American Music (NY), The Boys in the Backroom (Actors' Gang, Chicago).
PICTURES: Back to the Future (debut, 1985), Critters, Dead Calm, Back to the Future Part II, Megaville, Memphis Belle, Blood & Concrete: A Love Story, Millions, Femme Fatale, Sniper, Posse, Orlando, Flashfire, Tombstone, The Silence of the Hams, Cyborg Agent, Only You, Tales From the Crypt Presents Demon Knight, Reflections in the Dark, Danger Zone, The Phantom, Titanic, This World—Then the Fireworks, Head Above Water.
TELEVISION: *Series*: Twin Peaks. *Movie*: Brotherhood of Justice, The Case of the Hillside Stranglers, Lake Consequence, Running Delilah, The Set Up.

ZANUCK, LILI FINI
Producer, Director. b. Leominster, MA, April 2, 1954. e. Northern VA Community Coll. Worked for Carnation Co. in LA prior to entering film business. Joined Zanuck/Brown Company in 1978 working in development and various phases of production; 1984-present, prod. Made directorial debut in 1991 with Rush. Named Producer of the Year (1985) by NATO, along with Richard D. Zanuck and David Brown; Producer of the Year (1989) by Producers Guild of America, with Zanuck.
PICTURES: Cocoon, Cocoon: The Return, Driving Miss Daisy (Academy Award, Golden Globe & Natl. Board of Review Awards for Best Picture 1989), Rush (dir.), Rich in Love, Clean Slate, Wild Bill, Mulholland Falls, The Double, True Crime.
TELEVISION: *Movies*: Rush, Into Thin Air. *Mini-series*: From the Earth to the Moon.

ZANUCK, RICHARD DARRYL
Executive. b. Los Angeles, CA, Dec 13, 1934. e. Stanford U. 1952-56. Father was exec. Darryl Zanuck. Story dept., 20th Century Fox, 1954; NY pub. dept., 1955; asst. to prod.: Island in the Sun, The Sun Also Rises, The Longest Day; v.p. Darryl F. Zanuck Prods. 1958; first credit as prod. Compulsion (1959); president's prod. rep., 20th Century Fox Studio, 1963; v.p. charge prod., 20th Fox; pres., 20th Fox TV exec. v.p. chge. prod.; 1968 Chmn. of Bd., Television div., 20th Century Fox, 1969 Pres., 20th Century Fox Film Corp. Joined Warner Bros., 1971,

as sr. exec. v.p.; resigned 1972 to form Zanuck-Brown Production Company, Universal Pictures. Joined 20th Century-Fox, 1980-83. To Warner Bros., 1983. To MGM Entertainment, 1986. 1988, dissolved 16-year partnership with David Brown. Formed The Zanuck Company, 1989. Recipient: Irving Thalberg Award (1991).
PICTURES: Compulsion, The Chapman Report, Sssssssss, The Sting (Acad. Award for Best Picture, 1973), The Sugarland Express, Willie Dynamite, The Black Windmill, The Girl from Petrovka, The Eiger Sanction, Jaws, MacArthur, Jaws 2, The Island, Neighbors, The Verdict, Cocoon, Target, Cocoon: The Return, Driving Miss Daisy (Acad. Award for Best Picture, 1989), Rush, Rich in Love, Clean Slate, Wild Bill, Mulholland Falls.

ZEFFIRELLI, FRANCO
Director, Writer. b. Florence, Italy, Feb. 12, 1923. e. Florence Univ. Was stage director before entering film industry. Set designer 1949 -52 for Visconti plays (A Streetcar Named Desire, The Three Sisters). Worked as asst. dir. on La Terra Trema, Bellissima, Senso. Director of operas.
PICTURES: *Dir./Writer*. The Taming of the Shrew (also co-prod.), Romeo and Juliet (also exec. prod.), Brother Sun Sister Moon, The Champ (dir. only), Endless Love (dir. only), La Traviata (also prod. design), Othello, Young Toscanini (also story), Hamlet, Jane Eyre, Tea with Mussolini (also story).
TELEVISION: *Mini-Series*: Jesus of Nazareth.

ZELLWEGER, RENEE
Actress. b. Katy, TX, 1969. e. Univ. of Texas, Radio-Television-Film major, 1991.
PICTURES: A Taste for Killing, My Boyfriend's Back, Murder in the Heartland, Shake-Rattle and Rock!, The Return of the Texas Chainsaw Massacre, The Low Life, 8 Seconds, Reality Bites, Love and a .45, Empire Records, Jerry Maguire, The Whole Wide World, A Price Below Rubies, Liar, One True Thing.

ZELNICK, STRAUSS
Executive. b. Boston, MA, June 26, 1957. e. Wesleyan U. B.A., 1979 (Summa Cum Laude); Harvard Grad. School of Business Administration, M.B.A., 1983; Harvard Law School, J.D., 1983 (Cum Laude). 1983-86, VP Int'l. TV for Columbia Pictures. 1988-89, pres. & COO, Vestron, Inc.; 1989-93, pres. & COO, 20th Century Fox. CEO, Crystal Dynamics. Currently pres. & CEO of BMG Entertainment North America. Bd. member BMG Entertainment and Recording Industry Association of America.

ZEMECKIS, ROBERT
Director, Writer. b. Chicago, IL, May, 1951. e. U. of Film Awards sponsored by M.P. Academy of Arts & Sciences, plus 15 intl. honors. m. actress Mary Ellen Trainor. Has film editing background, having worked as cutter on TV commercials in Illinois. Also cut films at NBC News, Chicago, as summer job. After schooling went to Universal to observe on set of TV series, McCloud. Wrote script for that series in collab. with Bob Gale. Turned to feature films, directing I Wanna Hold Your Hand and co-writing s.p. with Gale.
PICTURES: *Director*: I Wanna Hold Your Hand (also co-s.p.), Used Cars (also co-s.p.), Romancing the Stone, Back to the Future (also co-s.p.), Who Framed Roger Rabbit, Back to the Future II (also story), Back to the Future III (also story), Death Becomes Her (also co-prod.), Forrest Gump (Acad. Award, Golden Globe & DGA Awards, 1994), Contact (also prod.). Co-*Writer*: 1941, Trespass. *Exec. Prod.*: The Public Eye, Tales From the Crypt Presents Demon Knight, Frighteners, Tales From the Crypt Presents Bordello of Blood.
TELEVISION: Amazing Stories, Tales From the Crypt (exec. prod.; also dir., All Through the House, You Murderer).

ZENS, WILL
Producer, Director. b. Milwaukee, WI, June 26, 1920. e. Marquette U.; USC, B.A., M.A. Wrote, prod. and dir. many TV shows. Formed Riviera Productions to prod. theatrical motion pictures, 1960.
PICTURES: Capture That Capsule, The Starfighters, To the Shores of Hell, Road to Nashville, Hell on Wheels, From Nashville with Music, Yankee Station, Help Me... I'm Possessed!, Hot Summer in Barefoot County, The Fix, Truckin' Man, The Satan Crossing (dir., s.p.), Death on the Carrier, Terror in the Streets.
TELEVISION: Punch & Trudy, Your Police, Aqua Lung Adventures, Teletunes, Sunday Drive.

ZERBE, ANTHONY
Actor. b. Long Beach, CA, May 20, 1936. Studied at Stella Adler Theatre Studio.
THEATER: *NY*: Solomon's Child, The Little Foxes.

PICTURES: Cool Hand Luke, Will Penny, The Liberation of L.B. Jones, The Molly Maguires, The Call Me Mister Tibbs, Cotton Comes to Harlem, The Omega Man, The Life and Times of Judge Roy Bean, The Strange Vengeance of Rosalie, The Laughing Policeman, Papillon, The Parallax View, Farewell My Lovely, Rooster Cogburn, The Turning Point, Who'll Stop the Rain, The First Deadly Sin, The Dead Zone, Off Beat, Opposing Force, Private Investigation, Steel Dawn, Listen to Me, See No Evil Hear No Evil, Licence to Kill, Touch, Star Trek: Insurrection.
TELEVISION: Series: Harry-O (Emmy Award, 1976), The Young Riders. Movies: The Priest Killer, The Hound of the Baskervilles, Snatched, She Lives, The Healers, In the Glitter Palace, KISS Meets the Phantom of the Park, Child of Glass, Attica, The Seduction of Miss Leona, Rascals and Robbers: The Secret Adventures of Tom Sawyer and Huck Finn, A Question of Honor, The Return of the Man from U.N.C.L.E., One Police Plaza, Independence, Baja Oklahoma, Onassis: The Richest Man in the World, Columbo: Columbo Goes to the Guillotine, To Save a Child, Treasure Island: The Adventure Begins, On Seventh Avenue. Mini-Series: Once an Eagle, Centennial, The Chisholms, George Washington, A.D., North and South II, Dream West, Asteroid.

ZHANG, YIMOU
Executive. b. 1950, Xi'An, Shaanxi, China.
PICTURES: Cinematographer: One and Eight, Yellow Earth, Old Well (also actor), The Big Parade. Writer: Soul of a Painter. Actor: Red Sorghum (also dir.), The Terracotta Warrior, Keep Cool (also dir.). Director: The Puma Action, Ju Dou, Raise the Red Lantern, The Story of Qiu Ju, Living, Lumiere and Company, Shanghai Triad.

ZIDE, LARRY M.
Executive. b. Flushing, NY, Oct. 16, 1954. 3rd generation in mp. industry. Started 1972 with American Intl. Pictures in sls. & adv.; 1973, named branch sls. mgr., Memphis. 1975, joined Dimension Pictures as print controller; 1978, formed Zica Films Co. serving m.p. industry; 1985, Zica merged with Filmtreat Intl. Corp; named pres., newly formed Filmtreat West Corp.

ZIDE, MICHAEL (MICKEY)
Executive. b. Detroit, MI, May 31, 1932. Joined m.p. ind. with American Intl. Pictures as print controller; 1962, promoted to asst. gen. sls. mgr. Named v.p., special projects, 1970; 1972, joined Academy Pictures as v.p. of prod. Later went with Zica Film Co.; 1985, named exec. v.p., Filmtreat West Corp.

ZIEFF, HOWARD
Director. b. Chicago, IL. e. Art Center School in Los Angeles. Started as artist and photographer, working as newsreel photographer for L.A. TV station. Went to N.Y. to do still photography; became top photo artist in advertising. Turned to film direction with Slither.
PICTURES: Slither (debut, 1973), Hearts of the West, House Calls, The Main Event, Private Benjamin, Unfaithfully Yours, The Dream Team, My Girl, My Girl 2.

ZIFKIN, WALTER
Executive. b. New York, NY, July 16, 1936. e. UCLA, A.B., 1958; USC, LL.B., 1961. CBS legal dept., 1961-63. William Morris Agency, exec. v.p.,1963-; also COO since 1989.

ZIMBALIST, EFREM, JR.
Actor. b. New York, NY, Nov. 30, 1923. e. Fay Sch., Southboro, MA; St. Paul's, Concord, NH; Yale. Son of violinist Efrem Zimbalist and opera singer Alma Gluck. Daughter is actress Stephanie Zimbalist. Studied drama, Neighborhood Playhouse. N.Y. Stage debut, The Rugged Path. Shows with American Repertory Theatre; Henry VIII, Androcles and the Lion, What Every Woman Knows, Yellow Jack, Hedda Gabler, Fallen Angels. Co-prod., The Medium, The Telephone, The Consul. Gave up acting after death of his wife and served as asst. to father, Curtis Inst. of Music for 4 years. Returned to acting, stock co., Hammonton, NJ, 1954.
PICTURES: House of Strangers (debut, 1949), Bombers B-52, Band of Angels, The Deep Six, Violent Road, Girl on the Run, Too Much Too Soon, Home Before Dark, The Crowded Sky, A Fever in the Blood, By Love Possessed, The Chapman Report, The Reward, Harlow, Wait Until Dark, Airport 1975, Elmira, Hot Shots!, Batman: Mask of the Phantasm (voice).
TELEVISION: Series: Concerning Miss Marlowe (daytime serial), 77 Sunset Strip, The FBI, Hotel, Spiderman the Series. Guest: Philco, Goodyear Playhouse, U.S. Steel Hour. Movies: Who Is the Black Dahlia?, A Family Upside Down, Terror Out of the Sky, The Best Place to Be, The Gathering Part II, Baby Sister, Shooting Stars. Host: You Are the Jury, The Tempest. Mini-Series: Scruples.

ZIMBALIST, STEPHANIE
Actress. b. New York, NY, Oct. 8. Father is actor Efrem Zimbalist Jr.; grandparents: violinist Efrem Zimbalist and soprano Alma Gluck; aunt: novelist Marcia Davenport.
THEATER: LA: Festival, The Tempest, American Mosaic, Love Letters, The Baby Dance, The Crimson Thread, AdWars, Sylvia. Williamstown Theatre Festival: Barbarians, Summer and Smoke, Threepenny Opera. Tours: My One and Only, Carousel. Regional: The Philadelphia Story, The Cherry Orchard, The Baby Dance.
PICTURES: The Magic of Lassie, The Awakening.
TELEVISION: Series: Remington Steele. Mini-Series: Centennial. Movies: Yesterday's Child, In the Matter of Karen Ann Quinlan, The Gathering, The Long Journey Back, Forever, The Triangle Factory Fire Scandal, The Best Place to Be, The Baby Sitter, The Golden Moment—An Olympic Love Story, Elvis and the Beauty Queen, Tomorrow's Child, Love on the Run, A Letter to Three Wives, Celebration Family, The Man in the Brown Suit, Caroline?, Personals, The Killing Mind, The Story Lady, Some Kind of Love, Breaking the Silence, Sexual Advances, Jericho Fever, Incident in a Small Town, Voices From Within, The Great Elephant Escape, Whose Daughter Is She? Stop the World—I Want to Get Off, Dead Ahead, Prison of Secrets.

ZIMMER, HANS
Composer. b. Germany. Member of the Buggles, producing hit song Video Killed the Radio Star. Pioneered use of digital synthesizers with computer technology and traditional orchestras. Establised Lillie Yard Studio in London. Received Grammy Award for best instrumental arragement with vocals and Golden Globe for best original score for The Lion King.
PICTURES: Burning Secret, A World Apart, Rain Man, Paperhouse, Wonderland, Black Rain, Driving Miss Daisy, Bird on a Wire, Days of Thunder, Pacific Heights, Green Card, Thelma & Louise, Backdraft, Radio Flyer, The Power of One, K-2, A League of Their Own, Toys, Younger and Younger, True Romance, Cool Runnings, I'll Do Anything, The House of the Spirits, Renaissance Man, The Lion King (Acad. Award, 1994), Drop Zone, Crimson Tide, Nine Months, Something to Talk About, Beyond Rangoon, Muppet Treasure Island, Broken Arrow, The Preacher's Wife.
TELEVISION: Two Deaths.

ZINNEMANN, TIM
Producer. b. Los Angeles, CA. e. Columbia U. Son of dir. Fred Zinnemann. Entered m.p. ind. as film editor; then asst. dir. on 20 films. Production mgr. for 5 projects; assoc. prod. on The Cowboys and Smile. Prod., Straight Time for Warners with Stanley Beck.
PICTURES: A Small Circle of Friends, The Long Riders, Tex, Impulse, Fandango, Crossroads, The Running Man, Pet Sematary (exec. prod.), Streetfighter, The Island of Dr. Moreau.
TELEVISION: The Jericho Mile, Lies of the Twins.

ZISKIN, LAURA
Producer. e. USC Cinema School. Worked as game show writer, development exec. before joining Jon Peters' prod. co. where she worked on A Star is Born, Eyes of Laura Mars (assoc. prod.). Formed Fogwood Films with Sally Field. Became pres. of company Fox 2000 Pictures.
PICTURES: Murphy's Romance, No Way Out, D.O.A., The Rescue, Everybody's All American, Pretty Woman (exec. prod.), What About Bob?, The Doctor, Hero (also co-story), To Die For, Courage Under Fire, As Good As It Gets.

ZITO, JOSEPH
Director. b. New York, NY, May 14, 1949. e. City Coll. of New York.
PICTURES: Abduction, The Prowler, Friday the 13th: The Final Chapter, Missing in Action, Invasion U.S.A., Red Scorpion.

ZSIGMOND, VILMOS
Cinematographer. b. Szeged, Hungary, June 16, 1930. e. National Film Sch. Began career photographing Hungarian Revolution of 1956. Later escaped from Hungary with friend Laszlo Kovacs, also a cinematographer. Winner of Academy Award and British Academy Award for cinematography, also several int'l and domestic awards as dir. of TV commercials.
PICTURES: The Time Travelers (1964), The Sadist, The Name of the Game Is Kill, Futz, Picasso Summer, The Monitors, Red Sky at Morning, McCabe and Mrs. Miller, The Hired Hand, The Ski Bum, Images, Deliverance, Scarecrow, The Long Goodbye, Cinderella Liberty, The Sugarland Express, The Girl From Petrovka, Sweet Revenge, Death Riders, Obsession, Close Encounters of the Third Kind (Academy Award, 1977), The Last Waltz, The Deer Hunter (BAFTA Award; Acad. Award nom.), Winter Kills, The Rose, Heaven's Gate, Blow Out, The Border, Jinxed, Table for Five, No Small Affair, The River (Acad. Award nom.), Real Genius, The Witches of Eastwick, Fat Man and Little Boy, The Two Jakes, Journey to Spirit Island, The Bonfire of the Vanities, The Long Shadow (dir.), Sliver, Intersection, Maverick (also actor), The Crossing Guard, Assassins, The Ghost and the Darkness (A.S.C. Award nom.).
TELEVISION: Flesh and Blood, Stalin (Emmy Award, ACE Award, ASC Award).

ZORADI, MARK
Executive. Began working for Disney in 1980, currently pres., Buena Vista International. Distributor of the Year, Cinema Expo International, 1996.

ZUCKER, DAVID
Producer, Director, Writer. b. Milwaukee, WI, Oct. 16, 1947. e. U. of Wisconsin, majoring in film. With brother, Jerry, and friend Jim Abrahams founded the Kentucky Fried Theatre in Madison in 1971 (moved theater to L.A. 1972); later wrote script for film of that name released in 1977.
PICTURES: The Kentucky Fried Movie (co-s.p., actor), Airplane! (co-s.p., co-dir., actor), Top Secret (co-dir., co-s.p., co-exec. prod.), Ruthless People (co-dir.), The Naked Gun: From the Files of Police Squad! (exec. prod., dir., co-s.p.), The Naked Gun 2 1/2: The Smell of Fear (dir., exec. prod., co-s.p., actor), Brain Donors (co-exec. prod.), The Naked Gun 33 1/3: The Final Insult (prod., co-s.p., actor), A Walk in the Clouds (co-prod.), High School High (prod., s.p.), Basketball.
TELEVISION: Police Squad (series), Our Planet Tonight (special).

ZUCKER, JERRY
Producer, Director. Writer. b. Milwaukee, WI, March 11, 1950. e. U. of Wisconsin, majoring in education. With brother, David, and friend Jim Abrahams founded the Kentucky Fried Theatre in Madison in 1970 and wrote script for film of that name released in 1977.
PICTURES: The Kentucky Fried Movie (co-s.p., actor), Airplane! (co-dir., co-s.p.), Top Secret (co-dir., co-s.p.), Ruthless People (co-dir.), The Naked Gun (exec. prod., co-s.p.), Ghost (dir.), The Naked Gun 2-1/2 (exec. co-prod.), Brain Donors (co-exec. prod.), My Life (co-prod.), Naked Gun 33-1/3 (co-exec. prod.), First Knight (dir., co-prod.), A Walk in the Clouds (co-prod.), First Knight, My Best Friend's Wedding, Toddlers, Imagining Nathan.
TELEVISION: Series: Police Squad! (co-exec. prod., dir.; co-wrote first episode).

ZUGSMITH, ALBERT
Producer, Director, Writer. b. Atlantic City, NJ, April 24, 1910. e. U. of VA. Pres. Intercontinental Broadcasting Corp.; ed. publ. Atlantic City Daily World; v.p. Smith Davis Corp.; chmn of bd., Continental Telecasting Corp., Television Corp. of America; assoc. ed. American Press; pres. World Printing Co.; exec. CBS; pres. American Pictures Corp.; pres. Famous Players Int'l Corp.
PICTURES: Producer: Invasion USA, Top Banana, Female on the Beach, Raw Edge, Written on the Wind, Man in the Shadow, Red Sundown, Star in the Dust, Tarnished Angels, The Incredible Shrinking Man, The Girl in the Kremlin, The Square Jungle, Female on the Beach, Touch of Evil, Captive Women, Sword of Venus, Port Sinister, Paris Model, Slaughter on Tenth Avenue, The Female Animal (also story), High School Confidential, Night of the Quarter Moon, The Beat Generation, The Big Operator, Girls Town, Violated!, Platinum High School,

Private Lives of Adam and Eve, Dondi (also dir., s.p.), College Confidential (also dir.), Confessions of an Opium Eater (also dir.), Sex Kitten Go to College (also dir., story), The Great Space Adventure, On Her Bed of Roses, Fanny Hill, The Rapist!, How to Break Into the Movies, Movie Star American Style: or LSA I Love You (dir., story, co- s.p.), The Chinese Room, Street Girl, The President's Girl Friend, The Phantom Gunslinger, Sappho Darling (s.p. only), Menage a Trois, Two Roses and a Goldenrod (dir., s.p. only), The Friendly Neighbors, Why Me God?, Tom Jones Rides Again.

ZUNIGA, DAPHNE
Actress. b. Berkeley, CA, 1962. e. UCLA.
PICTURES: Pranks (debut, 1982), The Dorm That Dripped Blood, The Initiation, Vision Quest, The Sure Thing, Modern Girls, Spaceballs, Last Rites, The Fly II, Gross Anatomy, Staying Together, Eight Hundred Leagues Down the Amazon.
TELEVISION: Movies: Quarterback Princess, Stone Pillow, Prey of the Chameleon. Series: Melrose Place. Guest: Family Ties, Nightmare Classics (Eye of the Panther).

ZWICK, EDWARD
Writer, Producer, Director. b. Chicago, IL, Oct. 8, 1952. e. Harvard U., B.A., 1974; American Film Inst. Center for Advanced Film Studies, M.F.A., 1976. Editor and feature writer, The New Republic and Rolling Stone magazines, 1972-74. Author: Literature and Liberalism (1975). Formed Bedford Falls Production Co. with Special Bulletin collaborator Marshall Herskovitz.
PICTURES: Director: About Last Night... (debut, 1986), Glory, Leaving Normal, Legends of the Fall (also co-prod.), Courage Under Fire, Against All Enemies.
TELEVISION: Series: Family (writer, then story editor, dir., prod., Humanitas Prize Award, 1980), thirtysomething (co-exec. prod.; Emmy Award, 1988), Dream Street (exec. prod.). Movies (dir.): Paper Dolls, Having It All, Extreme Close-Up (also co-exec. prod., co-story), Relativity. Special: Special Bulletin (dir., co-prod., co-story; 2 Emmy Awards, also DGA, WGA & Humanitas Prize Awards, 1983).

ZWICK, JOEL
Director. b. Brooklyn, NY, Jan. 11, 1942. e. Brooklyn Coll., B.A., M.A. Dir. film Second Sight.
THEATER: Dance with Me, Cold Storage, Esther, Cafe La Mama.
TELEVISION: Series: Laverne and Shirley, Mork and Mindy, It's a Living, America 2100, Goodtime Girls, Hot W.A.C.S. (also exec. prod.), Little Darlings, Joanie Loves Chachi, The New Odd Couple (also supv. prod.), Webster, Brothers (supv. prod.), Perfect Strangers (also pilot), Full House (also pilot), Getting By (also prod.). Pilots: Angie, Bosom Buddies, Struck by Lightning, Family Matters, Adventures in Babysitting, Morning Glory, Star of the Family, Up to No Good, Going Places, Hangin' With Mr. Cooper, Life Happens, On Our Own, Making Out, Nowhere Fast.

OBITUARIES

(OCT. 1, 1997 - SEPT. 30, 1998)

John Alland	Nov. 10, 1997
William H. Anderson	Dec. 28, 1997
John Ashley	Oct. 3, 1997
Lloyd Bridges	March 10, 1998
Saul Chaplin	Nov. 15, 1997
Dane Clark	Sept. 11, 1998
Joyce Compton	Oct. 13, 1997
Stanley Cortez	Dec. 23, 1997
John Denver	Oct. 12, 1997
Chris Farley	Dec. 18, 1997
Fred W. Friendly	March 3, 1998
Samuel Fuller	Oct. 31, 1997
Sheldon Gunsberg	June 18, 1998
Phil Hartman	May 28, 1998
Peter Lind Hayes	April 21, 1998
Juzo Itami	Dec. 20, 1997
Paul Jarrico	Oct. 28, 1997
Akira Kurosawa	Sept. 6, 1998

Jack Lord	Jan. 21, 1998
Wolf Mankowitz	May 20, 1998
E. G. Marshall	Aug. 24, 1998
Daniel Massey	March 25, 1998
Toshiro Mifune	Dec. 24, 1997
Gary Nardino	Jan. 31, 1998
Sydney Newman	Dec. 30, 1997
Thomas F. O'Neil	March 14, 1998
Maureen O'Sullivan	June 22, 1998
Roy Rogers	July 6, 1998
Henry G. Saperstein	June 24, 1998
Frank Sinatra	May 14, 1998
Dawn Steel	Dec. 20, 1997
J. T. Walsh	Feb. 27, 1998
Donald Woods	March 5, 1998
Marvin Worth	April 22, 1998
Robert Young	July 6, 1998

TELEVISION MOVIES AND MINISERIES

MOVIES AND MINISERIES, 1990-1997

MOVIES AND MINISERIES, 1997-1998

TV MOVIES AND MINISERIES

SEPTEMBER 1990 – AUGUST 1997

In the following listings, the network on which the movie first aired is followed by the original airdate, the director or producer (in parentheses) and cast. With the exception of movies shown on premium cable services, all running times include commercials. For movies and mini-series prior to 1990, see the 1996 Television & Video Almanac.

ABANDONED AND DECEIVED
ABC 3/20/95. (Joseph Dougherty), Lori Loughlin, Gordon Clapp, Brian Kerwin (2 hrs.).

ABDUCTED: A FATHER'S LOVE STORY
NBC. 5/26/97. (Zev Braun), Natalie Cole, Stepfanie Kramer, Loryn Locklin, Peter MacNicol, Christopher Noth.

THE ABDUCTION
LIF 7/7/96. Victoria Principal.

THE ABDUCTION OF INNOCENCE: A MOMENT OF TRUTH MOVIE
NBC. 10/7/96. (Michael O'Hara), Lucie Arnaz, Dirk Benedict, Lochlyn Munro, Katie Wright.

ABOUT US: THE DIGNITY OF CHILDREN
ABC. 3/29/97.

ABOVE SUSPICION
HBO 5/21/95. (Steven Schachter), Christopher Reeve, Joe Mantegna, Kim Cattrall (90 mins.).

ABRAHAM
TNT 4/3 & 4/4/94. (Joseph Sargent), Richard Harris, Barbara Hershey, Maximilian Schell (4 hrs.).

ABSOLUTE STRANGERS
CBS 4/14/91. (Gilbert Cates), Henry Winkler, Patty Duke, Richard Kiley (2 hrs.)

THE ABSOLUTE TRUTH
CBS. 4/30/97. (James Keach), Jane Seymour, Bruce Greenwood, Linda Purl, Sean McCann, Marina Palmier, Barbara Eve Harris.

THE ACCIDENT: A MOMENT OF TRUTH MOVIE
NBC. 9/15/97. (Tracey Jeffrey), Bonnie Root, Donna Bullock.

ACCIDENTAL MEETING
USA 3/17/94. (Michael Zinberg), Linda Gray, Linda Purl, Leigh J. McCloskey, Ernie Lively (2 hrs.)

ACTING ON IMPULSE
SHO 7/10/93. (Sam Irvin), Linda Fiorentino, C. Thomas Howell, Nancy Allen (2 hrs.)

ADRIFT
CBS 4/13/93. (Christian Duguay), Kate Jackson, Kenneth Welsh, Bruce Greenwood (2 hrs.)

THE AFFAIR
HBO 10/14/95. (Paul Seed), Courtney B. Vance, Kerry Fox, Leland Gantt, Beatie Edney, Ciraran Hinds, Ned Beatty.

AFTER THE SHOCK
USA 9/12/90. (Ross Gary Sherman), Rue McClanahan, Scott Valentine, Jack Scalia, Yaphet Kotto (2 hrs.)

AFTERBURN
HBO 5/30/92. (Robert Markowitz), Laura Dern, Robert Loggia, Vincent Spano, Michael Rooker (2 hrs.).

AFTERMATH: A TEST OF LOVE
CBS 3/10/91. (Glenn Jordan), Richard Chamberlain, Michael Learned, Zeljko Ivanek (2 hrs.).

AGAINST HER WILL: AN INCIDENT IN BALTIMORE
CBS 1/19/92. (Delbert Mann), Walter Matthau, Susan Blakely, Harry Morgan, Brian Kerwin (2 hrs.).

AGAINST HER WILL: THE CARRIE BUCK STORY
LIF 10/5/94. (John Coles), Marlee Matlin, Melissa Gilbert, Peter Frechette (2 hrs.).

AGAINST THE WALL
HBO 3/26/94. (John Frankenheimer), Kyle MacLachlan, Samuel L. Jackson, Clarence Williams III (2 hrs.).

AGAINST THEIR WILL: WOMEN IN PRISON
ABC 10/30/94. (Karen Arthur), Judith Light, Stacy Keach, Kay Lenz (2 hrs.).

ALIBI
ABC. 3/16/97. Jason Brooks, Tori Spelling.

ALIEN AVENGERS
SHO. 8/17/96. (Lev L. Spiro), Christopher Brown, Shanna Reed, George Wendt, Anastasia Sakelaris.

ALIEN NATION: DARK HORIZON
FOX 10/25/94. (Kenneth Johnson), Gary Graham, Eric Pierpoint, Michelle Scarabelli (2 hrs).

ALIEN NATION: THE ENEMY WITHIN
FOX. 11/12/96. Gary Graham, Joe Lando, Jeff Marcus, Eric Pierpoint, Michele Scarabelli, Sean Six, Terri Treas, Lauren Woodland.

ALIEN NATION: MILLENNIUM
FOX. 1/2/96. (Kenneth Johnson), Gary Graham, Eric Pierpoint, Michele Scarabelli, Terri Treas, Sean Six, Lauren Woodland.

ALIEN NATION: THE UDARA LEGACY
FOX. 7/29/97. (Kenneth Johnson), Gary Graham, Eric Pierpoint, Michele Scarabelli, Terri Treas, Lauren Woodland, Sean Six.

THE ALIEN WITHIN
SHO 7/16/95. (Scott Levy), Roddy McDowall, Alex Hyde-White, Melanie Shatner (90 mins.).

ALISTAIR MACLEAN'S NIGHT WATCH
USA 10/4/95. (David S. Jackson), Pierce Brosnan, Alexandra Paul, William Devane, Michael J. Shannon, Lim Kay Siu.

ALL LIES END IN MURDER
ABC. 1/19/97. (Daniel A. Sherkow), Kim Delaney.

ALL SHE EVER WANTED
ABC 4/14/96. Marcia Cross, James Marshall, Leila Kenzie, CCH Pounder.

ALL THE WINTERS THAT HAVE BEEN
CBS. 9/21/97. (Lamont Johnson), Richard Chamberlain, Karen Allen, Ben Cardinal, Sheila Tousey, Ken Pogue, Chris Martin, Hal Holbrook.

ALMOST GOLDEN: THE JESSICA SAVITCH STORY
LIF 9/4/95. (Peter Werner) Sela Ward, Ron Silver, Judith Ivey, Jeffrey DeMunn, William Converse-Roberts, Sean McCann.

ALWAYS REMEMBER I LOVE YOU
CBS 12/23/90. (Michael L. Miller), Patty Duke, Stephen Dorff, David Birney (2 hrs.).

AMANDA & THE ALIEN
SHO 8/20/95. (Jon Kroll), Nicole Eggert, Stacy Keach, Michael Bendetti (95 mins.).

AMELIA EARHART: THE FINAL FLIGHT
TNT 6/12/94. (Yves Simoneau), Diane Keaton, Rutger Hauer, Bruce Dern (2 hrs.).

THE AMERICAN CLOCK
TNT 8/23/93. (Bob Clark), Loren Dean, Mary McDonnell, Eddie Bracken, Darren McGavin (90 mins.).

AN AMERICAN STORY
CBS 11/29/92. (John Gray), Brad Johnson, Kathleen Quinlan, Tom Sizemore (2 hrs.).

AMERICA'S DREAM: LONG BLACK SONG
HBO 1/17/96. (Kevin Rodney Sullivan), Danny Glover, Tate Donovan, Tina Lifford, Daniel Tucker Kamin.

AMERICA'S DREAM: THE BOY WHO PAINTED CHRIST BLACK
HBO 1/17/96. (Bill Duke,) Wesley Snipes, Norman D. Golden II, Jasmine Guy, Rae'ven A'lyia Kelly.

AMERICA'S DREAM: THE REUNION
HBO 1/17/96. (Paris Barclay) Bennet Guillory, Carl Lumbly, Susanna Thompson, Lorraine Toussaint.

AMY FISHER: MY STORY
NBC 12/28/92. (Bradford May), Ed Marinaro, Noelle Parker, Boyd Kestner (2 hrs.).

THE AMY FISHER STORY
ABC 1/3/93. (Andy Tennant), Drew Barrymore, Anthony John Denison, Laurie Paton (2 hrs.).

AND THE BAND PLAYED ON
HBO 9/11/93. (Roger Spottiswoode), Matthew Modine, Alan Alda, Lily Tomlin, Ian McKellen, Saul Rubinek (141 mins.).

AND THE SEA WILL TELL
CBS 2/24 & 2/26/91. (Tommy Lee Wallace), Richard Crenna, Rachel Ward, Hart Bochner, James Brolin (4 hrs.).

... AND THEN SHE WAS GONE
NBC 9/29/91. (David Green), Robert Urich, Megan Gallagher, Brett Cullen, Vondi Curtis-Hall (2 hrs.).

AND THEN THERE WAS ONE
LIF 3/9/94. (David Jones), Amy Madigan, Dennis Boutsikaris, Jane Daly, Steven Flynn (2 hrs.).

ANDERSONVILLE
TNT 3/3-3/4/96. (John Frankenheimer).

THE ANDROID AFFAIR
USA 4/12/95. (Richard Kletter), Harley Jane Kozak, Griffin Dunne, Ossie Davis, Saul Rubinek (2 hrs).

ANGEL FLIGHT DOWN
ABC 4/29/96 (Charles Wilkinson) Patricia Kalember, David Charvet, Christopher Atkins, Garwin Sanford, Gary Graham.

ANGEL OF DEATH
CBS 10/2/90. (Bill L. Norton), Gregory Harrison, Jane Seymour, Brian Bonsall (2 hrs.).

ANNA LEE: DIVERSION
A&E 1/3/95. (Christopher King), Imogen Stubbs, Brian Glover, John Bird (2 hrs.).

ANNIE: A ROYAL ADVENTURE
ABC 12/18/95. (Ian Toynton), Ashley Johnson, Emily Ann Lloyd, Camilla Bell, George Hearn, Joan Collins.

ANOTHER PAIR OF ACES: THREE OF A KIND
CBS 4/9/91. (Bill Bixby), Willie Nelson, Kris Kristofferson, Joan Severance (2 hrs.).

ANOTHER WOMAN
CBS 10/2/94. (Allan Smythe), Justine Bateman, Peter Outerbridge, Ken Holcross (2 hrs.).

ANY PLACE BUT HOME
UPO. 3/5/97. Mary Page Keller, Joe Lando, Melissa McBride.

ANYTHING TO SURVIVE
ABC 2/5/90. (Zale Dalen), Robert Conrad, Emily Perkins, Matthew LeBlanc (2 hrs.).

APPEARANCES
NBC 6/17/90. (Win Phelps), Scott Paulin, Wendy Phillips, Ernest Borgnine, Matt McGrath (2 hrs.).

ARCHIE: TO RIVERDALE AND BACK AGAIN
NBC 5/6/90. (Dick Lowry), Christopher Rich, Lauren Holly, (2 hrs.).

ARE YOU LONESOME TONIGHT?
USA 1/22/92. (E.W. Swackhamer), Jane Seymour, Parker Stevenson, Beth Broderick, Joel Brooks (2 hrs.).

ARMED AND INNOCENT
CBS 1/4/94. (Jack Bender), Gerald McRaney, Kate Jackson, Cotter Smith, Andrew Starnes (2 hrs.).

AS GOOD AS DEAD
USA 5/10/95. (Larry Cohen), Judge Reinhold, Crystal Bernard, Traci Lords (2 hrs.).

ASSAULT AT WEST POINT
SHO 2/27/94. (Harry Moses), Samuel L. Jackson, Sam Waterston, Seth Gilliam, John Glover, Anthony Rapp (2 hrs.).

ASTEROID
NBC. 2/16 & 2/17/97. (Bradford May), Michael Biehn, Annabell Sciorra, Don Franklin, Anne-Marie Johnson, Anthony Zerbe.

ATTACK OF THE 50 FT. WOMAN
HBO 12/11/93. (Christopher Guest), Daryl Hannah, Daniel Baldwin, William Windom, Frances Fisher (2 hrs.).

AVALANCHE
FOX 11/1/94. (Paul Shapiro), Michael Gross, David Hasselhoff, Deanna Milligan, Myles Ferguson (2 hrs.).

THE AVENGING ANGEL
TNT 1/22/95. (Craig Baxley), Tom Berenger, James Coburn, Charlton Heston (2 hrs.).

AWAKE TO DANGER
NBC 3/13/95. (Michael Tuchner), Tori Spelling, Reed Diamond, Michael Gross (2 hrs.).

B

BABE RUTH
NBC 10/6/91. (Mark Tinker), Stephen Lang, Bruce Weitz, Donald Moffat, Lisa Zane (2 hrs.).

BABIES
NBC 9/17/90. (Michael Rhodes), Lindsay Wagner, Dinah Manoff, Marcy Walker, Adam Arkin (2 hrs.).

BABY BROKERS
NBC 2/21/94. (Mimi Leder), Cybill Shepherd, Nina Siemaszko, Tom O'Brien, Jeffrey Nordling (2 hrs.).

BABYLON 5
SYND 2/24/93. (Richard Compton), Michael O'Hare, Tamlyn Tomita, Jerry Doyle, Mira Furlan (2 hrs.).

BABYMAKER: THE DR. CECIL JACOBSON STORY
CBS 2/8/94. (Arlene Sanford), Melissa Gilbert, George Dzundza, Shanna Reed (2 hrs.).

THE BABYSITTER'S SEDUCTION
NBC. 1/22/96. (David Burton Morris), Keri Russel, Stephen Collins, Phylicia Rashad.

BACK TO HANNIBAL: THE RETURN OF TOM SAWYER AND HUCKLEBERRY FINN
DIS 10/21/90. (Paul Krasny), Raphael Sbarge, Mitchell Anderson, William Windom, Paul Winfield (2 hrs.).

BACK TO THE STREETS OF SAN FRANCISCO
NBC 1/27/92. (Mel Damski), Karl Malden, Debrah Farentino, Conor O'Farrell, Carl Lumbly (2 hrs.).

BACKFIELD IN MOTION
ABC 11/13/91. (Richard Michaels), Roseanne Arnold, Tom Arnold, Colleen Camp, Conchata Ferrell (2 hrs.).

BACKSTAB
WPIX 3/26/91. (Jim Kaufman), James Brolin, Meg Foster, Dorothee Berryman (2 hrs.).

BACKTRACK
SHO 12/14/91. (Dennis Hopper), Dennis Hopper, Jodie Foster, Dean Stockwell, Fred Ward (2 hrs.).

BAD ATTITUDES
FOX 9/16/91. (Alan Myerson), Richard Gilliland, Maryedith Burrell, Ethan Randall (2 hrs.).

BADGE OF BETRAYAL
ABC. 1/6/97. (Sandor Stern), Gordon Clapp, Michele Greene, Harry Hamlin.

BANGKOK HILTON
TBS 10/9 & 10/10/91. (Ken Cameron), Nicole Kidman, Denholm Elliott, Hugo Weaving (6 hrs.).

BARBARA TAYLOR BRADFORD'S "REMEMBER"
NBC 10/24 & 10/25/93. (John Herzfeld), Donna Mills, Stephen Collins, Derek De Lint, Ian Richardson (4 hrs.).

BARBARIANS AT THE GATE
HBO 3/20/93. (Glenn Jordan), James Garner, Jonathan Pryce, Peter Riegert, Joanna Cassidy (2 hrs.).

BARCELONA '92: 16 DAYS OF GLORY
DIS 8/15/93. (Bud Greenspan), Documentary (135 mins.).

BARE ESSENTIALS
CBS 1/8/91. (Martha Coolidge), Gregory Harrison, Mark Linn-Baker, Lisa Hartman (2 hrs.).

THE BAREFOOT EXECUTIVE
ABC 12/11/95 (Susan Seidelman), Jason London, Eddie Albert, Michael March, Terri Ivens, Jay Mohr, Ann Magnuson.

BASED ON AN UNTRUE STORY
FOX 9/20/93. (Jim Drake), Morgan Fairchild, Dyan Cannon, Robert Goulet, Harvey Korman, Ricki Lake (2 hrs.).

BATTLING FOR BABY
CBS 1/12/92. (Art Wolff), Suzanne Pleshette, Debbie Reynolds, Courteney Cox, Doug McClure (2 hrs.).

BEASTMASTER III: THE EYES OF BRAXUS
WB 4/27/96.Marc Singer, Casper Van Dien, David Warner, Tony Todd, Lesley-Anne Down.

BEAUTY AND THE BANDIT
SYND 3/30/94. Brian Bloom, Brian Krause, Henry Cho, Joe Cortese, Kathy Ireland (2 hrs.).

BECAUSE MOMMY WORKS
NBC 11/21/94. (Robert Markowitz), Anne Archer, John Heard, Ashley Crow (2 hrs.).

BED OF LIES
ABC 1/20/92. (William A. Graham), Susan Dey, Chris Cooper, G.W. Bailey, Mary Kay Place (2 hrs.).

BEFORE THE STORM
ABC 7/13/91. (Michael Fresco), Linda Purl, Anthony John Denison, Josef Sommer (2 hrs.).

BERMUDA GRACE
NBC 1/7/94. (Mark Sobel), Bill Sadler, David Harewood, Seran Scott Thomas. (2 hrs.).

BERMUDA TRIANGLE
ABC 4/4/96 (Ian Toynton), Lisa Jakub, David Gallagher, Susanna Thompson, Sam Behrens, Jerry Hardin.

BETRAYAL OF TRUST
NBC 1/3/94. (George Kaczender), Judith Light, Judd Hirsch, Betty Buckley, Jeffrey DeMunn (2 hrs.).

BETRAYED: THE STORY OF THREE WOMEN
ABC 3/19/95. (William Graham), Meredith Baxter, Swoosie Kurtz, Clare Carey (2 hrs.).

BETRAYED BY LOVE
ABC 1/17/94. (John Power), Mare Winningham, Steven Weber, Patricia Arquette, Perry Lang (2 hrs.).

BETTER OFF DEAD
LIF 1/12/93. (Neema Barnette), Mare Winningham, Tyra Ferrell, Kevin Tighe, Don Harvey (2 hrs.).

BETWEEN LOVE AND HATE
ABC 2/22/93. (Ron Hardy), Susan Lucci, Patrick Van Horn, Raymond J. Barry, Barry Bostwick (2 hrs.).

BETWEEN LOVE AND HONOR
CBS 2/14/95. (Sam Pillsbury), Grant Show, Robert Loggia, Maria Pitillo. (2 hrs.).

BEYOND BETRAYAL
CBS 10/11/94. (Carl Schenkel), Susan Dey, Richard Dean Anderson, Dennis Boutsikaris.(2 hrs.).

BEYOND OBSESSION
ABC 4/4/94. (David Greene), Emily Warfield, Victoria Principal, Henry Thomas (2 hrs.).

BEYOND SUSPICION
NBC 11/22/93. (William A. Graham), Markie Post, Corbin Bernsen, Kelsey Grammer, Don Swayze (2 hrs.).

BEYOND THE CALL
SHO 6/23/96. (Tony Bill) Sissy Spacek, David Strathairn, Arliss Howard, Janet Wright, Lindsay Murrell, Les Carlson.

BEYOND THE LAW
HBO 5/5/94. (Larry Ferguson), Charlie Sheen, Linda Fiorentino, Michael Madsen, Courtney Vance (2 hrs.).

**BIG DREAMS AND BROKEN HEARTS:
THE DOTTIE WEST STORY**
CBS 1/22/95. (Bill D'Elia), Michele Lee, Kenny Rogers, Larry Gatlin. (2 hrs.).

BIG ONE: THE GREAT LOS ANGELES EARTHQUAKE
NBC 11/11 & 11/12/90. (Larry Elikann), Joanna Kerns, Dan Lauria, Bonnie Bartlett, Ed Begley Jr. (4 hrs.).

BIONIC EVER AFTER
CBS 11/29/94. (Steve Stafford), Lindsay Wagner, Lee Majors, Richard Anderson. (2 hrs.).

THE BIRDS II: LAND'S END
SHO 3/19/94. (Alan Smithee), Brad Johnson, Chelsea Field, James Naughton, Tippi Hedren (2 hrs.).

BITTER VENGEANCE
USA 7/28/94. (Stuart Cooper), Virginia Madsen, Bruce Greenwood, Kristen Hocking (2 hrs.).

BLACK FOX
CBS 7/28/95. (Steven H. Stern), Chistopher Reeve, Tony Todd, Leon Goodstrike (2 hrs.).

BLACK FOX: GOOD MEN AND BAD MEN
CBS 8/11/95. (Steven H. Stern), Christopher Reeve, Tony Todd, Kim Coates.(2 hrs.).

BLACK FOX: THE PRICE OF PEACE
CBS 8/4/95. (Steven H. Stern), Christopher Reeve, Tony Todd, Raoul Trujillo (2 hrs.).

BLACK MAGIC
SHO 3/21/92. (Daniel Taplitz), Judge Reinhold, Rachel Ward, Anthony LaPaglia, Brion James (2 hrs.).

BLACK RAINBOW
SHO 8/17/91. (Mike Hodges), Rosanna Arquette, Jason Robards, Tom Hulce (2 hrs.).

BLACK SCORPION
SHO 8/22/95. (Jonathan Winfrey), Joan Severance, Bruce Abbott, Garrett Morris (90 mins.).

**BLACK WIDOW MURDERS:
THE BLANCHE TAYLOR MOORE STORY**
NBC 5/3/93. (Alan Metzger), Elizabeth Montgomery, David Clennon, John M. Jackson (2 hrs.).

BLACKMAIL
USA 10/23/91. (Ruben Preuss), Dale Midkiff, Susan Blakely, Beth Toussaint, Mac Davis (2 hrs.).

BLIND FAITH
NBC 2/11 & 2/13/90. (Paul Wendkos), Robert Urich, Joanna Kerns, Jay Underwood, Dennis Farina (4 hrs.).

BLIND MAN'S BLUFF
USA 2/19/92. (James Quinn), Robert Urich, Lisa Eilbacher, Patricia Clarkson, Ron Perlman (2 hrs.).

BLIND SIDE
HBO 1/30/93. (Geoff Murphy), Rutger Hauer, Rebecca DeMornay, Ron Silver (2 hrs.).

BLIND SPOT
CBS 5/2/93. (Michael Uno), Joanne Woodward, Laura Linney, Fritz Weaver, Reed Diamond (2 hrs.).

BLIND VENGEANCE
USA 8/22/90. (Lee Philips), Gerald McRaney, Lane Smith, Don Hood, Marg Helgenberger (2 hrs.).

BLINDFOLD: ACTS OF OBSESSION
USA 5/20/94. (Lawrence L. Simeone), Judd Nelson, Shannen Doherty, Kristian Alfonso (2 hrs.).

BLINDSIDED
USA 1/20/93. (Tom Donnelly), Jeff Fahey, Mia Sara, Ben Gazzara, Jack Kehler (2 hrs.).

BLOOD RIVER
CBS 3/17/91. (Mel Damski), Rick Schroder, Wilford Brimley, John P. Ryan, Adrienne Barbeau (2 hrs.).

BLOOD TIES
FOX 5/27/91. (Jim McBride), Harley Venton, Patrick Bauchau, Michelle Johnson (2 hrs.).

BLOODHOUNDS
USA 4/3/96 (Michael Katleman) Corbin Bernsen, Christine Harnos, Kirk Baltz, Markus Flanagan, Gina Mastrogiacomo.

BLOODLINES: MURDER IN THE FAMILY
NBC 3/1 & 3/2/93. (Paul Wendkos), Mimi Rogers, Elliott Gould, Clancy Brown, Kim Hunter (4 hrs.).

BLUE BAYOU
NBC 1/15/90. (Karen Arthur), Alfre Woodard, Mario Van Peebles, Roy Thinnes (2 hrs.).

BLUE RIVER
FOX 11/21/95. (Larry Elikann), Jerry O'Connell, Nick Stahl, Susan Dey, Sam Elliott, Jean Marie Barnwell.

BODY LANGUAGE
USA 7/15/92. (Arthur Allan Seidelman), Heather Locklear, Linda Purl, Edward Albert (2 hrs.).

BODY LANGUAGE
HBO 7/29/95. (George Case), Tom Berenger, Nancy Travis, Heidi Schanz (100 mins.).

BONANZA: THE RETURN
NBC 11/28/93. (Jerry Jameson), Ben Johnson, Richard Roundtree, Michael Landon Jr., Jack Elam (2 hrs.).

BONANZA: UNDER ATTACK
NBC 1/15/95. (Mark Tinker), Leonard Nimoy, Dirk Blocker, Dennis Farina (2 hrs.).

BONDS OF LOVE
CBS 1/24/93. (Larry Elikann), Treat Williams, Kelly McGillis, Steve Railsback, Hal Holbrook (2 hrs.).

BONNIE AND CLYDE: THE TRUE STORY
FOX 8/17/92. (Gary Hoffman), Tracey Needham, Dana Ashbrook, Doug Savant, Betty Buckley (2 hrs.).

BORIS AND NATASHA
SHO 4/17/92. (Charles Martin Smith), Sally Kellerman, Dave Thomas, Andrea Martin, Alex Rocco (100 mins.).

BORN FREE: A NEW ADVENTURE
ABC 4/27/96.Jonathan Brandis, Ariana Richards, Lea Moreno, Chris Noth.

BORN INTO EXILE
NBC. 3/17/97. (Eric Laneuville), Mark-Paul Gosselaar, Gina Philips, Talia Shire, Eddie Mills.

BORN TO RUN
FOX 8/2/93. (Albert Magnoli), Richard Grieco, Jay Acovone, Joe Cortese, Shelli Lether (2 hrs.).

BORN TOO SOON
NBC 4/24/93. (Noel Nosseck), Pamela Reed, Michael Moriarty, Terry O'Quinn, Joanna Gleason (2 hrs.).

THE BOYS
ABC 4/15/91. (Glenn Jordan), James Woods, John Lithgow, Joanna Gleason (2 hrs.).

THE BOYS NEXT DOOR
CBS 2/4/96. (John Erman), Tony Goldwyn, Michael Jeter, Nathan Lane, Robert Sean Leonard, Lynne Thigpen, Courtney B. Vance.

BRAM STOKER'S "BURIAL OF THE RATS"
SHO 8/8/95. (Dan Golden), Adrienne Barbeau, Maria Ford, Kevin Alber (90 mins.).

BREACH OF CONDUCT
USA 12/1/94. (Tim Matheson), Peter Coyote, Courtney Thorne-Smith, Tom Verica. (2 hrs.).

BREACH OF FAITH: FAMILY OF COPS II
CBS. 2/2/97. (Robert Lantos), Charles Bronson, Diane Ladd, Joe Penny, Sebastian Spence, Barbara Williams.

BREAKING THE SILENCE
CBS 1/14/92. (Robert Iscove), Gregory Harrison, Stephanie Zimbalist, Chris Young, Kevin Conway (2 hrs.).

BREAKING THE SURFACE: THE GREG LOUGANIS STORY
USA. 3/19/97. (Steven Hilliard Stern), Mario Lopez, Michael Murphy, Rosemary Dunsmore, Jeffrey Meek, Jonathan Scarfe, Fulvio Cecere.

BREAKING THROUGH
CBS. 10/30/96. (Fred Gerber), JoBeth Williams, Kellie Martin, Alan Rosenberg, Aaron Kubey, Thomas Kopache, Billy Jayne.

BREAST MEN
HBO. 12/97. David Schwimmer, Chris Cooper.

BREATHING LESSONS
CBS 2/6/94. (John Erman), James Garner, Joanne Woodward, Kathryn Erbe, Joyce Van Patten, Eileen Heckart (2 hrs.).

THE BRIDE IN BLACK
ABC 10/21/90. (James Goldstone), Susan Lucci, Reginald Vel Johnson, David Soul (2 hrs.).

BRIDGE OF TIME
ABC. 3/15/97. (Jorge Montesi), Susan Dey, Cotter Smith, Nigel Havers, Cicely Tyson, Josette Simon, Robert Whitehead, Todd Jensen.

THE BROKEN CHAIN
TNT 12/12/93. (Lamont Johnson), Eric Schweig, J. C. White Shirt, Wes Studi (2 hrs.).

THE BROKEN CORD
ABC 2/3/92. (Ken Olin), Jimmy Smits, Kim Delaney, Michael Spears, Raoul Trujillo (2 hrs.).

BROKEN PROMISES
CBS 12/26/93. (Donald Wrye), Cheryl Ladd, Robert Desiderio, Polly Draper (2 hrs.).

BROKEN PROMISES: TAKING EMILY BACK
CBS. 5/27/97. (Donald Wrye), Cheryl Ladd, Polly Draper, Robert Desiderio, D. David Morin, Kathleen Wilhoite, Ted Levine.

BROKEN TRUST
TNT 8/6/95. (Geoffrey Sax), Tom Selleck, Elizabeth McGovern, William Atherton (95 mins.).

A BROTHER'S PROMISE: THE DAN JANSEN STORY
CBS 2/14/96. (Bill Corcoran), Matt Keeslar, Jayne Brook, Christina Cox

BROTHERHOOD OF THE GUN
CBS 10/5/91. (Vern Gillum), Brian Bloom, Jamie Rose, David Carradine, Jorge Cervera Jr. (2 hrs.).

BROTHERS ON THE FRONTIER
ABC 4/6/96. Joey Lawrence, Matthew Lawrence, Andrew Lawrence.

BUFFALO GIRLS
CBS 4/30 & 5/1/95. (Rod Hardy), Anjelica Huston, Melanie Griffith, Gabriel Byrne (4 hrs.).

BUMP IN THE NIGHT
CBS 1/6/91. (Karen Arthur), Meredith Baxter-Birney, Christopher Reeve, Wings Hauser, Shirley Knight (2 hrs.).

THE BURDEN OF PROOF
ABC 2/9 & 2/10/92. (Mike Robe), Hector Elizondo, Brian Dennehy, Mel Harris, Stefanie Powers (4 hrs.).

BURIED ALIVE
USA 5/9/90. (Frank Darabont), Tim Matheson, Jennifer Jason Leigh, William Atherton (2 hrs.).

BURIED ALIVE II
UPO. February 4, 1997. (Tim Matheson), Stephen Caffrey, Brian Libby, Tim Matheson, Tracey Needham.

BURIED SECRETS
NBC. 11/4/96. (Michele Brustin, Richard Brams), Erika Flores, Channon Roe, Kelly Rutherford, Tiffani-Amber Thiessen.

BURNING BRIDGES
ABC 5/6/90. (Sheldon Larry), Meredith Baxter-Birney, Nick Mancuso, Derek de Lint (2 hrs.).

**A BURNING PASSION:
THE MARGARET MITCHELL STORY**
NBC 11/7/94. (Larry Peerce), Shannen Doherty, Rue McClanahan, Dale Midkiff (2 hrs.).

THE BURNING SEASON
HBO 9/17/94. (John Frankenheimer), Raul Julia, Sonia Braga, Kamala Dawson. (2 hrs.).

BUTTERBOX BABIES
A&E 8/9/96. (Don McBrearty), Susan Clark, Peter McNeill, Michael Riley, Catherine Fitch, Nicholas Campbell.

BY DAWN'S EARLY LIGHT
HBO 5/19/90. (Jack Sholder), Powers Boothe, Rebecca De Mornay, James Earl Jones (2 hrs.).

BYE BYE BIRDIE
ABC 12/3/95. (Gene Saks), Jason Alexander, Vanessa Williams, Chynna Phillips, George Wendt, Marc Kudisch, Tyne Daly.

CAFE SOCIETY
SHO 2/11/96. (Raymond De Felitta), Peter Gallagher, Frank Whaley, Lara Flynn Boyle, John Spencer, Anna Thomson.

CAGNEY & LACEY: THE RETURN
CBS 11/6/94. (James Frawley), Tyne Daly, Sharon Gless, James Naughton (2 hrs.).

CAGNEY & LACEY: TOGETHER AGAIN
CBS 5/2/95. (Reza Badiyi), Sharon Gless, Tyne Daly, James Naughton. (2 hrs.).

**CALENDAR GIRL, COP KILLER?
THE BAMBI BEMBENEK STORY**
ABC 5/18/92. (Jerry London), Timothy Busfield, Lindsay Frost, Linda Blair, John Karlen (2 hrs.).

CALL ME ANNA
ABC 11/11/90. (Gilbert Cates), Patty Duke, Timothy Carhart, Howard Hesseman, Karl Malden (2 hrs.).

THE CALL OF THE WILD
FAM. 10/22/97. (Peter Svatek), Rutger Hauer, Richard Dreyfuss, Robert Pierre Cote, Bronwen Booth, John Novak, Charles Powell.

CALL OF THE WILD
CBS 4/25/93. (Alan Smithee), Rick Schroder, Gordon Tootoosis, Duncan Fraser, Mia Sara (2 hrs.).

CALM AT SUNSET, CALM AT DAWN
CBS. 12/1/96. (Daniel Petrie, Richard Welsh), Jeremy Akerman, Michael Moriarty, Kate Nelligan.

CAMP CUCAMONGA
NBC 9/23/90. (Roger Duchowny), John Ratzenberger, Danica McKellar, Sherman Hemsley (2 hrs.).

CANDLES IN THE DARK
FAM 12/3/93. (Maximilian Schell), Chad Lowe, Alyssa Milano, Maximilian Schell (2 hrs.).

THE CANTERVILLE GHOST
ABC 1/27/96. (Syd Macartney), Patrick Stewart, Neve Campbell, Donald Sinden, Cherie Lunghi, Edward Wiley, Leslie Phillips.

THE CAPE
CBS 8/7/96. (Jan Toynton), Corbin Bernsen, Adam Baldwin, Cameron Bancroft, Bobby Hosea..

CAPTAINS COURAGEOUS
FAM CH. 4/21/96. (Michael Anderson), Robert Urich, Ken Vadas, Kaj-Erik Eriksen.

CAPTIVE
ABC 10/13/91. (Michael Tuchner), Joanna Kerns, Chad Lowe, John Stamos, Barry Bostwick (2 hrs.).

CAPTIVE HEART: THE JAMES MINK STORY
CBS 4/14/96. (Bruce Pittman), Louis Gossett, Jr., Kate Nelligan, Ruby Dee, Peter Outerbridge, Michael Jai White.

CAROLINA SKELETONS
NBC 9/30/91. (John Erman), Louis Gossett Jr., Bruce Dern, Melissa Leo, G.D. Spradlin (2 hrs.).

CAROLINE?
CBS 4/29/90. (Joseph Sargent), Stephanie Zimbalist, Pamela Reed, George Grizzard, Patricia Neal (2 hrs.).

A CASE FOR LIFE
ABC 2/18/96. Mel Harris, Valerie Bertinelli.

A CASE FOR MURDER
USA 5/19/93. (Duncan Gibbins), Peter Berg, Jennifer Grey, Belinda Bauer, Samantha Eggar (2 hrs.).

CAST A DEADLY SPELL
HBO 9/7/91. (Martin Campbell), Fred Ward, David Warner, Clancy Brown, Julianne Moore (2 hrs.).

CASUALTIES OF LOVE:
THE "LONG ISLAND LOLITA" STORY
CBS 1/3/93. (John Herzfeld), Alyssa Milano, Jack Scalia, Phyllis Lyons, Leo Rossi (2 hrs.).

A CASUALTY OF WAR
USA 3/14/90. (Tom Clegg), Shelley Hack, David Threlfall, Alan Howard (2 hrs.).

CAUGHT IN THE ACT
USA 7/22/93. (Deborah Reinisch), Gregory Harrison, Leslie Hope, Patricia Clarkson, Kimberly Scott (2 hrs.).

CAUTION:
MURDER CAN BE HAZARDOUS TO YOUR HEALTH
ABC 2/20/91. (Daryl Duke), Peter Falk, George Hamilton, Peter Haskell (2 hrs.).

CHALLENGER
ABC 2/25/90. (Glenn Jordan), Karen Allen, Barry Bostwick, Brian Kerwin, Joe Morton (3 hrs.).

CHANCE OF A LIFETIME
NBC 11/18/91. (Jonathan Sanger), Betty White, Leslie Nielsen, Ed Begley Jr., William Windom (2 hrs.).

A CHANGE OF PLACE
CBS 10/9/94. (Donna Deitch), Andrea Roth, Rick Springfield, Stephanie Beacham, Ian Richardson (2 hrs.).

CHANTILLY LACE
SHO 7/18/93. (Linda Yellen), Lindsay Crouse, Jill Eikenberry, Ally Sheedy, JoBeth Williams, Talia Shire (102 mins.).

CHARLES AND DIANA: UNHAPPILY EVER AFTER
ABC 12/13/92. (John Power), Catherine Oxenberg, Roger Rees, Benedict Taylor (2 hrs.).

CHARLES DICKENS' "DAVID COPPERFIELD"
NBC 12/10/93. (Don Arioli), Animated (2 hrs.).

THE CHASE
NBC 2/10/91. (Paul Wendkos), Casey Siemaszko, Ben Johnson, Gerry Bamman, Ricki Lake (2 hrs.).

CHASING THE DRAGON
LIFETIME 6/19/96. (Ian Sander), Markie Post, Noah Fleiss, Dennis Boutsikaris, Peter Frechette, Deirdre O'Connell.

CHERNOBYL: THE FINAL WARNING
TNT 4/22/91. (Anthony Page), Jon Voight, Jason Robards, Sammi Davis (2 hrs.).

THE CHEROKEE KID
HBO. 11/96. (Paris Barclay), Sinbad, A Martinez, James Coburn, Burt Reynolds.

CHILD IN THE NIGHT
CBS 5/1/90. (Mike Robe), JoBeth Williams, Tom Skerritt, Elijah Wood (2 hrs.).

A CHILD LOST FOREVER
NBC 11/16/92. (Claudia Weill), Beverly D'Angelo, Dana Ivey, Michael McGrady, Max Gail (2 hrs.).

CHILD OF DARKNESS, CHILD OF LIGHT
USA 5/1/91. (Marina Sargenti), Anthony John Denison, Sela Ward, Paxton Whitehead, Brad Davis (2 hrs.).

CHILD OF RAGE
CBS 9/29/92. (Larry Peerce), Mel Harris, Dwight Schultz, Ashley Peldon, Rosana DeSoto (2 hrs.).

A CHILD'S CRY FOR HELP
NBC 11/14/94. (Sandor Stern), Veronica Hamel, Pam Dawber, Daniel Hugh Kelly (2 hrs.).

A CHILD'S WISH
CBS. 1/21/97.\Anna Chlumsky, Bill Clinton, Tess Harper, John Ritter.

CHILDHOOD SWEETHEARTS?
3/18/97. (Marcus Cole), Melissa Gilbert-Boxleitner, Michael Reilly Burke, Ed Lauter, Leon Russom, Barbara Babcock, Ronny Cox.

CHILDREN OF THE BRIDE
CBS 10/5/90. (Jonathan Sanger), Rue McClanahan, Kristy McNichol, Patrick Duffy (2 hrs.).

CHILDREN OF THE DARK
CBS 4/17/94. (Michael Switzer), Peter Horton, Tracy Pollan, Roy Dotrice (2 hrs.).

CHILDREN OF THE DUST
CBS 2/26 & 2/28/95. (David Greene), Sidney Poitier, Michael Moriarty, Joanne Going. (4 hrs.).

THE CHINA LAKE MURDERS
USA 1/31/90. (Alan Metzger), Tom Skerritt, Michael Parks, Nancy Everhard (2 hrs.).

CHOICES OF THE HEART:
THE MARGARET SANGER STORY
LIF 3/8/95. (Paul Shapiro), Dana Delany, Henry Czerny, Rod Steiger. (2 hrs.).

THE CHRISTMAS BOX
UPN 12/17/96. Richard Thomas, Annette O'Toole, Maureen O'Hara, Kelsey Mulrooney.

CHRISTMAS IN CONNECTICUT
TNT 4/13/92. (Arnold Schwarzenegger), Dyan Cannon, Kris Kristofferson, Tony Curtis (2 hrs.).

CHRISTMAS ON DIVISION STREET
CBS 12/15/91. (George Kaczender), Fred Savage, Hume Cronyn, Badja Djola, Casey Ellison (2 hrs.).

A CHRISTMAS ROMANCE
CBS 12/18/94. (Sheldon Larry), Olivia Newton-John, Gregory Harrison, Chloe Lattanzi. (2 hrs.).

CHROME SOLDIERS
USA 5/6/92. (Thomas J. Wright), Gary Busey, Ray Sharkey, William Atherton, Yaphet Kotto (2 hrs.).

THE CISCO KID
TNT 2/6/94. (Luis Valdez), Jimmy Smits, Cheech Marin, Sadie Frost, Bruce Payne (2 hrs.).

CITIZEN COHN
HBO 8/22/92. (Frank Pierson), James Woods, Joe Don Baker, Lee Grant, Tovah Feldshuh (2 hrs.).

CITIZEN X
HBO 2/25/95. (Chris Gerolmo), Stephen Rea, Donald Sutherland, Jeffrey DeMunn, Joss Ackland, Max von Sydow. (2 hrs.).

CLARENCE
FAM 11/22/90. (Eric Till), Robert Carradine, Kate Trotter, Nicholas van Burek (2 hrs.).

CLASS OF '61
ABC 4/12/93. (Gregory Hoblit), Dan Futterman, Clive Owen, Joshua Lucas, Andre Braugher (2 hrs.).

CLONED
NBC. 9/28/97. (Paula Weinstein, Sid Feders), Elizabeth Perkins.

CLOSE RELATIONS
A&E 11/1/90. (Adrian Shergold), James Hazeldine, Clare Holman, Rosalind March (2 hrs.).

CLOSER AND CLOSER
LIF 96. (Fred Gerber), Kim Delaney, Anthony Sherwood, Peter MacNeill, Scott Kraft.

CLOVER
USA. 9/10/97. (Jud Taylor), Elizabeth McGovern, Ernie Hudson, Zelda Harris, Loretta Devine, Beatrice Winde, Ron Canada.

CO-ED CALL GIRL
CBS 2/6/96. (Michael Rhodes), Tori Spelling.

COINS IN THE FOUNTAIN
CBS 9/28/90. (Tony Wharmby), Loni Anderson, Stephanie Kramer, Shanna Reed (2 hrs.).

THE COLD HEART OF A KILLER
CBS 1/9/96. (Paul Schneider), Kate Jackson, Corbin Bernsen, Michael Damian.

THE COLONY
USA 9/13/95. (Rob Hedden), John Ritter, Mary Page Keller, Marshall Teague, Alexandra Picatto.

THE COLONY
ABC 7/13/96 (Tim Hunter), Brian Bloom, Michael Pare, Jennifer Guthrie, Alison Moir.

COLOR ME PERFECT
LIF. 11/96. (Michele Lee), Michele Lee, Robin Thomas, Stan Cahill, Nathaniel Deveaux.

COLOR OF JUSTICE
SHO. 9/7/97. (Jeremy Paul Kagan), Bruce Davison, F. Murray Abraham, Judd Hirsch, Gregory Hines.

COLUMBO: A BIRD IN THE HAND
ABC 11/22/92. (Vince McEveety), Peter Falk, Tyne Daly, Greg Evigan, Frank McRae (2 hrs.).

COLUMBO AND THE MURDER OF A ROCK STAR
NBC 4/29/91. (Alan J. Levi), Peter Falk, Dabney Coleman, Shera Danese (2 hrs.).

COLUMBO: BUTTERFLY IN SHADES OF GREY
ABC 1/10/94. (Dennis Dugan), Peter Falk, William Shatner, Molly Hagan (2 hrs.).

COLUMBO GOES TO COLLEGE
ABC 12/9/90. (E.W. Swackhamer), Peter Falk, Stephen Caffrey, Gary Hershberger (2 hrs.).

COLUMBO: IT'S ALL IN THE GAME
ABC 10/31/93. (Vincent McEveety), Peter Falk, Faye Dunaway, Claudia Christian (2 hrs.).

COLUMBO: NO TIME TO DIE
ABC 3/15/92. (Alan Levi), Peter Falk, Joanna Going, Thomas Calabro, Juliet Mills (2 hrs.).

COLUMBO: STRANGE BEDFELLOWS
ABC 5/8/95. (Vincent McEveety), Peter Falk, George Wendt, Jeff Yagher (2 hrs.).

COLUMBO: A TRACE OF MURDER
ABC. 5/19/97. (Vincent J. McEveety), Peter Falk, David Rasche, Shera Danese, Barry Corbin, Raye Birk.

COLUMBO: UNDERCOVER
ABC 4/2/94. (Vincent McEveety), Peter Falk, Ed Begley Jr., Burt Young (2 hrs.).

COME DIE WITH ME:
A MICKEY SPILLANE MIKE HAMMER MYSTERY
CBS 12/6/94. (Armand Mastroianni), Rob Estes, Pamela Anderson, Randi Interman, Darlanne Fluegel (2 hrs.).

COMMON GROUND
CBS 3/25 & 3/27/90. (Mike Newell), Jane Curtin, Richard Thomas, C.C.H. Pounder (4 hrs.).

THE COMPANION
USA 10/13/94. (Gary Fleder), Kathryn Harrold, Bruce Greenwood, Brion James (2 hrs.).

COMPLEX OF FEAR
CBS 1/12/93. (Brian Grant), Hart Bochner, Joe Don Baker, Chelsea Field, Brett Cullen (2 hrs.).

THE COMPUTER WORE TENNIS SHOES
ABC 2/18/95. (Peyton Reed), Kirk Cameron, Larry Miller, Jason Bernard, Jeff Maynard, Anne Marie Tremko (2 hrs.).

THE COMRADES OF SUMMER
HBO 7/11/92. (Tommy Lee Wallace), Joe Mantegna, Natalya Negoda, Michael Lerner (2 hrs.).

CONAGHER
TNT 7/1/91. (Reynaldo Villalobos), Sam Elliott, Katharine Ross, Barry Corbin (150 mins.).

CONDITION: CRITICAL
NBC 12/20/92. (Jerry Friedman), Christina Haag, Kevin Sorbo, Mark Blum, Joanna Pacula (2 hrs.).

CONFESSIONS OF A SORORITY GIRL
SHO 7/29/94. (Uli Edel), Jamie Luner, Alyssa Milano, Dani Wheeler, Brian Bloom (90 mins.).

CONFESSIONS: TWO FACES OF EVIL
NBC 1/17/94. (Gilbert Cates), Jason Bateman, James Wilder, James Earl Jones, Arye Gross (2 hrs.).

CONSPIRACY OF SILENCE
CBS 7/26 & 2/28/92. (Francis Makiewicz), Michael Mahonen, Stephen Quimette, Carl Marotte (4 hrs.).

CONTAGIOUS
USA. 1/22/97. (Maru Eilts), Lindsay Wagner.

CONUNDRUM
SHO 3/1 -3/3/96. (Douglas Barr) Marg Helgenberger, Michael Biehn, Ron White, Peter MacNeill.

CONVICT COWBOY
SHO 7/16/95. (Rod Holcomb), Jon Voight, Kyle Chandler, Marcia Gay Harden, Glenn Plummer, Ben Gazzara (2 hrs.).

CONVICTION: THE KITTY DODDS STORY
CBS 11/2/93. (Michael Tuchner), Veronica Hamel, Kevin Dobson, Lee Garlington (2 hrs.).

COOPERSMITH
CBS 7/31/92. (Peter Crane), Grant Show, Colleen Coffey, Clark Johnson (2 hrs.).

THE CORPSE HAD A FAMILIAR FACE
CBS 3/27/94. (Joyce Chopra), Elizabeth Montgomery, Dennis Farina, Lee Horsley, Yaphet Kotto (2 hrs.).

THE COSBY MYSTERIES
NBC 1/31/94. (Jerry London), Bill Cosby, James Naughton, Alice Playten, Richard Kiley (2 hrs.).

THE COUNTERFEIT CONTESSA
FOX 4/4/94. (Ron Lagomarsino), Tea Leoni, D.W. Moffett, David Beecroft (2 hrs.).

COUNTERFORCE
SYND 1/17/91. (J. Anthony Loma), George Rivero, George Kennedy, Andrew Stevens (2 hrs.).

THE COURT-MARTIAL OF JACKIE ROBINSON
TNT 10/15/90. (Larry Peerce), Andre Braugher, Ruby Dee, Stan Shaw, Daniel Stern (2 hrs.).

THE COVER GIRL MURDERS
USA 10/28/93. (James A. Contner), Lee Majors, Jennifer O'Neill, Beverly Johnson (2 hrs.).

CRACKER: BEST BOYS
A & E 8/6/96. (Charles McDougall), Robbie Coltrane, Geraldine Somerville, Liam Cunningham, John Simm, Ricky Tomlinson.

CRASH LANDING: THE RESCUE OF FLIGHT 232
ABC 2/24/92. (Lamont Johnson), Charlton Heston, Richard Thomas, James Coburn, Leon Russom (2 hrs.).

CRASH: THE MYSTERY OF FLIGHT 1501
NBC 11/18/90. (Philip Saville), Cheryl Ladd, Doug Sheehan, Jeffrey DeMunn (2 hrs.).

CRAZY FROM THE HEART
TNT 8/19/91. (Thomas Schlamme), Christine Lahti, Ruben Blades, William Russ (2 hrs.).

CRAZY HORSE
TNT 7/7/96. (John Irvin), Michael Greyeyes, Wes Studi, Irene Bedard, Lorne Cardinal, August Schellenberg, Ned Beatty.

CRAZY IN LOVE
TNT 8/10/92. (Martha Coolidge), Holly Hunter, Gena Rowlands, Frances McDormand, Bill Pullman (2 hrs.).

CRIES FROM THE HEART
CBS 10/16/94. (Michael Switzer), Patty Duke, Melissa Gilbert, Bradley Pierce, Marcus Flanagan (2 hrs.).

CRIES UNHEARD: THE DONNA YAKLICH STORY
CBS 2/1/94. (Armand Mastroianni), Jaclyn Smith, Brad Johnson, Hilary Swank, David Lascher (2 hrs.).

CRIME OF THE CENTURY
HBO. 9/96. (Mark Rydell), Stephen Rea, Isabella Rossellini, David Paymer, J.T. Walsh.

CRIMINAL BEHAVIOR
ABC 5/11/92. (Michael Miller), Farrah Fawcett, A. Martinez, Morgan Stevens, Dakin Matthews (2 hrs.).

CRIMINAL JUSTICE
HBO 9/8/90. (Andy Wolk), Forest Whitaker, Anthony LaPaglia, Jennifer Grey, Rosie Perez (90 mins.).

CRITICAL CHOICES
SHO. 12/8/96. (Claudia Weill), Lisa Repo-Martel, Betty Buckley, Diana Scarwid, Pamela Reed, Brian Kerwin.

CROSSING TO FREEDOM
CBS 4/8/90. (Norman Stone), Peter O'Toole, Mare Winningham, Susan Woodridge (2 hrs.).

CROWFOOT
CBS 6/7/95. (James Whitmore Jr.), Jim Davidson, Tsai Chin, Kate Hodge, Bruce Locke, Larry Manetti, Charles Ka'upu (2 hrs.).

CROWNED AND DANGEROUS
ABC. 9/21/97. (Christopher Leitch), Yasmine Bleeth, Cassidy Rae, Jill Clayburgh, Gates McFadden, Troy Evans, Lily Knight.

THE CRUCIFER OF BLOOD
TNT 11/4/91. (Fraser C. Heston), Charlton Heston, Richard Johnson, Susannah Harker, Edward Fox (2-1/2 hrs.).

CRUEL DOUBT
NBC 5/17 & 5/19/92. (Yves Simoneau), Blythe Danner, Matt McGrath, Gwyneth Paltrow, Ed Asner (4 hrs.).

CRY IN THE WILD: THE TAKING OF PEGGY ANN
NBC 5/6/91. (Charles Correll), David Morse, Megan Follows, David Soul (2 hrs.).

CURACAO
SHO 6/27/93. (Cark Schultz), George C. Scott, William Petersen, Julie Carmen, Dennis Christopher (2 hrs.).

CURIOSITY KILLS
USA 6/27/90. (Colin Bucksey), C. Thomas Howell, Rae Dawn Chong, Courteney Cox, Jeff Fahey (2 hrs.).

CURSE OF THE STARVING CLASS
SHO 2/4/95. (J. Michael McClary), James Woods, Kathy Bates, Henry Thomas, Louis Gossett Jr., Randy Quaid (2 hrs.).

CYBERJACK
SCI-FI 5/16/96. (Robert Lee), Michael Dudikoff, Suki Kaiser, Brion James.

D

DAD, THE ANGEL AND ME
FAM 3/12/95. (Rick Wallace), Judge Reinhold, Stephi Lineburg, Alan King, Carol Kane (2 hrs.).

DAISIES IN DECEMBER
SHO 12/3/95. (Mark Haber), Jean Simmons, Joss Ackland, Pippa Guard, Judith Barker, Barbara Lott, Muriel Pavlow.

DALLAS: J.R. RETURNS
CBS. 11/15/96. (Leonard Katzman), Rosalind Allen, Chris Demetral, Patrick Duffy, Linda Gray, Larry Hagman, Omri Katz.

DALVA
ABC 3/3/96. (Ken Cameron), Farrah Fawcett, Powers Booth, Peter Coyote.

DALZIEL AND PASCOE: A CLUBBABLE WOMAN
A&E 7/15/96. Warren Clarke, Colin Buchanan, Ralph Brown.

DAN TURNER, HOLLYWOOD DETECTIVE
SYND 8/22/90. (Christopher Lewis), Marc Singer, Tracy Scoggins, Nicholas Worth (2 hrs.).

DANCING IN THE DARK
LIF 7/5/95. (Bill Corcoran), Victoria Principal, Nicholas Campbell, Robert Vaughn, Dawn Greenhalgh (2 hrs.).

DANCING WITH DANGER
USA 4/22/94. (Stuart Cooper), Cheryl Ladd, Ed Marinaro, Miguel Sandoval (2 hrs.).

DANGER ISLAND
NBC 9/20/92. (Tommy Lee Wallace), Richard Beymer, June Lockhart, Kathy Ireland (2 hrs.).

THE DANGER OF LOVE
CBS 10/4/92. (Joyce Chopra), Jenny Robertson, Joe Penny, Richard Lewis, Joseph Bologna (2 hrs.).

A DANGEROUS AFFAIR
ABC 1/1/95. (Alan Metzger), Connie Sellecca, Gregory Harrison, Christopher Meloni, Rosalind Cash (2 hrs.).

DANGEROUS INTENTIONS
CBS 1/3/95. (Michael Toshiyuki Uno), Donna Mills, Corbin Bernsen, Allison Hossack, Sheila Larken, Ken Pogue, (2 hrs.).

DANGEROUS PASSION
ABC 3/25/90. (Michael Miller), Carl Weathers, Lonette McKee, Billy Dee Williams (2 hrs.).

DANGEROUS PURSUIT
USA 2/14/90. (Sandor Stern), Gregory Harrison, Alexandra Powers, Brian Wimmer (2 hrs.).

DANIELLE STEEL'S "CHANGES"
NBC 4/1/91. (Charles Jarrott), Cheryl Ladd, Michael Nouri, Christie Clark (2 hrs.).

DANIELLE STEEL'S "DADDY"
NBC 10/23/91. (Michael Miller), Patrick Duffy, Kate Mulgrew, Lynda Carter, John Anderson (2 hrs.).

DANIELLE STEEL'S "FAMILY ALBUM"
NBC 10/23/94. (Jack Bender), Jaclyn Smith, Michael Ontkean, Joe Flanigan, Kristin Minter, Leslie Horan, Tom Mason (2 hrs.).

DANIELLE STEEL'S "FINE THINGS"
NBC 10/16/90. (Tom Moore), D.W. Moffett, Tracy Pollan, Cloris Leachman (2 hrs.).

DANIELLE STEEL'S "FULL CIRCLE"
NBC 9/9/96. Teri Polo, Corbin Bernsen, Reed Diamond, Eric Lutes.

DANIELLE STEEL'S "HEARTBEAT"
NBC 2/8/93. (Michael Miller), Polly Draper, John Ritter, Nancy Morgan (2 hrs.).

DANIELLE STEEL'S "JEWELS"
NBC 10/18 & 10/20/92. (Roger Young), Annette O'Toole, Anthony Andrews, Jurgen Prochnow (2 hrs.).

DANIELLE STEEL'S "KALEIDOSCOPE"
NBC 10/15/90. (Jud Taylor), Jaclyn Smith, Perry King, Colleen Dewhurst (2 hrs.).

DANIELLE STEEL'S "MESSAGE FROM NAM"
NBC 10/17 & 10/19/93. (Paul Wendkos), Jenny Robertson, Billy Dee Williams, Rue McClanahan, Esther Rolle (4 hrs.).

DANIELLE STEEL'S "ONCE IN A LIFETIME"
NBC 2/15/94. (Michael Miller), Lindsay Wagner, Barry Bostwick, Duncan Regehr, Rex Smith (2 hrs.).

DANIELLE STEEL'S "PALOMINO"
NBC 10/21/91. (Michael Miller), Lindsay Frost, Lee Horsley, Eva Marie Saint, Rod Taylor (2 hrs.).

DANIELLE STEEL'S "A PERFECT STRANGER"
NBC 9/12/94. (Michael L. Miller), Robert Urich, Stacy Haiduk, Darren McGavin, Susan Sullivan, Holly Marie Combs (2 hrs.).

DANIELLE STEEL'S "SECRETS"
NBC 4/6/92. (Peter H. Hunt), Christopher Plummer, Stephanie Beacham, Linda Purl, Gary Collins (2 hrs.).

DANIELLE STEEL'S "STAR"
NBC 9/30/93. (Michael Miller), Jennie Garth, Craig Bierko, Terry Farrell (2 hrs.).

DANIELLE STEEL'S THE RING
NBC. 10/20 & 10/21/96. (Armand Mastroianni), Sheila Allen, Todd Boyce, Simon Burke, Christopher Canole, Leslie Caron.

DANIELLE STEEL'S "VANISHED"
NBC 4/3/95. (George Kaczender), George Hamilton, Lisa Rinna, Robert Hays, Maurice Godin, Alex D. Linz (2 hrs.).

DANIELLE STEEL'S "ZOYA"
NBC 9/17/96. (Richard Colla), Bruce Boxleitner, Philip Casnoff, Diana Rigg, Melissa Gilbert.

DARE TO LOVE
ABC 12/17/95. (Armand Mastroianni), Josie Bissett, Jason Gedrick, Jill Eikenberry, James B. Sikking, Lorri Lindberg.

DARK ANGEL
FOX 9/10/96. (Robert Iscove) Eric Roberts, Ashley Crow.

DARK AVENGER
CBS 10/11/90. (Guy Magyar), Leigh Lawson, Maggie Han, Robert Vaughn (2 hrs.).

DARK REFLECTION
FOX 1/10/94. (Jack Sholder), C. Thomas Howell, Lisa Zane, Miko Hughes, Ethan Phillips (2 hrs.).

DARKNESS BEFORE DAWN
NBC 2/15/93. (John Patterson), Meredith Baxter, Stephen Lang, Gwynyth Walsh, L. Scott Caldwell (2 hrs.).

DAUGHTER OF DARKNESS
CBS 1/26/90. (Stuart Gordon), Anthony Perkins, Mia Sara, Jack Coleman (2 hrs.).

DAUGHTER OF THE STREETS
ABC 2/26/90. (Ed Sherin), Jane Alexander, Roxana Zal, John Stamos (2 hrs.).

DAUGHTERS OF PRIVILEGE
NBC 3/17/91. (Michael Fresco), Dick Van Dyke, Daphne Ashbrook, Kate Vernon (2 hrs.).

DAVID
TNT. 4/6 & 4/9/97. (Robert Markowitz), Nathaniel Parker, Jonathan Pryce, Leonard Nimoy, Sheryl Lee.

DAVID'S MOTHER
CBS 4/10/94. (Robert Allan Ackerman), Kirstie Alley, Sam Waterston, Michael Goorjian (2 hrs.).

DAY MY PARENTS RAN AWAY, THE
FOX 12/13/93. (Martin Nicholson), Bobby Jacoby, Brigid Conley Walsh, Matt Frewer, Blair Brown (2 hrs.).

DAY OF RECKONING
NBC 3/7/94. (Brian Grant), Fred Dryer, Geoffrey Lewis, Patrick Bauchau (2 hrs.).

DAY-O
NBC 5/3/92. (Michael Schultz), Delta Burke, Elijah Wood, Carlin Glynn, Charles Shaughnessy (2 hrs.).

DAYBREAK
HBO 5/8/93. (Stephen Tolkin), Cuba Gooding Jr., Moira Kelly, John Cameron Mitchell, John Savage (90 mins.).

DEAD AHEAD
USA 4/17/96. (Stuart Cooper) Stephanie Zimbalist, Sarah Chalke, Brendan Fletcher, Andrew Airlie.

DEAD AHEAD: THE EXXON VALDEZ DISASTER
HBO 12/12/92. (Paul Seed), John Heard, Christopher Lloyd, Ron Frazier, David Morse, Bob Gunton (90 mins.).

DEAD AIR
USA 10/6/94. (Fred Walton), Gregory Hines, Deborah Farentino, Beau Starr, Gloria Reuben, Laura Harrington (2 hrs.).

DEAD AND ALIVE
ABC 11/24/91. (Peter Markle), Tony Danza, Ted Levine, Dan Lauria, Caroline Aaron (2 hrs.).

DEAD BEFORE DAWN
ABC 1/10/93. (Charles Correll), Cheryl Ladd, Jameson Parker, Hope Lange, Kim Coates (2 hrs.).

DEAD BY SUNSET
NBC 11/19 & 11/20/95. (Karen Arthur) Ken Olin, Lindsay Frost, Annette O'Toole, John Terry, Sally Murphy, Titan Crawford.

DEAD IN THE WATER
USA 12/4/91. (Bill Condon), Bryan Brown, Teri Hatcher, Veronica Cartwright, Anne DeSalvo (2 hrs.).

DEAD MAN'S REVENGE
USA 4/15/94. (Alan J. Levi), Bruce Dern, Michael Ironside, Keith Coulouris, Doug McClure (2 hrs.).

DEAD ON THE MONEY
TNT 6/17/91. (Mark Culllingham), Corbin Bernsen, Amanda Pays, John Glover (2 hrs.).

DEAD RECKONING
USA 5/23/90. (Robert Lewis), Cliff Robertson, Rick Springfield, Susan Blakely (2 hrs.).

DEAD SILENCE
FOX 8/26/91. (Peter O'Fallon), Renee Estevez, Lisanne Falk, Carrie Mitchum (2 hrs.).

DEAD SILENCE
HBO. 1/11/97. James Garner, Kim Coates, Charles Martin Smith, Lolita Davidovich, Marlee Matlin.

**DEADLINE FOR MURDER:
FROM THE FILES OF EDNA BUCHANAN**
CBS 5/9/95. (Joyce Chopra), Elizabeth Montgomery, Yaphet Kotto, Audra Lindley, Dean Stockwell, Evelyn Bakerges (2 hrs.).

DEADLOCK
HBO 9/28/91. (Lewis Teague), Rutger Hauer, Mimi Rogers, Joan Chen, Stephen Tobolowsky (2 hrs.).

DEADLOCKED: ESCAPE FROM ZONE 14
FOX 5/9/95. (Graeme Campbell), Esai Morales, Stephen McHattie, Jon Cuthbert, Sarah Strange, Douglas Arthurs, Nia Peeples (2 hrs.).

DEADLY BETRAYAL: THE BRUCE CURTIS STORY
NBC 2/2/92. (Graeme Campbell), Simon Reynolds, Jaimz Woolvett, Kenneth Welsh, Bruce Boa (2 hrs.).

DEADLY DESIRE
USA 1/29/91. (Charles Correll), Jack Scalia, Kathryn Harrold, Will Patton (2 hrs.).

DEADLY FAMILY SECRETS
NBC 12/4/95. (Richard T. Heffron), Loni Anderson, Gigi Rice, Greg Evigan.

DEADLY GAME
USA 7/10/91. (Thomas J. Wright), Roddy McDowall, Marc Singer, Michael Beck (2 hrs.).

DEADLY GAMES
UPN. 9/5/95. (Leonad Nimoy), Cynthia Gibb, James Calvert, Stephen T. Kay, Christopher Lloyd, Tom Rathman, Tony Carreiro.

DEADLY INTENTIONS... AGAIN?
ABC 2/11/91. (James Steven Sadwith), Harry Hamlin, Joanna Kerns, Conchata Ferrell (2 hrs.).

DEADLY INVASION: THE KILLER BEE NIGHTMARE
FOX 3/7/95. (Rockne S. O'Bannon), Robert Hays, Nancy Stafford, Dennis Christopher, Ryan Phillippe, Gina Philips.

DEADLY MATRIMONY
NBC 11/22 & 11/23/92. (John Korty), Brian Dennehy, Treat Williams, Embeth Davidtz, Susan Ruttan (4 hrs.).

DEADLY MEDICINE
NBC 11/11/91. (Richard Colla), Veronica Hamel, Susan Ruttan, Stephen Tobolowsky, Scott Paulin (2 hrs.).

DEADLY PURSUITS
NBC 1/8/96. (Felix Enriquez Alcala), Tori Spelling, Patrick Muldoon.

DEADLY RELATIONS
ABC 5/22/93. (Bill Condon), Robert Urich, Shelley Fabares, Gwyneth Paltrow, Georgia Emelin (2 hrs.).

DEADLY SURVEILLANCE
SHO 9/6/91. (Paul Ziller), Michael Ironside, Christopher Bondy, Susan Almgren, David Carradine (2 hrs.).

A DEADLY VISION
ABC. 4/21/97. Peter Boyle, Ellen Burstyn, Kristin Davis.

DEADLY VOWS
FOX 9/13/94. (Alan Metzger), Gerald McRaney, Peggy Lipton, Josie Bissett, Ric Reid, Michael MacRae, P. Lynn Johnson.

DEADLY VOYAGE
HBO 6/15/96. (John MacKenzie), Omar Epps, Sean Pertwee, Joss Ackland, David Suchet, Jean-Claude LaMarre.

DEADLY WEB
NBC 4/15/96. (Jorge Montesi), Gigi Rice, Ed Marinaro, John Wesley Shipp, Andrew Lawrence, Ted McGinley.

DEADLY WHISPERS
CBS 5/10/95. (Bill Norton), Tony Danza, Pamela Reed, Ving Rhames, Heather Tom, Sean Haberle (2 hrs.).

DEAN R. KOONTZ'S "SERVANTS OF TWILIGHT"
SHO 10/14/91. (Jeffrey Obrow), Bruce Greenwood, Belinda Bauer, Grace Zabriskie, Jarrett Lennon.

DEATH BENEFIT
USA 3/3/96. Peter Horton, Carrie Snodgress, Wendy Makkena.

DEATH DREAMS
LIF 6/25/91. (Martin Donovan), Christopher Reeve, Marg Helgenberger, Fionnula Flanagan (2 hrs.).

DEATH HITS THE JACKPOT
ABC 12/15/91. (Vince McEveety), Peter Falk, Rip Torn, Jamie Rose, Gary Kroeger (2 hrs.).

DEATH IN SMALL DOSES
ABC 1/16/95. (Sondra Locke), Richard Thomas, Tess Harper, Glynnis O'Connor, Shawn Elliott, Gary Frank, (2 hrs.).

THE DEATH OF THE INCREDIBLE HULK
NBC 2/18/90. (Bill Bixby), Bill Bixby, Lou Ferrigno, Elizabeth Gracen (2 hrs.).

DEATH TRAIN
SHO 4/14/93. (David Jackson), Pierce Brosnan, Patrick Stewart, Christopher Lee, Alexandra Paul (2 hrs.).

DECEPTION: A MOTHER'S SECRET
NBC 11/24/91. (Sandor Stern), Steven Weber, Katharine Helmond, Robert Hy Gorman, Mary Page Keller (2 hrs.).

DECEPTIONS
SHO 6/10/90. (Ruben Preuss), Harry Hamlin, Robert Davi, Nicollette Sheridan (2 hrs.).

DECONSTRUCTING SARAH
USA 6/17/94. (Craig R. Baxley), Sheila Kelley, Rachel Ticotin, A. Martinez, David Andrews (2 hrs.).

DECORATION DAY
NBC 12/2/90. (Robert Markowitz), James Garner, Bill Cobbs, Ruby Dee, Judith Ivey (2 hrs.).

DEEP FAMILY SECRETS
CBS. 4/15/97. Meg Foster, Molly Gross, Christie Lynn Smith.

DEEP TROUBLE
USA 7/8/93. (Armand Mastroianni), Robert Wagner, Ben Cross, Isabelle Pasco (2 hrs.).

DELIVER THEM FROM EVIL: THE TAKING OF ALTA VIEW
CBS 4/28/92. (Peter Levin), Harry Hamlin, Teri Garr, Terry O'Quinn, Gary Frank (2 hrs.).

THE DELIVERANCE OF ELAINE
4/10/96. Mare Winningham, Lloyd Bridges, Ron Lea, Chris Cooper.

DERBY
ABC 6/17/95. (Bob Clark), Joanne Vannicola, David Charvet, Leon Cariou, Darren McGavin, Felton Perry (2 hrs.).

DESCENDING ANGEL
HBO 11/25/90. (Jeremy Kagan), George C. Scott, Diane Lane, Eric Roberts (2 hrs.).

DESPERATE CHOICES: TO SAVE MY CHILD
NBC 10/5/92. (Andy Tennant), Joanna Kerns, Bruce Davidson, Joe Mazzello, Reese Witherspoon (2 hrs.).

DESPERATE JOURNEY: THE ALLISON WILCOX STORY
ABC 12/5/91. (Dan Lerner), Mel Harris, John Schneider, Dana Ashbrook (2 hrs.).

DESPERATE RESCUE: THE CATHY MAHONE STORY
NBC 1/11/93. (Richard Colla), Mariel Hemingway, Clancy Brown, Jeff Korber, James Russo (2 hrs.).

THE DESPERATE TRAIL
TNT 7/9/95. (P.J. Pesce), Sam Elliott, Linda Fiorentino, Craig Sheffer, Frank Whaley (2 hrs.).

DEVIL'S FOOD
LIF 9/2/96. (George Kaczender), Suzanne Somers, Dabney Coleman, William Katt, Charles R. Frank.

DEVLIN
SHO 9/12/92. (Rick Rosenthal), Bryan Brown, Roma Downey, Lloyd Bridges, Whip Hubley (2 hrs.).

DIAGNOSIS OF MURDER
CBS 1/5/92. (Chris Hilber), Dick Van Dyke, Mariette Hartley, Ken Kercheval, Bill Bixby (2 hrs.).

THE DIAMOND FLEECE
USA 6/1/92. (Al Waxman), Ben Cross, Kate Nelligan, Brian Dennehy, Tony Rosato (2 hrs.).

DIANA: HER TRUE STORY
NBC 4/4 & 4/5/93. (Kevin Connor), Serena Scott Thomas, David Threlfall, Elizabeth Garvie (4 hrs.).

DILLINGER
ABC 1/6/91. (Rupert Wainwright), Mark Harmon, Sherilyn Fenn, Will Patton, Patricia Arquette (2 hrs.).

DIRTY WORK
USA 7/22/92. (John McPherson), Kevin Dobson, John Ashton (2 hrs.).

THE DISAPPEARANCE OF CHRISTINA
USA 11/4/93. (Karen Arthur), John Stamos, Robert Carradine, Kim Delaney, C.C.H. Pounder (2 hrs.).

THE DISAPPEARANCE OF NORA
CBS 5/7/93. (Joyce Chopra), Veronica Hamel, Dennis Farina, Stephen Collins (2 hrs.).

THE DISAPPEARANCE OF VONNIE
CBS 9/27/94. (Graeme Campbell), Ann Jillian, Joe Penny, Kim Zimmer, Robert Wisden, Graham Beckel, Alexandra Purvis.

DISASTER IN TIME
SHO 5/9/92. (David H. Twohy), Jeff Daniels, Ariana Richards, Emilia Crow, Jim Haynie (2 hrs.).

THE DITCHDIGGER'S DAUGHTERS
FAM. 2/23/97. (Johnny E. Jensen), Carl Lumbly, Dule Hill, Victoria Dillard, Shelley Robertson, Adrienne Monique Coleman, Kimberly Elise.

DIVAS
FOX 9/19/96. (Thomas Carter), Khalil Kain, Nicole Parker, Tammy Townsend, Fatima Lowe.

DOCTOR WHO
FOX 5/14/96. (Geoffrey Sax), Paul McGann, Eric Roberts, Daphne Ashbrook, Sylvester McCoy, Yee Jee Tso, John Novak.

DOG'S BEST FRIEND
FAM. 3/23/97. (Marc Samuelson, Peter Samuelson, James Shavick), Adam Zolotin, Edward Asner, Meredith Baxter, Roger Clinton.

DOING TIME ON MAPLE DRIVE
FOX 3/16/92. (Ken Olin), William McNamara, James B. Sikking, Bibi Besch, James Carrey (2 hrs.).

DON KING
HBO. 11/97. Ving Rhames, Vondie Curtis Hall, Jeremy Piven, Darius McCrary, Keith David.

DON'T DRINK THE WATER
ABC 12/18/94. (Woody Allen), Woody Allen, Michael J. Fox, Mayim Bialik, Julie Kavner, Dom DeLuise (2 hrs.).

DON'T TALK TO STRANGERS
USA 8/11/94. (Robert Lewis), Pierce Brosnan, Shanna Reed, Terry O'Quinn, Keegan Macintosh (2 hrs.).

DON'T TOUCH MY DAUGHTER
NBC 4/7/91. (John Pasquin), Victoria Principal, Paul Sorvino, Jonathan Banks (2 hrs.).

DONATO AND DAUGHTER
CBS 9/21/93. (Rod Holcomb), Charles Bronson, Dana Delany, Xander Berkeley (2 hrs.).

DONOR
CBS 12/9/90. (Larry Shaw), Melissa Gilbert-Brinkman, Jack Scalia, Wendy Hughes (2 hrs.).

DOOMSDAY GUN
HBO 7/23/94. (Robert Young), Frank Langella, Kevin Spacey, Alan Arkin, Tony Goldwyn, Rupert Graves (2 hrs.).

DOUBLE DECEPTION
NBC 6/21/93. (Jan Egelson), James Russo, Alice Krige, Sally Kirkland, Burt Young (2 hrs.).

DOUBLE DOUBLE TOIL AND TROUBLE
ABC 10/30/93. (Stuart Margolin), Mary-Kate Olsen, Ashley Olsen, Cloris Leachman (2 hrs.).

DOUBLE EDGE
CBS 3/22/92. (Stephen Stafford), Susan Lucci, Robert Urich, Robert Prosky, Michael Woods (2 hrs.).

DOUBLE JEOPARDY
SHO 11/21/92. (Lawrence Schiller), Bruce Boxleitner, Rachel Ward, Sela Ward, Sally Kirkland (2 hrs.).

DOUBLE JEOPARDY
CBS 1/30/96. (Deborah Dalton), Brittany Murphy, Joe Penny, Teri Garr, Shawn Hatosy, Rutanya Alda, Ken James.

DOUBLECROSSED
HBO 7/20/91. (Roger Young), Dennis Hopper, Robert Carradine, Adrienne Barbeau (2 hrs.).

DOWN CAME A BLACKBIRD
SHO 10/22/96. (Jonathan Sanger), Raul Julia, Laura Dern, Vanessa Redgrave, Cliff Gorman, Sarita Choudhur.

DOWN, OUT AND DANGEROUS
USA 8/23/95. (Noel Nosseck), Richard Thomas, Bruce Davison, Cynthia Ettinger, George DiCenzo, Jason Bernard (2 hrs.).

DRAGSTRIP GIRL
SHO 9/2/94. (Mary Lambert), Mark Dacascos, Natasha Gregson Wagner, Maria Celedonio, Raymond Cruz, Traci Lords (90 mins.).

A DREAM IS A WISH YOUR HEART MAKES: THE ANNETTE FUNICELLO STORY
CBS. 1/26/97. Frankie Avalon, Len Cariou, Shelley Fabares, Annette Funicello, Eva LaRue, Linda Lavin, David Lipper.

THE DREAMER OF OZ
NBC 12/10/90. (Jack Bender), John Ritter, Annette O'Toole, Rue McClanahan, John Cameron Mitchell (2 hrs.).

DRIVE LIKE LIGHTNING
USA 1/8/92. (Bradford May), Steven Bauer, Cynthia Gibb, William Russ, Paul Koslo (2 hrs.).

DROP DEAD GORGEOUS
USA 8/7/91. (Paul Lynch), Jennifer Rubin, Peter Outerbridge, Sally Kellerman (2 hrs.).

DRUG WARS: THE COCAINE CARTEL
NBC 1/19 & 1/20/92. (Paul Krasny), Alex McArthur, Dennis Farina, Julie Carmen, John Glover (4 hrs.).

DRUG WARS: THE CAMARENA STORY
NBC 1/7, 1/8 & 1/9/90. (Brian Gibson), Steven Bauer, Elizabeth Pena, Craig T. Nelson (6 hrs.).

DUE SOUTH
CBS 4/23/94. (Fred Gerber), Paul Gross, David Marciano, Wendel Meldrum (2 hrs.).

DUEL OF HEARTS
TNT 2/24/92. (John Hough), Alison Doody, Michael York, Geraldine Chaplin, Billie Whitelaw (2 hrs.).

THE DUKES OF HAZZARD: REUNION
CBS. 4/25/97. (Lewis Teague), Tom Wopat, John Schneider, Catherine Bach, Denver Pyle, James Best, Ben Jones.

DUPLICATES
USA 3/18/92. (Sandor Stern), Gregory Harrison, Kim Griest, Cicely Tyson, Kevin McCarthy (2 hrs.).

DYING TO BE PERFECT: THE ELLEN HART PENA STORY
ABC. 11/24/96. (Jan Egleson), Crystal Bernard, Esai Morales, Casey Sander, Tom Atkins, Richard Jury, L. Scott Caldwell.

DYING TO BELONG
CBS. 2/24/97. (William A. Graham), Hillary Swank, Sarah Chalk, Jenna Van Oy, Tracy Middendorf.

DYING TO LOVE YOU
CBS 3/16/93. (Robert Iscove), Tim Matheson, Tracy Pollan, Christine Ebersole (2 hrs.).

DYING TO REMEMBER
USA 10/2/93. (Arthur Allan Seidelman), Melissa Gilbert, Ted Shackelford, Scott Plank (2 hrs.).

DYNASTY: THE REUNION
ABC 10/20 & 10/22/91. (Irving J. Moore), John Forsythe, Linda Evans, Joan Collins, Jeroen Krabbe (4 hrs.).

EARTH ANGEL
NBC 3/4/91. (Joe Napolitano), Cindy Williams, Cathy Podewell, Mark Hamill (2 hrs.).

ECHO
ABC. 1/5/97. Laurie Holden, Alexandra Paul, Kin Shriner, Jack Wagner.

ED MCBAIN'S 87TH PRECINCT
NBC 3/19/95. (Bruce Paltrow), Randy Quaid, Alex McArthur, Ving Rhames, Deanne Bray, Eddie Jones (2 hrs.).

ED MCBAIN'S 87TH PRECINT: HEATWAVE
NBC. 1/12/97. (Diana Kerew), Dale Midkiff, Paul Johannsen, Andrea Ferrell.

ED MCBAIN'S 87TH PRECINCT: ICE
NBC 2/18/96. (Bradford May), Dale Midkiff, Joe Pantoliano, Paul Johansson, Andrea Parker, Dean McDermott, Andrea Ferrell.

EDEN
USA 6/27/93. (Victor Lobl), Barbara Alyn Woods, Steve Chase, Jack Armstrong (2 hrs.).

83 HOURS 'TIL DAWN
CBS 11/11/90. (Donald Wrye), Peter Strauss, Robert Urich, Paul Winfield, Samantha Mathis (2 hrs.).

EL DIABLO
HBO 7/22/90. (Peter Markle), Anthony Edwards, Louis Gossett Jr., John Glover (2 hrs.).

ELMORE LEOMARD'S GOLD COAST
SHO. (Peter Weller), Marg Helgenberger, David Caruso, Jeff Kober, Barry Primus, Frederick Weller, Richard Bradford.

ELVIS AND THE COLONEL
NBC 1/10/93. (William A. Graham), Beau Bridges, Rob Youngblood, Dan Shor, Scott Wilson (2 hrs.).

ELVIS MEETS NIXON
SHO. 8/10/97. (Allan Arkush), Rick Peters, Bob Gunton, Alyson Court, Denny Doherty, Jackie Burroughs, Curtis Armstrong, Gabriel Hogan.

EMPTY CRADLE
ABC 10/3/93. (Paul Schneider), Kate Jackson, Lori Loughlin, Eric LaSalle, David Lansbury (2 hrs.).

END OF SUMMER
SHO. 2/2/97. (Linda Yellen), Jacqueline Bisset, Peter Weller, Julian Sands, Amy Locane, Elizabeth Shepherd, Michael Hogan.

ENDLESS GAME
SHO 1/21/90. (Bryan Forbes), Albert Finney, George Segal, Kristin Scott Thomas, Ian Holm (2 hrs.).

THE ENTERTAINERS
ABC 11/21/91. (Paul Schneider), Bob Newhart, Linda Gray, Richard Romanus, Bernie White (2 hrs.).

THE ERNEST GREEN STORY
DIS 1/17/93. (Eric Laneuville), Morris Chestnut, Ossie Davis, C.C.H. Pounder, Avery Brooks (2 hrs.).

ESCAPE FROM TERROR: THE TERESA STAMPER STORY
NBC 1/23/95. (Michael Scott), Maria Pitillo, Adam Storke, Cindy Williams, Tony Becker, Brad Dourif (2 hrs.).

ESCAPE TO WITCH MOUNTAIN
ABC 4/29/95. (Peter Rader), Robert Vaughn, Erik von Detten, Elisabeth Moss, Brad Dourif, Lynne Moody, Lauren Tom (2 hrs.).

EVERYTHING TO GAIN
CBS. 10/13/96. (Michael Miller), Sean Young, Jack Scalia, Charles Shaughnessy.

EVERY WOMAN'S DREAM
CBS. 10/15/96. (Steven Schachter), Kim Cattrall, Jeff Fahey, DeLane Matthews.

EVIL HAS A FACE
USA 3/20/96. Sean Young, William Moses.

EVOLVER
SCI-FI 2/10/96. (Mark Rosman), John de Lancie, Ethan Randall, Cassidy Rae, Paul Dooley, Cindy Pickett.

EXCLUSIVE
ABC 10/4/92. (Alan Metzger), Suzanne Somers, Michael Nouri, Ed Begley Jr., Joe Cortese (2 hrs.).

EXTREME CLOSE-UP
NBC 10/22/90. (Peter Horton), Craig T. Nelson, Blair Brown, Morgan Weisser, Samantha Mathis (2 hrs.).

EXTREME JUSTICE
HBO 6/26/93. (Mark L. Lester), Lou Diamond Phillips, Scott Glenn, Chelsea Field, Yaphett Kotto (2 hrs.).

EYE OF THE STALKER: A MOMENT OF TRUTH MOVIE
NBC 12/18/95. (Reza Badiyi), Brooke Langton, Jere Burns, Joanna Cassidy.

EYES OF A WITNESS
CBS 3/31/91. (Peter Hunt), Daniel J. Travanti, Jennifer Grey, Carl Lumbly (2 hrs.).

EYES OF TERROR
NBC 3/18/94. (Sam Pillsbury), Barbara Eden, Michael Nouri, Ted Marcoux (2 hrs.).

FACE OF A STRANGER
CBS 12/29/91. (Claudia Weill), Gena Rowlands, Tyne Daly, Cynthia Nixon, Harris Yulin (2 hrs.).

FACE OF EVIL
CBS 4/9/96. (Mary Lambert), Tracy Gold, Perry King, Shawnee Smith.

THE FACE OF FEAR
CBS 9/30/90. (Farhad Mann), Lee Horsley, Pam Dawber, Kevin Conroy (2 hrs.).

THE FACE ON THE MILK CARTON
CBS 5/24/95. (Waris Hussein), Kellie Martin, Sharon Lawrence, Jill Clayburgh, Edward Herrmann, Richard Masur (2 hrs.).

A FACE TO DIE FOR
NBC 3/11/96. (Jack Bender), Yasmine Bleeth, Robin Givens, James Wilder, Chandra West, Mary Ellen Trainor.

FACE TO FACE
CBS 1/24/90. (Lou Antonio), Elizabeth Montgomery, Robert Foxworth, Lou Antonio (2 hrs.).

FADE TO BLACK
USA 2/10/93. (John McPherson), Timothy Busfield, Heather Locklear, Cloris Leachman, Michael Beck (2 hrs.).

FALL FROM GRACE
NBC 4/29/90. (Karen Arthur), Bernadette Peters, Kevin Spacey, Richard Herd (2 hrs.).

FALL FROM GRACE
CBS 6/2 & 6/3/94. (Waris Hussein), Michael York, Gary Cole, Tara Fitzgerald, James Fox (4 hrs.).

FALL INTO DARKNESS
NBC. 11/25/97. (Ken Kaufman), Tatyana Ali, Jonathan Brandis, Sean Murray, Paul Scherrer, Marco Sanchez.

FALLEN CHAMP: THE UNTOLD STORY OF MIKE TYSON
NBC 2/12/93. (Barbara Kopple), Documentary.

FALLING FOR YOU
CBS 2/21/95. (Eric Till), Jennie Garth, Costas Mandylor, Billy Dee Williams, Peter Outerbridge, Helen Shaver (2 hrs.).

FALLING FROM THE SKY!: FLIGHT 174
ABC 2/20/95. (Jorge Montessi), William Devane, Shelley Hack, Scott Hylands, Mariette Hartley, Nicholas Turturro (2 hrs.).

FALSE ARREST
ABC 11/3 & 11/6/91. (Bill L. Norton), Donna Mills, Robert Wagner, Steven Bauer, Dennis Christopher (4 hrs.).

A FAMILY DIVIDED
NBC 1/22/95. (Donald Wrye), Faye Dunaway, Stephen Collins, Cameron Bancroft, Judson Mills, Aidan Pendleton, (2 hrs.).

A FAMILY FOR JOE
NBC 2/25/90. (Jeffrey Melman), Robert Mitchum, Chris Furrh, Maia Brewton (2 hrs.).

FAMILY OF SPIES
CBS 2/4 & 2/6/90. (Stephen Gyllenhaal), Powers Boothe, Lesley Ann Warren, Lili Taylor (5 hrs.).

FAMILY PICTURES
ABC 3/21 & 3/22/93. (Philip Saville), Anjelica Huston, Sam Neill, Kyra Sedgwick, Dermot Mulroney (4 hrs.).

FAMILY REUNION: A RELATIVE NIGHTMARE
ABC 4/1/95. (Neal Israel), Jason Marsden, Melissa Joan Hart, Susan French, David L. Lander, Joe Flaherty (2 hrs.).

A FAMILY TORN APART
NBC 11/21/93. (Craig R. Baxley), Neil Patrick Harris, Gregory Harrison, Johnny Galecki (2 hrs.).

FAST COMPANY
NBC 8/14/95. (Gary Nelson), Ann Jillian, Tim Matheson, Geoffrey Blake, Dex Elliott Sanders, Wendy Phillips (2 hrs.).

FATAL CHARM
SHO 2/22/92. (Fritz Kiersch), Christopher Atkins, Amanda Peterson, James Remar, Andrew Lowery (2 hrs.).

FATAL DECEPTION: MRS. LEE HARVEY OSWALD
NBC 11/15/93. (Robert Dornhelm), Helena Bonham Carter, Frank Whaley, Robert Picardo (2 hrs.).

FATAL EXPOSURE
USA 2/6/91. (Alan Metzger), Mare Winningham, Nick Mancuso, Christopher McDonald (2 hrs.).

FATAL FRIENDSHIP
NBC 12/1/91. (Bradford May), Kevin Dobson, Gerald McRaney, Kate Mulgrew, Patti Yasutake (2 hrs.).

THE FATAL IMAGE
CBS 12/2/90. (Thomas J. Wright), Michele Lee, Justine Bateman, Jean-Pierre Cassel (2 hrs.).

FATAL MEMORIES
NBC 11/9/92. (Daryl Duke), Shelley Long, Helen Shaver, Dean Stockwell (2 hrs.).

FATAL VOWS: THE ALEXANDRA O'HARA STORY
CBS 10/25/94. (John Power), John Stamos, Cynthia Gibb, David Faustino, Ben Gazzara, Sean McCann (2 hrs.).

FATHER AND SCOUT
ABC 10/15/95. (Richard Michaels), Bob Saget, Brian Bonsall, Troy Evans, Stuart Pankin, David Graf, Heidi Swedberg (2 hrs.).

FATHER & SON: DANGEROUS RELATIONS
NBC 4/19/93. (Georg Stanford Brown), Louis Gossett Jr., Blair Underwood, Rae Dawn Chong (2 hrs.).

A FATHER FOR CHARLIE
CBS 1/1/95. (Jeff Bleckner), Louis Gossett Jr., Joseph Mazzello, James Greene, Don Swayze, David Hart (2 hrs.).

FATHERLAND
HBO 11/26/94. (Christopher Menaul), Rutger Hauer, Miranda Richardson, Jean Marsh, Peter Vaughan, Michael Kitchen.

FEAR
SHO 7/15/90. (Rockne S. O'Bannon), Ally Sheedy, Lauren Hutton, Michael O'Keefe (90 mins.).

THE FEAR INSIDE
SHO 8/9/92. (Leon Ichaso), Christine Lahti, Dylan McDermott, Jennifer Rubin, David Ackroyd (2 hrs.).

FELLOW TRAVELER
HBO 3/4/90. (Philip Saville), Ron Silver, Hart Bochner, Imogen Stubbs (90 mins.).

FERGIE AND ANDREW: BEHIND CLOSED DOORS
NBC 9/28/92. (Michael Switzer), Pippa Hinchley, Sam Miller, Harold Innocent (2 hrs.).

FEVER
HBO 5/11/91. (Larry Elikann), Armand Assante, Sam Neill, Marcia Gay Harden (2 hrs.).

FIGHTING FOR MY DAUGHTER
ABC 1/9/95. (Peter Levin), Lindsay Wagner, Chad Lowe, Piper Laurie, Kirk Baltz, Deirdre O'Connell (2 hrs.).

FINAL APPEAL
NBC 9/26/93. (Eric Till), Brian Dennehy, JoBeth Williams, Tom Mason, Lindsay Crouse (2 hrs.).

THE FINAL CUT
PBS 2/4 & 2/5/96. (Mike Vardy), Ian Richardson, Diane Fletcher, Nick Brimble, Tom Easley, Erika Hoffman.

FINAL SHOT: THE HANK GATHERS STORY
SYND 4/1/92. (Chuck Braverman), Victor Love, Nell Carter, George Kennedy, Duane Davis (2 hrs.).

FINAL VERDICT
TNT 9/9/91. (Jack Fisk), Treat Williams, Glenn Ford, Olivia Burnette, Gretchen Corbett (2 hrs.).

FINDING THE WAY HOME
ABC 8/26/91. (Rod Holcomb), George C. Scott, Hector Elizondo, Julie Carmen (2 hrs.).

FIRE IN THE DARK
CBS 10/6/91. (David Jones), Olympia Dukakis, Lindsay Wagner, Jean Stapleton, Ray Wise (2 hrs.).

THE FIRE NEXT TIME
CBS 4/18 & 4/20/93. (Tom McLoughlin), Craig T. Nelson, Bonnie Bedelia, Richard Farnsworth, Jurgen Prochnow (4 hrs.).

FIRE! TRAPPED ON THE 37TH FLOOR
ABC 2/18/91. (Robert Day), Lisa Hartman, Peter Scolari, Lee Majors (2 hrs.).

FIRESTORM: 72 HOURS IN OAKLAND
ABC 2/7/93. (Michael Tuckner), Jill Clayburgh, LeVar Burton, Michael Gross, Keith Coulouris (2 hrs.).

FIRST DEGREE
HBO 8/20/95. (Jeff Woolnough), Rob Lowe, Leslie Hope, Tom McCamus, Joseph Griffin, Nadia Capone (100 mins.).

FIRST DO NO HARM
CBS. 2/16/97. Meryl Streep, Seth Adkins, Allison Janney, Fred Ward.

FLIGHT OF BLACK ANGEL
SHO 2/23/91. (Jonathan Mostow), Peter Strauss, William O'Leary, James O'Sullivan (2 hrs.).

THE FLOOD: WHO WILL SAVE OUR CHILDREN?
NBC 10/10/93. (Chris Thomson), Joe Spano, David Lascher, Michael Goorjian (2 hrs.).

FLYING BLIND
NBC 7/30/90. (Vince DiPersio), Richard Panebianco, Emily Longstreth, Frank Whaley (2 hrs.).

FOLLOW THE RIVER
ABC 4/22/95. (Martin Davidson), Sheryl Lee, Ellen Burstyn, Eric Schweig, Tim Guinee, Renee O'Connor (2 hrs.).

FOLLOW YOUR HEART
NBC 4/2/90. (Noel Nosseck), Patrick Cassidy, Catherine Mary Stewart, Jane Alexander (2 hrs.).

FOLLOWING HER HEART
NBC 11/28/94. (Lee Grant), Ann-Margret, Morgan Sheppard, Brenda Vaccaro, George Segal (2 hrs.).

FOR BETTER OR WORSE
TNT 2/18/96. (Jason Alexander), Jason Alexander, Lolita Davidovich, James Woods, Joe Mantegna, Jay Mohr.

FOR HOPE
ABC. 11/17/96. (David Paget.), Henry Czerny, Dana Delany.

FOR LOVE ALONE
CBS 1/5 & 1/7/96. Stephen Collins, Sanna Vraa, Trevor Eve, Brigitte Pacquette, Tom Rack, Madeline Kahn.

FOR LOVE AND GLORY
CBS 9/11/93. (Roger Young), Daniel Markel, Tracy Griffith, Zach Galligan, Kate Mulgrew (2 hrs.).

FOR MY DAUGHTER'S HONOR
CBS. 10/.20/96. Teddi Siddall, Nicholle Tom.

FOR RICHER OR POORER
HBO 2/29/92. (Jay Sandrich), Jack Lemmon, Talia Shire, Jonathan Silverman, Madeline Kahn (2 hrs.).

FOR THE FUTURE: THE IRVINE FERTILITY SCANDAL
LIF (David Jones), Marily Henner, Linda Lavin, Alicia Coppola.

FOR THE LOVE OF AARON
CBS 1/1/94. (John Kent Harrison), Meredith Baxter, Keegan Macintosh, Joanna Gleason (2 hrs.).

**FOR THE LOVE OF MY CHILD:
THE ANISSA AYALA STORY**
NBC 5/10/93. (Waris Hussein), Priscilla Lopez, Teresa Dispina, Tony Perez, Robin Thomas (2 hrs.).

FOR THE LOVE OF NANCY
ABC 10/2/94. (Paul Schneider), Tracey Gold, Jill Clayburgh, Cameron Bancroft, Mark-Paul Gosselaar (2 hrs.).

FOR THE VERY FIRST TIME
NBC 4/22/91. (Michael Zinberg), Corin Nemec, Cheryl Pollak, Madchen Amick (2 hrs.).

FOR THEIR OWN GOOD
ABC 4/5/93. (Ed Kaplan), Elizabeth Perkins, Laura San Giacomo, Charles Haid, C.C.H. Pounder (2 hrs.).

FORBIDDEN NIGHTS
CBS 4/10/90. (Waris Hussein), Melissa Gilbert, Robin Shou, Victor K. Wong (2 hrs.).

FOREIGN AFFAIRS
TNT 3/17/93. (Jim O'Brien), Joanne Woodward, Brian Dennehy, Eric Stoltz, Stephanie Beacham (2 hrs.).

FORGOTTEN PRISONERS: THE AMNESTY FILES
TNT 11/19/90. (Robert Greenwald), Ron Silver, Hector Elizondo, Roger Daltrey (2 hrs.).

FORGOTTEN SINS
ABC 3/7/96. (Dick Lowry), John Shea, Bess Armstrong, William Devane.

THE FOUR DIAMONDS
DIS 8/12/95. (Peter Werner), Thomas Guiry, Christine Lahti, Kevin Dunn, Jayne Brook, Sarah Rose Karr, Michael Bacall.

FOUR EYES AND SIX-GUNS
TNT 12/7/92. (Piers Haggard), Judge Reinhold, Fred Ward, Patricia Clarkson, Dan Hedaya (2 hrs.).

FOURTH STORY
SHO 1/19/91. (Ivan Passer), Mark Harmon, Mimi Rogers, Paul Gleason, Cliff De Young (2 hrs.).

FRAMED
A&E 9/19 & 9/20/93. (Geoff Sax), Timothy Dalton, Timothy West, David Morrissey (4 hrs.).

FRANK AND JESSE
HBO 4/22/95. (Robert Boris), Rob Lowe, Bill Paxton, Randy Travis, William Atherton, Dana Wheeler-Nicholson (110 minutes).

FRANKENSTEIN: THE COLLEGE YEARS
FOX 10/28/91. (Tom Shadyac), William Ragsdale, Vincent Hammond, Christopher Daniel Barnes (2 hrs.).

FREAKY FRIDAY
ABC 5/6/95. (Melanie Mayron), Shelley Long, Gaby Hoffmann, Alan Rosenberg, Sandra Bernhard, Carol Kane (2 hrs.).

FRENCH SILK
ABC 1/23/94. (Noel Nosseck), Susan Lucci, Lee Horsley, Shari Belafonte, R. Lee Ermey (2 hrs.).

FREQUENT FLYER
ABC 1/10/96. Jack Wagner, Shelley Hack, Nicole Eggert, Joan Severance, Kalen Mills, Elizabeth Ruscio, Mark Nutter.

A FRIEND TO DIE FOR
ABC 9/26/94. (William A. Graham), Kellie Martin, Tori Spelling, Valerie Harper, Terry O'Quinn, James Avery, Eugene Roche.

A FRIEND'S BETRAYAL
NBC 5/19/96. (Christopher Leitch), Brian Austin Green, Sharon Lawrence, Harley Jane Kozak, John Getz, Kataie Wright.

FRIENDS AT LAST
CBS 4/2/95. (John Coles), Kathleen Turner, Colm Feore, Faith Prince, Julie Khaner, Krista Marie Bonura (2 hrs.).

**FROM THE FILES OF JOSEPH WAMBAUGH:
A JURY OF ONE**
NBC 11/29/92. (Alan Metzger), John Spencer, Eddie Velez, Dan Lauria, Rachel Ticotin (2 hrs.).

**FROM THE MIXED-UP FILES OF
MRS. BASIL E. FRANKWEILER**
ABC 6/3/95. (Marcus Cole), Lauren Bacall, Jean Marie Barnwell, Jesse Lee, Miriam Flynn, Mark Taylor, M. Emmett Walsh (2 hrs.).

FRIENDS 'TIL THE END
NBC. 1/20/97. (Bonnie Raskin, Tana Nugent), Shannen Doherty, Jennifer Blanc, Jason London.

FUDGE-A-MANIA
ABC 1/7/95. (Anson Williams), Luke Tarsitano, Jake Richardson, Eve Plumb, Forrest Witt, Florence Henderson (2 hrs.).

FUGITIVE AMONG US
CBS 2/4/92. (Michael Toshiyuki Uno), Peter Strauss, Eric Roberts, Elizabeth Pena, Guy Body (2 hrs.).

FUGITIVE NIGHTS: DANGER IN THE DESERT
NBC 11/19/93. (Gary Nelson), Teri Garr, Sam Elliott, Thomas Haden Church (2 hrs.).

FULL BODY MASSAGE
SHO 12/5/95. (Nicolas Roeg), Mimi Rogers, Bryan Brown, Gareth Williams, Elizabeth Barondes, Christopher Burgard.

GALLOWGLASS
PBS 10/5, 10/12 & 10/19/95. (Tim Fywell), Michael Sheen, Paul Rhys, John McArdle, Arkie Whitely, Gary Waldhorn.

THE GAMBLER RETURNS: THE LUCK OF THE DRAW
NBC 11/3 & 11/4/91. (Dick Lowry), Kenny Rogers, Reba McIntire, Rick Rossovich, David Carradine (4 hrs.).

GAMBLER V: PLAYING FOR KEEPS
CBS 10/2/94. (Jack Bender), Kenny Rogers, Dixie Carter, Loni Anderson, Scott Paulin, Brett Cullen, Kris Kamm (2 hrs.).

THE GARDEN OF REDEMPTION
SHO. 5/25/97. (Thomas Michael Donnelly), James Acheson, Dan Hedaya, David Neal, Jorfg Sanf, Peter Firth.

GENERATION X
FOX 2/20/96. (Jack Sholder), Matt Frewer, Finola Hughes, Jeremy Ratchford, Heather McComb, Agustin Rodriguez.

GENGHIS COHN
A&E 11/4/94. (Elijah Moshinsky), Robert Lindsay, Diana Rigg, Antony Sher, John Wells (90 mins.).

GEORGE WALLACE
TNT. 8/24 & 8/26/97. (John Frankheimer), Gary Sinise, Mare Winningham, Clarence Williams III, Joe Don Baker, Angelina Jolie.

GERONIMO
TNT 12/5/93. (Roger Young), Joseph Running Fox, Nick Ramus, Michelle St. John (2 hrs.).

GETTING OUT
ABC 4/25/94. (John Korty), Rebecca De Mornay, Ellen Burstyn, Robert Knepper (2 hrs.).

GETTING UP AND GOING HOME
LIF 7/21/92. (Steven Schachter), Tom Skerritt, Blythe Danner, Roma Downey, Julianne Phillips (2 hrs.).

A GHOST IN MONTE CARLO
TNT 4/2/90. (John Hough), Sarah Miles, Oliver Reed, Christopher Plummer (2 hrs.).

GHOST MOM
FOX 11/1/93. (Dave Thomas), Jean Stapleton, Geraint Wyn Davies, Shae D'Lyn (2 hrs.).

THE GIFT OF LOVE
CBS 9/25/94. (Paul Bogart), Andy Griffith, Blair Brown, Olivia Burnette, Will Friedle, Joyce Van Patten (2 hrs.).

THE GIRL FROM MARS
FAM 3/16/91. (Neill Fearnley), Sarah Sawatsky, Edward Albert, Eddie Albert (2 hrs.).

THE GIRL FROM TOMORROW
DIS 10/23/91. (Kathy Muller), Katharine Cullen, Melissa Marshall, James Findlay (105 mins.).

THE GIRL WHO CAME BETWEEN THEM
NBC 4/1/90. (Mel Darnski), Cheryl Ladd, Anthony John Denison, Melissa Chan (2 hrs.).

GIRLS IN PRISON
SHO 8/19/94. (John McNaughton), Missy Crider, Ione Skye, Bahni Turpin, Anne Heche (90 mins.).

GOLDEN WILL: THE SILKEN LAUMANN STORY
DISNEY. (Eric Till), Nancy Anne Sakovich.

GONE IN THE NIGHT
CBS 2/25 & 2/27/96. (Bill L. Norton), Shannen Doherty, Edward Asner, Dixie Carter, Kevin Dillon, Michael Brandon.

GOOD COPS, BAD COPS
NBC 12/9/90. (Paul Wendkos), Edward Asner, Ray Sharkey, Steve Railsback (2 hrs.).

THE GOOD DOCTOR: THE PAUL FLEISS STORY
CBS 2/21/96. Michael Gross, Tricia Leigh Fisher, George Segal.

THE GOOD FIGHT
LIF 12/15/92. (John David Coles), Christine Lahti, Terry O'Quinn, Jonathan Crombie (2 hrs.).

GOOD KING WENCESLAS
FAM 11/26/94. (Michael Tuchner), Stefanie Powers, Perry King, Jonathan Brandis, Joan Fontaine, Leo McKern, (2 hrs.).

GOOD NIGHT, SWEET WIFE: A MURDER IN BOSTON
CBS 9/25/90. (Jerrold Freedman), Ken Olin, Margaret Colin, Annabella Price (2 hrs.).

THE GOOD OLD BOYS
TNT 3/5/95. (Tommy Lee Jones), Tommy Lee Jones, Terry Kinney, Frances McDormand, Sissy Spacek, Sam Shepard.

GOTTI
HBO 8/17/96. (Robert Harmon), Armand Assante, Anthony Quinn, William Forsythe, Richard S. Sarafian, Vincent Pastore.

GRAMPS
NBC 5/20/95. (Bradford May), Andy Griffith, John Ritter, Mary-Margaret Humes, Casey Moses Wurzbach (2 hrs.).

GRAND AVENUE
HBO 6/30/96. (Daniel Sackheim), A. Martinez, Irene Bedard, Tantoo Cardinal, Dianne Debassige, Sheila Tousey.

GRAND ISLE
TNT 7/14/92. (Mary Lambert), Kelly McGillis, Adrian Pasdar, Julian Sands, Glenne Headly (2 hrs.).

GRASS ROOTS
NBC 2/24 & 2/25/92. (Jerry London), Corbin Bernsen, Mel Harris, John Glover, Reginald Vel Johnson (4 hrs.).

GRAVE SECRETS: THE LEGACY OF HILLTOP DRIVE
CBS 3/2/92. (John Patterson), Patty Duke, David Selby, Blake Clark, David Soul (2 hrs.).

THE GREAT ELEPHANT ESCAPE
ABC 3/25/95. (George Miller),, Stephanie Zimbalist, Joseph Gordon-Levitt, Leo Burmester, Julian Sands (2 hrs.).

THE GREAT PRETENDER
NBC 4/14/91. (Gus Trikonis), Bruce Greenwood, Jessica Steen, Gregg Henry (2 hrs.).

GREEN DOLPHIN BEAT
FOX 6/27/94. (Tommy Lee Wallace), John Wesley Shipp, Jeffrey Sams, Miguel Sandoval (2 hrs.).

THE GREEN MAN
A&E 6/2/91. (Elijah Moshinsky), Albert Finney, Linda Marlowe, Sarah Berger (3 hrs.).

GREGORY K
ABC 2/8/93. (Linda Otto), Joseph Gordon-Levitt, Bill Smitrovich, Kathleen York, Robert Joy (2 hrs.).

GREYHOUNDS
CBS 6/24/94. (Kim Manners), James Coburn, Robert Guillaume, Pat Morita, Dennis Weaver (2 hrs.).

GRIDLOCK
NBC 1/14/96. David Hasselhoff, Kathy Ireland, Marc Strange, Miguel Fernandes, Tony Desantis.

GUESS WHO'S COMING FOR CHRISTMAS?
NBC 12/23/90. (Paul Schneider), Richard Mulligan, Barbara Barrie, Paul Dooley (2 hrs.).

GUILTY UNTIL PROVEN INNOCENT
NBC 9/22/91. (Paul Wendkos), Martin Sheen, Brendan Fraser, Caroline Kava, Zachary Mott (2 hrs.).

GUINEVERE
LIF 5/7/94. (Jud Taylor), Sheryl Lee, Sean Patrick Flannery, Noah Wyle, Brid Brennan (2 hrs.).

GULLIVER'S TRAVELS
NBC 2/4/96. (Charles Sturridge) Ted Danson, Mary Steenburgen, James Fox, Geraldine Chaplin, Edward Fox.

GUNCRAZY
SHO 10/17/92. (Tamra Davis), Drew Barrymore, James LeGros, Michael Ironside, Ione Skye (95 mins.).

GUNSMOKE: ONE MAN'S JUSTICE
CBS 2/10/94. (Jerry Jameson), James Arness, Bruce Boxleitner, Kelly Morgan (2 hrs.).

GUNSMOKE: THE LAST APACHE
CBS 3/18/90. (Charles Correll), James Arness, Richard Kiley, Michael Learned (2 hrs.).

GUNSMOKE: THE LAST RIDE
CBS 5/8/93. (Jerry Jameson), James Arness, James Brolin, Ali MacGraw, Amy Stock-Paynton (2 hrs.).

GUNSMOKE: TO THE LAST MAN
CBS 1/10/92. (Jerry Jameson), James Arness, Pat Hingle, Amy Stock-Poynton, Matt Mulhern (2 hrs.).

GYPSY
CBS 12/12/93. (Emile Ardolino), Bette Midler, Cynthia Gibb, Peter Riegert, Edward Asner (3 hrs.).

H

THE HABITATION OF DRAGONS
TNT 9/8/92. (Michael Lindsay-Hogg), Frederic Forrest, Brad Davis, Jean Stapleton, Pat Hingle (2 hrs.).

THE HALFBACK OF NOTRE DAME
SHO 1/21/96. (Rene Bonniere), Gabriel Hogan, Emmanuelle Vaugier, Allen Cutler, Scott Hylands, Sandra Nelson.

HANDS OF A MURDERER
CBS 5/16/90. (Stuart Orme), Edward Woodward, John Hillerman, Anthony Andrews (2 hrs.).

HARRISON: CRY OF THE CITY
UPN 2/27/96. (James Frawley) Edward Woodward, Jeffrey Nordling, Elizabeth Hurley, Cynthia Harris, Jude Ciccolella.

HART TO HART: CRIMES OF THE HART
NBC 3/25/94. (Peter Hunt), Robert Wagner, Stefanie Powers, Lionel Stander, John Stockwell (2 hrs.).

HART TO HART: HOME IS WHERE THE HART IS
NBC 2/18/94. (Peter Hunt), Robert Wagner, Stefanie Powers, Maureen O'Sullivan, Howard Keel (2 hrs.).

HART TO HART: OLD FRIENDS NEVER DIE
NBC 5/16/94. (Peter Hunt), Robert Wagner, Stefanie Powers, Mike Farrell, David Rasche (2 hrs.).

HART TO HART RETURNS
NBC 11/5/93. (Peter Hunt), Robert Wagner, Stefanie Powers, Lionel Stander, Mike Connors (2 hrs.).

HART TO HART: SECRETS OF THE HEART
NBC 3/6/95. (Kevin Connor), Robert Wagner, Stefanie Powers, Jason Bateman, Marion Ross, Wendie Malick (2 hrs.).

HARTS IN HIGH SEASON
FAM 3/24/96. Robert Wagner, Stefanie Powers, James Brolin.

HARVEST FOR THE HEART
FAM 4/16/94. (Michael Scott), Ted Shackelford, Ron White, Rebecca Jenkins (2 hrs.).

HARVEST OF FIRE
CBS 4/21/96. (Arthur Allan Seidelman), Lolita Davidovich, J.A. Preston, Jean Louisa Kelly, Tom Aldredge, James Read.

THE HAUNTED
FOX 5/6/91. (Robert Mandel), Sally Kirkland, Jeffrey DeMunn, Louise Latham (2 hrs.).

THE HAUNTING OF LISA
LIF 4/10/96. Cherly Ladd, Duncan Regehr.

HAVE YOU SEEN MY SON?
ABC 1/8/96. Lisa Hartman-Black, William Russ, Anne Francis.

HEADS
SHO 1/29/94. (Paul Shapiro), Jon Cryer, Edward Asner, Jennifer Tilly, Roddy McDowall (105 mins.).

HEART OF DARKNESS
TNT 3/13/94. (Nicolas Roeg), John Malkovich, Tim Roth, Isaach de Bankole, James Fox (2 hrs.).

HEART OF FIRE
CBS. 1/7/97. Patrick Duffy, Alex McKenna.

THE HEART OF JUSTICE
TNT 2/20/93. (Bruno Barreto), Eric Stoltz, Jennifer Connelly, Dermot Mulroney, Vincent Price, Keith Reddin (2 hrs.).

HEARTS ADRIFT
USA 8/7/96. (Vic Sarin), Ron McGee, Kathleen Noone, Nicholas Coster, Don Murray, Scott Reeves, Sydney Penny.

HEAT WAVE
TNT 8/13/90. (Kevin Hooks), Cicely Tyson, Blair Underwood, James Earl Jones (2 hrs.).

HEAVY WEATHER
PBS 2/18/96. Judy Parfitt, Richard Briers, Benjamin Soames, Richard Johnson.

HECK'S WAY HOME
SHO 3/8 & 3/10/96. Alan Arkin, Chad Krowchuck, Michael Riley, Shannon Lawson, Don Francks, Gabe Khouth.

HEIDI
DIS 7/18 & 7/19/93. (Michael Rhodes), Jason Robards, Jane Seymour, Noley Thornton, Patricia Neal (190 mins.).

THE HEIDI CHRONICLES
TNT 10/15/95. (Paul Bogart) Jamie Lee Curtis, Tom Hulce, Peter Friedman, Kim Cattrall, Eve Gordon, Sharon Lawrence.

HELD HOSTAGE: THE SIS AND JERRY LEVIN STORY
ABC 1/13/91. (Roger Young), Marlo Thomas, David Dukes, G.W. Bailey (2 hrs.).

HELL HATH NO FURY
NBC 3/4/91. (Thomas J. Wright), Barbara Eden, Loretta Swit, David Ackroyd (2 hrs.).

HER COSTLY AFFAIR
NBC. 10/28/96. (Sheldon Pinchuk), Bonnie Bedelia, Brian Austin Green, Joe Spano.

HER DEADLY RIVAL
CBS 9/19/96. (Jim Hayman), Harry Hamlin, Annie Potts, Lisa Zane, D.L. Anderson.

HER DESPERATE CHOICE
LIF. 10/96. (Julian Marks), Nigel Bennett, Faith Ford, Kyle Secor.

**HER FINAL FURY:
BETTY BRODERICK—THE LAST CHAPTER**
CBS 11/1/92. (Dick Lowry), Meredith Baxter, Judith Ivey, Ray Baker, Kelli Williams (2 hrs.).

HER LAST CHANCE
NBC 4/8/96. (Richard Colla), Kellie Martin, Patti Lupone, Devon Odessa, Jonathan Brandis, Jenna Elfman.

HER WICKED WAYS
CBS 1/1/91. (Richard Michaels), Barbara Eden, Tess O'Brien, Heather Locklear (2 hrs.).

HERCULES AND THE AMAZON WOMEN
SYND 4/30/94. (Christian Williams), Kevin Sorbo, Anthony Quinn, Roma Downey (2 hrs.).

THE HEROES OF DESERT STORM
ABC 10/6/91. (Don Ohlmeyer), Angela Bassett, Daniel Baldwin, Michael Allen Brooks, Kris Kamm (2 hrs.).

HI HONEY—I'M DEAD
FOX 4/22/91. (Alan Myerson), Curtis Armstrong, Catherine Hicks, Kevin Conroy (2 hrs.).

HIDDEN IN AMERICA
SHO. 12/1/96. (Martin Bell), Beau Bridges, Bruce Davison, Jena Malone, Shelton Dane, Alice Krige, Frances McDormand.

HIDDEN IN SILENCE
LIF 3/6/96. (Richard Colla), Kellie Martin, Gemma Coughlan, Marion Ross, Tom Radcliffe, Joss Ackland.

HIDDEN VIEW
WPIX 9/10/90. (Jag Mundhra), Andrew Stevens, Tanya Roberts, Warwick Sims (2 hrs.).

HIGH INCIDENT
ABC 3/4/96. (Charles Haid) Matthew Beck, Matt Craven, Cole Hauser, Catherine Kellner, Julio Oscar Mechoso.

HIGH STAKES
LIF. 4/7/97. Cynthia Gibb.

HIGHWAY HEARTBREAKER
CBS 3/29/92. (Paul Schneider), John Schneider, Linda Gray, Heather Locklear, Tracy Nelson (2 hrs.).

HIJACKED: FLIGHT 285
ABC 2/4/96. Anthony Michael Hall, James Brolin, Ally Sheedy, Michael Gross.

HIROSHIMA
SHO 8/6/95. (Roger Spottiswoode, Koreyoshi Kurahara), Kenneth Welsh, Wesley Addy, David Gow, Hisashi Igawa.

HIROSHIMA: OUT OF THE ASHES
NBC 8/6/90. (Peter Werner), Max von Sydow, Judd Nelson, Mako, Pat Morita (2 hrs.).

THE HIT LIST
SHO 1/17/93. (William Webb), Jeff Fahey, Yancy Butler, James Coburn (2 hrs.).

THE HIT MAN
ABC 6/29/91. (Gary Nelson), Dennis Boutsikaris, Daryl Anderson, Eagle Eye Cherry (2 hrs.).

HITLER'S DAUGHTER
USA 9/26/90. (James A. Contner), Patrick Cassidy, Melody Anderson, Veronica Cartwright (2 hrs.).

HOLIDAY AFFAIR
USA. 12/15/96. David James Elliott, Cynthia Gibb.

A HOLIDAY TO REMEMBER
CBS 12/12/95. Connie Sellecca, Rue McClanahan.

HOLLYROCK–A–BYE BABY
ABC 5/23/93. (William Hanna), Animated. (2 hrs.).

HOME FOR CHRISTMAS
LIF 12/6/90. (Peter McCubbin), Mickey Rooney, Simon Richards, Lesley Kelly (2 hrs.).

HOME INVASION
NBC. 1/13/97. (Michael Braverman), Veronica Hammel.

HOMECOMING
SHO 4/14/96. Kimberlee Peterson, Trever O'Brien, Hanna Hall.

HOMETOWN BOY MAKES GOOD
HBO 8/2/90. (David Burton Morris), Anthony Edwards, Cynthia Bain, Grace Zabriskie (90 mins.).

HOMEWRECKER
USA 12/17/92. (Fred Walton), Robby Benson, Sydney Walsh, Sarah Rose Karr, Kate Jackson (voice) (2 hrs.).

**HONOR THY FATHER AND MOTHER:
THE TRUE STORY OF THE MENENDEZ MURDERS**
FOX 4/18/94. (Paul Schneider), James Farentino, Jill Clayburgh, Billy Warlock, David Beron (2 hrs.).

HONOR THY MOTHER
CBS 4/26/92. (David Greene), Sharon Gless, William McNamara, Paul Scherrer, Brian Wimmer (2 hrs.).

A HORSE FOR DANNY
ABC 4/8/95. (Dick Lowry), Robert Urich, Ron Brice, Gary Basaraba, Eric Jensen, Leelee Sobieski (2 hrs.).

HOSTAGE FOR A DAY
FOX 4/25/94. (John Candy), George Wendt, John Vernon, Robin Duke, Peter Torkovei (2 hrs.).

HOSTAGES
HBO 2/19/93. (David Wheatley), Colin Firth, Ciaran Hinds, Natasha Richardson, Harry Dean Stanton, Kathy Bates.

HOSTILE ADVANCES: THE KERRY ELLISON STORY
SHO 5/27/96. (Allan Kroeker), Rena Sofer, Victor Garber.

HOSTILE WATERS
HBO. 7.25.97. (David Drury), Rutger Hauer, Max Von Sydow, Martin Sheen, Richard Graham, Rob Campbell, Colm Feore.

HOUSE OF SECRETS
NBC 11/1/93. (Mimi Leder), Melissa Gilbert, Bruce Boxleitner, Cicely Tyson, Kate Vernon (2 hrs.).

A HOUSE OF SECRETS AND LIES
CBS 9/27/92. (Paul Schneider), Connie Sellecca, Kevin Dobson, Grace Zibriskie, Georgann Johnson (2 hrs.).

THE HOUSE ON SYCAMORE STREET
CBS 5/1/92. (Christian I. Nyby II), Dick Van Dyke, Cynthia Gibb, Stephen Caffrey, Barry Van Dyke (2 hrs.).

HOW THE WEST WAS FUN
ABC 11/19/94. (Stuart Margolin), Mary-Kate Olsen, Ashley Olsen, Martin Mull, Michele Green, Patrick Cassidy (2 hrs.).

HOW TO MURDER A MILLIONAIRE
CBS 5/23/90. (Paul Schneider), Joan Rivers, Alex Rocco, Morgan Fairchild (2 hrs.).

HUCK AND THE KING OF HEARTS
SHO 10/7/94. (Michael Keusch), John Astin, Joe Piscopo, Dee Wallace Stone (2 hrs.).

A HUSBAND, A WIFE AND A LOVER
CBS 3/17/96. Judith Light, Jay Thomas, William Russo.

HUSH LITTLE BABY
USA 1/6/94. (Jorge Montesi), Diane Ladd, Wendel Meldrum, Geraint Wyn Davies (2 hrs.).

I

**I CAN MAKE YOU LOVE ME:
THE STALKING OF LAURA BLACK**
CBS 2/9/93. (Michael Switzer), Richard Thomas, Brooke Shields, Viveka Davis, William Allen (2 hrs.).

I KNOW MY SON IS ALIVE
NBC 2/20/94. (Bill Corcoran), Corbin Bernsen, Amanda Pays, Albert Schultz (2 hrs.).

I SPY RETURNS
CBS 2/3/94. (Jerry London), Robert Culp, Bill Cosby, George Newbern, Salli Richardson (2 hrs.).

I STILL DREAM OF JEANNIE
NBC 10/20/91. (Joseph Scanlan), Barbara Eden, Christopher Bolton, Bill Daly, Al Waxman (2 hrs.).

I YABBA DABBA DO!
ABC 2/7/93. (William Hanna), Animated (2 hrs.).

I'LL FLY AWAY: THEN AND NOW
PBS 10/11/93. (Ian Sander), Sam Waterston, Regina Taylor, Jason London (2 hrs.).

I'LL TAKE ROMANCE
ABC 11/25/90. (Piers Haggard), Linda Evans, Larry Poindexter, Tom Skerritt (2 hrs.).

I'M DANGEROUS TONIGHT
USA 8/8/90. (Tobe Hooper), Madchen Amick, Corey Parker, Anthony Perkins (2 hrs.).

IF SOMEONE HAD KNOWN
NBC 5/1/95. (Eric Laneuville), Kellie Martin, Kevin Dobson, Linda Kelsey, Ivan Sergei, Kristin Dattilo-Hayward.

ILLICIT BEHAVIOR
USA 12/9/92. (Worth Keeter), Robert Davi, Joan Severance, Jack Scalia, James Russo (2 hrs.).

THE IMAGE
HBO 1/27/90. (Peter Werner), Albert Finney, John Mahoney, Kathy Baker, Marsha Mason (2 hrs.).

IN A CHILD'S NAME
CBS 11/17 & 11/19/91. (Tom McLoughlin), Valerie Bertinelli, Michael Ontkean, Louise Fletcher, Timothy Carhart (4 hrs.).

IN BROAD DAYLIGHT
NBC 2/3/91. (James Steven Sadwith), Brian Dennehy, Cloris Leachman, Marcia Gay Harden (2 hrs.).

IN COLD BLOOD
CBS. 11/24 & 11/26/96. (Jonathan Kaplan), Anthony Edwards, Eric Roberts, Sam Neill, Kevin Tighe, Gillian Barber.

IN DEFENSE OF A MARRIED MAN
ABC 10/14/90. (Joel Oliansky), Judith Light, Michael Ontkean, Jerry Orbach (2 hrs.).

IN HIS FATHER'S SHOES
SHO. (Victor Sarin), Robert Richard, Louis Gossett, Jr., Barbara Eve Harris.

IN MY DAUGHTER'S NAME
CBS 5/10/92. (Jud Taylor), Donna Mills, Lee Grant, John Rubinstein, John Getz (2 hrs.).

IN PURSUIT OF HONOR
HBO 3/18/95. (Ken Olin), Don Johnson, Craig Sheffer, Gabrielle Anwar, Bob Gunton, Rod Steiger (2 hrs.).

IN SICKNESS AND IN HEALTH
CBS 3/8/92. (Jeff Bleckner), Lesley Ann Warren, Tom Skerritt, Marg Helgenberger, Ray Baker (2 hrs.)

IN THE ARMS OF A KILLER
NBC 1/5/92. (Robert Collins), Jaclyn Smith, John Spencer, Michael Nouri, Nina Foch (2 hrs.).

IN THE BEST INTEREST OF THE CHILD
CBS 5/20/90. (David Greene), Meg Tilly, Ed Begley, Jr., Michael O'Keefe (2 hrs.).

IN THE BEST INTEREST OF THE CHILDREN
NBC 2/16/92. (Michael Ray Rhodes), Sarah Jessica Parker, Sally Struthers, Elizabeth Ashley, Lexi Randall (2 hrs.).

**IN THE BEST OF FAMILIES:
MARRIAGE, PRIDE AND MADNESS**
CBS 1/16 & 1/18/94. (Jeff Beckner), Kelly McGillis, Harry Hamlin, Keith Carradine, Holland Taylor (4 hrs.).

IN THE BLINK OF AN EYE
ABC 3/24/96. Veronica Hamil, Mimi Rogers, Piper Laurie, Polly Bergen.

IN THE COMPANY OF DARKNESS
CBS 1/5/93. (David Anspaugh), Helen Hunt, Steven Weber, Jeff Fahey, Juan Ramirez (2 hrs.).

IN THE DEEP WOODS
NBC 10/26/92. (Charles Correll), Rosanna Arquette, Anthony Perkins, Will Patton, D.W. Moffet (2 hrs.).

IN THE EYES OF A STRANGER
CBS 4/7/92. (Michael Toshiyuki Uno), Justine Bateman, Richard Dean Anderson, Cynthia Dale, Colin Fox (2 hrs.).

IN THE GLOAMING
HBO. 4/20/97. (Christopher Reeve), Glenn Close, Bridget Fonda, David Strathairn, Whoopi Goldberg, Robert Sean Leonard.

IN THE HEAT OF THE NIGHT: A MATTER OF JUSTICE
CBS 10/21/94. (Reza Badiyi), Carroll O'Connor, George C. Scott, Carl Weathers, Joshua Lucas, Alan Autry, David Hart.

IN THE HEAT OF THE NIGHT: BY DUTY BOUND
CBS 2/17/95. (Harry Harris), Carroll O'Connor, Carl Weathers, Corbin Bernsen, John Calvin, Denise Nicholas (2 hrs.).

IN THE HEAT OF THE NIGHT: GROW OLD WITH ME
CBS 5/16/95. (Winrich Kolbe), Carroll O'Connor, Carl Weathers, Alan Autry, David Hart, Hugh O'Connor, Crystal Fox (2 hrs.).

IN THE HEAT OF THE NIGHT: WHO WAS GELI BENDL?
CBS 12/9/94. (Larry Hagman), Carroll O'Connor, Carl Weathers, Sydney Rome, Richard T. Jones, Arienne Battiste (2 hrs.).

IN THE LAKE OF THE WOODS
FOX 3/5/96. (Carl Schenkel) Peter Strauss, Peter Boyle, Kathleen Quinlan.

IN THE LINE OF DUTY: A COP FOR THE KILLING
NBC 11/25/90. (Dick Lowry), James Farentino, Steven Weber, Susan Walters (2 hrs.).

IN THE LINE OF DUTY: AMBUSH IN WACO
NBC 5/23/93. (Dick Lowry), Tim Daly, Dan Lauria, William O'Leary, Clu Gulager (2 hrs.).

IN THE LINE OF DUTY: BLAZE OF GLORY
NBC. 1/5/97. (Kenneth Kaufman), Lori Loughlin, Bruce Campbell, Bradley Whitford.

IN THE LINE OF DUTY: KIDNAPPED
NBC 3/12/95. (Bobby Roth), Dabney Coleman, Timothy Busfield, Lauren Tom, Tracey Walter, Barbara Williams (2 hrs.).

IN THE LINE OF DUTY: MANHUNT IN THE DAKOTAS
NBC 5/12/91. (Dick Lowry), Rod Steiger, Michael Gross, Gary Basaraba (2 hrs.).

IN THE LINE OF DUTY: SMOKE JUMPERS
NBC 2/11/96. (Dick Lowry) Adam Baldwin, Lindsay Frost.

IN THE LINE OF DUTY: STANDOFF AT MARION
NBC 2/10/92. (Charles Haid), Kyle Secor, Dennis Franz, Paul Le Mat, Tess Harper (2 hrs.).

IN THE LINE OF DUTY: STREET WAR
NBC 10/25/92. (Dick Lowry), Ray Sharkey, Peter Boyle, Mario Van Peebles, Courtney B. Vance (2 hrs.).

IN THE LINE OF DUTY: THE PRICE OF VENGEANCE
NBC 1/23/94. (Dick Lowry), Dean Stockwell, Michael Gross, Mary Kay Place (2 hrs.).

IN THE NAME OF LOVE: A TEXAS TRAGEDY
FOX 9/12/95. Michael Hayden, Richard Crenna, Bonnie Bartlett, Laura Leighton.

IN THE NICK OF TIME
NBC 12/16/91. (George Miller), Lloyd Bridges, Michael Tucker, Alison La Placa, Cleavon Little (2 hrs.).

IN THE PRESENCE OF MINE ENEMIES
SHO. 4/97. (Joan Micklin Silver), Armin Mueller-Stahl, Elina Lowensohn, Don McKeller, Charles Dance.

IN THE SHADOW OF A KILLER
NBC 4/27/92. (Alan Metzger), Scott Bakula, Lindsay Frost, Miguel Ferrer, Robert Clohessey (2 hrs.).

IN THE SHADOW OF EVIL
CBS 2/7/95. (Daniel Sackheim), Treat Williams, Margaret Colin, Joe Morton, William H. Macy, Timothy Busfield. (2 hrs.).

IN THE SHADOWS, SOMEONE'S WATCHING
NBC 10/4/93. (Richard Friedman), Joan Van Ark, Daniel Travanti, Christopher Noth, Rick Springfield (2 hrs.).

THE INCIDENT
CBS 3/4/90. (Joseph Sargent), Walter Matthau, Susan Blakely, Robert Carradine, Harry Morgan (2 hrs.).

INCIDENT AT DECEPTION RIDGE
USA 9/15/94. (John McPherson), Michael O'Keefe, Ed Begley Jr., Linda Purl, Miguel Ferrer, Michele Johnson (2 hrs.).

INCIDENT IN A SMALL TOWN
CBS 1/23/94. (Delbert Mann), Walter Matthau, Harry Morgan, Stephanie Zimbalist, Nick Stahl (2 hrs.).

AN INCONVENIENT WOMAN
ABC 5/12 & 5/13/91. (Larry Elikann), Jason Robards, Jill Eikenberry, Rebecca DeMornay, Chad Lowe (4 hrs.).

INDECENCY
USA 9/16/92. (Marisa Silver), Jennifer Beals, Sammi Davis-Voss, James Remar, Barbara Williams (2 hrs.).

INDICTMENT: THE MCMARTIN TRIAL
HBO 5/20/95. (Mick Jackson), James Woods, Mercedes Ruehl, Henry Thomas, Sada Thompson, Lolita Davidovich.

THE INFILTRATOR
HBO 6/24/95. (John Mackenzie), Oliver Platt, Arliss Howard, Tony Haygarth, Michael Byrne, Julian Glover, George Jackos.

THE INHERITANCE
CBS. 4/6/97. (Bobby Roth), Cari Shayne, Brigitta Dau, Paul Anthony Stewart, Max Gail, Tom Conti, Meredith Baxter.

THE INNOCENT
NBC 9/25/94. (Mimi Leder), Kelsey Grammer, Keegan Macintosh, Polly Draper, Dean Stockwell, Jeff Kober (2 hrs.).

INNOCENT VICTIMS
ABC 1/21 & 1/22/96. (Gilbert Cates), Rick Schroder, Hal Holbrook, Tom Irwin, Rue McClanahan, Howard Hesseman.

INSIDE
SHO 7/25/96. (Arthur Penn), Eric Stolz, Nigel Hawthorne, Louis Gossett Jr, Ian Roberts, Ross Preller.

INSIDE
SHO. 1/10/97. (Arthur Penn), Eric Stoltz, Nigel Hawthorne, Louis Gossett Jr., Ian Roberts, Janine Eser, Louis Van Niekerk.

INSPECTOR ALLEYN: HAND IN GLOVE
A&E 1/11/94. (Martyn Friend), Patrick Malahide, Belinda Lang, John Gielgud (2 hrs.).

INTENSITY
FOX. 8/5 & 8/6/97. (Yves Simoneau), John C. McGinley, Molly Parker, Tori Paul, Piper Laurie, Blu Mankuma, Lori Triolo.

INTO THE ARMS OF DANGER
NBC. 2/3/97. (Kristine Bamattre), Chandra West, Morgan Fairchild, Ricky Paull Goldin, Michael Woods, Venus Terzo.

INTO THE BADLANDS
USA 7/24/91. (Sam Pillsbury), Bruce Dern, Mariel Hemingway, Dylan McDermott (2 hrs.).

INTRUDERS
CBS 5/17 & 5/19/92. (Dan Curtis), Richard Crenna, Mare Winningham, Susan Blakely, Daphne Ashbrook (4 hrs.).

THE INVADERS
FOX 11/12/95. (Paul Shapiro), Scott Bakula, Elizabeth Pena, Richard Thomas, DeLane Matthews, Terence Knox.

INVASION OF PRIVACY
USA 10/7/92. (Kevin Meyer), Robby Benson, Jennifer O'Neill, Lydie Denier, Ian Ogilvy (2 hrs.).

INVESTIGATION: INSIDE A TERRORIST BOMBING
HBO 4/22/90. (Mike Beckham), John Hurt, Martin Shaw, Roger Allam (140 mins.).

IRAN: DAYS OF CRISIS
TNT 6/9/92. (Kevin Connor), Arliss Howard, Jeff Fahey, Alice Krige, Valerie Kaprisky (2 hrs.).

IRONCLADS
TNT 3/11/91. (Delbert Mann), Virginia Madsen, Alex Hyde-White, Reed Edward Diamond (2 hrs.).

IS THERE LIFE OUT THERE?
CBS 10/9/94. (David Jones), Reba McEntire, Keith Carradine, Genia Michaela, Mitchell Anderson (2 hrs.).

IT WAS HIM OR US
CBS 11/21/95. (Robert Iscove) Ann Jillian.

IT'S NOTHING PERSONAL
NBC 2/1/93. (Brandford May), Amanda Donohoe, Bruce Dern, Yaphet Kotto, Veronica Cartwright (2 hrs.).

J

JFK: RECKLESS YOUTH
ABC 11/21 & 23/93. (Harry Winer), Patrick Dempsey, Terry Kinney, Loren Dean, Andrew Lowery (4 hrs.).

JACK REED: DEATH AND VENGEANCE
NBC. 11/17/97. (Brian Dennehy), Brian Dennehy, Charles Dutton.

JACK HIGGINS' ON DANGEROUS GROUND
SHO 5/12/96. (Lawrence Gordon-Clark) Rob Lowe, Kenneth Cranham, Deborah Moore, Jurgen Prochnow.

JACK REED: A KILLER AMONGST US
NBC 1/7/96. (Brian Dennehy) Brian Dennehy, Charles S. Dutton, Susan Ruttan, Kevin Dunn, Suki Kaiser, Michael Talbott.

JACK REED: A SEARCH FOR JUSTICE
NBC 10/2/94. (Brian Dennehy), Brian Dennehy, Charles Dutton, Susan Ruttan, Joe Grifasi, Rex Linn, Miguel Ferrer (2 hrs.).

JACK REED: BADGE OF HONOR
NBC 11/12/93. (Kevin Connor), Brian Dennehy, Susan Ruttan, Alice Krige, R.D. Call (2 hrs.).

THE JACKSONS: AN AMERICAN DREAM
ABC 11/15 & 11/18/92. (Karen Arthur), Lawrence Hilton-Jacobs, Angela Bassett, Holly Robinson, Vannessa Williams (5 hrs.).

JACKIE COLLINS' "LADY BOSS"
NBC 10/11 & 12/92. (Charles Jarrott), Kim Delaney, Jack Scalia, David Selby, Vanity (4 hrs.).

JACKIE COLLINS' "LUCKY CHANCES"
NBC 10/7, 8 & 9/90. (Buzz Kulik), Nicollette Sheridan, Vincent Irizarry, Michael Nader (6 hrs.).

JACOB
TNT 12/4/94. (Peter Hall), Matthew Modine, Lara Flynn Boyle, Sean Bean, Joss Ackland, Juliet Aubrey, Irene Papas, Giancarlo Giannini (2 hrs.).

JAILBIRDS
CBS 5/16/91. (Burt Brinckerhoff), Dyan Cannon, Phylicia Rashad, David Knell (2 hrs.).

JAILBREAKERS
SHO 9/9/94. (William Friedkin), Shannen Doherty, Antonio Sabato Jr., Vince Edwards, Adrienne Barbeau, Adrien Brody (90 mins.).

JAKE LASSITER: JUSTICE ON THE BAYOU
NBC 1/9/95. (Peter Markle), Gerald McRaney, Robert Loggia, Tracy Scoggins, Daphne Ashbrook, James B. Sikking (2 hrs.).

JAMES A. MICHENER'S "TEXAS"
ABC 4/16 & 4/17/95. (Richard Lang), Stacy Keach, Patrick Duffy, Rick Schroder, Chelsea Field, Anthony Michael Hall (4 hrs.).

JANEK: A SILENT BETRAYAL
CBS 12/20/94. (Robert Iscove), Richard Crenna, Helen Shaver, Cliff Gorman, Philip Bosco, Gordon Currie, William Shatner.

JANEK: THE FORGET-ME-NOT MURDERS
CBS 3/29/94. (Robert Iscove), Richard Crenna, Tyne Daly, Helen Shaver, Cliff Gorman (2 hrs.).

JANE'S HOUSE
CBS 1/2/94. (Glenn Jordan), James Woods, Anne Archer, Missy Crider, Keegan MacIntosh (2 hrs.).

JEKYLL & HYDE
ABC 1/21/90. (David Wickes), Michael Caine, Cheryl Ladd, Joss Ackland (2 hrs.).

JOHN CARPENTER PRESENTS "BODY BAGS"
SHO 8/8/93. (John Carpenter, Tobe Hooper), Robert Carradine, Stacy Keach, Mark Hamill, Twiggy (90 mins.).

JOHN JAKES' HEAVEN AND HELL: NORTH AND SOUTH PART III
ABC 2/27, 2/28 & 3/2/94. (Larry Peerce), Lesley-Anne Down, James Read, Philip Casnoff, Peter O'Toole (6 hrs.).

JOHNNY & CLYDE
SHO 8/13/95. (Bill Bindley), John White, Michael Rooker, Diana Reis, Sam Malkin, Diane Douglass (2 hrs.).

JOHNNY RYAN
NBC 7/29/90. (Robert Collins), Clancy Brown, Bruce Abbott, Teri Austin (2 hrs.).

JONATHAN: THE BOY NOBODY WANTED
NBC 10/19/92. (George Kaczender), JoBeth Williams, Chris Burke, Madge Sinclair, Jeffrey DeMunn (2 hrs.).

JONNY'S GOLDEN QUEST
USA 4/4/93. (Mario Piluso, prod.), Animated.

JOSEPH
TNT 4/16 & 4/17/95. (Roger Young), Ben Kingsley, Paul Mercurio, Lesley Ann Warren, Martin Landau, Warren Clarke.

THE JOSEPHINE BAKER STORY
HBO 3/16/91. (Brian Gibson), Lynn Whitfield, Ruben Blades, David Dukes, Louis Gossett Jr. (135 mins.).

JOSHUA'S HEART
NBC 9/10/90. (Michael Pressman), Melissa Gilbert, Tim Matheson, Matthew Lawrence (2 hrs.).

JOURNEY
CBS 12/10/95. (Tom McLoughlin), Max Pomeranc, Jason Robards, Brenda Fricker, Meg Tilly, Eliza Dushku.

JOURNEY OF THE HEART
CBS. 3/2/97. Cassidy Rae, Stephen Lang, Cybill Shepherd.

JOURNEY TO THE CENTER OF THE EARTH
NBC 2/28/93. (Bill Dear), Jeffrey Nordling, Farrah Forke, John Neville, F. Murray Abraham (2 hrs.).

JUDGMENT
HBO 10/13/90. (Tom Topor), Keith Carradine, Blythe Danner, David Strathairn, Dylan Baker (90 mins.).

JUDGMENT DAY: THE JOHN LIST STORY
CBS 2/23/93. (Bobby Roth), Robert Blake, Carroll Baker, Beverly D'Angelo, David Caruso (2 hrs.).

JUDICIAL CONSENT
HBO 3/12/95. (William Bindley), Bonnie Bedelia, Dabney Coleman, Billy Wirth, Lisa Blount, Will Patton (2 hrs.).

JURY DUTY: THE COMEDY
ABC 1/14/90. (Michael Schultz), Bronson Pinchot, Lynn Redgrave, Heather Locklear (2 hrs.).

JUST ONE OF THE GIRLS
FOX 9/13/93. (Michael Keusch), Corey Haim, Nicole Eggert, Cameron Bancroft (2 hrs.).

JUSTICE FOR ANNIE: A MOMENT OF TRUTH MOVIE
NBC 1/15/96. Peggy Lipton, Danica McKellar, Susan Ruttan, Bruce Weitz, Terry David Mulligan, Gwynyth Walsh.

JUSTICE IN A SMALL TOWN
NBC 9/23/94. (Jan Egleson), Kate Jackson, John Shea, Dean Stockwell, Rand Courtney, Terry O'Quinn (2 hrs.).

K

K-9000
FOX 7/1/91. (Kim Manners), Chris Mulkey, Catherine Oxenberg, Dennis Haysbert (2 hrs.).

KANSAS
ABC 7/27/95. (Bob Mandel), Patricia Wettig, Jenny Robertson, Dierdre O'Connell, Scott Paulin, Luke Rossi (2 hrs.).

KEEP THE CHANGE
TNT 6/9/92. (Andy Tennant), William Petersen, Lolita Davidovich, Rachel Ticotin, Jack Palance (2 hrs.).

KEEPER OF THE CITY
SHO 1/25/92. (Bobby Roth), Louis Gossett Jr., Anthony LaPaglia, Peter Coyote, Renee Soutendijk (2 hrs.).

KEEPING SECRETS
ABC 9/29/91. (John Korty), Suzanne Somers, Ken Kercheval, Michael Learned, David Birney (2 hrs.).

KEEPING THE PROMISE
CBS. 1/5/97. (Sheldon Larry), Keith Carradine, Annette O'Toole, Brendan Fletcher, Gordon Tootoosis.

THE KENNEDYS OF MASSACHUSETTS
ABC 2/18, 2/19 & 2/21/90. (Lamont Johnson), William Petersen, Charles Durning, Campbell Scott (6 hrs.).

THE KEYS
NBC 4/12/92. (Richard Compton), Ben Masters, Brian Bloom, Scott Bloom, Barry Corbin (2 hrs.).

THE KID WHO LOVED CHRISTMAS
WPIX 12/14/90. (Arthur Allan Seidelman), Michael Warren, Cicely Tyson, Sammy Davis, Jr., Trent Cameron (2 hrs.).

A KIDNAPPING IN THE FAMILY
ABC 2/26/96. Tracey Gold, Kate Jackson, Robert Bishop.

KIDZ IN THE WOOD
NBC 5/25/96. (Neal Israel), Dave Thomas, Julia Duffy, Tatyana M. Ali, Darius McCrary, Candace Cameron.

A KILLER AMONG FRIENDS
CBS 12/8/92. (Charles Robert Carner), Patty Duke, Margaret Welsh, Loretta Swit (2 hrs.).

A KILLER AMONG US
NBC 10/29/90. (Peter Levin), Jasmine Guy, Anna Maria Horsford, Dwight Schultz (2 hrs.).

KILLER RULES
NBC 1/24/93. (Robert Ellis Miller), Jamey Sheridan, Sela Ward, Peter Dobson, Sam Wanamaker (2 hrs.).

KILLING IN A SMALL TOWN
CBS 5/22/90. (Stephen Gyllenhaal), Barbara Hershey, Brian Dennehy, Hal Holbrook (2 hrs.).

THE KILLING MIND
LIF 4/23/91. (Michael Ray Rhodes), Stephanie Zimbalist, Tony Bill, Daniel Roebuck (2 hrs.).

KILLING MR. GRIFFIN
NBC. 4/7/97. (Jack Bender), Jay Thomas, Mario Lopez, Amy Jo Johnson, Scott Bairstow, Joan McMurtrey, Scott Jaeck.

KINDRED: THE EMBRACED
FOX 4/2/96. (Peter Medak), E. Thomas Howell, Mark Frankel, Kate Vernon, Stacy Haiduk, Jeff Kober, Kelly Rutherford.

KINGFISH: A STORY OF HUEY P. LONG
TNT 3/19/95. (Thomas Schlamme), John Goodman, Matt Craven, Anne Heche, Jeff Perry, Ann Dowd, Bob Gunton (2 hrs.).

KISS AND TELL
ABC 1/15/96. (Andy Wolk), Cheryl Ladd, John Terry, Francie Swift, Barry Corbin, John Bedford Lloyd, Jack Gilpin.

KISS AND TELL
A&E. 6/15/97. (David Richards), Peter Howitt, Gillian Bevan, Danny Worters, Hilda Braid, Clare Cathcart, Rosie Rowell.

KISS OF A KILLER
ABC 2/1/93. (Larry Elikann), Annette O'Toole, Eva Marie Saint, Brian Wimmer, Gregg Henry (2 hrs.).

A KISS SO DEADLY
NBC. 10/14/96. (Chuck Bowman), Charles Shaughnessy, Dedee Pfeiffer, Tom Breznahan, Noelle Parker, Kerrie Keane.

A KISS TO DIE FOR
NBC 12/6/93. (Leon Ichaso), Tim Matheson, Mimi Rogers, William Forsythe, Carroll Baker (2 hrs.).

THE KISSING PLACE
USA 4/11/90. (Tony Wharmby), Meredith Baxter-Birney, David Ogden Stiers, Nathaniel Moreau (2 hrs.).

KISSINGER AND NIXON
TNT 12/10/95. (Daniel Petrie), Ron Silver, Beau Bridges, Matt Frewer, Ron White, George Takei.

KNIGHT RIDER 2010
SYND 2/9/94. (Sam Pillsbury), Richard Joseph Paul, Heidi Peick, Michael Beach (2 hrs.).

KNOT'S LANDING: BACK TO THE CUL-DE-SAC
CBS. 5/9 & 5/11/97. (Bill Corcoran), William Devane, Kevin Dobson, Michele Lee, Donna Mills, Ted Shackelford, Joan Van Ark.

KURT VONNEGUT'S "HARRISON BERGERON"
SHO 8/13/95. (Bruce Pittman), Sean Astin, Miranda DePencier, Christopher Plummer, Buck Henry, Howie Mandel (90 mins.).

L

L.A. JOHNS
FOX. 6/17/97. (Joyce Chopra), Thomas Calabro, Brittney Powell, John Terry, Curtis Armstrong, Brian Van Holt, Cress Williams.

LABOR OF LOVE: THE ARLETTE SCHWEITZER STORY
CBS 5/9/93. (Jerry London), Ann Jillian, Tracey Gold, Bill Smitrovich, Diana Scarwid (2 hrs.).

LADY AGAINST THE ODDS
NBC 4/20/92. (Bradford May), Crystal Bernard, Annabeth Gish, Rob Estes, Kevin Kilner, Roy Thinnes (2 hrs.).

LADY KILLER
CBS 4/5/95. (Steven Schachter), Judith Light, Tracey Gold, Jack Wagner, Ben Masters, Diana LeBlanc, J.R. Zimmerman (2 hrs.).

LADYKILLER
USA 8/19/92. (Michael Scott), Mimi Rogers, John Shea, Alice Krige, Bob Gunton (2 hrs.).

LAKE CONSEQUENCE
SHO 2/28/93. (Rafael Eisenman), Billy Zane, Joan Severance, Mary Karasun, Whip Hubley (2 hrs.).

LAKER GIRLS
CBS 4/3/90. (Bruce Seth Green), Tina Yothers, Paris Vaughan, Jean Simmons (2 hrs.).

LAKOTA WOMAN: SIEGE AT WOUNDED KNEE
TNT 10/16/94. (Frank Pierson), Irene Bedard, August Schellenberg, Joseph Runningfox, Floyd Red Crow Westerman.

LAND'S END
KCOP 9/22/96. (James Bruce) Fred Dryer, Geoffrey Lewis, Bryan Cranston, Rena Fiffel, Tim Thomerson, Pamela Bowen.

LANTERN HILL
DIS 1/27/90. (Kevin Sullivan), Sam Waterston, Marion Bennett, Sarah Polley (2 hrs.).

LARRY MCMURTRY'S DEAD MAN'S WALK
ABC 5/12 & 5/13/96. (Yves Simoneau), F. Murray Abraham, David Arquette, Keith Carradine, Patricia Childress.

LARRY MCMURTRY'S STREETS OF LAREDO
CBS 11/12/95. (Joseph Sargent), James Garner, Sissy Spacek, Sam Shepard, Ned Beatty, Randy Quaid, Wes Studi.

THE LAST BEST YEAR
ABC 11/4/90. (John Erman), Mary Tyler Moore, Bernadette Peters, Brian Bedford, Dorothy McGuire (2 hrs.).

THE LAST ELEPHANT
TNT 8/20/90. (Joseph Sargent), John Lithgow, Isabella Rosellini, James Earl Jones (2 hrs.).

LAST FLIGHT OUT
NBC 5/22/90. (Larry Elikann), Richard Crenna, James Earl Jones, Eric Bogosian (2 hrs.).

THE LAST FRONTIER
HBO 6/3/96. (Arlene Sanford), Anthony Starke, John Terlesky, Patrick Labyorteaux, David Kriegel, Jessica Tuck.

THE LAST HIT
USA 3/31/93. (Jan Egelson), Bryan Brown, Brooke Adams, Harris Yulin (2 hrs.).

LAST LIGHT
SHO 8/22/93. (Kiefer Sutherland), Forest Whitaker, Kiefer Sutherland, Amanda Plummer (2 hrs.).

THE LAST OF HIS TRIBE
HBO 3/28/92. (Harry Hook), Jon Voight, Graham Greene, David Ogden Stiers, Anne Archer (90 mins.).

THE LAST OUTLAW
HBO 10/30/93. (Geoff Murphy), Mickey Rourke, Dermot Mulroney, Steve Buscemi (2 hrs.).

THE LAST PROSTITUTE
LIF 9/11/91. (Lou Antonio), Wil Wheaton, Sonia Braga, Cotter Smith, David Kaufman (2 hrs.).

LAST STAND AT SABER RIVER
TNT. 1/19/97. (Dick Lowry), Tom Selleck, Suzy Amis, Rachel Duncan, Haley Joel Osment, Keith Carradine, David Carradine.

THE LAST TO GO
ABC 1/21/91. (John Erman), Tyne Daly, Terry O'Quinn, Annabeth Gish (2 hrs.).

LAST TRAIN HOME
FAM 3/2/90. (Randy Bradshaw), Noam Zylberman, Nick Mancuso, Ned Beatty (2 hrs.).

LAST WISH
ABC 1/12/92. (Jeff Bleckner), Patty Duke, Maureen Stapleton, Dwight Schultz, Lee Wallace (2 hrs.).

THE LAST WORD
SHO 8/27/95. (Tony Spiridakis), Timothy Hutton, Joe Pantoliano, Michelle Burke, Chazz Palminteri, Tony Goldwyn.

THE LATE SHIFT
HBO 2/24/96. (Betty Thomas), Kathy Bates, John Michael Higgins, Daniel Roebuck, Bob Balaban, Ed Begley Jr.

LAUREL AVENUE
HBO 7/10 & 11/93. (Carl Franklin), Mary Alice, Jay Brooks, Juanita Jennings, Dan Martin (3 hrs.).

LAVYRLE SPENCER'S HOME SONG
CBS 3/20/96. (Nancy Malone), Lee Horsley, Polly Draper, Deborah Raffin, Ari Meyers, Chris Martin, Stan Kirsch.

THE LAZARUS MAN
CBS 1/1/96. (Johnny E. Jensen), Robert Urich, Elizabeth Dennehy, David Marshall Grant, John Diehl.

LEAVE OF ABSENCE
NBC 5/11/94. (Tom McLoughlin), Brian Dennehy, Jacqueline Bisset, Blythe Danner, Polly Bergen (2 hrs.).

LEGACY OF LIES
USA 4/22/92. (Bradford May), Michael Ontkean, Martin Landau, Eli Wallach, Joe Morton (2 hrs.).

THE LEGEND OF GATOR FACE
SHO 5/19/96. Paul Winfield, John White, Dan Warry-Smith, Charlotte Sullivan, Matt Evans.

LEGEND OF THE LOST TOMB
SHO. Rick Rossovich, Stacy Keach, Brock Pierce, Kimberly Peterson.

LEGEND OF THE RUBY SILVER
ABC 1/13/96. (Charles Wilkinson), Bruce Weitz, Rebecca Jenkins, Jonathan Jackson, John Schneider.

LEONA HELMSLEY: THE QUEEN OF MEAN
CBS 9/23/90. (Richard Michaels), Suzanne Pleshette, Lloyd Bridges, Joe Regalbuto (2 hrs.).

LETHAL EXPOSURE
NBC 3/28/93. (Kevin O'Connor), Ally Sheedy, Francois Eric Gendron, Carmela Valente (2 hrs.).

LETTER TO MY KILLER
USA 8/9/95. (Janet Meyers), Mare Winningham, Nick Chinlund, Rip Torn, Josef Sommer, Eddie Jones (2 hrs.).

LIAR, LIAR
CBS 6/22/93. (Jorge Montesi), Art Hindle, Rosemary Dunsmore, Kate Nelligan (2 hrs.).

LIAR'S EDGE
SHO 12/4/92. (Ron Oliver), Nicholas Shields, David Keith, Joseph Bottoms, Shannon Tweed (2 hrs.).

LIE DOWN WITH LIONS
LIF 6/12/94. (Jim Goddard), Timothy Dalton, Marg Helgenberger, Nigel Havers (2 hrs.).

LIES AND LULLABIES
ABC 3/14/93. (Ron Hardy), Susan Dey, Lorraine Toussaint, D.W. Moffett, Piper Laurie (2 hrs.).

LIES BEFORE KISSES
CBS 3/3/91. (Lou Antonio), Jaclyn Smith, Ben Gazzara, Nick Mancuso (2 hrs.).

LIES HE TOLD
ABC. 3/17/97. (Larry Elikann), Gary Cole, Karen Sillas, Ron Lea, Nigel Bennett, Linda Sorensen, Teddi Siddall, George R. Robertson.

LIES OF THE HEART: THE STORY OF LAURIE KELLOGG
ABC 1/31/94. (Michael Uno), Jennie Garth, Gregory Harrison, Steven Keats (2 hrs.).

LIES OF THE TWINS
USA 8/21/91. (Tim Hunter), Aidan Quinn, Isabella Rossellini, Iman (2 hrs.).

A LIFE IN THE THEATRE
TNT 10/9/93. (Gregory Mosher), Jack Lemmon, Matthew Broderick (70 mins.).

THE LIFEFORCE EXPERIMENT
SCI 4/16/94. (Piers Haggard), Donald Sutherland, Corin Nemec, Mimi Kuzyk (2 hrs.).

LIFELINE
USA 5/15/96. Lorraine Bracco, Jean-Marc Barr.

LIFEPOD
FOX 6/28/93. (Ron Silver), Ron Silver, Robert Loggia, Jessica Tuck, C.C.H. Pounder (2 hrs.).

LIGHTNING FIELD
USA 9/11/91. (Michael Switzer), Nancy McKeon, Polly Bergen, Elpidia Carrillo, Miriam Colon (2 hrs.).

LIGHTNING IN A BOTTLE
LIF 2/20/96. Lynda Carter, Dee Wallace Stone, Martin Cove, Matt McCoy, Stuart Whitman.

LILY DALE
SHO 6/9/96. (Peter Masterson), Tim Guinee, Stockard Channing, Mary Stuart Masterson, Sam Shepard.

LILY IN WINTER
USA 12/8/94. (Delbert Mann), Natalie Cole, Brian Bonsall, Marla Gibbs, Dwier Brown, Cecil Hoffman, Monte Russell (2 hrs.).

THE LIMBIC REGION
SHO 6/30/96. (Michael Pattinson), Edward James Olmos, George Dzundza, Roger R. Cross, Gwynyth Walsh.

LINDA
USA 10/8/93. (Nathaniel Gutman), Virginia Madsen, Richard Thomas, Ted McGinley (2 hrs.).

LINE OF FIRE: THE MORRIS DEES STORY
NBC 1/21/91. (John Korty), Corbin Bernsen, Jenny Lewis, Sandy Bull (2 hrs.).

LITTLE GIRLS IN PRETTY BOXES
LIF. 1/19/97. Swoosie Kurtz, Philip Casnoff, Linda Hart, Jim Metzler, Mike Doukas, Lily Knight.

THE LITTLE KIDNAPPERS
DIS 8/17/90. (Donald Shebib), Charlton Heston, Bruce Greenwood, Leo Wheatley (95 mins.).

LITTLE LORD FAUNTLEROY
DIS 7/14/95. (Andrew Morgan), George Baker, Michael Benz, Betsy Brantly, John Castle, Bernice Stegers, Helen Lindsay.

A LITTLE PIECE OF HEAVEN
NBC 12/2/91. (Mimi Leder), Kirk Cameron, Cloris Leachman, Jenny Robertson, Chelsea Noble (2 hrs.).

LITTLE RIDERS
DISNEY 3/24/96. (Kevin Connor), Paul Scofield, Rosemary Harris, Noley Thornton, Malcolm McDowell, Benedick Blythe.

LIVE! FROM DEATH ROW
FOX 4/3/92. (Patrick Duncan), Bruce Davison, Joanna Cassidy, Jason Tomlins, Calvin Levels (2 hrs.).

LIVE SHOT
UPN 8/22/95. (Colin Bucksey) Sam Anderson, David Birney, Wanda De Jesus, Hill Harper, Spencer Klein, Bruce McGill.

LIVING A LIE
NBC 9/16/91. (Larry Shaw), Jill Eikenberry, Peter Coyote, Roxanne Hart, Jarred Blanchard (2 hrs.).

LIZ: THE ELIZABETH TAYLOR STORY
NBC 5/21 & 5/22/95. (Kevin Conner), Sherilyn Fenn, Angus MacFadyen, William McNamara, Nigel Havers.

LOCKED UP: A MOTHER'S RAGE
CBS 10/29/91. (Bethany Rooney), Cheryl Ladd, Jean Smart, Angela Bassett, Joshua Harris.

LONG ROAD HOME
NBC 2/25/91. (John Korty), Mark Harmon, Lee Purcell, Morgan Weisser (2 hrs.).

THE LOOKALIKE
USA 12/12/90. (Gary Nelson), Melissa Gilbert-Brinkman, Thaao Penghlis, Diane Ladd (2 hrs.).

LOSING CHASE
SHO 8/18/96. (Kevin Bacon), Helen Mirren, Kyra Sedgwick, Beau Bridges.

THE LOST CAPONE
TNT 9/10/90. (John Gray), Adrian Pasdar, Ally Sheedy, Eric Roberts (2 hrs.).

LOVE AND BETRAYAL: THE MIA FARROW STORY
FOX 2/28 & 3/2/95. (Karen Arthur), Patsy Kensit, Dennis Boutsikaris, Robert LuPone, Grace Una, Tovah Feldshuh.

LOVE AND CURSES... AND ALL THAT JAZZ
CBS 9/21/91. (Gerald McRaney), Gerald McRaney, Delta Burke, Elizabeth Ashley, Harold Sylvester (2 hrs.).

LOVE AND HATE: A MARRIAGE MADE IN HELL
NBC 7/15 & 7/16/90. (Francis Mankiewicz), Kate Nelligan, Kenneth Welsh, Leon Pownall (4 hrs.).

LOVE AND LIES
ABC 3/18/90. (Roger Young), Mare Winningham, Peter Gallagher, Tom O'Brien (2 hrs.).

THE LOVE BOAT: A VALENTINE VOYAGE
CBS 2/12/90. (Ron Satlof), Gavin McLeod, Tom Bosley, "Rowdy" Roddy Piper, Julia Duffy (2 hrs.).

LOVE CAN BE MURDER
NBC 12/14/92. (Jack Bender), Jaclyn Smith, Corbin Bernsen, Cliff DeYoung, Anne Francis (2 hrs.).

LOVE, CHEAT AND STEAL
SHO 12/5/93. (William Curran), John Lithgow, Eric Roberts, Madchen Amick, Richard Edson (95 mins.).

LOVE, HONOR & OBEY: THE LAST MAFIA MARRIAGE
CBS 5/23 & 5/25/93. (John Patterson), Eric Roberts, Nancy McKeon, Ben Gazzara, Dylan Baker (4 hrs.).

LOVE KILLS
USA 11/13/91. (Brian Grant), Virginia Madsen, Lenny Van Dohlen, Jim Metzler, Erich Anderson (2 hrs.).

LOVE, LIES & MURDER
NBC 2/17 & 2/18/91. (Robert Markowitz), Clancy Brown, Sheryl Lee, Moira Kelly (4 hrs.).

LOVE MATTERS
SHO 10/3/93. (Eb Lottimer), Griffin Dunne, Tony Goldwyn, Annette O'Toole, Kate Burton (96 mins.).

THE LOVE SHE SOUGHT
NBC 10/21/90. (Joseph Sargent), Angela Lansbury, Denholm Elliott, Cynthia Nixon (2 hrs.).

LOVE STRUCK
FAM. 6/1/97. (Larry Peerce), Cynthia Gibb, Costas Mandylor, Annabelle Gurwitch, Suzanne Somers, Mark Joy, Tyler Noyes.

LOVE'S DEADLY TRIANGLE: THE TEXAS CADET MURDER
NBC. 2/14/97. (Steve White), Holly Marie Combs, David Lipper, Cassidy Rae, Jack Landry, Dee Wallace-Stone.

LUCIFER'S CHILD
A&E 9/21/95. (Tony Abatemarco), Julie Harris.

LUCKY DAY
ABC 3/11/91. (Donald Wrye), Amy Madigan, Olympia Dukakis, Chloe Webb (2 hrs.).

LUCY & DESI: BEFORE THE LAUGHTER
CBS 2/10/91. (Charles Jarrott), Frances Fisher, Maurice Bernard, Robin Pearson Rose (2 hrs.).

LUSH LIFE
SHO 5/20/94. (Michael Elias), Jeff Goldblum, Forest Whitaker, Kathy Baker (105 mins.).

LYING EYES
NBC. 12/13/96. (Marina Sargenti), Cassidy Rae, Vincent Irizarry, Allison Smith, Jamie Rose, Ashlee Levitch, Sherry Hursey.

M

MACGYVER: LOST TREASURE OF ATLANTIS
ABC 5/14/94. (Michael Vegar), Richard Dean Anderson, Brian Blessed, Sophie Ward (2 hrs.).

MACGYVER: TRAIL TO DOOMSDAY
ABC 11/24/94. (Charles Correll), Richard Dean Anderson, Beatie Edney, Peter Egan, Alan Armstrong, Bob Sherman.

MACSHAYNE: THE FINAL ROLL OF THE DICE
NBC 4/29/94. (E.W. Swackhamer), Kenny Rogers, Maria Conchita Alonso, Wendy Phillips (2 hrs.).

MACSHAYNE: WINNER TAKES ALL
NBC 4/11/94. (E.W. Swackhamer), Kenny Rogers, Ann Jillian, John Karlen, Terry O'Quinn (2 hrs.).

MADONNA: INNOCENCE LOST
FOX 11/29/94. (Bradford May), Terumi Matthews, Wendie Malick, Jeff Yagher, Diana Leblanc, Dean Stockwell (2 hrs.).

MAID FOR EACH OTHER
NBC 1/13/92. (Paul Schneider), Nell Carter, Dinah Manoff, Joyce Van Patten, Garrett Morris (2 hrs.).

MAJORITY RULE
LIF 10/27/92. (Gwen Arner), Blair Brown, John Getz, Jensen Daggett, Donald Moffat (2 hrs.).

THE MAN FROM LEFT FIELD
CBS 10/15/93. (Burt Reynolds), Burt Reynolds, Reba McEntire, Joe Theismann (2 hrs.).

THE MAN NEXT DOOR
ABC 1/18/96. Michael Ontkean, Pamela Reed, Annette O'Toole, Sam Anderson, Richard Gilliland.

THE MAN UPSTAIRS
CBS 12/6/92. (George Schaefer), Katharine Hepburn, Ryan O'Neal, Helena Carroll (2 hrs.).

THE MAN WHO CAPTURED EICHMANN
TNT. 11/8/96. (William A. Graham), Robert Duvall, Arliss Howard, Jeffrey Tambor, Jack Laufer, Nicolas Surovy.

THE MAN WHO WOULDN'T DIE
ABC 5/29/95. (Bill Condon), Roger Moore, Malcolm McDowell, Nancy Allen, Michael Puttonen, Wendy Van Riesen (2 hrs.).

THE MAN WITH 3 WIVES
CBS 3/28/93. (Peter Levin), Beau Bridges, Pam Dawber, Joanna Kerns, Kathleen Lloyd (2 hrs.).

MANDELA AND DE KLERK
SHO. 2/16/97. (Joseph Sargent), Sidney Poitier, Michael Caine, Tina Lifford, Gerry Maritz, Ian Roberts, Ben Kruger.

MANTIS
FOX 1/24/94. (Eric Laneuville), Carl Lumbly, Bobby Hosea, Gina Torres, Steve James (2 hrs.).

MARILYN AND BOBBY: HER FINAL AFFAIR
USA 8/4/93. (Bradford May), Melody Anderson, James F. Kelly, Thomas Wagner, Richard Dysart (2 hrs.).

MARILYN AND ME
ABC 9/22/91. (John Patterson), Susan Griffiths, Jesse Dabson, Joel Grey, Sal Landi (2 hrs.).

MARIO PUZO'S THE LAST DON
CBS. 5/11, 5/13 & 5/14/97. (Graeme Clifford), Danny Aiello, Joe Mantegna, Daryl Hannah, Jason Gedrick, Penelope Ann Miller, Robert Wuhl, k. d. lang, Kirstie Alley.

MARK TWAIN AND ME
DIS 11/22/91. (Daniel Petrie), Jason Robards, Amy Stewart, Talia Shire, Fiona Reid (2 hrs.).

MARKED FOR MURDER
NBC 1/17/93. (Mimi Leder), Powers Boothe, Billy Dee Williams, Laura Johnson, Michael Ironside (2 hrs.).

THE MARLA HANSON STORY
NBC 2/4/91. (John Gray), Cheryl Pollak, Dale Midkiff, Kirk Baltz (2 hrs.).

MARY & TIM
CBS. 11/3/96. Candice Bergen, Roger Brooke, Richard Kiley, Shirley Knight, Louise Latham, Thomas McCarthy.

A MATCH MADE IN HEAVEN
CBS. 4/27/97. Olympia Dukakis, Della Reese, Kelly Rowan, John Stamos.

MATERNAL INSTINCTS
USA 1/17/96. (George Kaczender), Delta Burke, Beth Broderick, Tom Mason, Garwin Sanford, Sandra Nelson, Gillian Barber.

MATLOCK: THE VACATION
ABC 11/5/92. (Christopher Hillber), Andy Griffith, Brynn Thayer, Warren Frost (2 hrs.).

A MATTER OF JUSTICE
NBC 11/7 & 11/8/93. (Michael Switzer), Patty Duke, Martin Sheen, Alexandra Powers, Jason London (2 hrs.).

MATTERS OF THE HEART
USA 12/26/90. (Michael Rhodes), Jane Seymour, Chris Gartin, James Stacy (2 hrs.).

MAX AND HELEN
TNT 1/8/90. (Philip Saville), Treat Williams, Alice Krige, Martin Landau (2 hrs.).

MEMORIES OF MURDER
LIF 7/31/90. (Robert Lewis), Nancy Allen, Robin Thomas, Vanity (2 hrs.).

MELANIE DARROW
USA. 8/20/97. (Gary Nelson), Delta Burke, Brian Bloom, Christopher Birt, Jonathan Banks, Bruce Abbott.

THE MEMBER OF THE WEDDING
USA. 1/29/97. (Fielder Cook), Jack Landry, Anna Paquin, Alfre Woodward.

MEMPHIS
TNT 1/27/92. (Yves Simoneau), Cybill Shepherd, John Laughlin, J.E. Freeman, Moses Gunn (2 hrs.).

MEN DON'T TELL
CBS 3/14/93. (Harry Winer), Peter Strauss, Judith Light, Ashley Johnson, Michael Rand (2 hrs.).

MENENDEZ: A KILLING IN BEVERLY HILLS
CBS 5/22 & 5/24/94. (Larry Elikann), Edward James Olmos, Beverly D'Angelo, Damian Chapa (4 hrs.).

MENU FOR MURDER
(FORMERLY "MURDER AT THE PTA LUNCHEON")
CBS 12/90. (Larry Peerce), Julia Duffy, Morgan Fairchild, Marla Gibbs (2 hrs.).

MERCY MISSION: THE RESCUE OF FLIGHT 771
NBC 12/13/93. (Roger Young), Scott Bakula, Robert Loggia, Alan Fletcher (2 hrs.).

A MESSAGE FROM HOLLY
CBS 12/13/92. (Rod Holcomb), Lindsay Wagner, Shelley Long, Cotter Smith, MacDonald Carey (2 hrs.).

MIAMI HUSTLE
7/21/96. (Lawrence Lanoff), Kathy Ireland, Jon Enos, Audie England, Allan Rich, Richard Sarafian, Eduardo Yanez.

MIDNIGHT'S CHILD
LIF 4/21/92. (Colin Bucksey), Marcy Walker, Cotter Smith, Olivia D'Abo, Elissabeth Moss.

MILES FROM NOWHERE
CBS 1/7/92. (Buzz Kulik), Rick Schroder, James Farentino, Shawn Phelan, Melora Hardin (2 hrs.).

MILLION DOLLAR BABIES
CBS 11/20 & 11/22/94. (Christian Duguay), Beau Bridges, Kate Nelligan, Roy Dupuis, Celine Bonnier, Samantha Gilliland.

MIRACLE CHILD
NBC 4/6/93. (Michael Pressman), Crystal Bernard, Cloris Leachman, John Terry (2 hrs.).

MIRACLE IN THE WILDERNESS
TNT 12/9/91. (Kevin James Dobson), Kris Kristofferson, Kim Cattrall, John Dennis Johnston (2 hrs.).

MIRACLE LANDING
CBS 2/11/90. (Dick Lowry), Connie Sellecca, Wayne Rogers, Nancy Kwan (2 hrs.).

MIRACLE ON I-880
NBC 2/22/93. (Robert Iscove), Ruben Blades, David Morse, Len Cariou, Sandy Duncan (2 hrs.).

MISS AMERICA: BEHIND THE CROWN
NBC 9/21/92. (Richard Michaels), Carolyn Sapp, Ray Bumatai, Jack Blessing, Gedde Watanabe (2 hrs.).

MISS EVERS' BOYS
HBO. 2/22/97. (Kip Konwiser), Alfre Woodard, Laurence Fishburne, Craig Sheffer, Joe Morton, E. G. Marshall, Ossie Davis.

MISS ROSE WHITE
NBC 4/26/92. (Joseph Sargent), Kyra Sedgwick, Maximilian Schell, Amanda Plummer, D.B. Sweeney (2 hrs.).

MISSION OF THE SHARK
CBS 9/29/91. (Robert Iscove), Stacy Keach, Richard Thomas, Don Harvey, David Caruso (2 hrs.).

MIXED BLESSINGS
NBC 12/11/95. (Bethany Rooney), Gabrielle Carteris, Scott Baio, Bess Armstrong, Bruce Greenwood, James Naughton.

MODEL BY DAY
FOX 3/21/94. (Christian Duguay), Famke Janssen, Stephen Shellen, Clark Johnson, Shannon Tweed (2 hrs.).

MOLL FLANDERS
PBS. 10/13 & 10/14/96. (David Attwood), Alex Kingston, Daniel Craig, Diana Rigg, Colin Buchanan, Ian Driver, Caroline Harker.

A MOM FOR CHRISTMAS
NBC 12/17/90. (George Miller), Olivia Newton-John, Juliet Sorcey, Doug Sheehan (2 hrs.).

MOMENT OF TRUTH: A CHILD TOO MANY
NBC 10/11/93. (Jorge Montesai), Michelle Green, Conor O'Farrell, Nancy Stafford (2 hrs.).

MOMENT OF TRUTH: A MOTHER'S DECEPTION
NBC 10/17/94. (Chuck Bowman), Joan Van Ark, Stephen Macht, Daniel Hugh Kelly, Tom Kurlander, Brooke Langton (2 hrs.).

MOMENT OF TRUTH: BROKEN PLEDGES
NBC 4/11/94. (Jorge Montesai), Linda Gray, Leon Russom, David Lipper, Jane Galloway (2 hrs.).

MOMENT OF TRUTH: CAUGHT IN THE CROSSFIRE
NBC 9/14/94. (Chuck Bowman), Dennis Franz, Alley Mills, Daniel Roebuck, Anna Gunn, Ray McKinnon (2 hrs.).

MOMENT OF TRUTH: CRADLE OF CONSPIRACY
NBC 5/2/94. (Gabrielle Beaumont), Dee Wallace Stone, Danica McKellar, Kurt Deutsch (2 hrs.).

MOMENT OF TRUTH: MURDER OR MEMORY?
NBC 12/12/94. (Christopher Leitch), Leigh Taylor-Young, Karl David-Djerf, Michael Brandon, Louis Giambalvo (2 hrs.).

MOMENT OF TRUTH: STALKING BACK
NBC 10/18/93. (Corey Allen), Luanne Ponce, Shanna Reed, John Martin (2 hrs.).

MOMENT OF TRUTH: TO WALK AGAIN
NBC 2/16/94. (Randall Zisk), Blair Brown, Ken Howard, Cameron Bancroft (2 hrs.).

MOMENT OF TRUTH: WHY MY DAUGHTER?
NBC 4/28/93. (Chuck Bowman), Linda Gray, Jaimie Luner, Antonio Sabato Jr. (2 hrs.).

MONTANA
TNT 2/19/90. (William A. Graham), Gena Rowlands, Richard Crenna, Lea Thompson, Scott Coffey (2 hrs.).

MOONSHINE HIGHWAY
SHO 5/5/96. (Andy Armstrong), Kyle MacLachlan, Randy Quaid, Maria Del Mar.

THE MORRISON MURDERS
USA. 11/5/96. (Robert Cantos), Tanya Allen, Leana Brodie, John Corbett, Marc Donato, Shawn Lawrence, Jonathan Scarfe.

MORTAL SINS
USA 11/4/92. (Bradford May), Christopher Reeve, Roxanne Biggs, Francis Guinan (2 hrs.).

MOSES
TNT 4/7 & 4/8/96. (Roger Young), Ben Kingsley, David Suchet, Frank Langella, Christopher Lee, Anna Galiena.

MOTHER KNOWS BEST
ABC. 4/13/97. (Larry Shaw), Joanna Kerns, Christine Elise, Grant Show, David Spielberg, Kristen Dalton.

MOTHER OF THE BRIDE
CBS 2/27/93. (Charles Correll), Rue McClanahan, Kristy McNichol, Paul Dooley, Ted Shackelford (2 hrs.).

A MOTHER'S GIFT
CBS 4/16/95. (Jerry London), Nancy McKeon, Adrian Pasdar, Adam Storke, Dan Brook, Helen Cates, Gail Cronauer (2 hrs.).

A MOTHER'S INSTINCT
CBS 3/13/96. (Sam Pillsbury), Lindsay Wagner, Debrah Farentino, John Terry, Barbara Babcock, Lynn Thigpen.

A MOTHER'S JUSTICE
NBC 11/25/91. (Noel Nosseck), Meredith Baxter, G.W. Bailey, Carrie Hamilton, Blu Mankuma (2 hrs.).

A MOTHER'S PRAYER
USA 8/2/95. (Larry Elikann), Linda Hamilton, Noah Fleiss, Bruce Dern, Kate Nelligan, RuPaul, S. Epatha Merkerson (2 hrs.).

A MOTHER'S REVENGE
ABC 11/14/93. (Armand Mastroianni), Lesley Ann Warren, Bruce Davison, Missy Crider (2 hrs.).

A MOTHER'S RIGHT: THE ELIZABETH MORGAN STORY
ABC 11/29/93. (Linda Otto), Bonnie Bedelia, Terence Knox, Kenneth Welsh, Pam Grier (2 hrs.).

MOTORCYCLE GANG
SHO 8/5/94. (John Milius), Gerald McRaney, Elan Oberon, Carla Gugino (2 hrs.).

MR. AND MRS. LOVING
SHO 3/31/96. (Richard Friedenberg), Timothy Hutton, Lela Rochon, Ruby Dee, BillNunn, Corey Parker, Isaiah Washington.

MR. STITCH
SCI-FI 8/17/96. (Roger Avary), Wil Wheaton, Rutger Hauer, Nia Peeples, Michael Harris.

MRS. 'ARRIS GOES TO PARIS
CBS 12/27/92. (Allan King), Angela Lansbury, Diana Rigg, Omar Sharif, Lothaire Bluteau (2 hrs.).

MRS. LAMBERT REMEMBERS LOVE
CBS 5/12/91. (Charles Matthau), Ellen Burstyn, Walter Matthau, Ryan Todd (2 hrs.).

MRS. MUNCK
SHO 1/28/96. (Diane Ladd), Diane Ladd, Bruce Dern, Kelly Preston, Shelley Winters, Scott Fisher, Jim Walton.

MRS. SANTA CLAUS
CBS. 12/8/96. (Terry Hughes), Angela Lansbury, Charles Durning, Michael Jeter.

MURDER BETWEEN FRIENDS
NBC 1/10/94. (Waris Hussein), Timothy Busfield, Stephen Lang, Martin Kemp, Lisa Blount (2 hrs.).

MURDER C.O.D.
NBC 9/21/90. (Alan Metzger), Patrick Duffy, Chelsea Field, William Devane (2 hrs.).

MURDER AT MY DOOR
FOX. 10/8/97. (Eric Till), Johnny Galecki, Laura R. Harris, Vanessa King, Judith Light.

MURDER IN BLACK AND WHITE
CBS 1/7/90. (Robert Iscove), Richard Crenna, Diahann Carroll, Cliff Gorman, Fred Gwynne (2 hrs.).

MURDER IN HIGH PLACES
NBC 6/2/91. (John Byrum), Ted Levine, Adam Baldwin, Judith Hoag (2 hrs.).

MURDER IN MISSISSIPPI
NBC 2/5/90. (Roger Young), Tom Hulce, Jennifer Gray, Blair Underwood, Josh Charles (2 hrs.).

MURDER IN MY MIND
CBS. 2/19/97. David Kaye, Nicollette Sheridan.

**MURDER IN NEW HAMPSHIRE:
THE PAMELA SMART STORY**
CBS 9/24/91. (Joyce Chopra), Helen Hunt, Chad Allen, Ken Howard, Michael Learned (2 hrs.).

MURDER IN PARADISE
NBC 1/19/90. (Fred Walton), Kevin Kilner, Maggie Han, Mako (2 hrs.).

MURDER IN THE HEARTLAND
ABC 5/3 & 5/4/93. (Robert Markowitz), Tim Roth, Fairuza Balk, Kate Reid, Milo O'Shea (4 hrs.).

MURDER LIVE
NBC. 3/9/97. (Robert M. Sertner), David Morse, Marg Helgenberger, Peter Horton.

MURDER OF INNOCENCE
CBS 11/30/93. (Tom McLaughlin), Valerie Bertinelli, Stephen Caffrey, Graham Beckel (2 hrs.).

MURDER ONE: CHAPTERS 20 AND 21
ABC 4/22/96. (Marc Buckland), Daniel Benzali, Jason Gedrick, Barbara Bosson, Stanley Tucci, Mary McCormack.

MURDER 101
USA 3/20/91. (Bill Condon), Pierce Brosnan, Dey Young, Raphael Sbarge (2 hrs.).

MURDER TIMES SEVEN
CBS 10/14/90. (Jud Taylor), Richard Crenna, Susan Blakely, Cliff Gorman (2 hrs.).

**MURDER WITHOUT MOTIVE:
THE EDMUND PERRY STORY**
NBC 1/6/92. (Kevin Hooks), Curtis McClarin, Anna Maria Horsford, Carla Gugino, Guy Killum (2 hrs.).

MURDEROUS AFFAIR: THE CAROLYN WARMUS STORY
ABC 9/13/92. (Martin Davidson), Virginia Madsen, Chris Sarandon, Ned Eisenberg (2 hrs.).

MURDEROUS VISION
USA 2/20/91. (Gary Sherman), Bruce Boxleitner, Laura Johnson, Joseph d'Angerio (2 hrs.).

MY ANTONIA
USA 3/29/95. (Joseph Sargent), Jason Robards, Eva Marie Saint, Neil Patrick Harris, Elina Lowensohn, Jan Triska (2 hrs.).

MY BREAST
CBS 5/15/94. (Bett/ Thomas), Meredith Baxter, Jamey Sheridan, James Sutorius (2 hrs.).

MY BROTHER'S KEEPER
CBS 3/19/95. (Glenn Jordan), John Lithgow, Ellen Burstyn, Annette O'Toole, Veronica Cartwright, Richard Masur (2 hrs.).

MY NAME IS KATE
ABC 1/24/94. (Rod Hardy), Donna Mills, Daniel J. Travanti, Nia Peeples, Eileen Brennan (2 hrs.).

MY SON IS INNOCENT
ABC 5/6/96. Marilu Henner, Nick Stahl, Matt McCoy, Barry Corbin, John O'Hurley.

MY SON JOHNNY
CBS 11/10/91. (Peter Levin), Michele Lee, Rick Schroder, Corin Nemec, Rip Torn (2 hrs.).

MY STEPSON, MY LOVER
USA 4/25/97. Joshua Murrow, Terry O'Quinn, Rachel Ward.

MY VERY BEST FRIEND
CBS 3/27/96. Jill Eikenberry, Tom Irwin, Kim Wamat.

N

NYPD MOUNTED
CBS 8/3/91. (Mark Tinker), Dennis Franz, Dan Gautier, Cliff De Young (2 hrs.).

NAILS
SHO 7/25/92. (John Flynn), Dennis Hopper, Anne Archer, Tomas Milian, Cliff De Young (97 mins.).

NAOMI & WYNONA: LOVE CAN BUILD A BRIDGE
NBC 5/14 & 5/15/95. (Bobby Roth), Kathleen York, Viveka Davis, Megan Ward, Cari Shayne, Melinda Dillon (4 hrs.).

NED BLESSING: THE TRUE STORY OF MY LIFE
CBS 4/14/92. (Peter Werner), Daniel Baldwin, Chris Cooper, Luis Avalos, Rene Auberjonois (2 hrs.).

NEIL SIMON'S "BROADWAY BOUND"
ABC 3/23/92. (Paul Bogart), Anne Bancroft, Corey Parker, Jonathan Silverman, Hume Cronyn (2 hrs.).

NEIL SIMON'S "JAKE'S WOMEN"
CBS 3/3/96. (Glenn Jordan), Alan Alda, Anne Archer, Lolita Davidovich, Julie Kavner, Mira Sorvino, Joyce Van Patten.

NEIL SIMON'S "LONDON SUITE"
NBC 9/15/96. Michael Richards, Julie Hagerty, Jonathan Silverman, Julia Louis-Dreyfuss.

NEVER FORGET
TNT 4/8/91. (Joseph Sargent), Leonard Nimoy, Dabney Coleman, Blythe Danner (2 hrs.).

NEVER GIVE UP: THE JIMMY V STORY
CBS 4/2/96. Anthony LaPaglia, Ashley Crow.

NEXT DOOR
SHO 9/4/94. (Tony Bill), James Woods, Randy Quaid, Kate Capshaw, Lucinda Jenney, Miles Feulner (95 mins.).

NIGHTJOHN
DISNEY 6/1/96. Carl Lumbly, Allison Jones, Beau Bridges.

NIGHT OF THE FOX
SYND 11/26 & 11/27/90. (Charles Jarrott), George Peppard, Deborah Raffin, Michael York (4 hrs.).

NIGHT OF THE HUNTER
ABC 5/5/91. (David Greene), Richard Chamberlain, Diana Scarwid, Reid Binion (2 hrs.).

NIGHT OF THE TWISTERS
FAM 2/14/96. (Tim Bond), John Schneider, Devon Sawa, Amos Crawley, Laurie Betram, Helen Hughes.

NIGHT OWL
LIF 8/19/93. (Matthew Patrick), Jennifer Beals, James Wilder, Allison Hossack (2 hrs.).

NIGHTSCREAM
NBC. 4/14/97. (Robert M. Sertner), Denis Arndt, Candace Cameron Bure, Teri Garr, Bobby Hosea, Marie Stillin.

NIGHT SINS
CBS. 2/23 & 2/25/97. (Robert Allan Ackerman), Valerie Bertinelli, Harry Hamlin, Karen Sillas, Martin Donovan.

NIGHT VISIONS
NBC 11/30/90. (Wes Craven), Loryn Locklin, James Remar, Penny Johnson (2 hrs.).

NIGHT VISITORS
NBC. 10/13/96. (Jorge Montesi), Todd Allen, Charles Dutton, Faith Ford, Thomas Gibson, Christopher Gray.

THE NIGHTMAN
NBC 3/6/92. (Charles Haid), Jenny Robertson, Joanna Kerns, Ted Marcoux, Latanya Richardson (2 hrs.).

NIGHTMARE IN COLUMBIA COUNTY
CBS 12/10/91. (Roger Young), William Devane, Jeri Lynn Ryan, Michele Abrams, Nick Searcy (2 hrs.).

NIGHTMARE IN THE DAYLIGHT
CBS 11/22/92. (Lou Antonio), Jaclyn Smith, Christopher Reeve, Tom Mason, Eric Bell (2 hrs.).

NIGHTMARE ON THE 13TH FLOOR
USA 10/31/90. (Walter Grauman), Michele Greene, James Brolin, Louise Fletcher (2 hrs.).

NO CHILD OF MINE
CBS 10/31/93. (Michael Katleman), Patty Duke, Tracy Nelson, Susan Blakely (2 hrs.).

NO GREATER LOVE
NBC 12/29-12/31/95. (Richard Heffrom), Kelly Rutherford, Michael Landes, Simon MacCorkindale, Chris Sarandon.

NO ONE COULD PROTECT HER
ABC 2/11/96. (Larry Shaw) Anthony John Denison, Dan Lauria, Joanna Kerns, Lori Hallier.

NO ONE WOULD TELL
NBC 5/6/96. Fred Savage, Candace Cameron, Michelle Phillips, Heather McComb.

NOBODY'S CHILDREN
USA 3/3/94. (David Wheatley), Ann-Margret, Dominique Sanda, Jay O. Sanders (2 hrs.).

NORMA JEAN AND MARILYN
HBO 5/18/96. (Tim Fywell) Mira Sorvino, Ashley Judd, Josh Charles, Ron Rifkin, Peter Dobson, Lindsay Crouse.

NORTHERN LIGHTS
DIS. 8/23/97. (Linda Yellen), Diane Keaton, Maury Chaykin, Joseph Cross, Kathleen York, John Hoffman, Crystal Verge.

NOT A PENNY MORE, NOT A PENNY LESS
USA 4/24 & 4/25/90. (Clive Donner), Edward Asner, Ed Begley, Jr., Jenny Agutter (4 hrs.).

NOT IN MY FAMILY
ABC 2/28/93. (Linda Otto), Joanna Kerns, Michael Brandon, Shelley Hack, Tony Roberts (2 hrs.).

NOT LIKE US
SHO 8/15/95. (David Payne), Morgan Englund, Rainer Grant, Joanna Pacula, Peter Onorati (90 mins.).

NOT OF THIS WORLD
CBS 2/12/91. (Jon Daniel Hess), Lisa Hartman, A. Martinez, Pat Hingle, Luke Edwards (2 hrs.).

NOT OUR SON
CBS 1/31/95. (Michael Rhodes), Neil Patrick Harris, Gerald McRaney, Tom Verica, Cindy Pickett, Ari Myers (2 hrs.).

NOTHING BUT THE TRUTH
CBS 5/23/96. (Michael Switzer), Patricia Wettig, Ken Olin, Bradley Whitford, Harry Lennix, Katherine LaNasa.

NOTORIOUS
LIF 1/28/92. (Colin Bucksey), John Shea, Jenny Robertson, Jean-Pierre Cassel, Marisa Berenson (2 hrs.).

NOWHERE TO HIDE
ABC 10/9/94. (Bobby Roth), Rosanna Arquette, Scott Bakula, Max Pomeranc, Clifton Powell, Robert Wisden, Jenny Gago.

NURSES ON THE LINE: THE CRASH OF FLIGHT 7
CBS 11/22/93. (Larry Shaw), Lindsay Wagner, Robert Loggia, David Clennon (2 hrs.).

O

THE O.J. SIMPSON STORY
FOX 1/31/95. (Alan Smithee), Bobby Hosea, Jessica Tuck, David Roberson, James Handy, Bruce Weitz (2 hrs.).

O PIONEERS!
CBS 2/2/92. (Glenn Jordan), Jessica Lange, David Strathairn, Tom Aldredge, Reed Diamond (2 hrs.).

OBSESSED
ABC 9/27/92. (Jonathan Sanger), Shannen Doherty, William Devane, Clare Carey (2 hrs.).

THE ODD COUPLE: TOGETHER AGAIN
CBS 9/24/93. (Robert Klane), Tony Randall, Jack Klugman, Barbara Barrie (2 hrs.).

THE ODYSSEY
NBC. 5/22 & 5/23/97. (Andrei Konchalovsky), Armand Assante, Greta Scacchi, Geraldine Chaplin, Jeroen Krabbe, Isabella Rosellini, Eric Roberts, Bernadette Peters, Vanessa Williams.

THE OLD CURIOSITY SHOP
DIS 3/19/95. (Kevin Connor), Peter Ustinov, James Fox, Tom Courtenay, Julia McKenzie, Sally Walsh, Adam Blackwood.

OLD MAN
CBS. 2/13/97. (John Kent Harrison), Jeanne Tripplehorn, Arliss Howard, Jerry Leggio.

THE OLD MAN AND THE SEA
NBC 3/25/90. (Jud Taylor), Anthony Quinn, Gary Cole, Patricia Clarkson (2 hrs.).

OLDEST LIVING CONFEDERATE WIDOW TELLS ALL
CBS 5/1 & 5/3/94. (Ken Cameron), Diane Lane, Donald Sutherland, Cicely Tyson, Anne Bancroft, Blythe Danner (4 hrs.).

OMEN IV: THE AWAKENING
FOX 5/20/91. (Jorge Montesi, Dominique Othenin), Faye Grant, Michael Woods, Michael Lerner (2 hrs.).

ON PROMISED LAND
DIS 4/17/94. (Joan Tewksbury), Carl Lumbly, Joan Plowright, Norman D. Golden II, Judith Ivey (2 hrs.).

ON SEVENTH AVENUE
NBC 6/10/96. Wendy Makkena, Stephen Collins, Damian Chapa, Gene Saks, Alan Rosenberg, Liz Coke, Lara Harris.

ON THE EDGE OF INNOCENCE
NBC. 4/20/97. (Peter Werner), Kellie Martin, Jimmy Marsden, Karen Young, Lisa Jakub, Jamie Kennedy, Vince Vieluf.

ON THIN ICE: THE TAI BABILONIA STORY
NBC 11/5/90. (Zale Dalen), Rachel Crawford, Charlie Stratton, Denise Nicholas (2 hrs.).

ONE AGAINST THE WIND
CBS 12/1/91. (Larry Elikann), Judy Davis, Sam Neill, Denholm Elliott, Christien Anholt (2 hrs.).

ONE CHRISTMAS
NBC 12/19/94. (Tony Bill), Katharine Hepburn, Henry Winkler, Swoosie Kurtz, T.J. Lowther, Tonea Stewart (2 hrs.).

ONE MAN'S WAR
HBO 4/20/91. (Sergio Toledo), Anthony Hopkins, Norma Aleandro, Fernanda Torres (90 mins.).

ONE MORE MOUNTAIN
ABC 3/6/94. (Dick Lowry), Meredith Baxter, Chris Cooper, Larry Drake (2 hrs.).

ONE OF HER OWN
ABC 5/16/94. (Armand Mastroianni), Lori Loughlin, Martin Sheen, Greg Evigan (2 hrs.).

ONE SPECIAL VICTORY
NBC 12/8/91. (Stuart Cooper), John Larroquette, Kathy Baker, Christine Estabrook, Dirk Blocker (2 hrs.).

ONE WOMAN'S COURAGE
NBC 2/28/94. (Charles Robert Carner), Patty Duke, James Farentino, Keith Szarabajka, Dennis Farina (2 hrs.).

ONLY ONE SURVIVED
CBS 10/27/90. (Folco Quilici), Perry King, Michael Beck, Fabio Testi (2 hrs.).

THE ONLY WAY OUT
ABC 12/19/93. (Ron Hardy), John Ritter, Henry Winkler, Stephanie Faracy, Julianne Phillips (2 hrs.).

THE OPERATION
CBS 1/21/90. (Thomas J. Wright), Joe Penny, Lisa Hartman, Jason Beghe, Kathleen Quinlan (2 hrs.).

OPPOSITES ATTRACT
NBC 10/17/90. (Noel Nosseck), Barbara Eden, John Forsythe, Ilene Graff, Conchata Ferrell (2 hrs.).

ORANGES ARE NOT THE ONLY FRUIT
A&E 11/29/90. (Beeban Kidron), Geraldine McEwan, Kenneth Cranham, Charlotte Coleman (2 hrs.).

ORDEAL IN THE ARCTIC
ABC 2/15/93. (Mark Sobel), Richard Chamberlain, Melanie Mayron, Catherine Mary Stewart (2 hrs.).

ORIGINAL SINS
CBS 4/12/95. (Jan Egelson), Mark Harmon, Julianne Phillips, Sarah Trigger, David Clennon, Ron Perlman, Gus Johnson.

ORPHEUS DESCENDING
TNT 9/24/90. (Sir Peter Hall), Vanessa Redgrave, Kevin Anderson, Anne Twomey (2-1/2 hrs.).

THE OTHER MOTHER
NBC 4/17/95. (Bethany Rooney), Frances Fisher, Deborah May, Corrie Clark, Cameron Bancroft, Gwynth Walsh (2 hrs.).

THE OTHER WOMAN
CBS 3/26/95. (Gabrielle Beaumont), Jill Eikenberry, Laura Leighton, Rosemary Forsyth, Monica Parker (2 hrs.).

OTHER WOMEN'S CHILDREN
LIF 10/24/93. (Anne Wheeler), Melanie Mayron, Geraint Wyn Davies, Eric Pospisil (2 hrs.).

OUR SONS
ABC 5/19/91. (John Erman), Julie Andrews, Ann-Margret, Zeljko Ivanek, Hugh Grant (2 hrs.).

OUR SON, THE MATCHMAKER
CBS 5/8/96. (Lorraine Senna) Ann Jillian, Ellen Burstyn, Drew Ebersole, David Andrews, Linda Larkin.

OUT OF ANNIE'S PAST
USA 3/12/95. (Stuart Cooper), Catherine Mary Stewart, Scott Valentine, Dennis Farina, Carsten Norgaard, Ray Oriel (2 hrs.).

OUT OF DARKNESS
ABC 1/16/94. (Larry Elikann), Diana Ross, Ann Weldon, Rhonda Stubbins White (2 hrs.).

OUT THERE
SHO 11/19/95. (Sam Irvin) Bill Campbell, Wendy Schaal, Rod Steiger, Jill St. John, Bill Cobbs, Leslie Bevis, Paul Dooley.

OVEREXPOSED
ABC 10/11/92. (Robert Markowitz), Marcy Walker, Dan Lauria, Terence Knox (2 hrs.).

OVERKILL: THE AILEEN WUORNOS STORY
CBS 11/17/92. (Peter Levin), Jean Smart, Park Overall, Ernie Lively, Brion James (2 hrs.).

P

PAIR OF ACES
1/14/90. (Aaron Lipstadt), Willie Nelson, Kris Kristofferson, Helen Shaver, Rip Torn (2 hrs.).

PANDORA'S CLOCK
NBC. 11/10 & 11/11/96. (Eric Laneuville), Richard Dean Anderson, Daphne Zuniga, Jane Leeves, Richard Lawson.

PARALLEL LIVES
SHO 8/14/94. (Linda Yellen), James Belushi, Jill Eikenberry, Liza Minnelli, Ben Gazzara, JoBeth Williams (105 mins.).

PARIS TROUT
SHO 4/20/91. (Stephen Gyllenhaal), Dennis Hopper, Barbara Hershey, Ed Harris (100 mins.).

PARKER KANE
NBC 8/5/90. (Steve Perry), Jeff Fahey, Marisa Tomei, Drew Snyder, Amanda Pays (2 hrs.).

A PART OF THE FAMILY
LIF 7/6/94. (David Madden), Robert Carradine, Elizabeth Arlen, Ronny Cox (2 hrs.).

PARTNERS IN LOVE
FAM 11/27/92. (Eugene Levy), Eugene Levy, Linda Kash, John James (2 hrs.).

**A PASSION FOR JUSTICE:
THE HAZEL BRANNON SMITH STORY**
ABC 4/17/94. (James Keach), Jane Seymour, D.W. Moffett, Richard Kiley, Lou Walker (2 hrs.).

PASSPORT TO MURDER
NBC 3/7/93. (David Hemmings), Connie Sellecca, Ed Marinaro, Pavel Douglas (2 hrs.).

PAST TENSE
SHO 6/12/94. (Graeme Clifford), Scott Glenn, Anthony LaPaglia, Lara Flynn Boyle (2 hrs.).

PAST THE BLEACHERS
ABC 6/22/95. (Michael Switzer), Richard Dean Anderson, Barnard Hughes, Glynnis O'Connor, Ken Jenkins.

PATH TO PARADISE
HBO. 6/21/97. Peter Gallagher, Art Mallk, Ned Eisenberg, Marcia Gay Harden, Paul Guilfoyle, Andreas Katsulas.

PAYBACK
ABC. 2/14/97. (Ken Cameron), Mary Tyler Moore, Russ Fast, Fredric Lane, Edward Asner, Beverly Sanders, Denis Arndt.

PAYOFF
SHO 6/22/91. (Stuart Cooper), Keith Carradine, Harry Dean Stanton, Kim Greist (2 hrs.).

THE PEACOCK SPRING
PBS 5/19 & 5/26/96. (Christopher Morahan) Peter Egan, Hattie Morahan, Laura Barneby, Jennifer Hall, Naveen Andrews.

PERCY & THUNDER
TNT 9/7/93. (Ivan Dixon), James Earl Jones, Courtney B. Vance, Gloria Reuben, Gloria Foster (2 hrs.).

PERFECT BODY
NBC. 9/8/97. (Douglas Barr), Amy Jo Johnson, Brett Cullen, Wendie Malick, Ray Baker.

THE PERFECT BRIDE
USA 6/26/91. (Terrence O'Hara), Sammi Davis, Kelly Preston, Linden Ashby (2 hrs.).

PERFECT CRIME
USA. 7/9/97. Nick Seracy, Andrew Masset, Chuck Kinlaw, Mitzi Kapture, Jasmine Guy, Scott Allan Cambell,

THE PERFECT DAUGHTER
USA 8/21/96. (Harry Longstreet) Bess Armstrong, Mark Joy.

PERFECT FAMILY
USA 11/11/92. (E.W. Swackhamer), Bruce Boxleitner, Jennifer O'Neill, Joanna Cassidy (2 hrs.).

PERFECT HARMONY
DIS 3/31/91. (Will MacKenzie), Peter Scolari, Darren McGavin, Catherine Mary Stewart (2 hrs.).

THE PERFECT TRIBUTE
ABC 4/21/91. (Jack Bender), Jason Robards, Lukas Haas, Campbell Scott, Katherine Helmond (2 hrs.).

PERRY MASON: THE CASE OF THE DEFIANT DAUGHTER
NBC 9/30/90. (Christian I. Nyby II), Raymond Burr, Robert Culp, Robert Vaughn, Jere Burns (2 hrs.).

PERRY MASON:
THE CASE OF THE DESPERATE DECEPTION
NBC 3/11/90. (Christian I. Nyby II), Raymond Burr, Ian Bannen, Yvette Mimieux, Teresa Wright (2 hrs.).

PERRY MASON: THE CASE OF THE FATAL FASHION
NBC 9/24/91. (Christian I. Nyby II), Raymond Burr, Valerie Harper, Diana Muldaur, Scott Baio (2 hrs.).

PERRY MASON: THE CASE OF THE FATAL FRAMING
NBC 3/1/92. (Christian I. Nyby II), Raymond Burr, Barbara Hale, David Soul, John Rhys-Davies (2 hrs.).

PERRY MASON: THE CASE OF THE GLASS COFFIN
NBC 5/14/91. (Christian I. Nyby II), Raymond Burr, William R. Moses, Peter Scolari (2 hrs.).

PERRY MASON:
THE CASE OF THE HEARTBROKEN BRIDE
NBC 10/30/92. (Christian I. Nyby II), Raymond Burr, Ronny Cox, Linda Blair, Paul Dooley (2 hrs.).

PERRY MASON: THE CASE OF THE KILLER KISS
NBC 11/29/93. (Christian I. Nyby II), Raymond Burr, Barbara Hale, William R. Moses, Stuart Damon (2 hrs.).

PERRY MASON:
THE CASE OF THE MALIGNED MOBSTER
NBC 2/11/91. (Ron Satlof), Raymond Burr, Barbara Hale, Paul Anka, Howard McGillin (2 hrs.).

PERRY MASON: THE CASE OF THE MURDERED MADAM
NBC 10/4/87. (Ron Satlof), Raymond Burr, Daphne Ashbrook, Anthony Geary, Ann Jillian (2 hrs.).

PERRY MASON: THE CASE OF THE POISONED PEN
NBC 1/21/90. (Christian I. Nyby II), Raymond Burr, David Warner, William R. Moses, Cindy Williams (2 hrs.).

PERRY MASON: THE CASE OF THE RECKLESS ROMEO
NBC 5/5/92. (Christian I. Nyby II), Raymond Burr, Tracy Nelson, Geraldo Rivera, William R. Moses (2 hrs.).

PERRY MASON:
THE CASE OF THE RUTHLESS REPORTER
NBC 1/6/91. (Christian I. Nyby II), Raymond Burr, John James, Jerry Orbach, Mary Page Keller (2 hrs.).

PERRY MASON: THE CASE OF THE SILENCED SINGER
NBC 5/20/90. (Ron Satlof), Raymond Burr, Tim Reid, Vanessa Williams, Nia Peeples (2 hrs.).

PERRY MASON:
THE CASE OF THE SKIN-DEEP SCANDAL
NBC 2/19/93. (Christian I. Nyby II), Raymond Burr, Morgan Fairchild, Polly Bergen, David Warner (2 hrs.).

PERRY MASON MYSTERY, A:
THE CASE OF THE GRIMACING GOVERNOR
NBC 11/9/94. (Max Tash), Hal Holbrook, Barbara Hale, William R. Moses, Deborah Raffin, James Brolin (2 hrs.).

PERRY MASON MYSTERY, A:
THE CASE OF THE JEALOUS JOKESTER
NBC 4/10/95. (Vince McEveety), Hal Holbrook, Dyan Cannon, Tony Roberts, Victoria Jackson, David Rasche, Tina Yothers.

PERRY MASON MYSTERY, A:
THE CASE OF THE LETHAL LIFESTYLE
NBC 5/10/94. (Helaine Head), Hal Holbrook, Barbara Hale, William R. Moses, Dixie Carter (2 hrs.).

PERRY MASON MYSTERY, A:
THE CASE OF THE WICKED WIVES
NBC 12/17/93. (Christian I. Nyby II), Paul Sorvino, Barbara Hale, Maud Adams, Eric Braeden (2 hrs.).

PERSONALS
USA 2/28/90. (Steven H. Stern), Stephanie Zimbalist, Jennifer O'Neill, Robin Thomas (2 hrs.).

PETER BENCHLEY'S "THE BEAST"
NBC 4/28/96. (Jeff Bleckner), William Petersen, Karen Sillas, Charles Martin Smith, Ronald Guttman, Missy Crider.

THE PHANTOM OF THE OPERA
NBC 3/18 & 3/19/90. (Tony Richardson), Burt Lancaster, Charles Dance, Teri Polo, Adam Storke (4 hrs.).

PHAROAH'S ARMY
PBS 9/4/96. Chris Cooper, Kris Kristofferson.

THE PIANO LESSON
CBS 2/5/95. (Lloyd Richards), Charles Dutton, Alfre Woodard, Carl Gordon, Courtney B. Vance, Lou Myers, Tommy Hollis.

PIE IN THE SKY
HBO 8/23 & 8/25/96. (Bryan Gordon) Anne Heche, Josh Charles.

PINK LIGHTNING
FOX 7/8/91. (Carol Monpere), Sarah Buxton, Martha Byrne, Jennifer Blanc (2 hrs.).

PIRATE TALES
TBS. 8/24 & 8/31/97. (Kevin McCarey), Roger Daltrey, Richard Schumann, Antoinette Brennan, Raphael Alvarado, .

A PLACE FOR ANNIE
ABC 5/1/94. (John Gray), Sissy Spacek, Mary-Louise Parker, S. Epatha Merkerson, Jack Noseworthy (2 hrs.).

A PLACE TO BE LOVED
CBS 4/4/93. (Sandy Smolan), Tom Guiry, Richard Crenna, Rhea Perlman, Linda Kelsey (2 hrs.).

THE PLOT TO KILL HITLER
CBS 1/30/90. (Lawrence Schiller), Brad Davis, Madolyn Smith, Ian Richardson (2 hrs.).

PLYMOUTH
ABC 5/26/91. (Lee David Zlotoff), Cindy Pickett, Dale Midkiff, Richard Hamilton (2 hrs.).

POISONED BY LOVE: THE KERN COUNTY MURDERS
CBS 2/2/93. (Larry Peerce), Harry Hamlin, Helen Shaver, K.T. Oslin, Ed Lauter (2 hrs.).

THE POLITICIAN'S WIFE
PBS 1/7 & 1/14/96. (Graham Theakston).

POLLY-COMIN' HOME
NBC 11/18/90. (Debbie Allen), Keshia Knight Pulliam, Phylicia Rashad, Anthony Newley (2 hrs.).

POLTERGEIST: THE LEGACY
SHO 4/21/96. (Stuart Gillard) Derek de Lint, Helen Shaver, Robbi Chong, Martin Cummins, Patrick Fitzgerald.

THE PORTRAIT
TNT 2/13/93. (Arthur Penn), Gregory Peck, Lauren Bacall, Cecilia Peck, Paul McCrane (2 hrs.).

POSING: INSPIRED BY THREE REAL STORIES
CBS 11/5/91. (Stephen Stafford), Lynda Carter, Michele Greene, Amanda Peterson, Josie Bissett (2 hrs.).

THE POSITIVELY TRUE ADVENTURES OF THE ALLEGED TEXAS CHEERLEADER-MURDERING MOM
HBO 4/10/93. (Michael Ritchie), Holly Hunter, Beau Bridges, Swoosie Kurtz, Matt Frewer (2 hrs.).

THE POSSESSION OF MICHAEL D.
FOX 5/2/95. (Michael Kennedy), Stephen Lang, Sheila McCarthy, Michael Riley, Roger Rees, Phylicia Rashad (2 hrs.).

PRAYING MANTIS
USA 8/11/93. (James Keach), Jane Seymour, Barry Bostwick, Frances Fisher (2 hrs.).

PRECIOUS VICTIMS
CBS 9/28/93. (Peter Levin), Park Overall, Robby Benson, Richard Thomas, Frederic Forrest (2 hrs.).

THE PRESIDENT'S CHILD
CBS 10/27/92. (Sam Pillsbury), Donna Mills, William Devane, James Read (2 hrs.).

PREY OF THE CHAMELEON
SHO 2/7/92. (Fleming B. Fuller), Daphne Zuniga, James Wilder, Alexandra Paul, Don Harvey (90 mins.).

THE PRICE OF HEAVEN
CBS. 8/17/97. (Peter Bogdanovich), Grant Show, Cicely Tyson, Lori Loughlin, George Wendt, Cari Shayne, Allan Gurganus.

THE PRICE OF LOVE
FOX 11/28/95. (David Burton Morris) Peter Facinelli, Jay R. Ferguson, Laurel Holloman, Steven Martini, Alexis Cruz.

THE PRICE SHE PAID
CBS 3/31/92. (Fred Walton), Loni Anderson, Anthony John Denison, Stephen Meadows, Candy Clark (2 hrs.).

PRIDE AND EXTREME PREJUDICE
USA 1/17/90. (Ian Sharp), Brian Dennehy, Alan Howard, Lisa Eichhorn (2 hrs.).

PRIDE AND PREJUDICE
A&E 1/14 -1/16/96. (Simon Langton) Colin Firth, Jennifer Ehle, Alison Steadman, Julia Sawalha, Crispin Bonham-Carter.

PRIME SUSPECT: INNER CIRCLES
PBS 2/11/96. (Sarah Pia Anderson), Helen Mirren, Jill Baker, James Laurenson, Helene Kvale, Anthony Bate, Kelly Reilly.

PRIME SUSPECT: THE SCENT OF DARKNESS
PBS 5/5/96. Hellen Mirren, Tim Woodward, Stuart Wilson.

PRINCESS IN LOVE
CBS 5/15/96. (David Greene), Julie Cox, Christopher Bowen, Julia St. John.

PRISON OF SECRETS
LIF. 3/16/97. (Fred Gerber), Stephanie Zimbalist, Dan Lauria, Finola Hughes, Gary Frank, Rusty Schwimmer.

PRISON STORIES: WOMEN ON THE INSIDE
HBO 10/15/91. (Penelope Spheeris, Donna Deitch, Joan Micklin Silver), Rae Down Chong, Annabella Sciorra, Lolita Davidovich.

PRISONER OF HONOR
HBO 11/2/91. (Ken Russell), Richard Dreyfuss, Oliver Reed, Peter Firth, Jeremy Kemp (2 hrs.).

A PRIVATE MATTER
HBO 6/20/92. (Joan Micklin Silver), Sissy Spacek, Aidan Quinn, Estelle Parsons, Sheila McCarthy (90 mins.).

PROBABLE CAUSE
SHO 11/20/94. (Paul Ziller), Michael Ironside, Kate Vernon, James Downing, David Sivertsen, David McNally (95 mins.).

PROBLEM CHILD 3: JUNIOR IN LOVE
NBC 5/13/95. (Greg Beeman), William Katt, Jack Warden, Justin Chapman, Jennifer Ogletree, Gilbert Gottfried (2 hrs.).

PROJECT: ALF
ABC 96. (Dick Lowry) Martin Sheen, Jensen Daggett, William O'Leary, Paul Fusco, John Schuck.

A PROMISE KEPT: THE OKSANA BAIUL STORY
CBS 11/13/94. (Charles Jarrott), Miguel Ferrer, Monica Keena, Sonja Lanzener, Oksana Baiul, Susanna Thompson (2 hrs.).

A PROMISE TO CAROLYN
CBS 1/16/96. (Jerry London) Delta Burke, Swoosie Kurtz, Shirely Knight, Grace Zabriskie, Casey Biggs.

A PROMISE TO KEEP
NBC 10/1/90. (Rod Holcomb), Dana Delany, William Russ, Adam Arkin, Frances Fisher (2 hrs.).

PRONTO
SHO. 9/5/97.(Jim McBride), Peter Falk, Glenne Headly, Walter Olkewicz, Sergio Castellito, James LeGros.

PROPHET OF EVIL: THE ERVIL LEBARON STORY
CBS 5/4/93. (Jud Taylor), Brian Dennehy, William Devane, Tracey Needham, Danny Cooksey (2 hrs.).

THE PROSECUTORS
NBC. 12/2/96. (Lynda La Plante), Stockard Channing, Michelle Forbes, Judy Reyes.

PSYCHIC
USA 5/20/92. (George Mihalka), Zach Galligan, Catherine Mary Stewart, Michael Nouri, Albert Schultz (2 hrs.).

PSYCHO IV: THE BEGINNING
SHO 11/10/90. (Mick Garris), Anthony Perkins, Henry Thomas, Olivia Hussey (96 mins.).

QUEEN
CBS 2/14, 2/16 & 2/18/93. (John Erman), Ann-Margret, Jasmine Guy, Danny Glover, Madge Sinclair, Martin Sheen (6 hrs.).

QUICKSAND: NO ESCAPE
USA 3/4/92. (Michael Pressman), Donald Sutherland, Tim Matheson, Jay Acovone, Timothy Carhart (2 hrs.).

QUICKSILVER HIGHWAY
FOX. 5/13/97. (Mick Garris), Christopher Lloyd, Matt Frewer, Raphael Sbarge, Missy Crider, Silas Weir Mitchell, Bill Nunn.

QUIET KILLER
CBS 3/24/92. (Sheldon Larry), Kate Jackson, Howard Hesseman, Jeffrey Nordling, Chip Zien (2 hrs.).

A QUIET LITTLE NEIGHBORHOOD, A PERFECT LITTLE MURDER
NBC 10/14/90. (Anson Williams), Teri Garr, Robert Urich, Susan Ruttan, Tom Poston (2 hrs.).

RACE AGAINST TIME: THE SEARCH FOR SARAH
CBS 3/19/96. (Fred Gerber) Richard Crenna, Patty Duke, Katy Boyer, Jon Gries.

RACE TO FREEDOM: THE UNDERGROUND RAILROAD
FAM 2/19/94. (Don McBrearty), Janet Bailey, Courtney Vance, Dawn Lewis, Tim Reid (2 hrs.).

RADIANT CITY
ABC 3/31/96. (Robert Allan Ackerman), Kirstie Alley, Clancy Brown, Gil Bellows, Laraine Newman, Adam Lamberg.

RADIO INSIDE
SHO 10/21/94. (Jeffrey Bell), Elisabeth Shue, William McNamara, Dylan Walsh (2 hrs.).

THE RAILWAY STATION MAN
TNT 10/18/92. (Michael Whyte), Donald Sutherland, Julie Christie, John Lynch (2 hrs.).

RAINBOW DRIVE
SHO 9/8/90. (Bobby Roth), Peter Weller, Sela Ward, Henry Sanders, David Caruso (2 hrs.).

THE RANGER, THE COOK AND A HOLE IN THE SKY
ABC 6/15/95. (John Kent Harrison), Sam Elliott, Jerry O'Connell, Ricky Jay (2 hrs.).

THE RAPE OF DR. WILLIS
CBS 11/3/91. (Lou Antonio), Jaclyn Smith, Robin Thomas, Lisa Jakub, Holland Taylor (2 hrs.).

RASPUTIN
HBO 3/23/96. (Uli Edel), Alan Rickman, Greta Scacchi, Ian McKellen, David Warner, John Wood, James Frain, Diana Quick.

RATTLED
USA 2/14/96. (Tony Randel), William Katt, Shanna Reed.

RAY ALEXANDER: A MENU FOR MURDER
NBC 3/20/95. (Gary Nelson), Louis Gossett Jr., James Coburn, Tracy Nelson, Tony Colitti, Ossie Davis, Beverly Johnson.

RAY ALEXANDER: A TASTE FOR JUSTICE
NBC 5/13/94. (Gary Nelson), Louis Gossett Jr., James Coburn, Ossie Davis, Tracy Nelson, Ray Charles (2 hrs.).

REASON FOR LIVING: THE JILL IRELAND STORY
NBC 5/20/91. (Michael Rhodes), Jill Clayburgh, Lance Henriksen, Elizabeth Ashley (2 hrs.).

REASONS OF THE HEART
USA 10/2/96. (Rick Jacobson), Terry Farrell, Jim Davidson, Mimi Kennedy, Leon Russom, Gloria Dorson.

REBOUND: THE LEGEND OF EARL "THE GOAT" MANIGULT
HBO. 11/96. Don Cheadle, Eriq LaSalle, Loretta Devine, Forest Whitaker, Michael Beach, Monica Calhoun, James Earl Jones.

RED SHOE DIARIES
SHO 5/16/92. (Zalman King), David Duchovny, Brigitte Bako, Billy Wirth, Brenda Vaccaro (90 mins.).

RED WIND
USA 5/15/91. (Alan Metzger), Lisa Hartman, Philip Casnoff, Christopher McDonald (2 hrs.).

REDWOOD CURTAIN
ABC 4/23/95. (John Korty), Jeff Daniels, Lea Salonga, John Lithgow, Catherine Hicks, Debra Monk, Vilma Silva (2 hrs.).

RELENTLESS: MIND OF A KILLER
NBC 1/11/93. (John Patterson), Tim Matheson, Alberta Watson, Giancarlo Esposito (2 hrs.).

REMEMBER ME
CBS 11/19/95. Kelly McGillis, Cotter Smith.

THE RETURN OF ELIOT NESS
NBC 11/10/91. (James Contner), Robert Stack, Jack Coleman, Lisa Hartman, Philip Bosco (2 hrs.).

THE RETURN OF HUNTER: EVERYONE WALKS IN L.A.
NBC 4/30/95. (Bradford May), Fred Dryer, Barry Bostwick, Lisa Eilbacher, John C. McGinley, Beth Toussaint, Miguel Ferrer.

THE RETURN OF IRONSIDE
NBC 5/4/93. (Gary Nelson), Raymond Burr, Don Galloway, Perrey Reeves, Cliff Gorman (2 hrs.).

THE RETURN OF THE BORROWERS
TNT 4/6/96. (John Henderson), Ian Holm, Penelope Wilton, Rebecca Callard, Sian Phillips, Paul Cross, Ben Chaplin.

THE RETURN OF THE MUSKETEERS
USA 4/3/91. (Richard Lester), Oliver Reed, Michael York, C. Thomas Howell (2 hrs.).

THE RETURN OF THE NATIVE
CBS 12/4/94. (Jack Gold), Catherine Zeta Jones, Ray Stevenson, Clive Owen, Joan Plowright, Steven Mackintosh.

RETURN TO GREEN ACRES
CBS 5/18/90. (William Asher), Eddie Albert, Eva Gabor, Frank Cady, Henry Gibson (2 hrs.).

RETURN TO LONESOME DOVE
CBS 11/14, 11/16 & 11/18/93. (Mike Robe), Jon Voight, Barbara Hershey, Rick Schroder, Louis Gossett Jr., Oliver Reed (7 hrs.).

REUNION
CBS 12/11/94. (Lee Grant), Marlo Thomas, Peter Strauss, Frances Sternhagen, Leelee Sobiesky, Courtney Chase (2 hrs.).

REVEALING EVIDENCE
NBC 6/3/90. (Michael Switzer), Stanley Tucci, Mary Page Keller, Finn Carter (2 hrs.).

REVENGE OF THE NERDS III: THE NEXT GENERATION
FOX 7/13/92. (Roland Mesa), Robert Carradine, Curtis Armstrong, Ted McGinley, Morton Downey, Jr. (2 hrs.).

REVENGE OF THE NERDS IV: NERDS IN LOVE
FOX 5/9/94. (Steve Zacharias), Robert Carradine, Curtis Armstrong, Julia Montgomery (2 hrs.).

REVENGE ON THE HIGHWAY
NBC 12/6/92. (Craig R. Baxley), Stacy Keach, Tom Bower, Lisa Banes, Sandahl Bergman (2 hrs.).

REVOLVER
NBC 4/19/92. (Gary Nelson), Robert Urich, Dakin Matthews, Steve Williams, David Ryall (2 hrs.).

RICH MEN, SINGLE WOMEN
ABC 1/29/90. (Elliot Silverstein), Suzanne Somers, Heather Locklear, Joel Higgins, Larry Wilcox (2 hrs.).

RIDE WITH THE WIND
ABC 4/18/94. (Bobby Roth), Craig T. Nelson, Helen Shaver, Bradley Pierce, Max Gail (2 hrs.).

RIDERS OF THE PURPLE SAGE
TNT 1/21/96. (Charles Haid), Ed Harris, Amy Madigan, Henry Thomas, Robin Tunney, Norbert Weisser, G.S. Spradlin.

THE RIGHT CONNECTIONS
SHO. 8/15/97. (Chuck Vinson), M.C. Hammer, Belinda Metz, Meshach Taylor, Millissa Joan Hart.

THE RIGHT TO REMAIN SILENT
SHO 1/7/96. (Hubert de la Bouillerie), Lea Thompson, Robert Loggia, Larry Joshua, Joyce Sylvester, Mary Pat Gleason.

RING OF SCORPIO
USA 4/24 & 4/25/91. (Ian Barry), Catherine Oxenberg, Jack Scalia, Caroline Goodall (4 hrs.).

RIO SHANNON
ABC 8/14/93. (Mimi Leder), Blair Brown, Patrick Van Horn, Michael DeLuise, Jay O. Snaders (2 hrs.).

RIOT
SHO. 4/27/97. (Richard Di Lello), Mako, Luke Perry, Mario Van Peebles. Melvin Van Peebles, Cicely Tyson, Dante Basco.

RISE AND WALK: THE DENNIS BYRD STORY
FOX 2/28/94. (Michael Dinner), Peter Berg, Kathy Morris, Johann Carlo (2 hrs.).

RISING SON
TNT 7/23/90. (John David), Brian Dennehy, Matt Damon, Piper Laurie (2 hrs.).

RIVER OF RAGE: THE TAKING OF MAGGIE KEENE
CBS 10/3/93. (Robert Iscove), Victoria Principal, Peter Onorati, Sean Murray (2 hrs.).

THE ROAD TO GALVESTON
(Michael Toshiyuki Uno). Cicely Tyson, Tess Harper, Piper Laurie, James McDaniel, Starletta DuPois, Penny Johnson.

ROADRACERS
SHO 7/22/94. (Robert Rodriguez), David Arquette, Salma Hayek, John Hawkes (90 mins.).

ROBIN COOK'S "HARMFUL INTENT"
CBS 12/14/93. (John Patterson), Tim Matheson, Emma Samms, Robert Pastorelli, Alex Rocco (2 hrs.).

ROBIN COOK'S INVASION
NBC. 5/4 & 5/5/97. (Armand Mastroianni), Luke Perry, Kim Cattrall, Rebecca Gayheart.

ROBIN COOK'S "MORTAL FEAR"
NBC 11/20/94. (Larry Shaw), Joanna Kerns, Gregory Harrison, Max Gail, Tobin Bell, Katherine LaNasa, Judith Chapman.

ROBIN COOK'S "TERMINAL"
NBC 2/12/96. (Larry Elikann).

ROBIN COOK'S "VIRUS"
NBC 5/8/95. (Armand Mastroianni), Nicollette Sheridan, William Devane, Stephen Caffrey, Kurt Fuller, William Atherton (2 hrs.).

ROBIN HOOD
FOX 5/13/91. (John Irvin), Patrick Bergin, Uma Thurman, Jurgen Prochnow, Edward Fox (2-1/2 hrs.).

ROCK HUDSON
ABC 1/8/90. (John Nicolella), Thomas Ian Griffith, William R. Moses, Diane Ladd (2 hrs.).

THE ROCKFORD FILES: A BLESSING IN DISGUISE
CBS 5/14/95. (Jeannot Swarcz), James Garner, Richard Romanus, Joe Santos, Renee O'Connor, Ahron Ipale (2 hrs.).

THE ROCKFORD FILES: CRIME & PUNISHMENT
CBS. 10/16/96. (David Chase), James Garner, Kathryn Harrold, Joe Santos, Bryan Cranston, Vladimir Skomarovsky.

THE ROCKFORD FILES: FRIENDS AND FOUL PLAY
CBS 4/25/96. James Garner, Wendy Phillips, James Luisi, David Proval, Joe Santos, Gretchen Corbett, Stuart Margolin.

THE ROCKFORD FILES: GODFATHER KNOWS BEST
NBC 2/18/96. (Tony Wharmby), James Garner, Damian Chapa, Joe Santos, Barbara Carrera, Stuart Margolin, Al Mancini.

THE ROCKFORD FILES: I STILL LOVE L.A.
CBS 11/27/94. (James Whitmore Jr.), James Garner, Stuart Margolin, Joe Santos, Joanna Cassidy, Geoffrey Nauffts (2 hrs.).

THE ROCKFORD FILES: IF THE FRAME FITS
CBS 1/14/96. James Garner, Dyan Cannon, Joe Santos, Stuart Margolin, Gretchen Corbett, James Luisi, Tom Atkins.

THE ROCKFORD FILES: PUNISHMENT AND CRIME
CBS 9/18/96. James Garner, Richard Kiley, Bryan Cranston.

RONNIE & JULIE
SHO. (Philip Spink), Teri Garr, Josh Jackson, Margo Finlay.

ROOMMATES
NBC 5/30/94. (Alan Metzger), Randy Quaid, Eric Stoltz, Charles Durning, Elizabeth Pena (2 hrs.).

THE ROSE AND THE JACKAL
TNT 4/16/90. (Jack Gold), Christopher Reeve, Madolyn Smith Osborne, Carrie Snodgress (2 hrs.).

ROSE HILL
CBS. 4/20/97. (Christopher Cain), Jennifer Garner, Jeffrey D. Sams, Zak Orth, Justin Chambers, Tristan Tait, Casey Siemaszko.

ROSEANNE: AN UNAUTHORIZED BIOGRAPHY
FOX 10/11/94. (Paul Schneider), Denny Dillon, David Graf, John Karlen, John Walcutt, Judith Scarpone (2 hrs.).

ROSEANNE AND TOM: BEHIND THE SCENES
NBC 10/31/94. (Richard Colla), Patrika Darbo, Stephen Lee, Jan Hoag, Nancy Youngblut, Robert Neches (2 hrs.).

ROSWELL
SHO 7/31/94. (Jeremy Kagan), Kyle MacLachlan, J.D. Daniels, Doug Wert, Kim Griest, Martin Sheen (105 mins.).

ROUGH RIDERS
TNT. 7/20 & 7/21/97. (John Milius), Tom Berenger, Sam Elliott, Gary Busey, Brad Johnson, Illeana Douglas, Christopher Noth.

ROYCE
SHO 4/3/94. (Rod Holcomb), Jim Belushi, Peter Boyle, Miguel Ferrer, Chelsea Field (100 mins.).

RUBY JEAN AND JOE
SHO 8/11/96. (Geoffrey Sax), Tom Selleck, Jobeth Williams.

RUBY RIDGE: AN AMERICAN TRAGEDY
CBS 5/19 & 5/21/96. (Roger Young) Laura Dern, Randy Quaid, Diane Ladd, Kirsten Dunst, Darren Burrows, G.W. Bailey.

RUGGED GOLD
12/10/95. (Michael Anderson), Jill Eikenberry, Art Hindle, Graham Greene, Ari Madger (2 hrs.).

RUN FOR THE DREAM: THE GAIL DEVERS STORY
SHO 6/16/96. (Neema Barnette) Charlayne Woodard, Louis Gossett, Jr., Robert Guillaume, Jeffrey Sams.

RUNAWAY CAR
FOX. 12/21/97. Judge Reinhold, Brian Hooks, Alec Murdock, Nina Siemaszko.

RUNAWAY DAUGHTERS
SHO 8/12/94. (Joe Dante), Julie Bowen, Holly Fields, Jenny Lewis, Paul Rudd (90 mins.).

RUNAWAY FATHER
CBS 4/19/92. (John Nicolella), Donna Mills, Jack Scalia, Chris Mulkey, Jenny Lewis (2 hrs.).

RUNNING AGAINST TIME
USA 11/21/90. (Bruce Seth Green), Robert Hays, Catherine Hicks, Sam Wanamaker (2 hrs.).

RUNNING DELILAH
ABC 8/29/94. (Richard Franklin), Kim Cattrall, Billy Zane, Yorgo Voyagis, Diana Rigg (2 hrs.).

RUNNING MATES
HBO 10/4/92. (Michael Lindsay-Hogg), Diane Keaton, Ed Harris, Ed Begley Jr., Ben Masters (90 mins.).

SALT WATER MOOSE
SHO 6/2/96. (Stuart Margolin), Timothy Dalton, Lolita Davidovich, Johnny Morina, Katharine Isobel.

SAMSON AND DELILAH
TNT. 12/8 & 12/11/96. (Nicholas Roeg), Eric Thal, Elizabeth Hurley, Dennis Hopper, Michael Gambon.

SARAH: PLAIN AND TALL
CBS 2/3/91. (Glenn Jordan), Glenn Close, Christopher Walken, Lexi Randall, Margaret Sophie Stein (2 hrs.).

SAVED BY THE BELL: HAWAIIAN STYLE
NBC 11/27/92. (Don Barnhart), Mark-Paul Gosselaar, Dustin Diamond, Tiffani-Amber Thiessen (2 hrs.).

SAVED BY THE BELL: WEDDING IN LAS VEGAS
NBC 10/7/94. (Jeff Melman), Mark-Paul Gosselaar, Tiffani-Amber Thiessen, Mario Lopez, Dustin Diamond.

SAVED BY THE LIGHT
FOX 12/12/95. Eric Roberts, Lynette Walden, Don McManus.

SAWBONES
SHO 7/25/95. (Catherine Cyran), Nicholas Sadler, Nina Siemaszko, Barbara Carrera, Don Harvey, Adam Baldwin.

SCAM
SHO 5/22/93. (John Flynn), Christopher Walken, Lorraine Bracco, Miguel Ferrer (2 hrs.).

SCARLETT
CBS 11/13, 11/15, 11/16 & 11/17/94. (John Erman), Joanne Whalley-Kilmer, Timothy Dalton, Barbara Barrie, Ann-Margret, Sean Bean (8 hrs.).

SCATTERED DREAMS: THE KATHRYN MESSENGER STORY
CBS 12/19/93. (Neema Barnette), Tyne Daly, Gerald McRaney, Alicia Silverstone (2 hrs.).

THE SEA WOLF
TNT 4/18/93. (Michael Anderson), Charles Bronson, Christopher Reeve, Catherine Mary Stewart, Marc Singer.

SEARCH AND RESCUE
NBC 3/27/94. (Paul Krasny), Robert Conrad, Dee Wallace Stone, Chad McQueen (2 hrs.).

SEARCH FOR GRACE
CBS 5/17/94. (Sam Pillsbury), Lisa Hartman Black, Ken Wahl, Richard Masur, Don Michael Paul (2 hrs.).

A SEASON IN PURGATORY
CBS 3/5 & 3/7/96. (David Greene), Patrick Dempsey, Sherilyn Fenn, Craig Sheffer, Edward Herrmann, Bonnie Bedelia.

A SEASON OF GIANTS
TNT 3/17 & 3/18/91. (Jerry London), F. Murray Abraham, Steven Berkoff, Juliette Caton (4 hrs.).

A SEASON OF HOPE
CBS 1/8/95. (Marcus Cole), JoBeth Williams, Stephen Lang, Stephen Meadows, Jeremy London, Erik Von Detten (2 hrs.).

SEASONS OF THE HEART
NBC 5/22/94. (Lee Grant), Carol Burnett, George Segal, Malcolm McDowell, Eric Lloyd (2 hrs.).

SECOND CHANCES
CBS 12/2/93. (Sharron Miller), Connie Sellecca, Matt Salinger, Ronny Cox (2 hrs.).

THE SECOND CIVIL WAR
HBO. 3/17/97. (Joe Dante), Beau Bridges, Joanna Cassidy, Phil Hartman, Dan Hedaya, James Earl Jones, James Coburn.

THE SECRET
CBS 4/19/92. (Karen Arthur), Kirk Douglas, Bruce Boxleitner, Brock Peters, Laura Harrington (2 hrs.).

THE SECRET
NBC. 1/6/97. (Robert Greenwald, Kimberly Rubin), Soleil Moon Frye, Tess Harper, Mark Krassenbaum, Erika Flores, Ari Meyers.

A SECRET BETWEEN FRIENDS
NBC 2/15/96. Katie Wright, Marley Shelton, Lynda Carter.

THE SECRET LIFE OF ARCHIE'S WIFE
CBS 10/28/90. (James Frawley), Michael Tucker, Jill Eikenberry, Ray Wise, Elaine Stritch (2 hrs.).

THE SECRET LIFE OF IAN FLEMING
TNT 3/5/90. (Ferdinand Fairfax), Jason Connery, Kristin Scott Thomas, Joss Ackland (2 hrs.).

THE SECRET PASSION OF ROBERT CLAYTON
USA 6/3/92. (E. W. Swackhamer), John Mahoney, Scott Valentine, Eve Gordon, Kevin Conroy (2 hrs.).

THE SECRET SHE CARRIED
NBC. 10/27/96. (Joel S. Rice), Peri Gilpin, Jere Burns, D.W. Moffett.

SECRET SINS OF THE FATHER
NBC 1/9/94. (Beau Bridges), Beau Bridges, Lloyd Bridges, Lee Purcell, Frederick Coffin (2 hrs.).

SECRET WEAPON
TNT 3/20/90. (Ian Sharp), Griffin Dunne, Karen Allen, Jeroen Krabbe, Brian Cox (2 hrs.).

THE SECRETARY
CBS 9/12/96. (Andrew Lane), Sheila Kelley, Mel Harris, Rod McCary.

SECRETS
ABC 5/25/95. (Jud Taylor), Veronica Hamel, Richard Kiley, Shae D'Lyn, Thomas Gibson, Reed Diamond.

SEDUCED AND BETRAYED
NBC 4/24/95. (Felix Alcala), Susan Lucci, David Charvet, Gabrielle Carteris, Zach Glucksman, Peter Donat (2 hrs.).

SEDUCED BY EVIL
USA 8/25/95. (Tony Wharmby), Suzanne Sommers, John Vargas, James B. Sikking, Julie Carmen (2 hrs.).

SEDUCED BY MADNESS, THE DIANE BORCHARDT STORY
NBC 2/26/96. (John Patterson) Ann-Margret, Peter Coyote.

SEDUCTION IN A SMALL TOWN
ABC. 2/13/97. Joely Fisher, Melissa Gilbert-Boxleitner, Brian McNamara, Dennis Weaver.

A SEDUCTION IN TRAVIS COUNTY
CBS 5/19/91. (George Kaczender), Lesley Ann Warren, Peter Coyote, Jean Smart (2 hrs.).

SEDUCTION: THREE TALES FROM THE INNER SANCTUM
ABC 4/5/92. (Michael Ray Rhodes), Victoria Principal, John Terry, John O'Hurley, W. Morgan Sheppard (2 hrs.).

SEE JANE RUN
ABC 1/8/95. (John Patterson), Joanna Kerns, John Shea, Katy Boyer, Tiffany Taubman, Lee Garlington, Blaire Baron (2 hrs.).

SEPARATE BUT EQUAL
ABC 4/7 & 4/8/91. (George Stevens, Jr.), Sidney Poitier, Burt Lancaster, Richard Kiley, Lynne Thigpen (4 hrs.).

SEPARATED BY MURDER
CBS 4/12/94. (Donald Wrye), Sharon Gless, Steve Railsback, Ed Bruce (2 hrs.).

**SERVING IN SILENCE:
THE MARGARETHE CAMMERMEYER STORY**
NBC 2/6/95. (Jeff Bleckner), Glenn Close, Judy Davis, Jan Rubes, Wendy Wakkena, Susan Barnes, Colleen Flynn (2 hrs.).

THE SET UP
SHO 7/23/95. (Strathford Hamilton), Billy Zane, Mia Sara, James Russo, James Coburn (90 mins.).

SEX, LOVE AND COLD HARD CASH
USA 5/12/93. (Harry S. Longstreet), JoBeth Williams, Anthony John Denison, Richard Sarafian (2 hrs.).

SEXUAL ADVANCES
ABC 5/10/92. (Donna Deitch), Stephanie Zimbalist, William Russ, Terry O'Quinn, Patrick James Clarke (2 hrs.).

SHADOW OF A DOUBT
CBS 4/28/91. (Karen Arthur), Mark Harmon, Margaret Welsh, Diane Ladd (2 hrs.).

SHADOW OF A DOUBT
NBC (Brian Dennehy), Brian Dennehy, Bonnie Bedelia, Fairuza Balk, Kevin Dunn.

SHADOW OF A STRANGER
NBC 12/7/92. (Richard Friedman), Emma Samms, Parker Stevenson, Michael Easton, Joan Chen (2 hrs.).

SHADOW OF OBSESSION
NBC 4/10/94. (Kevin Connor), Veronica Hamel, Jack Scalia, Kim Miyori (2 hrs.).

SHADOW-OPS
UPN 12/ 23/95. Adam Baldwin.

SHADOWHUNTER
SHO 2/10/93. (J.S. Cardone), Scott Glenn, Angela Alvarado, Robert Beltran (107 mins.).

THE SHAGGY DOG
ABC 11/12/94. (Dennis Dugan), Ed Begley Jr., Scott Weinger, Sharon Lawrence, Jon Polito, James Cromwell (2 hrs.).

SHAKE, RATTLE AND ROCK
SHO 8/26/94. (Allan Arkush), Renee Zellweger, Jenifer Lewis, Max Perlich, John Doe (90 mins.)

SHAME
LIF 8/18/92. (Dan Lerner), Amanda Donohoe, Dean Stockwell, Fairuza Balk, Shelley Owens (2 hrs.).

SHAME II: THE SECRET
LIF 6/7/95. (Dan Lerner), Amanda Donohoe, Kay Lenz, George Wendt, Geoffrey Blake, David Andrews, Talia Balsam (2 hrs.).

SHAMEFUL SECRETS
ABC 10/10/93. (David Carson), Joanna Kerns, Tim Matheson, LaTanya Richardson, Ashley Peldon (2 hrs.).

THE SHAMROCK CONSPIRACY
UPN 3/7/95. (James Frawley), Edward Woodward, Jeffrey Nordling, Elizabeth Hurley, Nigel Bennett, Kim Coates (2 hrs.).

SHATTERED DREAMS
ABC 5/13/90. (Robert Iscove), Lindsay Wagner, Michael Nouri, Georgeann Johnson (2 hrs.).

SHATTERED IMAGE
USA 1/21/94. (Fritz Kiersch), Jack Scalia, Bo Derek, John Savage, David McCallum (2 hrs.).

SHATTERED MIND
NBC 5/27/96. (Stephen Gyllenhaal) Heather Locklear, Brett Cullen, Kevin Dunn, Richard Herd.

SHATTERED TRUST: THE SHARI KARNEY STORY
NBC 9/27/93. (Bill Corcoran), Melissa Gilbert, Kate Nelligan, Ellen Burstyn (2 hrs.).

SHE LED TWO LIVES
NBC 11/27/94. (Bill Corcoran), Connie Sellecca, Perry King, A. Martinez, Patricia Clarkson, J. Smith Cameron (2 hrs.).

SHE SAID NO
NBC 9/23/90. (John Patterson), Veronica Hamel, Judd Hirsch, Lee Grant, Ray Baker (2 hrs.).

SHE SAYS SHE'S INNOCENT
NBC 10/28/91. (Charles Correll), Katey Sagal, Charlotte Ross, Jameson Parker, Alan Rachins (2 hrs.).

SHE STOOD ALONE
NBC 4/15/91. (Jack Gold), Mare Winningham, Ben Cross, Taurean Blacque (2 hrs.).

SHE STOOD ALONE: THE TAILHOOK SCANDAL
ABC 5/22/95. (Larry Shaw), Gail O'Grady, Hal Holbrook, Rip Torn, Robert Urich, Bess Armstrong, James Marshall (2 hrs.).

SHE WOKE UP
NBC 1/19/92. (Waris Hussein), Lindsay Wagner, David Dukes, Frances Sternhagen, Maureen Mueller (2 hrs.).

SHE WOKE UP PREGNANT
ABC 4/28/96. (James Contner) Michele Greene, William R. Moses, Joe Penny, Theresa Saldana, Lynda Carter.

SHERLOCK HOLMES RETURNS
CBS 9/12/93. (Kenneth Johnson), Anthony Higgins, Debrah Farentino, Mark Adair Rios (2 hrs.).

SHIMMER
PBS 4/10/95. (John Hanson), Marcus Klemp, Elijah Shepard, Tom Bower, Clem Tucker Jr., Jake Busey, Mary Beth Hurt (90 mins.).

SHOOT FIRST: A COP'S VENGEANCE
NBC 3/24/91. (Mel Damski), Alex McArthur, Dale Midkiff, Terry O'Quinn (2 hrs.).

SIDNEY SHELDON'S "MEMORIES OF MIDNIGHT"
SYND 11/25 & 26/91. (Gary Nelson), Jane Seymour, Omar Sharif, Tato Penghlis, Stephen Macht (4 hrs.).

SIDNEY SHELDON'S "NOTHING LASTS FOREVER"
CBS 11/5 & 11/7/95. (Jack Bender) Gail O'Grady, Brooke Shields, Chris Noth, Vanessa Williams, Lloyd Bridges.

SIDNEY SHELDON'S "THE SANDS OF TIME"
SYND 11/23 & 24/92. (Gary Nelson), Deborah Raffin, Michael Nouri, Ramy Zada, Amanda Plummer (4 hrs.).

SIGHT UNSEEN
WPIX 4/18/91. (Greydon Clark), Susan Blakely, Edward Albert, Wings Hauser (2 hrs.).

SIGNS AND WONDERS
PBS 5/12-5/13/96. (Maurice Phillips), James Earl Jones, Jodhi May, David Warner, Prunella Scales, Michael Maloney.

SILENCE OF ADULTERY
LIF 8/9/95. (Stephen Stern), Kate Jackson, Robert Desiderio, Art Hindle, Patricia Gage, Kristin Fairlie, Tori McPetrie (2 hrs.).

SILENT CRIES
NBC 3/8/93. (Anthony Page), Gena Rowlands, Annabeth Gish, Chloe Webb, Clyde Kusatsu (2 hrs.).

SILENT MOTIVE
LIF 10/16/92. (Lee Philips), Patricia Wettig, Mike Farrell, Edward Asner, Rick Springfield (2 hrs.).

SILENT WITNESS
A&E 8/20/96. Amanda Burton.

SILENT WITNESS: WHAT A CHILD SAW
USA 7/14/94. (Bruce Pittman), Mia Korf, Bill Nunn, Clark Johnson (2 hrs.).

SILHOUETTE
USA 11/28/90. (Carl Schenkel), Faye Dunaway, David Rasche, John Terry, Talisa Soto (2 hrs.).

SIMON & SIMON: IN TROUBLE AGAIN
CBS 2/23/95. (John McPherson), Gerald McRaney, Jameson Parker, Tim Reid, Jeannie Wilson (2 hrs.).

SIN AND REDEMPTION
CBS 3/15/94. (Neema Burnette), Richard Grieco, Cynthia Gibb, Ralph Waite, Cheryl Pollack (2 hrs.).

SINATRA
CBS 11/8 & 10/92. (James Sadwith), Philip Casnoff, Olympia Dukakis, Rod Steiger, Marcia Gay Harden (5 hrs.).

SINS OF SILENCE
CBS 2/2/96. (Sam Pillsbury), Holly Marie Combs, Lindsay Wagner, Brian Kerwin.

SINS OF THE MIND
USA. 6/11/97. (James Frawley), Jill Clayburgh, Mike Farrell, Missy Crider, Cyia Batten, Michael Mantell, Robert Pine.

SINS OF THE MOTHER
CBS 2/19/91. (John Patterson), Dale Midkiff, Heather Fairchild, Elizabeth Montgomery (2 hrs.).

THE SISTER-IN-LAW
USA 7/12/95. (Noel Nosseck), Shanna Reed, Kate Vernon, Craig Wasson, Kent Williams, Kevin McCarthy, Tonea Stewart (2 hrs.).

THE SITTER
FOX 6/10/91. (Rick Berger), Kim Myers, Brett Cullen, Susan Barnes, Kimberly Cullum (2 hrs.).

SIX CHARACTERS IN SEARCH OF AN AUTHOR
BRAVO 4/2/96. (Bill Bryden), Brian Cox, John Hurt, Tara Fitzgerald, Susan Fleetwood, Rachel Robertson.

SKETCH ARTIST
SHO 6/27/91. (Phedon Papamichael), Jeff Fahey, Sean Young, Drew Barrymore (90 mins.).

SKETCH ARTIST II: HANDS THAT SEE
SHO 1/28/95. (Jack Sholder), Jeff Fahey, Courteney Cox, Michael Beach, Brion James, James Tolkan, Leilani Ferrer (2 hrs.).

SKYLARK
CBS 2/7/93. (Joseph Sargent), Glenn Close, Christopher Walken, Lexi Randall, Christopher Bell (2 hrs.).

SLAVE OF DREAMS
SHO 12/10/95. (Robert M. Young) Edward James Olmos, Sherilyn Fenn, Adrian Pasdar, Orso Maria Guerrini.

SLEEP, BABY, SLEEP
ABC 3/26/95. (Armand Mastroianni), Tracey Gold, Kyle Chandler, Missy Crider, Joe Minjares, Karla Tamburrelli (2 hrs.).

SLEEPING WITH THE DEVIL
CBS. 4/22/97. (William A. Graham), Tim Matheson, Shannen Doherty, Bonnie Bartlett, Steve Eastin, David Bowe.

THE SLEEPWALKER KILLING
NBC. 4/28/97. (John Cosgrove), Hilary Swank, Jeffrey Nordlling, Charles Esten, Natalia Nogulich, Lisa Darr, Sean Murray.

SNAPDRAGON
USA 7/20/94. (Worth Keeter), Steven Bauer, Pamela Sue Anderson (2 hrs.).

SNOW KILL
USA 7/25/90. (Thomas J. Wright), Terence Knox, Patti D'Arbanville, David Dukes (2 hrs.).

SNOW WHITE: A TALE OF TERROR
SHO. 8/24/97. (Michael Cohn), Sigourney Weaver, Sam Neill, Gil Bellows, Monica Keena, David Conrad, Miroslav Taborsky.

SNOWBOUND: THE JIM AND JENNIFER STOLPA STORY
CBS 1/9/94. (Christian Duguay), Neil Patrick Harris, Kelli Williams, Susan Clark, Michael Gross (2 hrs.).

SO PROUDLY WE HAIL
CBS 1/23/90. (Lionel Chetwynd), Edward Herrmann, David Soul, Chad Lowe, Raphael Sbarge (2 hrs.).

SODBUSTER
SHO 7/17/94. (Eugene Levy), Kris Kristofferson, John Vernon, Fred Willard (2 hrs.).

SOLOMON AND SHEBA
SHO 2/26/95. (Robert M. Young), Halle Berry, Jimmy Smits, Nicolas Grace, Kenneth Colley, Ruben Santiago Hudson (90 mins.).

SOMEBODY HAS TO SHOOT THE PICTURE
HBO 9/9/90. (Frank Pierson), Roy Scheider, Bonnie Bedelia, Robert Carradine, Andre Braugher (90 mins.).

SOMEBODY'S DAUGHTER
ABC 9/20/92. (Joseph Sargent), Nicollette Sheridan, Nick Mancuso, Boyd Kestner, Max Gail (2 hrs.).

SOMEONE ELSE'S CHILD
ABC 12/4/94. (John Power), Lisa Hartman Black, Bruce Davison, Whip Hubley, Ken Pogue, Glynn Turman (2 hrs.).

SOMEONE SHE KNOWS
NBC 10/3/94. (Eric Laneuville), Markie Post, Gerald McRaney, Jeffrey Nordling, Sharon Lawrence, Shawn Modrell (2 hrs.).

SOMETHING BORROWED, SOMETHING BLUE
CBS. 3/11/97/ (Gwen Arner), Connie Sellecca, Twiggy Lawson, Jameson Parker, Ken Howard, Shawnee Smith, Ricky Paul.

SOMETHING TO LIVE FOR: THE ALISON GERTZ STORY
ABC 3/29/92. (Tom McLaughlin), Molly Ringwald, Lee Grant, Martin Landau, Perry King (2 hrs.).

SON OF THE MORNING STAR
ABC 2/3 & 2/4/91. (Mike Robe), Gary Cole, Rosanne Arquette, Rodney A. Grant, David Strathairn (4 hrs.).

A SON'S PROMISE
ABC 3/5/90. (John Korty), Rick Schroder, Veronica Cartwright, Donald Moffat, Stephen Dorff (2 hrs.).

SOPHIE AND THE MOONHANGER
LIF 1/15/96. (David Jones), Patricia Richardson, Lynn Whitfield, Jason Bernard, Ja'net DuBois, David Andrews.

SOUL OF THE GAME
HBO 4/20/96. (Kevin Rodney Sullivan), Delroy Lindo, Mykelti Williamson, Edward Herrmann, Blair Underwood. R. Lee Ermey.

THE SOUND AND THE SILENCE
TNT 7/18 & 7/19/93. (John Kent Harrison), John Bach, Brenda Fricker, Ian Bannen, Vanessa Vaughan (4 hrs.).

SPACE: ABOVE AND BEYOND
FOX 9/24/95. (David Nutter), Morgan Weisser, Kristen Cloke, Rodney Rowland, Lanei Chapman, Joel de la Fuente.

SPACE MARINES
SHO 7/26 & 7/28/96. (John Weidner), Billy Wirth, Cady Huffman, Meg Foster, Edward Albert.

SPARKS: THE PRICE OF PASSION
CBS 2/25/90. (Richard Colla), Victoria Principal, Ted Wass, Ralph Waite, Hector Elizondo (2 hrs.).

SPENSER: CEREMONY
LIF 7/22/93. (Andrew Wild), Robert Urich, Avery Brooks, Barbara Williams (2 hrs.).

SPENSER: PALE KINGS AND PRINCES
LIF 2/2/94. (Vic Sarin), Robert Urich, Avery Brooks, Barbara Williams (2 hrs.).

SPENSER: THE JUDAS GOAT
LIF 12/12/94. (Jonas L. Scanlon), Robert Urich, Avery Brooks (2 hrs.).

THE SPIDER AND THE FLY
USA 5/13/94. (Michael Katleman), Mel Harris, Ted Shackleford, Peggy Lipton (2 hrs.).

SPOILS OF WAR
ABC 4/9/94. (David Greene), Kate Nelligan, John Heard, Tobey Maguire (2 hrs.).

SPRING AWAKENING
CBS 11/6/94. (Jack Gold), Sherilyn Fenn, Jamey Sheridan, Elizabeth Wilson, Sammi Davis, Philip Abbott (2 hrs.).

SPRING FLING!
ABC 4/15/95. (Chuck Bowman), James Eckhouse, Joyce DeWitt, Justin Burnette, Pat Harrington Jr., Billy Jayne (2 hrs.).

SPY GAMES
ABC 7/20/91. (Michael Fresco, Christopher Leitch), Linda Purl, Anthony John Denison, Josef Sommer (2 hrs.).

STALIN
HBO 11/21/92. (Ivan Passer), Robert Duvall, Julia Ormond, Maximilian Schell, Joan Plowright (3 hrs.).

STAND AGAINST FEAR: A MOMENT OF TRUTH MOVIE
NBC. 12/16/96. (Michael O'Hara), Sarah Chalke, Shanna Reed, Lochlyn Munro, Brigitta Dau, Gwynyth Walsh, Josh Taylor.

STAR COMMAND
UPN 3/11/96. (Jim Johnston), Chad Everett, Morgan Fairchild, Jay Underwood, Tembi Locke, Chris Conrad.

STAR STRUCK
CBS 10/30/94. (Jim Drake), Kirk Cameron, Chelsea Noble, D.W. Moffett, J.T. Walsh, Ned Eisenberg, Desiree Marie (2 hrs.).

STATE OF EMERGENCY
HBO 2/12/94. (Lesli Linka Glatter), Joe Mantegna, Lynn Whitfield, Melinda Dillon (2 hrs.).

STAY THE NIGHT
ABC 4/26 & 4/7/92. (Harry Winer), Barbara Hershey, Jane Alexander, Morgan Weisser, Fred Dalton Thompson (4 hrs.).

STAYING AFLOAT
NBC 11/26/93. (Eric Launeville), Larry Hagman, Dakin Matthews, Gregg Henry (2 hrs.).

STEEL CHARIOTS
FOX. 9/23/97. John Beck, Ben Browder, Kathleen Nolan, Randy Travis.

STEEL JUSTICE
NBC 4/5/92. (Christopher Crowe), Robert Taylor, J.A. Preston, Season Hubley, Roy Brocksmith (2 hrs.).

A STEP TOWARD TOMORROW
CBS. 11/10/96. Judith Light, Kendall Cunningham, Christopher Reeve, Tom Irwin.

STEPFATHER III
HBO 6/4/92. (Guy Mager), Robert Wightman, Priscilla Barnes, David Tom, Season Hubley (2 hrs.).

THE STEPFORD HUSBANDS
CBS 5/14/96. (Fred Walton) Donna Mills, Michael Ontkean, Cindy williams, Louise Fletcher, Sara Douglas, Jeffrey Pillars.

STEPHEN KING'S "IT"
ABC 11/18 & 20/90. (Tommy Lee Wallace), Dennis Christopher, Richard Thomas, John Ritter, Tim Reid (4 hrs.).

STEPHEN KING'S "SOMETIMES THEY COME BACK"
CBS 5/7/91. (Tom McLoughlin), Tim Matheson, Brooke Adams, Robert Rusler (2 hrs.).

STEPHEN KING'S "THE LANGOLIERS"
ABC 5/14 & 5/15/95. (Tom Holland), Dean Stockwell, Patricia Wettig, Mark Lindsay Chapman, Bronson Pinchot (4 hrs.).

STEPHEN KING'S "THE SHINING"
ABC. 4/27, 28 & 5/5/97. (Mick Garris), Rebecca De Mornay, Steven Weber, Courtland Mead, Melvin Van Peebles.

STEPHEN KING'S "THE STAND"
ABC 5/8, 9, 11 & 12/94. (Mick Garris), Gary Sinise, Molly Ringwald, Jamey Sheridan, Rob Lowe, Corin Nemec, Ruby Dee (8 hrs.).

THE STEPSISTER
USA. 5/7/97. Lynda Boyd, Linda Evans, Rena Sofer.

STILL NOT QUITE HUMAN
DIS 5/31/92. (Guy Mager), Alan Thicke, Jay Underwood, Betsy Palmer, Christopher Neame (2 hrs.).

STOLEN BABIES
LIF 3/25/93. (Eric Laneuville), Lea Thompson, Mary Tyler Moore, Kathleen Quinlan (2 hrs.).

**STOLEN MEMORIES:
SECRETS FROM THE ROSE GARDEN**
FAM 1/7/96. (Bob Clark), Nathan Watt, Mary Tyler Moore, Linda Lavin, Shirely Knight, Paul Winfield, Allison Mack.

STOLEN: ONE HUSBAND
CBS 2/27/90. (Catlin Adams), Valerie Harper, Elliott Gould, Brenda Vaccaro, Bruce Davison (2 hrs.).

STOLEN WOMEN, CAPTURED HEARTS
CBS. 3.16.97. (Jerry London), Janine Turner, Jean Louisa Kelly, Patrick Bergin, William Shockley, Michael Greyeyes.

STOMPIN' AT THE SAVOY
CBS 4/12/92. (Debbie Allen), Lynn Whitfield, Vanessa Williams, Jasmine Guy, Mario Van Peebles (2 hrs.).

STOP AT NOTHING
LIF 3/12/91. (Chris Thomson), Veronica Hamel, Lindsay Frost, David Ackroyd (2 hrs.).

STORM AND SORROW
LIF 11/22/90. (Richard Colla), Lori Singer, Todd Allen, Steven Anderson (2 hrs.).

STORMY WEATHERS
ABC 5/4/92. (Will Mackenzie), Cybill Shepherd, Tony LoBianco, Charlie Schlatter, Robert Beltran (2 hrs.).

THE STORY LADY
NBC 12/9/91. (Larry Elikann), Jessica Tandy, Lisa Jakub, Stephanie Zimbalist, Tandy Cronyn (2 hrs.).

THE STORY OF SANTA CLAUS
CBS. 12/4/96. Edward Asner, Tim Curry, Betty White.

THE STORY OF THE BEACH BOYS: SUMMER DREAMS
ABC 4/29/90. (Michael Switzer), Bruce Greenwood, Greg Kean, Arlen Dean Snyder (2 hrs.).

STRANGER AT MY DOOR
CBS 9/27/91. (Vincent McEveety), Robert Urich, Markie Post, Michael Beck, Ken Swofford (2 hrs.).

THE STRANGER BESIDE ME
ABC 9/17/96. Tiffani-Amber Thiessen, Eric Close, Gerald McRaney.

STRANGER IN MY HOME
CBS. 2/15/97. (Farhad Mann), Veronica Hamel, Robert Curtis-Brown, Michael Angarano, Joe Penny, Leigh Taylor-Young, Daniel Hugh-Kelly.

STRANGER IN THE FAMILY
ABC 10/27/91. (Donald Wrye), Teri Garr, Neil Patrick Harris, Randle Mell, Sierra Samuel (2 hrs.).

A STRANGER IN THE MIRROR
ABC 10/24/93. (Charles Jarrott), Perry King, Lori Laughlin, Christopher Plummer (2 hrs.).

A STRANGER IN TOWN.
CBS 3/29/95. (Peter Levin), Jean Smart, Gregory Hines, Jeffrey Nordling, Lucinda Jenney, Dave Florek (2 hrs.).

THE STRANGER WITHIN
CBS 11/27/90. (Tom Holland), Rick Schroder, Kate Jackson, Chris Sarandon (2 hrs.).

STRAPPED
HBO 8/21/93. (Forest Whitaker), Bokeem Woodbine, Michael Biehn, Kia Joy Goodwin (2 hrs.).

STRAYS
USA 12/18/91. (John McPherson), Timothy Busfield, Kathleen Quinlan, Heather Lilley, Jessica Lilley (2 hrs.).

STREET JUSTICE
SYND 9/18/91. (Bill Corcoran), Carl Weathers, Bryan Genesse, Michael A. Jackson, Kimberly Sheppard (2 hrs.).

THE SUBSTITUTE
USA 9/22/93. (Martin Donovan), Amanda Donohoe, Dalton James, Marky Mark, Natasha Gregson Wagner (2 hrs.).

SUBSTITUTE WIFE
NBC 5/23/94. (Peter Werner), Farrah Fawcett, Lea Thompson, Peter Weller (2 hrs.).

SUDDEN TERROR: THE HIJACKING OF SCHOOL BUS #17
ABC. 10/13/96. (Paul Schneider), Maria Conchita Alonso, Michael Paul Chan, Steven Bauer, Bruce Weitz.

SUDIE AND SIMPSON
LIF 9/11/90. (Joan Tewkesbury), Louis Gossett, Jr., Sara Gilbert, John Jackson, Frances Fisher (2 hrs.).

SUGARTIME
HBO 11/25/95. (John N. Smith) John Turturro, Mary-Louise Parker, Maury Chaykin, Elias Koteas, Louis Del Grande.

THE SUMMER MY FATHER GREW UP
NBC 3/3/91. (Michael Tuchner), John Ritter, Margaret Whitton, Karen Young, Joe Spano (2 hrs.).

THE SUMMER OF BEN TYLER
CBS. 12/15/96. (Arthur Allan Seidelman), James Woods, Elizabeth McGovern, Len Cariou, Charles Mattocks.

SUMMER OF FEAR
CBS 4/3/96. Gregory Harrison, Corin Nemec.

SUMMERTIME SWITCH
ABC 10/8/94. (Alan Metter), Rider Strong, Jason Weaver, Richard Moll, Teresa Ganzel, Soleil Moon Frye, Barry Williams.

SUNSTROKE
USA 9/23/92. (James Keach), Jane Seymour, Stephen Meadows, Steve Railsback, Ray Wise (2 hrs.).

SURVIVAL ON THE MOUNTAIN
NBC. 5/12/97. (Kevin Cooper), Dennis Boutsikaris, Markie Post, Katie Stuart.

SURVIVE THE NIGHT
USA 1/13/93. (Bill Corcoran), Stefanie Powers, Helen Shaver, Kathleen Robertson (2 hrs.).

SURVIVE THE SAVAGE SEA
ABC 1/6/92. (Kevin James Dobson), Robert Urich, Ali MacGraw, Danielle von Zerneck, Mark Ballou (2 hrs.).

SUSPECT DEVICE
SHO 7/11/95. (Rick Jacobson), C. Thomas Howell, Stacey Travis, Jed Allen, John Beck, Marcus Aurelius, Jonathan Fuller (90 mins.).

SWEET DREAMS
NBC. 10/14/96. Tiffani-Amber Thiessen, Amy Yasbeck.

SWEET POISON
USA 6/12/91. (Brian Grant), Steven Bauer, Edward Herrmann, Patricia Healy (2 hrs.).

SWEET REVENGE
TNT 7/9/90. (Charlotte Brandstrom), Carrie Fisher, Rosanna Arquette, John Sessions (2 hrs.).

SWEET TEMPTATION
CBS 3/6/96. (Ron Lagomarsino) Jenny Lewis, Beverly D'Angelo, Rob Estes.

THE SWITCH
CBS 1/17/93. (Bobby Roth), Gary Cole, Craig T. Nelson, Kathleen Nolan, Beverly D'Angelo (2 hrs.).

SWITCHED AT BIRTH
NBC 4/28 & 4/29/91. (Waris Hussein), Bonnie Bedelia, Brian Kerwin, Edward Asner, Caroline McWilliams (4 hrs.).

SWORN TO VENGEANCE
CBS 3/23/93. (Peter H. Hunt), Robert Conrad, William McNamara, Gary Bayer (2 hrs.).

T BONE N WEASEL
TNT 11/2/92. (Lewis Teague), Christopher Lloyd, Gregory Hines, Ned Beatty, Rip Torn (2 hrs.).

TAD
FAM 2/12/95. (Rob Thompson), Kris Kristofferson, Jane Curtin, Jean Louisa Kelly, Kieran Mulroney, Tyler Long (2 hrs.).

TAGGET
USA 2/14/91. (Richard T. Heffron), Daniel J. Travanti, William Sadler, Roxanne Hart (2 hrs.).

TAINTED BLOOD
USA 3/3/93. (Mathew Patrick), Raquel Welch, Joan Van Ark, Natasha Wagner (2 hrs.).

THE TAKE
USA 3/28/90. (Leon Ichaso), Ray Sharkey, R. Lee Ermey, Larry Manetti, Lisa Hartman (2 hrs.).

TAKE ME HOME AGAIN
NBC 12/18/94. (Thomas McLoughlin), Kirk Douglas, Craig T. Nelson, Bess Armstrong, Bonnie Bartlett, Richard Gilliland (2 hrs.).

TAKING BACK MY LIFE:
THE NANCY ZIEGENMEYER STORY
CBS 3/15/92. (Harry Winer), Patricia Wettig, Stephen Lang, Shelley Hack, Ellen Burstyn (2 hrs.).

TAKING THE HEAT
SHO 6/6/93. (Tom Mankiewicz), Tony Goldwyn, Lynn Whitfield, Alan Arkin, George Segal (2 hrs.).

TALK TO ME
ABC. 10/20/96. (Graeme Campbell), Yasmeen Bleethe, Ricky Paull Goldin, Veronica Hamel, Jenny Lewis, Peter Scolari.

TALL, DARK AND DEADLY
USA 1/24/95. (Kenneth Fink), Jack Scalia, Kim Delaney, Todd Allen, Gina Mastrogiacomo, Ely Pouget (2 hrs.).

TANGLED WEB
CBS. 11/13/96. Cheryl Ladd, Jarion Monroe.

TARGET OF SUSPICION
USA 6/9/94. (Bob Swaim), Tim Matheson, Lysette Anthony, Agnes Soral (2 hrs.).

A TASTE FOR KILLING
USA 8/12/92. (Lou Antonio), Jason Bateman, Henry Thomas, Michael Biehn, Blue Deckert (2 hrs.).

TEAMSTER BOSS: THE JACKIE PRESSER STORY
HBO 9/12/92. (Alastair Reid), Brian Dennehy, Jeff Daniels, Maria Conchita Alonso, Eli Wallach (2 hrs.).

TEARS AND LAUGHTER:
THE JOAN AND MELISSA RIVERS STORY
NBC 5/15/94. (Oz Scott), Joan Rivers, Melissa Rivers, Dorothy Lyman (2 hrs.).

TECUMSEH: THE LAST WARRIOR
TNT 6/4/95. (Larry Elikann), Jesse Borrego, David Morse, David Clennon, Tantoo Cardinal, Jeri Arredondo (2 hrs.).

TEKWAR
SYND 1/18/94. (William Shatner), Greg Evigan, Eugene Clark, Torri Higginson (2 hrs.).

TELL ME NO SECRETS
ABC. 1/20/97. (Bobby Roth), Lori Loughlin, Bruce Greenwood, Joe Flanigan, Wendy Gazelle, Nicole Mercurio, Lauren Tom.

TELLING SECRETS
ABC 1/17 & 18/93. (Marvin J. Chomsky), Cybill Shepherd, Ken Olin, Christopher McDonald, G.D. Spradlin (4 hrs.).

THE TEN MILLION DOLLAR GETAWAY
USA 3/6/91. (Christopher Canaan), John Mahoney, Karen Young, Tony LoBianco (2 hrs.).

TERROR IN THE FAMILY
FOX 4/16/96. Joanna Kerns, Hilary Swank, Dan Luria.

TERROR IN THE NIGHT
CBS 1/11/94. (Colin Bucksey), Joe Penny, Justine Bateman, Matt Mulhern (2 hrs.).

TERROR ON TRACK 9
CBS 9/20/92. (Robert Iscove), Richard Crenna, Swoosie Kurtz, Joan Van Ark, Cliff Gorman (2 hrs.).

TERROR STRIKES THE CLASS REUNION
SYND 5/27/92. (Clive Donner), Kate Nelligan, Jennifer Beals, Geraint Wyn Davies, Manfred Lehmann (2 hrs.).

TEXAS JUSTICE
ABC 2/12 & 13/95. (Dick Lowry), Peter Strauss, Heather Locklear, Dennis Franz, Lewis Smith, Susan Walters, Chris Mulkey (4 hrs.).

THANKSGIVING DAY
NBC 11/19/90. (Gino Tanasescu), Mary Tyler Moore, Jonathan Brandmeir, Tony Curtis (2 hrs.).

THEIR SECOND CHANCE
LIF. 2/9/97. (Andrea Baynes), Lindsay Wagner, Perry King, Tracy Griffith, Jerry Wasserman, Robin Douglas.

THERE ARE NO CHILDREN HERE
ABC 11/28/93. (Anita W. Addison), Oprah Winfrey, Mark Lane, Norman Golden II, Maya Angelou (2 hrs.).

THERE WAS A LITTLE BOY
CBS 5/16/93. (Mimi Leder), Cybill Shepherd, John Heard, Scott Bairstow (2 hrs.).

THEY
SHO 11/14/93. (John Korty), Vanessa Redgrave, Patrick Bergin, Valerie Mahaffey (2 hrs.).

THEY'VE TAKEN OUR CHILDREN:
THE CHOWCHILLA KIDNAPPING
ABC 3/1/93. (Vern Gillum), Karl Malden, Tim Ransom, Travis Fine, Julie Harris (2 hrs.).

THICKER THAN BLOOD
CBS 3/6/94. (Michael Dinner), Peter Strauss, Rachel Ticotin, Bob Dishy (2 hrs.).

THICKER THAN WATER
A&E 4/10/94. (Mark Evans), Theresa Russell, Jonathan Pryce, Robert Pugh (3 hrs.).

THIS CAN'T BE LOVE
CBS 3/13/94. (Anthony Harvey), Katharine Hepburn, Anthony Quinn, Jason Bateman, Jami Gertz (2 hrs.).

THIS GUN FOR HIRE
USA 1/9/91. (Lou Antonio), Robert Wagner, Nancy Everhard, John Harkins (2 hrs.).

THE THORN BIRDS: THE MISSING YEARS
CBS 2/11 & 2/13/96. (Kevin James Dobson) Richard Chamberlain, Amanda Donohoe, Simon Westaway, Julia Blake.

THOSE SECRETS
ABC 3/16/92. (David Manson), Blair Brown, Arliss Howard, Mare Winningham, Paul Guilfoyle (2 hrs.).

THE THREE LIVES OF KAREN
USA. 5/28/97. (David Burton Morris), Gail O'Grady, Dennis Boutsikaris, Tim Guinee, Bonnie Johnson, Ana Harrison.

THRILL
NBC 5/20/96. Antonio Sabato, Jr., Stepfanie Kramer, Christine Hamos, Ted Marcoux, Bill Cobbs, Maxxe Sternbaum.

THROUGH THE EYES OF A KILLER
CBS 12/15/92. (Peter Markle), Marg Helgenberger, Richard Dean Anderson, David Marshall Grant (2 hrs.).

TIDAL WAVE: NO ESCAPE
ABC. 5/9/97. (George Miller), Corbin Bernsen, Gene Wolande, Julianne Phillips, Wendy Schenker.

A TIME TO HEAL
NBC 4/18/94. (Michael Toshiyuki Uno), Nicollette Sheridan, Gary Cole, Mara Wilson, Annie Corley (2 hrs.).

THE TIN SOLDIER
SHO 3/22/95. (Jon Voight), Trenton Knight, Jon Voight, Ally Sheedy, Dom DeLuise, Bethay Richards, Aeryk Egan (2 hrs.).

TITANIC
CBS. 11/17 & 11/19/96. (Robert Lieberman), Peter Gallagher, George C. Scott, Catherine Zeta Jones, Eva Marie Saint.

TO BE THE BEST
CBS 8/2 & 4/92. (Tony Wharmby), Lindsay Wagner, Anthony Hopkins, Stephanie Beacham, Christopher Cazenove (4 hrs.).

TO BRAVE ALASKA
ABC. 11/3/96. (Bruce Pittman), Alyssa Milano, Cameron Bancroft, Duncan Fraser, Winston Rekart.

TO CATCH A KILLER
SYND 5/13 & 14/92. (Eric Till), Brian Dennehy, Michael Riley, Meg Foster, Margot Kidder (4 hrs.).

TO DANCE WITH OLIVIA
CBS. 3/9/97. (Bruce Pittman), Louis Gossett Jr., Joe Don Baker, Kathryne Dara Brown, Kathleen York, Robert C. Treveiler.

TO DANCE WITH THE WHITE DOG
CBS 12/5/93. (Glenn Jordan), Hume Cronyn, Jessica Tandy, Christine Baranski, Amy Wright, Frank Whaley (2 hrs.).

TO GRANDMOTHER'S HOUSE WE GO
ABC 12/6/92. (Jeff Franklin), Ashley Olsen, Mary-Kate Olsen, Rhea Perlman, Jerry Van Dyke (2 hrs.).

TOM CLANCY'S "OP CENTER"
NBC 2/26 & 27/95. (Lewis Teague), Harry Hamlin, Wilford Brimley, Rod Steiger, Carl Weathers, Patrick Bauachau (4 hrs.).

THE TOMMYKNOCKERS
ABC 5/9 & 5/10/93. (John Power), Jimmy Smits, Marg Helgenberger, Joanna Cassidy, John Ashton (4 hrs.).

TO MY DAUGHTER
NBC 11/26/90. (Larry Shaw), Rue McClanahan, Michele Greene, Ty Miller (2 hrs.).

TO MY DAUGHTER WITH LOVE
NBC 1/24/94. (Kevin Hooks), Rick Schroder, Linda Gray, Lawrence Pressman (2 hrs.).

TO SAVE A CHILD
ABC 4/8/92. (Robert Lieberman), Marita Geraghy, Shirley Knight, Anthony Zerbe, Peter Kowanko (2 hrs.).

TO SAVE THE CHILDREN
CBS 4/5/94. (Steven Stern), Richard Thomas, Robert Urich, Wendy Crewson (2 hrs.).

TO SIR WITH LOVE II
CBS 4/7/96. (Peter Bogdanovitch) Sidney Poitier, Daniel J. Travanti, Lulu, Judy Geeson, Christian Payton, Dana Eskelson.

TONYA & NANCY: THE INSIDE STORY
NBC 4/30/94. (Larry Shaw), Alexandra Powers, James Wilder, Heather Lagenkamp, Susan Clark (2 hrs.).

TOO CLOSE TO HOME
CBS. 4/29/97. (Bill Corcoran), Judith Light, Rick Schroder, Sarah Trigger, Dorothy Gordon.

TOO YOUNG TO DIE
NBC 2/26/90. (Robert Markowitz), Juliette Lewis, Michael Tucker, Brad Pitt, Michael O'Keefe (2 hrs.).

TORCH SONG
ABC 5/23/93. (Michael Miller), Raquel Welch, Jack Scalia, Alicia Silverstone, George Newbern (2 hrs.).

TORNADO
FOX 5/7/96. Bruce Campbell, Ernie Hudson, L.Q. Jones, Bo Easton.

THE TOWER
FOX 8/16/93. (Richard Kletter), Paul Reiser, Susan Norman, Richard Grant, Roger Rees (2 hrs.).

A TOWN TORN APART
NBC 11/30/92. (Daniel Petrie), Michael Tucker, Carole Galloway, Linda Griffiths, Jill Eikenberry (2 hrs.).

THE TRAGEDY OF FLIGHT 103: THE INSIDE STORY
HBO 12/9/90. (Leslie Woodhead), Ned Beatty, Peter Boyle, Vincent Gardenia, Michael Wincott (90 mins.).

TRAIL OF HOPE
PBS. 8/10/97. (Lee B. Groberg), (host) Hal Holbrook.

TREACHEROUS BEAUTIES
CBS 9/25/94. (Charles Jarrot), Emma Samms, Bruce Greenwood, Catherine Oxenberg, Tippi Hedren (2 hrs.).

TREACHEROUS CROSSING
USA 4/8/92. (Tony Wharmby), Lindsay Wagner, Angie Dickinson, Jeffrey DeMunn, Joseph Bottoms (2 hrs.).

TREASURE ISLAND
TNT 1/22/90. (Fraser C. Heston), Charlton Heston, Christian Bale, Oliver Reed, Christopher Lee (3 hrs.).

TRIAL & ERROR
USA 2/24/93. (Mark Sobel), Tim Matheson, Helen Shaver, Eugene Clark, Sean McCann (2 hrs.).

TRIAL: THE PRICE OF PASSION
NBC 5/3 & 4/92. (Paul Wendkos), Peter Strauss, Beverly D'Angelo, Ned Beatty, Jill Clayburgh (4 hrs.).

TRICK OF THE EYE
CBS 10/23/94. (Ed Kaplan), Ellen Burstyn, Meg Tilly, Barnard Hughes, Paxton Whitehead, Alastair Duncan (2 hrs.).

TRILOGY OF TERROR II
USA. 10/30/96. (Dan Curtis), Lysette Anthony, Geraint Wyn Davies, Matt Clark, Geoffrey Lewis, Blake Heron.

TRIPLECROSS
SHO 5/28/95. (Jeno Hodi), Patrick Bergin, Michael Pare, Ashley Laurence, Billy Dee Williams, Zachary Bogatz (2 hrs.).

TRIUMPH OF THE HEART: THE RICKY BELL STORY
CBS 4/2/91. (Richard Michaels), Mario Van Peebles, Lane Davis, Susan Ruttan (2 hrs.).

TRIUMPH OVER DISASTER:
THE HURRICANE ANDREW STORY
NBC 5/24/93. (Marvin J. Chomsky), Ted Wass, Brynn Thayer, Brian McNamara, Arnetia Walker (2 hrs.).

TROUBLESHOOTERS: TRAPPED BENEATH THE EARTH
NBC 10/3/93. (Bradford May), Kris Kristofferson, David Newsom, Leigh J. McCloskey (2 hrs.).

TRUE WOMEN
CBS. 5/22 & 5/24/97. (Karen Arthur), Dana Delany, Annabeth Gish, Angela Jolie, Michael York.

THE TUSKEGEE AIRMEN
HBO 8/26/95. (Robert Markowitz), Laurence Fishburne, Cuba Gooding Jr., Allen Payne, Malcolm Jamal Warner (2 hrs.).

12 ANGRY MEN
SHO. 8/17/97. (William Friedkin), Courtney B. Vance, Ossie Davis, George C. Scott, Armin Mueller-Stahl, Dorian Harewood, James Gandolfini, Tony Danza, Jack Lemmon, Hume Cronyn.

12:01
FOX 7/5/93. (Jack Sholder), Jonathan Silverman, Helen Slater, Nicolas Survoy, Robin Barlett (2 hrs.).

20,000 LEAGUES UNDER THE SEA
(Rod Hardy), Richard Crenna, Ben Cross, Paul Gross, Julie Cox, Michael Jayston, Jeff Harding, David Henry.

20,000 LEAGUES UNDER THE SEA
ABC. 5/11 & 5/12/97. (Michael Anderson), Michael Caine, Patrick Dempsey, Mia Sara, Bryan Brown, Kerry Armstrong.

TWILIGHT OF THE GOLDS
SHO. 9/24/97. (Ross Kagan Marks), Garry Marshall, Faye Dunaway, Jill Bernstein, Jennifer Beals, Brendan Fraser.

A TWIST OF THE KNIFE
CBS 2/13/93. (Jerry London), Dick Van Dyke, Suzanne Pleshette, Cynthia Gibb (2 hrs.).

TWISTED DESIRE
NBC 5/13/96. (Craig Baxley) Melissa Joan Hart, Daniel Baldwin, Isabella Hofmann, Jeremy Jordan, Meadow Sisto.

TWO FATHERS: JUSTICE FOR THE INNOCENT
NBC 1/14/94. (Paul Krasny), Robert Conrad, George Hamilton, Danny Goldring (2 hrs.).

TWO VOICES
LIF. 6/16/97. (Peter Levin), Mary McDonnell, Gail O'Grady, Richard Gilliland, Nicolas Surovy, Fredric Lane, Casey Biggs.

TYSON
HBO 4/29/95. (Uli Edel), Michael Jai White, George C. Scott, Paul Winfield, Malcolm Jamal Warner, Tony LoBianco (2 hrs.).

U

ULTIMATE BETRAYAL
CBS 3/20/94. (Donald Wrye), Marlo Thomas, Mel Harris, Eileen Heckart, Ally Sheedy (2 hrs.).

THE ULTIMATE LIE
NBC 3/18/96. (Larry Shaw) Michael Murphy, Blair Brown, George Eads, Kristin Davis, John Pennell.

UNDUE INFLUENCE
CBS. 9/15 & 9/17/97. (Bruce Pittman), Michael Ricupero, Patricia Richardson, Brian Dennehy, Peter Krantz, Laura Press.

AN UNEXPECTED FAMILY
USA. 12/4/96. Stockard Channing, Stephen Collins, Christine Ebersole, Noah Fleiss, Chelsea Russo.

AN UNFINISHED AFFAIR
ABC 5/5/96. Jennie Garth, Tim Matheson, Peter Facinelli.

UNFORGIVABLE
CBS 4/30/96. John Ritter, Harley Jane Kozak, Susan Gibney.

UNLIKELY ANGEL
CBS. 12/17/96. Roddy McDowall, Brian Kerwin, Allison Mack, Ely Marienthal, Dolly Parton.

UNNATURAL PURSUITS
A&E 1/23/94. (Christopher Morahan), Alan Bates, Paul Guilfoyle, Bob Balaban, Keith Szarabajka (2 hrs.).

UNTAMED LOVE
LIF 8/3/94. (Paul Aaron), Cathy Lee Crosby, Ashlee Lauren, John Getz, Gary Frank (2 hrs.).

US
CBS 9/20/91. (Michael Landon), Michael Landon, Casey Peterson, Barney Martin, Meg Wittner (2 hrs.).

V

VANISHING POINT
FOX. 1/7/97. (Charles Robert Carner), Christine Elise, Keith David, John Doe, Viggo Mortensen, Jason Priestley.

VANISHING SON
SYND 3/2/94. (John Nicolella), Russell Wong, Chi Muoi Lo, Rebecca Gayheart (2 hrs.).

VENDETTA: SECRETS OF A MAFIA BRIDE
SYND 5/20 & 21/91. (Stuart Margolin), Eric Roberts, Carol Alt, Eli Wallach, Burt Young (4 hrs.).

VENDETTA 2: THE NEW MAFIA
SYND 12/6 & 7/93. (Ralph Thomas), Carol Alt, Michael Ontkean, Eli Wallach (4 hrs.).

THE VERNON JOHNS STORY
SYND 1/17/94. (Kenneth Fink), James Earl Jones, Mary Alice, Cissy Houston (2 hrs.).

VESTIGE OF HONOR
CBS 12/30/90. (Jerry London), Gerald McRaney, Michael Gross, Season Hubley (2 hrs.).

VICTIM OF LOVE
CBS 5/5/91. (Jerry London), Pierce Brosnan, JoBeth Williams, Virginia Madsen (2 hrs.).

VICTIM OF LOVE: THE SHANNON MOHR STORY
NBC 11/9/93. (John Cosgrove), Sally Murphy, Dwight Schultz, Bonnie Bartlett, Andy Romano (2 hrs.).

VIRTUAL SEDUCTION
SHO 8/1/95. (Paul Ziller), Jeff Fahey, Ami Dolenz, Carrie Genzel, Emile Levisetti, Meshach Taylor, Rick Dean (90 mins.).

VISIONS OF MURDER
NBC 5/7/93. (Michael Rhodes), Barbara Eden, James Brolin, Terry O'Quinn (2 hrs.).

VOICE OF THE HEART
SYND 4/18 & 19/90. (Tony Whamby), Lindsay Wagner, James Brolin, Victoria Tennant (4 hrs.).

VOICES FROM WITHIN
NBC 10/10/94. (Eric Till), JoBeth Williams, Corbin Bernsen, Stephanie Zimbalist, Winston Rekert, Justin Louis (2 hrs.).

VOICES WITHIN: THE LIVES OF TRUDDI CHASE
ABC 5/20 & 21/90. (Lamont Johnson), Shelley Long, Tom Conti, John Rubinstein (4 hrs.).

VOLCANO: FIRE ON THE MOUNTAIN
ABC. 2/23/97. (Graeme Campbell), Dan Cortese, Cynthia Gibb, Brian Kerwin, Don S. Davis, Lynda Boyd, Colin Cunningham.

VOYAGE
USA 6/2/93. (John Mackenzie), Eric Roberts, Rutger Hauer, Karen Allen, Connie Nelson (2 hrs.).

VOYAGE OF TERROR: THE ACHILLE LAURO AFFAIR
SYND 5/1/90. (Alberto Negrin), Burt Lancaster, Eva Marie Saint, Robert Culp (4 hrs.).

W

A WALTON EASTER
CBS. 3/31/97. Michael Learned, Richard Thomas, Ralph Waite.

A WALTON WEDDING
CBS 2/12/95. (Robert Ellis Miller), Richard Thomas, Ralph Waite, Michael Learned, Kate McNiel, Jon Walmsley, Judy Norton (2 hrs.).

A WALTONS THANKSGIVING REUNION
CBS 11/21/93. (Harry Harris), Richard Thomas, Ralph Waite, Michael Learned, Kate McNeil (2 hrs.).

WASP WOMAN
SHO 8/29/95. (Jim Wynorski), Jennifer Rubin, Doug Wert, Daniel J. Travanti (90 mins.).

THE WATER ENGINE
TNT 8/24/92. (Steven Schachter), W.H. Macy, John Mahoney, Joe Mantegna, Patti LuPone (2 hrs.).

WE THE JURY
USA. 10/16/96. (Sturla Gunnarsson), Damir Andrei, Yank Azman, Tyrone Benskin, Dana Brooks.

WEAPONS OF MASS DISTRACTION
HBO. 5/17/97. (Steve Surjik), Gabriel Byrne, Ben Kingsley, Mimi Rogers, Jeffrey Tambor, Ileana Douglas.

WEB OF DECEIT
USA 10/17/90. (Sandor Stern), Linda Purl, James Read, Paul de Souza, Barbara Rush (2 hrs.).

WEB OF DECEPTION
NBC 4/25/94. (Richard Colla), Powers Boothe, Pam Dawber, Lisa Collins, Bradley Whitford (2 hrs.).

WEST SIDE WALTZ
CBS 11/23/95. (Ernest Thompson) Shirley MacLaine, Liza Minelli, Jennifer Grey, Robert Pastorelli, August Schellenberg.

THE WESTING GAME
SHO. 9/14/97. (Terry Winkless), Ray Walston, Diane Ladd, Sally Kirkland, Ashley Peidon.

WHAT EVER HAPPENED TO BABY JANE?
ABC 2/17/91. (David Greene), Vanessa Redgrave, Lynn Redgrave, John Glover (2 hrs.).

WHAT SHE DOESN'T KNOW
NBC 2/23/92. (Kevin James Dobson), Valerie Bertinelli, George Dzundza, Peter Dobson, David Marshall Grant (2 hrs.).

WHEELS OF TERROR
USA 7/11/90. (Chris Cain), Joanna Cassidy, Marcie Leeds, Arlen Dean Snyder (2 hrs.).

WHEN A STRANGER CALLS BACK
SHO 4/4/93. (Fred Walton), Jill Schoelen, Carol Kane, Charles Durning (96 mins.).

WHEN INNOCENCE IS LOST
LIF. 4/7/97. (Bethany Rooney), Jill Clayburgh, Keri Russell, Roberta Maxwell, Vince Corazza, Charlotte Sullivan.

WHEN LOVE KILLS: THE SEDUCTION OF JOHN HEARN
CBS 5/18/93. (Larry Elikann), Gary Cole, Marg Helgenberger, Julie Harris, Charles Hallahan (2 hrs.).

WHEN NO ONE WOULD LISTEN
CBS 11/15/92. (Armand Mastroianni), Michele Lee, James Farentino, Cicely Tyson (2 hrs.).

WHEN SECRETS KILL
ABC. 4/6/97. (Colin Bucksey), Gregory Harrison, Roxanne Hart, Timothy Busfield.

WHEN THE CRADLE FALLS
CBS. 3/4/97. Cathy Lee Crobsy, Linda Gray, Scott Reeves.

WHEN THE DARK MAN CALLS
USA 6/14/95. (Nathaniel Gutman), Joan Van Ark, James Read, Geoffrey Lewis, Chris Sarandon, Frances Hyland (2 hrs.).

WHEN WILL I BE LOVED?
NBC 12/3/90. (Michael Tuchner), Stefanie Powers, Katherine Helmond, Crystal Bernard (2 hrs.).

WHEN YOU REMEMBER ME
ABC 10/7/90. (Harry Winer), Fred Savage, Kevin Spacey, Ellen Burstyn, Dwier Brown (2 hrs.).

WHERE ARE MY CHILDREN?
ABC 9/18/94. (George Kaczender), Marg Helgenberger, Christopher Noth, Bonnie Bartlett, Corbin Bernsen (2 hrs.).

WHERE PIGEONS GO TO DIE
NBC 1/29/90. (Michael Landon), Art Carney, Cliff De Young, Michael Landon (2 hrs.).

WHERE'S THE MONEY, NOREEN?
USA 12/6/96. (Artie Mandelberg) Julianne Philips, A. Martinez.

THE WHEREABOUTS OF JENNY
ABC 1/14/91. (Gene Reynolds), Ed O'Neill, Debrah Farentino, Eve Gordon, Mike Farrell (2 hrs.).

WHICH WAY HOME
TNT 1/28/91. (Carl Schultz), Cybill Shepherd, John Waters, Peta Toppana (3 hrs.).

WHILE JUSTICE SLEEPS
NBC 12/5/94. (Ivan Passer), Cybill Shepherd, Tim Matheson, Karis Bryant, Dion Anderson, Kurtwood Smith (2 hrs.).

WHISKERS
SHO. 1/5/97. (Jim Kaufman), Michael Caloz, Jacob Tiemey, Laurel Paetz, Steve Adams, Suzanne Cloutier, Robert Higden.

WHITE DWARF
FOX 5/23/95. (Peter Markle), Beverly Mitchell, Roy Brocksmith, C.C.H. Pounder. (2 hrs.).

WHITE LIE
USA 9/25/91. (Bill Condon), Gregory Hines, Annette O'Toole, Bill Nunn, Gregg Henry (2 hrs.).

WHITE MILE
HBO 5/21/94. (Robert Butler), Alan Alda, Peter Gallagher, Robert Loggia, Bruce Altman (2 hrs.).

WHOSE CHILD IS THIS? THE WAR FOR BABY JESSICA
ABC 9/26/93. (John Kent Harrison), Susan Dey, Michael Ontkean, Amanda Plummer, David Keith (2 hrs.).

WIFE, MOTHER, MURDERER
ABC 11/10/91. (Mel Damski), Judith Light, David Ogden Stiers (2 hrs.).

WILD CARD
USA 10/28/92. (Mel Damski), Powers Boothe, Cindy Pickett, Rene Auberjonois, Terry O'Quinn (2 hrs.).

WILD JUSTICE
SYND 5/12 & 13/93. (Paul Madigan), Roy Scheider, Ted McGinley, Patricia Millardet, Sam Wanamaker (4 hrs.).

WILD PALMS
ABC 5/16 & 19/93. (Peter Hewitt), Keith Gordon, Kathryn Bigelow, Phil Joanou), James Belushi, Dana Delany, Angie Dickinson, Robert Loggia, Kim Cattrall (8 hrs.).

WILD TEXAS WIND
NBC 9/23/91. (Joan Tewkesbury), Dolly Parton, Gary Busey, Ray Benson, Dennis Letts (2 hrs.).

WILDFLOWER
LIF 12/3/91. (Diane Keaton), Patricia Arquette, William McNamara, Beau Bridges, Reese Witherspoon (2 hrs.).

WILLING TO KILL: THE TEXAS CHEERLEADER STORY
ABC 11/8/92. (David Greene), Lesley Ann Warren, Tess Harper, Dennis Christopher, William Forsythe (2 hrs.).

WISEGUY
ABC 5/2/96. (James Whitmore) Ken Wahl, Jonathan Banks, Jim Byrnes, Debrah Farentino, Ted Levine.

WITCH HUNT
HBO 12/10/94. (Paul Schrader), Dennis Hopper, Penelope Ann Miller, Eric Bogosian, Sheryl Lee Ralph, Julian Sands (2 hrs.)

WITH A VENGEANCE
CBS 9/22/92. (Michael Switzer), Melissa Gilbert-Brinkman, Michael Gross, Jack Scalia (2 hrs.).

WITH HOSTILE INTENT
CBS 5/11/93. (Paul Schneider), Melissa Gilbert, Mel Harris, Peter Onorati, Cotter Smith (2 hrs.).

WITH MURDER IN MIND
CBS 5/12/91. (Michael Tuchner), Elizabeth Montgomery, Robert Foxworth, Howard Rollins Jr. (2 hrs.).

WITHOUT A KISS GOODBYE
CBS 3/21/93. (Noel Nosseck), Lisa Hartman Black, Chris Meloni, Cloris Leachman (2 hrs.).

WITHOUT CONSENT
ABC 10/16/94. (Robert Iscove), Jennie Garth, Johnny Galecki, Jill Eikenberry, Tom Irwin, Gene Lythgow, Helen Shaver (2 hrs.)

WITHOUT HER CONSENT
NBC 1/14/90. (Sandor Stern), Melissa Gilbert, Scott Valentine (2 hrs.).

WITHOUT WARNING
CBS 10/30/94. (Sander Vanocur), Jane Kaczmarek, Bree Walker-Lampley, Ernie Anastos, Warren Olney (2 hrs.).

WITHOUT WARNING: THE JAMES BRADY STORY
HBO 6/16/91. (Michael Toshiyuki Uno), Beau Bridges, Joan Allen, Bryan Clark, Steve Flynn (90 mins.).

WITHOUT WARNING: TERROR IN THE TOWERS
NBC 5/26/93. (Alan Levi), George Clooney, Scott Plank, John Karlen, Susan Ruttan (2 hrs.).

WITNESS TO THE EXECUTION
NBC 2/13/94. (Tommy Lee Wallace), Tim Daly, Sean Young, Len Cariou, George Newbern (2 hrs.).

A WOMAN NAMED JACKIE
NBC 10/13 & 15/91. (Larry Peerce), Roma Downey, Stephen Collins, William Devane, Rosemary Murphy (6 hrs.).

A WOMAN OF INDEPENDENT MEANS
NBC 2/19, 20 & 22/95. (Preston Fischer), Sally Field, Ron Silver, Tony Goldwyn, Jack Thompson, Sheila McCarthy (6 hrs.).

WOMAN ON A LEDGE
NBC 3/15/93. (Chris Thomson), Leslie Charleston, Deidre Hall, Colleen Zenk Pinter (2 hrs.).

WOMAN ON THE RUN:
THE LAWRENCIA BEMBENEK STORY
NBC 5/16 & 17/93. (Sandor Stern), Tatum O'Neal, Bruce Greenwood, Peggy McCay, Colin Fox (4 hrs.).

WOMAN UNDONE
SHO 2/4/96. (Evelyn Purcell) Mary McDonnell, Randy Quaid, Sam Elliott, Jim Mercer, Charles Noland, Cheryl Anderson.

THE WOMAN WHO LOVED ELVIS
ABC 4/18/93. (Bill Bixby), Roseanne Arnold, Tom Arnold, Sally Kirkland, Cynthia Gibb (2 hrs.).

WOMAN WHO SINNED, THE
ABC 11/17/91. (Michael Switzer), Susan Lucci, Tim Matheson, Michael Dudikoff, John Vernon (2 hrs.).

WOMAN WITH A PAST
NBC 3/2/92. (Mimi Leder), Pamela Reed, Dwight Schultz, Richard Lineback, Carrie Snodgress (2 hrs.).

WOMEN & MEN: STORIES OF SEDUCTION
HBO 8/19/90. (Frederic Raphael, Ken Russell, Tony Richardson), Elizabeth McGovern, Peter Weller, James Woods (90 mins.).

WOMEN & MEN 2: IN LOVE THERE ARE NO RULES
HBO 8/18/91. (Walter Bernstein, Kristi Zea, Mike Figgis), Matt Dillon, Andie MacDowell, Scott Glenn (90 mins.).

THE WOMEN OF SPRING BREAK
CBS 1/10/95. (Bill Norton), Shelley Long, Mel Harris, DeLane Matthews, Ian Ziering, Francois-Eric Gendorn (2 hrs.).

WOOF RETURNS! A KID'S BEST FRIEND
DIS 3/30/95. (David Cobham), Edward Fidoe, Thomas Aldwinkle, John Ringham (2 hrs.).

WORKING TRASH
FOX 11/26/90. (Alan Metter), George Carlin, Ben Stiller, Buddy Ebsen (2 hrs.).

WORLD WAR II: WHEN LIONS ROARED
NBC 4/19 & 20/94. (Joseph Sargent), Michael Caine, Bob Hoskins, John Lithgow, Ed Begley Jr. (4 hrs.).

THE WORLD'S OLDEST LIVING BRIDESMAID
CBS 9/21/90. (Joseph L. Scanlon), Donna Mills, Brian Wimmer, Art Hindle, Beverly Garland (2 hrs.).

WOUNDED HEART
USA 8/16/95. (Vic Sarin), Paula DeVicq, Jon Hensley, Hank Stratton, Anita Barone, William Newman, Scott Stevens (2 hrs.).

WRITER'S BLOCK
USA 10/9/91. (Charles Correll), Morgan Fairchild, Michael Praed, Joe Regalbuto, Douglas Rowe (2 hrs.).

THE WRONG MAN
SHO 9/5/93. (Jim McBride), John Lithgow, Rosanna Arquette (2 hrs.).

THE WRONG WOMAN
CBS 3/26/96. Nancy McKeon, Chelsea Field, Michele Scarbelli.

X Y Z

XXX'S AND OOO'S
CBS 6/21/94. (Allan Arkush), Debrah Farentino, Andrea Parker, Nia Peeples (2 hrs.).

THE YARN PRINCESS
ABC 3/27/94. (Tom McLoughlin), Jean Smart, Robert Pastorelli, Dennis Boutsikaris (2 hrs.).

THE YEARLING
CBS 4/24/94. (Rod Hardy), Peter Strauss, Jean Smart, Wil Horneff, Philip Seymour (2 hrs.).

YES VIRGINIA, THERE IS A SANTA CLAUS
ABC 12/8/91. (Charles Jarrott), Richard Thomas, Charles Bronson, Katharine Isobel, Edward Asner (2 hrs.).

YOUNG AT HEART
CBS 3/12/95. (Allan Arkush), Olympia Dukakis, Joe Penny, Philip Bosco, Yannick Bisson, Louis Zorich, Audrey Landers (2 hrs.).

YOUNG CATHERINE
TNT 2/17 & 18/91. (Michael Anderson), Vanessa Redgrave, Julia Ormond, Christopher Plummer (4 hrs.).

YOUNG INDIANA JONES AND THE HOLLYWOOD FOLLIES
FAM 10/15/94. (Michael Schultz), Sean Patrick Flanery, Dana Gladstone, Allison Smith, Stephen Caffery, Bill Cusack (2 hrs.).

YOUNG INDIANA JONES: TRAVELS WITH FATHER
FAMILY 6/16/96. (Michael Schultz) Corey Carrier, Michael Gough, George Jackos, Lloyd Owen, George Yiasoumi.

ZELDA
TNT 11/7/93. (Pat O'Connor), Natasha Richardson, Timothy Hutton, Jon De Vries, Daniel Gerroll (2 hrs.).

ZOOMAN
SHO 3/19/95. (Leon Ichaso), Louis Gossett Jr., Charles S. Dutton, Cynthia Martells, C.C.H. Pounder (105 mins.).

TELEVISION MOVIES & MINI-SERIES

(OCTOBER 1, 1997—SEPTEMBER 30, 1998)

THE ADVOCATE'S DEVIL
Produced by Presto Productions in association with Columbia TriStar Television. Producers: Jeff Bleckner, Elon Dershowitz, Karen Moore. Director: Jeff Bleckner. Writers: Alan M. Dershowitz, Cyrus Nowrasteh, James Steven Sadwith. Shown Oct. 5, 1997.
Cast: Ken Olin, Mariska Hargitay, Gina Philips, Wendell Pierce, Jessica Tuck, Gary Basaraba, Gillian Barber, Scott Hylands.

ADDAMS FAMILY REUNION
Produced by Fox Family Films.
Cast: Tim Curry, Daryl, Hannah, Ed Begley Jr., Nicole Fugere, Alice Ghostley, Estelle Harris, Christopher Hart, Jerry Messing.

ALIEN ABDUCTION: INCIDENT IN LAKE COUNTY
Dick Clark Productions. Writer: Dean Alioto. Shown Jan 20, 1998.
Cast: Benz Antoinee, Kristian Ayre, Gillian Barber, Michael Buie, Emmanuelle Chriqui, Marva Belver, Katlyn Ducharme.

ALL THE WINTERS THAT HAVE BEEN
Jaffe/Braunstein Productions. Director: Jerry London, Writer: Linda Bergman. Shown on CBS, September 21, 1997.
Cast: Karen Allen, Sheila Tousey, Ben Cardinal, Richard Chamberlin, Hal Holbrook.

ALWAYS OUTNUMBERED
HBO NYC Productions and Palomar Pictures. Executive producers: Laurence Fishburne, Walter Mosley. Producers: Anne-Marie MacKay, Jonathon Key. Director: Michael Apted. Shown on HBO, March 21,1998.
Cast: Laurence Fishburne, Cicely Tyson, Bill Cobbs, Natalie Cole, Bill Duke, Laurie Metcalf, Bill Nunn, Isiah Washington.

ANGELS IN THE ENDZONE
Walt Disney Television in association with Arts & Leisure Corporation and Endzone Productions. Director: Gary Nadeau. Writers: Alan Eisenstock, Larry Mintz. Producers: Roger Birnbaum, Richard L. O'Connor.
Cast: Paul Dooley, Matthew Lawrence, David Gallagher, Christopher Lloyd, Lynda Boyd, Jack Coleman, Allan Zinyk.

AN UNEXPECTED LIFE
A Lee Rose production in association with Studios USA. Writer: Lee Rose. Shown on USA, June 24, 1998.
Cast: Stockard Channing, Stephen Collins.

ASSAULT ON DEVIL'S ISLAND
Alliance Entertainment in association with Turner Network Television and Ber/Schwartz/Bonann Productions. Producers: Kevin L. Beggs, Michael Berk, Eric Bischoff, Gregory J. Bonann, Paul Cajero, Bryan R Gawron, Joe Geus. Director: Jon Cassar. Writers: Michael Berk, Douglas Schwartz, Calvin Clements Jr., Steven McKay. Shown Oct. 28, 1997.
Cast: Hulk Hogan, Carl Weathers, Shannon Tweed, Martin Kove, Trevor Goddard, Chris Douglas, Mike White, Billy Banks.

THE BABY DANCE
An Egg Pictures Production in association with Pacific Motion Pictures. Director/Writer: Jane Anderson. Producers: Meg LeFauve, Vicky Herman. Executive producers: Jodie Foster, Robert Halmi Jr., Tony Allard, Matthew O'Connor. Shown on Showtime, Aug. 23, 1998.
Cast: Stockard Channing, Laura Dern, Richard Lineback, Peter Riegert, Laura Dern, Wally Dalton, Stephen E. Miller.

BAD AS I WANNA BE: THE DENNIS RODMAN STORY
Mandalay Television in association with Mandalay Sports Entertainment. Executive Producer: Tom Patricia. Producer: John Perrin Flynn. Director: Jean De Segonzac. Writers: John Miglis, Gary Haywood. Shown on ABC, Feb. 8, 1998.
Cast: Dwayne Adway, Daniel Hugh Kelly, Dee Wallace Stone, John Terry, Michael Galoz, Karen Robinson, Isys McKoy.

BARBARA TAYLOR'S LOVE IN ANOTHER TOWN
Alexander Adelson Entertainment. Director: Lorraine Senna. Writer: H Haden Yelin. Shown on CBS, Oct. 19, 1997.
Cast: Victoria Principal, Adrian Pasdar, Mary Kay Place.

BEFORE WOMEN HAD WINGS
Harpo Films. Director: Lloyd Kramer. Writer: Connie May Fowler. Producers: Jay Benson, Kate Forte, Oprah Winfrey, Shown Oct. 26, 1997.
Cast: Oprah Winfrey, Ellen Barkin, Tina Majorino, Julia Stiles, John Savage, Burt Young, William Lee Scott, Louis Crugnali.

BELLA MAFIA
Konigsberg Co in association with CBS Television. Executive Producer: Frank Konigsberg. Producer: Jack Clements, Director: David Greene. Shown on CBS, Nov. 16 & 18, 1997.
Cast: Vanessa Redgrave, Dennis Farina, Nastassja Kinski, Jennifer Tilly, Illena Douglas, Tony Lo Bianco, James Marsden.

BEST FRIENDS FOR LIFE
Hallmark Entertainment in association with Dan Paulson. Director: Michael Switzer. Writer: Cynthia Whitcomb. Shown on CBS, Jan. 18, 1998.
Cast: Gena Rowlands, Linda Lavin, Richard Farnsworth, Gwen Verdon, Helen Slater.

BLACKJACK
WCG Entertainment Productions in association with Baton Inc, Alliance Communications Corporation and USA Pictures. Producers: Terence Chang, Christopher Godsick, Peter Lance, John Ryan, John Woo, David Wu. Director: John Woo. Writer: Peter Lance. Shown on USA, June 1998.
Cast: Dolph Lundgren, Kate Vernon, Phillip Mackenzie, Kam Heskin, Fred Williamson, Padraign Murphy.

BLACKOUT EFFECT
Citadel Entertainment in association with First Street Films. Director: Jeff Bleckner. Writer: Matthew Bombeck. Shown Jan. 4, 1998.
Cast: Eric Stoltz, Charles Martin Smith, Leslie Hope, Lorraine Toussaint, Andy Comeau, Tucker Smallwood, Joe Guzaldo.

BLADE
Director: Ralph Hemecker. Writer: W Peter Iliff. Producers: Kim Fleary, Elliot Friedgen, W Peter Iliff, Robert Mickelson. Shown Aug. 12, 1998.
Cast: Yancey Arias, Kirk Baltz, Joy Bisco, Lori Heuring, Mushond Lee, Corin Nemec, David Sheinkopf, Michael Storm.

BLOOD ON HER HANDS
Robert Greenwald Productions Inc. Producers: Robert Greenwald, Helmut Huber, Philip K Kleinbart, Kimberly Rubin. Director: Steven Robman. Writers: Kenneth Berg, Steve Johnson. Shown March 22, 1998.
Cast: Susan Lucci, John O'Hurley, Lauren Collins, Philip Casnoff, Kamar De Los Reyes, Joe Grifasi, Nicholas Campbell.

BORROWED HEARTS
Atlantis Films in association with CTV. Producers: Gary Delfiner, Roma Downey, Ed Gernon, Mary Kahn. Director: Ted Kotcheff. Writers: Earl Wallace, Pamela Wallace. Shown Nov. 30, 1997.
Cast: Roma Downey, Eric McCormack, Shawn Thompson, Janet Bailey, Kevin Hicks, Barbara Gordon, Sarah Rosen.

BRAVE NEW WORLD
Filmed in Los Angeles by Michael Joyce Productions in association with Dan Wigutow Productions for USA Network Studios. Executive Producer: Dan Witgutow. Producer: Michael R. Joyce. Directors: Leslie Libman, Larry Williams. Writers: Dan Mazur, David Tausik. Shown on NBC, April 19, 1998.
Cast: Peter Gallagher, Leonard Nimoy, Tim Guinee, Rya Kihlstedt, Sally Kirkland, Miguel Ferrer.

BREAKFAST WITH EINSTEIN
Director: Craig Shapiro. Producer: Kelli Konop. Shown May 24, 1998.
Cast: Thomas Gottschalk, Priscilla Presley, Shia Lebeouf, Ben Foster, Jessica Bowman, Ben Stein.

BREAST MEN
Filmed by HBO Pictures. Executive Producer: Gar Lucchesi. Producer: Guy Roedel. Director: Lawrence O'Neil. Writer: John Stockwell. Shown on HBO, Dec. 13, 1997.
Cast: David Schwimmer, Chris Cooper, Emily Procter, Matt Frewer, Louise Fletcher.

A BRIGHT SHINING LIE
Filmed in Lompburi Thailand by HBO Pictures. Executive Producer: Lois Bonfiglio. Producer: Greg Ricketson. Director/Writer: Terry George. Shown on HBO, May 30 1998.
Cast: Bill Paxton, Amy Madigan, Vivian Wu, Donal Logue, Eric Bogosian, Kurtwood Smith, Robert J. Burke, James Rebhorn.

BUFFALO SOLDIERS
Trilogy group/Citadel Enterprise Productions. Executive producers: David R Ginsburg, John Watson, Pen Densham, Richard Lewis, Danny Glover. Director: Charles Haid. Writers: Frank Military, Susan Rhinehart.
Cast: Danny Glover, Lamont Bentley, Tom Bower, Timothy Busfield, Gabriel Casseus, Bob Gunton, Keith Jefferson.

BURIED ALIVE II
Produced by Universal Pictures in association USA Pictures. Director: Tim Matheson. Shown on USA, July 29, 1998.
Cast: Stephen Caffrey, Brian Libby, Tim Matheson, Tracey Needham, Ally Sheedy.

CASPER MEETS WENDY
Producer: Mike Elliott. Director: Sean McNamara. Writer: Jymm Magon. Shown Sept. 22, 1998
Cast: Shelley Duvall, Jeremy Foley, Blake Foster, Teri Garr, George Hamilton, Cathy Moriarty.

CHANCE OF A LIFETIME
Roaring Fork Productions in association with Citadel Entertainment. Director: Deborah Reinisch. Writers: Paul Morris, Renee Longstreet. Shown on CBS, March 29, 1998.
Cast: John Ritter, Katey Sagal, Jean Stapleton.

CHANGE OF HEART
A Freyda Rothstein Production in association with Hearst Entertainment. Executive producer: Freyda Rothstein. Director: Arvin Brown. Writer/Co-Producer: Aaron Mendelsohn. Shown on Lifetime, July 20, 1998.
Cast: Jean Smart, John Terry, Phillip Geoffrey, Shawna Waldron, Gretchen Corbett, George A Keller.

CIRCLE OF DECEIT
Produced by Andrea Baynes Productions in association with ABC Pictures. Producers: Karen Clark, Barbara Kelly, Janine Turner, Andrea Baynes. Director: Alan Metzger. Writer: Karen Clark. Shown on ABC, Jan. 29, 1998.
Cast: Janine Turner, Esai Morales, Joanna Cassidy, Tracy Griffith, Matthew Prior, Robert Wisden, Dean Wray.

THE CON
Wilshire Court Productions in association with Mi Sammy Productions. Director: Steven Schachter. Writers: William H Macy, Steven Schachter. Producers: Howard Griffith, Jeff Henry, Bob Rose.
Cast: William H. Macy, Rebecca De Mornay, Mike Naussbaum, Angela Paton, Frances Sternhagen, Tony Frank, Don Harvey.

CONVICTIONS
ABC Pictures in association with Lifetime Television. Producers: Anne Hopkins, Marian Rees. Director: Joyce Chopra. Writers: Phil Pennington, Ann Beckett. Shown on Lifetime, Nov. 10, 1997.
Cast: Blair Brown.

THE COWBOY AND THE MOVIE STAR
Saban Entertainment. Director: Mark Griffiths. Writers: Rob Gilmer, Michael Petryni. Producers: Mike Elliott, Lance H Robbins.
Cast: Sean Young, Perry King, Priscilla Barnes, David Groh, Michael Chieffo, Steve Kanaly, George Pilgrim.

CREATURE
Produced by Trilogy Entertainment Group/MGM Television. Producers: Brent-Karl Clackson, Robert Halmi Jr., Richard B. Lewis, Mark Stern, John Watson. Director: Stuart Gilliard. Writer: Peter Benchley, Rockne S. O'Bannon. Shown May 17, 1998.
Cast: Craig T Nelson, Kim Cattrall, Colm Feore, Cress Williams, Michael Reilly Burke, Michael Michele.

DALLAS: WAR OF THE EWINGS
Produced by Lakeside Productions Inc. in association with Warner Bros. Producers: Patrick Duffy, Elliot Friedgen, Larry Hagman, Rich Heller. Director: Michael Preece. Writers: Arthur Bernard Lewis, Julie Sayres.
Cast: Patrick Duffy, Linda Gray, Larry Hagman, Michele Johnson, Steve Kanaly, George Kennedy, Tracy Scoggins.

THE DEFENDERS: CHOICE OF EVILS
Produced by Stan Rogow Productions in association with Paramount Network Television, and Showtime Networks. Director: Andy Wolk. Writers: Reginald Rose, Andy Wolk, Peter Wolk. Shown on Showtime, Jan. 18, 1998.
Cast: Beau Bridges, E.G. Marshall, Martha Plimpton, Jon Polito, Lisa Gay Hamilton, David Hemblen.

DOGBOYS
Goodstuff Entertainment in association with Showtime Networks Inc. Director: Ken Russell. Writers: Dennis Kleinman, Hugh Martin, Rob Stork, David Taylor.
Cast: Bryan Brown, Dean Cain, Tia Carrere, Ken James, Sean McCann, Richard Chevolleau, Hardee T. Lineham, Von Flores.

DON KING:ONLY IN AMERICA
HBO Pictures in association with Thomas Carter Company. Executive producer: Thomas Carter. Producer: David Blocker. Director: John Herzfeld. Shown on HBO, Nov. 15, 1997.
Cast: Ving Rhames, Vondie Curtis-Hall, Jeremy Piven, Keith David, Darius McCrary, Bernie Mac Loretta Devine.

THE ECHO OF THUNDER
Produced by Hallmark Hall of Fame Productions Inc. Producers: Dorothea G Petrie, Brent Shields, Richard Welsh. Director: Simon Wincer. Writers: Libby Hathor, H. Haden Yelin. Shown on April 19, 1998.
Cast: Judy Davis, Jamey Sheridan, Lauren Hewett, Ernie Dingo, Emily Jane Browning, Chelsea Yates, Jamie Croft.

ELLEN FOSTER
Hallmark Productions. Executive Producer: Richard Welsh. Co-executive Producers: Brent Shields, Ruth Slawson. Producer/Director: John Erman. Writers: Maria Nation, William Hanley. Shown on CBS, Dec. 14, 1997.
Cast: Julie Harris, Jena Malone, Ted Levine, Glynnis O'Connor, Debra Monk, Barbara Garrick, Kate Burton, Zeljko Ivanek.

ESCAPE FROM WILCAT CANYON
Telescene Film Group Inc. Production for Showtime Original Pictures. Producer: Micheline Garant. Director: Marc F. Voizard, Writer: Robert Gosnell. Shown on Showtime, June 21, 1998.
Cast: Dennis Weaver, Michael Caloz, Peter Keleghan, Barbara Radecki.

ESCAPE: HUMAN CARGO
Produced by Neufeld Rehme Productions in association with Showtime Networks. Director: Simon Wince. Writers: John McDonald, Clyde Burelson, William Mickelberry, Dan Vining. Shown on Showtime, March 22, 1998.
Cast: Treat Williams, Stephen Lang, Sasson Gabai, Jack Adalist, Hamis Arbid, Johnny Arbid, Brandon Blue, Brent Bone.

EVERY MOTHER'S WORST FEAR
Produced by USA Pictures. Director: Bill Norton. Writer: John Robert Bensink. Shown Aug. 19, 1998.
Cast: Cheryl Ladd, Jordan Ladd.

EVERY NINE SECONDS
Freyda Rothstein Productions in association with Jean Abounader Productions and Hearst Entertainment. Producers: Jean Abounader, Adam Greenman, Lillie Morris, Freyda Rothstein, Deborah Wolsh. Director: Kenneth Link. Writer: Adam Greenman. Shown Oct. 12, 1997
Cast: Gail O'Grady, Amy Pietz, Michael Riley, Emily Hampshire, Scott Speedman, Djanet Sears.

EVERYTHING THAT RISES
Produced by Larry Levinson Productions in association with The Magnus Company and TNT. Producers: Mary Church, Frank Q Dobbs, Lincoln Lagesson, Larry Levinson, Joe Lunne, Jana Sue Memel. Director: Dennis Quaid. Writer: Mark Spragg. Shown on TNT, July 12, 1998.
Cast: Dennis Quaid, Mare Winningham, Harve Presnell, Meat Loaf, Ryan Merriman, Bruce McGill, Denise Durham.

EVIDENCE OF BLOOD
Produced by MGM Television. Director: Andrew Mondshein. Writers: Thomas H. Cook, Dalene Young. Producer: Becky Arntzen.
Cast: David Strathairn, Mary McDonnell, Sean McCann, Chris Wiggins, Jackie Burroughs, Nancy Beatty, Marnie McPhail.

FACE DOWN
Thom Eberhardt-Roni Weisberg Productions in association with Hallmark Entertainment Inc. Producer: Roni Weisberg. Director: Thom Eberhardt. Writer: Thom Eberhardt. Shown Nov. 15, 1997.
Cast: Joe Mantegna, Peter Riegert, Kelli Maroney, Cameron Thor, Adam Ant, J. K. Simmons, Shannon Lawson.

A FATHER FOR BRITTANY
Grossbart Barnett Productions. Writer: Scott Swanon. Director: Alan Metzger. Shown on CBS, March 15, 1998
Cast: Andrew McCarthy, Teri Polo, Michael Learned, Shirley Knight.

FIFTEEN AND PREGNANT
Hearst Entertainment in association with Lifetime Television. Producer: Diana Kerew. Director: Sam Pillsbury. Writer: Susan Cuscuna. Shown Jan. 19, 1998.
Cast: Kirsten Dunst, Park Overall.

FINAL DESCENT
Mandalay Television in association with Columbia TriStar Television. Producers: Michael O Gallant, Tom Patricia, Mike Robe. Director: Mike Robe. Writers: Robert P. Davis, Roger Young. Shown Oct. 12, 1997.
Cast: Robert Urich, Annette O'Toole, John De Lancie, Jim Byrnes, Ken Pogue, Blu Mankuma, Tom McBeath.

FINAL JUSTICE
Hearst Entertainment in association Lifetime Television. Producers: Chad Hoffman, Robert Schwartz. Director:Tommy Lee Wallace. Writer: Babs Greyhosky. Shown July 20, 1998.
Cast: Annette O'Toole, Micheal McKean

THE FIXER
Showtime Pictures. Director/Writer: Charles Robert Carner. Shown March 18, 1998.
Cast: Jon Voight, Brenda Bakke, J.J. Johnston, Miguel Sandoval, Jack Wallace, Barbara Gordon, Sara Botsford.

FLOATING AWAY
Director: John Badham. Writer: Tim Sandlin. Shown on Showtime, Aug. 30, 1998.
Cast: Rosanna Arquette, Paul Hogan, Judd Reinhold.

FOREVER LOVE
Longbow Productions in association with Starstruck Entertainment and Nassar Entertainment. Director: Michael Switzer. Writer: Joyce Heft Brotman. Shown on CBS, Sept. 27, 1998.
Cast: Reba McEntire, Tim Matheson, Bess Armstrong.

FUGITIVE MIND
Produced by Synthetic Film Works. Producers: Ashok Amritraj, Les Nordhauser, Fred Olen Ray, Andrew Stevens. Director: Fred Olen Ray.
Cast: Michael Dudikoff, Michele Green, Phil Hawn, David Hedison, Heather Langenkamp, Ian Ogilvy, Judson Scott.

THE GARBAGE PICKING FIELD GOAL KICKING PHILADELPHIA PHENOMENON
Produced by Walt Disney Television in association with Brillstein-Grey Entertainment. Director:Tom Kelleher. Writers: Greg Fields, Tom Kelleher. Shown Feb. 15, 1998.
Cast: Tony Danza, Jessica Tuck, Art LaFleur, Jaime Cardriche, Julie Stewart, Gil Filar, Al Ruscio, Ray Wise, Chris Berman.

GARGANTUA
Produced by Twentieth Century-Fox Film Corporation. Producers: Ronald Parker, Peter V Ware. Director: Bradford May. Writer: Ronald Parker. Shown on Fox, May 19, 1998.
Cast: Adam Baldwin, Julie Carmen, Emile Hirsch.

GET TO THE HEART: THE BARBARA MANDRELL STORY
Mandalay/Guber Productions. Director: Lamont Johnson. Writer: Quinton Peeple. Shown on CBS, Sept. 28, 1998.
Cast: Barbara Mandrell, Dolly Parton, Kenny Rogers, Maureen McCormack.

GIVE UP THE GHOST
ABC Pictures in association with Lifetime Television. Producers: Paula Weinstein, Anthea Sylbert. Director: Claudia Weil. Writers: Anthea Sylbert, Richard Romanus. Shown on Lifetime, Sept. 7, 1998.
Cast: Marg Helenberger, Alan Rosenberg.

GOLDRUSH: A REAL LIFE ALASKAN ADVENTURE
Director: John Power. Producers: Fitch Cady, Jeni Munn. Writers: Jacqueline Feather, David Seidler. Shown March 8, 1998.
Cast: Alyssa Milano, William Morgan Sheppard, Stan Cahill, Peter Flemming, Frank C. Turner, Tom Scholte.

HARLEQUIN'S, THE WAITING GAME
Alliance Communications/Second Wave Productions. Writers: Barbara O'Kelley, Jennifer Black, Peter Lauterman. Shown on The Movie Channel, Aug. 9, 1998.
Cast: Chandra West, Paula Abdul.

HEART FULL OF RAIN
CBS in association with Weiss/Moore Productions. Director: Roger Young. Writer: Quinton Peeples. Shown on CBS, Oct. 5, 1997.
Cast: Richard Crenna, Rick Schroder, Carroll Baker, Gabriel Mick, Kim Dickens.

THE HIRED HEART
Hearst Entertainment in association with Lifetime Television. Producer: Philip Roger. Director: Jeremy Kagen. Writer: Jeff Elison. Shown Oct. 13, 1997.
Cast: Penelope Ann Miller, Barry Corbin, Graham Greene, Brett Cullen.

HIS BODYGUARD
Distributed by Power Pictures in association with Wilshire Court Productions. Director: Artie Mandelberg. Producers: Julian Marks, Tracey Thompson, Mark Winemaker. Shown on USA, Aug. 1, 1998.
Cast: Robert Bockstael, Ho Chow, Michael Copeman, Elvis Dressler, T. L. Forsberg, Robin Gammell, Robert Guillaume.

HOLIDAY IN YOUR HEART
Von Zerneck Sertner Films in association with Stephanie Germaine Productions. Director: Michael Switzer. Writers: Tim Carter, LeAnn Rimes, Ellen Weston. Producers: Stephanie Germain, Robert M. Sertner, Randy Sutter, Frank von Zerneck. Shown Dec. 14, 1997.
Cast: LeAnn Rimes, Bernadette Peters, Rebecca Schull, Vernon Grote, Carol Farabee, Harlan Jordan, Rance Howard.

HOUSE OF FRANKENSTEIN
Big Productions Inc. and Michael R. Joyce Productions in association with Universal Televison Entertainment and HOF Productions Inc for NBC Entertainment. Executive Producer: David Israe. Producer: Michael R Joyce. Directors: Peter Werner. Writer: J.B. White. Shown on NBC, Nov. 2, 1997.
Cast: Adrian Pasdar, Greg Wise, Teri Polo, CCH Pounder, Miguel Sandoval, Jorja Fox, Peter Crombie.

THE HUNTED
Producers: Stuart Cooper, Jennifer Davis, Martin Ganz, Elke Keck, Doris Kirch, Colleen Nystedt. Director: Stuart Cooper. Writers: Bennett Cohen, David Ives. Shown April 28, 1998.
Cast: Madchen Amick, Harry Hamlin, Hannes Jaenicke, Enuka Okuma, Peter LaCroix, Terence Kelley.

I KNOW WHAT YOU DID
O'Hara/Horowitz Productions. Producers: Chuck Bowman, Rona Edwards, Lillian Gallo, Lawrence Horowitz, Tracey Jeffrey, Michael O'Hara, Nicholas Yellen. Director: Chuck Bowman. Writers: Tom Gates, Paul Stefaniak. Shown Jan. 11, 1998.
Cast: Rosanna Arquette, Steven Eckoldt, Lochlyn Munro, Teryl Rothery, Gary Chalk, Fulvio Cecere, Lawrence Monoson.

I'LL BE HOME FOR CHRISTMAS
Jaffe Braunstein Productions. Director: Jerry London. Writer: Darrah Cloud. Producers: Howard Braunstein, Darrah Cloud, Michael Jaffe, Susan Murdoch.
Cast: Ann Jillian, Robert Hays, Jack Palance, Tom Harvey, Linda Sorenson, Eric Peterson, Ashley Gorrell.

IN THE BEGINNING
Produced by Babylonian Productions. Director:Michael Vejar. Writer:J Michael Straczynski. Producers:John Copeland, Douglas Netter, Susan Norkin, J. Michael Straczynski. Shown Jan. 4, 1998. Shown Jan 4, 1998.
Cast:Bruce Boxleitner, Mira Furlan, Richard Biggs, Andreas Katsulas, Peter Jurasik, Theodore Bikel, Raynor Scheine.

IN THE DOUGHOUSE
Showtime Pictures in association Viacom Productions. Director: George Miller. Executive producer/Writer: Paul Bernbaum. Shown on Showtime, Sept. 6, 1998.
Cast: Matt Frewer, Rhea Pearlman, Trevor Morgan.

INDEFENSIBLE: THE TRUTH ABOUT EDWARD BRANNIGAN
Carla Singer Productions. Director: Brian Dennehy. Writer: Joe Cacaci. Shown on CBS, Nov. 23, 1997.
Cast: Brian Dennehy, Reed Diamond, Alice Krige, Lynn Redgrave.

INDISCREET
An Magic Hour Pictures Film Production. Director: Marc Bienstock. Based on a Vladimir Nemirovsky screenplay. Shown on HBO, Aug. 28, 1998.
Cast: Luke Perry, Gloria Reuben, Adam Baldwin, Peter Coyote, Lisa Edelstein.

INDISCRETION OF AN AMERICAN WIFE
ABC Pictures in association with Lifetime Televison. Director: George Kaczender. Writer: Emily Tracey. Producer: Lisa Demberg. Shown on Lifetime, March 9, 1998.
Cast: Anne Archer, Michael Murphy.

THE INSPECTORS
Logo Entertainment in association with Warren Weidman and New City Productions. Producers: Louis Gossett Jr., Dennis Considine, Colleen Nystedt. Director: Brad Turner. Writer: Bruce Zimmerman. Shown on Showtime, Sept. 18, 1998.
Cast: Louis Gossett Jr., Jonathan Silverman, Tobias Mehler, Gregory Thirloway, Samantha Ferris, Claire Riley.

INTO THIN AIR: DEATH ON EVEREST
Sofronski Productions in association with Columbia TriStar Television. Executive producer: Bernard Sofronski. Producer:Hans Proppe. Director: Robert Markowitz. Screenwriter: Robert J. Avrech. Shown on ABC, Nov. 9 1997.
Cast: Peter Horton, Christopher McDonald, Nathaniel Parker, Richard Jenkins, Tim Dutton, Pamela Gien, Peter J Lucas.

I'VE BEEN WAITING FOR YOU
Assistant Director: Wayne Bennett. Writer: Lois Duncan. Shown March 22, 1998.
Cast: Sarah Chalke, Markie Post, Ben Foster, Christian Campbell, Tom Dugan, Soleil Moon Frye.

JOE TORRE: CURVEBALLS ALONG THE WAY
British American Television in association with Norman Twain Productions, Hallmark Entertainment Inc and Showtime networks Inc. Producers: Bernard F. Conners, Steve Hewitt, Thomas F. Leahy, Norman Twain. Director: Sturla Gunnarsson. Writer: Philip Rosenberg. Shown on Showtime, Oct. 17, 1997.
Cast: Paul Sorvino, Robert Loggia, Barbara Williams, Gailard Sartain, Marilyn Chris, Eugene A. Clark, Kenneth Welsh.

JUST FRIENDS
A Five Sisters Production. Executive Producer: Bud Stone. Producers: Jordan Leibert, Kim Adelman. Director/Producer: Maria Burton. Writer: Chuck Rose. Shown on Romance Classics, Sept. 10, 1998.
Cast: Tony Palermo, Anita Barone, Hal Linden, Barbara Alyn Woods, Tim Bohn, Cameron Watson, Ursula Burton.

KISS AND TELL
Distributed by Phaedra Cinema. Producers: Delia Fine, Sally Head, Sarah Wilson. Directors: Jordan Alan, David Richards. Writers: Jordan Alan, Heidi Thomas. Shown Oct. 17, 1997.
Cast: Peter Howitt, Gillian Bevan, Danny Worters, Hilda Braid, Claire Cathcart, Rosie Rowell, Ralph Ineson, Daniel Craig.

LABOR OF LOVE
ABC Pictures in association with Lifetime Television. Writer: Nina Shengold. Director: Karen Arthur. Producer: Ken Raskoff. Premieres on Lifetime, May 4, 1998.
Cast: Marcia Gay Ilarden, David Marshall.

THE LAST DON II
Produced by Konigsberg-Sanitzky Productions. Director: Graeme Clifford. Shown May 3, 1998.
Cast: Jason Gedrick, Patsy Kensit, Kirstie Alley, David Marciano, James Wilder, Jason Isaacs, Michelle Thomas.

LEGALESE
New Line Television. Producers: Cindy Hornickel, Glenn Jordan. Executive Producer: J. Paul Higgins. Director: Glenn Jordan. Writer: Billy Ray. Shown on TNT, Oct. 4, 1998.
Cast: James Garner, Gina Gershon, Mary-Louise Parker, Ed Kerr, Kathleen Turner, Brian Doyle-Murray.

LEGION
Produced by Mahogonny Productions. Director: Jon Hess. Writer: Evan Spilotopoulos. Shown April 18, 1998.
Cast: Parker Stevenson, Terry Farrell, Corey Feldman, Rick Springfield, Troy Donahue, Audie England, Trevor Goddard.

LEGION OF FIRE:KILLER ANTS!
Producers: Rhonda Bloom, George Manasse, Irwin Meyer. Directors: Jim Charleston, George Manass. Writer: Wink Roberts. Shown June 24, 1998.
Cast: Eric Lutes, Julia Campbell, Mitch Pileggi, Jeremy Foley, Dallen Gettling.

LET ME CALL YOU SWEETHEART
Grosso-Jacobson Entertainment Corporation. Director: Bill Corcoran. Writers: Mary Higgins Clark, Christopher Lofton. Producers: Sonny Grosso, Lary Jacobson, Lisa Parasyn, Tony Thatcher. Shown Oct. 26, 1998.
Cast: Meredith Baxter, Victor Garber, Tony Lo Bianco, Colin Fox, Sophie Lang, Joe Lisi, Elizabeth Shepherd, Claire Celluci.

THE LONG ISLAND INCIDENT
Produced by Barwood Films. Director:Joseph Sargent. Writer:Maria Nation. Producers: Bob Christiansen, Cis Corman, Jordan Davis, Judy Miller, Rick Rosenberg, Barbra Streisand, Judith Verno, Rachel Verno. Shown April 19, 1998.
Cast: Laurie Metcalf, Mackenzie Astin, Tyrone Benskin, Cedric Smith, Elisa Moolecherry, Greg Ellwand, Lawrence Dane.

THE LONG WAY HOME
A Hallmark Entertainment Production. Executive Producers: Robert Halmi Sr., Lawrence Turman. Producer/Director: Glenn Jordan. Writers: Louise Vincent, Patrick Jamain. Shown on CBS, March 1, 1998.
Cast: Jack Lemmon, Sarah Paulson, Kristin Griffith, Garwin Sanford, Rosemary Dunsmore, Peter Dvorsky, Tom Butler.

THE LOVE LETTER
Hallmark Hall of Fame Production in association with Welsh/Raynor. Director: Dan Curtis. Writers: Jim Henderson, Pamela Gray. Shown on CBS, Feb. 1, 1998.
Cast: Campbell Scott, Jennifer Jason Leigh, Estelle Parsons.

THE MARRIAGE FOOL
Grossbart/Barnett Productions. Director: Charles Matthau. Writer: Richard Vetere. Shown on CBS, Sept. 20, 1998.
Cast: Walter Matthau, Carol Burnett, John Stamos, Teri Polo.

MEDUSA'S CHILD
Produced by The Comsky Group and Mandalay Televison in association with Columbia TriStar Television. Executive producer: Tom Patricia. Director: Larry Shaw. Writer/Co-Producer: Ellen Weston. Shown on ABC, Nov. 16 & 20, 1997.
Cast: Gail O'Grady, Christopher Noth, Vincent Spano, Lori Loughlin, Kevin Dillon, John Glover, Martin Sheen.

MERLIN II
Produced by Hallmark Entertainment Inc in association with NBC Entertainment. Director: Steve Barron. Writers: Edward Khmara, David Stevens, Peter Barnes. Shown April 26, 1998.
Cast: Sam Neill, Helena Bonham Carter, John Giegud, Rutger Hauer, James Earl Jones, Miranda Richardson.

METEORITES
Village Roadshow Productions in association with Wilshire Court Productions & USA Networks Inc. Producers: Brian Burgess, Jennifer Davis II. Shown on USA June 3, 1998.
Cast: Tom Wopat, Roxanne Hart, Abby Meates, Darrin Klimek, Pato Hoffman, Marshall Napier, Amiel Daemion, Leo Taylor.

MIND GAMES
Produced by Sarabande Productions. Producers: John Landgraf, Marcel Brassard, David Manson, Meredith Zamsky. Director: Jan Egleson. Writers: Arla Sorkin Manson, Paula Milne, Cynthia Saunders. *Cast:Jayne Brook, Kyle Secor, Lindsay Frost, William Greenblatt, Hayley Lochner, Marnie McPhail, Mark Wilson.*

MIRACLE IN THE WOODS
Patchett/Kaufman Production. Director: Arthur Allan Seidelman. Writer: Joe Slowensky. Shown on CBS, Oct. 26, 1997.
Cast: Della Reese, Meredith Baxter, Patricia Heaton, Anna Chlumsky.

MOBY DICK
Produced by Whale Productions Limited in association with USA Pictures, United Kingdom-Australia Co-Productions and Distributed by Hallmark Home Entertainment. Producers: Francis Coppola, Lulee Fisher, Fred Fuchs, Robert Haim Sr. Director: Franc Roddam. Writers: Herman Melville, Anton Diether, Franc Roddam. Shown on USA, March 15, 1998.
Cast: Patrick Stewart, Henry Thomas, Hugh Keays-Byrne, Ted Levine, Gregory Peck, Piripi Waretini, Shane Feeney-Connor.

MS. SCROOGE
Power Pictures in association with Wilshire Court Productions for USA Network. Producer: Julian Marks. Directed by John Korty. Teleplay: John McGreevey. Shown on USA, Dec. 10, 1997.
Cast: Cicely Tyson, Katherine Helmond, Michael Beach, John Bourgeois, Raevan Larrymore-Kelly, Karen Glave, Ken James.

MURDER SHE WROTE: SOUTH BY SOUTHWEST
Corymore Productions in association with Andrew Shaw and Angela Lansbury. Director: Anthony Shaw. Writer: Mark Burley. Shown on CBS, Nov. 2, 1997.
Cast: Angela Lansbury, Keith David, Mel Harris, Richard Riehl, John Vargas, Ray Baker, Harriet Harris.

MY OWN COUNTRY
Maintitles Pictures Productions. Director: Mira Nair. Writers: Jim Leonard Jr., Sooni Taraporevala, based on the best selling novel by Dr. Abraham Verghese. Shown on Showtime, July 12, 1998.
Cast: Naveen Andrews, Glenne Headly, Hal Holbrook, Marisa Tomei, Sean Hewitt.

NAKED CITY: JUSTICE WITH A BULLET
Showtime in association with Magnum Productions and Paramount Network Television. Director/Producer/Writer: Jeff Freilich. Shown on Showtime, Oct. 4, 1998.
Cast: Scott Glenn, Courtney B. Vance, Robin Tunney, Kathryn Erbe, Giancarlo Esposito.

NICHOLAS' GIFT
Produced by Lux Vide, Radiotelevisione Italiana, CBS Television, Five Miles River productions. Producers: Luca Bernabei, Marc Bruno, Russell Kagan, Paolo Lucidi, Lorenzo Minoli, Judd Parkin. Director: Robert Markowitz. Writer: Christine Berado. Shown on April 26, 1998.
Cast: Jamie Lee Curtis, Alan Bates, Hallie Kate Eisenberg, Gene Wexler, Isabella Ferrari, Anita Zagaria, Roberto Bisacco.

NICK FURY: AGENT OF S.H.I.E.L.D.
Produced by Fury Productions Limited Partnership in association with 20th Century Fox, National Studios Inc, Marvel Studios. Director: Rod Hardy. Writer: David Goyer. Producers: Avi Arad, Matthew Edelman, Tarquin Gotch, Stan Lee, Bob Lemchen, David Roessell. Shown May 26, 1998.
Cast: David Hasselhoff, Lisa Rinna, Sandra Hess, Neil Roberts, Gary Chalk, Tracey Waterhouse, Tom McBeath.

NIGHTMARE IN BIG SKY COUNTRY
Gaslight Pictures in association with ABC Pictures. Director: Alan Metzger. Writer: Sharon Elizabeth Doyle. Shown on Lifetime, Aug. 17, 1998.
Cast: Patricia Wettig.

NO LAUGHING MATTER
Produced by Universal TV in association with Great Falls Production. Producer: Jean Abounader. Director: Michael Elias. Writers: Michael Elias, Ted Kristian. Shown April 1, 1998.
Cast: Suzanne Somers, Chad Christ, Selma Blair, Robert Desiderio, Ann Bosler, Frank Gerrish, James Brewster.

NOBODY LIVES FOREVER
An O'Hara/Horowitz Production. Producers: Kristine Bamattre, Rick Blumenthal, Lawrence Horowitz, Tracey Jeffrey, Michael O'Hara. Director: Paul Wendkos. Writer: Edna Buchanan.
Cast: Greg Evigan, Brenda Bakke, Alexandra Powers, Kevin Dobson, Malcolm Stewart, Lynda Boyd, Gillian Barber.

OKLAHOMA CITY: A SURVIVOR'S STORY
ABC Pictures in association with Lifetime Television. Producer: Andrea Baynes. Director: John Korty. Writers: Sam Blackwell, Ara Watson. Shown, April 6, 1998.
Cast: Kathy Baker.

OLIVER TWIST
A Laurence Mark Production with Walt Disney Television. Executive Producers: Laurence Mark, John Baldecchhi. Producer: Steven North. Director: Tony Bill. Shown on ABC, Nov. 16, 1997.
Cast: Richard Dreyfuss, Elijah Wood, David O'hara, Alex Trench, Antoine Byrne, Olivia Caffrey, Anthony Finnegan.

ONE HOT SUMMER NIGHT
O'hara/Horowitz Productions. Producers: James A Contner, Michael Dougan, Lawrence Horowitz, Tracey Jeffrey, Michael O'Hara, Beth Schroeder. Director: James A. Contner. Writer: Michael O'Hara. Shown March 12, 1998.
Cast: Erika Eleniak, Brian Wimmer, Tobin Bell, Stephen Macht, Anne De Salvo, Lochlyn Munro, Christopher Darden.

ON THE LINE
Produced by All American Television Productions. Director: Elodie Keene. Writers: Walter Halsey Davis, Vickie Patik. Shown on ABC, Jan. 15, 1998.
Cast: Linda Hamilton, Jeff Fahey, Coolio, Jay Acovone, Marcia del Mar, Dan Ferro, Samaria Graham, Paul Herman.

ON THE SECOND DAY OF CHRISTMAS
ABC Pictures in association with Lifetime Television. Producer: Jane Goldenring. Director: James Frawley. Writer: Brian Hohlfeld. Shown Dec. 8, 1997.
Cast: Mark Ruffalo, Mary Stuart Masterson.

OPERATION DELTA FORCE:MAYDAY
Director: Yossi Wein. Writers: Danny Lerner, David Sparling. Shown April 22, 1998.
Cast: Michael McGrady, Simon Jones, Robert Patteri, Todd Jensen, Spencer Rochfort, Gavin Hood, J. Kenneth Campbell.

OUTRAGE
Polygram TV/American Zoetrope/Pacific Motion Pictures Corporation. Producers: Kevin Cooper, Francis Coppola, Preston Fischer, Fred Fuchs, Ellen Weston. Director: Robert Allan Ackerman. Writer: Ellen Weston. Shown Jan. 4, 1998.
Cast: Rob Lowe, Jennifer Gray, Eric Michael Cole, Shane Meier, Cyrus Theideke, Kathryn Harrold, Nathaniel Deveaux.

THE PATRON SAINT OF LIARS
Patchett Kaufman Entertainment. Producers: Ed Solorzano, Lynn Roth, Kenneth Kaufman, Stephen Gyllenhaal. Director: Stephen Gyllenhaal. Writers: Anne Patchett, Lynn Roth. Shown April 5, 1998.
Cast: Dana Delany, Sada Thompson, Clancy Brown, Ellen Burstyn, Nancy Moore Atchison, Jill Gascoine.

THE PENTAGON WARS
Howard Meltzer/The Entertainment Group in association with Jersey Films and HBO NYC. Executive producers: Danny DeVito, Michael Shamberg, Stacey Sher, Martyn Burke. Co- executive producer: Gail Lyon. Producer: Howard Meltzer. Director: Richard Benjamin. Writers: Jamie Malanowski, Martyn Burke. Shown on HBO, Feb. 28 1998.
Cast: Kelsey Grammer, Cary Elwes, Olympia Dukakis, Viola Davis, John C McGinley, Tom Wright, Clifton Powell.

THE PERFECT GETAWAY
Produced by Gaslight pictures in association with SRG Productions. Producers: Sandy Russell Gartin, Greg Gugliotta, Hans Proppe, Shanna Tyndall. Director: Armand Mastroianni. Writer: Tim Minear. Shown on HBO, Aug. 2, 1998.
Cast: Adrian Pasdar, Antonio Sabato Jr., Kelly Rutherford, Alicia Coppola, Nancy Linehan Charles, Loryn Locklin.

PLAYING TO WIN: A MOMENT OF TRUTH
An O'Hara-Horowitz Production. Producers: Lawrence Horowitz, Tracey Jeffrey, Michael O'Hara. Director: James A Contner. Writer: Sibyl Gardner. Shown Feb. 11, 1998.
Cast: Shelley Fabares, Lisa Dean Ryan, David Lascher, Gordon Currie, Kirby Morrow, Malcolm Stewart.

POODLE SPRINGS
Producer:Geoff Stier. Director: Bob Rafelson. Writers: Raymond Chandler, Robert B. Parker, Tom Stoppard.
Cast: Joe Don Baker, James Caan, David Keith, Dina Meyer, Tom Stoppard.

THE RANSOM OF RED CHIEF
Hallmark Entertainment. Director: Bob Clark III. Writers: O. Henry, Ed Naha. Shown Aug. 16, 1998.
Cast: Christopher Lloyd, Michael Jeter, Alan Ruck, Kaitlain Hopkins, Richard Riehle, Brent Hinkley, Sue Bugden.

THE RAT PACK
Produced by Home Box Office (HBO) pictures. Producer: Neal H Moritz. Director: Rob Cohen. Writer: Kario Salem. Shown on HBO.
Cast: Don Cheadle, Megan Dodds, Phil Hawn, Jim Jenkins, Ray Liotta, Angus MacFadyen,Joe Mantegna, Barbara Niven.

ROGERS AND HAMMERSTEIN'S CINDERELLA
Citadel Entertainment LP, Storyline Entertainment and Brownhouse productions in association with Walt Disney Television. Executive producers: Whitney Houston, Debra Martin Chase, Craig Zadan, Neil Meron, David R Ginsburg. Producer: Chris Montan. Director: Robert Iscove. Shown on ABC, Nov. 2, 1997
Cast: Brandy, Jason Alexander, Victor Garber, Whoopi Goldberg, Whitney Houston, Bernadette Peters, Jeanne Cox.

RUNNING WILD
Showtime in association with Hallmark Entertainment. A Save the Animals Production. Producer: Michael L. Games. Director: Timonthy Bond. Writer: Peter Welbeck. Shown on Showtime, July 26, 1998.
Cast: Gregory Harrison, Lori Hallier, Cody Jones, Brooke Nevin, Munyaradzi Kanaventi, Themba Ndaba.

SCATTERING DAD
Produced by Barbara Bosson Productions in association with Citadel Entertainment. Producers: Barbara Bosson, Karen Danaher-Dorr, David R. Ginsburg, Anthony Santa Croce. Director: Joan Tewkesbury. Writers: Barbara Bosson, Joan Tewkesbury. Shown Jan. 4, 1998.
Cast: Olympia Dukakis, Lucinda Jenney, Michelle Thomas, August Schellenberg, Andy Griffith, Jo Harvey Allen.

SECRET LIFE
Produced by Studios USA in association with USA Network. Executive Producer: Georgia Jeffries. Producer: Scott White. Director: Graeme Clifford. Writer: Georgia Jeffries.
Cast: Anne Archer, James Russo, Maria Conchita Alonso,

SHOT THROUGH THE HEART
Producers:Su Armstrong, Geogre Faber, Laszlo Helle, Robert Lantos, Francine Lefrak, Charles Pattinson. Director: David Attwood. Writer: Guy Hibbert. Shown Oct. 4, 1998.
Cast: Linus Roache, Vincent Perez,Lia Williams, Lothaire Bluteau, Adam Kotz, Soo Garay, Viktoria Bajza, Balazs Farkas..............

SILENCING MARY
Director: Craig R Baxley. Writer: Steve Johnson. Shown March 8, 1998.
Cast: Melissa Joan Hart, Corin Nemec, Lisa Dean Ryan, Peter MacNicol, James McDaniel, Josh Hopkins, Lochlyn Munro.

SINCE YOU'VE BEEN GONE
Producers: Richard N Gladstein, Brian Medavoy, Jeff Steinberg. Writer:Jeff Steinberg. Shown on April 18, 1998.
Cast: David Schwimmer, Laura Eason, Lara Flynn Boyle, Teri Hatcher, John Lehr, Molly Ringwald, Jerry Springer.

THE SPREE
Produced by Bona Fife Productions in association with MGM(Metro-Goldwyn-Mayer) and Pacific Motion Pictures. Producers: Albert Berger, Marcy Gross, Ann Weston, Ron Yerxa. Director: Tommy Lee Wallace. Writers: Percy Angress, Livia Linden. Shown on Showtime, April 18, 1998.
Cast: Jennifer Beals, Powers Boothe, Gary Chalk, John Cassini, Nathaniel Deveaux, Eric Keenley, Rita Moreno.

THE STAIRCASE
Produced by BWE Distribution in association with TeleVest and Craig Anderson Productions Inc. Executive: Craig Anderson, Jeffrey S Grant, Christopher Lofton, Marty Eli Schwartz. Director: Karen Arthur. Writer: Christopher Lofton. Shown April 12, 1998.
Cast: Barbara Hershey, William L Petersen, Diane Ladd, Justin Louis, David Clennon, Paul Robert Langdon, Anthony Ritter.

STILL HOLDING ON:
THE LEGEND OF CADILLAC JACK
Hallmark Entertainment in association with Davis Productions. Diretor: David Burton Morris. Writer: John Miglis. Shown on CBS, April 28, 1998.
Cast: Clint Black, Lisa Hartman, Mac Davis.

STORM CHASERS:REVENGE OF THE TWISTER
Distributed by the Family Channel Inc. Director: Mark Sobel. Shown on Family Channel, May 17, 1998.
Cast: Kelly McGillis, Wolf Larson, James MacArthur, Liz Torres, Adrian Zmed.

THE SUBSTITUTE 2: SCHOOL'S OUT
Produced by Shooting Gallery Films. Producers: Steven Bakalar, Devorah Cutler, Morrie Eisenman, Robert Salerno. Director: Steven Pearl. Writers: Roy Frumkes, Rocco Simonelli. Shown April 3, 1998.
Cast: Treat Williams, B.D. Wong, Angel David, Michael Michele, Larry Gilliard Jr. Susan May Pratt, Edoardo Ballerini.

THE TAKING OF PELHAM ONE TWO THREE,
Produced by Trilogy Entertainment Group in association with MGM Television. Producers: Pen Densham, Richard B Lewis, Karen Moore, John Watson. Director: Felix Enriquez Alcala. Writers: John Godey, Peter Stone, April Smith. Shown Feb. 1, 1998.
Cast: Edward James Olmos, Vincent D. Onofrio, Donnie Wahlberg, Richard Schiff, Lisa Vidal, Tara Rosling.

THE TALE OF SWEENEY TODD
Filmed in Dublin and at Ardmore Studios Ireland for Showtime Networks. Executive Producers: Peter Shaw, Gary Dartnall, Robert Halmi Jr. Producer: Ted Swanson. Director: John Schlesinger. Writer: Peter Buckman. Shown on Showtime April 19, 1998.
Cast: Ben Kingsley, Joanna Lumley, Campbell Scott, Selina Boyack, John Kavanagh, Katharine Schlesinger, David Wilmot.

TARGET EARTH
Director: Peter Markle. Writer: Michael Vickerman. Shown on Feb. 5, 1998.
Cast: Christopher Meloni, Marcia Cross, John C McGinley, Dabney Coleman, Courtney Crumpler, Chad Lowe, Barry Bell.

TEMPTING FATE
Produced by Singer/White Entertainment. Producers: Ron Gilbert, Sheri Singer, Steve White. Director: Peter Werner III. Writers: Gerald DiPego, Justin DiPego.
Cast: Tate Donovan, Abraham Benrubi, Matt Craven, Philip Baker Hall, Grace Phillips, Philip Casnoff, Ming-Na Wen.

THANKS OF A GRATEFUL NATION
Filmed in Toronto and in California by Adelson Entertainment, and by Tracey Alexander Productions. Executive producers: Tracey Alexander, Andrew Adelson, John Sacret Young. Producer: Lisa Niedenthal. Director: Rod Holcomb. Shown on Showtime, May 31, 1998.
Cast: Ted Danson, Jennifer Jason Leigh, Brian Dennehy, Marg Helgenberger, Steven Weber, Matt Keeslar, C. David Johnson.

THICKER THAN BLOOD
TNT Originals Production in association with Sarabande Productions. Producers: Charles Darby, Michael Hausman, David Manson. Director: Richard Pearce. Writer: Bill Cain. Shown on TNT, May 31, 1998.
Cast: Mickey Rourke, Dan Futterman, Carlo Alban, Lauren Velez, Josh Mostel, Peter Maloney, Vincent Laresca.

THIRDSPACE
Babylonian Productions. Producers: John Copeland, Douglas Netter, Susan Norkin, J. Michael Straczynski. Director: Jesus Salvador Trevino. Writer: J. Michael Straczynski. Shown July 19, 1998.
Cast: Bruce Boxleitner, Claudia Christian, Mira Furlan, Richard Biggs, Jeff Conaway, Stephen Furst, Patricia Tallman.

THE THIRD TWIN
A Jaffe/Braunstein films Ltd. in association with March Hare Entertainment production. Executive producers: Sally Jessy Raphael, Michael Jaffe, Howard Braunstein. Co-executive producer: Ellyn Williams. Producer: Christing Sacani. Director: Tom McLoughlin. Shown on CBS, Nov. 9 & 11 1997.
Cast: Kelly McGillis, Jason Gedrick, Larry Hagman, Regina Taylor, Lisa Vidal, Marion Ross, Jan Rubes, Kenneth Welsh.

A THOUSAND MEN AND A BABY
Finnegan-Pinchuk Company. Director: Marcus Cole. Writer: Richard Leder. Producers: Stephen Bedell, Dauri Chase-Slover, Lynn Danielson-Rosenthal, Sheldon Pincuk, Lori Etta Taub. Shown Dec 7, 1997.
Cast: Richard Thomas, Gerald McRaney, Jonathan Banks, Doris Roberts, Keith MacKechnie, Michael Woolson.

THE TIGER WOODS STORY
Produced by Paramount Network Television Productions/MTV Productions/Showtime Networks Inc. Producers: Jerry Goldman, Ken Mok, Dawn Parouse. Director: LeVar Burton. Writers: Takashi Bufford, John Strege.
Cast: Keith David, Khalil Kain, Freda Foh Shen, Gary LeRoi Gray, T.J. Hall, John Cho, Kathryne Dara Brown.

TIME TO SAY GOODBYE
Hearst Entertainment in association with Lifetime Television. Producer: Jimmy Schreckinger. Director: David Jones. Writers: Jacqueline Feather, David Seidler. Shown Sept. 21, 1997.
Cast: Eva Marie Saint, Richard Kiley, Margaret Colin.

TO LIVE AGAIN
Produced by Citadel Entertainment LP. Director: Steven Schachter. Shown on CBS, March 8, 1998.
Cast: Bonnie Bedelia, Annabeth Gish, Frances Sternhagen, Timothy Carhart.

TOOTHLESS

Walt Disney Television in association with Mandeville Films. Producers: David Hoberman, Mike Karz, Joan Van Horn. Director: Melanie Mayron. Writer: Mark S. Kaufman. Shown Oct. 5, 1997.
Cast: Kirstie Alley, Dale Midkiff, Ross Malinger, Daryl Mitchell, Lynn Redgrave, Melanie Mayron, Kimberly Scott.

TOWER OF TERROR

Producer: Iain Paterson. Director/Writer: D.J. MacHale. Shown Oct. 26, 1997.
Cast: Steve Guttenberg, Kirsten Dunst, Lela Ivey, Ben Kronen, Richard Minchenberg, Nia Peeples, Don Perry,.

THE TWILIGHT OF THE GOLDS

Below the Belt Entertainment, Regent Entertainment, and Showtime Networks Inc. Producers: Seth Bass, Charles H. Duggan, Stephen P. Jarchow, Garry Marshall, Valorie Massalas. Director: Ross Kagan Marks. Writers: Jonathan Tolins, Seth Bass. Shown Oct. 31, 1997.
Cast: Garry Marshall, Faye Dunaway, Jill Bernstein, Mark Shunkey, Jennifer Beals, Brendan Fraser, Jon Tenney.

TWO FOR TEXAS

Director: Rod Hardy. Writer: Larry Brothers. Shown Jan. 18, 1998.
Cast: Kris Kristofferson, Scott Bairstow, Irene Bedard, Tom Skerritt, Peter Coyote, Victor Rivers, Thomas Schuster.

UNIVERSAL SOLDIER II: BROTHERS IN ARMS

Executive Producer: John Laing. Director: Jeff Woolnough. Writers: Peter M. Lenkov, Kevin Gillis. Shown on The Movie Channel, Sept. 27, 1998.
Cast: Matt Battaglia, Burt Reynolds, Chandra West, Jeff Wincott.

UNWED FATHER

Brian Austin Green Productions in association with Dove Four Point Productions. Producers: Deborah Raffin, Ken Raskoff, Michael Viner, Ron Ziskin. Director: Michael Switzer. Writer: Nina Shengold. Shown Oct. 12, 1998.
Cast: Brian Austin Green, Nicholle Tom, Alan Rachins, Faye Grant, Isabella Hofmann, Ari Meyers, Cam Labine.

VIRTUAL OBSESSION

Produced by Von Zerneck-Sertner Films/Stephanie German Productions/Hallmark Entertainment Inc. Director: Mick Garris. Writers: Mick Garris, Peter James VIII, Preston Sturges II. Shown Feb. 26, 1998.
Cast: Peter Gallagher, Mimi Rogers, Jake Lloyd, Andy Comeau, Lee Garlington, Michael O'Neal Dan Martinell.

WHAT THE DEAF MAN HEARD

Hallmark Hall of Fame Productions. Producers: Tom Luse, Brent Shields, Richard Welsh. Director: John Kent Harrison. Writers: G.D. Gearino, Robert W. Lenski. Shown Nov. 23, 1997.
Cast: Matthew Modine, Claire Bloom, Judith Ivey, James Earl Jones, Jerry O'Connell, Bernadette Peters, Tom Skerritt.

WHEN HE DIDN'T COME HOME

Grossbart/Barnett Film Productions. Director: Paul Schnelder. Writer: John Miglis. Shown on CBS, May 19, 1998.
Cast: Patty Duke, Kelly Rowan, Robert Floyd.

WHEN HUSBANDS CHEAT

Produced by Brayton-Carlucci Productions in association with Hearst Entertainment Productions Inc. Producers: William J. Birnes, Marian Brayton, Anne Carlucci, Terry Gould, Alan Hines, Joe Lawler. Director: Richard A. Colla. Writer: Alan Hines. Shown Feb. 2 1998.
Cast: Patricia Kalember, Tom Irwin, Brenda Vaccaro, Gina Clayton, William Greenblatt, Robin Brule, Bobby Johnston.

WHEN THE TRUMPETS FADE

Citadel Entertainment-John Kemeny productions in association with Hofflund/Polone. Executive producers: David Ginsburg, Gavin Polone, Judy Hofflund. Producer: John Kemeny. Director: John Irvin. Writer: W.W. Vought. Shown on HBO, June 27, 1998.
Cast: Ron Eldard, Frank Whaley, Zak Orth, Dylan Bruno, Martin Donovan, Dwight Yoakam, Jeffrey Donovan.

WING AND A PRAYER A

USA Pictures. Director: Paul Wendkos. Shown April 22, 1998.
Cast: Claudia Christian, Jeff Yagher, Jessica Tuck, Christopher Cousins, Leon Russom, Jim Metzler, Judith Schoff.

WISHBONE'S DOG DAYS OF THE WEST

Big Feats Entertainment in association with Lyrick Studios. Director: Rick Duffield. Writers: Susan B. Chick, Rick Duffield, Steven Kavner, Michael Anthony Steele. Producers: Betty A. Buckley, Rick Duffield, Bert Guthrie, Steven Kavner. Shown March 29, 1998.
Cast: Larry Brantley, Christine Abbott, Brent Anderson, Sean Hennigan, Angee Hughes, Steven Kavner, Sean McGraw.

WITNESS TO THE MOB

Tribeca Productions/NBC Studios. Producers: Caroline Baron, Robert DeNiro, Brad Epstein, Jane Rosenthal. Director: Thaddeus O'Sullivan. Writer: Stanley Weiser. Shown May 10, 1998.
Cast: Nicholas Turturro, Tom Sizemore, Debi Mazar, Abe Vigoda, Philip Baker Hall, Adam J Roth, Frank Vincent.

BROADCAST NETWORKS

∎

TELEVISION STATIONS

NETWORK AFFILIATES

DIGITAL TELEVISION STATIONS

TOP TELEVISION GROUPS

STATE BROADCAST ASSOCIATIONS

MEDIA SALES REPRESENTATIVES

CORPORATE HISTORIES
OF THE NETWORKS

BROADCAST NETWORK
CORPORATE LISTINGS

TELEVISION PRODUCERS
AND DISTRIBUTORS

TELEVISION STATIONS

Stations are presented alphabetically by state, city and call letters. Stations are listed in the state and city in which they are licensed to broadcast. While most broadcasters maintain offices in the market the service, many stations are operated by corporations headquartered in other locales. In such cases, broadcast markets are indicated within the parenthesis. Satellite stations' listings will refer the reader to the parent station's listing. Where applicable, station manager's names can be found at the end of each entry.

ALABAMA

WJSU-TV, Channel 33, ABC
Radio Bldg., 1330 Noble St., Anniston, AL 36202-0040. (205) 237-8651. FAX: (205) 236-7336. Allbritton Communications Co.

WABM-TV, Channel 68, UPN
(see WBRC, Birmingham). Birmingham, AL. Sinclair Broadcast Group Inc.

WBIQ, Channel 10, PBS
2112 11th Ave., Suite 400, Birmingham, AL 35205. (205) 328-8756. FAX: (205) 251-2192. Alabama Educational Television Commission.

WBRC-TV, Channel 6, FOX
1720 Valleyview Dr., Birmingham, AL 35201. (205) 322-6666. FAX: (205) 583-4386. Fox Television Stations Inc. Stan Knott.

WIAT, Channel 42, CBS
2075 Goldencrest Dr., Birmingham, AL 35209. (205) 322-4200. FAX: (205) 320-2713. Media General Broadcast Group.

WTTO-TV, Channel 21, WB
651 Beacon Pkwy. W., Suite 105, Birmingham, AL 35209. (205) 290-2100. FAX: (205) 290-2114. Sinclair Broadcast Group Inc.

WVTM-TV, Channel 13, NBC
1732 Valley View Dr., Birmingham, AL 35209. (205) 933-1313. FAX: (205) 933-7389. Hicks, Muse, Tate & Furst Inc.

WIIQ, Channel 41, PBS
(see WBIQ, Birmingham). Demopolis, AL. Alabama Educational Television Commisson.

WDHN, Channel 18, ABC
PO Box 6237, Dothan, AL 36302-6237. (334) 793-1818. FAX: (334) 793-2623. Morris Network Inc.

WTVY, Channel 4, CBS
285 N. Foster St., Dothan, AL 36303. (334) 792-3195. FAX: (334) 793-3947. Benedek Broadcasting.

WDIQ, Channel 2, PBS
(see WBIQ, Birmingham). Dozier, AL. Alabama Educational Television Commission.

WFIQ, Channel 36, PBS
(see WBIQ, Birmingham). Florence, AL. Alabama Educational Television Commission.

WOWL-TV, Channel 15, NBC, WB
PO.Box 2220, 840 Cypress Mill Rd., Florence, AL 35630-0220. (205) 767-1515. FAX: (205) 764-7750. Rick Biddle.

WYLE, Channel 26, IND
4150 Underwood Mountain Rd., Florence, AL 35674. (205) 381-2600. FAX: (205) 383-3157. ETC Communications. Karen Snead.

WNAL-TV, Channel 44, CBS
PO Box 8249, Gadsden, AL 35902-8249. (205) 547-4444. FAX: (205) 547-1789. Fant Broadcasting. Jim Moss.

WPXH (Birmingham), Channel 44, IND
Gadsden, AL. (205) 547-4444. FAX: (205) 547-1789. Paxson Communications Corp.

WTJP, Channel 60, IND
313 Rosedale St., Gadsden, AL 35901-5361. (205) 546-8860, FAX: (205) 543-8623. All American TV Inc.

WAAY-TV, Channel 31, ABC, UPN
1000 Monte Sano Blvd S.E., Huntsville, AL 35801-6137. (205) 553-3131. FAX: (205) 533-6616. Smith Broadcasting Inc.

WAFF, Channel 48, NBC
Box 2116, Huntsville, AL 35804. (205) 533-4848. FAX: (205) 533-1337. Raycom Media Inc.

WHIQ, Channel 25, PBS
(see WBIQ, Burmingham). Huntsville, AL. Alabama Educational Television Commission.

WHNT-TV, Channel 19, CBS
200 Holmes Ave., Huntsville, AL 35801. (205) 533-1919. FAX: (205) 539-4503. The New York Times Co.

WZDX, Channel 54, IND
PO Box 3889, Huntsville, AL 35810-0889. (205) 859-5454. FAX: (205) 859-2194. Grant Communications.

WGIQ, Channel 43, PBS
(see WBIQ, Birmingham). Louisville, AL. Alabama Educational Television Commission.

WALA-TV, Channel 10, FOX
PO Box 1548, Mobile, AL 36633. (334) 434-1010. FAX: (334) 434-1073. USA Broadcasting Inc.

WEAR-TV (Mobile), Channel 3, ABC
PO Box 12278, Pensacola, FL 32581. (904) 456-3333. FAX: (904) 455-0159. Sinclair Broadcast Group Inc.

WEIQ, Channel 42, PBS
(see WBIQ, Birmingham). Mobile, AL. Alabama Educational Television Commission.

WKRG-TV, Channel 5, CBS
555 Broadcast Dr., Mobile, AL 36606-2936. (205) 479-5555. FAX: (205) 473-8130. Spartan Communications Inc.

WMPV-TV, Channel 21, TBN
120 Zeigler Circle E., Mobile, AL 36608-4829. (334) 633-2100. FAX: (334) 633-2174. All American TV Inc. Leslie McClure.

WPMI, Channel 15, NBC
PO Box 9038, Mobile, AL 36691-0038. (334) 602-1500. FAX: (334) 602-1515. Clear Channels Communications.

WAIQ, Channel 26, PBS
(see WBIQ, Birmingham). Montgomery, AL. Alabama Educational Television Commission.

WCOV-TV., Channel 20, FOX
1 WCOV Ave., Montgomery, AL 36111-2099. Woods Communications.

WHOA-TV, Channel 32, ABC
PO Box 3236, Montgomery, AL 36109. (334) 272-5331. FAX: (334) 271-6348. Media General Broadcast Group.

WMCF-TV, Channel 45, TBN
300 Mendel Pkwy. W., Montgomery, AL 36117. (334) 277-4545. FAX: (334) 277-6635. All American TV Inc.

WSFA, Channel 12, NBC
12 E. Delano Ave., Montgomery, AL 36105-2506. (334) 288-1212. FAX: (334) 613-8302. Cosmos Broadcasting Corp.

WCIQ, Channel 7, PBS
(see WBIQ, Birmingham). Mount Cheaha State Park, AL. Alabama Educational Television Commission.

WSWS-TV, Channel 66, WB
PO Box 870, 1800 Pepperell Pkwy, Opelika, AL 36801. (334) 749-5766. FAX: (334) 749-5583. Pappas Telecasting of Opelika.

WDFX-TV, Channel 34, FOX
Box 759, 318 El Palacio Plaza, Ozark, AL 36361. (334) 774-8000. FAX: (334) 774-1118. Woods Television Co.

WRJM (Troy), Channel 67, IND
409 E. Broad St., Ozark, AL 36360. (205) 774-9323. FAX: (205) 774-6450. H. Jack Mizell.

WAKA, Channel 8, CBS
3020 East Blvd., Selma, AL 36116. (334) 271-8888. FAX: (334) 271-6444. Bahakel Communications. Mark Smith.

WCFT-TV, Channel 40, ABC
4000 37th St E., Tuscaloosa, AL 35405-3543. (205) 553-1333. FAX: (205) 556-4814. Allbritton Communications Co. Phil Cox

WDBB, Channel 17, FOX, WB
5455 Jug Factory Rd., Tuscaloosa, AL 35403. (205) 345-1117. FAX: (205) 345-1173. Sinclair Broadcast Group.

ALASKA

KAKM, Channel 7, PBS
3877 University Dr., Anchorage, AK 99508. (907) 563-7070.
FAX: (907) 273-9192. Alaska Public Telecommunications. Susan
Reed.

KDMD, Channel 33, IND
6407 Brayton Dr., Ste. K, Anchorage, AK 99507. (907)
344-7817. FAX: (907) 344-7817. GREENTV Corp.

KIMO, Channel 13, ABC
2700 E. Tudor Rd., Anchorage, AK 99507-1136. (907) 561-1313.
FAX: (907) 561-1377. Smith Broadcasting Group Inc. Mark
Chassman.

KTBY, Channel 4, FOX
1840 S. Bragaw St., Ste. 101, Anchorage, AK 99508-3439. (907)
274-0404. FAX: (907) 264-5180. Grapevine Communications Inc.
Sean Bradley.

KTUU-TV, Channel 2, NBC
Tudor Park, Ste. 220, 701 E. Tudor Rd., Anchorage, AK 99510.
(907) 762-9202. FAX: (907) 561-0882. Zaser & Longston Inc.

KTVA, Channel 11, CBS
1007 W. 32nd Ave., Anchorage, AK 99503-3728. (907)
562-3456. FAX: (907) 562-0953. Northern TV Inc.

KYES, Channel 5, UPN
3700 Woodland Dr., Anchorage, AK 99517-2555. (907)
248-5937. FAX: (907) 243-0709. Jeremy Lansman & Carol
Schatz.

KZXC, Channel 9, IND
3211 Providence Rd., Anchorage, AK 99508. (907) 786-1626.
FAX: (907) 786-1027. University of Alaska.

KYUK-TV, Channel 4, PBS, CBS, ABC, NBC
Pouch 468, Bethel, AK 99559. (907) 543-3131. FAX: (907)
543-3130. Bethel Broadcasting Inc.

KATN, Channel 2, ABC
516 2nd Ave., #400, Fairbanks, AK 99701. (907) 452-2125. FAX:
(907) 456-8225. Smith Broadcasting Group of Alaska. John
Seekatz.

KFXF, Channel 7, FOX
3650 Bradock St., Ste. 2, Fairbanks, AK 99701. (907) 452-3697.
FAX: (907) 456-3428. Tanana Valley Television Co. William St.
Pierre.

KTVF, Channel 11, NBC
3528 International St., Fairbanks, AK 99701-7382. (907)
452-5121. FAX: (907) 452-5120. The Ackerley Group.

KUAC-TV, Channel 9, PBS
PO Box 755620, University of Alaska-Fairbanks, Fairbanks, AK
99775-5620. (907) 474-7491. FAX: (907) 474-5064. University of
Alaska. Jerry Brigham.

KJUD, Channel 8, ABC, NBC
175 S. Franklin, Juneau, AK 99801. (907) 586-3145. FAX: (907)
463-3041. Desert Communications, Inc.

KTOO-TV, Channel 3, PBS
360 Egan Dr., Juneau, AK 99801. (907) 586-1670. FAX: (907)
586-3612. Capital Community Broadcasting Inc. Jim Mahan

KJNP-TV, Channel 4, NFP
PO Box 56359, 2501 Mission Rd., North Pole, AK 99705. (907)
488-2216. FAX: (907) 488-5246. Alaska Missionary Fellowship
Julie K. Beaver.

KTNL, Channel 13, CBS
PO Box 1309, Sitka Professional Cre., Ste. 2F, 208 Lake St.,
Sitka, AK 99835-1309. (907) 747-6002. FAX: (907) 747-6003.
Wright Home Inc. Bill Wright.

ARIZONA

KMOH (Kingman), Channel 6, WB
2160 S. Hwy. 95, Bullhead City, AZ 86442. (520) 758-7333. FAX:
(520) 758-8139. Gannett Broadcasting.

KBPX (Phoenix) Channel 13, IND
Flagstaff, AZ. (520) 527-1300. FAX: (520) 527-1394. Paxson
Communications Corp.

KNAZ-TV, Channel 2, NBC
2201 N. Vickey St., Flagstaff, AZ 86004. (602) 526-2232. FAX:
(602) 526-8110. Gannett Co. Inc.

KTFL, Channel 4, IND
(see WTVA, Tupelo, MS). Flagstaff, AZ. WTVA Inc.

KWBF, Channel 13, IND
2158 N. 4th St., Flagstaff, AZ 86004. (520) 527-1300. FAX: (520)
527-1394. Paxson Communications Corp.

KAET, Channel 8, PBS
Arizona State University, Stauffer Hall B-wing, Phoenix, AZ
85287-1405. (602) 965-3506. FAX: (602) 965-1000. Arizona
Board of Regents. Beth Vershure.

KAJW (Tolleson), Channel 61, IND
11 W. Medlock, Phoenix, AZ 85013. (602) 277-8938. FAX: (602)
957-1354. Paxson Communications Corp.

KASW, Channel 61, WB
(see KTVK, Phoenix). Phoenix, AZ. Brooks Broadcasting.

KNXV-TV, Channel 15, ABC
4625 S. 33rd Place, Phoenix, AZ 85040-2861. (602) 243-4151.
FAX: (602) 304-3000. E. W. Scripps Co. Brad Nilsen.

KPAZ-TV, Channel 21, IND
3551 E.McDowell Rd., Phoenix, AZ 85008-3847. (602)
273-1477. FAX: (602) 267-9427. Trinity Broadcasting Networks.
Paul F. Crouch. Mrs. Billie Watts.

KPHO-TV, Channel 5, CBS
4016 N. Black Canyon, Phoenix, AZ 85017. (602) 264-1000.
FAX: (602) 263-8818. Meredith Broadcasting Group.

KPNX, Channel 12, NBC
1101 N. Central Ave., P. O. BOX 711, Phoenix, AZ 85004-1818.
(602) 257-1212. FAX: (602) 258-8186. Gannett Broadcasting.

KSAZ-TV, Channel 10, FOX
511 W. Adams St., Phoenix, AZ 85003-1608. (602) 257-1234.
FAX: (602) 262-0177.Fox Television Stations Inc.

KTVK, Channel 3, IND
5555 N. 7th Ave., Phoenix, AZ 85013. (602) 207-3333. Delbert
R. Lewis.

KTVW-TV, Channel 33, UNI
3019 E. Southern Ave., Phoenix, AZ 85040. (602) 243-3333.
FAX: (602) 276-8658. Univision Television Group, Inc.

KUTP, Channel 45, UPN
4630 S. 33rd St., Phoenix, AZ 85040-2812. (602) 268-4500.
FAX: (602) 276-4082. Chris Craft Industries Inc.

KAJW (Tolleson), Channel 51, IND
11 W. Medlock Dr., Phoenix, AZ 85013. (602) 957-1354. FAX:
(602) 468-1793. Paxson Communications Corp.

KUSK, Channel 7, IND
3211 Tower Rd., Prescott, AZ 86301-3734. (520) 778-6770. FAX:
(520) 445-5210.

KGUN, Channel 9, ABC
PO Box 17990, Tucson, AZ 85731-7990. (520) 722-5486. FAX:
(520) 290-7642. Lee Enterprises Inc.

KHRR, Channel 40, TEL
2919 Broadway, Garden Level, Tucson, AZ 85716. (520)
322-6888. FAX: (520) 881-7926. Jay S. Zucker.

KMSB-TV, Channel 11, FOX
1885 N. 6th Ave., Tucson, AZ 85705-5061. (520) 770-1123. FAX:
(520) 629-7185. A. H. Belo Corp.

KOLD-TV, Channel 13, CBS
7831 N. Business Park Drive, Tucson, AZ 85743. (520)
744-1313. FAX: (520) 744-5233. Raycom Media Inc.

KTTU-TV, Channel 18, UPN
1855 N. 6th Ave., Tucson, AZ 85705. (520) 624-0180. FAX: (520)
629-7185. Clear Channel Television License.

KUAS, Channel 27, PBS
University of Arizona, Tucson, AZ 85721. (520) 621-5828. FAX:
(520) 621-9105. Arizona Board of Regents.

KUAT-TV, Channel 6, PBS
(see KUAS-TV). Tucson, AZ. Arizona Board of Regents.

KVOA-TV, Channel 4, NBC
209 W. Elm St., Tucson, AZ 85705. (520) 792-2270. FAX: (520)
620-1309. Cordillera Communications Inc.

KSWT, Channel 13, CBS
PO Box 592, Yuma, AZ 85366-0592. (520) 782-5113. FAX: (520)
782-0320. Yuma Television Investments Inc. Michelle Dyer

KYMA Channel 11, NBC
1385 S. Pacific Ave., Yuma, AZ 85365-1725. (520) 782-1111.
FAX: (520) 782-5401. Sunbelt Communications Co.

ARKANSAS

KETG, Channel 9, PBS
(see KETS, Little Rock). Arkadelphia, AR. Arkansas Educational
TV Commission. Allen Weatherly.

KTVE (El Dorado), Channel 10, NBC
2909 Kilpatrick Blvd., Monroe, LA 71201-5120. (318) 323-1300.
FAX: (318) 322-9718. GOCOM Communications.

KAFT, Channel 13, PBS
(see KETS, Little Rock). Fayetteville, AR. Arkansas Educational
TV Commission. Allen Weatherly.

KFSM-TV, Channel 5, CBS
PO Box 369, Fort Smith, AR 72902-0369. (501) 783-3131. FAX:
(501) 783-3295. The New York Times Co.

KHBS, Channel 40, ABC
2415 N. Albert Pike Ave., Fort Smith, AR 72904-5617. (501)
783-4040. FAX: (505) 783-0550. Hearst-Argyle Television Inc.

KPOM-TV, Channel 24, NBC
PO Box 4610, Fort Smith, AR 72914-4610. (501) 785-2400.
Griffin Entities.

KAIT-TV, Channel 8, ABC
PO Box 790, Jonesboro, AR 72403-0790. (501) 931-8888. FAX:
(501) 933-8058. Cosmos Broadcasting Corp.

KTEJ, Channel 19, PBS
(see KETS, Little Rock). Jonesboro, AR. Arkansas Educational
TV Commission. Allen Weatherly.

KARK-TV, Channel 19, NBC
PO Box 748, Little Rock, AR 72203-0748. (501) 376-4444. FAX:
(501) 376-1852. Morris Network Inc.

KATV, Channel 7, ABC
PO Box 77, Little Rock, AR 72203-0077. (501) 324-7777. FAX:
(501) 324-7852. Allbritton Comunications Co.

KETS, Channel 2, PBS
350 S. Donaghey, Little Rock, AR 72033. (501) 450-1727. FAX:
(501) 682-4122. Arkansas Educational TV Commission. Allen
Weatherly.

KLRT, Channel 16, FOX
11711 W. Markham, Little Rock, AR 72221. (501) 225-0016.
FAX: (501) 225-0428. Clear Channel Communications.

KTHV, Channel 11, CBS
PO Box 269, Little Rock, AR 72203-0269. (501) 376-1111. FAX:
(501) 376-3719. Gannett Broadcasting.

KVTN (Pine Bluff), Channel 25, IND
PO Box 22007, Little Rock, AR 72221. (501) 223-2525. FAX:
(501) 225-3837. Agape Church Inc.

KVUT (Little Rock), Channel 42, IND
102 Fairmont Ctr., Daphne, AL 36526. (205) 626-3339. Paxson
Communications Corp.

KEMV, Channel 6, PBS
(see KETS, Little Rock). Mountain View, AR. Arkansas
Educational TV Commission. Allen Watherly.

KLEP, Channel 17, IND
1502 N. Hill St., Newark, AK 72562. (870) 799-8817. FAX: (870)
799-8647. Newark Public School System. Fre Ahlborn.

KASN, Channel 38, UPN
(see KLRT, Little Rock). Pine Bluff, AR. Mercury Broadcasting Co.

KFAA, Channel 51, NBC
1821 S. 8th St., Rogers, AR 72756. (501) 631-8851. FAX: (501)
631-1853. J.D.G. Television. Kathy Wilkerson

KSBN, Channel 57, IND
PO Box 6968, Springdale, AR 72766-6968. (501) 361-2900.
FAX: (501) 361-2323. Total Life Community Educational
Foundation.

CALIFORNIA

KBAK-TV, Channel 29, CBS
PO Box 2929, 1901 Westwind Dr., Bakersfield, CA 93303. (805)
327-7955. FAX: (805) 327-5603. Westwind Commu ications LLC.

KERO-TV, Channel 23, ABC
321 21st St., Bakersfield, CA 93301-4120. (805) 637-2323. FAX:
(805) 322-1701. McGraw-Hill Broadcasting Co.

KGET, Channel 17, NBC
2120 L St., Bakersfield, CA 93301. (805) 327-7511. FAX: (805)
283-1855. Ackerly Communications.

KUVI-TV, Channel 45, UPN
3223 Sillect Ave., Bakersfield, CA 93308. (805) 326-1011. FAX:
(805) 328-7576. Univision Television Group Inc.

KTSF (San Francisco), Channel 26, IND
100 Valley Dr., Brisbane, CA 94005-1350. (415) 468-2626. FAX:
(415) 467-7559. Lincoln Broadcasting Co.

KNBC, Channel 4, NBC
3000 W. Alameda St., Burbank, CA 91523. (818) 840-4444. FAX:
(310) 840-3535. NBC Inc.

KRCA (Riverside), Channel 62, IND
1813 Victory Place, Burbank, CA 91504. (818) 563-5722. FAX:
(818) 972-2694. Liberman Broadcasting Inc.

KCPM, Channel 24, NBC
180 E. 4th St., Chico, CA 95928. (916) 893-2424. FAX: (916)
893-1033. GOCOM Television.

KCVU (Paradise), Channel 30, FOX
300 Main St., Chico, CA 95928. (916) 893-1234. FAX: (916)
893-1266. Sainte Partners II L.P.

KHSL-TV, Channel 12, CBS
Chico, CA. (916) 342-0141. FAX: (916) 342-4905. Catamount
Broadcast Group.

KAIL (Fresno), Channel 53, UPN
1590 Alluvial Ave., Clovis, CA 93611. (209) 299-9753. FAX:
(209) 299-1523. Trans-America Broadcasting. Charles Williams.

KTNC-TV, Channel 42, IND
5101 Port Chicago Hwy., Concord, CA 94524. (510) 686-4242.
FAX: (510) 825-4242. Pappas Telecasting Companies. Frank
Savage.

KECY-TV, Channel 9, FOX
646 Main St., El Centro, CA 92243. (760) 353-9990. FAX: (760)
352-5471. Growth Cities Broadcasting.

KVYE, Channel 7, UNI
200 S. 5th St., El Centro, CA 92243. (760) 337-8707. FAX: (760)
337-8012. Entravision Communication Co.

KAEF (Arcata), Channel 23, ABC
540 E. St., Eureka, CA 95501. (707) 444-2323. FAX: (707)
445-9451. Lamco Communications.

KBVU, Channel 29, FOX
730 7th St., St.e 201, Eureka, CA 95501. (707) 442-2999. FAX:
(707) 441-0111. Sainte Partners II L.P. Doug Holroyd

KEET, Channel 13, PBS
7246 Humboldt Hill Rd., Eureka, CA 95503. (707) 445-0813.
FAX: (707) 445-8977. Redwood Empire Public TV.

KIEM-TV, Channel 3, NBC
5650 S. Broadway, Eureka, CA 95503. (707) 443-3123. FAX:
(707) 442-6084, Pollock Broadcasting Co.

KVIQ, Channel 6, CBS
1800 Broadway, Eureka, CA 95501. (707) 443-3061. FAX: (707)
443-4435. Ackerley Group.

KFWU, Channel 8, ABC
303B N. Main St., Fort Bragg, CA 95437. (707) 964-8888. FAX:
(707) 964-8150. Pappas Telecasting Companies.

KFSN-TV, Channel 30, ABC
1777 G. St., Fresno, CA 93706. (209) 442-1170. FAX: (209)
233-5844. ABC Inc

KFTV, Channel 21, UNI
3239 W. Ashlan Ave., Fresno, CA 93722. (209) 584-1800. FAX:
(209) 222-2890. Univision Television Group, Inc.

KGMC, Channel 43, WB
706 W. Herndon Ave., Fresno, CA 93650. (209) 432-4300. FAX:
(209) 435-3201. Gary Cocola.

KJEO, Channel 47, CBS
4880 N. First, Fresno, CA 93726. (209) 222-2411. FAX: (209)
221-6938. Retlaw Broadcasting Co.

KMPH (Visalia), Channel 26, FOX
5111 E. McKinley Ave., Fresno, CA 93727-2033. (209)
255-2600. FAX: (209) 255-0275. Pappas Telecasting Co.

KMSG-TV (Sanger), Channel 59, TEL
706 W. Herndon Ave., Fresno, CA 93650-1033. (209) 435-5900.
FAX: (209) 435-1448. Diane D. Dostinich. Lisa Nilmeier.

KNXT (Visalia), Channel 49, NFP
1550 N. Fresno St., Fresno, CA 93703. (209) 488-7440. FAX:
(209) 488-7444. Diocese of Fresno Education Corp.

KSEE-TV, Channel 24, NBC
5035 E. McKinley Ave., Fresno, CA 93727-1964. (209)
454-2424. FAX: (209) 454-2487. Granite Broadcasting Corp.

494

KVPT, Channel 18, PBS
1544 Van Ness, Fresno, CA 93721. (209) 266-1800. FAX: (209) 650-1880. Valley Public Television.

KVEA (Los Angeles), Channel 52, TEL
1130A Air Way, Glendale, CA 91201. (818) 502-5700. FAX: (818) 502-0029. Telemundo Group Inc.

KOCE-TV, Channel 50, PBS
15751 Gothard St., Huntington Beach, CA 92647. (714) 895-5623. FAX: (714) 895-0852. Coast Community College. Brue Reed.

KDOC-TV (Anaheim), Channel 56, IND
18021 Cowan, Irvine, CA 92714-6023. (714) 442-9800. FAX: (714) 261-5956. Golden Orange Broadcasting.

KABC, Channel 7, ABC
4151 Prospect Ave., Los Angeles, CA 90027. (310) 557-7777. FAX: (310) 557-5036. ABC Inc.

KAJB (Calipatria), Channel 54, IND
Ste. 590, 11990 Olympic Blvd., Los Angeles, CA 90064. (310) 820-5355. Entravision Communications Co. LLC.

KCAL, Channel 9, IND
5515 Melrose Ave., Los Angeles, CA 90038-3149. (213) 467-9999. FAX: (213) 460-6265. Young Broadcasting Inc..

KCBS-TV, Channel 2, CBS
6121 Sunset Blvd., Los Angeles, CA 90028. (213) 460-3431. FAX: (213) 460-3294. CBS Stations Inc. John Culliton.

KCET, Channel 28, PBS
4401 Sunset Blvd., Los Angeles, CA 90027. (213) 666-6500. FAX: (213) 665-6067. Community TV of Southern California.

KCOP, Channel 13, UPN
915 N. La Brea Ave., Los Angeles, CA 90038. (213) 851-1001. FAX: (213) 851-5197. Chris-Craft Industries, Inc.

KLCS, Channel 58, PBS
1061 Temple St., Los Angeles, CA 90012. (213) 625-6958. FAX: (213) 481-1019. Los Angeles Unified School District. Tom Mossman. Tom Mossman.

KMEX-TV, Channel 34, UNI
6701 Center Dr. West, Los Angeles, CA 90045-5073. (310) 216-3434. FAX: (310) 348-3459. Univision Television Group, Inc.

KTLA, Channel 5, WB
5800 Sunset Blvd., Los Angeles, CA 90028. (213) 460-5500. FAX: (213) 460-5405. Tribune Broadcasting.

KTTV, Channel 11, FOX
5746 W. Sunset Blvd., Los Angeles, CA 90028-8588. (213) 856-1000. Fox Television Stations Inc.Diana L. Vargas.

KWHY, Channel 22, IND
5545 Sunset Blvd., Los Angeles, CA 90028. (213) 993-2200. FAX: (213) 466-3613. Harriscope of Los Angeles.

KNSO (Merced), Channel 51, IND
PO Box 4159, c/o Chester Smith, Gen Ptnr., Modesto, CA 95352. (209) 529-5100. FAX: (209) 523-0839. Sainte Partners II L.P.

KUVS (Sacramento), Channel 19, UNI
PO Box 3689, Modesto, CA 95352. (209) 578-1900. FAX: (209) 527-2129. Univision Television Group, Inc.

KSMS-TV (Salinas), Channel 67, UNI
67 Garden Court, Monterey, CA 93940-5302. (408) 373-6767. FAX: (408) 373-6700. Entravision Communications Co.

KWOK, Channel 68 IND
c/o North Bay Television Inc., 7089 Redwood Blvd., Novato, CA 94945. (415) 892-8808. Christian Communications of Chicagoland Inc.

KHSC-TV (Los Angeles), Channel 46, HSN
3833 Ebony St., Ontario, CA 91761-1500. (909) 390-8846. FAX: (909) 390-8857. USA Broadcasting Inc.

KADY-TV, Channel 63, UPN
663 Maulhardt Ave., Oxnard, CA 93030. (805) 983-0444. FAX: (805) 485-6057. Biltmore Broadcasting LLC.

KESQ-TV (Palm Springs), Channel 42, ABC
42-650 Melanie Pl., Palm Desert, CA 92211. (619) 773-0342. FAX: (619) 773-5107. EGF Broadcasting.

KMIR-TV (Palm Springs), Channel 36, NBC
72920 Parkview Dr., Palm Desert, CA 92260. (760) 568-3636. FAX: (760) 568-1176. John & Sirpuhe Conte.

KPXF (Fresno), Channel 61, IND
1077 W. Morton Ave., Porterville, CA. (209) 781-6100. FAX: (209) 782-0364. Paxson Communications Corp.

KZKI (San Bernardino), Channel 30, IND
Ste. 155, 9229 Utica Ave., Rancho Cucamonga CA 91730. (909) 483-3030. FAX: (909) 483-0333. Paxson Communications Corp. Cecilia Nguyen.

KIXE, Channel 9, PBS
PO Box 9, Redding, CA 96099. (916) 243-5493. FAX: (916) 243-7443. Northern California Educational TV.

KRCR-TV, Channel 7, ABC
755 Auditorium Dr., Redding, CA 96001. (916) 243-7777. FAX: (916) 243-0217. Lamco Communications Inc.

KLXV-TV (San Jose), Channel 65, IND
660 Price Ave., #B, Redwood City, CA 94063. (415) 369-6565. FAX: (415) 369-4969. Paxson Communications Corp.

KRCB (Cotati), Channel 22, PBS
5850 Labath Ave., Rohnert Park, CA 94928. (707) 585-8522. FAX: (707) 585-1363. Rural California Broadcasting.

KCMY, Channel 29, IND
1029 Hook St., Suite 23, Sacramento, CA 95814-3815. (916) 443-2929. FAX: (916) 442-6414. Paxson Communications Corp.

KCRA-TV, Channel 3, NBC
3 Television Cir., Sacramento, CA 95814-0794. (916) 446-3333. FAX: (916) 325-3731. Kelly Media Corp. Harry Delaney.

KPWB, Channel 31, UPN
500 Media Pl., Sacramento, CA 95815. (916) 925-3100. FAX: (916) 920-1078. Paramount Stations Group Inc.

KQCA (Stockton), Channel 58, UPN
58 Television Cir., Sacramento, CA 95814. (916) 447-5858. FAX: (916) 554-4658. Wing K. Fat.

KTXL, Channel 40, FOX
4655 Fruitridge Rd., Sacramento, CA 95820. (916) 454-4422. FAX: (916) 739-1079. Tribune Broadcasting. Michael Fisher.

KVIE, Channel 6, PBS
Box 6, Sacramento, CA 95812. (916) 929-5843. FAX: (916) 929-7215. KVIE Inc.

KXTV, Channel 10, ABC
400 Broadway, Sacramento, CA 95818. (916) 441-2345. FAX: (916) 441-3054. A. H. Belo Corp.

KCBA, Channel 35, FOX
PO Box 3560, Salinas, CA 93912. (408) 422-3500. FAX: (408) 754-1120. Ackerley Communications Group, Inc.

KION-TV (Monterey), Channel 46, CBS
PO Box 3560, Salinas, CA 93912. (408) 784-1702. FAX: (408) 757-1766. Harron Television of Monterey

KSBW, Channel 8, NBC
238 John St., Salinas, CA 93901-3339. (408) 758-8888. FAX: (408) 424-3750. Hearst-Argyle Television Inc.

KPXN (Los Angeles), Channel 30, IND
San Bernardino, CA. (909) 483-3030. FAX: (909) 483-0333. Paxson Communications Corp.

KVCR-TV, Channel 24, PBS
701 S. Mt. Vernon Ave., San Bernardino, CA 92410. (909) 888-6511. FAX: (909) 885-2116. San Bernardino Community College District.

KFMB-TV, Channel 8, CBS
7677 Engineer Rd., San Diego, CA 92111. (619) 571-8888. FAX: (619) 569-4203. Midwest Television Inc.

KGTV, Channel 10, ABC
Box 85347, San Diego, CA 92186. (619) 237-1010. FAX: (619) 262-1302. McGraw-Hill Broadcasting Co. Ed Quinn.

KNSD, Channel 39, NBC
8330 Engineer Rd., San Diego, CA 92111. (619) 279-3939. FAX: (619) 279-1076. NBC Inc. Neil E. Derrough.

KPBS, Channel 15, PBS
5200 Camponile Rd., San Diego State University, San Diego, CA 92182-5400. (619) 594-1515. FAX: (619) 265-6417. Board of Trustees, CSU for SDSU. Doug Myrland.

KSWB (San Francisco), Channel 69, WB
7191 Engineer Rd, San Diego, CA 92111. (619) 492-9269. Tribune Broadcasting Co.

KUSI-TV, Channel 51, UPN
4575 Viewridge Ave., San Diego, CA 92123. (619) 571-5151. (FAX: (619) 505-5050. McKinnon Broadcasting Co.

XETV, Channel 6, FOX
8253 Ronson Rd., San Diego, CA 92111. (619) 279-6666. FAX: (619) 268-9388. Bay City Television.

XEWT, Channel 12, IND
Box 434537, San Diego, CA 92143. (619) 528-1212. FAX: (619) 280-9398. Televisa, S.A.

BAY-TV, Channel 35, NBC
(see KRON, San Francisco). San Francisco, CA. Chronicle Broadcasting Inc.

KBHK-TV, Channel 44, UPN
650 California St., San Francisco, CA 94108. (415) 249-4444. FAX: (415) 397-1924. Chris Craft Industries Inc.

KCNS, Channel 38, IND
1550 Bryant St., Ste 850, San Francisco, CA 94103-4832. (415) 863-3800. FAX: (415) 863-3998. Shop at Home, Inc.

KDTV, Channel 14, UNI
2200 Palou Ave., San Francisco, CA 94124. (415) 641-1400. FAX: (415) 641-8677. Univision Television Group, Inc.

KGO-TV, Channel 7, ABC
900 Front St., San Francisco, CA 94111-1427. (415) 954-7777. FAX: (415) 954-7294. ABC Inc.

KMTP-TV, Channel 32, PBS
211 Brannan St., San Francisco, CA 94107. (415) 777-3232. FAX: (415) 512-4379. Minority Television Project.

KOFY-TV, Channel 11, WB
2500 Marin St., San Francisco, CA 94124. (415) 821-2020. Granite Broadcasting Corp.

KPIX TV, Channel 5, CBS
855 Battery St., San Francisco, CA 94111-1503. (415) 362-5550. FAX: (415) 765-8844. CBS Stations Inc. Jerry Eaton.

KPST-TV (Vallejo), Channel 66, IND
Suite 700, 832 Folsom St., San Francisco, CA 94107. (415) 243-8866. FAX: (415) 547-1428. Whitehead Media. Martin Diaz.

KQED, Channel 9, PBS
2601 Mariposa St., San Francisco, CA 94110-1400. (415) 864-2000. FAX: (415) 553-2380. KQED Inc.

KRON-TV, Channel 4, NBC
1001 Van Ness Ave., San Francisco, CA 94109. (415) 441-4444. FAX: (415) 561-8136. Chronicle Broadcasting Inc. Al Holzer.

KTVU (Oakland), Channel 2, FOX
PO Box 22222, San Francisco, CA 94623-2222. (510) 834-1212. FAX: (510) 272-9957. Cox Broadcasting Inc. Jeff Block.

KICU-TV, Channel 36, IND
2102 Commerce Dr., San Jose, CA 95131. (408) 953-3636. FAX: (408) 953-3630. Ralph C. Wilson. James H. Evers.

KKPX, Channel 65, IND
San Jose, CA. (415) 369-6565. FAX: (415) 369-4969. Paxson Communications Corp.

KNTV (Salinas/Monterey), Channel 11, ABC
645 Park Ave., San Jose, CA 95110-2613. (408) 286-1111. FAX: (408) 295-5461. Granite Broadcasting Corp.

KSTS (San Francisco), Channel 48, TEL
2349 Bering Dr., San Jose, CA 95131-1125. (408) 435-8848. FAX: (408) 433-5921. Telemundo Group Inc.

KTEH, Channel 54, PBS
1585 Schallenburger Rd., San Jose, CA 95110-1301. (408) 437-5454. FAX: (408) 437-5469. KTEH-TV Foundation.

KFTL (Stockton), Channel 64, IND
403 McCormick St., San Leandro, CA 94577. (510) 632-5835. FAX: (510) 632-8943, Family Stations Inc. Matt Tuter.

KSBY, Channel 6, NBC
467 Hill St., San Luis Obispo, CA 93405. (805) 541-6666. FAX: (805) 541-5142. E.P. Communications Inc.

KCSM-TV, Channel 60, PBS
1700 W. Hillsdale Blvd., San Mateo, CA 94402. (415) 574-6586. FAX: (415) 574-6975. San Mateo Community College District.

KTBN-TV, Channel 40, IND
PO Box A, Santa Ana, CA 92711. (714) 832-2950. Trinity Broadcasting Co.

KEYT-TV, Channel 3, ABC
PO Box 729, Santa Barbara, CA 93102-0729. (805) 882-3933. FAX: (805) 882-3934. Smith Broadcasting Group Inc.

KCOY-TV, Channel 12, CBS
1211 W. McCoy Ln., Santa Maria, CA 93455. (805) 925-1200. FAX: (805) 922-9830. Benedek Broadcasting Corp.

KFTY, Channel 50, IND
PO Box 1150, Santa Rosa, CA 95402-1150. (707) 526-5050. FAX: (707) 526-7429. Ackerley Communications Inc.

KSTV-TV (Ventura), Channel 57, IND
Ste. A, 18344 Oxnard St., Tarzana, CA 91356. (310) 454-8637. FAX: (310) 454-4983. Costa de Oro Television Inc. Mike Seros

KVMD, Channel 31, IND
Desert 31 TV Inc., 66920 2 Mile Rd., Twentynine Palms CA 92277. (360) 825-1099. FAX: (360) 825-4517. Peoria Broadcasting Services Inc.

KHIZ (Barstow), Channel 64, IND
PO Box 6464, Victorville, CA 92393. (760) 241-5888. FAX: (760) 241-0056. Sunbelt Television.

KSCI (San Bernardino), Channel 18, IND
12401 W. Olympic, West Los Angeles, CA 90064. (310) 478-1818. FAX: (310) 479-8118. KSCI Inc.

KOVR, Channel 13, CBS
2713 KOVR Dr., West Sacramento, CA 95605. (916) 374-1313. FAX: (916) 374-1459. Sinclair Broadcast Group.

COLORADO

KRMT (Denver), Channel 41, IND
12014 W. 64th Ave., Arvada, CO 80004. (303) 423-4141. FAX: (303) 424-0571. Community Television Educators.

KKTV, Channel 11, CBS
PO Box 2110, Colorado Springs, CO 80901-2110. (719) 634-2844. FAX: (719) 632-0808. The Ackerley Group.

KOAA-TV, Channel 5, NBC
Box 195, 2200 7th Ave., Colorado Springs, CO 81003. (719) 544-5781. FAX: (719) 544-7733. Evening Post Publishing Co.

KRDO-TV, Channel 13, ABC
PO Box 1457, Colorado Springs, CO 80901-1457. (719) 632-1515. FAX: (719) 475-0815. Harry W. Hoth Jr.

KXRM-TV, Channel 21, FOX, UPN
PO Box 15789, Colorado Springs, CO 80935-5789. (719) 596-2100. FAX: (719) 591-4180. GOCOM Communications.

KBDI-TV, Channel 12, PBS
2900 Welton St., 1st Flr, Denver, CO 80205. (303) 296-1212. FAX: (303) 296-6650. Front Range Educational Media Corp.

KCEC, Channel 50, UNI
Ste. 110, 777 Grant St., Denver, CO 80203. (303) 832-0050. FAX: (303) 832-3410. Entravision Communications Co.

KCNC-TV, Channel 4, CBS
P. O. Box 5012, Denver, CO 80217. (303) 861-4444. FAX: (303) 830-6380. CBS Stations Inc. Marv Rockford.

KDVR, Channel 31, FOX
501 Wazee St., Denver, CO 80204-1858. (303) 595-3131. FAX: (303) 595-8312. Fox Television Stations Inc.

KMGH-TV, Channel 7, ABC
123 Speer Blvd., Denver, CO 80203. (303) 832-7777. FAX: (303) 832-0138. McGraw-Hill Broadcasting Co.

KRMA-TV, Channel 6, PBS
1089 Bannock St., Denver, CO 80204. (303) 892-6666. FAX: (303) 620-5600. Council for Public TV, Ch. 6 Inc.

KTVJ (Boulder), Channel 14, IND
2100 Downing St., Denver, CO 80205. (303) 832-1414. FAX: (303) 832-1561.Roberts Broadcasting of Denver Inc.

KUBD, Channel 59, IND
9805 E. Iliff, Denver, CO 80231. (303) 751-5959. FAX: (303) 751-5993. Paxson Communications Corp.

KUSA-TV, Channel 9, NBC
500 Speer Blvd., Denver, CO 80203. (303) 871-9999. FAX: (303) 871-1819. Gannett Broadcasting.

KFCT, Channel 22, FOX
(see KDVR, Denver). Durango, CO. Fox Television Stations Inc.

KREX-TV, Channel 6, CBS, NBC
PO Box 2508, Durango, CO 81302. (970) 259-6666. FAX: (970) 247-8472. Lee Enterprises Inc.

KTVD (Denver), Channel 20, UPN
PO Box 6522, Englewood, CO 80155-6522. (303) 792-2020. FAX: (303) 790-4633. Fred Eychaner.

KWGN-TV (Denver), Channel 2, WB
6160 S. Wabash Way, Englewood, CO 80111-5108. (303) 740-2222. FAX: (303) 740-2847. Tribune Broadcasting.

KWHD (Denver/Castle Rock), Channel 53, IND
Box 5321, Englewood, CO 80155. (303) 799-8853. FAX: (303) 773-9960. LeSea Broadcasting.

KJCT, Channel 8, ABC
PO Box 3788, Grand Junction, CO 81502. (970) 245-8880. FAX: (970) 245-8249. Pikes Peak Broadcasting Co. Jan Hammer.

KKCO, Channel 11, NBC
2325 Interstate Ave., Grand Junction, CO 81505. (970) 243-1111. FAX: (970) 243-1700. Eagle III, L.C.

KREG-TV (Glenwood Springs), Channel 3, CBS, NBC
PO Box 789, Grand Junction, CO 81502. (970) 963-3333. FAX: (970) 242-0886. Withers Broadcasting Co.

KREX-TV, Channel 5, CBS
PO Box 789, 345 Hillcrest Manor, Grand Junction, CO 81502. (970) 242-5000. FAX: (970) 242-0886. Withers Broadcasting Co

KDEN (Longmont, CO), Channel 25, IND
PO Box 984, Little Rock, AR, 72203. (501) 753-5338. Colorado Broadcasters.

KREY-TV, Channel 10, CBS, NBC
614 N. First, Montrose, CO 81401. (970) 249-9601. FAX: (970) 249-9610. Withers Broadcasting Co.

KFQX (Grand Junction), Channel 4, IND
PO Box 10, 800 Gold Creek Rd., Ohio City, CO 81237. John Harvey Reese.

KOAA-TV (Colorado Springs), Channel 5, NBC
PO Box 195, 2200 7th Ave., Pueblo, CO 81003. (719) 544-5781. FAX: (719) 544-7733. Evening Post Publishing Co.

KTSC, Channel 8, PBS
2200 Bonforte Blvd., Pueblo, CO 81001-4901. (719) 543-8800. FAX: (719) 549-2208. University of Southern Colorado.

KSBS-TV, Channel 24, IND
PO Box 582445, Steamboat Springs, CO 80488. (970) 870-6110. FAX: (970) 870-6210. Televerde Communications.

KTVS, Channel 3, CBS
PO Box 432, 9841 County Rd. 59, Sterling, CO 80751. (970) 522-5743. FAX: (970) 522-7813. Benedek Broadcating Corp.

CONNECTICUT

WEDH, Channel 24, PBS
PO Box 6240, 240 New Britain Ave., Hartford, CT 06106-0240. (860) 278-5310. FAX: (860) 278-2157. Connecticut Public Broadcasting.

WFSB, Channel 3, CBS
3 Constitution Plz., Hartford, CT 06103-1807. (860) 728-3333. FAX: (860) 247-8940. Meredith Broadcasting Group.

WHCT-TV, Channel 18, IND
Ste. 310. 345 N. Main St., W. Hartofrd, CT 06117. (860) 233-1865. FAX: (860) 233-1815. Astroline Communications Co. L.P.

WTIC-TV, Channel 61, FOX
One Corporate Ctr., Hartford, CT 06103. (203) 527-6161. Tribune Broadcasting.

WBNE-TV, Channel 59, WB
8 Elm St., New Haven, CT 06510. (203) 782-5900. FAX: (203) 782-5995. Hicks, Muse, Tate & Furst Inc.

WEDY, Channel 65, PBS
(see WEDH, Hartford). New Haven, CT. Connecticut Public Broadcasting.

WTNH-TV, Channel 8, ABC
PO Box 1859, 8 Elm St., New Haven, CT 06510. (203) 784-8888. FAX: (203) 784-2010. Hicks, Muse, Tate & Furst Inc.

WHPX, Channel 26, IND
New London, CT. (860) 444-2626. FAX: (860) 440-2601. D.P. Media.

WTWS, Channel 26, IND
Ste. 226, 3 Shaws Cove, New London, CT 06320. (860) 444-2626. FAX: (860) 440-2601. Roberts Broadcasting of Hartford.

WEDN, Channel 53, PBS
(see WEDH, Hartford). Norwich, CT. Connecticut Public Broadcasting.

WTXX (Waterbury), Channel 20, UPN
15 Peach Orchard Rd., Prospect, CT 06712-1052. (203) 575-2020. FAX: (203) 758-3908. Counterpoint Communications Inc.

WHAI-TV (Bridgeport), Channel 43, IND
80 Great Hill Rd., Seymour, CT 06483. (203) 734-6182. FAX: (203) 795-0061. Paxson Communications Corp.

WEDW (Bridgeport), Channel 49, PBS
307 Atlantic St., Stamford, CT 06901. (203) 965-0440. FAX: (203) 965-0447. Connecticut Public Broadcasting.

WVIT, Channel 30, NBC
1422 New Britain Ave., West Hartford, CT 06110-1632. (860) 521-3030. FAX: (860) 521-4860. NBC Inc.

DELAWARE

WDPB, Channel 64, PBS
(see WHYY, Wilmington). Seaford, DE. WHYY Inc.

WHYY-TV, Channel 12, PBS
625 Orange St., Wilmington, DE 19801. (302) 888-1200. FAX: (215) 351-0398. WHYY Inc.

WTGI-TV (Wilmington), Channel 61, IND
520 Columbus Blvd., Philadelphia, PA 19123. (215) 923-2661. FAX: (215) 923-2677. Paxson Communications Corp.

DISTRICT OF COLUMBIA

WDCA-TV (Washington), Channel 20, UPN
5202 River Rd., Bethesda, MD 20816. (301) 986-9322. FAX: (301) 654-3517. Paramount Stations Group Inc.

WBDC-TV, Channel 50, WB
Ste. 350, 2121 Wisconsin Ave NW, Washington, DC 20007. (202) 965-5050. FAX: (202) 965-0050. Tribune Broadcasting.

WETA-TV, Channel 26, PBS
PO Box 2626, Washington, DC 20013. (703) 998-2600. FAX: (703) 998-3401. Greater Washington Educational Telecom.

WHMM, Channel 32, PBS
2222 4th St. NW, Washington, DC 20059. (202) 806-3200. FAX: (202) 806-3300. Howard University.

WJLA-TV, Channel 7, ABC
3007 Tilden St. NW, Washington, DC 20008. (202) 364-7777. FAX: (202) 364-7922. Allbritton Communications Co.

WRC-TV, Channel 4, NBC
4001 Nebraska Ave. NW, Washington, DC 20016. (202) 885-4000. FAX: (202) 885-5022. NBC Inc.

WTTG, Channel 5, FOX
5151 Wisconsin Ave. NW, Washington, DC 20016. (202) 244-5151. FAX: (202) 244-1745. Fox Television Stations Inc.

WUSA, Channel 9, CBS
4100 Wisconsin Ave. NW, Washington, DC 20016. (202) 895-5999. FAX: (202) 966-7948. Gannett Broadcasting.

FLORIDA

WNTO (Orlando), Channel 26 IND
498 Palm Springs Dr., Altamonte, FL 32802. (407) 774-2626. FAX: (407) 830-7302. Jim McCotter.

WGCU-TV (Fort Myers), Channel 30, PBS
Channel 30 Dr., Bonita Springs, FL 33923. (941) 598-9737. FAX: (941) 598-2598. State Board of Regents, Florida. Kirk Lehtoman.

WTVK (Naples), Channel 46, WB
3451 Bonita Bay Blvd., Bonita Springs, FL 33923. (941) 498-4600. FAX: (941) 498-0146. Acme Television Holdings, LLC.

WZVN-TV (Naples), Channel 26, ABC
3719 Central Ave., Fort Myers, FL 33901. (941) 939-2020. FAX: (941) 939-4801. Lara Kunkler.

WXEL-TV (West Palm Beach), Channel 42, PBS
3401 S. Congress Ave., Boynton Beach, FL 33426. (561) 737-8000. FAX: (561) 369-3067. Barry Telecommunications, Inc.

WFCT, Channel 66, IND
Lakewood Business Park, Ste. E18, 4301 32nd St. W., Bradenton, FL 34205. (813) 747-2879. FAX: (813) 746-5053. Christian Network Inc.

WFTX (Fort Myers), Channel 36, FOX
621 S.W. Pine Island Rd., Cape Coral, FL 33991. (941) 574-3636. Fax: (941) 574-4803. Wabash Valley Broadcasting. Mark Pierce.

WCLF, Channel 22, IND
PO Box 6922, Clearwater, FL 33758 (813) 535-5622. FAX: (813) 531-2497. Christian Television Corp.

WBCC, Channel 68, IND
1519 Clearlake Rd., Cocoa, FL 32922. (407) 632-1111. FAX: (407) 634-3724. Brevard Community College.

WCEU (New Smyrna Beach), Channel 15, PBS
1200 W. International Speedway Blvd., Daytona Beach, FL 32124. (904) 254-4415. FAX: (904) 254-4427. Coastal Educational Broadcasters.

WBBH-TV, Channel 20, NBC
PO Box 7578, Fort Myers, FL 33911-7578. (941) 939-2020. FAX: (941) 939-4801. Waterman Broadcasting Corp. Laura Kunkler.

WINK-TV, Channel 11, CBS
2824 Palm Beach Blvd., Fort Myers, FL 33916-1503. (941)
334-1111. FAX: (941) 334-0744. Fort Myers Broadcasting Co.
Michael Castenegera.

WTCE, Channel 21, IND
3601 N. 25th St., Fort Pierce, FL 34946. (561) 489-2701. FAX:
(561) 489-6833. Jacksonville Educators Broadcasting.

WFGX-TV (Pensacola), Channel 35, WB
105 Beach Dr., Fort Walton Beach, FL 32547-2560. (904)
863-3235. FAX: (904) 862-7659. Sinclair Broadcast Group Inc.

WCJB, Channel 20, ABC
6220 N.W. 43rd St., Gainesville, FL 32653-3334. (352)
377-2020. FAX: (352) 373-6516. Diversified Communications.
Carolyn Catlin.

WGFL (High Springs), Channel 53, IND
c/o Budd Broadcasting Co., 4190 N.W. 93 Ave., Gainesville, FL
32653. (352) 375-5300. FAX: (352) 371-9353. Budd
Boradcasting Co. Inc.

WUFT, Channel 5, PBS
2200 Weimer, University of Florida, Gainesville, FL 32611. (352)
392-5551. FAX: (352) 392-5731. Florida Board of Regents.

WJXX (Orange Park), Channel 25, ABC
7025 A.C. Skinner Pkwy., Jacksonville, FL 32255. (904) 996-
0950. FAX: (904) 996-0959. Allbritton Communications Co. F.
Lewis Robertson.

WBFS-TV (Miami), Channel 33, UPN
16550 N.W. 52nd Ave., Hialeah, FL 33014-6214. (305)
621-3333. FAX: (305) 628-3448. Paramount Stations Group Inc.

WSCV (Miami/Ft. Lauderdale), Channel 51, TEL
2340 W. 8th Ave., Hialeah, FL 33010. (305) 888-5151. FAX:
(305) 889-7651. Telemundo Group Inc.

WDZL (Miami), Channel 39, WB
2055 Lee St., Hollywood, FL 33020-2410. (305) 925-3939. FAX:
(305) 949-3900. Tribune Broadcasting.

WHFT (Miami), Channel 45, IND
3324 Pembroke Rd., Pembroke Park, FL 33021-8320. (305)
962-1700. FAX: (305) 962-2817. Trinity Broadcasting Network.

WAWS, Channel 30, FOX
11700 Central Pkwy., Jacksonville, FL 32224. (904) 642-3030.
FAX: (904) 646-0115. Clear Channel Communications Inc.

WJCT, Channel 7, PBS
100 Festival Park Ave., Jacksonville, FL 32202. (904) 353-7770.
FAX: (904) 354-6846. WJCT Inc.

WJEB-TV, Channel 59, PBS
3101 Emerson Expwy., Jacksonville, FL 32207. (904) 399-8413.
FAX: (904) 399-8423. Jacksonville Educators Broadcasting.

WJWB, Channel 17, WB
9117 Hogan Rd., Jacksonville, FL 32216-4647. (904) 641-1700.
FAX: (904) 641-0306. Media General Broadcast Group.

WJXT, Channel 4, CBS
PO Box 5270, Jacksonville, FL 32247-5270. (904) 399-4400.
FAX: (904) 399-1828. Post-Newsweek Stations. Sherry Burns.

WTEV-TV, Channel 47, UPN
1170 Central Pkwy., Jacksonville, FL 32224. (904) 646-4747.
FAX: (904) 646-0115. RDS Broadcasting Inc.

WTLV, Channel 12, NBC
1070 E. Adams St., Jacksonville, FL 32202. (904) 354-1212.
FAX: (904) 633-8899. Gannett Broadcasting.

WEYS, Channel 22, IND
527 Southard St., Key West, FL 33040. (305) 296-4969. FAX:
(305) 296-1669. WEYS Television Corp. Kirk Sheldon.

WWFD, Channel 8, IND
5420 MacDonald Ave., Key West FL 33040. (305) 295-0084.
FAX: (305) 295-0132. Hispanic Keys Broadcasting Corp. Robert
Thompson.

WOFL (Orlando), Channel 35, FOX
35 Skyline Dr., Lake Mary, FL 32746. (407) 644-3535. FAX:
(407) 333-3535. Meredith Broadcasting Group.

WPXP (West Palm Beach), Channel 67, IND
Lake Worth, FL. (407) 478-9111. Paxson Communications Corp.

WIRB (Melbourne), Channel 56, IND
6525 Babcock St., Malabar, FL 32950. (407) 725-0056. FAX:
(407) 951-2669. The Christian Network. Dave Hall.

WBFS, Channel 33, IND
16550 N.W. 52nd Ave., Miami FL 33014. (305) 621-3333. FAX:
(305) 628-3448. Paramount Stations Group.

WBSF (Orlando), Channel 43, HSN
4450-L Enterprise Ct., Melbourne, FL 32934. (407) 254-4343.
FAX: (407) 242-0863. USA Broadcasting Inc.

WCTD, Channel 35, IND
One Datran Ctr., Ste. 1804, 9100 S. Dadeland Blvd., Miami, FL
33156. (305) 670-3535. FAX: (305) 670-0135. Paxson
Communications Corp.

WFOR-TV, Channel 4, CBS
8900 N.W. Terr., Miami, FL 33172. (305) 591-4444. FAX: (305)
639-4444. CBS Stations Inc. Allen Shaklan.

WLRN-TV, Channel 17, PBS
172 N.E. 15th St., Miami, FL 33132. (305) 995-2204. FAX: (305)
995-2299. School Board of Dade County.

WLTV, Channel 23, UNI
9405 N.W. 41st St., Miami, FL 33178. (305) 470-2323. FAX:
(305) 471-4236. Univision Television Group, Inc.

WPBT, Channel 2, PBS
14901 N.E. 20th Ave., Miami, FL 33181. (305) 949-8321. FAX:
(305) 944-4211. Community TV Foundation of Southern Florida.

WPLG, Channel 10, ABC
3900 Biscayne Blvd., Miami, FL 33137-3721. (305) 576-1010.
FAX: (305) 325-2480. Post-Newsweek Stations.

WSVN, Channel 7, FOX
1401 79th Street Causeway, Miami, FL 33141-4104. (305)
751-6692. FAX: (305) 757-2266. Edmund N. Ansin.

WTVJ, Channel 6, NBC
316 N. Miami Ave., Miami, FL 33128. (305) 379-6666. NBC Inc.

WYHS-TV (Miami), Channel 69,HSN
10306 USA Today Way, Miramar, FL 33025. (305) 435-6900.
FAX: (305) 435-7406. USA Broadcasting Inc.

WAWD (Fort Walton Beach), Channel 58, IND
5080 75th Ave. N.W., Ocala, FL 34482. (904) 622-7550. Wendell
M. Rowans Ministries Inc. Wendell M. Rowans

WOGX, Channel 51, FOX
PO Box 3985, Ocala, FL 34478-3985. (352) 873-6951. FAX:
(352) 237-5423. Meredith Broadcasting Group.

WFTV, Channel 9, ABC
PO Box 999, Orlando, FL 32802-0999. (407) 841-9000. FAX:
(407) 244-8302. Cox Broadcasting Inc.

WKCF, Channel 18, WB
Ste. 200, 602 Courtland St., Orlando, FL 32804. (407)
645-1883. FAX: (407) 647-4163. Press Communications.

WKMG-TV, Channel 6, CBS
4466 John Young Pkwy., Orlando, FL 32804. (407) 291-6000.
FAX: (407) 298-2122. Post-Newsweek Stations Inc.

WMFE-TV, Channel 24, PBS
11510 E. Colonial Dr., Orlando, FL 32817-4699. (407) 273-3200.
FAX: (407) 273-3613. Community Communications Inc.

WRBW, Channel 65, UPN
Suite 200, 2000 Universal Studios Plaza, Orlando, FL 32819.
(407) 248-6500. FAX: (407) 248-6520. Chris Craft Industries Inc.

WTGL-TV (Cocoa), Channel 52, IND
653 W. Michigan St., Orlando, FL 32805. (407) 423-5200. FAX:
(407) 422-0120. Good Life Broadcasting Inc.

WTVX (West Palm Beach), Channel 34, UPN
Ste. 7007, 3970 RCA Blvd., Palm Beach Garden, FL 33410.
(407) 694-2525. FAX: (407) 627-6738. Paramount Stations
Group Inc.

WPBF (West Palm Beach), Channel 25, ABC
Ste. 7007, 3970 RCA Blvd., Palm Beach Gardens, FL 33410. (407)
694-2525. FAX: (407) 627-6738.Hearst-Argyle Television Inc .

WFSG, Channel 56, PBS
(see WFSU, Tallahassee). Panama City, FL. Florida Board of
Regents, Florida State University.

WJHG-TV, Channel 7, NBC
8195 Front Beach Rd., Panama City, FL 32407. (904) 234-2125.
FAX: (904) 233-6647. Gray Communications Systems Inc. Terry
Cole.

WMBB, Channel 13, ABC
PO Box 1340, Panama City, FL 32402. (850) 769-2313. FAX:
(850) 769-8231. Spartan Communications Inc.

WPGX, Channel 28, FOX
Fox TV Center, 637 Luverne Ave., Panama City, FL 32401. (904)
784-0028. FAX: (904) 784-1773. Wicks Broadcast Group LP.
Patrick Quirk.

WPCT, Channel 46, IND
PO Box 9556, Panama City Beach, FL 32417. (904) 234-2773.
FAX: (904) 234-1179. Beach TV Properties Inc.

WHBR, Channel 33, IND
PO Box 2633, Pensacola, FL 32513. (850) 433-8633. FAX: (850)
433-8633. Christian TV of Pensacola/Mobile.

WJTC (Pensacola), Channel 44, UPN
661 Azalea Rd., Mobile, AL 36609. (334) 602-1544. FAX: (334)
602-1547. Mercury Broadcasting Co., Inc.

WPAN (Fort Walton Beach), Channel 53, IND
PO Box 18126, Pensacola, FL 32523. (904) 433-1776. FAX:
(904) 433-1641. John Franklin Ministries Inc.

WSRE, Channel 23, PBS
1000 College Blvd., Pensacola, FL 32504-8998. (904) 484-1200.
FAX: (904) 484-1255. Pensacola Jr. College Board of Trustees.

WRXY-TV (Tice), Channel 49, IND
40000 Horseshoe Rd., Punta Gorda, FL 33955. (941) 543-4173.
FAX: (941) 543-6800. Christian Television Network Inc.

WBSV-TV (Venice), Channel 62, IND
2065 Cantu Ct., Sarasota, FL 34232. (941) 379-0062. FAX: (941)
378-9224.Global Broadcasting Systems Inc.

WWSB, Channel 40, ABC
5725 Lawton Dr., Sarasota, FL 34233-2419. (941) 923-8840.
FAX: (941) 924-3971. Calkins Newspapers, Inc.

WBHS-TV (Tampa), Channel 50, HSN
Suite 301, 12425 28th St. N., St. Petersburg, FL 33716. (813)
573-5150. FAX: (813) 571-1931. USA Broadcasting Inc.

WTOG, Channel 44, UPN
365 15th Terr. N.E., St. Petersburg, FL 33716. (813) 576-4444.
FAX: (813) 577-1806. Paramount Stations Group Inc.

WCTV, Channel 6, CBS
PO Box 3048, Tallahassee, FL 32315-3048. (904) 893-6666.
FAX: (904) 893-5193. Gray Communications Systems Inc.

WFSU-TV, Channel 11, PBS
1600 Red Barber Plaza, Tallahassee, FL 32310. (904) 487-3170.
FAX: (904) 487-3093. Florida Board of Regents/ Florida State
University

WTLH, Channel 49, FOX
Ste. 501, 1203 Governors Square Blvd., Tallahassee, FL 32301.
(850) 942-4900. FAX: (850) 942-0062, Pegasus Broadcast TV
Inc. Gary Shipley.

WTWC, Channel 40, NBC
8440 Deerlake Road, Tallahassee, FL 32312. (904) 893-4140.
FAX: (904) 893-6974. Guy Gannett Communications.

WTXL-TV, Channel 27, ABC
8927 Thomasville Rd., Tallahassee, FL 32312-9761. (904)
893-3127. FAX: (904) 668-1460. Brian E. Cobb.

WEDU (Tampa), Channel 3, PBS
1300 North Blvd., Tampa, FL 33607. (813) 254-9338. FAX: (813)
253-0826. FL West Coast Pub. Broadcasting Inc.

WFLA-TV, Channel 8, NBC
905 E. Jackson St., Tampa, FL 33602-4117. (813) 228-8888.
FAX: (813) 221-5787. Media General Broadcast Group.

WFTS, Channel 28, ABC
4501 E. Columbus Dr., Tampa, FL 33605-3234. (813) 623-2828.
FAX: (813) 744-2828. E. W. Scripps Co.

WWWB-TV, Channel 32, IND
7201 E. Hillsborough Ave., Tampa, FL 33610. (813) 626-3232.
FAX: (813) 622-7732. Hearst-Argyle Television, Inc.

WTSP, Channel 10, CBS
11450 Gandy Blvd., Tampa, FL 33702. (813) 577-1010. FAX:
(813) 578-7637. Gannett Broadcasting.

WTTA, Channel 38, FOX
Ste. 38, 5510 W. Gray St., Tampa, FL 33609. (813) 289-3838.
FAX: (813) 289-0000. Bay Television Inc.

WTVT, Channel 13, FOX
PO Box 31113, Tampa, FL 33631-3113. (813) 876-1313. FAX:
(813) 875-8329. Fox Television Stations Inc.

WUSF-TV, Channel 16, PBS
Univ. of Southern FL, SVC 0001, 4202 Fowler Ave., Tampa, FL
33620. (813) 974-4000. FAX: (813) 974-4806. State Board of
Regents, Florida.

WFGC (Palm Beach), Channel 61, IND
Ste. 2, 2406 S. Congress Ave., W. Palm Beach, FL 33406. (561)
642-3361. FAX: (561) 967-5961. Christian TV of Palm Beach
County.

WHBI, Channel 67, IND
Centurion Tower, Suite 1200, 1601 Forum Place Blvd., W. Palm
Beach, FL 33401. (561) 478-9111. FAX: (561) 287-0512.
Hispanic Broadcasting Inc.

WFLX, Channel 29, FOX
4119 W. Blue Heron Blvd., West Palm Beach, FL 33404-4854.
(561) 845-2929. FAX: (561) 863-1238. Malrite Communications
Group Inc.

WPEC, Channel 12, CBS
PO Box 198512, West Palm Beach, FL 33419-8512. (561)
844-1212. FAX: (561) 842-1212. Freedom Communications Inc.

WPTV, Channel 5, NBC
622 N. Flagler Dr., West Palm Beach, FL 33401. (407)
655-5455. FAX: (407) 655-8947. E.W. Scripps Co.

WESH (Orlando), Channel 2, NBC
1021 N. Wymore Rd., Winter Park, FL 32789. (407) 645-222.
FAX: (407) 539-7812 Hearst-Argyle Television Inc.

GEORGIA

WALB, Channel 10, NBC
PO Box 3130, Albany, GA 31706-3130. (912) 883-0154. FAX:
(912) 434-8768. Liberty Corp.

WFXL, Channel 31, FOX
PO Box 4050, Albany, GA 31706-4050. (912) 435-3100. FAX:
(912) 435-0485. Wicks Broadcast Group LP, New York.

WAGA-TV, Channel 5, FOX
1551 Briarcliff Rd N.E., Atlanta, GA 30306-2217. (404)
875-5555. FAX: (404) 898-0277. Fox Television Stations Inc.

WATL (WB36), Channel 36, WB
1 Monroe Pl. N.E., Atlanta, GA 30324-4836. (404) 881-3600.
FAX: (404) 881-3748. Quest Broadcasting, LLC.

WGNX, Channel 46, CBS
PO Box 98097, Atlanta, GA 30359-1797. (404) 325-4646. FAX:
(404) 633-8358. Tribune Broadcasting.

WGTV (Athens), Channel 8, PBS
260 14th St., N.W., Atlanta, GA 30318. (404) 685-2400. FAX:
(404) 685-4476. GA Public Television Network.

WPBA, Channel 30, PBS
740 Bismark Rd. N.E., Atlanta, GA 30324. (404) 827-8900. FAX:
(404) 827-8956. Board of Ed., City of Atlanta.

WSB-TV, Channel 2, ABC
1601 W. Peachtree St. N.E., Atlanta, GA 30309-2641. (404)
897-7000. FAX: (404) 897-7525. Cox Broadcasting Inc.

WTBS, Channel 17, IND
1050 Techwood Dr. N.W., Atlanta, GA 30318. (404) 827-1717.
FAX: (404) 885-4947. Superstation Inc., Turner Broadcasting.

WUPA Channel 69, UPN
Suite A., 2700 Northeast Expwy., Atlanta, GA 30345. (404)
325-6969. FAX: (404) 633-4567. Paramount Stations Group Inc.

WXIA-TV, Channel 11, NBC
1611 W. Peachtree St. N.E., Atlanta, GA 30309. (404) 892-1611.
FAX: (404) 892-0182. Gannett Broadcasting.

WAGT, Channel 26, NBC
PO Box 1526, Augusta, GA 30903-1526. (706) 826-0026. FAX:
(706) 724-4028. Schurz Communications Inc.

WFXG, Channel 54, FOX, UPN
3933 Washington Rd., Augusta, GA 30907. (706) 650-5400.
FAX: (706) 650-8411. Galleria Broadcast Group.

WJBF, Channel 6, ABC
1001 Reynolds St., Augusta, GA 30901. (706) 722-6664. FAX:
(706) 722-0022. Spartan Radiocasting Company Inc.

WRDW, Channel 12, CBS
1301 Georgia Ave., N. Augusta, SC 29841. (803) 278-1212.
FAX: (803) 279-8316. Gray Communications Systems Inc.

WUBI-TV, Channel 34, UPN
PO Box 1080, E. Jekyll Rd., Baxley, GA 31513. (912) 367-3434.
FAX: (912) 367-5299. Southern TV Corp.

WNGM-TV (Atlanta), Channel 34, HSN
185 Ben Burton Cir., Bogart, GA 30622. (706) 353-3400. FAX:
(706) 549-5844. USA Broadcasting Inc.

WBSG-TV, Channel 21, ABC
7434 Blythe Island Hwy., Brunswick, GA 31525. (912) 267-0021.
FAX: (912) 267-9583. Allbritton Communications Co. Lewis
Robertson.

WCLP-TV, Channel 18, PBS
2765 Ft. Mountain State Park Rd., Chatsworth, GA 30705. (706)
695-2422. GA Public Telecomm. Commission.

WDCO-TV, Channel 29, PBS
PO Box 269, Salem Cary Rd., Cochran, GA 31014. (912)
934-2220. FAX: (912) 934-3646. GA Public Telecomm.
Commission.

WLTZ, Channel 38, NBC
PO Box 12289, 6140 Buena Vista Rd., Columbus, GA 31917.
(706) 561-3838. FAX: (706) 563-8467. Lewis Broadcasting Corp.

WRBL, Channel 3, CBS
PO Box 270, Columbus, GA 31902-0270. (706) 323-3333. FAX:
(706) 327-6655. TCS Management Corp. ML Media.

WTVM, Channel 9, ABC
PO Box 1848, Columbus, GA 31902-1848. (706) 324-6471. FAX:
(706) 322-7527. Raycom Media Inc.

WXTX, Channel 54, FOX, UPN
PO Box 12188, Columbus, GA 31917. (706) 561-5400. FAX:
(706) 561-6505. Galleria Broadcast Group.

WSST-TV, Channel 55, IND
PO Box 917, 112 S 7th St., Cordele, GA 31015. (912) 273-0001.
FAX: (912) 273-8894. P.A Streetman, William B. Goodson.

WHSG (Monroe), Channel 63, IND
1550 Agape Way, Decatur, GA 30035. (404) 288-1156. FAX:
(404) 288-5613. Trinity Broadcasting Network Inc.

WELF (Dalton), Channel 23, IND
384 S. Campus Rd., Lookout Mountain, GA 30750. (706)
820-1663. FAX: (706) 820-1735. All American Inc. Ray Guy.

WGNM Channel 64, UPN
2525 Beech Ave., Macon, GA 31204. (912) 746-6464. FAX:
(912) 745-2367. Good News Television. David Wood.

WGXA, Channel 24, FOX
PO Box 340, 599 Broadway., Macon, GA 31201. (912)
745-2424. FAX: (912) 750-4347. GOCOM Communications.

WMAZ-TV, Channel 12, CBS
PO Box 5008, Macon, GA 31213-8099. (912) 752-1313. FAX:
(912) 752-1331. Gannett Broadcasting.

WMGT, Channel 41, NBC
PO Box 4328, Macon, GA 31208-4328. (912) 745-4141. FAX:
(912) 742-2626. Morris Network Inc.

WTLK-TV (Rome), Channel 14, IND
Ste. 114, 200 N. Cobb Pkwy., Marietta, GA 30062. (770)
528-1400. FAX: (770) 528-1403. Paxson Communications Corp.

WATC-TV (Atlanta), Channel 57, IND
1862 Enterprise Drive, Norcross, GA 30093. (770) 30-9828.
FAX: (770) 300-9838. Community Television Inc.

WACS-TV (Dawson), Channel 25, PBS
Rt. 1, PO Box 75A, Parrott, GA 31777. (404) 756-2400. FAX: (404)
756-2617. GA Public Telecomm. Comm. Lewis C. Rickerson.

WABW-TV, Channel 14, IND
PO Box 249, Pelham, GA 31779. (912) 294-6501. GA Public
Telecomm. Commission.

WVAN-TV (Savannah), Channel 9, PBS
PO Box 367, 86 Vandiver St., Pembroke, GA 31321-0367. (912)
653-4996. FAX: (800) 222-6006. GA Public Telecomm.

WPGA-TV, Channel 58, ABC
PO Box 5858, Perry, GA 31208. (912) 745-5858. FAX: (912)
745-5800. Radio Perry Inc.

WPXA (Atlanta), Channel 14, IND
Rome, GA. (770) 528-1400. FAX: (770) 528-1403. Paxson
Communications Corp.

WJCL-TV, Channel 22, ABC
10001 Abercorn St., Savannah, GA 31406. (912) 925-0022.
FAX: (912) 925-8621. Grapevine Communications.

WSAV-TV, Channel 3, ABC
1430 E. Victory Dr., Savannah, GA 31404. (912) 651-0300. FAX:
(912) 651-0304. Media General Broadcast Group.

WTOC-TV, Channel 11, CBS
PO Box 8086, Savannah, GA 31412-8086. (912) 234-1111. FAX:
(912) 238-5133. Raycom Media Inc.

WNEG-TV, Channel 32, CBS
PO Box 907, 100 Blvd., Toccoa, GA 30577. (706) 886-0032.
FAX: (706) 886-7033. Roy E. Gaines.

WGVP, Channel 44, UPN
1202 B.W. Gordon St., Valdosta, GA 31602. (912) 253-9487.
FAX: (912) 241-0432. Venture Technologies Group of Florida
LLC.

WJSP-TV (Columbus), Channel 28, PBS
609 White House Pkwy., Warm Springs, GA 31830. (706)
655-2145. GA Public Telecomm. Commission.

WXGA-TV, Channel 8, PBS
PO Box 842, Waycross, GA 31502. (912) 283-4838. FAX: (912)
283-4838. GA Public Telecomm. Commission.

WCES-TV, Channel 20, PBS
PO Box 525, Wrens, GA 30833-0525. (706) 547-2107. FAX:
(706) 547-7290. GA Public Telecomm. Commission.

HAWAII

KGMD-TV, Channel 9, CBS
(see KGMB, Honolulu). Hilo HI. Lee Enterprises Inc.

KHBC-TV, Channel 2, NBC
(see KFVE, Honolulu). Hilo, HI (808) 847-3246. FAX: (808)
845-3616. A.H. Belo Corp.

KHVO, Channel 13, ABC
(see KITV, Honolulu). Hilo, HI. Hearst-Argyle Television, Inc.

KAII-TV (Wailuku), Channel 7, FOX
(See WHON, Honolulu) SF Broadcasting LLC.

KBFD, Channel 32, IND
1188 Bishop St., # PH-1, Honolulu, HI 96813-3301. (808)
521-8066. FAX: (808) 521-5233. Kea Sung Chung. Jeff Chung.

KFVE, Channel 5, UPN
150-B Puuhale Rd., Honolulu, HI 96819-2282. (808) 842-5555.
FAX: (808) 842-4594. Southern Media Inc.

KGMB, Channel 9, CBS
1534 Kapiolani Blvd., Honolulu, HI 96814. (808) 973-5462. FAX:
(808) 941-8153. Lee Enterprises Inc.

KHAW-TV (Hilo), Channel 11, FOX
1116 Auahi St., Honolulu, HI 96814-4907.(809) 591-2222. FAX:
(809) 591-9085. USA Broadcasting Inc.

KHET, Channel 11, PBS
2350 Dole St., Honolulu, HI 96822. (808) 973-1000. FAX: (808)
973-1090. Hawaii Public Broadcasting Authority.

KHNL, Channel 8, NBC
150-B Puuhale Rd., Honolulu, HI 96819-2282. (808) 842-5555.
FAX: (808) 842-4594. A.H. Belo Corp.

KHON-TV, Channel 2, FOX
1116 Auahi St., Honolulu, HI 36814. (808) 591-2222. FAX: (808)
591-9085. SF Broadcasting Inc.

KIKU, Channel 20, IND
Ste. 2021, 197 Sand Island Access Rd., Honolulu, HI 96819.
(808) 847-2021. FAX: (808) 841-3326. KHAI Inc.

KAAH, Channel 26, IND
Ste. 626, 875 Waimanu St., Honolulu, HI 96813. (808) 521-5826.
FAX: (808) 737-8959. Christopher J. Racine.

KITV, Channel 4, ABC
1290 Ala Moana Blvd., Honolulu, HI 96814. (808) 593-4444.
FAX: (808) 593-9446. Hearst-Argyle Television Inc.

KMEB (Wailuku), Channel 10, PBS
2350 Dole St., Honolulu, HI 96822. (808) 955-7878. FAX: (808)
949-7289. Hawaii Public Broadcasting Authority.

KWHE, Channel 14, WB
Century Sq., Suite 502, 1188 Bishop St., Honolulu, HI 96813.
(808) 538-1414. FAX: (808) 526-0326. LeSea Broadcasting
Corp.

KLEI (Kailua-Kona), Channel 6, IND
(see KOBN, Honolulu). Kailua-Kona, HI. Newport Broadcasting
Co.

KAPA-TV, Channel 66, Dark
Kaneohe/Honolulu, HI. Paxson Communications Corp.

KGMV, Channel 3, CBS
(see KGMB, Honolulu). Wailuku, HI. Lee Enterprises Inc.

KMAU, Channel 12, ABC
(see KITV, Honolulu). Wailuku, HI. Hearst-Argyle Television Inc.

KOGG, Channel 15, NBC
(see KFVE, Honolulu). Wailuku, HI. A.H. Belo Corp.

KWHM, Channel 21, IND
(see KWHE, Honolulu). Wailuku, HI. LeSea Broadcasting Corp.

IDAHO

KAID, Channel 4, PBS
1455 N. Orchard, Boise, ID 83706. (208) 373-7220. FAX: (208)
373-7245. Idaho State Board of Education.

KBCI-TV, Channel 2, CBS
140 N. 16th St., Boise, ID 83702. (208) 336-5222. FAX: (208)
336-9183. Retlaw Broadcasting Co.

KNIN-TV (Caldwell), Channel 9, WB, UPN
Ste. 402, 816 W. Bannock St., Boise, ID 83702. (208) 331-0909.
FAX: (208) 344-0119. Schuyler Broadcasting Corp.

KTVB, Channel 7, NBC
PO Box 7, Boise, ID 83707-0007. (208) 375-7277. FAX: (208)
378-1762. A. H. Belo Corp.

KIDK, Channel 3, CBS, FOX
PO Box 2008, Idaho Falls, ID 83403. (208) 522-1500. FAX: (208)
522-5103. Retlaw Enterprises Inc.

KIFI-TV, Channel 8, ABC
PO Box 2148, Idaho Falls, ID 83403. (208) 525-8888. FAX: (208)
522-1930. The Post Company.

KLEW, Channel 3, CBS
PO Box 615, 2626 17th St., Lewiston, ID 83501. (208)
746-2636. FAX: (208) 746-4819. Retlaw Enterprises Inc. Fred
Fickenwirth.

KCDT (Coeur d'Alene), Channel 26, PBS
Radio & Television Ctr., Univ. of Idaho, Moscow, ID 83844. (208)
765-9193. FAX: (208) 667-4689. Idaho State Board of Education.

KUID-TV, Channel 12, PBS
Radio-TV Ctr., Univ. of Idaho, Moscow, ID 83844-3101. (208)
885-1226. Idaho State Board of Education. Ken Segota.

KIVI, Channel 6, ABC
1866 E. Chisholm Dr., Nampa, ID 83687. (208) 336-0500. FAX:
(208) 381-6682. Cordillera Communications Inc.

KTRV, Channel 12, FOX
679 6th St S., Nampa, ID 83687. (208) 466-1200. FAX: (208)
467-6958. Blade Communications Inc.

KISU-TV, Channel 10, PBS
PO Box 8111, Bldg. 62, E. Derry at 19th, Pocatello, ID 83209-
0009. (208) 236-2857. FAX: (208) 236-2848. Idaho State Board
of Education. Marcia J. Hosking.

KPVI (Idaho Falls), Channel 6, ABC
902 E. Sherman, Pocatello, ID 83201. (208) 232-6666. FAX:
(208) 233-6678. Sunbelt Communications Co.

KBGH (Filer), Channel 19, IND
315 Falls Ave., Twin Falls, ID 83301. (208) 733-9554. FAX: (208)
736-3015. College of Southern Idaho.

KIPT, Channel 13, PBS
(see KAID Boise). Twin Falls, ID. Idaho State Board of Education.

KMVT, Channel 11, CBS
1100 Blue Lakes Blvd N., Twin Falls, ID 83301-3305. (208)
733-1100. FAX: (208) 733-4649. Catamount-Idaho License LLC.

KXTF, Channel 35, FOX, UPN
1061 Blue Lakes Blvd. N., Twin Falls, ID 83301. (208) 733-0035.
FAX: (208) 733-0160. Sunbelt Communications Co.

ILLINOIS

WYZZ-TV, Channel 43, FOX
2714 E. Lincoln St., Bloomington, IL 61704-6010. (309)
662-4373. FAX: (309) 663-6943. Sinclair Broadcast Group Inc.

WSIU-TV, Channel 8, PBS
1048 Communications Bldg., Southern Illinois University,
Carbondale, IL 62901-6602. (618) 453-4343. FAX: (618)
453-6186. Board of Trustess, Southern IL U.

KPOB-TV (Poplar Bluff, MO), Channel 15, ABC
Rt. 13, Carterville, IL 62918. (618) 985-2333. FAX: (618)
985-3709. Mel Wheeler Inc.

WCFN (Springfield), Channel 49, CBS
PO Box 20, 509 S. Neil St., Champaign, IL 61824-0020. (217)
356-8333. FAX: (217) 373-3648. Midwest Television Inc.

WCIA, Channel 3, CBS
Box 20, 509 S. Neil St., Champaign, IL 618204-0020. (217)
356-8333. FAX: (217) 373-3648. Midwest Television, Inc

WICD, Channel 15, NBC
250 S. County Fair Drive, Champaign, IL 61821. (217) 351-8500.
FAX: (217) 351-6056. Guy Gannett Communications.

WEIU-TV, Channel 51, PBS
Radio & TV Ctr., 139 Buzzard, Eastern Illinois University,
Charleston, IL 61920. (217) 581-5956. FAX: (217) 581-6650.
Eastern Illinois Univ.

WBBM-TV, Channel 2, CBS
630 N. McClurg Ct., Chicago, IL 60611-3007. (312) 944-6000.
FAX: (312) 440-0591. CBS Stations Inc. Hank Price.

WCFC-TV, Channel 38, IND
38 S. Peoria St., Chicago, IL 60607. (312) 433-3838. FAX: (312)
433-3839. Paxson Communications Corp.

WCIU-TV, Channel 26, WB
26 N. Halsted St., Chicago, IL 60661. (312) 705-2600. FAX:
(312) 705-2656. Howard Shapiro.

WEHS-TV, Channel 60, HSN
100 S. Sanagamon, Chicago, IL 60607. (312) 829-8860. FAX:
(312) 829-1059. USA Broadcasting Inc.

WFLD, Channel 32, FOX
205 N. Michigan Ave., Chicago, IL 60601-5925. (312) 565-5532.
FAX: (312) 819-0420. Fox Television Stations Inc.

WGBO-TV (Joliet), Channel 66, UNI
Suite 1100, 541 N. Fairbanks Ct., Chicago, IL 60611. (312)
670-1000. FAX: (312) 494-6492. Univision Television Group, Inc.

WGN-TV, Channel 9, WB
2501 W. Bradley Pl., Chicago, IL 60618-4701. (312) 528-2311.
FAX: (312) 528-6857. Tribune Broadcasting.

WLS-TV, Channel 7, ABC
190 N. State St., Chicago, IL 60601-3302. (312) 750-7777. FAX:
(312) 750-7015. ABC Inc. Joseph A. Ahern.

WMAQ-TV, Channel 5, NBC
454 N. Columbus Dr., Chicago, IL 60611. (312) 836-5555. FAX:
(312) 527-9072. NBC Inc.

WPWR-TV, Channel 50, UPN
2151 N. Elston Ave., Chicago, IL 60614-3903. (773) 276-5050.
FAX: (773) 276-6477. Newsweb Corp.

WSNS, Channel 44, TEL
430 W. Grant Pl., Chicago, IL 60614-3807. (312) 929-1200. FAX:
(312) 929-8153. Telemundo Group Inc.

WTTW, Channel 11, PBS
5400 N. St. Louis Ave., Chicago, IL 60625. (312) 583-5000. FAX:
(312) 583-3046. Window to the World Communications

WYCC, Channel 20, PBS
7500 S. Pulaski St., Chicago, IL 60652. (312) 838-7878. FAX:
(312) 581-2071. College Dist. #508, Cook County.

WAND, Channel 17, ABC
904 W. South Side Dr., Decatur, IL 62521-4022. (217) 424-2500.
FAX: (217) 422-8203. Hicks, Muse, Tate & Furst Inc.

WFHL, Channel 23, IND
2510 Pkwy. Ct., Decatur, IL 62526. (217) 428-2323. FAX: (217)
428-6455. Paxson Communications Corp.

WSIL-TV, Channel 3, ABC
(see KPOB, Carterville). Harrisburg, IL. Mel Wheeler Inc.

WSEC, Channel 14, PBS
Box 6248, Springfield, IL 62708. (217) 786-6647. FAX: (217)
786-7267. W Central IL Edu. Telecomm. Corp.

WMEC, Channel 22, PBS
Box 6248, Springfield, IL 62708. (217) 786-6647. FAX: (217)
786-7267. W. Central IL Edu. Telecomm. Corp.

WTCT, Channel 27, IND
PO Box 1010 Rt. 37 N., Marion, IL 62959. (618) 997-4700. FAX:
(618) 997-1859. Tri-State Christian T. Garth Coonce.

WQAD-TV, Channel 8, ABC
3003 Park 16th St., Moline, IL 61265. (309) 764-8888. FAX:
(309) 764-5763. The New York Times Co. Perry Chester.

WQPT-TV, Channel 24, PBS
6600 34th Ave., Moline, IL 61265. (309) 796-2424. FAX: (309)
796-2484. Black Hawk College. Charles Law.

WCEE, Channel 13, IND
125 N. 11th St., Mount Vernon, IL 62864. (618) 242-8813. FAX:
(618) 242-8643. DP Media Inc.

WUSI-TV, Channel 16, PBS
PO Box 430, Olney, IL 62450. (618) 754-3335. FAX: (618)
754-3330. Board of Trustees Southern IL Univ. Robert Gerig.

WWTO-TV (LaSalle), Channel 35, IND
420 E. Stevenson Rd., Ottawa, IL 61350. (815) 434-2700. FAX:
(815) 434-2458. All American TV Inc.

WEEK-TV, Channel 25, NBC
2907 Springfield Rd., Peoria, IL 61611-4878. (309) 698-2525.
FAX: (309) 698-9663. Granite Broadcasting Corp.

WHOI, Channel 19, ABC, UPN
500 N. Stewart St., Peoria, IL 61610. (309) 698-1919. FAX: (309)
698-4819. Benedek Broadcasting Corp.

WMBD-TV, Channel 31, CBS
3131 N. University St., Peoria, IL 61604-. (309) 688-3131. FAX:
(309) 686-8650. Midwest Television, Inc

WTVP, Channel 47, PBS
1501 W. Bradley Ave., Peoria, IL 61625. (309) 677-4747. (309)
677-3518. IL Valley Public Telecomm. Corp.

KHQA-TV, Channel 7, CBS
510 Maine St., Quincy, IL 62301. (217) 222-6200. FAX: (217)
228-3164. Benedek Broadcasting Co.

WGEM-TV, Channel 10, NBC
PO Box 80, 513 Hampshire, Quincy, IL 62306. (217) 228-6600.
FAX: (217) 228-6670. Quincy Newspapers Inc.

WQEC, Channel 27, PBS
Box 6248, Springfield, IL 62708. (217) 786-7267. FAX: (217)
786-7267. W. Central IL Edu. Telecomm. Corp.

WTJR, Channel 16, IND
PO Box 1189, 222 N. 6th St., Quincy, IL 62306. (217) 228-1616.
FAX: (217) 228-0966. Believers Broadcasting Corp.

WHBF-TV, Channel 4, CBS
231 18th St., Rock Island, IL 61201-8706. (309) 786-5441. FAX:
(309) 788-4975. Citadel Communications Co. Ltd.

WIFR (Freeport), Channel 23, CBS
Ste. 210, 308 W. State St., Rockford, IL 61101. (815) 987-5300.
FAX: (815) 965-0985. Benedek Broadcasting Co.

WQRF-TV, Channel 39, FOX
401 S. Main St., Rockford, IL 61101. (815) 987-3950. FAX: (815)
964-9974. Quorum Broadcasting.

WREX-TV, Channel 13, NBC
PO Box 530, Rockford, IL 61105. (815) 335-2213. FAX: (815)
335-1002. Quincy Newspapers Inc.

WTVO, Channel 17, ABC
1917 N. Meridian Rd., Rockford, IL 61101-9215. (815) 963-5413.
FAX: (815) 963-0201. Young Broadcasting Inc.

WICS, Channel 20, NBC
PO Box 3920, 2680 E. Cook St., Springfield, IL 62703. (217)
753-5620. FAX: (217) 753-8177. Guy Gannett Communications.
Jack Connors.

WRSP-TV, Channel 55, FOX, UPN
3003 Old Rochester Rd., Springfield, IL 62703. (217) 523-8855.
FAX: (217) 523-4410. Bahakel Communications.

Western Illinois Educational Television, PBS
PO Box 6248, Springfield, IL 62708. (217) 786-6647. FAX: (217)
786-7267. W. Central IL Edu. Telecomm. Corp.

WCCU, Channel 27, FOX
712 W. Killarney St., Urbana, IL 61801-1015. (217) 367-8827.
FAX: (217) 367-8839. Bahakel Communications.

WILL-TV, Channel 12, PBS
1110 W. Main St., Urbana, IL 61801. (217) 333-1070. FAX: (217)
244-6386. Board of Trustees, Univ. of Illinois. Ellis R. Bromberg.

INDIANA

WINM (Angola), Channel 63, IND
R.R. 1 State Line Rd., Edgerton, OH 43517. (419) 298-3703.
FAX: (419) 298-3707. Tri-State Christian Television.

WTIU, Channel 30, PBS
Radio-TV Bldg., Indiana University, Bloomington, IN 47405.
(812) 855-5900. FAX: (812) 855-0729. Trustees of Indiana
University.

WNIT-TV (South Bend), Channel 34, PBS
PO Box 3434, Elkhart, IN 46515. (219) 674-5961. FAX: (219)
262-8497. Michiana Public Broadcasting Corp.

WSJV (South Bend), Channel 28, FOX
58096 CR N. 7 South, Elkhart, IN 46517. (219) 679-9758. FAX:
(219) 294-1324. Quincy Newspapers Inc. Randy Angram.

WEHT, Channel 25, ABC
PO Box 25, Evansville, IN 47701-0025. (502) 826-9566. FAX:
(502) 826-6823. James S. Gilmore Stations.

WEVV, Channel 44, CBS
44 Main St., Evansville, IN 47708-1450. (812) 464-4444. FAX:
(812) 465-4559. WEVV Inc.

WFIE-TV, Channel 14, NBC
PO Box 1414, 1115 Mt. Auburn Rd., Evansville, IN 47720. (812)
426-1414. FAX: (812) 426-1945. Cosmos Broadcasting Group.

WNIN, Channel 9, PBS
405 Carpenter St., Evansville, IN 47708. (812) 423-2973. FAX:
(812) 428-7548. Tri-State Public Teleplex Inc.

WTVW, Channel 7, FOX
477 Carpenter St., Evansville, IN 47708. (812) 422-1121. FAX:
(812) 421-4040. Quorum Broadcasting.

WFTE (Salem), Channel 58, UPN
5257 S. Skyline Dr., Floyds Knobs, IN 47119. (812) 948-5841.
FAX: (812) 949-9365. Kentuckiana Broadcasting Inc.

WANE-TV, Channel 15, CBS
P. O. Box 1515, Fort Wayne, IN 46801-1515. (219) 424-1515.
FAX: (219) 424-1428. Hicks, Muse, Tate & Furst Inc.

WFFT-TV, Channel 55, FOX, UPN
3707 Hillegas Rd., Fort Wayne, IN 46808-1351. (219) 471-5555.
FAX: (219) 484-4331. Great Trails Broadcasting Corp.

WFWA, Channel 39, PBS
3632 Butler Rd., Fort Wayne, IN 46808. (219) 484-8839. FAX:
(219) 482-3632. Fort Wayne Public Television.

WKJG-TV, Channel 33, NBC
2633 W. State Blvd., Fort Wayne, IN 46808. (219) 422-7474.
FAX: (219) 422-9648. The Joseph R. Cloutier Trust.

WPTA, Channel 21, ABC
3401 Butler Rd., Fort Wayne, IN 46808. (219) 483-0584. FAX:
(219) 483-1835. Granite Broadcasting Corp. Tim Gilbert.

WCLJ (Bloomington), Channel 42, IND
2528 U.S. 31 S., Greenwood, IN 46143. (317) 535-5542. FAX:
(317) 535-8584. Trinity Broadcasting Network. Randall Lohr.

WYIN (Gary), Channel 56, PBS
8625 Indiana Pl., Merrillville, IN 46410. (219) 736-5656. FAX:
(219) 755-4312. Northwest Indiana Public Broadcasting Inc.

WFYI, Channel 20, PBS
1401 N. Meridian, Indianapolis, IN 46202. (317) 636-2020. FAX:
(317) 633-7418. Metro Indianapolis Public B'casting. Lloyd
Wright.

WISH-TV, Channel 8, CBS
PO Box 7088, 1950 N. Meridian St., Indianapolis, IN 46207.
(317) 923-8888. FAX: (317) 926-1144. Hicks, Muse, Tate & Furst
Inc.

WNDY, Channel 23, UPN
4555 West 16th St., Indianapolis, IN 46268. (317) 241-2388.
FAX: (317) 381-6975. Paramount Stations Group Inc.

WRTV, Channel 6, ABC
1330 N. Meridian St., Indianapolis, IN 46202-2303. (317)
635-9788. FAX: (317) 269-1400. McGraw-Hill Broadcasting Co.

WTBU, Channel 69, PBS
2835 N. Illinois, Indianapolis, IN 46208. (317) 940-9828. FAX:
(317) 940-5971. Butler University.

WTHR, Channel 13, NBC
1000 N. Meridian St., Indianapolis, IN 46204. (317) 636-1313.
FAX: (317) 636-3717. Dispatch Broadcast Group

WTTK (Kokomo), Channel 29, IND
3490 Bluff Rd., Indianapolis, IN 46217. (317) 782-4444. FAX:
(317) 780-5464. Sinclair Broadcast Group Inc.

WTTV-TV, Channel 4, UPN
3490 Bluff Rd., Indianapolis, IN 46217-3204. (317) 782-4444.
FAX: (317) 780-5464. Sinclair Broadcast Group Inc.

WXIN, Channel 59, FOX
1440 N. Meridian St., Indianapolis, IN 46202-2305. (317)
632-5900. FAX: (317) 687-6531. Tribune Broadcasting.

WIPB (also production facility), Channel 49, PBS
Edmund F. Ball Bldg., Ball State University Teleplex, Muncie, IN
47306. (317) 285-1249. FAX: (317) 285-5548. Ball State
University. Robert R. Smith.

WHMB-TV (Indianapolis), Channel 40, IND
10511 Greenfield Ave., Noblesville, IN 46060. (317) 773-5050.
FAX: (317) 776-4051. LeSea Broadcasting Corp. V.P.: Peter
Sumrall.

WKOI, Channel 43, IND
1702 S. 9th St., Richmond, IN 47374-7203. (317) 935-2390.
Trinity Broadcasting Network.

WHME-TV, Channel 46, WB
PO Box 12, 61300 S. Ironwood, South Bend, IN 46614. (219)
291-8200. FAX: (219) 291-9043. LeSea Broadcasting.

WNDU-TV, Channel 16, NBC
PO Box 1616, South Bend, IN 46634-1616. (219) 631-1616.
FAX: (219) 631-1600. Univ. of Notre Dame du Lac.

WSBT-TV, Channel 22, CBS
300 W. Jefferson Blvd., South Bend, IN 46601. (219) 233-3141.
FAX: (219) 288-6630. Schurz Communications Inc.

WBAK-TV, Channel 38, FOX
PO Box 719, Terre Haute, IN 47808-0719. (812) 238-1515. FAX:
(812) 235-3854. Bahakel Communications.

WTHI-TV, Channel 10, CBS
PO Box 1486, 918 Ohio St., Terre Haute, IN 47808. (812) 232-
9481. FAX: (812) 232-8953. Wabash Valley Broadcasting Corp.

WTWO, Channel 2, NBC
PO Box 299, Terre Haute, IN 47808. (812) 696-2121. FAX: (812)
696-2755. Nexstar Broadcasting Group.

WIIB (Bloomington), Channel 63, IND
Box 130, 2327 State Rd., 252 W., Trafalgar, IN 46181. (317)
878-5407. FAX: (317) 878-4458. Dr. David C. McCarus.

WVUT, Channel 22, PBS
David Hall, 1200 N. 2nd St., Vincennes, IN 47951. (812)
885-4345. FAX: (812) 882-2237. Vincennes University Trustees.

WLFI-TV (Lafayette), Channel 18, CBS
PO Box 2618, 2605 Yeager Rd., West Lafayette, IN 47906. (765)
463-1800. FAX: (765) 463-7979. The Block Family.

IOWA

KTVC-TV (Cedar Rapids), Channel 48, IND
1404 5th Ave S.E., Altoona, IA 50009-2027. (515) 967-6228.
Paxson Communications Corp.

KJMH (Burlington), Channel 26, FOX
(see KLJB, Davenport). Burlington, IA 52807. Quad Cities TV..

KCRG-TV, Channel 9, ABC
PO Box 816, Cedar Rapids, IA 52406-0816. (319) 398-8422.
FAX: (319) 398-8378. The Gazette Co.

KFXA, Channel 28, FOX
605 Boyson Rd. N.E., Cedar Rapids, IA 52402-7209. (319)
393-2800. FAX: (319) 395-7028. Second Generation of Iowa.

KGAN, Channel 2, CBS
PO Box 3131, Cedar Rapids, IA 52406-3131. (319) 395-9060.
FAX: (319) 395-0987. Guy Gannett Broadcasting Svc. Inc.

KBIN, Channel 32 (Council Bluffs), PBS
Box 6450, c/o Iowa Public TC., Johnston, IA. 50131. (515) 242-
3100. Iowa Public Broadcasting Board.

KLJB-TV, Channel 18, FOX
937 E. 53rd St., Ste D, Davenport, IA 52807-2614. (319)
386-1818. FAX: (319) 386-8543. Quad Cities. Kathy DeBoeuf.

KQCT, Channel 36 (Davenport), IND
6600 34th Ave., Moline, IA 61265. (309) 796-2424. FAX: (309)
796-2484. Black Hawk College.

KWQC-TV, Channel 6, NBC
805 Brady St., Davenport, IA 52803-5211. (319) 383-7000. FAX:
(319) 383-7165. Young Broadcasting Inc.

KCCI, Channel 8, CBS
888 9th St., Des Moines, IA 50309. (515) 247-8888. FAX: (515)
243-4931. Hearst-Argyle Television Inc.

KDSM-TV, Channel 17, FOX
4023 Fleur Dr., Des Moines, IA 50321-2321. (515) 287-1717.
FAX: (515) 287-0064. Sinclair Broadcast Group Inc.

WHO-TV, Channel 13, NBC
1801 Grand Ave., Des Moines, IA 50309. (515) 242-3500. FAX:
(515) 242-3797. New York Times Broadcast Group.

WOI-TV, Channel 5, ABC
300 E. Locust St., Des Moines, IA 50309. (515) 282-5555. FAX:
(515) 282-0716. Citadel Communications Company Ltd.

KFXB, Channel 40, FOX
PO Box 1090, Towns Clock Plaza, 744 Main St., Dubuque, IA
52001. (319) 556-4040. FAX: (319) 557-7101. Dubuque TV L.P.

KTIN, Channel 21, PBS
(see Iowa Public Television, Johnston). Fort Dodge, IA. Iowa
Public Broadcasting Board.

KIIN-TV, Channel 12, PBS
(see Iowa Public Television, Johnston). Iowa City, IA. Iowa Public
Broadcasting Board.

Iowa Public Television, PBS
PO Box 6540, Johnston, IA 50131. (515) 242-3100. Iowa Public
Broadcasting Board.

KDIN-TV (Des Moines), Channel 11, PBS
Box 6450, c/o Iowa Public TV, Johnston, IA 50131-6450. (515)
242-3100. Iowa Public Broadcasting Board.

KIMT, Channel 3, CBS
PO Box 620, 112 N. Pennsylvania Ave., Mason City, IA 50401.
(515) 423-2540. FAX: (515) 423-9309. Spartan Radiocasting
Co., Inc.

KYIN, Channel 24, PBS
(see Iowa Public Television, Johnston). Mason City, IA. Iowa
Public Broadcasting Board.

KYOU-TV, Channel 15, FOX, UPN
820 W. 2nd St., Ottumwa, IA 52501-2212. (515) 684-5415. FAX:
(515) 682-5173. Dean C. Engstrom.

KHIN, Channel 36, PBS
(see Iowa Public Television, Johnston). Red Oak, IA. Iowa Public
Broadcasting Board.

KCAU-TV, Channel 9, ABC
625 Douglas St., Sioux City, IA 51101. (712) 277-2345. FAX:
(712) 277-3733. Citadel Comm. Co./Coronet Comm. Co.

KMEG-TV, Channel 14, CBS
PO Box 657, Sioux City, IA 51102-0657. (712) 277-3554. FAX:
(712) 277-4732. Waitt Broadcasting. Fritz Miller.

KSIN, Channel 27, PBS
(see Iowa Public Television, Johnston). Sioux City, IA. Iowa
Public Broadcasting Board.

KTIV, Channel 4, NBC
3135 Floyd Blvd., Sioux City, IA 51105. (712) 239-4100. FAX:
(712) 239-2621. Quincy Newspapers Inc. Dave Madsen.

KRIN, Channel 32, PBS
(see Iowa Public Television, Johnston). Waterloo, IA. Iowa Public
Broadcasting Board.

KWWL, Channel 7, NBC
500 E. 4th St., Waterloo, IA 50703. (319) 291-1200. FAX: (319)
291-1255. Raycom Media Inc.

KANSAS

KOOD (Hays), Channel 9, PBS
PO Box 9, 604 Elm St., Bunker Hill, KS 67626. (913) 483-6990.
FAX: (913) 483-4650. Smoky Hills Public Television Corp.

KSWK (Lakin), Channel 3, IND
PO Box 9, 604 Elm St., Bunker Hill, KS 67626. (913) 483-6990.
FAX: (913) 483-4605. Smoky Hills Public Television Corp.

KLBY, Channel 4, IND
990 S. Range, Colby, KS 67701. (913) 462-8644. FAX: (913)
462-3522. Chronicle Broadcasting Co.

KBSD-TV (Ensign), Channel 6, CBS
PO Box 157, Dodge City, KS 67801. (316) 227-3121. FAX: (316)
225-1675. Spartan Radiocasting Company Inc.

KSNG, Channel 11, NBC
204 E. Fulton Terrace, Garden City, KS 67846-6151. (316)
276-2311. FAX: (316) 275-5076. Lee Enterprises.

KUPK-TV, Channel 13, ABC
2900 E. Schulman Ave., Garden City, KS 67846-2649. (316)
275-1560. FAX: (316) 275-1572. Chronicle Broadcasting Co.

KBSL-TV, Channel 10, CBS
PO Box 569, Broadcast Plaza, Goodland, KS 67735. (913) 899-
2321. FAX: (913) 899-3138. Spartan Radiocasting Company Inc.

KSNC, Channel 2, NBC
RR 5, PO Box 262, N. Hwy., Great Bend, KS 67530. (316)
793-7868. FAX: (316) 793-3079. Lee Enterprises Inc. Dan. L.
Bayes.

KBSH-TV, Channel 7, CBS
2300 Hall St., Hays, KS 67601. (913) 625-5277. FAX: (913)
625-1161. Spartan Radiocasting Company Inc. Wayne Roberts.

KMCI, Channel 38, NBC
2951 Four Wheel Dr., Lawrence, KS 66046. (785) 749-3388.
FAX: (785) 749-3377. Miller Broadcasting Inc. Doris J. Miller.

KOAM-TV, Channel 7, CBS
PO Box 659, 2950 N.E. Hwy. 69, Pittsburg, KS 66762-0659. (417)
624-0233. FAX: (417) 623-6111. Saga Communications Inc.

KAAS-TV, Channel 18, FOX
(see KSAS, Wichita). Salina, KS. Clear Channel Television.

KAKE-TV, Channel 10, ABC
1500 N. West, Wichita, KS 67203. (316) 943-4221. FAX: (316) 943-5160. Chronicle Broadcasting Co.

KSNT, Channel 27, NBC
PO Box 2700, Topeka, KS 66601-2700. (913) 582-4000. FAX: (913) 582-5283. Lee Enterprises Inc.

KTKA-TV, Channel 49, ABC
101 S.E. Monroe St., Topeka, KS 66603-3626. (913) 234-4949. FAX: (913) 234-5256. Marion Brechner, Berl Brechner.

KTWU, Channel 11, PBS
1700 College Ave., Topeka, KS 66621-1100. (913) 231-1111. FAX: (913) 231-1112. Washburn University of Topeka.Station.

WIBW-TV, Channel 13, CBS
5600 W. 6th St., Topeka, KS 66606. (913) 272-3456. FAX: (913) 272-0117. Stauffer Communications Inc.

KPTS (Hutchinson), Channel 8, PBS
320 W. 21st. N., Wichita, KS 67203. (316) 838-3090, Kansas Public Telecomm. Service Inc.

KSAS-TV, Channel 24, FOX, UPN
316 N. West St., Wichita, KS 67203-1205. (316) 942-2424. FAX: (316) 942-8927. Clear Channel Television.

KSNW, Channel 3, NBC
PO Box 333, Wichita, KS 67201-0333. (316) 265-3333. FAX: (316) 292-1197. Lee Enterprises Inc.

KWCH-TV (Hutchinson), Channel 12, CBS
2815 E. 37th St., Wichita, KS 67219. (316) 838-1212. FAX: (316) 838-6198. Spartan Radiocasting Co., Inc.

KWCV (Wichita), Channel 33, IND
R.R. 1, Box 203, Stockton, IA 52769. Wichita Communications.

KENTUCKY

WKAS, Channel 25, PBS
(see WKLE, Lexington). Ashland, KY. Kentucky Auth. for Educational TV.

WTSF, Channel 61, IND
PO Box 2320, 3100 Bath Ave., Ashland, KY 41105-2320. (606) 329-2700. FAX: (606) 324-9256. Tri-State Family Broadcasting Inc.

WLJC-TV, Channel 65, IND
Box 1129, 219 Radio Station Loop, Beattyville, KY 41311. (606) 464-3600. FAX: (606) 464-5021. Hour of Harvest, Inc.

WBKO, Channel 13, ABC
PO Box 13000, Bowling Green, KY 42102-9800. (502) 781-1313. FAX: (502) 781-1814. Benedek Broadcasting Group.

WKGB-TV, Channel 53, PBS
(see WKLE, Lexington). Bowling Green, KY. Kentucky Auth. for Educational TV.

WKNT, Channel 40, IND
810 Chestnut St., Bowling Green, KY 42101. (502) 781-2140. FAX: (502) 842-7140. Southeastern Communications Inc.

WKYU-TV, Channel 24, PBS
Academic Complex 153, Western Kentucky University, Bowling Green, KY 42101. (502) 745-2400. FAX: (502) 745-2084. Western Kentucky University. Jerry Barnaby.

WGRB, Channel 34, WB
PO Box 400, Campbellsville, KY 42719-0400. (502) 465-2223. FAX: (502) 384-6864. Jere Barton Davidson Sr.

WCVN, Channel 54, PBS
(see WKLE, Lexington). Covington, KY. Kentucky Auth. for Educational TV.

WKZT-TV, Channel 23, PBS
(see WKLE, Lexington). Elizabethtown, KY. Kentucky Auth. for Educational TV.

WAGV, Channel 44, NFP
(see Living Faith Ministries, Vansant, VA). Harlan, KY. Living Faith Ministries Inc.

WKHA, Channel 35, PBS
(see WKLE, Lexington). Hazard, KY. Kentucky Auth. for Educational TV.

WYMT-TV, Channel 57, CBS
PO Box 1299, Hazard, KY 41702-1299. (606) 436-5757. Gray Communications Systems.

WDKY-TV, Channel 56, FOX
836 Euclid Ave., Chevy Chase Plaza, Lexington, KY 40502-1509. (606) 269-5656. FAX: (606) 269-3774. Sinclair Broadcast Group Inc.

WKLE, Channel 46, PBS
600 Cooper Dr., Lexington, KY 40502. (606) 258-7000. FAX: (606) 258-7399. Kentucky Auth. for Educational TV.

WKYT-TV, Channel 27, CBS
PO Box 55037, Lexington, KY 40555-5037. (606) 299- 0411. FAX: (606) 299-2494. Gray Communications Systems Inc.

WLEX-TV, Channel 18, NBC
PO Box 1457, Lexington, KY 40591-1457. (606) 255-4404. FAX: (606) 255-2418. Bank One, Kentucky, NA. Marilyn Clark.

WTVQ-TV, Channel 36, ABC
PO Box 55590, Lexington, KY 40555. (606) 233-3800. FAX: (606) 293-5002. Media General Broadcast Group.

WAVE, Channel 3, NBC
725 S. Floyd St., Louisville, KY 40203-2337. (502) 585-2201. FAX: (502) 561-4115. Cosmos Broadcasting Corp.

WBNA, Channel 21, WB
3701 Fern Valley Rd., Louisville, KY 40219-1918. (502) 964-2121. FAX: (502) 966-9692. Word Broadcasting Network Inc.

WDRB-TV, Channel 41, FOX
One Independence Square, Louisville, KY 40203. (502) 584-6441. FAX: (502) 589-5559. Blade Communications Inc.

WHAS-TV, Channel 11, ABC
PO Box 1100, Louisville, KY 40201-1100. (502) 582-7840. FAX: (502) 582-7279. A. H. Belo Corp.

WKMJ, Channel 68, PBS
(see WKLE, Lexington). Louisville, KY. Kentucky Auth. for Educational TV.

WKPC-TV, Channel 15, PBS
(see WKLE, Lexington) Louisville, KY. Kentucky Authority for Educational Television.

WLKY, Channel 32, CBS
PO Box 6205, Louisville, KY 40206-0205. (502) 893-3671. FAX: (502) 897-2384. Hearst-Argyle Television Inc.

WKMA, Channel 35, PBS
(see WKLE, Lexington). Madisonville, KY. Kentucky Auth. for Educational TV.

WWAZ, Channel 19, IND
PO Box 1087, 27 Grapevine Rd., Madisonville, KY 42431-1087. (502) 821-5433. FAX: (502) 821-5343. South Central Communications Corp.

WAOM (Morehead), Channel 67, IND
c/o Garcia Communications, 1562 Oro Vista Rd., #282, San Diego, CA 92154-4043. Garcia Communications.

WKMR, Channel 38, PBS
(see WKLE, Lexington). Morehead, KY. Kentucky Auth. for Educational TV.

WKMU, Channel 21, PBS
(see WKLE, Lexington). Murray, KY. Kentucky Auth. for Educational TV.

WXIX-TV (Newport), Channel 19, FOX
635 W. 7th St., Cincinnati, OH 45203. (513) 421-1919. FAX: (513) 421-3105. Malrite Communications Group, Inc.

WKOH, Channel 31, PBS
(see WKLE, Lexington). Owensboro, KY. Kentucky Auth. for Educational TV.

WKON, Channel 52, PBS
(see WKLE, Lexington). Owenton, KY. Kentucky Auth. for Educational TV.

WKPD, Channel 29, PBS
(see WKLE, Lexington). Paducah, KY. Kentucky Auth. for Educational TV.

WDKA-TV (Paducah), Channel 49, UPN
400 Executive Ctr. Dr., # 210, West Palm Beach, FL 33401. (407) 640-3585. FAX: (407) 640-7699. Sinclair Broadcast Group Inc.

WPSD-TV, Channel 6, NBC
100 Television Lane, Paducah, KY 42003-5098. (502) 442-8214. FAX: (502) 442-2096. Paxton Media Group Inc.

WKPI, Channel 22, PBS
(see WKLE, Lexington). Pikeville, KY. Kentucky Auth. for Educational TV.

WKSO-TV, Channel 29, PBS
(see WKLE, Lexington). Somerset, KY. Kentucky Auth. for Ed. TV.

LOUISIANA

KALB-TV, Channel 5, NBC
605 Washington St., Alexandria, LA 71301-8028. (318) 445-2458. FAX: (318) 442-7427. Media General Broadcast Group.

KLAX-TV, Channel 31, ABC, UPN
PO Box 8818, Alexandria, LA 71303-1818. (318) 473-0031. FAX: (318) 442-4646. Pollack-Belz Communications Inc.

KLPA-TV, Channel 25, PBS
(see WLPB, Baton Rouge). Alexandria, LA. Louisiana Educational TV Authority.

WAFB, Channel 9, CBS
844 Government St., Baton Rouge, LA 70802-6030. (504) 383-9999. FAX: (504) 379-7891. Raycom Media Inc.

WBRZ, Channel 2, ABC
1650 Highland Rd., Baton Rouge, LA 70802. (504) 387-2222. FAX: (504) 336-2246. Louisiana Television Broadcasting.

WCCL (New Orleans), Channel 49, HSN
c/o Flinn Broadcasting Corp., 6080 Mount Moriah, Memphis, TN 38115. (901) 375-9324. FAX: (901) 795-4454. Paxson Comunications Corp.

WGMB, Channel 44, FOX
Stw. B, 5220 Essesn Lane, Baton Rouge, LA 70806. (504) 926-4444. FAX: (504) 926-9462. Com Corp. of Baton Rouge.

WLPB-TV, Channel 27, PBS
7733 Perkins Lane, Baton Rouge, LA 70810. (504) 767-5660. FAX: (504) 767-4277. Louisiana Educational TV Authority

WVLA, Channel 33, NBC
5220 Essen Ln., Baton Rouge, LA 70809-3542. (504) 766-3233. FAX: (504) 768-9191. White Knight Broadcating of El Paso Inc.

KADN, Channel 15, FOX
1500 Eraste Landry Rd., Lafayette, LA 70506-1925. (318) 237-1500. FAX: (318) 237-2237. KADN Broadcasting Inc.

KATC, Channel 3, ABC
PO Box 93133, Lafayette, LA 70509-3133. (318) 235-3333. FAX: (318) 235-9363. Cordillera Communications Inc.

KLFY-TV, Channel 10, CBS
2410 Eraste Landry Rd., Lafayette, LA 70509. (318) 981-4823. FAX: (318) 984-8323. Young Broadcasting Inc.

KLPB-TV, Channel 24, PBS
(see WLPB, Baton Rouge). Lafayette, LA. Louisiana Ed. TV Auth.

KLTL-TV, Channel 18, PBS
(see WLPB, Baton Rouge). Lake Charles, LA. Louisiana Educational TV Authority.

KPLC-TV, Channel 7, NBC
320 Division St., Lake Charles, LA 70601-4228. (318) 439-9071. FAX: (318) 437-7600. Cosmos Broadcasting Corp.

KVHP, Channel 29, FOX
129 W. Prien Lake Rd., Lake Charles, LA 70601-8570. (318) 474-1316. FAX: (318) 477-6795. National Communications Inc.

WUPL (New Orleans), Channel 54, UPN
Suite 454, 3850 N. Causeway Blvd., Metairie, LA 70002. (504) 828-5454. Paramount Stations Group Inc.

KLTM-TV, Channel 13, PBS
(see WLPB, Baton Rouge). Monroe, LA. Louisiana Educational TV Authority.

KNOE-TV, Channel 8, CBS
1400 Oliver Rd., Monroe, LA 71201. (318) 388-8888. FAX: (318) 388-0070. Noe Enterprises Inc.

WDSU, Channel 6, NBC
846 Howard Ave., New Orleans, LA 70113. (504) 679-0600. FAX: (504) 679-0745 Hearst-Argyle Television Inc.

WGNO, Channel 26, ABC
World Trade Center, Ste 2800, New Orleans, LA 70130-1408. (504) 581-2600. FAX: (504) 522-1885. Tribune Broadcasting.

WHNO, Channel 20, IND
1100 S. Jefferson Davis Pkwy., New Orleans, LA 70125. (504) 822-1920. FAX: (504) 822-2060. LeSea Broadcasting.

WLAE-TV, Channel 32, PBS
2929 S. Carrolton Ave., New Orleans, LA 70118. (504) 866-7411. FAX: (504) 861-5186. Educational Broadcasting Fdn. Inc. John Pela.

WNOL-TV, Channel 38, WB
1661 Canal St., New Orleans, LA 70112-2861. (504) 525-3838. FAX: (504) 569-0908. Qwest Broadcasting.

WVUE, Channel 8, FOX
1025 S. Jefferson Davis, Pkwy., New Orleans, LA 70125-1218. (504) 486-6161. FAX: (504) 483-1212. USA Broadcasting Inc.

WWL-TV, Channel 4, CBS
1024 N. Rampart St., New Orleans, LA 70116-2406. (504) 529-4444. FAX: (504) 592-1949. A.H. Belo Corp. Phil Johnson.

WYES-TV, Channel 12, PBS
916 Navarre Ave., New Orleans, LA 70124. (504) 486-5511. FAX: (504) 483-8408. Greater New Orleans Edu. TV Fdn.

KMSS, Channel 33, FOX
PO Box 30033, Shreveport, LA 71130-0033. (318) 631-5677. FAX: (318) 631-4195. Associated Broadcasters Inc.

KSHV, Channel 45, UPN, WB
3519 Jewella Ave., Shreveport, LA 71109. (318) 631-4545. FAX: (318) 431-4195. White Knight Holdings Inc.

KSLA-TV, Channel 12, CBS
PO Box 41812, Shreveport, LA 71134-1812. (318) 222-1212. FAX: (318) 677-6703. Raycom Media Inc.

KTAL-TV (Texarkana TX), Channel 6, NBC
3150 N. Market St., Shreveport, LA 71107-4005. (318) 425-2422. FAX: (318) 425-2488. KTAL-TV Inc.

KTBS, Channel 3, ABC
312 E. Kings Hwy., Shreveport, LA 71104-3504. (318) 861-5800. FAX: (318) 862-9434. Helen Wray & Florence H. Wray. George Sirven.

KLTS-TV (Shreveport), Channel 24, PBS
(see WLPB, Baton Rouge). Shreveport, LA. Louisiana Educational TV Authority.

KARD, Channel 14, ABC, UPN
Ste. 400, 102 Thomas Rd., West Monroe, LA 71291. (318) 323-1972. FAX: (318) 322-0926. Quorum Broadcasting.

KMCT-TV, Channel 39, IND
701 Parkwood Dr., West Monroe, LA 71291-5435. (318) 322-1399. FAX: (318) 323-3783. LA Christian Broadcasting Inc.

MAINE

WCBB, Channel 10, PBS
(see Maine Public TV, Lewiston). Augusta, ME. Maine Public Broadcasting Corp.

WABI-TV, Channel 5, CBS
35 Hildreth St., Bangor, ME 04401-5740. (207) 947-8321. FAX: (207) 941-9378. Diversified Communications Service.

WLBZ-TV, Channel 2, NBC
PO Box 315, Bangor, ME 04402-0315. (207) 942-4822. FAX: (207) 945-6816. Gannett Broadcasting.

WVII-TV, Channel 7, ABC
371 Target Industrial Cir., Bangor, ME 04401. (207) 945-6457. FAX: (207) 942-0511. Seaway Communications.

WMEA-TV, Channel 26, PBS
(see Maine Public TV, Lewiston). Biddeford, ME. Maine Public Broadcasting Corp.

WMED-TV, Channel 13, PBS
(see Maine Public TV, Lewiston). Calais, ME. Maine Public Broadcasting Corp.

Maine Public Television, PBS
1450 Lisbon St., Lewiston, ME 04240. (207) 783-9101. FAX: (207) 783-5193. Maine Public Broadcasting Corp.

WMEB-TV, Channel 12, PBS
(see Maine Public TV, Lewiston). Orono, ME. Maine Public Broadcasting Corp.

WCSH-TV, Channel 6, NBC
1 Congress Sq., Portland, ME 04101-3801. (207) 828-6666. FAX: (207) 828-6620. Gannett Broadcasting.

WGME-TV, Channel 13, CBS
PO Box 1731, Portland, ME 04104-5013. (207) 797-9330. FAX: (207) 878-3505. Guy Gannett Communications Group.

WMTW-TV (Poland Spring), Channel 8, ABC
PO Box 9501 D.T.S., 475 Congress St., Portland, ME 04112-9501. (207) 782-1800. FAX: (207) 783-7371. Harron Communications Corp.

WPXT, Channel 51, FOX, UPN
2320 Congress St., Portland, ME 04102. (207) 774-0051. FAX:
(207) 774-6849. Pegasus Broadcast TV.

WAGM-TV, Channel 8, ABC, CBS, NBC
PO Box 1149, Presque Isle, ME 04769. (207) 764-4461. FAX:
(207) 764-5329. Peter P. Kosloski.

WMEM-TV, Channel 10, PBS
(see Maine Public TV, Lewiston). Presque Isle, ME. Maine Public
Broadcasting Corp.

WPME (Lewiston), Channel 35, IND
Box 9421, Department 335, South Portland, ME 04116. (207)
774-0051. New England Television Inc.

MARYLAND

WMPT, Channel 22, PBS
(see WFPT, Owings Mills). Annapolis, MD. MD Public
Broadcasting Commission.

WBAL-TV, Channel 11, NBC
3800 Hooper Ave., Baltimore, MD 21211. (410) 467-3000. FAX:
(410) 338-6460. Hearst-Argyle Television, Inc.

WBFF, Channel 45, FOX
2000 W. 41st St., Baltimore, MD 21211. (410) 467-4545. FAX:
(410) 467-5090. Sinclair Broadcast Group Inc.

WHSW-TV, Channel 24, UPN
4820 Seton Dr., Ste M-N, Baltimore, MD 21215-3210. (410) 358-
2400. FAX: (410) 764-7232. Chris-Craft Industries Inc./BHC
Communications Inc./United Television Inc.

WJZ-TV, Channel 13, CBS
TV Hill, 3725 Malden Ave., Baltimore, MD 21211. (410)
466-0013. FAX: (410) 578-7502. CBS Stations Inc. Marcellus
Alexander.

WMAR-TV, Channel 2, ABC
6400 York Rd., Baltimore, MD 21212-2111. (410) 377-2222.
(410) 377-0493. E.W. Scripps Co.

WMPB, Channel 67, PBS
(see WFPT, Owings Mills). Baltimore, MD. MD Public
Broadcasting Commission.

WNUV-TV, Channel 54, WB
2000 W. 41st St., Baltimore, MD 21211. (410) 467-8854. FAX:
(410) 235-8450. Sinclair Broadcast Group Inc.

WJAL (Hagerstown), Channel 68, IND
Box 229, 229 Swamp Fox Rd., Chambersburg, PA 17201. (719)
375-4000. FAX: (719) 375-4052. Channel 68 Broadcasting.

WHAG-TV, Channel 25, NBC
13 E. Washington St., Hagerstown, MD 21740. (301) 797-4400.
FAX: (301) 733-1735. Great Trails Broadcasting Corp.

WWPB, Channel 31, PBS
(see WFPT, Owings Mills). Hagerstown, MD. MD Public
Broadcasting Commission.

WGPT, Channel 36, PBS
(see WFPT, Owings Mills). Oakland, MD. MD Public
Broadcasting Commission.

WFPT (Frederick), Channel 62, PBS
11767 Owings Mills Blvd., Owings Mills, MD 21117. (410)
356-5600. FAX: (410) 581-6579. MD Public Broadcasting Comm.

WBOC-TV, Channel 16, CBS
PO Box 2057, Salisbury, MD 21802-2057. (410) 749-1111. FAX:
(410) 749-2361. Draper Communications Inc.

WCPB, Channel 28, PBS
(see WFPT, Owings Mills). Salisbury, MD. MD Public
Broadcasting Commission.

WMDT, Channel 47, ABC, FOX, NBC
202 Downtown Plaza, Salisbury, MD 21801. (410) 742-4747.
FAX: (410) 742-5767. Delmarva Broadcasting Service G.P.

MASSACHUSETTS

WCDC Channel 19, ABC
(See WTEN, Albany, NY). Adams, MA. Young Broadcasting Inc.

WABU, Channel 68, IND
1660 Soldiers Field Rd., Boston, MA 02135. (617) 787-6868.
FAX: (617) 562-4280. BUCI Television. Will Meyl.

WBZ-TV, Channel 4, CBS
1170 Soldiers Field Rd., Boston, MA 02134-1092. (617)
787-7000. FAX: (617) 787-5969. CBS Stations Inc. Ed Goldman.

WCVB-TV, Channel 5, ABC
5 TV Pl., Needham Branch, Boston, MA 02194. (617) 449-0400.
FAX: (617) 433-4752. Hearst-Argyle Television, Inc.

WGBH-TV, Channel 2, PBS
125 Western Ave., Boston, MA 02134. (617) 492-2777. FAX:
(617) 787-0714. WGBH Educational Foundation.

WGBX-TV, Channel 44, PBS
(see WGBH, Boston). Boston, MA. WGBH Educational
Foundation.

WHDH-TV, Channel 7, NBC
7 Bulfinch Pl., Boston, MA 02114-2904. (617) 725-0777.
Sunbeam Television Corp.

WLVI-TV, Channel 56, WB
75 Morrissey Blvd., Boston, MA 02125. (617) 265-5656. FAX:
(617) 265-2538. Tribune Broadcasting.

WLWC-TV (New Bedford), Channel 28, UPN
76 Ashford St., Boston, MA 02134. (617) 782-6072. Paramount
Stations Group Inc.

WMFP (Lawrence), Channel 62, NBC
35th Fl., One Beacon St., Boston, MA 02108. (617) 720-1062.
FAX: (617) 720-0462. MFP Inc.

WSBK-TV (Boston), Channel 38, UPN
83 Leo Birmingham Pkwy., Brighton, MA 02135. (617) 783-3838.
FAX: (617) 783-1875. Paramount Stations Group Inc.

WFXT, Channel 25, FOX
PO Box 9125, 25 Fox Dr., Dedham, MA 02027-9125. (617) 467-
2525. FAX: (617) 467-7201. Fox Television Stations Inc.

WHSH-TV (Boston/Marlborough), Channel 66, HSN
71 Parmenter Rd., Hudson, MA 01749. (508) 562-0660. FAX:
(508) 562-1166. USA Broadcasting Inc.

WUNI, Channel 27, UNI
33 Fourth Ave., Needham, MA 02194. (617) 433-2727. FAX:
(617) 433-2750. JASAS Corp.

WBPX (Norwell), Channel 46, IND
c/o WTVE, 1729 N. 11th St., Reading, PA 19604. (610) 921-
9181. FAX: (610) 921-9139. DP Media Inc.

WGBY-TV, Channel 57, PBS
44 Hampden St., Springfield, MA 01103. (413) 781-2801. FAX:
(413) 731-5093. WGBH Educational Foundation.

WGGB-TV, Channel 40, ABC
PO Box 40, 1300 Liberty St., Springfield, MA 01102-0040. (413)
733-4040. FAX: (413) 781-1363. Guy Gannett Communications
Inc.

WWLP, Channel 22, NBC
PO Box 2210, Springfield, MA 01102-2210. (413) 786-2200.
FAX: (413) 786-7144. Brissette Broadcasting Corp. William M.
Pepin.

WZBU, Channel 58, IND
(see WABU, Boston). Vineyard Haven, MA. BUCI Television. Will
Meyl.

WYDN (Worcester), Channel 48, IND
PO Box 1975, San Benito, TX 78586. Worcester Educational
Corp. Inc.

MICHIGAN

WTLJ (Muskegon), Channel 54, IND
10294 48th Ave., Allendale, MI 49401. (616) 895-4154. FAX:
(616) 892-4401. Tri-State Christian TV Inc. Vic VanDeuenter.

WBKB-TV, Channel 11, CBS
1390 N. Bagley St., Alpena, MI 49707-8101. (517) 356-3434.
FAX: (517) 356-4188. Thunder Bay Broadcasting Corp.

WCML, Channel 6, PBS
(see WCMU, Mt. Pleasant). Alpena, MI. Central Michigan U.

WBSX (Detroit), Channel 31, IND
3975 Varsity Dr., Ann Arbor, MI 48108. (313) 973-7900. FAX:
(313) 973-7906. Paxson Communications Corp.

WOTV, Channel 41, ABC
Box 1616, 5200 W. Dickman Rd., Battle Creek, MI 49015-1033.
(616) 968-9341. FAX: (616) 966-6837. Hicks, Muse, Tate & Furst
Inc.

WCMV, Channel 27, PBS
(see WCMU, Mt. Pleasant). Cadillac, MI. Central Michigan U.

WGKI, Channel 33, FOX, UPN
7669 S. 45 Rd., Cadillac, MI 49601. (616) 775-9813. FAX: (616)
775-1898. GRK Production Inc. Julie Brinks.

WWTV, Channel 9, CBS
PO Box 627, Cadillac, MI 49601-0627. (616) 775-3478. FAX: (616) 775-3671. Heritage Broadcasting Co. of MI. William Kring

WTOM-TV, Channel 4, NBC
(see WBPN, Traverse City). Cheboygan, MI. Raycom Media Inc.

WADL (Mount Clemens), Channel 38, IND
22590 15 Mile Rd., Clinton Twp., MI 48035-2841. (810) 790-3838. FAX: (810) 790-3841. Adell Broadcasting Corp.

WDIV, Channel 4, NBC
550 W. Lafayette Blvd., Detroit, MI 48226-3123. (313) 222-0444. FAX: (313) 222-0471. Post-Newsweek Stations.

WTVS, Channel 56, IND
7441 Second Blvd., Detroit, MI 48202. (313) 873-7200. FAX: (313) 876-8118. Detroit Educational TV Foundation. Daniel Alpert.

WWJ-TV, Channel 62, CBS
300 River Place, Detroit, MI 48207. (313) 259-6288. FAX: (313) 259-8215. CBS Stations Inc. Jay Newman.

WKAR-TV, Channel 23, PBS
212 Communication Arts Bldg., East Lansing, MI 48824-1212. (517) 355-2300. FAX: (517) 353-7124. Michigan State Univ.

WJMN-TV, Channel 3, CBS
(see WFRV, Green Bay, WI). Escanaba, MI (906) 786-7767. FAX: (906) 474-6619. CBS Stations Inc.

WFUM, Channel 28, PBS
U. of Michigan-Flint, 1321 E. Court St., Flint, MI 48502-2186. (810) 762-3028. FAX: (810) 233-6017. Board of Regents, U. of MI. Jim Gaver.

WJRT-TV, Channel 12, ABC
2302 Lapeer Rd., Flint, MI 48503. (810) 233-3130. FAX: (810) 257-2834. ABC Inc.

WSMH-TV, Channel 66, FOX
G-3463 W. Pierson Rd., Flint, MI 48504. (810) 785-8866. FAX: (810) 785-8963. Sinclair Broadcast Group Inc.

WGVU-TV, Channel 35, PBS
301 W. Fulton St., Grand Rapids, MI 49504-6492. (616) 771-6666. FAX: (616) 771-6625. Board of Control, Grand Valley U.

WOOD-TV, Channel 8, NBC
PO Box B, Grand Rapids, MI 49501-4902. (616) 456-8888. FAX: (616) 771-9676. Hicks, Muse, Tate & Furst Inc.

WXMI Channel 17, FOX
3117 Plaza Dr N.E., Grand Rapids, MI 49505-2901. (616) 364-8722. FAX: (616) 364-8506. Tribune Co.

WZZM-TV, Channel 13, ABC
PO Box Z, Grand Rapids, MI 49501-4926. (616) 785-7373. FAX: (616) 785-1301. Gannett Broadcasting.

WILV (Battle Creek), Channel 43, IND
PO Box 907, Jenison, MI 49429-0907. (616) 457-7010. FAX: (616) 457-6949. DP Media Inc.

WGVK, Channel 52, PBS
(see WGVU, Grand Rapids). Kalamazoo, MI. Grand Valley State U.

WLLA, Channel 64, WB
PO Box 3157, Kalamazoo, MI 49003-3157. (616) 345-6421. Christian Faith Broadcasting Inc. Shelby Gillam.

WWMT (Grand Rapids), Channel 3, CBS
590 W. Maple St., Kalamazoo, MI 49008-1926. (616) 388-3333. FAX: (616) 388-8228. Granite Broadcasting Corp.

WDHS (Iron Mountain), Channel 8, IND
110 S. Elmhurst, Ave., Mt. Prospect, IL 60056. Kreb Christian Communications L.L.C.

WILX-TV (Onondaga), Channel 10, NBC
500 American Rd., Lansing, MI 48911. (517) 393-0110. FAX: (517) 393-8555. Benedek Broadcasting Corp.

WLAJ, Channel 53, ABC
5815 S. Pennsylvania Ave., Lansing, MI 48911-5230. (517) 394-5300. FAX: (517) 887-0077. Freedom Communications Inc..

WLNS-TV, Channel 6, CBS
2820 E. Saginaw St., Lansing, MI 48912-4240. (517) 372-8282. FAX: (517) 374-7610. Young Broadcasting Inc.

WSYM-TV, Channel 47, FOX
600 W. St. Joseph St., Lansing, MI 48933. (517) 484-7747. FAX: (517) 484-3144. Journal Broadcast Group Inc.

WCMW, Channel 21, PBS
(see WCMU, Mt. Pleasant). Manistee, MI. Central Michigan University.

WNMU-TV, Channel 13, PBS
Northern Michigan University, Marquette, MI 49855. (906) 227-1300. FAX: (906) 227-2905. Board of Control, N. Michigan U. Bruce S. Turner.

WCMU-TV, Channel 14, PBS
Central Michigan University, 3965 E. Broomfield Rd., Mt. Pleasant, MI 48859. (517) 774-3105. FAX: (517) 774-4427. Central Michigan University. Monte Higgins.

WLUC-TV (Marquette), Channel 6, NBC
177 U.S. Hwy. 41 E., Negaunee, MI 49866. (906) 475-4161. FAX: (906) 475-4824. Raycom Media Inc.

WAQP, Channel 49, IND
2865 Trautner Dr., Saginaw, MI 48604. (517) 249-5964. Tri- State Christian TV. Garth W. Coonce. Michael Socier.

WEYI-TV (Flint), Channel 25, NBC
Box 250, 2225 W. Willard Rd, Clio, MI 48420. (517) 755-0525. FAX: (810) 687-4925. Hicks, Muse, Tate & Furst Inc.

WNEM-TV (Flint/Bay City), Channel 5, CBS
107 N. Frankling St., Saginaw, MI 48606. (517) 755-8191. FAX: (517) 758-2110. Meredith Broadcasting Group.

WWUP-TV (Sault Ste. Marie), Channel 10, CBS
(see WWTV, Cadillac). Sault St. Marie, MI. Heritage Broadcasting Co. of MI.

WGTQ, Channel 8, ABC
300 Court St., Sault Ste. Marie, MI 49783. (616) 946-2900. FAX: (616) 946-1600. Scanlan Communications Inc.

WJBK-TV (Detroit), Channel 2, FOX
PO Box 2000, 16550 W. Nine Mile Rd., Southfield, MI 48037-2000. (248) 557-2000. FAX: (248) 552-0280. Fox Television Stations Inc.

WKBD (Detroit), Channel 50, UPN
PO Box 50, 26905 W. 11 Mile Rd., Southfield, MI 48037-0050. (248) 350-5050. FAX: (248) 355-2692. Paramount Stations Group Inc.

WXON (Detroit), Channel 20, WB
Ste. 1220, 27777 Franklin Rd., Southfield, MI 48034. (248) 355-2020. FAX: (248) 355-0368. Granite Broadcasting Corp.

WXYZ, Channel 7, ABC
PO Box 789, 207777 W, 10th Mile Rd., Southfield, MI 48037-0789. (248) 827-7777. FAX: (248) 827-4454. E. W. Scripps Co. Grace Gilchrist. John Lansing.

WGTU, Channel 29, ABC
201 E. Front St., Traverse City, MI 49684-2525. (616) 946-2900. FAX: (616) 946-1600. Scanlan Communications Inc. Todd Ruonavaara.

WPBN-TV, Channel 7, NBC
PO Box 546, Traverse City, MI 49685-0546. (616) 947-7770. FAX: (616) 947-0354. Raycom Media Inc.

WDCP (Bad Axe), Channel 35, PBS
University Ctr., Delta Rd., University City, MI 48710. (517) 686-9350. FAX: (517) 686-0155. Delta Collerge.

WDCQ-TV, Channel 19, PBS
WUCM Delta College Public Broadcasting, Delta and Mackinac Rds., University Center, MI 48710. (517) 686-9350. FAX: (517) 686-0155. Delta College.

WGKU, Channel 45, FOX
(see WGKI, Cadillac). Vanderbilt, MI. GRK Production Joint Venture.

MINNESOTA

KCCO-TV, Channel 7, CBS
720 Hawthorne St., Alexandria, MN 56308-1841. (612) 763-5166. FAX: (320) 763-1736. CBS Stations Inc. Ken Rees.

KRWF (Redwood Falls), Channel 43, ABC
PO Box 189, 415 Filmore, Alexandria, MN 56308. (320) 763-5729. FAX: (320) 763-4627. Hubbard Broadcasting Inc.

KWCM-TV/KSMN-TV, Channel 10, PBS
120 W. Schlieman, Appleton, MN 56208. (320) 289-2622. FAX: (320) 289-2634. W. Central MN Educational TV Co.

KAAL Channel 6, ABC
PO Box 577, 1701 10th Pl. N.E., Austin, MN 55912-0577. (507) 437-6666. FAX: (507) 433-9560. Grapevine Communications, Inc.

KSMQ-TV, Channel 15, PBS
2000 8th Ave N.W., Austin, MN 55912. (507) 433-0678. FAX: (507) 433-0670. Independent School District 492.

KPXM (St. Cloud), Channel 41, IND
Box 407, 22601 176th Str., Big Lake, MN 55309. (612) 263-8666. FAX: (612) 263-6600. Paxson Communications Corp. Dawn Hoglund.

KAWE, Channel 9, PBS
PO Box 9, BSU, 1400 Birchmont Dr., Bemidji, MN 56601. (218) 751-3393. FAX: (218) 751-3142. Northen MN Public TV Inc.

KXLT-TV (Rochester), Channel 47, IND
PO Box 407, 22601 176th St., Big Lake, MN 55309. (612) 263-8666. FAX: (612) 263-6600. Shockley Comm. Corp. Dawn Hoglund.

KAWB, Channel 22, PBS
(see KAWE, Bemidji). Brainerd, MN. Northern MN Public TV Inc.

KBJR-TV, Channel 6, NBC
230 E. Superios St., Duluth, MN 55802. (218) 727-8484. FAX: (218) 720-9699. Granite Broadcasting Corp.

KDLH, Channel 3, CBS
425 W. Superior St., Duluth, MN 55802-1511. (218) 727-8911. FAX: (218) 727-7515. Benedek Broadcasting Corp.

KNLD, Channel 21, IND
2001 London Rd., Duluth, MN 55802. (218) 728-6421. FAX: (218) 727-0562. Fant Broadcasting Co.

WDIO-TV, Channel 10, ABC
10 Observation Rd., Duluth, MN 55811-3506. (218) 727-6864. FAX: (218) 727-4415. Hubbard Broadcasting Inc.

WDSE-TV, Channel 8, PBS
1202 E. University Cir., Duluth, MN 55811-2420. (218) 724-8567. FAX: (218) 724-4269. Duluth Superior Area Educ. TV Corp.

KMSP-TV (Minneapolis) Channel 9, UPN
11358 Viking Dr., Eden Prairie, MN 55344-7258. (612) 944-9999. FAX: (612) 942-0286. Chris Craft Industries Inc.

WIRT (Hibbing), Channel 13, ABC
(see WDIO, Duluth). Hibbing, MN. Hubbard Broadcasting Inc.

WXOW-TV (La Crosse, WI), Channel 19, ABC
3705 County Hwy., La Crescent, MN 55947, 507-895-9969. FAX: 507-895-8124. Shockley Communications Corp

KEYC-TV, Channel 12, CBS
PO Box 128, Mankato, MN 56002-0128. (507) 625-7905. FAX: (507) 626-5745. United Communications Corp.

KARE, Channel 11, NBC
8811 Olson Memorial Hwy., Minneapolis, MN 55427-4762. (612) 546-1111. FAX: (612) 546-8590. Gannett Broadcasting.

WCCO-TV, Channel 4, CBS
90 S. 11th St., Minneapolis, MN 55403. (612) 339-4444. FAX: (612) 330-2603. CBS Stations Inc. Jan McDaniel.

WFTC, Channel 29, FOX
1701 Broadway St. N.W., Minneapolis, MN 55414. (612) 379-2929. FAX: (612) 379-2900. Clear Channel Television, Inc.

KTTC, Channel 10, NBC
601 1st Ave SW, Rochester, MN 55902-3334. (507) 288-4444. FAX: (507) 288-6324. Quincy Newspapers Inc.

KLGT-TV (Minneapolis), Channel 23, WB
1640 Como Ave., St. Paul, MN 55108. (612) 646-2300. FAX: (612) 646-1220. Sinclair Broadcast Group Inc.

KSTP-TV, Channel 5, ABC
3415 University Ave., St. Paul, MN 55114. (612) 646-5555. FAX: (612) 642-4172. Hubbard Broadcasting Inc.

KTCA-TV, Channel 2, PBS
172 E. 4th St., St. Paul, MN 55101. (612) 229-1717. FAX: (612) 229-1282. Twin Cities Public TV Inc.

KTCI-TV, Channel 17, PBS
(see KTCA St. Paul). St. Paul, MN. Twin Cities Public TV Inc.

KVBM-TV (Minneapolis) Channel 45, IND
Ste. 45, 1080 County Rd. E West., St. Paul, MN 55101. (612) 481-1717. FAX: (612) 481-1200. Dale Lang & Daniel Peters. Gary Kastner.

KBRR, Channel 10, FOX
(see KVRR, Fargo, ND). Thief River Falls, MN. Red River Broadcast Corp.

KCCW, Channel 12, CBS
(see KCCO Alexandria). Walker, MN 56308. CBS Stations Inc.

MISSISSIPPI

WLOX Television, Inc. Channel 13, ABC
PO Box 4596, 208 De Buys Rd., Biloxi, MS 39535-4596. (601) 896-1313. FAX: (601) 896-0749. Cosmos Broadcasting Corp.

WMAH-TV, Channel 19, PBS
(see WMAB, Jackson). Biloxi, MS. MS Authority for Educational TV.

WMAE-TV, Channel 12, PBS
(see WMAB, Jackson). Booneville, MS. MS Authority for Educational TV.

WMAU-TV, Channel 17, PBS
(see WMAB, Jackson). Bude, MS. MS Authority for Educational TV.

WBUY-TV (Holly Springs), Channel 40, IND
4240 Hwy. 309 N., Byhalia, MS 38611. (901) 521-9289. All American TV Inc. Ed Goetze.

WCBI-TV, Channel 4, CBS
PO Box 271, Columbus, MS 39703-0271. (601) 327-4444. FAX: (601) 329-1004. Imes Communication.

WXVT, Channel 15, CBS
3015 E. Reed Rd., Greenville, MS 38703-9452. (601) 334-1500. FAX: (601) 378-8122. Greenville Television Inc.

WABG-TV, Channel 6, ABC
PO Box 720, 2001 Garrard Ave., Greenwood, MS 38930. (601) 332-0949. FAX: (601) 334-6420. Bahakel Communications.

WMAO-TV, Channel 23, PBS
(see WMAB, Jackson). Greenwood, MS. MS Authority for Educational TV.

WXXV-TV, Channel 25, FOX
14351 Hwy. 49 N., Gulfport, MS 39503. (601) 832-2525. FAX: (601) 832-4442. Morris Newspaper Corp.

WDAM-TV, Channel 7, NBC
PO Box 16269, Hattiesburg, MS 39404-6269. (601) 544-4730. FAX: (601) 584-9302. Raycom Media Inc.

WHLT, Channel 22, CBS
Box 232, 990 Hardy St., Hattiesburg, MS 39401. (601) 545-2077. FAX: (601) 545-3589. Media General Broadcast Group.

WAPT, Channel 16, ABC
PO Box 10297, Jackson, MS 39289-0297. (601) 922-1607. FAX: (601) 922-1663.Hearst-Argyle Television Inc.

WDBD, Channel 40, FOX
PO Box 10888, Jackson, MS 39289-0888. (601) 922-1234. FAX: (601) 922-6752. Pegasus Broadcast Television Inc.

WJTV, Channel 12, CBS
PO Box 8887, Jackson, MS 39284-8887. (601) 372-6311. FAX: (601) 372-8798. Media General Broadcast Group.

WLBT, Channel 3, NBC
715 S. Jefferson St., Jackson, MS 39205. (601) 948-3333. FAX: (601) 960-4412. Civic Communication Corp.

WMAB-TV, Channel 2, PBS
3825 Ridgewood Rd., Jackson, MS 39211. (601) 982-6565. FAX: (601) 982-6746. Mississippi Authority for Ed. TV.

WMPN-TV, Channel 29, PBS
(see WMAB, Jackson). Jackson, MS. MS Authority for Educational TV.

WGBC, Channel 30, NBC
1151 Crestview Cir., Meridian, MS 39301. (601) 485-3030. FAX: (601) 693-9889. Global Communications.

WMAW-TV, Channel 14, PBS
(see WMAB, Jackson). Meridian, MS. Mississippi Authority for Ed. TV.

WMDN, Channel 24, IND
(see WTOK, Meridian). Meridian, MS. (601) 693-2424. FAX: (601) 693-7126. WMDN Inc.

WTOK-TV, Channel 11, ABC
PO Box 2424, Meridian, MS 39302. (601) 693-1441. FAX: (601) 483-3266. Benedek Broadcasting Co.

WNTZ, Channel 48, IND
PO Box 1836, Natchez, MS 39121. (601) 442-4800. FAX: (601) 446-7019. White Knight Broadcasting of Natchez License Corp.

WMAV-TV, Channel 18, PBS
(see WMAB, Jackson). Oxford, MS. Mississippi Authority for Ed. TV.

WTVA, Channel 9, NBC
PO Box 350, Tupelo, MS 38801. (601) 842-7620. FAX: (601) 844-7061. WTVA Inc. Frank K. Spain.

WLOV-TV (West Point), Channel 27, FOX, UPN
Box 1732, Tupelo, MS 38802. (601) 842-2227. FAX: (601) 844-7061. Jack Lingard. Jennifer Dennington.

MISSOURI

KBSI-TV, Channel 23, FOX
806 Enterprise St., Cape Girardeau, MO 63703-7516. (573) 334-1223. FAX: (573) 334-1208. Sinclair Broadcast Group Inc.

KFVS-TV, Channel 12, CBS
310 Broadway, Cape Girardeau, MO 63701. (573) 335-1212. FAX: (573) 335-6303. Raycom Media Inc.

KMIZ, Channel 17, ABC, FOX
501 Business Loop 70 E., Columbia, MO 65201. (573) 449-0917. FAX: (573) 875-7078. Benedek Broadcasting Co.

KOMU-TV, Channel 8, NBC
Hwy 63 S., Columbia, MO 65201. (573) 882-8888. FAX: (573) 884-8888. The Curators of the Univ of MO.

KRCG, Channel 13, CBS, FOX, UPN
PO Box 659, Jefferson City, MO 65102. (573) 896-5144. FAX: (573) 896-5193. Mel Wheeler Inc.

KODE-TV, Channel 12, ABC, FOX
Box 46, 1928 W. 13th St., Joplin, MO 64801-3839. (417) 623-7260. FAX: (417) 623-3736. Grapevine Communications, Inc.

KOZJ, Channel 26, PBS
PO Box 1226, Joplin, MO 64802. (417) 782-1226. FAX: (414) 782-7222. Ozark Public Telecommunications. Terry Stone.

KSNF, Channel 16, NBC
PO Box 1393, Joplin, MO 64802-1393. (417) 781-2345. Nexstar Broadcasting Group Inc.

KCPT, Channel 19, PBS
125 E. 31st Street, Kansas City, MO 64108. (816) 756-3580. FAX: (816) 931-2500. Public TV 19 Inc.

KCTV, Channel 5, CBS
PO Box 5555, Kansas City, MO 64109. (913) 677-5555. FAX: (913) 677-7284. Meredith Broadcasting Group.

KCWB, Channel 29, WB
Ste. 300, 605 W. 47th St., Kansas City, MO 64112. (816) 753-7201. FAX: (816) 753-5595. KCWB TV, Inc.

KMBC-TV, Channel 9, ABC
1049 Central St., Kansas City, MO 64105-1619. (816) 221-9999. FAX: (816) 760-9245. Hearst-Argyle Television, Inc.

KPXE, Channel 50, IND
Ste. 570, 3101 S. Broadway, Kansas City, MO 64111. (816) 924-5050. FAX: (913) 262-1782. Paxson Communications Corp.

KSHB, Channel 41, NBC
4720 Oak St., Kansas City, MO 64112-2236. (816) 753-4141. FAX: (816) 932-4122. E.W. Scripps Co.

KSMO-TV, Channel 62, WB
10 E. Cambridge Cir.Dr., Ste. 300, Kansas City, MO 66103. (913) 621-6262. FAX: (913) 621-4703. Sinclair Broadcast Group Inc.

WDAF-TV, Channel 4, FOX
Signal Hill, Kansas City, MO 64108. (816) 753-4567. FAX: (816) 932-3984. Fox Television Stations Inc.

KTVO (Ottumwa, IA), Channel 3, ABC
PO Box 949, Hwy. 63 N, Kirksville, MO 63501. (816) 627-3333. FAX: (816) 627-1885. Raycom Media Inc.

KNLJ (Jefferson City), Channel 25, WB
PO Box 2525, New Bloomfield, MO 65603. (573) 896-5105. FAX: (573) 896-4376. New Life Evangelistic Center, Inc.

KDEB-TV, Channel 27, FOX
3000 Cherry St., Springfield, MO 65802. (417) 862-2727. FAX: (414) 831-4209. Quorum Broadcasting.

KOLR-TV, Channel 10, CBS
PO Box 1716, Springfield, MO 65801. (417) 862-1010. FAX: (417) 862-6439. US Broadcast Group.

KOZK, Channel 21, PBS
PO Box 21, 821 N. Washington Ave., Springfield, MO 65801. (417) 865-2100. FAX: (417) 863-1599. Ozark Public Telecommunications Inc.

KSPR Channel 33, ABC
1359 St. Louis St., Springfield, MO 65802. (417) 831-1333. FAX: (417) 831-4125. GOCOM Television.

KYTV, Channel 3, NBC
999 W. Sunshine, Springfield, MO 65807. (417) 868-3800. FAX: (417) 868-3100. Schurz Communications Inc.

KQTV, Channel 2, ABC, FOX
PO Box 8369, 40th & Faraon Sts., St. Joseph, MO 64508. (816) 364-2222. FAX: (816) 364-3787. Nexstar Broadcasting Group.

KTAJ, Channel 16, IND
4410-B S. 40th St., St. Joseph, MO 64503. (816) 364-1616. FAX: (816) 364-6729. All-American TV.

KDNL-TV, Channel 30, ABC
1215 Cole St., St. Louis, MO 63106. (314) 436-3030. FAX: (314) 259-5763. Sinclair Broadcast Group Inc.

KETC, Channel 9, PBS
6996 Millbrook Blve., St. Louis, MO 63130. (314) 512-9000. FAX: (314) 512-9005. St. Louis Regional Ed. & Pub. TV.

KMOV, Channel 4, CBS
One Memorial Dr., St. Louis, MO 63102. (314) 621-4444. FAX: (314) 444-3367. A.H. Belo Corp.

KNLC, Channel 24, NFP
PO Box 924, St. Louis, MO 63188. (314) 436-2424. FAX: (314) 436-2434. New Life Evangelistic Center.

KPLR-TV, Channel 11, WB
4935 Lindell Blvd., St. Louis, MO 63108-1587. (314) 367-7211. FAX: (314) 454-6404. Acme Television Holdings LLC. Edward Kopler.

KSDK, Channel 5, NBC
TV Plaza, 1000 Market St., St. Louis, MO 63101. (314) 421-5055. FAX: (314) 444-5289. Gannett Broadcasting.

KTVI, Channel 2, FOX
5915 Berthold Ave., St. Louis, MO 63110. (314) 647-2222. FAX: (314) 644-7419. Fox Television Stations Inc.

WHSL (East St. Louis, IL), Channel 46, IND
Ste. 300, 1408 N. King's Hwy. Blvd., St. Louis, MO 63113. (314) 367-3600. FAX: (314) 367-0174. Home Shopping Network.

KMOS-TV (Sedalia), Channel 6, PBS
Central Missouri State Univ., Wood 11, Warrensburg, MO 64093. (816) 543-4155. FAX: (816) 543-8863. Central MO State Univ.

MONTANA

KHMT (Hardin) Channel 4, FOX
Box 23309, Ste. 404, 445 S. 24th St. W., Billings, MT 59104-3309. Wolf Mountain Broadcasting Inc. Pat Rookhuizen.

KSVI, Channel 6, ABC
PO Box 23309, 445 S. 24th St. W. Billings, MT 59104-3309. (406) 652-4743. FAX: (406) 652-6963. Great Trails Broadcasting Corp.

KTVQ, Channel 2, CBS
PO Box 2557, Billings, MT 59103. (406) 252-5611. FAX: (406) 252-9938. Cordillera Communications Inc.

KULR-TV, Channel 8, NBC
PO Box 80810, Billings, MT 59108-0810. (406) 656-8000. FAX: (406) 652-8207. Dix Communications.

KCTZ, Channel 7, FOX, UPN
PO Box 6040, Bozeman, MT 59715. (406) 586-3280. FAX: (406) 586-4135. Cordillera Communications Inc.

KUSM, Channel 9, PBS
Visual Communication Bldg, Mt. St. Univ., Rm 172, Bozeman, MT 59717. (406) 994-3437. FAX: (406) 994-6221. Montana State U.

KTVM, Channel 6, NBC
PO Box 3118, Ste. One, 750 Dewey Blvd., Butte, MT 59701. (406) 494-7603. FAX: (406) 494-2572. Lamco Communications Inc.

KXLF-TV, Channel 4, CBS
PO. Box 3500, 1003 S. Montana, Butte, MT 59701. (406) 782-0444. FAX: (406) 782-8906. Cordillera Communications Inc.

KXGN-TV, Channel 5, CBS, NBC
210 S. Douglas, Glendive, MT 59330. (406) 365-3377. FAX: (406) 365-2181. Stephen A. Marks.

KYUS-TV (Miles City), Channel 3, ABC, WB
210 S. Douglas, Glendive, MT 59330. (406) 232-3540. FAX: (406) 232-7345. Glendive Broadcasting Corp.

KFBB-TV, Channel 5, ABC, UPN
PO Box 1139, Great Falls, MT 59403. (406) 453-4377. FAX: (406) 727-9703. Dix Communications.

KRTV, Channel 3, CBS
PO Box 2989, Great Falls, MT 59403. (406) 791-5400. FAX: (406) 791-5479. Cordillera Communications Inc.

KWYB (Butte), Channel 18, ABC
118 Sixth St. S., Great Falls, MT 59405. (406) 761-8816. FAX: (406) 454-3484. Continental Television Network Inc. Aubrey Woods.

KTVH, Channel 12, NBC
PO Box 6125, Helena, MT 59604. (406) 443-5050. FAX: (406) 442-5106. Sunbelt Communications Co.

KCFW-TV, Channel 9, NBC
PO Box 857, 401 First Ave. E, Kalispell, MT 59901. (406) 755-5239. FAX: (406) 752-8002. Lamco Communications Inc.

KECI-TV, Channel 13, NBC
340 W. Main, Missoula, MT 59802. (406) 721-2063. FAX: (406) 721-2083. Lamco Communications Inc.

KPAX-TV, Channel 8, CBS
PO Box 4827, 2204 Regent St., Missoula, MT 59801. (406) 542-4400. FAX: (406) 543-7111. Cordillera Communications Inc.

KTMF, Channel 23, ABC
2200 Stephens Ave., Missoula, MT 59801. (406) 542-8900. FAX: (406) 728-4800. Continental Television Network Inc. Bob Ganzer.

KUFM-TV, Channel 11, PBS
Broadcast Media, PARTV 180, Missoula, MT 59812. (406) 243-4101. FAX: (406) 243-3299. University of Montana.

NEBRASKA

KSTF (Scottsbluff), Channel 10, CBS, FOX
3385 N. 10th St., Gering, NE 69341. (308) 632-6107. FAX: (308) 632-3470. Benedek Broadcating Corp

KGIN Channel 11, CBS
PO Box 1069, Grand Island, NE 68801. (308) 382-6100. FAX: (308) 382-3216. Gray Communications Systems Inc.

KTVG, Channel 17, FOX, UPN
PO Box 717, Grand Island, NE 68802-0717. (308) 384-1717. FAX: (308) 384-1986. Hill Broadcasting Inc.

KHAS-TV, Channel 5, NBC
PO Box 578, 6475 Osborne Dr. W., Hastings, NE 68901. (402) 463-1321. FAX: (402) 463-6551. North Platte Television Inc.

KWNB, Channel 6, ABC
(see KHGI, Kearney). Hayes Center, NE. Fant Broadcasting Co. of Nebraska.

KHNE-TV (Hastings), Channel 29, PBS
Box 83111, Lincoln, NE 68501. (402) 472-3611. FAX: (402) 472-1785. Nebraska Educ. Telecommunications.

KHGI-TV, Channel 13, ABC
PO Box 220, 13 S. Hwy 44, Kearney, NE 68848. (308) 743-2494. FAX: (308) 743-2644. Pappas Telecasting Co.

KLKE (Albion), Channel 24, ABC
c/o KLKN, 3240 S. 10th, Lincoln, NE 68502. (402) 434-8000. FAX: (914) 743-3693. Citadel Communications Co. Ltd.

KLKN, Channel 8, ABC
Citadel Comm. L.L.C., Ste. 1300, 3240 S. 10th, Lincoln, NE 68502. (402) 434-800. FAX: (402) 436-2236. Citadel Communications Co. Ltd.

KLNE-TV (Lexington), Channel 3, PBS
Box 83111, Lincoln, NE 68501. (402) 472-3611. FAX: (402) 472-1785. Nebraska Educ. Telecommunications.

KMNE-TV (Bassett), Channel 7, PBS
Box 83111, Lincoln, NE 68501. (402) 472-3611. FAX: (402) 472-1785. Nebraska Educ. Telecommunications.

KOLN, Channel 10, CBS
PO Box 30350, Lincoln, NE 68503. (402) 467-4321. FAX: (402) 467-9210. Gray Communications Systems Inc.

KRNE-TV (Merriman), Channel 12, PBS
Nebraska Telecommunications Ctr., 1800 N. 33rd St., Lincoln, NE 68503. (402) 472-3611. FAX: (402) 472-1785. Nebraska Educational Telecommunications Commission.

KUON-TV, Channel 12, PBS
Nebraska Telecommunications Ctr., 1800 N. 33rd St., Lincoln, NE 68503. (402) 472-3611. FAX: (402) 472-1785. Univ. of NE.

KXNE-TV (Norfolk), Channel 19, PBS
Box 83111, Lincoln, NE 68501. (402) 472-3611. FAX: (402) 472-1785. Nebraska Educ. Telecommunications.

KNOP-TV, Channel 2, NBC
PO Box 749, North Platte, NE 69103. (308) 532-2222. FAX: (308) 532-9579. Shively Communications.

KPNE-TV (North Platte), Channel 9, PBS
Box 83111, Lincoln, NE 68501. (402) 472-3611. FAX: (402) 472-1785. Nebraska Educ. Telecommunications.

KSNK (McCook), Channel 8, NBC
PO Box 238, W. Hwy. 36, Oberlin, KS 67749. (913) 475-2248. FAX: (913) 475-3944. Lee Enterprises Inc. Gloria Becker.

KETV, Channel 7, ABC
2665 Douglas St., Omaha, NE 68131-2699. (402) 345-7777. FAX: (402) 978-8931. Hearst-Argyle Television Inc.

KMTV, Channel 3, CBS
10714 Mockingbird Dr., Omaha, NE 68127. (402) 592-3333. FAX: (402) 592-4406. Lee Entrerprises Inc.

KPTM, Channel 42, FOX, UPN
4625 Farnam St., Omaha, NE 38132. (402) 558-4200. FAX: (402) 554-4290. Pappas Telecasting Companies.

KXVO, Channel 15, WB
4625 Farnam St., Omaha, NE 68132. (402) 554-1500. FAX: (402) 554-4290. Cocola Broadcasting Co.

KYNE-TV (Omaha), Channel 26, PBS
PO Box 83111, Lincoln, NE 68501. (402) 472-3611. FAX: (402) 472-1785. Nebraska Educ. Telecommunications

WOWT, Channel 6, NBC
3501 Farnam St., Omaha, NE 68131. (402) 346-6666. FAX: (402) 233-7888. Chronicle Broadcasting Co.

KDUH-TV, Channel 4, ABC
PO Box 1529, 1523 1st Ave., Scottsbluff, NE 69363-1529. (308) 632-3071. FAX: (308) 632-3596. Duhamel Broadcasting Enterprises.

KSNB-TV (Superior), Channel 4, ABC
Box 220, 13 S. Hwy. 44, Kearney, NE 68848-0220. (308) 743-2494. FAX: (308) 743-2644. Fant Broadcasting Co of Nebraska. Lee McAliley.

NEVADA

KENV, Channel 10, NBC
1025 Chilton, Elko, NV 89801. (702) 777-8500. FAX: (702) 777-7758. Sunbelt Communications Co.

KBLR (Paradise), Channel 39, TEL
5000 W. Oakey, Las Vegas, NV 89102. (702) 258-0039. FAX: (702) 258-0556. Summit Media Limited Partnership.

KFBT, Channel 33, WB
3840 S. Jones Blvd., Las Vegas, NV 89103. (702) 873-0033. FAX: (702) 873-6192. Sinclair Broadcast Group Inc.

KINC, Channel 15, UNI
Ste. D. 500 Pilot Rd., Las Vegas, NV 89119. (702) 434-0015. FAX: (702) 434-0527. Entravision Communications Co.

KLAS-TV, Channel 8, CBS
PO Box 15047, Las Vegas, NV 89114. (702) 792-8888. FAX: (702) 734-7437. Landmark Communications Inc.

KLVX, Channel 10, PBS
4210 Channel 10 Dr., Las Vegas, NV 89119. (702) 799-1010. FAX: (702) 799-5586. Clark City School District Bd. of Trustees.

KTNV, Channel 13, ABC
3355 S. Valley View Blvd., Las Vegas, NV 89102. (702) 878-1313. FAX: (702) 876-2237. Journal Broadcast Group Inc.

KUPN-TV, Channel 21, WB
920 S. Commerce, Las Vegas, NV 89106. (702) 382-2121. FAX: (702) 382-1351. Sinclair Broadcast Group Inc.

KVBC, Channel 3, NBC
1500 Foremaster Ln., Las Vegas, NV 89101. (702) 642-3333. FAX: (702) 657-3208. Valley Broadcasting Co.

KVVU-TV (Henderson), Channel 5, FOX
25 TV-5 Dr., Las Vegas, NV 89014. (702) 435-5555. FAX: (702) 451-4220. Meredith Broadcasting Group.

KWNV (Winnemucca), Channel 7, IND
c/o Sunbelt Broadcasting Co., 1500 Foremaster Ln., Las Vegas, NV 89101. (702) 642-3333. Sunbelt Broadcasting Co.

KAME-TV, Channel 21, UPN
4920 Brookside Way, Reno, NV 89502. (702) 856-2121. FAX: (702) 856-2100. Cox Broadcasting Co.

KNPB, Channel 5, PBS
1670 N. Virginia St., Reno, NV 89503. (702) 784-4555. FAX: (702) 784-1438. Channel 5 Public Broadcasting Inc.

KOLO-TV, Channel 8, ABC
PO Box 10000, Reno, NV 89510. (702) 858-8880. FAX: (702) 858-8855. Stephens Group Inc.

KREN-TV, Channel 27, UNI
961 Matley Ln., Ste. 130, Reno, NV 89502. (702) 333-2727. FAX: (702) 333-5264. Pappas Telecasting Companies. Elliott Troshinsky.

KRNV Channel 4, NBC
PO Box 7160, 1790 Vassar St., Reno, NV 89510. (702) 322-4444. FAX: (702) 785-1200. Sierra Broadcasting Co.

KRXI, Channel 11, FOX
4920 Brookside Way, Reno, NV 89502. (702) 856-1100. FAX: (702) 856-1101. Cox Broadcasting Inc.

KTVN, Channel 2, CBS
PO Box 7220, Reno, NV 89510. (702) 858-2222. FAX: (702) 858-2345. Sarkes Tarzian Inc.

NEW HAMPSHIRE

WNBU (Concord), Channel 21, IND
Boston Univ. Comm. Inc., 1660 Soldiers Field Rd., Boston , MA 02135. (617) 787-6868. FAX: (617) 562-4280. BUCI Television.

WNDS, Channel 50, IND
Box 50, 50 TV Place, Derry, NH 03038. (603) 434-8850. FAX: (603) 434-8627. Rachamim Anatian.

WENH-TV, Channel 11, PBS
PO Box 1100, 268 Mast Rd., Durham, NH 03824. (603) 868-1100. FAX: (603) 868-7552. University of New Hampshire.

WEKW-TV, Channel 52, PBS
(see WENH Durham). Keene, NH University of New Hampshire.

WLED-TV, Channel 49, PBS
(see WENH Durham). Littleton, NH. University of New Hampshire.

WMUR-TV, Channel 9, ABC
PO Box 9, 100 S. Commercial St., Manchester, NH 03105. (603) 641-9000. FAX: (603) 641-9065. Imes Communications.

WPXB (Merrimack), Channel 60, IND
Ste 501, One Sundial Ave., Manchester, NH 03103.. (603) 647-6060. FAX: (603) 644-0060. Paxson Communications Corp.

NEW JERSEY

WWAC-TV, Channel 53, IND
19 S., New York Ave., Atlantic City, NJ 08041. (609) 344-6800. FAX: (609) 347-4758. David W. Allen.

WNJS, Channel 23, PBS
(see WNJT, Trenton). Camden, NJ. New Jersey Public Broadcasting.

WMBC-TV (Newton), Channel 63, IND
PO Box 985, 500 Weldon Rd., Lake Hopatcong, NJ 07849-0156. (973) 697-0063. FAX: (973) 697-5515. Mountain Broadcasting Corp. Joon Joo.

WMGM-TV (Wildwood), Channel 40, NBC
1601 New Rd., Linwood, NJ 08221. (609) 927-4440. FAX: (609) 927-7014. The Green Group.

WNJN, Channel 50, PBS
(see WNJT, Trenton). Montclair, NJ. New Jersey Public Broadcasting.

WNJB, Channel 58, PBS
(see WNJT, Trenton). New Brunswick, NJ. New Jersey Public Broadcasting.

WHSE-TV, Channel 68, HSN
390 W. Market St., Newark, NJ 07105. (201) 643-6800. FAX: (201) 643-1903. USA Broadcasting Inc.

WNET (Newark), Channel 13, PBS
356 W. 58th St., New York, NY 10019. (212) 560-2000. FAX: (212) 560-3191. Educational Broadcasting Corp.

WHSP-TV (Vineland), Channel 65, HSN
4449 N. Delsea Dr., Newfield, NJ 08344. (609) 691-6965. FAX: (609) 691-2483. USA Broadcasting Inc.

WGTW (Burlington), Channel 48, IND
3900 Main St., Philadelphia, PA 19127. (215) 930-0482. FAX: (215) 930-0496. Brunson Commmunications, Inc.

WWOR-TV, Channel 9, UPN
9 Broadcast Plaza, Secaucus, NJ 07096. (201) 349-0009. FAX: (201) 330-2488. Chris-Craft Industries, Inc.

WXTV (New York), Channel 41, UNI
24 Meadowlands Pkwy., Secaucus, NJ 07094. (201) 348-4141. FAX: (201) 348-4104. Univision Television Group, Inc.

WNJU (Newark), Channel 47, TEL
47 Industrial Ave., Teterboro, NJ 07608. (201) 288-5550. FAX: (201) 288-5166. Telemundo Group Inc.

WNJB, Channel 58, PBS
(see WNJT, Trenton) New Brunswick, NJ. New Jersey Public Broadcasting.

WNJT, Channel 52, PBS
25 S. Stockton St., Trenton, NJ 08611. (609) 777-5000. FAX: (609) 633-2927. New Jersey Public Broadcasting.

WFME-TV (West Milford), Channel 66, IND
289 Mt. Pleasant Ave., West Orange, NJ 07052. (201) 736-3600. FAX: (510) 633-7983. Family Stations of NJ. Les Englehart.

NEW MEXICO

KASA-TV (Santa Fe), Channel 2, FOX
PO Box 25200, 13700 Univ. Blvd. N.E., Albuquerque, NM 87125. (505) 246-2222. FAX: (505) 242-1355. A. H. Belo Corp.

KASY-TV, Channel 50, UPN, WB
50 Broadcast Plaza S.W., Albuquerque, NM 87104. (505) 764-5279. FAX: (505) 767-9421. Ramar Communications, Inc. Dan Myers.

KAZQ-TV, Channel 32, IND
4501 Montgomery N.E., Albuquerque, NM 87109. (505) 884-8355. FAX: (505) 883-1229. Alpha-Omega Broadcasting of Albuquerque.

KCHF (Santa Fe), Channel 11, IND
PO Box 4338, Albuquerque, NM 87196. (505) 473-1111. FAX: (505) 345-5669. Son Broadcasting Inc.

KLUZ-TV, Channel 41, UNI
2725 F Broadbent Pkwy N.E. Albuquerque, NM 87107. (505) 342-4141. FAX: (505) 344-8714. Univision Television Group, Inc.

KNAT, Channel 23, IND
1510 Coors Rd. N.W., Albuquerque, NM 87121. (505) 836-6585. All American Network Inc.

KNME-TV, Channel 5, PBS
1130 University Blvd. N.E. Albuquerque, NM 87102. (505) 277-2121. FAX: (505) 277-6904. Regents of U of NM & Bd of Educ.

KOAT-TV, Channel 7, ABC
PO Box 25982, Albuquerque, NM 87125. (505) 884-7777. FAX: (505) 884-6282. Hearst-Argyle Television Inc.

KOB-TV, Channel 4, NBC
PO Box 1351, Albuquerque, NM 87103. (505) 243-4411. FAX: (505) 764-2522. Hubbard Broadcasting Inc

KRQE, Channel 13, CBS
PO Box 1294, Albuquerque, NM 87103. (505) 243-2285. FAX: (505) 248-1464. Lee Enterprises Inc. Loren Neuharth.

KOCT Channel 6, ABC
(see KOAT, Albuquerque). Carlsbad, NM. Hearst-Argyle Television Inc.

KVIH-TV, Channel 12, ABC
(see KVII, Amarillo, TX). Clovis, NM. Marsh Media Inc.

KMAZ (Las Cruces), Channel 48, TEL
10033 Carnegie, El Paso, NM 79925. (915) 591-9595. FAX: (915) 591-9896. Lee Enterprises Inc. Dan Kempner

KOBF, Channel 12, NBC
PO Box 1620, Farmington, NM 87499. (505) 326-1141. FAX: (505) 327-5196. Hubbard Broadcasting Inc.

KHFT (Hobbs), Channel 29, IND
5512 Rosewood Dr., Galveston, TX 77551-5556. (505) 392-2929. FAX: (505) 764-5279. Ramar Communications Inc.

KRWG-TV, Channel 22, PBS
PO Box 30001, MSCTV22, Las Cruces, NM 88003. (505) 646-2222. FAX: (505) 646-1924. Regents of New Mexico State Univ.

KENW, Channel 3, PBS
52 Broadcast Ctr, Portales, NM 88130. (505) 562-2112. FAX: (505) 562-2590. Regents of Eastern New Mexico Univ.

KBIM-TV, Channel 10, CBS
PO Box 910, 214 N. Main St., Roswell, NM 88201. (505) 622-2120. FAX: (505) 623-6606. Lee Enterprises Inc. Gene Munsey.

KOBR, Channel 8, NBC
124 E. 4th St., Roswell, NM 88201. (505) 625-8888. FAX: (505) 625-8866. Hubbard Broadcasting Inc.

KRPV, Channel 27, NFP
PO Box 967, 2606 S. Main, Roswell, NM 88201. (505) 622-5778. FAX: (505) 622-3424. Prime Time Christian Broadcasting. Dave Whitley.

KOVT, Channel 10, ABC
(see KOAT, Albuquerque). Silver City, NM. Pulitzer Broadcasting.

KAUO (Albuquerque), Channel 19, IND
3920 San Francisco Ct., St. Louis, MO 63115. (314) 261-5811. Acme Television.

NEW YORK

WNYT, Channel 13, NBC
PO Box 4035, 15 N. Pearl St., Albany, NY 12204. (518)
436-4791. FAX: (516) 436-8723. Hubbard Broadcasting.

WTEN, Channel 10, ABC
341 Northern Blvd., Albany, NY 12204. (518) 436-4822. FAX:
(518) 462-6065. Young Broadcasting Inc.

WXXA-TV, Channel 23, FOX
28 Corporate Cir., Albany, NY 12203. (518) 862-2323. FAX:
(518) 862-0865. Clear Channel Communications Inc.

WMGC-TV, Channel 34, ABC, UPN
203 Ingraham Hill Rd., Binghamton, NY 13903. (607) 723-7464.
FAX: (607) 723-1034. Ackerley Communications.

WSKG-TV, Channel 46, PBS
PO Box 3000, Binghamton, NY 13902. (607) 729-0100. FAX:
(607) 729-7328. WSKG Public Telecommuncations Council.

WNYE-TV, Channel 25, PBS
112 Tillary St., Brooklyn, NY 11201. (718) 250-5800. FAX: (718)
855-8865. Bd. of Education of the City of NY.

WGRZ-TV, Channel 2, NBC
259 Delaware Ave., Buffalo, NY 14202. (716) 849-2222. FAX:
(716) 849-7602. Gannett Broadcasting.

WIVB-TV, Channel 4, CBS
2077 Elmwood Ave., Buffalo, NY 14207. (716) 874-4410. FAX:
(716) 879-4896. Hicks, Muse, Tate & Furst Inc.

WKBW-TV, Channel 7, ABC
7 Broadcast Plaza, Buffalo, NY 14202. (716) 845-6100. FAX:
(716) 842-1855. Granite Broadcasting Corp.

WNED-TV, Channel 17, PBS
PO Box 1263, Buffalo, NY 14240. (716) 845-7000. FAX: (716)
845-7036. Western NY Public Broadcasting Assoc. Richard Daly.

WNEQ-TV, Channel 23, PBS
(see WNED, Buffalo). Buffalo, NY. Sinclair Broadcast Group Inc.

WNYO-TV, Channel 49, WB
Box 49, 699 Hertel Ave., Ste. 100, Buffalo, NY 14207. (716)
875-4919. Grant Television Inc.

WYDC Channel 48, FOX
33 E. Market St., Corning, NY 14830. (607) 937-6144. FAX:
(607) 937-6144. Standfast Broadcasting Corp.

WENY-TV, Channel 36, ABC
PO Box 208, Elmira, NY 14902. (607) 739-3636. The Green
Group. Meade Murtland.

WETM-TV, Channel 18, NBC
101 E. Water St., Elmira, NY 14901. (607) 733-5518. FAX: (607)
734-1176. Smith Television Investment Co.

WTBY (Poughkeepsie), Channel 54, IND
PO Box 534, Rt. 9 at Merrit Rd., Fishkill, NY 12524. (914) 896-
4610. FAX: (914) 896-4614. Trinity Broadcasting Network.

WUTV (Buffalo), Channel 29, FOX
951 Whitehaven Rd., Grand Island, NY 14072. (716) 773-7531.
FAX: (716) 773-5753. Sullivan Broadcast Group Inc.

WBNG-TV (Binghamton), Channel 12, CBS
PO Box 12, 12 Gateway Plz., Johnson City, NY 13790. (607)
729-8812. FAX: (607) 797-6211. Gateway Communications Inc.

WRNN-TV, Channel 62, IND
721 Broadway, Kingston, NY 12401-3449. (914) 339-6200. FAX:
(914) 339-6264. New Mass Media Partners L.P.

WABC-TV, Channel 7, ABC
7 Lincoln Sq., New York, NY 10023. (212) 456-7777. FAX: (212)
456-2290. ABC Inc.

WCBS-TV, Channel 2, CBS
524 W. 57 St., New York, NY 10019. (212) 975-4321. FAX: (212)
975-5656. CBS Stations Inc. Steve Friedman.

WNBC, Channel 4, NBC
30 Rockefeller Plaza, New York, NY 10112. (212) 664-4444.
FAX: (212) 664-6449. NBC TV Station Division.

WNYW, Channel 5, FOX
205 E. 67th St., New York, NY 10021. (212) 452-5555. FAX:
(212) 249-1182. Fox Television Stations Inc.

WPIX, Channel 11, WB
220 E. 42nd St., New York, NY 10017. (212) 949-1100. FAX:
(212) 986-1032. Tribune Broadcasting. Paul Bissonette.

WPXN-TV, Channel 43, IND
200 Liberty St., New York, NY 10281. (212) 416-2504. FAX:
(212) 416-2909. Paxson Communications Corp.

WNPI-TV, Channel 18, PBS
(see WNPE, Watertown). Norwood, NY. St. Lawrence Valley
Educational Television Council.

WNYB (Jamestown), Channel 26, IND
5775 Big Tree Rd., Orchard Park, NY 14127. (716) 662-2659.
Tri-State Christian TV Inc.

WLIW (Garden City), Channel 21, PBS
Box 21, 303 Sunnyside Blvd., Plainview, NY 11803. (516) 367-
2100. FAX: (516) 349-0760. Long Island Educational Television
Council Inc.

WCFE-TV, Channel 57, PBS
One Sesame St., Plattsburgh, NY 12901. (518) 563-9770. FAX:
(518) 561-1928. Mountain Lake Public Telecomm. Council.

WPTZ (North Pole), Channel 5, NBC
5 Television Dr, Plattsburgh, NY 12901. (518) 561-5555. FAX:
(518) 561-5940. Hearst-Argyle Television Inc.

WHEC-TV, Channel 10, NBC
191 East Ave., Rochester, NY 14604. (716) 546-5670. FAX:
(716) 454-7433. Hubbard Broadcasting.

WOKR, Channel 13, ABC
4225 W. Henrietta Rd., Rochester, NY 14602-0555. (716)
334-8700. FAX: (716) 359-1570. Guy Gannett Comm.

WROC-TV, Channel 8, CBS
201 Humboldt St., Rochester, NY 14610. (716) 288-8400. FAX:
(716) 288-7679. Hicks, Muse, Tate & Furst Inc.

WUHF-TV, Channel 31, FOX
360 East Avenue, Rochester, NY 14604. (716) 232-3700. FAX:
(716) 546-4774. Sinclair Broadcast Group Inc.

WXXI-TV, Channel 21, PBS
PO Box 21, Rochester, NY 14601. (716) 325-7500. FAX: (716)
258-0338. WXXI Public Broadcasting Council.

WRGB (Albany), Channel 6, CBS
1400 Balltown Rd., Schenectady, NY 12309. (518) 346-6666.
FAX: (518) 381-3721. Freedom Communications Inc.

WYPX (Albany). Channel 55, IND
165 Freeman's Bridge Rd., Scotia, NY 12302. (518) 372-8855.
FAX: (518) 372-1677. Paxson Communications Corp

WCNY-TV, Channel 24, PBS
PO Box 2400, Syracuse, NY 13220-2400. (315) 453-2424. FAX:
(315) 451-8824. Public Broadcasting Cncl of Central NY.

WIXT, Channel 9, ABC
PO Box 699, 5904 Bridge St., East Syracuse, NY 13057. (315)
446-4780. FAX: (315) 446-0045. Ackerley Communications Inc.
Stephen Kimatian.

WNYS-TV, Channel 43, UPN
1000 James St., Syracuse, NY 13203. (315) 471-4343. FAX:
(315) 471-8889. Sinclair Broadcast Group Inc.

WSTM-TV, Channel 3, NBC
1030 James St., Syracuse, NY 13203. (315) 477-9400. FAX:
(315) 474-5082. Raycom Media Inc.

WSYT-TV, Channel 68, FOX
1000 James St., Syracuse, NY 13203. (315) 472-6800. FAX:
(315) 471-8889. Sinclair Broacast Group Inc.

WTVH, Channel 5, CBS
980 James St., Syracuse, NY 13203. (315) 425-5555. FAX:
(315) 425-5513. Granite Broadcasting Corp.

WFXV-TV, Channel 33, FOX
33 Greenfield Rd., Utica NY 13440. (315) 337-3300. FAX: (315)
337-1862. Sinclair Broadcast Group Inc.

WKTV, Channel 2, NBC
PO Box 2, Utica NY 13503. (315) 733-0404. FAX: (315)
793-3498. Smith Broadcasting Group Inc.

WUTR, Channel 20, ABC
PO Box 20, Utica, NY 13503. (315) 797-5220. FAX: (315) 797-
5409. Utica Television Partners LLC. Paul R. Kennedy.

WICZ (Binghamton), Channel 40, FOX
PO Box 40, 4600 Vestal Pkwy. E., Vestal, NY 13850. (607)
770-4040. FAX: (607) 798-7950. Northwest Broadcasting. Jeff
Gray.

WNPE-TV, Channel 16, PBS
1056 Arsenal St., Watertown, NY 13601. (315) 782-3142. FAX:
(315) 782-2491. St. Lawrence Valley Educational Television
Council.

WWNY-TV (Carthage), Channel 7, CBS, NBC
120 Arcade St., Watertown, NY 13601. (315) 788-3800. FAX:
(315) 782-7468. United Communications Corp. Cathy Pircsuk.

WWTI, Channel 50, ABC, NBC
1222 Arsenal St., Watertown, NY 13601. (315) 785-8850. FAX: (315) 785-0127. Smith Broadcasting of Watertown.

WAQF (Batavia) Channel 51, IND
601 Clearwater Park Rd., West Palm Beach, FL 33401. (561) 659-4122. Paxson Communications Corp.

NORTH CAROLINA

WASV-TV, Channel 62, IND
Square Park Office, Ste. 12, 1293 Hendersonville Rd., Asheville, NC 28803. (704) 227-0902. Pappas Telecasting Companies.

WUNF-TV, Channel 33, PBS
(see University of NC, Research, Triangle Park). Asheville, NC. University of North Carolina. Gail Zimmermann.

WUNC-TV, Channel 4, PBS
(see University of NC, Research, Triangle Park). Chapel Hill, NC. University of North Carolina.

WBTV, Channel 3, CBS
One Julian Price Pl., Charlotte, NC 28208. (704) 374-3500. FAX: (704) 374-3885. Jefferson-Pilot Communication Co. Ron Miller.

WCCB, Channel 18, FOX
One TV Pl., Charlotte, NC 28205. (704) 372-1800. FAX: (704) 376-3415. North Carolina Broadcasting Prtnrs.

WCNC-TV, Channel 6, NBC
1001 Wood Ridge Center Dr., Charlotte, NC 28217-1901. (704) 329-3636. FAX: (704) 357-4980. A.H. Belo Corp.

WJZY (Belmont), Channel 46, UPN
PO Box 668400, Charlotte, NC 28266-8400. (704) 393-0046. FAX: (704) 393-8407. Capitol Broadcasting Co., Inc.

WSOC-TV, Channel 9, ABC
PO Box 34665, Charlotte, NC 28234. (704) 335-4999. FAX: (704) 335-4968. Cox Broadcasting Inc.

WTVI, Channel 42, PBS
3242 Commonwealth Ave., Charlotte, NC 28205. (704) 372-2442. FAX: (704) 335-1358. Charlotte-Mecklenburg Public Broadcasting.

WUND-TV, Channel 2, PBS
(see University of NC, Research, Triangle Park). Columbia, NC. University of North Carolina.

WUNG-TV, Channel 58, PBS
(see University of NC, Research, Triangle Park). Concord, NC. University of North Carolina.

WRAZ (Raleigh), Channel 50, WB
2337 Guess Road, Durham, NC 27704. (919) 383-5675. FAX: (919) 383-5710. Cotton Broadcasting Co.

WRDC-TV Channel 28, UPN
(see WLFL Raleigh). Durham, NC. Sinclair Broadcast Group Inc.

WTVD, Channel 11, ABC
PO Box 2009, Durham, NC 27702. (919) 683-1111. FAX: (919) 682-7225. ABC Inc. Emily L. Barr.

WKFT, Channel 40, IND
PO Box 2509, Fayetteville, NC 28302-2509. (910) 323-4040. FAX: (910) 323-3924. Bahakel Communications Ltd. Terri L. Byford.

WBFX (Lexington), Channel 20, IND
622-G Guilford College Rd., Greensboro, NC 27409. (910) 547-0020. Pappas Telecasting Companies.

WFMY-TV (High Point), Channel 2, CBS
PO Box TV2, Greensboro, NC 27420. (910) 379-9369. FAX: (910) 273-3444. Gannett Broadcasting.

WGPX (Burlington), Channel 16, IND
1114 N. O'Henry Blvd., Greensboro, NC 27405. (910) 272-9227. FAX: (910) 272-9298. Paxson Communications Corp.

WLXI-TV, Channel 61, IND
2109 Patterson St., Greensboro, NC 27407. (910) 855-5610. FAX: (910) 855-3645. Tri-State Christian Television.

WNCT-TV, Channel 9, CBS
PO Box 898, 3221 Evans St., Greenville, NC 27835-0898. (919) 355-8500. FAX: (919) 355-8568. Media General Broadcast Group.

WUNK-TV, Channel 25, PBS
(see University of NC, Research, Triangle Park). Greenville, NC. University of North Carolina.

WYDO, Channel 14, FOX
PO Box 2044, Greenville, NC 27836. (919) 746-8014. FAX: (919) 746-2555. GOCOM License L.L.C.

WHKY-TV, Channel 14, IND
PO Box 1059, Hickory, NC 28603. (704) 322-5115. FAX: (704) 322-8256. The Long Family Partnership.

WGHP-TV, Channel 8, FOX
2005 Francis St., High Point, NC 27263. (910) 841-8888. FAX: (910) 841-8050. Fox Television Stations Inc.

WUNM-TV, Channel 19, PBS
(see University of NC, Research, Triangle Park). Jacksonville, NC. University of North Carolina.

WAXN (Charlotte), Channel 64, IND
910 Fairview St., Kannapolis, NC 28083. (704) 933-9529. FAX: (704) 932-3880. Cox Broadcasting Inc. Mark Russell

WUNE-TV, Channel 17, PBS
(see University of NC, Research, Triangle Park). Linville, NC. University of North Carolina.

WFPX (Raleigh), Channel 62, IND
Drawer 62, Lumber Bridge, NC 28357. (910) 843-3884. FAX: (910) 843-2873. Paxson Communications Corp.

WRAY-TV (Raleigh/Durham), Channel 30, IND
Drawer 62, Lumber Bridge, NC 28357. (910) 843-3884. Shop at Home, Inc.

WUNU, Channel 31, IND
(see University of NC, Research, Triangle Park). Lumberton, NC. University of North Carolina.

WFXI, Channel 8, FOX
PO Box 2069, 5441 Highway 70, Morehead City, NC 28557. (919) 240-0888. FAX: (919) 240-2028. GOCOM Communications.

WCTI, Channel 12, ABC
PO Box 12325, New Bern, NC 28561. (919) 638-1212. FAX: (919) 637-4141. Lamco Communications Inc.

WLFL, Channel 22, FOX
3012 Highwoods Blvd., Raleigh, NC 27604. (919) 872-9535. Sinclair Broadcast Group Inc. Robert Gluck.

WNCN, Channel 17, NBC
1205 Front St., Raleigh, NC 27609. (919) 836-1717. FAX: (919) 836-1747. NBC Inc. Bud Polacek.

WRAL-TV, Channel 5, CBS
PO Box 12000, Raleigh, NC 27605. (919) 821-8555. FAX: (919) 821-8566. Capitol Broadcasting Co. Inc.

WRMY (Rocky Mount), Channel 47, IND
1507 Oakwood Ave., Raleigh, NC 27610. (919) 755-2277. FAX: (919) 755-1702. Paxson Communications Corp. Jack Hogan.

University of North Carolina, PBS
PO Box 14900, Reseach Triangle Pk, NC 27709-4900. (919) 549-7000. FAX: (919) 549-7201. Tom Howe.

WUNP-TV, Channel 36, PBS
(see University of NC, Research, Triangle Park). Roanoke Rapids, NC. University of North Carolina.

WITN-TV, Channel 7, NBC
PO Box 468, Hwy. 17 S, Washington, NC 27889. (919) 946-3131. FAX: (919) 946-9265. Gray Communications Systems Inc.

WECT Channel 6, NBC
PO Box 4029, Wilmington, NC 28406. (910) 791-8070. FAX: (910) 392-1509. Raycom Media Inc.

WSFX, Channel 26, FOX
1926 Oleander Dr., Wilmington, NC 28403. (910) 343-8826. FAX: (910) 251-0978. Robinson O. Everett.

WUNJ-TV, Channel 39, PBS
(see University of NC, Research, Triangle Park). Wilmington, NC. University of North Carolina.

WWAY, Channel 3, ABC
PO Box 2068, Wilmington, NC 28402. (910) 762-8581. FAX: (910) 762-8367. Kelso Investment Associates.

WUNL-TV, Channel 26, PBS
(see University of NC, Research, Triangle Park). Winston-Salem, NC. University of North Carolina.

WUPN-TV (Greensboro), Channel 48, UPN
3477 Myer Lee Drive, Winston-Salem, NC 27101. (910) 274-4848. FAX: (910) 722-6289. Sinclair Broadcast Group Inc. Ginny Brown.

WXII, Channel 12, NBC
PO Box 11847, 700 Coliseum Dr., Winston-Salem, NC 27116. (910) 721-9944. FAX: (910) 722-7685. Hearst-Argyle Televistion Inc.

WXLV-TV, Channel 45, ABC
3500 Myer-Lee Dr., Winston-Salem, NC 27101. (910) 722- 4545. FAX: (910) 723-8217. Sullivan Broadcasting Inc. Joe Koff.

NORTH DAKOTA

KBME Channel 3, PBS
(see KFME Fargo). Bismarck, ND Prairie Public Broadcasting Inc.

KBMY, Channel 17, ABC
PO Box 7277, Bismarck, ND 58507. (701) 223-1700. FAX: (701) 258-0886. Forum Publishing Co.

KFYR-TV, Channel 5, NBC
PO Box 1738, Bismarck, ND 58502. (701) 255-5757. FAX: (701) 255-8220. Sunrise Television Corp.

KQCD-TV (Dickinson), Channel 7, NBC
PO Box 1577, Bismarck, ND 58601. (701) 225-6843. FAX: (701) 225-8231. Sunrise Television Corp.

KXMA-TV (Dickinson), Channel 2, CBS
Drawer B, 119 2nd Ave., Bismarck, ND 58602. (701) 227-1400. FAX: (701) 227-8896. Chester Reiten & Family.

KXMB-TV, Channel 12, CBS
PO Box 1617, Bismarck, ND 58501. (701) 223-9197. FAX: (701) 223-3320. Reiten Television Inc.

WDAZ (Devils Lake), Channel 8, ABC
PO Box 12639, 2220 S. Washington, Grand Forks, ND. 58208, Forum Communications Co.

KDSE, Channel 9, PBS
(see KFME Fargo). Dickinson, ND. Prairie Public Broadcasting Inc.

KJRE, Channel 19, PBS
(see KFME Fargo). Ellendale, ND. Prairie Public Broadcasting Inc.

KFME Channel 13, PBS
PO Box 3240, 207 N. 5th St., Fargo, ND 58108-3240. (701) 241-6900. FAX: (701) 239-7650. Prairie Public Broadcasting Inc. Bruce Jacobs.

KVLY-TV, Channel 11, NBC
PO Box 1878, Fargo, ND 58107. (701) 237-5211. FAX: (701) 232-0493. Sunrise Television Corp.

KVRR, Channel 15, FOX
PO Box 9115, 4015 9th Ave. SW, Fargo, ND 58106. (701) 277-1515. FAX: (701) 277-1830. Red River Broadcast Group.

KXJB-TV, Channel 4, CBS
PO Box 10399, 4302 13th Ave. S., Fargo, ND 58106. (701) 282-0444. FAX: (701) 282-9331. North American Communication Corp. Paul Wickre.

WDAY-TV, Channel 6, ABC
PO Box 2466, Fargo, ND 58108. (701) 237-6500. FAX: (701) 241-5368. Forum Communications Co.

KGFE, Channel 2, PBS
(see KFME Fargo). Grand Forks, ND. Prairie Public Broadcasting Inc.

KJRR, Channel 7, IND
(see KVRR, Fargo). Jamestown, ND. Red River Broadcast Corp.

KMCY, Channel 14, ABC
PO Box 2276, Minot, ND 58702. (701) 838-6614. FAX: (701) 852-9315. Forum Publishing Co.

KMOT, Channel 10, NBC
PO Box 1120, 1800 S.W., Minot, ND 58702. (701) 852-4101. FAX: (701) 838-8195. Sunrise Television Corp.

KSRE, Channel 6, PBS
(see KFME Fargo). Minot, ND Prairie Public Broadcasting.

KXMC-TV, Channel 13, CBS
PO Box 1686, Minot, ND 58702. (701) 852-2104. FAX: (701) 838-9360. Reiten Family.

KNRR, Channel 12, FOX
(see KVRR, Fargo). Pembina, ND Red River Broadcast Group.

KUMV-TV, Channel 8, NBC
PO Box 1287, 602 Main St., Williston, ND 58801. (701) 572-4676. FAX: (701) 572-0118. Sunrise Television Corp.

KWSE, Channel 4, PBS
(see KFME Fargo). Williston, ND. Prairie Public Broadcasting Inc.

KXMD-TV, Channel 11, CBS
PO Box 790, Williston, ND 58801. (701) 572-2345. FAX: (701) 572-0658. Reiten Television Inc.

OHIO

WVPX, Channel 23, IND
26650 Renaissance Pkwy., Akron, OH 44128. (216) 831-2367. FAX: (216) 831-2676. Paxson Communications Corp.

WNEO, Channel 45, PBS
(see WEAO, Kent). Alliance, OH. Northeastern Educ. TV of Ohio Inc.

WOUB, Channel 20, PBS
9 S. College St., Athens, OH 45701. (614) 593-4555. FAX: (614) 593-0240. Ohio University. Assoc.

WOUC-TV, Channel 44, PBS
(see WOUB, Athens). Cambridge, OH. Ohio University.

WOAC, Channel 67, IND
26650 Emery Industrial Pkwy., Canton, OH 44718-2398. (561) 686-3434. FAX: (561) 691-1177. Shop at Home, Inc.

WGGN-TV (Sandusky) Channel 52, NFP
PO Box 247, 3809 Maple Ave., Castalia, OH 44824. (419) 684-5311. FAX: (419) 684-5378. Christian Faith Broadcasting Inc.

WWHO-TV, Channel 53, WB, UPN
1281 River Rd., Chillicothe, OH 45601. (614) 775-3578. FAX: (614) 775-3584. Paramount Stations Group Inc.

WCET, Channel 48, PBS
1223 Central Pkwy., Cincinnati, OH 45214-2890. (513) 381-4033. FAX: (513) 381-7520. Greater Cincinnati TV Educ. Foundation. Scott Elliott.

WCPO, Channel 9, ABC
500 Central Ave., Cincinnati, OH 45202. (513) 721-9900. FAX: (513) 721-6032. E. W. Scripps Co. J.B. Chase.

WKRC-TV, Channel 12, CBS
1906 Highland Ave., Cincinnati, OH 45219. (513) 763-5500. FAX: (513) 651-0704. Jacor Communications Inc.

WLWT, Channel 5, NBC
140 W. Ninth St., Cincinnati, OH 45202. (513) 352-5000. FAX: (513) 352-5028. Hearst-Argyle Television Inc.

WSTR-TV, Channel 64, WB
5177 Fishwick Dr., Cincinnati, OH 45216. (513) 641-4400. FAX: (513) 242-2633. Sinclair Broadcast Group Inc.

WBNX, Channel 55, IND
Box 91660, Cleveland, OH 44101. (216) 843-5555. FAX: (216) 843-7070. Winston Broadcasting Network Inc. Anne Catherine Keith.

WEWS, Channel 5, ABC
3001 Euclid Ave., Cleveland, OH 44115. (216) 431-5555. FAX: (216) 361-1762. E. W. Scripps Co.

WJW-TV, Channel 8, FOX
5800 S. Marginal Rd., Cleveland, OH 44103. (216) 431-8888. FAX: (216) 391-9559. Fox Television Stations Inc.

WKYC-TV, Channel 3, NBC
1403 E. 6th St., Cleveland, OH 44114. (216) 344-3333. FAX: (216) 344-3326. Gannett Broadcasting.

WOIO (Shaker Heights), Channel 19, CBS
1717 E. 12th St., Cleveland, OH 44114. (216) 771-1943. FAX: (216) 515-7185. Mairite Communications Group. Richard Sullivan.

WUAB (Lorain), Channel 43, UPN
1717 E.12th St., Cleveland, OH 44114. (216) 771-1943. FAX: (216) 515-7180. Cannell Communications L.P.

WVIZ-TV, Channel 25, PBS
4300 Brookpark Rd., Cleveland, OH 44134. (216) 398-2800. FAX: (216) 749-2560. Ed. TV Assoc. of Metro Cleveland.

WBNS, Channel 10, CBS
770 Twin Rivers Dr., Columbus, OH 43215. (614) 460-3700. FAX: (614) 460-2812. Dispatch Printing Co.

WCMH, Channel 4, NBC
PO Box 4, Columbus, OH 43216. (614) 263-4444. FAX: (614) 447-9107. NBC Inc.

WOSU, Channel 34, PBS
2400 Olentangy River Rd., Columbus, OH 43210. (614) 292-9678. FAX: (614) 688-3343. Ohio State University.

WSYX, Channel 6, ABC
1216 Dublin Rd., Columbus, OH 43215. (614) 481-6666. FAX: (614) 481-6624. Sinclair Broadcast Group Inc.

WTTE, Channel 28, FOX
PO Box 280, Columbus, OH 43216-0280. (614) 895-2800. FAX: (614) 895-3159. Sinclair Broadcast Group Inc.

WBNX (Akron), Channel 55, WB
2690 State Rd., Cuyahoga Falls, OH 44223. (216) 843-5555.
FAX: (216) 842-5597. Winston Broadcasting Network Inc.

WDTN, Channel 2, ABC
PO Box 741, Dayton, OH 45401. (937) 293-2101. FAX: (937)
294-6542. Hicks, Muse, Tate & Furst Inc.

WHIO-TV, Channel 7, CBS
PO Box 1206, Dayton, OH 45401. (937) 259-2111. FAX: (937)
259-2024. Cox Broadcasting Inc.

WKEF-TV, Channel 22, NBC
1731 Soldiers Home Rd., Dayton, OH 45418. (937) 263-2662.
FAX: (937) 268-2332. Sinclair Broadcast Group Inc.

WPTD, Channel 16, PBS
110 S. Jefferson St., Dayton, OH 45402-2415. (937) 220-1600.
FAX: (937) 220-1642. Greater Dayton Public TV Inc.

WRGT-TV, Channel 45, FOX
45 Broadcast Plaza, Dayton, OH 45408. (937) 263-4500. FAX:
(937) 268-5265, Sinclair Broadcast Group Inc.

WEAO (Akron), Channel 49, PBS
PO Box 5191, 1750 Campus Center Dr., Kent, OH 44240. (330)
677-4549. FAX: (330) 678-1656. Northeastern Educ. TV of Ohio Inc.

WLIO, Channel 35, NBC
1424 Rice Ave., Lima, OH 45805. (419) 228-8835. FAX: (419)
229-7091. Blade Communications Inc.

WTLW, Channel 44, NFP
1844 Baty Rd., Lima, OH 45807. (419) 339-4444. FAX: (419)
339-6812. American Christian Television Svcs.

WDLI (Canton), Channel 17, IND
6600 Atlantic Blvd., Louisville, OH 44641. (330) 875-5542. Trinity
Broadcasting Network.

WMFD-TV, Channel 68, IND
2900 Park Ave. W., Mansfield, OH 44906. (419) 529-5900. FAX:
(419) 529-2319. Mid-State Television Inc.

WSFJ, Channel 51, NFP
PO Box 770, 10077 Jacksontown Rd S.E., Newark, OH 43076.
(614) 833-0771. FAX: (614) 323-3242. Christian Television of Ohio.

WQHS-TV (Cleveland), Channel 61, HSN
2861 W. Ridgewood Dr., Parma, OH 44134. (216) 888-0061.
FAX: (216) 888-6551. USA Broadcasting Inc.

WPBO-TV, Channel 42, PBS
(see WOSU, Columbus). Portsmouth, OH. Ohio State University.

WDPX (Dayton), Channel 26, IND
Springfield, OH. (937) 323-0026. FAX: (937) 323-1912. Paxson
Communications Corp.

WTJC, Channel 26, IND
2675 Dayton Rd., Springfield, OH 45506. (937) 323-0026. FAX:
(937) 323-1912. Paxson Communications Corp.

WTOV-TV, Channel 9, NBC
PO Box 9999, Altamont Heights, Steubenville, OH 43952. (304)
232-6933. FAX: (614) 282-0439. Hicks, Muse, Tate & Furst Inc.

WGTE-TV, Channel 30, PBS
PO Box 30, 136 Huron St., Toledo, OH 43697. (419) 243-3091.
FAX: (419) 243-9711. Public Broadcasting Foundation of N.W. Ohio.

WLMB, Channel 40, IND
2757 Monroe St., Toledo, OH 43606. (419) 243-7005. FAX: (419)
243-5340. Dominion Broadcasting Inc.

WNWO-TV, Channel 24, NBC
300 S. Byrne Rd., Toledo, OH 43615. (419) 535-0024. FAX:
(419) 535-0202. Marlrite Communications Group Inc.

WTOL-TV, Channel 11, CBS
PO Box 1111, Toledo, OH 43699-1111. (419) 248-1111. FAX:
(419) 248-1177. Cosmos Broadcasting Corp.

WTVG, Channel 13, NBC
4247 Dorr St., Toledo, OH 43607. (419) 531-1313. FAX: (419)
531-1399. ABC Inc.

WUPW, Channel 36, FOX
Four SeaGate, Toledo, OH 43601. (419) 244-3600. FAX: (419)
244-8842. Sunrise Television Corp.

WFMJ-TV, Channel 21, NBC
PO Box 6230, Youngstown, OH 44501-6230. (330) 744-8611.
FAX: (330) 744-3402. WFMJ Television Inc.

WKBN-TV, Channel 27, CBS
3930 Sunset Blvd., Youngstown, OH 44512. (330) 782-1144.
FAX: (330) 782-3504. Youngstown Television License LLC.

WYTV, Channel 33, ABC
3800 Shady Run Rd., Youngstown, OH 44502. (330) 783-2930.
FAX: (330) 782-8154. Benedek Broadcasting Corp.

OKLAHOMA

KDOR (Bartlesville/Tulsa), Channel 17, IND
2120 N. Yellowood, Broken Arrow, OK 74012. (918) 250-0777.
All American TV Inc.

KWET, Channel 12, PBS
(see KETA, Oklahoma City). Cheyenne, OK Oklahoma
Educational TV Authority.

KRSC-TV, Channel 35, NFP
1701 W. Will Rogers Blvd., Claremore, OK, 74017-3252. (918)
343-7772. FAX: (918) 343-7952. Rogers State College.

KOET, Channel 3, PBS
(see KETA, Oklahoma City). Eufaula, OK. Oklahoma Educational
TV Authority.

KSWO-TV, Channel 7, ABC
PO Box 708, Hwy 7, Lawton, OK 73502. (405) 355-7000. R.H.
Drewry Group.

KETA, Channel 13, PBS
PO Box 14190, 7403 N. Kelley, Oklahoma City, OK 73113. (405)
848-8501. FAX: (405) 841-9282. Oklahoma Educational TV
Authority.

KFOR-TV, Channel 4, NBC
PO Box 14068, Oklahoma City, OK 73113. (405) 424-4444. FAX:
(405) 478-6206. The New York Times Company.

KOCB-TV, Channel 34, WB
PO Box 13034, Oklahoma City, OK, 73113. (405) 478-3434.
FAX: (405) 478-1027. Sinclair Broadcast Group Inc.

KOCO-TV, Channel 5, ABC
PO Box 14555, 1300 E. Britton Rd., Oklahoma City, OK, 73113.
(405) 478-3000. FAX: (405) 478-6675. Hearst-Argyle Television Inc.

KOKH-TV, Channel 25, FOX
PO Box 14925, Oklahoma City, OK, 73113. (405) 843-2525.
FAX: (405) 478-4343. Sinclair Broadcast Group Inc.

KOPX, Channel 62, IND
Oklahoma City, OK. (405) 751-6800. FAX: (405) 751-6867.
Paxson Communications Corp.

KSBI, Channel 52, IND
PO Box 26404, Oklahoma City, OK, 73126. (405) 631-7335.
FAX: (405) 631-7367. Locke Supply Co.

KTBO-TV, Channel 14, IND
3705 N.W. 63rd St., Oklahoma City, OK, 73116. (405) 848-1414.
Trinity Broadcasting Network.

KTLC, Channel 43, UPN
Box 14190, 11901 N. Eastern Ave., Oklahoma City, OK 73131.
(405) 478-4300. FAX: (405) 478-8716. Paramount Stations
Group Inc.

KWTV, Channel 9, CBS
PO Box 14159, Oklahoma City, OK 73113. (405) 843-6641. FAX:
(405) 841-9135. Griffin Television Inc.

KTPX (Okmulgee), Channel 44, IND
Ste. 101, 5800 W. Skelly Dr., Tulsa, OK 74135. (918) 664-1044.
Paxson Communications Corp.

KJRH, Channel 2, NBC
PO Box 2, 3701 S. Peoria, Tulsa, OK, 74105-3269. (918)
743-2222. FAX: (918) 748-1460. E.W. Scripps Co.

KOED-TV, Channel 11, PBS
811 N. Sheridan, Tulsa, OK, 74115. (918) 838-7611. FAX: (918)
838-1807. Oklahoma Educational TV Authority.

KOKI-TV, Channel 23, FOX
5416 S. Yale Ave., Ste. 500, Tulsa, OK 74135. (918) 491-0023.
FAX: (918) 491-6650. Clear Channel TV Licenses Inc.

KOTV, Channel 6, CBS
PO Box 6, Tulsa, OK 74101. (918) 582-6666. FAX:)918) 584-
5513. A.H. Belo Corp. Ron Longinotti.

KTFO, Channel 41, UPN
5416 S. Yale, Ste. 500, Tulsa, OK, 74135. (918) 491-6141. FAX:
(918) 491-6650. RDS Broadcasting Inc.

KTUL, Channel 8, ABC
PO Box 8, Tulsa, OK, 74101. (918) 445-8888. FAX: (918)
445-9316. Allbritton Communications Co.

KWHB, Channel 47, WB
11414 E. 58th Street, Tulsa, OK, 74146. (918) 250-9402. FAX:
(918) 254-5614. LeSea Broadcasting.

KWMJ, Channel 53, IND
7777 S. Lewis Ave., Tulsa, OK 74171. (918) 488-5300. FAX:
(918) 495-7388. University Broadcasting Inc.

OREGON

KWBP (Salem/Portland), Channel 32, WB
10255 S.W. Artic Dr., Beaverton, OR 97005. (503) 644-3232.
FAX: (503) 626-3576. Acme Television Holdings of Oregon.

KOAB-TV, Channel 3, PBS
PO Box 509., Bend, OR 97709. (503) 244-9900. FAX: (503)
293-1919. Charles J. Swindells.

KTVZ, Channel 21, NBC
PO Box 149, Bend, OR 97709. (541) 383-2121. FAX: (541)
382-1616. Northwest Broadcasting Inc.

KCBY-TV, Channel 11, CBS
PO Box 1156, Coalbank Slough Rd., Coos Bay, OR. 97420.
(541) 269-1111. FAX: (541) 269-7464. Northwest Television Inc.

KMTZ, Channel 23, NBC
(see KMTR, Springfield) Coos Bay, OR. Wicks Broadcast Group.

KOAC-TV, Channel 7, PBS
(see KOPB, Portland). Corvallis, OR.

KEPB-TV, Channel 28, PBS
(see KOPB, Portland). Eugene, OR.

KEVU, Channel 34, UPN
PO Box 10185, Eugene, OR 97401. (541) 342-3435. FAX: (541)
342-2818. California Oregon Broadcasting Inc.

KEZI, Channel 9, ABC
PO Box 7009, 2225 Coburg Rd., Eugene, OR 97401. (541)
485-5611. FAX: (541) 343-9664. Carolyn S. Chambers.

KLSR, Channel 34, FOX
888 Goodpasture Island Rd., Eugene, OR 97401. (541) 342-
3435. FAX: (541) 683-8016. California Oregon Broadcasting Inc.

KVAL-TV, Channel 13, CBS
PO Box 1313, Eugene, OR 97440. (541) 342-4961. FAX: (541)
342-2635. Retlaw Broadcasting Co.

KDKF, Channel 31, ABC
4509 S. 6th St., Suite 308, Klamath Falls, OR 97603. (541) 883-
3131. FAX: (541) 883-8931. Soda Mountain Broadcasting Inc.

KFTS, Channel 22, PBS
(see KSYS, Medford). Klamath Falls, OR. Southern Oregon
Public TV Inc.

KOTI, Channel 2, NBC
PO Box 2K, 222 S. 7th, Klamath Falls, OR 97601. (503)
882-2222. California Oregon Broadcasting Inc. Mark Logan.

KTVR, Channel 13, PBS
(see KOPB, Portland). La Grande OR. OR Public Broadcasting.

KDRV, Channel 12, ABC
1090 Knutson Ave., Medford, OR 97504. (503) 773-1212. FAX:
(503) 779-9261. Chambers Communications Corp.

KMVU, Channel 26, FOX, UPN
820 Crater Lake Ave., Medford, OR 97504. (541) 772-2600.
FAX: (541) 772-7364. Broadcasting Communications L.L.C.

KOBI, Channel 5, NBC
PO Box 5M, 125 S. Flr., Medford, OR 97501. (541) 779-5555.
FAX: (541) 779-5564. California Oregon Broadcasting Inc. Mark
Logan.

KSYS, Channel 8, PBS
34 S. Fir St., Medford, OR 97501. (541) 779-0808. FAX: (541)
779-2178. Southern Oregon Public TV Inc.

KTVL, Channel 10, CBS
PO Box 10, 1440 Rossanley Dr., Medford, OR 97501. (541)
773-7373. FAX: (541) 779-0451. Freedom Communications, Inc.

KATU, Channel 2, ABC
PO Box 2, Portland, OR 97207. (503) 231-4222. FAX: (503)
231-4233. Fisher Broadcasting Inc. Jan Allen.

KGW, Channel 8, NBC
1501 S.W. Jefferson St., Portland, OR 97201. (503) 226-5000.
FAX: (503) 226-4448. A. H. Belo Corp.

KNMT-TV, Channel 24, IND
432 N.E. 74Th Ave., Portland, OR 97213. (503) 252-0792. FAX:
(503) 256-4205. National Minority TV Inc.

KOIN, Channel 6, CBS
222 S.W. Columbia St., Portland, OR 97201. (503) 464-0600.
FAX: (503) 464-0717. Lee Enterprises Inc.

KOPB-TV, Channel 10, PBS
7140 S.W. Macadam Ave., Portland, OR 97219. (503) 244-9900.
FAX: (503) 293-1919. OR Public Broadcasting.

KPTV, Channel 12, UPN
211 S.E. Caruthers St., Portland, OR 97214. (503) 230-1200.
FAX: (503) 230-1065. Chris-Craft Industries, Inc.

KMTX-TV, Channel 46, NBC
(see KMTR, Springfield). Roseburg, OR. Wicks Broadcast
Group.

KPIC, Channel 4, CBS
PO Box 1345, 655 W Umpqua, Roseburg, OR 97470. (541)
672-4481. FAX: (541) 672-4482. California Oregon Broadcasting
Inc. Don Clithero.

KROZ, Channel 36, WB
931 N.W. Highland, Roseburg, OR 97470. (541) 673-3636. FAX:
(541) 673-1136. Johanna Broadcasting.

KBSP-TV, Channel 22, HSN
4923 Indian School Rd. N.E., Salem, OR 97305. (503)
390-2202. FAX: (503) 390-6829. Paxson Communications Corp.

KMTR (Eugene), Channel 16, NBC
3825 International Ct., Springfield, OR 97401. (503) 746-1600.
FAX: (503) 747-0866. Wicks Broadcast Group.

PENNSYLVANIA

WBPH-TV (Bethlehem), Channel 60, IND
813 N. Fenwyck St., Allentown, PA 18103. (610) 433-4400. FAX:
(610) 433-8251. Sonshine Family TV Inc.

WFMZ-TV, Channel 69, IND
300 E. Rock Rd., Allentown, PA 18103. (610) 797-4530. FAX:
(610) 791-2288. Richard C. Dean & others.

WATM-TV (Altoona), Channel 23, ABC
(see WWCP, Johnstown). Altoona, PA. Smith Broadcasting
Group Inc.

WKBS-TV, Channel 47, IND
1813 Valley View Blvd., Altoona, PA 16602. (814) 942-3400.
FAX: (814) 942-3400. Cornerstone Television Inc.

WTAJ-TV, Channel 10, CBS
PO Box 10, 5000 6th Ave., Commerce Park, Altoona, PA 16603.
(814) 942-1010. FAX: (814) 946-8746. Macromedia.

WCAU (Philadelphia), Channel 10, NBC
10 Monument Rd., Bala Cynwyd, PA 19004. (610) 668-5510.
FAX: (610) 668-7039. NBC Inc.

WLVT-TV (Allentown), Channel 39, PBS
1525 Mountain Drive N., Bethlehem, PA 18015. (610) 867-4677.
FAX: (610) 867-3544. Lehigh Valley Public Telecomm.

WJAL (Hagerstown, MD) Channel 68, WB
PO Box 229, 262 Swamp Fox Rd., Chambersburg, PA 17201.
(719) 375-4000. FAX: (719) 375-4052. Channel 68 Broadcasting
Corp. Todd Taylor.

WSWB-TV (Scranton), Channel 64, IND
PO Box 64, Clarks Summit, PA 18411.(717) 586-1744. Paxson
Communications Corp.

WPSX-TV, Channel 3, PBS
Wagner Annex, University Park, Clearfield, PA 16802-3899.
(814) 865-3333. FAX: (814) 865-3145. Pennsylvania State
University. Mark Erstling.

WFXP, Channel 66, FOX
3514 State St., Erie, PA 16508. (814) 454-5201. FAX: (814) 455-
0703. NV Acquisition Co.

WICU-TV, Channel 12, NBC
3514 State St., Erie, PA 16508. (814) 454-5201. FAX: (814)
455-0703. SJL Communications L.P.

WJET-TV, Channel 24, ABC
8455 Peach St., Erie, PA 16509. (814) 864-2400. FAX: (814)
868-3041. Nexstar Broadcasting Group Inc.

WQLN, Channel 54, PBS
8425 Peach St., Erie, PA 16509. (814) 864-3001. FAX: (814)
864-4077. Public Broadcasting of N.W. PA.

WSEE-TV, Channel 35, CBS
1220 Peach St., Erie, PA 16501. (814) 455-7575. FAX: (814)
454-5541. WSEE Holdings Inc.

WHP-TV, Channel 21, CBS
3300 N. Sixth St., Harrisburg, PA 17110. (717) 238-2100. FAX:
(717) 236-0198. Clear Channel Communications.

WHTM-TV, Channel 27, ABC
PO Box 5860, 3235 Hoffman St., Harrisburg, PA 17110-5860.
(717) 236-2727. FAX: (717) 232-5272. Allbritton Comm. Corp.

WITF-TV, Channel 33, PBS
PO Box 2954, Harrisburg, PA 17105. (717) 236-6000. FAX: (717)
236-4628. Eastern Education. Wick Woodford.

WLYH-TV (Lancaster), Channel 15, CBS
3300 N. Sixth St., Harrisburg, OA 17011. (717) 228-1500. FAX:
(717) 270-0901. Gateway Communications Inc. John Feeser III.

WWLF-TV, Channel 56, FOX
(see WOLF, Scranton). Hazleton, PA. Pegasus Broadcast
Television Inc.

WJAC-TV, Channel 6, NBC
1949 Hickory Lane, 49 Old Hickory Ln., Johnstown, PA 15905.
(814) 255-7600. FAX: (814) 255-3958. Hicks, Muse, Tate & Furst
Inc.

WWCP-TV, Channel 8, FOX, UPN
1450 Scalp Ave., Johnstown, PA 15904. (814) 266-8088. FAX:
(814) 266-7749. Peak Media.

WGAL, Channel 8, NBC
1300 Columbia Ave., Lancaster, PA 17603. (717) 393-5851.
FAX: (717) 383-9484. Hearst-Argyle Television Inc.

WNPA (Jeannette), Channel 19, IND
Ste. D, 50 Second St., Monroeville, PA 15143. (412) 374-2990.
FAX: (412) 374-2994. Leon A. Crosby.

WNEP-TV (Scranton), Channel 16, ABC
16 Montage Mountain Rd., Moosic, PA 18507. (717) 346-7474.
FAX: (717) 347-0359. The New York Times Co.

KYW-TV, Channel 3, CBS
101 S. Independence Mall E., Philadelphia, PA 19106. (215)
238-4700. FAX: (215) 238-4545. CBS Stations Inc. Alfred Bova.

WACI (Atlantic City, NJ), Channel 62, IND
400 W. Hortter, Philadelphia, PA 19123. (215) 848-5815. FAX:
(215) 848-9471. Garden State Communications.

WPHL-TV, Channel 17, WB
5001 Wynnefield Ave., Philadelphia, PA 19131. (215) 878-1700.
FAX: (215) 879-3665. Tribune Broadcasting.

WPPX-TV, Channel 61, IND
520 N. Delaware Ave., Philadelphia, PA 19123. (215) 923-2661.
FAX: (215) 923-2677. Paxson Communications Corp.

WPSG-TV, Channel 57, UPN
420 N. 20th St., Philadelphia, PA 19130. (215) 563-5757. FAX:
(215) 563-5786. Paramount Stations Group Inc. Walter
DeHaven.

WPVI-TV, Channel 6, ABC
4100 City Line Ave., Philadelphia, PA 19131. (215) 878-9700.
FAX: (215) 581-4515. ABC Inc.

WTFX-TV, Channel 29, FOX
330 Market St., Philadelphia, PA 19106. (215) 925-2929. FAX:
(215) 592-1535. Fox Television Stations Inc.

WYBE, Channel 35, PBS
PO Box 11896, Philadelphia, PA 19128-1604. (215) 483-3900.
FAX: (215) 483-6908. Independence Public Media of Phil.

KDKA-TV, Channel 2, CBS
One Gateway Ctr., Pittsburgh, PA 15222. (412) 575-2200. FAX:
(412) 575-3207. CBS Stations Inc. Gary Cozen.

WCWB-TV, Channel 22, WB
PO Box 2809, Pittsburgh, PA 15230. (412) 856-9010. FAX: (412)
856-0633. Sinclair Broadcast Group Inc.

WPGH-TV, Channel 53, FOX
750 Ivory Ave., Pittsburgh, PA 15214. (412) 931-5300. FAX:
(412) 931-8029. Sinclair Broadcast Group. Michael Wikff.

WPXI, Channel 11, NBC
11 Television Hill, Pittsburgh, PA 15214. (412) 237-1100. FAX:
(412) 323-8097. Cox Broadcasting Inc.

WQED, Channel 13, PBS
4802 Fifth Ave., Pittsburgh, PA 15213. (412) 622-1300. FAX:
(412) 622-1488. WQED Pittsburgh Public Broadcasting.

WQEX, Channel 16, PBS
(see WQED, Pittsburgh). Pittsburgh, PA. WQED Pittsburgh Inc.

WTAE-TV, Channel 4, ABC
400 Ardmore Blvd., Pittsburgh, PA 15221. (412) 242-4300. FAX:
(412) 244-4512. Hearst-Argyle Television, Inc. Joseph W.
Heston.

WVIA-TV, Channel 44, PBS
70 Old Boston Rd., Pittston, PA 18640. (717) 826-6144. FAX:
(717) 655-1180. Northeastern PA Education TV Assoc.

WTVE, Channel 51, IND
1729 N. 11th St., Reading, PA 19604. (610) 921-9181. FAX:
(610) 921-9139. Reading Broadcasting Inc. Daniel Bendetti.

WGCB-TV, Channel 49, IND
PO Box 88, 2900 Windsor Rd.,Red Lion, PA 17356. (717)
246-1681. FAX: (717) 244-9316. Red Lion Broadcasting Co.
John E. Stockstill.

WOLF-TV, Channel 38, FOX
916 Oak St., Scranton, PA 18508. (717) 347-9653. FAX: (717)
347-3141. KB Prime Media.

WQPX, Channel 64, IND
Box 764, Clarks Summit, Scranton, PA 18411. Paxson
Communications Corp.

WYOU, Channel 22, CBS
415 Lackawanna Ave., Scranton, PA 18503. (717) 961-2222.
FAX: (717) 342-1254. Nexstar Broadcasting Broup L.P..

WPCB-TV (Greensburg), Channel 40, IND
Signal Hill Dr., Wall, PA 15148-1499. (412) 824-3930. FAX: (412)
824-5442. Paxson Communications Corp.

WBRE-TV (Scranton), Channel 28, NBC
62 S. Franklin St., Wilkes-Barre, PA 18773. (717) 823-2828. FAX:
(717) 823-4523. Nexstar Broadcasting Group Inc.

WILF, Channel 53, FOX
(see WOLF, Scranton). Williamsport, PA. Pegasus Broadcast
Television Inc.

WPMT Channel 43, FOX
2005 S. Queen St., York, PA 17403. (717) 843-0043. FAX: (717)
843-9741. Tribune Broadcasting.

RHODE ISLAND

WJAR (Providence), Channel 10, NBC
23 Kenney Rd., Cranston, RI 02920. (401) 455-9100. FAX: (401)
455-9168. NBC Inc.

WLWC (Providence), Channel 28, IND
23 Kenney Rd., Cranston, RI 02920. (401) 455-9100. Fant
Broadcasting Inc.

WLNE Channel 6, ABC
10 Orms St., Providence, RI 02904. (401) 453-8000. FAX: (401)
453-8088. Freedom Communications Inc.

WNAC-TV, Channel 64, FOX
25 Catamore Blvd. E., Providence, RI 02914-1203. (401)
438-7200. FAX: (401) 434-3761. Hicks, Muse, Tate & Furst Inc.

WOST-TV (Block Island), Channel 69, IND
201 Power St., Providence, RI 02906. (401) 455-0162. FAX:
(401) 466-5222. Paxson Communications Corp.

WPRI-TV, Channel 12, CBS
25 Catamore Blvd., E. Providence, RI 02914-1203. (401)
438-7200. FAX: (401) 434-3761. Clear Channel
Communications.

WSBE-TV, Channel 36, PBS
50 Park Ln., Providence, RI 02907. (401) 277-3636. FAX: (401)
277-3407. Rhode Island Public Telecomm.

SOUTH CAROLINA

WFBC-TV, Channel 40, IND
(see WLOS-TV, Greenville). Anderson, SC. (864) 297-1313.
FAX: (864) 297-8085. Sinclair Broadcast Group Inc.

WJWJ-TV, Channel 16, PBS
PO Box 1165, Beaufort, SC 29901. (803) 524-0808. FAX: (803)
524-1016. South Carolina Educational Television Commission.
Michael Brannen.

WCSC-TV, Channel 5, CBS
PO Box 186, 485 E. Bay St., Charleston, SC 29402. (803)
723-8371. FAX: (803) 723-0074. William E. Blackwell.

WITV, Channel 7, PBS
(see South Carolina Educational Television Commission,
Columbia). Charleston, SC. South Carolina Educational TV Comm.

WTAT-TV, Channel 34, FOX
4301 Arco Ln., Charleston, SC 29418. (803) 744-2424. FAX:
(803) 554-9649. Sinclair Broadcast Group Inc.

WFVT (Rock Hill, SC), Channel 55, WB
3501 Performance Rd., Charlotte, NC 28214. (704) 398-0046.
FAX: (704) 393-6034. Wharton Winstead.

South Carolina Educational Television Commission, PBS
PO Box 11000, Columbia, SC 29211. (803) 737-3200. FAX:
(803) 737-5000. South Carolina Educational TV Comm.

WACH-TV, Channel 57, FOX
1400 Pickens St., Columbia, SC 29201. (803) 252-5757. FAX:
(803) 212-7270. Raycom Media Inc.

WEBA-TV (Allendale), Channel 14, IND
Box 11000, 1101 George Rogers Blvd., Columbia, SC 29211-
1000. (803) 737-3390. FAX: (803) 737-3542. SC Educational
Television Commission.

WIS, Channel 10, NBC
1111 Bull St., Columbia, SC 29201. (803) 799-1010. FAX: (803)
758-1155. Cosmos Broadcasting Corp.

WLTX, Channel 19, CBS
6027 DeVine St., Columbia, SC 29209. (803) 776-3600. FAX:
(803) 783-2971. Gannett Broadcasting.

WOLO-TV, Channel 25, ABC
5807 Shakespeare Rd., Columbia, SC 29240. (803) 754-7525.
FAX: (803) 754-6147. South Carolina Broadcasting Partners.

WRLK-TV, Channel 35, PBS
1101 George Rogers Blvd., Columbia, SC 29201. (803)
737-3200. FAX: (803) 737-3417. South Carolina Educational
Television Commission.

WHMC, Channel 23, PBS
(see South Carolina Educational Television Commission,
Columbia). Conway, SC. South Carolina Educational TV Comm.

WBTW, Channel 13, CBS, WB
3430 N. TV Rd., Florence, SC 29501-0013. (803) 317-1313.
FAX: (803) 317-1410. Spartan Radiocasting.

WJPM-TV, Channel 33, PBS
(see South Carolina Educational Television Comm., Columbia).
Florence, SC. South Carolina Educational Television Comm.

WPDE-TV, Channel 15, ABC
3215 S. Cashua Dr., Florence, SC 29501-6386. (803) 665-1515.
FAX: (803) 679-2723. Diversified Communications.

WWMB, Channel 21, UPN
3215 S. Cashua Dr., Florence, SC 29501. (803) 679-5487. FAX:
(803) 665-2709. C. Lenoir Sturkie.

WGGS-TV, Channel 16, IND
PO Box 1616, Greenville, SC 29602. (864) 244-1616. FAX: (864)
292-8481. James H. Thompson.

WHNS, Channel 21, FOX
21 Interstate Ct., Greenville, SC 29615. (864) 288-2100. FAX:
(864) 297-0728. Meredith Broadcasting Group.

WLOS-TV, Channel 13, ABC
288 Macon Ave., Greenville, SC 28804. (704) 255-0013. FAX:
(704) 255-4612. Sinclair Broadcast Group Inc.

WNTV, Channel 29, PBS
(see South Carolina Educational Television Commission,
Columbia). Greenville, SC. South Carolina Educational Television
Commission.

WSPA-TV, Channel 7, CBS
250 International Dr., Greenville, SC 29304. (864) 576-7777.
FAX: (864) 587-4480. Spartan Radiocasting Co.

WYFF, Channel 4, NBC
505 Rutherford St., Greenville, SC 29602. (864) 242-4404. FAX:
(864) 240-5329. Hearst-Argyle Television Inc.

WNEH, Channel 38, PBS
(see South Carolina Educational Television Commission,
Columbia). Greenwood, SC. South Carolina Educational
Television Commission.

WCBD-TV (Charleston), Channel 2, NBC
210 W. Coleman Blvd., Mt. Pleasant, SC 29464. (803) 884-2222.
FAX: (803) 881-3410. Media General Broadcast Group.

WCIV (Charleston), Channel 4, NBC
888 Allbritton Blvd., Mt. Pleasant, SC 29464. (803) 881-4444.
FAX: (803) 849-2507. Allbritton Communications Co.

WMMP-TV (Charleston), Channel 36, UPN
Bldg. A, 1558 Ben Sawyer Blvd., Mt. Pleasant, SC 29464. (803)
884-3185. FAX: (803) 849-1434. Sinclair Broadcast Group Inc.

WFXB, Channel 43, FOX
PO Box 8309, Myrtle Beach, SC 29578. (803) 828-4300. FAX:
(803) 828-4343. J.M.E. Media Inc.

WNSC-TV, Channel 30, PBS
PO Box 11766, Rock Hill, SC 29731. (803) 324-3184. FAX: (803)
324-0580. South Carolina Educational Television Commission.

WTGS (Hardeeville, SC), Channel 28, FOX
10001 Abercorn Street, Savannah, GA 31406. (912) 925-2287.
FAX: (912) 925-8621. Brissette Broadcasting of Savannah.

WRET-TV, Channel 49, PBS
PO Box 4069, Media Bldg., UCSC, 800 University Way,
Spartanburg, SC 29305-4069. (864) 503-9371. FAX: (864) 503-
3615. South Carolina Educational Television Commission.

WQHB, Channel 63, IND
500 Myrtle Beach Hwy., Sumter, SC 29150. (803) 775-2817.
McLaughlin Broadcasting Inc.

WRJA-TV, Channel 27, PBS
18 N. Marvin St., Sumter, SC 29150. (803) 773-5546. FAX: (803)
775-1059. South Carolina Educational Television Commission.

SOUTH DAKOTA

KABY-TV, Channel 9, ABC
PO Box 1520, Aberdeen, SD 57401. (605) 225-9200. FAX: (605)
225-9226. Raycom Media Inc.

KDSD-TV, Channel 16, PBS
(see KUSD, Vermillion). Aberdeen, SD. SD Board of Directors for
Educational Television.

KESD-TV, Channel 8, PBS
(see KUSD, Vermillion). Brookings, SD. SD Board of Directors for
Educational Television.

KPSD-TV, Channel 13, PBS
(see KUSD, Vermillion). Eagle Butte, SD. SD Board of Directors
for Educational Television.

KDLO-TV, Channel 3, CBS
(see KELO, Sioux Falls). Florence, SD. Young Broadcasting Inc..

KHSD-TV, Channel 11, ABC
(see KOTA, Rapid City). Lead, SD. Duhamel Broadcasting
Enterprises.

KIVV-TV, Channel 5, FOX
(see KEVN, Rapid City)., Lead, SD. USA Broadcasting Inc.

KQSD-TV, Channel 11, PBS
(see KUSD, Vermillion). Lowry, SD. SD Board of Directors for
Educational Television.

KZSD-TV, Channel 8, PBS
(see KUSD, Vermillion). Martin, SD. SD Board of Directors for
Educational Television.

KPRY-TV, Channel 4, ABC
(see KSFY, Sioux Falls). Pierre, SD. Raycom Media Inc.

KTSD-TV, Channel 10, PBS
(see KUSD Vermillion). Pierre, SD. SD Board of Directors for
Educational Television.

KBHE-TV, Channel 9, PBS
(see KUSD Vermillion). Rapid City, SD. SD Board of Directors for
Educational Television.

KCLO-TV, Channel 15, CBS
2497 W. Chicago St., Rapid City, SD 57702. (605) 341-1500.
FAX: (605) 348-5518. Young Broadcasting Inc.

KEVN, Channel 7, FOX
PO Box 677, Rapid City, SD 57709. (605) 394-7777. FAX: (605)
348-9128. USA Broadcasting Inc.

KOTA-TV, Channel 3, ABC
PO Box 1760, Rapid City, SD 57709-1760. (605) 342-2000. FAX:
(605) 342-7305. Duhamel Broadcasting Enterprises.

KPLO-TV, Channel 6, CBS
(see KELO, Sioux Falls). Reliance, SD. Young Broadcasting Inc..

KCSD-TV, Channel 23, PBS
(see KUSD Vermillion). Sioux Falls, SD. SD Board of Directors
for Educational Television.

KDLT (Mitchell), Channel 5, NBC
3600 S. Westport Ave., Sioux Falls, SD 57116-0196. (605)
361-5555. FAX: (605) 361-3982. Red River Broadcast Corp.

KELO-TV, Channel 11, CBS
501 S. Phillips, Sioux Falls, SD 57104. (605) 336-1100. FAX:
(605) 334-3447. Young Broadcasting Inc.

KSFY-TV, Channel 13, ABC
300 N. Dakota Ave., Ste. 1000, Sioux Falls, SD 57104. (605)
336-1300. FAX: (605) 336-3468. Raycom Media Inc.

KTTM (Huron), Channel 12, FOX
PO Box 5103, Sioux Falls, SD 57117-5103. (605) 338-0017.
FAX: (605) 338-7173. Independent Communications Inc.

KTTW, Channel 17, FOX, UPN
PO Box 5103, Sioux Falls, SD 57117-5103. (605) 338-0017.
FAX: (605) 338-7173. Independent Communications Inc. Ed
Hoffman.

KUSD-TV, Channel 2, PBS
PO Box 5000, Cherry & Dakota Sts., Vermillion, SD 57069-5000.
(605) 677-5861. FAX: (605) 677-5010. SD Board of Directors for
Educational Television.

TENNESSEE

WDEF-TV, Channel 12, CBS
3300 Broad St., Chattanooga TN 37408. (423) 785-1200. FAX:
(423) 785-1271. Media General Broadcast Group.

WDSI-TV, Channel 61, FOX
1101 E. Main St., Chattanooga, TN 37408. (615) 265-0061. FAX:
(615) 265-3636. Pegasus Broadcast TV Inc.

WRCB-TV, Channel 3, NBC
900 Whitehall Rd., Chattanooga, TN 37405-3247. (423)
267-5412. FAX: (423) 267-6840. Sarkes Tarzian Inc.

WTCI, Channel 45, PBS
4411 Amnicola Hwy., Chattanooga, TN 37406. (423) 629-0045.
FAX: (423) 698-8557. The Greater Chattanooga PTV Corp.

WTVC, Channel 9, ABC
PO Box 1150, Chattanooga, TN 37401. (423) 756-5500. FAX:
(423) 757-7400. Freedom Communications Inc.

WFLI-TV (Cleveland), Channel 53, UPN
PO Box 302, 4654 Cohutta-Varnell Rd., Cohutta, GA 30710,
(706) 694-3337. FAX: (706) 694-4112. Lambert Broadcasting of
Tennessee.

WCTE, Channel 22, PBS
PO Box 2040, Cookeville, TN 38502. (615) 528-2222. FAX: (615)
372-6284. Upper Cumberland Broadcast Council.

WBXX-TV, Channel 20, IND
PO Box 608, Crossville, TN 38555. (615) 484-6508. Acme
Television Licenses of Tennessee.

WPGD, Channel 50, IND
36 Music Village Blvd., Hendersonville, TN 37075. (615)
822-1243. FAX: (615) 822-1642. All American TV Inc.

WBBJ-TV, Channel 7, ABC, FOX
346 Muse St., Jackson, TN 38301. (901) 424-4515. FAX: (901)
424-9299. Tennessee Broadcasting Partners.

WPMC, Channel 54, NFP
PO Box 54, 231 Huddleston Cemetary Ln. Jellico TN 37762.
(423) 784-7854. FAX: (423) 784-9536. Global Broadcasting
Systems Inc.

WEMT-TV (Tri-Cities), Channel 39, FOX
3206 Hanover Rd., Johnson City, TN 37601. (423) 283-3900.
FAX: (423) 283-4938. Sinclair Broadcast Group Inc.

WJHL-TV, Channel 11, CBS
PO Box 1130, Johnson City, TN 37605. (423) 926-2151. FAX:
(423) 434-4537. Media General Broadcast Group.

WKPT-TV, Channel 19, ABC
222 Commerce St., Kingsport, TN 37660. (423) 246-9578. FAX:
(423) 246-6261. Glenwood Communications Corp. J. Raymond
Walker.

WATE-TV, Channel 6, ABC
PO Box 2349-37901, 1306 N.E. Broadway, Knoxville, TN 37917.
(423) 637-6666. FAX: (423 525-4091. Young Broadcasting Inc.

WBIR-TV, Channel 10, NBC
1513 Hutchison Ave., Knoxville, TN 37917. (423) 637-1010. FAX:
(423) 637-6280. Gannett Broadcasting.

WKOP-TV, Channel 15, PBS
1661 E. Magnolia Ave., Knoxville, TN 37917. (423) 595-0220.
FAX: (423) 595-0300. E. Tennessee Public Comm. Corp.

WTNZ, Channel 43, FOX
Bldg. D, Suite 300, 9000 Executive Park Dr., Knoxville, TN
37923. (423) 693-4343. FAX: (423) 691-6904. Raycom Media
Inc.

WVLT-TV, Channel 8, CBS
PO Box 59088, Knoxville, TN 37950. (423) 450-8888. FAX: (423)
450-8869. Gray Communications Systems Inc.

WJFB, Channel 66, IND
200 E. Spring St., Lebanon, TN 37087. (615) 444-8206. FAX:
(615) 444-7592. Bryant Communications Inc.

WLJT-TV (Lexington), Channel 11, PBS
U.T.-Martin, Clement Hall, Martin, TN 38238. (901) 587-7561.
FAX: (901) 587-7566. W. Tennessee Public TV Council Inc.

WFBI, Channel 50, HSN
c/o Film Broadcasting Corp., 6080 Mt. Mariah, Memphis, TN
38115. (901) 375-9324. FAX: (901) 795-4454. Paxson
Communications Corp.

WHBQ-TV, Channel 13, FOX
485 S. Highland St., Memphis, TN 38111. (901) 320-1313. FAX:
(901) 323-0092. Fox Television Stations Inc.

WKNO-TV, Channel 10, PBS
900 Getwell Rd., Memphis, TN 38111. (901) 458-2521. FAX:
(901) 452-2221. Mid-South Public Communications.

WLMT Channel 30, UPN
Clear Channel TV Ctr. 2701 Union Ext., Memphis, TN 38112.
(901) 323-2430. FAX: (901) 323-9503. Max Media.

WMC-TV, Channel 5, NBC
1960 Union Ave., Memphis, TN 38104. (901) 726-0555. FAX:
(901) 276-6851. Raycom Media Inc.

WMTU, (Jackson) Channel 16, FOX
2701 Union Extension, Memphis, TN 38112. (901) 323-2430.
FAX: (901) 323-9503. Max Media.

WPTY-TV, Channel 24, ABC
PO Box 42087, Memphis, TN 38174. (901) 323-2430. FAX: (901)
323-9503. Clear Channel Communications Inc.

WREG-TV, Channel 3, CBS
803 Channel 3 Drive, Memphis, TN 38103. (901) 543-2333. FAX:
(901) 543-2198. The New York Times Co. Ronald A. Walter.

WKZX (Cookeville), Channel 28, IND
9330 Sand Springs Church Rd., Monterey, TN 38574. (615) 839-
6173. FAX: (615) 839-6172. Paxson Communications Corp.

WDCN, Channel 8, PBS
PO Box 120609, Nashville, TN 37212-0609. (615) 259-9325.
FAX: (615) 248-6120. Metropolitan Board of Public Ed.

WKRN-TV, Channel 2, ABC
441 Murfreesboro Rd., Nashville, TN 37210. (615) 259-2200.
FAX: (615) 248-7298. Young Broadcasting Inc..

WNAB, Channel 58, WB
3201 Dickerson Pike, Nashville, TN 37207. (615) 650-5858. FAX:
(615) 650-5859. Lambert Broadcasting of Nashville.

WSMV, Channel 4, NBC
5700 Knob Rd., Nashville, TN 37209. (615) 353-4444. FAX:
(615) 353-2343. Meredith Broadcasting Group.

WTVF, Channel 5, CBS
474 James Robertson Pkwy., Nashville, TN 37219. (615)
244-5000. FAX: (615) 248-5353. Landmark Communications Inc.
Debbie Turner.

WUXP-TV, Channel 30, UPN
631 Mainstream Dr., Nashville, TN 37228. (615) 259-5630. FAX:
(615) 259-3962. Sinclair Broadcast Group Inc.

WZTV-TV, Channel 17, FOX
631 Mainstream Dr., Nashville, TN 37228. (615) 244-1717. FAX:
(615) 259-396. Sullivan Broadcasting Co Inc.

WHTN (Murfreesboro), Channel 39, IND
14346 Lebanon Rd., Old Hickory, TN 37138. (615) 754-0037.
FAX: (615) 754-0047. Christian Television Network. Phil Scott.

WSJK-TV, Channel 2, PBS
(see WKOP, Knoxville). Sneedville, TN. E. Tennessse Public
Communications.

TEXAS

KRBC-TV, Channel 9, NBC
PO Box 178, Abilene, TX 79604. (915) 692-4242. FAX: (915)
692-8265. Hicks, Muse, Tate & Furst Inc.

KTAB-TV, Channel 32, CBS, UPN
5401 S. 14th St., Abilene, TX 79606. (915) 695-2777. FAX: (915)
695-9922. Alta Communications VI L.P.

KTXS-TV (Sweetwater), Channel 12, ABC
PO Box 2997, Abilene, TX 79604. (915) 677-2281. FAX: (915)
676-9231.Lamco Communications.

KACV-TV, Channel 2, PBS
2408 S. Jackson, Amarillo, TX 79109. (806) 371-5222. FAX:
(806) 371-5258. Amarillo Junior College District.

KAMR-TV, Channel 4, NBC
PO Box 751, Amarillo, TX 79189. (806) 383-3321. FAX: (806)
381-2943. Darrold Cannan Communications Inc.

KCIT, Channel 14, FOX
PO Box 1414, 1015 S. Fillmore, Amarillo, TX 79105. (806)
374-1414. FAX: (806) 371-0408. WBG License Co., LLC, Ken
Bowman.

KFDA-TV, Channel 10, CBS
PO Box 10, Amarillo, TX 79105-0010. (806) 383-1010. FAX:
(806) 383-6397. R.H. Drewry Group.

KVII-TV, Channel 7, ABC
One Broadcast Center, Amarillo, TX 79101. (806) 373-1787. FAX: (806) 371-7329. Marsh Media Inc.

KEYE-TV, Channel 42, CBS
10700 Metric Blvd., Austin, TX 78758. (512) 835-0042. FAX: (512) 837-6753. Granite Broadcasting Corp.

KLRU-TV, Channel 18, PBS
PO Box 7158, Austin, TX 78713. (512) 471-4811. FAX: (512) 475-9090. Capital of TX Public Broadcasting. Bill Arhos.

KNVA-TV, Channel 54, WB
PO Box 684647, Austin, TX 78768. (512) 478-5400. FAX: (512) 476-1520. 54 Broadcasting Inc.

KTBC-TV, Channel 7, FOX
119 E. 10th St., Austin, TX 78701. (512) 476-7777. FAX: (512) 495-7001. Fox Television Stations Inc.

KVUE-TV, Channel 24, ABC
3201 Steck Ave., Austin, TX 78757. (512) 459-6521. FAX: (512) 467-7503. Gannett Broadcasting.

KXAN-TV, Channel 36, NBC
908 W. Martin Luther King Blvd., Austin, TX 78701. (512) 476-3636. FAX: (512) 476-1520. Hicks, Muse, Tate & Furst.

KBMT, Channel 12, ABC
PO Box 1550, 525 I-10 S. Beaumont, TX 77704. (409) 833-7512. FAX: (409) 833-4007. McKinnon Broadcasting Co.

KFDM-TV, Channel 6, CBS, UPN
PO Box 7128, 2955 I-10 E., Beaumont, TX 77726-7128. (409) 892-6622. FAX: (409) 892-6665. Freedom Communications Inc.

KWAB, Channel 4, IND
2500 Kentucky Way, Big Spring, TX 79720. (915) 263-4901. FAX: (915) 263-4901. Midessa Television. John Foster.

KVEO, Channel 23, NBC, UPN
394 N. Expressway, Brownsville, TX 78521. (956) 544-2323. FAX: (956) 544-4636. Tom Galloway.

KBTX-TV, Channel 3, CBS
Drawer 3730, 4141 E. 29th Str., Bryan, TX 77805. (409) 846-7777. FAX: (409) 846-1490. KWTX Broadcasting Co.

KYLE, Channel 28, FOX
Ste. B-101, 2402 Bradmoor Dr., Bryan, TX 77802. (409) 774-1800. FAX: (409) 774-1901. Comcorp of License Corp.

KAMU-TV, Channel 15, PBS
Texas A & M University, College Station, TX 77843. (409) 845-5611. FAX: (409) 845-1643. Texas A&M University. Rodney L. Zent.

KHIM-TV, Channel 55, IND
23 Deep Water, Conroe, TX 77356. Dowen Johnson.

KEDT, Channel 16, PBS
Ste. 38, 4455 S. Padre Island Dr., Corpus Christi, TX 78411. (512) 855-2213. FAX: (512) 855-3877. South Texas Public Broadcasting.

KIII, Channel 3, ABC
PO Box 6669, 4750 S. Padre Island Dr., Corpus Christi, TX 78466. (512) 854-4733. FAX: (512) 855-8419. McKinnon Broadcasting Co.

KORO, Channel 28, UNI
102 N. Mesquite, Corpus Christi, TX 78401. (512) 883-2823. FAX: (512) 883-2931. Entravision Communications Co. Suzel Meadieta.

KRIS-TV, Channel 6, NBC
PO Box 840, Corpus Christi, TX 78403. (512) 886-6100. FAX: (512) 887-6666. T. Frank Smith, Jr.

KZTV, Channel 10, CBS
PO Box TV-10, 301 Artesian, Corpus Christi, TX 78403. (512) 883-7070. FAX: (512) 882-8553. Corpus Christi Broadcasting Inc. James W. Bixler.

KDAF, Channel 33, WB
8001 Carpenter Fwy., Dallas, TX 75247. (214) 640-3300. FAX: (214) 640-3409. Tribune Broadcasting.

KDFI-TV, Channel 27, IND
400 N. Griffin St., Dallas, TX 75202. (214) 720-3849. FAX: (214) 720-3263. Fox Television Stations Inc. Mark Demopoulos.

KDFW-TV, Channel 4, FOX
400 N. Griffin St., Dallas, TX 75202. (214) 720-4444. FAX: (214) 720-3177. Fox Television Stations Inc.

KERA-TV, Channel 13, PBS
3000 Harry Hines Blvd., Dallas, TX 75201. (214) 871-1390. FAX: (214) 754-0635. North Texas Public Broadcasting Inc.

KMPX (Decatur), Channel 29, NFP
PO Box 612066, Dallas, TX 75261. (214) 432-0029. FAX: (214) 432-0650.Community Television Educators.

KTXA (Fort Worth), Channel 21, UPN
Ste. 700, 601 Pacific Ave., Dallas, TX 75202. (214) 743-2100. FAX: (214) 763-2121. Paramount Stations Group Inc.

KUVN, Channel 23, UNI
Ste. 1900, 2323 Bryan St., Dallas, TX 75201. (214) 758-2300. FAX: (214) 758-2324. Univision Television Group, Inc.

KXTX, Channel 39, IND
PO Box 190307, 3900 Harry Hines Blvd., Dallas, TX 75219. (214) 521-3900. FAX: (214) 533-5946. Hicks, Muse, Tate & Furst Inc.

WFAA-TV, Channel 8, ABC
Communication Ctr., 606 Young St., Dallas, TX 75202-4810. (214) 748-9631. FAX: (214) 977-6268. A.H. Belo Corp.

KTRG (Del Rio), Channel 10, IND
PO Box 276, River Road 1120, Concan, TX 78838. (210) 232-6700. FAX: (210) 232-6700. Thomas Gilchrist, Robert Gilchrist.

KTEN (Ada, OK), Channel 10, ABC
101 E. Main St., Denison, TX 75020. (903) 465-5836. FAX: (903) 465-5859. Channel 49 Acquisition Corporation.

KDTN, Channel 2, PBS
(see KERA, Dallas). Denton, TX. Community Board of Directors.

KVAW, Channel 16, IND
PO Box 788, Eagle Pass, TX 78852. (210) 757-0316. Juan Wheeler, Jr.

KCOS, Channel 13, PBS
Rm. 105 Education Bldg., Univ of Texas-El Paso, El Paso, TX 79902. (915) 747-6500. FAX: (915) 747-6605. El Paso Public TV Foundation.

KDBC-TV, Channel 4, CBS
2201 Wyoming, El Paso, TX 79903. (915) 532-6551. FAX: (915) 544-2591. Imes Communications. Jim Grimes.

KFOX-TV, Channel 14, FOX
6004 N. Mesa, El Paso, TX 79912. (915) 833-8585. FAX: (915) 833-8942. Cox Broadcasting Inc.

KINT-TV, Channel 26, UNI
5426 N. Mesa, El Paso, TX 79912. (915) 581-1126. FAX: (915) 581-1393. Entravision Comm. Co.

KKWB-TV, Channel 65, IND
5925 Cromo Dr., El Paso, TX 79912. (915) 833-0065. FAX: (915) 584-8005. White Knight Broadcasting.

KSCE, Channel 38, NFP
6400 Escondido Dr., El Paso, TX 79912. (915) 585-8838. FAX: (915) 533-7403. Channel 38 Christian Television.

KTSM-TV, Channel 9, NBC
801 N. Oregon St., El Paso, TX 79902. (915) 532-5421. FAX: (915) 532-6793. Associated Broadcasters Inc.

KVIA-TV, Channel 7, ABC
4140 Rio Bravo, El Paso, TX 79902. (915) 532-7777. FAX: (915) 532-0070. NPG of Texas L.P.

KTVT, Channel 11, CBS
5233 Bridge St., Fort Worth, TX 76103. (817) 451-1111. FAX: (817) 457-1897. Gaylord Broadcasting Co.

KXAS-TV (Dallas), Channel 5, NBC
3900 Barnett, Fort Worth, TX 76103. (817) 536-5555. FAX: (817) 654-6362. NBC Inc.

KTAQ, Channel 47, IND
PO Box 8547, Greeneville, TX 75404. (903) 455-8847. FAX: (903) 455-8891. Mike Simons.

KGBT-TV, Channel 4, CBS
9201 W. Expressway 83, Harlingen, TX 78552. (210) 421-4444. FAX: (210) 421-2318. Draper Communications Inc.

KLUJ, Channel 44, IND
1920 Al Coneway Dr., Harlingen, TX 78550. (956) 425-4225. FAX: (956) 412-1740. Community Educational TV Inc.

KMBH, Channel 60, PBS
1701 Tennessee St., Harlingen, TX 78550. (956) 421-4111. FAX: (956) 421-4150. RGV Educational Broadcasting Inc.

KETH, Channel 14, IND
10902 S. Wilcrest Dr., Houston, TX 77099. (281) 561-5828. FAX: (281) 561-9793. Community Educational TV of Houston.

KHOU-TV, Channel 11, CBS
1945 Allen Pkwy., Houston, TX 77019. (713) 526-1111. FAX: (713) 521-4326. A.H. Belo Corp.

KHSH-TV, Channel 67, HSN
10849 Kinghurst Dr., #130, Houston, TX 77099. (281) 933-8867.
USA Broadcasting Inc.

KHTV, Channel 39, WB
7700 Westpark Dr., Houston, TX 77063. (713) 781-3939. FAX:
(713) 781-3441. Tribune Broadcasting.

KLDT (Lake Dallas), Channel 55, IND
c/o KNWS-TV 8440 Westpark, Houston, TX 77063. (713) 974-
5151. Douglas Johnson.

KLTJ (Galveston), Channel 22, IND
1050 Gemini, Houston, TX 77058. (713) 212-1077. FAX: (713)
212-1022. GO Inc. Andrew Bless.

KNWS-TV (Katy), Channel 51, IND
8440 Westpark, Houston, TX 77063. (713) 974-5151. FAX: (713)
975-6397. Johnson Broadcasting

KPRC-TV, Channel 2, NBC
8181 Southwest Fwy., Houston, TX 77074. (713) 222-2222. FAX:
(713) 270-9334. Post-Newsweek Stations.

KPXB (Conroe), Channel 49, IND
Ste. 49, 256 N. Sam Pkwy. E, Houston, TX 77060. (281) 820-
4900. FAX: (281) 820-4048. Paxson Communications Corp.

KRIV, Channel 26, FOX
3935 Westheimer Rd., Houston, TX 77027. (713) 626-2610.
FAX: (713) 625-1907. Fox Television Stations Inc.

KTMD (Galveston), Channel 48, TEL
3903 Stoney Brook, Houston, TX 77063. (713) 974-4848. FAX:
(713) 974-5875. Telemundo Group Inc.

KTRK-TV, Channel 13, ABC
3310 Bissonnet Rd., Houston, TX 77005. (713) 666-0713. FAX:
(713) 668-0024. ABC Inc.

KTXH, Channel 20, UPN
8950 Kirby Dr., Houston, TX 77054. (713) 661-2020. FAX: (713)
665-3909. Paramount Stations Group Inc.

KUHT, Channel 8, PBS
4513 Cullen Blvd., Houston, TX 77004. (713) 748-8888. FAX:
(713) 749-8216. U of Houston, Board of Regents.

KVVV (Baytown), Channel 57, IND
1044 Hercules Ln., Houston, TX 77058. (713) 286-4245. FAX:
(713) 286-4541. VVI Baytown Inc.

KXLN-TV, Channel 45, UNI
9440 Kirby Dr., Houston, TX 77054. (713) 662-4545. FAX: (713)
668-9054. Univision Television Group, Inc.

KZJL, Channel 61, IND
1995 Ste. 1850, 1800 West Loop S., Houston, TX 77027. Urban
Broadcasting Systems Inc.

KDTX-TV (Dallas), Channel 58, IND
2823 W. Irving Blvd., Irving, TX 75061-4236. (214) 313-1333.
FAX: (214) 790-5853. Trinity Broadcasting of Texas Inc.

KFWD (Fort Worth), Channel 52, TEL
3000 W. Story Rd., Irving, TX 75038. (972) 255-5200. FAX: (972)
258-1770. Interspan Communications L.P.

KHSX-TV (Dallas), Channel 49, HSN
1957 E. Irving Blvd., Irving, TX 75060. (214) 579-4900. FAX:
(214) 579-1105. USA Broadcasting Inc.

KPXD (Arlington), Channel 68, IND
800 W Airport Fwy., Irving, TX 75062. (972) 438-6868. Paxson
Communications Corp.

KRRT-TV (San Antonio), Channel 35, WB
(see KABB-TV, San Antonio). Kerrville, TX. Glencairn Ltd..

KAKW, Channel 55, IND
904 E. Veterans Memorial Blvd., Killeen, TX 76542. (254) 554-
6266. FAX: (254) 554-6316. White Knight Broadcasting.

KNCT (Belton), Channel 46, PBS
PO Box 1800, Killeen, TX 76540-1800. (817) 526-1176. FAX:
(817) 526-4000. Central Texas College.

KGNS-TV, Channel 8, NBC, ABC, UPN
PO Box 2829, 120 W. Del Mar Blvd., Laredo, TX 78045. (210)
727-8888. FAX: (210) 727-5336. Malcolm Glazer Trust.

KLDO-TV, Channel 27, UNI
Riverdrive Mall, 1600 Water St., Laredo, TX 78040. (956) 727-0027.
FAX: (956) 727-2673. Entravision Communications Co.

KVTV, Channel 13, CBS
PO Box 2039, 2600 Shea & Ana, Laredo, TX 78041. (210)
723-2923. FAX: (210) 723-0474. K-SIX TV Inc.

KXAM-TV, Channel 14, NBC
Box 490, Austin, TX 78767. (512) 476-3636. FAX: (512) 476-
1520. KXAN Inc.

KFXK, Channel 51, FOX
701 N. Access Rd., Longview, TX 75602. (903) 236-0051. FAX:
(903) 753-6637. White Knight Broadcasting Inc.

KAMC, Channel 28, ABC
1201 84th St., Lubbock, TX 79423. (806) 745-2828. FAX: (806)
748-1080. McAlister TV Enterprises Inc. A.C. Wimberly.

KCBD-TV, Channel 11, NBC
5600 Avenue A, Lubbock, TX 79404. (806) 744-1414. FAX: (806)
744-0449. Holsum Inc. Craig Wells.

KJTV, Channel 34, FOX
9800 University Ave., Lubbock, TX 79423. (806) 745-3434. FAX:
(806) 748-1949. Raymar Communications Inc.

KLBK-TV, Channel 13, CBS
7400 S. University Ave., Lubbock, TX 79423. (806) 745-2345.
FAX: (806) 748-2250. Quorum Broadcasting.

KMZN (Farwell), Channel 18, IND
PO Box 3757, Lubbock, TX 79452. Ramar Communications Inc.

KTXT-TV, Channel 5, PBS
PO Box 42161, Tech Stn., 17th St. & Indiana Ave., Lubbock, TX
79409-2161. (806) 742-2209. FAX: (806) 742-1274. Texas Tech
University.

KTRE, Channel 9, ABC
PO Box 729, Lufkin, TX 75902. (409) 853-5873. FAX: (409)
853-3084. Civic Communication Corp.

KITU (Beaumont), Channel 34, IND
PO Box 158, Mauriceville, TX 77626. (409) 745-3434. FAX: (409)
745-4752. Community Educational TV Inc.

KNVO, Channel 48, UNI
Ste. 850, 1800 S. Main St., McAllen, TX 78503. (210) 687-4848.
FAX: (210) 687-7784. Entravision Communications Co.

KMID, Channel 2, ABC
PO Box 60230, 3200 Laforce Blvd., Midland, TX 79711. (915)
563-2222. FAX: (915) 563-5819. GOCOM Television.

KPCB (Snyder), Channel 17, IND
Box 61000, Midland, TX 79711-1000. (915) 573-9517. FAX:
(915) 573-9417. Prime Time Christian Broadcasting.

KPTB (Lubbock), Channel 16, NFP
PO Box 61000, Midland, TX 79711. Primetime Christian
Broadcasting.

KLSB-TV (Tyler/Longview), Channel 19, NBC
204 W. Main St., Nacogdoches, TX 75961. (409) 564-1911. FAX:
(409) 569-1595. Sinclair Broadcast Group Inc.

KMLM, Channel 42, NFP
PO Box 61000, Odessa, TX 79711. (915) 563-0420. FAX: (915)
563-1736. Prime Time Christian Broadcasting. Jeff Welter.

KOCV-TV, Channel 36, PBS
201 W. University, Odessa, TX 79764. (915) 335-6336. FAX:
(915) 339-0529. Odessa Junior College District.

KOSA-TV, Channel 7, CBS
1211 N. Whitaker, Odessa, TX 79760. (915) 580-5672. FAX:
(915) 580-8010. Benedek Broadcasting Corp.

KPEJ, Channel 24, FOX, UPN
1550 W. I-20, Odessa, TX 79763. (915) 337-2424. FAX: (915)
337-3707. Communications Corp. of America.

KWES-TV, Channel 9, NBC
PO Box 60150, 11320 County Rd., 127 W. Midland, Odessa, TX
79711-0150. (915) 567-9999. FAX: (915) 567-9992. R.H. Drewry
Group.

KJAC-TV (Beaumont), Channel 4, NBC
PO .Box 3257, Port Arthur, TX 77643. (409) 985-5557. FAX:
(409) 832-2444. Nexstar Broadcasting Management.

KACB-TV, Channel 3, NBC
(see KRBC, Abilene); San Angelo, TX. Hicks, Muse, Tate & Furst
Inc.

KIDY, Channel 6, FOX
406 S. Irving, San Angelo, TX 76903. (915) 655-6006. FAX:
(915) 655-8461. Dane Patricia Schinder.

KLST, Channel 8, CBS
2800 Armstrong, San Angelo, TX 76903. (915) 949-8800. FAX:
(915) 658-4006. Jewell Television Corp.

KABB-TV, Channel 29, FOX
4335 N.W. Loop 410, San Antonio, TX 78229-5168. (210)
366-1129. FAX: (210) 377-4758.Sinclair Broadcast Group Inc.

KENS-TV, Channel 5, CBS
5400 Fredericksburg Rd., San Antonio, TX 78229. (210) 366-5000. FAX: (210) 377-0740. A.H. Belo Corp.

KHCE, Channel 23, IND
326 Sterling Browning Dr., San Antonio, TX 78232. (210) 496-2323. Community Educational Television Inc.

KLRN, Channel 9, PBS
501 Broadway, San Antonio, TX 78215. (210) 270-9000. FAX: (210) 270-9078. Alamo Public Telecomm. Council.

KMOL-TV, Channel 4, NBC
1031 Navarro, San Antonio, TX 78205. (210) 226-4444. FAX: (210) 223-5693. Chris-Craft Industries, Inc./BHC Communications Inc./United Television Inc.

KSAT-TV, Channel 12, ABC
1408 N. St. Mary's St., San Antonio, TX 78215. (210) 351-1200. FAX: (210) 351-1297. Post-Newsweek Stations.

KVDA, Channel 60, TEL
6234 San Pedro, San Antonio, TX 78216. (210) 340-8860. FAX: (210) 341-3962. Telemundo Group Inc.

KWEX-TV, Channel 41, UNI
411 E. Durango Blvd., San Antonio, TX 78204. (210) 227-4141. FAX: (210) 227-0469. Univision Television Group, Inc.

KXII, Channel 12, CBS
PO Box 1175, 4201 Texoma Pkwy., Sherman, TX 75090. (903) 892-8123. FAX: (903) 893-7858. KXII Broadcasters Inc.

KCEN-TV, Channel 6, NBC
17 S. Third, Temple, TX 76501-6103. (817) 773-6868. FAX: (817) 770-0204. Anyse Sue Mayborn, Gayle Kiger.

KETK-TV (Jacksonville), Channel 56, NBC
4300 Richmond Rd., Tyler, TX 75703. (903) 581-5656. FAX: (903) 561-1648. Sinclair Broadcast Group Inc.

KLTV, Channel 7, ABC
105 West Ferguson, Tyler, TX 75702. (903) 597-5588. FAX: (903) 510-7847. Civic Communication Corp.

KAVU-TV, Channel 25, ABC
Box 4929, 3808 N. Navarro, Victoria, TX 77901. (512) 575-2500. FAX: (512) 575-2255.Saga Communications Inc.

KCTF, Channel 34, PBS
Sid Richardson Biology Bldg., Baylor Univ., Waco TX 76798. (254) 710-3472. FAX: (254) 710-3874. Brazos Valley Pub. Broadcasting.

KWKT, Channel 44, FOX
8803 Woodway Dr., Waco TX 76712. (254) 776-3844. FAX: (254) 776-8032. Communications Corp. of America.

KWTX-TV, Channel 10, CBS
6700 American Plaza, Waco TX 76712. (254) 776-1330. FAX: (254) 751-1088. KWTX Broadcasting Co.

KXXV, Channel 25, ABC
1909 S. New Rd., Waco TX 76711. (254) 754-2525. FAX: (254) 752-1002. R.H. Drewry Group.

KRGV-TV, Channel 5, ABC
900 E. Expwy. 83, Weslaco TX 78596. (956) 968-5555. FAX: (956) 973-5001. Manship Stations.

KAUZ-TV, Channel 6, CBS
One Broadcast Ave., Wichita Falls, TX 76307. (940) 322-6957. FAX: (940) 761-3331. Benedek Broadcasting Corp.

KFDX-TV, Channel 3, NBC
4500 Seymour Hwy., Wichita Falls, TX 76309. (940) 691-0003. FAX: (940) 691-0330. Nexstar Broadcasting Management.

KJTL, Channel 18, FOX
PO Box 4865, 3800 Call Field Rd., Wichita Falls, TX 76308. (817) 691-1808. FAX: (817) 696-5766. Wicks Broadcast Group.

KVCT (Victoria), Channel 29, FOX
980 FM 1746, Woodville, TX 75979-9609. (409) 429-3679. FAX: (409) 429-5257. Dana R. Withers.

UTAH

KOOG-TV, Channel 30, WB
1209 16th St., Ogden, UT 84404. (801) 621-3030. FAX: (801) 394-1451. Paxson Communications Corp.

KULC, Channel 9, PBS
(see KUED, Salt Lake City). Ogden, UT. (801) 581-4194. FAX: (801) 585-6105. Utah State Board of Regents.

KBYU-TV, Channel 11, PBS
2000 E. Ironto Blvd., Provo, UT 84606. (801) 378-8450. FAX: (801) 378-8478. Brigham Young University.

KJZZ-TV, Channel 14, UPN
5181 Amelia Earhart Dr., Salt Lake City, UT 84116. (801) 537-1414. FAX: (801) 238-6414. Larry H. Miller.

KSL-TV, Channel 5, NBC
PO Box 1160, KSL-TV, Broadcast House, Salt Lake City, UT 84110-1160. (801) 575-5500. FAX: (801) 575-5830. Bonneville International Corp.

KSTU, Channel 13, FOX
5020 W. Amelia Earhart Dr., Salt Lake City, UT 84116. (801) 532-1300. FAX: (801) 537-5335. Fox Television Stations Inc.

KTVX, Channel 4, ABC
1760 Fremont Dr., Salt Lake City, UT 84104. (801) 975-4444. FAX: (801) 975-4442. Chris-Craft Industries, Inc.

KUED, Channel 7, PBS
101 Wasatch Dr., Salt Lake City, UT 84112. (801) 581-7777. FAX: (801) 581-5620. University of Utah.

KUTV, Channel 2, CBS
2185 S. 3600 W., Salt Lake City, UT 84119. (801) 973-3000. FAX: (801) 973-3369. CBS Stations Inc. Dave Phillips.

KSGI-TV (Cedar City), Channel 4, IND
PO Box 1450, 210 N. 1000 E., St. George, UT 84771. (801) 628-1000. FAX: (801) 628-6636. E. Morgan Skinner Jr.

KUSG, Channel 12, CBS
(see KUTV, Salt Lake City). St. George, UT. (801) 973-3115. FAX: (801) 973-3387. KUTV L.P.

KZAR-TV (Salt Lake), Channel 16, IND
c/o WHSL, Ste. 300, 1408 N. Kings Hwy. Blvd., St. Louis, MO 63113. Acme Television.

VERMONT

WCAX-TV, Channel 3, CBS
PO Box 608, Burlington, VT 05402. (802) 658-6300. FAX: (802) 658-6319. S.T. Martin & Family.

WETK, Channel 33, PBS
(see Vermont Educational Television, Colchester). Burlington, VT. Vermont Educational Television Inc.

WVNY, Channel 22, ABC
PO Box 22, 100 Market Square, Burlington, VT 05401. (802) 658-8022. FAX: (802) 865-9976. Straight Line Communications.

Vermont Educational Television, PBS
88 Ethan Allen Ave., Colchester, VT 05446-3129. (802) 655-4800. FAX: (802) 655-6593. Vermont ETV Inc.

WFFF-TV (Burlington), Channel 44, FOX
45 Roosevelt Hwy., Colchester, VT 05446. (802) 655-0044. FAX: (802) 872-2841. STC Broadcasting Inc.

WVER, Channel 28, PBS
(see Vermont Educational Television, Colchester). Rutland, VT. Vermont Educational Television Inc.

WVTB, Channel 20, PBS
(see Vermont Educational Television, Colchester). St. Johnsbury, VT. Vermont Educational Television Inc.

WNNE-TV, Channel 31, NBC
PO Box 1310, White River Junction, VT 05001. (802) 295-3100. FAX: (802) 295-9056. STC Broadcasting Inc.

WVTA, Channel 41, PBS
(see Vermont Educational Television, Colchester). Windsor, VT. Vermont Educational Television Inc.

VIRGINIA

WLFG (Grundy), Channel 68, NFP
8594 Hidden Valley Rd., Abingdon, VA 24210. (540) 676-3806. FAX: (540) 676-3572. Tookland Pentecostal Church.

WTMW, Channel 14, IND
3565 Lee Hwy., Arlington, VA 22207. (703) 528-0051. FAX: (703) 528-2956. Theodore White.

WCYB-TV, Channel 5, NBC
101 Lee St., Bristol, VA 24201. (703) 645-1555. FAX: (703) 645-1553. Lamco Communications Inc.

WHTJ, Channel 41, PBS
PO Box 2021, 300 Preston Ave., 4th Fl., Charlottesville, VA 22902. (804) 320-1301. FAX: (804) 295-2813 Central Virginia Educational TV Communications. Connie Lombardo.

WVIR-TV, Channel 29, NBC
PO Box 769, 503 E. Market St., Charlottesville, VA 22902. (804) 977-7082. FAX: (804) 971-2800. Waterman Broadcasting Corp.

WNVC, Channel 56, IND
8101A Lee Hwy., Falls Church, VA 22042. (703) 698-9682. FAX: (703) 849-9796. Central Virginia Educational Television Communications.

WNVT Channel 53, PBS
8101A Lee Hwy., Falls Church, VA 22042. (703) 698-9682. FAX: (703) 849-9796. Central Virginia Educational Television Communications.

WVPY, Channel 42, PBS
(see WVPT, Harrisonburg), Front Royal, VA. Shenandoah Valley Educational Television Corp.

WJCB-TV (Norfolk), Channel 49, NFP
Suite 2C, 910 W. Mercury Blvd., Hampton, VA 23661. (757) 838-4949. FAX: (757) 838-4840. Paxson Communications Corp.

WHSV-TV, Channel 3, ABC
PO Box TV 3, Hwy. 33 W., Harrisonburg, VA 22801-0030. (540) 433-9191. FAX: (540) 433-4028. Benedek Broadcasting Co.

WVPT (Staunton), Channel 51, PBS
298 Port Republic Rd., Harrisonburg, VA 22801. (540) 434-5391. Shenandoah Valley Educational Television Corp.

WJPR, Channel 21, FOX
(see WFXR, Roanoke). Lynchburg, VA. Grant Broadcasting System II Inc.

WSET-TV, Channel 13, ABC
2320 Langhorne Rd., Lynchburg, VA 24501. (804) 528-1313. FAX: (804) 847-0458. Allbritton Communications Co.

WVVI, Channel 66, IND
9008 Center St., Manassas, VA 22110. (703) 631-2310. FAX: (703) 361-0795. Paxson Communications Corp.

WAVY-T, Channel 10, NBC
300 Wavy St., Norfolk, VA 23704. (804) 393-1010. FAX: (804) 399-7628. Hicks, Muse, Tate & Furst Inc.

WHRO-TV (Hampton-Norfolk), Channel 15, PBS
5200 Hampton Blvd., Norfolk, VA 23508. (757) 889-9400. FAX: (757) 489-0007. Hampton Roads Educ. Telecomm. Assn.

WTKR, Channel 3, CBS
720 Boush St., Norfolk, VA 23510. (757) 446-1000. FAX: (757) 622-1113. The New York Times Co.

WTVZ-TV, Channel 33, FOX
900 Granby St., Norfolk, VA 23510. (757) 622-3333. FAX: (757) 623-1541. Sinclair Broadcast Group Inc.

WVEC-TV, Channel 13, ABC
613 Woodis Ave., Norfolk, VA 23510. (804) 625-1313. FAX: (804) 628-6220. A.H. Belo Corp.

WGNT, Channel 27, UPN
1318 Spratley St., Portsmouth, VA 23704.(757) 393-2501. FAX: (757) 399-3303. Paramount Stations Group Inc.

WVBT-TV (Virginia Beach), Channel 43, WB, FOX
300 Way St., Portsmouth, VA 23704. (757) 393-4343. FAX: (757) 393-7615. Hicks, Muse, Tate & Furst Inc.

WCVE-TV, Channel 23, PBS
23 Sesame St., Richmond, VA 23235. (804) 320-1301. FAX: (804) 320-8729. Central VA Educational Telecomm Corp.

WCVW, Channel 57, PBS
(see WCVE, Richmond) Richmond, VA. Central VA Educational Telecomm. Corp.

WRIC-TV, Channel 8, ABC
301 Arboretum Pl., Richmond, VA 23236-3464. (804) 330-8888. FAX: (804) 330-8882. Young Broadcasting Inc.

WRLH-TV, Channel 35, FOX
1925 Westmoreland St., Richmond, VA 23230. (804) 358-3535. FAX: (804) 358-1495. Sinclair Broadcast Group Inc.

WTVR-TV, Channel 6, CBS
3301 W. Broad St., Richmond, VA 23230. (804) 254-3600. FAX: (804) 254-3699. Raycom Media Inc.

WUPV (Ashland), Channel 65, WB
4120 E. Parham Rd., Richmond, VA 23228. (804) 672-6565. FAX: (804) 672-6571. TV 65 Broadcasting L.C.

WWBT, Channel 12, NBC
5710 Midlothian Tpke., Richmond, VA 23225. (804) 230-1212. FAX: (804) 230-2500. Jefferson-Pilot Communications Co.

WBRA-TV, Channel 15, PBS
1215 McNeil Dr. S.W., Roanoke, VA 24015. (540) 344-0994. FAX: (540) 344-2148. Blue Ridge Public Television Inc.

WDBJ, Channel 7, CBS
2001 Colonial Ave., Roanoke, VA 24015. (540) 344-7000. FAX: (540) 344-5097. Schurz Communications Inc.

WDRL (Danville), Channel 24, UPN
5002 Airport Rd, Roanoke, VA 24014. (804) 791-2424. FAX: (804) 366-1660. Danville Television Partnership

WPXR, Channel 38, IND
612 Bullitt Ave. S.E., Roanoke, VA 24013. (540) 982-3696. FAX: (540) 345-8568. Paxson Communications Corp.

WFXR-TV, Channel 27, FOX
2618 Colonial Ave. SW, Roanoke, VA 24015. (540) 344-2127. FAX: (540) 345-1912. Grant Broadcasting System II Inc. Tony Kahl.

WMSY-TV (Marion), Channel 52, PBS
PO Box 13246, 1215 McNeil Dr., Roanoke, VA 24032. (540) 344-0991. FAX: (540) 344-2148. Blue Ridge Public Television Inc.

WSBN-TV (Norton), Channel 47, PBS
PO Box 13246, Roanoke, VA 24032. (540) 344-0991. FAX: (540) 344-2148. Blue Ridge Public Television Inc. Donald Piedmont.

WSLS-TV, Channel 10, NBC
401 3rd St. N.W., Roanoke, VA 24011. (703) 981-9110. FAX: (703) 343-3157. Media General Broadcast Group.

WASHINGTON

WBEH, Channel 51, IND
PO Box 3765, Bellevue, WA 98009-3765. African-American Broadcasting Co. of Bellevue Inc.

KBCB (Bellingham), Channel 24, IND
Ste. 211, 601 University Ave., Sacramento, CA 95825. (360) 647-8842. FAX: (916) 921-2085. Paxson Communications Corp.

KVOS-TV, Channel 12, IND
1151 Ellis St., Bellingham, WA 98225. (360) 671-1212. FAX: (604) 647-0824. Ackerly Communications Inc.

KCKA, Channel 15, PBS
(see KBTC, Tacoma). Centralia, WA. State Board, Community & Tech Coll.

KHCV (Seattle), Channel 45, IND
17221 Lido Lane, Huntington Beach, CA 92647. North Pacific International TV Inc.

KNDU (Richland), Channel 25, NBC
3312 W. Kennewick Ave., Kennewick, WA 99336. (509) 783-6151. FAX: (509) 783-3746. Raycom Media Inc. Dave Dalthrop.

KVEW, Channel 42, ABC
601 N. Edison, Kennewick, WA 99336. (509) 735-8369. FAX: (509) 735-7889. Morgan Murphy Stations.

KEPR-TV, Channel 19, CBS
2807 W. Lewis, Pasco WA 99301. (509) 547-0547. FAX: (509) 547-2845. Retlaw Broadcasting Co. Dick Drillant.

KWSU-TV, Channel 10, PBS
Murrow Communications Ctr., Washington State Univ., Pullman, WA 99164-2530. (509) 335-6511. FAX: (509) 335-3772. Washington State University.

KTNW, Channel 31, PBS
(see KWSU, Pullman). Richland, WA. Washington State U.

KBGE (Bellevue), Channel 33, IND
Ste. 4370, 701 5th Ave., Seattle, WA 98104. (206) 386-8033. FAX: (206) 386-5183. Paxson Communications Corp.

KCPQ (Tacoma), Channel 13, FOX, CBS, NBC
1813 Westlake Ave. N., Seattle, WA 98109 (206) 674-1313. FAX: (206) 674-1777. Kelly Broadcasting Co.

KCTS-TV, Channel 9, PBS
401 Mercer, Seattle, WA 98109. (206) 728-6463. FAX: (206) 443-6691. KCTS Television.

KCWT (Wenatchee), Channel 27, IND
1200 Westlake Ave. N., Seattle, WA 98109-3529. Bingham Communications Group.

KING-TV, Channel 5, NBC
333 Dexter Ave. N., Seattle, WA 98109. (206) 448-5555. FAX: (206) 448-3936. A.H. Belo Corp.

KIRO-TV, Channel 7, CBS
PO Box C 21326, 2807 3rd Ave., Seattle, WA 98111-7000. (206) 728-7777. FAX: (206) 441-4840. Cox Broadcasting Inc.

KOMO-TV, Channel 4, ABC
100 Fourth Ave. N., Seattle, WA 98109. (206) 443-4000. FAX: (206) 443-4014. Fisher Broadcasting Inc.

KONG (Everett), Channel 16, IND
333 Dexter Ave. N, Seattle, WA 98109. (206) 448-3166. Susan Vecker.

KSTW, Channel 11, CBS
2320 S. 19th St., Seattle, WA 98405. (206) 572-5789. FAX: (206) 272-7581. Paramount Stations Group Inc.

KTZZ-TV, Channel 22, WB
945 Dexter Ave. N., Seattle, WA 98109. (206) 282-2202. FAX: (206) 281-0207. Dudley Communications Corp.

KAYU-TV, Channel 28, FOX, UPN
PO Box 30028, S. 4600 Regal St., Spokane, WA 99223. (509) 448-2828. FAX: (509) 448-3815. Mountain Broadcasting LLC

KHQ-TV, Channel 6, NBC
4202 S. Regal Spokane, WA 99223-7738. (509) 448-6000. FAX: (509) 448-4694. James P. & William Stacey Cowles.

KREM-TV, Channel 2, CBS
4103 S. Regal Spokane, WA 99223. (509) 448-2000. FAX: (509) 448-2969. A. H. Belo Corp.

KSKN, Channel 22, IND
4103 S. Regal, Spokane, WA 99223. (509) 448-2000. FAX: (509) 443-9100. KSKN Inc.

KSPS-TV, Channel 7, PBS
3911 S. Regal, Spokane, WA 99223. (509) 353-5777. Spokane School District No. 81. Bill Stanley.

KXLY-TV, Channel 4, ABC
500 W. Boone Ave., Spokane, WA 99201. (509) 324-4000. FAX: (509) 328-5274. Morgan Murphy Stations.

KBTC-TV, Channel 28, PBS
1101 S. Yakima Ave., Tacoma, WA 98405. (206) 596-1528. FAX: (206) 596-1623. State Board, Community & Tech Coll.

KTBW-TV, Channel 20, IND
1909 S. 341st Pl., Federal Way, Tacoma, WA 98003. (253) 874-7420. FAX: (253) 874-7432. Trinity Broadcasting Network. Mary Jane Allen.

KWDK (Tacoma), Channel 56, NFP
Suite 571, 2166 W. Broadway, Anaheim, CA 92804. Korean American Missions Inc.

KPDX (Vancouver, WA), Channel 49, FOX
910 N.E. M.L. King Blvd., Portland, OR 97232. (503) 239-4949. FAX: (503) 239-6184. Meredith Broadcasting Group.

KAPP, Channel 35, ABC
1610 S. 24th Ave., Yakima, WA 98902. (509) 453-0351. FAX: (509) 453-3623. Apple Valley Broadcasting. Ron Simmons.

KIMA-TV, Channel 29, CBS
2801 Terrace Heights Dr., Yakima, WA 98901. (509) 575-0029. FAX: (509) 248-1218. Retlaw Broadcasting Corp.

KNDO, Channel 23, NBC
1608 S. 24th Ave., Yakima, WA 98902. (509) 248-2300. FAX: (509) 575-0266. Raycom Media Inc.

KYVE, Channel 47, PBS
1105 S. 15th Ave., Yakima, WA 98902. (509) 452-4700. FAX: (509) 452-4704. KCTS Television. Nancy Leahy.

WEST VIRGINIA

WSWP-TV (Grandview), Channel 9, PBS
PO Box A.H., Airport Rd., Beckley, WV 25802. (304) 255-1501. FAX: (304) 252-9797. WV Educational B'casting Auth.

WLFB, Channel 40, NFP
(see Living Faith Ministries, Vansant, VA). Bluefield, WV. Living Faith Ministries Inc.

WVVA Channel 6, NBC
PO Box 1930, Rt. 460 Bypass, Bluefield, WV 24701. (304) 325-5487. FAX: (304) 327-5586. Quincy Newspapers Inc.

WDTV (Weston), Channel 5, CBS
5 Television Dr., Bridgeport, WV 26330. (304) 623-5555. FAX: (304) 842-7501. Withers Broadcasting Co.

WCHS-TV, Channel 8, ABC
1301 Piedmont Rd., Charleston, WV 25301. (304) 346-5358. FAX: (304) 346-4765. Sinclair Broadcast Group Inc.

WKRP-TV, Channel 29, IND
10 Hail St., Charleston, WV 25323. Paxson Communications Corp.

WBOY-TV, Channel 12, NBC
904 W. Pike St., Clarksburg, WV 26301. (304) 632-3311. FAX: (304) 624-6152. Imes Communications. Gary R. Bowden.

WLYJ, Channel 49, NFP
PO Box 2544, 775 W. Pike St., Clarksburg, WV 26302. (304) 623-5784. FAX: (304) 623-9021. Channel 49 Acquisition Corp.

WVSX (Lewisburg), Channel 59, FOX
Box 509, 141 Old Cline Rd., Ghent, WV 25843. (304) 787-5959. FAX: (304) 787-2440. John Tupper & Bruce Fox. Stan Marinoff.

WOWK-TV, Channel 13, CBS
TV Center, 555 Fifth Ave., Huntington, WV 25701. (304) 525-1313. FAX: (304) 529-4910. Gateway Communications.

WPBY-TV, Channel 33, PBS
1615 Third Ave., Huntington, WV 25701. (304) 696-6630. FAX: (304) 696-4343. WV Educational Broadcasting Authority.

WSAZ-TV, Channel 3, NBC
PO Box 2115, 645 Fifth Ave., Huntington, WV 25721. (304) 697-4780. FAX: (304) 697-4325. Lee Enterprises Inc.

WVAH-TV (Charleston), Channel 11, FOX
11 Broadcast Plaza, Hurricane, WV 25526. (304) 757-0011. FAX: (304) 757-7533. Sinclair Broadcast Group Inc.

WSHE, Channel 60, IND
One Discovery Pl., Martinsburg, WV 25401. (304) 264-9960. FAX: (304) 264-4618. Paxson Communications Corp.

WNPB-TV, Channel 24, PBS
191 Scott Ave., Morgantown, WV 26505. (304) 293-6511. FAX: (304) 293-2642. WV Educational Broadcasting Authority. Al Prichard.

WOAY-TV, Channel 4, ABC
PO Box 251, Rte. 16 S., Oak Hill, WV 25901. (304) 469-3361. FAX: (304) 465-1420. Thomas Broadcasting Co.

WTAP-TV, Channel 15, NBC
One Television Plaza, Parkersburg, WV 26101. (304) 485-4588. FAX: (304) 422-3920. Benedek Broadcasting Corp.

WTRF-TV, Channel 7, CBS, ABC
96 16th St., Wheeling, WV 26003. (304) 232-7777. FAX: (304) 232-4975. Benedek Broadcasting Corp.

WISCONSIN

WYOW, Channel 34, ABC
Box 1952, Eagle River, WI 54521. Tel/FAX: (715) 477-8834. FAX: (715) 477-8834. Shockley Communications Corp.

WEAU-TV, Channel 13, NBC
1907 S. Hastings Way, Eau Claire, WI 54701. (715) 835-1313. FAX: (715) 832-0246. Gray Communications Systems Inc.

WEUX (Chippewa Falls), Channel 48, FOX
1324 W. Clairemont Ave., Eau Claire, WI 54701. (715) 831-2548. Aries Telecommunication Corp.

WQOW-TV, Channel 18, ABC
2881 S. Hastings Way, Eau Claire, WI 54701. (715) 835-1881. FAX: (715) 835-8009. Shockley Communications Corp.

WMMF-TV (Fond du Lac), Channel 68, IND
500 S. Chinowth Rd., Visalia, CA 93277. (209) 733-7800. FAX: (209) 627-5363. Harry J. & Stella A. Pappas.

WACY (Appleton), Channel 32, UPN, WB
PO Box 12328, Green Bay, WI 54307-2328. (414) 490-0320. FAX: (414) 494-7071. Ace TV Inc.

WBAY-TV, Channel 2, ABC
115 S. Jefferson, Green Bay, WI 54301. (920) 432-3331. FAX: (920) 432-7808. Young Broadcasting Inc.

WFRV-TV, Channel 5, CBS
1181 E. Mason St., Green Bay, WI 54307-9055. (920) 437-5411. FAX: (920) 437-4576. CBS Stations Inc. R. Perry Kidder.

WGBA, Channel 26, NBC
PO Box 19099, 1391 North Rd., Green Bay, WI 54313. (920) 494-2626. FAX: (920) 494-7071. DP & K Inc.

WLUK-TV, Channel 11, FOX
PO Box 19011, 787 Lombardi Ave., Green Bay, WI 54307-9011. (920) 494-8711. FAX: (920) 494-8782. USA Broadcasting Inc.

WPNE Channel 38, PBS
(see WI Educ. Comm. Bd., Madison). Green Bay, WI. Wisconsin Educational Communications Board.

WJNW (Janesville), Channel 57, IND
Box 5726,. Mulford Rd., Rockford, IL 61107. (815) 229-3600. FAX: (815) 229-9026. Puri Family LP.

WHKE, Channel 55, IND
4300 43rd Ave., Kenosha, WI 53144. (414) 657-9453. FAX: (414) 656-7664. Paxson Communications Corp.

WKBT, Channel 8, CBS
141 S. 6th St., La Crosse, WI 54601. (608) 782-4678. FAX: (608) 782-2892. Young Broadcasting Inc.

WLAX, Channel 25, FOX, UPN
1305 Interchange Pl., La Crosse, WI 54603. (608) 781-0025. FAX: (608) 781-1456. Grant Media Inc.

WHLA-TV, Channel 31, PBS
(see WI Educ. Comm. Bd., Madison). Lacrosse, WI. Wisconsin Educational Communications Board.

WWRS-TV (Mayville), Channel 52, IND
1750 W. Freedom Rd., Little Chute, WI 51540. (414) 687-0722. TV-52 Inc. Lyle R. Evans.

WHA-TV, Channel 21, PBS
821 University Ave., Madison, WI 53706. (608) 263-2121. FAX: (608) 263-9763. U. of Wisconsin Board of Regents.

WISC-TV, Channel 3, CBS, UPN
7025 Raymond Rd., Madison, WI 53744-4965. (608) 271-4321, FAX: (608) 271-0800. Morgan Murphy Stations.

WKOW-TV, Channel 27, ABC
5727 Tokay Blvd., Madison, WI 53719. (608) 274-1234. FAX: (608) 274-9514. Shockly Communications.

WMSN-TV, Channel 47, FOX
7847 Big Sky Dr., Madison, WI 53719. (608) 833-0047. FAX: (608) 833-5055. Sinclair Broadcast Group Inc.

WMTV, Channel 15, NBC
615 Forward Dr., Madison, WI 53711. (608) 274-1515. FAX: (608) 271-6110. Benedek Broadcasting Corp.

Wisconsin Educational Communications Bd., PBS
3319 W. Beltline Hwy., Madison, WI 53713. (608) 264-9600. FAX: (608) 264-9622. WI Educational Communications Board.

WHWC-TV, Channel 28, PBS
(see WI Educ. Comm. Bd., Madison). Menomonie, WI. Wisconsin Educational Communications Board. Byron Knight.

WCGV-TV, Channel 24, IND
4041 N. 35th St., Milwaukee, WI 53216. (414) 442-7050. FAX: (414) 874-1899. Sinclair Broadcast Group Inc.

WDJT-TV, Channel 58, CBS
Ste. 2500, 509 W. Wisconsin Ave., Milwaukee, WI 53203. (414) 271-5800. FAX: (414) 272-1368. Weigel Broadcasting.

WISN-TV, Channel 12, ABC
PO Box 402, Milwaukee, WI 53201. (414) 342-8812. FAX: (414) 342-6490. Hearst-Argyle Television, Inc.

WITI-TV, Channel 6, FOX
PO Box 17600, 9001 N. Green Bay Rd., Milwaukee, WI 53217-0600. (414) 355-6666. FAX: (414) 362-2141. Fox TV Stations Inc.

WMVS, Channel 10, PBS
1036 N. 8th St., Milwaukee, WI 53233-1400. (414) 271-1036. FAX: (414) 297-7536. Milwaukee Area Technical College.

WMVT, Channel 36, NFP
(see WMVS, Milwaukee). Milwaukee, WI. Milwaukee Area Technical College.

WTMJ-TV, Channel 4, NBC
720 E. Capitol Dr., Milwaukee, WI 53212. (414) 332-9611. FAX: (414) 967-5255. Journal Broadcast Group Inc.

WVCY, Channel 30, IND
3434 W. Kilbourn Ave., Milwaukee, WI 53208. (414) 935-3000. FAX: (414) 935-3015. VCY/America Inc. Vic Eliason.

WVTV, Channel 18, WB
4041 N. 35th St., Milwaukee, WI 53216. (414) 442-7050. FAX: (414) 874-1899. Sinclair Broadcast Group Inc. Eddie Edwards.

WJJA (Racine), Channel 49, IND
PO Box 92, 4311 E. Oakwood Rd., Oak Creek, WI 53154. (414) 764-4953. FAX: (414) 764-5190. TV-49 Inc.

WLEF-TV, Channel 36, PBS
(see WI Educ. Comm. Bd., Madison). Park Falls, WI. Wisconsin Educational Communications Board.

WJFW-TV, Channel 12, NBC
PO Box 858, S. Onieda Ave., Rhinelander, WI 54501. (715) 369-4700. FAX: (715) 369-1910. Seaway Holdings Inc.

WPXG, Channel 14, IND
(see WVCY, Milwaukee). Suring, WI 53208. Paxson Communications Corp. Vic Eliason.

WAOW-TV, Channel 9, ABC, UPN
1908 Grand Ave., Wausau, WI 54403-6897. (715) 842-2251. FAX: (715) 848-0195. Shockley Communications Corp.

WHRM-TV, Channel 20, PBS
(see WI Educ. Comm. Bd., Madison). Wausau, WI. Wisconsin Educational Communications Board.

WSAW-TV, Channel 7, CBS
1114 Grand Ave., Wausau, WI 54403. (715) 845-4211. FAX: (715) 845-2649. Benedek Broadcasting Corp.

WYOMING

KFNB-TV, Channel 20, ABC
1865 Skyview Dr., Casper, WY 82601. (307) 577-5923. FAX: (307) 577-5928. WyoMedia Corp.

KGWC-TV, Channel 14, CBS, FOX
304 N. Center, Casper, WY 86201. (307) 234-1111. (307) 234-2835. Benedek Broadcasting Corp. Ron Johnson.

KGWR-TV (Rock Springs), Channel 13, CBS
304 N. Center, Casper, WY 86201. (307) 234-1111. (307) 234-2835. Benedek Broadcasting Corp. Ron Johnson.

KTWO-TV, Channel 2, NBC, WB
4200 E. 2nd St., Casper, WY 82609. (307) 237-3711. FAX: (307) 234-9866. Grapevine Communications, Inc. Al Parsons.

KGWN-TV, Channel 5, CBS, ABC
2923 E. Lincolnway, Cheyenne, WY 82001. (307) 634-7755. FAX: (307) 637-8604. Benedek Broadcasting Corp.

KKTU, Channel 33, NBC, WB
422 E 2nd Str., Cheyenne, WY 82609. (307) 237-3711. (307) 234-9866. Grapevine Communications, Inc.

KLWY Channel 27, FOX
(see KFNB, Casper). Cheyenne, WY. WyoMedia Corp.

KJWY, Channel 2, NBC
PO Box 7454 Powder Horn, 970 N. Broadway, Jackson, WY 83002. (307) 733-2066. FAX: (307) 733-4834. Sunbelt Communications Co.

KGWL-TV, Channel 5, CBS
(see KGWC, Casper). Lander, WY. Benedek Broadcasting Corp. Ron Johnson.

KFNR, Channel 11, ABC
(see KFNB, Casper). Rawlins, WY. First National Broadcasting Corp. Mike McAuley.

KCWC-TV (Lander), Channel 4, PBS
Central Wyoming College, 2660 Peck Ave., Riverton, WY 82501. (307) 856-9291. FAX: (307) 856-3893. Central Wyoming College.

KFNE, Channel 10, ABC
(see KFNB, Casper). Riverton, WY. First National Broadcasting Corp.

KSGW-TV, Channel 12, ABC
(see KOTA, Rapid City SD). Sheridan, WY. Duhamel Broadcasting Enterprises.

AMERICAN SAMOA

KVZK-2 (Pago Pago), Channel 2, PBS
KVZK-TV, American Samoa, 96799. (684) 633-4191. FAX: (684) 633-1044. The Govt. of American Samoa.

KVZK-4 (Pago Pago), Channel 4, ABC
(see KVZK-TV 2). American Samoa. The Govt. of American Samoa.

KVZK-5 (Pago Pago), Channel 5, ABC, CBS
(see KVZK-TV 2). American Samoa. The Govt. of American Samoa.

GUAM

KGTF, Channel 12, PBS
PO Box 21449, Agana, GU 96921 (671) 734-2207. FAX: (671) 734-5483. Guam Educational Telecomm. Corp. Station.

KUAM-TV, Channel 8, CBS. NBC
PO Box 368, Agana, GU 96932. (671) 637-5826. FAX: (671) 637-9865. Micronesia Broadcasting Inc.

KTGM, Channel 14, ABC, FOX
Ste. 308, 692 N. Marine Dr., Tamuning, GU 96911. (671) 646-4873. FAX: (671) 649-0371. Island Broadcasting Inc.

PUERTO RICO

WQHA, Channel 50, NFP
Box 846, Aguada, PR 00602. Aurio Matos dba Channel 50 TV.

WVEO, Channel 44, IND
Box 55, Aguadilla, PR 00613. Southwestern Broadcasting Corp.

WTVC (San Juan), Channel 18, IND
Bori 1554 St. Urb Point, Antonsanti, PR 00927. (787) 274-1800. FAX: (787) 281-9758. International Broadcasting Corp.

WIRS (Yauco), Channel 42, NFP
PO Box 635, Bayamon, PR 00960. (787) 799-6400. FAX: (787) 797-7120. Maranatha Christian Network.

WRWR-TV (San Juan), Channel 30, IND
Calle No. One, No. 364 Hnas. Cavila, Bayamon, PR 00629. Ramon Rodriguez-Nieves.

WTIN (Ponce), Channel 14, IND
c/o Laura Nicolau, AS-15 Rio Orocovis St., Bayamon, PR 00961. (809) 795-4010. Laura Nicolau.

WECN (Naranjito), Channel 64, NFP
PO Box 310, Bayamon, PR 00960. (787) 799-6400. FAX: (787) 797-2450. Encuentro Christian Net.

WMEI-TV (Arecibo), Channel 60, IND
G.P. O. 7017, Caguas, PR 00726. Teleamerica Network Inc.

WCCV-TV (Arecibo), Channel 54, IND
PO Box 949, Kilo 92.6 Bo Membrillo, Carr. #2, Camuy, PR 00627. (787) 898-5120. FAX: (787) 262-0541. Asociacion Evan. Cristo Viene Inc.

WJPX (San Juan), Channel 24, IND
Box 1001, El CDommandate, Canovanas, PR 00729 . Paxson Communications Corp.

WDZE, Channel 52, IND
PO Box 1833, Carolina, PR 00984-1833. (809) 762-5500. FAX: (809) 752-1825. Enrique A. & Blanche Vidal Sanchez.

WUJA (Caguas), Channel 58, IND
PO Box 4039, Balle Arryba Heights Stn., Carolina, PR 00984. (787) 750-5858. FAX: (787) 257-9260. Community TV of Caguas.

WIDP (Guayama), Channel 46, IND
PO Box 501, Cidra, PR 00661. Bocanegra/Girlad B'casting Group.

WKPV (Ponce), Channel 20, IND
Box 3463, Carefree, AZ 85377. Paxson Communications Corp.

WRUA, Channel 34, IND
101 107th St., Villa Carolina, Fajardo, PR 00630. Damarys de Jesus.

WELU (Aguadilla), Channel 32, NFP
PO Box 530777, Harlingen, TX 78553. (210) 412 5600. FAX: (210) 428-7556. Healthy Christian Family Media, Inc.

WIPM-TV (Mayaguez), Channel 3, PBS
Box 190909, Hato Rey, PR 00919. (787) 834-0164. FAX: (787) 832-9139. PR Public Broadcasting Corp.

WIPR-TV (San Juan), Channel 6, PBS
PO Box 190909, Hato Rey, PR 00919. (787) 766-0505. FAX: (787) 763-9846. PR Public B'casting Corp.

WKAQ-TV (San Juan), Channel 2, TEL
383 Roosevelt Ave., Hato Rey, PR 00918. (787) 758-2222. FAX: (787) 759-9575. Telemundo Group Inc.

WDWL (Bayamon), Channel 36, NFP
PO Box 50615, Levittown, PR 00950. (787) 795-8181. FAX: (787) 795-8140. Bayamon Christian Network.

WNJX-TV, Channel 22, IND
PO Box 1030, Mayaguez, PR 00681-1030. (787) 831-2222. FAX: (787) 834-2222. Glenn A. Tyron & Ana J. Plaza.

WOLE-TV (Aguadilla), Channel 12, IND
PO Box 1200, Mayaguez, PR 00709-1200. (809) 833-1200. FAX: (809) 831-6330. Western Broadcasting Corp. of PR.

WORA-TV, Channel 5, TEL
PO Box 43, Mayaguez, PR 00681. (787) 831-5555. FAX: (787) 833-0075. Alfredo R. deArellano Jr. & Family.

WTRA (Mayaguez), Channel 16, IND
Box 980, Quebradillas, PR 00678. (809) 895-2725. Jose Arzuaga

WMTJ (Fajardo), Channel 40, IND
PO Box 21345, Rd. 176, Kilometer 3, Isoro Color, Cupey Bajo, Rio Piedras, PR 00928. (787) 766-2600. FAX: (787) 250-8546. Ana G. Mendez Educational Foundation.

WQTO (Ponce), Channel 26, IND
PO Box 21345, Rio Piedras, PR 00928. (787) 766-2600. FAX: (787) 250-8546. Fundacion Educativa Ana G. Mendez.

WAPA-TV, Channel 4, IND
State Rd. 19, San Juan, PR 00657. (787) 792-4444. FAX: (787) 782-4420. Pegasus Broadcasting of San Juan. Marguerita Millan.

WJWN-TV (San Sebastian), Channel 38, IND
PO Box 4522, San Juan, PR 00936. Paxson Communications Corp.

WLII (Caguas), Channel 11, NBC
Box 1000, San Juan, PR 00908-1000. (787) 724-1111. FAX: (787) 724-7071. Malrite Communications Group Inc.

WPRV-TV (Fajardo), Channel 13, IND
Arch of San Juan, Calle Simon Madera #10, San Juan, PR 00929. (787) 751-5300. FAX: (787) 276-1307. Catholic, Apostolic & Roman Church of PR.

WSTE (Ponce), Channel 7, IND
PO Box 15096, San Juan, PR 00902. (787) 724-7777. FAX: (787) 725-5870. Jerry B. & Esther M. Hartman.

WSUR-TV (Ponce), Channel 9, IND
PO Box 10000, San Juan, PR 00908-1000. (787) 724-1111. FAX: (787) 721-0777. Malrite Communications Group Inc.

WVOZ (Ponce), Channel 48
Bori 1554 St. Urb Point, Antonsanti, San Juan, PR 00927. (787) 274-1800. FAX: (787) 281-9758. International Broadcasting Corp.

U. S. VIRGIN ISLANDS

WSVI, Channel 8, ABC
PO Box 8ABC, Sunny Isle Shopping Ctr., Christiansted, VI 00823. (809) 778-5008. FAX: (809) 778-5011. Alpha B'casting Corp.

WVXF (U.S.V.I.), Channel 17, IND
PO Box 1605, Milwaukee, WI 53201. Atlantic Broadcasting Corp

WTJX-TV (Charlotte Amalie), Channel 12, PBS
158 Haypiece Hill, St. Thomas, VI 00801. (340) 774-6255. FAX: (340) 774-7092. Virgin Islands Public Television.

NETWORK AFFILIATES

ABC

ALABAMA

WJSU 33...................................Anniston
WDHN 18.....................................Dothan
*WAAY-TV 31.........................Huntsville
WEAR-TV 3......................................Mobile
WHOA-TV 32......................Montgomery
WCFT 40................................Tuscaloosa

ALASKA

KIMO 13...................................Anchorage
KYUK-TV 4..Bethel
KATN 2......................................Fairbanks
*KJUD 8...Juneau

ARIZONA

KNXV-TV 15...............................Phoenix
KGUN 9...Tucson

ARKANSAS

KHBS 40..................................Fort Smith
KAIT-TV 8..............................Jonesboro
KATV 7...................................Little Rock

CALIFORNIA

KAEF 23...Arcata
KERO-TV 23.........................Bakersfield
KFWU 8..................................Fort Bragg
KFSN-TV 30...................................Fresno
KABC 7...............................Los Angeles
KESQ-TV 42.....................Palm Springs
KRCR-TV 7....................................Redding
KXTV 10................................Sacramento
KNTV 11..Salinas
KGTV 10................................San Diego
KGO-TV 7.......................San Francisco
KEYT-TV 3.....................Santa Barbara

COLORADO

KRDO-TV 13.................Colorado Springs
KMGH-TV 7.....................................Denver
KJCT 8............................Grand Junction

CONNECTICUT

WTNH-TV 8.........................New Haven

DISTRICT OF COLUMBIA

WJLA-TV 7............................Washington

FLORIDA

WZVN-TV 26...........................Fort Myers
WCJB 20.................................Gainesville
WPLG 10...Miami
WZVN-TV 26.................................Naples
WJXX 25...........................Orange Park
WFTV 9..Orlando
WMBB 13......................Panama City
WWSB 40....................................Sarasota
WTXL-TV 27..........................Tallahassee
WFTS 28...Tampa
WPBF 25.....................West Palm Beach

GEORGIA

WSB-TV 2.......................................Atlanta
WJBF 6...Augusta
WBSG 21..................................Brunswick
WTVM 9.......................................Columbus
WPGA-TV 58...................................Perry
WSAV-TV 3............................Savannah

HAWAII

KHVO 13...Hilo
KITV 4..Honolulu
KMAU 12.......................................Wailuku

IDAHO

KIFI-TV 8..............................Idaho Falls
KPVI 6...................................Idaho Falls
KIVI 6..Nampa

ILLINOIS

KPOB-TV 15.........................Carterville
WLS-TV 7.....................................Chicago
WAND 17.......................................Decatur
WSIL-TV 3.............................Harrisburg
WQAD-TV 8.....................................Moline
WHOI 19...Peoria
WTVO 17.....................................Rockford

INDIANA

WEHT 25.....................................Evansville
WPTA 21.............................Fort Wayne
WRTV 6...............................Indianapolis

IOWA

KCRG-TV 9......................Cedar Rapids
WOI-TV 5...........................Des Moines
KTVO 3..Ottumwa
KCAU-TV 9...........................Sioux City

KANSAS

KUPK-TV 13.........................Garden City
KTKA-TV 49...................................Topeka
KAKE-TV 10................................Wichita

KENTUCKY

WBKO 13..........................Bowling Green
WTVQ-TV 36........................Lexington
WHAS-TV 11...........................Louisville

LOUISIANA

*KLAX-TV 31.........................Alexandria
WBRZ 2..............................Baton Rouge
KATC 3..Lafayette
WGNO 26.........................New Orleans
KTBS 3.................................Shreveport
KARD 14........................West Monroe

MAINE

WVII-TV 7...Bangor
WMTW-TV 8....................Poland Springs
*WAGM-TV 8......................Presque Isle

MARYLAND

WMAR-TV 2...............................Baltimore
*WMDT 47...................................Salisbury

MASSACHUSSETTS

WCDC 19..Adams
WCVB-TV 5....................................Boston
WGGB-TV 40......................Springfield

MICHIGAN

WOTV 41..............................Battle Creek
WJRT-TV 12..Flint
WZZM-TV 13...............Grand Rapids
WLAJ 53..Lansing
WGTQ 8.........................S. Ste. Marie
WXYZ-TV 7.................................Southfield
WGTU 29......................Traverse City

MINNESOTA

KAAL 6...Austin
WDIO-TV 10.................................Duluth
WIRT 13..Hibbing
KRWF 43......................Redwood Falls
KSTP-TV 5...................................St. Paul

MISSISSIPPI

WLOX 13...Biloxi
WABG-TV 6........................Greenwood
WAPT 16.......................................Jackson
WTOK-TV 11.............................Meridian

MISSOURI

*KMIZ 17.....................................Columbia
*KODE-TV 12.................................Joplin
KMBC 9................................Kansas City
KSPR 33...............................Springfield
KQTV 2...................................St. Joseph
KDNL-TV 30...............................St. Louis

MONTANA

KSVI 6...Billings
KWYB 18...Butte
*KFBB-TV 5.........................Great Falls
KYUS-TV 3............................Miles City
KTMF 23......................................Missoula

NEBRASKA

KCAN 8..Albion
KWNB 6.........................Hayes Center
KHGI-TV 13.................................Kearney
KLKN 8..Lincoln
KETV 7...Omaha
KDUH-TV 4.........................Scottsbluff
KSNB-TV 4.................................Superior

NEVADA

KTNV 13..................................Las Vegas
KOLO-TV 8..Reno

NEW HAMPSHIRE

WMUR-TV 9.........................Manchester

NEW MEXICO

KOAT-TV 7........................Albuquerque
KOCT 6..Carlsbad
KVIH-TV 12..Clovis
KOVT 10.............................Silver City

NEW YORK

WTEN 10..Albany
*WMGC-TV 34.....................Binghamton
WKBW-TV 7....................................Buffalo
WENY-TV 36....................................Elmira
WABC-TV 7.................................New York
WOKR 13....................................Rochester
WIXT 9..Syracuse
WUTR 20..Utica
WWTI 50...................................Watertown

NORTH CAROLINA

WSOC-TV 9.............................Charlotte
WTVD 11.......................................Durham
WCTI 12....................................New Bern
WWAY 3..................................Wilmington
WXLV-TV 45....................Winston-Salem

NORTH DAKOTA

KBMY 17.....................................Bismarck
WDAZ-TV 8......................Devils Lake
WDAY-TV 6..Fargo
KMCY 14..Minot

OHIO

WCPO 9....................................Cincinnati
WEWS 5................................Cleveland
WSYX 6...................................Columbus
WDTN 2..Dayton
WYTV 33.............................Youngstown

OKLAHOMA

KSWO-TV 7................................Lawton
KOCO-TV 5....................Oklahoma City
KTUL 8...Tulsa

OREGON

KEZI 9..Eugene
KDKF 31..........................Klamath Falls
KDRV 12..Medford
KATU 2...Portland

PENNSYLVANIA

WATM-TV 23.................................Altoona
WJET-TV 24...Erie
WHTM-TV 27......................Harrisburg
WPVI-TV 6.............................Philadelphia
WTAE-TV 4................................Pittsburgh
WNEP-TV16.............................Scranton

RHODE ISLAND

WLNE 6 ....Providence

SOUTH CAROLINA

WOLO-TV 25 ....Columbia
WPDE-TV 15................................Florence
WLOS 13 ....Greenville

SOUTH DAKOTA

KABY-TV 9................................Aberdeen
KHSD-TV 11.....................................Lead
KPRY-TV 4.......................................Pierre
KOTA-TV 3...............................Rapid City
KSFY-TV 13.............................Sioux Falls

TENNESSEE

WTVC 9................................Chattanooga
*WBBJ-TV 7.................................Jackson
WKPT-TV 19.............................Kingsport
WATE-TV 6................................Knoxville
WPTY-TV 24..............................Memphis
WKRN-TV 2.................................Nashville

TEXAS

KVII-TV 7...................................Amarillo
KVUE-TV 24....................................Austin
KBMT 12...................................Beaumont
KIII 3................................Corpus Christi
WFAA-TV 8.......................................Dallas
KTEN 10.....................................Denison

KVIA-TV 7....................................El Paso
KTRK-TV 13................................Houston
KGNS-TV 8....................................Laredo
KAMC 28...................................Lubbock
KTRE 9..Lufkin
KMID 2..Midland
KSAT-TV 12..........................San Antonio
KTXS-TV 12..........................Sweetwater
KLTV 7..Tyler
KAVU-TV 25................................Victoria
KXXV 25..Waco
KRGV-TV 5.................................Weslaco

UTAH

KTVX 4 ....Salt Lake City

VERMONT

WVNY 22 ....Burlington

VIRGINIA

WHSV-TV 3..........................Harrisonburg
WSET-TV 13.............................Lynchburg
WVEC-TV 13....................................Norfolk
WRIC-TV 8.................................Richmond

WASHINGTON

KVEW 42 ....Kennewick
KOMO-TV 4 ....Seattle
KXLY-TV 4 ....Spokane
KAPP 35 ....Yakima

WEST VIRGINIA

WCHS-TV 8................................Charleston
WOAY-TV 4....................................Oak Hill
WTRF-TV 7...................................Wheeling

WISCONSIN

WYOW 34................................Eagle River
WQOW-TV 18..........................Eau Claire
WBAY-TV 2............................Green Bay
WKOW-TV 27..............................Madison
WISN-TV 12..............................Milwaukee
*WAOW-TV 9...................................Wausau

WYOMING

KFNB-TV 20....................................Casper
*KGWN-TV 5.............................Cheyenne
KFNR 11..Rawlins
KFNE 10.......................................Riverton
KSGW-TV......................................Sheridan

AMERICAN SAMOA

KVZK 4 ....Pago Pago
*KVZK 5..................................Pago Pago

GUAM

*KTGM 14................................Tamuning

U.S. VIRGIN ISLANDS

WSVI 8................................Christiansted

CBS

ALABAMA

WIAT 42 ....Birmingham
WTVY 4..Dothan
WNAL-TV 44.................................Gadsden
WHNT-TV 19.............................Huntsville
WKRG-TV 5...................................Mobile
WAKA 8..Selma

ALASKA

KTVA 11 ....Anchorage
KYUK-TV 4......................................Bethel
KTNL 13..Sitka

ARIZONA

KPHO-TV 5...................................Phoenix
KOLD-TV 13.....................................Tucson
KSWT 13...Yuma

ARKANSAS

KFSM-TV 5.............................Fort Smith
KTHV 11 ....Little Rock

CALIFORNIA

KBAK-TV 29 ....Bakersfield
KHSL-TV 12 ....Chico
KVIQ 6..Eureka
KJEO 47..Fresno
KCBS-TV 2.........................Los Angeles
KION-TV 46...............................Monterey
KFMB-TV 8...............................San Diego
KCOY-TV 12.........................Santa Maria
KPIX-TV 5..Vallejo
KOVR 13 ....W. Sacramento

COLORADO

KKTV 11 ....Colorado Springs
KCNC-TV 4...................................Denver
*KREZ-TV 6.................................Durango
*KREG-TV 3.............Glenwood Springs
KREX-TV 6........................Grand Junction
KREY-TV 10.............................Montrose
KTVS 3..Sterling

CONNECTICUT

WFSB ....Hartford

DISTRICT OF COLUMBIA

WUSA ....Washington

FLORIDA

WINK-TV 11 ....Fort Myers
WJXT 4...................................Jacksonville
WFOR-TV 4......................................Miami
WKMG-TV 6..................................Orlando
WCTV 6.....................................Tallahassee

WTSP 10 ....Tampa
WPEC 12 ....West Palm Beach

GEORGIA

WGNX 46 ....Atlanta
WRDW-TV 12.................................Augusta
WRBL 3.......................................Columbus
WMAZ-TV 13....................................Macon
WTOC-TV 11..............................Savannah
WNEG-TV 32....................................Toccoa

HAWAII

KGMD-TV 9...Hilo
KGMB 9......................................Honolulu
KGMV 3...Wailuku

IDAHO

KBCI-TV 2...Boise
KIDK 3....................................Idaho Falls
KLEW 3.......................................Lewiston
KMVT 11.................................Twin Falls

ILLINOIS

WCFN 49.................................Champaign
WCIA 3......................................Champaign
WBBM-TV 2.................................Chicago
WIFR 23...Freeport
WMBD-TV 31....................................Peoria
KHQA-TV 7.....................................Quincy
WHBF-TV 4...........................Rock Island
WCFN 49....................................Springfield

INDIANA

WEVV 44.....................................Evansville
WANE-TV 15.............................Fort Wayne
WISH-TV 8............................Indianapolis
WSBT-TV 22.........................South Bend
WTHI-TV 10............................Terre Haute
WLFI-TV 18..........................W. Lafayette

IOWA

KGAN 2..............................Cedar Rapids
KCCI 8...................................Des Moines
KIMT 3....................................Mason City
KMEG-TV 14.............................Sioux City

KANSAS

KBSD-TV 6......................................Ensign
KBSL-TV 10..............................Goodland
KBSH-TV 7...Hays
KOAM-TV 7.................................Pittsburg
WIBW-TV 13...................................Topeka
KWCH-TV 12..................................Wichita

KENTUCKY

WYMT-TV 57....................................Hazard
WKYT-TV 27..............................Lexington
WLKY 32.....................................Louisville

LOUISIANA

WAFB 9 ....Baton Rouge
KLFY-TV 10................................Lafayette
KNOE-TV 8....................................Monroe
WHNO 20.............................New Orleans
WWL-TV 4...........................New Orleans
KSLA-TV 12..............................Shreveport

MAINE

WABI-TV 5..Bangor
WGME-TV 13.................................Portland
*WAGM-TV 8........................Presque Isle

MARYLAND

WJZ-TV 13................................Baltimore
WBOC-TV 16..............................Salisbury

MASSACHUSSETTS

WBZ-TV 4...Boston

MICHIGAN

WBKB-TV 11 ....Alpena
WWTV 9......................................Cadillac
WWJ-TV 62......................................Detroit
WJMN-TV 3.................................Escanaba
WNEM-TV 5..................Flint/Bay City
WWMT 3.....................................Kalamazoo
WLNS-TV 9.....................................Lansing
WWUP-TV 10......................S. St. Marie

MINNESOTA

KCCO-TV 7 ....Alexandria
KDLH 3..Duluth
KEYC-TV 12.................................Mankato
WCCO-TV 4.............................Minneapolis
KCCW 12..Walker

MISSISSIPPI

WCBI-TV 4..................................Columbus
WXVT 15...................................Greenville
WHLT 22..................................Hattiesburg
WJTV 12...Jackson

MISSOURI

KFVS-TV 12.......................Cape Girardeau
*KRCG 13.........................Jefferson City
KCTV 5...............................Kansas City
KOLR-TV 10.............................Springfield
KMOV 4.......................................St. Louis

MONTANA

KTVQ 2 ....Billings
KCTZ 7 ....Bozeman
KXLF-TV 4 ....Butte
KXGN-TV 5 ....Glendive
KRTV 3 ....Great Falls
KPAX-TV 8 ....Missoula

NEBRASKA

KGIN 11 ....Grand Island
KOLN 10................................Lincoln
KMTV 3...................................Omaha
*KSTF 10 ....Scottsbluff

NEVADA

KLAS-TV 8 ....Las Vegas
KTVN 2 ....Reno

NEW MEXICO

KRQE 13 ....Albuquerque
KBIM-TV 10 ....Roswell

NEW YORK

WRGB 6 ....Albany
WBNG-TV 12 ....Binghamton
WIVB-TV 4 ....Buffalo
WWNY-TV 7.........................Carthage
WCBS-TV 2 ....New York
WROC-TV 8 ....Rochester
WTVH 5 ....Syracuse

NORTH CAROLINA

WBTV 3 ....Charlotte
WNCT-TV 9 ....Greenville
WFMY-TV 2.......................High Point
WRAL-TV 5 ....Raleigh

NORTH DAKOTA

KXMB-TV 12 ....Bismarck
KXMA-TV 2 ....Dickinson
KXJB-TV 4.................................Fargo
KXMC-TV 13..............................Minot
KXMD-TV 11 ....Williston

OHIO

WKRC-TV 12 ....Cincinnati
WBNS 10............................Columbus
WHIO-TV 7............................Dayton
WOIO 19 ....Shaker Hts.
WTOL-TV 11 ....Toledo
WKBN-TV 2 ....Youngstown

OKLAHOMA

KWTV 9 ....Oklahoma City
KOTV 6.....................................Tulsa

OREGON

KCBY-TV 11 ....Coos Bay
KVAL-TV 13 ....Eugene
KTVL 10 ....Medford
KOIN 6...................................Portland
KPIC 4...................................Rosebug

PENNSYLVANIA

WTAJ-TV 10 ....Altoona
WSEE-TV 35................................Erie
WHP-TV 21 ....Harrisburg
WLYH-TV 15 ....Lancaster
KYW-TV 3........................Philadelphia
KDKA-TV 2 ....Pittsburgh
WYOU 22 ....Scranton

RHODE ISLAND

WPRI-TV 12 ....E. Providence

SOUTH CAROLINA

WCSC-TV 5 ....Charleston
WLTX 19.............................Columbia
*WBTW 13............................Florence
WSPA-TV 7 ....Spartanburg

SOUTH DAKOTA

KDLO-TV 3 ....Florence
KCLO-TV 15 ....Rapid City
KPLO-TV 6 ....Reliance
KELO-TV 11 ....Sioux Falls

TENNESSEE

WDEF-TV 12 ....Chattanooga
WJHL-TV 11.....................Johnson City
WVLT-TV 8 ....Knoxville
WREG-TV 3 ....Memphis
WTVF 5 ....Nashville

TEXAS

*KTAB-TV 32 ....Abilene
KFDA-TV 10 ....Amarillo
KEYE-TV 42 ....Austin
*KFDM-TV 6.......................Beaumont
KBTX-TV 3................................Bryan
KZTV 10 ....Corpus Christi
KDBC-TV 4 ....El Paso
KGBT-TV 4 ....Harlingen
KHOU-TV 11 ....Houston
KVTV 13 ....Laredo

KLBK-TV 13 (column 3)

KLBK-TV 13 ....Lubbock
KOSA-TV 7................................Odessa
KLST 8................................San Angelo
KENS-TV 5 ....San Antonio
KXII 12................................Sherman
KWTX-TV 10 ....Waco
KAUZ-TV 6 ....Wichita Falls

UTAH

KUTV 2...........................Salt Lake City
KUSG 12 ....St. George

VERMONT

WCAX-TV 3 ....Burlington

VIRGINIA

WTKR 3.................................Norfolk
WTVR-TV 6 ....Richmond
WDBJ 7 ....Roanoke

WASHINGTON

KEPR-TV 19 ....Pasco
KSTW 11..............................Tacoma
KCPQ 13................................Tacoma
KIRO-TV 7................................Seattle
KREM-TV 2 ....Spokane
KIMA-TV 29 ....Yakima

WEST VIRGINIA

WOWK-TV 13.......................Huntington
WDTV 5...................................Weston
WTRF-TV 7 ....Wheeling

WISCONSIN

WFRV-TV 5 ....Green Bay
WKBT 8................................La Crosse
*WISC-TV 3..........................Madison
WDJT-TV 58 ....Milwaukee
WSAW-TV 7 ....Wausau

WYOMING

*KGWC-TV 14............................Casper
*KGWN-T 5 ....Cheyenne
KGWL-TV 5 ....Lander
KGWR-TV 13 ....Rock Springs

U.S. TERRITORIES & POSSESSIONS

AMERICAN SAMOA

*KVZK 5 ....Pago Pago

GUAM

*KUAM-TV 8................................Agana

FOX

ALABAMA

WBRC 6 ....Birmingham
WALA 10.................................Mobile
WCOV-TV 20 ....Montgomery
WDFX-TV 34................................Ozark
*WDBB 17..............................Tuscaloosa

ALASKA

KTBY 4 ....Anchorage
KFXF 7 ....Fairbanks

ARIZONA

KSAZ-TV 10.............................Phoenix
KMSB-TV 11 ....Tucson

ARKANSAS

KLRT 16................................Little Rock

CALIFORNIA

KECY-TV 9 ....El Centro
KBVU 29...................................Eureka
KTTV 11................................Los Angeles
KTVU 2.................................Oakland
KCVU 30...............................Paradise
KTXL 40 ....Sacramento
KCBA 35 ....Salinas
XETV 6 ....San Diego
KMPH 26.................................Visalia

COLORADO

*KXRM-TV 21 ....Colorado Springs
KDVR 31.................................Denver
KFCT 22................................Durango

CONNECTICUT

WTIC-TV 61 ....Hartford

DISTRICT OF COLUMBIA

WTTG 5 ....Washington

FLORIDA

WFTX 36 ....Fort Myers
WAWS 30 ....Jacksonville
WOFL 35...............................Orlando
WSVN 7 ....Miami
WOGX 51..................................Ocala
WPGX 28 ....Panama City
WTLH 49.........................Tallahassee
WTTA 38 ....Tampa
WTVT 13...................................Tampa
WFLX 29 ....West Palm Beach

GEORGIA

WFXL 31 ....Albany
WAGA-TV 5 ....Atlanta
WFXG 54................................Augusta
*WXTX 54..............................Columbus
WGXA 24................................Macon
WPGA-TV 58 ....Perry

HAWAII

KHAW 11 ....Hilo
KHON 2...................................Honolulu
KAII 7.....................................Wailuku

IDAHO

KTRV 12................................Nampa
KXTF 35...............................Twin Falls

ILLINOIS

WYZZ-TV 43.......................Bloomington
WFLD 32 ....Chicago
WQRF-TV 39.........................Rockford
WRSP-TV 55 ....Springfield
WCCU 27................................Urbana

INDIANA

WSJV 28 ....Elkhart
WTVW 7 ....Evansville
WFFT-TV 55 ....Fort Wayne
WXIN 59 ....Indianapolis
WBAK-TV 38 ....Terre Haute

IOWA

KJMH 26................................Burlington
KFXA 28 ....Cedar Rapids
KLJB-TV 18.........................Davenport
KDSM-TV 17 ....Des Moines
KFXB 40................................Dubuque
*KYOU-TV 15 ....Ottumwa

KANSAS

KAAS-TV 18 ....Salina
*KSAS-TV 24 ....Wichita

KENTUCKY

WKNT 40....................................Bowling Green
WDKY-TV 56 ....Lexington
WDRB-TV 41................................Louisville
WXIX-TV 19 ....Newport

LOUISIANA

WGMB 44 ....Baton Rouge
KADN 15 ....Lafayette
KVHP 29....................................Lake Charles
WVUE 8 ....New Orleans
KMSS 33 ....Shreveport

MAINE

*WPXT 51 ....Portland

MARYLAND

WBFF 45 ....Baltimore
*WMDT 47 ....Salisbury

MASSACHUSSETTS

WFXT 25....................................Dedham

MICHIGAN

WGKI 33.....................................Cadillac
WJBK-TV 2..................................Detroit
WSMH 66...................................Flint
WXMI 17 ....Grand Rapids
WSYM-TV 47..............................Lansing
WGKU 45...................................Vanderbilt

MINNESOTA

WFTC 29....................................Minneapolis
KBRR 10....................................Thief River Falls

MISSISSIPPI

WXXV-TV 25...............................Gulfport
WDBD 40....................................Jackson
*WLOV-TV 27 ....West Point

MISSOURI

KBSI 23......................................Cape Girardeau
*KMIZ 17.....................................Columbia
*KRCG 13...................................Jefferson City
*KODE-TV 12 ....Joplin
WDAF-TV 4 ....Kansas City
KDEB 27....................................Springfield
KQTV 2......................................St. Joseph
KTVI 2..St. Louis

MONTANA

KCTZ 7......................................Bozeman
KHMT 4......................................Hardin

NEBRASKA

*KTVG 17 ....Grand Island
*KPTM 42...................................Omaha
*KSTF 10 ....Scottsbluff

NEVADA

KVVU-TV 5..................................Henderson
KRXI 11......................................Reno

NEW MEXICO

KASA-TV 2 ....Santa Fe

NEW YORK

WXXA-TV 23 ....Albany
WICZ-TV 40.................................Binghamton
WUTV 29....................................Buffalo
WYDC 48....................................Corning
WNYW 5.....................................New York
WUHF 31....................................Rochester
WSYT 68....................................Syracuse
WFXV 33....................................Utica

NORTH CAROLINA

WCCB 18....................................Charlotte
WYDO 14....................................Greenville
WGHP-TV 8.................................High Point
WFXI 8..Morehead City
WLFL 22.....................................Raleigh
WSFX 26.....................................Wilmington

NORTH DAKOTA

KVRR 15.....................................Fargo
KNRR 12.....................................Pembina

OHIO

WJW-TV 8...................................Cleveland
WTTE 28.....................................Columbus
WRGT-TV 45 ....Dayton
WUPW 36...................................Toledo

OKLAHOMA

KOKH-TV 25 ....Oklahoma City
KOKI-TV 23 ....Tulsa

OREGON

KLSR 34......................................Eugene
*KMVU 26....................................Medford

PENNSYLVANIA

WFXP 66....................................Erie
WWLF-TV 56 ....Hazleton
*WWCP-TV 8...............................Johnstown
WTXF-TV 29 ....Philadelphia
WPGH-TV 53...............................Pittsburgh
WOLF-TV 38 ....Scranton
WILF 53......................................Williamsport
WPMT 43....................................York

RHODE ISLAND

WNAC-TV 64 ....Providence

SOUTH CAROLINA

WTAT-TV 24................................Charleston
WACH 57....................................Columbia
WHNS 21....................................Greenville
WTGS 28....................................Hardeeville
WFXB 43.....................................Myrtle Beach

SOUTH DAKOTA

KTTM 12.....................................Huron
KIVV-TV 5....................................Lead
KEVN 7.......................................Rapid City
*KTTW 17....................................Sioux Falls

TENNESSEE

WDSI-TV 61 ....Chattanooga
WEMT 39....................................Greeneville
*WBBJ-TV 7.................................Jackson
WMTU 16....................................Jackson
WTNZ 43.....................................Knoxville
WHBQ-TV 13 ....Memphis
WZTV 17.....................................Nashville

TEXAS

KCIT 14.......................................Amarillo
KTBC-TV 7...................................Austin
KYLE 28......................................Bryan
KDFW-TV 4..................................Dallas
KFOX-TV 14.................................El Paso
KRIV 26.......................................Houston
KFXK 51......................................Longview
KJTV 34.......................................Lubbock
*KPEJ 24.....................................Odessa
KIDY 6..San Angelo
KABB 29......................................San Antonio
KWKT 44.....................................Waco
KJTL 18.......................................Wichita Falls
KVCT 19......................................Victoria

UTAH

KSTU 13......................................Salt Lake City

VERMONT

WFFF-TV 44 ....Colchester

VIRGINIA

WJPR 21.....................................Lynchburg
WTVZ 33.....................................Norfolk
*WVBT-TV 43...............................Portsmouth
WRLH-TV 35................................Richmond
WFXR-TV 27................................Roanoke

WASHINGTON

*KAYU-TV 28 ....Spokane
KCPQ 13.....................................Tacoma
KPDX 49.....................................Vancouver

WEST VIRGINIA

WVAH-TV 11 ....Charleston
WVSX 59.....................................Ghent

WISCONSIN

WEUX 48....................................Chippewa Falls
WLUK 11.....................................Green Bay
WLAX 25.....................................La Crosse
WMSN-TV 47 ....Madison
WITI-TV 6....................................Milwaukee

WYOMING

*KGWC-TV 14..............................Casper
KLWY 27.....................................Cheyenne

U.S. TERRITORIES & POSSESSIONS

GUAM

*KTGM 14 ....Tamuning

NBC

ALABAMA

WVTM-TV 13................................Birmingham
*WOWL-TV 15..............................Florence
WAFF 48.....................................Huntsville
WPMI 15......................................Mobile
WSFA 12.....................................Montgomery

ALASKA

KTUU-TV 2...................................Anchorage
KYUK-TV 4...................................Bethel
KTVF 11.......................................Fairbanks
*KJUD 8.......................................Juneau

ARIZONA

KNAZ-TV 2...................................Flagstaff
KPNX 12......................................Phoenix
KVOA-TV 4...................................Tucson
KYMA 11......................................Yuma

ARKANSAS

KTVE 10......................................El Dorado
KPOM-TV 24................................Fort Smith
KARK-TV 19.................................Little Rock
KFAA 51......................................Rogers

CALIFORNIA

KGET 17......................................Bakersfield
KNBC 4.......................................Los Angeles
KCPM 24.....................................Chico
KIEM-TV 3....................................Eureka
KSEE 24......................................Fresno
KMIR-TV 36..................................Palm Springs
KCRA-TV 3...................................Sacramento
KSBW 8.......................................Salinas
KNSD 39......................................San Diego
BAY-TV 35....................................San Francisco
KRON-TV 4...................................San Francisco
KSBY 6..San Luis Obispo

COLORADO

KOAA-TV 5...................................Colorado Springs
KUSA-TV 9...................................Denver
*KREZ-TV 6..................................Durango
KKCO 11.....................................Grand Junction
*KREG-TV 3..................................Glenwood Springs
KREY-TV 10..................................Montrose

CONNECTICUT

WVIT 30.......................................W. Hartford

DISTRICT OF COLUMBIA

WRC-TV 4....................................Washington

FLORIDA

WBBH-TV 20................................Fort Myers
WTLV 12......................................Jacksonville

WTVJ 6..Miami
WESH 2..Orlando
WJHG-TV 7..............................Panama City
WTWC 40......................................Tallahassee
WFLA-TV 8..Tampa
WPTV 5..........................West Palm Beach

GEORGIA

WALB 10..Albany
WXIA-TV 11....................................Atlanta
WAGT 26..Augusta
WLTZ 38..Columbus
WMGT 41..Macon

HAWAII

KHBC-TV 2..Hilo
KHNL 8..Honolulu
KOGG 15..Wailuku

IDAHO

KTVB 7..Boise

ILLINOIS

WICD 15....................................Champaign
WMAQ-TV 5....................................Chicago
WEEK-TV 25..Peoria
WGEM-TV 20......................................Quincy
WREX-TV 13....................................Rockford
WICS 20....................................Springfield

INDIANA

WFIE-TV 14....................................Evansville
WKJG-TV 33..............................Fort Wayne
WTHR 13..................................Indianapolis
WNDU-TV 16..............................South Bend
WTWO 2......................................Terre Haute

IOWA

KWQC-TV 6..................................Davenport
WHO-TV 13................................Des Moines
KTIV 4..Sioux City
KWWL 7..Waterloo

KANSAS

KSNG 11..................................Garden City
KSNC 2..Great Bend
KMCI 38..Lawrence
KSNT 27..Topeka
KSNW 3..Wichita

KENTUCKY

WLEX-TV 18..................................Lexington
WAVE 3..Louisville
WPSD-TV 6..Paducah

LOUISIANA

KALB-TV 5....................................Alexandria
WVLA 33..................................Baton Rouge
KPLC-TV 7..............................Lake Charles
WDSU 6....................................New Orleans

MAINE

WLBZ-TV 2..Bangor
WCSH-TV 6..Portland
*WAGM-TV 8..............................Presque Isle

MARYLAND

WBAL-TV 11....................................Baltimore
WHAG-TV 25..............................Hagerstown
*WMDT 47......................................Salisbury

MASSACHUSSETTS

WHDH-TV 7..Boston
WMFP 62..Lawrence
WWLP 22....................................Springfield

MICHIGAN

WTOM-TV 4..............................Cheboygan
WDIV 4..Detroit
WEYI-TV 25..Flint
WOOD-TV 8..........................Grand Rapids
WLUC 6......................................Marquette
WILX-TV 10....................................Onondaga
WPBN-TV 7..............................Traverse City

MINNESOTA

KBJR-TV 6..Duluth
KARE 11..................................Minneapolis
KTTC 10......................................Rochester

MISSISSIPPI

WDAM-TV 7..................................Hattiesburg
WLBT 3..Jackson
WGBC 30......................................Meridian
WTVA 9..Tupelo

MISSOURI

KOMU-TV 8......................................Columbia
KSNF 16..Joplin
KSHB 41....................................Kansas City
KYTV 3......................................Springfield
KSDK 5..St. Louis

MONTANA

KULR-TV 8..Billings
KTVM 6..Butte
KXGN-TV 5....................................Glendive
KTVH 12..Helena
KCFW-TV 9......................................Kalispell
KECI-TV 13..Missoula

NEBRASKA

KHAS-TV 5..Hastings
KSNK 8..McCook
KNOP-TV 2..................................North Platte
WOWT 6..Omaha

NEVADA

KENV 8..Elko
KVBC 3..Las Vegas
KRNV 4..Reno

NEW JERSEY

WMGM-TV 40............................Wildwood

NEW MEXICO

KOB-TV 4....................................Albuquerque
KOBF 12......................................Farmington
KOBR 8..Roswell

NEW YORK

WNYT 13..Albany
WGRZ-TV 2......................................Buffalo
WWNY-TV 7......................................Carthage
WETM-TV 18..Elmira
WNBC 4..New York
WPTZ 5......................................North Pole
WHEC-TV 10..................................Rochester
WSTM-TV 3......................................Syracuse
WKTV 2..Utica
WWTI 50..Watertown

NORTH CAROLINA

WCNC-TV 36....................................Charlotte
WNCN 17......................................Goldsboro
WITN-TV 7..................................Washington
WECT 6......................................Wilmington
WXII 12..............................Winston-Salem

NORTH DAKOTA

KFYR-TV 5..Bismarck
KQCD-TV 7....................................Dickinson
KVLY-TV 11..Fargo
KMOT 10..Minot
KUMV-TV 8......................................Williston

OHIO

WLWT 5......................................Cincinnati
WKYC-TV 3......................................Cleveland
WCMH 4......................................Columbus
WKEF 22..Dayton
WLIO 35..Lima
WTOV-TV 9..................................Steubenville
WNWO-TV 24..Toledo
WTVG 13..Toledo
WFMJ-TV 21..................................Youngstown
WHIZ-TV 18....................................Zanesville

OKLAHOMA

KFOR-TV 4..........................Oklahoma City
KJRH 2..Tulsa

OREGON

KTVZ 21..Bend
KMTZ 23..Coos Bay
KOTI 2................................Klamath Falls
KOBI 5..Medford
KGW 8..Portland
KMTX-TV 46......................................Rosebug
KMTR 16..Eugene

PENNSYLVANIA

WICU-TV 12..Erie
WJAC-TV 6..................................Johnstown
WGAL 8..Lancaster
WCAU 10..................................Philadelphia
WPXI 11..Pittsburgh
WBRE-TV 28......................Wilkes-Barre

RHODE ISLAND

WJAR 10......................................Cranston

SOUTH CAROLINA

WCBD-TV 2....................................Charleston
WCIV 4..Charleston
WIS 10..Columbia
WYFF 4..Greenville

SOUTH DAKOTA

KDLT 5..Mitchell

TENNESSEE

WRCB-TV 3..................................Chattanooga
WBIR-TV 10......................................Knoxville
WMC-TV 5..Memphis
WSMV-TV 4......................................Nashville

TEXAS

KRBC-TV 9..Abilene
KAMR-TV 4......................................Amarillo
KXAM-TV 14..Austin
KXAN-TV 36..Austin
*KVEO 23....................................Brownsville
KRIS-TV 6..............................Corpus Christi
KTSM-TV 9..El Paso
KXAS-TV 5....................................Fort Worth
KPRC-TV 2..Houston
KGNS-TV 8..Laredo
KCBD-TV 11..Lubbock
KLSB-TV 19..............................Nacogdoches
KWES-TV 9..Odessa
KJAC-TV 4..................................Port Arthur
KACB-TV 3..................................San Angelo
KMOL-TV 4..................................San Antonio
KCEN-TV 6..Temple
KTAL-TV 6....................................Texarkana
KETK-TV 56..Tyler
KFDX-TV 3................................Wichita Falls

UTAH

KSL-TV 5............................Salt Lake City

VERMONT

WNNE-TV 31..........White River Junction

VIRGINIA

WCYB-TV 5..Bristol
WVIR-TV 29......................Charlottesville
WAVY-TV 10..................................Portsmouth
WWBT 12......................................Richmond
WSLS-TV 10......................................Roanoke

WASHINGTON

KNDU 25..Richland
KING-TV 5..Seattle
KHQ-TV 6..Spokane
KCPQ 13..Tacoma
KNDO 23..Yakima

WEST VIRGINIA

WVVA 6..Bluefield
WBOY-TV 12..................................Clarksburg
WSAZ-TV 3......................................Huntington
WTAP-TV 15..................................Parkersburg

WISCONSIN

WEAU-TV 13....................................Eau Claire
WGBA 26....................................Green Bay
WMTV 15..Madison
WTMJ-TV 4......................................Milwaukee
WFJW-TV 12................................Rhinelander

WYOMING

*KTWO-TV 2..Casper
*KKTU 33......................................Cheyenne
KJWY 2..Jackson

U.S. TERRITORIES & POSSESSIONS

GUAM

*KUAM-TV 8..Agana

PUERTO RICO

WLII 11..Caguas

PBS

ALABAMA

WBIQ 10.............................Birmingham
WIIQ 41.................................Demopolis
WDIQ 2...Dozier
WFIQ 36.......................................Florence
WHIQ 25...................................Huntsville
WGIQ 43......................................Louisville
WEIQ 42..Mobile
WAIQ 26...............................Montgomery
WCIQ 7...................Mt. Cheaha St. Park

ALASKA

KAKM 7..................................Anchorage
KYUK-TV 4..................................Bethel
KUAC-TV 9................................Fairbanks
KTOO-TV 3..Juneau

ARIZONA

KAET 8...Phoenix
KOLD-TV 13.................................Tucson
KUAS 27...Tucson
KUAT-TV 6......................................Tucson

ARKANSAS

KETG 9....................................Arkadelphia
KAFT 13................................Fayetteville
KTEJ 19....................................Jonesboro
KETS 2.....................................Little Rock
KEMV 6..........................Mountain View

CALIFORNIA

KRCB 22...Cotati
KEET 13..Eureka
KVPT 18..Fresno
KOCE-TV 50............Huntington Beach
KCET 28.............................Los Angeles
KLCS 58.............................Los Angeles
KIXE 9...Redding
KVIE 6.....................................Sacramento
KVCR-TV 24.................San Bernardino
KPBS 15.................................San Diego
KMTP-TV 32.................San Francisco
KQED 9...........................San Francisco
KTEH 54...................................San Jose
KCSM-TV 60........................San Mateo

COLORADO

KBDI-TV 12.....................................Denver
KRMA-TV 6......................................Denver
KTSC 8..Pueblo

CONNECTICUT

WEDW 49................................Bridgeport
WEDH 24..Hartford
WEDY 65.............................New Haven
WEDN 53......................................Norwich

DELAWARE

WDPB 64.......................................Seaford
WHYY-TV 12.......................Wilmington

DISTRICT OF COLUMBIA

WETA-TV 26........................Washington
WHMM 32............................Washington

FLORIDA

WGCU-TV 30........................Fort Myers
WUFT 5....................................Gainesville
WJCT 7................................Jacksonville
WJEB-TV 59......................Jacksonville
WLRN-TV 17......................................Miami
WPBT 2..Miami
WCEU 15...............New Smyrna Beach
WMFE-TV 24..............................Orlando
WFSG 56.........................Panama City
WSRE 23..................................Pensacola
WFSU-TV 11...........................Tallahassee
WEDU 3...Tampa
WUSF-TV 16....................................Tampa
WXEL-TV 42..............West Palm Beach

GEORGIA

WGTV 8...Athens
WPBA 30...Atlanta
WCLP-TV 18...........................Chatsworth
WDCO-TV 29................................Cochran
WJSP-TV 28................................Columbus
WACS-TV 25...................................Dawson

WVAN-TV 9.................................Savannah
WXGA-TV 8................................Waycross
WCES-TV 20...................................Wrens

HAWAII

KHET 11......................................Honolulu
KMEB 10...Wailuku

IDAHO

KAID 4..Boise
KCDT 26.........................Coeur d'Alene
KUID-TV 12.................................Moscow
KISU-TV 10...............................Pocatello
KIPT 13..................................Twin Falls

ILLINOIS

WSIU-TV 8..............................Carbondale
WEIU-TV 51.............................Charleston
WTTW 11...Chicago
WYCC 20...Chicago
WSEC 14................................Jacksonville
WMEC 22.......................................Macomb
WQPT-TV 24.....................................Moline
WUSI-TV 16..Olney
WTVP 47..Peoria
WQEC 27...Quincy
WILL-TV 12......................................Urbana

INDIANA

WTIU 30...............................Bloomington
WNIN 9.....................................Evansville
WFWA 39............................Fort Wayne
WYIN 56..Gary
WFYI 20................................Indianapolis
WTBU 69...............................Indianapolis
WIPB 49...Muncie
WNIT-TV 34.......................South Bend
WVUT 22....................................Vincennes

IOWA

KBIN 32..............................Council Bluffs
KDIN-TV 11..........................Des Moines
KTIN 21................................Fort Dodge
KIIN-TV 12...............................Iowa City
KYIN 24..................................Mason City
KHIN 36...Red Oak
KSIN 27....................................Sioux City
KRIN 32..Waterloo

KANSAS

KOOD 9..Hays
KPTS 8....................................Hutchinson
KTWU 11...Topeka

KENTUCKY

WKAS 25......................................Ashland
WKGB-TV 53.................Bowling Green
WKYU-TV 24.................Bowling Green
WCVN 54.................................Covington
WKZT-TV 23.....................Elizabethtown
WKHA 36...Hazard
WKLE 46.....................................Lexington
WKMJ 68.....................................Louisville
WKPC-TV 15............................Louisville
WKMA 35.............................Madisonville
WKMR 38....................................Morehead
WKMU 21.......................................Murray
WKOH 31...................................Owensboro
WKON 52.....................................Owenton
WKPD 29.......................................Paducah
WKPI 22...Pikeville
WKSO-TV 29...............................Somerset

LOUISIANA

KLPA-TV 25............................Alexandria
WLPB-TV 27.....................Baton Rouge
KLPB-TV 24................................Lafayette
KLTL-TV 18......................Lake Charles
KLTM-TV 13....................................Monroe
WLAE-TV 32.......................New Orleans
WYES-TV 12......................New Orleans
KLTS-TV 24................................Shreveport

MAINE

WCBB 10.......................................Augusta
WMEA-TV 26.............................Biddeford
WMED-TV 13......................................Calais
WMEB-TV 12......................................Orono
WMEM-TV 10....................Presque Isle

MARYLAND

WMPT 22.................................Annapolis
WMPB 67.....................................Baltimore
WWPB 31.................................Hagerstown
WGPT 36...Oakland
WFPT 62............................Owings Mills
WCPB 28.....................................Salisbury

MASSACHUSETTS

WGBH-TV 2....................................Boston
WGBX-TV 44...................................Boston
WGBY-TV 57.........................Springfield

MICHIGAN

WCML 6..Alpena
WDCP 35..Bad Axe
WCMV 27.......................................Cadillac
WKAR-TV 23.....................East Lansing
WFUM 28...Flint
WGVU-TV 35.................Grand Rapids
WGVK 52...................................Kalamazoo
WCMW 21....................................Manistee
WNMU-TV 13...........................Marquette
WCMU-TV 14...................Mt. Pleasant
WDCQ-TV 19..............University Center

MINNESOTA

KWCM-TV/KSMN-TV 10.............Appleton
KSMQ-TV 15....................................Austin
KAWE 9...Bemidji
KAWB 22......................................Brainerd
WDSE-TV 8.......................................Duluth
KTCA-TV 2....................................St. Paul
KTCI-TV 17...................................St. Paul

MISSISSIPPI

WMAH-TV 19......................................Biloxi
WMAE-TV 12..............................Booneville
WMAU-TV 17.......................................Bude
WMAO-TV 23........................Greenwood
WMAB-TV 2....................................Jackson
WMPN-TV 29................................Jackson
WMAW-TV 14............................Meridian
WMAV-TV 18.....................................Oxford

MISSOURI

KOZJ 26...Joplin
KCPT 19................................Kansas City
KOZK 21..................................Springfield
KETC 9..St. Louis
KMOS-TV 6............................Warrenburg

MONTANA

KUSM 9.......................................Bozeman
KUFM-TV 11................................Missoula

NEBRASKA

KMNE-TV 7....................................Bassett
KHNE-TV 29................................Hastings
KLNE-TV 3.................................Lexington
KUON-TV 12...................................Lincoln
KRNE-TV 12.............................Merriman
KSNK 8..McCook
KXNE-TV 19...................................Norfolk
KPNE-TV 9............................North Platte
KYNE-TV 26.....................................Omaha

NEVADA

KLVX 10..................................Las Vegas
KNPB 5..Reno

NEW HAMPSHIRE

WENH-TV 11...................................Durham
WEKW-TV 52.....................................Keene
WLED-TV 49...................................Littleton

NEW JERSEY

WNJS 23...Camden
WNJN 50....................................Montclair
WNJB 58......................New Brunswick
WNET 13...Newark
WNJT 52..Trenton

NEW MEXICO

KNME-TV 5..........................Albuquerque
KRWG-TV 22........................Las Cruces
KENW 3..Portales

NEW YORK

WSKG-TV 46 ....Binghamton
WNYE-TV 25 ....Brooklyn
WNED-TV 17 ....Buffalo
WNEQ-TV 23 ....Buffalo
WLIW 21 ....Garden City
WNPI-TV 18 ....Norwood
WCFE-TV 57 ....Plattsburgh
WXXI-TV 21 ....Rochester
WCNY-TV 24...............................Syracuse
WNPE-TV 16 ....Watertown

NORTH CAROLINA

WUNF-TV 33 ....Asheville
WUNC-TV 4 ....Chapel Hill
WTVI 42 ....Charlotte
WUND-TV 2................................Columbia
WUNG-TV 58 ....Concord
WUNK-TV 25 ....Greenville
WUNM-TV 19 ....Jacksonville
WUNE-TV 17 ....Linville
WUNP-TV 36 ....Roanoke Rapids
WUNJ-TV 39...........................Wilmington
WUNL-TV 26 ....Winston-Salem

NORTH DAKOTA

KBME 3......................................Bismarck
KDSE 9 ....Dickinson
KJRE 19.....................................Ellendale
KFME 13...Fargo
KGFE 2 ....Grand Forks
KSRE 6 ....Minot
KWSE 4.....................................Williston

OHIO

WEAO 49 ....Akron
WNEO 45.......................................Alliance
WOUB 20 ....Athens
WOUC-TV 44 ....Cambridge
WCET 48 ....Cincinnati
WVIZ-TV 25 ....Cleveland
WOSU 34.................................Columbus
WPTD 16......................................Dayton
WPBO-TV 42..........................Portsmouth
WGTE-TV 30..................................Toledo

OKLAHOMA

KWET 12 ....Cheyenne
KOET 3 ....Eufaula
KETA 13 ....Oklahoma City
KOED-TV 11....................................Tulsa

OREGON

KOAB-TV 3 ....Bend
KOAC-TV 7 ....Corvallis
KEPB-TV 28 ....Eugene
KFTS 22.........................Klamath Falls
KTVR 13 ....La Grande
KSYS 8 ....Medford
KOPB-TV 10.................................Portland

PENNSYLVANIA

WLVT-TV 39 ....Allentown
WPSX-TV 3 ....Clearfield
WQLN 54...Erie
WITF-TV 33 ....Harrisburg
WYBE 35..............................Philadelphia
WQED 13 ....Pittsburgh
WQEX 16...............................Pittsburgh
WVIA-TV 44...............................Pittston

RHODE ISLAND

WSBE-TV 36 ....Providence

SOUTH CAROLINA

WJWJ-TV 16 ....Beaufort
WITV 7 ....Charleston
WRLK-TV 35 ....Columbia
WHMC 23 ....Conway
WJPM-TV 33 ....Florence
WNTV 29...................................Greenville
WNEH 38 ....Greenwood
WNSC-TV 30..............................Rock Hill
WRET-TV 49 ....Spartanburg
WRJA-TV 27 ....Sumter

SOUTH DAKOTA

KDSD-TV 16 ....Aberdeen
KESD-TV 8 ....Brookings
KPSD-TV 13 ....Eagle Butte
KQSD-TV 11 ....Lowry
KZSD-TV 8 ....Martin
KTSD-TV 10..................................Pierre
KBHE-TV 9 ....Rapid City
KCSD-TV 23 ....Sioux Falls
KUSD-TV 2 ....Vermillion

TENNESSEE

WTCI 45 ....Chattanooga
WCTE 22....................................Cookeville
WKOP-TV 15.............................Knoxville
WLJT-TV 11..............................Lexington
WKNO-TV 10............................Memphis
WDCN 8 ....Nashville
WSJK-TV 2 ....Sneedville

TEXAS

KACV-TV 2...................................Amarillo
KLRU-TV 18...................................Austin
KNCT 46...Belton
KAMU-TV 15 ....College Station
KEDT 16 ....Corpus Christi
KERA-TV 13 ....Dallas
KDTN 2 ....Denton
KCOS 13 ....El Paso
KMBH 60 ....Harlingen
KUHT 8...Houston
KTXT-TV 5.....................................Lubbock
KOCV-TV 36...............................Odessa
KLRN 9 ....San Antonio
KCTF 34 ....Waco

UTAH

KULC 9 ....Ogden
KBYU-TV 11...................................Provo
KUED 7 ....Salt Lake City

VERMONT

WETK 33 ....Burlington
WVER 28...................................Rutland
WVTB 20 ....St. Johnsbury
WVTA 41.......................................Windsor

VIRGINIA

WHTJ 41 ....Charlottesville
WNVT 53 ....Falls Church
WVPY 42...............................Front Royal
WHRO-TV 15..............Hampton-Norfolk
WMSY-TV 52 ....Marion
WSBN-TV 47 ....Norton
WCVE-TV 23 ....Richmond
WCVW 57...................University Park
WBRA-TV 15...............................Roanoke
WVPT 51 ....Staunton

WASHINGTON

KCKA 15..Centralia
KWSU-TV 10 ....Pullman
KTNW 31.....................................Richland
KCTS-TV 9 ....Seattle
KSPS-TV 7 ....Spokane
KBTC-TV 28.................................Tacoma
KYVE 47..Yakima

WEST VIRGINIA

WSWP-TV 9 ....Grandview
WPBY-TV 33 ....Huntington
WNPB-TV 24 ....Morgantown

WISCONSIN

WPNE 38...................................Green Bay
WHLA-TV 31 ....Lacrosse
WHA-TV 21 ....Madison
WHWC-TV 28 ....Menomonie
WMVS 10....................................Milwaukee
WLEF-TV 36 ....Park Falls
WHRM-TV 20 ....Wausau

WYOMING

KCWC-TV 4.....................................Lander

U.S. TERRITORIES & POSSESSIONS

AMERICAN SAMOA

KVZK-2 2...............................Pago Pago

GUAM

KGTF 12...Agana

PUERTO RICO

WIPM-TV 3...............................Mayaguez
WIPR-TV 6 ....San Juan

U.S. VIRGIN ISLANDS

WTJX-TV 12 ....Charlotte Amalie

TELEMUNDO

ARIZONA

KHRR 40...Tucson

CALIFORNIA

KMSG-TV 59..................................Fresno
KVEA 52..............................Los Angeles
WSTS 48 ....San Francisco

FLORIDA

WSCV 51 ....Ft. Lauderdale

ILLINOIS

WSNS 44 ....Chicago

NEVADA

KBLR 39 ....Las Vegas

NEW JERSEY

WNJU 47...Linden

NEW MEXICO

KMAZ 48 ....Las Cruces

TEXAS

KTMD 48..Galveston
KFWD 52..............................Fort Worth
KVDA 60..............................San Antonio

PUERTO RICO

WORA-TV 5 ....Mayaguez
WKAQ-TV 2 ....Hato Rey

UNIVISION

ARIZONA

KTVW-TV 33 ....Phoenix

CALIFORNIA

KVYE 7 ....El Centro
KFTV 21 ....Fresno
KMEX-TV 34 ....Los Angeles
KSMS-TV 67 ....Monterey
KUVS 19 ....Sacramento
KDTV 14...............................San Francisco

COLORADO

KCEC 50 ....Denver

FLORIDA

WLTV 23 ....Miami

ILLINOIS

WGBO-TV 66 ....Chicago

MASSACHUSSETTS

WUNI 27 ....Needham

NEVADA

KINC 15 ....Las Vegas
KREN-TV 27 ....Reno

NEW JERSEY

WXTV 41 ....Secaucus

NEW MEXICO

KLUZ-TV 41 ....Albuquerque

TEXAS

KORO 28 ....Corpus Christi
KINT-TV 26 ....El Paso
KUVN 23 ....Garland
KXLN-TV 45...................................Houston
KLDO-TV 27 ....Laredo
KNVO 48 ....McAllen
KWEX-TV 41 ....San Antonio

UPN

ALABAMA

WABM 68 ....Birmingham
*WAAY 31 ....Huntsville

ALASKA

KYES 5 ....Anchorage

ARIZONA

KUTP 45...Phoenix
KTTU-TV 18......................................Tucson

ARKANSAS

KASN 38.....................................Pine Bluff

CALIFORNIA

KUVI-TV 45 ....Bakersfield
KAIL 53 ....Fresno
KCOP 13..................................Los Angeles
KADY-TV 63..................................Oxnard
KCVU 30 ....Paradise
KPWB 31 ....Sacramento
KUSI-TV 51 ....San Diego
KBHK-TV 44 ....San Francisco
KQCA 58 ....Stockton

COLORADO

*KXRM-TV 21................Colorado Springs
KTVD 20 ....Denver

CONNECTICUT

WTXX 20 ....Waterbury

DISTRICT OF COLUMBIA

WDCA 20 ....Washington

FLORIDA

WBFS-TV 33 ....Miami
WTEV 47.................................Jacksonville
WRBW 65 ....Orlando
WTVX 34 ....West Palm Beach
WJTC 44..Pensacola
WTOG 44 ....St. Petersburg

GEORGIA

WUPA 69..Atlanta
*WFXG 54...................................Augusta
WUBI 34 ....Baxley
*WXTX 54...................................Columbus
WGNM 64...Macon
WGVP 44 ....Valdosta

HAWAII

KFVE 5...Honolulu

IDAHO

*KNIN 9..Caldwell
*KXTF 35....................................Twin Falls

ILLINOIS

WPWR-TV 50 ....Chicago
*WHOI 19...Peoria
*WRSP-TV 55 ....Springfield

INDIANA

*WFFT-TV 55 ....Fort Wayne
WNDY 23 ....Indianapolis
WTTV 4.....................................Indianapolis
WFTE 58..Salem

IOWA

*KYOU-TV 15.............................Ottumwa

KANSAS

*KSAS-TV 24...............................Wichita

KENTUCKY

WDKA-TV 49 ....Paducah

LOUISIANA

*KLAX-TV 31.........................Alexandria
WUPL 54...........................New Orleans
*KSHV 45 ....Shreveport
*KARD 14 ....West Monroe

MAINE

*WPXT 51 ....Portland

MARYLAND

WHSW-TV 24 ....Baltimore

MASSACHUSETTS

WSBK-TV 38.......................................Boston
WLWC-TV 28 ....New Bedford

MICHIGAN

*WGKI 33.......................................Cadillac
WKBD 50..Detroit

MINNESOTA

KMSP-TV 9 ....Minneapolis

MISSISSIPPI

*WLOV-TV 27.........................West Point

MISSOURI

*KRCG 13 ....Jefferson City

MONTANA

*KCTZ 7 ....Bozeman
*KFBB-TV 5 ....Great Falls

NEBRASKA

*KTVG 17 ....Grand Island
*KPTM 42..Omaha

NEVADA

*KAME-TV 21.................................Reno

NEW JERSEY

WWOR-TV 9 ....Secaucus

NEW MEXICO

*KASY-TV 50.....................Albuquerque

NEW YORK

*WMGC-TV 34 ....Binghamton
WNYS-TV 43 ....Syracuse

NORTH CAROLINA

WJZY 46...Belmont
WRDC 28 ....Durham
WUPN-TV 48 ....Greensboro

OHIO

WWHO-TV 53 ....Chilicothe
WUAB 43...Lorain

OKLAHOMA

KTLC 43 ....Oklahoma City
KTFO 41 ....Tulsa

OREGON

KEVU 34 ....Eugene
*KMVU 26 ....Medford
KPTV 12 ....Portland

PENNSYLVANIA

*WWCP-TV 8 ....Johnstown
WPSG-TV 57 ....Philadelphia

SOUTH CAROLINA

WMMP-TV 36 ....Charleston
WWMB 21.......................................Florence

SOUTH DAKOTA

*KTTW 17 ....Sioux Falls

TENNESSEE

WFLI-TV 53 ....Cleveland
WLMT 30 ....Memphis
WUXP-TV 30 ....Nashville

TEXAS

*KTAB-TV 32 ....Abilene
*KFDM-TV 6 ....Beaumont
*KVEO 23............................Brownsville
KTXA 21...................................Fort Worth
KTXH 20 ....Houston
*KGNS-TV 8..................................Laredo
*KPEJ 24 ....Odessa

UTAH

KJZZ-TV 14 ....Salt Lake City

VIRGINIA

WDRL 24...Danville
WGNT 27 ....Portsmouth

WASHINGTON

*KAYU-TV 28 ....Spokane

WISCONSIN

*WACY 32 ....Appleton
*WLAX 25...................................La Crosse
*WISC-TV 3 ....Madison
*WAOW-TV 9 ....Wausau

WB

ALABAMA

WTTO 21 ....Birmingham
*WOWL-TV 15............................Florence
WSWS-TV 66............................Opelika
*WDBB 17 ....Tuscaloosa

ARIZONA

KMOH 6 ....Kingman
KASW 61......................................Phoenix

CALIFORNIA

KGMC 43 ....Fresno
KTLA 5 ....Los Angeles
KOFY-TV 20 ....San Francisco
KSWB 69..........................San Francisco

COLORADO

KWGN-TV 2...................................Denver

CONNECTICUT

WBNE 59...............................New Haven

DISTRICT OF COLUMBIA

WBDC-TV 50 ....Washington

FLORIDA

WJWB 17.............................Jacksonville
WDZL 39...Miami
WTVK 46...Naples
WKCF 18...Orlando
WFGX 35...................................Pensacola

GEORGIA

WATL 36..Atlanta

IDAHO

*KNIN-TV 9.................................Caldwell

HAWAII

KWHE/KWHH 14 ....Honolulu

ILLINOIS

WCIU-TV 26.................................Chicago
WGN-TV 9 ....Chicago

INDIANA

WHME-TV 46 ....South Bend

KENTUCKY

WGRB 34.............................Cambellsville
WBNA 21..................................Louisville

LOUISIANA

WNOL-TV........................38 New Orleans
*KSHV 45 ....Shreveport

MARYLAND

WNUV-TV 54 ....Baltimore
WJAL 68 ....Hagerstown

MASSACHUSETTS

WLVI-TV 56...................................Boston

MICHIGAN

WXON 20 ....Detroit
WLLA 64 ....Kalamazoo

MINNESOTA

KLGT-TV 23 ....Minneapolis

MISSOURI

KNLJ 25 ....Jefferson City
KCWB 29 ....Kansas City
KSMO-TV 62 ....Kansas City
KPLR-TV 11 ....St. Louis

MONTANA

*KYUS-TV 3 ....Miles City

NEBRASKA

KXVO 15 ....Omaha

NEVADA

KFBT 33 ....Las Vegas
KUPN-21 ....Las Vegas

NEW MEXICO

*KASY-TV 50........................Albuquerque

NEW YORK

WNYO-TV 49 ....Buffalo
WPIX 11 ....New York

NORTH CAROLINA

WRAZ 50 ....Raleigh

OHIO

WBNX 55.......................................Akron
*WWHO 53............................Chillicothe
WSTR-TV 64 ....Cincinnati

OKLAHOMA

KOCB 34 ....Oklahoma City
KWHB 47..Tulsa

OREGON

KWBP 32 ....Salem/Portland
KROZ 36..................................Roseburg

PENNSYLVANIA

WPHL-TV 17 ....Philadelphia
WCWB-TV 22 ....Pittsburgh

SOUTH CAROLINA

*WBTW 13 ....Florence
WFVT 55....................................Rock Hill

TENNESSEE

WNAB 58.................................Nashville

TEXAS

KNVA 54..Austin
KDAF 33..Dallas
KHTV 39......................................Houston
KRRT 35............................San Antonio

UTAH

KOOG-TV 30 ....Ogden

VIRGINIA

WUPV 65 ....Ashland
*WVBT-TV 43...................Virginia Beach

WASHINGTON

KTZZ-TV 22 ....Seattle

WISCONSIN

*WACY 32 ....Appleton
WVTV 18...................................Milwaukee

WYOMING

*KTWO-TV 2................................Casper
*KKTU 33...................................Cheyenne

*indicates secondary affiliate.

535

DIGITAL TELEVISION STATIONS

In April 1998, ABC, CBS, FOX and NBC announced their format choices for digital transmission. The format is identified by the number of scanning lines (480, 720 or 1080) and by how the lines are presented on the screen (interlaced or progressive). Digital television stations broadcast the first digital signal in November 1998 with the NFL.

ATLANTA

WSB-TV, Channel 39, ABC
1601 W. Peachtree St. N.E., Atlanta, GA 30309-2641. (404) 897-7000. FAX: (404) 897-7525. Cox Broadcasting.

WXIA-TV, Channel 10, NBC
1611 W. Peachtree St. N.E., Atlanta, GA 30309. (404) 892-1611. FAX: (404) 892-0182. Gannett Broadcasting.

BOSTON

WCVB-TV, Channel 20, ABC
5 TV Pl., Boston, MA 02194. (617) 449-0400. FAX: (617) 433-4752. Hearst-Argyle Television, Inc.

WMUR-TV, Channel 59, ABC
P. O. Box 9, 100 S. Commercial St., Manchester, NH 03105. (603) 669-9999. FAX: (603) 641-9065. Imes Communications.

CHICAGO

WMAQ-TV, Channel 29, NBC
454 N. Columbus Dr., Chicago, IL 60611. (312) 836-5555. FAX: (312) 527-9072. NBC TV Stations Division.

DALLAS-FORT WORTH

KDFW-TV, Channel 35, FOX
400 N. Griffin St., Dallas, TX 75202. (214) 720-4444. FAX: (214) 720-3177. Fox Stations Group.

KXAS-TV, Channel 41, NBC
3900 Barnett, Fort Worth, TX 76103. (214) 745-5555. FAX: (817) 654-6362. LIN Television Corp.

WFAA-TV, Channel 9, ABC
Communication Ctr., 606 Young St., Dallas, TX 75202-4810. (214) 748-9631. FAX: (214) 977-6268. A.H. Belo Corp.

DETROIT

WJBK-TV, Channel 58, FOX
P. O. Box 2000, Southfield, MI 48037-2000. (810) 557-2000. FAX: (810) 552-0280. Fox Stations Group.

WWJ-TV, Channel 44, CBS
300 River Place, Detroit, MI 48207. (313) 259-6288. FAX: (313) 259-8215. CBS Station Group.

LOS ANGELES

KNBC, Channel 36, NBC
3000 W. Alameda St., Burbank, CA 91523. (818) 840-4444. FAX: (310) 840-3535. NBC TV Stations.

KABC, Channel 53, ABC
4151 Prospect Ave., Los Angeles, CA 90027. (310) 557-7777. FAX: (310) 557-5036. Capital Cities/ABC.

KTLA-TV, Channel 31, WB
5800 Sunset Blvd., Los Angeles, CA 90028. (213) 460-5500. FAX: (213) 460-5405. Tribune Broadcasting Co.

NEW YORK

WCBS-TV, Channel 56, CBS
524 W. 57 St., New York, NY 10019. (212) 975-7609. FAX: (212) 975-5656. CBS Station Group.

PHILADELPHIA

KYW-TV, Channel 26, CBS
101 S. Independence Mall E., Philadelphia, PA 19106. (215) 238-4700. FAX: (215) 238-4545. CBS Station Group.

WCAU, Channel 67, NBC 10
10 Monument Road, Bala Cynwyd, PA 19131. (610) 668-5510. FAX: (610) 668-7039. NBC TV Stations Division.

WPVI-TV, Channel 64, ABC
4100 City Line Ave., Philadelphia, PA 19131. (215) 878-9700. FAX: (215) 581-4515. ABC Broadcasting.

WTXF-TV, Channel 42, FOX
330 Market St., Philadelphia, PA 19106. (215) 925-2929. FAX: (215) 592-1535. Fox Television Stations Inc.

SAN FRANCISCO

KGO-TV, Channel 24, ABC
900 Front St., San Francisco, CA 94111-1427. (415) 954-7777. FAX: (415) 954-7294. Capital Cities/ABC Broadcast Group.

KPIX TV, Channel 29, CBS
855 Battery St., San Francisco, CA 94111-1503. (415) 362-5550. FAX: (415) 765-8844. CBS Station Group.

KRON-TV, Channel 57, NBC
1001 Van Ness Ave., San Francisco, CA 94109. (415) 441-4444. FAX: (415) 561-8136. Chronicle Broadcasting Inc.

WASHINGTON DC

WJLA-TV, Channel 39, ABC
3007 Tilden St. NW, Washington, DC 20008. (202) 364-7777. FAX: (202) 364-7922. Allbritton Communications Co.

WRC-TV, Channel 48, NBC
4001 Nebraska Ave. NW, Washington, DC 20016. (202) 885-4000. FAX: (202) 885-5022. NBC TV Stations Division.

WUSA, Channel 34, CBS
4100 Wisconsin Ave. NW, Washington, DC 20016. (202) 895-5999. FAX: (202) 966-7948. Gannett Broadcasting.

TOP NATIONAL TELEVISION GROUPS

Arranged alphabetically. These groups represent the largest holders of individual stations, and are not ranked by demographic areas covered. Holdings include part ownerships, local marketing agreements and time brokerage agreements. Number in parenthesis represents the number of owned stations.

A. H. BELO CORP. (17 stations)
400 South Record Street, Dallas, TX 75202. (214) 977-6606.
CHAIRMAN, PRESIDENT & CEO
Robert W. Decherd
VICE CHAIRMAN, CEO & PRESIDENT, BROADCAST DIVISION
Ward L. Huey
ABC: WFAA Dallas, KXTV Sacramento, WVEC Norfolk, WHAS Louisville.
CBS: KHOU Houston, KMOV St. Louis, KENS San Antonio, WWL New Orleans, KOTV Tulsa, KREM Spokane.
FOX: KASA Albuquerque, KMSB Tuscon.
NBC: KING Seattle, KGW Portland, WCNC Charlotte, KHNL Honolulu (satellites KHBC & KOGG), KTVB Boise.

FOX TELEVISION STATIONS INC. (23 stations)
(A subsidiary of News Corp.) Box 900, Beverly Hills, CA 90213. (310) 369-2300.
PRESIDENT & COO
Mitch Stern
CHAIRMAN & CEO
Chase Carey
FOX: WNYW New York, KTTV Los Angeles, WFLD Chicago, WTXF Philadelphia, WFXT Boston, WTTG Washington, KDFW Dallas, WJBK Detroit, WAGA Atlanta, KRIV Houston, WJW Cleveland, WTVT Tampa, KSAZ Phoenix, KDVR Denver, KTVI St. Louis, WDAF Kansas City, WITI Milwaukee, KSTU Salt Lake City, WHBQ Memphis, WGHP Greensboro, WBRC Birmingham, KTBC Austin, KDFI Dallas.

GANNETT BROADCASTING (19 stations)
(A subsidiary of Gannett Co.)11000 Wilson Blvd., Arlington, VA 22234. (703) 284-6760.
PRESIDENT
Cecil L. Walker
ABC: WZZM Grand Rapids, KVUE Austin.
CBS: WUSA Washington DC, WTSP Tampa, WFMY Greensboro, KTHV Little Rock, WLTX Columbia, WMAZ Macon.
NBC: WXIA Atlanta, WKYC Cleveland, KARE Minneapolis, KPNX Mesa/Phoenix (satellite KNAZ), KUSA Denver, KSDK St. Louis, WGRZ Buffalo, WTLV Jacksonville, WBIR Knoxville, WCSH Portland, WLBZ Bangor.
WB: (satellite) KMOH Kingman.

HEARST-ARGYLE TELEVISION INC. (16 stations)
959 Eight Ave., New York, NY 10019. (212) 649-2300.
VICE PRESIDENT
David Barrett
CHAIRMAN & CO-CEO
Bob Marbut
PRESIDENT & CO-CEO
John G. Conomikes
ABC: WCVB Boston, WTAE Pittsburgh, KMBC Kansas City, WISN Miwaukee, WPBF West Palm Beach, KOCO Oklahoma City, KITV Honolulu (satellites KHVO & KMAU), WAPT Jackson, KHBS Fort Smith (satellite KHOG).
IND: WWWB Tampa/St. Petersburg
NBC: WBAL Baltimore, WLWT Cincinnati, WPTZ Burlington (satellite WNNE), KSBW Salinas/Monterey.

HICKS, MUSE, TATE & FURST INC. (23 stations)
(Includes LIN TV Corp and Sunrise TV Corp.) 200 Crescent Court, Ste. 1600, Dallas, TX 75201. (214) 740-7300.
PRESIDENT, LIN TELEVISION
Gary R. Chapman
PRESIDENT, SUNRISE TELEVISION
Robert N. Smith
CHAIRMAN
Thomas O. Hicks
ABC: WTNH New Haven, WDTN Dayton, WAND Decatur, WOTV Battle Creek/Grand Rapids.
CBS: WISH Indianapolis, WIVB Buffalo, WROC Rochester, WANE Fort Wayne.
FOX: WNAC Providence.
IND: KXTX Dallas.
NBC: WOOD Grand Rapids, WAVY Norfolk, WVTM Birmingham, KXAN Llano/Austin, WEYI Flint/Saginaw, WJAC Johnstown, WTOV Wheeling/Steubenville, KRBC Abilene, KACB San Angelo.
WB: WBNE New Haven, WVBT Virginia Beach/Norfolk (WB/**Fox**), KNVA Austin.

PARAMOUNT STATIONS GROUP INC. (17 stations)
(Subsidiary of Viacom International Inc.) 5555 Melrose Ave., Hollywood, CA 90038. (213) 956-8100.
PRESIDENT
Anthony Cassara
CHAIRMAN, PARAMOUNT TV GROUP
Kerry McCluggage
UPN: WPSG Philadelphia, WSBK Boston, WDCA WAshington, KTXA Dallas, WKBD Detroit, WUPA Atlanta, KTXH Houston, KSTW Tacoma/Seattle, WTOG Tampa/St. Petersburg, WBFS Miami, KPWB Sacramento, WNDY Indianapolis, WGNT Norfolk/Portsmouth, WWHO Columbus (UPN/WB), WUPL New Orleans, KTLC Oklahoma City, WTVX West Palm Beach, WLWC New Bedford.

PAXSON COMMUNICATIONS CORP. (55 stations)
601 Clearwater Park, West Palm Beach, FL 33401. (561) 659-4122.
CHAIRMAN
Lowell W. Paxson
PRESIDENT, TV STATION GROUP
Jay Hoker
IND: WHAI New York, WPXN New York, KPXN Los Angeles, WCFC Chicago, WPPX Philadelphia, KKPX San Francisco, WPXB Boston, WPXW Washington, KPXD Dallas, WBSX Detroit, WPXA Atlanta, KPXB Houston, KWPX Seattle, WVPX Cleveland, KPXM Minneapolis, WXPX Tampa, WXPM Miami, KBPX Phoenix, KAJW Phoenix, KPXC Denver, WPCB Pittsburg, KCMY Sacramento, WOPX Orlando, WFPX Raleigh, KPXE Kansas City, WNPX Nashville, KUPX Salt Lake City, WPXV Norfolk, WAQF Buffalo, WPXP West Palm Beach, KOPX Oklahoma City, WGPX Greensboro, WQPX Wilkes Barre, WPXQ Providence, WPXH Birmingham, WYPX Albany, WDPX Dayton, KPXF Fresno, KVUT Little Rock, WKRP Charleston, KTPX Tulsa, WPXK Knoxville, WPXR Roanoke, WPXG Green Bay, KPXO Honolulu, WAQF Rochester, KTVC Cedar Rapids, WJWN San Sebastian, WKPV Ponce, WJPX San Juan, WBPX Boston, WHPX Hartford.
HSN: KBSP Salem/Portland, WCCL New Orleans, WFBI Memphis.

RAYCOM MEDIA INC (23 stations)
201 Monroe St., Ste. 710, Montgomery, AL 36104. (334) 206-1400.
PRESIDENT & CEO
John Hayes
CHAIRMAN
John Stein
ABC: KSFY Sioux Falls (satellites KABY & KPRY), WTVM Columbus, KTVO Ottumwa/Kirksville.
CBS: WTVR Richmond, KSLA Shreveport, KOLD Tucson, WAFB Baton Rouge, KFVS Cape Girardeau. WTOC Savannah.
FOX: WTNZ Knoxville, WUPW Toledo, WACH Columbia.
NBC: WMC Memphis, WSTM Syracuse, WAFF Huntsville, KWWL Cedar Rapids, WPBN Traverse City/Cadillac (satellite WTOM), KNDO Yakima (satellite KNDU), WECT Wilmington, WDAM Laurel/Hattiesburg, WLUC Marquette.

SINCLAIR BROADCAST GROUP INC. (56 stations)
2000 W. 41st St., Baltimore, MD 21211. (410) 467-5000.
PRESIDENT
David D. Smith
ABC: KDNL St. Louis, WLOS Asheville, WXLV Greensboro/Winston-Salem, WCHS Charleston,WEAR Mobile/Pensacola.
CBS: KOVR Sacramento.
FOX: WPGH Pittsburgh, WBFF Baltimore, WLFL Raleigh-Durham, WZTV Nashville, WUTV Buffalo, KOKH Oklahoma City, WRGT Dayton, WVAH Charleston, WRLH Richmond, WTTE Columbus, KABB San Antonio, WSMH Flint, WDKY Lexington, KDSM Des Moines, WSYT Syracuse, WUHF Rochester, KBSI Paducah/Cape Girardeau, WMSN Madison, WEMT Tri-Cities, WYZZ Peoria, WTAT Charleston, WFXV Utica.
IND: WTTV (satellite WTTK) Indianapolis, WCGV Milwaukee, WFBC Asheville, WABM Birmingham.
NBC: WKEF Dayton, KETK Tyler Longview (satellite KLSB).
UPN: WMMP Charleston, WRDC Raleigh/Durham, WUXP Nashville, WUPN Grennsboro/Winston-Salem, WNYS Syracuse, WDKA Paducah/Cape Girardeau.
WB: KLGT Minneapolis, WSTR Cincinnati, KSMO Kansas City, KOCB Oklahoma City, WTTO Birmingham, KUPN Las Vegas, WCWB Pittsburgh, WNUV Baltimore, WVTV Milwaukee, KRRT San Antonio, KFBT Las Vegas, WFGX Mobile, WDBB Tuscaloosa.

TRIBUNE BROADCASTING (19 stations)
435 N. Michigan Avenue, Ste. 1900, Chicago, IL 60611. (312) 222-3333.
PRESIDENT
Dennis FitzSimmons
ABC: WGNO New Orleans.
CBS: WGNX Atlanta.
FOX: KTXL Sacramento, WXIN Indianapolis, WTIC Hartford, WXMI Grand Rapids, WPMT Harrisburg.
WB: WPIX New York, KTLA Los Angeles, WGN Chicago, WPHL Philadelphia, WLVI Cambridge/Boston, WBDC Washington DC, KDAF Dallas/Fort Worth, KHTV Houston, KTTZ Seattle, WDZL Miami, KWGN Denver, KSWB San Diego.

State Broadcast Associations

ALABAMA BROADCASTERS ASSOCIATION
1316 Alford Ave., Suite 201, Birmingham AL 35226. (205) 979-1690. FAX: (205) 979-9981. URL: http://www.AL-Broadcasters.org
EXECUTIVE DIRECTOR
Ben K. McKinnon

ALASKA BROADCASTERS ASSOCIATION
Box 102424, Anchorage, AK 99510. (907) 258-2424. FAX: (907) 258-2414.
EXECUTIVE DIRECTOR
Robin Kornfield

ARIZONA BROADCASTERS ASSOCIATION
3800 N. Central Ave., Suite 1120, Phoenix, AZ 85012. (602) 274-1418. FAX: (602) 631-9853. URL: http://www.az.brdcstrs.com
EXECUTIVE DIRECTOR
Art Brooks

ARKANSAS BROADCASTERS ASSOCIATION
2024 Arkansas Valley Drive, Suite 201, Little Rock, AR 72212. (501) 227-7564. FAX: (501) 223-9798. email: aba@intellinet.com
PRESIDENT
Trey Stafford

CALIFORNIA BROADCASTERS ASSOCIATION
916 L St., Suite 1150, Sacramento, CA 95814. (916) 444-2237. FAX: (916) 444-2043. URL: http://www.cabroadcasters.org
EXECUTIVE DIRECTOR
Stan Statham

COLORADO BROADCASTERS ASSOCIATION
Five Points Floral Media Center, 2900 Welton St., Suite 320, Denver, CO 80205. (303) 293-2100. FAX: (303) 293-3835.
EXECUTIVE DIRECTOR
Douglas R. Wayland

CONNECTICUT BROADCASTERS ASSOCIATION
Box 678, Glastonbury, CT 06033. (860) 633-5031. FAX: (860) 657-2491. email: pktcba@aol.com
PRESIDENT
Paul K. Taff

FLORIDA ASSOCIATION OF BROADCASTERS, INC.
101 E. College Ave., Tallahassee, FL 32301. (850) 681-6444. FAX: (850) 222-3957. URL: http://www.fab.org
PRESIDENT
C. Patrick Roberts

GEORGIA ASSOCIATION OF BROADCASTERS, INC.
8010 Roswell Rd., Suite 260, Atlanta, GA 30350. (770) 395-7200. FAX: (770) 395-7235. email: sandersb@gab.org
URL: http://www.gab.org
EXECUTIVE DIRECTOR
William G. Sanders

HAWAII ASSOCIATION OF BROADCASTERS
Box 91049, Honolulu, HI 96835. (808) 591-4214. FAX: (808) 591-9085.
PRESIDENT
Susii K. Hearst
DIRECTOR
Greg Mueller

IDAHO STATE BROADCASTERS ASSOCIATION
2419 W. State St., Suite 5, Boise, ID 83702. (208) 345-3072. FAX: (208) 343-8046.
PRESIDENT
Connie Searles

ILLINOIS BROADCASTERS ASSOCIATION
1125 S. 5th St., Springfield, IL 62704. (217) 753-2636. FAX: (217) 753-8443. email: ilbrdcst@fgi.net. URL: http://www.ilba.org
EXECUTIVE VICE PRESIDENT
Wally Gair

INDIANA BROADCASTERS ASSOCIATION, INC.
11919 Brookshire Pkwy., Carmel, IN 46033. (317) 573-0119. FAX: (317) 573-0895.
EXECUTIVE DIRECTOR
Linda Compton
PRESIDENT, TV
John Newcomb

IOWA BROADCASTERS ASSOCIATION
Box 71186, Des Moines, IA 50325. (515) 224-7237. FAX: (515) 224-6560. email: iowaiba@dwy.com

KANSAS ASSOCIATION OF BROADCASTERS
1916 S.W. Sieben Ct., Topeka, 66611-1656. (785) 235-1307. FAX: (785) 233-3052. email: harriet@kab.net
URL: http://www.kab.net
PRESIDENT
Harriet J. Lange
CHAIRMAN
Joe Engel

KENTUCKY BROADCASTERS ASSOCIATION
Box 635, 1505 Twilight Trail, Frankfort, KY 40602. (502) 227-0157. FAX: (502) 227-0726.
EXECUTIVE DIRECTOR & TREASURER
Gary R. White
PRESIDENT
Wayne Martin

LOUISIANA ASSOCIATION OF BROADCASTERS
5425 Galeria, Suite F, Baton Rouge, LA 70816. (504) 295-1110. FAX: (504) 295-1159.
EXECUTIVE DIRECTOR
Louise Munson

MAINE ASSOCIATION OF BROADCASTERS
128 State St., Augusta, ME 04330. (207) 623-3870. FAX: (207) 621-0585.
EXECUTIVE DIRECTOR
Suzanne Goucher

MARYLAND-DISTRICT OF COLUMBIA-DELAWARE BROADCASTERS ASSOCIATION
1 E. Chase St., Suite 1129, Baltimore, MD 21202. (410) 385-0224. FAX: (410) 783-1875.
PRESIDENT
Chip Weinman

MASSACHUSETTS BROADCASTERS ASSOCIATION INC.
43 Riverside Ave., Suite 401, Medford, MA 02155. (800) 471-1875. FAX: (800) 471-1876.
PRESIDENT
B. Allan Sprague

MICHIGAN ASSOCIATION OF BROADCASTERS
819 N. Washington Ave., Lansing, MI 48906. (517) 484-7444. FAX: (517) 484-5810.
PRESIDENT
Karole White

MINNESOTA BROADCASTERS ASSOCIATION
Box 16030, 3517 Raleigh Ave. S., St. Louis Park, MN 55416-0030. (612) 926-8123. FAX: (612) 926-9761.email: idubois@minnesotabroadcasters.com. URL: http://www.min-nesotabroadcasters.com
PRESIDENT & CEO
Jim DuBois

MISSISSIPPI ASSOCIATION OF BROADCASTERS
15 Northtown Dr., Suite A, Jackson, MS 39211. (601) 957-9175. FAX: (601) 957-9121.
PRESIDENT
Jackie Lett

MISSOURI BROADCASTERS ASSOCIATION
P.O. Box 104445, 1803 Sun Valley Dr., Jefferson City, MO 65110-4445. (314) 636-6692. FAX: (314) 634-8258.
EXECUTIVE V.P.
Donald J. Hick

MONTANA BROADCASTERS ASSOCIATION
Box 503, Helena, MT 59624. (406) 442-3961. FAX: (406) 442-3987.
PRESIDENT
Dan Michael

NEBRASKA BROADCASTERS ASSOCIATION
12020 Shamrock Pl., Suite 200, Omaha, NE 68154. (402) 778-5178.
EXECUTIVE DIRECTOR
Richard Palmquist

NEVADA BROADCASTERS ASSOCIATION
2255-A Renaissance Dr., Las Vegas, NV 89119. (702) 891-0177. FAX: (702) 891-0203. email: RDFNBA@aol.com
PRESIDENT & CEO
Robert D. Fisher

NEW HAMPSHIRE ASSOCIATION OF BROADCASTERS
10 Chestnut Dr., Bedford, NH 03110. (603) 472-9800. FAX: (603) 472-9803.
PRESIDENT
B. Allan Sprague

NEW JERSEY BROADCASTERS ASSOCIATION
348 Applegate Rd., Cranbury, NJ 08512. (609) 860-0111. FAX: (609) 860-0110. email: proberts@njba.com. URL: http://www.njba.com
EXECUTIVE DIRECTOR
Phil Roberts

NEW MEXICO BROADCASTERS ASSOCIATION
Box 21760, Albuquerque, NM 87154-1760. (505) 881-4444. FAX: (505) 881-5353. email: pmaes@nmba.org. URL: http://www.nmba.org
EXECUTIVE DIRECTOR
Paula Maes

NEW YORK STATE BROADCASTERS ASSOCIATION, INC.
115A Great Oaks Blvd., Albany, NY 12203. (518) 456-8888. FAX: (518) 456-8943.
PRESIDENT
Joseph A. Reilly

NORTH CAROLINA ASSOCIATION OF BROADCASTERS
Box 627, Raleigh, NC 27602. (919) 821-7300. FAX: (919) 839-0304. email: ncbrdsast@aol.com
PRESIDENT
John Dawson

NORTH DAKOTA BROADCASTERS ASSOCIATION
Box 3178, Bismarck, ND 58502-3178. (701) 258-1332. FAX: (701) 258-1332. email: beth@ndba.org
EXECUTIVE DIRECTOR
Beth A. Helfrich

NORTHERN CALIFORNIA BROADCASTERS ASSOC.
131 Stewart St., Suite 301, San Francisco, CA 94105. (415) 546-NCBA. FAX: (415) 546-6290.
PRESIDENT
Thomas Martz

OHIO ASSOCIATION OF BROADCASTERS, INC.
88 E. Broad St., Suite 1180, Columbus, OH 43215. (614) 228-4052. FAX: (614) 228-8133. email: csoab@aol.com. URL: http://www.oabok.org
EXECUTIVE V.P.
Dale V. Bring

OKLAHOMA ASSOCIATION OF BROADCASTERS
6520 N. Western, Suite 104, Oklahoma City, OK 73116. (405) 848-0771. FAX: (405) 848-0772.
EXECUTIVE DIRECTOR
Carl C. Smith

OREGON ASSOCIATION OF BROADCASTERS
Box 449, 111 W. 7th St., Suite 320, Eugene, OR 97440-0449. (503) 343-2101. FAX: (503) 343-0662. email: theoab@ordata.com
EXECUTIVE DIRECTOR
Bill Johnstone

PENNSYLVANIA ASSOCIATION OF BROADCASTERS
475 W. Governor, Suite 3, Hershey, PA 17033. (717) 534-2504. FAX: (717) 533-1119. URL: http://www.pab.org
PRESIDENT
Richard E. Wyckoff

RHODE ISLAND BROADCASTERS ASSOCIATION
c/o WNRI Radio, 786 Diamond Hill Rd., Woonsocket, RI 02895. (401) 769-6925. FAX: (401) 762-0442.
EXECUTIVE DIRECTOR
Roger Bouchard

SOUTH CAROLINA BROADCASTERS ASSOCIATION
College of Journalism & Mass Communications, Univ. of South Carolina, Columbia, SC 29208. (803) 777-6783. FAX: (803) 777-8729. email: sunny@scba.net. URL: http://www.scba.net
EXECUTIVE MANAGER
Sunny Jewell

SOUTH DAKOTA BROADCASTERS ASSOCIATION
Box 1037, 106 W. Capital Ave., Pierre, SD 57501. (605) 224-1034. FAX: (605) 224-7426.
PRESIDENT
Steve Willard

TENNESSEE ASSOCIATION OF BROADCASTERS
Box 101015, Nashville, TN 37224-1015. (615) 399-3791. FAX: (615) 361-3488. email: tabspace@nc5.infi.net. URL: http://www.mainmenu.com/tab.html
EXECUTIVE V.P.
Whit Adamson
PRESIDENT
Gary Benton

TEXAS ASSOCIATION OF BROADCASTERS
1907 N. Lamar, Suite 300, Austin, TX 78705. (512) 322-9944. FAX: (512) 322-0522. email: tab@tab.org. URL: http://www.tab.org
PRESIDENT
Jane Wallace

UTAH BROADCASTERS ASSOCIATION
1600 S. Main St., Salt Lake City, UT 84115. (801) 486-9521. FAX: (801) 484-7294..
EXECUTIVE DIRECTOR
Dale O. Zabriskie

VERMONT ASSOCIATION OF BROADCASTERS
15 W. Patterson St., Barre, VT 05641. (802) 476-8789. FAX: (802) 479-5893.
EXECUTIVE DIRECTOR
Alan H. Noyes

VIRGINIA ASSOCIATION OF BROADCASTERS
630 County Green Lane, Charlottesville, VA 22902. (804) 977-3716. FAX: (804) 979-2439.
EXECUTIVE DIRECTOR
Peter Easter

WASHINGTON STATE ASSOCIATION OF BROADCASTERS
924 Capitol Way S., Suite 104, Olympia, WA 98501. (360) 705-0774. FAX: (360) 705-0873.
PRESIDENT & CEO
Mark Allen

WEST VIRGINIA BROADCASTERS ASSOCIATION
140 Seventh Ave., S. Charleston, WV 25303-1452. (304) 744-2143. FAX: (304) 744-1764. email: wvba@citynet.net
EXECUTIVE DIRECTOR
Michele Crist

WISCONSIN BROADCASTERS ASSOCIATION
44 E. Mifflin St., Suite 900, Madison, WI 53703. (608) 255-2600, (800) 236-1922. FAX: (608) 256-3986. email: krsf21a@prodigy.com
PRESIDENT
John Laabs

WYOMING ASSOCIATION OF BROADCASTERS
7217 Hawthorne Dr., Cheyenne, WY 82003. (307) 632-7622. FAX: (307) 638-3469. email: lgrott@wyld.state.wy.us
PRESIDENT
Kent Smith

A/D MEDIA SALES
2755 Franklin St., San Francisco, CA 94123, (415) 441-3955.
FAX: (415) 776-8305.
OWNER
Al Dougherty

HOWARD ANDERSON CO.
1705 S. 116th St., Omaha, NE 68144. (402) 333-2636. FAX:
(402) 333-2638.
PRESIDENT
Howard Anderson

JOHN BLAIR COMMUNICATIONS INC.
1290 Ave. of the Americas, New York, NY 10104. (212) 603-
5000. FAX: (212) 603-5453.
CHAIRMAN & CEO
Timothy M. McAuliff
EXECUTIVE V.P.
John B. Poor Jr.
V.P., DIRECTOR SALES ANALYSIS & PLANNING
Steven A. Murphy
V.P., DIRECTOR PROGRAMMING
Garnett Losak
V.P., DIRECTOR NETWORK SALES
Donald K. Williams
V.P., DIRECTOR RESERACH AMERICA
Eugene M. Cunningham
V.P., DIRECTOR RESEARCH USA
Alan B. Picozzi
PRESIDENT, BLAIR USA
Leo MacCourtney Jr.
VICE PRESIDENTS, SALES DIVISION
David R. Bisceglia
Charles W. Holmes
Peter Senseney
GROUP SALES MANAGERS
Julie Holmberg
Jane Zonino
David W. Abel
METS MANAGER
Vicki Garfield
V.P., GROUP SALES MANAGER
Jeff Lingg
PRESIDENT, BLAIR AMERICA
Floyd Gelini
V.P.'S, DIVISION SALES
David C. Crawford
Linda Scutari
Philip B. Kirk
GIANT MANAGER
Jeff Finkel
GROUP SALES MANAGER JETS
Nick Gardner

BRANCH OFFICES
5 Piedmont Ctr., Suite 72, Atlanta, GA 30305. (404) 239-6800.
FAX: (404) 239-6866.
V.P., MANAGER
Mike K. Mougey
V.P., SALES MANAGER, BLAIR TELEVISION
Michael K. Mougey
GROUP SALES MANAGER, BLAIR TELEVISION
Jeffrey P. Quick
1717 W. 6th St., Suite 470, Austin, TX 78703. (512) 457-1344.
FAX: (512) 457-1015.
SALES MANAGER & ACCOUNT EXEC.
Evan Papas
3 Copley Pl., Suite 301, Boston, MA 02116. (617) 375-9100.
FAX: (617) 375-0005.
V.P., SALES MANAGER
Carole J. Aaron
2101 Rexford Rd., Suite 119E, Charlotte, NC 28211, (704)
365-4747. FAX: (704) 365-8460.
SALES MANAGER
James T. Laura
445 N. Cityfront Plaza Dr., Suite 800, Chicago, IL 60611. (312)
321-6600. FAX: (312) 321-6797.
OFFICE MANAGER
Julie Holmberg
S.V.P., DIRECTOR REGIONAL SALES, BLAIR TELEVISION
Sidney C. Brown
GROUP SALES MANAGER, BLAIR TELEVISION
D. William Ross

5420 LBJ Fwy., Suite 530, Dallas, TX 75240. (972) 371-0330.
FAX: (972) 371-0331.
S.V.P. REGIONAL SALES
Sidney C. Brown
V.P., SOUTHWEST SALES, BLAIR TELEVISION
Michael D. Murphy
V.P., GROUP SALES MANAGER, BLAIR TELEVISION
James McGuire
Colorado Ctr., Tower I, 2000 S. Colorado Blvd., Suite 3300,
Denver, CO 80222. (303) 584-0787. FAX: (303) 584-0046.
V.P., SALES MANAGER
Scott Blackett
1000 Town Ctr., Suite 780, Southfield, MI 48075. (248) 827-
8600. FAX: (248) 827-8686.
V.P., SALES MANAGER
Kathy Zimmerman
GROUP SALES MANAGER, BLAIR TELEVISION
Linda Mitchell,
5 Post Oak Park, Suite 1740, Houston, TX 77027. (713) 552-
0600. FAX: (713) 552-1712.
V.P., SALES MANAGER
Barry Maxwell
Westwood Gateway Bldg., 11111 Santa Monica Blvd., Suite
1900, Los Angeles, CA 90025. (310) 444-3500. FAX: (310)
444-3666.
V.P. SALES WEST COAST
Nancy Dodson
SALES MANAGER, BLAIR TELEVISION
Stephanie Rosen
800 Corporate Dr., Suite 508, Fort Lauderdale, FL 33334.
(954) 351-7191. FAX: (954) 351-9169.
V.P., SALES MANAGER
Shelley Wright
60 S. 6th St., Suite 2450, Minneapolis, MN 55402. (612) 376-
7969. FAX: (612) 376-7970.
SALES MANAGER
Ileen Grace
1800 Kennedy Blvd., 4th Fl., Philadelphia, PA 19103. (215)
568-6540. FAX: (215) 568-1845.
V.P., SALES MANAGER
Alan Brittain
1501 S.W. Jefferson St., 2nd Fl., Portland, OR 97201. (503)
226-5090. FAX: (503) 220-1806.
V.P., SALES MANAGER
JoAnne James
The Equitable Bldg., 10 Broadway, Suite 1620, St. Louis, MO
63102. (314) 421-5262. FAX: (314) 421-6529
SALES MANAGER
Jim Hess
V.P., SALES MANAGER, BLAIR TELEVUSION
Glenna S. Pluchak
505 Sansome St., 4th Fl., San Francisco, CA 94111. (415)
434-2393. FAX: (415) 392-1943.
SALES MANAGER
Marilyn B. Citron
333 Dexter Ave. N., 5th Fl., Seattle, WA 98109. (206) 448-
3620. FAX: (206) 441-5620.
SALES MANAGER
Steven Linde
13577 Feathersound Dr., Suite 320, Clearwater, FL 34622.
(813) 572-7709. FAX: (813) 572-1193
V.P., SALES MANAGER
Sarah D. Tyrrell

BROADCAST REPRESENTATIVES RADIO & TV
1705 S. 116th St., Omaha, NE 68144. (402) 333-2363. FAX:
(402) 333-2638.
PRESIDENT
Howard Anderson

CBS/GROUP SPOT SALES
565 5th Ave., New York, NY 10017. (212) 856-8000. FAX: (212)
856-8144.
PRESIDENT
Richard Sheingold
V.P. NY SALES MANAGER
Bob Kaplan
NY SALES MANAGERS
Lisa Gottesman, Joe Oelvey
DIRECTOR, RESEARCH
Joseph Piccirillo

BRANCH OFFICES
1170 Soldiers Filed Rd., Boston, MA 02134. (617) 787-7000.
SALES MANAGER
Scott Brady

630 N. McClurg Cr., Chicago, IL 60611. (312) 944-6000.
OFFICE MANAGER
John Smith

6121 Sunset Blvd., Los Angles, CA 90028. (313) 352-2800.
OFFICE MANAGER
Julie Ballard

26877 Northwest Hwy., Southfield, MI 48037. (810) 647- 8960.
OFFICE MANAGER
Patricia Curry

Independence Mall E., Philadelphia, PA 19106. (215) 238-4700.
SALES MANAGER
Gary Herman

CABALLERO SPANISH MEDIA
261 Madison Ave., 18th fl., New York, NY 10016. (212) 697-4120. FAX: (212) 697-9151.
CEO
Eduardo Caballero
SENIOR V.P., NATIONAL SALES
Manny Ballastero
REGIONAL MANAGER
Eric Bench
ACCOUNT EXECUTIVES
Anne-Marie Diaz, Lisa Rodriguez
BRANCH OFFICES
205 N. Michigan Ave., Suite 2015, Chicago, IL 60601. (312) 616-7251. FAX: (312) 819-8371.
SALES DIRECTOR
Jan Emmelman Zablah
1300 Coral Way, Ste. 204, Miami, FL, 33145. (305) 285-3210. FAX: (305) 285-3215.
REGIONAL MANAGER
Veronica Falcon
3500 Maple Ave., Suite 1320, Dallas, TX 75219. (214) 522-1888. FAX: (214) 522-7406.
V.P., SOUTHERN REGIONAL SALES
Charles Crawford
10880 Wilshire Blvd., Suite 1000, Los Angeles, CA 90010. (310) 441-8190. FAX: (213) 441-8121.
V.P., WESTERN REGIONAL SALES
Leopoldo Ramos
118 Broadway, Ste. 617, San Antonio, TX 78205. (210) 220-3777. FAX: (210) 220-3555.
SALES DIRECTOR
Loretta Salazar

CABLE ADVANTAGE
(A Division of Holston Valley Broadcasting Corp.)
Box WKPT, Kingsport, TN 37662. (423) 246-9578. FAX: (423) 246-1863.
PRESIDENT & GENERAL MANAGER
George E. DeVault Jr.
EXECUTIVE V.P.
J. Raymond Walker

CABLE NETWORKS INC.
530 5th Ave., 6th floor, New York, NY 10036. (212) 382-5000. FAX: (212) 382-5055.
URL: http://www.rainbow-net-works.com.
PRESIDENT & COO
David Kline
SENIOR V.P.
Deborah Cuffaro
SALES DIRECTOR
Michael Labriola
DIRECTOR AFFILIATE SERVICES
Robert Ware
NATIONAL SALES MANAGER
Jim McDaniels
BRANCH OFFICES
7 Piedmont Ctr., Suite 420, Atlanta, GA 30305. (404) 266-3885. FAX: (404) 266-3938.
NATIONAL SALES MANAGER
Roger Stallard
Prudential Tower, 800 Boylston St., 15th floor, Boston, MA 02199. (617) 266-7711. FAX: (617) 266-7853.
NATIONAL SALES MANAGER
Bill Wayland
625 N. Michigan Ave., Suite 2101 Chicago, IL 60611. (312) 335-0870. FAX: (312) 335-5456.
NATIONAL SALES MANAGER
Nancy Benech

8150 Brookriver Dr., Suite S-608, Dallas, TX 75247. (214) 905-9966. FAX: (214) 688-7472.
NATIONAL SALES MANAGER
Ray Gaskin

2000 Town Center, Suite 1390, Southfield, MI 48075. (810) 356-0580. FAX: (810) 356-2018.
NATIONAL SALES MANAGER
Laura Blake

2425 W. Olympic Blvd., Suite 5050, Santa Monica, CA 90404. (310) 828-1142. FAX: (310) 828-1232.
DIRECTOR, WESTERN DIVISION
Ann Simley

6500 Rockside Rd., Suite 140, Independence, OH 44161. (216) 328-1214. FAX: (216) 328-1337.
NATIONAL SALES MANAGER
Tom Byrnes

353 Sacramento St., Suite 600, San Francisco, CA 94111. (415) 296-8222. FAX: (415) 296-9049.
NATIONAL SALES MANAGER
Catherine Berryessa

(Washington, DC Office), 8200 Greensboro Dr., Suire 1525, McLean, VA 22102. (703) 821-5477. FAX: (703) 821-5529.
NATIONAL SALES MANAGER
William Haight

CC/ABC NATIONAL TELEVISION SALES
77 W. 66 St., New York, NY 10023-6298. (212) 456-7777. FAX: (212) 456-7607.
PRESIDENT
John B. Watkins
VICE PRESIDENT
Phillip J. Sweenie
V.P., GENERAL SALES MANAGER
Ed Pearson
BRANCH OFFICES
190 N. State St., Chicago, IL 60601. (312) 899-4200.
SALES MANAGER
Scott Thomas
2020 Ave. of Stars, Los Angeles, CA 90067. (310) 557-6241.
SALES
Michael Jack
900 Front St., San Francisco, CA 94111. (415) 954-7810.
SALES
Gill Fitts
3000 Town Center, Ste. 2001, Detroit, MI 48075. (313) 355-4490.
SALES
Hyla Griesdorn
12222 Merit Dr., Ste. 1760, Dallas, TX 75251. (214) 960-7981.
SALES
Michael Irvine
3060 Peachtree Rd. N.W., Ste. 1470, Atlanta, GA 30305. (404) 266-1750.
SALES
Paul Courtney
One Exeter Plaza, Boston, MA 02116. (617) 262-8989.
SALES
Stewart Scott
6525 Morrison Blvd., #201, Charlotte, NC 28211. (704) 364-6767.
SALES
Scott Dempsey
4100 City Line Ave., Philadelphia, PA 19131. (215) 879-3100.
SALES
Kristin Long
One Metropolitan Sq., Suite 1630, St. Louis, MO 63102. (314) 231-6050.
SALES
Gene Reinhardt

COMMERCIAL MEDIA SALES INC.
1439 Denniston St., Pittsburgh, PA 15217. (412) 421-2600. FAX: (412) 421-6001. email: rafson@cmsradio.com.
URL: http://www.cmsradio.com
PRESIDENT
Roger Rafson

CREATIVE COMMUNICATORS INC.
4125 Victoria Dr., Fort Wayne, IN 46815. (219) 483-3882. FAX: (219) 484-2316.
PRESIDENT & GENERAL MANAGER
Eugene Pyle

CROASDELL & ASSOCIATES
1512 Charon Rd., Jacksonville, FL 32202. (904) 384-9980. FAX: (904) 384-4968.
PRESIDENT
Wayne Croasdell

DORA-CLAYTON AGENCY INC.
Box 33100, Decatur, GA 30033. (404) 373-2662. FAX: (404) 373-4658.
PRESIDENT
Daniel A. Haight Sr.
BRANCH OFFICES
20 N. Wacker Dr., Suite 562, Chicago, IL 60606. (312) 263-3340.
MANAGER
Howard Weiss

14330 Midway Rd., Suite 207, Dallas, TX 75234. (214) 788-1630. FAX: (214) 490-6438.
MANAGER
Jack Riley

21714 Lakeland, St. Clair Shores, MI 48081. (313) 445-0491.
MANAGERS
Ken Patt, Mike Martin

157 W. 57th St., New York, NY 10019. (212) 757-6868. FAX: (908) 233-0074.
MANAGER
Mel Williams

6326 Forward Ave., Pittsburgh, PA 15217. (412) 421-2600. FAX: (412) 421-6001.
MANAGER
Roger Rafson

559 Pacific Ave., #37, San Francisco, CA 94113. (415) 391-1984.
MANAGER
Sam Posner

EAGLE BROADCASTING GROUP, LTD.
2159 McCulloch Blvd., Lave Havasu, AZ 86403. (520) 855-9000. FAX: (520) 855-9445.
GENERAL MANAGER
Maury Cobum
MARKETING MANAGER
Joe Cairo
PROGRAM MANAGER
John Coburn
BRANCH OFFICES
711 California Ave., Parker, AZ 85344. (520) 669-5839.
STATION MANAGER
Jerry Hale

EMPIRE TIME SALES
9 Bard Ave., Red Hook, NY 12571. (914) 758-2680. FAX: (914) 758-2680.
PRESIDENT, GENERAL MANAGER
Dan Viles
INFO SYSTEMS
Jeremy Francis
OFFICE MANAGER
Francina Vantuyl

J.L. FARMAKIS INC.
Box 1004, New Canaan, CT 06840. (203) 966-1746. FAX: (203) 966-0473.
PRESIDENT
Jack Farmakis
V.P., GENERAL MANAGER
Jan Anderson
BRANCH OFFICES
Box 100, Mt. Vernon, IA 52314. (319) 895-6723.
VICE PRESIDENT
Russ Parker

J.C. GATES & CO.
3700 Las Vegas Blvd., Suite J, Las Vegas, NV 89109. (702) 795-7600. FAX: (702) 795-7132.
OWNER
James C. Gates
NATIONAL SALES MANAGER
Juanita Haddy Landon

HARRINGTON, RIGHTER & PARSONS INC.
805 Third Ave., New York, NY 10022. (212) 756-3600. FAX: (212) 756-3688.
PRESIDENT & COO
Peter F. Ryan
SR. V.P., SALES DIRECTOR
Murray L. Berkowitz
BRANCH OFFICES
3405 Peachtree Rd., Suite 400, Atlanta, GA 30305. (404) 237-7768. FAX: (404) 365-8139.
V.P., SOUTHEAST AREA SALES MANAGER
John Radovich

One Exeter Plaza, Boston MA 02116. (617) 247-4004. FAX: (617) 421-0933.
V.P., NORTHEAST AREA SALES MANAGER
Catherine Shaffer

6100 Fairview Rd., Suite 1460, Charlotte, NC 28210. (704) 553-7799. FAX: (704) 553-2824.
V.P., CHARLOTTE SALES MANAGER
Mark Chapman

500 N. Michigan Ave., Suite 800. Chicago, IL 60611. (312) 222-5500. FAX: (312) 222-4103.
SR. V.P., MIDWEST AREA SALES MANAGER
Steve Shadid

815 Superior Ave., Suite 1725, Cleveland, OH 44114. (216) 861-2265. FAX: (216) 861-5946.
V.P., CLEVELAND SALES MANAGER
Gerry Pas

8350 N. Central Expwy., Suite 325, Dallas, TX 75206. (214) 369-3925. FAX: (214) 373-3101.
V.P., DALLAS SALES MANAGER
Mike McAlone

4000 Town Ctr., Suite 202, Southfield, MI 48075. (810) 353-3370. FAX: (810) 353-9237.
V.P., DETROIT SALES MANAGER
Douglas Christie

8484 Wilshire Blvd., Suite 630, Los Angeles, CA 90211. (213) 653-5900. FAX: (213) 653-5995.
SENIOR V.P., LOS ANGELES SALES MANAGER
Jim Baral

105 S. 5th St., Suite 730, Minneapolis, MN 55402. (612) 332-2446. FAX: (612) 332-6741.
V.P., MINNEAPOLIS SALES MANAGER
Nan Diley

One Penn Ctr., 1617 JFK Blvd., Suite 1510, Philadelphia, PA 19103. (215) 557-2727. FAX: (215) 557-2720.
V.P., PHILADELPHIA SALES MANAGER
Michael D. Miglino

720 Olive St., Suite 2160, St. Louis, MO 63101. (314) 231-9797. FAX: (314) 231-5414.
V.P., ST. LOUIS SALES MANAGER
Bruce Butler

235 Montgomery St., Suite 925, San Francisco, CA 94104. (415) 781-4125. FAX: (415) 781-1908.
V.P., SAN FRANCISCO SALES MANAGER
William Wexelblatt

Plaza 600, 6th & Stewart Sts.,Suite 724, Seattle, WA 98101. (206) 443-1700. FAX: (206) 443-8859.
V.P., SEATTLE SALES MANAGER
Cara O'Donnell

4830 W. Kennedy Blvd., Suite 400, Tampa, FL 33609. (813) 287-0204. FAX: (813) 286-1465.
V.P., TAMPA SALES MANAGER
Ron Schrutt

1717 Saint James Pl., Suite 230, Houston, TX 77056. (713) 629-9705. FAX: (713) 629-9146.
V.P. HOUSTON SALES MANAGER
Mark Marino

HRP
Box 708, 27777 Franklin Rd., Suite 1220, Southfield, MI 48034. (248) 355-2020. FAX: (248) 355-0368.
GENERAL MANAGER
Marty Edelman
BRANCH OFFICES
212 E. 47th St., New York, NY 10017. (212) 888-7377; (800) 752-8320.
NATIONAL SALES MANAGER
Jack Dabbah

440 N. Wabash, Suite 3006, Chicago, IL 60611. (312) 923-0101, (800) 752-8321.
REGIONAL SALES MANAGER
Joseph Antelo

3131 Turtle Creek Blvd., Suite 1151, Dallas, TX 75219. (214) 521-5120; (800) 752-8554.
REGIONAL SALES MANAGER
Graham McKernan

HYETT/RAMSLAND INC.
120 S. 6th St., Suite 2240, Minneapolis, MN 55402. (612) 339-7179. FAX: (612) 339-7182.
PRESIDENT
James O. Ramsland

KATZ AMERICAN TELEVISION
125 W. 55 St., New York, NY 10019-5366. (212) 424-6330, 424-6010, 424-6789, 424-6250. FAX: (212) 424-6389, 424-6030, 424-6489, 424-6264.
PRESIDENT
Michael F. Hugger
V.P. & GENERAL SALES MANAGER
Swain Weiner
V.P. & NATIONAL MANAGER
Bruce Kallner
MANAGER (WHITE GROUP)
Sharon Korn
V.P., SALES DIRECTOR (BLUE GROUP)
Jay Zeitchick
MANAGER (BLUE GROUP)
Matt Curry

V.P., SALES DIRECTOR (WHITE GROUP)
Bob Scutari
V.P., DIRECTOR OF PROGRAMMING
Bill Carroll
V.P., SALES DIRECTOR (STARS GROUP)
Kenneth Perren
V.P. & DIRECTOR, (EAGLES GROUP)
Linda DeLaurentis
V.P. & MANAGER (STARS GROUP)
Rob Schu
MANAGER (EAGLES GROUP)
Michele Spector
V.P.& DIRECT-RESPONSE SALES DIRECTOR
Chickie Bucco
V.P. & RESEARCH DIRECTOR
Lisa Schoenback
KATZ CONTINENTAL TELEVISION
V.P. NATIONAL SALES MANAGER, EASTERN REGION
Chris Jordan
V.P., NATIONAL SALES MANAGER, SOUTHEASTER REGION
Peggy O'Neil
V.P., NATIONAL SALES MANAGER EAST CENTRAL REGION
Tom Stmler
V.P., GENERAL SALES MANAGER
Michael Spiesman
VICE PRESIDENTS, NEW YORK SALES MANAGERS
Tom Fury, Rich Yelner, Paul Bowlin
VICE PRESIDENTS, NATIONAL SALES MANAGERS
Ardie Bialek, Rich Schwartz,Mark Ryan
V.P. & DIRECT-RESPONSE SALES DIRECTOR
Chickie Bucco
V.P. & MARKETING SERVICES DIRECTOR
Jon Johannan
V.P., RESEARCH DIRECTOR
Michael Steinberg
KATZ DIMENSIONS
PRESIDENT
Bonnie Press
V.P. & MARKETING DIRECTOR
Ann Leary
V.P. & MANAGER
Patti Mrozowski
SR. V.P., KATZ DIMENIONS SPORTS
Stu Heifetz
V.P. & BUSINESS SYSTEMS MANAGER
Paula Sessa
KATZ HISPANIC MEDIA
PRESIDENT
Felix Perez
V.P., MARKETING EASTERN DIVISION
Laura Hagan
KATZ TELEVISION GROUP
PRESIDENT
Jim Beloyianis
PRESIDENT, MILLENIUM MARKETING
Jay Friesel
V.P. & PROGRAMMING DIRECTOR
Bill Carroll

BRANCH OFFICES
6 Piedmont Ctr., Suite 710, Atlanta, GA 30305-1579. (404) 365-3100. FAX: (404) 816-5503, 816-5509.
V.P. & MANAGER KATZ CONTINENTAL TELEVISION
Don Kirk
SALES MANAGER SPORTS
Philip Leopold

Statler Office Bldg., Suite 220, Boston, MA 02116-4396. (617) 542-5466, 542-5458. FAX: (617) 357-1677.
V.P. & MANAGER
Ruth Robertson
V.P. & MANAGER (KATZ CONTINENTAL TELEVISION)
David Henderson

5821 Fairview Rd., Suite 407, Charlotte, NC 28209-3514. (704) 553-0220. FAX: (704) 553-1547.
V.P. & MANAGER
Mark Turner

455 N. Cityfront Plaza Dr., Suite 1700, Chicago, IL 60611. (312) 755-3800, 755-3890, 755-3885. FAX: (312) 755-0872, 755-0870, 755-0874, 755-0887.
V.P., & MANAGER (RED GROUP)
Tom Morrissey
V.P. & MANAGER (EAGLE GROUP)
Robert Johnston
V.P. & MANAGER (SILVER TEAM)
Beth Wagner
V.P. & MANAGER (GOLD TEAM)
John Wall
V.P., REGIONAL MANAGER AGRI-MARKETING
Bob McArthur
SPORTS SALES MANAGER
Martin S. Berman
SALES MANAGER (KATZ HISPANIC MEDIA)
Jodi Desser

Keith Bldg., 1621 Euclid Ave., Suite 1718, Cleveland OH 44115-2107. (216) 621-7924. FAX: (216) 623-8363.
MANAGER
Ray Mendelsohn

300 Crescent Ct., Suite 400, Dallas, TX 75201-1817. (214) 999-2014, 999-2056, 999-2081, 999-2091. FAX: (214) 855-7801, 855-5320, 855-7854, 855-7853.
MANAGER
Don Adams
MANAGER (KATZ CONTINENTAL TELEVISION)
Tom Stemlar
MARKETING SALES MANAGER
Julie Lane
SALES MANAGER (KATZ HISPANIC MEDIA)
Leslie Falmar
MARKETING DIRECTOR (KATZ HISPANIC MEDIA)
Elias Lucero

One DTC, 5251 DTC Pkwy., PH5, Englewood, CO 80111-2702. (303) 740-8765. FAX: (303) 796-2930.
MANAGER
Tony McMahon

3310 W. Big Beaver Rd., Suite 501, Troy, MI 48084-2870. (313) 649-6390, 649-6381, 649-3900. FAX: (313) 649-2086, 643-0813.
V.P. & MANAGER
Karen Nielsen
V.P. & MANAGER (KATZ CONTINENTAL TELEVISION)
John Hoffman
MARKETING SALES MANAGER (KATZ DIMENSIONS)
Cheryl Kucken

2900 Wesleyan, Suite 625, Houston, TX 77027-5150. (713) 961-5195. FAX: (713) 961-5814.
MANAGER
Roger Ashley

1100 Main St., Suite 1890, Kansas City, MO 64105-2112. (816) 842-2606. FAX: (816) 221-7731.
V.P. & MANAGER
Peter A. Logli

6500 Wilshire Blvd., Suite 200, Los Angeles, CA 90048-4922. (213) 966-5000. FAX: (213) 658-6901, 658-6443, 852-1206, 655-5245.
MANAGER (RED GROUP)
Shelly Adrian
MANAGER (WHITE GROUP)
Dana Mulligan
NATIONAL SALES MANAGER (KATZ CONTINENTAL TV)
Rick Schwartz
V.P. & MANAGER (KATZ CONTINENTAL TV)
Terry Dreher
MANAGER (KATZ CONTINENTAL TV)
Greg O'Brien
SPORTS SALES MANAGER
Jim Austin
NETWORK SALES MANAGER
Lance Cerutti
V.P. & WESTERN DIVISION MANAGER (KATZ HISPANIC MEDIA)
Eduard D'Abate
SALES MANAGER (KATZ HISPANIC MEDIA)
Gabriela Donitz

3440 Hollywood Blvd., Suite 480, Hollywood, FL 33021-6927. (305) 961-3881. FAX: (305) 964-4518.
V.P. & MANAGER
Benjamin Wolf

Piper Jaffray Tower, Suite 2885, Minneapolis, MN 55402-3385. (612) 339-4405, 339-7711. FAX: (612) 339-1335.
V.P. & MANAGER
Debra Ryan
V.P. & MANAGER (KATZ CONTINENTAL TV)
John C. Aronson

1880 J.F. Kennedy Blvd., Philadelphia, PA 19103-2113. (215) 567-7590. FAX: (215) 567-6338.
MANAGER
Joe Eisberg

1500 S.W. 1st Ave., Suite 320, Portland, OR 97201. (503) 226-3973. FAX: (503) 228-4967.
V.P. & MANAGER
Jodi Rodaway
V.P. & SALES MANAGER (KATZ DIMENSIONS)
Dave Lichtman

10 S. Broadway, Suite 550, St. Louis, MO 63102-1795. (314) 231-1868. FAX: (314) 231-3620.
MANAGER
Gina Richardson
V.P. & MANAGER (KATZ CONTINENTAL TV)
Ed Adams

100 Spear St., Suite 1900, San Francisco, CA 94105-1575. (415) 777-3377. FAX: (415) 978-9657.
MANAGER
Sandy York
WESTERN DIVISION MARKETING & SALES MANAGER (KATZ HISPANIC MEDIA)
Doreen Cappelli

3131 Elliot Ave., Suite 620, Seattle, WA 98121. (206) 284-3088. FAX: (206) 284-5733.
V.P. & MANAGER
Kevin Cahill

Suite 450, 7650 W. Courtney Cambell Causeqay, Tampa, FL 33607. (813) 287-8686. FAX: (813) 287-0953.
MANAGER
Greg Goldman

1233 20th St., N.W., Suite 203, Washington, DC 20036-2304. (202) 872-5880. FAX: (202) 872-0263.
MANAGER
Cliff McKinney

2828 Coral Way, Miami, FL 33145. (305) 529-9279. FAX: (305) 529-9273.

Canadian Communications Co., Box 2384, 2300 Yonge St., Suite 807, Toronto, ON, Canada M4P IE4. (416) 488-6835. FAX: (416) 488-8283.
PRESIDENT & GENERAL MANAGER
Fraser Gordon

LANDIN MEDIA INC.
3033 N. 44th St., Suite 375, Phoenix, AZ, 85018-7229. (602) 553-4080. FAX: (602) 553-5090. E-mail: landin@ix.netcom.com.
PRESIDENT & CEO
Larry Cummings
V.P. & COO
Robert L. Dickinson
RELIGIOUS MEDIA MANAGER
Erich Lau
INFOMERCIAL MEDIA MANAGER
Scott Quen
ACCOUNT EXECUTIVES
Tricia Whipple, Dianna Lung, Rhonda VanLoon, Dan Beck
SHORT FORM MEDIA MANAGER
Terrye Gallegos
BRANCH OFFICES

344 Oakland Dr., Highland Park, IL 60035. (708) 926-9100. FAX: (708) 926-9101.
MIDWEST SALES MANAGER
Barry Lunenfeld

122 E. 42nd St., Suite 1107, New York, NY 10168. (212) 682-1515. FAX: (212) 949-7534.
GENERAL MANAGER
Jerry Wolff

BILL MASI NETWORK
1855 W. State Rd. 434, Suite 284, Longwood, FL 32750. (800) 275-6274, (407) 830-7060. FAX: (407) 830-7060.
CEO
Bill Masi
BUSINESS MANAGER
Wayne Burdick
SECRETARY
Linda Casalgrandi

MEDIA, INC.
650 5th Ave., New York, NY 10019. (212) 262-4141. FAX: (212) 262-1251.
EXECUTIVE V.P., MARKETING & SALES
Phlip Press
RESEARCH DIRECTOR
Joe Piccirillo
BRANCH OFFICES
11 Piedmont Ctr., Atlanta, GA 30305. (404) 261-2227.
OFFICE MANAGER
Lee Anderson

630 N. McClurg Ct., Chicago, Il 60611. (312) 944-6000.
OFFICE MANAGER
John Smith

1170 Soldiersfield Rd.,Boston, MA. (617) 787-7000.
OFFICE MANAGER
Scott Brady

545 E. John Carpenter Fwy., Suite 1540, Dallas, TX 75062. (214) 556-1245.
ACCOUNT EXECUTIVE
Laura Salzberger

26877 Northwest Hwy., Southfield, MI 48037. (810) 647-8960.
OFFICE MANAGER
Pat Curry

6121 Sunset Blvd., Los Angeles, CA 90028. (313) 352-2800.
OFFICE MANAGER
Julie Ballard

One Embarcadero Ctr., Suite 3237, San Francisco, CA 94111. (415) 433-0500.
OFFICE MANAGER
Craig McFarland

One Farragut Sq. S., 1634 One St. N.W., Suite 100, Washington, DC 2006. (202) 457-4509.
OFFICE MANAGER
Sonja Milliner

MEDIA WORKS
20 N. Walker Dr., Suite 562, Chicago, IL 60606. (312) 263-3343. FAX: (312) 263-8494.
PRESIDENT
Jeffrey Brunstein
BRANCH OFFICES
11 Penn Plaza, Suite 962, New York, NY 10001. (212) 239-3288. FAX: (212) 563-1301.
V.P., SALES
Joe Hoffman

Box 124, Los Angeles, CA 90274. (310) 377-8042. FAX: (310) 774-4889.
Paul Herzog

1705 S. 116th St., Omaha, NE 68144. (402) 333-2636. FAX: (402) 333-2638.
V.P., SALES
Howard Anderson

MEDIAONE
One Herald Sq., Suite 100, Fairborn, OH 45324. (513) 754-4700. FAX: (513) 754-4706.
GENERAL MANAGER
Tom Lemarche
SALES MANAGER
Clete Buddelmeyer
CLIENT SERVICES MANAGER
Cheri Linkous

MMT SALES, INC.
885 2nd Ave., New York, NY 10017. (212) 319-8008. FAX: (212) 319-5907
PRESIDENT
Jack Oken
SR V.P., & CFO
Bruce Mitchel
V.P. PROGRAMMING & RESEARCH
Cynthia Turner
SR V.P. & SALES DIRECTOR
David Pleger
SALES MANAGER
John McCann
BRANCH OFFICES
950 E. Paces Ferry Rd., Suite 2145. (404) 365-2088. FAX: (404) 365-2089.
V.P. & REGIONAL GROUP MANAGER
Kris Karavitis-Goff

20 Park Plaza. Suite 632, Boston, MA 02116. (617) 357-4950. FAX: (617) 357-4951.
BRANCH MANAGER
Mo Peck

2101 Rexford Rd., Suite 320 E, Charlotte, NC 28211. (704) 365-3900. FAX: (704) 365-4700.
BRANCH MANAGER
Katherine McKenzie

444 N. Michigan Ave., Suite 100, Chicago, Il 60611. (312) 467-9810. FAX: (312) 467-9808.
BRANCH MANAGER
Candace Rister

12790 Merit Dr., Suite 515, Dallas, TX 75251. (972) 980-9855. FAX: (972) 991-8479.
BRANCH MANAGER
Rick Thompson

50 W. Big Beaver Rd., Suite 250, Troy, MI 48084. (810) 680-1300. FAX: (810) 680-1867.
V.P. & BRANCH MANAGER
Steve Ryckman

5900 Wilshire Blvd., Suite 2130, Los Angeles, CA 90036. (213) 937-6434. FAX: (213) 939-2951.
BRANCH MANAGER
Jason Kleinhein

920 2nd Ave. S., Suite 1080, Minneapolis, MN 55402. (612) 339-7133. FAX: (612) 339-7277.
BRANCH MANAGER
DuAnn Surbaugh

One Boatman's Plaza, Suite 2160, St. Louis, MO 63101. (314) 421-5360. FAX: (314) 421-1733.
BRANCH MANAGER
Nivk Alivernia

10012 N. Dale Mabry, Suite 108, Tampla, FL 33618. (813) 264-1706. FAX: (813) 960-3549.
BRANCH MANAGER
Kitty Hutchens

180 Montgomery St., Suite 2380, San Francisco, CA 94104. (415) 434-9023. FAX: (415) 434-1358.
BRANCH MANAGER
Mary DiGiorgio

2 Penn Ctr., Suite 1004, Philadelphia, PA 19102. (215) 568-6570. FAX: (215) 568-2523.
BRANCH MANAGER
Jim Ross

NBC TV STATIONS SALES & MARKETING INC.
30 Rockefeller Plaza, 26th Flr., New York, NY 10112. (212) 664-4444, 664-2080. FAX: (212) 765-3869.
EXECUTIVE V.P., SALES & MARKETING
Ray Heacox
SR V.P.'s, SALES
Joanne Cini, Phil Sweenie
V.P., BUSINESS DEVELOPMENT
Gene Pizzolato
V.P., RESEARCH
William McDowell
DIRECTOR (EAST TEAM)
Kevyn Bymes
DIRECTOR (WEST TEAM)
Rich Mlotok
BRANCH OFFICES
1880 Century Park E., Suite 1104, Los Angeles, CA 90067. (310) 712-8000.
DIRECTOR
Craig Robinson

One Buckhead Plaza, 3060 Peachtree Rd., N.W., Suite 1020, Atlanta, GA 30305. (404) 848-0007.
MANAGER
Mike Panethere

100 Bush St., Suite 1725, San Francisco, CA 94104-3919. (415) 986-1397.
MANAGER
Bill Wexelblatt

WMAQ, 454 N. Columbus Dr., 4th Fl., Chicago, IL 60611. (312) 832-1871.
MANAGER
Jan Barkell

3131 McKinney Ave., Suite 270, Dallas, TX 75204. (214) 720-9211.
MANAGER
Dana Bell

WCAU, City Ave. & Monument Rd., Philadelphia, PA 19131. (610) 668-5629.
MANAGER
Maureen Duffin

376 Boylston St., Boston MA 02116. (617) 536-5226.
V.P. & MANAGER
Monte Newman

3001 W. Big Beaver Rd., Suite 310, Troy, MI 48084. (248) 649-4820.
MANAGER
Joe Trondle

NORTHWEST CABLE ADVERTISING
18 W. Mercer St., Suite 100, Seattle, WA 98119. (206) 286-1818. FAX: (206) 286-9010.
GENERAL MANAGER
Catherine McConnell
BRANCH OFFICES
2200 N. 30th St., Tacoma, WA 98403. (206) 572-1100.
SALES MANAGER
Keri Pickel

120 S. W. Everett Mall Way, #200, Everett, WA 98204. (206) 290-3400.
SALES MANAGER
Blaine Shepherd

PAN AMERICAN BROADCASTING
20410 Town Ctr. Ln., # 200, Cupertino, CA 95014-3230. (408) 996-2033. FAX: (408) 252-6855. email: pabcomain@aol.com.
CONTACTS
G. Bernard
C. Jung

PETRY, INC.
3 E. 54th St., New York, NY 10022. (212) 230-5600. FAX: (212) 230-5876.
PETRY CORPORATE
PRESIDENT & CEO
Thomas F. Burchill
EXEC. V.P. & CFO
CHMN PETRY VENTURES
James R. Ganley
PRESIDENT STATION SALES DIVISION
John I. Heise
PRESIDENT, PETRY NATIONAL TELEVISION
William R. Shaw
PRESIDENT PETRY COMMUNICATIONS
Harry R. Stecker
V.P., HUMAN RESOURCES
Stephanie B. Shaw

PETRY COMMUNICATIONS
PRES. & CEO, PETRY TELEVISION
Harry R. Stecker
V.P., PROGRAMMING DIRECTOR, PETRY NATIONAL
Jack Fentress
V.P., PROGRAMMING DIRECTOR, PETRY TELEVISION
Richard Kurlander
V.P., RESEARCH DIRECTOR, PETRY TELEVISION
Bob Hebenstreit
PROGRAMING DIRECTOR
Jennifer Getson
PETRY TELEVISION
PRESIDENT
John Heise
SR. V.P. & GENERAL SALES MANAGER
Jerry Linehan
SR V.P. & SALES DIRECTORS
Donald O'Toole, Kevin Nugent
V.P. & GROUP SALES MANAGER (FALCONS)
Susan Perelson
V.P., SALES DIRECTOR
Fran Gennarell
SR V.P. & REGIONAL AREA MANAGER (ALSO FOR PETRY NATIONAL)
Val Napolitano, Laverne Cole, Dan Mayasich
BRANCH OFFICES
706 2nd Ave. S., Suite 1138, Minneapolis, MN 55402-3092. (612) 339-6606. FAX: (612) 339-9330
V.P. & SALES MANAGER
James Ottolin

7 Penn Ctr., 1635 Market St., Suite 420, Philadelphis, PA 19103-2217. (215) 567-6005. FAX: (215) 567-5938.
V.P. & SALES MANAGER
Dave Bell

One S.W. Columbia, Suite 437, Portland, OR 97258-2005. (503) 228-0200. FAX: (503) 228-1060.
SALES MANAGER
Sunny Wetzel

10 S. Broadway, Suite 525, St. Louis, MO 63102-1732. (314) 241-2445. FAX: (314) 241-9215.
V.P. & SALES MANAGER
Bruce Farber

Spear Tower, One Market St., #1375, San Francisco, CA 94105-1313. (415) 442-1880. FAX: (415) 442-1846
V.P. & SALES MANAGER
Lori Gravino

2001 6th Ave., 1600 Westin Bldg., Seattle, WA 98121-3958. (206) 728-1747. FAX: (206) 728-4479.
SALES MANAGER
Ben Holland

888 Executive Ctr. Dr. W., Suite 108, St. Petersburgh, FL 33702-2402. (813) 576-1780. FAX: (813) 577-3911.
V.P. & SALES MANAGER
Mary Louise-Word

419 Boylston St., Boston, MA 02116-3305. (617) 353-1100. FAX: (617) 353-0280.
V.P. & SALES MANAGER
M.P. Kelleher

5950 Fairview Rd., Suite 804, Charlotte, NC 28210-3102. (704) 554-8134. FAX: (704) 553-0529.
V.P. & SALES MANAGER
Stockton Holt

1111 Superior Ave., Suite 970, Cleveland, OH 44114-2507. (216) 861-2252. FAX: (216) 861-0914.
SALES MANAGER
Paul Perozeni

2711 N. Haskell Ave., Suite 2000, LB#23, Dallas, TX 75204-2910. (214) 821-8200. FAX: (214) 821-4120.
SR V.P. & SALES MANAGER
Laverne Cole

6400 S. Fiddler's Green Cir., Suite 1860, Englewood, CO 80111-4961. (303) 773-9880. FAX: (303) 773-9420.
V.P., SALES MANAGER
Brook A. Willardsen

3221 W. Big Beaver Rd., Suite 102, Troy, MI 48084-2859. (810) 649-0100. FAX: (810) 649-0866.
V.P. & REGIONAL AREA MANAGER
Dan Mayasich

2800 Post Oak Blvd., 5220 TRANSCO Tower, Houston, TX 77056-6106. (713) 850-0194. FAX: (713) 850-8609.
SALES MANAGER
Miles Cathy

410 N. Michigan Ave., Suite 1180, Chicago, IL 60611-4243. (312) 644-9660. FAX: (312) 644-9774.
V.P., GENERAL MANAGER & REGIONAL SALES MANAGER
Bill Carney

8383 Wilshire Blvd., Suite 626, Beverly Hills, CA 90211-2405. (213) 655-3353. FAX: (213) 655-2862.
SR V.P. & REGIONAL AREA MANAGER
Richard Larcade

950 W. Paces Ferry Rd., Suite 2940, Atlanta, GA 30326-1115. (404) 237-5727. FAX: (404) 261-0586.
SR. V.P. & REGIONAL AREA MANAGER
Val Napolitano

RADIUS COMMUNICATIONS
1332 Enterprise Dr., Suite 300, West Chester, PA 19380. (610) 344-9000. FAX: (610) 344-9633.
PRESIDENT
Bill Stanfield
DIRECTOR NATIONAL & REGIONAL SALES
Phil W. Salas
RETAIL SALES DIRECTORS
Mike Wall, Nancy Fry
BRANCH OFFICES
960 Windham Ct., Boardman, OH 44512. (330) 629-8867.
2780 Beach Rd., Port Huron, MI 48060. (810) 989-9470.
160 S. River Rd., Bedford, NH 03110. (603) 622-8340.
1002 Firehouse Rd., Utica, NY 13502.
11676 Perry Hwy., Suite 3206, Wexford, PA 15090. (412) 934-5999.

RADIUS COMMUNICATIONS
49 E. Lancaster Ave., Malvern, PA 19355. (610) 725-0133. FAX: (610) 725-0419.
NATIONAL SALES MANAGER
Lee Stein
SALES DIRECTOR
Philip W. Salas

BRANCH OFFICES

Wexford Professional Bldg., #3, 11676 Perry Hwy., Suite 3206, Wexford, PA 15090. (412) 934-5999.

1000 Firehouse Rd., Utica, NY 13502. (315) 797-0037.
GENERAL SALES MANAGER
Joseph Noonan

RAINBOW SPORTS SALES
530 Fifth Ave., 6th Fl., New York, NY 10036. (212) 382-5200. FAX: (212) 382-6128.
PRESIDENT & COO
David Klein
SENIOR VICE PRESIDENT
Gerry Himmel
NATIONAL SALES MANAGER
Nick Langon
BRANCH OFFICES

625 N. Michigan Ave., Suite 1701, Chicago, Il 60611. (312) 335-0870. FAX: (312) 335-5456.
SALES MANAGER
John Hokin

2425 W. Olympic Blvd., Suite 5050, Santa Monica, CA 90404. (310) 453-1985. FAX: (310) 829-3765.
SALES MANAGER
Pat McCabe

Prudential Tower, 800 Boylston St., 11th Fl., Boston, MA 02199. (617) 266-7711. FAX: (617) 266-7853.
SALES MANAGER
Steve Baker

225 City Line Ave., Bala Cynwyd, PA 19004. (610) 668-2210. FAX: (610) 668-9499.
SALES MANAGER
Jon Seitz

901 Battery St., Suite 204, San Francisco, CA 94111. (415) 291-8352. FAX: (415) 291-8728.
SALES MANAGER
Arturo Riera

2000 Town Ctr., Suite 1390. Southfield, MI 48075. (810) 356-0550. FAX: (810) 356-2565.
NATIONAL SALES MANAGER
Jeff Edwards

11311 Cornell Park Dr., Suite 406, Cincinnati, OH 45242. (513) 469-2006. FAX: (513) 469-2007.
SALES MANAGER
Ned Paddock

REGIONAL REPS. CORP.
1100 Chester Ave. #100, Cleveland, OH 44115-1404. (216) 781-0030. FAX: (216) 781-7508.
PRESIDENT
Stuart J. Sharpe
SECRETARY & TREASURER
Rebecca L. Sharpe
BRANCH OFFICES
Holiday Park Tower, 644 Linn St., Cincinnati, OH 45203-1744. (513) 651-1511. FAX: 9513) 651-0174.
VICE PRESIDENT
Josph C. Hearn

1100 Chester Ave. #100, Cleveland, OH 44115-1404. (216) 781-0035. FAX: (216) 781-7508.
REGIONAL MANAGER
Douglas A. Trostler

4480 N. Shallowford Rd., Atlanta, GA 30338-6410. (770) 394-7377. FAX: (770) 394-0424.
REGIONAL MANAGER
Lazard "Buck" Blum

RILEY REPRESENTATIVES
14330 Midway Rd., Suite 216, Dallas, TX 75244. (214) 788-1630. FAX: (214) 490-6438.
OWNER
Jack Riley
BRANCH OFFICES
Drawer 33100, Decatur, GA 30033. (404) 633-9080.
CONTACT
Dan Height

20 N. Wacker Dr., Suite 540. Chicago, IL 60606. (312) 263-3340.
CONTACT
Howard Weiss

22971 Nine Mile Rd., St. Clair Shores, MI 48080. (313) 773-7700.
CONTACTS
Ken Patt, Mike Martin
6326 Forward Ave., Pittsburgh, PA 15217. (412) 421-2600.
CONTACT
Roger Rafson

559 Pacific Ave., San Francisco, CA 94133. (415) 391-1984.
CONTACT
Sam Posner

11 Penn Plaxa, New York, NY 10001. (212) 239-3288.

29209 Circle Dr., Los Angeles, CA 91301. (818) 707-9937.
CONTACT
Susan Laronge

SAVALLI RADIO & TV REPS.
11 Penn Plaza, Suite 962, New York, NY 10001. (212) 239-3288. FAX: (212) 563-1301.
SALES ACCOUNT EXECUTIVES
Howard Weiss, Tom Pazler, Shirley Rodriguez
GENERAL MANAGER
Joseph Hoffman

BRANCH OFFICES

20 N. Wacker Dr., Chicago, IL 60606. (312) 263-3340. FAX: (312) 263-8494. Howard Weiss.
14330 Midway Rd., Dallas, TX 75244. (214) 788-1630. FAX: (214) 490-6438. Jack Riley.

THE SANDEBERG-GLENN CO.
4426 Dumas Dr., Napa, CA 94558. (707) 226-8566. Ward Glenn

SELTEL, INC.
40 West 57 St., New York, NY 10019. (212) 632-9400. FAX: (212) 632-9770. URL: http://www.katz-media.com.
PRESIDENT
Jack Higgins
SR V.P. & SALES DIRECTOR (KNIGHTS TEAM)
Craig Boirman
V.P. & SALES DIRECTOR (WARRIORS TEAM)
Russell White
V.P. & SALES DIRECTOR (VOYAGERS TEAM)
Bob Webb
V.P. & SALES DIRECTOR (PATRIOTS TEAM)
Judy Kleinberger
V.P. & SALES DIRECTOR (GOVERNORS TEAMS)
Tom Motta
V.P. & SALES DIRECTOR (AMBASSADORS TEAM)
Steve Appel
V.P. & SALES DIRECTOR (GENERALS & SENATORS TEAMS)
Jeff Roberts
V.P. & SALES DIRECTOR (FEDERALS TEAM)
Barry Offitzer
V.P. & PROGRAMMING DIRECTOR
Janeen Bjork
V.P. & RESEARCH DIRECTOR
Richard Vogt

BRANCH OFFICES

3495 Piedmont Rd., Suite 205, Atlanta, GA 30305. (404) 233-3906. FAX: (404) 233-5440.
V.P. & GENERAL MANAGER
Dan Griffin

38 Newbury St., Suite 603, Boston, MA 02116. (617) 236-8666. FAX: (617) 236-4927.
V.P. & GENERAL MANAGER
Rose Marie Havens

5821 Fairview Rd., Suite 308, Charlotte, NC 28209. (704) 554-7124. FAX: (704) 553-7320.
V.P. & GENERAL MANAGER
Suzy Plettner

211 E. Ontario, Suite 700, Chicago, IL 60611. (312) 642-2450. FAX: (312) 642-1631.
V.P. & GENERAL MANAGER
Steve Henderson

1717 E. 9th St., Suite 1625, Cleveland, OH 44114. (216) 696-0500. FAX: (216) 696-0505.
GENERAL MANAGER
Chas Van Slyke

3131 McKinney Ave., Suite 240, Dallas, TX 75204. (214) 720-0070. FAX: (214) 720-0111.
GENERAL MANAGER
Angela Betasso

8101 E. Prentice Ave., Suite 701, Englewood, CO 80111. (303) 694-3317. FAX: (303) 694-2209.
GENERAL MANAGER
John Knippenberg

50 W. Big Beaver, Suite 460, Troy, MI 48084. (810) 524-0909. FAX: (810) 524-1760.

One Greenway Plaza, Suite 710, Houston, TX 77046. (713) 622-8122. FAX: (713) 622-4733.
GENERAL MANAGER
Jennifer Luke

6300 Wilshire Blvd., Suite #1700, Los Angeles, CA 90048. (213) 658-5022. FAX: (213) 658-5312.
V.P. & GENERAL MANAGER
Michael Girocco

6100 Blue Lagoon Dr., Suite 340, Miami, FL 33126. (305) 266-4066. FAX: (305) 266-7713.
GENERAL MANAGER
Enid Bluestone

120 S. 6th St., Suite 2005, Minneapolis, MN 55402. (612) 338-7017. FAX: (612) 349-6261.
GENERAL MANAGER
Essie Dalton

1760 Market St., 4th fl., Philadelphia, PA 19103. (215) 563-5400. FAX: (215) 563-2974.
GENERAL MANAGER
John Braun

1512 S.W. 18th Ave., Portland, OR 97201. (503) 226-1231. FAX: (503) 226-2935.
GENERAL MANAGER
Richard Gohlman

St. Louis Place, 200 N. Broadway, Suite 1620, St. Louis, MO 63102. (314) 241-4193. FAX: (314) 241-9849.
V.P., GENERAL MANAGER
Richard J. Quigley III

444 Market, Suite 1520, San Francisco, CA 94111. (415) 391-8890. FAX: (415) 391-4252.
GENERAL MANAGER
Frank DeMarco

211 6th Ave. N., Suite 200, Seattle, WA 98109. (206) 728-4277. FAX: (206) 441-0316.
GENERAL MANAGER
Bob Tacher

3507 Frontage Rd., Suite 130, Tampa, FL 33607. (813) 286-9686. FAX: (813) 282-3234.
V.P., GENERAL MANAGER
Steve Henderson

SJL BROADCAST MANAGEMENT CORP.
3203 3rd. Ave N., Billings, MT 59101. (406) 256-0705. FAX: (206) 252-9144.
PRESIDENT & TREASURER
George D. Lilly
V.P., SECRETARY & CFO
Dave McCurdy
BRANCH OFFICES
633 Picacho Ln., Montecito, CA 93108. (805) 969-9278. fAX: (805) 969-2399. George D. Lilly.

TCI MEDIA SERVICES
2940 Limited Ln. N.W., Olympia, WA 98502. (360) 754-7081. FAX: (360) 943-5911. E-mail: blk92@aol.com. URL: http://www.passnet.com.
OPERATIONS MANAGER
Kathryn Nevin
PRODUCTION MANAGER
Randall Knutson
INFOVISION MANAGER & SALES MANAGER
Brad Bradberry
BRANCH OFFICES
119 N. Commercial, #500, Bellingham, WA 98225. (360) 734-2150.
AREA SALES MANAGER
Bill Gorman

1100 Wheaton Way #B, Bremerton, WA 98310. (360) 479-8486.
AREA SALES MANAGER
Shirley Eclipse

117 N. First, Suite 7, Mount Vernon, WA 98273. (360) 336-2554.
AREA SALES MANAGER
Bill Groman

TELEREP, INC.
1 Dag Hammarskjold Plaza, 25th Fl., New York, NY 10017. (212) 759-8787. FAX: (212) 838-3814.
PRESIDENT & GENERAL MANAGER
Steven Herson
S.V.P., DIRECTOR OF PROGRAMMING
Jay Isabella
S.V.P., DIRECTOR OF SALES
Thomas Tilson
S.V.P., DIRECTOR OF BUSINESS ADMINISTRATION & HUMAN RESOURCES
Sandra McCourt
V.P. & CFP
Bob Drury
V.P., DIRECTOR OF INFORMATION SERVICES
Kerry Boehme
V.P., DIRECTOR OF TELEREP ENTERPRISES
Dave Hills

BRANCH OFFICES
3390 Peachtree Rd., N.E., Suite 210, Atlanta, GA 30326. (404) 848-0800.
SALES MANAGER
Ed Shaffer

399 Boylston St., #11F, Boston, MA 02116. (617) 247-2555.
V.P., EASTERN REGION MANAGER
Mary Jane Kelley

2 Fairview Plaza, 5950 Fairview Rd., Suite 705, Charlotte, NC 28210. (704) 552-8862.
SALES MANAGER
Patti Phillips

401 N. Michigan Ave., #1120, Chicago, IL 60611. (312) 329-1515.
OFFICE MANAGER
Todd Rohde

One Cleveland Ctr., 1375 E. 9th St., Suite 1970, Cleveland, OH 44114. (216) 566-8282.
SALES MANAGER
Tracy Benton

6500 Greenville Ave., # 770, Dallas, TX 75206. (214) 987-0991.
SALES MANAGER
Vickey Smith-Gist

1400 Fisher Bldg., Detroit, MI 48202. (313) 873-6664.
V.P., CENTRAL REGION MANAGER
Ed Kroninger

11 Greenway Plaza, # 510, Houston, TX 77046. (713) 627-7791.
SALES MANAGER
Charlene Salvato

5900 Wilshire Blvd., Suite 800, Los Angeles, CA 90036. (213) 937-4644.
V.P., WESTERN REGION MANAGER
Steve Bluestone

701 4th Ave. S., Minneapolis, MN 55415. (612) 332-7333.
SALES MANAGER
Marge Lewis

1601 Market St., Suite 1090, Philadelphia, PA 19103. (215) 564-1206.
SALES MANAGER
Joe Knauer

715 S.W. Morrison, Site 600, Portland, OR 97205. (503) 223-5038.
ACCOUNT EXECUTIVES
Karen Inman, Jim Cummings

50 California St., Suite 3145, San Francisco, CA 94111. (415) 433-1966.
SALES MANAGER
Betsy McReddie

Equitable Bldg., Suite 920, 10 S. Broadway, St. Louis, MO 63102. (314) 241-7979.
SALES MANAGER
Tim Jones

THOMPSON SOURCE, INC.
647 57th St., Des Moines, IA 50312. (515) 255-0254. FAX: (515) 255-4583.
PRESIDENT
Tommy Thompson
VICE PRESIDENT
Ellen Cleveland

UNITED TELEVISION BROADCASTING SYSTEMS, INC.
1670 W. Beverly Blvd., Los Angeles, CA 90026-5733. (213) 483-2929. FAX: (213) 483-3438.
CHAIRMAN
John Y. Haneda
PRESIDENT
Hisatake Shivuya

UNIVISION COMMUNICATIONS INC.

605 3rd Ave., 12th Fl., New York, NY 10158-0180. (212) 455-5200. FAX: (212) 867-6710. URL: http://www.univision.net.
CHAIRMAN & CEO
Joe Perenchio
PRESIDENT & COO
Ray Rodriguez
CO-PRES.
Tom McCarrity, Dennis McCauley
V.P., DIRECTOR SALES
Carlos Deschapelle
MANAGER NATIONAL SPOT SALES
Bill Acker
V.P. NEWS
Alina Falcon
EXEC. V. P.
Andrew Hobson

BRANCH OFFICES

30700 Telegraph Rd., Suite 3640, Bingham Farms, MI 48025. (810) 540-5705. FAX: (810) 540-2419.
SALES MANAGER
Mark Brown

541 N. Fairbanks Ct., Suite 1100, Chicago, IL 60611. (312) 494-5100. FAX: (312) 494-5115.
SALES MANAGER
Trisha Pray

2030 Main St., Suite 235, Irvine, CA 92714. (714) 474-8585. FAX: (714) 474-8385.
SALES MANAGER
Steve Mandala

600 E. Las Colinas Blvd., Suite 566, Irving, TX 75039. (214) 869-0202. FAX: (214) 869-2635.
SALES MANAGER
Jack Hobbs

6701 Center Dr. W., 15th Fl., Los Angeles, CA 90045. (310) 338-0700. FAX: (310) 348-3619.
SALES MANAGER
Steve Mandala

9405 N.W. 41st St., Miami, FL 33178. (305) 471-3900. FAX: (305) 471-4027.
SALES MANAGER
Evelyn Castillo

870 Market St., Suite 654, San Francisco, CA 94102. (415) 677-8730. FAX: (415) 772-9113.
SALES MANAGER
Doreen Cappelli

ADAM YOUNG, INC.

599 Lexington Ave.,47th Fl., New York, NY 10022. (212) 688-5100. FAX: (212) 758-5090.
PRESIDENT
Arthur W. Scott, Jr.

BRANCH OFFICES

1 Piedmont Center, Suite 502, Atlanta, GA 30305. (404) 261-8800. FAX: (404) 261-0015.
MANAGER
Tom Durr

31 St. James Ave., 9th fl., Boston, MA 02116. (617) 423-4987.
MANAGER
John D. Ketell

6100 Fairview Rd., Suite 625, Charlotte, NC 28210. (704) 643-0604. FAX: (704) 643-8202.
MANAGER
Gregory Mitchell

444 N. Michigan Ave., Suite 3470, Chicago, IL 60611. (312) 744-1313. FAX: (312) 744-0196.
V.P. & MANAGER
Lois Hamelin

3232 McKinney Ave., Suite 670, Dallas, TX 75204-2423. (214) 871-2988. FAX: (214) 871-2900.
MANAGER
Lynda Showtell

7853 E. Arapahoe Ct., Suite 2000, Englewood, CO 80112. (303) 779-4401. FAX: (303) 779-9733.

2855 Coolidge, Suite 210, Troy, MI 48084. (810) 649-3999. FAX: (810) 649-6455.
MANAGER
Allan Baur

6100 Wilshire Blvd., Suite 320, Los Angeles, CA 90048. (213) 938-2081. FAX: (213) 938-1483.
WEST COAST MANAGER
Lynda Shotwell

One Financial Plaza, 120 S. 6th St., Suite 2240, Minneapolis, MN 55402. (612) 339-3397. FAX: (612) 339-7182.
MANAGER
James O. Ramsland

4800 S.W. Macadam Ave., Suite 200, Portland, OR 97201. (503) 228-0914. FAX: (503) 228-0556.
MANAGER
Teddi Jones

CORPORATE HISTORIES
OF THE NETWORKS

ABC, INC.

ABC's predecessor, the Radio Corporation of America (RCA) owned two radio networks, the Blue and the Red. In 1941, the FCC decreed that the same company could not own two networks, so RCA incorporated the Blue under the name of American Broadcasting System and established it as an independent subsidiary. RCA then sold this network to Edward J. Noble, and in 1944, the name was changed to the American Broadcasting Company. ABC's first television broadcast was on April 19, 1948 with "On the Corner". Later in the year, ABC scored two "firsts": the live broadcast of an opera (Verdi's "Otello") from the Metropolitan Opera House in New York and a TV documentary, "The Marshall Plan." ABC merged with United Paramount Theatres in 1952. This merger was engineered by Leonard H. Goldenson, then the president of UPT. The new company was called American Broadcasting-Paramount Theatres, Inc. During the 1950's, ABC began to operate at a profit although it had to struggle fiercely to acquire new affiliates. In 1954, ABC made a deal with Walt Disney to acquire a 35% interest in Disneyland and all TV programs produced by Disney. The following year, ABC signed an exclusive rights contract with Warner Bros. for TV programming.

In the Fall of 1962, ABC introduced color programming for the fall season which was expanded in 1966 to include full color broadcasting. In 1965, AB-PT's name was changed to American Broadcasting Companies, Inc. The 1960's also introduced blockbuster theatrical movies to TV with spectacular rating results when "The Bridge on the River Kwai" was viewed (in 1966) by 60 million Americans. In 1967, the ABC evening news was expanded from 15 minutes to a half-hour, and Joey Bishop inaugurated ABC's late-night talk show programming.

In 1972, ABC was able to operate at a profit for the first time in ten years. In the 1976-77 season, ABC took first place in the ratings race for the first time. In 1976, Barbara Walters joined ABC, becoming the first anchorwoman in television history. The mini-series "Roots" appeared on ABC in 1977 and became the highest-rated program of all time. This helped immensely in the ratings race, and credit must go in large part to Fred Silverman who, two years before, had joined the company as president of ABC International. He left in 1978 to go to NBC.

The decade of the Eighties was a turbulent one for the networks as cable and home video began whittling away their audiences. In 1985, ABC agreed to be purchased by Capital Cities Communications. The merged company's name was changed to Capital Cities/ABC, Inc. ABC held second place in the ratings from 1979 to 1983 when it dropped to third position. It was unable to rise from third until 1987-88 when it displaced CBS in second place, primarily because of the World Series and the Superbowl. It remained second in 1988-89 and 1989-90. In the latter season, ABC had the distinction of broadcasting the most talked-about new series of the period, "Twin Peaks," and the highest-rated new series, "America's Funniest Home Videos." Daniel B

Burke replaced Frederick J. Pierce as president and chief operating officer. There were also sweeping reductions in personnel in the interests of economy and streamlining. Budget cuts notwithstanding, Capital Cities/ABC chairman Thomas Murphy pledged ABC would not scrimp on programming.

Profits at the end of 1990 rose about $70 million. Of the three networks, ABC won the ratings battle in news coverage of the war in the Persian Gulf. For two seasons in a row the network could boast having the only new series in the top ten: "America's Funniest People" (1990-91) and "Home Improvement" (1991-92). Capital Cities/ABC is a partner in ESPN, the highly successful cable TV sports channel and two other cable TV services—Arts & Entertainment and Lifetime. ABC was the only network in the 1992-93 season to gain ground, moving into second place behind CBS, from its previous third place standing. During the season, Robert A. Iger became the new network president. The network was the first to sign a deal with a cable operator (in this case Continental Cablevision) allowing its stations to be carried on cable without paying a fee. In 1994, the company signed an affiliation deal with E.W.Scripps Company to switch several of their stations over to ABC.

The big event of 1995 was the $19 billion acquisition of Capital Cities/ABC by the Walt Disney Company, said to be the second largest corporate takeover in history. In 1997, Ted Harbert resigned as entertainment chairman of ABC after 20 years with the network. At the end of the 1996-97 season, "Roseanne," one of ABC's sitcom staples, was discontinued after nine years on the air. The producers of ABC's "Home Improvement" sued the program's distributor, Walt Disney, alleging that a $3 million per episode renewal was in essence a sweetheart deal benefitting Disney. A lawsuit against the ABC news program Prime Time Live by the supermarket chain Food Lion for trespass, fraud and breach of fiduciary duty was decided in favor of the supermarket by a North Carolina jury. Producers for the evening news magazine were hired undercover as clerks by the chain in order to expose the sales of spoiled food and unsanitary food handling practices by Food Lion, which did not dispute the findings of the investigative report, but instead claimed that the practice of sending in undercover reporters constituted fraud.

ABC's ratings soared when it broke the news in January 1998, that sex-allegations were made by intern Monica Lewinsky involving President Clinton. Apparently continuing a trend started by the O.J. Simpson trial & elevated by the death of Princess Diana in September 1997, news proved very successful in attracting viewers. Despite its brief victory in the ratings war, the network was scheduled to go through a complete transformation for the 1998-99 season, after losing its number two slot among 18-49 year olds, to Fox. For the new season, the network was to introduce remakes of old shows such as "The Mary Tyler Moore Show" and "Fantasy Island," have "Sports Night" for male viewers, and air about 20 made for tv movies and miniseries.

RECENT ABC SERIES

1990-91: America's Funniest People, Dinosaurs.

1991-92: The Commish, Home Improvement, The Young Indiana Jones Chronicles

1992-93: Day One, Hangin' With Mr. Cooper.

1993-94: Grace Under Fire, Lois and Clark, NYPD Blue.

1994-95: My So-Called Life.

1995-96: Champs, Naked Truth.

1996-97: Spin City, Dangerous Minds.

1997-98: Cracker, Dharma & Greg.

1998-99: Fantasy Island, The Secret Lives of Men, Mr. Chapel.

CBS
(COLUMBIA BROADCASTING SYSTEM, INC.)

CBS began in 1927 as a radio network with 16 stations, United Independent Broadcasters, Inc., founded by Arthur Judson, a concert tour manager and backed by Louis Sterling, president of the Columbia Phonograph Company. Later other investors were invited in, the most prominent of whom was William S. Paley. On September 26, 1928, at the age of 27, Paley became president of the firm whose name was changed to the Columbia Broadcasting System. Paley introduced many innovations to radio broadcasting, the most significant of which was the signing of an agreement in 1931 with Paramount Pictures whereby film stars were heard on radio for the first time. This laid the groundwork for the CBS policy in television from the outset to feature shows built around stars (Ed Sullivan, Lucille Ball, Arthur Godfrey, Jack Benny, Burns & Allen, Garry Moore, etc.).

CBS was in TV as early as 1931 when it began regularly scheduled TV programming over experimental station W2XAB in New York City. In 1941, CBS began weekly broadcasts of black-and-white TV programming over WCBS-TV in New York. By 1948, it had 30 affiliated stations.

In 1951, CBS broadcast the first live coast-to-coast TV transmission between New York and San Francisco. 1951 was also the year that Bill Gordon designed the CBS Eye which was destined to become one of the most famous logos in the world.

In 1952, CBS opened Television City in Hollywood—the industry's first self-contained TV production facility. "Playhouse 90" made its debut in 1956, but the big event of the decade was the 1951 debut of "I Love Lucy", a series regarded as the progenitor of the situation-comedy. In the field of soap operas, CBS was both leader and winner, virtually monopolizing that market from 1951 to 1956. In 1951, it introduced "Search for Tomorrow," which was to become the longest-running show in that genre. This was followed by "Love of Life" (1951) and "The Guiding Light" (1952), both overnight hits.

In the late '50s and through the 60's and 70's, CBS reigned as king of prime time ratings, maintaining its long-running lead with such successes as "Gunsmoke" (1957), "The Defenders" (1961), "The Beverly Hillbillies" (1962), "All in the Family" (1972) and "Dallas" (1978). Also helping was "60 Minutes" the news-oriented show which, by 1995, had remained in the Top Ten prime time shows for 18 consecutive seasons.

CBS began the turbulent Eighties with a new president, Thomas Wyman (replacing John D. Backe). In 1985,

Ted Turner made an unfriendly bid for CBS, forcing the network to buy up 21% of its own stock to thwart the takeover. Laurence A. Tisch, a former theatre chain executive, had become the major stockholder in CBS when, in 1986, he instigated sweeping changes in the interests of cost-cutting and efficiency. 700 jobs were eliminated at the CBS Broadcast Group. Tisch also removed Wyman as president, named himself chief executive officer and induced founder William Paley to return to active duty as acting chairman of the board. It was quite a jolt to the company when, in 1985-86, it slipped to second place and stayed there through the following season. In 1987-88, CBS came in third for the first time in TV history. In 1988, Tisch shuffled executive ranks again, naming Howard Stringer, previously president of CBS News, president of the Broadcasting Group. The networks new management team sought to devise a strategy to pull the network out of its decline in the prime-time ratings. Jeff Sagansky, former head of Tri-Star Pictures, was brought in as president of the entertainment division in 1990.

Starting in 1991-92, CBS became the number one network for three years in a row based on the success of such shows as "60 Minutes" (the number one show for both '91-'92 and '92-'93), "Murphy Brown," "Murder She Wrote," and "Northern Exposure." CBS was hit hard by Fox's 1994 purchase of twelve stations from New World Communications, losing eight affiliates.

However, the following summer, Westinghouse Electric Corp. acquired the final independent network for $5.4 billion creating the largest collection of tv and radio stations in America. The 1994-95 season was a low point for the network as it plunged from number one to number three. By season's end, CBS had the dubious distinction of being the first of the three majors to fall into 4th place, coming in below Fox for the last week before the debut of the 1995-96 season. In late 1995, the venerable news program "60 Minutes" and CBS came under fire for refusing to air a controversial segment on the tobacco industry. Critics of CBS alleged that the network capitulated to the threat of legal action, rather than actual litigation. During this season the network placed third again. In 1997 CBS station group president Peter Lund was replaced by CBS radio president, Mel Karmazin.

Continuing the unpleasant trend of the last several years, CBS continued to lose viewers in all the age groups but the 60+. In the middle of 1998, Mel Karmazin made public the restructuring of CBS. Because of the network's failure to turn a profit, the radio and billboard companies which account for 60% of CBS' profits, were to be transferred into Infinity, thereby making the TV operations easier to sell, if need be. Infinity Broadcasting was sold by Karmazin to CBS in 1996 after trying to buy the Eye's radio stations himself. Two years later, the company is several times its former size, and it will have the cash to grow even more as a result of the CBS deal. Although the CBS president denied considering a TV sale, others have admitted that the sale has not been ruled out. Because of the network's questionable future, president & CEO of CBS TV, Leslie Moonves, was pressured to deliver successful primetime programming for the 1998-99 season. With the end of expensive shows such as "Cybill" and "Murphy Brown," Karmazin announced that the fall's lineup was considerably less costly than the previous year's. And, with shows such as "King of Queens" and "L.A. Docs" scheduled for the fall, analysts foresaw the possible resurrection of CBS.

RECENT CBS SERIES

1990-91: Evening Shade, The Trials of Rosie O'Neill.

1991-92: Brooklyn Bridge, Street Stories.

1992-93: Dr. Quinn: Medicine Woman, Picket Fences.

1993-94: Dave's World, Diagnosis Murder, The Nanny

1994-95: Chicago Hope, Cybill.

1995-96: Can't Hurry Love, If Not For You.

1996-97: Cosby, Pearl, Ink.

1997-98: Brooklyn South, Michael Hayes.

1998-99: Buddy Faro, L.A. Docs, Maggie Winters, King of Queens.

FOX BROADCASTING COMPANY

Fox Broadcasting, a subsidiary of Rupert Murdoch's News Company and owner of Twentieth Century-Fox, began broadcasting with the late night "Late Show with Joan Rivers" on October 9, 1986. The next year, on April 5, 1987, the fledgling network began prime-time broadcasts on Sunday nights only. The initial line-up consisted of "Married With Children" and "The Tracey Ullman Show", which featured animated interludes of a dysfunctional cartoon family named the Simpsons. Three new shows were added in the following weeks, including "21 Jump Street", which helped launch the career of actor Johnny Depp. In July of that year, Fox launched a Saturday night prime time line up. From 1989 to 1993, the network steadily added programming and expanded its prime time coverage to a full seven nights a week. Originally the network aimed its programming at a young urban demographic. Particular attention was given to African-American oriented programming, with comedy series such as "Roc", Martin", "Living Single" and "In Living Color" (a weekly comedy-variety show which showcased not only the talents of Keenan Ivory Wayans and his brother Damon Wayans, but also comedian Jim Carrey). The youth market was provided with its first soap opera with "Beverly Hills 90210", and its successful spin-off "Melrose Place". Fox consistently programmed "risky" shows, even in the face of boycotts, most notably aimed at "Married With Children" and "Beverly Hills 90210". The network, feeling strong about its programming, slotted "The Simpsons" against NBC's top-rated sitcom "The Cosby Show" in 1991.

The network was also actively pursuing sports programming. In 1993, Fox won the rights to NFL football for four years, including the rights to 1997's Super Bowl XXXI. In 1994, Fox acquired the rights to broadcast NHL hockey and in 1995, Fox signed an agreement with Major League Baseball to broadcast weekly games, the 1996, 1998 and 2000 World Series, and 1997 and 1999 All Star Games.

1994 saw the creation of FX Networks. In June, FX, a general entertainment basic cable network was launched, featuring marquee sports events, series and films. In October, fXM (Movies From Fox) was initiated to show Twentieth Century Fox films unedited and commercial free.

Also in 1994, Fox premiered "The X-Files", a fiction series dedicated to exploring the bizarre, the unusual and the paranormal, all with a slant aimed at conspiracy buffs. It took a season to achieve ratings success, but "The X-Files" has become one of the most popular series on Fox and is fast becoming the most imitated series on television. All of these programming decisions and experiments have paid off. In the 1994-95

broadcast season Nielsen ratings, Fox finished ahead of pioneer network CBS. Fox beat CBS yet again in November 1995. On October 7, 1996, Fox launched the new Fox News Channel on cable.

With the appointment of Richard Cronin as president and CEO of the Fox Kids Broadcast network and Fox Family Channel, Fox will be targeting young viewers with "quirky" programs. In its effort to increase its viewership by attracting young people, Fox hopes to also increase the number of older adults, watching along with the children. For the 1998-99 season, Fox moved up its primetime slot on the Fox Family channel, to begin at 6:00 p.m. instead of 8:00 p.m., and introduced four new dramas and two comedies, catering to the age group Fox is relying on to push its ratings up.

RECENT FOX SERIES

1991-92: Melrose Place, Roc

1992-93: Martin

1993-94: Living Single, The X-Files

1994-95: New York Undercover, Party of Five

1995-96: Space: Above and Beyond

1996-97: Millennium, Party Girl, Come Fly With Me.

1997-98: Ally McBeal, 413 Hope Street.

1998-99: Living In Captivity, Hollyweird, Brimstone.

NBC (NATIONAL BROADCASTING COMPANY)

NBC was an outgrowth of Radio Corp. of America, General Electric and Westinghouse. These three companies jointly launched a network in 1926 with 31 stations; 25 in a network called Red and 6 in a network called Blue. A year later, it was forced to sell the Blue network to ABC, keeping for itself the one known as Red. Television began for NBC in 1928, when on April 4, it acquired from the Federal Communications Commission a permit to operate an experimental station, W2XBS. Actual transmission from the Empire State Building did not begin until October 30, 1931. Eight years later, the network began broadcasting on a regular basis, beginning with the opening of the New York World's Fair on April 30, 1939.

NBC became a TV network on January 12, 1940, when two stations, WNBC-TV, New York, and WRGB-TV, Schenectady, New York, carried the first network programming. In June, 1941, the FCC granted NBC the first commercial TV license and a month later it had four advertisers signed up. After World War II, NBC scored two big "firsts." On June 19, 1946, Gillette became the first advertiser to sponsor a TV network show, the Joe Louis-Billy Conn boxing match. That same year, Bristol-Myers became the first sponsor of a network TV series, "Geographically Speaking." NBC can also claim to be the first to introduce coast-to-coast network TV coverage. On September 4, 1951, when the U.S.—Japanese peace treaty was signed in San Francisco, NBC cameras were on hand. In 1952, NBC pioneered early morning programming when it introduced "The Today Show." NBC can also claim the first regularly scheduled network color series "The Marriage," launched in 1954. That same year it achieved the first west-to-east TV transmission with the telecast of the Tournament of Roses Parade in color.

At the start of the 1965-66 season, NBC declared it was the "only all-color network." In 1968, NBC introduced new forms of TV programming with "The Name of the Game," a series that incorporated feature-film elements into a 90-minute show. This then spawned the "NBC Mystery Movie."

In 1972, NBC broke new ground again when it introduced "The Tomorrow Show" shown from 1:00 a.m. to 2:00 a.m. This was a talk program and it demonstrated that in the early hours of the morning something more than re-runs and old movies could be shown. In 1974, another late-night show called "Weekend" was begun. The 1976 NBC telecast of "Gone with the Wind" drew the largest audience to that date for an entertainment program. In 1978, "Holocaust" attracted 107 million viewers and won 21 major awards. Such programs helped NBC in the ratings, but in 1976-77 it fell to third place, where it stayed until 1983-84.

Along with the other networks, NBC moved into a period of turmoil during the decade of the Eighties, fighting off rising costs and competition from cable TV and home video. In 1986, General Electric Corporation purchased RCA (NBC's parent) for $6.28 billion; GE, it will be remembered, helped launch the radio network in 1926 which led to the development of NBC-TV. This brought personnel changes led by the replacement of Grant A. Tinker as NBC chief executive officer by Robert Wright, although Wright was not given Tinker's chairman title, that being taken by John F. Welch of GE. Instead, Wright was named president as well as chief executive officer. Along with its competition, NBC started cutting staff and budgets in 1986. In 1984-85, NBC edged up to second place, and the following year it was ranked number one in prime-time viewing for the first time in the three decades of Nielsen ratings.

NBC held on to its first place standing for the following five seasons, through 1990-91. Long-time hit series in the five-year period included "The Golden Girls," "Cheers," and "The Cosby Show." Despite the network's number one standing, figures showed a steady decline in viewers. In May of 1991, Brandon Tartikoff, credited with pulling the network up from third place 11 years earlier, departed from NBC to become head of Paramount Pictures. When "The Cosby Show" ran its final first run episode on April 30, 1992, it became NBC's highest-rated series finale episode ever. The 1992 Summer Olympics also gave the network its widest ratings margin of all time. The 1994-95 season found NBC on top with its popular sitcom "Seinfeld" and the two most highly rated new series, "ER" and "Friends", both placing in the top ten. During the 1995-96 season, NBC was again ranked the number one network, with four of its Thursday night shows ranking in the overall top five. In the summer of 1996, NBC, in association with software giant Microsoft, launched a 24 hour cable and Internet news channel.

In October 1997 the networks adopted an updated "voluntary" ratings system that uses the letters S, V, D, L, SV, which stand for sex, violence, suggestive dialogue, strong language and non-comedic fantasy violence in addition to the age rating. Only NBC and Black Entertainment Television refused to use the new system. Despite pressure from the White House, Congress and advocacy groups, the network had said that the ratings tread on its First Amendment right, and that there was no public outcry for the new system.

With its star show "Seinfeld" going off the air, NBC was faced in 1999 with the seemingly impossible task of finding a replacement. The network did manage to keep "ER" its other highly successful show, albeit at a draining cost of $13 million per episode. Keeping in line with the demand for news television, NBC's Dateline showed 6 1/2 hrs. of programming about Princess Diana and her fatal accident.

RECENT NBC SERIES

1990-91: Fresh Prince of Bel Air, Law & Order.
1991-92: I'll Fly Away.
1992-93: Homicide, Mad About You
1993-94: Frasier, The John Larroquette Show.
1994-95: Amazing Grace, ER, Friends.
1995-96: Caroline in the City, Third Rock From the Sun.
1996-97: Men Behaving Badly, Suddenly Susan.
1997-98: Veronica's Closet, Working, Jenny.
1998-99: Will & Grace, Encore! Encore!, Trinity.

PAX TV

August 31st, 1998 marked the debut of PAX TV, the nation's seventh and newest broadcast network committed to airing family-friendly programming that includes original live-action series, daily entertainment and information shows, children's programming, as well as popular movies and off-network shows with proven audience appeal. PAX TV is a wholly-owned service of Paxson Communications Corp., a broadcasting company whose principal business is the ownership and operation of the largest broadcast television station group in the United States. Paxson Communications Corp. was an outgrowth of Paxson Broadcasting founded in 1991 by Lowell W. "Bud" Paxson, the co-founder and past president of the Home Shopping Network, Inc., who had been involved in the radio and electronic retailing business for nearly 40 years. Paxson Broadcasting, a Florida-based radio group, initially purchased four radio stations in the fourth quarter of 1991-AM/FM combos in Jacksonville and Tampa. Over the course of several years, the Company assembled a substantial statewide radio broadcasting group, and as a result of agreements it had in place on radio stations prior to 1993's FCC rule change permitting radio duopolies, the Company was among the first to exercise its options and expand its duopoly holdings.

By 1994, the company sought to replicate in television its success in radio. Paxson looked to acquire two types of television properties: underperforming, undermanaged network affiliates and independent stations in major markets which broadcast long-form paid programming. In April 1994, the company purchased the equipment and acquired an option to buy its first television property, an independent TV station in Miami. Paxson took his company public in November m1994, through a reverse merger with the American Network Group, Inc., and subsequently moved the new company, Paxson Communications Corp. to the American Stock Exchange. By December of that same year, Paxson had owned or operated four stations, airing a variety of infomercial and long form programming which by January 1995, became known as the Infomall TV Network ("IN TV"). By purchasing independent television stations, entering into time brokerage agreements, affiliating with stations and extending its broadcast reach on cable via "must carry" requirements, Paxson created a national television broadcasting distribution infrastructure providing long form programming.

In March 1997, the Supreme Court upheld the "must carry" legislation, and as a result, all of the company's broadcast stations were suddenly viable as a network and would remain accessible to cable television audiences. In June 1997, the company sold its entire radio interest to Clear Channel Communications in a tax-advantaged transaction, and also during that month, acquired The Travel Channel of which it in turn sold an interest to Discovery Communications, Inc. later that year. The company announced in November 1997 that it would launch the seventh broadcast television network, at that time branded as PAX NET, on August 31st the following year. The network would feature off-network runs of popular shows including the CBS hit series, "Touched By An Angel," "Dr. Quinn, Medicine Woman," and "Diagnosis Murder," in addition to a number of original programs and theatrical and made-for-television movies.

Between the November announcement of PAX NET and August 31st launch of PAX TV, the company acquired additional television stations and expanded its distribution through cable agreements. The company also added popular off-network and original shows, and hired a number of executives and hundreds of new employees. In May 1998, the company announced the appointment of former CBS president, Jeff Sagansky, to the post of president & CEO and the election of William E. Simon, Jr. to the position of vice chairman for Paxson Communications Corp. Paxson also announced that the Simon family would make an equity investment in the company, and one month later, announced the completion of its offering of $275 million of Preferred Stock.

With PAX TV maintaining positive ratings, Paxson Communications Corp. will continue to focus on enhancing the distribution of its network and the quality of PAX TV's programming.

RECENT PAX TV PROGRAMS

1998-99: Little Men, Flipper: The New Adventures, Neon Rider, It's a Miracle.

PUBLIC BROADCASTING SERVICE

In 1948, the FCC stopped issuing new television station licenses. American educators, fearful of the impact of unrestricted commercial broadcasting, pushed for the Commission to hold open channel slots for non-commercial, educational television broadcasts. In 1952, when the FCC freeze was lifted, 242 channels were reserved for educational television. America's first non-commercial educational television station was KUHT in Houston, started in 1953. By 1962, 75 educational stations were broadcasting around the country. As these stations shared roughly the same programming interests, a loose distribution network evolved, allowing locally-produced programs like "Children's Corner" to be circulated among these stations. Most of the programming was produced on a shoestring budget. In 1962, the federal government authorized $32 million in matching funds for the construction of new educational television broadcasting facilities. In 1967, a blue ribbon panel urged local and state governments to increase their financial support of "public television" and recommended that the federal government participate in the production of programming. To this end, the first Public Broadcasting Act was enacted. This law also created the Corporation for Public Broadcasting, a non-profit "steward" of the public funds committed to public broadcasting, and, not incidentally, a barrier against government interference in programming decisions. In

1969, the Public Broadcasting Service's charter was signed, with its main intent the establishment of a nation-wide program distribution service. 1969 saw the premiere of an hour long, daily children's variety show, named "Sesame Street", which targeted pre-schoolers with fast-paced educational programming and featured live performers, cartoons and Muppets developed exclusively for the show by Jim Henson.

In 1970, PBS' first year as a "network", its programming included series as widely varied as "Washington Week in Review", "Civilisation", "The French Chef" and "Soul!" By 1973, PBS had more than 1 million individual subscribers. PBS and its member stations were responsible for bringing to U.S. audiences critically acclaimed BBC programming under the flag of "Masterpiece Theatre", which included such classics of television as "Upstairs Downstairs" and "I, Claudius". In 1976, PBS began broadcasting closed-captioned programming for the hearing impaired. In 1978, PBS became the first American network to distribute its programs by satellite.

Although some portion of PBS and its member stations' budgets are provided by federal and state government funding and corporate gifts, PBS and its member stations have continued to rely upon the contributions of individual viewers to stay afloat. In the late 1980's and early 1990's, PBS and the CPB suffered an enormous amount of criticism by government officials for an alleged "liberal" bias, and later in the 90's, for not being "self sufficient". Although a notable few PBS series have achieved some financial success in other areas (primarily children's' programming in the home video and product licensing fields), it is important to note that the production of most of the all-important local educational and public affairs programming never breaks even. In the face of continuing cuts in government funding, PBS programmers have accepted what may have been inevitable, the inclusion of commercial sponsorship (and actual commercials) in programming.

In the wake of the government threat of fund cuts, PBS increased its effort to achieve financial independence. In 1997, PBS president Ervin Duggan announced that the network would use its recognizable brand to market products and services, such as educational videos and distance learning programs. With this approach as well as using the internet to sell its products and investing in new programming, PBS experienced a total revenue for the 1997 fiscal year of $239 million; $15 million more than its target.

UPN (UNITED PARAMOUNT NETWORKS)

UPN began broadcasting on January 16, 1995 as a joint venture between United Television/Chris Craft Industries, Inc. and Paramount Television/ Viacom Inc. The fledgling network's first official hit was the newest entry in the long-lived Star Trek franchise, "Star Trek: Voyager." Paramount TV executive Lucy Salhany was named president of the network. UPN currently broadcasts two nights of prime-time programming weekly, a Saturday afternoon movie, and plans to add an afternoon children's programming block. In the 1995-96 season, UPN debuted 8 new prime time series. Lucy Salhany, president and CEO of the fledgling UPN network, announced that she would not renew her contract when it expired in September of 1997.

Led by the newly appointed CEO, Dean Valentine, UPN's management team had the difficult task of giving the sagging network a face-lift. Not unlike the other networks, UPN had to struggle to keep its viewers in 1998.

The network's audience, consisting largely of black viewers, was angered when in an effort to attract a broad Middle American audience, UPN cancelled most of the shows that appealed to black viewers. And, in what seemed like a second slap, the network premiered the sitcom "The Secret Diary of Desmond Pfeiffer," despite protests from black activists claiming that the show trivialized slavery.   As explained by Mr. Valentine, it appeared that UPN's problem was with its specific programming, which does not attract the female or suburban viewer.

RECENT UPN SERIES

1994-95: Star Trek: Voyager.

1995-96: Moesha, Nowhere Man, Paranormal Borderline.

1996-97: Good Behavior, An American Family, Homeboys in Outer Space.

1997-98: Seventh Heaven, Dawson's Creek, Three Buffy the Vampire Slayer.

1998-99: Guys Like Us, Love Boat: The Next Wave.

WARNER BROTHERS TELEVISION

In the 1950's when other studios were setting their eyes on television, Jack Warner was not interested in doing the same. But in 1955, the television network ABC managed to make a deal with Warner and create the studio's first pact. The agreement entailed a Tuesday night one-hour drama program on ABC, called "Warner Brothers Presents." Three rotating series were featured: "King's Row," "Casablanca," and the TV Western that lasted for eight seasons, "Cheyenne." "Maverick" starring James Garner, was introduced in 1957. The western proved popular with both viewers and critics, finishing sixth in the 1958-59 season ratings and being awarded the Best Western Series for the 1958-59 season, giving Warner Bros. TV its first Emmy award.

Although WB produced and created its share of shows in the 1960s, such as "Room for One More" (the first situation comedy produced by the studio),

"The Bugs Bunny Show" (TV's first animated series), and "The F.B.I." (WB's most popular primetime show of the late 1960s), TV production began drying up. With the appointment in 1969 of Gerald Leider as president of WB TV, the studio went through a revival with such shows as "Alice," "Kung Fu," and "The Dukes of Hazzard." The studio also acquired the rights to "Chico and the Man" and "Welcome Back, Kotter" already successful sitcoms, and the dramatic miniseries depicting the lives of African slaves, "Roots."

In 1988 WB acquired Lorimar Television absorbing the series "Dallas," "Knots Landing," "Falcon Crest," "Full House," "I'll Fly Away" and others. By 1989, Lorimar Television & Warner Bros. TV represented the biggest supplier of primetime TV programming to the networks. With the start of a new decade, the Warner Bros. studio appeared to be in good shape. But, the end of the Financial Interest rules, which limited the broadcast networks' ownership in programming and their ability to also produce, put WB in a less than perfect position as supplier. With the fear of falling victim to the networks, newly empowered by the FCC decision, WB began considering a network of its own. The first effort resulted in PTEN, which presented series as a syndicated block offered to stations. In January 1995 and in partnership with Tribune Broadcasting, the WB network took off.

The budding network will be reaching 90% of the country in the 1998-99 season, with five nights of primetime programming. While CBS and ABC have lost audience members in the 18-49 demographic group, and Fox and NBC have experienced only slight growth, WB has continued on its upward swing and increased its viewership by this (most desirable) demographic group, by 60%.

WARNER BROS. NETWORK SERIES

1995-96: Kirk, The Parent 'Hood, The Wayans Bros, Unhappily Ever After.

1997-98: Dawson's Creek.

1998-99: Felicity, The Army Show.

BROADCAST NETWORKS

See also, Index: Producers & Distributors, Services, Cable Networks, Cable Program Suppliers, Direct Broadcast Satellite & Wireless System Broadcasters.

ABC, INC.
(A Subsidiary of the Walt Disney Company.) 77 W. 66th St., New York, NY 10023. (212) 456-7777.
2040 Avenue of the Stars, Century City, CA 90067. (213) 557-7777.
PRESIDENT
Robert A. Iger
PRESIDENT, ABC TV NETWORK
Patricia Fili-Krushel
CHAIRMAN,
Stuart Bloomberg
PRESIDENT & CEO, ESPN
Steven M. Bornstein
S.V.P. & GENERAL COUNSEL
Alan N. Braverman
PRESIDENT, ABC RADIO
Robert F. Callahan
PRESIDENT, WALT DISNEY TELEVISION INTERNATIONAL
Etienne de Villiers
S.V.P., ABC, INC., & CHAIRMAN OF THE BOARD, ESPN
Herbert A. Granath
PRESIDENT DISNEY/ABC CABLE NETWORKS & PRESIDENT, DISNEY CHANNEL
Anne Sweeney
CHAIRMAN, BUENA VISTA TELEVISION
Walter C. Liss
S.V.P., COMMUNICATIONS
Patricia J. Matson
PRESIDENT, ABC OWNED TELEVISION STATIONS
Lawrence J. Pollock
S.V.P
Laurie Younger
V.P., HUMAN RESOURCES
Jeffrey S. Rosen
S.V.P., MEDIA DEV'T., BRAND MANAGEMENT & RESEARCH
Alan Wurtzel

ABC TELEVISION NETWORK GROUP
PRESIDENT, ABC TV NETWORK
Patricia Fili-Krushel
PRESIDENT, ABC TV NETWORK ADMINISTRATION & OPERATIONS
Alex Wallau
EXEC. V.P., MARKETING
Alan Cohen
EXEC. V.P., FINANCE
John J. Wolters
CHAIRMAN, ABC ENTERTAINMENT
Stuart Bloomberg
PRESIDENT, ABC ENTERTAINMENT
Jamie Tarses
EXEC.V.P., BUSINESS AFFAIRS & ADMINISTRATION
Mark Pedowitz
PRESIDENT, ABC DAYTIME
Angela Shapiro
S.V.P. & GENERAL MANAGER, CHILDREN'S PROG.
Jonathan Barzilay
CHAIRMAN, ABC NEWS & S.V.P., ABC, INC.
Roone Arledge
PRESIDENT, ABC NEWS
David Westin
EXEC. V.P., ABC NEWS
Shelby Coffee III
PRESIDENT, SALES & MARKETING
Marvin F. Goldsmith
EXEC.V.P., MARKETING & GENERAL SALES MANAGER & EXEC. V.P., NFL SALES
Lawrence Fried
S.V.P., AFFILIATE RELATIONS
John L. Rouse
PRESIDENT, BROADCAST OPERATIONS & ENGINEERING
Preston A. Davis
S.V.P., ADMINISTRATION
Richard E. Hockman
EXEC.V.P., & GENERAL MANAGER, ABC SPORTS
Brian McAndrews
V.P., NETWORK COMMUNICATIONS
Edward Dandridge

AFFILIATE RELATIONS
SENIOR V.P., AFFILIATE RELATIONS
John L. Rouse
V.P. & DIRECTOR OF AFFILIATE OPERATIONS
William (Buzz) Mathesius
V.P., AFFILIATE MARKETING & RESEARCH SERVICES
Mike Nissenblatt

TELEVISION NETWORK SALES
PRESIDENT, SALES & MARKETING
Marvin F. Goldsmith
EXECUTIVE V.P., NATIONAL SALES MANAGER
Roger Sverdlik
EXECUTIVE V.P., GENERAL SALES MANAGER
Lawrence S. Fried
SENIOR V.P., FINANCE & ADMINISTRATION
Robert S. Wallen
V.P., EASTERN SALES
Mark C. Mitchell
V.P., PRIMETIME SALES PROPOSAL
Peter Scanlon
V.P., CENTRAL SALES
Edward J. Wollock
V.P. & DIRECTOR, CENTRAL DIVISION
Michael R. Rubin
V.P., DETROIT SALES MANAGER
Mary Ellen Holahan
V.P., WESTERN DIVISION SALES
Charles W. Clark
V.P., SALES DEVELOPMENT & MARKETING SERVICES
Charles A. Gabelmann
V.P., SALES MARKETING
Madeline C. Nagel
V.P., PROMOTIONAL SALES & ACCOUNT DEVELOPMENT
Harry H. Factor
V.P., SPORTS SALES
Brian C. Sikorski
V.P. & DIRECTOR, SPORTS SALES
Ronald H. Furman
V.P., SPORTS SALES ADMINISTRATION
Michael Kay
V.P., DAYTIME SALES
Daniel Barnathan
V.P. & DIRECTOR, DAYTIME SALES
Gail A. Sullivan
V.P., NEWS & EARLY MORNING SALES
Cynthia Ponce Abrams
V.P. & DIRECTOR, NEWS, EARLY MORNING & LATE NIGHT SALES
Patrick J. McGovern
V.P., REVENUE PLANNING & ADMINISTRATION
John J. Abbattista

NETWORK COMMUNICATIONS
SENIOR V.P., NETWORK COMMUNICATIONS
Sherrie S. Rollins
V.P., MEDIA RELATIONS
Janice Gretemeyer
V.P., NETWORK COMMUNICATIONS
Mark R. Johnson
V.P., PHOTOGRAPHY
Peter Murray

ABC ENTERTAINMENT
CHAIRMAN
Stuart Bloomberg
PRESIDENT
Jamie Tarses
EXECUTIVE V.P., PRIME TIME
Stuart Bloomberg
SENIOR V.P., TALENT & CASTING
Donna L. Rosenstein
V.P., COMEDY SERIES DEVELOPMENT
Kim Fleary
V.P., DRAMATIC SERIES DEVELOPMENT
Greer Shepherd
SENIOR V.P., PROGRAM PLANNING & SCHEDULING
Alan Sternfeld
SENIOR V.P., VARIETY & SPECIAL EVENTS
John Hamlin
V.P., CURRENT SERIES PROGRAMS
Jeffrey D. Bader

SENIOR V.P., MOTION PICTURES FOR TELEVISION
Judd Parkin
V.P., MOTION PICTURES FOR TV & MINI-SERIES
Barbara Lieberman
SENIOR V.P., CONCEPT SPECIALS
Mark C. Zakarin
V.P., ON-AIR PROMOTION
Stuart L. Brower
V.P., SPECIAL PROJECTS
Geoffrey S. Calnan
V.P., MARKETING
Chris Carlisle
V.P., ON-AIR GRAPHICS
Barbara Eddy
SENIOR V.P., FINANCE & ADMINISTRATION
P. Thomas Van Schaick
V.P., FINANCE & ADMINISTRATION, WEST COAST
Eric Beattie

BUSINESS AFFAIRS
EXECUTIVE V.P., BUSINESS AFFAIRS & CONTRACTS
Ronald V. Sunderland
V.P., BUSINESS AFFAIRS, WEST COAST
Barry Gordon
V.P., BUSINESS AFFAIRS ADMINISTRATION, WEST COAST
Ronald Pratz
V.P., MUSIC & BUSINESS AFFAIRS
David L. Sherman
V.P., BUSINESS AFFAIRS, EAST COAST
Anthony S. Farinacci

DAYTIME, CHILDREN'S & LATE NIGHT ENTERTAINMENT
PRESIDENT, ABC DAYTIME
Pat Fili-Krushel
SENIOR V.P., DAYTIME PROGRAMMING
Maxine Levinson
V.P., DAYTIME PROGRAMMING, WEST COAST
Tom Campbell
SENIOR V.P., MARKETING & PROMOTION, ABC DAYTIME
Angela Shapiro
V.P., PRODUCTION, EAST COAST
Dominick J. Nuzzi
V.P., PRODUCTION, WEST COAST
Edgar Hirst
V.P., ABC CHILDREN'S ENTERTAINMENT
Linda H. Steiner

ABC SPORTS, INC.
PRESIDENT, SPORTS
Dennis Swanson
SENIOR V.P., PRODUCTION
Dennis Lewin
EXECUTIVE PRODUCER OF ABC SPORTS
Jack O'Hara
SENIOR V.P., PROGRAMMING
David Downs
SENIOR V.P., FINANCIAL & ADMINISTRATION
Robert H. Apter
V.P., PRODUCTION PLANNING
Jonathan Leess
V.P., MARKETING
Keith Ritter
V.P., ADVERTISING & PROMOTION
Tom Remiszewski
V.P., PROGRAMMING
Lydia Stephans
V.P., PROGRAMMING
Tony Petitti

ABC NEWS
CHAIRMAN, ABC NEWS
Roone Arledge
PRESIDENT, ABC NEWS
David Westin
EXECUTIVE V.P.
Paul Friedman
SENIOR V.P. FOR HARD NEWS
Robert J. Murphy
SENIOR V.P., FINANCE
William N. Temple
SENIOR V.P. OF EDITORIAL QUALITY
Richard Wald
SENIOR V.P. NEWS MAGAZINE, LONG FORM PROGRAM-
MING & EARLY MORNING PROGRAMMING
Alan Wurtzel
V.P. FOR BUSINESS DEVELOPMENT & MARKETING
William Abrams
V.P., OPERATIONS
Michael Duffy
V.P., NEWS OPERATIONS, WASHINGTON
Glenwood Branche
V.P., BUSINESS AFFAIRS
Steven Sadicurio
V.P., AFFILIATE NEWS SERVICE
Donald Dunphy

V.P. & WASHINGTON BUREAU CHIEF
Robin Sproul
EXECUTIVE PRODUCER, "20/20"
Victor Neufeld
EXECUTIVE PRODUCER, "PRIME TIME LIVE"
Phyllis McGrady
V.P., PRODUCTION CONTROL
William Nagy
V.P & ASSISTANT TO THE PRESIDENT
Joanna E. Bistany
V.P., TALENT RECRUITMENT & DEVELOPMENT
Amy Entelis
V.P., NEWS COVERAGE
Mimi Gurbst
EXECUTIVE PRODUCER OF "WORLD NEWS TONIGHT
WITH PETER JENNINGS"
Richard N. Kaplan
EXECUTIVE PRODUCER
Eleanor Prescott
SENIOR BROADCAST PRODUCER "WORLD NEWS TONIGHT
WITH PETER JENNINGS"
Robert Roy
EXECUTIVE PRODUCER "NIGHTLINE"
Tom Bettag

BROADCAST OPERATIONS & ENGINEERING
PRESIDENT
Preston A. Davis
SENIOR V.P., BUSINESS AFFAIRS
Michael Lang
V.P., ENGINEERING SERVICES, EAST COAST
David Elliott
V.P. & DIRECTOR, PROGRAM ADMINISTRATION
Maureen P. Domal
V.P., TELEVISION OPERATIONS, EAST COAST
Diane M. Tryneski
V.P., PROGRAM OPERATIONS
Stephen K. Nenno
V.P., POST PRODUCTION & SPECIAL PROGRAMS
Elliott Reed

ABC BROADCAST GROUP
PRESIDENT
Michael P. Mallardi
PRESIDENT, CABLE & INTERNATIONAL BROADCAST
GROUP
Herbert A. Granath
PRESIDENT, ABC DISTRIBUTION CO.
Joseph Y. Abrams
PRESIDENT, CAPITAL CITIES/ABC OWNED TELEVISION
STATIONS
Lawrence J. Pollock
PRESIDENT, CAPITAL CITIES/ABC NATIONAL TELEVISION
SALES
John B. Watkins
PRESIDENT, CAPITAL CITIES/ABC RADIO
James B. Arcara
PRESIDENT, CAPITAL CITIES/ABC OWNED RADIO STA-
TIONS—GROUP I
Don P. Bouloukos
PRESIDENT, CAPITAL CITIES/ABC OWNED RADIO
STATION—GROUP II
Norman S. Schrutt
PRESIDENT, ABC RADIO NETWORKS
Robert Callahan, Jr.

ABC NATIONAL TELEVISION SALES
PRESIDENT
John B. Watkins

ABC-OWNED TELEVISION STATIONS
PRESIDENT
Lawrence J. Pollock
VICE PRESIDENT
Robert O. Niles

DISNEY/ABC CABLE & INTERNATIONAL TELEVISION
PRESIDENT
Herbert A. Granath
PRESIDENT, ABC INTERNATIONAL OPERATIONS & EXECU-
TIVE V.P., ABC CABLE BROADCAST/EUROPEAN OPERA-
TIONS
John T. Healy
PRESIDENT, ABC EUROPEAN OPERATIONS
Richard F. Spinner
V.P., ABC CABLE INTERNATIONAL BROADCAST/EURO-
PEAN OPERATIONS
Emon Amselem
SENIOR V.P., FINANCE & ADMINISTRATION
Jeremiah G. Sullivan
V.P., FINANCIAL CONTROLS & ACCOUNTING
James R. Waltz

556

ABC DISTRIBUTION CO.
PRESIDENT
Joseph Y. Abrams
V.P., INTERNATIONAL TELEVISION SALES
Maria D. Komodikis
V.P., THEATRICAL/HOME VIDEO MARKETING
Michael J. Dragotto
V.P., SALES ADMINISTRATION & OPERATIONS
Carol Brokaw

ABC MULTIMEDIA GROUP
PRESIDENT
Stephen A. Weiswasser
EXECUTIVE V.P.
Bruce Maggin
V.P., FINANCE & ADMINISTRATION
Robert J. Ackley
V.P., PRODUCTION & TECHNOLOGY
Katherine Dillon

ABC VIDEO PUBLISHING
PRESIDENT
Jon R. Peisinger
V.P., PROGRAMMING & ACQUISITIONS
Cindy Bressler
V.P., FINANCE & OPERATIONS
Peter Fifield
V.P., SALES & MARKETING
Mark Gilula

CBS, INC.
51 W. 52 St., New York, NY 10019. (212) 975-4321.
CBS Television City, 7800 Beverly Blvd., Los Angeles, CA
90036. (213) 852-2345.
CHAIRMAN & CEO
Michael H. Jordan (resigned 10/98)
PRESIDENT & COO
Mel Karmazin
PRESIDENT, CBS NEWS
Andrew Heyward
PRESIDENT, CBS NEW MEDIA
Derek Reisfield
PRESIDENT, CBS SPORTS
Sean McManus
PRESIDENT, CBS CABLE
Donald Mitzner
PRESIDENT, CBS TV STATIONS & GENERAL MANAGER
Jonathan Klein
PRESIDENT, CBS RADIO
Dan Mason
PRESIDENT & CEO, CBS TELEVISION
Leslie Moonves
PRESIDENT, CBS ENTERTAINMENT
Nancy Tellem
PRESIDENT, CBS ENTERPRISES
Ed Wilson
PRESIDENT, STUDIO CENTER
Michael Klausman
EXECUTIVE V.P. & CFO
Fred Reynolds
EXECUTIVE V.P., INDUSTRIAL RELATIONS
James Sirmons
EXECUTIVE V.P., GENERAL COUNSEL
Louis Briskman
S.V.P. TECHNOLOGY
Joseph Flaherty
S.V.P., FINANCE, CBS CORP. & S.V.P. & CFO, CBS STATION
GROUP
Farid Suleman
S.V.P., & GENERAL MANAGER, EAST COAST BROADCAST
OPERATIONS
Jay Fine
S.V.P., WEST COAST OPERATIONS AND ENGINEERING
Charles Cappleman
S.V.P., CBS CORPORATION & PRESIDENT,CBS FOUNDATION
Martin Franks
S.V.P., COMMUNICATIONS
Gil Schwartz
S.V.P., COMMUNICATIONS, CBS ENTERTAINMENT
Chris Ender
S.V.P., COMMUNICATIONS, CBS CABLE
Cheryl Daly
S.V.P., HUMAN RESOURCES
David Zemelman
S.V.P'S., DEPUTY GENERAL COUNSEL
Martin P. Messinger
Susan J. Holliday
S.V.P. NEW VENTURES & BUSINESS DEVELOPMENT
Derk Zimmerman
MANAGING DIRECTOR, ASSISTANT TREASURER
Kenneth Hill
V.P., CONTROLLER
Robert Freedline

V.P., FINANCE, CBS TELEVISION NETWORK
James A. DePalma
V.P., FINANCE WEST COAST
Gary McCarthy
V.P., FINANCIAL PLANNING
Bruce Taub
V.P., BUSINESS PROCESS ANALYSIS
Donald W. Janson
V.P., GENERAL TAX COUNSEL
J. Phillip Adams
V.P., FINANCE
Carol Savage
V.P., & GENERAL MANAGER, CBS NEW MEDIA
Dean Daniels
V.P., MARKETING, CBS NEW MEDIA
Debra Zeyen
V.P., ENGINEERING
Howell Mette
V.P., ENGINEERING/ADVANCED TECHNOLOGY
Robert Seidel
V.P., TECHNICAL SERVICES
Shane O'Donoghue
V.P., ENTERTAINMENT PRODUCTION SERVICES
David Conant
V.P., NEWS PRODUCTION SERVICES
Bob Ross
V.P., BROADCAST DISTRIBUTION
Brent Stranathan
V.P., SPORTS PRODUCTION SYSTEMS
Ray Potter
V.P., PROGRAM PRODUCTION SERVICES
Steve Schilfrin
V.P., STAGE OPERATIONS
Harvey Holt
TECHNICAL OPERATIONS & ENGINEERING
Berry Zegel
V.P., CHIEF INFORMATION OFFICER
David Zink
V.P., INFORMATION SERVICES
John Difronzo
V.P., INFORMATION SYSTEMS, WEST COAST
Michael Vinyard
V.P., TELECOMMUNICATIONS
Thomas Maile
V.P., RISK MANAGEMENT
Dennis D'Oca
V.P., DIRECTOR, REAL ESTATE
Elliott Matz
V.P., WASHINGTON
John S. Orlando
V.P., FEDERAL POLICY
Gail MacKinnon
V.P., EXECUTIVE DIRECTOR, CBS FOUNDATION
Helene Blieberg
V.P., PROGRAM PRACTICES, EAST COAST
Matthew Margo
V.P., PROGRAM PRACTICES, WEST COAST
Carol Altieri
V.P., PUBLICITY, PRIMETIME SERIES
Theresa Corigliano
V.P., PUBLICITY, TELEVISION MOVIES, MINI-SERIES, SPE-
CIALS AND CHILDREN'S PROGRAMMING
Nancy Carr
V.P., COMMUNICATIONS, CBS NEWS
Sandra Genelius
V.P., COMMUNICATIONS, CBS SPORTS
LeslieAnne Wade
V.P., COMMUNICATIONS, EYEMARK ENTERTAINMENT
Andi Sporkin
V.P., COMPENSATION & POLICY
Karen Beldegreen
V.P., PERSONNEL BENEFITS
Anthony Ambrosio
V.P., FACILITIES OPERATIONS
Kenneth Cooper
V.P., INDUSTRIAL RELATIONS
Ed Yergeau
V.P., INDUSTRIAL RELATIONS, EAST COAST
Leon Schulzinger
V.P., INDUSTRIAL RELATIONS, WEST COAST
John McLean
V.P., HUMAN RESOURCES, WEST COAST
Lynn Hemont
V.P., ASSOCIATE GENERAL COUNSEL, LITIGATION
Susanna M. Lowy
ASSOCIATE GENERAL COUNSEL, LICENSING
Howard F. Jaeckel
ASSOCIATE GENERAL COUNSEL, LABOR
Mark W. Engstrom
ASSOCIATE GENERAL COUNSEL, CONTRACTS, RIGHTS
DEVELOPMENT
Sanford I. Kryle
ASSOCIATE GENERAL COUNSEL, WASHINGTON
Mark W. Johnson
ASSOCIATE GENERAL COUNSEL, GWSC
Jane R. Cottrell

CBS NEWS DIVISION
PRESIDENT
Andrew Heyward
EXECUTIVE V.P.
Jonathan C. Klein
V.P., PUBLIC AFFAIRS
Linda Mason
V.P., NEWS COVERAGE
Marcy McGinnis
V.P., PRIME TIME
Betsy West
V.P., PROGRAM PLANNING
Ted Savaglio
V.P., NEWS, CBS RADIO
Harvey Nagler
V.P., LONDON BUREAU CHIEF
John Paxson
V.P., NEWS SERVICES
John Frazee
V.P., OPERATIONS
Frank Governale
V.P., FINANCE & ADMINISTRATION
James McKenna
V.P., BUSINESS AFFAIRS
Josie Thomas

CBS SPORTS DIVISION
PRESIDENT
Sean McManus
SENIOR V.P., BUSINESS AFFAIRS & PROGRAMMING
Tony Petitti
S.V.P., OPERATIONS & TECHNICAL PLANNING
Ken Aagaard
S.V.P., MARKETING
Keith Ritter
V.P., PROGRAMMING
Michael L. Aresco
V.P., PROGRAMMING
Robert Correa
EXECUTIVE PRODUCER
Terry Ewert
V.P., BUSINESS AFFAIRS
Julie Wolf
V.P., BUSINESS PLANNING
Raymond Harmon
V.P., PRODUCTION SERVICES & ADMINISTRATION
James Harrington

CBS CABLE
PRESIDENT, CBS CABLE
Donald Mitzner
PRESIDENT, CBS EYE ON PEOPLE
Geoffrey Darby
PRESIDENT, CBS TELENOTICIAS
Francisco De la Torre
PRESIDENT, TNN & CMT
David Hall
PRESIDENT, GROUP W. NETWORK SERVICES
Altan Stalker
EXECUTIVE V.P., SALES & MARKETING
Lloyd Werner
SENIOR V.P., ADVERTISING SALES
Peter Weisbard
SENIOR V.P., AFFILIATE RELATIONS
Steve Soule
SENIOR V.P., COMMUNICATIONS
Cheryl Daly
V.P & GENERAL MANAGER, CMT
Paul Hastaba
V.P., PROGRAMMING, TNN
Brian Hughes
V.P., GENERAL MANAGER, HOME TEAM SPORTS
Jody Shapiro
V.P., GENERAL MANAGER, MIDWEST SPORTS CHANNEL
Kevin Cattoor
V.P., GENERAL MANAGER, INTERACTIVE MEDIA
Martin Clayton
V.P., FINANCE
Roy Coulter
V.P., GENERAL COUNSEL
Jane Cottrell
V.P., MARKETING SERVICES
Steve Yanovsky

CBS TELEVISION
PRESIDENT, SALES
Joseph D. Abruzzese
S.V.P. & CREATIVE DIRECTOR, ADVERTISING & PROMOTION
Ron Scalera
S.V.P., GENERAL MANAGER, AFFILIATE RELATIONS
Peter K. Schruth
EXECUTIVE V.P., PLANNING & RESEARCH
David Poltrack
EXECUTIVE V.P., MARKETING & COMMUNICATIONS
George Schweitzer

V.P., NATIONAL SALES MANAGER
Daniel J. Koby
V.P'S., DIRECTORS, SALES & MARKETING
Martin Daly
Michael Guariglia
John O'Sullivan
Duncan Ryder
Christopher Simon
V.P., WEST COAST SALES
John Gray
V.P., DETROIT SALES
Richard E. Masilotti
V.P., CENTRAL SALES
John F. Lee
V.P., PRIME TIME SALES/CENTRAL SALES
Mark Tupper
V.P., PROGRAM SALES
William Cecil
V.P., DAYTIME & CHILDREN'S SALES
Louis Jerome
V.P., SPORTS SALES
Scott McGraw
V.P & DIRECTOR, SPORTS SALES
John K. Brooks
V.P., NEWS SALES
Michael Nowacki
V.P., NEW BUSINESS DEVELOPMENT & MEDIA PLANNING RELATIONS
Elizabeth Rockwood-Fulton
V.P., MARKET RESOURCES
Tom Delaney
V.P., PRIMETIME, LATE NIGHT SALES
JoAnn Ross
V.P., GROUP HEAD, SALES PLANNING & ADMINISTRATION
Dean Kaplan
V.P., DIRECTOR, PRIMETIME & LATE NIGHT SALES
Linda Rene
V.P., SALES PLANNING
Russ Behrman
V.P., SALES SERVICES
Ann E. Harkins
V.P., TELEVISION AUDIENCE MEASUREMENT
Gregory Kasparian
V.P., TELEVISION RESEARCH, LOS ANGELES
Adam Gold
V.P., CREATIVE DIRECTOR, ADVERTISING & PROMOTION
Jeff Kreiner
V.P., ADVERTISING & CREATIVE SERVICES
Ileene Mittelman
V.P., ON-AIR PROMOTION
Jack Parmeter
V.P., PRINT ADVERTISING
Katherine Broyles
V.P., AFFILIATE ADVERTISING, PROMOTION & NETWORK PROJECTS
Brad Crum
V.P., PROMOTION MARKETING & EVENTS
Anne O'Grady
V.P., MARKETING OPERATIONS
Kathleen Culleton
V.P'S., DIRECTORS, AFFILIATE RELATIONS
Preston Farr
Frances Eigendorff

CBS ENTERTAINMENT DIVISION
PRESIDENT
Nancy Tellem
S.V.P., PROGRAM PLANNING & SCHEDULING
Kelly Kahl
S.V.P., MOVIES FOR TELEVISION & MINISERIES
Sunta Izzicupo
S.V.P., CURRENT PROGRAMS & SPECIALS
Terry Botwick
S.V.P., COMMUNICATIONS
Chris Ender
S.V.P., TALENT & CASTING
Peter Golden
S.V.P., BUSINESS AFFAIRS
Marc J. Graboff
S.V.P., DAYTIME/CHILDREN'S PROGRAMS & SPECIAL PROJECTS
Lucy Johnson
S.V.P., PROGRAMMING, EAST COAST
Mitchell R. Semel
S.V.P., COMEDY SERIES DEVELOPMENT
Gene Stein
S.V.P., DRAMA SERIES DEVELOPMENT
Nina Tassler
S.V.P., COMEDY, CBS PRODUCTIONS
Maria Crenna
S.V.P., PRODUCTION, CBS PRODUCTIONS
Robert Gros
V.P., PUBLICITY, PRIMETIME SERIES
Theresa Corigliano

V.P., PUBLICITY, TV-MOVIES, MINISERIES, SPECIALS & CHILDREN'S PROGRAMMING
Nancy Carr
V.P., SPECIALS
Jack Sussman
V.P., BUSINESS AFFAIRS, PROGRAMS & RIGHTS NEGOTIATIONS
Martin Garcia
V.P., BUSINESS AFFAIRS
Gary Silver
V.P., TALENT & GUILD NEGOTAIONS, BUSINESS AFFAIRS, CBS PRODUCTIONS
Leola Gorius
V.P., BUSINESS AFFAIRS, LONGFORM CONTRACTS & ACQUISITIONS
Sidney H. Lyons
V.P., MOVIES FOR TELEVISION, CBS PRODUCTIONS
Michael Wright
V.P., CHIDLREN'S PROGRAMS
Brian O'Neal
V.P., CREATIVE SERICES/ARTIST RELATIONS
Madeline Peerce
V.P., SPECIAL COMEDY PROGRAMS & DIRECTOR, COMEDY DEVELOPMENT
Wendi Goldstein
V.P., DRAMA DEVELOOPMENT
David Zucker
V.P., DRAMA CBS PRODUCTIONS
Jeff Eckerle

CBS ENTERPRISES
PRESIDENT, CBS ENTERPRISES
Ed Wilson
EXECUTIVE V.P'S., CBS ENTERPRISES
Bob Cook
Marvin Shirley
Rainer Siek
PRESIDENT, EYEMARK ENTERTAINMENT
Ed Wilson
EXECUTIVE V.P'S., EYEMARK ENTERTAINMENT
Bob Cook
Marvin Shirley
EXECUTIVE V.P., SYNDICATION
Barry Wallach
SENIOR V.P., BUSINESS & PROGRAM DEVELOPMENT
Robb Dalton
SENIOR V.P., PROGRAMMING & DEVELOPMENT
Jim Dauphinee
SENIOR V.P., EASTERN SALES
Joe DiSalvo
SENIOR V.P., BUSINESS AFFAIRS
Jon Hookstratten
SENIOR V.P., MARKET DEVELOPMENT
Nancy Widmann
V.P., EASTERN SALES
Sid Beighley
V.P., SOUTHWESTERN SALES
Nancy Cook
V.P., OPERATIONS
Sam Cue
V.P., SALES SERVICES
Suni Deskin
V.P., RESEARCH
Peggy Filis-Burkhardt
V.P., SOUTHEASTERN SALES
John Holdridge
V.P., MARKETING SERVICES
Mary Beth McAdaragh
V.P., MIDWESTERN SALES
Sean O'Boyle
V.P., WESTERN SALES
Peter Preis
V.P., COMMUNICATIONS
Andi Sporkin
PRESIDENT, EYEMARK MEDIA SALES
Dan Cosgrove
V.P., MIDWEST/WEST COAST SALES MANAGER
Patricia Brown
V.P. & GENERAL MANAGER, EYEMARK VIDEO SERVICES
George Kieffer
PRESIDENT, CBS BROADCAST INTERNATIONAL
Rainer Siek
V.P., WORLDWIDE SALES
Scott Michels
MANAGING DIRECTOR, EUROPE
Sonja Mendes
MANAGING DIRECTOR, ASIA
Yuet-fung Ho
SENIOR V.P., INTERNATIONAL MEDIA SALES
Bill Kunkel
V.P., BUSINESS AFFAIRS & OPERATIONS
Judith Bass
V.P., MARKETING & GENERAL MANAGER, CBS VIDEO
Kenneth Ross

CBS STATION GROUP
CHAIRMAN & CEO
Mel Karmazin
SENIOR V.P., & CFO
Faird Suleman
V.P., PERSONNEL
John Moran
PRESIDENT, CBS TELEVISION STATIONS
Jonathan Klein
EXECUTIVE V.P., SALES
Joseph Berwanger
PRESIDENT, CBS RADIO
Dan Mason

CBS OWNED TELEVISION STATIONS
PRESIDENT, CBS TELEVISION STATIONS & GENERAL MANAGER
Jonathan Klein
PRESIDENT, CBS SPOT SALES
Richard Sheingold
V.P., PROGRAMMING & RESEARCH
Ben Zurier
V.P., MARKETING
Licia Hahn
V.P., FINANCE & PLANNING
Anton Guitano
V.P., CONTROLLER
MIke Wittman
V.P., OPERATIONS & ENGINEERING
Paul Puccio

FOX BROADCASTING COMPANY
(A Subsidiary of the News Corporation.) 10201 West Pico Blvd., Los Angeles, CA 90035. (310) 369-1000. FAX: (310) 203-1454.
Mailing address: P.O. Box 900, Beverly Hills, CA 90213.
New York office: 1211 Avenue of the Americas, 3rd fl., New York, NY 10036. (212) 556-2400. URL: http://www.foxnews.com
Chicago office: 444 N. Michigan Ave., Chicago, IL 60611. (312) 494-2800.
CHAIRMAN & CEO, NEWS CORPORATION
K. Rupert Murdoch
CHAIRMAN & CEO, FOX BROADCASTING CO.
David Hill
CHAIRMAN & CEO, FOX NEWS
Roger Ailes
PRESIDENT & COO, NEWS CORPORATION
Peter Chernin
PRESIDENT, FOX TELEVISION NETWORK
Larry Jacobson
PRESIDENT, FOX ENTERTAINMENT GROUP
Peter Roth
PRESIDENT, NETWORK DISTRIBUTION
Lana Corbi
PRESIDENT, SALES, FOX BROADCASTING CO.
Jon Nesvig
PRESIDENT, FOX TELEVISION STUDIOS
David Grant
CO-CHIEF OPERATION OFFICER, NEWS CORPORATION
Chase Carey
CHIEF FINANCIAL OFFICER, NEWS CORP.
David F. DeVoe
GROUP GENERAL COUNSEL, NEWS CORP.
Arthur Siskind
EXEC. V.P.'S, NEWS CORPORATION, NEWS CORP
Leon Hertz
Martin Pompadur
EXEC. V.P., HUMAN RESOURCES, NEWS CORP
Bill O'Neill
EXEC. V.P., MARKETING, FOX BROADCASTING CO.
George Greenberg
EXEC. V.P., SALES, FOX BROADCASTING CO.
Jean Rossi
EXEC. V.P., LEGAL AFFAIRS, FOX BROADCASTING CO.
Eric Yeldell
EXEC. V.P., PROGRAM ENTERPRISES, FOX TV STUDIOS
Mindy Herman
EXEC. V.P., CREATIVE AFFAIRS, FOX TV STUDIOS
Lisa Berger
S.V.P., PUBLICITY & CORPORATE COMMUNICATIONS, FOX BROADCASTING CO.
Christina Kounelias
S.V.P., MARKETING, FOX BROADCASTING CO.
Ira Kurgan
S.V.P., CORPORATE AFFAIRS, NEWS CORP.
James Platt
S.V.P., MARKETING, NEWS CORP.
Roger Fishman
S.V.P., FINANCE, NEWS CORP.
John Nallen
S.V.P., FINANCE & INVESTOR RELATIONS, NEWS CORP.
Bill Sorenson

S.V.P., CORPORATE AFFAIRS, NEWS CORP.
James Platt
S.V.P., GOVERNMENT RELATIONS
Peggy Binzel
S.V.P., PROGRAMMING, FOX NEWS
Chet Collier
S.V.P., AFFILIATE SALES & MARKETING, FOX NEWS
Betsy Dirnberger
V.P., INVESTOR RELATIONS, NEWS CORP
Reed Nolte
V.P., CORPORATE COMMUNICATIONS, FOX TV STUDIOS
Tom Tyrer
V.P., GOVERNMENT RELATIONS
Steve Vest
V.P., REGULATORY & GOVERNMENT AFFAIRS
Maureen O'Connell, Esquire
V.P., FINANCE & ADMINISTRATION, FOX NEWS
Jack Abernethy
V.P., NEWS GATHERING, FOX NEWS
Brian Jones
V.P., NEWS EDITORIAL, FOX NEWS
John Moody
V.P., ADVERTISING SALES, FOX NEWS
Paul Rittenberg
V.P., OPERATIONS & ENGINEERING, FOX NEWS
Gerald O'Sullivan
V.P., MEDIA RELATIONS, FOX NEWS
Brian Lewis

FOX SPORTS
5746 Sunset Blvd., Sunset Bldg., Los Angeles, CA 90028.
(213) 856-1234.
1440 South Sepulveda, 2nd Flr., Los Angeles, CA 90025. (310)
444-8123. URL: http://www.foxsports.com
PRESIDENT
David Hill
PRESIDENT & CEO, FOX SPORTS NET
Tony Ball
PRESIDENT, SALES, FOX SPORTS NET
Lou Lattore
EXEC. V.P. & EXECUTIVE PRODUCER
Edward Goren
EXEC. V.P., BUSINESS OPERATIONS
Larry Jones
EXEC. V.P., MARKETING, FOX SPORTS & COO, FOX
SPORTS NET
Tracy Dolgin
EXEC. V.P.
George Krieger
EXEC. V.P. & HEAD OF BUSINESS OPERATIONS, FOX
SPORTS NET
Jim Martin
EXEC. V.P., PROGRAMMING & PROD., FOX SPORTS NET
Arthur Smith
EXEC. V.P., RIGHTS ACQUISITIONS, FOX SPORTS NET
Bob Thompson
S.V.P., MARKETING, FOS SPORTS NET
Peter Liguori
S.V.P., FINANCE, FOX SPORTS NET
Jeff Shell
S.V.P., SPORTS SALES
Jim Burnette
S.V.P., MARKETING
Neal Tiles
S.V.P., PROGRAM PLANNING & AFFILIATE RELATIONS
Victoria Quoss
S.V.P., MEDIA RELATIONS
Vince Wladika
V.P., MEDIA RELATIONS
Lou D'Emilio

FOX TELEVISION STATIONS, INC.
1999 S. Bundy Drive, Los Angeles, CA 90025. (213) 584-2000.
PRESIDENT & CHIEF OPERATING OFFICER
Mitchell Stern
EXECUTIVE V.P.'S.
Tom Herwitz
Mark Pearlman
EXECUTIVE V.P., ENGINEERING & OPERATIONS
Dick Slenker
S.V.P., LEGAL AFFAIRS
Gerry Firedman
V.P., CORPORATE & LEGAL FCC
Molly Pauker
V.P., FINANCE
Betsy Swanson
V.P., CONTROLLER
Kathy Maloney
V.P., PERSONNEL
Jean Fuentes
V.P., PROGRAMMING
Frank Cicha
V.P., ADVERTISING & PROMOTION
Leslie Lyndon
V.P., IS & FACILITIES
Alec Pettersen

TWENTIETH CENTURY FOX TELEVISION
PRESIDENT
Sandy Grushow
EXECUTIVE V.P.
Gary Newman
EXECUTIVE V.P., PRODUCTION & FINANCE
Charlie Goldstein
EXECUTIVE V.P., BUSINESS & LEGAL AFFAIRS
Howard Kurtzman
SENIOR V.P., TELEVISION PRODUCTION
Joel Hornstock
SENIOR V.P., CURRENT PROGRAMMING
Ken Horton
SENIOR V.P., FINANCE
Robert Barron
SENIOR V.P., TELEVISION POST-PRODUCTION
Edward Nassour
SENIOR V.P., TALENT & CASTING
Randy Stone
SENIOR V.P., CREATIVE AFFAIRS
Dawn Tarnofsky
SENIOR V.P., DRAMA
Dana Walden
SENIOR V.P., COMEDY
Mindy Schutheis
V.P., MEDIA RELATIONS, 20TH CENTURY FOX TELEVISION
Sarah Goldstein

INTERNATIONAL
PRESIDENT, INTERNATIONAL TV
Mark Kaner
EXECUTIVE V.P., INTERNATIONAL TV
Marion Edwards
EXECUTIVE V.P., INTERNATIONAL SALES & DISTRIBUTION
Julian Levin
SENIOR V.P., MARKETING, PROMOTION & PUBLICITY
Suzanne Krajewski
SENIOR V.P., INTERNATIONAL MARKETING
Scott Neeson
SENIOR V.P., EUROPEAN/NEAR EAST & AFRICA
Jorge Canizares
SENIOR V.P., INTERNATIONAL TV
Ken Bettsteller

NATIONAL BROADCASTING COMPANY, INC. (NBC)
30 Rockefeller Plaza, New York, NY 10112. (212) 664-4444.
Registered Telegraphic Address: NAT-BROCAST, NY.
3000 W. Alameda Blvd., Burbank, CA 91523. (818) 840-4444.
4001 Nebraska Ave., NW, Washington, DC 20001. (202) 885-
4000.
Government Relations & Law Offices: 1299 Pennsylvania Ave.
N.W., 11th fl., Washington, DC 20004. (202) 833-3600.
CHAIRMAN
John F. Welch Jr.
PRESIDENT & CEO
Robert Wright
PRESIDENT, NBC TELEVISION NETWORK
Neil Braun
S.V.P., CORP. COMMUNICATIONS & MEDIA RELATIONS
Beth Comstock
EXEC.V.P. & GENERAL COUNSEL
Richard Cotton
PRESIDENT, NBC SPORTS & S.V.P., NBC NEWS
Dick Ebersol
S.V.P. & COO
John Eck
PRESIDENT, BROADCAST & NETWORK OPERATIONS
Randy Falco
PRESIDENT, NBC NEWS
Andrew Lack
PRESIDENT, NBC ENTERTAINMENT
Warren Littlefield
PRESIDENT, NBC WEST COAST
Don Ohlmeyer
PRESIDENT, NBC CABLE & NEW BUSINESS DEV'T.
Thomas S. Rogers
PRESIDENT, NBC TELEVISION STATIONS
Scott Sassa
EXEC. V.P., EMPLOYEE RELATIONS
Edward L. Scanlon
PRESIDENT, CABLE DISTRIBTUTION, NBC
David M. Zaslav

NBC, WEST COAST
PRESIDENT, NBC WEST COAST
Don Ohlmeyer
PRESIDENT, NBC TELEVISION NETWORK
Neil Braun
PRESIDENT, NBC SPORTS
Dick Ebersol

PRESIDENT, BROADCAST NETWORK OPERATIONS &
OLYMPICS
Randall Falco
PRESIDENT, NETWORK SALES
Larry Hoffner
PRESIDENT, NBC NEWS
Andrew Lack
PRESIDENT, NBC CABLE & BUSINESS DEVELOPMENT
Thomas Rogers
PRESIDENT, NBC TELEVISION STATIONS
John Rohrbeck
PRESIDENT, NBC DESKTOP VIDEO
Michael Wheeler
PRESIDENT, CABLE DISTRIBUTION, NBC
David Zaslav
EXECUTIVE V.P., BUSINESS AFFAIRS & ADMINISTRATION,
NBC ENTERTAINMENT AND NBC STUDIOS
Harold Brook
EXECUTIVE V.P., BROADCAST STANDARDS & PRACTICES
Dr. Rosalyn Weinman
EXECUTIVE V.P., NBC ENTERPRISES
Jerry Petry
EXECUTIVE V.P., ADVERTISING & PROMOTION
John Miller
SENIOR V.P., ADVERTISING & PROMOTION
Vince Manze
SENIOR V.P., BUSINESS AFFAIRS
Dondal Gadsden
SENIOR V.P., BUSINESS AFFAIRS —NBC STUDIOS
Stephen Sass
S. V.P., PRODUCTION BUSINESS AFFAIRS —NBC STUDIOS
Lorna Bitensky
SENIOR V.P., DAYTIME PROGRAMS
Susan Lee
SENIOR V.P., EMPLOYEE RELATIONS —NBC STUDIOS
Brian McNamee
V.P., ADVERTISING & PROMOTION
Frank Radice
V.P. & CREATIVE DIRECTOR, ON-AIR PROMOTION
Ron Hayes
V.P., PRINT ADVERTISING
Jennifer Brewer
V.P., MEDIA, PRODUCTION SERVICES & AFFILIATE PRO-
MOTION SERVICES
Deborah Hamberlin
V.P., ON-AIR PROMOTION
Rick Oulette
V.P., DAYTIME PROGRAMS
Annamarie Kostura
V.P., PROGRAM RESEARCH
Susan Lee
Eric Cardinal
V.P., ENTERTAINMENT PRESS & PUBLICITY
Patricia Schultz
V.P., ENTERTAINMENT ELECTRONIC PUBLICITY & TALENT
RELATIONS
Kathleen Tucci
V.P., PROGRAM & TALENTS CONTRACTS
Richard Nathan
V.P.'S, BUSINESS AFFAIRS
Marjorie Neufeld
Nicole Ungerman

NBC ENTERTAINMENT
PRESIDENT, NBC ENTERTAINMENT
Warren Littlefield
EXECUTIVE V.P., MINI-SERIES & MOTION PICTURES FOR
TV, NBC ENTERTAINMENT & LONGFORM PROGRAMS, NBC
STUDIOS
Lindy DeKoven
SENIOR V.P., PROGRAM PLANNING & SCHEDULING
Preston Beckman
SENIOR V.P., PRIME TIME SERIES
Karey Burke
SENIOR V.P., SPECIALS, PRIME TIME SERIES, & LATE
NIGHT PROGRAMS
Richard Ludwin
SENIOR V.P., PRIME TIME SERIES
David Nevins
SENIOR V.P., PRIME TIME SERIES, NBC STUDIOS
David Bartis
SENIOR V.P., TALENT & CASTING
Lori Openden
SENIOR V.P., ENTERTAINMENT PROGRAMS, EAST COAST
Bridget Potter
V.P., PRIME TIME SERIES, NBC STUDIOS
JoAnn Alfano
VICE PRESIDENTS, MOVIES & MINISERIES
Joanna Brockway
Bari Carrelli
V.P., MOVIES & MINISERIES, NBC STUDIOS
Angela Bromstead

V.P., PRIME TIME SERIES, NBC STUDIOS
Michael Forman
V.P., STORY & WRITER DEVELOPMENT
Geoffrey Harris
V.P., MOVIES & MINISERIES
Gary Kessler
V.P.'S, PRIME TIME SERIES
Kate Juergens
John Landgraf
Robert Levy
Shelley McCrory
Charisse McGhee-Lazarou
Stephen McPherson
Flody Suarez
Ted Frank
V.P., CASTING
Jeff Meschel
V.P., PRIME TIME SERIES & SATURDAY AM PROGRAMS
Robin Schwartz

NBC CABLE & BUSINESS DEVELOPMENT
PRESIDENT & EXECUTIVE V.P.
Thomas Rogers
PRESIDENT, CNBC
Albert Barber

NBC TV NETWORK
PRESIDENT
Neil Braun
PRESIDENT, NETWORK SALES
Larry Hoffner
V.P., EASTERN SALES
Mel Berning
V.P. & GENERAL MANAGER, EASTERN SALES
Mike Mandelker
SENIOR V.P., MARKETING
Andrew Capone
SENIOR V.P., NETWORK DEVELOPMENT
Robert Niles
SENIOR V.P., AFFILIATE RELATIONS
John Damiano
SENIOR V.P., RESEARCH
Nicholas Schiavone
V.P., NETWORK SALES PLANNING & PRICING
William Caulfield
V.P., AFFILIATE RELATIONS EAST & MARKETING
Jean Dietz
V.P., TV NETWORK OPERATIONS
John Dewald
V.P., CENTRAL NATIONAL SALES
Richard Schade
V.P., DETROIT SALES
J. Nicholls Spain Jr.
V.P., AFFILIATE RELATIONS (MOUNTAIN & PACIFIC),
ENTERTAINMENT
William Fouch
V.P., SPORTS SALES
Keith Turner
V.P., AFFILIATE RELATIONS (CENTRAL), SPORTS
Carl Schweinler
V.P., NETWORK MARKETING
Barry Goodman
V.P., WEST COAST SALES
Steve Agase

NBC WASHINGTON GOVERNMENT RELATIONS
V.P., WASHINGTON
James H. Rowe III
V.P., GOVERNMENT RELATIONS
Terence P. Mahony

LEGAL
EXECUTIVE V.P. & GENERAL COUNSEL
Richard Cotton
V.P., LEGAL POLICY & PLANNING
Ellen Agress
SENIOR V.P., LAW, NEW YORK
Steve Stander
V.P., LAW, WEST COAST
Anne Egerton

NEWS DIVISION
PRESIDENT, NBC NEWS
Andrew Lack
PRESIDENT, NBC NEWS CHANNEL
Robert Horner
SENIOR V.P. & WASHINGTON BUREAU CHIEF
Timothy J. Russert
VICE PRESIDENTS, NBC NEWS
Bill Wheatley
Cheryl Gould
David Corvo
V.P., TALENT DEVELOPMENT
Elena Nachmanoff
DIRECTOR, SPECIAL PROJECTS
Lloyd Siegal

BROADCAST & NETWORK OPERATIONS

PRESIDENT, BROADCAST & NETWORK OPERATIONS
Randall Falco
V.P., BROADCAST & ENTERTAINMENT OPERATIONS
Frank Accarrino
V.P., NETWORK NEWS FIELD OPERATIONS
Stacy Brady
V.P., BROADCAST & NETWORK ENGINEERING
Charles Jablonski
V.P., BROADCAST & NETWORK FACILITIES PLANNING
Crawford McGill
V.P., SPORTS OPERATIONS & NETWORK TRANSMISSION
Michael Meehan
V.P., ENTERTAINMENT PRODUCTION OPERATIONS,
WEST COAST
James Powell
V.P., PRODUCTION & NETWORK SYSTEMS
David Rabinowitz
V.P., NEWS PRODUCTION OPERATIONS
David Schmerler

TECHNOLOGY DIVISION

EXECUTIVE V.P., SOURCING, REAL ESTATE & FACILITIES
Michael Sherlock
V.P., TECHNOLOGY
Peter Smith

PERSONNEL & LABOR RELATIONS

EXECUTIVE V.P., EMPLOYEE RELATIONS, NBC
Edward Scanlon
V.P., EMPLOYEE RELATIONS, WEST COAST
Wayne Rickert
V.P., LABOR RELATIONS, WEST COAST
Bernard Gehan
V.P., ORGANIZATION & MANAGEMENT RESOURCES
PLANNING
Jeffrey Trullinger
V.P., LABOR RELATIONS
Day Krolik, III
V.P., EMPLOYEE RELATIONS, CNBC
Adria Alpert Romm

CORPORATE COMMUNICATIONS

V.P., TALENT RELATIONS & MEDIA SERVICES, WEST
COAST
Kathleen Tucci
V.P., CORPORATE & MEDIA RELATIONS, WEST COAST
Patricia Schultz

SPORTS

PRESIDENT
Dick Ebersol
VICE PRESIDENT
Gary Zenkel
V.P., OLYMPIC PROGRAMMING
Peter Diamond
SENIOR V.P.
Jonathan Miller
V.P., SPORTS NEGOTIATIONS
John Ertmann
V.P., AFFILIATE SERVICES & PROGRAMMING
Mike Meehan
V.P., AFFILIATE SERVICES & PROGRAM PLANNING
Richard Hussey

TELEVISION STATIONS

PRESIDENT, NBC TELEVISION STATIONS
Scott Sassa
V.P., FINANCE & OPERATIONS
Robert Finnerty
PRESIDENT & GENERAL MANAGER, WMAQ-TV, Chicago
Lyle Banks
GENERAL MANAGER, WCAU-TV, Philadelphia
Pat Wallace
PRESIDENT & GENERAL MANAGER, KNBC-TV, Los Angeles
Carole Black
PRESIDENT & GENERAL MANAGER, WNBC4-TV, New York
Dennis Swanson
PRESIDENT & GENERAL MANAGER, WRC-TV, Washington DC
Allan Horlick
PRESIDENT & GENERAL MANAGER, WTVJ, Miami
Don Brown
PRESIDENT & GENERAL MANAGER, KCNC, Denver
Roger Ogden
V.P., TVSD RESEARCH
Barbara Tenney

NBC PRODUCTIONS

PRESIDENT, CREATIVE AFFAIRS
Michael Zinberg
EXECUTIVE V.P., NBC STUDIOS
Gary Considine
V.P., CURRENT SERIES
Joann Alfano
V.P., PRODUCTION BUSINESS AFFAIRS
Lorna Bitensky
V.P., CREATIVE AFFAIRS
Michael Browne
V.P., POST PRODUCTION
Joe Dervin
V.P., MOVIES & MINISERIES
Laurie Goldstein
V.P., TAPE PRODUCTION
Nina Lederman
V.P., PRODUCTION & MARKETING BUSINESS AFFAIRS
Albert Spevak
V.P., FILM PRODUCTION
Jim McGee
V.P., FILM PRODUCTION
Johanna Persons
V.P., PRODUCTION & MARKETING BUSINESS
Albert Spevak

NBC ENTERPRISES

EXECUTIVE V.P., NBC ENTERPRISES
Jerry Petry
V.P., FINANCE & NBC STUDIOS PRODUCTION
Jerry Dicanio
V.P., POSTPRODUCTION
Joe Dervin
SENIOR V.P., BUSINESS AFFAIRS
Joe Bures
V.P'S., PRODUCTION
Nina Lederman
James McGee
Nora Reynolds
V.P., NBC ENTERPRISES — STRATEGIC VENTURES
David Eun
V.P., INTERNATIONAL SALES & DEVELPOMENT
Sergio Getzel
V.P., NBC ENTERPRISES — BUSINESS AFFAIRS
Rhonda Troutman

FINANCE

SENIOR V.P. & CFO
Warren C. Jenson
PRESIDENT, TREASURY & ADMINISTRATION
Arthur Angstreich
V.P., CORPORATE EVENTS & TRAVEL SERVICES
Victor Garvey
V.P., FORECASTING
Edward Swindler
V.P. NEWS & FINANCE
Daniel J. Renaldo
CFO, NBC INTERNATIONAL
John W. Eck
V.P., CORPORATE FINANCE
Lawrence R. Rutkowski
V.P., BROADCAST & NETWORK OPERATIONS
Peter J. Haas

PAXSON COMMUNICATIONS CORP.

601 Clearwater Park, West Palm Beach, FL 33401. (561) 659-4122. FAX: (561) 659-4252. URL: http://www.paxson.com
CHAIRMAN
Lowell Bud Paxson
PRESIDENT & CEO
Jeff Sagansky
PRESIDENT, PAXSON COMMUNICATIONS CORP.
Jim Bocock
PRESIDENT, PAXSON TELEVISION STATION GROUP
Jay Hoker
PRESIDENT, PAX TV
Dean Goodman
PRESIDENT, PROGRAMMING, PAX NET
Bill Scott
PRESIDENT, MARKETING & PUBLICITY, PAX NET
Steve Sohmer
CFO
Arthur D. Tek
S.V.P., PROGRAMMING, PAX NET
Tim Johnson
S.V.P., NETWORK/NATIONAL SALES
Karen Schmidtke-Lincoln
S.V.P., MARKETING & PUBLIC RELATIONS
Lea Sloan
S.V.P., INVESTOR & CORPORATE DEVELOPMENT
Seth Grossman
V.P., RESEARCH, PAX NET
Richard M. Hebenstreit

V.P., EASTERN REGION
Lewis Freifeld
V.P., WESTERN REGION
Robert Hyland
V.P., SOUTHERN REGION
Michael Schweitzer
V.P., MIDWEST REGION
Dennis Thatcher
V.P., NETWORK SALES, NEW YORK
Michael Gannon
DIRECTOR, PUBLIC RELATIONS
Nancy David Udell
SALES MANAGER, NEW YORK
Kenneth Gelb
SALES MANAGER, LOS ANGELES
Lee Warpack
SALES MANAGER, CHICAGO
Jon Kleinman
SALES MANAGER, PHILADELPHIA
Bill Macready
SALES MANAGER, SAN FRANCISCO
Stephen Ullman
SALES MANAGER, DALLAS
Brian J.D. Duffy
SALES MANAGER, DETROIT
Jennifer Buda
SALES MANAGER, WEST PALM BEACH
Susan Patton

PUBLIC BROADCASTING SERVICE (PBS)

1320 Braddock Place, Alexandria, VA 22314-1698. (703) 739-5000.
1790 Broadway, 16th floor, New York, NY 10019-1412. (212) 708-3000.
5757 Wilshire Blvd., Suite 639, Los Angeles, CA 90036. (213) 965-5265.
PRESIDENT & CEO
Ervin S. Duggan
CHAIRMAN
Colin G. Campbell
VICE CHAIRMEN
Hope S. Green
Marshall Turner
EXECUTIVE V.P, PBS SYSTEM SERVICE & COO
Robert G. Ottenhoff
EXECUTIVE V.P., PBS LEARNING VENTURES
John Hollar
EXECUTIVE V.P., PROGRAMMING & CHIEF PROGRAMMING EXECUTIVE
Kathy Quattrone
EXECUTIVE V.P., LEARNING SERVICES
Sandra H. Welch
SENIOR V.P., DEVELOPMENT & CORPORATE RELATIONS
Jonathan C. Abbott
SENIOR V.P., PROGRAM BUSINESS AFFAIRS
M. Peter Downey
SENIOR V.P., ADVERTISING, PROMOTION & CORPORATE COMMUNICATIONS
Carole Feld
SENIOR V.P., LEARNING SERVICES
Jinny Goldstein
SENIOR V.P., GENERAL COUNSEL & CORPORATE SECRETARY
Paula A. Jameson
SENIOR V.P., PBS LEARNING MEDIA
Eric L. Sass
SENIOR V.P., CFO & TREASURER, FINANCE & ADMINISTRATION
Elizabeth A. Wolfe
V.P., FINANCE & TREASURER
Nanette Dudar
SENIOR V.P., BROADCAST & OPERATIONS ENGINEERING
Edward Caleca
V.P., DEPUTY GENERAL COUNSEL & CORPORATE SECRETARY
Sherri N. Blount

TELEMUNDO

(43 affiliated broadcast stations)
2290 W. Eighth Ave., Hialeah, FL 33010. (305) 884-8200. FAX: (305) 889-7980.
PRESIDENT & CEO
Peter Tortoricci
PRESIDENT OF ENTERTAINMENT
Nely Galan
COO
Alan Sokol
EXECUTIVE V.P., MARKETING
Rachel Welss

UNITED PARAMOUNT NETWORK (UPN)

11800 Wilshire Blvd., Los Angeles, CA 90025. (310) 575-7000.
PRESIDENT & CEO
Dean Valentine
SENIOR EXECUTIVE V.P.
Len Grossi
EXECUTIVE V.P., ENTERTAINMENT
Tom Nunan
EXECUTIVE V.P., BUSINESS OPERATIONS
Layne Leslie Britoon
V.P., DRAMA DEVELOPMENT
Maira Suro
V.P., COMEDY DEVELOPMENT
Kelley Edwards
V.P., CHILDREN'S PROGRAMMING
Ellen Levy-Sarnoff
V.P., BUSINESS AFFAIRS & LEGAL
Barry Gordon
V.P., FINANCE & ADMINISTRATION
Barbara Mannina
SENIOR V.P.'S, MARKETING & ADVERTISING
Joe Passarella
Dylan Gerber
SENIOR V.P., MEDIA & TALENT RELATIONS
Penelope Levey
EXECUTIVE V.P., NETWORK DISTRIBUTION
R. Kevin Tannehill
V.P.'S., NETWORK DISTRIBUTIONS
Sandy Pastoor
Rich Iazetta
V.P., AFFILIATE MARKETING
Marna Grantham
V.P., RESEARCH
Beth O'Connor
SENIOR V.P., NETWORK SALES
Perri Stein Procida

UNIVISION, INC.

605 Third Ave., 12th floor, New York, NY 10158-0180. (212) 455-5200. FAX: (212) 867-6710.
URL: http://www.univision.net
CHAIRMAN & CEO
A. Jerrold Perenchio
PRESIDENT & COO, NETWORK
Ray Rodriguez
EXECUTIVE V.P.
Andrew Hobson
V.P., DIRECTOR OF RESEARCH
Doug Darfield
V.P., DIRECTOR OF OPERATIONS & SPORTS
Tony Oquendo
V.P. & NEWS DIRECTOR
Alina Falcon
V.P., NY SALES MANAGER
Judith Kenny
CO-PRESIDENT, NETWORK SALES
Thomas McGarrity
CO-PRESIDENT, NETWORK SALES
Dennis McCauley

UNIVISION NETWORK

9405 N.W. 41st St., Miami, FL 33178. (305) 471-3900. FAX: (305) 471-4065.
PRESIDENT & COO
Ray Rodriguez
V.P., PROGRAMMING
Mario Rodriguez
PROGRAMMING ADMINISTRATION
Valeria Palazio

UNIVISION COMMUNICATIONS, INC.

6701 Center Drive West, 15th floor, Los Angeles, CA 90045. (310) 216-3434. FAX: (310) 348-3698.
PRESIDENT & COO
Henry Cisneros
EXECUTIVE V.P.
Andrew Hobson

UNIVISION REGIONAL SALES OFFICES

WEST
6701 Centre Drive West, 15th floor, Los Angeles, CA 90045. (310) 338-0700. FAX: (310) 348-3626.
V.P., & GENERAL SALES MANAGER
Jim Baral

50 Fremont St., 41st floor, San Francisco, CA 94105. (415) 677-8094.
SALES MANAGER
Doreen Capelli

MIDWEST
541 N. Fairbanks Court, 11th Floor, Chicago, IL 60611. (312) 494-5100. FAX: (312) 494-5115.
NETWORK SALES MANAGER
Trisha Pray
SPOT SALES
Chris Joyce
3155 West Big Beaver Rd., Suite 105, Troy, MI 48084. (810) 643-1921. FAX: (810) 643-7993.
SALES MANAGER
Mark Brown
SOUTH
9405 N.W. 41st St., Miami, FL 33178. (305) 471-3900. FAX: (305) 471-4027.
V.P. & REGIONAL SALES MANAGER
Nick Valls
SALES MANAGER
Evelyn Castillo
1 Buckhead Plaza, Suite 1340, 3060 Peachtree Rd. NW, Atlanta, GA 30305. (404) 264-8660. FAX: (404) 264-8661.
SPOT SALES MANAGER
Tammy Heinen
2323 Bryan Str., Ste. 1900, Dallas, TX 75201-2646. (214) 758-2400. FAX: (214) 758-2410.
V.P. & REGIONAL NATIONAL SALES MANAGER
Jack Hobbs
SALES MANAGER
Michael Burch

THE WB TELEVISION NETWORK

4000 Warner Blvd., Building 34R, Burbank, CA 91522. (818) 954-6000.
?CEO, THE WB TELEVISION NETWORK
Jamie Kellner
PRESIDENT, PROGRAMMING
Garth Ancier
EXECUTIVE V.P., PROGRAMMING
Susanne Daniels

EXECUTIVE V.P., NETWORK DISTRIBUTION
Ken Werner
SENIOR V.P., DEVELOPMENT
Jordan Levin
SENIOR V.P., CURRENT PROGRAMMING
John Litvack
SENIOR V.P., TALENT
Kathleen Letterie
SENIOR V.P., BUSINESS AFFAIRS
Michael A. Ross
EXECUTIVE V.P., MARKETING
Bob Bibb
EXECUTIVE V.P.
Lewis Goldstein
PRESIDENT, WARNER BROS. TV ANIMATION
Jean MacCurdy
SENIOR V.P., PUBLICITY
Brad Turell
V.P.'S, KIDS' WB! MARKETING
Betsy McGowen
Dave Dore
V.P., PRIMETIME PUBLICITY
Janine Jones
V.P., ON-AIR PROMOTION
Steve Domier
V.P., AFFILIATE SERVICES
Andy Crittenden
V.P., PRINT CREATIVE SERVICES
Suzanne Kolb
SENIOR V.P., MEDIA SALES
Jed Petrick
SENIOR V.P. & GENERAL COUNSEL
John Maata
SENIOR V.P., FINANCE & ADMINISTRATION
Mitch Nedick
SENIOR V.P., AFFILIATE RELATIONS
Hal Protter
V.P., BROADCAST STANDARDS & PRACTICES
Rick Mater

PRODUCERS AND DISTRIBUTORS

Where available, television products have been listed. For additional companies, please see Broadcast Networks and Cable Networks.

A.B. ENTERPRISES, INC./BECK INTERNATIONAL CORP.

Box 1228, Scarsdale, NY 10583. (914) 472-5908. FAX: (914) 472-6564.
CHAIRMAN
Alexander Beck
PRESIDENT
Shirley Beck
EXEC. V.P. & HOUSE COUNSEL
Kenneth A. Beck

ABRAMS/GENTILE ENTERTAINMENT

244 W. 54th St., 9th floor, New York, NY 10019. (212) 757-0700. FAX: (212) 765-1987.
Series: Dragonflyz (26 x 23 mins.), Guardian Angels: The TV Series (13 x 44 mins.), The Hammer Horror Zone (26 x 23 mins.), Happy Ness: The Secret of The Loch (13 x 23 mins.), Jelly Bean Jungle (13 x 23 mins.), Paparazzi Samurai (26 x 23 mins.), Sky Dancers (26 x 23 mins.), Van-pires (26 x 23 mins.), Open Call ((13 x 23 mins.), Di Resta (13 x 23 mins.), Micronauts (26 x 23 mins.).

ACT III TELEVISION

1999 Ave. of the Stars, Suite 500, Los Angeles, CA 90067. (310) 553-3636.
CHAIRMAN
Norman Lear
PRESIDENT
John Baskin

ADLER MEDIA, INC.

6849 Old Dominion Dr., Suite 360, McLean, VA 22101. (703) 556-8880. FAX: (703) 556-9288. email: adlermedia@aol.com
PRESIDENT
Larry Adler
DIRECTOR, INT'L SALES & ACQUISITIONS
Ingrid Enzelsberger

ALICE ENTERTAINMENT, INC.

1539 Sawtelle Blvd., #4, Los Angeles, CA 90025. (310) 231-1050. FAX: (310) 231-1159. email: aliceranch@aol.com
PRESIDENT
Alice Donenfeld
VICE PRESIDENT
Harry Donenfeld
HEAD OF LATIN AMERICAN SALES
Carmela Spencer
HEAD OF NORTHERN EUROPEAN SALES
Pieter L.E. Gosselaar
Series: Bingo & Molly (26 x 30 mins.), Global Business 2000 (26 x 30 mins.), Guardians of the Truth (10 x 30 mins.), The Walker's Cay Chronicles (52 x 30 mins.), Antoine... Once Upon an Island (12 x 1hr.), over 1,000 hrs. of hunting & fishing shows.

ALL AMERICAN TELEVISION

1325 Avenue of the Americas, 6th floor, New York, NY 10019. (212) 541-2800. FAX: (212) 541-2810.
2114 Pico Blvd., Santa Monica, CA 90405. (310) 450-3193.
PRESIDENT & CEO
Larry Lamattina
CHAIRMAN, DISTRIBUTION
George Back
Series: Baywatch.

ALLIANCE COMMUNICATIONS CORPORATION

920 Yonge St., Suite 400, Toronto, Ontario, Canada M4W 3C7. (416) 967-1174. FAX: (416) 960-0971.
301 N. Canon Dr., Suite 321, Beverly Hills, CA 90210. (310) 275-5501. FAX: (310) 275-5502.
CHAIRMAN
Robert Lantos
CHAIRMAN, ALLIANCE TELEVISION
Todd Leavitts
S.V.P., BUSINESS & LEGAL AFFAIRS, ALLIANCE TV
John Morayniss
PRESIDENTS, ALLIANCE TELEVISION
Michael Weisbarth
Andras Hamori

PRESIDENT, ALLIANCE PICTURES INTERNATIONAL
Mark Horowitz
EXECUTIVE V.P., ALLIANCE TELEVISION
Laurie Pozmantier
V.P., CREATIVE AFFAIRS, ALLIANCE TELEVISION
Ted Gold
V.P., CREATIVE AFFAIRS, ALLIANCE TELEVISION PROD.
Noreen Halpern
V.P., SALES, INTERNATIONAL TELEVISION
Guy Petty
Series: Blanche (11 x 60 mins.), Bordertown (78 x 30 mins.), Counterstrike (66 x 60 mins.), Due South (1 x 2 hrs. & 40 x 60 mins.), E.N.G. (2 hr, pilot & 94 x 60 mins.), Fly By Night (13 x 60 mins.), Mount Royal (2 hr. pilot & 15 x 60 mins.), North of 60 (64 x 60 mins.), Stuntmasters (22 x 60 mins.), Taking The Falls (13 x 60 mins.).
Children's Series: The Adventures of The Black Stallion (78 x 30 mins.), Beast Wars (26 x 30 mins.), Max Glick (26 x 30 mins.), The Mighty Jungle (26 x 30 mins.), Mirror Mirror (20 x 30 mins.), The Odyssey (39 x 30 mins.), ReBoot Season II (10 x 30 mins.), Straight Up (6 x 30 mins.).
Mini-series: The Boys of St. Vincent (4hrs.), Shehaweh (5 hrs.), Woman On The Run: The Lawrencia Bembenek Story (4 hrs.).
TV Movies: Craque La Vie (2 hrs.), L'Enfant Sur Le Lac, Family of Strangers (2 hrs.), Frostfire (2 hrs.), Golden Will: The Silken Laumann Story (2 hrs.), Gridlock (2 hrs.), Harlequin Romance Movies (6 x 2 hrs.), L'Homme De Reve, Justice On Wheels: The Diana Kilmury Story (2 hrs.), Model By Day (2 hrs.), Nenette, Once A Thief (2 hrs.), Solo, Trial And Error (2 hrs.), Un Leger Vertige.
Documentaries/Docu-Dramas: Scales of Justice (5 x 60 mins, & 2 x 2 hrs.), The Valour And The Horror (3 x 2 hrs.).

AMBLIN ENTERTAINMENT

100 Universal Plaza, Bungalow 477, Universal City, CA 91608. (818) 777-4600.
One Hour: seaQuest 2032, ER.
Half-Hour: Amazing Stories, Fudge, Harry & the Hendersons.
Animation: Animaniacs, Back to the Future, Fievel's American Tales, Tiny Toon Adventures, A Wish for Wings That Work, Tiny Toons: How I Spent My Vacation.
Movies of the Week: The American Clock, Class of '61, Cooperstown, Fudge-a-Mania, Habitation of Dragons, Heart of Justice, Percy and Thunder, The Water Engine.

ANIMATED PRODUCTIONS, INC.

1600 Broadway, New York, NY 10019. (212) 265-2942. FAX: (212) 265-2944.
PRESIDENT
Al Stahl
VICE PRESIDENT
Richard Stahl
PRODUCTION DIRECTOR
Shirlee Debrier
EXECUTIVE DIRECTOR
Peter Puzzo

ARTISAN ENTERTAINMENT

2700 Colorado Ave., 2nd Flr., Los Angeles, CA 90404. (310) 449-9200.
CHAIRMAN
Roger A. Burlage
CEO
Mark Curcio
PRESIDENT, DISTRIBUTION & MARKETING
Amir Malin
V.P., LEGAL & BUSINESS AFFAIRS
Karen Levin
V.P., TV & NEW MEDIA
Gary Rubin

ASSOCIATED PRESS BROADCAST DIVISION

AP Broadcast News Center, 1825 K Street, N.W., Suite 710, Washington, DC 20006-1253. (202) 736-1100, (800) 821-4747. FAX: (202) 736-1124.
V.P. & DIRECTOR
Jim Williams

ASSOCIATED TELEVISION INTERNATIONAL

36 W. 44 St., #1400, New York, NY 10036. (212) 764-6060.
6290 Sunset Blvd., 12th Fl., Hollywood, CA 90028. (213) 871-1340. FAX: (213) 469-6048.
CEO
Paul Sharratt
PRESIDENT
David McKenzie
SENIOR VICE PRESIDENT
James Romanovich
V.P., BUSINESS AFFAIRS
Richard Casares
V.P., MARKETING
Howard Coleman

Series: Miracles (3 x 60 mins.), Mysteries, Magic & Miracles (65 x 30 mins.), Safari (78 x 30 mins.), Petersen's American Adventures (39 x 30 mins.), Crime Strike (26 x 30 mins.).

ATA TRADING CORP.

50 W. 34th St., Suite 5C6, New York, NY 10001. (212) 594-6460.
FAX: (212) 594-6461.
PRESIDENT
Harold G. Lewis
HEAD OF PRODUCTION
Phil Saunders
DIRECTOR OF SALES
Luci Lo Russo

Children's Series: Champs (13 x 30 mins.), Zoo Stories (13 x 30 mins.).
Documentary: Space: Beyond the Final Frontier (13 x 60 mins.).

ATLANTIS FILMS/ATLANTIS RELEASING

65 Heward Ave., Toronto, Ontario, Canada M4M 2T5. (416) 462-0246. 227 Broadway, #300, Santa Monica, CA 90401. (310) 576-7719. FAX: (310) 576-0799.
PRESIDENT
Michael MacMillan
VICE PRESIDENTS, TV & FILM PRODUCTION
Seaton McLean
Peter Sussman
Ted Riley

Series: The Adventures of Sinbad, Flash Forward, My Life As A Dog, The Outer Limits, Psi Factor, Traders.

BALTIMORE PICTURES, INC.

c/o Warner Bros., 4000 Warner Blvd., Burbank, CA 91522.
(818) 954-2666. FAX: (818) 954-2693.
DIRECTOR, WRITER, EXEC. PRODUCER
Barry Levinson

Series: Homicide: Life on the Street.

BOB BANNER ASSOCIATES, INC.

10350 Santa Monica Blvd., Suite 290, Los Angeles, CA 90025.
(310) 557-1800. FAX: (310) 557-1880.
EXECUTIVE PRODUCER & V.P.
Bob Banner
DIRECTOR OF DEVELOPMENT
Ben Caswell

Series: Amazing Music, It's Showtime At The Apollo.

BEN BARRY & ASSOCIATES, INC.

10246 Briarwood Dr., Los Angeles, CA 90077. (310) 274-1523.
FAX: (310) 274-1523.
PRESIDENT
Mimi Barry
CHAIRMAN
Ben Barry

Feature films include: Blood on the Arrow, Death Rage, The Devil's Rain, Eyes Behind the Stars, Human Factor, The Inheritance, Shattered, Swiss Conspiracy.

Feature films under House of Horrors heading include: Children Shouldn't Play with Dead Things, Invaders From Mars, Magnificent Matador, Restless Breed, Swingin' Summer.
Samuel Fuller classics: Naked Kiss, Shock Corridor.

BBC WORLDWIDE AMERICAS

747 Third Ave., 7th floor, New York, NY 10017. (212) 705-9406.
FAX: (212) 705-9332.
Series: Absolutely Fabulous (18 x 30 mins.), Being There (6 x 30 mins.), Dr. Who (86 x 100 mins.), Fawlty Towers (12 x 30 mins.) Keeping Up Appearances (43 x 30 mins.), Madison's Adventures: Growing Up Wild (200 x 30 mins.), Nostromo (6 x 50 mins.), Perceptions (6 x 50 mins.), Pride & Prejudice (6 x 50 mins.), Prohibition (3 x 60 mins.), Stephen Hawking's Universe (6 x 50 mins.), Wallace & Gromit (3 x 30 mins.).

BBC WORLDWIDE TELEVISION

Woodlands, 80 Wood Lane, London W12 OTT. (44181) 576-2000. FAX: (44181) 749-0538.
Series: David Attenborough's Life of Birds (10 x 50 mins.), Oh, Doctor Beechin (8 x 30 mins.), Prohibition (3 x 60 mins.), The Sculptress (4 x 50 mins.).

BEHAVIOUR WORLDWIDE

1925 Century Park East, Ste. 1700, Los Angeles, CA 90067.
(310) 226-8300. FAX: (310) 226-8850.
CHAIRMAN & CEO
Lawrence Goebel
S.V.P., WORLDWIDE DISTRIBUTION
Rob Aft

TV-Movies: Daddy's Girl, The Nurse, The Secretary, Stranger In The House, The Wrong Woman, Table For One.

BELISARIUS PRODS.

c/o Paramount TV, 5555 Melrose Ave., Clara Bow Bldg., #204, Los Angeles, CA 90038. (213) 956-8660. FAX: (213) 956-0250.
Series: Jag.

BELL-PHILLIP TV PRODS.

7800 Beverly Blvd., Suite 3371, Los Angeles, CA 90036. (323) 575-4138. FAX: (323) 655-8760.
EXECUTIVE PRODUCERS
William J. Bell
Lee Phillip Bell
Bradley Bell

Series: The Bold and the Beautiful.

BICKLEY/WARREN PRODS.

c/o Warner Bros. TV, 4000 Warner Blvd., Producers 9, #159, Burbank, CA 91522. (818) 954-2782. FAX: (818) 954-4326.
EXECUTIVE PRODUCER
William Bickley

Series: Family Matters, Hangin' With Mr. Cooper, Kirk, Step by Step.

THE BIG FIGHTS INC.

9 E. 40 St., New York, NY 10016. (212) 532-1711.
PRESIDENT
William D. Cayton

Products: Big Fights of the Decades Series, Knockout (750 x 2 mins.).

Features: A.K.A. Cassius Clay, Grudge Fights, Heavyweight Championship, Jack Johnson, Legendary Champions, The Middleweight Championship, Muhammad Ali: Skill Brains & Guts, Olympic Highlights of '72, Sugar Ray Robinson.

Quarter-Hours: Madison Square Garden Spots Programs 1951-56, Most Famous Fights of the Golden Era of Boxing.

Half-Hours: Big Fights Inc. Olympic Film and Tape Library, Bill Cayton's Greatest Knockouts, Boxing's Best, Boxing's Greatest Champions, Great Fights of the 70's and 80's, Guinness Book of World Records Film, Main Event Series, Mike Tyson Fights, Olympic Glory: The Golden Years, etc., Pocket Billiards Library.

BIG TICKET TELEVISION

(A unit of Spelling Entertainment Group, Inc.)
5700 Wilshire Blvd. #575, Los Angeles, CA 90036. (213) 860-7400. FAX: (213) 468-4176.
PRESIDENT
Larry Lyttle
SENIOR V.P., CREATIVE AFFAIRS
Bill Sanders
V.P. & CONTROLLER
Fed Paccone
V.P., CURRENT PROGRAMMING
Deborah Curtain

BLACK/MARLENS COMPANY

17351 Sunset Blvd., Suite 504, Pacific Palisades, CA 90272.
(310) 772-8264.
Series: Ellen.

STEVEN BOCHCO PRODUCTIONS

10201 W. Pico Blvd., Los Angeles, CA 90035. (310) 369-2400.
FAX: (310) 369-3941.
CHAIRMAN & CEO
Steven Bochco
PRESIDENT, TV PRODUCER
Dayna Flanagan
PRESIDENT & CFO
Franklin B. Rohner

Current Series: Brooklyn South, Murder One, NYPD Blue, Total Security.

BRIGHT-KAUFFMAN-CRANE PRODUCTIONS

300 S. Lorimar Plaza, Bldg. 140, Rm. 130, Burbank, CA 91522.
(818) 977-7777. FAX: (818) 977-7711.
EXECUTIVE PRODUCERS
Kevin S. Bright
Marta Kauffman
David Crane
EXECUTIVE ASSISTANT
Adrienne Turner

Series: Dream On, Friends, Veronica's Closet.

BRILLSTEIN-GREY ENTERTAINMENT

9150 Wilshire Blvd., Suite 350, Beverly Hills, CA 90212. (310) 275-6135. FAX: (310) 275-6180.
CEO & CHAIRMAN
Brad Grey
PRESIDENT
Lloyd Braun
CONSULTANT
Bernie Brillstein
S.EXECUTIVE V.P.
Sanford Wernick
EXECUTIVE V.P. & CO-PRESIDENT, MANAGEMENT DIV.
Marc Gurvitz
CO-PRESIDENT, MANAGEMENT DIVISION
Cynthia Pett
EXECUTIVE V.P., TELEVISION
Kevin Reilly
SENIOR V.P.
Michael Rosenfeld
SENIOR V.P.'S, TELEVISION
Susie Fitzgerald
Peter Traugott
V.P., PRODUCTION, TELEVISION
Tony Carey
V.P., BUSINESS AFFAIRS
Michael Tenzer

Series: Alright Already, C-16: FBI, Def Comedy Jam, The Jeff Foxworthy Show, The Larry Sanders Show, The Naked Truth, NewsRadio, The Steve Harvey Show.

BROADWAY VIDEO ENTERTAINMENT

1619 Broadway, 9th floor, New York, NY 10019. (212) 603-0648. FAX: (212) 582-8097.
PRESIDENT
Eric Ellenbogen
V.P., INT'L CO-PRODUCTIONS & PROGRAM DISTRIBUTION
Alexander Drosin
MANAGER, PROGRAM DISTRIBUTION
Ted S. Lehman

Animated Series: Felix The Cat (26 x 30 mins.), Kid Power (17 x 30 mins.), King Kong (26 x 30 mins.), The Mighty Hercules (26 x 30 mins.), The New Adventures of Pinocchio (130 x 5 mins.), The Reluctant Dragon and Mr. Toad (17 x 30 mins.), Smokey The Bear (17 x 30 mins.), Tales Of the Wizard Of Oz (8 hrs.), The Underdog Show (65 x 30 mins.).

Animated Specials: Broadway Video Holiday Classics: Frosty The Snowman (30 mins.), Candle, Family Classics (20 x 30 mins.), Frosty Returns (30 mins.), Here Comes Peter Cottontail (1 hr.), The Little Drummer Boy (30 mins.), Mad Mad Monsters (1 hr.), Mouse On the Mayflower (1 hr.), Red Baron (1 hr.), Return To Oz (1 hr.), Rudolph The Red-Nosed Reindeer (1 hr.), Santa Claus Is Coming To Town (1 hr.), Snow and Mistletoe (1 hr.), Willie Mays And The Say-Hey Kid (1 hr.), Willie McBean And His Magic Machine (94 mins.), The Wizard Of Oz (1 hr.).

Comedy Series: The Abbott and Costello Show (52 x 30 mins.), The Kids In The Hall (110 x 30 mins.), Saturday Night Live (133 x 30 mins., 400 x 60 mins., 420 x 90 mins.).

Comedy Specials: Best Of the Blues Brothers (1 hr.), Best of Dan Ackroyd (1 hr.), Best of Gilda Radner (1 hr.), Best of John Belushi (1 hr.), Diary Of A Young Comic (67 mins.), Saturday Night Live Christmas Past (90 mins.), Saturday Night Live Election Day Special (2 hrs.), Saturday Night Live Goes Commercial (1 hr.), Saturday Night Live Halloween Special (1 hr.), Saturday Night Live Mother's Day Specials (2 x 2hrs.), Saturday Night Live Sports Extra (90 mins.).

Family Series: Lassie (374 x 30 mins. b&w, 204 x 30 mins., 17 x 90 mins.), The Lone Ranger (182 x 30 mins. b&w, 39 x 30 mins., 13 x 90 min. features), Sergeant Preston Of The Yukon (78 x 30 mins.).

Family Specials: Lassie Unleashed (1 hr.).

Sports Series: Greatest Sports Legends (206 x 30 mins., 65 x 60 mins.).

Variety/Music Series: Night Music (40 x 60 mins.).

Variety/Music Specials: Neil Young In Berlin (1 hr.), Night Music Specials (4 x 60 mins.), The Paul Simon Special (1 hr.), Randy Newman At The Odeon (1 hr.), The Rutles (1 hr.).

Over 150 Theatrical and TV Features including: Abroad With Two Yanks, America at the Movies, The Autobiography of Miss Jane Pittman, The Balcony, Black Like Me, Born Innocent, The Christmas Tree, Chu Chu and the Philly Flash, The Coca-Cola Kid, Coffee Tea or Me?, Consenting Adult, The Count of Monte Cristo, Deadly Harvest, A Doll's House, The Family Rico, Four Feathers, Gargoyles, Glass House, Ghidrah the 3-Headed Monster, Godzilla vs. the Sea Monster, Goodbye Raggedy Ann, Gravy Train, I Heard the Owl Call My Name, I Want to Keep My Baby, In This House of Brede, Jolly Bad Fellow, Juliet of the Spirits, Lady Caroline Lamb, Last Ten Days of Hitler, Luck of Ginger Coffey, The Magic of Lassie, Miss Annie Rooney, My Bodyguard, Negatives, Oliver Twist, On the Right Track, Pretty Boy Floyd, Private's Progress, Queen of the Stardust Ballroom, Revenge of the Stepford Wives, Ride in the Whirlwind, Room at the Top, September Storm, The Shooting, Slaves, Son of Godzilla, South of Pago Pago, A Taste of Honey, Tell Me Where It Hurts, Three for Bedroom C, Tillie's Punctured Romance, Trans-Atlantic Merry-Go-Round, Up in Mabel's Room, A War of Children, White Orchid, Zorro the Gay Blade.

BUENA VISTA INTERNATIONAL, INC.

(A subsidiary of The Walt Disney Company.)
350 S. Buena Vista St., Burbank, CA 91521. (818) 972-3553.
PRESIDENT, BV INTERNATIONAL
Mark Zoradi
PRESIDENT, BV WORLDWIDE MARKETING
Robert Levin

Animated Series: 101 Dalmations (65 x 30 mins.), Mummies (42 x 30 mins.)

Specials: The Academy Awards 1998.

Hour Series: Honey, I Shrunk the Kids (22 x 60 mins.).

Movies: Jitters (2 hrs.).

BUENA VISTA TV

(A subsidiary of The Walt Disney Company.)
500 S. Buena Vista St., Burbank, CA 91521. (818) 560-5000. FAX: (818) 566-7412.
CHAIRMAN
Walter Liss
PRESIDENT
Mort Marcus
EXECUTIVE V.P., SALES
Janice Marinelli
EXECUTIVE V.P., AD SALES
Mike Shaw
S.V.P., DEVELOPMENT, BUENA VISTA PRODUCTIONS
Michael Davies
S.V.P, CURRENT PROGRAMMING/PRODUCTION
Mary Kellogg
SENIOR V.P., BUSINESS AFFAIRS
Don Loughery
S.V.P. & GENERAL SALES MANAGER, WEST COAST
Jim Packer
SENIOR V.P., ADVERTISING & CREATIVE SERVICES
Sal Sardo
V.P., AFFILIATE RELATIONS
Sandra Brewer
V.P., SOUTHEAST REGIONAL MANAGER
John Bryan
V.P., RESEARCH
Frances Calfo
V.P. & GENERAL SALES MANAGER, EAST COAST
Tom Cerio
V.P. & GENERAL MANAGER, PAY TELEVISION
Dan Cohen
V.P., AD SALES, MIDWEST
Jim Engleman
V.P., OPERATIONS & SALES DEVELOPMENT
Helen Faust
V.P., PUBLICITY
Kim Harbin
V.P., EASTERN REGIONAL MANAGER
Lloyd Komesar
V.P.'S, AD SALES
Norman Lesser
Howard Levy
V.P., FINANCE, PLANNING & DISTRIBUTION
Andrew Lewis
V.P., CREATIVE SERVICES
Peter Martin
V.P., MIDWEST REGIONAL MANAGER
David McLeod
V.P., DEVELOPMENT, BUENA VISTA PRODUCTIONS
Suzy Polse-Unger
V.P., PRODUCTION
Hayma (Screech) Washington
V.P., SOUTHEAST REGION
Rod Winterrowd

Series: The Disney Afternoon (Darkwing Duck, Disney's Alladin, Gargoyles, Mighty Ducks, Quack Pack, Timon & Pumbaa), Disney Presents Bill Nye The Science Guy, Disney's Sing Me A Story: With Belle, Home Improvement, LIVE! With Regis & Kathie Lee, Siskel & Ebert.

Film Packages: Buena Vista II, Buena Vista III, Disney Imagination 3.

BURRUD PRODUCTIONS, INC.

16902 Bolsa Chica St., #203, Huntington Beach, CA 92649-3590. (714) 846-7174. FAX: (714) 846-4814.
PRESIDENT & CEO
John Burrud
V.P., ADMINISTRATION
Linda Karabin-Hecomovich
V.P., BUSINESS AFFAIRS
Stanley Green
V.P., PRODUCTION
Drew Horton
PRODUCER
Bill MacDonald

Series: Animal Odyssey, Beyond Bizarre, Family Theatre, Jean-Michel Cousteau Presents Stories of the Sea, New! Animal World, Return to Tarawa, Seals Whales & Dolphin Tales, Treasure!, True Adventure, Shark! The Silent Savage, Wildlife Adventure, Wonders of America, Young Explorer's Club.

B.V.T.V., INC.
PO Box 749, 20 Rascally Rabbit Rd., Marstons Mills, MA 02648. (508) 428-3171. FAX: (508) 428-3179.
Series: Bob Vila's Home Again.

CAMELOT ENTERTAINMENT SALES
1700 Broadway, New York, NY 10019. (212) 315-4747.
PRESIDENT
Steve Hirsch
Series: American Journal, Inside Edition, Jeopardy!, The Oprah Winfrey Show, The Rolanda Watts Show, Showtime at the Apollo, Wheel of Fortune.

CANDID CAMERA, INC.
P.O. Box 827, Monterey, CA 93942. (408) 625-3788.
Candid Camera: All-Time Funniest Moments, Candid Camera (385 x 30 mins.), Candid Camera (35 x 30 mins. "adult"), Candid Camera Specials.

STEPHEN J. CANNELL PRODS.
7083 Hollywood Blvd., Hollywood, CA 90028. (213) 465-5800. FAX: (213) 856-7454.
Products: The A-Team (NBC), Booker (FBC), Broken Badges (CBS), The Commish (synd.), Hardcastle & McCormick (ABC), Hat Squad (CBS), Hawkeye, Hunter (NBC), J.J. Starbuck (NBC), The Last Precinct (NBC), Missing Persons, Personals (CBS), Renegade (Synd.), Riptide (NBC), Scene of the Crime (CBS), Silk Stalkings (CBS), Sonny Spoon (NBC), Stingray (NBC), Street Justice (Synd.), Thunder Boat Row (ABC), Top of the Hill (CBS), 21 Jump Street (FBC), Unsub (NBC), Wiseguy (CBS).

CANNELL DISRIBUTION COMPANY
7083 Hollywood Blvd., 4th fl., Hollywood, CA 90028. (213) 465-5800. FAX: (213) 856-7987.
PRESIDENT
Patrick J. Kenney
PRESIDENT, INTERNATIONAL
Herb Lazarus
DIRECTOR, DISTRIBUTION
Jerry Leifer
V.P. SALES
Ed Youngmark

CAROLINE FILM PRODUCTIONS
12711 Ventura Blvd., #210, Los Angeles, CA 91604. (818) 508-3420. FAX: (818) 508-3464.
Series: Touched by an Angel, Promised Land

CARSEY-WERNER PRODUCTIONS
4024 Radford Ave., Bldg. 3, Studio City, CA 91604. (818) 655-5598. FAX: (818) 655-6236.
OWNERS/EXECUTIVE PRODUCERS
Marcy Carsey
Tom Werner
VICE CHAIRMAN & CEO
Stuart Glickman
PRESIDENT
Caryn Mandabach
PRESIDENT, CARSEY-WERNER DISTRIBUTION, LLC
Joe Zaleski
PRESIDENT, CARSEY-WERNER INTERNATIONAL
Herb Lazarus
EXECUTIVE V.P. & CFO
Bob Dubelko
EXECUTIVE V.P., BUSINESS & LEGAL AFFAIRS
Dirk Van De Bunt
EXECUTIVE V.P., PRODUCTION
Courtney Conte
S.V.P., CREATIVE AFFAIRS
David Tochterman
S.V.P., FINANCE
Brett Sarnoff
S.V.P., PUBLICITY & PUBLIC RELATIONS
James Anderson
S.V.P., ART DEPARTMENT & PRODUCTION DESIGNER
Garvin Eddy
Series: Cosby, Feelin' Alright, 3rd Rock From the Sun.

CARSON PRODUCTIONS GROUP
3110 Main St., #200, Santa Monica, CA 90405. (310) 314-8784. FAX: (310) 314-8797.
Series: The Tonight Show (1980–1994).

CASTLE HILL TELEVISION
1414 Ave. of the Americas, New York, NY 10019. (212) 888-0080. FAX: (212) 644-0956.
CEO
Julian Schlossberg
PRESIDENT, MARKETING & DISTRIBUTION
Mel Maron
VICE PRESIDENT
Milly Sherman
V.P., SALES
Barbara Karmel
DIRECTOR, ADVERTISING & CLIENT SERVICES
Dawn Attridge
DIRECTOR, DISTRIBUTION
Ivory Harris
Volume III (package of feature films): An American Summer, Control, Defense Play, Double Edge, A Fine Romance, The Imagemaker, Innocent Victim, In the Spirit, Iron Maze, Julia & Julia, Paper Mask, Prayer of the Roller Boys, Primary Motive, Voyager, White Light.
Volume IV (package of feature films): Alan & Naomi, A Climate for Killing, Desire & Hell at Sunset Motel, Honor Among Thieves, Matewan, Rider on the Rain, The Secret Rapture, The Seventh Coin, Sweet Justice, Tim.
Volume V (package of feature films, current and future availability): Andy Warhol Presents Dracula, A Business Affair, Cannibal Women In The Avocado Jungle of Death, Concrete War, A Day In October, Deadly Advice, Hell's Angels On Wheels, The Lost Honor Of Kathryn Beck, Puppetmaster, A Reason To Believe, The Sailor Who Fell From Grace With The Sea.
Made in Hollywood (package of films): Blockade, The Crystal Ball, 52nd Street, Foreign Correspondent, History Is Made at Night, The House Across the Bay, I Married a Witch, The Long Voyage Home, A Night in Casablanca, Stagecoach, To Be or Not to Be, Vogues of 1938, You Only Live Once.

CASTLE ROCK ENTERTAINMENT
335 N. Maple Dr., Ste. 135, Beverly Hills, CA 90210. (310) 285-2300. FAX: (310) 285-2345.
Series: Boston Common, Lazarus Man, Seinfeld, The Single Guy.

CBC INTERNATIONAL SALES
1801 Century Park East, Suite 2250, Los Angeles, CA 90067. (310) 229-3600. FAX: (310) 229-3604.
P.O. Box 500, Station A, Toronto, Ontario, M5W 1E5, Canada. (416) 205-3500. FAX: (416) 205-3482.
email: cbcis@toronto.cbc.ca
43/51 Great Titchfield Rd., London W1P 8DD, UK. (44171) 412-9200. FAX: (44171) 323-5658.
MANAGER, US SALES & CO-PRODUCTIONS
Dina Vangelisti
SALES EXECUTIVE, LOS ANGELES
Katherine Kaufman
SENIOR DIRECTOR, INT'L CO-PRODUCTIONS, SALES & ACQUISITIONS, TORONTO
Thomas Howe
DEPUTY DIRECTOR, INT'L SALES & CO-PRODUCTIONS, TORONTO
Criss Hajek
SALES EXEC., TORONTO
Randi Rose
MANAGER, MARKETING & CREATIVE SVC'S., TORONTO
Emily Donaldson
SENIOR SALES EXECUTIVE, LOS ANGELES
Veronique Verges
HEAD OF INTERNATIONAL SALES, LONDON
Susan Hewitt
SENIOR SALES EXECUTIVE, LONDON
Michelle Payne
SALES EXECUTIVE, LONDON
Janice Russell
Features: Anne's Story (90 mins.), And Then You Die (115 mins.), Best Of Both Worlds (88 mins.), Coming Out Alive (73 mins.), The Cuckoo Bird (75 mins.), Dangerous Offender (120 mins.), The Diary of Evelyn Lau (90 mins.), Family Reunion (98 mins.), Gentle Sinners (106 mins.), Getting Married In Buffalo Jump (98 mins.), Giant Mine (91 mins.), Grand Larceny (94 mins.), I'll Never Go To Heaven (92 mins.), Last Season (150 mins.), Liar Liar (90 mins.), Little Criminals (92 mins.), Mama's Going To Buy You A Mockingbird (97 mins.), A Nest Of Singing Birds (98 mins.), Net Worth (95 mins.), 9B (The Movie) (98 mins.), Sarah (85 mins.), Shellgame (101 mins.), Skate! (99 mins.), Small Gifts (90 mins.), Turning To Stone (98 mins.), War Brides, Wojeck: Out Of Fire (88 mins.), For Those Who Hunt the Wounded Down (120 mins), In This Corner (60 mins.), Nights Below Station Street (120 mins.), Peacekeepers (120 mins.), White Lies (120 mins).

Mini-Series: Chasing Rainbows (14 hrs.), Conspiracy Of Silence (4 hrs.), Dieppe: The Politics of War (4 hrs.), Empire Inc. (6 hrs.), Love And Hate (4 hrs.), Love And Larceny (3 hrs.), The Other Kingdom (3 hrs.), Riel (3 hrs.), Vanderburg (4 hrs.).

Drama Series: The Beachcombers (88 x 30 mins. & 2 x 60 mins.), Danger Bay (123 x 30 mins.), Ekhaya: A Family Chronicle (13 x 60 mins.), Gift To Last (22 x 60 mins.), Home Fires (13 x 60 mins.), The King of Kensington (55 x 30 mins.), Material World (32 x 30 mins.), Moments In Time (15 x 60 mins.), 9B–The Series (5 x 45 mins.), Side Effects: Season 1 (13 x 60 mins.), Season 2 (16 x 60 mins.), Street Legal: Season 1 (6 x 60 mins.), Season 2 (13 x 60 mins.), Season 3 (19 x 60 mins.), Season 4 (16 x 60 mins.), Season 5 (16 x 60 mins.), Season 6 (18 x 60 mins.), Season 7 (18 x 60 mins.), Season 8 (18 x 60 mins. & Last Rights–Finale 93 mins.).

Comedy/Music/Variety: AIDScare (60 mins.), Anne Murray In Nova Scotia (60 mins.), Anne Murray's Classic Christmas (48 ins.), Back To The Beanstalk (60 mins.), Brian Orser: Blame It On The Blues (60 mins.), Bryan Adams: Waking Up The World (60 mins.), Buffy Sainte-Marie: Up Where We Belong (47 mins.), Colin James Presents The Blues Masters (60 mins.), Comics! (72 x 30 mins.), Elvis Incognito (45 mins.), Kurt Browning: You Must Remember This (60 mins.), Martini & Underhill: Leap of Faith (47 mins.), Michelle (60 mins.), Michelle Wright: Songs & Secrets (46 mins.), Rita McNeil: Once Upon A Christmas (60 mins.), The Newsroom (12 x 30 mins. & 1 x 60 mins.), Speak Low, Swing Hard (31 mins.), The Trial Of Red Riding Hood (60 mins.), Wayne & Shuster (80 x 30 mins.), Wayne & Shuster: Once Upon A Giant (90 mins.), The Wayne & Shuster Years (90 mins.), Classic Comics! Volume I (60 mins.), Christmas With the Vestibules (30 mins.), Masterschtick Theatre (60 mins.), More Tears (6 x 30 mins.), Diana Thorneycroft: More Than Skin Deep (54 mins.), Herman Scherchen In Rehearsal (60 mins.), John Vickers & Boehm In Concert (60 mins.), Norma, The Man Behind the Words: Michael Tremblay (53 mins.), Tom Cochrane: Solo (60 mins.).

Cultural Programming: Adrienne Clarkson Presents: All About Yves (23 mins.), Artemisia (48 mins.), Arthur Erickson: Conversations With An Architect (45 mins.), Attila Richard Lukacs (30 mins.), The Boundless Sea (15 mins.), Canvas of Conflict: Art of the Great War (53 mins.), Children of Terezin (45 mins.), Evergon: Making Homo Roccoco (43 mins.), Freeman Patterson Up Close (22 mins.), The Gift of Messiah (44 mins.), He Who Dreams: Michael Greyeyes (54 mins.), Jessye Norman (21 mins.), Kokoro Dance (19 mins.), La La Lock (18 mins.), The Lust of His Eye–Vision of J.W. Morrice (36 mins.), Making of the English Patient (53 mins.), Mark Morris Choreographer (45 mins.), Mastersinger Paul Frey (45 mins.), Moxy Früvous World (23 mins.), Mump & Smoot (24 mins.), Nigel Kennedy (9 mins.), Noranda Man (21 mins.), Pavarotti (11 mins.), Piano Man–John Kimura Parker (46 mins.), Pinteresque (29 mins.), Robertson Davies (24 mins.), Sir Yehudi Menuhin (13 mins.), Sophia Loren (9 mins.), Sounding A Legacy: Metis Fiddlers (26 mins.), Squeeze Box Stories (23 mins.), Tafelmusik Plays Wassermusik (45 mins.), Travels With Germaine (22 mins.), Views Of A Room (19 mins.), The World of Janina Fialkowska (44 mins.), Big Life (30 mins.), Love of Gardening (30 mins.), Star News (30 mins.), Travels With Mom (30 mins.).

Arts: Alarmel Valli (30 mins.), Anton Kuerti & Yo-Yo Ma (30 mins.), Birds In Art (30 mins.), Degas (60 mins.), Figure Of A Spirit: Kimiko Koyanagi (30 mins.), Giselle (90 mins.), Glenn Gould Plays Beethoven (60 mins.), Grand Piano (60 mins.), Grizzly Kingdom: An Artists's Encounter (60 mins.), Hand & Eye (7 x 60 mins.), Homage To Chagall (90 mins.), Karsch: The Searching Eye (90 mins.), Keewatin Arts & Crafts Festival (34 mins.), Lucy Maud Montgomery: The Road To Green Gables (90 mins.), Margie Gillis: Wild Hearts in Strange Times (60 mins.), To Mend The World (87 mins.), The Mystery of Henry Moore (90 mins.), The Quilt As Art (30 mins.), Scented Treasures (18 mins.), The Sleeping Beauty (90 mins.), Tennessee Williams' South (80 mins.), Vivaldi (2 x 53 mins.), The Stratford Collection (13 perfs.).

Stratford Performances: As You Like It (158 mins.), Comedy of Erros (90 mins.), The Gondoliers (154 mins.), H.M.S. Pinafore (90 mins.), Iolanthe (150 mins.), The Mikado (150 mins.), Much Ado About Nothing (180 mins.), Pirates of Penzance (150 mins.), Romeo And Juliet (180 mins.), The Taming of the Shrew (163 mins.), The Tempest (150 mins.), Three Musketeers (120 mins.), Twelfth Night (150 mins.).

Continuing Series: Fashion File (52 per year x 30 mins.), The Fifth Estate, 50/Up (30 mins.), Future World (30 mins.), The Health Show (30 mins.), Life & Times (60 mins.), Man Alive (30 mins.), Market Place (15-30 mins.), The National (15-30 mins.), On The Road Again (30 mins.), Spilled Milk (30 mins.), Undercurrents (30 mins.), Venture (15-30 mins.), Witness (weekly x 60 mins.).

Children's Series: Degrassi Between Takes (30 mins.), Fred Penner's Place (15 mins.), The Friendly Giant (123 x 15 mins.), Guess What (80 x 15 mins.), Jonovision (40 x 30 mins.), Mr. Dressup (65 x 30 mins.), Painting Pictures (20 x 3 mins.), Travels With Mom (25 x 30 mins.), Wonderstruck (52 x 30 mins.), Artifacts (20 x 3 mins.), Sariwan and the Animals (30 mins.).

Documentary: Amazonia (2 hrs.), Battle Diary: A Day In the Life of Charlie Martin (60 mins.), A Climate For Change (2 hrs.), The Damned (2 hrs.), Dealing With Drugs (2 hrs.), Drums (2 hrs.), Food or Famine (2 hrs.), Great Northern Forest (120 mins.), Indonesia (6 x 30 mins.), Labrador: Home of the Spirits (120 mins.), Mah Jong Orphan (60 mins.), The Man Who Hid Anne Frank (60 mins.), Marconi (60 mins.), Mr. Yao & The Crocodiles (30 mins.), The National Dream (6 x 60 mins.), The Nature Of Things (95 x 60 mins. & 38 x 30 mins.), Prophecy (90 mins.), Return To Saigon: Two Viet Kieu (60 mins.), Sea of Slaughter (95 mins.), A Secret Underground (30 mins.), The Seeds Of Terror (60 mins.), The Shadow & The Spirit (60 mins.), Temples of Glory (30 mins.), The Third Angel (60 mins.), Timelines (30 x 60 mins.), Trading Futures: Living In The Global Economy (2 hrs.), Voices In the Forest (2 hrs.), The War Against the Indians (143 mins.), Water: To the Last Drop (2 hrs.), Fisheries: Beyond the Crisis (60 mins.), The Friendly Atom (60 mins.), The Green Zone (60 mins.), Little Brother Watches Back (60 mins.), Lost In the Suburbs (60 mins.), Menopause/Hot Flashes (60 mins.), Not So Sweet: Living With Diabetes (60 mins.), Out of the Shadows (60 mins.), Way of the Caribous (60 mins.), Ask a Silly Question (60 mins.), Between Here and Heaven (60 mins.), In Security (60 mins.), Quake Hunters (60 mins.), Carpe Diem: Transplant Olympics (30 mins.), Mother Courage (30 mins.), Opposing Missions (30 mins.), Return to Everdale (30 mins.), Sleeping Children (30 mins.), Voluntary Simplicity (30 mins.), Broken Hearts (24 mins.), Dog I.Q. (17 mins.), Goose Hunters (16 mins.), Hostage: Jamie's Story (38 mins.), In Harm's Way (38 mins.), Little Short of Magic (21 mins.), Moral Authority (30 mins.), Ratline to Canada (38 mins.), Remarkable Case of John/Joan (30 mins.), Thin Ice Update (27 mins.), Sleep Room (21 mins.), Virus SV40 (24 mins.), The Day—the Night and the Dead (30 mins.), Grizzlies of the Canadian Rockies (60 mins.), Life & Times: Ben Wicks (60 mins.), Life & Times: Glenn Gould (60 mins.), National Magazine: Forget Me Not, National Magazine: Freon, Sense of History (30 x 30 mins.).

CBS ENTERTAINMENT PRODUCTIONS

(For a complete listing of CBS executives and subsidiaries, please see the Broadcast Network section of this book.)
7800 Beverly Blvd., Los Angeles, CA 90036. (213) 852-2345.
PRESIDENT, CBS ENTERTAINMENT
Leslie Moonves
S.V.P., PROGRAMMING
Steve Warner
V.P., SERIES DEVELOPMENT
Kelly Goode
V.P., CURRENT PROGRAMS
Maddy Horne
Series: Can't Hurry Love, Central Park West, Dave's World, Dr. Quinn–Medicine Woman, Early Edition, The Gordon Elliott Show, Moloney, Promised Land, Rescue 911, Touched by an Angel, Walker–Texas Ranger.

CBS NEWS

524 W. 57 St., New York, NY 10019. (212) 975-4321.
Series: 48 Hours, 60 Minutes.

CEL COMMUNICATIONS, INC.

460 Park Ave. So., New York, NY 10016. (212) 953-4650.
CHAIRMAN & CEO
Peter Collins
Series: America the Way We Were: The Home Front, 1940-45 (Discovery Channel), Animal Express (syndicated by 20th Century Fox), Biography–Hosted by Peter Graves (A&E Network), Class of the 20th Century–Hosted by Richard Dreyfuss (A&E), Creativity with Bill Moyers (PBS), Dining in France (13 x 30 mins.), John F. Kennedy: A Celebration of His Life & Times (Discovery Channel), Legends in Love (Lifetime), The Magic Years in Sports (ESPN), A Walk Thru the 20th Century with Bill Moyers (PBS), World War II: A Personal Journey– Hosted/Narrated by Glenn Ford (Disney Channel).

THE CHICAGO PRODUCTION CENTER AT WTTW

5400 N. Saint Louis Ave., Chicago, IL 60625. (773) 583-5000.
FAX: (773) 583-3046.
SENIOR VICE PRESIDENT
Mary Beth Hughes
Series: About Your House with Bob Yapp, Handy Ma'am with Beverly DeJulio, The Americas' Family Kitchen, The McLaughlin Group, McLaughlin One on One.

CHILDREN'S TELEVISION WORKSHOP

1 Lincoln Plaza, New York, NY 10023. (212) 595-3456.
CHAIRMAN—EXECUTIVE COMMITTEE
Joan Ganz Cooney
PRESIDENT & CEO
David V. B. Britt
EXECUTIVE V.P.
Emily Swenson
SENIOR V.P., PRODUCTION/PROGRAMMING
Marjorie Kalins
OPERATIONS
Gary E. Knell
PRESIDENT, COMMUNITY EDUCATION SERVICES
Digna Sanchez
SENIOR V.P., MARKETING & COMMUNICATIONS
Allyson Kossow Felix
SENIOR V.P. & PUBLISHER, CTW PUBLISHING GROUP
Nina B. Link
V.P. & TREASURER
Wayne W. Luteran
V.P., INTERACTIVE TECHNOLOGY
Robert L. Madell, Phd.
V.P., HUMAN RESOURCES
Lavera Johnson
SENIOR V.P., CTW INTERNATIONAL PRODUCT LICENSING &
TELEVISION GROUP
J. Baxter Urist

CINAR FILMS, INC.

1055 Rene Levesque Blvd. East. Montreal, Quebec H2L 4S5,
Canada. (514) 843-7070. FAX: (514) 843-7080.
CHAIRMAN & CO-CEO
Micheline Charest
PRESIDENT & CO-CEO
Ronald A. Weinberg
CFO & PRESDIENT, CINAR EDUC.
Hasanain Panju
V.P. & GENERAL COUNSEL
Marie-Josee Corbeil
V.P., ANIMATION PRODUCTION & DEVELOPMENT
Cassandra Schafhausen
V.P. ANIMATION & V.P. OPERATIONS
Lesley Taylor
V.P., LIVE-ACTION PRODUCTION & DEVELOPMENT
Patricia Lavole
V.P., CINAR STUDIOS
Francois Deschamps
V.P., DISTRIBUTION & MARKETING
Louis Fournier
V.P., FINANCE-PRODUCTION
Andrew Porporino
V.P., CINAR EUROPE & MANAGING DIRECTOR, FILMFAIR
David Ferguson
V.P., COMMUNICATIONS
Louise Sansregret
New Products: The Adventures of Padington Bear (26 x 30
mins.), Animal Crackers (26 x 30 mins.), Arthur (65 x 30 mins.),
The Best Bad Thing (1 x 90 mins.), The Busy World of Richard
Scarry (65 x 30 mins.), Caillou (65 x 5 mins.), The Country
Mouse & City Mouse Adventures (52 x 30 mins.), Doctor Xargie
(13 x 30 mins.), Emily of the New Moon (39 x 60 mins.), Ivanhoe
(52 x 30 mins.), Lassie (52 x 30 mins.), The Little Lulu Show (52
x 30 mins.), The Sleep Room (2 x 2 hrs.), Space Cases (27 x 30
mins.), Wimzie's House (112 x 30 mins.), The Wombles (26 x 10
mins.).
Other Series: Albert the 5th Musketeer (26 x 30 mins.), Are You
Afraid of the Dark? (65 x 30 mins.), Astrofarm (53 x 10 mins.),
Babaloos (13 x 30 mins.), Bangers & Mash (25 x 5 mins.), The
Blunders (30 x 5 mins.), Bonjour Timothy (1 x 90 mins.), Brown
Bear's Wedding (1 x 60 mins.), A Bunch of Munsch (7 x 30
mins.), Chris Cross (13 x 30 mins.), C.L.Y.D.E. (26 x 30 mins.),
Cat Tales (15 x 30 mins.), Dirty Beasts and Revolting Rhymes (2
x 30 mins.), Energy (1 x 60 mins.), A Gift of Munsch (1 x 60
mins.), Gingerbread Man (13 x 10 mins.), Happy Castle (13 x 30
mins.), Hattytown (39 x 11 mins.), The Herbs (13 x 13 mins.),
Huxley Pig (26 x 10 mins.), The Intrepids (26 x 30 mins.),
Juniper Jungle (13 x 10 mins.), Legend of White Fang (26 x 30
mins.), Madeline (6 x 30 mins.), The Making of Million Dollar
Babies (1 x 60 mins.), Million Dollar Babies (2 x 2 hrs.),
Moschops (13 x 11 mins.), Nellie the Elephant (30 x 5 mins.),
The New Adventures of the Intrepids (26 x 30 mins.), New Shoe
People (26 x 11 mins.), Nighthood (26 x 30 mins.), Paddington
Bear (56 x 5 mins.), Papa Beaver Storytime (26 x 30 mins.),
Parsley the Lion (32 x 5 mins.), The Perishers (20 x 5 mins.),
Portland Bill (50 x 5 mins.), The Real Story (13 x 30 mins.),
Robinson Crusoe (26 x 30 mins.), Rod 'n' Emu (13 x 10 mins.),
Shoe People (26 x 5 mins.), Simon In the Land of Chalk
Drawings (26 x 5 mins.), Stand-In for Danger (1 x 60 mins.),
Stop the Smoggies (52 x 30 mins.), Treasure Island (13 x 30
mins.), White Bear's Secret (1 x 60 mins.), The Whole of the
Moon (1 x 90 mins.), Windfalls (26 x 5 mins.), Wonderful Wizard
of Oz (60 x 30 mins.), Young Robin Hood (26 x 30 mins.).

Features: Adventures in Odyssey (6 x 30 mins.), Clown White (60
mins.), Hockey Night (77 mins.), Peter and the Wolf (85 mins.).

CINETEL PRODUCTIONS

9701 Madison Ave., Knoxville, TN 37932. (423) 690-9950. FAX:
(423) 693-6576.
EXECUTIVE V.P. & GENERAL MANAGER
Jim Zarchin
Series: Club Dance, Crafts & Co., Easy Does It, Remodeling &
Decorating Today, Shadetree Mechanic, Home Wise, Interiors by
Design, Sew Perfect, The Fix.
Specials: America's Castles, Circus, Freeze Frame, America's
Most Endangered, Great Trials in History, Country at Home.

CITADEL ENTERTAINMENT

301 N. Cannon Dr., Ste. 321, Beverly Hills, CA 90210. (310)
477-5112. FAX: (310) 312-9781.
PRESIDENT
David Ginsburg

DICK CLARK PRODUCTIONS, INC.

3003 W. Olive Ave., Burbank, CA 91505. (818) 841-3003.
CHAIRMAN & CEO
Dick Clark
PRESIDENT & COO
Francis La Maina
Products: Academy of Country Music Awards, American
Music Awards, Golden Globe Awards, Rockin' New Years
Eve, Tempestt Bledsoe Show, TV's All-Star Censored Bloopers.

CNBC: CONSUMER NEWS & BUSINESS CHANNEL

2200 Fletcher Ave., Ft. Lee, NJ 07024. (201) 585-2622. URL:
http://info@cnbc.com
Series: Business Insiders, The Dick Cavett Show, Equal Time,
Money Tonight, Rivera Live, Talk Live.

COLUMBIA PICTURES TELEVISION
(A SONY PICTURES ENTERTAINMENT COMPANY)

10202 W. Washington Blvd., Culver City, CA 90232-3195. (310)
244-8000.
Series: Courthouse, Days of Our Lives, First Time Out,
Married... With Children, NewsRadio, Party of Five, Walker–
Texas Ranger, The Young and the Restless.

COLUMBIA TRISTAR TELEVISION GROUP
(A SONY PICTURES ENTERTAINMENT COMPANY)

9336 W. Washington Blvd., Culver City, CA 90232. (310) 202-1234.
SONY PICTURES ENTERTAINMENT
PRESIDENT & COO
John Calley
CO-PRESIDENT
Jeff Sagansky
EXECUTIVE V.P.
Yuki Nozoe
C0-PRESIDENT & CHIEF CORPORATE OPERATIONS
Robert Wynne
EXECUTIVE V.P. & CFO
Ted Howells, Jr.
EXECUTIVE V.P.
Jon Feltheimer
EXECUTIVE V.P., HUMAN RESOURCES
Beth Berke
EXECUTIVE V.P., GENERAL COUNSEL & CORPORATE
SECRETARY
Ronald Jacobi
EXECUTIVE V.P., CORPORATE DEVELOPMENT &
STRATEGIC PLANNING
Yair Landau
SENIOR V.P., CORPORATE COMMUNICATIONS &
EXTERNAL AFFAIRS
Bruce Redditt
V.P. & TREASURER
Joe Kraft
VICE PRESIDENT
Robert M. Moses
COLUMBIA TRISTAR TELEVISION GROUP
PRESIDENT
Jon Felteimer
EXECUTIVE V.P. & PRESIDENT, INTERNATIONAL
Andrew Kaplan
SENIOR V.P., MEDIA RELATIONS
Justin Pierce

COLUMBIA TRISTAR TELEVISION

PRESIDENT
Eric Tannenbaum
EXECUTIVE V.P.
Helene Michaels
EXECUTIVE V.P., ADVERTISER SALES
Chris Kager
EXECUTIVE V.P., PRODUCTION
Edward Lammi
EXECUTIVE V.P., CHILDREN'S PROGRAMMING
Sander Schwartz
EXECUTIVE V.P., BUSINESS AFFAIRS
Sandra Stern
EXECUTIVE V.P., MOVIES & MINISERIES
Helen Verno
SENIOR V.P., PROGRAMMING
Jeanie Bradley
SENIOR V.P., INTERACTIVE PROGRAMMING
Richard Glosser
SENIOR V.P., COMEDY DEVELOPMENT
Kim Haswell
SENIOR V.P., TALENT
Ruth-Ann Huvane
SENIOR V.P., BUSINESS AFFAIRS
Beverly Nix
SENIOR V.P., DRAMA DEVELOPMENT
Sarah Timberman
V.P., MEDIA RELATIONS/PROMOTIONS
Paula Askanas
V.P., ANIMATION PRODUCTION
Peggy Becker
V.P., DRAMA DEVELOPMENT
Carolyn Bernstein
V.P., POST PRODUCTION
Christina Friedgen
V.P., INTERNATIONAL PROGRAM DEVELOPMENT & FORMAT SALES
Paul Gilbert
V.P., BUSINESS AFFAIRS
Amy Gittelsohn
V.P., PRODUCTION OPERATIONS
David Holman
V.P., PRODUCTION
Andy House
V.P., TELEVISION MUSIC
Robert Hunka
V.P., TECHNOLOGY & PRODUCTION, INTERACTIVE
Steven Katz
V.P'S, BUSINESS AFFAIRS
Michael Kohn
Joanne Mazzu
V.P., FILM PRODUCTION
John Morrissey
V.P., PRODUCTION
John Spector
V.P., TECHNICAL OPERATIONS
Phil Squyres
V.P., ONLINE PROGRAMMING
Robert Tercek
V.P., MOVIES & MINISERIES
Winifred White Neisser

COLUMBIA TRISTAR TELEVISION DISTRIBUTION

10202 W. Washington Blvd., Culver City, CA 90232. (310) 244-4000.
PRESIDENT
Barry Thurston
EXECUTIVE V.P., PROGRAMMING
Russ Krasnoff
EXECUTIVE V.P., PLANNING & OPERATIONS
David Mumford
SENIOR V.P., BUSINESS AFFAIRS
Richard Frankie
SENIOR V.P., MARKETING
John Moczulski
SENIOR V.P., SYNDICATION
Steve Mosko
SENIOR V.P., FIRST-RUN PROGRAMMING
Alan Perris
V.P., DISTRIBUTION OPERATIONS, DOMESTIC SYNDICATION
Francine Beougher
V.P., MEDIA RELATIONS
Steve Coe
V.P., DEVELOPMENT
Melanie Chilek
V.P., CREATIVE SERVICES
Alan Daniels
V.P., DRAMA DEVELOPMENT, FIRST RUN
Paul Frank
V.P., RESEARCH
Doug Roth

COLUMBIA TRISTAR TELEVISION DISTRIBUTION REGIONAL OFFICES

10202 West Washington Blvd., Culver City, CA 90232. (310) 244-8550. FAX (310) 244-1798.
V.P. WESTERN REGION
John Weiser
2859 Paces Ferry Rd., Suite 1130, Atlanta, GA 30339. (770) 434-5400. FAX: (770) 431-0202.
V.P., SOUTHERN REGION
Joe Kissack
V.P., SOUTHEASTERN REGION
Steve Maddox
455 N. Cityfront Plaza Drive, Suite 3120, Chicago, IL 60611. (312) 644-0770. FAX (312) 644-0781.
V.P., MIDWESTERN REGION
Tom Warner
8117 Preston Rd., Suite 510, Dallas, TX 75225. (214) 987-3671. FAX (214) 987-3675,
V.P., SOUTHWESTERN REGION
Dirk Johnston
550 Madison Ave., 8th Fl., New York, NY 10022. (212) 833-8350. FAX (212) 833-8360.
SENIOR V.P., EASTERN REGION MANAGER
John Rohrs, Jr.
V.P., AD SALES & MARKETING
Chris Kager
V.P., EASTER REGION, AD SALES
Barbara Baugher
VICE PRESIDENTS, NORTHEASTERN REGION
David Ozer
Jeff Wolf

COLUMBIA TRISTAR INTERNATIONAL TELEVISION

10202 W. Washington Blvd., Culver City, CA 90232. (310) 244-4000.
PRESIDENT, CTIT
Michael Grindon
PRESIDENT, SPEJ—Japan
Yoshiyuki (Jack) Isomura
PRESIDENT, COLUMBIA TRISTAR FILMS OF KOREA
Hyuk-Jo Kwon
SENIOR V.P., LONDON OFFICE
Leslie Tobin Bacon
SENIOR V.P., INTERNATIONAL PRODUCTION (BERLIN)
John Barber
SENIOR V.P., INTERNATIONAL NETWORKS
Lauren Cole
SENIOR V.P. & GENERAL MANAGER, EUROPE
Florent Gaignault
SENIOR V.P., INTERNATIONAL NETWORKS
George Leitner
SENIOR V.P., SALES PLANNING
John McMahon
SENIOR V.P. & MANAGING DIRECTOR, ASIA
William Pfeiffer
SENIOR V.P., INTERNATIONAL PRODUCTION (MUNICH)
Ludwig zu Salm
SENIOR V.P., WORLDWIDE PAY TV
Lawrence Smith
DIVISION MANAGER, JAPAN
Kunikazu Sogabe
SENIOR V.P. & GENERAL MANAGER, LATIN AMERICA
Dorien Sutherland
SENIOR V.P., MARKETING & SALES SUPPORT
Rachel Wells
V.P. & GENERAL MANAGER, CHINA
Mishka Chen
V.P., SOUTHERN EUROPEAN PRODUCTION
Nathalie Civrais
V.P., PRODUCTION, LATIN AMERICA
Iona deMaceda
V.P. & MANAGING DIRECTOR, AUSTRALIA
Jack Ford
V.P., INTERNATIONAL PAY TV
Peter Iacono
V.P. & REGIONAL DIRECTOR, INDIA
Sujit Kumar
V.P., CHANNEL MARKETING & PROMOTIONS
Donald Meek
V.P., SALES, NORTHERN EUROPE
Mark O'Connell
V.P., CONTROLLER
Michael Pangas
V.P., SALES
Simon Pollock
V.P., SALES PLANNING & ADMINISTRATION
Natalie Pratico
V.P., CREATIVE SERVICES
Mark Santo
V.P., BUSINESS AFFAIRS & ACQUISITIONS
Paul Bresburger
V.P., INTERNATIONAL CHANNELS
Theodore Schultz
V.P., NEW BUSINESS DEVELOPMENT
Patrice Van De Walle

COLUMBIA TRISTAR INTERNATIONAL TELEVISION OFFICES

ARGENTINA

Columbia TriStar Films of Argentina, Inc., Ayacucho 533, (1026) Buenos Aires, Argentina. (541) 954 3820. FAX: (541) 954 3819.

AUSTRALIA

Columbia TriStar Television Pty., Ltd., Level 30, 1 Market St., Sydney, NSW 2000, Australia. (612) 9272 2900. FAX: (612) 9272 2997.

BRAZIL

Columbia TriStar International Television, Edificio Plaza Centenario, Av. Das Nacoes Unidas, 12.995, 12 Andar, Vila Almeida, Sao Paulo, SP 04578-000, Brazil. (5511) 5505 3828. FAX: (5511) 5505 3814.

CANADA

Columbia Tristar Media Group of Canada, 365 Bloor St. East, Suite 1602, Toronto, Ontario, M4W 3L4. (416) 962 5490. FAX: (416) 962 5496.

CHINA

Sony Pictures Entertainment (China), Inc., Representative Office, Room 50530 Beijing Friendship Hotel, No. 3 Bai Shi Qiao Rd., Haisian District, Beijing 100873, China. (8610) 6849-8600. FAX: (8610) 6849-8628.

FRANCE

Columbia Tristar International Television, 131 Avenue de Wagram, 75017 Paris, France. (331) 4440 6300. FAX: (331) 4440 6301.

GERMANY

Columbia Tristar Film-Und Fernseh Produktions Gmbh, An Der Hasenkaule 22, 50354 Huerth, Germany. (492233) 518 100. FAX: (492233) 518 119.

HONG KONG

Columbia Tristar International Television, 35/F Bank of China Tower, No. 1 Garden Rd., Central, Hong Kong. (852) 2913 3788. FAX: (852) 2913 3733.

JAPAN

Sony Pictures Entertainment (Japan) Inc., Columbia Tristar Television Division, Hamamatsucho TS Build., 5th Floor, 8-14, Hamamatsucho, 2-Chome Minato-Ku Tokyo 105, Japan. (813) 3431 1372. FAX: (813) 3438 2970.

KOREA

Columbia TriStar Films of Korea, Inc., 8th floor, Kyungahm Building, 157-27 Samsung-dong, Kangnam-gu, Seoul 135 090, Korea. (822) 563 4000. FAX: (822) 539 1221.

MEXICO

Columbia Tristar Films De Mexcio, SA, Edificio Plaza Reforma, Prolong, Paseo de la Reforma #600, Penthouse Cuerpo D, Mexico D.F. 01210. (525) 258 2700. FAX: (525) 57 0740.

UNITED KINGDOM

Columbia TriStar International Television, Sony Pictures Europe House, 25 Golden Square, London W1R 6LU. (44171) 533 1500. FAX: (44171) 533 1235.

COLUMBIA TRISTAR HOME VIDEO

10202 W. Washington Blvd. Culver City, CA 90232. (310) 244-4000. FAX: (310) 244-2626.
PRESIDENT
Ben Feingold
EXECUTIVE VICE PRESIDENT
William Chardavoyne
EXECUTIVE V.P., NORTH AMERICA
Paul Culberg
EXECUTIVE V.P., OPERATIONS & EUROPEAN SUPERVISOR
Alan Pritchard
SENIOR V.P., CONTROLLER
Robert Houseal
SENIOR V.P., BUSINESS AFFAIRS & ACQUISITIONS
Peter Schlessel
SENIOR V.P., SALES, U.S.
Ralph Wallin
V.P., SPECIAL MARKETS
Betsy Caffrey
V.P., MANUFACTURING & PRODUCTION
Walt Engler
V.P., SALES
Mike Evans
V.P., SALES, CANADA
Marshall Forster
V.P., WORLDWIDE PUBLICITY
Fritz Friedman
V.P., SALES, RETAIL, U.S.
John Reina
V.P., LICENSING, FAR EAST
Janet Robertson
V.P., INTERNATIONAL MARKETING
Lexine Wong
V.P., MARKETING
Nancy Harris

COLUMBIA TRISTAR TELEVISION PRODUCT

New Series: Between Brothers, Dawson's Creek, The Gregory Hines Show, Head Over Heels, Michael Hayes, Over The Top, Sleepwalkers, The Tony Danza Show.

Series/First Run: Boston Common, Come Fly With Me, Dark Skies, The Dating/Newlywed Hour, Days of Our Lives, Early Edition, High Tide,. Hightower 411, Hudson Street, The Jeff Foxworthy Show, Just Shoot Me, The Larry Sanders Show, Mad About You, Malcolm and Eddie, Maloney, Married...With Children, The Naked Truth, The Nanny, Ned and Stacey, News Radio, Party of Five, Ricki Lake, Seinfeld, The Single Guy, The Young & The Restless.

Children's Programming: Beakman's World, Jumanji: The Animated Series, Project Geeker, Super Ghostbusters.

TV Movies: Born Free: A New Adventure, Cadillac Desert, To Sir With Love II.

Syndication Feature Film Packages: Columbia Gems I (6 titles), Columbia Gold (24 titles), Columbia Gold II (34 titles), Columbia Night at the Movies (ad hoc quarterly barter network), Columbia Showcase I (22 titles), Columbia Showcase II (25 titles), Embassy II (20 titles), Embassy III (20 titles), Entertainer of the Year (4 titles), TV I (20 titles), TV 20 (20 titles), Volume IV (9 titles), Volume V (16 titles), Volume VI (18 titles), Pegasus I (20 titles), Pegasus II (21 titles), Pegasus III (24 titles), Showcase III (26 titles), Tri-Star Showcase (ad hoc monthly barter network).

Syndication Off-Network Comedy Series: All in the Family (207 x 30 mins.), Archie Bunker's Place (97 x 30 mins.), Barney Miller (170 x 30 mins.), Benson (158 x 30 mins.), Carson's Comedy Classics (130 x 30 mins.), Carter Country (44 x 30 mins.), Designing Women (164 x 30 mins.), Diff'rent Strokes (189 x 30 mins.), The Facts of Life (209 x 30 mins.), Fish (35 x 30 mins.), Good Times (133 x 30 mins.), The Jeffersons (253 x 30 mins.), Married . . . With Children (131 x 30 mins.), Maude (141 x 30 mins.), My Two Dads (60 x 30 mins.), One Day at a Time (209 x 30 mins.), Parker Lewis (73 x 30 mins.), Punky Brewster (88 x 30 mins.), Sanford & Son (136 x 30 mins.), Seinfeld (108 x 30 mins.), Silver Spoons (116 x 30 mins.), Soap (93 x 30 mins.), That's My Mama (39 x 30 mins.), The Three Stooges (190 x 30 mins.), 227 (116 x 30 mins.), Who's the Boss? (196 x 30 mins.).

Syndication Off-Network Drama Series: Charlie's Angels (115 x 60 mins.), Fantasy Island (200 x 30 mins., 152 x 60 mins.), Hart to Hart (112 x 60 mins.), Hunter (129 x 60 mins.), Police Story (105 x 30 mins.), Police Woman (91 x 60 mins.), S.W.A.T. (37 x 60 mins.), Starsky and Hutch (92 x 60 mins.), T.J. Hooker (90 x 60 mins.).

COMMUNICATION COMMISSION OF THE NATIONAL COUNCIL OF THE CHURCHES OF CHRIST IN THE USA

475 Riverside Dr., Rm. 856, New York, NY 10115-0050. (212) 870-2574. FAX: (212) 870-2030. email: randy@ncccusa.org
DIRECTOR OF COMMUNICATION
Randy Naylor

COPRODUCERS CORPORATION

2670 N.E. 24th St., Pompano Beach, FL 33064. (954) 781-2627. FAX: (954) 781-2627.
PRESIDENT
John F. Rickert
SECRETARY/TREASURER
Ildiko M. Rickert
25 Theatrical Features.

COSGROVE-MEURER PRODUCTIONS, INC.

4303 W. Verdugo Ave., Burbank, CA 91505. (818) 843-5600. FAX: (818) 843-8585.
Series: Unsolved Mysteries.

THE CRAMER CO.

4605 Lankershim Blvd., Suite 617, North Hollywood, CA 91602. (213) 877-0150. FAX: (213) 877-0159.
PRESIDENT
Douglas S. Cramer
DIRECTOR OF DEVELOPMENT
Grady Hall
Features: Danielle Steel's "The Ring", Danielle Steel's "Vanished", Danielle Steel's "Zoya", Family of Cops.

BING CROSBY PRODUCTIONS, INC.

2401 Colorado Ave., Building A, 2nd floor, Santa Monica, CA 90404-3567. (310) 309-5775. FAX: (310) 309-5205.
PRESIDENT
Nicholas D. Trigony
VICE PRESIDENTS
J. Randall Stargel
Preston B. Barnett
Series: Ben Casey, Bing Crosby Show, Breaking Point, Hogan's Heroes, The Queen and I, Slattery's People.

CRYSTAL PICTURES, INC.

1560 Broadway, Suite 503, New York, NY 10036-1525. (212) 840-6181. FAX: (212) 840-6182.
9 Pack Sq., Asheville, NC 28801. (828) 285-9996. FAX: (828) 285-9997. email: cryspic@aol.com
URL: www.ivyvideo.com
PRESIDENT
Joshua Tager

DE PASSE ENTERTAINMENT, INC.

5750 Wilshire Blvd., Ste. 640, Los Angeles, CA 90036. (213) 965-2580. FAX: (213) 965-2598.
CHAIRMAN & CEO
Suzanne de Passe
PRESIDENT
Suzanne Coston

Series: Lonesome Dove: The Outlaw Years, Lupe Solano, Nite Time, Sister Sister, The Smart Guy.

Specials: Motown 25: Yesterday Today Forever, Motown Goes To The Apollo, Motown 30: What's Goin' On.

Movies: Someone Else's Child.

Miniseries: Buffalo Girls, Dead Man's Walk, The Jacksons: An American Dream, Lonesome Dove, Return To Lonesome Dove, Small Sacrifices, Streets of Laredo.

Upcoming Products: Courage of Conviction: The Martha Bethel Story, Five Smooth Stones, The Kindness of Strangers, Motown Presents, The Ronnie Spector Story, Without A Choice.

VIN DI BONA PRODUCTIONS

12233 W. Olympic Blvd., Suite 170, Los Angeles, CA 90064. (310) 442-5600. FAX: (310) 442-5604.

Series: America's Funniest Home Videos, Sherman Oaks.

DIC ENTERTAINMENT, INC.

303 N. Glenoaks Blvd., Burbank, CA 91505. (818) 955-5400. FAX: (818) 955-5696.
PRESIDENT
Andy Heyward
EXECUTIVE V.P., OPERATIONS & COO
Jeff Wernick
EXECUTIVE V.P., CREATIVE AFFAIRS
Robby London
S.V.P., LEGAL & BUSINESS AFFAIRS, CORP. SECRETARY
Greg Payne
SENIOR V.P. & CFO
Bill Cooper
S.V.P., DEVELOPMENT
Michael Maliani
SENIOR V.P., TALENT
Marsha Goodman
V.P., POSTPRODUCTION
Kevin McLaughlin
V.P., PRODUCTION
Stacey Gallishaw
V.P., ADMINISTRATION
Tricia Piascik

Series: Adventures of the Sonic Hedgehog, Dennis the Menace, Double Dragon, Gadget Boy's Adventures in History, Hurricane, Inspector Gadget's Field Trip, Madeline, Mummies, Tex Avery Theatre.

DISCOVERY COMMUNICATIONS

(For a complete listing, see Cable Networks.)
7700 Wisconsin Ave., Bethesda, MD 20814. (301) 986-0444. FAX: (301) 986-4826. URL: http://www.discovery.com

New Products: The Roots of Evil, Ancient Inventions, Wild Discovery, Sci-Trek, Byzantium: The Lost Empire, Great Books.

THE WALT DISNEY COMPANY

500 S. Buena Vista St., Burbank, CA 91521. (818) 560-1000.
CHAIRMAN OF THE BOARD, PRESIDENT & CEO
Michael D. Eisner
EXECUTIVE V.P. & CHIEF STRATEGIC OFFICER
Lawrence P. Murphy
EXECUTIVE V.P., LAW & HUMAN RESOURCES/ CHIEF OF CORPORATE OPERATIONS
Sanford Litvack
EXECUTIVE V.P., CORPORATE AFFAIRS
John F. Cooke
SENIOR V.P. & CFO
Thomas Staggs
V.P., PLANNING & CONTROL
John Garand
CORPORATE SECRETARY
Marsha L. Reed

WALT DISNEY TELEVISION & TOUCHSTONE TELEVISION

(See separate Touchstone listing for product.)
500 South Buena Vista St., Burbank, CA 91521. (818) 560-5000.
PRESIDENT, WALT DISNEY TELEVISION
Charles Hirschhorn
EXECUTIVE V.P., TELEVISION PRODUCTION
Mitch Ackerman
SENIOR V.P., BUSINESS AFFAIRS & LEGAL AFFAIRS
Alan Duke
SENIOR V.P., TELEVISION PRODUCTION FINANCE
Walter O'Neal
VICE PRESIDENT, CASTING
Gail Levin
VICE PRESIDENTS, PRODUCTION
Peter Green
Leah Keith
V.P., TELEVISION POST PRODUCTION
Grady Jones
V.P., ADVERTISING, PUBLICITY & PROMOTION
Heidi Trotta
VICE PRESIDENT, FINANCE
Joanna Spak

WALT DISNEY TELEVISION ANIMATION

500 South Buena Vista St., Burbank, CA 91521. (818) 560-5000.
PRESIDENT
Charles Hirschhorn
EXECUTIVE VICE PRESIDENTS
Barry Blumberg
Sharon Morrill
V.P., INTERNATIONAL PRODUCTION
Lenora Hume
S.V.P., BUSINESS & LEGAL AFFAIRS
Mark Kenchelian
V.P., FINANCE
Joanna Spak
V.P., POST PRODUCTION
Cheryl Murphy
V.P., TV PRODUCTION
Barbara Ferro
V.P., MUSIC
Bambi Moc
S.V.P., JUMBO PICTURES
Bill Gross
V.P., PUBLICITY & SYNERGY
Laurel Whitcomb

Series: Disney's Aladdin, Duck Daze, Gargoyles, The Lion King's Timon & Pumbaa.

BUENA VISTA TELEVISION

500 South Buena Vista St., Burbank, CA 91521. (818) 560-5000.
CHIARMAN
Walter C. Liss, Jr.
PRESIDENT
Mort Marcus
V.P., AFFILIATE RELATIONS
Sandra Brewer
V.P., RESEARCH
Francie Calfo
S.V.P. & GENERAL SALES MANAGER, EAST
Tom Cerio
V.P., & GENERAL MANAGER, PAY TV
Dan Cohen
V.P., WESTERN REGION
Jed Cohen
S.V.P., DEVELOPMENT
Stephanie Drachkovitch
V.P., OPS & SALES DEVELOPMENT
Helen Faust
V.P., PUBLICITY
Kim Harbin
V.P., FINANCE
Jim Hedges
V.P., DEVELOMENT
Brooke Karzen
S.V.P., PRODUCTION
Mary Kellogg-Joslyn
V.P., PRINT ADVERTISING
Jimmy Lee
S.V.P., BUSINESS AFFAIRS
Don Loughery
EXEC.V.P., SALES
Janice Marinelli
V.P., CREATIVE SERVICES
Peter Martin
V.P., PROMOTIONS
Meredith Momoda
S.V.P., GENERAL SALES MANAGER
Jim Packer
V.P., RESEARCH
Julie Piopenkotter
V.P., DISTRIBUTION & BUSINESS AFFAIRS
Bill Rogers
EXEC.V.P., AD SALES
Mike Shaw
V.P., PRODUCTION
Screech Washington

WALT DISNEY INTERNATIONAL TELEVISION

3 Queen Caroline Street, Hammersmith, London W6 9PE. (44 181) 222-1000. FAX: (44 181) 222-1122.
PRESIDENT
Etienne de Villiers
SENIOR V.P. & GENERAL MANAGER, BROADCASTING
David Hulbert
SENIOR V.P. & MANAGING DIRECTOR, ASIA PACIFIC
Ed Borgerding
S. V.P., EUROPEAN SALES BUSINESS & LEGAL AFFAIRS
Sally Davies
SENIOR V.P., MARKETING & RESEARCH
Selby Hall
V.P. TELEVISION, CANADA
Orest Olijnyk
SENIOR V.P. & MANAGING DIRECTOR, LATIN AMERICA
Simon Kenny
SENIOR V.P., PROGRAMMING & CREATIVE DEVELOPMENT
David Snyder
V.P. & MANAGING DIRECTOR, PRODUCTION
Mike Watts
V.P., MARKETING/COMMUNICATIONS
Diane Digit-Rebouche
V.P., SALES, LATIN AMERICA
Bettina Bose
V.P., SALES, ASIA PACIFIC
Sophia Evans

D.L.T. ENTERTAINMENT

31 W. 56 St., New York, NY 10019. (212) 245-4680. FAX: (212) 315-1132.
188 Century Park E, Los Angeles, CA 90067. (213) 937-1144. FAX: (213) 937-5095.
PRESIDENT
Donald L. Taffner
V.P., INTERNTIONAL SALES
Nigel Emery
Series: Love On A Branch (4 x 60).
Comedy: As Time Goes By (54 x 30 mins.), After Henry (19 x 30 mins.), A Kind of Living (13 x 30 mins.), All at #20 (12 x 30 mins.), Benny Hill (111 x 30 mins.), Bloomin' Marvelous (8 x 30 mins.), Chances in a Million (18 x 30 mins.), Executive Stress (19 x 30 mins.), Ffizz (12 x 30 mins.), French Fields (27 x 30 mins.), Fresh Fields (27 x 30 mins.), Never the Twain (42 x 30 mins.), Never the Twain (42 x 30 mins.), No Job for a Lady (12 x 30 mins.), The Russ Abbot Show (65 x 30 mins.), Shelley (58 x 30 mins.), Thames Comedy Originals (156 x 30 mins.).
Animated: Animated Family Classics (29 hours).
Series/Off Network: Check It Out (66 x 30 mins.), Three's Company (222 x 30 mins.), Too Close for Comfort (129 x 30 mins.), The Ropers (26 x 30 mins.), Three's a Crowd (22 x 30 mins.).
Children's Programs: Wind in the Willows (65 x 30 mins.).
Features/Packages: Dick Francis Mysteries (2 hrs. each), The Saint (6 films, 2 hrs. each), Selling Hitler (5 one-hrs.).
Specials: Benny Hill Specials (18 hrs.), The Heat is On, Miss Saigon (60 or 90 mins.)
Game Shows: Talkabout (260 x 30 mins.), 5432 Run (34 x 30 mins.)
Drama: The Bill (65 x 30 mins.), Capitol City (23 hrs.), Danger: UXB (13 hrs.), Hannay (13 hrs.), London Embassy (6 hrs.), Lytton's Diary (13 hrs.), Mr. Palfrey of Westminster (10 hrs.), Minder (13 hrs.), The One Game (4 hrs.), Reilly: Ace of Spies (11 hrs. and 1 x 90 mins.), Rock Follies (12 hrs.), Unnatural Causes (7 hrs.).
Documentaries: Cambodia Year Ten (60 mins.), Charles Rennie Mackintosh: A Modern Man (1 x 60 mins.), Cinema Europe: The other Hollywood (6 x 60 mins.), Destination America (9 x 60 mins.), Holiday World (52 x 30 mins.), Hollywood (13 x 60 mins.), Killiam Collection (13 x 5 mins.), Nature Watch (27 x 30 mins.), The World at War (36 hrs.).

DREAMWORKS SKG

100 Universal City Plaza, Bldg. 477, Universal City, CA 91608. (818) 733-7000.
PRINCIPALS
Steven Spielberg
Jeffrey Katzenberg
David Geffen
HEAD OF TELEVISION
Dan McDermott
HEAD OF MARKETING & PUBLIC RELATIONS
Terry Press

E! ENTERTAINMENT TELEVISION

(For executives, please see Cable Networks.)
5670 Wilshire Blvd., Los Angeles, CA 90036. (213) 954-2400. FAX: (213) 954-2620. URL: http://www.eonline.com
Series: Behind the Scenes, Coming Attractions, E! News Daily, Fashion File, The Gossip Show, Howard Stern, Melrose Place, On E! Specials, Q & E!, Talk Soup, ThE! Movie, Uncut, Mysteries & Scandals, Fashion Emergency, Celebrity Profile.

RALPH EDWARDS/STU BILLETT PRODUCTIONS

6922 Hollywood Blvd., #415, Hollywood, CA 90028. (213) 851-1500.
OWNER
Ralph Edwards
Syndication: Family Medical Center, Love Stories, The People's Court, Superior Court, This is Your Life, Truth or Consequences.

ENTERTAINMENT PRODUCTIONS, INC.

2118 Wilshire Blvd., Suite 744, Santa Monica, CA 90403. (310) 456-3143. FAX: (310) 456-8950.
PRESIDENT & PRODUCER
Edward Coe
Series: Bankruptcy Fever, Las Vegas Shows, That's Lawyer Talk.
Specials: Alien Kid, Bankruptcy Exposed, Kidsville, Mama Hanukkah and Santa Claus–A Joint Adventure.

EYEMARK ENTERTAINMENT

(a unit of CBS Enterprises.)
10877 Wilshire Blvd., 9th floor, Los Angeles, CA 90024. (310) 446-6000. FAX: (310) 446-6066.
51 W. 52nd. St., New York, NY 10019. (212) 975-4321. FAX: (212) 975-9174.
PRESIDENT
Ed Wilson
EXECUTIVE VICE PRESIDENT
Robert A. Cook
EXECUTIVE V.P., SYNDICATION
Barry Wallach
S.V.P., BUSINESS & PROGRAM DEVELOPMENT
Robb E. Dalton
S.V.P., BUSINESS & PROGRAM DEVELOPMENT
Jim Dauphinee
Series: Bob Vila's Home Again, The George Michael Sport Machine, Martha Stewart Living, Pensacola: Wings of Gold, Psi Factor: Chronicles of the Paranormal, Wild Wild Web, The Dr. Joy Browne Show, Peter Benchley's Amazon, The Howard Stern Show.

FILM ROMAN, INC.

12020 Chandler Blvd., #200, N. Hollywood, CA 91607. (818) 761-2544. FAX: (818) 761-0844.
PRESIDENT & CE)
David Pritchard
SENIOR VICE PRESIDENT
Jon F. Vein
PRODUCER
Andi Copley and Danica Katz
Series: The Mr. Potato Head Show, Shamu and Crew.

FILMROOS, INC.

8899 Beverly Blvd., 6th fl., Los Angeles, CA 90048. (310) 205-5490. FAX: (310) 205-0217. email: info@filmroos.com
PRESIDENT & EXECUTIVE PRODUCER
Bram Roos
EXECUTIVE ASSISTANT
Morgan Bateman
SUPERVISING PROD. & DIR. OF OPERATIONS & DEV'T.
Yun Lingner
CONTROLLER
Ellen Curtis
SUPERVISING PRODUCER
Liz Newstat
Series: Ancient Mysteries, Biography, Mysteries of the Bible, In Search of History.

FINNEGAN-PINCHUK CO.

4225 Coldwater Canyon, Studio City, CA 91604. (818) 508-5614.

44 BLUE PRODUCTIONS, INC.

4040 Vineland Ave., Ste. 105, Studio City, CA 91604. (818) 760-4442. FAX: (818) 760-1509.
PRESIDENT & EXECUTIVE PRODUCER
Rasha Drachkovitch
Series: All-Americans, Bob Uecker's Wacky World of Sports, The Christopher Lowell Show, Discovery Sport, Future Stars, Men's World, Offbeat Sportsbeat, Those Who Dare, World of Valor.
Features: And Now This: with Rosie O'Donnell, Behind Bars, Betty Boop, Bigfoot, Copworld, Elite Choppers: Birds of Prey, Flash Gordon, The History of College Football and Basketball, Journeys to Remember, The Keepers, Red Light Districts, Special Report: Journey to Mars, Trophy Kill: America's Poacher Wars.

FOUR STAR INTERNATIONAL, INC.

1440 S. Sepulveda, Los Angeles, CA 90025. (310) 444-8400.
PRESIDENT
Lennart Ringquist
Series: Big Valley, Detectives, Honey West, Rouges.
Movies: Cisco Kid Features (13 features) Dick Tracy (8 features) No Restrictions (13 new films), Star One (15 new films), Star Two (15 new films).

FOX BROADCASTING CO.

(For officers and personnel see listing under Networks.)
P.O. Box 900, Beverly Hills, CA 90213. (310) 277-2211. FAX: (310) 369-1000.

Series/First Run: Chicago Hope, Cleghorne!, The Crew, A Current Affair (daily live 30 mins.), NYPD Blue, Picket Fences, The Preston Episodes, The Simpsons, Space: Above and Beyond, The X-Files.

Series/Off-Network: Circus (52 x 30 mins.), That's Hollywood (74 x 30 mins.), Adventures in Paradise (91 x 60 mins.), Animal Express (130 x 30 mins.), The Ann Sothern Show (93 x 30 mins.), Audubon Wildlife Theater (78 x 30 mins.), Batman (120 x 30 mins.), Bracken's World (41 x 60 mins.), Broken Arrow (72 x 60 mins. b&w), Circus (52 x 30 mins.), Daniel Boone (120 x 60 mins.), Dobie Gillis (147 x 60 mins. b&w), Dynasty (198 hours), Expedition Danger (26 x 30 mins.), Fall Guy (112 hours), The Ghost and Mrs. Muir (50 x 30 mins.), Green Hornet (26 x 30 mins.), Incredible World of Adventure (31 x 30 mins.), Jackie Gleason Show (100 x 30 mins.), Judd for the Defense (50 x 60 mins.), Julia (86 x 30 mins.), Lancer (51 x 60 mins.), Land of the Giants (51 x 60 mins.), Lost in Space (83 x 50 mins., 54 color), M*A*S*H (255 x 30 mins.), Miller's Court (52 x 30 mins.), The Monroes (26 x 60 mins.), Movin' On (44 x 60 mins.), Mr. Belvedere (95 x 30 mins.), 9 to 5 (85 x 30 mins.), Nanny and the Professor (54 x 30 mins.), Peyton Place (247 x 30 mins. color & 267 x 30 mins. b&w), Private Secretary (104 x 60 mins.), Room 222 (113 x 60 mins.), Small Wonder (96 x 30 mins.), That's Hollywood (74 x 30 mins.), Trapper John (151 x 60 mins.), 12 O'Clock High (78 x 60 mins., 17 color, 61 b&w), The Untamed World (156 x 30 mins.), Vegas (68 x 60 mins.), Voyage to the Bottom of the Sea (111 x 60 mins., 78 color, 32 b&w).

Specials: Anatomy of a Crime (1 hr.), Assassins Among Us (1 hr.), Blind Alley (1 hr.), The Cancer Confrontation (1 hr.), Charles Dickens' Classics (8 hrs.), Divorce, Kids in the Middle (1 hr.), Fox Movietone News (520 newsreels), Future Shock (1 hr.), Gudonov - The World to Dance In (1 hr.), Hollywood: The Gift of Laughter (3 hrs.), Inside Russia (1 hr.), Jane Goodall and the World of Animal Behavior (4 hrs.), The Making of M*A*S*H (1), The President's Command Performance (2 hrs.), Sex, Teenage Style (1 hr.), Summer Solstice (1 hr.), Time of Man (1 hr.), The Undersea World of Jacques Cousteau (36 hrs.), War to End all Wars (1 hr.).

Features/Packages: Big 36 (36 titles, 5 color, 29 b&w), Carry On (11 titles), Century 5, 6, 7, 8, 9, 20, 22, 23 (total of 220 titles, 212 color and 8 b&w), Century 13 (26 titles), Century 14 (20 titles, includes Aliens, Black Widow, Cocoon, The Fly, The Jewel of the Nile, The Name of the Rose), Fox Premiere Movies (9 titles, includes: Enemy Mine, The Name of the Rose, Project X), Fox Mini-Series I (4 titles: Tender Is the Night, Jamaica Inn, Little Gloria, Evergreen), Fox IV, V & VI (102 color, 102 b&w), Fox Mystery Theatre (13 titles, 90-min. specials), Fox Hollywood Theatre '89 - 90 (7 titles including: Miracle on 34th Street, Almost You, Eating Raoul, Kidco), Golden Century (49 titles b&w), Special 41 (41 titles, 26 color, 15 b&w), Mark I (10 titles), Mark II (16 titles), Mark III (25 titles), MPC-20 (20 titles), Planet of the Apes (5 hrs.), Premiere I (20 titles), Premium Plus (28 titles), Premiere II (22 titles), Premiere III (20 titles), Super 65 (48 color, 17 b&w), Time Tunnel (5 hrs.).

Domestic Late-Night Network: The New Avengers (26 hours).

Domestic Miniseries: Empire, Inc. (6 hrs.), The Far Pavilions (6 hrs.), Mussolini and I (4 hrs.), Roughnecks (4 hrs.), Sara Dane (8 hrs.), Spearfield's Daughter (6 hrs.), Wild Times (4 hrs.).

Domestic Cartoons: Crusader Rabbit (13 color hrs., 260 x 4 mins. 195 x 4 mins., b & w), Doctor Doolittle (17 x 30 mins.), Fantastic Voyage (17 x 30 mins.), Groovie Goolies & Friends (104 x 30 mins.), The Hardy Boys (17 x 30 mins.), Journey to the Center of the Earth (17 x 30 mins.), Return to the Planet of the Apes (13 x 30 mins.).

FOX LORBER ASSOCIATES INC.

419 Park Ave. South, 20th Floor, New York, NY 10016. (212) 686-6777. FAX: (212) 685-2625.
PRESIDENT & CEO
Richard Lorber
V.P., WORLDWIDE PROGRAM SALES
Sherri Levine

New Entertainment Series: Circus Around the World, Life on the Digital Edge, Models Profiles and Fantasies, Out of Control, Tilt 23 1/2.

Documentary Series: The Directors, Space Tech.

FOX SPORTS NEW YORK

4 Penn Plaza, 4th Fl., New York, NY 10001. (212) 465-5926. FAX: (212) 465-6024.
PRESIDENT & CEO
David W. Checketts
EXECUTIVE PRESIDENT
Joseph M. Cohen
S.V.P. PRODUCTION AND EXECUTIVE PRODUCER
Mike McCarthy
V.P. MARKETING
Greg Brosdky

Live Events: College basketball and football, pro-boxing, New York Mets baseball, New Jersey Nets basketball, New Jersey Devils hockey, New York Islanders hockey, New Jersey Red Dogs Arena football, Grand Prix auto racing, thoroughbred horse racing, English Premier League soccer, NFL Europe, Golf.

FOXLAB

5746 Sunset Blvd., Los Angeles, CA 90028-8588. (213) 856-1000.
Series: America's Most Wanted, Cops, Final Justice, Liars, Manhunter, Not Just News.

THE FREMANTLE CORPORATION

660 Madison Ave., 21st floor, New York, NY 10021. (212) 421-4530. FAX: (212) 207-8357.
Fremantle of Canada, Ltd., 23 Lesmill Rd., Suite 201, Don Mills, Ontario M3B 3P6. (416) 443-9204. FAX: (416) 443-8685.
PRESIDENT & CEO
Paul Talbot
SECRETARY & TREASURER
Fannie Mack
SENIOR VICE PRESIDENT
Josh Braun
V.P., INT'L SALES, LATIN AMERICA, HOME VIDEO
Julie Zuleta-Corbo
V.P., CHINA SALES
Dianbo Xie
DIRECTOR, NEW PROGRAM DEVELOPMENT
Keith Talbot
V.P., SALES, CANADA
Frank Braun
MANAGING DIRECTOR, UK
Tony Gruner
DIRECTOR OF PROGRAM SALES, UK
Veronique Heim
CHAIRMAN, AUSTRALIA
Russell Becker
MANAGING DIRECTOR, AUSTRALIA
Richard Becker
SALES AGENT, SPAIN
Antoinetta Brughera

INTERNATIONAL BRANCHES

AUSTRALIA

Fremantle Productions Pty., Ltd., 2nd floor, 486 Pacific Highway, St. Leonards, Autralia NSW 2065. (612) 438-3377. FAX: (612) 439-1827.

SPAIN

Fremantle de Espana, Ltd., Sacedilla 13-13, Bajahonda, Madrid, Spain 28220. (341) 639 2688. FAX: (341) 639 4025.

UNITED KINGDOM

The Fremantle Corporation Ltd., Unit 2, Water Lane, Kentish Town Rd., London, England NW1 8NZS. (44171) 284-0880. FAX: (44171) 209-2294.

INTERNATIONAL PRODUCT

Series: The Anti-Gravity Room (26 x 30 mins.), Baywatch (155 hrs. & 7 2 hr. movies), The Baywatch Summerfest Special (1 hr.), The Best of Baywatch Special (1 hr.), The Campbells (100 x 30 mins., Years I, II, III, IV), Candid Camera (385 x 30 mins., 7 hr. specials, 7 x 30 mins. specials, 35 x 30 mins. "Adult" versions), The City (30 mins. strip), The Conspiracy Tapes (12 hrs.), Davis Rules (29 x 30 mins.), Family Theater (31 hrs.), Fire Rescue (24 x 30 mins.), Frannie's Turn (6 x 30 mins.), Funny People (6 hrs.), The Galloping Gourmet (595 x 30 mins.), Grace Under Fire (123 x 30 mins.), Loving (30 min. strip), Makin 8 (27 x 30 mins./25 hrs. & 1 hr. special), Mysterious Island (22 hrs./44 x 30 mins.), Raising Miranda (9 x 30 mins.), Save Our Streets (46 hrs.), She TV (6 hrs.), Swiss Family Robinson (26 x 30 mins.), Take Kerr (155 5 mins.), TV 101 (17 hrs.), The Tripods (25 x 30 mins.) 3rd Rock From The Sun (19 x 30 mins.), The Van Dyke Show (9 x 30 mins.), Warriors Of Wrestling (52 hrs.), You Bet Your Life (195 x 30 mins.).

Animated Series: The Happy Circus (Le Cirque Bonheur) (10 x 8 mins.), In The Beginning: Stories From The Bible (26 x 30 mins.), Miss Peach: "Career Day At The Kelly School" (1 hr.).

Animated Specials: Family Circus (3 x 30 mins.), Little Orphan Annie's A Very Animated Christmas (1 half hr.), The Mousehole Cat (1 half hr.), On Christmas Eve (1 half hr.), Snowman (1 half hr.).

TV Movies: Can You Feel Me Dancing (2 hrs., NBC), Cat On A Hot Tin Roof (150 mins.), A Fight For Jenny (2 hrs., NBC), Half Slave Half Free (2 hrs., PBS), The Killing Floor (2 hrs. PBS), The Last Days Of Frank And Jesse James (2 hrs., ABC), Loving (2 hrs., ABC), Manhunt For Claude Dallas (2 hrs., CBS), On Fire (2 hrs., ABC), Special People (2 hrs., CBS), Still Watch (2 hrs., CBS), Strange Possession Of Mrs. Oliver (2 hrs.), Vanishing Act (2 hrs., ABC), We Are The Children (2 hrs., ABC).

Specials: American Comedy Awards (2 hrs.), An All-Star Tribute To Rosemary Clooney (90 mins.), An All-Star Word From Our Sponsor (1 hr.), The All-Star Christmas Concert (1 hr.), Celebrity First Loves (2 hrs.), Comedy Hall Of Fame (2 hrs.), Country Comes Home 1 & 2 (2 hrs. each), Daredevils (2 hrs.), Jazz In America, The Kennedy Center Honors (2 hrs.), Las Vegas 75th Anniversary (2 hrs.), Magic With The Stars (2 hrs.), Muhammad Ali's 50th Birthday Celebration (2 hrs.), A Party For Richard Pryor (2 hrs.), Penn & Teller: Don't Try This At Home (1 hr.), Roy Acuff: The King Of Country Music (2 hrs.), Rowan & Martin's Laugh-In: 25th Anniversary (2 hrs.), Past Christmas Present (1 hr.), Romance, Love Sex And Marriage (1 hr.), Sammy Davis Jr's 60th Anniversary Celebration (2.5 hrs.), Seven Wonders Of The Circus World (1 hr.), The 75th Anniversary Of Beverly Hills (1 hr.), Tony Awards (2 hrs.), A Word From Our Sponsor I & II (1 hr. each).

Documentaries: Erich Von Stroheim–The Man You Loved To Hate (90 mins.), Russia's War: Blood Upon The Snow (10 hrs.), Wild Westerns (9 hrs.), Wildlife International I & II (34 x 30 mins.).

CHUCK FRIES PRODUCTIONS, INC.

6922 Hollywood Blvd., Los Angeles, CA 90028. (213) 466-2266. FAX: (213) 465-7835. email: cwfries@ix.netcom.com.

THE GAME SHOW NETWORK

10202 W. Washington Blvd., Culver City, CA 90232. (310) 244-2222. FAX: (310) 244-2080.
3390 Peachtree Rd. NE, Ste. 1000, Atlanta, GA 30326. (404) 364-6506. FAX: (404) 364-6512.
Three Forest Plaza, 12221 Merit Drive, Ste. 1065, Dallas, TX 75251. (972) 404-0506. FAX: (972) 404-1935.
1625 Larimer, #2603, Denver, CO 80202. (303) 722-7337. FAX: (303) 722-5932.
550 Madison Ave., 12th Flr., New York, NY 10022. (212) 833-8727. FAX: (212) 833-8711.
PRESIDENT
Michael Fleming
S.V.P., SALES & AFFILIATE MARKETING
Elaine Parrish
V.P., BUSINESS AFFAIRS
Kim Cunningham
V.P.'S, NATIONAL ACCOUNTS
Anne Droste
Sandy McGill
Sydney McQuoid
V.P., SALES
Dena Kaplan
V.P., PROGRAMMING
Ryan Tredinnick

GENESIS ENTERTAINMENT

1440 South Sepulveda Blvd., Los Angeles, CA 90025. (310) 444-8344, (818) 706-6341. FAX: (310) 231-1633.
625 Madison Ave., 11th fl., New York, NY 10022. (212) 527-5400. FAX: (212) 527-6401.
PRESIDENT & CEO
Wayne Lepoff
S.V.P., WEST COAST SALES
Ed Wasserman
EXECUTIVE V.P., NEW YORK
Phil Oldham
S.V.P., DOMESTIC SALES, NEW YORK
Barry Wallach
Series: Biker Mice from Mars (65 x 30 mins.), Emergency Call (104 x 30 mins.), Fantastic Four (26 x 30 mins.), Juvenile Justice (210 x 30 mins.), Marvel Action Universe—Iron Man (26 x 30 mins.), The Mark Walberg Show (195 hours), Real Stories of the Highway Patrol (325 x 30 mins.).
Syndicated: Tales From The Crypt, Top Cops.

GOLDWYN ENTERTAINMENT COMPANY (A METROMEDIA ENTERTAINMENT GROUP COMPANY)

10203 Santa Monica Blvd., Suite 500, Los Angeles, CA 90067. (310) 552-2255. FAX: (310) 284-8493.
560 W. 43rd St. Ste., 32E, New York, NY 10036. (212) 594-3334. FAX: (212) 268-9289.
CHAIRMAN & CEO
Samuel Goldwyn, Jr.
PRESIDENT & CEO
Meyer Gottlieb
HEAD OF MARKETING & DISTRIBUTION
Jeff Lipsky
V.P., ACQUISITIONS & PRODUCTION
John Manulis
DIRECTOR, ACQUISITIONS & PRODUCTION
Monica Chuo

SAMUEL GOLDWYN TELEVISION

10203 Santa Monica Blvd., Los Angeles, CA 90067. (310) 552-2255. FAX: (310) 284-8493.
888 Seventh Ave., #2901, New York, NY 10106. (212) 315-3030.
625 Center St., Elgin, IL 60120. (708) 468-0468.
760 S. Waukegan Rd., Lake Forest, IL 60045. (708) 735-9041.
PRESIDENT, TV
Dick Askin

GOODSON PRICE PRODUCTIONS/TPIR, LLC

5750 Wilshire Blvd., Ste. 206, Los Angeles, CA 90036. (323) 965-6500. FAX: (323) 965-6527.
SENIOR VICE PRESIDENT
Michael S. Brockman
CFO
Alan R. Sandler
Products: The Price Is Right.

GOTHIC RENAISSANCE PRODUCTIONS

1223 N. 23rd St., Wilmington, NC 28404. (910) 251-2211.
Series: American Gothic.

GRACIE FILMS

c/o Sony Film Corp., 10202 W. Washington Blvd., Culver City, CA 90232. (310) 244-4222. FAX: (310) 244-1530.
Current Series: The Simpsons.

GRANADA ENTERTAINMENT USA

The Lantana Center, 3000 West Olympic Blvd., Suite 1100, Santa Monica, CA 90404. (310) 689-4787.
PRESIDENT
Scott Siegler

GRAY-SCHWARTZ ENTERPRISES, INC.

Teleflix Division, 4507 Park Allegra, Calabasas, CA 91302-1759. (818) 222-6500. FAX: (818) 222-6501.
PRESIDENT
Marv Gray
Series: Cimarron Strip.

GRB ENTERTAINMENT

12001 Ventura Pl., #600, Studio City, CA 91604, (818) 753-3400. FAX: (818) 753-3401. email: info@grbtv.com. URL: http://www.grbtv.com
PRESIDENT & CEO
Gary G. Benz
V.P., INT'L DISTRIBUTION & BUSINESS DEVELOPMENT
Kim Relick
Series: Movie Magic, Anatomy of Disaster, Storm Warning!, AXN-TV, What Went Wrong?, Inferno, TAC-1, Mega Movie Mag.
Specials: Action Awards, World's Wildest Daredevils.

GREYSTONE COMMUNICATIONS, INC.

5161 Lankershim Blvd., 2nd Fl., North Hollywood, CA 91601. (818) 762-2900. FAX: (818) 762-1626. URL: www.greystoneonline.com.
PRESIDENT
Craig A. Haffner
EXECUTIVE VICE PRESIDENT
Donna E. Lusitana
V.P. PRODUCTION
Brad Wilson
Series: Ancient Mysteries, Biography, The Life and Times of...

MERV GRIFFIN ENTERPRISES

3000 31st St., Santa Monica, CA 90405. (310) 664-3000. FAX: (310) 664-3001.
CHAIRMAN & CEO
Merv Griffin
PRESIDENT & COO
Robert J. Murphy
Series: Jeopardy!, Wheel of Fortune.

GRUB STREET PRODS.

c/o Paramount TV, 5555 Melrose Ave., Wilder #101, Los Angeles, CA 90038-3197. (213) 956-4657.
CREATORS
Peter Casey
David Lee
David Angell
EXECUTIVE PRODUCER
Chris Lloyd
Series: Frasier.

ALFRED HABER DISTRIBUTION, INC.

321 Commercial Ave., Palisades Park, NJ 07650. (201) 224-8000. FAX: (201) 947-4500.
Alfred Haber
EXEC. V.P.
Robert Kennedy
Series: Jack Hanna's Animal Adventures (123 x 30 mins), Beyond Belief (32 x 60 mins.).
Specials: The World's Scariest Police Chases (6 x 60 mins.).

HALLMARK ENTERTAINMENT

1325 Avenue of the Americas, 21st floor, New York, NY 10019. (212) 977-9001. FAX: (212) 977-9049.
3/5 Bateman St., 2nd floor, London W1V 5TT. (44171) 439 0633. FAX: (44171) 439 0644.
Suite 9 Level 9, 100 Walker St., Sydney, NSW 2060, Australia. (02) 9957 2999. FAX: (02) 9957 2247.
Hallmark Entertainment Network: 5670 Greenwood Plaza Blvd., Penthouse, Englewood, CO 80111. (303) 220-7990. FAX: (303) 220-7660.
CHAIRMAN
Robert Halmi, Sr.
PRESIDENT & CEO
Robert Halmi, Jr.
EXECUTIVE V.P., & COO
Peter von Gal
EXECUTIVE PRODUCER
Steve Hewitt
PRESIDENT & CEO HALLMARK ENTERTAINMENT NETWORK
George Stein
S.V.P., MANAGING DIRECTOR INT'L SALES
Joel Denton
PRESIDENT, PRODUCTION WORLDWIDE
David V. Picker
EXECUTIVE V.P., PRODUCTION
Dan Martin
V.P.'S, INTERNATIONAL SALES
Erik Pack
Bonnie Low
DIRECTOR OF MARKETING
Donna Cornwell
DIRECTOR OF BUSINESS DEVELOPMENT
Whitney Vliet
S.V.P., MARKETING & ANCILLARY RIGHTS
Liz Sheppard
Products: Merlin (NBC, 4 hrs.), The Long Way Home (CBS, 2 hrs.), The Love Letter (CBS, 2 hrs.), A Christmas Memory (CBS, 2 hrs.), The Echo of Thunder ((CBS, 2 hrs.), Ellen Foster (CBS, 2 hrs.), What the Dead Man Heard (CBS, 2 hrs.), Rose Hill (CBS, 2 hrs.), Ken Follett's The Third Twin (CBS, 4 hrs.), Mother Theresa: In the Name of God's Poor (FAM, 2 hrs.), Clover (USA, 2 hrs.), In His Father's Shoes (SHO, 2 hrs.), True Woman (CBS, 4 hrs.), The Odyssey (NBC, 4 hrs.), To Dance With Olivia (CBS, 2 hrs.), Mandela and DeKlerk (SHO, 2 hrs.), William Faulkner's Old Man (CBS, 2 hrs.), Member of the Wedding (USA, 2 hrs.), The Summer of Ben Taylor (CBS, 2 hrs.), Mrs. Santa Claus (CBS, 2 hrs.), Calm at Sunset (CBS, 2 hrs.), Hidden In America (SHO, 2 hrs.), In Cold Blood (CBS, 4 hrs.), Titanic (CBS, 4 hrs.), Mary and Tim (CBS, 2 hrs.), Inside (SHO, 2 hrs.), Captive Heart: The James Mink Story (CBS, 2 hrs.), Gulliver's Travels (NBC, 4 hrs.), The Canterville Ghost (ABC, 2 hrs.), Journey (CBS, 2 hrs.), Bye Bye Birdie (ABC, 2 hrs.), Larry McMurtry's Streets of Laredo (CBS, 3 hrs.), My Brother's Keeper (CBS, 2 hrs.), The Piano Lesson (CBS, 2 hrs.), Scarlett (CBS, 8 hrs.), Breathing Lesson (CBS, 2 hrs.), Gypsy (CBS, 2 hrs.), To Dance With the White Dog (CBS, 2 hrs.), The Incident (CBS, 2 hrs.), Lonesome Dove (CBS, 8 hrs.).

HAMDON ENTERTAINMENT

12711 Ventura Blvd., Suite 300, Studio City, CA 91604. (818) 753-6363. FAX: (818) 753-6388.
CEO
Stephen Davis
100 TV Movies including: Before Women Had Wings, Change of Heart, Love In Ambush, Love After Death, Love Murder and Deceit, Murder At Devil's Glen, Narrow Escape, The Wedding.

HANNA-BARBERA CARTOONS, INC.

(A subsidiary of Turner Broadcasting System, Inc.)
3400 Cahuenga Blvd., Hollywood, CA 90068. (818) 977-7500. FAX: (213) 969-1201.
CO-CHAIRMAN & FOUNDER
Joseph Barbera
CO-CHAIRMAN & FOUNDER
William Hanna
PRESIDENT
Fred Seibert
EXECUTIVE PRODUCER, TV
Buzz Potamkin
V.P., DEVELOPMENT & PROGRAMMING
Jeff Holder

Animated Series: Dumb & Dumber, The New Adventures of Captain Planet, The Real Adventures of Jonny Quest.
Animated Specials: Babe He Calls Me, Bloo's Gang, Boid 'n' Woim, Cow and Chicken, Dexter's Laboratory, Dino: The Great Egg-scape, Help?, Hillbilly Blue, Johnny Bravo and the Amazon Women, Mina and the Count, Pfish and Chip II, Pizza Boy, Podunk Possom, Strange Things, Tales of Worm Paranoia.

DEAN HARGROVE PRODUCTIONS

(Producer in assoc. with Fred Silverman Co. & Viacom Prods.)
7700 Balboa Blvd., Van Nuys, CA 91406. (818) 756-1340. FAX: (818) 756-1343.
Series/TV Movies: Diagnosis Murder, Matlock, Perry Mason Movies.

HARMONY GOLD U.S.A.

7655 Sunset Blvd., Los Angeles, CA 90046. (213) 851-4900. FAX: (213) 851-5599.
CHAIRMAN & CEO
Frank Agrama
PRESIDENT, INTERNATIONAL TV
Colleen Morris
S.V.P., SALES & ACQUISITIONS
Alan Letz
Animation: Adventures on Rainbow Pond (26 x 30 mins.), Animation Adventure Theatre (3 features), Robotech (85 x 30 mins.).
Miniseries: Around the World in 80 Days (6 hrs.), Confessional (4 hrs.), Heidi (4 hrs.), The King of the Olympics (4 hrs.), The Man Who Lived at the Ritz (4 hrs.), Shaka Zulu (10 hrs.), Sherlock Holmes & the Leading Lady (4 hrs.), Sherlock Holmes: Incident at Victoria Falls (4 hrs.).
Series: Animals of Africa (52 x 30 mins.), Cobra (22 x 60 mins.), Masters of War (13 x 60 mins.), Rin Tin Tin (65 x 30 min.), Walking After Midnight (26 x 30 min.).
Features/Specials: American Strays (90 mins.), Cannibals (1 hr.), Fire Attack (1 hr.), The Lost World (2 hrs.), Return to the Lost World (2 hrs.), The Secret Identity of Jack the Ripper (live special event).

HARPO ENTERTAINMENT GROUP

110 N. Carpenter St., Chicago, IL 60607. (312) 633-1000.
CHAIRMAN & CEO
Oprah Winfrey
PRESIDENT & COO
Jeffrey Jacobs
PRESIDENT, HARPO PRODUCTIONS
Tim Bennet
EXECUTIVE PRODUCER
Dianne Atkinson Hudson
EXECUTIVE V.P., HARPO FILMS
Kate Fort
Series: The Oprah Winfrey Show.

HBO DOWNTOWN PRODUCTIONS

1100 Ave. of the Americas 13th Fl., New York, NY 10023. (212) 512-8900. FAX: (212) 512-8969.
S.V.P.
Nancy Geller
V.P., PRODUCTION
John Fisher
HEAD OF DEVELOPMENT
Nina Rosenstein
Series: Dr. Katz: Professional Therapist, Politically Incorrect with Bill Maher, Comedy Showcase, The Chris Rock Show.

HBO INDEPENDENT PRODUCTIONS.

2049 Century Park E., Ste. 4200, Los Angeles, CA 90067. (310) 201-9200.
Series: Martin.

HEARST ENTERTAINMENT, INC.

235 E. 45 St., New York, NY 10017. (212) 455-4000. FAX: (212) 983-6379. Telex: 7105812391.
136 Sloane Street, London, England SW1X 9AY. (44 171) 565-6666. FAX: (44 171) 565-6675.
PRESIDENT, HEARST ENT. INC.
Bruce L. Paisner
PRESIDENT, HEARST ENT. DISTRIBUTION & PRESIDENT, HEARST ANIMATION PRODS.
William E. Miller
SENIOR V.P., INTERNATIONAL SALES
TOM DEVLIN
V.P., INTERNATIONAL SALES, (LONDON OFFICE)
Michael Doury
Distributor of Reality Series, Movies of the Week, Animation & Specials.

JIM HENSON PRODUCTIONS

117 E. 69th St., New York, NY 10021. (212) 794-2400. FAX: (212) 570-1147.
c/o Raleigh Studios, 5358 Melrose Ave., West Office Building, 3rd Floor, Hollywood, CA 90038. (213) 960-4096. FAX: (213) 960-4935.
1(B) Downshire Hill, Hampstead, London NW3 1NR, England. (44171) 431 2818. FAX: (44171) 431 3737.
Product: Jim Henson's Animal Show with Stinky and Jake.

HILL/FIELDS PRODUCTIONS

4500 Wilshire Blvd., Los Angeles, CA 90010. (213) 954-4500. FAX: (213) 954-4550.
EXECUTIVE PRODUCERS
Leonard Hill
Joel Fields
DIRECTOR, DEVELOPMENT
Alys Shanti

IFEX INTERNATIONAL

(A Subsidiary of Cifex Corp.), 1 Peconic Hills Court, Southampton, NY 11968-1650. (516) 283-9454. FAX: (516) 283-4210.
EXECUTIVE OFFICERS
Gerald J. Rappoport
Beulah Rappoport

IFM FILM ASSOCIATES, INC.

1541 N. Gardner St., Los Angeles, CA 90046. (323) 874-4249. FAX: (323) 874-2654. email: ifmfilm@aol.com
PRESIDENT & CEO
Antony I. Ginnane
EXEC. V.P
Ann Lyons
SALES A`SSISTANT
Anthony J. Lyons

IMAGINE TELEVISION

1925 Century Park East., Ste. 2300, Los Angeles, CA 90067. (310) 277-1665. FAX: (310) 785-0107.
CO-CHAIRMEN
Brian Grazer
Ron Howard
Tony Krantz
SENIOR V.P., BUSINESS AFFAIRS
Skip Chasey
SENIOR V.P.
Nena Rodrigue
VICE PRESIDENT
Sally Desipio
CREATIVE EXECUTIVE
Cambi Clark

INDEPENDENT-INTERNATIONAL PICTURES CORP.

400 Perrine Rd., Old Bridge, NJ 08857. (732) 727-8500. FAX: (732) 727-8881.
PRESIDENT
Samuel M. Sherman
CHAIRMAN
Daniel Q. Kennis
EXECUTIVE VICE PRESIDENT
Jeffrey C. Hogue, J.D., L.L.M.
Current productions: Beyond This Earth, The Edwards Air Force Base Encounter.
Feature packages: Action Group: The Gun Riders, Mission to Death, The Fakers, Queen of Sheba, The Barbarians, Submarine Attack, Fighting Rats of Tobruk, Money.
Scream Showcase: Beyond the Living, Demons of the Dead, Doctor Dracula, Exorcism at Midnight, In Search of Dracula, Man with the Synthetic Brain, Ship of Zombies, Terror of Frankenstein, Vampire Men of the Lost Planet, Hand of Power, Night Fiend, Horror of the Werewolf, Voice from the Grave.
Drive In Theatre: The Murder Gang, Intrigue in the Orient, Blazing Stewardesses, The Naughty Stewardesses, Trapped in the Desert, The Smiling Maniacs, Syndicate Sadists.
Cult Movie Classic: The Al Adamson Collection.

MICHAEL JACOBS PRODUCTIONS

c/o Walt Disney Studios, 500 South Buena Vista St., Animation 2A, Burbank, CA 91521. (818) 560-2160. FAX: (818) 567-0415.
CEO
Michael Jacobs
Series: Boy Meets World, Zoe Bean.

JEF FILMS, INC.

Film House, 143 Hickory Hill Circle, Osterville, MA 02655-1322. (508) 428-7198. FAX: (508) 428-7198. Organized 1973. Branches: Los Angeles (Film Classic Exchange), Australia, New Zealand, England, France, Spain, Portugal, Greece, Canada, Fiji, Switzerland, Austria, West Germany, Italy, Monaco, Ireland, Denmark, Finland, Sweden, Norway, Belgium, Luxembourg, Algeria, Morocco, Tunisia, South Korea.
CEO
Jeffrey H. Aikman
VICE PRESIDENT
Elsie Aikman
SALES MANAGER
Jo-Ann Pollack
Product: A library of over 30,000 films from the following libraries: Film Classic Exchange, XTC Video, WHAM!, VIP Video, JEF Video line, JEF Films International, PHD Video, The Stock Exchange.

QUINCY JONES/DAVID SALZMAN ENTERTAINMENT

3800 Barham Blvd., #503, Los Angeles, CA 90068. (213) 874-2009. FAX: (213) 874-3363.
CEO
Quincy Jones
David Salzman
EXECUTIVE PRODUCER
Jerry Gottlieb
V.P., TV DEVELOPMENT
Debra Langford
Series: Fresh Prince of Bel Air, In the House, Jenny Jones.

KELLER ENTERTAINMENT GROUP

14225 Ventura Blvd., Sherman Oaks, CA 91423. (818) 981-4950. FAX: (818) 501-6224. email: crddouglas@aol.com
CHAIRMAN & OWNER
Max Keller
PRESIDENT & CEO
Micheline Keller
VICE PRESIDENT
Jeannine A. Imperiale
V.P., DISTRIBUTION
Cord Douglas
V.P., ADMINISTRATION
Carol Rossi

DAVID E. KELLEY PRODUCTIONS

c/o Twentieth Century Fox, 10201 W. Pico Blvd., Bldg. 80, Los Angeles, CA 90035-2651. (310) 369-4570. FAX: (310) 369-1000.
PRESIDENT
Jeffrey Kramer
WRITER/EXECUTIVE PRODUCER
David E. Kelley
Series: Ally McBeal, Chicago Hope, Picket Fences.

KINGWORLD PRODUCTIONS, INC.

1700 Broadway, 33rd floor, New York, NY 10010. (212) 315-4000. FAX: (212) 459-3738.
12400 Wilshire Blvd., Suite 1200, Los Angeles, CA 90025. (310) 826-1108. FAX: (310) 207-2179.
455 N. City Front Plaza Dr., Suite 2910, Chicago IL 60611. (312) 644-7500.
CHAIRMAN
Roger M. King
VICE CHAIRMAN & CEO
Michael G. King
PRESIDENT & COO
Julie Haimovitz
PRESIDENT, KING WORLD INTERNATIONAL
Fred Cohen
PRESIDENT, KING WORLD VENTURES
Michael Spiessbach
PRESIDENT, DOMESTIC TELEVISION SALES
J. Stuart Stringfellow
ACTING PRESIDENT, KING WORLD DIRECT
Jacob Weisbarth
EXECUTIVE V.P., PROGRAMMING & PRODUCTION
Andy Friendly
S.V.P., BUSINESS AFFAIRS & GENERAL COUNSEL
Jonathan Birkhahn
S.V.P., CORPORATE RESEARCH & SALES MARKETING
Moira Farrell

S.V.P., NETWORK PROGRAMMING
Merrill Karpf
S.V.P., STRATEGIC PLANNING & ACQUISITIONS
Robert King
S.V.P. & CFO
Steven A. Locascio
S.V.P., CORPORATE COMMUNICATIONS
Arthur R. Sando
S.V.P., ADVERTISING & PROMOTION
Donald Prijatel
V.P., CONTRACT ADMINSTRATION
Patsy Bundy
V.P., FINANCE & TREASURER
Leonard Spilka
V.P. & SECRETARY
Diana King
BRANCHES
EAST

1700 Broadway, 33rd floor, New York, NY 10019. (212) 315-4000. FAX: (212) 582-9255.
V.P., SALES
Fred Petrosino
V.P., EASTERN DIVISION MANAGER
Lee Leddy
ACCOUNT EXECUTIVE
Lee Villas
WEST

12400 Wilshire Blvd., Suite 1200, West Los Angeles, CA 90025. (310) 826-1108. FAX: (310) 207-2179.
S.V.P., SALES WEST
Randy Hanson
V.P., WESTERN SALES DIVISION MANAGER
Larry Hutchings
SOUTH

15303 Dallas Parkway, Suite 1280, Dallas, TX 75248. (214) 960-1996. FAX: (214) 934-0418.
V.P., SOUTHWEST DIVISION
Stephen N. Hackett
ACCOUNT EXECUTIVE
D. Kevin Frady, Jr.
MIDWEST

455 North City Front Plaza Dr., Suite 2910, Chicago, IL 60611. (312) 644-7500. FAX: (312) 644-7506.
V.P., CENTRAL DIVISION
Lee Kiersted
V.P., MIDWEST SALES
Mike Stornello
ACCOUNT EXECUTIVE
Christopher Rooke
SOUTHEAST

1 Boca Raton Pl., 2255 Glades Rd., Suite 212E, Boca Raton, FL 33431. (407) 998-3097. FAX: (407) 993-4312.
V.P., SOUTHEAST REGION
Jim Farah

Half Hour Strips: American Journal, C.O.W.Boys of MooMesa, Inside Edition, Jeopardy!, Wheel of Fortune, Wild West.

Movie Packages: Classic Detectives (34), Epics (5), Popcorn Theatre (15), Spotlight 10 (10).

Off-net: Branded, Guns of Will Sonnett, Topper.

One Hour Strips: The Oprah Winfrey Show, Rolonda.

THE KONIGSBERG COMPANY

7919 Sunset Blvd., 2nd flr., Los Angeles, CA 90046. (213) 845-1000. FAX: (213) 845-1020.
EXECUTIVE PRODUCER
Frank Konigsberg
Mini-series: Titanic (4 hrs.), Children of the Dust.

STEVE KRANTZ PRODUCTIONS

166 Groverton Pl., Los Angeles, CA 90077. (213) 549-6940. FAX: (213) 937-3161.
PRESIDENT
Steve Krantz
Animated Features: Fritz The Cat (75 minutes), Heavy Traffic (75 minutes).

SID & MARTY KROFFT PICTURES CORP.

419 N. Larchmont Blvd., Suite 11, Los Angeles, CA 90004. (213) 467-3125. FAX: (213) 932-6332.
PRESIDENT
Marty Krofft
EXECUTIVE VICE PRESIDENT
Sid Krofft

Series: Land of the Lost (69 episodes).

THE KUSHNER-LOCKE COMPANY

11601 Wilshire Blvd., Ste. 2030, Los Angeles, CA 90025. (310) 445-1111. FAX: (310) 445-1181.
CO-CHAIRMEN
Peter Locke
Donald Kushner
PRESIDENT & COO
Bruce Lilliston
PRESIDENT
Pascal Borno
PRESIDENT, TELEVISION
Marvinia Anderson
PRESIDENT, TELEVISION
Andrew Steinberg
S.V.P., FEATURES & BUSINESS AFFAIRS & FEATURES
Richard Marks
S.V.P., FEATURES
Phil Mittleman
V.P., MARKETING
Wendy Reeds
V.P., CONTRACTS & SALES ADMINISTRATION
D'Arcy Conrique
V.P., CASTING
Annette Benson
V.P., PRODUCTION FINANCE
Steve Rosen
V.P., POSTPRODUCTION
Bob Wenokur
V.P., THEATRICAL (U.K.)
Eleanor Powell
Series: Cracker.

1996-1997 TV Movies: Echo (ABC), Every Woman's Dream (CBS), Gun (CBS), Innocent Victims (ABC), Jack Reed: One of Our Own (NBC), Jack Reed 5 (NBC), Princess In Love (CBS), A Strange Affair (CBS).

Past Products: Brave Little Toaster (animated movie), Carolina Skeletons (NBC movie), Cops Are Robbers (NBC movie), Father & Son (NBC), Fire in the Dark (CBS), 1st & Ten (HBO), Getting Gotti (NBC movie), Harts of the West (CBS), Murder C.O.D. (NBC movie), Night Games (CBS), Sweating Bullets (CBS), Sweet Bird of Youth (NBC), To Save the Children (CBS), Your Mother Wears Combat Boots (NBC).

THE LANDSBURG COMPANY, INC.

11811 W. Olympic Blvd., Los Angeles, CA 90064. (310) 478-7878. FAX: (310) 477-7166, (310) 473-6776.
email: tlcpix@aol.com
CHAIRMAN
Alan Landsburg
PRESIDENT
Howard Lipstone
V.P., DEVELOPMENT
Linda Otto
MANAGER, DEVELOPMENT
Gloria Morris
MANAGER, BUSINESS AFFAIRS
Diane Skwarek
V.P., ADMINISTRATION
Virginia Levy

TV Movies: Adam: His Song Continues, Country Justice, In Defense Of A Married Man, The Diamond Fleece, The George McKenna Story, If Someone Had Known, Long Gone, A Mother's Right, The Elizabeth Morgan Story, Nightmare In Columbia County, The Parent Trap II, Quiet Victory: The Charlie Wedemeyer Story, The Ryan White Story, A Stoning In Fulham County, Strange Voices, Terror In The Night, Too Young The Hero, Triumph Of The Heart: The Ricky Bell Story, Unspeakable Acts, The Lottery.

Series: High Risk.

Specials: Destined To Live, Maggie's Secret, A Place At The Table, To Protect The Children, The Secret Of..., Wanted: A Room With Love.

LANGLEY PRODUCTIONS, BARBOUR/LANGLEY PRODUCTIONS

2225 Colorado Ave., Santa Monica, CA 90404. (310) 449-5300. FAX: (310) 449-5330.
URL: http://www.tvcops.com
EXECUTIVE PRODUCER
John Langley
EXECUTIVE ASSISTANT
Elena Lobito
Series: Code 3, Cops, Cop Files.

LEACH ENTERTAINMENT ENTERPRISES

c/o 885 Second Ave., 25th Floor, New York, NY 10017. (212) 759-8787. FAX: (212) 838-4364.
EXECUTIVE PRODUCER
Robin Leach
PRODUCERS
Rob Hess
Nick La Penna

Series: Gourmet Getaways, Heroes America, Lifestyles of the Rich & Famous (synd.), Miracles and Wonders, Runaway With the Rich and Famous (synd.), Travel Secrets, World Class Cuisine.

HERBERT B. LEONARD PRODUCTIONS

2240 Manzanita Lane, Reno, NV 89509-7004. (702) 829-0192. FAX: (702) 829-7099.
PRESIDENT
Herbert B. Leonard
SECRETARY
James P. Tierney

Series: Naked City (138 x 30 mins.), Rin Tin Tin (164 x 30 mins.), Route 66 (116 x 30 mins.).
Features: Going Home, Rin Tin Tin—The Movie, Route 66 (remake).

LEVINSON ENTERTAINMENT VENTURES INTER-NATIONAL, INC.

1440 Veteran Ave., Suite 650, Los Angeles, CA 90024. (323) 663-6940. FAX: (323) 663-2820.
PRESIDENT
Robert S. Levinson
VICE PRESIDENT
Sandra S. Levinson
DIRECTOR OF DEVELOPMENT
Jed Leland, Jr.

Products: The Hollywood Press Club Awards, A Tribute To The Institute Of The American Musical, The Aggie Gold Seminars.

LIBERTY INTERNATIONAL ENTERTAINMENT INC.

1990 Westwood Blvd., Penthouse, Los Angeles, CA 90025. (310) 479-6755. FAX: (310) 474-7455.
CHAIRMAN
Irv Holender
PRESIDENT
Randy Naft
VICE PRESIDENT
Sy Samuels

Animated Series: The New Three Stooges (52 x 30 min.).
Series: The Achievers (13 x 30 min.), The Magic & Beyond (26 x 30 min.), Phenomenon Archives (13 x 60 min.), Religions of the World (13 x 60 min.).
Movie Madness I & II, over 50 motion pictures and MOW's.

LONGBOW PRODUCTIONS

4181 Sunswept Dr., Suite 100, Studio City, CA 91604-2335. (818) 762-6600.
CHAIRMAN
Richard Kughn
PRESIDENTS
Ronnie D. Clemmer
Bill Pace
V.P., DEVELOPMENT
Sharon Cicero

TV Movies: Dream Of Murder, Journey Of Heart.

MADISON SQUARE GARDEN NETWORK

4 Penn Plaza, 4th Fl., New York, NY 10001. (212) 465-5926. FAX: (212) 465-6024. URL: http://www.msgnetwork.com
PRESIDENT & CEO
David W. Checketts
EXECUTIVE PRESIDENT
Joseph M. Cohen
S.V.P. PRODUCTION & EXECUTIVE PRODUCER
Mike McCarthy
V.P. MARKETING
Greg Brodsky

Live Events: College football and basketball, pro boxing, track and field, tennis, Metro Stars soccer, New York Knickerbockers & New York Liberty basketball, New York Rangers hockey, New York Yankees baseball, New York Cityhawks Arena football.

JEFF MARGOLIS PRODUCTIONS

1401 Westwood Blvd., 3rd floor, Los Angeles, CA 90024. (310) 235-1030. FAX: (310) 235-1032.
Productions: The Miss America Pageant (ABC), A Gala For the President at Ford's Theater (ABC), Ebony's 50th Anniversary (ABC), Country Fest '96 (CBS), Quincy Jones' 50th Anniversary (ABC).

MEDALLION TV ENTERPRISES, INC.

8831 Sunset Blvd., W. Hollywood, CA 90069. (310) 652-8100. FAX: (310) 659-8512.
PRODUCTION
Lise H. Ettlinger
FINANCE
Linda L. Brooks

METRO-GOLDWYN-MAYER STUDIOS, INC.

2500 Broadway St., Santa Monica, CA 90404-3061. (310) 449-3000. FAX: (310) 449-3100.
1350 Avenue of the Americas, New York, NY 10019-4870. (212) 708-0300. FAX: (212) 708-0337.
CHAIRMAN OF THE BOARD & CEO, MGM STUDIOS INC.
Frank Mancuso
VICE CHAIRMAN, MGM STUDIOS, INC.
A. Robert Pisano
SENIOR EXECUTIVE V.P. & CFO, MGM STUDIOS, INC.
Daniel Taylor
SENIOR EXECUTIVE V.P., MGM STUDIOS, INC.
William A. Jones
PRESIDENT, MGM WORLDWIDE TELEVISION GROUP
John P. Symes
PRESIDENT, MGM DOMESTIC TELEVISION DISTRIBUTION, MGM WORLDWIDE TELEVISION GROUP
Sid Cohen
PRESIDENT, INT'L TELEVISION DISTRIBUTION & MGM NETWORKS, MGM WORLDWIDE TELEVISION GROUP
James Griffiths
PRESIDENT, MGM HOME ENTERTAINMENT & CONSUMER PRODUCTS GROUP
Richard Cohen
PRESIDENT, MGM HOME ENTERTAINMENT
David Bishop
PRESIDENT, WORLDWIDE THEATRICAL DISTRIBUTION, MGM DISTRIBUTION CO.
Larry Gleason
PRESIDENT, WORLDWIDE MARKETING, MGM DISTRIBUTION CO.
Gerry Rich
EXECUTIVE V.P., MGM MUSIC
Michael Sandoval
EXECUTIVE V.P., CONSUMER PRODUCTS
Linda Berman
EXECUTIVE V.P., FINANCE & CORPORATE DEVELOPMENT
Charles E. Cohen
SENIOR V.P., WORLDWIDE MKT'G., MGM HOME ENT.
Blake Thomas
SENIOR V.P., LABOR RELATIONS
Mark Crowley
SENIOR V.P., WORLDWIDE PUBLICITY, MGM DISTRIBUTION
Amanda Marashinsky
EXECUTIVE V.P., ADMINISTRATION
Richard Parness
SENIOR V.P. & DEPUTY GENERAL COUNSEL
Mark Fleischer
SENIOR V.P. & DEPUTY GENERAL COUNSEL
Robert Brada
SENIOR V.P. & DEPUTY GENERAL COUNSEL
Rebecca Laurie Ford
SENIOR V.P., CORPORATE COMMUNICATIONS & INVESTOR RELATIONS
Craig Parsons
EXECUTIVE V.P., STUDIO FINANCE & OPERATIONS
Daniel J. Rosett
V.P., INFORMATION SERVICES
Kim Spenchian
S.V.P. & ASSISTANT SECRETARY
Maria Angeletti
V.P., TAXES
Deborah J. Arvesen

MGM WORLDWIDE TELEVISION GROUP INC.

2500 Broadway St., Santa Monica, CA 90404-3061. (310) 449-3000.
PRESIDENT, MGM WORLDWIDE TELEVISION GROUP
John P. Symes
PRESIDENT, INTERNATIONAL TELEVISION DISTRIBUTION & MGM NETWORKS
James Griffiths
SENIOR V.P., MGM ANIMATION
Jay Fukuto
SENIOR V.P., BUSINESS AFFAIRS, MGM WORLDWIDE TELEVISION GROUP
Albert Spevak
EXECUTIVE V.P., CREATIVE AFFAIRS
Hank Cohen
EXECUTIVE V.P., TELEVISION FINANCE & ADMINISTRATION
Thomas Malanga
EXECUTIVE V.P., PRODUCTION
Mel Swope

V.P., TELEVISION SALES, CANADA
Tony Leadman
SENIOR V.P., BUSINESS DEVELOPMENT
John Pike
SENIOR V.P., MARKETING, MGM WORLDWIDE TELEVISION GROUP
Dea Shandera

MGM DOMESTIC TELEVISION DISTRIBUTION
1200 North Federal Highway, Suite 200, Boca Raton, FL 33432. (561) 391-1655. FAX: (561) 391-7173.

6133 North River Rd., Suite 320, Rosemont, IL 60018. (847) 518-0500. FAX: (847) 518-0013.

2500 Broadway St., Santa Monica, CA 90404-3061. Domestic TV: (310) 449-3000. Int'l TV: (310) 449-3767.

1350 Ave. of the Americas, New York, NY. (212) 708-0300
PRESIDENT, MGM DOMESTIC TELEVISION DISTRIBUTION
Sid Cohen
EXECUTIVE V.P. & GENERAL SALES MANAGER, MGM DOMESTIC TELEVISION DISTRIBUTION
Noranne Frisby
V.P., SOUTHEAST DIVISION, MGM DOMESTIC TV DIST.
Phil Smith
SENIOR V.P., EASTERN REGIONAL MANAGER, MGM DOMESTIC TELEVISION
Jacqueline E. Comeau
SENIOR V.P., CENTRAL REGIONAL MANAGER, DOMESTIC TELEVISION DISTRIBUTION
Steven Hodder
V.P., WESTERN REGIONAL MANAGER, DOMESTIC TELEVISION DISTRIBUTION
Donald Golden
V.P., SOUTHWESTERN DIVISION MANAGER, DOMESTIC TELEVISION DISTRIBUTION
Frank Hussey
V.P.'S, EASTERN DIVISION, DOMESTIC TV DISTRIBUTION
Glen P. Hagen
Lyle Foster
S.V.P., ADVERTISER SALES, MGM DOMESTIC TV DIST.
Michael Daraio

INTERNATIONAL OFFICES

AUSTRALIA
MGM International TV–United Artists (Australia) Pty. Ltd., Level 19, AGL Centre, 111 Pacific Highway, North Sydney, NSW 2060. (612) 9966 1711. FAX: (612) 9966 1969.
Mailing address: P.O. Box 6125, Shopping World, North Sydney, NSW 2060.

FRANCE
MGM International Distrbution France, SARL, 25 rue de Marignan, Paris 75008. Fax: (331) 5383 9740. Free TV FAX: (331) 4562 6204. Pay TV Fax: (331) 5383 9750.

INTERNATIONAL PRODUCT
One-hr. Series: Against The Law (17), The Aquanauts (32), The Bradshaw Difference (195), Cutter To Houston (9), Dark Shadows (11 & 2 hr. pilot), The Dirty Dozen (11 & 2 hr. pilot), Dream Street (5 & 90 min. pilot), East Side/West Side (24), Fame (135), For Love and Honor (11 & 2hr. pilot), Freshman Dorm (5), In The Heat Of The Night (137 & 8 2 hr. & 2 hr. pilot), Jack and Mike (17 & 90 min. pilot), Knightwatch (9), Lady Blue (13 & 2 hr. pilot), Nightmare Cafe (6), The Outer Limits–New (47), The Outer Limits–Original (49), Paper Dolls (12 & 2 hr. pilot), Poltergeist: The Legacy (44), Seven Brides...Seven Brothers (21 & 90 min. pilot), Stoney Burke (32), thirtysomething (85), The Young Riders (68).
Half-hr. Series: Adventures At Scott Island (26), All Dogs Go To Heaven (13), Baby Boom (13), Bat Masterson (108), Bold Venture (39), Boson Blackie (58), Case Of The Dangerous Robin (38), Cesar's World (39), Circus Parade (26), Dial 999 (39), Doctor Christian (39), The Edge (3), The Everglades (38), Favorite Story (78), Group One Medical (130), Harbor Command (39), Hello Kitty: Furry Tale Theatre (13), Hey, Landlord (31), Highway Patrol (156), Hollywood & The Stars (31), Home Run Derby (26), Hudson's Bay (39), I Led Three Lives (117), It's About Time (26), James Bond, Jr. (65), Karen's Song (13), Keyhole (38), Kids, Inc. (149), King Of Diamonds (38), LAPD (365), Lee Marvin Presents Lawbreaker (32), Lock-Up 1 (78), Love Me, Love Me Not (130), Mackenzie's Raiders (39), Man And The Challenge (36), The Man Called X (39), Men Into Space (38), Men Of Annapolis (39), Mona McClusky (26), Mr. District Attorney (78), My Mother, The Car (30), The New Adventures of Martin Kane (39), The New Phil Silvers Show (30), The New Pink Panter Show (60), The Patty Duke Show (104), Pink Panther & Sons (13), Rat Patrol (58), Ripcord (76), Rough Riders (39),

Science Ficion Theatre (78), Sea Hunt (155), Sea Hunt–1987 (22), The Story Of... (38), Straight To The Heart (50), Super President (15), The Super Six (20), Target (38), This Man Dawson (39), Tombstone Territory (91), The Twilight Zone (94), The Unexpected (39), We Got It Made (24).
TV Movies: Broken Angel, Convict Cowboy, Cry For The Strangers, The Defiant Ones, The Dirty Dozen: Deadly Mission, The Dirty Dozen: Fatal Mission, The Escape, Escape Clause, Extreme Close-Up, Fatal Memories, Finding The Way Home, Have You Seen My Son?, Hot Paint, I Take These Men, I Want To Live, If It's Tuesday It Still..., In The Arms Of A Killer, Inherit The Wind, Johnny Ryan, The King Of Love, Lady Against The Odds, The Limbic Region, The Man Who Fell To Earth, Marian Rose White, Marshal Law, Mercy Or Murder?, Miss America: Behind The Crown, Moving Target, My Father My Son, Police Story: The Freeway Killings, Prime Target, Red River, Separate Tables, She Knows Too Much, The Silver Strand, Sketch Artists II: Hands That See, The Tenth Man, Those Secrets, Trenchcoat In Paradise, Witness For The Prosecution, Women Of San Quentin.
Miniseries: George Washington I (8 hrs.), George Washington II (4 hrs.), Studs Lonigan (6 hrs.).
Specials: Happy Anniversary 007 (60 mins.), A Funny Thing Happened... (90 mins.), The Insider (60 mins.), Iron Men (60 mins.), James Cagney: Yankee Doodle (75 mins.), James Stewart: Wonderful Life (98 mins.), The Joy Of Socks (104 mins.), The Kids From Fame (60 mins.), The Making Of A President–1964 (90 mins.), Minnelli On Minnelli (70 mins.), The Olympinks (30 mins.), Pink At First Sight (30 mins.), A Pink Christmas (30 mins.), Reckless Valor (2 rs.), Shari Lewis: Have I Got A Story For You (60 mins.), Shari Lewis: Kooky Classics (54 mins.), Shari Lewis: You Can Do It (60 mins.), That's Panthertainment (60 mins.), A Thousand Days (90 mins.), 7 Days...Life Of The President (90 mins.).

MG/PERIN
21 E. 40 St., New York, NY 10016. (212) 447-5600. FAX: (212) 447-9320. email: MGPERIN@worldnet.att.net
Specials: Mi Gente–My People
Series: Homer's Workshop, America' s Black Forum

MILLER/BOYETT PRODUCTIONS
c/o Warner Bros., 4000 Warner Blvd., Bldg. #1, Burbank, CA 90048. (818) 954-7700. FAX: (818) 954-7712.
Series: Angie, Bosom Buddies, The Family Man, Family Matters, Full House, Getting By On Our Own, Going Places, Goodtime Girls, Happy Days, The Hogan Family, Joanie Loves Chachi, Laverne & Shirley, Perfect Strangers, Petrocelli, Step by Step.

MOFFITT-LEE PRODUCTIONS
c/o Sunset-Gower Studios, 1438 N. Gower St., Suite 250, Hollywood, CA 90028. (213) 463-6646. FAX: (213) 467-2946.
CO-OWNERS/EXECUTIVE PRODUCERS/DIRECTORS
John Moffitt
Pat Tourk Lee
SUPERVISING PRODUCER
Nancy Kurshner
New Products: Thirty Seconds Over Washington (HBO), Not Neccessarily The Election (HBO).

KATHY MORGAN INTERNATIONAL
12262 Sky Lane, Los Angeles, CA 90049. (310) 440-1019. FAX: (310) 472-8530. email: kmisky@aol.com
URL: http://kmi@primenet.com
PRESIDENT & CEO
Kathy Morgan
DIRECTOR, MARKETING & PUBLICITY
Lori Yeakel
DIRECTOR, SALES & ACQUISITIONS
Matt McCombs

MOTION PICTURE CORPORATION OF AMERICA (A METROMEDIA ENTERTAINMENT GROUP CO.)
1401 Ocean Ave., #301, Santa Monica, CA 90401. (310) 319-9500. FAX: (310) 319-9501.
CO-PRESIDENT & TREASURER
Brad Krevoy
CO-PRESIDENT & TREASURER
Steven B. Stabler
EXECUTIVE V.P.
Jeffrey Ivers
SENIOR V.P. & ASSISTANT SECRETARY
John W. Hester
EXECUTIVE V.P., TELEVISION
Paul Frank

MP CONSULTING INTERNATIONAL, INC.
947 Second Ave., Suite #2, New York, NY 10022. (212) 223-4112. FAX: (212) 421-9187. email: mpinyc@aol.com
PRESIDENT
Alex Massis
V.P., SALES & ACQUISITIONS
Christopher White
Series: Salty the Lion (20 x 25 mins.), Super Kid (52 x 25 mins.).
Features: Au Pair, Bang the Drum Slowly, Closer and Closer Apart, The Comedian, Days of Wine and Roses, Dear Darwin, Facing the Forest, Gimlet, Hungry Heart, Jigsaw, A Kink in the Picasso, The Lady From the Movie, Liquid Sky, Marty, No Time For Sergeants, O'Hara's Wife, Patterns, Premeditated Murder, Provocateur, Puppet On a Chain, Radio Moscow, Requiem For a Heavyweight, Return From the River Kwai, Running, The Still Point, Scent of Gardenia, Shampoo Horns, St. Helens, A Sting In the Tale, Triangle of Death, Women, A Wind From the South, Super Kid, Salty the Sea Lion.

MTG MEDIA PROPERTIES, LTD.
805 Third Ave., 8th floor New York, NY 10022. (212) 755-4742. FAX: (212) 755-4628.
PRESIDENT
Joseph E. Kovacs
VICE PRESIDENT
Steven Nurkin
DIRECTOR, INTERNATIONAL SALES
Almira R. Malyshev
DIRECTOR, OPERATIONS
Donna Tracey
Over 450 theatrical motion pictures, including Dirty Dancing, Dune, The Dead Zone, Earth Girls Are Easy, 8 Million Ways to Die, Return of the Secaucus Seven, Steel Dawn, etc.
Made for TV movies including Disaster in Time, Double Jeopardy, Fourth Story, O'Hara's Wife, Past Tense, St. Helen's, Taking the Heat, etc.

MTM ENTERTAINMENT, INC.
12700 Ventura Blvd., Suite 200, Studio City CA 91604. (818) 755-2400. FAX: (818) 755-2448.
CEO
Anthony Thomopoulos
PRESIDENT, WORLDWIDE DISTRIBUTION
Charles Larsen
PRESIDENT, MTM TV
Michael Ogiens
Syndication: America's Funniest Home Videos, Dr. Quinn–Medicine Woman, Rescue 911.

MTV
(For a complete listing see Cable Networks.)
1515 Broadway, New York, NY 10036. (212) 258-8000. FAX: (818) 505-7800.
CHAIRMAN & CEO, MTV NETWORKS
Thomas E. Freston
PRESIDENT, MTV NETWORK
Judy McGrath
Series: Beavis and Butt Head, Daria, The Grind, House of Style, Jenny McCarthy Show, MTV Beach House, MTV Oddities, MTV Unplugged, Oddville MTV, The Real World, Road Rules, Sandblast, Singled Out, Yo! MTV Raps.
Specials: Freaks Nerds and Weirdos, MTV Music Video Awards, Movie Awards, NBA's Slam N' Jam, Rock n' Jock.

MULLER MEDIA
11 E. 47th St., 3rd Flr., New York, NY 10017. (212) 317-0175. FAX: (212) 317-0102. email: mullermedia@juno.com
PRESIDENT
Robert Muller
EXECUTIVE V.P.
Dan Mulholland
CLIENT SERVICES
Dolly Cirona
REGIONAL MARKETING DIRECTOR
Greg Muller
Series: Scratch (65 x 30 mins.).
Feature Packages: Classic Gold (12), Godzilla All-Stars (12), Night Raiders I (15), Night Raiders II (12), Prime Targets (17), Prime Targets II (15), Prime Targets III (15), Prime Target IV, (18), Smoke Screens (10), Smoke Screen II (12), This Day in History (365), Wild Ones (10), Weapons (6).

MULTIMEDIA ENTERTAINMENT
45 Rockefeller Plaza, 35th Floor, New York, NY 10111. (212) 391-1111. FAX: (212) 332-2010.
Multimedia Television Production, 8439 Sunset Blvd., Suite 200, Los Angeles, CA 90069. (213) 656-9756. FAX: (213) 656-1693.
PRESIDENT
Robert L. Turner
S.V.P. & DIRECTOR, STATION SALES
Thomas F. Shannon

EXECUTIVE VICE PRESIDENT
Richard C. Coveny
V.P., BUSINESS AFFAIRS & GENERAL COUNSEL
Elizabeth Allen
S.V.P., INTERNATIONAL SALES
John Ranck
S.V.P., PROGRAMMING
Richard C. Thrall, Jr.
Series: Donahue, Rush Limbaugh, Jerry Springer, Sally Jessy Raphael, Susan Powter, Dennis Prager, Inside the Vatican with Sir Peter Ustinov, Mysteries of the Ancient World.
Specials: Children's Plus Network (67 x 30 mins.).

NBC ENTERPRISES
(For a complete listing of officers, see NBC under Networks.)
3500 Olive Drive, 15th floor, Burbank, CA 91505. (818) 526-6903. FAX: (818) 526-6921.
EXECUTIVE V.P., NBC ENTERPRISES
Jerry Petry
V.P., FINANCE & NBC STUDIOS PRODUCTION
Jerry Dicanio
V.P., POSTPRODUCTION
Joe Dervin
V.P.'S, PRODUCTION
James McGee
Nora Reynolds
V.P., INTERNATIONAL SALES & DEVELOPMENT
Sergio Getzel
V.P., BUSINESS AFFAIRS
Rhonda Troutman
Hour Series: Amazing Grace (5 x 50 mins.), Father Murphy (35 x 60 mins.), I Witness Video (54 x 60 mins.), Late Night With Conan O'Brien, Later With Bob Costas, Later With Greg Kinnear, Mancuso FBI (20 x 60 mins.), Profiler (22+ x 60 mins.), Secret Service (22 x 60 mins.), Shannon's Deal (16 x 60 mins.), Supertrain (10 x 30 mins.), The Tonight Show With Jay Leno, True Blue (13 x 60 mins.).
Half Hour Series: A Family For Joe (13 x 30 mins.), Generations (470 x 30 mins.), Here & Now (13 x 30 mins.), Hot Pursuit (13 x 30 mins.), Man Of The People (12 x 30 mins.), Mr. Rhodes (18 x 30 mins.), Out All Night (20 x 30 mins.), Sara (8 x 30 mins.), Saved By The Bell: College Years (19 x 30 mins.).
Childrens' Series: Brains & Brawn (15 x 30 mins.), California Dreams (78 x 30 mins.), Go Show (28 x 30 mins.), Gravedale High (13 x 30 mins.), The Guys Next Door (14 half rs.), Hang Time (26 x 30 mins.), Kissyfur (26 x 30 mins.), Name Your Adventure (40 x 30 mins.), Punky Animated (21 x 30 mins.), Punky Brewster (88 x 30 mins.), Running The Halls (13 x 30 mins.), Saved By The Bell (86 x 30 mins.), Saved By The Bell: The New Class (91 x 30 mins.), USA High (30+ x 30 mins.).
Movies Of The Week: A Burning Passion: The Margaret Mitchell Story, The Abduction of Kari Swenson, Assault & Matrimony, Awake To Danger, Bermuda Grace, Blue Deville, Bonanza: The Return, Bonanza: Under Attack, Born Into Exile, CAT Squad I: Stalking Danger, CAT Squad II: Python Wolf, Chameleons, Childsaver, Convicted: A Mother's Story, Christmas Eve, Class Reunion, Danger Island, Double Deception, An Early Frost, Express To Terror, Fall From Grace, A Family For Joe, Father's Homecoming, Fight For Justice, Flying Blind, Follow Your Heart, Friends 'Til the End, The Gifted One, The Good Family, Her Hidden Truth, Her Last Chance, Hot Pursuit, How I Spent My Summer, Hurricane Andrew, I'll Be Home For Christmas, In The Best Interest Of The Children, In the Shadow Of A Killer, The Keys To The Kingdom, Killing Mr. Griffin, The Last Flight Out, The Last Ride Of The Dalton Gang, The Little Match Girl, Loneliest Runner, Love On The Run, Marked For Murder, Mothers, Daughter & Lovers, Mrs. R.'s Daughter, Murder In High Places, Murder Live!, Night Visitors, One Special Victory, One Woman's Courage, Perfect Body, Poison Ivy, Roe vs. Wade, Roseanne & Tom: A Hollywood Marriage, Saved By The Bell: Hawaiian Syle, Saved By The Bell: A Wedding In Vegas, The Secret of Lake Success, The Secret She Carried, Shadow Of A Stranger, Shannon's Deal I, Shannon's Deal II, She Fought Alone, Sleeping With The Devil, The Story Lady, Sweet Dreams, Take My Daughters–Please, Those She Left Behind, Thrill, A Time To Heal, Tonya & Nancy: The Inside Story, True Blue, Turn Back The Clock, Wait Till Your Mother Gets Home, While Justice Sleeps, Winnie.
Danielle Steel Movies: Changes (2 hrs.), Daddy (2 hrs.), Family Album (4 hrs.), Fine Things (3 hrs.), Full Circle (2 hrs.), Heartbeat (2 hrs.), Kaleidoscope (2 hrs.), Message From Nam (4 hrs.), Mixed Blessings (2 hrs.), Once In A Lifetime (2 hrs.), Palomino (2 hrs.), Perfect Stranger (2hrs.), Remembrance (2 hrs.), The Ring (4 hrs.), Secrets (2 hrs.), Star (2 hrs.), Vanished (2 hrs.), Zoya (4 hrs.).
Mini-Series: Asteroid (4 hrs.), Blind Faith (4 hrs.), The Brotherhood Of The Rose (4 hrs.), Celebrity (6 hrs.), Cruel Doubt (4 hrs.), Devil's Cargo (4 hrs.), Fatal Vision (4 hrs.), The Favorite Son (6 hrs.), Lucky/Chances (6 hrs.), Pandora's Clock (4 hrs.), Princess Daisy (4 hrs.), Sidney Sheldon's Rage Of Angels I (4 hrs.), Sidney Sheldon's Rage Of Angels II (4 hrs.), Remember (4 hrs.), The Secret Of Lake Success (6 hrs.), Seduced By Madness (4 hrs.), Tradewinds (6 hrs.), A Woman On The Run (4 hrs.).
Specials: Abbot & Costello (1 hr.), Bonanza: A Retrospective (1 hr.), Life In The Fast Lane II (1 hr.), The Martin Short Show (9 1hrs.), Show Formally Known as the Martin Short Show (90 mins.), Too Good To Be True (2 hrs.), Toscanini: The Television Concerts (10 x 60 mins.).

NBC NEWS VIDEO ARCHIVES

30 Rockefeller Plaza, 2nd Flr., New York, NY 10112. (212) 664-3797. FAX: (212) 957-8917.
Complete archives of NBC News.

NBC STUDIOS

(For a complete listing, see Broadcast Networks.)
3000 W. Alameda Ave., Suite 124, Burbank, CA 91523. (818) 840-7500.
Series: Homicide: Life on the Street, In the House, Late Night with Conan O'Brien, The Pretender, Profiler, The Tonight Show with Jay Leno, The Tony Danza Show, Working.

NELVANA COMMUNICATIONS, INC.

4500 Wilshire Blvd., Los Angeles, CA 90010. (213) 549-4222. FAX: (213) 549-4232.
c/o 32 Atlantic Ave., Toronto, Ontario, Canada M6K 1X8. (416) 588-5571. FAX: (416) 588-5588.
CO-CHIEF EXECUTIVE OFFICERS
Patrick Loubert
Michael Hirsh
EXECUTIVE V.P.
Clive Smith
PRESIDENT
Toper Taylor
Animated Series: Franklin, Sam & Max, Pippi Longstocking, Ned's Newt, Little Bear, Blazing Dragons, Donkey Kong Country, Rupert, Scholastic's The Magic School Bus.
Animated Features: Babar—The Movie, Pippi Longstocking, The Care Bears Adventure in Wonderland.

NEW LINE TELEVISION

888 Seventh Ave., New York, NY 10106. (212) 649-4900. FAX: (212) 956-1941
PRESIDENT, NEW LINE TELEVISION
Robert Friedman
EXECUTIVE V.P., DOMESTIC TELEVISION DISTRIBUTION
David Spiegelman
EXECUTIVE V.P., INTERNATIONAL TELEVISION
Diane Keating
EXEC. V.P., FRANCHISE PROGRAMMING & MARKETING
Christopher Russo
EXEC. V.P., LICENSING & MERCHANDISING
David Imhoff
SENIOR V.P., SALES ADMINISTRATION
Vicky Gregorian
V.P., TELEVISION & ANCILLARY ACCOUNTING
Frank Buquicchio
S.V.P.'S, PRODUCTION & DEVELOPMENT
Laura Armstrong
Tom Campbell
V.P., PRODUCTION & DEVELOPMENT
Pat Moran

NEWSTAR MEDIA, INC.

8955 Beverly Blvd., Los Angeles, CA 90048. (310) 786-1600. FAX: (310) 246-6544.
PRESIDENT & CEO
Ron Lightstone
CFO
Neil Topham
V.P., SALES & ACQUISITIONS
Gene George
PRESIDENT, NEWSTAR TELEVISION
Ron Ziskin
V.P., DEVELOPMENT
Dave Collins

NICKELODEON/NICK AT NITE

(For complete listing, please see Cable Networks.)
1515 Broadway, New York, NY 10036. (212) 258-7500.
Nickelodeon: AAAHH!! Real Monsters, The Adventures of Pete & Pete, The Adventures of Tin Tin, All That, The Alvin Show, Alvin & the Chipmunks, Allegra's Window, Are You Afraid of the Dark?, Beetlejuice, Bullwinkle's Moose-a-Rama, Cable in the Classroom, Clarissa Explains It All, Doug, Eureeka's Castle, Flipper, Gullah Gullah Island, Gumby, Hey Dude, Lassie, Launch Box, Legends of the Hidden Temple, Looney Tunes, Jim Henson's Muppet Babies, Mr. Wizard's World, The Muppet Show, My Brother & Me, Nick Arcade, Nick News, Nickelodeon Guts U to U, Nickelodeon Special Edition, Nickelodeon Weinerville, Nickelodeon Wild Side Show, Ren & Stimpy Show, Rocko's Modern Life, Roundhouse, Rugrats, Salute Your Shorts, The Secret World of Alex Mack, Welcome Freshmen, What Would You Do?, Wild & Crazy Kids, The World of David the Gnome.
Nick at Nite: The Adventures of Superman, Bewitched, The Bob Newhart Show, The Dick Van Dyke Show, Dragnet, F Troop, Get Smart, I Dream of Jeannie, I Love Lucy, The Lucy & Desi Comedy Hour, The Lucy Show, The Mary Tyler Moore Show, Mork & Mindy, The Munsters, Taxi, Welcome Back Kotter, The White Shadow.

FIMA NOVECK PRODUCTIONS

161 E. 61 St., New York, NY 10021. (212) 751-2329.
432 N. Palm Dr., Beverly Hills, CA 90210. (310) 273-1933. FAX: (310) 273-1933.
PRESIDENT
Fima Noveck
Productions: Disappearance, Fellons, Blood Feud, The Inheritance, Joshua Tree, Love and Anarchy, Men of War, No Way Out, Rasputin, Save Me, Swept Away ..., Trouble With Spies, Utamaro's World, Viper.

O'HARA-HOROWITZ PRODUCTIONS

16633 Ventura Blvd., Suite 1330, Encino, CA 91436-1840. (818) 986-7150. FAX: (818) 986-8226.
EXECUTIVE PRODUCERS
Michael O'Hara
Lawrence Horowitz
DIRECTOR OF DEVELOPMENT
Robert Shaw
DEVELOPMENT COORDINATOR
Dara Collins
TV Movies: A Child's Wish, Crimes of Passion Series, Moment of Truth Series.

PACIFIC INTERNATIONAL ENTERPRISES, INC.

1133 S. Riverside Ave., Suite #1, P.O. Box 1727, Medford, OR 97501. (541) 779-0990. FAX: (541) 779-8880. email: pie@wave.net.
PRESIDENT & PRODUCER
Arthur R. Dubs
V.P. SALES & ACQUISITIONS
Arn S. Wihtol
SECRETARY & TREASURER
Barbara J. Brown
Features: Across the Great Divide, The Adventures of the Wilderness Family, American Wilderness, Aravaipa Desert Bighorn, Blue Fin, Challenge To Be Free, Cold River, The Dream Chasers, The Fourth Wish, Great Adventure, Land of Kilimanjaro, Mountain Family Robinson, Mystery Mansion, Sacred Ground, Vanishing Wilderness, Wilderness Family Part 2, Windwalker, Wonder of It All, Young and Free.

PAPAZIAN-HIRSCH ENTERTAINMENT, INC.

2401 Colorado Ave., Suite 200, Santa Monica, CA 90404. (310) 471-2332. FAX: (310) 471-3352.
EXECUTIVE PRODUCERS
Robert Papazian
Jim Hirsch
Series: Nash Bridges (CBS), The Burning Zone (UPN).
TV Movies: Dead Man's Island (CBS), Hart to Hart (NBC, 5 x 2 hr. features), The Invaders (Fox, 4 hr. miniseries).

PARAMOUNT TELEVISION GROUP

(A division of Paramount Pictures.)
5555 Melrose Ave., Hollywood, CA 90038-3197. (213) 956-5000.
CHAIRMAN, PARAMOUNT TELEVISION GROUP
Kerry Mc Cluggage
PRESIDENT, NETWORK TV
Garry Hart
CO-PRESIDENTS, DOMESTIC TELEVISION
Frank Kelly
Meryl Cohen
EXECUTIVE V.P., BUSINESS AFFAIRS/FINANCE, DOMESTIC TELEVISION
Robert Sheehan
EXECUTIVE V.P., BUSINESS AFFAIRS
Jake Jacobson
EXECUTIVE V.P., CURRENT PROGRAMMING & STRATEGIC PLANNING
Tom Mazza
EXECUTIVE V.P., TELEVISION GROUP
Richard Lindheim
EXECUTIVE V.P. & CHIEF ADMINISTRATIVE OFFICER, TELEVISION GROUP
Steve Goldman
EXECUTIVE V.P., MARKETING, NETWORK PROGRAMMING & MEDIA RELATIONS
John A. Wentworth
SENIOR V.P., PROGRAMMING, DOMESTIC TELEVISION
Larry Forsdick
S.V.P., PROGRAMMING (EAST), DOMESTIC TELEVISION
Bobbee Gabelmann
S.V.P., GROUP OPERATIONS, DOMESTIC TELEVISION
Phillip Murphy
SENIOR V.P., RESEARCH, DOMESTIC TELEVISION
Mike Mellon

S.V.P., BUSINESS & LEGAL AFFAIRS, DOMESTIC TV
Bruce Pottash
SENIOR V.P., COMEDY DEVELOPMENT
Dan Fauci
SENIOR V.P., DRAMA DEVELOPMENT
Kathy Lingg
SENIOR V.P., LEGAL-NETWORK TV
Milinda McNeely
SENIOR V.P., TALENT & CASTING
Helen Mossler
S.V.P., PRODUCTION
Reid Shane
V.P., PROGRAMMING, DOMESTIC TELEVISION
Dawn Abel
V.P., DEVELOPMENT, DOMESTIC TELEVISION
Clancy Collins
V.P., ADVERTISING & PROMOTION, DOMESTIC TELEVISION
Lynn Davis
V.P., BUSINESS AFFAIRS ADMINISTRATION, DOMESTIC TV
Lynn Fero
V.P., CABLE SALES, DOMESTIC TELEVISION
Robert Friedman
V.P., BUSINESS AFFAIRS, DOMESTIC TELEVISION
Peter Kane
V.P., FINANCE, DOMESTIC TELEVISION
Karen Kanemoto
V.P., EASTERN REGIONAL SALES MANAGER, DOMESTIC
TELEVISION
Scott Koondel
V.P., BUSINESS AFFAIRS, DOMESTIC TELEVISION
Robert Mendez
V.P., LEGAL, DOMESTIC TELEVISION
Cynthia Teele
V.P., TV MUSIC
David Grossman
V.P., MEDIA RELATIONS
Trisha Drissi
V.P., MEDIA RELATIONS
Michelle Hunt
V.P., POST PRODUCTION
Hal Harrison
V.P., PRODUCTION FINANCE
Eileen Ige-Wong
V.P., CURRENT PROGRAMS
Brett King
V.P., BUSINESS AFFAIRS
J.R. McGinnis
V.P., COMEDY DEVELOPMENT
Rose Catherine Pinkney
V.P., BUSINESS AFFAIRS
Cheryl Birch Rothschild
V.P., LONG-FORM PROGRAMMING
Tom Russo
V.P., CURRENT PROGRAMS
Steve Stark
V.P., DRAMA DEVELOPMENT
Scott Vila
V.P., LEGAL
Jody Zucker

INTERNATIONAL TELEVISION DIVISION
PRESIDENT, INTERNATIONAL TELEVISION
Gary Marenzi
SENIOR V.P., INTERNATIONAL DISTRIBUTION
Joseph Lucas
V.P., PPI (CANADA)
Alastair Banks
V.P., LATIN AMERICA SALES
Susan Bender
V.P., TELEVISION SALES, INTERNATIONAL TV (CANADA)
Malcolm Orme
V.P., EUROPEAN SALES (CANADA)
Patrick Stambaugh

INTERNATIONAL SALES OFFICES

AUSTRALIA
Paramount Pictures Pty., Ltd., Suite 3209, Australia Square, Box 4272 GPO, Sydney, 2001, N.S.W. Australia.
V.P., AUSTRALIA & FAR EAST SALES
Stephen Carey

BERMUDA
Paramount International Television, Sales Headquarters, P.O. Box 704, 1 Parliament St, Hamilton HM CX, Bermuda.
CONSULTANT
Bruce Gordon

CANADA
Paramount Pictures Corp. Ltd., 146 Bloor Street W., Toronto, Ontario M5S 1M4, Canada.
V.P., CANADIAN SALES
Malcolm Orme
V.P., MANAGING DIRECTOR, CANADA
Alaastair Banks
DIRECTOR, SYNDICATED SALES, CANADA
Kevin Keeley

ENGLAND
Paramount TV Ltd., 49 Charles St., London, W1X 8LV, England.
DIRECTOR OF SALES, U.K. & EUROPE
Stephen Tague
MANAGER, EUROPE & MIDDLE EAST SALES
David Coombes
CONSULTANT
Patrick Stambaugh

PARAMOUNT NETWORK TELEVISION PRODUCTIONS

Series: Almost Perfect, Clueless, Fired Up, Frasier, George & Leo, Hitz, The Home Court, JAG, Leeza, The Marshal, Sister Sister, Star Trek: Deep Space Nine, Star Trek: Voyager, Three, Wings.

Series/First Run: Entertainment Tonight (5 x 30 mins., weekend hr., 2 x 60 mins./week), Geraldo (5 x 60 mins./week), Hard Copy (5 x 30 mins./week), Maury, Montel, Nick News, Sightings, This Morning's Business.

Hour Series: The Complete Star Trek (127+ hrs.), Mannix (130 hrs.), Mission: Impossible (171 hrs.), The Untouchables (114 hrs.).

Half Hour Series: Brothers (116 x 30 mins.), Cheers (146+ x 30 mins.), Family Ties (154+ x 30 mins.), Happy Days (255 x 30 mins.), Love American Style (224 x 30 mins.), The Lucy Show (156 x 30 mins.), Taxi (114 x 30 mins.), Webster (150 x 30 mins., until 9/99).

Features/Packages: Marquee II (17), Marquee III (18), Portfolio XI (22), Portfolio XII (26), Portfolio XIII (27), Preview II (16), Preview III (20), Preview IV (18), Special Edition I (50), Special Edition II (40), Special Edition III (55), The Untouchables (3).

Mini-Series: Shogun (12-hrs.), Space (10 hrs.), Wallenburg (4 hrs.), Winds of War (10-hrs.).

PATCHETT KAUFMAN ENTERTAINMENT
8621 Hayden Pl., Culver City, CA 90232. (310) 838-7000. FAX: (310) 838-8430.
CHAIRMAN
Tom Patchett
PRESIDENT
Kenneth Kaufman

PEARSON TELEVISION NORTH AMERICA
808 Wilshire Blvd., Los Angeles, CA 90401. (310) 656-1100. FAX: (310) 656-7422.
PRESIDENT & CEO (LA & UK)
Tony Cohen
COO (LA)
William Lincoln
PRESIDENT & COO, PEARSON ALL AMERICAN
Myron Roth
PRESIDENT, ALL AMERICAN PRODUCTION, INC. (LA)
David Gerber
SENIOR EXEC. V.P., ALL AMERICAN COMMUNICATIONS
Syd Vinnedge
EXECUTIVE V.P., PEARSON TELEVISION INTERNATIONAL
Matt Loze
EXECUTIVE V.P., ALL AMERICAN PRODUCTION, INC.
Jamie Waldron
SENIOR V.P.'S, NON-FICTION PROGRAMING,
ALL AMERICAN TELEVISION PRODUCTION, INC.
Paul Buccieri
Robert Weiss
SENIOR V.P., LEGAL & BUSINESS AFFAIRS,
PEARSON TELEVISION PRODUCTIONS NORTH AMERICA
Richard Gire
SENIOR V.P., GRUNDY LATIN AMERICA (CHILE)
Peter Pinne
SENIOR EXEC. PRODUCER, ALL AMERICAN FREMANTLE INTERNATIONAL, INC.
Howard Huntridge
V.P., PROGRAMMIING, PEARSON TELEVISION
Juliet Blake
V.P., WORLDWIDE MARKETING, PEARSON TELEVISION
Pauline Bohm
V.P., GRUNDY LATING AMERICA (CHILE)
Carlos Gonzales
V.P., ALL AMERICAN TELEVISION PRODUCTION, INC.
Gaby Johnson
V.P., MEDIA RELATIONS, PEARSON ALL AMERICAN DOMESTIC DISTRIBUTION
Paul Nichols
V.P., OPERATIONS, PEARSON TELEVISION INT'L.
Jennifer Phillips
V.P., PROD., ALL AMERICAN TELEVISION PROD., INC.
Loren Salob
V.P., DEV'T., ALL AMERICAN TELEVISION PROD., INC.
Geoff Silverman
DIR'S., PROGRAM DEVELOPMENT, PEARSON TELEVISION
Ruth Caruso
Jill Schwartz
MANAGER, MARKTING & VISUAL COMMUNICATIONS,
PEARSON TELEVISION
Gregory Calvosa

PLAYBOY ENTERTAINMENT GROUP

9242 Beverly Blvd., Beverly Hills, CA 90210. (310) 246-4000. (310) 246-4050.
PRESIDENT
Anthony J. Lynn
PRESIDENT, PLAYBOY NETWORKS WORLDWIDE
Jim Enalisno

Products: Hot Rocks, Night Call, Playboy's Really Naked Truth, Take Five, Women of Color, World of Playboy, Sex Court, Naughty Amateur Home Videos.

POLYGRAM TELEVISION

9333 Wilshire Blvd., Beverly Hills, CA 90210. (310) 385-4200. FAX: (310) 385-4201.
PRESIDENT & CEO
Jules Haimovitz
SENIOR VICE PRESIDENT
Michael Birnbaum
EXECUTIVE V.P., ITC DISTRIBUTION
Les Haber
V.P. & GENERAL SALES MANAGER, DOMESTIC TV
Mike Russo

Feature Films: Volume 10 (32 features including: Young Doctors in Love, Stepfather 2, Sex Lies and Videotape), Movie of the Month Network 4 (12 features including: Doppelganger, Whispers, David Hardware, Rage in Harlem and Trouble Bound), Volume 9 (8 features including: Better Off Dead, Jacknife and Without a Clue).
Series: Motorweek, Madison's Adventures: Growing Up Wild.
Mini-Series: Night of the Fox, People Like Us, Touch and Die.

POLYGRAM TELEVISION ENTERTAINMENT

10 Livonia St., London, England W1V 3PH. (44171) 800-1339. FAX: (44171) 800-1337.
Series: The Big Easy–The Series (22 x 60 mins.), Charlotte Sophie Bentinick (6 x 52 mins.).

THE PROGRAM EXCHANGE

(A Division of Saatchi & Saatchi North America, Inc.)
375 Hudson St., New York, NY 10014-3620. (212) 463-3900. FAX: (212) 463-2662.
PRESIDENT
Allen Banks
EXECUTIVE V.P. & DIRECTOR, MEDIA OPERATIONS
Jack Irving
MANAGING DIRECTOR
Christopher Hallowell
V.P., DIRECTOR, STATION RELATIONS
Beth Kempner

Series: Three's Company (174 x 30 mins.), Too Close For Comfort (129 x 30 mins.), Webster (150 x 30 mins.), Bosom Buddies (37 x 30 mins.), Dear John (90 x 30 mins.), Amen (110 x 30 mins.), Charles in Charge (126 x 30 mins.), Abbott & Costello (52 x 30 mins.), Leave It to Beaver (234 x 30 mins.).
Features: The Bad News Bears, Murder on the Orient Express, The Presidio.
Children's Series: The Wacky World of Tex Avery (65 x 30 mins.), The Real Adventures of Johnny Quest (52 x 30 mins.), Garfield and Friends (73 x 30 mins.), Sailor Moon (82 x 30 mins.), Super Mario Brothers Supershow (52 x 30 mins.), Dennis the Menace (78 x 30 mins.), The Bullwinkle Show (98 x 30 mins.), Rocky and His Friends (156 x 15 mins.),The Underdog Show (62 x 30 mins.), Uncle Waldo's Cartoon Show (52 x 30 mins.), Tennessee Tuxedo and His Tales (140 x 30 mins.), Dudley Do Right and Friends (38 x 30 mins.), Young Samson (20 x 30 mins.), Space Kidettes (20 x 30 mins.), King Leonardo (38 x 30 mins.), Dinobabies (26 x 30 mins.).

MARIAN REES ASSOCIATES, INC.

3708 Vantage Ave., Studio City, CA 91604. (818) 508-5599. FAX: (818) 508-8012.
EXECUTIVE PRODUCER
Marian Rees
ASSISTANT TO EXEC. PROD.
Jenny Cowan
V.P., DEVELOPMENT
Anne Hopkins
ASSISTNAT TO V.P., DEVELOPMENT
Carin Chapin

REPUBLIC PICTURES CORPORATION

6311 Romaine St., Los Angeles, CA 90038. (213) 463-2141.
Series/Off Network: Beauty & the Beast (56 hours), Bonanza (260 hours), Car 54 Where Are You? (60 half hours), Get Smart (138 half hours), High Chaparral (98 hours), My World and Welcome To It (26 half hours).
Film Packages: Action-Packed Package (28 features), All Nite Movies (5 nights per week), Animated Features (5 features), Cartoons (15), Christmas Features (4 features), Classic Comedy (13 features), Color movies (quarterly), Hollywood Stars (16 features), Hollywood 1-2-3 (89 features), Home of the Cowboys (22 features), The John Wayne Collection (16 features), Republic Premiere Four (12), Serial Movies (26 features), Showcase One (8), Take 3 (6).

RUBY-SPEARS PRODUCTIONS, INC.

710 S. Victory Blvd., #201, Burbank, CA 91502-2425. (818) 840-1234. FAX: (818) 840-1258. email: rubyspears@earthlink.net
PRESIDENT
Joe Ruby
VICE PRESIDENT
Ken Spears

Series: Mega Man, Skysurfer: Strike Force.

RYSHER ENTERTAINMENT

2401 Colorado Ave., Ste. 200, Santa Monica, CA 90404. (310) 309-5200. FAX: (310) 309-5215.
PRESIDENT & CEO
Tim Helfet
PRESIDENT, CREATIVE AFFAIRS
Rob Kenneally
S.V.P., BUSINESS & LEGAL AFFAIRS
Jeff Matloff
S.V.P., TV BUSINESS & LEGAL AFFAIRS
Barbara Rubin
CFO & S.V.P., FINANCE
Franklin Johnson
S.V.P., PRODUCTION
Mel Efros
S.V.P., CABLE PROGRAM SALES
Tim Mudd
S.V.P., RESEARCH
George Gubert
V.P., INTERNATIONAL THEATRICAL SALES
Adam Wright
V.P'S., INTERNATIONAL TV SALES
Cathie Trotta
Giannina Antola
V.P., POSTPRODUCTION
Ned Humphreys
V.P., WESTERN SALES
Paul Danylik
V.P., DOMESTIC MARKETING
Paul Eagleton

Series: Fire House (13 x 1 hr.), FX The Series (20 x 1hr.), Highlander The Series (110 x 1 hr.), Live Shot (13 x 1 hr.), Nash Bridges (13 x 1 hr.), Soldier of Fortune (19 x 1 hr.), Strange Universe (195 x 30 mins.), Strangers (13 x 30 mins.).
TV Movies: Body Language (2 hrs.), Citizen X (2 hrs.), Gunfigter's Moon (2 hrs.), Her Deadly Rival (2 hrs.), A Kidnapping In The Family (2 hrs.), The Prosecutor (2 hrs.), Sugartime (2 hrs.), Urban Legend (2 hrs.).

SABAN ENTERTAINMENT, INC.

10960 Wilshire Blvd., Los Angeles, CA 90024. (310) 235-5100. FAX: (310) 235-5102.
CHAIRMAN & CEO
Haim Saban
PRESIDENT & COO
Mel Woods
PRESIDENT, SABAN INTERNATIONAL
Stan Golden
PRESIDENT, PRODUCTION & MUSIC
Shuki Levy
PRESIDENT, MOTION PICTURES & TELEVISION
Lance Robbins
PRESIDENT, SABAN ENTERPRISES INTERNATIONAL
Michel Welter
EXECUTIVE V.P., MARKETING & ADVERTISING
Elie Dekel
EXECUTIV V.P., MUSIC
Ron Kenan
EXECUTIVE V.P., PRODUCTION & POSTPRODUCTION
Eric Rollman
EXECUTIVE V.P., DOMESTIC DISTRIBUTION
Peter Schmid
SENIOR V.P., DEVELOPMENT
Joel Andrye
SENIOR V.P., CREATIVE SERVICES
Russell Hicks
SENIOR V.P., FINANCE
Mark Ittner
SENIOR V.P., BUSINESS AFFAIRS & GENERAL COUNSEL
Bill Josey
SENIOR V.P., LICENSING & MERCHANDISING
Susanne Lee
SENIOR V.P., POSTPRODUCTION
Clive Mizumoto
SENIOR V.P., CORPORATE COMMUNICATIONS
Barry Stagg
V.P., CASTING
Julie Ashton

V.P., ANIMATION PRODUCTION
Dana Booton
V.P., MARKETING SERVICES
Lou Bortone
V.P., INTERNATIONAL SALES
Eugenia Briseno
V.P., PRODUCTION
Abbie Charette
V.P., ADMINISTRATION & HUMAN RESOURCES
Beth Cleary
V.P., ACQUISITIONS
Susan Cooper
V.P., CREATIVE AFFAIRS
Ron Coro
V.P., MIS
Tina Delgado
V.P., ENGINEERING
Denny Densmore
V.P. & CONTROLLER, FINANCE
Jon Dyer
V.P., BUSINESS & LEGAL AFFAIRS, LICENSING & MERCHANDISING
Greg Economos
V.P., INTERNATIONAL CO-PRODUCTIONS & ACQUISITIONS
Sam Ewing
V.P., CREATIVE SERVICES
Jorge Ferreiro
V.P., PUBLICITY
Carol Holdsworth
V.P., PROMOTIONS
George Leon
V.P., INTERNATIONAL BUSINESS AFFAIRS
Cheryl McDermott
V.P., INTERNATIONAL BUSINESS & LEGAL AFFAIRS
Judith Merians
V.P., FINANCIAL PLANNING
Bill Nault
V.P., MUSIC ADMINISTRATION
Teri Nelson
V.P., MIDWEST SALES
Tim Newman
V.P., PRODUCTION OPERATIONS
Bob Palmer
V.P., SPECIAL PROJECTS
Mark Pinsker
V.P., LEGAL AFFAIRS
Angie Small

Branch Offices: Sydney, Toronto, London, Paris, Cologne, Zurich and Tel Aviv.

Live-action series: Beetleborgs Metalix (FOX), Breaker High (UPN), Goosebumps (Fox), Mad Scientist Toon Club (synd.), Ninja Turtles: The Next Mutation, Power Rangers Turbo (Fox), Saban's Masked Rider (Fox), Saban's Mighty Morphin Power Rangers (Fox), Saban's VR Troopers (synd.), Sweet Valley High (synd.), Unsolved Mysteries.

Features/2-hour movies: Abduction of Innocence, Addicted to Love, An Innocent Heart, Baby Face Nelson, Badge of Betrayal, Behind Closed Doors, Blindfold: Acts of Obsession, Born Bad, Brothers' Destiny, Cadillac Girls, Chantilly Lace, Cheyenne Warrior, Criminal Affairs, Criminal Hearts, Criminal Pursuit, Deadly Sins, Edge of Deception, Exception to the Rule, Falling for You, False Pretense, Fight for Justice, Flashpoint, Guns of Honor, Hard Evidence, Honor Thy Father and Mother: The Menendez Killings, Hostile Intentions, Jailbreak, Last Exit to Earth, Midnight Heat, Mind Breakers, No Dessert Dad, 'Til You Mow the Lawn, Not Like Us, Not of This Earth, One Hot Summer Night, Overdrive, Parallel Lives, Prescription for Murder, The Protector, Quest for Justice, Random Encounter, Running Wild, Samurai Cowboy, Seeds of Doubt, Shadow of Obsession, Someone to Die For, Someone's Watching, Suspicious Agenda, Terminal Voyage, Termination Man, To Catch a Killer, Trapped and Deceived, Too Much Trouble, Under Oath, Unlawful Intent, With Harmful Intent.

Animated Series: Battletech (synd.), Bobby's World (Fox), Bureau of Alien Detective, Camp Candy (NBC), Captain N: The Game Master (NBC), Casper, Creepy Crawlers (synd.), Eagle Riders, Eek! Stravaganza (Fox), Grimm's Fairy Tales (Nick.), Honey Bee Hutch, Iznogoud, Jin Jin and the Panda Patrol, Journey to the Heart of the World, Life With Louie, Little Shop (synd.), Mouse & the Monster, Ninja Turtles: The Next Mutation (13 x 30 mins.), Noozles, Oliver Twist, Princess Sissi, Saban's Adventures of Oliver Twist, Saban's Adventures of the Little Mermaid (synd.), Saban's Around the World in 80 Dreams (synd.), Saban's Gulliver's Travels (synd.), Saban's Little Mouse on the Prairie, Saban's Power Rangers Turbo (50 x 30 mins.), Samurai Pizza Cats (synd.), Space Strikers—changed from 20,000 Leagues Into Space (UPN), Sugar Pig, Teknoman (UPN), Tenko and the Guardians of the Magic (synd.), Video Power (synd.), Walter Melon, Why Why Family, X-Men (Fox).

EDGAR J. SCHERICK ASSOCIATES

1950 Sawtelle Blvd., Suite 282, Los Angeles, CA 90025. (310) 996-2376. FAX: (310) 996-2392.
EXECUTIVE PRODUCER & PRESIDENT
Edgar J. Scherick
V.P., DEVELOPMENT
Liza Leeds
EXECUTIVE DIRECTOR, DEVELOPMENT
Matthew Burns

Productions: Ruby Ridge: An American Tragedy (CBS, 4 hrs), Tyson (HBO, 2 hrs.), The Wall (Showtime, 2 hrs.)

GEORGE SCHLATTER PRODUCTIONS

8321 Beverly Blvd., Los Angeles, CA 90048. (213) 655-1400.
FAX: (213) 852-1640.
PRESIDENT
George H. Schlatter
VICE PRESIDENT
Jolene B. Schlatter

Products: American Comedy Awards–Years 1-12, American Television Awards, Ceasar's Palace 30th Anniversary Celebration, American Comedy Honors, Frank Liza & Sammy: The Ultimate Event, Laugh-In, Meaning of Life, Muhammad Ali's 50th Birthday, People's Choice Awards, Real People, Sammy Davis Jr.'s 60th Anniversary Celebration, She TV, Sinatra 80 Years My Way, Sinatra Duets, USO 50th Anniversary, Welcome Home America.

SFM ENTERTAINMENT

1180 Ave. of the Americas, New York, NY 10036. (212) 790-4888. FAX: (212) 790-4852.
PRESIDENT
Stanley Moger
EXECUTIVE V.P., BUSINESS AFFAIRS
Jordan Ringel
V.P., PRODUCTION SERVICES
Dewey Wigod

Features: Instant Love, Jungle Book, A Time to Remember, Witness to the Execution.

Animation: Dennis the Menace, Here Comes the Grump, Rose Petal Place, The Yum Yums.

Documentaries: A Beautiful Friendship: Claude Rains and the Movies, Benny Carter: A Symphony in Riffs, Crusade in Europe, Moshe Dayan: A Warrior's Story, Dayan's Israel, Deal, George Stevens: D-Day to Berlin, George Stevens: A Filmaker's Journey, The Harry Hausen Chronicles, The Indomitable Teddy Roosevelt, The Made-for-TV Election, Pillar of Fire, Visions of Light.

Children's: Alice Through the Looking Glass, Zoobilee Zoo.

Series: The Adventures of Jim Bowie, The American Craftsman, The Barbara Stanwyck Theater, Cooking with Dione Lucas, The Flip Wilson Show, Industry on Parade, The Joey Bishop Show, The Life and Legend of Wyatt Earp, Love & Marriage, The Marriage Counselor, Open Book, The Real McCoys, Wichita Town.

Specials: American Film Institute Life Achievement Award Special, Breaking the Screen Barrier: The Making of Terminator 2-3D, Country Music Hall of Fame 25th Anniversary Special, Everybody Rides the Carousel, The Family Film Awards, Fear: The Universal Monster, Gift of the Magi, Jaws: The Last Dragon, Just the Facts!, THe Making of Jurassic Park: The Ride, One Hundred Years... One Hundred Movies, A Sea World/Busch Gardens Adventure (14 shows), Songs and Visions.

ARNOLD SHAPIRO PRODUCTIONS

520 Broadway, Suite 220, Santa Monica, CA 90401. (310) 451-6270. FAX: (310) 451-4634.
PRESIDENT
Arnold Shapiro

Series: Rescue 911.

SHUKOVSKY ENGLISH ENTERTAINMENT (SEE)

CBS Studio Center, 4024 Redford Ave., Studio City, CA 91604. (818) 760-6100. FAX: (818) 760-5527.
PARTNERS & EXECUTIVE PRODUCERS
Diane English
Joel Shukovsky
EXECUTIVE V.P., LEGAL COUNSEL
John Drinkwater
EXECUTIVE IN CHARGE OF PRODUCTION
John Whitman

Series: Double Rush, The Louie Show, Love and War, Murphy Brown.

THE FRED SILVERMAN COMPANY

12400 Wilshire Blvd., Suite 920, Los Angeles, CA 90025. (310) 826-6050.
PRESIDENT
Fred Silverman
Products: Bedtime, Bone Chillers, Diagnosis Murder, In the Heat of the Night, Matlock, Perry Mason movies.

RICK SPALLA VIDEO PRODUCTIONS

1622 North Gower St., Hollywood, CA 90028. (323) 469-7307. FAX: (323) 469-8251.
301 W. 45 St., New York, NY 10036. (212) 765-4646.
PRESIDENT
Rick Spalla
VICE PRESIDENT
Anthony J. Spalla
PRODUCTION SUPERVISOR
Richard Spalla

TV Products: Century of Fashion...in Motion Pictures, The Great Getaway, High Road to Danger, Hobby Nobbing...with the Stars, Holiday on Wheels, Hollywood Backstage... The Sensational Sixties (115 x 30 mins.), Hollywood Newsreel Stock Footage Library... Stars/Premieres/Parties, Hollywood's Fantastic Artists' and Models' Ball, Hollywood Star Newsreel, Kay Crawford's Pep Arts Training Series (14 hrs.), Miss California International Beauty Pageant (2 hours—Annual Competition in April), The Open Road, Portrait: The New Breed, Portrait of a Star, The Wild...Wild...World of Spirit, Academy Awards—The Behind the Scenes World of the Stars.

SPECTACOR FILMS

9000 Sunset Blvd., Suite 1550, Los Angeles, CA 90069. (310) 271-9990. FAX: (310) 247-0412.
PARTNER
Ed Snider
TV Movies: The Invader, Johnny 2.0

SPELLING ENTERTAINMENT GROUP INC.

5700 Wilshire Blvd., 5th Fl., Suite 575, Los Angeles, CA 90036. (213) 965-5700. (213) 965-5895.
PRESIDENT
Peter Bachmann
SENIOR V.P., HUMAN RESOURCES
Cecelia Holloway
SENIOR V.P., PRODUCTION & PROGRAMMING
Karen Miller
S.V.P., GENERAL COUNSEL & CORPORATE SECRETARY & LEGAL SERVICES
Sallu Suchil
V.P., CORPORATE COMMUNICATIONS
Nancy Bushkin
V.P., BUSINESS & LEGAL AFFAIRS
Karen Green
V.P., PARTICIPATIONS & RESIDUALS
Kevin Gunn
V.P., FINANCE & TAX
Ross Landsbaum
V.P., RISK MANAGEMENT
Eugene Mellevold
V.P., HUMAN RESOURCES
Tim McDonald
V.P. & CONTROLLER, CONTROLLER & FINANCE ADMINISTRATION
James Miller
V.P., ACCOUNTING & FINANCE
Lise Schneider
SPELLING TELEVISION INC.
CHAIRMAN & CEO
Aaron Spelling
VICE CHAIRMAN
E. Duke Vincent
PRESIDENT
Jonathan C. Levin
EXECUTIVE V.P.
James Conway
S.V.P., ADMINISTRATION & OFFICE SERVICES
Renate Kamer
SENIOR V.P., POST PRODUCTION
Kenneth Miller
SENIOR V.P., PRODUCTION & PROGRAMMING
Gail Patterson
V.P., MOW & MINISERIES
Kathryn McCardle

V.P., BUSINESS & LEGAL AFFAIRS
Lougenia A Patrick
V.P., STI TALENT
Pamela Shae
V.P., DAYTIME CURRENT PROGRAMMING
Kristina Smith
V.P., STI CURRENT PROGRAMMING
Steve Tann
Series: Beverly Hills 90210, Melrose Place, Savannah, Seventh Heaven.

SANDE STEWART TELEVISION, INC.

5525 Oakdale Ave, #275, Woodland Hills, CA 91364. (818) 313-9394. FAX: (818) 313-9514.
PRESIDENT
Sande Stewart

THE SULLIVAN COMPANY

4024 Radford Ave., Studio City, CA 90212. (818) 991-7564. FAX: (818) 991-7619.
EXECUTIVE PRODUCER
Beth Sullivan
Series: Dr. Quinn—Medicine Woman.

SUNBOW PRODUCTIONS

100 Fifth Ave., New York, NY 10011. FAX: (212) 366-4242.
CO-CHAIRMEN
Thomas L. Griffin
Joe Bacal
PRESIDENT & C.O.O.
C.J. Kettler
C.F.O.
Andrew Karpen
S.V.P., PRODUCTION
Carole Weitzman
S.V.P., SALES
Jane Smith
S.V.P., DEVELOPMENT
Nina Hahn

Series: Bigfoot (9 x 7 mins.), Bucky O'Hare (13 x 30 mins.), Cartoon Capers (17 x 30 mins.), Conan & The Young Warriors (13 x 30 mins.), Conan The Adventurer (65 x 30 mins.), G.I. Joe: Extreme (26 x 30 mins.), G.I. Joe: Original (95 x 30 mins.), G.I. Joe (199 & 300 series, 44 x 30 mins.), Glorfiends (26 x 10 mins.), Great Space Coaster (52 x 30 mins.), Inhumanoids (13 x 30 mins.), Jem (65 x 30 mins.), Littlest Pet Shop (40 x 30 mins.), Moondreamers (16 x 10 mins.), My Little Pony N'Friends (65 x 30 mins.), My Little Pony: Original (32 x 30 mins.), My Little Pony Tales (13 x 30 mins.), The Nudnik Show (13 x 30 mins.), The Puzzle Place (65 x 30 mins.), Robotix (15 x 7 mins.), Transformers Generation 2 (52 x 30 mins.), Transformers Takara (115 x 30 mins.), Transformers: Original (98 x 30 mins.), Visionaries (13 x 30 mins.).
Family Features: A Matter of Conscience (60 mins.), All That Glitters (60 mins.), Flour Babies (60 mins.), Private Affairs (60 mins.).

TAFFNER ENTERTAINMENT, LTD.

1888 Century Park East, 19th fl., Los Angeles, CA 90067. (213) 937-1144. FAX: (213) 937-5095.
EXECUTIVE VICE PRESIDENT
Don Taffner Jr.
V.P., BUSINESS AFFAIRS
Emmet G. Lavery, Jr.
Products: Cinema Europe: The Other Hollywood (6 hrs.), Rumpole of the Bailey, Three's Company, Too Close for Comfort.

TELEVISION REPRESENTATIVES, INC.

9911 W. Pico Blvd., Suite PH-E, Los Angeles, CA 90035. (310) 552-2660. FAX: (310) 552-9039.
CHAIRMAN
Alan Silverbach
DIRECTOR, DOMESTIC SYNDICATION
Betty Jane Metz
Features: The Best Christmas Pageant Ever, The Video History of the Civil War: Gettysburg.

TELEWORLD, INC.

1780 Broadway, Suite 804, New York, NY 10019. (212) 489-9310. FAX: (212) 262-9395.
PRESIDENT
Robert Seidelman
Mini-Series: Kennedy (7 hrs.), Mistral's Daughter (8 hrs.).
Features/Packages: Spiderman movie specials (7 live-action features), Teleworld's Top 50 (chiller & action features), 17 AIP Science Fiction Classics.

TOUCHSTONE TELEVISION

(For executves, see Walt Disney Company listing.)

TRANS WORLD INTERNATIONAL

(A division of IMG, Inc.)
IMG Center, 1360 E. 9, Ste. 100, Cleveland, OH. (216) 522-1200. FAX: (216) 522-1145.
Branch offices in Auckland, Barcelona, Budapest, Hamburg, Hong Kong, Johannesburg, London, Milan, Paris, Stockholm, Sydney, Tokyo, Toronto.
CHAIRMAN, PRESIDENT & CEO, IMG
Mark H. McCormack
SENIOR EXECUTIVE V.P., IMG
Alastair J. Johnson
SENIOR GROUP V.P.
Barry Frank
V.P., ACQUISITIONS & DISTRIBUTION
Hillary Mandel
PROGRAM COORDINATOR, TWI
Katie Boes
EXECUTIVE PRODUCER
Brian Williams
Series: Futbol Mundia, Transworld Sport.

Features: The Greatest Moments In Sports–Vol 1, High Five Series Three, College Bowl Preview, College Football Special, Escape From Alcatraz Triathlon, NFL Pre-Season Special, TV.COM, AVD Pro Beach Volleyball, Hawaiian Holiday Celebrity Sports Spectacular, Golden Moments of the Winter Games, Golden Moments on Ice, Academy Awards, A Year in Review, Images 1997, Winter Celebrity Sports Invitational.

Athletics: Chemical Bank Millrose Games, Mobil Invitational, New York City Marathon (1996, 1997, 1998), Reno Indoor Games, Uncle Toby's Ironman & Devondale Ironwoman Super Series, USA Indoor Track & Field Championships, Weetabix New Zealand Ironman Triathlon.

Badminton: Ciba Asia Cup Badminton, Seiko Asian Badminton Championships, Thomas Uber Cup Qualifier & Finals, World Cup Badminton Championships.

Cricket: India vs. South Africa, Indian Domestic Cricket, Pakistan Domestic Cricket, West Indies vs. New Zealand Cricket.

Figure Skating: Canadian Pro Figure Skating Championships, European Speed Skating Championships, European Figure Skating Championships, Junior World Figure Skating Championships, Stars On Ice, World Junior Speed Skating Championships, World Junior Track Speed Skating, World Pro Figure Skating, World Short Track Speed Skating Championships, World Single Distance Championships, World Speed Skating Championships, World Sprint Speed Skating Championships.

Men's Golf: Alfred Dunhill Cup, Alfred Dunhill Masters, Alfred Dunhill South African PGA Championship, Anderson Consulting World Championship, AT&T Australian Skins Game, Australian Masters, Benson & Hedges International Open, BMW International Open, Cannes Open, Canon European Masters, Chemapol Trophy Czech Open, Collingtree British Masters, Deutsche Bank Open TPC of Europe, Dubai Desert Classic, Dutch Open, English Open, Epson Singapore Open, FNB Players Championship, German Masters, Heineken Classic, Hohe Brucke Open, Italian Open Golf Championship, Johnnie Walker Asian Classic, Loch Lomond World Invitational, Madeira Island Open, Moroccan Open, Murphy's Irish Open, The 125th British Open Golf Championships –1996, The 126th British Open Golf Championships–1997, 127th British Open Golf Championships–1997, Peugeot Open de Espana, Peugeot Open de France, Portugese Open, The Ryder Cup–1997, The Scottish Open, The Senior British Open Golf Championship–1996, Smurfit European Open, Toyota World Match Play, Trophée Lancôme, Turespana Masters, Turespana Open Mediterrania, US Open Golf Championship –1996, US PGA Championship–1996, US PGA Championship –1997, Volvo German Open, Volvo PGA Championship, Volvo MastersVolvo Scandinavian Masters, World Championship of Golf, YPF Argentine Republic Open Golf Championship.

Women's Golf: Chick-fil-A Charity Championship, Chrysler-Plymouth Tournament of Champions, Compaq Open, Fieldcrest Cannon Classic, Healthsouth Inaugural, JAL Big Apple Classic, Jamie Farr Kroger Classic, Ping/AT&T Wireless Services, Ping/Welch's Championship, Rochester International, SAFECO Classic, Sara Lee Classic, ShopRite LPGA Classic, Spint Titleholders Championship, Star Bank LPGA Classic, State Farm Rail Classic, Trygg-Hansa Ladies Open, US Women's Open Golf Championship, Women's British Open Golf Championship – (1996, 1997, 1998, 1999, 2000), Youngstown-Warren LPGA Classic.

Motor Sports: Brickyard 400, Daytona 500, Die Hard 500 (Talladega), Indy Racing League: Indy 200 at Walt Disney World, Indianapolis 500, Las Vegas 200, New England 200, Phoenix 200, Trans Am Racing (includes 12 different venues/races).

Olympic Programming: 1996 Olympic Trials (includes Men's Marathon, Swimming, Boxing, Track & Field, Basketball, Gymnastics), The Olympic Century — Program One: The Olympic Spirit, Program Two: The Pursuit of Excellence, Program Three: The Future of The Games, The Olympic Series — Volume I: Golden Moments of The Olympic Games, Volume II: Road To Glory, Volume III: The Dream Team 1992, Volume IV: The Olympic Spirit.

Rugby: European Rugby Club Championships for the Heineken Cup, World Rugby Cup Championships.

Sports Series: Coca-Cola World of Cricket, Finish Line, Ian Botham's Dream Team, Survival of The Fittest.

Snooker: B&H Irish Masters, British Open Snooker, International Open Snooker, Regal Welsh Open Snooker, Thailand Open Snooker.

Soccer: Chinese Soccer, Indian Soccer.

Tennis: Australian Open Tennis–1996 & 1997, Colonial Classic, Peters International, Wimbledon Lawn Tennis Championships–1996 & 1997, WTA Tour 1996 (Acura Classic, Advanta Championships, Ameritech, Bank of The West Classic, Bausch & Lomb, Citizen Cup, Direct Line Insurance Championships, German Open, Italian Open, Lipton Championships, Nicherei International Ladies Championships, Open Ford International Championships, Open Gaz de France, State Farm Evert Cup, Toshiba Tennis Classic, WTA Tour Championships).

Other Programming: Chinese Basketball, Indian Hockey (Field Hockey), Thai Kickboxing, Nobel Prize Awards Ceremony, Rodeo Showdown, World Bull Riding Championships, Whitbread Around the World Race (Sailing), World's Strongest Man, Qatar Table Tennis.

TRANSVUE TV INTERNATIONAL CO.

5131 Colbath Ave., Sherman Oaks, CA 91423. (818) 990-5600.
PRESIDENT
Herbert B. Schlosberg
Assorted features including Disco Godfather, Petey Wheatstraw, Seven Wonders of the West.

TRIBUNE ENTERTAINMENT COMPANY

435 N. Michigan Ave., Suite 1800, Chicago, IL 60611. (312) 222-4441. FAX: (312) 222-9065.
PRESIDENT & CEO
Rick Jacobson
S.V.P., GENERAL SALES MANAGER
Steve Mulderrig
Talk: Geraldo, The Charles Perez Show.

Series/First Run: Out of the Blue, Soul Train, U.S. Farm Report.

Movies/Mini-Series: To Catch a Killer, Final Shot: The Hank Gathers Story, Sidney Sheldon's Sands of Time, Vendetta II, The Vernon Johns Story, Wild Justice.

Specials: Hollywood Christmas Parade, Macy's Fourth of July Fireworks Spectacular.

Variety/Music/Comedy: Soul Train Lady of Soul Awards, Soul Train Music Awards.

Sports: Chicago Cubs TV Network.

TURNER TELEVISION

(A division of Time-Warner)
One CNN Center, P.O. Box 105366, Atlanta, GA 30348-5366.
PRESIDENT & CEO
Terence McGuirk

TURNER INTERNATIONAL

One CNN Center, P.O. Box 105366, Atlanta, GA 30348-5366.
(404) 827-5639. FAX: (404) 827-3224.
CORPORATE V.P., WORLDWIDE DISTRIBUTION
William H. Grumbles
SENIOR V.P., SYNDICATE SALES
Michael Byrd

CNN NEWS SOURCE SALES

One CNN Center, 12th floor, P.O. Box 105366, Atlanta, GA 30348-5366. (404) 827-2085. FAX: (404) 827-2373.
PRESIDENT
Susan Grant
S.V.P., CNN TELEVISION
Gary Anderson
S.V.P. MARKETING & SALES STRATEGY
Meade Camp
V.P., WORLDWIDE DUSTRIBUTION, TBS INC.
Jonathon Katz

Children's Programming: Feed Your Mind (52 x 30 mins.), The Flintstones (100+ strips), The Flintstones & The Jetsons (26 each), The New Adventures Of Captain Planet (52 x 30 mins.), Tom And Jerry (100 x 30 mins.), Warner Bros. Cartoons (301 segments).

Hanna-Barbera Specials: Arabian Nights (90 mins.), A Flintstones Christmas Carol (90 mins.), The Halloween Tree (90 mins.), I Yabba-Dabba Do! (120 mins.), Johnny's Golden Quest (120 mins.), Tom And Jerry–The Movie (120 mins.), Yogi–The Easter Bear (60 mins.).

Series/Off Network: Chips (138 one hr.), Gilligan's Island (98 x 30 mins.), The Wonder Years (115 x 30 mins.).

Series/First-Run: Lauren Hutton And... (260 x 30 mins.), The Lazarus Man (22 x 1 hr.), National Geographic On Assignment (12 x 1 hr.), WCW Wrestling, Wild! Life Adventures (12 x 1 hr.).

Features/Packages: Turner Pictures III—The Legends (24 movies), Turner Pictures IV—The Legends (24 mvies), New World I-IV (76 titles), New World: TV Gold (10 titles), New World: Pretty Smart (10 titles).

CNN Television: Headline News Programs, Syndicated News Service, Turner Entertainment Report.

20TH CENTURY FOX INTERNATIONAL TELEVISION
P.O. Box 900, Beverly Hills, CA 90213. (310) 369-1000. FAX: (310) 369-4611.
PRESIDENT, INTERNATIONAL TV
Mark Kaner
EXECUTIVE V.P., INTERNATIONAL TV
Marion G. Edwards
V.P., WORLDWIDE PAY TV & PAY PER VIEW
Ken Bettsteller

Animated Series: King of the Hill (35 x 30mins.).

Half Hour Series: Sercret Service Guy (7 x 30 mins.).

Hour Series: The Practice (13 x 30 mins.)

UNIVERSAL TELEVISION GROUP
(A Division of Universal Studios, Inc.) 100 Universal City Plaza, Universal City, CA 91608. (818) 777-1000.
445 Park Ave., New York, NY 10022. (212) 759-7500.
CHAIRMAN & CEO, UNIVERSAL STUDIOS
Frank J. Biondi, Jr.
PRESIDENT & COO, UNIVERSAL STUDIOS
Ron Meyer
EXECUTIVE V.P. & CFO, UNIVERSAL STUDIOS
Bruce L. Hack
EXECUTIVE V.P., CORPORTE OPERATIONS, UNIVERSAL STUDIOS
Howard L. Weitzman
SENIOR V.P., HUMAN RESOURCES, UNIVERSAL STUDIOS
Kenneth L. Kahrs
SENIOR V.P., CHIEF TECHNOLOGY OFFICER, UNIVERSAL STUDIOS
Alice H. Lusk
SENIOR V.P., INTERNATIONAL BUSINESS DEVELOPMENT
J. Brian McGrath
SENIOR V.P., CORPORATE DEVELOPMENT & STRATEGIC PLANNING, UNIVERSAL STUDIOS
Brian C. Mulligan
SENIOR V.P. & GENERAL COUNSEL, UNIVERSAL STUDIOS
Karen Randall
SENIOR V.P., CORPORATE COMMUNICATIONS & PUBLIC AFFAIRS, UNIVERSAL STUDIOS
Deborah S. Rosen
SENIOR V.P.
Hellene H. Runtagh
V.P., WORLDWIDE ANTI-PIRACY
Karen Elliott
V.P., CORPORATE COMMUNICATIONS & PUBLIC AFFAIRS
Susan Nahley Fleishman
V.P., PUBLIC POLICY
Matthew Gerson
V.P., NETWORK & TELECOMMUNICATIONS SERVICES, UNIVERSAL INFORMATION SERVICES
Noubar Ghazarossian
V.P., HUMAN RESOURCES DEVELOPMENT
Mark Halacy
V.P., HUMAN RESOURCES
Janet Iannessa
V.P., UNIVERSAL STUDIOS
Steven W. Lew
V.P., TELEVISION GROUP SYSTEMS, INFORMATION SVCS.
Naz Nicolian
V.P., GOVERNMENT AFFAIRS
Ann M. O'Connon
V.P., PRODUCT DEVELOPMENT, UIS ADMINISTRATION
Andrew J. Sells
V.P., CONTROLLER
William Sutman

UNIVERSAL TELEVISION
PRESIDENT
Ken Solomon
EXECUTIVE V.P.
Ned Nalle
EXECUTIVE V.P., PROGRAMMING
Charles Engel
EXECUTIVE V.P., PRODUCTION
Matt Herman
SENIOR V.P., CURRENT PROGRAMMING
Cheryl Bloch
SENIOR V.P., DRAMATIC DEVELOPMENT
Dan Filie

SENIOR V.P., DRAMATIC DEVELOPMENT
William Hamm
SENIOR V.P., CASTING
Nancy Perkins
SENIOR V.P., MUSIC
Derek Platt
V.P., TELEVISION PRODUCTION MANAGEMENT
David Beanes
V.P., BUSINESS AFFAIRS
James Brock
V.P., CURRENT PROGRAMMING
Peter Jankowski
V.P., LEGAL AFFAIRS
Stephen Sass
V.P., PUBLICITY
Neil Schubert
V.P., DRAMA DEVELOPMENT
Pat Wells

UNIVERSAL TELEVISION ENTERPRISES
EXECUTIVE V.P.
Steve Rosenberg
SENIOR V.P., EASTERN SALES
Arthur Hasson
V.P., MANAGER, SOUTHWEST REGION SALES
Cameron Hutton
V.P., MANAGER, SOUTHEAST REGION SALES
Michael Howard
V.P., MIDWEST REGION
Phil Martzolf

UNIVERSAL INTERNATIONAL TELEVISION
PRESIDENT
Armando Nunex, Jr.
EXECUTIVE V.P.
Peter G. Hughes
V.P., LATIN AMERICA
Alejandro Garcia-Ramon
MANAGING DIRECTOR, UNIVERSAL INTERNATIONAL TELEVISION
Michael Brodie

UNIVERSAL TELEVISION ENTERTAINMENT
PRESIDENT
Barbara Fisher
EXECUTIVE V.P., UNIVERSAL CARTOON STUDIO
Nancy Steingard
EXECUTIVE V.P.
Bob Kelley
SENIOR V.P., CREATIVE AFFAIRS
Randy Levinson

Series/First Run: Coach (152 x 30 mins.), Hercules (35 x 60 mins.), Vanishing Son (35 x 60 mins.), Xena: Warrior Princess (22 x 60 mins.).

One-hour Series/Off-Network: Airwolf (80), Alfred Hitchcock Hour (93), Alias Smith And Jones (43), The A-Team (98), B.J./Lobo (85 x 30 mins. or 80 hours), Baretta (82), The Bionic Woman (58), Black Sheep Squadron (35), The Bold Ones (98), Buck Rogers (37), Emergency (136), The Equalizer (88), Five Star Mystery: Delvecchio/Ellery Queen/Mrs. Columbo/O'Hara (87), The Incredible Hulk (85), Ironside (198), It Takes A Thief (65), Knight Rider (90), Kojak (118), Magnum P.I. (162), Marcus Welby M.D. (172), Miami Vice (114), Northern Exposure (85), Quincy (148), Rockford Files (125), Run For Your Life (85), Simon & Simon (156), The Six Million Dollar Man (108), Thriller (67).

Half-hour Series: Alfred Hitchcock Presents (268), Amen (110), Bachelor Father (157), Charles in Charge (126), The Deputy (76), Gimme a Break (137), Harper Valley PTA (29), Harry and The Hendersons (72), House Calls (57), The Jack Benny Show (104), Kate and Allie (122), Leave It To Beaver (234), Love That Bob (173), Major Dad (96), McHale's Navy (138), Mickey Spillane's Mike Hammer (78), The Munsters Today (72), The Munsters (70), My Secret Identity (72), The New Dragnet (52), New Leave It To Beaver (105), The New Adam 12 (52), The New Lassie (48), Operation Petticoat (32), Out Of This World (96), Rod Serling's Night Gallery (97), That's Incredible (165), What A Dummy (24)

90 Min. Series: Banacek (16), Men From Shiloh (23), Mystery Movie: Columbo/McCloud/McMillan (124), The Name of The Game (76), The Virginian (225), Wagon Train (32).

Features/Packages: Abbott and Costello (29), Comedy Festival I (26), Dead End Kids Movies, Diabolic Dozen (12), List of a Lifetime I, List of a Lifetime II, Ninety Minute Movies (49 Made-For-TV), Paramount Pre'48 (196), Paramount Select (100), Reserve (169), Universal 53 (50), Universal 123 (114), Universal Color 100 (99), Universal Grand 50 (48 features), Universal Marvelous 10 (10 TV movies), Universal Network Movies 85 (52-2 hours, 33-90 minutes), Universal Pictures Debut Network (33 features), Universal Pictures Debut Network II (35 features), Universal Pictures Debut Network III (29 features), Universal Pictures Debut Network IV (19 features), Universal Pictures Debut Network V (19 features), Universal Pictures Debut Network VI (24 titles).

UPA PRODUCTIONS OF AMERICA

8640 Wilshire Blvd., Beverly Hills, CA 90211. (310) 659-6004.
FAX: (310) 659-4599.
PRESIDENT
Henry G. Saperstein
Series: Dick Tracy, Gerald McBoing-Boing, Godzilla, Mr. Magoo, Rodan.

VH-1

(For officers, please see listing under Cable Networks.)
1515 Broadway, New York, NY 10036. (212) 258-7800.
PRESIDENT
John Sykes
Products: Big Eighties, Crossroads, Flix, Four on the Floor, Top 21 Countdown, The Midnight Special, The Rupaul Show, Storytellers, VH-1 Archives, VH-1 Video Hall of Fame.

VIACOM INC.

1515 Broadway, New York, NY 10036. (212) 258-6000.
CHAIRMAN OF THE BOARD & CEO
Sumner M. Redstone
CEO, SHOWTIME NETWORKS, INC.
Matthew Blank
SENIOR V.P.
Martin Shea
PRESIDENT, PARAMOUNT PARKS
Jane Cooper
DEPUTY CHAIRMAN, EXECUTIVE V.P., GENERAL COUNSEL & CHIEF ADMINISTRATIVE OFFICER
Philippe P. Dauman
CHAIRMAN & CEO, VIACOM ENTERTAINMENT GROUP
Jonathan L. Dolgen
DEPUTY CHAIRMAN, EXECUTIVE V.P., FINANCE, CORPORATE DEVELOPMENT & COMMUNICATIONS
Thomas E. Dooley
CHAIRMAN & CEO, BLOCKBUSTER ENTERTAINMENT GROUP
John Antioco
SENIOR V.P., CORPORATE RELATIONS
Carl D. Folta
CHAIRMAN & CEO, MTV NETWORKS
Thomas E. Freston
SENIOR V.P., LEGAL & DEPUTY COUNSEL GENERAL
Michael D. Fricklas
SENIOR V.P., CORPORATE DEVELOPMENT
Rudolph L. Hertlein
CHAIRMAN, MOTION PICTURE GROUP, PARAMOUNT PICTURES
Sherry Lansing
PRESIDENT, NICKELODEON/NICK AT NITE
Herb Scannell
CHAIRMAN, TELEVISION GROUP, VIACOM ENTERTAINMENT GROUP
Kerry McCluggage
PRESIDENT & CEO, SIMON & SCHUSTER
Jonathan Newcomb
SENIOR V.P., HUMAN RESOURCES & ADMINISTRATION
William A. Roskin
First Run Programs: Montel Williams Show (daily x 60 mins.), Nick News (wkly x 30 mins.).
Series/Off-Network: The Adventures of Superboy (100 x 30 mins.), All in the Family (207 x 30 mins.), The Andy Griffith Show (249 x 30 mins.), The Beverly Hillbillies (274 x 30 mins.), Cannon (122 x 60 mins.), Clint Eastwood in Rawhide (144 x 60 mins.), The Cosby Show (200 x 30 mins.), A Different World (144 x 30 mins.), Family Affair (138 x 30 mins.), Gomer Pyle U.S.M.C. (150 x 30 mins.), Gunsmoke (402 x 60 mins.), Hawaii Five-O (282 x 60 mins.), Hogan's Heroes (168 x 30 mins.), The Honeymooners (107 x 30 mins.), I Love Lucy (179 x 30 mins., & 26 x 30 mins. of We Love Lucy), The Life and Times of Grizzly Adams (35 hours, 2 x 90 min. specials), Marshall Dillon (233 x 30 mins.), Matlock (177 hours), My Three Sons (160 x 30 mins.), Perry Mason (271 hours), Petticoat Junction (148 x 30 mins.), The Phil Silvers Show, Rawhide (73 x 60 mins.), The Rookies (90 x 60 mins.), Roseanne (147 x 30 mins.), The Twilight Zone (136 x 30 mins. & 18 x 60 mins.), The Wild Wild West (104 x 60 mins.).
Animated: The Alvin Show (26 x 30 mins.), Harlem Globetrotters (22 x 30 mins.), Terrytoons (689 cartoon units).
Feature Packages: Black Magic, Exploitables, Exploitables III, Exploitables IV, Family Entertainment, Gasp Horror, Gasp Science Fiction, Guts and Glory, The Legend Group, Perry Mason Features, Thematics: TV Net (Tonight Only), Thematics 2: Stories for Men, Stories for Women, Viacom Features I through 14, Viacom Movie Greats, Young and Reckless.

VIACOM PRODUCTIONS

c/o Colossal Pictures, 10 Universal City Plaza, Universal City, CA 91608-1002. (818) 505-7500. FAX: (818) 505-7599.
Current Series: Deadly Games.

JEFF WALD ENTERTAINMENT

12424 Wilshire Blvd., Suite 840, Los Angeles, CA 90025. (310) 820-9897.
PRESIDENT
Jeff Wald

WARNER BROS. TELEVISION ANIMATION

15303 Ventura Blvd., #1200, Sherman Oaks, CA 91403. (818) 977-8534. FX: (818) 977-8252.
PRESIDENT, WARNER BROS. TELEVISION ANIMATION
Jean McCurdy
S.V.P., & GENERAL MANAGER
Andy Lewis
SENIOR V.P., CLASSIC ANIMATION
Katherine Helppie-Shipley
Series: The Adventures of Batman and Robin, Steven Spielberg Presents Animaniacs, The Bugs Bunny & Tweety Show, Freakazoid, Pinky and the Brain, The Sylvester & Tweety Mysteries, That's Warner Bros.

WARNER BROS. TELEVISION

(For the WB Network, please see Broadcast Networks.)
(A subsidiary of Time Warner, Inc.)
4000 Warner Blvd., Burbank CA 91522. (818) 954-6000. FAX: (818) 954-4539. Telex: 4720389.
75 Rockefeller Plaza, New York, NY 10019. (212) 484-8000.

WARNER BROS. INC.

75 Rockefeller Plaza, New York, NY 10019. (212) 484-8000.
640 Fifth Ave., New York, NY 10019. (212) 903-5500.
4000 Warner Blvd., Burbank, CA 91522. (818) 954-6000.
CHAIRMAN OF THE BOARD & CO-CEO
Robert A. Daly
CHAIRMAN OF THE BOARD & CO-CEO
Terry Semel
EXECUTIVE V.P. & COO
Barry A. Meyer
EXECUTIVE V.P., BUSINESS & ACQUISITIONS
James R. Miller
EXECUTIVE V.P., INTERNATIONAL THEATRICAL ENTERPRISES
Richard J. Fox
EXECUTIVE V.P., MARKETING & PLANNING
Sanford E. Reisenbach
EXECUTIVE V.P & GENERAL COUNSEL
John Schulman
S.V.P., CORPORATE COMMUNICATIONS
Barbara S. Brogliatti

WARNER BROS. TELEVISION

PRESIDENT
Tony Jonas
EXECUTIVE V.P., BUSINESS AFFAIRS
Craig Hunegs
EXECUTIVE V.P., CREATIVE AFFAIRS
Gary Levine
SENIOR V.P., PRODUCTION
Andrew Ackerman
SENIOR V.P., ADMINISTRATION
Geriann Geraci
SENIOR V.P., COMEDY DEVELOPMENT
Maria Grasso
SENIOR V.P., MOVIES & MINI-SERIES
Gregg Maday
SENIOR V.P., TALENT & CASTING
Barbara Miller
SENIOR V.P., CURRENT PROGRAMMING
David Sacks
SENIOR V.P., LABOR RELATIONS
Hank Lachmund
SENIOR V.P., STUDIO GENERAL COUNSEL
Marjorie Neufeld
SENIOR V.P., COMEDY & DRAMA PRODUCTION
Judith Zaylor
SENIOR V.P., DRAMA DEVELOMENT & CURRENT PRO-GRAMMING
Steve Pearlman
SENIOR V.P., PUBLICITY, ADVERTISING & PROMOTION
David Stapf

WARNER BROS. DOMESTIC TELEVISION DISTRIBUTION

4001 N. Olive Ave., 4th Flr., Burbank, CA 91522. (818) 954-5652. FAX: (818) 954-5697.
PRESIDENT
Dick Robertson
EXECUTIVE V.P.
Scott Carlin
EXECUTIVE V.P./GENERAL SALES MANAGER
Dan Greenblatt
V.P., FINANCIAL OPERATIONS
David Cooper
VICE PRESIDENTS, CONTRACT ADMINISTRATION
Dan McRae
Brad Horner
VICE PRESIDENTS, WESTERN SALES
Mark O'Brien
Chris Smith
NEW YORK OFFICE
1325 Avenue of the Americas, 31st Flr., New York, NY 10019. (212) 636-5102. FAX: (212) 636-5380.
VICE PRESIDENTS, EASTERN SALES
Andrew Weir
Bill Marcus
Eric Strong
MANAGER, NORTHEASTERN SALES
John Buckholtz
SENIOR V.P., MEDIA SALES
Julie Kantrowitz
V.P., MEDIA SALES, EAST COAST SALES MANAGER
Paul T. Montoya
V.P., MEDIA SALES RESEARCH
Jean Goldberg
DIR., SALES PLANNING & BUSINESS DEVELOPMENT
Clifford Brown
DIRECTOR, MEDIA SALES
Roseann Cacciola
CHICAGO OFFICE
645 N. Michigan Ave., Ste. 1050, Chicago, IL 60611. (312) 440-9696. FAX: (312) 440-0949.
V.P. & CENTRAL SALES MANAGER
Mark Robbins
V.P., CENTRAL SALES
Jeff Hufford
MANAGER, CENTRAL SALES
James Knopf
V.P., MEDIA SALES
Jean Medd
SALES PLANNER
Jean Medd
ATLANTA OFFICE
One CNN Center North Tower, Ste. 908, Atlanta, GA 30303. (404) 525-4300. FAX: (404) 525-4336.
V.P., SOUTHEASTERN SALES MANAGER
Mary Voll
MANAGER, SOUTHEASTERN SALES
Marlynda Salas Lecate
DALLAS OFFICE
8144 Walnut Hill Lane, Ste. 500, Dallas, TX 75231. (214) 360-3016. FAX: (214) 369-4889.
V.P., SOUTHWESTERN SALES MANAGER
Jacqueline Hartley
MANAGER, SOUTHWESTERN SALES
Jim Kramer

DOMESTIC PRODUCT

Continuing Series: Bless This House, Charlie Grace, The Drew Carey Show, ER, Family Matters, Friends, The Jamie Foxx Show, Living Single, Murphy Brown, Nick Freno: Licensed Teacher, The Parent 'Hood, Sisters, Step by Step, Suddenly Susan, The Wayans Bros.

Series: Alvin & the Chipmunks (65 x 30 mins.), Carnie, EXTRA, Getting Even (260 x 30 mins.), History of Rock & Roll, Island City, Jenny Jones (170 x 60 mins.), The Jesse Jackson Show (40 x 60 mins.), Love Connection (195 x 30 mins.), Love Stories (170 x 60 mins.), Merrie Melodies Starring Bugs Bunny & Friends (65 x 30 mins.), P-TEN (Kung Fu: The Legend Continues, Time Trax, Pointman and Babylon 5), The People's Court (195 x 30 mins.), The Rosie O'Donnell Show, Tiny Toon Adventures (65 x 30 mins.), Trump Card (170 x 30 mins.).

Miniseries: Bare Essence (4 x 60 mins. or 4 x 30 mins.), Hollywood Wives (6 hrs.), The Thorn Birds (10 hrs.), "V" (10 hrs.).

Series/Off-Network: ALF, Alice (202 x 30 mins.), Batman/Superman/Aquaman (69 animated x 30 mins.), The Blue Knight (23 x 60 mins.), Chico and the Man (88 x 30 mins.), Dallas (330 x 60 mins.), The Dukes of Hazzard (147 x 60 mins.), Eight is Enough (112 x 30 mins.), Family Matters, The FBI (234 x 60 mins.), The Fresh Prince of Bel-Air, F-Troop (65 x 30 mins.), Full House, Growing Pains, Harry-O (44 x 60 mins.), Head of the Class, Here's Lucy (144 x 30 mins.), The Hogan Family, It's a Living, Knots Landing (276 x 60 mins.), Kung Fu (62 x 60 mins.), Mama's Family, Matt Houston (68 x 60 mins.), Maverick (124 x 60 mins.), More Real People, Murphy Brown, My Favorite Martian (107 x 30 mins.), The New Dick Van Dyke/Mayberry R.F.D., Night Court, Perfect Strangers, Private Benjamin (39 x 30 mins.), Scarecrow and Mrs. King (88 x 60 mins.), Superman (104 x 30 mins.), Tarzan (57 x 60 mins.), The Waltons (221 x 60 mins.), Welcome Back, Kotter (95 x 30 mins.), Wonder Woman (61 x 60 mins.).

Features/Packages: Bomba the Jungle Boy (13 features), The Bowery Boys (48 features), Classic Thrillers (13 features), Classic Thrillers II (13 features), Cowboys and Indians (32 westerns from Allied Artists), Easy Eight (8 features), Encore One (53 features), The FBI Story (4 features), Lorimar I (21 features), Lorimar II (22 features), Masters of Fury (15 martial arts films), Mint Edition (23 features), Power Package I (13 titles), Premiere Edition (15 titles), Premiere Edition (10 titles), Premiere Edition 2 (25 made-for-TV movies), Sci-Fi Horror (33 features), Starlite 3 (30 features, 19 in color), Starlite 4 (30 features, 16 in color), Starlite 5 (28 features, 18 in color), Starlite 6 (26 features, 12 in color), Tarzan Features (32 features, 9 in color), Telepictures 1 (14 features), Telepictures 2 (27 made-for-TV movies), Telepictures 3 (24 features), TVI (13 features), TV2 (13 features), TV3 (13 features), TV4 (13 features), 22 Karat (24 features), Ultra 4 (30 features), Volume 1-A (24 features, 17 in color), Volume 13 (25 features, 17 in color), Volume 14-15 (13 features, 12 in color), Volume 16 (18 features, 16 in color), Volume 17 (23 features, 21 in color), Volume 18 (28 features, 25 in color), Volume 19 (29 features, 28 in color), Volume 20 (30 features), Volume 21 (26 features), Volume 22 (38 features), Volume 23 (20 features), Volume 24 (18 features), Volume 25 (24 features), Volume 26 (24 features), Volume 27 (18 features), Volume 28 (28 features), Volume 29 (20 features), Volume 30 (29 titles), Volume 31 (53 titles), Volume 2-A (22 features, 13 in color).

Cartoons: Bugs Bunny & Friends (100 cartoons), Porky Pig & Friends (156 cartoons).

WARNER BROS. CORP. MARKETING & ADVERTISING

4001 N. Olive Ave., Burbank, CA 91522. (818) 954-5652. FAX: (818) 954-5925.
SENIOR V.P.
Jim Moloshok
V.P., MARKETING & ADVERTISING
Yelena Garofolo
EXECUTIVE, STATION MARKETING
Gene Steinberg
DIRECTOR, MEDIA SERVICES
Wendy Ehrlich
DIRECTORS, VIDEO SERVICES
Judi Stewart
Lauren Dansey

WARNER BROS. CORPORATE MEDIA RESEARCH

4001 N. Olive Ave., Burbank, CA 91522. (818) 954-5652. FAX: (818) 954-5882.
SENIOR V.P.
Bruce K. Rosenblum
VICE PRESIDENTS
Wayne Neiman
Liz Huszarik
Kurt Bensmiller
V.P., RESEARCH & NEW MEDIA DEVELOPMENT
Robert Jennings
DIRECTORS
Karen Barcheski
David Sommerville
MANAGER
Mark Howard
SUPERVISOR
Jamie Euster
SENIOR ANALYSTS
Dika Ryan
Mary McIlrath
Carolyn Stys
Sharon Maroof
ANALYSTS
Tanysha Laney
Julia Olson
Liz Militello

TELEPICTURES PRODUCTIONS

3500 W. Olive Ave., Suite 1000, Burbank, CA 91505. (818) 972-0777. FAX: (818) 972-0706.
PRESIDENT
Jim Paratore
SENIOR V.P., PROGRAMMING
Alan Perris
LEGAL & BUSINESS AFFAIRS
Alan Saxe
SENIOR V.P., PRODUCTION
Kevin Fortson
VICE PRESIDENTS, DEVELOPMENT
David Auerbach
Lisa Hackner-Goldberg

TIME TELEPICTURES TELEVISION

3500 W. Olive Ave., Suite 1000, Burbank, CA 91505. (818) 972-0778. FAX: (818) 954-0706.
PRESIDENT, TELEPICTURES PRODUCTIONS
Jim Paratore
V.P., CURRENT PROGRAMMING, TIME TELEPICTURES TV
David Goldberg

TELEPICTURES DISTRIBUTION

4001 N. Olive Ave., 4th Flr., Burbank, CA 91522. (818) 954-5728. FAX: (818) 954-7295.
EXECUTIVE V.P.
Scott Carlin
SENIOR V.P.
Vince Messina
ACCOUNT EXECUTIVE
John Martinelli
NEW YORK OFFICE
1325 6th Ave., #1st Flr., New York, NY 10019. (212) 636-5102. FAX: 9212) 636-5380.
SENIOR V.P.
Damiam Riordan
MANAGER, EASTERN SALES
Joel Lewin
ACCOUNT EXECUTIVE
Pat McDonald
CHICAGO OFFICE
645 N. Michigan Ave., Ste. 1050, Chicago, IL 60611. (312) 440-9696. FAX: (312) 440-0949.
V.P., CENTRAL SALES MANAGER
Bill Hague
ACCOUNT EXECUTIVE
Matt Wasserlauf
ATLANTA OFFICE
One CNN Center North Tower, Ste. 908, Atlanta, GA 30303. (404) 525-4300. FAX: (404) 525-4336.
V.P., SOUTHEASTERN SALES
Chuck Self

PAY TV, CABLE & NETWORK FEATURES

75 Rockefeller Center, New York, NY 10020. (212) 484-8000. FAX: (212) 397-0728.
PRESIDENT
Edward Bleier
V.P., MARKETING
Eric Frankel
VICE PRESIDENT
Jeffrey Calman

WARNER BROS. INTERNATIONAL TELEVISION DISTRIBUTION

4000 Warner Blvd., Bldg. 118, Burbank, CA 91522. (818) 954-5491. FAX: (818) 954-4040.
PRESIDENT
Jeffrey R. Schlesinger
SENIOR V.P.
Kevin Byles
SENIOR V.P., ADMINISTRATION & OPERATIONS
Mauro Sardi
SENIOR V.P., INTERNATIONAL TV OPERATIONS
Annette Bouso
SENIOR V.P., PAY TV, INTERNATIONAL DISTRIBUTION
Malcolm Dudley-Smith
SENIOR V.P., INTERNATIONAL TV PRODUCTION
Catherine Malatesta
SENIOR V.P., LEGAL & BUSINESS AFFAIRS, INTERNATIONAL TV DISTRIBUTION
Ron Miele

FOREIGN SALES OFFICES

AUSTRALIA & FAR EAST

Warner Bros. Int'l, Level 22, 8-20 Napier St., N. Sydney, NSW 2060, Australia. (612) 957 3899. FAX: (612) 956 7788.
V.P., MANAGING DIRECTOR, AUSTRALIA/ ASIA PACIFIC
Wayne Broun
V.P., ASIA
Greg Robertson

CHINA

100 Canton Road, 7th Floor, Tsimshatsui, Kowloon, Hong Kong. (852) 376 3963. FAX: (852) 376 1302.
DIRECTOR, BUSINESS DEVELOPMENT, ASIA
Robert Wood

FRANCE

67 Avenue de Wagram, 75017 Paris, France. (331) 4401 4999. FAX: (331) 4401 4968.
VICE PRESIDENT
Michel LeCourt

CANADA

Warner Bros. TV, 4576 Yonge St., 2nd floor, North York, Ontario, Canada, M2N 6P1. (416) 250 8384. FAX: (416) 250 8930.
V.P., OPERATIONS
Kevin Byles

ITALY

Warner Bros. Italia, Via G. Avezzana #51, Rome 00195, Italy. (396) 321 7779. FAX: (396) 321 7278.
MANAGING DIRECTOR
Rosario Ponzio

SPAIN, PORTUGAL, MALTA & GIBRALTAR

Warner Bros. TV, 28014 Madrid, Spain. (341) 522 2906. FAX: (341) 532 9869.
MANAGING DIRECTOR V.P., BUSINESS DEVELOPMENT, EUROPE
Josh Berger

JAPAN

Warner Bros. Intl. TV Distribution, 1-2-4 Hamamatsu-Cho, Minato-Ku, Tokyo 105 Japan. (813) 5472 8340. FAX: (813) 5472 6343.
MANAGING DIRECTOR
Teruji Mochimaru

LATIN AMERICA

Warner Bros. (Mexico) S.A., Acapulco 37, Mexico 7 D.F., Mexico C.D. 06140. (525) 211 3353. FAX: (525) 553 2822.
VICE PRESIDENT
Jorge Sanchez

UNITED KINGDOM TERRITORIES, SCANDINAVIA & BENELUX, AFRICA, MIDDLE EAST

Warner Bros. Intl. TV, 135 Wardour Street, London W1V 4AP England. (4471) 494 3710. FAX: (4471) 287 9086.
V.P., U.K. TERRITORIES
Richard Milnes
V.P., PAY-TV & NEW TECHNOLOGY LICENSING
Malcolm Dudley-Smith
SALES DIRECTOR, SCANDINAVIA & BENELUX
Donna Brett
SALES EXECUTIVE, MIDDLE EAST & AFRICA
Tim Horan
DIRECTOR, MARKETING & PROMOTION, U.K. TERRITORIES
Shelley Groves

INTERNATIONAL PRODUCT

New One Hour Series: Hungry For Survival (ABC), Leaving LA, Prince Street, Police Academy: The Series (Synd.), Spy Game.

New Half Hour Series: Built to Last (NBC), Meego (CBS), Rewind (FOX), The Secret Lives of Men (ABC), Veronica's Closet (NBC), You Send Me (NBC), You're the One (WB).

New Half Hour Animated Series: Johnny Bravo (Cartoon Network), Zorro (Synd.).

New Made-For-Television Movies: Babylon 5: In the Beginning (TNT), Babylon 5: Thirdspace (TNT), L.A. Johns (FOX), Path to Paradise: The Untold story of the World Trade Center Bombing (HBO), The Second Civil War (HBO), The Underworld (NBC).

New Specials: 1998 Goodwill Games (TNT), HBO Boxing Special Events, HBO World Boxing, World Championship Wrestling (TNT).

Animated Series: ALF (26 x 30 mins.), ALF Tales (21 x 30 mins.), Alvin and the Chipmunks (65 x 30 mins.), Aquaman (18 x 30 mins.), Batman (17 x 30 mins.), Batman: The Animated Series (85 x 30 mins.), Beetlejuice (94 x 30 mins.), Beverly Hills Teens (65 x 30 mins.), The Botts (65 x 30 mins.), Bugs Bunny and Tweety Show (26 x 30 mins.), Bugs Bunny Show (78 x 30 mins.), Bumpety Boo (43 x 30 mins.), C.O.P.S. (65 x 30 mins.), Camp Candy (39 x 30 mins.), Captain N (26 x 30 mins.), Care Bears (36 x 30 mins.), Cats & Company (86 x 30 mins.), Challenge of Superfriends (16 x 30 mins.), Comic Strip-Karate Kat (13 x 30 mins.), Comic Strip-Monsters (13 x 30 mins.), Comic Strip-Street Frogs (13 x 30 mins.), Comic Strip-Tiger Sharks (26 x 30 mins.), Cow & Chicken, Dennis the Menace (65 x 30 mins.), Dexter's Laboratory, The Dukes (20 x 30 mins.), Fairy Tale Favorites (5 x 30 mins.), Fat Albert and the

Cosby Kids (60 x 30 mins.), Gepetto's Music Shop (13 x 30 mins.), Get Along Gang (13 x 30 mins.), Grendizier Raids (52 x 30 mins.), Gumby (32 x 30 mins.), Inspector Gadget (21 x 30 mins.), Jayce and the Wheeled Warriors (65 x 30 mins.), Kid 'n Play (13 x 30 mins.), Lassie's Rescue Rangers (17 x 30 mins.), Little Women (48 x 30 mins.), Marine Boy (78 x 30 mins.), Mask (75 x 30 mins.), Maxie's World (16 x 30 mins.), Merrie Melodies (24 x 30 mins.), New Adventures of Batman (16 x 30 mins.), New Adventures of Superman (34 x 30 mins.), The New Archies (13 x 30 mins.), The New Gumby (33 x 30 mins.), Photon (26 x 30 mins.), Pole Position (13 x 30 mins.), Police Academy: The Animated Series (65 x 30 mins.), Popples (23 x 30 mins.), Porky Pig Show (26 x 30 mins.), Rainbow Brite (13 x 30 mins.), Roadrunner Show (26 x 30 mins.), Rubik: The Amazing Cube (13 x 30 mins.), Sanybelle (47 x 30 mins.), Silverhawks (65 x 30 mins.), Spiral Zone (65 x 30 mins.), Starcom (26 x 30 mins.), Steven Spielberg Presents Animaniacs (65 x 30 mins.), Tiny Toon Adventures (96 x 30 mins.), Super Mario Brothers (65 x 30 mins.), Superfriends (77 x 30 mins.), Superman Animated (13 x 30 mins.), Sylvanians (13 x 30 mins.), Tarzan: Lord of the Jungle (34 x 30 mins.), Taz-Mania (65 x 30 mins.), Thundercats (130 x 30 mins.), Tiny Toons Adventures–The Looney Beginning (1 x 30 mins.), TV Funnies (16 x 30 mins.), Wolfrock TV (13 x 30 mins.), Zoobilee Zoo (65 x 30 mins.).

Miniseries: A.D. (12 hrs.), Alcatraz: The True Story (4 hrs.), The Awakening Land (7 hrs.), Bare Essence (4 hrs.), Blind Ambition (8), Blood & Orchids (4), Blood Red Roses (4), Bloodlines: Murder in the Family (4 hrs.), Born to the Wind (4 hrs.), The Bourne Identity (4 hrs.), Casanova (4 hrs.), Christopher Columbus (6 hrs.), Common Ground (4 hrs.), Crossings (6 hrs.), Deadly Intentions (4 hrs.), A Death in California (4 hrs.), The Deliberate Stranger (4 hrs.), Dream West (7 hrs.), Dress Gray (4 hrs.), Eleanor and Franklin (4 hrs.), Ellis Island (7 hrs.), Eureka Stockade (4 hrs.), For Those I Loved (8 hrs.), Golden Moment: Olympic Love Story (4 hrs.), Guyana Tragedy (4 hrs.), Hanging by a Thread (4 hrs.), Haywire (4 hrs.), Heaven and Hell (6 hrs.), Hollywood Wives (6 hrs.), I Know My First Name Is Steven (4 hrs.), IT (4 hrs.), Jack the Ripper (4 hrs.), Lace (5 hrs.), Lace II (4 hrs.), Liberty (4 hrs.), A Man Called Intrepid (6 hrs.), Maria Chapdelaine (4 hrs.), Mino (6 hrs.), Moviola (4 hrs.), Mr. Horn (4 hrs.), Murder in Texas (4 hrs.), The Mystic Warrior (5 hrs.), Napoleon and Josephine: A Love Story (9 hrs.), Night the Bridge Fell Down (4 hrs.), North and South - I (12 hrs.), North and South - II (12 hrs.), Nutcracker: Money, Madness and Murder (6 hrs.), Pearl (6 hrs.), Pirate (4 hrs.), Queen (6 hrs.), Race for the Bomb (6 hrs.), Roots (12 hrs.), Roots: The Next Generation (14 hrs.), Roses Are for the Rich (4 hrs.), The Sacketts (4 hrs.), Salem's Lot (4 hrs.), Sands of Time (4 hrs.), Scruples (6 hrs.), Sinatra (5 hrs.), The Sophisticated Gents (4 hrs.), Stalin (4 hrs.), Strong Medicine (4 hrs.), Studs Lonigan (6 hrs.), The Thorn Birds (10 hrs.), Thornbirds: The Missing Years (6 hrs.), The Two Mrs. Grenvilles (4 hrs.), "V" (10 hrs.), The Wild West (10 hrs.), World War III (4 hrs.).

One-Hour Series: Aaron's Way (14), The Adventures of Brisco County Jr. (26), Against the Grain (8), The Alaskans (36), American Detective (4), Angel Street (3), Babylon 5 (22), Banyon (15), Bare Essence (11), Berrenger's (13), The Best Times (6), Big Shamus Little Shamus (10), Billy Crystal Show (6), Bodies of Evidence (16), Booker (13), Boone (13), Bourbon Street Beat (39), Bourbon Street Parade (26), Bridges to Cross (6), Bronco (68), California Fever (10), Casablanca (5), Cheyenne (107), China Beach (62), Cobra (22), Code R (13), The Colbys (49), Crossroads (12), D.E.A. (11), The Dakotas (19), Dark Justice (66), Delphi Bureau (8), Detective in the House (6), Dial M for Murder (13), Diamonds (44), Divine Obsession (122), Double Dare (6), Dramas I & II (42), Dukes of Hazard (147), Enos (17), Eye to Eye (6), Falcon Crest (209), The F.B.I. (238), La Femme Nikita, Finder of Lost Loves (23), Fitzpatricks (13), The Flash (21), Freddy's Nightmares (22), Freebie and the Bean (9), Gabriel's Fire (22), Gallant Men (25), Games People Play (25), Glitter (13), Going to Extremes (17), Guns of Paradise (13), Harry O (44), Hawaiian Eye (134), Heartbeat (17), Hearts Are Wild (7), High Performance (4), Hollywood Beat (14), Homefront (42), Hot House/The Clinic (6), Hotel (124), How'd They Do That? (23), Hulk Hogan's Rock and Wrestling (13), Human Target (7), Hunter (153), I Had Three Wives (6), I'll Fly Away (37), In Concert (78), Island Son (18), Jenny Jones III (170), Jesse Jackson Show/Voices of America (40), Knots Landing (303), Kung Fu (62), Kung Fu: The Legend Continues (42), Life Goes On (61), Life on Earth (13), Lois & Clark: The New Adventures of Superman (20), MacGruder and Loud (13), A Man Called Hawk (13), Maria Maria (198), Matt Houston (66), Maverick (124), Max Headroom (14), Midnight Caller (61), The Mississippi (23), Morningstar/Eveningstar (6), New Adventures of Wonder Woman (46), The New Land (13),

Nichols (24), Nightingales (12), Ohara (28), Our Family Honor (12), Our House 46), Paradise (44), Pros and Cons (13), Rafferty (13), Real People (105), Reasonable Doubts (44), Renegade (44), Roaring 20's (45), Scarecrow and Mrs. King (88), Search (23), Secrets of Midland Heights (10), 77 Sunset Strip (205), Shadow Chasers (12), Shell Game (6), Sisters (75), Skag (5), Sonny Spoon (15), Spenser: For Hire (64), Spies (6), Studio 5-B (10), Sugarfoot (69), Surfside Six (74), Tarzan (57), Three Kingdoms (26), Time Express (4), Time Trax (42), Top of the Hill (12), The Tribal Eye (7), Two Marriages (9), Under Cover (12), Unsub (8), "V" (19), The Waltons (219), Wizards and Warriors (8), Wonder Woman (13), Wonderworks (21), World Entertainment (156), The Yeagers (4), The Yellow Rose (22), Young Maverick (6).

Half-Hour Series: Love, Sidney (44), Off the Rack (7), A.E.S Hudson Street (5), ALF (100), All New Let's Make a Deal (170), American Detective (43), Another Day (13), At Ease (14), B.C. Archaeology of Bible Lands (12), Beetlejuice (21), Behind the Screen (13), Best of the Worst (14), Better Days (12), Bill & Ted's Excellent Adventures (7), Billy/Immediate Family (13), Bourbon Street Parade (26), Brian Keith Show (22), Buffalo Bill (26), Cafe Americain (18), Caribbean Nights (13), Catch Phrase (65), The Challengers (9), Chicago Teddy Bears (13), Chico and the Man (88), College Madhouse (26), Colt .45 (67), The Cowboys (12), Dave Thomas Comedy Show (6), Days and Nights of Molly Dodd (65), Detective School (13), Dorothy (4), Down the Shore (29), Dreams (12), The Drew Carey Show, F Troop (65), Family Album (13), Family Man (22), Family Matters (144), Family Medical Center (170), Fantasy Theatre (39), Flatbush (7), Flo (29), Fresh Prince of Bel Air (98), Frontier Adventures (63), Full House (168), Fun House (331), Game of the Century World Cup (6), George Carlin (14), Getting By (31), Gigi (52), Going Places (19), Good Sports (15), Goodnight Beantown (18), Growing Pains (176), Hail to the Chief (7), Hangin' With Mr. Cooper (44), Head of the Class (90), Heavenly Days (4), Here's Lucy (144), Hitchhiker (65), Hogan Family (110), In Concert III (26), It Had to Be You (9), It's a Living (93), Jackie Thomas Show (18), Jimmy Stewart Show (24), John Larroquette Show (22), Just in Time (6), Just Our Luck (13), Just the Ten of Us (47), Last Frontier (100), Laugh-In (130), Lawman (156), Life With Lucy (13), Little Kids Dynamite All-Star Band (13), Little People (24), Little Women (48), Living Single (49), Look at Us (24), Lorne Greene's Wild Wilderness (94), Love Connection (2,118), Love Stories (85), Love Sidney (44), Lulabelle (52), Maggie Briggs (6), Magic Star Traveler (39), Mama's Family (95), Martin (54), Mayberry RFD (78), Me and Maxx (10), Mednews and Family News (170), Mednews II (312), Memories of a Fairy Godmother (13), Molloy (6), More Real People (130), Mr. Moon's Magic Circus (13), Mr. Roberts (30), Murphy Brown (175), My Favorite Martian (107), My Kind of Town (7), My Pet Monster (13), My Sister Sam (44), Mysteries of the Indigo Depths (39), Nearly Departed (6), New Dick Van Dyke Show (72), Night Court (180), No Time for Sergeants (34), Oceanquest (6), Off the Rack (7), One Big Family (25), $1,000,000 Chance of a Lifetime (285), Parenting Network (312), Park Place (5), People Next Door (10), People's Court (over 2,000 episodes), Perfect Couples (80), Perfect Strangers (144), Private Benjamin (39), The Professionals (13), The Redd Foxx Show (13), Roc (72), Rollergirls (4), Room for One More (26), Room for Two (26), Scorch (6), Shaky Ground (17), Shazam! (28), She's the Sheriff (44), Six O'Clock Follies (6), Slap Maxwell (22), Step by Step (69), Sugar Time (13), Superior Court (510), Tales From the Crypt (21), Tales From the Darkside (90), Tall Hopes (6), Television Parts (8), Third Degree (170), Tom (12), The Trouble With Larry (6), Waverly Wonders (9), Welcome Back Kotter (95).

90 minute series: King's Crossing (10).

One-Hour Specials: Abracadabra: It's Magic, ALF's Christmas Special, All-Star Tribute to Jazz, All-Star Toast to Improv, Andrew Dice Clay: For Ladies Only, Annual Young Comedians Specials (13 episodes), Bernstein at 70, Bill Hicks: Revelations, Blockheads, Boo, Brotherhood, Carly Simon: Coming Around Again, Cinemax Sessions (12), Concert of the World, Damon Wayans, Debby Boone Special, Dennis Miller: Live From Washington D.C., Different Worlds, Dionne Warwick in Concert, Dummies: Third Annual Adult Ventriloquism Show, Entertainment Weekly (91), Evening With Alan King, Garry Shandling: Stand-Up, Garry Trudeau Rap Master, George Burns in Concert, Grammy Hall of Fame, HBO Comedy Hour (3), HBO Magic Show, HBO Presents EMO, International Emmy Awards, Karmon Israeli Dancers, Larry Miller: Just Words, Little River Band in Australia, Loretta Lynn Special, Louie Anderson: Comedy on Canvas, Luciano Pavarotti at Via Reggio, Made in Italy With Irene Cara, Made in Italy With Lola Falana, Manhattan Transfer Special, Martin Mull on Location, Mumbo Jumbo: It's Magic, Pat Benetar, Paul Reiser: Out on a Whim, Paul Shaffer: Viva Shaf Vegas, Paula Poundstone: Cats Cops and Stuff, Pee-wee Herman Show, People Magazine (3), People of the Year I, Presto Chango: It's Magic, Richard Lewis: I'm Exhausted, Rita Rudner: Born to Be Mild, Robert Townsend & His Partners in Crime, Robin Williams on Location, Sinbad: Brain Dead, Sports

Illustrated Swimsuit (4), Stand Up at 40, Superman's 50th Anniversary Special, A Very Special Christmas, Whoopi Goldberg: Fontaine...Why Am I Straight?, Women of the Night (3), Woodstock: Return to the Planet of the 60's, World Entertainment: Road to the 1992 Academy Awards, World Figure Skating Champions Salute Dorothy Hamill, A Year Without Santa Claus, 15th Annual Young Comedians Show.

Half-Hour Specials: Alexander and the Terrible No Good Very Bad Year, Ann Magnuson's Vandemonium, Bat Cat and the Penguin, Big Apple Circus, Braingames, Earthday Birthday, Hardcore IV, Hollywood Dog, Jackie Bison Show, Kids on Kids on Kids, Little Drummer Boy Book II, New Home Owner's Guide to Happiness, Norman's Corner, One-Night Stand (38), Paula Poundstone Show, Rock the House, The Wickedest Witch.

Long-form Specials: Barbara Walters 50th Anniversary Special, Boxing Event: Mancini vs. Camacho, Billy Crystal: Midnight Train to Moscow, Diana Ross in Concert, Exploring the Unknown (74 mins.), Gladys Knight and the Pips, Guilt or Innocence: The Trial of James Earl Ray, Here's Looking at You Warner Bros., Presidential Inaugural Gala, Special Olympics, St. Mark's Gospel, Earth Day Special, You Can't Take It With You.

WEISS GLOBAL ENTERPRISES

2055 S. Saviers Rd., Suite 12, Oxnard, CA 93033-3693. (805) 486-4495. FAX: (805) 487-3330
PRESIDENT/TREASURER
Adrian Weiss
VICE PRESIDENT
Karen R. Engelhardt
SECRETARY
Ethel L. Weiss
INFORMATION SERVICES
Alex Gordon
Features: Galaxy "15" (15 features including: Ginger in the Morning, Lovers Like Us, Molly and Lawless John), Impact "120" (120 features prod. by Robert L. Lippert including: Baron of Arizona, I Shot Jesse James, King Dinosaur, Sins of Jezebel, Steel Helmet), Bride & The Beast, Westerns: (60 action features starring Johnny Mack Brown, Harry Carey, Fred Kohler, Jr., Rex Lease, Buddy Roosevelt and Bob Steele), Vintage Flicks (24 features from the 30's and 40's).
Serials: The Black Coin (15 episodes), The Clutching Hand (15 episodes), Custer's Last Stand (15 episodes).
Series: Kids Say the Darndest Things (500 x 5 min. each), The Stan Kann Show (52 x 30 mins.).
Off-Network Series: The Adventures of Jim Bowie (76 x 30 mins.), Craig Kennedy, Criminologist (26 x 30 mins.), I Married Joan (98 x 30 mins.), Make Room For Daddy (161 x 30 mins.), My Little Margie (126 x 30 mins.), Rocky Jones–Space Ranger (39 x 30 mins.), Thrill of Your Life (13 x 30 mins.), Waterfront (78 x 30 mins.).
Comedy Shorts: The Chuckle Heads (150 x 5 mins.).
Cartoons: Alice by Walt Disney (10 Alice cartoons), Krazy Kid Kartunes (4 x 6 mins.), Nursery Rhymes (6 x 1.5 mins.).

WILSHIRE COURT PRODUCTIONS

1840 Century Park East, Suite 400, Los Angeles, CA 90067. (310) 557-2444. FAX: (310) 557-0017.
PRESIDENT
John J. McMahon
V.P., PRODUCTION
Ed Milkovich

WIND DANCER PRODUCTION GROUP

500 S. Buena Vista, Prod. Bldg., 3rd floor, Burbank, CA 91521-2215. (818) 560-5715. FAX: (818) 563-9654.
152 W. 57th St., New York, NY 10019. (212) 830-5820. FAX: (212) 830-5838.
EXECUTIVE PRODUCERS
Matt Williams
David McFadzean
Carmen Finestra
Series: Home Improvement, Soul Man.

WITT-THOMAS PRODUCTIONS

c/o Sunset-Gower Studios, 1438 N. Gower St., Bldg. 35, 4th fl., Hollywood, CA 90028. (213) 464-1333. FAX: (23) 957-9886.
PARTNERS
Paul Junger Witt
Tony Thomas
Series: Brotherly Love, The John Larroquette Show, Pearl, Common Law.

FRED WOLF FILMS

4222 W. Burbank Blvd., Burbank, CA 91505. (818) 846-0611.
Animated Series: Teenage Mutant Ninja Turtles, Dino Babies.

WOLF FILMS INC.

c/o Universal TV, 100 Universal City Plaza, Bldg. 69-F, Universal City, CA 91608-1085. (818) 777-3131. FAX: (818) 866-1446
EXECUTIVE PRODUCER, PRESIDENT
Dick Wolf
DIRECTOR, DEVELOPMENT, TV
Adam Borstein
Series: Law & Order, New York Undercover.

THE WOLPER ORGANIZATION

4000 Warner Blvd., Bldg. 14, #X, Burbank, CA 91522-0001. (818) 954-1421. FAX: (818) 954-1593.

WORLDVISION ENTERPRISES, INC.

(A Unit of Spelling Entertainment, Inc.)
1700 Broadway, 10th floor, New York, NY 10019-5992. (212) 261-2700. FAX: (212) 261-2788.
PRESIDENT & CEO
John D. Ryan
EXECUTIVE V.P. & COO
Bert Cohen
S.V.P., FINANCE & CFO
Tony Colabraro
S.V.P., LEGAL & BUSINESS AFFAIRS
Philip Marella
S.V.P., MARKETING
Gary G. Montanus
S.V.P., OPERATIONS
Charles Quinones
S.V.P., DOMESTIC SALES
Robert E. Raleigh
V.P., ADVERTISER SALES
Robert Chernoff
V.P., CABLE/NEW TECHNOLOGIES
Bill Baffi
V.P., EASTERN DIVISION MANAGER
Frank L. Browne
V.P., EASTERN DIVISION
Brian O'Sullivan

INTERNATIONAL BRANCHES

AUSTRALIA

Worldvision Enterprises of Australia Pty. Ltd., 5-13 Northcliff St., Milsons Point 2061, Sydney. (612) 922 4722. FAX: (612) 955 8207.
SALES
Brian Rhys-Jones

BRAZIL

Worldvision Filmes do Brasil Ltd., Rua Macedo Sobrinho 50, Botafogo, CEP 22271, Rio de Janeiro. (5521) 286 8992. FAX: (5521) 266 4737.
SALES
Raymundo Rodriguez

CANADA

Worldvision Enterprises of Canada, 1200 Bay St., Suite 203, Toronto M5R 2A5, Ontario. (416) 967 1200. FAX: (416) 967 0521.
SALES
Bruce Swanson

FRANCE

Worldvision Enterprises S.A.R.L., 28 rue Bayard 75008, Paris. (331) 4723 3995. FAX: (331) 4070 9269.
SALES
Mary Jane Fourniel

ITALY

Worldvision Enterprises, Inc., Adalia Anstalt, Via Del Corso, 22/Interno 10, 00186, Rome.
SALES
Michael Kiwe

JAPAN

Worldvision Enterprises, Inc., Tsukiji Hamarikyu Bldg., 7th Floor, 5-3-3, Tsukiji, Chou-ku, Tokyo 104. (813) 3545 3978. FAX: (813) 3545 3964.
SALES
Yukie Kumagai

LATIN AMERICA

Worldvision Enterprises Latin America, Inc., 400 Perimeter Center Terrace, Suite 150, Atlanta, GA 30346. (404) 394 3967. FAX: (404) 394 9002.

UNITED KINGDOM

Worldvision Enterprises, U.K. Ltd., 54 Pont St., London, SW 1X OAE, England. (44171) 584 5357. FAX: (44171) 581 3483.
SALES
William Peck
Janice Wilson
Zsuzsanna Jung
DOMESTIC PRODUCT
First Run Series: Hot Bench, Jim J. & Ann, Night Stand.

First Run Theatrical Features: Carolco III (20 theatrical releases), Carolco IV (20 theatrical releases), Fantastic Fantasies (4 family-oriented features), Showcase Network II (15 theatrical releases), Worldvision 1 (18 theatrical films), Worldvision 2 (18 theatrical films), Worldvision 3 (26 theatrical films).

Off-Network Hour Series: Barnaby Jones (177), Ben Casey (153), Beverly Hills 90210 (108), Combat (152), The Invaders (43), Little House on the Prairie (216.5), Love Boat (140), Love Boat II (115), Mod Squad (124), Night Heat (96), Streets of San Francisco (119).

Half-Hour Series: Adventures of Champion (26), After Hours (120), Almost Alive (65), Annie Oakley (80), Buffalo Bill, Jr. (40), Come Along (13), Dark Shadows (1,245), Dickens & Fenster (32), Doris Day Show (128), Douglas Fairbanks Presents (115), Emergency (6), F.D.R. (27), Flying "A" Series (222), High Road (36), It Pays to Be Ignorant (39), Love Boat II (115), Man With Camera (29), Mickey Rooney (17), Next Step Beyond (24), N.Y.P.D. (49), On the Mat (52), One Step Beyond (94), People's Choice (104), Range Rider (76), The Rebel (76), Starring the Actors (13), Starting From Scratch (22), Take My Word for It (130), Tales From the Dark Side (90), Tarzan (25), That Girl (136), Throb (48), Wendy and Me (34), You Again? (26).

Mini-Series: Double Take (4 hrs.), Four Minute Mile (4 hrs.), Hands Of A Stranger (4 hrs.), Holocaust (10 hrs.), Internal Affairs (4 hrs.), Key to Rebecca (4 hrs.), Love, Lies & Murder (4 hrs.), On Wings of Eagles (5 hrs.), Return to Eden (6 hrs.), Separate But Equal (4 hrs.), Son of the Morning Star (4 hrs.), Sword of Honor (6 hrs.), Voice of the Heart (4 hrs.).

Features: Prime VIII (20 color features), Prime Time All the Time (16 theatricals and made-for-tv), Shark's Paradise (2 hr. movie), Star Performers (12 made-for-tv movies).

Children's Programs: Camp Candy (40 x 30 mins.), The Jackson Five (23 x 30 mins.), The Jerry Lewis Show (17 x 30 mins.), King Kong (26 x 30 mins. & 78 6–8 mins.), Lancelot Link (17 x 30 mins.), Milton the Monster (78 6–8 min. & 26 x 30 mins.), Professor Kitzel (104 4 1/2 mins.), The Reluctant Dragon & Mr. Toad (17 x 30 mins.), Smokey the Bear (51 6–8 min. & 17 x 30 mins.), George of the Jungle (17 x 30 mins. & 51 6–8 mins.), Discovery (103 x 30 mins.).

Specials: Amahl & the Night Visitors (1 hr.), Baseball Our Way (90 mins.), The Bay City Rollers (1 hr.), The Bobby Vinton Show (1 hr.), Candid Camera Specials (5 x 60 mins.), Children of the Gael (1 hr.), Chris Evert Specials (1 hr.), Christmas Memory (90 mins.), A Christmas Carol (30 mins.), Cliffhanger Serial Specials (4 x 60 mins.)Dick Smith: Master of Make-Up (30 mins.), Echo 1 (17 x 60 mins.), An Evening with Irish Television (1 hr.), The Fabulous Sixties (10 x 60 mins.), Frankenstein (1 hr.), Greatest American Film (2 hrs.), Herbie Mann/Roland Kirk (30 mins.), Hollywood Mavericks (2 hrs.), Irish Rovers Special (1 hr.), Is It Christ? (1 hr.), Jack Nicklaus at the Home of Golf (3 x 90 mins.), The Last Nazi (1 hr.), The Musical Ambassadors (1 hr.), The New Fangled Wandering Minstrel Show (1 hr.), The Night the Animals Talked (30 mins.), Raphael (30 mins.), Roberta Flack/Donny Hathaway (30 mins.), Ron Luciano's Lighter Side of Sports (30 mins.), Russian Festival of Music and Dance (1 hr.), Sunshine Specials (8 x 60 mins.), Tennis Our Way (90 mins.), Thank You Mr. President (90 mins.), Wedding Planner—Marion Ross (1 hr.), The World of Miss World (1 hr.).

Additional Feature Packages: Animated Features (5), Animated Cartoons (500), Champions (152), Color Movies 3 (11), Color Movies 4 (6), Color Movies 5 (13), Hollywood Stars (17), John Wayne Collection (16), Prime I (10), Prime II (16), Prime III (16), Prime IV (26), Prime V (26), Prime VI (19), Prime VII (18), Prime VIII (20), Republic Premiere One (12), Republic Premiere Two (12), Republic Premiere Three (12), Republic Premiere Four (12), Showcase One (8), Take 3 (6), Theatrical Cartoons (100).

Additional Hour Series/Specials/Mini-Series: American Chronicles (13), Cowboy in Africa (26), Dan August (26), The Fugitive (120), The Heights (13), Momentous Events (6), Most Deadly Game (12), The Round Table (15), Twin Peaks (30), 2000 Malibu Road (6), Urban Anxiety (6).

INTERNATIONAL PRODUCT

Series: The Addams Family (64 x 30 mins, b&w), All My Children, American Chronicle (13 x 30 mins.), The Andros Targets (13 x 60 mins.), Barnaby Jones (177 x 60 mins.), Beverly Hills 90210 (Years 1-6, 177 x 60 mins.), Beauty & The Beast (56 x 60 mins.), Bellevue Emergency (6 x 30 mins.), Ben Casey (153 x 60 mins, b&w), Burke's Law (27 x 60 mins.), Charles Perez (260 x 60 mins.), Combat (152 x 60 mins.), Cowboy In Africa (26 x 60 mins.), Dallas (357 x 60 mins.), Dan August (26 x 60 mins.), The Doris Day Show (128 x 30 mins.), Eight Is Enough (112 x 60 mins.), The Fugitive (120 x 60 mins.), Garrison's Gorrilas (26 hrs.), General Hospital, Geraldo (260 x 60 mins./yr.), Heaven Help Us (13 x 60 mins.), The Heights (13 x 60 mins.), Highway To Heaven (111 x 60 mins.), Hunter (13 x 60 mins.), The Invaders (43 x 60 mins.), Kaz (22 x 60 mins.), Kindred: The Embraced, The Love Boat (255 x 60 mins.), The Lucie Arnaz Show (6 x 30 mins.), Malibu Shores, Madman of The People (16 x 30 mins.), Little House On The Prairie (216 x 60 mins.), Married: The First Year (4 x 60 mins.), Melrose Place (Years 1-4, 131 x 60 mins.), Mod Squad (124 x 60 mins.), Models Inc. (29 x 60 mins.), Moesha, Monsters (72 x 30 mins.), Most Wanted (22 x 60 mins.), The Next Step Beyond (24 x 30 mins.), Night Stand (26 x 60 mins.), On The Air (7 x 30 mins.), One Life To Live, Project UFO (26 x 60 mins.), Pruitts of Southhampton (30 x 30 mins.), Return To Eden (22 x 60 mins.), The Road (21 x 60 mins.), Robin's Hoods (22 x 60 mins.), The Round Table (8 x 60 mins.), Savannah, Sidney (13 x 30 mins.), Spencer's Pilots (11 x 60 mins.), Starring The Actors (13 x 30 mins.), Starting From Scratch (22 x 30 mins.), Streets of San Francisco (119 x 60 mins.), That Girl (136 x 30 mins.), Throb (48 x 30 mins.), Thunder (12 x 30 mins.), Twin Peaks (32 x 60 mins.), University Hospital (9 x 60 mins.), Urban Anxiety (7 x 30 mins.), Winnetka Road (6 x 60 mins.), You Again? (26 x 30 mins.).

Republic International Series: Over 3,000 hrs. of off-network programming including: The Bill Cosby Show (52 x 30 mins.), Bonanza (430 x 60 mins.), Dr. Kildare (58 x 30 mins, 142 x 60 mins.), Get Smart (117 x 30 mins.), The High Chaparral (98 x 60 mins.).

TV Movies (2 hrs.): Angel In Green, Armed And Innocent, Back To The Streets of San Francisco, Conviction of Kitty Dodd, David Lynch's Hotel Room, A Deadly Business, Fatal Vows: The Alexandra O'Hara Story, Final Appeal, Forget-Me-Not-Murders, Green Dolphin Beat, The High Price of Passion, Jailbirds, Jane's House, Kids Like These, Kiss And Tell, The Love Boat–Valentine Voyage, Love On The Run, Murder In Black & White, Murder Times Seven, My Two Loves, Night of Courage, Precious Victims, Rich Men, Sam's Son, Single Women, Sexual Advances, Shark's Paradise, Sidney Sheldon's A Stranger In The Mirror, A Silent Betrayal, The Stepford Children, The Stone Fox, Stones For Ibarra, Stranger In My Bed, Stranger On My Land, Terror on Track 29, Unholy Matrimony, The Vernon Johns Story, Welcome Home Bobby, When The Bough Breaks, Wild Texas Wind.

Mini-series: Doubletake (4 hrs.), Dynasty: The Reunion (4 hrs.), Grass Roots (4 hrs.), Hands Of A Stranger (4 hrs.), Home Fires (4 hrs.), Internal Affairs (4 hrs.), The Invaders (4 hrs.), Key To Rebecca (4 hrs.), Love, Lies and Murder (4 hrs.), On Wings Of Eagles (5 hrs.), A Season In Purgatory (4 hrs.), Separate But Equal (4 hrs.), Son Of The Morning Star (4 hrs.), Stephen King's Golden Years (8 hrs.), Stephen King's The Langoliers (4 hrs.), Stephen King's The Stand (8 hrs.), Texas (4 hrs.), 2000 Malibu Road (6 hrs.).

Specials: AFI Lifetime Acheivement Awards: Kirk Douglas (90 mins.), Clint Eastwood (2 hrs.), David Lean (90 mins.), Jack Nicholson (2 hrs.), Gregory Peck (90 mins.), Sidney Poitier (90 mins.), Steven Spielberg (2 hrs.), Elizabeth Taylor (90 mins.), Dick Smith: Master of Make-Up (30 mins.), Dracula: Fact or Fiction (1 hr.), Halloween With the Addams Family (90 mins.), Hollywood Mavericks (2 hrs.), Momentous Events: Russia In The 90's (5 x 60 mins.), 1995 Hollywood Christmas Parade (2 hrs.), 1995 Soul Train Lady of Soul Awards (2 hrs.), 1995 Soul Train Music Awards (2 hrs.), Pope John Paul II (3 hrs.), Soul Train 25th Anniversay Hall of Fame Special (2 hrs.).

Special Presentation Programming: An Act of Love: The Patricia Neal Story (2 hrs.), Candid Camera Specials (5 x 60 mins.), Freedom Road (4 hrs.), The Holocaust (9 x 30 mins.), The Last Nazi (90 mins.), Little House on the Prairie (Three Special Presentations: Bless All the Dear Children, Look Back to Yesterday & The Last Farewell, 2 hrs. each), Little Mo (3 hrs.), The Ordeal of Patty Hearst (3 hrs.), Reincarnation (2 hrs.), Russian Festival of Music and Dance (1 hr.), The Trial of Lee Harvey Oswald (4 hrs.), Worldvision Dramatic Specials (7 x 60 mins.).

Paragon Features: Over 90 color features. Stars include Robert Preston, Patty Duke, Valerie Perrine, Dom DeLuise, Patricia Elliott, Gary Coleman, Mickey Rooney, George C. Scott, Henry Fonda, James Whitmore, Dennis Weaver, David Janssen, James Woods, Lee Majors, James Earl Jones, Ed Asner, Suzanne Pleshette, William Devane.

ABC Pictures: Cabaret, They Shoot Horses Don't They?, Charly, Take the Money and Run, Straw Dogs, For Love of Ivy, Song of Norway, The Killing of Sister George, and Krakatoa East of Java, (all in color).

Prestige Features: 21 features in color including: I Will I Will ... For Now, Night Watch, A Touch of Class, Hedda, Baker's Hawk, Black Market Baby, Breakthrough, Book of Numbers, Fingers, Cry For Me Billy, Sweet Hostage, Nasty Habits, and Thieves.

Prestige II Features: 10 features including A Killing Affair, Bad Guys, Dirt Bike Kid, Vasectomy, Wizards of the Lost Kingdom, and Hurry Up or I'll Be 30.

Selznick Classics: 22 films including Intermezzo, Duel in the Sun, Notorious, Spellbound, Rebecca, The Spiral Staircase, Portrait of Jenny, The Farmer's Daughter, The Garden of Allah, Bill of Divorcement, Made For Each Other, and The Wild Heart.

Republic Pictures, over 1,000 Feature Films including, It's A Wonderful Life, The Quiet Man, High Noon, The Bells of St. Mary's, Sands of Iwojima, Father Goose, Indiscrete, That Touch of Mink, The Republic Library also includes 47 John Wayne films, plus features starring Cary Grant, Marlon Brando, James Cagney, Gary Cooper, Grace Kelly, Ingrid Bergman, Kirk Douglas, James Stewart, Bing Crosby, Gene Kelly, Natalie Wood, and many others.

Children's Programming: Alvin & The Chipmunks (52 x 30 mins.), Bugaloos (17 x 30 mins.), George of The Jungle (17 x 30 mins.), Hot Wheels (17 x 30 mins.), Hugo The Hippo (90 mins.), Jackson 5 (23 x 30 minsw.), The Jerry Lewis Show (17 x 30 mins.), King Kong (26 x 30 mins.), Krofft Superstar Hour Starring The Bay City Rollers (13 x 60 mins.), Lancelot Link (17 x 30 mins.), Land Of The Lost (69 x 30 mins.), Lidsville (17 x 30 mins.), Milton The Monster (26 x 30 mins.), The Point (90 mins.), Professor Kitzel (104 x 4.5 mins.), Reluctant Dragon & Mr. Toad (17 x 30 mins.), Sigmund & The Sea Monster (29 x 30 mins.), Skyhawks (17 x 30 mins.), Smokey The Bear (17 x 30 mins.).

Holiday Specials: Alvin & The Chipmunks Reunion (30 mins.), Amahl and the Night Visitors (1 hr.), A Christmas Memory (1 hr.), A Christmas Carol (30 mins.), I Love the Chipmunks Valentine Special (30 mins.), The Night the Animals Talked (30 mins.).

WORLDWIDE PANTS, INC.

1697 Broadway, New York, NY 10019. (212) 975-5300. FAX: (212) 975-4760.
7716 Beverly Blvd., #25B, Los Angeles, CA 90036. (213) 852-4475. FAX: (213) 852-2885.
Series: Late Show With David Letterman, Everybody Loves Raymond.

WORLDWIDE TELEVISION NEWS

(A division of ABC in the U.S.)
1995 Broadway, New York, NY 10023. (212) 362-4440. FAX: (212) 496-1269.
The Interchange, Oval Road, Camden Lock, London NW1 7DZ. (44171) 410-5200. FAX: (44171) 413-8302.
PRESIDENT
Robert Burke
BUREAU CHIEF, NY
Dave Modrowski
SALES, NORTH AMERICA
Scott Michaeloff
SALES, SOUTH AMERICA
Dolores Wilson

ZM ENTERTAINMENT

3131 Cahuenga Blvd. West, Ste. 300, Los Angeles, CA 90068. (213) 436-2300. FAX: (213) 436-2399.

CABLE AND SATELLITE TELEVISION

CABLE NETWORKS

MULTIPLE SYSTEM CABLE OPERATORS

DIRECT BROADCAST SATELLITE SYSTEMS OPERATORS

WIRELESS CABLE SYSTEMS

———————————

■

CABLE NETWORKS

Premium cable services and pay-per-view services are designated as such. All others are basic cable services. Regional news and sports programming is excluded. Most programming is also available on selected satellite broadcasting services.

A & E TELEVISION NETWORK/THE HISTORY CHANNEL
(A joint venture of Hearst Corp., ABC and NBC)
235 E. 45 St., New York, NY 10017. (212) 661-4500. FAX: (212) 949-7147.
PRESIDENT & CEO
Nickolas Davatzes
EXECUTIVE V.P., CFO, ADMINISTRATIVE OFFICER A & E NETWORKS, EXECUTIVE V.P., & GENERAL MANAGER THE HISTORY CHANNEL INTERNATIONAL
Seymour H. Lesser
EXECUTIVE V.P., SALES & MARKETING
Whitney Goit II
EXECUTIVE V.P. & GENERAL MANAGER, A & E
Brooke Bailey Johnson
EXECUTIVE V.P., & GENERAL MANAGER THE HISTORY CHANNEL
Daniel E Davids
S.V.P., PROGRAMMING, THE HISTORY CHANNEL
Abbe Raven
S.V.P., SALES
Ronald M Schneier
S V P FINANCE
Gerald Gruosso
V.P., PROGRAMMING A& E NETWORKS
Michael Cascio
V.P., HISTORICAL PROGRAMMING, THE HISTORY CHANNEL
Charles Maday
V.P., & GENERAL COUNSEL
Anne Atkinson
V.P., HUMAN RESOURCES
Rosalind Clay Carter
V.P., CORPORATE BUSINESS DEVELOPMENT
Joseph Warren
V.P., PUBLIC AFFAIRS & COMMUNICATIONS
Gary Morgenstein

AMERICAN MOVIE CLASSICS (AMC)
Rainbow Programming Service Holdings Inc., 150 Crossways Park W., Woodbury, NY 11797. (516) 364-2222. FAX: (516) 364-8929.
CEO, RAINBOW PROGRAMMING SERVICE HOLDINGS & PRESIDENT, NATIONAL SERVICES
Joshua Sapan
PRESIDENT & GENERAL MANAGER, AMC & ROMANCE CLASSICS
Kate McEnroe

BLACK ENTERTAINMENT TELEVISION (BET)
One Bet Plaza, 1900 W Place N.E., Washington, D.C. 20018-1211. (202) 608-2000.
CHAIRMAN & CEO
Robert L. Johnson
PRESIDENT & COO
Debra Lee
PRESIDENT, BET NETWORKS
Jefferi K. Lee
EXECUTIVE V.P., BET NETWORKS
Maurita Coley
EXECUTIVE V.P., ,CFO & TREASURER
William T. Gordon III
EXECUTIVE V P, MEDIA SALES
James A Ebron
EXECUTIVE V P, CORPORATE AFFAIRS
Shiela Crump Johnson
EXECUTIVE V P, AFFILIATE SALES & MARKETING, COO, BET ACTION PAY PER VIEW & PRESIDENT, BET INTERNATIONAL
Curtis Symonds
V.P., PROGRAMMING
Lydia Cole
V.P., NEWS ENTERTAINMENT & SPORTS
Deborah Tang
V.P., DEVELOPMENT & SPECIAL PROJECTS
Cindy Mahmoud
V.P., AFFILIATE MARKETING
Joe Lawson

BRAVO
Rainbow Programming Holdings Inc., 150 Crossways Park West, Woodbury, NY 11797. (516) 364-2222. FAX: (516) 364-7638.
PRESIDENT
Kathleen Dore
S.V.P., PROGRAMMING
Jonathan Sehring

BUENA VISTA PAY TELEVISION
(also see the Disney Channel)
350 South Buena Vista St., Burbank, CA 91521. (818) 560-1000.
CHAIRMAN
Walter C. Liss, Jr.
SENIOR V.P., BUSINESS & LEGAL AFFAIRS
John J. Reagan
V.P., BUSINESS & LEGAL AFFAIRS
Dennis Dort
V.P., PAY TV
Wendy Ferren
V.P., SALES & OPERATIONS, PAY TV
Julie Jenkins

CONSUMER NEWS & BUSINESS CHANNEL (CNBC)
2200 Fletcher Ave., Ft. Lee, NJ 07024. (201) 585-2622. FAX: (201) 585-6482.
PRESIDENT
Bill Dolster

C-SPAN CABLE SATELLITE PUBLIC AFFAIRS NETWORK (C-SPAN/C-SPAN 2)
400 N. Capitol St., N.W., Suite 650, Washington, DC 20001. (202) 737-3220. FAX: (202) 737-3323.
CHAIRMAN & CEO
Brian P. Lamb
EXECUTIVE V.P. & CO-COO
Robert Kennedy
EXECUTIVE V.P. & CO-COO
Susan Swain
V.P. OF PROGRAMMING
Terence Murphy

CABLE NEWS NETWORK (CNN) & HEADLINE NEWS
Turner Broadcasting System, One CNN Center, P.O. Box 105366, Atlanta, GA 30348-5366. (404) 827-1700. FAX: (404) 523-8517. Headline News: (404) 827-1500.
CHAIRMAN
Thomas Johnson
PRESIDENT, CNN NEWSGROUP
Rich Kaplan
PRESIDENT, INT'L NETWORK & GLOBAL NEWS GATHERING
Ethan Jordan
EXECUTIVE V.P.
John Petrovich

CARTOON NETWORK
(A subsidiary of TBS and Time Warner, Inc.)
1050 Techwood Dr. N.W., Atlanta, GA 30318. (404) 885-2263. FAX: (404) 885-4301.url http://www.cartoonnetwork.com
PRESIDENT
Betty Cohen
GENERAL MANAGER
Rob Sorcher
S.V.P., MARKETING
Craig McAnsh
S.V.P., PROGRAMMING
Mike Lazzo
S.V.P., CREATIVE DIRECTOR
Michael Ouweleen
S.V.P., GLOBAL BRAND MANAGEMENT
Lisa Fernow
S V P, GENERAL MANAGER, CARTOON NETWORK ENTERPRISES
Kim McQuilken
DIRECTOR, PUBLIC RELATIONS
Joseph Swaney
V.P., PUBLIC RELATIONS
Mike Manning
V.P., ORIGINAL ANIMATION
Linda Simensky
V.P., BUSINESS OPERATIONS
Mark Norman
V.P., & CONTROLLER
Becky Courson

CHRISTIAN BROADCASTING NETWORK
977 Centerville Tpke., Virginia Beach, VA 23463-0001. (757)
579-7000. FAX: (757) 579-2017.
FOUNDER & CEO
M.G. (Pat) Robertson

CINEMAX
(See Home Box Office Listing)

COMEDY CENTRAL
1775 Broadway, New York, NY 10019. (212) 767-8600. FAX:
(212) 767-8592.
PRESIDENT & CEO
Doug Herzog
EXECUTIVE V P, ADVERTISING SALES
Larry Divney
CFO & S V P, FINANCE
John Cucci
S.V.P., PROGRAMMING
Eileen Cats
S V P, AFFILIATE RELATIONS
Brad Samuels
S.V.P., MARKETING & NEW BUSINESS DEVELOPMENT
Bert Gould
S.V.P., CORPORATE COMMUNICATIONS
Anthony Fox
GENERAL COUNSEL & V.P., LEGAL & BUSINESS AFFAIRS
Shari Patrick

COUNTRY MUSIC TELEVISION
2806 Opreyland Dr., Nashville, TN 37214. (615) 871-5831.
FAX: (615) 871-5830
PRESIDENT
David Hall

DISCOVERY COMMUNICATIONS, INC.
7700 Wisconsin Ave., Bethesda, MD 20814. (301) 986-1999.
FAX: (301) 986-4826. URL: http://www.discovery.com
CHAIRMAN & CEO
John S. Hendricks
PRESIDENT & CHIEF EDITORIAL & CREATIVE OFFICER
Gregory Moyer
PRESIDENT, DISCOVERY NETWORKS.
Donald Wear
PRESIDENT & COO
Judith McHale
PRESIDENT, DISCOVERY ENTERPRISES WORLDWIDE
Michela English
S.V.P., DISCOVERY NETWORKS INTERNATIONAL
Dom Fioravanti
S.V.P., DAYTIME PROGRAMMING
Chuck Gingold
S.V.P., ADVERTISING SALES
Bill McGowan
S.V.P., DISCOVERY LATIN AMERICA
Dawn McCall
S.V.P., BUSINESS AFFAIRS
Dara Altman
S.V.P., DISCOVERY ASIA
Kevin-John McIntyre
S.V.P., BUSINESS DEVELOPMENT DISCOVERY ENTER-
PRISES WORLDWIDE & GENERAL MANAGER, HOME
VIDEO
Raymond Cooper
S.V.P., MARKETING
Chris Mosely
S.VP AFFILIATE SALES & MARKETING
Bill Goodwin
S.V.P., INTERACTIVE MEDIA
Andrew Sharpless
S.V.P., GENERAL COUNSEL
Mark Hollinger
V.P., RESEARCH & PLANNING
Sandy Wall

DISNEY CHANNEL
(A basic cable service of the Walt Disney Company)
3800 West Alameda Ave., Burbank, CA 91505. (818) 569-
7500. FAX: (818) 588-1241.
PRESIDENT, DISNEY/ABC CABLE NETWORKS &
PRESIDENT, DISNEY CHANNEL
Anne Sweeney
S.V.P., MARKETING
Eleo Hensleigh
S.V.P., BUSINESS & LEGAL AFFAIRS
Frederick Kuperberg
S.V.P., FINANCE & ADMINISRATION
Patrick T. Lopker
S.V.P., SALES & AFFILIATE MARKETING
Charlie Nooney
S.V.P., PROGRAMMING & PRODUCTION
Rich Ross

SENIOR V.P., ORIGINAL PROGRAMMING
Gary K. Marsh
V.P., CREATIVE AFFAIRS
Peggy J. Christianson
V.P., SALES, STRATEGY & PLANNING
Peter Cullen
V.P., ENGINEERING & OPERATIONS
Vincent H. Roberts
V.P., ACQUIRED PROGRAMMING
Carol Sussman
V.P., PROGRAM PLANNING
Jill Casagrande
V.P., PRODUCTION
Susette Hsiung
V.P., MEDIA RELATIONS
Shirley Powell
V.P., MARKETING
Adam Sanderson
V.P., EASTERN REGION
Kenneth Crooks
V.P., CENTRAL REGION
David Daniels
V.P., SOUTHEASTERN REGION
Deborah Shay
V.P., PLANNING & CONTROL
Jewell Engstrom
V.P., SOUTHWEST REGION
Rob Evanko
V.P., NATIONAL MARKETING
Ned Hickok
V.P., CREATIVE SERVICES
Maria Josey
V.P., BUSINESS AFFAIRS
Chuck Kent
V.P., NATIONAL ACCOUNTS, EAST
Maureen Lane
V.P., NATIONAL ACCOUNTS, WEST
Ann Swanson
V.P., AFFILIATE SERVICES
Douglas K. Miller
V.P., WESTERN REGION
Ben Pyne

E! ENTERTAINMENT TELEVISION
5670 Wilshire Blvd., Los Angeles, CA 90036-3709. (213) 954-
2400. FAX: (213) 954-2661.
PRESIDENT & CEO
Lee Masters
S.V.P. & CFO
Bill Keenan
S.V.P., INTERNATIONAL DEVELOPMENT
Chris Fager
S.V.P., PROGRAMMING
Fran Shea
S.V.P., MARKETING
Dale Hopkins
S.V.P., AFFILIATE RELATIONS
Debra Green
S.V.P., HUMAN RESOURCES
Patti Robinson
S.V.P., ADVERTISING SALES
Dave Cassaro
S.V.P., BUSINESS & LEGAL AFFAIRS
Mark Feldman

**ENTERTAINMENT & SPORTS PROGRAMMING
NETWORK, INC. (ESPN)**
935 Middle st Bristol CT 06010 (860) 585-2000. FAX: (860)
585-2213.
605 Third Ave., New York, NY 10158-0180. (212) 916-9200.
PRESIDENT & CEO ESPN INC, PRESIDENT ABC SPORTS
Steve Bornstein
EXECUTIVE V.P. ADMINISTRATION
Ed Durso
EXECUTIVE V.P., SALES & MARKETING
George W Bodenheimer
EXECUTIVE V.P., OPERATIONS, ENGINEERING & NEW
TECHNOLOGY
Reginald R Thomas
S.V.P., PROGAMMING & DEVELOPMENT
Len De Luca
EXECUTIVE V.P., PRODUCTION
Howard C Katz
S.V.P., & CFO
Christine F Driessen
S.V.P., ESPN ENTERPRISES
Richard K Glover

S.V.P., & MANAGING DIRECTOR ESPN INTERNATIONAL
David F Zucker
S.V.P., PROGRAMMING
John Wildhack
S.V.P., INTERGRATED SALES & MARKETING
Michael Chico
S.V.P., ADVERTISING SALES
Jeffrey S Mahl
S.V.P., PROGRAMMING & TALENT NEGOTIATIONS
Betsy Goff
S.V.P., OPERATIONS & ENGINEERING PROJECT DEVELOP-
MENT
Chuck Pagano
S.V.P., & GENERAL COUNSEL
David Pahl

ENCORE
(A premium cable service)
5445 Denver Tech. Center Parkway, #600, Engelwood, CO
80111-3051. (303) 771-7700. FAX: (303) 741-3067.
CHAIRMAN & CEO
John J. Sie
V.P., PLANNING & SCHEDULING
David Salinger

FAITH & VISION (F & V)
74 Trinity Pl., Suite 915, New York, NY 10006. (212) 964-1663.
FAX: (212) 964-5966.
S.V.P., PROGRAMMING
Mary Silverman
DIRECTOR, ACQUISITIONS
Anne Morgan

FOX FAMILY CHANNEL
International Family Entertainment, 2877 Guardian Lane,
Virginia Beach, VA 23452. (757) 459-6000. FAX: (757) 459-
6425.
CEO & PRESIDENT
Rich Kronin
DIRECTOR, PROGRAMMING
Tom Halleen
V.P., MARKETING
Doug Symons

FOX NEWS CHANNEL
(A subsidiary of Fox, Inc.)
1211 Ave. of the Americas, Concourse Level, New York, NY
10036. (212) 556-2500. FAX: (212) 819-0816.
CHAIRMAN & CEO
Roger Ailes
V.P., FINANCE & ADMINISTRATION
Jack Abernethy
NEWS DIRECTOR
Janet Alshouse
V.P., NEWSGATHERING
George Case
S.V.P., PROGRAMMING
Chet Collier
V.P., OPERATIONS
Anthony Fragetti
V.P., NEWS AFFILIATES
Brian Jones
V.P., MEDIA RELATIONS
Brian Lewis
V.P., NEWS EDITORIAL
John Moody
V.P., CREATIVE DIRECTOR
Richard O'Brien
V.P., ADVERTISING SALES
Paul Rittenberg

FX NETWORKS INC.
(A subsidiary of Fox, Inc.)
1440 S. Sepulveda Blvd., Los Angeles, CA 90025. (310) 444-
8594. FAX: (310) 235-2853.
PRESIDENT
Peter Liguori
EXECUTIVE V.P., ENTERTAINMENT SALES
Guy Sousa
S.V.P., MARKETING & ADVERTISING
Gavin Harvey
S.V.P., AFFILIATE RELATIONS
Tim Krauss
V.P., AFFILIATE RELATIONS NATIONAL ACCOUNTS
Janice Arouh
V.P., PROGRAMMING
Chuck Salter
V.P., DEVELOPMETNT & PRODUCTION
Bob Boden
V.P., AFFILIATE RELATIONS NATIONAL ACCOUNTS
Ray Hopkins

V.P., SALES OPERATIONS
Kathy Trullender
V.P., AFFILIATE BUSINESS AFFAIRS
Bill Bridgen
V.P., AFFILIATE BUSINESS DEVELOPMENT
Steve Carcano
V.P. FINANCE
Christy Kirchner
V.P., BUSINESS & LEGAL AFFAIRS
Mark DeVitre
V.P., COMMUNICATIONS
Ellen Cooper
DIRECTOR, RESEARCH
Mindy Hahn
DIRECTOR, DEVELOPMENT & PRODUCTION
Chris Fahland

FXM
(Please see FX Networks, Inc.)

GALAVISION
(Spanish language)
605 Third Ave., 12th Floor, New York, NY 10158. (212) 455-
5200. FAX: (212) 455-5327.
PRESIDENT & COO
Javier Saralegui
V.P., PROGRAMMING & OPERATIONS
Alex Hadad

HOME BOX OFFICE, INC. & CINEMAX
(A premium service and subsidiary of Time Warner, Inc.)
1100 Ave. of the Americas, New York, NY 10036. (212) 512-
1000. FAX: (212) 512-5517.
2049 Century Prk East, Suite 4100, Los Angeles, CA 90067-
3215. (310) 201-9200. FAX: (310) 207-9310.
PRESIDENT CHAIRMAN & CEO, HOME BOX OFFICE
Jeffrey L. Bewkes
PRESIDENT, HBO PICTURES & HBO NYC PRODUCTIONS
John Matoian
PRESIDENT, HBO INTERNATIONAL
Steven Rosenberg
PRESIDENT, ORIGINAL PROGRAMMING & HBO INDEPEN-
DENT PRODUCTIONS
Chris Albrecht
PRESIDENT, U S NETWORK GROUP
John Billock
PRESIDENT, FILM PROGRAMMING VIDEO & ENTERPRISES
Steve Scheffer
EXECUTIVE V.P. & GENERAL COUNSEL
John S. Redpath, Jr.
EXECUTIVE V.P., & CFO
Bill Nelson
EXECUTIVE V.P., HBO INTERNATIONAL
William Hooks
EXECUTIVE V.P., HBO NYC PRODUCTIONS
Colin Callender
EXECUTIVE V.P., CREATIVE AFFAIRS
Lowell Mate
EXECUTIVE V.P., BUSINESS AFFAIRS
Russell Schwartz
EXECUTIVE V.P., & PRESIDENT TIME WARNER SPORTS
Seth Abraham
S.V.P., BUSINESS AFFAIRS
Harold Akselrad
S.V.P., PROGRAM PLANNING, HBO & CINEMAX
David Baldwin
S.V.P., SATELLITE SERVICES
Vinton H. Bauer
S.V.P., INFORMATION TECHNOLOGY
Albert Collins, Jr.
S.V.P., HUMAN RESOURCES & ADMINISTRATION
Shelley D. Fischel
S.V.P., AFFILIATE RELATIONS
Robert S. Grassi
S.V.P. TIME WARNER SPORTS PRODUCTION & HBO
SPORTS
Ross Greenburg
S.V.P., HBO MARKETING
Eric Kessler
S.V.P. & PRESIDENT, HBO HOME VIDEO
Henry McGee
S.V.P., FILM PROGRAMMING
Leslie Jacobson
S.V.P., DOCUMENTARY & FAMILY PROGRAMMING
Shiela Nevins
S.V.P., CORPORATE COMMUNICATIONS
Richard Plepler
S.V.P., STUDIO & BROADCAST OPERATIONS
Dominic Serio
S.V.P., TECHNOLOGY OPERATIONS
Robert M. Zitter
CFO & S.V.P., OPERATIONS TIME WARNER SPORTS
Mark Taffert

HOME SHOPPING NETWORK INC.
1 (HSN) Home Shopping Network Plaza St Petersburg FL 33729 (813) 572-8585. FAX: (813) 539-8137.
PRESIDENT & CEO
James Held
EXECUTIVE V.P., BROADCASTING & ENGINEERING
Mark Bozek

INDEPENDENT FILM CHANNEL
(A premium cable service.)
Rainbow Programming Holdings Inc., 150 Crossways Park West, Woodbury, NY 11797. (516) 396-3000. FAX: (516) 364-7638, (516) 364-7684. email: BravoTV@ad.com
PRESIDENT, THE INDEPENDENT FILM CHANNEL, BRAVO, MUCH MUSIC
Kathleen Dore
V P, PROGRAMMING & ACQUISITION
Caroline Kaplan
V.P., PROGRAMMING
Frances Berwick
DIRECTOR, ACQUISITION
George Lentz

INTERNATIONAL CHANNEL
5445 DTC Parkway Ste 600 Englewood CO 80111 (303)267-4000 FAX: (303)267-5840.
12401 West Olympic Blvd Los Angeles CA 90064(310)826-4777 FAX: (310)447-7906
PRESIDENT
Kent Rice
V.P., SALES & MARKETING
Victoria Kent
EXECUTIVE V.P.,
Rosemary Danon

KTLA
(United Video Television)
7140 S. Lewis Ave., Tulsa, OK 74136-5422. (800) 331-4806. FAX: (918) 488-4295, (918) 488-4278.
SENIOR V.P.
Ray Duffy
DIRECTOR OF PROGRAMMING
Derk Tenzythoff

KALEIDOSCOPE TELEVISION (KTV)
(Programming for Americans with disabilities.)
1777 N.E. Loop 410, Suite 300, San Antonio, TX 78217. (210) 824-7446. (210) 824-1666. FAX: (210) 829-1388.
PRESIDENT & CEO
Dr. Bill Nichols
EXECUTIVE V.P., PROGRAMMING & PRODUCTION
Ron Dixon

THE LEARNING CHANNEL
Discovery Communications Inc., 7700 Wisconsin Ave., Bethesda, MD 20814. (301) 986-1999.
PRESIDENT, DISCOVERY NETWORKS, U.S.
Jonathan Rodgers
S.V.P. & GENERAL MANAGER, DAYTIME PROGRAMMING, DISCOVERY NETWORKS, U.S.
Charles Gingold
S.V.P. & GENERAL MANAGER
John B. Ford
S.V.P., AFFILIATE SALES & MARKETING
Bill Goodwin
S.V.P., ADVERTISING & PROMOTION
Chris Moseley
S.V.P., ADVERTISING SALES
Bill McGowan
V.P., RESEARCH
Steve McGowan

LIFETIME
(Lifetime Entertainment Services)
Worldwide Plaza, 309 W. 49th St., New York, NY 10019. (212) 424-7000. FAX: (212) 424-4264.
PRESIDENT & CEO
Douglas W. McCormick
EXECUTIVE V.P. ADMINISTRATION
Jane Tollinger
S.V.P., PROGRAMMING & PRODUCTION
Patrick Guy
S.V.P., AFFILIATE RELATIONS
William Padalino
S.V.P., PRICE & PLANNING
Richard Basso
S.V.P., SALES
Lynn Picard

MSNBC
(A joint venture of NBC and Microsoft)
2200 Fletcher Ave., Ft. Lee, NJ 07024. (201) 583-5010.
Internet programming: http://www.msnbc.com
PRESIDENT, NBC NEWS
Andrew Lack
V.P. & GENERAL MANAGER, MSNBC
Eric Sorenson
PRESIDENT, NBC CABLE & BUSINESS DEVELOPMENT
Tom Rogers
V.P., STATEGIC PARTNERSHIPS
Peter Neupert
V.P., MSNBC MEDIA RELATIONS
Cory Shields

MTV NETWORKS, INC.
(A subsidiary of Viacom, Inc.)
1515 Broadway, New York, NY 10036. (212) 258-7800. FAX: (212) 258-8358.
CHAIRMAN & CEO
Thomas E. Freston
PRESIDENT & COO
Mark C. Rosenthal
PRESIDENT, ADVERTISING & PROMO SALES, WORLDWIDE
Harvey Ganot
EXECUTIVE V.P., ADVERTISING SALES
John J. Popkowski
EXECUTIVE VICE PRESIDENT
James M. Shaw
EXECUTIVE V.P., AFFILIATE SALES & MARKETING
Nicole A. Browning
EXECUTIVE V.P., RESEARCH & DEVELOPMENT
Betsy Frank
EXECUTIVE V.P., CORPORATE
Gregory J. Ricca

MTV
PRESIDENT/WORLDWIDE CREATIVE DIRECTOR
Judy McGrath
PRESIDENT, MTV INTERNATIONAL
William Roedy
PRESIDENT, MTV LATIN AMERICA
Tom Hunter
PRESIDENT, MTV ANIMATION
Albert Terkuhle
EXECUTIVE V.P., PROGRAMMING
Brian Graden
GENERAL MANAGER, MTV
Van E. Toffler
EXECUTIVE V.P., BUSINESS OPERATIONS
Richard Eigendorff
EXECUTIVE V.P., MTV NEWS & SPECIALS
David A. Sirulnick
S.V.P., CREATIVE & ON-AIR, MTV EUROPE
Peter D. Dougherty
S.V.P., MARKETING
T. Allen Broce
S.V.P., PROGRAMMING, PRODUCTION, PROMOTION
Robert W. Kusbit
S.V.P., DEVELOPMENT ORIGINAL PROGRAMMING
Lisa K. Berger
S.V.P., MTV FILMS
David M. Gale

VH-1
PRESIDENT, VH-1
John Sykes
S.V.P., PROGRAMMING & PRODUCTION
Jeffrey M. Gaspin
S.V.P., PROMOTIONS & PROGRAM PLANNING
Michael D. Benson
S.V.P., MARKETING & COMMUNICATIONS
Joshua M. Katz

NICKELODEON & NICK AT NITE
PRESIDENT, NICKELODEON & NICK AT NITE
Herb Scannell
PRESIDENT, NICK FEATURES
Deborah Beece-May
EXECUTIVE V.P. & COO
Jeffrey D. Dunn
S.V.P., CREATIVE DIRECTOR & CHIEF OF STAFF
Lisa Judson
S.V.P., NETWORK MARKETING/ASSOCIATE WORLDWIDE CREATIVE DIRECTOR
Thomas P. Harbeck
S.V.P., WORLDWIDE PRODUCTION
Alan Hecht
S.V.P., PROGRAM ENTERPRISES
Kathleen M. Hricik
S.V.P., PROGRAMMING, NICK AT NITE'S TV LAND
Diane L. Robina
S.V.P., PROGRAMMING & NETWORK MANAGEMENT
Cyma Zarghami
S.V.P., STRATEGY, RESEARCH & FINANCE
Ann M. Sarnoff

NICKELODEON
(See MTV Network listing above)

NOSTALGIA TELEVISION
(Good Life television Network)
650 Massachusetts Ave. NW, Washington, DC 20001. (202) 289-6633. FAX: (202) 289-6632. URL: http://www.nostalgiatv.com
PRESIDENT & CEO
Squire Rushnell
DIRECTOR, PROGRAMMING & PRODUCTION
Mark Ringwald

PLAYBOY TV
(A pay-per-view cable service)
9242 Beverly Blvd., Beverly Hills, CA 90210. (310) 246-4000. FAX: (310) 246-4050.
PRESIDENT
Jim English
DIRECTOR, PROGRAMMING & ACQUISITIONS
Claire Zrimc
DIRECTOR, DEVELOPMENT & PRODUCTION
Tammara Wells

PREVUE NETWORK
(Program listings for cable.)
One Technology Plaza, 7140 S. Lewis Ave., Tulsa, OK 74136-5422. (918) 488-4450. FAX: (918) 488-4638.
PRESIDENT & CEO
Gary Howard
S.V.P., PRODUCTION
Madeleine Forrer

QVC
Goshen Corporate Park, 1365 Enterprise Dr., West Chester, PA 19380. (610) 701-1000. FAX: (610) 701-8170.
PRESIDENT
Doug Briggs
EXECUTIVE V.P., MARKETING, BUSINESS DEVELOPMENT & PROGRAMMING
Irv Kalick
S.V.P., PROGRAMMING
Robert Cadigan
S.V.P., MARKETING
Fred Seigel

REQUEST TELEVISION
(A pay-per-view cable service)
4700 S. Syracuse St., Suite 100, Denver CO 80237. (303) 267-6100. FAX: (303) 267-6195.
PRESIDENT & CEO
Hugh Panero
V.P., PROGRAMMING
Debbie Barackman
V.P., MARKETING
Laurie Lawrence

THE SCI-FI CHANNEL
(See USA Network)

SHOWTIME NETWORKS, INC.
(A premium cable service and a subsidiary of Viacom, Inc.)
1633 Broadway, New York, NY 10019. (212) 708-1600. FAX: (212) 708-1530.
10880 Wilshire Blvd., Suite 1600, Los Angeles, CA 90024. (310) 234-5200.
CHAIRMAN & CEO
Matthew C. Blank
PRESIDENT, PROGRAMMING
Jerry Offsay
EXECUTIVE V.P., ADMINISTRATION & GENERAL COUNSEL
H. Gwen Marcus
EXECUTIVE V.P. CREATIVE/MARKETING
Len Fogge
EXECUTIVE V.P. BUSINESS AFFAIRS & PRODUCTION
Melinda Benedeck
EXECUTIVE V.P., BUSINESS DEVELOPMENT
Larry Aidem
EXECUTIVE V.P., FINANCE & OPERATIONS
Jerry Cooper
EXECUTIVE V.P., SALES & AFFILIATE MARKETING
Jeff Wade
EXECUTIVE V.P., CORPORATE MARKETING & COMMUNICATION
Mark Greenberg
EXECUTIVE V.P., ORIGINAL PROGRAMMING
Mark Zakarin
S.V.P., PROGRAM ACQUISITIONS & PLANNING
Matthew Duda
S.V.P., CREATIVE AFFAIRS, MOTION PICTURE
Joan Boorestein

S.V.P., NEW MEDIA & TECHNOLOGY DEVELOPMENT
Jeff Morris
S.V.P., PROGRAMMING ENTERPRISES & DISTRIBUTION
Matt Riklin
S.V.P., SPORTS & EVENT PROGRAMMING
Jay Larkin
S.V.P., OPERATIONS & ENGINEERING
Richard Keatinge
S.V.P., INFORMATION SYSTEMS
Tom Espeland

SPICE
(A pay-per-view cable service)
536 Broadway, 7th fl., New York, NY 10012. (212) 941-1434. FAX: (212) 941-4746.
PRESIDENT
Roger Ferry

TBS
Turner Broadcasting System, 1050 Techwood Drive, N.W., Atlanta, GA 30318. (404) 827-1700. FAX: (404) 827-2437.
CHAIRMAN PRESIDENT & CEO
Terence McGuirk
CHAIRMAN & CEO, CABLE NEWS NETWORK
Tom Johnson
PRESIDENT TBS
Bill Burke
PRESIDENT NEWS & OPERATION TURNER BROADCASTING SALES INC
Larry Goodman
PRESIDENT CNN
Richard Kaplan
PRESIDENT TURNER NETWORK TELEVISION
Brad Siegel
PRESIDENT, TIME INC/TURNER ORIGINAL PRODUCTIONS
Patricia Mitchell

(TNN) THE NASHVILLE NETWORK
(A service of Opryland USA, Inc. and Group W Satellite Communications.)
Box 10210, 250 Harbor Dr., Stamford, CT 06904-2210. (203) 965-6000.
Production Center: 2806 Opryland Dr., Nashville, TN 37214. (615) 889-6840. FAX (615) 871-6944.
PRESIDENT
Don Mitzner
EXECUTIVE V.P.
Lloyd Werner
V.P., PROGRAMMING
Brian Hughes

(TNT) TURNER NETWORK TELEVISION
1050 Techwood Dr., N.W., P.O. Box 105366, One CNN Center, Atlanta, GA 30318. (404) 885-4538. FAX: (404) 885-4947.
1888 Century Park East, 14th Fl., Los Angeles, CA 90067 (310) 551-6341. FAX (310) 551-6634.
EXECUTIVE V.P., ORIGINAL PROGRAMMING
Allen Sabinson
S.V.P., BUSINESS AFFAIRS
Susan Oman Gross
V.P., PROGRAM DEVELOPMENT
Howard Cohen
V.P., PROGRAM DEVELOPMENT
Betsy Newman

THE TRAVEL CHANNEL
2690 Cumberland Pkwy., Suite 500, Atlanta, GA 30339. (770) 801-2400. FAX: (770) 801-2441.
S.V.P., ADVERTISING SALES
William C. Wiehe
V.P., NEW MEDIA
Mike Carey
V.P., PROGRAMMING & PRODUCTION
Gail Gleeson
V.P., MARKETING
Thomas Lucas
V.P., AFFILIATE SALES
Dana Michaelis
V.P., PUBLIC RELATIONS
Gillian Renault

TRINITY BROADCASTING NETWORK
2823 W. Irving Blvd., Irving, TX 75061. (972) 313-1333.
PRESIDENT
Paul F. Crouch
DIRECTOR, NATIONAL CABLE MARKETING
Bob Higley

USA NETWORK

1230 Ave. of the Americas, New York, NY 10020. (212) 408-9100. FAX: (212) 408-3606.
2049 Century Park East, Suite 2550, Los Angeles, CA 90067. Programming: (310) 201-2335; Ad Sales: (310) 201-2345.
PRESIDENT, PROGRAMMING & MARKETING
Stephen Chao
PRESIDENT, OPERATIONS
Stephen Brenner
EXECUTIVE V.P., NETWORK DISTRIBUTION & AFFILIATE RELATIONS
Douglas Holloway
EXECUTIVE V.P., AD SALES
John Silvestri
CFO & S V P., ADMINISTRATION
Douglas Hamilton
S V P. CORPORATE COMMUNICATIONS & PUBLIC AFFAIRS
Iris Burnett
S V P. RESEARCH
Tim Brooks
S.V P. PROGRAMMING USA NETWORK
Neil Hoffman
V P. ORIGINAL PROGRAMMING & INTERNATIONAL CO PRODUCTIONS
Monia Joblin
S.V.P., PRODUCTION & SPORTS
Gordon Beck
S.V P. CURRENT PROGRAMMING & USA NETWORK ORIGININAL PRODUCTIONS
Bonnie Hammer
S.V.P., NETWORK OPERATIONS
Richard Ross

UVTV

A UVSG Company, 7140 S. Lewis Ave., Tulsa, OK 74136-5422. (800) 331-4806. FAX: (918) 488-4928.
ACTING PRESIDENT
Ray Duffy
PROGRAMMING
Derk Tenzthythoff

VH-1

(Please see MTV Networks)

VIEWER'S CHOICE

(A pay-per-view cable service.)
909 Third Ave., 21st fl., New York, NY 10022. (212) 486-6600. FAX: (212) 688-9497.

PRESIDENT
James O. Heyworth
EXECUTIVE V.P., SALES & MARKETING
J. Robert Bedell
S.V.P., FINANCE & ADMINISTRATION
Samuel Yates
S.V.P., PROGRAMMING
Michael Klein
V.P., TECHNOLOGY & OPERATIONS
John Vartanian
V.P. & GENERAL COUNSEL
Sandra E. Landau, Esq.
V.P. AFFILIATE RELATIONS
Terry Taylor
V.P,.VIDEO PROMOTION
Leigh Bolton
V.P., RESEARCH
Anthony White
V.P., BUSINESS AFFAIRS
David Meyer

WPIX

United Video, Inc., A UVSG Company, 7140 S. Lewis Ave., Tulsa, OK 74136-5422. (918) 488-4000. FAX: (918) 488-4250.
PRESIDENT & CEO
Gary Howard
COO
Peter Boylan

WWOR TV

Advance Entertainment Corporation, 5015 Campuswood Dr., E., Syracuse, NY 13057 (315) 455-5955. (800) 448-3322. FAX: (315) 433-2342.
MARKETING MANAGER
Betsy Bianco

THE WEATHER CHANNEL

300 Interstate N. Pkwy., Atlanta, GA 30339. (770) 226-0000. FAX: (770) 226-2930.
CEO
Michael J. Eckert
S.V.P., PROGRAMMING & OPERATIONS
Stan Hunter
S.V.P., ADVERTISING SALES
William Wiehe
V.P., AFFILIATE SALES
Dana Michaelal

Major U.S. Multiple Cable System Operators

ADELPHIA COMMUNICATIONS CORP.
85 Cable Systems, 1.9 million subscribers.
Box 472, 5 West Third St., Coudersport, PA 16915. (814) 274-9830. FAX: (814) 274-8631.
PRESIDENT, CHAIRMAN & CEO
John Rigas
CFO
Timothy J. Rigas
V.P., OPERATIONS
Michael Rigas

AMERICAN CABLE ENTERTAINMENT
24 Cable Systems, 76,000 subscribers.
4 Landmark Sq., Suite 302, Stamford, CT 06901. (203) 323-1100. FAX: (203) 325-3110.
CEO & PRESIDENT
Bruce Armstrong
CFO
John Flanagan

ARMSTRONG GROUP OF COLORADO
20 Cable Systems, 195,804 subscribers.
One Armstrong Pl., Butler, PA 16001. (412) 283-0925. FAX: (412) 283-2602.
CEO & PRESIDENT
Jay Sedwick
CFO
Kirby Campbell

BAY CABLE INC.
23 Cable Systems, 14,500 subscribers
2444 Solomons Island Rd., Ste. 202, Annapolis, MD 21401. (410) 266-9393. FAX: (410) 266-9054.

BRESNAN COMMUNICATIONS
16 Cable Systems, 777,000 subscribers.
709 Westchester Ave., White Plains, NY 10604. (914) 993-6624. FAX: (914) 993-6601.
PRESIDENT
William J. Bresnan

BUFORD TELEVISION INC.
270 Cable Systems, 153,432 Subscribers.
P.O. Box 9090, Tyler, TX 75711. (903) 561-4411. FAX: (903) 561-4031.
PRESIDENT & CEO
Ben Hooks
CHAIRMAN
Robert Buford
CFO
Thomas Seals

C-TEC CABLE SYSTEMS INC.
78 Cable Systems, 367,192 subscribers.
150 Carnegie Center, Princeton, NJ 08540. (609) 734-3716. FAX: (609) 734-3717.
CEO
David Mc Court
PRESIDENT
Mike Mahoney
CFO
Bruce Godfrey

CABLE AMERICA CORPORATION
21 Cable Systems, 72,069 subscribers.
2720 E. Camelback Rd., Ste. 200, Phoenix, AZ 85016. (602) 957-2500. FAX: (602) 952-0458.
CEO & PRESIDENT
William G. Jackson
CFO
Christopher Dyrek

CABLE MANAGEMENT
22 Cable Systems, 46,200 subscribers.
Box 802068, Noel Rd., Dallas, TX 75380. (972) 233-9616. FAX: (972) 701-8332.
CHAIRMAN
Nathan A. Levine
PRESIDENT
Doug Bridges

CABLE ONE INC.
63 Cable Systems, 632,430 Subscribers
4742 N. 24th St., Ste. 270, Phoenix, AZ 85016. (602) 468-1177. FAX: (602) 468-9216.
PRESIDENT
Thomas O. Might

CABLEVISION INDUSTRIES INC.
81 Cable Systems, 1.4 million subscribers.
One Cablevision Ctr., Box 311, Liberty, NY 12754. (914) 292-7550. FAX: (914) 295-2761.
CHAIRMAN & CEO
Alan Gerry
CFO
Keith Suehnholz
V.P., OPERATIONS
Fred H. Schulte

CABLEVISION SYSTEMS CORPORATION
30 Cable Systems, 2.6 million subscribers.
One Media Crossways, Woodbury, NY 11797. (516) 364-8450. FAX: (516) 496-1780.
CEO
James Dolan
CHAIRMAN
Charles F. Dolan
CFO
William J. Bell
V.P., OPERATIONS
Rudy Welter

CENTURY COMMUNICATIONS CORP.
70 Cable Systems, 1.25 million subscribers.
50 Locust Ave., New Canaan, CT 06840. (203) 972-2000. FAX: (203) 966-9228.
CHAIRMAN & CEO
Leonard Tow
PRESIDENT
Bernard P. Gallagher
CFO & V.P.
Scott Schneider

CHARTER COMMUNICATIONS
74 Cable Systems, 1 million subscribers.
12444 Powerscourt Dr., Suite 400, St. Louis, MO 63131. (314) 965-0555. FAX: (314) 965-8793.
CEO & PRESIDENT
Jerad I. Kent
CHAIRMAN
Barry L. Babcock

CLASSIC CABLE INC.
278 Cable Systems, 166,526 subscribers.
515 Congress St., #2626, Austin, TX 78701. (512) 476-9095. FAX: (512) 476-5204.
CHAIRMAN & CEO
J. Merritt Berlisle
PRESIDENT & CFO
Steven Seach

COMCAST CABLE COMMUNICATIONS, INC.
74 Cable Systems, 4.3 million subscribers.
1500 Market St., Philadelphia, PA 19102. (215) 665-1700. FAX: (215) 981-7790.
PRESIDENT
Thomas G. Baxter

COMMUNITY COMMUNICATIONS CO.
35 Cable Systems, 14,544 subscribers.
Box 558, 1920 Hwy., 425 N. Monticello, AR 71656-0558. (870) 367-7300. FAX: (870) 367-9770.
PRESIDENT
Paul Gardner
VICE PRESIDENT
Bill Copeland

CONTINENTAL CABLEVISION, INC./U. S. WEST
144 Cable Systems, 4.9 million subscribers.
The Pilot House, Lewis Wharf, Boston, MA 02110. (617) 742-9500. FAX: (617) 742-0530.
CHAIRMAN & CEO
Amos B. Hostetter, Jr.
PRESIDENT
Chuck Lillis

COX COMMUNICATIONS INC.
25 Cable Systems, 3.3 million subscribers.
(A division of Cox Enterprises, Inc.)1400 Lake Hearn Dr., Atlanta, GA 30319. (404) 843-5000. FAX: (404) 843-5777.
PRESIDENT & CEO
James O. Robbins
CFO
Jimmy Hayes
V.P., OPERATIONS
Maggie Bellville

DOUGLAS COMMUNICATIONS CORPORATION II
60 Cable Systems, 23,250 subscribers.
201 Rock Rd., Glen Rock, NJ 07452. (201) 444-1700. FAX: (201) 444-5092.
CEO & PRESIDENT
Douglas H. Dittrick
CHAIRMAN
Jay E. Ricks

FALCON CABLE TV
366 Cable Systems, 1.1 million subscribers.
10900 Wilshire Blvd., 15th floor, Los Angeles, CA 90024. (310) 824-9990. FAX: (310) 208-3655.
CHAIRMAN & CEO
Mark Nathanson
V.P., OPERATIONS
John Johnson

FANCH COMMUNICATIONS INC.
280 Cable Systems, 275,000 subscribers.
1873 S. Bellaire St., Suite 1550, Denver, CO 80222. (303) 756-5600. FAX: (303) 756-5774.
CEO & CHAIRMAN
Robert C. Fanch
PRESIDENT
Jack Pottle
CFO
Rich Halle
V.P., OPERATIONS
Bruce Tinney

FIBERVISION INC.
13 Cable Systems, 17,020 Subscribers
Box 427, 222 W. First St., Laurel, MT 59044. (406) 628-2100. FAX: (406) 628-8181.
PRESIDENT
L.P. Hillard
V.P., OPERATIONS
Ken Young

GALAXY CABLEVISION
500 Cable Systems, 200,000 subscribers.
1220 North Main, Sikeston, MO 63801. (573) 472-8200. FAX: (573) 471-0119.
CEO
Thomas L. Gleason, Jr.
PRESIDENT
Jim Gleason
CFO
Keith Davidson

GREAT PLAINS CABLE TV
27 Cable Systems, 7,000 subscribers
Box 600, 1635 Front St., Blair, NE 68008. (402) 426-9511. FAX: (402) 426-6475.
VICE PRESIDENT
Timothy J. Garrigan

GREAT SOUTHERN
4 Cable Systems, 100,000 Subscribers.
438 W. Patrick St., Frederick, MD 21701. (301) 662-6822. FAX: (301) 662-1307. URL: http://www.gscommunications.com
PRESIDENT
Robert W. Cole

HARRON COMMUNICATIONS CORP.
9 Cable Systems, 252,000 subscribers.
70 E. Lancaster Ave., Frazer, PA 19355. (610) 644-7500. FAX: (610) 644-2790.
PRESIDENT & CEO
Paul F. Harron Jr.
CFO
John F. Quigley

HELICON CORPORATION
8 Cable Systems, 155,000 Subscribers.
630 Palisades Ave., Engelwood Cliffs, NJ 07632. (201) 568-7720. FAX: (201) 568-6228.
CHAIRMAN & CEO
Theodore Baum
CFO
Herbert J. Roberts
V.P., OPERATIONS & V.P., PROGRAMMING
David M. Baum

HORIZON CABLEVISION INC.
9 Cable Systems, 31,990 subscribers.
2598 Lansing Rd., Charlotte, MI 48813, (517) 543-1245. FAX: (517) 543-8057.
CHAIRMAN
Glenn Friedly
VICE PRESIDENT
Alan Baird

INDEPENDENT COMPANY CABLE TV INC.
22 Cable Systems, 10,139 subscribers
Box 3799, 2700 N. St. Louis St., Batesville, AR 72501. (501) 793-4174. FAX: (501) 793-7439.
PRESIDENT
J.D. Pierce
VICE PRESIDENT
Boyce E. Barnett

INSIGHT COMMUNICATIONS CO.
9 Cable Systems, 180,000 subscribers.
126 E. 56 St., New York, NY 10022. (212) 371-2266. FAX: (212) 935-2575.
CHAIRMAN
Sidney R. Knafel
PRESIDENT
Michael S. Willner
CFO
Kim D. Kelly
V.P., OPERATIONS
James Stewart Jr.

INTERMEDIA PARTNERS
17 Cable Systems, 937,000 subscribers.
235 Montgomery St., San Francisco, CA 94104. (415) 616-4600. FAX: (415) 397-3406.
CEO
F. sTeven Crawford
CFO
Edon V. Hartley
V.P., OPERATIONS
Terry Cotton

JAMES CABLE PARTNERS L.P.
9 Cable Systems, 79,427 subscribers.
710 N. Woodward Ave., Ste. 180, Bloomfield Hills, MI 48304. (248) 647-1080. FAX: (248) 647-1321.
CEO
William R. James
CFO
Daniel K. Shoemaker
V.P., OPERATIONS
TImothy Trenary

JONES INTERCABLE, INC.
30 Cable Systems, 1.4 million subscribers.
9697 East Mineral Ave., Englewood, CO 80112. (303) 792-3111. FAX: (303) 799-1644.
CHAIRMAN & CEO
Glenn R. Jones
PRESIDENT
James B. O'Brien
CFO
Kevin Coyle
V.P., OPERATIONS
Ruth Warren

MARCUS CABLE PARTNERS L.P.
200 Cable Systems, 1.24 million subscribers.
2911 Turtle Creek Blvd., Suite 1300, Dallas, TX 75219. (214) 521-7898. FAX: (214) 526-2154. URL: www.marcuscable.com.
PRESIDENT & CEO
Jeffrey A. Marcus

MEDIA GENERAL INC.
2 Cable Systems, 230,000 subscribers.
Box 85333, Richmond, VA 23293. (804) 649-6000.
PRESIDENT & CEO
J. Stewart Bryan III

MEDIAONE, INC.
10 Cable Systems, 558,000 Subscribers.
2925 Courtyard Dr., Norcorss, GA 30071. (770) 613-2424. FAX: (770) 395-1124.
PRESIDENT
John Ridall
CFO
Mike Ricks
V.P., OPERATINS
Ellen Filipiak

MIDCONTINENT CABLE CO.
174 Cable Systems, 135,030 subscribers.
24 First Ave. N.E., Box 910, Aberdeen, SD 57402. (605) 229-1775. FAX: (605) 229-0478.
CHAIRMAN & CEO
N.L Bentson
PRESIDENT
Joseph H. Floyd

MOFFAT COMMUNICATIONS LTD.
8 Cable Systems, 216,972 subscribers.
Box 220, Station L, Winnipeg, Manitoba, Canada R3H 0Z5.
(204) 788-3440. FAX: (204) 956-2710.
PRESIDENT & CEO
Randall L. Moffat
CFO
William A. Davis

MULTIMEDIA CABLEVISION
44 Cable Systems, 460,000 subscribers.
701 E. Douglas, Box 3027, Wichita, KS 67201. (316) 262-4270.
PRESIDENT & CEO
Mike Burrus

NORTHLAND COMMUNICATIONS CORP.
40 Cable Systems, 210,000 subscribers.
1201 Third Ave., Suite 3600, Seattle, WA 98101. (206)
621-1351. FAX: (206) 674-3950.
PRESIDENT & CEO
John S. Whetzell
CFO
Gary S. Jones
V.P., OPERATIONS
Richard J. Dyste

NOVA CABLE MANAGEMENT INC.
20 Cable Systems, 6,767 subscribers
Box 793, 228-1/2 Washington Ave., Grand Haven, MI 49417.
(616) 847-0072. FAX: (616) 847-9409.
PRESIDENT
Gary Van Volkenburg

OMEGA COMMUNICATION INC.
11 Cable Systems, 50,000 subscribers.
Box 1766, 29 E. Maryland St., Indianapolis, IN 46206. (317)
264-4000. FAX: (317) 264-4020.
CEO & PRESIDENT
Robert E. Schloss
CFO
James Jones

ONE POINT COMMUNICATIONS
100 Cable Systems, 40,372 subscribers.
5335 Wisconsin Ave. N.W., Ste. 750, Washington, DC 20015.
(202) 364-3511. FAX: (202) 364-3520.
CEO & PRESIDENT
John C. Norcutt
CFO
John H. Long
V.P., OPERATIONS
Joan H. MIller

PENCOR SERVICES
34 Cable Systems, 164,000 subscribers.
471 Delaware Ave., Box 215, Palmerton, PA 18071. (610)
826-2551. FAX: (610) 826-7626.
PRESIDENT & CEO
Donald Reinhard
V.P., OPERATIONS
Frederick Reinhard

PHOENIX CABLE INC
47 Cable Systems, 35,000 subscribers.
10 S. Franklin Tpk., Ramsey, NJ 07446. (201) 825-9090. FAX:
(201) 825-8794.
PRESIDENT
James H. Fenney
V.P., OPERATIONS
Charles Himelrick Jr.

PINE STATE MANAGEMENT
12 Cable Systems, 8,800 subscribers.
724 W. Lancaster Ave., Ste. 233, Wayne, PA 19087. (610) 688-
6051. FAX: (610) 975-0123.
CEO & PRESIDENT
Walter Kemmerer
V.P., OPERATIONS
Thomas Cataldo

POST-NEWSWEEK CABLE
54 Cable Systems, 570,000 subscribers.
(A subsidiary of The Washington Post Co.) 4742 N. 24th St.,
#270, Phoenix, AZ 85016. (602) 468-1177. FAX: (602) 468-9216.
PRESIDENT
Thomas O. Might

PREMIERE CABLE II LTD.
58 Cable Systems, 18,648 subscribers
1104 Ironwood Dr., Coeur d'Alene, ID 83814. (208) 664-3370.
FAX: (208) 664-5888.
CEO & PRESIDENT
Ted Hughett
CFO
Bob Sprigli

PRESTIGE CABLE TV, INC.
10 Cable Systems, 138,000 Subscribers.
156 Morningside Drive, Cartersville, GA 30120. (770) 382-
0531. FAX: (770) 386-2540.
PRESIDENT & CEO
Jon Oscher

PRIME CABLE
5 Cable Systems, 820,000 subscribers.
1 American Center, 600 Congress Ave, Suite 3000, Austin, TX
78701. (512) 476-7888. FAX: (512) 476-4869.
CEO
Gregory Marchbanks
CHAIRMAN
Robert W. Hughes

RAPID COMMUNICATIONS PARTNERSHIP L.P. DBA RAPID CABLE
52 Cable Systems, 14,000 subscribers.
2620 S. Parker Rd., Ste. 355, Aurora, CO 80014-1651. (303)
751-5333. FAX: (303) 751-5221.
CEO, CHAIRMAN & PRESIDENT
Thomas Semptimphelter

REGIONAL CABLE TV
90 Cable Systems, 25,000 subscribers.
68 S. Park Blvd., Greenwood, IN 46143. (317) 865-2400. FAX:
(317) 865-2426.
PRESIDENT
Paul Scott

RIFKIN & ASSOCIATES
80 Cable Systems, 312,082 subscribers.
360 S. Monroe St., Suite 600, Denver, CO 80209. (303) 333-
1215. FAX: (303) 322-3553.
CHAIRMAN & CEO
Monroe M. Rifkin
PRESIDENT
Jeffrey D. Bennis
CFO
Dale P. Wagner

ROGERS CABLESYSTEMS LIMITED
50 Cable Systems, 2.5 million subscribers.
One Valleybrook Dr., 5th Flr., Toronto, ON M3B 2S7. (416)
447-5500. FAX: (416) 391-7247.
CEO
Jos Wintermans
CFO
Allen Horn

SATELLITE CABLE SERVICES INC.
57 Cable Systems, 9,885 subscribers.
Drawer U, De Smet, SD 57231. (605) 854-9133. FAX: (605)
854-9122.
PRESIDENT
Richard Cutler
VICE PRESIDENT
Doug Bierschbach

SAVAGE COMMUNICATIONS INC.
12 Cable Systems, 5,100 subscribers.
206 Power Ave. N., Hainckley, MN 55037. (320) 384-7442.
FAX: (320) 384-7446.
PRESIDENT
Ron Savage

SJOBERG'S CABLE TV INC.
13 Cable Systems, 8,000 subscribers.
315 N. Main Ave., Thief River Falls, MN 56701. (218) 681-
3044. FAX: (218) 681-6801.
PRESIDENT
Richard Sjoberg
VICE PRESIDENT
Stan Sjoberg

SOUTH DAKOTA CABLE INC.
9 Cable Systems, 16,500 subscribers.
Box 309, R.R. 8C55, Sturgis, SD 57785. (605) 347-3090. FAX:
(605) 347-3499.
PRESIDENT
William Duhamel Jr.
V.P., OPERATIONS
Steve Duffy

STAR CABLE ASSOCIATES
38 Cable Systems, 42,404 subscribers.
381 Mansfield Ave., Ste. 100, Pittsburgh, PA 15220. (412)
937-0099. FAX: (412) 937-0145.
CEO
James C. Roddey
PRESIDENT
Michael R. Haislip
CFO
Richard W. Talarico

STATE CABLE TV CORP.
11 Cable Systems, 63,500 subscribers.
Box 1076, Augusta, ME 04332. (207) 623-5145. FAX: (207) 623-3407.
CEO & PRESIDENT
Michael Angelakis
CHAIRMAN
Edward Barlow
CFO
Kenneth E. Danielson
V.P., OPERATIONS
Kathleen Hounsell

SUBURBAN CABLE TV CO., INC.
13 Cable Systems, 994,339 subscribers.
Box 989, 200 Cresson Blvd., Oaks, PA 19456. (610) 650-1000. FAX: (610) 650-3011.
PRESIDENT, CHAIRMAN & CEO
H. F. Lenfest
CFO
Harry Brooks

SUMMIT COMMUNICATIONS INC.
31 Cable Systems, 39,000 subscribers.
3633 136th Pl. S.E., Ste. 107, Bellevue, WA 98006. (206) 747-4600. FAX: (206) 644-4621.
CEO
James H. HIrschfield
CFO
Robert Erickson
V.P., OPERATIONS
Steve Weed

SUSQUEHANNA CABLE CO.
7 Cable Systems, 148,000 Subscribers.
140 East Market St., York, PA 17401. (717) 848-5500.
CHAIRMAN
Louis Appell, Jr.

TCA CABLE TV
64 Cable Systems, 640,000 subscribers.
Box 130489, 3015 E.S.E. Loop 323, Tyler, TX 75713-0489. (903) 595-3701. FAX: (903) 595-1929.
CEO
Robert M. Rogers
PRESIDENT
Fred Nichols
CFO
Jimmy Taylor
V.P., OPERATIONS
Randy Goad

TELE-COMMUNICATIONS, INC.
692 Cable Systems, 14 million subscribers.
5619 DTC Parkway, Englewood, CO 80111-3000. Mailing: P.O. Box 5630, Denver, CO 80217. (303) 267-5500. FAX: (303) 488-3210.
CEO
Leo Hindrey
PRESIDENT
John C. Malone

TELE-MEDIA CORPORATION OF DELAWARE
45 Cable Systems, 274,086 subscribers.
320 West College Ave., P.O. Box 5301, Pleasant Gap, PA 16823. (814) 359-3481. FAX: (814) 359-5390.
CHAIRMAN & CEO
Robert Trudek
PRESIDENT
Everett I. Mundy
V.P., OPERATIONS
Frank R. Vicente

THOMPSON CABLEVISION CO INC.
10 Cable Systems, 15,977 subscribers.
Box 13309 Sissonville, WV 25360. (304) 984-0025. FAX: (304) 984-0002.
PRESIDENT
Allen D. Thompson
VICE PRESIDENT
Anthony Cochran

TIME WARNER CABLE
117 Cable Systems, 11.7 million subscribers.
(A Time Warner Entertainment Company) 290 Harbor Dr., Stamford, CT 06902. (203) 328-0600. FAX: (203) 328-0692.
CHAIRMAN & CEO
Joseph J. Collins
PRESIDENT
James Doolittle
CFO
Tom Harris

TRIAX TELECOMMUNICATIONS CORP.
483 Cable Systems, 447,377 subscribers.
100 Fillmore St., Suite 600, Denver, CO 80206. (303) 333-2424. FAX: (303) 333-1110.
CHAIRMAN & CEO
James DeSorrento
PRESIDENT
Jay Busch
CFO
Christopher O'Toole

US CABLE CORPORATION
35 Cable Systems, 240,000 subscribers.
28 W. Grand Ave., Montvale, NJ 07645. (201) 930-9000. FAX: (201) 930-9232.
CHAIRMAN
Stephen E. Myers
PRESIDENT
James D. Pearson
V.P., OPERATIONS
Joseph Appio

WEHCO VIDEO, INC.
14 Cable Systems, 117,000 Subscribers.
P.O. Box 2221, Little Rock, AR 72203. (501) 378-3529. FAX: (501) 376-8594.
CEO
Walter E. Hussman, Jr.
V.P., OPERATIONS
Jim Wilbanks

Direct Broadcast Satellite Systems Operators

ALPHASTAR DIGITAL TELEVISON
55,000 subscribers
88 South Water St., Greenwich, cT 06830. (203) 531-7272.
FAX: (203) 531-6903.
PRESIDENT
Mahmound A. Wahba

CANADIAN SATELLITE COMMUNICATIONS, INC.
50 Burnhamthorpe Rd. W., 10th Floor, Mississauga, Ontario,
L5B 3C2 Canada. (905) 272-4960. FAX: (905) 272-3399.
PRESIDENT & CEO
Alain Gourd

DIRECTV INC.
(A subsidiary of Hughes Electronics Corp.)
2.7 million subscribers.
2230 E. Imperial Highway, El Segundo, CA 90245. (310) 535-5113. FAX: (310) 535-5225.
PRESIDENT
Eddy Hartenstein
EXECUTIVE V.P.'S
Bill Butterworth
Jim Ramo
S.V.P., MARKETING
Steve Ste. Marie

EXPRESSVU INC.
115 Scarsdale Rd., North York, Ontario, M3B 2R2 Canada. (416) 383-6600. FAX: (416) 383-6692. URL: http://www.expressvu.com
PRESIDENT & CEO
Michael Neuman
V.P., MARKETING & SALES
Michael Skea
V.P., TECHNOLOGY
Terry Snazel
V.P., GOVERNMENT & REGULATORY AFFAIRS
Chris Frank

FORT WAYNE TELSAT (DBA CHOICE TV)
4,000 subscribers
1909 Production Rd., Fort Wayne, IN 46808. (219) 471-2324.
FAX: (219) 471-5406.
PRESIDENT
James F. Simon
V.P. & GENERAL MANAGER
William A. Millett
OPERATIONS MANAGER
Michelle L. Sweeney

GBI/GEAR BROADCASTING INTERNATIONAL INC.
94 Calvary St., Providence, RI 02908. (401) 331-6072. FAX: (401) 274-5508.
CHAIRMAN & PRESIDENT
Edward R. Robalisky
EXECUTIVE V.P.
Jack G. Thayer

PRIMESTAR PARTNERS
1.9 million subscribers.
3 Bala Plaza West, Suite 700, Bala Cynwyd, PA 19004. (610) 617-5300. FAX: (610) 617-5312.
CHAIRMAN & CEO
James Gray
PRESIDENT
Dan O'Brien

UNITED STATES SATELLITE BROADCASTING CO., INC.
1.36 million subscribers.
3415 University Ave., St. Paul, MN 55114. (612) 645-4500.
FAX: (612) 642-4578.
CHAIRMAN
Stanley S. Hubbard
PRESIDENT & CEO
Stanley E. Hubbard
EXECUTIVE VICE PRESIDENT
Robert Hubbard
S.V.P., MARKETING
Mary Pat Ryan

WORLD SPACE MANAGEMENT CORP.
2400 N St. N.W., Washington, DC 20037. (202) 884-7800. FAX: (202) 884-7900.
URL: http://www.worldspace.com
CHAIRMAN & CEO
Noah A. Samara
PRESIDENT
John Cusick
GENERAL COUNSEL/SECRETARY
James R. Laramie
CFO
Heinz Stubblefield

WIRELESS CABLE SYSTEMS

AMERICAN TELECASTING, INC.
4065 N. Sinton Rd., Suite 201, Colorado Springs, CO 80907.
(719) 632-5544. FAX: (719) 632-5549
PRESIDENT & CEO
Brian Gast

BELLSOUTH ENTERTAINMENT
660 Hembree Parkway, Suite 120, Roswell, GA 30076.
6767 Bundy Road, Room 103, New Orleans, LA 70127.
Atlanta: (770) 360-4990; Orlando: (877) 463-4448; New
Orleans: (504) 245-2700;Alabama: (800) 509-2278.

CAI WIRELESS SYSTEMS, INC.
18 Corporate Woods Blvd., 3rd Fl., Albany, NY 12211. (518)
462-2632. FAX: (518) 462-3045.
CEO
Jared E. Abbruzzese
PRESIDENT & COO
John J. Prisco

CFW CABLE
401 Spring Lane, Suite 300, P.O Box 1990, Waynesboro,
Virginia 22980. (540) 946-3500.
PRESIDENT & CEO
James S. Quarforth

C.S. WIRELESS
(Popvision) 3115 N. Sillect Ave., Bakersfield, CA 93308-6339.
(805) 638-2222. FAX: (805) 638-2223.

COMMUNICATIONS INTERNATIONAL
13-15 Fair Lawn Ave., Fair Lawn, NJ 07410. (201) 794-1506.
FAX: (201) 794-1970. email: videotel@aol.com
CEO
Scott Lagrosa

FORT WAYNE TELSAT INC.
(dba choice TV) 1909 Production Rd., Fort Wayne, IN 46808.
(219) 471-2324. FAX: (219) 471-5406.
VICE PRESIDENT & GENERAL MANAGER
William A. Millett

GEAR WIRELESS CABLE
Box 28404, Smith St., Providence, RI 02908. (401) 331-6072.
PRESIDENT & CEO
Jack G. Thayer

HEARTLAND WIRELESS COMMUNICATIONS, INC.
200 Chisholm Place, Suite 200, Plano, TX 75075. (972) 633-
4000, (972) 423-9494. FAX: (972) 633-0074.
email: hwireless@aol.com.
URL: http://www.heartlandwireless.com
PRESIDENT/CHMN/CEO
Caroll D. McHenry

LIBERTY CABLE TELEVISION
575 Madison Ave., New York, NY 10022. (212) 891-7701. FAX:
(212) 891-7790.
PRESIDENT
P. Price

NEW YORK CHOICE TELEVISION
140 Broadway. 29th Flr., New York, NY 10005. (201) 808-3700.
FAX: (201) 227-2612.
GENERAL MANAGER & VICE PRESIDENT
Robert Bauman

PEOPLE'S CHOICE TV CORP.
Two Corporate Drive, Suite 249, Shelton, CT 06484-6239.
(203) 925-7900. FAX: (203) 929-1454.
CHAIRMAN & CEO
Matthew Oristano

TEL-COM WIRELESS CABLE CORP
1506 NE 162nd St., North Miami BEach, FL 33162. (305) 947-
3010. FAX: (305) 945-9974.
CEO
Melvin Rosen
CFO
James R. Pekarek

TV COMMUNICATIONS NETWORK
10020 E. Girard Ave., Ste. 300, Denver, CO 80231. (303) 751-
2900. FAX: (303) 751-1081
2775 Arnold, Ste. B, Salina, KS 67401. (913) 827-5551.
CHAIRMAN OF THE BOARD, PRESIDENT & CEO
Omar A. Duwalk

VIDEOTEL
13-15 Fairlawn Ave., Fairlawn, NJ 07410. (201) 794-1506. FAX:
(201) 794-1970. email: videotel@aol.com
PRESIDENT
Scott Lagrosa

WIRELESS ADVANTAGE
2155 Main St., Sarasota, FL 34237. (941) 955-0065. FAX:
(941) 955-6586.
PRESIDENT
David Bednarsh

WIRELESS CABLE INTERNATIONAL, INC.
67-A Mountain Blvd. Extension, Warren, NJ 07059. (908) 271-
4880. FAX: (908) 469-8778.
PRESIDENT & CEO
George M. Ring

WIRELESS ONE
2506 Lakeland Drive, Suite 600, Jackson, Mississippi 39208.
(601) 936-1515.
PRESIDENT & CEO
Henry M. Burkhalter

PRODUCTION SERVICES

Advertising & Publicity

BOB ABRAMS AND ASSOCIATES
2030 Prosser Ave., Los Angeles, CA 90025. (310) 475-7739.
FAX: (310) 475-7739.
Bob Abrams

ADSPOSURE ADVERTISING SPECIALTIES
209 W. Alameda Ave., Ste. 102, Burbank, CA 91502. (818)
559-6304. FAX: (818) 563-6423. email: mimivh@aol.com
URL: http://adsposure.com
PRESIDENT
Mimi Van Horn

AD 2, INC.
2118 Wilshire Blvd., Ste. 205, Santa Monica, CA 90403. (310)
394-8379. FAX: (310) 451-0966. URL: http://www.ad2.com
PRESIDENT
Brad Mooberry

AIR CREATIVE GROUP INC.
731 N. Fairfax Ave., Los Angeles, CA 90046. (213) 966-3900.
FAX: (213) 966-3975.
PRESIDENT & CREATIVE DIRECTOR
Stephan Gerber
SENIOR V.P., FINANCE & ADMINISTRATION
Barbara Breest

**AMERICAN ASSOCIATION OF ADVERTISING AGENCIES,
INC. (A.A.A.A.)**
130 Battery St., Ste. 330, San Francisco, CA 94111. (415) 291-
4999. FAX: (415) 291-4995. email: aaaawest1@aol.com
URL: http://www.comercepark.com/aaaa/aaaa.html
EXECUTIVE V.P.
Jerry L. Gibbons

AMOROSANO ASSOCIATES
411 N. Central Ave., STe. 230, Glendale, CA 91203. (818) 247-
2900. FAX: (818) 247-3927. email: amorprla@aol.com
CONTACT
Ken Amorosano

THE ANGELLOTTI COMPANY
12413 Ventura Court, Suite 200, Studio City, CA 91604. (818)
506-7887. FAX: (818) 506-8822. email: Tony@angelco.clrs.com
PRESIDENT
Tony Angellotti
V.P. & SENIOR PUBLICIST
Karen Fried

ASTHER/GOULD ADVERTISING, INC.
5900 Wilshire Blvd., 31st Flr., Los Angeles, CA 90036. (213)
931-4151. FAX: (213) 931-4548.

AXIS MEDIA
289 S. Robertson Blvd., Ste. 489, Beverly Hills, CA 90211.
(310) 478-4944. FAX: (310) 478-3036.
URL: http://www.axismedia.com
CONTACT
Sean Olson

JANE AYER PUBLIC RELATIONS, INC.
3204 Ocean Park Blvd., Suite 240, Santa Monica, CA 90405.
(310) 581-1330. FAX: (310) 581-1335. email: japr@aol.com

N.W. AYER & PARTNERS
Worldwide Plaza, 825 Eighth Ave., New York, NY 10019-7498.
(212) 474-5000. FAX: (212) 474-5400.
CEO
Mary Lou Quinlan

BABLOVE AGENCY INC.
2980 N. Campbell St., Ste. 190, Tucson, AZ 85719, (520) 322-
9060.

BACKER, SPIELVOGEL, BATES INC.
2010 Main St., Ste. 700, Irvine, CA 92614. (714) 261-0330.
FAX: (714) 261-6565.

BAKER, WINOKUR, RYDER
405 S. Beverly Dr., 5th floor, Beverly Hills, CA 90212. (310)
277-6200.
250 W. 57 St., #1610, New York, NY 10017. (212) 582-0700.
FAX: (212) 582-0490.

BALLARD COMMUNICATIONS
1850 E. Flamingo Rd., Ste. 120, Las Vegas, NV 89119. (702)
836-3000, (800) 864-2792. FAX: (702) 836-3003.

BARCLAY COMMUNICATIONS
3550 N. Central, Ste. 915, Phoenix, AZ 85012. (602) 277-3550.
FAX: (602) 277-1217. email: Barclay@netzone.com

BARTEL DESIGN GROUP
2820 Glendale Blvde., Los Angeles, CA 90039. (213) 662-
6869. FAX; 9213) 662-2026. email: jane@barteldesign.com
URL: http://www.barteldesign.com
PRESIDENT & CREATIVE DIRECTOR
Jane Bartel

BBDO LOS ANGELES
10960 Wilshire Blvd., # 1600, Los Angeles, CA 90024. (310)
444-4500. FAX: (310) 444-7581.

BBDO WORLDWIDE
1285 Avenue of the Americas, New York, NY 10019. (212) 459-
5000.

BEAR ADVERTISING INC.
32121 Lindero Canyon Rd., Ste. 200, Westlake Village, CA
91361. (818) 865-6464. FAX: (818) 865-6499.

BENDER, GOLDMAN & HELPER
11500 W. Olympic Blvd., Suite 655, Los Angeles, CA 90064.
(310) 473-4147.
400 Madison Ave., New York NY 10017. (212) 371-0798. FAX:
(212) 754-4380.

WALTER F. BENNETT COMMUNICATIONS
7111 Valley Green Rd., Ste. 220, Fort Washington, PA 19034.
(215) 836-2727. FAX: (215) 836-2726.
PRESIDENT
Robert H. Straton

BIEDERMAN, KELLY & SHAFFER INC.
475 Park Ave. South, New York, NY 10016. (212) 213-5500.
FAX: (212) 213-4775.
CHAIRMAN
Barry Biederman

MARION BILLINGS PUBLICITY LTD,
250 W. 57 St., #2420, New York, NY 10107. (212) 581-4493.

RALPH BING ADVERTISING CO.
16109 Selva Dr., San Diego, CA 92128. (714) 487-7444.
PRESIDENT
Ralph Bing

THE BLAINE GROUP
7465 Beverly Blvd., Los Angeles, CA 90036. (213) 938-2577.
FAX: (213) 939-7701. email: blaine@pacificnet.net
PRESIDENT & CEO
Devon Blaine

BLOCK-KORENBROT PUBLIC RELATIONS
8271 Melrose Ave., Rm. 115, Los Angeles, CA 90046. (213)
655-0593. FAX: (213) 655-7302. email: classicpr@aol

MICHELLE BOLTON & ASSOCS.
100 S. Doheny Dr., #420, Los Angeles, CA 90048. (310) 273-
4030. FAX: (310) 273-2640.
CONTACT
Michelle Bolton

BOZELL WORLDWIDE.
40 W. 23 St., New York, NY 10010. (212) 727-5000. FAX: (212)
645-9262. email: dbell@newyork.com
PRESIDENT & CEO
David A. Bell

BRAGMAN HYMAN CAFARELLI
9171 Wilshire Blvd., Penthouse, Beverly Hills, CA 90210. (310)
274-7800. FAX: (310) 274-7838. email:
dharris.bnc@mcimail.com
V.P., ENTERTAINMENT MARKETING
Debi Farkas Harris

THE BROKAW COMPANY
9255 Sunset Blvd., #804, Los Angeles, CA 90069. (310) 273-
2060. FAX: (310) 276-4037. email: brokawc@aol.com
PARTNERS
David Brokaw
Sanford Brokaw

BUMBLE WARD & ASSOCIATES
6426 W. 82nd, St., Los Angeles, CA 90045. (310) 645-8517.
FAX: (310) 645-3001

611

LEO BURNETT COMPANY, INC.
35 W. Wacker, Chicago, IL 60601. (312) 220-5959. FAX: (312) 220-3299.
10900 Wilshire Blvd., Ste. 700, Los Angeles, CA 90024. (310) 443-2000. FAX: (310) 208-5984.
CHAIRMAN & CEO
Richard Fizdale
PRESIDENT
Jim Oats

BURSON-MARSTELLER
230 Park Ave. South, New York, NY 10003-1566. (212) 614-4000. FAX: (212) 598-6942.
1800 Century Park E. Ste. 200, Los Angeles, CA 90067. (310) 226-3000. FAX: (310) 226-3030.
CHAIRMAN
Harold Burson

THE BUTLER GROUP
4444 Lankershim Blvd., Ste. 202, North Hollywood, CA 91602. (818) 623-9780. FAX: (818) 623-9785. email: butlergrp@aol.com
CREATIVE DIRECTOR
Michael Masterson

CAPSTONE FILM CO.
29 W 74th St., Ste. 3B, New York, NY 10023. (212) 362-9828. FAX: (212) 580-5661.

THE CATANIA GROUP
520 Washington Blvd., Ste. 641, Marina Del Rey, CA 90292. (310) 827-6810. FAX: (310) 827-6480. email: catania@ix.net-com.com
PRESIDENT
Cirina Catania

CITIGATE, ALBERT, FRANK LAW INC.
850 3rd Ave., New York, NY 10022. (212) 755-6841.
CHAIRMAN
Gary Goldstein
PRESIDENT
James H. Feeney

CLEIN & WHITE, INC.
8584 Melrose Ave., 2nd Flr., W. Hollywood, CA 90069. (310) 659-4141. FAX: (213) 659-3995.
33 W. 54th St., New York, NY 10019. (212) 247-4100.

CLOCK-WISE
2661 S. Gravenstein Hyw., Unit 102, Sabastopol, CA 95472. (800) 969-8463, (707) 823-1382. FAX: (707) 823-8251.
email: jcl@sonic.net
URL: http://www.clockwise.com
PRESIDENT
Jon Liebling

CMG WORLDWIDE
10500 CrossPoint Blvd., Indianapolis, In 46256. (317) 570-5000. FAX: (317) 570-5500.
CHARIMAN & CEO
Mark Roesler

COMMUNICATIONS PLUS INC.
102 Madison Ave. S., New York, NY 10016. (212) 686-9570.

CONSOLIDATED ADVERTISING DIRECTORS INC.
8060 Melrose Ave., ste. 300, los Angeles, CA 90046. (213) 653-8060. FAX: (213) 655-9452.

CREATIVE PRODUCTIONS
1850 Redondo Ave., Ste. 104, Long Beach, CA 90804. (562) 985-1363. FAX: (562) 985-1365. email: cpnow@aol.com
URL: http://www.creativeproductions.com

CREATIVE RESOURCE MAVEN
PO Box 191183, Dallas, TX 75219. (972) 438-4085. FAX: (972) 438-5090.

AARON D. CUSHMAN & ASSOCIATES, INC.
35 E. Wacker Dr., Ste. 850, Chicago, IL 60601. 9312) 263-2500. FAX: (312) 263-1197.
380 Lexington, Ste. 1700. New York, NY 10168. 92120 856-0100. FAX: (212) 551-1001.

D'ARCY, MASIUS, BENTON & BOWLES
1675 Broadway, New York, NY 10019-5809. (212) 468-3622. FAX: (212) 468-4385.
6500 Wilshire Blvd., Los Angeles, CA 90048. (213) 658-4500.
CEO
Roy J. Bostock
PRESIDENT
John Farrell

DAVIS, BALL & COLOMBATTO ADVERTISING, INC.
865 S. Figueroa St., 12th Flr., Los Angeles, CA 90017. (213) 688-7000. FAX: (213) 688-7288.

DAZU
4705 Laurel Canyon Blvd., Valley Village, CA 91607. (818) 752-2800.

DENNIS DAVIDSON & ASSOCS. INC.
5670 Wilshire Blvd., Suite 700, Los Angeles, CA 90036. (213) 954-5858. FAX: (213) 954-5850.
1776 Broadway, New York, NY 10019. (212) 246-0500. FAX: (212) 246-8918.
PRESIDENT (CA)
Melanie Hodal
CONTACTS (NY)
Jeremy Walker
Mary Flanagan

DDB NEEDHAM WORLDWIDE INC.
437 Madison Ave., New York, NY 10022. (212) 415-2000. FAX: (212) 415-3591.
CHAIRMAN/CEO
Keith Reinhard
PRESIDENT, NY
Ken Kaes

SAMANTHA DEAN & ASSOCS.
36 W. 44 St., Ste. 1401, New York, NY 10036. (212) 391-2675. FAX: (212) 391-4913.

DENTSU, INC.
120 Broadway, Ste. 220, Santa Monica, CA 90401. (310) 899-1113. FAX: (310) 899-0113.

DOREMUS & COMPANY
200 Varick St., 11th & 12th floors, New York, NY 10014. (212) 366-3000. FAX: (212) 366-3632.
12100 Wilshire Blvd., Ste. 400, Los Angeles, CA 90025. (310) 207-3210. FAX: (310) 207-5444. email: cparsons@pondel.com
CONTACT (CA)
Craig A. Parsons
PRESIDENT
Carl Anderson
EXECUTIVE V.P., WORLDWIDE CREATIVE DIRECTOR
Rebecca Tudor-Foley

LARRY DORN ASSOCS. INC.
5820 Wilshire Blvd., Suite 306, Los Angeles, CA 90036. (213) 935-6266. FAX: (213) 935-9523.
PRESIDENT
Larry Dorn
CONTACTS
Linda Dorn-Wallerstein
Lucy Kohn

EDELMAN PUBLIC RELATIONS WORLDWIDE
5670 Wilshire Blvd., #1500, Los Angeles, CA 90036. (213) 857-9100. FAX: (213) 857-9117. email: gdrucker@la.edelman.com
URL: http://www.edelman.com
CONTACT
George Drucker

MAX EISEN
234 W. 44 St., New York, NY 10036. (212) 391-1072. FAX: (212) 391-4004.

EMA MULTIMEDIA, INC.
11911 San Vicente Blvd., Ste. 230, Los Angeles, CA 90049. (310) 440-3355. FAX: (310) 440-3340.
email: pace@emamulti.com
URL: http://www.emamulti.com
CREATIVE DIRECTOR & CO
Michael Pace

EMERITUS PUBLIC RELATIONS
PO Box 292362, Penthouse, Beverly Hills, CA 90212. (213) 860-8822. email: mheath@boxtop.com
CONTACTS
Michael Hearth
Robbie Horwitz

JOHN EMMERLING PRODUCTION
415 Madison Ave., New York, NY 10017. (212) 753-4700. FAX: (212) 753-4996.

EMPTY STREET PRODUCTIONS
4872 Topanga Canyon Blvd., Ste. 343, Woodland Hills, CA 91364. (818) 887-4940. FAX: (818) 340-1838.
email: pattrex@emptystreet.com
URL: http://www.emptystreet.com
CREATIVE DIRECTOR
Pat Ortman

ENCORE INTERNATIONAL GROUP
280 S. Beverly Dr., Penthouse, Beverly Hills, CA 90212. (310) 246-0688. FAX: (310) 246- 9038.
CONTACT
Jerry Pam

ENTERTAINMENT COMMUNICATIONS NETWORK
4370 Tujunga Ave., 2nd Flr., Studio City, CA 91604. (818) 752-1400.

EURO RSCG TATHAM
980 N. Michigan Ave., Chicago, IL 60611. (312) 337-4400. FAX: (312) 337-5930.
CHAIRMAN, CHIEF CREATIVE OFFICER
Robert H. Welke

EVANS GROUP
110 Social Hall Ave., Salt Lake City, UT 84111. (801) 364-7452. FAX: (801) 364-7484.
5757 Wilshire Blvd., Ste. 240, Los Angeles, CA 90036. (213) 954-3000. FAX: (213) 931-1257.
CHAIRMAN/CEO
Dave Thomas

FELDMAN PUBLIC RELATIONS
9220 Sunset Blvd., #230, Los Angeles, CA 90069. (310) 859-9062.
CONTACT
Brenda Feldman

FOOTE, CONE & BELDING COMMUNICATIONS, INC.
101 East Erie Street, Chicago, IL 60611-2897. (312) 425-7000. FAX: (312) 425-5010.
CHAIRMAN & CEO
Bruce Mason

B. D. FOX & FRIENDS, INC. ADVERTISING
1111 Broadway, Santa Monica, CA 90401. (310) 394-7150. FAX: (310) 393-1569. URL: http://www.bdfox.com
PRESIDENT & CEO
Brian D. Fox.

GELFOND, GORDON ASSOCIATES
11500 Olympic Blvd., Suite 350, Los Angeles, CA 90064. (310) 478-3600. FAX: (310) 477-4825. email: ggelfond@aol.com
PRESIDENT
Gordon Gelfond

GERBER ADVERTISING AGENCY
209 S.W. Oak St., Portland, OR 97204. (503) 221-0100. FAX: (503) 228-5315.
PRESIDENT & CEO
Duncan Strang

GOLIN/HARRIS COMMUNICATIONS
601 W. 5th St., 4th Flr., Los Angeles, CA 90071. (213) 623-4200. FAX: (213) 895-4745.
500 N. Michigan Ave., Chicago, IL 60611. (312) 729-4000.
CHAIRMAN
Al Golin
PRESIDENT & CEO
Rich Jernstedt

GOOD WAG MERCHANDISING, INC.
80 8th Ave., Ste. 303, New York, NY 10011. (212) 807-5728. FAX: (212) 242-4287.

GRACE UNDER PRESSURE
23 Lavelle Ave., New Fairfield, CT 06812. (203) 746-9177.

GREY ADVERTISING, INC.
777 Third Ave., New York, NY 10017. (212) 546-2000. FAX: (212) 546-1495.
6100 Wilshire Blvd., 9th Flr., Los Angeles, CA 90048. (213) 936-6060.
CHAIRMAN & CEO
Edward H. Meyer

GREY ENTERTAINMENT & MEDIA
875 Third Ave., New York, NY 10022. (212) 303-2400. FAX: (212) 418-3950.

GRIFFIN BACAL INC.
130 5th Ave., New York, NY 10011. (212) 337-6300.

GS ENTERTAINMENT MARKETING GROUP
522 N. Larchmont Blvd., Los Angeles, CA 90004. (213) 860-0270. FAX: (213) 860-0279.
CONTACT
Steven Zeller

GUTTMAN ASSOCIATES
118 S. Beverly Dr., Suite 201, Beverly Hills, CA 90212. (310) 246-4600. FAX: (310) 246-4601.

HAMMER FILMS
6311 Romaine St., Ste. 7316, Hollywood, CA 90038. (213) 463-9156. FAX: (213) 463-8130. email: hammerfilm@aol.com
FACILITY COORDINATOR
Tracey Buscaglia

HANSON & SCHWAM
9350 Wilshire Blvd., Suite 315, Beverly Hills, CA 90212. (310) 248-4488. FAX: (310) 248-4499.

HENNESSEY ENTERTAINMENT, LTD.
PO Box 481164, Los Angeles, CA 9048. (213) 874-4700. FAX: (213) 436-0091. email: thefixer@webtv.net.
URL: http://www.geocities.com/hollywood/lot/5967
CEO
Ellis A. Cohen

HILL & NOLTON
466 Lexington Ave., New York, NY 10017. (212) 885-0300.

HILTON CREATIVE AGENCY, INC.
PO Box 2026, Toluca Lake, CA 91610. (213) 851-6532. FAX: (213) 851-6532.

HODES, BERNARD, ADV. INC.
555 Madison Ave., New York, NY 10022. (212) 758-2600. FAX: (212) 751-6278.
PRESIDENT & CEO
Bernard S. Hodes

THE HOLLYWOOD-MADISON GROUP
11684 Ventura Blvd., Ste. 258, Studio City, CA 91604. (818) 762-8008. FAX: (818) 762-8089.
email: hollywood-madison@worldnet.att.net
CONTACT
Lori Popovich

HORIZON MEDIA, INC.
1801 Century Park East, Ste. 480, Los Angeles, CA 90067. (310) 282-0909. FA: (310) 277-9692.

HUTCHINS/YOUNG & RUBICAM
400 Midtown Tower, Rochester, NY 14604. (716) 546-6480. FAX: (716) 325-0360.
PRESIDENT & CEO
M.A. Sapos

IMAGEMAKERS
2341-1/2 San Marco Dr., Los Angeles, CA 90068. (213) 467-0240. FAX: (213) 467-1679.

INDEPENDENT MEDIA WEST, INC.
10100 Santa Monica Blvd., Ste. 270, Los Angeles, CA 90067. (310) 556-2455. FAX: (310) 556-2164.

INTER/MEDIA ADVERTISING
15910 Ventura Blvd., Ste. 1010, Encino, CA 91435. (818) 995-1455.

INTERNATIONAL COMMUNICATIONS GROUP, INC.
1925 Century Park East, Ste. 1850, Los Angeles, CA 90067. (310) 557-2585. FAX: (310) 557-3009.
URL: http://icg-media.com
CONTACT
Andrew Butcher

JENSEN COMMUNICATIONS INC.
230 E. Union St., Pasadena, CA 91101. (626) 585-9575. FAX: (626) 564-8920.

K. MEDIA RELATIONS
1710 Hillhurst Ave., Ste. 204, Los Angeles, CA 90027. (213) 644-3700. FAX: (213) 644-3705. email: kmediapr@aol.com
URL: http://www.kmediapublicrelations.com
PRESIDENT
Tara Kolla

KAISER MCEUEN INC.
1631 Pontius Ave., Los Angeles, CA 90025. (310) 479-8999. FAX: (310) 479-8006.

KAUFER MILLER COMMUNICATIONS
1750 112th Ave., NE, Ste. D-154, Bellevue, WA 98004. (206) 450-9965. FAX: (206) 450-9963. email: marketing@kmcomm.com
URL: http://kmcomm.inter.net
V.P., MARKETING
Rusty Citron

HENRY J. KAUFMAN & ASSOCIATES, INC.
2233 Wisconsin Ave. NW, Washington, DC 20007. (202) 333-0700.
PRESIDENT & CEO
Michael G. Carberry

KETCHUM COMMUNICATIONS, INC.
Six PPG Place, Pittsburgh, PA 15222. (412) 456-3500.
11755 Wilshire Blvd., Ste. 1900, Los Angeles, CA 90025. (310) 444-5000.

LANDIN MEDIA INC.
3033 N. 44 St., #375, Phoenix, AZ 85018-7229. (602) 348-9225. FAX: (602) 553-4090.
PRESIDENT & CEO
Larry L. Cummings

BILL LANESE ADVERTISING & PUBLIC RELATIONS
33 New Montgomery, Ste. 1200, San Francisco, CA 94105.
(415) 543-8000. FAX: (415) 543-7765.
1809 7th Ave. Ste. 1008, Seattle, WA 98101. (206) 343-8000.
FAX: (206) 682-2877.

LEE & ASSOCIATES INC.
145 S. Fairfax Ave., Los Angeles, CA 90036. (213) 938-3300.
CONTACT
Leo Pearlstein

LETTER EXCELLENCE INC.
16300 Stagg St., Van Nuys, CA 91406. (818) 909-4444. FAX:
(818) 909-4433. email: info@letterx.com
URL: http://www.letterx.com
V.P., SALES & MARKETING
Kelly Bennett

LEVINSON ASSOCIATES
1440 Veteran Ave., Ste. 650, Los Angeles, CA 90024. (213)
460-4545. FAX: (213) 663-2820. email: leviinc@aol.com

LIPPIN GROUP INC.
6100 Wilshire Blvd., #400, Los Angeles, CA 90048. (213) 965-
1990. FAX: (213) 965-1993.

LOIS—EJL
5700 Wilshire Blvd., 6th floor, Los Angeles, CA 90036. (213)
932-1234. FAX: (213) 965-6134.
PRESIDENT
Denis Coe

TED LOR ENTERTAINMENT MARKETING
4465 Nogales Dr., Tarzana, CA 91356. (818) 776-8035. FAX:
(818) 776-8108. email: tc4troy@aol.com
PRESIDENT
Eugene Cofsky

THE LYON GROUP, INC.
PO Box 158, Malibu, CA 90265. (310) 456-3199. FAX: (310)
456-8019. email: LyonGrp@aol.com

MARCUS ADVERTISING INC.
Landmark Center, 25700 Science Park Dr., Cleveland, OH
44122. (216) 292-4700. FAX: (216) 831-6189.
CHAIRMAN & CEO
Donald M. Marcus

MARKETING COMMUNICATIONS SERVICES
5217 Oliva Ave., Lakewood, CA 90712. (562) 630-8439. FAX:
(562)-546-3018.
PRESIDENT
Bill Ormsby

MARKHAM/NOVELL COMMUNICATIONS, LTD.
4311 Wilshire Blvd., Ste. 419, Los Angeles, CA 90010. (213)
634-5434. FAX: (213) 634-5420. email: mnovella@aol.com
VICE PRESIDENT
Patricia O'Brien Fine
211 E. 43rd St., Ste. 1102, New York, NY 10017. (212) 687-
1765, (800) 762-4761. FAX: (212) 687-1978.
CONTACT
Arthur Novell

MARLIN ENTERTAINMENT GROUP
767 3rd Ave., 14th Flr., New York, NY 10017. (212) 888-5890.
FAX: (212) 888-5896.

MATSON ADVERTISING
1304 Desoto Ave., Ste. 400, Tampa, FL 33606. (813) 254-
8610. FAX: (813) 253-0858. email: matson@gte.net
URL: http://www.matsonadagency.com

McCANN-ERICKSON, INC.
750 Third Ave., New York, NY 10017. (212) 697-6000.
6300 Wilshire Blvd., Ste. 2100, Los Angeles, CA 90048. (213)
655-9420.
CHAIRMAN
John Dooner
PRESIDENT, NORTH AMERICA
Don Dillon

MINDSHARE MEDIA
201 Wilshire Blvd., Ste. A-19, Santa Monica, CA 90401. (310)
656-0790. FAX: (310) 656-0791. email: info@msmedia.com
URL: http://www.mindsharemedia.com
PRESIDENT
Thom Kozik

DAVID MIRISCH
2824 La Costa Ave., Rancho La Costa, CA 92009. (760) 632-
7770. FAX: (760) 632-5408. URL: http://www.davidmirisch.com

MOMENTUM INTERNATIONAL MARKETING MANAGEMENT
P.O. Box 5889, Sherman Oaks, CA 91413. (818) 752-4500.
FAX: (818) 752-4554.

MOROCH & ASSOCIATES
3625 N. Hall St., #1200, Dallas, TX 75219. (214) 520-9700.
FAX: (214) 520-6464.
CHAIRMAN
Tom Moroch

MOTION PICTURE PLACEMENT
10 Universal City Plaza, Ste. 2000, Universal City, CA 91608.
(310) 858-1173. FAx: (818) 754-0048. JHenrie@msn.com
PRINCIPAL
Joel Henrie

JULIAN MYERS PUBLIC RELATIONS
2040 Ave. of the Stars, 4th floor, Century City, 90067. (310)
557-1525. FAX: (310) 557-0133. email: jmyerspr@soca.com
CEO & OWNER
Julian Myers

MYRIAD ENTERTAINMENT
8170 Beverly Blvd., Ste. 106, Los Angeles, CA 90048. (213)
651-5001. FAX: (213) 651-3323. email: myriad-la@msn.com
VICE PRESIDENT
Steven Jensen

NATIONWIDE ADVERTISING SERVICE, INC.
15303 Ventura Blvd., Ste. 1050, Sherman Oaks, CA 91403.
(818) 906-3313.

NEALE ADVERTISING ASSOCIATES
10201 Riverside Dr., Ste. 200, Toluca Lake, CA 91602. (818)
508-7003. FAX: (818) 508-3141. email: Neale9@idt.net
PRESIDENT
Ted Neale

N.W. AYER
825 8th Ave., New York, NY 10019. (212) 474-5000.

OGILVY & MATHER INC.
309 W. 49 St., New York, NY 10019. (212) 237-4000. FAX:
(212) 237-5123.
11766 Wilshire Blvd., Ste. 900, Los Angeles, CA 90025. (310)
996-0400. FAX: (310) 996-0492.
CHAIRMAN EMERITUS
Charlotte Beers

OLMOS MARKETING
1551 4th Ave., Ste. 503, San Diego, CA 92101. (619) 238-
1239. FAX: (619) 238-9878. email: elichavez@aol.com
PRESIDENT
Elida Chavez

DALE C. OLSON & ASSOCS.
6310 San Vicente Blvd., #340, Los Angeles, CA 90048. (213)
932-6026. FAX: (213) 932-1989. email: dolson2000@aol.com
PRESIDENT
Dale Olson

PARROT COMMUNICATIONS INTERNATIONAL INC.
2917 N. Ontario St., Burbank, CA 91504. (818) 567-4700. FAX:
(818) 567-4699. email: geemail@aol.com
URL: http://www.parrotmedia.com

PASADENA ADVERTISING
51 W. Dayton St., Ste. 100, Pasadena, CA 91105. (626) 584-
0011. FAX: (626) 584-0907. email: accts@pasadenaadv.com
URL: http://www.pasadenaadv.com

PLA MEDIA WEST
11959 Hatteras St., North Hollywood, CA 91607. (818) 761-
7171. FAX: (818) 761-7175. email: plamediaw@aol.com
URL: http://www.plamedia.com
1303 16th Ave., South Nashville, TN 37212. (615) 327-0100.
FAX: (615) 320-1061.

PMK INC.
955 Carrillo Dr., Ste. 200, Los Angeles, CA 90048. (213) 954-
4000. FAX: (213) 954-4011.
1775 Broadway, New York, NY 10019. (212) 582-1111. FAX:
(212) 582-6666.

THE POLLACK PR MARKETING GROUP
1901 Avenue of the Stars, Suite 1040, Los Angeles, CA 90067.
(310) 556-4443. FAX: (310) 286-2350.
PRESIDENT
Noemi Pollack.

PORTER/NOVELLI
10960 Wilshire Blvd., #800, Los Angeles, CA 90024. (310)
444-7000.
437 Madison Ave., 12th Flr., New York, NY 10022. (212) 872-
8000.

MYRNA POST ASSOCIATES
1650 Broadway, Ste. 1507, New York, NY 10019. (212) 757-
5021. FAX: (212) 541-5463.

P.O.V.
12248 Santa Monica Blvd., Ste. B, Los Angeles, CA 90025.
(310) 207-8584. FAX: (310) 207-8524. email: 1pov@earthlink.net
PRESIDENT
Duane Meltzer

PR NEWSWIRE
865 S. Figueroa St., Ste. 2310, Los Angeles, CA 90017. (800)
321-8169, (213) 626-5500. FAX: (213) 488-1152.
email: lisa_lamprich@prnewswire.com
URL: http://www.prnewswire.com
NATIONAL MARKET MANAGER, ENTERTAINMENT
Lisa Lamprich

PUBLIC RELATIONS ASSOCIATES
557 Norwich Dr., Los Angeles, CA 90048. (310) 659-0380.
FAX: (310) 659-5270.

THE RALEIGH GROUP
1223 Wilshire Blvd., Ste. 502, Santa Monica, CA 90403. (310)
209-0990

RESPONSE MARKETING
32123 W. Lindero Canyon Rd., 3rd Flr., Westlake Village, CA
91364. (818) 224-2050. email: info@responsemarketing.com
URL: http://www.responsemarketing.com
PRESIDENT
Robert Haukoos

RNF MEDIA CORPORATION INC.
9440 Santa Monica Blvd., Ste. 710, Beverly Hills, CA 90210.
(310) 273-2912. FAX: (310) 276-8950.

ROGERS & COWAN
1888 Century Park East, Suite 500, Los Angeles, CA 90067-
1709. (310) 201-8800. FAX: (310) 552-0412.
475 Park Ave. S., 32nd floor, New York, NY 10016. (212) 779-
3500. FAX: (212) 447-9630.

STAN ROSENFIELD PUBLIC RELATIONS, LTD
2029 Century Park East, Ste. 1240, Los Angeles, CA 90067.
(310) 286-7474. FAX: (310) 286-2255.
375 Greenwich St., Ste. 700, New York, NY 10013. (212) 941-
3999. FAX: (212) 941-3997.

ROSKIN-FRIEDMAN ASSOCS., INC.
8425 W. 3rd St., #309, Los Angeles, CA 90048. (213) 385-
0005. FAX: (213) 385-0951.
PRESIDENT
Monroe Friedman.
20 Vesey St., Penthouse, New York, NY 10007. (212) 385-
0005. FAX: (212) 385-0951.
PRESIDENT
Sheldon Roskin

SAATCHI & SAATCHI ADVERTISING
375 Hudson St., New York, NY 10014-3620. (212) 463-2000.
FAX: (212) 463-9855.
CEO, WORLDWIDE
Kevin Roberts
CHAIRMAN & CEO, NORTH AMERICA
Jennifer Lang

SAATCHI & SAATCHI/THE SAATCHI ENTERTAINMENT GROUP
3501 Sepulveda Blvd., Torrance, CA 90505. (310) 214-6000.
FAX: (310) 214-6160.
PRESIDENT
Scott Gilbert

SAGON-PHIOR GROUP
13425 Ventura Blvd., 2nd Flr., Shermon Oaks, CA 91423. (818)
380-0280. FAX: (818) 380-0325.

SAM COMMUNICATIONS
5252 Coldwater Canyon. Ste. 208, Sherman Oaks, CA 91401.
(818) 762-0068. FAX: (818) 506-8571.

SCHNEIDER DESIGN
6777 Hollywood Blvd., 10th flr., Hollywood, CA 90028. (213)
467-6141. FAX: (213) 467-6143.

SCREENVISION CINEMA NETWORK
6601 Center Dr. West, Ste. 500, Los Angeles, CA 90045. (310)
342-8240.
597 5th Ave., 7th Flr., New York, NY 10017. (212) 752-5774.
FAX: (212) 752-0086.

NANCY SELTZER & ASSOCS.
1775 Broadway, New York, NY 10019. (212) 307-0117. FAX:
(212) 307-0182.

SGI MARKETING
18034 Ventura Blvd., Ste. 275, Encino, CA 91316. (818) 343-
3669.
PRESIDENT
Brian Scott

SMOKE & MIRRORS PUBLIC RELATIONS
2121 Princeton Ave., Los Angeles, CA 90026. (213) 953-0063.
FAX: (213) 953-0064. email: smokemirrors@earthlink.net
OWNER
Richelle Winters

SOUTH BAY STUDIOS
20434 S. Santa Fe Ave., Long Beach, CA 90810. (310) 762-
1360.
CONTACT
Dana Bromley

THE SPARK FACTORY
1601 Colorado Ave., Santa Monica, CA 90640. (310) 829-
4549. FAX: (310) 829-4539.
PRODUCER
Robert Teimowitz

SPELLING COMMUNICATIONS
1180 S. Beverly Dr., Ste. 401, Los Angeles, CA 90035. (310)
277-8811. FAX: (310) 277-8106. email: spellcom@aol.com
URL: http://www.emoon.com/service/la/spelling
CEO
Daniel Spelling

SSA PUBLIC RELATIONS
16027 Ventura Blvd., Ste. 206, Encino, CA 91436. (818) 501-
0700. FAX: (818) 501-7216. email: ssapr@ssapr.com
URL: http://ssapr.com
245 5th Ave., Ste. 903, New York, NY 10016. (212) 679-4750.
FAX: (212) 679-4725.
PRESIDENT
Steve Syatt

SUDLER & HENNESSEY INC.
1633 Broadway, New York, NY 10019. FAX: (212) 969-5991.
FAX: (212) 969-5991.
CHAIRMAN & CEO
Jed Beitler
PRESIDENT
Barbara Renta

TANZANITE PRODUCTIONS
2118 Wilshire Blvd., Ste. 176, Santa Monica, CA 90403. (310)
281-8139. FAX: (310) 828-0427.
SENIOR V.P., SALES & DEVELOPMENT
Maria Laing

TARGET ENTERPRISES
16501 Ventura Blvd., Ste. 515, Encino, CA 91436. (818) 905-
0005. FAX: (818) 905-1444.

T.G.I.F. PRODUCTIONS
1410 2nd St., Ste. 310, Santa Monica, CA 90401. (310) 314-
1111. FAX: (310) 314-1115.
CONTACT
Grant Simmons

TH&M ADVERTISING, INC.
14988 Sand Canyon Ave., Ste. 16, Irvine, CA 92618. (714)
559-4554. FAX: (714) 559-9680. th~m@ix.netcom.com
CONTACT
Jera Meren

30SIXTY DESIGN, INC.
2801 Cahunega Blvd. West, Los Angeles, CA 90068. (213)
850-5311.

J. WALTER THOMPSON COMPANY
466 Lexington Ave., New York, NY 10017. (212) 210-7000.
FAX: (212) 210-6889.
6500 Wilshire Blvd., Ste. 2100, Los Angeles, CA 90048. (213)
951-1500.
CHAIRMAN & CEO
Chris Jones

TIERNEY & PARTNERS
200 S. Broad St., Philadelphia, PA 19102. (215) 790-4100.
FAX: (215) 790-4363.
PRESIDENT & CEO
Brian P. Tierney
S.V.P., MEDIA DIRECTOR
Molly K. Watson

TIGERMARK—THE DISPLAY SOURCE, INC.
188 W. Techonology, Ste. D, Irvine, CA 92618. (714) 557-7779, (800) 972-3022. FAX: (714) 557-7837.
PRESIDENT
Marie L. Titolo

TMG INTERNATIONAL
499 N. Canon Dr., Penthouse, Beverly Hills, CA 90210. (310) 887-7077. FAX: (310) 887-7078.

TRACY-LOCKE ADVERTISING INC.
200 Crescent Ct., PO Box 50129, Dallas, TX 75250. (214) 969-9000.
PRESIDENT & CEO
Bruce Orr

TRC CONSULTANTS, INC.
105 E. Jefferson Blvd., Ste. 800, South Bend, IN 46601. (219) 287-7070. FAX: (219) 232-7337. email: trc@celebrity~network.com
URL: http://www.celebrity~network.com
PRESIDENT & CEO
Rita J. Runyon

TRI-ELITE ENTERTAINMENT LTD.
9244 Wilshire Blvd., Beverly Hills, CA 90212. (310) 285-9743.
FAX: (310) 285-9770.
PRESIDENT
Jarvee E. Hutcherson

TUCKER WAYNE/LUCKIE & CO.
1100 Peachtree St., N.E., Suite 1800, Atlanta, GA 30309. (404) 347-8700. FAX: (404) 347-8800.
CHAIRMAN & CEO
Knox Massey, Jr.
PRESIDENT
Sidney L. Smith

VANGUARD PRODUCTIONS
PO Box 931497, Hollywood, CA 90093. (310) 772-8212.
DIRECTOR, PROMOTION & PUBLICITY
Maverick

VENTURE ENTERTAINMENT GROUP, INC.
PO Box 55113, Sherman Oaks, CA 91413. (800) 981-8433.
FAX: (818) 981-3466. email: Venture818@aol.com
URL: http://Venture818.com
PRESIDENT
Leigh Leshner

VISTA GROUP
805 S. San Fernando Blvd., Burbank, CA 91502. (818) 840-6789.
FAX: (818) 840-6880. email: ericdahlquistjr@vistagroupsa.com
URL: http://www.vistagroupusa.com
DIRECTOR OF CLIENT SERVICES
Eric Dahlquist, Jr.

MORTON D. WAX PUBLIC RELATIONS
1560 Broadway, New York, NY 10019. (212) 302-5360. FAX: (212) 302-5364. email: mortwax@worldnet.att.net
PRESIDENT
Morton D. Wax

WESTERN PRODUCT PLACEMENT
8544 Sunset Blvd., Los Angeles, CA 90069. (310) 854-4894.
FAX: (310) 659-0271. email: andrewv@winc.com
VICE PRESIDENT
Andrew Varela

WOLF GROUP
1350 Euclid Ave., Cleveland, OH 44115. (216) 241-2141. FAX: (216) 479-2437.
PRESIDENT & EXECUTIVE CREATIVE DIRECTOR
Jerry Preyss
V.P., DIRECTOR OF BROADCAST PRODUCTION
Ginny Carmichael

WORD OF MOUTH CREATIVE
19 W. 21st St., Ste. 1105, New York, NY 10010. (212) 924-8359. FAX: (212) 924-8426.
PRESIDENT
Olivia Olkowski

WORTH MENTIONING PUBLIC RELATIONS
8231 De Longpre Ave., Ste. 1, West Hollywood, CA 90046.
(213) 656-6545.

W3 PUBLIC RELATIONS
8380 Melrose Ave., Ste. 105, Los Angeles, CA 90069. (213) 852-1043. FAX: (213) 852-7127.

YM&B
685 3rd Ave., 22nd Flr., New York, NY 10017. (212) 986-3333.

YOUNG & RUBICAM INC.
285 Madison Ave., New York, NY 10017-6486. (212) 210-3000.
FAX (212) 490-9073.
CHAIRMAN & CEO
Edward Vick

ZERO 2 60
121 W. 27th St., New York, NY 10001. (212) 807-7123.

ANIMATION HOUSES

ABBY LOU ENTERTAINMENT
1411 Edgehill Pl., Pasadena, CA 91103. (818) 795-7334. FAX: (818) 795-4013. email: ALE@Full-Moon.com
PRESIDENT & CEO
George LaFave

ABRAMS/GENTILE ENTERTAINMENT
244 W. 54th St., 9th floor, New York, NY 10019. (212) 757-0700.
FAX: (212) 765-1987.
PRESIDENT
John Gentile

ACME FILMWORKS
6525 Sunset Blvd., Garden Ste 10, Hollywood, CA 90028.
(213) 464-7805. FAX: (213) 464-6614. email: ron@awm.com
URL: http://www.awm.com/acmefilmworks
EXECUTIVE PRODUCER
Ron Diamond

ACORN ENTERTAINMENT
1800 N. Vine, Ste. 305, Hollywood, CA 90028. (818) 340-5272.
email: info@acornentertainment.com URL: http://www.acornentertainment.com
PRESIDENT
Thad Weinlein

ADVANCED MEDIA SYSTEMS
4348 Van Nuys Blvd., Ste. 207, Sherman Oaks, CA 91403.
(818) 461-1899. FAX: (818) 461-1890. email: tmedia2514@aol.com URL: http://home.earthlink.net/~tmedia2514/
V.P. & DIRECTOR OF OPERATIONS
Richard Zarro

ALICE ENTERTAINMENT
2986 Baseline Ave., Santa Ynez, CA 93460. (805) 688-1523.
FAX: (805) 688-7934. email: aliceranch@aol.com
1539 Sawtelle Blvd., Ste. 4, Los Angeles, CA 90025. (310) 231-1050. FAX: (310) 231-1159.
PRESIDENT & CEO
Alice Donenfeld

DAVID ALLEN PRODUCTIONS
(Miniatures, puppet and object stop-motion animation)
918 W. Oak St., Burbank, CA 91506. (818) 845-9270. FAX: (818) 567-4954.
OWNER
David Allen

AMBLIMATION
(see Dreamworks)

ANGEL FILMS
967 Highway 40, New Franklin, MO 65274-9778. (573) 698-3900. FAX: (573) 698-3900. email: AngelFilm@aol.com
CHAIRMAN/OWNER
William H. Hoehne, Jr.
PRESIDENT
Arlene Hulse
CEO/CFO
Joyce L. Chow
V.P., PRODUCTION
Matthew P. Eastman

ANIMOTION
501 W. Fayette St., Syracuse, NY 13204. (315) 471-3533. FAX: (315) 471-2730. email: animotion@aol.com
CONTACTS
David Hicock
Larry Royer.

ASTRALTECH, INC.
2101 rue Ste. Catherine Ouest, Montreal, Quebec, H3HY 1M6. (514) 939-5060. FAX: (514) 939-5070.
email: belleros@astral.com
PRESIDENT
Hubert Harel
VICE PRESIDENT
Michel Deslisle
DIRECTOR, MARKETING, SALES & CUSTOMER SERVICE
Paul Bellerose

ATOMIX, INC.
1800 North Vine Street, Suite 310, Hollywood, CA 90028. (310) 962-4745. FAX: (213) 962-3206. email: mail@tomix.com
URL: http://www.tomix.com
PRESIDENT & CEO
Chris Mitchell

BACKGROUND ANIMATION
720 N. Franklin, Ste. 400, Chicago, IL 60610. (312) 664-4580.
EXECUTIVE PRODUCER
Harriet Katz

BAER ANIMATION COMPANY INC.
3765 Cahuenga Blvd. West, Studio City, CA 91604. (818) 760-8666. FAX: (818) 760-9698. email: baer@baeranimation.com
URL://http.baeranimation.com
PRESIDENT
Jane Baer

BAGDASARIAN PRODUCTIONS
1192 East Mountain Drive, Montecito, CA 93108. (805) 969-3349. FAX: (805) 969-7466.
CHAIRMAN & CEO
Ross Bagdasarian

BBC WORLDWIDE AMERICAS
747 3rd Ave., 6th Flr., New York, NY 10017. (212) 705-9300.
VICE PRESIDENT
Rick Singleton

BLUE PEACH PRODUCTIONS
10201 W. Pico Blvd., Bldg. 769, Los Angeles, CA 90035. (310) 369-5623. FAX: (310) 369-8633.
PRESIDENT
Mireille Soria

BLUR STUDIO INC.
1130 Abbot Kinney Blvd., Venice, CA 90291. (310) 581-8848. FAX: (310) 581-8850. email: cat@blur.com
URL: http://www.blur.com
EXECUTIVE PRODUCER
Cat Chapman

BOBTOWN
2003 Canyon Drive, Hollywood, CA 90068. (213) 462-6116.
PRESIDENT
John Lamb

BOHBOT ENTERTAINMENT
41 Madison Ave., 26th Flr., New York, NY 10010. (212) 213-2700. FAX: (212) 685-8332.
PRESIDENT & CEO
Allen J. Bohbot

BOYINGTON FILM PRODUCTIONS
5907 W. Pico Blvd., Los Angeles, CA 90035. (213) 933-7500. FAX: (213) 930-3255.
OWNER
Paul Boyington

BROADWAY VIDEO DESIGN
1619 Broadway, 10th Flr., New York, NY 10019. (212) 265-7600.
V.P., SALES
Bob Koch

BUZZCO ASSOCIATES INC.
33 Bleecker St., New York, NY 10012. (212) 473-8800. FAX: (212) 473-8891. email: info@BUZZZCO.com
URL: http://www.buzzzco.com
CONTACT
Candy Kugel

CALABASH ANIMATION
657 West Ohio St., Chicago, IL 60610. (312) 243-3433. FAX: (312) 243-6227.
EXECUTIVE PRODUCER
Monica Kendall

CALICO CREATIONS, LTD.
9340 Eton Ave., Chatsworth, CA 91311-5879. (818) 407-5200. FAX: (818) 407-5323.
PRESIDENT & CEO
Tom Burton

THE CALVERT GROUP
5050 Tujunga Ave., Ste. 5, North Hollywood, CA 91601. (818) 760-8700.
PRESIDENT
Fred Calvert

CARLTON ENTERTAINMENT
18201 Erwin St., Reseda, CA 91335. (818) 705-3100. FAX: (818) 705-0174.

CELLULOID STUDIOS
2128 15th Street, Denver, CO 80202. (303) 595-3152.
EXECUTIVE PRODUCER
Olivier Katz

CHARACTER BUILDERS, INC.
1115 20th St., Ste. 3, Santa Monica, CA 90403. (310) 315-9990. FAX: (310) 315-9344. email: cbuilders@cbuilders.com
URL: http://www.cbuilders.com
PRODUCER
Leslie Hough

CHILDREN'S MEDIA PRODUCTIONS
PO Box 40400, Pasadena, CA 91114. (626) 797-5462. FAX: (626) 797-7524.
CONTACT
C. Ray Carlson

CHIODO BROTHERS PRODUCTIONS, INC.
110 W. Providencia Ave., Burbank, CA 91502. (818) 842-5656. FAX: (818) 848-0891.
PRESIDENT
Stephen Chiodo

CINAR ANIMATION (US) INC.
1055 Rene Levesque Blvd. E., Montreal, Quebec, Canada H2L 4S5. (514) 843-7070. FAX: (514) 843-7080. email: info@cinar.com
URL: http://www.cinar.com
PUBLICITY & PROMOTION COORDINATOR
Katina Katadotis

CINEPIX FILM PROPERTIES
561 Broadway, Ste. 12B, New York, NY 10012. (212) 966-4670.
SENIOR V.P.
Mike Paseornek

CINEVOX ENTERTAINMENT
9000 Sunset Blvd., Ste. 1010, Los Angeles, CA 90069. (310) 273-1460. FAX: (310) 273-9420.
HEAD OF INTERNATIONAL
Sigrid Ann Davison

CLASS 6 ENTERTAINMENT
6777 Hollywood Blvd., 7th floor, Hollywood, CA 90028. (213) 465-0300.

COFFEY/BALLANTINE
10202 W. Washington Blvd., SPP 3650, Culver City, CA 90232. (310) 280-6585.
CONTACTS
Vanessa Coffey
Jim Coffey

COLOSSAL PICTURES
2800 3rd. St., San Francisco, CA 94107. (415) 643-1799.
PRESIDENT
Drew Takahashi

CPC ENTERTAINMENT
840 N. Larabee St., Ste. 2322, Los Angeles, CA 90069. (310) 652-8194. FAX: (310) 652-4998.
email: 7415.1117@compuserve.com
353 W. 57th St., Ste. 2411, New York, NY 10019. (212) 554-6447. FAX: (310) 652-4998.
PRODUCER & DIRECTOR
Peggy Chase

CREATIVE INTERESTS
146 Main St., Ste. 205, Los Altos, CA 94022. (415) 948-5650. FAX: (415) 948-1315.

CREATIVE VISIONS MIAMI INC.
260 Crandon Blvd., Ste. 32-160, Key Biscayne, FL 33149.
(305) 880-7228. FAX: (954) 989-7268. email: tarzan@safari.net

CURIOUS PICTURES
440 Lafayette, New York, NY 10003. (212) 674-1400. FAX:
(212) 674-0081. email: rwink5@aol.com
URL:http://www.curiouspix.com
1360 Mission St., Ste. 201, San Francisco, CA 94103. (415)
437-1400. FAX: (415) 437-1408.
PRESIDENT
Steve Oakes
EXECUTIVE PRODUCER
Richard Winkler

DADDY-O PRODUCTIONS
22616 Erwin St., Woodland Hills, CA 91367. (818) 598-8784.
CONTACT
Tom McLaughlin

DANGER PRODUCTIONS
305 San Anselmo Ave., Ste. 203, San Anselmo, CA 94960.
(415) 256-8850.
CONTACT
Ken Pontac

DIC ENTERTAINMENT, L.P.
303 N. Glen Oaks Blvd., Burbank, CA 91502. (818) 955-5400.
FAX: (818) 955-5696.
PRESIDENT
Andy Heyward

DIGITAL CONSORTIUM
470 3rd St., Ste. 212, San Francisco, CA 94102. (415) 357-2121.
FAX: (415) 357-2122. URL: http://www.digitalconsortium.com

DIGITAL CREATIVE
1112 N. Tamarind Ave., Hollywood, CA 90038. (800) 94M-
EDIA. (213) 993-9570. FAX: (213) 962-3446.
email: webmaster@digitalcreative.com
PRESIDENT
Brian Patterson

DIGITAL DOMAIN
300 Rose Ave., Venice, CA 90291. 9310) 314-2800. FAX:
(310) 314-2888.
PRESIDENT
Scott Ross

WALT DISNEY FEATURE ANIMATION
500 S. Buena Vista St., Burbank, CA 91521. (818) 560-
1000. FAX: (818) 560-8899.
PO Box 10200, Lake Buena Vista, FL 32830. (407) 560-
4968.

WALT DISNEY TELEVISION ANIMATION
5200 Lankershim Blvd., North Hollywood, CA 91601. (818)
754-7100. FAX: (818) 752-9835.
PRESIDENT
Peter Schneider

DLT ENTERTAINMENT LTD.
31 W. 56th St., New York, NY 10019. (212) 245-4680. FAX:
(212) 315-1132.

DNA PRODUCTIONS INC.
5950 Cedar Springs Rd., Ste. 250, Dallas, TX 75235. (214) 352
-4696. FAX: (214) 352-4696. email: dnahelix@dnahelix.com
CONTACT
Keith Alcorn

DREAM QUEST IMAGES
2635 Park Center Dr., Simi Valley, CA 93065. (805) 578-3100.
FAX: (805) 583-4673. email: talent@dqimages.com
DIRECTOR OF PUBLIC AFFAIRS
Mary Reardon

DREAM THEATER
21345 Lassen St., Ste. 200, Chatsworth, CA 91311. (818) 773-
4979. FAX: (818) 773-8314. email: darren@dreamtheater.com
URL: http://www.dreamtheater.com
MANAGER
Darren Chuckry

DREAMWORKS SKG FEATURE ANIMATION
3801 Barham Blvd., Los Angeles, CA 90068. (818) 733-7000.
FAX: (818) 733-3036.
HEAD OF FEATURE ANIMATION
Bonne Radford

DREAMWORKS SKG TELEVISION ANIMATION
16030 Ventura Blvd., 4th Flr., Encino, CA 91436. (818) 733-
6600.
HEAD OF TV ANIMATION
David Simon

DUCK SOUP PRODUCKTIONS, INC.
2205 Stoner Ave., Los Angeles, CA 90064. (310) 478-0771.
FAX: (310) 478-0773. URL: http://www.ducksoupla.com
EXECUTIVE PRODUCER
Mark Medernach

ELECTRIC MACHINE ENTERTAINMENT
1930 Purdue Ave., Ste. 6, los Angeles, CA 90025. (310) 330-
8841. FAX: (310) 477-7292. email: emeprods@aol.com
CONTACT
Clive Milton

ENCORE ENTERPRISES
25510 Stanford Ave., Suite 101, Valencia, CA 91355. (805)
295-0677. FAX: (805) 295-0680. email: encore@ecom.net
PRESIDENT
Bill Hutten

ENGINEERING ANIMATION, INC. (EAI)
100 Wilshire Blvd., 18th Flr., Santa Monica, CA 90401. (310)
656-9500, (800) 324-6777. FAX: (310) 656-9501.
URL: http://www.eai.com
EXECUTIVE DIRECTOR, BUSINESS DEVELOPMENT
Julie A. Weitzell

ENOKI FILMS U.S.A., INC.
16501 Venture Blvd., Suite 306, Encino, CA 91436. (818)
907-6503.
V.P., DISTRIBUTION
Ricky Ames

EYEMARK ENTERTAINMENT
10877 Wilshire Blvd., Los Angeles, CA 90024. (310) 446-6000.
FAX: (310) 446-6066.
PRESIDENT
Ed Wilson

RUSS FARBER
19324 Oxnard St., Tarzana, CA 91356. (818) 882-8220.
email: jfmusic@primenet.com

FARMHOUSE FILMS, INC.
4399 Irvine Ave., Studio City, CA 91604. (818) 760-8700.
PRESIDENT
Fred Calvert

FILM ROMAN INC.
12020 Chandler Blvd., Suite 200, North Hollywood, CA 91607.
(818) 761-2544.
CHAIRMAN/FOUNDER
Phil Roman
PRESIDENT
David Pritchard

FILM VENTURES INTERNATIONAL
1640 S. Sepulveda Blvd., Ste. 520, Los Angeles, CA 90025.
(310) 479-6755. FAX: (310) 479-3475.

FLAMDOODLE ANIMATION
6 Cuesta lane, Santa Fe, NM 87505. (505) 466-3525. FAX:
(505) 466-3475. email: jeff@flamdoodle.com
PRESIDENT
Jeff LaFlamme

FLEISCHER STUDIOS, INC.
10160 Cielo Dr., Beverly Hills, CA 90210. (310) 276-7503. FAX:
(310) 276-1559. email: stanhandmans@msn.com
PRESIDENT
Richard Fleischer

FLINT PRODUCTIONS INC.
1015 N. Orlando, Los Angeles, CA 90069. (213) 654-0503.
FAX: (213) 848-9637.
Roger Flint

FLIP YOUR LID ANIMATION STUDIOS
650 N. Bronson Ave., Ste. 223, Hollywood, CA 90004. (213)
960-1306. FAX: (213) 461-4202. email: flip4rlid@aol.com
CREATIVE DIRECTOR & ANIMATOR
Jay Jacoby

FLYING FOTO FACTORY, INC.
PO Box 1166, Durham, NC 27702. (919) 682-3411. FAX: (919)
688-7886. email: fffinc@aol.com
URL: http://www.flyingfoto.com
V.P., SALES & MARKETING
Kathy Bennett

FOX ANIMATION STUDIOS
2747 E. Camelback Rd., Phoenix, AZ 85016. (602) 808-4600.
EXECUTIVE V.P.
Steve Brian

GALAXY WORLD INC.
216 S. Jackson St., Glendale, CA 91205. (818) 265-5600. FAX: (818) 265-1200. email: rag39@rainbow.idt.net
PRODUCTION MANAGER
Jonathan Kang

GRACIE FILMS
10202 W. Washington Blvd., Sidney Poitier Bldg., #2221, Culver City, CA 90232. (310) 244-4222. FAX: (310) 244-1530.
CONTACT
Maria Kavanaugh

GREATEST TALES
22477 MacFarlane Dr., Woodland Hills, CA 91364. (818) 225-9545.
PRESIDENT
Fred Ladd

GREEN GRASS BLUE SKY COMPANY
10700 Ventura Blvd., Studio City, CA 91604. (818) 763-4182. FAX: (818) 763-4625. email: frankcatalano@msn.com
WRITER & PRODUCER
Frank Catalano

GUNTHER-WAHL PRODUCTIONS
26500 W. Agoura Blvd., Ste. 210, Calabasas, CA 91302. (818) 776-9200. FAX: (818) 776-9293.
PRESIDENT & CEO
Michael Wahl

HALLMARK ENTERTAINMENT
1235 Avenue of the Americas, 21st floor, New York, NY 10019. (212) 977-9001. FAX: (212) 977-9049.
S.V.P., WORLDWIDE MARKETING
Donna Cornwell

HANDS-ON BROADCAST
124 W. 24th St., Ste. 6B, New York, NY 10011. 9212) 924-5036. FAX: (212) 604-9036. email: bgspeed@aol.com
URL: http://www.jobopts.com
PRESIDENT
Lorraine Rebe

HANNA-BARBERA PRODUCTIONS
15303 Ventura Blvd., # 1400, Sherman Oak, CA 91403. (818) 977-7500.
PRESIDENT
Fred Seibert

HARVEY ENTERTAINMENT
1999 Ave. of the Stars, #2050, Los Angeles, CA 90067. (310) 789-1990.
PRESIDENT
Jeffrey Montgomery

HBO ANIMATION
2049 Century Park East, Ste. 4100, Los Angeles, CA 90067. (310) 229-1100. URL: http://www.hbo.com
VICE PRESIDENT
Catherine Winder

HEARST ENTERTAINMENT, INC.
1640 S. Sepulveda Blvd., 4th Flr., Los Angeles, CA 90025. (310) 478-1700. FAX: (310) 478-2203.
235 E. 45th St., New York, NY 10017. (212) 455-4000. FAX: (212) 983-6379.
PRESIDENT
William Miller

HEART OF TEXAS PRODUCTIONS
3006 Bee Caves Rd., Suite A-340, Austin, TX 78746. (512) 329-8262.
PRESIDENT
Don Smith

JIM HENSON PRODUCTIONS
c/o Raleigh Studios, 5358 Melrose Ave., West Bldg., 3rd Flr., Hollywood, CA 90038. (213) 960-4096. FAX: (213) 960-4935.
CONTACT
Nicole Chiasson

HUBLEY STUDIO
2575 Palisade Ave., Riverdale, NY 10463. (718) 543-5958.
Faith Hubley

HYPERION STUDIOS
111 N. Maryland Ave., Suite 200, Glendale, CA 91206. (818) 244-4704. FAX: (818) 244-4713.
PRESIDENT
Tom Wilhite

ICE TEA PRODUCTIONS
160 E. 38 St., #15-G, New York, NY 10016. (212) 557-8185.
PRESIDENT
Richard Durkih

IF/X PRODUCTION INC.
3522 Knobhill Dr., Sherman Oaks, CA 91423. (818) 501-1822. FAX: (818) 501-4526. email: ifx@aol.com
PRESIDENT
George Dougherty

IMAGINAMATION STUDIOS
11684 Ventura Blvd., Suite 144, Studio City, CA 91604. (213) 991-0831. email: danaoostudios@msn.com
URL: http://www.rockyrabbit.com
PRODUCER & CEO
Dana Blanchard

IMAGINATION FACTORY
9340 Eton Ave., Chatsworth, CA 91311. (818) 993-4448.
PRESIDENT
Stanford Blum

THE INK TANK
2 W. 47th St., New York, NY 10036. (212) 869-1630. FAX: (212) 764-4169
EXECUTIVE PRODUCER
Brian O'Connell

INVENTION ENTERTAINMENT
3177 Cahuenga Blvd. West, Los Angeles, CA 90068. (213) 850-1713. FAX: (213) 851-8855. email: ijshow@aol.com
CEO
Rocky Gamad

INVISION ENTERTAINMENT
3000 Ocean Park Blvd., Ste. 3045, Santa Monica, CA 90405. 9310) 452-3555. FAX: (310) 452-1550.
EXECUTIVE V.P.
Michael Hack

ITC ENTERTAINMENT
9100 Wilshire Blvd., 600 West, Beverly Hills, CA 90212. (310) 724-8100. FAX: (310) 274-7849.
PRESIDENT & CEO
Jules Haimovitz

ITZAWRAP, INC.
PO Box 993, Homewood, IL 60430. (708) 335-3538. FAX: (708) 335-3999. email: jdmc@juno.com
EXECUTIVE PRODUCER
Christine McClenahan

JETLAG PRODUCTIONS
15315 Magnolia Blvd., Suite 310, Sherman Oaks, CA 91403. (818) 385-3400. FAX: (818) 385-1610.
PRESIDENT
Jean Chalopin

JUMBO PICTURES
161 6th Ave., 14th Flr., New York, NY 10013. (212) 337-0077. FAX: (212) 337-0437.
OWNER
Jim Jinkins

JIM KEESHEN PRODUCTIONS
1950 Sawtelle Blvd., Ste. 220, Los Angeles, CA 90025. (310) 478-7230. FAX: (310) 478-5142. email: animatics@aol.com
URL: http://www.jfkproductions.com
PRESIDENT
Jim Keeshan

KLASKY CSUPO, INC.
1139 N. Highland Ave., Hollywood, CA 90038. (213) 957-4183. FAX: (213) 462-6745. email: kccomm@earthlink.net
EXECUTIVE PRODUCER
Tim Bloch

KLEISER-WALCZAK CONSTRUCTION COMPANY
6105 Mulholland Hwy., Hollywood, CA 90068. (213) 467-3563. FAX: (213) 467-3583.
PRESIDENT
Jeff Kleiser

GENE KRAFT PRODUCTIONS
29 Calvados, Newport Beach, CA 92657. (714) 721-0609.

THE KRISLIN COMPANY
23901 Calabasas Road, Suite 1051, Calabasas, CA 91302. (818) 222-0555.
PRESIDENT
Walt Kubiak

KURTZ & FRIENDS
2312 W. Olive Ave., Burbank, CA 91506. (818) 841-8188. FAX: (828) 841-6263.
PRESIDENT
Bob Kurtz

L.A. ANIMATION
23501 Park Sorrenta, Ste. 207, Calabasas, CA 91302. (818) 224-4888. FAX: (818) 224-4148.
PRESIDENT
Lyn Henderson

LAMB & COMPANY
650 3rd Ave. South, 17th Flr., Minneapolis, MN 55402. (612) 333-8666. FAX: (612) 333-9173. email: larry@lamb.com
URL: http://www.lamb.com
CONTACT
Larry Lamb

LANDMARK ENTERTAINMENT GROUP
5200 Lankershim Blvd., North Hollywood, CA 91601. (818) 753-6700. FAX: (818) 753-6767.

LEPREVOST CORPORATION
6781 Wildlife Rd., Malibu, CA 90265. (310) 457-3742. FAX: (310) 457-6142. email: leprevost@aol.com
V.P., MARKETING
John H. LePrevost

JERRY LIEBERMAN PRODUCTIONS
76 Laight Street, New York, NY 10013. (212) 431-3452. FAX: (212) 941-8976.
Jerry Lieberman

LIBERTY INTERNATIONAL ENTERTAINMENT INC.
1990 Westwood Blvd., Penthouse, Los Angeles, CA 90025. (310) 479-6755. FAX: (310) 474-7455.
CEO
Irv Hollender

LION'S DEN ANIMATION, INC.
PO Box 7368, Northbridge, CA 91327. (818) 772-7234.
VICE PRESIDENT
Milton Gray

LIVE WIRE PRODUCTIONS & VFX
28631 S. Western Ave., Ste. 101, Rancho Palos Verdes, CA 90275. (310) 831-6227. FAX: (310) 547-3456.
VISUAL-EFFECTS PRODUCER
Kristen Simmons

WARREN LOCKHART PRODUCTIONS INC.
PO Box 11629, Marina Del Rey, CA 90295. (310) 306-4661. FAX: (310) 301-0536. email: WarrenLockhartFilms@compuserve.com
PRESIDENT
Warren L. Lockhart

LUMENI PRODUCTIONS, INC.
1632 Flower St., Glendale, CA 91201. (818) 956-2200. FAX: (818) 956-3298. email: lumeni@aol.com

MANGA ENTERTAINMENT
727 N. Hudson St., Ste. 100, Chicago, IL 60610. (312) 751-0020. FAX: (312) 751-2483. email: manga@manga.com
URL: http://www.manga.com/manga
CEO
Marvin Gleicher

MARVEL FILMS ANIMATION
1440 S. Sepulveda Blvd., Los Angeles, CA 90025. (310) 444-8644. FAX: (310) 444-8168.
PRESIDENT
Avi Arad

MASS. ILLUSION
30 Riverview Rd., Lenox, MA 01240. (413) 637-4500. FAX: (413) 637-0054. email: diane@mass-illusion.com
EXECUTIVE PRODUCER
Diane Pearlman

MATINEE ENTERTAINMENT
345 N. Maple Dr., Suite 285, Beverly Hills, CA 90210. (310) 246-9044. FAX: (310) 246-9066.
PRESIDENT
Michael I. Yanover

MATTHEWS PRODUCTIONS
P.O. Box 74, Cedar Glen, CA 92321. FAX: (909) 867-5068.
PRODUCER
John Clark Matthews

MAX INK CAFE
3015 Ocean Front Walk, Studio 1, Venice, CA 90291. (213) 962-3953. FAX: (213) 962-3913. email: maxinkcafe@aol.com
URL: http://www.maxinkcafe.com
EXECUTIVE PRODUCER
Jennifer A. Chamagne

MEDIALAB PRODUCTIONS
301 N. Canon Dr., Ste. 228, Beverly Hills, CA 90210. (310) 247-0994. URL: http://www.medialab3d.com
SENIOR V.P. OF CREATIVE AFFAIRS
Carole Kirschner

MEDIAMAX PRODUCTIONS
9538 Brighton Way, Beverly Hills, CA 90210. (310) 285-0550.
PRESIDENT
Frederick Ittah

MEGA ENTERTAINMENT
156 W. 95th St., Ste. B, New York, NY 10025. (212) 678-4421. FAX: (212) 865-3411. email: mega-int@msn.com
MARKETING & SALES
Nancy Oster

BILL MELENDEZ PRODUCTIONS
439 N. Larchmont Ave., Los Angeles, CA 90004. (213) 463-4101. FAX: (213) 469-0195.
PRESIDENT
Bill Melendez

LEE MENDELSON FILM PRODUCTIONS
330 Primrose Rd., Ste. 310, Burlingame, CA 94010. (415) 342-8284. FAX: (415) 342-6170.
CONTACT
Glenn Mendelson

METROLIGHT STUDIOS
5724 W. 3rd St., Suite 400, Los Angeles, CA 90036-3078. (323) 932-0400. FAX: (323) 932-8440. email: sales@metrolight.com
PRESIDENT
James W. Kristoff

METROPOLIS DIGITAL
12 S. 1st St., 11th Flr., San Jose, CA 95113. (408) 286-2900. (408) 286-2970. email: degrande@metrosd.com
URL: http://www.metrosd.com
EXECUTIVE PRODUCER
Ken DeGrande

MGM ANIMATION INC.
1545 26th St., 2nd Flr., Santa Monica, CA 90404. (310) 449-3250. FAX: (310) 449-3251.
EXECUTIVE PRODUCER
Jonathan Dern

MODERN CARTOONS
228 Main St., Ste. 12, Venice, CA 90291. (310) 396-9066.
PRODUCER
Aaron Slavin

MOON MESA MEDIA
14945 Ventura Blvd., Ste. 300, Sherman Oaks, CA 91408. (818) 528-1455. FAX: (818) 528-1467.
PRESIDENT
Sheryl Hardy

MORGAN CREEK PRODUCTIONS
4000 Warner Blvd., Bldg. 76, Burbank, CA 91522. (818) 954-4800.
CONTACT
Brian Robinson

MORNING SUN ANIMATION GROUP, INC.
8642 Melrose Ave., Ste. 200, Los Angeles, CA 90069. (310) 854-3510. FAX: (310) 854-1881. email: smsla@earthlink.net
CONTACT
Alexis Wallrich

MOTION CITY FILMS
1847 Gentinela Ave., Santa Monica, CA 90404. (310) 264-4870. FAX: (310) 264-4871. email: witt@motioncity.com
URL: http://www.motioncity.com
CONTACT
Jerry Witt

M3D STUDIOS, INC.
15820 Arminta St., Van Nuys, CA 91406. (818) 785-6662. FAX: (818) 785-6810. email: m3d@m3dstudios.com
URL: http://www.m3dstudios.com
CEO
Marcel Nottea

MTM ENTERPRISES
12700 Ventura Blvd., Studio City, CA 91604. (818) 755-2400.
CEO
Anthony D. Thomopolous

MTV ANIMATION
1633 Broadway, 31st Flr., New York, NY 10019. (212) 654-3600. FAX: (212) 654-4701.

MUSIVISION
185 E. 85th St., New York, NY 10028. (212) 860-4420.
CONTACT
Fred Kessler

NELVANA COMMUNICATIONS, INC.
4500 Wilshire Blvd., 1st floor, Los Angeles, CA 90010. (213) 549-4222. FAX: (213) 549-4232.

NEST ENTERTAINMENT
6100 Colwell Blvd., Irving, TX 75039. (214) 402-7100. FAX: (214) 402-7181.

NEW HOLLYWOOD INC.
1302 N. Cahuenga Blvd., Hollywood, CA 90028. (213) 466-3686. email: 76231.1032@compuserve.com
CONTACT
Ozzie Zornizer

NEW WORLD ANIMATION
3340 Ocean Park Blvd., Santa Monica, CA 90405. (310) 444-8113.
PRESIDENT
Rick Unger

NICKELODEON
1515 Broadway, New York, NY 10036. (212) 258-7500.

NICKTOONS ANIMATION
4040 Vineland Ave., Ste. 105, Studio City, CA 91604. (818) 753-3255.

ODYSSEY PRODUCTIONS
4413 Ocean Valley Lane, San Diego, CA 92130. (619) 793-1900. FAX: (619) 793-1942.

OPTICAM INC.
810 Navy St., Santa Monica, CA 90405. (310) 396-4665, (800) 345-6394. FAX: (310) 452-0040. email: opcam@aol.com

ORBIT PRODUCTIONS
726 14th St., Ste. F, Modesto, CA 95354. (209) 529-4835. FAX: (209) 571-2307. email: kevin@orbitproductions.com
URL: http://www.orbitproductions.com
CONTACT
Kevin Orbit

OVATION/ANIMATION
9 Caccamo St., Westport, CT 06880. (203) 227-9346.
CONTACT
Art Petricone

PACHYDERM ENTERTAINMENT
8899 Beverly Blvd., Ste. 502, Los Angeles, CA 90048. (310) 777-8387. FAX: (310) 777-8381.

PACIFIC DATA IMAGES
3101 Park Blvd., Palo Alto, CA 94306. (650) 846-8100. FAX: (650) 846-8101. email: info@pdi.com
URL: http://www.pdi.com
CONTACT
Judy Conner

PARAGON ENTERTAINMENT
11300 W. Olympbic Blvd., Ste. 800, Los Angeles, CA 90064. (310) 478-7272. FAX: (310) 479-2314.
CEO
Jon Slan

PERENNIAL PICTURES FILM CORP.
2102 E. 52nd St., Indianapolis, IN 46205. (317) 253-1519.
PRESIDENT
Jerry Reynolds

PHOENIX ENTERTAINMENT
2222 Linstromeberg Rd., Beaufort, MO 63013. (573) 484-4599.
CHAIRMAN & CEO
Ed Ascherman

PINNACLE EFX
2334 Elliott Ave., seattle, WA 98121. (206) 441-9878. FAX: (206) 728-2266.

PIXAR ANIMATION STUDIOS
1001 W. Cutting Blvd., Se. 200, Richmond, CA 94804. (510) 236-4000. (510) 236-0388.
EXECUTIVE VICE PRESIDENT
Ed Catmull

PLAYHOUSE PICTURES
1401 N. La Brea Ave., Hollywood, CA 90028. (213) 851-2112.
email: playpix@aol.com
PRESIDENT & PRODUCER
Ted Woolery
DIRECTORS
Sam Cornwell
Todd Shaller
Gerry Woolery

POLESTAR FILMS
231 W. 29th St., Suite 203, New York, NY 10001. FAX: (212) 268-2088.
CONTACTS
Don Duga
Irra Verbitsky

PORCHLIGHT ENTERTAINMENT
11828 LaGrange Ave., Los Angeles, CA 90025. (310) 477-8400.
PRESIDENT
Bruce Johnson
EXECUTIVE V.P. & CFO
William T. Bauman
V.P., POST PRODUCTION
Tom Gleason
V.P., ANIMATION
Fred Schaefer

PROTOZOA, INC.
2727 Mariposa, Ste. 100, San Francisco, CA 94110. (415) 522-6500. FAX: (415) 522-6522. email: info@protozoa.com
URL: http://www.protozoa.com
EXECUTIVE PRODUCER
Jane White

PULSE ENTERTAINMENT
2444 Wilshire Blvd., Ste. 303, Santa Monica, CA 90403. (310) 264-8320. FAX: (310) 264-8321. email: pulse@loop.com
CEO
Ron Layton

PUPPET STUDIO
c/o The Taft Building, 1680 Vine St., Ste. 506, Hollywood, CA 90028. (213) 461-1415. FAX: (213) 461-1415.
email: shermboy@aol.com
CONTACT
Steve Sherman

PYROS PICTURES
1201 Dove St., Ste. 550, Newport Beach, CA 92660. (714) 833-0334. FAX: (714) 833-8655.

QUARTER STAR PRODUCTIONS
7216 Park Rd., Charlotte, NC 28210. (704) 554-7127.
PRESIDENT
Patrick W. May

RAINMAKER DIGITAL PICTURES
178 South Victory Blvd., Suite 108, Burbank, CA 91502. (818) 526-1500. FAX: (818) 953-5051. email: info@rainmaker.com
50 West 2nd Ave., Vancouver, B.C. V5Y 1B3. (604) 874-8700. FAX: (604) 874-1719.
PRESIDENT (CA)
Peter Sternlicht
PRESIDENT (CANADA)
Bob Scarabelli

RANKIN/BASS
24 W. 55th St., new York, NY 10019. (212) 582-4017. FAX: (212) 582-0937.

R & B FILMS
7001 Melrose Ave., Hollywood, CA 90038. (213) 933-5703. FAX: (213) 933-4911.

REALITY CHECK INC.
723 N. Cahuenga Blvd., Hollywood, CA 90038. (213) 465-3900. FAX: (213) 465-3600. email: andrew@realityx.com
URL: http://www.realityx.com
PRESIDENT
Andrew Heimbold

REMBRANDT FILMS
BallyHack Rd., Brewster, NY 10509. (914) 279-4158.
PRESIDENT
Adam Snyder

REMOTE CONTROL PRODUCTIONS
1547 14th St., Santa Monica, CA 90404. (310) 260-3172. FAX: (310) 260-3172. email: jweiss@rcprods.com
PRODUCER
Karla Murray

RENEGADE ANIMATION
204 N. San Fernando Rd., Burbank, CA 91502. (818) 556-3395. FAX: (818) 556-3398.
EXECUTIVE PRODUCER
Ashley Quinn

RICK REINERT PICTURES, INC.
32107 Lindero Canyon Rd., Suite 224, Westlake Village, CA 91361. (818) 889-8977. FAX: (818) 889-9097.
PRESIDENT
Rick Reinert
ART DIRECTOR
Dave Bennett

RHYTHM N HUES
5404 Jandy Place, Los Angeles, CA 90066. (310) 448-7500. FAX: (310) 448-7600. email: suze@rhythm.com
URL: http://www.rhythm.com
ADVERTISING & PUBLICITY DIRECTOR
Suzanne Datz

RICH ANIMATION STUDIO
333 N. Glenoaks Blvd., 3rd floor, Burbank, CA 91502. (818) 846-0166.
CONTACT
Tom Tobin

RUBY-SPEARS PRODUCTIONS
710 S. Victory Blvd., # 201, Burbank, CA 91502. (818) 840-1234. FAX: (818) 840-1258. email: rubyspears@earthlink.net
PRESIDENT
Joe Ruby

SABAN ENTERTAINMENT
10960 Wilshire Blvd., Suite 2400, Los Angeles, CA 90024. (310) 235-5100. FAX: (310) 235-5102.
PRESIDENT
Haim Saban

SAN MARCO FILMS
PO Box 1170, Studio City, CA 91614. (818) 508-1215.
EXECUTIVE PRODUCER
Cheryl Abood

SCHOLASTIC PRODUCTIONS
555 Broadway, New York, NY 10012. (212) 343-7500. FAX: (212) 343-7570. URL: http://www.scholastic.com

SCHWARTZBERG & COMPANY
12700 Ventura Blvd., 4th Flr., Studio City, CA 91604. (818) 508-1833. FAX: (818) 508-1253.

J.J. SEDELMAIER PRODUCTIONS, INC.
199 Main St., 10th Flr., White Plains, NY 10601. (914) 949-7979. FAX: (914) 949-7989. email: sedelmaier@aol.com
PRESIDENT & DIRECTOR
J.J. Sedelmaier

7TH LEVEL, INC.
900 Allen Ave., Glendale, CA 91201. (818) 547-1955. FAX: (818) 246-5198.
S.V.P., OPERATIONS
Veronica Murdock

SHANGHAI MORNING SUN ANIMATION CO. LTD.
8642 Melrose Ave., Ste. 200, Los Angeles, CA 90069. (310) 854-3510. FAX: (310) 854-1881.
CONTACT
Faith DeVeaux

SHERER DIGITAL ANIMATION
71-956B Magnesia Falls Dr., Rancho Mirage, CA 92270. (760) 346-7234. FAX: (760) 340-3170. URL: http://www.shererdesign.com
PRESIDENT & CEO
Steve Sherer

SHERWOOD ANIMATION
31324 Via Colinas, ste. 117, Westlake Village, CA 91362. (818) 879-1668. FAX: (818) 879-8192.

SILVERLINE PICTURES
11846 Ventura Blvd., Suite 100, Studio City, CA 91604. (818) 752-3730.
PRESIDENT
Axel Munch
CEO
Leman Cetiner

SINGLE FRAME FILMS
437-1/2 N. Genessee Ave., Los Angeles, CA 90036. (213) 655-2664.
CONTACT
Gary Schwartz

SIX FOOT TWO PRODUCTIONS
1011 Magnolia Ave., Larkspur, CA 94939. (415) 925-9909. FAX: (415) 925-9922. email: animate@sixfoottwo.com
EXECUTIVE PRODUCER
Suzanne Atherly

SMITHGROUP COMMUNICATIONS
614 SW 11th Ave., Ste. 405, Portland, OR 97205. (513) 224-1905. FAX: (503) 224-5548. email: smithgrp@smithgrp.com
PRESIDENT
Phil Bevans

SONY PICTURES IMAGEWORKS
9050 W. Washington Blvd., Culver City, CA 90232. (310) 840-8000. FAX: (310) 840-8100. email: don@spimageworks.com
URL: http://www.spiw.com
EXECUTIVE DIRECTOR OF PUBLICITY, PROMOTIONS & ADVERTISING
Don Levy

MICHAEL SPORN ANIMATION LTD.
632 Broadway, 4th floor, New York, NY 10012. (212) 228-3372.
PRESIDENT
Michael Sporn

SPUMCO INC.
5625 Melrose Ave., 2nd Flr., Hollywood, CA 90038. (213) 462-2943. FAX: (213) 957-1128. email: spumcoinc@aol.com
URL: http://www.spumco.com
PRESIDENT
John Kricfalusi

ST PRODUCTIONS
2041 Manning St., Burbank, CA 91505. (818) 846-3939. FAX: (818) 846-2530. email: stprods@indycine.com
URL: http://home.earthlink.net/~stprods

STARTOONS INTERNATIONAL
P.O. Box 1232, Homewood, IL 60430. (708) 335-3535. FAX: (708) 339-3999. email: star2ns@aol.xom
URL: http://www.startoons
GENERAL MANAGER
Terry Hamilton
EXECUTIVE PRODUCER
Christine McClenahan
PRESIDENT
Jon McClenahan
VICE PRESIDENT
Ravi Yanamadula

DAVID STIPES PRODUCTIONS, INC.
685 Glenandale Ter., Glendale, CA 91206. (818) 243-1442.
CONTACT
David A. Stipes

STOKES/KOHNE ASSOCIATES, INC.
742 Cahuenga Blvd., Hollywood, CA 90038. (213) 468-2340. FAX: (213) 468-2345. email: djkohne@aol.com

STORYOPOLIS
116 N. Robertson Blvd., Plaza A, Los Angeles, CA 90048. (310) 358-2525.
PRESIDENT
Fonda Snyder

BERT STRATFORD PRODUCTIONS
221 W. 57th St., 10th Flr., New York, NY 10019. (212) 757-2211. FAX: (212) 757-2213.

STREAMLINE PICTURES
8624 Wilshire Blvd., Beverly Hills, CA 90211. (310) 659-7690. FAX: (310) 659-9798.
PRESIDENT
Carl Macek

STRIBLING PRODUCTIONS
6528 Camellia Ave., N. Hollywood, CA 91606. (818) 509-0748. FAX: (818) 509-1966.
PRESIDENT
Mike Stribling

STUDIO PRODUCTIONS
650 N. Bronson Ave., Ste. 223, Hollywood, CA 90004. (213) 856-8048. FAX: (213) 461-4202. email: vizualman@aol.com
EXECUTIVE PRODUCER
Steve Soffer

SUNBOW ENTERTAINMENT
100 Fifth Ave., New York, NY 10011. (212) 886-4900. FAX:
(212) 366-4242. email: cj-kettler@sunbow.com
CHIEF FINANCIAL OFFICER
Andrew Karpen
PRESIDENT
C.J. Kettler

TAWEEL LOOS & CO. ENTERTAINMENT
CBS Studio Center, 4024 Radford Ave., Studio City, CA
91604. (818) 655-6155. FAX: (818) 655-6254.
email: TLCE@aol.com
OWNERS
George Taweel
Rob Loos

THRESHOLD ENTERTAINMENT
1649 11th St., Santa Monica, CA 90404. (310) 452-8899. FAX:
(310) 452-0736.

TLC ENTERTAINMENT/THE MINI-MOVIE STUDIO
c/o CBS Studios, 4024 Radford Ave., Studio City, CA 91604.
(818) 760-6155. FAX: (818) 760-6254. email: TLCE@aol.com
CONTACT
George Taweel

TMS/KYOKUICHI CORPORATION
15760 Ventura Blvd., Ste. 700, Encino, CA 91436. (818)
905-8881. FAX: (818) 905-0815.
L.A. DIRECTOR OF OPERATIONS
Andrew Berman

TOEI ANIMATION CO., LTD.
444 W. Ocean Blvd., Ste. 1000, Long Beach, CA 90802. (310)
901-2444.
VICE PRESIDENT
Mary Jo Winchester

TOON MAKERS INC.
16007 Knapp St., North Hills, CA 91343. (818) 895-2995. FAX:
(818) 893-4888. email: cartoonmkr@aol.com
EXECUTIVE PRODUCER
Rocky Solotoff

THE TOONIVERSAL COMPANY, INC.
6324 Variel Ave., Suite 318, Woodland Hills, CA 91367. (818)
884-2374. FAX: (818) 884-2259.
PRESIDENT
Igor Meglic

TROON LTD.
914 Colorado Ave., Santa Monica, CA 90401. (310) 394-3946.
FAX: (310) 394-1224. email: troon@troon.com

TURNER FEATURE ANIMATION
611 B. Brand Blvd., 5th Flr., Glendale, CA 91203. (818) 553-
5500. FAX: (818) 553-4930.

TWILIGHT ENTERTAINMENT FILMS
c/o Todd Calhoun, PO Box 76196, Los Angeles, CA 90076.
(213) 387-6267.
PRODUCER, ACTOR & FOUNDER
Todd Calhoun

UNITED MEDIA
330 Primrose Rd., Suite 310, Burlingame, CA 94010. (415)
342-8284.
DIRECTOR
Lee Mendelson

UNIVERSAL CARTOON STUDIOS
100 Universal City Plaza, Universal City, CA 91608. (818)
777-1000.
PRESIDENT
Jeff Segal

UPA PRODUCTIONS OF AMERICA
8640 Wilshire Blvd., Beverly Hills, CA 90211. (310) 659-
6004. FAX: (310) 659-4599.
PRESIDENT
Hank Saperstein

VIDE-U PRODUCTIONS
9976 West Wanda Dr., Beverly Hills, CA 90210. (310) 276-
5509. FAX: (310) 276-1183. email: brad3845@aol.com
CONTACT
Bradley Freeman

VIEWPORT IMAGES
109 N. Naomi St., Burbank, CA 91505. (818) 559-8705. FAX:
(818) 559-5453.
PRESIDENT
John Howard

WILL VINTON STUDIOS
1400 N. W. 22nd Ave., Portland, OR 97210. (503) 225-1130.
FAX: (503) 226-3746.
CONTACT
Will Vinton

VISUAL IMPULSE PRODUCTIONS (V.I.P.)
10850 Wilshire Blvd., Ste. 380, Los Angeles, CA 90024.
(310) 441-2556. FAX: (310) 441-2558.

WARNER BROS. CLASSIC ANIMATION
15303 Ventura Blvd., Ste. 1200, Sherman Oaks, CA 91403.
(818) 977-8534. FAX: (818) 977-8252.

WARNER BROS. FEATURE ANIMATION
500 N. Brand St., Ste. 1800, Glendale, CA 91203-1923. (818)
977-7600, (800) 286-0868. FAX: (818) 977-7111.
PRESIDENT
Max Howard

WARNER BROS. TELEVISION ANIMATION
15303 Ventura Blvd., Suite 1200, Sherman Oaks, CA 91403.
(818) 977-8700.
PRESIDENT
Jean MacCurdy

WHAMO ENTERTAINMENT
1850 S. Sepulveda Blvd., Ste. 201, Los Angeles, CA 90025.
(310) 477-0338.
CHAIRMAN & CEO
Myles Spector

WILD BRAIN INC.
2650 18th St., Sam Francisco, CA 94110. (415) 553-8000.
FAX: (415) 553-8009. email: jeff@wildbrain.com
URL: http://www.wildbrain.com
CEO
Jeff Fino

FRED WOLF FILMS
4222 W. Burbank Blvd., Burbank, CA 91505. (818) 846-0611.
PRESIDENT
Fred Wolf

WORLD EVENTS PRODUCTIONS, LTD.
4935 Lindell Blvd., Saint Louis, MO 63108. (314) 454-6475.
FAX: (314) 454-6428. email: world_events@mail.KPLR.com
URL: http://www.wep.com
MANAGING DIRECTOR
Kevin Harlan

MIKE YOUNG PRODUCTIONS
20335 Ventura Blvd., Suite 225, Woodland Hills, CA 91364.
(818) 999-0062. FAX: (818) 999-0172.
CONTACT
Liz Young

ZEN ENTERTAINMENT
1620 26th St. Ste. 250, Santa Monica, CA 90404. (310)
315-4166. FAX: (310) 315-4171.
CONTACT
Peter Keefe

CASTING AGENTS

ACCESS CASTING
16209 Victory Blvd., Suite 225, Van Nuys, CA 91406. (818) 908-9213. FAX: (818) 884-9886.
CASTING DIRECTOR
Joseph Grant

JANE ALDERMAN CASTING
1633 N. Halstead, Chicago, IL 60614. (312) 397-0123. FAX: (312) 397-0126. email: jalderman@condor.depaul.edu

SANDY ALLISON
1759 Orchid Ave., Los Angeles, CA 90028. (213) 874-3631.

ANDERSON/MCCOOK/WHITE CASTING INC.
451 N. La Cienega Blvd., ste. 2, Los Angeles, CA 90048. (310) 659-5535. FAX: 9310) 659-5007.

ANTOINETTE MOTION PICTURE PRODUCTION & CASTING SERVICE
8306 Wilshire Blvd., Ste. 900, Beverly Hills, CA 90211. (310) 323-9028.

DEBORAH AQUILA
Feature Casting, Paramount Pictures, 5555 Melrose Avenue, Bob Hope Bldg. #206, Los Angeles, CA 90038. (213) 956-5444. FAX: (213) 862-1371.

ARTZ & COHEN CASTING
5225 Wilshire Blvd., Suite 624, Los Angeles, CA 90036. (213) 938-1043. FAX: (213) 938-1046.
CONTACT
Mary Gail Artz

THE ASIANCY
6671 W. Sunset Blvd., Ste. 1535, Hollywood, CA 90028. (213) 957-7117. FAX: (213) 957-1657. email: theasiancy@aol.com
OWNER
Rhonda Dea

RISE BARISH CASTING
21920 Lamplighter Lane, Malibu, CA 90265. (310) 456-9018. FAX: 9310) 456-9718.

BARTON G. CREATIVE PRODUCTIONS
400 N.E. 67th St., Miami, FL 33138. (305) 576-8888. FAX: (305) 751-0040.

FRAN BASCOM & ASSOC.
3400 Riverside Dr., Suite 765, Burbank, CA 91505. (818) 972-8339. FAX: (818) 972-0295.

PAMELA BASKER
Warner Bros. Casting, 300 Television Plaza, Bldg. 140, Room #148, Burbank, CA 91505. (818) 954-4291. FAX: (818) 954-2748.

DONNA BELAJAC CASTING
109 Market St., Second F, Pittsburgh, PA 15222. (412) 391-1005. FAX: (412) 560-1005.

ANNETTE BENSON
c/o Kushner-Locke Co., 11601 Wilshire Blvd., 21st Flr., Los Angeles, CA 90025. (310) 445-1111. FAX: (310) 445-1191.

TERRY BERLAND CASTING
2050 S. Bundy Dr., Los Angeles, CA 90025. (310) 571-4141. FAX: (310) 820-5408.

BOSTON CASTING
JFK PO Box 9067, Boston, MA 02114. (617) 437-6600. FAX: (617) 437-6677.
DIRECTORS
Angela Peri
Lisa Lobel

BRAMSON & ASSOC.
7400 Beverly Blvd., Los Angeles, CA 90036. (213) 938-3595. FAX: (213) 938-0852.

BROWN/WEST CASTING
7319 Beverly Blvd., Ste. 10, Los Angeles, CA 90036. (213) 938-2575. FAX: (213) 938-2755.

BUCK/EDELMAN CASTING CO.
4045 Radford Ave., Ste. B, Studio City, CA 91604. (818) 506-7328.

CATHI CARLTON CASTING
2050 S. Bundy Dr., Los Angeles, CA 90025. (310) 827-5641.

THE CASTING COMPANY
7461 Beverly Blvd., Penthouse, Los Angeles, CA 90036-2704. (213) 938-0700.

THE CASTING CREW, INC.
1948 Tyler St., Hollywood, FL 33020. (954) 927-2329. FAX: (954) 927-2371/

CASTING SOCIETY OF AMERICA
606 N. Larchmont Blvd., #4B, Los Angeles, CA 90004. (213) 463-1925. FAX: (213) 463-5753.
AGENTS
Julie Alter, Maureen Arata, Simon Ayer, Lisa Beach, Juel Bestrop, Susan Bluestein, Jacklynn Briskey, Jackie Burch, Irene Cagen, Marta Carlson, Ferne Cassel, Alice Cassidy, Fern Champion, Ellen Chenoweth, Andrea Cohen, Barbara Cohen, Mary Colquhoun, Leslee Dennis, Dick Dinman, Dorian Dunas, Howard Feuer, Nancy Foy, Gerald Franks, Carrie Frazier, Jean Sarah Frost, Risa Bramon Garcia, Melinda Gartzman, Alixe Gordon, Harriet Greenspan, Tory Herald, Vicki Huff, Steven Jacobs, Amy Klein, Nancy Klopper, Allison Kohler, Carol Lewis, Terry Liebling, Lisa London, Jackie Margey, Valorie Massalas, Lisa Mionie, Patrick Mock, Roger Mussneden, Robin Nassif, Mark Paladini, Linda Phillips Palo, Pamela Rack, Joe Reich, Gretchen Rennell, Eleanor Ross, Renee Rousselot, Julie Selzer, Bill Shepard, Jennifer Shull, Margaret Simkin, Catheribe Stroud, Joel Thurm, Mark Tillman, Rosemary Weldon, Susan Wieder, Geri Windsor, Liz Woodman, Ronnie Yeskel, Debra Zane, Gary Zuckerbroad.

CENTRAL CASTING/CENEX CASTING
1700 W. Burbank Blvd., Burbank, CA 91506. (818) 562-2700. FAX: (818) 562-2786.

CIRCUIT RIDER TALENT & MANAGEMENT
120 Walton Ferry Rd., Hendersonville, TN 37075. (615) 824-1947, (800) 420-8568. FAX: (615) 264-0462.
email: dotwool@bellsouth.net
PRESIDENT
Linda Dotson

BARBARA CLAMAN CASTING
10834 Burbank Blvd., North Hollywood, CA 91601. (818) 755-9235.

MARGIE CLARK CASTING
9636 Heather Rd., Beverly Hills, CA 90210. (310) 859-2807. FAX: (310) 858-0926.

LORI COBE CASTING
2005 Palo Verde Ave., Ste. 306, Long Beach, CA 90815. (562) 596-7406.

ANNELISE COLLINS CASTING
1103 N. El Centro Ave., Los Angeles, CA 90038. (213) 962-9562. FAX: (213) 460-6871.

COMMUNICATIONS CORP. OF AMERICA
2501 N. Sheffield Ave., Chicago, IL 60614. (773) 348-0001. FAX: (773) 472-7398.
EXECUTIVE PRODUCER
Fred Strauss

COPELAND CREATIVE TALENT
4140-1/2 Grand Ave., Des Moines, IA 50312. (515) 271-5970. FAX: (515) 277-0770. email: copetalent@aol.com
CONTACT
Deb Copeland

RICHARD DELANCY & ASSOCIATES
12240 Ventura Blvd., Ste. 103, Studio City, CA 91604. (818) 760-3110. email: rdelancy@juno.com
URL: http://www.satorucom/delancy/

DIPRIMA CASTING
1688 Meridian Ave., Ste. 418, Miami Beach, FL 33139. (305) 672-9232. FAX: (305) 672-9020. email: diprima@aol.com
CASTING DIRECTOR
Barbara DiPrima

DIVISEK CASTING & ASSOCIATES
6420 Wilshire Blvd., LL 100, Los Angeles, CA 90048. (213) 655-7766. FAX: (213) 822-2199.

PAM DIXON
PO Box 672, Beverly Hills, CA 90213. (818) 954-3928.

DONNA ECKHOLDT
20th Century Fox, 10201 W. Pico Blvd., Trailer 730, Los Angeles, CA 90035. (310) 202-5527. FAX: (310) 369-8926.

DONOVAN/FOLEY CASTING
12716 Riverside Dr., Ste. 100, North Hollywood, CA 91607. (818) 985-9902. FAX: (818) 753-9322.

MICK DOWD/TOM REUDY CASTING
5724 W. 3rd St., Ste. 508, Los Angeles, CA 90036. (213) 665-1776, (213) 954-0007. FAX: (213) 913-9379.

ENTERTAINMENT PARTNERS
2835 N. Naomi St., Burbank, CA 90510-7836. (818) 955-6000. FAX: (818) 845-6507. URL: http://www.ep/services.com
CONTACT
Albeth Grass

STEVEN ERDEK/STACEY HERMAN CASTING
2050 S. Bundy Dr., Los Angeles, CA 90025. (310) 820-9200.

THE ERICKSON AGENCY
1491 Chain Bridge Rd., Ste. 200, McLean, VA 22101. (703) 356-0040, (703) 356-4251. FAX: (703) 442-0055.
email: talent@ericksonagency.com
URL: http://www.ericksonagency.com
BRANCHES
7201 Glen Forest Dr., Ste. 201, Richmond, VA 23226. (804) 673-4182. FAX: (804) 673-1708.
1447 York Rd., Ste. 502, Towson, MD 21093. (410) 366-7727.

MEGAN FOLEY CASTING
12716 Riverside Dr., Ste. 100, N. Hollywood, CA 91607. (818) 755-9455. FAX: 9818) 753-9322.

EDDIE FOY, III, CASTING
3003 W. Olive Ave., Burbank, CA 91505. (818) 841-3003. FAX: (818) 954-8609.

JEFF GERRARD CASTING
13107 Ventura Blvd., Studio City, CA 91604. (818) 906-7800. FAX: (818) 906-7892.

PETER GOLDEN
CBS Entertainment, 7800 Beverly Blvd., Los Angeles, CA 90036. (213) 852-2335. FAX: (213) 852-2279.

DANNY GOLDMAN & ASSOCIATES CASTING
1006 N. Cole Ave., Los Angeles, CA 90038. (213) 463-1600. FAX: (213) 463-3139.

JEFF GREENBERG
Paramount, 5555 Melrose Ave., Marx Brothers Bldg., #102, Los Angeles, CA 90038. (213) 956-4886. FAX: (213) 862-1368.

AARON GRIFFITH CASTING
8424-A Santa Monica Blvd., Ste. 517, Los Angeles, CA 90069. (310) 659-6412.

IRIS GROSSMAN
Turner Netowrk Television, Inc., 1888 Century Park East, 14th floor, Los Angeles, CA 90067. (310) 551-6352. FAX: (310) 551-6383.

THEODORE HAHN
Warner Bros. Television Prods., 300 Television Plaza, Bldg. 140, 1st floor, Burbank, CA 91505. (818) 954-7642. FAX: (818) 954-7678.

ROBERT HARBIN
c/o Twentieth Century Fox, 10201 W. Pico Blvd., Los Angeles, CA 90035. (310) 369-3847. FAX: (310) 369-1914.

JANET HIRSHENSON
7461 Beverly Blvd., Penthouse, Los Angeles, CA 90036. (213) 938-0700.

BETH HOLMES CASTING
11331 Ventura Blvd., Ste. 201, Studio City, CA 91604. (818) 752-8100.

DONNA ISAACSON
20th Century Fox, 10201 W. Pico Blvd., Bldg. 12, Room 201, Los Angeles, CA 90035. (310) 369-1824. FAX: (310) 369-1469.

JOHNSON/LIFF CASTING
1501 Broadway, Ste. 1400, New York, NY 10036. (212) 391-2680. FAX: (212) 840-0691.

CARO JONES CASTING
PO Box 3329, Los Angeles, CA 90078. (213) 664-0460. FAX: (213) 664-0463.

EILEEN KNIGHT
12009 Guerin St., Studio City, CA 91604. (818) 752-1994.

DEBORAH KURTZ CASTING
1345 Abbot Kinney Blvd., Venice, CA 90291. (310) 452-6800.

ROSS LACY CASTING
9899 Santa Monica Blvd., Ste. 270, Beverly Hills, CA 90212. (310) 358-7558. FAX: (310) 393-4806. email: rmmlacy@aol.com

AL LAMPKIN CASTING/ENTERTAINMENT
359-B.F. Magnolia Blvd., Burbank, CA 91502. (818) 846-4951. FAX: (818) 846-5908. email: lampkin@earthlink.net
URL: http://www.allampkin.com

JUDY LANDAU CASTING
1453 7th St., Santa Monica, CA 90401. (213) 932-6886.

BARBARA LAUREN CASTING
11684 Ventura Blvd., Ste. 311, Studio City, CA 91604. (213) 932-1113. FAX: (818) 506-6111.

LEAR CASTING
1112 S. 3rd St., Las Vegas, NV 89104. (702) 385-9000. FAX: (702) 474-6352.

HOLLY LEE CASTING
1241 Johnson Ave., Ste. 314, San Luis Obispo, CA 93401. (805) 773-8664. FAX: (805) 541-1228. email: slofilm@thegrid.net

LEGACY CASTING
6671 W. Sunset Blvd., Ste. 1535, Hollywood, CA 90028. (213) 957-7117. FAX: (213) 957-1657. email: legacycast@aol.com

JOHN LEVEY
c/o Warner Bros., 300 Television Plaza, Bldg. 140, Rm. 138, Burbank, CA 91505. (818) 954-4080.

LIBERMAN/HIRSHFELD CASTING
4311 Wilshire Blvd., Ste. 606, Los Angeles, CA 90010. 9213) 525-1381.

MICHAEL LIEN CASTING
7461 Beverly Blvd., Ste. 203, Los Angeles, CA 90036. (213) 937-0411.

MACDONALD-BULLINGTON CASTING
1645 N. Vine St., 9th Flr., Hollywoood, CA 90028. (213) 468-0599. FAX: (213) 468-0598.

MAGIC CASTING INC.
1660 Cougar Ridge Rd., Buellton, CA 93427. (805) 688-3702.

MALI FINN CASTING
c/o MGM/UA 2500 Broadway, Ste E-5014, Santa Monica, CA 90404. (310) 586-8220. FAX: (310) 586-8221.

MAMBO KASTING
8679 W. Olympbic Blvd., Los Angeles, CA 90035. (310) 657-6108. email: mambo2@mail.idt.net
CASTING DIRECTOR
Orlette Ruiz

SHEILA MANNING CASTING
508 S. San Vicente Blvd., Los Angeles, CA 90048. (213) 852-1046. email: samanning@earthlink.net

MAXANN'S CASTING CO.
PO Box 4137, Rock Hill, SC 29732. (803) 328-3420. FAX: (803) 328-2173.

MEDIA ACCESS OFFICE, INC.
4640 Lankershim Blvd., North Hollywood, CA 91602. (818) 752-1196. FAX: (818) 506-7352. email: maocasting@aol.com

MEDIA CASTING
23391 Mulholland Dr., #477, Woodland, CA 91364. (800) 859-8422.

SANDRA MERRILL CASTING
6671 Sunset Blvd., Bldg. 1509, Ste. 101, Hollywood, CA 90028. (213) 465-9898.

ANN MILLER CASTING
PO Box 5273, North Hollywood, CA 91616. (818) 506-8922. FAX: (818) 506-8922.

MIMI WEBB MILLER
171 Pier Ave., Santa Monica, CA 90405. (310) 452-0863.

NANCY NAYOR
c/o Universal Studios, 100 Universal City Plaza, Bldg. 507/3A, Universal City, CA 91608. (818) 777-3566. FAX: (818) 866-3319.

NEVADA CASTING GROUP, INC.
100 Washington St., Ste. 100, Reno, NV 89503. (702) 322-8187. FAX: (702) 322-0161.

DAVID O'CONNOR CASTING COMPANY
1017 W. Washington Blvd., Ste. 2A, Chicago, IL 60607. (312) 226-9112. FAX: (9312) 226-9921.

LORI OPENDEN
c/o NBC Network, 3000 W. Alameda Ave., Ste. 231, Burbank, CA 91523. (818) 840-3774. FAX: (818) 840-4412.

JESSICA OVERWISE
17250 Sunset Blvd., Ste. 304, Pacific Palisades, CA 90272. (310) 459-2686. FAX: (310) 459-0961.

PAGANO/MANWILLER CASTING
c/o 20th Century Fox, 10201 W. Pico, Trailer 776, Los Angeles, CA 90035. (310) 369-3153. FAX: (310) 369-3572.

MARVIN PAIGE CASTING
PO Box 69964, West Hollywood, CA 90069. (818) 760-3040.

PARADOXE CASTING
PO Box 691037, West Hollywood, CA 90069. (310) 552-8257.

LINDA PHILLIPS PALO
225 Santa Monica Blvd., 7th Flr., Santa Monica, CA 90401. (310) 394-4699. FAX: (310) 394-3052.

CAMILLE H. PATTON
Witt-Thomas Prods., 1438 N. Gower St., Bldg. 35, Suite 155, Los Angeles, CA 90028. (213) 960-8276. FAX: (213) 960-8311.

PRIME CASTING
7060 Hollywood Blvd., #1025, Hollywood, CA 90028. (213) 962-0377, (213) 962-0378. FAX: (213) 465-1600.
email: Extracast@aol.com
CASTING DIRECTOR
Peter Alwazzan

KATHY LEIGH PRYOR
PO Box 458113, San Antonio, TX 78280. (210) 692-3664. FAX: (210) 647-4119.

QUANTUM CASTING & PRODUCTION SERVICES
8586 Miramar Pl., San Diego, CA 92121. (619) 623-8116.

R & M CASTING
451 N. La Cienega Blvd., Los Angeles, CA 90048. (310) 939-3388.

RAINBOW CASTING
12501 Chandler Blvd., #204, N. Hollywood, CA 91607. (818) 752-2278. FAX: (818) 752-6580.
OWNER
Terry Zarchi

REAL PEOPLE CASTING
4732-D Villa Marina, Marina Del Rey, CA 90292. (310) 827-9498.

REEL SOUTHERN CASTING
c/o CRTM-123 Walton Ferry Rd., 2nd Flr., Hendersonville, TN 37075. (800) 420-8568. FAX: (615) 264-0462.
email: dotwool@bellsouth.net
PRESIDENT
Linda Dotson

CHARLES ROSEN CASTING
2633 34th St., Santa Monica, CA 90405. (310) 314-3348.

DONNA ROSENSTEIN
c/o ABC Entertainment, 2040 6th Ave., 5th Flr., Century City, CA 90067. (310) 557-6532. FAX: (310) 557-6928.

MARCIA ROSS
Disney Studios, 500 S. Buena Vista St., Frank G. Wells Bldg., Rm. 1088, Burbank, CA 91521. (818) 560-7510. FAx: (818) 563-3719.

GABRIELLE SCHARY CASTING
1418 Abbot Kinney Blvd., Venice, CA 90291. (310) 450-0835.

TINA SEILER CASTING
PO Box 46321, Los Angeles, CA 90046. (818) 382-7929.

LILA SELIK CASTING
1551 S. Robertson Blvd., Ste. 202, Los Angeles, CA 90035. (310) 556-2444. FAX: (310) 556-3266.

AVA SHEVITT
Village Studio, 519 Broadway, Santa Monica, CA 90401. (310) 656-4600. FAX: (310) 656-4610.

SHOOTING FROM THE HIP CASTING
c/o Second Story Studios, 13107 Ventura Blvd., Studio City, CA 91604. (818) 783-8900. FAX: (818) 783-3831.
CASTING DIRECTOR
Francene Selkirk

SLATE PLEASE CASTING
4047 Radford Ave., Studio City, CA 91604. (818) 785-9568. FAX: (818) 785-7965.

MARY JO SLATER CASTING
2425 Colorado, Ste. 204, Santa Monica, CA 90404. (310) 449-3685. FAX: (310) 449-3685.
CONTACTS
Tim Michals
Camila Rhodes

DON SLATON CASTING
2323 Delaware St., Ste. 1, Huntington Beach, CA 92648. (714) 969-4348. FAX: (714) 969-4348. email: gatbar1@aol.com

RON SMITH CELEBRITY LOOK-ALIKES
7060 Hollywood Blvd., #1215, Hollywood, CA 90028. (213) 467-3030. FAX: (213) 467-6720.

LYNN STALMASTER, & ASSOCIATES
500 S. Sepulveda Blvd., Suite 600, Los Angeles, CA 90049. (310) 552-0983.

STUART STONE CASTING
2050 N. Bundy Dr., Los Angeles, CA 90025. (213) 650-4463. FAX: (310) 820-5408. email: stonecast1@aol.com

STUDIO TALENT GROUP
1328 12th St., Ste. 3, Santa Monica, CA 90401. (310) 393-8004. FAX: (310) 393-2473. email: stgactor@gte.net

YUMI TAKADA CASTING
1830 The Strand, Ste. 3, Hermosa Beach, CA 90254. (310) 372-7287. FAX: (310) 937-4813.
email: bananaco@eartlinlink.net

MARK TAPER FORUM CASTING
601 W. Temple St., Ste. 112, Los Angeles, CA 90012. (213) 972-7374. FAX: (213) 972-7645.

TREADWELL & ASSOCIATES
427 W. Spazier Ave., Burbank, CA 91506. (818) 846-1666. FAX: (818) 846-1668.

SUSAN TYLER CASTING
c/o 2nd Story Studio, 13107 Ventura Blvd., Studio City, CA 91604. (818) 506-0400.

VOICECASTER
1832 W. Burbank Blvd., Burbank, CA 91506-1348. (818) 841-5300. FAX: (818) 841-2085. email: casting@voicecaster.com
URL: http://www.voicecaster.com
MANAGING DIRECTOR
Lisa Dyson

DONNA WAUHOB AGENCY
3135 Industrial Rd., Ste. 234, Las Vegas, NV 89109. (702) 733-1017. FAX: (702) 733-1215. email: dwahob@wizard.com

TOM WEBB
PO Box 15328, Atlanta, GA 30333. (770) 621-4601.

WISE & ASSOCIATES
18034 Ventura Blvd., Ste. 403, Encino, CA 91316. (818) 343-8936. FAX: (818) 345-1792. email: castwise@aol.com
PRESIDENT
Peter Wise

KEITH WORLFE CASTING
1438 N. Gower, Ste. 39, Hollywood, CA 91605. (213) 469-5595. FAX: (213) 957-1872.
URL: http://www.directcast.com/castings

LORI WYMAN CASTING
16499 N.E. 19th Ave., Ste. 203, North Miami Beach, FL 33162. (305) 354-3901. FAX: (305) 354-3970.

CONSULTANTS & TECHNICAL ADVISORS

A & C HARBOUR LITES, LTD.
(Marine consultants)
8819 Dehaviland Ave., Los Angeles, CA 90045. (310) 641-9566. FAX: (310) 641-9566. email: captsetu1@aol.com
PRESIDENT
Seth Chcase

ACADEMY OF THEATRICAL COMBAT
6109 Pickford Pl., Los Angeles, CA 90035. (213) 939-7345.
URL: http://www.catalog.com/academy/
CONTACT
Dan Speaker

ACCOMMODATING IDEAS, INC.
(Sign-language consultants.)
11650 Riverside Dr., Ste. 4, North Hollywood, CA 91602. (818) 752-3320. FAX: (818) 752-3323.

ADVANCED FIRE & RESCUE SERVICES
10044 Columbus Ave., Mission Hills, CA 91345. (818) 837-7336. FAX: (818) 830-9221. URL:
http://www.wwfire~ems.net/firedept/view/missionhillsca

AERIAL ACTION ADVENTURES
(Skydiving, Hang Gliding and Aerial Stunts)
30251 Golden Lantern, Ste. E-518, Laguna Niguel, CA 92677. (714) 495-6325, (714) 443-6422. FAX: (714) 249-6945.

AERIAL FOCUS PRODUCTIONS
(Aerial, Skydiving, Base Jumps, Hang Gliding)
8 Camino Verde, Santa Barbara, CA 93103. (805) 962-9911.
FAX: (805) 962-9536. email: aerialfcs@aol.com
URL: http://www.aerialfocus.com

AIMPRO
(Firearms and Law-Enforcement Consultants)
5004 Newcastle Ave., Encino, CA 91316. (213) 303-2965.

ALEXANDER TECHNIQUE/PERFORMANCE WORKSHOPS
(Animal Behavior & Morphology)
PO Box 9812, Beverly Hills, CA 90212. (310) 277-0009. FAX: (310) 277-0009. email: jeanlouis@aol.com
DIRECTOR OF TRAINING
Jean-Louis Rodrigue

AVIATION IN ENTERTAINMENT CONSULTANTS
(Airline & Military Aircraft, Pilots, Procedure)
21521 Hummingbird St., Trabuco Canyon, CA 92679. (714) 888-0550. FAX: (714) 888-0099.
PRESIDENT
John T. Durkin

BEE PEOPLE UNLIMITED
(Insect Handlers, Trainers and Research Services)
P.O. Box 343, Claremont, CA 91711. (909) 626-2929, (800) 924-3097. FAX: (909) 869-7391.

BIGGS-ADAMS
(Union Labor Consultant)
8019 Corbin Ave., Canoga Park, CA 91306. (818) 349-4057.
FAX: (818) 993-8642.

BLACKSTONE MAGIK ENTERPRISES, INC.
(Magic Technical Advisers, Consultants)
12800 Puesta Del Sol, Redlands, CA 92373. (909) 792-1227.
FAX: (909) 794-2737. URL: http://BlackstoneMagik.com

BOOZ, ALLEN & HAMILTON INC.
(Strategy, reorganization for companies)
Four Wood Hollow Road, Parsippany, NJ 07054-2814. (973) 630-7600.

BRAVO HELICOPTERS
(Aerial Technical Advisers)
3401 Airport Dr., Torrance, CA 90505. (310) 325-9565, (800) 77F-LYNN. FAX: (310) 325-9856. URL: http://www.bravoair.com
OWNER & CHIEF PILOT
Robin Petgrave

BRIGHT & ASSOCIATES
(Identity Design & Consultants)
4223 Glencoe Ave., Ste. A-223, Marina Del Rey, CA 90292.
(310) 305-2565. FAX: (310) 305-2566.

BROADCAST BUSINESS CONSULTANTS, LTD.
(Talent payment and residuals)
317 Madison Ave., New York, NY 10017. (212) 687-3525. FAX: (212) 949-9143.

PAUL BRONSTON, M.D.
(Medical Adviser)
1 Jib St., #202, Marina Del Rey, CA 90292. (310) 301-9426.
FAX: (310) 823-2433.

BUDGETS BY DESIGN
(Schedules & Budgets)
428 Spencer St., Glendale, CA 91202. (818) 507-4449. FAX: (818) 507-4464. email: budgets@earthlink.net. URL: http://www.budgetsbydesign.com
CONTACT
Robert Schneider

**CALIFORNIA HISTORICAL GROUP
WWII LIVING HISTORY ASSOCIATION**
(World War II Technical Advice)
PO Box 1950, Costa Mesa, CA 92628. (714) 641-3421, (310) 479-5943. FAX: (714) 546-9035. email: roberte@wgn.net.
URL: http://www.wgn.net/~roberte/chg
CHAIRMAN
Stan Wolcott

CALIFORNIA SAILING ACADEMY
14025 Panay Way, Marina Del Rey, CA 90292. (310) 821-3433.
FAX: (310) 821-4141. email: rusus@ucla.edu
PRESIDENT
Paul Miller

CALIFORNIA YACHTING SERVICES
520 Washington Blvd., Ste. 369, Marina Del Rey, CA 90292.
(310) 391-6652. FAX: (310) 397-8763.
PRESIDENT
Rosalin Jarrett de Ruyter

CALL THE COPS
(Police Tactics, Homicide Procedures)
PO Box 911, Agoura Hills, CA 91376. (805) 245-2677, (818) 595-5125. FAX: (805) 245-2677. URL: http://www.callthecops.com

RICHARD G. CASTANON, M.D., F.A.C.S.
(Medical Adviser)
17822 Beach Blvd., Ste. 325, Huntington Beach, CA 92647.
(714) 842-2596. FAX: (714) 841-5413.

THE CHARTER CONNECTION
(Marine Coordination & Consulting)
5015 Pacific Ave., Marina Del Rey, CA 90292. (310) 827-4105.
FAX: (310) 827-0381.
CONTACT
Bertram McCann

CHEQUERED FLAG INTERNATIONAL, INC.
(Classic European Cars, Technical Advisers)
4128 Lincoln Blvd., Marina Del Rey, CA 90292. (310) 827-8665. FAX: (310) 821-1272.

CONSULTANTS FOR TALENT PAYMENT INC.
(Talent payment and residuals)
22 W. 27 St., New York, NY 10001. (212) 696-1100. FAX: (212) 545-0607.

COUNCIL OF CONSULTING ORGANIZATIONS
521 Fifth Ave., 35th floor, New York, NY 10175. (212) 697-8262.

DALE SYSTEM INC.
(Security Consultants)
1101 Stewart Ave., Garden City, NY 11530. (516) 794-2800.
FAX: (516) 542-1063.
250 W. 57 St., New York, NY 10107. (212) 586-1320.
2440 Whitney Ave., Hamden, CT 06518. (203) 288-7933.
PRESIDENT
Harvey M. Yaffe

CURT DECKERT ASSOCS. INC.
(Technical management consultants)
18061 Darmel Pl., Santa Ana, CA 92705. (714) 639-0746.
FAX: (714) 639-0746.

DEWITT MEDIA INC.
(Media consulting, advertising planning and buying)
460 Park Ave. S., 10th floor, New York, NY 10106. (212) 545-0120.
Angela Linsell

JOSEF DOLEZAL, CZECH SLOVAK CONSULTING SVCS.
(Consulting Services for Czech Rep. & Eastern Europe)
9025 Wilshire Blvd., Ste. 301, Beverly Hills, CA 90211. (310) 281-8042. FAX: (310) 281-8021.

ELECTROFEX
(Entertainment Industry Electronics Support)
1146 N. Central, Ste. 231, Glendale, CA 91202. (818) 775-
3838. email: bat2@flash.net

DONALD M. FAXON
(Historic Architecture & Transportation Adviser)
365 Mariposa Ave., Unit D, Sierra Madre, CA 91024. (626)
355-1826.

FIRE PROTECTION SPECIALISTS/DAN GOLD
(Fire & Rescue Advice)
260 S. Lake Ave., Ste. 169, Pasadena, CA 91101. (800) 327-
1239, (310) 502-9389. email: FranMC@aol.com
CONTACTS
Dan Gold
Fran Couzens

THE FISH DOCTOR
(Aquatic Consultants)
PO Box 138, La Jolla, CA 92038. (310) 273-6640. FAX: (503)
650-4123. email: fshdr@aol.com

FLORIDA FILM CARS/CLASSIC VEHICLE RENTALS
(Advisers for Vehicles for Film)
4691 University Dr., Ste. 204, Coral Springs, FL 33067. (954)
340-3013, (800) 746-9140.

NINA FOCH STUDIOS
(Creative consultant)
P.O. Box 1884, Beverly Hills, CA 90213. (310) 553-5805. FAX:
(310) 553-6149.
CONTACT
Maud Valot

DODI FROMSON
(Art Consultant)
PO Box 49808, Los Angeles, CA 90049. (310) 451-1110.

GARY GANG STABLES
(Western period Livestock, Firearms)
13801 Gladstone, Sylmar, CA 91342. (818) 362-4648.

IRA A. GREENBERG, PH.D/GROUP HYPNOSIS CENTER
8939 S. Sepulveda Blvd., Ste. 318, Los Angeles, CA 90045.
(310) 568-0022. FAX: (310) 568-0011.

LARTEC SYSTEMS
(Studio Design and Wiring)
4201 W. Burbank Blvd., Burbank, CA 91505. (818) 972-1070.
FAX: (818) 845-2414.

LENA PRODUCTION SERVICES
(Initial budgets, breakdowns and invoicing)
11700 Iowa Ave., Suite 203, Los Angeles, CA 90025. (310)
207-5362. FAX: (310) 826-5362.

LEXINGTON SCENERY & PROPS
10443 Arminta St., Sun Valley, CA 91352-4109. (818) 768-
5768. FAX: (818) 768-4217. email: lexscene@earthlink.net.
URL: http://www.lexingtonscenery.com
OWNERS
John Wright, Frank Bencivengo

LIN-DEL ASSOCIATES
(Consultants on Period Props)
13601 Ventura Blvd., Ste. 359, Sherman Oaks, CA 91423.
(310) 453-0193, (516) 374-0173. FAX: (310) 453-0193.

WARREN LOCKHART CONSULTING
(Film & TV Production Consultants)
4333 Admiralty Way, Ste. 10BP on the Promenade, Marina Del
Rey, CA 90292. (310) 821-1414. FAX: (310) 301-0536.
email: WarrenLockhartFilms@compuserve.com
CONTACT
McKenzie Allen

MARSHALL/PLUMB RESEARCH ASSOCIATES
(Legal research, script clearances)
4150 Riverside Dr., # 209, Burbank, CA 91505. (818) 848-7071.

MEDIA CITY TELEPRODUCTION
(Technical Advisers)
2525 N. Naomi St., Burbank, CA 91504. (818) 848-5800. FAX:
(818) 848-6454. email: tvburbank@aol.com
URL: http://www.mediacitystudios.com

MIRIMAR ENTERPRISES
(Script consultants)
P.O. Box 4621, N. Hollywood, CA 91607. (818) 784-4177. FAX:
(818) 990-3439.
CONTACT
Mirk Mirkin

LARRY MOSS SPEECH & DIALECT SERVICES
(Dialect, Diction & Speech)
855 3rd St., Suite 305, Santa Monica, CA 90403. (310) 395-
4284.

PANPIPES MAGICKAL MARKETPLACE
(Occult Technical Advisers)
1641 N. Cahuenga Blvd., Hollywood, CA 90028. (213) 462-
7078. FAX: (213) 462-6700.
GENERAL MANAGER & PRACTITIONER
George H. Derby

PRODUCTION CONSULTANTS
(Production Consulting, Budgets & Schedules)
(213) 350-3456. email: filmmaking@aol.com
URL: http://members.aol.com/filmaking

PROFESSIONAL FORCE SECURITY CONSULTANTS
(Police Technical Adviser)
(800) 662-7372. FAX: (800) 662-7372. email: rjnla@earthlink.net
PRESIDENT
Ron Boyd

SANTA ANITA PARK
(Technical Advisers, Horse Racing)
285 W. Huntington Dr., Arcadia, CA 91007. (626) 574-6394.
FAX: (626) 574-5074. email: santaanita@aol.com
URL: http://www.santaanita.com

SECOND LINE SEARCH
(Stock footage researchers)
1926 Broadway, New York, NY 10023. (212) 787-7500.

KATHRYN SEGURA'S PHD ANIMALS
(Animal Coordinator)
11179 Aqua Vista St., Studio City, CA 91604. (818) 508-8353.
FAX: (818) 508-6732.

THE SIGN LANGUAGE COMPANY
(Sign Language Consultants, Interpreters & Tutors)
14203 Califa St., Van Nuys, CA 91401. (818) 782-6002. FAX:
(818) 994-3214. email: scriptla@aol.com
CONTACT
Bill Pugin

SOUTH FORK PRODUCTIONS
(Sports-Media Consultants)
PO Box 1935, Santa Monica, CA 90406. (310) 829-5029. FAX:
(310) 829-5029.

THRILLSEEKERS UNLIMITED, INC.
(Extreme Sports Cons. for Film, TV and S.A.G. Stuntpersons)
3172 N. Rainbow Blvd., Suite 321, Las Vegas, NV 89108. (702)
699-5550, (813) 201-1251 (Florida). email: thrillrich@aol.com
URL: http://www.thrillnet.com/richh.htm.
CEO & DIRECTOR OF OPERATIONS
Rich Hopkins

II JAM PRODUCTIONS
(Sports related Technical Advice)
12531 Chanute St., Pacoima, CA 91331. (310) 246-8267. FAX:
(818) 834-4515. email: nmiguel@aol.com
COORDINATOR
Nigel Miguel

MADEMOISELLE IRENE UJDA
(Period Re-enactment & Historical Consultant)
2546-1/2 Corralitas Dr., Los Angeles, CA 90039. (213) 664-
0227, (310) 244-8028.

U.S. FILM FORCE
(Military & Government Coordination, Technical Advice)
8306 Wilshire Blvd., Ste. 2659, Beverly Hills, CA 90211. (213)
468-0282. FAX: (213) 651-0380. email: filmforce@aol.com
PRESIDENT
David Georgi

VENTURA COUNTY PRODUCTION SERVICES
(Advisor on Court & Law Pratice)
6633 Telephone Rd., Suite 213, Ventura, CA 93003. (805) 650-
8368, (805) 650-6411. FAX: (805) 650-6411.
PRESIDENT & ESQUIRE
David L. Hames

VETS MILITARY TECHNICAL ADVISORS
PO Box 7004, Santa Monica, CA 90406. (213) 739-4039.

MICHAEL WIESE PRODUCTIONS
11288 Ventura Blvd., ste. 821, Studio City, CA 91604. (818)
379-8799. FAX: (818) 986-3408. email: kenlee@earthlink.net
URL: http://websites.earthlink.net/~mwp

THE WING GALLERY
13520 Ventura Blvd., Sherman Oaks, CA 91423. (818) 981-
9464. FAx: (818) 981-2787. URL: http://www.winggallery.com
OWNER
Mark Dietrich

COSTUME & PROP RENTALS

ABC COSTUME SHOP
3704 N.E. 2nd Ave., Miami, FL 33137. (305) 573-5657. FAX: (305) 573-5758.

ABRAHAM RUGS GALLERY
525 N. La Cienega Blvd., Los Angeles, CA 90048. (310) 652-6520. (800) 222-RUGS. FAX: (310) 652-6594.

ADELE'S OF HOLLYWOOD
5034 Hollywood Blvd., Los Angeles, 90027. (213) 663-2231. FAX: (213) 663-2232.

AGAPE UNIFORM CO.
3606 W. Washington Blvd., Los Angeles, CA 90018. (213) 731-0621. FAX: (213) 731-0690.

AIM PROMOTIONS
37 35th Ave., #11, Astoria, NY 11101. (718) 729-9288.

ALLAN UNIFORM RENTAL SERVICE INC.
121 E. 24 St., 7th Flr., New York, NY 10010. (212) 529-4655.

ALTERED ANATOMY, INC.
7125 Laurel Canyon Blvd., Suite A, North Hollywood, CA 91605. (818) 765-1992. FAX: (818) 765-5147.

ALTMAN LUGGAGE
135 Orchard St., New York, NY 10002. (212) 254-7275.

AMERICAN COSTUME CORP.
12980 Raymer St., North Hollywood, CA 91605. (818) 764-2239. FAX: (213) 765-7614.

ANIMAL MAKERS
2250 Turquoise, Unit B, Newbury Park, CA 91320. (805) 499-9779. URL: http://www.animalmakers.com

ANIMAL OUTFITS FOR PEOPLE CO.
2255 Broadway, New York, NY 10024. (212) 877-5085.

ANTIQUARIAN TRADERS
9031 W. Olympic Blvd., Beverly Hills, CA 90211. (310) 247-3900. FAX: (310) 247-8864. email: antiques@antiquariantraders.com URL: http://www.antiquariantraders.com

ANTIQUE & CLASSIC CAR RENTALS
611 1/2 W. Vernon Ave., Los Angeles, CA 90037. (213) 232-7211.

ANTIQUE & CLASSIC VEHICLES
811 Union St., Brooklyn, NY 11215. (718) 788-3400.
CONTACT
Leonard Shiller

ANTIQUE GUILD
8800 Venice Blvd., Los Angeles, CA 90034. (310) 838-3131. FAX: (310) 287-2486.

ARTS & CRAFTERS INC.
175 Johnson St., Brooklyn, NY 11201. (718) 875-8151.

BEDFELLOWS
12250 Ventura Blvd., Sherman Oaks, CA 91604. (818) 985-0500. FAX: (818) 985-0617.

THE BRUBAKER GROUP
10560 Dolcedo Way, Los Angeles, CA 90077. (310) 472-4766.

BUENA VISTA STUDIOS
500 S. Buena Vista St., Burbank, CA 91521. (818) 560-1056.

CAL-EAST IMPORTS
232 S. Beverly Dr., #211, Beverly Hills, CA 90212. (310) 270-4720.. FAX: (310) 278-4761.

CAMERA READY CARS
11161 Slater Ave., Fountain Valley, CA 92708. (714) 444-1700.

CENTRAL PROPERTIES
514 W. 49 St., 2nd floor, New York, NY 10019. (212) 265-7767. FAX: (212) 582-3746.

CENTRE FIREARMS CO, INC.
10 W. 37 St., New York, NY 10018. (212) 244-4040, (212) 244-4044. FAX: (212) 947-1233.

CINEMAFLOAT
1624 W. Ocean Front, Newport Beach, CA 92663. (714) 675-8888.

C.J.S. FILM STUDIOS
2005 N. 103rd Ave., Avondale, AZ 85323. (602) 264-2539. FAX: (602) 936-7015.

CLASSIC CAR SUPPLIERS
1905 Sunset Plaza Dr., W. Hollywood, CA 90069. (310) 657-7823.

CLASSIC CARS LEASING CO.
500 Park Ave., New York, NY 10022. (212) 752-8080.

CONTINENTAL SCENERY
7802 Clybourn Ave., Sun Valley, CA 91352. (213) 461-4139.

COOPER FILM CARS
132 Perry, New York, NY 10014. (212) 929-3909.

COSTUME ARMOUR INC.
2 Mill St., Cornwall, NY 12518. (914) 534-9120.

THE COSTUME PLACE
3117 Hamilton Way, Los Angeles, CA 90029. Tel/FAX: (213) 661-2597.

COSTUME RENTALS CO.
11149 Vanowen St., North Hollywood, CA 91605. (818) 753-3700. FAX: (818) 753-3737.

ELIZABETH COURTNEY COSTUMES
4019 Tujunga Ave., Studio City, CA 91604. (818) 763-8615.

CREATIVE COSTUME CO.
242 West 36th St., 8th Fl., New York, NY 10018. (212) 564-5552. FAX: (212) 564-5613.

CUSTOM CHARACTERS
621 Thompson Ave., Glendale, CA 91201-2032. (818) 507-5940. FAX: (818) 507-1619.

DAVID'S OUTFITTERS, INC.
36 W. 20 St., New York, NY 10011. (212) 691-7388.

THE WALT DISNEY STUDIOS
500 S. Buena Vista St., Burbank, CA 91521. (818) 560-0044.

DOMSEY INTERNATIONAL SALES CORP.
431 Kent Ave., Brooklyn, NY 11211. (800) 221-RAGS. (718) 384-6000.

DOZAR OFFICE FURNITURE
9937 Jefferson Blvd., Ste. 100, Culver City, CA 90232. (310) 559-9292. FAX: (310) 559-9009.

E. C. 2 COSTUMES
4019 Tujunga Ave., Studio City, CA 91604. (818) 506-7695. FAX: (818) 506-0772.

EASTERN COSTUME
7243 Coldwater Canyon, N. Hollywood, CA 91605. (818) 982-3611.

EAVES-BROOKS COSTUME CO., INC.
21-07 41st Ave., Long Island City, NY 11101. (718) 729-1010.

ECLECTIC ENCORE PROPERTIES INC.
620 W. 26 St., 4th floor, New York, NY 10001. (212) 645-8880. FAX: (212) 243-6508.
James Gill

ELLIS MERCANTILE CO.
169 N. La Brea Ave., Los Angeles, CA 90036. (213) 933-7334. FAX: (213) 930-1268.

ENVIRION VISION
3074 Whaleneck Dr., Merrick, NY 11566. (516) 378-2250.

EYES ON MAIN
3110 Main St., #108, Santa Monica, CA 90405. (310) 399-3302. FAX: (310) 399-7682.

LARRY FIORITTO SPECIAL EFFECTS SERVICES
1067 E. Orange Grove, Burbank, CA 91501. (818) 954-9829.

FUN ANTIQUES & COLLECTIBLES
1101 First Ave., New York, NY 10021. (212) 838-0730. FAX: (212) 838-3617. email: george@fun-antiques.com URL: http:// www.fun-antiques.com

GARY GANG STABLES
13801 Gladstone, Sylmar, CA 91342. (818) 362-4648.

PETER GEYER ACTION PROPS & SETS
8235 Lankershim Blvd., Suite G, N. Hollywood, CA 91605. (818) 768-0070.

GLENDALE COSTUMES
746 W. Doran St., Glendale, CA 91203. (818) 244-1161. FAX: (818) 244-8576.

GLOBAL EFFECTS INC.
7115 Laurel Canyon Blvd., N. Hollywood, CA 91605. (818) 503-9273. FAX: (818) 503-9459.

GROSH SCENIC STUDIOS
4114 Sunset Blvd., Los Angeles, CA 90029. (213) 662-1134. FAX: (213) 664-7526.

HAND PROP ROOM, INC.
5700 Venice Blvd., Los Angeles, CA 90019. (213) 931-1534.
FAX: (213) 931-2145.

HOLLYWOOD BREAKAWAY
15125-B Califa St., Van Nuys, CA 91411. (818) 781-0621.

HOLLYWOOD CENTRAL PROPS
9171 San Fernando Rd., Sun Valley, CA 91352-1414. (818)
394-4504. FAX: (818) 394-4509.
V.P. & GENERAL MANAGER
Rick Caprarelli

HOLLYWOOD TOYS & COSTUMES
6600 Hollywood Blvd., Hollywood, CA 90028. Tel/FAX: (213) 464-
4444. URL: http://www.hollywoodtoys.com

HOUSE OF COSTUMES LTD.
166 Jericho Turnpike, Mineola, NY 11501. (516) 294-0170.

HOUSE OF PROPS
1117 Gower St., Hollywood, CA 90038. (213) 463-3166. FAX:
(213) 463-8302.

IMAGE ENGINEERING, INC.
733 N. Reese Place, Burbank, CA 91505. (818) 840-1444.
CONTACT
Peter Chesney

IN COSTUME
37 W. 20 St., New York, NY 10011. (212) 255-5502. FAX: (212)
255-3788.

INDEPENDENT STUDIO SERVICES
11907 Wicks St., Sun Valley, CA 91352. (818) 764-0840, (818)
768-6320.

INTERNATIONAL COSTUME
1423 Marcellina Ave., Torrance, CA 90501. (310) 320-6392.
FAX: (310) 320-3054.

IWASAKI IMAGES OF AMERICA
(Food Replicas)
20460 Gramercy Pl., Torrance, CA 90501. (310) 328-7121.
FAX: (310) 618-0876. email: iwasaki@iwasaki-images.com
URL: http://www.iwasaki-images.com

IZQUIERDO STUDIOS
118 W. 22 St., New York, NY 10011. (212) 807-9757.

KREISS COLLECTION
8619 Melrose Ave., Los Angeles, CA 90069-5010. (310) 657-3990.

KUTTNER PROP RENTALS INC.
56 W. 22 St., New York, NY 10010. (212) 242-7969. FAX: (212)
247-1293.
CONTACT
Barbara Guest

L.A. EYEWORKS
7407 Melrose Ave., Los Angeles, CA 90046. (213) 653-8255.
FAX: (213) 653-8176.

LILLIAN COSTUME CO. OF L.I. INC.
226 Jericho Turnpike, Mineola, NY 11501. (516) 746-6060.

MERCURY NEON LIGHTING & SIGN UNLIMITED
104 E. 7 St., New York, NY 10009. (212) 473-NEON.

MODERN PROPS
5500 W. Jefferson Blvd., Los Angeles, CA 90016. (213) 934-
3000. FAX: (213) 934-3155. URL: modernprops.com

NATIONAL HELICOPTER SERVICE
16800 Roscoe Blvd., Van Nuys, CA 91406. (818) 345-5222.
FAX: (818) 782-0466. URL: http://www.nationalhelicopter.com
CONTACT
Richard Hart

A NEON SHOP
13026 Saticoy St., N. Hollywood, CA 91605. (818) 764-7181.

NICCOLINI ANTIQUES
19 W. 21 St., New York, NY 10010. (212) 243-2010. (800) 734-9974.

NIGHTS OF NEON
7442 Varna Ave., N. Hollywood, CA 91605. (818) 982-3592.
FAX: (818) 503-1090.

NORCOSTCO, INC.
3606 W. Magnolia Blvd., Burbank, CA 91505. (818) 567-0753,
(800) 220-6915. FAX: (818) 567-1961.
GENERAL MANAGER
Wayne Thonrton

OMEGA CINEMA PROPS
5857 Santa Monica, Blvd., Los Angeles, CA 90038. (213) 466-
8201. FAX: (213) 461-3643.

ONE NIGHT AFFAIR GOWN RENTAL
2370 Westwood Blvd., #H, W. Los Angeles, CA 90064-2120.
(310) 474-7808. FAX: (310) 474-6543.

PALACE COSTUME COMPANY
835 N. Fairfax Ave., Los Angeles, CA 90046. (213) 651-5458.
FAX: (213) 658-7133.

PARAMOUNT COSTUME DEPARTMENT
5555 Melrose Ave., Hollywood, CA 90038. (213) 956-5288.
FAX: (213) 956-2342.

PERIOD PROPS
235 W. Olive Ave., Burbank, CA 91502. (818) 848-PROP. (818)
41S-ERVE. FAX: (818) 843-4745.

PICTURE CARS, EAST, INC.
72 Huntington St., Brooklyn, NY 11231. (718) 852-2300.

PROP MASTERS, INC.
912 W. Isabel St., Burbank, CA 91506. (818) 846-3915, (818)
846-3957. FAX: (818) 846-1278.

PROP SERVICES WEST INC.
915 N. Citrus Ave., Los Angeles, CA 90038. (213) 461-3371.
FAX: (213) 461-4571.

PROPS DISPLAYS & INTERIORS, INC.
132 W. 18 St., New York, NY 10011. (212) 620-3840. FAX:
(212) 620-5472.

PROPS FOR TODAY
330 W. 34th St. New York, NY 10001. (212) 244-9600. FAX:
(212) 244-1053. email: prophouse@aol.com

R/C MODELS
P.O. Box 6026, San Pedro, CA 90734. (310) 833-4700.

RUBIE'S COSTUME CO., INC.
120-08 Jamaica Ave., Richmond Hill, Queens, NY 11418. (718)
846-1008.

SCENIC HIGHLIGHTS
4640 Sperry St., Los Angeles, CA 90039. (818) 956-3610.
FAX: (818) 956-3616.

SCHOEPFER STUDIOS
138 W. 31 St., New York, NY 10001. (212) 736-6939.

SONY PICTURES STUDIOS WARDROBE
10202 W. Washington Blvd., Culver City, CA 90232. (310) 280-7260.

STICKS & STONES
(Specialty props, costume design, not a rental co.)
12990 Branford St., Suite M, Arleta, CA 91331. (818) 252-
2088. FAX: (818) 252-2087. email: jemrtb@aol.com
CONTACTS
Rob Burman, Jennifer E. McManus

STUDIO PICTURE VEHICLES
5418 Fair Ave., N. Hollywood, CA 91601. (818) 765-1201,
(818) 781-4223. FAX: (818) 506-4789.

THE STUDIO WARDROBE DEPT.
1125 N. Highland, Los Angeles, CA 90038. (818) 503-1490,
(213) 467-9455.

TRIANGLE SCENERY/DRAPERY/LIGHTING CO.
1215 Bates Ave., Los Angeles, CA 90029. (213) 662-8129.

20TH CENTURY PROPS
11651 Hart St., N. Hollywood, CA 91605-5802. (818) 759-
1190. FAX: (818) 759-0081.

UNIVERSAL FACILITIES RENTAL
100 Universal City Plaza, #480-3, Universal City, CA 91608.
(818) 777-3000, (800) 892-1979. FAX: (818) 733-1579.

URSULA'S COSTUMES INC.
2516 Wilshire Blvd., Santa Monica, CA 90403. (310) 582-8230.
FAX: (310) 582-8233.

VISUAL SERVICES
40 W. 72 St., New York, NY 10023. (212) 580-9551.

WARNER BROS. STUDIOS
4000 Warner Blvd., Burbank, CA 91522. (818) 954-2923.

WAVES
(Antique radios)
110 W 25th St., New York, NY 10001. (212) 989-9284.

WEAPONS SPECIALISTS LTD.
33 Greene St., 1-W, New York, NY 10013. (212) 941-7696.
(800) 878-7696. FAX: (212) 941-7654.
Rick Washburn

WESTERN COSTUME CO.
11041 Van Owen St., N. Hollywood, CA 91605. (818) 760-0902.

WONDERWORKS
7231 Remmet Ave., #F, Canoga Park, CA 91303. (818) 992-
8811. FAX: (818) 347-4330.

ADRIA ZIMMERMAN
5 Park Village Ct., Greensboro, NC 27455. (910) 288-4736.
FAX: (910) 288-4736.

FILM PRESERVATION, PROCESSING, REPAIR & STORAGE

AFD/PHOTOGRAD FILM COATING LAB
1015 N. Cahuenga Blvd., Hollywood, CA 90038. (213) 469-8141. FAX: (213) 469-1888.

ALLIED'S NEW INDEPENDENTS LAB
6305 North O'Connor Road, Bldg. 4, #111, Irving, TX 75039. (972) 869-0100. FAX: (972) 869-2117.
email: txdmaye@allied.mhs.compuserve.com

ALPHA CINE LABORATORY INC.
1001 Lenora St., Seattle, WA 98121. (206) 682-8230. FAX: (206) 682-6649. email: jean@alphacine.com
CONTACTS
Roberta Ukura
Jean Fee

AMERICAN ARCHIVES, INC.
2636 North Ontario, Burbank, CA 91504. (818) 558-6995. FAX: (818) 558-7791.

ASTRO COLOR LAB
61 W. Erie St., Chicago, IL 60610. (312) 280-5500.

AVALON STAGES
6918 Tujunga Ave., N. Hollywood, CA 91605. (818) 508-0505. FAX: (818) 508-5581.

BARTCO CO.
924 N. Formosa, Hollywood, CA 90046. (213) 851- 5411.

BENTON FILM FORWARDING CO.
150 Great Southwest Pkwy., Atlanta, GA 30336. (404) 699-2020. FAX: (404) 699-5588.
CONTACT
Lucy Benton

BONDED FILM STORAGE
550 Main St., Fort Lee, NJ 07024. (201) 944-3700.

BONDED SERVICES
3205 Burton Ave., Burbank, CA 91504. (818) 848-9766.

BRAMBLES INFORMATION MANAGEMENT
P.O. Box 128, Sun Valley, CA 91353. (800) 310-DATA. (818) 504-0252. FAX: (818) 504-6918.
CONTACT
Reed E. Irvin

CHACE PRODUCTIONS, INC.
201 S. Victory Blvd., Burbank, CA 91502. (818) 842-8346. FAX: (818) 843-8353.
PRESIDENT
Robert Heiber

CINE MAGNETICS FILM & VIDEO
100 Business Park Dr., Armonk, NY 10504. (914) 273-7500.

CINE MOTION PICTURE SERVICE LAB
377 Court St., Bldg. 3, Plymouth, MA 02360. (508) 746-3085. email: cinelab@aol.com

CINEFILM/CINETRANSFER
2156 Faulkner Rd., N.E., Atlanta, GA 30324. (404) 633-1448, (800) 633-1448. FAX: (404) 633-3867.

CINESITE
1017 N. Las Palmas Ave., Suite 300, Hollywood, CA 90038. (212) 468-4400. FAX: (213) 468-4404.

CONSOLIDATED FILM INDUSTRIES (CFI)
959 N. Seward St., Hollywood, CA 90038. (213) 960-7444.

CONTINENTAL FILM LABS, INC.
1998 NE 150 St., N. Miami, FL 33181. (305) 949-4252, (800) 327-8396. FAX: (305) 949-3242.
CONTACT
Vincent Hogan

7675 Currency Drive, Orlando, FL 33181. (407) 856-8958. FAX: (407) 856-4070.
CONTACT
A. J. Robbins

CREST NATIONAL VIDEO FILM LABS
1141 N. Seward St., Hollywood, CA 90038. (213) 466-0624, (213) 462-6696. FAX: (213) 461-8901.
1000 N. Highland Ave., Los Angeles, CA 90038. (213) 466-0624.

DELTA PRODUCTIONS
3333 Glendale Blvd., Suite 3, Los Angeles, CA 90039. (213) 663-8754. FAX: (213) 663-3460.

DELUXE LABORATORIES, INC.
1377 N. Serrano Ave., Hollywood, CA 90027. (213) 462-6171, (800) 2DE-LUXE. FAX: (213) 461-0608.
URL: http://www.deluxe-ent.com

DU ART FILM LABORATORIES
245 W. 55 St., New York, NY 10019. (212) 757-4580.

FILM CRAFT LAB
23815 Industrial Park Drive, Farmington Hills, MI 48335. (248) 474-3900. FAX: (248) 474-1577.

FILM PRESERVE
2 Depot Plaza, #202-B, Bedford Hills, NY 10507. (914) 242-9838. FAX: (914) 242-9854.
Robert A. Harris

FILM TECHNOLOGY COMPANY INC.
726 N. Cole Ave., Hollywood, CA 90038. (213) 464-3456. FAX: (213) 464-7439.

FILMACK STUDIOS
1327 S. Wabash Ave., Chicago, IL 60605. (312) 427-3395, (800) FILMACK. FAX: (312) 427-4866.
OWNER
Robert Mack

FILMLIFE INC. AMERICAN FILM REPAIR INSTITUTE
P.O. Box 604, Lake Worth, FL 33460. (561) 582-0700. FAX: (561) 582-3535.
CHAIRMAN & CEO
Marvin A. Bernard
S.V.P., PRODUCTION
Jeremy D. Bernard
COMPUTER GRAPHICS V.P., DESIGN ENGINEER
Rachel D. Bernard
V.P. WORLD-WIDE OPERATIONS
Milton Miller

FILMTREAT INTERNATIONAL CORP.
42-24 Orchard St., Long Island City, NY 11101. (718) 784-4040. FAX: (718) 784-4677.
CONTACTS
Y. W. Mociuk
Sam Borodinsky

FILMTREAT WEST CORP.
10810 Cantara St., Sun Valley, CA 91352. (818) 771-5390.

FORDE MOTION PICTURE LABS
306 Fairview Ave. N., Seattle, WA 98109. (206) 682-2510. (800) 682-2510.

FORT LEE FILM STORAGE & SERVICE
1 Mt. Vernon, St., Ridgefield Park, NJ 07660. (201) 440-6200. FAX: (201) 440-5799.
EXECUTIVE VICE PRESIDENT
Patricia Miller

FOTO-KEM FOTO-TRONICS, FILM-VIDEO LAB
2800 W. Olive Ave., Burbank, CA 91505. (818) 846-3101.(818) 846-9350. FAX: (818) 841-2130.

FOUR MEDIA COMPANY
2813 W. Alameda Ave., Burbank, CA 91505. (818) 840-7000. FAX: (818) 840-7195.

GUFFANTI FILM LABORATORIES INC.
630 Ninth Ave., New York, NY 10036. (212) 265-5530.

HIGHLAND LABORATORIES
747 Front St., #202, San Francisco, CA 94111. (415) 981-5010.

HOLLYWOOD FILM & VIDEO INC.
6060 Sunset Blvd., Hollywood, CA 90028. (213) 464-2181. FAX: (213) 464-0893.

HOLLYWOOD FILM CO.
826 Seward St., Hollywood, CA 90038. (213) 462-1971, (213) 462-3284. FAX: (213) 263-9665.

HOLLYWOOD VAULTS, INC.
Vault: 742 N. Seward St., Hollywood, 90038. (213) 461-6464. Office: 1780 Prospect Ave., Santa Barbara, CA 93103. (805) 569-5336. FAX: (805) 569-1657. email: vault@hollywoodvaults.com
URL: http://www.hollywoodvaults.com

FRANK HOLMES LABORATORIES
140 E. Providencia Ave., Burbank, CA 91502. (818) 558-1139.

ICS SERVICES, INC.
920 Allen Ave., Glendale, CA 91201. (818) 242-3839. FAX:
(818) 242-1566. email: Intercine@aol.com
URL: http://members.aol.com/INTERCINE

IRON MOUNTAIN RECORDS MANAGEMENT
6190 Boyle Ave., Vernon, CA 90058-3952. (213) 466-9271.
FAX: (213) 467-8068.

LAB LINK, INC.
115 W. 45 St., New York, NY 10036. (212) 302-7373.

LASER-PACIFIC MEDIA CORP.
809 N. Cahuenga Blvd., Hollywood, CA 90038. (213) 462-
6266. FAX: (213) 464-3233.
540 N. Hollywood Way, Burbank, CA 91505. (818) 842-1111.

KEN LIEBERMAN LABORATORIES INC.
118 W. 22 St., New York, NY 10011. (212) 633-0500. FAX:
(212) 675-0500.
Ken Lieberman

LIPSNER-SMITH COMPANY
4700 Chase, Lincolnwood, IL 60646-1689. (847) 677-3000, FAX:
(847) 677-1311, (800) 784-6733. email: sales@rtico.com
URL: http://www.rtico.com
6 Swan Wharf, Waterloo Road, Uxgridge UB8 2RA, England.
(01895) 252191. FAX: (01895) 274692.
email: rtiuk@cix.compulink.co.uk
PO Box 387, Miranda NSW 2228, Australia. (612) 9524 3991.
FAX: (612) 9524 6635. email: rtiaus@acay.com.au

LUCASFILM LTD.
P.O. Box 2009, San Rafael, CA 94912. (415) 662-1800.

MAGNO SOUND INC.
729 Seventh Ave., New York, NY 10019. (212) 302-2505. FAX:
(212) 819-1282.

MAGNO VISUALS
115 W. 45 St., New York, NY 10036. (212) 575-5162, (212)
575-5159. FAX: (212) 719-1867.

METRO BUSINESS ARCHIVES
609 W. 51 St., New York, NY 10019. (201) 333-3033.

MILLENNIUM FILM WORK SHOP
66 E. 4 St., New York, NY 10003. (212) 673-0090.

MOTION PICTURE LABORATORIES, INC.
781 S. Main St., Memphis, TN 38106. (901) 774-4944, (800)
4MP-LMPL.

NATIONAL PHOTOGRAPHIC LABORATORIES
1926 W. Gray, Houston, TX 77019. (713) 527-9300. FAX: (713)
528-2584.

NEWELL COLOR LAB
221 N. Westmoreland Ave., Los Angeles, CA 90004. (213) 380-2980.

NEWSFILM & VIDEO LABORATORY, INC.
516 N. Larchmont Blvd., Hollywood, CA 90004. (213) 462-6814.

PACIFIC TITLE ARCHIVES
4800 San Vicente Blvd., Los Angeles, CA 90019. (213) 938-
3711. FAX: (213) 938-6364.
CONTACT
David Weeden
561 Mateo St., Los Angeles, CA 90013. (213) 617-8650. FAX:
(213) 617-7876.
10717 Vanowen St., N. Hollywood, CA 91605. (818) 760-4223.
FAX: (818) 760-1704.
900 Grand Central Ave., Glendale, CA 91201. (818) 547-0090.
FAX: (818) 548-7990.
CONTACT
Dan Gentile

PACIFIC TITLE & ART STUDIO
6350 Santa Monica Blvd., Los Angeles, CA 90038. (213) 464-0121.

PRODUCERS COLOR SERVICE
2921 E. Grand Blvd., Detroit, MI 48202. (313) 874-1112.

PRODUCERS FILM CENTER
948 N. Sycamore Ave., Hollywood, 90038. (213) 851-1122.

RGB COLOR LAB
816 N. Highland Ave., Los Angeles, CA 90038. (213) 469-1959.

RAINMAKER DIGITAL PICTURES
50 West 2nd Ave., Vancouver, B.C. V5Y 1B3. (604) 874-8700.
FAX: (604) 874-1719. email: info@rainmaker.com
PRESIDENT
Bob Scabarelli

SPECTRUM MOTION PICTURE LAB
399 Gundersen Dr., Carol Stream, IL 60188. (708) 665-4242,
(800) 345-6522.

SPORTS FILM LAB
361 W. Broadway, South Boston, MA 02127. (617) 268-8388.
FAX: (617) 268-8390.

TECHNICOLOR INC.
Professional Film Division, 4050 Lankershim Blvd., North
Hollywood, CA 91608. (818) 769-8500.
321 W. 44 St., New York, NY 10036. (212) 582-7310.

TITRA FILM CALIFORNIA INC.
733 Salem St., Glendale, CA 91203. (818) 244-3663. FAX:
(818) 244-6205.

TRACK WISE, INC.
123 W. 18 St., New York, NY 10011. (212) 627-7700.
MANAGER
Fran Bowen

FILM STOCK

DR. RAWSTOCK
6916 Santa Monica Blvd., Ste. A, Los Angeles, CA 90038.
(213) 960-1781. FAX: (213) 960-1780. email: filmsell@aol.com
PRESIDENT
Lowell Kay

EASTMAN KODAK COMPANY
343 State St., Rochester, NY 14650-0310. (716) 724-4000.
6700 Santa Monica Blvd., Hollywood, CA 90038. (213) 464-
6131. FAX: (213) 468-1568.
360 W. 31 St., New York, NY 10001. (212) 631-3450.
4 Concourse Parkway, Suite 300, Atlanta, GA 30328.
Information: (800) 800-8398; MP Film Orders: (800) 621-FILM.
CHAIRMAN & CEO
George M.C. Fisher
PRESIDENT & COO
Daniel Carp
PRESIDENT, ENTERTAINMENT IMAGING
Joerg D. Agin
COO, PROFESSIONAL MOTION IMAGING
Richard P. Aschman

FILM EMPORIUM
17 E. 45th St., New York, NY 10017. (800) 371-2555. FAX:
(212) 681-6920. URL: http://www.filmemporium.com
CEO
Laird R. Criner

FILM STOCK EXCHANGE
1041 N. Formosa Ave., Hollywood, CA 90046

FUJI PHOTO FILM U.S.A., INC.
555 Taxter Rd., Elmsford, NY 10523. (914) 789-8100. (800)
755-3854. FAX: (770) 789-8295.
1285 Hamilton Pkwy., Itasca, IL 60143. (800) 877-0555,
(630) 773-7200. FAX: (630) 773-6266.
1628 W, Crobsy Rd., Ste. 100, Carrollton, TX 75006. (800)
927-3854, (214) 466-9200. FAX: (214) 446-1329.
2450 Satellite Blvd., Duluth, GA 30136. (800) 366-3854,
(770) 813-5100. FAX: (770) 813-5166.

ILFORD IMAGING U.S.A., INC..
W. 70 Century Rd., Paramus, NJ 07653. (201) 265-6000.

RAW STOCK
1133 Broadway, 5th Flr., New York, NY 10010. (212) 255-0445.

RESEARCH TECHNOLOGY, INC.
4700 Chase Ave., Lincolnwood, IL 60646. (847) 677-3000. **STEA-
DI SYSTEMS**
1014 N. Highland Ave., Los Angeles, CA 90038. (213) 993-
3031. FAX: (213) 461-8915. URL: http://www.steadi.com

STUDIO FILM & TAPE INC.
1215 N. Highland, Hollywood, CA 90038. (213) 466-8101,
(800) 824-3130. FAX: (213) 466-6815.
630 Ninth Ave., New York, NY 10036. (212) 977-9330, (800)
444-9330. FAX: (212) 586-2420.

SUPER8 SOUND
2805 W. Magnolia Blvd., Burbank, CA 91505. (818) 848-5522.
FAX: (818) 848-5956. email: s8s@worldnet.att.net

FINANCIAL SERVICES

AFRA FILM ENTERPRISES, INC.
137 S. Robertson Blvd., Suite 254, Beverly Hills, CA 90211-2831. (310) 785-6671. FAX: (310) 785-6683.
PRESIDENT
Anatoly A. Fradis

BANK OF AMERICA NT & SA/COMMERCIAL BANKING ENTERTAINMENT OFFICE
2049 Century Park E., #200, Los Angeles, CA 90067. (310) 785-6071. FAX: (310) 785-6100.
VICE PRESIDENT
Fred Denitz

BANK OF CALIFORNIA
Entertainment Division, 9401 Wilshire Blvd., 6th Flr., Beverly Hills, CA 90212. (310) 273-7200. FAX: (310) 273-9030.

BANK OF NEW YORK
530 Fifth Ave., New York, NY 10036. (212) 852-4099.

BANKERS TRUST CO.
Entertainment Division, 300 S. Grand Ave., 41st Flr., Los Angeles, CA 90071. (213) 620-8200. FAX: (213) 620-8484.

BANQUE PARIBAS
2029 Century Park East, #3900, Los Angeles, CA 90067. (310) 551-7399. FAX: (310) 556-3145. email: rene_turin@paribas.com
ENTERTAINMENT COORDINATOR
Rene Turin

CALIFORNIA UNITED BANK
16030 Ventura Blvd., Suite 650, Encino, CA 91436-4487. (818) 379-1249. FAX: (818) 907-9132.
SENIOR MARKETING DIRECTOR
Steve Ellis

CHASE SECURITIES INC./ENTERTAINMENT INDUSTRIES GROUP
c/o The Chase Manhattan Bank, 1800 Century Park E., #400, Los Angeles, CA 90067. (310) 788-5600. FAX: (310) 788-5628.
CONTACT
Ken Wilson

CINE FIN CORP
11601 Wilshire Blvd., Suite 500, Los Angeles, CA 90025. (310) 575-4808. FAX: (310) 575-1890.

CITICORP
725 S. Figueroa St., Los Angeles, CA 90025. (310) 575-4808. FAX: (310) 575-1890/

CITY NATIONAL BANK
Entertainment Division, 400 N. Roxbury Dr., 4th Flr., Beverly Hills, CA 90210. (310) 888-6200. FAX: (310) 888-6157.

CREATIVE MANAGEMENT AGENCY, INC.
1 Penn Plaza, Suite 1910, New York, NY 10119. (212) 239-0804. FAX: (212) 239-9417.
PRESIDENT & CPA
Rick Gould

DAI-ICHI MOTION PICTURES CORP.
2106 Mt. Olympus Dr., Los Angeles, CA 90046. (213) 850-1157. FAX: (213) 850-1398.

DE WITT STERN GROUP INC.
(Insurance Services)
420 Lexington Ave., New York, NY 10170. (212) 867-3550.

DELOITTE & TOUCHE
2029 Century Park E., #300, Los Angeles, CA 90067. (310) 551-6705. FAX: (310) 284-9029.

ENTERTAINMENT COALITION
(Completion Bonds, Entertainment Insurance)
10 Universal City Plaza, 28th floor, Universal City, CA 91608. (818) 505-5900. FAX: (818) 505-5999.
PRESIDENT & CEO
Donna Smith

ENTERTAINMENT FINANCIERS INTERNATIONAL
2049 Century Park East, Suite 350, Los Angeles, CA 90067. (310) 229-2612. FAX: (310) 785-1760. email: efi2@juno.com
CONTACT
Rick Norris

FILM CAPITAL CORP.
2533 N. Carson St., Suite 2212, Carson City, NV 89706. (800) 337-2916, (702) 885-2070. FAX: (702) 883-4874.
email: mmend77777@aol.com
URL: http://members.aol.com/mmend77777/index.htm
CONTACT
Marlene Mendozal

FILM FINANCES INC.
9000 Sunset Blvd., Suite 1400, Los Angeles, CA 90069. (310) 275-7323. FAX: (310) 275-1706. email: ffl@ffl.com
URL: http://www.filmfinances.com

FIRST CHARTER BANK N.A.
Entertainment Division, 265 N. Beverly Drive, Beverly Hills, CA 90210. (310) 278-7200. FAX: (310) 278-9543.

LEWIS HORWITZ ORGANIZATION
1840 Century Park East, Los Angeles, CA 90067. (310) 275-7171. FAX: (310) 275-8055.

IMPERIAL BANK
Entertainment Banking, 9777 Wilshire Blvd., Beverly Hills, CA 90212. (310) 281-2400. FAX: (310) 281-2476.

INTERNATIONAL FILM GUARANTORS
10940 Wilshire Blvd., Suite 2010, Los Angeles, CA 90024. (310) 208-4500. FAX: (310) 443-8998.

MARATHON NATIONAL BANK
Entertainment Division, 11150 W. Olympia Blvd., W. Los Angeles, CA 90064. (310) 996-9100. FAX: (310) 996-9113.

MERCANTILE NATIONAL BANK
Entertainment Industries Division, 1840 Century Park East, 2nd Flr., Los Angeles, CA 90067. (310) 277-2265.

THE MOTION PICTURE BOND COMPANY
1901 Avenue of the Stars, #2000, Los Angeles, CA 90067. (310) 551-0371. FAX: (310) 551-0518.

THE MOVIE GROUP
1900 Ave. of the Stars, Ste. 1425, Los Angeles, CA 90067. (310) 556-2830. FAX: (310) 277-1490.

NEAR NORTH INSURANCE BROKERAGE INC-. ENTERTAINMENT INDUSTRIES DIVISION
55 E. 52nd St., Suite 3100, New York, NY 10055-0002. (212) 935-7373, (800) 795-8075. FAX: (212) 702-3333.
email: rcohen@nnng.com
URL: http://www.nnng.com
PRESIDENT, ENTERTAINMENT DIVISION
Ron Cohen

1840 Century Park East, Suite 1100, Los Angeles, CA 90067.
email: doliver@nnng.com
SENIOR VICE PRESIDENT
David Oliver

OCEAN CAPITAL CORP.
6500 Wilshire Blvd., Suite 500, Los Angeles, CA 90048. (213) 653-3600. FAX: (213) 653-3834.

PERCENTERPRISES COMPLETION BONDS
1901 Ave. of the Stars, Suite 2000, Los Angeles, CA 90067. (310) 551-0371. FAX: (310) 551-0518.

PLATINUM FILM INVESTMENTS
2269 Chestnut St., Suite 315, San Francisco, CA 94123. (415) 885-0100. FAX: (415) 292-4464. email: platinum@sprynet.com

D. R. REIFF & ASSOCIATES
41 W. 83 St., New York, NY 10024. (212) 877-1099.

RUBEN, ALBERT G., & CO.
48 West 25 St., 12th floor, New York, NY 10010. (212) 627-7400.

SILICON VALLEY BANK
Entertainment Division, 10585 Santa Monica Blvd., Ste. 135, Los Angeles, CA 90025. (310) 234-3580. FAX: (310) 234-3589.
email: pwyckoff@svbank.com
CONTACT
Paul Wyckoff

TRIDENT FILM FINANCING
P.O. Box 388, Burbank, CA 91503. (818) 382-4568.

UNION BANK OF CALIFORNIA ENTERTAINMENT GROUP
Communications/Media Division, 445 S. Figueroa, 15th floor, Los Angeles, CA 90071. (213) 236-7001. FAX: (213) 236-5747.
VICE PRESIDENT & MANAGER
Joseph S. Woolf

WESTERN SECURITY BANK
Entertainment Division, 4100 W. Alameda Ave., Burbank, CA 91505. (213) 849-3200.

MARKET RESEARCH & ANALYSIS

A.C. NIELSEN COMPANY
150 N. Martingale Rd., Schaumburg, IL 60173. (708) 605-5000.
731 Wilshire Blvd., #940, Los Angeles, CA 90010. (213) 386-7316. FAX: (213) 386-7317.
299 Park Ave., New York, NY 10171. (212) 708-7500.

A.C. NIELSEN COMPANY— EDI
(Provides daily box-office information for exhibition and distribution. On-line access to data.)
8350 Wilshire Blvd., #210, Beverly Hills CA 90211. (213) 658-8300.
PRESIDENT
Marcy Polier
SENIOR V.P.
Philip Garfinkle

ASI ENTERTAINMENT
101 N. Brand Blvd., #1700, Glendale, CA 91203-2619. (818) 637-5611. FAX: (818) 637-6408. email: lenburg@asientertainment.com
URL: http://www.asientertainment.com
EXECUTIVE V.P.
Paul Lenburg

AMERICAN MARKETING ASSOCIATION
(310) 568-5713.

BJK&E MEDIA GROUP
40 W. 23rd St., New York, NY 10010. (212) 727-5000.

BRAMSON & ASSOCIATES
7400 Beverly Blvd., Los Angeles, CA 90036. (213) 938-3595.

ROBERT A. BRILLIANT, INC.
(TV, Film & Promotion Research)
13245 Riverside Dr., #530, Sherman Oaks, CA 91423. (818) 386-6600. FAX: (818) 990-9007. email: rabinc@earthlink.net.
PRESIDENT
Robert Brilliant

CERTIFIED MARKETING SERVICES, INC. (CMS)
Route 9, Kinderhook, NY 12106. (518) 758-6405.

CERTIFIED REPORTS (CRI) EAST
(Theatre checking open, blind and trailer checking nationwide.)
7 Hudson St., Kinderhook NY 12106. (518) 758-6400. FAX: (518) 758-6451.
CHAIRMAN OF BOARD
Jack J. Spitzer
PRESIDENT
Bill Smith
EXECUTIVE VICE PRESIDENT
Bryan Zweig
VICE PRESIDENT
Elizabeth Stevens
VICE PRESIDENT, ADMINISTRATION & FINANCE
Michael F. Myers

CERTIFIED REPORTS INC. (CRI) WEST
PO Box 208670, Northridge CA 91325. (818) 727-0929. FAX: (818) 727-7426.
VICE PRESIDENT
Elizabeth Stevens

CINEMA CONSULTANTS GROUP
9903 Santa Monica Blvd., Suite 831, Beverly Hills, CA 90212-1671. (310) 470-2295. FAX: (310) 470-2975.
email: Goldmanmf@aol.com
PRESIDENT
Michael F. Goldman

CINEMASCORE
8524 Sahara Blvd., P.O. Box 173, Las Vegas, NV 89117. (702) 255-9963.

CONSUMERS PERSPECTIVE
1456 Canfield Ave., Los Angeles, CA 90035. (310) 556-3006. FAX: (310) 556-3002.

DALE SYSTEM INC., THEATRE DIVISION
1101 Stewart Ave., Garden City, NY 11530. (516) 794-2800. FAX: (516) 542-1063.

EXHIBITOR RELATIONS CO., INC.
116 N. Robertson Blvd., Suite 606, Los Angeles CA 90048. (310) 657-2005. FAX: (310) 657-7283.
PRESIDENT
Paul Dergarabedian

THE GALLUP ORGANIZATION
47 Hulfish St., Princeton, NJ 08542. (609) 924-9600. FAX: (609) 924-0228.

HANOVER SECURITY REPORTS
952 Manhattan Beach Blvd., Suite 250, Manhattan Beach CA 90266. (310) 545-9891. (800) 634-5560. FAX: (310) 545-7690.
EXECUTIVE VICE PRESIDENT
Nancy Stein

HISPANIC ENTERTAINMENT SPECIALIST
3726 Laurel Canyon Blvd., Studio City, CA 91604. (818) 766-9100. FAX: (818) 766-9201.

IMAGE ANALYSTS ALL-MEDIA
P.O. Box 1587, Santa Monica, CA 90406. (310) 458-0503.

INTERNATIONAL RESEARCH & EVALUATION,
21098 IRE Control Ctr., Eagan, MN 55121-0098. (612) 888-9635. FAX: (612) 888-9124.
CONTACT
Rick Kenrick

PAUL KAGAN ASSOCIATES INC.
(Research and analysis of entertainment, communications and media industries.)
126 Clock Tower Place, Carmel CA 93923-8734. (408) 624-1536. FAX: (408) 625-3225. email: info@kagan.com
URL: http://www.pkbaseline.com
PRESIDENT
Paul Kagan

KINDERHOOK RESEARCH, INC.
(Distributor & exhibitor open and blind checking; industry research; housekeeping/integrity surveys.)
PO Box 589, Kinderhook, NY 12106. (518) 758-1492. FAX: (518) 758-9896.
PRESIDENT
Andrea Koppel

McCANN-ERICKSON INC.
6420 Wilshire Blvd., Los Angeles, CA 90048. (213) 655-9420.

MARKET RESEARCH CORP. OF AMERICA
819 S. Wabash, Chicago, IL 60605. (708) 480-9600.
2215 Sanders Road, Northbrook, IL 60062. (708) 480-9600.

MOMENTUM INTERNATIONAL
(Media & Entertainment Consulting Services)
P.O. Box 5889, Sherman Oaks, CA 91413. (818) 752-4500. FAX: (818) 752-4554.

CHARLES A. MOSES
3211 W. Alameda Ave., Suite A, Burbank, CA 91505-4412. (818) 848-0513. FAX: (818) 848-4977.

OPINION RESEARCH CORP. INTL.
P.O. Box 183, Princeton, NJ 08542-0183. (609) 924-5900. FAX: (609) 908-5103.

JOAN PEARCE RESEARCH ASSOCS.
8111 Beverly Blvd., #308, Los Angeles, CA 90048. (213) 655-5464. FAX: (213) 655-4770.

PREMIER DATA VISION (P.D.I.)
(Collects and distributes ShowTime information; ShowTime packaging and resale; Ad-Gen–theatre directories)
1536 Cole Blvd., Suite 340, Golden, CO 80401.
PRESIDENT & CEO
Blaine Newton
DIRECTOR, RESEARCH & DEVELOPMENT
Gordon Hoak

PROFESSIONAL RESEARCH ASSOCIATES
6255 Sunset Blvd., #1515, Los Angeles, CA 90028. (213) 466-6124.

R. SELTZER ASSOCIATES
15445 Ventura Blvd., #14, Sherman Oaks, CA 91413. (818) 888-8450. FAX: (818) 888-8446.

SINDLINGER & CO., INC.
405 Osborne St., Wallingford, PA 19086. (610) 565-0247.

JANET SNOW & ASSOCIATES
327 Reeves Dr., Beverly Hills, CA 90212. (310) 552-0082.

VIDEO MONITORING SERVICES OF AMERICA
6430 W. Sunset Blvd., #504, Los Angeles, CA 90028. (213) 993-0111.

WABASH ASSOCIATES
201 N. Wells, Suite 2010, Chicago, IL 60606. (312) 251-1920. FAX: (312) 251-1921.
Barry S. Schain
Daniel Porter

Sound Studios & Services

AB AUDIO DESIGN STUDIOS
3765 Marwick Ave., Long Beach, CA 90808. (562) 429-1042.
FAX: (562) 429-2401. email: sound@abaudio.com
URL: http://www.abaudio.com
PRESIDENT
Arlan H. Boll
STUDIO MANAGER
Linda Rippee

ACCLAIM STUDIOS
12002 Ventura Pl., Ste. 300, Studio City, CA 91604. (818) 752-
5900, (310) 207-3319. FAX: (818) 752-5917.

ADVANTAGE AUDIO
1026 Hollywood Way, Burbank, CA 91505. (818) 566-8555.
email: aai242@idt.net
PRESIDENT
Bill Koepnick
VICE PRESIDENT
Jim Hodson
STUDIO MANAGER
Tammy Crosby

A & J RECORDING STUDIOS, INC.
225 W. 57 St., New York, NY 10019. (212) 247-4860.

JOHN ERIC ALEXANDER MUSIC INC.
8 John Walsh Blvd., Suite 400, Peekskill, NY 10566. (914) 736-
2829. FAX: (914) 736-3134. email: jeamusic@westnet.com
CONTACT
John Alexander

ALL POST, INC.
1133 N. Hollywood Way, Burbank, CA 91505. (818) 556-5700.
FAX: (818) 556-5748.
SENIOR V.P., SALES & SERVICE
Ben "Ponz" Ponzio

ASSOCIATED PRODUCTION MUSIC
6255 Sunset Blvd., Suite 820, Hollywood, CA 90028. (213)
461-3211, (800) 543-4276. FAX (213) 461-9102.
URL: http://www.apmmusic.com
PRESIDENT
Bill Brooks
WEST COAST SALES DIRECTOR
Tia Sommer
EAST COAST SALES DIRECTOR
Marla Mauer

ASTRALTECH, INC.
2101 St. Catherine West, Montreal, Quebec H3H 1M6. (514)
939-5060. FAX: (514) 939-5070. email: belleros@astral.com
PRESIDENT
Hubert Harel
VICE PRESIDENT
Michel Deslisle
DIRECTOR, MARKETING, SALES & CUSTOMER SERVICE
Paul Bellerose

THE AUDIO DEPARTMENT
119 W. 57 St., 4th Flr., New York, NY 10019. (212) 586-3503.

AUDIO MECHANICS
6735 Forest Lawn Dr., #200, Los Angeles, CA 90068. (213) 874-
4422. FAX: (213) 874-8413. email: info@audiomechanics.com
URL: http://www.audiomechanics.com

AUDIO SERVICES COMPANY
353 West 48th St., New York, NY 10036. (212) 977-5150. FAX:
(212) 262-5150. email: mtopham@msn.com
URL: http://www.audioservicesco.com
PRESIDENT
Marva Topham
VICE PRESIDENT
Ron Topham

AVID TECHNOLOGY
Metropolitan Technology Park, 1 Park West, Tewksbury, MA
01876. (508) 640-6789. FAX: (508) 640-1366.
115 N. 1st St., Ste. 208, Burbank, CA 91502. (818) 557-2520.
FAX: (818) 557-2558.

THE BAKERY RECORDING STUDIO
10709 Burbank Blvd., North Hollywood, CA 91601. (818) 508-
7800. FAX: (818) 508-7122. email: chrisaustin@bakerystudio.com
PRESIDENT
Andre Watterman
STUDIO MANAGER & CONTACT
Chris Austin

BLUEFIELD MUSIC DESIGN
1006 E. Cooper St., Aspen, CO 81611. (970) 925-2202. FAX:
(970) 825-2202. email: dblue@rof.net
URL: http://www.clazzax.com
PRESIDENT
David Bluefield

WALLY BURR RECORDING
1126 Hollywood Way, #203, Burbank, CA 91505. (818) 845-0500.

CAPITOL STUDIOS
1750 N. Vine St., Hollywood, CA 90028. (213) 871-5001. FAX:
(213) 871-5058. email: paula@capitolstudios.com
STUDIO DIRECTOR
Paula Salvatore

CHACE PRODUCTIONS, INC.
201 S. Victory Blvd., Burbank, CA 91502-2349. (818) 84A-
UDIO, (818) 842-8346. FAX: (818) 842-8353.
email: b_heiber@chace.com
CONTACT
Robert Heiber

CINESOUND
915 N. Highland Ave., Hollywood, CA 90038. (213) 464-1155.
FAX: (213) 464-1820.

CLAY DIGITAL SOUND
3151 Cahuenga Blvd. West, Ste. 105, Los Angeles, CA 90068.
(818) 769-8778. FAX: (213) 876-1132.

CONCEPT PLUS
1132 Vine St., Hollywood, CA 90038. (213) 466-2066. FAX:
(213) 466-2717. email: onstott@faithlink.net
VICE PRESIDENT
Brad Onstott

CORELLI-JACOBS RECORDING INC.
25 W. 45 St., New York, NY 10036. (212) 382-0220. FAX: (212)
382-0220.
CONTACT
Andrew Jacobs

CREATIVE MEDIA RECORDING
11105 Knott Ave., Ste. G, Cypress, CA 90630. (714) 892-9469.
email: KeenanCM@worldnet.att.net
OPERATIONS DIRECTOR
Tim Keenan
STUDIO MANAGER
Linda Keenan

CRESCENDO STUDIOS
615 Battery St., San Francisco, CA 94111. (415) 834-0580.
FAX: (415) 834-0599.
DIRECTOR OF OPERATIONS
Cindy McSherry

DB SOUND & MUSIC
4176 Arch Street, Suite 310, Studio City, CA 91604-3295.
Tel/FAX: (818) 753-4954. email: bondelev@usc.edu
PRESIDENT
David J. Bondelevitch

DIGITAL MASTERS
13848 Ventura Blvd., 12nd Flr., Sherman Oaks, CA 91423.
(818) 386-9172. FAX: (818) 386-9646. email: digitalm@earth-
link.net
CONTACT
Galen Walker

DIGITAL THEATER SYSTEMS
5171 Clareton Dr., Agoura Hills, CA 91301. (818) 706-3525, (800)
959-4109. FAX: (818) 706-1868. email: info@dtsonline.com
URL: http://www.dtsonline.com
CHAIRMAN & FOUNDER
Terry Beard
VICE CHAIRMAN & CEO
Dan Slusser
PRESIDENT & COO
Bill Neighbors
DIRECTOR WORLDWIDE SALES
Jim Murray

DIRECTORS SOUND & EDITORIAL SERVICE
1150 W. Olive Ave., Burbank, CA 91506. (818) 843-0950. FAX:
(818) 843-0357.

DISNEY I.D.E.A.S. AT THE DISNEY MGM STUDIOS
Roy O. Disney Production Ctr., Lake Buena Vista, FL 32830.
(407) 560-5600. FAX: (407) 560-5483.
CONTACT
Jamie Fuehner

DOLBY LABORATORIES, INC.
3375 Barham Blvd., Los Angeles, CA 90068. (213) 845-1880.
FAX: (415) 863-1373.
CONTACT
Liza Pano

100 Portrero Ave., San Francisco, CA 94103. (415) 558-0200.
75 S. Hill Court, Brisbane, CA 94005. (415) 715-0200.
1350 Ave. of the Americas, 28th floor, New York, NY 10019-
4703. (212) 767-1700.

ECHO SOUND SERVICES, INC.
4119 Burbank Blvd., Burbank, CA 91505. (818) 841-4114.
FAX: (818) 841-5038.
CONTACTS
Joe Melody
Russ Tinsley

EDS DIGITAL STUDIOS
3575 Cahuenga Blvd. West, Ste. 675, Los Angeles, CA 90068.
(213) 850-1165. FAX: (213) 850-6151.

EFX
919 N. Victory Blvd., Burbank, CA 91502. (818) 843-4762.
FAX: (818) 843-4029. URL: http://www.efx.com
PRESIDENT
Rick Stevens
VICE PRESIDENT
John O'Connor
STUDIO MANAGER
Lisa Ramirez

ALAN ETT MUSIC GROUP
12711 Ventura Blvd., Suite 110, Studio City, CA 91604. (818)
955-7010. FAX: (818) 955-7088.
PRESIDENT
Alan Ett
VICE PRESIDENT
Scott Liggett
CONTACT
Jim Faraci

FIESTA SOUND
1655 S. Compton Ave., Los Angeles, CA 90021. (213) 748-
2057. FAX: (213) 748-5388.
CONTACT
R. G. Robeson

FOUR MEDIA COMPANY
2813 W. Alameda Ave., Burbank, CA 91505-4455. (818) 840-
7100. FAX: (818) 846-5197. URL: http://www.4mc.com
CEO
Robert T. Walston
HUMAN RESOURCES
Kristi Kleckner

GELULA & CO., INC.
8421 Wilshire Blvd., Ste. 205, Beverly Hills, CA 90211. (213)
651-1167. FAX: (213) 651-3612.
PRESIDENT
Elio Zarurati

GNOME PRODUCTIONS
3610 W. Magnolia Blvd., Burbank, CA 91505. (818) 558-5088.
FAX: (818) 558-5817. email: gnome@magnoliastudios.com
URL: http://www.magnoliastudios.com/~gnome
CONTACT
Bruce Nazarian

GRM PRODUCTIONS
5914 Tuxedo Terrace, Los Angeles, CA 90068. (213) 462-3220.
FAX: (213) 462-0656. email: glandress@aol.com
PRESIDENT
George Landress

INTELLIGENT MEDIA INC.
1350 Abbot Kinney Blvd., #203, Venice, CA 90291. (310) 581-
8840. FAX: (310) 581-8844. email: mail@intelligentmedia.com
URL: http://intelligentmedia.com
PRESIDENT
Ron Marbolis

IF/X DIGITAL INC.
3522 Knobhill Dr., Sherman Oaks, CA 91423. (818) 501-1822.
FAX: (818) 501-4526. email: IFXdig@aol.com
URL: http://www.IFX.com
PRESIDENT
George Daugherty

JOHN HILL MUSIC
116 E. 37 St., New York, NY 10016. (212) 683-2273. FAX:
(212) 683-2546.
CONTACT
Rosemary Rogers

INTELLIGENT MEDIA INC.
1350 Abbott Kinney Blvd., Ste. 203, Venice, CA 91367. (310)
581-8840. FAX: (310) 581-8844. email: iweinc@earthlink.net.
URL: http://www.interweaveinc.com
PRESIDENT
Ron Marbolis

INTERLOCK AUDIO POST
6520 Sunset Blvd., Los Angeles, CA, 90028. (213) 469-3986.
FAX: (213) 469-8507.
GENERAL MANAGER
Lisa Pegnato

INTERSOUND, INC.
8746 Sunset Blvd., Los Angeles, CA 90069. (310) 652-3741.
FAX: (310) 854-7290. email: admin@wedubem.com
URL: http://www.netcom.com/~ispost
PRESIDENT
Kent Harrison Hayes

INTERWEAVE ENTERTAINMENT
22723 Berdon St., Woodland Hills, CA 91367. (818) 883-1920.
FAX: (818) 883-9650. email: iweinc@earthlink.net.
URL: http://www.interweaveinc.com
CONTACT
Lynne Weaver

KILLER MUSIC
30 Kewen Place, San Marino, CA 91108. (626) 792-0540. FAX:
(626) 792-0545.
PRESIDENT
Ron Hicklin

LARSON SOUND CENTER
4109 W. Burbank Blvd., Burbank, CA 91505. (818) 845-4100.
FAX: (818) 845-2414.

LASER PACIFIC MEDIA CORP., SOUND SERVICES
809 N. Cahuenga Blvd., Los Angeles, CA 90038. (213) 462-
6266. FAX: (213) 466-5047. email: info@laserpacific.com
URL: http://www.laserpacific. com
PRESIDENT
Emory Cohen
EXEC. V.P. SALES & MARKETING
Leon Silverman
DIRECTOR, SOUND SERVICES
Ed Fassl

540 N. Hollywood Way, Burbank, CA 91505. (818) 842-0777,
(213) 462-6266. FAX: (818) 566-9834.
VICE PRESIDENT OF OPERATIONS
Steve Mitchell

823 N. Seward Ave., Hollywood, CA 90038. (213) 469-4040,
(213) 462-6266. FAX: (213) 466-5047.
GENERAL MANGER
Ethan Bush

LITTLE GEMSTONE MUSIC/24 CARAT PRODUCTIONS
P.O. Box 1703, Fort Lee, NJ 07024. (201) 488-8562.
Kevin D. Noel

LOOK INC.
168 5th Ave., New York, NY 10010. (212) 627-3500. FAX: (212)
633-1980.
Jeanne Look

LUCASFILM LTD. (THX DIVISION)
P.O. Box 10327, San Rafael, CA 94912. (415) 492-3900. FAX:
(415) 492-3973.
DIRECTOR
Kurt Schwenk
DIRECTOR, THEATRE ALIGNMENT
Tim Schafbuch
DIRECTOR, CUSTOMER RELATIONS
Tim Schafbuch
MANAGERS, INTL SALES
Lawrence Cervantes
Martin Dew

MAD DOG STUDIOS & SOUTH LAKE STAGE
291-293 S. Lake St., Burbank, CA 91502. (818) 557-0100.
FAX: (818) 557-6383. email: mdogstudio@aol.com
OWNERS
Dusty Wakeman
Michael Dumas
STUDIO MANAGER
Mark Harvey

LEE MAGID INC.
P.O. Box 532, Malibu, CA 90265. (213) 463-5998. FAX: (310) 457-8891.
PRESIDENT
Lee Magid
VICE PRESIDENT
Adam Magid

CHRIS MANY MUSIC/SILVERSTORM STUDIOS
907 S. Victory Blvd., Burbank, CA 91508. (818) 953-5126. FAX: (818) 953-5140.
PRESIDENT
Chris Many
STUDIO MANAGER
Jim Kee

MARCLAND INTERNATIONAL COMMUNICATIONS
P.O. Box 3100, Burbank, CA 91508. (818) 557-6677. FAX: (818) 567-0568. email: info@marcland.com
URL: http://www.marcland.com
CEO
Alfredo Marco Fulchignoni

MCA MUSIC MEDIA STUDIOS
5161 Lankershim Blvd., Ste.201, North Hollywood, CA 91601. (818) 777-9200. FAX: (818) 777-9235.

MEDIA CITY SOUND
12711 Ventura Blvd., Suite 110, Studio City, CA 91604. (818) 955-7010. FAX: (818) 955-7088.
PRESIDENT
Alan Ett
SENIOR VICE PRESIDENT
Scott Liggett
VICE PRESIDENT, OPERATIONS
Donna Walker

MOVIE TECH STUDIOS
832 N. Seward St., Hollywood, CA 90038. (213) 467-8491. FAX: (213) 467-8471.

MUSIC ROOM PICTURES, PRODUCTIONS & PUBLISHING
PO Box 219,, Redondo Beach, CA 90277. (310) 316-4551. FAX: (310) 540-3532. email: MRP@aol.com
PRESIDENT
John Reed

N.T. AUDIO VIDEO FILMS LABS
1833 Centinela Ave., Santa Monica, CA 90404. (310) 828-1098. FAX: (310) 828-9737. email: jon@ntaudio.com
URL: http://www.ntaudio.com
PRESIDENT
Tom McCormick
STUDIO MANAGER
Jon Seifert

NAMRAC MUSIC/SOUCI MUSIC
15456 Cabrito Road, Van Nuys, CA 91406. (213) 873-7370, (818) 787-6436. FAX: (818) 787-3981.
PRESIDENT
Tommy R. Skeeter

NOVASTAR DIGITAL SOUND
6430 Sunset Blvd., #103, Hollywood, CA 90028. (213) 467-5020. FAX: (213) 957-8707. email: bsky@novastarpost.com
URL: http://www.novastarpost.com
V.P. & GENERAL MANAGER
Bob Sky
MANAGER, CLIENT SERVICES/SCHEDULING
Scott Sonderegger

OF SOUND MIND, INC.
356 E. Olive Ave., Burbank, CA 91502. (818) 558-3950. FAX: (818) 295-2910.
PRESIDENT
Patrick M. Griffith
GENERAL MANAGER
Donald Carruthers

PARAMOUNT RECORDING STUDIOS
6245 Santa Monica Blvd., Hollywood, CA 90038. (213) 465-4000. FAX: (213) 469-1905. email: calrocker@earthlink.net
URL: http://teaminfinity.com/Paramount.html
CONTACTS
Adam L. Beilenson
Michael Kerns

PLUS THREE POST
3610 W. Magnolia Blvd., Burbank, CA 91505. (818) 558-5088. FAX: (818) 558-5817.

RALEIGH SOUND
650 N. Bronson Ave., Hollywood, CA 90004. (213) 960-4720. FAX: (213) 871-5629.
CONTACT
Keith Stephenson

RUSSIAN HILL RECORDING
1520 Pacific Ave., San Francisco, CA 94109. (415) 474-4520. FAX: (415) 474-7190. email: russian@rhrnet.com
STUDIO MANAGER
Lucrezia Conklin

RYDER SOUND SERVICES, INC.
1147 N. Vine St., Hollywood, CA 90038. (213) 469-3511. FAX: (213) 461-8057.

SCREENMUSIC STUDIOS
11700 Ventura Blvd., Studio City, CA 91604. (818) 753-6040. FAX: (818) 508-4870. email: jkaufman@earthlink.net
COO
Jay R. Kaufman

SEVEN TORCH MUSIC
12932 Huston St., Sherman Oaks, CA 91423. (818) 789-7568. FAX: (818) 784-2570. email: steverino@earthlink.net
URL: http://www.7torch.home.ml.org
PRESIDENT
Steven Orich
CONTACT
Judy Halpert

SKYVIEW FILM & VIDEO
541 N. Fairbanks, Ste. 2200, Chicago, IL 60611. (312) 670-2020. FAX: (312) 670-3010.
PRESIDENT
Jack Tohtz
STUDIO MANAGER
Bill Reis
SALES
Al Nolan-Cohn

SONY PICTURES STUDIOS
10202 W. Washington Blvd., Culver City, CA 90232. (310) 244-5523. FAX: (310) 204-2123. email: steven_cohen@spe.sony.com
V.P., SALES & DEVELOPMENT
Steven B. Cohen

SOUND MASTER AUDIO/VIDEO
10747 Magnolia Blvd., Los Angeles, CA 91601. (213) 650-8000.

SOUND THINKING MUSIC RESEARCH
1534 N. Moorpark Rd., #333, Thousand Oaks, CA 91360. (805) 495-3306. FAX: (805) 495-3306. email: cginell@gte.net
URL:http://www.success.edu/ncginell
CONTACT
Cary Ginell

SOUNDCASTLE RECORDING STUDIO
2840 Rowena Ave., Los Angeles, CA 90039. (213) 665-5201. FAX: (213) 662-4273.
CONTACT
Candace Corn

SOUNDELUX/SOUNDELUX MEDIA LABS
7060 Hollywood Blvd., 7th Flr., Hollywood, CA 90028. (213) 463-3855. FAX: (213) 463-1977. email: cmeister@soundelux.com
URL: http://www.soundelux.com
PRESIDENT
Charlie Meister

SOUNDELUX SHOWORKS
4401 Vineland Rd., Ste. 117, Orlando, FL 32811. (407) 345-1555. FAX: (407) 345-0014.
CONTACTS
John Miceli
Tony Miceli

SOUNDSCAPE PRODUCTIONS
3614 Overland Ave., Los Angeles, CA 90034. (310) 202-9989. FAX: (310) 202-6088. email: dubscape@pacbell.net
CHIEF ENGINEER
Gregg Hall

SOUNDZ NU
95 Madison Ave., New York, NY 10016. (212) 684-7222. FAX: (212) 689-5084.
PRESIDENT
Elvis Herbert
VICE PRESIDENT
Adam Charity

SOUTHERN LIBRARY OF RECORDED MUSIC
4621 Cahuenga Blvd., Toluca Lake, CA 91602. (818) 752-
1530. FAX: (818) 508-0213.
PRESIDENT
Ralph Peer II
MANAGER
Roy Kohn

STARDUST FILM, INC.
7510 Sunset Blvd., #240, Hollywood, CA 90046. (310) 288-
7889. FAX: (818) 763-5886. email: pvmstardustfilm@msn.com
PRESIDENT
Peter V. Meiselmann, C.A.S.

STUDIO 56
7000 Santa Monica Blvd., Hollywood, CA 90038. (213) 464-7747.

STUDIO M PRODUCTIONS UNLIMITED
4032 Wilshire Blvd., #403, Los Angeles, CA 90010. (213) 389-
7372, (888) 389-7372. FAX: (213) 389-3299.
email: studiom@pacbell.net
URL://www.mandy.com/stuoo1.html

8715 Waikiki Station, Honolulu, HI 96830. (808) 734-3345,
(888) 734-3345. FAX: (808) 521-0919.
OWNER
Senator Mike Michaels, C.A.S.

SUNSET SOUND RECORDERS
6650 Sunset Blvd., Hollywood, CA 90028. (213) 469-1186.
FAX: (213) 465-5579. URL: http://www.sunsetsound.com
CONTACT
Lisa Matthews

SUPERLOOPERS
P.O. Box 341678, Los Angeles, CA 90034. (310) 839-0895, (310)
395-1830. FAX: (310) 839-0896. email: ThursdaysChild@juno.com
PRESIDENT
DeVera Marcus
CONTACT
Norman Marcus

TODD-AO/EDITWORKS
3399 Peachtree Rd. N.E., Suite 200, Atlanta, GA 30326. (404)
237-9977. FAX: (404) 237-3923.
V.P., SALES & MARKETING
Mike Hoff

TODD-AO STUDIOS
900 N. Seward St., Hollywood, CA 90038. (213) 962-4000.
FAX: (213) 466-2327.
PRESIDENT
Christopher Jenkins

TODD-AO STUDIOS EAST
259 W. 54th St., New York, NY 10019. (212) 265-6225. FAX:
(212) 247-5206.
PRESIDENT & GENERAL MANAGER
Stephen Castellano

TODD-AO STUDIOS WEST
3000 Olympic Blvd., Bldg. One, Santa Monica, CA 90404.
(310) 315-5000. FAX: (310) 315-5099.
1861 S. Bundy Dr., West Los Angeles, CA 90025. (310) 315-
5200. FAX: (310) 315-5399.
PRESIDENT
Richard Hassanein

TOM THUMB MUSIC/ RUTH WHITE FILMS
(Divisions of Rhythms Productions) Box 34485, Los Angeles,
CA 90034-0485. (310) 836-4678.
PRESIDENT
Ruth White
EXECUTIVE PRODUCER
David White
ART DIRECTOR
Lotte Cherin

ULTRA STEREO LABS INC.
18730 Oxnard St., Ste. 208, Tarzana, CA 91356. (818) 609-
7405. FAX: (818) 609-7408.
181 Bonetti Dr., San Luis Obispo, CA 93401. (805) 549-0161.
FAX: (805) 549-0163.

UNIVERSAL STUDIOS
100 Universal City Plaza, Universal City, CA 91608. (818) 777-
0169. FAX: (818) 866-1494. email: TamiLozano@unistudios.com
URL: http://www.universalstudios.com/studio
DIRECTOR, SOUND FACILITIES
Tami Hulcher

VOICES
16 E. 48 St., New York, NY 10017. (212) 935-9820. FAX: (212)
755-1150.
CONTACT
Richard Leonai

WARNER BROS. STUDIOS FACILITIES
4000 Warner Blvd., Burbank, CA 91522. (818) 954-3000. FAX:
(818) 954-2677. email: wbsf@warnerbros.com
URL: http://www.wbsf.com
CONTACT
Tracy Balsz

WARNER HOLLYWOOD STUDIOS
1041 N. Formosa, Los Angeles, CA 90046. (213) 850-2500.
FAX: (213) 850-2839.

WAVES SOUND RECORDERS
1956 N. Cahuenga Blvd., Hollywood, CA 90048. (213) 466-
6141. FAX: (213) 466-3751.

WEST PRODUCTIONS, INC.
2921 W. Olive Ave., Burbank, CA 91505. (818) 841-4500. FAX:
(818) 567-1820.
PRESIDENT
David Rawlinson
CEO
David West

WESTLAKE AUDIO
7265 Santa Monica Blvd., Los Angeles, CA 90046. (213) 851-
9800. FAX: (213) 851-9386.
8447 Beverly Blvd., Los Angeles, CA 90048. (213) 654-2155.
OWNER
Glen Phoenix
STUDIO MANAGER
Steve Burdick

WORKSHIRT MUSIC
6083 Selma Ave., Hollywood, CA 90083. (213) 466-6046.

ZACUTO AUDIO
1316 3rd St., Ste. 109, Santa Monica, CA 90401. (310) 394-
4932. FAX: (310) 458-7802. email: zacz@earthlink.net
URL: http://zacuToaudio.com
PRESIDENT
Gary Zacuto
STUDIO MANAGER
Martin Royer

SAUL ZAENTZ FILM CENTER
2600 Tenth St., Berkeley, CA 94710. (510) 486-2100, (800)
227-0466. FAX: (510) 486-2115. email: shurtzs@aol.com
CONTACT
Steve Shurtz

SPECIAL EFFECTS

A & A SPECIAL EFFECTS
7021 Hayvenhurst Ave., Van Nuys, CA 91406. (818) 909-6999. FAX: (818) 782-0635.

ACCLAIM STUDIOS
12001 Ventura Pl., Suite 300, Studio City, CA 91604. (818) 752-5900. FAX: (818) 752-5917.
CONTACT
Andy Maisner

ADVANCED CAMERA SYSTEMS
16117 Cohasset St., Van Nuys, CA 91406-2908. (818) 989-5222. FAX: (818) 994-8405.

ADVANCED FIRE & RESCUE SERVICES
16205 Lost Canyon Road, Santa Clarita, CA 91351. (818) 837-7336, (805) 299-4801. FAX: (805) 298-3069.
CONTACTS
Craig Sanford
Mark Pedro

ADVANCED MEDIA SYSTEMS
4348 Van Nuys Blvd., Ste. 207, Sherman Oaks, CA 91403. (818) 461-1899. FAX: (818) 461-1890. email: tmedia2514@aol.com
URL: http://home.earthlink.net/~tmedia2514/
CONTACT
Richard Zarro

ALIAS/WAVEFRONT
11835 W. Olympic Blvd., Suite 350, Los Angeles, CA 90064. (310) 914-1566. FAX: (310) 914-1580. URL: http://www.aw.sgi.com

ALL EFFECTS COMPANY, INC.
7915 Ajay Dr., Sun Valley, CA 91352. (818) 768-2000. FAX: (818) 768-2312.

DAVID ALLEN PRODUCTIONS
918 W. Oak St., Burbank, CA 91506. (818) 845-2970. FAX: (818) 567-4954.
CONTACT
David Allen

ALTERIAN STUDIOS
1107 S. Mountain Ave., Monrovia, CA 91016. (626) 932-1488. FAX: (626) 932-1494.
PRESIDENT
Tony Gardner

AMALGAMATED DYNAMICS
20100 Plummer St., Chatsworth, CA 91311. (818) 882-8638. FAX: (818) 882-7327.

ANATOMORPHEX
8210 Lankershim, Suite 14, North Hollywood, CA 91605. (818) 768-2880. FAX: (818) 768-4808.
CONTACTS
Robert Devine
James Clark

HOWARD A. ANDERSON CO.
100 Universal City Plaza, #504-3, Universal City, CA 19608. (818) 777-2402, (818) 777-2779. FAX: (818) 733-1118.
5418 McConnell Ave., Los Angeles, CA 90066. (805) 823-5511. FAX: (805) 823-5501.

ANIMUS FILMS
2 W. 47 St., New York, NY 10036. (212) 391-8716.

APA STUDIOS
500 S. Lakeview Dr., Lake Helen, FL 32744. (904) 228-2144. FAX: (904) 228-2155. URL: http://www.A-P-A.com

ARTEFFEX
5419 Clean St., North Hollywood, CA 91601. (818) 506-5358. FAX: (818) 506-3171.
CONTACT
Dann O'Quinn

AVAILABLE LIGHT, LTD.
1125 Flower S. St., Burbank, CA 91502. (818) 842-2109. FAX: (818) 842-0661. email: avlight@availablelightltd.com
OWNER & PRESIDENT
John VanVliet
OWNER & CFO
Katherine Kean

BALSMEYER & EVERETT, INC.
459 W. 15th St., New York, NY 10011. (212) 627-3430. FAX: (212) 989-6528. email: randyb@balsmeyer-everett.com
URL: http://www.balsmeyer-everett.com
3000 W. Olympbic Blvd., Santa Monica, CA 90404. (310) 264-4115. FAX: (31) 264-4116.

BANNED FROM THE RANCH ENTERTAINMENT
2048 Broadway, Santa Monica, CA 90404. (310) 449-1313. FAX: (310) 449-1315.
CONTACT
Casey Cannon

BIFROST LASERFX
6733 Sale Ave., Wesy Hills, CA 91307. (818) 704-0423. FAX: (818) 704-4629. email: bifrost@earthlink.com

BIGGER THAN LIFE INC.
1327 Fayette St., El Cajon, CA 92020. (800) 383-9980. FAX: (619) 449-8299. URL: http://www.biggerthanlife.com
email: bgrnlife@ix.netcom.com
PRESIDENT
R.T. "Dick" Dickson
CEO
Mark Bachman
MARKETING MANAGER
Connie Clark

BILLY SKY PRODUCTIONS
1739 Berkeley St., Ste. 101, Santa Monica, CA 90404. (310) 264-7800. FAX: (310) 828-2404. email: staff@bigskypost.com
URL: http://www.bigskypost.com
OPERATIONS MANAGER
Michael Davis

BIOVISION
44-460 Indian Wells Lane, Indian Wells, CA 92210. (760) 341-5007, (888) bio-vision. FAX: (760) 773-4004.
email: sportscenter@earthlink.net
URL: http://www.biovisionsp.com
DIRECTOR & CEO
Ken Kline

BLACKSHEAR COMMUNICATIONS
6922 Hollywood Blvd., Suite 923, Hollywood, CA 90028. (213) 466-6412. FAX: (213) 466-1557.
PRESIDENT
Dwight A. Blackshear

BLACKSTONE MAGIK ENTRPRISES, INC.
12800 Puesta Del Sol, Redlands, CA 92373-7408. URL: http://www.blackstone.org

BLUE SKY/VIFX
5333 McConnell Ave., Los Angeles, CA 90066. (310) 822-8872. FAX: (310) 821-1012. URL: http://www.vifx.com
1 South Rd., Harrison, NY 10528. (914) 381-8400. FAX: (914) 381-9790.

BLUR STUDIO, INC.
1130 Abbot Kinney Blvd., Venice, CA 90291. (310) 581-8848. FAX: (310) 581-8850. email: cat@blur.com
URL: http://www.blur.com
EXECUTIVE PRODUCER
Cat Chapman

BODYTECH
13659 Victory Blvd., Suite 145, Van Nuys, CA 91401. (818) 385-0633.

BOOM BOOM EFFECTS
17402 Chase St., Northridge, CA 91325. (818) 345-7703. FAX: (818) 365-0882.

BRANAM ENTERPRISES, INC.
20675 Bahama St., Chatsworth, CA 91311. (818) 709-8787. FAX: (818) 717-9898. email: branam@gte.net
PRESIDENT
Joe Branam
CONTACT
Randy Beckman

BROOKLYN MODEL WORKS
60 Washington Ave., Brooklyn, NY 11205. (718) 834-1944. FAX: (718) 596-8934. email: bromowo@inch.com
PRESIDENT
John Kuntzsch

THE BRUBAKER GROUP
10560 Dolcedo Way, Los Angeles, CA 90077. (310) 472-4766.

BRYANT & JOHNSEN
210 N. Pass Ave., Suite 106, Burbank, CA 91505. (818) 557-7495. FAX: (818) 557-7498.

BUENA VISTA IMAGING
500 South Buena Vista St., Burbank, CA 91521-5073. (818) 560-5284. FAX: (818) 842-0532.
CONTACT
John Chambers

BURMAN STUDIOS INC.
4706 W. Magnolia Blvd., Burbank, CA 91505. (818) 980-6587. FAX: (818) 980-6589.
CONTACT
Bari Dreiband-Burman

MICHAEL BURNETT PRODUCTIONS
9848 Glenoaks Blvd., Sun Valley, CA 91352. (818) 768-6103. FAX: (818) 768-6136.

CACIOPPO PRODUCTION DESIGN INC.
928 Broadway, Suite 1204, New York, NY 10010. (212) 777-1828. FAX: (212) 777-1847.

CALIBAN FILMWORKS
454 S. Robertson Blvd., Ste. D, Los Angeles, CA 90048. (310) 281-2511. FAX: (310) 281-2512.
EXECUTIVE V.P.
Lena Evans

CALICO ENTERTAINMENT
9340 Eton Ave., Chatsworth, CA 91311-5879. (818) 407-5200. FAX: (818) 407-5323.
PRESIDENT & CEO
Tom Burton

THE CHARACTER SHOP INC.
9033 Owensmouth Ave., Canoga Park, CA 91304-1417. (818) 718-0094. FAX: (818) 718-0967.
CONTACT & PRESIDENT
Rick Lazzarini

CHARLEX, INC.
2 W. 45 St., New York, NY 10036. (212) 719-4600.

CHIODO BROS. PRODUCTIONS INC.
110 W. Providencia Ave., Burbank, CA 91502. (818) 842-5656. FAX: (818) 848-0891.
PRESIDENT
Stephen Chiodo

CIMMELLI INC.
16 Walter St., Pearl River, NY 10965. (914) 735-2090.

CINEMA ENGINEERING COMPANY
7243 Atoll Ave., Suite A, N. Hollywood, CA 91605-4105. (818) 765-5340. FAX: (818) 765-5349. email: CineEng@aol.com

CINEMORPH EFFECT S GROUP
3123 Livonia Ave., Los Angeles, CA 90034. (310) 287-1674.

CINENET (CINEMA NETWORK, INC.)
1350 Los Angeles Ave., 3rd floor, Simi Valley, CA 93065. (805) 527-0093. FAX: (805) 527-0305. URL: http://www.cinenet.com

CINESITE DIGITAL FILM CENTER
1017 N. Las Palmas Ave., Suite 300, Hollywood, CA 90038. (213) 468-4400. FAX: (213) 468-4404.

CINEVISION ENTERTAINMENT
1111 S. Victory Blvd., Burbank, CA 91502. (818) 566-4917. FAX: (818) 566-6639.
PRESIDENT
Philip Jones

CINNABAR
2840 N. Hollywood Way, Burbank, CA 91505. (818) 842-8190. FAX: (818) 842-0563. email: info@cinnabar.com
URL: http: www.cinnabar.com
CONTACTS
Doug Morris
Ann Mitchell

COLLINS ENTERTAINMENT CONCEPTS CORP.
2715,Culver Ave., Kettering, OH 45429. (513) 293-0040. FAX: (513) 293-4431.

COMPOSITE IMAGE SYSTEMS
1144 N. Las Palmas Ave., Hollywood, CA 90038. (213) 463-8811.

THE COMPUTER FILM COMPANY
8522 National Blvd., Suite 103, Culver City, CA 90232. (310) 838-3456. FAX: (310) 838-1713 email: info@cfla.com
URL: http://www.cfla.com
PRESIDENT
Donald R. Fly

CREATIVE CHARACTER ENGINEERING
16110 Hart St., Van Nuys, CA 91406. (818) 901-0507. FAX: (818) 901-8417. email: andyCCE@earthlink.net
CREATIVE DIRECTOR
Andrew Clement

CREATIVE EFFECTS, INC.
760 Arroyo Ave., San Fernando, CA 91340-2222. (818) 365-0655. FAX: (818) 365-0651.

THE CREATIVE GROUP
305 E. 46th St., 12th Flr., New York, NY 10017. (212) 935-0145. FAX: (212) 838-0853.
PRESIDENT
Linda Ardigo

CRISWEEL PRODUCTIONS
16535 Gault St., Van Nuys, CA 91406. (818) 781-7739. FAX: (818) 781-7759.

CRUSE & COMPANY, INC.
7000 Romaine St., Hollywood, CA 90038. (213) 851-8814. FAX: (213) 851-8788.

CUBENA RESEARCH CORP./DIGITAL RESOLUTION
6860 Lexington Ave., Hollywood, CA 90038. (213) 460-4111. FAX: (213) 463-2483.
V.P., MARKETING & SALES
John Haggar

CURIOUS PICTURES CORPORATION
440 Lafayette, 6th Flr., New York, NY 10003. (212) 674-1400. FAX: (212) 674-0081. email: rwink5@aol.com
URL: http://www.curiouspix.com
EXECUTIVE PRODUCER
Richard Winkler
1360 Mission St., Ste. 201, San Francisco, CA 94103. (415) 437-1400. FAX: (415) 437-1408.

DAVE'S MARINE SERVICES INC.
1438 W. 14th St., Long Beach, CA 90813. (562) 437-4772. FAX: (562) 503-0848.
CONTACT
David W.L. Hilchey

DAY SHADES
6859 Leetsdale Dr., Suite 202, Denver, CO 80224. (303) 399-8889. FAX: (303) 399-8881.
CONTACT
Craig T. Jones

DE LA MARE ENGINEERING, INC.
1908 1st St., San Fernando, CA 91340-2610. (818) 365-9208. FAX: (818) 365-8775.

DIGISCOPE
2308 Broadway, Santa Monica, CA 90034. (310) 315-6060. FAX: (310) 828-5856. email: m_stuart@digiscope.com
URL: http://www.digiscope.com
CONTACT
Mary Stuart

DIGITAL DOMAIN
300 Rose Ave., Venice, CA 90291. (310) 314-2800. FAX: (310) 314-2888.
PRESIDENT
Scott Ross

DIGITAL MAGIC COMPANY
3000 W. Olympic Blvd., 2nd Flr., Santa Monica, CA 90404. (310) 315-4720. FAX: (310) 315-4721.

DISNEY I.D.E.A.S. AT THE DISNEY MGM STUDIOS
Roy O. Disney Production Center, Lake Buena Vista, FL 32830. (407) 560-5600. FAX: (407) 560-5483.
CONTACT
Jamie Fuehner

WALT DISNEY IMAGINEERING
1401 Flower St., P.O. Box 25020, Glendale, CA 91221-5020. (818) 544-6500.

DISNEY-MGM STUDIOS
PO Box 10200, Film-TV Dept., Bungalow 2, Lake Buena Vista, FL 32830. (407) 560-5736. FAX: (407) 827-5168.

THE WALT DISNEY STUDIOS
500 S. Buena Vista St., Burbank, CA 91521. (818) 560-1000.
CONTACT
Tony Richards

DREAM QUEST IMAGES
(Feature Film visual effects division of Walt Disney Co.)
2635 Park Center Dr., Simi Valley, CA 93065. (805) 578-3100. FAX: (805) 583-4673.

DREAM THEATER
21345 Lassen St., Suite 200, Chatsworth, CA 91311. (818) 773-4979. FAX: (818) 773-4970. email: darren@dreamtheater.com
URL: http://www.dreamtheater.com
CONTACT
Darren Chuckry

DUCK SOUP PRODUCKIONS, INC.
2205 Stoner Ave., Los Angeles, CA 90064. (310) 478-0771.
FAX: (310) 478-0073. URL: http://www.ducksoupla.com
EXECUTIVE PRODUCER
Mark Medernach

DYNACS DIGITAL STUDIOS
572 E. Green St., Ste. 204, Pasadena, CA 91101. (818) 449-7385, (818) 725-3899. FAX: (818) 449-7432.
email: javiben@dynacs.com
URL: http://www.dynacsdigital.com
PRESIDENT
Javier E. Benavente

EAI
100 Wilshire Blvd., 18th Flr., Santa Barbara, CA 90401. (310) 260-5050. FAX: (310) 260-5051. URL: http://www.eai.com
CONTACT
Julie A. Weitzell

EDS DIGITAL STUDIOS
3575 Cahuenga Blvd. W., Ste. 675, Los Angeles, CA 90068.
(213) 850-1165. FAX: (213) 850-6151.

EDITEL LOS ANGELES
729 N. Highland Ave., Hollywood, CA 90038-3437. (213) 931-1821. FAX: (213) 931-7771.

EFEX SPECIALISTS
43-17 37th St., Long Island City, NY 11101. (718) 937-2417.

EFFECTIVE ENGINEERING
6727 Flanders Dr., Suite 106, San Diego, CA 92121. (619) 450-1024. FAX: (619) 452-3241. email: mlipsky@effecteng.com
URL: http//www.effecteng.com/mlipsky
CONTACT
Mark Lipsky

THE EFFECTS HOUSE
111 8th Ave., Suite 914, New York, NY 10011. (212) 924-9150.
FAX: (212) 924-9193.

EFILM
1146 N. Las Palmas, Hollywood, CA 90038. (213) 463-7041.
FAX: (213) 465-7342. email: info@efilm.com
URL: http://www.efilm.com
CONTACT
David Hays

ELECTRIC MACHINE ENTERTAINMENT
1930 Purdue Ave., Suite 6, Los Angeles, CA 90025. (310) 330-8841. FAX: (310) 473-7317. email: emeinc@earthlink.net
CONTACT
Clive Milton

E=MC² INC.
710 W. Ivy Street, Glendale, CA 91204. (818) 243-2424. FAX: (818) 243-5126.
CONTACT
Bob Morgenroth

ELECTROFEX
1146 N. Central, Suite 231, Glendale, CA 91202. (818) 775-3838.
email: bat2@flash.net

ENCORE VISUAL EFFECTS
702 Arizona Ave., Santa Monica, CA 90401. (310) 656-7663.
FAX: (310) 656-7699. URL: http://www.encorevideo.com
6344 Fountain Ave., Hollywood, CA 90028. (213) 466-7663.
FAX: (213) 467-5539. email: jwarren@encorevideo.com
CONTACT
Jan Warren

ENERGY FILM LIBRARY
12700 Ventura Blvd., 4th Flr., Studio City, CA 91604. (818) 508-1444, (800) IMAGERY. FAX: 818-508-1293.
CONTACT
Joan Sargent

EUE/SCREEN GEM PRINTS
222 E. 44 St., New York, NY 10017. (212) 867-4030.

F-STOP INC.
120 S. Buena Vista St., Burbank, CA 91505. (818) 843-7867.
FAX: (818) 842-7706.

FX ZONE—SPECIAL EFFECTS
Jamboree Center, 1 Park Plaza, 6th floor, Irvine, CA 92614.
(714) 852-7375. FAX: (714) 434-2776.
CONTACT
Jeff T. Miller

FANTASY II FILM EFFECTS
504 S. Varney St., Burbank, CA 91502. (818) 843-1413. FAX: (818) 848-2824.
CONTACT
Leslie Huntley

RUSS FARBER
19324 Oxnard St., Tarzana, CA 91356-1123. (818) 882-8220.
FAX: (818) 708-8113. email: jfmusic@primenet.com

FILM EAST
9 E. Stow Rd., Ste. A, Marlton, NJ 08053. (609) 810-1090.
FAX: (609) 810-1077. URL: http://www.filmeast.com

FILM TECHNICAL SERVICES/SPECIAL EFFECTS
11118 Ventura Blvd., Studio City, CA 91604. (818) 508-1094.

FILMTRIX, INC.
P.O. Box 715, N. Hollywood, CA 91603-0715. (818) 980-3700.
FAX: (818) 980-3703. email: filmtrix@aol.com
CONTACT
Kevin Pike

FINE ART PRODUCTIONS/TICHIE SURACI PICTURES
67 Maple St., Newburgh, NY 12550-4034. (914) 542-1585.
FAX: (914) 561-5866. email: rs7.fap@mhv.net
URL: http://www.geopages.com/Hollywood/1077

FINE LINE GRAPHICS
PO Box 441, Madison, OH 44057. (216) 428-7332. FAX: (216) 428-7332. email: finelinegr@aol.com
CEO
Rick Fike

LARRY FIORITTO SPECIAL EFFECTS SERVICES
1067 E. Orange Grove, Burbank, CA 91501. (818) 954-9828.
FAX: (818) 954-9828.
Larry Fioritto

525 POST PRODUCTION
6424 Santa Monica Blvd., Hollywood, CA 90038. (213) 525-1234. FAX: (213) 467-1589. email: irichards@525post.com
URL: http://www.525post.com

FLAT EARTH
4405 Riverside Dr., Ste. 205, Burbank, CA 91505. (818) 563-6419. FAX: (818) 563-5218. email: flatearth@aol.com
97 Wooster St., 6th Flr., New York, NY 10012. (212) 750-7029.
FAX: (212) 343-3178.
CONTACT
Michael Schertz

4-WARD PRODUCTIONS
2801 Hyperion Ave., Studio 104, Los Angeles, CA 90027. (213) 660-2430. FAX: (213) 660-2445.

FRAMEWORK
3000 W. Olympic Blvd., Ste. 1369, Santa Monica, CA 90404.
(310) 449-4033. FAX: (310) 449-4037.
email: maliboo812@aol.com
EXECUTIVE PRODUCER
Ziv Givron

GALAXIE ENTERTAINMENT CO.
PO Box 8523, Universal City, CA 91618. (818) 362-6005.
email: galaxie@loop.com
CONTACT
Dave Gregory

JOHN GATI FILM EFFECTS, INC.
6456 83rd Pl., Middle Village, NY 11379. (718) 894-5753.

GEAR PRODUCTIONS
6404 Hollywwod Blvd., Ste. 424, Hollywood, CA 90028. (213) 466-GEAR. FAX: (213) 466-0546. URL: http://www.gearprod.com
PRESIDENT
David Kim

PETER GEYER ACTION PROPS & SETS
8235 Lankershim Blvd., Suite G, North Hollywood, CA 91605.
(818) 768-0070.

GILDERFLUKE & COMPANY INC.
820 Thompson Ave., Ste. 35, Glendale, CA 91201. (818) 546-1618. FAX: (818) 546-1619. URL: http://www.gilderfluke.com
CONTACT
Doug Mobley

GLOBAL EFFECTS INC.
7119 Laurel Canyon Blvd., Unit 4, North Hollywood, CA 91605.
(818) 503-9273. FAX: (818) 503-9459.

GLOBUS STUDIOS, INC.
44 W. 24 St., New York, NY 10010. (212) 243-1008.

RICHARD HAAS PHOTO IMAGERY LTD.
P.O. Box 8385, Universal City, CA 91618. (818) 248-8696, (818) 417-2064. FAX: (818) 549-0616.

HANSARD ENTERPRISES INC.
P.O. Box 469, Culver City, CA 90232. (310) 840-5660. FAX: (310) 840-5662. email: hansard@earthlink.net.
CONTACT
William Hansard

HBO STUDIO PRODUCTIONS
120-A E. 23rd St., New York, NY 10010. (212) 512-7800. FAX:
(212) 512-7788. email: hsp@hsptv.com
CONTACT
Judy Glassman

HFWD VISUAL EFX
5634 Melrose Ave., Hollywood, CA 90038. (213) 962-2225.
FAX: (213) 962-2220. email: HFWDefx@aol.com
URL: http://www.hfwd-vfx.com
CONTACTS
Jayelle Sargent
Gretchen Shronts
Celia Falkin

JIM HENSON'S CREATURE SHOP
2821 Burton Ave., Burbank, CA 91504. (818) 953-3030. FAX:
(818) 953-3039. email: mbritton@la.creature.henson.com
CONTACT
Matt J. Britton

HILL PRODUCTION SERVICE, INC.
6902 W. Sunset Blvd., Hollywood, CA 90028. (213) 463-1182.
FAX: (213) 463-2862.

HOLLYWOOD DIGITAL
6690 Sunset Blvd., Hollywood, CA 90028. (213) 465-0101.
FAX: (213) 469-8055.

HOLOGRAPHIC STUDIOS
240 E. 26 St., New York, NY 10010. (212) 686-9397.

HOLY COW! VISUAL EFFECTS
3763 Valleybrink Rd., Los Angeles, CA 90039. (213) 913-7913.
FAX: (213) 913-9113. email: Leslie@holycowfx.com
PRESIDENT
Leslie Merkovich

HOUSE OF MOVES MOTION CAPTURE STUDIOS, LLC
711 Hampton Dr., Venice, CA 90291. (310) 399-2485. FAX:
(310) 399-9115.email: motion@moves.com
URL: http://www.moves.com/motion
CONTACT
Tom Tolles

HUNTER GRATZNER INDUSTRIES INC.
4107 Redwood Ave., Los Angeles, CA 90088. (310) 578-9929.
FAX: (310) 578-7370. email: hgimodels@aol.com
PARTNERS
Matthew Gratzner
Ian Hunter
Shannon Blake Gans

IF/X DIGITAL INC.
3522 Knobhill Dr., Sherman Oaks, CA 91423. (818) 501-1822.
FAX: (818) 501-4526. email: IFXdig@aol.com
URL: http://www.IFX.com
PRESIDENT
George Dougherty

ILLUSIONS
21205 Georgetown Dr., Santa Clarita, CA 91350. (805) 296-
9620. FAX: (818) 387-1994. email: bwdm98a@prodigy.com
CONTACT
Dave Simmons

IMAGE CREATORS INC.
2712 6th St., Santa Monica, CA 90405. (310) 392-3583. FAX:
(310) 396-6972. email: creators@flash.net
URL: http://www.image creators. com
OWNER & CEO
Fred Spencer
CFO
Karen Brooks

IMAGE ENGINEERING INC.
736 N. Reese Place, Burbank, CA 91506. (818) 840-1444.

IMAGINE THAT
28064 Avenue, Unit K, Valencia, CA 91355. (805) 294-0061.

INDUSTRIAL F/X PRODUCTIONS INC.
5103 Gloria St., Encino, CA 91436. (818) 501-1822. FAX: (818)
501-4526.

INDUSTRIAL LIGHT & MAGIC (ILM)
P.O. Box 2459, San Rafael, CA 94912. (415) 258-2000.
URL:http://www.ilm-jobs.com
PRESIDENT
Jim Morris

INTELLIGENT MEDIA INC.
1350 Abbot Kinney Blvd., Ste. 203, Venice, CA 90291. (310)
581-8840. FAX: (310) 581-8844.
email: mail@intelligentmedia.com
URL: http://intelligentmedia.com
PRESIDENT
Ron Marbolis

INTERNATIONAL CREATIVE EFFECTS
401 S. Flower St., Burbank, CA 91502. (818) 840-8338. FAX:
(818) 840-8023. email: icefx@primenet.com
URL: http://www.primenet.com/nicefx
CHAIRMAN
Lawrence E. Benson

INTROVISION INTERNATIONAL
1011 N. Fuller Ave., Hollywood, CA 90046. (213) 969-1930.
FAX: (213) 969-9360.

JEX FX
47 Paul Dr., #9, San Rafael, CA 94903. (415) 499-9477. FAX:
(415) 499-0911. URL: http://www.jexfx.com

STEVE JOHNSON'S X/FX INC.
320 S. Flower St., Burbank, CA 91502. (818) 504-2177. FAX:
(818) 531-1525.

THE JONES EFFECTS STUDIO
26007 Huntington Lane, Suite 9, Santa Clarita, CA 91355-
2746. (805) 294-9159. FAX: (805) 294-9689.
CONTACT
Andrew Jones

KNB EFFECTS
20830 Dearborn St., Chatsworth, CA 91311. (818) 341-1484.
CONTACT
Greg Nicotero

GENE KRAFT PRODUCTIONS
29 Calvados, Newport Beach, CA 92657. (714) 721-0609.
OWNER
Gene Kraft

L.A. VIDEOGRAMS
3203 Overland Ave., Ste. 6157, Los Angeles, CA 90034. (310)
836-9224. email: LExplore1@aol.com
CONTACT
Larry Rosen

LASER-PACIFIC MEDIA CORP.
540 N. Hollywood Way, Burbank, CA 91505. (818) 842-0777,
(213) 462-6266. FAX: (818) 566-9834.
809 N. Cahuenga Blvd., Hollywood, CA 90038. (213) 462-6266.
fax: (213) 464-3233. email: info@laserpacific.com
URL: http://www.laserpacific.com

DANIEL LEVY
408 E. 13 St., New York, NY 10009. (212) 254-8964.

LEXINGTON SCENERY & PROPS
10443 Arminta St., Sun Valley, CA 91352-4109. (818) 768-5768.
FAX: (818) 768-4217. email: lexscene@lexingtonscenery.com
URL: http://www.lexingtonscenery.com

LIBERTY STUDIOS, INC.
238 E. 26 St., New York, NY 10010. (212) 532-1865.

LINKER SYSTEMS
13612 Onkayha Circle, Irvine, CA 92620. (949) 552-1904. FAX:
(949) 552-6985. email: linker@linker.com
URL: http://www.linker.com

LIVE WIRE PRODUCTIONS & VFX
28631 S. Western Ave., Suite 101, Rancho Palos Verdes, CA
90275-0800. (310) 831-6227.
VISUAL EFFECTS PRODUCER
Kris Simmons

LOWTECH
11825 Major St., Suite 8, Culver City, CA 90230. (310) 398-7094.

LUCASFILM, LTD.
(see Industrial Light & Magic)

LUMENI PRODUCTIONS, INC.
1632 Flower Street, Glendale, CA 91201-2357. (818) 956-
2200. FAX: (818) 956-3298. email: lumeni@aol.com

MAGIC CRAFT
5722-A Union Pacific Ave., Commerce, CA 90022. (213) 724-2279.

MAGICAL MEDIA INDUSTRIES, INC.
12031 Vose St., North Hollywood, CA 91605. (818) 765-6150.

MAKEUP & EFFECTS LABORATORIES, INC. (M.E.I.)
7110 Laurel Canyon Blvd., Unit E, N. Hollywood, CA 91605.
(818) 982-1483. FAX: (818) 982-5712.

MAKEUP & MONSTERS
1012 Fair Oaks, #271, South Pasadena, CA 90130. (818) 886-
6587. FAX: (818) 709-6587. email: afryt4u@earthlink.net

MANHATTAN TRANSFER/EDIT/DIGITAL
545 5th Ave., New York, NY 10017. (212) 687-4000. FAX: (212)
687-2719. email: info@mte.com
CONTACTS
Joanne Gross, Steve Coffey

PAUL MANTELL STUDIO
16 Yale Ave., Jersey City, NJ 07304. (212) 966-9038.

MASS-ILLUSION
30 Riverview Rd., Lenox, MA 01240. (413) 637-4500. FAX:
(413) 637-0054. email: diane@mass-illusion.com
EXECUTIVE PRODUCER
Diane Pearlman

MASTERSFX, INC
10312 Norris Ave., Unit D, Arleta, CA 91331. (818) 834-3000.
email: mastersfx@prodigy.net
URL: http://mastersfx.com
PRESIDENT
Todd Masters

MATTE WORLD DIGITAL
24 Digital Dr., Ste. 6, Novato, CA 94949. (415) 382-1929. FAX:
(415) 382-1999. email: info@matteworld.com
URL: http://www.matteworld.com
CONTACT
Krystyna Demkowicz

MAX INK CAFE
3015 Ocean Front Walk, Studio 2, Venice, CA 90291. (310)
827-5351. FAX: (310) 827-5651. email: info@mediacap.com
URL: http://www.mediacap.com
VICE PRESIDENT
Bob Skibinski

MCCOURRY & ROBIN, INC.
22647 Ventura Blvd., Suite 240, Woodland Hills, CA 91364.
(888) 932-8113. FAX: (818) 386-2113.

MEDIA FABRICATORS INC.
5067 W. Washington Blvd., Los Angeles, CA 90016. (213) 937-
3344. FAX: (213) 937-1142. email: info@mediafab.com
URL: http://mediafab.com
PRESIDENT
Barry Flustier

MEDIALAB PRODUCTIONS/MEDIALAB STUDIO L.A.
301 N. Canon Dr., Ste. 228, Beverly Hills, CA 90210.
URL: http://www.medialab3d.com
S.V.P., CREATIVE AFFAIRS
Carole Kirschner
2130 N. Hollywood Way, Burbank, Ca 91505. (818) 973-2037.
FAX: (818) 973-2033. email: medialave@4mc.com
EXECUTIVE PRODUCER
Mackenzie Waggaman

MELROSE TITLES & OPTICAL EFFECTS
(213) 469-2070. FAX: (213) 469-7088.

METROLIGHT STUDIOS
5724 W. 3rd St., Ste. 400, Los Angeles, CA 90036. (213) 932-
0400. FAX: (213) 932-8440.
PRESIDENT
James W. Kristoff

BILL MILLAR
116 S. Buena Vista St., Burbank, CA 91505. (818) 848-3300.
FAX: (818) 848-3301.

MILLER IMAGING INTERNATIONAL, INC.
2401 West Olive Ave., Burbank, CA 91506. (818) 972-1440.
FAX: (818) 972-2098. email: info@millercd.com
URL: http://www. millercd.com
CONTACT
Steve Miller

DAVID MILLER CREATIONS
14141 Covello, Van Nuys, CA 91406. (818) 782-5615.

MODUS EFX PRODUCTIONS
11535 Tuxford St., Sun Valley, CA 91352. (818) 771-0016. FAX:
(818) 771-0017.

MONSTER MECANIX
13958 Huston St., Sherman Oaks, CA 91423. (818) 995-0271.
CONTACT
Jurgen Heimann

MOTION CITY FILMS
1847 Centinela Ave., Santa Monica, CA 90404. (310) 264-
4870. FAX: (310) 264-4871. email: witt@motioncity.com
URL: http://www.motioncity.com
CONTACT
Jerry Witt

MOVIE TECH STUDIOS
832 N. Seward St., Hollywood, CA 90038. (213) 467-8491.
FAX: (213) 467-8471.
Ewing M. "Lucky" Brown

NETWORK ART SERVICE
630 S. Mariposa St., Burbank, CA 91506. (818) 843-5078.
FAX: (818) 843-2528.

NOVOCOM
5401 Beethoven St., Playa Vista, CA 90066-7016. (310) 448-
2500 FAX: (310) 448-2525. URL: http://www.novo.com
CONTACT
Tami Clark

OCS/FREEZE FRAME/PIXEL MAGIC
10635 Riverside Dr., Toluca Lake, CA 91602. (818) 760-0862.
FAX: (818) 760-0483.
CONTACTS
Ray McIntyre Jr.
Dave Fiske

JAMES O'NEIL & ASSOCIATES
725 N. Western Ave., Suite 109, Los Angeles, CA 90029. (213)
464-2995. FAX: (213) 464-2994.
Jim O'Neil

OPTIC NERVE STUDIOS
9818 Glenoaks Blvd., Sun Valley, CA 91352. (818) 771-1007.
FAX: (818) 771-1009. email: JohnVulich@aol.com
PRESIDENT
John Vulich

OWEN MAGIC SUPREME
734 N. McKeever Ave., Azusa, CA 91702. (626) 969-4519.
FAX: (626) 969-4614.

PACIFIC DATA IMAGES
3101 Park Blvd., Palo Alto, CA 94306. (650) 846-8100. FAX:
(650) 846-8101. email: info@pdi.com
URL: http://www.pdi.com
CONTACT
Judy Conner

PACIFIC ENTERTAINMENT GROUP
21462 Pacific Coast Hwy., Unit 36, Huntington Beach, CA
92648. (714) 667-2897. FAX: (714) 775-1732.
email: automated_hd@earthlink.net
URL: http://home.earthlink.net/~automated_hd

PACIFIC TITLE/MIRAGE
6350 Santa Monica Blvd., Los Angeles 90038. (213) 464-0121.
email: ksmith@pactitle.com

PACIFIC TITLE MIRAGE STUDIO
1149 N. Gower, Los Angeles, CA 90038. (323) 769-3700. FAX:
(323) 769-3701.

PERFORMANCE WORLD SPECIAL EFFECTS
416 S. Victory Blvd., Burbank, CA 91502. (818) 845-2704. FAX:
(818) 846-1145.
PRESIDENT
Jerry Williams

PERPETUAL MOTION PICTURES
24730 Tibbets Avenue, Ste. 160, Valencia, CA 91355-3449.
(805) 294-0788. FAX: (805) 294-0786.
email: rmpmp@aol.com
CONTACT
Richard Malzahn

PINNACLE EFX
2334 Elliot Ave., Seattle, WA 98121. (206) 441-9878. FAX:
(206) 728-2266.
EXECUTIVE PRODUCER
Karen Olcott

PLAYHOUSE PICTURES
1401 N. La Brea Ave., Hollywood, CA 90028-7505. (213) 851-
2112. FAX: (213) 851-2117.
CONTACT
Ted Woolery

POLAR TECHNOLOGIES USA
P.O. Box 1515, Folsom, CA 95763. (916) 677-4484. FAX: (916)
677-4485.
PRESIDENT & MANAGING DIRECTOR
Steve Carey
V.P./DIRECTOR OF OPERATIONS
Joe Ippolito

POST EDGE
1111 Lincoln Rd., Ste. 700, Miami Beach, FL 33139. (305)
674-0700. FAX: (305) 674-8900.
400 Hollywood Blvd., Ste. 180-N, Hollywood, FL 33021. (954)
894-9900. FAX: (954) 894-8600.

PYROS PICTURES
1201 Dove St., Suite 550, Newport Beach, CA 92660. (949)
833-0334. FAX: (949) 833-8655. email: gpyros@pyros.com
URL: http://www.pyrospictures.com

QUANTEL
28 Thorndale Circle, Darien, CT 06820. (203) 656-3100. FAX:
(203) 656-3459. URL: http://www.quantel.com

R/C MODELS
803 Channel St., San Pedro, CA 90731. (310) 833-4700. FAX: (310) 833-9167.

RGA/LA
6526 Sunset Blvd., Los Angeles, CA 90028. (213) 957-6868. FAX: (213) 957-9577.

RAINMAKER DIGITAL PICTURES
178 S. Victory Blvd., Ste. 108, Burbank, CA 91502. (818) 526-1500. FAX: (818) 953-5051. email: info@rainmaker.com
URL: http://www.rainmaker.com
PRESIDENT (CA)
Peter Sternlicht

RANDO PRODUCTIONS
1829 Dana St., Glendale, CA 91201. (818) 552-2900. FAX: (818) 552-2388.
CONTACT
Joe Rando

REEL EFX
5539 Riverton Ave., N. Hollywood, CA 91601. (818) 762-1710.

REELISTIC FX
21318 Hart St., Canoga Park, CA 91312. (818) 346-2484. FAX: (818) 346-2710.

RHYTHM & HUES STUDIOS
5404 Jandy Pl., Los Angeles, CA 90066. (310) 448-7500. FAX: (310) 448-7600. email: suze@rhythm.com
URL: http://www.rhythm.com
ADVERTISING & PUBLICITY DIRECTOR
Suzanne Datz

ROARING MOUSE ENTERTAINMENT
1800 Bridgegate St., Ste. 103, Westlake Village, CA 91361. (805) 373-8131. FAX: (805) 373-8133.

SFX-STARLIGHT EFFECTS
9142 1/2 Del Arroyo Drive., La Tuna Canyon, Los Angeles, CA 91352. (818) 771-9206. FAX: (818) 771-9208.
email: kimsfx@aol.com

SAFARI ANIMATION & EFFECTS
10845 Van Owen St., Unit E, N. Hollywood, CA 91605. (818) 762-5203. FAX: (818) 762-3709.

SCENIC TECHNOLOGIES
4170 W. Harmon Ave., Suite 6, Las Vegas, NV 89103. (702) 876-1451. FAX: (702) 876-2795.
CONTACT
Robert Mealmear

SCHWARTZBERG & COMPANY
12700 Ventura Blvd., 4th floor, Studio City, CA 91604. (818) 508-1833. FAX: (818) 508-1253.

SCREAMING MAD GEORGE, INC.
11750 Roscoe Blvd., Suite 11, Sun Valley, CA 91352. (818) 767-8587. FAX: (818) 768-3968.

SIDESHOW PRODUCTIONS
31364 Via Colinas, Suite 106, Westlake Village, CA 91362. (818) 879-1996. FAX: (818) 879-1603.

SIGHT EFFECTS
321 Hampton Rd., Venice, CA 90291. (310) 392-0999. FAX: (310) 392-7112.
PRODUCER
Jeff Blodgett

SINGLE FRAME FILMS
437-1/2 N. Genesee Ave., Los Angeles, CA 90036. (213) 655-2664.
CONTACT
Gary Schwartz

SLAGLE MINIMOTION, INC.
39 E. Walnut St., Pasadena, CA 91103. (626) 584-4088. FAX: (626) 584-4099.

SOLDIERS OF LIGHT PRODUCTIONS
P.O. Box 16354, Encino, CA 91416-6354. (818) 345-3866.

ELAN SOLTES FX & DESIGN
2745 Angelo Dr., Los Angeles, CA 90077-2101. (310) 858-3170. FAX: (310) 278-2356. email: elanfx@earthlink.net
OWNER
Elan Soltes

SONY PICTURES IMAGEWORKS
9050 W. Washington Blvd., Culver City, CA 90232. (310) 840-8000. FAX: (310) 840-8100. email: don@spimageworks.com
URL: http://www.spiw.com
CONTACT
Don Levy

S.O.T.A. FX
7338 Valjean Ave., Van Nuys, CA 91406. (818) 780-1003. FAX: (818) 780-4315.

SPECIAL EFFECTS SYSTEMS
PO Box 220-399, Santa Clarita, CA 91322-0399. (805) 251-1333, (213) 462-2301. FAX: (805) 255-1723.
CONTACT
Christina Knipe

SPECIAL EFFECTS UNLIMITED, INC.
1005 Lillian Way, Los Angeles, CA 90038. (213) 466-3361. FAX: (213) 466-5712.
CONTACT
Lorraine Fadden

SPECTAK PRODUCTIONS
222 N. Sepulveda Blvd., Suite 2000, El Segundo, CA 90245. (310) 335-2038.

STAGE 18
18 Leonard St., Norwalk, CT 06850. (203) 852-8185. FAX: (203) 838-3126.

STICKS & STONES
12990 Branford St., Suite M, Arleta, CA 91331. (818) 252-2088. FAX: (818) 252-2087.
CONTACT
Rob Burman
Jennifer E. McManus

DAVID STIPES PRODUCTIONS, INC.
685 Glenandale Ter., Glendale, CA 91206. (818) 243-1442.
CONTACT
David Stipes, III

STOKES/KOHNE ASSOCIATES, INC.
742 Cahuenga Blvd., Hollywood, CA 90038. (213) 468-2340. FAX: (213) 468-2345.

STUDIO PRODUCTIONS
650 N. Bronson Ave., Suite 223, Hollywood, CA 90004. (213) 856-8048. FAX: (213) 461-4202. email: Vizualman@aol.com
EXECUTIVE PRODUCER
Steve Soffer

SUNSET POST, INC.
1813 Victory Blvd., Glendale, CA 91201. (818) 956-7912. FAX: (818) 545-7586.

T.E.S.T. KREASHENS
26536 Golden Valley Rd., Suite 612, Saugus, CA 91350. (805) 251-6466. FAX: (805) 251-1153.

T & T OPTICAL EFFECTS
1619 1/2 S. Victory Blvd., Glendale, CA 91201. (818) 241-7407. FAX: (818) 241-7207.

TANZINITE PRODUCTIONS
2118 Wilshire Blvd., Ste. 176, Santa Monica, CA 90403. (310) 281-8139. FAX: (310) 828-0427.
S.V.P., SALES & DEVELOPMENT
Maria Laing

TECHNICREATIONS
2328 N. Batavia, Suite 106, Orange, CA 92865. (714) 282-8423. FAX: (714) 282-7853. email: tcreate@deltanet.com
URL: http://www.netpage.com/technicreations.html
CONTACT
Terry Carrigan

THIRD DIMENSION EFFECTS
427 W. Alameda Ave., Burbank, CA 91506-3201. (818) 842-5665. FAX: (818) 842-9132.

3-D VIDEO
5240 Medina Rd., Woodland Hills, CA 91364-1913. (626) 722-8425. FAX: (818) 592-0987. email: mr3d@3dcompany.com
URL: http://www.3dcompany.com
PRESIDENT
Dan Symmes

TITLE HOUSE INC./TITLE HOUSE DIGITAL EFFECTS
738 N. Cahuenga Blvd., Los Angeles, CA 90038. (213) 469-8171. FAX: (213) 469-0377.
PRESIDENT
Keith Allan
VICE PRESIDENT
Mark Allan
DIRECTOR OF SALES
Ridge Blackwell

TODD-AO DIGITAL IMAGES
6601 Romaine St., Hollywood, CA 90038. (213) 962-4141. FAX: (213) 466-7903.
PRESIDENT
Brian Jennings

TRIBAL SCENERY
3216 Vanowen St., Burbank, CA 91505. (818) 558-4045.

TRI-ESS SCIENCES, INC.
1020 W. Chestnut St., Burbank, CA 91506. (818) 848-7838.
FAX: (818) 848-3521. email: pyro@tri-sss.com
CONTACT
Kim Greenfield

MIKE TRISTANO WEAPONS & SPECIAL EFFECTS
14431 Ventura Blvd., Suite 185, Sherman Oaks, CA 91423.
(818) 888-6970. FAX: (818) 888-6447.

TWO HEADED MONSTER
6161 Santa Monica Blvd., Suite 100, Los Angeles, CA 90038.
(213) 957-5370. FAX: (213) 957-5371.
email:thmonster@aol.com
CONTACT
Ruth Schiller

ULTIMATE EFFECTS
642 Sonora Ave., Glendale, CA 91201. (818) 547-4743.

UNITEL VIDEO
729 N. Highland Ave., Los Angeles, CA 90038. (213) 878-
5800. FAX: (213) 931-7771. URL: http://www.univid.com
515 W. 57th St., New York, NY 10019. (212) 265-3600. FAX:
(212) 765-5801.

THE VIDEO AGENCY
10900 Ventura Blvd., Studio City, CA 91604. (818) 505-8300.
FAX: (818) 505-8370. email: TVA@pacbell.net
CONTACT
Jeffrey Goddard

VIDEO DIMENSIONS, INC.
6922 Hollywood Blvd., #921, Hollywood, CA 90028. (213) 466-
6412. FAX: (213) 466-1557. email: dwight@blackshearcomm.com
URL: http://www.blackshearcomm.com
PRESIDENT
Dwight Blackshear

VIDEO POST & TRANSFER, INC.
2727 Inwood Rd., Dallas, TX 75235. (214) 350-2676. FAX:
(214) 352-1427. email: sference@cyberramp.net
EXECUTIVE DIRECTOR OF BUSINESS DEVELOPMENT
Steve Ference

VIEW POINT STUDIOS
162 Columbus Ave., Boston, MA 02116. (617) 338-1113. FAX:
(617) 423-1481. email: imendez@viewpointstudios.com
URL: http://www.viewpointstudios.com
BROADCAST MARKET COORDINATOR
Liz Mendez

VIEW STUDIO, INC.
6715 Melrose Ave., Hollywood, CA 90038. (213) 965-1270.
FAX: (213) 965-1277.

VIEWPOINT DATA LABS
625 S. State Street, Orem, UT 84058. (801) 229-3000. FAX:
(801) 229-3300. email: vpia@viewpoint.com
4223 Glencoe Ave., Ste. C-100, Los Angeles, CA 90292. (310)
578-6997, (888) 773-7276. FAX: (310) 578-9867.
URL: http://www.viewpoint.com
CONTACT
Steve Skinner

VIEWPORT IMAGES
109 N. Naomi St., Burbank, CA 91505. (818) 559-8705. FAX:
(818) 559-5453.
PRESIDENT
John Howard

VISION ART DESIGN & ANIMATION
3025 Olympic Blvd., Santa Monica, CA 90404. (210) 264-5566.
FAX: (310) 264-5572.

VISUAL CONCEPT ENGINEERING (VCE)
13300 Ralston Ave., Sylmar, CA 91342-7608. (818) 367-9187.
FAX: (818) 362-3490. email: vceinc@aol.com
URL: http://www.vce.com
CONTACT
Peter Kuran

VISION CREW UNLIMITED
5939 Rodeo Rd., Los Angeles, CA 90016. (310) 558-0450.
FAX: (310) 558-0437. email: visioncrew@visioncrew.com
URL: http://www.visioncrew.com
EXECUTIVE PRODUCER
Evan Jacobs

VISUAL FX.COM
8129 Willow Glen Rd., Los Angeles, CA 90046. (213) 650-
0772. FAX: (213) 650-7209.email: rohaver@earthlink.com URL:
http://www.visualfx.com

VISUAL IMPULSE PRODUCTIONS (V.I.P.)
10850 Wilshire Blvd., Suite 380, Los Angeles, CA 90024. (310)
441-2556. FAX: (310) 441-2558.

DON WAYNE MAGIC EFFECTS
10929 Hartsook St., N. Hollywood, CA 91601. (818) 763-3192.
FAX: (818) 985-4953.

WILDFIRE, INC. LIGHTING & VISUAL EFFECTS
5200 W. 83rd St., Los Angeles, CA 90045. (310) 645-7787,
(800) 937-8065. FAX: (310) 645-9009.
CONTACT
Richard Gleen

STAN WINSTON STUDIO
7032 Valjean Ave., Van Nuys, CA 91406. (818) 782-0870.

WONDERWORKS, INC.
7231 Remmet Ave., Canoga Park, CA 91303. (818) 992-8811.
FAX: (818) 347-4330. email: WndrWrksEt@aol.com
URL: http://www.wonderworks.web.com

WORKS NEW YORK, INC.
180 Varick St., New York, NY 10014. (212) 229-0741.

WORLDS, INC.
605 Market St., 14th floor, San Francisco, CA 94105 (415)
281-1300.

STEVE WRIGHT DIGITAL FX, INC.
2206 Carnegie Lane, Ste. A, Redondo Beach, CA 90278. (310)
374-4164. FAX: (310) 374-7574. email: swdfx@cyberverse.com
CONTACT
Steve Wright

WUNDERFILM DESIGN
7700 W. Sunset Blvd., Los Angeles, CA 90046. (213) 845-
4100. FAX: (213) 845-4101. email: jerry@wunderfilm.com
URL: http://wunderfilm.com
OWNER
Jerry Jaskulski

XAOS
444 De Harrow St., Ste. 222, San Francisco, CA 94107. (415)
558-9267. FAX: (415) 558-9160.

X-STREAM POST (LAUBE-ROTH INC.)
7025 Santa Monica Blvd., Hollywood, CA 90038. (213) 464-
7337. FAX: (213) 856-9934. email: Xstreampo@aol.com
PRESIDENT
Greg Laube
CONTACT
Sherry Howell

Y.L.S. PRODUCTIONS
P.O. Box 34, Los Alamitos, CA 90720. (562) 430-2890. FAX:
(562) 596-9563.

KEVIN YAGHER PRODUCTIONS
6615 Valjean Ave., Van Nuys, CA 91406. (818) 374-3210. FAX:
(818) 374-3214.

GENE YOUNG EFFECTS
517 W. Windsor Street, Glendale, CA 91204. (818) 243-8593.

STOCK SHOTS

ACADEMY OF MOTION PICTURE ARTS & SCIENCES
333 S. La Cienega Blvd., Beverly Hills, CA 90211. (310) 247-3020, (310) 247-3000. FAX: (310) 657-5193.

AMERICAN FILM INSTITUTE LIBRARY
2021 N. Western Ave., Los Angeles, 90027. (213) 856-7600.

AMERICAN STOCK PHOTOGRAPHY
6255 Sunset Blvd., #716, Los Angeles, CA 90028. (213) 469-3900. FAX: (213) 469-3909.

ARCHIVE FILMS/ARCHIVE PHOTOS
530 W. 25 St., New York, NY 10001. (212) 822-7800, (800) 876-5115. FAX: (212) 645-2137. email: sales@archivefilms.com
URL: http//:www.archivefilms.com
VICE PRESIDENT, SALES
Eric Rachlis

ARCHIVE SERVICES
2830 Waverly Dr., Los Angeles, CA 90069. (213) 665-2456.
OWNER
Charles Phoenix

ASSOCIATED MEDIA IMAGES, INC.
650 N. Bronson, Suite 300, Los Angeles, 90004. (213) 871-1340. FAX: (213) 469-6048.

THE BBC WORLDWIDE AMERICAS/THE BBC LIBRARY
3500 W. Olive Ave., Ste. 110, Burbank, CA 91505. (818) 840-9770, (800) 966-5424. FAX: (818) 840-9779.
email: lals@bbcfootage.com

BEST SHOT INC.
4726 N. Lois Ave., Ste. A, Tampa, FL 33614. (813) 877-2118. FAX: (813) 874-3655. email: bestshot@cyberspy.com
URL: http://www.cyberspy.com/bestshot
CONTACT
Peter Klein

BLOOMING PARADISE PRODUCTIONS
5202 Edgewood Pl. #B, Los Angeles, CA 90019. Tel/FAX: (213) 937-0432.

THE BRIDGEMAN ART LIBRARY INTERNATIONAL
65 E. 93rd St., New York, NY 10128. (212) 828-1238. FAX: (212) 828-1255. email: lori@bridgemanart.com
URL: http://www.bridgeman.co.uk
PICTURE MANAGER
Lori Bridgeman

BRITANNICA FILMS
310 S. Michigan, Chicago, IL 60604. (312) 347-7400, ext. 6512, (800) 554-9862.

BUDGET FILMS
4427 Santa Monica Blvd., Los Angeles, 90029. (213) 660-0187. FAX: (213) 660-5571.

BUENA VISTA IMAGING (DISNEY)
500 S. Buena Vista St., Burbank, 91521. (818) 560-1270. FAX: (818) 842-9454.
CONTACT
Ben F. Hendicks, Jr.

CAMEO FILM LIBRARY, INC.
10760 Burbank Blvd., North Hollywood, 91601. (818) 980-8700. FAX: (818) 980-7113.
LIBRARIANS
Marilyn Chielens
Steve Vrabel

CHERTOK ASSOCIATES, INC.
100 S. Main St., New City, NY 10956. (914) 639-4238.

DICK CLARK MEDIA ARCHIVES
3003 W. Olive Ave., Burbank, CA 91505. (818) 841-3003. FAX: (818) 954-8609.

CLASSIC IMAGES
1041 N. Formosa Ave., W. Hollywood, CA 90046. (213) 850-2980, (800) 949-CLIP. FAX: (213) 850-2981.
email: sales@classicimg.com
URL: http://www.classicimg.com
PRESIDENT
Marcie Alexander

THE CLIP JOINT FOR FILM
833-B N. Hollywood Way, Burbank, CA 91505. (818) 842-2525. FAX: (818) 842-2644.

LARRY DORN ASSOCS. INC.
5820 Wilshire Blvd., #306, Los Angeles, CA 90036. (213) 935-6266. FAX: (213) 935-9523.
STOCK FOOTAGE LIBRARIAN
Linda Dorn Wallerstein

EASTMAN KODAK COMPANY
343 State St., Rochester, NY 14650. (800) 242-2424.

ENERGY FILM LIBRARY
12700 Ventura Blvd., 4th Flr., Studio City, 91604. (818) 508-1444, (800) IMAGERY. FAX: (818) 508-1293.
email: rob@digital-energy.com
URL: http://www.digital-energy.com
DIRECTOR OF LIBRARY SALES, WEST COAST
Joan Sargent

404 Park Ave. South, Ste. 1304, New York, NY 10016. (212) 686-4900. (800) IMAGERY. FAX: (212) 686-4998.
DIRECTOR OF LIBRARY SALES, EAST COAST
Larry K. Aubrey

F.I.L.M. ARCHIVES, INC.
432 Park Ave. S., New York, NY 10016. (212) 696-2616. FAX: (212) 696-0021. email:fastimages@compuserve.com
URL: http://www.fastimages.com

FILM & VIDEO STOCK SHOTS, INC.
10442 Burbank Blvd., N. Hollywood, CA 91601-2217. (888) 4-FOOTAGE, (818) 760-2098. FAX: (818) 760-3294.
email: stockshot@earthlink.net
PRESIDENT
Stephanie Siebert

FILM BANK
425 S. Victory Blvd., Burbank, CA 91502. (818) 841-9176. FAX: (818) 567-4235. email: filmbank@primenet.com
URL: http://www.filmbank.com
PRESIDENT
Paula Lumbard
SALES REPRESENTATIVES
Carol Martin
Barry Dagestino

GORDY COMPANY MEDIA LIBRARY
6255 Sunset Blvd., #1800, Los Angeles, CA 90028. (213) 856-3500. FAX: (213) 962-3054.

GREAT WAVES FILM LIBRARY
483 Mariposa Dr., Ventura, CA 93001-2230. (805) 653-2699.

HALCYON DAYS PRODUCTIONS
1926 Broadway, #302, New York, NY10023. (212) 724-2626. FAX: (212) 724-4239.

HOLLYWOOD NEWSREEL SYNDICATE INC.
1622 N. Gower St., Hollywood, CA 90028. (213) 469-7307. FAX: (213) 469-8251.

THE IMAGE BANK/THE IMAGE BANK WEST
111 Fifth Ave., New York, NY 10003. (212) 539-8300. FAX: (212) 539-8370.
2400 Broadway, #220, Santa Monica, CA 90404. (310) 264-4850. FAX: (310) 453-1482.

INTERNATIONAL COLOR STOCK, INC.
3841 N.E. 2nd Ave., Ste. 304, Miami, FL 33137-3639. (305) 573-5200. email: ins@mindspring.com
CONTACT
R. Taylor

INTERVIDEO INC.
1500 N. Burbank Blvd., Burbank, CA 91506-1309. (818) 843-3624, (800) 843-3626. FAX: (818) 843-6884.

JALBERT PRODUCTIONS, INC.
775 Park Ave., Huntington, NY 11743. (516) 351-5878.

KESSER STOCK LIBRARY
21 S.W. 15th Rd., Miami, FL 33129. (305) 358-7900, (800) 785-3843. FAX: (305) 358-2209. email: kesser@icanect.net
URL: http://www.kesser.com

CLAY LACY AVIATION INC.
7435 Valjean Ave., Van Nuys, CA 91406. (818) 989-2900. FAX: (818) 909-9537. URL: http://www.claylacy.com
ADMINISTRATIVE DIRECTOR
Tina Gossman

LIBRARY OF MOVING IMAGES INC.
6671 Sunset Blvd., #1581, Hollywood, CA 90028. (323) 469-7499. FAX: (323) 469-7559.
OWNER
Michael Peter Yakaitis

MACGILLIVRAY FREEMAN FILMS
P.O. Box 205, Laguna Beach, CA 92652. (714) 494-1055. FAX: (714) 494-2079.
STOCK LIBRARIAN
Robert Walker

MUSEUM OF MODERN ART FILM LIBRARY
11 W. 53 St., New York, NY 10019. (212) 708-9400.

MUSEUM OF NATURAL HISTORY FILM ARCHIVES
Central Park W. at 79th St., New York, NY 10024. (212) 769-5419.

NBC NEWS ARCHIVES
30 Rockefeller Plaza, Rm. 280-E, New York, NY 10112. (212) 664-3797. FAX: (212) 957-8917.

NATIONAL GEOGRAPHIC FILM LIBRARY
1145 17th St. NW, Washington, DC 20036. (202) 857-7659., (202) 775-6167. FAX: (202) 429-5755.
NATIONAL SALES MANAGER
Sally Russell

4370 Tujunga Ave., Ste. 300., Studio City, CA 91604. (818) 506-8300. FAX: (818) 506-8200.
CONTACT
Robyn Paul

1251 6th Ave., 17th Flr., New York, NY 10020. (212) 221-5842. FAX: (212) 221-5815.
CONTACT
Erica Sashin

PALISADES WILDLIFE LIBRARY
1205 S. Ogden Dr., Los Angeles, CA 90019. (213) 931-6186.

PARAMOUNT PICTURES STOCK FOOTAGE LIBRARY
5555 Melrose Ave., Hollywood, CA 90038. (213) 956-5510, (888) 264-9009. FAX: (213) 862-1833, (888) 264-9011
email: Pat Harris@Paramount.com
URL: http://www.Paramountstock.com
HEAD LIBRAIAN
Pat Harris

PASSPORT INTERNATIONAL PRODUCTIONS
10520 Magnolia Blvd., North Hollywood, CA 91601. (818) 760-1500. FAX: (818) 760-1532. email: passport4@earthlink.net
VICE PRESIDENT OF OPERATIONS
Jeanette Pugliese

PRODUCERS LIBRARY SERVICE
1051 N. Cole Ave., Hollywood, CA 90038. (213) 465-0572. FAX: (213) 465-1671. email: stockftg@primenet.com
URL: http://www.filmfootage.com
OWNER
Jeff Goodman

PYRAMID FILM & VIDEO
2801 Colorado Ave., Santa Monica, 90404. (310) 828-7577. FAX: (310) 453-9083. email: info@pyramidmedia.com
URL: http:// www.pyramidmedia.com
PRESIDENT
Randy Wright

A RETROSPECT FILM ARCHIVE
11693 San Vicente Blvd., #111, Los Angeles, CA 90049. (310) 471-1906, (415) 948-7526. FAX: (310) 471-1430
URL: http://nettwork@hotmail.com
DIRECTOR
Patrick Netter

REUTERS NEWMEDIA INC.
1700 Broadway, 15th Flr., New York, NY 10019. (212) 603-3850. FAX: (212) 397-3003.

RO-MA STOCK
1003 S. Los Robles Ave., Pasadena, CA 91106-4332. (818) 799-7733. FAX: (818) 799-6622. email: romastock@aol.com
PRESIDENT
Robert Marien

SECOND LINE SEARCH
1926 Broadway, 5th Flr., New York, NY 10023. (212) 787-7500. FAX: (212) 787-7636. email: clips@secondline.com
CONTACT
Eileen Kelly

THE SOURCE STOCK FOOTAGE
738 N. Constitution Dr., Tucson, AZ 85748. (520) 298-4810. FAX: (520) 290-8831. email: Requests@sourcefootage.com
URL: http://www.sourcefootage.com
LIBRARY MANAGER
Don French

SPECTRAL COMMUNICATIONS
178 S. Victory Blvd., #106, Burbank, CA 91502. (818) 840-0111. FAX: (818) 840-0618.

THE STOCK HOUSE
6922 Hollywood Blvd., Ste. 621, Los Angeles, 90028. (213) 461-0061. FAX: (213) 461-2457.
VICE PRESIDENT OF OPERATIONS
Allison Hopeland

TOTAL RESEARCH/ANDREA SCHARF
(213) 933-2200. FAX: (213) 933-2818. email: andscharf@aol.com
URL: http://footage.net

UCLA FILM & TELEVISION ARCHIVE
1015 N. Cahuenga Blvd., Hollywood, CA 90038. (213) 466-8559. FAX: (213) 461-6317.
CONTACT
Howard Hays

UNIVERSAL STOCK FOOTAGE LIBRARY
100 Universal City Plaza, Bldg. 99, Rm. 213, Universal City, 91608. (818) 777-3000. FAX: (818) 733-1579.
email: jzwilli@unistudios.com
URL: http://www.universalstudios.com
HEAD LIBRARIAN
John Willison

VIDEO TAPE LIBRARY, LTD.
1509 N. Crescent Heights Blvd. #2, Los Angeles, 90046. (323) 656-4330. FAX: (323) 656-8746. email: vtl@earthlink.net
URL: http://www.videotapelibrary.com
PRESIDENT
Melody St. John

WISH YOU WERE HERE FILM & VIDEO
1455 Royal Blvd., Glendale, CA 91207. (818) 243-7043. FAX: (818) 241-1720.

Studio & Equipment Rentals

Including Editing equipment and Services

ACCLAIM WEST
2046 Armacost Ave., West Los Angeles, CA 90025. (310) 207-3319.

THE ACTOR AGENCY
7000 E. Tanque Verde, Ste. 17, Tucson, AZ 85715. (520) 721-9582. FAX: (520) 751-7589.

ADVENTURE FILM STUDIOS
40-13 104 St., Queens, NY 11368. (718) 478-2639.

THE ALLIED NETWORK
7355 N.W. 41st St., Miami, FL 33166. (305) 532-2410.

AMS PRODUCTIONS
13709 Gamma Rd., Dallas, TX 75244. (972) 701-0878.

HOWARD A. ANDERSON COMPANY
100 Universal City Plaza, Ste. 504-3, Universal City, CA 91608. (818) 777-2402. FAX: (818) 733-1118.

5418 McConnell Ave., Los Angeles, CA 90066. (805) 823-5511. FAX: (805) 823-5501.

APOLLO THEATRE FOUNDATION, INC.
253 W. 125 St., New York, NY 10027. (212) 222-0992. FAX: (212) 749-2743.
CONTACT
Charlotte Sutton

APRICOT ENTERTAINMENT, INC.
940 N. Oragne Dr., Hollywood, CA 90038. (213) 469-4000. FAX: (213) 469-5809.

ATELIER CINEMA VIDEO STAGES
295 W. 4 St., New York, NY 10014. (212) 243-3550.

AVALON STAGES
6918 Tujunga Ave., N. Hollywood, CA 91605. (818) 508-0505. FAX: (818) 508-5581.

AVID TECHNOLOGY
115 N. First ST., Suite 208, Burbank, CA 91502. (818) 557-2520. FAX: (818) 557-2558.
REGIONAL SALES MANAGER
Michael Piccus

THE BARKER HANGAR/SANTA MONICA AIR CENTER
3021 Airport Ave., Ste. 203, Santa Monica, CA 90405-6117. (310) 390-9071, (310) 262-4144. FAX: (310) 391-8824.

BC STUDIOS
152 W. 25 St., New York, NY 10001. (212) 242-4065.

BIG VALLEY STAGE
7311 Radford Ave., N. Hollywood, CA 91605. (818) 340-1256.

BIRNS & SAWYER, INC.
1026 N. Highland Ave., Hollywood, CA 90038. (213) 466-8211. FAX: (213) 466-7049. email: INFO@BIRNSandSAWYER.com
PRESIDENT
Marvin Stern
RENTAL MANAGER
Mark Schweickart

BOKEN SOUND STUDIO
513 W. 54 St., New York, NY 10019. (212) 581-5507

BROADWAY STUDIOS STAGE A
25-09 Broadway, Astoria, NY 11106. (718) 274-9121. FAX: (718) 274-8510

BURBANK MEDIA CENTER
2801 W. Olive Ave., Burbank, CA 91505. (818) 845-3531.

CAMERA SERVICE CENTER INC.
(Rentals: 16mm, 35mm, 65mm cameras, lighting & grip equipment, cranes, dollies, trucks and generators)
619 W. 54 St., New York, NY 10019. (212) 757-0906. FAX: (212) 713-0075. URL: http://www.cameraservice.com
V.P., OPERATIONS
Hardwrick Johnson

THE CANNELL STUDIOS
7083 Hollywood Blvd., Hollywood, CA 90028. (213) 465-5800. FAX: (213) 463-4987.

CARMAN PRODUCTIONS INC.
15456 Cabrito Rd., Van Nuys, CA 91406. (818) 787-6436. FAX: (818) 787-3981.
CONTACT
Tom Skeeter

CARTHAY STUDIOS, INC.
5907 W. Pico Blvd., Los Angeles, CA 90035. (213) 938-2101. FAX: (213) 936-2769.

CBS STUDIO CENTER
4024 N. Radford Ave., Studio City, CA 91604. (818) 760-5000. FAX: (818) 760-5048.

CBS TELEVISION CITY
7800 Beverly Blvd., Los Angeles, CA 90036. (213) 852-2345.

CECO INTERNATIONAL CORP.
440 W. 15 St., New York, NY 10011. (212) 206-8280. FAX: (212) 727-2144.
CONTACT
Jody Baran

CFI (CONSOLIDATED FILM INDUSTRIES)
959 Seward St., Hollywood, CA 90038. (213) 960-7444. FAX: (213) 460-4885.

CHAMBERS MEDIA CENTER
2975 Chad Dr., Eugene, OR 97408. (541) 485-5611. FAX: (541) 342-1568. email: dlarson@cmc.net
URL: http://www..cmc.net/~cpc
FACILITIES MANAGER
Dave Larson

CHANDLER TOLUCA LAKE STUDIOS
11405 Chandler Blvd., N. Hollywood, CA 91601. (818) 763-3650. FAX: (818) 990-4755.

CHAPLIN STAGE
1416 N. La Brea Ave., Hollywood, CA 90028. (213) 856-2682. FAX: (213) 856-2795.

THE CHICAGO PRODUCTION CENTER
5400 N. St. Louis Ave., Chicago, IL 60625-4698. (773) 509-5555. FAX: (773) 583-3046. URL: http://www.wttw.com

CINEMA SERVICES OF LAS VEGAS
4445 South Valley View Blvd., #7 & 8, Las Vegas, NV 89103. (702) 876-4667. FAX: (702) 876-4542.

CINEWORKS-SUPERSTAGE
1119 N. Hudson Ave., Los Angeles, CA 90038. (213) 464-0296. FAX: (213) 464-1202.

PETER COHN/SOLAR STUDIOS
1601 S. Central Ave., Glendale, CA 90214. (818) 240-1893.

COLUMBIA COLLEGE, HOLLYWOOD
18618 Oxnard St., Tarzana, CA 91356-1411. (213) 851-0550. FAX: (213) 345-9053.

Dep't. of Cinema, 925 N. La Brea Ave., Hollywood, CA 90038. (213) 851-0550. FAX: (213) 851-6401.

THE COMPLEX
6476 Santa Monica Blvd., Hollywood, CA 90038. (213) 465-0383. FAX: (213) 469-5408.

THE CULVER STUDIOS
9336 W. Washington Blvd., Culver City, CA 90230. (310) 202-1234. FAX: (310) 202-3272.
CONTACT
Jack Kindberg

DELFINO STUDIOS
12501 Gladstone Ave., Sylmar, CA 91342. (818) 361-2421. FAX: (818) 361-5891.

THE WALT DISNEY STUDIOS
500 S. Buena Vista St., Burbank, CA 91521. (818) 560-5151, (818) 560-1000. FAX: (818) 560-1930.

WALT DISNEY/MGM STUDIOS
3300 N. Bonnett Creek Rd., Lake Buena Vista, FL 32830. (407) 560-5353. (407) 560-6188.

DOCTORIAN ENTERTAINMENT
814 E. Claremont St., Pasadena, CA 91104. (626) 794-7747. FAX: (626) 794-7737.

DOS CARLOS STAGES & STANDING SETS
1360 E. 6th St., Los Angeles, CA 90021. (310) 306-4555. FAX: (213) 627-5950. email: dcstagecss@aol.com
CONTACT
Diane Markoff

EDIT DECISIONS, LTD.
311 W. 43 St., New York, NY 10036. (212) 757-4742. FAX: (212) 757-5258.

EDIT POINT POST PRODUCTION SYSTEMS
620 N. Victory Blvd., Burbank, CA 91502. (818) 841-7336. FAX: (818) 841-7378.

THE EDITING COMPANY
8300 Beverly Blvd., Los Angeles, CA 90048. (213) 653-3570. FAX: (213) 653-8855.

EDITING CONCEPTS
7 W 22nd St., New York, NY 10010. (212) 367-7373.

THE EDITING MACHINE, INC.
630 Ninth Ave., New York, NY 10036. (212) 757-5420.

EMPIRE BURBANK STUDIOS
1845 Empire Ave., Burbank, CA 91504. (818) 840-1400. FAX: (818) 567-1062.
CONTACTS
Don Buccola
Felix Girard

ENTITY PRODUCTIONS, INC.
106 N. Glendale Blvd., #216, Glendale, CA 91206. (818) 562-4311.
PRESIDENT
Mark Enzenauer

FARKAS FILMS, INC.
385 Third Ave., New York, NY 10016. (212) 679-8212. FAX: (212) 889-8354. URL: http://www.non-stop.com/farkas
F. E. Robinson

GLENDALE STUDIOS
1239 S. Glendale Ave., Glendale, CA 91205. (818) 502-5300, (818) 502-5500. FAX: (818) 502-5555. email: glenstudio@aol.com URL: http://www.glendalestudios.com
CONTACTS
Steven Makhanian

GLOBECAST
3872 Keystone Ave., South Culver City, CA 90232. (310) 845-3900. FAX: (310) 845-3904. URL: http://www.globecast.com
6430 Sunset Blvd., Ste. 1400, Los Angeles, CA 90028. (213) 467-8900. FAX: (213) 465-8750.

GLOBUS STUDIOS
44 W. 24 St., New York, NY 10011. (212) 243-1008.

GMT STUDIOS
5751 Buckingham Parkway, Unit C, Culver City, CA 90230. (310) 649-3733. FAX: (310) 216-0056.

ALAN GORDON ENTERPRISES, INC.
1430 Cahuenga Blvd., Hollywood, CA 90028. (213) 466-3561. FAX: (213) 871-2193. email: info@alangordon.com
PRESIDENT
Grant Louks
VICE PRESIDENT
Don Sahlein
GENERAL MANAGER
Wayne Loucks

GREENWICH STUDIOS, INC.
12100 Ivanvan Tors Blvd., North Miami, FL 33161. (305) 899-9467. FAX: (305) 895-0560.

GTE VISNET
112 Lakeview Canyon Rd., Thosand Oaks, CA 91362. (800) 626-3150. FAX: (805) 372-5727. email: visnet@gte.sprint.com URL: http://www.gtevisnet.com

HARPO STUDIOS
1058 W. Washington Blvd., Chicago, IL 60607. (312) 633-1000.

HAYVENHURST STUDIOS
7017 Hayvenhurst Ave., Van Nuys, CA 91406. (818) 909-6999. FAX: (818) 782-0635.

HBO STUDIO PRODS.
120 E. 23 St., New York, NY 10010. (212) 512-7800.

HERO PRODUCTIONS
7291 N.W. 74th St., Miami, FL 33166. (305) 887-1600. FAX: (305) 887-4121.

HI-TECH RENTALS
(Video/audio equipment rental, production, presentation, staging services.)
2907 W. Olive Ave., Burbank, CA 91505. (213) 469-9000, (800) 954-3000. FAX: (818) 848-0112.
URL: http://www.hitechrentals.com
CONTACT
Andrew Bruce Overton

HOLLYWOOD CENTER STUDIOS, INC.
1040 N. Las Palmas Ave., Los Angeles, CA 90038. (213) 860-0000. FAX: (213) 860-8105. email: rschnyder@hollywoodcenter.com URL: http://www.hollywoodcenter.com
CONTACT
Richard Schnyder

HOLLYWOOD NATIONAL STUDIOS
1043 N. Seward, Hollywood, CA 90038. (213) 467-6272.

THE HOLLYWOOD STAGE
6650 Santa Monica Blvd., Los Angeles, CA 90038. (213) 466-4393. FAX: (213) 463-5514. email: hwdstage@worldnetaccescc.com URL: http://www.studiorental.com

HORVATH & ASSOCIATES STUDIOS LTD.
744 Greenwich St., New York, NY 10014. (212) 367-7550.

THE IMAGE GROUP
401 5th Ave., New York, NY 10016. (212) 592-0600.

INC PRODUCTIONS
12401 W. Olympic Blvd., Los Angeles, CA 90064. (310) 893-2371. FAX: (310) 447-7906. email: icnproductions@i-channel.com URL: http://www.i-channel.com

INTER VIDEO, INC.
1500 W Burbank Blvd Burbank CA 91506 (818) 843-3633, (818) 569-4000. FAX: (818) 843-6884.

INTERSOUND INC.
8746 Sunset Blvd., Los Angeles, CA 90069. (310) 652-3741. FAX: (310) 854-7290. email: kent@intersound.com
CONTACT & PRESIDENT
Kent Harrison Hayes

KAUFMAN ASTORIA STUDIOS
34-12 36th St., Astoria, NY 11106. (718) 392-5600. FAX: (718) 706-7733.

KCET STUDIOS
4401 W. Sunset Blvd., Los Angeles, CA 90027. (213) 953-5258, (213) 666-6500. FAX: (213) 953-5496.

BEN KITAY STUDIOS STAGES TEN & FIFTEEN
1015 N. Cahuenga Blvd., Stage 15, Hollywood, CA 90038. (213) 466-9015. FAX: (213) 466-4421.

LIGHTING & PRODUCTION EQUIPMENT, INC.
1379 Logan Circle NW Atlanta GA 30318 (404) 352-0464.

LIFETIME STUDIOS
34-12 36th St., Astoria, NY 11106. (718) 706-3600. FAX: (718) 706-3500. email: brill@lifetimetv.com

LIGHTING SERVICES, INC.
241 S. Cherokee St., Denver, CO 80223. (303) 722-4747. FAX: (303) 722-4537.

LOS ANGELES THEATRE CENTER
514 S. Spring St., Los Angeles, CA 90013. (213) 627-6500. FAX: (213) 847-3169.

MAGNO SOUND INC.
729 Seventh Ave., New York, NY10019. (212) 302-2505.

MELROSE STAGE
1215 Bates Ave., Los Angeles, CA 90029. (213) 660-8466.

MOLE-RICHARDSON CO.
937 N. Sycamore Ave., Los Angeles 90038. (213) 851-0111.

MODERN TELECOMMUNICATIONS/MTI
1 Dag Hammarskjold Pl., New York, NY 10017. (212) 355-0510.

MORO-LANDIS
10960 Ventura Blvd., Studio City, CA 91604. (818) 753-5081. FAX: (818) 752-1689.

MOTHERS FILM STAGE
210 E. 5 St., New York, NY 10003. (212) 529-5097.

MOVIE TECH STUDIOS
832 N. Seward St., Hollywood, CA 90038. (213) 467-8491. FAX: (213) 467-8471.

NATIONAL VIDEO CENTER/RECORDING STUDIOS, INC.
460 W. 42 St., New York, NY 10036. (212) 279-2000.

NBA ENTERTAINMENT, INC.
450 Harmon Meadow Blvd., Secaucus, NJ 07094. (201) 865-1500. FAX: (201) 974-6159.

NBC TELEVISION
3000 W. Alameda Ave., Burbank, CA 91523. (818) 840-4444.

NEW JERSEY PRODUCTION CENTER
PO Box 777, Trentaon, NJ 08625-0777. (609) 777-5200. FAX: (609) 633-2932. email: fred_litwinowicz@njn.pbs.org

NEW MEXICO FILM OFFICE
PO Box 20003, Santa Fe, NM 87504-5003. (800) 545-9871.
FAX: (505) 827-9799. email: film@edd.state.nm.us
URL: http://www.edd.state.nm.us
DIRECTOR
Linda Taylor Hutchinson

NORTHWEST TELEPRODUCTIONS
142 E. Ontario, Ste. 300, Chicago, IL 60611. (312) 337-6000.
FAX: (312) 337-0500.

OCCIDENTAL STUDIOS
201 N. Occidental Blvd., Los Angeles, CA 90026. (213) 384-
3331. FAX: (213) 384-2684. email: oxy@earthlink.net
URL: http://www.netzonecom/~realss/oxstudio.html

THE PALACE
1735 N. Vine St., Hollywood, CA 90028. (213) 462-6031. FAX:
9213) 462-0579.

PANAVISION
6219 De Soto Ave., Woodland Hills, CA 91367. (818) 316-
1000. FAX: (818) 316-1111.

PASADENA PRODUCTION STUDIOS
39 E. Walnut St., Pasadena, CA 91103-3832. (626) 584-4090.
FAX: (626) 584-4099.

PARAMOUNT STUDIO GROUP
5555 Melrose Ave., Los Angeles, CA 90038. (213) 956-5000.

PATCHETT KAUFMAN ENTERTAINMENT
8621 Hayden Place, Culver City, CA 90232. (310) 838-7000.

PC&E PRODUCTION CONSULTANTS & EQUIPMENT
2335 De Foor Hills Rd., NW Atlanta, GA 30318. (800) 537-
4021. FAX: (404) 609-9926.

PRIMALUX VIDEO PRODUCTION, INC.
30 W. 26 St., New York, NY 10010. (212) 206-1402. FAX: (212)
206-1826.
CONTACT
Judy Cashman

RALEIGH STUDIOS
5300 Melrose Ave., Los Angeles, CA 90038. (213) 466-3111.
FAX: (213) 871-5600.
CONTACT
Sharon Bode

REMOTE IMAGES
3206 W. Lake Ave., Glenview, IL 60025. (847) 729-8070.

REN-MAR STUDIOS
846 North Cahuenga Blvd., Los Angeles, CA 90038. (213) 463-
0808. FAX: (213) 465-8173.

SANTA CLARITA STUDIOS
25135 Anza Dr., Santa Clarita, CA 91355. (805) 294-2000.
FAX: (805) 294-2020

SCREEN JUMP STUDIOS
1223 N. 23 St., Wilmington, NC 28405. (910) 343-3500.

SCREENLAND STUDIOS, INC.
3800 W. Burbank Blvd., Burbank, CA 91505. (818) 843-2262.
FAX: (818) 843-2261.

SCREENLAND STUDIOS II
10501 Burbank Blvd., North Hollywood, CA 91601. (818) 508-
2288. FAX: (818) 753-8953.

MACK SENNETT STAGE
1215 Bates, Los Angeles, CA 90029. (213) 660-8466. FAX:
(213) 953-1706.

SHINBONE ALLEY STAGE
680 Broadway, New York, NY 10012. (212) 420-8463.

SILVERCUP STUDIOS
42-22 22nd St., Long Island City, NY 11101. (718) 784-3390,
(212) 349-9600.

S.I.R. STUDIOS
8660 Hayden Pl., Culver City, CA 90232. (310) 287-3600. FAX:
(310) 287-3608.

SONY PICTURES STUDIOS
10202 W. Washington Blvd., Culver City, CA 90232. (310) 280-
6926. FAX: (310) 244-8090.

SOURCE FILMS STUDIOS
1150 S. La Brea Ave., Los Angeles, CA 90019. (213) 938-
4762. FAX: (213) 931-9565.

SOUTH LAKE STAGE
293 S. Lake, Burbank, CA 91502. (818) 953-8400. FAX: (818)
956-0268.

STUDIO AKIVA/AKIVA FILMS
31 Washington St., Brooklyn, NY 11201. (718) 802-0531. FAX:
(718) 834-0025.

SUNSET-GOWER STUDIOS LTD.
1438 N. Gower St., Los Angeles, CA 90028. (213) 467-1001.
FAX: (213) 467-2717.

TELETECHNIQUES, INC.
1 W. 19 St., New York, NY 10011. (212) 206-1475.

TELEVISION CENTER
6311 Romaine St., Los Angeles, CA 90038. (213) 464-6638.

3-G STAGE CORP.
236 W. 61 St., New York, NY 10023. (212) 247-3130.

TWENTIETH CENTURY FOX FILM CORP
10201 W. Pico Blvd., Los Angeles, CA 90035. (310) 369-3762.
FAX: (310) 369-8858.
DIRECTOR OF PROD. FACILITIES & SPECIAL EVENTS
Wil Guido

UFO DOWNTOWN
2476 Hunter St., Los Angeles, CA 90021. (213) 694-0556.

UNITEL VIDEO
515 W. 57 St., New York, NY 10019. (212) 265-3600. FAX:
(212) 765-5801.

UNIVERSAL STUDIOS
100 Universal City Plaza, Universal City, CA 91608. (800) 892-
1979. FAX: (818) 866-0293..

UNIVERSAL STUDIOS FLORIDA
1000 Universal Studios Plaza, Orlando, FL 32819. (407) 363-8400.

VANCO LIGHTING SERVICES
1902 Cypress Lake Dr Ste 100., Orlando, FL 32837. (407)
855-8060. FAX: (407) 855-8059.

VERITAS STUDIOS
527 W. 45 St., New York, NY 10036. (212) 581-2050.

VIDEO PLANNING INC.
250 W. 57 St., New York, NY 10019. (212) 582-5066.

VISION CREW UNLIMITED
5939 Rodeo Rd., Los Angeles, CA 90016. (310) 558-0450.
FAX: (310) 558-0437. email: visioncrew@visioncrew.com
URL: http://www.visioncrew.com

VPS STUDIOS
800 N. Seward St., Hollywood, CA 90038. (213) 469-7244.
FAX: (213) 463-7538.

WARNER BROS. STUDIOS FACILITIES
4000 Warner Blvd., Burbank, CA 91522. (818) 954-3000, (818)
954-2577. FAX: (818) 954-2677. email: wbsf@warnerbros.com
URL: http://www.wbsf.com
CONTACT
Tracy Balsz

THE WARNER DRIVE WAREHOUSE
8461 Warner Dr., Culver City, CA 90232. (310) 841-6572. FAX:
(310) 559-7362.

WARNER HOLLYWOOD STUDIOS
1041 N. Formosa Ave., W. Hollywood, CA 90046. (213) 850-
3180. FAX: (213) 850-3189.
URL: http://www.warnerhollywood.com

JOHN WARREN ENTERTAINMENT, INC.
25241 Ave. stanford Valencia, CA 91355. (805) 257-9292. FAX:
(805) 257-1963. email: info@warrenent.com
URL: http://www.warrenent.com

WESLEY MORRIS ENTERTAINMENT
6711 Valjean, Van Nuys, CA 91406. (818) 909-9600. FAX:
(818) 909-4111.

WHITEFIRE THEATRE, THE SOUNDSTAGE RENTAL
13500 Ventura Blvd., Sherman Oaks, CA 91423. (818) 989-
9146.
Dan Hirsch

WTN-WORLDWIDE TV NEWS PRODS.
1995 Broadway, New York, NY 10023. (212) 362-4440. FAX:
(212) 446-1269.

Subtitles & Captions

BERLITZ TRANSLATION CENTER
525 Broadway, St.e 300, Santa Monica, CA 90401. (310) 260-7100. FAX: (310) 260-7185.

CAPTION CENTER
(Closed Captions, Subtitles, Dual-Languge Captioning)
610 N. Hollywood Way, Ste. 350, Burbank, CA 91505. (818) 562-3344. FAX: (818) 562-3388.
MARKETING REPRESENTATIVE
Michelle Maddalena

125 Western Ave., Boston, MA 02134. (617) 492-9225. FAX: (617) 582-0590. URL: http://www.wgbh.org/caption
MANAGER, NEW BUSINESS DEVELOPMENT
Margaret Albright

475 Park Ave. S., 10th floor, New York, NY 10016. (212) 223-4930. FAX: (212) 688-2181.
MARKETING MANAGER
Donna Horn

CAPTIONMAX
(Closed-Captioning/Foreign Language Captioning)
708 N. 1st St., Suite 238, Minneapolis, MN 55401. (800) 822-3566. FAX: (612) 341-2345. URL: http://www.captionmax.com

CAPTIONS, INC.
(Closed-Captions, Subtitles, Translations)
5744 San Fernando Rd., Glendale, CA 91202. (818) 500-7301. FAX: (818) 500-7023. email: rob_troy@captionsinc.com
SALES MANAGER
Robert Troy

619 W. 54th St., 5th Flr., New York, NY 10019. (212) CAP-TION. FAX: (212) 262-4855.
CONTACT
John Baxter

541 N. Fairbanks Ct., Ste. 2030, Chicago, IL 60611. (773) CAP-TION. FAX: (773) 527-0948.
CONTACT
Marko Iglendza

CINETYP, INC.
843 Seward St., Hollywood, CA 90038. (213) 463-8569. FAX: (213) 463-4129. email: cinetyp@aol.com
PRODUCTION MANAGER
Dave Margolis

CREST NATIONAL DIGITAL MEDIA COMPLEX
1000 N. Highland Ave., Hollywood, CA 90038. (213) 860-1300. FAX: (213) 466-7128. email: John_Walker@crestnational.com
URL: http://www.crestnational.com
EXECUTIVE V.P. OF SALES & MARKETING
John Walker

1141 N. Seward, Hollywood, CA 90038. (213) 462-6696. FAX: (213) 462-5039.

DEVLIN VIDEO SERVICE
1501 Broadway, Suite 408, New York, NY 10036. (212) 391-1313.

FOREIGN LANGUAGE GRAPHICS
12517 Chandler Blvd., #102, Valley Village, CA 91607. (818) 753-9584. FAX: (818) 753-9617. URL: http://www.ISItrans.com

GELULA & CO., INC.
8421 Wilshire Blvd., Ste. 205, Beverly Hills, CA 90211. (213) 651-1167. FAX: (213) 651-3612. email: gelula@compuserve.com
URL: http://www.gelula.com
PRESIDENT
Elio Zarurati

GLOBAL LANGUAGE SERVICES
(Translation Services & Foreign Language Supervision)
2027 Las Lunas, Pasadena, CA 91107. (626) 792-0862, (626) 792-0576. FAX: (818) 792-8793. email: globallang@aol.com
URL: http://aebi@hss.caltech.edu
CONTACT
Dr. Andreas Aebi

HOMER AND ASSOCIATES, INC.
Sunset Gower Studios, 1420 N. Beachwood Dr., Hollywood, CA 90028. (213) 462-4710.

INTEX AUDIOVISUALS
9021 Melrose Ave., Suite 205, Los Angeles, CA 90069. (310) 275-9571. FAX: (310) 271-1319.

LASER VIDEO TITRES INC.
375 Greenwich St., New York, NY 10013. (212) 343-1910. FAX: (212) 965-1338.
CHAIRMAN
Denis Auboyer
DIRECTOR, DEVELOPMENT
Valerie Gorge

LINGUATHEQUE OF L.A.
13601 Ventura Blvd., #102, Sherman Oaks, CA 91423. (818) 995-8933. FAX: (818) 995-1228.
CONTACT
Karen Delaney

MARCLAND INTERNATIONAL COMMUNICATIONS
P.O. Box 3100, Burbank, CA 91508. (818) 557-6677. FAX: (818) 567-0568. email: info@marcland.com
URL: http://www.marcland.com
CEO
Alfredo Marco Fulchignoni

MASTERWORDS
(Subtitles, Dialogue, Continuity)
1512 Eleventh St., #205, Santa Monica, CA 90401-2907. (310) 390-1033. FAX: (310) 394-7954.

NATIONAL CAPTIONING INSTITUTE
(Closed-Captioning, Subtitling)
303 N. Glenoaks Blvd., Ste. 200, Burbank, CA 91502. (818) 238-0068. FAX: (818) 238-4266. email: dougroberts@earthlink.net
URL: http://www.ncicap.org/nci
MARKETING DIRECTOR
Doug Roberts

545 5th Ave., Ste. 1101, New York, NY 10017. (212) 557-7011. FAX: (212) 557-6975. email: mail@ncicap.org
V.P. OF MARKETING
Betty Hallman

1900 Gallows Rd., Suite 3000, Vienna, VA 22182. (703) 917-7600. FAX: (703) 917-9853.

PACIFIC TITLE & ART STUDIO
6350 Santa Monica Blvd., Los Angeles, CA 90038. (213) 464-0121. FAX: (213) 938-6364.

P.F.M. DUBBING INTERNATIONAL
1007 Montana Ave., Ste. 306, Santa Monica, CA 90403. (310) 451-6068. FAX: (310) 451-6058.
PRESIDENT
Andre Guimond

JOY RENCHER'S EDITORIAL SERVICE
738 Cahuenga Blvd., Hollywood, CA 90038. (213) 463-9836. FAX: (213) 469-0377.

STS FOREIGN LANGUAGE SERVICES
(Foreign Language Translations, Subtitling, Voice-Overs)
P.O. Box 10213, Burbank, CA 91510. (818) 508-1454.
email: STSMedia@aol.com

SOFTNI SUBTITLING & DUBBING INTERNATIONAL
11444 W. Olympic Blvd., #200, Los Angeles, CA 90064. (310) 312- 9558. FAX: (310) 445-8800. email: info@softni.com
URL: http://www.softni.com
PRESIDENT
Jose M. Salgado

TITLE HOUSE INC.
738 N. Cahuenga Blvd., Los Angeles, CA 90038. (213) 469-8171. FAX: (213) 469-0377.

TITRA CALIFORNIA, INC.
(Laser Subtitles)
733 Salem St., Glendale, CA 91203. (818) 244-3663. FAX: (818) 244-6205. email: lalaser@aol.com
URL: http://www.titra.com
MANAGING DIRECTOR
Daniele Allen

285 W. Broadway, Ste. 560, New York, NY 10013. (212) 334-6927. FAX: (212) 334-6935. email: raoulny@aol.com
CONTACT
Justin King

V.I.T.A.C.
4450 Lakeside Dr., Ste. 250, Burbank, CA 91505. (818) 295-2490. FAX: (818) 295-2494. email: vitacla@aol.com

WORDS IN PICTURES
1028 S. Alfred, Los Angeles, CA 90035. (213) 655-9221. FAX: (213) 655-3350.

TALENT AGENCIES

ABRAMS ARTISTS AGENCY
9200 Sunset Blvd., 11th Flr., Los Angeles, CA 90069. (310) 859-0625. FAX: (310) 276-6193.
420 Madison Ave., Ste. 1400, New York, NY 10017. (212) 935-8980. FAX: (212) 935-2862.

ABRAMS, RUBALOFF & LAWRENCE.
8075 West 3rd, Ste. 303, Los Angeles, CA 90048. (213) 935-1700. FAX: (213) 932-9901.

ABOVE THE LINE AGENCY
9200 Sunset Blvd., #401, Los Angeles, CA 90069. (310) 859-6115.
AGENT
Rime Greer

ACME TALENT & LITERARY
6310 San Vicente Blvd., Ste. 520, Los Angeles, CA 90048. (213) 954-2263.

ACTORS ETC. INC.
2620 Foutainview, Ste. 210, Houston, TX 77057. (713) 785-4495. FAX: (713) 785-2641. email: actoretc@insync.net.
AGENT
Denise Coburn

ACTORS GROUP AGENCY
8730 Sunset Blvd., Ste. 220 W., Los Angeles, CA 90069. (310) 657-7113. FAX: (310) 657-1756.
157 W. 57 St., Ste. 211, New York, NY 10019. (212) 245-2930. FAX: (212) 245-7096.
CONTACT
Pat House

BRET ADAMS LTD.
448 W. 44th St., New York, NY 10036. (212) 765-5630. FAX: (212) 265-2212.

THE AGENCY
1800 Avenue of the Stars, #400, Los Angeles, CA 90067. (310) 551-3000. FAX: (310) 551-1424.
AGENTS
Elime Gladstone, Jerry Zeitman, Walter Van Dyke, Walter Morgan, Nick Mechanic

AGENCY FOR THE COLLABORATIVE ARTS
132 W. 22nd St., 4th Flr., New York, NY 10011. (212) 807-8344.

AGENCY 2 TALENT AGENCY
2425 San Diego Ave., Ste. 211, San Diego, CA 92110-2876. (619) 291-9556. FAX: (619) 291-4952.
URL: http://www.showbizdatabase.com/A2
AGENTS
Lois Ringe, Terry Ringe

AGENTS FOR THE ARTS
203 W. 23rd St., 3rd Flr., New York, NY 10011. (212) 229-2562.

AIMEE ENTERTAINMENT ASSOCIATION
1500 Ventura Blvd., Ste. 340, Sherman Oaks, CA 91403. (818) 783-9115. FAX: (818) 783-8308.

AKO PRODUCTIONS
20531 Plummer St., Chatsworth, CA 91311. (818) 998-0443. FAX: (818) 998-2537.

ALLIANCE TALENT INC.
9171 Wilshire Blvd., Ste. 441, Beverly Hills, CA 90210. (310) 858-10190.
1501 Broadway, # 404, New York, NY 10036. (212) 840-6868

THE ALPERN GROUP
4400 Coldwater Canyon, Ste. 125, Studio City, CA 91604. (818) 752-1877. FAX: (818) 752-1859.

CARLOS ALVARADO AGENCY
8455 Beverly Blvd., Ste. 406, Los Angeles, CA 90048-3416. (213) 655-7978.

MICHAEL AMATO THEATRICAL AGENCY
1650 Broadway, Ste. 307, New York, NY 10019. (212) 247-4456.

AMBROSIO/MORTIMER & ASSOCS. INC.
5757 Wilshire Blvd., Ste. 512, Beverly Hills, CA 90036. (213) 954-1888. FAX: (213) 954-1666.
165 W. 46th St., Ste.1214, New York, NY 10036. (212) 719-1677. FAX: (212) 768-9361.

AMERICAN INTERNATIONAL TALENT AGENCY
303 W. 42 St., Ste. 608, New York, NY 10036. (212) 245-8888. FAX: (212) 245-8926.

AMSEL, EISENSTADT & FRAZIER, INC.
5757 Wilshire Blvd. #510, Los Angeles, CA 90036. (213) 939-1188. FAX: (213) 939-0630.
CO-OWNERS/THEATRICAL AGENTS
Michael Eisenstadt, John Frazier

ANDREADIS TALENT AGENCY, INC.
119 W. 57th St., Ste. 711, New York, NY 10019. (212) 315-0303. FAX: (212) 315-0311.

BEVERLY ANDERSON
1501 Broadway, New York, NY 10036. (212) 944-7773.

ANIIMANAGEMENT
245 E. Olive Ave., Ste. 400, Burbank, CA 91502. (818) 526-7600. FAX: (818) 526-7606.

APA/AGENCY FOR THE PERFORMING ARTS
9200 Sunset Blvd., Ste. 900, Los Angeles, CA 90069. (310) 273-0744. FAX: (310) 888-4242.
888 Seventh Ave., Ste 602, New York, NY 10106. (212) 582-1500. FAX: (212) 245-1647.
3322 West End Ave., Ste. 520, Nashville, TN 37203. (615) 297-0100. FAX: (615) 297-5434.
PRESIDENT
James H. Goswell

ARIA MODEL & TALENT MANAGEMENT
1017 W. Washington, Ste. 2-C, Chicago, IL 60607. (312) 243-9400. FAX: (312) 243-9020. URL: http://www.ariamodel.com
DIRECTOR
Mary Boncher

ARTIST MANAGEMENT AGENCY
835 5th Ave., Ste. 411, San Diego, CA 92101. (619) 233-6655. FAX: (619) 233-5332.
PRESIDENT
Nanci Washburn

ARTIST NETWORK
8438 Melrose Pl., Los Angeles, CA 90039. (213) 651-4244. FAX: (213) 651-4699.
Debra Hope

THE ARTISTS AGENCY
10000 Santa Monica Blvd., Ste. 305, Los Angeles, CA 90067. (310) 277-7779. FAX: (310) 785-9338.
LITERARY AGENTS, PARTNERS
Mickey Friedberg, Richard Shepherd, Merrily Kane
TALENT AGENT, PARTNER
Jim Cota

THE ARTISTS GROUP LTD.
1930 Century Park W., # 403, Los Angeles, CA 90067. (310) 552-1100. FAX: (310) 277-9513.
1650 Broadway, Ste. 711, New York, NY 10036. (212) 586-1452. FAX: (212) 586-0037.
AGENTS
Art Rutter, Susan Grant, Hal Stalmaster

ASSOCIATED BOOKING CORP.
1995 Broadway, New York, NY 10023. (212) 874-2400.

RICHARD ASTOR
250 W. 57th St., New York, NY 10107. (212) 581-1970

ATKINS & ASSOCS.
303 S. Crescent Heights Blvd., Los Angeles, CA 90048. (213) 658-1025.

BADGLEY/CONNOR
9229 Sunset Blvd., #311, Los Angeles, CA 90069. (310) 278-9313. FAX: (310) 278-4128.

BALDWIN TALENT, INC.
1640 5th St., Ste. 201, Los Angeles, CA 90049. (310) 899-1166.

BAUMAN, HILLER & ASSOCS.
5757 Wilshire Blvd., PH 5, Los Angeles, CA 90036. (213) 857-6666. FAX: (213) 857-0368.
250 W. 57 St., #2223, New York, NY 10019. 757-0098. (212) 757-0098. FAX: (212) 489-8531.

BENNETT AGENCY
150 S. Barrington Ave., Suite 1, Los Angeles, CA 90049. (310)
471-2251. FAX: (310) 471-2254.

THE SARA BENNETT AGENCY
6404 Hollywood Blvd. Ste. 316, Hollywood, CA 90028. (213)
965-9666.

BERMAN, BOALS AND FLYNN, INC.
225 Lafayette St., Ste. 1207, New York, NY 10012. (212) 966-
0339.

BERZON TALENT AGENCY
336 E. 17th St., Costa Mesa, CA 92627. (714) 631-5936.
email: marian@berzon.com
URL: http://www.berzon.com

THE BLAKE AGENCY
415 N. Camden Dr., Ste. 111, Beverly Hills, CA 90210. (310)
246-0241. FAX: (310) 246-0244.
CONTACTS
Merritt Blake, Niki Mirisch

BLOOM AT FORD
8826 Burton Way, Beverly Hills, CA 90211. (310) 859-9300.

J. MICHAEL BLOOM & ASSOC.
9255 Sunset Blvd., Ste. 710, Los Angeles, CA 90069. (310)
275-6800. FAX: (310) 275-6941.

THE BOHRMAN AGENCY
8489 W. 3rd St., Los Angeles, CA 90048. (213) 653-6701. FAX:
(213) 653-6702.

BONTALENT, INC.
146 Great Oak Dr., Hapstead, NC 82443. (910) 270-9413.
FAX: (910) 270-9490.
PRESIDENT
John Bonitz

BORINSTEIN ORECK BOGART AGENCY
8271 Melrose Ave., Ste. 110, Los Angeles, CA 90046. (213)
658-7500. FAX: (213) 658-8866.

THE BRANDT COMPANY
15250 Ventura Blvd., #720, Sherman Oaks, CA 91403. (818)
783-7747. FAX: (818) 784-6012. email: brandtco@aol.com
CONTACT
Geoffrey Brandt

BRESLER KELLY & ASSOCIATES
15760 Ventura Blvd., #1730, Encino, CA 91436. (818) 905-1155.

BREVARD TALENT GROUP, INC.
405 Palm Springs Blvd., Indian Harbour Beach, FL 32937. (407)
773-1355. FAX: (407) 773-1842. email: brevtalent@aol.com
PRESIDENT
Traci Danielle

CURTIS BROWN, LTD.
10 Astor Pl., 3rd Flr., New York, NY 10003. (212) 473-5400.

DON BUCHWALD & ASSOCIATES
9229 Sunset Blvd., Ste. 710, Los Angeles, CA 90069. (310)
278-3600. FAX: (213) 278-4099.
AGENT
Tim McNeil

10 E. 44th St., New York, NY 10017. (212) 867-1200.
AGENT
Traci Chung

BURKETT TALENT AGENCY
27001 La Paz Rd., #41800, Mission Viejo, CA 92691. (714)
830-6300. FAX: (714) 830-6399.
AGENT
Nancy Burkett
Jackie Ashman

DON BURNS TALENT AGENCY
478 Severn, Tampa, FL 33606. (813) 251-5882. FAX: (813)
253-2363

IRIS BURTON AGENCY
PO Box 15306, Beverly Hills, CA 90219. (310) 288-0121. FAX:
(310) 274-4882.

CAA/CREATIVE ARTISTS AGENCY
9830 Wilshire Blvd., Beverly Hills, CA 90212. (310) 288-4545.
FAX: (310) 288-4800.
AGENTS
Mike Ovitz, Bill Haber, Ron Meyer, Rowland Perkins, Todd
Smith, David O'Connor, David Tenzer, Michael Menchel, Adam
Krentzman, Glenn Bickel, Sonya Rosenfield, Jack Rapke, Rand
Holston, Jane Sindell, Rosalie Swedlin, David Lonner, Joe
Rosenberg, Brian Lourd, Justin Connolly

THE CAMPBELL AGENCY
3906 Lemmon Ave., Ste. 200, Dallas, TX 75219. (214) 522-8991.

CAPITOL ARTISTS
(213) 658-8118. FAX: (213) 658-7871.
CONTACTS
Nancy Delafuente
Gloria Hinojosa

WILLIAM CARROLL AGENCY
139 N. San Fernando Blvd., Ste. A, Burbank, CA 91502. (818)
848-9948. FAX: (818) 845-1769.

CARRY CO. TALENT REPS.
1501 Broadway, Ste. 1410, New York, NY 10036. (212) 768-
2793. FAX: (212) 768-2713.

CARSON ADLER AGENCY, INC.
250 W. 57th St., Ste. 808, New York, NY 10107. (212) 307-
1842. FAX: (212) 541-7008.
PRESIDENT
Nancy Carson
SENIOR AGENTS
Bonnie Deroski, Shirley Faison

CASSELL-LEVY, INC.
843 N. Sycamore Ave., Los Angeles, CA 90038. (213) 461-
3971. FAX: (213) 461-1134.

CAVALERI & ASSOCIATES
405 Riverside Dr., Ste. 200, Burbank, CA 91506. (818) 955-
9300. FAX: (818) 955-9399.
Ray Cavaleri

CENTURY ARTISTS, LTD.
3511 Sealedge Lane, Santa Barbara, CA 93109. (310) 395-
3800. FAX: (310) 393-7988.

THE CHASIN AGENCY
8899 Beverly Blvd., Ste. 716, Los Angeles, CA 90048. (310)
278-7505. FAX: (310) 275-6685.

CINEMA TALENT AGENCY
8033 W. Sunset Blvd., #808. Los Angeles, CA 90046. (213)
656-1937. FAX: (213) 654-4678.

CIRCLE TALENT AGENCY
433 N. Camden Dr., #400, Beverly Hills, CA 90210. (310) 285-
1585.

CIRCUIT RIDER TALENT & MANAGEMENT
123 Walton Ferry Rd., Hendersonville, TN 37075. (615) 824-
1947. FAX: (615) 264-0462. email: dotwool@bellsouth.net.com
PRESIDENT
Linda S. Dotson
SENIOR AGENT
Doreen Patten

W. RANDOLPH CLARK COMPANY
13415 Ventura Blvd., Suite 3, Sherman Oaks, CA 91423. (818)
385-0583. FAX: (818) 385-0599.
PRESIDENT
W. Randolph Clark
V.P.,TALENT
Arlene Tsurutani

CLINC TALENT AGENCY
843 N. Sycamore Ave., Los Angeles, CA 90038. (213) 461-
3971. FAX: (213) 461-1134.
PRESIDENT
Leanna Levy
SENIOR AGENTS
Richard Ohanesian, Ed Ilsen

COAST TO COAST TALENT GROUP, INC.
4942 Vineland Ave., Ste. 200, North Hollywood, CA 91601.
(818) 762-6278. FAX: (818) 762-7049.

COLLEEN CLER AGENCY
178 S. Victory Blvd., #108, Burbank, CA 91502. (818) 841-
7943. FAX: (818) 841-4541.

COLOURS TALENT AGENCY
8344-1/2 W. 3rd St., Los Angeles, CA 90048. (213) 658-7072.

COMMERCIALS UNLIMITED, INC.
9601 Wilshire Blvd., #620, Los Angeles, CA 90210. (310) 888-
8788. FAX: (310) 888-8712.

CONTEMPORARY ARTISTS LTD. TALENT AGENCY
1317 5th St., #200, Santa Monica, CA 90401. (310) 395-1800.
FAX: (310) 394-3308.

COPELAND CREATIVE TALENT
4140 1/2 Grand Ave., Des Moines, IA 50312. (515) 271-5970.
FAX: (515) 277-0770. email: copetalent@aol.com
OWNER
Debra Copeland

CORALIE JR. AGENCY
4789 Vineland Ave., #100, N. Hollywood, CA 91602. (818) 766-9501.
AGENT, ACTORS & ACTRESSES
Stuart Edward
LITERARY AGENT
Gary Dean

THE COSDEN AGENCY
3518 Cahuenga Blvd. West., Ste. 216, Los Angeles, CA 90068. (213) 874-7200.

THE CRAIG AGENCY
8485 Melrose Pl., Ste. E, Los Angeles, CA 90069. (213) 655-0236. FAX: (213) 655-1491.

CUNNINGHAM, ESCOTT, DIPENE & ASSOC.
10635 Santa Monica Blvd., Los Angeles, CA 90025-4900.
Commercial: (310) 475-2111; Children's: (310) 475-3336. FAX: (310) 475-1929.
257 Park Ave. South, New York, NY 10010. Comerical: (212) 477-1666; Children's: (212) 477-6622. FAX: (212) 979-2011.
One East Superior St., Suite 505, Chicago, IL 60611. (312) 944-5600. FAX: (312) 944-5694.

DADE/SCHULTZ ASSOCS.
12302 Sarah St., Studio City, CA 91604. (818) 760-3100. FAX: (818) 760-1395.

D.D.K.
9744 Wilshire Blvd., Ste. 203, Beverly Hills, CA 90212. (310) 274-9356.
16 W. 22nd St., 7th Flr., New York, NY 10010. (212) 727-7820.

DH TALENT AGENCY
1800 N. Highland Ave., Ste. 300, Los Angeles, CA 90028. (213) 962-6643.

DIAMOND ARTISTS AGENCY, LTD.
215 N. Barrington Ave., Los Angeles, CA 90049. (310) 472-7579. FAX: (310) 472-2687.

DOUGLAS, GORMAN, ROTHACKER & WILHELM
1501 Broadway, Ste. 703, New York, NY 10036. (212) 382-2000.

DURKIN ARTISTS AGENCY
127 Broadway, Ste. 210, Santa Monica, CA 90401. (310) 458-5377. FAX: (310) 458-5337.

DUVA-FLACK ASSOCIATES INC.
200 W. 57th St., Ste. 1008, New York, NY 10019. (212) 957-9600. FAX: (212) 957-9606.

DYTMAN & ASSOCIATES
9200 Sunset Blvd., Ste. 809, Los Angeles, CA 90069. (310) 274-8844.

ELITE CASTING
2820 Eagle St., New Orleans, LA 70118. (504) 861-0245.

ELLIS TALENT GROUP
6025 Sepulveda Blvd., Ste. 201, Van Nuys, CA 91411. (818) 997-7447.

ENDEAVOR
9701 Wilshire Blvd., 10th Flr., Beverly Hills, CA 90212. (310) 248-2000. FAX: (310) 248-2020.

ENTERTAINMENT ENTERPRISES
1680 Vine St. Ste. 519, Los Angeles, CA 90028. (213) 462-6001, (213) 462-6002. FAX: (213) 462-6003.

EPSTEIN-WYCKOFF & ASSOCIATES
311 W. 43rd St., Ste. 304, New York, NY 10036. (212) 586-9110. FAX: (212) 586-8019.

CAROL FAITH AGENCY
280 South Beverly Dr., Suite 411, Beverly Hills, CA 90212. (310) 274-0776. FAX: (310) 274-2670. email: carolatcfa@aol.com
PRESIDENT
Carol Faith

E. FARRELL/C.COULTER TALENT AGENCY
PO Box 15189, North Hollywood, CA 91615. (818) 765-0400. FAX: (818) 765-0153.

FAVORED ARTISTS
122 S. Robertson Blvd., #202, Los Angeles, CA 90048. (310) 247-1040. FAX: (310) 247-1048.
AGENTS
Amy Mackie, Peter Albers
230 W. 55th St., Ste. 29-D, New York, NY 10019. (212) 245-6960. FAX: (212) 333-7420.

FERRAR MAZIROFF ASSOCIATES
8430 Santa Monica Blvd., Ste. 220, West Hollywood, CA 90069. (213) 654-2601. FAX: (213) 654-2979.

THE FIELD-COCH AGENCY INC.
12725 Ventura Blvd., Ste. D, Studio City, CA 91604. (818) 980-2001. FAX: (818) 980-0754.

LIANA FIELDS AGENCY
7081 N. Marks Ave., #104-175, Fresno, CA 93711-0232. (213) 487-3656.

FILM ARTISTS ASSOCIATES
13563 Ventura Blvd., 2nd floor, Sherman Oaks, CA 91423. (818) 386-9669. FAX: (818) 386-9363.
CEO
Cris Dennis
PRESIDENT
Penrod Dennis

FILM MUSIC ASSOCS.
6525 W. Sunset Blvd., 3rd Flr., Hollywood, CA 90028. (213) 463-1070. FAX: (213) 463-1077.
SENIOR AGENTS
John Tempereau, Michael Horner

FIRST ARTISTS AGENCY
10000 Riverside Dr., Ste. 10, Toluca Lake, CA 91602. (818) 509-9292. FAX: (818) 509-0523.

FLASHCAST ET AL.
Centrum Towers, Ground floor, 3575 Cahuenga Blvd. West, Universal City, CA 90068. (818) 760-7986, (800) 273-9008. FAX: (818) 760-6792.
OWNER
Carl Carranza
CONTACT & ACCOUNTING MANAGER
Richard Weiner

FLICK EAST-WEST TALENTS INC.
9057 Nemo St., Suite A, W. Hollywood, 90069. (310) 247-1777. FAX: (310) 858-1357.
Carnegie Hall Studio 1110, 881 Seventh Ave., New York, NY 10019. (212) 307-1850.

FOLKLORE PRODUCTIONS, INC.
1671 Appian Way, Santa Monica, CA 90401. (310) 451-0767. FAX: (310) 458-6005. email: 71222.2600@compuserve.com
URL: http://www.rootsworld.com/folklore/

THE BARRY FREED COMPANY
2049 Century Park E. Ste. 1200, Los Angeles, CA 90067. (310) 277-1260. FAX: (310) 277-3865.

ALLIE FRIES AGENCY
1927 Vista Del Mar Ave., Hollywood, CA 90068. ((213) 464-6491.

FRONTIER BOOKING INTERNATIONAL
1560 Broadway, Ste 1110, New York, NY 10036. (212) 221-0220.

THE GAGE GROUP
9255 Sunset Blvd., Ste. 515, Los Angeles, CA 90069. (310) 859-8777. FAX: (310) 859-8166.
315 W. 57 St., Ste. 4H, New York, NY 10019. 541-5250. FAX: (212) 956-7466.

GARBER TALENT AGENCY
2 Pennsylvania Plaza, Ste. 1910, New York, NY 10121. (212) 292-4910.

DALE GARRICK INTL. AGENCY
8831 Sunset Blvd., #402, Los Angeles, CA 90069. (310) 657-2661.

GEDDES AGENCY
8430 Santa Monica Blvd. #200, W. Hollyood, CA 90069. (213) 848-2700.
PRINCIPLE
Ann Geddes
AGENTS
Anne Margaret Tower
Glenn Hughes III
AGENT, LITERARY
Dana Wright

DON GERLER TALENT AGENCY
3349 Cahuenga Blvd. West, Ste. 1, Los Angeles, CA 90068. (213) 850-7386. FAX: (213) 850-7490.

THE GERSH AGENCY
232 N. Canon Dr., Beverly Hills, CA 90210. (310) 274-6611. FAX: (310) 274-4035.
AGENTS
Phil Gersh, David Gersh, Nancy Nigrosh, Maryann Kellt, Lee Keele, Jim Lefkowitz, Richard Arlook
130 W. 42 St., #2400, New York, NY 10036. (212) 997-1818. FAX: (212) 391-8459.
AGENTS
David Guc, Scott Yoselow

THE GILCHRIST TALENT GROUP
630 9th Ave., Ste. 800, New York, NY 10036. (212) 692-9166.

GILLA ROOS LTD.
9744 Wilshire Blvd., #203, Beverly Hills, CA 90212. (310) 274-9356. FAX: (310) 274-3604.

GOLD/MARSHAK/LIEDKE ASSOCIATES
3500 W. Olive, Ste. 1400, Burbank, CA 91505. (818) 972-4300. FAX: (818) 955-6411.

THE GOLDEY COMPANY
1156 S. Carmelina, Los Angeles, CA 90049. (310) 447-6611. FAX: (310) 447-6616.

GORFAINE/SCHWARTZ AGENCY INC.
13245 Riverside, Ste. 450, Sherman Oaks, CA 91423. (818) 461-9600. FAX: (818) 461-9622.

GOTHIC ARTIST AGENCY
699 Bay St., Santa Monica, CA 90405. (310) 581-9102. FAX: (310) 581-9383. email: megaent@aol.com
PRESIDENT
Diane Anderson

MARY GRADY AGENCY
4444 Lankershim Blvd., Ste. 207, North Hollywood, CA 91602. (818) 766-4414. FAX: (818) 766-3860.

GREEN & ASSOCIATES
8899 Beverly Blvd., Ste. 705, Los Angeles, CA 90048. (310) 288-2100. FAX: (310) 274-3835.

LARRY GROSSMAN & ASSOCIATES
211 S. Beverly Dr., St.e 206, Beverly Hills, CA 90212. (310) 550-8127. FAX: (310) 550-8129.

THE HAEGGSTROM OFFICE
6404 Wilshire Blvd., Ste. 1100, Los Angeles, CA 90048. (213) 658-9111. FAX: (213) 658-5518. email: idyshark@wavenet.com

BUZZ HALLIDAY & ASSOCIATES
8899 Beverly Blvd., Ste. 715, Los Angeles, CA 90048. (310) 275-6028. FAX: (310) 275-8514.

HAMILBURG AGENCY
292 S. La Cienega, Suite 312, Beverly Hills, CA 90211. (310) 657-1501.

VAUGHN D. HART
8899 Beverly Blvd., Ste. 815, Los Angeles, CA 90048. (310) 273-7887. FAX: (310) 273-7924.

MICHAEL HARTIG
156 Fifth Ave., New York, NY 10010. (212) 929-1772.

BEVERLY HECHT AGENCY
12001 Ventura Pl., Ste. 320, Studio City, CA 91604. (818) 505-1192. FAX: (818) 505-1590.

HENDERSON/HOGAN AGENCY
247 S. Beverly Dr., #102, Beverly Hills, CA 90212. (310) 274-7815. FAX: (310) 274-0751.
850 Seventh Ave., New York, NY 10019. (212) 765-5190. (212) 586-2855.

THE HOUSE OF REPRESENTATIVES
400 S. Beverly Dr., Ste. 101, Beverly Hills, CA 90212. (310) 772-0772. FAX: (310) 772-0998.

HOWARD TALENT WEST
11712 Moorpark St., Ste. 205B, Studio City, CA 91604. (818) 766-5300. FAX: (818) 760-3328. email: me10u90@wavenet.com

H.W.A. TALENT REPRESENTATIVES
1964 Westwood Blvd., Ste. 400, Los Angeles, CA 90025. (310) 446-1313.
36 E. 22nd St., 3rd Flr., New York, NY 10010. (212) 529-4555.

IFA TALENT AGENCY
8730 Sunset Blvd., #490, Los Angeles, CA 90069. (310) 659-5522. FAX: (310) 659-3344.

INNOVATIVE ARTISTS
1999 Ave. of the Stars, Suite 2850, Los Angeles, CA 90067-6082. (310) 553-5200. FAX: (310) 557-2211.
141 5th Ave., Ste. 3S, New York, NY 10010. (212) 253-6900. FAX: (212) 253-1198.
OWNER
Scott Harris

INTERNATIONAL CREATIVE MANAGEMENT
8942 Wilshire Blvd., Beverly Hills, CA 90211. (310) 550-4000. FAX: (310) 550-4100.
AGENTS
Alan Greenspan, Michael Black, Bill Douglas, Barbara Dreyfus, Richard Feldman, Diane Cairns, Mitch Douglas, Lee Gabler, Tony Howard, Scott Amovitz, Steve Rabineau, Joe Rosenberg, Scott Schwartz, Jim Wiatt, David Lonner, Bob Gumer, Dave Wirtschafter, Alan Berger, Nancy Josephson, Jeff Berg, Lou Pitt.
40 W. 57 St., New York, NY 10019. (212) 556-5600. (212) 556-5665.
AGENTS
Sam Cohn, Lisa Loosemore, Boaty Boatwright, Paul Martino, Andrea Eastman, Sue Leibaman.

IT MODEL MANAGEMENT
526 N. Larchmont Blvd., Los Angeles, CA 90004. (213) 962-9564. FAX: (213) 962-3087.

JACKMAN & TAUSSIG ENTERTAINMENT
1815 Butler Ave., Ste. 120, Los Angeles, CA 90025. (310) 478-6641. FAX: 9310) 444-8935.

JACKSON ARTISTS CORP.
7251 Lowell Dr., Overland Park, Ste. 200, KS 66204. (913) 384-6688. FAX: (913) 384-5353.
CEO
Dave Jackson
SENIOR AGENTS
Jean Newland, Tom Zang

JAN J. AGENCY
365 W. 34 St., New York, NY 10001. (212) 967-5265.

THE GEORGE JAY AGENCY
6269 Selma Ave., Hollywood, CA 90028. (213) 466-6665. FAX: (213) 462-6197.
AGENTS
George Jay, Anthony Freeman

JORDAN, GILL & DORNBAUM
156 Fifth Ave., #711, New York, NY 10010. (212) 463-8455. FAX: (212) 691-6111.

KAPLAN-STAHLER-GUHMER AGENCY
8383 Wilshire Blvd., #923, Beverly Hills, CA 90211. (213) 653-4483. email: TKSA@aol.com
PARTNERS
Mitchell T. Kaplan, Elliot J. Stahler, Robert Guhmer

KAZARIAN AND SPENCER AND ASSOCS. INC.
11365 Ventura Blvd., #100, Studio City, CA 91604. (818) 769-9111. FAX: (818) 769-9840.

KELMAN/ARLETTA AGENCY
7813 Sunset Blvd., Los Angeles, CA 90046. (213) 851-8822. FAX: (213) 851-4923.

TYLER KJAR AGENCY
10643 Riverside Dr., Toluca Lake, CA 91602. (818) 760-0321.
PRESIDENT
Tyler Kjar
SENIOR AGENTS
Brandon Kjar, Candy Potter, Julie Edwards

THE ERIC KLASS AGENCY
144 S. Beverly Dr., Beverly Hills, CA 90212. (310) 274-9169.

PAUL KOHNER AGENCY
9300 Wilshire Blvd., #555, Beverly Hills, CA 90212. (310) 550-1060. FAX: (310) 276-1083.

THE KRAFT-BENJAMIN AGENCY
345 N. Maple Dr., Suite 385, Beverly Hills, CA 90210. (310) 247-0123. FAX: (310) 247-0066. email: kbagency@aol.com
CONTACTS
Richard Kraft, Lyn Benjamin, Laura Engel

THE KRASNY OFFICE
1501 Broadway, Ste. 1303, New York, Ny 10036. (212) 730-8160. FAX: (212) 768-9379.

L.A. ARTISTS AGENCY
606 Wilshire Blvd., #416, Santa Monica, CA 90401. (310) 395-9589.

L.A. TALENT
8335 Sunset Blvd., 2nd Flr., Los Angeles, CA 90069. (213) 656-3722. FAX: (213) 650-4272. email: general@lamodels.com
URL: http://www.lamodels.com

CANDACE LAKE AGENCY
9229 Sunset Blvd., Ste. 320, Los Angeles, CA 90069. (310) 247-2115. FAX: (310) 247-2116.

LALLY TALENT AGENCY
630 9th Ave., Ste. 800, New York, NY 10036. (212) 974-8718.

STACEY LANE TALENT AGENCY
13455 Ventura Blvd., Ste. 240, Sherman Oaks, CA 91423. (818) 501-2668. FAX: (818) 501-0765.

SUSAN LANE MODEL & TALENT AGENCY, INC.
14071 Windsor Pl., Santa Ana, CA 92705. (714) 731-1420. FAX: (714) 731-5223.
PRESIDENT & CEO
Susan Lane
MANAGING DIRECTOR
Grace Berukoff
ASSISTANT DIRECTOR
Sharon Moiseiff

THE LANTZ OFFICE
888 Seventh Ave., #2500, New York, NY 10106. (212) 586-0200. FAX: (212) 262-6659.

LIONEL LARNER LTD.
119 W. 57 St., Suite 1412, New York, NY 10019. (212) 246-3105. FAX: (212) 956-2851.

JACK LENNY ASSOCIATES
9454 Wilshire Blvd., Ste. 600, Beverly Hills, CA 90212. (310) 271-2174. FAX: (310) 271-3540.

BUDDY LEE ATTRACTIONS, INC.
38 Music Square East, Nashville, TN 37203. (615) 244-4336. FAX: (615) 726-0429. email: blanash@aol.com
PRESIDENT
Tony Conway
S.V.P.
John Sachel
VICE PRESIDENTS
Paul Lohr, Kevin Neal

THE LEVIN AGENCY
8484 Wilshire Blvd., Ste. 745, Beverly Hills, CA 90211. (213) 653-7073. FAX: (213) 653-0280.

ROBIN LEVY & ASSOCIATES
9220 Sunset Blvd., Ste. 305, Los Angeles, CA 90069. (310) 278-8748. FAX: (310) 278-8767.

TERRY LICHTMAN COMPANY
4439 Wortser Ave., Studio City, CA 91604. (818) 783-3033. FAX: (818) 783-3009.

THE ROBERT LIGHT AGENCY
6404 Wilshire Blvd., Ste. 900, Los Angeles, CA 90048. (213) 651-1777. FAX: (213) 651-4933. email: rlatalent@aol.com

KEN LINDNER & ASSOCIATES INC.
2049 Century Park East., Ste. 2750, Los Angeles, CA 90067. (310) 277-9223. FAX: (310) 277-5806.

LOOK TALENT
166 Geary St., San Francisco, CA 94108. (415) 781-2841. FAX: (415) 781-5722.

LOVELL & ASSOCIATES
7095 Hollywood Blvd., Los Angeles, CA 90028. (213) 462-1672.

JANA LUKER TALENT AGENCY
1923 1/2 Westwood Blvd., Suite 3, Los Angeles, CA 90025. (310) 441-2822. FAX: (310) 441-2820.
PRESIDENT
Jana Luker
SENIOR AGENT
Kathy Keeley

LYNNE & REILLY AGENCY
10725 Vanowen St., Ste. 113, N. Hollywood, CA 91605. (213) 850-1984.

THE LYONS/SHELDON AGENCY
800 S. Robertson Blvd., Los Angeles, CA 90035. (310) 652-8778. FAX: (310) 652-8772..

SANDRA MARSH MANAGEMENT
9150 Wilshire Blvd., #220, Beverly Hills, CA 90210. (310) 285-0303. FAX: (310) 285-0218.

MARTIN & DONALDS TALENT AGENCY INC.
1915-A Hollywood Blvd., Hollywood, FL 33020. (954) 921-2427. FAX: (954) 921-7635.

JOHNNIE MARTINELLI ATTRACTIONS, INC.
888 Eighth Ave., New York, NY 10019. (212) 586-0963. FAX: (212) 581-9362.
PRESIDENT
John Martinelli
TALENT DEVELOPMENT
Hyun Mi Lee

MARGE McDERMOTT
216 E. 39 St., New York, NY 10016. (212) 889-1583.

MCQUEENEY MANAGEMENT, INC.
10279 Century Woods Dr., Los Angeles, CA 90067. (310) 277-1882.

MEDIA ARTISTS GROUP
8383 Wilshire Blvd., Ste. 954, Beverly Hills, CA 90211-2408. (213) 658-5050. FAX: 9213) 658-7871.

MERIDIAN TALENT AGENCY
499 N. Cannon Dr., Ste. 313, Beverly Hills, CA 90210. (310) 887-7034. FAX: (310) 887-7009.
OWNER/CONTACT
Dorothy Day Otis

METROPOLITAN TALENT AGENCY
4526 Wilshire Blvd., Los Angeles, CA 90010. (213) 857-4500. FAX: (213) 857-4599. URL: http://www.mta.com
PRESIDENT
Christopher Barrett

MIRAMAR TALENT AGENCY
7400 Beverly Dr., Ste. 220, Los Angeles, CA 90036. (213) 934-0700.

THE MIRISCH AGENCY
10100 Santa Monica Blvd., #700, Los Angeles, CA 90067. (310) 282-9940. FAX: (310) 282-0702. email: mirischagy@aol.com
PRESIDENT
Lawrence A. Mirisch
SENIOR AGENTS
Penny Key, Robin Schreer

MITCHELL TALENT MANAGEMENT
323 Geary St., Ste. 302, San Francisco, CA 94102. (514) 395-9475. FAX: (415) 395-9301.

PATTY MITCHELL AGENCY
4605 Lankershim Blvd., Ste. 408, N. Hollywood, CA 91602. (818) 508-6181.

MONTANA ARTISTS
625 Montana Ave., 2nd Flr., Santa Monica, CA 90403. (310) 576-3456. FAX: (310) 576-7840.

WILLIAM MORRIS AGENCY
151 El Camino Dr., Beverly Hills, CA 90212. (310) 859-4000. FAX: (310) 859-4462.
1325 Ave. of the Americas, New York, NY 10019. (212) 586-5100. FAX: (212) 246-3583.
2100 West End Ave., Ste. 100, Nashville, TN 37203. (615) 963-3000. FAX: (615) 963-3090.
AGENTS
Jeff Hunter, Gene Parseghian, Lee Rosenberg, John Riley, Scott Zimmerman, Leonard, Hirshan, Arthur Axelman, Ala Izeman, Jeff Field, Rich Hess, George Lane, Mary Meagher, John Burnham, Bill Butler, Johnny Planco, Frank Frataroli, Dave Phillips, Emily Gerson, Joan Fields, Chris Simonian, John Sheinberg, Greg LIpstone, Larry Taube.

H. DAVID MOSS & ASSOCIATES
733 N. Seward St., Penthouse, Hollywood, CA 90038. (213) 465-1234. FAX: (213) 465-1241.

MOTION ARTISTS, INC.
1400 N. Hayworth Ave., Ste. 36, Los Angeles, CA 90046. (213) 851-7737. FAX: (213) 851-7649.
PRESIDENT
Philip Mittell

NATIONWIDE ENTERTAINMENT SERVICES
2756 N. Green Valley Pkwy., #449, Las Vegas, NV 89014. (702) 451-8090. URL: http://www.EntertainmentServices.com
PRESIDENT
A.J. Sagman
AGENTS
S. Rosenthal, Deb Manning

OMNIPROP INC. TALENT AGENCY WEST
10700 Ventura Blvd., 2nd Flr., Studio City, 91604. (818) 980-9267. FAX: (818) 980-9371.
55 W. Old Country Rd., Hicksville, NY 11801. (516) 937-6011. FAX: (516) 937-6209.

OPPENHEIM-CHRISTIE ASSOC.
13 E. 37 St., New York, NY 10016. (212) 213-4330.

FIFI OSCARD AGENCY
24 W. 40 St., New York, NY 10018. (212) 764-1100.

DOROTHY DAY OTIS & ASSOCIATES
499 N. Canon St., Ste. 313, Beverly Hills, CA 92120. (310) 887-7028. FAX: (310) 887-7009.

OTTO MODEL & TALENT AGENCY
1460 N. Sweetzer Ave., West Hollywood, CA 90069. (213) 650-2200. FAX: (213) 650-1134. URL: http://www.quikpage.com/o/ottomod
PRESIDENT
Jason C. Otto

PAKULA/KING & ASSOCIATES
9229 Sunset Blvd., Ste. 315, Los Angeles, CA 90069. (310) 281-4868. FAX: (310) 281-4866.

DOROTHY PALMER TALENT AGENCY INC.
235 W. 56th St., Ste. 24-K, New York, NY 10019. (212) 765-4280.

PARADIGM A TALENT & LITERARY AGENCY
10100 Santa Monica Blvd., 25th Flr., Los Angeles, CA 90067. (310) 277-4400. FAX: (310) 277-7820.
200 W. 57th St., Ste. 900, New York, NY 10019. (212) 246-1030.
AGENTS
Ken Gross, Bernard Weintraub, Gary Pearl, Stu Robinson, Doug Brodex, Kerry Jones, Lucy Stille

PINE MOUNTAIN TALENT AGENCY
1042 Willow Creek Rd., Ste A-111-125, Prescott, AZ 86301. (520) 771-1380. FAX: (520) 445-4090.

THE PLAYERS TALENT AGENCY
8770 Shoreham Dr., Ste. 2, West Hollywood, CA 90069. (310) 289-9797. FAX: (310) 289-8779.

RICHARD POIRIER MODEL & TALENT AGENCY
3575 Cahuenga Blvd., West. Ste. 254, Los Angeles, CA 90068. (213) 969-9990. FAX: (213) 850-3382.

PREFERRED ARTISTS
16633 Ventura Blvd., Ste. 1421, Encino, CA 91436. (818) 990-0305. FAX: (818) 990-2736.
AGENTS
Lew Weitzman, Roger Strull, Sylvia Hirsch, Susie Weissman

PREMIER TALENT AGENCY
3 E. 54 St., New York, NY 10022. (212) 758-4900. FAX: (212) 755-3251.

PREMIERE ARTISTS AGENCY
8899 Beverly Blvd., #510, Los Angeles, CA 90048. (310) 271-1414. FAX: (310) 205-3981.

JIM PREMINGER AGENCY
1650 Westwood, Ste. 201,Los Angeles, CA 90024. (310) 475-9491. FAX: (310) 470-2934.
AGENTS
Jim Preminger, Harvey Harrison, Monica Riordan

PRIVILEGE TALENT AGENCY
9229 Sunset Blvd., Ste. 414, West Hollywood, CA 90069.

PRODUCERS & CREATIVES GROUP INC.
7060 Hollywood Blvd., Ste. 1025, Los Angeles, CA 90028. (213) 465-5475. FAX: (213) 461-2967.

PROGRESSIVE ARTISTS AGENCY
400 S. Beverly Dr., Ste. 216, Beverly Hills, CA 90212. (310) 553-8561. FAX: (310) 553-4726.

GORDON RAEL COMPANY
9229 Sunset Blvd., Ste. 310, Los Angeles, CA 90069. (310) 285-0572.

RENAISSANCE
(310) 858-5365. FAX: (310) 858-5389.
email: renaissance@earthlink.net
PARTNERS
Alan Nevins, Irv Schwartz, Joel Gotler

THE RICHLAND AGENCY
11777 San Vicente Blvd., Ste. 702, Los Angeles, CA 90049. (310) 571-1833. FAX: (310) 571-1834.

THE ROBERTS COMPANY
10345 W. Olympic Blvd., PH, Los Angeles, CA 90064. (310) 552-7800. FAX: (310) 552-9324.

THE MARION ROSENBERG OFFICE
8428 Melrose Pl., Suite B, Los Angeles, CA 90069. (213) 653-7383. FAX: (213) 653-9268.
AGENT
Matthew Lesher

THE ROTHMAN AGENCY
9465 Wilshire Blvd., Ste. 840, Beverly Hills, CA 90212. (310) 247-9898. FAX: (310) 247-9888.

THE SANDERS AGENCY LTD.
8831 Sunset Blvd., Suite 304, Los Angeles, CA 90069. (310) 652-1119. FAX: (310) 652-7810. email: snadersla@aol.com
1204 Broadway, Suite 306, New York, NY 10001. (212) 779-3737.
PRESIDENT & OWNER
Honey Sanders, Gretchen Osmond
TV & MP, EQUITY, NY
Barbara Sanders, Leo Simard

THE SAVAGE AGENCY
6212 Banner Ave., Los Angeles, CA 90038. (213) 461-8316. FAX: (213) 461-2417.

IRV SCHECTER COMPANY
9300 Wilshire Blvd., #400, Beverly Hills, CA 90212. (310) 278-8070. FAX: (310) 278-6058. email: iscagency@aol.com
AGENTS
Irv Schechter, Victorya Michaels, Debbee Klein, Don Klein, Charlotte Savavi, Debra Lieb, Andrea Simon, Michael Magules

SCHULLER TALENT
276 Fifth Ave., New York, NY 10001. (212) 532-6005.

WILLIAM SCHILL AGENCY
250 W. 57th St., Ste. 2402, New York, NY 10107. (212) 315-5919. FAX: 9212) 397-7366.

DON SCHWARTZ & ASSOC.
6922 Hollywood Blvd., #508, Los Angeles, CA 90028. (213) 464-4366. FAX: (213) 464-4661.

SEVEN SUMMITS PICTURES & MANAGEMENT
8447 Wilshire Blvd., Ste. 206, Beverly Hills, CA 90211. (213) 655-0101.

DAVID SHAPIRA ASSOCIATES, INC.
15301 Ventura Blvd., Ste. 345, Sherman Oaks, CA 91403. (818) 906-0322. FAX: (818) 783-2562.
AGENTS
David Shapira, Mike Wise, Peter Giagni, Dan Schrierm Bobby Litman

SILVER, MASSETTI & SZATMARY, LTD.
8730 Sunset Blvd., Ste. 480, Los Angeles, CA 90069. (310) 289-0909. FAX: (310) 289-0990.
PARTNERS
Monty Silver, Donna Massetti, Marilyn Szatmary

RICHARD SINDELL & ASSOCIATES
8271 Melrose Ave., Ste. 202, Los Angeles, CA 90046. (213) 653-5051.

MICHAEL SLESSINGER & ASSOCS.
8730 Sunset Blvd., #270 West, Los Angeles, CA 90069. (310) 657-7113. FAX: (310) 657-1756.

SUSAN SMITH & ASSOCIATES
121 N. San Vicente Blvd., Beverly Hills, CA 90211. (310) 852-4777. FAX: (213) 658-7170.
AGENTS
Peter Donaldson, JOanne Roberts, Lisa Helsing

STARWIL TALENT AGENCY CO. INC.
6253 Hollywood Blvd., Ste. 730, Los Angeles, CA 90028. (213) 874-1239. FAX: (213) 464-2813.

STEVENS & ASSOCIATES
9454 Wilshire Blvd., 6th Flr., Beverly Hills, CA 90212. (310) 275-7541. FAX: (310) 275-5929.

STONE/MANNERS AGENCY
8091 Selma Ave., Los Angeles, CA 90046. (213) 654-7575.

SUITE A. MANAGEMENT
1728 S. La Cienega Blvd., Ste. A, Los Angeles, CA 90035. (310) 558-3820. FAX: (310) 558-4440.
OWNER
Lloyd D. Robinson

THE SUN AGENCY
8961 Sunset Blvd., Ste. V, Los Angeles, CA 90069. (310) 888-8737. FAx: (310) 888-7721.

SUTTON, BARTH & VENNARI, INC.
145 S. Fairfax Ave., #310, Los Angeles, CA 90036. (213) 938-6000. FAX: (213) 935-8671.
PARTNERS
Vic Sutton
Rita Vennari

H. N. SWANSON
8523 Sunset Blvd., Los Angeles, CA 90069. (310) 652-5385.

TALENT GROUP INC.
6300 Wilshire Blvd., Ste. 2110, Los Angeles, CA 90048. (213) 852-9559. FAX: 9213) 852-9579.

TALENT REPS., INC.
20 E. 53 St., New York, NY 10022. (212) 752-1835.

TALENT TREK AND NASHVILLE
2021 21st Ave. S., Suite 102, Nashville, TN 37212. email: tal-entrek@mindspring.com
PARNTERS
Jaunell Walker
Charlotte Dennison
AGENTS
Evelyn Foster
Sharon D. Smith

THE TANTLEFF OFFICE
375 Greenwich St., Ste. 700, New York, NY 10013. (212) 941-3939. FAX: (212) 941-3948.

TISHERMAN AGENCY INC.
6767 Forest Lawn Dr., Ste. 101, Los Angeles, CA 90068. (213) 850-6767. FAX: (213) 850-7340.
 URL: http://www.tishermanagency.com

TURNING POINT MANAGEMENT TALENT AGENCY
6601 Center Dr. West, Ste. 500, Los Angeles, CA 90445.(310) 348-8171. FAX: 9310) 348-0174.
AGENT
Cheryl Downs

THE TURTLE AGENCY
12456 Ventura Blvd., Ste. 1, Studio City, CA 91604. (818) 506-6898. FAX: (818) 506-1723. email: cturtlewal@aol.com

TWENTIETH CENTURY ARTISTS
4605 Lankershim Blvd., Ste. 305, N. Hollywood, CA 91602. (818) 980-5118.
PRESIDENT
Diane Davis
ADULT THEATRICAL MP, TV, STAGE, CHOREOGRAPHERS, STAGE DIRECTORS
Jae Ross
ADULT THEATRICAL MP, TV LITERARY, TV DIRECTORS
David Ankrum

UNITED TALENT AGENCY
9560 Wilshire Blvd., #500, Beverly Hills, CA 90212. (310) 273-6700. FAX: (310) 247-1111.
AGENTS
Robert Stein, James Berkus, Gary Cosay, Marty Bauer, David Kanter, Robb Rothman, Toby Jaffe, Risa Gertner, David Schiff, Peter Benedek, Jeremy Zimmer, Martin Hurwitz, Marty Adelstein, Judy Hofflund, Pat Dollard, Karen Russell, Chris Buchanan, Christopher Harbert, Dana Cioffi, Ilene Feldman.

ANNETTE VAN DUREN AGENCY
925 N. Sweetzer Ave., Ste. 12, Los Angeles, CA 90069. (213) 650-3643. FAX: (213) 654-3893.

SHIRLEY WILSON AGENCY
5410 Wilshire Blvd., Ste. 227, Los Angeles, CA 90036. (213) 857-6977. FAX: (213) 857-6980.

WARDLOW & ASSOCIATES
1501 Main St., #204, Venica, CA 90291. (310) 452-1292. FAX: (310) 452-9002.
PRINCIPAL/OWNER
David Wardlow
LITERARY
Jeff Ordway

RUTH WEBB ENTERPRISES, INC.
13834 Magnolia Blvd., Sherman Oaks, CA 91423. (818) 905-7000. FAX: (213) 874-1860.
AGENTS
Scott Stander
Ruth Webb

HANNS WOLTERS THEATRICAL AGENCY
10 W. 37 St., New York, NY 10018. (212) 714-0100. FAX: (212) 643-1412.

WORLD CLASS SPORTS
880 Apollo St., El Segundo, CA 90245. (310) 535-9120. FAX: (310) 535-9128.
SENIOR AGENTS
Andrew Woolf, Don Franken

CARTER WRIGHT TALENT AGENCY
6513 Hollywood Blvd., Ste. 210, Los Angeles, CA 90028. (213) 469-0944.

WRITERS & ARTISTS AGENCY
924 Westwood Blvd., Ste. 900, Los Angeles, CA 90024. (310) 824-6300.
19 W. 44 St., #1000, New York, NY 10036. (212) 391-1112. FAX: (212) 398-9877.
AGENTS
Lisa Feinstein, Beill Carver, Scott Hudson

FEDERAL COMMUNICATIONS COMMISSION

FEDERAL GOVERNMENT OFFICES AND FILM AND MEDIA SERVICES

GUILDS AND UNIONS

ORGANIZATIONS

STATE AND CITY FILM COMMISSIONS

TRADE PRESS

■

FEDERAL COMMUNICATIONS COMMISSION

FEDERAL COMMUNICATIONS COMMISSION
1919 M Street NW, Washington, DC 20554. (202) 418-0200.
FAX: (202) 418-0999. FCC NATIONAL CALL CENTER:1-888-
Call FCC (1-888-225-5322).

OFFICE OF THE CHAIRMAN
1919 M Street NW, Rm. 814, Washington, DC 20554. (202)
418-1000.
CHAIRMAN
William Kennard
COMMISSIONERS
Harold Furchtgott-Roth
Gloria Tristani
Michael K. Powell
Susan Ness

OFFICE OF PLANS AND POLICY
1919 M Street NW, Rm. 822, Washington, DC 20554. (202)
418-2030.
CHIEF
Robert M. Pepper

OFFICE OF PUBLIC AFFAIRS
1919 M Street NW, Rm. 202, Washington, DC 20554. (202)
418-0500.
ACTING DIRECTOR
Elizabeth Rose
DEPUTY DIRECTORS
David H. Fiske
Maureen P. Perantino
PRESS SECRETARY
Audrey J. Spivack
PUBLIC SERVICE DIVISION
Rm. 242, (202) 418-0260.
CHIEF
Martha Contee
PUBLIC INQUIRIES BRANCH
Rm. 254, (202) 418-0190.
CHIEF
Sharon Jenkins
REFERENCE OPERATIONS DIVISION
Rm. 242, (202) 418-0267.
CHIEF
William Cline
MASS MEDIA/ADJUDICATION BRANCH
Rm. 242, (202) 418-0272.
LIBRARY BRANCH
Rm. 639, (202) 418-0450.
CHIEF
Gloria Thomas
FCC REFERENCE CENTER
Rm. 239, (202) 418-0270.
OWNERSHIP REPORTS
Rm. 221, (202) 418-0258.
RECORDS IMAGING PROC. SYSTEM
Rm. 230, (202) 418-0029.
TARIFF PUBLIC REFERENCE
Rm. 250, (202) 418-1933.
CALL SIGN INFORMATION
Rm. 230, (202) 418-0270.
CABLE FILES
2033 M. Street, Rm. 333, (202) 418-0919.

OFFICE OF LEGISLATIVE & INTERGOVERNMENTAL AFFAIRS
1919 M Street NW, Rm. 808, Washington, DC 20554. (202)
418-1900
DIRECTOR
Sheryl J. Wilkerson

OFFICE OF COMM. BUSINESS OPPORTUNITIES
1919 M Street NW, Rm. 644, Washington, DC 20554. (202)
418-0990
DIRECTOR
Catherine Sandoval

OFFICE OF ADMINISTRATIVE LAW JUDGES
2000 L Street, Rm. 224, Washington, DC 20554. (202) 418-
2250
CHIEF JUDGE
Vacant

OFFICE OF GENERAL COUNSEL
2000 L. Street NW, Rm. 614, Washington, DC 20554. (202)
418-1700
GENERAL COUNSEL
Christopher J. Wright
LITIGATION DIVISION
Rm. 602, (202) 418-1740.
ASSOCIATE GENERAL
Daniel M. Armstrong
ADMINISTRATIVE LAW DIVISION
Rm. 622, (202) 418-1720.
ASSOCIATE GENERAL
Susan H. Steinman
COMPETITION DIVISION
Rm. 658, (202) 418-1880.
ACTING CHIEF
Lawrence Strickling

OFFICE OF INSPECTOR GENERAL
Rm. 752, (202) 418-0470.
INSPECTOR GENERAL
H. Walker Feaster

OFFICE OF WORKPLACE DIVERSITY
2000 M. Street, Rm. 250, Washington, DC 20554. (202) 418-
1799.
DIRECTOR
Jack W. Gravely

OFFICE OF MANAGING DIRECTOR
2000 M. Street, Rm. 852, Washingon, DC 20554. (202) 418-
1919
MANAGING DIRECTOR
Andrew S. Fishel
THE SECRETARY
Rm. 222, (202) 418-0300.
SECRETARY
Magalie Roman
HUMAN RESOURCES MANAGEMENT
Rm. 212, (202) 418-0100.
ASSOCIATE MANAGING DIRECTOR
Michelle A. Oppenheimer
PERSONNEL RESOURCES DIVISION
Rm. 212, (202) 418-0137.
CHIEF
Michele C. Sutton
LABOR RELATIONS AND WORKFORCE EFFECTIVENESS
DIVISION
Rm. 206, (202) 418-0113.
CHIEF
Stephen E. Schumacher
INFORMATION TECHNOLOGY CENTER
Rm. 418, (202) 418-2022.
DIRECTOR
Ronald Stone
NETWORK DEVELOPMENT GROUP
Rm. 424, (202) 418-1823.
CHIEF
Spencer Hyndman
PLANNING AND SUPPORT GROUP
Rm. 420, (202) 418-1812.
CHIEF
Edward J. McCarthy
OPERATIONS GROUP
Rm. 438D, (202) 418-7505.
CHIEF
Dave Sequeira

ASSOCIATE MANAGING DIRECTOR, OPERATIONS
Rm. 848, (202) 418-1925.
ACTING ASSOCIATE MANAGING DIRECTOR, OPERATIONS
Thomas M. Holleran
FINANCIAL OPERATIONS DIVISION
Rm. 414, (202) 418-1970.
CHIEF
Linda King
OPERATIONS MANAGEMENT AND SERVICES DIVISION
Rm. 404, (202) 418-1950.
CHIEF
Jeffrey R. Ryan

OFFICE OF ENGINEERING AND TECHNOLOGY
2000 M Street, Rm. 480, Washington, DC 20554. (202) 418-2470.
CHIEF
Richard M. Smith
POLICY AND RULES DIVISION
Rm. 480, (202) 418-2472.
CHIEF
Lynn Remly
SPECTRUM POLICY
Rm. 480, (202) 418-2473.
CHIEF
Charles J. Iseman
TECHNICAL RULES BRANCH
Rm. 480, (202) 418-2474.
CHIEF
Karen Rackley
ALLOCATIONS AND STANDARDS DIVISION
Rm. 230, (202) 418-2475.
CHIEF
Robert M. Bromery
SPECTRUM UTILIZATION AND ECONOMICS
Rm. 230, (202) 418-2476.
CHIEF
Fred Thomas
STANDARDS DEVELOPMENT
Rm. 230, (202) 418-2477.
CHIEF
James R. Burtle
NEW TECHNOLOGY DEVELOPMENT
Rm. 230, (202) 418-2478.
CHIEF
Lawrence P. Petak
EXPERIMENTAL LICENSING BRANCH
Rm. 230, (202) 418-2479.
CHIEF
Paul Marrangoni
ENGINEERING & TECHNOLOGY—TECHNICAL BRANCHES
P. O. Box 250, Columbia, MD 21045-9998. (301) 725-1585.
CHIEF
David L. Means

CABLE SERVICES BUREAU
2033 M Street NW, Rm. 918, Washington, DC 20554. (202) 418-7200.
CHIEF
Meredith Jones
FINANCIAL ANALYSIS AND COMPLIANCE DIVISION
Rm. 804, (202) 418-2296.
CHIEF
Elizabeth Beaty
CONSUMER PROTECTION AND COMPETITITION DIVISION, Rm. 700, (202) 418-1029.
CHIEF
Gary Laden
POLICY AND RULES DIVISION
Rm. 406, (202) 418-7034
CHIEF
JoAnn Lucanik
ENGINEERING AND TECHNICAL SERVICES DIVISION
Rm. 201, (202) 418-7000.
CHIEF
John Wong

COMMON CARRIER BUREAU
2033 M Street, Rm. 500, Washington, DC 20554. (202) 418-1500.
CHIEF
A. Richard Metzger
NETWORK SERVICES DIVISION
200 M Street., Rm. 230, Washington, DC 20554. (202) 418-2320.
CHIEF
Gerald Matise

ENFORCEMENT DIVISION
2025 M. Street, Rm. 6008, Washington, DC 20554. (202) 418-0700.
ACTING CHIEF
Robert W. Spangler
INDUSTRY ANALYSIS DIVISION
2033 M. Street, Rm. 500, Washington, DC 20554. (202) 418-0940.
CHIEF
Peyton L. Wynns
COMPETITIVE PRICING DIVISION
Rm. 518. (202) 418-1520.
CHIEF
James D. Schlichting
POLICY AND PROGRAM PLANNING DIVISION
Rm. 544. (202) 418-1580.
ACTING CHIEF
Carol Mattey

COMPLIANCE AND INFORMATION BUREAU
2033 M Street, Rm. 734, Washington, DC 20554. (202) 418-1100.
CHIEF
Richard Lee
OFFICE OF MANAGEMENT AND RESOURCES
Rm. 728. (202) 418-1135.
ASST. BUREAU CHIEF FOR MANAGEMENT AND RESOURCES
Robert W. Crisman
DIRECTOR, RESOURCES GROUP
Gkebba F. Werking
DIRECTOR, MANAGEMENT & SYSTEMS GROUP
Wayne T. Toivanen
DIRECTOR, COMMUNICATIONS & CRISIS GROUP
David T. Prescott
OFFICE OF INFORMATION RESOURCES
Rm. 734. (202) 418-1100.
ASSISTANT BUREAU CHIEF FOR INFORMATION RESOURCES
John R. Winston
COMPLIANCE DIVISION
Rm. 744. (202) 418-1160
ACTING CHIEF
Pamela D. Hairston
TECHNOLOGY DIVISION
Rm. 720. (202) 418) 1210.
CHIEF
Kenneth R. Nichols

INTERNATIONAL BUREAU
2000 M Street, Rm. 800, Washington, DC 20554. (202) 418-0420.
CHIEF
Regina Keeney
TELECOMMUNICATIONS DIVISION
Rm. 800. (202) 418-1470.
CHIEF
Diane J. Cornell
SATELLITE & RADIOCOMMUNICATION DIVISION
Rm. 800, (202) 418-0719.
CHIEF
Thomas Tycz
PLANNING AND NEGOTIATIONS DIVISION
Rm. 800, (202) 418-2150.
CHIEF
Richard B. Engelman

MASS MEDIA BUREAU
2000 M. Street, Rm. 314, Washington, DC 20054. (202) 418-2600.
CHIEF
Roy J. Stewart
AUDIO SERVICES DIVISION
Rm. 302, (202) 418-2780.
CHIEF
Linda Blair
ENFORCEMENT DIVISION
2025 M Street, Rm 8202, Washington, DC 20554. (202) 418-1420.
CHIEF
Charles W. Kelley
EQUAL EMPLOYMENT OPPORTUNITY BRANCH
Rm. 7218, (202) 418-1450.
CHIEF
Paulette Laden

POLICY AND RULES DIVISION
ACTING CHIEF
2000 M Street, Rm. 536, Washington, DC 20554. (202) 418-2120.
Charles W. Logan
LEGAL BRANCH
Rm. 556, (202) 418-2130.
CHIEF
Charles W. Logan
ENGINEERING POLICY BRANCH
Rm. 536, (202) 418-2120.
ACTING CHIEF
Bruce A. Romano
POLICY AND INDUSTRY ANALYSIS BRANCH
Rm. 536, (202) 418-2170.
CHIEF
Judith Herman
VIDEO SERVICES DIVISION, TELEVISION BRANCH
Rm. 702, (202) 418-1600.
CHIEF
Clay Pendarvis
LOW POWER TELEVISION BRANCH
Rm. 702, (202) 418-1600.
CHIEF
Mary M. Fitzgerald

WIRELESS TELECOMMUNICATIONS BUREAU
2025 M Street, Rm. 5002, Washington, DC 20554. (202) 418-0660
CHIEF
Daniel Phythyon

COMMERCIAL WIRELESS DIVISION
2100 M. Street, Rm. 700, Washington, DC 20554. (202) 418-0620.
CHIEF
David Furth
POLICY AND RULES BRANCH
Rm. 7130.
CHIEF
Ramona Melson
LICENSING AND TECHNICAL ANALYSIS BRANCH
Rm. 8643A.
CHIEF
Roger Noel
LICENSING SECTION
Rm. 8028, (202) 418-1334.
CHIEF
Pearl McGinnis
ENFORCEMENT AND CONSUMER INFORMATION DIVISION
2025 M. Street, Rm. 8308, Washington, DC 20054. (202) 418-0569.
CHIEF
Howard C. Davenport
POLICY DIVISION
Rm. 7002, (202) 418-1310.
CHIEF
John Cimko
INFORMATION TECHNOLOGY DIVISION
Gettysburg, PA. (717) 338-2510.
CHIEF
John Chudovan

FEDERAL GOVERNMENT OFFICES AND FILM & MEDIA SERVICES

EXECUTIVE DEPARTMENTS

DEPARTMENT OF AGRICULTURE
VIDEO AND TELECONFERENCE AND RADIO DIVISION
Office of Public Affairs, 1614 South Bldg., USDA, Washington,
DC 20250-1300. (202) 720-6072. FAX: (202) 720-5773.
DIRECTOR
Larry Quinn

DEPARTMENT OF COMMERCE
OFFICE OF PUBLIC AFFAIRTS—MEDIA SECTION
Office of the Secretary, 14th St. & Constitution Ave., Rm. 5056,
Washington, DC 20230. (202) 482-3140. FAX: (202) 482-2639.
PRODUCER & DIRECTOR
J.R. Olivero

INTERNATIONAL TRADE ADMINISTRATION—OFFICE OF
SERVICE INDUSTRIES
Information Industries Division—Motion Picture & Recorder
Music, 14th St. and Constitution Ave., Rm. H-1114,
Washington, DC 20230. (202) 482-4781. FAX: (202) 482-2669.
SENIOR INTERNATIONAL TRADE SPECIALIST
John Siegmund

NATIONAL TELECOMMUNICATIONS AND INFORMATION
ADMINISTRATION
Main Commerce Bldg., 1401 Constitution Ave., Washington,
DC 20230. (202) 482-1840. FAX: (202) 482-1635.
ASST. SECRETARY, COMMUNICATIONS & INFORMATION
Larry Irving

NATIONAL TECHNICAL INFORMATION SERVICE
5282 Port Royal Rd., Springfield, VA 22161. (800) 553-6847.
FAX: (703) 321-8547.
ACTING DIRECTOR
Donald Corrigan

DEPARTMENT OF DEFENSE
SPECIAL ASSISTANT (AUDIOVISUAL)
Office of the Assistant Secretary of Defense (Public Affairs),
The Pentagon, Room 2E789, Washington, DC 20301. (703)
695-2936. FAX: (703) 695-1149.
HEAD OF DIVISION
Philip M. Strub

BROADCAST PICTORIAL BRANCH
Office of the Assistant Secretary of Defense (Public Affairs),
The Pentagon, Room 2E765, Washington, DC 20301. (703)
695-0168. FAX: (703) 697-3501.
BRANCH CHIEF
Jim Kout

MILITARY SERVICES
SECRETARY OF THE AIR FORCE
Office of Public Affairs, The Pentagon, Room 5C887,
Washington, DC 20330-1000. (703) 697-2769. FAX: (703) 614-
7486.
CHIEF OF DIVISION
Lt. Col. Bob Williams

SECRETARY OF THE ARMY
Media Relations Division, Army Public Affairs, The Pentagon,
Room 2E641, Washington, DC 20310-1500, (703) 697-2564.
FAX: (703) 657-2159.
CHIEF OF DIVISION
Col. John A. Smith

DEPARTMENT OF THE NAVY
Chief of Information, The Pentagon, Room 4A686, Washington,
DC 20350-1200. (703) 697-4627.
DIRECTOR
Rear Admiral Thomas J. Jurkowsky

HEADQUARTERS, U.S. MARINE CORPS.
Media Branch Public Affairs Division, Code PAM, The
Pentagon, Washington, DC 20380. (703) 614-8010. FAX: (703)
697-5362.
CHIEF OF BRANCH
Lt. Col. Pat Messer

DEPARTMENT OF EDUCATION
OFFICE OF PUBLIC AFFAIRS
Audiovisual Division, 600 Independence Ave. SW, Rm. 2200,
Washington, DC 20202. (202) 401-1576. FAX: (202) 401-3130.
AUDIOVISUAL OFFICER
Sherry Sweitzer
OFFICE OF SPECIAL EDUCATION AND REHABILITATION
SERVICES
Office of the Asst. Secretary, 330 C St. SW, Ste. 3006,
Sweitzer Bldg., Washington, DC 20202-2500. (202) 205-5465.
FAX: (202) 205-9252.
BRANCH CHIEF, CAPTIONING
Judith Hewmann

DEPARTMENT OF ENERGY
OFFICE OF PUBLIC AFFAIRS—MEDIA & MP DIVISION
Forrestal Bldg.,1000 Independence Ave. SW, CP41, Room
IE200, Washington, DC 20585. (202) 586-6250. FAX: (202)
586-7303.
DIRECTOR
Pinny Adams

DEPARTMENT OF HEALTH AND HUMAN SERVICES
OFFICE OF PUBLIC AFFAIRS
200 Independence Ave. SW, Room 647D, Washington, DC
20201. (202) 690-7850. FAX: (202) 690-5673.
DIRECTOR OF COMMUNICATIONS
Campbell Garnett

ADMINISTRATION FOR CHILDREN & FAMILY
370 L'Enfant Promenade SW, 7th floor, Washington, DC 20447.
(202) 401-9215. FAX: (202) 205-9688.
DIRECTOR
Michael Kharfen

HEALTH CARE FINANCING ADMINISTRATION
200 Independence Ave. SW, Room 314G, Washington, DC
20201. (202) 690-6113. FAX: (202) 690-6262.
ADMINISTRATOR
Nancy Ann De Parle

SOCIAL SECURITY ADMINISTRATION OFFICE OF PUBLIC
AFFAIRS
4200 West High Rise, 6401 Security Blvd., Baltimore, MD
21235. (401) 965-1720. FAX: (401) 965-3903.
DIRECTOR
Joan Wainwrithe

DEPARTMENT OF HOUSING AND URBAN DEVELOPMENT
OFFICE OF PUBLIC AFFAIRS
HUD Bldg., 451 7th St. SW, Rm. 10132, Washington, DC
20410. (202) 708-0980. FAX: (202) 619-8153.
ASSISTANT SECRETARY
Karen Hinton

DEPARTMENT OF THE INTERIOR
OFFICE OF PUBLIC INFORMATION, AUDIOVISUAL
PROGRAMS
1849 C St. NW, Washington, DC 20240. (202) 501-9649. FAX:
(202) 208-64116.
MANAGER OF AUDIOVISUAL PROGRAMS
Steve Brooks

DEPARTMENT OF JUSTICE
AUDIOVISUAL SERVICES
10th St. & Pennsylvania Ave., Rm. 1313, Washington, DC
20530. (202) 514-4387. FAX: (202) 514-6741.
SUPERVISOR
Joe Keyerleber

DEPARTMENT OF LABOR
AUDIOVISUAL AND PHOTOGRAPHIC SERVICES BRANCH
Audiovisual Division, 200 Constitution Ave. NW, N6311,
Washington, DC 20210. (202) 219-7910. FAX: (202) 219-4788.
DIRECTOR
Meg Ingold
EXECUTIVE PRODUCER
Stan Hankin

DEPARTMENT OF STATE
INTERNATIONAL COMMUNICATIONS AND INFORMATION
POLICY
Department of State, Rm. 4826, 2201 C St. NW, Washington,
DC 20520. (202) 647-5212. FAX: (202) 647-5957.
DEPUTY ASST. SECRETARY
Ambassador Vonya B. McCann

OFFICE OF INTERNATIONAL TRADE CONTROL
Department of State, 1700 N. Lynn St., Rm. 200, Arlington, VA
22209. (703) 875-6644. FAX: (703) 0875-6647.
DIRECTOR OF STAFF
William Lowell

OFFICE OF PRESS RELATIONS
Department of State, Rm. 2109-A, Washington, DC 20520.
(202) 647-0874. FAX: (202) 647-0244.
DIRECTOR OF STAFF
Jeff Margino

DEPARTMENT OF TRANSPORTATION
FEDERAL HIGHWAY ADMINISTRATION AUDIOVISUAL AND
VISUAL AIDS
400 7th St. SW, Rm. 4429, HMS51, Washington, DC 20590.
(202) 366-0481.
AUDIOVISUAL CHIEF
Colonel Giles

NATIONAL HIGHWAY AND TRAFFIC SAFETY ADMINISTRATION
Public Affairs, Audiovisual Section, 400 7th St. SW, Rm. 5232,
Washington, DC 20590. (202) 366-9550. FAX: (202) 366-5962.
PUBLIC AFFAIRS SPECIALIST
Tina Foley

U.S. COAST GUARD MOTION PICTURE & TELEVISION
LIAISON OFFICE
10880 Wilshire Blvd., Ste. 1210, Los Angeles, CA 90024. (310)
235-7817. FAX: (310) 235-7851.
LIAISON OFFICERS
Cmdr. Dwight McGee, CWO Alastair Worden, CWO Lance
Jones

U.S. COAST GUARD MEDIA RELATIONS BRANCH
2100 2nd St. SW, Washington, DC 20593. (202) 267-1587.
(202) 267-4307.
CHIEF OF DEPARTMENT
Mike Lapinski

U.S. COAST GUARD AUDIOVISUAL BRANCH
(202) 267-0923. FAX: (202) 267-4307.
AUDIOVISUAL SPECIALIST
Wayne Paugh

DEPARTMENT OF TREASURY
OFFICE OF PUBLIC AFFAIRS
1500 Pennsylvania Ave. NW, Rm. 3442, Washington, DC
20220. (202) 622-2960. FAX: (202) 622-2808.
ASSISTANT SECRETARY
Howard Schloss

EXECUTIVE AGENCIES

ENVIRONMENTAL PROTECTION AGENCY
AUDIOVISUAL DIVISION
401 M St. SW, North Conference, Washington, DC 20460.
(202) 260-6735. FAX: (301) 585-7976.
DIRECTOR
Mawell Jama

FEDERAL COMMUNICATIONS COMMISSION
(For an expanded listing, please see the section entitled Federal
Communications Commission beginning on page 628).
1919 M St. NW, Washington, DC 20554. (202) 418-0200. FAX:
(202) 418-0999.

FEDERAL TRADE COMMISSION
Press Office, 6th St. and Pennsylvania Ave. NW, Washington,
DC 20580. (202) 326-2180. FAX: (202) 326-3676.
CHAIRMAN
Robert Pitofsky

LIBRARY OF CONGRESS
COPYRIGHT OFFICE
Madison Bldg., Rm. 403, Washington, DC 20540. (202) 707-
8350. FAX: (202) 707-8366.
REGISTER OF COPYRIGHTS
Marybeth Peters

COPYRIGHT CATALOGING DIVISION
Madison Bldg., Rm. 513. (202) 707-8040. FAX: (202) 707-8049.
CHIEF OF DIVISION
William Collins

MOTION PICTURE, BROADCASTING AND RECORDED
SOUND DIVISION
Madison Bldg., Rm. 338, Washington, DC 20540. (202) 707-
5840. FAX: (202) 707-2371.
CHIEF OF DIVISION
David Francis

NATIONAL AERONAUTICS & SPACE ADMINISTRATION
NASA VIDEO LIBRARY
Code AP42, Bldg. 423, Johnson Space Center, Houston, TX
77058. (281) 483-2973. FAX: (281) 483-2848.
DIRECTOR
Jody Russel

NATIONAL ARCHIVES AND RECORDS ADMINISTRATION
MOTION PICTURE, SOUND AND VIDEO BRANCH
8601 Adelphi Rd., College Park, MD 20740. (703) 713-7050.
BRANCH CHIEF
Jack Saunders
PRESIDENTIAL LIBRARIES CENTRAL OFFICE
7th St. & Pennsylvania Ave. NW, Rm. 104, Washington, DC
20408. (202) 501-5700. FAX: (202) 501-5709.
DIRECTOR
David Peterson

NATIONAL ENDOWMENT FOR THE ARTS
CREATION & PRESENTATION—MEDIA ARTS PROGRAM
1100 Pennsylvania Ave. NW, Rm. 726, Washington, DC 20506.
(202) 682-5452. FAX: (202) 682-5721.
MEDIA ARTS DIRECTOR
Brian O'Doherty

NATIONAL ENDOWMENT FOR THE HUMANITIES
HUMANITIES PROJECTS IN MEDIA—DIVISION OF PUBLIC
PROGRAMS
1100 Pennsylvania Ave. NW, Rm. 426, Washington, DC 20506.
(202) 606-8278. FAX: (202) 606-8557.
PROGRAM OFFICER
James Dougherty

SECURITIES AND EXCHANGE COMMISSION
DIVISION OF CORPORATE FINANCE
450 5th St. NW, Washington, DC 20549. (202) 942-8088.
Radio, Television, and Telegraph
Rm. 3113. (202) 942-1900. FAX: (202) 942-9525.
ASSISTANT DIRECTOR
H. Christopher Owings

MOTION PICTURES
Rm. 3134. (202) 942-1800.
ASSISTANT DIRECTOR
James Daly

SMITHSONIAN INSTITUTION
FILM ARCHIVES
Archives Division, National Air and Space Museum,
Washington, DC 20560. (202) 357-3133. FAX: (202) 786-2835.
FILM ARCHIVIST
Mark Taylor

TELECOMMUNICATIONS OFFICE
National Museum of American History, Rm. BB40, Washington,
DC 20560. (202) 357-2984. FAX: (202) 357-1565.
DIRECTOR
Paul Johnson

U.S. INFORMATION AGENCY
TELEVISION AND FILM OFFICE
601 D St. NW, Rm. 5000, Washington, DC 20547. FAX: (202)
501-6664.
DIRECTOR
Charles W. Fox

U.S. INTERNATIONAL TRADE COMMISSION
OFFICE OF THE SECRETARY
500 E Street, Rm. 112, Washington, DC 20436. (202) 205-
2000. FAX: (202) 205-2104.
SECRETARY
Donna R. Koehnke

MILITARY FILM LIAISONS

ARMY CHIEF OF PUBLIC AFFAIRS
10880 Wilshire Blvd., Room 10104, Los Angeles, CA 90024-
3688. (310) 235-7621. FAX: (310) 235-6075.
CHIEF OF PUBLIC AFFAIRS
Ann. K. Canham
TECHNICAL ADVISOR
Deputy Chief—Maj. Beni C. Frazier
PUBLIC INFORMATION OFFICER
Kathy Canham Ross

MARINE CORPS PUBLIC AFFAIRS
10880 Wilshire Blvd., Ste. 1230, Los Angeles, CA 90024. (310)
235-7272. FAX: (310) 235-7274.
OFFICER IN CHARGE
Major T.V. Johnson

U. S. AIR FORCE, MOTION PICTURE AND TELEVISION
LIAISON OFFICE
10880 Wilshire Blvd., Room 10114, Los Angeles, CA 90024.
(310) 235-7522. FAX: (310) 235-7500.
CHIEF, ENTERTAINMENT LIAISON
Charles E. Davis

U. S. COAST GUARD, MOTION PICTURE AND
TELEVISION OFFICE
10880 Wilshire Blvd., Ste. 1210, Los Angeles, CA 90024. (310)
235-7817. FAX: (310) 235-7851.
LIAISON OFFICERS
Cmdr. Dwight McGee, CWO Alastair Worden, CWO Lance
Jones

GUILDS AND UNIONS

**ACTORS' EQUITY ASSOCIATION
(AAAA-AFL-CIO-CLC)**
(Organized May 26, 1913. Membership: 38,000.)
National/Eastern Regional Office: 165 W. 46th St., New York, New York 10036. (212) 869-8530; FAX (212) 719-9815.
Central Regional Office: 203 N. Wabash Ave., Suite 1700, Chicago, IL 60601. (312) 641-0393; FAX (312) 641-6365.
Western Regional Office: 5757 Wilshire Boulevard, Suite One, Los Angeles, CA 90036. (323) 634-1750. FAX (323) 634-1777.
San Francisco Office: 235 Pine Street, Suite 1200, San Francisco, CA 94104. (415) 391-3838. FAX (415) 391-0102.
Orlando Office: 10319 Orangewood Blvd., Orlando, FL 32821. (407) 345-8600. FAX (407) 345-1522
PRESIDENT
Ron Silver
FIRST VICE PRESIDENT
Patrick Quinn
SECOND VICE PRESIDENT
Richard Warren Pugh
THIRD V.P. & EASTERN REGIONAL V.P.
Donald Christy
CENTRAL REGIONAL V.P.
Madeleine Fallon
WESTERN REGIONAL V.P.
Carol Swarbrick
EASTERN REGIONAL V.P.
Arne Gundersen
SECRETARY & TREASURER
Conard Fowkes
COUNSEL
Spivak, Lipton, Watanabe, Spivak (NY)
Taylor, Roth, Bush & Geffner (L.A.)

AFFILIATED PROPERTY CRAFTSMEN LOCAL 44 (IATSE-AFL-CIO), HOLLYWOOD
11500 Burbank Blvd. N. Hollywood, CA 91601. (818) 769-2500. FAX: (818) 769-1739.
SECRETARY
Walter Keske
BUSINESS AGENT
Ronald Cunningham

AMERICAN CINEMA EDITORS
(Organized 1950. Membership: 450.)
1041 N. Formosa Ave., W. Hollywood, CA 90046. (323) 850-2900. FAX: (323) 850-2922.
PRESIDENT
Mark Goldblatt
VICE PRESIDENT
Tina Hirsch
SECRETARY
Christopher Cooke
TREASURER
Jack Tucker

**AMERICAN FEDERATION OF MUSICIANS
(AFL-CIO)**
(Organized October, 1896. Membership: 150,000.)
1501 Broadway, New York, NY 10036. (212) 869-1330. FAX: (212) 764-6134.
PRESIDENT
Steve Young
VICE PRESIDENT
Tom Lee, 4400 MacArthur Blvd. NW, Washington, DC 20001.
CANADIAN V.P.
David Jandrisch, 75 The Donway West, Suite 1010, Don Mills, Ontario, Canada M3C 2E9.
SECRETARY-TREASURER
Stephen R. Sprague
EXECUTIVE BOARD
Thomas C. Bailey ,Edward Kirk, Tammy Kirk, Tim Shea, Kenneth B. Shirk

AMERICAN FEDERATION OF TELEVISION AND RADIO ARTISTS (AAAA-AFL-CIO)
(Organized August, 1937. Membership 80,000)
260 Madison Ave., 7th Fl., New York, NY 10016. (212) 532-0800.
NATIONAL PRESIDENT
Shelby Scott
FIRST VICE PRESIDENT
Denny Delk
SECOND VICE PRESIDENT
Ray Bradford
VICE PRESIDENTS
Susan Boyd, Belva Davis, Bob Edwards, J. R. Horne, Dave Corey, Jimmie Wright, Reed Farrell

TREASURER
Mitch McGuire
RECORDING SECRETARY
Bernie Alan
NATIONAL REPRESENTATIVES
Jonathan Dunn-Rankin, Stan Farber, Peter Cleaveland, Ann Chaitovitz, Dominique Bravo, David M Besbris.

**AMERICAN GUILD OF MUSICAL ARTISTS, INC.
(AFL-CIO, AAAA)**
(Organized 1936. Membership: 5,500.)
1727 Broadway, New York, NY 10019-5284. (212) 265-3687. FAX: (212) 262-9088.
PRESIDENT
Gerald Otte
FIRST VICE PRESIDENT
Linda Mays
SECOND VICE PRESIDENT
Pamela Warrick-Smith
THIRD VICE PRESIDENT
Burman Timberlake
FOURTH VICE PRESIDENT
John Coleman
TREASURER
Deborah Williams
NATIONAL EXECUTIVE SECRETARY
Louise J. Gilmore
COUNSEL
Cohen, Weiss & Simon
MEMBERSHIP SUPERVISOR
Vincent Brown
RECORDING SECRETARY
Candace Itow
NATIONAL MANAGER OF ADMIN. & OPERATIONS
Dianne James

**AMERICAN GUILD OF VARIETY ARTISTS
(AAAA AFL-CIO)**
(Organized July 14, 1939. Registered Membership: 78,000.)
184 Fifth Ave., New York, NY 10010. (212) 675-1003.
4741 Laurel Canyon Blvd., #208, N. Hollywood, CA 91607.
(818) 508-9984. FAX: (818) 508-3029. email: AGVANY@aol.com
PRESIDENT
Rod McKuen
EXECUTIVE SECRETARY-TREASURER
Frances Gaar
EXECUTIVE VICE PRESIDENT
David J. Cullen
HONORARY PRESIDENT
Phyllis Diller
HONORARY FIRST VICE PRESIDENT
Rip Taylor
HONORARY THIRD VICE PRESIDENT
Gloria DeHaven
REGIONAL VICE PRESIDENTS
Emelise Aleandri, Bobby Brookes, Mary Lynn Cullen, Susanne Doris, Larry Dorn, John Eaden, Wayne Hermans, Elaine Jacovini, Dee Dee Knapp-Brody, Paula Lane, Judy Little, Tina Marie, Stafford Mills, Victoria Reed, Dorothy Stratton, Dorothy Zuckerman.

AMERICAN SOCIETY OF CINEMATOGRAPHERS
1782 N. Orange Dr., Hollywood, CA 90028. (323) 876-5080. FAX: (323) 882-6391.
PRESIDENT
Woody Omens
FIRST VICE PRESIDENT.
Victor J. Kemper
SECOND VICE PRESIDENT
Steven B. Poster
THIRD VICE PRESIDENT
Laszlo Kovacs
TREASURER
Howard A. Anderson, Jr.
SECRETARY
John Bailey
SERGEANT AT ARMS
Gerald P. Finnerman

ART DIRECTORS, LOCAL 876 (IATSE) HOLLYWOOD
11365 Ventura Blvd. #315, Studio City, CA 91604. (818) 762-9995. FAX: (818) 762-9997.
SECRETARY
Frank Pezza

ASSOCIATED ACTORS AND ARTISTS OF AMERICA (AAAA)-AFL-CIO
(Organized July 18, 1919. Membership: 93,000.)
165 W. 46 St., New York, NY 10036. (212) 869-0358. FAX: (212) 869-1746.
PRESIDENT
Theodore Bikel
VICE PRESIDENTS
Carl Harns
Rod McKuen
Kendall Orsatti
Seymour Rexite
Bruce York
TREASURER
Thomas Jamerson

ASSOCIATED MUSICIANS OF GREATER NEW YORK LOCAL 802 AFM (NEW YORK)
(Organized August 27, 1921. Membership: 15,000.)
322 W. 48 St., New York, NY 10036-1308. (212) 245-4802. FAX: (212) 489-6030.
PRESIDENT
William Moriarity
FINANCIAL V.P.
Mary Landolfi
RECORDING V.P.
Erwin Price

ASSOCIATION OF TALENT AGENTS
(Organized April, 1937. Official organization of talent agents.)
9255 Sunset Blvd., Suite 930, Los Angeles, CA 90069. (310) 274-0628. FAX: (310) 274-5063. email: agentassoc@aol.com
EXECUTIVE DIRECTOR
Karen Stuart
FIRST VICE PRESIDENT
Sandy Bresler
VICE PRESIDENTS
Sid Craig
T. J. Escott
Sheldon Sroloff
Sonjia Warren Brandon
SECRETARY & TREASURER
Martin Gage

AUTHORS GUILD, INC.
(Membership: 7,000.)
330 W. 42 St., 29th Floor, New York, NY 10036-6902. (212) 563-5904. FAX: (212) 564-8363. email: staff@authorsguild.org. URL: http://www.authorsguild.org.
PRESIDENT
Letty Cottin Pogrebin
VICE PRESIDENT
James Gleick
SECRETARY
Pat Cummings
TREASURER
Peter Petre
EXECUTIVE DIRECTOR
Paul Aiken

AUTHORS LEAGUE OF AMERICA, INC., THE
(Membership: 15,000.)
330 W. 42 St., 29th Floor, New York, NY 10036. (212) 564-8350.
PRESIDENT
Garson Kanin
ADMINISTRATOR
Paul Aiken

CATHOLIC ACTORS GUILD OF AMERICA
(Organized April, 1914. Membership: 700.)
1501 Broadway, Suite 510, New York, NY 10036. (212) 398-1868.
PRESIDENT
William J. O'Malley
TREASURER
Martin Kiffel

COSTUME DESIGNERS GUILD LOCAL 892
13949 Ventura Blvd., Suite 309, Sherman Oaks, CA 91423. (818) 905-1557. FAX: (818) 905-1560.
SECRETARY
Dan Moore

DIRECTORS GUILD OF AMERICA, INC. (DGA)
7920 Sunset Blvd., Los Angeles, CA 90046. (310) 289-2000. FAX: (323) 289-2029.
110 W. 57 St., New York, NY 10019. (212) 581-0370.
400 N. Michigan Ave., # 307, Chicago, IL 60611. (312) 644-5050.
330 N. Federal Hwy., Hollywood, FL 33020. (954) 927-3338. FAX: (954) 923-8737.
PRESIDENT
Jack Shea
NATIONAL VICE PRESIDENT
Edwin Scherin

VICE PRESIDENTS
Larry Auerbach
Robert Butler
Martha Coolidge
John Frankenheimer
Nancy Littlefield
Max A. Schindler
SECRETARY & TREASURER
Gilbert Cates
EXECUTIVE DIRECTOR
J. Roth

THE DRAMATISTS GUILD, INC.
1501 Broadway, Suite 701, New York, NY 10036. (212) 398-9366. FAX: (212) 944-0420.
PRESIDENT
Peter Stone
VICE PRESIDENT
Terrence McNally
SECRETARY
Arthur Kopit
TREASURER
Richard Lewine
ACTING EXECUTIVE DIRECTOR
Chrisopher C. Wilson
COUNSEL
Cahill, Gordon & Reindel
MEMBERSHIP COORDINATOR
Douglas Green

EPISCOPAL ACTORS GUILD OF AMERICA, INC.
(Organized 1923. 550 members.)
1 E. 29 St., New York, NY 10016. (212) 685-2927. FAX: (212) 682-8793.
EXECUTIVE SECRETARY
Mart Hulfwit
PRESIDENT
Barnard Hughes
VICE PRESIDENT AND WARDEN
Rev. Norman J. Catir, Jr.
VICE PRESIDENTS
Robert Aberdeen
Peter Harris
Cliff Robertson
Eugene Smith
Joan Warren

FIRST AID EMPLOYEES, LOCAL 767 (IATSE), LOS ANGELES
243 S. Beachwood Dr., Burbank, 91506-2419. (818) 845-2907. FAX: (818) 846-0727
SECRETARY
Michael A. Kemp
BUSNESS AGENT
Rana Jo Platz Peterson, (310) 532-1345

INTERNATIONAL ALLIANCE OF THEATRICAL STAGE EMPLOYEES & MOVING PICTURE MACHINE OPERATORS OF THE U.S. AND CANADA (AFL-CIO, CLC)
(Organized nationally, July 17, 1893; internationally, October 1, 1902. The Alliance comprises approximately 800 local unions covering the United States, Canada and Hawaii.)
1515 Broadway, Suite 601, New York, NY 10036-5741. (212) 730-1770. FAX: (212) 921-7699.
INTERNATIONAL PRESIDENT
Thomas C. Short
GENERAL SECRETARY & TREASURER
Michael W. Proscia
FIRST V.P.
John J. Nolan
SECOND V.P.
Edward C. Powell
THIRD V.P.
Daniel J. Kerins
FOURTH V.P.
Rudy N. Napoleone
FIFTH V.P.
Carmine A. Palazzo
SIXTH V.P.
Jean Fox
SEVENTH V.P.
Ben F. Lowe
EIGHTH V.P.
Timothy Magee
NINTH V.P.
James Wood
TENTH V.P.
Michael J. Sullivan
ELEVENTH V.P.
Michael Barnes
INTERNATIONAL TRUSTEES
Ada S. Philpot
Ron Cunningham
Thomas M. Riley
AFL-CIO DELEGATES
Stephen R. Flint
Nancy Manganelli-Bues
CLC DELEGATE
C. Gus Bottas

INTERNATIONAL CINEMATOGRAPHERS GUILD, IATSE LOCAL 600, HOLLYWOOD
7715 Sunset Blvd., Suite 300, Hollywood, CA 90046. (213) 876-0160. FAX: (213) 876-6383.
WESTERN REGION DIRECTOR
Steve Flint

INTERNATIONAL CINEMATOGRAPHERS GUILD, IATSE LOCAL 600, NEW YORK
80 Eighth Ave., 14th Floor, New York, NY 10011. (212) 647-7300. FAX: (212) 647-7317.
EASTERN REGION DIRECTOR
Chris Lomolino

INTERNATIONAL CINEMATOGRAPHERS GUILD, IATSE LOCAL 600, ORLANDO
7463 Conroy-Windermere Rd., Suite A, Orlando, FL. (407) 295-5577. FAX: (407) 295-5335
CENTRAL REGION DIRECTOR
Larry Gianneschi

INTERNATIONAL BROTHERHOOD OF ELECTRICAL WORKERS (AFL-CIO, CFL)
(Organized November 28, 1891. Membership: over 1 million.)
1125 15th St. NW, Washington, DC 20005. (202) 833-7000.
INTERNATIONAL PRESIDENT
John J. Barry
INTERNATIONAL SECRETARY
Jack Moore
INTERNATIONAL TREASURER
Thomas Van Arsdale
ALABAMA: Melvin Horton, No. 2 Metroplex Dr., Suite 304, Birmingham, AL 35209-6899. CALIFORNIA: Michael Mowrey, 150 N. Wiget Lane, Suite 100, Walnut Creek, CA 94598-2494. CANADA: Ken Woods, 45 Sheppard Ave. East, Suite 401, Willowdale, Ont. M2N 5Y1. IDAHO: Jon Walters, 330 Shoup Ave., Suite 204, P.O. Box 51216, Idaho Falls, ID 83405. ILLINOIS: James P. Conway, 2200 S. Main St., Suite 303, Lombard, IL 60148. MASSACHUSETTS: Paul A. Loughran, Batterymarch Park, Quincy, MA 02169. NY: Edwin D. Hill, 16 Computer Dr. West, Suite C, Albany, NY 12205. MISSOURI: Ray Edwards, 300 S. Jefferson, Suite 300, Springfield, MO 65806. OHIO: Paul J. Witte, 7710 Reading Rd., Suite 9, Cincinnati, OH 45237. OKLAHOMA: Orville A. Tate, Jr., 4400 Will Rogers Pkwy., #309, Oklahoma City, OK 73108. PITTSBURGH: Lawrence Rossa, 200 Corporate Center Dr., Suite 301, Coriopolis, PA 15108. TENNESSEE: Carl Lansden, 500 Franklin Bldg., Suite 500, Chattanooga, TN 37411.

MOTION PICTURE STUDIO TEACHERS AND WELFARE WORKERS, LOCAL 884 (IATSE) HOLLYWOOD
P.O. Box 461467, Los Angeles, CA 90046. (213) 650-3792.
SECRETARY
Jim Hartz
BUSINESS AGENT
Polly Businger

PRODUCER-WRITERS GUILD OF AMERICA PENSION PLAN
1015 N. Hollywood Way, Burbank, CA 91505. (818) 846-1015, (800) 227-7863. FAX: (818) 566-8445.
CHAIRMAN
Richard Mittleman
VICE-CHAIRMAN
Jonathan Rintels, Jr.
SECRETARY
Bernard Gehan
VICE SECRETARY
Helayne Antler

PRODUCERS GUILD OF AMERICA
(Founded 1950. Membership: 500.)
400 S. Beverly Dr., Suite 211, Beverly Hills, CA 90212. (310) 557-0807. FAX: (310) 557-0436.
PRESIDENT
Thom Mount
VICE PRESIDENT
Marian Rees
SECRETARY
Charles Floyd Johnson
TREASURER
Joel Freeman
EXECUTIVE DIRECTOR
Charles B. FitzSimons

PRODUCTION OFFICE COORDINATORS, ACCOUNTANTS & ART DEPT. COORDINATORS GUILD LOCAL 717
13949 Ventura Blvd., Suite 306, Sherman Oaks, CA 91423. (818) 906-9986. FAX: (818) 990-8287.
BUSINESS AGENT
Deirdre Floyd

PROFESSIONAL MUSICIANS, LOCAL 47, (AFM,AFL-CIO)
(Organized October 30, 1894. Membership: 10,000.)
817 Vine St., Hollywood, CA 90038. (323) 462-2161. FAX: (323) 461-5260, (323) 466-1289, (323) 461-3090.
PRESIDENT
Bill Peterson
VICE PRESIDENT
Hal Espinosa

SECRETARY
Serena Kay Williams
TREASURER
Richard Totusek
TRUSTEES
Vince Trombetta
Abe Most
Irving Bush
DIRECTORS
William (Buddy) Collette
Art Davis
Vince DiBari
Lyle (Spud) Murphy
Jay Rosen
Ann Stockton

PUBLICISTS, LOCAL 818 (IATSE), HOLLYWOOD
13949 Ventura Blvd., Suite 302, Sherman Oaks, CA 91423. (818) 905-1541. FAX: (818) 905-6944
SECRETARY
Jess Garcia
BUSINESS AGENT
Marlene Mattaschiam

SCENIC & TITLE ARTISTS, LOCAL 816 (IATSE) LOS ANGELES
13949 Ventura Blvd., Suite 308, Sherman Oaks, CA 91423. (818) 906-7822. FAX: (818) 906-0481.
SECRETARY
Lisa Frazza
BUSINESS AGENTS
Gavin J. Koon

SCREEN ACTORS GUILD (AAAA-AFL-CIO)
(Organized July 1933. Membership: 95,000.)
5757 Wilshire Blvd., Los Angeles, CA 90036. (213) 954-1600. FAX: (213) 549-603. Website: http://www.sag.com.
PRESIDENT
Richard Masur
FIRST VICE PRESIDENT
Amy Aquino
THIRD VICE PRESIDENT
Paul Napier
FOURTH VICE PRESIDENT
Kim Sykes
FIFTH VICE PRESIDENT
Mary Seibel
SIXTH VICE PRESIDENT
Chuck Dorsett
TREASURER
F.J. O'Neil
NATIONAL EXECUTIVE DIRECTOR
Ken Orsatti
ASSOCIATE NATIONAL EXECUTIVE DIRECTOR
John McGuire
DIRECTOR, COMMUNICATIONS
Katherine Moore
COUNSEL
Leo Geffner
DISTRICT OFFICES
ARIZONA: 1616 East Indian School Rd., Suite 330, Phoenix, AZ 85016. (602) 265-2712. CALIFORNIA: San Diego: 7827 Convoy Court, #400, San Diego, CA 92111. (619) 278-7695. San Fransico: 235 Pine St., 11th fl., San Francisco, CA 94104. (415) 391-7510. COLORADO: 950 South Cherry Street, Suite 502, Denver, CO 80222. (303) 757-6226. FLORIDA: 7300 N. Kendall Dr., #620, Miami, FL 33145. (305) 444-7677. GEORGIA: 455 E. Paces Ferry Rd., NE, #334, Atlanta, GA 30305. (404) 239-0131. HAWAII: 949 Kapiolani Boulevard, Suite 105, Honolulu, HI 96814. (808) 596-0388. ILLINOIS: 1 E. Erie St., Suite 650, Chicago, IL 60611. (312) 573-0318. MASSACHUSETTS: 11 Beacon St., Rm. 512, Boston, MA 02108. (617) 742-2688. MICHIGAN: 27770 Franklin Rd., Southfield, MI 48034. (248) 355-3105. NEW YORK: 1515 Broadway, 44th Floor, New York, NY 10036. (212) 944-1030. PENNSYLVANIA: 230 South Broad Street, 10th Floor, Philadelphia, PA 19102. (215) 545-3150. TENNESSEE: 1108 7th Ave. S., Nashville, TN 37212. (615) 327-2958. TEXAS: Dallas: 6060 N. Central Expressway, #302, LB 604, Dallas, TX 75206. (214) 363-8300. Houston: 2400 Augusta Dr., Suite 264, Houston, TX 77057. (713) 972-1806. WASHINGTON DC/MARYLAND: 4340 East West Hwy., Suite 204, Bethesda, MD 20814. (301) 657-2560.

SCRIPT SUPERVISORS, LOCAL 871 (IATSE), HOLLYWOOD
13111 Ventura Boulevard, Suite 105, Studio City, CA 91604. (818) 995-6195. FAX: (818) 995-0814
SECRETARY
Melanie Mander
BUSINESS AGENT
Lainie Miller

SET DESIGNERS AND MODEL MAKERS, LOCAL 847 (IATSE), HOLLYWOOD
13949 Ventura Blvd., Suite 301, Sherman Oaks, CA 91423. (818) 784-6555. FAX: (818) 784-2004.
SECRETARY
Suzanne Feller-Otto

667

THE SONGWRITERS GUILD OF AMERICA
1500 Harbor Blvd., Weehawken, NJ 07087-6732. (201) 867-7603. FAX: (201) 867-7335.
1560 Broadway, Room 1306, New York, NY 10036. (212) 768-7902. FAX: (212) 768-9048.
6430 Sunset Blvd., Suite 1011, Hollywood, CA 90028. (213) 462-1108. FAX: (213) 462-5430.
1222 16th Avenue South, Suite 25, Nashville, TN 37212. (615) 329-1782. FAX: (615) 329-2623.
PRESIDENT
George David Weiss
EXECUTIVE DIRECTOR
Lewis M. Bachman

STORY ANALYSTS, LOCAL 854 (IATSE), HOLLYWOOD
13949 Ventura Blvd., Suite 301, Sherman Oaks, CA 91423. (818) 784-6555. FAX: (818) 784-2004.
SECRETARY
Calvin T. Yocum

STUDIO MECHANICS, LOCAL 52 (IATSE), NEW YORK
326 W. 48 St., New York, NY 10036. (212) 399-0980. FAX: (212) 741-1073.
SECRETARY
Robert F. Reilly
BUSINESS AGENT
George DeTitta

STUDIO MECHANICS, LOCAL 209 (IATSE) OHIO
1468 W. 9th St., Room 435, Cleveland, OH 44113. (216) 621-9537. FAX: (216) 621-3518.
SECRETARY
Timothy Woods
BUSINESS AGENT
Dale W. Short

STUDIO MECHANICS, LOCAL 477 (IATSE) N. MIAMI
10705 N.W. 33th Street - Suite 110, Miami, FL 33172. (305) 594-8585. FAX: (305) 597-9278.
SECRETARY
Norman Zuckerman
BUSINESS AGENT
Ben F. Lowe

STUDIO MECHANICS, LOCAL 479 (IATSE) ATLANTA
P.O. Box 78757, Atlanta, GA 30357. 404-885-9134. FAX: (404) 367-0240.
SECRETARY
Suzanne L. Carter
BUSINESS AGENT
Hilary Henkin

STUDIO MECHANICS, LOCAL 480 (IATSE) SANTA FE
1274 Calle de Comercio, Santa Fe, NM 87506. (505) 473-5100. FAX: (505) 424-0100.
SECRETARY
S. R. Pollard
BUSINESS AGENT
Stephen Mullen

STUDIO MECHANICS, LOCAL 484 (IATSE) TEXAS
440 Louisiana, Suite 480, Houston, TX 77002. (713) 229-8357. FAX: (713) 229-8138.
SECRETARY
Tom Sprague
BUSINESS AGENT
Mark B. Quick

STUDIO MECHANICS, LOCAL 485 (IATSE) TUCSON
P.O. Box 5705, Tucson, AZ 85704-5705. (602) 579-0088. FAX: (602) 579-0089.
SECRETARY
Rose Lujan
BUSINESS AGENT, NORTH
William J. Randall, 602-827-9907
BUSINESS AGENT, SOUTH
Scott Stravitz, 520-733-3691

STUDIO MECHANICS, LOCAL 812 (IATSE) DETROIT
20017 Van Dyke, Detroit, MI 48234. (313) 368-0825. FAX: (313) 368-1151.
SECRETARY, BUSINESS AGENT
Timothy F. Magee

STUNTMEN'S ASSOCIATION
(Organized 1961.)
4810 Whitsett Ave., North Hollywood, CA 91607. (818) 766-4334. FAX: (818) 766-5943.
PRESIDENT
George Marshall Ruge

TELEVISION BROADCASTING STUDIO EMPLOYEES, LOCAL 794 (IATSE), NEW YORK
P.O. Box 154, Lenox Hill Sta., New York, NY 10021-0012. (516) 724-4815. FAX: (516) 724-4815.
SECRETARY
Maria Smiley
BUSINESS AGENT
David Hodges

THEATRICAL WARDROBE UNION LOCAL 764 (IATSE), NEW YORK
151 W. 46 St., 8th fl., New York, NY 10036. (212) 221-1717. FAX: (212) 302-2324.
SECRETARY
Jenna Krempel
BUSINESS AGENTS
Stage: J. Raymond Polgar
Film: Jim Hurley

THEATRICAL WARDROBE ATTENDANTS, LOCAL 768 (IATSE), LOS ANGELES
13949 Ventura Blvd., Suite 307, Sherman Oaks, CA 91423. (818) 789-8735. FAX: (818) 905-6297.
SECRETARY
Mary B. Seward
BUSINESS AGENT
Dorothy Priest

THEATRICAL WARDROBE ATTENDANTS, LOCAL 769 (IATSE), CHICAGO
1220 Hawkins Ct., Bartlett, IL 60103. (630) 289-4568. FAX: (630) 289-4568.
SECRETARY
Cheryl Ryba
BUSINESS AGENT
Hugh Pruett, 3500 North Lake Shore Drive, Chicago, IL 60657. (773) 477-4952

WRITERS GUILD OF AMERICA, EAST, INC.
555 W. 57 St., New York, NY 10019. (212) 767-7800. FAX: (212) 582-1909.
PRESIDENT
Herb Sargent
VICE PRESIDENT
Albert Rubin
EXECUTIVE DIRECTOR
Mona Mangan

WRITERS GUILD OF AMERICA, WEST, INC.
7000 W. 3rd St., Los Angeles, CA 90048. (323) 951-4000. FAX: (323) 782-4800.
PRESIDENT
Daniel Petrie, Jr.
VICE PRESIDENT
John Wells
SECRETARY & TREASURER
Michael Mahern
EXECUTIVE DIRECTOR
Brian Walton

ORGANIZATIONS

ACADEMY OF TELEVISION ARTS AND SCIENCES
(Formed in 1948 to advance the arts and sciences of television. Awards Emmys for nighttime programming and publishes Emmy Magazine.)
5220 Lankershim Blvd., No. Hollywood, CA 91601. (818) 754-2800. FAX: (818) 761-2827. URL: http://www.emmys.org
PRESIDENT
Meryl Marshall
VICE PRESIDENT
Nancy Bradley Wiard
SECOND VICE PRESIDENT
George Sunga
V.P., LOS ANGELES
Nelson Davis
SECRETARY
Sheila Manning
TRESURER
Lee Miller
EXECUTIVE COMMITTEE
Chris Albrecht, Leo Chaloukian, Jeffrey Cole, Mark Allen Itkin, Robert H. Levi, David A. Neuman, Peter Roth, Thomas W. Sarnoff, John S. Shaffner.
EXECUTIVE DIRECTOR
James Loper
DIRECTOR, AWARDS
John Leverence
DIRECTOR, MEMBERSHIP/ACTIVITIES
Linda Loe
BOARD OF GOVERNORS
Janet Ashikaga A.C.E., Conrad Bachmann, Bob Baker, Patricia Barry, Daniel Birman, Robert Boden, Beth Bohn, Janice Brandow, James Castle, Leo Chaloukian C.A.S., Marcy DeVeaux, Maura Dunbar, Hal Eisner, Alan Fama, Geriann Geraci, Mark Glamack, Ron Grant, Jack Grossbart, Vince Gutierrez, Michael Hoey A.C.E., Robert Holmes, Caro Jones C.S.A., Paula Kaatz, Teresa Koenig, Richard Larson, Alfred Lehman, Robert Liu A.S.C., Isidore Makofsky A.S.C., Sheila Manning, David Michaels, Bill Millar, Lee Miller, Deborah Miller, Donna Mitroff, John Moffitt, Irene Nachreiner, Meryl O'Loughlin C.S.A., Barbara Rubin, Socorro Serrano, John Shaffner, Nancy Steingard, George Sunga, Peter Tolan, Mathew Tombers, Heidi Trotta, Patricia van Ryker, Mark Watters, William Wistrom, Robert Wollin, Bryce Zabel.

THE ADVERTISING COUNCIL
261 Madison Ave., 11th floor, New York, NY 10016-2303. (212) 922-1500. FAX: (212) 922-1676. email: info@adcouncil.org
URL: http://www.adcouncil.org
CHAIRMAN
Gregory G. Coleman
PRESIDENT & CEO
Ruth A. Wooden
EXECUTIVE VICE PRESIDENT & COO
S. Murray Gaylord
EXECUTIVE VICE PRESIDENT & CFO
Arie Weissman
S.V.P., CORPORATE COMMUNICATIONS
Paula A. Veale

ADVERTISING RESEARCH FOUNDATION
641 Lexington Ave., New York, NY 10022. (212) 751-5656. FAX: (212) 319-5265.
CEO & PRESIDENT
Jim Spaeth
S.V.P., RESEARCH DIRECTOR
Gabe Samuels
S.V.P., COMM. MEMBER RELATIONS
William Cook

ALLIANCE FOR COMMUNITY MEDIA
666 Eleventh St., NW, Suite 806, Washington, DC 20001-4542. (202) 393-2650. FAX: (202) 393-2653.
EXECUTIVE DIRECTOR
Bunnie Riedel

ALLIANCE OF MOTION PICTURE AND TELEVISION PRODUCERS
(Membership: Major studios, independent production companies and film processing laboratories.)
15503 Ventura Blvd., Encino, CA 91436-3140. (818) 995-3600.
PRESIDENT
J. Nicholas Counter III

S.V.P., LEGAL & BUSINESS AFFAIRS
Carol A. Lombardini
CFO
Kathy Grotticelli
V.P., LEGAL AFFAIRS
Helayne Antler

AMERICAN ADVERTISING FEDERATION
1101 Vermont Ave., NW, Suite 500, Washington, DC 20005. (202) 898-0089. FAX: (202) 898-0159.
PRESIDENT & CEO
Wallace Snyder
V.P., PUBLIC AFFAIRS
Marjorie Valin
V.P., MARKETING SERVICES
Christine Hilferty

AMERICAN ASSOCIATION OF ADVERTISING AGENCIES
405 Lexington Ave., New York, NY 10174-1801. (212) 682-2500. FAX: (212) 682-8391.
URL: http://www.commercepark.com/AAAA
CHAIRMAN
David Bell, Bozell Worldwide, Inc. (NY)
VICE CHAIRMAN
Ralph W. Rydholm, Tatham EURO RSCG (Chicago)
SECRETARY & TREASURER
Byron Lewis, UniWorld Group, Inc. (NY)
-PRESIDENT & CEO
O. Burtch Drake, A.A.A.A. (NY)
EXECUTIVE V.P., CONSULTING
Harry Paster
SENIOR VICE PRESIDENTS
Marilyn Bockman
Michael D. Donahue
Robert J. Finn
Joyce Harrington
James C. Martucci Jr.

AMERICAN HUMANE ASSOCIATION
(Organized 1877. Liaison with the television and motion picture industry as supervisors of animal action in television and motion picture production.)
15366 Dickens Str., Sherman Oaks, CA 91403. (818) 501-0123. email: ahawest@aol.com
National Headquarters: 63 Inverness Dr. E., Englewood, CO 80112. (303) 792-9900.
NATIONAL PRESIDENT
Richard Glance
NATIONAL EXECUTIVE DIRECTOR
Robert F.X. Hart
TREASURER
Timothy O'Brien
DIRECTOR, WESTERN REGIONAL OFFICE
Gini Barrett

AMERICAN SOCIETY OF COMPOSERS, AUTHORS AND PUBLISHERS (ASCAP)
(Organized February 13, 1914. Membership: 39,000 Music Writers, 18,000 Publishers.)
One Lincoln Plaza, New York, NY 10023. (212) 621-6000. FAX: (212) 724-9064.
7920 Sunset Blvd., Suite 300, Hollywood, CA 90046. (213) 883-1000. FAX: (213) 883-1049.
Two Music Square W., Nashville, TN 37203. (615) 742-5000. FAX: (615) 742-5020.
2690 Cumberland Pkwy., Ste. 490, Atlanta, GA 30339. (770) 805-3400. FAX: (770) 916-0232.
1608 W. Belmont Ave., Ste. 200, Chicago, IL 60657. (773) 472-1157. FAX: (773) 471-1158.
PRESIDENT & CHAIRMAN
Marilyn Bergman
CEO
John A. LoFrumento
COO
Al Wallace
CFO
Jim Collins
VICE CHAIRMEN
Cy Coleman
Jay Morgenstern
S.V.P., DIRECTOR OF MARKETING
Todd Brabec

SECRETARY
Arthur Hamilton
TREASURER
Arnold Broido
COUNSEL
I. Fred Koenigsberg
BOARD OF DIRECTORS
Marilyn Bergman, John Bettis, Freddy Bienstock, Joanne Boris, Leon J. Brettler, Arnold Broido, John Cacavas, Cy Coleman, Hal David, John L. Eastman, Nicholas Firth, Arthur Hamilton, Donna Hilley, Wayland Holyfield, Jimmy Jam, Dean Kay, Leeds Levy, Johnny Mandel, Jay Morgenstern, Stephen Paulus, David Raksin, Irwin Z. Robinson, Mary Rodgers, Kathy Spanberger.

ASIAN CINEVISION, INC.
(A not-for-profit organization dedicated to encouraging Asian and Asian-American media arts.)
32 East Broadway, New York, NY 10002. (212) 925-8685. FAX: (212) 925-8157.
EXECUTIVE DIRECTOR
Bill J. Gee

ASSOCIATION OF AMERICA'S PUBLIC TELEVISION STATIONS
(Organized 1979. Research, planning and representation for member public television stations throughout the U.S.)
1350 Connecticut Ave. NW, Suite 200, Washington, D.C. 20036. (202) 887-1700. FAX: (202) 293-2422.
email: info@apts.org
URL: http://www.apts.org
PRESIDENT
David J. Brugger
BOARD OF TRUSTEES
Keith Alexander, Steve Bass, Ronald Becker, Howard W. Bell Jr., Mary Bitterman, Richard Bodorff, David J. Brugger, Beth Courtney, Susan Farmer, Elsie Garner, James Morgese, Steven Newberry, Allen Pizzato, William Reed, Karen Sherrin, Smauel Smith, Jerry Wareham, Viviane Warren, Caroline Whitson.

ASSOCIATION OF CINEMA & VIDEO LABORATORIES, INC.
(Organized 1953. Publishes *ACVL Handbook*.)
7095 Hollywood Blvd., #751, Hollywood, CA 90028.
Correspondence only, no phone number.
PRESIDENT
Frank Ricotta, Technicolor, Inc.
FIRST VICE PRESIDENT
George Hutchison, Consolidated Film Industries
SECOND VICE PRESIDENT
Jim George, Deluxe Laboratories
TREASURER
Richard Vedvick, Forde Motion Picture Labs
SECRETARY
Robert Smith, Duart Film Laboratories

ASSOCIATION OF INDEPENDENT COMMERCIAL PRODUCERS
(Organized 1972.)
P.O. Box 2007, San Francisco, CA 94126-2007. (415) 642-8595. FAX: (415) 861-4212.
PRESIDENT
Tony Hurd, Six Foot Two Productions
PAST PRESIDENT
Marcia Herman McLean, Marcia Can, Inc.
TREASURER
Rachel Leibert, Red Sky Films
SECRETARY
Michelle Dennis, Phoenix Editorial Services
VICE PRESIDENTS
Lori Anderson (Varitel Video)
Deborah Giarratana (Pacific Data Images)
Shari Hanson (Industrial Light & Magic)
Larry Walsh (Hammond Martin Walsh & Smith)
BRANCHES
New York, Chicago, Denver, Miami, Atlanta, Dallas, Seattle, Los Angeles

ASSOCIATION OF INDEPENDENT VIDEO & FILMMAKERS, INC.
(A national membership organization dedicated to the growth of independent media. Publishes *The Independent Magazine*.)
304 Hudson Str., 6th Flr. N, New York, NY 10013. (212) 807-1400. FAX: (212) 463-8519.
EXECUTIVE DIRECTOR
Ruby Lerner
DIRECTOR OF PROGRAMS & SERVICES
Pamela Calvert
EDITOR
Pat Thompson
MANAGING EDITOR
Michele Shapiro
BOARD OF DIRECTORS
Joe Berlinger, Melissa Burch, Loni Ding, Barbara Hammer, Ruby Lerner, James Klein, Diane Markrow, Meni Matias, Robb Moss, Robert Richter, James Schamus, Norman Wang, Burton Wiess

ASSOCIATION OF LOCAL TELEVISION STATIONS
1320 19th St., Suite 300, Washington, DC 20036. (202) 887-1970. FAX (202) 887-0950.
PRESIDENT
James B. Hedlund
CHAIRMAN
Michael Eigner
VICE CHAIRMAN
Stuart Swartz
V.P., LEGAL & LEGISLATIVE AFFAIRS
David L. Donovan
V.P. & GENERAL COUNSEL
James Popham
V.P., FINANCE
Al Petrionio
DIRECTOR, CONGRESSIONAL RELATIONS
Angela Giroux
TREASURER
David Pulido
ASSISTANT TO PRESIDENT
Susan Baurenfeind

ASSOCIATION OF NATIONAL ADVERTISERS, INC.
708 3rd Ave., New York, NY 10017. (212) 697-5950. FAX: (212) 661-8057.
PRESIDENT & CEO
John J. Sarsen, Jr.
SENIOR VICE PRESIDENTS
Robert Liodice
Phil Shyposh
Robin Webster

ASSOCIATION OF TALENT AGENTS
(Organized April, 1937. Official organization of talent agents in Hollywood.)
9255 Sunset Blvd., Suite 318, Los Angeles, CA 90069. (310) 274-0628. FAX: (310) 274-5063. email: agentassoc@aol.com
EXECUTIVE DIRECTOR
Karen Stuart
FIRST VICE PRESIDENT
Sandy Bresler
VICE PRESIDENTS
Sid Craig
T. J. Escott
Sheldon Sroloff
Sonjia Warren Brandon
SECRETARY & TREASURER
Martin Gage

BMI (BROADCAST MUSIC, INC.)
320 W. 57 St., New York, NY 10019. (212) 586-2000. FAX: (212) 245-8986. email: newyork@bmi.com. URL: http://bmi.com
V.P., WRITER/PUBLISHER RELATIONS, NEW YORK
Charlie S. Feldman
8730 Sunset Blvd., 3rd fl. West, Los Angeles, CA 90069. (310) 659-9109. FAX: (310) 657-6947. email: losangeles@bmi.com
V.P., WRITER/PUBLISHER RELATIONS, LOS ANGELES
Rick Riccobono
10 Music Square E., Nashville, TN 37203. (615) 401-2000. FAX: (615) 401-2707. email: nashville@bmi.com
V.P., WRITER/PUBLISHER RELATIONS, NASHVILLE
Roger Sovine
5201 Blue Lagoon Dr., Ste. 310, Miami, FL 33126. (305) 266-3636. FAX: (305) 266-2442. email: miami@bmi.com
CONTACT
Diane Almodovar
255 Ponce de Leon, East Wing, Ste. !-262, Royal Bank Center, Hato Rey, PR 00917. (787) 754-6490. FAX: (787) 753-6765. email: latin@bmi.com
CONTACT
Joey Mercado
84 Harley House, Marylebone Rd., London NW1 5HN, England. (44 171) 935-2037. FAX: (44 171) 224-1046. email: london@bmi.com
CONTACT
Phil Graham
CHAIRMAN OF THE BOARD
Phil Jones
PRESIDENT & CEO
Frances W. Preston

THE BROADCASTERS' FOUNDATION
296 Old Church Rd., Greenwich, CT 06830. (203) 862-8577. FAX: (203) 629-5739.
PRESIDENT & CEO
Gordon Hastings

CABLE TELECOMMUNICATIONS ASSOCIATION (CATA)
3950 Chain Bridge Rd., Fairfax, VA 22030. (703) 691-8875.
FAX: (703) 691-8911. email: acowan@catamail.org. URL:
http://www.catanet.org
PRESIDENT
Stephen R. Effros
EXECUTIVE VICE PRESIDENT
James H. Ewalt
V.P., COMMUNICATIONS
Anne Cowan

CABLE TELEVISION ADVERTISING BUREAU
830 Third Ave., New York, NY 10022. (212) 508-1200. FAX:
(212) 832-3268.
CHAIRMAN
Theodore Cutler
PRESIDENT & CEO
Joseph Ostrow
VICE CHAIRMEN
Robert H. Atler
Michael J. Eckert
TREASURER
Douglas McCormick
BOARD OF DIRECTORS
Robert H. Alter, Allan Barnes (Prime Cable), Thomas G. Baxter
(Comcast Cable Communications), George Bodenheimer (ESPN),
William J. Bresnan (Bresnan Communications), Michael C. Burrus
(Multimedia Cablevision), F. Steven Crawford (Intermdia Partners),
Theodore J. Cutler (Time Warner Cable), Ajit Dalvi (Cox Cable
Communications), Michael J. Eckert (Landmark Communications),
Ed Frazier (Liberty Sports), Tom Freston (MTV Networks),
Whitney Goit (Arts & Entertainment Cable Network), Daniel E.
Gold (Century Communications), Erica Gruen (TV Food Network),
Steven J. Heyer (Turner Broadcasting System), Frank J. Intiso
(Falcon Cable TV), Kay Koplovitz (USA Network), Marvin Jones
(Tele-Communications Inc.), Greg Liptak (Jones International),
Jeff Marcus (Marcus Communications), Lee Masters (E!
Entertainment), Douglas W. McCormick (Lifetime Entertainment),
Judith McHale (Discovery Networks, Inc.), Donald Mitzner (CBS
Cable), Joseph W. Ostrow (CAB), John J. Rigas (Adelphia
Communications Corp.), Timothy B. Robertson (International
Family Entertainment), Tom Rogers (NBC Cable & Business
Development), Joel Rudich (Coaxial Communications), Bill
Stanfield (Radius Communications), Robert A Stengel (Media
One), Curtis Symonds (Black Entertainment TV).

CABLE TELEVISION INFORMATION CENTER (CTIC)
(Organized 1972. Provides community governments and con-
sumers with objective information about the cable industry.)
1700 Shaker Church Rd., Olympia, WA 98502. (206) 866-2080.
PRESIDENT
Harold E. Horn

CATHOLIC ACTORS GUILD OF AMERICA
(Organized April, 1914. Membership: 550.)
1501 Broadway, # 510, New York, NY 10036. (212) 398-1868.
PRESIDENT
William J. O'Malley

COMMUNICATION COMMISSION OF THE NATIONAL
COUNCIL OF THE CHURCHES OF CHRIST IN THE USA
475 Riverside Dr., Room 856, New York, NY 10115. (212) 870-
2574. FAX: (212) 870-2030. email: davepomeroy@ecunet.org
CHAIRMAN
Eric Shafer
DIRECTOR OF ELECTRONIC MEDIA
David W. Pomeroy

CORPORATION FOR PUBLIC BROADCASTING
901 E St., N.W. Washington, DC 20004. (202) 879-9600. FAX:
(202) 783-1019. URL: http://www.cpb.org
PRESIDENT & CEO
Robert T. Coonrod
EXECUTIVE VICE PRESIDENT
Cynthia Browne
Frederick L. DeMarco
GENERAL COUNSEL/CORPORATE SECRETARY
Kathleen Cox
V.P., PROGRAMMING
Katherine R. R. Carpenter
V.P., COMMUNICATIONS
Charles B. Fancher Jr.
V.P., GOVERNMENT RELATIONS
David Guhse
V.P., RADIO
Richard H, Madden
V.P., EDUCATION
Peggy O'Brien
V.P., TELEVISION OPERATIONS
Douglas A. Weiss
MEMBERS
Katherine M. Anderson, Ritajean H. Butterworth, Christy
Carpenter, Henry J. Cauthen, Winter Horton, Heidi Schulman.

COUNCIL ON INTERNATIONAL NON-THEATRICAL EVENTS
(Organized 1957. CINE selects and enters theatrical short
subjects and tv products in 120 film & video competitions.)
1001 Connecticut Ave. NW, Suite 625, Washington, DC 20036.
(202) 785-1136. (202) 785-1137. FAX: (202) 785-4114.
PRESIDENT
Rob Gardner

ELECTRONIC INDUSTRIES ALLIANCE
2500 Wilson Blvd., Arlington, VA 22201. (703) 907-7500. FAX:
(703) 907-7501.
CHAIRMAN OF THE BOARD
John Major
PRESIDENT
Peter F. McCloskey
V.P., PUBLIC AFFAIRS
Mark V. Rosenker

ELECTRONIC MEDIA RATING COUNCIL
200 W. 57th St., Suite 204, New York, NY 10019. (212) 765-
0200. FAX: (212) 765-1868.
EXECUTIVE DIRECTOR
Richard Weinstein
CHAIRMAN
Tim Brooks

FILM/VIDEO ARTS
(Organized 1968. Provides independents with training, equip-
ment rental and editing services.)
817 Broadway, 2nd Flr., New York, NY 10003. (212) 673-9361.
FAX: (212) 475-3467.
EXECUTIVE DIRECTOR
Frank Millspaugh
HEAD OF DEVELOPMENT & PUBLIC RELATIONS
Duana C. Butler
HEAD OF EDUCATION
Matt Lavine

INSTITUTE OF ELECTRICAL AND ELECTRONICS
ENGINEERS, INC.
345 E. 47 St., New York, NY 10017-2394. (212) 705-7900.
email: j.bordogna@ieee.org
PRESIDENT
Dr. Joseph Bordogna
EXECUTIVE DIRECTOR
Daniel J. Senese

INTERACTIVE TELEVISION ASSOCIATION
1030 Fifteenth St. N.W., Suite 1053, Washington, DC 20005
(202) 408-0008. FAX: (202) 408-0111.
PRESIDENT
Andrew L. Sernovitz
EXECUTIVE VICE PRESIDENT
Peter C. Waldheim
MEMBERSHIP
Yasha M. Harari
MEMBER SERVICES
Mathew I. Laurencelle
RESEARCH AND PUBLICATIONS
Philip R. Strohi

INTERNATIONAL COUNCIL OF THE NATIONAL ACADEMY
OF TELEVISION ARTS AND SCIENCES
(Awards the International Emmy in recognition of excellence in
television programs produced and broadcast outside the U.S.)
142 W. 57 St., 16th fl., New York, NY 10019. (212) 489-6969.
FAX: (212) 489-6557. email: intcouncil@aol.com
URL: http://www.intlemmys.org
PRESIDENT
Kay Koplovitz
CHAIRMAN
Tom Rogers
VICE CHAIRMAN, INTERNATIONAL
Robert Phillis
VICE CHAIRMAN, US
Larry Gershman
EXECUTIVE DIRECTOR
Georges Leckre
GENERAL MANAGER
Linda Alexander

INTERNATIONAL DOCUMENTARY ASSOCIATION
1551 S. Robertson Blvd., Suite 201, Los Angeles, CA 90035.
(310) 284-8422. FAX: (310) 785-9334. email: idf@netcom.com
PRESIDENT
David Haugland
FIRST V.P.
Lisa Leeman
SECOND V.P.
Steven Roche

SECRETARY
Richard L. Samuels
TREASURER
Mitchell Block
EXECUTIVE DIRECTOR
Betsy A. McLane
LEGAL COUNSEL
Michael Donaldson
BOARD OF DIRECTORS
Mitchell Block, Nicholas Clapp, Carol L. Fleisher, Lyn Goldfarb, Marina Goldovskaya, David Haugland, Carol Munday Lawrence, Lisa Leeman, Lynne Littman, John Mason, Steven Ogden, Richard Propper, Steven Roche, Richard L. Samuels, Joan Sekler, Michael Tobias, Lance Webster.
REGIONAL MEMBERS
John Alonzo (Mobile), Henry Hampton (Boston), Len McClure (Hong Kong), Michael Rabiger (Chicago), Harry Rasky (Toronto), Andre Singer (London), Marc Weiss (New York), Frederick Wiseman (Boston)

INTERNATIONAL RADIO AND TELEVISION SOCIETY FOUNDATION
420 Lexington Ave. Suite 1714, New York, NY 10170-0101. (212) 867-6650. FAX: (212) 867-6653. URL: http://www.irts.org
PRESIDENT
Joyce M. Tudryn
SENIOR DIRECTOR, PROGRAM ADMINISTRATION
Maria De Leon-Fisher
DIRECTOR, SPECIAL PROJECTS
Marilyn Ellis
DIRECTOR, MARKETING
Maggie Davis

MEDIA RATING COUNCIL
200 W. 57th St., Ste. 204, New York, NY 10019. (212) 765-0200. FAX: (212) 765-1868.
EXECUTIVE DIRECTOR
Richard Weinstein
EX-OFFICIO
Tim Brooks
CHAIRMAN
David Potrack
CHAIRMAN, RADIO COMMITTEE
Ron Werth
CHAIRMAN, CABLE COMMITTEE
Barry Kresch
CHAIRMAN, TV COMMITTEE
Leigh Graham

MOTION PICTURE AND TELEVISION FUND
23388 Mulholland Drive, Woodland Hills, CA 91364. (818) 876-1888.
Bob Hope Health Center, 335 N. LaBrea Ave., Los Angeles, CA 90036. (213) 634-3850.
Toluca Lake Health Center, 4323 Riverside Dr., Burbank, CA 91505. (818) 556-2700.
Westside Health Center, 1950 Sawtelle Blvd., Suite 130, Los Angeles, CA 90025. (310) 996-9355.
Samuel Goldwyn Foundation Children's Center, 2114 Pontius Ave., Los Angeles, CA 90025. (310) 445-8993.
CHAIRMAN
Roger L. Mayer
VICE CHAIRS
Robert Blees
Irma Kalish
Michael Wayne
TREASURER
Marshall Wortman
SECRETARY
Gloria Palazzo
PRESIDENT/CEO
William F. Haug
V.P., PROFESSIONAL SERVICES
Timothy M. Lefevre, M.D.

THE MUSEUM OF TELEVISION AND RADIO
(Formerly the Museum of Broadcasting. Founded in 1976, the museum houses a permanent collection of over 75,000 television and radio programs and commercials.)
25 W. 52 St., New York, NY 10019. (212) 621-6600. FAX: (212) 621-6700.
465 N. Beverly Dr., Beverly Hills, CA 90210. (310) 786-1000.
CHAIRMAN
Frank A. Bennack
PRESIDENT
Robert M. Batscha

THE NATIONAL ACADEMY OF TELEVISION ARTS AND SCIENCES
(Organized 1947. Awards Emmys for daytime programming. Publishers of *Television Quarterly*.)
National Office: 111 W. 57 St., New York, NY 10019. (212) 586-8424. FAX: (212) 246-8129.
CHAIRMAN OF THE BOARD
Charles F. Dolan
PRESIDENT
John Cannon
VICE CHAIRMAN
Malachy Wienges
VICE PRESIDENT
Darryl B. Cohen
NATIONAL AWARDS DIRECTOR
Trudy Wilson
PUBLIC RELATIONS
Robert F. Blake
Robert H. Christie
MEMBERSHIP INFORMATION
Michael Grigaliunas
EDITOR OF TELEVISION QUARTERLY
Richard Pack

NATIONAL ASIAN AMERICAN TELECOMMUNICATIONS (NAATA)
(Distributes Asian Pacific American media productions and provides techinal assistance and funding to media arts.)
S.F. International Asian American Film Festival, 346 Ninth Street, 2nd Flr., San Francisco, CA 94103. (415) 863-0814. FAX: (415) 863-7428. E-,ail: naata@naatanet
URL: http://www.naatanet.org
EXECUTIVE DIRECTOR
Eddie Wong
MEDIA FUND DIRECTOR
Janice Sakamoto
FESTIVAL DIRECTOR
Corey Tong
PROGRAMMING DIRECTOR
Donald Young

NATIONAL ASSOCIATION OF BROADCASTERS
(Organized 1922.)
1771 N St. N.W., Washington, DC 20036-2891. (202) 429-5300. (202) 429-5651.
PRESIDENT & CEO
Edward O. Fritts
EXECUTIVE V.P. & ASSISTANT TO PRESIDENT
Rory Benson
EXECUTIVE V.P., & CFO
Kenneth D. Almgren
EXECUTIVE V.P., OPERATIONS & INTERNATIONAL BUSINESS DEVELOPMENT
Jack Knebel
EXECUTIVE V.P., GOVERNMENT RELATIONS
James C. May
EXECUTIVE V.P. & GENERAL COUNSEL
Henry L. "Jeff" Baumann
S.V.P., OPERATIONS & INTERNATIONAL BUSINESS DEVELOPMENT
Terri Rabel
S.V.P., MEETINGS & CONFERENCE SERVICES
Kathy Muller
S.V.P., ADVERTISING & SERVICES GROUP
David Dziedzic
S.V.P., CONVENTIONS & EXPOSITIONS
Haidee Calore
S.V.P., CORPORATE COMMUNICATIONS
Dennis Wharton
S.V.P., RESEARCH & INFORMATION GROUP
Richard Ducey
S.V.P., SCIENCE & TECHNOLOGY
Lynn Claudy
S.V.P., TELEVISION
Charles E. Sherman
DIRECTOR OF SALES
Jodi McMannis
DIRECTOR OF SERVICES
Daryl Everett
DIRECTOR, MARKETING & RESEARCH
Lisa O'Bara

TELEVISION BOARD OF DIRECTORS
James G. Babb Jr., L. Martin Brantly, Elizabeth Murphy Burns, John Conomikes, W. Don Cornwell, Richard Cotton, Nick Evans Jr., Michael Finkelstein, Dennis J. FitzSimons, Martin D. Franks, Ralph W. Gabbard, John Hayes, Philip A. Jones, Amy McCombs, Howard W. Meagle Jr., Thomas A. Oakley, Preston Padden, Clyde Payne, Bill Pitts, G. William Ryan, Patricia C. Smullin, Bill Sullivan, Nick Trigony, John P. Zanotti

NATPE (NATIONAL ASSOCIATION OF TELEVISION PROGRAM EXECUTIVES)

2425 Olympic Blvd., #550-E, Santa Monica, CA 90404. (310) 453-4440. FAX: (310) 453-5258. URL: http://www.natpe.org
454 Oakleigh Rd. N., London, England N2O 0RZ. (44181) 361-3793. FAX: (44181) 368-3824.
32 Buccaneer Court, Paradise Waters, Queensland 4210, Australia. (617) 5532-1046. FAX: (617) 591-4035.
CHAIRMAN
Greg Meidel
FIRST VICE CHAIRMAN
Nick Trigony
IMMEDIATE PAST CHAIRMAN
Jayne Adair
MEMBER REPRESENTATIVE
Brooke Bailey Johnson
PRESIDENT & CEO
Bruce Johansen
S.V.P., CONFERENCES & SPECIAL EVENTS
Nick Orfanopoulos
S.V.P., MARKETING
Ron Gold
V.P., CREATIVE SERVICES
Beth Braen
V.P., FINANCE
Ron Dobkin
PRESIDENT, NATPE EDUCATIONAL FOUNDATION
Lew Klein
EUROPEAN DIRECTOR
Pam Smithard
PACIFIC RIM REPRESENTATIVE
Nick McMahon

NATIONAL CABLE TELEVISION ASSOCIATION

(Organized 1951. Trade association that lobbies for cable television interest.)
1724 Massachusetts Ave. N.W., Washington, DC 20036. (202) 775-3550.
PRESIDENT & CEO
Decker Anstrom
EXECUTIVE V.P. & COO
June E. Travis
V.P., GOVERNMENT RELATIONS
Pamela J. Turner
V.P., LAW & REGULATORY POLICY
Daniel L. Brenner
V.P., ASSOCIATION AFFAIRS
Jadz Janucik
V.P., INDUSTRY AFFAIRS
Barbara York
V.P., PUBLIC AFFAIRS
Victoria Clarke
CHAIRMAN
Robert Miron
TREASURER
James O. Robbins
SECRETARY
Leo J. Hindery
IMMEDIATE PAST CHAIRMAN
R.E. "Ted" Turner
MEMBERS OF THE BOARD
Barry L. Babcock, Jeffrey D. Bennis, Jeffrey L. Bewkes, Matthew C. Blank, Steven M. Bornstein, William J. Bresnan, Peter P. Brubaker, Michael C. Burrus, Scott D. Chambers, Joseph J. Collins, Nickolas Davatzes, James L. Dolan, Frank M. Drendel, John M. Egan, John D. Evans, Joseph S. Gans III, John S. Hendricks, Glenn R. Jones, Marvin L. Jones, Kay Koplovitz, Charles M. Lillis, Jerry D. Lindauer, Jeffrey A. Marcus, Thomas O. Might, James A. Monroe, Marc B. Nathanson, John J. Rigas, Brian L. Roberts, Timothy B. Robertson, Paul F. Schonewolf, Michael S. Willner, John O. Wynne.

NATIONAL CABLE TELEVISION COOPERATIVE, INC.

14809 W. 95th St., Lenexa, KS 66215. (913) 599-5900. FAX: (913) 599-5903. URL: http://www.cabletvco-op.org
PRESIDENT
Michael L. Pandzik
S.V.P., OPERATIONS
David M. Clark
S.V.P., PROGRAMMING
Frank J. Hughes
V.P., MEMBER SERVICES
Daniel P. Mulveron

NATIONAL VIDEO RESOURCES

73 Spring St., #606, New York, NY 11238. (212) 274-8080. FAX: (212) 274-8081. email: NVRInfo@nvr.org
EXECUTIVE DIRECTOR
Timothy Gunn
DIRECTOR OF PLANNING AND COMMUNCATIONS
Lisa B. Segal
ASSOCIATE DIRECTOR
Tania Blanich

NEW YORK FOUNDATION FOR THE ARTS

155 Ave. of the Americas, 14th Flr., New York, NY 10013. (212) 366-6900. FAX: (212) 366-1778.
URL: http://www.artswire.org/nyfa
EXECUTIVE DIRECTOR
Theodore Berger
DIRECTOR, ARTISTS' SERVICES
Penelope Dannenberg

NEW YORK STATE COUNCIL ON THE ARTS

915 Broadway, 8th Flr., New York, NY 10010, (212) 387-7000. FAX: (212) 366-7168. email: nysca@interport.net
URL: http://www.artswire.org/~nysca
DIRECTOR, INDIVIDUAL ARTISTS PROGRAM
Gary Schiro
DIRECTOR, ELECTRONIC MEDIA & FILM PROGRAM
Deborah Silverfine

NEW YORK WOMEN IN FILM & TELEVISION

6 East 39th St., 12th floor, New York, NY 10016-0112. (212) 679-0870. FAX: (212) 679-0899. email: staff@nywift.org
URL: http://www.nywift.org
PRESIDENT
Ellen Geiger
VICE PRESIDENT
Vanessa Cordova Corwin
SECRETARY
Alice Elliott
TREASURER
Laverne Berry
EXECUTIVE DIRECTOR
Terry Lawler
PROGRAM COORDINATOR
Jenny Fox
ADVISORY BOARD
Jeanne Betancourt, Mirra Bank Brockman, Grace Blake, Karen Cooper, Beth Dembitzer, Linda Elerbee, Nora Ephron, Pat Fili-Krushel, Gail Frank, Harlene Freezer, Linda Gottlieb, Pat Herold, Charlayne Hunter-Gault, Marjorie Kalins, Kay Koplovitz, Geraldine Laybourne, Eileen Newman, Jane Pauley, Peggy Rajski, Cokie Roberts, Jane Rosenthal, Thelma Schoonmaker, Susan Seidelman, Joan Micklin Silver, Diane Sokolow, Juliet Taylor, Patrizia von Brandenstein.

PERMANENT CHARITIES COMMITTEE OF THE ENTERTAINMENT INDUSTRIES

11132 Ventura Blvd., Suite 401, Studio City, CA 91604-3156. (818) 760-7722. FAX: (818) 760-7898.
CHAIRMAN OF THE BOARD
Earl Lestz
PRESIDENT & CEO
Lisa Paulsen
FIRST V.P.
Harry J. Floyd
SECOND V.P.
Roger L. Mayer
SECRETARY
T. J. Baptie
TREASURER
Robert S. Colbert, CPA
V.P., ADMINISTRATION
Marilyn Augustine
V.P., COMMUNICATIONS & CORPORATE RELATIONS
Danielle M. Guttman

RADIO-TELEVISION NEWS DIRECTORS ASSOCIATION

100 Connecticut Ave. N.W., Suite 615, Washington, DC 20036. (202) 659-6510. FAX: 9202) 223-4007. email: rtnda@rtnda.org
URL: http://www.rtnda.org
CHAIRWOMAN
Lucy Riley
CHAIRMAN-ELECT
John Sears

SESAC, INC.

(A music licensing organization.)
55 Music Square East, Nashville, TN 37203. (800) 826-9996. FAX: (615) 329-9627.
CHAIRMEN
Freddie Gershon
Ira Smith
Stephen Swid
PRESIDENT & COO
Bill Velez

SOCIETY OF COMPOSERS & LYRICISTS

400 South Beverly Dr., Suite 214, Beverly Hills, CA 90212.
(310) 281-2812. FAX: (818) 990-0601.
URL: http://www.filmscore.org
PRESIDENT
Joy Chattaway
FIRST V.P.
Charles Bernstein
VICE PRESIDENT
Alex Shapiro
SECRETARY/TREASURER
Gary Woods
ADVISORY BOARD
Alan Bergman, Marilyn Bergman, Elmer Bernstein, Bill Conti,
Jerry Goldsmith, James Newton Howard, Quincy Jones,
Peter Matz, Alan Menken, David Raksin, Lalo Schifrin, Marc
Shaiman, Howard Shore, Alan Silvestri, Patrick Williams,
Hans Zimmer
BOARD OF DIRECTORS
Steven Bramson, Alf Clausen, Ray Colcord, Cliff Eidelman,
Dan Foliart, Jerry Grant, Ron Grant, Laura Karpman,
Hummie Mann, Michael McCuistion, Marc Parmet, Dennis
Spiegel, Mark Watters, Jonathan Wolff, Christopher Young.

SOCIETY OF MOTION PICTURE AND TELEVISION ENGINEERS

(Organized 1916. Membership: 9,700.)
595 W. Hartsdale Ave., White Plains, NY 10607-1824. (914)
761-1100. FAX: (914) 761-3115.
PRESIDENT
David L. George
PAST PRESIDENT
Stanley N. Baron
EXECUTIVE VICE PRESIDENT
Charles H. Jablonski
V.P., ENGINEERING
William C. Miller
V.P., EDITORIAL
Robert B. Kisor
V.P., FINANCE
Gavin Shutz
V.P., CONFERENCE
John L. Mason
SECRETARY/TREASURER
Thomas M. Jordan
EXECUTIVE DIRECTOR
Frederick C. Motts
MARKETING COORDINATOR
Linda Alexander

EDITOR/PUBLISHER
Jeffrey Freidman
PRODUCTION/GRAPHICS SUPERVISOR
Mathew v. Kuriakose
PRODUCTION EDITOR
MaryAnn Frusciante
ASSISTANT EDITOR
Jermaine Hall

STATION REPRESENTATIVES ASSOCIATION, INC.

16 W. 77th St., New York, NY 10024-5126. (212) 362-8868.
FAX: (212) 362-4995.
PRESIDENT
Jack Ocken
V.P. & SECRETARY, TELEVISION
John Heise
TREASURER
James Beloiyanis
MANAGING DIRECTOR
Jerry Feniger

TELEVISION BUREAU OF ADVERTISING

(Organized 1954.)
850 Third Ave., 10th floor, New York, NY 10022. (212) 486-
1111. FAX: (212) 935-5631. URL: http://www.tvb.org
PRESIDENT
Ave Butensky
S.V.P., STRATEGIC PLANNING
Joseph C. Trinato
S.V.P., MARKETING
Thomas A. Conway
V.P., MARKETING COMMUNICATIONS
Gary Bells
V.P., RESEARCH
Harold Simpson

UNITED STATES CATHOLIC CONFERENCE, DEPARTMENT OF COMMUNICATION—OFFICE FOR FILM & BROADCASTING

Suite #1300, 1011 First Ave., New York, NY 10022. (212) 644-
1894. FAX: (212) 644-1886.
DIRECTOR, OFFICE FOR FILM & BROADCASTING
Henry Herx

WOMEN IN COMMUNICATIONS

1244 Ritchie Hwy., Arnold, MD 21012-1887. (410) 544-7442.
FAX: (410) 544 4640. email: womcom@aol.com
EXECUTIVE DIRECTOR
Patricia Troy

STATE & CITY FILM COMMISSIONS

ALABAMA

ALABAMA FILM OFFICE
401 Adams Ave., Montgomery, AL 36130. (800) 633-5898, (334) 242-4195. FAX: (334) 242-2077.
URL: http://www.telefilm-south.com/Alabama/Alabama.html
EXECUTIVE DIRECTOR
Michael Boyer

ALASKA

ALASKA FILM OFFICE
Frontier Bldg., 3601 "C" St., Suite 700, Anchorage, AK 99503. (907) 269-8137. FAX: (907) 269-8136.
COORDINATOR
Mary Pignalberi

ARIZONA

ARIZONA FILM COMMISSION
3800 N. Central Ave., Bldg. D, Phoenix, AZ 85012. (602) 280-1380, (800) 523-6695. FAX: (602) 280-1384.
DIRECTOR
Linda Peterson Warren

CITY OF PHOENIX FILM OFFICE
200 W. Washington, 10th fl., Phoenix, AZ 85003. (602) 262-4850. FAX: (602) 534-2295
PROGRAM MANAGER
Luci Fontanilla

CITY OF SCOTTSDALE
3939 Civic Center Blvd., Scottsdale, AZ 85251. (602) 994-2636. FAX: (602) 994-7780
FILM LIAISON
Jan Horne

ARKANSAS

ARKANSAS FILM OFFICE
One State Capitol Mall, 4th floor, Little Rock, AR 72201. (501) 682-7676. FAX: (501) 682-FILM. email: phohnbaum@aedc.state.ar.us
FILM & VIDEO PROMOTIONS SPECIALIST
Prisca Hohnbaum

CALIFORNIA

CALIFORNIA FILM COMMISSION
7080 Hollywood Blvd., Suite 900, Hollywood, CA 90028. (800) 858-4PIX. FAX: (213) 860-2972. email: filmca@commerce.ca.gov
DIRECTOR
Patti Stolkin Archuletta

COUNTY OF LOS ANGELES
Entertainment Industry Development Corp., Los Angeles Film Office, 7083 Hollywood Blvd., Suite 500, Los Angeles, CA 90028. (213) 957-1000. FAX: (213) 962-4966.
PRESIDENT
Cody Cluff

CITY OF SAN DIEGO
San Diego Film Commission, 1010 Second Ave, Suite 1600, San Diego, CA 92101-4912. (619) 234-3456. FAX: (619) 234-4631.
FILM COMMISSIONER
Cathy Anderson

CITY OF SAN FRANCISCO
San Francisco Film and Video Arts Commission, 401 Van Ness Ave., Rm. 417, San Francisco, CA 94102. (415) 554-6244. FAX: (415) 554-6503
DIRECTOR
Robin Eickman

CITY OF SAN JOSE
San Jose Film & Video Commission, 333 W. San Carlos St., Suite 1000, San Jose, CA 95110. (408) 295-9600, (800) SAN-JOSE. FAX: (408) 295-3937. email: jokane@sanjose.org
URL: http://www.sanjose.org
EXECUTIVE DIRECTOR
Joe O' Kane

MONTEREY COUNTY
Monterey County Film Commission, P.O. Box 111, Monterey, CA 93942-0111. (408) 646-0910. FAX: (408) 655-9244. email: mryfilm@aol.com; URL: http://tmx.com/mcfilm
EXECUTIVE DIRECTOR
Karen Nordstrand

COLORADO

COLORADO MOTION PICTURE & TV COMMISSION
1625 Broadway, Suite 1700, Denver, CO 80202. (303) 620-4500, (800) SCO-UTUS. FAX: (303) 620-4545. email: staff@coloradofilm.org; URL: http://www.coloradofilm.org
DIRECTOR
Michael Klein

BOULDER COUNTY FILM COMMISSION
2440 Pearl St., Boulder, CO 80302. (303) 442-1044. FAX: (303) 938-8837.
DIRECTOR
Shelly Helmerick

COLORADO SPRINGS FILM COMMISSION
Colorado Springs Convention & Visitors Bureau, 104 S. Cascade Ave., #104, Colorado Springs, CO 80903. (719) 635-7506 x131. FAX: (719) 635-4968.
DIRECTOR
Edwina Foreman

CONNECTICUT

CONNECTICUT FILM OFFICE
505 Hudson St., Hartford, CT 06106. (860) 270-8084. FAX: (860) 270-8077.
DIRECTOR
Katherine Ray

DELAWARE

DELAWARE FILM OFFICE
Delaware Tourism Office, 99 Kings Highway, Dover, DE 19901. (302) 739-4271. FAX: (302) 739-5749.
FILM COMMISSIONER
Jennifer Hastings

DISTRICT OF COLUMBIA

MAYOR'S OFFICE OF TV & FILM
410 Eighth St., NW., Washington, D.C. 20004. (202) 727-6608/6607. FAX: (202) 727-3787.
DIRECTOR
Crystal Palmer

FLORIDA

FORT LAUDERDALE AREA/BROWARD COUNTY
Motion Picture & TV Office, Broward Economic Development Council, 200 E. Las Olas Blvd., Suite 1850, Fort Lauderdale, FL 33301. (954) 524-3113. FAX: (954) 524-3167. email: BEDC@safari.net
DIRECTOR
Elizabeth Wentworth

CITY OF JACKSONVILLE
Jacksonville Film & TV Office, 128 E. Forsythe St., # 505, Jacksonville, FL 32202. (904) 630-2522. FAX: (904) 630-1485. email: HBS@mail.itd.ci.jax.fl.us
URL: http://www.ci.jax.fl.us/pub/film/film.html
DIRECTOR
Todd Roobin

MIAMI-DADE COUNTY
Miami-Dade Office of Film, TV & Print, 111 Northwest 1st Street, Suite 2510, Miami, FL 33128. (305) 375-3288. FAX: (305) 375-3266.
DIRECTOR
Jeff Peel

OCALA/MARION COUNTY FILM COMMISSION
Chamber of Commerce, 110 East Silver Springs Blvd., Ocala, FL 34470. (352) 629-8051, x25. FAX: (352) 629-7651.
DIRECTOR
Jude Hagin

ORLANDO/CENTRAL FLORIDA FILM & TV OFFICE
200 E. Robinson St., Suite 600, Orlando, FL 32801-1950. (407) 422-7159. FAX: (407) 843-9514. email: filminfo@film-orlando.org; URL: http://www.film-orlando.org
DIRECTOR
Katherine Ramsberger

PALM BEACH COUNTY FILM & TV COMMISSION
1555 Palm Beach Lakes Blvd., Suite 414, West Palm Beach, FL 33401. (800) 745-FILM, (561) 233-1000. FAX: (561) 683-6857. URL: http://www.co.palmbeach.fl.us/film
FILM COMMISSIONER
Chuck Eldred

GEORGIA

GEORGIA FILM & VIDEOTAPE OFFICE
285 Peachtree Center Avenue, NW, Suite 1000, Atlanta, GA 30303. (404) 656-3591. FAX: (404) 651-9063. email: Film@itt.state.ga.us; URL: http://www.Georgia-on-my-mind.org
DIRECTOR
Greg Torre

HAWAII

HAWAII FILM OFFICE
P.O. Box 2359, Honolulu, HI 96804. (808) 586-2570. FAX: (808) 586-2572.
MANAGER
Georgette T. Deemer

IDAHO

IDAHO FILM BUREAU
700 W. State St., Box 83720, Boise, ID 83720. (208) 334-0093, (800) 942-8338. FAX: (208) 334-2631.
DIRECTOR
Peg Owens

ILLINOIS

ILLINOIS FILM OFFICE
100 W. Randolph, Suite 3-400, Chicago, IL 60601. (312) 814-3600. FAX: (312) 814-8874.
DIRECTOR
Ron Ver Kuilen

CITY OF CHICAGO FILM OFFICE
One North LaSalle, Suite 2165, Chicago, IL 60602. (312) 744-6415. FAX: (312) 744-1378.
DIRECTOR
Richard M. Moskal

INDIANA

INDIANA DEPARTMENT OF COMMERCE
1 N. Capitol Ave., Suite 700, Indianapolis, IN 46204-2288. (317) 233-8829. FAX: (317) 233-6887. email: idoc70@indyvax.iupui.edu
URL: http://www.a1.com/derringer/filmcomm.html
DIRECTOR
Jane Rulon

IOWA

IOWA FILM OFFICE
200 E. Grand Ave., Des Moines, IA 50309. (515) 242-4726. FAX: (515) 242-4859.
DIRECTOR
Wendol Jarvis

KANSAS

KANSAS FILM COMMISSION
700 SW Harrison St., Suite 1300, Topeka, KS 66603-3712. (785) 296-4927. FAX: (785) 296-6988. TTY: (785) 296-3487.
FILM COMMISSIONER
Vicky Henley

KENTUCKY

KENTUCKY FILM COMMISSION
Capitol Plaza Tower, 500 Mero St., 22nd floor, Frankfort, KY 40601. (800) 345-6591. FAX: (502) 564-7588.
DIRECTOR
Russ Slone

LOUISIANA

LOUISIANA FILM COMMISSION
P.O. Box 44320, Baton Rouge, LA 70804-4320. (504) 342-8150. FAX: (504) 342-7988. (area code will change to 225 in April, 1999) URL: http://www.state.la.us
DIRECTOR
Peter Loop II

CITY OF NEW ORLEANS FILM AND VIDEO COMMISSION
1515 Poydras St., New Orleans, LA 70112. (504) 565-8104. FAX: (504) 565-0801.
Kimberly Carbo

MAINE

MAINE FILM OFFICE
Station 59, Augusta, ME 04333-0059. (207) 287-5703. FAX: (207) 287-8070. URL: http://www.state.me.us/deed/film/mainefilm.htm
DIRECTOR
Lea Girardin

MARYLAND

MARYLAND FILM OFFICE
217 E. Redwood St., 9th floor, Baltimore, MD 21202. (410) 767-6340, (800) 333-6632. FAX: (410) 333-0044.
DIRECTOR
Michael Styer

MASSACHUSETTS

MASSACHUSETTS FILM OFFICE
10 Park Plaza, Suite 2310, Boston, MA 02116. (617) 973-8800. FAX: (617) 973-8810.
DIRECTOR
Robin Dawson

MICHIGAN

MICHIGAN FILM OFFICE
201 N. Washington Sq., Lansing, MI 48913. (517) 373-0638, (800) 477-3456. FAX: (517) 373-0059.
email: lockwoodj@state.mi.us
DIRECTOR
Janet Lockwood

MINNESOTA

MINNESOTA FILM BOARD
401 N. Third St., Suite 460, Minneapolis, MN 55401. (612) 332-6493. FAX: (612) 332-3735.
DIRECTORS
Randy Adamsick, Kelly Heikkila

MISSISSIPPI

MISSISSIPPI FILM OFFICE
550 High St., Walter Sillers Blsg., Suite 1100, Jackson, MS 39205-0849. (601) 359-3297. FAX: (601) 359-5757.
email: wemling%gw@decd.state.ms.us
DIRECTOR
Ward Emling

CITY OF COLUMBUS
Columbus Film Commission, P.O.Box 789, Columbus, MS 39703. (601) 329-1191, (800) 327-2686. FAX: (601) 329-8969.
DIRECTOR
Carolyn Denton

CITY OF NATCHEZ
Natchez Film Commission, P.O. Box 1485, Natchez, MS 39121. (601) 446-6345, (800) 647-6724. FAX: (601) 442-0814.
DIRECTOR
Laura Godfrey

MISSOURI

MISSOURI FILM OFFICE
301 West High, Room 720, P.O. Box 118, Jefferson City, MO 65102. (573) 751-9050. FAX: (573) 751-7384.
URL: http://www.ecodev.state.mo.us/film
MANAGER
Richard Smreker

MONTANA

MONTANA FILM OFFICE
1424 Ninth Ave., Helena, MT 59620.
(406) 444-3762, (800) 553-4563. FAX: (406) 444-4191.
email: montanafilm@travel.state.mt.us
URL: http://montanafilm.mt.gov
DIRECTOR
Lonie Stimac

CITY OF BILLINGS FILM LIAISON OFFICE
P.O. Box 31177, Billings, MT 59107. (406) 245-4111, (800) 711-2630. FAX: (406) 245-7333.
DIRECTOR
John Brewer

CITY OF BUTTE FILM LIAISON OFFICE
1000 George St., Butte, MT 59701. (406) 723-3177.
FILM LIAISON TO STATE COMMISSIONER
Connie Kenney

GREAT FALLS REGIONAL FILM LIAISON
710 First Ave. N., Great Falls, MT 59401. (406) 761-4434, (800) 735-8535. FAX: (406) 761-6129.
FILM COMMISSIONER
Peggy Gentry

NEBRASKA

NEBRASKA FILM OFFICE
P.O. Box 94666, Lincoln, NE 68509-4666. (402) 471-3680,
(800) 228-4307. FAX: (402) 471-3026.
email: laurier@ded2.ded.state.ne.us
URL: http://www.ded.state.ne.is/film
DIRECTOR
Laurie J. Richards

OMAHA FILM COMMISSION
6800 Mercy Rd., Suite 202, Omaha, NE 68106. (402) 444-
7736. FAX: (402) 444-4511.
DIRECTOR
Julie Ginsberg

NEVADA

NEVADA ECONOMIC DEVELOPMENT COMMISSION
3770 Howard Hughes Pkwy., Suite 295, Las Vegas, NV 89109.
(702) 486-7150, (702) 791-0839 (after hours and holidays).
FAX: (702) 486-7372.
MOTION PICTURE DIVISION/C.E.D.
Robert Hirsch

NEW HAMPSHIRE

NEW HAMPSHIRE FILM & TELEVISION BUREAU
Box 1856, 172 Pembroke Rd., Concord, NH 03302-1856. (603)
271-2598. FAX: (603) 271-2629.
DIRECTOR
Laura Simoes

NEW JERSEY

NEW JERSEY MOTION PICTURE & TV COMMISSION
P.O. Box 47023, 153 Halsey St., 5th floor, Newark, NJ 07101.
(973) 648-6279. FAX: (973) 648-7350. email: njfilm@nj.com
URL: http://www.nj.com/njfilm
DIRECTOR
Joseph Friedman

NEW MEXICO

NEW MEXICO FILM OFFICE
P.O. Box 20003, Santa Fe, NM 87504-5003. (505) 827-9810, (800)
545-9871. FAX: (505) 827-9799. email: film@edd.state.nm.us
DIRECTOR
Linda Taylor Hutchison

CITY OF ALBUQUERQUE
Albuquerque TV & Film Office, Albuquerque Convention &
Visitor's Bureau, Box 26866, Albuquerque, NM 87125. (505)
842-9918, (800) 733-9918. FAX: (505) 247-9101.
email: barnhill@abqcvb.org
DIRECTOR OF TOURISM SERVICES
Shannon Barnhill

NEW YORK

**NEW YORK STATE GOVERNOR'S OFFICE FOR MOTION
PICTURE & TELEVISION DEVELOPMENT**
633 Third Ave., 33rd floor, New York, NY 10017. (212) 803-
2330. FAX: (212) 803-2339.
email: NYFILM@empire.state.ny.us
DEPUTY COMMISSIONER & DIRECTOR
Pat Swinney Kaufman

**CITY OF NEW YORK MAYOR'S OFFICE OF FILM,
THEATRE & BROADCASTING**
1697 Broadway, 6th floor, New York, NY 10019. (212) 489-
6710. FAX: (212) 307-6237. FAXBACK SVC: (212) 262-8825.
URL: http://www.ci.nyc.ny.us/html/filmcom/
COMMISSIONER
Patricia Reed Scott

NASSAU COUNTY FILM OFFICE
1550 Franklin Ave., Rm. 207, Mineola, NY 11501. (516) 571-
4160. FAX: (516) 571-4161.
email: debfilm@aol.com
DIRECTOR
Debra Markowitz

SUFFOLK COUNTY MOTION PICTURE & TV OFFICE
Dennison Bldg., 2nd floor, 100 Veterans Memorial Highway,
NY 11788-0099. (516) 853-4800, (800) 762-GROW. FAX: (516)
853-4888.
COMMISSIONER
Alice A. Amrhein

NORTH CAROLINA

NORTH CAROLINA FILM COMMISSION
301 N. Wilmington St., Raleigh, NC 27601. (919) 733-9900,
(800) 232-9227. FAX: (919) 715-0151. email:
barnold@travel.commerce.state.nc.us
DIRECTOR
William Arnold

NORTH DAKOTA

NORTH DAKOTA FILM OFFICE
604 E. Blvd., 2nd floor, Liberty Memorial Bldg., State Capitol,
Bismarck, ND 58505. (701) 328-2525, (800) 328-2871. FAX:
(701) 328-4878. email: phertz@state.nd.us
FILM COMMISSIONER
Pat Hertz

OHIO

OHIO FILM COMMISSION
77 S. High St., 29th Floor, Columbus, OH 43216-1001. (614)
466-2284, (800) 230-3523. FAX: (614) 466-6744.
MANAGER
Eve Lapolla

GREATER CINCINNATI FILM COMMISSION
602 Main St., Suite 712, Cincinnati, OH 45202. (513) 784-
1744. FAX: (513) 768-8963.
email: info@film-cincinnati.org
EXECUTIVE DIRECTOR
Lori Holladay
PRODUCTION DIRECTOR
Kristen Erwin

OKLAHOMA

OKLAHOMA FILM COMMISSION
440 S. Houston, Suite 304, Tulsa, OK 74127. (800) 766-3456,
(918) 581-2660. FAX: (918) 581-2244.
URL: http://www.otrd.state.ok/filmcommission
DIRECTOR
Robert M. Davis

OREGON

OREGON FILM & VIDEO OFFICE
One World Trade Center, 121 S.W. Salmon St., Suite 1205,
Portland, OR 97204. (503) 229-5832. FAX: (503) 229-6869.
email: shoot@oregonfilm.org
EXECUTIVE DIRECTOR
David Woolson

PENNSYLVANIA

PENNSYLVANIA FILM OFFICE
Department of Commerce, 200 N. 3rd St., Suite 901,
Harrisburg, PA 17101. (717) 783-3456. FAX: (717) 772-3581.
DIRECTOR
Timothy D. Chambers

GREATER PHILADELPHIA FILM OFFICE
1600 Arch St., 12th Floor, Philadelphia, PA 19103, (215) 686-
2668. FAX: (215) 686-3659. email: mail@film.org
URL: http://www.film.org
EXECUTIVE DIRECTOR
Sharon Pinkelson

RHODE ISLAND

RHODE ISLAND FILM & TV OFFICE
7 Jackson Walkway, Providence, RI 02903. (401) 222- 3456.
FAX: (401) 277-2102.
DIRECTOR
Richardson Smith

SOUTH CAROLINA

SOUTH CAROLINA FILM OFFICE
P.O. Box 7367, Columbia, SC 29202. (803) 737-0490. FAX:
(803) 737-3104
DIRECTOR
Isabel Hill

SOUTH DAKOTA

SOUTH DAKOTA FILM COMMISSION
711 E. Wells Ave., Pierre, SD 57501-3369. (605) 773-3301.
FAX: (605) 773-3256. email: garyk@goed.state.sd.us.
FILM OFFICE COORDINATOR
Gary Keller

TENNESSEE

TENNESSEE FILM, ENTERTAINMENT & MUSIC COMMISSION
Rachel Jackson Bldg., 320 Sixth Ave. N., 7th floor, Nashville, TN 37243-0790. (615) 741-3456, (800) 251-8594. FAX: (615) 741-5544.
EXECUTIVE DIRECTOR
Anne Pope

MEMPHIS-SHELBY CO. FILM/TAPE/MUSIC COMMISSION
Beale St. Landing, 245 Wagner Pl., Suite 4, Memphis, TN 38103-3815. (901) 527-8300. FAX: (901) 527-8326.
EXECUTIVE DIRECTOR
Linn Sitler

TEXAS

TEXAS FILM COMMISSION
P.O. Box 13246, Austin, TX 78711. (512) 463-9200. FAX: (512) 463-4114. email: film@governor.state.texas.us
URL: http://www.governor.state.tx.us/film
EXECUTIVE DIRECTOR
Tom Copeland

AMARILLO FILM OFFICE
1000 S. Polk St., Amarillo, TX 79101. (806) 374-1497. FAX: (806) 373-3909.

EL PASO FILM COMMISSION
One Civic Center Plaza, El Paso, TX 79901. (915) 534-0698, (800) 351-6024. FAX: (915) 532-2963.
DIRECTOR
Charles Meeks

HOUSTON FILM COMMISSION
801 Congress, Houston, TX 77002. (800) 365-7575, (713) 227-3100 x615. FAX: (713) 223-3816.
DIRECTOR
Rick Ferguson

IRVING TEXAS FILM COMMISSION
6309 N. O'Connor Rd., Suite 222, Irving, TX 75039-3510. (972) 869-0303, (800) 247-8464. FAX: (972) 869-4609. email: itfc@airmail.net
DIRECTOR
Ellen Mayers

DALLAS/FORT WORTH REGIONAL FILM COMMISSION
P.O. Box 610246, DFW Airport, TX 75261. (972) 621-0400, (800) 2FILM99. FAX: (972) 929-0916. email: 2filmdfwtexas@ntc-dfw.org
DIRECTORS
Roger Burke
Sarah Bruce Craft

SAN ANTONIO FILM COMMISSION
P.O. Box 2277, San Antonio, TX 78230. (210) 270-8700. FAX: (210) 270-8782.

UTAH

UTAH FILM COMMISSION
324 South State, Suite 500, Salt Lake City, UT 84114. (801) 538-8740. FAX: (801) 538-8886.
EXECUTIVE DIRECTOR
Leigh von der Esch

MOAB TO MONUMENT VALLEY FILM COMMISSION
50 East Center, #1, Moab, UT 84532. (801) 259-6388. FAX: (801) 259-6399.
EXECUTIVE DIRECTOR
Bette L. Stanton

PARK CITY FILM COMMISSION
P.O. Box 1630, Park City, UT 84060. (800) 453-1360. FAX: (801) 649-4132, (801) 649-6100.
URL: http://www.netpp.com/parkcity
COMMISSIONER
Mary Bradley

VERMONT

VERMONT FILM BUREAU
Agency of Development and Community Affairs, 134 State St., VT 05601-1471. (802) 828-33847. FAX: (802) 828-3233. email: ggerdel@dca.state.vt.us
DIRECTOR
J. Gregory Gerdel

VIRGINIA

VIRGINIA FILM OFFICE
901 E. Byrd St., Richmond, VA 23219. (804) 371-8204. FAX: (804) 371-8177. email: vafilm@vedp.state.va.us
URL: http://www.film.virginia.org
DIRECTOR
Rita McClenny
LOCATION MANAGER
Andrew Edmonds

WASHINGTON STATE

WASHINGTON STATE FILM OFFICE
2001 6th Ave., Suite 2600, Seattle, WA 98121. (206) 464-7148. FAX: (206) 464-7222.
DIRECTOR
Suzy Kellett

WEST VIRGINIA

WEST VIRGINIA FILM OFFICE
State Capitol Complex, Building 6, Rm. 525, Charleston, WV 25305. (304) 558-2234. FAX: (304) 558-1189, (800) 982-3386.
DIRECTOR
Mark McNabb

WISCONSIN

WISCONSIN FILM OFFICE
Department of Tourism, 123 W. Washington Ave., 6th floor, Madison, WI 53702-0001. (608) FILM-WIS, (800) FILM-WIS. FAX: (608) 266-3403. email: ssolheim@mail.state.wi.us.
URL: http://www.film.state.wi.us
DIRECTOR
Stanley Solheim

WYOMING

WYOMING BUSINESS COUNSEL FILM OFFICE
Interstate 25 at College Dr., Cheyenne, WY 82002-0240. (800) 458-6657, (307) 777-3400. FAX: (307) 777-6904. email: omarti@missc.state.wy.us
MANAGING DIRECTOR
Michell Phelan

JACKSON HOLE FILM COMMISSION
P.O. Box E, Jackson, WY 83001. (307) 733-3316. FAX: (307) 733-5585.
DIRECTOR
Deborah Supowit.

U.S. TERRITORIES & PROTECTORATES

PUERTO RICO FILM COMMISSION
355 F. D. Roosevelt Ave., Fomento Bldg., Suite 106, San Juan, PR 00918. (787) 758- 4747, ext. 2250-2255. FAX: (787) 756-5706. URL: http://www.prfilm.com

U.S. VIRGIN ISLANDS FILM PROMOTION OFFICE
78 Contant 1-2-3, St. Thomas, U.S.V.I. 00804. (340) 774-8784, (340) 775-1444. FAX: (340) 774-4390.
DIRECTOR
Manny Centeno

TRADE PUBLICATIONS

QUIGLEY PUBLISHING COMPANY
Publishers of International Motion Picture Almanac (Annual),
International Television and Video Almanac (Annual) and
Quigleys Entertainment Industry Reference CD-ROM.
Corporate: 159 W. 53 St., New York, NY 10019. (212) 247-
3100. FAX: (212) 489-0871. email: QUIGLEYPUB@aol.com
URL: http://members.aol.com/quigleypub/home.html
Editorial: 6639 La Jolla Blvd., La Jolla, CA 92037. (619) 459-
1159. FAX: (619) 459-1590.
Sales: P.O. Box 1952, La Jolla, CA 92038-1952. (800) 231-
8239.
PRESIDENT AND PUBLISHER
Martin Quigley
VICE PRESIDENT
Katherine D. Quigley
VICE PRESIDENT & EDITORIAL DIRECTOR
Tracy Stevens
EDITOR
Patricia K. Nicolescu
CANADIAN BUREAU
Patricia Thompson, Editor. Box 152; Toronto, Ont. M4G 3Z3,
Canada. (416) 696-2382. FAX: (416) 696-6496.
FOREIGN CORRESPONDENTS
U.K.: Nimra Bucha, 68 Kensington Hgts, Campden Hill Rd,
London W87 BD England (011 44 171) 792 3469..
GREECE: Rena Velissariou, 32, Kolokotroni Str., Aguia
Paraskevi, Attikis, Athens. 153 42, Greece. (65) 67 665.
INDIA: B. D. Garga, 11 Verem Villas, Reis Magos, Bardez, Goa
403114 India. FAX: (91 832) 43433.
PAKISTAN: A.R. Slote, P.O. Box 7426, Karachi, 74400, Pakistan.

INTERNATIONAL MOTION PICTURE ALMANAC
Editorial: 6639 La jolla Blvd., La Jolla, CA 92037. (619) 459-
1159. FAX: (619) 459-1590.
Sales: P.O. Box 1952, La Jolla, CA 92038-1952. (800) 231-8239.
email: QUIGLEYPUB@aol.com
URL: http://members.aol.com/quigleypub/qp.html
Corporate: 159 W. 53 St., New York, NY 10019. (212) 247-
3100. FAX: (212) 489-0871.
EDITORIAL DIRECTOR
Tracy Stevens
EDITOR
Patricia K. Nicolescu
CANADIAN EDITOR
Patricia Thompson
BRITISH EDITOR
Nimra Bucha

INTERNATIONAL TELEVISION & VIDEO ALMANAC
Editorial: 6639 La jolla Blvd., La Jolla, CA 92037. (619) 459-
1159. FAX: (619) 459-1590.
Sales: P.O. Box 1952, La Jolla, CA 92038-1952. (800) 231-8239.
email: QUIGLEYPUB@aol.com
URL: http://members.aol.com/quigleypub/qp.html
Corporate: 159 W. 53 St., New York, NY 10019. (212) 247-
3100. FAX: (212) 489-0871.
EDITORIAL DIRECTOR
Tracy Stevens
EDITOR
Patricia K. Nicolescu
CANADIAN EDITOR
Patricia Thompson
BRITISH EDITOR
Nimra Bucha

ACADEMY PLAYERS DIRECTORY
(Tri-Annual) Academy of Motion Picture Arts & Sciences, 8949
Wilshire Blvd., Beverly Hills, CA 90211-1972. (310) 247-3000.
FAX: (310) 550-5034.
EDITOR
Keith W. Gonzales

ADVERTISING AGE
(Weekly) 740 N. Rush St., Chicago, IL 60611. (312) 649-5200.
220 E. 42 St., New York, NY 10017. (212) 210-0100.
CHAIRMAN
Keith Crain
PUBLISHING DIRECTOR
Joe Cappo
PUBLISHER
Ed Erhardt
PRESIDENT & EDITOR-IN-CHIEF
Rance Crain

THE AMERICAN CINEMATOGRAPHER
(Monthly) Published by American Society of
Cinematographers, Inc., P.O. Box 2230, Hollywood, CA 90078.
(213) 969-4333. FAX: (213) 876-4973.
PUBLISHER
Jim McCullaugh
EDITOR
Stephen Pizzello
ASSOCIATE EDITOR
David E. Williams
ASSISTANT EDITOR
Andrew O. Thompson
CIRCULATION MANAGER
Saul Molina

AMERICAN PREMIERE MAGAZINE
(Bi-monthly) 8421 Wilshire Blvd., Penthouse, Beverly Hills, CA
90211. (213) 852-0434.
PUBLISHER & EDITOR
Susan Royal
ASSISTANT EDITOR
Dawn Brooks

ANNUAL INDEX TO MOTION PICTURE CREDITS
(Annual compilation of feature film credits) Academy of Motion
Picture Arts and Sciences, 8949 Wilshire Blvd., Beverly Hills,
CA 90211. (310) 247-3000. FAX: (310) 859-9619.
EXECUTIVE DIRECTOR
Bruce Davis
EDITOR
Byerly Woodward

AV GUIDE: THE LEARNING MEDIA NEWSLETTER
(Monthly) 380 Northwest Highway, Des Plaines, IL 60016-
2282. (847) 298-6622. FAX: (847) 390-0408.
PUBLISHER
H. S. Gillette
EDITOR
Natalie Ferguson
CIRCULATION DIRECTOR
Linda Lambdin

BILLBOARD
(Weekly) 5055 Wilshire Blvd., Los Angeles, CA 90036-4396.
(213) 525-2300. FAX: (213) 525-2394.
1515 Broadway, New York, NY 10036. (212) 764-7300. FAX:
(212) 536-5358.
49 Music Square W., Nashville, TN 37203. (615) 321-4290.
FAX: (615) 327-1575.
806 15 St., NW, Washington, D.C. 20005. (202) 783-3282. FAX:
(202) 737-3833.
23 Ridgmount St., 3rd fl., London WC1E 7AH. (01 71) 323-
6686. FAX: (01 71) 631-0428.
PRESIDENT & PUBLISHER
Howard Lander
EDITOR-IN-CHIEF
Timothy White
MANAGING EDITOR
Susan Nunziata
ASSOCIATE PUBLISHER, MARKETING & SALES
Gene Smith

BOXOFFICE
6640 Sunset Blvd., #100, Hollywood, CA 90028. (213) 465-
1186. FAX: (213) 465-5049. Published by RLD
PO Box 25485, Chicago, IL 60625. (773) 338-7007.
email: boxoffice@earthlink.net
URL: http://www.boxoffice.com
PUBLISHER
Robert L. Dietmeier
EDITOR-IN-CHIEF
Kim Williamson
NATIONAL AD DIRECTOR
Robert M. Vale

**BROADCASTING & CABLE—THE NEWS WEEKLY OF
TELEVISION AND RADIO**
(Weekly) 1705 DeSales St., NW, Washington, DC 20036. (202)
659-2340. FAX: (202) 429-0651.
245 W. 17 St., New York, NY 10011. (212) 645-0067. FAX:
(212) 337-7028.
5700 Wilshire Blvd., #120, Los Angeles, CA 90036. (213) 549-
4100. FAX: (213) 937-4240.
28310 Pine Dr., Evergreen, CO 80439. (303) 670-4124. FAX:
(303) 670-1082.
V P GROUP PUBLISHER
Peggy Conlon
SENIOR VICE PRESIDENT & EDITOR
Donald V. West

BROADCASTING & CABLE YEARBOOK
(Annual)R. R. Bowker, 121 Chanlon Rd., New Providence, NJ 07974
VICE PRESIDENT GROUP PUBLISHER
Pegggy Conlon.
VICE PRESIDENT, DATABASE PUBLISHING
Leigh C. Yuster-Freeman
EDITORIAL DIRECTOR
Elizabeth A. Kizar

CELEBRITY SERVICE INTERNATIONAL
Publisher of Celebrity Bulletin (daily).and Celebrity Service International Contact Book (semi-annual).250 W 57th St, New York, NY 10107. (212) 757-7979. FAX: (212) 582-7701.
8833 Sunset Blvd., Los Angeles, CA 90069. (310) 652-1700. FAX: (310) 652-9244.
EDITOR, CELEBRITY BULLETIN (NY)
Bill Murray
EDITOR, CELEBRITY BULLETIN (LA)
Todd Longwell
EDITORS, CELEBRITY SERVICE INTERNATIONAL CONTACT BOOK
Vicki Bagley, Mark Kerrigan

CINEFEX
(Quarterly) P.O. Box 20027, Riverside, CA 92516.
PUBLISHER
Don Shay
EDITOR
Jody Duncan

COMING ATTRACTIONS
(Monthly) Connell Communications Inc., 86 Elm St., Peterborough, NH 03458. (603) 924-7271. FAX: (603) 924-7013.
EXECUTIVE PUBLISHER
Jim Connell

COSTUME DESIGNERS GUILD DIRECTORY
(Annual) c/o Costume Designers Guild, 13949 Ventura Blvd., #309, Sherman Oaks, CA 91423. (818) 905-1557. FAX: (818) 905-1560.

DAILY VARIETY
(Daily) 5700 Wilshire Blvd., Suite 120, Los Angeles, CA 90036. (213) 857-6600. FAX: (213) 857-0494.
SPECIAL EDITIONS EDITOR
Steven Gaydos
MANAGING EDITOR
Jonathan Taylor
NATIONAL SALES MANAGER
Charles Koones
PRODUCTION MANAGER
Bob Butler

EDITOR & PUBLISHER
(Weekly) 11 W. 19 St., New York, NY 10011. (212) 675- 4380. FAX: (212) 929-1259.
PRESIDENT & EDITOR
Robert U. Brown
MANAGING EDITOR
George Garneau

ELECTRONIC MEDIA
(Weekly.) 740 N. Rush St., Chicago, IL 60611, (312) 649-5293. FAX: (312) 649-5465.
VICE PRESIDENT, PUBLISHER & EDITORIAL DIRECTOR
Ron Alridge
EDITOR
P. J. Bednarski

ELECTRONICS
(Monthly) Penton Publishing, 1100 Superior Ave., Cleveland, OH 44114. (216) 696-7000.
PUBLISHER/EDITOR
Jonah McLeod

ELECTRONICS NOW
(Monthly) 500 Bi-County Blvd., Farmingdale, NY 11735. (516) 293-3000. FAX: (516) 293-3115. URL: http://www.gernsback.com
PUBLISHER
Larry Steckler
EDITOR
Carl Laron

FILM & VIDEO MAGAZINE
(Monthly) Organized 1983. 8455 Beverly Blvd., #508, Los Angeles, CA 90048-3416. (213) 653-8053. FAX: (213) 653-8053.
ASSOCIATE PUBLISHER/EDITOR
Paula Swartz
ASSOCIATE PUBLISHER
Debbie Vodenos
SENIOR EDITOR
Cristina Clapp
ASSOCIATE EDITOR
Katie Makal

FILM JOURNAL INTERNATIONAL
(Monthly) 244 W. 49 St., Suite 200, New York, NY 10019. (212) 246-6460. FAX: (212) 265-6428.
PUBLISHER-EDITOR
Robert H. Sunshine
ASSOCIATE PUBLISHER
Jimmy Sunshine
MANAGING EDITOR
Kevin Lally
ASSOCIATE EDITORS
Ed Kelleher, Mitch Neuhauser
DIRECTOR OF ADVERTISING/SALES
Jim Merck
WEST COAST EDITOR
Peter Henne
CIRCULATION MANAGER
Michelle Lederkramer

FILM QUARTERLY
University of California Press, 2120 Berkeley Way, Berkeley, CA 94720. (510) 601-9070. FAX: (510) 601-9036.
EDITOR
Ann Martin
Films in Review
P.O. Box 589, New York, NY 10021. (212) 628-1594.
EDITOR
Robin Little

HOLLYWOOD CREATIVE DIRECTORY
(Annual) 3000 W Olympic Blvd.Ste 2525, Santa Monica, CA 90404. (310) 315-4815.FAX: (310)315-4816. email: hcd@online.com

THE HOLLYWOOD REPORTER
(Daily) 5055 Wilshire Blvd., Los Angeles, CA 90036. (213) 525-2000, (213) 525-2068 (editorial). FAX: (213) 525-2377 (editorial), (213) 525-2372 (advertising), (213) 525-2390 (special issues). URL: http://www.hollywoodreporter.com
1515 Broadway, New York, NY, 10036. (212) 536-5344, (212) 536-5325 (editorial). FAX: (212) 536-5345.
733 15th St., N.W. Suite 510, Washington, DC 20005. (202) 737-2828. FAX: (202) 737-3833.
23 Ridgemont St, London WC1E 7AH England. (01 71) 323-6686. FAX: (01 71) 323-5513.
PUBLISHER & EDITOR-IN-CHIEF
Robert J. Dowling
EDITOR
Alex Ben Block
MANAGING EDITOR
Howard Burns

I.A.T.S.E. OFFICIAL BULLETIN
(Quarterly) 1515 Broadway, Suite 601, New York, NY 10036. (212) 730-1770. FAX: (212) 921-7699.
EDITOR
Michael W. Proscia
ASSISTANT EDITOR
Mary Ann Kelly

IN MOTION FILM & VIDEO PRODUCTION MAGAZINE
(Monthly) Phillips Business Information, 1201 Seven Locks Rd., Suite 300, Potomac, MD 20854. (301) 340-1520.
PUBLISHER
Roscoe C Smith
MANAGING EDITOR
Cristina Brooks Clapp
EDITOR
Rita Street

INTERNATIONAL DOCUMENTARY ASSOCIATION
1551 S. Robertson Blvd., Suite 201, Los Angeles, CA 90035. (310) 284-8422. FAX: (310) 785-9334.
EDITOR
Diana Rico

INTERNATIONAL PHOTOGRAPHER
(Monthly) 7715 Sunset Blvd., Suite 300, Hollywood, CA 90046. (213) 876-0160.
PUBLISHER
International Photographers Guild
EDITOR-IN-CHIEF
George Spiro Dibie, ASC
EDITOR
Suzanne R. Lezotte

JOURNAL OF THE SYD CASSYD ARCHIVES ACADEMY OF TELEVISION ARTS & SCIENCES/HOLLYWOOD REPORT
(Quarterly) 917 S. Tremaine, Hollywood 90019, CA. (213) 939-2345.
FOUNDER
Syd Cassyd

MARKEE— REGIONAL AMERICA'S MAGAZINE FOR FILM AND VIDEO PRODUCTION
366 E Graves Ave. Suite D., Orange City, FL 32763. (904) 774-8881. FAX: (904) 774-8908.
PUBLISHER
John Hutchinson
Janet Karcher
EDITOR
Janet Karcher

MEDIA WEEK
(Weekly) BPI Communications. 1515 Broadway, New York, NY 10036. (212) 536-5336.
EDITOR IN CHIEF
Sid Holt
EDITOR
William F Gloede
EXECUTIVE EDITOR
Brian Moran
MANAGING EDITOR
Dwight Cunningham

MILLIMETER
(Monthly) 122 E. 42 St., #900, New York, NY 10168. (212) 309-7650. Fax: (212) 867-5893.
5300 Melrose Ave., # 219E, Hollywood, CA 90038. (213) 960-4050. FAX: (213) 960-4059.
PUBLISHER
Sam Kintzer
EDITOR
Bruce Stockler

PACIFIC COAST STUDIO DIRECTORY
(3 times per year) P.O. Box V, Pine Mountain, CA 93222-4921. (805) 242-2722. FAX: (805) 242-2724.
PUBLISHER
Jack Reitz

PERFORMANCE MAGAZINE
(Weekly) 2049 Century Park E., Suite 1100, Los Angeles, CA 90067. (310) 552-3118. FAX: (310) 286-1990.
PUBLISHER
Pete Clay
L.A. SENIOR EDITOR
Stann Findelle
MANAGING EDITOR
Jane Cohen

PRODUCER'S MASTERGUIDE
(Annual) 60 E. 8th St., 34st Floor, New York, NY 10003. (212) 777-4002. FAX: (212) 777-4101.
URL: http://www.producers.masterguide.com
PUBLISHER
Shmuel Bension

THE REEL DIRECTORY
(Annual) P.O. Box 866, Cotati, CA 94931. (707) 584-8083.
PUBLISHER & EDITOR
Bonnie Carroll

SCREEN ACTOR/CALL SHEET
(Bi-Monthly) 5757 Wilshire Blvd., Los Angeles, CA 90036. (213) 549-6652. FAX: (213) 549-6656.

SHOOT
(Weekly) 1515 Broadway, New York, NY 10036. (212) 764-7300. FAX: (212) 536-5321.
5055 Wilshire Blvd., Los Angeles, CA 90036. (213) 525-2262. FAX: (213) 525-0275.
Merchandise Mart Plaza, #936, Chicago, IL 60654. (312) 464-8555. FAX: (312) 464-8550.
PUBLISHER
Roberta Griefer
EDITOR
Bob Goldrich

SHOT IN LA
(Monthly) Louisiana Production & Entertainment Magazine. 207 W Hanson Ave., New Orleans, LA 70124. (504) 486-3112. FAX: (504)486-3354. email: editor@shotinla.com
http://www.shotinla.com
PUBLISHER/EDITOR
Elisabeth M. Deluna
ART DIRECTOR
Christy Scacia
DIRECTOR MARKETING
Marcy Hatch

SMPTE JOURNAL (SOCIETY OF MOTION PICTURE AND TELEVISION ENGINEERS)
(Monthly) 595 West Hartsdale Ave., White Plains, NY 10607. (914) 761-1100. FAX: (914) 761-3115.
EDITOR
Jeffrey B. Friedman
DIRECTOR OF MARKETING & COMMUNICATIONS
John Izzo

TAPE/DISC BUSINESS
(Monthly) Knowledge Industry Publications, Inc., 701 Westchester Ave., White Plains, NY 10604-3098. (914) 328-9157. FAX: (914) 328-9093.
EDITOR
Tom O'Reilly
CIRCULATION DIRECTOR
Jeff Hartford

TELEVISION & CABLE FACTBOOK
(Annual) Warren Publishing, Inc., 2115 Ward Court, N.W., Washington, DC 20037. (202) 872-9200. FAX: (202) 293-3435.
EDITOR & PUBLISHER
Albert Warren
MANAGING EDITOR
Michael C. Taliaferro
EDITORIAL DIRECTOR
Richard Kochl

TELEVISION DIGEST WITH CONSUMER ELECTRONICS
(Weekly) Warren Publishing, Inc., 2115 Ward Court, N.W., Washington, DC 20037. (202) 872-9200. FAX: (202) 293-3435.
EDITOR & PUBLISHER
Albert Warren
EDITORIAL DIRECTOR
David Lachenbruch
EXECUTIVE EDITOR
Dawson B. Nail
SENIOR EDITOR & EXECUTIVE PUBLISHER
Paul Warren
SENIOR EDITOR & ASSOCIATE PUBLISHER
Daniel Warren

TELEVISION INDEX
40-29 27th St., Long Island City, NY 11101-3869, (718) 937-3990.
EDITOR & PUBLISHER
Jonathan Miller

TELEVISION QUARTERLY
(Quarterly) National Academy of Television Arts & Sciences, 111 W. 57 St.ste 1020, New York, NY 10019. (212) 586-8424.
EDITOR
Richard Pack
ADVERTISING
Trudy Wilson

TV GUIDE
(Weekly) News America Publications, Inc., 100 Matsonford Rd., Radnor, PA 19088. (610) 293-8500.
EDITOR-IN-CHIEF
Steven Reddicliffe
PRESIDENT/CEO
David Steward
PUBLISHER/SENIOR VICE PRESIDENT
Dick Porter
MANAGING EDITOR-PROGRAMMING
Steve Sonsky

VARIETY
(Weekly) Reed Publishing, Inc., 245 W. 17 St., New York, NY 10011. (212) 645-0067. FAX: (212) 337-6977.
5700 Wilshire Blvd., Suite #120, Los Angeles, CA 90036, (323) 857-6600. FAX: (323) 857-0494, (323) 932 0393 (advertising).
Chicago: (847) 615-9742. FAX: (847) 615-9743.
Washington: (202) 861-0852. FAX: (202) 861-0853.
Italy: Lungotevere Flaminio 22, Rome 00196. (39-6) 361-3103.
England: 6 Bell Yard, London WC2A 2JR. (44171) 520-5222 FAX: (44171) 520-5219
Madrid: (34 91) 766-1356. FAX: (34 91) 383-8671.
Sydney:(612) 9422 8630. FAX: (612) 9419-8632.
Latin America: (341) 576-4262. FAX: (341) 575-9390.
France: (331) 41 90 46 77. FAX: (331) 41 90 46 79..
PRESIDENT/CEO
Bruce Barnet
VICE PRESIDENT, PUBLISHING OPERATIONS
Gerard A. Byrne
VICE PRESIDENT, EDITOR IN CHIEF
Peter Bart
MANAGING EDITOR
Elizabeth Guider
EUROPEAN EDITOR
Adam Dawtrey

VARIETY'S ON PRODUCTION
5700 Wilshire Blvd., Suite 120, Los Angeles, CA 90036. (213) 857-6600. FAX: (213) 549-4184. email: America Online, onprodmag@aol.com
PUBLISHER
Jerry Brandt
EDITOR
Gregory Solman

VIDEO

Hachette Filipacchi Magazines, Inc., 1633 Broadway, 45th Floor, New York, NY 10019. (212) 767-6020. FAX: (212) 767-5615. email: VideoMag@aol.com
GROUP PUBLISHER
Tony Catalaro
EDITOR-IN-CHIEF
Bill Wolfe

VIDEO BUSINESS

(Weekly) Chilton Publications, 825 Seventh Ave., New York, NY 10019. (212) 887-8400.
PUBLISHER
John Gaffney
EDITOR
Bruce Apar
ADVERTISING DIRECTOR
Stacy Kelly
ADVERTISING SALES
Andi Elliott, Linda Buckley

VIDEO STORE MAGAZINE

(Weekly) 201 E. Sandpointe Ave., Ste. 600, Santa Ana, CA 92707. (714) 513-8400, (800) 854-3112. FAX: (714) 513-8403.
PRESIDENT OF PUBLICATIONS
Brian Nairn
GROUP VICE PRESIDENT
Glenn Rogers
PUBLISHER
Don Rosenberg
EDITOR IN CHIEF
Thomas K. Arnold
ASSOCIATE PUBLISHER
Anne Sadler
MARKET RESEARCH DIRECTOR
Judith McCourt

VIDEO SYSTEMS MAGAZINE

(Monthly) 9800 Metcalf Ave., Overland Park, KS 66212-2215. (913) 341-1300. FAX: (913) 967-1898.
PUBLISHER
Judd Alford
GROUP VICE PRESIDENT
Cameron Bishop
MARKETING DIRECTOR
Eric Proffitt
AD PRODUCTION COORDINATOR
Pat Eisenman

VIDEO WEEK

(Weekly) Warren Publishing, Inc. 2115 Ward Court N.W., Washington, DC 20037-1213. (202) 872-9200. FAX: (202) 293-3435.

VIDEOGRAPHY MAGAZINE

(Monthly) 276 Fifth Avenue Ste 1111, New York, NY 10001. (212) 686-5410. FAX: (212) 889-5097
PUBLISHER/EDITOR
Cindy Spielvogel

GREAT BRITAIN

BROADCAST

(Published weekly).EMAP Media Ltd., 33-39 Bowling Green Lane, London, EC1R ODA. (44171) 505 8014. FAX: (44171) 505 8050.
EDITOR
Steve Clarke

IMAGE TECHNOLOGY

Journal of the BKSTS—The Moving Image Societ, 63-71 Victoria House, Vernon Place, London, WC1B 4DA, England. (44171) 242-8400. FAX: (44171) 405 3560.
MANAGING EDITOR
Jim Slater

KEMPS FILM, TV & VIDEO HANDBOOK

(Annual) Reed Information Services, Windsor Court, East Grinstead House, East Grinstead, West Sussex, RH19 1XA England. (44342) 326 972.
PUBLISHER
Richard Woolley
PRODUCT MANAGER
Sara Tyler
EDITOR
Claire Crossfield

SCREEN INTERNATIONAL

(Published weekly). Published by EMAP Media, 33-39 Bowling Green Lane, London EC1R 0DA, England. (44171) 505-8080. FAX: (44171) 505-8050.
EDITOR
Boyd Farrow

TELEVISUAL

(Published monthly). Centaur Communications, St. Giles House, 50 Poland St., London, W1V 4AX. (44171) 439 4222. FAX: (44171) 287 0768.
PUBLISHER
Morag Armand Addey
EDITOR
Mundy Ellis

CANADA

FILM CANADA YEARBOOK

Box 152, Toronto, Ont. M4G 3Z3, Canada. (416) 696-2382. FAX: (416) 696-6496.
Editor
Patricia Thompson

FRANCE

LE FILM FRANCAIS

(Weekly) 103 Blvd. St. Michel, Paris, France, 75005. (331) 4329 4090. FAX: (331) 4329 1405.
PUBLISHER
Claude Pommereau
EDITOR
Marie-Claude Arbaudie

HOME VIDEO

HOME VIDEO COMPANIES

VIDEO DISTRIBUTORS

A & E HOME VIDEO/HISTORY CHANNEL HOME VIDEO
235 E. 45th St., New York, NY 10017. (212) 210-1319. FAX:
(212) 210-1326.

A & M VIDEO
1416 N La Brea Ave., Hollywood, CA 90028. (213) 856-2767.
FAX: (213) 856-2778.
SENIOR DIRECTOR OF VIDEO PROMOTIONS
Emily Wittman
NATIONAL MANAGER OF VIDEO PROMOTIONS
Sergio Silva

A-PIX ENTERTAINMENT
(a division of Unapix) 200 Madison Ave., 24th floor, New York,
NY 10016. (212) 252-7711. FAX: (212) 252-7626.
PRESIDENT
Robert Baruch
V. P., NORTH AMERICAN TELEVISION
Rob Miller
PRESIDENT & CEO, UNAPIX
David Fox

ACTIVE HOME VIDEO
12121 Wilshire Blvd., Suite 200, Los Angeles, CA 90025. (310)
447-6131. FAX: (310) 207-0411.
GENERAL MANAGER
Ron Levanson
CREATIVE SERVICES DIRECTOR
Juanita Weber
SALES
Alice de Buhr

ADMIT ONE VIDEO PRESENTATIONS
P.O. Box 66 Station "O", Toronto, Ontario, Canada M4A 2M8.
(416) 463-5714.

ANCHOR BAY ENTERTAINMENT
500 Kirts Blvd., Troy, MI 48084.

ASTRAL HOME ENTERTAINMENT
(An Astral Communications Company) 889 Montee de Liesse,
Ville Saint-Laurent, QC H4T 1P5. (51 4) 734-2500. FAX: (514)
734-2501.
PRESIDENT, ASTRAL HOME
Randal Pallach
PRESIDENT, ASTRAL TECH & TECHNICAL SVC'S. DIVISION
Sidney Greenberg
NATIONAL SALES MANAGER
Barry Brooker
DIRECTOR OF PURCHASING
Randy Greenberg

BFS LIMITED
360 Newkirk Road North, Richmond Hill, Ontario, Canada L4C
3G7. (905) 884-2323. FAX: (905) 884-8292.
PRESIDENT
Denis Donnelly

BMG VIDEO
1540 Broadway, New York, NY 10036. (212) 930-4607. FAX:
(212) 930-7043.
PRESIDENT
Alvin B. Reuben
V.P., SALES
Gene Fink
V.P., ACQUISITIONS
Susan Rosenberg

BUENA VISTA HOME VIDEO
350 S. Buena Vista St., Burbank, CA 91521. (818) 560-1000.
(Distributor of Walt Disney, Touchstone, Hollywood Pictures,
Jim Henson, DIC Toon-Time, Miramax, Dimension and Buena
Vista Home Video lines.)
PRESIDENT, HOME VIDEO WORLD WIDE
Michael Orlin Johnson
SENIOR V.P., MARKETING
Dennis Rice
V.P., RETAIL MARKETING
Kelley Avery
SENIOR V.P., SALES
Dennis Maguire
V.P., SALES
Matt Brown
SENIOR V.P., BUSINESS AFFAIRS & ACQUISITIONS
Jere Hausfater

CABIN FEVER ENTERTAINMENT
1 Sound Shore Dr., Greenwich, CT 06830. (203) 863-5200.
FAX: (203) 863-5258.
PRESIDENT
Tom Molito

CABLE FILMS & VIDEO
7171 County Club Station, Kansas City, MO 64113. (913) 362-
2804, (800) 514-2804. FAX: (913) 341-7365.
email: movies@onlineworld.com
URL: http://onlineworld.com/movies
PRESIDENT
Herb Miller
GENERAL MANAGER
Todd Randall

CAPITOL RECORDS VIDEO
1750 North Vine St., Tower-6, Hollywood, CA 90028. (213)
871-5180.
V.P., VIDEO PRODUCTION & DEVELOPMENT
Michelle Peacock

CBS FOX VIDEO
1330 Ave. of the Americas, New York, NY 10019-5402. (212)
373-4800. FAX: (212) 373-4803. (Partnership between CBS,
Inc./Fox Film Corp.)
SENIOR V.P., PROGRAM ACQUISITIONS
Steven Poe
V.P., SPORTS & FITNESS MARKETING
Kevin Conroy
V.P., NON-THEATRICAL MARKETING
Mindy Pickard
V.P., PROGRAM ACQUISITIONS
Ken Horowitz
V.P., BUSINESS AFFAIRS/GENERAL COUNSEL
Curtis Roberts
CONTROLLER
Louis Polenta

CC STUDIOS/CHILDREN'S CIRCLE
389 Newtown Turnpike, Weston, CT 06883. (203) 222-0002,
(800) 457-0686. FAX: (203) 226-3818.
PRESIDENT & TREASURER
Morton Schindel
VICE PRESIDENT
Linda Lee

CINEVISTA
1680 Michigan Ave., Suite 1106, Miami Beach, FL 33139.
(305) 532-3400. FAX: (305) 532-0047.
PRESIDENT
Rene Fuentes-Chao
EDITOR-IN-CHIEF, CINEVISTA NEWS
Susan M. Alvarez

COLUMBIA TRISTAR HOME VIDEO
10202 W. Washington Blvd., Culver City, CA 90232. (310) 280-8000.
PRESIDENT
Ben Feingold
EXECUTIVE V.P.
William Chardavoyne
EXECUTIVE V.P., NORTH AMERICA
Paul Culberg
EXECUTIVE V.P., OPERATIONS & EUROPEAN SUPERVISION
Alan Pritchard
SENIOR V.P., LEGAL
Kim Lynch
SENIOR V.P., BUSINESS AFFAIRS & ACQUISITIONS
Peter Schlessel
SENIOR V.P., SALES, U.S.
Ralph Walin
V.P., LICENSING, FAR EAST
Janet Almroth Robertson
V.P., MANUFACTURING & PRODUCTION
Walt Engler
V.P., SALES, CANADA
Marshall Forster
V.P., WORLDWIDE PUBLICITY
E. Fritz Friedman
V.P., SALES, RENTAL, U.S.
Jeff Rabinowitz
V.P., SALES, RETAIL, U.S.
John Reina
V.P., LICENSING, LATIN AMERICA
Rodolfo Vila
V.P., MARKETING, NORTH AMERICA
Lon Von Hurwitz
V.P., INTERNATIONAL MARKETING
Lexine Wong

CORONET/MTI FILMS & VIDEO
2349 Chaffe Dr., St. Louis, MO 63146. (314) 569-0211, (800) 221-1274. FAX: (314) 569-2834. email: phoenixfilms@att.net
MARKETING COORDINATOR
Tom Ambroson

ENGELWOOD ENTERTAINMENT LLC
10917 Winner Road, Independence, MO 64052. (816) 252-4288. FAX: (816) 836-2400.
URL: http://www.englewd.com
OWNER
Ben Mossman

FIRST RUN FEATURES/ICARUS FILMS
153 Waverly Pl., Sixth floor, New York, NY 10014. (212) 727-1711.FAX: (212) 989-7649. email: frif@echonyc.com
PRESIDENTS
Jonathan Miller
Seymour Wishman

FOX VIDEO
2121 Avenue of the Stars, #2500, Los Angeles, CA 90067. FAX: (310) 203-3318.
PRESIDENT
Robert DeLellis
SENIOR V.P., ADMINISTRATION & OPERATIONS
David Goldstein
SENIOR V.P., MARKETING
Bruce Psander
SENIOR V.P., SALES
Vince Larinto

FOX/LORBER ASSOCIATES, INC.
419 Park Ave. South, 20th Floor, New York, NY 10016. (212) 686-6777. FAX: (212) 685-2625.
PRESIDENT & CEO
Richard Lorber
V.P., ACQUISITIONS
Krysanne Katsoolis

FULL MOON HOME VIDEO
3030 Andrita St., Los Angeles, CA 90065. (213) 341-5959. FAX: (213) 341-5960.
DIRECTOR OF VIDEO MARKETING & DISTRIBUTION
Dwight Krizman

GOLDEN BOOK VIDEO
11444 W. Olympic Blvd., 10th fl., Los Angeles, CA 90064. (310) 445-8877.

GOODTIMES HOME VIDEO
16 E. 40 St., New York, NY 10016. (212) 951-3000.
PRESIDENT
Joseph Carey
SENIOR V.P., THEATRICAL ACQUISITIONS
Jeff Baker

HBO VIDEO
1100 Ave. of the Americas, New York, NY 10036. (212) 512-7400. FAX: (212) 512-7458.
PRESIDENT
Henry McGee
DIRECTOR, SALES—RENTAL
Michael Vassen
DIRECTOR, SALES—SELL-THROUGH
Bob Cowan

JIM HENSON VIDEO
Raleigh Studios, 5358 Melrose Ave., Hollywood, CA 90038. (213) 960-4096. FAX: (213) 960-4935.

HOME VISION PUBLIC MEDIA INC.
4411 N. Ravenswood, Chicago, IL 60640. (773) 878-2600. FAX: (773) 878-8406.
PRESIDENT, PUBLIC MEDIA INC.
Adrianne Furniss
SENIOR V.P., SALES
Jeff McGuire
CHAIRMAN OF PUBLIC MEDIA, INC.
Charles Benton

IRS VIDEO
3520 Hayden Ave., Culver City, CA 90232. (310) 841-4100. 594 Broadway, #901, New York, NY 10012. (212) 334-2173.

KINO ON VIDEO
333 West 39th St., Suite 503, New York, NY 10018. (212) 629-6880. FAX: (212) 714-0871. URL: http://www.kino.com
PRESIDENT
Don Krim

KULTUR INTERNATIONAL FILMS/WHITE STAR VIDEO
195 Highway 36, West Long Branch, NJ 07764. (800) 458-5887. FAX: (908) 229-0066.
PRESIDENT
Dennis M. Hedlund
VICE PRESIDENT
Pearl Lee
MANAGING DIRECTOR & ACQUISITIONS DIRECTOR
Ronald F. Davis
SALES EXECUTIVE
Leslie Cohen Murray

LIVE ENTERTAINMENT
15400 Sherman Way, Suite 500, Van Nuys, CA 91406. (818) 908-0303. FAX: (805) 908-0320.
PRESIDENT & COO
Roger Burlage
EXECUTIVE V.P., DISTRIBUTION & MARKETING
Elliot Slutzky
SENIOR V.P., PRODUCTION & ACQUISITION
Paul Almond
SENIOR V.P., SALES & DISTRIBUTION
Jeffrey Fink
SENIOR V.P. & GENERAL MANAGER INTERNATIONAL
Edwin Friendly

LYONS GROUP
2000 E Bethany, Allen, TX 75002. (972) 390-6000. FAX: (972) 390-6190.
V.P., COMMUNICATIONS
Sue Bristol

MANGA ENTERTAINMENT
c/o Polygram Home Video. Worldwide Plaza, 825 8th Ave., New York, NY 10019. (212) 333- 8000.

MCA/UNIVERSAL HOME ENTERTAINMENT
70 Universal City Plaza, #435, Universal City, CA 91608. (818) 777-2100. FAX: (818) 733-1483.

MGM/UA HOME VIDEO, INC.
2500 Broadway St., Santa Monica, CA 90404. (310) 449-3000.
PRESIDENT, HOME ENTERTAINMENT DIVISION
David Bishop
PRESIDENT & COO, HOME ENT. CONSUMER PRODUCT
Richard Cohen
S.V.P., WORLDWIDE MKTG., MGM HOME ENTERTAINMENT
Blake Thomas
S.V.P., SALES, MGM HOME ENTERTAINMENT
Robert Wittenberg
V.P., MARKETING
Corie Tappin

MPI HOME VIDEO
16101 S. 108th Ave., Orland Park, IL 60467. (708) 460-0555. FAX: (708) 460-0175.
CEO
Waleed B. Ali
VICE PRESIDENT
Malik B. Ali
MARKETING DIRECTORS
Nasser Zegar
Sam Citro
MARKETING DIRECTOR, WEST COAST
Richard Shenson

NATIONAL GEOGRAPHIC SOCIETY
1145 17th St., N.W., Washington, D.C. 20036. (202) 857-7680. FAX: (202) 775-6590.
Los Angeles TV Office: 4370 Tujunga Ave., #300, Studio City, CA 91604. (818) 506-8300.
PRESIDENT
Tim Kelly

NEW LINE HOME VIDEO
888 Seventh Ave., 20th fl., New York, NY 10106. (212) 649-4900. FAX: (212) 956-1941.
PRESIDENT & COO
Stephen Einhorn

NEW WORLD VIDEO
1440 S. Sepulveda Blvd., Los Angeles, CA 90025. (310) 444-8100. FAX: (310) 444-8101.
SENIOR V.P., SALES AND MARKETING
Rex Bowring
EXECUTIVE DIRECTOR, CREATIVE SERVICES
Jerry Zanitsch

NEW YORKER VIDEO
16 W. 61 St., New York, NY 10023. (212) 247-6117, (800) 447-0196. FAX: (212) 307-7855.
PRESIDENT
Daniel Talbot
V.P. & DIRECTOR OF HOME VIDEO
Jose Lopez

PARAMOUNT HOME VIDEO
5555 Melrose Ave., Los Angeles, CA 90038. (213) 956-5000.
PRESIDENT, WORLDWIDE VIDEO
Eric Doctorow
SENIOR V.P., SALES
Meegan Burrows
EXECUTIVE V.P., SALES & MARKETING
Jack Kanne
SENIOR V.P., MARKETING
Michael Arkin

PBS HOME VIDEO
1320 Braddock Pl., Alexandria, VA 22314-1698. (703) 739-5380, (800) 424-7963.

POLYGRAM HOME VIDEO
Worldwide Plaza, 825 8th Ave., New York, NY 10019. (212) 333- 8000. FAX: (212) 333-8225.

PRISM ENTERTAINMENT CORPORATION
1888 Century Park E., Suite 350, Los Angeles, CA 90067. (310) 277-3270. FAX: (310) 203-8036.
PRESIDENT & CEO
Barry Collier
PRESIDENT, PRISM PICTURES
Barbara Jamvitz
SENIOR V.P., SALES
Joe Petrone

RANDOM HOUSE, INC.
201 E. 50 St., New York, NY 10022. (212) 751-2600. FAX: (212) 940-7640. URLl: www.randomhouse.com
PRESIDENT, JUVENILE DIVISION
Harold Clarke

REPUBLIC PICTURES HOME VIDEO
(A subsidiary of Spelling Entertainment) 5700 Wilshire Blvd., #575, Los Angeles, CA 90036. (213) 965-5700. URL: http://www.republic-pictures.com

RHINO HOME VIDEO
10635 Santa Monica Blvd., Los Angeles, CA 90025-4900. (310) 474-4778. FAX: (31) 441-6573
S.V.P. & GENERAL MANAGER
Arny Schorr

SINISTER CINEMA
P.O. Box 4369, Medford, OR 97501-0168. (541) 773-6860. FAX: (541) 779-8650. URL: http://www.cinemaweb.com/sinister

SOMETHING WEIRD VIDEO
P. O. Box 33664, Seattle, WA 98133. (206) 361-3759. FAX: (206) 364-7526.

TAI SENG VIDEO
170 South Spruce Ave., Suite 200, South San Francisco, CA 94080. (650) 871-8118, (888) 668-8338. FAX: (650) 871-2392. email: webstaff@taiseng.com. URL: http://www.taiseng.com
GENERAL MANAGER
Helen K. Soo

TELEVISION REPRESENTATIVES, INC.
9911 W. Pico Blvd., PH-E, Los Angeles, CA 90035. (310) 552-2660. FAX: (310) 552-9039.
CHAIRMAN
Alan Silverbach
GENERAL MANAGER
Betty Jane Metz

TROMA TEAM VIDEO
733 Ninth Avenue, New York, NY 10019. URL: http://www. troma.com/home
PRESIDENT
Lloyd Kaufman

TURNER HOME ENTERTAINMENT
P.O. Box 105366, Atlanta, GA 30348-5366. (404) 827-3261.

UNIVERSAL STUDIOS HOME VIDEO
70 Universal City Plaza, #435, Universal City, CA 91608. (818) 777-2100. FAX: (818) 733-1483.

VCI & LIBERTY HOME VIDEO
11333 East 60th Place, Tulsa, OK 74146. (918) 254-6337, (800) 331-4077. FAX: (918) 254-6117. URL: http://www.vcihomevideo.com

VIDMARK, INC.
2644 30th St., Santa Monica, CA 90405-2906. (310) 399-8877, (800) 424-7070. FAX: (310) 392-0252.
CHAIRMAN & CEO
Mark Amin

WEA CORP. (WARNER/ELEKTRA/ATLANTIC)
(A subsidiary of Warner Bros. Inc., a Time Warner company.)
111 N. Hollywood Way, Burbank, CA 91505-4356. (818) 843-6311. FAX: (818) 840-6212.
CHAIRMAN & CEO
Dave Mount
EXECUTIVE V.P., MARKETING
George Rossi
SENIOR V.P., SALES
Fran Aliberte

WARNER HOME VIDEO INC.
(A subsidiary of Warner Bros. Inc., a Time Warner company)
3903 W. Olive Ave., Burbank, CA 91522. (818) 954-6000.
PRESIDENT
Warren N. Lieberfarb
EXECUTIVE V.P. & GENERAL MANAGER, INTERNATIONAL
Edward J. Byrnes
EXECUTIVE V.P., NORTH AMERICA
James F. Cardwell
EXECUTIVE V.P., WORLDWIDE BUSINESS AFFAIRS
Marsha King
S.V.P., WORLDWIDE MARKETING & DEVELOPMENT
Tom Lesinski
S.V.P., DOMESTIC SALES
John Quinn

WEST GLEN COMMUNICATIONS, INC.
1430 Broadway, 9th Flr., New York, NY 10018. (212) 921-2800, (800) 325-8677. FAX: (212) 944-9055.
PRESIDENT
Stanley S. Zeitlin
SENIOR V.P., PRODUCTION
John Summerlin

WESTERN PUBLISHING CORPORATION
1220 Mound Ave., Racine, WI 53404-3336. (414) 633-2431. FAX: (414) 631-1854.
PRESIDENT & CEO
Richard Snyder

MAJOR VIDEO WHOLESALERS

BAKER & TAYLOR ENTERTAINMENT
8140 N. Lehigh Ave., Morton Grove, IL 60053. (847) 965-8060. FAX: (847) 470-7860.
EXEC. V.P., & GENERAL MANAGER
Richrad Czuba

BUDGET VIDEO INC.
9830 Charleville Blvd., Beverly Hills, CA 90212.

THE CINEMA GUILD
1697 Broadway, Suite 506, New York, NY 10019-5904. (212) 246-5522. email: TheCinemaG@aol.com
CHAIRPEOPLE
Philip Hobel & Mary-Ann Hobel
PRESIDENT
Gary Crowdus
DISTRIBUTION MANAGER
Heather Alvevras
SALES DIRECTOR
Marlene Graham

ETD ENTERTAINMENT DISTRIBUTING
7171 Grand Blvd., Houston, TX 77054. (713) 748-2520, (800) 892-5055. FAX: (713) 748-2617.
PRESIDENT
Ron Eisenberg
MARKETING & SALES
Dan Malaguilla

FIRST VIDEO EXCHANGE
13722 Harvard Pl., Gardena, CA 902498. (310) 516-6422, (800) 247-2351. FAX: (310) 516-6654.
PRESIDENT
Jeff Leyton

INGRAM ENTERTAINMENT, INC.
2 Ingram Blvd., La Vergne, TN 37086-1986. (615) 287-4000. (800) 759-5000. FAX: (615) 793-3875.
PRESIDENT & CEO
David Ingram
SENIOR V.P., SALES & MARKETING
Vern Fross
V.P., OPERATIONS & PURCHASING
Robert Webb

M.S. DISTRIBUTING CO.
6405 Muirfield Dr., Hanover Park, IL 60103. (630) 582-2888.
FAX: (630) 582-8448.
PRESIDENT
Tony Dalesandro
EXECUTIVE V.P.
John Salstone
MARKETING & SALES
Rick Chrzan

RENTRAK HOME ENTERTAINMENT
7700 NE Ambassador Plaza, Portland, OR 97220. (503) 284-
7581. FAX: (503) 288-1563.
PRESIDENT
Ron Berger
V.P., SALES
Chris Roberts
SENIOR V.P., MARKETING
Michael R. Lightbourne

SIGHT AND SOUND DISTRIBUTORS
2055 Walton Rd., St. Louis, MO 63114. (314) 426-2388, (800)
388-6601. FAX: (314) 426-1307.
CEO
Jim Former

VIDEO DIMENSIONS
208 West 30th St., New York, NY 10001. Tel/FAX: (212) 216-9628.
GENERAL MANAGER
Victor Kalart

VIDEO MARKETING & DISTRIBUTING INC.
4301 Hwy. 7, St. Louis Park, MN 55416. (612) 920-8400. FAX:
(612) 920-8474.
PRESIDENT
Mark Saliterman

WAX WORKS/VIDEO WORKS
325 E. 3rd St., Owensboro, KY 42303. (800) 825-8558. (502)
926-0008. FAX: (502) 685-0563.
URL: http://www.waxworksonline.com
4477 Winchester Rd., Ste. 1, Memphis, TN 38118. (800) 888-
4088, (901) 366-4088. FAX: (901) 366-0555.
530 Lakeview Plaza Blvd., Worthington, OH 43085.(800) 816-
6843, (614) 848-6440. FAX: (614) 848-6490.
PRESIDENT
Terry Woodward
VICE PRESIDENT
Noel Clayton
VICE PRESIDENT, MARKETING
Kirk Kirkpatrick

MAJOR VIDEO DIRECT MARKETERS

BOOK-OF THE MONTH CLUB, INC.
1271 Avenue of the Americas, 3rd fl., New York, NY 10020.
(212) 522-4200.
V.P., NEW BUSINESS DEVELOPMENT
Steve Frary

COLUMBIA HOUSE VIDEO
1400 N. Fruitridge Ave., Terre Haute, IN 47811. (800) 457-
0866.
Executive offices: 1221 Avenue of the Americas, New York,
NY 10020-1090. (212) 596-2691. FAX: (212) 596-2740.
EXECUTIVE V.P., COLUMBIA HOUSE VIDEO
Brian Wood
V.P., COLUMBIA HOUSE VIDEO LIBRARY
Harry Elias

DISCOUNT VIDEO TAPES, INC./HOLLYWOOD'S ATTIC
P.O. Box 7122, Burbank, CA 91510. (818) 843-3366. FAX:
(818) 843-3821. email: jr@discountvideotapes.com
URL: http://www.discountvideotapes.com
BUYER/PRESIDENT
Woody Wise

PBS DIRECT
2800 28th St., Suite 310, Santa Monica, CA 90405. (310) 581-
3700. FAX: (310) 581-3707.
SALES MANAGER
Harry Haber

SPECIAL INTEREST VIDEO
1717 Darby Rd., Sebastopol, CA 95472. (707) 829-0127. FAX:
(707) 829-9542.
PRESIDENT
Michael Heumann

TIME-LIFE HOME VIDEO/TIME-LIFE KIDS
2000 Duke St., Alexandria, VA 22314. (703) 838-7000.

VIDEO ORGANIZATIONS

VSDA/VIDEO SOFTWARE DEALERS OF AMERICA
16530 Ventura Blvd., Suite 400, Encino, CA 91436. (818) 385-
1500. FAX: (818) 385-0567.
PRESIDENT
Jeffrey P. Eves

Video Retailers

Figures for the number of retail outlets and 1997 revenue, where present, are courtesy of *Video Store Magazine*.

BLOCKBUSTER ENTERTAINMENT GROUP
3,343 corp. owned video stores & 697 franchises; $2,584 million.
1201 Elm St., Dallas, TX 75270. (800) 800-6767.
PRESIDENT & CEO
John Antioco

BLOWOUT ENTERTAINMENT, INC.
125 outlets; $60 million.
P.O. Box 13280, Portland, OR 97213. (503) 331-2729. FAX: (503) 331-2730.
CEO
Steve Berns

CIANCI VIDEOLAND
73 outelts; $29 million.
7929 South West Burns Way, Wilsonville, OR 97070. (503) 682-3262. FAX: (503) 682-6786.
CEO
Jim Nowodworski

EASY VIDEO
42 outlets; $23 million.
515 Plainfield Ave,. Edison, NJ 08817. (732) 248-1550. FAX: (732) 248-1647.
CEO
John Howell

FAMILY VIDEO
125 outlets; $60 million.
1022 E. Adams, Springfield, IL 62703. (217) 544-2001. FAX: (217) 544-8416.
CEO
Keith Hoogland

HOLLYWOOD ENTERTAINMENT
901 outlets; $490 million.
25600 SW Pkwy. Center Dr., Wilsonville, OR 97611. (503) 570-1600. FAX: (503) 570-1701.
PRESIDENT
Doug Gordon

MOOVIES INC.
267 outlets; $110 million.
201 Brookfield Pkwy., Suite 200, Greenville, SC 29607. (864) 213-1700. FAX: (864) 213-1702.
CEO
John Bedaro

THE MOVIE EXCHANGE
1000 outlets.
705 General Washington Ave., Suite 300, Norristown PA 19403. (610) 631-9180. FAX: (610) 631-9359.
CHAIRMAN
Lamont T. Bbitts
BUYER
Dale Cooper

THE MOVIE GALLERY
970 outlets; $257 million.
739 West Main St., Dothan, AL 36301. (334) 677-2108. FAX: (334) 677-7169.
CEO
J. Steven Roy

MR. MOVIES, INC.
73 outlets; $23.4 million.
7625 Parklawn Ave., Suite 200, Edina, MN 55435. (612) 835-3321. FAX: (612) 855-1144.
CEO
Bill Kaiser

PIC-A-FLICK
41 outlets; $11.7 million.
120 Garner Rd., Spartanburg, SC 29303. (864) 585-1533. FAX: (864) 591-0767.
CEO
Jan Keith

PLANET VIDEO, INC.
34 outlets; $16.7 million
W222 N615 N. Cheaney Dr., Waukensha, WI 53186. (414) 544-9100. FAX: (414) 544-9100.
CEO
Charles J. Wyse

SUNCOAST MOTION PICTURE CO.
409 outlets in the U.S. and Puerto Rico; $420 million.
(A subsidiary of Music Land Group), 10400 Yellow Circle Dr., Minnetonka, MN 55343. (612) 931-8000. FAX: (612) 931-8300.
CHAIRMAN
Brant K. Skogrand
CEO
Jack Eugster
BUYER
Peter Busch

TOTAL ENTERTAINMENT CENTER/VIDEO BUYERS GROUP
39 outlets; $13.3 million.
199 Coon Rapids Blvd., Suite 208, Minneapolis, MN 55433-5860. (612) 780-6012. FAX: (612) 780-6039.
CEO
Ted Engen

TOWER RECORDS/VIDEO
100 outlets; $50 million.
2500 Delmonte, Building C, West Sacramento, CA 95827. (916) 373-2500. FAX: (916) 373-2429.
CEO
John Thrasher

20/20 VIDEO
26 outlets; $9.1 million.
1901 S. Pontius Ave., West Los Angeles, CA 90025. (310) 829-2020. FAX: (301) 445-0935.
CEO
Maurice Shab

VIDEO CITY
24 outlets; $12.4 million.
6840 District Blvd., Bakersfield, CA 93313. (805) 397-7955. FAX: (805) 397-5982.
CEO
Craig Kelly

VIDEO TYME, INC.
22 outlets; $12 million.
3463 S. Jones Blvd., Las Vegasm NV 89102. (702) 251-8900. FAX: (702) 251-4961.
CEO
Andrew Barufi

VIDEO UPDATE, INC.
445 outlets; $124 million.
3100 World Trade Center, 30 E. 7th St., St. Paul, MN 55101-4913. (612) 222-0006. FAX: (612) 229-9666.
CEO
John Bedaro

WEST COAST ENTERTAINMENT
600 outlets; $137 million.
1 Summit Sq., Ste. 200, Langhorne, PA 19047. (800) 433-5171; (215) 968-4318. FAX: (215) 497-5988.
CEO
Steve Apple

WEST COAST VIDEO ENTERPRISES, INC.
9990 Global Rd., Philadelphia, PA 19115. (215) 677-1000.
350 outlets.
BUYER
Tom Foltz

THE WORLD MARKET

GREAT BRITAIN

EUROPE, CANADA, LATIN AMERICA, AFRICA, ASIA AND THE PACIFIC

BRITISH TELEVISION & VIDEO
YEAR IN REVIEW

Digital television has arrived in Britain at a time when Britons are beginning to switch off. According to polls conducted in the early summer, average daily viewing has dropped by 18 minutes a day in the past six years. Tuning in time has fallen from 4.13 to 3.84 hours per person. Longer working hours, other leisure options and boredom with the standard TV fare could be the factors responsible for the decline in viewership.

This is particularly bad news for the non BBC channels which make their revenue by advertising. In that respect, digital television could help boost flagging interest by offering audiences more choice and more control over the programs that they watch. But digital television is an expensive option. The costs for the hardware alone - set-top decoder boxes, satellite dishes ,widescreen TV - start at around 200 pounds, and the subscriptions anywhere from 7.99 to thirty pounds per channel. The hardware for Ondigital and Skydigital, the two digital companies so far, is not compatible so there are added costs for viewers to gain access to both.

The launch of digital television was not coordinated properly with the sale of the hardware in the market and there is still very little knowledge about digital television in general and how it will change the way we watch TV. Not enough information has been passed on to the public to enable them to make a complete switch from analogue to digital. The government believes that it will take a maximum of seven to eight years for people to upgrade their televisions to digital and for the analogue spectrum to be sold off but BBC figures suggest a more realistic time span of fourteen to fifteen years. The National Consumer Council (NCC) has also called upon the government to protect consumers from making expensive mistakes in a rush to get hooked on to a system which they might not even want; the NCC stated that there was no proof that people wanted to switch to digital TV. It said that there were real doubts about the cost and accessibility of the new system and there was no guarantee that the new service would deliver quality programmes. The government has proposed to make the analogue switch off by 2012 but the NCC says that that must only be done only if digital tv is reaching 99 per cent of the public by that time.

Polls suggest that viewing habits are becoming increasingly fickle and programmes and personalities fall out of favour rather quickly. Even so some programmes stand the test of time - "Only Fools and Horses", for example has been rated the best comedy year after year and the veteran "This is Your Life" has risen by a third in ratings. By the end of 1997, one-third of Britain was buying non-terrestrial TV but very few had installed the whole gamut of satellite channels. According to Broadcast magazine, only half of television owners are tuned in to Channel 5 let alone satellite. Last year Channel 4 and BBC2 had more viewers than all the satellite channels put together. In BARB Weekly Network Report's Autumn 1997 compilation of top 50 programmes it emerged that drama serials had doubled in popularity rising from three to six entries while game and quiz shows had dropped from 12 to eight entries having lost their audience to documentary productions.

The funeral of Diana Princess of Wales on 6th September 1997 became the most watched special transmission on television with a single-channel record of 19.3 million viewers. Animal programmes, like "Animal Hospital" and "Vets in Practice" rate very highly among factual programmes so every channel has its own version of the rescued animal programme.

Despite the onslaught of sex on television and the channels trying to outdo each other in squeezing nudity into their transmissions, it does not seem to be a reliable audience-puller. The BBC's "Teletubbies" have spawned a mega industry since the first Teletubby dolls came out and have perhaps become Britain's most popular export since the royal family but BBC is still struggling to compete with channels such as Nickleodeon, Cartoon Network and Fox Kids Network. The BBC is planning to invest eight million pounds a year on a separate public service channel for children on digital television. BBC One is planning to meet the digital challenge by dishing out an extra 20 million pounds. The channel controller for Channel One claimed that in a multi-channel environment, BBC One would remain the channel to bring people together. He cited Princess Diana's funeral, "Eurovision Song Contest", "Ballykissangel" and "Eastenders" as examples of programmes that had viewers across the cross-section of society. BBC America has also proved a popular export for the BBC with cable and satellite subscribers adding up to over two million.

Sports has become an expensive proposition on British television since the arrival of Sky. The professional bodies that demand huge fees usually get it and it is very difficult for BBC with its limited license fee revenue to compete with other channels for sports coverage. Its credibility as a primary public broadcaster is threatened by its failure to provide some of the major sporting events for its license-fee paying audience.

— Nimra Bucha

COMMERCIAL BROADCASTERS AND GOVERNMENT UNITS

BRITISH BROADCASTING CORPORATION TELEVISION SERVICE
Television Centre, Wood Lane, London W12 7RJ. Tel: (0181) 743 8000. FAX: (0181) 576 1865.
DIRECTOR GENERAL
John Birt
DEPUTY DIRECTOR GENERAL & CHIEF EXECUTIVE, BBC WORLDWIDE
Bob Phillis
CHIEF EXECUTIVE, BBC BROADCAST
Will Wyatt
CHIEF EXECUTIVE, BBC PRODUCTION
Ronald Neil
CHIEF EXECUTIVE, BBC NEWS
Tony Hall
CHIEF EXECUTIVE, BBC RESOURCES
Rod Lynch
DIRECTOR OF PERSONNEL
Margaret Salmon
DIRECTOR OF FINANCE & INFORMATION TECHNOLOGY
Rodney Baker-Bates
DIRECTOR OF POLICY & PLANNING
Patricia Hodgson CBE
DIRECTOR OF CORPORATE AFFAIRS
Colin Browne
BBC BROADCAST
DIRECTOR OF TELEVISION
Alan Yentob
DIRECTOR OF RADIO
Matthew Bannister
DIRECTOR OF REGIONAL BROADCASTING
Mark Byford
DIRECTOR OF EDUCATION
Jane Drabble
BBC WORLDWIDE
MANAGING DIRECTOR, WORLD SERVICE
Sam Younger
BBC WORLDWIDE
Woodlands, 80 Wood Lane, London W12 0TT. Tel: (0181) 576 2000. FAX: (0181) 749 0538.
CHIEF EXECUTIVE
Bob Phillis
CHIEF OPERATING OFFICER
Dick Emery
DIRECTOR, RIGHTS AGENCY
Mike Phillips
DIRECTOR, FINANCE & INFORMATION TECHNOLOGY
Peter Teague
COMMERCIAL DIRECTOR & MANAGING DIRECTOR BBC WORLD
Mark Young
DIRECTOR, INTERNATIONAL & GLOBAL BRAND DEVELOPMENT
Jeff Taylor
MANAGING DIRECTOR, UK DIVISION
Peter Phippen
DIRECTOR, NEW MEDIA
Jeremy Mayhew
DIRECTOR, STRATEGY
Carolyn Fairbairn
DIRECTOR, MARKETING
Simon Sudbury
DIRECTOR, PERSONNEL
Bob McCall
HEAD OF CORPORATE AFFAIRS
Ian Hunter
HEAD OF PRESS & PUBLIC RELATIONS
Janie Ironside-Wood

BRITISH SKY BROADCASTING
Grant Way, Isleworth, Middlesex, TW7 5QD. Tel: (0171) 705 3000. FAX: (0171) 705 3030. http://www.sky.co.uk
CHIEF EXECUTIVE & MANAGING DIRECTOR
Mark Booth
DEPUTY MANAGING DIRECTOR
David Chance
DIRECTOR OF MULTI-CHANNEL CO-VENTURES
James Ackerman
HEAD OF PROGRAMMING
James Baker
HEAD OF LEGAL & BUSINESS AFFAIRS
Deanna Bates
GROUP FINANCE DIRECTOR
Rickard Brooke
CHIEF FINANCIAL OFFICER
Nick Carrington
DIRECTOR OF PROGRAMMES & GENERAL MANAGER, BROADCASTING
Elisabeth Murdoch
DIRECTOR OF PROMOTIONS & CREATIVE SERVICES
Bruce Dunlop
DIRECTOR OF PROMOTIONS & PUBLICITY
Raymond Jaffe
DIRECTOR OF DISTRIBUTION
Jon Florsheim
DIRECTOR OF PUBLIC AFFAIRS
Ray Gallagher
DIRECTOR OF ENGINEERING & SERVICES
Geoff Walters
DIRECTOR OF SALES
Peter Shea
DIRECTOR OF DIGITAL & BUSINESS DEVELOPMENT
Ian West
DIRECTOR OF TECHNOLOGY DEVELOPMENT
Robin Crossley
DIRECTOR OF MOVIES & PAY PER VIEW
Bruce Steinberg
GROUP HEAD OF PERSONNEL
Cynthia Guthrie
HEAD OF PRESS & PUBLICITY
Chris Haynes
MARKETING DIRECTOR
Jim Hytner
GENERAL MANAGER & COMPANY SECRETARY
Chris Mackenzie
HEAD OF NEWS
Nick Pollard
CONTROLLER OF SKY CHANNELS
Les Sampson
GROUP HEAD OF INFORMATION TECHNOLOGY
Rob Shepherd
GROUP SALES & MARKETING DIRECTOR
Tony Vickers
HEAD OF SPORT
Vic Wakeling
STATION MANAGER
David Butorac

INDEPENDENT TELEVISION COMMISSION (ITC)
Founded in 1991, the ITC was created by Parliament under the terms of the Broadcasting Act 1990 to license and regulate all commercially-funded television in the United Kingdom, whether delivered terrestrially (i.e. ITV, Channel 4 and Channel 5) or by cable or satellite, public teletext and certain other text and data services. The ITC regulates these services through license conditions and through its various codes on program content, advertising, sponsorship and technical standards.

33 Foley Street, London, WIP 7LB. Tel: (0171) 255 3000. FAX: (0171) 306 7800.
CHAIRMAN
Sir Robert Biggam
CHIEF EXECUTIVE
Peter Rogers
DIRECTOR OF PROGRAMMES
Clare Mulholland
DIRECTOR OF CABLE & SATELLITE
Jon Davey
DIRECTOR OF ADVERTISING & SPONSORSHIP
Frank Willis
DIRECTOR OF PUBLIC AFFAIRS
Sarah Thane
DIRECTOR OF ENGINEERING
Gary Tonge

DEPARTMENT FOR CULTURE, MEDIA & SPORT
4th Floor, 2-4 Cockspur Street, London, SWIY 5DH. Tel: (0171) 211 6000. FAX: (0171) 211 6210.
CONTACT
Paul Wright

COMMERCIAL BROADCASTERS

(Appointed by the Independent Television Commission (ITC)).

ANGLIA TELEVISION LTD.

Registered office: Anglia House, Norwich, NR1 3JG. Tel: (01603) 615 151. Telex: 97424. FAX: (01603) 631 032. London Office: 48 Leicester Square, London, WC2H 7FB. Tel: (0171) 389 8555. FAX: (0171) 493 7677.
EAST OF ENGLAND LICENCE
CHAIRMAN
D. S. McCall, CBE
MANAGING DIRECTORS
M. Wall
M.J. Hughes
Lord Hollick
Sir David Puttnam, CBE
P. G. Sharman
P. Hickson
R. Laughton
Lord Eatwell

ANGLIA TELEVISION BROADCASTING DIVISION
DIRECTOR OF PROGRAMMES
Graham Creelman
DEPUTY DIRECTOR OF PROGRAMMES
Malcolm Allsop
DIRECTOR OF FINANCE
Brian Bolt
DIRECTOR OF FACILITIES
Debbie Hills
DIRECTOR OF PERSONNEL & ADMINISTRATION
Peter Meier
CONTROLLER OF PROGRAMME PLANNING
Steve West
CONTROLLER, NEWS
Mike Read
EDITOR, ANGLIA NEWS EAST
David Jennings
EDITOR, ANGLIA NEWS WEST
Guy Adams
SPORT EDITOR
Kevin Piper
HEAD OF PRESS & PUBLIC RELATIONS
Martin Morrall
TECHNICAL CONTROLLER
Tim Dye
PRODUCTION CONTROL MANAGER
Chris Wilden
POST PRODUCTION MANAGER
David Brackenbury
NEWS OPERATIONS MANAGER
Roger Beavis
ADMINISTRATION MANAGER
Gina Boltwood
BUSINESS AFFAIRS & PROGRAM CONTRACTS MANAGER
Paddy Burns
COMMUNITY EDUCATION OFFICER
Cathy Mason

ANGLIA TELEVISION ENTERTAINMENT LTD.
CHAIRMAN
David McCall, CBE
MANAGING DIRECTOR
Sarah Lawson
CONTROLLER OF PRODUCTION & PROGRAMME FINANCE
David Fitzgerald

SURVIVAL ANGLIA LTD.
CHAIRMAN
David McCalle CBE
EXECUTIVE PRODUCERS
Graham Creelman
Sir David Puttnam, CBE
Roger Laughton
Alan Root
Petra Regent
PRODUCTION CONTROLLER
Peter Schofield

BORDER TELEVISION

(Borders and Isle of Man Licence). The Television Centre, Carlisle, CA1 3NT, Cumbria. Tel: (01228) 25101. FAX: (01228) 41384.
CHAIRMAN
James L. Graham
MANAGING DIRECTOR
P. Brownlow
DIRECTORS
A. Quinn
M. Sutherland
M. Hartley
Dr. June Paterson-Brown
Sir David Steel
Robin Burgess

CONTROLLER OF PROGRAMMES
N. Robinson
DIRECTOR OF BROADCASTING
Kath Worrall

CARLTON TELEVISION

(London and South East Weekday Licence). 101 St. Martin's Ln., London, WC2N 4AZ. Tel: (0171) 240 4000. FAX: (0171) 240 4171.
Productions: 35-38 Portman Square, London W1H 9FH. Tel: (0171) 486 6688. FAX: (0171) 486 1132.
Carlton Studios, Lenton Lane, Nottingham NG7 2NA. Tel: (0115) 986 3322. FAX: (0115) 964 5552.
Westcountry: Language Science Park, Western Wood Way, Banham, Plymouth PL7 5BG. Tel: (01752) 333 333. FAX: (01752) 333 444.
CHAIRMAN
Nigel Walmsley
CHIEF EXECUTIVE & CHAIRMAN, WESTCOUNTRY
Clive Jones
DIRECTOR OF PROGRAMMES
Andy Allan
MANAGING DIRECTOR, CARLTON SALES
Martin Bowley
FINANCE DIRECTOR
Mike Green
BUSINESS AFFAIRS DIRECTOR
John Egan
CONTROLLER OF REGIONAL & PUBLIC AFFAIRS
Hardeep Karsi
CONTROLLER OF COMPLIANCE & LEGAL AFFAIRS
Don Christopher
DIRECTOR OF PROGRAMMES
Andy Allan
CONTROLLER OF BROADCASTING
Coleena Reid
MANAGING DIRECTOR, CARLTON STUDIOS
Ian Squires

CENTRAL BROADCASTING

(Operated by Carlton UK Television)
(East, West and South Midlands Licence). Central Court, Broad Street, Birmingham B1 2JP. Tel: (0121) 643 9898. FAX: (0121) 643 4897.
CHAIRMAN
Nigel Walmsley
MANAGING DIRECTOR
Ian Squires

CHANNEL FOUR TELEVISION

124 Horseferry Road, London, SW1P 2TX. Tel: (0171) 396 4444. FAX: (0171) 306 8353.
CHAIRMAN
Sir Michael Bishop, CBE
CHIEF EXECUTIVE
Michael Jackson
DIRECTOR OF PROGRAMMES
John Willis
CONTROLLER OF ARTS/ENTERTAINMENT
Stuart Cosgrove
CONTROLLER OF FACTUAL
Karen Brown
HEAD OF FILM
David Aukin
DIRECTOR OF FINANCE
David Scott
DIRECTOR OF ACQUISITION
Colin Leventhal
DIRECTOR & GENERAL MANAGER
Frank McGettigan

CHANNEL FIVE BROADCASTING LTD.

(National Network). 22 Long Acre, London, WC2E 9LY. Tel: (0171) 550 5555. FAX: (0171) 550 5554.
CHIEF EXECUTIVE
Ian Ritchie
DIRECTOR OF PROGRAMMES
Dawn Airey
DIRECTOR OF BROADCASTING
Warren Breach
CONTROLLER, FEATURES AND ARTS
Michael Atwell
CONTROLLER, CURRENT AFFAIRS/DOCUMENTARIES
Tim Gardam
CONTROLLER, ENTERTAINMENT
Alan Nixon
CONTROLLER OF ENGINEERING OPERATIONS
Chris Collingham
DIRECTOR OF MARKETING & COMMUNICATIONS
David Brook

CHANNEL TELEVISION CHANNEL ISLANDS.
(Serves the Bailiwicks of Jersey and Guernsey as well as several smaller islands).
The Television Centre, St. Helier, Jersey, JE2 3ZD, Channel Islands. Tel: (01534) 816 816. FAX: (01534) 816 817.
The Television Centre, St. George's Place, St. Peter Port, Guernsey, GY2 4LA, Channel Islands. Tel: (01481) 723 451. FAX: (01481) 710 739.
CHAIRMAN
John Riley
MANAGING DIRECTOR
John Henwood
DIRECTOR OF SALES & MARKETING
Bob Jones
DIRECTOR OF FINANCE
Charles Day
DIRECTOR OF TELEVISION
Michael Lucas
DIRECTOR OF OPERATIONS
Roy Manning
DIRECTOR OF TELEVISION
Michael Lucas
GUERNSEY OFFICE MANAGER
Roger Bowns
HEAD OF PROGRAMME DEVELOPMENT
Frank Hayes

DATA BROADCASTING INTERNATIONAL LTD.
(Commercial Additional Services Licence). Allen House, Station Road, Egham, Surrey TW20 9NT. Tel: (01784) 471515. FAX: (01784) 438732.
CHIEF EXECUTIVE
P. W. H. Mason
CHAIRMAN
G. J. P. Cadbury

GMTV LTD.
(National breakfast-time licence. 7 days weekly, 6:00-9:25 am.).
The London
Television Centre, Upper Ground, London SE1 9TT. Tel: (0171) 827 7000. FAX:
(0171) 827 7001.
MANAGING DIRECTOR
Christopher Stoddart
CHAIRMAN
Charles Allen
DIRECTOR OF PROGRAMMING
Peter McHugh
MANAGING EDITOR, REUTERS
Henry Clark
MANAGING EDITOR, GMTV
John Scammell
EDITOR
Gerry Melling

GRAMPIAN TELEVISION PLC.
Queen's Cross, Aberdeen AB15 4XJ, Scotland. Tel: (01224) 846 560. FAX:
(01224) 846 800.
Albany House, 68 Albany Road, West Ferry, Dundee DD5 1NW, Scotland. Tel:
(01382) 739 363. FAX: (01382) 480 230.
23-25 Huntly Street, Inverness IV3 5PR, Scotland. Tel: (01463) 242 624.
FAX: (01463) 242 624.
Seaforth House, Stornoway HS1 25D, Scotland. Tel: (01851) 704 433. FAX:
(01851) 706 406.
46 Albany Street, Edinurgh EH1 3QR. Tel: (0131) 557 8668. FAX: (0131) 557
6676.
DIRECTORS
CHAIRMAN
Dr. Calum A. Macleod, CBE, LLD
DEPUTY CHAIRMAN
Donald H. Waters, OBE CA
DIRECTOR OF TELEVISION
Robert L. Christie
DIRECTOR OF FINANCE/COMPANY SECRETARY
Graham Good, C.A.
DIRECTOR OF PROGRAMS
George W. Mitchell
HEAD OF NEWS AND CURRENT AFFAIRS
Alistair Gracie
HEAD OF GAELIC
Bob Kenyon
HEAD OF PUBLIC RELATIONS
Michael J. McLintock, M.A., D.I.P. C.A.M.

GRANADA TELEVISION LTD.
(Northwest England Licence). Granada TV Centre, Quay Street, Manchester M60
9EA. Tel: (0161) 832 7211. FAX: (0161) 832 7211.
36 Golden Square, London W1R 4AH. Tel: (0171) 734 8080.
News Centre, Albert
Dock, Liverpool L3 4BA.
News Centre, White Cross, Lancaster LA1 4XQ.
News Centre, Bridgegate House, Chester and Daisfield Business Centre,
Blackburn BB1 3BL.
CHAIRMAN
Charles L. Allen
CHIEF EXECUTIVE
Steve Morrison
MANAGING DIRECTOR, GRANADA TV
David Fraser
COMMERCIAL DIRECTOR
Kate Stross
DIRECTOR OF PROGRAMMES
Peter Salmon
JOINT MDS GRANADA PRODUCTIONS
Jules Burns, Andrea Wonfor
DIRECTOR OF SALES
Michael Desmond
DIRECTOR OF RESOURCES
Brenda Smith
DIRECTOR OF BROADCASTING
Julia Lamaison
HEAD OF DRAMA
Sally Head
CONTROLLER OF ENTERTAINMENT & COMEDY
Andy Harries
CONTROLLER OF FACTUAL PROGRAMMES
Dianne Nelmes
HEAD OF SPORT
Paul Doherty
CONTROLLER OF PROGRAMME SERVICES & PERSONNEL
David Fraser
HEAD OF PROGRAMME PUBLICITY
Ian Haworth
DIRECTOR OF PUBLIC AFFAIRS
Chris Hopson
CONTROLLER OF ENTERTAINMENT & COMEDY
Andy Harries
HEAD OF CHILDREN'S PROGRAMMES
Ed Pugh
HEAD OF CURRENT AFFAIRS AND DOCUMENTARIES
Charles Tremayne
HEAD OF REGIONAL PROGRAMMES
Jeff Anderson
HEAD OF FEATURES
James Hunt
HEAD OF GRANADA TV FACTUAL DRAMA
Ian McBride

HTV GROUP PLC.
(Wales and West of England Licence). Television Centre, Culverhouse Cross,
Cardiff CF5 6XJ, Wales. Tel: (01222) 590 590. FAX: (01222) 597183.
HTV West Ltd., Television Centre, Bath Road, Bristol BS4 3HG. Tel: (01179)
722 722. Fax (01179) 722 400
CHAIRMAN HTV GROUP PLC
Louis Sherwood
CHIEF EXECUTIVE, HTV GROUP PLC
Christopher Rowlands
GROUP DIRECTOR OF BROADCASTING
Ted George
COMMERCIAL DIRECTOR, BROADCASTING
Simon Forrest

ITN LTD.
200 Gray's Inn Rd., London WC1X 8XZ. Tel: (0171) 833 3000. FAX: (0171) 430
4016. Telex: 22101.
CHAIRMAN
Sir David English
CHIEF EXECUTIVE
Stewart Purvis
EDITOR-IN-CHIEF
Richard Tait

LWT (LONDON WEEKLY TELEVISION)

(London Licence—Friday 5:15 p.m. to Monday 6:00 a.m.).
The London Television Centre, Upper Ground, London SE1
9LT. Tel: (0171) 620
1620. FAX: (0171) 261 1290.
CHIEF EXECUTIVE
Steve Morrison
MANAGING DIRECTOR
Eileen Gallagher
DIRECTOR OF PROGRAMMES
Simon Shaps
CHAIRMAN OF LNN
Clive Jones
MANAGING DIRECTOR OF THE LONDON STUDIOS
Harry Urquhart
DIRECTOR OF PROGRAMMES, GTP
Peter Salmon
MANAGING DIRECTOR, PRODUCTION RESOURCES
Brenda Smith
COMMERCIAL & MEDIA DEVELOPMENT DIRECTOR
Kate Stross
DIRECTOR OF BUSINESS & LEGAL AFFAIRS
Paul Taylor
JOINT MANAGING DIRECTOR
Andrea Wonfor
DEPUTY CHAIRMAN, LWT & MANAGING DIRECTOR, GUKB
David Liddiment
DIRECTOR OF BROADCASTING
Liam Hamilton
DIRECTOR OF PRODUCTION MANAGEMENT
Terri Jones
HEAD OF PRODUCTION MANAGEMENT, ENTERTAINMENT
Vijay Amarnani
HEAD OF LICENSING & MARKETING
Richard Cox
HEAD OF ENTERTAINMENT FEATURES
Lorna Dickinson
DIRECTOR OF OPERATIONS, TLS
Kate Hynes
CONTROLLER OF ARTS
Melvyn Bragg
CONTROLLER OF DRAMA
Sally Head
HEAD OF MUSIC
Rachel Williams
HEAD OF POST PRODUCTION
Dougie Robinson

MERIDIAN BROADCASTING LTD

(South, Southeast England Licence). Television Centre,
Northam, Southampton
S014 OPZ. Tel: (01703) 222 555. FAX: (01703) 335 050.
CHAIRMAN
Bill Cotton, OBE
MANAGING DIRECTOR
Mary McAnally
FINANCE DIRECTOR
Tim Rickets
DIRECTOR OF BROADCASTING
Richard Platt
DIRECTOR OF NEWS, SPORT AND CURRENT AFFAIRS
Jim Raven
CONTROLLER OF PROGRAMMES & PRODUCTION
Richard Simons
PERSONNEL
Peter Ashwood

RADIO TELEFIS EIREANN

(National Network of the Republic of Ireland). Donnybrook,
Dublin 4,
Ireland. Tel: (3531) 208 3111.
Ireland House, 150 New Bond Street, London, W1Y OHD. Tel:
(0171) 233 3382.
CHAIRMAN
Farrel Corcoran
DIRECTOR-GENERAL
Bob Collins
ASST. DIRECTOR-GENERAL
Adrian Moynes
DIRECTOR OF TELEVISION PROGRAMMES
David Blake Knox
DIRECTOR OF RADIO PROGRAMMES
Helen Shaw
DIRECTOR OF NEWS
Ed Muhall

S4C

Parc Ty Glas, Llanishen, Cardiff CF4 5DU, Wales. Tel: (01222)
747 444. Telex: 94017032 SIAN G. FAX: (01222) 741 457.
THE WELSH FOURTH CHANNEL AUTHORITY
CHAIRMEN
Prys Edwards
Janet Lewis-Jones
Janice Rowlands
Peter Davies, CBE
Dr. Gwenllian Awbery
CHIEF EXECUTIVE
Huw Jones
DIRECTOR OF PRODUCTION
Huw Eirug
DIRECTOR OF BROADCASTING
Dafydd Rhys
CHIEF ENGINEER
Rodger Fuse
DIRECTOR OF ANIMATION
Christopher Grace
HEAD OF FINANCE
Kathryn Morris
HEAD OF MARKETING
Menna Lewis
HEAD OF PRESS & PUBLIC RELATIONS
David Meredith

SCOTTISH TELEVISION, PLC

(Central Scotland Licence). Cowcaddens, Glasgow, G2 3PR,
Scotland. Tel: (0141) 300 3000. FAX: (0141) 300 3030.
The Gateway, Edinburgh EH7 4AH, Scotland. Tel: (0131) 557
4020. FAX: (0131) 557 9199.
CHAIRMAN
Gus Macdonald
DIRECTOR OF BROADCASTING
Blair Jenkins
MANAGING DIRECTOR
Andrew Flanagan
CHIEF EXECUTIVE OF SCOTTISH TV ENTERPRISES
Alistair Moffat
FINANCE DIRECTOR
Gary Hughes
COMPANY SECRETARY/HEAD OF LEGAL & BUSINESS
AFFAIRS
Sheelagh Lawrie
HEAD OF NEWS
Mark Smith
HEAD OF SPORT
Ian Crawford
HEAD OF NEWS
Mark Smith
HEAD OF CURRENT AFFAIRS
Alan Smart
HEAD OF PUBLIC AFFAIRS
Bob Tomlinson
HEAD OF PERSONNEL
Christine Walsh
CONTROLLER OF PRODUCTION
Ron Ferguson
HEAD OF TECHNICAL OPERATIONS
Tom Gallagher
BROADCAST SERVICES MANAGER
Carol Sinclair
PRODUCTION MANAGER, TECHNICAL OPERATIONS
Steve Dunlop

SCOTTISH TELEVISION ENTERPRISES
DEPUTY CHIEF EXECUTIVE
Sandy Ross
GENERAL MANAGER
Liz Moriarty
DIRECTOR OF BUSINESS DEVELOPMENT
Darrel James
CONTROLLER OF DRAMA
Robert Love
HEAD OF PROGRAMME SALES
Anita Cox
HEAD OF CHILDREN'S PROGRAMMING
Elizabeth Partyka

TELETEXT LTD.
(Holder of the public service licence for Teletext on ITV and Channel 4).
101 Farm Lane, London, SW6 1QJ. Tel: (0171) 386 5000; FAX: (0171) 386 5002.
MANAGING DIRECTOR
Mike Stewart
EDITOR-IN-CHIEF
Graham Lovelace
COMMERICAL DIRECTOR
Lawrence Lawson

TYNE TEES TELEVISION LTD.
(North East England Licence). The Television Centre, City Road, Newcastle upon Tyne, NE1 2AL. Tel: (0191) 261 0181. FAX: (0191) 261 2302.
15 Bloomsbury Square, London, WC1A 2LJ. Tel: (0171) 312 3700. FAX: (0171) 242 2441.
CHAIRMAN
Sir Ralph Carr-Ellison
MANAGING DIRECTOR
Tony Brill
CONTROLLER OF NEWS & CURRENT AFFAIRS
Graeme Thompson
CONTROLLER OF FEATURES
Malcolm Wright
HEAD OF YOUNG PEOPLE'S PROGRAMMES
Lesley Oakden
HEAD OF SPORT
Roger Thames
DEPUTY GROUP DIRECTOR OF RESOURCES
Margaret Fay
DIRECTOR OF FINANCE
Nick Castro
PUBLIC RELATIONS
Ruth Laing

ULSTER TELEVISION PLC
(Northern Ireland Licence). Havelock House, Ormeau Road, Belfast BT7 1EB, Ireland. Tel: (01232) 328 122. Telex: 74654. FAX: (01232) 246 695.
CHAIRMAN
J. B. McGuckian B.Sc. (Econ.)
MANAGING DIRECTOR
J.D. Smyth, B.Sc, F.C.A., F.R.T.S
GENERAL MANAGER
John McCann
CONTROLLER OF PROGRAMMING
Alan Bremner
DIRECTORS
R.E. Benner, O.B.E.
The Earl of Antrim
Lady McCollum
E. J. O'Driscoll
A. Bremner, B.A., Med
H. McClure
R.E. Bailie, O.B.E.
J. McCann, B.Sc. FCA
CORPORATE AFFAIRS
Michael McCann

WESTCOUNTRY TELEVISION LTD.
(South-West England Licence). Western Wood Way, Language Science Park,
Plymouth, PL7 5BG. Tel: (01752) 333 333. FAX: (01752) 333 444.
CHAIRMAN
Sir John Banham
MANAGING DIRECTOR
John Prescott Thomas
CONTROLLER OF NEWS & CURRENT AFFAIRS
Brad Higgins
DIRECTOR OF PROGRAMMES
Jane McCloskey
PUBLIC AFFAIRS
Mark Clare

YORKSHIRE TELEVISION LTD.
(Yorksire Contractor). The Television Centre, Leeds, LS3 1JS. Tel: (01132) 438 283. FAX: (01132) 445 107.
Television House, 15 Bloomsbury Square, London WC1A 2LJ. Tel: (0171) 312 3700. FAX: (0171) 242 2441.
Charter Square, Sheffield, S1 3EJ. Tel: (01142) 723 262.
88 Bailgate, Lincoln, LN1 3AR. Tel: (01522) 530 738.
8 Coppergate, York Y01 1NR. Tel: (01904) 610 066.
GROUP CHAIRMAN & CHIEF EXECUTIVE
G.E. Ward Thomas, CBE, D.F.C., CdG
CHAIRMAN
Victor Watson
CHIEF EXECUTIVE
Bruce Gyngell
GROUP DIRECTOR OF RESOURCES
Tony Brill
GROUP FINANCIAL DIRECTOR
Nick Castro
NON-EXECUTIVE DIRECTOR
Kenneth Dixon CBE, DL
MANAGING DIRECTOR OF BROADCASTING
Richard Gregory
MANAGING DIRECTOR OF GROUP PROGRAMME PROD.
David Holdgate
CONTROLLER OF BROADCASTING
Bob Bairstow
HEAD OF REGIONAL PRODUCTION
Mike Best
GROUP CONTROLLER OF FACTUAL PROGRAMMES
Chris Bryer
GROUP COMPANY SECRETARY
Simon Carlton
HEAD OF RELIGION
Pauline Duffy
CONTROLLER OF PROPERTY MANAGEMENT
Peter Fox
HEAD OF NEWS & CURRENT AFFAIRS
Calre Morrow
GROUP CONTROLLER OF ENTERTAINMENT
David Reynolds
GROUP CONTROLLER OF DRAMA
Keith Richardson
HEAD OF CHILDREN'S & EDUCATION
Patrick Titley

Satellite and Cable Systems Operators

ABERDEEN CABLE SERVICES
303 King Street, Aberdeen, AB2 3AP. Tel: (01224) 649 444. FAX: (01224) 645 372.

ANGLIA CABLE
17-19 Rayntham Rd., Bishops Stortford, Hertf., CM23 5PB. Tel: (01279) 867 000. FAX: (01279) 866 000.

BELL CABLEMEDIA EASTERN REGION, NORWICH
31 King St., Norwich NR3 2AZ. Tel: (01603) 445 000. FAX: (01603) 448 900.

BELL CABLEMEDIA NORTHEAST REGION
Ring Rd., Seacroft, Leeds LS14 1NH. Tel: (01132) 932 000. FAX: (01132) 932 111.

BELL CABLEMEDIA SOUTHERN REGION
Bell Cablemedia House, 5 Limeharbour, London. E14 9TY. Tel: (0171) 363 2000. FAX: (0171) 363 3500.

BIRMINGHAM CABLE LTD.
CablePhone House, Small Heath Business Park, Talbot Way, Small Heath, Birmingham B10 0HJ. Tel: (0121) 628 1234. FAX: (0121) 628 4321.

BT NEW TOWNS SYSTEMS (IRVINE)
15 Mackintosh Place South, Newmoor, Irvine KA11 1BR. Tel: (01294) 218 218. FAX: (01294) 216 631.

BT NEW TOWNS SYSTEMS (MILTON KEYNES)
51 Alston Dr., Bradwell Abbey, Milton Keynes MK13 9HB. Tel: (01908) 322 522. FAX: (01908) 319 802.

BT NEW TOWNS SYSTEMS (WASHINGTON)
Suite 10, Coniston House, Washington NE38 7RN. Tel: (0191) 415 0604. FAX: (0191) 417 7763.

CABLECOM INVESTMENTS LTD.
Surtees House, The Market Pl., Maidenhall, Suffolk 1P28 7EF. Tel: (01638) 711 345. FAX: (01638) 711 074.

CABLE CORPORATION LTD.
Cable House, Waterside Dr., Langley, Berkshire SL3 6EZ. Tel: (01753) 810 810. FAX: (01753) 810 818.

CABLE LONDON Plc.
2 Stephen St., London W1 1PL. Tel: (0171) 911 0555. FAX: (0171) 209 8459.

CABLE & TELECOM UK LTD.
P.O. Box 319, Whipsnade, Dunstable, LU6 2LT. Tel: (01582) 873 006. FAX: (01582) 873 003.

CABLETEL BEDFORDSHIRE LTD.
CableTel House, 2-8 Laporte Way, Luton, Befdordshire LU4 8RJ. Tel: (01582) 610 000. FAX: (01582) 610 100.

CABLETEL GLASGOW
40 Anderson Quay, Glasgow G3 8DA. Tel: (0141) 564 0000. FAX: (0141) 564 0100.

CABLETEL KIRKLEES
CableTel House, Market St., Huddersfield, Yorkshire HD1 2EH. Tel: (01484) 438 700. FAX: (01484) 438 777.

CABLETEL PORT TALBOT
Network House, Baglan Industrial Park, Baglan, Port Talbot SA12 7DJ. Tel: (01639) 899 999. FAX: (01639) 891 100.

CABLETEL SOUTH WALES LTD.
Colchester House, Colchester Ave., Cardiff CF3 7RR. Tel: (01222) 456 644. FAX: (01222) 456 645.

CABLETEL SURREY LTD.
CableTel House, Reading North Rd., Fleet, Hants, GU13 8XR. Tel: (01252) 652 000. FAX: (01252) 652 100.

CABLEVISION (WELLINGBOROUGH OFFICE LTD.)
c/o Mobile Radio Services Ltd., Centre Hall Buildings, Wellingborough, NN8 4HT. Tel: (01933) 222 078. FAX: (01933) 223 890.

CAMBRIDGE CABLE GROUP OF COMPANIES
1st floor, Block D, Westbrook Centre, Cambridge CB4 1YG. Tel: (01223) 567 200. FAX: (01223) 567 200.

COMCAST—TEESSIDE
Roberts House, DeHavilland Ave., Preston Farm Business Park, Stockton-on-Tees, TS18 3TH. Tel: (01642) 642 600. FAX: (01642) 626 648.

COMTEL ANDOVER
284 Wethill Rd., Andover, Hants, SP10 1YB. Tel: (01264) 401 402. FAX: (01264) 401 403.

COVENTRY CABLE
Whitley Village, London Road, Coventry, West Midlands CV3 4HL. Tel: (01203) 505 345. FAX: (01203) 505 445.

DIAMOND CABLE LTD.
Regency House, 2a Sherwood Rise, Nottingham NG7 6JN. Tel: (01159) 522 240. FAX: (01159) 522 211.

EUROBELL (SOUTH WEST) LTD.
Multimedia House, Abbey Court, Eagle Way, Sowton Industrial Estate, Exeter, EX2 7HY. Tel: (01392) 200 222. FAX: (01392) 200 220.

HARRIS OF SALTCOATS
104-106 Dockhead St., Saltcoats, Strathclyde KA21 5EL. Tel: (01294) 646 330. FAX: (01294) 466 665.

JERSEY CABLE LTD.
2 Colomberie, St. Hellier, Jersey JE2 4QB. Tel: (01534) 66555. FAX: (01534) 66681.

MEDWAY CABLEVISION LTD.
2-4 William St., Sittingbourne, Kent ME10 1HR. Tel: (01795) 429 711. FAX: (01795) 422 807.

METRO CABLE TELEVISION.
Unit 12, Park Royal Road, London, NW10 7JH. Tel: (0181) 961 6776. FAX: (0181) 961 6776.

METRO CABLE TELEVISION (ENGLAND)
Unit 17 Weltech Centre, Ridgeway, Welwyn Garden City, Hertf. AL7 2AA. Tel: (01707) 372 631. FAX: (01707) 325 621.

METRO CABLE TELEVISION (MID GLAMMORGAN)
Patridge Rd., Llwynpia, Rhondda, Mid Glammorgan CF40 2SH. Tel: (01443) 440 270. FAX: (01443) 435 700.

METRO CABLE TELEVISION (NORTH MIDLANDS)
Unit 1, 40 Commercial Square, Freemans Common, Leicester LE2 7SR. Tel: (01162) 550 824. FAX: (01162) 546 351.

METRO CABLE TELEVISION (OXFORD)
Nuttfield Press Site, Hollow Way, Coweley, Oxford OX4 2PH. Tel: (01865) 711 108. FAX: (01865) 77159.

METRO CABLE TELEVISION (SE REGION)
Bentalls, Basildon, Essex SS14 3BY. Tel: (01268) 526 841. FAX: (01268) 527 797.

METRO CABLE TELEVISION (WALES)
5 Penrice Court, Fendrod Business Park, Enterprise Park, Morriston, Swansea SA6 8QW. Tel: (01792) 701 601. FAX: (01792) 702 510.

METRO CABLE TELEVISION (WALES—DYFED OFFICE)
Unit 6, Honeyborough Industrial Estate, Dyfed. Tel: (01646) 601 494. FAX: (01646) 600 804.

METRO CABLE TELEVISION (WALES—GWENT OFFICE)
Bridge Terrace, Newbridge, Gwent NP1 5FE. Tel: (01495) 247 595. FAX: (01495) 246 095.

MULTICHANNEL TELEVISION LTD. (NORTHERN)
Reservoir Rd., Clough Rd., Hull HU6 7QD. Tel: (01482) 470 805. FAX: (01482) 470 806.

MULTICHANNEL TELEVISION LTD. (SOUTHERN)
Summerland St., Exeter EX1 2AT. Tel: (01224) 646 644.

NYNEX CABLECOMMS (BROMLEY OFFICE)
NYNEX House, 2a Farwig Lane, Bromley, Kent BR1 3QS. Tel: (0181) 402 2000. FAX: (0181) 402 9090.

NYNEX CABLECOMMS (MIDLAND REGION)
Kedleston House, Prime Business Centre, Aspen Dr., Raynesway, Derby DE21 7SG. Tel: (01332) 380 038. FAX: (01332) 661 431.

NYNEX CABLECOMMS (N.W. BOLTON OFFICE)
25-30 Queensbrook, Bolton Technology Exchange, Spa Rd., Bolton BL1 4AY. Tel: (01204) 365 111. FAX: (01204) 365 417.

NYNEX CABLECOMMS (N.W. MACNHESTER OFFICE)
NYNEX House, Timpson Rd., off Southmoor Rd., Baguley, Manchester M23 9WX. Tel: (0161) 946 0388. FAX: (0161) 945 6932.

NYNEX CABLECOMMS (SOLENT)
Unit c, Wellington Gate, Silverthorne Way, Waterlooville, Hampshire P07 7XY. Tel: (01705) 610 061. FAX: (01705) 230 548.

NYNEX CABLECOMMS (SOUTHERN REGION)
Langbourne House, Randalls Way, Leatherhead, Surrey KT22 7TW. Tel: (01372) 360 844. FAX: (01372) 360 605.

NYNEX CABLECOMMS (SUSSEX—HEAD END)
South Wharf House, Basin Road South, Aldrington Basin, Hove BN41 1WF. Tel: (01273) 413 021. FAX: (01273) 416 081.

OXFORD CABLE LTD.
c/o IVS Cable Services, 284 Weyhill Rd., Andover, Hampshire SP10 1YB. Tel: (01264) 334 697. FAX: (01264) 332 071.

SALFORD CABLE TELEVISION
Unit 5, (Shopping Giant) 385 Bolton Rd., Irlam, O'Th Heights, Salford M6 7NL. Tel: (0161) 737 9313. FAX: (0161) 736 9313.

STAFFORD COMMUNICATIONS LTD.
c/o IVS Cable Services, 284 Weyhill Rd., Andover, Hampshire SP10 1YB. Tel: (01264) 334 607. FAX: (01264) 332 071.

SWINDON CABLE
Newcombe Dr., Hawksworth Estate, Swindon, Wiltshire SN2 1TU. Tel: (01793) 480 482. FAX: (01793) 619 535.

TAWD VALLEY CABLE LTD.
82 Sandy Lane, Skelmersdale, Lancashire WN8 8LQ. Tel: (01695) 51000. FAX: (01695) 51315.

TELCENTIAL COMMUNICATIONS, NORTHANTS
11 Duncan Close, Moulton Park, Northampton NN3 1WL. Tel: (01604) 451 111. FAX: (01604) 451 126.

TELECENTIAL COMMUNICATIONS, THAMES VALLEY
Imperial Way, Reading RG2 0BS. Tel: (01734) 544 000. FAX: (01734) 544 001.

TELECENTIAL COMMUNICATIONS, WEST HERTS.
Unit 1A, Centro, Maxted Rd., Hemel Hempstead, Hertf. HP2 7EF. Tel: (01442) 369 111. FAX: (01442) 368 100.

THOMSON (RELAY) LTD.
27 Auld Lea Rd., Beith, Ayrshire KA15 2DA. Tel: (01505) 502 118.

UNITED ARTISTS COMMUNICATIONS, AVON
700 Waterside Dr., Aztec West, Almondsbury, Bristol BS12 4ST. Tel: (01179) 839 000. FAX: (01179) 839 966.

UNITED ARTISTS COMMUNICATIONS, COTSWOLDS
The Network Centre, Staverton Technology Park, Staverton, Cheltenham GL51 6TQ. Tel: (01452) 535 353. FAX: (01452) 535 399.

UNITED ARTISTS COMMUNICATIONS, SCOTLAND WEST
Unit 7, Bothwell Industrial Estate, Uddingston, Glasgow G71 6NX. Tel: (01689) 322 322. FAX: (01689) 322 213.

UNITED ARTISTS, DUNDEE
Tat Works, Brown St., Dundee DD1 5EF. Tel: (01382) 322 220. FAX: (01382) 322 225.

UNITED ARTISTS, GLENROTHES
4 Bankhead Ave., Bankhead Industrial Estate, Glenrothes KY7 6JG. Tel: (01592) 595 857. FAX: (01592) 590 001.

UNITED ARTISTS, LONDON SOUTH
Communications House, 5 Factory Lane, Croydon, CR9 3RA. Tel: (0181) 760 0222. FAX: (0181) 681 2340.

UNITED ARTISTS, NORTHEAST
Communications House, 1 Dukesway West, Team Valley, Gateshead NE11 0PN. Tel: (0191) 420 2000. FAX: (0191) 420 2001.

UNITED ARTISTS, PERTH
13 Canal St., Perth PH2 84Q. Tel: (01763) 838 794. FAX: (01763) 36867.

UNITED ARTISTS, SCOTLAND
1 South Gyle Crescent Lane, Edinburgh EH12 9EG. Tel: (0131) 539 0002. FAX: (0131) 539 0003.

UNITED ARTISTS, SOUTHEAST
Unit 1, Scimitar Park, Basildon, Essex SS1 1ND. Tel: (01268) 471 000. FAX: (01268) 470 199.

VIDEOTRON CORPORATION
London Division, Viedoetron House, 76 Hammersmith Rd., London, WI4 8UD. Tel: (0181) 244 1234. FAX: (0181) 244 1232.

VIDEOTRON CORPORATION LTD., SOUTHAMPTON
Hampshire Division, Ocean House, West Quay Rd., Southampton, Hants SO1 0XL. Tel: (01703) 315 000. FAX: (01703) 315 002.

WESSEX CABLE LTD.
c/o IVS Cable Services, 284 Weyhill Rd., Andover, Hampshire SP10 1YB. Tel: (01264) 334 607. FAX: (01264) 332 071.

WESTMINSTER CABLE TELEVISION
87-89 Baker Street, London, W1M 1AJ. Tel: (0171) 935 4400. FAX: (0171) 486 9447.

YORKSHIRE CABLE COMMUNICATIONS LTD.
Communications House, Mayfair Business Park, Broad Lane, Bradford BD4 8PW. Tel: (01274) 828 282. FAX: (01274) 828 400.

NYNEX CABLECOMMS SUSSEX
Wharf House, Basin Road South, Portslade, Brighton BN41564
1W. Tel: (01273) 880 278.
EXECUTIVE DIRECTOR OPERATIONS
Peter Morse

NYNEX CABLECOMMS CHESHIRE
NYNEX House, Timpson Road off Southmoor Road, Manchester
M23 9WX. Tel: (0161) 946 0388.
EXECUTIVE DIRECTOR OPERATIONS
Carl Grose

NYNEX CABLECOMMS DERBY
Unit A, Chequers Business Park, Derby DE2 6AW. Tel:
(01332) 200 002.
EXECUTIVE DIRECTOR OPERATIONS
Carl Grose

NYNEX CABLECOMMS SOLENT
Unit C. Wellington Gate, Silverthorne Way, Waterlooville PO7
7XY. Tel: (01705) 266 555.
EXECUTIVE DIRECTOR OPERATIONS
Carl Grose

NYNEX CABLECOMMS BROMLEY
NYNEX House, 51-67 Farwig Lane, Bromley BR1 2WD.
Tel: (0181) 402 2000.
EXECUTIVE DIRECTOR OPERATIONS
Carl Grose

NYNEX CABLECOMMS WESSEX
SEB Offices, 25 Bourne Valley Road, Bournemouth BH12 1HH.
Tel: (01202) 760 856.
EXECUTIVE DIRECTOR OPERATIONS
Carl Grose

SHROPSHIRE CABLE AND TELECOMS
US Cable Corporation, UK Division, PO Box 319, Whipsnade
LU6 2LT. Tel: (01582) 873 006.
MANAGING DIRECTOR
Philip Morgan

SOUTHERN EAST ANGLIA CABLE
Westbrook Centre, Milton Road, Cambridge CB4 1YG. Tel:
(01223) 567 200.
MANAGING DIRECTOR
Frank Cullen

SWINDON CABLE
Newcome Drive, Hawksworth Estate, Swindon SN2 1TU. Tel:
(01793) 480 482.
GENERAL MANAGER
Phil Holmes

TAMWORTH CABLE COMMUNICATIONS
The Green, Wolverhampton Road, Stafford ST17 4BL. Tel:
(01785) 601 602.
GENERAL MANAGER
Ian Renshaw

TELECENTIAL COMMUNICATIONS
Wharfedale Road, Winnersh, Woningham RG41 ST2. Tel: (0118)
9540 4000.

TELECENTIAL COMMUNICATIONS NORTHANTS
11 Duncan Close, Moulton Park, Northampton NN1 1WL. Tel:
(01604) 451 111.
GENERAL MANAGER
Roger Bell

TELECENTIAL COMMUNICATIONS THAMES VALLEY
Imperial Way, Reading, Berkshire RG2 OXT. Tel: (01734) 544 000.
GENERAL MANAGER
Kelvin Fogwill

TELECENTIAL COMMUNICATIONS WARWICKSHIRE
Unit 11, Stoneleigh Deer Park, Stareton, Warwickshire CV8 2LY.
Tel: (01203) 531 333.
TECHNICAL SERVICES MANAGER
Mick Kelley

TELECENTIAL COMMUNICATIONS WEST HERTFORDSHIRE
Unit 1A Centro, Maxted Road, Hemel Hempstead HP2 7EF. Tel:
(01442) 396 111.
ACTING GENERAL MANAGER
Stewart Redman

TELEWEST AVON
700 Waterside Drive, Aztec West, Almondsbury, Bristol BS2 4ST.
Tel: (0117) 983 9000.
MANAGING DIRECTOR
Mark Wynn

TELEWEST COTSWOLDS
The Network Centre, Staverton Technology Park, Staverton
GL41 6TQ. Tel: (01452) 535 353.
MANAGING DIRECTOR
Alex Heath

TELEWEST LONDON SOUTH
Communications House, 5 Factory Lane, Croydon CR9 3RA. Tel:
(0181) 760 0222.
MANAGING DIRECTOR
Alex Heath

TELEWEST NORTH EAST
1 Dukesway West, Team Valley, Gateshead NE11 0PN. Tel:
(0191) 420 2000.
MANAGING DIRECTOR
David Thomas

TELEWEST SCOTLAND
Unit 7, Bothwell Industrial Park, Uddingston, Glasgow G71 6NX.
Tel: (01698) 322 332.

Fowler Court, Fowler Road, West Pitkerro Industrial Estate,
Dundee DDS 3RU. Tel: (01382) 322 123.
1 South Gyle Crescent Lane, Edinburgh EH12 9EG. Tel: (0131)
539 0002.
Unit 4. Bankhead Avenue, Bankhead Industrial Estate,
Glenrothes KY7 6JG. Tel: (01592) 595 857.
13 Canal Street, Perth PH2 8LQ. Tel: (01738) 38794.
MANAGING DIRECTOR
Bart Bonsall

TELEWEST SOUTH EAST
Unit 1, Scimitar Park, Courtauld Road, Basildon SS1 1ND. Tel:
(01268) 471 000.
MANAGING DIRECTOR
Andrew Ballard

TELEWEST SOUTHPORT
2-8 Frenchwood Avenue, Preston PR1 4QF. Tel: (01772)
832 888.
GENERAL MANAGER
Ian Fishwick

VIDEOTRON
76 Hammersmith Road, London W14 8UD. Tel: (0181) 244 1234.
MANAGING DIRECTOR
David Colley

VIDEOTRON
Ocean House, West Quay Road, Southampton SO1 0XL. Tel:
(01703) 315 000.
DIRECTOR OF OPERATIONS
Suzanne Thomas

WESTMINSTER CABLE COMPANY
87-89 Baker Street, London W1M 1AJ. Tel: (0171) 935 4400.
MANAGING DIRECTOR
Andy Lockwood

YORKSHIRE CABLE COMMUNICATIONS
Communications House, Mayfair Business Park, Broad Lane,
Broadford BD4 8PW. Tel: (01274) 828 282.
MANAGING DIRECTOR
Bruce Massey

SATELLITE CHANNELS

3+
Scandinavia 3+ Ltd., Broadcast Centre, Horton Road, West Drayton, Middlesex UB7 8JD. Tel: (01895) 433 327.
MANAGING DIRECTOR
Annie Warner

ACE TV
7 Peregrine Way, London SW19 4RN. Tel: (0181) 947 8841.
CONTACT
Kalid Saeed

THE ADULT CHANNEL
Home Video Channel Ltd., Aquis House, Station Road, Hayes UB3 4DX. Tel: (0181) 581 7000.
CHIEF EXECUTIVE
Chris Yates

AG VISION
PO Box 10, Banbury Stockyard, Banbury, Oxon OX16 8EP. Tel: (01295) 250 501.
GENERAL MANAGER
Jane Wood

AMC (ASIAN MUSIC CHANNEL)
Vis Television, Productions Ltd., 25-27 Bede Street, Leicester LE3 5LD. Tel: (0116) 233 5599.
DIRECTOR
Satish Visavadia

ANIMAL PLANET
Discovery Communications Europe, 160 Great Portland Street, London W1N 5TB. Tel: (0171) 462 3600.
MANAGING DIRECTOR
Joyce Taylor

ASIANET
Elliott House, Victoria Road, London NW10 6NY. Tel: (0181) 867 9111.
EXECUTIVE DIRECTOR
G.F. Pitman

BABYLON BLUE
Rolldale Ltd., 82 Berwick Street, London W1V 3PS. Tel: (0171) 287 6623.
MANAGING DIRECTOR
Derek Hanlon

BLOOMBERG INFORMATION TELEVISION
City Gate House, 39-45 Finsbury Square, London EC2A 1PX. Tel: (0171) 330 7500.
HEADS OF OPERATIONS
Gerald Walker
Katherine Oliver

BRAVO
9-13 Grape Street, London WC2H BDR. Tel: (0171) 813 7000.
MANAGING DIRECTOR
Franklin Getchell

CHINESE NEWS AND ENTERTAINMENT
China News Europe, Marvick House News, Bishop's Road, London SW6 7AD. Tel: (0171) 610 3880.
GENERAL MANAGER
Betty Yao

CNN INTERNATIONAL
Turner Broadcasting Systems, CNN House, 19-22 Rathbone Place, London W1P 1DF. Tel: (0171) 637 6700.
MANAGING DIRECTOR
Phil Kent

CNBC
4th Floor, 3 Shortlands, London W6 8BX. Tel: (0181) 600 6600.
DIRECTOR
Peter Bullard

CARLTON FOOD NETWORK/SELECT
45 Foubert Place, London W1V 2DN. Tel: (0171) 432 9000.
MANAGING DIRECTOR
Janet Goldsmith

CARTOON NETWORK
Turner Entertainment, Network Ltd., 18 Soho Square, London W1V 5FD. Tel: (0171) 478 1000.
MANAGING DIRECTOR
Andy Bird

CATHOLIC TELEVISION TRUST LTD
Castle Craig, Blyth Bridge, West Linton, Peebleshire EH46 7DH. Tel: (017217) 52625.
DIRECTOR
Peter J. McCann

CHALLENGE TV
Vinters Park, Maidstone, Kent ME14 5NZ. Tel: (01622) 69111.
DIRECTOR OF PROGRAMMES
Nigel Pickard

CHAND TELEVISION
4 Bourne Street, Dudley DY2 7HL. Tel: (0973) 481 104.
MANAGING DIRECTOR
M. Jamil

CHANNEL ONE
60 Charlotte Street, London W1P 2AX. Tel: (0171) 209 1234.
DIRECTOR
Julian Aston

THE CHINESE CHANNEL
30-31 Newman Street, London W1P 3PE. Tel: (0171) 636 6818.
GENERAL MANAGER
Thomas Li

CHRISTIAN COMMUNICATION NETWORK
646 Shore Road, Whiteabbey, Coounty Antrim BT37 OPR. Tel: (01232) 853 997.
MANAGING DIRECTOR
Cecil Stewart

THE COMPUTER CHANNEL
British Sky Broadcasting, 6 Centaurs Business Park, Grant Way, Isleworth TW7 5QD. Tel: (0171) 705 3000.
GENERAL MANAGER
Elisabeth Murdoch

CULTURAL TELEVISION
CTV International Ltd., Bowercombe House, Great Burches Road, Thundersly, Essex SS7 3NA. Tel: (01268) 775 362.
MANAGING DIRECTOR
Chris Dandridge

DISCOVERY CHANNEL EUROPE
Discovery Communications, 160 Great Portland Street, London W1N 5TB. Tel: (0171) 462 3600.
MANAGING DIRECTOR
Joyce Taylor

DISCOVERY HOME AND LEISURE
160 Great Portland Street, London W1N 5TB. Tel: (0171) 462 3600.
GENERAL MANAGER
Nick Comer-Calder

THE DISNEY CHANNEL UK
The Walt Disney Company Ltd., Beaumont House, Kensington Village, Avonmore Road, London W14 8TS. Tel: (0171) 605 1300.
MANAGING DIRECTOR
Tom Wszalek

DRAGON
Chinasat, China European Satellite Ltd., 1st Floor, 2 Waterloo Street, Manchester M1 6HY. Tel: (0161) 236 3557.
CHIEF EXECUTIVE
Peter Chui

EBN (EUROPEAN BUSINESS NEWS)
European Business News Partners, 10 Fleet Place, London EC4M 7RB. Tel: (0171) 653 9300.
MANAGING DIRECTOR
Michael Connor

EDTV
Wealden Space Services Ltd., 12 Church Leys, Evenley, Northants NN13 5SX. Tel: (01403) 217 727.
DIRECTOR
Michael Genner

EUROPEAN NETWORK BROADCASTING
2nd Floor, 22 Greek St., London, W1V 5LF. Tel: (0171) 287 4908.
CONTACT
Jonathan Roberts

EVENT ONLINE
Eurocity Television Ltd., 34 Kingly Court, Kingly Street, London W1R 5LE.
CONTACT
Alistair Symon

THE FANTASY CHANNEL
Portland Enterprises Ltd., Portland House, London E14 9TN. Tel: (0171) 712 0800.
PROGRAMME CONTROLLER
Peter Farrell

FOX KIDS NETWORK
Fox Kids (UK), 6 Centaurs Business Park, Grant Way,
Isleworth TW7 5QD. Tel: (0171) 705 3000.
HEAD OF PROGRAMMING
Michael Yorrick

GOODLIFE TV
Goodlife TV Ltd., 82 Berwick Street, London W1V 3PS. Tel:
(0171) 287 6623.
MANAGING DIRECTOR
Christina Shepherd

GRANADA GOOD LIFE/MEN + MOTORS/PLUS/TALK TV
Granada Sky Broadcasting Ltd., Franciscan Court, 16
Hatfields, London SE1 8DJ. Tel: (0171) 578-4040.
CHIEF EXECUTIVE
Stuart Prebble

GSTV
GSTV (UK) Ltd., 29 Old Gloucester Street, London WC1N
3XX. Tel: (0171) 404 5014.
DIRECTOR
R. Jackson

HBO
HBO Communications (UK) Ltd., Ashurst Morris Group,
Broadwalk House, 5 Appold Street, London EC2A 2HA. Tel:
(0171) 972 7310.
CONTACT
Tony Ghee

HET WEER KANAAL
64 Newman Street, London W1P 3PG. Tel: (0171) 665 0600.
CONTACT
Annemieke Wapperom

THE HISTORY CHANNEL
British Sky Broadcasting, 6 Centaurs Business Park, Grant
Way, Isleworth TW7 5QD. Tel: (0171) 705 3000.
GENERAL MANAGER
Elisabeth Murdoch

HOME ORDER TELEVISION
Home Order Television, c/o Stringer Saul, Marcol House, 293
Regent Street, London W1R 7PD. Tel: (0171) 631 4048.

HOME SHOPPING NETWORK
160 Great Portland Street, London W1N 5TB. Tel: (0171) 299
5000.
DIRECTOR
Roger Luard

HVC - HOME VIDEO CHANNEL
Aquis House, Station Road, Hayes UB3 4DX. Tel: (0181) 581
7000.
CHIEF EXECUTIVE
Christopher Yates

INTERSHOP
Interwood Marketing plc, Ilex House, Twickenham TW1 4HF.
Tel: (0181) 891 2202.
DIRECTOR
Nigel Mott

JAPANSAT
Japan Satellite TV (Europe) Ltd., 3rd Floor, Quick House, 65
Clifton Street, London EC2A 4JE. Tel: (0171) 426 7330.
MANAGING DIRECTOR
Norio Shimamura

JONES COMPUTER NETWORKS
Jones Educational Networks, 60 Charlotte Street, London W1P
2AX. Tel: (0171) 209 1234.
MANAGING DIRECTOR
Dennis Garrison

KANAL 5
Kanal 5 Limited, c/o Ahurst Morris Group, Broadwalk House, 5
Appold Street, London EC2A 2HA. Tel: (0171) 972 7310.
CONTACT
Tony Ghee

THE LANDSCAPE CHANNEL
Landscape Channel Ltd., Landscape Studios, Crowhurst, East
Sussex TN33 9BX. Tel: (01424) 830 688.
CHAIRMAN
Nick Austin

LIVE TV
Mirror Television Ltd., 1 Canada Square, Canary Wharf,
London E14 5AP. Tel: (0171) 293 3900.
MANAGING DIRECTOR
Kelvin Mackenzie

MED TV
MED Broadcasting Ltd., Room 232, The Linen Hall, 162-168
Regent St., London W1. Tel: (0171) 284 7777.
PRESIDENT
Peter Einstein

MEDIASHOP TELEVISION
19 Norfolk Road, London NW8 6HG. Tel: (0171) 722 0242.
CONSULTANT
Anthony Pole

MIDDLE EAST BROADCASTING
80 Silverhorne Road, London SW8 3XA. Tel: (0171) 501 1111.
HEAD OF MARKETING
Mamdouth Abougabal

MINAJ BROADCAST INTERNATIONAL
Minaj (UK) Ltd., Berkeley Square House, Berkeley House,
London W1X 5LE. Tel: (0171) 491 2393.
DIRECTORS
Mr. & Mrs. Ajegbo

THE MOVIE CHANNEL
British Sky Broadcasting Ltd., 6 Centaurs Busines Park, Grant
Way, Isleworth TW7 5QD. Tel: (0171) 705 3000.
GENERAL MANAGER
Elisabeth Murdoch

MUSLIM TELEVISION AHMADIYYA
16 Gressenhall Road, London SW18 5QL. Tel: (0181) 870
8517.
CO-ORDINATOR
Said Jaswal

NBC EUROPE
3 Shorlands, London W6 8BX. Tel: (0181) 600 6100.
MANAGING DIRECTOR
Tim Ogden

NAMASTE
Namaste Asia TV, 77/87 River Road, Barking, Essex IG11
OE2. Tel: (0181) 507 8292.
DIRECTOR
Atul Gandhi

NICKELODEON/NICKELODEON SCANDINAVIA
Nickelodeon International UK, 15-18 Rathbone Place, Londonn
W1P 1DF. Tel: (0171) 462 1000.
MANAGING DIRECTOR
Janie Grace
MANAGING DIRECTOR
Jon Miller

NOVASHOP ONE/NOVASHOP TWO
Quantum International Ltd., Manor House, 21 Soho Square,
London W1V 6HN. Tel (0171) 465 1234.
INTERNATIONAL MARKETING DIRECTOR
Penny Heyes

THE PARAMOUNT CHANNEL
15-18 Rathbone Place, London W1P 1DF. Tel: (0171) 462
1000.
DEPUTY MANAGING DIRECTOR
John Partridge

THE PARLIAMENTARY CHANNEL
160 Great Portland Street, London W1 5TB. Tel: (0171) 299
5000.
HEAD OF OPERATIONS
Charles Willby

THE PENTHOUSE CHANNEL
Home Video Channel Ltd., Aquis House, Station Road, Hayes
UB3 4DX. Tel: (0181) 581 7000.
CHIEF EXECUTIVE
Chris Yates

PERFORMANCE THE ARTS CHANNEL
Arts and Entertaiment Ltd., 60 Charlotte Street, London W1P
1LS. Tel: (0171) 209 1234.
DIRECTOR
Julia Aston

PLAYBOY TV
160 Great Portland St., London W1 5TB. Tel: (0171) 299 5000.
MANAGING DIRECTOR
Jessica Cox

PRO SIEBEN
Pro Sieben, Media AG, Medienallee 7, D-85767 Unterfoehring,
Germany. Tel: (0089) 9507 1590.
CONTACT
Gary Howes

Q24
21 Soho Square, London W1V 6HN. Tel: (0171) 465 1234.
INTERNATIONAL MARKETING DIRECTOR
Penny Heyes

QVC DEUTSCHLAND/THE SHOPPING CHANNEL
QVC International Ltd., Marco Polo House, 346 Queenstown
Road, London SW8 4NQ. Tel: (0171) 705 5600.
CHIEF EXECUTIVE OFFICER
Mark Suckle

QUANTUM HOME SHOPPING
Quantum International Ltd., Manor House, 21 Soho Square, London W1V 6HN. Tel: (0171) 465 1234.
INTERNATIONAL MARKETING DIRECTOR
Penny Heyes

RACENET
Oakhill Communications Ltd., Isleworth Studios, Studio Parade, 484 London Road, Isleworth TW7 4DE. Tel: (0181) 568 3511.
CONTACT
Geoff Scofield

THE RACING CHANNEL
Satellite Information Services Ltd., 17 Corsham Street, London N1 6DR. Tel: (0171) 696 8704.
DIRECTOR OF PROGRAMMING
George Irvine

RAINBOW TELEVISION NETWORK
Rainbow Television Network Ltd., 40 Bolinbroke Grove, London SW11 6EH. Tel: (0171) 328 1566.
CONTACT
G. Cooper

REGAL SHOP
5-7 Carnaby Street, London W1V 1PG. Tel: (0171) 434 0567.
DIRECTOR
Richard Whinfrey

SAT 1
SAT 1, Satellite Fernsehen GmbH, c/o Ahurst Morris Group, Broadwalk House, 5 Appold Street, London EC2A 2HA. Tel: (0171) 972 7310.
CONTACT
Tony Ghee

SATELLITE INFORMATION SERVICES
Satellite Information Services Ltd., Satellite House, 17 Corsham Street, London N1 6DR. Tel: (0171) 696 8704.
DIRECTOR OF PROGRAMMING
George Irvine

SCI-FI CHANNEL EUROPE
77 Charlotte Street, London W1P 2DD. Tel: (0171) 805 6100.
MANAGING DIRECTOR
David Woodman

SELL-A-VISION SHOPPING
Quantum International Ltd., Manor House, 21 Soho Square, London W1V 6HN. Tel: (0171) 465 1234.
INTERNATIONAL MARKETING DIRECTOR
Penny Heyes

SHOWTIME - THE MOVIE CHANNEL
Paramount British Pictures Ltd., 180 Oxford Street, London W1N 0DS. Tel: (0171) 478 6800.
MANAGING DIRECTOR
Eddie McGrath

SIMA TV
Trafalgar House, Grenville Pl., London NW7 3SA. Tel: (0181) 959 3611.
CONTACT
S. M. Komari

SKY MOVIES GOLD/SKY MOVIES/SKY NEWS/ SKY ONE/SKY SCOTTISH /SKY SOAP/SKY SPORTS/ SKY SPORTS 2/SKY SPORTS 3/SKY TRAVEL/SKY TWO
British Sky Broadcasting Ltd., 6 Centaurs Business Park, Grant Way, Isleworth TW7 5QD. Tel: (0171) 705 3000.
GENERAL MANAGER
Elisabeth Murdoch

STEP-UP
Satellite Uplink, Room 8, Scott Building, University of Plymouth, Drake Circus, Plymouth PL4 8AA. Tel: (01752) 232 701.
SATELLITE PROJECTS CO-ORDINATOR
R. Winders

SUPERSHOP
Quantum International Ltd., Manor House, 21 Soho Square, London W1V 6HN. Tel: (0171) 465 1234.
INTERNATIONAL MARKETING DIRECTOR
Penny Heyes

TCC
160 Great Portland St., London W1N 5TB. Tel: (0171) 299 5000.
GENERAL MANAGER
Franklin Getchell

TESUG TV
The European Satellite User Group, PO Box 576, Orpington, Kent BR6 9WY. Tel: (01689) 817 487.
DIRECTOR
Eric Wiltsher

THAIWAVE
Thaiwave International Broadcasting Company Ltd., Haupstrasse 100, 76461 Muggensturm, Germany.
MANAGING DIRECTOR
W. Chandanahom

TLC
160 Great Portland St., London W1N 5TB. Tel: (0171) 462 3600.
GENERAL MANAGER
Nick Comer-Calder

TNT CLASSIC MOVIES
Turner Entertainment Network Ltd., 18 Soho Square, London W1V 5FD. Tel: (0171) 478 1000.
MANAGING DIRECTOR
Andy Bird

TV LAND
Gulf DTH Production, 180 Oxford Street, London W1N 9DH. Tel: (0171) 478 6800.
MANAGING DIRECTOR
Dr. John Tydeman

THE TRAVEL CHANNEL
Landmark Travel Channel Ltd., 66 Newman Street, London W1P 3LA. Tel: (0171) 636 5401.
DIRECTOR OF PROGRAMMING
Alison Rice

THE TRAVEL INDUSTRY CHANNEL
11 Marlborough Place, Brighton BN1 1UB. Tel: (01273) 728 809.
MANAGING DIRECTOR
Sean Mahoney

TV SHOP/TV SHOP SPORT
19 Norfolk Road, London NW8 6HG. Tel: (0171) 722 0242.
CONSULTANT
Anthony Pole

TV3 DENMARK/TV3 NORWAY/TV3 SWEDEN
TV3 Broadcasting Centre, Horton Road, West Drayton UB7 8JD. Tel: (01895) 433 327.
PRESIDENT
Per Bystedt

THE UK CHANNEL
Polygram International, 76 Oxford Street, London W1R 1TA. Tel: (0171) 307 1300.
LEGAL ADVISER
Geraldine Atlee

UK GOLD/UK LIVING
Flextech TV, 160 Greek Portland Street, London W1N 5TB. Tel: (0171) 299 5000.
CHIEF EXECUTIVE
Bruce Steinberg

VH1
UK House, 180 Oxford Street, London W1N 0DS. Tel: (0171) 478 6245.
PRESIDENT
Peter Einstein

VEDIC TELEVISION
50 Penywern Road, London SW5 9SX. Tel: (0171) 370 2255.
CHAIRMAN
G. K. Warrior

VISUAL ARTS
Polygram International, 76 Oxford Street, London W1R 1TA. Tel: (0171) 307 1300.
LEGAL ADVISER
Geraldine Atlee

VT4
VT4 Ltd., Suite 1, 87 Cadogan Gardens, London SW3 2RD. Tel: (0171) 584 9761.
MANAGING DIRECTOR
Karlo Gepts

THE WEATHER CHANNEL
64 Newman Street, London W1P 3PG. Tel: (0171) 665 0600.
MANAGING DIRECTOR
Patrick Scott

WHAT'S IN STORE/WHAT'S IN STORE 2
Quantum International Ltd., Manore House, 21 Soho Square, London W1V 6HN. Tel: (0171) 465 1234.
INTERNATIONAL MARKETING DIRECTOR
Penny Heyes

X1
ICS Broadcasting Ltd., 17 Blackstone Road, London NW2 6DA. Tel: (0171) 452 6213.
MANAGING DIRECTOR
Erich Cagran

ZEE TV
Unit 7, Belevue Business Centre, Belevue Road, Northolt UB5 5QQ. Tel: (0181) 841 5112.
CHIEF EXECUTIVE OFFICER
Rajan Singh

CABLE & COMMUNITY CHANNELS

ATM
Asian Television Marketing Ltd., 68 George Street, Oldham
OL1 1LS. Tel: (0161) 627 1207.
CHIEF EXECUTIVE
Shaafat A. Chaudhry

THE ADAM AND EVE CHANNEL
PO Box 3BD, London W1A 3BD. Tel: (0171) 286 4738.
DIRECTOR
Ray Millar

AFRICA TV
Africa TV Limited, PO Box 395, Wallington SM6 7QX. Tel:
(0181) 395 4014.
CHIEF EXECUTIVE
Bernard Ampaw

THE AFRO-CARIBBEAN CHANNEL
Takerak Ltd., 81 Seaford Road, London N15 5DX. Tel: (0181)
802 4576.
DIRECTOR
Vernon King

AIRPORT TELEVISION
Concourse Communications Ltd., The Old Dairy, 470 London
Road, Slough SL3 8QY. Tel: (01753) 580 233.
DIRECTOR
Anthony Max

ANDOVER NOW
ComTel Andover Ltd., 284 Weyhill Road, Andover SP10 3LS.
Tel: (01264) 401 402.
GENERAL MANAGER
Ken Ayling

ARCADE (AVON)
Telewest Avon, 700 Waterside Drive, Aztec West, Almondsbury,
Bristol BS12 4ST. Tel: (01484) 612 290.
MANAGING DIRECTOR
Mark Wynn

ARCADE (COTSWOLDS)
Telewest Cotswolds, The Network Centre, Staverton
Technology Park, Staverton GL41 6TQ. Tel: (01452) 535 353.
MANAGING DIRECTOR
Alex Heath

ARCADE (SCOTLAND)
Telewest Scotland, 1 South Gyle Crescent Lane, Edinburgh
EH12 9EG. Tel: (0131) 539 0002.
MANAGING DIRECTOR
Bart Bonsall

ARCADE (SOUTH EAST)
Telewest South Eat, Unit 1, Scimitar Park, Courtauld Road,
Basildon SS1 1ND. Tel: (01268) 471 000.
MANAGING DIRECTOR
Andrew Ballard

ARCADE (LONDON SOUTH)
Telewest London South, Communications House, 5 Factory
Lane, Croydon CR9 3RA. Tel: (0181) 760 0222.
MANAGING DIRECTOR
Alex Heath

BET INTERNATIONAL
Kershaw House, Great West Road, Hounslow, Middlesex TW5
0BU.
DIRECTOR
Lawrence Nugent

BLACK MUSIC TELEVISON
Mapleglass Ltd., 86 Adelaide Grove, London W12 0JL. Tel:
(0181) 740 5505.
PRODUCER/DIRECTOR
Howard Johnson

THE BOX
The Box, Imperial House, 11-13 Young Street, London W8
5EH. Tel: (0171) 376 2000.
MANAGING DIRECTOR
Vincent Monsey

BRADFORD FESTIVAL NEWS
Carlisle Road Business Centre, Carlisle Road, Bradford BD8
8BD. Tel: (01274) 223 219.
SENIOR CURATOR
John Trenouth

BRADFORD FESTIVAL TELEVISION
Yorkshire Community TV Ltd., The Hammerhead Partnership,
Town End Road, Bradford BD14 6BN. Tel: (01274) 884 863.
DIRECTOR
Andrew Sugden

BRITISH GREEK COMMUNITY CHANNEL
13 Lancing Gardens, London N9 9ET. Tel: (0181) 807 6035.
DIRECTOR GENERAL
Floros Theodorou

BVTV
1st Floor, 57 Bellview Grove, Welling, Kent DA16 3PV. Tel:
(0181) 301 0250.
DIRECTOR
Michael Mowatt

CLTV
Cable London Plc, 2 Stephen Street, London W1 1PL. Tel:
(0171) 911 0555.
MANAGING DIRECTOR
Neil Johnson

CSV MEDIA
CSV Media (Yorkshire), Lloyds Bank Chambers, Hustlergate,
Bradford BD1 1NT. Tel: (01274) 736 413.
CSV MEDIA REGIONAL OFFICER (NORTH)
Sue Ostler

CABLE DAILY - MILTON KEYNES
Cable Daily, 3 Chaple Street, Coventry CN1 4AB. Tel: (01203)
231 099.
MANAGING EDITOR
Roger Monkman

CABLE 17
Telewest Communications Cable Plaza, Waterfront West,
Brierley Hill, West Midlands DY5 1LW. Tel: (01384) 867 889.
CHANNEL CO-ORDINATOR
James Pearson

CABLE 10
Cabletel South Wales, Network House, Baglan Industrial Park,
Port Talbot, West Glamorgan SA12 7DJ. Tel: (01639) 899 999.
SALES AND MARKETING MANAGER
Nigel J. Griffiths

CABLE VIDEO STORE
CVS Partners, 14785 Preston Road, Suite 174, Dallas, TX
75240. Tel: (972) 980 0002.
PRESIDENT
Barry Goldberg

THE CAMBRIDGE INTERACTIVE TV SERIES
Cambridge Cable, 1st Floor, Block D, Westbrook Centre, Milton
Road, Cambridge CB4 1YG. Tel: (01223) 567 200.
MANAGING DIRECTOR
Frank Cullen

CHANNEL GUIDE
Picture Applications Ltd., Yeoman's Court, Wave Road,
Hertford SG13 7HJ. Tel: (01992) 500 016.
MANAGING DIRECTOR
Geoff Bush

CHANNEL SEVEN
Cable Midlands, Cable House, The Waterfront, Dudley DY5
1XJ. Tel: (01384) 838 483.
MARKETING DIRECTOR
Mark Cullen

CHANNEL 17
Telewest London South, Communications House, 5 Factory
Lane, Croydon CR9 3RA. Tel: (0181) 760 0222.
MANAGING DIRECTOR
Alex Heath

CHANNEL 10
Aberdeen Cable Services, 303 King Street, Aberdeen AB24
5AP. Tel: (01224) 649 444.
CHIEF EXECUTIVE
Graham Duncan

CLYDE CABLEVISION (LOCAL)
CableTel Glasgow, 60 Maxwell Road, Glasgow G41 1PR. Tel:
(0141) 564 0000.
MANAGING DIRECTOR
Doug Gieson

COLT TV
Coventry Cable, London Road, Coventry CV3 4HL. Tel: (01203) 505 345.
PROGRAMME CONTROLLER
Joan Skidmore

COMMUNITY CHANNEL
Bell Cablemedia, Westfield Road, Peterborough PE3 9TJ. Tel: (0113) 293 2000.
GENERAL MANAGER
Stuart Curtis

DIAMOND CABLE 7
Diamond Cable Communications (UK), Diamond Plaza, Daleside Road, Nottingham NG2 3GG. Tel: (0116) 233 4100.
CHANNEL MANAGER
Jenny Ludlam

DUBAI
Westminster Cable Commpany, 87-89 Baker Street, London W1M 1AJ. Tel: (0171) 935 6699.
HEAD OF PROGRAMMING
Sue Royle

EAST
HDS Studios, Springfield Road, Hayes, Middlesex UB4 0LE. Tel: (0181) 573 4000.
MANAGING DIRECTOR
Handial Singh Bhabra

EDINBURGH TELEVISION
TU/TV Ltd., 3 Belvue Place, Edinburgh EH7 4BS. Tel: (0131) 557 8610.
DIRECTOR
Dave Rushton

EDUCATION AND TRAINING CHANNEL
University of Sunderland, Langham Tower, Ryhope Road, Sunderland SR2 7EE. Tel: (0191) 515 2070.
ASSISTANT POLYTECHNIC SECRETARY
David William Penn

THE EDUCATION CHANNEL
Open Campus Television, Blackburn College, Fielden Street, Blackburn BB2 1LH. Tel: (01254) 55144.
CABLE CHANNEL MANAGER
Brian Kelly

THE FOOD CHANNEL
The Food Channel Ltd., 34 The Old Woodyard, Hagley Hall, Stourbridge DY9 9LG. Tel: (01562) 882 633.
CHIEF EXECUTIVE
Richard Patching

HAVERING COMMUNITY CHANNEL
Bell Cablemedia, 5 Limeharbour, London E14 9TY. Tel: (0171) 363 2000.
CO-ORDINATOR
Marcus Marcu

HELLENIC TELEVISION
50 Clarendon Road, London N8 0DG. Tel: (0181) 292 7037.
CHAIRMAN
Dr. C. N. Fellas

ICE TV
The Cable Corporation Ltd., Cable House, Waterside Drive, Langley, Berks SL3 6EZ. Tel: (01753) 810 810.
MANAGING DIRECTOR
Andy Linton

THE INTERACTIVE CHANNEL
Videotron, 76 Hammersmith Road, London W14 8UD. Tel: (0181) 244 1234.
HEAD OF INTERACTIVE TV
Andrew Curry

INTERACTIVE LONDON NEWS NETWORK
London News Network Limited, The London Television Centre, Upper Ground, London SE1 9LT. Tel: (0171) 827 7700.
COMPANY SECRETARY
Denise Harker

INTERACTIVE MULTIMEDIA SERVICES
British Telecommunications Ltd., Room 502, Holborn Centre, 120 Holborn, London EC1N 5ET. Tel: (0171) 492 2935.
DIRECTOR OF MULTIMEDIA SERVICES
Rupert Gavin

KNOWLEDGE TV
Jones Educational Networks, 60 Charlotte Street, London W1P 2AX. Tel: (0171) 209 1234.
MANAGING DIRECTOR
Dennis Garrison

LEICESTER COMMUNITY CHANNEL
Leicester Communications Ltd., 28-29 Oswin Road, Leicester LE3 1HR. Tel: (0116) 233 400.
CHIEF EXECUTIVE
Daniel Breen

LIVE TV
Mirror Television Ltd., 1 Canada Square, Canary Wharf, London E14 5AP. Tel: (0171) 293 3900.
MANAGING DIRECTOR
Kelvin MacKenzie

LTT - LONDON TURKISH TV
34 Cottersmore Avenue, Ilford 1G5 0TG. Tel: (0181) 550 5195.
MANAGING DIRECTOR
Hatice Arslan

METROVISION COMPANY
Westminster Cable, 87-89 Baker Street, London W1M 1AJ Tel: (0171) 935 6699.
HEAD OF PROGRAMMING
Sue Royle

THE MULTI-SCREEN CHANNEL (AVON)
Telewest Avon, 700 Waterside Drive, Aztec West, Almondsbury, Bristol BS12 4ST. Tel: (01454) 612 290.
MANAGING DIRECTOR
Mark Wynn

THE MULTI-SCREEN CHANNEL (COTSWOLDS)
Telewest Cotswolds, The Network Centre, Staverton Technology Park, Staverton GL41 6TQ. Tel: (01459) 535 353.
MANAGING DIRECTOR
Alex Heath

THE MULTI-SCREEN CHANNEL (NORTH EAST)
Telewest North East, 1 Dukesway West, Team Valley, Gateshead NE11 0PN. Tel: (0191) 420 2000.
MANAGING DIRECTOR
David Thomas

THE MULTI-SCREEN CHANNEL (SOUTH EAST)
Telewest South East, Unit 1, Scimitar Park, Courtauld Road, Basildon, Essex SS1 1ND. Tel: (01268) 471 000.
MANAGING DIRECTOR
Andrew Ballard

THE MULTI-SCREEN CHANNEL (SCOTLAND)
1 South Gayle, Crescent Lane, Edinburgh EH12 9EG. Tel: (0131) 539 0002.
MANAGING DIRECTOR
Bart Bonsall

NYNEX COMMUNITY TELEVISION
Nynex Cablecomms, The Metal Box, Gardener Road, Portslade, Hove, East Sussex BN41 1QP. Tel: (01273) 413 021.
EXECUTIVE DIRECTOR OPERATIONS
Peter Morse

NYNEX COMMUNITY TELEVISION
Nynex House, Timpson Road off Southmoor Road, Manchester M23 9WX. Tel: (0161)946 0388.
EXECUTIVE DIRECTOR
Carl Grose

NETWORK 021
Birmingham Cable Ltd., Cablephone House, Talbot Way, Small Heath Business Park, Birmingham B10 0HR. Tel: (0121) 628 1234.
MANAGING DIRECTOR
Frank Webb

PERFORMANCE - THE ARTS CHANNEL
Arts and Entertainment Programmes Ltd., 60 Charlotte Street, London W1P 1LS. Tel: (0171) 209 1234.
MANAGING DIRECTOR
Julian Aston

THE PREVIEW CHANNEL
52/54 North Lane, Leeds LS6 3HU. Tel: (0113) 230 5105.
MANAGING DIRECTOR
R. N. K. Sian

PTV (THE PERSIAN CHANNEL)
Rangami, 160 Clitterhouse Street, London NW2 1DN. Tel: (0181) 455 0413.
MANAGING DIRECTOR
Mahmood Taghi Sarabi

REDBRIDGE COMMUNITY CHANNEL
Bell Cablemedia, 2 Limeharbour, London E14 9TE. Tel: (0171) 363 2000.
CO-ORDINATOR
Marcus Marcu

ROYAL OPERA HOUSE CHANNEL
Royal Opera House, Floral Street, London WC2E 9DD. Tel: (0171) 240 1200.
PROJECTS MANAGER
Cormack Simms

SHEFFIELD LOCAL CABLE
5 Brown Street, Sheffield S1 2BS. Tel: (0114) 281 2661.
CONTACT
John Gray

THE SKELMERSDALE LOCAL CHANNEL
Tawd Valley Cable Ltd., 82 Sandy Lane, Skelmersdale, Lancs
WN8 8LQ. Tel: (01695) 51000.
MANAGING DIRECTOR
James O'Shea

SILVERSTONE TV
Silverstone Circuits Ltd., 8-9 Bulstrode Place, London W1M
5FW. Tel: (0171) 487 2641.
CONTACT
Barrie Woolston

SWINDON LOCAL
Swindon Cable Television Ltd., Newcome Drive, Hawksworth
Estate, Swindon SN2 1TU.Tel: (01793) 615 601.
GENERAL MANAGER
Nigel Kidd

TELEWEST CHANNEL
Cable House, 2-8 Frenchwood Avenue, Preston PR1 4QF. Tel:
(01772) 90288.
MANAGING DIRECTOR
Ian Fishwick

TELLYWEST
Telewest Communications, 700 Waterside Drive, Aztec West,
Almondsbury, Bristol BS12 4ST.
MANAGING DIRECTOR
Mark Wynn

TOWER HAMLETS/NEWHAM
Bell Cablemedia, 2 Limeharbour, London E14 9TE. Tel: (0171)
363 2000.
CO-ORDINATOR
Marcus Marcu

VIDEONET INTERACTIVE TELEVISION
Video Networks, Gate House, Fretherne Road, Welwyn Garden
City, Herts AL8 GNS. Tel: (01707) 362 5000.
CHAIRMAN
Simon Hochester

VIDEOTRON CHANNEL
Videotron, 76 Hammersmith Road, London W14 8UD. Tel:
(0181) 244 1234.
MANAGING DIRECTOR
David Colley

THE VISION CHANNEL
Vision Broadcasting Commmunications, Rochester House, 27
Victoria Road, Swindon SN1 3AW. Tel: (01793) 511 244.
CHIEF EXECUTIVE
Fran Wildish

WALTHAM FOREST
Bell Cablemedia, 5 Limeharbour, London E14 9TY. Tel: (0171)
363 2000.
CO-ORDINATOR
Marcus Marcu

WEST HERTS TV
Telecential Communications, Unit 1A Centro, Maxted Road,
Hemel Hempstead, Hertfordshire HP2 7EF. Tel: (01442) 369 111.
LOCAL PROGRAMMING MANAGER
Keith Jefferies

WESTMINSTER CABLE INTERACTIVE SERVICES
87-89 Baker Street, London W1M 2LP.
HEAD OF PROGRAMMING
Sue Royle

WILLIAMS WORLDWIDE TELEVISION
1-4 Argyll Street, London W1V 1AD. Tel: (0171) 734 7010.
VICE PRESIDENT
Pippa Alexander

YCTV - YOUTH CABLE
YCTV Ltd., 85 Barlby Rd., London W10 6AZ. Tel: (0181) 964 4646.
PROJECT DIRECTOR
Sabrina Guinness

Television Producers and Distributors

AARDMAN ANIMATIONS
Gas Ferry Rd., Bristol BS1 6UN. Tel: (0117) 984 8485. FAX: (0117) 984 8486.
CONTACT
Michael Rose

ABACUS PRODUCTIONS LTD.
40 St Martin=9s Lane, London, WC2N 4ER. Tel: (0171) 240 1277. FAX: (0171) 836 7014.
DIRECTORS
Abbie Gache
Ron Trainer

ABBEY BROADCAST COMMUNICATIONS
53 Abbey Rd., London, NW8 OAD. Tel: (0171) 372 0752. FAX: (0171) 372 0887.

ABC INTERNATIONAL
54 Portland Place, London, WIN 4DY. Tel: (0171) 636 4225. FAX: (0171) 636 4159.
CONTACT
Wendy Hallam

ABC SPORTS
8 Carburton Street, London, W1P 7DT. Tel: (0171) 636 7366. Telex: 23625 ABC5PT G. FAX: (0171) 323 4986.

ACI INTERNATIONAL
Lee House, 109 Hammersmith Rd., London, WI4 0QH. Tel: (0171) 602 7020. FAX: (0171) 371 3679.
CONTACT
Brian Harris

ADN ASSOCIATES/HOLLYWOOD CLASSICS
8 Cleveland Gardens, London, W2 6HA. Tel: (0171) 262 4646. FAX: (0171) 262 3242.
CONTACTS
Pano A. Alafouzo
Joe Dreier
John Flynn (USA)

AEROFILMS
Gate Studios, Station Rd., Boreham Wood, Herts., WD6 1EJ. Tel: (0181) 207 0666. FAX: (0181) 207 5433.
MANAGING DIRECTOR
Lindsay Simmons

AGRAN BARTON TELEVISION LTD.
The Yacht Club, Chelsea Harbour, London, SW10 OXA. Tel: (0171) 351 7070. FAX: (0171) 352 3528.
JOINT CHIEF EXECUTIVES
Linda Agran
Mick Barton

ALLIED TELEVISION
The Glassworks, 3-4 Ashland Place, London, W1M 3JH. Tel: (0181) 423 9888. FAX: (0181) 423 9333.
MANAGING DIRECTOR
Peter McRae

ALLIED TROMA LTD
4 Warner House, Harruvian Centre, Business Village, Bessborough Rd. Harrow HA1 3EX Tel: (0171) 333 0100. FAX: (0171) 973 6590.
HEAD OF FILM, VIDEO & BROADCASTING
Rodney Wilson

ALPHA FILMS LTD.
Unit 1, McKay Trading Estate, Kensal Rd., London, W10 5BX. Tel: (0181) 960 8211. Telex: 291877 Vision G.

ANIMAL ARK
The Studio, 29 Somerset Rd., Brentford, Middlesex TW8 8BT. Tel: (0181) 560 3029. FAX: (0181) 560 5762.
MANAGER
David Manning

ANIMATION LINK
7 Baron's Gate, 33/35 Rothschild Rd., Chiswick, London, W4 5HT. Tel: (0181) 995 5080. FAX: (0181) 747 9452.
CONTACT
Jane Garner

ANTELOPE FILMS LTD.
29 B, Montague Street London, WC1B 5BH. Tel: (0171) 209 0099. FAX: (0171) 209 0098.
CONTACT
Mick Csaky

ANVIL POST PRODUCTION LTD.
Denham Studios, North Orbital Rd., Denham, Nr. Uxbridge, Middx. UB9 5HL. Tel: (01895) 833 522. Telex: 934704. FAX: (01895) 835 006.
CONTACT
Ken Somerville, Alan Snelling

AUSTRALIAN BROADCASTING CORPORATION
54 Portland Place, London, W1N 4DY. Tel: (0171) 631 4456. Telex: 263897.FAX: (0171) 323 1125 (News), (0171) 323 0059 (Admin).
HEAD OF OPERATIONS
Alan Stephenson

AUTOCUE LTD.
Autocue House, 265 Merton Rd., London, SW18 5JS. Tel: (0181) 870 0104. FAX: (0181) 874 3726.
CONTACTS
Mick Gould
Brian Ravter

BBC WORLDWIDE TELEVISION
Woodlands, 80 Wood Lane, London, W12 0TT. Tel: (0181) 576 2000. FAX: (0181) 749 0538.
MANAGING DIRECTOR
Dr. John Thomas

BFI FILM & VIDEO LIBRARY
21 Stephen St., London, W1P 1PL. Tel: (0171) 255 1444. FAX (0171) 436 0165.
CONTACT
Heather Stewart

JANE BALFOUR FILMS LTD.
Burghley House, 35 Fortress Rd., London, NW5 1AD. Tel: (0171) 267 5392. FAX: (0171) 267 4241.
CONTACT
Mary Barlow

BLUE DOLPHIN FILM PRODUCTIONS LTD.
40 Langham Street, London, W1N 5RE. Tel: (0171) 255 2494. FAX: (0171) 580 7670.
CONTACT
Joseph D'Morais

BOULTON-HAWKER FILMS LTD.
Hadleigh, Ipswich, Suffolk, IP7 5BG. Tel: (01473) 822 235. FAX: (01473) 824 519.
DIRECTORS
K.P. Boulton
M.J. Boulton
N.H.L. Rea
D.A. Boulton

BRAVEWORLD LTD.
Multimedia House, Trading Estate Rd., Park Royal, London NW10 7NA. Tel: (0181) 961 0011. FAX: (0181) 961 1413.
MANAGING DIRECTOR
Colin Bayliss

BRITE
(The International sales representatives of LWT, Granada TV and Yorkshire Tyne-Tees Television).
The London Television Centre, Upper Ground, London SE1 9LT. Tel: (0171) 737 8603. FAX: (0171) 261 8162.
MANAGING DIRECTOR
Nadine Nohr

BRITISH LION
Pinewood Studios, Pinewood Rd., Iver, Bucks, FL0 0NH. Tel: (01753) 651 700. Telex: 847505. FAX: (01753) 656 391.
CHAIRMAN & CHIEF EXECUTIVE
Peter R. E. Snell

BRITISH MOVIETONEWS LTD.
North Orbital Rd., Denham, Uxbridge, Middx., UB9 5HQ. Tel: (01895) 833 071. FAX: (01895) 834 893.
MANAGING DIRECTOR
Barry S. Florin

BRITISH SCREEN FINANCE
14/17 Wells Mews, London, W1P 3FL. Tel: (0171) 323 9080. FAX: (0171) 323 0092.
CHIEF EXECUTIVE
Simon Perry

BRITISH SKY BROADCASTING LTD.
Grant Way, Isleworth, Middx: TW7 5QD. Tel: (0171) 705 3000.
FAX: (0171) 705 3030.
CHIEF EXECUTIVE & MANAGING DIRECTOR
Sam Chisolm
DEPUTY MANAGING DIRECTOR
David Chance
DIRECTOR OF PROGRAMMES
Elisabeth Murdoch
DIRECTOR OF SALES
Peter Shea

BRITISH UNIVERSITIES FILM & VIDEO COUNCIL
77 Wells St., London, W1P 3RE. Tel: (0171) 393 1500. FAX:
(0171) 393 1555.
DIRECTOR
Murray Weston

BROOK PRODUCTIONS LTD.
21-24 Bruges Place, Randolph Street, London NW1 0TF. Tel:
(0171) 428 3100. FAX: (0171) 284 0626.
CONTACT
Anne Lapping

BRYON PARKIN ASSOCIATES LTD.
37 Dover Street, London, W1X 3RA. Tel: (0181) 950 5151.

BUENA VISTA PRODUCTIONS LTD.
Beaumont House, Kensington Village, Avonmore Rd., London,
WI4 8TS. Tel: (0181) 222 2795. FAX: (0181) 222 1000.
MANAGING DIRECTOR
David Simon

CBC TV PROGRAM SALES
43-51 Great Titchfield Street, London W1P 8DD. Tel: (0171)
580 0336. FAX: (0171) 323 5658.
CONTACT
Susan Hewitt Jolley

C.T.S. STUDIOS LTD.
Engineers Way, Wembley, Middlesex, HA9 0DR. Tel: (0181) 903
4611. FAX: (0181) 903 7130.
CONTACT
Adrian Kerridge

CTVC
Hillside Studios, Merry Hill Rd., Bushey, Watford, WD2 1DR.
Tel: (0181) 950 4426. FAX: (0181) 950 1437.
HEAD OF FACILITIES
David Hillier

CABLE CONNECTIONS TELEVISION LTD.
201 Holland Park Avenue, London, W11 4UN. Tel: (0171) 603
4500. Telex: 8950117 AZITAP G. FAX: (0171) 603 1830.
HEAD OF SALES
Sue Hewitt

CANADIAN BROADCASTING CORPORATION
43-51 Great Titchfield Street, London, W1P 8DD. Tel: (0171)
412 9200. FAX: (0171) 323 5658.

CAPITAL GROUP STUDIOS
13 Wandsworth Plain, London, SW18 1ET. Tel: (0181) 874
0131. FAX: (0181) 871 9737. Telex: 929509.
CONTACT
Sally Trickett

CARLTON UK PRODUCTIONS
35-38 Portman Square, London W1H 9FH. Tel: (0171) 486
6688. FAX: (0171) 486 1132.
MANAGING DIRECTOR
Andy Allan

CASTLE COMMUNICATIONS PLC.
A29 Barwell Business Park, Leatherhead Rd., Chessington,
Surrey KT9 2NY. Tel: (0181) 974 1021. FAX: (0181) 974 2674.
MANAGING DIRECTOR
Geoff Kempin

CASTLE ROCK INTERNATIONAL
8 Queen Street, Mayfair, London, W1X 7PH. Tel: (0171) 409
3532. FAX: (0171) 499 9885.
PRESIDENT
Mashmo Grabosi
V.P., MARKETING & PUBLICITY
Lindsey Stride

CBS BROADCAST INTERNATIONAL
10 Dover Street, London, W1X 3PH. Tel: (0171) 355 4422.
FAX: (0171) 355 4429
CONTACT
Katie Allen.

CENTRAL OFFICE OF INFORMATION
Hercules Rd., London, SE1 7DU. Tel: (0171) 261 8495. FAX:
(0171) 261 8874.
DIRECTOR, FILM, TV & RADIO DIVISION
Ian Hamilton

CHEERLEADER PRODUCTIONS
3rd floor, 141-143 Drury Lane, London WC2B ST8. Tel: (0171)
240 5389. FAX: (0171) 240 5391.
MANAGING DIRECTOR
Charles Thompson

CHANNEL 4 INTERNATIONAL LTD.
124 Horseferry Rd., London, SW1P 2TX. Tel: (0171) 396 4444.
FAX: (0171) 306 8363.

CHATSWORTH TELEVISION
97-99 Dean Street, London, W1V 5RA. Tel: (0171) 734-4302.
FAX: (0171) 437 3301.
MANAGING DIRECTOR
Malcolm Heyworth

CHILDREN'S CHANNEL
9-13 Grape Street, London, WC2H 8DR. Tel: (0171) 240 3422.
FAX: (0171) 497 9113.
CONTACT
Ann Cook

CHRYSALIS GROUP PLC
The Chrysalis Bldg., Bramley Rd., London, W10 6SP. Tel:
(0171) 221 2213. FAX: (0171) 221 6455.

CINE ELECTRA
110 Gloucester Avenue, Primrose Hill, London, NW1 8HX.
Tel/FAX: (0171) 586 2780.
INTERNATIONAL COORDINATOR
Anne Billard
MANAGING DIRECTOR
Julia Kennedy

CINEMA VERITY PRODUCTIONS LTD.
The Mill House, Millers Way, 1A Shepherds Bush Rd., London,
W6 7NA. Tel: (0181) 749 8485. FAX: (0181) 743 5062.
EXECUTIVE PRODUCER
Verity Lambert

CINESOUND EFFECTS LIBRARY LTD.
Imperial Studios, Maxwell Rd., Elstree Way, Boreham Wood,
Herts., WD6 IWE. Tel: (0181) 953 5837 and 5545, 1587, 4904.
FAX: (0181) 207 1728.
CONTACTS
Mike Rogers
Angela Marshall

BRIAN CLEMENS ENTERPRISES LTD.
Park Farm Cottage, Ampthill Beds. Tel: (01525) 402 215. FAX:
(01525) 402 954.
DIRECTORS
John Simmons
Cecilia Simmons

CLIP SHOP
47 Dean St., London W1V 5HL. Tel: (0171) 287 1808. FAX:
(0171) 287 1454.
DIRECTORS
Helen Bennitt
Jenny Morgan

COLSTAR INTERNATIONAL
11 Wythburn Place, London, WIH 5WL. Tel: (0171) 437 5725.
FAX: (0171) 706 1704.
CONTACT
Steve Goddard

COLUMBIA TRISTAR INTERNATIONAL TELEVISION
A Division of Sony Pictures Entertainment, St. Margaret's
House, 19/23 Wells Street, London, W1P 4DH. Tel: (0171) 580
2090. FAX: (0171) 436 0323.
CROWN TELEVISION
Crown House, 72 Hammersmith Rd., London W14 8YE. Tel:
(0171) 371 6060. FAX: (0171) 371 2727.
CONTACT
Bruce Todd

CTE
35-38 Portman Square, London W1H 9FH. Tel: (0171) 224
3339. FAX: (0171) 486 1707.
MANAGING DIRECTOR
Philip Jones

CTVC
Hillside Studios, Merry Hill Rd., Bushey, Watford, WD2 1DR.
Tel: (0181) 950 4426. FAX: (0181) 950 1437.
CONTACT
Peter Davies

CYGNET VIDEO & FILM
Communication Business Centre, Blenheim Rd., High
Wycombe, Bucks., HP12 3RS. Tel: (01494) 450541. FAX:
(01494) 462154.
MANAGING DIRECTOR
D. N. Plunket
PRODUCER
Philip Lee

DANDELION DISTRIBUTION LTD.
5 Churchill Court Station Rd., North Harrow, Middx. HA2 7SA.
Tel: (0181) 863 1888. FAX: (0181) 863 0463
SALES DIRECTOR
John Clutten.

D B POST SOUND STUDIOS LTD.
27-29 Berwick Street, London, W1V 3RF. Tel: (0171) 437 0136.
FAX: (0171) 439 2012.
DIRECTORS
Richard Daniel
Kevin Brazier

DE LANE LEA SOUND CENTRE
75 Dean Street, London, W1V 5HA. Tel: (0171) 439 1721. FAX:
(0171) 437 0913. CONTACT
Richard Paynter

DE WOLFE LTD.
2nd Floor East, Shropshire House, 11-20 Caper Street
London, W1V 3LF. Tel: (0171) 631 3600. FAX: (0171) 631
3700.
DIRECTORS
James de Wolfe
Warren de Wolfe

WALT DISNEY COMPANY LTD.
Beaumont House, Kensington Village, Avonmore Rd., London,
WI4 8TS. Tel: (0171) 605 2400. FAX: (0171) 605 2593.
MANAGING DIRECTOR
Etienne de Villiers

DL TAFFNER UK
10 Bedford Square, London WC1B 3RA. Tel: (0171) 631 1184.
FAX: (0171) 636 4571.
MANAGING DIRECTOR
John Reynolds

DRAKE VIDEO SERVICES
89 St. Fagans Rd., Fairwater, Cardiff CF5 3AE, Wales.
MANAGING DIRECTORS
R. G. Drake
H. Drake

DRUMMER FILMS LTD.
14 Haywood Close, Pinner, Middx., HA5 3LQ. Tel: (0181) 866
9466. FAX: (0181) 866 9466.
MANAGING DIRECTOR
Martin M. Harris (Producer)

DUCK LANE FILM PRODUCTIONS LTD.
8 Duck Lane, London, W1V 1FL Tel: (0171) 439 3912. FAX:
(0171) 437 2260.
DIRECTOR
Rigby Andrews

EATON FILMS LTD.
10 Holbein Mews, London, SW1W 8NN. Tel: (0171) 823 6173.
FAX: (0171) 823 6017.
CONTACTS
Judith Bland
Liz Cook

EDUCATIONAL & TELEVISION FILMS LTD.
247a Upper Street, London, N1 1RU. Tel: (0171) 226 2298.
FAX: (0171) 226 8016.
GENERAL MANAGER
Stanley Forman

ELECTRONIC PUBLISHING CO. LTD.
68-70 Wardour Street, London, W1V 3HP. Tel: (0171) 734
4609. Telex: Peclon 25554. FAX: (0171) 437 1366.

ENTERTAINMENT FILM PRODUCTIONS LTD.
27 Soho Square, London, W1V 7HU. Tel: (0171) 439 1606.
FAX: (0171) 734 2483. Telex: 262428 ENT VIF. DIRECTORS
Michael L. Green
Nigel G. Green
Trevor H. Green

ENTERTAINMENT PRODUCTIONS
3 Fitzroy Square, London, W1P 5AH. Tel: (0171) 388 1234.
FAX: (0171) 387 5789.
CONTACT
Tony Fitzpatrick

EPA INTERNATIONAL DISTRIBUTORS
31-A Regents Park Rd., London NW1 7TL. Tel: (0171) 267
9198. FAX: (0171) 267 8852.

EUREKA LOCATION MANAGEMENT
51 Tonsley Hill, London, SW18 1BW. Tel: (0181) 870 4569.
FAX: (0181) 871 2158.
HEAD OF OPERATIONS
Suzannah Holt

EUSTON FILMS LTD.
Pinewood Studios, Iver Heath, Bucks, SL0 0NH. Tel: (01753)
650222. FAX: (01753) 650222.
CONTACT
John Hambley

EYELINE FILM AND VIDEO LTD.
77 Dean Street, London, W.1. Tel: (0171) 734 3391. Telex:
265351. FAX: (0171) 437 2095.
DIRECTORS
Harold Orton
Jacki Roblin

F.I.L.M.S. LTD.
2 Savile Row, London W1X 1AF. Tel: (0171) 434 0340. FAX:
(0171) 434 0442.

FILM AND GENERAL PRODUCTIONS LTD.
10 Pembridge Place, London, W2 4XB. Tel: (0171) 221 1141.
FAX: (0171) 792 1167.
DIRECTORS
Clive Parsons
Davina Belling
Richard Whatmore

FILM FAIR LTD.
1-4 Jacobs Wells Mews, London, W1H 5PD. Tel: (0171) 935
1596.
MANAGING DIRECTOR
Lewis Rudd

FILM FOUR INTERNATIONAL
124 Horseferry Road, London SW1P 2TX Tel: (0171) 396
4444. FAX: (0171) 306 8361.
DIRECTOR OF SALES
Bill Stephens
FILM SALES MANAGER
Heather Playford-Denman

FIRST INDEPENDENT FILMS LTD.
99 Baker Street, London W1M 1FB. Tel: (0171) 317 2500. FAX:
(0171) 317 2502/2503.
MANAGING DIRECTOR
Michael Myers

MARK FORSTATER PRODUCTIONS LTD.
27 Lonsdale Road, London NW6 6RA. Tel: (0171) 624 1123.
FAX: (0171) 624 1124.
DIRECTOR
Mark Forstater

FOWLER-CHAPMAN COMPANY LTD.
28 Saint Mary Park Court, Albert Bridge Rd., London, SW11
4PJ. Tel: (0171) 223 0034. FAX: (0892) 784023.
MANAGING DIRECTOR
Roy Fowler

FOX VIDEO
31-32 Soho Square, London, WIV 6AP. Tel: (0171) 753 8686.

FRIDAY PRODUCTIONS LTD.
23a St. Leonards Terrace, London SW3 4QG. Tel: (0171) 730
0608. FAX: (0171) 730 0608.

FTS BONDED
Heston Industrial Estate, Aerodrome Way, Cranford Lane,
Hounslow, Middx., TW5 9QB. Tel: (0181) 897 7973. Telex:
21747 FILM BO G. FAX: (0181) 897 7979.
SALES DIRECTOR
John Reeves

G.H.W. PRODUCTIONS LTD.
52 Queen Anne Street, London, W1M 9LA. Tel: (0171) 935
1186.
DIRECTORS
Peter Rogers
Betty E. Box, O.B.E.
D.G. Truscott.

GAINSBOROUGH (FILM & TV) PICTURES LTD.
The Groom Cottage, Pinewood studios, Pinewood Lane, Iver
Heath, Iver, Bucks SLO ONH. Tel: (0171) 409 1925. FAX:
(0171) 408 2042.

GANNET FILMS LTD.
88 Gresham Rd., Staines, Middx., TW18 2AE. Tel: (01784) 453
912.
DIRECTORS
Bob Kellett
Anne Kellett

JAMES GARRETT & PARTNERS LTD.
25 Bruton Street, London, W1X 7DB. Tel: (0171) 499 6452.
Telex: 261163. FAX: (0171) 409 1797.
DIRECTORS
J. L. M. P. Garrett
M. Gilmour
D. T. Cromwell
M. Garrett

JOHN GAU PRODUCTIONS LTD.
Burston House, 1 Burston Rd., Putney, London, SW15 6AR.
Tel: (0181) 788 8811. FAX: (0181) 789 0903. email: John
Gau@aol.com

NOEL GAY TELEVISION
1 Albion Court, Gelene Road, Hammersmith, London W6 0QT.
Tel: (0181) 600 5200. FAX: (0181) 600 5222.
OWNERS
Charles Armitage
Alex Armitage

GENERAL SCREEN ENTERPRISES
Highbridge Estate, Oxford Rd., Uxbridge, Middx., UB8 1LX. Tel:
(01895) 231 931. FAX: (01895) 235 335.
DIRECTOR & GENERAL MANAGER
Fred Chandler

GFD COMMUNICATIONS LTD
Unit 15A, Parkmore Industrial Estate, Longmile Rd., Dublin 12,
Ireland. Tel: (3531) 569 500. FAX: (3531) 569 342.

WILLIAM GILBERT ASSOCIATES LTD.
16 Brook Mews North, London, W2 3BW. Tel: (0171) 258 3620.
Telex: 264826 RKOINT. FAX: (0171) 723 5100.
CONTACT
William Gilbert

GINGER TV
39-41 Hanover Steps, St. George's Fields, Albion St., London,
W2 2YG. Tel: (0171) 577 7100. Telex: 896559 Gecoms G. FAX:
(0171) 262 5736.
CONTACT
Brian Jackson

GLOBAL ENTERTAINMENT MANAGEMENT LTD.
22 Wadsworth Rd., Perivale, Middx. UB6 7JD. Tel: (0181) 991
5051. FAX: (0181) 998 3521.
CHIEF EXECUTIVE
Claude Heilman
DIRECTOR
P. Kotak

GLOBO INTERNATIONAL (LONDON) LTD.
29 Princes St., London, W1R 7RG. Tel: (0171) 409 1712. FAX:
(0171) 491 3167.
CONTACT
Roberto Filippelli

BOB GODFREY FILMS LTD
199 Kings Cross Road London WC1X 9DB Tel: (0171) 278
5711 FAX: (0171) 278 6809.

GOLDCREST FILMS AND TELEVISION LTD.
65-66 Dean Street, London, WIV 5HD. Tel: (0171) 437 8696.
FAX: (0171) 437 4448.
CHIEF EXECUTIVE
John Quested

GOLDWYN FILMS
10 Stephen Mews, London, W1P 1PP. Tel: (0171) 333 8877.
FAX: (0171) 333 8878.
CONTACT
Wendy Palmer

SAMUEL GOLDWYN COMPANY
St. George's House, 14-17 Wells Street, London, W1P 3FP. Tel:
(0171) 436 5105. FAX: (0171) 580 6520.

THE GRADE COMPANY
34 Grosvenor St., Mayfair, London, W1X 9FG. Tel: (0171) 409
1925. FAX: (0171) 408 2042.
DIRECTOR
Lord Grade

GRANADA LWT INTERNATIONAL LTD.
The London Television Centre, Upper Ground, London, SE1
9LT. Tel: (0171) 737 8681/8682. FAX: (0171) 928 8476.
HEAD OF SALES
Nadine Nohr

GREEN & HEATON LTD.
37 Goldhwak Rd., London W12 8QQ. Tel: (0181) 749 0315.
FAX: (0181) 749 0318.
DIRECTORS
Carol Heaton
Timothy Webb

GRUNDY WORLDWIDE LTD.
Grundy House/Barge House CRESCENT, 34 Upper Ground,
London, SE1 9PD. Tel: (0171) 928 8942. FAX: (0171) 928
8417.

HALLIFORD STUDIOS LTD
Manygate Lane, Shepperton, Middx., TW17 9EG. Tel: (01932)
226 341. FAX: (01932) 246 336.
STUDIO MANAGER
Allan d'Aguiar

HAMMER FILM PRODUCTIONS LTD.
Millenium Studios, Elstree Way, Boreham Wood, Herts. WD6
1SF. Tel: (0181) 207 4011. FAX: (0181) 905 1127.
DIRECTORS
Roy Skeggs
Andrew Mitchell

HAMPDEN GURNEY STUDIOS, LTD.
39-41 Hanover Steps, St. George's Fields, Albion Street,
London, W2 2YG. Tel: (0171) 402 7543. Telex: 896559
GECOMS G. FAX: (0171) 262 5736.

STEWART HARDY FILMS LTD.
2-4 Wigton Gardens, Stanmore, Middx., HA7 18G. Tel: (0181)
204 4153.
DIRECTOR
J. R. Williams

HAT TRICK PRODUCTIONS
10 Livonia Street, London, W1V 3PH. Tel: (0171) 434 2451.
FAX: (0171) 287 9791.
CONTACT
Denise O'Donoghue

HEMDALE HOLDINGS
10 Avenue Studio, Sydney Close, Chelsea London SW3 6HW.
Tel: (0171) 581 9734. FAX: (0171) 581 9735.
CONTACT
John Smallcombe

JIM HENSON PRODUCTIONS
30 Oval Road Camden London NW1 7DE Tel: (0171) 428
4000. FAX: (0171) 428 4001.

HIGH POINT FILM AND TV
25 Elizabeth Mews, London, NW3 4UH. Tel: (0171) 586 3686.
FAX: (0171) 586 3117.

HIT ENTERTAINMENT PLC
The Pump House, 13-16 Jacobs Well Mews, London, W1H
5PD. Tel: (0171) 224 1717. FAX: (0171) 224 1719.
MANAGING DIRECTOR
Peter Orton

GERARD HOLDSWORTH PRODUCTIONS LTD.
140 Buckingham Palace Rd., London, SW1W 95A. Tel: (0171)
824 8770. FAX: (0171) 824 8762.
DIRECTORS
P. H. Filmer-Sankey
A.M.V. Brunker

MICHAEL HURLL TELEVISION
8-12 Broadwick Street, London, W1V 1FH. Tel: (0171) 287
4314. FAX: (0171) 287 4315.

INDEPENDENT COMMUNICATIONS ASSOCIATES
20-28 Dalling Rd., London, W6 0JB. Tel: (0181) 748 0160. FAX:
(0181) 748 0160.
CONTACT
Richard Melman

INIMITABLE LTD.
Greenman, Highmoor, Henley-on-Thames, Oxfordshire, RG9
5DH. Tel: 01491 641140. FAX: 01491 641080.
CONTACT
Gerry Anderson

INITIAL FILM & TV LTD.
74 Black Lion Lane, Hammersmith, London, W6 9BF. Tel:
(0181) 741 4500. FAX: (0181) 741 9416.
CONTACT
Malcolm Gerrie

ISLAND WORLD PRODUCTIONS
12-14 Argyll St., London, W1V 1AB. Tel: (0171) 734 3536. FAX:
(0171) 734 3585.

ITC ENTERTAINMENT GROUP LTD.
33 Foley St., London, W1. Tel: (0171) 255 3000. Telex: 912121.
FAX: (0171) 306 7800.
S.V.P., INTERNATIONAL
Lynden Parry

ITC HOME VIDEO (UK)
161-167 Oxford St., London W1R 1TA. Tel: (0171) 439 3000.
FAX: (0171) 437 4370.

ITEL
48 Leicester Square, London, WC2H 7FB. Tel: (0171) 491
1441. FAX: (0171) 493 7677.
MANAGING DIRECTOR
Andrew MacBean

IVS ENTERPRISES LTD.
54 Warwick Square, London, SW1V 2AJ. Tel: (0171) 834 6012. Telex: 27151. FAX: (0171) 630 6270.

ITN LTD.
200 Gray's Inn Rd., London, WC1X 8XZ. Tel: (0171) 833 3000. FAX: (0171) 430 4016.
CHAIRMAN
Gerry Robinson
CHIEF EXECUTIVE
Stewart Purvis
EDITOR-IN-CHIEF
Richad Tait

ITV NETWORK ACQUISITIONS
ITV Network Centre, 200 Gray's Inn Rd., London, WCIX 8X2. Tel: (0171) 843 8120. Telex: 262988. FAX: (0171) 843 8160.
CONTROLLER OF ACQUISITIONS
Pat Mahoney

J & M ENTERTAINMENT
2 Dorset Square, London, NW1 6PU Tel: (0171) 723 6544. Telex: 298538 FILMING. FAX: (0171) 724 7541.
CONTACTS
Julia Palau
Michael Ryan

BRIAN JACKSON FILMS LTD.
39-41 Hanover Steps, St. Georges Fields, Albion Street, London, W2 2YG. Tel: (0171) 402 7543 and (0171) 262 5736. FAX: (0171) 262 5736. Telex: 896559 GECOMS-G.

JARAS ENTERTAINMENTS LTD.
Broughton House, 3rd fl., 6-8 Sackville St., London, W1X 1DD. Tel: (0171) 287 4601. FAX: (0171) 287 9652.

CYRIL JENKINS PRODUCTIONS LTD.
7 Coniston Court, Carlton Drive, London, SW15 2BZ. Tel: (0181) 788 2733.
DIRECTORS
Cyril G. Jenkins
J.M. Jenkins

KAVUR PRODUCTIONS LTD.
14 Lownes Square, London, SW1X 9HB. Tel: (0171) 235 4602. FAX: (0171) 235 5215.

KILROY TELEVISION COMPANY LTD.
Unit 1 Warston Court, Warstone Road, Hockley, Birmingham B18 6JQ. Tel: (0121) 693 5515. FAX: (0121) 693 5525.
CONTACT
Robert Strange

LITTLE KING PRODUCTIONS LTD.
Greek Court, 14a Old Compton St., London W1V 5PE. Tel: (0171) 437 1772. FAX: (0171) 437 1782.

LONDON FILMS
35 Davies Street London W1Y 1FN. Tel: (0171) 499 7800 FAX(0171) 499 7994.

LUCIDA PRODUCTIONS LTD.
53 Greek Street, London, WIV 5LR. Tel: (0171) 437 1140. FAX: (0171) 287 5335.
DIRECTORS
Paul Joyce
Chris Rodley

LWT INTERNATIONAL
London Television Centre, London, SE1 9LT. Tel: (0171) 620 1620. FAX: (0171) 430 4016.

MAJESTIC FILMS AND TELEVISION INTERNATIONAL
P.O. Box 13, Gloucester Mansions, Cambridge Circus, London, WC2H 8XD. Tel: (0171) 836 8630. FAX: (0171) 836 5819. Telex: 46601 BTGKAG.
CHIEF EXECUTIVE
Guy East

MIKE MANSFIELD TELEVISION LTD.
5-7 Carnaby Street, London, W1V 1PG. Tel: (0171) 494 3061. FAX: (0171) 494 3057.

MARK I PRODUCTIONS LTD.
Lee International Studios, 128 Wembley Park Drive, Wembley, Middlesex, HA9 8JE. Tel: (0181) 902 1262.

MCA TV INTERNATIONAL
1 Hamilton Mews, London, W1V 9FF. Tel: (0171) 491 4666. FAX: (0171) 493 4702.

McCANN INTERNATIONAL PROGRAMME MARKETING LTD.
88-94 Tottenham Court Rd., London, W1P 9HE. Tel: (0171) 323 4641.

MECCA INTERNATIONAL PRODUCTIONS LTD
14 Oxford Street, London, W1N 0HL. Tel: (0171) 637 9401.

M.C.E.G. VIRGIN VISION
Atlantic House, 1 Rockley Rd., Shepherd's Bush, London, W14 ODB. Tel: (0181) 740 5500. FAX: (0181) 967 1360.
DIRECTORS
Bill Tennant
Julian Portman
Angus Margerison
Peter Coles

MEDIA RELEASING DISTRIBUTORS LTD.
27 Soho Square, London, W1V 5FL. Tel: (0171) 437 2341. Telex: 943763 CROCOM G(MRD). FAX: (0171) 734 2483.
DIRECTORS
Trevor H. Green
J. Green

MEDUSA COMMUNICATIONS LTD.
Regal Chambers, 51 Bancroft, Hitchin, Herts., SG5 1LL. Tel: (01462) 421 818. FAX: (01462) 420 393.

MENTORN BARRACLOUGH CAREY
Mentorn House, 140 Wardour Street, London, W1V 3AV. Tel: (0171) 287 4545. FAX: (0171) 287 3728. CONTACT
Tom Gutteridge
John Needham

MGM/UA HOME VIDEO (UK) LTD
Glenthorne House, Hammersmith Grove, London . Tel: (0181) 563 8383. FAX: (0181) 563 2896.
CONTACT
Jonathan Cocker

MIRACLE COMMUNICATIONS LTD.
69 New Oxford St., London, W1A 1DG. Tel: (0171) 528 7767. FAX: (0171) 528 7770.
CONTACT
Michael Myers

THE MOVING PICTURE COMPANY
25 Noel Street, London, W1V 3RD. Tel: (0171) 434 3100. FAX: (0171) 287 5187.
MANAGING DIRECTOR
David Jeffers

MTM INTERNATIONAL
180 Oxford Street London W1N ODS. Tel: (0171) 284 7777. FAX: (0171) 284 7778.
CONTACT
Greg Phillips

MTV EUROPE
Hawley Crescent, London, NW1 8TT. Tel: (0171) 284 7777. FAX: (0171) 284 7788.
DIRECTOR OF CORPORATE COMMUNICATIONS
Monique Amaudry

MUSEUM OF THE MOVING IMAGE
South Bank, Waterloo, London, SE1 8XT. Tel: (0171) 928 3535. FAX: (0171) 815 1378.

MUSIC BOX
247-257 Euston Rd., London NW1 2HY. Tel: (0171) 287 5700. FAX: (0171) 387 9106.
MANAGING DIRECTOR
John Leach

NBC EUROPE
3 Shortlands, Hammersmith, London, W6 8BX. Tel: (0181) 600 6600. FAX: (0181) 600 6278.
MANAGING DIRECTOR
Patrick Cox

NBD TELEVISION
Unit 2, Royalty Studios, 105 Lancaster Rd., London, WII 1QF. Tel: (0171) 243 3646. FAX: (0171) 243 3656.
CONTACTS
Nicky Davies Williams
Maro Korkou
Carolyne Waters

N.F.H. LTD.
37 Ovington Square, London SW3 1LJ. Tel: (0171) 584 7561. FAX: (0171) 589 1863.
MANAGING DIRECTOR
Norma Heyman

NAMARA LTD.
51 Beak Street, London, W1R 3LF. Tel: (0171) 437 9524. FAX: (0171) 734 1844.
EXECUTIVE PRODUCER
Naim Attaliah

NATIONAL FILM AND TELEVISION SCHOOL
Beaconsfield Studios, Station Rd., Beaconsfield, Bucks, HP9 1LG. Tel: (01494) 671234. FAX: (01494) 674042. DIRECTOR
Henning Camre

NATIONAL SCREEN
2 Wedgwood Mews, Greek Street London, W1V 6BH. Tel:
(0171) 437 4851. FAX: (0171) 287 0328.
Studios: 15 Wadsworth Rd., Greenford, Middx., UB6 7JN. Tel:
(0181) 998 2851. FAX: (0181) 997 0840.
DIRECTORS
John Mahony
Norman Darkins
Brian McIlmail

NIXPARGO ANIMATIONS
Maidensgrove, Nr. Henley-on-Thames, Oxon., RG9 6EZ. Tel:
(0149) 163 286.
PRODUCERS
Nicholas Spargo
Mary Spargo

OPEN MEDIA
9 Leamington Rd., Villas, W11 1HS. Tel: (0171) 229 5416. FAX:
(0171) 221 4842.

OVERVIEW FILMS LTD.
16 Brook Mews North, London, W2 3BW. Tel: (0171) 258 3620.
FAX: (0171) 723 5100. Telex: 264826 RKOINT G. CONTACT
William G. Gilbert

OXFORD SCIENTIFIC FILMS
Lower Rd., Long Hanborough, Oxon, OX8 8LL. Tel: (01993)
881 881. FAX: (01993) 882 808.
45-49 Mortimer Street, London W1N 7TD. Tel: (0171) 323
0061. FAX: (0171) 323 0161.

DAVID PARADINE PRODUCTIONS LTD.
5 St. Mary Abbots Place, Kensington, London, W8 6L5. Tel:
(0171) 371 3111. FAX: (0171) 602 0411.

PAVILION INTERNATIONAL
(A part of Circle Communications)
45-49 Mortimer Street, London W1N 7TD. Tel: (0171) 636
9421. FAX: (0171) 436 7426.

PEARL & DEAN LTD.
Woolverstone House, 61-62 Berners Street, London, WIP 3AE.
Tel: (0171) 636 5252. FAX: (0171) 637 3191. MANAGING
DIRECTOR
Peter Howard Williams

PIZAZZ PICTURES
S30 Berwick Street, London, W1V 3RF. Tel: (0171) 434 3581.
FAX: (0171) 437 2309.
PRODUCER
Pamela Dennis

PLANET 24 LTD.
Norex Court, Thames Quay, 195 Marsh Wall, London, E14
9SG. Tel: (0171) 345 2424. FAX: (0171) 345 9400.
DIRECTORS
Waheed Alli
Bob Geldof
Charlie Parsons

PLATO FILMS LTD.
247A Upper Street, London, N1 1RU. Tel: (0171) 226 2298.
FAX: (0171)226 2046
MANAGING DIRECTOR
Stanley Forman

POLYGRAM FILM INTERNATIONAL
76 Oxford St., London W1N 0HQ. Tel: (0171) 307 1300. FAX:
(0171) 307 1355.
PRESIDENT
Aline Perry

POLYMUSE INTERNATIONAL TELEVISION
22 Cleveland Square, London, W2. Tel: (0171) 402 9066.
PORTMAN INTERNATIONAL
Advance House, 95 Ladbroke Grove, London W11 1PG. Tel:
(0171) 468 3400. FAX: (0171) 468 3499.
CONTACT
Victor Glynn

PORTMAN ZENITH GROUP LTD.
43-45 Dorset Street, London, W1H 4AB. Tel: (0171) 224 3344.
FAX: (0171) 224 1057.
DIRECTORS
Victor Glynn
John Hall
John Sivers
Simon Cox
Andrew Warren
Scott Meek
Dorothy Berwin
Ivan Rendall
Richard Leworthy

PORTOBELLO PICTURES
14-18 D, 92 Arblay Street, London, W1V 3YF. Tel: (0171) 379
5566. FAX: (0171) 379 5599. Telex: 268388 PORTO G.
EXECUTIVE PRODUCER & DIRECTOR
Eric Abraham

POST OFFICE FILM & VIDEO UNIT
(Archival Material) P.O. Box 145, Sittingbourne, Kent ME10
1NH. Tel: (01795) 426 465. FAX: (01795) 474 871.
CONTACT
Alma Headland

RICHARD PRICE TELEVISION ASSOCIATES LTD
Seymour Mews House, Seymour Mews, Wigmore St., London,
W1H 9PE. Tel: (0171) 935 9000. FAX: (0171) 935 1992.
DIRECTORS
Richard Price
Richard Leworthy
Simon Willock

PRIMETIME TELEVISION LTD.
Seymour Mews House, Seymour Mews, Wigmore St., London,
W1H 9PE. Tel: (0171) 935 9000. FAX: (0171) 935 1992.
CONTACTS
Richard Price
Ian Gordon

PRIMROSE FILM PRODUCTIONS LTD.
61 Regents Park Rd., London, NW1. Tel: (0171) 722 7475.
DIRECTORS
Louis Hagen
Anne Hagen

PROSPECT PICTURES
30-32 Mortimer St., London, W1N 7RA. Tel: (0171) 636 1234.
MANAGING DIRECTOR
Tony McAvoy

QUADRANT TELEVISION
17 West Hill, Wandsworth, London SW18 1RB. Tel: (0181) 870
9930. FAX: (0181) 870 7172.

RADIO LUXEMBOURG (LONDON) LTD.
38 Hertford Street, London, W1V 8BA. Tel: (0171) 493 5961.
DIRECTOR OF SALES & MARKETING
Brian Mellor

RADIUS TELEVISION PRODUCTION
Glenageary Office Park, Dun Laoghaire Co., Dublin, Ireland.
Tel: (3531) 285 6511. FAX: (3531) 285 6831.

RANDOM FILM PRODUCTIONS LTD.
Unit 2, Cornwall Works, Cornwall Avenue, Finchley, London,
N3 1LD. Tel: (0181) 349 9155.
DIRECTORS
F.G. Woosnam-Mills
M.R. Woosnam-Mills
M.P. Molloy

RANK FILM DISTRIBUTORS LTD.
127 Wardour Street, London, WIV 4AD. Tel: (0171) 437 9020.
Telex: 262556. FAX: (0171) 434 3689.
MANAGING DIRECTOR
F. P. Turner
HEAD OF INTERNATIONAL SALES
Nicole MacKey

RANK VIDEO SERVICES LTD.
Phoenix Park, Great West Rd., Brentford, Middlesex, TW8 9PL.
Tel: (0181) 568 4311. Telex: 22345. FAX: (0181) 847 4032.
MANAGING DIRECTOR
Peter Pacitt

RECORDED PICTURE CO. LTD.
24 Hanway St., London, W1P 9DD. Tel: (0171) 636 2251. FAX:
(0171) 636 2261.
DIRECTORS
Jeremy Thomas

REDIFFUSION FILMS LTD
P.O. Box 451, Buchanan House, 3 St. James's Square,
London, SW1Y 4LS. Tel: (0171) 925 0550. Telex: 919673.
Cables: Rediffuse. FAX: (0171) 839 7135.
PRODUCTION EXECUTIVE
Jelte Bonnevie

**RED ROOSTER FILM & TELEVISION ENTERTAINMENT
LTD.**
29 Floral Street, London, WC2E 9DP. Tel: (0171) 379 7727.
FAX: (0171) 379 5756.
CONTACT
Grainne Marmion

REGENT PRODUCTIONS
The Mews, 6 Putney Common, London, SW15 1HL. Tel: (0181)
789 5350. FAX: (0181) 789 5332
CONTACT
William G. Stewart

REUTERS TELEVISION LTD.
85 Fleet Street, London EC4P 4AJ. Tel: (0171) 250 1122. FAX: (0171) 542 4995.
DIRECTOR
Enrique Jara
HEAD OF NEWS
Stephen Claypole
FACILITIES MANAGER
Howard Barrow

REVELATION FILM GROUP
5-6 Parkside, Ravenscourt Park, Hammersmith, London. Tel: (0181) 741 2203. FAX: (0181) 741 2204.

REX ROBERTS STUDIOS LTD.
22 Glasthule Rd., Dun Laoghaire, Co. Dublin, Ireland. Tel: (3531) 808305.

RIGHT ANGLE PRODUCTIONS LTD.
31 Ransome's Dock, 35 Parkgate Rd., London, SW11 4NP. Tel: (0171) 228 9968. FAX: (0171) 223 8116.
CONTACT
Anise Driessen

PETER ROGER PRODUCTIONS LTD.
Pinewood Studios, Iver Heath, Bucks 5CO ONH. Tel: (01753) 651 700. FAX: (01753) 656 844.
DIRECTORS
Peter Rogers
B.E. Rogers
G.E. Malyon

ROYAL SOCIETY FOR THE PROTECTION OF BIRDS (RSPB)
Film and Video Unit, The Lodge, Sandy, Beds. SG19 2DL. Tel: (01767) 680 551. Telex: 82469 RSPB. FAX: (01767) 692 365.
FILM & VIDEO MANAGER
Colin Skevington

SAGITTA PRODUCTIONS LTD.
c/o Pamela Gillis Management, 46 Sheldon Avenue, London, N6 4JR. Tel: (0181) 340 7868.
MANAGING DIRECTOR
John Hawkesworth

SAMUELSON FILM SERVICE LTD.
21 Derby Rd., Metropolitan Centre, Greenford, Middx., UB6 8US. Tel: (0181) 578 7887. FAX: (0181) 575 2733.
MANAGING DIRECTOR
Barry Measure

SCORES FILM & TELEVISION
44 Great Marlborough St., London, W1V 1DB. Tel: (0171) 439 0225. FAX: (0171) 734 5288.

CINEMA SEVEN PRODUCTIONS LTD.
Pinewood Studios, Iver Heath, Bucks SL0 0NH. Tel: (01753) 651 700. FAX: (01753) 652 525.
DIRECTORS
Cassian Elwes
George Pappas
CONTACT
Chantal Ribeiro

SILVERBACH LAZARUS LTD.
South Bank TV Centre, Upper Ground, London, SE1 9LT. Tel: (0171) 261 1284. FAX: (0171) 633 0412. CONTACT
George Blaug

SETANA STUDIOS LTD.
Ardmore Studios, Herbert Rd., Bray Co. Wicklow, Ireland. Tel: (3531) 286 2971. FAX: (3531) 286 1894. CONTACT
Tracey Richardson

SKREBA FILMS LTD.
5a Noel St., London, W1V 3RB. Tel: (0171) 437 6492. FAX: (0171) 437 0644.
PRODUCERS
Ann Skinner
Simon Relph

SOVEREIGN PICTURES INC.
10 Greek Street, London, W1V 5LE. Tel: (0171) 494 1010. FAX: (0171) 494 3949. Telex: 261564 SOVE G.

SPITTING IMAGE PRODUCTIONS
4 Nice St., London, N1. Tel: (0171) 251 2626. FAX: (0171) 251 2066.
MANAGING DIRECTOR
Joanna Beresford

SR PROGRAMS INTERNATIONAL LTD.
Broadfield House, 22 Wilton Rd., Beaconsfield, Bucks HP9 2DE. Tel: (01494) 670 100. FAX: (01494) 670 101.

STRAIGHT FORWARD FILM & TV PRODUCTIONS LTD.
Crescent Studios, 18 High Street, Holywood Co. Down BT18 9AD. Tel: (01232) 427 697. FAX: (01232) 422 289. CONTACT
Moya Neeson

SUMMIT ENTERTAINMENT
18 Broadway St., London W1V 1FG. Tel: (0171) 494 1724. FAX: (0171) 494 1725.
CONTACT
David Garrett

SUNSET & VINE PLC
30 Sackville Street, London, WIX 1DB. Tel: (0171) 287 5700. FAX: (0171) 287 6524.
CONTACT
Colin Frewin

SURVIVAL ANGLIA LTD.
Anglia House, Norwich, NR1 3JG. Tel: (01603) 615 151.
EXECUTIVE PRODUCER
Graham Creelman

SWIFT FILM PRODUCTIONS
1 Wool Rd., Wimbledon, London, SW20. Tel: (0181) 946 2040.
DIRECTOR
T. Peter Hadingham, M.B.K.S.

SWINDON CABLE LTD.
Newcome Drive, Hawksworth Estate, Swindon, SN2 1TU. Tel: (01793) 615601.

TKO FILM & TELEVISION LTD.
P.O. Box 130, Hove, East Sussex, BN3 6QU. Tel: (01273) 550088. Telex: 877050. FAX: (01273) 540969.
DIRECTOR
J.S. Kruger
R. Kruger

TV CARTOONS
39 Grafton Way, London, W1P 5LA. Tel: (0171) 388 2222. FAX: (0171) 383 4192.
CONTACT
John Coates

TV SALES COMPANY
3 Derby Street, Mayfair, London, WIY 7HD. Tel: (0171) 355 2868. FAX: (0171) 495 3310.
CONTACT
Nick Witkowski

TVI LTD.
142 Wardour Street, London, W1V 3AU. Tel: (0171) 434 2141. Telex: 268208. FAX: (0171) 439 3984.
MANAGING DIRECTOR
Debbie Hills

TALBOT TELEVISION LTD.
57 Jamestown Rd., London, NWI 7DB. Tel: (0171) 284 0880. FAX: (0171) 916 5511.
MANAGING DIRECTOR & CHIEF EXECUTIVE
David Champtaloup
CHAIRMAN
Anthony Gruner
EXECUTIVE PRODUCER
Howard Huntridge
CHIEF OF FINANCE
Susan Sharples

TELECINE
Video House, 48 Charlotte Street, London, W1P 1LX. Tel: (0171) 916 3711. FAX: (0171) 916 3700. CONTACT
Sian Morgan

TELEFILM CANADA
22 Kingly Court, London, W1R 5LE. Tel: (0171) 437 8308. FAX: (0171) 734 8586.
INTERIM DIRECTOR
Bill Niven

TELEVENTURES
19/23 Wells Street, London, W1P 3FP. Tel: (0171) 436 5720.
CONTACT
Ray Lewis

THAMES TELEVISION INTERNATIONAL
Broom Rd., Teddington Lock, Teddington, Middlesex TW11 9NT. Tel: (0181) 614 2800. FAX: (0181) 943 0344.

TIGER FILM
65 Portland Rd., London W11 4LQ. Tel: (0171) 727 9810. FAX: (0171) 243 2940.
DIRECTORS
Angela Cheyne
Carole Rousseau

TRANSATLANTIC FILMS
Studio 1, 3 Brackenbury Road, London W6. Tel: (0171) 727 0132. FAX: (0171) 727 2293.
MANAGING DIRECTOR
Revel Guest

TRANSWORLD INTERNATIONAL (UK) INC.
TWI House, 23 Eyot Gardens, London W6 9TR. Tel: (0181) 233 5400. FAX: (0181) 233 5401.

TURNER INTERNATIONAL
CNN House, 19-22 Rathbone Place, London, W1P 1DF. Tel: (0171) 637 6900. FAX: (0171) 637 6713.

TWICKENHAM FILM STUDIOS LTD.
St. Margarets, Twickenham, Middlesex, TW1 2AW. Tel: (0181) 892 4477. FAX: (0181) 891 0168.
DIRECTORS
G. Humphreys
M. Landserger
N. Daou
S. J. Mullens

TYNE TEES ENTERPRISES LTD.
15 Bloomsbury Square, London, WC1A 2LJ. Tel: (0171) 405 8474. FAX: (0171) 242 2441.
INTERNATIONAL SALES MANAGER
Ann Gillham

UNICORN ORGANISATION
Pottery Lane Studios, 34a Pottery Lane, Holland Park, London W11 4LZ. Tel: (0171) 229 5131 FAX: (01710 229 4999.

UNION PICTURES
36 Marshall Street, London, W1V 1LL. Tel: (0171) 287 5100. FAX: (0171) 287 3770.
DIRECTORS
Brad Adams
Franc Roddam
Geoff Deeham

UNITED ARTISTS PROGRAMMING
Twyman House, 16 Bonny Street, London, NW1 9PG. Tel: (0171) 482 4824. FAX: (0171) 284 2042.
DIRECTORS
Trevor Fetter
Brian Yell
CONTACT
Paul Hudson

UNITED INTERNATIONAL PICTURES
(A subsidiary of United International Pictures B.V., Postbus 9255, 1006 AG Amsterdam, The Netherlands).
Mortimer House, 37-41 Mortimer Street, London W1A 2JL. Tel: (0171) 636 1655. FAX: (0171) 636 4118

UNITED TELEVISION ARTISTS LTD.
15-17 St Cross Street, London EC1N 8UN. Tel: (0171) 287 2727. FAX: (0171) 287 5053.
CONTACT
Bill Kerr Elliott

UNITED VIDEO INTERNATIONAL
54 Warwick Square, London, SW1V 2AJ. Tel: (0171) 834 6012.
VATV LTD.
60-62 Margaret St., London, W1N 7FJ. Tel: (0171) 636 9421. FAX: (0171) 436 7426.

VCI PROGRAMME SALES LTD.
Royalty House, 72-74 Dean Street, London W1V 5HB. Tel: (0171) 470 6666. FAX: (0171) 470 0006.
CONTACT
Karen Chillery

VOICE OF LONDON LTD.
245 Old Marylebone Rd., London, NW1 5RT. Tel: (0171) 402 8385.
STUDIO MANAGER
Miss Pat Smith

WALPORT INTERNATIONAL LTD.
(Subsidiary of Novo Communications), 15 Park Rd., London, NW1 6XH. Tel: (0171) 258 3477. FAX: (0171) 723 9568.
CONTACT
Mark O' Brien

WATERLOO PRODUCTIONS
1 Lower James Street, London, W1. Tel: (0171) 734 8311.

WESTCOUNTRY TELEVISION LTD.
Western Wood Way, Language Science Park, Plymouth PL7 5BG. Tel: (01752) 333 333. FAX: (01752) 333 444.

WITZEND PRODUCTIONS LTD.
6 Derby Street, Mayfair, London, W1Y 7HD. Tel: (0171) 355 2868. FAX: (0171) 629 1604.

WORLD AUDIO VISUAL ENTERTAINMENT PLC
18 Great Marlborough Street, London, W1V 1AF. Tel: (0171) 439 9596. Telex: 264036 WAVE G.

WORLDMARK PRODUCTIONS LTD.
7 Cornwall Crescent, London W11 1PH. Tel: (0171) 792 9800. FAX: (0171) 792 9801.

WORLD WIDE GROUP
21-25 St. Anne's Court, London, W1V 3AW. Tel: (0171) 434 1121. FAX: (0171) 734 0169.
CONTACT
Ray Townsend
Chris Courtenay-Taylor
Paul Verbruggen

WORLDWIDE TELEVISION NEWS
The Interchange, Oval Rd., Camden Lock, London, NW1 7EP. Tel: (0171) 410 5200. Telex: 23915. FAX: (0171) 413 8302.
MARKETING MANAGER
Lorrie Graham Morgan

WYATT CATTANEO PRODUCTIONS LTD.
Charing Cross Rd., London, WC 2. Tel: (0171) 379 6444.

YO YO FILMS LTD.
79 Dean Street, London W1 5HA. Tel: (0171) 642 8954. FAX: (0171) 287 1072. email: yoyofilms@compuserve.com
CONTACT
Lauren C. Postma
Phillip Bartlett

ZENITH PRODUCTIONS LTD.
43-45 Dorset Street, London, W1H 4AB. Tel: (0171) 224 3194. FAX: (0171) 224 2440.
DIRECTOR OF PRODUCTION
Scott Meek

ZIERLER MEDIA
19 Greenwood Place, London NW5 1LB. Tel: (0171) 284 2848. FAX: (0171) 485 7089.
CHIEF EXECUTIVE
Gerald Zierler

HOME VIDEO DISTRIBUTORS

ABBEY HOME ENTERTAINMENTS
1 Sussex Place, Hammersmith, London, W6 9XS. Tel: (0181) 910 5424 FAX: (0181) 910 5425.

ART HOUSE PRODUCTIONS
39-41 North Road, Islington London N7 9DP Tel: (0171) 700 0068 FAX: (0171) 609 2249.

BBC VIDEO
Woodlands, 80 Wood Lane, London, W12 0TT. Tel: (0181) 576 2236. FAX:(0181)743 0393.

BLUE DOLPHIN FILM & VIDEO
40 Langham Street, London W1N 5RG Tel: (0171) 255 2494. FAX:(0171) 580 7670.

BUENA VISTA HOME ENTERTAINMENT
Beaumont House, Kensington Village, Avonmore Road, London W14 8TS. Tel: (0171) 605 2400. FAX:(0171)605 2795.

CARLTON HOME ENTERTAINMENT LTD
The Water Front, Elstree Road, Elstree, Herts WD6 3EE. Tel: (0181) 207 6207. FAX (0181) 207 5789.

CIC VIDEO
Glenthorne House, 5-17 Hammersmith Grove, London. W6 0ND. Tel (0181) 846 9433. FAX:(0181) 741 9773.

CHANNEL FOUR VIDEO
124 Horseferry Road, London SW1P 2TX. Tel: (0171) 306 8687.

COLUMBIA TRISTAR HOME VIDEO
Sony Pictures Europe House, 25 Golden Square, London W1R 6LV. Tel: (0171) 533 1200. FAX:(0171) 533 1105.

CTE (CARLTON)
35-38 Portian Square, London, W1H 9FH. Tel: (0171) 224 3399.

DD VIDEO
5 Churchill Court, 58 Station Rd., North Harrow, Middlesex HA2 75A. Tel: (0181) 863 8819. FAX (0181) 863 0463.

ENTERTAINMENT IN VIDEO
27 Soho Square, London W1V 5FL Tel:(0171) 439 1979 FAX:(0171) 734 2483.

FILM FOUR DISTRIBUTORS LTD.
Castle House, 75-76 Wells St., London W1O 3RE. Tel: (0171) 436 9944.

FIRST INDEPENDENT FILMS LTD.
99 Baker St., London W1H 1FB. Tel: (0171) 317 2500. FAX:(0171) 317 2502/2503.

HIGH FLIERS DISTRIBUTION LTD.
16 Hethfield Terrace, Chiswick, London W4 4JE. Tel: (0181) 742 2023.

HIT ENTERTAINMENT
3rd floor, The Pump House, 13-16 Jacobs Well Mews, London W1H 5PD. Tel: (0171) 299 9000. FAX (0171) 224 1719.

MAINLINE PICTURES
37 Museum Street, London WC1A 1LP. Tel: (0171) 242 5523. FAX: (0171) 430 0170.

MANGA ENTERTAINMENT LTS.
Essex Place Chiswick W4 5UT. Tel: (0181) 987 5900. FAX: (0181) 987 5945.

MGM HOME ENTERTAINMENT (EUROPE) LTD.
Ground floor, South Wing, Glenthrone House, Hammersmith Grove, London W6 0ND. Tel: (0181) 563 8383. FAX:(0181) 563 2896.

ODYSSEY VIDEO
15 Dufours Place, London, W1V IFE. Tel: (0171) 437 8251. FAX: (0171) 734 6941.

PEARSON ENTERTAINMENT
1 Stephen Street, London W1P 8AR. Tel: (0171) 691 6000.

POLYGRAM FILMED ENTERTAINMENT
P.O. Box 1425, Chancellors House, 72 Chancellors Road, Hammersmith, London, W6 9QB. Tel: (0181) 910 5000. FAX:(0181) 910 5901.

SIG VIDEO GEMS LTD
The Coach House, The Old Vicarage, 10 Church Street, Rickmansworth Herts WD3 1BS Tel: (01923) 710 599. FAX:(01923) 710 549.

SONY MUSIC U.K. LTD.
Rabans Lane, Aylesbury, Bucks, HP19 3BX. Tel: (01296) 426151. (01296) 395 551.

TELSTAR VIDEO INTERACTIVE ENTERTAINMENT
The Studio, 5 King Edwards Mews, Byfield Gardens, Barnes, London SW13 9HP. Tel: (0181) 846 9946. FAX:(0181) 741 5584.

THAMES VIDEO LTD.
Pearson Television International, 1 Stephen Street, London W1P 1PJ. Tel: (0171) 691 6000. FAX (0171) 691 6079.

TWENTIETH CENTURY HOME ENTERTAINMENT
31-32 Soho Square, London, W1V 6AP. Tel: (0171) 753 8686. (0171) 434 2170.

VIDEO COLLECTION INTERNATIONAL.
Royalty House, 72-74 Dean St., London, W1V 5HB. Tel: (0171) 470 6666. FAX:(0171) 470 0006.

WARNER HOME VIDEO
135 Wardour Street, London, W1V 4AP. Tel: (0171) 494 3441. FAX: (0171) 494 3297.
CONTACT
Mike Heap

WARNER VISION
35-38 Portman Sq., London W1H 0EU. Tel: (0171) 467 2566.

ANIMATION

A FOR ANIMATION LTD.
Unit 3A, The Old Malthouse, Little Anne St., Bristol BS2 9EW.
Tel: (0117) 955 0611. FAX: (0117) 955 0600.
CONTACT
Mark Taylor

AARDMAN ANIMATIONS
Gas Ferry Rd., Bristol, Avon BS1 6UN. Tel: (0117) 984 8485.
FAX: (0117) 984-8486.
CONTACT
Lisa Murphy

THE ANIMATION PARTNERSHIP LTD.
77 Dean St., London W1V 5HA. Tel: (0171) 636 3300. FAX:
(0171) 580 9153.

THE ANIMATION PEOPLE LTD.
5/7 Kean St., London WC2B 4AT. Tel: (0171) 836 1623. FAX:
(0171) 836 4130.
CONTACT
Brian Larkin

ANIMATION SERVICES LTD.
9 Bourlet Close, London W1P 7PJ. Tel: (0171) 436 0426. FAX:
(0171) 436 0428.

ANIMATION WORKS
10 Stokes Court, Diploma Ave., London N2 N8X. Tel: (0181)
883 3402.
CONTACT
Lee Stork

ANTICS WORKSHOP
42 Champion Hill, Camberwell, London SE5 8BS. Tel/FAX:
(0171) 274 0135.

BARE BOARDS PRODUCTIONS LTD.
Studio 6, Commercial Wharf. 6 Commercial St., Manchester
M15 467. Tel/FAX: (0161) 834 5406.

BERMUDA SHORTS LTD.
1 Lower John St., London W1R 3PD. Tel: (0171) 437 7335.
FAX: (0171) 437 7334.
CONTACT
Maria Manton

BOLEXBROTHERS LTD.
3-6 Brunel Lock Development, Cumberland Basin, Bristol BS1
6SE. Tel: (0117) 985 8000. FAX: (0117) 985 8899.

BROOKE EDWARDS ANIMATION
21 Kingly St., London W1R 5LB. Tel: (0171) 734 9384. FAX:
(0171) 734 9385.
CONTACT
Lee Hill

BUMPER FILMS LTD.
Unit 15, Bridgewater Ct., Oldmixon Crescent, Weston-super-
Mare, N. Somerset BS24 9AY. Tel: (01934) 418 961. FAX:
(01934) 624 494. email: bumper@ibm.net
CONTACT
John Walker

CARTWN CYMRU
Screen Centre, Llantrisant Rd., Cardiff, South Glamorgan CF5
2PU. Tel: (01222) 575 999. FAX: (01222) 575 919.
CONTACT
Naomi Jones

CELL LTD.
28-30 Osnaburgh St., London NW1 3ND. Tel: (0171) 208 1500.
FAX: (0171) 208 1501.

CFX ASSOCIATES LTD.
16-18 Ramillies St., London W1V 1DL. Tel: (0171) 734 3155.
FAX: (0171) 494 3670.
ANIMATORS
Craig Zerouni, Chris Briscoe

THE COMPUTER FILM COMPANY
19-23 Wells St., London W1P 3FP. Tel: (0171) 344 8000. FAX:
(0171) 344 8001.
CONTACT
Rosy Burnie

CONCEPT MEDIA LTD.
Orwell Place, 172 Tunbridge Rd, Wateringbury Kent ME18
5NS. Tel/FAX: (01622) 817 178.
CONTACT
Denise Peckham

TONY CUTHBERT PRODUCTIONS
7A Langley St., London WC2H 9JA. Tel: (0171) 437 8884. FAX:
(0171) 734 6579.
CONTACT
Susanna Balson

WALT DISNEY PRODUCTIONS LTD.
Beaumont House, Kensington Village, Avonmore Rd., London
W14 8TS. Tel: (0171) 605 2400. FAX: (0171) 605 2795.

EALING ANIMATION
302 Canalot Production Studios, 222 Kensal Rd., London W10
5BN. Tel: (0181) 960 8188. FAX: (0181) 964 9917.

EAST ANGLIAN PRODUCTIONS
Frinton-on-Sea, Essex CO13 0AA Tel: (01255) 676 252. FAX:
(01255) 850 528.
CONTACT
Ray Anderson

EDITPOINT
SM House, 26-27 West St., Horsham, West Sussex RH20 3BX.
Tel: (01403) 241 345. FAX: (01403) 269 264.

ELECTRIC IMAGE LTD.
7-11 Lexington St., London W1R 3HQ. Tel: (0171) 287 8800.
FAX: (0171) 287 3750.

FAIRWATER FILMS LTD.
68 Vista Rise, Llandaff, Cardiff CF5 2SD. Tel/FAX: (01222) 578
488.
ANIMATOR
Tony Barnes

FILMFAIR ANIMATION LTD.
106 Gloucester Place,London W1H 3DB. Tel: (0171) 935 1596.
FAX: (0171) 935 0229.

FLICKS FILMS LTD.
101 Wardour St., London W1V 3TD. Tel: (0171) 734 4892. FAX:
(0171) 287 2307.
CONTACT
Tracy Cook

FRAMELINE
33-34 Rathbone Pl., London W1P 1AD. Tel: (0171) 636 1301.
FAX: (0171) 436 8878.

FUNNY BUSINESS LTD.
61 Connaught St., London W2 2AE. Tel: (0171) 402 9281. FAX:
(0171) 402 2643.

G&M PRODUCTIONS
3 Carlisle St., London W1 5RH. Tel: (0171) 439 6936. FAX:
(0171) 439 0280.
CONTACT
Mike Wallis

BOB GODFREY FILMS
199 Kings Cross Rd., London WC1X 9DB. Tel: (0171) 278
5711. FAX: (0171) 278
6809.
CONTACT
Bob Godfrey

GRAND SLAMM PARTNERSHIP LTD.
22 Bloomsbury St., London WC1B 3QJ. Tel: (0171) 436 1982.
FAX: (0171) 323 0183.

HIBBERT RALPH ANIMATION LTD.
10 D'Arblay St., London W1V 3FP. Tel: (0171) 494 3011. FAX:
(0171) 494 0383.
CONTACTS
Maddy Sparrow, Bernadette Hannon, John Woolley

HONEYCOMB ANIMATION STUDIOS
Lower Westown Studio, Hemyock, Cullompton, Devon EX15
3RN. Tel: (01823) 680 383. FAX: (01823) 681026.

ICE PICS
111A Wardour St., London W1V 3TD. Tel: (0171) 437 3505.
FAX: (0171) 287 0393.
CONTACT
Mike Davis

KING ROLLO PRODUCTIONS
Dolphin Court, High Street, Honiton Devon EX14 8LS
Tel:01404 45218 FAX: 01404 45328

KLACTOVEESEDSTEENE ANIMATIONS
49/50 Great Marlborough St., 2nd floor, London W1V 1DB. Tel: (0171) 439 1420. FAX: (0171) 434 0410.
CONTACT
Sue Hicks

LEEDS ANIMATION WORKSHOP
45 Bayswater Row, Leeds LS8 5LF. Tel: (0113) 248 4997. FAX: (0113) 248 4997.
CONTACT
Jane Bradshaw

MAGNETIC IMAGE GRAPHICS
6 Grand Union Centre, West Row, North Kensington, London W10 5AS. Tel: (0181) 964 5000. FAX: (0181) 964 4110.

MATTES AND MINIATURES
Bray Studios, Water Oaklet, Windsor, Berks SL4 5UG. Tel: (01628) 622111, ext. 126. FAX: (01628) 778 872.
CONTACT
Leigh Took

MELENDEZ FILMS
33 Gresse St., London W1P 2AH. Tel: (0171) 323 2311. FAX: (0171) 323 2331.

TJFX DEPARTMENT
40-41 Great Marlborough St., London W1V 1DA. Tel: (0171) 287 4041. FAX: (0171) 287 8393.
CONTACTS
Dave Levy
Dave Throssell

HILL ROBERTS FILMS
Unit 2, 81 Southern Row, London W10 5AL. Tel: (0181) 964 0234. FAX: (0181) 968 7710
CONTACT
Julian Roberts

RAY MOORE ANIMATION LTD.
Animation Centre, 113 Humber Rd., London SE3 7LW. Tel: (0181) 853 1164. FAX: (0181) 853 3043.
CONTACT
Ray Moore

NISSELL LTD.
Maxted Close, Hemel Hempstead, Herts HP2 7BS. Tel: (01422) 69101. FAX:(01422) 211 804.

PASSION PICTURES LTD.
25-27 Riding House St. London W1P 7PB. Tel: (0171) 323 9933. FAX: (0171) 323 9030.
CONTACT
Sian Rees

PEARCE STUDIOS LTD.
Old Lodge Farm, Coningsby Lane, Fifield, Maidenhead, Berks SL6 2PF. Tel: (01628) 627032. FAX: (01628) 777 343.
CONTACT
Rod Lord

PICASSO PICTURES LTD.
7 D'arblay St., London W1V 4FD. Tel: (0171) 437 9888. FAX: (0171) 437 9040.
CONTACT
Jane Bolton

PIZAZZ PICTURES
30 Berwick St., London W1V 3RF. Tel: (0171) 434 3581. FAX: (0171) 437 2309.
CONTACT
Pam Dennis

PUPPET VISUALS
60 Catton Chase, Old Catton, Norwich, Norfolk NR6 7AS. Tel: (01603) 482513.

RAGDOLL PRODUCTIONS
11 Chapel Street, Stratford upon Avon, Warwickshire CV 37 6EP. Tel: (01789) 262 772 FAX: (01789) 262 773

ROCKY ROAD PRODUCTIONS LTD.
The Studio, 221B Upper Richmond Rd., Putney, London SW15 6SQ. Tel: (0181) 789 9277. FAX: (0181) 788 3752.
CONTACT
John Ley

SCENE 2
72 Campbell Rd., Woodley, Reading RG5 3PG. Tel/FAX: (01734) 268144.

SIMONETTI PRODUCTIONS LTD.
9 1/2 Charlotte Mews, London W1P 1LN. Tel: (0171) 636 2164. FAX: (0171) 636 6739.
PRODUCER
Malcolm Bubb

SIRIOL PRODUCTIONS
Phoenix Buildings, 3 Mount Stuart Square Butetown, Cardiff CF1 6RW. Tel: (01222) 488400 FAX: (01222)485962

SOHO 601
71 Dean St., London W1V 5HB. Tel: (0171) 439 2730. FAX: (0171) 734 3331.
CONTACT
John Roberts-Cox

SPEEDY FILMS LTD.
8 Royalty Mews, Dean St., London W1V 5AW. Tel: (0171) 494 4043. FAX: (0171) 434 0830.

STARDUST PICTURES
58-59 Highgate, Westhill., London N6 4RT. Tel: (0181).342 9444.
CONTACT
Gayle Martin

BRIAN STEVENS ANIMATED FILMS LTD.
11 Charlotte Mews, London W1P 1LN. Tel: (0171) 637 0535. FAX: (0171) 323 3892.
CONTACT
Brian Stevens

STOP FRAME LTD.
46 Fortrose St., Glasgow, Strathclyde G11 5LP. Tel: (0141) 334 2577. FAX: (0141) 334 8990.
CONTACT
Beart Ross

SUPER-VISIONS 3D COMPUTER ANIMATION
84A Telephone Pl., London SW6 1TH. Tel/FAX: (0171) 385 2848.
CONTACT
Gordon Tait

GORDON TAIT MODEL FX
84A Telephone Pl., London SW6 1TH. Tel/FAX: (0171) 385 2848.

RICHARD TAYLOR CARTOON FILMS
76 Dukes Ave., London N10 2QA. Tel: (0181) 444 7547. FAX: (0181) 444 7218.

TELLY GRAPHICS LTD.
The Pictures, 5th floor, 41 St. Vincent's Place,. Glasgow G1 2ER. Tel: (0141) 226 2201. FAX: (0141) 248 1022.
CONTACT
David Long

TOUCH ANIMATIONS LTD.
44 Earlham St., London WC2H 9LA. Tel: (0171) 379 6247. FAX: (0171) 379 5210.
CONTACT
Jo Manser

TRIFFIC FILMS
114 High St., Stony Stratford, Milton Keynes, Bucks MK11 1AY. Tel: (01908) 261 234. FAX: (01908) 263 050.
CONTACT
Tim Searle

TV CARTOONS
39 Grafton Way, London W1P 5LA. Tel: (0171) 388 2222. FAXL (0171) 383 4192.
CONTACTS
John Coastes, Claire Jennings

WARDOUR MOTION PICTURES LTD.
Flint Studios Knatts Valley Nr Brands Hatch, Sevenoaks, Kent TN15 6XY. Tel & FAX: (0147) 485 3538

WILL VINTON PRODUCTIONS
10 D'Arblay St., London W1V 3FP. Tel: (0171) 613 3740. FAX: (0171) 494 0383.

WIZARD ANIMATION
Geller House, 51 Hoxton Sq., London N1 6PB. Tel/FAX: (0171) 613 3740.

WOODLAND ANIMATIONS LTD.
58 Queens Gate Mews, London SW7 5QN. Tel: (0171) 589 7584. FAX: (0171) 584 1790.
CONTACT
Mrs JO Wood

?Z ANIMATION
8 Royalty Mews, Dean St., London W1V 5AW. Tel: (0171) 439 8653. FAX: (0171) 437 4518.

COSTUME SUPPLIERS

ANGELS & BERMANS
40 Camden Street, London, NW1 0EN. Tel: (0171) 387 0999.
FAX: (0171) 383 5603.
119 Shaftesbury Avenue, London, WC2H 8AE. Tel: (0171) 836
5678. FAX: (0171) 240 9527.
CONTACTS
Tim Angel, Jonathan Lipman

THE ANTIQUE CLOTHING SHOP
282 Portobello Rd., London W10. Tel: (0181) 993 4162.
CONTACT
Sandy Stagg

ARMS & ARCHERY
The Coach House, London Road, Ware, Herts, SG12 9QU. Tel:
(01920) 460 335. FAX: (01920) 461 044.
CONTACT
Terry Goulden

CARLO MANZI RENTALS
32 33 Liddell Road, London, NW6 2EW. Tel: (0171) 625 6391.
FAX: (0171) 625 5386.

COSPROP LTD.
26 28 Rochester Place, London, NW1 9JR. Tel: (0171) 485
6731. FAX: (0171) 485 5942.
CONTACT
Bernie Chapman

THE COSTUME STUDIO
Montgomery House, 159-161 Balls Pond Rd., Islington N1
4BS Tel: (0171) 388 4481. FAX: (0171) 837 6576
CONTACTS
Rupert Clive, Richard Dudley

M.B.A. COSTUMES
Good year House, 52-56 Osnaburgh St., London NW1 3ND.
Tel: (0171) 388 4994. FAX: (0171) 383 2038.
CONTACTS
Noel Howard, Fred Brazier

PULLONS PM PRODUCTIONS
St. Georges Studio, Wood End Lane, Fillongley, Coventry,
Warks CV7 8DF. Tel: (01676) 541 390. FAX: (01676) 542 438.

ROYAL NATIONAL THEATRE
1-3 Brixton Rd., London SW9 6DE. Tel: (0171) 820 1358. FAX:
(0171) 820 9324.

ROYAL SHAKEPEARE COMPANY
Timothy's Bridge Rd., Sratford Upon Avon, Warks CV37 9UY.
Tel: (01789) 25920. FAX: (01789) 205 920.
CONTACT
Alison Mitchell

TORBAY COSTUME HIRE
31 Market St., Torquay, Devon TQ1 3AW. Tel: (01803) 211 930.
FAX: (01803) 293 554.
CONTACT
Lionel Digby

EDITING SERVICES

124 FACILITIES
124 Horseferry Rd., London SW1P 2TX. Tel: (0171) 306 8040.
FAX: (0171) 306 8041.
CONTACTS
Carolyn Heald, Tracy Smith

BBC RESOURCES SCOTLAND
Broadcasting House, Queen Margaret Dr., Glasgow G12 8DG.
Tel: (0151) 338 2020. FAX: (0141) 338 2335.
MARKETING & BUSINESS DEVELOPMENT MANAGER
Jim Douglas

BLUE POST PRODUCTION
58 Old Compton St., London W1V 5PA. Tel: (0171) 437 2626.
FAX: (0171) 439 2477.
CONTACTS
Samantha Greenwood

CAPITAL TELEVISION
13 Wandsworth Plain, London SW18 1ET. Tel: (0181) 874
0131. FAX: (0181) 877 0234.
CONTACT
Clare Phillips

CFX ASSOCIATES
16-18 Ramillies St., London W1V 1DL. Tel: (0171) 734 3155.
FAX: (0171) 494 3670.
CONTACT
Alison Thompson

CHRYSALIS TODD-AO EUROPE
Hawley Crescent, Kindin NW1 8NP. Tel: (0171) 284 7900. FAX:
(0171) 485 3667.
CONTACTS
Carolyn McManus, Kerry Aspinal

D6 POST PRODUCTION
8 Golden Sq., London W1R 3AF. Tel: (0171) 734 6434. FAX:
(0171) 734 7414.

DIGITAL ARTS
9-11 Richmond Buildings, Dean St., London W1V 5AF. Tel:
(0171) 439 0919. FAX: (0171) 427 1146.
CONTACT
Geoff Axtell

ELECTRIC IMAGE
7-11 Lexington St., London W1R 3HQ. Tel: (0171) 287 8800.
FAX: (0171) 287 3750.
CONTACT
Jay Williams

ESSENTIAL PICTURES
Canalot Studios, 222 Kensal Rd., London W10 5BN. Tel: (0181)
969 7017. FAX: (0181) 960 8201.
CHIEF EXECUTIVE
John Martineau, Robin Clarkson

THE FILM EDITORS
6-10 Lexington St., London W1R 3HS. Tel: (0171) 437 6409.
FAX: (0171) 751 1119
CONTACT
Pam Power

FILM MEDIA SERVICES LTD.
Unit 8, Spacewaye, North Feltham Trading Est., Feltham,
Middlesex TW14 0TH. Tel: (0181) 890 8780.
CONTACT
Brian Gilmore

FOUNTAIN TELEVISION STUDIOS
Cocks Crescent, New Malden, Surrey KT3 4TA. Tel: (0181) 942
6633. FAX: (0181) 949 7911.
CONTACT
Bobbi Johnstone

GENERAL SCREEN ENTERPRISES
Unit 9, Highbridge Estate, Oxford Rd., Uxbridge, Middlesex
UB8 1LX. (01895) 231 931. FAX: (01895) 235 335.
CONTACT
Fred Chandler

HOLLOWAY FILM & TELEVISION
68-70 Wardour St., London W1V 3HP. Tel: (0171) 494 0777.
FAX: (0171) 494 0309.
CONTACT
David Holloway

SHEILA LOGIE
2 Westbourne House, Mount Park Rd., Harrow-on-the-Hill,
Middlesex HA1 3JT. Tel: (0181) 422 8378.

LONDON POST
34-35 Dean St., London W1V 5AP. Tel: (0171) 439 9080. FAX: (0171) 434 0714.
MARKETING DIRECTOR
Andy Newman

THE LONDON STUDIOS
The London Television Centre, Upper Ground, London SE1 9LT. Tel: (0171) 261 3473. FAX: (0171) 633 9703.
CONTACT
Charlotte Bernard, Ed Harvey

THE MILL
40-41 Great Marlborough St., London W1V 1DA. Tel: (0171) 287 4041. FAX: (0171) 287 8393.
HEAD OF PRODUCTION
Derryn Clarke

MOLINARE
34 Fouberts Pl., London W1V 2BH. Tel: (0171) 439 2244. FAX: (0171) 734 6813.
CONTACTS
Kate George, Simon Gosling

OBE PARTNERSHIP LTD.
16 Kingly St., London W1R 5LD. Tel: (0171) 734 3028. FAX: (0171) 734 2830.
CONTACT
Clare House

PARALLAX PICTURES LTD.
7 Denmark St, London WC2H 8LS. Tel: (0171) 836 1478. FAX: (0171) 497 8062.
CONTACT
Angela Murray

PICTURE POST PRODUCTION
13 Manette St., London W1V 5LB. Tel: (0171) 439 1661. FAX: (0171) 494 1661.

PINEWOOD STUDIOS LTD.
Pinewood Rd., Iver, Bucks SL0 0NH. Tel: (01753) 651 700. FAX: (01753) 656 844.
CONTACT
David Lance

QUANTEL LTD.
Turnpike Rd., Newbury, Berks RG14 2NE. Tel: (01635) 48222. FAX: (01635) 31776.
CONTACT
Roger Thornton

RAZOR
3 Newburgh St., London W1V 1LH. Tel: (0171) 439 1037. FAX: (0171) 287 0973.

RED POST PRODUCTION
Hammersly House, 5-8 Warwick St., London W1R 6JD. Tel: (0171) 439 1449. FAX: (0171) 439 1339.
PRODUCER
Carl Grinter

SHEARS POST PRODUCTION SERVICES
Warwick House, Shapone Pl., Dean St., London W1V 5AJ. Tel: (0171) 437 8182. FAX: (0171) 437 8183.
CONTACT
Steve Shears

SOHO IMAGES LTD.
71 Dean St., London W1V 5HB. Tel: (0171) 437 0831. FAX: (0171) 734 9471.

TANGRAM POST PRODUCTIONS
5 Sherwood St., London W1V 7RA. Tel: (0171) 437 8710. FAX: (0171) 439 0491.
CONTACT
Simon or Laurence

TV MEDIA SERVICES LTD.
3rd floor, 420 Suchiehall St., Glasgow G2 3JD. Tel: (0141) 331 1993. FAX: (0141) 332 9040.
CONTACT
Charles Chalmers

THE WHITEHOUSE POST PRODUCTION
12-13 Kingly St., London W1R 5LD. Tel: (0171) 287 3404. FAX: (0171) 287 9670.
EDITORS
Andrea MacArthur
Rick Lawley
John Smith
Russel Icke
Jinx Godfrey
Jim Weedon

WORKHOUSE LTD.
Granville House, St. Peter St., Winchester, Hants SO23 8BP. Tel: (01962) 626 400. FAX: (01962) 626 401.
CONTACT
Sarah Carroll

FILM & VIDEO LABORATORIES

BUCKS MOTION PICTURE LABORATORIES LTD.
714 Banbury Avenue, Slough, Berks., SL1 4LH. Tel: (01753) 576 611. FAX: (01753) 691 762. Harry Rushton, Mike Bianchi.

COLOUR FILM SERVICES LTD.
22-25 Portman Close, Baker Street, London, W1A 4BE. Tel: (0171) 486 2881. Telex: 24672.
10 Wadsworth Road, Perivale, Greenford, Middx., UB6 7JX. Tel: (0181) 998 2731.

COLOUR VIDEO SERVICES LTD.
10 Wadsworth Rd., Perivale, Greenford, Middlesex UB6 7JX. Tel: (0181) 998 2731. FAX: (0181) 997 8738.

FILMATIC LABORATORIES LTD.
16 Colville Road, London, W11 2BS. Tel: (0171) 221 60181. FAX: (0171) 229 2718.
CHAIRMAN & MANAGING DIRECTOR
D. L. Gibbs
ASSISTANT MANAGING DIRECTOR
I. Magowan

HALLIFORD STUDIOS
Manygate Lane, Shepperton, Middlesex. Tel: (01932) 226 341. FAX: (01932) 246 336.
STUDIO MANAGER
Allan d'Aguiar

METROCOLOR LONDON LTD.
22 Soho Square, London, W1V 5FL. Tel: (0171) 437 7811.
91/95 Gillespie Road, Highbury, London, N5 1LS. Tel: (0171) 226 4422. FAX: (0171) 359 2353.
MANAGING DIRECTOR
K. B. Fraser

PORTLAND RECORDING STUDIOS LTD.
35 Portland Place, London, W1N 3AG. Tel: (0171) 637 2111.

RANK FILM LABORATORIES LTD.
Denham, Uxbridge, Middlesex, UB9 5HQ. Tel: (01895) 832 323. Telex: 934704. FAX: (01895) 833 617.
MANAGING DIRECTOR
T. A. McCurdie
DIRECTOR OF SALES
David Dowler

SOHO IMAGES GROUP LTD.
8-14 Meard Street, London, W1V 3HR. Tel: (0171) 437 0831. FAX: (0171) 734 9471.
MANAGING DIRECTOR
Ray Adams

TECHNICOLOR LTD.
Bath Road, West Drayton, Middx., UB7 0DB. Tel: (0181) 759 5432. FAX: (0181) 897 2666.
MANAGING DIRECTOR
Ashley Hopkins

TWICKENHAM FILM STUDIOS, LTD.
St. Margarets, Twickenham, Middlesex, TW1 2AW. Tel: (0181) 892 4477. FAX: (0181) 891 0168.

UNITED MOTION PICTURES (LONDON) LTD.
3 and 36/38 Fitzroy Square, London, W.1. Tel: (0171) 580 1171, (0171) 388 1234.

WORLD WIDE GROUP
21-25, St. Anne's Court, London, W1V 3AW. Tel: (0171) 434 1121. Telex: 269271. FAX: (0171) 734 0619.

Financial Services

AON ENTERTAINMENT LTD. INSURANCE SERVICES
9th floor, Minster Court, Mincing Lane, London EC3R 7AA.
Tel: (0171) 283 1033. FAX: (0171) 283 1077.

BARCLAYS BANK PLC
The Media Section, Barclays Business Centre, 27 Soho
Square, London, W1A 4WA. Tel: (0171) 439 6851. FAX:
(0171) 434 9035.

BRITISH & COMMONWEALTH MERCHANT BANK PLC
62 Cannon Street, London, EC4N 6AE. Tel: (0171) 248 0900.

COMPLETION BOND COMPANY INC.
Pinewood Studios, Iver Heath, Bucks., SL0 0NH. Tel: (01753)
652 433. Telex: 849003 CPLBND G. FAX: (01753) 655 697.

CONSOLIDATED ARTISTS
Strachans Somerville, Phillips Street, St. Helier, Jersey,
Channel Islands. Tel: (01534) 71505. FAX: (01534) 23902.

CONTRACTS INTERNATIONAL LTD.
13-14 Golden Square, London, W1R 3AG. Tel: (0171) 287
5800. FAX: (0171) 287 3779. Telex: 295835.

ERNST & YOUNG
Beckett House, 1 Lambeth Palace Road, London, SE1 7EU.
Tel: (0171) 928 2000. FAX: (0171) 401 2136.

EUROPEAN SCRIPT FUND
39c Highbury Place, London, N5 1QP. Tel: (0171) 226 9903.

GENERAL ENTERTAINMENT INVESTMENTS
65-67 Ledbury Road, London, W11 2AD. Tel: (0171) 221
3512. Telex: 28604. FAX: (0932) 868 989.

GUARANTORS INTERNATIONAL INC.
5 Carlton Gardens, Pall Mall, London, SW1Y 5AD. Tel:
(0171) 839 9355. FAX: (0171) 839 1774.

GUINNESS MAHON & CO. LTD.
32 St. Mary at Hill, London, EC3P 3AJ. Tel: (0171) 623 9333.
FAX: (0171) 283 4811.

INTERNATIONAL COMPLETION INC.
Pinewood Studios, Pinewood Road, Iver Heath, Bucks SL0
0NH. Tel: (01753) 651 700. FAX: (01753) 656 564.

KPMG PEAT MARWICK
1 Puddle Dock, Blackfriars, London, EC4V 3PD. Tel: (0171)
236 8000. FAX: (0171) 248 6552.

PARMEAD INSURANCE BROKERS LTD.
Lyon House, 160-166 Borough High Street, London, SE1
1JR. Tel: (0181) 467 8656. FAX: (0181) 295 1659.

PRODUCTION PROJECTS FUND
BFI, 29 Rathbone Place, London, WIP 1AG. Tel: (0171) 636
5587. FAX: (0171) 780 9456.

ROLLINS BURDICK HUNTER (INTERNATIONAL) LTD.
Braintree House, Braintree Road, Ruislip, Middx., HA4 0YA.
Tel: (0181) 841 4461. FAX: (0181) 842 2124.

RUBEN SEDGWICK INSURANCE SERVICES
Pinewood Studios, Pinewood Road, Iver, Bucks., SL0 0NH.
Tel: (01753) 654 555. FAX: (01753) 653 152

SAMUEL MONTAGU & CO. LTD.
10 Lower Thames Street, London, EC3 R6AE. Tel: (0171)
260 9000. FAX: (0171) 488 1630.

SARGENT-DISC LTD.
Pinewood Studios, Pinewood Road, Iver, Bucks. Tel: (01753)
656 631. FAX: (01753) 655 881.

SPECTRUM ENTERTAINMENT GROUP PLC
The Pines, 11 Putney Hill, London, SW15 6BA. Tel: (0181)
780 2525. FAX: (0181) 780 1671. Telex: 262433.

STOY HAYWARD
8 Baker Street, London, WIM 1DA. Tel: (0171) 486 5888.
FAX: (0171) 487 3686.

TOUCHE ROSS
Hill House, 1 Little New Street, London, EC4A 3TR. Tel:
(0171) 936 3000. FAX: (0171) 583 8517.

UNITED MEDIA LTD.
2nd fl., Broadwick House, 8 12 Broadwick St., London, W1V
4EQ. Tel: (0171) 434 3501. FAX: (0171) 734 8893.

WILLIS WRIGHTSON LONDON LTD.
Willis Wrightson House, Wood Street, Surrey KT1 1UG. Tel:
(0171) 860 6000. Telex: 929606. FAX: (0181) 943 4297.

PRODUCTION EQUIPMENT AND SUPPLIES

ABEKAS COX ELECTRONICS
Hanworth Trading Estate, Feltham TW13 6DH. Tel: (0181) 894 5622. FAX: (0181) 898 0298.

ACMADE INTERNATIONAL
Studio 64, Shepperton Studios, Studios Road, Shepperton, Middlesex, TW17 QD. Tel: (01932) 562 611. FAX: (01932) 568 414.

ADVANCED VIDEO HIRE LTD.
51 The Cut, London, SE1 8LF. Tel: (0171) 928 1963.

ADVENT COMMUNICATIONS LTD.
Watermeadow House, Watermeadow Chesham, Bucks. HP5 1LF. Tel: (01494) 774 400.

AGFA-GEVAERT (MOTION PICTURE DIVISION)
27 Great West Road, Brentford, Middlesex, TW8 9AX. Tel: (0181) 231 4310. FAX: ((0181)) 231 4315.
DIVISIONAL MANAGER
Ken Biggins

AMPEX MEDIA EUROPA
Unit 3, Commerce Park, Brunel Road, Reading, Berks, RG7 4AB. Tel: (01734) 302 208. FAX: (01734) 800 521 773.

AMSTRAD plc
Brentwood House, 169 Kings Road, Brentwood, Essex, CM14 4EF. Tel:(01277) 228888.

ASTON ELECTRONIC DEVELOPMENTS, LTD.
125 Deepcut Bridge Road, Deepcut, Camberley, Surrey. Tel: (01251) 66221.

AUTOCUE LTD.
265 Merton Road, London, SW18 5JS. Tel: (0181) 870 0104. FAX: (0181) 874 3726. Telex: Autocue Telexir 885039 Autocu
G. Sarah Lewis, Mick Gould

AV DISTRIBUTORS (LONDON) LTD.
21 22 St. Albans Place, Upper Street, Islington Green, London N1 0NX. Tel: (0171) 226 1508.

BAL COMPONENTS LTD.
Bermuda Park, Nuneaton, Warwickshire, CV10 7QF. Tel: (01203) 341 111. Telex: 311563.

F. W. O. BAUCH LTD.
49 Theobald Street, Boreham Wood, Herts., WD6 4RZ. Tel: (0181) 953 0091. Telex: 27502. FAX: (0181) 207 5970.

R. R. BEARD LTD.
110 Trafalgar Avenue, London, SE15 6NR. Tel: (0171) 703 3136.

STUART BELL & PARTNERS LTD.
40 Frith Street, London, W1V 5TF. Tel: (0171) 439 2700.

BETTER SOUND LTD.
35 Endell Street, London, WC2. Tel: (0171) 836 0033.

CAMERON VIDEO SYSTEMS LTD.
Burnfield Road, Glasgow G46 7TH, Scotland. Tel: (0141) 633 0077. FAX: (0141) 633 1745.

CANON (UK) LTD.
TV Products Dept., Canon House, 2 Manor Rd., Wallington, Surrey, SM6 0BW. Tel: (0181) 773 3173. FAX: (0181) 773 2851.

CFS EQUIPMENT HIRE LTD.
10 Wadsworth Road, Perivale, Greenford, Middx., UB6 7JX. Tel: (0181) 998 2731. FAX: (0181) 997 8738.

CINESOUND INTERNATIONAL LTD.
Imperial Studios, Maxwell Road, Boreham Wood, Herts., LWD6 1WE. Tel: (0181) 953 5387. FAX: (0181) 207 1728.
DIRECTORS
Mike Rogers
Angela Marshall

CINETECHNIC LTD.
169 Oldfield Lane, Greenford, Middlesex. Tel: (0181) 578 1011. 35 Briardale Gardens, London, NW3 7PN. Tel: (0171) 435 2289.

CINEVIDEO LTD.
7 Silver Road, White City Industrial Park, Wood Lane, London, W12 7SG. Tel: (0181) 743 3839. FAX: (0181) 743 8417. Telex: 915 282 CINEGP G.

DESISTI LIGHTING (UK) LTD.
15 Old Market Street, Thetford, Norfolk IP24 2EQ. Tel: (01842) 752 909. FAX: (01842) 753 746.

DOLBY LABORATORIES INC.
Interface Park, Wootton Bassett, Wiltshire, SN4 8QJ. Tel: (01793) 842 100. FAX: (01793) 842 101.
Catherine Unwin

JOE DUNTON CAMERAS LTD.
Wycombe Road, Wembley, Middlesex, HA0 1QN. Tel: (0181) 903 7933. Telex: 291843.

EDRIC AUDIO VISUAL LTD.
34-36 Oak End Way, Gerrard's Cross, Bucks, SL9 8BR. Tel: (01753) 884 646.

ENGLISH ELECTRIC VALVE COMPANY LTD.
Waterhouse Lane, Chelmsford, Essex. Tel: (01245) 493 493. Telegrams: Enelectico, Chelmsford. Telex: 99103.

FAMILY CHANNEL STUDIOS
Vinters Park, Maidstone, ME14 5NZ. Tel: (01622) 691 111. FAX: (01622) 684 456.

FUJI PHOTO FILM (UK) LTD.
Fuji Film House, 125 Finchley Road, London, NW3 6JH. Tel: (0171) 586 5900. FAX: (0171) 722 4259, Telex: 8812995.
DIVISIONAL MANAGER
E. J. Mould

GE THORN LAMPS LTD.
Miles Road, Mitcham, Surrey CR4 3YX. Tel: (0181) 640 1221. FAX: (0181) 640 9760.

GEC LAMPS & LIGHTING LTD.
P.O. Box 17, East Lane, Wembley, Middlesex HA9 7PG. Tel: (0181) 904 4321.

GTE LIGHTING LTD.
Otley Rd., Charleston, Shipley, West Yorkshire. Tel: (01274) 595 921.

HARKNESS HALL LTD.
Gate Studios, Station Road, Boreham Wood, Herts., WD6 1DQ. Tel: (0181) 953 3611. FAX: (0181) 207 3657.

HAYDEN LABORATORIES LTD.
Hayden House, Chiltem Hill, Chalfont St. Peter, Gerrards Cross, Bucks., SL9 9UG. Tel: (01753) 888 447. FAX: (01753) 880 109.

HENDON STUDIO
2 Victoria Road, London, NW4 2BE. Tel: (0181) 203 4206. FAX: (0181) 203 7377.

HITACHI DENSHI (UK) LTD.
13-14 Garrick Ind. Centre, Irving Way, Hendon, London, NW9 6AZ. Tel: (0181) 202 4311. FAX: (0181) 202 2451.

I.C. EQUIPMENT LTD.
Unit 1 3, The Robert Elliot Center, 1 Old Nichol Street, Shoreditch, London, E2 7HR. Tel: (0171) 739 4800. FAX: (0171) 729 2154.

INTERNATIONAL VIDEO CORPORATION
10 Portman Road, Reading, Berks., RG3 1JR. Tel: (01734) 585 421. Telex: 847579.

ITN LTD.
200 Gray's Inn Road, London, WC1X 8XZ. Tel: (0171) 833 3000. FAX: (0171) 430 4016. Telex: 22101.
CHIEF EXECUTIVE
Stewart Purvis

JVC PROFESSIONAL PRODUCTS (UK) LTD.
Alperton House, Bridgewater Road, Wembley, Middx. HA0 1EG. Tel: (0181) 902 8812. FAX: (0181) 900 0941.

KEM ELECTRONIC LTD.
24 Vivian Avenue, Hendon Central, London, NW4 3XP. Tel: (0181) 202 0244. Telex: 28303.

KODAK LTD.
Professional Motion Imaging, P.O. Box 66, Kodak House, Station Road, Hemel Hempstead, Herts., HP1 1JU. Tel: (01442) 61122. FAX: (01442) 844458.
DIRECTOR & GENERAL MANAGER
John Parsons-Smith
NATIONAL SALES MANAGER
Denis Kelly

LEE COLORTRAN LTD.
Ladbroke Hall, Barlby Rd., London, W10 5HH. Tel: (0181) 968 7000.

LEE FILTERS LTD.
Central Way, Walworth Industrial Estate, Andover, Hants., SP10 5AN. Tel: (01264) 66245. Telex: 477259.

LEE LIGHTING
Wycombe Road, Wembley, Middlesex, HA0 1QD. Tel: (0181) 900 2900. FAX: (0181) 902 5500.

LIGHTHOUSE EDITING SYSTEMS LTD.
38 Soho Square, London, W1V GLE. Tel: (0171) 494 3084. FAX: (0171) 437 3570.

LIMEHOUSE TELEVISION LTD.
The Trocadero, 19 Rupert Street, London, W1V 7FS. Tel: (0171) 287 3333. FAX: (0171) 287 1998.
CONTACT
A. Goddard

MALHAM PHOTOGRAPHIC EQUIPMENT LTD.
65 67 Malham Road, London, SE23 1AJ. Tel: (0181) 699 0917. FAX: (0181) 699 4291.

MARCONI COMMUNICATION SYSTEMS LTD.
Marconi House, Chelmsford, Essex, CM1 1PL. Tel: (01245) 353 221.

MITCHELL CAMERAS
Wycombe Road, Wembley, Middx. HA0 1QN. Tel: (0181) 903 7933. FAX: (0181) 902 3273.

NEILSON-HORDELL LTD.
Unit 18, Central Trading Estate, Staines, Middlesex, TW18 4XE. Tel: (01784) 456 456. FAX: (01784) 459 657.

OPTEX
22 26 Victoria Road, New Barnet, Herts. EN4 9PF. Tel: (0181) 441 2199. FAX: (0181) 449 3646.

OSRAM (GEC) LTD.
P.O. Box 17, East Lane, Wembley, Middlesex HA9 7PG. Tel: (0181) 904 4321.

OTARI ELECTRIC (UK) LTD.
22 Church Road, Slough, Berks, SL1 1PT. Tel: (01753) 822 381. FAX: (01753) 83707.

PANASONIC BROADCAST EUROPE
117-119 Whitby Road, Slough, Berks, SL1 3DR. Tel: (01753) 692 442. FAX: (01753) 512 705.

PANAVISION (UK)
Wycombe Rd., Stonebridge Park, Wembley, Middx. HA0 1QN. Tel: (0181) 903 7933. FAX: (0181) 902 3273.

PHILIPS LIGHTING LTD.
City House, 420 430 London Road, Croydon, Surrey CR9 3QR. Tel: (0181) 689 2166. FAX: (0181) 665 5102.

PHOENIX VIDEO
Unit 4, Denham Way, Maple Cross, Herts., WD3 2AS. Tel: (01923) 777 782. FAX: (01923) 772 163.

PHOTOMEC (LONDON) LTD.
Valley Road Industrial Estate, St. Albans, Herts, AL3 6NU. Tel: (01727) 501 711. FAX: (01727) 43991.

RADAMEC EPO LTD.
Bridge Road, Chertsey, Surrey, KT16 8LJ. Tel: (01932) 561 181. FAX: (01932) 568 775. Telex: 929945 RADEPOG.

RANK CINTEL
Watton Road, Ware, Herts, SG12 0AE. Tel: (01895) 463 939. Telex: 81415. FAX: (01895) 460 803.
MANAGING DIRECTOR
Jack R. Brittain

RANK TAYLOR HOBSON LTD.
P.O. Box 36, 2 New Star Road, Leicester, LE4 7JQ. Tel: (01533) 763 771. Telex: 342338. Cables: Metrology Lestr. FAX: (01533) 740167.
MANAGING DIRECTOR
Richard Freeman

PHILIP RIGBY & SONS LTD.
14 Creighton Avenue, Muswell Hill, London, N10 1NU. Tel: (0181) 883 3703. FAX: (0181) 444 3620.

RONFORD-BAKER
Braziers, Oxhey Lane, Watford, Herts., WD1 4RJ. Tel: (0181) 428 5941. FAX: (0181) 428 4743.

RONFORD LTD.
Shepperton Film Studios, P. O. 30, Studio Road, Shepperton, Middx. TW17 0QD. Tel: (01932) 564 111. FAX: (01932) 561 423.

SAMUELSON FILM SERVICE LONDON LTD.
21 Derby Road, Metropolitan Centre, Greenford, Middx., UB6 8UQ. Tel: (0181) 578 7887. FAX: (0181) 578 2733.

MICHAEL SAMUELSON LIGHTING LTD.
Pinewood Studios, Iver Heath, Bucks. SL0 0NH. Tel: (01753) 631 133. FAX: (01753) 630 485.

SET PARTNERS
13 D'Arblay Street, London, W1V 3FP. Tel: (0171) 734 1067. FAX: (0171) 494 0197.

SHURE ELECTRONICS LTD.
Eccleston Rd., Maidstone, Kent, ME15 6AU. Tel: (01622) 59881.

SIGMA FILM EQUIPMENT LTD.
Unit K, Chantry Lane, Industrial Estate, Storrington, West Sussex, RH20 4AD. Tel: (019066) 3382.

SONY BROADCAST LTD.
Jay Close, Viables, Basingstoke, Hants, RG22 4SB. Tel: (01256) 474 011. FAX: (01256) 474 585.

SOHO IMAGES GROUP LTD.
8-14 Meard Street, London, W1V 3HR. Tel: (0171) 437 0831. FAX: (0171) 734 9471.
MANAGING DIRECTOR
Ray Adams

STRAND LIGHTING
Grant Way, Off Syon Lane, Isleworth, Middx. TW9 5QD. Tel: (0181) 560 3171. FAX: (0181) 490 0002.

SYSTEM VIDEO LTD.
Venture House, Davis Rd., Chessington, Surrey KT9 1TT. Tel: (0181) 391 5678. FAX: (0181) 391 5522.

TECHNOVISION CAMERAS LTD.
Unit 4, St. Margaret's Business Centre, Drummond Place, Twickenham, Middlesex, TW1 1JN. Tel: (0181) 891 5961. Telex: 917408 TECNOV G. FAX: (0181) 744 1154.

VARIAN TUT LTD.
P.O. Box 41, Coldhams Lane, Cambridge, CB1 3JU. Tel: (01223) 245 115. Telex: 81342. VARTUT G.. FAX: (01223) 214 632.

VIDEO TIME
22/24 Greek Street, London, W1V 5LG. Tel: (0171) 439 1211. Telex: 27256. FAX: (0171) 439 7336.

VIEWPLAN
1 Syon Gateway, Great West Road, Brentford, Middx., TW8 9DD. Tel: (0181) 847 5771.

VINTEN BROADCAST
Western Way, Bury St. Edmunds, Suffolk, IP33 3TB. Tel: (01284) 752 121. Telex: 81176 VINTEN G. FAX: (01284) 750 560.

WESTAR SALES & SERVICES LTD.
Unit 7, Cowley Mill Trading Estate, Longbridge Way, Uxbridge, Middx., UB8 2YG. Tel: (01895) 34429. Telex: 8954169.

WOTAN LAMPS LTD.
1 Gresham Way, Durnsford Road, London, SW19 8HU. Tel: (0181) 947 1261. FAX: (0181) 947 5132.

ZONAL LTD.
Holmethorpe Avenue, Redhill, Surrey, RH1 2NX. Tel: (01737) 767 171. FAX: (01737) 767 610.

PRODUCTION FACILITIES AND SERVICES

CENTRAL TELEVISION FACILITIES
Central House Broad Street, Birmingham, B1 2JP. Tel: (0121) 643 9898. FAX: (0121) 633 4473.

CHERRILL, ROGER LTD.
65-66 Dean Street, London, W1V 6PL. Tel: (0171) 437 7972. FAX: (0171) 437 6411.

CINEBUILD LTD.
1 Wheatsheaf Hall, Wheatsheaf Lane, London SW8. Tel: (0171) 582 8750.

CINEVIDEO LTD.
7 Silver Road, White City Industrial Park, Wood Lane, London, W12 7SG. Tel: (0181) 743 3839. Telex: 915 282 CINEGP G. FAX: (0181) 749 3501.

NIKKI CLAPP
18 Cresswell Road, East Twickenham, Middx., TW1 2DZ. Tel: (0181) 891 0054.

COMBINED PRINTS & PRODUCTION SERVICE LTD.
65-66 Dean Street, London, W1V 5HD. Tel: (0171) 437 7972. FAX: (0171) 437 6411.

COMPLETE VIDEO
3 Slingsby Place, London, WC2E 9AB. Tel: (0171) 379 7739.

COMPONENT GROUP
1 Newman Passage, London, W1P 3PF. Tel: (0171) 631 4400. FAX: (0171) 580 2890.

CROW FILM & TV SERVICES LTD.
12 Wendell Road, London, W12 9RT. Tel: (0181) 749 6171. FAX: (0181) 740 0785.

DIGITAL FILM
5 D'Arblay Street, London, W1V 3FD. Tel: (0171) 434 3100. FAX: (0171) 287 3191.
CONTACT
Matthew Holben

EDINBURGH FILM & TV STUDIOS
Nine Mile Burn, by Penicuik, Midlothian, EH 26 9LT. Tel: (01968) 72131.

THE FRAME SHOP
33 Great Pulteney Street, London, W1R 3DE. Tel: (0171) 439 1267. FAX: (0171) 439 0129.

FRONTLINE TELEVISION SERVICES
44 Earlham Street Covent Garden, London, WC2H 9LA. Tel: (0171) 836 0411. FAX: (0171) 379 5210.

FOUNTAIN TELEVISION
Cocks Crescent, New Malden, Surrey, KT3 4TA. Tel: (0181) 942 6633. FAX: (0181) 949 7911.

CHARLES H. FOX LTD.
22 Tavistock Street, Covent Garden, London WC2E 7PY. Tel. (0171) 240 3111.

GENERAL SCREEN ENTERPRISES
Highbridge Estate, Oxford Road, Uxbridge, Middlesex, UB8 1LX. Tel: (01895) 231 931. FAX: (01895) 235 335.

HAMLET TELEVISION LTD.
28 Denmark Street, London, WC2H 8NJ. Tel: (0171) 240 9(0181). FAX: (0171) 836 5358.

INFOVISION LTD.
Bradley Close, White Lion Street, London, N1 9PN. Tel: (0171) 837 0012. Telex: 299800 ACTION.

LWT PRODUCTION FACILITIES
South Bank TV Centre, London, SE1 9LT. Tel: (0171) 261 3683. Telex: 91823.

LEGEND TELEVISION
Pinewood Studios, Pinewood Road, Iver Heath, Bucks SL0 0NH. Tel: (01753) 656 027. FAX: (01753) 656 028.

LIMEHOUSE TELEVISION LTD.
The Trocadero, 19 Rupert Street, London, W1V 7FS. Tel: (0171) 287 3333. FAX: (0171) 287 1998.
CONTACT
A. Goddard

LOUIS ELMAN + LEAH INTERNATIONAL PRODUCTIONS LTD.
Denham Studios, Denham, Nr. Uxbridge, Middlesex. Tel: (01895) 833 036, 853 522. Telex: 934704.

METRO VIDEO
The Old Bacon Factory, 57-59 Great Suffolk Street, London, SE1 0BS. Tel: (0171) 929 2088.

MOLINARE
34 Fouberts Place, London, W1V 2BH. Tel: (0171) 439 2244. FAX: (0171) 734 6813. Telex: 299200 MOLI G.

NORWOOD STUDIOS LTD.
147 Victoria Road, Leeds, LS6 1DU. Tel: (01532) 787 539.

OASIS TELEVISION LTD.
76a Wardour Street, London, W1V 3LF. Tel: (0171) 434 4133. FAX: (0171) 494 2843.

ONE INCH VIDEO COMPANY
11/13 Neal's Yard, Covent Garden, London, WC2H 9LZ. Tel: (0171) 831 1900. FAX: (0171) 836 0914. Telex: 22125 VIDEO G.

PMPP FACILITIES
69 Dean Street (Entrance Meard Street), London, W1V 5HB. Tel: (0171) 437 0979.

PEERLESS CAMERA CO.
15 Neals Yard, London, WC2H 9DP. Tel: (0171) 836 3367.

PRATER AUDIO VISUAL LTD.
7A College Approach, Greenwich, London, SE10 9HY. Tel: (0181) 858 8939. FAX: (0181) 305 1537.

RANK VIDEO SERVICES LTD.
Phoenix Park, Great West Road, Brentford, Middlesex, TW8 9PL. Tel: (0181) 568 4311. Telex: 22345. FAX: (0181) 847 4032.
MANAGING DIRECTOR
Peter Pacitt

REUTERS TELEVISION LTD.
40 Cumberland Avenue, London, NW10 7EN. Tel: (0181) 965 7733. FAX: (0181) 965 0620.
DIRECTOR
Enrique Jara

RUSHES
66 Old Compton Street, London, W1V 5PH. Tel: (0171) 437 8676. FAX: (0171) 734 2519.

SAMUELSON COMMUNICATIONS BROADCAST
Unit 20, Fairway Drive, Fairway Industrial Estate, Greenford, Middx., UB6 8PW. Tel: (0181) 566 6444. FAX: (0181) 566 6365.

SET PARTNERS
13 D'Arblay Street, London, W1V 3FP. Tel: (0171) 734 1067.

SOLUS ENTERPRISES
35 Marshall Street, London, W1V 1LL. Tel: (0171) 734 0645 and (0171) 734 3384/5.

SPITFIRE TELEVISION PLC
19 Hatton Street, London, NW8 8PR. Tel: (0171) 724 7544. FAX: (0171) 724 2058.

SVC TELEVISION
142 Wardour Street, London, W1V 5PH. Tel: (0171) 734 1600. FAX: (0171) 437 1854.

TABS
63 Stirling Ct., Marshall St., London W.1. Tel: (0171) 734 3356.
CONTACT
Janet Easton

TELEVISUAL LTD.
58 Kew Road, Richmond, Surrey, TW9 2PQ. Tel: (0181) 940 1155.

THAMES TELEVISION PLC
Broon Road, Teddington Lock, Teddington, Middx. TW11 9NT. Tel: (0181) 614 2800.

VIDEO EUROPE
31 Ransome's Dock, Parkgate Road, Battersea, London, SW11 4NP. Tel: (0171) 585 0555.

VIDEO ROOM
155-157 Oxford Street, London, W1R 1TB. Tel: (0171) 434 0724.

WEST 1 TELEVISION
10 Bateman Street, London, W1V 5TT. Tel: (0171) 437 5533. FAX: (0171) 287 8621.

WSTV PRODUCTION LTD.
159-163 Great Portland Street, London, W1N 5FD. Tel: (0171) 580 5896.

Sound Services

ABBEY ROAD STUDIOS
3 Abbey Rd., St. John's Wood, London NW8 9AY. Tel: (0171) 266 7000. FAX: (0171) 266 7250.

ADMUSIC
Shepperton Studios, Studio No. 94, Studios Rd., Shepperton, Middlesex TW17 0QD. Tel: (01932) 572 266. FAX: (01932) 572 265.

ANVIL FILM & RECORDING GROUP LTD.
Denham Studios, North Orbital Rd., Denham, Nr. Uxbridge, Middlesex UB9 5HL. Tel: (01895) 833 522. FAX: (01895) 835 006.
CONTACT
Ken Somerville, Alan Snelling

APS LTD.
4 Lapwing Lane, West Didsbury, Manchester M20 8WS. Tel: (0161) 448 9990. FAX: (0161) 448 2023.

BACKYARD RECORDING STUDIOS
Units 405, Willowbrook Industrial Estate, Crickhowell Rd., St. Mellons, Cardiff. Tel: (01222) 777 739. FAX: (01222) 798 901.

BOUNDARY ROW STUDIOS
1-7 Boundary Row, London SE1 8HP. Tel: (0171) 633 9629. FAX: (0171) 928 6082.

CINELINGUAL SOUND STUDIOS
27-29 Berwick St., London W1V 3RF. Tel: (0171) 437 0136. FAX: (0171) 439 2012.

CTS STUDIOS LTD.
Engineers Way, Wembley, Middlesex HA9 0DR. Tel: (0181) 903 4611. FAX: (0181) 903 7130.

D B POST PRODUCTIONS LTD.
1-8 Batemans Buildings, South Soho Square, London W1V 5TW. Tel: (0171) 434 0097. FAX: (0171) 287 9143.

DE LANE LEA SOUND CENTRE LTD.
75 Dean St., London W1V 5HA. Tel: (0171) 439 1721. FAX: (0171) 437 0913.

DELTA SOUND SERVICES
Shepperton Studios, Studios Rd., Shepperton, Middlesex TW17 0QD. Tel: (01932) 562 045. FAX: (01932) 572 396.

THE DIGITAL AUDIO COMPANY
3 Carleton Business Park, Carleton New Rd., Skipton, N. Yorkshire BD23 2AA. Tel: (01756) 797 100. FAX: (01756) 797 101.

DIGITAL SOUND HOUSE
14 Livonia St., London W1V 3PH. Tel: (0171) 434 2928. FAX: (0171) 287 9110.

THE FACILITY
Ravenhill Business Park, Ravenhill Rd., Belfast BT6 8AW. Tel: (01232) 450 231. FAX: (01232) 459 499.

FLAMINGO PRODUCTIONS
25-26 Poland St., London W1V 3DB. Tel: (0171) 437 2243. FAX: (0171) 437 0410.

FOUNTAIN TELEVISION LTD.
Cocks Crescent, New Malden, Surrey KT3 4TA. Tel: (0181) 942 6633. FAX: (0181) 949 7911.

G WHIZ TELEPRODUCTION
22 Chervil Way, Burghfield Common, Reading Berks RG7 3YX. Tel: (01734) 832 232. FAX: (01734) 831 295.

GATEWAY AUDIO VISUAL & VIDEO
472 Green Lanes, Palmers Green, London N13 5XF. Tel: (0181) 872 054. FAX: (0181) 882 4131.

GWBB AUDIOVISION
2 Silver Rd., White City, London W12 7SG. Tel: (0181) 746 2000. FAX (0181) 746 0180

INDUSTRIAL ACOUSTICS CO. LTD. (STUDIO DIVISION)
IAC House, Moorside Road, Winchester SO23 7US TW18 4XB. Tel: (01962) 873 000. FAX: (01962) 873 111

INHOUSE PRODUCTIONS LTD.
3rd floor, Canada House, Chepstow St., Manchester M1 6FQ. Tel: (0161) 228 0366. Fax: (0161) 236 3056.

LANSDOWNE MUSIC PUBLISHING LTD.
Lansdowne House, Lansdowne Rd., London W11 3LP. Tel: (0171) 727 0041. FAX: (0171) 792 8904.

MAGMASTERS POST PRODUCTIONS
20 St. Annes Court, London W1V 3AW. Tel: (0171) 437 8273. FAX: (0171) 494 1281.

MATINEE SOUND & VISION
132 Oxford St., Reading, Berks RG1 7NL. Tel: (0118) 958 4934. FAX: (0118) 959 4936.

NINTH WAVE AUDIO
PO Box 5517 Birmingham B13 8QB. Tel: (0121) 442 2276. FAX: (0121) 689 1902.

PERFECT PITCH
The Studio, 39 Landser Rd., London N19 4JU. Tel: (0171) 272 9456.

PINEWOOD SOUND DEPARTMENT
Pinewood Studios, Pinewood Rd., Iver, Bucks SL0 0NH. Tel: (01753) 656 301. FAX: (01753) 656 014.

RED BUS RECORDING & VIDEO STUDIOS LTD (BROADLEY ENTERTAIMNMENT GROUP LTD.).
Broadley House, 48 Broadley Terrace, London NW1 6UL. Tel: (0171) 258 0324. FAX: (0171) 724 2361.

THE SOUND COMPANY LTD.
23 Gosfield St., London W1P 7HP. Tel: (0171) 580 5880. FAX: (0171) 580 6454.

THE SOUND DESIGNERS
11 Wardour Mews., London W1V 3FF. Tel: (0171) 437 7161. FAX: (0171) 437 3667.

THE SOUND HOUSE SCOTLAND
Forth House, Forth St., Edinburgh EH1 3LF. Tel: (0131) 557 1557. FAX: (0131) 557 3899. email: lorna@thesoundhouse.com

THE SOUND STUDIO LTD.
17 St. Annes Court, London W1V 3AW. Tel/FAX: (0171) 734 6198.

THE SOUNDHOUSE LTD.
Unit 11, Goldhawk Industrial Estate, 2A Brackenbury Rd., Shepherds Bush, London W6 0BA. Tel: (0181) 743 2677. FAX: (0181) 740 9122.

STEREO FILM SOUND
3 Sterndale Rd., London W14 0HT. Tel: (0171) 603 7401. FAX: (0171) 359 4027. email: Johnl@alchemea.demon.co.uk

STUDIO SOUND (PART OF IBF)
15 Monmouth Street, London WC2H 9DA. Tel: (0171) 497 1515. FAX: (0171) 379 8562

SYNCHRO SONICS LTD.
5 Richmond Mews, Richmond Building, London W1V 5AG. Tel: (0171) 437 3361. FAX: (0171) 437 0913.

TARAN STUDIOS
Cardiff Workshops, Lews Rd., Cardiff CF1 5EJ. Tel: (01222) 484 298. Fax: (01222) 451 200.

UNIVERSAL SOUND
16 Aintree Rd., Perivale, Middlesex UB6 7LA. Tel: (0181) 998 1619. FAX: (0181) 991 9461.

VIDEOLONDON SOUNDSTUDIOS
16-18 Ramillies St., London W1V 1DL. Tel: (0171) 734 4811. FAX: (0171) 494 2553. email: info@videolon.ftech.co.uk

VIDEOSONICS LTD.
13 Hawley Crescent, London NW1 8NP. Tel: (0171) 482 2855. FAX: (0171) 482 0849.

WARWICK DUBBING THEATRE
111 A Wardour St., London W1V 3TD. Tel: (0171) 437 5532. FAX: (0171) 439 0372.

WILD TRACKS AUDIO STUDIOS LTD.
2nd floor, 55 Greek St., London W1V 5LR. Tel: (0171) 734 6331. FAX: (0171) 734 6195.

YORKSHIRE TYNE TEES TELEVISION
The Television Centre, Leeds LS3 1JS. Tel: (0113) 234 1293.
CONTACT
John Surtees

ZIPPER MOBILE STUDIO
272 Cricklewood Lane, Cricklewood, London NW2. 2PU. Tel/FAX: (0181) 450 4130.

Special Effects

AARDMAN ANIMATIONS LTD.
Gas Ferry Rd., Bristol, Avon BS1 6UN. Tel: (0117) 984 8485.
FAX: (0117) 984 8486.

ALBATROSS MODELS, SETS, EFFECTS
Unit 2, Beckett's Wharf, Lower Teddington Rd., Hampton Wick, Kingston-upon-Thames, Surrey KT1 4ER. Tel: (0181) 943 4720. FAX: (0181) 977 0854.

ANIMATED EXTRAS
Buiding 13/24a, Shepperton Film Studios, Studios Rd., Shepperton, Middlesex TW17 0QD. Tel: (01932) 562 611, ext. 2347. FAX: (01932) 569 605.

ANY EFFECTS
64 Weir Rd., London SW19 8UG. Tel :(0181) 944 0099. FAX: (0181) 944 6989.

ARTEM VISUAL EFFECTS
Perivale Industrial Park, Horsenden Lane, South Perivale, Middlesex UB6 7RH. Tel: (0181) 997 7771. FAX: (0181) 997 1503.

CINE IMAGE FILM OPTICALS
7A Langley St., Covent Garden, London WC2H 9JA. Tel: (0171) 240 6222. FAX: (0171) 240 6242.

CHRIS CORBOULD
Rustling, 4 Tudor Close, Great Bookham, Surrey, KT23 3DP
Tel/FAX:01372 454088

CRAWLEY CREATURES
The Lime Studio, East St., Fritwell, Oxon OX6 9QF. Tel: (01869) 345 208. FAX: (01869) 345 639.

DIGITAL ARTS LTD.
39 Beak Street London W1R 3LD. Tel: (0171) 439 0919. FAX: (0171) 437 1146.
CONTACT
Graham Brown-Martin

THE DEFINITIVE SPECIAL PROJECTS LTD
P. O. Box 169 Stevenage SG2 7SG Tel: 01438 869 005 FAX: (01438) 869 006

EFFECTS ASSOCIATES LTD.
Pinewood Studios, Pinewood Rd., Iver Heath, Bucks SL0 0NH. Tel: (01753) 652 007. FAX: (01753) 630 127.
CONTACTS
Martin Gutteridge, Elaine Wishart

ELECTRIC IMAGE
7-11 Lexington St., London W1R 3HQ. Tel: (0171) 287 8800. FAX: (0171) 287 3750.

ENTERPRISES UNLIMITED SPECIAL EFFECTS
Unit 6, Cowbridge Business Park, Cowbridge, Boston, Lincs PE22 7DJ. Tel: (01205) 310 440. FAX: (01205) 310 450.

GENERAL SCREEN ENTERPRISES
Denham Media Park North Orbital Road Denham, Middlesex UB9 5HG. Tel: (01895) 831931. FAX: (01895) 835338.

DAVID HARRIS SPECIAL EFFECTS
Shepperton Studios, Studios Rd., Shepperton, Middlesex TW17 0QD. Tel: (01932) 562 611, ext. 2378. FAX: (01932) 572 377.

IMAGE ANIMATION
Pinewood Studios, Pinewood Rd., Iver, Bucks SL0 0NH. Tel: (01753) 656 962. FAX: (01753) 630 394.

LASER CREATIONS INTERNATIONAL LTD.
55 Merthyr Terrace, Barnes, London SW13 9DL. Tel: (0181) 741 5747. FAX: (0181) 748 9879.

LIQUID IMAGE
1 Park Circus, Charing Cross, Glasgow, G3 6AX Tel: 0141 353 2455 FAX: 0141 353 2466

LYONS MODEL EFFECTS
85 Bell Barn Rd., Stoke Bishop, Bristol BS9 2DF. Tel: (0117) 987 3699. FAX: (0117) 987 3698.

THE MAGIC CAMERA COMPANY LTD.
Box 42, Shepperton Studios, Studios Rd., Shepperton, Middlesex TW17 0QD. Tel: (01932) 572 424. FAX: (01932) 568 944.

OPTICAL FILM EFFECTS
Pinewood Studios, Pinewood Rd., Iver, Bucks SL0 0NH. Tel: (01753) 655 486. FAX: (01753) 656 844.

OTTER EFFECTS
Pinewood Film studios, Pinewood Rd., Iver, Bucks SL0 0NH. Tel: (01753) 656 430. FAX: (01753) 656 844.

OXFORD SCIENTIFIC FILMS LTD.
Lower Rd, Long Hanborough, Oxford OX8 8LL. Tel: (01993) 881 881. FAX: (01993) 882 808.

PERDIX FIREARMS LTD.
P.O. Box 1670 Sasbury SP4 6QL, Avon BA2 4RL. Tel: (01722) 782 402. FAX: (01722) 782 790

QUANTEL LTD.
Turnpike Rd., Newbury, Berkshire RG14 2NE. Tel: (01635) 48222. FAX: (01635) 31776.

BRYAN SMITHIES SPECIAL EFFECTS
No 1Lyne Close Cottages, Lyne Close, Virginia Water Surrey GU25 4EA. Tel: (01344) 843 251. FAX: (01344) 843 337

SNOW BUSINESS
56 Northfield Road, Tetbury, Gloucestershire, GL8 8HQ
Tel/FAX: 01666 502 857

UNDIVIDED LTD/KIT WEST PRODUCTIONS
12 Gilpin Ave., East Sheen, London SW14 8QY. Tel: (0181) 878 6745. FAX: (0181) 392 2948.

IAN WINGROVE
Park House, Wash Hill, Woburn Green, Bucks HP10 0JA. Tel/FAX: (016285) 21356.

STUDIO FACILITIES

ARDMORE STUDIOS LTD.
Herbert Road, Bray, Co. Wicklow, Ireland. Tel: (0404) 416 2971.
Telex: 91504 PATT E1. FAX: (0404) 416 1894.

BRAY STUDIOS
Windsor Road, Windsor, Berks SL4. Tel: (01628) 22111. FAX:
(01628) 770 381.

CAPITAL GROUP STUDIOS
13 Wandsworth Plain, London, SW18 1ET. Tel: (0181) 874
0131. FAX: (0181) 871 9737.

CENTRAL TELEVISION STUDIOS
Lenton Lane, Nottingham NG7 2NA. Tel: (01602) 863 322.
FAX: (01602) 435 142.

EALING STUDIOS
Ealing Green, Ealing, London, W5 5EP. Tel: (0181) 567 6655.

FOUNTAIN TELEVISION
128 Wembley Park Drive, Wembley, Middlesex HA9 8HQ. Tel:
(0181) 900 1188. FAX: (0181) 900 2860.

HAMPDEN GURNEY STUDIOS LTD.
39/41 Hanover Steps, St. George's Fields, Albion Street,
London, W2 2YG. Tel: (0171) 402 7543. FAX: (0171) 262 5736.

HILLSIDE STUDIOS
Merry Hill Road, Bushey, Watford WD2 1DR. Tel: (0181) 950
7919. FAX: (0181) 950 1437.

LIMEHOUSE STUDIOS
The Trocadero, 19 Rupert Street, London, W1V 7FS. Tel:
(0171) 287 3333. FAX: (0171) 287 1998.

THE LONDON STUDIOS
The London Television Centre, Upper Ground, London SE1
9LT. Tel: (0171) 737 8888. FAX: (0171) 928 8405.

PARAMOUNT CITY TV THEATRE
Great Windmill St., London, W1V 7PH. Tel: (0171) 722 8111.

PINEWOOD STUDIOS
Pinewood Rd., Iver Bucks., SL0 0NH. Tel: (01753) 651 700. FAX:
(01753) 656 844.
MANAGING DIRECTOR
Steve Jaggs

PROSPECT STUDIOS LTD.
High Street, Barnes, London, S.W.13. Tel: (0181) 876 6284.

REEL TV STUDIOS
19 Derry's Cross, Plymouth, PL1 2SP. Tel: (01752) 255 529.
FAX: (01752) 255 531.
Tim Watson

SHEPPERTON STUDIOS
Studios Road, Shepperton, Middlesex, TW17 0QD. Tel: (01932)
562 611. FAX: (01932) 568 989.

TEDDINGTON STUDIOS
Broom Road, Teddington Lock, Middx., TW11 9NT. Tel: (0181)
977 3252. FAX: (0181) 943 4050.

TWICKENHAM
St. Margaret's, Twickenham, Middlesex, TW1 2AW. Tel: (0181)
892 4477. FAX: (0181) 891 0168.

WORLD WIDE GROUP
21-25 St. Anne's Court, London, W1V 3AW. Tel: (0171) 434
1121. FAX: (0171) 734 0619.

BRITISH TRADE ORGANISATIONS AND GOVERNMENT UNITS

THE ADVERTISING ASSOCIATION
(The Advertising Association is the federated organisation representing the shared advertising interests of advertisers, agencies and
the media. It is the central spokesman for the UK advertising business at national and international levels, and as such, maintains a
continuing programme of research and information retrieval. It is
responsible for the collection and dissemination of the UK statistics
on advertising expenditure, and runs an annual programme of seminars and courses for people in the communications business.)
Abford House, 15 Wilton Road, London SW1V 1NJ. Tel:
(0171) 828 2771. FAX: (0171) 931 0376.
DIRECTOR GENERAL
Andrew Brown

**ADVERTISING FILM & VIDEOTAPE PRODUCERS
ASSOCATION (AFVPA)**
26 Noel Street, London W1V 3RD. Tel: (0171) 434 2654.
FAX: (0171) 434 9002.
CHIEF EXECUTIVE
Cecilia Garnett

THE ADVERTISING STANDARDS AUTHORITY
Brook House, 2-16 Torrington Place, London, WC1E 7HN.
Tel: (0171) 580 5555. FAX: (0171) 631 3051.

AMALGAMATED ENGINEERING & ELECTRICAL UNION
(The Union represents electrical lighting operatives engaged
in production.)
Hayes Court, West Common Road, Bromley, BR2 7AU. Tel:
(0181) 462 7755. FAX: (0181) 462 4959.

ARTS COUNCIL OF ENGLAND
14 Great Peter Street, London, SW1P 3NQ. Tel: (0171) 333
0100. FAX: (0171) 973 6590.
CONTACT
Rodney Wilson

**ASSOCIATION OF PROFESSIONAL RECORDING
SERVICES LTD.**
2 Windsor Square, Silver Street, Reading, Berks. RG1 2TH. Tel:
(0118) 975 6218. FAX: (0118) 975 6216.
CHIEF EXECUTIVE
Philip Vaughan

ASSOCIATION OF PROFESSIONAL VIDEO DEALERS LTD.
P.O. Box 25, Godalming, Surrey, GU7 1PL. Tel: (014868) 23429.
DIRECTOR & SECRETARY
Charles Potter, M.B.E.

AUSTRALIAN FILM COMMISSION
2nd Floor, Victory House, 99 101 Regent Street, London, W1R
7HB. Tel: (0171) 734 9383. FAX: (0171) 434 0170.
CONTACT
Pressanna Vasudevan

BRITISH ACADEMY OF FILM AND TELEVISION ARTS
(The British Academy of Film and Television Arts exists in order
to promote, improve and advance original and creative work
amongst people engaged in film and television production.)
195 Piccadilly, London, W1V 0LN. Tel: (0171) 734 0022. FAX:
(0171) 734 1792.
PRESIDENT
H.R.H. The Princess Royal
VICE PRESIDENT
David Puttnam, C.B.E.
CHAIRMAN
Tim Angel

BRITISH ACTORS' EQUITY ASSOCIATION
(Incorporating the Variety Artistes Fed.), Guild House, Upper
St. Martins Lane, London, WC2H 9EG. Tel: (0171) 379 6000.
FAX: (0171) 379 7001.
GENERAL SECRETARY
Ian McGarry

BRITISH BOARD OF FILM CLASSIFICATION
3 Soho Square, London, W1V 5DE. Tel: (0171) 439 7961. FAX:
(0171) 287 0141.
DIRECTOR
James Ferman

BRITISH FILM COMMISSION
70 Baker Street, London, W1M 1DJ. Tel: (0171) 224 5000. FAX:
(0171) 224 1013.
COMMISSIONER
Steve Morris

BRITISH COUNCIL
Events Section, Films, Television and Video Department, 11 Portland Place, London, W1N 4EJ. Tel: (0171) 389 3063. Telex: 8952201 BRICON G. FAX: (0171) 389 3041.

BRITISH FILM DESIGNERS GUILD
9 Elgin Mews South, London, W9 1JZ. Tel: (0171) 286 6716. FAX: (0171) 286 6716.
EXECUTIVE CONSULTANT
John French

BRITISH FILM INSTITUTE
(The BFI exists to encourage the development of film, television and video in the UK and to promote knowledge, understanding and enjoyment of the culture of the moving image. The Board of Governors is appointed by the Minister for National Heritage. Two are selected by a poll of the membership. The BFI's divisions include BFI South Bank (National Film Theatre Museum of the Moving Image), and London Film Festival Research, Exhibition & Distribution, the National Film Archive, Publishing including Sight & Sound, Library and Information Services, Planning and Production.)
21 Stephen Street, London, W1P 1PL. Tel: (0171) 255 1444. Telex: 27624 BFILDNG. FAX: (0171) 436 7950.
CHAIRMAN
Alan Parker

BRITISH INDEPENDENT TELEVISION ENTERPRISES
London Television Centre, Upper Ground, London SE1 9LT. Tel: (0171) 737 8603. FAX: (0171) 261 8162.
MANAGING DIRECTOR
Nadine Nohr

BRITISH KINEMATOGRAPH SOUND AND TELEVISION SOCIETY
(Founded in 1931, the Society was incorporated in 1946 to service the industries of its title, encouraging technical and scientific progress. To further these aims, the Society disseminates to its Members information on technical developments within these industries, arranges technical lectures, international conferences, and demonstrations, and encourages the exchange of ideas. The broad nature of its purpose is made possible by the subscriptions of its members and by its freedom from political or commercial bias. The BKSTS Journal, Image Technology, is published and sent free to all members.)
63-71 Victoria House, Vernon Place, London, WC1B 4DF. Tel: (0171) 242 8400. FAX: (0171) 405 3560.
EXECUTIVE DIRECTOR
Anne Fenton

BRITISH MUSIC INFORMATION CENTRE
(Reference library of works by 20th Century British composers.)
10 Stratford Place, London, W1N 9AE. Tel: (0171) 499 8567. FAX: (0171) 499 4795.

THE BRITISH RADIO AND ELECTRONIC EQUIPMENT MANUFACTURERS' ASSOCIATION
Landseer House, 19 Charing Cross Road, London, WC2H 0ES. Tel: (0171) 930 3206. Telex: 296215 BREMA G.
DIRECTOR
H. Peltor.
SECRETARY
H. H. Skinner.

BRITISH SOCIETY OF CINEMATOGRAPHERS LTD.
(To promote and encourage the pursuit of the highest standards in the craft of motion picture photography.)
Tree Tops, 11 Croft Road, Chalfont St. Peter, Gerrards Cross, Bucks., SL9 9AE. Tel: (01753) 888 052. FAX: (01753) 891 486.
SECRETARY & TREASURER
Frances Russell

BRITISH VIDEO ASSOCIATION LTD.
167 Great Portland Street, London, W1M 5FD. Tel: (0171) 436 0041. FAX: (0171) 436 0043.
DIRECTOR GENERAL
Mrs. Lavinia Carey
BROADCAST ADVERTISNG CLEARANCE CENTRE
200 Gray's Inn Rd., London WC1X 8HF. Tel: (0171) 843 8265. FAX: (0171) 923 5484.
HEAD OF CLEARANCE
Uisdean Macclean

BROADCASTERS AUDIENCE RESEARCH BOARD LTD.
Glenthorne House, Hammersmith Grove, London W6 0ND. Tel: (0181) 741 9110. FAX: (0181) 741 1943.

BROADCASTING ENTERTAINMENT CINEMATOGRAPH AND THEATRE UNION
111 Wardour Street, London, W1V 4AY. Tel: (0171) 437 8506. FAX: (0171) 437 8268.
GENERAL SECRETARY
Roger Bolton

BROADCASTING STANDARDS COUNCIL
7 The Sanctuary, London, SW1P 3JS. Tel: (0171) 233 0544. FAX: (0171) 233 0397.
CHAIRMAN
The Lady Howe

CABLE COMMUNICATIONS ASSOCIATION
(The Cable Communications Association is the trade body representing the interests of companies with an interest in the provision of cable communications in the United Kingdom.
Fifth Floor, Artillery House, Artillery Row, London, SW1P 1RT. Tel: (0171) 222 2900. FAX: (0171) 799 1471.
CHIEF EXECUTIVE
Bob Frost

CENTRAL CASTING LTD.
(Licensed annually by the Dept. of Employment.)
162-170 Wardour Street, London, W1V 3AT. Tel: (0171) 437 1881. FAX: (0171) 437 2614.
MANAGING DIRECTOR
B. T. Yeoman

CHILDREN'S FILM & TELEVISION FOUNDATION LTD.
Elstree Studios, Boreham Wood, Herts., WD6 1JG. Tel: (0181) 953 0844. FAX: (0181) 207 0860.
CHIEF EXECUTIVE
Stanley T. Taylor

CINEMA AND TELEVISION BENEVOLENT FUND
(The Fund gives relief by financial grants and allowances to needy members or ex-members of the film industry or independent TV, and their widows. Convalescence is available to assist in recovery after illness or operations at "Glebelands," Wokingham, Berks.)
22 Golden Square, London, WIR 4AD. Tel: (0171) 437 6567. FAX: (0171) 437 7186.
EXECUTIVE DIRECTOR
S. D. Hunsley.
APPEALS & P.R. OFFICER
Sandra Bradley

CINEMA AND TELEVISION VETERANS
166 The Rocks Road, East Malling, Kent, ME19 6AX. Tel: (01732) 843 291.
PRESIDENT
Roger Bennett
SECRETARY
K. M. Morgan

COMPOSERS' GUILD OF GREAT BRITAIN
34 Hanway Street, London, W1P 9DE. Tel: (0171) 436 0007. FAX: (0171) 436 1913.
GENERAL SECRETARY
Heather Rosenblatt

DEPARTMENT FOR CULTURE MEDIA AND SPORT
Room 203, 2-4 Cockspur Street, London, SW1Y 5DH. Tel: (0171) 211 6000. FAX: (0171) 211 6249.
CONTACT
Diana Brown

DIRECTORS GUILD OF GREAT BRITAIN
15-19 Great Titchfield Street, London, W1P 7FB. Tel: (0171) 436 8626. FAX: (0171) 436 8646.
CONTACT
Kate Hillman

THE ENTERTAINMENT AGENTS' ASSOCIATION (GREAT BRITAIN)
54 Keyes House, Dolphin Square, London, SW1V 3NA. Tel: (0171) 834 0515. FAX: (0171) 821 0261.

FEDERATION AGAINST COPYRIGHT THEFT (FACT)
7 Victory Business Centre, Worton Road, Isleworth, Middlesex, TW7 6DB. Tel: (0181) 568 6646. FAX: (0181) 560 6364.
DIRECTOR GENERAL
R. Dixon

FILM ARTISTES' ASSOCIATION
111 Wardour Street, London W1V 4AY. Tel: (0171) 937 4567. FAX: (0171) 937 0790.
GENERAL SECRETARY
Spencer MacDonald

FILM INSTITUTE OF IRELAND
Irish Film Centre, 6 Eustace Street, Dublin 2, Republic of Ireland. Tel: (353 1) 679 5744. FAX: (353 1) 677 8755.
DIRECTOR
Sheila Pratschke

GENERAL MUNICIPAL BOILERMAKERS & ALLIED TRADES UNION
Thorne House, Ruxley Ridge, Claygate, Esher, Surrey. Tel: (01372) 620 181. Telex: 27428.
GENERAL SECRETARY
John Edmonds

GUILD OF BRITISH CAMERA TECHNICIANS
5 11 Taunton Road, Metropolitan Centre, Greenford, Middx., UB6 8UQ. Tel: (0181) 578 9243. FAX: (0181) 575 5972.
CONTACT
Maureen O'Grady

GUILD OF FILM PRODUCTION EXECUTIVES
Pinewood Studios, Iver, Bucks. Tel: (01753) 656 428 FAX: (01753) 656 850
CONTACT
Ann Runeckles

GUILD OF FILM PRODUCTION ACCOUNTANTS AND FINANCIAL ADMINISTRATORS
Pinewood Studios, Pinewood Road, Iver, Bucks. SL0 0NH. Tel: (01753) 656 473. FAX: (01753) 656 850.
CONTACT
Ann Runeckles

GUILD OF LOCAL TELEVISION (GLT)
16 Fountain Road, Edgbaston, Birmingham B17 8NL. Tel: (0121) 429 3706. FAX: (0121) 429 3706.
CHAIRMAN
Richard Patching

ITV NETWORK CENTRE
(The ITV Network Centre, wholly owned by the ITV companies, independently commissions and schedules the television programmes which are shown across the ITV network.)
200 Gray's Inn Road, London, WC1X 8HF. Tel: (0171) 843 8000. FAX: (0171) 843 8158.
NETWORK DIRECTOR
Marcus Plantin
DIRECTOR, ITV ASSOCIATION
Barry Cox

THE INCORPORATED SOCIETY OF BRITISH ADVERTISERS LTD.
44 Hertford Street, London W1Y 8AE. Tel: (0171) 499 7502.
DIRECTOR GENERAL
John Hooper

INSTITUTE OF PRACTITIONERS IN ADVERTISING
44 Belgrave Square, London, SW1X 8QS. Tel: (0171) 235 7020. FAX: (0171) 245 9904.
DIRECTOR GENERAL
Nick Philips

INDEPENDENT FILM DISTRIBUTORS' ASSOCIATION
10A Stephen Mews, London, W1A 0AX. Tel: (0171) 957 8957. FAX: (0171) 957 8968.

INTERNATIONAL ANIMATED FILM ASSOCIATION
61 Railwayside, Barnes, London, SW13 OPQ. Tel: (0181) 878 4040. FAX: (0181) 675 8499.
VICE PRESIDENT
Pat Raine Webb

INTERNATIONAL ASSOCIATION OF BROADCASTING MANUFACTURERS
4B, High St., Burnham, Slough SL1 7JH. Tel: (01628) 667 633. FAX: (01628) 665 882.
SECRETARIAT
Brenda White

INTERNATIONAL VISUAL COMMUNICATION ASSOCIATION (IVCA)
Bolsover House, 5 6 Clipstone Street, London, W1P 7EB. Tel: (0171) 580 0962. FAX: (0171) 436 2606.
CHIEF EXECUTIVE
Wayne Drew

IRISH ACTORS EQUITY GROUP
Liberty Hall, Dublin 1, Republic of Ireland. Tel: (353 1) 874 0081. FAX: (353 1) 874 3691.
GROUP SECRETARY
Gerard Browne

LONDON NEWS NETWORK
London Television Centre, Upper Ground, London SE1 9LT. Tel: (0171) 827 7700. FAX: (0171) 827 7720.
MANAGING DIRECTOR
Geoff Henry

MECHANICAL COPYRIGHT PROTECTION SOCIETY LTD. (MCPS)
Elgar House, 41 Streatham High Road, London, SW16 1ER. Tel: (0181) 769 4400. FAX: (0181) 769 8792. Telex: 946792 MCPS G.
CONTACT
Adrian Crrooke

MUSICIANS' UNION
60 62 Clapham Road, London, SW9 0JJ. Tel: (0171) 582 5566. FAX: (0171) 582 9805.
CONTACT
Don Smith

NATIONAL FILM AND TELEVISION SCHOOL
Beaconsfield Studios, Station Road, Beaconsfield, Bucks., HP9 1LG. Tel: (01494) 671 234. FAX: (01494) 674 042.
DIRECTOR
Henning Camre

NATIONAL TRANSCOMMUNICATIONS LTD.
Crawley Court, Winchester S021 2QA. Tel: (01962) 823 434. FAX: (01962) 822 378.
CHIEF OPERATING OFFICER
Leigh Wood

PACT Ltd.
(Producers Alliance for Cinema and Television)
45 Mortimer Street, London W1N 7 TD. Tel: (0171) 331 6700. FAX: (0171) 233 8935.
CHIEF EXECUTIVE
John Woodward
MEMBERSHIP OFFICER
David Alan Mills

THE PERFORMING RIGHT SOCIETY LTD. (PRS)
29 33 Berners Street, London, W1P 4AA. Tel: (0171) 580 5544. FAX: (0171) 306 4050.
GENERAL MANAGER
John Axon
PUBLIC AFFAIRS CONTROLLER
Terri Anderson

THE PERSONAL MANAGERS' ASSN. LTD.
Rivercroft, One Summer Road, East Molesey, Surrey KT8 9LX. Tel: (0181) 398 9796. FAX: (0181) 398 9796.
SECRETARY
Angela Adler

PHONOGRAPHIC PERFORMANCE LTD.
(A company founded by the British recording industry to own and exercise the public performance and broadcasting rights in sound recordings in the U.K. and to issue licences for public performances and broadcasting.)
Ganton House, 14/22 Ganton Street, London, W1V 1LB. Tel: (0171) 437 0311.
CHAIRMAN
J. A. Brooks
MANAGING DIRECTOR
J. V. Love

THE RADIO, ELECTRICAL AND TELEVISION RETAILERS' ASSOCIATION (RETRA) LTD.
RETRA House, St. Johns' Terrace, 1 Ampthill Street, Bedford, MK42 9EY. Tel: (01234) 269 110. FAX: (01234) 269 609.
CHIEF EXECUTIVE
J. Scott

THE RADIO INDUSTRY COUNCIL
Landseer House, 19 Charing Cross Road, London, WC2H 0ES. Tel: (0171) 930 3206. Telex: 296215 BREMAG.
DIRECTOR
O. P. Sutton, C.B.E.
SECRETARY
R. B. S. Purdy, O.B.E.

RADIO SOCIETY OF GREAT BRITAIN
Lambda House, Cranborne Road, Potters Bar, Herts., EN6 3JE.
CHIEF EXECUTIVE & SECRETARY
David A. Evans

ROYAL TELEVISION SOCIETY
Holborn Hall, 100 Gray's Inn Road, London, WC1X 8AL. Tel: (0171) 430 1000. FAX: (0171) 430 0924.
EXECUTIVE DIRECTOR
Michael Bunce

SATELLITE AND CABLE BROADCASTER GROUP
34 Grand Avenue, London N10 3BP. Tel: (0181) 444 4891. FAX: (0181) 444 6473.
CHAIRMAN
Rosemary Stock

SCREEN ADVERTISING WORLD ASSOCIATION LTD.
103A Oxford Street, London, W1R 1TF. Tel: (0171) 734 7621.
SECRETARY GENERAL
Charles Sciberras

SOCIETY OF AUTHORS BROADCASTING GROUP
84 Drayton Gardens, London, SW10 9SB. Tel: (0181) 363 6642.

SOUND AND COMMUNICATIONS INDUSTRIES FEDERATION
4-B, High Street, Burnham, Slough, SL1 7JH. Tel: (01628) 667 633. FAX: (01628) 665 882.
CHIEF EXECUTIVE
Ken Walker, M.B.E.

VARIETY CLUB OF GREAT BRITAIN
St Martin's House, 139 Tottenham Court Road, LondonW1P 9 LN.
CONTACT
Christian Jenner

VIDEO STANDARDS COUNCIL
Research House, Fraser Rd., Perivale, Middlesex UB6 7AQ. Tel: (0181) 566 8272. FAX: (0181) 991 2653.
SECRETARY GENERAL
Laurie Hall

GOVERNMENT DIVISIONS ON FILM AFFAIRS

AUSTRALIAN FILM COMMISSION
2nd Floor, Victory House, 99 101 Regent Street, London, W1R 7HB. Tel: (0171) 734 9383. FAX: (0171) 434 0170.
CONTACT
Pressanna Vasudevan

BRITISH COUNCIL EVENTS SECTION
Film, TV and Video Department, 11 Portland Place, London, W1N 4EJ. Tel: (0171) 389 3063/4. FAX: (0171) 389 3041. Telex: 8952201 BRICON G.
FESTIVALS OFFICERS
Kevin Franklin, Satwant Gill
OTHER EVENTS
Geraldine Higgins, Jo Maurice

THE BRITISH DEFENCE FILM LIBRARY
SSVC Chalfont Grove, Chalfont St. Peter, Gerrerds Cross, Bucks, SL9 8TN. Tel: (01494) 878 278. FAX: (01494) 878 007.
PATRON
H.R.H. The Princess Margaret
MANAGING DIRECTOR
Air Vice Marshall David Crwys Williams, CB FIPM, FIMGT, RAR
FILM & VIDEO DEPARTMENT
Renate Foster

BRITISH FILM COMMISSION
70 Baker Street, London W1M 1DJ. Tel: (0171) 224 5000. FAX (0171) 224 1013. email: info@britfilmcom.co.uk
http:// www.britfilmcom.co.uk
BRITISH FILM COMMISSIONER
Steve Norris
EVENTS AND DEVELOPMENT MANAGER
Krysia Rozanska

BRITISH FILM INSTITUTE (BFI)
(The BFI's divisions and departments include: BFI on the South Bank (National Film Theatre, Museum of the Moving Image and London Film Festival); Research (Research and Education, Book Publishing and "Sight and Sound" magazine); the National Film and Television Archive; Exhibition and Distribution; Library and Information Services; Planning Unit; BFI Production.)
21 Stephen Street, London, W1P 1PL. Tel: (0171) 255 1444. FAX: (0171) 436
7950. Telex: 27624 BFILDNG.
CHAIRMAN
Alan Parker

INFORMATION MANAGER
Joanna Dewar Gibb
PRESS AND PUBLICATIONS MANAGER
Tina McFarling
PRESS AND PUBLICATIONS COORDINATOR
Paula Smith

BRITISH SCREEN ADVISORY COUNCIL
19 Cavendish Square, London W1M 9AB. Tel: (0171) 304 0040. FAX: (0171) 306 0329.
CHAIRMAN
David Elstein
DIRECTOR
Fiona Clarke Hackslor

CENTRAL OFFICE OF INFORMATION
Hercules Road, London, SE1 7DU. Tel: (0171) 261 8500. FAX: (0171) 928 5637.
DIRECTOR OF FILMS, TELEVISION & RADIO DIVISION
Ian Hamilton

DEPARTMENT FOR CULTURE, MEDIA AND SPORT
Room 203, 2 4 Cockspur Street, London, SWIY 5DH. Tel: (0171) 211 6000. FAX: (0171) 211 6249.
CONTACT
Diana Brown

LONDON FILM COMMISSION
c/o Carnival Films, 12 Raddington Rd., Ladbroke Grove, London, W10 5TG. Tel: (0181) 968 0968. FAX: (0181) 968 0177.
CONTACT
Christabel Alberty

NATIONAL FILM AND TELEVISION SCHOOL
Beaconsfield Studios, Station Road, Beaconsfield, Bucks., HP9 1LG. Tel: (01494) 671 234. FAX: (01494) 674 042.
CONTACT
Hilary Thomas

THE SERVICES SOUND & VISION CORPORATION
Chalfont Grove, Chalfont St. Peter, Gerrards Cross, Bucks., SL9 8TN. FAX: (01494) 872 982.
PATRON
H.R.H. The Princess Margaret
BOARD OF MANAGEMENT CHAIRMAN
Gen. Sir Geoffrey Howlett, K.B.E. M.C.
MANAGING DIRECTOR
Air Vice Marshal David Crwys Williams, CB FIPM, FIMGT, RAR
ASSISTANT DIRECTOR, MARKETING
Renate Foster

TV, Cable, Satellite & Video
World Market

AFGHANISTAN

Population: 31.876 million.
TV Sets: 100,000.
Video Standard: PAL
Television is under the control of fundamentalist Islamic forces.

RADIO-TELEVISION OF AFGHANISTAN
Post Office Box 544, Kabul. 9 Stations. Tel: (93) 25460.

ALBANIA

Population: 3.50 million.
TV Sets: 300,000.
Video Standard: PAL.

RADIOTELIVISIONE SHQIPTAR
Rruga Ismail Qemali 11, Tirana. Tel: (35542) 27512. FAX: (35542) 23650.

ALGERIA

Population: 30.50 million.
TV Sets: 2 million
Video Standard: PAL.

ENTERPRISE NATIONALE DE TELEVISION
21 Boulevard des Martyrs, Algiers 16000. Tel: (2132) 780 310. FAX: (2132) 601 922.

ANGOLA

Population: 10.90 million.
TV Sets: 50,500.
Video Standard: PAL.

TELEVISAO POPULAR DE ANGOLA
Avenida Ho-Chi-Minh, PO Box 2604, Luanda. Tel: (2442) 320 025. FAX: (2442) 391 091.

ARGENTINA

Population: 35 million.
TV Sets: 9.80 million
Cable Subscribers: 5 million.
Satellite Homes: 7,500.
Estimated Piracy Level: 40%
Video Standard: PAL.
A decree signed by Argentine President Carlos Menem will initiate the process for deregulation of the country's telecommunications industry.

BROADCASTERS

ASOCIACION DE TELERADIODIFUSORAS (ATV)
Av. Cordoba 323, 6to., 1054 Buenos Aires. Tel: (541) 312 4208. FAX: (541) 312 4208.

ARGENTINA TELEVISORA COLOR (ATC)
Avda. Figueroa Alcorta 2977, 1425 Buenos Aires. Tel: (541) 802 6001/6. Telex: 22916 TVCOL AR. FAX: (541) 802 9878

CANAL 2 DE LA PLATA (LS 86)
Calle 36 entre 2 y 3, 1900 La Plata, Prov. Buenos Aires. Tel: (54 21) 24 4270. Telex: 23517 TVPLA AR.

CANAL 2 DE LA PLATA (LS 86)
Cerrito 1266, Piso 11, 1010 Buenos Aires. Tel: (541) 313 6879, 393 9186, 393 9270, 393 9388, 393 9430.

CANAL 5 DE ROSARIO (LT 84)
Belgrano 1055, 2000 Rosario, Prov. Santa Fe. Tel: (44638) 245 236, 245 332, 245 457. Telex: 41810. FAX: (44638) 259 698.

CANAL 8 DE MAR DEL PLATA (LRI 486)
Avda. Pedro Luro 2907, 7600 Mar del Plata, Prov. Buenos Aires. Tel: (5423) 232 3046/8.

CANAL 9 (BUENOS AIRES) LS 83
Pasaje Gelly 3378, 1425 Buenos Aires. Tel: (541) 801 3065, 801 3072, 801 3075. Telex: 22132 LIBER AR.

CANAL 9 DE BAHIA BLANCA (LU 80)
Sarmiento 54, 8000 Bahia Blanca, Prov. Buenos Aires. Tel: (091) 550 946. Telex: 81826 CANUEVE AR.

CANAL 11 (BUENOS AIRES) LS 84
Pavon 2444, 1248 Buenos Aires. Tel: (541) 941 2448, 941 9231, 948 9351. Telex: 22780 DICON AR.

PROARTEL (CANAL 13 LS 85)
Avda. San Juan 1170, 1147 Buenos Aires. Tel: (541) 27 0321, 27 3601, 27 3605. Telex: 21762 PATEL AR.

TELEVISION LITORAL SA
San Martin S.A., Av. Godoy 8101, 2000 Rosario, Pcia, Santa Fe. Tel: (1) 394 2576, 394 6115.

CABLE AND SATELLITE

AVELLANEDA TELEVISION SA
España 130, 1870 Avellaneda, Prov. Buenos Aires. Tel: (541) 201 0134, 201 3432, 201 4331, 201 4718.

CABLEVISION
Bonpland 1773, 1414 Buenos Aires. Tel: (541) 771 6021, 775 3090, 775 3190, 775 3290, 775 3390, 775 3490, 775 3590. Telex: 18390 UZAL AR.

CABLEX
C. Pellegrini 1029, Corrientes 3400. Tel: (0783) 22 922.

CV CABLEVISION
Departamento Comercial, Honduras 5667, Buenos Aires 1414. Tel: (1) 771 2058.

VIDEO CABLE COMUNICACION SA
Cuba 2370, 1428 Buenos Aires. Tel: (541) 782 0237, 782 0364, 782 0413, 783 0465, 782 0565. Telex: 26284 AR.

VIDEO ORGANIZATIONS

ASSOCIATION OF ARGENTINEAN INDEPENDENT VIDEO EDITORS
Ayacucho 457, Piso 2/21, 1026 Buenos Aires. Tel: (541) 953 7336.

ARGENTINEAN VIDEO UNION
Planta baja, Viamonte 2095, 1056 Buenos Aires. Tel: (541) 46 8248.

VIDEO DISTRIBUTORS

FILMARTE
Ayacucho 595, Buenos Aires, Tel: (541) 459945. FAX: (541) 403662.

FILMEX
Lavalle 17-18 9 A, Buenos Aires. Tel: (541) 814 3048. FAX: (541) 9533654.

GRECIAN FILMS
Lavalle 2047, Buenos Aires, Tel/FAX: (541) 954 0850.

MUNDIAL FILMS
Lavalle 2024 piso 8, Buenos Aires. Tel: (541) 953 1793.

TRANSEUROPA
Ayacucho 586, Buenos Aires, Tel: (541) 492 653.

UNITED INTERNATIONAL PICTURES
Ayacucho 520, Buenos Aires, Tel/FAX: (541) 490 261.

WARNER BROS.
Tucuman 1938, Buenos Aires. Tel: (541) 456 094.

ARMENIA

Population: 3.6 million.
TV Sets: 866,000
Video Standard: SECAM

ARMENIAN TELEVISION
Alek Manukyan 5, 375025 Yerevan, ALBANIA. (3742) 552 502. FAX: (3742) 551 513.

AUSTRALIA

Population: 18.26 million.
VCR Homes: 8.3 million.
Video Standard: PAL-B

In spite of efforts by the local production industry to raise quotas, Australia's government will continue to support an eforcetable code requiring 10% of pay television programming to contain local content. Local fare is dominant in Australia with current affairs, lifestyle, infotainment, sports and drama programs outrating their foreign counterparts. Only "ER", "The Simpsons", "Friends" and "Veronica's Closet" are regularly in the Top 15.

The Federal government announced that it will allocate a digital spectrum at no cost to free television providers for eight years after the introduction of digital television on January 1, 2001. The government also promised to bar entry to any new free-to-air networks until December, 2008. In order to protect the pay television sector, the networks will not be permitted to introduce subscription services for multichanneling.

SportsVision Australia, a provider of four channels to Optus Vision, will shut down the company with the aid of a court provided liquidator. The company had incurred substantial losses and had run out of funding.

Pay television in general is still oeprating at a loss in Australia. That said, it has one of the world's fastest take-up rates of 15% and has signed up almost a million sibscribers since its inception in 1995.

BROADCASTERS

ABD DARWIN
PO Box 9994, Darwin 0801, Northern Territory. Tel: (6189) 823 222.

ABN 2 SYDNEY
221 Pacific Highway, Gore Hill 2065, New South Wales. Tel: (2) 9950 4500. FAX: (2) 9950 4504.

ABQ 2 BRISBANE
600-612 Coronation Drive, Toowong 4066, Queensland. Tel: (617) 3377 5222. FAX: (617) 3377 5307.

ABS 2 ADELAIDE
85 North East Rd., Collinswood 5081, South Australia. Tel: (618) 343 4000. FAX: (618) 343 4026.

ABT 2 HOBART
ABC Centre, Railway Roudnabout, Hobart TAS 7000. Tel: (3) 6235 3333. FAX: (3) 6235 3661.

ABV 2 MELBOURNE
8 Gordon St., Elsternwick 3185, Victoria. Tel: (3) 9528 4444. FAX: (3) 9524 2504.

ABW 2 PERTH
GPO Box 9994, Perth 6001, Western Australia. Tel: (619) 326 0222.

ADS 10 ADELAIDE
125 Strangways Terrace, Adelaide 5006, South Australia. Tel: (618) 877 7777. FAX: (618) 877 7888.

ATN 7 SYDNEY
TV Centre, Mobbs Lane, Epping 2121, New South Wales. Tel: (612) 9877 7777. FAX: (612) 877 7888.

AUSTRALIAN BROADCASTING CORPORATION
GPO Box 9994, Sydney 2001, New South Wales. Tel: (612) 437 8000. FAX: (612) 9950 3055.

AUSTRALIAN CAPITAL TELEVISION
Aspinall St., Watson 2602, ACT. Tel: (616) 242 2400. FAX: (616) 241 7230.

BTQ 7 BRISBANE
Sir Samuel Griffiths Drive, Mount Coot-tha 4000, Queensland. Tel: (617) 3368 7211. FAX: (617) 3368 6410.

GOLDEN WEST NETWORK
30 Kings Park Rd., West Perth 6005, Western Australia. Tel: (619)481 0050. FAX: (619) 321 2470.

HSV 7 MELBOURNE
119 Wells St., South Melbourne 3205, Victoria. Tel: (613) 9697 7777. FAX: (613) 9697 7888.

IMPARJA TELEVISION PTY LTD.
14 Leichhardt Terrace, NT 0871, Alice Springs. Tel: (6189) 527 3744. FAX: (6189) 531 014.

NBN 3 NEWCASTLE
11-17 Mosbri Crescent, Newcastle 2300, New South Wales. Tel: (6149) 292 933. FAX: (6149) 263 629.

NETWORK TEN AUSTRALIA
Northern Star Holdings, GPO Box 10, Sydney 2007, New South Wales. Tel: (612) 887 0222.

NEW 10 PERTH
Cottonwood Crescent, Dianella Heights 6062, Western Australia. Tel: (619) 345 1010. FAX: (619) 345 2210.

NINE NETWORK AUSTRALIA
PO Box 27, Willoughby 2068, New South Wales. Tel: (612) 430 0444. FAX: (612) 436 2193.

NTD 8 DARWIN
Blake St., Gardens Hill, Darwin 0820, Northern Territory. Tel: (6189) 818 888. FAX: (6189) 816 802.

NWS 9 ADELAIDE
202-208 Tynte St., North Adelaide 5006, South Australia. Tel: (618) 267 0111. FAX: (618) 267 3996.

PRIME TELEVISION ORANGE
P.O. Box 465, Orange 2800, New South Wales. Tel: (6163) 622 288. FAX: (6163) 631 889.

QTQ 9 BRISBANE
Sir Samuel Griffith Drive, Mount Coot-tha 4066, Queensland. Tel: (617) 369 9999. FAX: (617) 369 3512.

QTV ROCKHAMPTON
Acquatic Place, North Rockhampton 4700, Queensland. Tel: (6179) 261 155. FAX: (6179) 261 931.

QTV TOWNSVILLE
Telecasters North Queensland, 12 The Strand, Townsville 4810, Queensland. Tel: (6177) 213 377. FAX: (6177) 211 705.

SAS 7 ADELAIDE
45 Park Terrace, Gilberton 5081, South Australia. Tel: (618) 342 7777. FAX: (618) 342 7717.

SEVEN NETWORK
Television Centre, Mobbs Lane, Epping, NSW 2121. Tel: (612) 858 7777. FAX: (612) 858 7888.

SOUTHERN CROSS TELEVISION (TNT 9)
36 Watchom St., Launceston 7250, Tasmania. Tel: (6103) 6344 0202. FAX: (6103) 6343 0340.

SPECIAL BROADCASTING SERVICE
Locked Bag 028, Crows Nest, NSW 2065, New South Wales. Tel: (612) 9430 2828. FAX: (612) 9430 3700.

SUNSHINE TELEVISION
140-142 Horton Parade, Maroochydore, QLD 4558. Tel: (74) 439 444. FAX: (74) 439 373.

TASMANIAN TELEVISION
48-52 New Town Rd., Hobart 7008, Tasmania. Tel: (3) 6278 0612. FAX: (3) 6228 1835.

TEN 10 SYDNEY
44 Bay Street, Sydney 2001, New South Wales. Tel: (612) 9844 1010. FAX: (612) 844 1368.

TVQ 10 BRISBANE
Sir Samuel Griffith Drive, Mt. Coot-tha 4066, Queensland. Tel: (617) 3368 1010. FAX: (617) 3369 3786.

TVW7
Osborne Road, Dianella, WA 6060. Tel: (9) 344 0777. FAX: (9) 344 0670.

THE UNEXPECTED FILM COMPANY PTY.
6/52 Beach Street, Coogee, NSW 2034. Tel: (2) 9644 1889. FAX: (2) 9319 8240.

VIC TV BALLARAT
PO Box 464, Ballarat, VIC 3350. Tel: (53) 201 366. FAX: (53) 331 598.

VIDEO ORGANIZATION

VIDEO INDUSTRY DISTRIBUTORS ASSOCIATION
302 Pitt St., Sydney 2000, New South Wales. (612) 264 3411. FAX: (612) 267 9581.

VIDEO DISTRIBUTORS

AAV AUSTRALIA
180 Bank St., South Melbourne 3205, Victoria. Tel: (613) 9699 1844. FAX: (613) 9690 3734.

ABC ENTERPRISES
PO Box 9994, Sydney 2001, New South Wales. Tel: (612) 9950 3999. FAX: (612) 9950 3888.

ALL MEDIA INTERNATIONAL
643 Chapel St., South Yarra 3141, Victoria. Tel: (613) 926 3637. FAX: (613) 824 0370.

ANJOHN INTERNATIONAL
19/151 Bayswater Rd., Rushcutters Bay 2011, New South Wales. Tel: (612) 9361 6536. FAX: (612) 9361 6521.

ATLANTIS RELEASING
Suite 4, 65 Military Rd., Neutral Bay 2089, New South Wales. Tel: (612) 9953 2999. FAX: (612) 9953 3248.

AUSTRALIAN BROADCASTING AUTHORITY
Level 15, Darling Park, 201 Sussex St., Sydney, NSW 2000. Tel: (2) 9334 7700. FAX: (2) 9344 7799.

AUSTRALIAN FILM INSTITUTE DISTRIBUTION
49 Eastern Rd., South Melbourne 3205, Victoria. Tel: (613) 696 1844. FAX: (613) 696 7972.

AUSTRALIAN VISUAL PRODUCTIONS
13/63 Crown Rd., Queenscliff, NSW 2096. Tel: (2) 9905 3407.

AUSTRALIAN WORLD ENTERTAINMENT
202 Tynte St., North Adelaide 5006, South Australia. Tel: (618) 267 3644. FAX: (618) 267 3996.

BUSINESS FILMS
43 Davey St., Frankston 3199, Victoria. Tel: (613) 866 8735. FAX: (613) 770 1650.

COLIN MCCLENNAN AND ASSOCIATES
13 Napier St., North Sydney 2060, New South Wales. Tel: (612) 955 5122. FAX: (612) 957 3550.

COLUMBIA TRISTAR HOYTS HOME VIDEO
42-46 Longueville Rd., Lane Cove 2066, New South Wales. Tel: (612) 911 3300. FAX: (612) 911 3333.

D. L. TAFFNER AUSTRALIA
Unit 20, Greenwich Square, 130-134 Pacific Highway, Greenwich 2065, New South Wales. Tel: (612) 439 5699. FAX: (612) 439 4501.

DENDY FILMS
19 Martin Pl., Sydney, NSW 2000. Tel: (2) 9233 8558. FAX: (2) 9232 3841.

DISCOVERY INTERNATIONAL
PO Box 550, Malvern 3144, Victoria. Tel: (613) 9563 9344. FAX: (613) 9563 9885.

FIELD ASSOCIATES (AUSTRALIA)
Suite 4, 2nd Floor, 118 Willoughby Rd., Crows Nest 2065, New South Wales. Tel: (612) 439 4730. FAX: (612) 439 3103.

FIRST RELEASE HOME ENTERTAINMENT
9th Fl., 42-46 Longueville Rd., Lane Cove 2066, New South Wales. Tel: (612) 9911 3300. FAX: (612) 9911 3333.

HOYTS FOX COLUMBIA TRI-STAR FILMS
490 Kent St., Sydney 2000, New South Wales. Tel: (612) 261 7800. FAX: (612) 283 2191.

M.C. STUART AND ASSOCIATES
88 Highett Street, Richmond 3121, Victoria. Tel: (613) 429 8666. FAX: (613) 429 1839.

MCA
1st Fl., MCA Universal House, 23 Pelican Street, Sydney 2010, New South Wales. Tel: (612) 9267 9844, 9267 9032. FAX: (612) 264 1742.

NETWORK ENTERTAINMENT
2B Woodcock Place, Lane Cove, 2066 New South Wales. Tel: (612) 418 8099. FAX: (612) 418 8598.

NEW VISION FILM DISTRIBUTORS
2nd Floor, 254 Bay Street, Port Melbourne 3207, Victoria. Tel: (613) 646 5555. FAX: (613) 646 2411.

OPEN EYE (FILM & TV)
1/87 Bent St., North Sydney 2060, New South Wales. Tel: (612) 9954 3626. FAX: (612) 9959 3253.

OTHER FILM DISTRIBUTION
89 High St., Northcote 3070, Victoria. Tel: (613) 9489 1741. FAX: (613) 9481 5618.

PACIFIC LINK COMMUNICATIONS
2A Eltham St., Gladesville 2111, New South Wales. Tel: (612) 817 5055. FAX: (612) 879 7297.

R A BECKER AND CO./FREEMANTLE INTERNATIONAL PRODUCTIONS
486 Pacific Highway, St. Leonards 2065, New South Wales. Tel: (612) 9438 3377. FAX: (612) 9439 1827.

RONIN FILMS
PO Box 1005, Civic Square 2068, ACT. Tel: (616) 248 0851. FAX: (616) 249 1640.

SHARMILL FILMS
Suite 4, 200 Toorak Rd., South Yarra 3141, Victoria. Tel: (613) 826 9077. FAX: (613) 826 1935.

SHOWBIZ VIDEO
183 Harris St., Pyrmont 2009, New South Wales. Tel: (612) 660 8999. FAX: (612) 660 7916.

SMART ST. FILMS
3/30 Lamrock Ave., Bondi Beach 2026, New South Wales. Tel: (612) 360 8429. FAX: (612) 365 3195.
CONTACTS
Cai Steele
Haydn Keenan.

SOUTH AUSTRALIAN FILM CORPORATION
3 Butler Dr., Hendon, SA 5014. Tel: (618) 8348 9300. FAX: (618) 8347 0385.

SOUTHERN STAR INTERNATIONAL
10th Floor, 8 West St., North Sydney 2060, New South Wales. Tel: (612) 957 2788. FAX: (612) 956 6918.

VIRGIN VISION AUSTRALIA
99 Victoria St., Potts Point 2011, New South Wales. Tel: (612) 368 1700.

WARNER HOME VIDEO
Level 7, 116 Military Rd., Neutral Bay 2089, New South Wales. Tel: (612) 9908 3088. FAX: (612) 9909 8494.

WORLD VISION ENTERPRISES
2nd Floor, 5-13 Northcliff Street, Milsons Point 2061, New South Wales. Tel: (612) 922 4722. FAX: (612) 955 8207.

AUSTRIA

Population: 8.02 million.
TV Sets: 2.706 million.
VCR Homes: 1.9 million.
Home Cable Service: 1.32 million
Home Satellite Service: 520,000.
Video Standard: PAL

BROADCASTERS

3SAT
Wuerzburggasse 30, Vienna 1136. Tel: (431) 878 782 386. FAX: (431) 878 783 688.

OSTERREICHISCHER RANDFUNK—ORF-ZENTRUM WIEN
Wurzburggasse 30, Vienna A-1136. Tel: (431) 87878, 2228. FAX: (431) 878 78, 2387. 24 stations.

CABLE SERVICES

BKS BERGENLANDSCHERS KABELFERNSEHEN
Kasernenstrasse 9, Eisenstadt A-7001. Tel: (432682) 170 1471. FAX: (432682) 170 1480.

KABLE TV VIENNA
Hofzeile Strasse 3, Vienna. Tel: (431) 363 4240

PREMIERE
Neubaugasse 25, Vienna A-1070. Tel: (431) 52127. FAX: (431) 523 8253.

HOME VIDEO DISTRIBUTORS

BMG ARIOLA
Erlachgasse 134-8, Vienna A-1010. Tel: (431) 60154. FAX: (431) 60154 139.

CCS MEDIENPRODUKTION
Stolzenthalergasse 14, Vienna A-1080. Tel: (431) 408 6198.

COLUMBIA TRISTAR
Wallgasse 21/1/1/9, Vienna A-1080. Tel: (431) 597 1515. FAX: (431) 597 1516.

EMI AUSTRIA
Webgasse 43, Vienna A-1060. Tel: (431) 599 890. FAX: (431) 596 9336.

MEDIENWERKSTAT
Neubaugasse 40A, Vienna A-1070. Tel: (431) 526 3667. FAX: (431) 526 7168.

PAUKER
Ortsstrasse 18, Voesendorf A-2331. Tel: (431) 881 149.

POLYGRAM
Edelsinnstrasse 4, Vienna A-1120. Tel: (431) 811 210. FAX: (431) 813 1300.

PREISER
Fischerstiege 9, Vienna A-1010. Tel: (431) 533 6228.

RAINBOW VIDEO
Tetmajergasse 5A, Vienna. Tel: (431) 2701 8230. FAX: (431) 270 6278.

VIDEO MARKET
Ortsstrasse 18, Vosendorf A-2331. Tel: (431) 692 593. FAX: (431) 6295 9315.

VIDEO VERTRIEB
Webgasse 43, Vienna A-1060. Tel: (431) 597 9795. FAX: (431) 596 8111.

WARNER BROS.
Zieglergasse 10/2, Vienna A-1072. Tel. (431) 523 8626. FAX: (431) 523 8626 31.

AZERBAIDZHAN

Population: 7.67 million.
Video Standard: SECAM

BROADCASTERS

AZERBAYCAN RESPUBIKASI RABITA NAZIRLIYI
Azerbaycan pr. 33, Bake 370139. Tel: (99412) 930 004. FAX: (99412) 983 325.

AZERBAYCAN RADIOTELEVIZIYA SIRKETL
Medhi Huseyn kucasi 1, Baki 370000. Tel: (99412) 398 585. FAX: (99412) 395 452.

TELERADIO
Azerbaycan pr. 33, 370139, Baki. (99412) 988 066. FAX: (99) 983 325.

BAHAMAS

Population: 266,000
TV Sets: 57,000.
Video Standard: NTSC

BROADCASTERS

BAHAMAS TELEVISION
Broadcasting Corp. of the Bahamas, PO Box N-1347, Nassau. Tel: (809) 322 4623. FAX: (809) 322 3924.

ZNS 1 & 2 RADIO & TELEVISION STATION
3rd Terrace Centreville, PO Box N-1347, Nassau. Tel: (809) 322 4623. FAX: (809) 322 3924.

BAHRAIN

Population: 590,000.
TV Sets: 295,000.
Video Standard: PAL.

BROADCASTER

BAHRAIN TV
PO Box 1075, Manama, Bahrain. Tel: (973) 781 888. FAX: (973) 681 544.

BANGLADESH

Population: 137 million.
TV Sets: 365,500.
Video Standard: PAL.

BROADCASTER

NATIONAL BROADCASTING AUTHORITY, BANGLADESH TV
Television Bhaban, PO Box 456, Rampura, Dhaka 1219. Tel: (8802) 400 131. FAX: (8802) 832 927.

BARBADOS

Population: 260,000.
TV Sets: 65,000.
Video Standard: NTSC.

BROADCASTERS

CARIBBEAN BROADCASTING UNION (CBU)
Wanderers Gap, Dayrells Road, Christ Church, Barbados. Tel: (809) 429 9146. Telex: 2569.

CARIBBEAN BROADCASTING CORP.
P.O.Box 900, Bridgetown. Tel: (809) 429 2041. FAX: (809) 429 4795.

BELARUS

Population: 10.44 million.
TV Sets: 3.6 million.
Video Standard: SECAM.

BROADCASTER

BELARUSKAE TELEBACHANNE
Makaenka 9, Miensk, 220807. Tel: (375172) 649 286. FAX: (375172) 648 182.

TELEVISION BROADCASTING NETWORK (TBN)
15a F. Skariny Street, Miensk 22072. (375172) 394 171.FAX: (375172) 394 171. E-mail: mmc@glas.apc.org

VIDEO DISTRIBUTOR

FOBOS S
P/B 490, Minsk 220050, Belarus. Tel: (375172) 393 383. FAX: (375172) 393 383.

BELGIUM

Population: 10.17 million.
TV Sets: 4.2 million.
VCR Homes: 2.28 million.
Home Cable Service : 4.02 million.
Home Satellite Service: 40,000.
Video Standard: PAL.

ASSOCIATIONS

EUROPEAN SATELLITE TELEVISION ASSOCIATION (ESTA)
Esselte pay TV-Tollaan 95, Avenue de Paige 95, Brussels, B-1940 Belgium. Tel: (322) 725 0650. FAX: (322) 720 2449.

EUROAIM
rue des Minimes Brussels, B-1000, Belgium. Tel: (322) 518 1460. Telex: 64917.

BROADCASTERS

ARBELTSGEMELNSCHAFT DER OFFENTIICHEN RUND-FUNKANSTALTEN DER BUNDESREPUBLIK DEUTSCH-LAND (ARD)
Wetstraat 223-225, B-1040 Brussels. Tel: (322) 230 48 77.

BELGISCHE RADIO EN TELEVISIE (BRTN)
Boulevard August Reyerslaan 52, B-1043 Brussels. Tel: (322) 742 5215. FAX: (322) 734 9351.

BRITISH BROADCASTING CORPORATION (BBC)
Karel de Grotelaan 1, Box 50, B-1040 Brussels. Tel: (322) 230 2120.

RADIO TELEVISION LUXEMBOURGEOISE-TELEVISION INDEPENDANTE (RTL-TVI)
1 Ave. Ariane, 1210 Brussels. Tel: (322) 640 5150. FAX: (322) 737 4357.

RADIO-TELEVISION BELGE DE LA COMMUNAUTE CUL-TURELLE FRANCAISE (RTBF)
Boulevard August Reyerslaan 52, B-1044 Brussels. Tel: (322) 737 2111. FAX: (322) 733 4357.

RADIOTELEVISIONE ITALIANA UNO (RAI-1) & DUE (RAI-2)
Karel de Grotelaan 1, Box 13, B-1040 Brussels. Tel: (RAI-1) (322) 238 09 30; (RAI-2) (322) 238 08 14.

RTL-TVI
1051 Brussels. (322) 640-5150. FAX: (322) 640 9307.

TELE BRUXELLES
Avenue Louise 166, Brussels 1050. Tel: (322) 640 6645. FAX: (322) 640 8583.

TV5
(See RTBF listing above.)

VLAAMSE RADIO EN TELEVISIE (VTR)
1043 Brussels. Tel: (322) 741 3111. Fax: (322) 734 9351.

VTM (VLAAMSE TELEVISIE MAATSCHAPPIJ)
1 Medialaan, 1818 Vilvoorde. (322) 254 5611. FAX: (322) 252 5016.

ZWEITES DEUTSCHES FERNSEHEN (ZDF)
Wetstraat 223, Box 5, B-1040 Brussels. Tel: (322) 230 0814.

CABLE SERVICES

ANTENNE CENTRE TELEVISION
Rue de la Tombelle 92, B-7110 Houdeng-Aimeries. Tel: (3264) 281 542, 281 106. FAX: (3264) 285 644.

ASSOC. OF PRIVATE EUROPEAN CABLE OPERATORS
1 Boulevard Anspach, Box 25, B-1000 Brussels. Tel: (322) 229 2885. FAX: (322) 229 2889.

ASSOC. INTERCOMMUNALE
(Pour Le Developpement Economique Et L'Amenagement Des Regions Du Centre Et Du Borinage-Idea)
74 Rue de Paturages, B-7300 Quaregnon. Tel: (3265) 665 701. FAX: (3265) 665 769.

ASSOCIATION LIEGOISE D'ELECTRICITE-ALE
95 Rue Louvrez, B-4000 Liege. Tel: (3241) 201 211. FAX: (3241) 201 363.

BRUTELE
29-31 Rue de Naples, B-1050 Brussels. Tel: (322) 511 6543.

CANAL C
Rue Des Relis, 5000 Namurwes 1. Tel: (3281) 741 000. FAX: (3281) 740 946.

CANAL PLUS
656 Chaussee de Lauvain, B-1050 Brussels. Tel: (322) 730 0211. FAX: (322) 732 1848.

CANAL PLUS BELGIUM
656 Chaussee de Louvain, B-1030 Brussels. Tel: (322) 732 0211. FAX: (322) 732 1848.

CANAL ZOOM
5 Place Du Sablon, 5030 Gembloux. Tel: (3281) 610 017. FAX: (3281) 612 999.

CODITEL BRABANT
26 Tweerkerkenstraat, B-1040 Brussels. Tel: (322) 226 5211.

ELECTRABEL
271 Mechelsesteenweg, 2018 Antwerp. Tel: (323) 280 0211. FAX: (323) 218 7788.

GASELWEST
57 Ryselstraat, 8500 Kotrijk. Tel: (3256) 369 211. FAX: (3256) 369 360.

HAVI TV
10 Noordkustlaan, 1702 Groot-Bijgaarden. Tel: (322) 466 2222. FAX: (322) 466 4202.

INTERELECTRA
8 Trichterheideweg, 3500 Hasselt. Tel: (3211) 221 171. FAX: (3211) 266 910.

NO TELE
2 Blvd. des Freres Rimbaut, 7500 Tournai. Tel: (3269) 210 691. FAX: (3269) 215 383.

RADIO PUBLIC
140 Ave. Chazel, B-1030 Brussels. Tel: (322) 240 0800. FAX: (322) 240 0801.

RTC TELE LIEGE
Rue de Rotterdam 33, 4000 Liege. Tel: (3241) 524 077. FAX: (3241) 520 353.

TELE MONS BORINAGE
8 Rue des Arbalestriers, 7000 Mons. Tel: (3265) 353 552. FAX: (3265) 346 241.

TELESAMBRE
Espace Sud, Route de Philipeville, 6010 Charleroi. Tel: (3271) 473 737. FAX: (3271) 473 838.

TELEVESDRE
Rue Neufmoulin 3, 4820 Dison. Tel: (3287) 337 625. FAX: (3287) 338 263.

TEVE WEST
56 Scheepsdalelaan, 8000 Brugge. Tel: (3250) 440 811. FAX: (3250) 440 905.

TV COM
7 Chaussee de la Croix, 1340 Ottignies. Tel: (3210) 410 196. FAX: (3210) 414 168.

TV-5
(See TV-5 listing under Broadcasters.)

VIDEOSCOPE
1 Place de la Gare, 5580 Rochefort. Tel: (3284) 211 572. FAX: (3284) 221 102.

VTM
(See VTM listing under Broadcasters.)

WOLU-TV
399 Avenue Georges Henri, 1200 Brussels. Tel: (322) 736 8733. FAX: (322) 733 7881.

SATELLITE BROADCASTERS

EURATEL BRUSSELS
12 Ave. Ariane, B-1200 Brussels. Tel: (322) 736 1795. FAX: (322) 773 4895.

FILMNET BELGIUM
Tollaan 97, St. Stevens Woluwe, B-1932 Brussels. Tel: (322) 714 1818. FAX: (322) 714 1814.

VIDEO ORGANIZATIONS

BELGIAN VIDEO FEDERATION
Jozef Mertensstraat 46, B-1702 Groot-Bijgaarden. Tel: (322) 463 1812. FAX: (322) 46 31481.

VIDEO DISTRIBUTORS

BAETEN & DE MUNCK-BDM
Box 12, 70 Barklaan, 9100 St Nicholas. Tel: (323) 766 4800. FAX: (323) 766 1004.

BELGIAN PRODUCTION VIDEO-BPV
5 Rue de College, 6000 Charleroi. Tel: (3271) 322 733. FAX: (3271) 325 012.

BMG ARIOLA
Square F, Riga 30, B-1030 Brussels. Tel: (322) 240 2863. (322) 737 1750.

BUENA VISTA INTERNATIONAL
Romeinsesteenweg 486, B-1853 Grimbergen. Tel: (322) 263 1711. FAX: (322) 263 1797.

C.T.V. CENTRE D'ACTION ET DE DOCUMENTATION POUR LA TELEVISION
Ave. des Nerviens 3, B-1040 Brussels. Tel: (322) 735 22 77.

CANAL C
1 Rue Res des Relis Namurwes, 5000 Namur. Tel: (3281) 741 000. FAX: (3281) 740 946.

CINELIBRE
Chaussee de Haecht, 270, B-1030 Brussels. Tel: (322) 245 8700. FAX: (322) 210 2575.

CONCORDE VIDEO
130 Hulpa, 1050 Brussels. Tel: (322) 675 2050. FAX: (322) 675 3076.

ECVD
7 Rue de Chatelet, 6030 Marchienne-au-Pont. Tel: (3271) 517 984. FAX: (3271) 519 410.

METEOR HOME VIDEO
Box 40, 1 Doornveld, 1731 Zellik. Tel: (322) 463 1775. FAX: (322) 466 5456.

OCIC
Rue de L'Orme 8, B-1040 Brussels. Tel: (322) 734 4294. FAX: (322) 734 3207.

PAULINE PICTURES
159 Berkendaelstraat, 1060 Brussels. Tel: (322) 347 5846. FAX: (322) 347 2462.

POLYGRAM VIDEO
34 Blvd. de la Woluwe, Woluwedal, B-1200 Brussels. Tel: (322) 775 8140. FAX: (322) 770 7691.

SUPER CLUB
110 Van Kerckhovenstraat, 2880 Bornem. Tel: (323) 890 4811. FAX: (323) 890 4800.

SUPER PRODUCTION VIDEO BELGIUM
241 Rue Royale, 1210 Brussels. Tel: (322) 218 7280.

VDM VIDEO
Box 12, 70 Parklaan, 9100 Sint-Niklaas. Tel: (323) 766 4800. FAX: (323) 766 1004.

VIDEO PLAY
14 Rue de la Neuville, 6000 Charleroi. Tel: (3271) 330 701. FAX: (3271) 332 224.

VIDEOPOOL
Rue de Il'Inquisition 21, B-1040 Brussels. Tel: (322) 736 1185. FAX: (322) 736 8200.

WARNER HOME VIDEO
42-44 Boulevard Brand Whitlock, B-1200 Brussels. Tel: (322) 735 1791. FAX: (322) 736 2318.

BELIZE

Population: 230,000.
TV Sets: 24,000.

BROADCASTER

TROPICAL VISION
48 Albert Cattouse Bldg., Regent St., Belize City. Tel: (5012) 77246. FAX: (5012) 75040.

BENIN

Population: 5.71 million.
TV Sets: 30,000.

BROADCASTER

OFFICE DE RADIODIFFUZION ET TV DE BENIN (ORTB)
PO Box 366, Cotonou. Tel: (229) 301 0628.

BERMUDA

Population: 61,600.
TV Sets: 50,000.
Video Standard: NTSC.

BROADCASTER

ZBM-ZFB RADIO & TELEVISION
PO Box HM 452, Hamilton. Tel: (809) 295 2828.

BHUTAN

Population: 1.65 million

Since 1989, all TV antennas and satellite dishes have been dismantled by order of law. Private television reception is against the law.

BOLIVIA

Population: 7.680 million.
TV Sets: 805,000.
Cable Subscribers: 55,000.
Satellite Dishes: under 1,000.
Video Standard: NTSC.

MAJOR BROADCASTERS

TV POPULAR
Calle Juan de la Riva 1527, Casilla 8704, La Paz.

GALAVISION
Cas. 495, Santa Cruz.

AMERICA TV
Cas. 10076, Santa Cruz.

EMPRESA NACIONAL DE TV
Cas. 900, La Paz.

REDE ATB
Ave. 6 de Agnosto 2972, La Paz.

TELEANDINA
Cas. 1665, La Paz.

TV UNIVERSTARIA
Cas. 21982, La Paz.

TECNITRON
Cas. 4410, La Paz.

BOSNIA-HERZEGOVINA

Population: 3.265 million.
TV Sets: 1.1 million.
Video Standard: PAL

BROADCASTER

RADIO TELEVIZIJA BOSNE I HERCEGOVINE
VI Prolerterske Brigade 4, 71000 Sarajevo. Tel: (3871) 522 333.

BOTSWANA

Population: 1.49 million.
TV Sets: 13,800.
Video Standard: PAL.

BROADCASTER

BOP-TV MMABATHO
P.O. Bag X 2150, Mmabatho. Tel: (27140) 289 111. FAX: (27140) 26009.

GABORONE TELEVISION CORP.
Private Bag 0060, Gaborone. Tel: (267) 352 541. FAX: (267) 357 138.

BRAZIL

Population: 161.65 million.
TV Sets: 34 million.
Cable Subscribers: 1.6 million.
Satellite Dishes: 2.75 million.
VCR Penetration: 35%.
Video Stores: 10,500.
Video Standard: PAL-M.

TV Record, a Sao Paulo based network may be taking over the number two spot long held by SBT. Record attributes its ratings surge to a reduction of religious programming, an increase in American products and family-oriented telenovelas. While SBT and TV Record wrangle for second place, Globo is still the top ranked network, leading by a wide margin.

ASSOCIATIONS

ASSOCIACAO BRASILEIRA DE EMISORAS DE RADIO E TELEVISAU (ABERT)
Hotel Nacional, s/5 a 8, C.P.040-280, 70322-900 Brasilia, DF. Tel: (5561) 224 4600. FAX: (5561) 321 7583.

BROADCASTERS

REDE MANCHETE DE TELEVISTAO
Rua do Russel 766, 22210 Rio de Janeiro. Tel: (5521) 285 0033. Telex: 21 21525.

REDE BANDEIRANTES DE TELEVISTAO
Rua Radiantes 13, 05699 Sao Paulo. Tel: (5511) 842 3011. Telex 11 81680.

SISTEMA BRASILEIRO DE TELEVISTAO
Rua Dona Sta Veloso 575, 02050 Sao Paulo. Tel: (5511) 292 9044. Telex: 11 63892.

TV CULTURA (SAO PAULO)
Rua Ceno Sbrighi 378, 05099 Sao Paulo. Tel: (5511) 263 9111. Telex :11 82052.

TV EDUCATIVA (FEDERAL)
Av. Gomes Freire 474, 20231 Rio de Janeiro. Tel: (5521) 221 2227. Telex: 21 22609

TV GAZETA
Av Paulista 900, 01310 Sao Paulo. Tel: (5511) 287 4322. Telex: 11 35914.

TV GLOBO LTDA. (GLOBO TV NETWORK)
Rua Lopes Quintas, 303, 22460-10 Rio de Janeiro-RJ. Tel: (21) 274 5322. Telex: 2123131, 2131775. FAX: (21) 259 3348.

TV RECORD
Av. Miruna 713, 04084 Sao Paulo. Tel: (5511) 240 1633. Telex: 11 22245.

TV RIO
Rua Miguel de Frias 57, 20211 Rio de Janeiro. Tel: (5521) 293 0012. Telex: 21 38183.

CABLE OPERATORS

GLOBO CABO S.A.
Av. Rio Branco, 1-6th Fl., Rio de Janeiro 20090-003. Tel: (5521) 276 6000. FAX: (5521) 283 1886.
URL: http://www.multicanal.com.br
CEO
Moyses Pluciennik
CFO:
Roberto Waddington

VIDEO ORGANIZATIONS

BRAZIL VIDEO UNION
Rua Mexico 31/603, Rio de Janeiro. Tel: (5521) 240 2326.

BRUNEI DARUSSALAM

Population: 316,000.
TV Sets: 95,000.
Video Standard: PAL.

BROADCASTER

RADIO TV BRUNEI
Jabatan Perdana Menteri, Bander Seri Begawan 2042, Negara Brunei Darussalam. (6732) 243 1111. FAX: (6732) 241 882.

BULGARIA

Population: 8.963 million.
TV Sets: 3.127 million.
Cable Subscribers: 500,000.
Satellite Subscribers: 100,000.
Video Standard: SECAM.

"Hushove", a highly rated satire that attracted over 4 million viewers per week was cancelled following spoofs in early 1998 of the countrys president, minister of foreign affairs and prime minister. The cancellation led to protests in Sofia that led to police intervention.

BROADCASTER

BULGARSKA TELEVIZIJA

Ul, San Stefano Str 29, 1504 Sofia. Tel. (3592) 446 329. FAX: (3592) 662 388.

NOVA TV

16 Sveta Nedelja Sq, 1000 Sofia. (3592) 805025. FAX: (3592) 870 298.

BURKINA FASO

Population: 11.32 million.
TV Sets: 45,500.
Video Standard: SECAM.

BROADCASTER

TÉLÉVISION NATIONALE BURKINA

B.P. 1 2530, Ougadougou. Tel: (226) 354 773.

CAMBODIA

Population: 10.86 million.
TV Sets: 80,000.
Video Standard: PAL.

BROADCASTER

CAMBODIAN TV

19, Street 242, Chaktomuk, Daun Penh, Phnom Penh. Tel: (8552983) 22349.

INTERNATIONAL BROADCASTING CORP. LTD.

Borei Keila St. No. 169, Sangkat Vealvong, Phnom Penh City. Tel: (85523) 66061, 66064. FAX: (85523) 66063.

CAMEROON

Population: 14.74 million
TV Sets: 15,000.
Video Standard: PAL.

BROADCASTER

CAMEROON RADIO AND TELEVISION

P.O. Box 1634, Yaoundé. Tel: (237) 426 060. FAX: (237) 204 340.

CANADA

Population: 28.8 million
TV Sets: 12 million
Cable households: 11,580 million
VCRs: 9.8 million
Video Standard: NTSC
(All following figures in Canadian dollars)

TV REVENUES

The total revenue of the broadcasting industry (television and radio) in 1995, including the Canadian Broadcasting Corporation (CBC), was $C2.67 billion. The television operating revenues of the CBC were $363.364 million in 1995, and its program expenses increased by 1.8% from $968.5 million in 1994 to $985.8 million in 1995. These figures represent 276.5% and 270.2% of total CBC revenue. The net cost of CBC operations decreased 0.8% from $1,122 million in 1994 to $1,112 million in 1995. CBC expenses increased 2.3% in 1995, and were 417.8% of its revenue for 1995 compared to 425.5% in 1994.

For the year ended August 31, 1995, total operating revenue of $2.31 billion was received by the private broadcasters, up 2.2% from the $2.26 billion for the same period in 1994. In 1995, total program expenses of private television broadcasters totalled $825 million. Total expenses for private stations which include departmental expenses, depreciation and interest expense increased 0.6% from $2.19 billion in 1994 to $2.20 billion in

1995, and represented 95.3% of total 1995 revenue compared to 97.0% in 1994. Net profit after tax for private stations increased with a profit of $39.9 million in 1995 compared to $7.1 million in 1994.

Excluding the CBC, there were 100 licensed TV stations, with 99 in operation in 1995.

NUMBER OF TV SETS

In 1996 colour televisions were in 11,246 million households. 5,873 million homes had two or more colour sets - 51.5%, a big jump from 23.8% a decade ago. In 1996 the province of Ontario again led with estimates of 1,978 million households owning one television and 2,169 million owning two or more (compared to 2,023 million with one and 2,060 million with two or more in 1995). The province of Québec followed with estimates of 1,419 million owning one television and 1,540 million with two or more (compared to 1,398 million owning one television and 1,505 million with two or more in 1995).

TELEVISION VIEWING

Recent television viewing data showed that, while average viewing time increased 30 mins. per week between 1994 and 1995, it was still an hour less than a decade ago. This increase in 1995 viewing time was attributed to the introduction of cable speciality channels.

The net cost of the Canadian Broadcasting Corporation (CBC) operations increased 10.9% from $1,112 million in 1995 to $1,234 million in 1996, and its expenses decreased 1.6% in this year. CBC expenses were 326.0% of its revenue for 1996 compared to 417.8% in 1995. Program expenses decreased by 2.4% from $985.8 million in 1995 to $962.2 million in 1996. These figures represent 270.2% and 209.2% of total CBC revenue

The total air time sales for the broadcasting industry (television and radio)reached $2.6 billion for the year ended August 31/96 (a 5.8% increase from 1995) and air time sales for television increased 5.7%. The CBC had an increase of 19.6% in 1996 for air time sales over 1995 and acounted for 13.0% of industry air time sales. Air time sales represented 91.8% of revenues received by broadcasting systems. For the same period, a total operating revenue of $2.39 billion was received by the private broadcasters, up 3.4% from the $2.31 billion for the same period in 1995.

In 1996 total program expenses of private television broadcasters totalled $861.9 million. Of this amount 90.7% or $782 million was accounted for by programs telecast which were 56.2% Canadian and 34.5% non Canadian. Total expenses for private stations, which include departmental expenses, depreciation and interest expense increased 2.6% from $2.20 billion in 1995 to $2.26 billion in 1996, and represented 94.5% of total 1996 revenue compared to 95.3% in 1995. Net profit after tax for private stations decreased to $27.1 million in 1996 from $39.9 million in 1995.

Excluding the CBC, there were 102 licensed and operating TV stations in 1996.

In 1982 almost 85% of homes had a colour television, but only 12% had two or more colour sets. By 1997 virtually every home had a colour set and 51.9% of households had two or more. The proportion for black and white sets had tumbled to 12.4% in 1997 from 42.7% in 1982.

In 1997 a total of 11.58 households owned television sets, with one colour television in 4,920 households, and 6,562 million homes had two or more colour sets (contrasting with 1,334 million owning one black-and-white television, and 107,000 owning two). In 1997 the province of Ontario again led with estimates of 1.738 million households owning one television and 2.459 million owning two or more (compared to 1.978 million with one and 2.169 million with two or more in 1996). The province of Québec followed with estimates of 1.374 million owning one television and 1.675 million with two or more (compared to 1.419 million owning one television and 1.540 million with two or more in 1996).

CABLE

Revenues for the entire cable television industry totalled $2,679.0 million in 1996, an increase of 5.8% over 1995. Basic tier cable television revenues in 1966 were $1,903.6 million. Discretionary and other services earned revenue of $775.4 million in 1996, an increase of 13.0% from 1995. Expenses for the industry were $1,999.8 million in 1996, a 5.3% increase over 1995. Net profit after income taxes for the cable television industry was $148.9 million in 1996, an increase of 54.3% over 1995.

There were 7,346,725 subscribers and 520,115 indirect subscribers in 1996 compared to 7,231,028 and 560,078 in 1995, representing an overall increase of 1.0% in subscribers over the previous year.

Cable television penetration increased steadily between 1982 and 1997, from 59.1% to 73.7%. In 1997, the proportion of households with cable is highest in British Columbia (83.9%) and lowest in Saskatchewan (61.0%)

In 1997 there were 2,076 cable television systems licensed by the Canadian Radio-Television and Telecommunications Commission (CRTC) broken down by province as follows: Alberta 199, British Columbia 159, Manitoba 103, New Brunswick 118, Newfoundland 276, Nova Scotia 81, North West Territories 43, Ontario 376, Prince Edward Island 17, Québec 435, Saskatchewan 263, Yukon Territory 6

VIDEO

Out of 11.58 million households sampled in 1997, 7.456 million owned one VCR, and 2.352 million owned two or more. The province of Ontario led with an estimated 2.758 million households owning one VCR and 899,000 households with two or more, out of 4.227 million reponding. Québec followed with an estimated 1.932 million households owning one VCR and 530,000 households with two or more, out of 3.062 million responding. Since 1983, when data were first collected, the percentage of households with a VCR has soared from 6.4% to 84.7%, and one in five homes report having two or more VCRs in 1997.

GOVERNMENT AGENCY

CANADIAN RADIO-TELEVISION AND TELECOMMUNICATIONS COMMISSION (CRTC)
(The CRTC is an independent authority responsible for regulating all broadcasting in Canada, including AM and FM radio, TV, cable television, specialty services and pay-TV. The CRTC is also responsible for the regulation, mainly with respect to rates and terms of service, of Canada's federally-regulated telecommunications carriers.)
Ottawa, ON K1A 0N2. (819) 997-0313.
CHAIRMAN
Françoise Bertrand
VICE-CHAIRMAN, BROADCASTING
Fernand Belisle
VICE-CHAIRMAN, TELECOMMUNICATIONS
David Colville

TV CORPORATIONS

ACCESS – THE EDUCATION STATION
3720 - 76 Ave., Edmonton, AB T6B 2N9. (403) 440-7777. FAX:: (403) 440-8899.

CABLE PULSE 24
(24-hour local news) 299 Queen St. W.Toronto, ON M5V 2Z5. (416) 591-5757. FAX:: (416) 591-0080.

CANADIAN BROADCASTING CORPORATION
250 Lanark Ave., P.O. Box 3220, Stn. C, Ottawa, ON K1Y 1E4 (613) 724-1200.
English Networks
P.O.Box 500, Stn. A, Toronto, ON M5W 1E6. (416) 205-3311.
French Networks
1400 René Lévesque Blvd. E., P.O.Box 6000, Montréal, QC. (514) 597-5970.

CFMT INTERNATIONAL
(A multilingual television broadcaster serving more than 18 ethnic communities)
545 Lakeshore Blvd.W., Toronto, ON M5V 1A3. (416) 260-0047. Fax: (416) 260-3621.

CITY-TV
299 Queen St. W.Toronto, ON M5V 2Z5. (416) 591-5757, Fax, News: (416) 593-6397. FAX:, Sales: (416) 591-7792.

CTV TELEVISION NETWORK
BATON / CTV
P.O.Box 9, Stn. O, Toronto, ON M4A 2M9. (416) 299-2000. FAX:: (416) 299-2643.

GLOBAL COMMUNICATIONS LIMITED/GLOBAL TELEVISION NETWORK/CAN WEST GLOBAL SYSTEM
81 Barber Greene Rd., Don Mills, ON M3C 2A2. (416) 446-5311. FAX:: (416) 446-5543.

GROUPE TVA INC.
1600 de Maisonneuve est., Montréal, QC H2L 4P6. (514) 526-9251/598-2869. FAX:: (514) 598-6073.

ITV
5325 Allard Way, Edmonton, AB T6H 5B8. (403) 436-1250. FAX:: (403) 438-8448.

KNOWLEDGE NETWORK / OPEN LEARNING AGENCY
(Educational) 4355 Mathissi Pl., Burnaby, BC V5G 4S8. (604) 431-3000. FAX:: (604) 431-3333.

SASKATCHEWAN COMMUNICATIONS NETWORK (SCN)
(Educational) 2440 Broad St., North Block, Regina, SK S4P 3V7. (306) 787-0490. FAX:: (306) 787-0496.

TVONTARIO
(Educational) 2180 Yonge St., Toronto, ON M4S 2B9. (416) 484-2600. FAX:: (416) 484-6285.

WIC/WESTERN INTERNATIONAL COMMUNICATIONS
1960 - 505 Burrard St., Vancouver, BC V7X 1M6. (604) 687-2844. Fax: (604) 687-1651.

WIC ENTERTAINMENT LTD.
5325 Allard Way, Edmonton, AB T6H 5B8. (403) 438-8555. FAX:: (403) 438-8495.

PAY-TV

ASTRAL BROADCASTING GROUP INC.
An Astral Communications Company, 2100, rue Sainte-Catherine Ouest, bur. 900, Montréal, QC H3H 2T3. (514) 939-5000. Fax: (514) 939-1515.

CTV PAY-PER-VIEW SPORTS
P.O.Box 9, Stn. O, Toronto, ON M4A 2M9. (416) 299-2072. FAX:: (416) 299-2076.

THE FAMILY CHANNEL INC.
BCE Place, 181 Bay St., P.O.Box 787, Toronto, ON M5J 2T3. (416) 956-2030. FAX:: (416) 956-2035.

MOVIEPIX
BCE Place, 181 Bay St., P.O. Box 787, Toronto, ON M5J 2T3. (416) 956-2010. Fax: (416) 956-2012.

LES RESEAUX PREMIER CHOIX INC.: CANAL D
LES RESEAUX PREMIER CHOIX INC.: CANAL FAMILLE
LES RESEAUX PREMIER CHOIX INC.: SUPER ECRAN
(Astral Communications Companies) 2100, rue Sainte-Catherine Ouest, bur. 800, Montréal, QC H3H 2T3. (514) 939-3150 . FAX:: (514) 939-3151.

VIEWER'S CHOICE CANADA
BCE Place, 181 Bay St., Ste. 100, P.O. Box 787, Toronto, ON M5J 2T3. (416) 956-2010. FAX:: (416) 956-2015.

WIC PREMIUM TELEVISION LIMITED
(Superchannel, Family Channel, Movie Max, Teletoon Pay-Per-View Home Theatre)
5324 Calgary Trail S., Ste. 200, Edmonton, AB T6H 4J8 (403) 430-2800. Fax: (403) 437-3188.

SPECIALTY CHANNELS

BRAVO!
299 Queen St. W., Toronto, ON M5V 2Z5. (416) 591-5757. FAX:: (416) 591-8497.

LE CANAL NOUVELLES
(Headline news) 1600 de Maisonneuve E., 10th Fl., Montréal, QC H2L 4P2. (514) 598-2858. FAX:: (514) 598-6071.

LE CANAL VIE
(Life/health/outdoors) 1717 Rene Levesque Blvd. E., Ste. 050, Montreal, QC H2L 4T9. (514) 529-3233. FAX:: (514) 529-3236.

CBC NEWSWORLD
(News & information 24-hours) P.O. Box 500, Stn. A, Toronto, ON M5W 1E6. (416) 205-2950. FAX:: (416) 205-2894.

CMT - COUNTRY MUSIC TELEVISION
630 - 3rd Ave. S.W., Ste. 100, Calgary, AB T2P 4L4. (403) 716-6500. Fax: (403) 716-6599.
Toronto: (416) 534-1191. FAX:: (416) 530-5206

THE COMEDY NETWORK
P.O. Box 9, Stn. O, Toronto, ON M4A 2M9. (416) 299-2626. FAX:: (416) 299-2653.

CTV NEWS 1
P.O.Box 9, Stn. O, Toronto, ON M4A 2M9. (416) 609-7400. FAX:: (416) 291-5337.

CTV SPORTSNET
P.O.Box 9, Stn. O, Toronto, ON M4A 2M9. (416) 332-4300. FAX:: (416) 299-2076.

DISCOVERY CHANNEL
2225 Sheppard Ave. E., Ste. 100, North York, ON M2J 5C2. (416) 494-2929. FAX:: (416) 490-7067.

FAIRCHILD TV
Production: 525 W. Broadway, Ste. B8, Vancouver, BC V5Z 4K5. (604) 708-1313. FAX:: (604) 708-1300.

HEADLINE SPORTS TELEVISION NETWORK
370 King St. W., Toronto, ON M5V 1J9. (416) 977-6787. FAX:: (416) 977-0238.

HISTORY TELEVISION INC.
121 Bloor St. E., Ste. 200, Toronto, ON M4W 3M5. (416) 967-0022. FAX:: (416) 967-0044.

HOME & GARDEN TELEVISION / LIFE NETWORK
1155 Leslie St., Toronto, ON M3C 2J6. (416) 444-9494. FAX:: (416) 444-0018.

MUCHMOREMUSIC
(Adult contemporary music videos) 299 Queen St. W., Toronto, ON M5V 2Z7. (416) 591-5757. FAX:: (416) 591-9317.

MUCHMUSIC NETWORK
299 Queen St. W., Toronto, ON M5V 2Z5. (416) 591-5757. FAX:: (416) 591-6824.
EXEC. PRESIDENT & EXEC. PRODUCER:
Moses Znaimer

OUTDOOR LIFE NETWORK
P.O.Box 9, Stn. O, Toronto, ON M4A 2M9. (416) 299-2640. FAX:: (416) 299-2641.

SHOWCASE TELEVISION INC.
121 Bloor St. E., Ste. 200, Toronto, ON M4W 3M5. (416) 967-0022. FAX:: (416) 967-0044.

SPACE - THE IMAGINATION STATION
299 Queen St. W., Toronto, ON M5V 2Z5. (416) 591-5757. FAX:: (416) 591-6619.

T.L.N. TELEVISION (TELELATINO NETWORK INC.)
(24-hour programming in Italian, Spanish & English) 5125 Steeles Ave. W., Weston, ON M9L 1R5. (416) 744-8200, (800) 551-8401. Fax: (416) 744-0966.
800 boul. Langelier, bur. 410, Ville St-Léonard, QC H1P 3K2. (514) 324-4231. FAX:: (514) 324-8098.

TELETOON
(All animation/English & French) BCE Place, 181 Bay St., P.O.Box 787, Toronto, ON M5J 2T3. (416) 956-2060. FAX:: (416) 956-2070.

TREEHOUSE TV
(Pre-schoolers, six years and younger) 64 Jefferson Ave., Unit 18, Toronto, ON M6K 3H3. (416) 534-1191. FAX:: (416) 544-0346.

TSN - THE SPORTS NETWORK
2225 Sheppard Ave. E., Ste. 100, North York, ON M2J 5C2. (416) 494-1212. FAX:: (416) 490-7010.

VISION TV
(Alternative, multicultural and multi-faith national satellite to cable) 80 Bond St., Toronto, ON M5B 1X2 (416) 368-3194. Fax: (416) 368-9774.

WTN - WOMEN'S TELEVISION NETWORK
1661 Portage Ave., Ste. 300, Winnipeg, MB R3J 3T7. (204) 783-5116. FAX:: (204) 774-3227.

YTV CANADA INC.
(Youth network) 64 Jefferson Ave., Unit 18, Toronto, ON M6K 3H3. (416) 534-1191. FAX:: (416) 533-0346.

GOVERNMENT AGENCY

CANADIAN RADIO-TELEVISION AND TELECOMMUNICA-TIONS COMMISSION (CRTC)
(The CRTC is an independent authority responsible for regulating all broadcasting in Canada, including AM and FM radio, TV, cable television, specialty services and pay-TV. The CRTC is also responsible for the regulation, mainly with respect to rates and terms of service, of Canada's federally-regulated telecommunications carriers.)
Ottawa, ON K1A 0N2 Tel: (819) 997-0313.
CHAIRMAN
Françoise Bertrand
VICE-CHAIRMAN, BROADCASTING
Fernand Belisle
VICE-CHAIRMAN, TELECOMMUNICATIONS
David Colville

TV CORPORATIONS

ACCESS—THE EDUCATION STATION
3720 76 Ave., Edmonton, AB T6B 2N9. Tel: (403) 440-7777. FAX: (403) 440-8899.

CANADIAN BROADCASTING CORPORATION
250 Lanark Ave. PO Box 3220, Stn. C, Ottawa, ON K1Y 1E4. Tel: (613) 724 1200.
English Networks: PO Box 500, Stn. A, Toronto, ON M5W IE6. Tel: (416) 205-3311.
French Networks: 1400 René-Lévesque Blvd. E., P.O. Box 6000, Montréal, QC H3C 3A8. Tel: (514) 597-5970

CFMT INTERNATIONAL
(A multilingual TV station serving 21 ethnic communities) 545 Lakeshore Blvd.W., Toronto, ON M5V 1A3. Tel: (416) 260-0047. FAX: (416) 260-3621

CITY-TV
299 Queen St. W., Toronto, ON M5V 2Z5. Tel: (416) 591-5757. FAX: Executive office (416) 340-7005

CTV TELEVISION NETWORK LTD.
250 Yonge St., Ste. 1800, Toronto, ON M5B 2N8. Tel: (416) 595-4100. FAX: (416) 595-1203

GLOBAL COMMUNICATIONS LIMITED/GLOBAL TELEVI-SION NETWORK/CANWEST GLOBAL SYSTEM
81 Barber Greene Rd., Don Mills, ON M3C 2A2. Tel: (416) 446-5311. FAX: (416) 446-5543.

KNOWLEDGE NETWORK/OPEN LEARNING AGENCY
(Educational, adults & children) 4355 Mathissi Pl., Burnaby, BC V5G 4S8. Tel: (604) 431-3000. FAX: (604) 431-3333

SASKATCHEWAN COMMUNICATIONS NETWORK (SCN)
(Educational) 2440 Broad St., North Block, Regina, SK S4P 3V7. Tel: (306) 787-0490. FAX: (306) 787-0496

TVONTARIO
(Educational) 2180 Yonge St., Toronto, ON M4S 2B9. Tel: (416) 484-2600. Toll free: (800) INFO-TVO. FAX: (416) 484-6285

PAY TV

ALLARCOM PAY TELEVISION LTD.
5324 Calgary Trail S., Ste. 200, Edmonton, AB T6H 4J8. Tel: (403) 430-2800. FAX: (403) 437-3188.

ASTRAL COMMUNICATIONS INC.
(MOVIEPIX, TMN—THE MOVIE NETWORK, VIEWER'S CHOICE CANADA)
BCE Place, 181 Bay St., BCE Place, 181 Bay St., PO Box 787, Toronto, ON M5J 2T3. Tel: (416) 956-2010. FAX: (416) 956-2012.

THE FAMILY CHANNEL INC.
BCE Place, 181 Bay St., P.O. Box 787, Toronto, ON M5J 2T3. Tel: (416) 956-2030. FAX: (416) 956-2035

LES RESEAUX PREMIER CHOIX INC.(CANAL D, CANAL FAMILLE, SUPER ECRAN)
(Astral Communications Inc. companies) 2100, rue Ste-Catherine Ouest, bur. 800, Montréal, QC H3H 2T3. Tel: (514) 939-3150. FAX: (514) 939-3151.

SPECIALTY CHANNELS

BRAVO!
299 Queen St. W., Toronto, ON M5V 2Z5. Tel: (416) 591-5757. FAX: (416) 591-8497.

CBC NEWSWORLD
P.O. Box 500, Stn. A, Toronto, ON M5W 1E6. Tel: (416) 205-2950. FAX: (416) 205-6080.

CMT COUNTRY MUSIC TELEVISION
49 Ontario St., Toronto, ON M5A 2V1. Tel: (416) 360-4626. FAX: (416) 360-6263.

THE DISCOVERY CHANNEL
2225 Sheppard Ave. E., Ste. 100, North York, ON M2J 5C2. Tel: (416) 494-2929. FAX: (416) 490-7067

FAIRCHILD TV
Production: 525 W. Broadway, Ste. B8, Vancouver, BC V5Z 4K5. Tel: (604) 708-1313. FAX: (604) 708-1300.

LIFE NETWORK
1155 Leslie St.Toronto, ON M3C 2J6. Tel: (416) 444-9494. FAX: (416) 444-0018.

MUCHMUSIC NETWORK
299 Queen St. W., Toronto, ON M5V 2Z5. Tel: (416) 591-5757. FAX: (416) 591-6824.

SHOWCASE
160 Bloor St. E., Ste. 1000, Toronto, ON M4W 1B9. Tel: (416) 967-0022. FAX: (416) 967-0044.

TELELATINO NETWORK INC.
5125 Steeles Ave. W., Weston, ON M9L 1R5. Tel: (416) 744-8200. FAX: (416) 744-0966. (Approx. 100 hours weekly of Spanish & Italian programming)

VISION TV
80 Bond St., Toronto, ON M5B 1X2. Tel: (416) 368-3194. FAX: (416) 368-9774. (Alternative, multicultural and multi-faith national satellite to cable)

WTN WOMEN'S TELEVISION NETWORK
1661 Portage Ave., Ste. 300, Winnipeg, MB R3J 3T7. Tel: (204) 783-5116. FAX: (204) 774-3227

YTV CANADA INC.
64 Jefferson Ave., Unit 18, Toronto, ON M6K 3H3. Tel: (416) 534-1191. FAX: (416) 533-0346.

INDUSTRY ORGANIZATIONS

ACADEMY OF CANADIAN CINEMA AND TELEVISION
158 Pearl St., Toronto, ON M5H 1L3 (416) 591-2040 FAX: (416) 591-2157.
3375 boul. St-Laurent, bur.709, Montréal, QC H2X 2T7 (514) 849-7448. FAX:: (514) 849-5069.
1385 Homer St., Vancouver, BC V6B 2S2 (604) 684-4528. FAX:: (604) 684-4574.
Halifax, NS, c/o 158 Pearl St., Toronto, ON M5H-1L3 (800) 644-5194
Los Angeles Division: (800) 644-5194

ACTRA PERFORMERS GUILD (CLC, FIA)
National Office, 2239 Yonge St., Toronto, ON M4S 2B5 (416) 489-1311 . FAX:: (416) 489-1435.

ASSOCIATION DES PRODUCTEURS DE FILMS ET DE TELEVISION DU QUEBEC (APFTQ)
740 St-Maurice, bur. 408, Montréal, QC H3C 1L5 (514) 397-8600. FAX:: (514) 392-0232.

ASSOCIATION QUEBECOISE DES REALISATEURS ET REALISATRICES DE CINEMA ET DE TELEVISION
3480 rue Saint-Denis, Montréal, QC H2X 3L3 (514) 842-7373. FAX::(514) 842-6789.

CANADIAN CABLE TELEVISION ASSOCIATION
360 Albert St., Ste. 1010, Ottawa, ON K1R 7X7 (613) 232-2631 FAX: (613) 232-2137.

CANADIAN FILM & TELEVISION PRODUCTION ASSOCIATION (CFTPA)
175 Bloor St. E., North Tower, Ste. 806, Toronto, ON M4W 3R8 (416) 927-8942. FAX:: (416) 922-4038.
130 Albert St., Ste. 514, Ottawa, ON K1P 5G4 (613) 233-1444. FAX:: (613) 233-0073. (800) 656-7440.
BC Producers Branch, 1431 Howe St., Vancouver, ON V6Z 1R9 (604) 682-8619. FAX: (604) 684-9294.

WOMEN IN FILM AND TELEVISION – TORONTO (WIFT-T)
20 Eglinton Ave.W., Ste. 902, Toronto, ON M4R 1K8 (416) 322-3430, fax: (416) 322-3703.

WOMEN IN FILM & VIDEO VANCOUVER
P.O.Box 1238, Stn. A, Vancouv er, BC V6C 2T1 (604)685-1151. FAX:: (604) 685-1124.

VIDEO TRADE ASSOCIATION

VIDEO SOFTWARE DEALERS ASSOCIATION (VSDA)
Canadian office: 40 Sheppard Ave. W., 8th.Fl., North York, ON M2N 6K9. Tel: (416) 733-2294. FAX: (416) 730-8591.

VIDEO DIRECT DISTRIBUTION

ASTRAL HOME ENTERTAINMENT/CINE-MAISON ASTRAL
An Astral Communications Company, 889 Montée de Liesse, Ville St-Laurent, QC H4T 1P5 (514) 734-2500. FAX:: (514) 734-2501.
1185 Caledonia Rd, North York, ON M6A 2X1 (416) 785-5580, (800) 263-2974. FAX:: (416) 785-1219.
889 Montée de Liesse.Ville Saint-Laurent, QC H4T 1P5 (514) 734-2500, (800) 361-3320. FAX:: (514) 734-2503.
2058 Alpha St., Burnaby, BC V5C 5K7 604) 299-8484. (800)663-4559. FAX:: (604) 299-8494.
11486 - 149th St., Edmonton, AB T5M 1W8 (403) 453-3007, (800) 252-7907. FAX:: (403) 452-8026.
6130 - 4th St. E., Unit 12, Calgary, AB T2H 2H9 (403) 258-2131 (800) 352-8296,(800) 661-1545. FAX:: (403) 253-3455.
1555 Dublin Ave., Unit 7, Winnipeg, MB R3E 3M8 (204) 772-0050, (800) 665-8012. FAX:: (204) 786-0076.
201 Brownlow Ave., Ste. 16, Dartmouth, NS B3B 1W2 (902) 468-3393. FAX:: (902) 468-3197.

FIDELITY HOME ENTERTAINMENT
5600 Ambler Dr., Mississauga, ON L4W 2K9. (905) 625-7333. FAX:: (905) 625-70541.
#215 - 2550 Boundary Rd., Burnaby, BC V5M 3Z3 (604) 438-4336. FAX:: (604) 438-4337.

VIDEO ONE CANADA LTD.
5600 Ambler Dr., Mississauga, ON L4W 2K9. (905) 624-7337. FAX:: (905) 624-7310.
105 - 2250 Boundary Rd., Burnaby, BC V5M 3Z3 (604) 437-4473/(800) 242-0648. FAX:: (604) 432-6926.
6023 – 4th St.S.E., Calgary, AB T2H 2A5, (403) 258-3880/(800) 352-8245. FAX:: (403) 252-3176.
11133 – 156th St., Edmonton, AB T5M 1X9, (403) 451-9060/(800) 661-9635. FAX:: (403) 452-1763.
Bay D - 2220 Northridge Dr., Saskatoon, SK S7L 6X8 (306) 933-4930. FAX:: (306) 933-4139.
1821 King Edward, Unit 12, Winnipeg, MB R2R 0N1 (204) 694-6007. FAX:: (204) 694-0928.
647 Wilton Grove Rd. W., Units 1 & 2, London, ON N6A 4C2 (519) 685-1502/(800) 265-6054. FAX:: (519) 668-2059.
5600 Ambler Dr., Mississauga, ON L4W 2K9 (905) 624-4330. FAX:: (905) 624-9077.
105 Scarsdale Rd., Toronto, ON M3B 2R2 (416) 447-9600/(800) 387-0184. FAX:: (416) 447-7775.
380 Terminal Rd., Ottawa, ON K1G 0Z3 (613) 244-0000. FAX:: (613) 244-1230.
10 Morris Dr., Unit 40, Dartmouth, NS B3B 1K8 (902) 468-6661. FAX:: (902) 468-2260.
21 Mews Pl., St. John's, NF A1B 3V8, (709) 754-3437. FAX:: (709) 754-3230.

VIDEO GLOBE 1
398 Isabey, Ville St-Laurent, QC H4T 1V3 (514) 738-6665/(800) 361-7151. FAX:: (514) 738-3923.

WHOLESALERS

R.O.W. ENTERTAINMENT
255 Shields Ct., Markham, ON L3R 8V2 (905) 475-3550. FAX:: (905) 475-4163.

THE SHANNOCK CORPORATION
4222 Manor St., Burnaby, BC V5G 1B2 (604) 433-3331/(800) 665-9767. FAX:: (604) 433-4815.
10 - 6120 3rd St. S.E., Calgary, AB T2H 1K4 (403) 253-2113/(800) 661-1636. FAX: (403) 255-3359.
14944 - 121 Ave., Edmonton, AB T5V 1A3 (403) 453-1986/(800) 661-6969. FAX:: (403) 451-0401.
First Business Centre, 901 1st Ave., Saskatoon, SK S7L 6C4 (306) 652-3553. FAX:: (306) 652-2726.
1692 Dublin Ave., Unit 2, Winnipeg, MB R3H 0H1, (204) 632-0581. FAX:: (204) 632-7855.
6305 Danville Rd., Unit 1, Mississauga, ON L5T 2H7 (905) 565-0812, (800) 665-9417. FAX:: (905) 565-0819.
109 Ilsley Ave., Unit 15, Dartmouth, NS B3B 1S8 (902) 468-2868,(800) 565-0668. FAX:: (902) 468-2814.
8569 Dalton Rd., Ville Mont-Royal, QC H4T 1V5 (514) 344-4424. FAX:: (514) 344-4461.

SMA DISTRIBUTION
A division of the Shannock Corporation. 6305 Danville Rd., Unit 1B, Mississauga, ON L5T 2H7 (905) 565-0822, (800) 267-1216. FAX:: (905) 565-0830.

VIDEO DISTRIBUTION

ALLIANCE COMMUNICATIONS CORPORATION
Home Video Division. 5 Place Ville-Marie, Montréal, QC H3G 2G2 (515) 878-2282. FAX:: (514) 878-2419.

BEHAVIOUS DISTRIBUTION
Montréal, QC H3C 1Y1 (514) 879-3339. FAX:: (514) 879-0152
2221 Yonge St., Ste. 400, Toronto, ON (416) 4800453. FAX:: (416) 480-0501.

CYCLOPS COMMUNICATIONS CORPORATION
44 Gibson Ave., Toronto, ON M5R 1T5 (416) 926-8981. FAX:: (416) 926-9878.

FRANCE FILM COMPANY INC./ COMPAGNIE FRANCE FILM INC.
505 Sherbrooke St.E., Ste.2401, Montr<130>al, QC H2L 4N3 (514) 844-0680.

NORTH AMERICAN RELEASING INC.
808 Nelson St., Ste.2105, Vancouver, BC V6Z 2H2 (604) 681-2165. FAX:: (604) 681-5538.

POLYGRAM FILMED ENTERTAINMENT
4100 Yonge St., Ste. 302, Toronto, ON (416) 733-9001. FAX:: (416) 733-9905.

TELEGENIC VIDEO DISTRIBUTORS INC.
20 Holly St., Ste. 300, Toronto, ON M4S 3B1 (416) 484-8000.
FAX:: (416)484-8001.

TSC FILM DISTRIBUTION CORP.
4222 Manor Rd., Burnaby, BC V5G 1B2 (604) 439-2563. FAX::
(604) 433-0269

VIDEOVILLE SHOWTIME INC.
4610 Côte Vertu, Ville St.-Laurent, QC H4S 1C7 (514) 336-
0038. FAX:: (514) 745-4274.

PATRICIA THOMPSON

CANARY ISLANDS

Population: 1.7 million
TV Sets: 240,000
Video Standard: PAL

BROADCASTERS

ANTENA 3 TELEVISION
Eduardo Benot 3, Santa Cruz de Tenerife. (3422) 275 242.

CANAL BUENAS NUEVAS
Calle Sao Paulo 45, Santa Cruz de Tenerife. (3422) 279 442.

CANARYVISION
Calle Arequipa 10, Santa Cruz de Tenerife. (3422) 470 366.

LIBERTAD TELEVISION
Avda. Escaleritas 112, Escaleritas. (3422) 251 440.

ONDA TELEVISION MASPALOMAS (OTM 6)
Calle Galdar 48, San Agustin, Playa del Ingles. (3422) 772
445.

TELE GRAN CANARIA
Calle Sao Paulo 46, Santa Cruz de Tenerife. (3422) 464 722.

TELEVISION ESPANOLA EN CANARIAS
69 Calle Buenos Aires, Santa Cruz de Tenerife. (3422) 216
200.

CENTRAL AFRICAN REPUBLIC

Population: 3.27 million.
TV Sets: 7,800.
Video Standard: SECAM.

BROADCASTER

RADIODIFFUSION TELEVISION CENTRAFRIQUE
PO Box 940, Bagui. Tel: (236) 613 342.

CHAD

Population: 6.98 million.
TV Sets: 50,000.
Video Standard: SECAM.

BROADCASTER

TELECHAD
B.P. 74, N'Djamena. Tel: (235) 512 923.
DIRECTOR
Hourmadji Houssa Doumgor.

CHILE

Population: 14.3 million.
TV Sets: 3.5 million
Cable Subscribers: 600,000.
Satellite Dishes: 2,500.
Number of VCRs: 1.1 million.
Retail Price Per Video: US$19.00.
Rental Price Per Video: US$2.00.
Blank Tape: US$5.00.
Video Standard: NTSC.

HBO Ole, Cinemax, the Warner Channel and Sony Entertainment
blacked out signals to Chile's 2 largest cable companies, citing
non-payment of fees.

BROADCASTERS

CANAL 13 CORP DE TELEVISION
Ines Matte Urrejola 0848, Providencia, Santiago. Tel: (562) 251
4000. FAX: (562) 735 2955.

CORP UNIV CATOLICA DE CHILE TV
13 Dover 9478, Santiago. Tel: (562) 251 4000. FAX: (562) 737
1441.

**LA RED (GLOBAL CAN-WEST, CANADA/COPESA-
BANCOSORNO), CHANNEL 4**
Av. Maquehue Sur 1201, Las Condes, Santiago. Tel: (562) 212-
1111.

**MEGAVISIÓN (TELEVISA MEXICO/RICARDO CLARO
GROUP), CHANNEL 9**
Av. Vicuna Mackenna 1348, Santiago. Tel: (562) 555-5400.

ROCK & POP (RADIO COOPERATIVA), CHANNEL 2
Antonio Bellet 223, Providencia, Santiago. Tel/FAX: (562) 236
0066.

TELEVISIÓN NACIONAL DE CHILE, CHANNEL 7
Bellavista 0990, Santiago. FAX: 735-3000.

UNIVERSIDAD CATÓLICA DE VALPARAISO, CHANNEL 5
Aqua Santa 2455, Via del Mar. Tel: (Santiago) (562) 231-8950.

CABLE & PAY TV

ALPHACOMM
Apoquindo 6415, of. 92, Las Condes. Tel: (562) 229 7735.

CABLE HOGAR
Pajaritos 5717, Maipe. Tel/FAX: (562) 743 1998.

CABLEXPRESS
Salesianos 1140, Santiago. Tel: (562) 554 4500. FAX: (562)
551 9050.

INTERCOM
Manquehue Sur 520, Las Condes. Tel: (562) 224 5150. FAX:
224 5830.

KUHN LTDA.
Marin 097, Santiago. Tel: (562) 222 6451. FAX: (562) 634 4631.

METROPOLIS
Irarrazaval 4760 Vicuna. Tel: (562) 237 1010.

MARKET RESEARCH AND RATINGS

HERNANDO DE AGUIRRE
111, Providencia. Tel: (562) 231 5064. FAX: (562) 233 5599.

REGULATORY BODY

CONSEJO NACIONAL DE TELEVISION
Moneda 1020, Santiago.

VIDEO RETAILERS

BLOCKBUSTER CHILE
Colon 3494, Las Condes. Tel: (562) 207 1427. FAX: (562) 208
7698.

VIDEO DISTRIBUTORS

TRANSANDIA
Rancagua 0226, Santiago. Tel: (562) 699 1239. FAX: (562) 698
9692. (Twentieth-Century Fox)

TRANSEUROPA
General del Canto 10, 3rd flr., Providencia. Tel: (562) 235
5683. FAX: (562) 235 2399. (New Line)

VIDEO CHILE
Colon 3494, Las Condes. Tel: (562) 207 1427. FAX: (562) 208
7698. (Cinea International, Paramount, Warner Bros.,
Touchstone and Walt Disney).

VIDEO LKTEL
Alameda 1146, 3rd Flr., sector B, Santiago. Tel: (562) 696
9814. FAX: (562) 698 7100 (for Columbia, Orion and Tri Star).

CHINA

MAINLAND CHINA
Population: 1.21 billion.
TV Sets: 300 million.
Video Standard: PAL.
Home Cable Service: 10 million.
Video Outlets: 100,000.
Cable: CGTV Beijing.

HONG KONG

Population: 6.3 million.
TV sets: 1.75 million.
Cable Homes: 340,000.
Satellite dish homes: 360,000.
VCR Homes: 1.25 million.

Chinese national broadcaster, Beijing Television, will include cartoon programs from Germany's EMTV & Merhcandising group in its lineup. The "Kid's TV Clube", "Tabaluga", "Flipper" and "Lapitch" will air on Chinese TV in 1999.

Hong Kong is still relatively healthy when compared with other economies in Asia, however TVB and ATV both say that they will be financially conservative throughout 1998. Both will benefit from Asia's economic downturn to the extent that there will be a decrease in competition for programming, as other countries find themselves without means to bid for product.

ATV has had success with "surprise" prgramming of feature films while TVB is having some success with U.S. series such as "Friends" and "NYPD Blue".

With the launch of the world's first video-on-demand system, competition for first-run movies will increase. Both networks are experimenting with series in their daily 9:30 p.m. slots as replacements for primetime features.

New deregulation in Hong Kong has benefited Rupert Murdoch's STAR TV. The digital satellite platform hasd been granted full ownership of its uplink license as well as a reduction in annual license fees from $600,000 to $6,666. The government has also announced that STAR TV will be allowed to rollout pay tv services. All of this means that Hong Kong's Wharf Cable TV is for the first time facing competition for its 400,000 subscribers. In an effort to meet the video-on-demand challenge, Wharf TV has added 24 hour channels such as Discovery, TNT, The Cartoon Netowrk and MGM Gold. Wharf also offers a package fo Cineplex pay-per0view channels which will offer considerable competition for video-on-demand.

BROADCASTERS

ASIA TELEVISION LTD. (ATV)
81 Broadcast Dr., Kowloon. Tel: (852) 2992 8888. FAX: (852) 2338 0438.

CHINA CENTRAL TELEVISION (CCTV)
11 Fuxing Lu Road, Haidan, Beijing 100859. Tel: (8610) 850 0000. FAX: (8610) 851 3025.

RADIO TELEVISION HONG KONG
Broadcasting House, 30 Broadcast Drive, Kowloon. (852) 2339 3600. FAX (852) 2338 0279.

TELEVISION BROADCASTS LTD. (TVB)
TV City, Clear Water Bay Rd., Kowloon. (852) 2719 4828. FAX: (852) 2358 1337.

CABLE & SATELLITE

ASIA SATELLITE TELECOMMUNICATIONS CO. LTD. (ASIASAT)
23-24/F East Exchange Tower, 38-40 Leighton Road, Causeway Bay, Hong Kong. Tel: (852) 805 6666. Telex: 68345 ASAT HX. FAX: (852) 576 4111.

RCP-TV/CHINA CABLEVISION LTD.
1 Suffolk Rd., Kowloon Tong. Tel: (852) 338 3641.

STAR TV (SATELLITE TELEVISION ASIAN REGION LTD.)
12th Fl., Hutchison House, 10 Harcourt Road. Tel: (852) 524 4093.

COLOMBIA

Population: 36.8 million.
TV Households: 7 million.
Cable Subscribers: 200,000.
Satellite Dishes: 30,000.
VCR Ownership level: 24%.
Estimated Piracy Level: 40%
Video Standard: NTSC.

Start -up private TV networks from Caracol and RCN have been plagued by technical problems resulting in transmission difficulties to over half their target households. The Colombian government set a $95 million license fee for the two start-up private TV companies. While both networks are backed by industrial groups who have pledged to invest over $300 million in the first year, profits will be a long time coming. TV in Colombia has a disproportionately small share of advertising revenue and, as of yet, advertisers have not augmented their television budgets to include the new networks.

TELEVISION COMPANIES

AMD TELEVISION
Cra 30 No 90-54, Bogota. Tel: (571) 610 1155. FAX: (571) 236 1601.

AUDIOVISUALES
Edificio Murillo Toro, Piso 4, Bogota. Tel: (571) 283 4325.

JORGE BARON TELEVISION
Centro Jorge Baron, Ave. 15 No 123-31, Torre A, Bogota. Tel: (571) 215 0211.

CARACOL TELEVISION
Calle 19 No 3-16, Piso 3, PO Box 26484, Bogota. Tel: (571) 281 7900. FAX: (571) 286 3160. Telex: 41480.

COESTRELLAS SA
Tr 6 No 51A-25, Bogota. Tel: (571) 288 7154. FAX: (571) 288 5443. Telex: 45611.

COLOMBIANA DE TELEVISION
Calle 92 No 9-17, PO Box 7661, Bogota. Tel: (571) 236 9267. FAX: (571) 218 1775. Telex: 45614.

INSTITUTO NACIONAL DE RADIO Y TELEVISION (INRAVISION)
National Radio and Television Institute, Centro Administrativo Nacional CAN, Bogota. Tel: (571) 222 0700. Telex: 43311.

PRODUCCIONES JES
Calle 21 No 42A-10, PO Box 28508, Bogota. Tel: (571) 268 5500. FAX: (571) 269 9473. Telex: 42072.

PRODUCCIONES PUNCH
Calle 43 No 27-47, Bogota. Tel: (571) 269 4711. FAX: (571) 269 3539.

PRODUCCIONES TEVECINE LTDA
Cra 18 No 80-15, Bogota. Tel: (571) 218 4799. FAX: (571) 211 1924.

RCN TELEVISION
Ave. de la Americas No 65-82, PO Box 35800, Bogota. Tel: (571) 290 6088. FAX: (571) 260 0924. Telex: 45470.

RTI
Calle 19 No 4-56, Piso 2, PO Box 7808, Bogota. Tel: (571) 282 7700. FAX: (571) 284 9012. Telex: 43294.

TELEANTIOQUIA
Calle 41 NO 25-28 (Piso 3), Medellin. Tel: (574) 262 0311.

TELECARIBE
Cra 54 No 72-142, Piso 10, Barranquilla. Tel: (5753) 582 297. FAX: (58) 560 924.

TELEPACIFICO
Calle 5 No 38A-14. Of 308, Centro Comercial Imbanaco, Cali. Tel: (5723) 575 014.

VIDEO DISTRIBUTORS

BATI VIDEOS DE COLOMBIA
Calle 91, 8-69, Bogota. Tel: (571) 218 9800. FAX: (571) 218 8841.

MAGNUM VIDEO
Transversal 42B, 99-A66, Bogota. Tel: (571) 245 3060. FAX: (571) 287 7795.

VIDEO IMPACTO
Carrera 13, 77-31, Bogota. Tel: (571) 623 7083. FAX: (571) 610 3692.

CONGO

Population: 2.53 million.
TV sets: 8,500.
Video Standard: SECAM.

BROADCASTER

ANTENNE A
Av. du Port 4, Building Forescom 2e Floor, Kinshasa/ Gombe. (243) 21736.

CANAL Z
6 av. du Port, Kinshasa Gombe. (243) 20239.

OZRT
P. 1717, Kinshasas, Gombe 3164. (243) 23171.

RADIODIFFUSION TELEVISION CONGOLAISE
B.P. 2241, Brazzaville. Tel: (242) 814 574, 814 273.

COSTA RICA

Population: 3.46 million.
TV Sets: 360,000.
Video Standard: NTSC.

BROADCASTERS

CORP. COSTARICENSE DE TELEVISION
P.O. Box 2860, San Jose 1000. Tel: (506) 312 222.

MULTIVISION
Apt 4666, San Jose 1000. Tel: (506) 334 444.

REDE NACIONAL DE TELEVISION
Apt. 7-1980, San Jose 1000. Tel: (506) 200 071.

TELEVISORA DE COSTA RICA
Apt. 3786, San Jose 1000. Tel: (506) 322 222.

UNIVERSIDAD DE COSTA RICA
San Pedro, Montes de Doa, San Jose 1000.Tel.: (506) 340
463. FAX: (506) 256 950.

CROATIA

Population: 5 million.
TV Sets: 950,000
Satellite Dishes: 400,000.
Video Standard: PAL.

BROADCASTERS

HRVATSKA TELEVIZIJA (HTV)
PrisavlJe 3, Zagreb 10000. Tel: (3851) 616 3366. FAX: (3851)
616 3392. URL: http: //www.hrt.hr

OTV
Teslina 7, Zagreb 10000. Tel: (3851) 424 124. FAX: (3851) 455
1386.

SLAVONSKA TELEVISIJA OSIJEK
Hrvatske Republike 20, Osijek 31000. Tel: (38531) 124 666.
FAX: (38531) 124 111.

TV MARJAN
Savska bb, Split 21000. Tel: (38521) 364 525. FAX: (38521)
523 455.

VINKOVACKA TELEVIZIJA
Genschera 2, Vinkovci 32000. Tel: (38532) 331 990. FAX:
(38532) 331 985.

ZADARSKA TELEVISIJA
Molotska bb, Zadar 23000. Tel: (38523) 311 791. FAX: (38523)
314 749.

VIDEO DISTRIBUTORS

BLITZ FILM & VIDEO
Sv Mateja 121-04, Zagreb 10000. Tel: (3851) 687 541. FAX:
(3851) 692 814.

CONTINENTAL FILM
Sostariceva 10, Zagreb 10000. Tel: (3851) 421 312. FAX:
(3851) 428 247.

JADRAN FILM DD
Oporovecka 12, Zagreb 10000. Tel: (3851) 298 7222. FAX:
(3851) 251 394.

MOVIE PRODUCTION
Frankopanska 3, Osijek 31000. Tel: (38531) 559 704. FAX:
(38531) 559 730.

ORLANDO FILM
Nasicka 14, Zagreb 10000. Tel: (2851) 334 587. FAX: (3851)
170 167.

POLYBROS
Draganicka 19, Zagreb 10000. Tel: (3851) 563 236. FAX:
(3851) 563 236.

ZAUDER FILM
Jablanicka 1, Zagreb 10040. Tel: (3851) 245 724. FAX: (3851)
245 973.

CUBA

Population: 11 million.
TV Sets: 2.5 million.
Video Standard: NTSC.

BROADCASTERS

**INSTITUTO CUBANO DE RADIODIFUSION (TV
NACIONAL/CUBA VISION)**
Calle M, No. 313, Vedado, Havana.

TELE REBELDE
Mazon # 52, Vedado, Havana. Tel: (53732) 3369.

CYPRUS

Population: 756,000.
TV Sets: 276,000.
Video Standard: PAL.

BROADCASTER

**BAYRAK RADIO & TELEVISION CORP (NORTHERN
CYPRUS)**
Yeni Organize Sanayi Bolgesi, Lefkosa via Mersin 10, Turkey.
(90392) 228 5555.

BFBS
BFPO 57, Dhekelia Mil 381. (357474) 8518.

CYPRUS BROADCASTING CORPORATION
P.O. Box 4824, 1397 Nicosia. Tel: (3572) 422 231. FAX: (3572)
314 055.

LOGOS TV
20 St. Avgoustinou, Archangelos, Nicosia. (3572) 355 595.
FAX: (3572) 355 737.

LUMIERE TELEVISION
Papabisiliou Bldg., 70 Kennedy Ave, Nicolsia. (3572) 311 080.
FAX: (3572) 415 767.

CZECH REPUBLIC

Population: 10.51 million
TV Homes: 3.8 million.
VCR Penetration: 33%.
Cable Service : 650,000
Home Satellite Service: 511,000.
Video Standard: SECAM.

ASSOCIATIONS & ORGANIZATIONS

CZECH CABLE TV ASSOCIATION
Novodvorska 994, 14000 Prague 4. Tel: (422) 373 690. FAX:
(422) 381 157.

CZECH PRODUCERS ASSOCIATION
Krizeneckeho Nam 322, Prague 5. Tel: (422) 6709 1111.

CZECH TELEVISION
Kavcihory, 14070 Prague 4. Tel: (422) 6113 1111. FAX: (422)
692 7202. URL: http://www.czech-tv.cz

FITES-UNION OF TV AND FILM
Pod Nuselskymi Schody 3, 12000 Prague 2. Tel: (422) 691
0310. FAX: (422) 691 1375.

MINISTRY OF CULTURE
Valdstejnske Nam 4, 11000 Prague 1. Tel: (422) 513 1111.
FAX: (422) 536 322.

RADA CESKE TELEVIZE
Na Hrebenech 2, 14070 Prague 4. Tel/FAX: (422) 420 997.

BROADCASTERS

CZECH TELEVISION
Kavcihory, 140 70 Prague 4. Tel: (422) 6113 1111. FAX: (422)
421 562.

NOVA
Vladislavova 20, 11313 Prague 1. Tel: (422) 2110 0111. FAX:
(422) 2110 0565.

PREMIERA TV
Dukelskych Hrdinu 47, Prague 7. Tel. (422) 430 1147. FAX:
(422) 430 1115.

LOCAL CABLE OPERATORS

CABLE PLUS
28 Rijna 124, 70924 Ostrava. Tel: (4269) 217 4202. FAX:
(4269) 644 5441.

CODIS
Novodvorska 994, 14221 Prague 4. Tel: (422) 354 893. FAX:
(422) 356 734.

HBO
Pod Visnovicou 21, 14000 Prague 4. Tel: (422) 472 1347. FAX:
(422) 472 2749.

KABEL NET
Pod Visnovkou, 14000 Prague 4. Tel: (422) 425 145. FAX: (422) 472 2242.

VIDEO ORGANIZATIONS

UNION OF VIDEO DISTRIBUTORS (ANTI-PIRACY SECTION)
Thamova 7, 11000 Prague 8. Tel: (422) 2426 0340.

VIDEO DISTRIBUTORS

ARTEMIS
Masaraykova 179/656, PO Box 1, Usti Nad Lebem 400 13. Tel/FAX: (47) 62049.

BONTON HOME VIDEO
Ostrov Stvanice 858, 17021 Prague 7. Tel: (422) 381 020, 373 959. FAX: (422) 381 020.

FILM VIDEO STUDIO PRAGUE
Vycpalkova 368, 14000 Prague 4. Tel/FAX: (422) 793 1317.

FILMEXPORT HOME VIDEO
Na Morani 5, 12800 Prague. Tel: (422) 293 275. FAX: (422) 293 312.

LUCERNA FILM VIDEO
Narodni Trida 28, 11121 Prague. Tel: (422) 261 341. FAX: (422) 236 6903.

TRANSPRESS
Starochodovska 1098, PO Box 62, 14900 Prague. Tel: (422) 763 161. FAX: (422) 763 176.

WARNER HOME VIDEO
Karlovo Namesti 7, Prague 12000. Tel: (2) 212 3406. FAX: (2) 296 639.

DENMARK

Population: 5.25 million.
TV Sets: 2.7 million.
VCR Homes: 1.5 million.
Home Cable Service: 1.47 million
Home Satellite Service: 340,000
Video Standard: PAL.

BROADCASTERS

DANMARKS RADIO
TV-Byen, DK-2860 Soborg. Tel: (4535) 203 040. FAX: (4535) 202 644.

KANAL 2 PRIME TIME
Mileparken 20A, Skovlunde DK-2740. Tel: (4542) 916 699. FAX: (4542) 841 360.

TELECOM A/S
Telegade 2, DK-2630 Taastrup. Tel: (4542) 529 111. FAX: (4542) 529 331.

TV MIDT-VEST
Sovej 2, Box 1460, Holstebro DK-7500. Tel: (4597) 403 300. FAX: (4597) 401 444.

TV NORD
Soparken 2, Aabybro DK-9440. Tel: (4598) 244 600. FAX: (4598) 244 698.

TV SYD A/S
Laurids Skausgade 12, Haderslev DK-6100. Tel: (4574) 530 511. FAX: (4574) 532 316.

TV 2
Rugaardsvej 25, Odense C DK-5100. Tel: (4565) 911 244. FAX: (4565) 913 322.

TV3
Overgaden Oven Vandet 10, Copenhagen K DK-1415. Tel: (4531) 573 080. FAX: (4531) 578 081.

CABLE SERVICES

TELE DANMARK
Kannikegade 16, Aarhus DK-8000. Tel: (4580) 808 080. FAX: (4589) 337 719.

TELE DENMARK
Norregarde 21, Copenhagen DK-0900. Tel: (4580) 808 080. FAX: (4533) 118 050.

TELE DENMARK KTAS
Rosenbaengets Alle 11, Copenhagen DK-2100. Tel: (4533) 993 399.

SATELLITE

TV3
Indiakaj 6, Copenhagen DK-2100. Tel. (4535) 439 600. FAX: (4535) 439 606.

VIDEO DISTRIBUTORS

BMG ARIOLA
Overgaden Neden, Vandat 17, Copenhagen DK 1414. Tel: (4533) 157 922.

BUENA VISTA INTERNATIONAL
Ostergade 24B, 3rd Floor, Copenhagen DK-1100. Tel: (4533) 120 800. FAX: (4533) 124 332.

DANSK MANAGEMENT CENTER (DMC)
Kristianiagade 7, Copenhagen DK-2100. Tel: (4531) 389 777. FAX: (4531) 420 056.

IRISH VIDEO
Haandvaerkerbyen 7, Greve DK-2670. Tel: (4542) 902 700. FAX: (4542) 900 053.

KRAK VIDEO
Virumsgardvej 21, Virum DJ-2830. Tel: (4545) 836 600. FAX: (4545) 831 011.

METRONOME VIDEO
Sondermarksvej 16, Valby DK-2500. Tel: (4531) 467 755. FAX: (4531) 173 453.

NORDSIK FILM ACQUISITION
Skelbaekgade 1, Copenhagen DK-1717. Tel: (4531) 232 488. FAX: (4531) 230 488. email: nikki@inet.uni-c.dk

POLYGRAM
Emdrupvej 115A, Copenhagen NK-2400. Tel: (4539) 692 522. FAX: (4539) 694 616.

REGINA FILM IMPORT
Bregnegaardsvej 7, Charlottenlund DK-2920. Tel: (4531) 629 640.

SAGA FILM INTERNATIONAL
Soendergada 5, Hjorring DK-9800. Tel: (4598) 922 199. FAX: (4598) 900 439.

SATURN FILMS
V/Knud Thieme, Naerum Husvej 9, Naerum DK 2850. Tel: (4542) 800 869.

SCANBOX DANMARK
Hirsemarken 3, Farum DK-3520. Tel: (4544) 996 200. FAX: (4542) 951 786.

SFC
Vestergade 27, Copenhagen P DK-1456. Tel: (4533) 132 686. FAX: (4533) 130 203.

SONET/DANSK FILM APS
Sndermarksvej 16, Valby DK-2500. Tel: (4536) 467 755. FAX: (4536) 440 969.

UNITED INTERNATIONAL PICTURES
Hauchsvej 13, Frederiksberg C DK-1825. Tel: (4531) 312 330. FAX: (4531) 233 420.

WARNER BROS. INTERNATIONAL
(see Metronome Film listing.)

DJIBOUTI

Population: 575,000.
TV Sets: 13,000.

BROADCASTER

RADIO TELEVISION DE DJIBOUTI
PO Box 97, Malabo Bioko Norte, Djibouti. Tel: (253) 352 294.

DOMINICAN REPUBLIC

Population: 8 million.
TV Sets: 728,000.
Video Standard: NTSC.

BROADCASTERS

CANAL 6
Circuito Independencia C-A, Mariano Cestero esq. Enrique Henriquez, Santo Domingo. Tel: (809) 689 8151.

CANAL 7 CIBAO
Edificio Banco Universal, Calle Sol, Santiago. Tel: (809) 583 0421.

COLOR VISION
(Corp. Dominicana de Radio & Television) Emilio Morel esq.
Lulu Perez, Ens. La Fe, Santo Domingo. Tel: (809) 556 5876.

RADIOTELEVISION DOMINICA
Dr. Tejeda Florentino 8, Santo Domingo. Tel: (809) 689 2120.

RAHINTEL
Av. Independencia, Centro de los Heroes, Santo Domingo. Tel:
(809) 532 2531.

TELEANTILLAS
Autopista Duarte Km. 7, Santo Domingo. Tel: (809) 567 7751.

TELESISTEMA
27 de Febrero, Santo Domingo. Tel: (809) 567 1251.

TV 13
Av. Pasteuresq, Santiago, Santo Domingo. Tel: (809) 687 9161.

ECUADOR

Population: 12 million.
TV Sets: 9600,000.
Cable Subscribers: 85,000.
Satellite Dishes: under a thousand.
Video Standard: NTSC.

BROADCASTERS

CANAL 2 QUITO
Murgeon 732, Quito. Tel: (5932) 540 877.

CANAL 4 GUAYAQUIL S.A.
9 de Octobure 1200, Guayaquil. (5934) 308 914.

CANAL 8 ESMERELDAS
Cas. 108, Esmeraldas. Tel: (5932) 710 090.

CANAL 10
Casilla 673, Guayaquil. Tel: (5934) 391-555.

CANAL 13 QUITO
Rumipampa 1039, Quito. Tel: (5932) 242 758.

CORPORACION ECUATORIANA DE TELEVISION
Casilla 1239, Guayaquil. Tel: (5934) 300 150. FAX: (5934) 303 677.

MANAVISION S.A.
Apt. 50, Portoviejo.

TELEAMAZONAS
Av. Diguja 529 y Brazil, Quito. Tel: (5932) 430 313.

TELECUENCA
Canal Universidad Catolica, Casilla 400, Cuenca. (593) 827 862.

TELEVISORA NACIONAL
Bosmediano 447 y Jose Carb, Quito.

EGYPT

Population: 63.57 million.
TV sets: 7 million.
Video Standard: PAL.

ASSOCIATION

ARAB STATES BROADCASTING UNION (ASBU)
22 a Taha Hussein St, Zannalek, Cairo. Tel: (202) 805 825.
Telex: 347 ASBUUN.

BROADCASTER

EGYPTIAN RADIO AND TV UNION
TV Building, Cornish El-Nil, Maspero, Cairo. (202) 757 155.
(Channel 1: National; Channel 2: News—Arabic, English and
French; Channel 3: Greater Cairo—Cairo, Giza and El-
Qaliubia: Channel 4: Suez Canal Zone—Port Said, Ismailia and
Suez: Channel 5: Alexandria—Alexandria and El-Beheira;
Channel 6: The Nile Delta; Channel 7: Upper Egypt; The
Information Channel: Teletext service.)

SATELLITE BROADCASTER

EGYPTIAN SPACE CHANNEL
P.O. Box 1886, Cairo. Tel: (202) 574 6881. FAX: (202) 749 310.

EL SALVADOR

Population: 5.9 million.
TV Sets: 530,000.
Video Standard: NTSC.

BROADCASTERS

CANAL CUATRO
(See Canal Dos below). Tel: (503) 244 633.

CANAL DOS SA
Ap. Postal 720, San Salvador. Tel: (503) 236 744.

CANAL SEIS
Km. 6, Carretera Panamericana a Santa Tecla, San Salvador.
Tel: (503) 235 122.

TELEVISION CULTURAL EDUCATIVA
Ap. Postal 4, Santa Tecla. Tel: (503) 280 499.

EQUATORIAL GUINEA

Population: 453,803.
TV Sets: 2,500.
Video Standard: SECAM.

BROADCASTER

TELEVISION NACIONAL
MaloboBioko Norte, Malobo.
DIRECRTOR
Antonio Nkulu Oye

ESTONIA

Population: 1.48 million.
TV Sets: 615,000.
Cable Service: 180,000.
Satellite Service: 25,000.
Video Standard: PAL/SECAM.

GOVERNEMENT AGENCIES

ESTONIAN CULTURAL ENDOWMENT
Suur-Karja 23, Tallinn EEOOO1. Tel: (2) 446 922. FAX: (2) 446
983.

MINISTRY OF CULTURE OF THE ESTONIAN REPUBLIC
Suur-Karja 23, Tallinn EEOOO1. Tel: (6) 282 257. FAX: (6) 282
202.

ASSOCIATIONS & ORGANIZATIONS

ESTONIAN ACTORS' UNION
Uus 5, Tallinn EEOOO1. Tel: (2) 446 868. FAX: (2) 443 584.

ESTONIAN ASSOCIATION OF VIDEO PRODUCTION CO.
Narva Mnt 11, Tallinn EEOOO1. Tel: (6) 408 391. FAX: (6) 408
392.

ESTONIAN FILMAKERS' ASSOCIATION
Uus 3, Tallin EEOOO1. Tel: (2) 445 337. FAX: (2) 601 423.

NETWORKS

BFD REKLAAMIKLUBI
Raekoja Plats 15, Tallinn EEOOO1. Tel: (2) 446 922. FAX: (2)
446 983.

EVTV/ESTONIAN VIDEO & TELEVISION
Peterburi Mnt 81, Tallinn 0014. Tel (2726) 328 228. FAX: (3726)
323 650.

KANAL KAKS
9 Harju St, Tallinn 0001. Tel: (3722) 442 356. FAX: (3722) 446
862.

REKLAAMITELEVISIOON LTD (RTV LTD)
3 Endla St, Tallinn 0001. Tel: (3722) 666 743. FAX: (3726) 311
077.

TALLINN EESTI TELEVISIOON
12 Faehlmanni St., Tallinn EE 0100. Tel. (3722) 434 101. FAX:
(3722) 434 155. E-mail: etv@etv.ee. URL:http://www.etv.ee.

TIPP TV
Regali Pst 1-6, Tallinn 0019. Tel: (3722) 238 535. FAX: (3722)
238 555.

ETHIOPIA

Population: 61.33 million.
TV Sets: 150,000.
Video Standard: PAL.

BROADCASTER

ETHIOPIA TELEVISION
Post Office Box 5544, Addis Ababa. Tel: (2511) 116 701.

FIJI

Population: 782,381.
TV Sets: 12,000.
Video Standard: NTSC.

BROADCASTER

FIJI TELEVISION
GPO Box 2442, Suva. Tel: (679) 305 100. FAX: (679) 305 077.
email: fijitv@is.com.fj

FINLAND

Population: 5 million.
TV Sets:2.08 million.
VCR Homes: 1.4 million.
Cable Service: 828,000.
Satellite Service: 65,000.
Video Standard: PAL.

BROADCASTERS

CHANNEL THREE FINLAND/OY KOLMOSTELEVISIO
Ilmalanakatu 2 C, Helsinki. 00240. Tel: (3580) 150 01. FAX
(3580) 150 0677.

THE FINNISH BROADCASTING COMPANY
Head Office, P.O. Box 10,Yliesradio, Helsinki 00241. Tel: (3580)
14801. Telex: 121270. FAX: (3580) 1480 3390.
Radio and TV Centre: Pasilankatu 39, SF-0240 Helsinki, Tel:
(3580) 15001.

MTV OY
00033 MTV3, Finland. Tel: (3580) 15001. FAX: (3580) 150
0707.

TV 2, YLE
Yleisradio, Tohloppinrata 31, Tampere 33270. Tel: (35831) 345
6111. FAX: (35831) 345 6891.

YLEISRADIO OY
TV-1, Box 96, FIN-0024, Yleisradio, Filnland. (3580) 14801.

CABLE

HAMEEN PUHELIN
P.O. Box 94, Hameenlinna SF-13101. Tel: (35817) 614 4204.
FAX: (35817) 612 1005.

HTV PRODUCTION
Ratamestarinkaty 11, Helsinki SF-00520. Tel: (3580) 15651.
FAX: (3580) 140 487.

KAJAANI TV
Pohgolakatu 20, Kajaani, SF-87100. Tel: (35886) 613 0070.
FAX: (35886) 617 7255.

CABLE SYSTEMS

HAMEEN PUHELIN
P.O. Box 94, Hameenlinna 13101. Tel: (35817) 614 4204. FAX:
(35817) 612 1005.

HTV PRODUKTION
Ratamestarinkaty 11, Helsinki 00520. Tel: (3580) 156 51. FAX:
(3580) 140 487.

KAJAANI TV
Pohgolakatu 20, Kajaani 87100. Tel: (35886) 613 0070. FAX:
(35886) 617 7255.

SATELLITE

FINNISH BROADCASTING AUTHORITY
(see Finnish Broadcasting listing under Broadcasters.)

VIDEO DISTRIBUTORS

BMG ARIOLA
PO Box 173, Helsinki 00211. Tel: (3580) 613 201. FAX: (3580)
6132 0299.

DOUBLECHECK
Askoukatou 5, Lahti SF-15100. Tel: (35818) 783 2077. FAX:
(35818) 752 1958.

EL-KO FILMS OY
Kavallintie 23A, Kauniainen SF-02700. Tel: (3580) 505 2600.

ERIKSSON ENTERTAINMENT
Kaisaniemenkatu 2B, Helsinki SF-00100. Tel: (3580) 1311
9377. FAX: (3580) 1311 9444.

EUROPA VISON
Koivuvaarakuja 2, Vantaa 01640. Tel: (3580) 852 711. Telex:
121616. FAX: (3580) 853 2183.

FINNKINO
Kaisaniemenkatu 2B, Helsinki SF-0100. Tel: (3580) 131 191.
FAX: (3580) 1311 9300.

VIPVISION FINLAND
Kapytie 6A, Tampere SF-33180. Tel: (35831) 253 4466. FAX:
(35831) 253 3366.

WARNER HOME VIDEO
Kaisaniemenkatu 1b A 73, Helsinki SF-00100. Tel: (3580) 638
192. FAX: (3580) 638 289.

FRANCE

Population: 58.9 million.
TV Sets: 29.3 million.
Cable Service : 1.42 million.
Home Satellite Service: 1.5 million.
VCR Households: 15 million.
Video Standard: SECAM.

Herve Berger, the Conseil Superieur de l'Audiovisuel gave some
indication that the current quota restricting non-European productions to 40% of films aired on French TV will be eased by the
year 2000.

CanalSatelilite, the digital arm of Canal Plus, began broadcasting its new sports channel L'Equipe TV in September. The channel is also carried by NumeriCable (a Canal Plus subsidiary)
and Reseaux Cables de France. Digital provider TPS began
broadcasting its sports channel, Infosports, in July.

The number of subscribers to cable, pay television and satellite
reached the 6 million mark in 1998. Most of the subscriber
growth is attributed to new subscriptions to the Canal Satellite
platform.

Canal Plus and Info grames Entertainment are launching
Europe's first video game channel that will be broadcast all over
Europe by Canal Satellite.

France counted its largest ever television audience for the World
Cup soccer final. More than 23 million viewers tuned in for the
July sporting event.

ASSOCIATIONS & ORGANIZATIONS

ASSOCIATION OF COMMERCIAL TELEVISION IN EUROPE (ACT)
17 rue de l'arrive, Montparnasse, 75015 France. Tel: (33142)
751 234.

CONSEIL SUPERIEURE DE L'AUDIOVISUEL
39 Quai Andre Citroen, Paris 75015. Tel: (331) 4058 3800.
FAX: (331) 4579 0006.

EUTELSAT
33 Avenue de Maine, Paris, Cedex 15-15 France. Tel: (331)
4538 4757. FAX: (331) 4538 3700. Telex: 203823.

OBSERVATOIRE DE L'AUDIOVISUEL
76 allee de la Robertsan, Strasbourg 67000. Tel: (3388) 144
400. FAX: (3388) 144 419.

PRODUCTEURS DE FILM ET DE PROGRAMMES AUDIOVISUELLES
50 Ave. Marcel, Paris 75008. Tel: (331) 4723 7910. FAX: (331)
4723 9157.

SYNDICAT FRANCAIS DES ARTISTES
21 bis rue Victor Masse, Paris 75009. Tel: (331) 4285 8811.
FAX: (331) 4526 4721.

BROADCASTERS

ARTE
2A rue de la Fonderie, 67080 Strasbourg Cedex. Tel: (333)
8814 2222. FAX: (333) 8814 2200.
PRESIDENT
Jerome Clement

ARTE GEIE
2 Rue de le Fonderie, Strasbourg 6700. Tel: (3388) 52247.

CANAL J
91 Rue de Cherche Midi, Paris 75286. Tel. (331) 4954 5454.
FAX: (331) 4222 8717.

CANAL PLUS
85/89 Quai Andre Citroen, Paris Cedex 75015. Tel: (331) 4425
1000. FAX: (331) 4425 1234.
DIRECTOR
Pierre Lescure

LA CINQUIEME
10 Rue Horace-Vesnet, 92130 Issy les Moulineaux. Tel: (331) 4146 5555. FAX: (331) 4108 0222.
PRESIDENT
Jean-Marie Cavada

EUROSPORT
1 quai du Point du Jour, Boulogne 92100. Tel: (331) 4141 2820. FAX: (331) 4141 1953.

FRANCE TELEVISION
42 Ave. d'Iena, Paris 75008. Tel: (331) 4431 6000. FAX: (331) 4720 2454.
PRESIDENT
Xavier Goyou-Beauchamps

FRANCE 2
21 Ave Montaigne, Paris 75008. Tel: (331) 4421 4242. FAX: (331) 4421 5145.

FRANCE 3
116 Avenue de President Kennedy, Paris 75016. Tel: (331) 4230 1313. FAX: (331) 4289 0327.

METROPOLE TELEVISION (M6)
16 Cours Albert Premier, Paris 75008. Tel: (331) 4421 6666. FAX: (331) 4563 7852.
PRESIDENT
Jean Drucker

TELEVISION FRANCAISE 1 (TF1)
Societe TF1, 1 quai de Pont du Jour, Boulogne 92100. Tel: (331) 4141 1234. FAX: (331) 4141 3400.
CHAIRMAN
Patrick LeFay

CABLE

ALCATEL
30 Rue des Chassees, P.O. Box 309, Clichy 92111. Tel: (331) 4756 6900.

CANAL J
(See Canal J listing under Broadcasters.)

ELLIPSE CABLE/CANAL PLUS
(See Canal Plus listing under Broadcasters.)

LA CHAINE INFO
33 Rue Vaugelas, Paris 75015. Tel: (331) 4045 2345. FAX: (331) 4045 2362.

LYONNAISE COMMUNICATIONS
6 Villa Thoreton, Paris 75015. Tel: (331) 4425 8181. FAX: (331) 4425 8140.

TDF
21-27 rue d'Oradour-sur-Glane, Paris 75732. Tel: (331) 4095 4000. FAX: (331) 4663 3203.

TDF CABLE
21-27 rue Barbes BP-518, Montrouge 92524. Tel: (331) 4965 1000. FAX: (331) 4965 2046.

TELE SHOPPING
30-32 Rue Proudhon, La Plaine Street, Denis 93214. Tel: (331) 4917 7600. FAX: (331) 4917 0395.

TV5
174 Rue de la Universite, Paris 75007. Tel: (331) 4556 0080. FAX: (331) 4556 0004.

SATELLITE BROADCASTERS

CANAL COURSES
83 rue de la Boutie, Paris 75008. Tel: (331) 4953 3900. FAX: (331) 4289 0895.

CANAL FRANCE INTERNATIONALE
59 Boulevard Exelmans, Paris 75016. Tel: (331) 4067 1177. FAX: (331) 4071 1171.

CANAL JEUNESSE
(See Canal J listing under Broadcasters.)

CANAL JIMMY
305 Rue le jour se leve, Boulogne-Cedex 92654. Tel: (331) 4425 1129.

CANALSATELLITE
(See Canal Plus listing under Broadcasters.)

EUTELSAT
Tour Maine Montparnasee, 33 Ave. du Maine, Paris 75755. Tel. (331) 4538 4757. FAX: (331) 4538 3700.

FRANCE TELECOM
6, Place d'Allenery, F-75740, Paris Cedex 15. Tel: (331) 4444 2222. FAX: (331) 4531 5211. http://www.francetelecom.com

LA CHAINE INFO
33 Rue Vaugelas, Paris 75015. Tel: (331) 4045 2345. FAX: (331) 4045 2362.

TV-5 EUROPE
174 rue de l'Universite, Paris 7507. Tel: (331) 4556 0080. FAX: (331) 4556 0004.

CABLE AND SATELLITE PROGRAM SUPPLIERS

ARTE GEIE
(See Arte Geie listing under Broadcasters.)

EURONEWS
60 Chemin des Monilles, Ecully 69130. Tel: (3372) 1881 06. FAX: (3372) 1893 71.

EUROSPORT
54 avenue de la Voie Lactee, Boulogne 92100. Tel: (331) 4141 1234. FAX: (331) 4141 2485.

FRANCE SUPERVISION
22 Ave. Montaigne, Paris 75008. Tel: (331) 4421 4514. FAX: (331) 4421 4481.

MCM EUROMUSIQUE
109 Rue de Fauborg Ste. Honore, Paris 75008. Tel: (331) 4495 9100. FAX: (331) 4495 9125.

MULTIVISION
6 Villa Thorepon, Paris 75015. Tel: (331) 4425 8181. FAX: (331) 4425 8940.

RFO
5 Ave.du Recteur Poincare, Paris 75016. Tel: (331) 4524 7100. FAX: (331) 4524 9596.

SERIE CLUB
16 Cours Albert, Paris 75008. Tel: (331) 4256 7666. FAX: (331) 4256 9666.

TELE MONTE CARLO
16 Blvd. Princesse Charlotte, Monte Carlo 98000. Tel: (3393) 151 415.

TV-SPORT
305 Avenue Le Jour se Leve, Boulogne-Billancourt 92657. Tel: (331) 4694 6100. FAX: (331) 4761 0030.

VIDEO DISTRIBUTORS

ALPHA VIDEO
126 Rue la Boetie, Paris 75008. Tel: (331) 4563 4411.

ATOLL VIDEO
18-20 Rue Borrego, Paris 75003. Tel: (331) 4366 6922. FAX: (331) 4366 5221.

CENTRE NATIONALE DE DOCUMENTATION PEDA-GOGIQUE
29 Rue D'IUlm, Paris 75230 Cedex 5. Tel: (331) 4634 9000. FAX: (331) 4634 5544.

CIC VIDEO
1 bis Rue du Petit Clamart, PO Box 13, Velizy 78149. Tel: (331) 4094 1020. FAX: (331) 4094 1004.

CINEMADIS FILMS
78 Ave. des Champs Elysees, Paris 75008. Tel: (331) 4562 8287. FAX: (331) 4289 2198.

CONCORDE
276 Rue des Pyrenees, Paris 75020. Tel: (331) 4797 3374. FAX: (331) 4797 7259.

DCX
31 Rue Rennequin, Paris 75017. Tel: (331) 4267 3037. FAX: (331) 4267 0278.

EMI FRANCE
43 rue camille Desmoulins, Issy-les-Moulineaux 92130. Tel: (331) 4629 2020. FAX: (331) 4629 2121.

FFCM VIDEO
126 Rue la Boetie, Paris 75008. Tel: (331) 4256 1642.

FILM OFFICE
63 Champs-Elysees, Paris 75008. Tel: (331) 5377 1800. FAX: (331) 4256 0375.

LES FILMS ARIANE/REVCOM INTERNATIONAL
62 Rue Louis Bleriot, Boulogne Billancourt 92641 Tel: (331) 4110 5000. FAX: (331) 4110 5025.

LES FILMS VERTS
La Tissote, Mondragon 84430. Tel: (3390) 406 211. FAX: (3390) 406 639.

FRANCE TELEVISION DISTRIBUTION
(See France 2 listing under Broadcasters.)

GAUMONT COLUMBIA TRISTAR HOME VIDEO
31 rue Louis Pasteur, Boulogne-Billancourt, 92100. Tel: (331) 4684 1919. FAX: (331) 4604 2818.

HEURE EXQUISE
Rue de Normandie Le Fort BP 113, Mons en Bareuil 59370. Tel: (3320) 432 432. FAX: (3320) 432 433.

K-FILMS
15 Rue Saintonges, Paris 75003. Tel: (331) 4274 7014. FAX: (331) 4274 7024.

LAURA VIDEO PRODUCTION
64 Blvd. Voltaire, Paris 75011. Tel: (331) 4355 8805. FAX: (331) 4355 0190.

LA MEDIATHEUE DES TROIS MONDES
63 bis Rue due Cardinal Lemoine, Paris 75005. Tel: (331) 4354 3338. FAX: (331) 4634 7019.

POLYGRAM VIDEO
107 Blvd Periere, Paris 75017. Tel: (331) 4415 6615. FAX: (331) 4415 9588.

RENE CHATEAU VIDEO
72 Rue Lariston, Paris 75116. Tel: (331) 4727 9968. FAX: (331) 4704 5980.

SONY MUSIC
131 Avenue de Wagram, Paris 75017. Tel: (331) 4440 6905. FAX: (331) 4440 6666.

TF1 VIDEO
1 quai de Point du Jour, Boulogne Cedex 92656. Tel: (331) 4141 2416. FAX: (331) 4141 2929.

TWENTIETH CENTURY FOX
8 Rue Bellini, Paris 75116. Tel: (331) 4434 6000. FAX: (331) 4434 6105.

VAUBAN PRODUCTIONS
9 Avenue Franklin D. Roosevelt, Paris 75008. Tel: (331) 4225 6604. FAX: (331) 4953 0491.

WARNER BROS.
67 Ave. de Wagram, Paris 75017. Tel: (331) 4401 4999. FAX: (331) 40547193.

GABON

Population: 1.3 million.
TV sets: 40,000.
Video Standard: PAL-B.

BROADCASTER

RTG TV GABON
PO Box 10150, Libreville. Tel: (241) 732 152. FAX: (241) 732 153.

GAMBIA

Population 1.2 million
TV sets: 6000
Video Standard: PAL-B.

BROADCASTERS

INFORMATION AND BROADCASTING SERVICE
19 Hagan St. Banjul. Tel: (220) 27230.

RADIO GAMBIA
Mile 7, Banjul. Tel: (220) 495 101. FAX: (220) 495 102.

GEORGIA

Population 5.37 million
TV sets: N/A
Video Standard: SECAM

GEORGIAN TELEVISION
M. KOstavas 68, 380071 Tbilisi. (78832) 362 294. FAX: (78832) 362 319.

GERMANY

Population: 82 million.
TV Sets: 32.7 million.
Home Cable Service : 19.5 million.
Home Satellite Service: 6.5 million.
VCR Homes: 50 million (62%)
Video Stores: 6,200
Video Standard: PAL
Video Rental: $395.5 million
Video Sales: $522 million

In March of 1998, the EEC blocked the proposed merger of two pay TV powerhouses, Kirch Group and the Bertelsmann affiliated CLT-UFA.

Investment in domestic programming has risen in the past year. ZDF produced over 90 original movies in 1998 and ARD increased its local investment by more than $30 million. Not to be outdone, ProSieben and Sat ! have announced that they too will invest more money German productions. ZDF has set up a new production arm, Network Movie Film-und-Fersehenproduktion, to produce programming for the German market with production set to begin in 1999.

CLT-UFA production arm, UFA Film and TV, is expanding its international TV co-production by creating deals with HBO, Warner Bros. and Paramount.

Helmut Thoma, the managing director of RTL, retired at the end of 1997. He is largely redited with the success of RTL whose advertising revenues were a record $1.27 billion in 1997, yielding $96 million in profit. RTL broadcasts "Gute Zeiten, Sclechte Zeiten", the most popular soap opera on German television.

German public television network, ARD, has changed its programming on its member stations to compete more directly with the commercial

British TV producer, Granada Prods., is setting up a subsidiary in Germany on the strength of its deal with RTL to produce one miniseries and two series locally.

A commission designed to evaluate regulations for digital pay tv has mandated that sporting events such as the Olympics, the Tour de France and World Cup Soccer, must first be shown on free television before being aired on pay TV

Further evidence that the German pay TV market is tough to penetrate came in May when Viacom's Nickelodeon channel in Germany closed its doors. Viacom had invested more that $66 million in the failed venture. As a result, other pay tv providers are re-evaluating the risks of entering the German market. Another failed venture was Landmark Communications Weather Channel. It is estimated that by the end of 1998, total start-up losses for German TV channels will be $4.2 billion. Since private television was legalized in Germany 12 years ago, total profits are only $643 million. Based on these figures, it is likely that several more channels will flounder in the near future.

German music channel Viva is prouducing foreign-language programming for international broadcast. Beginning in 1999, Viva will add a Polish language, Polish music and Polish VJ broadcast.

Shock television is alive and well in Germany with the ProSieben channel daytime talk show "Arabella". The DLM, a conference of Germany's 11 regional media authorities and MABB, the Berlin based media authority have received and are considering acting upon the numerous complaints about the sexual nature of Arabella's programming. There are several similar shows on German television, but Arabella has been singled out, perhaps because it is a youth-oriented talk show.

BROADCASTERS

ANTENNE BAYERN
Munchner Str 20, 85774 Unterfohring. Tel: (89) 992 770. FAX: (89) 9927 7209.

ARD
Arnulfstrasse 42, 80335 Munich. (4989) 590 001. FAX: (4989) 5900 3249.

ARTE DEUTSCHLAND TV GMBH
Schutzenstr 1, 76530 Baden-Baden. Tel: (7221) 93690. FAX: (7221) 936 950.

BAYERISCHER RUNDFUNK FERNSEHEN
Rundfunkplatz 1, 80300 Munich. Tel: (4989) 590 001. FAX: (4989) 5900 2375. Telex: 521070.

DER KABELKANAL-DKK
Bahnhofstrasse 28, Unterfohring 85774. Tel: (4989) 950 8070. FAX: (4989) 950 80714.

DEUTSCHE WELLE
Raderberggurtel 50, 50968 Cologne. Tel: (221) 3890. FAX: (221) 389 3000.

DEUTSCHES SPORTFERNSEHEN
Bahnhofstrasse 27, 8774 Unterfohring. (4989) 950 002. FAX: (4989) 9500 2392.

FRANKEN FUNK U. FERNSEHEN GMBH
Weinstr 70, 91058 Erlangen. Tel: (9131) 6090. FAX: (9131) 609 217.

HESSICHER RUNDFUNK FERNSEHEN
Bertramstrasse 8, Frankfurt am Main 60320. Tel: (4969) 1551. FAX: (4969) 155 2900.

MDR FERNSEHEN
Kantstr 71-73, 04275 Leipzig. Tel: (49341) 22760. FAX: (49341) 566 3544.

MTV MUSIC TELEVISION
Widenmayerstr 18, 80538 Munich. Tel: (89) 212 3060. FAX: (89) 298 777.

NBC SUPER CHANNEL
Praunheimer Landstr 50, 60488 Frankfurt/Main. Tel: (69) 9760 7319. FAX: (69) 9760 7671.

NDR FERNSEHEN
Rothenbaumchaussee 132, 20149 Hamburg. Tel: (4940) 4131. FAX: (4940) 447 602.

NORDOSTDEUTSCHE VERLAGSGESSELSCHAFT
Domhof 24, 31139 Hildesheim. Tel: (495121) 169 253. FAX: (495121) 169 259.

N-TV
Taubenstr 1, 10117 Berlin. Tel: (30) 201 900. FAX: (20) 2019 0775.

OSTDEUTSCHER RUNDFUNK BRANDENBURG
August-Bebel-strasse 25-53, 14482 Postdam-Babelsberg. Tel: (49331) 723 600. FAX: (49331) 77395.

PREMIERE MEDIEN GMBH & CO KG
Am Stadtrand 52, 22047 Hamburg. Tel: (40) 694 450. FAX: (40) 6944 5199.

PRIVATE BAYRISCHE AV UND TV GESELLSCHAFT (PRIB-AG)
Binsberg 28, 85658 Egmating. Tel: (4980) 95751. FAX: (4980) 95753.

PRO-SIEBEN
Bahnhofstrasse 27a, Unterfohring 85774. Tel: (4989) 9507 1000.

RTL FERNSEHEN
Aachener Str 1036, 50858 Cologne. Tel: (49221) 4560. FAX: (49221) 456 4290.

RTL 2
Bavariafilmplatz, 82031 Gruunewald. Tel: (4989) 6418 50. FAX: (4989) 6418 5999.

RTL 2 FERNSEHEN GMBH & CO KG
Max Planck Str. 39, 50850 Cologne. (492234) 95880. FAX: (492234) 958 896.

SAARLANDISCHER RUNDFUNK FERNSEHEN (SR)
Funkhaus Halberg, 66100 Saarbruken. Tel: (49681) 6020. FAX: (49681) 602 3874.

SAT 1
Martin Luther Str 1, 10777 Berlin. (4930) 212 410 FAX: (4930) 2124 1140.

SENDER FREIES BERLIN (SFB)
Masurenallee 8-14, W-14057 Berlin. Tel: (4930) 30310. FAX: (4930) 301 5062.

SUDDEUTSCHER FUNDFUNK (SDR)
Neckarstr 230, 70190 Stuttgart. Tel: (49711) 9291. FAX: (49711) 929 2600.

SUDWESTFUNK (SWF)
Hans-Bredow Str., 76530 Baden-Baden. Tel: (497221) 920. FAX: (497221) 922 013.

SUPER CHANNEL
Goethestr 8/V, 80336 Munich. Tel: (89) 597 988. FAX: (89) 554 190.

SUPER RTL
Richard-Byrd-Strasse 6, D-50829, Cologne. (49221) 91550.

TD1 GMBH
Pankstr 54, 13357 Berlin. Tel: (30465) 201 114. FAX: (30465) 3787.

3 SAT
Postfach 4040, Essenheimere Landstr, 55128 Mainz. Tel: (6131) 701.

VIVA TV
Clausius-Dornier Str 5b, 50829 Cologne. Tel: (221) 956 820. FAX: (221) 956 8282.

VOX
Richard Byrd Strasse 6, D-50829 Cologne. (49221) 953 40. FAX: (49221) 953 4400.

WDR FERNSEHEN
Appelhofplatz 1, D-50667 Cologne. Tel: (49221) 2201. FAX: (49221) 2204 800.

ZWEITES DEUTSCHES FERNSEHEN (ZDF)
P.O. Box 4040, ZDF Strasse 1, 55100 Mainz. Tel: (496131) 7011. FAX: (496131) 702 157.

CABLE SERVICES

DER KABELKANAL-DKK
Bahnhofstrasse 28, 85774 Unterfohring. Tel: (4989) 950 8070. FAX: (4989) 950 80714.

DEUTSCHE TELEKOM
Postfach 2000, 33105 Bonn. Tel: (49228) 181 4949. FAX: (49228) 181 8941.

ENGELS TELEVISION
Berlinstrasse 12, 36270 Niederaula. Tel: (49662) 592 130. FAX: (49662) 570 60.

KOMMUNAL BAU RHEINLAND-PFALZ
Hindenburgplatz 7, 55188 Mainz. Tel: (49613) 123 490. FAX: (49 613) 123 4949.

PREMIERE MEDIEN GMBH & CO KG
Am Stadtrand 52, 22047 Hamburg. Tel: (40) 694 450. FAX: (2234) 958 896.

SATELLITE

AFN-TELEVISION EUROPE
Bertramstrasse 6, 60320 Frankfurt am Main. Tel: (4969) 1568 8262. FAX: (4969) 1568 3800.

ARD
(See ARD listing under Broadcasters.)

DEUTSCHE BUNDESPOST TELEKOM
Heinrich-von-Stephan Strasse, 53175 Bonn. Tel: (49228) 140. FAX: (49228) 148 872.

DEUTSCHES SPORTFERNSEHEN
Bahnhofstrasse 27, 8774 Unterfohring. Tel: (4989) 950 020. FAX: (4989) 950 02392.

DEUTSCHE WELLE
Raderberggurtel 50, 50968 Cologne. Tel: (49 221 3890 FAX: (49 221 3893 000.

KABAL 1
Bahnhofstrasse 28, 85774 Unterfohring. Tel: (4989) 950 8070 FAX: (4989) 9508 8044.

N-TV
Taubenstrasse 1, 10117 Berlin. Tel: (4930) 2312 5500. FAX: (4930) 2312 5505.

RTL-FERNSEHEN
(see RTL listing under Broadcasters.)

RTL NORD
Jenfelder Allee 80, 22045 Hamburg. Tel: (4940) 6688 4350. FAX: (4940) 6688 4400.

SAT
Otto Schott Str 13, 55127 Mainz. Tel: (6131) 9000.

SWF
Hans Bredow Strasse, PO Box 820, 76522 Baden Baden. Tel: (497221) 920. FAX: (497221) 922 010.

VOX
Richard Byrd Strasse 6, D-50829 Cologne. Tel: (49221) 95340. FAX: (49221) 953 4800.

WDR-3 KOLN
Appellhofplatz 1, 50667 Cologne. Tel: (49221) 160 2132. FAX: (49221) 160 2135.

VIDEO DISTRIBUTORS

ATLAS FILM UND AV GMBH & CO. KG
Ludgeristrasse 14-16, 47057 Duisburg. Tel: (49203) 378 6201. FAX: (49203) 378 6200.

BAVARIA FILM
Bavariafilmplatz 7, 82031 Geiselgasteig. Tel: (4989) 64990. FAX: (4989) 6492507.

BMG VIDEO
Kastenbauer Strasse 2, 81677 Munich. Tel: (4989) 413 6687.
FAX: (4989) 413 6130.

BUENA VISTA
Kastenbauer Strasse 2, 81677 Munich. Tel: (4989) 9934 0270.
FAX: 9934 0139.

COLUMBIA TRISTAR HOME VIDEO
Ickstatt Strass 1, 80469 Munich. Tel: (4989) 230 370. FAX:
(4989) 2303 7400.

CONCORDE-CASTLE ROCK-TURNER VIDEO
Rosenheimer Strasse 143b, 90600 Frankfurt. Tel: (4969) 450
6100. FAX: (4969) 4506 1092.

CONCORDE VIDEO
Stefan-George-Ring 23, 81929 Munich. Tel: (4989) 930 950.

CONSTANTIN VIDEO
Kaiserstrasse 39, 80801 Munich 80801. Tel: (4989) 386 090.
FAX: (4989) 3860 9242.

EMI ELECTROLA
Maarweg 149, 50825 Cologne. Tel: (49221) 49020. FAX:
(49221) 497 2335.

EUROVIDEO BILDPROGRAM
Oskar Messterstrasse 15, Ismaning 85737. Tel: (4989) 9624
4432. FAX: (4989) 9642 4450.

FIPRO/VMP
Taunusstrasse 51, Munich 80807. Tel: (4989) 350940. FAX:
(4989) 3509 4101.

FOX VIDEO
Am Forsthaus Gravenbruh 7, Neue Isenberg. Tel: (496102)
50040. FAX: (496102) 5550.

HIGHLIGHT FILMVERLEIH
Herkomerplatz 2, 82131 Stockdorf. Tel: (4989) 895 6170. FAX:
(4989) 8956 1730.

HVW FOCUS FILMVERTRIEBS
Industrie Strasse 49, 41564 Kaarst. Tel: (4921) 3160 4041.
FAX: (4921) 316 3290.

INTER-PATHE GMBH & CO. KG
Bolongarostrasse 141, 65929 Frankfurt am Main. Tel: (4969)
304 043. FAX: (4969) 311 091.

KIRCHGRUPPE/MDM
2 Robert Buerkle Strasse, 85737 Munich. Tel: (4989) 9956
2422. FAX: (4989) 9956 2640.

MERKUR FILM AGENCY
Isarstrasse 6, 82065 Baierbrunn. Tel: (4989) 793 7879. FAX:
(4989) 793 7970.

PHILIPS MEDIA
Alexander Strasse 1, 20099 Hamburg. Tel: (4940) 2852 1401.
FAX: (4940) 2852 1402.

POLYGRAM VIDEO
Glockengiesserwalle 2, 20095 Hamburg. Tel: (4940) 308 7740.
FAX: (4940) 308 7436.

ROTAVISION FILMHANDEl
Postfach 1701, Koblenz 56015. Tel: (49261) 18888. FAX:
(49261) 18868.

SONY MUSIC ENTERTAINMENT
Stephan Strasse 15, 60313 Frankfurt. Tel: (4969) 138 880.
FAX: (4969) 1388 8440.

SPRINGER-VERLAG GMBH & CO. KG
Heidelbergerplatz 3, 14197 Berlin. Tel: (4930) 82071. FAX:
(4930) 820 7821.

UNIVERSUM FILM GMBH (UFA)
Kastenbauer Strasse 2, 81677 Munich. Tel: (4989) 413 6671.
FAX: (4989) 413 6870.

VIPRO VIDEO VERTRIEBS UND PRODUKTIONS
Taunusstrasse 51, 80807 Munich. Tel: (4989) 350 940. FAX:
(4989) 3509 4101.

VPS FILM-ENTERTAINMENT
Waldmeisterstrasse 72, 80935 Munich. Tel: (4989) 3548 4154.
FAX: (4989) 3548 4160.

GHANA

Population: 19.4 million.
TV Sets: 800,000.
Video Standard: PAL-B.

BROADCASTER

GHANA BROADCASTING CORPORATION
Broadcast House, P.O. Box 1633, Accra. (23321) 221 161.
FAX: (23321) 773 240.

GREECE

Population: 10.5 million, plus 500,000 immigrants from Balkan
countries.
TV homes: 3.5 million.
Pay TV Homes: No specific figures available.
Satellite Dishes: 10,000.
VCR Households: 2 million
VCR Penetration: 50%
Video Prices: $3.50—$5.50
Video Standard: PAL

The number of TV viewers fropped again this year in favour of
the movies as a result of the low quality of local TV production.
By order of the Nationl Audiovisual Council, many illegal channels stationed across the country ceased oepration. The Council
also imposed fines on legal channels for violations including
exceeding the lawful time allowed for commercials and programming the included violent and/or hocking scenes. A draft of
a new law covering the above mentioned violations as well as
programming containing "insulting scenes" or segments that
endanger human rights in "reality shows" will be debated by
Parilament.

Though the income from commercials was over $23 billion this
year, all channels are in the red. Besides the State channels ET
1 and Net stationed in Athens and ET 3 which broadcasts from
Thessaloniki, there are more than 300 other legal and illegal private channels operating across the country.

It is likely that digital broadcasts will begin in 1999.

Due to the steps taken by the Society for Protection of
Audiovisual Works, the piracy level dropped in 1998. Many
regional TV channels were prosecuted for airing and distributing
illegal video cassettes.

STATE BROADCASTERS

ET1 AND NET
431 Messoguion St., Athens 153 42.Tel: (301) 638 0390. FAX:
(301) 689 0652.

ET 3
20 Evagkelaki St., Thessaloniki 632 26. Tel: (3031) 264 800.
FAX: (3031) 236 466.

PRIVATE BROADCASTERS

ANTENNA 1
10-12 Kifissias Str., Athens 151 29. Tel: (301) 685 3370. FAX:
(301) 681 0128.

CHANNEL 5
31 Demetros St., Tavros Athens. Tel: (301) 342 4090. FAX:
(301) 341 2608.

FILMNET CABLE CHANNEL
144 Kifissias St., Athens. Tel: (301) 672 3110. FAX: (301) 671
9926.

MEGA CHANNEL
Alamanas and Delphi St., Athens 104 41. Tel: (301) 618 1207.
FAX: (301) 879 9016.

NEW CHANNEL
9-11 Pireaus St., Athens 10 53. Tel: (301) 524 3823. FAX: (301)
524 4514.

SEVEN X CHANNEL
27 Demetros Str., Tavros, Athens 151 25. Tel: (301) 689 7604.
FAX: (301) 689 7608.

SKY CHANNEL
6 Philellinon Str., Athens 105 57. Tel: (301) 422 2002. FAX:
(301) 412 7628.

STAR CHANNEL
22 Demetros St., Tavros, Athens 177 78. Tel: (301) 342 1301.
FAX: (301) 342 7816.

TELECITY CHANNEL
22 Vassileos Constantinou St., Athens 116 35. Tel: (301) 937
6400. FAX: (301) 956 3545.

TELETORA CHANNEL
15 Elia Eliou St., Neos Kosmos, Athens.

TV 100
1 Nikolaou Germanou St., Thessalonki 546 21. Tel: (3031) 265 828.

CABLE AND SATELLITE

ANTENNA TV
(See listing for Antenna under Broadcasters)

FILMNET CABLE TV
(See listing for Filmnet under Broadcasters)

VIDEO DISTRIBUTORS

AUDIOVISUAL ENTERPRISES
32 Sochou St., Athens 115 25. Tel: (301) 666 8824. FAX: (301) 666 6996.

CBS-FOX VIDEO
311 Missogioun St., Chalandri, Athens 152 31. Tel: (301) 647 7727. FAX: (301) 672 7728.

HOME VIDEO HELLAS
276 Missoguion St., Athens 152 31. Tel: (301) 647 7727. FAX: (301) 647 7728.

VIDEOSONIC
1 Evrydamantos Str, Athens 117 34. Tel: (301) 924 2200. FAX: (301) 924 7388.

—RENA VELISSARIOU

GUADELOUPE

Population: 430,000.
TV Sets: 150,000.
Video Standard: NTSC.

BROADCASTERS

ARCHIPEL 4
ResidenceLes Palmiers, Gabarre 2, 97110. Tel: (590) 836 350.

CANAL ANTILLES (PAY TV)
2 lot. Les Jardins de Houelbourg, 97122 Baie Mahault. Tel: (590) 268 179.

RFO GUADALOUPE
P.O. Box 402, F-97163, Point-a-Pitre. Tel: (590) 939 696. FAX: (590) 939 682.

GUATEMALA

Population: 11.3 million.
TV Sets: 513,000.
Video Standard: NTSC.

BROADCASTERS

RADIO TELEVISON GUATEMALA
Apt. 1367, Guatemala. Tel: (5022) 922 491.

TELEVISIETE
Apt. Postal 1242., Guatemala. Tel: (5022) 62216.

TELEVISION CULTURAL EDUCATIVA
4a Calle 18-38, Zona 1, Guatemala. Tel: (5022) 531 913.

TELEONCE
Ca. 20, 5-02, Zona 10, Guatemala. Tel: (5022) 682 165.

TRECEVISION
3a Calle 10-70, Zona 10, Guatemala. Tel: (5022) 63266.

GUINEA

Population: 7.4 million.
TV Sets: 65,000.
TV Standard: PAL.

BROADCASTER

RADIODIFFUSION TELEVISION GUINIEENNE
B.P. 391, Conraky. Tel: (224) 442 205.

GUYANA

Population: 713,000
TV Sets: 15,000.
Video Standard: NTSC.

BROADCASTER

GUYANA TELEVISION
68 Hadfield St., Lodge Georgetown. Tel: (5922) 69231.

HAITI

Population: 6.76 million.
TV Sets: 25,000.
Video Standard: NTSC.

BROADCASTERS

TELEVISON NATIONALE D'HAITI
P.O. Box 13400 Delmas 33, Port-au-Prince. (5091) 63324.

TELE HAITI
P.O. Box 1126, Port-au-Prince. (5091) 23000.

HONDURAS

Population: 5.6 million.
TV Sets: 170,000.
Video Standard: NTSC.

BROADCASTERS

COMPANIA BROADCASTING
Apt. Postal 882, Bariio Rio Pedras.

COMPANIA CENTROAMERICANA DE TV
Apt. Postal 68, Tegucigalpa.

CORP. CENTROAMERICANA DE COMMUNICACIONES, S.A.
Apt. Postal 120, San Pedro Sula.

CRUCENA DE TELEVISON
Casilla 3424, Tegucigalpa.

TELESISTEMA HONDURENO
Apt. Postal 734, Tegucigalpa. Tel: (50432) 7835.

HUNGARY

Population: 10.325 million.
TV Sets: 4.26 million.
Cable Service: 1.4 million.
Satellite Service: 424,000.
VCR Homes: 1.3 million.
Video Standard: PAL.

Hungarian cable operator, KabelKom, which is partly owned by Time Warner, will be challenged in the coming yesar by a start-up organization delivering cable programming to a projected 40,000 subscribers. The new cabler is owned by Hungarian telecommunications company, MATAV.

ORGANIZATIONS

ASSOCIATION OF FILM & TV MAKERS
Gorkij Fasor 38, H-1068 Budapest. Tel: (361) 142 5756.

BROADCASTERS

ATV LTD
Konyves K Krt 13-15, Budapest 1097. Tel: (361) 215 6213. FAX: (361) 215 7754.

MAGYAR TELEVIZLO (MTV 1 & 2)
Szabadsag Ter 17, H-1810 Budapest. Tel: (361) 111 4059. FAX: (361) 1157 4979.

PRIVATE BROADCASTERS

NAP-TV
Angol Ut 13, H-1149 Budapest. Tel: (361) 251 0490. FAX: (361) 251 3371.

A3 (PEST-BUDA TV)
Rona utca 140, 1147 Budapest. (361) 251 4749.

TV3 BUDAPEST
Budakeszi utca 51, 1021 Budapest. Tel: (361) 275 1800. FAX: (361) 275 1801.

SIO TELEVISIO
Fo ter 2, 8600 Siofok. (3684) 317 111. FAX: (3684) 310 887.

CABLE

GLOBAL KABELTELEVISIO
Csik-Hegyek U 18, Budapest 1118. Tel: (361) 736 250. FAX: (361) 736 252.

HBO HUNGARY/KABELKOM/SPEKTRUM
Budafoki Ut 59, H-1111 Budapest. Tel: (361) 165 2466. FAX: (361) 181 2377

SATELLITE BROADCASTERS

ALFA TV
Vadrosligeti Fusor 38, H-1068 Budapest. Tel. (361) 351 7762. FAX: (361) 351 7768.

DUNA TV
Rona Ut 174, H-1145 Budapest. Tel: (361) 562 449. FAX: (361) 558 458.

VIDEO DISTRIBUTORS

BEST HOLLYWOOD
P.O. Box 1167, H6701 Szeged. Tel: (3662) 202 4697.

CINE-ART LTD

CINEMAGYAR KFT (HUNGAROFILM EX)
Batori u 10, H-1054 Budapest. Tel: (361) 111 4614. FAX: (361) 153 1317.

DUNA/UIP DANUBE
Tarogato u 24, H-1021 Budapest. Tel: (361) 174 7291. FAX: (361) 176 7291.

FLAMEX
Labanc u 22B, Budapest H-1021. Tel: (361) 176 1543. FAX: (361) 176 0596.

INTERCOM
Rona Ut 174, H-1145 Budapest. Tel: (361) 467 1400. FAX: (361) 252 2736.

MOKEP
Bathori u 10, Budapest H-1054. Tel: (361) 111 2097. FAX: (361) 153 1613.

VIDEO RENT
Szepvigyi Ut 128, H-1025 Budapest. Tel: (361) 250 4523. FAX: (361) 250 4106.

ICELAND

Population: 273.407.
TV sets: 92,595.
Cable households: 28,000.
Satellite Subscribers: 3,000.
Video households: 53,000.
Video Standard: PAL.

BROADCASTERS

IRIKISUTVARPID - SJONVARP
ICELANDIC NATIONAL BROADCASTING SERVICE
Laugavegi 176, Reykjavik 105. Tel: (354) 515 3900. FAX: (354) 515 3008.
Icelandic National Broadcasting Service Television (RUV). Tel: (3541) 515 6000. FAX: (3541) 515 6800.

ICE-TV CHANNEL 3
Laufey Gudjonsdottir, Kringlan 7, Reykjavik 103. (3541) 533 5633. FAX: (3541) 533 5699.

STOD 2 & STOD 3
Krokhals 6, 112 Reyjavik. (354) 515 6000 (Stod 2), (354) 533 5600 (Stod 3). FAX: (354) 533 5699.

INDIA

Population: 916 million.
TV Homes: 55 million.
Pay TV Homes: Metro only; 20.
VCR Homes: 15 million.
Average Video Price: Rs.250.
Rental: 40 cents (overnight rental).
Legal Home Video Distributors: 2000.
Estimated Piracy level: 60%
Video Standard: PAL.

India's state controlled television known as Doordarshan is among the premier TV organizations in the world, with 34 pro-gramme production centres and as many as 656 TV transmitters of varying power covering over 85 percent of the population. Viewership surveys have shown that feature films, film based programmes and sponsored serials are popular all over the country, cutting across regional and linguistic barriers. India is the most desired satellite 'footprint' among international media moguls. The result of so many contenders in the Indian televi-sion industry has been the cutting into each others profit margin.

In an odd development, Indian court issued a warrant for the arrest of Rupert Murdoch in July. Murdoch's STAR-TV Network is accused of showing obscene films in India.

BROADCASTERS

ASIANET
Center Plaza, Vezhutacaud, Trivandrum 14 (Kerala). Tel: (91471) 085 03; FAX: (91471) 685 63.

ATN
Jal Building, Nehru Rd, Off Western Express Highway, Ville Parle (E), Bombay 400057. Tel: (9122) 610 4617. FAX: (9122) 287 2753

BBC WORLD LTD
AIFACS Bldg, 1 Rafi Marg, New Delhi 110001. Tel: (9111) 335 5751. FAX: (9111) 335 5673.

CNN
Taj Mahal Hotel, Suite 1112, 1 Mansingh Road, New Delhi. Tel: (9111) 601 6162. FAX: (9111) 301 9480.

DOORDARSHAN
Mandi House, Copernicus Marg, New Delhi 110001. Tel: (9111) 338 3394. FAX: (9111) 338 6507.

ESPN
Modi Entertainment Network: c-44/32 Okhla Industrial Area-Phase II, New Delhi 20. Tel: (9111) 683 3409. FAX: (9111) 684 7605.

JAIN SATELLITE TELEVISION
Jain Studio Campus, Scindia Villa, Ring Rd, New Delhi 23.

NEPC COMMUNICATIONS
GR Complex Annex, 3rd floor, 407-408 Anna Salai, Nandanam, Madras 400 035. Tel: (9144) 433 0489. FAX: (9144) 433 1029.

SONY TV
Plot 23, Shah Industrial Estate, Off Veera Desai Road, Andheri (West) Bombay 400 058. Tel: (9122) 633 1729. FAX: (9122) 731 7836

STAR TV
News TV India Ltd, 3rd Floor, Sanghrajka House, 431 Lamington Road, Bombay 400 004. Tel: (9122) 382 7878.

SUN TV
268/269, 3rd floor, Anna Salai, Teynampeh, Madras 600018. Tel: (9144) 457 424. FAX: (9144) 825 1266.

WHAT'S IN MUMBAI (HINDUJAS)
Sind Mercantile Bldg., Hindujas College Compound, Charni Road, Bombay 400 004. Tel: (9122) 386 0404. FAX: (9122) 383 3232.

ZEE TV
Continental Bldg, 135 D.R. A.B.Rd., Worli, Bombay 400 018. Tel: (9122) 492 5723. FAX: (9122) 493 1938.

—B.D. GARGA

INDONESIA

Population: 203.6 million.
TV sets: 11 million.
Average Daily TV Viewing: 3.7 hours
Cable Homes: 30,000.
Satellite Dish Homes: 300,000.
Video Standard: PAL-B.

In 1997, Indonesia, with one of the most robust economies in Asia, had $302 million in television advertising revenues. With the economic woes of 1998, advertising revenues have decreased substantially and SCTV, one of the country's five pri-vate networks, has begun large scale layoffs. The production of sinetrons (local teleplectures) has been curtailed and transmis-sion hours of the networks have been cut.

BROADCASTERS

ANTEVE
Mulia Center Building, 19th Floor, Jl. HR Rasuna Said Kav., X-6, No. 8, Jakarta 12940. Tel: (6221) 522-2084. FAX: (6221) 522-2087.
GENERAL MANAGER
Dennis Cabalfin

PT RAJAWALI CITRA TELEVISI INDONESIA (RCT)
J1 Raya Perjuangan, No. 3, Jeruk, Jakarta 11000. Tel: (6221) 5303 540. FAX: (6221) 5493 852.
MANAGING DIRECTOR
Azis Husein

PT SURYA CITRA TELEVISI (SCTV)
JL Raya Darma Permai III, Surabaya 60189. (6231) 714 567. FAX: (6231) 717 723.

PT CIPTA TELEVISI PENDIDKAN INDONESIA (TPI)
Jalan Pintu II, Taman Mini Indonesian Indah, Podok Gede, Jakarta Timur 13810. (6221) 841 2473. FAX: (6221) 841 2740.

TELEVISI REPUBLIK INDONESIA (TVRI)
Jalan Jerbang Pemuda, Senayan, Jakarta. Tel: (6221) 573 3135. FAX: (6221) 573 2408.

SATELLITE

INDOVISION
Gedung Elektrino, Lantai 7 & 8, J1 Kuningan Barat # 8, Jakarta 12710.

IRAN

Population: 69.16 million.
TV Sets: 7.7 million.
Number of VCRs: 2.5 million.
Satellite Dishes: 800,000—900,000.
Video Standard: SECAM

Satellite dishes are illegal in Iran, due to the "corrupting influences" of the programs they receive. Hence, the nearly one million dishes in Iran are very well hidden.

BROADCASTER

ISLAMIC REPUBLIC OF IRAN BROADCASTING
Post Office Box 19395, 1774 Tehran. Tel: (9821) 298 053. FAX: (9821) 295 056.

IRAQ

Population: 23 million.
TV sets: 1 million.
Video Standard: SECAM B.

Iraq welcomed its first satellite TV channel that will broadcast for three hours daily. The programming will be sent to various Middle Eastern countries as part of the celebrations surrounding 30 years of Baath Party rule. Hummam Abdul-Khaliq, the nation's Minister of Culture, said that the service will reflect the negative impact of UN imposed sanctions on Iraq. Whether he was referring to the quality of the programming or the use of the channel as a medium for disseminating propaganda is unclear.

While Iraq is broadcasting to other Arab nations, the penalty for possessing a satellite dish in Iraq is an indefinite term of imprisonment.

BROADCASTER

IRAQI BROADCASTING AND TV ESTABLISHMENT
Salihiya Blvd., Karkh, Baghdad. Tel: (9641) 884 4412. FAX: (9641) 541 0480.

IRELAND

Population: 3.585 million.
TV sets: 1 million.
Cable Subscribers: 490,000.
Satellite Dishes: 75,000.
Video Standard: PAL.

For information regarding Ireland, see the British Television and Video section of this book.

RADIO TELEFIS EIREANN
Donnybrook, Dublin 4. (3531) 208 3111. FAX: (3531) 208 3080.
URL: http://www.rte.ie/tv/

ISRAEL

Population: 5.67 million.
TV sets: 1.5 million.
Cable homes: 1.2 million.
Video Standard: PAL.

BROADCASTERS

CHANNEL 2
97 Jaffa St., Jerusalem 94340. Tel: (9722) 242 776. FAX: (9722) 242 720.

ISRAEL BROADCASTING AUTHORITY (IBA)
P.O. Box 7139, Jerusalem 91071. Tel: (9722) 291 888. FAX: (9722) 292 944.

ISRAEL BROADCASTING AUTHORITY TELEVISION ROMENA
P.O. Box 7139, Jerusalem 91905. Tel: (9722) 557 111.

ISRAEL EDUCATIONAL TV
14 Klausner St., Tel Aviv 690011. Tel: (9723) 543 4343. FAX: (9723) 642 9291.

ISRAEL TV
1 B.A. Television House, Romema, Jerusalem. Tel: (9722) 301 333. FAX: (9722) 380 751.

KESHET BROADCASTING LTD.
65 Derech Patach Tikva, Tel Aviv 61202. Tel: (9723) 561 6007. FAX: (9723) 561 6002.

PALESTINIAN BROADCASTING CORP.
Police Headquarters, Jericho. Tel: (9722) 656 4017. FAX: (9722) 656 4029.

THE SECOND TV & RADIO AUTHORITY
3 Kanfei Nesharim St., Jerusalem 95464. Tel: (9722) 510 222. FAX: (9422) 513 443.

CABLE/TV STUDIO

ISRAEL CABLE PROGRAMMING
128 Jabotinsky St., Ramat Gan 52522. Tel: (9723) 575 4682. FAX: (9273) 575 4688.

JERUSALEM CAPITAL STUDIOS LTD.
P.O. Box 13172, 206 Jaffa Rd., Jerusalem 91131. Tel: (9722) 701 711.

VIDEO DISTRIBUTORS

FORUM FILM
11 Pinsker St., Tel Aviv 63421. Tel: (9723) 528 6211. FAX: (9723) 528 0313.

SHAPIRA FILMS
34 Allenby Rd., P.O. Box 4842, Tel Aviv 63325.

TAMUZ FILMS
5 Pinsker St., Tel Aviv. FAX: (9723) 528 1564.

ITALY

Population: 57.88 million.
TV sets: 16.9 million.
Cable Households: 820,000.
Satellite households: 680,000.
Video households: 9.9 million.
Video Standard: PAL

Stream, a company established by Telecom Italia to exploit the cable industry with pay-per-view and video-on-demand services, has accumulated a $220 million loss since 1993, while reaching only 56,000 subscribers. Stream has decided to focus on satellite, providing new decoders that offer access to the basic TV package as well as interactive services.

Mediaset and public broadcaster RAI took a combined 90% of the Italian tv audience. RAI's audience share for its three channels was 47.3% while Mediaset brought in a healthy 42.6% for its three channels. Mediaset's Canale-5 beat rival RAI-1 in television ratings for the first time in two years.

RAI and Telecom Italia plan to launch a pay TV platform by early 1999 in which Cecchi Gori will have a stake in exchange for providing content.

Italian television viewers have begun to express more enthusiasm for local product. While U.S. movies still garner healthy ratings, Italian and European miniseries, serials and soaps have attracted considerable primetime viewership. This change is attributed to the improved quality of European production.

Mediaset and RAI have budgeted more funds for production than ever before, and have entered into international production partnerships. Mediaset has a three year deal with U.S. Hallmark Entertainment while RAI has secured a committment from Polygram.

BROADCASTERS

CANALE 5
Viale Europa 48, Cologno Monzese, Milan 20093. Tel: (392) 251 41. FAX: (392) 2162 8951.

ITALIA 1
Viale Europa 48, Cologno Monzese, Milan 20093. Tel: (392) 251 41. FAX: (392) 2514 6599.

ITALIA 7
Via Turati 3, Milan 20121. Tel: (392) 659 8238.

ITALIA 3
Consorzio Televisivo Italiano, Via Velletri 30, Rome 00198. Tel: (396) 844 2873.

ITALIA NOVE NETWORK
Via Settala 57, Milan 20124. Tel: (392) 221 964.

JUNIOR TV
Corso Garibaldi 3, Milan 20122. Tel: (392) 805 5820. FAX: (392) 864 2343.

MEDIASET
Viale Europa 48, 20093 Cologno Monzese, Milan. Tel: (392) 998 221.

R.T.I.
Viale Europa 48, Cologno Monzese, Milan 20093. Tel: (392) 2102 8460.

RADIOTELEVISIONE ITALIANA (RAI UNO, DUE & TRE)
Viale Mazzini 14, Rome 00195. Tel: (396) 38781. FAX: (396) 322 6070.

RETE A
Viale Morelli 165, Milan 20099. Tel: (392) 247 7241. FAX: (392) 240 1630.

RETECAPRI
Via Li Campi 19, Capri 80073. Tel: (3981) 837 0144. FAX: (3981) 837 0421.

RETEQUATTRO
Viale Europa 48, Cologno Monzese, Milan 20093. Tel: (392) 25141. FAX: (392) 2162 8951.

TELEMONTECARLO-TV INTERNAZIONALE
Piazza della Balduina 49, Rome 00136. Tel: (396) 355 841. FAX: (396) 3558 4227.

TELEVENEZIA
Via Piraghetto 86, Mestre (VE) 30173. Tel: (3941) 931 183. FAX: (3941) 932 326.

TIVUITALIA
Via S. Senatore 6/1, Milan 20122. Tel: (392) 8901 0772. FAX: (392) 890 0987.

TV ELEFANTE
Via Villa Nuova 38, Rocandelle, Brescia 25030. Tel: (3930) 258 2611. FAX: (3930) 258 3341.

TVA VICENZA
Via del Commercio 17, Vicenza 36100. Tel: (39444) 562 355. FAX: (39444) 960 883.

TVRS
Via Politi 27, Recanati (MC) 65019. Tel: (3971) 757 0002. FAX: (3971) 982 463.

VCO
Via S. Antonio 11, Domodossola 28037. Tel: (39324) 45454. FAX: (39324) 45457.

VIDEO BOX
Via F. Bazzaro 6, Milan 20128. Tel: (392) 257 1688.

CABLE

TELEPIU PRIMA TV
Via Piranesi 46, Milan 20124. Tel: (392) 7009 7387.

SATELLITE BROADCASTERS

ORBIT COMMUNICATIONS
Sapienza Network Centre, Via Raffaele, Costi 60, Rome. Tel: (396) 2254 3615. FAX: (396) 225 4639.

R.T.I. SPA
Palazzo del Cigni, Segrate 20090, Milan 2. Tel: (392) 216 001. FAX: (392) 213 8090.

RAI INTERNATIONAL
Saxa Ruba, L'Go Villy De Luca, Rome 00188. Tel: (396) 3317 2270. FAX: (396) 3317 1885.

RAISAT
via del Babuino 9, Rome 00187. Tel: (396) 368 62276. FAX: (396) 322 0390.

SILVIO BERLUSCONI COMMUNICATIONS
Palazzo Michelangelo, Via Cassanese 224, Segrate 20090. Tel: (392) 21621. FAX: (392) 2162 8724.

TELESPACIO/ITALSAT
Via Alberto Bergamini 50, Rome 00159. Tel: (396) 406 931.

VIDEO DISTRIBUTORS

A B FILM DISTRIBUTORS
Via Monte Zebio 28, Rome 00195. Tel: (396) 321 9554. FAX: (396) 361 3641.

AVO FILM
Via C. Ravizza 20, Milan 20149. Tel: (392) 4801 2727. FAX: (392) 4801 2737.

BMG
Via S Alessandro 7, Rome 00131. Tel: (396) 4199 51. FAX: (396) 4199 5235.

BLACK HORSE
C. so Rosmini 8, Rovereto 38068. Tel: (3946) 443 1313. FAX: (3946) 443 1314.

BUENA VISTA HOME VIDEO
Via Sandro Sandri, Milan 20121. Tel: (392) 290 851. FAX: 2908 5650.

CECCHI GORI EDITORIA ELETTRONICA
Via Tornabuoni 17, Florence 50123. Tel: (3955) 218 131. FAX: (3955) 217 543.

CINEHOLLYWOOD EDUCATIONAL VIDEO
Via Reguzzoni 15, Milan 20125. Tel: (392) 643 9042. FAX: (392) 6610 3899.

COLUMBIA TRISTAR HOME VIDEO
Via Flaminia, 872, Rome 00191. Tel: (396) 3330 180. FAX: (396) 3330 174.

EAGLE PICTURES
Via M Buonarroti 5, Milan 20149. Tel: (392) 481 4169. FAX: (392) 481 3389.

EMI
Via Bergamo 315, Caronno Pertusella 21042. Tel: (39322) 96511. FAX: (39322) 965 6002.

FOX HOME VIDEO
Piazza Fontana 6, Milan 20123. Tel: (392) 723 251. FAX: (392) 805 1371.

IMPACT FILM GROUP
Via Bertoloni 41, Rome 00197. Tel: (396) 803 2235. FAX: (396) 808 8166.

MCA
Corso Matteotti 3, Milan 20121. Tel: (392) 760 321. FAX: (392) 7603 2502.

MONDADORI VIDEO
Via Mondadori 1, Segrate MI 75421. Tel: (392) 7542 2060. FAX: (392) 7542 3230.

POLYGRAM
Via Carlo Tenca 2, Milan 20124. Tel: (392) 67961. FAX: (392) 679 6471.

RCS HOME VIDEO
Via Mecenate 91, Milan 20138. Tel: (392) 50951. FAX: (392) 5095 5576.

SONY MUSIC VIDEO
Via Amedei 9, Milan 20161. Tel: (392) 85361. FAX: (392) 860 175.

STARLIGHT
Via Bellerio 30, Milan 20161. Tel: (392) 646 6441. FAX: (392) 6620 4483.

VIDEO DIRECT MARKETING
Via P. Amedeo 25, Bari 70121. Tel: (3980) 524 5325. FAX: (3980) 524 3216.

VIDEOEVENT
Via Zamenhoff 21, Milan 20136. Tel: (392) 837 3551. FAX: (392) 837 5852.

WARNER HOME VIDEO
Via U. Foscolo 1, Milan 20121. Tel: (392) 721 281. FAX: (392) 7212 8200.

IVORY COAST

Population: 14.8 million.
TV sets: 810,000.
Video Standard: SECAM.

BROADCASTER

TELEVISION IVOIRIENNE
08 B.P. 883, Abidjan 08. Tel: (225) 439 039. FAX: (225) 222 297.

JAMAICA

Population: 2.6 million.
TV sets: 500,000.
Number of VCRs: 235,000.
Video Standard: NTSC.

BROADCASTER

JAMAICA BROADCASTING CORP.
P.O. Box 100, Kingston 10. Tel: (809) 926-5620. FAX: (809) 929 1069.

JAPAN

Population: 125.86 million.
TV Sets: 104 million.
Average Daily TV Viewing: 4 hours
Video Standard: NTSC.

Direct-to-home digital service is off to a slow start in Japan, with SkyPerfecTV attaining 800,000 subscribers and DirecTV Japan enrolling 140,000 subscribers. In an attempt to increase sales, DirecTV plans to add 25 new channels including 5 movie channels, four animation pay-per-view channels and new sports offerings.

Japan's Education Ministry has set up a committee designed to evaluate and potentially restrict the exposure of youths to sexual and violent material on television, in video games and publications.

ASSOCIATION

THE NATIONAL ASSOCIATION OF COMMERCIAL BROADCASTERS IN JAPAN
3-23, Kioi-Cho, Chiyodaku, Tokyo 102. Tel: (813) 5213 7700. FAX: (813) 5213 7701.

BROADCASTERS

ASAHI NATIONAL BROADCASTING (TV ASAHI OR ANB)
1-1, Roppongi, 1-chome, Minato-ku, Tokyo 106. Tel: (813) 3587 5111 (Intl Dept.). FAX: (813) 3505 3539 (Int'l Dept.).

FUJI NEWS NETWORK/FUJI TELEVISION NETWORK
3-1, Kawada-cho, Shinjuku-ku, Tokyo 106. Tel: (813) 3353-1111. FAX: (813) 3358-1747.

NHK (JAPAN BROADCASTING CORPORATION)
2-2-1 Jinnan, Shibuya-ku, Tokyo 105-01. Tel: (813) 3485 6517. FAX: (813) 3481 1362.

NIPPON TELEVISION NETWORK CORPORATION
14, Niban-cho, Chiyoda-ku, Tokyo 102 40. Tel: (813) 5275 1111. FAX: (813) 5275 4008.

TOKAY TELEVISION BROADCASTING CO. LTD
1-14-27 Higashsakura, Higashi-ku, Nagoya, Aichi. Tel: (052) 951 2511. Telex: 4447355 JOFXTV J. FAX: (052) 962 7640.

TOKYO BROADCASTING SYSTEM/JAPAN NEWS NETWORK
5-3-6 Akasaka 5-chome, Minato-ku, Tokyo 107 06. Tel: (813) 3746 1111. Telex: 24883. FAX: (813) 3588 6378.
CHAIRMAN
Hiroshi Shiho
PRESIDENT
Yukio Sunahara
PROGRAM DIRECTOR
Kenichi Sato
BUSINESS DEVELOPMENT DIRECTOR
Hiroshi Ikeda
HEAD OF CO-PRODUCTIONS AND ACQUISITIONS
Yukio Kinugasa

TXN NETWORK/TELEVISION TOKYO
3-12, Toranomon 4-chome, Minato-ku, Tokyo 105-12. Tel: (813) 3432-1212. FAX: (813) 5473 3447.

SATELLITE

CNN
2-23, Roppongi 6-Chome, Minato-ku, Tokyo. Tel: (813) 3405 3186. FAX: (813) 3405 5454.

CTV
2-23, Roppongi 6-Chome, Minato-ku, Tokyo. Tel: (813) 3405 3186. FAX: (813) 3405 5454.

JAPAN DIGITAL COMMUNICATIONS
Tel: (813) 5571 2260.
PRESIDENT
Soya Hikita

JAPAN SATELLITE BROADCASTING, INC. (JSB)
No. 6 Central Building, 1-19-10, Toranomon, Minato-ku, Tokyo.

NATIONAL SPACE DEVELOPMENT AGENCY OF JAPAN (NASDA)
World Tade Center Building 2-4-1, Hamamatsu-cho, Minato-ku Tokyo 105, Japan. Tel: (813) 5470 4111. Telex: J28424. FAX: (813) 3433 0796. http://www.goin.nasda.go.jp/

NHK (JAPAN BROADCASTING CORPORATION)
(see Japan Broadcasting Corp. listing under Broadcasters.)

STAR CHANNEL
4-17-7 Akasaka, Mianto-ku 107, Tokyo. Tel: (813) 5563 0438. FAX: (813) 5563 0440.

STUDIOS

AVACO CREATIVE STUDIOS
2-3-18 Nishi-Waseda Shinjuku-ku, Tokyo 169. Tel: (813) 3203 4181. FAX: (813) 3207 1398.

IMAGICA CORPORATION
2-14-1, Higashigotanda, Shinagawa-ku, Tokyo 141. Tel: (813) 3280 1280. FAX: (813) 3280 1364.

NATIONAL PANASONIC
National No. 1 Bldg., 1-2, 1-Chome, Shiba-Koen, Minato-ku 105, Tokyo. Tel: (813) 578 1237. FAX: (813) 437 2776.

NIKKATSU CORPORATION
3-28-12, Hongou, Bunkyo-ku, Tokyo. Tel: (813) 5689 1019. FAX: (813) 5689 1043.

SONY CORPORATION
6-7-35, Kitashinagawa, Shinagawa-ku 141, Tokyo. Tel: (815) 448 2200. FAX: (815) 448 3061.

TOHOKUSHINSHA FILM CORP.
17-7 Akasaka, 4-chome, Minato-ku, Tokyo 107. Tel: (813) 3582 0211. FAX: (813) 3584 2824.

VIDEO DISTRIBUTORS

BUENA VISTA JAPAN
DK Bldg., 7-18-23 Roppongi 106, Minato-ku, Tokyo. Tel: (813) 3746 5009. FAX: (813) 3746 0009.

DISC CENTER
C.P.O. Box 874, Osaka 530-91. Tel: (816) 323 6350. FAX: (816) 323 0249.

GAGA COMMUNICATIONS
Step Roppongi Bldg., 6-8-10 Rappongi, Minato-ku, Tokyo 106. Tel: (813) 5410 3507. FAX: (813) 5410 3558.

MITSUBISHI CORPORATION
3-1, Marunouchi 2-Chome, Chiytoda-ku, Tokyo 100-86. Tel: (813) 3210 7795. FAX: (813) 3210 7397.

NEW SELECT
Nakamura Bldg., 7th Floor, 5-9-13 Ginza, Ghuo-ku. Tel: (813) 3573 7571. FAX: (813) 3572 0139.

PONY CANYON
4-3-31 Kudan Kita, Chiyoda ku 102, Tokyo. Tel: (813) 3221 3155. FAX: (813) 3221 3168.

TIME WARNER ENTERTAINMENT
1-2-4 Hama matsu-Cho, Minato-ku 105, Tokyo. Tel: (813) 5472 8000. FAX: (813) 5472 8029.

TOEI COMPANY
2-17, 3-Chome, GinzaJapan, Chuo-ku 104, Tokyo. Tel: (813) 535 4641.

TOHO INTERNATIONAL
(A Division of Toho) 1-8-1, Yurakucho, Chiyoda-ku, Tokyo 100. Tel: (813) 3213 6821. FAX: (813) 3213 6825.

TOHO TOWA COMPANY
6-4, Ginza 2-Chome, Chuo-ku, Tokyo 104. Tel: (813) 3562 0109. FAX: (813) 3535 3656.

20TH CENTURY FOX (FAR EAST)
Fukide Bldg. 4-1-13 Toranomon, Minato-ku, Tokyo. Tel: (813) 3436 3421. FAX: (813) 3433 5322.

UNITED INTERNATIONAL PICTURES (FAR EAST)
Riccar Kaikan Bldg. 6-2-1 Ginza, Choo-ku 104, Tokyo. Tel: (813) 3248 1771. FAX: (813) 3248 6274.

VICTOR CO. OF JAPAN
4-8-14 Nihon Bashi-Honcho, Chuo-ku 103, Tokyo. Tel: (813) 3246 1254. FAX: (813) 3246 1254.

JORDAN

Population: 4.44 million.
TV Sets: 250,000.
Video Standard: PAL-B

BROADCASTER

JORDAN RADIO & TELEVISION CORPORATION
Post Office Box 1041, Amman. Tel: (9626) 773 111. FAX: (9626) 751 503.

KAZHAKSTAN

Population: 16.92 million.
TV Sets: 4.7 million.
Video Standard: SECAM.

BROADCASTER

KAZHAKHSTAN TELEVISION
Jeltoksan Kosesi 175, Alma Ata 480013. Tel: (73272) 695 188. FAX: (73272) 631 207.

VIDEO DISTRIBUTORS

ORKEN-FILM
Abai St. 10, Apartment 213, Alma-Ata 480000, Kazakhstan.
Tel: (73272) 691 697. FAX: (73272) 632 249.

KENYA

Population: 29.68 million.
TV Sets: 500,000.
Video Standard: PAL B.

BROADCASTER

KENYA BROADCASTING CORP.
P.O. Box 30456, Nairobi, Tel: (2542) 334 567. FAX: (2542) 220 675.

KEYNA TELEVISION NETWORK
PO Box 56985, Nairobi. (2542) 227 122. FAX: (2542) 214 467.
URL: http://www.knyeaweb.com/ktn/ktn.html

NORTH KOREA

Population: 23.9 million.
TV Sets: 2.07 million reported.
Video Standard: PAL/NTSC.

Television sets in North Korea are constructed to receive only domestic programming signals. Only members of the "political elite" can access foreign media broadcasts.

BROADCASTER

RADIO AND TELEVISION BROADCASTING OF THE REPUBLIC OF KOREA.
Chonsung-dong, Moranbong District, Pyongyang. Tel. (8502) 816 035. FAX: (8502) 812 100.

SOUTH KOREA

Population: 46.4 million.
TV Homes: 2.97 million.
Multiset Homes: 2.85 million.
Average Daily TV Viewing: 2.2 hours
Cable Subscrobers 80,000.
Dish Homes: 400,000.
VCR Homes: 2.6 million.
Video Standard: NTSC.

Advertising revenues have dropped by over 30% in 1998, largely due to the country's economic woes and the fact that the Korea Broadcasting Advertising Corporation, the government agency authorized to sell airtime, has not dropped rates.

Foreign programming is limited to 20%, although the terrestrial networks usually show about 10% foreign product.

ORGANIZATION

KOREAN CABLE TV ASSOCIATION
KPC Building, 7th floor, 122-1 Chucksun-dong, Chongno-ku, Seoul. Tel: (822) 398 5344. FAX: (822) 735 6514.
PRESIDENT
Jongsoo Choi

INTERNATIONAL BROADCASTING SOCIETY
c/o KBS, 18 Yoidi-dong, Youngdungpo-gu, Seoul, South Korea. Tel: (822) 780 3636. Telex: K24599.

MINISTRY OF CULTURE AND TOURISM
82-1 Sejong-ro, Jongro-gu, Seoul 110-703. Tel: (822) 720 3802. FAX: (822) 720 2546.
MINISTER
Nakyun Shin

BROADCASTERS

EDUCATION BROADCASTING SYSTEM
92-6, Umyeon-dong, Seocho-gu, Seoul 137-791. Tel: (822) 521 1586. FAX: (822) 521 0241.

KOREAN BROADCASTING SYSTEM
18, Yoido-dong, Youngdungpo-gu, Seoul 150-790. Tel: (822) 781 2001. FAX: (822) 781 2099.

MUNHWA TV-RADIO BROADCASTING CORP.
31, Yoido-dong, Youngdungpo-gu, Seoul, 150-728. Tel: (822) 789 2851. FAX: (822) 782 3094.

SEOUL BROADCASTING SYSTEM
10-2, Yoido-dong, Youngdungpo-gu, Seoul 150-010. Tel: (822) 786 0792. FAX: (822) 785 6171.

KUWAIT

Population: 2.255 million.
TV Sets: 975,000.
Video Standard: PAL.

BROADCASTER

KUWAIT TELEVISION
P.O. Box 193, 13007 Safat, Kuwait. Tel: (96524) 150 301. FAX: (96524) 34511.

LAOS

Population: 4.96 million.
TV Sets: 84,000.
Video Standard: PAL-B.

BROADCASTER

LAO NATIONAL TELEVISION
P.O. Box 310, Vientiane. Tel: (856) 4475.

LATVIA

Population: 2.51 million.
TV Sets: 1.23 million.
Cable Subscribers: 57,800.
Satellite Dishes: 91,000.
Video Standard: SECAM/PAL.

BROADCASTER

LATVIJAS TELEVIZIJA
Zakusalas krastmala 3, Riga LV-1509. Tel: (3712) 200 314.
FAX: (3712) 200 0025.

LEBANON

Population: 3.93 million.
TV Sets: 2.36 million.
Video Standard: SECAM.

BROADCASTERS

FUTURE TELEVISION
White House, Rue Spears, Sanayeh, Beirut, Lebanon. Tel: (9611) 347 121, 340 303, 341 303. FAX: (9611) 602 310.

LEBANESE BROADCASTING CORP.
PO Box 16-5853, Beirut. Tel: (9619) 938 938. FAX: (9619) 937 916.

MIDDLE EAST TELEVISION
PO Box 5689, Nicosia, Cyprus.

MURR TELEVISION (MTV)
Fouad Chehab Ave, PO Box 166000, Fassouh, MTV Bldg. Tel: (9611) 217 000. FAX: (9611) 423 121

TELE-LIBAN
B.P. 115054, Hazmieh, Beirut. Tel: (9611) 405 100. FAX: (9611) 457 253.

LESOTHO

Population: 2.14 million
TV sets: 250,000
Video Standard: PAL

LESOTHO NATIONAL BROADCASTING SERVICES
PO Box 552, Maseru 100. (266) 323 561. FAX: (266) 310 003.

LIBERIA

Population: 2.95 million.
TV Sets: 45,000.
Video Standard: PAL.

BROADCASTER

LIBERIAN BROADCASTING CORPORATION
PO Box 594, Monrovia. Tel: (231) 271 250.

LIBYA

Population: 5.45 million.
TV Sets: 550,000.
Video Standard: PAL.
Libyan TV broadcasts 7 hours daily on Arabsat.

BROADCASTER

PEOPLES REVOLUTION BROADCASTING
P.O. Box 333, Tripoli 1.

LITHUANIA

Population: 3.72 million.
TV Sets: 1.57 million.
Cable Subscribers: 145,000.
Satellite Dishes: 25,000.
Video Standard: PAL

BROADCASTERS

AIDAS
Birutes 42, LT-4050 Trakai. (37038) 52480/

BALTIJOS TELEVIZIJA
Laisves pr.60, LT-2044 Vilnius. Tel: (3702) 417 134. FAX: (3702) 428 907

5 KANALAS
Vanagupes 20, LT-5720 Palanga. Tel: (37036) 51131. FAX: (37036) 52878.

KAUNAS PLIUS
PD 2040, LT-3000 Kaunas. (3707) 220 650. FAX: (3707) 220 640.

KEDAINIU KRASTO TV
Valdybos Culturos Centras, Radvilu 5, LT-5030 Kedainiai. (37057) 53947. FAX: (37057) 65894.
DIRECTOR
Vytoldas Burneika

KLAIPEDOS TV
Vilties 12, LT-5800, Klaipeda. (37061) 11701.

LIETUVOS RADIJAS IR TELEVIZIJA
Konarskio 43, IT-2674, Vilnius. Tel: (3702) 637 961. FAX: (3702) 263 282.

LNK (LITPOLINTER TV)
Laisvas Nepriklausomas Kanalas, Mazosios Lapes, Kauno raj. (3707) 531 269. FAX: (3707) 712 444.
DIRECTOR
Audrius Girzadas

MARIJAMPOLES TELEVIZIJA
Kauno 13, LT-4520 Mirijampole. (37043) 51687. FAX: (37043) 50606.

PAN-TV
Laisves a. 26, LT-5300 Panevezys. (37054) 62121. FAX: (37054) 64980.
DIRECTOR
Saulius Bukelis

SIALIU TV
Ausros al. 48, LT-5400 Siauliai. (37014) 25211. FAX: (37014) 25211.

TAURAGES TV-3
Vytauto 16, LT-5900 Taurage. (37046) 54503.
DIRECTOR
Liudas Urbonas

TELES-3
Kalvariju 35, LT-2000 Vilnius. Tel: (3702) 752 533. FAX: (3702) 355 032.

VILNIAUS TV
Vivulskio 25, LT-2600 Vilnius. Tel: (3702) 661 560.
DIRECTOR
Vytautas Kvietkauskas

LUXEMBOURG

Population: 416,000.
TV Sets: 100,500
Cable Subscribers: 140,000.
Satellite Dishes: 4,000.
Video Standard: PAL/SECAM.

CLT-UFA's major European networks include RTL 4, Veronica, and RTL 5, all in the Netherlands, Belgium's RTL TVI, France's M6 and Germany's RTL.

BROADCASTERS

CLT-UFA
45 Blvd. Pierre Frieden, Luxembourg-Kirchberg L-2850. Tel: (352) 42142. FAX: (352) 42142 2760. http://ww.cltmulti.com

RTL LUXEMBOURG
177, rue de Luxembourg, L-8077 Bertrange. Tel: (352) 252 7251. FAX: (352) 2527 25431.

CABLE

ASTRA/SOCIETE EUROPEENNE DES SATELLITES (SES)
Chateau Betzdorf, Betzdorf 6815. Tel: (352) 7172 51. FAX: (352) 7172 5324.

ELTRONA
4-6 Rue de l'Acierie L-1010. Tel: (352) 499 4661. FAX: (352) 499 4661.

MEDIAPORT LUXEMBOURG
5 Rue Large, Luxembourg L-1917. Tel: (352) 478 2160. FAX: (352) 475 662.

SATELLITE BROADCASTERS

ASTRA
(See Astra listing under Cable.)

RTL-4
Villa Louvigny, Allee Marconi, Luxembourg L-2850. Tel: (352) 4766 2933. FAX: (352) 4766 2744.

VIDEO DISTRIBUTORS

CINE UTOPIA
16 Ave.de Faiencerie, Luxembourg L-1510. Tel: (352) 464 902.

PAUL THILTGES DIST.
1 Rue de Nassau, Luxembourg L1510. Tel: (352) 442 429.

MACAU

Population: 491,000.
TV Sets: 70,300.
Video Standard: PAL.

Macau, currently a Portuguese possession, will revert to Chinese control in 1999.

BROADCASTER

TELEDIFUSAO MACAU
P.O. Box 446, Macau. Tel: (853) 520 204. FAX: (853) 520 208.

MACEDONIA

Population: 2.2 million.
TV Sets: 345,000.
Video Standard: PAL.

BROADCASTER

TELEVIZIJA MAKEDONIJE
Dolno Nerezi bb, 9100 Skopje. Tel: (3891) 258 230.

MADAGASCAR

Population: 14.35 million.
TV Sets: 130,000.
Video Standard: SECAM.

BROADCASTER

RADIO TELEVISION MADAGASY
P.O. Box 442, Antananarivo. Tel: (2612) 21784.
DIRECTOR
M. Rabesahala

MALAYSIA

Population: 21 million.
TV Sets: 9.4 million.
Average Daily TV Viewing: 2.2 hours
Home Satellite Service:
Video Standard: SECAM K.

GOVERNMENT AGENCIES

ASIA-PACIFIC BROADCASTING UNION (ABU)
PO Box 1964, Jalan Pantai Bhary, Kuala Lumpur, 59700 Malaysia. Tel: (603) 274 3592. FAX: (603) 274 0761. Telex: 32227.

**ASIA-PACIFIC INSTITUTE
FOR BROADCASTING DEVELOPMENT**
PO Box 1137, Pantai, Kuala Lumpur, 59700 Malaysia. Tel: (603) 274 4618. Telex: MA 30083.

MULTIMEDIA DEVELOPMENT CORPORATION

1st Floor, Bangunan Getah Asli, 148 Jalan Ampang, 50450 Kuala Lumpur, Malaysia. Tel: (603) 262-9599. FAX: (603) 262-9400. URL: http://www.mdc.com.my

BROADCASTERS

METROVISION
33 Jin Delima 1/3 Subnag, Hi-Tec Industrial Park 40000, Shahalam. (603) 732 8000. FAX: (603) 732 8932.

RADIO TELEVISION MALAYSIA (RTM)
Department of Broadcasting, Angkasapuri, Kuala Lumpur 50614. Tel: (603) 282 5333. FAX: (603) 282 4735.

TV MALAYSIA SABAH AND SARAWAK
PO Box 1016, 88614 Kota Kinabalu. Tel: (6088) 52711.

SYSTEM TV MALAYSIA BERHAD (TV3)
Sri Pentas, Ground Floor, South Wing, No. 3, Persiaran Banjar Urama, 47800 Petaling Jaya Selangor Darul Ehsan, Malaysia. Tel: (603) 716 6333. FAX: (603) 716 133.

SATELLITE

ASTRO
Technology Park Malaysia, Kuala Lumpur.

MALI

Population: 10.21 million.
TV Sets: 11,000.
Video Standard: SECAM K.

BROADCASTERS

RADIODIFFUSION TELEVISION DU MALI
P.O. Box 171, Bamako. Tel: (22322) 20192 24308.

MALTA

Population: 377,988
TV Sets: 145,300.
Video Standard: PAL

BROADCASTERS

MELITA CABLE TELEVISION LTD
High Rise, Triq L-Imradd, Ta'Xbiex. Tel: (343) 5470. FAX: (343) 5435.

PUBLIC BROADCASTING SERVICES LTD/TELEVISION MALTA
PO BOX 82, Valetta. Tel: (356) 225 051. FAX: (356) 244 601.

SUPER 1 TELEVISION
St Luke's Rd, G'Mangia. Tel: (22) 5051. FAX: (24) 4601.

CABLE

MELITA CABLE TELEVISION LTD
(see Melita Cable Television Ltd listing under broadcasters)

MAURITANIA

Population: 2.34 million.
TV Sets: 2,000.
Video Standard: SECAM.

BROADCASTER

TV NATIONALE MAURITAINE
B.P. 2000, Nouakchott.

MAURITIUS

Population: 1.157 million.
TV Sets: 157,850.
Video Standard: SECAM

BROADCASTER

MAURITIUS BROADCASTING CORP.
1 Louis Pasteur St., Forest Side. Tel: (230) 675 5001. FAX: (230) 675 7332.

MEXICO

Population: 96 million.
TV Sets: 14.5 million.
Cable Subscribers: 1.7 million.
Home Satellite Service: 1.6 million.
VCR Homes: 6 million.
Video Standard: NTSC.

Mexico's basic cable market is led by Multivision, USA and Antena 3, the most watched networks.

In June, 1998, the president of the Mexican Association of Hotels and Motels admitted that as many as 30% of hotels were pirating the multichannel cable TV services in guest rooms. They are in talks with the cable industry to reach an "economic agreement" that will presumably compensate the cable providers for lost revenue.

TELEVISION BROADCASTERS

CANAL 3
Miguel Hidalgo No 105, Col Cuahutemoc, CP 62220, Octobec, Morelos. Tel: (73) 136 714. FAX: (73) 115 154.

CANAL 8
Plutarco Elisa Calles No 714, Col Club de Golf, CP 32050, Cuernavaca, Morelos. Tel/FAX: (73) 127 104.

CANAL 11
Prolongacion Carpio 475, Col. Casco de Santos Tomas, 11340 Mexico, DF. Tel: (525) 396 8177. Telex: 1777554. FAX: (525) 341 1813

CANAL 22
Atletas No 2, Col Country Club, Mexico DF 04220. Tel: (525) 5538 3535. FAX: (525) 5538 3935.

CORTV
Calz Modero Esq, Av Tecnologico s/n, Oaxaca. Tel: (951) 46952. FAX: (951) 63646.

DIRECCION GENERAL DE TELEVISION UNIVERSITARIA
Circuito Mario de la Cueva sin numero, Ciudad Universitaria, 04510 Mexico, DF. Tel: (525) 622 6461.

IMAGEN OCHO
Av Mzexico 51, Col. Hipodromo Condesa, 06100 Mexico, DF. Tel: (525) 286 3581.

IMEVISION
Periferico Sur 4121, 01420 Mexico, DF. Tel: (525) 652 0973. FAX: (525) 652 0803.

MEDIOS PRODUCCION DE COMUNICACION
Sacramento 121, Col. Del Valle, 03100 Mexico, DF. Tel: (525) 543 6780.

MVS MULTIVISION
Blvd Puerto Aereo No 486, Col Montezuma, Mexico DF 15500. Tel: (5) 762 9680. FAX: (5) 762 0607.

TELEMEDIA
Romulo O'Farril 535, Col. Las Aguilas, 01710 Mexico, DF. Tel: (525) 6780 4399, 651 0096, 651 0097. Telex: 1777202 MTSA ME. FAX: (525) 680 0984.

TELEREY
Blvd Puerto Aereo 486, Col. Moctezuma, 15500 Mexico, DF. Tel: (525) 762 1155.

TELEVISA
Av Chapultepec 28, Col. Doctores, 11520 Mexico, DF. Tel: (525) 709 3333. FAX: (525) 709 3021.

TELEVISION AZTECA
Periferico Sur No. 4121, Mexico DF 14141. Tel: (525) 420 1313. FAX: (525) 420 1400.

TELEVISION DE TLAXCALA SE DE CV
Hidalgo No 17, San Pablo Apetatitlan, CP 90600, Tlaxcala. Tel: (246) 44424. FFAX: (246) 44427.

VIDEO OMEGA
Monte Elbruz 145, Col. Lomas de Chapultepec, 11000 Mexico, DF. Tel: (525) 281 2887, 281 3287, 281 3420. FAX: (525) 280 5590.

XHDF (CANAL 13)
Av. Periferico Sur 4121, Mexico City 12 DF.

XEOK TV CANAL
Av Circunvalacion Dr Atl 2, Guadalajara 44340. Tel: (363) 70100.

XETV (CANAL 6, FOX, TIJUANA)
8253 Ronson Rd., San Diego, CA 92111. Tel: (619) 279-6666. FAX: (619) 268-9388. Bay City Television.

XEWT-TV (CANAL 12, TIJUANA)
P. O. Box 434537, San Diego, CA 92143. Tel: (619) 528-1212.
FAX: (619) 280-9398. Televisa S.A.

XHBO TELETRE DE OAXACA
Via Nicolas Copernico s/n, Cerro del Fortin, Oaxaca. Tel: (951)
43777. FAX: (951) 62426.

XHIJ (CANAL 44, TELEMUNDO, CIUDAD JUAREZ)
Suite 200, 1790 Lee Trevino, El Paso, TX 79936. Tel: (915)
598-0440. FAX: (915) 598-1485. Arnoldo Cabada De la O.
Sergio Cabada.

CABLE AND SATELLITE

CABLEVISION
Dr Rio de la Loza 190, Colonia Doctores, 06720 Mexico, DF.
Tel: (525) 588 2200. FAX: (525) 588 1474.

MULTIVISION
Blvd Puerto Aereo 486, Col Moctezuma, 15500 Mexico, DF.
Tel: (525) 785 4230.

MICRONESIA

Population: 125,000
TV Sets: 8,000.
Video Standard: NTSC

BROADCASTERS

TV STATION POHNPEI
KPON-TV, Central Micronesian Communications, P.O. Box 460,
Kolonia, Pohnpei FSM 96941.
PRESIDENT
Bernard Hegenberger

TV STATION TRUK
Truk State, FSM 96942.

TV STATION YAP
WAAB, Yap State FSM 96943.

MOLDOVA

Population: 4.5 million.
Video Standard: SECAM.

BROADCASTER

VTV
Str. Hinncesti 61, Chisinau 277028.

MONACO

Population: 31,000
TV Sets: 20,000.
Video Standard: SECAM.

BROADCASTER

TELE MONTE CARLO
16 Blvd. Princess Charlotte, MC 98090 Monaco-Cedex. Tel:
(3393) 505 940. FAX: (3393) 250 109.
URL: http://www.cecchigori.com/tv/
PRESIDENT
Jean-Louis Medecin

MONGOLIA

Population: 2.69 million.
TV Sets: 139,000.
Video Standard: SECAM.

BROADCASTER

RADIO-TV MONGOLIA
Mongolian TV Centre, Huvisgalyn Zalm 3, P.O. Box, Ulan Bator.
Tel: (9761) 328 939. FAX: (9671) 237 234.

MOROCCO

Population: 29.8 million.
TV Sets: 1.21 million.
Video Standard: SECAM.

BROADCASTERS

RADIODIFFUSION TELEVISION MAROCAINE
1 rue Al Brihi, Rabat. Tel. (2127) 704 963. FAX: (2127) 722
047.

2M INTERNATIONAL
KM7, 300 route de Rabat, Casablanca. (2122) 354 444.

MOZAMBIQUE

Population: 19.72 million.
TV Sets: 36,000.
Video Standard: PAL.

BROADCASTER

TELEVISAO DE MOCAMBIQUE TVM
P.O. Box 2675, Mabuto. Tel: (258) 744 788.

MYANMAR

Population: 46 million.
TV Sets: 1 million.
Video Standard: NTSC.

BROADCASTER

TV MYANMAR
P.O. Box 1432, Yangon. Tel: (951) 31355. FAX: (951) 30211.

NAMIBIA

Population: 1.82 million.
TV Sets: 38,500.
Video Standard: PAL.

BROADCASTER

NAMIBIA BROADCASTING CORP.
P.O. Box 321, Windhoek 9000. Tel: (26461) 215 811. FAX:
(26461) 291 2291.

NAURU

Population: 11,000.
Video Standard: NTSC.

BROADCASTER

NAURU TELEVISION
Republic of Nauru, Central Pacific. (674) 444-3190.

NEPAL

Population: 23.168 million.
TV Sets: 283,000.
Video Standard: PAL.

BROADCASTER

NEPAL TELEVISION CORPORATION
P.O. Box 3826, Singha Durbar, Kathmandu. Tel: (9771) 227
290. FAX: (9771) 228 312.

THE NETHERLANDS

Population: 15.4 million
TV Sets: 6.5 million
Cable Subscribers: 5.8 million.
Satellite Dishes: 300,000.
VCR homes: 3.8 million
A2000, the only cable operator in Amsterdam, has alienated
CNN International, MTV Europe, Eurosport and the Discovery
Channel. All of these providers have elected to withdraw their
feeds to Amsterdam due to unreasonable renewal conditions
imposed by A2000. The cable operator was charging $360,000
in carriage fees per year. Accordingly, Amsterdam will be the
only major capital in Western Europe without CNN.

BROADCASTERS

AVRO
P.O. Box 2, 1200 JA Hilversum. Tel: (3135) 671 7911. FAX:
(3135) 671 7439.

E.O.
P.O. Box 21000, 1202 BB Hilversum. Tel: (3135) 688 2411.
FAX: (3135) 688 2685.

EURO 7
PO Box 1594, Hilversum 1200 BN. Tel: (35) 621 0799. FAX:
(35) 621 1374.

HOLLAND MEDIA GROUP (RTL 4, RTL 5, VERONICA)
Franciscusweg 219, Hilversum 1216 SE. Tel: (3135) 671 8718.
FAX: (3135) 623 6892.

HUMANISTISCH VERBOND (CHANNEL 1)
Borneolaan 17, Hilversum 1217 GX. Tel: (35) 628 4689. FAX:
(35) 621 8019.

IKON TELEVISION
Berweg 16, Hilversum 1217 SE. Tel: (3135) 623 3841. FAX:
(3135) 621 5100. Telex: 43974 IKON NL.

KRO TELEVISION
P.O. Box 23000, 1202 EA Hilversum. Tel: (3135) 671 3911.
FAX: (3135) 623 7345. Telex: 43534.

NCRV
P.O. Box 25000, 1202 HB Hilversum. Tel: (3135) 671 9911.
FAX: (3135) 671 9285.

NCVR
P.O. Box 121, 1200 JE Hilversum. Tel: (3135) 671 9325. FAX:
(3135) 671 9445.

**NEDERLANDSE OMROEPPROGRAMMA STICHTING
(NOS)**
P.O. Box 26600, 1202 JT Hilversum. Tel: (3135) 677 9222. FAX:
(3135) 677 2649.

NEDERLANDSE PROGRAMMA STICHTING (NPS)
P.O. Box 29000, 1202 MA Hilversum. Tel: (3135) 677 9333.
FAX: (3135) 677 4517.

NETHERLANDS BROADCASTING SERVICE
P.O. Box 10, 1200 JB Hilversum. Tel: (3135) 677 5445.

NOT (EDUCATIONAL - CHANNEL 2)
PO Box 1070, Hilversum 1200 BB. Tel: (35) 672 3611. FAX:
(35) 621 0143.

OMROEP HINDOE MEDIA
Koninginneweg 8, Hilversum 1217 KX. Tel: (35) 624 8784. FAX:
(35) 628 0843.

RVU (EDUCATIONAL - CHANNEL 3)
PO Box 1950, Hilversum 1200 BZ. Tel: (35) 624 0551. FAX:
(35) 624 0555.

STER
PO Box 344, Hilversum 1200 AH. Tel: (35) 672 5500.

TELEAC (EDUCATIONAL - CHANNEL 2)
PO Box 2414, Ultrecht 3500 GK. Tel: (30) 295 6911. FAX: (30)
294 1411.

TROS
PO Box 28450, 1202 LL Hilversum. Tel: (3135) 671 5715. FAX:
(3135) 671 5236.

TV PLUS
PO Box 427, 1200 AK Hilversum. Tel: (3135) 677 3840. FAX:
(3135) 677 3770.

TV PLUS SELECT
PO Box 427, 1200 AK Hilversum. Tel: (3135) 630 0180.

VARA
PO Box 175, 1200 AD Hilversum. Tel: (3135) 671 1999. FAX:
(3135) 671 1333.

VERONICA (CHANNEL 2)
Laapersveld 75 1213 VB Hilversum. Tel: (3135) 671 6716. FAX:
(3135) 624 9771.

VPRO
PO Box 11, 1200 JC Hilversum. Tel: (3135) 671 2911. FAX:
(3135) 671 2254.

CABLE

CNN INTERNATIONAL SALES
Kolfweg 10, 3255 BK Oude Tonge. Tel: (3118) 741 522.

ENECO
P.O. Bax 1313, 3000 DE Rotterdam. Tel: (3110) 457 5157. FAX:
(3110) 457 5281.

E.O.
(See E.O. listing under Broadcasters.)

KABEL TV AMSTERDAM
Willem de Zwygerlaan 350, 1055 RD Amsterdam. Tel: (3120)
584 8801. FAX: (3120) 400 3025.
KBN Kabel
Tel: (3120) 584 8888. FAX: (3120) 682 0992.
KTA Amsterdam
Tel: (3120) 686 8691.

NOS
(See NOS listing under Broadcasters.)

NUON
Paramariboweg 65, 7333 BR Appeldorn. Tel: (3155) 265 173.

REMU
P.O. Box 8888, 3503 SG Utrecht. Tel: (3130) 297 5911. FAX:
(3130) 294 1631.

SATELLITE

EURO 7
Lorentzweg 46, 1221 EH Hilversum. Tel: (3135) 646 4646. FAX:
(3135) 646 4600.

KINDERNET
Joan Muyskenweg 42, 1099 CK Amsterdam. Tel: (3120) 665
9576. FAX: (3120) 692 8772.

RTL 4 AND 5
Franciscusweg 219, 1216 SE Hilversum. Tel: (3135) 671 8709.
FAX: (3135) 621 0942. Telex: 43079.

VIDEO DISTRIBUTORS

BUENA VISTA HOME ENTERTAINMENT
Postbus 891, 1170 AH Badhoevedorp. Tel: (3120) 658 0300.
FAX: (3120) 659 3836.

CIC VIDEO BV
Ampereweg 13, 3442 AB Woerden. Tel: (313480) 66 900. FAX:
(313480) 10 576.

CINEMA INTERNATIONAL
PO Box 9228, 1006 AE Amsterdam. Tel: (3120) 617 7575. FAX:
(3120) 617 7434.

CINEMIEN FILM AND VIDEO DISTRIBUTORS
Entrepotdok 66, 1018 AD Amsterdam. Tel: (3120) 625 8857.
FAX: (3120) 620 9857.

CONCORDE FILM BENELUX
Lange Voorhout 35, 2514 EC Den Haag. Tel: (3170) 360 5810.
FAX: (3170) 360 4925.

FOX VIDEO
PO Box 1213, 1200 NL Hilversum. Tel: (3135) 222 111. FAX:
(3135) 222 190.

POLYGRAM
Mozartlaan 27, 1200 CM Hilversum. Tel: (3135) 261 740. FAX:
(3135) 281 474.

20TH CENTURY FOX VIDEO
Mozartlaan 27, 1200 CM Hilversum. Tel: (3135) 622 2111. FAX:
(3135) 622 2190.

WARNER BROS. HOLLAND
De Boelelaan 16 3H, 1083 HJ Amsterdam. Tel: (3120) 541
1211. FAX: (3120) 644 9001.

NEW ZEALAND

Population: 3.55 million.
TV Sets: 1.1 million.
VCRs: 870,000.
Video Standard: PAL-B.

New Zealand's newest and fifth free network, Prime TV, premiered in September.

Telecom Corp. has decided to close its First Media pay TV unit
and will instead concentrate on Internet services. In spite an
investment of $36 million, Telecom has reached only 3,000 of its
targeted 75,000 homes. New Zealand has two remaining pay TV
providers, Sky TV and Saturn Communications.

ORGANIZATION

INTERNATIONAL TV ASSOCIATION OF NEW ZEALAND
PO Box 10092, Wellington. Tel: (644) 385 8055. FAX: (644) 385
8055.

BROADCASTERS

ACTION TV
PO Box 388-99 ,Wellington. Tel. (644) 576 6999. FAX: (644)
576 6942.

CANTERBURY TELEVISION
P.O. Box 3741, 196 Gloucester St., Christchurch.

SKY NETWORK TV (PAY-TV)
P.O. Box 9059, New Market, Auckland. Tel: (649) 525 5555.
FAX: (649) 555 5725.

TELEVISION NEW ZEALAND
PO Box 3819, Auckland. Tel: (649) 377 0630. FAX: (649) 375 0918.

TV3 NETWORK (TV 4)
PO Box 5185, Auckland. Tel: (649) 377 9730. FAX: (649) 366 7029.

VIDEO ORGANIZATION

VIDEO ASSOCIATION
125 Vincent St., Auckland. Tel: (649) 308 9421.

VIDEO DISTRIBUTORS

EVERARD FILMS
PO Box 3664, Auckland 1. Tel: (649) 302 1193. FAX: (649) 302 1192.

HOYTS CORPORATION (NZ)
PO Box 6445, Auckland. Tel: (649) 303 2739. FAX: (649) 307 0011.

KONTACT VIDEO SERVICES
PO Box 25156, Auckland. Tel: (649) 575 8238.

UNITED INTERNATIONAL PICTURES
PO Box 105263, Auckland. Tel: (649) 379 6269. FAX: (649) 379 6271.

WARNER BROS. (NZ)
PO Box 8687, Mt. Eden, Auckland. Tel: (649) 377 5223. FAX: (649) 309 2795.

NICARAGUA

Population: 4.27 million.
TV Sets: 214,000.
Video Standard: NTSC.

BROADCASTER

SISTEMA SANDINISTA DE TELEVIAION (GOV.)
Km 31/2 Carretera Sur, Contigo Shell, Las Palmas, Managua. Tel: (5052) 660 028. FAX: (5052) 662 411.

NIGER

Population: 9.11 million.
TV Sets: 26,000.
Video Standard: SECAM.

BROADCASTER

TELE-SAHEL
PO Box 309, Niamey. Tel: (227) 723 155. FAX: (227) 723 548.

NIGERIA

Population: 122.84 million.
TV Sets: 6.1 million.
Video Standard: PAL.

BROADCASTER

NIGERIAN TELEVISION AUTHORITY
Television House, PMB 120005, Victoria Island, Lagos. Tel: (2341) 614 966. FAX: (2341) 261 0289.

NORWAY

Population: 4.33 million.
TV Sets: 2 million.
Cable Subscribers: 800,000.
Satellite Dishes: 270,000.
VCR Homes: 54,000.
Video Standard: PAL.

ASSOCIATION

INTERNATIONAL MASS MEDIA INSTITUTE
PO Box 7084, Kongsgaard N-4602, Kristiansand S, Norway. Tel: (47) 429 8811. Telex: 21281.

BROADCASTERS

NORSK RIKSKRINGKASTING (NRK)
Bjrnstjerne Bjrnsons Plass 1, N-0340 Oslo 1. Tel: (4722) 459 050. FAX: (4722) 457 440.

QUIVE A/S
Postbox 1604, Sandefjord 3207. Tel: (33) 479 930. FAX: (33) 479 933.

TV2 AS
P.O. Box 2, Verfsgt 2c, Bergen 5002. Tel: (4755) 908 070. FAX: (4755) 908 090.

TV3
Karl Johansgt 12J, N-0154 Oslo. Tel: (47) 2242 3030. FAX: (47) 2242 5029.

ZTV
Maridalsvn 139 A, N-0406. Tel: (47) 2271 4000. FAX: (47) 2271 6550.

CABLE

ASKER OG BAERUM LOKAL TV
Industrivn 33, Sandvika 1300. Tel: (67) 565 667.

FREDRIKSTAD NAERINGKASTIG
Postboks 1185, N-1601, Fredrikstad. Tel: (47) 6931 9030. FAX: (47) 6931 9280.

HOLMLIA KABEL TV
Postboks 69, Holmlia, Oslo N 1201. Tel: (22) 616 635, 619 057.

TV HALDEN
Os Alle P.O. Box 623 Busterud, N-1754 Halden. Tel: (47) 6917 5310. FAX: (47) 6918 7913.

TV HEDMARK
Elvarheimgt 10, N-2400 Elverum. Tel: (47) 6241 3555. FAX: (47) 6241 3375.

TV HELGELAND
Handverksgt 5, Mo 8610. Tel: (75) 155 022. FAX: (75) 132 286.

TV INNLANDET HAMAR A/S
Kornsilovn 62, Hamar 2300. Tel: (62) 530 760. FAX: (62) 534 845.

TV NORDMORE
Idustrivn 18, N-6500 Kristiansund. Tel: (47) 7158 4922. FAX: (47) 7158 3755.

TV 1000 NORGE AS
Nedre Slottsgt 8, N-0157 Oslo. Tel: (47) 2241 1000. FAX: (47) 2242 2715.

TV PLUS
Grensen 15, P.O. Box 289, Sentrum, N-0103 Oslo. Tel: (47) 2286 4150. FAX: (47) 2286 4430.

TV TROMSO A/S
Sondre Tollbugt 17, Tromso 9000. Tel: (77) 683 333. FAx: (77) 683 533.

TV3
(See TV3 listing under Broadcasters.)

SATELLITE

SCANSAT BROADCASTING TV3
Bogstadveien 8, N-0355 Oslo. Tel: (47) 2260 1860. FAX: (47) 2260 1310.

TV 1000 NORGE AS
(See TV 100 listing under Cable.)

TV2 AS
(See TV2 listing under Broadcasters.)

TV3
(See TV3 listing under Broadcasters.)

TVNORGE AS
Sagveien 17, N-0458 Oslo. Tel: (47) 2235 0350. FAX: (47) 2235 1000.

VIDEO DISTRIBUTORS

ACTION FILM
Valerenggata 47, PO Box 9343,Valerenga, Oslo N-0610. Tel: (47) 2267 3131. FAX: (47) 2267 3005.

BUENA VISTA HOME VIDEO
PO Box 164, Stabekk N-1320. Tel: (47) 6756 3609. FAX: (47) 6758 3709.

BV FILM INTERNATIONAL
PO Box 17, Avaldnsnes, Oslo N-4262. Tel: (47) 5284 3544. FAX: (47) 5284 3575.

CCC VIDEO
PO Box 95, Alnabru, Oslo N-0614. Tel: (47) 2264 7770. FAX: (47) 2264 2122.

CIC VIDEO NORWAY
Gjerdrumsvel 21, PO Box 38, Tasen, Oslo N-0801. Tel: (47) 2223 2500. FAX: (47) 2223 2599.

EGMONT FILM
PO Box 417, Asker N-1370. Tel: (47) 6690 4121. FAX: (47) 6690 4175.

FILMCO
Profdaohlsegt 8, Oslo N-03554262. Tel: (47) 2646 4000.

HOLLYWOOD FILM
Baneviksgt 7, Stavanger N-4014. Tel: (47) 5153 4045. FAX: (475152) 7398.

NORSK FILM DISTRIBUTION
Stortingsgt 12, Oslo N-0161. Tel: (47) 2242 3600. FAX: (47) 2242 2313.

NOVIO
Nes Terrasse 45, Nesbru N-1360. Tel: (47) 6684 9160. FAX: (47) 6698 0342.

POLYGRAM
Drammensvn 88B, Oslo N-4262. Tel: (47) 2243 6060. FAX: (47) 2243 4430.

SF NORGE
Box 6868, St Olavs Plass, Oslo N-0614. Tel: (47) 2233 4750. FAX: (47) 2242 4430.

TOUR DE FORCE
Georgemes V 3, Bergen N-5011. Tel: (47) 5532 2590. FAX: (47) 5532 3740.

WARNER HOME VIDEO
Oscargate 55, Oslo N-0258. Tel: (47) 2243 1800. FAX: (47) 2255 4683.

OMAN

Population: 2.19 million.
TV Sets: 1.56 million
Video Standard: PAL.

BROADCASTER

SULTANATE OF OMAN TELEVISION
PO Box 600, Muscat 113. (968) 603 222. FAX: (968) 602 381.

PAKISTAN

Population: 141.5 million
TV Sets: 9 million
Licensed TV Sets: 1.2 million
VCRs/VCPs: 2.3 million
VCR/VCP Households: 40% approximately
VCR Prices: $200–$275
VCP Prices: $100
Estimated Piracy level: 70% (Video is an illegal business under Pakistani laws.)
Video Standard: PAL.

All of the five centers of Pakistan Television Corporation Ltd. (PTV), Lashore, Karachi, Islamabad, Peshawar and Quetta, produce and transmit color programs, including foreign films about 20 hours per day. Three centers of Shalimar Television Co., (which is also a state-controlled network) are leased out to a private company, NTM, for five hours from 7 to 12 pm. The remaining time is fed by CNN live. One more channel, PTV World, is liekely to go on satellite feed in 1998. Shalimar TV may be closed down beofre the end of 1998.

The main source of income for PTV are commercials, license fees and export of programmes to those countries where large numbers of Pakistanis live. The license fee is Rs 250 for domestic and Rs 500 for commercial sets per year. Due to ongoing heavy losses, PTV now sells play time to private parties. All PTV programs are now telecast via satellite and can be seen in 38 neighboring countries. The second channel, described as ETC or PTV2, went on the air in 1995 and is likely to be leased out to private parties. There is an Academy for the training of artistes and technicians within Pakistan and neighboring countries.

Cable operators have strongly affected the VCR/VCP and dish business, as the price of cable technology has gone down considerably. Monthly rent is between Rs 50 and Rs 300 while a registration fee of Rs 2,000 is imposed on dish antennas by the government, although few pay.

There are two kinds of video shops—one deals in sales, the other in rentals only. The number of video distributors is countless, but there are about a dozen big ones, who 'import' video films from all countries except India. Their primary business comes from Indian films pictures with highly sexual content. Because of strict censorship, moviegoers cannot see such films in cinemas. Therefore, pirated uncensored videos are popular.

BROADCASTERS

NETWORK TELEVISION MARKETING (PVT) LTD.
43/15 F Block No. 6, PECHS., Karachi. Tel: (9221) 454 1170. FAX: (9221) 454 5538.

PAKISTAN TELEVISION CORPORATION LTD.
Federal TV Complex, Constituion Ave., Islamabad. Tel: (9251) 920 8651, 920 2194, 920 3062. FAX: (9251) 920 2202, 920 3406.

PTV-LAHORE
21 Mehmood Ghaznavi Road, Lahore 6. Tel: (9242) 920 0651. FAX: (9242) 920 0612.

PTV-KARACHI
Stadium Road, Karachi 5. Tel: (9221) 493 1001. FAX: (9221) 493 1000.

PTV-PESHAWAR
58 Shahrah-e-Quaide Azam, Peshawar Cantt. Tel: (9291) 279 100, 279 116. FAX: (9291) 278 550.

PTV-QUETTA
Shahrah-e-Hali, Quetta. Tel: (9281) 920 2461. FAX: 920 2125.

SHALIMAR TELEVISION CO.
PTV Center, Islamabad. Tel: (9251) 827 119.

—A.R. SLOTE

PANAMA

Population: 2.66 million.
TV Sets: 204,000.
Video Standard: NTSC.

BROADCASTER

PANAVISION
Apt. 6-2605, El Dorado, Panama 1.

RPC TELEVISION
Apt. 1795, Panama 1.

SISTEMA DE TV EDUCATIVA
Estafeta Universitaria, Universidad de Panama.

TELEMETRO
P.O. Box 8-116, Panama 8.

TELEVISION NACIONAL
Apr. 6-3092, El Dorado, Panama.

PAPUA NEW GUINEA

Population: 4.597 million.
TV Sets: 100,000.
Video Standard: PAL.

BROADCASTER

EMTV
PO Box 443 Boroko. Tel: (675) 325 7322. FAX: (675) 325 4450.

PARAGUAY

Population: 5.5 million.
TV Sets: 393,000.
Pay-TV Subscribers: 150,000.
Satellite Dishes: Under one thousand.
Video Standard: PAL.

BROADCASTER

CANAL 9 TV CERRO CORA S.A.,
Avenida Carlos Antonio Lopez 572, Asuncion. Tel: (59584) 222 26. Tel: (59584) 498 911.

TELEDIFUSORA PARAGUAYA S.A.
8 Proy Lambare, Asuncion. Tel: (59521) 443 093.

TELEVISION ITAPUA
Avda. Irrazabal 25 de Mayo, Encarnacion.

TELEVISORA DEL ESTE
Area 5, Cd. Puerto Stroessner.

PERU

Population: 25 million.
TV Sets: 2.23 million.
Pay-TV Subscribers: 110,000.
Satellite Dishes: 2,000.
Video Standard: NTSC.

BROADCASTERS

ANDINA DE TELEVISION/CANAL 9
Arequipa 3570, San Isidro, Apartado 270077, Lima.

CANAL 11
Avenido Manca Capac 333, La Victoria, Lima.

CANAL 4
Montero Rosas 1099, Santa Beatriz, Lima.

CANAL 13
Jiron Huarez 1098, Pueblo Libre, Lima.

COMPANIA LATINOAMERICANA DE RADIODIFUSION S.A/CANAL 2
San Felipe 968, Jesus Maria, Lima 11. Tel: (5114) 707 272. FAX: (5114) 712 688.

COMPANIA PERUANA DE RADIODIFUSION
Cas. 1192, Lima.

DIFUSORA UNIVERSAL DE TELEVISION
Paseo de la Republica 6099, San Antonio, Miraflores, Lima.

EMPRESA DE CINE, RADIO Y TELEVISION PERUANA/CANAL 7
Jose Galvez 1040, Lima.

EMPRESA RADIODIFUSORA 1160 TV
Apt. Postal 2355, Lima.

PANAMERICANA DE TELEVISION/CANAL 5
Av Arequipa 1110, Lima.

RBC TELEVISION
Juan de la Fuente 453, Miraflores, Lima.

PHILIPPINES

Population: 74.48 million.
TV Sets: 7.6 million.
Average Daily TV Viewing: 3.5 hours
Cable Homes: 200,000.
Video Standard: NTSC.

The Disney Channel will luanch a customized version of their channel for Philippine audiences. The Disney Channel-Philippines will be distributed through Cable Boss. Service will be 24 hours, with international animation, live action series and features as well as local programming.

NATIONAL TELECOMMUNICATIONS COMMISSION
865 Vibal Bldg., Esda Corner Times Str., Quezon City.

BROADCASTERS

ABS-CBN BROADCASTING CORP.
Mother Ignacia Street, Dilliman, Quezon City, Metro Manila. Tel: (2) 924 4101, 924 2762. FAX: (2) 924 1506.

ASSOCIATED BROADCASTING CO.
726 Quirino Highway, Quezon City, Metro Manila. Tel: (2) 936 2551.

BANAHAW BROADCASTING CORP.
Broadcast City Complex, Quezon City, Metro Manila. Tel: (2) 931 5080.

INTERCONTINENTAL BROADCASTING CORP. TV 13
Broadcast City, Quezon City, Metro Manila. Tel: (2) 931 8928

PEOPLE'S TELEVISION NETWORK, INC.
Broadcast Complex, Visayas Avenue, Quezon City 1100. Tel: (632) 921 2344. FAX: (632) 921 1777.

RADIO PHILLIPPINES NETWORK (RPN-9)
P.O. Box 1574, Broadcast City, Capitol Hills, Quezon City, Metro Manila. Tel: (632) 931-5080. FAX: (632) 931-8618.
PRESIDENT
Rex D. Lores

REPUBLIC BROADCASTING SYSTEM INC (GMA 7)
RBS Building, EDSA, Quezon City, Metro Manila. Tel: (2) 928 5041, 928 7021.

POLAND

Population: 38.64 million.
TV Households: 10 million.
Cable Subscribers: 2.5 million
Satellite Subscribers: 1.4 million.
Video Standard: PAL.

@Entertainment has launched Poland's first digital platform with 14 of a possible 16 channels already on air. Poland's second digital platform will be a joint venture established by public broadcaster TVP, premium channel Canal Plus Polska, telcom operator TP S.A. and Commercial network, Polsat.

BROADCASTERS

LODZKIE CENTRUM FILMOWE
Lakowa 29, Lodz 90 554. Tel: (4842) 367 500, 362 589. FAX: (4842) 360 487.

POLSAT (POLSAT 1 & 2)
Al. Stanow Zjednoczonych 53, Warsaw 04-028. Tel: (4822) 135-824. FAX: (4822) 134 295.
PRESIDENT
Zygmunt Solarz-Zak
PROGRAM DIRECTOR POLSAT 1
Barbara Trzeciak-Pietkiewicz
PROGRAM DIRECTOR POLSAT 2
Boguslaw Chrabota

TELEWIZJA POLSKA SA
Woronicza 17, Warsaw 00 999. Tel: (4822) 433 361, 445 432. FAX: (4822) 447 419. URL: http://www.tvp.com.pl

TELEWIZJA WISLA
Plk. Dabka 2, Krakow 30 995. Tel: (4812) 255 272. FAX: (4812) 255 221.

TV POLONIA
JP Woronicza 17, Warsaw 00-999. Tel: (4822) 647-8444, 647 6211. FAX: (4822) 440 779
PRESIDENT
Ryszard Miaszek
DIRECTOR OF FILM PRODUCTION
Miroslaw Bork

TV POLSAT
Marchakovska 83, P-00517, Warsaw 84. (4822) 295 684.

TV WROCLAW
Ul Karkonoska 8/10, Wroclaw 53/015. Tel: (4871) 684 300. FAX: (4871) 679 454.

TVN
Powsinska Str 4, Warsaw 02920. Tel: (4822) 640 4420. FAX: (4822) 640 4456.
PRESIDENT
Mariusz Walter

WARSZAWKI OSRODEK TEWIZYJNY (WOT)
Jasna 14/16, Warsaw 00 041. Tel: (4822) 278 429. FAX: (4822) 273 808.

PAY-TV

CANAL PLUS POLSKA
Kawalerii 5, Warsaw 00468. Tel: (4822) 657 0900.
PRESIDENT
Lew Rywin

HBO POLSKA
Wilcza Str 8/3, Warsaw. Tel: (4822) 651 1116. FAX: (4822) 651 1117.
MANAGING DIRECTOR
Slawomir Suss

TV POLONIA/TYLKO MUZYKA
Woronicza 17, Warsaw 00999. Tel: (4822) 476 013. FAX: (4822) 434 833.

VIDEO DISTRIBUTORS

ANWA FILM INTERNATIONAL
Smolensk 27/3, Krakow 30960. Tel: (4812) 215 634.

ARATHOS
Lakowa Str 29, Lodz 90554. Tel: (4842) 362 592. FAX: (4842) 360 487.

ARTVISION
Smocza 18, Warsaw 01034. Tel: (4822) 382 407.

BEST FILM
Ul Twarda 16a, Warsaw 00105. Tel: (4826) 201 207. FAX: (4826) 201 203.

BOOM-FILM
Os Plastow 12C, Krakow 31410. Tel/FAX: (4812) 486 802.

DEMEL
Al Stanow Zjednoczonych, Pawilon, C3, Warsaw 04028. Tel:
(4826) 101 854. FAX: (4823) 103 074.

EUROKADR
Potocka Str 14, Warsaw 01639. Tel/FAX: (4822) 332 491.

EUROPOL
Chelmzynska 180, Warsaw 01639. Tel: (4822) 611 1140. FAX:
(4822) 610 8717.

FILM STUDIO HELIOS.
Przybyszewskiego 167, Lodz 93120. Tel: (4842) 417 510. FAX:
(4842) 417 367.

IFDF MAX
Jagelionska Str 26, Warsaw 03719. Tel: (4826) 190 481. Tel:
(4826) 191 209.

IMP
Ul Hoza 66, Warsaw 00950. Tel: (4826) 226 819. FAX: (4826)
226 821.

IMPERIAL ENTERTAINMENT
Przasnysla 9, Warsaw 01756. Tel: (4822) 637 871. FAX: (4822)
637 884.

ITI HOME VIDEO
Klobucka 23, Warsaw 02699. Tel: (4822) 430 506. FAX: (4822)
430 506.

MARIANNE
Al Lotnikow 1, Warsaw 02668. Tel: (4822) 431 406. Tel: (4822)
434 492.

MUVI ENTERTAINMENT GROUP
Rovbrat St 44, Warsaw 00-419. Tel: (4822) 629 2664. FAX:
(4822) 629 5911.

NEPTUN VIDEO CENTER
Sapiezynska 10, Warsaw 00131. Tel: (4826) 359 276. FAX:
(4826) 359 276.

PELOGRAF
Pl Mirowski 14, Warsaw 00135. Tel: (4822) 205 1260. FAX:
(4822) 208 342.

SALOPAN
Ul Krakowskie Przedmiescie 21/23, Warsaw 00071. Tel: (4822)
226 3335. FAX: (4822) 635 0044.

SILESIA-FILM
Kosciuszki 88, Katowice 40041. Tel: (4832) 512 248. Tel: (4832)
512 284.

STUDIO KINEO
Ul Zlota 7/9, Warsaw 00019. Tel: (4822) 272 906. FAX: (4822)
266 468.

SYRENA ENTERTAINMENT GROUP
Marszalkowska 115, Warsaw 00950. Tel: (4822) 275 204. Tel:
(4822) 275 648.

TOP VIDEO
Ul Frankuska 11, Warsaw 03906. Tel: (4826) 174 082. FAX:
(4822) 241 762.

VIM
Ul Wspolna 30a, Warsaw 00930. Tel: (4822) 623 2155. FAX:
(4822) 623 2157.

WARNER HOME VIDEO
Ks J Popieluszki Str 16, Warsaw 01590. Tel: (4822) 339 808.
FAX: (4822) 335 497.

PORTUGAL

Population: 10.676 million.
TV sets: 3 million.
Cable Subscribers: 150,000.
Satellite Dishes: 300,000.
Video Standard: PAL.

BROADCASTERS

RTP (PORTUGUESE RADIOTELEVISION)
Av 5 de Outubro, 197, Lisbon 1000. Tel: (3511) 793 1774.
Telex: 14527 (INT. REL/EV). FAX: (3511) 793 1758.

SIC (SOCIEDADE INDEPENDENTE DE COMMUNICACAO)
Estrada da Outurela 119, Camaxide 2795, Linda-A-Velha,
Lisboa. Tel: (3511) 417 3138. FAX: (3511) 418 7156.

TVI (INDEPENDENT TELEVISION)
Edificio Altejo, rua 3 da Martinha, 6 piso, Lisboa 1900. Tel:
(3511) 434 7500. FAX: (3511) 435 5075.

VIDEO DISTRIBUTORS

ACTUAL-VIDEO
Campo Grande 30, 3 F, Lisbon 1700. Tel: (3511) 793 6726.
FAX: (3511) 797 8816.

ATALANA FILMS
Av Joao Crisostomo, 38C-1, Escrittorio 3, Lisbon 1000. Tel:
(3511) 353 1616. FAX: (3511) 353 1636.

BMG ARIOLA
Rua Joao Chagas, N-53-1, Alges 1495. Tel: (3511) 414 8020.
FAX: (3511) 414 2959.

CASTELO LOPES
Rua de St Amaro Estrela, 17A, Lisbon 1200. Tel: (3511) 395
5955. FAX: (3511) 395 5924/5.

COMPETIVIDEO
Rua da Trinidad, 12-2, Lisbon 1000. Tel: (3511) 346 6971. FAX:
(3511) 346 6967.

DEVA VIDEO
Av Duque de Loule 75 8 dto 1000. Tel: (3511) 573 698.

ECOVIDEO EDICOES VIDEO
Estrada de Benifica 407 1 dto, Lisbon 1500. Tel: (3511) 778
1921.

EDIVIDEO
Rua Manual Ferreira Andrade, B, Lisbon 1500. Tel: (3511) 778
3158. FAX: (3511) 778 0661.

EMI-VALENTIM DE CARVALHO
Rua Cruz dos Polais 111, Lisbon 1200. Tel: (3511) 600 111.
FAX: (3511) 395 7074.

FANTAS VIDEO
Rua Diogo Brandao 87, Porto 4000. Tel: (3512) 320 759. FAX:
(3512) 383 679.

FILITALUS
Rua Alexandre Herculano 2, Lisbon 1150. Tel: (3511) 547 988.
Tel: (3511) 524 674.

FILMAYER ALFA
Praca de Alegria 22-1, Lisbon 1250. Tel: (3511) 347 4561. FAX:
(3511) 346 5349.

LUSOMUNDO
Praca de Alegria 22, Lisbon 1250. Tel: (3511) 347 4561. FAX:
(3511) 346 5349.

MUNDIAL VIDEO
Rua Luciano Cordeiro 113 7 Esq, Lisbon 1100. Tel: (3511) 315
0860.

POLYGRAM DISCO
Rua Prof Reinaldo dos Santos 12, Lisbon 1200. Tel: (3511)
778 7101. FAX: (3511) 778 0212.

PRISVIDEO EDICOES VIDEOGRAF
Durbalino Neves, Rua Bartolomeu Dias, PO Box 207, S Joao
Madeira Codex 3701. Tel: (3515) 688 1992. FAX: (3515) 688
1923.

ROMALUSA
Rua Alexandre Herculano 2 Lisbon 1150. Tel: (3511) 354 7142.
FAX: (3511) 352 4674.

TRANSVIDEO
Rua dos Soeiros 317 A, Lisbon 1500. Tel: (3511) 726 2510. Tel:
(3511) 726 9579.

UNITED KING VIDEO
E. N. 2494, Km 7, 4, Abobada, Parede 2775. Tel: (3514) 444
324. FAX: (3514) 443 892.

VERA VIDEO
Alameda das Linhas de Torres, 104, 1 Esq, Lisbon 1700. Tel:
(3511) 759 0591. FAX: (3511) 353 5630.

VISAO VIDEO
Rua de Santa Marta21, 1 dto, Lisbon 1100. Tel: (3511) 353
0736. FAX: (3511) 315 5630.

QATAR

Population: 605,000.
TV sets: 250,500.
Video Standard: PAL.

BROADCASTER

QATAR TELEVISION SERVICE
Min. of Information and Culture, QTV, PO Box 1944, Doha. Tel:
(974) 894 444. FAX: (974) 864 511.

ROMANIA

Population: 23.2 million.
TV Sets: 7.277 million.
Cable Subscribers: :2 million.
Satellite Dishes: 300,000.
Video Standard: PAL.

RADIOTELIVIZIUNEA ROMANA
191 Calea Dorobanti, 79756 Bucuresti, Tel: (401) 212 0290.
FAX: (401) 312 0381.

PRIVATE BROADCASTERS

ANTENA 1
Ploesti 25-27, 70000 Bucurest. Tel: (401) 212 0619. FAX: (401) 212 0188.

CANAL 31
155 Piata Victoriei Di, Etaj 7, 70411 Bucuresti. Tel: (401) 210 6628.

CANALUL DE STIRI
Calea Victoriei 133-5, s 1, Bucuresti. Tel: (401) 312 4348. FAX: (401) 312 0349.

PRO TV
Bd Carol 1 109, Etaj s2, Bucuresti. Tel: (401) 312 4218. FAX: (401) 312 4228.

TELE AMERICA
Blvd. Armata Poporului 1-3, s6, Bucuresti. Tel: (401) 311 0419. FAX: (401) 311 0417.

TELE EUROPA NOVA
Dr. Lister 6, s5, Bucuresti. Tel: (401) 623 6661. FAX:(401) 312 1324.

TELE 7 ABC
Christo Botev 8, s3, Bucuresti. Tel: (401) 312 1695. FAX: (401) 611 6576.

TV SIGMA
Blvd. Armata Poporului 1, Complex Leu-Facultatea de Electronic Crp A, Etaj 8, Bucuresti. Tel: (401) 631 4734.

RUSSIAN FEDERATION

Population: 148.18 million.
TV sets: 50 million.
Video Standard: SECAM.

MTV is launching a customized service for the Russian market that will feature Russian hosts and local artists. The new channel is the first western network channel to be tailored to the Russian market and will be supported by advertiser revenue.

Russia's national TV channels, ORT and NTV did not carry Boris Yeltsin's annual address to the nation in 1998, electing to air sorts and a game show, respectively. Only state-owned Radio Television Russia carried the address.

BROADCASTERS

AS BAIKAL TV—TV & RADIO
6 Shelehov, Shelehov 666020. Tel: (7395) 109 3303. FAX: (7395) 103 1917

ARKHANGELSKAYA TV COMPANY
Levachov St. 17, Cor 2, Arkhangelsk 163020, Russia. Tel: (7818) 002 7777.

BRYANSK STATE TV
Stanice Dmitrov Propsect 77, Bryansk 241033, Russia. Tel: (7832) 212 661.

CHANNEL 5/6TR PETERSBURG
6 Chapygina Str., St Petersburg 197022. Tel: (7812) 234 3763. FAX: (7812) 234 1416.

EVRASIA TV
Lesvaya St. 63/43, Moscow 103055, Russia. Tel: (7095) 250 1248. FAX: (7095) 973 1216.

FILMEXPORT
27 Lesnaya St, Moscow 125047. Tel: (095) 251 3507. FAX: (095) 251 2910.

HBC
8a Suvorovski Blvd, Moscow 121019.Tel: (095) 291 1784.

INDEPENDENT BROADCASTING SYSTEM (MVS)
Suite 303, 8A, Suvoroysky Blvd., Moscow 121019. Tel: (7095) 291 1787. FAX: (7095) 291 2174.

KALININGRAD STATE TV & RADIO
19 Klinicheskaja Str., Kaliningrad 136016. Tel: (70112) 452 700. FAX: (70112) 452 233.

KOSMOS TV-1
ul. Akad Koroleva 12, Moscow 127000. Tel: (095) 217 7133, 217 7359. FAX: (095) 215 8257.

LENINGRAD REGION TV
Uritskogo Str 2, St Petersburg 188350. Tel: (7812) 274 3536. FAX: (7812) 274 4470.

MOSCOW TV
12 Akademika Korolyova Str., Moscow 127000. Tel: (7095) 217 5298. FAX: (7095) 216 5401.

MOSCOW TV 6
Ilyinka 15, Moscow. Tel: (7095) 206 8423. FAX: (7095) 206 8886.

NTV
Novyi Arbat Str 36, Moscow 121102. Tel: (7095) 290 7077. FAX: (7095) 290 9757.

ORT/OSTANKINO STATE
12 Akademika Korolyova St., Moscow 127000. (7095) 217 7898. FAX: (7095) 255 9542.

OSTANKINO
12 Korolyov, Moscow 127000. Tel: (095) 215 5446. Telex: 411340. FAX: (095) 288 9508, 288 9510.

PETERSBURG - CHANNEL 5 (RUSSIAN RADIO & TV CO)
Italianskaya ul 27, St Petersburg 191011. Tel: (812) 233 1443, 234 0716. FAX: (812) 234 1510.

REGIONAL TELEVISION
Akademika Pavlova Str 3, St Petersburg 197022. Tel: (7812) 238 6073. FAX: (7812) 238 5807.

ROSSYIA (II TELEKANAL)
5a Yamskogo Poya ul 19/21, Moscow 125124. Tel: (095) 214 0655. FAX: (095) 973 2069.

RTR (ALL RUSSIAN STATE TV & RADIO CO)
Leningradsky pr 22, Moscow 125040. Tel: (095) 214 4817, 214 4978. FAX: (095) 921 2526, 973 2080.

RTR (CHANNEL 2)
5th Ulitza Yamskogo Polya 19/21, Moscow 125124. Tel: (7095) 250 0511. FAX: (7095) 250 0105.

RUSSIAN INSTITUTE FOR CULTURAL RESEARCH
20 Bersenevskaya Nab, Moscow 109072. Tel: (7095) 230 0177. FAX: (7095) 230 0822.

RUSSIAN UNIVERSITY CHANNEL
5 Yamskogo Polya 19/21, Moscow 125124. Tel: (7095) 213 1754. FAX: (7095) 213 1436.

RUSSKOYE VIDEO—CHANNEL 11
Malaya Nevka 4, St Petersburg 197022. Tel: (7812) 234 4207. FAX: (7095) 234 0088.

SOVINTERFEST
10 Khohlovsky per, Moscow 109028. Tel: (095) 917 2486. FAX: (095) 917 8628.

STATE NATIONAL TV COMPANY OF SAKHA REPUBLIC
Ordjokinidze St. 48, Yakutsk 677892, Russia. Tel: (7411) 225 3169. FAX: (7411) 225 3176.

TELEKANAL 2X2
ul Akad Koroleva 12, Moscow 127000. Tel: (7095) 217 7094. FAX: (095) 215 2063.

TELEXPRESS—CHANNEL 31
12 Alademika Korolyova Str., Moscow 127000. Tel: (7095) 282 4260. FAX: (7095) 276 8892.

TV CENTER
Korolyova St 12, Moscow 127000. Tel: (7095) 217 7094. FAX: (7095) 215 2063.

TV COMP FOURTH CHANNEL
PO Box 751, Yekaterinburgh 620069. Tel: (73432) 232 041. FAX: (73432) 236 033.

TV 6 MOSCOW
Ilinka 15-I, Moscow 103070. Tel: (095) 206 0331, 206 8423. FAX: (095) 290 8594..

2 X 2 TV CHANNEL
12 Ulitza Akademika Korolyeva, Moscow 127000. Tel: (095) 215 9690. FAX: (095) 283 8814.

VGTRK
Jamskogo polja 5-ja ul. 19/12, Moskow 124124. (7095) 217 9981. FAX: (7095) 250 0506.

SATELLITE

INTERSPUTNIK
2 Smolensky Lane 1/4, Moscow 1210 99, Russia. Tel: (7095) 224 0333. FAX: (7095) 253 9906.

KOSMOS TV
Akademika Kovoleva UL 15, Moscow. Tel: (7095) 282 3360. FAX: (7095) 286 2631

NTV PLUS
Novyi Arbat Str 36, Moscow 121102. Tel: (7095) 290 7077. FAX: (7095) 290 9757.

OSTANKINO TV-1
Piatickaia 25, Moscow 113326. Tel: (7095) 217 7260. FAX: (7095) 215 1324

RTR NETWORK
5YA Yamskogo Polya 19/21, Moscow 125124. Tel: (7095) 213 4052. FAX: (7095) 213 6081

RUSSIA TV-2
12 Korolyov Street, Moscow 127000. Tel: (7095) 2177 898. FAX: (7095) 2889 508.

CABLE

TELESET
Soretskaya st 80, P/B55, Moscow 105037. Tel: (7095) 166 9763. FAX: (7095) 166 1436.

VIDEO DISTRIBUTORS

ATLANT CO
9A Kirovogradskaya St, Moscow 113587. Tel: (7095) 312 5203. FAX: (7095) 312 8127.

EKATERINBURG ART
Chebyshev Str., 5th Fl., Ekaterinburg 620062. Tel: (73432) 442 1120. FAX: (73432) 442 343.

GEMINI FILM
Bldg 6, 40 Myasnitskaya Str., Moscow 101000. Tel: (7095) 921 0854. FAX: (7095) 921 2394.

KINOTON
16 Okruzhnoy Proyezd, Moscow 101000. Tel: (7095) 290 3412. FAX: (7095) 200 5612.

KREDO-ASPEK
Novy Arbat St 11, Moscow 121019. Tel: (7095) 291 7269. FAX: (7095) 219 6880.

MOST MEDIA
Maly Gnezdnikovsky, Moscow 103877. Tel: (7095) 229 1172. FAX: (7095) 229 1274.

PARADISE LTD AGENCY
12a Christoprudny Blvd, Suite 601, Moscow, 101000. Tel: (7095) 916 9220. FAX: (7095) 924 1331.

SKIP CENTRE FILM
2 Filevskaya Str 7/19, Moscow 121096. Tel: (7095) 145 2459. FAX: (7095) 145 3355.

SOVEXPORTFILM
14 Kalashny Pereulok, Moscow 103009. Tel: (7095) 290 2053. FAX: (7095) 200 1256.

STUDIO PYRAMID
8 K-1, Ak Koroleva Str., Moscow. Tel: (7095) 216 4778. FAX: (7095) 216 4778.

VARUS VIDEO
1-st Veshnyakovsky Proezd 1, Moscow 109456. Tel: (7095) 170 9629. FAX: (7095) 170 5738.

SAN MARINO

Population: 24,521.
TV Sets: 7,000.
Video Standard: PAL.

BROADCASTER

SAN MARINO RTV SPA
Via le J. F. Kennedy, 13-Citta, San Marino. Tel: (39549) 882-000.

SAUDI ARABIA

Population: 19.4 million.
TV sets: 6.06 million.
Video Standard: SECAM & PAL

BROADCASTERS

ARABSAT
PO Box 1038, Riyadh. Tel: (9661) 464 6666. FAX: (9661) 465 6983.

BSKSA SAUDI ARABIA
PO Box 57137, Riyadh 11574. Tel: (9661) 401 040. FAX: (9661) 404 4192.

CHANNEL 3TV
Bldg. 3030, LIP, Dhahran, Saudi Arabia.

ISLAMIC STATES BROADCASTING SERVICES ORGANIZATION
PO Box 6351, Jeddah, Saudi Arabia.

SAUDI ARABIAN TELEVISION
Ministry of Information, PO Box 57317, Riyadh 11574. (9661) 401 4440. FAX: (9661) 404 4192.

SENEGAL

Population: 9.1 million.
TV sets: 61,000.
Video Standard: SECAM.

ORGANIZATION

UNION OF NATIONAL RADIO & TELEVISION ORGANIZATIONS OF AFRICA (URTNA)
101 Rue Carnot, BP 3237 Dakar, Senegal. Tel: (221) 211 625.

BROADCASTER

CANAL HORIZONS
31 ave. Albert Sarraut (B.P. 1390), Dakar. (221) 232 525. FAX: (221) 233 030.

RADIODIFFUSION TELEVISION SENEGALAISE
B.P. 1765, Dakar. (221) 21780. FAX: (221) 223490.

SENEGAL TELEVISION
Radiodiffision Television Senegalaise (RTS), Triangle Sud B.P. 1765 Dakar. Tel: (221) 2178 7801. FAX: (221) 223 490.

SIERRA LEONE

Population: 4.79 million.
TV Sets: 27,000.
Video Standard: PAL.

BROADCASTER

SIERRA LEONE TV SERVICE
New England, Private Mail Bag, Freetown. (23222) 40403.

SINGAPORE

Population: 3.4 million.
TV Sets: 1.06 million.
Video Standard:
Pay TV Subscribers: 47,000.
VCR Homes: 90%.

BROADCASTERS

SINGAPORE CABLEVISION (SCV)
150 Beach Road, #30-00, Singapore 0718. Tel: (65) 299 8500. FAX: (65) 299 6313

TELEVISION CORPORATION OF SINGAPORE (TCS)
Caldecott Mill, Andrew Rd., 29938. Tel: (65) 256 0401.

TELEVISION TWELVE (TV-12)
12 Prince Edward Road, #05-00 Bestway Bldg., Singapore 0207. Tel: (65) 225 8133. FAX: (65) 220 3881.

SLOVAKIA

Population: 5.4 million.
TV sets: 1.8 million.
Cable Subscribers: 450,000.
Satellite Dishes: 150,000.
Video Standard: PAL/SECAM.

BROADCASTERS

DANUBIUS TV
Brectanova 1, Bratislava 83007. Tel: (427) 371 801. FAX: (427) 371 801.

MARKYZA
Palisady 39, Bratislav 81106. (427) 531 6610. FAX: (427) 531-4061.
CEO
Pavel Rusko

SLOVAK TELEVISION
Mlynska Dolina 28, Bratislava 84545. (427) 727 448. FAX: (427) 729 440.

SATELLITE

DANUBIUS CABLE TV
Brectanova 1, Bratislava 83007. Tel: (427) 371 801. FAX: (427) 371 801.

MARKYZA
Palisady 39, Bratislava 81106. Tel: (427) 531 6610. FAX: (427) 531 4061.

VIDEO DISTRIBUTORS

DAVAY
Trnavska 67, PO Box 15, Bratislava 82101. Tel: (427) 294 645. FAX: (427) 294 677.

INTERSONIC TAUNUS PRODUCTIONS
Stare Grunty 36, Bratislava 84225. Tel: (427) 571 1176. FAX: (427) 571 1181.

SLOVENIA

Population: 2 million.
TV Sets: 600,000.
Cable Subscribers: 2.95 million
Satellite Dishes: 160,000.
Video Standard: PAL.

TELEVIZJA SLOVENIJA
Tavcarjeva 17, 6100 Ljubljana. Tel: (3861) 311 922.

PRIVATE BROADCASTERS

KANAL A
Tivolska 50 pp 44, 61101 Ljubljana. Tel: (38661) 133 4133. FAX: (3861) 133 4222.

MMTV
Zorgova 70, 61231 Ljubljana. Tel: (38661) 161 2525. FAX: (38661) 374 5541.

PRO PLUS/POP TV
Kranjecva 26, 611113 Ljubljana. Tel: (38661) 189 3200. FAX: (38661) 189 3204.

SOMALIA

Population: 11.387 million.
Video Standard: PAL.

MINISTRY OF INFORMATION
P. O. Box 1748, Mogadishu.

SOUTH AFRICA

Population: 44 million.
TV sets: 3.485 million.
Video Standard: PAL.

ASSOCIATIONS & ORGANIZATIONS

AFRICAN FILM AND TELEVISION COLLECTIVE
P.O. Box 42723, Fordsbury 2033. Tel: (2711) 804 5186. FAX: (2711) 838 3034.

ASSOCIATION OF ADVERTISING AGENCIES
5 Tyrwhitt Ave., AAA House, Rosebank, P.O. Box 2302, Parklands 2121. Tel: (2711) 880 3908. FAX: (2711) 447 1147.

SOUTH AFRICAN FILM AND TELEVISION INSTITUTE
P.O. Box 3512, Halfway House 1685. Tel: (2711) 315 0140.

BROADCASTERS

BOPHUTATSWANA TELEVISION & RADIO
Private Bag X2150, Mnbatho 8681. Tel: (14) 089 711.

CCV-TV
PO Box 2491, Johannesberg 2000.

INDEPENDENT BROADCASTING AUTHORITY
28 Baker Street, Rosebank 2196, Private Bag x31, Parklands 2121. Tel: (44) 76180, 76187. FAX: (44) 76788, 76789.

M-NET TELEVISION
PO Box 4950, Randburg, Johannesburg 2125. Tel: (2711) 329 5156. FAX: (2711) 329 5166.

SENTECH (PTY) LTD.
Private Bag XO6, Honeydew 2040. (2711) 475 1596. FAX: (2711) 475 5112. URL: http://www.sentech.co.za

SOUTH AFRICAN BROADCASTING
PO Box 2551, Cape Town 8000. Tel: (21) 434 1155.

SOUTH AFRICAN BROADCASTING CORPORATION
Private Bag X41, Auckland Park, Johannesberg 2006. Tel: (2711) 714 9111. FAX: (2711) 714 3106.

CABLE

FRAMEWORK TELEVISION
PO Box 5200, Horizon 1730. Tel: (2711) 475 4220. FAX: (2711) 475 5333.

STUDIOS: FILM & TV

FRAMEWORK TELEVISION
PO Box 5200, Horizon 1730. Tel: (2711) 475 4220. FAX: (2711) 475 5333.

SONNEBLOM FILM PRODUCTIONS
PO Box 3940, Honeydew 2040. Tel: (2711) 794 2100. FAX: (2711) 794 2061.

SONOVISION STUDIOS
PO Box 783133, Sandton 2146. Tel: (2711) 783 1100. FAX: (2711) 883 3834.

TELENEWS VIDEO STUDIO
13-2nd Ave., Houghton. Tel: (2711) 728 4450.

TORON INTERNATIONAL
PO Box 89271, Lyndhurst 2106. Tel: (2711) 786 2360.

SPAIN

Population: 39.4 million.
TV homes: 12 million.
Cable homes: 400,000
DTH homes: 760,000 digital; 600,000 analog.
Video households: 64%
Avergae video rental price: $2
Rental revenue: $194 million
Video Standard: PAL.

Spain's two private television networks, Antena 3 and Tele 5 have joined to create the Union of Free Commercial TV designed to pressure the government to regulate public spending on public channels and helping private channels improve their access to the marketplace

In 1997, TVE-1 held 25.1% of market share, followed by Antena 3 with 22.7%, Tele 5 with 21.5%, regional (FORTA) with 17.4%, TVE-2 with 8.9% and Canal Plus Spain (pay) with 2.5%.

Antena 3 Internacional and the state-owned Radio Television Espanol (RTVE) plan to stregthen their position in the Latin American market. With 100 million television homes, 15.2 million of which are pay tv homes, both are tailoring programming to Latin American viewers.

Antena 3 is currently seen in 18 Latin American countries where it claims some 5 million subscribers. Its most popular programs are "Sopresa, Sopresa" and "La Paroldia Nacional".

RTVE has traditionally broadcast one channel, TVE America, to 9 million people through cable packages offered by local carriers. Recentaly, RTVE has signed new territory agreements that will increase its penetration in the Latin American market. By changing its signal on the Hispasat satellite to digital, RTVE has been able to multiplex, adding three new channels: 24 Horas, Euronews and Hispanavision. RTVE has also signed a deal with US MSO Tele-Communications Inc. to broadcast its channels to 1 million South Florida homes as part of local basic cable.

ORGANIZATION

AHCIET
Vitruvio 7, Madrid, 28006 Spain. Tel: (34144) 9500. FAX: (34144) 9821. Telex: 46183 AH-E.

BROADCASTERS

ANTENA 3 TV
Avda. Isla Graciosa s/n, San Sebastian de los Reyes, Madrid 18013. Tel: (341) 623 0500.

CANAL PLUS
Gran Via, 32/3a planta, Madrid 28013. Tel: (341) 396 5500.
FAX: (341) 396 5600.

CANAL PLUS SOCIEDAD ESPANOLA DE TELEVISION
Torre Picasso Pl., Complejo Azca, Madrid 28020. Tel: (341)
396 5500. FAX: (341) 556 4253.

EUSKAL TELEBISTA (ETB)
Basque Country, 48278 Iurreta. Tel: (344) 620 3000. FAX: (344)
681 6526.

GESTEVISION-TELECINCO
Plaza Pablo Ruiz Picasso s/n, Torre Picasso, Plantz 36, Madrid
28020. Tel: (341) 396 6100. FAX: (341) 555 0044, 555 0306.

RADIOTELEVISION ESPANOLA SA (RTVE—TVE1, TVE 2)
Prado del Rey, Pozuelo, Madrid 28023. Tel: (341) 346 8754.
FAX: (341) 581 7125. URL: http://www.rtve.es/rtve/
DIRECTOR
Jordi Garcia Candau
EXECUTIVE DIRECTOR
Ramon Colom Esmatges

RETEVISION
Paseo de La Castellana 83-85, Madrid 28046. Tel: (341) 556
0214. FAX: (341) 555 5892.

TELECONCO
Carretera Irun KM 11, 700, Madrid 28049. Tel: (341) 396 6100.
FAX: (341) 555 0044.

TELEMADRID (TM-3)
Zurbano 70, Madrid 28010 Madrid. Tel: (341) 308 3188. FAX:
(341) 308 3811.

TELETRES MURCIA
Plateria 44 2 C, Murcia 300001 Murcia. Tel: (3468) 212 270.
FAX: (3468) 212224.

TELEVISIO DE CATALUNYA
s/n 08970 Sant Joan Despi, Catalunya. Tel: (349) 3499 9333.
FAX: (349) 3473 1964.
DIRECTOR
Jaume Ferrus i Estopa

TELEVISIO VALENCIANA (CANAL 9)
s/n, Burjassot 46100, Valencia. Tel: (346) 364 1100. FAX: (346)
363 9516.

TELEVISION ANDALUCIA (RTVA/CANAL SUR)
Apartado 132, 419 20 San Juan de Asnalfarach. Tel: (345) 560
7777. FAX: (345) 560 7799.

TELEVISION DE GALICIA (TVG)
Apt de Corrces 707, San Marcos, Santiago de Compostela,
15080. Tel: (3481) 565 141. FAX: (3481) 562 886.
DIRECTOR
Herardo R. Rodriguez

TELEVISION MURCIANA
Plateraa 44, 23001 Murcia. (3468) 212 224. FAX: (3468) 214
673.

TV 3
Televisio de Catalunya, Independent Network, Mossen Jacint,
Verdeguer, s/n, Sant Joan Despi, Barcelona 08970. Tel: (343)
473 0333. FAX: (343) 473 1563.

TV VASCA-EUSKAL TELEVISTA
Barria Lurreta, 48200 Durango. (3494) 681 6600. FAX: (3494)
681 6526.
DIRECTOR
Koldo Anasagasti

CABLE

CABLE DEVELOPMENT & SYSTEMS
Vincente Blasco Ibanez 27, Elche 03201. Tel: (346) 546 1850.
FAX: (346) 667 3874

CABLEDIS
Guipozo Kalea 15, Zarautz 20800. Tel: (3443) 131 650. FAX:
(3443) 133 079.

CABLEVISION
Gral Marinez Campos 53, Madrid 28010. Tel: (341) 310 2008.
Tel: (341) 310 4789.

CALVIA 2000
Lisboa 6, Santa Fonca 07180. Tel: (3471) 693 652. FAX: (3471)
693 507.

CARTAGENA DE COMUNICACIONES
Carmen Conde 4, Cartagena 30204. Tel: (3468) 310 304. FAX:
(3468) 310 204.

CREVISIO
Rey Jamie 11, Crevillente 03330. Tel: (346) 540 4634. FAX:
(346) 540 1649.

DTC
Antonio Machado 5, Arnedo 26580. Tel: (3441) 381 677. FAX:
(3441) 384 070.

EUROPEAN CANAL & TV
Paseo de la Castellan 9, Madrid 28046. Tel: (341) 308 1819.
FAX: (341) 308 2023.

GALAVISION TELEVICINE ESPANA
Arrastaria s/n Ctra de Barcelona Km, 11.300, Poligono de Las
Mercedes, Madrid 28022. Tel: (341) 329 0369. FAX: (341) 747
6463.

GENERAL DE SERVICIOS DE COMMUNICATION
Consell de Cent 303 pral, Barcelona 08007. Tel: (343) 323
5654. FAX: (343) 323 7596

HISPASAT
Gobelas 41-45 2, La Florida, Madrid 28023. Tel: (341) 372
9000. FAX: (341) 307 6683.

MULTIMEDIA TELECOM SERVICES
Graal Peron 38 pl 11, Madrid 28020. Tel: (341) 584 8125. FAX:
(341) 584 8127.

MULTITEL
Marques de Cubas 21, Madrid 28014. Tel: (341) 429 1222.
FAX: (341) 420 3755.

MUNDICABLE
San Valeriano 1, Torrent 46900. Tel: (346) 155 6050. FAX:
(346) 156 3524.

RADIO TELEVISION ESPANOLA SA (TELEDEPORTE,
CANAL CLASICO, HISPAVISION, TVE INTERNACIOAL)
Prado del Rey, Pozuelo, Madrid 28023. Tel: (341) 346 4000.

TDC SANLUCAR
Infanta Beatriz 24, Sanlucar de Barrameda 11540. Tel: (3456)
365 077. FAX: (3456) 367 771.

TELECABLE MENORCA
Deya 2 Bajo, Mahon 07701. Tel: (3471 365 065. FAX: (3471
354 839.

TELECABLE SALAMANCA
Aliso 2 Jajo, Salamanca 37004. Tel: (3423) 121 455. FAX:
(3423) 121 466.

TELEON
Covadonga 4, Bajo D, Leon 24004. Tel: (3487) 212 200. FAX:
(3487) 261 184.

TELEVIDEO COSTA BLANCA
San Policarpo 41, Torrevieja 03180. Tel: (346) 571 5392. FAX:
(346) 571 5392.

VICOSAT
Plaza de las Farolas, 1 Bajo, Mula 30170. Tel: (3468) 662 411.
FAX: (3468) 662 160.

SATELLITE

ANTENA TRES TV/RADIO
Carretera San Sebastian de los Reyes, Madrid 28700. Tel:
(341) 632 0500. FAX: (341) 632 7144

CANAL PLUS ESPANA
Gran Via 32, 3rd floor, Madrid 28103. Tel: (341) 396 5500. FAX:
(341) 396 5600

COTELSAT
Gran Via 32, Madrid 2844. Tel: (341) 521 0729. FAX: (341) 521
7846.

DOCUMANIA SOGECABALE
Gran Via 32 3 Piso, Madrid 28103. Tel: (341) 396 5687. FAX:
(341) 396 5484

GALAVISION
(See Galavision listing under Cable.)

HISPASAT
PO Box 95000, Madrid 28080. Tel: (341) 372 9000. FAX: (341)
307 6683

CSD
Torre Picasso, Plaza Ruiz Picasse, Madrid E-28020. Tel: (341)
3965 514.

VIDEO DISTRIBUTORS

BMG VIDEO SPAIN
27 Avda. de los Madronos, Parqu Conde Orgaz, Madrid 28043. Tel: (341) 388 0002. FAX: (341) 759 0135.

BUENA VISTA HOME VIDEO
Jose Berdasamo Baos 9, Madrid 28016. Tel: (341) 383 0312. FAX: (341) 308 3152.

CIC VIDEO Y CIA
Albacete 5 3, Planta, Edificio AGF, Madrid 28027. Tel: (341) 326 0120. FAX: (341) 326 5823.

CINE COMPANY
Zurbano 74, Madrid 28010. Tel: (341) 442 2944. FAX: (341) 441 0098.

COLUMBIA TRISTAR VIDEO
Albacete 5 4, Madrid 28027. Tel: (341) 326 4362. FAX: (341) 409 9458.

CYB VIDEO
Mn Cinto Verdaguer 185, Sant Vincent Vicena dels Horts, Barcelona 08620. Tel: (343) 656 3361. FAX: (343) 656 1817.

DISTER GROUP
Caidos de la Division Azul, 22-B, Madrid 28016. Tel: (341) 250 3900. FAX: (341) 250 3904.

DOBLE A FILMS AND TAPES
Quinonnes 2, Madrid 28015. Tel: (341) 594 2059. FAX: (341) 594 2709.

ESPACIO P
Nunezde Arce 11, Madrid 28012. Tel: (341) 531 3111.

EUROVENTANILLA
Plaza de la Constitucion 9, Malaga 29008. Tel: (345) 222 0959. FAX: (345) 222 0936.

EX LIBRIS VIDEO
C Rossello 17, 1er 1a, Barcelona 08029. Tel: (343) 410 0556. FAX: (343) 419 0262.

FILM INTERNATIONAL
Arda Burgos, 8-A planta 10-1, Madrid 28036. Tel: (341) 383 0265. FAX: (341) 383 0845.

FOREM
Longares 6-8, Madrid 28002. Tel: (341) 324 0119. FAX: (341) 306 9193.

FOX VIDEO ESPANOLA
Avida de Burgos 8a Pllz 11, Madrid 28036. Tel: (341) 343 4640. Tel: (341) 343 4655.

FRAN-EL
Villa Tibidado, Colonia Tibidado 14, Barcelona 08023. Tel: (343) 212 5965. FAX: (341) 212 7503.

FURA DELS BAUS
Diputacio 291-2n, Barcelona 08009. Tel: (343) 487 5982. FAX: (343) 487 6776.

G & CM INTERNACIONAL
Sagasta 15.5 Izq, Madrid 28004. Tel: (341) 447 7100. FAX: (341) 593 3886.

GESTMUSIC
Santa Elionor 3, Barcelona 08024. Tel: (343) 210 5666. Tel: (343) 219 4797.

GRUP CONTINENTAL
Victor Chavarri 19-1, Ovideo 33001. Tel: (3485) 222 971. FAX: (3485) 227 952.

INTEGRA MULTIMEDIA
Parque Tecnologico 103-2 Planta, Samupio 48016. Tel: (344) 420 9812. Tel: (344) 420 9813.

INTERACCION
c/o Enrique Granados, 125 Entio 1, Barcelona 08008. Tel: (343) 415 3204. FAX: (343) 415 3215.

INTERNATIONAL FILM GROUP
Gran Via de las Cortes Catalanas 1176, Barcelona. Tel: (343) 305 3605. FAX: (341) 305 3259.

JMM INVEST (WANDA FILMS)
Avda. de Europa 9, Portal 3 Bajoc, Madrid 28224. Tel: (341) 352 8466. FAX: (341) 352 8371.

KALENDER VIDEO
Pintor Juan Gris 5 1B, Madrid 28020. Tel: (341) 555 4477. Tel: (341) 597 3807.

LAUREN FILMS VIDEO HAGAR
Balmes 87, Barcelona 08008. Tel: (343) 451 7189. FAX: (343) 323 6155.

MGM UA
Doce de Octubre 28, Madrid 28009. Tel: (341) 574 9008. FAX: (341) 574 9005.

MUNDOGRAFICO
Marin Baldo 1-Bajo, Murcia 30001. Tel: (34968) 210 561. Tel: (34968) 221 271.

MUSIDORA FILMS
Calle Princess 17, Madrid 30001. Tel: (341) 541 6869. FAX: (341) 541 5482.

POLYGRAM IBERICA
Suero de Quinnones 38, Madrid 28002. Tel: (341) 564 3310. FAX: (341) 564 3235.

PRIME FILMS
Padre Xitre 5-7C, Madrid 28002. Tel: (341) 519 0181. Tel: (341) 413 0772.

PROFILMAR
Rambla Cataluna 50-1, Barcelona 08007. Tel: (343) 488 0180.

SELECTA VISION
Calle Roma 4-Bajos, Barcelona 08023. Tel: (343) 418 5300. FAX: (343) 418 8811.

TRI PICTURES
Doce de Octubre 28, Madrid 28009. Tel: (341) 574 9008. FAX: (341) 574 9005.

VIDEO COLLECTION
Crta Boadilla a, 28220. Tel: (341) 639 5562. FAX: (341) 639 5456.

VIDEO MERCURY FILMS
Fernan Gonzalez 28, Madrid 28009. Tel: (341) 431 4790. FAX: (341) 431 7555.

VIDEOMAN INTERNATIONAL
Doce de Octubre 28, Madrid 28009. Tel: (341) 574 9008. FAX: (341) 574 9005.

VISUAL EDICIONES
Paravincinos 16-1 Planta, Madrid 28039. Tel: (341) 450 0750. FAX: (341) 450 0877.

WARNER HOME VIDEO ESPANOLA
Angel Munoz 14-16, Entreplanta, Madrid 28043. Tel: (341) 413 0543. FAX: (341) 519 5759.

SRI LANKA

Population: 19 million.
TV sets: 1.5 million.
Video Standard: PAL-B

BROADCASTERS

EAP NETWORK
676 Galle Rd., Colombo 3. (941) 503 819. FAX: (941) 503 788.

INDEPENDENT TELEVISION NETWORK (ITN)
Wickremasinghepura, Battaramulla. Tel/FAX: (941) 864 591.

MTV CHANNEL
109 Collets Bldg., Rt. Hon. D.S. Senanayake Mawatha, Colombo 8. Tel: (941) 689 324. FAX: (941) 689 328.

SRI LANKA BROADCASTING CORPORATION
P.O. Box 574, Colombo 7. Tel: (941) 696 140.

SRI LANKA RUPAVAHINI CORPORATION
PO Box 2204, Colombo 7. Tel: (941) 580 136. FAX: (941) 580 929.

TELESHAN TV NETWORK CHANNEL 21
Innagale Estate Dampe-Piliyandala. Tel: (941) 575 436. FAX: (941) 575 436.

PRODUCERS

FILMTEL
81/3 Isipathana Mawatha, Colombo 5. Tel: (941) 585 573.

TELECINE LTD.
43 Hyde Park Corner, Colombo 2, Sri Lanka. Tel: (941) 23909.

TELESHAN LTD.
1st Floor, Vogue Buiding, 528 Galle Road, Colombo 3. Tel: (941) 575 436.

SELACINE
2 Gregory's Avenue, Colombo 7. Tel: (941) 596 926.

WORLDVIEW FOUNDATION
8 Kinross Avenue, Colombo 4. Tel: (941) 589 225.

SUDAN

Population: 32.294 million.
TV sets. 300,000.
Video Standard: PAL.

BROADCASTER

SUDAN TELEVISION
P.O. Box 1094, Omdurman. Tel: (24911) 55022.

SURINAME

Population: 436,000.
TV sets: 45,,000.
Video Standard: NTSC.

BROADCASTERS

ALTERNATIEVE TELEVISIE VERZORGING
Adrianusstraat 1, Paramaribo. Tel: (597) 410027. FAX: (597) 470 425.

SURINAAMSE TELEVISIE STICHTING (STVS)
P.O. Box 535, Paramaribo. Tel: (597) 473 100. FAX: (597) 477 216.

SWAZILAND

Population: 1.06 million.
TV sets: 12,500.
Video Standard: PAL.

BROADCASTER

SWAZILAND TELEVISION AYTHORITY
Swazi TV, PO Box A146, Mbabane. Tel: (268) 43036. FAX: (268) 42093.

SWEDEN

Population: 8.975 million.
TV Sets: 3.75 million.
Cable Service: 2.05 million
Satellite Service: 328,000.
VCRs: 2.41 million.
Video Standard: PAL.
Scandinavian Broadcasting System revenues increased 59% by mid 1998 as a result of the increased strength of uropean television as a whole, and SBS' expansion into Northern, Western and Central Europe.

ASSOCIATION

NORDISK FILM/TV UNION, SVERIGE
Stig Palm, Swedish Television-Training, Centre, Stockholm S-10510. Tel: (468) 784 4403. FAX: (468) 667 4466.

BROADCASTERS

SCANSAT BROADCASTING LTD
PO Box 2094, Stockholm 103 13. Tel: (468) 103 333.

SVERIGES TELEVISION
Oxenstiernsgatan 26-32, Stockholm S-105 10. Tel: (468) 784 6001. FAX: (468) 784 6010. URL: http://www.svt.se
CHAIRMAN
Anna-Greta Leijon

SVERIGES TV—GOTHENBURG
Gothenburg S-405 13. Tel: (4631) 837 000. FAX: (4631) 401 741

SVERIGES TV—MALMO
Malmo S-212 01. Tel: (4640) 227 000. FAX: (4640) 227 020

TV4 NORDISK TELEVISION CO.
S-115, Stockholm 79. Tel: (468) 644 4400. FAX: (468) 644 4440. URL: http://www.tv4.se
CHAIRMAN
Erik Belfrage

TERACOM SVENSK RUNDRADIO
PO Box 17666, Stockholm S-118 92. Tel: (468) 671 2000. FAX: (468) 671 2001.
CEO
Valdemar Persson

CABLE

FILM NET TV
PO Box 5165, Stockholm S-102 44. Tel: (468) 660 2700. FAX: (468) 660 9218.

SETH'S KABEL-TV
Box 104, Kallered 430 50. Tel: (31) 954 400.

TELEVERKET KABEL-TV
Box 1389, Solna 171 27. Tel: (468) 764 9300. FAX: (468) 288 482.

SATELLITE

FILMMAX
PO Box 2133, Stockholm 10314. Tel: (468) 100 019. FAX: (468) 243 840.

TERRACOM SVENSK RUNDRADIO
PO Box 17666, Stockholm S-118 92. Tel: (468) 671 2000. FAX: (468) 671 2401.

TV-4 NORDISK TELEVISION
Storangskroken 10, Stockholm 11479. Tel: (468) 644 4400. FAX: (468) 644 4440.

TV-1000 SUCCE KANALEN (SCANSAT)
Skeppsbron 44, PO Box 2133, Stockholm 10314. Tel: (468) 100 019. FAX: (468) 243 840.

TV-3 (SCANSAT)
P.O. Box 2094, Stockholm 10313. Tel: (468) 403 333. FAX: (468) 216 564.

VIDEO ORGANIZATION

FILM-OCH VIDEOBRANCHENS SAMAR, FILM AND VIDEO JOINT INDUSTRY
PO Box 49084, Stockholm S-100 28. Tel: (468) 785 0400. FAX: (468) 653 2425.

VIDEO DISTRIBUTORS

ATLANTIC FILM
Norra Stationsgatan, PO Box 21112, Stockholm S-100 86. Tel: (468) 305 230. FAX: (468) 305 280.

BUENA VISTA HOME ENTERTAINMENT
PO Box 5631, Stockholm S-114 86. Tel: (468) 679 1550. FAX: (468) 678 0728.

BUENA VISTA INTERNATIONAL
PO Box 5631, Stockholm S-114 86. Tel: (468) 679 1550. FAX: (468) 678 0728.

CIC
Lilla Bommen, Gothenborg 411 04. Tel: (4631) 771 2450. FAX: (4631) 152 455.

EGMONT FILM
PO Box 507, Taby S-183 25. Tel: (468) 510 10050. FAX: (468) 510 12046.

FILM AB CORONA
Brantingsgatan 35, Stockholm S-115 35. Tel: (468) 661 0509. FAX: (468) 663 3595.

FILMCO
PO Box 11128, Bromma S-161 11. Tel: (468) 285 111. FAX: (468) 284 111.

FILMGORLAGET
PO Box 27066, Stockholm S-102 52. Tel: (468) 665 1100. FAX: (468) 661 1053.

FILMO
Skulptorvagen 25, Stockholm S-121 43. Tel: (468) 772 9510. FAX: (468) 772 9966.

FILMPARTNER
Lilla Verkstadsgaten 7, Kungsbacka S-434 42. Tel: (46) 3007 0010. FAX: (46) 3007 0241.

FOX FILM
Box 9501, Stockholm S-102 74. Tel: (468) 658 1144. FAX: (468) 841 204.

LUDAVDELNINGEN
Kummelnasvagen 74, Saltsjo-Boo S-132 37. Tel: (468) 747 9367. FAX: (468) 747 9367.

NORDISK FILM & TV DISTRIBUTION
PO Box 45437, Stockholm S-104 31. Tel: (468) 440 9070. FAX: (468) 440 9080.

PICKWICK
PO Box 1150, Boras S-501 11. Tel: (4633) 116 800. FAX: (4633) 100 588.

POLYGRAM
PO Box 20510, Bromma S-161 02. Tel: (468) 629 5300. FAX: (468) 764 5688.

SANDREW FILM & TEATER
Box 5612, Stockholm S-114 86. Tel: (468) 234 700. FAX: (468) 103 850.

SF VIDEO
Soder Malarstrand 27, Stockholm S-117 88. Tel: (468) 658 7500. FAX: (468) 658 3705.

SONET FILM
PO Box 20105, Bromma S-161 20. Tel: (468) 799 7700. FAX: (468) 285 834.

SVENSK FILMINDUSTRI
Suder Malerstrand 27, Stockholm S-127 83. Tel: (468) 680 3500. FAX: (468) 710 4460.

WARNER HOME VIDEO SWEDEN
Hornsbruksgatan 19, Stockholm S-117 34. Tel: (468) 616 7240. FAX: (468) 844 078.

WENDROS
PO Box 5100, Huddinge S-141 05. Tel: (468) 774 0425. FAX: (468) 779 8316.

SWITZERLAND

Population: 7.2 million.
TV Sets: 2.6 million.
Cable Subscribers: 2.08 million.
Satellite Subscribers: 200,000.
Video Standard: PAL.
The nation's first 100% privately owned TV network, Tele 24, is due May 1999.

ORGANIZATIONS

EUROPEAN BROADCASTING UNION (EBU)
Case Postale 67, Grand Sacounex, Geneva, CH-1218 Switzerland. Tel: (4122) 798 7766. FAX: (4122) 985 897. Telex: 415700.

INTERNATIONAL TELECOMMUNICATIONS UNION (ITU)
Place des Nations, Geneva 20, CH-1211 Switzerland. Tel: (4122) 730 5111. FAX: (4122) 733 7256. Telex: 421000 UIT CH.

WORLD INTELLECTUAL PROPERTY ORGANIZATION (WIPO)
32, Chemin des Colom Bettes, 1211 Geneva.

BROADCASTERS

SCHWEIZ 4/SUISSE 4/SVIZZERA 4
Giacomettistrasse 1, CH-3000 Bern 15, Switzerland. (4131) 350 9444 FAX: (4131) 350 9725.
DIRECTOR
Dario Rabbiani

SCHWEIZER FERNSEHEN DRS
Fernsehstrasse 1-4, Postfach, CH-8052 Zurich. Tel: (411) 305 6611. FAX: (411) 305 5660.

SWISS BROADCASTING CORPORATION (SBC)
Giacomettistrasse 3, CH-3000 Bern 15. Tel: (4131) 350 9111. Telex: 911590 SSRCH. FAX: (4131) 350 9256.
PRESIDENT
Eric Lehmann

TELEVISION DE LA SUISSE ROMANDE (TSR)
20, quai Ernest-Ansermet, Case postale 234, CH-1211 Geneve 8. Tel: (4122) 708 99 11. FAX: (4122) 329 41144.

TELEVISIONE DELLA SVIZZERA ITALIANA (TSI)
Casella postale, CH-6903 Lugano. Tel: (4191) 585 111. FAX: (4191) 58 53 55.

CABLE

ASCOM TELEMATIC
Raugistr 71, CH-8048 Zurich. Tel: (411) 631 2111. FAX: (411) 405 2103.

BALLCAB
Postfach, CH-4058 Basel. Tel: (4161) 691 9151. FAX: (4161) 691 9147.

LOKALFERNSEHEN DIESSENHOFEN
Gabenstr 26, CH-8253 Dissenhofen. Tel: (4153) 373 890.

REDIFFUSION
Postfach, CH-8021 Zurich. Tel: (411) 277 9111. FAX: (411) 272 8184.

SERVICE DE L'ELECTRICITE DE LA VILLE DE LAUSANNE
Case Postale 836, CH-1000 Lausanne. Tel: (4121) 315 8111. FAX: (4121) 315 8456.

TELE M1
Stadtturmstrasse 19, CH-5401 Baden. Tel: (411) 209 410. FAX: (411) 209 409.

022 TELEGENEVE
Quai Ernest Ansermet 20, CH-1211 Geneva. Tel: (4122) 781 1222. FAX: (4122) 329 8804.

VIDEO DISTRIBUTORS

ADO FILM
Stollenraen 4, CH-4144 Arlesheim. Tel: (4161) 701 3756. FAX: (4161) 701 3711.

ATLANTIC FILM
Munchhaldenstrasse 10, PO Box 322, CH-8034 Zurich. Tel: (411) 422 3832. FAX: (411) 422 3793.

ATLAS
Munchhaldenstrasse 10, Postfach 322, CH-8034 Zurich. Tel: (411) 422 3833. FAX: (411) 422 3383.

BERNARD LANG
Dorf Str 14D, Freienstein, CH-8427 Zurich. Tel: (411) 865 6627. Tel: (411) 865 6629.

BUENA VISTA INTERNATIONAL
Am Schanzengraben 27, CH-8427 Zurich. Tel: (411) 201 6655. FAX: (411) 201 7770.

EFFECTRONIC
Schindellegistrasse 57, CH-8808 Pfaffikon. Tel: (4155) 415 4550. FAX: (4155) 415 4051.

ELITE FILM
Molkenstrasse 21, CH-8026 Zurich. Tel: (411) 242 8822. FAX: (411) 241 2123.

LES FILMS ROGER WEIL
Ave.Leon Gaud 5, CH-1206 Geneva. Tel: (4122) 346 9532. Tel: (4122) 781 0676.

FOX VIDEO
Rte des Acacias 52, CH-1211 Geneva. Tel: (4122) 343 3315. FAX: (4122) 343 9255.

HOME MOVIES
Stegackerstrasse 6, CH-8409 Winterthur. Tel: (4152) 233 6822. FAX: (4152) 233 6830.

IMPULS VIDEO & HANDELS
Sumpf Str 28, 6302 Zug. Tel: (4142) 417 171. Tel: (4142) 417 174.

PRIMEFILMS
Via Tamporiva 3, CH-6976 Castagnola-Lugano. Tel: (4191) 972 9630. FAX: (4191) 972 9632.

LES PRODUCTIONS JMH
Ave.de Beaumont 70, CH-1010 Lausanne. Tel: (4121) 653 6550. FAX: (4121) 653 6553.

RAINBOW VIDEO
Netziboden Str 23B, 2133 Prattein. Tel: (4161) 811 4480. FAX: (4161) 811 4490.

REGINA FILM
4 Rue de Rive, CH-1204 Geneva. Tel: (4122) 310 8136. FAX: (4122) 310 9476.

RIALTO VIDEO
Munchalden Str 10, 8048 Zurich. Tel: (411) 422 3831. FAX: (411) 422 3793.

SCHMALFILM
Badenstrasse 342, PO Box 182, CH-8040 Zurich. Tel: (411) 491 2727. Tel: (411) 492 4046.

STELLA VIDEO
Munchhalden Str 10, PO Box 322, CH-8034 Zurich. Tel: (411) 422 3831. FAX: (411) 422 3793.

SWISS FILM INSTITUTE
Erlachstrasse 21, CH-3000 Berne. Tel: (4131) 301 0831. FAX: (4131) 301 2860.

VIDEO-T-RONIC
Allmend Str 29, 8320 Fehraltori. Tel: (411) 955 1020. FAX: (411) 955 0010.

VIDEOPHON
Badner Str 555, CH-8048 Zurich. Tel: (411) 491 3545. FAX: (411) 401 4420.

WARNER HOME VIDEO
Studerweg 3, CH-8802 Kilchberg. Tel: (411) 715 5752. FAX: (411) 715 3451.

SYRIA

Population:15.6 million.
TV sets: 780,000.
Video Standard: PAL.

BROADCASTER

SYRIAN ARAB TELEVISION (GOV.)
Ommayyad Square, Damascus. Tel/FAX: (96311) 720 700.

TAIWAN

Population: 21.47 million.
TV sets: 7.15 million
Average Daily TV Viewing: 2 hours
Cable Penetration : 75%
Video Standard: NTSC.

Taiwan has the highest cable penetration in Asia - 75%. Asian movie channel MGM Gold Networks has launched a film channel that will feature action movies.

BROADCASTERS

CHINA TELEVISION COMPANY
No. 120 Chung Yang Rd., Nankang Dist., Taipei. (8862) 783 8308. FAX: (8862) 782 6007.

CHINESE TELEVISION SERVICE
100 Kuang Fu South Rd., Taipei. (8862) 751 0321. FAX: (8862) 751 6019.

TAIWAN TELEVISION ENTERPRISE
No. 120, Pa Te Rd., Section 3, Taipei 10560. (8862) 771 1515. FAX: (8862) 741 3626.

TAJIKISTAN

Population: 5.9 million.
TV sets: 894,000.
Video Standard: SECAM.

BROADCASTER

TAJIK TELEVISION
Behzod kuca 7, 734013 Dushanbe. Tel: (73772) 224 357.

TANZANIA

Population: 30.95 million.
TV sets: 80,000.
Video Standard: PAL.

BROADCASTER

TELEVISION ZANZIBAR TVZ
PO Box 314, Zanzibar. Tel: (25554) 32816.

THAILAND

Population: 60.3 million.
Number of TV Sets: 3.6 million.
Cable Homes: 150,000.
Video Standard: PAL.

Thailand's two major cable companies, International Broadcasting Corp. and United Television, merged in February of 1998. In response to this merger in an effort to gain more leverage with the government and foreign program distributors, 90 small cable TV operators have joined together as the Thailand Cable TV Association. The Association plans to license programs from HBO, STAR TV and Discovery. Currently, only IBC and UTV have access to this programming.

Subscription fees for cable television are low in Thailand, about $3.75 per month, although IBC and UTV charge about $20 per month to their metropolitan Bagkok subscriber base.

BROADCASTERS

BANGKOK BROADCASTING & TV CO (BBTV)
998/1 Phaholyothjn Rd., PO Box 4-56, Bangkok. Tel: (662) 278 1255. FAX: (662) 270 1976.

BANGKOK ENTERTAINMENT CO. (CHANNEL 3)
Vanit Bldg., 1126/1 New Petchburi Rd., Phayathal, Bangkok 10400. Tel: (662) 253 9970. FAX: (662) 253 9978.

MASS COMMUNICATION ORGANIZATION OF THAILAND
222 Thanon Asok-Dindang Rd., Bangkok 10310. Tel: (662) 245 0700. Telex: 84577.

TELEVISION OF THAILAND
Public Rel Dept/. 26th Flr., Fortune Town Bldg., Ratchadamoen Rd., Huay Khwang, Bangkok 10310. Tel/FAX: (662) 248 1601.

TELEVISION OF THAILAND (CHANNEL 11)
New Petchburi Rd., Phayathal, Bangkok 1030. Tel: (662) 318 3330. FAX: (662) 318 2991.

TOGO

Population: 4.4 million.
TV sets: 150.000.
Video Standard: SECAM.

BROADCASTER

TELEVISION TOGOLAISE
B.P. 3286, Lome. Tel: (228) 215 357. FAX: (228) 215 786

TRINIDAD AND TOBAGO

Population: 1.27 million.
TV sets: 250,000.
Video Standard: NTSC.

BROADCASTER

TRINIDAD & TOBAGO TELEVISION CO., LTD.
Television House, 11A Maraval Rd., PO Box 665, Port of Spain. Tel: (809) 622 4141. FAX: (809) 622 0344.

TUNISIA

Population: 9.02 million.
TV sets: 694,000.
Video Standard: SECAM.

BROADCASTERS

ARAB STATES BROADCASTING UNION (ASBU)
17 rue el-Mansoura, el-Mennsah 4, BP 66, Tunis 1014. Tel: (2161) 238 828. FAX: (2161) 766 551.

ENTERPRISE DE LA RADIODIFFUSION TELEVISION TUNISIENNE
71 Ave. de la Liberte, 1002 Tunis Belvedere. (2161) 287 300. FAX: (2161) 781 058.

RTT TUNISIA
71 Avenue de la Liberte, Tunis 1002. Tel: (2161) 287 300. FAX: (2161) 781 058.

TURKEY

Population: 62.53 million.
TV sets: 10.77 million.
Video Standard: PAL-B.

Intellectual copyright piracy is a $190 million industry in Turkey.

BROADCASTERS

ATV, SATEL TELEVIZYON PRODUKSIYON
Basin Express Yolu, Media Plaza, Gunesli, Istanbul. Tel: (901) 550 4900. FAX: (901) 502 8468, (901) 502 8233.

CINE 5, CINE 5 FILMCILIK & YAPIMCILIK
Hurriyet Medya Towers, 34540 Gunesli, Istanbul. Tel: (901) 655 8822, (901) 655 9860. FAX: (901) 655 9867.

DTV HABER & GORSEL YAYINCILIK
Yuzyil Mahallesi, Mahmutbey Viyadugu Alti, Milliyet Tesisleri, 4. Kat Ikitelli, Istanbul. Tel: (901) 512 1107, 513 6100. FAX: (901) 505 6509.

EKO RADIO & TELEVISION
Nakkastepe Azizbey Sokak No. 1, 81207 Kuzguncuk, Istanbul. Tel: (901) 341 8523. FAX: (901) 343 1944.

HAS BILGI BIRIKIM TELEVIZYON
Yeni Bosna Asfalti, Bahcelievler, Isanbul. Tel: (901) 281 4800. FAX: (901) 281 4808.

INTERSTAR
Basin Expres Yolu, Medya Print Binasi No. 2, Gunesli 34540, Istanbul. Tel: (901) 698 4901. FAX: (901) 698 4957, (901) 698 4934.

KANAL 6, ARTI YAYINCILIK & FILMCILIK
Imam Cesme Caddesi, G 48 Sok. No. 12, Seyrantepe, Levent 4, Istanbul. Tel: (901) 285 1250. FAX: (901) 286 0073.

SHOW TV, AKS TELEVIZYON REKLAMCILIK & FILMCILIK
Hurriyet Medya Towers, 34540 Gunesli, Istanbul. Tel: (901) 655 1111. FAX: (901) 515 5128.

TGRT, IHLAS FILM PRODUKSIYON
Sanayi Caddesi No. 17, Yenibosna, Istanbul. Tel: (901) 652 2560. FAX: (901) 652 2592.

TRT, THE TURKISH RADIO-TV CORP.
Oran Sitesi, Oran, Ankara. Tel: (90312) 490 3884. FAX: (90312) 490 4985.

TURKISH RADIO & TELEVISION CORP.
TRT TV Dept., TRT Sitesi Katib Ablok Oran 06450, Ankara. (90312) 490 4983. FAX: (90313) 490 4985.

VIDEO DISTRIBUTORS

ATV
Medya Plaza Basin Express Yolu, Gunesli 34540. Tel: (901) 603 9006. FAX: (901) 502 8802.

BARLIK FILM
Ahududu Cad 32/3, Beyoglu, Istanbul 80060. Tel: (901) 2441542. FAX: (901) 2510386.

HBB TV
Buyukdere Cad 187, Levent, Istanbul. Tel: (90212) 281 4800.
FAX: (90212) 281 4808.

INTERSTAR (AKK)
Divan Yolu Turbedar Sok 2, Iketelli Gunesli, Istanbul. Tel:
(90212) 698 4901. FAX: (90212) 698 4970.

KILIC FILM
Yesilcam SK 26/2, Beyoglu, Istanbul 80070. Tel: (901) 249
5804. FAX: (901) 244 1612.

SHOW TV
Halaskargazi Cad 180, Istanbul. Tel: (901) 246 1260. FAX:
(901) 247 5778.

TURKMENISTAN

Population: 4.57 million.
Video Standard: SECAM.

BROADCASTER

TURKMEN TELEVISION
Machtumkuli 89, 744000 Asgabat. Tel: (73632) 251 515. FAX:
(73632) 251 412.

UGANDA

Population: 29.92 million.
TV sets: 128,000.
Video Standard: PAL.

BROADCASTER

UGANDA TELEVISION
PO Box 7142, Kampala. Tel: (25641) 254 461.

UKRAINE

Population: 51.27 million.
TV Sets: 7.58 million.
Satellite Subscribers: 500,000.
Video Standard: SECAM.

BROADCASTER

UKRAJINSKA TELEBACENNJA
vul. Chrescatik 26, 252001 Kiev. (38044) 229 0638. FAX:
(38044) 229 6945.

VIDEO DISTRIBUTORS

ADONIS
40 Letiya Oktyabrya Prospect 116, Kiev 252127.

ALAN
Sevastopolskaya St 8, Simeropol 333005.

UNITED ARAB EMIRATES

Population: 3.06 million.
TV sets: 235,000.
Video Standard: PAL.
BROADCASTERS

EDTV/UAE RADIO & TELEVISION
PO Box 1695, Dubai. Tel: (9714) 470 255. FAX: (9714) 371 079.

SHARJAH TV
PO Box 111, Sharjah. Tel: (9716) 547 755.

U.A.E. RADIO & TELEVISION-DUBAI
PO Box 1695, Dubai. Tel: (9714) 470 255.

URUGUAY

Population: 3.24 million.
TV sets: 611,000.
Pay TV Subscribers: 260,000.
Satellite Subscribers: 5,000
Video Standard: PAL.

ASSOCIATION

INTERNATIONAL ASSOCIATION OF BROADCASTING (IAB)
25 de Mayo 520, Montevideo, Uruguay. Tel: (598) 295 8141.
FAX: (598) 296 1703. Telex: 23225 Air UY.

BROADCASTERS

CANAL 8 TV MELO
18 de Julio 572, 37000 Melo, Cerro Largo.

CANAL 11 PUNTADEL ESTE
Cantegril Country Club, 20100 Punta del Este, Maldonado.

CANAL 5 S.O.D.R.E.
Bul Artigas 2552, 11600 Montevideo. Tel: (442) 470 507, 474 129.

CANAL 9 DEL ESTES TV COLOR
Av. Artigas 879, 20000 Maldonado.

CANAL 7 CERRO PAN DE AZUCAR
L Carnelli 1223, Montevideo. Tel: (442) 493 666, 496 828.

CANAL 12 RIO URUGUAY
Cno, San Salvador s/n 65000 Fray Bentos, Rio Negro.

MELO TV
Castellanos 723, 37000 Melo, Cerro Largo.

MONTE CARLO TV COLOR
Paraguay 2253, 11800 Montevideo.

RADIOTELEVISION "ZORILLA DE SAN MARTIN"
18 de Julio 302, 45000 Tucuarenbo.

RED TELEVISION COLOUR
E Martinez 1337, Montevideo. Tel: (442) 232 425, 232 426.

RIO DE LOS PAJAROS TV
Av. Espana 1629, 6000 Paysandu.

SAETA TV CANAL 10
Dr. Lorenzo Carnelli 1234, 11200 Montevideo. Tel: (442) 402 120.

TELE-ARTIGAS
Lecueder 291, 55000 Artigas.

TELEDIEZ
General Rivera s/n 55100 Bela Union Artigas.

TELEDOCE CANAL 12
Enriqueta Compte y Rique 1276, 11800 Montevideo. Tel: (442)
283 363, 239 771.

TELEVISORA COLONIA
W. Barbot 172, 70000 Colonia.

TELIVISORA SALTO GRANDE
Av Vieta 1280, 50000 Salto.

TELEVISORA TREINTA Y TRES
Pablo Zufriategui 226, Treinta y Tres, 9700 Durazno.

TV CERRO DEL VERDUN
Treinta y Tres 632, 30000 Minas Lavalleja.

UZBEKISTAN

Population: 23.42 million.
TV sets: 3.7 million.
Video Standard: SECAM.

BROADCASTER

UZBEK TELEVISION
Navoii kucasi 69, 700011 Taskent. Tel: (73712) 495 214.

VENEZUELA

Population: 21.98 million.
TV Sets: 3.85 million.
Pay-TV Subscribers: 180,000.
Satellite Subscribers: 75,000.
Video Standard: NTSC.

BROADCASTERS

AMAVISION
Calle Selesiano, Colegio Pio XI, Puerto Ayacucho.

CAMARA VENEZOLANA DE LA TELEVISION
Ap. 60423, Chacao, Caracas 1010-A. Tel: (582) 781 4608.

CANAL METROPOLITANO DE TELEVISION
Av. Circumvalacion El Sol, Centro Professional Santa Paula,
Torre B. Piso 4, Santa Paula, Caracas. Tel: (582) 987 6190.
FAX: (582) 985 4856.

CANAL 10
Av. Francisco de Miranda, con Principal de los Ruices, Centro
Empresaria Miranda PHD, Caracas. Tel: (582) 239 8697. FAX:
(582) 239 7757.

CORPORACIO TELEVEN CANAL 10
C.C. Los Chaguaramos, Piso 4, Caracas. Tel: (582) 661 7511.
Tel: (582) 662 7279.

NCTV
Urv. La Paz, Avenida 57 y Maracaibo, Maracaibo. Tel: (5861)
512 662. FAX: (5861) 512 729.

OMNIVISION
Calle Milan, Edif. Omnivision, Los Ruices Sur, Caracas. Tel:
(582) 256 3586. Tel: (582) 256 4482.

RADIO CARACAS TELEVISION RCTV
Edif Empresas 1 BC, Los Cotijos De Lourdes, Caracas. Tel: (2) 256 3411. FAX: (2) 256 2672.

TELE BOCONO
Calle 3, Qta. Caleuche, El Saman, Bocono. Tel: (5872) 52127. FAX: (5872) 52485.

TELECENTRO
Avenida Pedro Leon Torres, Esquina de la Calle 47, Edificio Telecentro, Barquisimeto.

TELESOL
Calle Sucre no 15, Cuman, Sucre. Tel: (5893) 662 059. FAX: (5893) 662 775.

TELEVISORA ANDINA DE MERIDA
Av. Bolivar, Calle 23 entre Av. 4-5, Merida 5101. Tel: (5874) 525 785. FAX: (5874) 520 098.

TELIVISORA DE ORIENTE, TVO
Puerto la Cruz, Anzoategui. Tel: (5882) 662 163.

TELEVISORA NACIONAL-CHANNEL 5 & 8
Apt. 3979, Caracas.

TELEVISORA REGIONAL DEL TACHIRA
Av. Libertador, edif. Servicios Unidos, Piso 3, San Cristobal, Tachira. Tel: (5876) 447 366. Tel: (5876) 465 277.

TV GUAYANA
Puerto Ordaz, Bolivar Caracas. Tel: (5886) 229 908.

VENEVISION
Apartado 6674, Caracas 1010-A. Tel: (2) 708 9444. FAX: (2) 782 2132.

VENEZOLANA DE TELEVISION
Edif Venezolana de Television, Los Ruices, Caracas. Tel: (2) 235 0361. FAX: (2) 239 4472.

VENEZOLANA DE TELEVISION 5
Ap. 2739, Caracas 1010-A. Tel: (582) 239 9811. FAX: (582) 35734.

VENEZOLANA DE TELEVISION 8
Ap. 2739, Caracas 1010-A. Tel: (582) 349 571.

VENMISION CHANNEL 4
PO Box 75705, Caracas. Tel: (2) 781 1734.

VIDEO DISTRIBUTORS

ABD VIDEO
Calle Los Cerritos Edo ADB, Urb Bello Monte, Caracas. Tel: (582) 762 9572.

AUDIO VIDEO MISION
Av Varsovia, Casa Parroquial, La California Sur, Caracas. Tel: (582) 214 117.

BOLIVAR FILMS VIDEO
Av Luis Guillermo Villegas B, Edificio Bolivar Films, Santa Euvigis, Caracas. Tel: (582) 283 5177.

DISTRIBUIDORA SONIA
Marron a Cuji, Edificio Aldomar, Caracas. Tel: (582) 561 9359.

PRODUCCIONES VIDEO LASER
Av La Salle, Edif Mengal, piso 4, Ofic, 4-C, los Caobos, Caracas. Tel: (582) 781 8107.

RENT-A-EQUIPO
Av San Marino, Quinta Pena Fiel, Country, Club, Caracas. Tel: (582) 323 380. FAX: (582) 284 7801.

3M DE VENEZUELA
Puente Brion a Luis Razetti, Edificio 3M, Caracas. Tel: (582) 572 8074.

VIDEO GRABACIONES MERVIN
Professional La Urbina, Calle 3-A, Caracas. Tel: (582) 241 9015. FAX: (582) 241 3475.

VIDEO RODVEN
Centro Comercial Concresa, piso 2, Ofic 422, Prados del Este, Caracas. Tel: (582) 979 5742.

VIDEOMAX
Av Urdaneta, Esquina Urapal, Edificio, Centro Urapal, Piso 17, Oficina 17-10, Caracas. Tel: (582) 573 4020. FAX: (582) 575 2309.

VIETNAM

Population: 77.8 million.
TV Sets: 2.55 million.
Video Standard: NTSC/SECAM.

BROADCASTER

TELEVISION VIETNAM
59 Giang Vo St., Hanoi. (8443) 43188. FAX: (8443) 55332.

YEMEN

Population: 14.7 million.
TV sets: 433,000.
Video Standard: PAL & NTSC.

BROADCASTER

YEMEN RADIO & TV CORP.
PO Box 2182, Sana'a. Tel: (9671) 230 654. FAX: (967) 230 761. Telex: 2645 YARTV.

YUGOSLAVIA

Population: 14 million.
TV sets: 1.6 million.
Cable Subscribers: 150,000.
Satellite Subscribers: 220,000.
Video Standard: PAL

BROADCASTERS

NTV STUDIO B
Masarikova 5, 11000 Belgrade.

TELEVIZIJA CRNE GORE
Cetinski put bb. 81000 Podgorica. Tel: (38181) 41 529.

TELEVIZIJA SRBIJE NOVI SAD
Kamenicki put 45, 21000 Novi Sad. Tel: (38121) 56855

TELEVIZIJA SRBIJE PRISTINA
Beograd 66m 38000 Pristina. Tel: (38138) 31 211.

TELEVIZIJA SRBIJE/TELEVIZIJIA BEOGRAD
Takovska 10, 11000 Belgrade. Tel: (38111) 342 001.

TV ART CHANNEL
VI Kovacevica6, 1000 Belgrade.

TV PALMA
Banijska 2, 11080 Belgrade.

TV POLITIKA
Makedonska, 11000 Belgrade.

UDRUZENJE JUGOSLOVENSKIH RADIOTELEVIZIJA D.O.O. (JRT)
JRT Permanent Series—Television Department Hartvigova 70/I, 11000 Beograd. Tel: (38111) 434 910.

ZAIRE

Population: 44 million.
TV sets: 22,000.
Video Standard: SECAM

BROADCASTERS

ANTENNE A
Av. du Port 4, Building Forescom, 2nd Floor, Kishasa, Gombe. Tel: (243) 21736, 24818, 25308.

CANAL Z
6 av. du Port, PO Box 614, Kinshasa. Tel: (243) 20239.

ZAMBIA

Population: 10.23 million.
TV sets: 200,000
Video Standard: PAL.

BROADCASTER

TELEVISION ZAMBIA
Broadcasting House, P.O.Box 50015, Lusaka 229648. Tel: (2601) 220 864.

ZIMBABWE

Population: 11.745 million.
TV sets: 375,000.
Video Standard: PAL.

BROADCASTER

ZIMBABWE BROADCASTING CORP.
P.O. Box H.G. 444, Highlands, Harare. Tel: (2634) 498 659. FAX: (2634) 498 613.

ALPHABETICAL INDEX OF SUBJECTS

This index lists selected companies from major sections of the book. If the company you are looking for is not in the index, please find the company in alphabetical order within the relevant section.

A

B

C

D

E

F

G

H

K

L

M

S

T

W

X Y Z

Souled Out?

How Blacks Are Winning and Losing in Sports

Shaun Powell

HUMAN KINETICS

Library of Congress Cataloging-in-Publication Data

Powell, Shaun, 1960-
  Souled out? : how blacks are winning and losing in sports / Shaun Powell.
    p. cm.
  Includes index.
  ISBN-13: 978-0-7360-6750-8
  ISBN-10: 0-7360-6750-7
  1. African American athletes. 2. African American athletes--Social
conditions. 3. Sports--Social aspects--United States. I. Title.
  GV706.32.P69 2008
  796.089'96073--dc22

                                    2007019299

ISBN-10: 0-7360-6750-7
ISBN-13: 978-0-7360-6750-8

Developmental Editor: Leigh Keylock; **Assistant Editor:** Christine Horger; **Copyeditor:** John Wentworth; **Proofreader:** Bethany J. Bentley; **Indexer:** Craig Brown; **Permission Manager:** Carly Breeding; **Graphic Designer:** Nancy Rasmus; **Graphic Artist:** Tara Welsch; **Cover Designer:** Keith Blomberg; **Photographer (cover):** Neil Bernstein; **Photo Asset Manager:** Laura Fitch; **Photo Office Assistant:** Jason Allen; **Printer:** Edwards Brothers Inc.

Human Kinetics books are available at special discounts for bulk purchase. Special editions or book excerpts can also be created to specification. For details, contact the Special Sales Manager at Human Kinetics.

Printed in the United States of America   10 9 8 7 6 5 4 3 2 1

Human Kinetics
Web site: www.HumanKinetics.com

United States: Human Kinetics
P.O. Box 5076
Champaign, IL 61825-5076
800-747-4457
e-mail: humank@hkusa.com

Canada: Human Kinetics
475 Devonshire Road Unit 100
Windsor, ON N8Y 2L5
800-465-7301 (in Canada only)
e-mail: orders@hkcanada.com

Europe: Human Kinetics
107 Bradford Road
Stanningley
Leeds LS28 6AT, United Kingdom
+44 (0) 113 255 5665
e-mail: hk@hkeurope.com

Australia: Human Kinetics
57A Price Avenue
Lower Mitcham, South Australia 5062
08 8372 0999
e-mail: info@hkaustralia.com

New Zealand: Human Kinetics
Division of Sports Distributors NZ Ltd.
P.O. Box 300 226 Albany
North Shore City
Auckland
0064 9 448 1207
e-mail: info@humankinetics.co.nz

For my brother Scott, who went from 9/11 to heaven, and my daughter Victoria, who's heaven-sent.

Contents

CHAPTER 1

Generational–Cultural Differences

Seeking Common Ground 1

CHAPTER 2

Black Athlete Activism

Has the Last Militant Left the Stage? 25

CHAPTER 3

Home Is the City

Metro Dares and Small-Town Stares 49

CHAPTER 4

Academic Divide

Old School, New School, No School 71

CHAPTER 5

Basketball Score

*Jumping Through Hoops or
Just Growing Up?* 93

CHAPTER 6

Baseball Bygones

Going Soft on Hardball 117

Acknowledgments

This labor of love on a subject I felt qualified to write about would not have been possible without the help of several individuals whose input was priceless. I must begin with Ted Miller. He approached me about this project and made a mighty fine pitch, because at first I did not feel compelled to write this book. I thank Ted for his persistence, his criticism, his wisdom, his suggestions, and for showing the utmost confidence in a first-time author. Also, Brian Holding lent much support; thanks, Brian. A shout out goes to Leigh Keylock, Patty Lehn, Christine Horger, and Chad Hoffman for their efforts in seeing this book to the finish line. Much props to them.

Larry Lundy, whom I regard as a friend and now a business partner, was helpful in various ways. So were Art Powell, Erick Irvis, Dave Wiggins, Gary Spencer, Leon Carter, Bryan Burwell, Steve Ruinski, J.A. Adande, Terence Moore, Rick Telander, the late great Ralph Wiley, and the editors at *Newsday*, led by John Mancini, who were gracious to me during the process of writing the book. I've never had what I would call a true mentor, but two others have helped mold me as a writer in ways they will never know: Mike Bevans and the late Shelby Strother. Thanks to you all.

I'd also like to thank everyone who agreed to be interviewed for the book for putting up with my line of questioning. I learned a lot from them all. I'm a smarter man today as a result.

Terry Powell is a mighty fine woman to have in your corner. Her support, compassion, understanding, and love were unwavering throughout. Finally, I thank my mother, Cathy Powell, who is an inspiration to all of her children.

Introduction
Setting the Stage

It was the summer of '68, and I wanted to beat the hell out of a white boy, any white boy.

Sorry if that offends anyone. That's just how I felt back then, filled with rage just months before turning the innocent age of eight, all because two men rammed their fists through our family's 13-inch black-and-white Zenith. They weren't just any fists. They belonged to Tommie Smith and John Carlos, and though they were thrust into the smoggy Mexico City air, they were somehow clearly visible for all of black America to see thousands of miles away. Those fists were squeezed inside black gloves tighter than the ones O.J. Simpson later wore in an L.A. courtroom, gloves so tight the knuckles were aching to pop through the leather. Two black sprinters at the Summer Olympics stood on the medal podium during the national anthem and gave a four-knuckle salute to the white oppressors back home, and in my household, anyway, the hands on the clock just stopped cold.

You know how life sometimes brings moments that tingle and send a shiver? Like, right after you kiss your first love, or after a president gets shot, or after an earthquake hits? Well, Smith and Carlos in '68 was a mother of a moment for dark-skinned people from San Diego to Maine, if any lived in Maine.

Someone in our living room, maybe it was my father or one of my uncles, finally broke the dead air by saying, with mock disbelief, "I know they didn't."

Then he said it again, slowly, with emphasis: "I . . . know . . . they . . . did-int."

Oh, yes they did.

Plenty of whooping and hollering and shouts of "you damn right!" followed. And swept up in the emotional whirlwind was a little boy who felt a bolt of black pride for the first time.

You had to understand the day and age. That was the year black folks finally woke up and rose up. This was the painful and exhausting stretch run of the Civil Rights era. The blood of Martin Luther King Jr. was still damp on the balcony of a Memphis hotel, and his assassination was followed by violence and anger from a fed-up race of people who had had enough. Some adults in my family were into the whole black power thing, going to marches, joining demonstrations, nodding their heads to the rhetoric from the street poets, taking leaflets and buying newspapers from the bow-tied robots of the Nation of Islam. Their view of the world turned radical; their view of the establishment turned suspicious. They cleared room in their closets for a more Afrocentric wardrobe, trimmed with kinte cloth, which they wore proudly.

This was done in part because Smith and Carlos seized an opportunity and forevermore became synonymous with free speech and the most prestigious sporting event in the world. They used the international glare of the Olympics and the platform of sports to punctuate a Rosa Parks–like message that was far greater, and proved more valuable, than the Olympic awards that hung around their necks. This was a risk well worth taking, judging from the overwhelming response from the black community—including the rousing approval of a certain little boy who would soon devote his lifetime to watching and dissecting sports for a living.

Just before bedtime, I remember rummaging through my closet and finding one of my winter gloves and putting it on. It felt snug. I felt powerful. And after making a fist, I wanted to find a white kid and punch him right in the face, except none lived in my neighborhood.

Then to my surprise, only days later, I felt like hitting George Foreman instead.

Foreman won the gold medal in boxing, which in itself was a bigger deal in urban America than winning a race, because boxing was ruled by blacks and represented strength and ferocity and fire and unapologetic violence, all the things that percolated inside black America in the searing summer of '68. But what does Foreman do? He grabs a tiny American flag and waves it while grinning, walking around the ring and taking these obedient bows.

John Dominis/Time & Life Pictures/Getty Images

John Carlos and Tommie Smith, courageously taking a stand for equality, justice, and more.

Once again, stone silence fell in our living room. Then someone said, "I know he didn't." Oh, yes. He did.

With an uppercut that nobody saw coming, Foreman sucker-punched lots of black folks with that flag that day. He swiftly became, in the eyes of a good many, the definition of a sellout. In the wake of Carlos and Smith and the riots and the rage, he picked the absolute wrong time to smile and show his patriotic side. His attempt to heal the wounds caused by the strife of the '60s was viewed as brave by some in white society but cowardly by a good segment of black society, given the bold risk taken by Smith and Carlos. Foreman made a conscious decision to conform to society, quite the opposite of Smith and Carlos, who made it very evident on which side they stood. One Olympic winner embraced what the country stood for. Two others railed against it. One seemed to say everything was cool back home. Two wanted to distance themselves from a mainstream that discriminated against them and their people.

Over a span of several years, the image of blacks in sports was changing, and not just because of the 1968 Olympic Games. The all-black line-up of Texas Western conquered basketball king Kentucky for the 1966 national championship. Bruising USC fullback Sam "Bam" Cunningham ran roughshod over traditional football power Alabama in 1970. First, eyes opened, and soon thereafter minds and doors opened to the recruitment of black athletes in the South. The NBA was in its final seasons in which the league would be at least half white. And then there was Muhammad Ali, fresh off a boxing exile for refusing to serve in the war because "no Viet Cong never called me nigger," fighting his way back into the consciousness of a wary sporting America. Damn, as a growing black boy sucking in all the history and flavor, this was incredible to witness and feel and breathe.

It was easy to root for and identify with the rebels back then. They said something and stood for something, whereas O.J. just wanted people to rent cars. Jim Brown made a bunch of really bad movies, the kind that would go straight to video, except he always played threatening black men who didn't take any lip and kicked plenty of ass. Hank Aaron saw letters in his mailbox that were a lot less inviting than bills, and he brought them to our attention while remaining classy and professional. And every now and then, somebody would say or do something profound that reeked of pride and freedom and made everyone, not just black people, know what's up.

Then the inevitable yet startling evolution arrived—for me, for the athletes, for the country. Integration and jobs and tolerance turned a hose on anger, defiance, and the most serious racial issues, and the face of blacks in sports was altered forever. White America began gravitating without hesitation toward large black men, at least those wearing jerseys. The level of fear and distrust between white and black society decreased significantly, though not entirely. Helped partly by the media spotlight and the unifying power of sports, Madison Avenue sold black culture to Nebraska. In certain circles, and in certain doses, black people and particularly black culture became chic and acceptable. It began to influence popular culture, music, fashion, television, and even speech. Quite obviously, the impact in sports became considerable. For those whites who didn't live next door to blacks or spend time around them, big-time sports were their only window into a strange and foreign world, and some drew their beliefs on race from how those athletes talked and walked.

The rebels were still around, but I felt a sudden disconnection from them. Our ideas no longer meshed, which gave me a terrible case of heartache.

On my end, age, maturity, wisdom, and the realization that I didn't need to fight the same battles as my parents and grandparents softened my view of the world. No question about that. As an adult, my neighborhood and circle of friends have changed drastically from what I knew at eight years old and now include people of all races and backgrounds, giving me a healthier understanding and respect for all cultures. And I've since jumped to the other side of the generational line. Fair enough. But on their end, the rebels stopped having anything significant to say. Their words and actions weren't uplifting and positive anymore. Instead, the tone of their rebellion became more reckless, self-defeating, deflating, disturbing, and, dare I say, downright embarrassing. They began defying authority not necessarily because authority was unfair and discriminatory and deserved a black-gloved salute. This is where we are today. Some black athletes defy authority and reject the notion of proper behavior because they weren't raised properly, or because they lack social skills, or because they weren't educated, or because they don't subscribe to personal discipline. The only encouraging sign is that, thankfully, there seems to be change on the horizon.

The reasons for this type of rebellion are obvious enough. Many black athletes are products of the worst places to live in America, and a fair share carry this baggage into college (for those who decide to go), onto the professional level (for those lucky enough to go), and even throughout their lives. It's not totally their fault. Plenty of forces are at work against them, both forces that they created themselves and forces that were created specifically for them, rooted in racism. The combination of some being raised by single mothers (and sometimes grandmothers), poverty, poor role models, laughable post–Civil Rights leadership, absentee fathers, impressionistic gangsta rap, crumbling city schools, and a sense of entitlement because of their athletic ability has managed to warp the character of the rebels. They're caught in this vicious cycle that keeps spinning and snatching the next unfortunate generation of ballplayers. Some recover before it's too late and assimilate fairly smoothly into society. Others don't. Given the enormous pub they get, sometimes for the wrong reasons, they're a burden for those of us who strive to present a balanced view of black people to America. This is important because we're the only race on the planet that too often gets snapshots taken of our bad side instead of our good.

Here's what I mean. In the mid-1990s, the campaign to sell overpriced basketball sneakers became intense, with at least a half-dozen companies fighting among themselves for the right pro athlete to snatch a healthy slice of the market, which was mostly geared to teenagers. The competition included two very interesting pitchmen: David Robinson and Allen Iverson. They were both super-stars, highly visible, and tremendously successful. But even Stevie Wonder could see they were about as different as possible in every way other than skin color.

Robinson was lucky enough to come from a two-parent household. He grew up middle class, was educated at the prestigious Naval Academy, and was about as hip as C-SPAN. Nike gave him a commercial, but Robinson wanted control of the content, and the two sides agreed on "Mr. Robinson's Neighborhood," playing off the "Mr. Rogers" children's show. Near the end of the commercial, which was mostly done tongue in cheek, Robinson turned serious. He said, "Mr. Robinson doesn't like garbage in his shoes. If you're into drugs, don't come into my neighborhood. Mr. Robinson doesn't like garbage in his neighborhood."

The ad didn't sell many shoes. No surprise there because neither Robinson nor his well-meaning message could resonate with an audience that craved the street credibility that Iverson exuded. Almost as soon as he signed his first pro contract, Iverson was blessed with the worship of fans who liked their ballplayers with attitude. And Iverson, who unveiled cornrowed hair a few years later at the All-Star Game and set off a mad rush to the salons, was the Tupac Shakur of the courts. He clearly met the insatiable demand for a hip-hop hoops messiah. He was born to a teenaged mother who raised him alone, was arrested for inciting a riot inside a bowling alley, left Georgetown University after his sophomore year, and

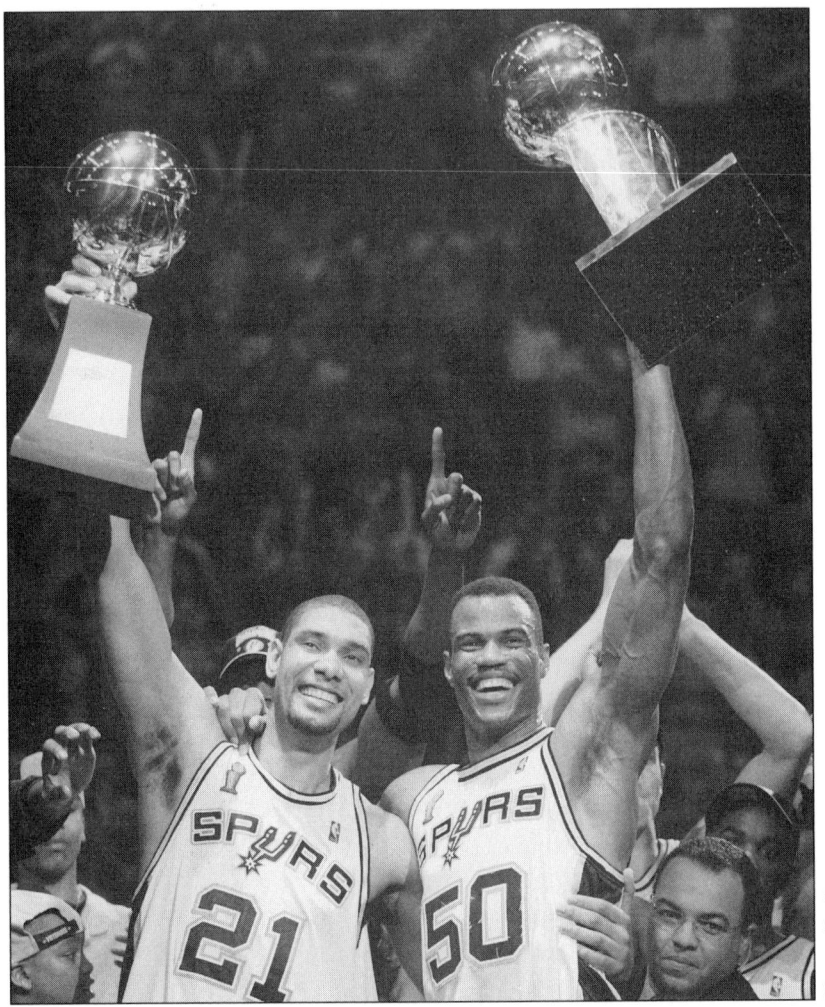

David Robinson (right), with teammate Tim Duncan, was blessed with a stable household and a Naval Academy education, but he had zero street credibility.

then had a string of run-ins (though none serious) with the law and his coaches in the NBA.

This only made his popularity soar, of course, and his $100 sneakers also flew off the shelves.

Gregg Popovich, who coached Robinson with the San Antonio Spurs, once wondered aloud why Robinson didn't connect, "since he's exactly the kind of example you'd want your kids to follow." But everyone knew the answer to that. Robinson's body didn't have a single tattoo, he spoke eloquently, he was a family man who embraced his religious faith, and he was strongly critical of certain lifestyle choices of kids. That didn't exactly endear him to the sneakers-buying public.

A touch of danger, a healthy dose of defiance, and anything else that frightens authority is exactly what strikes a nerve among those young black kids who reject any thoughts of joining the mainstream, along with those wanna-be-def white kids from the suburbs. And who better to deliver those goods than a rebellious black athlete with nothing constructive to say or do except, you know, keep it real?

Most disappointing about the rebel today is how he shows no interest in speaking out about the last stubborn remnant of racism in sports: hiring practices. The average sports fan couldn't care less, but anyone who subscribes to fairness should be appalled by what goes on outside the view of the spectators. On the fields and courts, it's all about talent and skill, and the best player reaps the rewards largely without regard to color. It's big business, with billions on the line, and money trumps all else. Owners have too much on the line to construct barriers, and if a multicolored martian could thread a football through a tire from 100 yards away, every team in the NFL would find a spot and a locker and a salary for him.

That's not the case behind the scenes. Not even close.

The percentage of blacks playing football and basketball should roughly be reflected by the numbers that coach and manage football and basketball teams. But it doesn't, because that's where politics and networking and connections come into play, and black folks are left out of the loop. Very few are groomed for jobs, or have the advantage of being blessed with a mentor, or get to rub shoulders with the owners and school presidents. Even worse, black players don't bother to demand changes in the coaching and administrative ranks. Many of the black pro superstars, who at least have power and clout in their organizations to promote change, just shrug and collect their oversized paychecks on the 1st and 15th.

Trust me, after more than two decades of interviewing athletes from a number of pro, college, and amateur sports in my job as a newspaper reporter, I'm fully aware that ignorance and fools come in all colors. Nobody has a monopoly on this. Cheaters, drug addicts, woman beaters, criminal behavior, and good old idiocy aren't confined within a single racial boundary. Not as much as the media would like us to believe. But that's not entirely the issue here. This book isn't a multicultural examination of sports or a higher-than-thou morality play; I'll leave that to the critics who demand perfection from a portion of the human race that's relentlessly hyped yet hopelessly flawed. Nor is it just about the rebels and their silly and destructive idea of radicalism. This is about the fascinating modern-day American black athlete, the burden he carries, the racism he gets and the racism he imagines, the image he gives, the image the media gives him, his triumphs and failures, his friends and enemies, and why he's the only one dancing in the end zone. Basically, this is about how the black athlete has evolved since John Carlos and Tommie Smith, for better and for worse.

It is quite possible that everyone and everything around him has Souled Out. Yes, a few words about the title and the variety of definitions it assumes for this book. These are no longer the 1960s or '70s, when a stronger sense of unity and pride existed among a struggling race of people who, for the most part, followed a more positive culture, purpose, and leadership. A sizeable group of young athletes today, because they were born later, have no concept of history or the athletes who paved the way for them to make millions and enjoy a better lifestyle. That, in a sense, suggests modern-day black society has lost some soul in the process of switching from one generation to the next.

But it goes deeper. Those misguided black athletes who religiously follow a thug mentality and show no inclination to reform have Souled Out. Black people with athletic backgrounds are being Souled Out of good administrative jobs throughout sports by white power brokers. Young black male athletes from poor backgrounds are being Souled Out of a quality education by their teachers and coaches. Blacks are being systematically kept out and Souled Out of influential positions in the major media companies that, for the most part, control the sports leagues and the images we get on TV and in print. Title IX was supposed to be a boon to women in sports, and yet the system has Souled Out black women while white women benefit. Highly paid black athletes are too busy hiding behind their precious public profiles and endorsement deals to lend a voice to activism, which means they've Souled Out in their worship of the almighty dollar. We'd like to say blacks have Souled Out of golf, but blacks were never souled in, even with Tiger Woods. But given the steady decline of American black faces in our national pastime over the last three decades, isn't it clear by now that blacks have voluntarily Souled Out of baseball for good?

So the real reason for the question mark in *Souled Out?* isn't to express doubt. The real issue is whether we— blacks, whites, everyone—continue to support behaviors that undermine our movement from here. This book will explain the obstacles, both self-imposed and external, and present ways to overcome them.

Speaking of transformation, how 'bout that George Foreman? Vilified by a good number of black folks upon returning home from Mexico City, he initially retreated into a cantankerous shell. He turned sullen and moody and eventually got rope-a-doped by Ali in a fight that nobody outside Foreman's family wanted Foreman to win. He retired, saw his money vaporize, and then reinvented himself as a triple-cheeseburger-eating, G-rated man who struck a chord with a public that could relate. After winning the heavyweight title in what now amounts to a bogus sport, Big George then cashed in big time with his own grilling machine. And he's still grinning like he did in '68.

Most amazingly, he's not the one I wanna punch anymore.

CHAPTER 1

Generational–
Cultural Differences
Seeking Common Ground

Most people admire him professionally and like him personally. Those who know him best speak highly of him. Twenty-plus years of honorable service to the National Basketball Association as a player and coach will do that for a man's reputation. It almost guarantees the opinions of Maurice Cheeks will reek of respect. "Professional" is a word commonly used to describe him, and so is "quiet." Billy Cunningham, who coached Cheeks with the Philadelphia 76ers, had a habit of calling him "smart," the ultimate compliment for a point guard, the position of leadership that Cheeks played. Then there's the word "classy." Over the years, Cheeks heard that one a lot, too.

And early one afternoon, he heard something else: the N-word.

Obviously, Cheeks was surprised. That was a new one. But just when he thought his ears had deceived him, he heard it again, according to those who witnessed the scene. That was the kind of angry talk that belonged in the 1920s from someone wearing a white hood, but this incident happened in 2005, and the offender was wearing a do-rag. He was Darius Miles, who, like Cheeks, is black.

The day after a loss to the Dallas Mavericks was not one to remember for the Portland Trail Blazers. Cheeks, the head coach, had seen enough from his dysfunctional team. He wasn't the only one with a beef. Miles was irritated after being yanked in and out of games by Cheeks, and he was fed up, too. They had a testy relationship, which isn't uncommon between players and coaches in professional sports. But this one erupted into an ugly, frothy mess after Cheeks angrily singled out Miles while the team watched film in a meeting. That's when Miles used specific words, none of which were "professional" or "quiet" or "smart" or "classy" or any of the usual descriptions directed toward a man with 20-plus years of honorable service to the NBA.

If the shouting from Miles toward Cheeks was alarming, the aftermath was most interesting. When details of their confrontation were leaked and became public, the media didn't know what to do with them. Had Miles been a white player and angrily dropped N-bombs on his black head coach, the national reaction would have been understandably volcanic. Newspapers and magazines and talk radio and Internet sites would have barbequed Miles over an open flame of strong opinions. His reputation would have been destroyed. His family members would have drawn the window curtains in shame, crawled under beds, and changed their home telephone number, if not their last name. That makes sense. Given the racist origin of the word, a white player would receive his comeuppance for daring to use it.

But because Miles was black, the watchdog media performed a collective shrug, sensing the public was okay with blacks calling each other *that word*. The morning newspapers did mention that Miles "repeatedly used a racial epithet" but mostly left it at that. The local NAACP chapter did not picket or demand an apology. Jesse Jackson did not order a march on Portland, Oregon. Miles' black teammates did not whip his ass or demand his immediate removal from the team, as they certainly would've done had he been white. They brushed the incident aside and remained quite friendly with him.

And the Trail Blazers organization suspended Miles for only two games without pay while pleading with him to behave in a more civil manner. The only person outraged was Cheeks.

"Years ago, you would never think about talking to someone like that," Cheeks said later, when he confirmed the altercation with Miles. "I don't think anything would trigger that kind of response. But it's different now, you know. It's different."

The difference certainly wasn't evident on the surface between the two men. They were born on opposite ends of Illinois but essentially in the same world. Cheeks came from the hard side of Chicago, Miles from East St. Louis, a town sucker-punched for decades by corruption and

Sam Forencich/NBAE via Getty Images

The wisdom of Maurice Cheeks did not rub off in generous doses to Darius Miles during their days with the Portland Trail Blazers.

drugs and so strapped for funds that it once had to surrender City Hall to settle a lawsuit. As city kids often do,
Cheeks and Miles gravitated to the basketball courts to
escape the constant knocks of the hard life. They quickly
developed a passion for the game and began dribbling
their way to a velvet-rope lifestyle that neither could
fathom as children. They beat the incredible odds and
reached the NBA and by chance ended up in the same
locker room—Miles as a player and Cheeks now as a
coach.

And that was the extent of their shared experiences.
Their backgrounds were also "different," as Cheeks mentioned, primarily because of their eras. As a child of the
1970s, Cheeks did not enjoy the same perks of instant
fame that some teenage basketball stars do today. His
high school basketball games weren't televised nationally. Dick Vitale, the hyper basketball commentator, did
not foam at the mouth at the mention of Cheeks. Small
and skinny, he was never given free sneakers or fancy
warm-up suits by the shoe companies that constantly
stock AAU teams today. All he received was a scholarship to West Texas State, a tumbleweed school in the
bushes, and only because a high school teammate, the
player West Texas really wanted, asked to bring Cheeks
along. Cheeks called home during his freshman year and
begged to return to Chicago. His mother told him she
would simply drive him right back to Texas. So he stayed,
and he prospered, and he earned his degree, making his
family proud. He was a second-round draft choice by the
Sixers, and his first contract paid him roughly what current NBA stars spend on their monthly cell phone bills.
He learned about the NBA world from the lap of Julius
Erving, the great and eloquent Dr. J, and stayed clear of
controversy or trouble.

"If Billy Cunningham told me to stand on top of that
backboard," said Cheeks, "I'd be on top of that backboard. Or I'd keep jumping until I got there. There'd be
no hesitation. Nowadays, you ask them to do that, they

say, 'Why?' I was taught to respect coaches and people in authority and to carry myself a certain way."

Miles was an only child raised by his mother, Ethel, who drove a bus. For a while the family lived near drug dealers. He grew quickly, and by his early teens he was already the most celebrated prep basketball player ever raised in hardscrabble East St. Louis, America's murder capitol in 1992 though only 50,000 people lived there. He was mentioned in several national magazines. After his junior year in high school, he knew he was on the fast track to the NBA and put his schoolwork second. When he failed to meet the minimum score on his college entrance exam to attend St. John's University, fans at a rival high school cruelly mocked him by chanting, "S-A-T!" They were quickly drowned out by supporters yelling back, "N-B-A!" Anyway, whether or not he met the grade meant nothing. There would be no leafy college campus or thesis papers or long nights with baggy red eyes spent in the library for Miles—only basketball games played in plush professional arenas filled with adoring and sellout crowds. The Los Angeles Clippers made him the third selection overall in the 2000 NBA draft. At the time he was the highest high school graduate taken in draft history.

Miles was certainly ready physically for the sometimes punishing grind of the NBA schedule. His body was already long and lean, and he could jump in quick, powerful bursts. But he was far from being ready mentally to carry himself like an adult, mainly because he wasn't one. He was a teenager raised by a mother in the 'hood. For too many young black men, athletically gifted or not, such an upbringing isn't a recipe for success in today's America. In a grown-up world that was new and unfamiliar, Miles was affable and polite and grounded in some ways, but he was immature in others. He was suddenly his own boss. He had a measure of celebrity and money and bling and cheering fans and new friends and few serious worries. On the court, his work ethic and motivation were questioned. Eventually, the Clippers traded him to Cleveland, which sent him to Portland, where he used a word in his vocabulary to address his coach, a proud black man from a different era.

It's not that Cheeks had never seen a black player cop an attitude in his day. Of course he had. But none with the backing of Madison Avenue, which markets and exploits the most destructive force known to poor black kids: street credibility.

What Cheeks experienced was an up-close and very personal brush with one side of a growing division in black society. One group includes individuals who will reject the notion of conforming to mainstream America and will dress and behave and do whatever they please, regardless of what you and I think or what message it might send. When he was young and reckless and not nearly as wise as he is today, Charles Barkley once boldly announced himself as "a '90s nigger. We do what we want." The other side of the divide embraces a more conventional way of life and distances itself from any behavior or lifestyle that feeds the tired images that lump together an entire race. Incidentally, Barkley, a devoted father and celebrated deep thinker, is now clearly on this side.

With the influx of athletes in professional sports becoming younger each year, the size of the nonconforming group gets bigger. Understand that this has nothing to do with cornrows and tattoos, the street-fashion choice among young black athletes. Please, let's not make too much out of that. To judge people solely on a fashion statement is racial stereotyping at its worst. Those are harmless cosmetic trends that mean nothing, really. What we're talking about is character—about conduct and vision and lifestyle choices.

Allen Iverson is a hero to fans of all colors, and not only because he's a terrific scorer, exciting player, and courageously sacrifices his body every night. He has also developed a cult status because of the way he looks and speaks and the way he thumbed his nose at authority a few times. His element of defiance is offensive to some but revered by others. Randy Moss gets high marks for many of the same reasons. Latrell Sprewell, after he choked his coach, became a martyr when he was slapped with a season-long suspension by the white commissioner of the NBA, and later a fan favorite at Madison Square Garden when he played for the Knicks. The core audiences for those players would struggle to make a deep spiritual connection with, let's say, Greg Oden.

We've seen other scattered examples, where some athletes "entertain" for their applauding white audiences. We're very familiar with the orchestrated and over-the-top celebrations, especially in football, where white players, with few exceptions, rarely do much more than toss the ball to the referee. We know about the in-your-face confrontations, done with little or no regard for sportsmanship. We've endured several incidents of crimes involving black players in the NFL during a particularly troublesome stretch between 2005 and 2007, most famously by the Cincinnati Bengals and Pacman Jones, which forced the league to institute a strict behavior policy. These are the images commonly attached to black athletes, only because a few are willing to play those roles. When they do, they cultivate stereotypes. They give ammunition to the bigots and the ignorant.

The real shame is when this behavior becomes confused with culture, because in fact this type of behavior and character has little to do with color or culture. It has everything to do with environment and circumstance. Which means, if you're influenced a certain way in this day and age, you tend to carry yourself that way, whether you are white or black or born in the housing projects or on a tree-lined cul-de-sac. Of course, environment and circumstance are working against many in urban America, where black athletes continue to be produced at a disproportionate rate, where positive role models are scarce, where discipline and education and morality aren't always prioritized. Still, whatever image they project is not a reflection on all black people or even all black athletes. It's not cultural. If this were understood, there wouldn't be sweeping generalizations made or beliefs held about an entire race.

"Image is exceedingly important," said Dave Bing, the NBA Hall of Famer, "and the image of a lot of our young black athletes today is negative. Even though these guys are wealthy, they will never be accepted into the mainstream. We've got to start letting these guys know we have another generation that we've got to worry about. I think things have gotten out of hand. We just don't have the same respect for each other that we had in years past."

Bing stressed that only a small number of young black athletes insist on carrying this burden. He's right, of course. I'm reassured that this wedge within the race isn't entirely generational. It can't be, because too many black athletes over the last dozen years have done nothing to fall into racial typecasting. They've managed to conform to the norms while not losing sight of who they are or where they're from. They're the ones who provide a more accurate barometer for how blacks think and act and carry themselves in this society, both in and out of sports.

David Robinson is one of the most honorable men I've ever met, in and out of sports. He created, with his time, money, faith, and connections, a charter school in the most depressing section of San Antonio, where hope rarely reached children, mostly black, until Robinson magically appeared in their lives. Michael Jordan, lucky for us, was about as graceful as he was good. He has touched the lives of young black people in ways that you can't imagine. Kevin Garnett went straight to the NBA from high school and never experienced the bumpy transition some feared when, as a 19-year-old, he was showered with the intoxicating trappings of money and fame. He showed more maturity than teammates 10 years older.

James Blake has an Arthur Ashe–like aura and is exactly the kind of representative we need, not only in tennis but in sports, period. Warrick Dunn, Tracy McGrady, Shaquille O'Neal, Ray Allen, Ken Griffey Jr., LaDainian Tomlinson, Jermaine Dye, Torii Hunter—the list is long and reassuring and filled with current-generation players who represent themselves well. But if these black athletes deserve a salute just for being responsible people, which is what we all should be, then what amount of scolding is proper for those who play to stereotypes?

"I've seen some situations that make you proud," said former Packers great Willie Davis, the Hall of Famer. "Dwyane Wade, for example, is the kind of athlete you'd want to represent you in every way. He conducts himself well, and his performance is unbelievable. And then you have others who upset me because they don't do anything to promote and build on what has been accomplished by those who came before them. These bad actors are demeaning, and they set an example that I'd rather not see from our people. I also get upset when, proportionately, black athletes seem more likely to get caught up in bad situations away from the field, crime and things like that. The bad actors are constantly in and out of trouble."

Davis and Bing speak for the proud old-school, the great pioneers who fought the very stereotypes that are flaunted today by those who insist on being ignorant and self-serving. "I was always very concerned about image, both on the field and off, when I played," said Davis, with a heavy sigh. "I'm not saying every guy needs to be like that. But the bad actors need to think twice about what they're doing."

Obviously, every race has its conventional and unconventional types. White athletes get suspended, flunk out of college, and curse their coaches, too. Nobody has a monopoly on counterculture behavior. But the issue is which race of people is harmed most by this, in terms of public perception. There's no question or debate about that. It's not even close. If a fair number of whites carry themselves a certain, off-centered way, nobody is chalking it up to white culture. But blacks stand more to lose, image wise, when a street mentality is perpetuated by someone who's black. When that happens, sweeping indictments are made, widely held beliefs are reinforced, and black culture takes another unfair hit.

This isn't restricted to sports. This strikes a nerve throughout black society and forces a race to conduct a much-needed self-inspection. It's what encouraged Bill Cosby to switch from comedian to passionate community leader who lectured blacks on their ideas about raising children and conducting their lifestyle. The tendency of some blacks to embrace the very worst stereotypes was also captured with clever brilliance by comedian Chris Rock with his riff about how "I love black people, but I am tired of niggas," who Rock says "ruin it for everybody."

These prickly observations met with backlash, as expected, by some in a black society who are dead-set against airing dirty laundry in public and would rather keep attention focused on the white power structure. Cosby, in particular, was savaged by a number of blacks. They thought he was harping mainly on the downtrodden, who are powerless and vulnerable. But there was also a silent majority in the black community that took notice and lent support. Cosby became a refreshing voice, especially when compared to the dreadful collection of self-appointed black leaders who are fearful of criticizing the people they claim to represent. Cosby's take was applauded by black teachers and scholars and parents, and he found himself besieged by invitations to spread the gospel in the places that need to hear it most. Arguably, Bill Cosby became the most important black man in America the moment he started preaching self-responsibility. Rock's "I love black people" sketch, performed before a mostly black audience, drew an ovation that was louder than the laughter. Not only was it funny, it was approved.

Clearly, these two entertainers are not the only people in black America who take offense at those who feed the harmful stereotypes and images. With so many governmental and societal forces against black people, why do some insist on being a force against themselves? Why, for example, has some popular black music been degraded by platinum-selling gangsta rappers, who glorify the N-word and the ghetto in their tacky videos and gush about their bitches and ho's? Rap is certainly well-represented in my iPod by those artists who are positive and thoughtful. But somewhere, after KRS-One and Public Enemy and other great godfathers of hip-hop and rap, the lyrics and the message took a serious turn for the worse, to the point where it goes through heavy screening before it reaches my grade-school daughter. This music is quite a comedown from the romantic soul of Sam Cooke and inspirational vibe of Earth, Wind & Fire. And why has the black community as a whole endorsed this not only through silence, but in sales? Tell me: Did Dr. King really die just so some of us could breathe life into the very racist images he tried to destroy?

"Not everyone is into that hip-hop lifestyle," said Len Elmore, the former NBA player, Harvard Law grad, and current broadcaster who grew up in working-class Brooklyn. "But if you go into certain areas, yes, that's about all they have to hold onto. There's not a lot of hope there. Some use that as an anthem and guiding force in their lives."

Because sports often reflect society, and because of the high status and media visibility we give athletes, their behavior cuts deeper and reaches farther. That's not particularly fair; all they do is play ball. But such is the celebrity-worshipping world we created. Given a choice, I'd rather have the eye of America trained on the legions of blacks from all walks who nourish their children, elevate their communities, and show a willingness to mesh comfortably into the mainstream while staying true to their heritage. You can imagine my horrific reaction, for instance, while watching the men's 4 × 100-meter relay team at the Sydney Olympics, the biggest televised sports event of the year, conduct the longest and silliest victory lap in history. Suddenly, stereotypical misbehavior went global. As they danced around the track, Maurice Greene, Jon Drummond, Bernard Williams III, and Brian Lewis wrapped the flag over their heads, under their arms, and around their waists while making muscle poses, facial contortions, and even wearing their medals as monocles. They claimed they were only having fun. They admitted their mistake, and we must judge them on their body of work, not on a moment. But on that day, I could only shake my head and wonder what the world thought about us now. Until then, we had the good sense to confine that act to the States.

Both sides of the great black racial divide were played prominently and intensely during a turbulent 2005 season for the Philadelphia Eagles. Several months

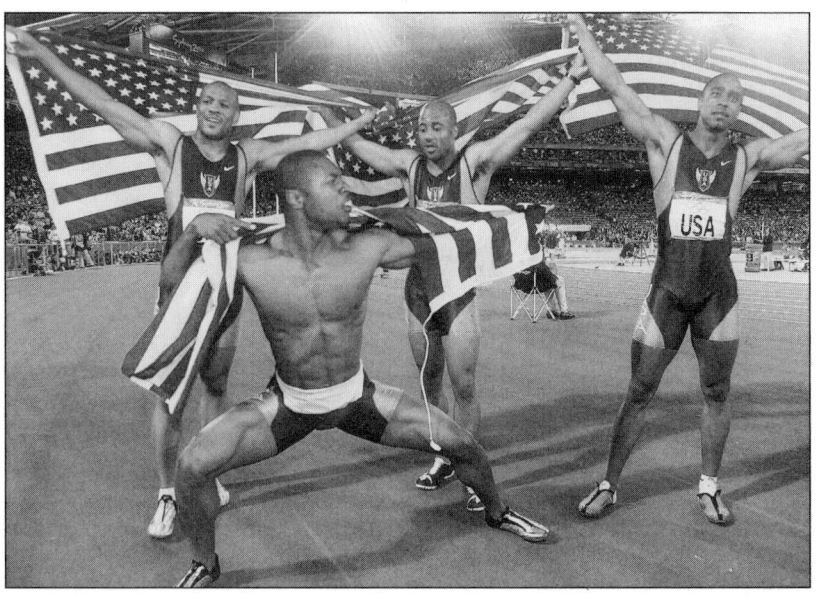

©Reuters/Corbis

The U.S. men's 4 × 100-meter relay team at the 2000 Sydney Olympics was accused of over-the-top celebration.

before, they lost the Super Bowl to the New England Patriots, a better team, but not before two interesting developments took place. The first was the courageous effort by receiver Terrell Owens, who managed to play the entire game and strike fear into the Patriots despite a sore ankle he seriously damaged late in the regular season. The second was the astonishing final-minute meltdown by quarterback Donovan McNabb, who looked sluggish and unsure in the huddle and at the line of scrimmage while the Eagles tried in vain to mount a comeback.

Owens and McNabb didn't have the best of relationships, and the reasons were evident enough. They had different personalities; McNabb was quiet by comparison, though personable and easy going, whereas Owens was gregarious and outrageous. The other reason was jealousy. McNabb had a contract worth over $100 million. Owens was one year into a contract he thought was already outdated and unfit for a player who clearly helped the Eagles reach the Super Bowl.

Despite the differences, McNabb never held a beef with Owens and even invited Owens to the annual parties held at the quarterback's New Jersey mansion. But that wasn't enough to pacify T.O., who mentioned how he "wasn't the guy who got tired in the Super Bowl," an obvious slap at McNabb. Owens later called McNabb a "hypocrite" and then seemed to question, in a thinly disguised way, McNabb's blackness.

First, Owens charged McNabb with being a "company man." Now that can be construed in a few ways. Either McNabb was simply loyal to an Eagles management that awarded him the big money and promoted him as the team's star. Or McNabb was a house Negro. Owens left it up to us to decide. Then came an Owens interview with Michael Irvin, then a guest commentator for ESPN and a silly-acting player in his own right during an otherwise great career with the Dallas Cowboys. With McNabb struggling to perform through an abdominal injury, Irvin wondered if the Eagles would be better off with Brett

Favre as the quarterback, a suggestion wholeheartedly endorsed by Owens. With Favre being white, this struck a sensitive nerve with McNabb, who played a position once considered beyond the intelligence of blacks.

McNabb felt betrayed by Irvin but mostly by Owens. He wondered if their attacks amounted to a "black-on-black crime," an unfortunate choice of words given that nobody was murdered, which happens far too often in urban America. But McNabb simply echoed the same phrase used earlier by Sam McNabb in a spirited defense of his son in a *Philadelphia Daily News* story. And no matter how clumsy either McNabb response was, their disappointment was understandable. It only deepened when the publisher of the *Philadelphia Sun*, who also happened to be president of the Philadelphia branch of the NAACP, did a racial pile-on.

J. Whyatt Mondesire criticized McNabb for abandoning the scrambling ability that made him an extra threat, all for the intentional purpose of escaping the stereotype of the running black quarterback. Once again, McNabb's authenticity as a black man was questioned, and once again by someone who was black.

The racial implications were obvious. A quarterback who has conducted himself professionally even during times of crisis, who obviously is intelligent, who was raised by both parents under one roof, whose style of play began to lean toward a more conventional manner for an NFL quarterback, and whose personality and character is more befitting of someone in mainstream America was somehow less black. Meanwhile, a flamboyant, mouthy, and belligerent receiver who can't resist putting on a freak show in the end zone was somehow more black.

This kind of warped thinking supports a decades-old and self-defeating attitude in parts of black society, that someone who speaks good English and is educated and may even prefer rock music over rap has hopelessly lost his racial identity, if not his mind. His "blackness" comes into question, as if there's a company manual on how to be black. It's just another reason why black society should be sensitive about self-created images and the astonishing value placed on street cred, which celebrates stupidity and self-destructive behavior. Get this: Owens acts a certain way and therefore he's definitely a black man; McNabb doesn't and therefore he's not black enough. That's another way of suggesting that one side of the great black divide is 100 percent pure, while the other Souled Out.

Nobody ever mentioned the word "sellout" and Allen Iverson in the same breath. The graphic story of how Iverson's basketball skills helped him escape extreme poverty and danger in Hampton, Virginia, is so worn that it's bald. How he was born to a 15-year-old single mother. How his family's house sat above the city's sewer line, which broke often and filled the floor with a layer of sludge, making his younger sister sick. How his natural father mainly stayed in jail and out of Iverson's life. How a bowling-alley brawl at age 17 nearly halted his athletic career at the high school level until an intervention by Governor Douglas Wilder reduced Iverson's jail time to only four months. How he went to Georgetown and became a star. How he unveiled a head full of cornrows at the NBA All-Star Game, starting a follicle trend, which further endeared him to teenage fans in urban America and wannabes from the suburbs. He is truly an American success story.

But because of his grim background and his disregard for the mainstream, Iverson made no apologies for tweaking authority figures, especially coaches, or being cited for carrying a concealed weapon, or being accused of threatening to kill a family member during a domestic spat. He felt he owed it to himself to be himself, no matter what images it sent, and also owed it to the many kids in Hampton who grew up like him. Even when Iverson turned 30 and the media, anxious for a new angle, started applauding Iverson's delayed maturity, he suffered embarrassing lapses. Shortly after being named captain of the 2004 Olympic team, he missed practice, and two years later he arrived late the night of the 76ers' final home game, which was Fan Appreciation Night.

In one sense, Iverson's willingness to inspire black kids who have little or nothing is commendable. He did not dump his friends from Hampton once he made the NBA. He showed the neighborhood kids an honorable way to make good money. Ask any of his teammates, past and present, in the NBA, and they'll tell you Iverson is one of the most genuine people they've ever met, that he has a good soul underneath the tattoos. Feel free to wonder if Iverson blew a big chance to be a trailblazer, given his clout in urban America. Wouldn't it have been helpful had he returned to college to get his degree or if he demonstrated the importance of being prompt? And not gone on a silly rant about "practice," as he did when his coach merely asked him to attend a few? Or not mocked the NBA's dress code, which was only meant to make young black men keep their oversized shirts and bling and baggy pants at home and appear presentable and respectable while on the job? Wouldn't the kids in Hampton, almost none of whom have any chance of being NBA stars themselves, gain more from that? Wouldn't they adopt those critical life lessons and apply them in school and beyond? Or would Iverson lose his authenticity and connection and street cred with that audience?

On that latter note, Iverson definitely stood to suffer, in terms of bankability, on Madison Avenue had he gone mainstream and, in effect, sold out. The companies that flocked to Iverson did so largely because he was a thrilling player to watch and a tough little guy who constantly scored against bigger and stronger players. No question. But there was the other side of Iverson they wanted to exploit, too. He reflected well on the street. In that regard, he wouldn't have nearly as much appeal if, let's suppose, he wore a corporate haircut or constantly preached religion. He could not be the basketball version of Will Smith.

The footwear of choice for many of Iverson's followers was sneakers, and it made him Reebok's biggest basketball spokesman. Like other professional athletes, he couldn't touch Michael Jordan for sales, but Iverson, much edgier than Jordan, managed to tap into another vein nonetheless. A company whose financial health depended in part on the image it sent to urban kids and suburban wannabes had its Basketball Jesus, someone who gave Reebok street cred. And regardless of any negative connotations that came with that, street cred meant money, and no company ever turned down the chance to make as much bank as possible.

In a sense, the professional sports leagues are capitalizing on bad behavior by all athletes, especially the stereotypical kind by blacks. It was no coincidence that Randy Moss had the highest-selling NFL jersey in the 2005 season, his first with the Raiders, even though it was a noticeably poor season by Moss' standards and the Raiders were losers. Even without scoring tons of touchdowns, Moss still had a street image that he cultivated the moment he entered the NFL, and that image stayed with him from Minnesota to Oakland. Iverson's jersey is a big seller for the NBA, and in an interesting twist, Kobe Bryant's jersey sold briskly the year after a rape charge was brought against him, a charge that ultimately fizzled and was settled out of court. Then there's the pot of gold created by video game cartridges, some of which emphasize end-zone dancing and hip gyrating done primarily by digitally enhanced black cartoon characters. Yes, stereotypical behavior has gone cyberspace in a big and profitable way.

What the sports leagues have discovered, to the delight of their financial health, is that the same black athletes the leagues claim to distance themselves from are making millions for the leagues by way of licensed apparel, the cash cow of the new millennium.

"The athlete in the 21st century has become completely commodified," said Harry Edwards, the sports sociologist. "He has become a marketing vehicle to sell the game and the products. The dancing and acting up in the end zone, the NFL doesn't want it to go too far, but if they wanted to eliminate it, they could. They want the athlete out there doing it because of the marketing success, the jerseys that it will sell, and the people who will be talking about it in the office the next day."

Thankfully, there are limits to commercialism, which explains why Ron Artest wasn't exactly overwhelmed with endorsement offers after he punched his way through the stands and instigated the NBA's saddest hour, the infamous brawl that interrupted the Pacers–Pistons game in 2004. In the span of roughly 20 raw minutes, the disturbing images of large black men committing acts of violence were replayed before a country too often bombarded by such nonsense on the 6 o'clock news. A few black men gave fodder to popular attitudes within a society that makes the connection between thuggish tendencies and black males.

An unnecessarily hard foul from Artest on Ben Wallace resulted in Wallace shoving Artest by the throat, and then Artest retreating to a scorer's table, where he lay down, seemingly in an effort to mock and inflame the situation. This certainly was nothing new for Artest. In short time, he replaced Dennis Rodman for stupidity and nuttiness by bashing a TV camera and hurling small TV sets from courtside tables at Madison Square Garden, by giving cheap shot fouls, and by other unsportsmanlike behavior that managed to suck thousands of dollars in fines from his wallet.

Artest came from the Queensbridge projects just across the East River in New York, where he was viewed as a saint by people who knew firsthand about his soft and caring side. True enough, Artest was almost childlike in nature, naïve to a degree about the real world, which amused his teammates and coaches, first at St. John's and then in the NBA. But Artest clearly had anger issues, and they flared once again when a dim-witted fan at the Palace in suburban Detroit approached and hurled a cup of liquid onto Artest's chest.

In a reflex action, Artest charged through the stands and began throwing roundhouse rights at the person he thought was guilty, thus starting the madness. Even more inexcusable than Artest was Stephen Jackson, his teammate, who went looking to make blood, not peace. Funny thing about Jackson—two years later he was cited for firing his gun in the air outside a nightclub in Indianapolis, forcing NBA commissioner David Stern to issue a plea to his players: "Leave your guns at home." The mob mentality at the chaotic Palace also sucked in Jermaine O'Neal, who didn't have anywhere near the rap

AP Photo/Duane Burleson

Ron Artest sparked a nasty scene when he charged after a fan into the stands during a game between the Indiana Pacers and Detroit Pistons.

sheet of Artest but who nonetheless applied one of the most vivid shots of the night when he cold-cocked a fan who made the mistake of venturing onto the court, looking for a piece of the action. Lost in the reaction to the riot was the fact that several black athletes and coaches desperately tried to police the situation in a responsible manner—but by then, it was too late. The images were already packed and gift-wrapped and ready to be spread by a media age that gravitated toward shocking footage. The black athlete was again under siege, partly by his own doing.

Not surprisingly, Artest wasn't universally condemned over the ensuing days by his fellow black athletes. Not wanting to risk alienating themselves from the fraternity, most repeated the company line, saying, "I would've done the same thing had I been under attack," even though a cup of liquid barely constitutes being under attack. Any criticism of Artest by other NBA players was mildly placed. Few dismissed Artest and the others for perpetuating yet another round of stereotypes that a weary black society had to deal with. Instead of blaming the people responsible for sending a bad message, most critics inside and outside the NBA blamed anyone in the sports world who dared to make any racial leap of faith.

Not until the following season, when Artest selfishly asked for more shots and played the victim in an interview with the *Indianapolis Star* newspaper that ultimately got him traded to Sacramento, did his teammates finally take a tough stand. And it came from O'Neal, who lost hundreds of thousands of dollars in fines and suspensions when he blindly followed Artest into the riot. O'Neal said he was through making sacrifices for Artest, and you only wonder what took him so long.

The only other good news to emerge from the spectacle was that even the hip-hop community, quite literally, wasn't buying Artest. When he showed poor judgment by using the media storm to promote a group of singers he bankrolled, the tactic didn't work, and the CD didn't sell.

And then, after being sent to the Sacramento Kings in 2007, Artest was charged in a domestic spat. He couldn't run from trouble, or hide.

What players like Artest fail to show a suspicious America is that most blacks in this country aren't poverty stricken or severely challenged educationally. Far from it, actually. Fact is, the black middle class is booming, larger than ever before. There are swelling suburban pockets outside Atlanta and Washington and New York that are filled with Huxtables, the fictional yet functional family from *The Cosby Show*. Test scores for black students in all walks of society are up (though not at the levels of whites or Asian-Americans) as are the numbers enrolling in college. The American Dream, once sheer fantasy for a majority of blacks during Jim Crow and even as recent as the late 1960s in this country, is not only well within reach, it's being squeezed in some cases.

When raised in a caring, two-parent household, exposed to a wide variety of educational experiences, and properly taught how to conduct themselves in a reasonable manner by responsible role models, these black kids have the same cheery outlook as their white neighbors. What a surprise. Of course, that doesn't come with a guarantee. It doesn't mean some kids won't drift and become socially inept. It doesn't mean they won't become unwed teenage parents. It doesn't mean they won't go on a killing spree in a shopping mall. But with only 13 percent of juvenile delinquents coming from families with the biological mother and father in the house, it does reduce the odds somewhat significantly. That's what a firm foundation does for children. It gives them a tremendous head start to succeed in society as adults. It prepares them for life's challenges and teaches them how to handle a variety of tricky situations.

And then there are the blacks left behind in our rotting, neglected urban communities, such as Queensbridge. They never recovered from the white man's racism. They're still largely victimized by substandard educational opportunities, drugs, alcoholism, crime, menial jobs, limited motivation, absentee fathers, and teenage mothers. And bigotry—because they are the most vulnerable blacks and thus the easiest to discriminate against.

This doesn't mean a kid raised by an overwhelmed mother in the projects will definitely become a criminal. It doesn't mean he or she will drop out of high school and become a teenage parent. It doesn't mean this kid will drift from one dead-end job to another and be sentenced to a life of living paycheck to paycheck. But 85 percent of teenage prisoners grew up in fatherless homes, so it increases the odds somewhat significantly. That tends to happen to the average black child tagged with these disadvantages. In the race of life, they're five paces behind at the start and will pick up too much heavy baggage along the way to catch up to the pack.

The options for these kids, as they grow, are limited because of their circumstances. There will be no weekend trips to Disney World, nights at the opera, or summers spent in Paris visiting the Louvre. Most days, for the boys anyway, it's an afternoon spent on the football fields or basketball courts. Their parents, or parent in most cases, may struggle to pass down the gift of knowledge, unlike middle-class black parents, who tend to be college educated themselves. Too often, poor single teenage mothers who don't have a firm grip on life, or haven't experienced much life, are burdened with the task of being the primary role model for their kids. Therefore, kids aren't being raised by adults. Kids are being raised by kids. Babies are teaching babies.

This is the incubator in which black athletes, those who reach the professional level or simply play in college, are created. They're not flooding the NCAA or NBA or NFL from suburbia. They're coming straight off the unforgiving streets. They're poor and desperate. This is no surprise or revelation. This has been going on for decades.

But there's an interesting new twist. The black athletes who reach the pros in this era tend to be younger than ever before. Teenagers are being thrust into an adult world and told to act like one, or expected to, anyway. That's just not reasonable for some. That often means even with the small army of advisors and counselors assigned to that young pro player, he might stick with the habits he learned from the streets.

"You have to understand," said Kenny Smith, the ex-NBA player turned TV personality, "the people who are mentors can teach these athletes a lot of things, but they can't teach them how to be a star and deal with a lot of money. They can't show them how to deal with those vices and the availabilities that athletes have. The fame. The number of women. The new friends. The luxuries. Doors are open that aren't normally open. Not only are they opened, they're kicked in. You're exposed to a world that really is a music video. And nobody can prepare someone for that, unless they've been there before. Most haven't."

Another factor is money. A big factor, actually. When it appears a teenager might be talented enough to play sports for a living, he becomes instantly empowered. In poor families, which obviously are quite common in urban America, he's suddenly seen as the breadwinner, the provider, the winning lottery ticket. That changes the attitude of people around him, especially if those people have dreams of becoming dependent on him for their own welfare. At 17 and 18, an age when he should be getting advice, he's giving it. He's suddenly the boss of the house, and everyone tells him what he wants to hear.

Perhaps this was the case with Darius Miles, who had tremendous athletic ability in his favor but almost no idea at first how to balance it with maturity and wisdom. Truth is, Miles should never even have been a member of the Trail Blazers, should never have been in a position to cuss at his coach and use the N-word. He was supposed to have a long career with the team that drafted him, the Clippers. But weary of waiting for Miles to mature on and off the court, the Clippers gave up on him fairly quickly, unusual for someone drafted so high and considered to be a big part of the team's future. Curiously, Miles became expendable the year after the Clippers, in perhaps their wisest decision in franchise history, traded for Elton Brand.

Brand was raised in Peekskill, New York, a town 25 miles north of New York City that's a suburb in name only. Peekskill is strictly blue collar with gritty streets and a healthy population of poor blacks, which makes it decidedly unique in upscale Westchester County, peppered with estates and old money.

Like Miles, Brand was mostly raised by his mother, a shy woman who nonetheless demanded and received respect from her son. As he grew tall and strong, Brand began taking daily train trips south to New York to play summer-league basketball, and he ultimately made his high school team a state power. But most impressive about Brand very early was his character. The rough side of Peekskill couldn't touch that. There was no nonsense about him or a hint of trouble. He went to Duke and in two years became the finest basketball player in the country and the top draft pick overall by Chicago. When the Bulls foolishly traded him, Brand quickly became the graceful face of the Clippers franchise, someone who combined charm and intelligence and leadership with solid play to gain respect. He took it upon himself to join UNICEF and fight AIDS. In that sense, as a success story and inspiration to those who share his background, Brand became the ultimate stereotype-buster. He proved that not every black athlete raised poor by a single parent will turn out alike.

While Brand helped lead the Clippers to the playoffs in the 2005-2006 season, Miles lapsed into another irrational act of defiance. He changed into street clothes at halftime during a game late in the season. This irritated Nate McMillan, who had replaced Maurice Cheeks as coach prior to the season, and who also happened to be black. But at least Miles showed progress, in one regard. The only N-word McMillan heard was Nate.

CHAPTER 2

Black Athlete Activism

Has the Last Militant Left the Stage?

Amazing, when you think about it, how one of the loudest protests in the history of mankind, and definitely the loudest in the history of sports, was done very quietly. It was so silent, in fact, inside Olympic Stadium in Mexico City on a summer night in 1968 that you could hear a thousand jaws drop.

All Tommie Smith and John Carlos did was raise their hands on the medal stand. Many years later, their victory salute has stood the test of time because it was original. They didn't storm some political headquarters and shoot pistols in the air, the protest of choice in many turbulent countries during a coup. They didn't march down a wide avenue with signs and megaphones and shout for justice, the protest of choice for many special interest groups. Nor did they refuse to report to work and thereby screw thousands of innocent people, the protest of choice by sanitation workers and the police force and other public service organizations. They clenched a fist but didn't punch anyone, the protest of choice by hoodlums looking for street justice.

They just stood up, literally, for what they believed in.

"Human rights," said Carlos.

That raises another point about the protest. Smith and Carlos weren't just promoting black power; they weren't that selfish. They were promoting equality for all. The source of their protest was indeed based on the plight of black people back home who were getting lynched and hosed and kicked in the behind by an oppressive white society. But, indirectly, they also spoke for the poor and downtrodden, for women trying to adjust in a man's world, for blue-collar workers looking for an honest day's pay. Also, Carlos and Smith weren't radicals or trouble-makers or rabble-rousers, all the labels given to them in the aftermath of their protest. They were ordinary human beings and American citizens asking for fairness.

"It was done in the name of pride, freedom, and equality," said Smith.

Until then, athletes didn't have much of a platform because the media was a fraction of what it is today. And athletes certainly didn't carry any clout or credibility when it came to issues beyond sports. The jock was best seen and not heard because society had decided he was sorely lacking in intelligence, socialization, and sophistication. And the black athlete, most definitely, was told to know his place and remain there. He kept his mouth shut and chose not to rock the boat. That made Smith and Carlos a pair of originals, along with Muhammad Ali. Each was willing to put his career on the line by being an outspoken black man, and all three sacrificed a good bit of those careers, not for money or fame, but for justice and their beliefs. Their agenda was pure, honorable, respectful, and terribly important.

"It had to be done because we were dealing with life and trying to change society," said Smith. "It was not about the dollar bill. That never entered our minds."

Smith and Carlos were black athletes of a different era, cut from a different mold, because money is most certainly on the mind of the typical professional black athlete today. He has a comfortable standard of living, a fair degree of fame, a healthy amount of respect from the public, and because he doesn't want to jeopardize any of that, he also has a severe case of laryngitis. Today's black athlete is not a crusader who presses for change and dares to speak out against injustice and racism and the crippling conditions that choke urban America, which is ironic in that the urban setting serves as the maternity ward for black athletes.

With millions at stake in endorsement money and an unwillingness to be misinterpreted by the media, and because of the simple fact that they didn't grow up in the smoldering '60s as Smith and Carlos did, black athletes today sidestep issues as easily as they would a clumsy linebacker. If there's a political pulse, few show it. If they have a passion for social topics within and beyond sports, it remains insulated. Regarding the lack of blacks in management and other positions of power, black athletes either don't care enough, would rather not discuss it, or simply give the subject a quick nod without dwelling too long.

Nothing seems to anger the rebellious black athlete today except playing time, contract status, and bad press. This disinclination to attack sensitive issues is an attitude that stretches from one end of the player spectrum to the other. It muffles the player on the bench, who would just as soon slap his coach than say something inflammatory and endanger his flimsy spot on the team. And it presses the mute button on Michael Jordan, who was said to snicker and reply, "Republicans buy sneakers, too," while explaining his initial refusal to publicly endorse Harvey Gantt, a black Democratic candidate from Jordan's home state of North Carolina who twice ran for the Senate against Jesse Helms.

Rather than raise hell when hell is needed, most black athletes are content to let the politically correct media rail against issues and do the dirty work that the athletes feel would only backfire on them if they spoke up. Because most athletes, even the ordinary ones, enjoy a plush standard of living that's beyond the scope of the average person, you must question whether there's any fire in their bellies. They have no personal stake in tackling social matters. Better to just leave things be.

Of course, there's the question of why *any* athlete, black or white, should weigh in on anything. It's not as though society is sitting on the edge of their seats and salivating while awaiting Joe Quarterback's take on the tense situation in the Middle East. There are certainly enough Hollywood types, actually too many, who eagerly serve up their political views for free visibility and plastic surgery for the ego. You'd think the last thing the world needs is another celebrity activist with an agenda, and from an uninformed jock at that. Well, no, the revolution will not suffer if the athlete refuses to chime in on national, world, and social issues. True, the athlete's job is to perform; he owes us nothing more, just as a dentist owes us nothing more than a pain-free tooth pull. And yes, nobody ever wonders aloud why white athletes don't speak out; they're never held to the same activist standard. That's all well and good, and it also totally misses the central point.

Activism has helped the black athlete get where he is today. That's what sets him apart from the white athlete in this discussion. Activism by Curt Flood and John Mackey, pioneers in free agency, made baseball and football players rich. Activism by Jim Brown and Bill Russell and other black athletes pushed the envelope and racial boundaries, broke barriers, created awareness, shattered myths and stereotypes, held white folks accountable, and essentially boosted and improved sports in general for the black man. Russell, in particular, staged two silent protests; he refused to appear at Boston Garden when his jersey was retired and also when he was inducted into the Basketball Hall of Fame in 1975. It was a payback for the insensitivity shown by the city of Boston toward Russell when he played there, and also for the Hall of Fame, which hadn't inducted a black player until Russell was voted in. It would be a shame, therefore, if black athletes continued to abandon this precious tool. His voice might actually echo farther than he thinks, especially in troublesome urban America, where sports and pro athletes enjoy a healthy (maybe unhealthy) status. And how much longer must we wait before a black athlete with clout shows enough guts to take management to task for its front-office hiring practices?

"I don't criticize a guy if he doesn't want to get in that arena," said Joe Morgan, the baseball Hall of Famer. "The athlete today is a little different. We can all be who we are. But one of these days we have to look in the mirror and say, 'Did I do all that I could do to make this better?' If Jackie Robinson looked in that mirror, the mirror would smile back at him. Some of these guys who don't want to get involved, one of these days, it's going to happen. They're going to look in that mirror, and that mirror is going to say, 'Why didn't you?'"

The last world-class black athlete to attach himself to social and political causes was Arthur Ashe, the most important black athlete since Robinson, someone whose identity was tied more to what he did away from the tennis court than what he did in the game. I suspect Ashe's legacy will live forever in this 60-40 imbalance between social causes and sport, even though he won three Grand Slam tournaments. Just to make sure, I checked his obituary, the best way to measure a man's impact in this world, and sure enough, the opening paragraph in the *New York Times* read, "Arthur Ashe, a tennis champion who spent his years in the sport fighting discrimination and then spent the final year of his life seeking to broaden public awareness on the subject of AIDS, died Saturday. He was 49." For an athlete, this was a distinguished obituary because it emphasized the character inside of the man, the depth of his influence, and his attempt to improve the world. Notice there was no mention of his U.S. Open, Australian Open, and Wimbledon titles until later in the story. And the monument of Ashe near downtown Richmond, Virginia, his hometown, fittingly shows him holding books higher in his right hand than

AP Photo/Lana Harris

Arthur Ashe, one of the greatest humanitarians in sports, used his athletic ability and fame to attract attention for social causes, such as education, AIDS, and, shown here, apartheid.

the tennis racket in his left, thereby stressing education, which was dear to Ashe's heart, over athletics.

The possibility of backlash is what frightens those black athletes who do have a social pulse. And yet, you wonder why. Although it's true that the activist pioneers who risked their public image did pay a price for doing so, history ultimately pardoned them and repaid them handsomely. Paul Robeson, the great football player at Rutgers, was essentially run out of the country for speaking out well before his time. Carlos and Smith were flogged immediately by the U.S. Olympic establishment and again when they returned home; there was no endorsement pot of gold awaiting these two winning sprinters, who were deemed too uppity for white America. Muhammad Ali was sucker punched for famously refusing to serve his country in Vietnam, poetically explaining that "No Viet Cong never called me nigger," simultaneously hitting the bull's-eye on the war and racism, twin targets in a turbulent time. His subsequent suspension erased a portion of his prime in the ring.

But without activism, the names of these four men wouldn't carry the cache they do today. Robeson is hailed by scholars and historians for his bravery. Carlos and Smith are immortalized on the campus of San Jose State by a statue depicting their salute. And the value given to Ali by activism can't be measured. In his postretirement, Ali was recognized by huge crowds in far away places not only for his swift hands but also for his courage, conviction, and sacrifice. He became so much more than a boxer, and in life, don't we all strive to be applauded for who we are rather than what we do? Given this unconventional road to respect that he took, you'd think others would follow down the same path, but instead, the opposite has happened. Rather than copy Ali, legions of black athletes today have allowed him to walk that road virtually alone.

The times have changed, obviously, and many battles fought by Ali and Ashe and the others have been won. No doubt about that. Nobody's lynching black folks or forcing them to sip from separate fountains. The sports landscape, for the most part, has embraced the black athlete, but primarily because he means tremendous bank for basketball and to a large degree football, two of the three cash-cow sports in America in which blacks are concentrated. By pacifying him with millions of dollars and a large dose of conditional love, society has softened him, even homogenized him. He sees no evil, hears no evil, and therefore suspects no evil. He's secure inside the gated suburban compound in which he lives, where there are no gang issues, rotting neighborhoods, sub-standard schools, and in-your-face racism. Well, here's a bit of reality for him to swallow: There's a grim world beyond his velvet lawn, one he knew not long ago, except now, based on his silence on the issues, you wonder if he ventures inside urban America only long enough to get a haircut and a plate of soul food to go.

"I don't have anything against them," said Tommie Smith, when asked his opinion on the silent black athlete. "I pray for them."

Every now and then, a few black athletes will show a crusading pulse. Etan Thomas, a forward with the Washington Wizards, used his voice and his proximity to the White House to protest the policies of George Bush, spoke at an antiwar rally, and published a book of socially relevant poems. In a guest column in the *Washington Post* in 2005, Thomas wrote, "There is simply too much going on to keep me silent. I have a voice and I have to use it. In the same way as Muhammad Ali, Bill Russell, Jim Brown, Tommie Smith and John Carlos used their positions as platforms, I feel obligated to speak out. All my life, my mother has told me: To whom much is given, much is expected."

But the general rule among black athletes is to be seen and not heard. Smith says the reason for what he calls "the passivication of the black athlete" is obvious enough.

"The road has been paved for these black athletes to become great financially," he said. "The social and political wars have been fought, and now, they have an avenue with no stop signs. Basically, we were their agents. We allowed them to make money, and now, it's much easier for them to make money and be quiet. There's too much at stake."

Michael Jordan illustrated this point on the medal stand at the 1992 Barcelona Olympics, where protest and the black athlete took an interesting turn. Just 24 years after Carlos and Smith raised a fist and spoke for those without a voice back home, Jordan struck a pose for the almighty dollar. When he draped an American flag over his shoulder to conceal the Reebok logo on his Dream Team warm-up, a strategy copied by fellow teammates and Nike pitchmen Scottie Pippen and Charles Barkley, the symbolism was just as striking as it was in 1968. As the undisputed endorsement king in sports, pre-Tiger Woods, Jordan was clearly protecting his interests. He was literally covering his own assets. For Jordan, money and image resonated just as strongly as racism did with

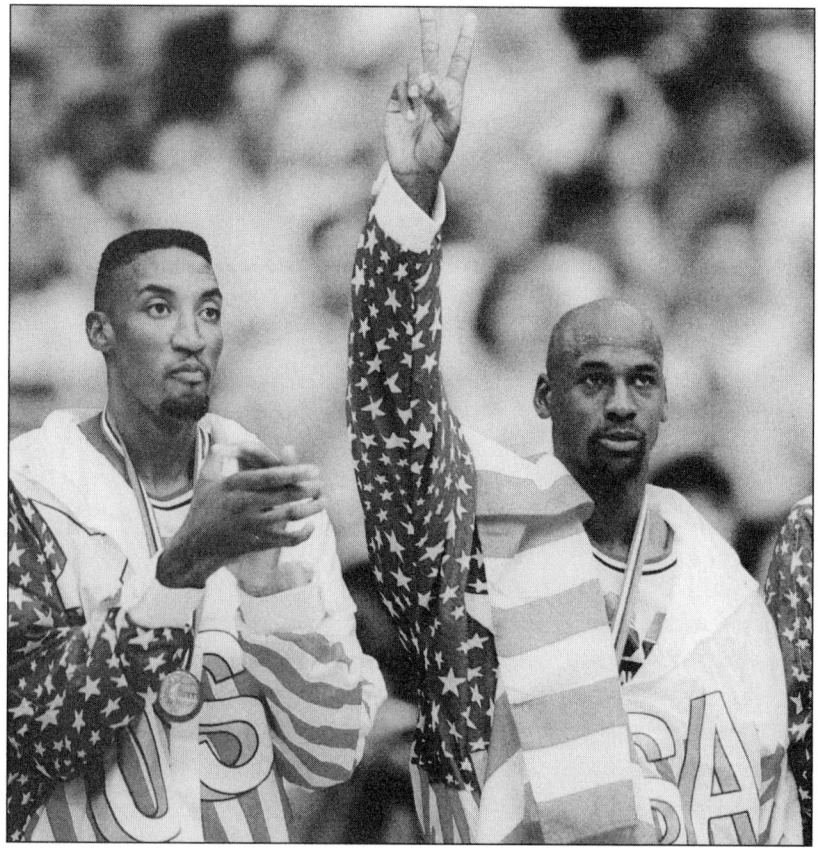

Mike Powell/Getty Images

Michael Jordan always kept his eye on the almighty dollar, which was supplied generously by Nike, the company that did not outfit the 1992 Olympic basketball team. Money made from endorsements has silenced many black athletes from speaking out about sensitive issues.

Carlos and Smith. But unlike Smith and Carlos, Jordan knew he wouldn't be accused of embarrassing his own country. True enough, he wasn't yanked off the podium and told to go home. He didn't receive anywhere near the flak that Smith and Carlos did when he arrived back in the States. Jordan did what 99 out of 100 Americans probably would have done.

No, Jordan wasn't going to throw away millions by using the Olympic platform to bring attention to sweat-shop conditions in Asia, where Nike products were made. Had he done so, his courage would have been applauded (and maybe his sanity questioned). But the greatest player in NBA history didn't need a fawning society to gush in awe of his courage; he already had tons of fans kneeling at his feet for what he did on the basketball court and how he carried himself away from it. Money and Nike clout, that's what Jordan needed. Therefore, throughout his career, Jordan did not commit financial suicide. He wasn't about to attack the establishment; hell, he was part of the establishment. So he continued serving as a slave to the swoosh and kept his mouth shut, speaking only when given the cue by Spike Lee in the Nike commercials.

Clearly, Jordan's method of activism wasn't with a clenched fist in the air but with a clenched fist full of money. His goal was to build as much capital for himself as possible, done mainly through endorsements, which represented the bulk of his fortune. And in order to get the endorsement money, Jordan had to be appealing to the masses, which ruled out any activism. That was considered too risky, too hot-button. With an equal mix of money and celebrity, Jordan had the right cocktail to empower himself and make his own rules. And it worked, because Jordan created the kind of wealth that no black athlete before him could comprehend, not even The Greatest. Remember, for all his magnetic appeal, Ali was forced to keep fighting as an ailing old man because he was just about flat broke. Then Ali spent much of his retirement as a sad mute, a walking museum piece for hire, partly because of Parkinson's and partly because he had no solid business plan in place during the prime of his career, when he blew his chance to make a ton in endorsements. That lesson was not lost on Jordan. He knew the golden rule: He who has the gold rules.

By selling his image to corporate America, though, Jordan wasted an enormous opportunity to lend his voice to great causes. That's because no black athlete in American history was equally welcomed in black and white households quite like Jordan. Even when illness left Ali in a crippled state and ironically rendered him speechless, he was still frowned upon in some unsympathetic corners of the country by those who'll always remember how he turned down Uncle Sam. But Jordan? Jordan was America's Guest in red and blue states alike. Jordan was nonthreatening, noncontroversial, and nonpolitical and in many ways didn't belong to one culture or another. Jordan wasn't a radical. Jordan made a movie with Bugs Bunny. Who wouldn't want to be like Mike? Who didn't like Mike?

Jordan knew the power of his voice, though; he wasn't that naïve. If Jordan took a public stand on a serious issue, he would have the media groveling at his feet and society cupping its ear, straining to listen. That's how much weight he carried in mainstream America during the prime of his career when he was dunking and winning championships. And yet Jordan recognized early on, even before we knighted him an icon, that it's probably safe to play it straight down the middle in public and thereby reap all the benefits of that, financial and otherwise. He also contributed, both publicly and privately, a great deal of money to charities, and while that doesn't necessarily fall under the umbrella of activism, he should and must receive tremendous applause for that. Still, the only time Jordan flashed a fighter's determination in public was the 1998-99 season in the labor battle between players and owners, or the haves and the have-mores. Otherwise, he refused any and every chance to lend his considerable name and public clout to any major cause. For example, if Jordan had a love for cute animals and nature, sorry, he wouldn't campaign to Save the Whales or even Hug a Tree. He had clearly made up his mind. The only aggressive stance he would take was against any fool who dared to guard him one on one.

"It's heavy duty to try to do everything and please everybody," Jordan explained in a *60 Minutes* interview conducted by Ed Bradley, who usually grills world leaders and corporate crooks but went soft with Jordan on the subject of activism.

Jordan even skipped a perfect chance to tee off against violence when it struck close to home. In the summer of 1993, while driving alone in rural North Carolina, a weary James Jordan pulled his white Lexus over and took a nap. Two young thugs with mayhem on their minds saw the shiny car sitting all alone, a diamond waiting to be heisted. They shot James Jordan dead in the chest, stole the car purchased through his son's wealth, made calls on his cell phone, and even ripped one of Jordan's championship rings off James Jordan's cold fingers.

You would think, then, that Michael Jordan finally had a cause that tugged at his heartstrings, a cause that every man and woman in America could relate to, a cause that absolutely no one would hold against him, a cause that might even result in a hefty spike in sales of Air Jordans had he taken an antiviolence stance in his next commercial. How many young men who idolized Jordan, especially those in gang-laced urban America, would have shed a tear, reached for their pistols, and thrown them in the river after listening to a plea to stop the violence from their emotional hero? How many potential lives might have been saved? How many other James Jordans would've been spared? But just as he did on the final possession of his spellbinding 55-point game in New York, the famous "double nickel" performance shortly after his return to basketball, Jordan decided to pass.

Say this about Jordan: He was no Craig Hodges. Not even close. In terms of basketball ability, these two men were on another planet, which wasn't that unusual, since Jordan really didn't have any peer and Hodges was a backup guard, barely over 6 feet tall with a gift only for shooting three-pointers. But in the game of activism and social causes, Hodges ran laps around Jordan, his former teammate with the Bulls. Hodges was never one to turn down an opportunity to vent, especially during the team's White House visit in 1992, when he famously handed the President a list of grievances that ultimately punched his own ticket out of the NBA for good.

Hodges was a Muslim who occasionally tried in vain to get his teammates to hear Louis Farrakhan. He went to the poorest communities in Chicago and held court with black kids, once saying he was "one of the few brothers" in the NBA who spoke up against racism and preached self-help to black communities. He was also the Bulls' representative to the player's union and constantly knocked the league for hiring practices. Amazingly, he was constantly warned by his black teammates, as well as other black players around the league, to "cool it." These same athletes, especially the famous ones, were taken to task by Hodges for their refusal to adopt the black community as a cause. This was largely considered a slap against Jordan.

Then came the White House visit, which Jordan curiously skipped to play golf. Hodges wore African garb and a dashiki and passed George H.W. Bush a handwritten note, asking the President to act more aggressively in matters regarding the black community. Word quickly reached Hodges that the Bulls as well as the NBA were embarrassed.

"I was speaking on behalf of poor people who didn't have the chance to meet the president," Hodges explained at the time. As for receiving any uneasy vibes from the Bulls' traveling party, Hodges did notice how "the black players were more uncomfortable than the white players."

The Bulls released him shortly after, although Hodges figured he'd simply find another team. He was 33 and his skills were clearly declining, but he still had enough of a touch from the three-point line to be used as a specialist off the bench. The careers of shooters usually last two or three more years compared to big men. When no NBA teams called, Hodges began to suspect the reason was deeper than his inability to play solid defense. He sued the NBA, charging a conspiracy to blackball him for being outspoken and a "rabble-rouser who posed a threat." In the lawsuit, Hodges anointed himself as someone who sought to slow "the breakdown of the African-American family" and once again knocked black athletes "who failed to use their considerable wealth and influence to assist the poor and disenfranchised."

The lawsuit was silly, really; sports owners don't conspire to do anything except make money. They had nothing against Hodges' beliefs, only his fading skills. Hodges had no proof of a conspiracy and therefore no case, which fizzled anyway when the two-year statute of limitations expired. Hodges never played again and didn't find steady work in the NBA until Phil Jackson, a rebel himself with a soft spot for activism, hired Hodges as a shooting coach with the Lakers. Not surprisingly, black athletes have steered as far away as possible from Hodges' example ever since. It makes you wonder if somebody whispered Hodges' name to Steelers linebacker Joey Porter.

After saying, "I've got something to tell Bush," before the 2006 Super Bowl champs paid a visit to the White House, Porter insisted he was only joking and backpedaled faster than a defensive back. Instead of going hard after the President, Porter saved his best punch for Bengals lineman Levi Jones when they tangled in a Las Vegas nightclub in 2007. It proved that there are plenty more Joey Porters in sports than Alis and Ashes and Hodgeses. Rather than address the needs of urban America and press those who hold the public's trust for change, some athletes today have decided to direct their venting elsewhere. They're more likely to lash out at coaches or teammates or fans or the media or anyone else who rubs them the wrong way. And others have confused acting foolishly with activism.

"What you have," said Harry Edwards, the Berkeley sociologist who inspired the Mexico City salute, "are certain athletes who are focused on themselves, who draw tremendous attention not necessarily to a greater cause, but to themselves."

The overall apathy toward serious social and political causes in and out of sports was intriguing to an NBA player who, by comparison with his black teammates, was from another world. True enough, Adonal Foyle, the center for the Golden State Warriors, is from a faraway land that most people can't spell or pronounce and probably never heard of, which is understandable. Canouan might even cause problems for MapQuest. It's an island in the Caribbean roughly the size of a salt crystal, the little brother of St. Vincent and the Grenadines. To say people in Canouan live simple lives would be an understatement; most are farmers, few have electricity, and only a fair number have outdoor toilets and kitchens. To say the residents of Canouan are kept uninformed by their isolation, however, would be wrong.

"Everyone listens to the news," said Foyle. "Everyone is very versed on local and international affairs, from the shop owners to the cab drivers. You have to be, because of the political system in the country. People want to know about their government so they're not left in the dark about matters that are important to them. If you didn't take care of political matters, it would come back to bite you."

Foyle was raised by his grandmother and an aunt, who grew peanuts. He mainly did chores in and around the house after school. He loved soccer, but he quickly grew too big and tall to play the sport very well against smaller and more nimble kids. He didn't touch a basketball until he turned 15, and just by chance, was playing in a local youth league when Jay and Joan Mandle, a white husband and wife team of college professors from the States, were on the island. They took notice of the friendly overgrown kid and were struck by his level of intelligence and curiosity and raw basketball ability. The Mandles asked permission to take Foyle back to America, where he might accelerate his basketball skills and perhaps gain a college scholarship. Foyle arrived and adapted well, both on the court and off. Because he didn't grow up in America, he wasn't spoiled by the system, which coddles teenagers who show special talent while ignoring their social and academic growth. After two years of high school, Foyle received offers from a number of good basketball schools.

But Foyle chose Colgate, a small liberal arts college not exactly known for flooding the professional sports leagues with star athletes, partly because the Mandles taught there and also because he was drawn to the academic climate, which challenged him. While he eventually graduated magna cum laude, his education at Colgate wasn't just limited to the classroom.

"Our dinners at home were interesting," Foyle said. "I couldn't get a word in at the table because my foster parents would invite other professors over and it would be one big debate hour. It's not like I wasn't invited to share my views. But you sit there, waiting for a chance to jump in, and those chances didn't come around much. Still, I learned to articulate what I wanted to say in an environment that wasn't hostile, but competitive."

Foyle did well enough in three years at Colgate to draw considerable attention from the NBA and was the eighth pick in the 1997 draft. Gradually, some of the suspicions held by wary scouts came true; the level of competition Foyle saw at Colgate hardly prepared him to become a star in the NBA. His offensive skills remained robotic, his rebounding numbers were mild for someone 6 feet, 10 inches, and only his defensive ability made him a functional player. Foyle received more respect for his intellect and passion for political reform, so much that his teammates called him "senator" and predicted his true calling would come away from the NBA.

He openly questioned the reasons for the Iraq War. He formed a group called Democracy Matters in an effort to jolt political awareness among young people and help them gain a voice in the political system. Oddly enough, a certain "other" group of young people, who played basketball for a living, who were blessed with a platform and a megaphone, chose not to use their voice. Foyle said he was "a little amused and annoyed" about the lack of an activism pulse in NBA locker rooms, until he took a closer inspection of the landscape and understood the reason for silence.

"They want to do good but don't have the tools," Foyle said. "They're not trained for anything by the time they get to this level. It's more of an issue of the culture we created. They haven't been in a situation where they learned how to make an argument. You're talking about guys who never even had a checking account before they came to the NBA. When an athlete is thrown on this stage and then asked to make an argument, well, it's hard to speak on an issue because you have to be well-versed, or you'll get destroyed in the public eye. That's just too much work for a lot of people, who don't think it's worth it."

Foyle wasn't trying to be holier than thou; he was merely stating fact. Jay and Joan Mandle, who had raised him since high school, were educated; many black athletes are raised by single mothers who never went to college. The Mandles were active in the Civil Rights and antiwar movements in the 1960s and handed their gift for awareness to Foyle. The average black athlete, meanwhile, was educated by deficient schools and grew up in a household where the parent was just trying to pay the rent.

Foyle expressed sympathy for Michael Jordan's corporate prison, but only to a point. "He was told along the way to 'have a squeaky clean image, play great basketball, and you'll become a millionaire. If you do this, you'll be successful. This is the American dream.' So you have to look at him in the social context," said Foyle. "Maybe we need to change our definition of 'making it.' For me, I've always known that I'm never going to have a lot of endorsements. But I'm always going to speak my mind. If that means I'm not going to be appealing to a lot of people, then so be it.

That's a decision that came out of the environment I was raised in, where people taught me to question everything or at least have an argument about it."

Foyle said he would speak his mind and reveal his beliefs even if he were an All-Star and blessed with endorsements. At the very least, Foyle would be on the cover of *Time* magazine if he were a star; this much is very clear. He'd be hailed as the black Bill Bradley. And if the Warriors ever won a championship, Foyle would salivate at the thought of receiving one of the perks given to all champions: the White House visit. Foyle insists he would not pull a Craig Hodges when given an audience with the President; at the same time, he wouldn't be Joey Porter, either. "He may not take me seriously, but I'd ask a question or two and make a statement," said Foyle. "Everyone has the responsibility to be involved in a democracy. Politics are not just for politicians. Everyone should be heard, including athletes."

That's certainly what Harry Edwards believed as soon as his young mind became more aware. From the start, Edwards tried to change the world's thinking, even if he couldn't change the world. He was one of eight kids and grew up in East St. Louis, Illinois, in the 1950s and '60s, raised by a father with an eighth-grade education who made $65 a week. While serving time in Joliet for burglary, Harry Sr. learned how to box. He gave his son a pair of boxing gloves at age three and told him boxing was the only way a black man could get respect in white America. Edwards eventually gravitated to football and basketball and as a teenager joined the first group of black students to integrate East Side, the all-white high school in town. There, Edwards first felt the sting of racism and felt the tug of activism.

"My father always pushed Joe Louis and Jackie Robinson as examples of what we can do and what we can be if we demonstrate how we can perform with anybody else," he said. "When I went to East Side, I found that this wasn't the case. When you were on the field, you were in one world. Once you left the field, it was something different altogether. You were just like the janitor. A Negro was a Negro was a Negro. That's when I began to wake up. I saw an all-white faculty and an all-white coaching staff and an all-white administration, and they didn't know how to deal with Negroes. I got a right hook to the chops at 13. By the time I left, I was angry about a lot of things."

He went to Fresno City College, then San Jose State. It was purely by coincidence that Edwards landed in the Bay area in the '60s, where activism and free speech converged. Fueled by discrimination and a desire to create change, he shook up the San Jose State campus in 1967 when, as a part-time teacher, he approached the administration on behalf of black students and athletes with a list of grievances. Edwards charged the university with practicing housing discrimination and dragging its feet on hiring black faculty members and recruiting black students. If their demands weren't met, Edwards told the university, the football season opener would be disrupted.

The opener was canceled, and Edwards swiftly became a voice to be heard in the collegiate sports community. He wore black shades and a black leather jacket, which scared the hell out of some people and made others listen. He constantly approached athletes from other schools in an effort to roust their support for a national movement. He successfully encouraged black athletes not to compete at a track meet held at Madison Square Garden sponsored by the New York Athletic Club, which Edwards cited for discriminatory practices. He fought other causes with Stokely Carmichael and H. Rap Brown and soon joined them on the FBI's list of troublemakers and potential threats to society. Back in East St. Louis, his father was sure Edwards would return home in a body bag.

With the feds constantly monitoring him by now, Edwards called for a black boycott of the Mexico City Olympics in '68. That same year, a watershed moment for black America, the country endured a long, hot summer, with riots in all the major cities as a response to the

murder of Martin Luther King Jr. and pent-up animos-
ity toward a country that had been dragging its feet on
issues regarding equality. The U.S. Olympic Committee
made it clear that Edwards was not invited to Mexico City
and was not to infiltrate the athletes' village. Plus, his
confidants warned him against making the trip, out of
fear for his safety. No matter; in his absence, his message
was delivered in black-gloved, two-fisted style, famously
raised by John Carlos and Tommie Smith, a pair of San
Jose State sprinters, on the victory stand.

At the time, the salute was met with tremendous outrage within the Olympic community and parts of America,
but over time the protest burned itself into a respectable
place in history. In a curious twist, some 35 years later,
San Jose State honored Smith and Carlos by recaptur-
ing the victory stand salute with twin statues placed on
campus. As for Edwards, he weighed tryout offers from
the Minnesota Vikings and San Diego Chargers against
a full scholarship ride to Cornell.

"There was a white lineman from San Jose State who
played for the Dallas Cowboys," said Edwards. "He came
back to campus during the off-season to get some rehab.
He said, 'Harry, I see the way black guys are treated in
this league. They're treated like dogs. If I had what you
have going for you, with your intellectual ability, I would
go to Cornell and never look back.' And this was a white
guy saying this."

Edwards went the intellectual route and spent his
sports career as a deep-thinking, fiery-speaking sociologist from his base as a professor at Berkeley. Curiously,
the same establishments that came under fierce attack
by Edwards began to lean on him to enforce change
within their own walls. Bill Walsh brought him to the
49ers during their Super Bowl dynasty to counsel players. Major League baseball sought his advice, and he
heard a calling in the NCAA, where black athletes are
many but black coaches and athletic directors are few.
And he racked up frequent flier miles through speaking

engagements across the country. The establishment was basically telling Edwards he was right all along.

Another forecast by Edwards also seems to be deadly accurate. Just before the turn of the century, he noticed a trend in sports and concluded that the golden age of black participation was over. The rapid and stark decline of American blacks in baseball, Latinos emerging as the dominant ethnic group in boxing, and an influx of European players into the NBA told him so. And the reasons lie in a shift within the black community.

"We are in a diminishing age of black athletic involvement," said Edwards. "We are disqualifying our potential athletes. The black working class has always produced the athletes, not the underclass, which tended to send kids to the military or jail. The working class was stable enough to keep their kids in school. But with globalization and technology eliminating jobs, the working class began pushing into the lower class. When that happened, the athletes would not be in school but on the street, trading team colors for gang colors, especially with the elimination of the military draft. So what institutions pick them up? The jails do. The collapse of the working class has resulted in a diminishing of the athletic pool. More potential players have ended up in jail or the cemetery, confined to the trash bin of American society."

Those who argue that a reduction of blacks in sports might be a good thing are missing the point, Edwards said. Any time an avenue to employment is pinched or closed, it's never good for black society. Especially because, in many instances, black teenagers who compete in athletics become the first from their families to attend college and get a degree.

These are issues that could and maybe should have the voice of a prominent black athlete, but today, he is mostly the silent type. When he talks, he usually isn't saying much, at least nothing of significance. That's why there's a generational detachment in the black athletic community, with the new athlete barely knowing, or caring about, those who suffered before him.

The mantle of leadership and activism is a heavy one; not everyone is qualified, not everyone can articulate such concerns or possess the charisma to pull it off, and not everyone is willing to put themselves on the line. So what does this bode for the future of sports and activism? Well, the one most likely to offer a refreshing twist is Joakim Noah, son of tennis great Yannick Noah, who refused to follow the hushed athletic crowd during his outspoken college days at Florida. Born to a father of Cameroon and French blood and a mother of Swedish ancestry, Noah understandably emerged as a worldly thinker at a young age. That alone set him apart from the usual American athletes of color. At Florida, he earned a reputation as a rebel and eagerly took the Bush administration to task regarding the Iraq War and the response to Hurricane Katrina. Now that he's free from overly protective college administrators, and if he feels compelled, Noah should be even more outspoken with regard to world and social issues, and he has the opportunity to be a modern-day trailblazer in that regard.

An NBA journeyman became an unlikely activist leader in 2007 when Ira Newble adopted Darfur as a cause. The region in Sudan, gripped by conflict, has suffered over half a million deaths. A number of governments have classified it as genocide. Newble was so disturbed by the horrors that he created a letter, addressed to China, which did big business with the Sudanese government. The letter was a plea to China, which hosts the 2008 Olympic Games in Beijing, to help end the destruction in Darfur. Then Newble rounded up his Cleveland Cavaliers teammates in the spring of 2007 and asked them to sign the letter.

Most players did, with one interesting omission. LeBron James said he needed "time" to study the situation more closely, but it should be said that James, as a Nike pitchman, did big business in China and, clearly, there was a conflict. If business indeed kept James from endorsing the movement, then once again, a heavily-endorsed superstar athlete put money ahead of his convictions.

Magic Johnson has intentionally targeted urban America for his thriving businesses, which is not only an admirable effort, but a smart and profitable one as well. He brought movie theaters and coffee shops to places that historically never had either. He has also been an advocate for finding medical advances to cure the virus that causes AIDS, a cause that, unfortunately, is very personal to him. One day, Magic might be remembered almost as much for his social consciousness as for his basketball ability. Knowing him as I do, after covering him for half his career, I know he would be enormously pleased with that.

The heartfelt effort by NFL running back Warrick Dunn to bring stability into the lives of single mothers can also be considered activism to an extent. Dunn operates more

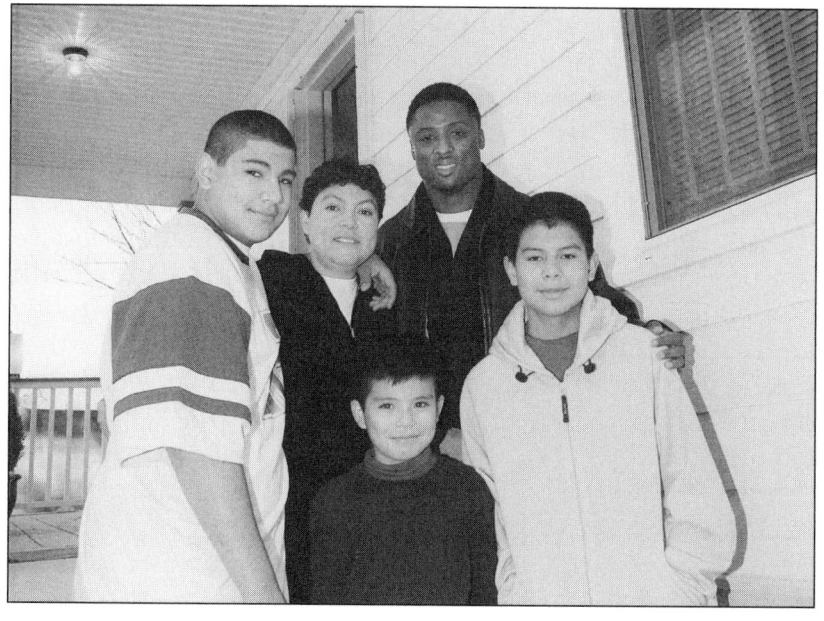

Photo by John Curry

Warrick Dunn, shown helping a single mother and her children, is one of the more giving professional athletes and is regarded as a saint by single mothers, who have received brand new homes courtesy of the generous NFL player.

through his deeds than words by building homes for such mothers, and his charity hits close to home; he was raised by a single mother himself. Dunn's work is certainly commendable, but he could take it even a step further by educating young black women on the importance of making better choices when it comes to partners, and by showing young black men the destruction they cause by impregnating women and having children before they're mature enough to be fathers and secure enough to support a family. This way, Dunn's cause would address the root of the problem of single parenting, not just the problem itself.

Anyway, Tommie Smith said he is rarely approached by a black athlete today and besides, he says, any conversation probably would be awkward. "What are we going to talk about?" Smith said, not with bitterness, but with sadness. "Their education? Eight out of ten don't have one beyond high school. Sports? The issues? I know what's inside of them, and I know what was inside us, and it's different. The pride of the man is different."

Any concerns about the plight of the black community and racism are being voiced almost exclusively by Smith, Carlos, Edwards, a few sports sociologists, a smattering of media people, and every once in a while, a lonely cry in the wilderness from the rare black athlete who chooses to speak out on issues. Otherwise, muffled by wealth and softened by a fawning society, black athletes today share a common role model and mentor. They'd rather not be like Tommie Smith or John Carlos. They'd rather be like Mike.

CHAPTER 3

Home Is the City

Metro Dares and Small-Town Stares

Every year my family takes a ski trip to Utah, and every time we reach the slopes, we get the same greeting. People stare. Not for long. Not with the same intensity Beyoncé might get if she walked into a frat house. But people stare. They stared the first time we went, and they stared the last time. Some visits had more stares than others. In that microsecond or two when the eyes of white strangers tattooed us for no other apparent reason, we knew exactly what was being processed in their brains. We knew how we stood out to them, black skin against white snow and standing in an all-white line at the chair lift. We knew they wondered if we took a wrong turn in Denver. We knew we were aliens to them.

It's more amusing than offensive. Any black person who ventures into remote areas of the country has stories to tell. Our most extreme fish-out-of-water tale happened back in 1989 on a hiking trip to Glacier National Park in Montana, where a startled middle-aged white woman came upon my wife on a trail and suddenly felt the need to approach. "Well," said the lady, eyes wide, expressing shock. "I have never seen a black person at this park before."

That same year, while working as a reporter from Miami and attending a Utah Jazz game in Salt Lake City, I stayed at the same hotel as the visiting team, the Miami Heat. After I stepped off the elevator and into the lobby, a small group of autograph-seeking kids studied my face closely and then began shuffling their basketball cards, looking for a match. Obviously, it never dawned on them that I might be a salesman from Chicago. Those local kids, who probably went days without seeing a black person, just assumed.

You couldn't fault them. Salt Lake City is one of two professional sports towns (Green Bay the other) with the smallest amount of blacks living in the area. The black population in the entire state of Utah is less than 1 percent, and blacks are less than 2 percent of greater Salt Lake. The 2000 census put Green Bay's black population at 1.4 percent. Most whites in those towns don't see many blacks or live next door to blacks or work with blacks. Their kids don't attend school with many black kids. Thus, their attitudes about race are shaped partly, if not mostly, by what they absorb from secondary sources, such as TV, movies, pop culture, music, and finally, sports. Definitely sports.

Whatever biases or ignorance these whites might harbor toward blacks gets tucked away when it comes to the Jazz and Packers, two teams smothered with love. But let us define love as it relates to sports. Love is purely conditional, and the condition is that the teams win and the players score touchdowns and hit jump shots or home runs. In Salt Lake and Green Bay, the most racially homogenous cities in professional sports, the local population professes their conditional love in gushing doses, without regard to a player's color or background. The small town does tend to enjoy a more intimate relationship with its sports teams and players than that of the large city, mainly because these towns have entire identities tied to "their team." What would Green Bay be without the Packers? With few other entertainment options, going to a game becomes a major social event on the calendar.

The team enjoys a special status. The players are godlike, almost mythical figures who have rose petals tossed at their feet by adoring and star-struck fans.

All this makes for an interesting case study in racial attitudes. The people in these overwhelmingly white towns, who would probably cast a wary eye toward some of the ordinary black citizens, suddenly are the most colorblind people on Earth when it comes to their black athletes. A player such as Reggie White, for instance, never saw a Packer fan who didn't love him. But there always seems to be a catch. The small-town teams also tend to have a fair number of white players, sometimes

Photo courtesy of the Milwaukee Journal Sentinel.

Reggie White at a press conference announcing his choice of Green Bay over several other NFL cities as a free agent in 1993. White became such an admired force on the field, in the locker room, and throughout the community that the Packers retired his jersey in 2005, only the fifth player in the storied franchise's history to receive that honor.

more than most other teams, raising the suspicion that management tries to appease the ticket-buying fan base whenever possible. And those white players are promoted to the hilt. Brett Favre, for example, is viewed as the Greatest Packer Ever based on the degree of love shown him by the media and local fans, and yet if you ask black NFL players, Favre is the most overhyped Packer ever. He has one less Super Bowl ring than Willie Davis. And any misbehavior by a black athlete often weighs heavier in smaller cities, where tolerance has its limits.

No small-market team in professional sports has suffered from an image problem as severely as the Portland Trail Blazers over the last few years. The city of Portland, Oregon, developed a fondness for its NBA team almost from the franchise's birth in 1970. Long considered a refuge for hippies and flower-power children of the '60s, Portland was unusually liberal for a city of its size and location in the Northwest—so much that a good many black players from the '70s continued to live in Portland long after their careers ended. The love affair for the basketball team was strong and devoted. The community felt a connection with the Blazers, and the city's identity was tied to the team. It helped that the Blazers in their championship era had Bill Walton, a white marquee player, along with a handful of white role players often described as "smart" and "crafty" and "hard working," the buzz words usually associated with white players who lack tremendous talent. But Maurice Lucas and Lionel Hollins and other black players were revered just as well. Later, even though the Blazers lacked a white star in the '90s, the same amount of respect was extended to Clyde Drexler, Jerome Kersey, and Terry Porter.

However, Drexler, Kersey, and Porter were professional, sociable, and approachable and mainly free of controversy. And they won. That formula was not followed by their successors. The best player was suddenly Rasheed Wallace, who was paranoid, antisocial, and distrustful in public, along with being famously whiny and quick tempered with the referees. He also was busted for weed, as was Damon Stoudamire, the local kid who had a mostly unhappy and unproductive homecoming after he arrived from Toronto. Darius Miles was young and immature; Ruben Patterson came to Portland carrying a sex rap from his days in Seattle; and Zach Randolph had frequent run-ins with the law. The Blazers also struggled to win. Fed up with the thug behavior by their heroes, annoyed by the losing, and disconnected from the team they once knew as being the soul of the community, the fans began tuning out the Blazers, who played before sparse home crowds.

Because of the depressing lack of a cultural connection with these types of towns, many black players hardly crave working in small markets, or Hootervilles. The small-market city suffers in any popularity contest under most conditions, but the racial stigma goes deeper in Salt Lake and Green Bay, especially Salt Lake. A 2006 *Sports Illustrated* survey of 248 NBA players revealed the Jazz as the team they'd least like to play for, by a wide margin. Well, the reason couldn't be that the franchise was a hapless loser or fraught with instability, because the Jazz hold the NBA record for consecutive playoff appearances with 20 straight and changed coaches only twice in a quarter-century. Basically, the reason is cultural and racial. The heavy-handed influence of the LDS Church and its racist history, the lack of a social life, and the overwhelming whiteness simply doesn't appeal to black players, especially younger ones. And those concerns are seconded by black wives of NBA players; more than a few have cried upon learning the news that their families were headed to Salt Lake. As Derek Harper, the former Dallas Mavericks guard, explained when he nixed a trade, "You go live in Utah."

"Players struggle with it even now," said Ron Boone, who played for the Utah Stars of the ABA and serves as a TV analyst for the Jazz. "They don't want to make the adjustment, even though, when you think about it, you're in the city for only a certain number of days during the season, with all the travel."

We're all creatures of habit, and just as some whites might initially feel uneasy about being surrounded by a large number of blacks, the same is true vice versa. Believe me, if Salt Lake had the same demographic as Atlanta, but without the perennial futility and growing pains suffered yearly by the Hawks, Utah would be top 10 on the NBA players' wish list. "When you look at where most of these players grew up, in the inner city, it becomes understandable why there's a hesitancy to play for the Jazz," said Thurl Bailey, who played nine seasons in Utah. "We like to be around people that are most like us."

Curiously, the Jazz franchise was created in 1974 in New Orleans, which was (and remains) overwhelmingly black, the polar opposite of their present home. Even then, racial politics were hard at work. Before the first season began, the owners had the good sense to trade for Pete Maravich, the floppy-socked basketball wizard who played college ball up the road at LSU. Most important, Maravich was the flashy white star that many NBA teams craved in the 1970s, when the complexion of the NBA began to darken and owners started to worry about the league's image. Maravich gave the Jazz everything they wanted; he scored in bunches, made fancy passes, and drew fans to the Superdome. He just couldn't help the team win. The Jazz lost the first 11 games and never played .500 ball in New Orleans.

The team was badly mismanaged, both business-wise and basketball-wise. There always seemed to be cash-flow issues. Truck Robinson, their star power forward, was essentially sold. This was also a franchise that drafted a woman, obviously as a gimmick, only to later learn that Lucy Harris was pregnant. Barry Mendelson, the team's promotions guy, became the general manager, and his signature personnel move was surrenduring a number 1 pick to the Lakers for an aging Gail Goodrich, another white shooter. That number 1 pick became Magic Johnson. Sensing financial doom in New Orleans, and smelling the untapped potential of Salt Lake City, owner Sam Battistone, who also happened to be Mormon, hastily moved the team in 1979 to the smallest market in the country.

Battistone had other business interests in and around Salt Lake, too. He was the cofounder of Sambo's, a popular family restaurant chain with a name you wouldn't holler in a roomful of angry black people. Sambo was a children's book written in 1899 by Helen Bannerman, who centered her story around a boy in India. The dark-skinned boy ventures into the jungle, becomes victimized by man-eating tigers, who then turn to butter and are used by the boy on his pancakes. Decades later, Battistone and his business partner, Newell Bohnett, opened a restaurant in California in the '50s and agreed to name it Sambo's, a take on Battistone's first name and "Bo," the nickname for Bohnett. Sam-Bo. But by then, Bannerman's book had been Americanized, and the dark Indian boy became a black boy. The *Little Black Sambo* book series was a hit in the States in the 1930s and '40s until civil rights groups finally and rightfully made a stink about the insulting and degrading images, which were being absorbed by innocent kids.

That didn't faze Battistone, who either didn't care about the complaints or wasn't sensitive to them. The walls of some restaurants were filled with drawings of the Indian boy and tigers. Battistone kept the name and saw the chain grow to 1,200 stores right around the time the Jazz moved from New Orleans. Thankfully, the chain soon collapsed, partly due to competition, but also to political correctness, according to industry experts. The restaurant business was only slightly better than the basketball business for Battistone. Shortly after moving to Salt Lake, the Jazz once again needed cash. The financial straits of the franchise were revealed when they drafted and then sold Dominique Wilkins to the Hawks. Battistone eventually bailed and sold the Jazz to Larry Miller.

Salt Lake City wasn't exactly some backwater town when it came to basketball and black players. The Utah Stars of the old ABA were fondly embraced in the early 1970s, and most of the large universities throughout the Rockies integrated their sports teams long before schools in the Deep South. Still, the racial tolerance of Salt Lake City was put to the test almost immediately by the Jazz. Early in their first season in Utah, the Jazz cut Maravich, who was hobbling with a bad knee and had nothing left. They replaced him with Adrian Dantley, obtained from the Lakers, who scored as much as Maravich did but offered none of Maravich's flair. Dantley was also black, as was Ron Boone, a holdover from the old Utah Stars of the ABA, and Bernard King, a troubled scorer from Brooklyn. In theory, a new team in a new town with no other professional team and scarcely few entertainment options could expect brisk business, even if the team was a loser on the court.

But that wasn't the case in Salt Lake. There was no crush at the turnstiles. There was no honeymoon period. The first year attendance averaged 7,821, among the lowest in the league, and that number was inflated by giveaways. The next season, attendance dropped to 7,508, despite the addition of Darrell Griffith, the exciting college basketball player of the year from Louisville, where he won a national title. Attendance rose only slightly to 7,655 the following season and 8,679 in 1982-83. In those four years, the Jazz played to roughly 60 percent capacity at the Salt Palace arena, and while they averaged only 27 wins a season over that time, which was a big issue, they also had no white stars. That undoubtedly was an issue, too. Whether a virtually all-white town would embrace a mostly black team, especially one that didn't win much, became a legitimate concern. The overall apathy toward the NBA at that time wasn't just a Salt Lake phenomenon, however; the new commissioner, David Stern, even wondered if the waning public interest was caused by a league considered to be "too black and too drug infested."

That was a curious choice of words by Stern, because they summed up the early years of the Jazz. In the team's first season in Salt Lake, on New Year's Day, police barged into Bernard King's apartment and slapped him with five felony sex charges. They also found drugs in his apartment, which really wasn't much of a surprise; King had been dogged by marijuana use stemming back to his college days at Tennessee, and a haze of rumored drug use followed him into the NBA. But the felony sex charges hit the Salt Lake community like a June blizzard. Suddenly, every white parent's greatest fear regarding black men was realized. According to a local white woman, King asked her to his apartment, then forced her to perform various sexual acts. Already dealing with losing games and sparse attendance, the Jazz were in no mood to give him a second chance. There was too much at stake. They immediately cut ties with King, even after the charges were reduced and he pled guilty to attempted forcible sexual abuse, a misdemeanor. He never played another game for the Jazz, and that fall they traded him to Golden State for backup center and second-round pick Wayne Cooper, a measly return for someone like King who was usually good for 22 points a night.

Five months after King's arrest, another black Jazz player, Terry Furlow, died in a car accident, and cocaine was found in his system. Then in 1982, John Drew, a player the Jazz received in return for Dominique Wilkins, went into rehab, the start of a downward drug spiral for him. Drew had been constantly monitored by the Hawks regarding his rumored drug use, and the Jazz suspected Drew was dirty when they gave up Wilkins. But Battistone needed the cash that came in the deal, so it was done.

The less controversial black Jazz players from the early days were mostly welcomed in and around Salt Lake by white fans, who couldn't resist the powerful pull of celebrity when confronted by it. Dantley was embraced by his suburban neighbors the day he moved next door. He was constantly approached on the street, which hardly caught him by surprise; after all, he was black and tall and tended to stand out. The Salt Lake demographics didn't bother Dantley. He was born in Washington, D.C., but attended mostly white DeMatha High School, a basketball power in the Maryland suburbs. Then he played college ball at Notre Dame. "I was prepared for Utah, you could say," said Dantley.

That wasn't the case for most of his black teammates, especially Darrell Griffith, raised in a black section of Louisville before going to an urban university. Griffith remembers traveling to Salt Lake for a game during his senior year at Louisville, and while eating dinner, telling his teammates, "I never want to come back to this place." He said it mainly because Louisville lost the game and slipped in the national ranking, but also because Salt Lake was a different world. A few months after he was drafted by the Jazz, Griffith saw a black man park at a downtown convenience store. Griffith ran up to him, excitedly struck up a conversation with the stranger, and asked where the black people hung out. The man shook his head. "Bruh, I'm just passing through and getting some gas," he said, before driving off in his Seville with California plates.

In the first few years, the players knew of only one man, named Billy, who cut black hair; and a church group from Indianapolis ran the city's only soul food restaurant, where the local black players and the visiting players felt welcomed. The visiting players always made it clear to Griffith and Dantley that they never wanted to be their teammates. The idea of being traded to Utah sent a chill through many black players around the league. "You just had to see the expression on Dominique Wilkins' face when we drafted him," said Griffith. "And then again when we announced we were trading him to Atlanta." It was even more frightful for the black wives of players, who also had hair issues, shared little in common with potential white female friends, and constantly worried about sending their kids to all-white schools.

Griffith grew to love playing in Utah, where he was always greeted warmly, in stores, at gas stations, and at the mall. Of course, he knew the deal. "As ballplayers," he said, "we're viewed differently. People want to see us and talk to us."

Another player fresh off a national championship college basketball team arrived in 1983, and Thurl Bailey would not have as rough a transition as Griffith. Bailey was indeed from a poor Washington, D.C., family, but he escaped the usual trappings that claimed other boys. He was bused to a more racially mixed school and took steps to ensure he would not be your typical basketball-playing kid from the ghetto. He performed in the school band and sang in the choir. He made the National Honor Society, counted as many white friends as black, and became the first black kid at the school to be voted student body president. He was also popular on the North Carolina State campus, where he mingled with all students, not just the athletes. "Once I got to Utah," Bailey said, "I was open to learning about my surroundings. I wasn't closed to anything."

Of course, there's still the culture shock associated with a black athlete arriving in Utah, and it was no different with Bailey. Every morning, he took the same route from home to basketball practice, and every morning he'd see the same two or three black people on their way to work, which made him feel like Bill Murray in *Groundhog Day*. Much more grounded than the average professional athlete, Bailey mingled with the locals and made friends with some of the few blacks in Salt Lake. He knew, as a Jazz player, that he lived in a different world, where celebrity trumps everything else, where the red-carpet welcome he received from white strangers was certainly different from that given to the average black person.

"I never sensed there were any serious racial problems suffered by other African Americans, mainly because there weren't many blacks," said Bailey. "But some of the ones I've gotten to know have felt it, mostly through racial profiling, getting pulled over for no apparent reason, things like that."

Bailey was immune from those life hassles in Salt Lake, partly because he was an upstanding citizen, but mostly because he was a rich and famous Jazz player. In addition to making the NBA all-rookie team and being a quality player for the Jazz, Bailey became a magnet in the Salt Lake community, frequently making hospital appearances, giving speeches to high schools, and going beyond the usual number of public appearances that players are required to make. In a franchise known for stability, Bailey fit right in; he loved playing for the Jazz and living in Utah and, like most black athletes, living in a world where his color rarely, if ever, became an issue.

While holding his annual basketball camp late in his career, Bailey became friendly with a Utah woman named Sindi, who was raised on a ranch in the country and came from a strict Mormon family. She had no black friends and rarely even saw black people for much of her life, which wasn't too unusual for most in Utah. They began seeing each other, and when their relationship took a serious turn, that's when the Teflon coat of celebrity was stripped away from Bailey. For the first time since becoming a professional basketball player, he became an ordinary black man in a suspicious white society.

Sindi's parents drew the line. They made it clear they didn't approve of Bailey. Her mother was so troubled by the relationship that she stopped speaking to her daughter. And there would be no contact between the parents and Bailey. Suddenly, the hospital trips and high school speeches and tireless charity work and his NBA citizenship award didn't matter. In every which way, Bailey displayed the values and personality and character that would easily win over the parents of any daughter. But Bailey was a black man, and you can imagine how many white parents, especially those in overwhelmingly white cities and towns, will never look past that.

Bailey was troubled by this and began writing heartfelt letters to Sindi's mother, Sue. He begged for a chance, asking the family to meet him and get to know him before passing judgment. "I was hoping she was a Jazz fan," Bailey said. "So in my early letters, I played up my basket-

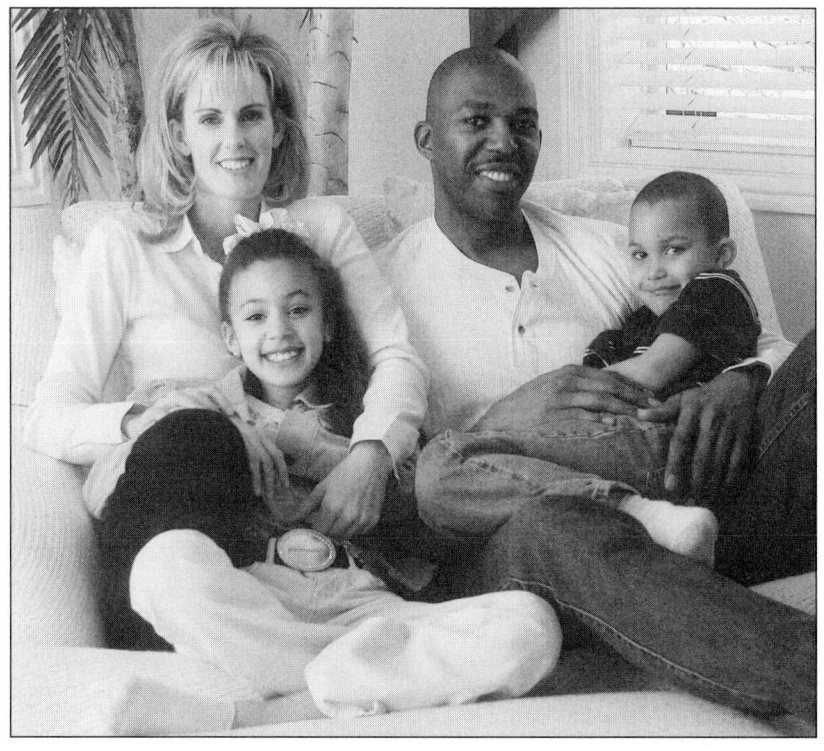

Deseret Morning News

Thurl Bailey made the transition to Utah more smoothly than many black athletes, despite a few negative incidents, including initial rejection by his wife Sindi's family.

ball career. I said, 'This is who I am and how many points I scored.' I hoped these letters would break the ice, but it didn't happen. Then I began to talk about myself and who I was and how strongly I felt about their daughter. This is a family-oriented place, and I knew how important that was to many people. And I still didn't hear back from them. Everything on my end was exhausted."

Bailey even drove up to the house on a whim but was stopped at the door and told not to bother; nobody wanted to see him. Sindi insisted her parents would eventually come around, but he began to weaken and wonder if their relationship was worth the trouble. He thought back to his childhood, in D.C., where whites live near blacks and work with blacks, and to his high school, where a mostly white student body judged him on his character when they voted him president. "A lot of people in Utah have only been in Utah," Bailey said. "We're afraid of what we don't know and don't understand. We go on stereotypes and hearsay. We don't go outside of that. My parents were at the Monument when Martin Luther King made his speech. But they never came home with a negative word about white people. They wanted us to treat people like we wanted to be treated."

Bailey married Sindi without the approval of her parents. He also made another life-altering decision. Nearing the end of his professional career, he played in Italy, and while there, he decided to convert to the Church of Jesus Christ of Latter-day Saints. It was a spiritual awakening for him and also gave him a firmer connection with Sindi. As for the other connection, between Bailey and the LDS church, that was even stranger. Black faces are extremely rare in the church, which until recently held a racist attitude toward blacks. It was long believed by the church that blacks received their dark skin as a curse from God. The church founder, Brigham Young, ruled that "no person having the least particle of Negro blood can hold the priesthood." In 1954, during a speech at BYU, Mormon elder Mark E. Peterson said: "We are willing that the Negro have the highest education. I would be willing to let the Negro drive a Cadillac if they could afford it. I would be willing that they have all the advantages they can get out of life in the world. But let them enjoy these things among themselves. I think the Lord segregated the Negro. [However] if a Negro is faithful all his days, he can and will enter the celestial kingdom. He will go as a servant, but he will get his celestial glory."

Eventually, as times changed in society, so did the church. And this change was forced in part through pressure provided by sports. In the late 1960s, teams from other universities threatened to cancel events at BYU because the church refused to distance itself from comments made by its leaders and still barred blacks from entering the priesthood. And BYU, which took massive pride in its sports teams, especially the football team, stood little to no chance of recruiting black athletes, who began to change the face of college athletics and strengthened Division I football programs around that time. Predictably enough, in 1978 the LDS church received this update from God: "All worthy male members of the church may be ordained to the priesthood, without regard for race or color."

The arrival of the Baileys' two children, BreElle and Brendan, began to melt away any sensitive feelings between Sindi's family and Bailey. Three years after she rejected him, Sindi's mother dealt with a lot of guilt once she got to know her son-in-law. She saw how he was an in-demand motivational speaker, a recording artist who performed with the Utah Symphony, a businessman with diversified interests, a frequent speaker at fireside conferences during church services on Sunday, and how he treated her daughter. She began to apologize constantly, writing the same emotional letters that Bailey once sent her, although Bailey didn't think it was necessary and never held a grudge. He understood. "She had to get past the stereotypes," Bailey said. "She only knew about us from what she heard and what she suspected. She wasn't the only one who learned from this. It taught me about forgiveness and tolerance. And it also gave me two of the greatest grandparents my kids could ever have. I love both of Sindi's parents to death."

Sindi's mother was hardly the only person who had to overcome the sight of a black husband and white wife. While vacationing in Las Vegas, the Baileys went to a food court in a shopping mall. While getting food, Bailey noticed a small group of black women, who noticed him. They exchanged smiles and hellos. Then the pleasantries disappeared. "When they realized I was with this white girl, things changed," Bailey said. "All of a sudden, I wasn't this tall, nice, well-mannered black guy."

On their way to their table, one of the women in the group walked by the Baileys' table, said something to Sindi, and kicked her chair. When Bailey returned, Sindi said nothing, but Bailey noticed something was wrong. The mood of his family had changed. Finally, Brendan, their son, told his father what happened. "My heart dropped to my chest," said Bailey. "On one hand, I knew why this happened. I knew why they felt this way, but I think they crossed the line when they invaded my personal space."

He walked over to the group of women and demanded answers. He lectured them on their childish behavior and their beliefs, and then he noticed that one of the women was a mother. "Is this how you treat your children? Is this how you raise them?" he asked her. He began to leave, but then took the cup of drink in his hand, poured it on the woman who kicked Sindi's chair and said, "Next time you do that, somebody might have a gun. Just be thankful this is a drink."

Bailey has never forgotten the episode, for a few reasons. One, it was out of character for him, but he felt he needed to take a stand, in the name of his family. Two, it proved to him that people of all colors and backgrounds have their own prejudices, not just whites. And, finally, it gave him something to discuss and rail against when speaking with groups about bigotry and bias and the importance of judging character over color.

"I'm proud of my black heritage, and I make sure my kids are proud of theirs," Bailey said. "I'm encouraged that our future generations will become better when dealing with this. My kids are special because they have the best of both worlds."

The real litmus test for basketball and Utah arrived in the form of a burly country boy from Louisiana named Karl Malone. Rather than recoil at the thought of starting his career in Utah, Malone, like Bailey, liked the idea almost immediately. He was uncomfortable in big cities. The easy pace and outdoorsy feel of Salt Lake and the nearby Wasatch Mountains agreed with Malone, and when he quickly became a star, Salt Lake agreed with him. At first he spent his off-seasons in Dallas, but eventually Malone became one of the few black Jazz players to live year-round in Salt Lake. He evolved into a black Paul Bunyan, larger than life, elevated to icon status by a white community that couldn't get enough of the Mailman.

This amused many black players around the league, who couldn't comprehend the level of love given to Malone in Salt Lake. It made Malone an outcast of sorts among black players. Malone wasn't one of them. He didn't dress the way they dressed; he loved country music, 10-gallon hats, belt buckles, and cowboy boots. He had very few black friends on other teams, and he adored Salt Lake. More than a few black players would joke how Utah stripped Malone of his identity, once again buying into the notion that all black people must follow a specific guidebook. After a brief scuffle with Malone on the court, for example, Nets forward Derrick Coleman called Malone an "Uncle Tom." Many things are said in the heat of battle, but the Uncle Tom comment was a first and was clearly meant to mock Malone's connection with Salt Lake. Coleman, you suspect, would not have said that to Moses Malone.

"Karl embraced Utah, and Utah embraced him," said Bailey. "There probably aren't that many black superstar players who could've done that."

The ascent by Malone to All-Stardom coincided with the rise in popularity of the Jazz in Salt Lake, but this process had help. The Jazz began to win, and they also began to whiten. John Stockton quickly became one of the best passing point guards in NBA history and made a career-long connection with Malone. The Jazz also had Mark Eaton, a lumbering, clumsy center whose ability to block shots prevented him from becoming a car mechanic, the career he figured he'd have when he left UCLA. Bobby Hansen and Kelly Tripucka assumed major roles, followed by Jeff Hornacek, and the Jazz bench stayed stocked with white players. The team moved to a new home, and the Delta Center was filled to 95 percent capacity through much of the mid to late '90s. Clearly, the city had taken to a team that constantly won and reached the playoffs.

The retirement of Stockton and Malone's departure to the Lakers left the Jazz without their twin stars, and understandably, they began to lose. After making the playoffs for 20 straight years, the Jazz missed the post-season for the third straight year in 2005-06. But this presented a twist. Instead of deserting a losing team, as it did in the early days, Salt Lake stayed loyal. The Jazz continued to play at 90 percent capacity, and it should be mentioned that four of the top five players in average minutes played in 2005-06 were white, and in 2006-07, their best season since Malone and Stockton retired, six of the 13 players on the roster were white.

Before Salt Lake, there was Green Bay, thrust into the upper right-hand corner of Wisconsin, distant and barren and cold. And very white. The 1960 census showed that Brown County, Wisconsin, was less than 1 percent black. Forty years later, that percentage crept to almost 2 percent. In most cities, that's a crawl. In Green Bay, that's progress.

There were four blacks on the Packers in '60, and they unintentionally became museum pieces for the whites in town, many of whom had never seen a black person before. Whenever he was approached on the street, Willie Davis, the great defensive lineman, always knew when he was The First. It was the stare, the distinctive look on the white person's face that told him so. "I can't tell you how many times I was the first black person that some of them ever talked to," said Davis, years later.

In these often awkward situations, Davis, Emlen Tunnel, Willie Wood, and Paul Winslow tried to deflate the situation as much as possible. "We were very cautious dealing with people," Davis said. "We didn't know how to anticipate what people thought about us. But I think the whites were more concerned than we were. They didn't want to make us feel unwanted. They went out of their way to make us feel at home. Sometimes they didn't know whether to address you as black or colored or Negro or what. But I do know this. I never heard the N-word in Green Bay. Never. Of course, I did in other places, including Dallas, especially when we beat the Cowboys."

Socially, life in Green Bay was the pits for the black players. They were aliens in an alien place. They couldn't hear their music on the radio, or eat the kind of food they grew up with, or converse with people who knew how to talk the talk. It was especially tough on Davis, who played at Grambling State and started his career in Cleveland, where he could unwind at a number of spots after a game. He obviously was not a racial outcast in Cleveland; he had friends and hangouts and no concern whatsoever about where to go. That changed in Green Bay, where whites would be so sympathetic that they would apologize for not having more blacks for Davis to meet. Later in the '60s, when the Packers added more blacks, some of the single players would date local white women, but always discreetly. "It was the fear of not knowing how the community would react," said Davis. "It was better to keep those relationships tucked away."

The black players in the '60s also had a powerful ally. Vince Lombardi, according to Davis, would not stand for bigotry, not in town, not in his own locker room. Davis said Lombardi once, and only once, gave a speech before the team and said that any name calling or examples of racism would be dealt with harshly. Everyone got the message. Davis saw no racial tensions on the Packers; if anything, the blacks and whites mingled more frequently among the Packers than they did on other teams. Lombardi's voice also resonated in Green Bay, which revered the great coach, and the locals met his demands for a prejudice-free environment for his black players, as well as players with religious beliefs. Lombardi also warned hotels in the South that the Packers wouldn't stay there unless his black players were as welcome as his white players, according to Davis. Strangely, Lombardi had a brush with racism himself. In the book *When Pride Still Mattered*, a biography of Lombardi, author David Maraniss told the story of how Lombardi, the son of Italian immigrants, went to a restaurant while the Packers prepared for an exhibition game in Winston-Salem, North Carolina. The hot sun during training camp gave Lombardi's skin an olive color, and he was refused service by a waitress who obviously mistook him for a black man.

Lombardi was so concerned about the plight of his black players in Green Bay that he allowed them frequent trips to Milwaukee, 90 minutes south, where they could enjoy soul food and mingle with blacks. "When we played some of our games in Milwaukee, he would not force the black players to come back right away," said Davis. "We had talked to him about our unique problems, and he agreed on this solution. That showed you what type of man he was."

Lombardi also insisted that black and white players share rooms. This made the Packers a team with no racial hang-ups or cliques. Paul Hornung would eat with the black players, and it wasn't seen as unusual. Davis said Lombardi preached togetherness in practice, meetings, and road trips and theorized that this would make the Packers more of a cohesive team on Sundays. After winning two Super Bowls, who could argue?

The racial spirit of Lombardi carried on long after he left and was evident when Reggie White chose Green Bay, of all places, when he became a free agent. He turned into a local folk hero and was embraced, even after his racially-charged comments to the Wisconsin Legislature when he made stereotypical remarks about a variety of ethnicities.

Lee Remmel, the longtime public relations man for the Packers whose link to the organization predates Vince Lombardi, said about the Legislature flap: "That was a media concern more than a fan concern. The people never lost sight of who Reggie White was and what he did for the community while he was here. To some extent, given the racial makeup of the town, the level of acceptance in Green Bay regarding African-American players through-out the history of the organization may seem surprising. But it's a welcoming place in general. There has never been a problem or an incident. Our citizens judge the players based on their conduct on and off the field."

Maybe the amount of respect given to black players in Salt Lake and Green Bay is equal to the respect given in return. Rather than allow stereotypes to dictate attitudes and fears, both sides saw each other as people first, and foremost.

CHAPTER 4

Academic Divide

Old School, New School, No School

This uniquely urban American tale begins on an outdoor basketball court filled with cracks in the pavement, rust on the rim, and kids with dreams. One of the boys is faster, stronger, and slicker with the ball than the others. He stands out, and because basketball is a big status symbol in his poor and troubled neighborhood where there are precious few other options for kids, everyone notices him.

As he gets older, he gets better. His dribble is tight, his hands are quick, his shot is sure. Once he reaches junior high, the whispers begin. People say he's going places. They say basketball will make him rich and famous some day. He's gonna be on TV! He hears, he listens, he believes. He locks himself into the game, plays it almost 24-7, and pushes everything else aside. His grades are average and his study habits nonexistent, but other than an occasional scolding from the coach and the guidance counselor, nobody really holds it against him. By this time, everybody's too much in love with his potential in basketball to take issue—including his family.

He's now a senior in high school. He signs his first autograph. His mother, who raised him alone, is approached by street hustlers claiming to represent agents. They're already scouting him for NBA potential. The newspapers are now writing gushing stories about her son, raising his profile, swelling his head, increasing his hopes. He has another terrific season, and the letters from colleges are starting to give the mailman a hernia. Head coaches from top 20 college basketball programs are sprinkled in the bleachers, sending a buzz through the gym. Heads turn, voices gush: "Do you see Coach So-and-So from State U.? He's sitting right over there."

He graduates, but in all honesty, he never tackled complicated courses in high school and was never benched because of grades. Somehow, he gets pushed through the commencement line anyway, to a rousing ovation. He is voted Most Likely to Succeed by his awe-struck classmates. The teachers, the ones who ignored his academic struggles because they didn't want to hold him back and cause problems, line up for pictures. Everyone smiles.

He gets into State U., partly because the coach, who's under pressure to win and keep his job and shoe contract, did some minor arm-twisting to get the administration to admit the kid, with the promise that every effort will be made to boost his grades. "If you bar this kid," the coach argues, "you'll put him on the street, and society will lose another black teenager. That's racist." The kid is admitted, with strings attached. He is assigned regular visits to the "academic counselor," which are quite common in athletic departments around the country. He spends most of his time around other jocks instead of meshing with the student body.

He stays away from the majors that are considered academically rigorous. He takes just the required number of credits and receives the bare minimum grades required to stay eligible. His classroom attendance is also the barest minimum. He has no real interest in school, no desire to rise early and walk across campus to class, no motivation to do anything more than what's necessary to suit up and play ball. Speaking of basketball, he discovers, to his surprise, that he's no longer the best player on his team. He's not even in the starting lineup every game. Actually, he's somewhat of a disappointment at the college level. His senior year is a blur and passes quickly. The last game he plays for the university is also the last game he plays for any team. His eligibility is up. Basketball is over.

And so is his college experience. He flunks out, packs up, moves on. He's back home, in the old neighborhood, this time without much hope or a future. His name carries no special cache anymore, not like before. He's only a fuzzy memory to those who knew him four years earlier. Anyway, there's a new kid now. Somebody else is a star at the high school, hearing the cheers, getting the mail, signing the autographs. Somebody else is preparing to go through the system. Meanwhile, he's suddenly an adult who's short on cash and has no training to compete in a competitive, high-tech world. He prepares to go through a string of menial jobs. He swears he had it and lost it, but in reality, he never really had it. He never had a chance. He only had a brief, shining moment as a high school basketball star, a fleeting memory that will serve as the high point of his entire life.

His disturbing story is not rare among those athletes from urban America who don't treat academics with the same intensity as they do basketball or football. We saw it in Maurice Clarett, the former Ohio State star who ran into trouble with the law, left after his freshman year of college, and then had no academic cushion when his chances to play professionally went poof. Same, too, for Brien Taylor; he was the highly touted 1991 first round pick of the New York Yankees who blew out his throwing arm in a fight, never pitched a single inning for the organization, never went to college, and began drifting from one menial job to another. And Korleone Young, who foolishly declared for the NBA draft straight out of a Wichita high school in 1989 and played a total of three games; he was sentenced to spending the rest of his youth bouncing from one bush league to the next, mainly overseas. And those are just the semivisible names; a vast majority of black athletes like them, or worse off, are complete unknowns.

We're often bombarded with success stories about rich black athletes living straight out of an episode of *Cribs*. They're all true, and thankfully, a good many return to their birth home and become great role models for the neighborhood kids. Dwyane Wade, for example, makes a point of stressing education whenever he speaks to young athletes back home, which is often. Then there are the athletes who had short or no professional careers but at least made enough of an effort to return to school, grab their degrees, and become successful businessmen, community leaders, teachers, and so forth. There's a good number of those examples, too. Unfortunately, there's

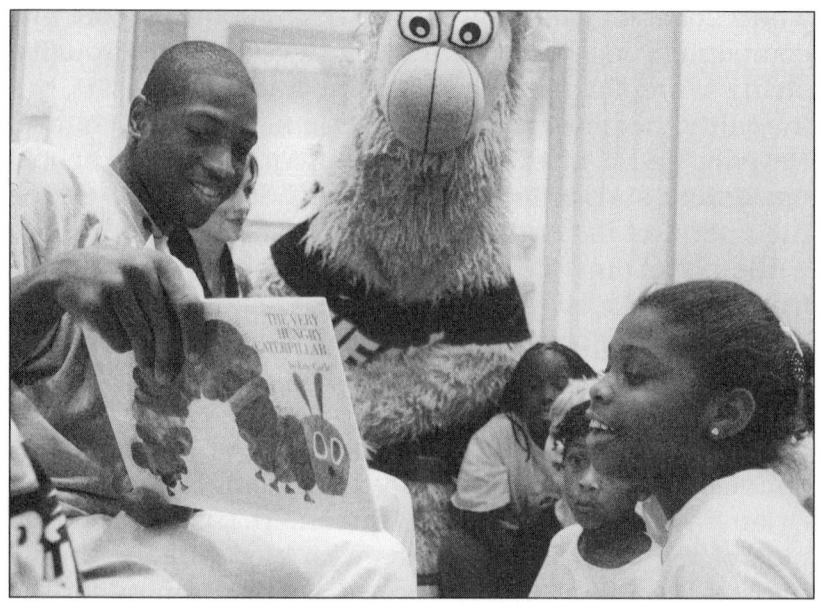

Victor Baldizon/NBAE/Getty Images

Dwyane Wade, realizing that 99 percent of young black athletes will never match his achievements on the basketball court, stresses education to children instead, as he does here at an NBA Read-to-Achieve event. Wade credits his sister, Tragil, as instrumental in his completing high school and receiving an opportunity to attend Marquette University.

also the grim reality of athletes we don't see, the ones hidden under the carpet of success. They couldn't cut it in the pros or the classroom, and they're stuck in low-paying, blue-collar, dead-end jobs. They once had an opportunity to grab a college education and a better life for themselves, but they either weren't prepared for the rigors of college or didn't care enough to work toward a degree, or both. Then there are other athletes whose high school grades were so bad they were forced to go to junior college first, but then showed no interest there, either, and never earned the necessary credits to jump to a Division I school.

This is tragic for black America, which is perpetually reeling from educational issues that handcuff the race and prevent them from moving up the ladder in society. And it enhances the cliché-ridden and rather tired notion that sports is "the only way out" for many young black men, when in truth, reading a textbook would actually help them find the exit faster than throwing a football. Really, now: There are only a few hundred NBA players but hundreds of thousands of black doctors, teachers, and similar professionals. As Harvard scholar Henry Louis Gates once recalled his father saying, as they rode past an outdoor court filled with black kids: "If our people studied calculus like we studied basketball, we'd be running MIT!"

The proof of a lax academic attitude among black athletes can be found among those who drop out of school or fail to take advantage of the benefits of attending school. It presents a skewed perception of a great number of black athletes and nonathletes who were educated properly by the system. What it also does is feed the suspicion that a good number just went to school to play ball, and the school, in turn, merely took advantage of their skills to win a few games.

When this happens, the blame is thick enough to spread around the many guilty parties who made it happen. The larger issue, obviously, is the state of poor black America, where a quality education is a yearly challenge for all students, not just athletes. The schools in our worst neighborhoods are fighting an uphill battle because of funding, which is always in short supply, and the neighborhood, which is rotting and not geared toward academics. Many teachers, bless their underpaid souls, certainly give their best, but some turn soft when the star athlete headed for big-time college sports struggles to pass the core courses. Finally, and most important, the athlete's household must encourage and demand effort in the classroom; if not, the kid won't have a prayer.

"There's a whole process involved here," said Richard Lapchick, who has spent a lifetime charting and analyzing academic performance among racial groups. "There's the withdrawing of emphasis on academics in some communities of color, which see a limited number of opportunities in the world. There's the emphasis on developing physical skills and a de-emphasis on developing academic skills. There's also the way they see role models on television in sports, sitcoms, music, and drama, very few of which stress academic performance."

The definition of a proper education is a murky one. It does not mean that every man and woman would benefit from college, which isn't for everyone. History is filled with college dropouts who followed their instincts and became major contributors to society; at the top of the list is Bill Gates, who had enough of Harvard. Millions more didn't even bother with college and wound up changing the worlds of fashion, art, design, music, even business. And sprinkled among our precious professional sports leagues are athletes who saw no need for a degree; LeBron James, you suspect, might survive without one.

Well, yes, if an individual is blessed with an amazing skill or talent that will promise him a comfortable life, the value of an advanced education isn't as important. But those people are gifted prodigies. They're exceptions. They're the fortunate and lucky few who can afford to take an academic shortcut down the road to personal and professional success. If they have common sense and a sharp intuition and surround themselves with competent people, their educational gaps can be minimized. But the overwhelming number of athletes don't become set-for-life superstars. For the rest of us, especially in urban America and particularly black athletes who aren't gifted enough to enjoy a long professional career, the smarter we are, the better off we are. And according to the annual and exhaustive research done by Lapchick, a black athlete in this country needs to tuck a textbook under his arm, not a football.

According to Lapchick's studies and other reliable studies, troubling graduation rates for black athletes are mainly concentrated in football and basketball, the two revenue-generating sports in college and the sports where colleges are more likely to gamble and accept risky students for the sake of winning. You don't find many blacks on the swim team or tennis team or track team flunking out of school in startling numbers or percentages, because colleges don't accept risky athletes for those sports. The academic problems revolve around only two sports; however, those are the sports in which black participation is highest.

"I remain alarmed at the persistent gap between African-American and white basketball student–athletes," Lapchick said. "And men's basketball traditionally has the worst record for graduating rates."

Lapchick found that only 47 percent of the black football players in Division I graduated compared to 63 percent of their white teammates in 2005. In basketball, in 2007, 51 percent of black players graduated (a depressing figure considering black players comprise 62 percent of basketball teams), compared to 76 percent of white players. Overall, the failure rate for black athletes is dropping steadily, but slowly. The NCAA graduation rates don't include athletes who leave early for the pros, as long as they were eligible when they departed. It does, however, include transfers' graduation rates, something the federal government rates don't take into account. A

2006 report showed a discrepancy of 14 percent overall between federal and NCAA graduation rates. Also, black athletes tend to have higher graduation rates than black nonathletes, but this is a bit misleading. Keep in mind that athletes are often assigned a small army of academic babysitters, and athletes have other advantages that normal students don't.

"On college campuses," said Lapchick, the director for the Institute for Diversity and Ethics in Sport, "some African-American athletes aren't prepared to compete academically, and in too many cases it becomes a self-fulfilling prophesy. They don't think they can cut it, and they take less rigorous courses. The rules put in place by the NCAA, where schools are punished for not meeting certain standards, have helped improve the situation, and things are getting better. But too often, the under-privileged student–athletes, by the time they report to college, are so far behind the typical student. They are intimidated by the environment, just as they intimidate their competition on the football fields and basketball courts."

Too often when it comes to education, college is being used as a starting line by black athletes when in reality it's the finish line. For all but a few, their sports careers will end right there. The odds of striking it rich in the lottery are greater than becoming a Pro Bowl player. Some black athletes are poorly prepared for college, and that's why I don't fault the NCAA more than I do the public school system and the households and environments where these athletes are raised. How can anyone grasp higher education and compete on campus when they barely competed in grade school and high school? How can that kid compete when there's little or no academic structure in his home? I remember how one college coach responded when a high school recruit's mother told the coach to make sure her son became a great student. The coach basically told her he couldn't undo what she failed to do for 18 years. It's a sad situation that you wonder will ever be fixed in poor America, which presents little hope for kids. The root of the problem begins shortly after birth and grows rapidly once athletic ability becomes evident.

Black kids aren't born dumb, which bigots and crackpot anthropologists want us to believe. Instead, poor black people are saddled with the other D: disadvantaged. Almost from birth, they'll fight steep odds to become winners in life. They're behind the eight-ball before they turn eight. That doesn't mean they won't beat the odds. It means they'll struggle. The gap between whites and blacks in standardized test scores is less a measurement of intelligence than a commentary on the public school system in poor communities. As Earl Smith, a sociology professor at Wake Forest, said: "This isn't an issue of intelligence. A lot of these players come from families and neighborhoods that don't place them in the best academic situations."

One obstacle in urban America is the misguided idea among grade school kids that speaking properly and going to class and raising your hand means you're talking white, acting white, and being white. Peer pressure actually encourages these black kids to "dummy down" as much as possible in order to blend in and be "authentic." Those who refuse to play by the rules of this stupid game run the risk of being outcasts and rejected, and what boy or girl who craves acceptance wants to deal with that? It's a warped way of thinking, and it certainly doesn't encourage or stimulate academic progress in places that need it most, but it's real. Black kids in city schools everywhere are teased unmercifully by their classmates if they use proper pronunciation and keep their vocabulary Ebonics-free. They're not called a teacher's pet; they're called a "white boy." If it's difficult being a nerd in a suburban school, imagine being one in the toughest, bleakest schools in black communities. Then, it's downright hell.

"Fortunately, with the ascent of the black middle class, we're growing out of that mentality in some areas," said Len Elmore, a former NBA player who's now a senior counsel with a New York law firm. "But kids trapped in those other schools, subconsciously, they know they're going nowhere, and they don't want others to go anywhere, either. So they apply that peer pressure to anyone who is seen trying to climb out of that pot."

Parents shape the academic climate for their kids, although it would be terribly unfair to characterize all parents in urban America as negligent on the subject of caring about education. That is simply not correct. No mother or father wants their child to lead a life of ignorance. The real issue is whether single moms, who head most black households, are equipped to provide the proper academic atmosphere at home. First and foremost, they work full time, and some are forced to work two jobs. It's an effort to juggle the job and the household, especially when many of these single mothers don't get home until dinnertime. How many have the energy to cope with the demands of family five exhausting days a week? And then there's the question of how many of those same working mothers have an advanced education themselves. Some may feel too self-conscious to get involved. Do they sit with their children and spend an hour on homework and problem solving, for example, or do they leave the task of educating their children to the school?

Not every black athlete in urban America can grow up like Elmore, who was raised in the Brooklyn projects and then in working-class Queens, and who eventually earned a Harvard Law degree after his NBA playing career. He had both parents in the house, which helped. His father, who had a ninth-grade education and worked for the sanitation department, installed a small library in the basement of the Queens home and went into debt buying a set of encyclopedias. The turning point in Elmore's life happened when a fourth grade teacher, who was white, asked students to reveal their ideal future occupation and Elmore said he wanted to be a lawyer. He watched *Perry Mason* and noticed how lawyers were champions of those who couldn't help themselves. He liked how lawyers spoke for the inarticulate.

"That's really nice, Leonard," his teacher said, "but more realistically, you should think about being a plumber, being a carpenter, or something like that, working with your hands." Elmore was bothered enough by her response that he went home and told his mother. She dragged him back to the school, found the teacher, and laid into her, chastising the teacher for limiting her son's dreams and destroying his hope. "That stuck with me for the rest of my life," said Elmore, many years later. "That's a gift that will never leave me, to see my mother stand up for my dreams. So how could I disappoint her by doing poorly in school?"

The black school-age athlete from urban America must deal with more educational obstacles than the average student at his school. In some cases, he has adults in his life who don't behave like adults when it comes to his skills in sports and his status in the community. Some of these adults evolve into fans, who cheer him on, who give him far more rope in the classroom than they would an ordinary student. He is deemed "special" and therefore exempt from certain rules. He's coddled, told how much he means to the school and community, and elevated to a status far above that of the straight-A student. A sense of entitlement is introduced into his life. He notices how athletic stardom, not academic performance, is rewarded. In the case of the athlete who lacks the inner strength to do the right thing, he concentrates on sports and goes through the motions in the classroom.

"In America, you put stuff in his head and tell him he's special and make it clear he doesn't need the vigorous academic training," said Adonal Foyle, the Golden State Warriors center and Colgate grad who grew up in the Grenadines. "You don't make the parallel that, for all the effort he puts on the basketball court, he needs to put in the classroom as well. You make that kid in seventh grade think he's a superstar and stuff is going to be given to him. And everyone wants to curry favor; nobody wants to be a parent to these kids. With no demands placed on them, where are they going to learn that stuff? If they don't have the morals and virtues at that point, then you can't expect them to learn it later on. We're stifling them. Sports has created this carrot and nothing else seems to matter."

These black athletes notice how their role models in the NBA and the NFL get commercials and endorsements and are even hired to work as TV announcers. Therefore, they wonder, why bother to study hard? Why bother with such annoyances as ancient history and complicated laboratory experiments? Just take care of business on the field or the court, and business will eventually take care of you—that's what sports society often teaches.

Well-meaning administrators have taken steps over the years to rectify the obvious problem, mostly by linking eligibility to grade-point averages. Still, many of these reforms lack bite, and most demand the barest minimum from the athletes. Some even have loopholes that are routinely exploited, just to keep certain star athletes on the field. "Of all the things I've been involved in," said Richard Lapchick, "the one where I've faced the most opposition is trying to get the C average on the high school level. In the state of Massachusetts, where I worked, a high school basketball player could play for four years and not only not get a C average, but not get a C in any single course. I would tell the people there, 'What are we preparing the athlete to do?' The coaches would actually say to me, 'At least these kids will have the memory of being successful athletes while they were in high school. Don't take that away from them.' Well, how are they going to be happy in their lives if they can't get jobs and can't speak or write well enough to improve their lifestyles and the lives of their families later on?"

From his office in Washington, D.C., where too many examples of young black athletes without proper education occur annually, Robert Woodson doesn't paint a much better picture. As a community activist who runs the National Center for Neighborhood Enterprise, Woodson says the mentality in some communities is flawed. "We don't lionize kids whose achievement is tied to academics, but we do lionize the athletes," he said. "We say the way to get out of the ghetto is to rap or dribble a ball. Well, I do some speaking inside prisons, and most of my work takes me into poor communities, and I tell them all the time how it's fascinating that a kid can stand at the free throw line with thousands of people cheering or booing him with two seconds left on the clock. There are people waving banners, trying to distract him, and yet he can control himself and hit two free throws. I tell them that if they applied the same amount of discipline to mathematics and English, they would achieve the same way."

Woodson is disturbed whenever the conversation shifts to the role of the school district and local government, because he says a certain amount of personal accountability and responsibility must be demanded and expected.

"We say the reason our athletes are flunking out is because of racism," Woodson said. "We keep finding ways to excuse behavior. We are playing into the stereotype. Yet when others try to stereotype us, we get annoyed."

As a sports columnist for *Newsday*, the largest newspaper on Long Island, I took great interest in the amazing high school career of Jason Gwaltney, a black football player from the racially mixed working class town of North Babylon. For four years this kid, powerful and strong and fast and blessed with balance, evoked the memory of the last running back from the Island who owned Friday nights, a guy named Jim Brown. Gwaltney was so big and strong that some kids didn't want to tackle him, and those who did either went for a ride on his jersey or grabbed an armful of air. Gwaltney rushed for a total of 7,800 yards, scored 135 touchdowns, 828 points, and mostly sat the final minutes of most games in his senior year. He was mentioned in all of the national high school publications and made the All-America teams and heard from just about every college in the country. Pete Carroll, the coach of national champion USC, recruited him hard, but Gwaltney went to West Virginia in a package deal with his half-brother, who also played for North Babylon High.

No doubt, Gwaltney was a load on the field, but he also had issues. Some were behavioral, and he was reprimanded for that. Most were academic, and you wonder if he was punished severely enough for that. You wonder if adults at the high school, fearful of disrupting the career of perhaps the greatest high school football player in Long Island history, went great lengths to cover for his problems. I didn't personally know how Gwaltney was treated, but one way or another, the truth would eventually emerge, I figured, after a few years in college. But I was wrong in that estimation. The truth took only a few months.

By December of his freshman year, Gwaltney was gone from West Virginia. He did suffer a minor knee injury, which cut short his mild performance on the field, although that wasn't his main problem. He wasn't prepared to compete in a college environment. Everyone shared in this failure, from his teachers back in high school who didn't raise enough red flags or much of a stink; his principal; his coach, who kept Gwaltney on the field with a football tucked under his arm; and, of course, Gwaltney himself. He transferred to a small school back home in an effort to resuscitate his football career, but the same habits followed Gwaltney from West Virginia to Nassau Community College. He never went to class and left that school, too. He re-enrolled at West Virginia, but his history of academic neglect will follow him wherever he ends up until he resolves it.

"I told him he would never be able to graduate here," said John Anselmo, the Nassau coach. "He withdrew with Ws. I even gave him a W in my physical education class. Sooner or later he better wake up and smell the coffee and realize he has to go to school if he wants to play. I'm disappointed for the kid. I'd truly like to see him get it straight."

In the ground-breaking sports documentary *Hoop Dreams*, which was filmed in a tough part of Chicago, the two main characters, William Gates and Arthur Agee, were obviously basketball talents. The film made that very apparent. But the essence of the film was the lives these teenagers lived. That's why the film was so brilliant. Aside from the basketball and family pressures faced by Gates and Agee, the role of academics was captured, and the suspicions about black athletes in urban America were confirmed. When it came to basketball and academics, one was clearly superior to the other, an imbalance largely caused by circumstances in the home.

"There was a desire from the parents that their kids be educated," said Steve James, the director who spent months in the homes and schools of Gates and Agee. "William's mother really wanted him to go to college because nobody else in the family had done that. Arthur's parents wanted him to go to college. But the practical reality is there aren't a lot of homes with books because the parents never made it to college and in some cases didn't graduate from high school. How do they model themselves for their kids? In a lot of ways they can't help with homework and things like that. We noticed when we were in the homes that there weren't books. When we filmed Arthur's little brother, we noticed there weren't kid's books, the kind of thing you typically see in homes where parents are more affluent and educated."

Of course, when it comes to education, there's also self-responsibility, which is hard for some black athletes in poor neighborhoods to grasp because little is demanded from them beyond the field. So why should anyone be surprised when not much effort is given? "One of the things we found out while filming was that the talented African-American players were like Jekyll and Hyde," said James. "In class, they'll sit back, won't raise their hand, and certainly won't volunteer answers. They just hope to disappear back there because they had no real confidence in that setting. Then when school ends, and they're on the court, suddenly they're Mr. Hyde, brimming with confidence. They're completely different guys. Suddenly, when it came to sports, they were confident."

In the movie, Gates met with a guidance counselor, who took one look at his transcript from grammar school and told Gates he must be "one heck of a basketball player." In his brief stay in college, Gates noticed how all the players on the basketball team took a basketball class. "He also said they had tutors whose job technically was helping the players do work," said James, "although the line between helping the players and doing it yourself is very thin indeed. There's no question that athletes, especially the very promising ones, get a message early on that they're going to be treated differently and not going to be held accountable academically."

After spending so much time in the company of athletes and schools and families, James was given an intimate look at the vicious system and how it exploits athletic ability while neglecting, for the most part, to properly educate black athletes. James found himself feeling disturbed, sad, and frustrated. "We have a tendency to view African-American players and say, 'How can they think basketball is going to be their ticket out when it's like winning the lottery?' Well, these players aren't that naïve. They know that. But I tell people that they don't see any other options where they can be successful. They don't say they're going to grow up and be an architect. They do see basketball and football players on TV, and often they know somebody from their neighborhood who made it in those sports. They don't know anyone from their neighborhood who became an architect or lawyer or doctor."

Fact is, some athletes of all races want no part of college. College has too many demands, in terms of games, travel, and practice, for them to place the same emphasis on education that most normal students can. They feel they don't belong there, aren't made to feel comfortable there, and quite honestly, don't want to be there. They mainly go to college to prepare themselves for the professional leagues or to play in the NCAA basketball tournament or a major bowl game. They stay just long enough to become eligible for the draft or to play their way into the draft. O.J. Mayo, a talented basketball player who skipped between high schools from Cincinnati to Huntington, West Virginia, took a scholarship to USC in 2007, not for USC's fine academic reputation, but mainly to take advantage of the exposure he'd get in Los Angeles in preparation for an NBA career someday. You see this attitude every spring when dozens of college basketball undergrads declare themselves for the NBA draft, even those who are given a small chance of actually getting drafted. They make themselves available for the NBA because, for all practical purposes, they're done with college and studying. They're so fed up with the idea of going to class that they will take a one-in-a-million chance in the draft and risk losing their remaining collegiate eligibility, provided they sign with an agent. Some of these kids would rather forfeit the remaining time left on their scholarships, their free meal tickets, and best chances at success, rather than spend another year or two on campus.

The pro sports leagues, worried that their game would soon become overpopulated by raw and unprepared athletes, took steps to plug the dike. The NFL will not allow college football players to turn pro before their junior seasons and successfully took troubled former Ohio State star Maurice Clarett to court to uphold the rule. The NBA allowed high school players to make the jump until forging a compromise with the union in 2005; now, players must be at least 19, which means they must spend a year in college first. The response, especially with regard to the NBA, was predictable. Indiana Pacers forward Jermaine O'Neal, one of the last high schoolers to jump before the rule change, publicly wondered why tennis players and golfers aren't urged by society to attend college, implying that the world is exclusively picking on poor black basketball players. His view was shared by many, including Jack Keefer, the boy's coach at Lawrence North in Indianapolis. Keefer coached Greg Oden, the country's top high school player in 2005-06, an excellent student and a center who would've been among the top players chosen in the 2006 draft if not for the age limit. Instead, Oden went to Ohio State. Keefer called the rule "racist" and unfair. "Greg is going to college because he can handle college," he said, "but Greg and other high school players should have a choice, and in this case, the NBA took that choice away."

Well, first of all, it's awfully hard to conclude that the NBA, which employs more blacks in front office and management positions than any sports league, is a racist organization. Those who share the opinion of Keefer and O'Neal are implicating David Stern in this discussion, and the commissioner, who pushed hard for the rule, is more colorblind than a dog. His impeccable track record on racial matters speaks for itself. Plus, the age reform was done with the cooperation of the NBA union, which is run by Billy Hunter, a black man. So much for the racial angle. I will give the critics this much: There's a noticeable lack of fuss regarding Michelle Wie and white hockey players and white tennis players who don't bother with college. Did anyone ever raise this issue when Andy Roddick turned pro? Pete Sampras? Andre Agassi?

However, the NBA's age-limit rule was put into place purely for economic and competitive reasons, not racial reasons. When a player is drafted in the first round, that team must pay him guaranteed money for five years. That amounts to millions of dollars, and in the case of high school players, NBA scouts simply aren't given much history to work with to allow them to make an intelligent choice. It becomes an expensive gamble. A great high school player can become an average NBA player in a flash. Kwame Brown, anyone?

And on a personal note, I couldn't care less that no noise is ever made about Roddick and the rest of the white high school phenoms. Given the alarming state of academics in the black community, why should anyone, for any reason, even suggest that it's okay for black people to skip school? What kind of message does that send to those athletes in urban America looking for any reason not to study or take school seriously? What kind of message does that send to society? You'd think critics of the NBA rule would pause and weigh the repercussions of their criticism. Is there a double standard when it comes to gifted white teenage athletes and black teenage athletes? Perhaps. Should there be a double standard? Damn right. At least as long as black academic achievement continues to trail white academic achievement by a wide and shameful margin. Also, consider this: Chances are pretty good that if tennis or golf doesn't work out for the white teenaged player, his family likely has the financial ability to send him to college and give him a soft landing cushion. Or he'll simply go to work for his father in the family business. If basketball doesn't work out for the poor black teenager, well, you can only imagine what happens next.

Billy Hawkins, a sports sociologist at the University of Georgia, did a study that showed black athletes graduated with a potential earning power of $10,000 less than white athletes. He blames that partially on what he calls "academic clustering," where athletes are steered toward "open majors" that don't lead to the best-paying jobs and have less stringent requirements. It's sort of a legal method of academic fraud. One of the worst recent examples of real academic fraud among black athletes was the scandal involving the University of Minnesota basketball team. The Gophers went to the 1997 Final Four, and yet none of their starters that year went on to graduate. And later, we discovered why; an investigation by the *St. Paul Pioneer Press* in 1999 revealed that a whistle-blowing office manager claimed to write over 400 papers for 20 players over a four-year period in the early '90s. There was also a pattern of intimidation from the men's basketball office toward faculty members.

While that was disturbing enough, Jan Ganglehoff, the office manager, maintained that Clem Haskins, the coach, was fully aware of this. If so, and a subsequent university investigation supported her theory, then Haskins deserves double shame. First, for his role in academic fraud. Second, for being a black man and stunting the academic progress of his black players. According to the newspaper's investigation, one of those players, Voshon Lenard, couldn't correctly answer a professor who asked why George Washington is considered a Founding Father.

"Athletic departments are in the business of making money," said Hawkins. "The educational mission doesn't fall on their radar scope. When you think about the amount of money generated and the amount of money needed to keep those sports programs going, the goal is to put the best athletes on the field. Some of those athletes are at great academic risk. As long as there is this drive to accumulate capital, they're going to be tempted to bring these athletes in."

There's also a fear among college coaches and administrators that the NCAA's attempts to get tough and introduce stronger academic standards might be counterproductive, that athletes will choose easier majors just to stay eligible. Then there would be students armed with Basket Weaving degrees flooding the job market.

"Should we challenge our athletes to take more rigorous fields of study? Absolutely," said Elmore. "It disheartens me because they don't see themselves as I see them, as having the potential to be captains of industry. To achieve on that level requires a strong work ethic, perseverance, and poise under pressure, all the things they used to become outstanding athletes. But again, I feel that by the time these kids get to college, they might not be up to the challenge in this area. There are so many kids who come in and aren't equipped to be literature majors or computer and technology majors."

The proper role model for all teenage black athletes to follow is sitting right now in a Minnesota courtroom. Alan Page was one of the best three or four linemen in

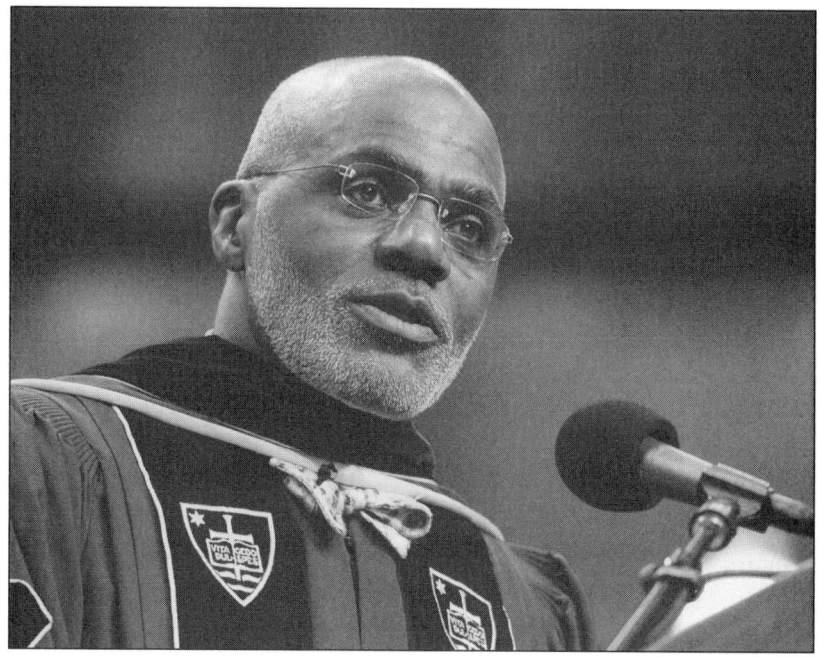

AP Photo/Joe Raymond

Now an Associate Justice on the Minnesota Supreme Court, Alan Page presents the commencement address at his alma mater, Notre Dame. Page, the first defensive player ever to win the NFL MVP award, has demonstrated how a similar passion for educational pursuits can make an athlete even more successful when his playing days are through.

NFL history. He was the soul of the Purple People Eaters, the respected defensive line of the Minnesota Vikings during the 1960s and '70s, and once was named MVP of the league. As terrific as Page was during his Hall of Fame career, his true calling arrived after he was through with football. Always an advocate of education, Page worked his way through law school and up the judicial ladder, climbing high enough to become a judge on the Minnesota Supreme Court. His story is one that should resonate through the minds of young athletes from all backgrounds. His story should be copied to the hilt, because Page followed one career with an even greater one. And he couldn't have done it without education and without attacking the classroom with the same intense aggression as he used when chasing running backs, which was considerable.

According to all the research, too many black student–athletes leave college without all the necessary tools to compete in a highly competitive world. Some do. And the extremely lucky ones, those who last long enough in the pros to earn a decent living and build a nest egg for themselves, manage to escape the trap. Still, every now and then, their lack of proper education comes back to haunt them as adults in a variety of embarrassing ways. There is little that Vince Young, for instance, can do in the NFL to erase the stigma created by the poor Wonderlic score he reportedly received before the draft. That tends to stick and reflect what an athlete did, or didn't do, during his time in college.

A number of black athletes in recent years have made a point of returning to school after their playing careers to complete their degrees or to obtain a master's degree. Troy Vincent, a former star defensive back, has led the cause. Vincent encourages former athletes to enhance their education as well as their business knowledge through a program at the Wharton School at Penn, where Kenneth Shropshire, the director of the sports business initiate there, is a professor and mentor.

For the athlete who doesn't place an emphasis on education, he should know that, eventually, the knees and the ankles give way to Father Time. Meanwhile, education and achievements off the playing field, as evidenced by Alan Page and others like him, enhance an athlete's opportunities for a lifetime. So, isn't it time student–athletes grasp this to see that scores in the classroom are more significant in the long run than scores on a stat sheet? Which is the better choice for both personal and professional success?

CHAPTER 5

Basketball Score

Jumping Through Hoops or Just Growing Up?

The commissioner of the NBA does not, to anyone's knowledge, subscribe to *Vibe* magazine or keep his car radio locked on the local hip-hop station or spend his afternoons watching music videos on BET and MTV. Therefore, David Stern in 2000 was among the last to know about an up-and-coming rapper named Jewelz, but he was certainly not the last to wince at what Jewelz rapped about.

In the song "40 Bars," a clumsy if ambitious first swing at a music career, Jewelz was tough, Jewelz was dirty, Jewelz was nasty, Jewelz was hardcore, and Jewelz was dangerous, all of which are necessary for anyone trying to keep it real and sell records in the image-conscious gangsta rap game. Jewelz came hard with these lyrics: "Get murdered in a second in the first degree, come to me with faggot tendencies." He also said, "See, dem bitch azz niggaz y'all killin' don't amaze us" and "Everybody stay fly, get money, kill and fuck bitches." He mentioned "AKs, rifles, and nines." Also, in a salute to his home state, Jewelz added this: "Va.'s finest fillin' up ditches, where niggaz turn to bitches."

Throughout the song, which was a rambling if barely coherent rant about Lord knows what, Jewelz referred to women as "bitches," used the N-word 13 times (in variations of "nigger," "nigga," and "niggaz"), and made 13 references to violence. Of course, in the music world, where almost anything is excused in the name of art, a rapper could get a glowing review in *Rolling Stone* and props in the *New York Times* arts section for his "gritty" and "compelling" language. But from the man who runs the NBA, Jewelz got a Stern request: Stick to your day job.

Jewelz was better known as Allen Iverson, arguably the most exciting player in the league, a determined player shaped like a Twizzler who managed to flourish in a game made for giants. When he arrived to the NBA, Iverson almost instantly developed a rapport with basketball fans, who admired his toughness and intensity. He also earned a large following of teenagers who made a connection to his inner rebel. Iverson didn't just have street credibility, he oozed it and embraced it. The tattoos, cornrows (a trend he reintroduced to urban society at the 2001 All-Star Game), baggy pants, overgrown shirts, and custom-made diamond necklaces were all apparent with Iverson, who made no apologies for how he looked and talked and the image he projected. The idea of making a rap CD, therefore, appealed to him, while any public concerns over the lyrics did not.

Stern, incidentally, was not completely white bread, nor was he a starched corporate shirt who was hopelessly out of touch with a new generation. Stern grew up in the politically charged and free-love 1960s and spent much of his childhood and adult life in and around the cultural melting pot of New York City. He was commissioner of a league that had been over 70 percent black since 1983. He had a closer relationship with more NBA players than most commissioners had with players in their leagues. Stern is staunchly liberal and certainly an advocate of free speech. But Iverson's lyrics didn't strike Stern as creative or constructive, just needlessly mean spirited and homophobic and sexist and racist. As someone who was sensitive to the image of the league he had nurtured into great financial health, Stern couldn't sit still and say nothing, even if he risked being called out of touch with today's young black males.

At first, he wanted to punish Iverson with a fine or a suspension. But after realizing the words Iverson used were quite common in the gangsta rap game, Stern simply admonished Iverson and then issued a statement, calling the lyrics "coarse, offensive, and antisocial" and adding that Iverson "has done a disservice to himself, the Philadelphia 76ers, his teammates, and perhaps all NBA

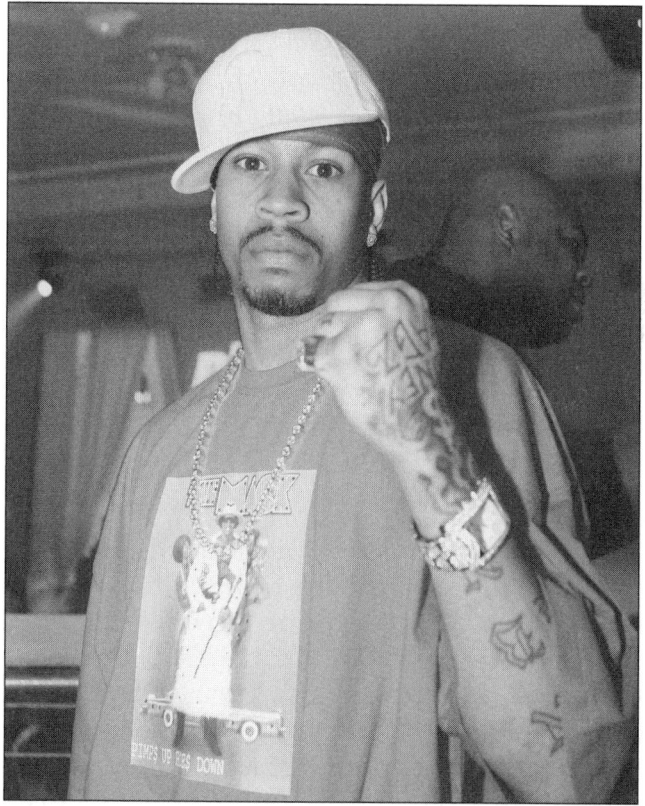

Sandra Rose/Getty Images

Iverson once had his tattoos airbrushed away by image-conscious PR people before they placed his picture in a league publication.

players." Stern conceded that the NBA should probably not regulate artistic expression, "no matter how repugnant."

As a frequent critic of poisonous lyrics that leave nothing to the imagination, that wrongly influence children and degrade black culture, I developed sore hands in my applauding of Stern for being as hard on Iverson as Iverson was on his CD. Finally, I figured, somebody gets it. Some versions of rap had gone from socially relevant to self-loathing. Finally, someone with a high public profile took notice and spoke up. My only disappointment was that it took a white sports commissioner, not one of our black leaders, to come out publicly and aggressively and intensely against such garbage. I realized Stern walked a fine line and risked alienating a fair amount of black NBA players, many of whom held much love for Iverson. But it was worth it. Stern didn't really have a choice; besides, he truly seemed to be annoyed that an NBA player would attach himself to words that would get most of us fired if we ever used them on the job. My appreciation of Stern grew, at least until a few years later, when he literally sold out.

The next episode involving the NBA and "coarse, offensive, and antisocial" lyrics happened when this particular rapper with NBA ties recorded this piece of poetry: "Motherfuckers wanna act loco, hit 'em wit numerous shots with the fo fo, faggots wanna talk po po's, smoke em like cocoa." And this: "Stop your bullshittin', glock with the full clip/Motherfuckers better duck when the fool spit/One shot could make a nigga do a full flip/See the nigga layin' shocked when the bullet hit." Then, another rapper in the NBA family chimed in with this: "See now you could be a lady or a bitch, girl/Still you're a thicky thicky thicky thick girl/Lookin' like a lollipop waitin' for the lick girl."

The lyrics created by the first rapper in question were in the song "Nigga What, Nigga Who" and the next rapper sang his lyrics on "Thicky Thick Girl." The first rapper was Jay-Z, the other Nelly. Both rap stars, giants in the industry, had used a portion of the enormous earnings made from selling black street culture to buy their way into the NBA, Jay-Z as part owner of the Nets and Nelly as a partner with the Bobcats. The raw and obscene side of the hip-hop culture, the same kind Stern had come out so vehemently against in the Iverson episode, was now sitting in the boardroom of the NBA. And not only did Stern do nothing to prevent these two from buying into the NBA, this time he said nothing about the choice of lyrics used by Jay-Z and Nelly who, as owners, were essentially Stern's bosses.

If the commissioner needed support, he would have found it from a group of brave black women who had seen and heard enough. Nelly and his idea of romantic music was rejected by a historically black college shortly before he was accepted by the NBA. The proud black women of Spelman College refused a request by Nelly to hold a bone marrow drive on campus in 2004. The women were appalled by his video for "Tip Drill" in which nearly nude women (several of them black) danced around provocatively. In one sequence, Nelly swiped a credit card between the crack of a woman's behind. The Spelman women wanted Nelly to answer for this. He couldn't. Asha Jennings, then the president of the Spelman student government, told the *Atlanta Journal-Constitution* newspaper, "We can't continue to support artists and images that exploit our women and put us out there as oversexed, non-intelligent human beings."

Stern's silence illustrated just how handcuffed he was. He chose not to attack two artists who were enormously popular in locker rooms around the NBA; Jay-Z counted many players as friends that he frequently entertained in his Manhattan club 40-40, named after the baseball feat of hitting 40 homers and stealing 40 bases. Also, the principal owner of the Charlotte Bobcats was Robert Johnson, the first black man to run a professional sports franchise, whose appointment was a proud moment on Stern's watch. Johnson is also one of the most forward-thinking black businessmen ever; during the infancy of cable TV, he seized the idea of creating a station with mainly black programming. Black Entertainment Television carved a niche in the industry and gave tremendous exposure to news and entertainment catering to black audiences. A good bit of BET's shows were community oriented and geared toward enhancing the lives of people. A healthy portion of programming, however, was exploitative gangsta rap videos that ran almost as constantly as infomercials. Thus, a portion of Johnson's $1 billion fortune, courtesy of BET's sale to Viacom that enabled Johnson to buy into the NBA, came from those videos. Before he cashed in, Johnson's network had come under criticism by some in the black community for its imbalance between Snoop Dogg videos and more mainstream programming. Thus, the problem—how could Stern take a defiant stand against Nelly and Jay-Z without someone making a link to Johnson?

Robert Johnson and Nelly are two NBA owners with a link to controversial music videos.

Clearly, Stern had these unique issues to tackle in the new generation NBA. There was a growing perception that the NBA was embracing an edgy culture and a certain image. Well, let's stop with the buzzwords and cut to the chase: The NBA, in the minds of some, was becoming too ghetto. "The word 'image' is just a buzzword for black professional basketball players," said Billy Hunter, the executive director of the player's union.

The influx of young players barely out of their teens, some of whom were immature and socially awkward, had given the league a different flavor. Most quickly embraced the idea of professionalism and meshed comfortably, without problems. A few behaved and dressed and spoke and carried themselves differently. Their attitude was quickly labeled "hip-hop," a reflection not only of their taste in music but also the lifestyle seen in the music videos.

The evidence of this began to surface in various ways in the early 2000s. Young black players began appearing on the covers of sports magazines and basketball magazines dressed in gold chains, flashing their tattoos, and rarely if ever smiling. It made them seem menacing, always a heavy image burden for black men in America. In televised press conferences after playoff games, players wore sunglasses and oversized baseball caps and the ever-present thick gold chains with medallions as big as Delaware. Those who were too injured to play often sat on the team bench in baggy pants, big shirts, and hiking boots. More sneaker companies began making commercials that connected the NBA player with the street in order to tap into a certain demographic. Carmelo Anthony, one of the NBA's most precious new stars, made a cameo in a homemade film that featured a reputed drug dealer. Anthony and a few other players openly rebelled against coach Larry Brown during the 2000 Olympics, where the U.S. team of NBA players finished a disastrous third, taking the bronze, mainly because few players could make an open jump shot. Ron Artest ignited the infamous brawl in Auburn

Hills where black players swung away at white fans and began a national dialogue on race and sports. The NBA began booking rappers and hip-hoppers to entertain at NBA functions during All-Star weekend and used their music in promotional commercials and during timeouts in the arenas. Finally, the game itself began to show signs of slippage, with palming and traveling violations that went unpunished, with an emphasis on "athletes" instead of pure basketball players, and with an overall decrease in scoring.

The real question was whether this had any effect on business. By the late 1990s, right around the time Michael Jordan wrapped up his sixth and final championship, the Golden Age was clearly over for the NBA. The league was no longer lava hot, as it was in the '80s with Magic Johnson and Larry Bird and the promise of classic rivalries. Stern and the owners, perhaps reading too much into the league's popularity, stretched the product thin through expansion. Suddenly, instead of having three or four outstanding players, most contending teams had one or two. Television ratings dropped to pre-Magic and Bird levels, even for the NBA Finals. Attendance in Portland, where the Blazers always enjoyed incredible support, plunged in part because of the bad attitudes and decisions of certain Blazer players, all of them black. A good number of those expansion cities began to struggle, too; the NBA failed in Vancouver, saw sparse crowds in New Orleans even before Hurricane Katrina hit, and the honeymoon for Bob Johnson's team in Charlotte lasted about a year. Clearly, the NBA wasn't so fantastic anymore.

Strangely enough, right around this time, the NBA started doing big business with the street. It was a move that smacked of desperation by a league that needed to tap into another audience and to stay hip and relevant among a new generation of fans. When the league began licensing and selling throwback jerseys, it discovered gold. Throwbacks hit the pavement like a fresh pair of Timberlands. Kids everywhere, but especially in urban

America, had to have them. It didn't matter if the jerseys sold for roughly $350 each or that some kids who bought them hardly knew the players who once wore them; they became a cult status symbol. The NBA put a high-tech store in the high-rent district of Fifth Avenue in Manhattan, just down the street from Saks, mainly to hawk those jerseys and other licensed apparel that was constantly worn by teenagers. The NBA Store owes much of its success to the street.

So, if you're David Stern, do you really make a public stink about the rap lyrics of two of your owners, the way you once did with Iverson? Do you risk alienating a new audience? Maybe not.

"The league is trying to promote and enhance the next generation of consumers," said Dave Bing, voted one of the 50 greatest players. Bing graduated from Syracuse, played for the Pistons, and knows something about consumers. He formed his own business late in his career and gradually built Bing Steel into one of the most successful black-owned businesses in history. By any and all accounts, Bing is one of the best role models in NBA history. "The leadership in this league, I don't think, really likes it. But they've got to play that game, because if they don't, they lose a potential customer. It's all about business, so they don't want to let that happen. It's a fine line. I know David, and he stands up for what he believes in, but you can't satisfy everybody."

Stern did put his foot down when he slapped NBA players with a dress code just before the 2005-06 season. He took a stance that he knew would be unpopular with many of the league's young black players, and I couldn't thank him enough. Bothered by footage of NBA players dressed like the thugs you see in music videos, Stern decided a standard uniform was in order, and certain items and accessories were off-limits on NBA property. No more gold ropes and hats and do-rags and Gucci sunglasses while sitting on the benches; players now had to wear a sports jacket or face a fine. When representing their team, they had to appear business-like because, after all, the NBA was a business. Nothing wrong with that, right? We all must conform to a dress code on the job, so why should NBA players be any different? And since the players proudly wore a custom-made suit the day they were drafted, when they shook Stern's hand and pointed the bill of their team cap straight ahead instead of wearing it backward, what was the big deal?

Well, it was a big deal to many players who complained loudly. It even smacked of racism, they felt. Iverson chimed in, "Just because you put a guy in a tuxedo, it doesn't mean he's a good guy. It sends a bad message to kids. If you don't have a suit on when you go to school, is the teacher going to think you're a bad kid? I never wore a suit in any park I ever went to when I was growing up."

Of course, there's a big difference between going to the park and going to work, which was the whole point behind the dress code. Once again, some players just didn't get it. They didn't understand the reach of their influence, which was perhaps too powerful, with kids who hoped to one day grow up to be them. And they either refused to comprehend the importance of image or were simply ignorant about image. As for their weak whine about racism, it was laughable. Exactly who was promoting racism: Stern, who simply wanted young black men to appear presentable in public, or those specific black players who insisted on dressing stereotypically? Suppose things were reversed and Stern, a white man in charge of a black league, demanded his players wear gold ropes, baggy jeans, and baseball hats cocked to the side at all times? Can you imagine the ensuing storm if that were to happen?

"I was in total disagreement with the position that a lot of the players took," said Bing. "I respect freedom, but the NBA has expectations in terms of how their players look, how they act, how they talk. All those things are part of the package, and a lot of the young guys couldn't relate to that."

Regina H. Boone/Detroit Free Press

Because of his success in basketball and later in business, Bing is one of the most important figures in NBA history. He also gives back to society—here he visits a Detroit neighborhood he helped to rehabilitate.

There were whispers inside the NBA offices and in business circles that Stern created the dress code because he had become too concerned about his corporate sponsors, who attached their products to the NBA and put their clients in luxury suites in NBA arenas. That's probably not entirely true because a fair number of the sponsors did business with the NBA primarily because they wanted to reach a young audience and take advantage of the astonishing market value of street credibility. However, Stern was first and foremost a marketing genius who knew the power of image, and he wanted the league to resonate in all households, like any businessman would. There was a middle ground, and by asking his players to be more conservative in their appearance, Stern reached for it.

"There have been efforts made by the league to distance itself from hip-hop and that element," said union chief Billy Hunter. "I agree that there are some negatives and a lot of things that our guys do that you don't like. I would say, however, that that's not the majority. And the issues we're talking about with the league are no different than the issues we're dealing with in society in general."

Hunter and Stern form one of the most ideal commissioner–labor leader combinations in sports, if not sports history. Both men deeply admire one another. They share the same taste in politics, both being staunchly liberal. Their legal backgrounds are also similar, and quite clearly, they have a love for basketball, the health of the league, and the players themselves. Given that, their squabbles seem petty, if almost forced. You almost get the idea that when they disagree on certain issues, it's only because common sense says they can't agree on everything. But if you press both men on their philosophies about what's best for the NBA, one would be almost a carbon copy of the other.

Hunter played football at Syracuse, and his biggest victory came when he united the team's other black players and told the athletic administration that they would not play against those schools in the Deep South where segregation was practiced. Later, as a highly regarded litigator based in the Bay Area, he encouraged Jimmy Carter to free Patty Hearst. Hunter is well-respected both within the NBA office and among the players because he's tough yet fair. It doesn't hurt that he's also a black man representing a league that's overwhelmingly black.

"I bring certain experiences to the job," he said, unapologetically.

As a black man who grew up in the old-school '50s and '60s, Hunter must somehow bridge the gap and connect with those black athletes whose values and culture and lifestyle are different than the ones he knew at their age. It's his job to fight for the players' rights. But that doesn't mean Hunter finds every issue worth battling. For example, he agreed with Stern on the dress code and thus clashed with many of the members of his union. And, like Stern, he was disturbed by the role the Pistons and Pacers players took in their infamous fight at the Palace in Auburn Hills; Hunter really didn't fault Stern when the punishments came down with the swiftness and weight of a falling anvil. What troubled Hunter was the rash of rule changes that took place in such a short period of time, all designed to keep the NBA player in his place. The league even enforced an on-court mandate that jerseys must be tucked into the shorts at all times.

"I don't know if they're trying to sanitize the league or what," Hunter said. "I understand our players have an obligation to conform their conduct. Just the same, you can't put them in a straight-jacket."

But Hunter knew the purpose behind the rules. The NBA is a business, above all, and Stern is out to protect the investments of his (mostly) white owners by keeping the league valuable in the eyes of its corporate sponsors. When the popularity of the NBA began to dip following Michael Jordan's retirement, the league already had a performance crisis; what it couldn't afford was an image crisis as well. Also, when young and immature players began flowing into the league at an epidemic rate, Stern wanted to lay down the law to players who simply didn't know how to conduct themselves as professionals or, to some extent, as adults.

If nothing else, the dress code and other hot-button NBA topics fed newspapers and sports radio shows and TV talk shows that feasted on the controversy, to Stern's amusement. All he wanted to do was see his players dress for business; meanwhile, society saw a cultural clash with hip-hop black athletes lashing out against the establishment, an establishment that made them millionaires, by the way. The issue of race, still a hot-button topic in white and black households alike, was analyzed and dissected like a laboratory frog. For the first time since Jordan retired, mainstream America was buzzing about the NBA again, and with a drop-off in TV ratings and attendance in some NBA cities, there was no such thing as bad publicity.

When it came to race, the NBA had suffered through enough bad publicity before. Most NBA rosters remained at least half white until the early 1970s, when the demographics changed for good. Then, when black players became more prominent in the game, the NBA couldn't attract a large casual fan base. In the late 1970s, even after the merger brought Julius Erving and others from the ABA, the NBA remained a niche sport. It was a league that knew its place, which was a distant third after professional baseball and football, even though basketball was a more popular recreational sport in America than either baseball or football. The league desperately craved an audience beyond the hardcore crowd but couldn't make the connection mainly because NBA stars didn't resonate as well as NFL and baseball stars. Everyone had their suspicions. Few NBA players had endorsement deals beyond a sneaker contract; there was no NBA version of O.J. Simpson running through airports and selling rental cars. The league's most dominant player was fortunate enough to play in big-market Los Angeles, but Kareem Abdul-Jabbar was moody and icy and, as a Muslim, embraced a religion considered extreme and radical. Other than Erving, a personable player and true ambassador of the game, the NBA lacked a mass-marketable black player.

The league's relationship with national television was poor, even for the pre-cable TV age; national games on CBS during the regular season weren't even picked up by affiliates in certain markets. As a kid who lived in Pittsburgh during the '70s, the NBA was a myth to me, mostly because I saw few games on TV, and when the games were shown, it was mainly the Celtics, Lakers, or Knicks. Even in the years immediately after Larry Bird and Magic Johnson arrived to save the league, the NBA experienced sluggish growth and then a major embarrassment. The 1980 NBA Finals between the Lakers and

Sixers, Magic and Erving, were shown on tape delay, right after the 11 o'clock news in the East.

The NBA went from mostly white to mostly black in less than two decades, and you wondered then if the country was ready for that transition in the beginning. Basketball fans really didn't care; they just wanted to see the game. But the casual fan wasn't rushing to the ticket window or the TV, and I suspect it was racial to an extent. Even Stern's racial antenna detected some disturbing signals when he became commissioner in 1984 and said the public considered the NBA to be "too black, too drug-infested." It didn't help, image-wise, when a pair of violent episodes involving black players tarnished the game during this low period. Kermit Washington nearly killed Rudy Tomjanovich with a vicious punch, and Darryl Dawkins threw up his dukes during the 1977-78 finals. If the casual fan wanted another reason to tune out the NBA, he had one.

Magic and Bird have largely been credited for rescuing the game and giving the NBA an enormous popularity boost, and to an extent, this is true. Magic came into the NBA with a smile to match his talent, making him nonthreatening and refreshing, an extreme contrast to his more accomplished teammate, Abdul-Jabbar. Bird was the coveted white star, the most anticipated since Pete Maravich. Millions watched Magic and Bird in the 1979 Final Four, and that audience simply followed them to the NBA, curious to see if a rivalry would develop. Lucky for the league, Magic went to big-market L.A., and Bird joined the most storied franchise in the NBA, and both teams were transformed into instant winners. When the Celtics and Lakers squared off during their classic championship matches in the 1980s, garnished by a celebrity mascot named Jack Nicholson, the league had finally piqued the interest of casual fans and secured a spot in prime-time television.

"Magic couldn't have done that by himself," said Walt "Clyde" Frazier, the Hall of Fame guard who starred with the Knicks. "He needed Bird. We needed Bird. Basketball needed a white superstar at that time, and you could say it still does now. It's human nature. You need someone to identify with, and Larry identified with the people who bought all the tickets, just like Pistol Pete Maravich. Nobody wanted to come right out and say it, but everyone knew how much Bird meant to the league at that time, because of his race. Basketball was in trouble. Nobody was making money. Franchises were selling for a fraction of what they'd get today. We had no corporate sponsors. A lot of southern cities didn't even pick up the game of the week on their TV affiliates. When I left the league, I thought it was going to fold."

Totally lost among the theories to explain the increase in NBA popularity was the increase in acceptance of black culture by white America. Music that was almost exclusively consumed by blacks found its way to the suburbs, where white kids gorged themselves on hip hop and rap, and was suddenly played over the loudspeakers at NBA arenas. Street fashion also found a huge market beyond the city limits, where jeans became baggier. Bo Derek wore her hair in braids in the movie *10*. The white kids of the 1960s, who witnessed and felt the social transformation caused by integration and the Civil Rights Movement, were now adults, and they brought less racial baggage home to their kids. It was far more acceptable for whites in this new era to relate to black culture and even, to an extent, identify with it as best they could; plenty of white teenagers developed their rebellion by embracing any and all things black. Major corporations that wouldn't even consider using blacks in their advertising campaigns just a few decades earlier were suddenly hiring, especially in sports. All of this had a profound effect on the NBA and how America began to view a game dominated by blacks. Suddenly, the NBA was chic and NBA players were idols.

Bolstered by Stern's marketing skills, the NBA was suddenly flush with success, which reflected in attendance, merchandise sales, and TV ratings. The golden goose was growing, and the league never felt so healthy in terms of perception and revenue and its place in the American sports landscape. No other professional team sports, not even the NFL, experienced the kind of growth in the mid-1980s as the NBA did. With the change in racial attitudes, a league once considered "too black" was now too good to be true. NBA owners saw their investments multiply many times over, and NBA players became among the richest pro athletes in the country. This could not have happened unless the consumer, which was still overwhelmingly white inside the arenas, accepted black athletes. And it also helped that the black stars with the most visibility were "white friendly," meaning they were very mainstream and very nonthreatening.

Julius Erving spoke like a Harvard literature professor and reeked of class. Magic Johnson remained congenial and upbeat throughout his career, and even survived an out-of-character episode when he openly rebelled against Paul Westhead and got the Laker coach fired. Moses Malone gave white America an early Ebonics lesson when he predicted the 1983 Sixers would win each playoff series in "fo, fo, and fo."

The only time racial boundary lines were drawn was during the Lakers–Celtics championship grudge matches in the '80s. Whites tended to identify more with the Celtics because of Bird and a roster that held more white players than most teams, while blacks sided with the up-tempo Lakers and their fast-break mentality. This dynamic was exploited by Spike Lee in *Do the Right Thing,* in which Lee strategically placed a Bird jersey on a white worker in an Italian pizza shop in a black neighborhood. The reasons for those racial alliances, however, didn't hold much credibility beyond the surface. The Celtics were coached by K.C. Jones, then one of only a handful of black coaches, while Pat Riley coached the Lakers. Also, the Celtics were historically a leader when it came to integration in pro sports. They were among the first to welcome black players; Bill Russell became the first black coach of a pro franchise in 1969; and Celtics boss Red Auerbach insisted that wherever the Celtics played, especially in the Deep South, his black players be treated fairly.

The Celtics were only guilty of playing in a northern city that often held Dixie attitudes about blacks, especially during forced busing. The city was especially cool initially toward Russell, who jump-started the Celtics' string of championships. The reasons for this were undoubtedly racial, given that a white star of Russell's magnitude would have enjoyed a much more comfortable association with fans and the media. In some ways, given the attitudes of Boston in the 1950s and '60s and Russell, a clash was inevitable. By the time he arrived in Boston, Russell was already hardened by discrimination he and his family felt in Louisiana, where he was born, and later in Oakland, where he was raised. In Boston, despite being a star, Russell was subjected to housing discrimination, developed a strained relationship with the media, and suffered in popularity when compared to Ted Williams and Bobby Orr, the only two Boston athletes on Russell's level. Russell, who once insisted he didn't play for Boston—"I played for the Celtics"—refused to attend his own jersey retirement ceremony at Boston Garden and also his Hall of Fame induction in 1975. Many years later, and only after he received encouragement from his daughter, Russell softened toward the city and made public appearances there. Russell never cited any problems with his teammates or Auerbach, however. Therefore, given their progressive attitudes about blacks, which weren't popular at the time in Boston, the Celtics deserved plenty of respect, not scorn, from the black community.

The litmus test for black players and widespread public acceptance was provided by Michael Jordan. He showed star potential on the court almost immediately. But almost just as quickly, he became a national commercialized phenomenon. With the country embracing the concept of fitness in the late 1980s, Nike made Jordan the face of the company, and it was a marriage made in Madison Avenue heaven. Not only did Jordan show well on TV, he was colorless. He was packaged for mass-market appeal, and he cut through all racial barriers. In public at least, Jordan was a man for all people, someone who didn't attach himself to a particular cause or racial identity. His image-spinners cast him as someone who could relate to a Harlem playground or a La Jolla country club, which wasn't much of a stretch at all; in reality, Jordan was an icon in any setting.

The biggest winner in Jordan's widespread appeal was the NBA. With Nike essentially doing the marketing for the league, the NBA reaped all the rich benefits at the box office, and in a change of fortune, the league suddenly had leverage in contract talks with the networks. Less than a decade after the NBA finals were shown on tape-delay, the championship round was suddenly doing big numbers in prime time, and NBA regular-season games were shown on cable and network TV. This certainly was a 180-degree change. Also, the image of the typical NBA player changed, in an interesting way: Stern likened his players to Disney characters who were loved by people of all ages and races. On the court and off, life for the NBA was rich and rewarding.

Prosperity came with a price. The average salary for NBA players began to dwarf those in other sports, and some Joe Fans couldn't relate to the paychecks or the idea of those oversized checks going to black men. There was an undercurrent of racial resentment between white fan and black athlete that didn't reflect at the box office but instead on talk radio and inside the arenas, where discontent was frequently heard. Given the kind of money they made, which the average fan couldn't relate to, black players in certain situations found themselves walking a fine line, and if they ever got out of line, they ran the risk of fan backlash. Charles Barkley accidentally spitting on a little innocent white girl would not be tolerated, nor would the most glaring act of defiance: Latrell Sprewell choking his white coach.

When Sprewell grabbed P.J. Carlesimo by the throat and squeezed, it was more than insubordination. It was a player, one making millions of dollars a year, who couldn't take orders from a coach who simply asked that Sprewell "put some mustard" on his passes. The incident happened out of sight and spared America countless replays on TV, but it did give the country a reason to gripe and maybe conjure up old and stereotypical images of black men bent on violence. True enough, Sprewell choking his white coach was something straight out of a blaxploitation movie, where the angry black man takes out his frustration on the white establishment. And this wasn't merely a lapse by a mainstream black athlete; this was a player with an edge going on a rampage. This was hard for conservative America to swallow, and so was a subsequent press conference held by Sprewell, where he was "supported" in the background by some of his team-mates, none of whom were white. It seemed to smack of race, when in reality Sprewell had simply behaved like all idiots do when they feel their manhood is questioned.

It was fairly evident that the NBA had a growing problem as the new millennium approached. A fair amount of teenage players, almost all of them black, were coming into the league carrying maturity issues. Stern had tried to institute an age limit, and he was finally successful in 2005 in barring players from the draft until they turned 19 or were one year removed from high school. But a good number of teenagers arrived before the age limit. A majority managed to mesh comfortably in an adult world, a lot better than some young NFL players did. Some hadn't mastered the skill of conducting themselves as professionals. Their arrival was not lost on Rasheed Wallace, a veteran who went on a mindless rant about race in a 2003 interview with the *Oregonian* newspaper.

Wallace said, "They just want to draft niggers who are dumb and dumber, straight out of high school. That's why they're drafting all these high school cats, because they come into the league and they don't know no better. . . . They look at us black athletes like we're dumb-ass niggers. It's as if we're just going to shut up and sign for the dollars and do as they say."

It wasn't the most ignorant thing to come out of an athlete's mouth, but close enough. Truthfully, the NBA didn't want high school players to be eligible for the draft; that was a desire of the player's union, not the commissioner or the general managers, who hated the risks

AP Photo/Ben Margot

Latrell Sprewell, playing for the New York Knicks against the Golden State Warriors, two years after choking his former coach P.J. Carlesimo, who is on the sidelines to the right.

involved in drafting teenagers. Wallace was simply being Wallace, someone who, given his history of arguing with referees and getting busted with reefer, needed maturity lessons himself. Wallace was Exhibit A in the theory that not everyone famous deserves a platform. Not surprisingly, when I asked black players about Wallace's profane argument, they had no comment, none of them willing to publicly disagree with a fellow black player about race.

Richard Jefferson, a thoughtful young forward with the New Jersey Nets who, as a kid, went to Africa with his parents on a missionary journey, said accountability was definitely in order. "Whenever you start to be portrayed as thugs," said Jefferson, "the NBA has to change the way the game is viewed. I don't blame the commissioner for trying to clean up the image. But if individuals don't take into account what they're doing, it doesn't matter."

Jefferson was quick to state the obvious, that a majority of black players in the NBA conduct themselves as professionals. "We just have the three or four percent who keep getting into trouble. I'm not going to knock someone who wasn't as fortunate as I was, in terms of socioeconomic backgrounds. It all comes down to maturity and personal responsibility."

The NBA did receive a kiss from the basketball gods just before the age-limit rule was put in place. The NBA got LeBron James. He was the rare team-sport athlete who was nationally famous while in high school. He made the cover of *Sports Illustrated* in his junior year, and by the following year, the boys' team at St. Vincent–St. Mary in Akron, Ohio, played a national traveling schedule to sold-out gyms and was on ESPN. James also grew up poor in Akron and was raised by a single mother. And this is where the NBA got lucky. James managed to steer clear of the usual trappings that follow plenty of kids like him, and he came into the NBA with a mental maturity to match his physical maturity. He surrounded himself with the right people, said the right things, conducted himself the right way, radiated the right image. Even at the raw age of 18, James was wise enough to know the enormous stakes and the importance of image and conduct for someone who had heavy influence among kids and teenagers. In that sense, he was a lot like Kevin Garnett, another teenager from a less than ideal background who made a bump-free transition from high school to the NBA.

To the delight of Stern and others, LeBron wasn't the second coming of Iverson or Rasheed; he was mainstream, with just enough cool to connect with teenagers. Even the popular Nike commercials featuring the "LeBrons," his fictional family, walked the fine line between mainstream and street. The characters in the commercials, all played by James, included a graying old man from the '60s, a young kid, a hip-talking smoothie constantly on a cell phone, and the real-life LeBron. The music played in the background was exclusively old school. Not only were the commercials catchy, they appealed to everyone and offended no one. They spanned generations. LeBron's TV image was one that parents and their kids could agree on, much the same as Michael Jordan commercials, and the image seemed fairly accurate to his true personality and values.

"It just felt right for me," said LeBron. "A little bit of me is in all of those characters. I'm a businessman, a kid, I like old school, and I'm a basketball player. That's all of my personalities."

As the commercials and LeBron's performances began to overwhelm the NBA, another startling transformation began taking place. A one-time gangsta rapper turned 30 and got wiser. Allen Iverson confessed he "made some mistakes" back when he was young and stubborn and owned the kind of generational appeal that LeBron does today. At the risk of destroying all of the street credibility he built up over the years, Iverson admitted he'd do a few things differently.

He made this admirable and refreshing admission in the fall of 2006, shortly before paying for the funeral of a Philadelphia boy, a robbery victim who was murdered for not handing over an Iverson jersey. The jerseys are hot sellers among kids because Iverson, through his own recklessness, transformed himself into an urban Jesus long ago. Evidently, by killing in order to get one, some thug wanted that jersey to make a connection to an idol, a basketball player once worshipped for reasons other than his ability to shoot a jumper.

CHAPTER 6

Baseball Bygones

Going Soft on Hardball

On a typical weekend morning in the summertime, in a front yard near you, a father and son will each grab a leather glove and toss a ball back and forth for maybe an hour. They will laugh, they will talk, and most of all, they will bond, all because of this simple and innocent game of catch. Then they'll hop into the car, head to the ballpark, buy some peanuts and popcorn and two colas, sit in the bleachers, and spend the rest of the glorious day watching baseball. This is where it begins, where baseball is passed from one generation to the next, where the love of the game creeps into the blood of the kid and remains until he becomes a father and the cycle repeats itself.

This time-honored ritual is older than Wrigley Field and stronger than the smell of spilt beer at the concession stand. It captures the essence of a sport that in turn captures the imagination of America and strengthens American families. Baseball bonds loved ones and creates simple yet special and priceless moments. Baseball doesn't get any purer than the sight of Senior and Junior enjoying a special moment at the ballpark on a lazy Sunday afternoon, sharing a red hot with mustard, and taking home an everlasting memory, maybe even a foul ball if they're lucky. This is how millions of kids become hooked on baseball. This is how they start playing baseball. And this is where baseball loses black America, which has turned its back on the pastime with the swiftness and sureness of Jackie Robinson stealing home.

The baseball fields in many parts of urban America are mostly well worn and trampled, not by wide-eyed Little Leaguers toting their Louisville Sluggers and leather gloves, but by glassy-eyed drunks holding their half-empty bottles. That's how Willie Randolph, the manager of the New York Mets, recalled some of the ballparks where he grew up in Brooklyn, which aren't much different than those in other cities. In these urban towns, baseball fields are barely more than glorified public parks badly in need of TLC. With the municipal funding for parks and recreation departments plummeting about as low as a slider, these fields are literally diamonds in the rough, complete with dandelions in the patchy outfield grass and rusted poles holding up decrepit dugouts. There is little money or incentive to repair them, and therefore, little reason for kids to use them. In some urban areas, baseball fields have become urban cow pastures, neglected and unused, just a swatch of dirt and grass that also lacks the one necessity to play the game: bases.

Then there's the absence of the father, which today is sadly a grim statistic in poor black America, where the majority of families are run by single mothers, bless their overstressed hearts. In order to survive and flourish, baseball needs fathers almost as much as kids need fathers. He's baseball's best ambassador, keeper of the flame. He brings baseball into the home, buys the first bat and glove, and introduces the kid to the innocent and wonderful game of catch. He takes pride in his role as a sports father and considers baseball a sworn duty. Throughout suburbia, this is common and widespread. The father is in his kid's life 24/7. But in other households where the father is present, the ball tossed back and forth by the father is either bright orange, or brown with laces. He's throwing a basketball or football because his generation also tuned out baseball, you see, and he can only teach what he knows and loves. There is the very real chance that baseball has now lost at least two generations of blacks.

Black America, as a whole, doesn't care deeply about baseball and never will, no matter how hard baseball tries to seduce the race. A Harris poll in 2005 confirmed this; only 6 percent of blacks polled selected baseball as their favorite sport, compared to 47 percent for football. The decaying baseball fields in the 'hood and the diminishing number of active fathers who are willing to pass the game to their sons are just two reasons why blacks have tuned out baseball. There are others. "This is the result of a perfect storm created by a lot of different things that took place, and that are taking place," admits Jimmie Lee Solomon, the Major League executive in charge of reinventing baseball in the city.

Solomon is right. Kids can't just show up and start playing baseball. The sport requires equipment, which makes it difficult for young boys to play on a whim and too expensive for the poor. Some kids will have gloves, some won't. Most catchers can't afford a mask. Nobody has a uniform or cleats. And if the bat breaks, the game is over. In basketball and football, all they need is the ball. There's the argument that baseball was expensive several decades ago, when the Negro Leagues were in business, and that never stopped black kids from playing. Well, there were few other athletic options then. Football and basketball hadn't achieved the popularity they enjoy today, and when those sports took off, so did plenty of black kids after them.

Baseball also has no street credibility. Black kids in urban America don't gain status among their peers by playing baseball; if anything, they lose it by messing around with what is perceived as a "white man's sport" or a "Latino sport." Baseball has no transcendent black star who carries clout among black kids. Baseball is also slow and boring and simply doesn't trigger the imagination of city kids who gravitate to the excitement of basketball and the danger of football. Finally, playing baseball doesn't solve the poverty problem quickly enough for poor kids looking to cash in right away. Nobody can get rich fast by playing baseball. The typical Major Leaguer spends years in the minors before getting called up, and once he makes the bigs, he still doesn't get the set-for-life contract right away. Kids from the city don't read about 19-year-old baseball players pulling $15 million a year. But they do know what LeBron James makes.

There's also the issue of college scholarships, or the lack of them. Only 11.78 baseball scholarships are allotted per school. Thus, only a handful of players in each Division I school earn full rides, because baseball isn't a revenue-producing sport at the college level. The incentive to play high school baseball in order to attend college for free doesn't exist among poor blacks. This is a big factor that cannot be underestimated or disputed.

"Baseball has become a rich person's game," said Hall of Famer Joe Morgan. "Colleges don't give you scholarships, so you play basketball instead. Or football. If you need a full ride to college, you're going to play basketball. Baseball doesn't do that, so your parents have to be rich enough to pay your way to college, just so you'll have the opportunity to play baseball."

Did we list enough factors working against baseball's effort to generate interest among black kids?

"It's not just the game," said Willie Randolph of the Mets, who became the first black manager of a New York team. "It's also the kids today. Some just aren't patient enough anymore. They don't work as hard as we used to. They'll try baseball for a while, then leave and never come back."

Inside his office at Shea Stadium, Randolph has built a shrine that honors a legacy of a woebegone era. The walls are nearly covered with pictures of Negro League players. Clearly, the history of the black baseball player lives and

©Rob Tringali/SportsChrome/Getty Images

Willie Randolph celebrates with one of his New York Mets players following a win over the Los Angeles Dodgers in the 2006 National League Division Series. Randolph, who is from the Bronx and played and coached for the New York Yankees before becoming manager of the Mets, is the rare exception today as a black player born and raised on baseball in the big city.

breathes inside Randolph, once a standout player himself on every level. He takes pride in the game and his culture and will never forget the people who made it possible for him to make a comfortable living through baseball. But when Randolph walked through his own clubhouse on Opening Day 2007, he saw just two American-born black players. Combined with the Yankees, the New York baseball teams had only three African-American players on their active rosters for Opening Day, and that's counting Derek Jeter, whose father is black and mother is white and who's technically biracial. The Cardinals won the 2006 World Series with two American-born blacks. And as miniscule as that number seems, it's about average for Major League rosters in this millennium. The number of African-American players was 8 percent in 2006. When Randolph played for the great Yankee teams in the late 1970s, the number was roughly 27 percent. Therefore, the wishful idea that blacks are trying baseball for a while and then dropping it, as Randolph suggested, isn't entirely accurate. Many aren't trying at all.

The source for this can be found in the attitude and culture of the big city. The majority of blacks in the minor and major leagues aren't coming from Chicago or New York City or Los Angeles, the breeding ground for a fair number of pro and college black athletes. They're coming from the middle-class suburbs where the game is organized, or small-town America where there are fields aplenty and the game still has clout among country kids. The same big cities that send scores of players to the NBA and professional football are weakly represented in Major League baseball. These kids aren't involved in the game, nor is there great effort made by adults to get them involved. The playing fields are substandard when compared to those in the suburbs, and the community doesn't have the passion or the patience to teach these kids how to play properly. Therefore, these kids are growing up with other sports. Baseball is badminton to them.

Veteran outfielder Cliff Floyd, that lone American-born black member of the Mets on Opening Day 2006, was a rare example of a city kid who not only loved baseball but chose the sport over basketball and football. He grew up in Chicago and played on the same high school basketball team as Michael Finley, who went to the NBA. He eventually chose a path barely traveled. After basketball season, when Floyd went out for baseball, he was the only black player on the team. "All my black friends, they thought I was wasting my time, they thought I was crazy," Floyd recalled. "I played baseball, and they went to McDonald's."

Most of the young black athletes in urban America who are physically gifted will steer away from baseball. And that hurts baseball's chances of finding and developing the next black Hall of Fame player. "There are no tall black players in the Majors," said Mookie Wilson, the former Mets star. "There are no more Dave Winfields and Dave Parkers, two guys who could have played professional football or basketball if they wanted. Those athletes don't stick with baseball anymore. If there's a guy who's six-four or six-five, you know baseball's not going to get him. And if the guy is strong and weighs 240, baseball's not going to get him, either. One is going to basketball, and the other's going to football. There are so many great athletes that could help take baseball to another level. But we lost them."

Down in the Caribbean, where the Major Leagues get most of their players of color, the process is completely reversed. Poor kids do nothing but play baseball. It's the activity of choice in the streets of the Dominican Republic and Cuba and Puerto Rico, where kids begin playing baseball as soon as they can walk. With so much talent and money at stake, these places have sprouted baseball factories, lavishly supported and funded by Major League teams, where future shortstops and second basemen learn the nuances of the game early and perfect it before they reach high school. It's a pipeline that leads directly to Major League rosters; thus, professional teams place a higher priority on getting talent from Latin America than from urban America. The Major League teams know they're getting players who are hungry and motivated and have already figured out the nuances of the game by the time they reach their teens. Therefore, there's no comparison between the 'hood in Latin America and that in America. One place has a commitment and a Jones for baseball; the other place would rather shoot hoops.

"Nobody goes to the 'hood anymore to search for ballplayers," said Gary Sheffield, born and raised on the hard side of Tampa. "I know it's dangerous in there, but still, you'd think baseball would have the courage to go in there and get something started. You don't see anyone going to L.A. and finding another Eddie Murray or Ozzie

Smith. They don't go there anymore. I don't think there's much effort being made to grow our own players."

It's not totally baseball's fault. Again, this is a business. The scouts will only look for talent where talent lies, and, contrary to what Sheffield said, they go wherever there's an abundance of talent, same as football and basketball scouts do. Problem is, baseball talent isn't thick in south-central L.A. or the north side of St. Louis. The search now extends overseas, to Japan and Korea, to countries with the same passion for baseball as white America and Latin America.

At first, the Asian countries sent only pitchers to the Majors, but now position players are becoming plentiful and successful. Just as in the Dominican Republic, the Asian countries have strong baseball factories in place to train talent and keep kids interested in the game. There's also a vibrant professional league in Japan, where talent is almost on par with the Major Leagues. Urban America can't compete with that. Baseball did open a development factory in Compton in 2006, in an effort to revive the game in an area that once produced a respectable number of Major League players. And another organization, called RBI, for Reviving Baseball in Inner Cities, is active and optimistic. But those are exceptions. Those are two positive developments facing a multitude of negative forces against change. It isn't unusual for city high schools to drop baseball altogether, citing budget problems and waning interest. Therefore, for various reasons, urban America is forcing scouts to fly 5,000 miles, instead of a few hundred miles, to find the next great ballplayer, and you can't fault baseball entirely for that. This is a business.

The ultimate irony, of course, is Jackie Robinson and how he endured threats and taunts and became one of the most important if not beloved athletes in sports history when he broke the color line. Some 60 years later, his impact is reflected everywhere but in the game he changed. This is the saddest trend in the history of baseball, if not all sports. No one could have predicted such a near mass exodus by an entire race. Thanks to Robinson, there are more black bankers and lawyers and doctors and CEOs and quarterbacks and coaches than ever before, a more satisfying impact, in my opinion, in the big picture. But baseball has roughly the same number of blacks in the Majors now as when Robinson played. And in 1997, on the 50th anniversary of Robinson's historic feat, the Dodgers had only one black player on the roster, and he was a backup.

"Jackie is turning in his grave," said Mookie Wilson, who's outraged by the rapidly invisible black player, but not surprised. This reversal has been a steady work in progress. The disconnection began in the early 1980s and appears permanent. There is no hint of a major reversal, or a complete change in attitude, or a sharp rising infatuation for baseball among black kids. There is nothing but abandonment. You might not buy Reggie Jackson's bold assertion that "some day soon, there might be more blacks in the NHL," but the point is made. There is a considerable lack of black faces at all playing levels of baseball, there is little fire inside the belly of blacks to play baseball, and there's ample evidence that blacks will never return to baseball in great numbers.

"Jack expected more," said Rachel Robinson, speaking of her husband. "We're all disappointed that it has come to this."

Actually, the whole notion that blacks were hopelessly addicted to baseball is debatable. At best, blacks did hold baseball in high esteem during the peak years of the Negro Leagues. At worst, black passion for baseball is largely a myth, perhaps inflamed by Robinson and integration and the hope that blacks would adopt the sport because of him. There are no credible statistics taken that support either assertion. This much we do know: The barnstorming teams of the Negro Leagues certainly played to ample audiences in the South and certain parts of the Northeast and Midwest. But those games also served as social chitchats, much the same as football games at historically black colleges do today. On those campuses, the football game is secondary to mingling, making plans to party that night, and, of course, the spirited halftime battle of the marching bands. As an alum of Howard University and someone who chronicled countless games for the campus newspaper, I can tell you that very few people actually go to the stadium strictly for football.

In the Negro Leagues, fans congregated partly to see Josh Gibson and Satchel Paige, no doubt, but also to exchange gossip and catch up on the times. Understand that social options for blacks back then were limited, especially in the South, because of Jim Crow. Going to the movie theater or the beach or the racetrack was out of the question in these small towns. Television was in its infancy then, and owning TV sets was beyond the scope and reach of poor blacks, anyway. Therefore, baseball was the primary source of entertainment, almost by default. Along with the church, the baseball park served as the black community's town hall, a chance to see a game and enjoy an afternoon without worrying about sitting in the whites-only section. When integration came to the Major Leagues, the Negro Leagues died, and so did baseball in urban America, for the most part.

When Robinson arrived in the Majors, scores of blacks began showing up at ballparks in a show of support at first. But if you went strictly on sightings at the ballparks, their numbers, interestingly, seemed to dwindle just as the number of black players began to multiply. That wasn't because of economics, because baseball has always been priced right for families and lower-income fans. Baseball was (and is) affordable, and blacks still didn't go in droves. That in itself was proof that blacks never loved the game all that much from the get-go. Black fans came to root for black players, not necessarily to root for baseball. When the novelty of seeing black players in baseball began to wear off, gradually, the attention span of the black sports fan shifted to football and basketball in the 1960s, and it stayed there.

History has distorted the scope of Robinson in regard to popularizing baseball among blacks. Truthfully, Robinson could only do so much. Decades of racism and the barring of blacks from the Major Leagues proved far more powerful than Robinson. Baseball is built on tradition and history and a romantic look at yesteryear, and for many blacks who were lynched and beaten and

Jackie Robinson conquered many obstacles in paving the way for all people, not just blacks, to play baseball. No doubt he'd be saddened to see so few of today's black athletes taking advantage of his trail-blazing efforts and sacrifices.

discriminated against, there's no such thing as the good old days. Blacks know how baseball felt about the race for a long time. A level of distrust developed in black society during segregation, and generations of blacks therefore refused to embrace the game. Baseball never took root in the black community in the early 1900s, not the way boxing did. Boxing was where a black man could whup a white man in the ring and not get arrested or shot for it. Notice how boxing is still popular today in the black community. Meanwhile, the passive attitude regarding baseball was in the blood almost from the start, you might say, and stayed there, even after Robinson broke the color barrier.

Wisely, other professional sports saw the black race push away from baseball and seized the opportunity to tap into a new audience. The NBA began to aggressively push basketball and its stars to black audiences in the 1980s. The league became chic in the 'hood and, most important, had credibility. Kids found they could gain status among their peers by playing basketball, so more kids spent hours playing the game. And then came Michael Jordan, a gift from Madison Avenue, a one-man marketing giant. When Jordan came and grabbed the sports fan by the throat, he also assured that baseball would never approach basketball in terms of popularity in the black community. "Michael Jordan killed baseball," said Cliff Floyd.

When the number of black baseball players began to decline in the '80s, the black community had yet another reason to tune out the sport. Black kids simply didn't have enough role models to dream about. Baseball has always struggled with black idols over the last few decades, and for that reason, black baseball stars never carried as much clout in the black community as basketball or football stars did. Unlike in the NFL and the NBA, a Major League roster has never been majority black or strongly identified with the black community. Major League baseball has never had a team that developed a large and loyal following in black America like John Thompson's basketball teams at Georgetown, or the Showtime Lakers, or Doug Williams and the Redskins. Only a handful of championship baseball teams have even had more than two or three high-profile black players. Despite the greatness of Bob Gibson, for example, black pitchers have always been scarce, and today a black starting quarterback is more common. The biggest baseball stars in the post–Willie Mays era mainly saw their appeal limited to the cities their teams represented. They managed to spread their influence only to an extent in the black community, and certainly not at the level of the elite players in the two other major sports.

Mays was indeed the last black baseball player who had no competition from black players in other professional sports because he had flair and he connected with kids, although arguably his following was bigger among white kids. Mays also was popular strictly based on his ability. He did not radiate beyond baseball. He could be gruff and surly in public, which often overshadowed the image he created by playing stickball with kids in the streets of New York. He also played baseball well before the golden age of athletic endorsements and thus didn't have the benefit of having his image spun and polished through crafty commercials and advertisements. That's what Nike and other companies did with Bo Jackson, who often tended to be grumpy in public except in the Bo Knows commercials, where he was magically transformed into lovable and cuddly.

That introduces another factor. If Jordan didn't kill baseball, then Nike did. The company that was formed in white-bread Oregon strictly as a footwear supplier to runners had no pulse in the urban community. Nike was for Yuppie white people who loved to jog. But then, Phil Knight, the cofounder, decided to branch out into apparel and basketball and made the brilliant decision to hire not a lumbering seven-foot center who couldn't jump more than two inches off the floor but a young, handsome, gravity-defying guard to hawk warm-up suits and hi-tops. Knight did more to bring the NBA into the 'hood than David Stern did. The Nike commercials helped make the NBA cool in the 1980s. Jordan and his line of sneakers changed the way kids dressed, especially black kids in the city. Yet another spike was driven into the heart of baseball.

"Sneakers evolved from a performance item to a fashion item," said Jimmie Lee Solomon. "If you couldn't play like Mike, you could still look like Mike. Baseball couldn't compete with that. You can't wear cleats to school."

Baseball made a few desperate and somewhat transparent attempts to make a play for the black audience, like hiring LL Cool J to rap in promotional commercials, a blatant (and clumsy) reach for street credibility. But baseball was already too late coming to the marketing game, and far too behind basketball and football to produce any drastic change. A handful of hip-hop commercials could not and would not reverse what years of neglect did to baseball among blacks. Baseball's image was already set in granite, and that image didn't endear the game to the masses.

Joe Morgan, a Hall of Famer and frequent critic of baseball's marketing efforts in the past, said sarcastically, "We woke up one morning and realized there weren't any African Americans playing."

As the Major Leagues try to devise new marketing methods, it's interesting how baseball's players aren't tremendous assets to this effort. It's just baseball's rotten luck that the biggest black star of the last dozen years is Barry Bonds. It's as if the sports gods played a rotten trick on baseball. Why else would the same heavens that blessed basketball with Jordan and football with LaDainian Tomlinson dump a suspected steroid cheat and a jerk on baseball, the sport that needs a black star the most? It just doesn't seem fair, but such is the cursed plight of baseball.

Bonds is one of the top dozen sports stars of this generation, and yet he became a colossal and toxic public relations waste. In his prime, Bonds was the closest baseball came to having its very own Jordan. He had the talent to transcend his sport, or at least come close, which is the kind of athlete that every sport needs to convince casual fans to join the hardcore crowd. In his prime, Bonds had style—he played a glamour position, crushed pitches, and was a terrific all-around player. He also was a nightmare away from the field. Bonds certainly had a soft side, but in public he was too unpredictable and surly and a big turnoff. In urban America, he was about as invisible as a star of his magnitude could get. Plus, there was nothing genuine about him, in the street sense, because he grew up a privileged child of a former ballplayer. Poor black kids couldn't relate to Bonds. "Barry," said Torii Hunter, the Gold Glove outfielder for the Twins, "is not one of us."

There were no Nike commercials made by Spike Lee for Bonds, even before the drug allegations. Bonds couldn't capitalize from Madison Avenue the way his peers did in other sports. Even before the steroid cloud followed him later in his career, he had no magnetism among the baseball world at large during his early days with the Pirates. Then, when he began winning MVPs and hitting home runs at a record pace, his appeal was limited to San Francisco, and only because he starred for the home team. In his prime, then, Bonds had zero clout on Madison Avenue, amazing given his accomplishments in baseball, but understandable considering the drug associations and his sour attitude.

You would think, however, that given these bad-boy elements, Bonds would at least have credibility with the counter-culture, in a warped, Dennis Rodman sort of way. That never happened, and the public verdict was unanimous: Bonds wasn't welcomed anywhere. Even stranger, when Bonds tried to play the role of victim as the drug noise increased, he introduced the issue of race. He tried to portray himself as the persecuted black man who was being dogged by injustice. This was hysterical. Here was Bonds, who never attached himself to a single social cause and never was a presence in the black communities of San Francisco or Pittsburgh, suddenly fitting himself for an Afro. Bryan Burwell, a journalist from St. Louis, said it best when he wrote this: "Bonds is a brother of convenience." Bonds followed the same formula as Marion Barry and other black politicians and celebrities did when confronted by trouble they caused themselves—he played the race card. The black community as a whole didn't throw itself in support of Bonds. Besides, Bonds played baseball, largely ignored by the people he claimed to represent.

But Bonds wasn't the only black baseball star who struggled to find a sizable black audience in his prime. Ken Griffey Jr., smart and charitable and someone who respects the black pioneers who paved the way, had the best chance but always came off as shy in public. He lacked the charisma of Torii Hunter, but Hunter spent much of his career in small-market Minnesota, and although a terrific player, he was never MVP talent. Dontrelle Willis and Derek Jeter represent the best package of talent and visibility. But compared to their equals in basketball and football, they too fall short.

We should pause for this clarification: Truthfully, the perception that baseball is lacking in urban America isn't totally accurate. Baseball is lacking among urban black kids. The game still thrives in the 'hood with Latin-born parents, especially in the pockets of New York City, which produced Manny Ramirez among others. In the Latin neighborhoods of large Northeast cities, baseball is king. Scores of black kids don't even bother trying out for those school teams.

The most encouraging success story in urban America regarding black kids and baseball occurred in 1989 when Josh Raiford, an eight-year-old from Harlem, came home one day and told his parents he wanted to play Little League baseball like his classmates at a private school he attended outside of Harlem. Dwight and Iris Raiford discovered, to their disappointment, that Little League had

Mitchell Layton/Getty Images

Barry Bonds might be Major League baseball's all-time home run hitter and one of the top black athletes in history, but his circumstantial link to steroids and off-putting personality have made him a hard sell on Madison Avenue. Even the body armor he wears to bat seems like another barrier between him and fans.

deserted Harlem some 20 years earlier. So the Raifords applied for and received a Harlem chapter and began the chore of creating a slice of youth baseball heaven amid the asphalt and often dangerous streets of the world's most famous black neighborhood.

Dwight Raiford is Ivy League educated and works as a financial planner in Manhattan and also grew up with a love for baseball in rural North Carolina. He quickly became a beacon for the national Little League headquarters because of his color, his background, and his love for his community. He was exactly what Little League was looking for, and within four years, Raiford was elected to chairman of the board for the organization on the strength of his work with the Harlem chapter, which had a storybook start.

The initial response from Harlem to Little League baseball was overwhelming, in terms of participation and favorable media coverage and community involvement. It became a wonderful urban success story. Local businesses and private donations covered the start-up costs. People throughout New York gravitated to one of the more positive events regarding youth and Harlem to happen in years. It conspired to remove the political red tape surrounding the acquisition of playing fields and public funding to insure that the Harlem Little League would be nothing short of a resounding smash. So many kids signed up that a waiting list was issued.

"We had families coming out who had lived in the same building but didn't even know each other," said Raiford. "They found each other through Little League baseball. It broke down the whole idea about New York City people not looking anyone in the eye. It became a duty for the community, and it gave black parents something to engage their kids."

The problems that destroy most urban youth baseball programs before they get started did not ruin the Harlem effort. Raiford even noticed how fathers, some of whom didn't live in the same house as their kids, actually became more involved in their sons' lives once their kids started playing. "Baseball helped strengthen the family," Raiford said. "Baseball brought out the dads, who came out of the woodwork to participate. They look for ways to engage in activities with their kids, and baseball gave them one. Dads came out in great numbers and asked how they could get involved."

Not even the Raifords could comprehend the impact of winning, however. When the Harlem team reached the semifinals of the 2002 Little League World Series, baseball had the moment that it craved for decades, ever since Hank Aaron passed Babe Ruth. Finally, something was happening in baseball that made the black community take notice. The Harlem team returned home to a parade and a hero's welcome, and baseball actually registered a pulse among a large segment of blacks. But even the continued success of the Harlem chapter isn't enough to convince Raiford that baseball's problem in the black community is over.

"I think baseball is viewed as a white sport," he said. "It has a white culture, and it's not inviting to African Americans. It's hostile to African Americans. You go to basketball and football games, for example, and listen to the music that's being played. It's not the same music played at baseball games. It's subtle, but it's part of the culture of the sport. Baseball has been traditionally white, and even with the rise of black athletes it has not welcomed black athletes."

The Harlem team did, however, raise the consciousness of the Little League and started a push to improve youth baseball in the bigger cities. In that sense, David James might have the toughest job in baseball. He's in charge of raising interest in areas where there's little or no interest in baseball. As the Director of the Urban Initiative Program, James understands the task at hand. He realizes nothing will change overnight, if it changes at all. But he refuses to concede defeat, even when many signs suggest that defeat is inevitable.

"Kids want to play," he said. "There are many challenges in getting them to play and keeping them interested. That's where the obstacles lie. But I believe kids want to play and will play baseball if we overcome those obstacles."

When the program began in 2000, the group conducted a national study of Little League participation, which merely confirmed the obvious. Black kids don't play baseball, nor do they have much incentive to play. There are over 200 Little League programs in about 80 cities, but the healthiest leagues and teams were those beyond the city limits, especially the biggest cities. "We saw holes across the country in places like St. Louis and Kansas City and saw numbers diminishing in Los Angeles," he said. "You do the research and find that these places have high numbers of African Americans. I can't say that I was surprised, but I certainly was disappointed. It was worse than I suspected."

The biggest problems facing Little League baseball in poor black communities are facilities and organization. Both areas are beyond the control of kids who otherwise would play baseball and might even choose baseball over other sports. But facilities and organization depend on the cooperation of parents and local businesses and politicians. The infrastructure of these Little League sites is a wreck compared to those in the more affluent and whiter suburbs. It's really no contest. The big cities can't compete with the small towns and suburbs, which place a greater priority on developing baseball players and building youth sports teams in general. Those places have the money and the commitment and the passion and the sites, and therefore they have the attention and participation of the kids.

The public baseball fields in Camden, New Jersey, are often left lonely from neglect while the nearby basketball courts require heavy maintenance from overuse. On one sunny weekend during the summer of 2006, while my eight-year-old daughter and others competed in a track meet in Camden Park, the baseball field next door was used by dogs for exercise and by cars as a parking lot. At the Schools Stadium in Newark, which is used by over 20 teams during the summer, there are no batting cages or bullpens, and the field is often used by soccer play-ers. Like most cities that are strapped for funds, Newark cannot and will not prioritize the maintenance of baseball fields over fixing the schools or aiding the elderly. There's simply only so much money to spread around.

"Some city leagues don't own facilities, so they have to apply for permits for usage of time," said James. "They have to compete with other organizations and sometimes with other sports. That's not easy."

Youth baseball is mainly run by volunteers, and in that area, the city leagues also run a distant second to the suburbs. Parents and community leaders lack the time or interest, or both, to show up in force and lend the amount of support needed to successfully run a league. Finding enough baseball coaches is a problem, partly because a good number of adults in black communities didn't grow up playing baseball themselves. By contrast, there's never a problem finding adults to teach and supervise basketball teams or football teams in the city. Also, money is a major factor in certain areas. This is an era in which youth baseball teams travel constantly in the summer to compete in top-level tournaments and gain valuable experience and instruction. It's not unusual for white families to spend thousands of dollars on travel costs and fees, and poor families from the city can't scratch up that kind of money on a yearly basis. Also, outfitting teams and stockpiling first-rate equipment is beyond the reach of most city-funded clubs and leagues.

"The kids aren't the problem," said James. "Our biggest problem is the adults. The number of adult volunteers directly impacts the number of kids they can serve. The kids just aren't getting enough support. They want to play. They want to experience it. But the assistance from adults in many areas just isn't there. Meanwhile, the affluent communities have more volunteers than they know what to do with."

Another major difference in city versus suburbia is the presence of fathers. James was introduced to the game by his father, and in turn, James taught his son how to throw and catch. Both generations of the James family followed baseball tradition and passed on the love of the game, a process that repeats itself in millions of families. But when he travels the country and studies the state of youth baseball in urban areas, he notices a disturbing pattern.

"When the kids come to sign up," James said, "it's usually with a mom or a grandmother. Most of these kids were never introduced to the game by a male."

The problem hit youth baseball close to home during the last decade, when the league that serves the black section of Williamsport, Pennsylvania, the headquarters for Little League baseball, began showing an overall decline in participation. The Maynard league eventually closed because of problems with funding and field maintenance and volunteers, all of which steered kids in other directions. The league was restarted in 2004 when the community became involved and took action.

"The minute we redid the field," said James, "the numbers shot up. Kids began showing up. That was important, because for something like this to happen in Williamsport, it really was a little embarrassing."

In an effort to stimulate a passion for baseball among kids in urban America, James and his group bring 10 teams to Williamsport for a special tournament during the summer. A collective effort by a handful of Major Leaguers, led by Torii Hunter, have agreed to sponsor four teams to play exhibition games during the Little League World Series. The Major Leaguers pay for everything: housing, food, and, most of all, the experience. James is hoping the exposure to youth baseball that only Williamsport can provide will change attitudes and lead to a more active participation in urban areas. He thinks the big cities and poor black neighborhoods are missing the positive aspects that baseball can provide.

"The local Little League program is the rallying point of most communities around the country," he said. "It's the point where you meet and greet. You get parents and adults mingling and talking about their day, or about their kids. In some communities, that's needed, something positive instead of the negative things that are taking place."

You almost want to root for baseball to find a substantial black audience if only to validate the valiant effort by

Hunter. There just aren't many black athletes like him with the same level of social consciousness, energy, pride in his people, and love for his sport. Bringing baseball to urban America has become a cause for Hunter, who uses his time, money, and energy to introduce the game to young black kids and asks for nothing in return except that these kids expand their interests.

"I'd never left Pine Bluff, Arkansas, when I was a kid until I traveled with my youth baseball team," Hunter said. "When you take a kid out of his environment, he sees a way to change. It pushed me to go to school and get my grades. It made me take a different road than everyone else around me. I wanted to do something different. And now, I want to get these kids out of their environment and see something different, like I did."

Deep inside, Hunter knows he's fighting a lost battle. He realizes he can't change the attitude of a game or an entire race overnight, and probably not at all. He just wants to do his part, and if that results in getting one black kid into the Majors, he's fine with it. Or if a black kid tries baseball and doesn't like it but becomes an astronaut simply because he wanted to take a different path the way he did with baseball, Hunter sees that as a victory as well.

Throughout his baseball life, Hunter grew weary of being one of the few black players on his team. Sometimes he was the only black player. He decided early on that once he made a Major League roster and established himself, he would try to alter the racial makeup of the game. Since he began his crusade, he enlisted the help of many professional players, white as well as black, to raise the awareness of baseball among blacks. He didn't know how difficult the task was until he gave one of many speeches to kids. "I asked if they knew who Hank Aaron was," said Hunter. "They looked at me real funny."

Hunter has somewhat harsh words for Major League baseball and its efforts to promote the game among blacks. He believes the effort and the methods need to improve. "If Derek Jeter wasn't in New York winning championships, you wouldn't even know Derek Jeter," Hunter said. "Major League baseball doesn't market us enough. We're not household names in the places where we need to be household names. We're losing these kids to the other sports. All the youth coaches want to put these kids in basketball or football, and the parents are thinking that way, too. They're saying, 'I want my son to be like LeBron, or I want him to be like Iverson.' You don't hear them saying they want their sons to be like Torii Hunter or Ken Griffey Jr."

And Hunter doesn't limit his disappointment to Major League baseball. "It starts with the parents," he said. "They don't take their kids to practice. And the organization of baseball in the inner city needs to improve. Practices don't start on time. Or parents bring their kids late, because they can't get off from work in time. Hey, I know it's hard, especially for the single mothers. In the suburbs, the mother doesn't work. But it all comes down to the parents."

Hunter personally knows of one parent who tried to get his son to play baseball and failed.

"My own son said baseball wasn't for him," Hunter said, speaking of Torii Jr., a 12-year-old. "He calls baseball a 'punk sport.' He said football and basketball are more fun. Can you believe that?"

Hunter laughed. "This is happening in my own household."

It's even happening in the backyard of the black community. A good number of the baseball teams at historically black colleges and universities, especially those on the East Coast, are white, a racial sign of the apocalypse if there ever was one. And this isn't a recent phenomenon. While attending Howard University in the early 1980s, I was struck by the stark racial difference of our basketball and football teams compared to our baseball team, which incidentally was coached by Rock Newman, who later managed Riddick Bowe's boxing career. Shortly after I left Howard, the school dropped the baseball program because of a lack of facilities, although I suspect Howard would have kept baseball and found a suitable field if the campus demanded it. But there was no outcry from the students or faculty. Once again, baseball didn't matter to black people.

Without a rich pool of black players to choose from, the Major Leagues eventually wind up receiving a smattering of blacks from the minors each year. Mookie Wilson has managed the Mets' farm team in Kingsport, Tennessee, and he does a double-take whenever a black prospect walks into the clubhouse. "My first year, we had three black players," he said. "The next year, we had none. In three years of managing in the minors, I've coached six black players. It gets to the point where you're surprised if you see more than two on a minor league team."

If you see more than two on a Major League team today, that's unusual. But get used to it. Blacks aren't coming back to baseball, at least not in droves, and quite honestly, blacks never had a passionate love affair with baseball to begin with. On the contrary, blacks had a love affair with a special man who once played baseball.

"When it comes to getting us to play baseball, every-thing Jackie Robinson went through was for nothing," said Torii Hunter. "Nothing."

CHAPTER 7

Golf Gulf

The Lonesome King of Cablinasia

There are several dozen golfers competing at the 2007 Masters, but only one is followed from hole to hole by a smattering of black fans. When he pushes the tee into the soft ground, they peek down. When he swings his club and sends the ball whistling through the steamy Georgia air, they squint into the distance. When he begins the slow walk toward the next shot, they don't wait for the next group of golfers to come through; they move, too. They aren't especially loud, unlike other fans, and they don't push toward the ropes. Most are fairly content to stand quietly in the background, often in clusters, whispering, making eye contact with other black fans and exchanging an obligatory nod. It's a show of ethnic loyalty that's unlike anything seen in sports today, where a specific group of American fans totally tunes out every other player in the game but one. For all of his enormous popularity, the 2006 Masters champion Phil Mickelson, for example, almost never saw a black face rooting him on in Augusta.

No, all black folks on the golf course at the Masters or any given tournament are there for Tiger Woods only. Obviously, as the number 1 attraction in sports, fans of all colors follow Woods. His appeal knows no racial boundaries. He's a player who gives credibility and box office appeal to any event he enters, and who's on a first-name basis with the world. Greatness is guaranteed a widespread audience, and to that end, Woods delivers. But black fans, more than others, seem to bond exclusively with him, seem to congregate around him for reasons other than his ability to strike a golf ball better than any mortal. And the answer to that is obvious enough. They feel he represents them.

For sure, nobody in the history of golf has broadened the racial scope of the constituency more than Tiger Woods. It's generally accepted and understood that, if not for Tiger, golf would have the same appeal today in the black community as it did when Bobby Jones played. The smattering of black boys and girls you see on the pitch-and-putt courses and the driving range were led there largely by Tiger. Or their parents nudged them in that direction because of Tiger. His dominance in golf helped introduce the game to a segment of the population that hardly knew it existed. His youthful appeal, helped largely by Nike support, made him a beacon for black kids, especially those who aren't tall or fast or big enough to play basketball or football.

In another bygone era, back when golf restricted blacks to the kitchen and the caddie shack, the affections of black fans were reserved for a boxer. Whenever Joe Louis fought, it was a holiday in black communities. Families would gather in a room and press their ears to a radio that crackled with static but also buzzed with anticipation and mostly good news. In the 1930s and '40s, during his prime, Louis had that much racial clout and pull, perhaps more than anyone else in America. He was a black man getting paid great sums of money to pummel white people, during a time when an ordinary black man faced the potential of death if he raised his voice to a white man on the street. In that sense, Louis was the original sports Pied Piper for blacks, someone who generated a great following and could roust tremendous racial joy and pride with a single well-placed right hook to the chin. Black people felt good about themselves whenever Louis leveled a white man, and again decades later, when Woods destroyed the mostly-white field at a golf tournament.

The difference between Louis and Woods is the degree and depth of black support. There's no comparison, really. Poor blacks, better-off blacks, and blacks who weren't even heavily into sports all connected with Louis for a number of reasons. He was a black role model at a time when blacks were barred from competing against whites in many sports. He was boxer, a popular sport among blacks. His ability to be violent toward whites was viewed by blacks as a way for them to strike back against the oppression and racism of the era. He was a man of the people, someone who lived in the black community, socialized in the black community, and felt a strong connection with the black community. And whenever he fought, Louis felt he represented all of black America, which saw him as a hero.

As for the "Cablinasian" golfer with Thai, Chinese, Native American, black, and white DNA, he is a product of another era, another time, and another world. The racial connection between black America and Woods is thus much more complicated. He plays a game with a terrible history with blacks and a game that still, to this day, caters to privileged America. He's not in basketball or football, the sports of choice among black kids. He's a bowl of ethnic gumbo who doesn't belong to a specific race, not officially anyway; he's more qualified to check the box that says "other." Neither he nor his agency promotes him as a sports hero of black people; he prefers to set an example for all people and all cultures. And, finally, he doesn't publicly embrace one race over another. Tiger is more neutral than Switzerland in a time of war. From the very start, Tiger never identified with typical black culture. As he once told Oprah Winfrey, in one of the few times he has addressed the subject of race, "I'm just who I am. What you see in front of you, that's what you got."

Tiger can't be pigeonholed, and judging by his actions, he doesn't want to be, either. As a person of mixed race, his life, not surprisingly, is seen and experienced through one big kaleidoscope. His father was half-black, one-fourth Chinese, and one-fourth Indian. His mother is half-Thai, one-fourth Chinese, and one-fourth white. His close friends from college come from all backgrounds. His agent and right-hand-man is white. His wife is Swedish. His caddie is a Kiwi. His rich neighbors behind the security gate in Florida are white CEOs mixed with a few black professional ballplayers. And other than hearing a racial taunt on his first day of kindergarten, Tiger has never given any indication he tasted poverty or lived the kind of life struggle that most black people experienced at one time or another while growing up. He's from middle-class Orange County, he was raised on golf, he was blessed to have both parents under one roof, he went to Stanford, and he snaps his fingers to Nickleback. A fair number of black people, as you might imagine, can't relate to that. The child on the south side of Chicago, for example, who never goes to the golf course and doesn't dream of being a golfer, is certainly impressed by Woods, but he's more blown away by Dwyane Wade.

Woods' popularity among blacks is primarily a result of the desire of black people to ignore his multiethnicity and claim him as "one of us." That's a common reflex reaction in black America when it comes to biracial celebrities. The other 50 percent of their ethnicity is always buried or rejected, because a portion of society still blindly follows the racist "one-drop rule" of slavery days, when anyone born with even the slightest trace of black blood was considered black. White people created that rule, and as racist as it is, black people amazingly embrace it and accept the rule on principle. Colin Powell, who grew up in Queens but whose lineage is West Indian, even said, "In America, when you look like me, you're black."

Even today, in a world rapidly becoming more mixed in race by the minute, where multiple ethnicity doesn't carry the negative stigma it once did, some of us still have our heads stuck in the 1800s. Halle Berry was raised primarily by her white mother and never even had a relationship with her black father, and yet she was saluted by black society as the first black woman to win the Oscar for Best Actress. Well, strictly from a biological standpoint, it hasn't happened yet. Barack Obama is the son of an African father and a white mother from Kansas and grew up in Hawaii but is considered a black politician, not a biracial politician. After winning the Super Bowl MVP, Hines Ward took an emotional trip to Korea, where his mother was born and raised and met his father, who was stationed there. Ward was abandoned by his black father and mostly raised by his mother in the States. And yet Ward, along with Berry and Obama and Woods, for whatever reason, is still forced by society to choose one race over another instead of being who he is.

Other than black golf fans, who finally have someone of color to root for, and blacks who want to claim him simply because he's famous, Woods doesn't appear to have much of a connection with black society. His reach in the black community definitely doesn't go as deep as that of the legendary black sports stars.

"I don't know that he has the significant influence among African Americans that my father had, only because my father was their hope," said Joe Louis Barrow. Barrow has a unique and exclusive perspective on Woods and Louis because of lineage, obviously, and also because Barrow is the executive director of The First Tee program, which is geared to generate interest in golf among kids in urban America. He knows first-hand about his father's impact, and through The First Tee, he sees Tiger's impact. And he knows the difference. "Times have changed," Barrow said. "My father came along when there were no other black sports figures. Tiger must compete with the NBA and the NFL. Even as great as Tiger is and even as much as he means to golf, that's a lot."

Even Tiger himself realized early that attempting to attach himself exclusively to the black community felt awkward. As a kid, he was told by his parents to be exactly who he is. That persuaded Woods to create a racial designation for himself: Cablinasian. Growing

Jon Levy/AFP/Getty Images

Tiger Woods enjoyed a strong bond with his father, Earl, who taught and encouraged his son to play golf but never forced him into the sport. Tiger's relationship with black America has been much more complex throughout his amazing career.

up as a future phenom, back in 1995, Tiger said, "I'm mostly Asian but early on I've been labeled black. I don't consider myself a great black hope. It's hard to classify me as black because I'm not really all black."

His initial advertising campaign for Nike, the company he joined when he turned pro, made a statement with its three-word slogan: "I Am Tiger." The early ad was filled with utopian pictures and images and words, with Tiger surrounded by kids of various colors and shades, very Benetton-like, and the multirace theme was designed to reflect a multiracial golfer. Clearly, Tiger and Nike were following the law laid by Earl and Tida when they told their son to be exactly who he is. Earl even joined the marketing effort with this sly pitch: "When you're in America, be black. When you're in the Orient, be Asian."

One of his first Nike commercials tried to paint a young Tiger as someone who, despite his growing fame and fortune, was vulnerable to racism, just like any ordinary black person. In the rather grim commercial, Woods spoke in a serious tone about golf and barriers and how there were courses in America where even he could not play. Which, of course, was silly. By virtue of being the face of golf, and soon the biggest name in sports on the planet, Woods could show up unannounced at the exclusive golf club of his choice and someone would scurry to find him a tee time and maybe even shine his shoes. He is not like the ordinary black man on 125th Street, in that sense, because we live in a celebrity-crazed world where doors are swung open to the famous and privileged, even those of color. Nike had the good sense to pull the absurd commercial after only a few airings, probably at the request of Tiger.

As a concession, Woods seemed to adopt the responsibility of generating an awareness of golf among black kids, but even that campaign lost steam. Eventually Tiger settled on a strategy that seemed to come from the heart, a cause that was more genuine. He went back to what his parents taught him about himself. He would serve as an inspiration to all kids, regardless of color or culture or religion. He would indeed be true to himself. Suddenly, in the commercials that promoted his charity alliance with Target, black kids and white kids and Latino kids and Asian kids all received equal face time as Tiger spoke in unifying terms and described the importance of helping kids who need it most.

Once Tiger began to win tournaments, societal pressure regarding his racial designation began to push harder and press him for an answer. This was especially the case after the 1997 Masters, which changed his life forever. The tournament and the golf club itself were known for being off limits to black players until Lee Elder finally accepted an invitation in 1975. In 1962, Charlie Sifford shot a 67 to take the lead of the Canadian Open in the second round. Legend has it that the tournament received an urgent phone call from the organizers of the Masters, announcing an abrupt change in plans: "The Masters will not offer an automatic invitation to the winner." Therefore, given the racial hurdles placed in front of those people of color who played before him, Tiger's victory was steeped in historical significance. But he continued to stay true to his parents' wishes. When asked by TV announcer Jim Nantz if he had an obligation to minority kids, Tiger responded, "No, I have an obligation to all kids."

The reviews of Tiger's victory and what it meant swirled through the country. Newspaper columnists and TV commentators, flush by the moment, drew parallels with MLK and Jackie Robinson. By chance, Tiger's victory came the day before Robinson was honored by Major League baseball on the 50th anniversary of breaking the color barrier. Bill Clinton was moved enough by the victory that he invited Woods to attend the ceremony. Woods declined and instead took a brief vacation with his buddies, then helped open a sports-themed restaurant. The President didn't take offense; in his speech at the Robinson gala he called Tiger "Jackie's brilliant successor."

The race questions persisted. Tiger appeared on Oprah and tried to put them to rest by revealing his "Cablinasian" choice, which was rejected by blacks who began accusing him of being a sellout. Suddenly, Tiger was under siege and being chided for committing one of the worst crimes a black person could be accused of: not being "black enough." During a good-natured TV promotion for the Byron Nelson Classic, announcer Curtis Strange asked, "Tiger, you have a multiethnic background. Is there a group you wish you were part of?" And Tiger's reply: "I guess Boyz II Men."

Having failed to diffuse the situation through humor, Tiger turned serious and issued a stern and pointed statement, which he claimed would be the "final and only comment I will make on the issue." The statement read, "My parents have taught me to always be proud of my ethnic background. Please rest assured that is and will always be the case. Truthfully, I feel very fortunate, and EQUALLY PROUD, to be both African American and Asian! The critical and fundamental point is that ethnic background and/or composition should NOT make a difference. It does NOT make a difference to me. The bottom line is that I am an American . . . and proud of it! That is who I am and what I am. Now, with your cooperation, I hope I can just be a golfer and a human being."

White society seemed to accept this. But a portion of the black community, staying true to the one-drop rule and wanting Tiger as a member of the frat, rolled its eyes. The racial tug-of-war ensued while Tiger kept toeing the racial line. In 2000, the NAACP asked him to boycott all golf tournaments held in South Carolina, which still recognized the Confederate flag. Tiger's response: "I'm a golfer. That's their deal, not mine." His close friend, Charles Barkley, all but ordered Woods to declare himself black. "They don't send Asian people hate mail," reasoned Sir Charles. "Only black people get hate mail."

The call for Tiger to be an agent for social change continued when women's rights activist Martha Burk suggested he boycott the Masters, or at least pressure the Augusta National Golf Club to start admitting women. Tiger's response: "I'm not a member." Only when the agenda-pushing media kept pressing did Woods finally concede the club should welcome women, which prompted a stern rebuttal from club chairman Hootie Johnson, who said he will not tell Woods how to play golf, "if he doesn't tell me how to run my golf club." When Woods refused to take the club or the tournament to task, that was not good enough for some media watchdogs, who felt he was letting his considerable power go to waste. Clarence Page of the *Chicago Tribune,* one of the more respected black columnists, wrote, "If there's anybody who could do something to help the world of men-only country clubs catch up with the new century, it is Tiger Woods."

By forming the Tiger Woods Foundation, designed to enrich the lives of underprivileged children, Woods armed himself with considerable ammunition in any battle against those who questioned whether he had a social pulse. The foundation became his defense mechanism and the perfect disarming tool. Woods could always point to the foundation and the millions he raised to support it as proof of his desire to help humanity and, through extension, poor kids from the black community.

But in one area, he refused to surrender. He would not be pigeonholed to a single racial group. Nor should he. To those who have a problem with that, here's a simple question: Why should a man of many races be a spokesman for only one of them?

Tiger should be free to decide who he wants to be, and all of society, black and white and whatever, should accept it and respect his desire. Notice how you didn't hear white people call Halle Berry a "sellout" after her Oscar speech, when she paid respect only to black actresses. That was her choice, and it was respected. Tiger, meanwhile, somehow qualifies as a racial sellout in the minds of some black extremists. The biggest misconception of Tiger is that he wants nothing to do with his black heritage. That is absolutely incorrect. Woods doesn't ignore his black side; he just embraces all of his "sides." It hurt, for example, when Fuzzy Zoeller made the "fried chicken or collard greens or whatever" comment regarding Woods' choice for the menu at the annual

Masters' champions dinner. Many thought that would be the moment when Woods discovered he really was black; but in truth, Woods refused to allow an ignorant fool the opportunity to classify him racially. Only a weaker person would have shifted course and ignored their true heritage. Woods did not.

It's not Tiger who has a problem with his racial identity; it's those who want to designate one for him. He shouldn't be assigned the burden of carrying black America any more than he should have the responsibility of carrying Asia. Tiger is a product of a middle-class multicultural upbringing in modern-day America. Why must his adult life reflect typical black America when he never truly lived the experience as a kid? He can't be expected to have the same feelings and outlook as his father, who was born and raised in another world. When you spoke to Earl Woods, you felt a different vibe when it came to race, because he experienced things that his son never did or had to. Earl Woods had to stay in separate hotels from his Kansas State teammates when he played college baseball. Earl Woods, you can imagine, might have reacted differently had Zoeller said what he said to him.

However, Earl always recognized that he and his son saw the world differently and grew up differently, and when asked how we should see Tiger, Earl answered, "As an American." Just like Tiger preferred, regardless of whether it's realistic or not in a society that's still racist.

My hunch is Tiger either followed his instincts or the example of Michael Jordan when it came to race. Jordan made a conscious decision to stay mainstream in public, perhaps for economic reasons. By appealing to a wide audience, instead of attaching himself to a specific audience, Jordan sold more sneakers and Gatorade. He didn't frighten middle America. He was everybody's hero. And he turned sports fans colorblind. That's the way Jordan wanted it, and that's how Tiger wants it, too.

The bond between Woods and the black community had always been a bit overstated, I thought, since his victory at the 1997 Masters. That was supposed to be a watershed moment for blacks in sports, a snapshot frozen in time and never to be thawed. Certainly, the sight of a kid with copper skin shaking a triumphant fist on a golf course with a racist history was something to behold and one of the truly great coincidences in sports history. One of sports' last remaining racial barriers, along with decades of ignorance, was shattered to pieces. The national media, no surprise, reached deep into the thesaurus to spin the right words and perspective after Tiger's 12-stroke victory. "Historic" and "social" and "monumental" were the adjectives used most. There was a heated rush to make a connection between Tiger winning the Masters and social change. Some of Augusta's black caddies, who were used exclusively for the tournament until recently, were interviewed. Tiger mentioned Elder and Sifford and Teddy Rhodes, three black golfers who experienced real racism on tour, in his victory speech. It was the biggest-played sports story of the year.

No doubt, it was a dizzying 48-hour period, filled with racial and historical connotations, and in hindsight, probably more than the moment deserved.

Why President Clinton mentioned Tiger and Robinson in the same breath, I'll never know. Maybe Clinton, like everyone else, was caught up in the fumes of the Masters victory. But winning a golf tournament and breaking the color barrier in baseball are achievements several worlds apart. Not only did Robinson integrate baseball, he opened the door for integration everywhere, in the workforce and schools and public facilities and all other sports. Robinson also endured threats and taunts and took unimaginable abuse and endured it all. Woods went through none of that; he won the Masters in a far more accepting atmosphere than the one Robinson knew. Woods wasn't refused a place to stay; a number of Augustans were all too willing to rent their mansions to him. Nobody tried to deny Woods the right to play at Augusta; hell, the golf club rolled out the red carpet for him. As Earl Woods, Tiger's father, once told me, "The members treated us right from the day we stepped foot there."

Golf clubs and tournaments weren't turning Woods away when he showed up at the clubhouse; on the contrary, his arrival was widely anticipated and eagerly awaited. The people who run golf knew Tiger meant money, and money tends to make folks colorblind. They knew he had crossover appeal and would expose the game to a younger audience that would allow golf to tap into another demographic. They knew a young, multicultural golfer with once-in-a-lifetime skills would only make the game more popular and valuable than ever before, and they were right. Tiger meant millions, maybe billions, to golf. Everyone benefited financially from having Tiger around, from the tournaments to the tour to the players to the sponsors. Everyone wanted more Tiger, not less.

Of course, the acceptance of Woods by the golfing establishment was mainly because of money. But not among the fans. They didn't stand to make money, and therefore, their intentions were genuine and free of any racial hang-ups. Huge galleries, a large percentage of them white, swelled around Tiger from one hole to the next, all supportive and cheering and applauding and showing much love. Jackie Robinson never saw that—not at first, anyway. These Tiger Woods fans looked past the color and chose instead to study the golfer and the greatness he was capable of achieving. Thus to equate what Tiger did at Augusta to what Robinson did in 1947 is to commit the most glaring and unforgivable form of blasphemy.

In fact, much of the groundwork for Tiger's arrival was done by others, namely Sifford, who was treated terribly by the golf establishment in the 1950s and '60s, along with Elder and Calvin Peete, who were skilled enough to enjoy respectable careers in a more receptive atmosphere. But Joe Louis also played a part, of all people. Golf was Louis' passion, not boxing, and he played whenever he could. He was a three-handicap who mostly played on public courses, because not even an ex-heavyweight champ was invited to private clubs. And then Louis received a sponsor's exemption for the San Diego Open in

©Bettmann/Corbis

Lee Elder turned pro in 1959 and was the first black to play in the Masters (1975) and on the U.S. Ryder Cup Team (1979). His pioneering efforts, however, have hardly led to mass black participation in golf, as many factors still make it less accessible than other sports.

1952. The tournament officials forgot about the whites-only rule on tour, and Louis was asked to qualify for the tournament, which he did. "He played as an amateur under the exemption and became the first black person to play a PGA event," said Barrow. "He helped move golf along for blacks."

In retrospect, Tiger's impact on the black community, in terms of generating more potential professional golfers, was inflated and overdramatized in the immediate aftermath of the '97 Masters. Too many people made too many bold and unrealistic projections and predictions.

True, the initial ripple effect was considerable. Almost overnight, public courses filled up with black adults. Black kids began showing up at golf camps and clinics. Inspired by Woods, they gave junior golf, long a haven for suburban white kids, a different complexion. Stunned by the numbers and the potential, golf experts and the media began a massive rush to judgment and reached the conclusion that golf, in due time, would soon see the result caused by the Masters victory, or the "Tiger effect." Once again, folks were guilty of breathing 1997 vapors.

Ten years after Tiger's win, golf at the highest level had fewer blacks than it did in the 1960s with Sifford and Elder. Woods remained the only golfer with African-American blood on tour in 2007. Even Tiger admitted, "I thought there would be more of us out here." More telling was miniscule numbers of blacks playing the Nationwide Tour, and those who tried to make qualifying school, and those competing at the major college level, all of which guarantees very few, if any, blacks on the PGA tour in 2008 or the near future. If you argue that the kids who were motivated by Woods' win in '97 are now in their late teens, then the numbers should reflect as much on the high school level. But even there, especially in urban America, golf among teenage blacks remains as foreign as cricket and as popular as country music. Those lofty and ambitious predictions in 1997 neglected these important factors: Golf is still for the middle class and wealthy, Tiger doesn't have the appeal of basketball or football stars among most black kids, and drastic change cannot and will not happen in a snap, if it happens at all.

In his work with The First Tee, Joe Louis Barrow concedes that most of the minority golfers in the program are Latino and Hispanic. The hardest obstacle facing young black kids who try golf, Barrow said, is getting them to stay with it. A good many soon begin to lose interest, or find it too difficult, or don't find it exciting enough. They also don't get the same level of encouragement from their parents to stick it out as white kids get from their parents. Also, peer pressure sometimes comes into play. If their friends aren't into golf, or if their friends spend more time in other sports, chances are good that the black kid will gravitate elsewhere.

"The question is whether we'll ever see numbers that will have the skills and desire to achieve at the highest level," Barrow said. "Getting them to start hasn't been that much of a problem, but it takes a strong commitment to see the process through. Tiger has certainly done his part in exposing the game to kids of all backgrounds. You couldn't ask someone like him to do more. Ultimately, that kid must have the desire to stick with the game and improve his skills to the point where he can play on the upper levels."

My guess is Tiger will have far less influence among blacks, when it comes to golf, than many originally thought. He will not single-handedly change the complexion of the game, as some claimed he did years ago. That's not because he hasn't done his part. It's because he plays a sport that never was popular among black kids and, my hunch says, never will be. Remember, Jackie Robinson's breakthrough in 1947, as historic as it was, never encouraged blacks to pour into baseball in great numbers. Roughly 20 years after Robinson's achievement, the game was bigger among Latinos than among blacks. And right now, the number of black Major League players is less than 7 percent. Baseball is not a game that blacks care deeply about. Althea Gibson had a similar breakthrough in tennis in the 1950s, and yet tennis remained a country club sport that never attracted hordes of boys and girls from urban America. Tennis and baseball are much cheaper to play than golf and yet, for whatever reason, tennis and baseball lack a strong pulse in the black community. Thus, if Robinson and Gibson and later Arthur Ashe couldn't create a passion for their sports in the black community, it makes you wonder why people thought Tiger would in his. Again, his 1997 victory at the Masters prompted wishful thinking, not realistic thinking.

Golf is simply not accessible enough to black kids. Public courses usually don't allow any kids to play, and private courses are for the rich and the white. Most urban schools don't have golf teams. Some kids who normally would give golf a try aren't aware of The First Tee or other city golf programs. Even if a number of black kids get hooked on the game and stay with it, they stand a better chance of becoming President than posing a challenge to Woods. That's because a kid must make it through junior golf and show tremendous promise. That's the easy part. He must then work his way through state, sectional, national, college, and amateur golf, and then play on the minitours before he can even think about getting his PGA tour card. A huge number of very talented white players don't reach the finish line, so how realistic is it to think that someone from a small pool of black players will taste a professional career?

If anything, the ethnic group most influenced by Tiger is Asian. The next wave of minority golfers will come from his Asian side. Already, Korean golfers and American kids of Korean descent are filling up and even dominating the women's game, and they're in abundance in junior golf, so it's only a matter of time before the PGA tour gets a share. Unlike black culture, Korean culture has adopted golf as its primary sport; parents don't need to push golf onto their kids because the kids are anxious to play. Even though South Korea has golf academies, it's not uncommon for parents to move entire families from that country, where golf courses are scarce and tee times expensive, to America to give their children a better chance to master the game. At the very least, their kids will get college scholarships; at most, they'll be on tour. There's a bigger pool of Korean kids than black kids playing golf, and therefore a greater chance for Koreans to represent on the highest level of golf.

At the same time, though, it would be a shame if current and future generations of black kids weren't motivated by Woods. All things considered, he is the complete package, the kind of example you'd like your kid to follow. There are just too many positives a kid, especially someone from urban America, can take from Woods. There's the education factor. Woods was not a one-track athlete while growing up. He had balance and knew the importance of doing well in sports and academics. He was bright enough in high school to get into Stanford, and as an adult, he's smart enough to turn himself into a global money-making machine. He has made many good decisions, in terms of friends, people to trust for his inner circle, companies that he represents, and charities that bear his name. He doesn't have even the slightest whiff of scandal. He knew how to deal with the temptations that come with being famous. And he's eloquent, comes across great in public, and is as humble as the world's greatest golfer can possibly be. There is nothing not to like, in terms of role model material.

And he plays golf, a game that doesn't lend itself to most black kids. Perfect. Tiger represents a refreshing change from the usual menu of football and basketball stars who keep a hypnotic spell over black children. In poorer communities, these kids lack choices in their lives, from activities to friends to education. These kids don't need another Kobe Bryant or LeBron James. They need a golfer, along with a violinist, an artist, a corporate lawyer, an astronaut, and a mountain climber. They need to be exposed to events and places and occupations and types of people that don't enter their lives very often, if at all. Tiger gives them a different look and something else to consider.

"My gosh," said an incredulous Jack Nicklaus, when told of the discontent generated by Woods. "He has done so much just by being Tiger Woods. What more do people want from him?"

The notion that black kids should gravitate toward athletes who look exactly like them is tiresome and stereotypical. Funny how you always hear the media and otherwise well-meaning experts always pair up black kids with someone black. That's saying black children can't be motivated by someone white or Latino or Asian or Mexican. Well, why can't the black kid gravitate toward Tom Brady instead of Donovan McNabb, if he chooses?

And that's no knock against McNabb, either; it's just a vote for variety. Why was a black kid considered a sellout if he admitted to liking Larry Bird over Magic Johnson? As a society, we really need to quit thinking inside the box in this regard and open up. That kind of thinking is limiting the possibilities for black children, who need as many positive reinforcements as they can get, especially those black children who aren't surrounded by much hope. For those children, the race or gender or ethnic background of their motivational role model shouldn't matter. What counts isn't what that person looks like, it's the example that person leads. And in that regard, Woods' multiculturalism and upbringing, which is in contrast to most kids from urban America, is definitely a good thing. He's not a hardcore gangsta rapper, and thank goodness for that. Urban America has enough of those.

The main problem with black kids in bad situations is that their world is so limited. Their parents, most likely, live within limits, as do their relatives, and their neighbors. A kid needs as many options as possible so he can choose wisely and find a goal and path in life. And if that path is unconventional or different than the one usually traveled, even better. That was the path laid out for Tiger by Earl and Tida Woods, and he blazed it.

There's something else about Woods. He also gets it. He has the perfect charity project with the Tiger Woods Learning Center. Instead of using his money to build a football field or a weight room or a sparkling new gym for the local high school sports teams, Woods created an environment that stresses academic and social development over sports development. That's an example of creative thinking by an athlete who realizes the chances of a kid being a professional athlete are about nil. He understands that the best way to help a kid isn't by teaching him how to throw a football but how to read a book or do research on a computer. Other than sitting next to a golf course, and bearing the name of the golfer who came up with the idea (along with his father), the Learning Center is decidedly nonsports.

One hopes that the Learning Center will encourage the kids, especially poor kids, to recognize the academic side of Tiger as well as the athletic side. He had superb parents who weren't so anxious to expose their son to golf that they neglected everything else. They taught Tiger the benefits of having balance in his young life, even though he clearly adopted golf as his passion. And they emphasized the importance of school. Even with his golf skills, which were obviously amazing at a very young age, Woods would not have gotten into Stanford unless he showed the ability to handle the academic workload. The Learning Center will achieve its goal by helping kids learn how to make good choices, become better students, and shape their priorities in life. If they also figure out how to hit a golf ball squarely on the club face, that's a bonus.

Unlike other wealthy athletes, Woods is contributing a significant amount of his money to a greater cause. Of course, that's easy for him to do. He has more money than any current athlete. Woods donating a half-million dollars is like Oprah giving every audience member a free TV set. He won't exactly feel the pinch. And since he's staring at another 25-plus years of golf, he's on track to be the first billionaire athlete. With his financial clout and charitable heart, Woods may become the Bill Gates of sports by creating a philanthropic machine unlike any seen by his peers. He has mentioned his desire to be known for more than just golf, and while that's unlikely, he could come close.

Regardless of his racial identity and where he stands on race, Woods has been good for golf, good for sports, and good for those who use him as motivation. He may not register like Jordan and Kobe in certain households, and because of his refusal to take a stand on sensitive political and social issues ("I just hit a little white ball into a little round hole," he once said), he isn't following Arthur Ashe, either. But the Tiger Woods before us is impressive in his own way. As he famously told Oprah, what you see is what you get.

CHAPTER 8

Show Time

Ali Started It,
NFL Exhibitionists Ruined It

Even now, it seems such an unlikely birthplace for trash talking. And in a sense, it was chosen by chance. A major heavyweight championship fight was scheduled to take place in Boston in November of 1964, but an injury to the champ delayed the event, and then the absence of a promoter's license for Massachusetts forced a drastic change of venue. Thus, the second Muhammad Ali–Sonny Liston fight was moved north to the unassuming town of Lewiston, Maine, which, true to its reputation, was mostly sleepy on the night of May 25, 1965, until Ali pierced the air and the ears by running his mouth.

At St. Dominic's Arena, before an attendance of 2,434, which remains the smallest crowd to witness a heavyweight championship fight, a controversial straight right to the head dropped Liston to the canvas in the first round. What happened next was a moment that refuses to be erased by time. The champ did not retreat to a neutral corner and obey the rules of boxing, something that fighters have followed since the bare-knuckle brawl days. On this night, the so-called phantom punch that floored Liston wasn't enough to bring satisfaction to Ali. It could not clinch victory or bring closure. No, on this night, Ali wanted to inflict more damage on Liston. He wanted to humiliate Liston.

He stood over Liston's body, glowering, gesturing, gloating. He motioned with his twirling right arm and clenched right glove and, further proof that nobody or nothing could keep Ali from talking back then, managed to be heard clearly despite wearing a mouthpiece.

"Git up and fight, sucka."

It was not the first or the last time Ali mocked an opponent, just the most famous. The scene was captured perfectly by the lens of Neil Leifer, a ringside photographer who worked for *Sports Illustrated*, and the still image is perhaps the most famous photo in sports history. The picture is one of the few taken that doesn't need a caption to explain what you're seeing. Amazingly, even those who weren't born in 1965 are well aware of the man standing and the message he was trying to get across that night, even if his exact words have withstood several version changes over the years.

Even more interesting is how the immortalized moment has not only endured time but has been adored over time by millions around the world. From Pakistan to Punxsutawney and Kenya to Kalamazoo, the image of Ali verbally stomping on a beaten Liston brings a flush feeling of admiration and adulation from those who take just a quick, casual glance; no need to stare too long. People are drawn by the strength and the emotion and the sheer overall impact of the photo, and Ali has drawn raves for projecting "courage" and "power" and "conquest."

Nobody, at least to my knowledge, accused Ali of being "unsportsmanlike."

After taunting Liston, Ali still refused to return to his corner. He never did, actually. Next, he began dancing around the ring, arms held high. His legs moved swiftly, with a slight touch of rhythm and a total cockiness about them. Later in his career, Ali would refine the technique and make it an instrumental part of his in-fight strategy and overall ring showmanship. It became the "Ali Shuffle." Before Liston rose from the canvas, the fight was over

©Bettmann/Corbis

The mouth that roared. Ali, in his famous May 1965 defeat of Sonny Liston, taunts his opponent openly and, rather unknowingly, begins a trend in sports.

and a phenomenon was born. Or, more accurately, it was popularized. Before long, trash talking and showboating were an accepted part of sports, much like uniforms and sweat.

"We were watching a football game in a hotel lobby back in 1997 on Thanksgiving Day," recalled Thomas Hauser, Ali's biographer. "One of the players on the Lions scored and started dancing. And then Muhammad turned to me and said, 'I started that.' He loves the fact that he started it."

Truth be known, the seeds of this culture weren't planted by Ali. He wasn't the first boxer to provoke the other corner. In this regard, Jack Johnson was decades ahead of his time. Even more dangerous than publicly flaunting his white women in an era in which black men were shot just for looking at one, Johnson constantly teased and taunted the "White Hopes" who tried to steal his championship belt. After pummeling them to the floor, Johnson would often release a deep, hearty laugh. Then he'd warn those fighters about the potential hazard of rising to their feet, according to the historians, and enduring another beating. He did this at great risk of being lynched by a racist mob, which means Johnson was either crazy or courageous or both.

But Johnson fought before the video age, so his bombast in the ring was limited to a grainy and flickering silent movie. Unlike Ali, he was hardly a photogenic national sports hero, either, at least beyond the black community; therefore his words and gestures did not stand the test of time, nor did they make more than a ripple in overall sports society at the time. Boxing historians rarely mentioned Johnson's trash talking in their reports from the ring. Anyway, boxing, while known today for being half-sport and half-spectacle, safely returned to stability and serenity soon after Johnson left for good, with only the occasional lapse of bombast.

The other sports during that era were rather tame, too, with athletes collectively and obediently following a certain standard of conduct, Ty Cobb being one of the few exceptions. As an unabashed racist and all-around bad guy, Cobb had a prickly personality, and baseball historians have more than once noted his eagerness to speak his mind during the game. But again, he was a rarity, and for the most part, athletes in the pre-Ali days played their sport with few or no public acts of verbal unprofessionalism or sensationalism. That behavior was totally frowned on and greeted with disgust by the athletes themselves, who policed one another. One of the worst things in sports then was to be called a "hot dog." If someone celebrated or teased another player or team, they were an instant outcast. Many would rather live their professional life as a benchwarmer than carry that burden and reputation. Only the Harlem Globetrotters could get away with it, and only because they played for laughs.

That all changed when Cassius Clay won an Olympic gold medal. Even as a teenager, Ali was brash, but again, he was largely unknown and had no media panting after him and recording every boastful word. Even when Ali slowly rose in the heavyweight ranks in the early 1960s, he was seen as a novelty, a goofball, nothing more, and hardly taken seriously by the public and the sporting press. He wasn't even considered a threat to the championship belt, just a squeaky wheel who was desperate for attention.

Two events changed Ali and sports forever. The first came when Ali, about a year before the first Liston fight, listened to a radio interview with Gorgeous George, the Liberace of pro wrestlers, whose career was winding down (and also his life; he died two years after the interview). George Wagner was a white man from Nebraska who was rather mediocre in the ring; he stood only 5 feet, 9 inches, and wasn't terribly strong, nor much in demand in the world of wrestling, which had only a limited audience in the 1940s and '50s. Wagner tried to change that. He grew his hair long, dyed it blond, and tied it back with gold bobby pins. He had friends act as valets, and their job was to escort him from the dressing room to the ring while music blared over the loudspeakers. He wore sequined robes and became a smash hit as wrestling's original ring villain. His theatrics made pro wrestling a mild if infectious hit on the relatively new medium called television.

Gorgeous George also talked a good game, which only created interest in his matches, and he screamed and bragged and ranted in this particular radio interview overheard by a young and impressionable Ali. At that point, Ali was hooked. He was already famous for predicting the round of his knockouts, but after taking a cue from Gorgeous George, he turned up the volume on his prefight taunts. And that led to the second and final event that changed Ali and sports forever: Ali started backing up his talk.

Had Liston given Ali a whipping either in their first fight or the second, trash talking would have died a rather quick death, and maybe Ali's career would have as well. Had Liston gotten up from that canvas in Lewiston and rammed his Everlast down Ali's throat, which was nearly hoarse from overuse, then perhaps a sports culture would have ended before it began. But it all came together in Lewiston: the skill, the mouth, the showmanship. Ali was a lot closer to being "the greatest," his boast, than the boxing experts originally thought. The complete package was rather irresistible, especially to TV and the media, and it conspired to turn Ali from a boxing champ to an international icon and today, a saint, especially after his dramatic lighting of the Olympic flame in Atlanta. That wasn't so bad; for the most part, Ali did his shtick with a tongue firmly planted in his cheek. What followed decades later, however, was a trend that sank deep into the fabric of black culture. What Ali unknowingly did by shouting "git up" in Lewiston was cause the decay and decline of sportsmanship. He did this by inspiring poor imitators, with black athletes making up a disproportionate amount, to the point where today, talking smack and shuffling and dancing is shrugged off by the public as part of the black experience.

It must be told that black athletes do not own a monopoly on this; their vast numbers only make it seem that way. Larry Bird was a legendary trash talker, always quick with the lip after he dropped a three-point shot on a defender who was two steps too late. Mark Gastineau and his sack dance became a fixture each time he threw the quarterback for a big loss, even during games in which the Jets trailed badly and any celebration was considered over the top and self-centered. More recently, Jeremy Shockey, the tight end for the Giants, just can't resist making a scene after every catch, no matter how few yards he gains on the play.

There are other white players who play the role, but they're exceptions, and most of their acts are spontaneous, not choreographed. The vast majority of players who feel compelled to gyrate their hips in the end zone are not white. White football players did not gather in a tight circle after one scored a touchdown and perform a group leap into the air; that was the Fun Bunch with the Redskins in the 1980s. The U.S. players who grabbed their crotch and banged their chest and screamed after dunking the ball at the 1994 World Basketball Championships weren't white. Nor was a receiver for the Saints who famously pulled a hidden cell phone from under the goal post and began dialing after he scored.

In the specific sports in which whites are the clear majority, these clownish antics are either few or non-existent, and mainly confined to the goons who patrol hockey, and often soccer; French soccer star Zinedine Zidane lost his head after hearing smack talk from Italy's Marco Materazzi in the 2006 World Cup final. Tennis has more temper tantrums than trash talking. Golfers are mature men in their 30s and 40s who religiously follow the game's proper etiquette. Baseball has rather strict codes for showing up the opposition, and many players of all races, respectful of the tradition, follow it or else feel the sting of a well-placed brushback pitch. The only place where white spectacle is common and heavy is in pro wrestling, where spectacle is required and where, thanks to Gorgeous George, it all began.

What's mostly depressing is not the percentage of black athletes who submit to the stereotype but how this behavior is generally demanded by the mainly white public and rewarded by Madison Avenue and, sadly, copied to the hilt. And don't underestimate the role television plays in fanning the flames of this behavior. Most of today's athletes are children of the 24-hour TV sports age, where unsportsmanlike conduct and selfish look-at-me displays get tremendous air time and publicity for the instigators and rubs off on the next generation, much like Gorgeous George rubbed off on Ali. Television also tends to ignore

AP Photo/Andrew Cohoon

In one of the most blatant pre-planned exhibitions in NFL history, Joe Horn uses a cell phone that he had stashed in the goal post padding after scoring on a touchdown pass during the 2003 season.

the good and healthy portion of black athletes who carry themselves in a dignified, pre-Ali manner and simply toss the football to the referee after reaching the end zone, or head back up court after dunking the ball, or congratulate their teammates. When that happens, however, the TV camera doesn't focus on the player; he's considered, well, too boring and white bread and not ethnic enough.

"It was in the 1980s when a lot of the stuff you see started getting tremendous attention," said Julius Erving, who never celebrated a dunk, no matter how spectacular. "Players just started bringing attention to themselves. I never felt a reason to conduct myself that way. I've always been success driven but never ego driven. Even though I was a high flier and did innovative dunks, I was never doing it to bring attention to myself. I got enjoyment out of completing the play. When ego doesn't play a role, then there's no need to celebrate the play. I didn't have to taunt or tease anyone or flagrantly go outside of my character. My attitude on spectacular plays was do it, and once it's done, let's see what comes next."

The attitude of the University of Miami football players in the 1991 Cotton Bowl was this: talk smack, then apply a smackdown. The Hurricanes were determined not only to beat the University of Texas on the annual New Year's Day game but also to explain in unsavory terms how they were going to beat them. They taunted Texas from the time they jogged onto the field until they left, victorious by the punishing final score of 46-3 and also by the swagger they demonstrated throughout. The Hurricanes ran up the yards, the score, and also the penalties, amassing 202 yards on infractions, most of them for unsportsmanlike conduct, and all nine players flagged were black.

This didn't exactly catch the country by surprise. By then, Miami had earned a reputation for being an outlaw school that talked trash and laughed at the thought of sportsmanship. Once, in a much-hyped game between Miami and Notre Dame, where "Catholics vs. Convicts" shirts sold briskly, Miami players were in the ear of eventual Heisman Trophy winner Tim Brown constantly, to the point where Brown said later, "They bring your mama into every conversation." The 'Canes arrogantly dressed in military fatigues in preparation for the 1987 Fiesta Bowl, essentially flaunting their "war" image to the hilt and flashing their middle fingers to anyone who took exception. Amazingly, their behavior was tolerated by officials at a school of higher learning that placed a premium on winning and running a rather loose ship.

And after the Cotton Bowl, even the team's spiritual advisor at the time, Father Leo Armbrust, remarked how black players have "a way of expressing their values, personalities, and culture that a large part of American society does not approve of" and mentioned how black people in general were simply more expressive than whites. Now counseling at-risk kids in Palm Beach County, the Roman Catholic priest believes the expressive behavior favored by some black athletes is rooted in the church, mainly gospel music.

"You can go to a lot of white churches that don't have the same enthusiasm," he explained. "I wish I could go to white churches that have the verve and zeal of worship as African-American churches. I see that kind of environment in black athletes, who have no fear in expressing themselves to society. We are all unique, and to blend us all together is to ignore what makes us different."

Well, the Miami performance in the Cotton Bowl was hardly considered saintly. But you could see it coming. Days after the game, Arthur Ashe wrote an op-ed piece in the *Washington Post,* saying in effect that the behavior of the Miami players was years in the making.

"What the Miami players did was disgraceful on its merits but it was learned behavior," wrote Ashe. "Somehow, somewhere, when they were younger, they concluded that these acts were not only condoned, but acceptable and laudatory."

Trash talking took a curious turn for the worse when Joey Porter, a loud-mouthed linebacker who played for the Steelers and signed in 2007 with the Dolphins, exchanged taunts with the Bengals' Levi Jones in a Las Vegas casino. It led to a wrestling match and did nothing for the image of Porter, nor the Bengals, who had nine players arrested in a nine-month period. Not surprisingly, Porter and Jones had a prior history of trash talking to each other on the field.

Trash talking wasn't just born out of the second Ali–Liston fight; it was also a byproduct of the times. Ali's profile was created by the 1960s, a very turbulent era in America, the first in which the ideas of one generation clashed violently with the next. For those who came of age during that time, it was about free love and loud expression and living spontaneously, consequences be damned. Militancy and rebellion was the order of the day. Kids born to soldiers who returned from World War II sought a new lifestyle as teenagers, one that was drastically different from their parents'. On all levels and within all ethnic groups, a younger generation did whatever it could to shake up society. The Rolling Stones were the top act in rock music partly because they were viewed as edgier and sexier than the Beatles.

On the social front, the Civil Rights Movement was already raging in major cities, and the black community, once largely silent and powerless on issues of inequality, suddenly felt a strong need to be loudly heard. The antiviolence stance of Martin Luther King was considered soft and viewed with a skeptical eye in poorer neighborhoods that were growing weary with the slow rate of change. In those areas, a radical voice and fresh set of ideas made more sense, and suddenly the Black Panther Party and similar groups had the ear of the young and restless and angry. Counterculture behavior was being embraced by a new generation, and anyone who told the establishment where to stick it was embraced as a hero. Thus, Ali, with a mouth that roared, became the symbol of a new generation.

"Some time in the 1960s, sports lost their original moral bearings that frequently were violated in the past," wrote Ashe. "But at least there was clarity and universal agreement in the United States as to how sports heroes should conduct themselves."

In addition, the '60s were the dawn of a new media age. Television, once considered a luxury for the wealthy, began multiplying in households and became part of the family. Slowly, the medium took a liking to sports and athletes and made them larger than life, putting them on the same celebrity level as singers and actors. They were seen as entertainers. Newspapers, too, began devoting more coverage and entire sections to sports. The media needed someone to create buzz and give viewers and readers a reason to stay interested, and in Ali, brash and bold and boastful, they had their man. Ali would either enrage fans or satisfy fans; one way or another, he was not to be ignored.

"Ali came into a new arena," said Earl Smith, a sociology professor at Wake Forest. "He had a way of communicating that was quite different than many we saw before him. Ali was able to convince people that this was an art form and people needed to listen to it. Which they did. The media liked his line. He had an audience. Not all of that audience was behind him. A lot of people, even in the black community, didn't like Ali. I would even go as far to say he wasn't as popular at the time as people think. But he made people listen."

In almost every way, Ali was drastically different from any sports star who preceded him. He wasn't guarded or wary around the press, like Joe DiMaggio was. With DiMaggio, the media had limits, especially about his personal life and Marilyn Monroe; Ali placed no such barriers on the media. Whenever he trained, the doors were open, and the more press, the better. Ali was more accessible than any major star, before or since. He gave interviews on the spot and spoke at great length. He was entertaining, effervescent, and intoxicating to the media. After arriving in town, he would often call newspapers or TV stations and invite reporters en masse to lunch or dinner, making himself available in ways that Michael Jordan would never do. Ali loved the media, and he enjoyed making the media's job easy. He would often give interviews until late at night, when he sometimes fell asleep in the middle of a thought.

Ali also made the media feel at ease. There was seldom any tension around Ali, unlike Mickey Mantle, for instance. Mantle could be rude and crass and insensitive, especially around reporters he didn't like. Ali enjoyed the media so much that he even spoke to those who knocked him in the press, which happened often early in his career. Gradually, a new generation of sportswriters made a strong connection with Ali and was mesmerized by his considerable charm. His fights were always heavily covered by the national media.

It helped tremendously that Ali was quite funny and quick with a quip. He made people laugh. He entertained. He had the sharp wit and sense of humor to draw a crowd and make people enjoy being around him. A good many of Ali's clever lines and poems were given to him, however, by Bundini Brown, the jester in Ali's entourage. It was Brown who coined the phrase "float like a butterfly, sting like a bee," but it took someone with the charisma and delivery of Ali to pull it off, much like Johnny Carson took the jokes written for him by gag writers and brought them to life.

Finally, Ali had a "purty face" and his leading-man looks only enhanced his image. Society is naturally drawn to attractive people, and once again, Ali fit the bill. His looks, charm, and ability to provoke and entertain guaranteed him a massive audience and the media's attention. His playful relationship with Howard Cosell, the legendary television announcer, made for must-see TV, especially when they traded good-natured barbs and put-downs, which was often. They were a comedy troupe, the Laurel and Hardy of sports, and were parodied by comedians long after both retired.

Basically, a number of circumstances both within and beyond his control created a national stage for Ali. And because boxing depends heavily on promotion to make money, Ali was a very willing one-man circus act who breathed life into the sport and at the gate by talking as much trash as possible about the other fighter. It made him popular, controversial, and most of all, extremely rich.

"He understood the game of salesmanship," said Jerry Izenberg, the long-time sports columnist with the *Star-Ledger* in New Jersey and a constant presence in Ali's camp. "I thought a lot of the stuff he said was funny. A lot of people did. I laughed. Everyone around him laughed. He had fun. Sometimes he came up with stuff, sometimes the guys in his camp came up with it. He was a performer, in and out of the ring."

He was not Joe Louis. That was evident. Louis was serious and stoic. Louis was as mainstream as it gets. He did not rock the boat or constantly lash out against the establishment. He depicted himself as America's heavyweight champ, not just black America's. Again, like Ali, Louis was a product of his time. The 1930s and '40s were not the ideal era for a black man who beat up white men to brag about it or become a lightning rod, certainly not like Jack Johnson a few decades before. Louis remained proper and polite without being a sellout. He didn't date white women. He stayed in Harlem. His views on race and racism, at least in public, were rather docile; Louis would not be confused with Marcus Garvey. Because of this, Louis enjoyed a measure of comfort with white America, about as much comfort as a black man could have during that time. When he beat Max Schmeling, a symbol of Hitler's Nazi Germany, his triumph was largely viewed as a victory for America, and Louis was painted as a red, white, and blue man, not just an ordinary black man. Even though Louis battered white men in the ring, he was nonthreatening, the first black athlete whom white parents allowed their sons to admire and consider a worthy role model. Later in life, Louis would openly express his displeasure at Ali's trash talking and even made disparaging comments when Ali, unlike Louis, famously refused to serve in the military.

After Louis came Floyd Patterson, who was cut much in the same mold. Patterson was open minded on issues of race and did not embrace the philosophies of Elijah Muhammad and the Nation of Islam, the extremist organization that had Ali under its thumb. Patterson did not hate white people, or see them as devils, or blame them for all the evil in the world, which was some of the rhetoric that seeped from that organization. Because Patterson was clearly his opposite on almost all things racial and social, Ali took great pleasure in pitting the black community against Patterson, calling him an "Uncle Tom," a charge that Ali levied frequently against his black opponents.

This is where Ali's trash talking and taunting turned sinister, ugly, totally unacceptable. Until the Patterson fight, Ali's barbs were laced with humor and good-natured teasing, the childlike provoking you see on every playground. He crossed the line, however, when he tried to turn another black fighter into an outcast and a sellout. He cast them as tools of white America, the ruthless oppressors, and turned the black community against these fighters. Ali did this not only with Patterson but more aggressively with Ernie Terrell, who drew Ali's anger by playfully calling the champ by his given name of Cassius Clay.

"I had less respect for him as a person at that point," said Izenberg, "because of his behavior toward Terrell. It was mean-spirited."

Ali did seem to have a particular beef with black fighters, starting with Liston. He seldom, if ever, said anything racially inflammatory toward his white opponents, which was interesting because Ali never passed up a chance to poke white society in his political rants. One by one, from Joe Bugner to Chuck Wepner to Jerry Quarry, white boxers drew mostly silence and a fair amount of respect from Ali during the prefight hype. History in general and black society in particular gave Ali a pass for this double standard. Nobody raised the issue or took Ali to task for demeaning black men who did nothing to deserve it other than step into the ring.

But you can understand why. At that point in the smoldering '60s, when black pride came of age, Ali was too strong a symbol against racial inequity. He was too bullet-proof among a new generation and among a growing number of militant blacks who blindly sided with him without bothering to study the character of the black fighters he accused of being racial traitors. None of the so-called leaders in the black community dared to demand that Ali cease with the slander. To speak out against Ali would be the equivalent of speaking out against black America and risking being called a sellout. No black politician or leader would kill their careers and credibility in the community just to defend an opponent who wasn't going to whip Ali anyway. It was better to keep quiet and let Ali do his thing. Therefore, without any resistance from the community or media, Ali continued with his character assassinations while everyone laughed and nodded their heads. A black opponent was a Tom. A white opponent was just another fighter to be treated with respect.

The most vivid example of this came against Joe Frazier. Born in rural Beaufort, South Carolina, as the son of a bootlegger and raised on the hard side of Philadelphia, Frazier was about as genuinely black as one could get in America, given his life experiences. His roots were in the Deep South, where there was rampant racism, and his personality was formed in the heart of the big city, under the suffocating presence of severe poverty. Racism and poverty are the double-barreled evils that black people have dealt with constantly, and it was very much a part of Frazier's life. He found salvation in the boxing ring, however, where he groomed his vicious left hook by pounding meat in a Philly slaughterhouse and developed tremendous courage to become one of the greatest fighters of all time.

In a sense, Ali had a smoother life than Frazier, who, contrary to the racial portrayal given to him by Ali, had a lot more in common with the black experience than his more famous rival. Ali's upbringing in Louisville was somewhat middle class and mild compared to the lives of the majority of blacks in the '50s. Ali had the benefit of being raised by both parents. Like Frazier, Ali won Olympic gold but earned a shot at the heavyweight title and big money much earlier. Also, Ali was fair-skinned and handsome, therefore much easier to digest by a country obsessed with a celebrity's looks. Frazier had a flat nose and dark skin, and when he stood next to Ali for publicity shots, all the old and tired stereotypes within the black community came into play: dark skin and thick hair equal ugly, and light skin and "good" hair equal attractive.

Amazingly, given all this, Ali was able to successfully cast Frazier as being less than black. Ali's unfair characterization of Frazier lasted five years, from their first fight, the extravagantly hyped showdown at Madison Square Garden in 1971, to the last, the Thrilla in Manila in 1975. During his bombastic rants, Ali called Frazier an "Uncle Tom" and mentioned how Frazier was "too dumb" and "too ugly" to beat him. Ali added, "Ninety-eight percent of (black) people are for me. They identify with my struggle. If I win, they win. If I lose, they lose." That was the mantra Ali created and clung to in preparation for the first fight. En route to Manila, Ali mocked again, "It will be a killa and a chilla and a thrilla when I get the gorilla in Manila!" And then, before the fight, Ali squeezed a prop, a toy gorilla, which stood for Frazier, and began pounding it with his fist. "C'mon gorilla," Ali yelled. "We in Manila."

How much deeper into the stereotypical bag could Ali reach? Once again, he was quick with the "Tom" charge when it came to a black fighter. He also raised the issue of intelligence, a racial ball and chain that blacks have dragged around for years. He compared another black man to an ape and, appallingly, no one raised a stink. He spoke unflatteringly about Frazier's looks, again essentially degrading a man with darker skin and thicker hair. Had a white fighter said the same about Frazier, that fighter would've been correctly branded a racist of the worst kind. But when Ali said these things, it was greeted by the masses with a typical response: laughter, hysterical and unapologetic laughter.

For much of his career, Ali's trash talking was rationalized by those who said he was merely "selling tickets." That's a joke. Most of Ali's fights were sold out within moments of their announcement. Plus, his purse was guaranteed months before the fight. He didn't need to "sell" his fights for them to be successful, but he chose to play the role, anyway, particularly in the 1970s, his heyday in the sport. If anything, Ali was selling himself to the public and doing a wonderful job of it; gradually, he became one of the most recognized people on the planet. By then, Ali had opened the door for trash talking and showboating and weakened the resistance in sports toward it. On schoolyard basketball courts, mostly in urban America, not only was it suddenly trendy to trash talk, it was accepted as part of the sport. It was also taken for granted that whoever lost a game would hear about it. Kids in the '70s grew up with this mentality. The goal in certain sports was to win and then emphasize what you just did. It was to provoke, humiliate, taunt, tease, and strip the loser of all dignity. It became a psychological tool to be used to a player's advantage, a way of putting someone in his place. And above all, society collectively looked the other way, in essence accepting such behavior as part of the black culture, if not the sports culture.

Sometimes there is a tolerance level, thank goodness. Sometimes, the desire for good taste produces sound reasoning and change. This was the case following the 1994 World Basketball Championships, where some members of Team USA used every conceivable trick to mock their overmatched opponents. They went Ali on teams that just wanted to play basketball. They brought boorish behavior to the world stage and basically made fools of themselves. Even worse, after watching the spectacle, people in faraway places with little or no contact with American blacks likely came away with an unflattering image based on the actions of a few mindless basketball players after scoring baskets and grabbing rebounds. Shawn Kemp dunked with one hand and grabbed his crotch with the other. Larry Johnson screamed at the top of his lungs after scoring a basket and rubbed his hands on his face and his jersey. Alonzo Mourning and Derrick

Coleman also postured and hollered. This was no Dream Team; this was the Scream Team. There were incidents of chest-thumping and preening and posing, and it was all done by black players. Johnson even proudly announced that he and his fellow instigators were members of the "All Principal's Office Team."

That was enough for the executives who selected the USA team; the president, C.M. Newton, had an announcement of his own, saying the next team would be made up of "character, not characters" and had the good sense to put David Robinson and Grant Hill, among others, on the 1996 Olympic team.

Still, the action taken by Newton was a severe case of too little, too late. The trend created by Ali was rolling downhill, and there was no stopping it. This stereotype was rock solid well before director Ron Shelton created the characters for one of his most successful sports movies. So it came as no surprise that the role played by Wesley Snipes in *White Men Can't Jump* was the mouthy and trash-talking black basketball player, whereas his basketball partner, Woody Harrelson, mainly shut up and played, like a typical suburban, well-mannered white guy. Did anyone expect otherwise? Almost all the playground scenes in the movie showed black players as trash-talking, foul-mouthed, cackling agitators who can't resist a chance to verbally attack one another, typical of the culture that suffocates street ball.

The same racial lines were drawn in *Jerry Maguire,* in which Tom Cruise played a preppy and paranoid white sports agent, and his best client was a black football player who, you guessed it, ran his mouth and even danced while telling Cruise over the telephone, "Show me the money!" Cuba Gooding Jr. won an Oscar for portraying Rod Tidwell, a mouthy, stereotypical new-school black athlete, a role Hollywood evidently approved.

Around the time of the third Ali–Frazier fight, two new words appeared in the sports dictionary: shuckin' and jivin'. These racial code words were created by white people and used by white people to describe the behavior of black people. Even now, they are never, ever directed toward a white person. For example, as silly as comedian Jim Carrey sometimes acts, nobody ever accuses him of shuckin' or jivin'. Also, these words never appear by themselves. If a black person is shuckin', then he must be jivin'.

These racist words made their way into sports and stayed when the black athlete took a tip from Ali and began celebrating after touchdowns. The Ali copycats began strutting their stuff rather innocently in the mid-'60s, led by a New York Giants receiver named Homer Jones who slammed the football to the ground after scoring—or rather, he spiked it. Once again, scoring points and beating the other team wasn't enough; the achievement had to be emphasized and driven home by pounding the ball. But the watershed moment arrived on November 18, 1973, when Elmo Wright, a receiver for the Kansas City Chiefs, stumbled a few yards from the end zone. He instantly leaped from the turf and started high-stepping, and then he spiked the ball. Because it happened live on national television, Wright's high-step caused an instant sensation and changed football forever, something that Wright didn't expect.

What Wright did was the football equivalent of the Ali shuffle with hands held high. The stereotypical copy machine was warming up once again, with mainly black athletes conducting a can-you-top-this celebration contest. Butch Johnson of the Cowboys performed the "quake" after catching touchdown passes, and others tried to be just as creative. Whereas most players did variations of the spike or the latest dance craze of the moment, the unofficial winner in the 1970s was Billy "White Shoes" Johnson, who slowly flapped his knees in the end zone. The next decade, it was Ickey Woods, a running back with the Bengals, who did a choreographed stutter-step after scoring, a hopping and twirling dance routine, which he called the Ickey Shuffle. After a knee injury cut his career short, Woods sold meat door to door and even shuffled on the front steps of his customers if they asked.

At least Johnson and Sanders waited until they scored; once the '90s arrived, players started dancing after five-yard gains. It was suddenly chic to celebrate everything and self-promote endlessly, no matter the circumstances. This created the phenomenon named Deion Sanders, an All-Pro at showcasing himself. He refused to wait until he scored. He made a habit of holding the ball with one hand while high-stepping 30 yards away from the end zone, then performing a jig once he arrived.

These flamboyant displays are often passed off as innocent forms of expression and a way to get the crowd excited, which is strange because touchdowns and big plays usually generate excitement by themselves. Plus, you wonder why black players in the past were never compelled to behave like this. Yet they were created out of the demand for them in today's society. That's the only reason these acts began to multiply and become common. When black athletes first did their thing, the white audience applauded and laughed and begged for more. It was a mutual cooperation on both sides, and everybody ignored the obvious racial messages being sent and the stereotypes they formed. Depending on the performer, the white audience, which comprises the vast majority of fans in football stadiums, looked forward to the touchdown celebrations more than the touchdowns themselves. Basically, white people liked certain black athletes to shuck, and these black athletes in turn were anxious to jive.

The mutual acceptance from players and fans was so strong that there was outrage when the NFL, in a well-intended attempt to return to simpler times, tried to outlaw most end-zone celebrations. The "Fun Bunch" group-touchdown hug by the Redskins forced the NFL's hand, and in 1984 the league outlawed what it called "excessive celebration." The media, mostly white, and ticket-buying fans, also mostly white, demanded the return of their shuckin' and jivin' black athletes. Someone mocked the NFL as the "No Fun League," and suddenly, not wanting to be seen as stuffy old white men totally out of touch with the times, league executives caved. They didn't erase the rule from the books, but when dancing and choreography snuck back into the end zone, they looked the other way. Very rarely since 1984 has a player been flagged for excessive celebration, and you wonder how much of this is because of the almighty dollar. The last thing the NFL wants is to fail to give the public what it craves, and in the case of black football players, the public wants dancing, and the funkier, the better.

Another half-hearted response from the league was to institute a no-taunting rule in 1991. Again, the NFL refused to police the rule very strongly, except in flagrant instances. The mere act of spiking the ball next to an opposing player is a taunt in itself, however mildly. No matter how it's disguised, the entire culture is designed to show up the other guy, to rub your success in his face, to tell the world how great you are. Just as Ali famously did decades ago.

The irony, cruel as it may be, is that the man who spawned legions of poor imitators can no longer imitate his own art. Part of Ali's legacy lies with Parkinson's and how the disease stole his ability to express himself, which only further endeared him to the world and increased his sainthood and the sympathy he received. It was the equivalent of Beethoven turning deaf, or Ted Williams losing his flexibility to swing, or Jesse Owens being confined to a wheelchair, or Julia Child suddenly losing her sense of taste.

In his later years, all Muhammad Ali could do was point to a TV screen on a Thanksgiving Day, silently chuckle at a dancing black football player in the end zone, and whisper proudly about creating a phenomenon. No doubt, purely as a boxer and activist, Ali created change in sports. As for his other claim to originality, we must seriously begin to wonder if that change was for the better.

CHAPTER 9

Media Madness

The Price of (Not) Dancing to Their Tune

Immortality doesn't always wait until death. In sports, immortality happens while a certain athlete is very much alive and doing quite well, actually. Immortality arrives once a week, in the shape of a glossy sheet of paper 8 inches wide and 10.5 inches long, and it brings the athlete the kind of fame he never imagined. For that moment, when immortality hits and transforms him forever, he becomes the center of the sports universe. He's guaranteed a place in sports history.

That's because athletes become immortalized once they make the cover of *Sports Illustrated* magazine, still after 50 years the most prestigious publication devoted to fun and games. While the cover of *Rolling Stone* inspired a folk song, the cover of *Sports Illustrated* inspired legions of athletes to do whatever possible to get their face on it and to get their piece of immortality. Ask any first-time coverboy or covergirl, and they'll tell you it was almost an out-of-body experience. Ask anyone lucky enough to appear on the cover more than once, and they'll say it never gets old. They'll take one look at themselves on the front of the magazine and time almost freezes, sort of like my expression after I pulled the November 13, 1989, issue from my mailbox and saw who made the cover.

It was Deion Sanders, the supreme cornerback for Atlanta at the time, but he wasn't wearing his Falcons uniform. No, Deion was very much out of uniform. He wore a supple leather jacket, unzipped to show a bare chest and a sparkling collection of gold and silver ropes, chains, and medallions from the Mr. T jewelry line. On his wrists was even more ice, enough to cool Bangladesh. He wore a black hat and was using his fingers to gently lower his Wayfayer sunglasses in a Tom Cruise-in-*Risky Business*-like manner. And he had a grin.

The headline screamed almost as loud as he looked. "Atlanta's Neon Deion Sanders," it said. "Prime Time Live."

It was a good thing the headline revealed the man behind the shades. Otherwise, everyone would've wondered what I wondered: What's a street pimp doing on the cover of *Sports Illustrated?*

A good many of *Sports Illustrated's* covers are action photographs taken of the previous week's big game, and those pictures capture a particular moment or theme addressed inside the magazine. Maybe a game-winning goal, or a slick move on the field, the thrill of victory or the agony of defeat. That sort of picture. Sometimes the magazine will conduct a photo shoot with the chosen player and get creative in order to convey a message about the player. The athlete has no control over the action shot taken at a game. But he can decide what he will or will not do in a photo shoot, and for this particular cover, Sanders was anxious to play the role for a magazine that used him for shock appeal.

Certainly, *Sports Illustrated* had shown the black athlete in a gazillion different ways over the decades, almost always honorable or respectable or decent. The magazine does not have a history, shameful or otherwise, of exploiting the black athlete negatively. Muhammad Ali, for example, the most covered athlete in the magazine's history, could usually be seen as the essence of black power, putting a fist to someone's face. Michael Jordan, number 2 on the list, was the picture of grace and greatness. And so on. But along came Deion Sanders, with all his blinging and jingling, and *Sports Illustrated* couldn't resist. Sanders wasn't about to be caught dead in a Brooks Brothers suit, although that certainly would have been a twist for him at that time in his professional life. Deion had to be neon. He had to be true to the game. He had to keep it real. And *Sports Illustrated* had to have that cover.

It didn't matter that Sanders dressed the way most drug dealers dressed, or once did anyway, back in his humble Fort Myers, Florida, neighborhood. Sanders was

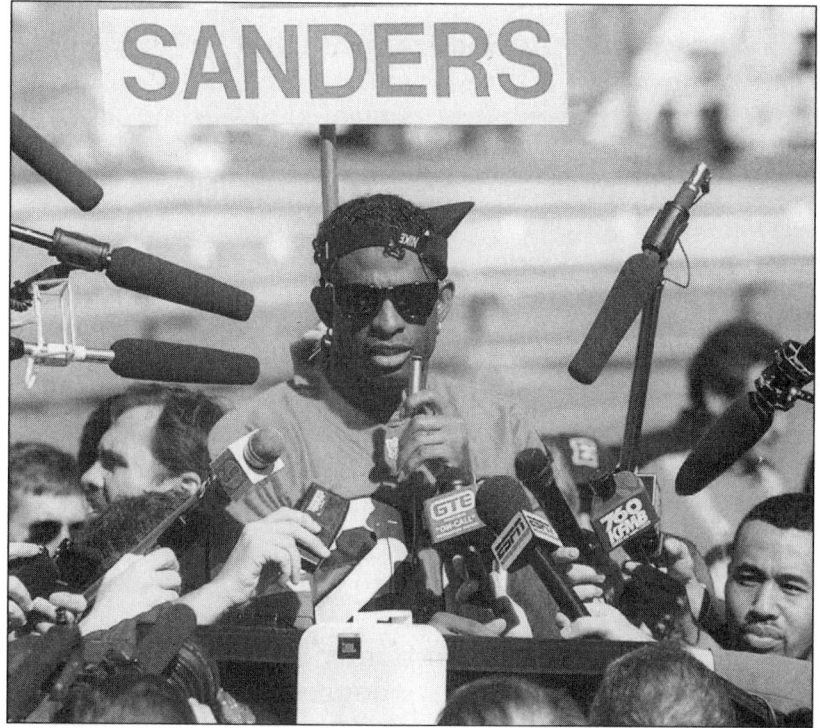

Deion Sanders created a character, Neon Deion, to bring attention to himself and increase his marketability. Obviously, it worked, as reflected by the hoards of media surrounding Sanders in January 1995, prior to Super Bowl XXIX.

all about living up to a cartoonish character he created for the purpose of self-promotion and making money, and selfishly, he posed in a way to flaunt this image. And *Sports Illustrated*, given the green light by Sanders, a black man, figured everything was okay. It was a partnership, then. An immature black athlete, blinded by fame, chose to dress this way. A magazine, looking for a provocative cover that would catch the eye, tried to capture the essence of the subject at hand.

Each benefited from the other, and in the process, the sensitive image of the black athlete, if not the black race, took another kick in the groin.

Is this being too harsh, judgmental, and hypersensitive? Well, to an extent, maybe. Some of what we get from athletes is goofy fun, nothing intentionally meant to harm anyone. And Sanders was never charged with a double murder or hitting a woman or caught sucking on a crack pipe. He was never convicted of a crime or guilty of doing anything more felonious than dumping a tub of ice water on the head of TV broadcaster Tim McCarver, who had the audacity to take Deion to task over the airwaves. In the broader picture, though, the black community is overrepresented by athletes and entertainers in the mainstream media, and therefore, their visibility runs deeper. That's not their fault. They'd have competition from judges and CEOs and university presidents if decades of racism and poverty didn't keep blacks from ascending to those visible and far more important jobs in greater numbers. Unfortunately, when it comes to the black community, the mainstream media doesn't have the same number of options to choose from as it does with white America.

"No one complains about Homer Simpson on TV being an idiotic Anglo male who's a danger to all Anglo males," said Robert Thompson, a professor at Syracuse University who studies popular television, "but you can see how images are so crucial to African Americans. Each image tends to stand for so much because there aren't that many out there being shown through the media."

If nothing else, the Deion Sanders cover provided an interesting look at the mainstream media's role in depicting the black athlete. Usually, the media serves up a fairly limited scope, mainly confined to the typical rags-to-riches tale, in which the athlete survived the mean streets of the ghetto, saw his best friends either shot or taken to jail, and finally made the pros and bought his mother a house. The media also provides nonstop, exhausting coverage of the loudest and flashiest black athlete to see how far he can push the envelope. The first option is somewhat (and regrettably) necessary simply because some football and basketball players came from tough places. The second option is purely for entertainment purposes; the athlete provides a self-serving minstrel show, and the media happily goes along for the ride in order to get a strong reaction from the (mostly white) public and fill airtime on TV or space in newspapers and magazines.

The second option wasn't even an option until roughly 30 years ago, when TV turned even athletes with mediocre talent into instant celebrities, and later, when Madison Avenue began rewarding these amateur entertainers with endorsement deals. Thus, funky end-zone dancing and finger pointing and taunting and chest pounding entered into the sports culture for good, no matter how much (or little) the sports leagues tried to tone it down. Controversy sells almost as well as sex, and with money and ratings at stake, the media and attention-starved athletes began a partnership to help each other out. Of course, this came at a price. Sportsmanship began to erode quickly on the professional level, and a fresh set of stereotypes was dumped on the black community, because a good many of these entertainers were black.

"Clearly, when it comes to certain black athletes, the media's doing double duty," Thompson said. "One, to show the sports performer, and two, to show the jesters in this new pantheon of celebrity in our society. An awful lot of these black athletes are being cast in jester and comic roles, much the same as Jimmy J.J. Walker, or to go a step further, to even more demeaning TV and movie roles of a long time ago. Dennis Rodman in a wedding dress, for example. The media couldn't resist."

The media has an interesting and complex historical relationship with the black athlete, much of it mired in blatant racism and utter ignorance. It began deep in the previous century, when boxer Jack Johnson was basically compared by a biased media to a wild beast that needed to be tamed by a good, well-meaning white man who would become a Great White Hope. Later, when an assortment of black boxers began rising to prominence, they were characterized by the media for their appetite for violence and savagery, arousing fear among whites, who during this time learned to be troubled by the sight of big black men.

When Jackie Robinson broke the color barrier, the coverage of the event by the media hardly matched the social significance; a number of newspapers and magazines didn't even bother sending reporters to his first game, and only Wendell Smith, a black reporter from the *Pittsburgh Courier* and constant traveling companion of Robinson, provided in-depth coverage that year. John Carlos and Tommie Smith were seen as troublemakers by some media commentators in 1968. When blacks began to increase in dramatic numbers in football and basketball, TV commentators developed a racial code—the black athlete was a "natural," whereas the white athlete was applauded for being "smart." And now, the black athletes who receive an unhealthy portion of coverage are those who clown or disrupt or self-promote, even though their behavior does not represent the majority of blacks who participate in sports; it only seems that way.

If the media did its job correctly and portrayed everyone accurately, Deion Sanders never would have been cast as a loud-mouthed buffoon. Truthfully, Sanders was a mama's boy who liked to fish. He was quiet as a kid, never caused trouble, and was a decent student. When he wasn't on the football field, he could be quite nerdy, in fact. Only when he went to Florida State and got a taste of fame did he behave out of character. To keep the media's attention trained on him, which is tough for a cornerback to do, Sanders created Neon Deion, a dancing smack talker who said and did anything to get his name in the paper and face on TV. He was the black version of "The Boz," the alter-ego of Brian Bosworth, the Oklahoma All-America linebacker.

The difference is white America could afford to have a Boz because white America, through the media, has so many examples of white people who aren't like Boz at all. Nobody ever attached Boz to white culture. That's not always the case in black America, where the media keeps such a narrow view of black people and has a skewed idea of black behavior and culture. Therefore, when Neon Deion started shuckin' and jivin', his behavior was somehow lumped with black culture, as though black folks have been doing it since slavery.

"Whenever there's a story done on Tim Duncan, it always comes with a preface: That Tim isn't like the rest of those guys, he's not from Harlem. He's from the Caribbean," said Earl Smith, a professor at Wake Forest, where Duncan attended college. "I would argue that Tim Duncan, who's plain vanilla, has no media appeal. I don't think the media is looking for that kind of black athlete. If they scratch the surface, they're supposed to find something. You know, 'he came from a single parent household, ran with a gang, raised by adoptive white parents,' something like that. When they don't find that person, they take a pass, because nobody wants to read about those folks. So I always wonder, Where's the story about the player who doesn't carry all that baggage?"

As for those black athletes who willingly play the role, Smith doesn't spare any sympathy. "I call it the Self-Promotion Showmanship Syndrome," he said. "These guys are socialized early on about the concept of self-promotion. Everything we learned from Lombardi and all the other coaches who said it was 'always about the team,' well, players bought into that at first. And now, these guys are saying it belongs to me. It's learned behavior, not genetic behavior."

Sanders refused to kill off his character because it gave him so much, in terms of attention, social status, and of course money. He was elevated to a rock-star level, which is very difficult for anyone to pull off in football unless they're a Super Bowl–winning white quarterback. Pure greed kept Neon Deion alive. He knew that, in a celebrity-crazed America that keeps Paris Hilton on radar, personality and showmanship were rewarded almost as much as athletic talent, and in some cases, even more. And who could blame him? He grew up in an MTV age in which singers of modest ability could sell millions of records based partly on their ability to shake booty in their music videos. A woman these days doesn't need the pipes of Ella Fitzgerald to go platinum in pop music; all she needs is a good beat playing in the background, a cute face, a killer body, and the right camera angle. Therefore, Sanders wasn't content with being merely the best cover cornerback of his generation, maybe of all time. He had to give what the public wanted and even came to expect from certain black athletes. He had to clown.

In his book, *Power, Sex and Money: How Success Almost Ruined My Life,* Sanders concedes as much. "Everybody wanted to see this flamboyant, egotistical, arrogant, outspoken young man, and they didn't realize that it was all an act," he wrote. "Prime Time was a character—a caricature of this cocky black football dude that I had created. But the fans and media were totally captivated by it. . . . If the press bought all the stuff I was doing out there as Prime Time, then I had manipulated the heck out of them. In fact, I think that's the main reason so many of them hate me today. They finally realized they were letting themselves be manipulated."

Sanders used the press, the press used Sanders, and this is how it usually works when it comes to athletes who insist on being like Neon Deion. Sadly, the media was (and still is) too white at the top levels of decision making to realize the image it sent by going overboard on Deion. And Sanders was too hell-bent on generating star power for himself to understand the ramifications of his actions. Neither side took into account the imagery and how it could influence a great number of young and impressionable black kids to start high-stepping down the field and dancing like Bill "Bojangles" Robinson after a touchdown and speaking outrageously because it worked for their sports hero, Neon Deion. Obviously, neither the media nor Sanders had an obligation to raise anyone else's kids. And thus, that's why there's a problem with imagery in sports: Nobody cares enough to change it.

"The media, by choosing these types of athletes to promote, are guilty," said Professor Thompson of Syracuse. "But they're only part of the shaping process. The athletes are their own co-conspirators because they keep giving the media this material. They keep it coming. It's a role they've learned to play and play very well. When we're writing fiction, we have our fictional characters doing outrageous things. If the networks have real fictional characters doing outrageous things, they're not going to turn away. Instead, it's up to the athlete. He should look in the mirror and wonder, What exactly am I saying about myself?"

Every so often, the media must find a lightning rod to exploit to the hilt, all for the sake of ratings or newsstand sales, and once again, these roles are often occupied by black athletes to various degrees. It's Dennis Rodman one moment, Deion Sanders the next, and perhaps the most exploited of them all: Terrell Owens. In each case, the media assumes the position of 24-hour watchdog, giving us a constant diet of outrageous behavior, even though most of us get our fill pretty quickly. Or do we? There must be a reason why the cable news channels find a sensational subject, usually a white woman in distress who died a shocking death, and squeeze every last second of coverage, to the point that it becomes a parody. Usually, these causes are driven by high ratings, or else no media outlet in its right mind would give it more than a minute of airtime. Maybe the problem is us. Maybe we as a society simply developed bad taste and are addicted to it.

That's about the only possible explanation for the media's infatuation with Owens. Magazines and television, especially ESPN, couldn't get enough of Owens and sent a steady stream of T.O. tales to the public during his last season with the Philadelphia Eagles and his first season with the Dallas Cowboys. We saw Owens give constant tongue-lashings on the sideline to various coaches and teammates. We saw Owens doing push-ups on the front lawn of his New Jersey mansion. We saw Owens give a stammering apology to Eagles quarterback Donovan McNabb. We saw Owens deny a suicide attempt, a soap opera that was treated on live TV like a presidential kidnapping or the O.J. white Bronco chase. It was Owens this, Owens that. It was enough to make you scream. But because this obnoxious black athlete refused to shut up and go away, TV refused to stop showing him, and society was subjected to a daily serving of a freak show.

"When I see Terrell Owens on TV," said Gregg Popovich, the coach of the San Antonio Spurs, "I turn it off. I'm sick of it. Who gives a damn what Terrell Owens thinks or does, with his antics? He's what people teach their kids how not to act. But who do you see on TV all the time? People just like him. And who put him there? Adults put him there. So how can we be surprised when our kids follow that stuff?"

If anything, we should have seen the Deion Sanders magazine cover coming our way. Magazines have always been under pressure to run a splashy and often controversial cover that allows the publication to stand out from the rest on the news racks. *Sports Illustrated* was one of the few exceptions because of its dominance in the market. But that dominance began to wane in the late 1980s. With the expansion of the cable networks, primarily ESPN, the magazine suddenly had competition for the young demographic. Before ESPN, sports fans usually waited two or three days for *Sports Illustrated* to recap the previous week's major events. Once the 24-hour network started showing highlights and in-depth coverage on the spot, a weekly publication such as *Sports Illustrated* was in danger of being obsolete by the time it hit the stands. Too often, the magazine covered yesterday's news. It was filled with stories about an event that happened the previous weekend, and by the time the magazine was published, everyone already knew who won and lost and had already heard from the athletes and coaches in those events.

A new generation of sports fans was younger and less inclined to wait. In an era of instant news, a weekly magazine had to be awfully special and cutting edge to maintain circulation, much less experience any dramatic increase in sales. While readers have always shown an appreciation for the finely crafted story and special investigation, two trademarks of *Sports Illustrated,* those readers were getting older. The younger generation, according to studies, wanted stories about people who connected with their generation. *Sports Illustrated,* while excellent, was in danger of being your father's magazine, according to industry experts.

This was the central selling point for the biggest threat yet to *Sports Illustrated: ESPN The Magazine.* The new publication promised catchy covers and creative photos designed to captivate younger readers, and it delivered. In a climate of declining circulation in the publishing industry, *ESPN Magazine* was an instant success, partly because of its link to the network, but also because of its Generation X layout and philosophy. To catch the eye of the reader, the magazine stuck to a consistent trend: It often featured athletes on the cover in moments of expression that were acceptable to young readers. These covers were meant to pique the interest of a young culture. Kansas City Chiefs running back Larry Johnson, for example, didn't wear an ordinary baseball cap for his cover, with the interesting headline: "Got Cred?" His cap was worn backward.

Just like *Sports Illustrated, ESPN Magazine* depicted athletes of all races in many different ways, not just one. On some *ESPN* covers, though, the athletes tended to have attitude. Terrell Owens posed with his tongue hanging out next to the headline "Shock Therapy." Randy Moss, another infamous bad boy, wore a backward cap while flexing a muscle. Amare Stoudemire, the Phoenix Suns player, and Nelly, the rapper, were both shown on the cover devoted to a story linking hip-hop and the NBA.

All of this clearly caused *Sports Illustrated* to stray from its comfort zone and attempt to change with the times in a rather clear if not desperate effort to grab the young demographic. You wonder if twenty years ago the magazine would have had a basketball player pose the way New Jersey Nets player Kenyon Martin did in 2002. For that cover, Martin wore an angry scowl and pulled back his jersey far enough to reveal a tattoo on the right side of his chest that read, "Bad Ass Yellow Boy." The headline was "Bad Boy." Given the nasty brawl the following season in Detroit between the Pistons and Pacers, that cover certainly had to make NBA commissioner David Stern cringe.

It can be argued that the bad-boy coverboy phenomenon featuring famous blacks was a creation of *The Source* and *Vibe* and other hip-hop magazines, which spent a great deal of creativity in finding new ways to make rappers appear angry. Once again, it was all about imagery and the magazine's desire to be seen as cool and hip by a young generation that put heavy emphasis on street credibility. And when those magazines saw their circulations soar, the white-owned media companies took notice, and one enterprising publisher in particular saw an opportunity to take the cover concept a step further.

Dennis Page, an executive with Harris Publications and founder of *Guitar World* and *XXL*, a rap magazine, was also a huge basketball fan, and he wanted to link the music and basketball worlds with a magazine that would satisfy both audiences.

"The light bulb went off," he said. "I just said, 'Why don't we do a hip basketball magazine?' I was enamored with *Vibe* because it was done in a hip way, written in street language, which had never been done before in the industry. You know, a lot of the stories were 'Yo-dis, yo-dat,' the language of the street. My magazine would be about rappers who were into basketball and vice versa. You take the rap world, and the basketball world, coupled with sneaker ads and combine all that, and you have *Slam*."

Slam magazine made no pretense about itself, and from the very first issue, the publication cut right to the chase: This was not going to be a white-bread magazine, not on the cover, not in the ads, not even in the stories themselves. While the magazine was religiously and exclusively devoted to basketball, John Stockton was never going to appear on the pages. As Page said, "There are *Slam* guys and non-*Slam* guys."

Translation: Any basketball player who did not exude the 'hood was treated by *Slam* as a badminton player.

And neither Page nor *Slam* make any apologies for the urban slang and Ebonics prose that flow through many of the feature stories. These stories are filled with grammar purposely written in such a way to connect with the intended audience, just like *Golf Digest* speaks the language of its white-collar subscription base. "Younger high school kids had never seen a magazine speak in the language of the sport," explained Page. Well, that language would get a high school kid an F in English class if he used it on a term paper, but in *Slam,* such language is not only accepted by the editors, it's encouraged. And as for the N-word, Page said, "If a player used it in conversation, I wouldn't edit it out."

Interestingly, Page and most of the writers and editors on a small staff that puts out the magazine from its headquarters in Manhattan are white. In 2002, a former creative director for Harris Publications filed a

$15 million lawsuit in U.S. District Court, claiming Page and company honcho Stanley Harris, who's also white, commonly used the N-word when referring to blacks. The charges made by Donald Morris, who filed the suit, were denied by Page and Harris. The company characterized Morris as a disgruntled ex-employee who didn't receive the promotion he desired. Morris also said Page and Harris created a racially demeaning caricature of Dennis Rodman and passed it around the offices. The lawsuit was settled out of court.

Evan Agostini/Getty Images

Dennis Rodman was a good enough player to be an integral part of five NBA Championship teams and for the Detroit Pistons and Chicago Bulls to put up with his antics. Rodman would stop at nothing—not even a wedding dress, which he dons here during a book promotion—in seeking to shock and gain attention.

For sure, the *Slam* staff writers are instantly recognized and graciously welcomed by black players throughout the NBA and college, and even on the high school level. You might say *Slam* not only has street cred, it has locker-room cred. It also has a circulation of roughly 200,000 and is widely read by young black men who play basketball both recreationally and for a living.

The biggest appeal and impact of *Slam*, obviously, is the cover, which goes straight for shock appeal. Since the magazine is geared toward basketball, the vast majority of the coverboys are black. Allen Iverson has had multiple covers and is clearly the ideal player to promote, in the view of *Slam*. Page said, "He resonates with our readers. He's so hip-hop. He doesn't conform. He's an outlaw, and *Slam* has always been known as an outlaw publication."

In no specific terms, when it comes to the cover, anything goes, and players are encouraged to be themselves, as long as they don't smile. That goes against the image that *Slam* is all about.

"We try to capture the true essence of the player and the game," said Page. "That's not to say all black people got anger, but they got attitude. When they pose for the cover, we don't tell the players, 'Be angry.' They just come in with a game face. We want to capture that soul. We continue to try to do that. Smiling is not what we do."

Given the license to express themselves in ways that probably would be out of place in the mainstream media, many of the young black players let their hair down, so to speak, in the presence of *Slam*. They decide to be angry and threatening. They also choose to wear bowling ball–sized diamond earrings, droopy jeans falling toward their ankles, and of course, a frown. Showing off tattoos is also a must. So is the ever-present gold necklace.

"Big necklaces, that's who they are," said Page. "*Slam* is very much true to the culture. We tell the player, 'Be who you are, do your thing.' That's important to the identity of *Slam*."

The magazine is strictly nonconforming and makes no secret about it. The cover of *Slam* and the stories inside are all about attitude and street credibility. The larger issue, of course, is the stereotype of the angry and materialistic black athlete that *Slam* eagerly promotes. But altering this philosophy, according to Page, is not negotiable. In this day and age, people aren't offended by the image that *Slam* lives and breathes, he believes.

"Maybe the older folks," he said. "But the kids, I don't think so."

And what if he were told by adults or special interest groups to change the focus of the magazine?

"I wouldn't even listen," he said.

Despite its role as a niche magazine, *Slam* has influenced the sports-publishing landscape more than the mainstream magazines care to acknowledge. *ESPN Magazine,* with vastly superior resources, began running bold, creative covers to great success, and *Sports Illustrated* made a drastic effort to break from tradition and become edgier and flashier, all in the name of capturing a younger audience.

"I believe *Slam* single-handedly changed the landscape of sports magazines," said Page. "We are the first hip sports magazine. All the rest tried to take a lot of elements of *Slam.*"

If certain magazine covers are guilty of enhancing the supposed modern-day young black athlete, the video game business is the undisputed king and ruler of exploiting stereotypes in the media industry. Once again, the lucrative youth audience is at stake, and video programmers spare no pixels in their attempt to go cyberhood. The enormously popular Grand Theft Auto series is the most flagrant example, where black (and Latino) gang members wearing scarves and baggy clothes and tattoos engage in mayhem. All this does, obviously, is promote minorities as gang-bangers, thugs, and menaces to society, quite a contrast to the abundance of real minorities in this country, who struggle to make ends meet and deal with an oppressive society that doesn't do them any favors.

Even more disturbing is that these games end up in the hands of children, including preteenagers, despite the mature rating. These impressionable young minds are being polluted with the very worst images that black people constantly must battle against, but are mostly powerless to prevent, because a study showed that 80 percent of the video programmers are white. That 2001 examination, "Fair Play? Violence, Gender and Race in Video Games," done by Children Now, also noted that of 1,500 video game characters surveyed, 288 were black males and 83 percent of those males were athletes.

Many of these black cyber-athletes had huge biceps and chests, thereby upholding the image of the black super-athlete, who has a superior body type and more raw athletic ability than white athletes. David Leonard, a Washington State assistant professor, found that black competitors in video games are more prone to aggressive behavior than their white counterparts. One of the more popular characters found in video games is a black boxer who wears an Afro and talks plenty of trash to his opponents.

Most of the black characters are confined to basketball and football, in such games as Streetball, NBA Live, and the Madden football series. The characters in Streetball are precisely what you'd expect: jive-talking, flashy basketball players who tend to dunk a lot. In the NBA Ballers game, which carries an all-ages rating, the players do plenty of showboating and strutting, while gamers also get to experience the off-the-court life of these computer creations, which includes riding in Cadillac Escalades with big rims.

Although the overwhelmingly white video game programmers are being insensitive, at the very least, for enhancing these images, the consumers can't be excused. Evidently, with video game sales reaching $7 billion, plenty of gamers either don't care about the images or they endorse them by exercising their spending power. And none of our so-called black leaders raise any stink about it. Once again, the cooperative effort of whites in power and a silent black community allow these images to live and breathe.

The goliath of media players is television, obviously, because of its ability to reach and influence generations through the use of images and commentary. And when it comes to portraying the black athlete, we've witnessed the good and bad. There were two watershed moments in TV on the subject of black athletes and image: one, when sports bettor Jimmy "The Greek" Snyder made a clumsy attempt at dissecting the black athletic family tree, and two, when Dodgers executive Al Campanis became an expert on the mental capacity of black people.

Both men took those episodes to their graves, but more important, their rambling demonstrated the power of TV and reflected what some whites believe about black people. Aside from his comments regarding the ana-tomical advantages of black athletes ("big thighs which allow them to run faster and jump higher"), Snyder said something more damaging that was lost in the reaction. He also noted how whites were holding for dear life onto their coaching jobs because, with the ascent of the black athlete, management is all they had left. Which basically meant the black man shouldn't expect to enjoy the same gains in the front office as he has on the field.

The Snyder and Campanis episodes shook fear into the TV networks. Suddenly, they were exposed to their own shortcomings and insensitivities regarding black athletes. The shortcomings were caused by the lack of blacks in upper management and decision-making positions. The insensitivities were caused by the ignorant beliefs held by sports commentators regarding the physical ability of black athletes. You cannot put a number on how many times white TV commentators have marveled about a black athlete's "natural ability" while complimenting the "intelligence" of white athletes. As Smith, the Wake Forest professor, said, "The media will go about it in different ways nowadays, but they still spin the story about the super black athlete who rolled out of the womb. It keeps coming back to that."

That's precisely what Isiah Thomas wondered with his racially charged comment-in-passing about how Larry Bird would be "just another athlete" in the minds of the media if he were black. No doubt, black players respected Bird, but just the same, they were weary about the media's infatuation with Bird's intelligence, as if Bird were Einstein. Thomas never heard the TV experts rave about his own intelligence when, in fact, Thomas was one of the smartest athletes in any sport who ever lived. But being a black athlete in the TV world, it goes with the territory.

Television executives have since gone great lengths to diversify their on-air talent, and yet this gives the misleading indication that blacks hold positions of great power in the industry, when in fact blacks do not. No black man or woman has ever run a sports division at the major networks, and the producer roles are largely white. Plus, much of the black on-air talent is reserved for former players, who are asked to do nothing more than ramble about the game. And some don't do that very well. Michael Irvin pulled a "Greek" when he said Cowboys quarterback Tony Romo has "some brother" in him and wondered if a patriarch woman in Romo's family history "pulled one of those studs up out of the barn" during slavery days and, well, got busy.

In response to Irvin's attempt at being funny, ESPN executive Norby Williamson said, "Any time you generalize on racial matters, it can be damaging, dangerous, and inappropriate. You learn from such mistakes and move on." Actually, it's not wrong to hold a conversation on racial matters; the more, the better. It's just dumb to say something you know nothing about. Honest, candid, and informed commentary should be welcome, not discouraged, in any appropriate forum. But Michael Irvin, last anyone knew, was an ex-football player who knew how to catch passes, not a physiologist who did extensive research on human development. He soon became an ex-ESPN employee when the network refused to extend his contract for 2007.

Aside from their inability to keep their mostly white commentators from sounding foolish (Howard Cosell's "monkey" characterization of Redskins receiver Alvin Garrett comes to mind), the networks have a knack for bringing out unsportsmanlike behavior from athletes. About a decade ago, after one too many fans jumped from the stands and disrupted a baseball or football game in progress, the networks came together and created an unwritten rule: No longer would they show a fan running on the field. The networks sensed that TV was the problem, that fans wanted to see themselves on TV so badly they would risk getting arrested (or tackled by an angry football player) just for that 15 seconds of fame. Rather than encourage this behavior, the networks decided to turn their cameras away from the fan until security dragged him from the field. It was unusual for competing networks to agree on what should or should not be covered, and even though the audience usually was amused by streakers or disrupters, viewers understood. This was probably best for everyone.

Not surprisingly, the TV networks refused to follow their own principle when it came to the people who belong on the field. Not only do the cameras show every touchdown celebration or other display of self-promotion, they even show a replay, sometimes in slow motion. Chest-thumping, jersey-tugging, dancing, you name it, the camera will find it, and the players know this. Some genius TV producer in the control truck is constantly monitoring the benches for something outrageous to show the folks at home. In football, hand-held cameras are even stationed by the benches solely for the purpose of encouraging players to do or say something. And when someone scores a touchdown, cameras descend quickly in the end zone, like a pack of paparazzi outside a trendy Hollywood club, waiting for a show to begin.

"It's just that swagger we got," explained receiver Plaxico Burress of the New York Giants. "It's an urban thing. Most of us have a lot of rhythm, and we want to show it off. Who wouldn't want to entertain? To try and be like a rock star? That's the way I am. I'm thinking I'm the best player on the field and I can't wait until Sunday to prove it. I know I'm going to do something that even I didn't think I could do, and after I do it, I'm going to celebrate it."

Television is constantly trying to find new ways to bring us closer to the game and to capture the essence of a game, but by doing this, television encourages acts of outrageousness. Television turns players into more than athletes; it makes them entertainers. Why else would Chad Johnson of the Bengals spend precious time agonizing over new ways to dance after scoring a touchdown? Or why would any number of athletes decide to play to the cameras? If you ask the TV producers, they all say the same thing: This is entertainment and this is what the audience wants. Once again, our tastes have changed. Before, we were content to allow the game itself to entertain us. Today, the audience (mostly white) wants to see a show from athletes who are willing to provide one.

Just a hunch, but if TV applied the same principle to showboating athletes as it does to disruptive fans, we would see far fewer acts of unsportsmanlike conduct and egotistical displays. More than half of these athletes want to see themselves on the highlight shows anyway, so if the networks agreed to stop showing it, how often would they be compelled to do it? Of course it would take a cooperative effort on both sides, but if TV decided to confine itself to the game only, the entertainment beyond the game would die a slow death.

The reason TV goes beyond the game is money. Until the 1970s, the rights fees that TV paid to televise sporting events were reasonable. Then those fees tripled almost overnight because of competition from cable networks, especially when the fourth major network, Fox, began spending heavily. The NFL television package is well over $1 billion today. Suddenly, to make the numbers work and keep the ratings high, TV wanted more than just the game. For NFL games, they added pregame shows that stretched from 30 minutes to over an hour. And they turned athletes into superstar celebrities to be packaged and sold to the public. Suddenly, the Packers didn't play the Cowboys; according to the TV buildup, it was Brett Favre versus Terrell Owens. And the Lakers didn't play the Heat—it was Kobe versus Shaq.

"These networks have to squeeze out every dollar they can," said Thompson, the Syracuse professor. "So, in presenting a game, they've got to make sure they can put on a show. You've got to goose that up by finding drama. If you can identify a few stars or players who do eccentric things, then great. Terrell Owens is a telecaster's dream come true. These players realize the role they're being telecast and they completely cooperate."

The reason for this cooperation may even go beyond an athlete's desire to get noticed. Rather than be seen as an obedient black man who dutifully follows the rules put in place by white society and white sports owners, he decides to become a rebel. Instead of falling in line, he eagerly falls out of line and follows his own rules and regulations, all in the name of defiance.

"A lot of this behavior by certain African-American athletes is designed to be threatening," Thompson said, "because they know America is just uncomfortable seeing black men in nonsubservient roles. So some of these athletes are being defiant because of that. They're like, 'What, should we just go back to acting like we're in the 1950s when white America wanted us sitting in the back of the bus and knowing our place? Isn't that what America wants us to do?' I can see why some athletes see the appeal in that, where today's young African-American male decides to take a different route than what society found acceptable from them once before, when it was yes sir, no sir."

For sure, there is no turning back the clock for the media and the modern-day athlete, one phenomenon still learning about the other, even now. It's a marriage that continues to exist, some ways for the better, some for the worse.

CHAPTER 10

Leadership Positions

Hitting the Cement Ceiling

In the spring of 2003, he was removed from his coaching job with the Toronto Raptors, which surprised absolutely no one, including him. He knew the end was coming. The winds of change were swirling long before the pink slip arrived, which is common in these situations. In the days and weeks leading to the end, there was tension in the locker room. His team finished dead last in the division and obviously didn't reach the playoffs. His star player, hurt most of the year, did not give him much support. Other players tuned him out. The fans grew restless, as did upper management, finally concluding that he was part of the problem, not the solution.

He knew the deal. He knew he was getting fired. He'd been around long enough, had seen it happen to others and to him. That's coaching. That's sports.

He turned to his passion, which was golf, playing almost daily that summer and into early fall, both for the pleasure and the challenge it gave him but also because it filled the enormous void left by basketball, which had been part of his life for six decades. That was over now, or so he thought. Right then and there on the course, in the still air, drowning out the chirping of swallows, his cell phone rang. Or rather, opportunity knocked. Again. After six head coaching jobs, Lenny Wilkens had another. He was still a wanted man.

When he joined the New York Knicks just months after being unceremoniously dumped by Toronto, 10 years after his last division title and 25 years after his one and only NBA title, it was truly a remarkable moment in the business. That's because a black man had the honor of officially becoming the senior member of the recycled coaches club, a distinguished if crude badge of honor rarely granted to men of color in sports.

It showed progress in sports, how a coach whose teams did not win big or challenge for a championship was still employable. Plus, he was black. True, Wilkens was the winningest coach in league history and knew basketball, yet the results were no longer in his favor. Men like him were usually tossed in the coaching scrap heap as relics of a bygone era. Clearly, Wilkens still had a measure of respect among the people in power, and this is where his story gets an interesting twist.

The people in power with the Knicks at the time were Steve Mills, the team's chief operating officer, and Isiah Thomas, the team president, also both black. The most valuable if not prestigious franchise in the NBA was headed by three black men, which was bold both in statement and fact. Forget for a moment that the trifecta was short-lived; Wilkens was removed the very next year. And put aside, for now, that the Knicks endured a tough stretch on the court initially with these men in control. Rather, ponder the significance of the situation. Three black men were in charge of a major professional sports franchise and society barely noticed. And when they failed to win, there were no serious repercussions, not in the big picture. It was not a devastating setback for an entire race. Employment opportunities for black men in coaching and management in the NBA didn't suddenly dry up faster than a bead of sweat in the Sahara. This atmosphere was quite a change from 1969, when

Wilkens first landed an NBA coaching job. There were no blacks then in head coaching or management in the NFL or Division I sports, only one other black coach in the NBA, and none in Major League baseball. Sports looked like a sundae: white on top.

The Knicks trifecta was made possible because of trust and familiarity and connections. In layman's terms, they knew one another. Mills worked in the NBA office as an executive when he first met Thomas, and when Mills originally tried to hire Magic Johnson to run the Knicks, he eagerly settled on Thomas partly because of Magic's recommendation. Thomas was a long-time admirer of Wilkens back when they competed against each other frequently, Thomas as a Hall of Fame point guard with the Pistons and Wilkens as coach of the Cavaliers. It also didn't hurt that they shared the same agent years later. It all fit together nicely.

In any business where much is at stake, including reputations and money and prestige, people tend to surround themselves with those they trust and know. And that, perhaps more than blatant racism, is why the upper echelon of sports organizations today is thick with white males. White owners and power brokers most likely have long-standing and very close associations with other whites; thus, their top management staffs tend to be white. And as in the case of the Knicks, when given positions of power, blacks can and do tend to hire people they've known and trusted most of their lives, too. Those people tend to be black.

An even better example of this happened in Charlotte, shortly after the NBA made history and awarded a new franchise to Robert Johnson, who became the first black person to own a major sports franchise. Almost immediately, Johnson surrounded himself with those he knew from his days as the creator of Black Entertainment Television. His team president became Ed Tapscott, an appointment that looked surprising on the surface. Tapscott had little experience in upper management in pro sports, and his brief stint as a decision maker with the Knicks ended when he drafted Frederic Weis, a lightly regarded Frenchman who never made the team. But Tapscott was also a former coach at American University in Washington, D.C., where BET was based, and his wife was a former high-level BET executive under Johnson. Tapscott and Johnson hired Bernie Bickerstaff as the team's first head coach. Again, this was mildly surprising; Bickerstaff hadn't coached in the NBA in five years and wasn't on any team's radar. But he knew Tapscott and Johnson for years back when he was an assistant and later coach of the Bullets in Washington.

The expansion Charlotte Bobcats, therefore, began their inaugural season with a black owner, president, and coach, an achievement far more revealing than anything they did on the court that season. It was the old-boy network at work again, this time with a different complexion.

For decades, racism was alive and well in organized sports, just like everywhere else in society. Gradually, the desire to win, along with social change, erased some of that from the field. Sam Cunningham, the former Southern Cal running back, did almost as much for race relations in the Deep South as any Civil Rights leader when he blasted through the all-white Alabama defense in 1970. Suddenly, in order for teams on all levels to compete, mindsets had to change. Today, you can't find too many teams that would rather use an inferior white player over a superior black player and risk losing games simply because the coach or athletic director or owner doesn't like blacks. We live in different times, and besides, in sports, everyone likes to win. And make money. When it comes to sports, those twin forces are far more powerful than racism.

Taken at its most basic form, sports is truly a meritocracy, one of the few we have in society, where talent is the ultimate decision maker in many cases. If you're good, you play. It's really that simple. An athlete's ability

Photo courtesy of University of Southern California.

USC fullback Sam Cunningham did more than shred the Alabama defense in a September 1970 game featuring two of the nation's biggest college football powers; his dominant performance prompted 'Bama coach Bear Bryant and others to integrate football in the South.

to do the job outweighs his skin color. There's too much at stake, financially and otherwise, for professional sports teams to operate in a racially sinister and undercover manner. So, we can safely assume that racism doesn't exist to the degree it once did between the lines on the court or the field. That battle, led by General Cunningham, has been mostly won.

The only area where race and ignorance can play a role, and still do, is beyond the field. That's because talent doesn't always decide who gets the job. Other issues creep into play and become factors. Again, because society is more flexible on matters of race, even the most skeptical must concede that blatant racism isn't keeping blacks from holding positions of power in most areas of sports.

There's no Oz wearing a white hood, hiding behind a curtain, preventing black folks from all the good jobs. There is no collusion or conspiracy among all teams in all sports to reserve these jobs for whites only, as much as black folks love racial conspiracy theories. As Stan Wilcox, a past president of the Black Coaches Association admitted, "From what I've found, it's not the racism we've come to know from the '60s."

Then what accounts for the paucity of black head coaches in Division I football well into the middle of this decade? And why are black faces hard to find in the executive suites of NFL stadiums and on the sideline? And what about the administrative positions in the league offices and college conferences? Why do these areas continue to be disproportionately white even when the number of black athletes in the major revenue-producing sports of football and basketball are often overwhelmingly black? Why does true power, which is confined to decision-making positions on all levels, still largely escape blacks in sports?

"When I see some of these basketball games, especially on the college level, it looks like Ghana vs. Nigeria," said Earl Smith, a professor of sociology at Wake Forest. "But when you look at the top, everything is nearly lily white. Something's wrong with that. Something's not right."

Is it racism? Well, yeah, to an extent. In some cases, it would be very hard for anyone to say that racism does not play a role beyond the field. At Alabama, the same school that was trampled on by Cunningham back in 1970, Sylvester Croom was not given the head coaching job that went to Mike Shula, son of Don, the Hall of Famer. This caught the attention of many blacks in the South, who felt 'Bama simply wasn't ready to give a black man the chance to run the football program and hold one of the most prestigious jobs in the state, if not the South. It didn't matter that Croom was an Alabama assistant, or that his father was once the team chaplain when 'Bama was coached by Paul "Bear" Bryant. For a school immersed in tradition, Alabama decided to go outside the "family" to find a coach. This was a slap in the face for those who saw 'Bama blow a chance to show a different mindset and make a statement, in addition to hire someone who was clearly ready to become a head coach. As it turned out, Croom was hired by Mississippi State, becoming the first black head coach in the SEC conference; Shula was fired after the 2006 season when he failed to restore the Alabama football program to the country's elite.

Although racism could not be proven in the Alabama case, it was the kind of situation that made blacks wonder if race played a role. Such is the dilemma for any black person, when it comes to jobs we don't get: You simply don't know when you've been hoodwinked or not. As long as blacks are unable to hold true power in sports, the issue of hiring will remain, because the real roadblock is the inability to break through the buddy-buddy network, which is controlled by whites. This creates a racial imbalance that makes everyone losers, because somewhere out there, a black man who could be the Shula or Riley or Auerbach will probably never get the chance, denying both himself and the unlucky team that missed out.

Again, people tend to hire those they're comfortable with, and in sports, like society, whites and blacks still aren't as comfortable with each other as they should be.

Take the typical white athletic director at a major university. He was not raised in a black neighborhood, did not have many, if any, blacks as friends and frequent house guests while growing up, did not have blacks as fraternity brothers, and did not break into the business with many black coworkers. Again, we're talking the typical white AD, not all white ADs. His circle of close friends is mostly all white. Maybe he developed a level of ignorance when it came to black people, who were foreign to him. Maybe he bought into the damaging stereotypes when it came to black people. Because of circumstances within and beyond his control, he lived in a different world and still does.

Now, take the typical black applicant for a job in sports. His world was a lot blacker, in terms of where he was born and raised, his life experiences, the people he associated with, and the people he connected with. Even as an adult, those in his social circle probably look a lot like him, not like the people who do the hiring.

Basically, these two typical individuals are complete strangers whose lives and worlds never crossed with any regularity or permanence. What's more, you must wonder if either side goes out of his way to make this critical connection. The typical white person doing the hiring—does he cross over much into the other world? What about vice versa? The white person in charge probably makes little or no effort to honestly extend his search to black candidates; meanwhile, feel free to question whether the typical black candidates apply enough shoulder-rubbing with those who can give them that coveted job. This is a problem mainly in college sports but in professional sports as well. White power brokers and black hopefuls rarely connect, and often when they do, it's awkward and even forced.

Therefore, whites in power tend to rely on a tired formula: Go with whom you know. This happens often in the professional ranks, where there are little or no regulations about the hiring process. In college, a job must be posted, and a good number of universities have hiring guidelines that at least open the door to black applicants. Even then, whites in power, for the most part, already have their minds made up, sometimes before the job becomes vacant.

It's not a very fair process, but then, few are in society. Jobs don't always go to the most deserving. The people doing the hiring don't always extend their search into the cracks and crevices. They look for the easier or safest way out. In that sense, whites in power are some of the laziest creatures on Earth. They don't care to venture far beyond their own limited world, to explore new possibilities, to tap into another talent pool. Or they'll just consider the same handful of recycled black candidates. Obviously, nobody is willing or able to interview 5,000 people for a job. They create a set number to consider for the position and then stick to it. But that number doesn't include very many blacks because, again, those worlds seldom collide.

"For a long time, the ADs hired people they knew or their colleagues recommended," said Wilcox, now an athletic department administrator at Notre Dame. "The vast majority of ADs were white males, and they were hiring from that pool. The only way you were going to make change is to break down the old-boy network and make sure hiring was fair across the board. You had to slow down the process. They had to do like they were hiring a provost and expand their search. If your sphere is not open wider, then your ability to bring minorities will be limited."

Just the same, if the other sphere is limited, job possibilities will be, too. A fair number of blacks who aspire to be coaches probably aren't too skilled at the networking game, or would rather not play it, or aren't encouraged to play it. When it comes to getting the good jobs, where competition is fierce, often it becomes a game of who you know. It's fair, then, to ask some of these candidates who whine about jobs whether their social and professional networks reach far and wide and well into the other world. These candidates may be equipped to do the job, but their inability to market themselves and make an impression on the people who hire will ultimately doom their chances of getting one.

Although the Black Coaches Association was formed to serve as a necessary watchdog in college sports, and while many universities have hiring procedures in place, athletic directors are wary when forced to hire someone. There must be a degree of comfort and a sense of knowledge about that person on the list. Above all, there must be a gut feeling that this is the right man or woman for the job. That's where black candidates can pull their end of the deal, by making enough connections to break down that wall of ignorance.

"They have to make an effort to widen their associations of people that they will ultimately associate with," said Wilcox. "It goes both ways."

While the BCA's mission is a noble one, it can also lead to sham interviews, where blacks are brought in just to satisfy hiring guidelines and to mute the watchdogs. Wilcox prefers to look at the positives; at least the candidate can reap the benefit of the interview itself, which can lead to a word-of-mouth recommendation from one AD to another. In that sense, the black candidate assures himself of a place in the pipeline and on the list of schools who may have an opening in the future.

"It starts the process of these athletic directors or school presidents having contact with a minority coach that they otherwise wouldn't have," Wilcox said.

But this can lead to awkward moments. In 2002, a pair of attorneys, Johnnie Cochran and Cyrus Mehri, who won millions in judgments against some of the country's biggest corporations in civil rights cases, struck fear into the NFL. They examined hiring practices in the coaching ranks and released "Black Coaches in the National Football League: Superior Performance, Inferior Opportunities." The report began by mentioning the faulty hiring practices by major corporations who were successfully sued and exposed by the attorneys. Then the report stated this: "The parallels between the struggles of African Americans at those companies and within the NFL coaching ranks are striking." Cochran and Mehri's decision to lump the NFL with companies with racist hiring practices was certainly not a mistake, and the implication was the NFL was not beyond being hit with a lawsuit, either.

This sent a shiver through NFL headquarters. The gist of the report was that black coaches, although doing a slightly better job of coaching than whites at the time based on overall average of wins, still had trouble landing jobs. The report also concluded that blacks mainly inherited crummy teams, while the glamour teams in pretty good shape were mostly handed to white coaching candidates. Cochran and Mehri even went as far as asking the NFL to reward teams with a draft pick when diversity hires were made and to punish those teams that don't hire blacks by taking picks from them.

The reaction by the NFL was nervous, the kind of knee-buckling that Cochran and Mehri saw from the Fortune 500 companies they sued. The league swiftly created a Workforce Diversity Committee, chaired by Steelers owner Dan Rooney, and mandated that all teams must interview at least one minority candidate for every head coaching vacancy. The gesture had good intentions but eventually proved to be problematic for teams as well as for the black candidates.

A year after the "Rooney Rule" went into effect, Detroit Lions GM Matt Millen wanted to hire Steve Mariucci, and everyone knew this. He reached out to five black candidates, and they basically told him not to bother; they wanted no part of a dog and pony show and to serve as someone's "minority interview." Millen shrugged and hired Mariucci and was fined $200,000, basically for not wasting everyone's time and interviewing people the Lions had no plans to hire. And you could see why the Rooney Rule can have a stigmatizing effect on black candidates. Nobody wants to be the token "candidate" flown in and basically used by a team to satisfy the Rooney Rule, then given a condescending handshake and shown the door. The Rooney Rule, again despite its good intentions, is further proof that you can't legislate hiring because, ultimately, owners and GMs cannot be told whom to hire. Regardless of any watchdog group or hiring procedure, people will ultimately settle on the person they're most comfortable with.

Another issue, mainly at the college level, is a black candidate's desire to work virtually anywhere in the country. Trying to land a job near Atlanta or Chicago or another ideal place for blacks to live is one thing. But a willingness to work in, say, Manhattan, Kansas, is another. Some schools located in distant outposts have approached candidates in the past about openings, not necessarily in the football and basketball programs, only to discover that some weren't anxious to start out in Boondoggle, Idaho, or move their families there.

A constant topic in both pro and college concerns the size of the pool of black candidates. This is where the entire issue of hiring gets sticky. Organizations are always citing pool size as a reason for the absence of black faces in many jobs, which is both a legitimate excuse and a cop-out. There are fewer blacks for most of the jobs that carry high visibility and power because few blacks are groomed for those jobs. Once again, the white power structure usually goes hunting in its own world when looking for apprentices. Young men and women apprentices tend more often to be white, and a team president or general manager or athletic director will nurture and guide that person, giving him or her valuable experience to use as an advantage when the time comes to get the big break. In some cases, a fortunate black person will be chosen to be groomed for the future; Ernie Accorsi personally greased the way for Jerry Reese to be his successor as New York Giants general manager in 2007. However, the typical black person left out of the loop and looking for a top position in a sports organization can't compete with this system, which can be construed as institutional-ized racism. This guarantees the black talent pool will never be the size of the white pool, and thus, more often than not, blacks will be judged as unqualified for certain jobs. The smaller the black talent pool, the more likely the stigma of qualifications will never be removed. That must change somehow, because the fewer excuses that blacks can give the white establishment for not hiring them, the better.

Black faces are needed and necessary in positions of power and influence for two very important reasons. One, black labor, in the form of players, helped build major college sports and certain pro sports into the multibillion-dollar businesses they've become. And two, without blacks in these positions, it sends a not-so-subtle message that blacks lack the intelligence and organizational skills needed for the job. It all comes back to the question of qualifications, the racial code word that's always tossed about when black people are considered for jobs and seldom heard when whites apply for jobs. Yet, isn't it strange how qualifications can be a barrier for aspiring black coaches, who have played their sport almost their entire lives? How can a former football player be unqualified to become a head coach? In the case of someone who has been around the game his entire life, it's not a matter of what he doesn't know; rather, what can he possibly not know?

The coaching picture for blacks at the major college football level is by far the most disgraceful and unforgivable in sports. Only 5 of the 119 Division I programs had black coaches during the 2006 season. And that was actually an upgrade from previous years. But it gets worse: Only 12 athletic directors at major colleges were black, and in the ultimate test of power, only 4 school presidents were black, and none at the universities with the biggest budgets for football and basketball, the major revenue-producing sports in which black athletes are abundant. It all comes back to power, and whether those who hold such power see the advantages of a diverse workforce.

A seldom explored possibility for the lack of black college football coaches lies with the alums, who hold considerable power in the hiring process. There's the widely held suspicion among aspiring black coaches that alums don't want a black man serving as the symbol of the program, believing he would negatively affect fund raising. If true, this is blatant racism, but again, racism that would be hard to prove.

The only guaranteed method for increasing the number of black coaches in major sports on every level is to increase the number of blacks doing the hiring. For some reason, the emphasis has always been on putting more blacks in coaching than in executive positions, where the real influence lies. This is a considerable misstep by black special interest groups. Nobody had the foresight to form a Black Athletic Directors Association, for example, before creating a Black Coaches Association. Wouldn't that make more sense? Isn't that a better way of prioritizing? In the NFL, there is much bellyaching among black assistant coaches, who complain about not seeing enough Tony Dungys. Meanwhile, other than the NFL's workforce committee, hastily formed at the threat

Scott Halleran/Getty Images

It took 41 years for a black head coach to have an opportunity to lead a team into a Super Bowl. And when it finally happened in 2007, one wasn't enough, as long-time friends Tony Dungy and Lovie Smith brought their Indianapolis Colts and Chicago Bears teams to sports' most celebrated annual event.

of a lawsuit from Johnnie Cochran's firm, there's little or no visible movement afoot to get blacks into the general manager's chair or the team president's office. The priorities are all wrong. There would not be a handful of Division I black football coaches and a smattering of black NFL coaches if more athletic directors and general managers were black. Once blacks move into these positions of power, where they can hire coaches, the coaching issue will take care of itself.

Sadly, black representation in these areas is abysmal, with little or no chance of drastic change in the near future. Here's why: Most blacks in sports aspire to be coaches, where visibility and money is greater in most cases. There's more of a desire to be closer to the action, in the locker room and on the sidelines, than behind a desk. In addition, with most of the minority hiring efforts concentrated toward coaching, whites in power don't feel any outside pressure to put blacks in the front office. Very few blacks are encouraged by the power structure to chase jobs on the administrative level, the one place in sports that's almost reserved for whites. It's a major fallacy on both sides.

No matter how blacks get any job in sports, the pressure to be twice as good as whites is always present. Almost every black person in a decent job will tell you that. There's usually more at stake when a black person gets a visible job in sports, if only because it seems everyone's looking and drawing certain conclusions.

"On the college basketball side," said Wilcox, "things were dismal until we had an African American win a championship. Once that happened with John Thompson at Georgetown, the floodgates opened. People in charge saw an African-American man make his mark, and it opened their minds. When you see the same thing happen in football, things will change pretty quickly, the way it did in basketball, because everybody wants to win."

A sore subject among black coaches is the apathy toward the subject shown by black players. With very few exceptions, black players don't use their voice to demand more black coaches, and in some instances, black players don't go the extra mile to support black coaches. One example occurred when Byron Scott was forced out of New Jersey despite reaching the NBA Finals twice, and Jason Kidd was largely reported to be behind Scott's ouster. Scott was replaced by Lawrence Frank, a white assistant coach, who subsequently did not take the Nets as far as Scott took them. Also, Joe Morgan, the baseball Hall of Famer, was disturbed by the lack of effort by some black Raiders players, which spelled doom for Art Shell in 2006 after one season in Oakland.

"The people he had a problem with in Oakland were African American," said Morgan. "There's something wrong with that. I played for white managers all my life until I played for Frank Robinson in 1981. That was one of the proudest and happiest days of my life, to run out on that field on Opening Day knowing a black manager was in the dugout. That's all I would ask of African-American athletes. You should want to do whatever you can to give him a chance to be successful. All black managers and coaches aren't great. But give them that chance to be great."

One of the more groundbreaking achievements, in terms of racial progress, somehow escaped the attention of the sports world when the Chicago White Sox won the 2005 World Series. The White Sox became champions for the first time in several decades, one of the driest stretches in sports, certainly a cause for celebration. Lost in the hoopla was another historical event. The team was quietly built by Ken Williams, then the only black general manager in a sport that hasn't seen too many. Williams made clever moves, mixed veterans with young players, kept his payroll to a reasonable figure to guarantee profits, and hired Ozzie Guillen, who became the first Venezuelan manager in the Majors, bucking the old-boy trend. In a nutshell, Williams brought intelligence and organization skills, thereby dismissing the old stereotypes about the qualifications of blacks. Yet his work went largely unapplauded by the media, historians, and those who shape the perceptions of Major League baseball.

Nobody rushed to brand Ken Williams a "genius" or "deep thinker" or any other buzzword of high praise often extended to anointed boy wonders in sports who happen to be white. On the contrary: Williams heard himself labeled as "unqualified" and a "yes man" to White Sox owner Jerry Reinsdorf when he was given the job at age 36.

"I ran the minor league operation for the White Sox for five years," Williams said, with a heavy sigh. "I played the game before that. The day I was hired, all of that was ignored. Instead, I was overmatched, I was hired only because I was black, and I was Jerry Reinsdorf's

Ken Williams is one of the few black executives in professional team sports, but he quickly made his mark and his reputation as a sharp baseball talent evaluator. Here he celebrates the fruits of his labor, the 2005 World Series trophy, with MLB commissioner Bud Selig, Chicago White Sox Chairman Jerry Reinsdorf, and manager Ozzie Guillen.

ass kisser. People around here lobbied for someone else. But Jerry went against the grain. He saw my work ethic early on, even when I was a player, so when I was done playing, he saw I would be an easy fit on the other side of the field."

Williams was chosen over Dan Evans, a white man and the team's long-time assistant general manager, who promptly quit in protest. Almost immediately, the whispers of "reverse racism" were heard in the baseball world, and some quietly wondered what the outcry would have been had the races been reversed and the White Sox chose a white person over a seasoned black executive. Jesse Jackson, whose Operation PUSH is based in Chicago, wouldn't have to travel far for his next protest site, some snickered. Yet, in this rare instance, a white power broker hired someone he was comfortable with, and that someone happened to be black. Williams had a 20-year relationship with Reinsdorf, first as a player for the White Sox and later as a scout, special assistant, and farm system chief.

Williams was also Stanford-educated, destroying any myths about intelligence and organization skills. And during his first few years on the job, he was a risk taker. He was hired because of his background in the farm system, yet his best work was done through trades and free agency. He traded for Jose Contreras, who had flopped in big moments with the Yankees, and saw Contreras deliver big time in the championship postseason for the Sox. He took a chance on Carl Everett, a slugger with an attitude problem, and catcher A.J. Pierzynski, one of the most disliked players in baseball. He also added Jermaine Dye, who received heavy MVP consideration in 2006 and Scott Podsednik, who brought speed to the team.

When the White Sox won a championship with these players, the noise during the victory celebration was louder than the ruckus caused by Williams' surprise hiring. It confirmed everything Reinsdorf knew, and what

Williams tried to convey from his first day on the job. "All I could do," he said, "was give it my best and let my accomplishments speak for themselves. The only way I could make it better for people who will follow me was to win and do it with dignity."

Williams came to baseball with an interesting link to black sports history. Born in Berkeley and raised on the Black Nationalist movement in the Bay Area during the turbulent 1960s, he's the godson of black-fisted Olympic sprinter John Carlos, a friend of his father, who was forced to sue San Jose for racial discrimination in order to become one of the city's first black firefighters. Therefore, Williams gained the kind of education they don't teach in schools, not even Stanford, the kind of education that served him well when he followed Bill Lucas and Bob Watson as black general managers in the Majors.

The poor record of hiring blacks in positions of power, on every level of sports, is not lost on Williams. He often wonders whether his championship will open doors for others, the way doors opened in college basketball after John Thompson won at Georgetown. He's not too optimistic.

"I feel sad about it," he said, "but that's the way it is when you're a black man in America. There are plenty of examples of success, given the opportunity, but not enough examples of opportunity being given. Consequently, you have a bunch of guys sitting on the sideline having to watch. I think in the distant future, society is going to look back at the last 60 years and be astonished at the tremendous amount of change that's apparent everywhere, except in certain areas."

No organization in sports can match the NBA's track record for hiring blacks in meaningful positions, a crusade of David Stern ever since he became commissioner in 1983. In that sense, Stern has done more for black progress in sports than anyone since Branch Rickey. Working the corporate backrooms skillfully, like the litigator he once was before joining the league, Stern sold most of his owners on the benefits of diversity in coaching and the front office, to the point where today diversity is hardly an issue. However, it never *should* be an issue in a league that's roughly 75 percent black on the court.

For a long time in the NBA, the math didn't always add up. Even in the late 1960s, when the demographics began to change drastically, front-office jobs for blacks were nonexistent. Dave Bing, voted one of the 50 greatest players in NBA history, remembers getting no response when he tried for positions of power. This was surprising, how there was no room in the front offices for a bright, ambitious, Syracuse-educated man from Washington who could connect with Wall Street types as well as the common man on the street. "It wasn't there for me," Bing said. "No general managing, no team president, nothing. It forced me to look in another direction."

Strangely, racism and the old-boy network led to Bing becoming one of the wealthiest black people in America. Turned away by the NBA, Bing used his business connections in Detroit, where he enjoyed a Hall of Fame playing career, to form Bing Steel, a supplier to automobile and other companies. It wasn't long before Bing realized his blessing in disguise. The NBA actually did him a favor, because Bing Steel gradually became one of the country's true success stories among black-owned businesses. Since its inception, Bing Steel has generated over $1 billion in revenue, which demonstrates how the old-boy network can be counterproductive to those who run it. If Bing had the wisdom and energy to form his own company and turn it into a goliath, what could he have done with an NBA team? Bing didn't lose in this deal; the NBA lost. Sadly, because of the old-boy network, some NBA team likely missed a chance on hiring the next great team president or chief operating officer.

Instead of Bing, the honor of being the first black executive in sports went to Wayne Embry when he was hired to run the Milwaukee Bucks in 1972. This was two years before Hank Aaron broke Babe Ruth's home run record, but in some ways the elevation of Embry held a more important if quieter distinction. Finally, a black man was trusted with a franchise, and for the most part, the announcement was met with little backlash, except for a handful of hate letters. Wes Pavalon, the Bucks' owner, was close friends with many prominent blacks in and out of sports, including the author Alex Haley and Muhammad Ali, so he carried none of the racial hang-ups that would have prevented the hiring. The most pressure Embry faced was the pressure he placed on himself.

"It was very important to succeed," he said, "because you're carrying the torch for a lot of people. You don't want to fail. That was a fear at the time."

After an ownership change, Embry eventually lost a power struggle with Don Nelson, a former teammate Embry hired and later accused of backstabbing. While he and Nelson were still civil, Embry recalled he wanted to give an assistant coaching position to Paul Silas, their old teammate with the Celtics, but he said Nelson nixed the idea, claiming Silas was unqualified. Embry thought this comment was strange because Nelson didn't have any coaching experience, and Embry had hired him anyway.

"We're all stigmatized," Embry said. "It's going to be there when our names come up."

Embry's most awkward moment in management happened when he interviewed for his next job, in Cleveland. One of the board members wondered if Embry planned to hire a black coach. Embry said he would hire the best coach, regardless of color, and if he happened to be black, so be it. After sleeping on the question overnight, Embry was bothered by the implication and the line of questioning and decided to remove his name from consideration for the job. After some further arm-twisting by the Cavaliers, he reconsidered and became their general manager; at that time he was only the second black person, along with Elgin Baylor, in management in the NBA.

In time, the numbers improved in the NBA, although Embry is not encouraged by what he sees beyond professional basketball. He agrees that whites in power and blacks who aspire for front-office jobs are virtually out of touch with each other.

"There's built-in isolation among us, because of our backgrounds," Embry said. "We don't belong to the country clubs. They do. We don't have those all-important contacts that land the jobs. And even when you do get the jobs, there's still isolation. I remember when the son of Gordon Gund, the owner of the Cavs, got married. Well, you go to the wedding, and you're the only black person there. And that struck me. These people don't have relationships with black folks, here in the 21st century. That blows my mind. I've sat on five boards of some important companies and never saw one African American come before us for important jobs.

"It's hard to call it outright racism. I'd like to think we've made big progress in that area. I just think it's because of several built-in factors, and two in particular: the isolation between us, the people who do the hiring, and the pool. When it comes to some positions, I think the pool is shrinking, which scares me. In the NBA, very few athletes have degrees. Well, if you're going to be a manager, you need managing skills and a solid educational background. You can't expect a person who doesn't have an intellectual background to be able to manage. There are things, financial and otherwise, that they must comprehend."

There's still plenty of work to be done on both sides. Black candidates must look beyond coaching and reach for real positions of power, where they can set hiring policies that will include everyone. And the white power structure must allow this to happen. There are two worlds that could solve the hiring problem if they ever agreed to become one.

CHAPTER 11

The Feminine Side
You Go, Girl, But How Far?

Rarely is a black woman called anything but strong when times get tough. That's because the description fits. Black women, as a whole, have required more strength than any human being in this country with the possible exception of Native Americans. It's not easy being a woman in America, and it's not easy being black in America. Do the math. That's two strikes.

Historically, black women have not been treated fairly or justly by white or black men. The black woman has dealt with discrimination, sexism, and abandonment, all while handling the tremendous responsibility of raising a family under extreme and trying conditions in most cases. In a modern-day black society in which households are more likely to be headed by a single parent, the black woman must often be the bread winner, housekeeper, cook, mother, handywoman, transporter, bookkeeper, soft shoulder, disciplinarian, inspiration, role model, and mentor. She has held the lower paying positions in the workforce. This requires the kind of strength you don't see in the Olympic weightlifting competition.

It's no surprise, then, that black women must also summon the necessary amount of strength for sports.

Because of circumstances mostly beyond her control, she's concentrated into two sports, basketball and track and field; faces competition from both men and other women for the top jobs in sports; and deals with the usual gender issues that confront all women in sports. Plus, in poor areas, black females must cope with the typical hazards of poverty.

All of this tends to escape a society that sees the enormous success of Serena and Venus Williams in a country club sport and figures everything is swell. Indeed, athletic opportunities for all women have significantly improved since the inception of Title IX. The number of girls at the junior levels of sports has multiplied many times over. The number of athletic choices for girls in high schools is greater than their grandmothers knew. On the college level, the popularity of women's sports, especially among a handful of Division I basketball schools, often rivals that of the men. Women can earn a modest living playing basketball both in America and abroad. The prize money and sponsorship deals in women's golf have increased, and in professional tennis, women are making as much as the men in major tournaments and more, in some cases, through endorsements. A pretty face and a wicked backhand can make the cash register ring loudly, as Maria Sharapova can tell you.

And yet, black women in sports lag behind their white counterparts in various ways, which suggests they not only share some of the same problems of black men, but also problems unique to them.

The funneling effect is the most obvious one. Black female athletes are being ghettoed into basketball and track, in which they are served well compared to other sports, in which they are aliens. In this sense, black women are not the ones getting the most out of Title IX, which takes good care of rich white girls from prep schools. A 2001 study conducted by the *Chronicle of Higher Education* found that of the women holding athletic scholarships in Division I sports other than basketball and track, only 3 percent were black. The minor sports at historically black colleges and universities have plenty of black women on the team, obviously, but those schools aren't flush with the kind of money, facilities, and exposure you see at the traditional schools. If you erased basketball and track from State U., the campus would have the look and feel of a typical white suburban soccer league, minus the moms and minivans.

The reason is as simple as one plus one. "It's a matter of opportunity and finances," said Tina Sloan Green, the first black woman to coach Division I lacrosse. "No need to look any deeper than that."

Richard Williams' youngest daughters had neither while growing up in South-Central Los Angeles. Their father made a meager living, and their neighborhood had no organized tennis program, which is typical of many urban communities that cling to cheap, easy-to-play sports. That's what makes the professional careers of Venus and Serena so unconventional and unlikely—nothing short of amazing, really. The story of how Richard Williams discovered tennis for his "ghetto princesses" has been retold so often that it's now folklore. He watched a pro match, saw how much prize money the winner earned, and saw a ticket out of the neighborhood for his daughters. He became a coach by reading books on tennis and watching how-to VHS tapes. He swept the broken glass off the neglected and crumbling courts in Compton and shooed away the winos and gang members who appeared at dusk. He gave Venus a hand-me-down racket. He had her hit balls for hours with Serena. They bypassed the juniors, which is the baseball equivalent of skipping the minors, and took the hard road. They moved to Florida, briefly joined an academy, and then they changed women's tennis.

"They came from nowhere to get somewhere," Richard Williams once said of his daughters. "The ghetto to the penthouse. But they had to pay the price. They didn't have anything handed to them. They did it the hard way, straight from the streets."

Ken Levine/Allsport

The Williams sisters, along with their nurturing father Richard, shook up tennis and became two of the sport's all-time greats. And they started young, as shown here at a tennis camp in Florida in 1992 when Venus was 11 and Serena 10.

Only Zina Garrison, the Wimbledon finalist who rose through the parks and rec program in Houston, compares. Tennis is unforgiving when it comes to widespread black participation, to the point that only the middle class can even dream about a professional career. Even Althea Gibson, who came from humble beginnings, had the help of business leaders from within the black community who passed around the hat to keep her going. But what the Williamses did was demonstrate the power of opportunity and why the lack of opportunity remains the most dominant factor in terms of limits placed on the black and poor. Once opportunity was given to them,

Venus and Serena had to provide only the determination. Once they began to rise, the money and support quickly followed from companies anxious to exploit these fish out of water and their true American success tale.

The Williams sisters meshed quickly and rather effortlessly into a tennis world that often comes across as stoic and upper crust. They elevated interest in a sagging sport, especially on the women's side, and even carried tennis briefly when Pete Sampras and Andre Agassi entered the twilight of their careers. In their prime, Venus and Serena were the marquee names in whatever tournament they entered. Most refreshingly, they proved far wiser and savvier than some of their peers, who grew up on tennis and little else and turned into tennis robots. This was the greatest gift their parents, Richard Williams and Oracene Price, lavished on their daughters. They taught Venus and Serena the value of having a life beyond tennis, to the extent that Richard even hoped they'd retire in their early 20s. Well, good thing they didn't take all of his advice, for not only were Venus and Serena responsible for bringing tennis into black households, they brought tennis into young households, regardless of race. They had the eye and ear of another generation, which made them valuable commodities to tournament officials across the globe. When Venus made her first U.S. Open final, watching from one of the luxury suites at Arthur Ashe Stadium was Donald Trump, Lenny Kravitz, and P. Diddy. One woman was responsible for that.

But if tennis was indeed a realistic option for poor urban girls, then Venus and Serena would have plenty of company on tour right now. Instead, the smattering of black faces that followed the Williams sisters on the professional level came straight from middle- and upper-class homes. When they were young and showed promise, the parents of these new girls could afford to hire private coaches or send them to academies. They had the money for pricey lessons. This continues to send black females from poor households looking elsewhere for athletic glory. Basketball and track are the cheapest to play and therefore the most logical option, or the only option, for them. Meanwhile, the vast majority of sports that cater to women are preppy club sports that not only require money, but they don't always lead to scholarships or lucrative professional opportunities. You can certainly understand why a poor girl and her family would take a pass on ice skating, for example.

So don't anticipate an influx of black lacrosse players any time soon. Or field hockey players. Or softball players or volleyball players or synchronized swimmers or, in the case of Wendy Hilliard, a rhythmic gymnast, even though she has tirelessly tried to introduce her sport to a new audience.

Hilliard runs a gymnastics center in Brooklyn, which is both a labor of love and gives her a sense of purpose. Over 5,000 girls, many of them black, some of them homeless, have passed through her annual summer camps in Harlem. Her foundation sponsors teams that compete in national tournaments and even abroad, giving some girls their very first plane ride. The idea of bringing gymnastics to the city energized Hilliard and became a passion soon after she stopped competing in the sport. She was born and raised in Detroit and soon found herself as the first black woman to represent the United States in rhythmic gymnastics. There, she won gold medals and served as team captain and even coach.

She was also exposed to an uncomfortable aspect of some unconventional sports: the selection process. In gymnastics, club soccer, and a few other sports for women, the elite teams are chosen by coaches and panels. It's a very selective procedure and opens the door for other deciding factors, such as favoritism and who you know and even racism. After training in Europe, Hilliard returned home and found herself left off the team, although she was ranked higher than girls who were selected. The explanation? Her routine wasn't traditional enough. After her family and some colleagues took a furious stand, not only was Hilliard appointed to the team, she remained for several years and became one of the more decorated gymnasts. "I had to take a stand," she said, "and I had to go against the establishment to do it."

She was attracted to rhythmic gymnastics partly because "it was a nontraditional sport, and the challenge of not having any blacks ahead of me made me determined to succeed." She eventually understood why her road was mostly a lonely one. "The sport is small and relatively expensive," she said. "You have to have a large amount of parental involvement. It's not found in the public school, either. In basketball and track, the system is at the school. Your kid learns it there. Gymnastics is not in the school. You have to take your kid to class. And parents don't see the immediate benefits in most cases. They'll say, 'Why invest all this money and you can't even get a college scholarship from it?' It makes it more difficult to get more girls involved and stay involved. As an instructor, it takes a lot more effort on my part."

That never discouraged Hilliard from starting her foundation and using her time and even her own money to create awareness for gymnastics among girls who normally would never receive exposure to it. As much as Hilliard would love to find the next Dominique Dawes, she's more interested in how gymnastics can open new possibilities for her campers and teach them the wonders of exploring unconventional options.

"The lifelong lessons from the sport would benefit them in the long run in academics and in school," said Hilliard, who became an honors graduate of New York University. "You have to have a broader vision and see the benefits that way. The motivation can't be about money in the nontraditional sports. It's about trying something different and striving to get better."

Tina Sloan Green also took a different route in Philadelphia when, because of her favorable academic scores, she was bused to Girls High, which had 20 blacks in the entire class. There it was another world in many ways, even in sports. She was encouraged by her mostly white teachers to try field hockey, then volleyball. "At first, I was out of my league socially, but I was accepted because of sports," she said. "It just proved that once girls are exposed and get proper training, they can excel, no matter where they're from."

Not only did she become a standout field hockey player at West Chester State, she went to Temple and coached the field hockey and lacrosse teams, the latter to three national championships and 11 NCAA appearances. But, again, she saw very few who looked like herself, either on the playing field or, later, in coaching. In fact, many of the influential black women in sports came up through the prep-school sports even though they weren't prep-school students. Purely by chance, while in college in Connecticut, Anita DeFrantz happened to come upon a man carting some rowing equipment, and she asked what it was. The rowing coach invited her to give the sport a try, mainly because he figured DeFrantz, at a lean 5 feet, 11 inches, had the perfect body type for it. Three years later she won a bronze medal at the Montreal Games, and she eventually became the first black member of the International Olympic Committee. Because she specialized in an unconventional sport for black women, and was surrounded by white men in the IOC, she embraced the doctrine that blacks in these situations must be "twice as good" as whites just to be considered equals.

There are other scattered examples of black women finding homes in unconventional sports and even excelling. U.S. Olympian Danielle Scott became one of the best middle blockers in the world and also blessed volleyball with her amazingly down-to-earth persona and grace. In a more visible sport, she would serve as a perfect mentor and role model for girls who look like her. However, with the lack of organization, parental involvement, and money available at the ground level in many black communities, these sports are shunned if not totally dismissed by girls and their families. Also, there is no peer pressure

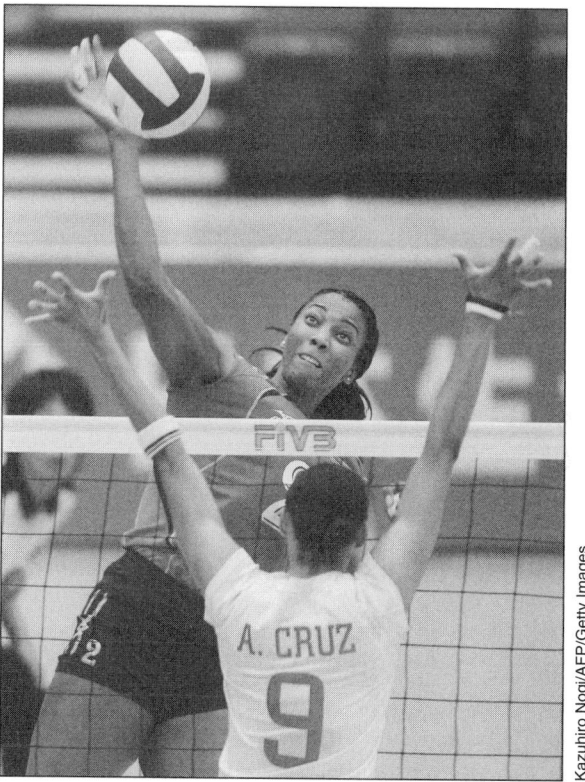

Kazuhiro Nogi/AFP/Getty Images

Danielle Scott has been an elite player for many years in a sport that could be, but isn't, one in which a large number of black women participate. Scott started playing volleyball in school in her hometown of Baton Rouge, Louisiana, then went on to achieve great success at Long Beach State and on international teams.

to encourage girls to try them; if anything, peer pressure discourages black girls from playing what is perceived as sports for white girls. So these girls stick to basketball and track. Call it "funnel vision." Simply based on the way these nontraditional sports are structured, with the clubby atmosphere and the steep financial commitment and the glaring absence of blacks coaching them, they emit classism if not racism. And maybe it's being done unintentionally, but these sports are not placing a welcome mat or sending out a frantic search party for poor black girls, who hardly know they exist.

Title IX, then, brings a mixed bag to women. It serves to remove gender discrimination and level the playing field for women in sports while locking the door on most minority women, not just blacks. Buffy from the suburbs can ride Title IX to a free ride in college, but Shaniqua from the 'hood can't, unless she's into basketball or track and field. The girl who badly needs a college scholarship isn't the one getting it, unless she beats out another poor black girl for a starting spot on the school basketball team. Rather than these basketball-dribbling girls branching out and trying something new, they must compete against each other because of the lack of opportunity in the non-traditional sports on the ground level. And unless they get training on that level, they're at a severe competitive disadvantage once they reach their teens if they finally give those sports a try. World-class tennis players don't begin playing the sport when they're 15, and the same goes for golfers. By then, it's too late.

All told, the limits placed on poor female athletes of color is a cooperative effort by urban schools that lack certain programs, by the massive difference in earning power between whites and blacks, and by the absurd yet popular notion that black women should really stick to the sports they know best.

"Tiger Woods is good, and why is that?" asks C. Vivian Stringer, the basketball coach at Rutgers. "Because he was exposed to golf early on. I wasn't exposed to a swimming pool until I was in college. So I would venture to say that within many black communities, there isn't a YMCA, there's certainly not a home swimming pool, and there's not the opportunity to get training. So it just makes sense. My niece was one of the top tennis players in the country because her mother got her involved. Had Richard Williams not thrown himself into tennis, Venus and Serena wouldn't have become who they are. It's the same effect as a parent who takes the time to prepare his son or daughter to become a doctor."

Fred Thompson left a law career in the 1960s to devote himself to running an all-girls track club in Brooklyn and serving as host to the annual Colgate Women's Games, the country's largest continuous amateur indoor meet. In a perfect world, Thompson would have the resources to give city girls more than just track, even though his program has produced Olympians, national champions, and NCAA All-Americans.

"One of the tragedies in our communities is every time we put something up, it's a basketball court," said Thompson. "I'm so sick of it. My dream has always been to put up a multipurpose building, where kids can go swimming at 6 in the morning, the way they do in California. There'd be a kitchen where they can have breakfast before going to school. On another floor, we'd have a running track. On another floor, a basketball court, then upstairs, a room for gymnastics and fencing. Outside, we'd have soccer. This would go a long way into breaking down the stereotypes we so often see attached to black women. Don't tell me we don't have girls in our communities that can't do these sports. Give these girls the chance."

The disparity of black women at the playing level has had the expected impact at the coaching level. Basically, there aren't many Tina Sloan Greens leading Division I lacrosse teams, or any other preppy sports teams. Black women hold jobs in the usual sports, except there's a cruel twist: She must compete with white women, white men, and black men for those coaching jobs, an irony that Sloan Green calls "a triple jeopardy."

"Now that there's money in these jobs, men all of a sudden want to coach women," she said. "It wasn't like that in my day. Unfortunately, in a lot of coaching situations, men are automatically given credibility over women. It's just another obstacle women must face, especially black women. There's a lot that needs to be done in that area."

In the late '90s, less than 2 percent of the women's teams in the NCAA were coached by black women. That number has improved slightly but is still unacceptable for black women looking for a fair shot or at least a fairer distribution, percentage-wise, of the jobs in coaching. In 2005, according to research done by sociologist Richard Lapchick, 43 percent of Division I women's college basketball players were black, but only 9 percent of Division I coaching positions were held by black women. There were also no black female athletic directors in major colleges that year and a smattering of associate ADs. Overall, men held the clear majority of coaching jobs in college athletics.

"Other than college football on the Division I level," said Lapchick, "the worst situation for people of color is in women's college basketball."

The silver lining in black female participation in athletics involves education and priorities. Because there aren't any million-dollar contracts or lucrative professional careers waiting for women unless they beat the incredible odds in golf or tennis, the ticket-out-of-the-ghetto syndrome doesn't apply to them. Candace Parker, the gifted center for the 2007 national champion Tennessee Volunteers, is the only player capable of leaving school early to play professionally for big money. Parker not only has the ability but also the "wow" factor needed to draw fans and generate interest and money for a pro team. But she is clearly the exception in women's team sports. These women play sports strictly for enjoyment, love of the game, and, if they're exceptional, a chance at a college degree. Those who are gifted enough athletically quickly realize their athletic skills are useless without good grades. In a sense, they're not distracted like a number of poor black high school boys who focus more on the NBA or NFL than the books. The system corrupts boys by dangling the irresistible pull of instant riches, even though the odds of these boys actually making the NBA or NFL are stacked against them. That's why the ghetto graveyard is filled with black males who came up short and, without a degree, were sentenced to working menial jobs and living with the regret of not taking care of schoolwork first.

Poor black females understand the deal very early. They aren't hypnotized by the sight of women playing for the Lakers or lining up at quarterback for the Eagles or making several dozen Nike commercials, because women aren't doing any of that. In a warped way, the lack of professional sports opportunities actually helps high school girls place a great value on education and concentrate on what's important. You don't see them looking for shortcuts. They aren't pampered at an early age just because they can dribble or run fast or spike a volleyball. It's certainly no accident that black female college athletes graduate at a considerably higher rate than black males. They use sports as a way to get college degrees and become doctors instead of using sports to play one or two years of college ball, then pray they get drafted. By comparison, the black female is a more genuine student–athlete than the black male.

There are also fewer outside influences. The black female basketball star in high school doesn't deal with agents, flunkies, and leeches. Their recruiting process goes a lot smoother and more honestly, without all the tricks and games and sneaker representatives. She isn't poisoned by a fawning society and in most cases doesn't develop an inflated opinion of herself. The reduced level of attention paid to women's sports allows her to function in a more normal manner than male athletes.

Athletics also serve as an effective tool in steering black females away from typical teen issues, including pregnancy, which is the surest way to remain locked in poverty for poor black girls. White girls from the suburbs can absorb teen pregnancy much easier because chances are good they have a support system from their parents and family, and they have the resources that poor black girls lack. Very likely, they can still go to college, whereas the poor girl can't. With the percentage of black single mothers still beyond that of whites, sports is one of the best weapons available to be used against one of the plagues facing the black community. You might say sports are a pretty good contraceptive.

"Sports tends to take up a lot of time," said Wendy Hilliard. "It gives you a different respect and understanding and protection of your body. Once girls are into sports, they think of a lot of things they can do with their body other than becoming pregnant. A lot of teen pregnancy situations come from wanting to be loved. Well, sports provides the social group for the athlete so she doesn't have to go looking for that in the wrong places."

Sports gives females of all races more goals to shoot for and more reasons to treat their bodies like their most precious possession. Hours are spent in training and preparation for the season. There's the state championships to focus on and college scholarships to be earned. From a practical standpoint, they realize it makes no sense to put themselves, their bodies, or their futures in jeopardy through unprotected sex. Not only does sports steer them away from possible situations that could invite pregnancy, it forces them to follow a proper diet and improves self-esteem, two additional issues that constantly confront young people stuck in poverty.

"Women are more likely to be assertive," said Vivian Stringer, the Rutgers coach. "Women are more likely to go to college. And when they're involved in sports they know how to function in difficult situations and how to handle adversity. Too often, people think sports is just about winning and losing, but there's more than that. It's about the opportunity to participate in something that's organized, to be disciplined and learn about discipline, to work hard and see improvements, and to develop the necessary characteristics that one needs to make it as a leader. The exposure and opportunities that one can receive when traveling and playing is beyond words."

Fortunately, young black girls with athletic aspirations have positive examples, such as Stringer. Like them, she wasn't born with all the comforts in life, other than a loving family. A coal miner's daughter, her father lost both legs to diabetes and died young. Stringer played sports back in "the tea and cookies days" for female athletes,

Photo by Grant Halverson.

C. Vivian Stringer, shown here cutting down the net in celebrating her Rutgers University team's winning the Greensboro, North Carolina, regional championship in 2007, has been a leading force in women's basketball for four decades. Stringer, who has taken three schools to the Final Four (Cheyney in 1982, Iowa in 1993, and Rutgers in 2000 and 2007), eagerly serves as a mentor and role model for black female athletes and coaches.

when athletic scholarships weren't available. She was lucky enough to try a variety of sports anyway, and later, as a teacher at Cheyney State, a predominately black college outside Philadelphia, she was asked to coach a few of them, without receiving any extra pay, of course.

Then Title IX came along, and pretty soon Stringer was able to round up enough local talent to turn Cheyney into a power, good enough to reach the Final Four. That would be next to impossible today because the large schools have a monopoly on the best talent. But it did get Stringer to Iowa and then to Rutgers, where she upgraded the programs at both schools and also took them to the Final Four, becoming the first to do so in women's college basketball. Stringer also speaks her mind, is fiercely protective of her players, is a fighter for women's rights, and is, unfortunately, a survivor for all the wrong reasons.

Stringer's daughter, Nina, was born with spinal meningitis and can't walk or talk. Her husband, Bill, died from a heart attack on Thanksgiving Eve in 1992. One son was cleared of wrongdoing in the death of a classmate, and another suffered a serious car accident at age 16. Finally, a nephew, the great Minnesota Vikings tackle Korey Stringer, collapsed and died during training camp in 2001. After every episode, Stringer picked herself off the ground, patched together her shattered emotions, and summoned the strength to move on, difficult as it was.

When she left Iowa for Rutgers, it became a victory of sorts for women, and especially black women. Not only did Rutgers make her the highest paid coach in women's sports, the school paid her more than the men's basketball and football coaches. Although those programs were mostly lousy at the time, it was nonetheless a statement and struck a powerful chord for equal rights. It also raised the salary bar for female coaches around the country. After a struggle the first two years and having to listen to whispers on campus and in the media, Stringer turned Rutgers around and turned herself into a trail-blazing Hall of Famer. She also opened the door for black women in coaching, and a good many of them, including Dawn Staley at Temple, owe their opportunities in part to her.

Stringer and her players reached the women's Final Four in 2007, despite playing five freshmen and losing more games than they won during the first few weeks of the season. It was a tremendous accomplishment that was applauded by all except Don Imus, the long-time morning political DJ who mocked them by calling them "nappy-headed ho's" while one of Imus' coworkers compared the Rutgers team to the Toronto Raptors. Once again, black women received a slap in the face by males, although the real enemy wasn't only Imus but a gangsta, hip-hop culture that created and cultivated such attitudes toward women and especially women of color. Really, now—where did an old white guy like Imus get the word "ho"? My guess is he borrowed it from Snoop Dogg.

"We don't have the civility in this society that we need," said Stringer. "Have we lost our sense of moral fiber? It's time for everybody to reflect and understand what's going on. We all need to make changes. Do we understand what's going on in society?"

Anyway, given all the positives of Stringer and others like her, black girls still don't see enough black female athletes cornering the market in endorsements. Some of this is understandable, because Madison Avenue doesn't pay much respect to female athletes in general; only about a dozen can command significant commercial air time and dollars. And many of those women are playing in the country-club sports: Mia Hamm and Julie Foudy in soccer, Annika Sorenstam in golf, Sharapova in tennis. The obvious exclusion is professional female basketball players. They suffer in part because the WNBA appeals only to a niche audience, and also because of the lesbian factor. That scares away most major companies who don't want their products associated with anyone who embraces a counterculture lifestyle. For all of her tennis brilliance, for example, Martina Navratilova, who was open about her homosexuality, couldn't touch Chris Evert, portrayed as the All-American girl, in endorsement earning power.

In a sense, Venus and Serena Williams can relate to Navratilova. It's not that the Williams sisters haven't enjoyed commercial success; on the contrary, their prize money pales in comparison to what Nike and the other companies throw into the kitty. There's no need to cry for a pair of multimillionaires who are hardly lacking in exposure. But despite their success in the Grand Slams, they ran a distant third and fourth to Anna Kournikova and Maria Sharapova when it came to making money away from tennis. The Williams sisters could win as many titles as possible, but they couldn't turn white and blonde. They couldn't give the major companies the "look" that much of society equates with beauty. For centuries, black women have dealt with that. Not only were they told, in no uncertain terms, that their skin was too dark, they also heard their body types—thick hips and legs, mainly—weren't what society considered attractive. For many years, black women were missing from the pages of the *Sports Illustrated* swimsuit issue, and when they finally appeared, the black models had more in common with white models from a body standpoint.

In addition, Serena Williams constantly heard snide comments from TV commentators, all of them white, that she wasn't in shape. That was an assumption based on her body type only, because the commentators had no clue about Serena's training habits, and they somehow ignored her ability to chase baseline shots and muster the energy to capture dramatic third sets. Their view of Serena probably had little or nothing to do with racism, but clearly the commentators hadn't seen anyone like Serena in tennis before.

And most likely, they won't see many like her again, unless a swelling of middle-class black girls begin adopting tennis instead of spending their time becoming entrepreneurs or lawyers or developing some other career. Even now, even with the success of the Williams sisters, the time and money it takes to create a tennis star is beyond the scope and imagination of many in the black community.

Because of funnel vision, black girls remain on a direct path to basketball and track, with an occasional detour to volleyball. Strange, but while black girls are headed in one direction, there is one sport that's seeing a drastic influx of minorities: golf. The mothers and fathers of Korean and Japanese girls are budgeting their money toward giving their kids as much exposure to golf as possible, and they're doing it early. Some of these families aren't well-to-do, either, but they don't see themselves competing for starting positions or scholarships in the other, more traditional American sports. They practice their own funnel vision and are slowly influencing golf the way black girls influence basketball and track. Just witness the Asian influence in the LPGA and the NCAA. Gradually, golf has become part of the culture for many Asian Americans.

"I think exposure creates opportunity, and when opportunity and exposure come together, it makes for the kind of end result we have," said Stringer.

What we have is a tremendous number of black women making strides in sports in terms of participation and coaching, just not significant strides, in many ways. Based on circumstances created by a world that does her few favors, a black woman brings plenty of toughness, and considering what she's up against, she certainly needs it.

CHAPTER 12

Natural Athleticism

Where Science Ends and Bias Begins

Blacks aren't ruling sports. Blacks aren't controlling sports. Blacks certainly aren't the face of sports. It's only made to seem that way.

It's the biggest misconception in sports, that blacks dominate the playing courts and playing fields while white people are stuck with supporting roles and crumbs from the sports dinner table. In reality, nothing can be further from the truth. Here in the 21st century, the more appropriate question is this: Whatever happened to the black athlete? On just about all levels, black participation is either waning or stagnant. He isn't exactly extinct, but he is shrinking in stature, a strange phenomenon considering the widely held assumption that black people are more naturally qualified than any race on the planet to run faster, jump higher, and of course, dribble adeptly with the left hand and the right.

What a shock, then, to notice how the NBA, the so-called black man's game, is siphoning talent at a rapid rate from Germany, France, Italy, Spain, and Croatia. And in boxing, where black faces once ruled the upper divisions for decades, we see a sudden influx of heavy-weight champions and contenders from Russia and other

Eastern European countries, while boxers of Latin American descent have taken over the middle and lower divisions. The "new minorities" in baseball hail from Japan, Korea, Cuba, the Dominican Republic, and various South American baseball gardens, while a number of linemen with Oceanic lineage is on the increase in the NFL.

Have we covered everything? Oh, how could we forget? Professional golf still has only one player with African blood on tour, despite all the knee-jerk projections in 1997 that claimed Tiger Woods, after his record win at the Masters tournament, would change the complexion of the sport with a few inspirational swings of his 3-iron.

Here's the final result, then: White people still own, and have always owned, baseball, golf, tennis, skiing, cycling, swimming, diving, surfing, hockey, soccer, volleyball, softball, skating, cricket, fencing, every event at the X-Games and the Winter Olympics, and, in suburbs everywhere, T-ball. And this doesn't include white dominance in such borderline sports as auto racing, horse racing, bowling, and trophy hunting. Also, based on sheer numbers, starting with youth and including recreational leagues, white participation in basketball and football is higher than that of blacks. To paraphrase Jimmy the Greek, the white is bred to be the dominant athlete.

Nobody bothers to examine that, however. When it comes to sports, the image of the Super Negro is all the rage among fans, media, and those who practice junk science in a flawed attempt to explain something that really isn't true: that blacks are superior in athletics.

Rather, blacks are retreating from athletics. The steady, if not drastic, decline is caused by several factors but can be directly linked to the rise of the black middle class. In the early 1980s, children of the Civil Rights era became adults blessed with college degrees and helped by Affirmative Action and a more tolerant (if not racist-free) white society. That gave them advantages, educationally, financially, and otherwise, that blacks from previous generations never realized, and it created the most startling contrast in America: black people with white picket fences. Rather than repeat the vicious poverty cycle of their parents and great-grandparents, these Civil Rights benefactors left the ghetto, broke the mold, traveled a different path, and ventured into lifestyles that put them more in touch with the typical white family of four. The new Norman Rockwell portrait required several hasty strokes of brown paint, because the Huxtables moved next door to the Brady Bunch.

In many instances, the sons and daughters of porters, domestic workers, and laborers grew up to become doctors, CEOs, and administrators, thanks to the blood of Martin Luther King and the courage of Rosa Parks. The outlook on life for these Civil Rights babies changed as well. This segment of black society saw a multitude of options for themselves and their own children, and it altered every single phase of their lives: how they socialized, viewed other cultures, and simply existed day to day. It was a complete upgrade from the prehistoric way their parents and grandparents lived. For example, generations of blacks never invested in the stock market or real estate, preferring to tie their modest nest eggs in insurance, an ordinary checking account, or in a sack under the bed. That all changed with the new generation. The Civil Rights babies also developed a more worldly outlook toward the arts, education, science, and many other areas. They used this heightened awareness not only to enhance themselves but also their families.

Meaning: Their children wouldn't be limited the way some poor children are in urban America.

Black middle-class children have options besides sports, just as white middle-class children do. They're more likely to join the debate team, play a musical instrument, do social work, learn the family business, or just go in a different direction from poor black children. The suburbanization of black kids hasn't increased black participation in sports; it has helped to shallow the pool.

These kids aren't as singularly focused on sports as certain kids are in urban America, and they therefore don't place much emphasis on developing the athletic skills needed for long-term success. Not only has this led a new generation of blacks away from sports and toward white-collar occupations, it also disputes the myth that blacks are uniquely gifted to dominate certain sports. And it perfectly illustrates the importance of weighing environment when determining why blacks are superior in the few sports in which blacks are large in number.

In poor neighborhoods, there just aren't as many doors that kids can open. If the only outlets are sports and trouble, these kids will find sports and trouble. It really isn't that complicated. Many of our inner cities are overloaded with basketball courts, so that's what kids will do. You don't see baseball fields on every corner, or tennis courts, or volleyball nets, or golf courses, or ice rinks, or wrestling mats, or equestrian courses. For decades, city parks and recreation departments went the inexpensive route and simply paved basketball courts and put up nets, thereby dictating what poor black kids did with their spare time and excess energy. These park and rec departments also assumed this is what the neighborhood wanted, rather than give the neighborhood other venues and alternatives to explore. That's why basketball became the black man's game. It wasn't necessarily his choice. It was the choice he was given.

On the flip side, black middle-class kids aren't as confined because such limits aren't placed on them. Their parents are taking them to the ballet and the opera and directing them to the soccer field and giving them the resources to do whatever strikes their interest. If you gave the typical poor black kid these same advantages, basketball courts would empty in a hurry, if not completely. So it's no accident that the decline of blacks in sports coincided with the rise of the black middle class.

Excuse me if I don't shed plenty of tears over the decline of black participation in sports, either. Harry Edwards, the Berkeley sociologist, said in an interview for this book that any trend that results in fewer blacks reaching the big time is not a very good thing. On that point, we agree; success is success, no matter how it's accomplished, as long as it's done legally and honorably. And success is always welcomed by a race of people that constantly struggles to find it.

But the high visibility of blacks in our most popular sports always tugged me in opposite directions. On one hand, black athletes do provide an ego boost and a sweeping sense of pride for the black community. Also, a good many athletes have helped unite a racially mixed and sports-mad country in ways that those in other professions can't. And yet, a race that suffers from an unhealthy emphasis on athletes and entertainers needs to be recognized and respected for its ability to produce leaders in all fields, not just a few.

All this tends to do is give a skewed image of blacks as being physically more gifted than whites, when in reality, blacks simply don't have as many opportunities to prove themselves as superior dentists, doctors, administrators, TV producers, computer analysts, university professors, and yes, sports authors. If a healthy number of poor whites were led to sports, and just two sports in particular, then those sports would be dominated by whites.

Anyway, the notion of blacks as being better athletes is faulty purely by definition. Exactly what is an athlete? Someone who runs fast and jumps high? If so, then that discounts anyone who can swim. Or hurl a heavy object. Or twirl on a razor-thin blade while skating around ice. Basically, the term "athlete" is far-reaching and includes, but is not limited to, running and jumping. Even then, the definition of running and jumping is a broad one. Do we mean sprinting or distance running? Jumping high or jumping far? According to the popularly held perception, nobody on the planet can run faster, or run over greater distances, or jump higher vertically or farther horizontally, than the black man. And we know, based on results, that blacks do not dominate every one of these areas.

Then we must break down the black man himself. Do we mean Africans? African Americans? South Africans or West Africans or East Africans? Central Africans? All of the above? The continent, like its people, is so diverse. The variables that go into producing and defining a great athlete are broad and complex and numerous and confusing. Greatness is not limited to genes and certainly not exclusively tied to race. Therefore, here's the most responsible way to explain why blacks appear to dominate certain athletic movements: I don't know, and neither do you.

That doesn't make it wrong to wonder why. After taking a 48-10 beating from Texas Christian University in 2004, Fisher DeBerry, the coach of a virtually all-white Air Force team, chalked it up to race. "We must get the black athlete if we're going to compete," he said. "It's very obvious to me that the other team had a lot more Afro-American players than we did, and they ran a lot faster than we did. It just seems to be that way, that Afro-American kids can run very, very well. That doesn't mean Caucasian kids and other descendants can't run, but it's very obvious to me they run extremely well."

DeBerry was gently reprimanded by his superiors at Air Force for being insensitive, which was a typical response in a politically correct world. And it further illustrated how uncomfortable people get when it comes to honest and thoughtful discussion on a rather obvious sight in sports. It's just one of those topics that most people would prefer to whisper about by the water cooler. Whites are afraid of coming off as racist. Blacks are afraid where the conversation might lead—maybe to assumptions that physical superiority somehow translates to inferior intelligence.

Floyd Keith, the executive director of the Black Coaches Association, turned huffy at DeBerry's remarks. "If the coach wanted to say something, he should say something in regard to his lack of speed and the need to upgrade his skill and left out race," Keith said. "To draw any kind of inference that blacks were faster and whites slower, that's a subject as a coach you don't go. It should've been left alone."

You had to question whether DeBerry's rather candid, if not totally scientific, observation about whites and blacks in athletics was actually racist, though. Plenty of black athletes believe there's something about their makeup that's different than the makeup of their white counterparts. Plenty of black coaches (and members of Keith's organization, the BCA) feel the same way about black athletes and speed. Same goes for many white coaches, except they keep it on the hush-hush. In fact, you can't find many athletes or football coaches, black or white, who don't believe what DeBerry said. He thought his Air Force team lacked speed because it lacked black players. He did properly acknowledge that some whites and members of other racial groups can run fast, but blacks tend to reach the finish line a few steps ahead. Again: racist? You decide. DeBerry was only late with his "Afro-American" designation, which went out of style with bell-bottom jeans and eight-track tapes. But what do you expect from a guy who was 67 years old when he made these comments?

Some 40 years earlier, Bear Bryant said the same thing when his Alabama team was shredded by Sam Cunningham, the great black tailback from USC. Bryant wasn't labeled a racist for essentially admitting that 'Bama needed to get some speed; he was applauded by blacks (and, grudgingly, by southern whites) and hailed by integrationists. The administration at Alabama didn't rap Bryant on the knuckles, the way Air Force did with DeBerry; the administration simply gave the green light to integrate the football team and get some speed.

Keith's reply, on the other hand, is exactly what whites fear: being taken out of context, and being misunderstood, by blacks when discussing race in an honest forum. Why was DeBerry better off, as Keith said, leaving it alone? Why is anybody? What message does that send to a society that struggles with the topic of race and needs more conversation, instead of less? We should not just shut up, stop searching for answers, and keep living in a cesspool of ignorance.

DeBerry did not say blacks made better football players. That would have been wrong and a stretch, because speed doesn't automatically make someone a better player. And it would have insinuated that blacks emerge from the womb with the ability to sack quarterbacks and throw tight spirals and make one-handed catches. As we know, skills are developed through years of hard work and devotion, not inside a mother's belly. Skills are developed by poor blacks who have precious few options other than playing pickup basketball and backyard football. Environment and circumstance don't always determine who runs faster, but it does often decide who'll go farther.

Two black athletes who were labeled as naturally gifted were never given their due for their hard work and the attention they paid to detail. Jesse Owens won races and stole the 1936 Olympics partly because of speed, but he was a true student of track and field. He knew the proper way to sprint out of the blocks, how to use flawless form on the track, and also how to buy extra inches in the long jump with his leaping technique. Bo Jackson was a two-time state decathlon champ before he became an All-Star in both pro football and baseball, and it requires plenty of time to master the different aspects of those sports. Interestingly, Jackson became a successful businessman in Chicago with diversified assets, meaning he applied the same approach to building a business empire as he did his athletic career.

Months before DeBerry made his comments, Paul Hornung tried to explain in an interview why his alma mater, the great Notre Dame, wasn't winning more football games. He said Notre Dame couldn't "stay as strict as we are, as far as the academic structure is concerned, because we've got to get the black athlete." This was more

©Bettmann/Corbis

After Hitler's claim of German athletic superiority, Jesse Owens embarrassed the Nazi leader with an awesome performance in the 1936 Olympic Games. And to the host Hitler's dismay, many in attendance cheered Owens as he won gold medals in 100-meter and 200-meter dashes, the long jump, and the 4 × 100-meter relay. And, as a reflection of the historic significance of his feat, Berlin named a street in Owens' honor in 1984.

damaging. Clearly, Hornung was attaching intelligence to athletic ability when it came to black players. This was a racial comment, and possibly racist, although it probably wasn't the point Hornung meant to make. After briefly making exceptions for a handful of players who were borderline academically, some of them black, Notre Dame stiffened its requirements and lost players who easily met the grade, for instance, at Alabama. Notre Dame, Duke, Stanford, and other schools with standards higher than most colleges face challenges when recruiting a number of poor black kids, as well as white kids, who can't cut it academically.

But like many people, Hornung forgot to explain the reasons behind the racial inequities when it came to the poor black players he wanted Notre Dame to recruit. Yes, the achievement scores of black high school kids, and therefore black high school players, are lower on average than those of whites. But look at the challenges some of these black kids face. Look at their environment and their circumstances. They are victims of a long racist society. Many grew up poor, came from single-parent households (where education isn't always stressed), received a public school education in some of our worst districts, and didn't have as many primary role models in their lives. Put that same child in the suburbs, give him the same advantages both at home and in school as white kids have, and test scores wouldn't be an issue.

This is why blacks are often sensitive and defensive when the topic is so-called black athletic superiority. It allows racists to chuckle and crackpots to reach certain conclusions about black intelligence without any reliable research done to support the notion. All the scientific attempts and Bell Curve analysis that tried to determine differences among racial groups came away with inconclusive data and far-reaching theories containing loopholes and faulty logic and arguments. And those studies didn't properly weigh environment and circumstance.

This even extends to the widely accepted belief that North American blacks with West African ancestry are the fastest species on the planet. You have to only open your eyes to see the overwhelming evidence of this. John Hoberman, a professor and chair in the department of Germanic Studies at the University of Texas and author of *Darwin's Athlete: How Sports Has Damaged Black America and Preserved the Myth of Race*, cites the 100- and 200-meter dash lists. Only men of West African ancestry have run under 10 seconds in the 100, and only three nonblacks have broken 20 seconds in the 200.

"There is a segment of people with West African origin capable of taking it another step," he said. "That's just a fact. And it would be irresponsible to claim otherwise. Ever since electronic timing began, we have 30 years of evidence that one group is running faster than the most gifted representatives of all other groups."

Studies by Japanese scientists determined that Africans had stiffer muscles than whites, which the Japanese used to explain sprinting and jumping performance by blacks. In America, research by various health organizations showed black men had greater bone density and lower body fat ratios than whites. In the last century, scientists from Scandinavia and Asia and the Americas studied the black athletic phenomenon and mostly told us that what we see in track meets is true. Relying on a variety of biological factors, Jon Entine concluded blacks were genetically superior to whites in *Taboo: Why Black Athletes Dominate Sports and Why We're Afraid to Talk About It*, a book widely discussed with a mixture of acceptance, suspicion, and scorn when it was published in 2001.

In football, blacks totally control the speed positions of receiver, cornerback, and running back. The NFL didn't have a full-time white starter at cornerback during the 2006 season. Only one white sprinter, quarter-mile specialist Jeremy Wariner of Texas, has consistently won the 100, 200, or 400 sprints in world-class meets this decade, although Liu Xiang of China did become the world-record holder in the 110-meter hurdles. But these generalizations about black athletes, although hard to dismiss given the evidence on the field, courts, and track stadiums, still fail to answer some fundamental questions. That's why Entine's project was fraught with too many holes in its arguments. If people of West African descent are so superior genetically, why aren't sprinters from Liberia, Mali, Senegal, and other West African countries dominating the sprints in the Olympics? It would make sense, given the purity of their genetic makeup, that they would breeze past North American blacks on the track, right?

Also, if we were to subscribe to the theory of muscle fibers and fast-twitch, why haven't blacks dominated the Tour de France and other world-class cycling events that require strength in the thighs? The race would seem to be a natural for black athletes. Well, blacks are not only failing to accumulate yellow jerseys, they aren't even entering the race. Is that because blacks aren't big on cycling, or because blacks aren't good at cycling? Also, if Michael Jordan was such a great natural athlete, why couldn't he flick a switch and chase down fly balls with DiMaggio-like ease when he tried baseball? And if we are to believe blacks are superior athletes, then why in the name of Rafer Johnson don't blacks dominate the decathlon in Olympic competition?

Then there's the perception that white men can't jump. Well, then why do whites stand a good chance of winning high-jump events on every level in competitive track and field? This goes for males and females. Strange, but while the NBA was growing in popularity in the 1970s (by leaps and bounds, quite literally) and pushing the white player down the end of the bench, Dwight Stones was setting world records in the high jump and winning Olympic medals. Certainly, a degree of technique is involved in the high jump, compared to the act of jumping for a rebound, where any powerful burst of spring will do. Still, that doesn't fully explain the discrepancy and inconsistency.

Finally, in a sport in which speed goes a long way, soccer is ruled by multiple ethnicities, not just one. You can find fast players of every ethnicity on soccer teams throughout the world. In this sense, speed knows no racial boundary. The African countries don't hold a spell over the sport, not like European countries and South American countries, certainly. And the makeup of most top-flight American teams is mainly white. Yet, nobody cites white dominance in soccer or even wonders, with some surprise, why blacks aren't filling out the rosters of the American teams and pushing whites to try something else, like bowling. Well, here's the reason: Soccer isn't big in urban America, at least not with blacks. It's a suburban sport played by whites, who begin to master it at an early age. White dominance is a result of circumstance and chance, the same rationale we can apply to blacks and basketball.

What the scientists, anthropologists, and other physiological experts fail to concede is how African-American blood has been diluted since slavery, thereby destroying Jimmy the Greek's ambitious but clumsy assertion about selective mating. You'd be pressed to find a single black person in America who is completely pure of white blood. That, more than anything else, makes it very difficult for so-called experts to measure athletic superiority based exclusively on race and purely on genetics. Other factors must be considered: cultural, environmental, and so forth. Also, why do so many gifted black sprinters come from the South, the Far West, and the Caribbean, where warm weather can dictate physical development? If blacks are so much more advanced as a group, why don't we see blacks from Chicago and Boston breaking all the sprint records? Isn't that additional proof of how environment plays a role in determining speed?

It's not uncommon for little boys in Kenya to cover great distances while running errands and going back and forth to school. Over time, the effects of how this changes the body and muscular structure must be considered when determining why Kenyans are big winners in the distance events and marathon races. Again, it's a matter of

Mike Powell/Getty Images

One of the greatest athletes of our time, Bo Jackson worked hard to make himself a star in both football and baseball. Whether it was carrying the ball as he did for four seasons in the NFL or hitting it as he did for eight seasons in the Major Leagues, Jackson often struck fear into his opponents and produced awe among fans.

environment. In any sport that requires constant training, certain muscle groups are strengthened over time. Just observe the physical transformation (or lack of it, in most cases) of little girls who practice gymnastics for hours every day. Or the chests of male gymnasts who specialize on the rings. Or the torsos of rowers and the legs and thighs of figure skaters and speed skaters. In each case, overworked muscles, more than genetics or race, lead to athletic success.

As you see, there are more open-ended questions than researchers, the responsible ones anyway, that can answer with any relevancy to reach indisputable conclusions.

It is not a crime, or even racist, to acknowledge basic physical differences and characteristics among the races. That's what makes us unique. We all have different shaped eyes, noses, lips, hips, and feet, and we have differences in the texture of our hair. Certain races have more tall people than others. Some have shorter and thicker people. And so on and so forth. I'm certainly not qualified to understand why, but given that the earth's people originated in strategic spots around the globe, environment and culture had a huge say in the evolution of our physical development.

The danger occurs when uninformed and unqualified people conclude that a so-called superior physical human being translates into a limited human being intelligence wise. What I find insulting is how only blacks have been cited in this regard. If a human being with tremendous physical gifts somehow has less intelligence, then why doesn't the same philosophy apply to weightlifters from the Middle East, Russia, or Nordic countries? Has anyone ever questioned their mental capacity? Once again, these inconsistencies are proof that you can't trust anyone's judgment in this area, no matter how qualified their credentials may be. And still nobody has explained why physical ability and intelligence must somehow be tied to one another, as though someone who is physically gifted must be a born idiot.

"The old saying that 'you pay in brain what you gain in brawn' is what drives people to make such assumptions," said John Hoberman, the University of Texas professor. "This is why you must be careful, because we have been frequently misled by folklore on this subject. A lot of things that people think about race is still centralized in the 19th century. There is very little good science on the whole topic."

The faulty logic and science, along with the obvious sensitivity expressed by black people, is precisely why most people would rather leave enough alone. Those in the sports world would rather touch a hot stove than the topic of physical differences among black athletes; chances are the burn from the stove would be less harmful. Because of white liberal guilt and politically correct times, the elephant in the room becomes ignored or dismissed as trivial. Nobody who's white wants to hear from Jesse Jackson or Floyd Keith, and most definitely, nobody wants to meet the same fate as Jimmy the Greek Snyder or Al Campanis, the twin poster boys for this subject and why folks subscribe to the theory that "it's better to just say nothing."

Snyder was a jovial oddsmaker who picked winners on the CBS pregame football shows and served as a Jesus to gamblers everywhere. He brought no sheer expertise to the program in terms of football knowledge; he was, for lack of a better description, a TV bookie. Among others, the CBS show had Phyllis George, a former Miss America who was mostly eye candy for the male audience; Irv Cross, a smart former football star who was miscast as the token black face on the show; and The Greek. The show was pure entertainment before kickoff and The Greek, like the others, brought something to the mix.

He had the good sense not to enjoy a glass of wine during the show, but this wasn't the case when a local TV reporter innocently approached Snyder having a meal at Duke Zeibert's in Washington, D.C., on Martin Luther King's birthday and asked The Greek why the modern black athlete was so dominant.

At that moment, Snyder became afflicted with a condition that many TV analysts suffer from: know-it-all disease. His word was gospel on Sunday afternoons, so rather than politely explain that he had done no research on the subject and had no educated opinion, Snyder started ranting. He talked about slaves and of how plantation masters carefully matched their "big black with his big black woman so he could have a big black kid," and so on. Then he resumed eating and drinking.

All hell broke loose within days, when CBS began receiving calls and Jesse Jackson saw another chance to appear before the cameras and justify his self-appointed role as spokesman for all black people. Top executives at the network, all of them white, quivered in their three-piece suits during the fallout and finally gave Snyder the boot when the howl became deafening. The NAACP feared Snyder set "race relations back 100 years or more" when in reality, Snyder forced companies such as CBS to look closer at diversity and make efforts to hire more blacks in meaningful positions. Rather than hold forthright discussion about race and sports, most of America condemned Snyder as an amateur physiologist and called his comments "stupid," another way of saying he should have said nothing. Others simply criticized our PC times and lack of freedom of speech. Nobody actually addressed the topic, at least not in depth or with any honesty, with an audience composed of whites, blacks, and specialists.

At least Snyder didn't bring intelligence into the discussion. He left that to Campanis who, a year earlier, agreed to appear with Ted Koppel on *Nightline* to discuss the 40th anniversary of Jackie Robinson's Major League debut. Campanis was a former teammate of Robinson's in the minor leagues and briefly in the Majors; he knew Robinson well and considered him a friend. At the time of the interview, Campanis was a general manager of the Dodgers who held decision-making power, which made his thought process and comments on black intelligence all the more alarming and damaging. After Campanis said many blacks didn't pay enough dues to become managers, Koppel pressed on.

"Yeah, but you know in your heart of hearts, you know that's a lot of baloney," he said. "I mean, there are a lot of black players, there are a lot of great black baseball men who would dearly love to be in managerial positions, and I guess what I'm really asking you is to, you know, peel it away a little bit. Just tell me why you think it is. Is there still that much prejudice in baseball today?"

Campanis: "No, I don't believe it's prejudice. I truly believe that they may not have some of the necessities to be, let's say, a field manager or perhaps a general manager."

Koppel: "Do you really believe that?"

Campanis: "Well, I didn't say all of them, but they are certainly short. How many quarterbacks do you have? How many pitchers do you have that are black?"

Campanis further buried himself by adding that blacks lack "the buoyancy" to become great swimmers, again, all done without research or any expertise. At worst, Campanis truly thought black folks were born dumb and was a racist of the worst kind, a characterization dismissed by Don Newcombe, one of the pioneering black Major League players who knew Campanis personally. At best, Campanis was just ignorant and misinformed, a product of his day. Anyway, after Campanis and Snyder, any attempt at dialogue on the subject of blacks in sports came off awkwardly. The public flogging they received was enough for plenty of people in the industry. Fearing for their jobs, commentators on TV shied away from the topic, which was airbrushed from the airways. Most attempts to publicly explore why blacks appeared to have slight advantages in certain sports was done very gingerly and without much expert analysis. Mainly people were left with their uneducated guesses and wild assumptions. Again, people took the safe route because most scientific study in this area has proved to be inconclusive, and also because they knew they were being watched by the heavily armed PC police.

Any discussion of blacks and physical differences must include the hours and dedication and hard work that's put into becoming a great athlete. That's where many blacks feel shortchanged on the subject of their so-called superiority. The perception of black dominance doesn't give black athletes enough credit for their training and implies that blacks use brawn whereas whites use intelligence to get ahead in sports. This is laughable.

This comes as a surprise to anyone who watched Magic Johnson, never considered the fastest runner or highest jumper, but unquestionably one of the smartest NBA players ever. Johnson's ability to read defenses, anticipate tendencies, understand his opponent, and figure out the other coach was virtually unmatched in his day, perhaps in NBA history. It also helped that he was 6 feet, 9 inches, and knew how to use his body effectively against smaller players. Meanwhile, TV commentators raved instead about the mental capacity of his biggest rival, Larry Bird. Black audiences held nothing against Bird; they were simply irritated by the media's constant emphasis on Bird's intelligence while failing to recognize the intelligence of great black players. It implied the obvious. As sociologist and commentator Thomas Sowell noted: "To be an outstanding basketball player means to out-think opponents consistently in these split-second decisions while under stress."

It's rather astonishing, with so many blacks playing point guard, how intelligence is often missing from the accolades handed out when it comes to black athletes. That has enraged plenty of black players, past and present, who rightly view any discussion about natural athletic ability with a skeptical eye. Fact is, blacks in basketball and football are forced to work as hard if not harder than anyone else in sports, mainly because they're competing against each other and against whites. Also, the competition for college scholarships and professional jobs is steep in these high-revenue sports. This goes counter to the racist notion that blacks are inherently lazy. Actually, poor black kids will spend hours practicing in all kinds of weather, partly for their love of the game, partly because of a desire to mimic their role models, partly to achieve a degree of status in the neighborhood, and partly because they see these sports as their only chance to get rich. That's a tremendous amount of desire, much more desire than many kids show in anything, sports or otherwise. This kind of singular focus is what creates great players and, unfortunately, sends legions of poor black kids careening to a dead-end when their singular pursuits don't lead to a pot of gold.

This focus also scares away potential players, which leads to another explanation of so-called black dominance. Very often, white boys are discouraged by their parents or coaches from playing certain sports and certain positions for fear that these kids can't adequately compete against black kids. Subsequently, the white kid in some cases is nudged away from tailback in football or playing in the outfield in baseball, positions that will be controlled by faster players (read: black players). In more extreme cases, white kids begin leaving mainstream sports altogether to participate in sports that are beyond the reach and interest of urban black kids. This has created the winter sports spectacle known as the X Games, more cynically described as the annual white man's Olympic festival.

Speaking of the Winter Olympics, Bryant Gumbel caused a stir in 2006 when he essentially dismissed the event as just that: the White Man's Games. "So try not to laugh," Gumbel said on his HBO show, "when someone says these are the world's greatest athletes, despite a paucity of blacks that makes the Winter Games look like a GOP convention." In his obvious thirst to degrade the Games, Gumbel inferred that blacks are superior athletes, thus falling into the same trap as the masses. Does this mean *Dancing With the Stars* was bogus because most of the contestants weren't black?

But just like dance, athleticism takes on so many forms and involves so many people that nobody can rightly claim overall dominance. Someone who can tango can't necessarily breakdance, for example. You get the gist.

Overall, the topic is a fascinating one to some people, especially when the Summer Olympics surface every four years. As they crouch in the starting blocks, most if not all, of the finalists for the 100-meter dash, which produces the World's Fastest Man, will be black. As will the winner. But just the same, the winner of the 1,600 meters might be someone from Morocco or England or heaven knows where. Just as the winner of the 100 can't claim to be the world's best athlete, neither can the 1,600 winner, or the gold-medal winner in the pole vault or high jump. The decathlon winner can make the best argument for being the best athlete, and the 2004 winner of the decathlon was a white man from the Czech Republic who beat, imagine this, a black man from America.

Well, actually, Brian Clay's father is black, and his mother is Japanese–American, which is a genetic way of explaining how no single racial group can claim owner-ship in athletics.

Closing

Solutions Start at Home

While America was consumed by gluttony, Reaganomics, and a pair of cable TV start-ups called ESPN and MTV that would soon change the culture, another phenomenon was developing in the 1980s. Three men who had never met were about to make their mark on society just by doing what fathers do.

One of the men was purely fictional, although Heathcliff Huxtable appeared almost lifelike to a record number of devoted watchers of *The Cosby Show,* the highest-rated sitcom of the decade. The others were Earl Woods and Richard Williams, a pair of Southern California dads who would meet with Huxtable-like comparison soon enough. These three men had their own distinct personalities, occupations, and outlooks, and even their family situations were diverse: The Huxtables were New York upper-middle-class, the Woodses were typical Orange County suburbanites, and the Williams family lived on the rough edges of Los Angeles.

Most important, though, is what the men did share. They were black fathers living with their young kids and were devoted to raising them properly.

In each instance, the impact was considerable. Bill Cosby's TV character awakened America to the realization that, surprise, there are black families headed by highly educated parents with professional jobs. Earl Woods stuck a toy golf club in the crib of his infant son Eldrick and laid the foundation that created a golf legend. Richard Williams hustled home from work every day and hit tennis balls with his two youngest daughters until Venus and Serena grew up and changed the sport. Certainly in the case of the real-life dads, the sports world would now be a lot poorer had Woods and Williams fallen victim to a destructive trend in black America and become disinterested or absentee fathers. Those who really benefited, though, were Tiger Woods and the Williams sisters, who are a lot richer today for having dads in their lives—and not just richer financially.

Any examination of the state of blacks in sports, or blacks in general, starts with the father. Many of the problems currently faced by black athletes, along with solutions for those problems, can be attached to him. When he is involved in the lives of his children, the result will be mostly positive. When he is a ghost who fades in and out of the lives of his children, the result is mostly negative. We can list all the evils of black society and rail against drugs, unemployment, and racism until our vocal chords snap. But the most critical issue by far is the health of the black family, which depends heavily on the father and whether he handles his business.

Too often, he doesn't handle his business in poor black America, from where we get most of our black athletes, where too many fathers are jackasses who flee once they become fathers with the swiftness of LaDainian Tomlinson in the open field. And then, when their sons are ready to hit the sports jackpot, they magically reappear with ready-made excuses for their failures as fathers. Usually, the deadbeat will blame it on society, or the white man, or the inability to keep a job, all legit excuses to a degree. But the real reason is he was simply unwilling to spend his time with one woman or work out any problems they may have had. He was unprepared to be a father in the first place, and when he became one, he turned coward and looked for the easy way out instead of owning up and manning up to his responsibilities.

The number of black athletes raised primarily by their mothers (or grandmothers, in some extreme cases) is staggering and sickening. It's beyond the crisis stage, beyond tragedy. It's officially a plague that society has grown to accept, ever so ignorantly. Roughly 55 percent of black kids in this country grow up fatherless. There aren't any hard statistics to tell us how this situation cripples black athletes specifically. But in a sense, numbers aren't necessary. We see the problem clearly reflected in a variety of ways among some, though not all, athletes. We see it in behavior. We see it in the athletes who think they're men but have no idea how to be a man. We see it in how they treat women. We see it in the males who become fathers before they turn 20, and when that happens, we see them becoming part-time dads themselves. We see it in a vicious cycle that keeps spinning and chewing up one generation after another, spitting out more potential misguided souls who do nothing to improve the image of black society.

We see it in the black athletes who lean on their coaches, especially on the high school and college levels, to be "father figures" because their own father is a rumor who lives strictly in their imagination. While a number of men have done incredible jobs as fill-in replacements, Uncle Bob is just that, an uncle. Coach John Doe is nothing more than a paid teacher who's with a kid a few hours a day at practice after school. Although their intentions are good, these men aren't waking up in the same house or helping with homework or expressing love to the mother, all things kids need to see, feel, and experience from real fathers. Kids aren't stupid. They know the difference. They see the bond enjoyed by their more fortunate friends who do have involved fathers, and they know they're missing out because that bond can be made possible only by one man.

Let's make one thing clear. There's no question that a black kid is better off without a natural father if that natural father is a worthless bum. Shaquille O'Neal perfectly captured his situation in a raw and angry ode titled "Biological Didn't Bother," a rap song written from the (broken) heart, and it became an appropriate anthem for those like him in modern-day sports who could relate. Biological doesn't play catch with his young boy, and the result is that blacks are no longer falling in love with baseball. Biological isn't taking his son back and forth to practice. Biological isn't teaching his boy how to act after scoring a touchdown or dunking on someone's head. Biological isn't around when the flesh-peddling agents come knocking at the front door to buy naïve boys in what has become a shady slave trade. Biological isn't keeping his kid from playing ball when the grades suffer. Biological isn't helping the kid decide which college to attend and what to look for. Biological often does show up eventually, however . . . when the first paycheck arrives. Lucky for him and us, Phil Harrison stepped in, as many stepfathers often do, and provided Shaq the necessary guidance for success. Shaq also became a doting father himself and did not repeat the sins of his biological father.

This is a good opportunity to salute the real heroes in these situations: black women. For much too long, she's had to deal with discrimination, abandonment, and mistreatment from men of all races. In the cases of single-parent households, she somehow manages to keep her sanity and her family together, as best as possible, given the challenging circumstances. She must wear so many hats in order to give her children the best chance for survival and prosperity. We all know the story of Mary Thomas and how she was the toughest human being in the Chicago neighborhood where her son, Isiah, grew up to become a Hall of Fame point guard. She shooed all of the negative influences away from her son so he could realize his dream. Fact is, there are many mothers like Mary Thomas in the black community, only they don't get the publicity and honor they deserve, except from their children, who remain eternally grateful. Still, in a perfect world, single mothers would have help, in the form of the fathers of their children.

Yes, in that ideal world, the number of responsible black fathers would soar. He would love his woman, demonstrate a work ethic, provide for the family, and teach his boy what it takes to be a man. Decades ago, this was the case more often than not. Decades ago, you saw legions of men take fatherhood very seriously. He was very much a part of the family, even in poor communities, and his touch and guidance helped a good number of black athletes lead productive and professional lives both during and after their playing careers. Those athletes carried themselves with dignity during a racist era, paving the way for black athletes of today, who enjoy a much higher standard of living and fame.

But society changed. Morals changed. Lifestyles changed. Mindsets changed. Some black mothers stopped forcing the fathers of their children to meet their responsibilities. They began to accept the father's absence and take it on themselves to raise their children alone, without seeing this as a problem. And because they were no longer being held to a high standard, black fathers accepted their part-time status, too. This only increased the chances of their children developing behavior problems, flunking out of school, having children out of wedlock, and flooding into mainstream America without the social or educational skills needed to flourish.

Listen to what Bo Jackson said in his autobiography, *Bo Knows Bo*, about growing up as an unruly child: "We never had enough food. But at least I could beat on other kids and steal their lunch money and buy myself something to eat. But I couldn't steal a father. I couldn't steal a father's hug when I needed one. I couldn't steal a father's whipping when I needed one." Jackson didn't meet his real father until he was 11; fortunately, Bo eventually became a model father of three.

We can only imagine how some black athletes would have turned out if they had a responsible father in their lives. And this doesn't just include the lucky athletes who made it to the big leagues. The real body count lies among the tremendous number of athletes who don't get beyond high school. What about them? After their athletic ability gets them nothing more than a varsity lettermen's jacket and a few memories, what becomes of them? If they had a responsible father in their lives, would they have studied harder in school and copped an academic scholarship to college or learned a trade from their old man? Those athletes are the real tragedies, not the athletes who make millions.

Another lifestyle choice that's far too popular is the part-time dad syndrome. These fathers have children without being married to the mother, and because they provide financially and see their kids on the weekends or during the off-season, they figure everything's okay. They're being men and taking care of their responsibilities, or so they think. Meanwhile, they continue enjoying the perk of being a professional athlete by staying single and hitting the clubs. This, too, is nothing but a cop-out, a cowardly way of trying to have it all. One of the more tragic stories recently in sports involved Derrick Thomas, the great Kansas City Chiefs linebacker who died on an icy road while still in his prime as a great football player and beloved human being. Following that tragedy came a disturbing epilogue: Thomas was revealed to have had multiple children by multiple mothers, and his estate had to be divided up like your mother's apple pie on Thanksgiving. Thomas is hardly alone; some of our finest black athletes, for whatever reason, behave just like their own fathers did, although they have the means to do much better in the important job of fatherhood. The best way to raise a kid is not by sending home a paycheck and popping in every now and then—but these fathers just don't get it. In some ways, because they tease their children by entering and exiting their lives so often, they're almost as bad as absentee fathers. Some of these kids see their ball-playing fathers more on TV than in person.

Overall, black athletes who grew up without active fathers have done well, if only because they've had strong and dependable mothers in their lives, and in certain cases, solid support systems provided by other family members as well. As I said in the opening chapter, there are far more examples of professional, hard-working, caring, and intelligent black athletes than there are knuckleheads. That includes pretty much all the blacks currently on the tennis tour, and a good number in Major League baseball. The NBA has programs designed to teach professionalism to the player who comes into the league much too young. And commissioner Roger Goodell's season-long punishment of Pacman Jones should straighten the ship in a hurry in the NFL.

Let us hold off on extended applause for professional leagues and college programs, though, until they properly address other glaring issues. Chief among them is seeing that the percentage of black coaches and executives matches the percentage of players in these sports, especially in college football, where the administrative situation is a joke. There needs to be more progressive thought given to leveling the playing field in that area. Also, the media needs to take a closer look at its depiction of the black athlete. This would be best done by finding more people who specialize in communications and who bring considerable qualifications and putting them into decision-making positions.

Black athletes should use the public forum our sports-crazed society offers to help stimulate these and other such positive changes in the system. We're all responsible for making things better. When it comes to serving people, one hopes that more black athletes will follow the lead of New York Knicks guard Stephon Marbury, who hooked up with Steve & Barry's, a budget clothing store, and launched a line of sneakers that cost under $15. This was a cause that hit Marbury close to home; he remembered while growing up being too poor to afford the $150 sneakers worn on the feet of his NBA heroes. Not only did Marbury help in virtually all phases of his signature, ground-breaking sneaker, he wore a pair of the shoes throughout the 2006-2007 season. This terrific gesture was rewarded when the shoes flew off the shelves. In an era when black kids are killed over their Nikes, this was a crusade from the soul, or should we say the sole, by Marbury. While other sports stars were busy endorsing sneakers with huge mark-up costs, Marbury made affordable sneakers and took less money in return. Let's hope Marbury helps revolutionize the entire billion-dollar sneaker industry and forces companies to take a closer look at their mark-up tactics, considering that many of these sneakers are coveted by poor black kids.

Of course, there's always resistance to changing the status quo, particularly when the status quo feathers one's considerable wallet. When Marbury came out with his budget-priced sneakers, other NBA stars were forced to defend their choices to endorse shoes that often run $150 and up. LeBron James was one of them. When asked about James, one of Nike's highly rewarded pitchmen, Marbury thought for a moment, then said, "I'd rather own than be owned." Perfect.

The future of blacks in sports can be changed for the better in other ways. Black females should be encouraged to try other sports, especially in suburbia, where the black middle class is swelling. City schools should recheck their budgets and introduce nonmainstream sports. Finally, high school coaches and teachers should do more to prepare athletes for college in order to improve the statistics in Richard Lapchick's annual studies regarding race and academic progress. Maybe one day test scores for black athletes will equal that of white athletes, and Lapchick will need to find other work. If that happens, he'll be very glad to go searching.

As for the role of the father, I personally know one who had better stay true to his responsibilities: me. My daughter has shown amazing athletic potential in two and possibly three sports while still in grade school. One thing she'll never need to worry about is my involvement. She'll either be a model student (first) and athlete (distant second), or I'll die trying. Not that I deserve some award for that; it's simply part of the job.

Look, Earl Woods and Richard Williams were no saints. Same goes for Bill Cosby and his TV character, Cliff Huxtable. They all had their issues and their crosses to bear. As his daughters scaled the ladders in tennis,

Richard Williams had a tendency to make nutty statements and behave like a goofball. Earl Woods had left his previous family to remarry and raise Tiger. But these men took fatherhood seriously. Don't diminish that. The sports stars they helped bring into this world and nurture into great athletes are proof enough. Remember that Tiger Woods was good enough academically to attend Stanford, and he oversees a fortune that could generate billions. He's more than a great sportsman. Venus and Serena Williams, although lacking in formal education, are intelligent and dignified and very much a boost for tennis. The sisters are well-rounded people, not robotic tennis machines. And they would not be who they are without their father's helping hand.

In a neat coincidence, Earl Woods and Richard Williams also steered their kids toward sports that lack black faces. It means more to black society that Tiger Woods and the Williams sisters shook up a pair of country-club sports instead of joining the crowd in basketball or football. By going the unconventional route for black athletes, they had an impact that soared beyond sports. They were able to shatter myths and educate the predominately white crowds that follow golf and tennis. They also challenged black kids, parents, and urban communities to think out of the box and consider other types of sports, not just the handful that round up the black athletes. If the prosperity of Woods and the Williams sisters doesn't result in greater numbers of black kids filling these sports, fine; at least the examples they set can motivate in other areas, such as education and the arts. It's unrealistic to think many black kids will rip 300-yard drives like Tiger or whip backhands across the net like Serena or Venus. But they can match their work ethic and dedication and apply it elsewhere.

Anyway, the question is not whether the next generation of potential black athletes can copy Tiger Woods or the Williams sisters—the critical question is whether their fathers can copy those fathers.

Reference Points

Most of the quotations used in this book come from first-hand interviews with the subjects that I conducted from February 2006 through April 2007. I thank these people for their time, their cooperation, their kindness, and most of all, for their depth and honesty. Some subjects were quoted in other publications, and in many cases, those publications were credited following the quotation.

Most of the statistics gathered for this book were pulled from a variety of respected sources, and, again, those sources were credited within the text. What follows are the most significant quotes and reference sources used but not credited within the text. Given below are the page numbers and beginnings of the sentences in which the quotes or statistics appear.

Chapter 1

Page 6: "When he was young and reckless and not . . .": Charles Barkley, in 1992, to a group of reporters in Philadelphia, in defense of a missed shot.

Page 10: "The tendency by some blacks to embrace . . .": Chris Rock, in "Bring the Pain," HBO special.

Page 13: "But that wasn't enough to pacify T.O. . . .": Terrell Owens, in an interview with ESPN.com, 2005.

Page 14: "He wondered if their attacks . . .": Donovan McNabb, in an interview with Michael Smith of ESPN.com, 2006.

Page 17: "It was no coincidence that Randy Moss . . .": Source: NFL.

Page 20: "When he showed poor judgment by using the media . . .": Ron Artest's debut album, *Chapter III*, performed by Allure, ranked 13,565th on Amazon.com after the first week of release.

Page 21: "But with only 13 percent of juvenile delinquents . . .": Wisconsin Department of Health and Social Sciences, 1994.

Page 22: "But 85 percent of teenage prisoners . . .": Fulton County, Georgia, jail populations, Texas Department of Corrections, 1992.

Chapter 2

Page 29: "Just to make sure, I checked his obituary . . .": *New York Times*, February 8, 1993.

Page 35: "He knew the golden rule . . .": *Forbes Magazine* estimated Michael Jordan's net worth at $398 million in 2006.

Chapter 3

Page 62: "In 1954, during a speech at BYU . . .": Mark E. Petersen, "Race Problems: As They Affect the Church," delivered August 1954.

Chapter 4

Page 75: "As Harvard scholar Henry . . .": Henry Louis Gates, Jr., in an op-ed piece, *New York Times*, August 1, 2004.

Chapter 5

Page 102: "Iverson chimed in . . .": Allen Iverson, in an interview with the *Philadelphia Daily News*, October 2005.

Chapter 6

Page 120: "Only 11.78 baseball scholarships are allotted . . .": Source: NCAA manual.

Page 122: "When Randolph played for the great . . .": Source: Major League Baseball.

Page 122: "The majority of blacks in the minor and major . . .": Source: Major League Baseball Opening Day rosters 2006.

Page 131: "Bonds couldn't capitalize from Madison Avenue . . .": Barry Bonds did not serve as a spokesperson for a Fortune 500 company in 2006.

Page 135: "There are over 200 Little League programs . . .": Source: Little League Baseball.

Chapter 7

Page 149: "Earl even joined the marketing effort . . .": Earl Woods, as told to *Golf Digest*, November 2002.

Page 150: "In 1962, Charlie Sifford shot a 67 . . .": Charlie Sifford's recollection to *Golf Digest*, December 2002.

Page 150: "When asked by TV announcer . . .": Tiger Woods, interviewed by Jim Nantz, 1996.

Page 157: "Even Tiger admitted . . .": Woods, June 2005, at the U.S. Open.

Chapter 8

Page 179: "Ali added, 'Ninety-eight percent . . .'": Muhammad Ali, various press conferences, 1971-1975.

Chapter 9

Page 195: "In a climate of declining circulation . . .": *ESPN Magazine* launched in March 1998 with a circulation of 350,000. In the period from 2004 to 2005, according to *Advertising Age*, the circulation went from 1.7 million to 1.9 million.

Chapter 10

Page 213: "As it turned out, Croom was hired . . .": Alabama did not compete for the NCAA national college football championship during Shula's tenure.

Chapter 12

Page 250: "The steady, if not drastic, decline . . .": Black median household income in 2000 quadrupled since 1965, according to the U.S. Census Bureau.

Index

About the Author

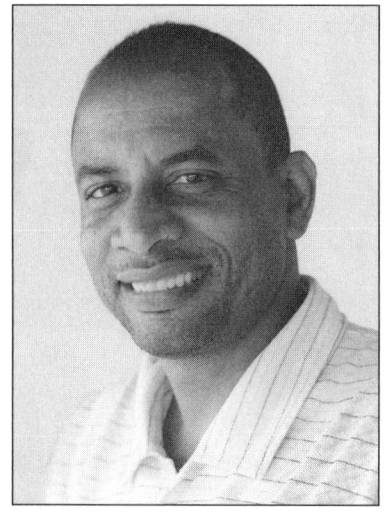

Shaun Powell is a sports columnist for *Newsday*, a New York-based newspaper renowned for its local, national, and international coverage. He has worked at the newspaper since September 1993. Powell is a distinguished writer and has been honored by the Associated Press Sports Editors, the New York Associated Press, the New York Deadline Club, the Basketball Writers Association, the United States Tennis Writers Association, and the National Association of Black Journalists.

Powell has worked in various sports-writing capacities at *Newsday*, *Miami Herald*, *Dallas Times Herald*, *St. Louis Globe-Democrat*, and *Washington Post*. His assignments have taken him to Japan, Australia, South Africa, England, Scotland, Greece, and Italy, among other international sites, to cover a variety of events and sports, including the Olympics, Super Bowl, World Series, Masters, Wimbledon, NBA Finals, NCAA championships, and world championship boxing matches. He has appeared numerous times on local and national broadcast outlets, including CNN and ESPN TV and radio.

Powell currently resides in New Jersey. He was born in Pittsburgh in 1960 and earned a journalism degree from Howard University in 1983. He and his wife have a daughter.